"The I.A.P.N. dealer, your guide to the world of numismatics"

More than one hundred of the world's most respected coin dealers are members of the I.A.P.N. (International Association of Professional Numismatists). I.A.P.N. members offer the collector an exceptional selection of quality material, expert cataloguing, outstanding service and realistic pricing. The I.A.P.N. also maintains the International Bureau for the Suppression of Counterfeit Coins (I.B.S.C.C.) which for a fee can provide expert opinions on the authenticity of coins submitted to it.

A booklet listing the names, addresses and specialties of all I.A.P.N. members is available without charge by writing to the I.A.P.N. General Secretary, Jean-Luc Van der Schueren, 14 rue de la Bourse, B-1000 BRUXELLES, Belgium. Tel: +32-2-511 0400; Fax: +32-2-512 2528; E-mail: iapnsecret@compuserve.com; Web site: http://www.iapn-coins.org

AUSTRALIA
DOWNIES Coins Pty. Ltd.
Mr. Ken Downie
P.O. Box 888, ABBOTSFORD, VIC.3067
NOBLE NUMISMATICS Pty Ltd
Mr. Jim Noble
169 Macquarie Street
SYDNEY, NSW 2000
AUSTRIA
HERINEK, Gerhard
Herr Gerhard Herinek
Josefstädterstrasse, 27, 1080 WIEN
MOZELT Christine Numismatik
Herr Erich Mozelt
Postfach 19
1043 WIEN
BELGIUM
FRANCESCHI & FILS, B.
M. Druso Franceschi
Rue de la Croix-de-Fer, 10
1000 BRUXELLES
VAN DER SCHUEREN, Jean-Luc
M. Jean-Luc Van der Schueren
Rue de la Bourse, 14
1000 BRUXELLES
CANADA
RANDY WEIR NUMISMATICS Ltd
Mr. Randy Weir
P.O. Box 64577
UNIONVILLE, ONT. L3R 0M9
EGYPT
BAJOCCHI JEWELLERS
Cav. Uff. Pietro Bajocchi
Abdel Khalek Sarwat Street, 45
CAIRO 11511
FRANCE
BOURGEY, Sabine
Mme Sabine Bourgey
Rue Drouot, 7, 75009 PARIS
BURGAN, Claude - Maison FLORANGE
M. Claude Burgan
Rue du 4 Septembre, 8
75002 PARIS
LA PARPAÏOLLE
M. Robert Le Guen
B.P. 06
13191 MARSEILLE
MAISON PLATT S.A.
M. Gérard Barré
B.P. 2612
75026 Cedex 01 PARIS
NUMISMATIQUE & CHANGE DE PARIS
Mme Annette Vinchon
Rue de la Bourse, 3
75002 PARIS
O.G.N.
M. Pierre Crinon
Rue de Richelieu, 64
75002 PARIS
POINSIGNON-NUMISMATIQUE (A.)
M. Alain Poinsignon
Rue des Francs Bourgeois, 4
67000 STRASBOURG
SAIVE, Philippe
M. Philippe Saive
Rue Dupont des Loges, 18
57000 METZ
SILBERSTEIN, Claude, COMPTOIR de NUMISMATIQUE
M. Claude Silberstein
Rue Vivienne, 39
75002 PARIS
VINCHON-NUMISMATIQUE
Mme Françoise Berthelot-Vinchon
Rue de Richelieu, 77
75002 PARIS
GERMANY
DILLER, Johannes
Herr Johannes Diller
Postfach 70 04 29
81304 MÜNCHEN
FRITZ RUDOLF KÜNKER MÜNZENHANDLUNG
Herr Fritz Rudolf Künker
Gutenbergstrasse, 23
49076 OSNABRÜCK
GERHARD HIRSCH NACHF.
Frau Dr. Francisca Bernheimer
Promenadeplatz, 10/II
80333 MÜNCHEN
GORNY & MOSCH, GIESSENER MÜNZENHANDLUNG GmbH
Maximiliansplatz, 20
80333 MÜNCHEN
JACQUIER, Paul-Francis
Herr Paul-Francis Jacquier
Honsellstrasse, 8
77694 KEHL am RHEIN
KRICHELDORF NACHF. (H.H.)
Herr Volker Kricheldorf
Günterstalstrasse,16
79102 FREIBURG i. Br.
KURPFÄLZISCHE MÜNZHANDLUNG oHG - KPM
Herr Helmut Gehrig
Augusta-Anlage, 52
68165 MANNHEIM
LEIPZIGER MÜNZHANDLUNG und AUKTION
Mrs. Heidrun Höhn
Nicolaistrasse 25
04109 LEIPZIG
MANFRED OLDING MÜNZENHANDLUNG
Herr Manfred Olding
Goldbreede 14
49078 OSNABRÜCK
MEISTER, Michael
Herr Michael Meister
Moltkestrasse 6
71634 LUDWIGSBURG

MÜNZEN- UND MEDAILLENHANDLUNG STUTTGART
Herr Stefan Sonntag
Charlottenstrasse, 4
70182 STUTTGART
NEUMANN GmbH (Ernst)
Herr Ernst Neumann
Wätteplatz, 6
89312 GÜNZBURG
NUMISMATIK LANZ
Dr. Hubert Lanz
Luitpoldblock - Maximiliansplatz 10
80333 MÜNCHEN
PEUS NACHF. (Dr. Busso)
Herr Christoph Raab
Bornwiesenweg, 34
60322 FRANKFURT / M
RITTER MÜNZHANDLUNG GmbH
Herr J. Ritter
Postfach 24 01 26
40090 DÜSSELDORF
Rüdiger KAISER MÜNZEN-FACHGESCHÄFT
Herr Rüdiger Kaiser
Mittelweg, 52
60318 FRANKFURT
TIETJEN + Co
Herr Detlef Tietjen
Spitalerstrasse, 30
20095 HAMBURG
WESTFÄLISCHE AUKTIONSGESELLSCHAFT
Herr Udo Gans
Nordring 22
59821 ARNSBERG
HUNGARY
Numismatica EREMBOLT
Mr. László Nudelman
Vörösmarty Tèr 6
1051 BUDAPEST
ITALY
BARANOWSKY s.a.s.
Dott. Vincenzo Filonardi
Via del Corso, 184
00187 ROMA
CRIPPA NUMISMATICA S.A.S.
Sign. Paolo Crippa
Via Cavalieri del S. Sepolcro, 10
20121 MILANO
DE FALCO, Alberto
Sign. Alberto de Falco
Corso Umberto, 24
80138 NAPOLI
FALLANI
Dott. Carlo-Maria Fallani
Via del Babuino, 58
00187 ROMA
GIULIO BERNARDI S.R.L.
Sign. Gianni Paoletti
Casella Postale 560
34121 TRIESTE
PAOLUCCI Numismatica sas
Sign. Andrea Paolucci
Via San Francesco, 154
35121 PADOVA
RANIERI Numismatica srl
Sign. Marco Ranieri
Piazza de Calderini 2/2
40124 - BOLOGNA
RINALDI, Marco
Sign. Marco Rinaldi
Via Cappello, 23 (Casa di Giulietta)
37121 VERONA
VARESI Numismatica s.a.s.
Sign. Alberto Varesi
Viale Montegrappa 3
27100 PAVIA
JAPAN
DARUMA INTERNATIONAL GALLERIES
Mr. Yuji Otani
2-16-32-701, Takanawa, Minato-ku
TOKYO 108-0074
WORLD COINS JAPAN
Mr. Eiichi Ishii
1-15-5, Hamamatsu-cho, Minato-ku
TOKYO 105-0013
MONACO
EDITIONS VICTOR GADOURY
M. Francesco Pastrone
57 rue Grimaldi, "Le Panorama"
98000 MONACO
NETHERLANDS
LAURENS SCHULMAN BV
Mr. Laurens Schulman
Willemslaan 34
1406 LZ BUSSUM
MEVIUS NUMISBOOKS INTERNATIONAL BV
Mr. Johan Mevius
Oosteinde, 97
7671 AT VRIEZENVEEN
SCHULMAN BV
Mr. Eddy Absil
P.O. Box 346
1400 AH BUSSUM
VERSCHOOR Munthandel
Mr. Dim Verschoor
P.O. Box 5803
3290 AL STRIJEN
WESTERHOF, Jille Binne
Mr. Jille Binne Westerhof
Trekpad, 38-40
8742 KP BURGWERD
NORWAY
OSLO MYNTHANDEL AS
Mr. Gunnar Thesen
Postboks 2745 Solli
0204 OSLO

PORTUGAL
NUMISPORTO LDA
Mr. Jose Manuel Ferreira Leite
Av. Combatentes Grande Guerra 610 Lj6
4200-186 PORTO
SPAIN
AUREO & CALICO
Señor Don Xavier Calicó
Plaza del Angel, 2
08002 BARCELONA
CAYON - JANO S.L.
Mr. Juan R. Cayon
Calle Orfila 10
28010 MADRID
Jesús VICO S.A.
Mr. Jesús Vico
Jorge Juan n 83 Duplicado
28009 MADRID
SEGARRA, Fernando P.
Señor Don Fernando P. Segarra
Plaza Mayor 26
28012 MADRID
SWEDEN
NORDLINDS MYNTHANDEL AB
Mr. Hans Hirsch
P.O. Box 5132
102 43 STOCKHOLM
SWITZERLAND
ADOLPH HESS AG
Herr H.J. Schramm
Postfach 7070
8023 ZÜRICH
HESS-DIVO AG
Mr. Ulf Künker
Postfach 7070
8023 ZÜRICH
LHS NUMISMATIK
Herr Heiner Stotz
Postfach 2553
8022 ZÜRICH
NUMISMATICA ARS CLASSICA NAC AG
Mr. Roberto Russo
Postfach 2655
8022 ZÜRICH
NUMISMATICA GENEVENSIS S.A.
Mr. Alain Baron
1 Rond-Point de Plainpalais
1205 GENEVE
THAILAND
HOUSE of the GOLDEN COIN
Mr. Jan Olav Aamlid
P.O. Box 31, Jomtien
20261 - CHONBURI
UNITED KINGDOM
A.H. BALDWIN & SONS Ltd
Mr. A.H.E. Baldwin
Adelphi Terrace, 11
LONDON, WC2N 6BJ
DAVIES Paul Ltd
Mr. Paul Davies
P.O. Box 17
ILKLEY, W.York., LS29 8TZ
DIX NOONAN WEBB
Mr. Christopher Webb
16 Bolton Street, Piccadilly
LONDON, W1J 8BQ
EIMER, Christopher
Mr. Christopher Eimer
P.O. Box 352
LONDON, NW11 7RF
FORMAT OF BIRMINGHAM Ltd
Mr. Garry Charman
18 Lower Temple Street, Unit K, Burlington Court
BIRMINGHAM, B2 4JD
KNIGHTSBRIDGE COINS
Mr. Stephen C. Fenton
Duke Street, 43, St. James's
LONDON, SW1Y 6DD
LUBBOCK & SON Ltd
Mr. Richard M. Lubbock
P.O. Box 35732
LONDON, E14 7WB
Mark RASMUSSEN "Numismatist"
Mr. Mark Rasmussen
P.O. Box 42
BETCHWORTH, RH3 7YR
RUDD Chris
Mr. Chris Rudd
P. O. Box 222
AYLSHAM, Norfolk, NR11 6TY
Douglas SAVILLE Numismatic Books
Mr. Douglas Saville
Chiltern Thameside, 37c St Peters Avenue, Caversham
READING, Berkshire, RG4 7DH
SPINK & SON Ltd
Mr. Paul Dawson
69 Southampton Row, Bloomsbury
LONDON, WC1B 4ET
USA
BASOK Alexander
Mr. Alexander Basok
1954 First Street # 186
HIGHLAND PARK, IL.60035
BERK Ltd. (Harlan J.)
Mr. Harlan J. Berk
North Clark Street, 31
CHICAGO, IL.60602
BULLOWA, C.E. - COINHUNTER
Mrs. C.E. Bullowa (Mrs. Earl E. Moore)
1616 Walnut Street, Suite 2112
PHILADELPHIA, PA.19103
CEDERLIND, TOM
P.O. Box 1963
PORTLAND, OR 97207

CLASSICAL NUMISMATIC GROUP
Mr. Victor England
P.O. Box 479
LANCASTER, PA.17608-0479
COIN & CURRENCY INSTITUTE Inc
Mr. Arthur Friedberg
P.O. Box 1057
CLIFTON, N.J.07014
COIN GALLERIES
Mr. Jan Eric Blamberg
123 West 57th Street
NEW YORK, NY. 10019
DAVISSON'S LTD.
Allan Davisson, Ph.D.
COLD SPRING, MN.56320-1050
Dmitry MARKOV COINS & MEDALS
Mr. Dmitry Markov
P.O. Box 950
NEW YORK, NY.10272
DUNIGAN, Mike
Mr. Mike Dunigan
5332 Birchman
FORT WORTH, TX.76107
FREEMAN & SEAR
Mr. Robert D. Freeman
P.O. Box 641352
LOS ANGELES, CA.90064-6352
FROSETH INC. (K.M.)
Mr. Kent Froseth
P.O. Box 23116
MINNEAPOLIS, MN.55423
GILLIO INC. (Ronald J.) - GOLDMÜNZEN INTERNATIONAL
8 West Figueroa Street
SANTA BARBARA, CA.93101
HARVEY, Stephen
Mr. Stephen Harvey
P.O. Box 3778
BEVERLY HILLS, CA.90212
JENCEK, JOHN
205 De Anza Blvd., #119
San Mateo, CA 94402
JONATHAN K. KERN Co
Mr. Jonathan K. Kern
441 South Ashland Avenue
LEXINGTON, KY.40502-2114
KOLBE,George Frederick
Mr. George F. Kolbe
P.O. Drawer 3100
CRESTLINE, CA.92325-3100
KOVACS, Frank L.
Mr. Frank L. Kovacs
P.O. Box 7150
CORTE MADERA, CA.94976
KREINDLER, B. & H.
Mr. H. Kreindler
236 Altessa Blvd.
MELVILLE, N.Y.11747
MALTER GALLERIES, Inc.
Mr. Michael Malter
17003 Ventura Boulevard, Suite 205
ENCINO, CA.91316
MARGOLIS, Richard
Mr. Richard Margolis
P.O. Box 2054
TEANECK, NJ.07666
MILCAREK, Dr. Ron
Dr. Ron Milcarek
P.O. Box 1028
GREENFIELD, MA.01302
PEGASI Numismatics
Mr. Eldert Bontekoe
P.O. Box 131040
ANN ARBOR, MI. 48113
PONTERIO & ASSOCIATES, INC.
Mr. Richard Ponterio
1818 Robinson Avenue
SAN DIEGO, CA.92103
RARCOA, INC.
Mr. Edward Milas
6262 South Route 83, Suite 200
WILLOWBROOK, IL.60527-2998
STACK'S
Mr. Harvey Stack
123 West 57th Street
NEW YORK, NY.10019
STEPHENS INC. (Karl)
Mr. Karl Stephens
P.O. Box 3038
FALLBROOK, CA.92088
SUBAK INC.
Mr. Carl Subak
79 West Monroe Street, Room 1008
CHICAGO, IL.60603
TELLER NUMISMATIC ENTERPRISES
Mr. M. Louis Teller
16055 Ventura Boulevard, Suite 635
ENCINO, CA.91436
WADDELL, Edward J. Ltd.
Mr. Edward J. Waddell Jr.
P.O. Box 3759
FREDERICK, MD.21705-3759
WORLD-WIDE COINS OF CALIFORNIA
Mr. James F. Elmen
P.O. Box 3684
SANTA ROSA, CA.95402
VENEZUELA
NUMISMATICA GLOBUS
Señor Antonio Alessandrini
Apartado de Correos 50418
VEN - CARACAS 1050

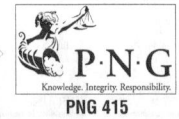

2010 Standard Catalog of®

WORLD COINS

1901-2000

37th OFFICIAL Edition

Thomas Michael
Market Analyst

George Cuhaj
Editor

Harry Miller
U.S. Market Analyst

Merna Dudley
Coordinating Editor

Deborah McCue
Database Specialist

Kay Sanders
Editorial Assistant

Special Contributors

Serge Huard

Craig Keplinger

Rudi Lotter

Juozas Minikevicius

Bullion Value (VB) Market Valuations

Valuations for all platinum, gold, palladium and silver coins of the more common, basically bullion types, or those possessing only modest numismatic premiums are presented in this edition based on the market ranges of:

$1,000 - $1,200 per ounce for **platinum** $850 - $950 per ounce for **gold**

$200 - $225 per ounce for **palladium** $12.50 - $15.00 per ounce for **silver**

©2009 Krause Publications, Inc., a subsidiary of F+W Media, Inc.

Published by

A subsidiary of F+W Media, Inc.

700 East State Street • Iola, WI 54990-0001
715-445-2214 • 888-457-2873
www.krausebooks.com

Our toll-free number to place an order or obtain
a free catalog is (800) 258-0929.

ISSN 1939-814X
ISBN-13: 978-0-89689-814-1
ISBN-10: 0-89689-814-8

Designed by: Stacy Bloch
Edited by: Debbie Bradley

Printed in the United States of America

TABLE OF CONTENTS

Introduction.. 4

Acknowledgments.. 5

How To Use The DVD.. 6

How To Use This Catalog 8

Submitting Electronic Image Guide 12

Standard International Numeral Systems 13

Country Index 14

Hejira Date Chart.. 17

Foreign Exchange 18

THANKS FOR YEARS OF SERVICE

The numismatic editorial staff at Krause Publications would like to recognize the recent retirement of two key contributors to the *Standard Catalog of World Coins* catalogs.

Colin R. Bruce II joined the Krause Publications numismatics staff in April 1974. Prior to joining KP, he had worked as a full-time dealer in world coins and paper money. He is an expert on modern Eastern/Oriental coinages and paper money, which was a valuable asset in developing the *Standard Catalog of World Coins* into four successful century editions. From these we developed the *Standard Catalog of World Gold Coins, Collecting World Coins* and other more specialized titles.

Colin R. Bruce II

Fred Borgmann joined Krause Publications on Aug 2, 1976, as a new issues editor and a numismatic jack-of-all-trades. He has been involved with the *Standard Catalog of World Coins* as a contributor since its inception. Previously, he was a coin cataloger for Jess Peters Inc.

Colin and Fred, thank you for your years of dedication to the hobby and to the Krause Publications vast database of world coins.

Fred Borgmann

INTRODUCTION

You hold in your hands the latest in the long series of *Standard Catalog of World Coin* books. This new edition of the longest running annual world coin catalog represents a great deal of hard work, dedication and years of development from hundreds of loyal contributors comprised of coin collectors, coin dealers, editors, researchers, photographers, programmers and designers.

Beginning with the ideas of original authors Chester L. Krause and Clifford Mishler, the *Standard Catalog of World Coins* was brought into our hobby in 1972 as the largest and most comprehensive world coin reference available. Those first few editions in the early 1970s offered world coin data for all countries from the mid-1800s to the then current day. There were photographs of many of the coins, plenty of information on metal content, descriptions of types and varieties, date listings and of course values presented in multiple grades of preservation. It was all that a hobbyist could want, in one complete package.

But of course, the burgeoning expanse of the world coin hobby brought with it new requirements for added data. Over time we found that collectors wanted information on earlier time periods, and so our database of information was developed and expanded to include coin listings first from the 1700s, then the 1600s and now even some listings into the mid-1500s. Related areas to circulating coins were also researched developed and rolled into our base of knowledge. Patterns, pieforts, trial strikes and essais were added to many countries offering steps of information towards the regular issue coins we had come to know so well. Tokens and medallic issues were compiled for eras and areas where regular issue coinage was scarce or non-existent.

Many experts leant their knowledge and time to these various expansions and to them our hobby is most indebted. Many editors came and went over the years; our staff of experts has over time included some of the most interesting and well-known people one could ever hope to meet. The broader base of those contributing advice and expertise from the field has been a vibrant ray of sunshine, with so many brilliant people stepping forward that it makes our minds spin. Along the way the primary concern for everyone has always been to expand our base of available knowledge and to present as much of what we have learned as possible in an affordable and manageable book form for all to use and enjoy.

Over the years this base of knowledge has come to encompass a full four hundred years of world coinage in four catalog volumes, plus a newly developed edition covering the fledgling 21st century. These five volumes represent the most cost effective and complete numismatic library available in the world today! In that we can all take a moment of pride and honor.

However, we should never pause for very long, as there are always new territories to conquer. As in the past, when we found a need to offer more specialized catalogs such as the landmark *Standard Catalog of German Coins* and *Standard Catalog of World Crowns and Talers*, the classic *Standard Guide to South Asian Coins and Paper Money* and *Standard Catalog of World Coins – Spain, Portugal and the New World*, the refined *Standard Catalog of World Gold Coins*, the streamlined *Collecting World Coins*, our geographic *North American Coins & Prices*, the distinctive *Unusual World Coins*, our innovative *Coins & Currency of the Middle East*, or the most recent geographically oriented *Coins of Northern Europe and Russia*, we are always looking for new ways to better serve our shared hobby.

Our Web design team has developed NumisMaster, the first-ever online version of the Standard Catalog, which can be found at www.numismaster.com. This is due, in large part, to the enthusiastic input of our dedicated readers. Keep writing, we love to hear from you!

As we look towards the future, this new edition completed and out in use, we would like to take a moment to ask a favor of you, our readers. While you are using the various volumes of the Standard Catalog series, please keep in mind that this ever changing, developing and expanding series of numismatic reference books is really a living, breathing entity. It's a book that requires your attention and nurture. Watch over it carefully, keep and eye out for possible mistakes, errors and omissions. Look for an opportunity to participate in its expansion and refinement. Contact the editorial staff with your observations, additions and ideas.

Be a part of your hobby through the pages of the most recognized and respected world coin reference on the planet!

Best Wishes,
The Editorial Staff of the
Standard Catalog of World Coins

ACKNOWLEDGMENTS

Many individuals have contributed countless changes, which have been incorporated into previous and now this thirty seventh edition. While all may not be acknowledged, special appreciation is extended to the following who have exhibited a special enthusiasm for this edition.

Dr. Lawrence A. Adams
David Addey
Esko Ahlroth
Stephen Album
Antonio Alessandrini
Paul Baker
Oksana Bandrivska
Mitchell A. Battino
Albert Beck
Richard Benson
Peter N. Berger
Allen G. Berman
Joseph Boling
Al Boulanger
Klaus Bronny
Colin R. Bruce II
Mahdi Bseiso
John T. Bucek
Chris Budesa
Doru Calin
Charles R. Carlson
Henry K. H. Chan
Peter A. Chase
Scott E. Cordry
Luis V. Costa
Freeman Craig Jr.
Jerry Crain
Vincent Craven-Bartle
Jed Crump
Raymond E. Czahor
Howard A. Daniel III
Eric G. Dawson, M.D.
Konstantinos Dellios
Jean-Paul Divo
Yossi Dotan

James R. Douglas
Dr. Jan M. Dyroff
Stephen Eccles
Wilhelm R. Eglseer
Esko Ekman
Daniil Fishteyn
Andrzej Fischer
Thomas F. Fitzgerald
Joe Flores
Eugene Freeman
Arthur M. Friedberg
K. M. Froseth
Tom Galway
Dennis Gill
David R. Gotkin
Marcel Häberling
Flemming Lyngbeck Hansen
David Harrison
Martin Rodney Hayter
Istvan Hegedus
Anton Holt
Serge Huard
Nelva G. Icaza
Ton Jacobs
A. K. Jain
Hector Carlos Janson
Robert W. Julian
Børge R. Juul
Alex Kaglyan
John K. Kallman
Melvyn Kassenoff
Craig Keplinger
George Katsikis
Ronachai Krisadaolarn
Matti Kuronen

Samson Kin Chiu Lai
Joseph E. Lang
Thomas Lautz
Alex Lazarovici
Nirat Lertchitvikul
Richard Lobel
Rudi Lotter
Ma Tak Wo
Miguel Angel Pratt Mayans
Jürgen Mikeska
Juozas Minikevicius
Robert Mish
Ing. Benjamin M. Mizrachi R.
Dr. Richard Montrey
Paul Montz
Edward Moschetti
Horst-Dieter Müller
Arkady Nakhimovsky
N. Douglas Nicol
Michael G. Nielsen
Bill Noyes
Gus A. Pappas
Janusz Parchimowicz
Frank Passic
Marc Pelletier
Juan Pena
Jens Pilegaard
Gastone Polacco
Luis R. Ponte Puigbo
Richard Ponterio
Kent Ponterio
Martin Purdy
Frank Putrow
Yahya Qureshi
Mircea Raicopol

Dr. Dennis G. Rainey
Tony Raymond
Dana Roberts
William M. Rosenblum
Egon Conti Rossini
Remy Said
Leon Saryan
Erwin Schäffer
Gerhard Schön
Dr. Wolfgang Schuster
Alexander Shapiro
F. Ferreira da Silva
Ladislav Sin
Ole Sjoelund
Jorgen Sømod
Benjamin Swagerty
Steven Tan
Mehmet Tolga Taner
M. Louis Teller
Tonin Thaci
Frank Timmermann
Anthony Tumonis
J. J. Van Grover
Erik J. Van Loon
Carmen Viciedo
Wakim Wakim
Justin Wang
Paul Welz
Stewart Westdal
J. Brix Westergaard
J. Hugh Witherow
Joseph Zaffern

AUCTION HOUSES

Dixon-Noonan-Webb
Heritage World Coin Auctions
Hess-Divo Ltd.
Gerhard Hirsch

Thomas Høiland Møntauktion
Fritz Rudolf Künker
Leu Numismatik AG

Münzenhandlung Harald Möller, GmbH
Noble Numismatics, Pty. Ltd.
Ponterio & Associates

Stack's
UBS, AG
World Wide Coins of California

INTERNATIONAL SOCIETIES AND INSTITUTIONS

American Numismatic Association

American Numismatic Society
British Museum

Numismatics International

Smithsonian Institution

WORLD MINTS, CENTRAL BANKS AND DISTRIBUTORS

Austrian Mint
Banco de Mexico
Banque Centrale Du Luxembourg
Casa de la Moneda de Cuba
Central Bank of D.P.R. Korea - Kumbyol Trading Corp.
Central Bank of the Russian Fed.
CIT
Czech National Bank
Educational Coin Company
Faude & Huguenin
Global Coins & Medals Ltd. - Official Sales Company of the Bulgarian Mint
Imprensa Nacional - Casa da Moeda, S.A.

Israel Coins & Medals Corp.
Istituto Poligrafico e Zecca dello Stato I.p.A.
Jablonex Group - Division of Czech Mint
Japan Mint
Kazakhstan Mint
KOMSCO - South Korea
Latvijas Banka
Lietuvos Bankas
Lithuanian Mint
Magyar Penzvero Zrt.
MDM
Mennica Polska
Mincovna Kremnica
Mint of Finland, Ltd.
Mint of Norway

Monnaie de Paris
Moscow Mint
National Bank of the Republic of Belarus
National Bank of Ukraine
New Zealand Mint
New Zealand Post
Numiscom
Numistrade Gmbh & Co. kg.
Omni Trading B.V.
Perth Mint
Pobjoy Mint
Real Casa de la Moneda - Spain
Royal Mint
Royal Australian Mint
Royal Belgian Mint

Royal Canadian Mint
Royal Dutch Mint
Royal Thai Mint
Servei D'Emissions Principat D'Andorra
Singapore Mint
South African Mint
Staatliche Munze Berlin
Staatliche Munze Baden-Wurttemberg
Talisman Coins
Thailand Treasury Department
Ufficio Filatelico e Numismatico - Vatican
United States Mint

HOW TO USE THE CD

This CD is PC and Macintosh® compatible when used with Adobe Acrobat Reader® version 6.0 or later. A step-by-step free download of Adobe Acrobat Reader® 8 is available at www.adobe.com. Adobe Reader® 8 was used in creating the instructions that follow.

To help you successfully navigate through the PDF document, several types of searches are available.

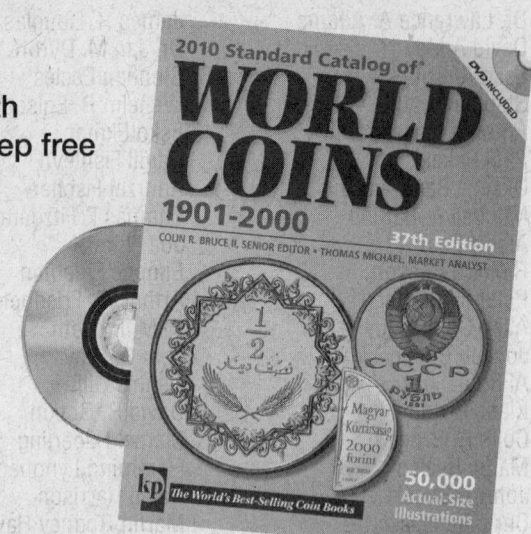

USING BOOKMARKS

Click on the Bookmarks icon to open the Bookmarks window. Use these links to go to specific points of interest. To scroll through pages in each section, use the arrows at the top of the screen (see next page for instructions to find page navigators).

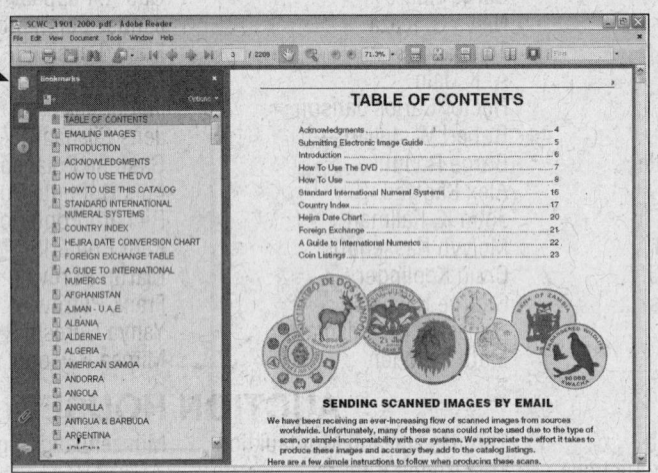

USING THE FIND BOX

Locate the find box in the tool bar and enter the word(s) you are searching for.

To navigate through the results of your search, use the Find Next icon.

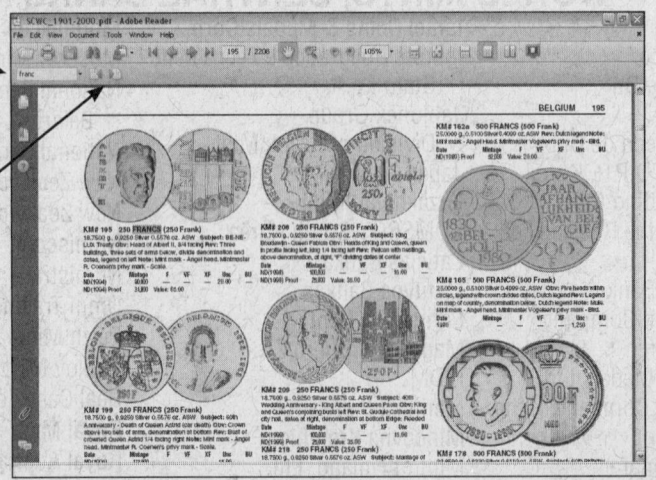

USING THE SEARCH OPTION

Locate the Search button by choosing Customize Toolbars in the Tools pull-down menu. Check Search (binocular icon) to have the Search option available in the toolbar.

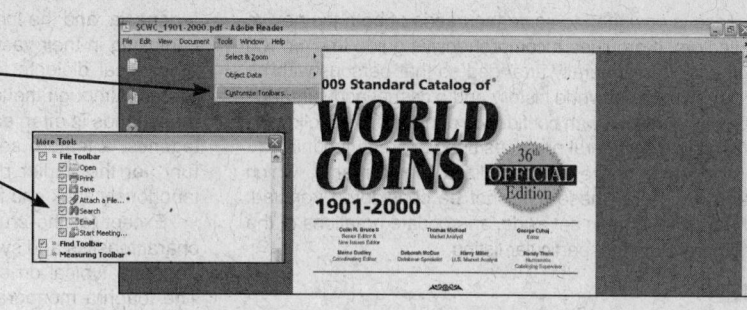

Click on the Search icon to open the Search dialog box.

In the Search dialog box, enter the word(s) you are searching for and click on the Search button.

The list of results will appear in the dialog box. Click on the listings to view each page that contains your searched word(s).

To begin a new word search, click on the New Search button.

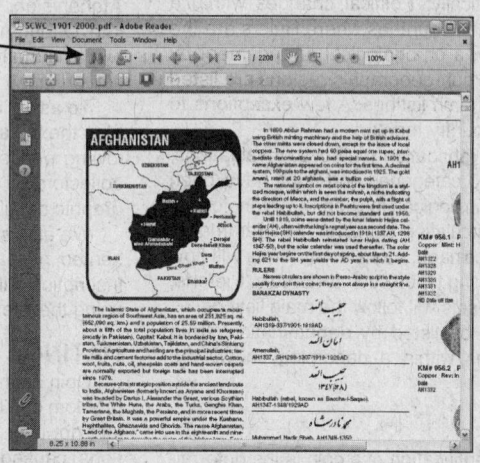

USING PAGE NAVIGATORS

Activate the Page Navigator Toolbar by choosing Customize Toolbars in the Tools pull-down menu. Check each tool as shown at right. You are now able to page through the PDF document by using the arrows at the top of the screen or by entering a page number you wish to view.

The Table of Contents is on page 3 and the Country Index starts on page 17.

You may also enlarge the images of the coins up to 400% for easy viewing

HOW TO USE THIS CATALOG

This catalog series is designed to serve the needs of both the novice and advanced collectors. It provides a comprehensive guide to over 100 years of world coinage. It is generally arranged so that persons with no more than a basic knowledge of world history and a casual acquaintance with coin collecting can consult it with confidence and ease. The following explanations summarize the general practices used in preparing this catalog's listings. However, because of specialized requirements, which may vary by country and era, these must not be considered ironclad. Where these standards have been set aside, appropriate notations of the variations are incorporated in that particular listing.

ARRANGEMENT

Countries are arranged alphabetically. Political changes within a country are arranged chronologically. In countries where Rulers are the single most significant political entity, a chronological arrangement by Ruler has been employed. Distinctive sub-geographic regions are listed alphabetically following the country's main listings. A few exceptions to these rules may exist. Refer to the Country Index.

Diverse coinage types relating to fabrication methods, revaluations, denomination systems, non-circulating categories and such have been identified, separated and arranged in logical fashion. Chronological arrangement is employed for most circulating coinage, i.e., Hammered coinage will normally precede Milled coinage, monetary reforms will flow in order of their institution. Non-circulating types such as Essais, Pieforts, Patterns, Trial Strikes, Mint and Proof sets will follow the main listings.

Within a coinage type coins will be listed by denomination, from smallest to largest. Numbered types within a denomination will be ordered by their first date of issue.

IDENTIFICATION

The most important step in the identification of a coin is the determination of the nation of origin. This is generally easily accomplished where English-speaking lands are concerned, however, use of the country index is sometimes required. The coins of Great Britain provide an interesting challenge. For hundreds of years the only indication of the country of origin was in the abbreviated Latin legends. In recent times there have been occasions when there has been no indication of origin. Only through the familiarity of the monarchical portraits, symbols and legends or indication of currency system are they identifiable.

The coins of many countries beyond the English-language realm, such as those of French, Italian or Spanish heritage, are also quite easy to identify through reference to their legends, which appear in the national languages based on Western alphabets. In many instances the name is spelled exactly the same in English as in the national language, such as France; while in other cases it varies only slightly, like Italia for Italy, Belgique or Belgie for Belgium, Brasil for Brazil and Danmark for Denmark.

This is not always the case, however, as in Norge for Norway, Espana for Spain, Sverige for Sweden and Helvetia for Switzerland. Some other examples include:

DEUTSCHES REICH - Germany 1873-1945

BUNDESREPUBLIC DEUTSCHLAND - Federal Republic of Germany.

DEUTSCHE DEMOKRATISCHE REPUBLIK -
German Democratic Republic.

EMPIRE CHERIFIEN MAROC - Morocco.

ESTADOS UNIDOS MEXICANOS - United Mexican States (Mexico).

ETAT DU GRAND LIBAN - State of Great Lebanon (Lebanon).

Thus it can be seen there are instances in which a little schooling in the rudiments of foreign languages can be most helpful. In general, colonial possessions of countries using the Western alphabet are similarly identifiable as they often carry portraits of their current rulers, the familiar lettering, sometimes in combination with a companion designation in the local language.

Collectors have the greatest difficulty with coins that do not bear legends or dates in the Western systems. These include coins bearing Cyrillic lettering attributable to Bulgaria, Russia, the Slavic states and Mongolia; the Greek script peculiar to Greece, Crete and the Ionian Islands; the Amharic characters of Ethiopia; or Hebrew in the case of Israel. Dragons and sunbursts along with the distinctive word characters attribute a coin to the Oriental countries of China, Japan, Korea, Tibet, Viet Nam and their component parts.

The most difficult coins to identify are those bearing only Persian or Arabic script and its derivatives, found on the issues of nations stretching in a wide swath across North Africa and East Asia, from Morocco to Indonesia, and the Indian subcontinent coinages which surely are more confusing in their vast array of Nagari, Sanskrit, Ahom, Assamese and other local dialects found on the local issues of the Indian Princely States. Although the task of identification on the more modern issues of these lands is often eased by the added presence of Western alphabet legends, a feature sometimes adopted as early as the late 19th Century, for the earlier pieces it is often necessary for the uninitiated to laboriously seek and find.

Except for the cruder issues, however, it will be found that certain characteristics and symbols featured in addition to the predominant legends are typical on coins from a given country or group of countries. The toughra monogram, for instance, occurs on some of the coins of Afghanistan, Egypt, the Sudan, Pakistan, Turkey and other areas of the late Ottoman Empire. A predominant design feature on the coins of Nepal is the trident; while neighboring Tibet features a lotus blossom or lion on many of their issues.

To assist in identification of the more difficult coins, we have assembled the Instant Identifier and Monogram sections presented on the following pages. They are designed to provide a point of beginning for collectors by allowing them to compare unidentified coins with photographic details from typical issues.

We also suggest reference to the Index of Coin Denominations presented here and also the comprehensive Country Index, where the inscription will be found listed just as it appears on the coin for nations using the Western alphabet.

DATING

Coin dating is the final basic attribution consideration. Here, the problem can be more difficult because the reading of a coin date is subject not only to the vagaries of numeric styling, but to calendar variations caused by the observance of various religious eras or regal periods from country to country, or even within a country. Here again, with the exception of the sphere from North Africa through the Orient, it will be found that most countries rely on Western date numerals and Christian (AD) era reckoning, although in a few instances, coin dating has been tied to the year of a reign or government. The Vatican, for example dates its coinage according to the year of reign of the current pope, in addition to the Christian-era date.

Countries in the Arabic sphere generally date their coins to the Muslim era (AH), which commenced on July 16, 622 AD (Julian calendar), when the prophet Mohammed fled from Mecca to Medina. As their calendar is reckoned by the lunar year of 354 days, which is about three percent (precisely 2.98%) shorter than the Christian year, a formula is required to convert AH dating to its Western equivalent. To convert an AH date to the approximate AD date, subtract three percent of the AH date (round to the closest whole number) from the AH date and add 622. A chart converting all AH years from 1010 (July 2, 1601) to 1450 (May 25, 2028) may be found elsewhere in the catalog under the name Hejira Date Chart.

The Muslim calendar is not always based on the lunar year (AH), however, causing some confusion, particularly in Afghanistan and Iran, where a calendar based on the solar year (SH) was introduced around 1920. These dates can be converted to AD by simply adding 621. In 1976 the government of Iran implemented a new solar calendar based on the foundation of the Iranian monarchy in 559 BC. The first year observed on the new calendar was 2535 (MS), which commenced March 20, 1976. A reversion to the traditional SH dating standard occurred a few years later.

Several different eras of reckoning, including Christian and Muslim (AH), have been used to date coins of the Indian subcontinent. The two basic systems are the Vikrama Samvat (VS), which dates from Oct. 18, 58 BC, and the Saka era, the origin of which is reckoned from March 3, 78 AD. Dating according to both eras appears on various coins of the area.

Coins of Thailand (Siam) are found dated by three different eras. The most predominant is the Buddhist era (BE), which originated in 543 BC. Next is the Bangkok or Ratanakosindsok (RS) era, dating from 1781 AD; followed by the Chula-Sakarat (CS) era, dating from 638 AD. The latter era originated in Burma and is used on that country's coins.

Other calendars include that of the Ethiopian era (EE), which commenced seven years, eight months after AD dating; and that of the Jewish people, which commenced on Oct. 7, 3761 BC. Korea claims a legendary dating from 2333 BC, which is acknowledged in some of its coin dating. Some coin issues of the Indonesian area carry dates determined by the Javanese Aji Saka era (AS), a calendar of 354 days (100

Javanese years equal 97 Christian or Gregorian calendar years), which can be matched to AD dating by comparing it to AH dating.

The following table indicates the year dating for the various eras, which correspond to 2009 in Christian calendar reckoning, but it must be remembered that there are overlaps between the eras in some instances.

Christian era (AD)	-2009
Muslim era (AH)	-AH1430
Solar year (SH)	-SH1387
Monarchic Solar era (MS)	-MS2568
Vikrama Samvat (VS)	-VS2066
Saka era (SE)	-SE1931
Buddhist era (BE)	-BE2552
Bangkok era (RS)	-RS228
Chula-Sakarat era (CS)	-CS1371
Ethiopian era (EE)	-EE2002
Korean era	-4342
Javanese Aji Saka era (AS)	-AS1942
Fasli era (FE)	-FE1419
Jewish era (JE)	-JE5769
Roman	-MMIX

Coins of Asian origin - principally Japan, Korea, China, Turkestan and Tibet and some modern gold issues of Turkey - are generally dated to the year of the government, dynasty, reign or cyclic eras, with the dates indicated in Asian characters which usually read from right to left. In recent years, however, some dating has been according to the Christian calendar and in Western numerals. In Japan, Asian character dating was reversed to read from left to right in Showa year 23 (1948 AD).

More detailed guides to less prevalent coin dating systems, which are strictly local in nature, are presented with the appropriate listings.

Some coins carry dates according to both locally observed and Christian eras. This is particularly true in the Arabic world, where the Hejira date may be indicated in Arabic numerals and the Christian date in Western numerals, or both dates in either form.

The date actually carried on a given coin is generally cataloged here in the first column (Date) to the right of the catalog number. If this date is by a non-Christian dating system, such as 'AH' (Muslim), the Christian equivalent date will appear in parentheses(), for example AH1336(1917). Dates listed alone in the date column which do not actually appear on a given coin, or dates which are known, but do not appear on the coin, are generally enclosed by parentheses with 'ND' at the left, for example ND(1926).

Timing differentials between some era of reckoning, particularly the 354-day Mohammedan and 365-day Christian years, cause situations whereby coins which carry dates for both eras exist bearing two year dates from one calendar combined with a single date from another.

Countermarked Coinage is presented with both 'Countermark Date' and 'Host Coin' date for each type. Actual date representation follows the rules outlined above.

NUMBERING SYSTEM

Some catalog numbers assigned in this volume are based on established references. This practice has been observed for two reasons: First, when world coins are listed chronologically they are basically self-cataloging; second, there was no need to confuse collectors with totally new numeric designations where appropriate systems already existed. As time progressed we found many of these established systems incomplete and inadequate and have now replaced many with new KM numbers. When numbers change appropriate cross-referencing has been provided.

Some of the coins listed in this catalog are identified or cross-referenced by numbers assigned by R.S. Yeoman (Y#), or slight adaptations thereof, in his Modern World Coins, and Current Coins of the World. For the pre-Yeoman dated issues, the numbers assigned by William D. Craig (C#) in his Coins of the World (1750-1850 period), 3rd edition, have generally been applied.

In some countries, listings are cross-referenced to Robert Friedberg's (FR#) Gold Coins of the World or Coins of the British World. Major Fred Pridmore's (P#) studies of British colonial coinage are also referenced, as are W.H. Valentine's (V#) references on the Modern Copper Coins of the Mohammedan States. Coins issued under the Chinese sphere of influence are assigned numbers from E. Kann's (K#) Illustrated Catalog of Chinese Coins and T.K. Hsu's (Su) work of similar title. In most cases, these cross-reference numbers are presented in the descriptive text for each type.

DENOMINATIONS

The second basic consideration to be met in the attribution of a coin is the determination of denomination. Since denominations are usually expressed in numeric rather than word form on a coin, this is usually quite easily accomplished on coins from nations which use Western numerals, except in those instances where issues are devoid of any mention of face value, and denomination must be attributed by size, metallic composition or weight. Coins listed in this volume are generally illustrated in actual size. Where size is critical to proper attribution, the coin's millimeter size is indicated.

The sphere of countries stretching from North Africa through the Orient, on which numeric symbols generally unfamiliar to Westerners are employed, often provide the collector with a much greater challenge. This is particularly true on nearly all pre-20th Century issues. On some of the more modern issues and increasingly so as the years progress, Western-style numerals usually presented in combination with the local numeric system are becoming more commonplace on these coins.

Determination of a coin's currency system can also be valuable in attributing the issue to its country of origin. A comprehensive alphabetical index of currency names, applicable to the countries as cataloged in this volume, with all individual nations of use for each, is presented in this section.

The included table of Standard International Numeral Systems presents charts of the basic numeric designations found on coins of non-Western origin. Although denomination numerals are generally prominently displayed on coins, it must be remembered that these are general representations of characters, which individual coin engravers may have rendered in widely varying styles. Where numeric or script denominations designation forms peculiar to a given coin or country apply, such as the script used on some Persian (Iranian) issues. They are so indicated or illustrated in conjunction with the appropriate listings.

MINTAGES

Quantities minted of each date are indicated where that information is available, generally stated in millions or rounded off to the nearest 10,000 pieces when more exact figures are not available. On quantities of a few thousand or less, actual mintages are generally indicated. For combined mintage figures the abbreviation "Inc. Above" means Included Above, while "Inc. Below" means Included Below. "Est." beside a mintage figure indicates the number given is an estimate or mintage limit.

MINT AND PRIVY MARKS

The presence of distinctive, but frequently inconspicuously placed, mintmarks indicates the mint of issue for many of the coins listed in this catalog. An appropriate designation in the date listings notes the presence, if any, of a mint mark on a particular coin type by incorporating the letter or letters of the mint mark adjoining the date, i.e., 1950D or 1927R.

The presence of mint and/or mintmaster's privy marks on a coin in non-letter form is indicated by incorporating the mint letter in lower case within parentheses adjoining the date; i.e. 1927(a). The corresponding mark is illustrated or identified in the introduction of the country.

In countries such as France and Mexico, where many mints may be producing like coinage in the same denomination during the same time period, divisions by mint have been employed. In these cases the mint mark may appear next to the individual date listings and/or the mint name or mint mark may be listed in the Note field of the type description.

Where listings incorporate mintmaster initials, they are always presented in capital letters separated from the date by one character space; i.e., 1850 MF. The different mintmark and mintmaster letters found on the coins of any country, state or city of issue are always shown at the beginning of listings.

METALS

Each numbered type listing will contain a description of the coins metallic content. The traditional coinage metals and their symbolic chemical abbreviations sometimes used in this catalog are:

Platinum - (PT)	Copper - (Cu)
Gold - (Au)	Brass -
Silver - (Ag)	Copper-nickel- (CN)
Billion -	Lead - (Pb)
Nickel - (Ni)	Steel -
Zinc - (Zn)	Tin - (Sn)
Bronze - (Ae)	Aluminum - (Al)

During the 18th and 19th centuries, most of the world's coins were struck of copper or bronze, silver and gold. Commencing in the early years of the 20th century, however, numerous new coinage metals, primarily non-precious metal alloys, were introduced. Gold has not been widely used for circulation coinages since World War I, although silver remained a popular coinage metal in most parts of the world until after World War II. With the disappearance of silver for circulation coinage, numerous additional compositions were introduced to coinage applications.

Most recent is the development of clad or plated planchets in order to maintain circulation life and extend the life of a set of production dies as used in the production of the copper-nickel clad copper 50 centesimos of Panama or in the latter case to reduce production costs of the planchets and yet provide a coin quite similar in appearance to its predecessor as in the case of the copper plated zinc core United States 1983 cent.

Modern commemorative coins have employed still more unusual methods such as bimetallic coins, color applications and precious metal or gem inlays.

OFF-METAL STRIKES

Off-metal strikes previously designated by "(OMS)" which also included the wide range of error coinage struck in other than their officially authorized compositions have been incorporated into Pattern listings along with special issues, which were struck for presentation or other reasons.

Collectors of Germanic coinage may be familiar with the term "Abschlag" which quickly identifies similar types of coinage.

PRECIOUS METAL WEIGHTS

Listings of weight, fineness and actual silver (ASW), gold (AGW), platinum or palladium (APW) content of most machine-struck silver, gold, platinum and palladium coins are provided in this edition. This information will be found incorporated in each separate type listing, along with other data related to the coin.

The ASW, AGW and APW figures were determined by multiplying the gross weight of a given coin by its known or tested fineness and converting the resulting gram or grain weight to troy ounces, rounded to the nearest ten-thousandth of an ounce. A silver coin with a 24.25-gram weight and .875 fineness for example, would have a fine weight of approximately 21.2188 grams, or a .6822 ASW, a factor that can be used to accurately determine the intrinsic value for multiple examples.

The ASW, AGW or APW figure can be multiplied by the spot price of each precious metal to determine the current intrinsic value of any coin accompanied by these designations.

Coin weights are indicated in grams (abbreviated "g") along with fineness where the information is of value in differentiating between types. These weights are based on 31.103 grams per troy (scientific) ounce, as opposed to the avoirdupois (commercial) standard of 28.35 grams. Actual coin weights are generally shown in hundredths or thousands of a gram; i.e., 0.500 SILVER 2.9200g.WEIGHTS AND FINENESSES

As the silver and gold bullion markets have advanced and declined sharply over the years, the fineness and total precious metal content of coins has become especially significant where bullion coins - issues which trade on the basis of their intrinsic metallic content rather than numismatic value - are concerned. In many instances, such issues have become worth more in bullion form than their nominal collector values or denominations indicate.

Establishing the weight of a coin can also be valuable for determining its denomination. Actual weight is also necessary to ascertain the specific gravity of the coin's metallic content, an important factor in determining authenticity.

TROY WEIGHT STANDARDS
24 Grains = 1 Pennyweight
480 Grains = 1 Ounce
31.103 Grams = 1 Ounce

UNIFORM WEIGHTS
15.432 Grains = 1 Gram
0.0648 Gram = 1 Grain

AVOIRDUPOIS STANDARDS
27-11/32 Grains = 11 Dram
437-1/2 Grains = 1 Ounce
28.350 Grams = 1 Ounce

BULLION VALUE

The simplest method for determining the bullion value of a precious metal coin is to multiply the actual precious metal weight by the current spot price for that metal. Using the example above, a silver coin with a .6822 actual silver weight (ASW) would have an intrinsic value of $7.85 when the spot price of silver is $11.50. If the spot price of silver rose to $17.95 that same coins intrinsic value would rise to $12.25.

HOMELAND TYPES

Homeland types are coins which colonial powers used in a colony, but do not bear that location's name. In some cases they were legal tender in the homeland, in others not. They are listed under the homeland and cross-referenced at the colony listing.

COUNTERMARKS/COUNTERSTAMPS

There is some confusion among collectors over the terms "countermark" and "counterstamp" when applied to a coin bearing an additional mark or change of design and/or denomination.

To clarify, a countermark might be considered similar to the "hall mark" applied to a piece of silverware, by which a silversmith assured the quality of the piece. In the same way, a countermark assures the quality of the coin on which it is placed, as, for example, when the royal crown of England was countermarked (punched into) on segmented Spanish reales, allowing them to circulate in commerce in the British West Indies. An additional countermark indicating the new denomination may also be encountered on these coins.

Coin Alignment   **Medal Alignment**

COIN vs MEDAL ALIGNMENT

Some coins are struck with obverse and reverse aligned at a rotation of 180 degrees from each other. When a coin is held for vertical viewing with the obverse design aligned upright and the index finger and thumb at the top and bottom, upon rotation from left to right for viewing the reverse, the latter will be upside down. Such alignment is called "coin rotation." Other coins are struck with the obverse and reverse designs mated on an alignment of zero or 360 degrees. If such an example is held and rotated as described, the reverse will appear upright. This is the alignment, which is generally observed in the striking of medals, and for that reason coins produced in this manner are considered struck in "medal rotation". In some instances, often through error, certain coin issues have been struck to both alignment standards, creating interesting collectible varieties, which will be found noted in some listings. In addition, some countries are now producing coins with other designated obverse to reverse alignments which are considered standard for this type.

Countermarks are generally applied singularly and in most cases indiscriminately on either side of the "host" coin.

Counterstamped coins are more extensively altered. The counterstamping is done with a set of dies, rather than a hand punch. The coin being counterstamped is placed between the new dies and struck as if it were a blank planchet as found with the Manila 8 reales issue of the Philippines. A more unusual application where the counterstamp dies were smaller than the host coin in the revalidated 50 centimos and 1 colon of Costa Rica issued in 1923.

PHOTOGRAPHS

To assist the reader in coin identification, every effort has been made to present actual size photographs of every coinage type listed. Obverse and reverse are illustrated, except when a change in design is restricted to one side, and the coin has a diameter of 39mm or larger, in which case only the side required for identification of the type is generally illustrated. All coins up to 60mm are illustrated actual size, to the nearest 1/2mm up to 25mm, and to the nearest 1mm thereafter. Coins larger than 60mm diameter are illustrated in reduced size, with the actual size noted in the descriptive text block. Where slight change in size is important to coin type identification, actual millimeter measurements are stated.

TRADE COINS

From approximately 1750-1940, a number of nations, particularly European colonial powers and commercial traders, minted trade coins to facilitate commerce with the local populace of Africa, the Arab countries, the Indian subcontinental, Southeast Asia and the Far East. Such coins generally circulated at a value based on the weight and fineness of their silver or gold content, rather than their stated denomination. Examples include the sovereigns of Great Britain and the gold ducat issues of Austria, Hungary and the Netherlands. Trade coinage will sometimes be found listed at the end of the domestic issues.

VALUATIONS

Values quoted in this catalog represent the current market and are compiled from recommendations provided and verified through various source documents and specialized consultants. It should be stressed, however, that this book is intended to serve only as an aid for evaluating coins, actual market conditions are constantly changing and additional influences, such as particularly strong local demand for certain coin series, fluctuation of international exchange rates, changes in spot price of precious metals and worldwide collection patterns must also be considered. Publication of this catalog is not intended as a solicitation by the publisher, editors or contributors to buy or sell the coins listed at the prices indicated.

All valuations are stated in U.S. dollars, based on careful assessment of the varied international collector market. Valuations for coins priced below $100.00 are generally stated in full amounts - i.e. 37.50 or 95.00 - while valuations at or above that figure are rounded off in even dollars - i.e. $125.00 is expressed 125. A comma is added to indicate thousands of dollars in value.

For the convenience of overseas collectors and for U.S. collectors doing business with overseas dealers, the base exchange rate for the national currencies of approximately 180 countries are presented in the Foreign Exchange Table.

It should be noted that when particularly select uncirculated or proof-like examples of uncirculated coins become available they can be expected to command proportionately high premiums. Such examples in reference to choice Germanic Thalers are referred to as "erst schlage" or first strikes.

MEDALLIC ISSUES

Medallic issues are similar to coin-type issues and can generally be identified as commemoratives produced to the country's established coinage standards but without the usual indicator of denomination. These pieces sometimes feature designs adapted from the country's regular issue or commemorative coinage, and occassionally have been issued in conjunction with related coinage issues. Medallic issues,

though bearing these similarites to coinage issues, are not coins and therefore are **not** listed in this catalog, but can be found in the companion catalog Unusual World Coins.

RESTRIKES, COUNTERFEITS

Deceptive restrike and counterfeit (both contemporary and modern) examples exist of some coin issues. Where possible, the existence of restrikes is noted. Warnings are also incorporated in instances where particularly deceptive counterfeits are known to exist. Collectors who are uncertain about the authenticity of a coin held in their collection, or being offered for sale, should take the precaution of having it authenticated by the American Numismatic Association Authentication Bureau, 818 N. Cascade, Colorado Springs, CO 80903. Their reasonably priced certification tests are widely accepted by collectors and dealers alike.

NON-CIRCULATING LEGAL TENDER COINS

Coins of non-circulating legal tender (NCLT) origin are individually listed and integrated by denomination into the regular listings for each country. These coins fall outside the customary definitions of coin-of-the-realm issues, but where created and sold by, or under authorization of, agencies of sovereign governments expressly for collectors. These are primarily individual coins and sets of a commemorative nature, marketed at prices substantially in excess of face value, and usually do not have counterparts released for circulation.

EDGE VARIETIES

NEW ISSUES

All newly released coins dated up to the year 2000 that have been physically observed by our staff or identified by reliable sources and have been confirmed by press time have been incorporated in this edition. Exceptions exist in some countries where current date coin production lags far behind or information on current issues is less accessible.

SETS

Listings in this catalog for specimen, proof and mint sets are for official, government-produced sets. In many instances privately packaged sets also exist.

Mint Sets/Fleur de Coin Sets: Specially prepared by worldwide mints to provide banks, collectors and government dignitaries with examples of current coinage. Usually subjected to rigorous inspection to insure that top quality specimens of selected business strikes are provided. One of the most popular mint set is that given out by the monarch of Great Britain each year on Maunday Thursday. This set contains four special coins in denominations of 1, 2, 3 and 4 pence, struck in silver and contained in a little pouch. They have been given away in a special ceremony for the poor for more than two centuries.

The Paris Mint introduced polyvinyl plastic cases packed within a cardboard box for homeland and colonial Fleur de Coin sets of the 1960s. British colonial sets were issued in velvet-lined metal cases similar to those used for proof sets. For its client nations, the Franklin Mint introduced a sealed composition of cardboard and specially molded hard clear plastic protective container inserted in a soft plastic wallet. Recent discovery that soft polyvinyl packaging has proved hazardous to coins has resulted in a change to the use of hard, inert plastics for virtually all mint sets.

Some of the highest quality mint sets ever produced were those struck by the Franklin Mint during 1972-74. In many cases matte finish dies were used to strike a polished proof planchet. Later on, from 1975, sets contained highly polished, glassy-looking coins (similar to those struck by the Bombay Mint) for collectors over a period of 12 years.

Specimen Sets: Forerunners of today's proof sets. In most cases the coins were specially struck, perhaps even double struck, to produce a very soft or matte finish on the effigies and fields, along with high, sharp, "wire" rims. The finish is rather dull to the naked eye.

The original purpose of these sets was to provide VIPs, monarchs and mintmasters around the world with samples of the highest quality workmanship of a particular mint. These were usually housed in elaborate velvet-lined leather and metal cases.

Proof-like Sets are relatively new to the field of numismatics. During the mid 1950s the Royal Canadian Mint furnished the hobby with specially selected early business strike coins that exhibited some qualities similar to proof coinage. However, the "proof-like" fields are generally flawed and the edges are rounded. These pieces are not double struck. These are commonly encountered in cardboard holders, later in soft plastic or pliofilm packaging. Of late, the Royal Canadian Mint packages such sets in rigid plastic cases.

Many worldwide officially issued proof sets would in reality fall into this category upon careful examination of the quality of the coin's finish.

Another term encountered in this category is "Special Select," used to describe the crowns of the Union of South Africa and 100-schilling coins produced for collectors in the late 1970s by the Austrian Mint.

Proof Sets: This is undoubtedly among the most misused terms in the hobby, not only by collectors and dealers, but also by many of the world mints.

A true proof set must be at least double-struck on specially prepared polished planchets and struck using dies (often themselves polished) of the highest quality.

Modern-day proof quality consists of frosted effigies surrounded by absolute mirror-like fields.

Listings for proof sets in this catalog are for officially issued proof sets so designated by the issuing authority, and may or may not possess what are considered modern proof quality standards.

It is necessary for collectors to acquire the knowledge to allow them to differentiate true proof sets from would-be proof sets and proof-like sets which may be encountered.

CONDITIONS/GRADING

Wherever possible, coin valuations are given in four or five grades of preservation. For modern commemoratives, which do not circulate, only uncirculated values are usually sufficient. Proof issues are indicated by the word "Proof" next to the date, with valuation proceeded by the word "value" following the mintage. For very recent circulating coins and coins of limited value, one, two or three grade values are presented.

There are almost no grading guides for world coins. What follows is an attempt to help bridge that gap until a detailed, illustrated guide becomes available.

In grading world coins, there are two elements to look for: 1) Overall wear, and 2) loss of design details, such as strands of hair, feathers on eagles, designs on coats of arms, etc.

The age, rarity or type of a coin should not be a consideration in grading.

Grade each coin by the weaker of the two sides. This method appears to give results most nearly consistent with conservative American Numismatic Association standards for U.S. coins. Split grades, i.e., F/VF for obverse and reverse, respectively, are normally no more than one grade apart. If the two sides are more than one grade apart, the series of coins probably wears differently on each side and should then be graded by the weaker side alone.

Grade by the amount of overall wear and loss of design detail evident on each side of the coin. On coins with a moderately small design element, which is prone to early wear, grade by that design alone. For example, the 5-ore (KM#554) of Sweden has a crown above the monogram on which the beads on the arches show wear most clearly. So, grade by the crown alone.

For **Brilliant Uncirculated** (BU) grades there will be no visible signs of wear or handling, even under a 30-power microscope. Full mint luster will be present. Ideally no bags marks will be evident.

For **Uncirculated** (Unc.) grades there will be no visible signs of wear or handling, even under a 30-power microscope. Bag marks may be present.

For **Almost Uncirculated** (AU), all detail will be visible. There will be wear only on the highest point of the coin. There will often be half or more of the original mint luster present.

On the **Extremely Fine** (XF or EF) coin, there will be about 95% of the original detail visible. Or, on a coin with a design with no inner detail to wear down, there will be a light wear over nearly all the coin. If a small design is used as the grading area, about 90% of the original detail will be visible. This latter rule stems from the logic that a smaller amount of detail needs to be present because a small area is being used to grade the whole coin.

The **Very Fine** (VF) coin will have about 75% of the original detail visible. Or, on a coin with no inner detail, there will be moderate wear over the entire coin. Corners of letters and numbers may be weak. A small grading area will have about 66% of the original detail.

For **Fine** (F), there will be about 50% of the original detail visible. Or, on a coin with no inner detail, there will be fairly heavy wear over all of the coin. Sides of letters will be weak. A typically uncleaned coin will often appear as dirty or dull. A small grading area will have just under 50% of the original detail.

On the **Very Good** (VG) coin, there will be about 25% of the original detail visible. There will be heavy wear on all of the coin.

The **Good** (G) coin's design will be clearly outlined but with substantial wear. Some of the larger detail may be visible. The rim may have a few weak spots of wear.

On the **About Good** (AG) coin, there will typically be only a silhouette of a large design. The rim will be worn down into the letters if any.

Strong or weak strikes, partially weak strikes, damage, corrosion, attractive or unattractive toning, dipping or cleaning should be described along with the above grades. These factors affect the quality of the coin just as do wear and loss of detail, but are easier to describe.

In the case of countermarked/counterstamped coins, the condition of the host coin will have a bearing on the end valuation. The important factor in determining the grade is the condition, clarity and completeness of the countermark itself. This is in reference to countermarks/counterstamps having raised design while being struck in a depression.

Incuse countermarks cannot be graded for wear. They are graded by the clarity and completeness including the condition of the host coin which will also have more bearing on the final grade/valuation determined.

SENDING SCANNED IMAGES BY EMAIL

We have been receiving an ever-increasing flow of scanned images from sources worldwide. Unfortunately, many of these scans could not be used due to the type of scan, or simple incompatability with our systems. We appreciate the effort it takes to produce these images and accuracy they add to the catalog listings.

Here are a few simple instructions to follow when producing these scans. We encourage you to continue sending new images or upgrades to those currently illustrated and please do not hesitate to ask questions about this process.

- Scan all images within a resolution range of 200 dpi to 300 dpi
- Size setting should be at 100%
- Scan in true 4-color
- Save images as 'jpeg' or 'tif' and name in such a way,

which clearly identifies the country of origin and diameter size of coin in millimeters (mm)

- Please email with a request to confirm receipt of the attachment
- Please send images to Tom.Michael@fwpubs.com

STANDARD INTERNATIONAL NUMERAL SYSTEMS

Prepared especially for the *Standard Catalog of World Coins*© 2008 by Krause Publications

Western	0	½	1	2	3	4	5	6	7	8	9	10	50	100	500	1000
Roman			I	II	III	IV	V	VI	VII	VIII	IX	X	L	C	D	M
Arabic-Turkish	٠	١/٢	١	٢	٣	٤	٥	٦	٧	٨	٩	١٠	٥٠	١٠٠	٥٠٠	١٠٠٠
Malay-Persian	۰	١/٢	۱	۲	۳	۴	۵	۶	۷	۸	۹	۱۰	۵۰	۱۰۰	۵۰۰	۱۰۰۰
Eastern Arabic	٥	½	١	٢	٣	٤	٥	٦	٧	٩	٩	١٠	٥١٠	١٠٠	٥١٠٠	١٠٠٠
Hyderabad Arabic	٥	١/٢	١	٢	٣	٤	٥	٤	٧	٨	٩	١٠	٥٠	١٠٠	٥٠٠	١٠٠٠
Indian (Sanskrit)	०	½	१	२	३	४	५	६	७	८	९	१०	५०	१००	५००	१०००
Assamese	০	d/2	১	২	৩	৪	৫	৬	৭	৮	৯	১০	৫০	১০০	৫০০	১০০০
Bengali	০	১/২	১	২	৩	৪	৫	৬	৭	৮	৯	১০	৫০	১০০	৫০০	১০০০
Gujarati	૦	૧/૨	૧	૨	૩	૪	૫	૬	૭	૮	૯	૧૦	૪૦	૧૦૦	૪૦૦	૧૦૦૦
Kutch	૦	½	૧	૨	૩	૪	૫	૬	૭	૮	૯	૧૦	૪૦	૧૦૦	૪૦૦	૧૦૦૦
Devavnagri	०	½	१	२	३	४	५	६	७	८	९	१०	४०	१००	४००	१०००
Nepalese	०	½	१	२	३	४	५	६	७	८	९	१०	४०	१००	४००	१०००
Tibetan	༠	½	༡	༢	༣	༤	༥	༦	༧	༨	༩	༧༠	༤༠	༧༠༠	༤༠༠	༧༠༠༠
Mongolian	༠	½	༡	༢	༣	༤	༥	༦	༧	༨	༩	༡༠	༥༠	༡༠༠	༥༠༠	༡༠༠༠
Burmese	၀	⅔	၁	၂	၃	၄	၅	၆	၇	၈	၉	၁၀	၅၀	၁၀၀	၅၀၀	၁၀၀၀
Thai-Lao	๐	½	๑	๒	๓	๔	๕	๖	๗	๘	๙	๑๐	๕๐	๑๐๐	๕๐๐	๑๐๐๐
Lao-Laotian	໐		໑	໒	໓	໔	໕	໖	໗	໘	໙	໑໐				
Javanese	꧐		꧑	꧒	꧓	꧔	꧕	꧖	꧗	꧘	꧙	꧑꧐	꧕꧐	꧑꧐꧐	꧕꧐꧐	꧑꧐꧐꧐
Ordinary Chinese Japanese-Korean	零	半	一	二	三	四	五	六	七	八	九	十	十五	百	百五	千
Official Chinese			壹	貳	叁	肆	伍	陸	柒	捌	玖	拾	拾伍	佰	佰伍	仟
Commercial Chinese			〡	〢	〣	〤	〥	〦	〧	〨	〩	十	〥十	一百	〥百	一千
Korean		반	일	이	삼	사	오	육	칠	팔	구	십	오십	백	오백	천

Georgian

	1	2	3	4	5	6	7	8	9	10	50	100	500	1000
	ა	ბ	გ	დ	ე	ვ	ზ	ჱ	თ	ი	ნ	რ	ჩ	ჰ
	11 ⟨20⟩	20	30	40	60	70	80	90	200	300	400	600	700	800

Ethiopian

0	1	2	3	4	5	6	7	8	9	10	50	100	500	1000
◆	፩	፪	፫	፬	፭	፮	፯	፰	፱	፲	፶	፻	፭፻	፲፻
	20 ፳	30 ፴	40 ፵	60 ፷	70 ፸	80 ፹	90 ፺							

Hebrew

1	2	3	4	5	6	7	8	9	10	50	100	500	1000
א	ב	ג	ד	ה	ו	ז	ח	ט	י	נ	ק	תק	תת
20 כ	30 ל	40 מ	60 ס	70 ע	80 פ	90 צ	200 ר	300 ש	400 ת	600 תר	700 תש	800 תת	

Greek

1	2	3	4	5	6	7	8	9	10	50	100	500	1000
Α	Β	Γ	Δ	Ε	Ζ	Η	Θ	Ι	Ν	Ρ	Φ	Α	
20 Κ	30 Λ	40 Μ	60 Ξ	70 Ο	80 Π	200 Σ	300 Τ	400 Υ	600 Χ	700 Ψ	800 Ω		

COUNTRY INDEX

Afghanistan ... 19	British Honduras ... 246	Danzig ... 664
Aguascalientes ... 1467	British North Borneo ... 248	Darfur ... 1959
Ajman ... 31	British Virgin Islands ... 248	Datia ... 1060
Albania ... 34	British West Africa ... 262	Denmark ... 665
Alderney ... 41	Brunei ... 267	Dewas ... 1060
Algeria ... 43	Brunswick-Wolfenbuttel ... 837	Djibouti ... 677
American Samoa ... 48	Bukhara ... 352	Dominica ... 679
Ametlla del Valles ... 1944	Bulgaria ... 271	Dominican Republic ... 681
Andorra ... 49	Bundi ... 1058	Dungarpur ... 1060
Angola ... 60	Burundi ... 287	Durango ... 1469
Anguilla ... 63	Cambay ... 1059	East Africa ... 688
Anhalt-Dessau ... 833	Cambodia ... 289	East Caribbean States ... 692
Anhwei Province ... 378	Cameroon ... 292	East Hopei ... 448
Antigua & Barbuda ... 65	Canada ... 295	Ecuador ... 696
Antigua ... 65	Canada, Newfoundland ... 335	Egypt ... 700
Arahal ... 1944	Cape Verde ... 337	El Salvador ... 736
Arenys de Mar ... 1944	Catamarca ... 73	Empire ... 368
Argentina ... 65	Cayman Islands ... 340	Equatorial African States ... 741
Armavir ... 1791	Cazalla De La Sierra ... 1945	Equatorial Guinea ... 741
Armenia ... 73	Central African Republic ... 350	Eritrea ... 749
Aruba ... 77	Central African States ... 351	Estonia ... 752
Ascension Island ... 79	Central Asia ... 352	Ethiopia ... 754
Asturias & Leon ... 1944	Ceylon ... 355	Euzkadi ... 1945
Australia ... 81	Chad ... 358	Faeroe Islands ... 759
Austria ... 122	Chekiang Province ... 380	Falkland Islands ... 759
Azerbaijan ... 144	Chihli Province ... 381	Fengtien Province ... 384
Azores ... 145	Chihuahua ... 1468	Fiji ... 767
Baden ... 834	Chile ... 360	Finland ... 774
Bahamas ... 146	China ... 368	France ... 783
Bahawalpur ... 1057	China, Japanese Puppet States ... 448	French Afars & Issas ... 816
Bahrain ... 162	China, People's Republic ... 450	French Equatorial Africa ... 817
Bangladesh ... 164	China, Republic ... 437	French Indo-China ... 817
Barbados ... 166	Chinese Soviet Republic ... 518	French Oceania ... 820
Baroda ... 1057	Colombia ... 521	French Polynesia ... 820
Bavaria ... 835	Comoros ... 531	French Somaliland ... 822
Belarus ... 172	Congo Free State ... 533	French West Africa ... 823
Belgian Congo ... 175	Congo Republic ... 533	Fujairah ... 823
Belgium ... 177	Congo, Democratic Republic ... 537	Fukien Province ... 385
Belize ... 194	Cook Islands ... 542	Gabon ... 825
Benin ... 202	Costa Rica ... 572	Gambia ... 826
Bermuda ... 205	Crete ... 580	Georgia ... 831
Bhaunagar ... 1058	Croatia ... 581	German, Democratic Republic ... 884
Bhutan ... 214	Cuba ... 588	German East Africa ... 832
Biafra ... 222	Culion Island ... 1667	German States ... 833
Bohemia & Moravia ... 223	Curacao ... 637	Germany, Empire ... 850
Bolivia ... 223	Cyprus ... 638	Germany, Federal Republic ... 864
Bosnia-Herzegovina ... 226	Czech Republic ... 644	Germany, Third Reich ... 860
Botswana ... 231	Czechoslovakia ... 648	Germany, Weimar Republic ... 854
Brazil ... 234	Dahomey ... 661	Ghana ... 896
Bremen ... 838	Danish West Indies ... 663	Ghent ... 193

Gibraltar 898
Gratallops 1945
Great Britain 952
Greece 977
Greenland 985
Grenada 987
Guadeloupe 987
Guatemala 987
Guernsey 993
Guerrero 1470
Guinea 1001
Guinea-Bissau 1005
Guyana 1008
Gwalior 1060
Haiti 1010
Hamburg 838
Heilungkiang Province 387
Hejaz & Nejd Sultanate 1843
Hejaz & Nejd 1843
Hejaz 1019
Hesse-Darmstadt 839
Honan Province 387
Honduras 1020
Hong Kong 1023
Hsiang-o-hsi Soviet 519
Hunan Province 390
Hunan Soviet 519
Hungary 1029
Hupeh Province 395
Hupeh-Honan-Anwhei Soviet 519
Hyderabad 1061
Ibi 1945
Iceland 1051
India, British 1081
India, Portuguese 1079
India, Princely States 1056
India, Republic 1090
Indonesia 1109
Indore 1064
Iran 1113
Iraq 1130
Ireland (Eire) 1135
Irian Barat 1112
Isle of Man 1139
Israel 1212
Italian Somaliland 1238
Italy 1239
Ivory Coast 1255
Jaipur 1065
Jalisco 1473
Jamaica 1255
Japan 1269
Jersey 1281

Jodhpur 1067
Jordan 1289
Junagadh 1069
Kansu Province 398
Katanga 1295
Kazakhstan 1295
Keeling (Cocos) Islands 1298
Kelantan 1400
Kenya 1299
Khiva 353
Kiangnan Province 399
Kiangsi Province 403
Kiangsu-Chingkiang Province 405
Kiangsu-Kiangsoo Province 406
Kiau Chau 1301
Kiribati 1301
Kirin Province 407
Kishangarh 1070
Korea 1304
Korea-North 1306
Korea-South 1322
Kotah 1071
Kutch 1071
Kuwait 1329
Kwangsi-Kwangsea 410
Kwangtung Province 411
Kweichow Province 412
Kyrgyzstan 1332
La Rioja 73
Lao 1332
Latvia 1338
Lebanon 1342
Leper Colonies of Venezuela 2207
Lesotho 1344
Liberia 1349
Libya 1376
Liechtenstein 1378
Lippe-Detmold 839
Lithuania 1379
Lora del Rio 1945
Lubeck 840
Lunavada 1074
Luxembourg 1383
Macao 1388
Macedonia 1393
Madagascar 1395
Madeira Islands 1397
Malawi 1397
Malay Peninsula 1400
Malaya & British Borneo 1402
Malaya 1401
Malaysia 1403
Maldive Islands 1408

Maler Kotla 1074
Mali 1413
Malta 1414
Manchoukuo 448
Manchurian Provinces 413
Marchena 1945
Marshall Islands 1422
Martinique 1441
Mauritania 1441
Mauritius 1442
Mecklenburg-Schwerin 840
Mecklenburg-Strelitz 841
Meng Chiang 450
Menorca 1945
Mewar 1075
Mexico 1446
Mexico, Estado de 1473
Mexico, Revolutionary 1467
Moldova 1480
Monaco 1481
Mongolia 1484
Montenegro 1494
Montserrat 1496
Morelos 1475
Morocco 1496
Mozambique 1504
Muscat & Oman 1509
Myanmar 1511
Nagorno-Karabakh 1514
Namibia 1515
Nauru 1516
Nepal 1517
Netherlands Antilles 1551
Netherlands East Indies 1556
Netherlands 1541
Newfoundland 335
New Caledonia 1558
New Guinea 1559
New Hebrides 1560
New Zealand 1561
Nicaragua 1576
Niger 1582
Nigeria 1583
Niue 1584
North Korea 1306
North Viet Nam 2209
Norway 1592
Nulles 1946
Oaxaca 1475
Oldenburg 841
Olot 1946
Oman 1602
P'ing Chiang County Soviet 519

Pakistan	1609	Saxe-Meiningen	844	Tatarstan	1999
Palau	1614	Saxe-Weimar-Eisenach	845	Thailand	1999
Palestine	1618	Saxony	846	Thule-Kap York	986
Palo Seco	1630	Schaumburg-Lippe	848	Tibet	2022
Panama	1619	Schleswig-Holstein	848	Timor	2030
Papua New Guinea	1630	Schwarzburg-Rudolstadt	848	Togo	2031
Paraguay	1634	Schwarzburg-Sondershausen	848	Tokelau Islands	2032
Patiala	1076	Segarra de Gaia	1946	Tonga	2035
Peru	1645	Senegal	1847	Tonk	1077
Philippines	1657	Serbia	1848	Tonkin	2047
Pitcairn Islands	1668	Seychelles	1849	Transnistria	2047
Poland	1669	Shansi Province	414	Travancore	1077
Portugal	1713	Shantung Province	414	Trengganu	1401
Provisional Govt. Of China	450	Sharjah	1857	Trinidad & Tobago	2047
Prussia	842	Shensi Province	415	Tristan da Cunha	2053
Puebla de Cazalla	1946	Shensi-North Soviet	519	Tunisia	2054
Puebla	1479	Sierra Leone	1858	Turkey	2063
Qatar & Dubai	1731	Sinaloa	1449	Turkmenistan	2091
Qatar	1730	Singapore	1866	Turks & Caicos Islands	2094
Ras al-Khaimah	1731	Sinkiang Province	415	Tuvalu	2110
Reformed Govt. of China	450	Slovakia	1877	Uganda	2113
Reunion	1734	Slovenia	1882	Ukraine	2120
Reuss	844	Socialist Republic of Vietnam	2210	Umm Al Qaiwain - U.A.E.	2129
Reuss-Obergreiz	844	Soloman Islands	1885	United Arab Emirates	2129
Rhodesia & Nyasaland	1736	Somalia	1891	United Kingdoms	1844
Rhodesia	1735	Somaliland	1900	United States	2133
Riau Archipelago	1113	South Africa	1900	Uruguay	2168
Romania	1737	South Arabia	1920	Uzbekistan	2175
Ruanda-Urundi	176	South Georgia and the		Valdivia	367
Russia	1747	South Sandwich Islands	1921	Vanuatu	2176
Russian Caucasia	1791	Southern Rhodesia	1921	Vatican City	2179
Rwanda & Burundi	1793	South Korea	1322	Venezuela	2201
Rwanda	1792	South Viet Nam	2213	Vietnam	2208
Saarland	1794	Spain Civil War	1944	Waldeck-Pyrmont	848
Saharawi Arab Democratic		Spain	1924	Wan-Hsi-Pei-Soviet	521
Republic	1794	Spitzbergen	1946	West African States	2215
Sailana	1076	Sri Lanka	1947	Wurttemberg	849
Saint Helena & Ascension	1799	Straits Settlements	1950	Yemen Arab Republic	2222
Saint Helena	1798	Sudan	1952	Yemen Eastern Aden	
Saint Kitts & Nevis	1801	Suiyuan Province	428	Protectorate	2226
Saint Lucia	1802	Suriname	1960	Yemen Republic	2226
Saint Pierre & Miquelon	1803	Swaziland	1964	Yemen	2216
Saint Thomas & Prince Island	1803	Sweden	1967	Yemen, Democratic	
Saint Vincent	1809	Switzerland	1977	Republic of	2227
Samoa	1810	Syria	1990	Yugoslavia	2227
San Marino	1818	Szechuan Province	428	Yunnan Province	434
Santander, Palencia & Burgos	1946	Szechuan-Shensi Soviet	520	Yunnan-Szechuan	437
Sarawak	1842	Taiwan	445	Zaire	2240
Saudi Arabia	1843	Tajikistan	1994	Zambia	2241
Saxe-Altenburg	844	Tannu Tuva	1994	Zanzibar	2253
Saxe-Coburg-Gotha	844	Tanzania	1994	Zimbabwe	2254

HEJIRA DATE CONVERSION CHART

JEHIRA DATE CHART

HEJIRA (Hijira, Hegira), the name of the Muslim era (A.H. = Anno Hegirae) dates back to the Christian year 622 when Mohammed "fled" from Mecca, escaping to Medina to avoid persecution from the Koreish tribemen. Based on a lunar year the Muslim year is 11 days shorter.

*=Leap Year (Christian Calendar)

AH Hejira	AD Christian Date
1010	1601, July 2
1011	1602, June 21
1012	1603, June 11
1013	1604, May 30
1014	1605, May 19
1015	1606, May 19
1016	1607, May 9
1017	1608, April 28
1018	1609, April 6
1017	1608, April 28
1018	1609, April 6
1019	1610, March 26
1020	1611, March 16
1021	1612, March 4
1022	1613, February 21
1023	1614, February 11
1024	1615, January 31
1025	1616, January 20
1026	1617, January 9
1027	1617, December 29
1028	1618, December 19
1029	1619, December 8
1030	1620, November 26
1031	1621, November 16
1032	1622, November 5
1033	1623, October 25
1034	1624, October 14
1035	1625, October 3
1036	1626, September 22
1037	1627, Septembe 12
1038	1628, August 31
1039	1629, August 21
1040	1630, July 10
1041	1631, July 30
1042	1632, July 19
1043	1633, July 8
1044	1634, June 27
1045	1635, June 17
1046	1636, June 5
1047	1637, May 26
1048	1638, May 15
1049	1639, May 4
1050	1640, April 23
1051	1641, April 12
1052	1642, April 1
1053	1643, March 22
1054	1644, March 10
1055	1645, February 27
1056	1646, February 17
1057	1647, February 6
1058	1648, January 27
1059	1649, January 15
1060	1650, January 4
1061	1650, December 25
1062	1651, December 14
1063	1652, December 2
1064	1653, November 22
1065	1654, November 11
1066	1655, October 31
1067	1656, October 20
1068	1657, October 9
1069	1658, September 29
1070	1659, September 18
1071	1660, September 6
1072	1661, August 27
1073	1662, August 16
1074	1663, August 5
1075	1664, July 25
1076	1665, July 14
1077	1666, July 4
1078	1667, June 23
1079	1668, June 11
1080	1669, June 1
1081	1670, May 21
1082	1671, may 10
1083	1672, April 29
1084	1673, April 18
1085	1674, April 7
1086	1675, March 28
1087	1676, March 16*
1088	1677, March 6
1089	1678, February 23
1090	1679, February 12
1091	1680, February 2*
1092	1681, January 21
1093	1682, January 10
1094	1682, December 31
1095	1683, December 20
1096	1684, December 8*
1097	1685, November 28
1098	1686, November 17
1099	1687, November 7
1100	1688, October 26*
1101	1689, October 15
1102	1690, October 5
1103	1691, September 24
1104	1692, September 12*
1105	1693, September 2
1106	1694, August 22
1107	1695, August 12
1108	1696, July 31*
1109	1697, July 20
1110	1698, July 10
1111	1699, June 29
1112	1700, June 18
1113	1701, June 8
1114	1702, May 28
1115	1703, May 17
1116	1704, May 6*
1117	1705, April 25
1118	1706, April 15
1119	1707, April 4
1120	1708, March 23*
1121	1709, March 13
1122	1710, March 2
1123	1711, February 19
1124	1712, Feburary 9*
1125	1713, January 28
1126	1714, January 17
1127	1715, January 7
1128	1715, December 27
1129	1716, December 16*
1130	1717, December 5
1131	1718, November 24
1132	1719, November 14
1133	1720, November 2*
1134	1721, October 22
1135	1722, October 12
1136	1723, October 1
1137	1724, September 19
1138	1725, September 9
1139	1726, August 29
1140	1727, August 19
1141	1728, August 7*
1142	1729, July 27
1143	1730, July 17
1144	1731, July 6
1145	1732, June 24*
1146	1733, June 14
1147	1734, June 3
1148	1735, May 24
1149	1736, May 12*
1150	1737, May 1
1151	1738, April 21
1152	1739, April 10
1153	1740, March 29*
1154	1741, March 19
1155	1742, March 8
1156	1743, Feburary 25
1157	1744, February 15*
1158	1745, February 3
1159	1746, January 24
1160	1747, January 13
1161	1748, January 2
1162	1748, December 22*
1163	1749, December 11
1164	1750, November 30
1165	1751, November 20
1166	1752, November 8*
1167	1753, October 29
1168	1754, October 18
1169	1755, October 7
1170	1756, September 26*
1171	1757, September 15
1172	1758, September 4
1173	1759, August 25
1174	1760, August 13*
1175	1761, August 2
1176	1762, July 23
1177	1763, July 12
1178	1764, July 1*
1179	1765, June 20
1180	1766, June 9
1181	1767, May 30
1182	1768, May 18*
1183	1769, May 7
1184	1770, April 27
1185	1771, April 16
1186	1772, April 4*
1187	1773, March 25
1188	1774, March 14
1189	1775, March 4
1190	1776, February 21*
1191	1777, February 91
1192	1778, January 30
1193	1779, January 19
1194	1780, January 8*
1195	1780, December 28*
1196	1781, December 17
1197	1782, December 7
1198	1783, November 26
1199	1784, November 14*
1200	1785, November 4
1201	1786, October 24
1202	1787, October 13
1203	1788, October 2*
1204	1789, September 21
1205	1790, September 10
1206	1791, August 31
1207	1792, August 19*
1208	1793, August 9
1209	1794, July 29
1210	1795, July 18
1211	1796, July 7*
1212	1797, June 26
1213	1798, June 15
1214	1799, June 5
1215	1800, May 25
1216	1801, May 14
1217	1802, May 4
1218	1803, April 23
1219	1804, April 12*
1220	1805, April 1
1221	1806, March 21
1222	1807, March 11
1223	1808, February 28*
1224	1809, February 16
1225	1810, Febauary 6
1226	1811, January 26
1227	1812, January 16*
1228	1813, Janaury 5
1229	1813, December 24
1230	1814, December 14
1231	1815, December 3
1232	1816, November 21*
1233	1817, November 11
1234	1818, October 31
1235	1819, October 20
1236	1820, October 9*
1237	1821, September 28
1238	1822, September 18
1239	1823, September 18
1240	1824, August 26*
1241	1825, August 16
1242	1826, August 5
1243	1827, July 25
1244	1828, July 14*
1245	1829, July 3
1246	1830, June 22
1247	1831, June 12
1248	1832, May 31*
1249	1833, May 21
1250	1834, May 10
1251	1835, April 29
1252	1836, April 18*
1253	1837, April 7
1254	1838, March 27
1255	1839, March 17
1256	1840, March 5*
1257	1841, February 23
1258	1842, February 12
1259	1843, February 1
1260	1844, January 22*
1261	1845, January 10
1262	1845, December 30
1263	1846, December 20
1264	1847, December 9
1265	1848, November 27*
1266	1849, November 17
1267	1850, November 6
1268	1851, October 27
1269	1852, October 15*
1270	1853, October 4
1271	1854, September 24
1272	1855, September 13
1273	1856, September 1*
1274	1857, August 22
1275	1858, August 11
1276	1859, July 31
1277	1860, July 20*
1278	1861, July 9
1279	1862, June 29
1280	1863, June 18
1281	1864, June 6*
1282	1865, May 27
1283	1866, May 16
1284	1867, May 5
1285	1868, April 24*
1286	1869, April 13
1287	1870, April 3
1288	1871, March 23
1289	1872, March 11*
1290	1873, March 1
1291	1874, February 18
1292	1875, Feburary 7
1293	1876, January 28*
1294	1877, January 16
1295	1878, January 5
1296	1878, December 26
1297	1879, December 15
1298	1880, December 4*
1299	1881, November 23
1300	1882, November 12
1301	1883, November 2
1302	1884, October 21*
1303	1885, October 10
1304	1886, September 30
1305	1887, September 19
1306	1888, September 7*
1307	1889, August 28
1308	1890, August 17
1309	1891, August 7
1310	1892, July 26*
1311	1893, July 15
1312	1894, July 5
1313	1895, June 24
1314	1896, June 12*
1315	1897, June 2
1316	1898, May 22
1317	1899, May 12
1318	1900, May 1
1319	1901, April 20
1320	1902, april 10
1321	1903, March 30
1322	1904, March 18*
1323	1905, March 8
1324	1906, February 25
1325	1907, February 14
1326	1908, February 4*
1327	1909, January 23
1328	1910, January 13
1329	1911, January 2
1330	1911, December 22
1331	1912, December 11
1332	1913, November 30
1333	1914, November 19
1334	1915, November 9
1335	1916, October 28*
1336	1917, October 17
1337	1918, October 7
1338	1919, September 26
1339	1920, September 15*
1340	1921, September 4
1341	1922, August 24
1342	1923, August 14
1343	1924, August 2*
1344	1925, July 22
1345	1926, July 12
1346	1927, July 1
1347	1928, June 20*
1348	1929, June 9
1349	1930, May 29
1350	1931, May 19
1351	1932, May 7*
1352	1933, April 26
1353	1934, April 16
1354	1935, April 5
1355	1936, March 24*
1356	1937, March 14
1357	1938, March 3
1358	1939, February 21
1359	1940, February 10*
1360	1941, January 29
1361	1942, January 19
1362	1943, January 8
1363	1943, December 28
1364	1944, December 17*
1365	1945, December 6
1366	1946, November 25
1367	1947, November 15
1368	1948, November 3*
1369	1949, October 24
1370	1950, October 13
1371	1951, October 2
1372	1952, September 21*
1373	1953, September 10
1374	1954, August 30
1375	1955, August 20
1376	1956, August 8*
1377	1957, July 29
1378	1958, July 18
1379	1959, July 7
1380	1960, June 25*
1381	1961, June 14
1382	1962, June 4
1383	1963, May 25
1384	1964, May 13*
1385	1965, May 2
1386	1966, April 22
1387	1967, April 11
1388	1968, March 31*
1389	1969, march 20
1390	1970, March 9
1391	1971, February 27
1392	1972, February 16*
1393	1973, February 4
1394	1974, January 25
1395	1975, January 14
1396	1976, January 3*
1397	1976, December 23*
1398	1977, December 12
1399	1978, December 2
1400	1979, November 21
1401	1980, November 9*
1402	1981, October 30
1403	1982, October 19
1404	1983, October 8
1405	1984, September 27*
1406	1985, September 16
1407	1986, September 6
1409	1987, August 26
1409	1988, August 14*
1410	1989, August 3
1411	1990, July 24
1412	1991, July 13
1413	1992, July 2*
1414	1993, June 21
1415	1994, June 10
1416	1995, May 31
1417	1996, May 19*
1418	1997, May 9
1419	1998, April 28
1420	1999, April 17
1421	2000, April 6*
1422	2001, March 26
1423	2002, March 15
1424	2003, March 5
1425	2004, February 22*
1426	2005, February 10
1427	2006, January 31
1428	2007, January 20
1429	2008, January 10*
1430	2008, December 29
1431	2009, December 18
1432	2010, December 8
1433	2011, November 27*
1434	2012, November 15
1435	2013, November 5
1436	2014, October 25
1437	2015, October 15*
1438	2016, October 3
1439	2017, September 22
1440	2018, September 12
1441	2019, September 11*
1442	2020, August 20
1443	2021, August 10
1444	2022, July 30
1445	2023, July 19*
1446	2024, July 8
1447	2025, June 27
1448	2026, June 17
1449	2027, June 6*
1450	2028, May25

FOREIGN EXCHANGE TABLE

The latest foreign exchange rates below apply to trade with banks in the country of origin. The left column shows the number of units per U.S. dollar at the official rate. The right column shows the number of units per dollar at the free market rate.

Country	Official #/$	Market #/$
Afghanistan (New Afghani)	52	–
Albania (Lek)	102	–
Algeria (Dinar)	72	–
Andorra uses Euro	.788	–
Angola (Readjust Kwanza)	75	–
Anguilla uses E.C. Dollar	2.7	–
Antigua uses E.C. Dollar	2.7	–
Argentina (Peso)	3.63	–
Armenia (Dram)	359	–
Aruba (Florin)	1.79	–
Australia (Dollar)	1.55	–
Austria (Euro)	.788	–
Azerbaijan (New Manat)	.81	–
Bahamas (Dollar)	1.0	–
Bahrain Is. (Dinar)	.377	–
Bangladesh (Taka)	69	–
Barbados (Dollar)	2.0	–
Belarus (Ruble)	2,870	–
Belgium (Euro)	.788	–
Belize (Dollar)	1.95	–
Benin uses CFA Franc West	517	–
Bermuda (Dollar)	1.0	–
Bhutan (Ngultrum)	51	–
Bolivia (Boliviano)	7.02	–
Bosnia-Herzegovina (Conv. marka)	1.54	–
Botswana (Pula)	8.28	–
British Virgin Islands uses U.S. Dollar	1.0	–
Brazil (Real)	2.37	–
Brunei (Dollar)	1.54	–
Bulgaria (Lev)	1.54	–
Burkina Faso uses CFA Fr. West	517	–
Burma (Kyat)	6.43	1,250
Burundi (Franc)	1,234	–
Cambodia (Riel)	4,124	–
Cameroon uses CFA Franc Central	517	–
Canada (Dollar)	1.28	–
Cape Verde (Escudo)	87	–
Cayman Islands (Dollar)	0.82	–
Central African Rep.	517	–
CFA Franc Central	517	–
CFA Franc West	517	–
CFP Franc	94	–
Chad uses CFA Franc Central	517	–
Chile (Peso)	607	–
China, P.R. (Renminbi Yuan)	6.84	–
Colombia (Peso)	2,549	–
Comoros (Franc)	388	–
Congo uses CFA Franc Central	517	–
Congo-Dem.Rep. (Congolese Franc)	774	–
Cook Islands (Dollar)	1.99	–
Costa Rica (Colon)	566	–
Croatia (Kuna)	5.85	–
Cuba (Peso)	1.00	27.00
Cyprus (Euro)	.788	–
Czech Republic (Koruna)	21.7	–
Denmark (Danish Krone)	5.87	–
Djibouti (Franc)	177	–
Dominica uses E.C. Dollar	2.7	–
Dominican Republic (Peso)	35.4	–
East Caribbean (Dollar)	2.7	–
Ecuador (U.S. Dollar)	1.00	–
Egypt (Pound)	5.59	–
El Salvador (U.S. Dollar)	1.00	–
Equatorial Guinea uses CFA Franc Central	517	–
Eritrea (Nafka)	15	–
Estonia (Kroon)	12.3	–
Ethiopia (Birr)	11.1	–
Euro	.788	–
Falkland Is. (Pound)	.709	–
Faroe Islands (Krona)	5.87	–
Fiji Islands (Dollar)	1.88	–
Finland (Euro)	.788	–
France (Euro)	.788	–
French Polynesia uses CFP Franc	94	–
Gabon (CFA Franc)	517	–
Gambia (Dalasi)	26	–
Georgia (Lari)	1.69	–
Germany (Euro)	.788	–
Ghana (New Cedi)	1.39	–
Gibraltar (Pound)	.709	–
Greece (Euro)	.788	–
Greenland uses Danish Krone	5.87	–
Grenada uses E.C. Dollar	2.7	–
Guatemala (Quetzal)	8.01	–
Guernsey uses Sterling Pound	.709	–
Guinea Bissau (CFA Franc)	517	–
Guinea Conakry (Franc)	4,955	–
Guyana (Dollar)	204	–
Haiti (Gourde)	39.7	–
Honduras (Lempira)	18.88	–
Hong Kong (Dollar)	7.75	–
Hungary (Forint)	246	–
Iceland (Krona)	112	–
India (Rupee)	51.7	–
Indonesia (Rupiah)	12,010	–
Iran (Rial)	9,916	–
Iraq (Dinar)	1,169	–
Ireland (Euro)	.788	–
Isle of Man uses Sterling Pound	.709	–
Israel (New Sheqalim)	4.24	–
Italy (Euro)	.788	–
Ivory Coast uses CFA Franc West	517	–
Jamaica (Dollar)	88	–
Japan (Yen)	97	–
Jersey uses Sterling Pound	.709	–
Jordan (Dinar)	.71	–
Kazakhstan (Tenge)	150	–
Kenya (Shilling)	79.8	–
Kiribati uses Australian Dollar	1.55	–
Korea-PDR (Won)	2.2	142
Korea-Rep. (Won)	1,543	–
Kuwait (Dinar)	.29	–
Kyrgyzstan (Som)	41	–
Laos (Kip)	8,568	–
Latvia (Lats)	.558	–
Lebanon (Pound)	1,503	–
Lesotho (Maloti)	10.4	–
Liberia (Dollar)	65	–
Libya (Dinar)	1.32	–
Liechtenstein uses Swiss Franc	1.15	–
Lithuania (Litas)	2.72	–
Luxembourg (Euro)	.788	–
Macao (Pataca)	7.98	–
Macedonia (New Denar)	48	–
Madagascar (Franc)	1,975	–
Malawi (Kwacha)	140	–
Malaysia (Ringgit)	3.71	–
Maldives (Rufiya)	12.8	–
Mali uses CFA Franc West	517	–
Malta (Euro)	.788	–
Marshall Islands uses U.S.Dollar	1.00	–
Mauritania (Ouguiya)	263	–
Mauritius (Rupee)	34	–
Mexico (Peso)	15.2	–
Moldova (Leu)	10.7	–
Monaco uses Euro	.788	–
Mongolia (Tugrik)	1,570	–
Montenegro uses Euro	.788	–
Montserrat uses E.C. Dollar	2.7	–
Morocco (Dirham)	8.72	–
Mozambique (New Metical)	27.25	–
Namibia (Rand)	10.41	–
Nauru uses Australian Dollar	1.55	–
Nepal (Rupee)	82.7	–
Netherlands (Euro)	.788	–
Netherlands Antilles (Gulden)	1.79	–
New Caledonia uses CFP Franc	94	–
New Zealand (Dollar)	1.99	–
Nicaragua (Cordoba Oro)	20	–
Niger uses CFA Franc West	517	–
Nigeria (Naira)	147	–
Northern Ireland uses Sterling Pound	.709	–
Norway (Krone)	7.04	–
Oman (Rial)	.385	–
Pakistan (Rupee)	80	–
Palau uses U.S.Dollar	1.00	–
Panama (Balboa) uses U.S.Dollar	1.00	–
Papua New Guinea (Kina)	2.83	–
Paraguay (Guarani)	5,135	–
Peru (Nuevo Sol)	3.2	–
Philippines (Peso)	48	–
Poland (Zloty)	3.7	–
Portugal (Euro)	.788	–
Qatar (Riyal)	3.64	–
Romania (New Leu)	3.38	–
Russia (Ruble)	36	–
Rwanda (Franc)	568	–
St. Helena (Pound)	.709	–
St. Kitts uses E.C. Dollar	2.7	–
St. Lucia uses E.C. Dollar	2.7	–
St. Vincent uses E.C. Dollar	2.7	–
San Marino uses Euro	.788	–
Sao Tome e Principe (Dobra)	17,474	–
Saudi Arabia (Riyal)	3.75	–
Scotland uses Sterling Pound	.709	–
Senegal uses CFA Franc West	517	–
Serbia (Dinar)	74.9	–
Seychelles (Rupee)	16.77	–
Sierra Leone (Leone)	3,087	–
Singapore (Dollar)	1.5	–
Slovakia (Sk. Koruna)	23.7	–
Slovenia (Euro)	.788	–
Solomon Islands (Dollar)	8.11	–
Somalia (Shilling)	1,415	–
Somaliland (Somali Shilling)	1,800	4,000
South Africa (Rand)	10.4	–
Spain (Euro)	.788	–
Sri Lanka (Rupee)	114	–
Sudan (Pound)	2.3	–
Surinam (Dollar)	2.74	–
Swaziland (Lilangeni)	10.4	–
Sweden (Krona)	9.18	–
Switzerland (Franc)	1.15	–
Syria (Pound)	47	–
Taiwan (NT Dollar)	34.7	–
Tajikistan (Somoni)	3.74	–
Tanzania (Shilling)	1,304	–
Thailand (Baht)	36	–
Togo uses CFA Franc West	517	–
Tonga (Pa'anga)	2.24	–
Transdniestra (Ruble)	–	–
Trinidad & Tobago (Dollar)	6.26	–
Tunisia (Dinar)	1.45	–
Turkey (New Lira)	1.78	–
Turkmenistan (Manat)	14,250	–
Turks & Caicos uses U.S. Dollar	1.00	–
Tuvalu uses Australian Dollar	1.56	–
Uganda (Shilling)	2,000	–
Ukraine (Hryvnia)	7.85	–
United Arab Emirates (Dirham)	3.67	–
United Kingdom (Sterling Pound)	.709	–
Uruguay (Peso Uruguayo)	23.9	–
Uzbekistan (Sum)	1,413	–
Vanuatu (Vatu)	120	–
Vatican City uses Euro	.788	–
Venezuela (New Bolivar)	2.15	5.7
Vietnam (Dong)	17,481	–
Western Samoa (Tala)	3.07	–
Yemen (Rial)	200	–
Zambia (Kwacha)	5,540	–
Zimbabwe (Dollar)	–	–

AFGHANISTAN

The Islamic State of Afghanistan, which occupies a mountainous region of Southwest Asia, has an area of 251,825 sq. mi. (652,090 sq. km.) and a population of 25.59 million. Presently, about a fifth of the total population lives in exile as refugees, (mostly in Pakistan). Capital: Kabul. It is bordered by Iran, Pakistan, Turkmenistan, Uzbekistan, Tajikistan, and China's Sinkiang Province. Agriculture and herding are the principal industries; textile mills and cement factories add to the industrial sector. Cotton, wool, fruits, nuts, oil, sheepskin coats and hand-woven carpets are normally exported but foreign trade has been interrupted since 1979.

Because of its strategic position astride the ancient land route to India, Afghanistan (formerly known as Aryana and Khorasan) was invaded by Darius I, Alexander the Great, various Scythian tribes, the White Huns, the Arabs, the Turks, Genghis Khan, Tamerlane, the Mughals, the Persians, and in more recent times by Great Britain. It was a powerful empire under the Kushans, Hephthalites, Ghaznavids and Ghorids. The name Afghanistan, "Land of the Afghans," came into use in the eighteenth and nineteenth centuries to describe the realm of the Afghan kings. For a short period, this mountainous region was the easternmost frontier of the Iranian world, with strong cultural influences from the Turks and Mongols to the north and India to the south.

Afghanistan's traditional coinage was much like that of its neighbors Iran and India. There were four major mints: Kabul, Qandahar, Balkh and Herat. The early Durranis also controlled mints in Iran and India. On gold and silver coins, the inscriptions in Persian (called Dari in Afghanistan) included the name of the mint city and, normally, of the ruler recognized there, but some issues are anonymous. The arrangement of the inscriptions, and frequently the name of the ruler, was different at each mint. Copper coins were controlled locally and usually did not name any ruler. For these reasons the coinage of each mint is treated separately. The relative values of gold, silver, and copper coins were not fixed but were determined in the marketplace.

In 1890 Abdur Rahman had a modern mint set up in Kabul using British minting machinery and the help of British advisors. The other mints were closed down, except for the issue of local coppers. The new system had 60 paisa equal one rupee; intermediate denominations also had special names. In 1901 the name Afghanistan appeared on coins for the first time. A decimal system, 100 puls to the afghani, was introduced in 1925. The gold amani, rated at 20 afghanis, was a bullion coin.

The national symbol on most coins of the kingdom is a stylized mosque, within which is seen the mihrab, a niche indicating the direction of Mecca, and the minbar, the pulpit, with a flight of steps leading up to it. Inscriptions in Pashtu were first used under the rebel Habibullah, but did not become standard until 1950.

Until 1919, coins were dated by the lunar Islamic Hejira calendar (AH), often with the king's regnal year as a second date. The solar Hejira (SH) calendar was introduced in 1919 (1337 AH, 1298 SH). The rebel Habibullah reinstated lunar Hejira dating (AH 1347-50), but the solar calendar was used thereafter. The solar Hejira year begins on the first day of spring, about March 21. Adding 621 to the SH year yields the AD year in which it begins.

RULERS

Names of rulers are shown in Perso-Arabic script in the style usually found on their coins; they are not always in a straight line.

BARAKZAI DYNASTY

Habibullah,
AH1319-337/1901-1919AD

Amanullah,
AH1337, SH1298-1307/1919-1929AD

Habibullah (rebel, known as Baccha-i-Saqao),
AH1347-1348/1929AD

Muhammed Nadir Shah, AH1348-1350,
SH1310-1312/1929-1933AD

Muhammad Zahir Shah,
SH1312-1352/1933-1973AD

Republic, SH1352-1358/1973-1979AD
Democratic Republic, SH1358-1373/1979-1994 AD
Islamic Republic, SH1373-1381/1994-2002AD

MINT NAMES

Coins were struck at numerous mints in Afghanistan and adjacent lands. These are listed below, together with their honorific titles, and shown in the style ordinarily found on the coins.

افغانستان
Afghanistan

غزني
Ghazni

هراة هرات
Herat

كابل
Kabul

قندهار
Qandahar

MINT EPITHETS

دار الملك
"Dar al-Mulk"
Abode of the King

دار النصرات
"Dar al-Nusrat"

KINGDOM

Abdur Rahman
AH1297-1319 / 1880-1901AD
MILLED COINAGE

10 Dinar = 1 Paisa; 5 Paise = 1 Shahi; 2 Shahi = 1 Sanar; 2 Sanar = 1 Abbasi; 1-1/2 Abbasi = 1 Qiran; 2 Qiran = 1 Kabuli Rupee; 1 Tilla = 10 Rupees

KM# 831   1/2 RUPEE (Qiran)
4.6500 g., 0.5000 Silver 0.0747 oz. ASW **Obv:** Toughra
Rev: Crossed cannons below mosque, wreath surrounds **Mint:** Afghanistan

Date	Mintage	VG	F	VF	XF	Unc
AH1319	—	20.00	40.00	75.00	125	—

Habibullah
AH1319-1337 / 1901-1919AD
LOCAL COINAGE

KM# 957   PAISA
Copper **Mint:** Herat **Note:** Counterstruck over Iran, 50 Dinars, Y#4.

Date	Mintage	Good	VG	F	VF	XF
AH1322	—	4.00	6.50	12.50	18.00	—
AH1328	—	3.00	5.00	10.00	16.00	—

KM# 956.1   PAISA
Copper **Mint:** Herat **Note:** Round or irregular flan.

Date	Mintage	Good	VG	F	VF	XF
AH1322	—	2.50	4.00	7.50	12.50	—
AH1328	—	2.50	4.00	7.50	12.50	—
AH1329	—	2.50	4.00	7.50	12.50	—
AH1330	—	2.50	4.00	7.50	12.50	—
AH1331	—	2.50	4.00	7.50	12.50	—
AH1332	—	2.50	4.00	7.50	12.50	—
ND Date off flan	—	1.50	2.50	5.00	8.00	—

KM# 960.4   PAISA
Copper **Rev:** Mosque **Mint:** Qandahar **Note:** Counterstruck on British East India Co., 1/4 Anna.

Date	Mintage	Good	VG	F	VF	XF
AH1322	—	4.00	7.50	12.50	20.00	—
AH1330	—	4.00	7.50	12.50	20.00	—

KM# 960.2   PAISA
Copper **Rev:** Mosque **Mint:** Qandahar **Note:** Counterstruck on Iran 50 dinars, Y#4.

Date	Mintage	Good	VG	F	VF	XF
AH1321	—	3.00	5.00	8.00	15.00	—
AH1322	—	3.00	5.00	8.00	15.00	—

KM# 956.2   PAISA
Copper **Rev:** In a rayed circle **Mint:** Herat

Date	Mintage	Good	VG	F	VF	XF
AH1332	—	3.00	5.00	8.50	15.00	—

KM# 956.3   PAISA
Copper **Obv:** Scroll symbol **Mint:** Herat

Date	Mintage	Good	VG	F	VF	XF
AH1325	—	3.00	5.00	8.50	15.00	—

KM# 960.1   PAISA
Copper **Rev:** Mosque **Mint:** Qandahar **Note:** Dump.

Date	Mintage	Good	VG	F	VF	XF
AH1322	—	4.50	7.50	12.50	17.50	—

KM# 960.3 PAISA
Copper Rev: Mosque Mint: Qandahar Note: Counterstruck on Muscat and Oman, 1/4 Anna, KM#4.

Date	Mintage	Good	VG	F	VF	XF
AH1322	—	3.75	6.50	10.00	16.00	—

KM# 960.5 PAISA
Copper Rev: Mosque Mint: Qandahar Note: Overstruck on Oman, 1/4 Anna, KM#3.1.

Date	Mintage	Good	VG	F	VF	XF
AH1322	—	3.75	6.50	10.00	16.00	—

KM# 963 PAISA
Copper Obv: Text Rev: Star with five points within wreath Mint: Ghazni Note: Struck over British East India Co., 1/4 Anna.

Date	Mintage	Good	VG	F	VF	XF
AH1322	—	10.00	20.00	35.00	75.00	—

KM# 958.1 PAISA
Copper Obv: "Dar al-Nusrat" added above date Rev: Mosque Mint: Herat

Date	Mintage	Good	VG	F	VF	XF
AH1331	—	2.50	4.00	7.50	12.50	—

KM# 958.2 PAISA
Copper Rev: Date below mosque Mint: Herat

Date	Mintage	Good	VG	F	VF	XF
AH1331	—	3.50	5.00	8.50	15.00	—

KM# 964 PAISA
Copper Obv: Text Rev: Mosque Mint: Qandahar

Date	Mintage	Good	VG	F	VF	XF
AH1333	—	2.00	3.50	6.00	10.00	—
AH1334	—	2.00	3.50	6.00	10.00	—

KM# 973 PAISA
Copper Mint: Kabul

Date	Mintage	Good	VG	F	VF	XF
ND	—	—	—	—	—	—

KM# 959 2 PAISE
Copper Mint: Without Mint Name Note: Similar to Paisa, KM#965 but inscribed "Do Paisa" below mosque.

Date	Mintage	Good	VG	F	VF	XF
AH1329	—	3.00	5.00	8.50	15.00	—

MILLED COINAGE

10 Dinar = 1 Paisa; 5 Paise = 1 Shahi; 2 Shahi = 1 Sanar; 2 Sanar = 1 Abbasi; 1-1/2 Abbasi = 1 Qiran; 2 Qiran = 1 Kabuli Rupee; 1 Tilla = 10 Rupees

KM# 848 PAISA
Bronze Or Brass, 20 mm. Obv: Text within beaded circle Rev: Mosque Mint: Afghanistan

Date	Mintage	VG	F	VF	XF	Unc
AH1329	—	6.00	12.00	25.00	45.00	—
AH1329/17	—	8.00	16.00	35.00	60.00	—

Note: On KM#828 obverse die

KM# 849 PAISA
Brass, 21 mm. Obv: Text Rev: Mosque within 8-pointed star Mint: Afghanistan

Date	Mintage	VG	F	VF	XF	Unc
AH1329	—	2.00	4.00	7.50	15.00	—
AH1331	—	2.00	4.00	7.50	15.00	—
AH1332	—	—	—	—	—	—

KM# 849a PAISA
Bronze, 21 mm. Obv: Text Rev: Mosque within 8-pointed star Mint: Afghanistan

Date	Mintage	VG	F	VF	XF	Unc
AH1334	—	3.00	6.00	11.50	20.00	—

KM# 854 PAISA
Bronze Or Brass, 19 mm. Obv: Text within circle Rev: Mosque within 8-pointed star, circle surrounds Mint: Afghanistan Note: Thick flan, reduced size.

Date	Mintage	VG	F	VF	XF	Unc
AH1336	—	3.00	6.00	12.00	25.00	—

KM# 855 PAISA
Bronze Or Brass Mint: Afghanistan Note: Thin flan.

Date	Mintage	VG	F	VF	XF	Unc
AH1336	—	6.50	10.00	20.00	35.00	—
AH1337	—	2.00	4.00	8.00	16.00	—

KM# 858 PAISA
Bronze Or Brass, 19-20 mm. Mint: Afghanistan Note: Thin flan. Size varies.

Date	Mintage	VG	F	VF	XF	Unc
AH1337 (1918)	—	3.00	6.00	10.00	20.00	—

Note: Three varieties are known dated AH1337

KM# 857 PAISA
Bronze Or Brass, 20 mm. Obv: Text within wreath Rev: Mosque within 8-pointed star Mint: Afghanistan Note: Thin flan.

Date	Mintage	VG	F	VF	XF	Unc
AH1337	—	6.50	10.00	20.00	35.00	—

KM# 846 SANAR (10 Paisa)
1.5500 g., 0.5000 Silver 0.0249 oz. ASW, 13 mm. Rev: Mosque above crossed cannons and swords, wreath surrounds Mint: Afghanistan

Date	Mintage	VG	F	VF	XF	Unc
AH1325	—	10.00	20.00	35.00	60.00	—
AH1326	—	5.00	7.50	12.50	22.50	—
AH1328	—	5.00	7.50	12.50	22.50	—
AH1329	—	5.75	8.50	14.00	25.00	—

KM# 850 SANAR (10 Paisa)
1.5500 g., 0.5000 Silver 0.0249 oz. ASW, 13 mm. Obv: Text and date Rev: Mosque within 7-pointed star Mint: Afghanistan Note: Coins dated AH1333 and 1337 are known in two varieties.

Date	Mintage	VG	F	VF	XF	Unc
AH1329	—	4.00	7.00	12.00	22.00	—
AH1330	—	3.00	6.00	10.00	20.00	—
AH1331	—	3.00	6.00	10.00	20.00	—
AH1332	—	3.00	6.00	10.00	20.00	—
AH1333	—	3.00	5.00	9.00	16.00	—
AH1335	—	3.00	5.00	9.00	16.00	—
AH1337	—	3.00	6.00	10.00	20.00	—

KM# 863 3 SHAHI (15 Paisa)
Copper, 32-33 mm. Obv: Without "Al-Ghazi" Rev: Mosque within 8-pointed star inside circle, stars surround Mint: Afghanistan Note: Size varies.

Date	Mintage	VG	F	VF	XF	Unc
AH1337 (1918)	—	5.00	12.00	22.00	40.00	—

Note: Three varieties are known

KM# 869 3 SHAHI (15 Paisa)
Copper Obv: "Shamsi" left and below date Rev: Mosque within 8-pointed star within circle, stars surround Mint: Afghanistan

Date	Mintage	VG	F	VF	XF	Unc
SH1298 (1919)	—	2.00	4.00	10.00	20.00	—

Note: Shamsi (Solar) is an additional word written on some of the coins dated SH1298, to show the change from a lunar to solar calendar

KM# 837 ABBASI (20 Paisa)
3.1100 g., 0.5000 Silver 0.0500 oz. ASW, 16 mm. Obv: Tughra within wreath Rev: Mosque above crossed cannons and swords, wreath surrounds Mint: Afghanistan

Date	Mintage	VG	F	VF	XF	Unc
AH1320	—	30.00	60.00	100	225	—

KM# 845 ABBASI (20 Paisa)
3.1100 g., 0.5000 Silver 0.0500 oz. ASW, 17 mm. Obv: Tughra within wreath Rev: Mosque above crossed cannons and swords, wreath surrounds Mint: Afghanistan

Date	Mintage	VG	F	VF	XF	Unc
AH1324	—	35.00	70.00	125	250	—
AH1328	—	35.00	70.00	125	250	—
AH1329	—	50.00	100	175	300	—

KM# 851 ABBASI (20 Paisa)
3.1100 g., 0.5000 Silver 0.0500 oz. ASW, 17 mm. Obv: Tughra within wreath Rev: Mosque above crossed cannons and swords, wreath surrounds Mint: Afghanistan

Date	Mintage	VG	F	VF	XF	Unc
AH1329	—	6.00	11.00	16.00	24.00	—
AH1330	—	6.00	11.00	16.00	24.00	—
AH1333	—	5.00	10.00	15.00	22.50	—
AH1334	—	5.00	10.00	15.00	22.50	—
AH1335	—	5.00	10.00	15.00	22.50	—
AH1337	—	5.00	10.00	15.00	22.50	—

KM# 838 1/2 RUPEE (Qiran)
4.6500 g., 0.5000 Silver 0.0747 oz. ASW, 19 mm. **Obv:** Toughra divides date **Rev:** Mosque above crossed cannons and swords, wreath surrounds **Mint:** Afghanistan

Date	Mintage	VG	F	VF	XF	Unc
AH1320	—	25.00	45.00	85.00	140	—
AH1325	—	20.00	40.00	75.00	125	—

Note: Two varieties of the AH1325 date are known

KM# 841 1/2 RUPEE (Qiran)
4.6500 g., 0.5000 Silver 0.0747 oz. ASW, 19 mm. **Obv:** Date at upper right of toughra **Rev:** Mosque above crossed cannons and swords, wreath surrounds, dated AH1320 **Mint:** Afghanistan

Date	Mintage	VG	F	VF	XF	Unc
AH1321	—	25.00	45.00	85.00	140	—
AH1323	—	30.00	55.00	100	170	—

KM# 844.1 1/2 RUPEE (Qiran)
4.6500 g., 0.5000 Silver 0.0747 oz. ASW, 19 mm.
Obv: Inscription and date within wreath **Rev:** Frozen date AH1320 split above mosque, crossed cannons and swords below, wreath surrounds **Mint:** Afghanistan

Date	Mintage	VG	F	VF	XF	Unc
AH1323	—	6.00	9.00	16.00	28.00	—
AH1324	—	6.00	9.00	15.00	25.00	—
AH1326	—	6.00	9.00	15.00	25.00	—
AH1327/6	—	6.00	9.00	15.00	25.00	—
AH1327	—	6.00	9.00	15.00	25.00	—

KM# 844.2 1/2 RUPEE (Qiran)
4.6500 g., 0.5000 Silver 0.0747 oz. ASW, 19 mm. **Obv:** Inscription and date within wreath **Rev:** Mosque above crossed cannons and swords, wreath surrounds, actual date at top **Mint:** Afghanistan

Date	Mintage	VG	F	VF	XF	Unc
AH1326/3	—	25.00	45.00	75.00	135	—

Note: AH1326/0 for actual date on reverse

AH1328	—	25.00	45.00	75.00	135	—
AH1329	—	25.00	45.00	75.00	135	—

KM# 852 1/2 RUPEE (Qiran)
4.6000 g., 0.5000 Silver 0.0739 oz. ASW, 20 mm. **Obv:** Text within wreath **Rev:** Mosque within 8-pointed star, wreath surrounds **Mint:** Afghanistan

Date	Mintage	VG	F	VF	XF	Unc
AH1329	—	3.50	5.50	8.50	16.00	—
AH1333	—	3.50	5.50	8.50	16.00	—
AH1334	—	4.50	7.50	12.50	22.50	—
AH1335	—	4.50	7.50	12.50	22.50	—
AH1337	—	3.50	5.50	8.50	16.00	—

KM# 864 1/2 RUPEE (Qiran)
5.0000 g., Silver **Obv. Leg.:** "Habibullah" **Rev:** Star of Solomon **Mint:** Afghanistan

---

Date	Mintage	VG	F	VF	XF	Unc
AH1335	—		300	500		—

KM# 865 1/2 RUPEE (Qiran)
Silver **Obv:** Uncircled inscription **Rev:** Mosque within 8-pointed star, wreath surrounds **Mint:** Afghanistan

Date	Mintage	VG	F	VF	XF	Unc
AH1337 (1918)	—		4.00	9.00	15.00	25.00

Note: Five varieties are known

KM# 832 RUPEE
9.2000 g., 0.5000 Silver 0.1479 oz. ASW, 25 mm. **Obv:** Toughra of Habibullah in wreath, star above **Rev:** Mosque above crossed swords and cannons, wreath surrounds **Mint:** Afghanistan

Date	Mintage	VG	F	VF	XF	Unc
AH1319	—	8.00	12.00	25.00	70.00	—

Note: Two varieties are known

KM# 833.1 RUPEE
9.2000 g., 0.5000 Silver 0.1479 oz. ASW, 25 mm.
Obv: "Afghanistan" above small toughra, star at right **Rev:** Mosque above crossed swords and cannons, large inverted pyramid dome **Mint:** Afghanistan

Date	Mintage	VG	F	VF	XF	Unc
AH1319	—	4.00	5.50	10.00	25.00	—
AH1320	—	4.00	5.50	8.50	20.00	—
AH1325	—	7.00	15.00	25.00	50.00	—

KM# 833.2 RUPEE
9.2000 g., 0.5000 Silver 0.1479 oz. ASW, 25 mm. **Obv:** Tughra within wreath, without star **Rev:** Swords and cannons crossed below mosque, wreath surrounds **Mint:** Afghanistan

Date	Mintage	VG	F	VF	XF	Unc
AH1319	—	4.00	5.50	10.00	25.00	—
AH1325	—	7.00	15.00	25.00	50.00	—

KM# 839 RUPEE
9.2000 g., 0.5000 Silver 0.1479 oz. ASW, 25 mm. **Obv:** "Afghanistan" divided by a star above large toughra **Rev:** Swords and cannons below mosque, wreath surrounds **Mint:** Afghanistan

Date	Mintage	VG	F	VF	XF	Unc
AH1320	—	4.00	6.00	10.00	20.00	—

KM# 840.1 RUPEE
9.2000 g., 0.5000 Silver 0.1479 oz. ASW, 25 mm. **Obv:** Tughra within wreath **Rev:** Small dome mosque above weapons within wreath **Mint:** Afghanistan

Date	Mintage	VG	F	VF	XF	Unc
AH1320	—	5.00	8.00	15.00	35.00	—

KM# 840.2 RUPEE
9.2000 g., 0.5000 Silver 0.1479 oz. ASW, 25 mm. **Obv:** Date in loop of toughra, wreath surrounds **Rev:** Mosque above weapons within wreath **Mint:** Afghanistan

Date	Mintage	VG	F	VF	XF	Unc
AH1321	—	10.00	15.00	25.00	50.00	—

KM# 842.1 RUPEE
9.2000 g., 0.5000 Silver 0.1479 oz. ASW, 25 mm. **Obv:** Text within wreath **Rev:** "Afghanistan" above mosque, crossed swords and cannons below, wreath surrounds **Mint:** Afghanistan

Date	Mintage	VG	F	VF	XF	Unc
AH1321	—	4.00	7.00	11.00	22.50	—

Note: Two varieties exist for AH1321 date

AH1322	—	4.00	7.00	11.00	22.50	—

KM# 842.2 RUPEE
9.2000 g., 0.5000 Silver 0.1479 oz. ASW, 25 mm. **Obv:** Text within wreath **Rev:** Mosque above crossed cannons, wreath surrounds **Mint:** Afghanistan

Date	Mintage	VG	F	VF	XF	Unc
AH1322	—	4.00	5.00	9.00	20.00	—
AH1324	—	4.00	5.00	9.00	20.00	—
AH1325	—	5.00	8.00	12.00	25.00	—
AH1326	—	4.00	6.00	10.00	20.00	—
AH1327/6	—	6.00	8.00	15.00	30.00	—
AH1327	—	4.00	6.00	10.00	20.00	—
AH1328	—	6.00	8.00	15.00	30.00	—

Note: Two varieties exist for AH1328 date.

AH1329	—	6.00	8.00	15.00	30.00	—

KM# 847.1 RUPEE
9.2000 g., 0.5000 Silver 0.1479 oz. ASW, 25 mm. **Obv:** Date divided 13 Arabic "j" 28 **Rev:** Large dome mosque without "Afghanistan" **Mint:** Afghanistan

Date	Mintage	VG	F	VF	XF	Unc
AH1328	—	7.00	15.00	25.00	50.00	—

KM# 847.2 RUPEE
9.2000 g., 0.5000 Silver 0.1479 oz. ASW, 25 mm. **Obv:** Date divided 132 Arabic "j" 8 **Rev:** Mosque above weapons, wreath surrounds **Mint:** Afghanistan

Date	Mintage	VG	F	VF	XF	Unc
AH1328	—	10.00	20.00	30.00	60.00	—

KM# 853 RUPEE
9.2000 g., 0.5000 Silver 0.1479 oz. ASW, 25-26 mm. **Obv:** Name and titles of Habibullah within wreath **Rev:** Mosque within 8-pointed star, wreath surrounds **Mint:** Afghanistan **Note:** Size varies. Two varieties exist for AH1330, 1331, and 1337 and three varieties exist for AH1333; thickness of obverse inscription and size of mosque dome on reverse vary.

Date	Mintage	VG	F	VF	XF	Unc
AH1329	—	4.00	6.00	10.00	20.00	—
AH1330	—	4.00	6.00	9.00	18.50	—
AH1331/0	—	4.00	6.00	9.00	18.60	—
AH1331	—	4.00	6.00	9.00	18.50	—
AH1332	—	4.00	6.00	9.00	18.50	—
AH1333	—	4.00	6.00	9.00	18.50	—
AH1334	—	4.00	6.00	9.00	18.50	—
AH1335	—	4.00	6.00	9.00	18.50	—
AH1337	—	4.00	6.00	10.00	20.00	—

Note: Two varieties of the AH1337 date exist, with either crossed cannons or a six-pointed star below the mosque

KM# 853a   RUPEE
10.0500 g., 0.9000 Gold 0.2908 oz. AGW, 26 mm. **Obv:** Name and titles within wreath **Rev:** Mosque within 8-pointed star, wreath surrounds

Date	Mintage	F	VF	XF	Unc	BU
AH1334	—				1,625	—

KM# 834.1   5 RUPEES
45.6000 g., 0.9000 Silver 1.3194 oz. ASW, 46 mm. **Obv:** Tughra divides date, wreath surrounds **Rev:** Similar to KM#826 **Mint:** Afghanistan

Date	Mintage	VG	F	VF	XF	Unc
AH1319	—	28.00	45.00	90.00	175	—

KM# 834.2   5 RUPEES
45.6000 g., 0.9000 Silver 1.3194 oz. ASW, 46 mm. **Obv:** Date at left of tughra, wreath surrounds **Mint:** Afghanistan

Date	Mintage	VG	F	VF	XF	Unc
AH1319	—	28.00	45.00	90.00	175	—

KM# 843   5 RUPEES
45.6000 g., 0.9000 Silver 1.3194 oz. ASW, 45 mm. **Obv:** Wreath surrounds text **Rev:** Mosque within beaded circle, wreath surrounds **Mint:** Afghanistan **Note:** Most dates are recut dies. Two varieties are known for each date, AH1324 and 1327.

Date	Mintage	VG	F	VF	XF	Unc
AH1322	—	27.50	32.50	50.00	100	—
AH1324	—	27.50	30.00	45.00	90.00	—
AH1326	—	27.50	30.00	45.00	90.00	—
AH1327/6	—	27.50	30.00	45.00	90.00	—
AH1328	—	30.00	35.00	55.00	120	—
AH1329	—	27.50	40.00	70.00	145	—

KM# 835   TILLA (10 Rupees)
4.6000 g., 0.9000 Gold 0.1331 oz. AGW, 21 mm. **Obv:** Star above toughra within wreath **Rev:** Flags flank mosque above weapons, wreath surrounds **Mint:** Afghanistan

Date	Mintage	VG	F	VF	XF	Unc
AH1319	—	125	140	175	240	—

KM# 836.1   TILLA (10 Rupees)
4.6000 g., 0.9000 Gold 0.1331 oz. AGW, 21 mm. **Obv:** Legend divided by star above toughra, wreath surrounds **Obv. Leg.:** "Afghanistan" **Rev:** Flags flank mosque above weapons, wreath surrounds **Mint:** Afghanistan

Date	Mintage	VG	F	VF	XF	Unc
AH1319	—	.130	145	185	250	—

KM# 836.2   TILLA (10 Rupees)
4.6000 g., 0.9000 Gold 0.1331 oz. AGW, 21 mm. **Obv:** Legend above toughra with star to right, wreath surrounds **Obv. Leg.:** "Afghanistan" **Rev:** Flags flank mosque above weapons, wreath surrounds **Mint:** Afghanistan

Date	Mintage	VG	F	VF	XF	Unc
AH1320	—	130	145	185	250	—

KM# A856   TILLA (10 Rupees)
4.6000 g., 0.9000 Gold 0.1331 oz. AGW, 21 mm. **Obv:** Date divided **Mint:** Afghanistan

Date	Mintage	VG	F	VF	XF	Unc
AH1325	—		450	650	900	—

KM# 856   TILLA (10 Rupees)
4.6000 g., 0.9000 Gold 0.1331 oz. AGW, 21 mm. **Obv. Leg.:** Habibullah... **Mint:** Afghanistan

Date	Mintage	VG	F	VF	XF	Unc
AH1335	—	170	200	260	330	—
AH1336	—	125	140	175	240	—
AH1337	—	130	145	180	245	—

KM# 879   2 TILLAS (20 Rupees)
9.2000 g., 0.9000 Gold 0.2662 oz. AGW, 22 mm. **Obv:** Text above date, wreath surrounds **Rev:** Mosque within 8-pointed star, denomination above, wreath surrounds **Mint:** Afghanistan

Date	Mintage	F	VF	XF	Unc	BU
SH1298 (1919)	—		BV	275	400	550

KM# 889   5 AMANI (50 Rupees)
23.0000 g., 0.9000 Gold 0.6655 oz. AGW, 34 mm. **Obv:** Tughra within wreath, Persian "5" above tughra; "Al Ghazi" at right **Rev:** Legend above mosque within 7-pointed star, wreath surrounds **Rev. Leg.:** "Amaniya" **Mint:** Afghanistan

Date	Mintage	VG	F	VF	XF	Unc
SH1299 (1920)	—	BV	650	750	1,500	—

KM# 890   5 AMANI (50 Rupees)
23.0000 g., 0.9000 Gold 0.6655 oz. AGW, 34 mm. **Obv:** Star above toughra within wreath **Rev:** Mosque within 7-pointed star, wreath surrounds, persian "5" above mosque **Mint:** Afghanistan

Date	Mintage	VG	F	VF	XF	Unc
SH1299	—	BV	600	750	1,500	—

Amanullah
AH1337-1348 / 1919-1929AD
LOCAL COINAGE

KM# 965   PAISA
Copper, 20 mm. **Obv:** Denomination "Yek Paisa" **Mint:** Without Mint Name **Note:** Crudely struck. Believed to be struck at Kabul.

Date	Mintage	Good	VG	F	VF	XF
SH1298 (1919)	—	4.50	7.50	12.50	22.00	—
SH1299 (1920)	—	4.50	7.50	12.50	22.00	—

KM# 966   PAISA
Copper **Mint:** Without Mint Name **Note:** Crudely struck; without mint name, believed to be struck at Kabul.

Date	Mintage	Good	VG	F	VF	XF
SH1299 (1920)	—	6.00	10.00	16.50	27.50	—

KM# 967   SHAHI (5 Paise)
Copper **Rev:** Both denominations **Mint:** Without Mint Name **Note:** Crudely struck; without mint name, believed to be struck at Kabul.

Date	Mintage	Good	VG	F	VF	XF
AH1338 - SH1298 (1919)	—	6.00	10.00	16.50	27.50	—
AH1338 - SH1299 (1920)	—	7.50	12.50	20.00	35.00	—
AH1339 - SH1299 (1920)	—	6.00	10.00	16.50	27.50	—

KM# A846   10 PAISE
Copper **Mint:** Without Mint Name **Note:** Crudely struck; believed to be struck at Kabul.

Date	Mintage	Good	VG	F	VF	XF
SH1299 (1920)						

Note: Reported, not confirmed

MILLED COINAGE

10 Dinar = 1 Paisa; 5 Paise = 1 Shahi; 2 Shahi = 1 Sanar; 2 Sanar = 1 Abbasi; 1-1/2 Abbasi = 1 Qiran; 2 Qiran = 1 Kabuli Rupee; 1 Tilla = 10 Rupees

KM# 880   PAISA
Bronze Or Brass, 20 mm. **Mint:** Afghanistan

Date	Mintage	VG	F	VF	XF	Unc
SH1299 (1920)	—	2.50	5.50	12.00	22.50	—
SH1300 (1921)	—	3.50	7.00	15.00	25.00	—
SH1301 (1922)	—	3.50	7.00	15.00	25.00	—

Note: Two varieties are known dated SH1301

| SH1302 (1923) | — | 2.50 | 5.50 | 12.00 | 22.50 | — |
| SH1303 (1924) | — | 2.50 | 5.50 | 12.00 | 22.50 | — |

KM# 859   SHAHI (5 Paise)
Copper Or Brass, 25 mm. **Mint:** Afghanistan **Note:** Thick flan.

Date	Mintage	VG	F	VF	XF	Unc
AH1337	—	12.00	22.00	40.00	70.00	—

KM# 860   SHAHI (5 Paise)
Copper Or Brass, 25 mm. **Mint:** Afghanistan **Note:** Thin flan.

Date	Mintage	VG	F	VF	XF	Unc
AH1337	—	10.00	20.00	35.00	55.00	—

KM# 861   SANAR (10 Paisa)
Copper Or Brass, 29-30 mm. **Obv:** Text within inner circle, stars surround **Rev:** Mosque within 8-pointed star, within circle, stars surrounds **Mint:** Afghanistan **Note:** Thick flan. Size varies.

Date	Mintage	VG	F	VF	XF	Unc
AH1337	—	10.00	17.50	30.00	55.00	—

KM# 862   SANAR (10 Paisa)
Copper Or Brass, 29-30 mm. **Mint:** Afghanistan **Note:** Thin flan. Size varies.

Date	Mintage	VG	F	VF	XF	Unc
AH1337	—	9.00	14.00	20.00	35.00	—

KM# 881   3 SHAHI (15 Paisa)
Copper, 33 mm. **Obv:** Stars surround inner circle, without "Shamsi" **Rev:** Mosque within 7-pointed star, within circle, stars surrounds **Mint:** Afghanistan **Note:** Four varieties for date SH1299 and three varieties for date SH1300 are known.

Date	Mintage	VG	F	VF	XF	Unc
SH1298 (1919)	—	4.00	15.00	22.00	40.00	—
AH1299 (1920)	—	1.50	3.50	8.00	17.00	—
AH1300 (1921)	—	1.50	3.50	8.00	17.00	—

KM# 870   3 SHAHI (15 Paisa)
Copper, 32-33 mm. **Obv:** "Al-Ghazi", without "Shamsi" by date **Rev:** Mosque within 8-pointed star, within circle, stars surrounds **Mint:** Afghanistan **Note:** Size varies.

Date	Mintage	VG	F	VF	XF	Unc
SH1298 (1919)	—	3.00	5.00	10.00	20.00	—
SH1299 (1920)	—	3.00	5.00	10.00	20.00	—

Note: 2 varieties of SH1299 exist

KM# 871.1   3 SHAHI (15 Paisa)
11.5000 g., Copper, 33 mm. **Obv:** "Al-Ghazi, Shamsi" **Rev:** Mosque within 8-pointed star, within circle, stars surrounds **Mint:** Afghanistan **Note:** Thick flan.

Date	Mintage	VG	F	VF	XF	Unc
SH1298 (1919)	—	10.00	15.00	22.00	40.00	—

KM# 871.2   3 SHAHI (15 Paisa)
9.0000 g., Copper, 33 mm. **Obv:** "Al-Ghazi, Shamsi" **Rev:** Mosque within 8-pointed star, within circle, stars surrounds **Mint:** Afghanistan **Note:** Thin flan.

Date	Mintage	VG	F	VF	XF	Unc
SH1298 (1919)	—	2.00	4.00	9.00	18.00	—

Note: Two reverse varieties with 10 or 11 circular stars exist

KM# 872   3 SHAHI (15 Paisa)
Copper, 33 mm. **Obv:** "Shamsi" **Rev:** Mosque in seven-pointed star **Mint:** Afghanistan

Date	Mintage	VG	F	VF	XF	Unc
SH1298 (1919)	—	2.00	4.00	9.00	18.00	—

KM# 881a   3 SHAHI (15 Paisa)
Brass, 33 mm. **Obv:** Stars surround inner circle, without "Shamsi" **Rev:** Mosque within 7-pointed star, within circle, stars surrounds **Mint:** Afghanistan **Note:** Prev. KM#892.

Date	Mintage	VG	F	VF	XF	Unc
SH1300 (1921)	—	4.00	8.00	15.00	30.00	—

KM# 893   3 SHAHI (15 Paisa)
Copper, 33 mm. **Obv:** Tughra, stars surround **Rev:** Mosque within 7-pointed star, within circle, stars surrounds **Mint:** Afghanistan

Date	Mintage	VG	F	VF	XF	Unc
SH1300 (1921)	—	1.50	3.50	8.00	17.00	—
SH1301 (1922)	—	1.50	3.50	8.00	17.00	—

Note: 2 varieties of SH1301 exist

SH130x (1923) (error)	—	—	—	—	—	—
SH1303 (1924)	—	1.50	3.50	8.00	17.00	—

KM# 891   3 SHAHI (15 Paisa)
Brass **Obv:** Eight stars around perimeter **Rev:** Eight stars around perimeter **Mint:** Afghanistan

Date	Mintage	VG	F	VF	XF	Unc
SH1300 (1921)	—	—	—	—	—	—

KM# 874   ABBASI (20 Paisa)
Copper Or Billon, 20 mm. **Obv:** Text within circle, stars surround **Rev:** Mosque within 8-pointed star, within circle, stars surrounds **Mint:** Afghanistan

Date	Mintage	VG	F	VF	XF	Unc
SH1298 (1919)	—	50.00	75.00	90.00	150	—

KM# 882   ABBASI (20 Paisa)
Copper Or Billon, 25 mm. **Mint:** Afghanistan

Date	Mintage	VG	F	VF	XF	Unc
SH1299 (1920)	—	15.00	30.00	50.00	75.00	—

KM# 883   ABBASI (20 Paisa)
Copper Or Billon, 25 mm. **Obv:** Tughra, stars surround **Rev:** Mosque within 7-pointed star, stars surrounds **Mint:** Afghanistan

Date	Mintage	VG	F	VF	XF	Unc
SH1299 (1920)	—	2.00	6.00	15.00	30.00	—
SH1300 (1921)	—	2.00	6.00	15.00	30.00	—
SH1301 (1922)	—	2.00	6.00	15.00	30.00	—

Note: Two varieties for date SH1301 exist

SH1302 (1923)	—	2.00	6.00	15.00	30.00	—
SH2031 (1923) Error	—	7.00	15.00	30.00	50.00	—
SH1303 (1924)	—	2.00	6.00	15.00	30.00	—

KM# 866   1/2 RUPEE (Qiran)
Silver **Obv:** Legend within circle and wreath **Rev:** Mosque within 8-pointed star, wreath surrounds **Mint:** Afghanistan

Date	Mintage	VG	F	VF	XF	Unc
AH1337 (1918)	—	150	300	500	725	—

KM# 875   1/2 RUPEE (Qiran)
4.7500 g., 0.5000 Silver 0.0764 oz. ASW, 20 mm. **Obv:** Star above inscription, "Shamsi" **Rev:** Mosque within 8-pointed star, wreath surrounds **Mint:** Afghanistan

Date	Mintage	VG	F	VF	XF	Unc
SH1298 (1919)	—	3.00	6.00	10.00	20.00	—

Note: Two varieties are known

KM# 876   1/2 RUPEE (Qiran)
4.7500 g., 0.5000 Silver 0.0764 oz. ASW, 20 mm. **Obv:** "Al-Ghazi" above inscription, "Shamsi" **Rev:** Mosque within 8-pointed star, wreath surrounds **Mint:** Afghanistan

Date	Mintage	VG	F	VF	XF	Unc
SH1298 (1919)	—	15.00	30.00	50.00	75.00	—

KM# 884   1/2 RUPEE (Qiran)
4.7500 g., 0.5000 Silver 0.0764 oz. ASW, 20 mm. **Obv:** Without "Shamsi" **Mint:** Afghanistan

Date	Mintage	VG	F	VF	XF	Unc
SH1299 (1920)	—	3.00	4.00	7.00	15.00	—

Note: Two varieties are known dated 1299

SH1300 (1921)	—	3.00	4.00	7.00	15.00	—

KM# 894   1/2 RUPEE (Qiran)
4.7500 g., 0.5000 Silver 0.0764 oz. ASW, 20 mm. **Obv:** Tughra within wreath **Rev:** Mosque within 7-pointed star, wreath surrounds **Mint:** Afghanistan

Date	Mintage	VG	F	VF	XF	Unc
SH1300 (1921)	—	2.00	4.00	7.00	12.00	—
SH1301 (1922)	—	2.00	4.00	7.00	12.00	—
SH1302 (1923)	—	2.00	4.00	7.00	12.00	—
SH1303 (1924)	—	2.00	4.00	7.00	12.00	—

KM# 867   RUPEE
9.2000 g., 0.5000 Silver 0.1479 oz. ASW, 25 mm. **Obv:** Name and titles of Amanullah, star above inscription **Rev:** Mosque within 8-pointed star, wreath surrounds **Mint:** Afghanistan

Date	Mintage	VG	F	VF	XF	Unc
AH1337 (1918)	—	6.00	10.00	18.00	30.00	—

Note: Seven varieties are known

KM# 877   RUPEE
9.0000 g., 0.9000 Silver 0.2604 oz. ASW, 25 mm. **Obv:** "Al-Ghazi" above inscription **Rev:** Mosque within 8-pointed star, wreath surrounds **Mint:** Afghanistan

Date	Mintage	VG	F	VF	XF	Unc
SH1298 (1919)	—	5.00	6.50	10.00	18.50	—

Note: Four varieties are known for date SH1298

SH1299 (1920)	—	5.00	6.50	10.00	18.50	—

Note: Two varieties are known for date SH1299

KM# 885   RUPEE
9.2500 g., 0.9000 Silver 0.2676 oz. ASW, 27 mm. **Obv:** Toughra of Amanullah **Rev:** Mosque within 7-pointed star, wreath surrounds **Mint:** Afghanistan

Date	Mintage	VG	F	VF	XF	Unc
SH1299 (1920)	—	5.25	6.50	8.00	16.50	—
SH1300 (1921)	—	5.25	6.50	8.00	16.50	—
SH1301 (1922)	—	5.25	6.50	8.00	16.50	—
SH1302/1 (1923)	—	5.25	6.50	8.00	16.50	—
SH1302 (1923)	—	5.25	6.50	8.00	16.50	—
SH1303 (1924)	—	5.25	6.50	8.00	16.50	—

KM# 878   2-1/2 RUPEES
22.9200 g., 0.9000 Silver 0.6632 oz. ASW, 34 mm. **Obv:** Tughra

above date within wreath **Rev:** Mosque within 7-pointed star, wreath surrounds **Mint:** Afghanistan **Note:** Two varieties each are known for dates SH1298-1300.

Date	Mintage	VG	F	VF	XF	Unc
SH1298 (1919)	—	12.50	16.50	20.00	45.00	—
SH1299 (1920)	—	9.50	12.50	17.50	40.00	—
SH1300 (1921)	—	9.50	12.50	17.50	40.00	—
SH1301 (1922)	—	9.50	12.50	15.00	35.00	—
SH1302 (1923)	—	9.50	12.50	15.00	35.00	—
SH1303 (1924)	—	9.50	12.50	15.00	35.00	—

KM# 886   1/2 AMANI (5 Rupees)
2.3000 g., 0.9000 Gold 0.0665 oz. AGW, 16 mm. **Obv:** Tughra within wreath **Rev:** Mosque within 7-pointed star, wreath surrounds **Mint:** Afghanistan

Date	Mintage	VG	F	VF	XF	Unc
SH1299 (1920)	—	65.00	75.00	95.00	135	—

KM# 868.1   TILLA (10 Rupees)
4.6000 g., 0.9000 Gold 0.1331 oz. AGW, 21 mm. **Obv:** Text within wreath **Obv. Leg.:** "Amanullah..." **Rev:** Mosque within 8-pointed star, crossed swords below mosque, wreath surrounds **Mint:** Afghanistan

Date	Mintage	VG	F	VF	XF	Unc
AH1337 (1918)	—	125	140	165	225	—

KM# 868.2   TILLA (10 Rupees)
4.6000 g., 0.9000 Gold 0.1331 oz. AGW, 21 mm. **Obv:** Text within wreath **Rev:** Mosque within 8-pointed star, 6-pointed star below mosque, wreath surrounds **Mint:** Afghanistan

Date	Mintage	VG	F	VF	XF	Unc
AH1337 (1918)	—	125	150	175	250	—

KM# 887   AMANI (10 Rupees)
4.6000 g., 0.9000 Gold 0.1331 oz. AGW, 22 mm. **Obv:** Tughra above date within wreath **Rev:** Mosque within 7-pointed star, wreath surrounds **Mint:** Afghanistan

Date	Mintage	VG	F	VF	XF	Unc
SH1299 (1920)	—	—	BV	135	175	—

KM# 888   2 AMANI (20 Rupees)
9.2000 g., 0.9000 Gold 0.2662 oz. AGW, 24 mm. **Obv:** Tughra above date within wreath **Rev:** Mosque within 7-pointed star, wreath surrounds **Mint:** Afghanistan

Date	Mintage	VG	F	VF	XF	Unc
SH1299 (1920)	—	—	BV	260	285	320
SH1300 (1921)	—	—	BV	260	285	320
SH1301 (1922)	—	—	BV	260	285	320
SH1302 (1923)	—	—	BV	260	285	320
SH1303 (1924)	—	—	BV	260	285	320

KM# 900   HABIBI (30 Rupees)
4.6000 g., 0.9000 Gold 0.1331 oz. AGW **Obv:** Small star replaces "30 Rupees" in legend **Rev:** Value stated as "Habibi"

Date	Mintage	VG	F	VF	XF	Unc
AH1347	—	BV	135	200	325	—

DECIMAL COINAGE

100 Pul = 1 Afghani; 20 Afghani = 1 Amani

KM# 905   2 PUL
2.0000 g., Bronze Or Brass, 18 mm. **Obv:** Tughra within inner circle, spray below **Rev:** Denomination within inner circle, spray below **Mint:** Afghanistan

Date	Mintage	F	VF	XF	Unc	BU
SH1304 (1925)	—	3.00	5.00	9.00	15.00	—
SH1305 (1926)	—	3.00	5.00	9.00	15.00	—

KM# 906   5 PUL
3.0000 g., Bronze Or Brass, 22 mm. **Obv:** Tughra within inner circle, spray below **Rev:** Denomination within inner circle, spray below **Mint:** Afghanistan

Date	Mintage	F	VF	XF	Unc	BU
SH1304 (1925)	—	1.75	3.50	6.00	14.00	—
SH1305 (1926)	—	1.50	3.00	5.50	14.00	—

KM# 907   10 PUL
6.0000 g., Copper, 24 mm. **Obv:** Tughra within inner circle, spray below **Rev:** Denomination within inner circle, spray below **Mint:** Afghanistan

Date	Mintage	F	VF	XF	Unc	BU
SH1304 (1925)	—	2.00	4.00	6.00	15.00	—
SH1305 (1926)	—	2.50	4.50	7.00	20.00	—
SH1306 (1927)	—	2.50	4.50	7.00	20.00	—

KM# 908   20 PUL
2.0000 g., Billon, 19 mm. **Obv:** Tughra within inner circle, spray below **Rev:** Denomination within inner circle, spray below **Mint:** Afghanistan **Note:** Varieties exist.

Date	Mintage	F	VF	XF	Unc	BU
SH1304 (1925)	—	50.00	75.00	100	170	—
SH134 (1925) Error	—					
ND(ca.1926)	—	35.00	60.00	90.00	160	—

KM# 909   1/2 AFGHANI (50 Pul)
5.0000 g., 0.5000 Silver 0.0804 oz. ASW, 25 mm. **Obv:** Tughra, date and spray below **Rev:** Mosque with flags flanking within wreath **Mint:** Afghanistan

Date	Mintage	F	VF	XF	Unc	BU
SH1304/7 (1925)	—	2.00	3.50	6.50	18.50	—
Note: Two varieties are known dated SH1304						
SH1305/8 (1926)	—	2.00	3.50	6.50	18.50	—
SH1306/9 (1927)	—	2.00	3.50	6.50	18.50	—

KM# 915   1/2 AFGHANI (50 Pul)
5.0000 g., 0.5000 Silver 0.0804 oz. ASW, 25 mm. **Obv:** Date below mosque **Mint:** Afghanistan

Date	Mintage	F	VF	XF	Unc	BU
SH1307/10 (1928)	—	3.00	6.00	12.00	35.00	—

KM# 910   AFGHANI (100 Pul)
10.0000 g., 0.9000 Silver 0.2893 oz. ASW, 29 mm. **Obv:** Date below toughra **Mint:** Afghanistan **Note:** Two varieties each are known for dates SH1305-06.

Date	Mintage	F	VF	XF	Unc	BU
SH1304/7 (1925)	—	6.00	7.00	12.50	28.00	—
Note: Three varieties are known for date SH1304						
SH1305/8 (1926)	—	6.00	7.00	12.50	28.00	—
SH1305/9 (1926)	—	6.00	7.00	12.50	28.00	—
SH1306/9 (1927)	—	6.00	7.00	12.50	28.00	—

KM# 913   2-1/2 AFGHANIS
25.0000 g., 0.9000 Silver 0.7234 oz. ASW, 38 mm. **Obv:** Tughra within wreath **Rev:** Mosque within wreath **Mint:** Afghanistan **Note:** Two varieties are known for each date.

Date	Mintage	F	VF	XF	Unc	BU
SH1305/8 (1926)	—	15.00	25.00	50.00	125	—
SH1306/9 (1927)	—	15.00	20.00	40.00	90.00	—

KM# 911   1/2 AMANI (5 Rupees)
3.0000 g., 0.9000 Gold 0.0868 oz. AGW, 18 mm. **Mint:** Afghanistan

Date	Mintage	VG	F	VF	XF	Unc
SH1304/7 (1925)	—	—	BV	95.00	120	165
SH1305/8 (1926)	—	—	BV	95.00	120	165
SH1306/9 (1927)	—	—	BV	95.00	120	165

KM# 912   AMANI
6.0000 g., 0.9000 Gold 0.1736 oz. AGW, 23 mm. **Mint:** Afghanistan

Date	Mintage	F	VF	XF	Unc	BU
SH1304/7 (1925)	—	—	BV	170	185	250
SH1305/8 (1926)	—	—	BV	170	220	300
SH1306/9 (1927)	—	—	BV	170	185	250

KM# 914   2-1/2 AMANI
15.0000 g., 0.9000 Gold 0.4340 oz. AGW, 29 mm. **Obv:** Tughra above date within wreath **Rev:** Mosque within wreath **Mint:** Afghanistan

Date	Mintage	F	VF	XF	Unc	BU
SH1306/9 (1927)	—	—	—	5,000	7,000	—

Habibullah Ghazi
Rebel; AH1347-1348 / 1929AD; Struck in the name of Baccha-i-Saqao

LOCAL COINAGE

KM# 969   5 PAISE
Brass **Mint:** Herat

Date	Mintage	Good	VG	F	VF	XF
AH1347	—	5.00	8.50	15.00	25.00	—

KM# 970.1 10 PAISE
Brass **Rev:** Denomination "Dah" written above "Paisa" **Mint:** Herat

Date	Mintage	Good	VG	F	VF	XF
AH1347	—	6.00	10.00	16.50	27.50	—

KM# 970.2 10 PAISE
Brass **Rev:** Denomination "Dah" written at right of "Paisa" **Mint:** Herat

Date	Mintage	Good	VG	F	VF	XF
AH1347	—	7.50	12.50	20.00	35.00	—

KM# 972 20 PAISE
Brass **Mint:** Herat

Date	Mintage	Good	VG	F	VF	XF
AH1347	—	7.50	12.50	20.00	35.00	—
AH1348	—	10.00	15.00	25.00	40.00	—

Muhammed Nadir Shah
AH1348-1350 / 1929-1933AD

MILLED COINAGE

10 Dinar = 1 Paisa; 5 Paise = 1 Shahi; 2 Shahi = 1 Sanar; 2 Sanar = 1 Abbasi; 1-1/2 Abbasi = 1 Qiran; 2 Qiran = 1 Kabuli Rupee; 1 Tilla = 10 Rupees

KM# 901 10 PAISE
4.1000 g., Copper, 22 mm. **Obv:** Text above spray **Rev:** Mosque within 8-pointed star, spray below **Mint:** Afghanistan

Date	Mintage	VG	F	VF	XF	Unc
AH1348	—	6.00	12.00	20.00	40.00	—

KM# 895 20 PAISE
5.7000 g., Bronze Or Brass, 25 mm. **Obv:** Text within wreath **Rev:** Mosque within 8-pointed star, wreath surrounds **Mint:** Afghanistan

Date	Mintage	VG	F	VF	XF	Unc
AH1347	—	3.00	5.00	7.50	18.00	—

KM# 896 1/2 RUPEE (Qiran)
4.7000 g., 0.5000 Silver 0.0756 oz. ASW, 21 mm. **Obv:** Text within wreath **Rev:** Value (Qiran) above mosque within 8-pointed star, wreath surrounds **Mint:** Afghanistan

Date	Mintage	VG	F	VF	XF	Unc
AH1347	—	4.00	7.00	12.00	20.00	—

KM# 902 1/2 RUPEE (Qiran)
4.7000 g., 0.5000 Silver 0.0756 oz. ASW, 21 mm. **Obv:** Text within wreath **Rev:** Value (Qiran) above mosque within 8-pointed star, wreath surrounds **Mint:** Afghanistan

Date	Mintage	VG	F	VF	XF	Unc
AH1348	—	12.00	20.00	32.00	50.00	—

KM# 897 RUPEE
9.1000 g., 0.9000 Silver 0.2633 oz. ASW, 25 mm. **Obv:** Name and titles of Amir Habibullah (The Usurper) **Rev:** Mosque within 8-pointed star, wreath surrounds **Mint:** Afghanistan

Date	Mintage	VG	F	VF	XF	Unc
AH1347	—	5.00	9.00	15.00	25.00	—

KM# 898 RUPEE
9.1000 g., 0.9000 Silver 0.2633 oz. ASW, 26 mm. **Obv:** Title in circle **Rev:** Mosque within 8-pointed star, wreath surrounds **Mint:** Afghanistan

Date	Mintage	VG	F	VF	XF	Unc
AH1347	—	25.00	35.00	55.00	90.00	—

KM# 899 HABIBI (30 Rupees)
4.6000 g., 0.9000 Gold 0.1331 oz. AGW, 21 mm. **Obv:** Value text within wreath **Rev:** Mosque within 8-pointed star, wreath surrounds, value stated as Habibi (2 values on coin) **Mint:** Afghanistan

Date	Mintage	VG	F	VF	XF	Unc
AH1347	—	BV	140	200	325	—

DECIMAL COINAGE

100 Pul = 1 Afghani; 20 Afghani = 1 Amani

KM# A922 PUL
1.0000 g., Bronze Or Brass, 15 mm. **Obv:** Text, stars surround **Rev:** Denomination within inner circle, stars surround **Mint:** Afghanistan

Date	Mintage	F	VF	XF	Unc	BU
AH1349 (1930)	—	0.75	1.25	1.75	2.50	—

KM# 922 PUL
Bronze Or Brass, 15 mm. **Obv:** Toughra **Rev:** Denomination within inner circle **Mint:** Afghanistan

Date	Mintage	F	VF	XF	Unc	BU
AH1349 (1930)	—	100	250	300	400	—

KM# 917 2 PUL
2.0000 g., Bronze Or Brass, 18 mm. **Obv:** Tughra within inner circle **Rev:** Denomination within inner circle, spray below **Mint:** Afghanistan

Date	Mintage	F	VF	XF	Unc	BU
AH1348 (1929)	—	1.25	2.50	3.50	8.00	—
AH1349/8 (1930)	—	1.25	2.50	3.50	8.00	—

KM# 923 5 PUL
3.0000 g., Bronze Or Brass, 22 mm. **Obv:** Tughra within inner circle, wreath surrounds **Rev:** Denomination within inner circle, spray below **Mint:** Afghanistan

Date	Mintage	F	VF	XF	Unc	BU
AH1349 (1930)	—	1.75	2.75	4.50	12.50	—

Date	Mintage	VG	F	VF	XF	Unc	BU
AH1350 (1931)	—	1.25	2.25	3.50	12.50	—	

Note: Two varieties are known dated AH1350

KM# 929 5 PUL
3.0000 g., Bronze Or Brass, 21 mm. **Obv:** Text within beaded circle, wreath surrounds **Rev:** Denomination within beaded circle, spray below **Mint:** Afghanistan

Date	Mintage	F	VF	XF	Unc	BU
SH1311 (1932)	—	2.50	5.50	9.00	20.00	—
SH1312 (1933)	—	2.50	5.50	9.00	20.00	—
SH1313 (1934)	—	2.50	5.50	9.00	20.00	—
SH1314 (1935)	—	2.50	5.50	9.00	20.00	—

KM# 918 10 PUL
5.8000 g., Copper Or Brass, 25 mm. **Obv:** Tughra within circle **Rev:** Denomination within circle **Mint:** Afghanistan **Note:** Illustration shows an example struck off-center; prices are for properly struck specimens.

Date	Mintage	F	VF	XF	Unc	BU
AH1348 (1929)	—	2.00	3.50	5.00	15.00	—
AH1349 (1930)	—	2.25	4.00	5.50	15.00	—

Note: Small or large letters, weight varies: 5.8 or 5.3

KM# 930 10 PUL
Bronze Or Brass, 23 mm. **Obv:** Text within beaded circle, spray below **Rev:** Denomination within small beaded circle, spray below **Mint:** Afghanistan

Date	Mintage	F	VF	XF	Unc	BU
SH1311 (1932)	—	1.50	2.50	4.00	15.00	—
SH1312 (1933)	—	1.50	2.50	4.00	15.00	—
SH1313 (1934)	—	1.50	2.50	4.00	15.00	—
SH1314 (1935)	—	1.50	2.50	4.00	15.00	—

KM# 919 20 PUL
5.5589 g., Copper Or Brass, 25 mm. **Obv:** Tughra within inner circle, wreath surrounds **Rev:** Denomination within circle, wreath surrounds **Mint:** Afghanistan

Date	Mintage	F	VF	XF	Unc	BU
AH1348 (1929)	—	2.00	4.00	10.00	22.00	—
AH1349 (1930)	—	3.00	5.00	12.00	25.00	—

KM# 924 25 PUL
6.0000 g., Copper Or Brass, 25 mm. **Obv:** Tughra within circle, wreath surrounds **Rev:** Denomination within circle, wreath surrounds **Mint:** Afghanistan **Note:** 2 varieties of letters

Date	Mintage	F	VF	XF	Unc	BU
AH1349	—	2.50	5.00	10.00	20.00	—

Note: Two varieties are known dated AH1349.

134x	—	2.50	5.00	10.00	20.00	—

KM# 920 1/2 AFGHANI (50 Pul)
5.0000 g., 0.5000 Silver 0.0804 oz. ASW, 24 mm. **Obv:** Mosque above date within wreath **Mint:** Afghanistan **Note:** Prev. KM#919.

Date	Mintage	F	VF	XF	Unc	BU
AH1348/1 (1929)	—	1.75	2.50	5.00	14.00	—
AH1349/2 (1930)	—	1.75	2.50	5.00	14.00	—
AH1350/3 (1931)	—	1.75	2.50	5.00	14.00	—

KM# 926 1/2 AFGHANI (50 Pul)
1.8000 g., 0.5000 Silver 0.0289 oz. ASW, 24 mm. **Obv:** Text within beaded circle, wreath surrounds **Rev:** Mosque within wreath **Mint:** Afghanistan

Date	Mintage	F	VF	XF	Unc	BU
SH1310 (1931)	—	2.00	3.00	5.50	15.00	—
SH1311 (1932)	—	1.75	2.25	4.50	12.50	—
Note: Two die varieties exist						
SH1312 (1933)	—	2.00	3.00	5.50	15.00	—

Note: With and without diamond-shaped dot beneath the wreath on the obverse

KM# 921 AFGHANI (100 Pul)
9.9500 g., 0.9000 Silver 0.2879 oz. ASW, 30 mm. **Obv:** Tughra within wreath **Rev:** Mosque within wreath **Mint:** Afghanistan

Date	Mintage	F	VF	XF	Unc	BU
AH1348 (1929)	—	6.00	7.00	9.00	16.50	—
AH1349 (1930)	—	6.00	7.00	9.00	16.50	—
AH1350 (1931)	—	6.00	7.00	9.00	16.50	—

KM# 927 AFGHANI (100 Pul)
10.0000 g., 0.9000 Silver 0.2893 oz. ASW, 27 mm. **Obv:** Text within beaded circle, wreath surrounds **Rev:** Mosque within wreath **Mint:** Afghanistan

Date	Mintage	F	VF	XF	Unc	BU
SH1310 (1931)	—	—	—	125	200	—

KM# 927.2 AFGHANI (100 Pul)
10.0000 g., 0.9000 Silver 0.2893 oz. ASW, 27 mm. **Obv:** Text within beaded circle, wreath surrounds **Rev:** Mosque within wreath **Mint:** Afghanistan **Note:** Thick flan.

Date	Mintage	F	VF	XF	Unc	BU
SH1310 (1931)	—	—	—	—	—	—
Rare						

KM# 925 20 AFGHANIS
6.0000 g., 0.9000 Gold 0.1736 oz. AGW, 22 mm. **Mint:** Afghanistan

Date	Mintage	F	VF	XF	Unc	BU
AH1348	—	BV	175	200	300	400
AH1349	—	—	BV	170	240	325
AH1350	—	—	BV	170	240	325

Muhammed Zahir Shah
SH1312-1352 / 1933-1973AD
DECIMAL COINAGE
100 Pul = 1 Afghani; 20 Afghani = 1 Amani

KM# 928 2 PUL
2.0000 g., Bronze Or Brass, 18 mm. **Obv:** Text within beaded circle, wreath surrounds **Rev:** Denomination within beaded circle, wreath surrounds **Mint:** Afghanistan

Date	Mintage	F	VF	XF	Unc	BU
SH1311 (1932)	—	2.00	3.00	4.00	12.00	—
SH1312 (1933)	—	1.50	2.25	3.00	10.00	—
SH1313 (1934)	—	1.75	2.75	3.75	10.00	—
SH1314 (1935)	—	2.00	3.00	4.00	12.00	—

KM# 936 2 PUL
2.0000 g., Bronze, 15 mm. **Obv:** Arms within wreath, radiant background **Rev:** Denomination within inner circle, wreath surrounds, radiant background **Mint:** Afghanistan

Date	Mintage	F	VF	XF	Unc	BU
SH1316 (1937)	—	0.15	0.20	0.35	1.00	—

KM# 937 3 PUL
2.5000 g., Bronze, 16 mm. **Obv:** Arms within wreath, radiant background **Rev:** Denomination within inner circle, radiant background **Mint:** Afghanistan

Date	Mintage	F	VF	XF	Unc	BU
SH1316 (1937)	—	0.35	0.50	0.75	2.00	—

KM# 938 5 PUL
3.0300 g., Bronze, 17.1 mm. **Obv:** Arms within wreath, radiant background **Rev:** Denomination within inner circle, radiant background **Mint:** Afghanistan

Date	Mintage	F	VF	XF	Unc	BU
SH1316 (1937)	—	0.35	0.50	0.75	2.00	—

KM# 939 10 PUL
2.5000 g., Copper-Nickel, 18 mm. **Obv:** Arms within wreath, radiant background **Rev:** Denomination within inner circle, radiant background **Mint:** Afghanistan

Date	Mintage	F	VF	XF	Unc	BU
SH1316 (1937)	—	0.40	0.65	1.00	3.00	—

KM# 931 25 PUL
7.0000 g., Bronze Or Brass, 24-25 mm. **Obv:** Text within beaded circle, wreath surrounds **Rev:** Denomination within inner circle, wreath surrounds **Mint:** Afghanistan **Note:** Size varies.

Date	Mintage	F	VF	XF	Unc	BU
SH1312 (1933)	—	2.00	4.00	12.00	25.00	—
SH1313 (1934)	—	2.00	4.00	12.00	25.00	—
SH1314 (1935)	—	2.00	4.50	14.00	28.00	—
SH1316 (1937)	—	2.00	4.50	14.00	28.00	—

KM# 940 25 PUL
2.9000 g., Copper-Nickel, 20 mm. **Obv:** Text within inner circle, text surrounds **Rev:** Arms within wreath **Mint:** Afghanistan

Date	Mintage	F	VF	XF	Unc	BU
SH1316 (1937)	—	0.60	0.75	1.50	3.50	—

KM# 941 25 PUL
3.0000 g., Bronze, 20 mm. **Obv:** Text within inner circle, text surrounds **Rev:** Arms within wreath **Mint:** Afghanistan

Date	Mintage	F	VF	XF	Unc	BU
SH1330 (1951)	—	0.30	0.50	0.75	2.50	—
SH1331 (1952)	—	0.30	0.50	0.75	2.50	—
SH1332 (1953)	—	0.30	0.50	0.75	2.50	—
SH1333 (1954)	—	1.00	2.00	3.50	6.00	—

KM# 943 25 PUL
3.0000 g., Nickel Clad Steel **Edge:** Reeded **Mint:** Afghanistan

Date	Mintage	F	VF	XF	Unc	BU
SH1331 (1952)	—	1.00	2.00	3.50	7.00	—
SH1332 (1953)	—	1.50	3.00	5.00	9.00	—

KM# 944 25 PUL
3.0000 g., Nickel Clad Steel **Edge:** Plain **Mint:** Afghanistan

Date	Mintage	F	VF	XF	Unc	BU
SH1331 (1952)	—	0.35	0.65	1.00	3.00	—
SH1332 (1953)	—	0.35	0.65	1.00	3.00	—
SH1333 (1954)	—	0.35	0.65	1.00	3.00	—
SH1334/2 (1955)	—	1.50	3.00	5.00	9.00	—
SH1334 (1955)	—	0.35	0.65	1.00	3.00	—

KM# 945 25 PUL
Aluminum, 24 mm. **Obv:** Text within inner circle, text surrounds **Rev:** Arms within wreath **Mint:** Afghanistan **Note:** Struck on oversize 2 Afghani KM#949 planchets in 1970.

Date	Mintage	F	VF	XF	Unc	BU
SH1331 (1952)	—	0.50	1.00	3.00	10.00	—

KM# 932.1 1/2 AFGHANI (50 Pul)
4.7500 g., 0.5000 Silver 0.0764 oz. ASW, 24 mm. **Obv:** Smaller dotted circle within wreath **Rev:** Arms within wreath **Mint:** Afghanistan

Date	Mintage	F	VF	XF	Unc	BU
SH1312 (1933)	—	1.75	3.00	6.00	16.00	—

KM# 932.2 1/2 AFGHANI (50 Pul)
4.7500 g., 0.5000 Silver 0.0764 oz. ASW, 24 mm. **Obv:** Large dotted field in circle within wreath **Rev:** Arms within wreath **Mint:** Afghanistan

Date	Mintage	F	VF	XF	Unc	BU
SH1313 (1934)	—	1.75	3.00	6.00	16.00	—
Note: 60 dots in circle						
SH1314 (1935)	—	1.75	3.00	6.00	16.00	—
Note: 60 dots in circle						
SH1315 (1936)	—	1.50	2.50	5.50	15.00	—
Note: 40 dots in circle						
SH1316 (1937)	—	1.50	2.50	5.50	15.00	—
Note: 40 dots in circle						

KM# 947   1/2 AFGHANI (50 Pul)
5.0000 g., Nickel Clad Steel, 22.3 mm. **Obv:** Value on coin is
"50 Pul" in Pashto. **Rev:** Arms within wreath **Mint:** Afghanistan

Date	Mintage	F	VF	XF	Unc	BU
SH1331 (1952)	—	0.50	1.00	2.00	4.00	—
SH133x (1953)	—	5.00	7.50	12.50	20.00	—

KM# 942.1   50 PUL
4.8000 g., Bronze, 22.5 mm. **Obv:** Denomination in numerals
Rev: Arms within wreath **Mint:** Afghanistan

Date	Mintage	F	VF	XF	Unc	BU
SH1330 (1951)	—	0.50	1.00	2.00	4.00	—
SH133x (1951)	—	1.50	3.00	5.00	9.00	—

KM# 942.2   50 PUL
Bronze, 24 mm. **Obv:** Denomination in numerals **Rev:** Arms
within wreath **Mint:** Afghanistan

Date	Mintage	F	VF	XF	Unc	BU
SH1330 (1951)	—	20.00	30.00	40.00	50.00	—

KM# 946   50 PUL
5.0000 g., Nickel Clad Steel, 22.3 mm. **Obv:** Denomination
within inner circle **Rev:** Arms within wreath **Mint:** Afghanistan

Date	Mintage	F	VF	XF	Unc	BU
SH1331 (1952)	—	0.20	0.35	0.65	2.00	—
SH1332 (1953)	—	0.20	0.35	0.65	2.00	—
SH1333 (1954)	—	1.00	2.00	3.50	6.00	—
SH1334/2 (1955)	—	0.40	0.65	1.00	2.50	—
SH1334 (1955)	—	0.20	0.35	0.65	2.00	—

KM# 953   AFGHANI (100 Pul)
4.0000 g., Nickel Clad Steel, 23 mm. **Obv:** Three wheat sprigs
Rev: Denomination and stars **Edge:** Reeded **Mint:** Afghanistan

Date	Mintage	F	VF	XF	Unc	BU
SH1340 (1961)	—	0.20	0.35	0.60	1.25	—

KM# 949   2 AFGHANIS
2.5000 g., Aluminum **Obv:** Arms within wreath, circle surrounds
Rev: Denomination within inner circle **Mint:** Afghanistan
Note: This issue was withdrawn and demonetized due to
extensive counterfeiting.

Date	Mintage	F	VF	XF	Unc	BU
SH1337 (1958)	—	0.60	1.00	1.50	2.50	—

KM# 954.1   2 AFGHANIS
5.3000 g., Nickel Clad Steel, 25.1 mm. **Obv:** Radiant eagle
statue, with wings spread **Rev:** Wheat sprig left of denomination
Edge: Plain **Mint:** Afghanistan **Note:** Coin turn.

Date	Mintage	F	VF	XF	Unc	BU
SH1340 (1961)	—	0.25	0.45	0.85	2.00	—

KM# 954.2   2 AFGHANIS
5.3000 g., Nickel Clad Steel, 25.1 mm. **Obv:** Radiant eagle
statue, with wings spread **Rev:** Wheat sprig left of denomination
Mint: Afghanistan **Note:** Medallic die orientation.

Date	Mintage	F	VF	XF	Unc	BU
SH1340 (1961)	—	0.75	1.25	2.25	5.00	—

Note: Some evidence indicates that this variety was the first
Republican issue struck in 1973

KM# 950   5 AFGHANIS
3.0000 g., Aluminum **Obv:** Tughra within beaded circle
Rev: Arms within beaded circle, denomination below
Mint: Afghanistan **Note:** This issue was withdrawn and
demonetized due to extensive counterfeiting.

Date	Mintage	F	VF	XF	Unc	BU
SH1337 (1958)	—	1.00	2.00	3.50	5.00	—

KM# 955   5 AFGHANIS
8.0400 g., Nickel Clad Steel, 29.2 mm. **Obv:** Bust 3/4 right
divides dates **Rev:** Wheat sprigs flank denomination
Edge: Reeded **Mint:** Afghanistan

Date	Mintage	F	VF	XF	Unc	BU
SH1340 (1961)	—	0.35	0.75	1.50	3.00	—

KM# 948   10 AFGHANIS
Aluminum **Obv:** Tughra within beaded circle, denomination below
Rev: Arms within wreath, date below, stars flank **Mint:** Afghanistan

Date	Mintage	F	VF	XF	Unc	BU
SH1336 (1957)	—	—	—	—	900	—

KM# 935   4 GRAMS
4.0000 g., 0.9000 Gold 0.1157 oz. AGW, 19 mm. **Mint:** Afghanistan

Date	Mintage	F	VF	XF	Unc	BU
SH1315 (1936)	—	—	BV	125	175	225
SH1317 (1938)	—	—	BV	125	175	225

KM# 933   TILLA
6.0000 g., 0.9000 Gold 0.1736 oz. AGW, 22 mm. **Mint:** Afghanistan

Date	Mintage	F	VF	XF	Unc	BU
SH1313 (1934)	—	BV	165	185	275	375

KM# 934   8 GRAMS
8.0000 g., 0.9000 Gold 0.2315 oz. AGW, 22 mm. **Mint:** Afghanistan

Date	Mintage	F	VF	XF	Unc	BU
SH1314 (1935)	—	—	BV	225	275	350
SH1315 (1936)	—	—	BV	225	275	350
SH1317 (1938)	—	—	BV	225	275	350

KM# 952   8 GRAMS
8.0000 g., 0.9000 Gold 0.2315 oz. AGW, 22 mm. **Obv:** Tughra
Rev: Eagles divide date and flank figure above horse within
cornucopias **Mint:** Afghanistan

Date	Mintage	F	VF	XF	Unc	BU
SH1339-AH1380 (1960)	200	—	—	375	800	—

Note: Struck for royal presentation purposes. Specimens
struck with the same dies (including the "8 grams", the
"8" having been effaced after striking), but on thin
planchets weighing 3.9-4.0 grams, exist, they are regarded as "mint sports". Market value $275.00 in Unc

REPUBLIC
SH1352-1357 / 1973-1978AD
STANDARD COINAGE

KM# 975   25 PUL
2.5200 g., Brass Clad Steel **Obv:** National arms
Rev: Denomination, six stars

Date	Mintage	F	VF	XF	Unc	BU
SH1352(1973)	45,950,000	0.25	0.50	1.00	2.00	—

KM# 976   50 PUL
Copper Clad Steel, 21 mm. **Obv:** National arms
Rev: Denomination, six stars **Edge:** Plain

Date	Mintage	F	VF	XF	Unc	BU
SH1352(1973)	24,750,000	0.50	1.00	2.00	4.00	—

KM# 977   5 AFGHANIS
Copper-Nickel Clad Steel **Obv:** National arms
Rev: Denomination within stylized grain sprig wreath

Date	Mintage	F	VF	XF	Unc	BU
SH1352(1973)	34,750,000	1.75	3.50	5.00	10.00	—

KM# 978   250 AFGHANIS
28.5700 g., 0.9250 Silver 0.8496 oz. ASW, 38.5 mm. **Subject:**
Conservation **Obv:** National arms **Rev:** Snow Leopard

Date	Mintage	F	VF	XF	Unc	BU
1978	4,370	—	—	—	32.00	—

KM# 979   250 AFGHANIS
28.2800 g., 0.9250 Silver 0.8410 oz. ASW **Subject:**
Conservation **Obv:** National arms **Rev:** Snow Leopard

Date	Mintage	F	VF	XF	Unc	BU
1978 Proof	4,387	Value: 40.00				

KM# 980   500 AFGHANIS
35.3000 g., 0.9250 Silver 1.0498 oz. ASW, 42 mm. **Subject:**
Conservation **Obv:** National arms **Rev:** Siberian Crane

Date	Mintage	F	VF	XF	Unc	BU
1978	4,374	—	—	—	25.00	—

KM# 981   500 AFGHANIS
35.0000 g., 0.9250 Silver 1.0408 oz. ASW **Series:** Conservation
Subject: Siberian Crane **Obv:** National arms, date below
Rev: Crane and denomination

Date	Mintage	F	VF	XF	Unc	BU
1978 Proof	4,218			Value: 35.00		

KM# 982   10000 AFGHANIS
33.4370 g., 0.9000 Gold 0.9675 oz. AGW **Subject:**
Conservation **Obv:** National arms **Rev:** Marco Polo Sheep

Date	Mintage	F	VF	XF	Unc	BU
1978	694				950	
1978 Proof	181			Value: 1,150		

DEMOCRATIC REPUBLIC
SH1358-1371 / 1979-1992AD
STANDARD COINAGE

KM# 990   25 PUL
Aluminum-Bronze **Obv:** National arms **Rev:** Value at center

Date	Mintage	F	VF	XF	Unc	BU
SH1357 (1978)	—	0.25	0.50	1.00	2.00	—

KM# 996   25 PUL
2.3000 g., Aluminum-Bronze, 19 mm. **Obv:** National arms **Rev:**
Value at center

Date	Mintage	F	VF	XF	Unc	BU
SH1359 (1980)	—	0.20	0.35	0.70	1.50	—

KM# 992   50 PUL
3.1000 g., Aluminum-Bronze, 20.9 mm. **Obv:** National arms
Rev: Value at center

Date	Mintage	F	VF	XF	Unc	BU
SH1357 (1978)	—	0.50	0.80	1.50	2.50	—

KM# 997   50 PUL
3.1600 g., Aluminum-Bronze, 21 mm. **Obv:** National arms
Rev: Value at center

Date	Mintage	F	VF	XF	Unc	BU
SH1359 (1980)	—	0.25	0.50	1.00	2.00	—

KM# 993   AFGHANI
4.6000 g., Copper-Nickel, 23 mm. **Obv:** National arms
Rev: Value at center

Date	Mintage	F	VF	XF	Unc	BU
SH1357 (1978)	—	0.60	1.00	2.00	4.00	

KM# 998   AFGHANI
6.1800 g., Copper-Nickel **Obv:** National arms **Rev:** Value at center

Date	Mintage	F	VF	XF	Unc	BU
SH1359 (1980)	—	0.50	0.80	1.50	2.50	—

KM# 994   2 AFGHANIS
6.0000 g., Copper-Nickel, 25 mm. **Obv:** National arms
Rev: Value at center

Date	Mintage	F	VF	XF	Unc	BU
SH1357 (1978)	—	1.00	1.50	2.00	4.00	—
SH1358 (1979)	—	1.00	1.50	2.00	4.00	—

KM# 999   2 AFGHANIS
6.2100 g., Copper-Nickel **Obv:** Similar to 1 Afghani, KM#998

Date	Mintage	F	VF	XF	Unc	BU
SH1359 (1980)	—	0.60	1.00	1.50	3.00	—

KM# 995   5 AFGHANIS
7.4000 g., Copper-Nickel **Obv:** National arms **Rev:** Value at center

Date	Mintage	F	VF	XF	Unc	BU
SH1357 (1978)	—	1.00	2.00	4.00	6.50	—

KM# 1000   5 AFGHANIS
7.4000 g., Copper-Nickel

Date	Mintage	VG	F	VF	XF	Unc
SH1359	—		1.00	1.50	2.00	4.00

KM# 1001   5 AFGHANIS
Brass **Series:** F.A.O. **Subject:** World Food Day **Obv:** National
arms **Rev:** FAO logo

Date	Mintage	F	VF	XF	Unc	BU
SH1360 (1981)	—	0.25	0.50	1.00	1.75	—

KM# 1015   10 AFGHANIS
Brass **Subject:** 70th Anniversary of Independence **Obv:** Arch
Rev: Bank logo

Date	Mintage	F	VF	XF	Unc	BU
1989	—				3.50	

KM# 1016   50 AFGHANIS
Copper-Nickel **Subject:** 100 Years of the Automobile
Obv: National arms **Rev:** Ferrari

Date	Mintage	F	VF	XF	Unc	BU
ND(1986)	—		—	—	14.00	—

KM# 1006   50 AFGHANIS
Copper-Nickel **Subject:** World Wildlife Fund **Obv:** National arms
Rev: Leopard

Date	Mintage	F	VF	XF	Unc	BU
1987	28,000		—	—	15.00	—

KM# 1024   50 AFGHANIS
29.7000 g., Copper, 38 mm. **Subject:** Prehistoric Animals
Obv: National arms **Rev:** Deinotherium-Elephant

Date	Mintage	F	VF	XF	Unc	BU
1993	—	—	—	—	25.00	—

KM# 1032   50 AFGHANIS
Copper **Subject:** Prehistoric Animals **Obv:** National arms
Rev: Ankylosaurus

Date	Mintage	F	VF	XF	Unc	BU
1995 Proof	100			Value: 65.00		

KM# 1014   100 AFGHANIS
15.1000 g., Copper-Nickel, 31.1 mm. **Series:** World Soccer
Championship **Subject:** Italy to U.S.A. **Obv:** Bank logo **Rev:**
World Football Championship

Date	Mintage	F	VF	XF	Unc	BU
1990 Proof	10,000	—			Value: 14.00	

KM# 1017   250 AFGHANIS
20.3100 g., 0.9250 Silver 0.6040 oz. ASW **Subject:**
Conservation **Obv:** National arms **Rev:** Snow Leopard

Date	Mintage	F	VF	XF	Unc	BU
1978 4 known	—	—	—	—	500	—

KM# 1018   500 AFGHANIS
35.4400 g., 0.9250 Silver 1.0539 oz. ASW **Subject:**
Conservation **Obv:** National arms **Rev:** Siberian Crane

Date	Mintage	F	VF	XF	Unc	BU
1978 4 known	—	—	—	—	500	—

KM# 1002   500 AFGHANIS
9.0600 g., 0.9000 Silver 0.2621 oz. ASW **Series:** F.A.O.
Subject: World Food Day **Obv:** National arms **Rev:** FAO

Date	Mintage	F	VF	XF	Unc	BU
SH1360(1981) Proof	—	Value: 25.00				

KM# 1003   500 AFGHANIS
12.0000 g., 0.9990 Silver 0.3854 oz. ASW **Series:** 100th
Anniversary of the Automobile **Rev:** Ferrari

Date	Mintage	F	VF	XF	Unc	BU
ND(1986)	2,000	—			40.00	—

KM# 1004   500 AFGHANIS
12.0000 g., 0.9990 Silver 0.3854 oz. ASW **Subject:** 1988 Winter
Games, Calgary **Obv:** National arms **Rev:** Ice dancers

Date	Mintage	F	VF	XF	Unc	BU
ND(1986)	10,000	—			35.00	—

KM# 1005   500 AFGHANIS
12.0000 g., 0.9990 Silver 0.3854 oz. ASW **Subject:** Wildlife
Preservation **Obv:** National arms **Rev:** Leopard

Date	Mintage	F	VF	XF	Unc	BU
1986	5,000	—			35.00	—

KM# 1010   500 AFGHANIS
12.0000 g., 0.9990 Silver 0.3854 oz. ASW **Series:** 1988
Summer Olympics **Subject:** Volleyball **Obv:** National arms above
denomination **Mint:** Havana, Cuba

Date	Mintage	F	VF	XF	Unc	BU
1987 (k)	10,000	—			25.00	—

KM# 1007   500 AFGHANIS
12.0000 g., 0.9990 Silver 0.3854 oz. ASW **Subject:** European
Soccer Championship - West Germany **Obv:** National Arms **Rev:**
European Football Championship **Mint:** Havana, Cuba

Date	Mintage	F	VF	XF	Unc	BU
1988 (k)	Est. 5,000	—			37.50	—

KM# 1009   500 AFGHANIS
16.0000 g., 0.9990 Silver 0.5139 oz. ASW **Series:** 1986 World
Soccer Championship - Mexico **Obv:** National Arms **Rev:** World
Football Championship-Mexico 86

Date	Mintage	F	VF	XF	Unc	BU
ND(1988)	5,000	—			32.00	—

KM# 1008.1   500 AFGHANIS
16.0000 g., 0.9990 Silver 0.5139 oz. ASW **Series:** 1992 Winter
Olympics **Subject:** Bobsledding **Obv:** Short thick letters
Rev: Bobsled between legends, date at right

Date	Mintage	F	VF	XF	Unc	BU
1989 Proof	Est. 10,000				Value: 30.00	

KM# 1008.2   500 AFGHANIS
16.0000 g., 0.9990 Silver 0.5139 oz. ASW **Series:** 1992 Winter
Olympics **Subject:** Bobsledding **Obv:** National arms above
denomination, tall thin letters **Rev:** Bobsled between legends,
date at right

Date	Mintage	F	VF	XF	Unc	BU
1989 Proof	Inc. above				Value: 35.00	

KM# 1011   500 AFGHANIS
16.0000 g., 0.9990 Silver 0.5139 oz. ASW **Series:** 1990 World
Soccer Championship **Obv:** National Arms **Rev:** World Football
Championship-Italy 1990

Date	Mintage	F	VF	XF	Unc	BU
1989 Proof	10,000				Value: 30.00	

KM# 1012   500 AFGHANIS
16.0000 g., 0.9990 Silver 0.5139 oz. ASW **Series:** 1992
Summer Olympics **Subject:** Field Hockey **Obv:** National Arms
Rev: XXV Olympic Games-Barcelona-Date, field hockey players
between dates

Date	Mintage	F	VF	XF	Unc	BU
1989 Proof	10,000				Value: 30.00	

KM# 1013   500 AFGHANIS
12.0000 g., 0.9990 Silver 0.3854 oz. ASW **Series:** 1994 World
Cup Soccer Games U.S.A. **Obv:** National Arms **Rev:** XV World
Cup across top - United States of America; date across bottom

Date	Mintage	F	VF	XF	Unc	BU
1991	—	—	—	—	30.00	—

KM# 1022   500 AFGHANIS
20.0000 g., 0.9990 Silver 0.6423 oz. ASW **Series:** 1994 World
Cup Soccer Games - U.S.A. **Obv:** National Arms **Rev:** XV World
Cup across top-soccer player with date, USA in center

Date	Mintage	F	VF	XF	Unc	BU
1992 Proof	—	Value: 45.00				

KM# 1020   500 AFGHANIS
16.0000 g., 0.9990 Silver 0.5139 oz. ASW **Subject:** Prehistoric
Animals **Obv:** National Arms **Rev:** Deinotherium-Elephant

Date	Mintage	F	VF	XF	Unc	BU
1993 Proof	—	Value: 50.00				

KM# 1021   500 AFGHANIS
16.0000 g., 0.9990 Silver 0.5139 oz. ASW **Subject:** Prehistoric
Animals **Obv:** National Arms **Rev:** Styracosaurus

Date	Mintage	F	VF	XF	Unc	BU
1994 Proof	—	Value: 45.00				

KM# 1035   500 AFGHANIS
16.0000 g., 0.9990 Silver 0.5139 oz. ASW **Subject:** Prehistoric
Animals **Obv:** National arms **Rev:** Ankylosaurus

Date	Mintage	F	VF	XF	Unc	BU
1995 Proof	—	Value: 50.00				

KM# 1023   500 AFGHANIS
20.0000 g., 0.9990 Silver 0.6423 oz. ASW **Series:** 1996
Olympics **Obv:** National Arms **Rev:** Three runners and building,
small date under building, large date under runners **Rev. Leg.:**
FROM ATHENS TO ATLANTA

Date	Mintage	F	VF	XF	Unc	BU
1995 Proof	15,000	Value: 22.50				

KM# 1019   10000 AFGHANIS
33.6600 g., 0.9000 Gold 0.9739 oz. AGW **Subject:**
Conservation **Obv:** National Arms **Rev:** Marco Polo Sheep

Date	Mintage	F	VF	XF	Unc	BU
1978 4 known	—	—	—	—	2,000	—

ISLAMIC STATE
SH1373-1381 / 1994-2002AD
STANDARD COINAGE

KM# 1026   50 AFGHANIS
28.6800 g., Copper-Nickel, 38.5 mm. **Series:** 50th Anniversary
- United Nations **Obv:** National symbol, denomination below
Rev: Meditating figure with three doves

Date	Mintage	F	VF	XF	Unc	BU
ND(1995)	—	—	—	—	8.50	—

KM# 1030   50 AFGHANIS
25.9500 g., Copper-Nickel, 37.8 mm. **Series:** World Food Summit
Obv: National symbol, denomination below **Rev:** Gate of Zafar

Date	Mintage	F	VF	XF	Unc	BU
1996	—	—	—	—	8.50	—

KM# 1037   50 AFGHANIS
Copper-Nickel **Series:** Sydney Olympics 2000 **Obv:** National
symbol, denomination below **Rev:** Equestrian event

Date	Mintage	F	VF	XF	Unc	BU
1999	10,000	—	—	—	7.50	—

KM# 1031   500 AFGHANIS
28.4300 g., 0.9250 Silver 0.8455 oz. ASW **Series:** 50th
Anniversary United Nations **Obv:** National symbol, denomination
below **Rev:** Meditating figure with three doves

Date	Mintage	F	VF	XF	Unc	BU
ND(1995) Proof	—	Value: 35.00				

KM# 1025   500 AFGHANIS
20.0000 g., 0.9990 Silver 0.6423 oz. ASW **Subject:** Multicolor Lynx
Obv: National symbol, denomination below **Rev:** Multicolor Lynx

Date	Mintage	F	VF	XF	Unc	BU
1996 Proof	—	Value: 50.00				

KM# 1027   500 AFGHANIS

20.0000 g., 0.9990 Silver 0.6423 oz. ASW **Subject:** XVI World Cup Soccer - France **Obv:** National symbol, denomination below **Rev:** Soccer player going for goal

Date	Mintage	F	VF	XF	Unc	BU
1996	100				100	—
1996 Proof	—	Value: 45.00				

KM# 1028   500 AFGHANIS

20.1300 g., 0.9990 Silver 0.6465 oz. ASW **Subject:** World Food Summit - Rome **Obv:** National symbol, denomination below **Rev:** Zafar Gate, F.A.O. logo, dates

Date	Mintage	F	VF	XF	Unc	BU
1996 Proof	—	Value: 45.00				

KM# 1036   500 AFGHANIS

20.3100 g., 0.9990 Silver 0.6523 oz. ASW **Series:** Sydney Olympics 2000 **Obv:** National symbol, denomination below **Rev:** Winged goddess bearing torch, Greek temples behind

Date	Mintage	F	VF	XF	Unc	BU
1996 Proof	500	Value: 40.00				

KM# 1040   500 AFGHANIS

20.0000 g., 0.9990 Silver 0.6423 oz. ASW, 38 mm. **Subject:** World Cup Soccer **Obv:** National symbol, denomination below **Rev:** Multicolor soccer players, flags and ball **Edge:** Reeded **Mint:** Havana, Cuba

Date	Mintage	F	VF	XF	Unc	BU
1996 Proof	—	Value: 35.00				

KM# 1029   500 AFGHANIS

14.9500 g., 0.9990 Silver 0.4802 oz. ASW **Series:** World of Adventure **Obv:** National symbol, denomination below **Rev:** Multicolor enamel airplane and statue, cameo portrait

Date	Mintage	F	VF	XF	Unc	BU
1996 Proof	—	Value: 45.00				

KM# 1039   500 AFGHANIS

15.0000 g., 0.9990 Silver 0.4818 oz. ASW **Subject:** 16th World Cup - Soccer **Obv:** National symbol, denomination below **Rev:** Soccer player superimposed on ball **Edge:** Plain

Date	Mintage	F	VF	XF	Unc	BU
1997 Proof	—	Value: 37.50				

KM# 1036a   500 AFGHANIS

15.0000 g., 0.9990 Silver 0.4818 oz. ASW **Series:** Sydney Olympics 2000 **Obv:** National symbol, denomination below **Rev:** Winged Goddess bearing torch, Greek temples behind

Date	Mintage	F	VF	XF	Unc	BU
1998 Proof	7,500	Value: 27.50				

KM# 1033   500 AFGHANIS

20.0000 g., 0.9990 Silver 0.6423 oz. ASW **Series:** Sydney Olympics 2000 **Obv:** National symbol, denomination below **Rev:** Javelin thrower

Date	Mintage	F	VF	XF	Unc	BU
1998 Proof	5,000	Value: 37.50				

KM# 1034   500 AFGHANIS

20.0000 g., 0.9990 Silver 0.6423 oz. ASW **Subject:** Fauna of Asia **Obv:** National symbol, denomination below **Rev:** Marco Polo Sheep

Date	Mintage	F	VF	XF	Unc	BU
1998	100	—	—	—	75.00	—

KM# 1038   500 AFGHANIS

20.0000 g., 0.9990 Silver 0.6423 oz. ASW **Subject:** Sydney Olympics - 2000 - XXVII Olympiad **Obv:** National symbol, denomination below **Rev:** Equestrian event

Date	Mintage	F	VF	XF	Unc	BU
1999 Proof	5,000	Value: 30.00				

KM# 1041   500 AFGHANIS

14.9000 g., 0.9990 Silver 0.4785 oz. ASW, 35 mm. **Subject:** Third Millennium **Obv:** National symbol, denomination below **Rev:** Millennium change design **Edge:** Plain

Date	Mintage	F	VF	XF	Unc	BU
ND(1999) Proof	—	Value: 30.00				

KM# 1042   500 AFGHANIS

15.0000 g., 0.9990 Silver 0.4818 oz. ASW, 35 mm. **Obv:** National symbol, denomination below **Rev:** Snow Leopard **Edge:** Plain

Date	Mintage	F	VF	XF	Unc	BU
2000 Proof	—	Value: 35.00				

KM# 1047   5000 AFGHANIS

503.0000 g., 0.9990 Silver 16.155 oz. ASW, 85 mm. **Subject:** XXVII Olympic Games - Sydney Olympics 2000 **Obv:** State emblem **Rev:** Wrestling, winged goddess bearing torch, 2 wrestlers

Date	Mintage	F	VF	XF	Unc	BU
1999						

PATTERNS
Including off metal strikes

KM#	Date	Mintage	Identification	Mkt Val
Pn1	SH1310	—	1/2 Afghani. Silver. 4.7500 g.	
Pn2	SH1336	—	5 Afghanis. Silver. Legend within off-center circle, denomination. National emblem with wreath, date.	350
Pn3	SH1336	—	10 Afghanis. Silver. Toughra within off-center circle, denomination. National emblem with wreath, date.	350

PIEFORTS

KM#	Date	Mintage	Identification	Mkt Val
P1.1	1989	110	500 Afghanis. 0.9990 Silver. National Arms. XVI Winter Olympic Games, bobsled 1989 in center, Albertville date at bottom. KM#1008.2	85.00
P1.2	1989	—	500 Afghanis. 0.9990 Silver. KM#1008.2, pine tree without needles	125
P1.3	1989	—	500 Afghanis. 0.9990 Silver. KM#1008.2, pine tree with sagging branches	85.00
P1.4	1989	—	500 Afghanis. 0.9990 Silver. KM#1008.2, pine tree with uplifted branches	85.00
P2	1996	—	500 Afghanis. Silver. KM#1029	65.00
P3	1998	—	500 Afghanis. Silver. KM#1033	120
P4	1999	—	500 Afghanis. Silver. KM#1038	80.00

AJMAN - U.A.E.

Ajman is the smallest and poorest of the emirates in the United Arab Emirates. It has an estimated area of 100 sq. mi. (250 sq. km.) and a population of 6,000. Ajman's first act as an autonomous entity was entering into a treaty with Great Britain in 1820. On December 2, 1971 Ajman became one of the 6 original members of the United Arab Emirates.

TITLE

عجمان

Ajman

RULERS
Abdul Aziz Bin Humaid al-Naimi, 1900-1908
Humaid Bin Abdul Aziz al-Naimi, 1908-1928
Rashid Bin Hamad al-Naimi, 1928-1981
Humaid Bin Rashid al-Naimi, 1981--

MONETARY SYSTEM
100 Dirhams = 1 Riyal

UNITED ARAB EMIRATE

NON-CIRCULATING
LEGAL TENDER COINAGE

KM# 1.1   RIYAL
3.9500 g., 0.6400 Silver 0.0813 oz. ASW **Ruler:** Rashid Bin Hamad al-Naimi 1928-1981 **Obv:** Denomination within circle **Rev:** Chicken below state emblem, two dates

Date	Mintage	F	VF	XF	Unc	BU
AH1389 - 1969	20,000	—	—	—	8.00	12.00
AH1389 - 1969 Proof	1,200	Value: 45.00				

KM# 1.2   RIYAL
3.9500 g., 0.6400 Silver 0.0813 oz. ASW **Ruler:** Rashid Bin Hamad al-Naimi 1928-1981 **Obv:** Denomination within circle **Rev:** Chicken below state emblem, three dates

Date	Mintage	F	VF	XF	Unc	BU
AH1390 - 1970	—	—	—	—	20.00	22.50

KM# 2.1   2 RIYALS
6.4500 g., 0.8350 Silver 0.1731 oz. ASW **Ruler:** Rashid Bin Hamad al-Naimi 1928-1981 **Obv:** Denomination within circle **Rev:** Chicken below state emblem, two dates

Date	Mintage	F	VF	XF	Unc	BU
AH1389-1969	20,000	—	—	—	17.50	20.00
AH1389-1969 Proof	1,200	Value: 55.00				

KM# 2.2   2 RIYALS
6.4500 g., 0.8350 Silver 0.1731 oz. ASW **Ruler:** Rashid Bin Hamad al-Naimi 1928-1981 **Obv:** Denomination within circle **Rev:** Chicken below state emblem, three dates

Date	Mintage	F	VF	XF	Unc	BU
AH1390-1970	—	—	—	—	30.00	32.50

KM# 3.1   5 RIYALS
15.0000 g., 0.8350 Silver 0.4027 oz. ASW **Ruler:** Rashid Bin Hamad al-Naimi 1928-1981 **Obv:** Denomination within circle **Rev:** Chicken below state emblem, two dates

Date	Mintage	F	VF	XF	Unc	BU
AH1389-1969	10,000	—	—	—	22.50	25.00
AH1389-1969 Proof	1,200	Value: 60.00				

KM# 3.2   5 RIYALS
15.0000 g., 0.8350 Silver 0.4027 oz. ASW **Ruler:** Rashid Bin Hamad al-Naimi 1928-1981 **Obv:** Denomination within circle **Rev:** Chicken below state emblem, three dates

Date	Mintage	F	VF	XF	Unc	BU
AH1390-1970	—	—	—	—	50.00	55.00
AH1390-1970 Proof	—	Value: 90.00				

KM# 12   5 RIYALS
15.0000 g., 0.9250 Silver 0.4461 oz. ASW. **Ruler:** Rashid Bin Hamad al-Naimi 1928-1981 **Subject:** Death of Gamal Abdel Nassar **Obv:** State emblem divides denomination **Rev:** Head left divides dates.

Date	Mintage	F	VF	XF	Unc	BU
AH1390-1970 Proof	5,000	Value: 30.00				

KM# 17   5 RIYALS
15.0000 g., 0.9250 Silver 0.4461 oz. ASW **Ruler:** Rashid Bin Hamad al-Naimi 1928-1981 **Obv:** State emblem, denomination above **Rev:** Head left, denomination below

Date	Mintage	F	VF	XF	Unc	BU
ND(1970) Proof	1,175	Value: 75.00				

KM# 18   5 RIYALS
15.0000 g., 0.9250 Silver 0.4461 oz. ASW **Ruler:** Rashid Bin Hamad al-Naimi 1928-1981 **Obv:** State emblem, denomination above **Rev:** Head left, denomination below

Date	Mintage	F	VF	XF	Unc	BU
ND(1970) Proof	1,175	Value: 75.00				

KM# 19   5 RIYALS
15.0000 g., 0.9250 Silver 0.4461 oz. ASW **Ruler:** Rashid Bin Hamad al-Naimi 1928-1981 **Obv:** State emblem, denomination above **Rev:** Head left, denomination below

Date	Mintage	F	VF	XF	Unc	BU
ND(1970) Proof	1,175	Value: 75.00				

KM# 20   5 RIYALS
15.0000 g., 0.9250 Silver 0.4461 oz. ASW **Ruler:** Rashid Bin Hamad al-Naimi 1928-1981 **Obv:** State emblem, denomination above **Rev:** Head left, denomination below

Date	Mintage	F	VF	XF	Unc	BU
ND(1970) Proof	1,175	Value: 75.00				

KM# 21   5 RIYALS
15.0000 g., 0.9250 Silver 0.4461 oz. ASW **Ruler:** Rashid Bin Hamad al-Naimi 1928-1981 **Obv:** State emblem, denomination above **Rev:** Head 3/4 left, denomination below

Date	Mintage	F	VF	XF	Unc	BU
ND(1970) Proof	1,175	Value: 75.00				

KM# 22   5 RIYALS
15.0000 g., 0.9250 Silver 0.4461 oz. ASW **Ruler:** Rashid Bin Hamad al-Naimi 1928-1981 **Obv:** State emblem, denomination above **Rev:** Head left, denomination below

Date	Mintage	F	VF	XF	Unc	BU
ND(1970) Proof	1,175	Value: 75.00				

KM# 23   5 RIYALS
15.0000 g., 0.9250 Silver 0.4461 oz. ASW **Ruler:** Rashid Bin Hamad al-Naimi 1928-1981 **Obv:** State emblem, denomination above **Rev:** Head 3/4 right, denomination below

Date	Mintage	F	VF	XF	Unc	BU
ND(1970) Proof	1,175	Value: 75.00				

KM# 24   5 RIYALS
15.0000 g., 0.9250 Silver 0.4461 oz. ASW **Ruler:** Rashid Bin Hamad al-Naimi 1928-1981 **Obv:** State emblem, denomination above **Rev:** Head 3/4 left, denomination below

Date	Mintage	F	VF	XF	Unc	BU
ND(1970) Proof	1,175	Value: 75.00				

KM# 26   5 RIYALS
15.0000 g., 0.9250 Silver 0.4461 oz. ASW **Ruler:** Rashid Bin Hamad al-Naimi 1928-1981 **Series:** F.A.O. **Obv:** State emblem, denomination above **Rev:** Open hands holding grain divide dates, F.A.O. below

Date	Mintage	F	VF	XF	Unc	BU
AH1390-1970 Proof	2,000	Value: 85.00				

Note: This issue is not recognized by the F.A.O.

KM# 27   5 RIYALS
15.0000 g., 0.9250 Silver 0.4461 oz. ASW **Ruler:** Rashid Bin Hamad al-Naimi 1928-1981 **Subject:** Save Venice **Obv:** State emblem, denomination above, bust below **Rev:** Denomination, symbols and legend

Date	Mintage	F	VF	XF	Unc	BU
ND(1971) Proof	4,800	Value: 135				

KM# 5   7-1/2 RIYALS
23.0000 g., 0.9250 Silver 0.6840 oz. ASW **Ruler:** Rashid Bin Hamad al-Naimi 1928-1981 **Subject:** Rashid bin Humaid al-Naimi **Obv:** State emblem, denomination above, bust below **Rev:** Bonefish right, denomination below, circle surrounds

Date	Mintage	F	VF	XF	Unc	BU
AH1389-1970	4,350			55.00	65.00	
AH1389-1970 Proof	650	Value: 90.00				

KM# 6   7-1/2 RIYALS
23.0000 g., 0.9250 Silver 0.6840 oz. ASW **Ruler:** Rashid Bin Hamad al-Naimi 1928-1981 **Obv:** Bust facing divides dates, circle surrounds **Rev:** Barbary Falcon right, denomination above, circle

Date	Mintage	F	VF	XF	Unc	BU
AH1389-1970	4,350			55.00	65.00	
AH1389-1970 Proof	650	Value: 90.00				

KM# 7   7-1/2 RIYALS
23.0000 g., 0.9250 Silver 0.6840 oz. ASW **Ruler:** Rashid Bin Hamad al-Naimi 1928-1981 **Obv:** Bust facing divides dates, circle surrounds **Rev:** Gazelle left, denomination above within circle

Date	Mintage	F	VF	XF	Unc	BU
AH1389-1970	4,350			60.00	70.00	
AH1389-1970 Proof	650	Value: 95.00				

KM# 13   7-1/2 RIYALS
23.0000 g., 0.8350 Silver 0.6174 oz. ASW **Ruler:** Rashid Bin Hamad al-Naimi 1928-1981 **Subject:** Death of Gamal Abdel Nassar **Obv:** State emblem divides denomination **Rev:** Head left divides dates

Date	Mintage	F	VF	XF	Unc	BU
AH1390-1970 Proof	6,000	Value: 50.00				

KM# 9.1   10 RIYALS
30.0000 g., 0.9250 Silver 0.8921 oz. ASW **Ruler:** Rashid Bin Hamad al-Naimi 1928-1981 **Obv:** State emblem, denomination above **Rev:** Head left, denomination at left

Date	Mintage	F	VF	XF	Unc	BU
ND(1970) Proof	—	Value: 175				
ND(1970) Matte	—					175

KM# 9.2   10 RIYALS
30.0000 g., 0.9250 Silver 0.8921 oz. ASW **Ruler:** Rashid Bin Hamad al-Naimi 1928-1981 **Obv:** State emblem, denomination above, PROOF added **Rev:** Head left, denomination at left

Date	Mintage	F	VF	XF	Unc	BU
ND(1970) Proof	3,200	Value: 50.00				

KM# 28   25 RIYALS
5.1750 g., 0.9000 Gold 0.1497 oz. AGW **Ruler:** Rashid Bin Hamad al-Naimi 1928-1981 **Obv:** State emblem, denomination above **Rev:** Head left, denomination below

Date	Mintage	F	VF	XF	Unc	BU
ND(1970) Proof	—	Value: 165				

KM# 29   25 RIYALS
5.1750 g., 0.9000 Gold 0.1497 oz. AGW **Ruler:** Rashid Bin Hamad al-Naimi 1928-1981 **Obv:** State emblem, denomination above **Rev:** Head left, denomination below

Date	Mintage	F	VF	XF	Unc	BU
ND(1970) Proof	—	Value: 165				

KM# 30   25 RIYALS
5.1750 g., 0.9000 Gold 0.1497 oz. AGW **Ruler:** Rashid Bin Hamad al-Naimi 1928-1981 **Obv:** State emblem, denomination above **Rev:** Head left, denomination below

Date	Mintage	F	VF	XF	Unc	BU
ND(1970) Proof	—	Value: 165				

KM# 31   25 RIYALS
5.1750 g., 0.9000 Gold 0.1497 oz. AGW **Ruler:** Rashid Bin Hamad al-Naimi 1928-1981 **Obv:** State emblem, denomination above **Rev:** Head left, denomination below

Date	Mintage	F	VF	XF	Unc	BU
ND(1970) Proof	—	Value: 165				

KM# 32   25 RIYALS
5.1750 g., 0.9000 Gold 0.1497 oz. AGW **Ruler:** Rashid Bin Hamad al-Naimi 1928-1981 **Obv:** State emblem, denomination above **Rev:** Head 3/4 left, denomination below

Date	Mintage	F	VF	XF	Unc	BU
ND(1970) Proof	—	Value: 165				

KM# 33   25 RIYALS
5.1750 g., 0.9000 Gold 0.1497 oz. AGW **Ruler:** Rashid Bin Hamad al-Naimi 1928-1981 **Obv:** State emblem, denomination above **Rev:** Head left, denomination below

Date	Mintage	F	VF	XF	Unc	BU
ND(1970) Proof	—	Value: 165				

KM# 34   25 RIYALS
5.1750 g., 0.9000 Gold 0.1497 oz. AGW **Ruler:** Rashid Bin Hamad al-Naimi 1928-1981 **Obv:** State emblem, denomination above **Rev:** Head 3/4 right, denomination below

Date	Mintage	F	VF	XF	Unc	BU
ND(1970) Proof	—	Value: 165				

KM# 35   25 RIYALS
5.1750 g., 0.9000 Gold 0.1497 oz. AGW **Ruler:** Rashid Bin Hamad al-Naimi 1928-1981 **Obv:** State emblem, denomination above **Rev:** Head 3/4 left, denomination below

Date	Mintage	F	VF	XF	Unc	BU
ND(1970) Proof	—	Value: 165				

KM# 15   25 RIYALS
5.1750 g., 0.9000 Gold 0.1497 oz. AGW **Ruler:** Rashid Bin Hamad al-Naimi 1928-1981 **Subject:** Death of Gamal Abdel Nassar **Obv:** State emblem divides denomination **Rev:** Head left divides dates **Note:** Some examples have a serial number on the obverse below the bust.

Date	Mintage	F	VF	XF	Unc	BU
AH1390 Proof	1,100	Value: 150				

KM# 36   25 RIYALS
5.1750 g., 0.9000 Gold 0.1497 oz. AGW **Ruler:** Rashid Bin Hamad al-Naimi 1928-1981 **Rev:** Two men ringing large bell **Rev. Leg.:** Save Venice

Date	Mintage	F	VF	XF	Unc	BU
ND(1971) Proof	—	Value: 200				

KM# 16   50 RIYALS
10.3500 g., 0.9000 Gold 0.2995 oz. AGW **Ruler:** Rashid Bin Hamad al-Naimi 1928-1981 **Subject:** Death of Gamal Abdel Nassar **Obv:** State emblem divides denomination **Rev:** Head left divides dates **Note:** Some examples have a serial number below the bust on the obverse

Date	Mintage	F	VF	XF	Unc	BU
AH1390 Proof	700	Value: 275				

KM# 39   50 RIYALS
10.3500 g., 0.9000 Gold 0.2995 oz. AGW **Ruler:** Rashid Bin Hamad al-Naimi 1928-1981 **Subject:** Save Venice **Obv:** State emblem, denomination above, bust below **Rev:** Stallion divides denomination

Date	Mintage	F	VF	XF	Unc	BU
ND(1971) Proof	—	Value: 375				

KM# 41   75 RIYALS
15.5300 g., 0.9000 Gold 0.4494 oz. AGW **Ruler:** Rashid Bin Hamad al-Naimi 1928-1981 **Series:** F.A.O.

Date	Mintage	F	VF	XF	Unc	BU
AH1389-1969 Proof	—	Value: 450				

KM# 10   100 RIYALS
20.7000 g., 0.9000 Gold 0.5989 oz. AGW **Ruler:** Rashid Bin Hamad al-Naimi 1928-1981 **Obv:** State emblem, denomination above **Rev:** Head left, denomination at left

Date	Mintage	F	VF	XF	Unc	BU
ND(1970) Proof	1,000	Value: 550				

KM# 40   100 RIYALS
20.7000 g., 0.9000 Gold 0.5989 oz. AGW **Ruler:** Rashid Bin Hamad al-Naimi 1928-1981 **Subject:** Save Venice **Obv:** State emblem, denomination above, bust below **Rev:** Courthouse, denomination lower left

Date	Mintage	F	VF	XF	Unc	BU
ND(1971) Proof	—	Value: 600				

ESSAIS
With Assay or Proof

KM#	Date	Mintage	Identification	Mkt Val
E1	1969	1,250	Riyal. Silver. Denomination within circle. Chicken below state emblem, two dates.	40.00
E2	1969	1,250	2 Riyals. Silver. Denomination within circle. Chicken below state emblem, two dates.	50.00
E3	1969	1,250	5 Riyals. Silver. Denomination within circle. Chicken below state emblem, two dates.	55.00
E4	1970	100	Riyal. Denomination within circle. Chicken below state emblem, three dates.	50.00
E5	1970	100	2 Riyals. Denoimination within circle. Chicken below state emblem, three dates.	60.00
E6	1970	100	5 Riyals. Denomination within circle. Chicken below state emblem, three dates.	80.00
E7	1970	—	5 Riyals. Aluminum. State emblem divides denomination. Head left divides dates.	40.00
E8	1970	—	7-1/2 Riyals. Silver. Denomination above state emblem, bust below divides dates. Fish above denomination, circle surrounds.	100
E9	1970	—	7-1/2 Riyals. Silver. Bust facing divides dates, circle surrounds. Barbary Falcon right, denomination above, circle surrounds.	100
E10	1970	—	7-1/2 Riyals. Aluminum. Bust facing divides dates, circle surrounds. Gazelle left divides denomination, circle surrounds.	120

KM#	Date	Mintage Identification				Mkt Val
E11	1970	— 7-1/2 Riyals. Aluminum. State emblem divides denomination. Head left divides dates.				60.00
E12	ND(1970)	800 10 Riyals. KM#9.2				80.00

PATTERNS
Including off metal strikes

KM#	Date	Mintage Identification				Mkt Val
Pn1	1970	— 100 Dirhams. Copper-Nickel.				

MINT SETS

KM#	Date	Mintage Identification	Issue Price	Mkt Val
MS1	1969 (3)	— KM#1.1-3.1	—	55.00
MS2	1970 (3)	4,350 KM#5-7	—	200

PROOF SETS

KM#	Date	Mintage Identification	Issue Price	Mkt Val
PS1	1969 (3)	1,200 KM#1.1-3.1	11.22	160
PS2	1970 (8)	1,175 KM#17-24	—	600
PS3	1970 (8)	— KM#28-35	—	1,320
PS4	1970 (4)	— KM#12, 13, 15, 16	—	500
PS5	1970 (3)	100 KM#E4-6	—	190
PS6	1970 (3)	650 KM#5-7	19.50	275
PS7	1970 (3)	— KM#E9, E7, 10	—	700
PS8	1970 (2)	800 KM#E7, 10	—	600
PS9	1970 (2)	5,000 KM#12, 13	9.50	80.00
PS10	1970 (3)	— KM#12, 13, 15	—	225
PS11	1970 (3)	— KM#9.1, 9.2, 10	—	775
PS12	1971 (4)	— KM#27, 36, 39, 40	—	1,300

ALBANIA

The Republic of Albania, a Balkan republic bounded by Macedonia, Greece, Montenegro, and the Adriatic Sea, has an area of 11,100 sq. mi. (28,748 sq. km.) and a population of 3.49 million. Capital: Tirane. The country is predominantly agricultural, although recent progress has been made in the manufacturing and mining sectors. Petroleum, chrome, iron, copper, cotton textiles, tobacco and wood products are exported.

Independence was re-established by revolt in 1912, and the present borders established in 1913 by a conference of European powers, which, in 1914, placed Prince William of Wied on the throne; popular discontent forced his abdication within months. In 1920, following World War I occupancy by several nations, a republic was set up. Ahmed Zogu seized the presidency in 1925, and in 1928 he proclaimed himself king with the title of Zog I. King Zog fled when Italy occupied Albania in 1939 and enthroned King Victor Emanuel of Italy. Upon the surrender of Italy to the Allies in 1943, German troops occupied the country. They withdrew in 1944, and communist partisans seized power, naming Gen. Enver Hoxha provisional president. In 1946, following a victory by the communist front in the 1945 elections, a new constitution modeled on that of the USSR was adopted. In accordance with the constitution of Dec. 28, 1976, the official name of Albania was changed from the Peoples Republic of Albania to the Peoples Socialist Republic of Albania.

Albania's former communists were routed in elections. March 1992, amid economic collapse and social unrest, Sali Berisha was elected as the first non-communist president since World War II. Rexhep Mejdani, elected president in 1997, succeeds him.

RULERS
Ahmed Bey Zogu - King Zog I, 1928-1939
Vittorio Emanuele III, 1939-1943

MINT MARKS
L – London
R - Rome
V – Vienna

MONETARY SYSTEM
100 Qindar Leku = 1 Lek
100 Qindar Ari = 1 Frang Ar = 5 Lek

KINGDOM
STANDARD COINAGE

KM# 1   5 QINDAR LEKU
Bronze **Ruler:** Ahmed Bey Zogu - King Zog I **Obv:** Lion head left **Rev:** Value above oak branch

Date	Mintage	F	VF	XF	Unc	BU
1926R	512,000	22.00	60.00	95.00	210	—

KM# 2   10 QINDAR LEKU
Bronze **Obv:** Eagle's head right **Rev:** Value between olive branches

Date	Mintage	F	VF	XF	Unc	BU
1926R	511,000	16.00	50.00	85.00	165	—

KM# 14   QINDAR AR
Bronze **Ruler:** Ahmed Bey Zogu - King Zog I **Obv:** Two headed Eagle **Rev:** Value above oak leaves and acorn

Date	Mintage	F	VF	XF	Unc	BU
1935R	2,000,000	2.50	7.00	16.00	38.00	—

KM# 15   2 QINDAR ARI
Bronze **Ruler:** Ahmed Bey Zogu - King Zog I **Obv:** Two headed Eagle **Rev:** Value above oak leaves

Date	Mintage	F	VF	XF	Unc	BU
1935R	1,500,000	3.50	11.00	20.00	42.00	—

KM# 3   1/4 LEKU
Nickel **Obv:** Lion advancing left **Rev:** Oak branch above value

Date	Mintage	F	VF	XF	Unc	BU
1926R	506,000	3.50	8.00	25.00	52.00	60.00
1927R	756,000	3.50	8.00	18.00	40.00	55.00

KM# 4   1/2 LEK
6.0700 g., Nickel, 23.96 mm. **Obv:** Two headed Eagle **Rev:** Hercules wrestling Nemean lion

Date	Mintage	F	VF	XF	Unc	BU
1926R	1,002,000	3.00	6.00	15.00	32.00	—

KM# 13   1/2 LEK
Nickel **Ruler:** Ahmed Bey Zogu - King Zog I **Obv:** Kings arms **Rev:** Hercules wrestling Nemean lion

Date	Mintage	F	VF	XF	Unc	BU
1930V	500,000	3.00	6.00	19.00	30.00	—
1931L	500,000	3.00	6.00	19.00	30.00	—
1931L Proof	—	Value: 220				

KM# 5   LEK
8.0000 g., Nickel, 26.7 mm. **Obv:** Head right **Rev:** Caped man on horse right

Date	Mintage	F	VF	XF	Unc	BU
1926R	1,004,000	2.00	4.00	10.00	26.00	—
1927R	506,000	3.00	7.00	18.00	38.00	—
1930V	1,250,000	1.50	3.00	7.00	24.00	—
1931L	1,000,000	2.00	4.00	10.00	26.00	—
1931L Proof	—	Value: 230				

KM# 6   FRANG AR
5.0000 g., 0.8350 Silver 0.1342 oz. ASW, 23 mm. **Obv:** Helmeted head right **Rev:** Prow of ancient ship

Date	Mintage	F	VF	XF	Unc	BU
1927R	100,000	70.00	140	220	400	—
1928R	60,000	70.00	150	240	430	—

KM# 16   FRANG AR
5.0000 g., 0.8350 Silver 0.1342 oz. ASW, 23.20 mm. **Ruler:** Ahmed Bey Zogu - King Zog I **Obv:** Head right, date below **Rev:** Kings arms

Date	Mintage	F	VF	XF	Unc	BU
1935R	700,000	5.00	10.00	24.00	65.00	—
1937R	600,000	5.00	12.00	30.00	75.00	—

KM# 18   FRANG AR
5.0000 g., 0.8350 Silver 0.1342 oz. ASW, 23 mm. **Ruler:** Ahmed Bey Zogu - King Zog I **Subject:** 25th Anniversary of Independence **Obv:** Head right, date below **Rev:** Kings Arms

Date	Mintage	F	VF	XF	Unc	BU
1937R	50,000	8.00	16.00	36.00	95.00	—

KM# 7   2 FRANGA ARI
10.0000 g., 0.8350 Silver 0.2684 oz. ASW, 28 mm. **Obv:** Standing eagle with wings spread divides denomination **Rev:** Seed sower

Date	Mintage	F	VF	XF	Unc	BU
1926R	50,000	60.00	130	250	420	—
1927R	50,000	70.00	150	270	420	—
1928R	60,000	60.00	130	250	410	—

KM# 17   2 FRANGA ARI
10.0000 g., 0.8350 Silver 0.2684 oz. ASW **Ruler:** Ahmed Bey Zogu - King Zog I **Obv:** Head right, date below **Rev:** Kings Arms

Date	Mintage	F	VF	XF	Unc	BU
1935R	150,000	10.00	30.00	75.00	135	—

KM# 19   2 FRANGA ARI
10.0000 g., 0.8350 Silver 0.2684 oz. ASW **Ruler:** Ahmed Bey Zogu - King Zog I **Subject:** 25th Anniversary of Independence **Obv:** Head right, date below **Rev:** Kings arms

Date	Mintage	F	VF	XF	Unc	BU
1937R	25,000	15.00	30.00	80.00	160	—

KM# 8.1   5 FRANGA ARI
25.0000 g., 0.9000 Silver 0.7234 oz. ASW **Ruler:** Ahmed Bey Zogu - King Zog I **Obv:** Head right **Rev:** Man with plow left, value below

Date	Mintage	F	VF	XF	Unc	BU
1926	60,000	100	220	460	800	—
1927	Est. 40,000	—	—	—	—	—

Note: Only exist as provas

KM# 8.2   5 FRANGA ARI
25.0000 g., 0.9000 Silver 0.7234 oz. ASW **Ruler:** Ahmed Bey Zogu - King Zog I **Obv:** Hed right, star below head **Rev:** Man with plow left, value below

Date	Mintage	F	VF	XF	Unc	BU
1926R	Inc. above	130	300	490	800	—

KM# 9   10 FRANGA ARI
3.2258 g., 0.9000 Gold 0.0933 oz. AGW **Ruler:** Ahmed Bey Zogu - King Zog I **Obv:** Head left **Rev:** Double imperial eagle divides denomination below

Date	Mintage	F	VF	XF	Unc	BU
1927R	6,000	160	180	290	400	—

KM# 10   20 FRANGA ARI
6.4516 g., 0.9000 Gold 0.1867 oz. AGW, 21 mm. **Ruler:** Ahmed Bey Zogu - King Zog I **Obv:** Head left **Rev:** Double imperial eagle divides denomination below

Date	Mintage	F	VF	XF	Unc	BU
1926R	—	BV	190	280	380	—
1927R	6,000	BV	185	270	390	—

KM# 12   20 FRANGA ARI
6.4516 g., 0.9000 Gold 0.1867 oz. AGW, 21 mm. **Subject:** George Kastrioti "Skanderbeg" **Obv:** Lion of St. Mark right divides denomination, date below **Rev:** Bust right

Date	Mintage	F	VF	XF	Unc	BU
1926R	5,900	BV	200	330	450	—
1926 Fasces	100	—	—	4,200	6,600	—

Note: 90 pieces were reported melted

| 1927V | 5,053 | BV | 180 | 290 | 400 | — |

KM# 20   20 FRANGA ARI
6.4516 g., 0.9000 Gold 0.1867 oz. AGW, 21 mm. **Ruler:** Ahmed Bey Zogu - King Zog I **Subject:** 25th Anniversary of Independence **Obv:** Head right, date below **Rev:** Kings arms, denomination below

Date	Mintage	F	VF	XF	Unc	BU
1937R	2,500	—	225	350	500	—

KM# 22   20 FRANGA ARI
6.4516 g., 0.9000 Gold 0.1867 oz. AGW, 21 mm. **Ruler:** Ahmed Bey Zogu - King Zog I **Subject:** Marriage of King Zog to Countess Geraldine Apponyi, April 27, 1938 **Obv:** Head right, date below **Rev:** Kings arms, denomination below

Date	Mintage	F	VF	XF	Unc	BU
1938R	2,500	—	225	360	520	—

KM# 24   20 FRANGA ARI
6.4516 g., 0.9000 Gold 0.1867 oz. AGW, 21 mm. **Ruler:** Ahmed Bey Zogu - King Zog I **Subject:** 10th Anniversary - Reign of King Zog **Obv:** Head right, date below **Rev:** Kings arms, denomination below

Date	Mintage	F	VF	XF	Unc	BU
1938R	1,000	—	250	400	600	—

Note: Pieces struck in 1969 from new dies

KM# 25   50 FRANGA ARI
16.1290 g., 0.9000 Gold 0.4667 oz. AGW **Ruler:** Ahmed Bey Zogu - King Zog I **Subject:** 10th Anniversary - Reign of King Zog **Obv:** Head right, date below **Rev:** Kings Arms, denomination below

Date	Mintage	F	VF	XF	Unc	BU
1938R	600	—	600	900	1,650	—

Note: Pieces struck in 1969 from new dies

KM# 11.1   100 FRANGA ARI
32.2580 g., 0.9000 Gold 0.9334 oz. AGW, 35 mm. **Ruler:** Ahmed Bey Zogu - King Zog I **Obv:** Head left **Rev:** Biga right, denomination below

Date	Mintage	F	VF	XF	Unc	BU
1926R	6,614	—	900	1,100	1,650	—

Note: Mintage figures includes provas, Pr7-9

KM# 11.2   100 FRANGA ARI
32.2580 g., 0.9000 Gold 0.9334 oz. AGW, 35 mm. **Ruler:** Ahmed Bey Zogu - King Zog I **Obv:** Head left, star below **Rev:** Biga right, denomination below

Date	Mintage	F	VF	XF	Unc	BU
1926R	Inc. above	—	925	1,200	1,800	—

KM# 11.3   100 FRANGA ARI
32.2580 g., 0.9000 Gold 0.9334 oz. AGW, 35 mm. **Ruler:** Ahmed Bey Zogu - King Zog I **Obv:** Head left, two stars below **Rev:** Biga right, denomination below

Date	Mintage	F	VF	XF	Unc	BU
1926R	Inc. above	—	925	1,200	1,800	—

KM# 11a.1   100 FRANGA ARI
32.2580 g., 0.9000 Gold 0.9334 oz. AGW, 35 mm. **Ruler:** Ahmed Bey Zogu - King Zog I **Obv:** Head left **Rev:** Biga right, denomination below

Date	Mintage	F	VF	XF	Unc	BU
1927R	5,000	—	900	1,100	1,500	—

Note: Mintage figure includes provas, Pr17-19

KM# 11a.2   100 FRANGA ARI
32.2580 g., 0.9000 Gold 0.9334 oz. AGW **Ruler:** Ahmed Bey Zogu - King Zog I **Obv:** Head left, star below **Rev:** Biga right, denomination below

Date	Mintage	F	VF	XF	Unc	BU
1927R	Inc. above	—	950	1,200	2,100	—

KM# 11a.3   100 FRANGA ARI
32.2580 g., 0.9000 Gold 0.9334 oz. AGW **Ruler:** Ahmed Bey Zogu - King Zog I **Obv:** Head left, two stars below **Rev:** Biga right, denomination below

Date	Mintage	F	VF	XF	Unc	BU
1927R	Inc. above	—	950	1,250	2,200	—

KM# 21   100 FRANGA ARI
32.2580 g., 0.9000 Gold 0.9334 oz. AGW, 35 mm. **Ruler:** Ahmed Bey Zogu - King Zog I **Subject:** 25th Anniversary of Independence **Obv:** Head right, date below **Rev:** Kings arms divide denomination below

Date	Mintage	F	VF	XF	Unc	BU
1937R	500	—	1,000	1,600	2,350	—

KM# 23   100 FRANGA ARI
32.2580 g., 0.9000 Gold 0.9334 oz. AGW, 35 mm. **Ruler:** Ahmed Bey Zogu - King Zog I **Subject:** Marriage of King Zog to Countess Geraldine Apponyi, April 27, 1938 **Obv:** Head right, date below **Rev:** Kings Arms divide denomination below

Date	Mintage	F	VF	XF	Unc	BU
1938R	500	—	1,000	1,600	2,350	—

KM# 26   100 FRANGA ARI
32.2580 g., 0.9000 Gold 0.9334 oz. AGW, 35 mm.
Ruler: Ahmed Bey Zogu - King Zog I **Subject:** 10th Anniversary
- Reign of King Zog **Obv:** Head right, date below **Rev:** Kings Arms
divide denomination below

Date	Mintage	F	VF	XF	Unc	BU
1938R	500	—	1,000	1,600	2,350	

Note: Pieces restruck in 1969 from new dies

ITALIAN OCCUPATION WWII
STANDARD COINAGE

KM# 27   0.05 LEK
Aluminum-Bronze **Ruler:** Vittorio Emanuele III **Obv:** Head right
Rev: Value below oak branch

Date	Mintage	F	VF	XF	Unc	BU
1940R	1,400,000	3.00	6.00	16.00	32.00	—
1941R Rare	200,000	100	150	330	570	—

KM# 28   0.10 LEK
Aluminum-Bronze **Ruler:** Vittorio Emanuele III **Obv:** Head left
Rev: Value below olive branch

Date	Mintage	F	VF	XF	Unc	BU
1940R	550,000	4.00	8.00	22.00	38.00	—
1941R	250,000	18.00	50.00	100	170	—

KM# 29   0.20 LEK
4.0000 g., Stainless Steel, 21.7 mm. **Ruler:** Vittorio Emanuele III
Obv: Helmeted head right **Rev:** Double eagle between columns,
value below

Date	Mintage	F	VF	XF	Unc	BU
1939R	900,000	1.00	4.00	8.00	15.00	—

Note: 1939 dated coins exist in 2 varieties, magnetic and non-magnetic

1940R	700,000	1.00	2.00	7.00	18.00	—
1941R	1,400,000	1.00	2.00	5.00	14.00	—

KM# 30   0.50 LEK
Stainless Steel **Ruler:** Vittorio Emanuele III **Obv:** Helmeted
head left **Rev:** Double eagle between columns, value below

Date	Mintage	F	VF	XF	Unc	BU
1939R	100,000	2.00	5.00	12.00	30.00	—

Note: 1939 dated coins exist in two varieties, magnetic and non-magnetic

1940R	500,000	1.50	3.00	7.00	18.00	—
1941R	—	1.50	3.50	8.00	20.00	—

KM# 31   LEK
Stainless Steel **Ruler:** Vittorio Emanuele III **Obv:** Helmeted
head right **Rev:** Double eagle between columns, value below
Note: Coins dated after 1939 were not struck for circulation.

Date	Mintage	F	VF	XF	Unc	BU
1939R	2,100,000	1.50	2.50	5.00	16.00	—

Note: 1939 dated coins exist in two varieties, magnetic and non-magnetic

1940R Rare	1,500,000	—	—	—	—	—

Note: The official mintage figure is large, but few examples are known

| 1941R Rare | 1,000,000 | — | — | — | — | — |

Note: The official mintage figure is large, but few examples are known

KM# 32   2 LEK
Stainless Steel **Ruler:** Vittorio Emanuele III **Obv:** Helmeted
head left **Rev:** Double eagle between columns,value below
Note: Coins dated after 1939 were not struck for circulation.

Date	Mintage	F	VF	XF	Unc	BU
1939R	1,300,000	2.00	4.00	9.00	22.00	—

Note: 1939 dated coins exist in 2 varieties, magnetic and non-magnetic

Date	Mintage	F	VF	XF	Unc	BU
1940R Rare	—	—	—	—	—	—
1941R Rare	—	—	—	—	—	—

KM# 33   5 LEK
5.0000 g., 0.8350 Silver 0.1342 oz. ASW **Ruler:** Vittorio
Emanuele III **Obv:** Head left **Rev:** Double eagle between columns,
value

Date	Mintage	F	VF	XF	Unc	BU
1939R	1,350,000	6.00	12.00	35.00	75.00	—

KM# 34   10 LEK
10.0000 g., 0.8350 Silver 0.2684 oz. ASW **Ruler:** Vittorio
Emanuele III **Obv:** Head right **Rev:** Double eagle between
columns, value

Date	Mintage	F	VF	XF	Unc	BU
1939R	175,000	40.00	70.00	120	220	—

PEOPLE'S SOCIALIST REPUBLIC
1945 - 1990
STANDARD COINAGE

KM# 39   5 QINDARKA
0.7500 g., Aluminum, 18 mm. **Obv:** National Arms, date below
Rev: Five stars across top, value in center of wheat

Date	Mintage	F	VF	XF	Unc	BU
1964	—	0.10	0.25	0.50	1.25	1.50

KM# 44   5 QINDARKA
0.8000 g., Aluminum, 18 mm. **Subject:** 25th Anniversary of
Liberation **Obv:** National Arms, two dates below **Rev:** Five stars
across top, value in center of wheat

Date	Mintage	F	VF	XF	Unc	BU
ND (1969)	—	0.10	0.20	0.30	0.85	1.25

KM# 71   5 QINDARKA
Aluminum **Obv:** National Arms, date below **Rev:** Value between
wheat **Edge:** Plain

Date	Mintage	F	VF	XF	Unc	BU
1988	—	—	—	0.20	0.65	1.00

KM# 40   10 QINDARKA
1.0900 g., Aluminum, 17.95 mm. **Obv:** National Arms, date
below **Rev:** Five stars across top, value at center between wheat

Date	Mintage	F	VF	XF	Unc	BU
1964	—	0.15	0.30	0.60	1.50	1.75

KM# 45   10 QINDARKA
1.2000 g., Aluminum, 20 mm. **Subject:** 25th Anniversary of
Liberation **Obv:** National Arms, two dates **Rev:** Five stars across
top, value at center between wheat

Date	Mintage	F	VF	XF	Unc	BU
ND (1969)	—	0.10	0.20	0.35	1.00	1.25

KM# 60   10 QINDARKA
Aluminum, 20 mm. **Obv:** National Arms, date below **Rev:** Value
at center between wheat **Edge:** Plain

Date	Mintage	F	VF	XF	Unc	BU
1988	—	—	—	0.30	0.80	1.25

KM# 41   20 QINDARKA
1.5000 g., Aluminum, 22 mm. **Obv:** National Arms, date below
Rev: Five stars across top, value at center between wheat

Date	Mintage	F	VF	XF	Unc	BU
1964	—	0.20	0.40	0.60	1.75	2.00

KM# 46   20 QINDARKA
1.6000 g., Aluminum, 22 mm. **Subject:** 25th Anniversary of
Liberation **Obv:** National Arms, two dates **Rev:** Five stars across
top, value at center between wheat

Date	Mintage	F	VF	XF	Unc	BU
ND (1969)	—	0.15	0.30	0.50	1.25	1.50

KM# 65   20 QINDARKA
Aluminum **Obv:** National Arms, date below **Rev:** Value at center
between wheat

Date	Mintage	F	VF	XF	Unc	BU
1988	—	—	—	0.20	0.80	1.25

KM# 42   50 QINDARKA
2.0000 g., Aluminum, 24.49 mm. **Obv:** National Arms, date
below **Rev:** Five stars across top, value at center between wheat

Date	Mintage	F	VF	XF	Unc	BU
1964	—	0.50	0.75	2.00	4.00	6.00

KM# 47   50 QINDARKA
2.0000 g., Aluminum, 24.4 mm. **Subject:** 25th Ann. of Liberation
Rev: Two half-length figures holding torch aloft, value below

Date	Mintage	F	VF	XF	Unc	BU
ND (1969)	—	0.30	0.50	1.00	2.00	3.00

KM# 72 50 QINDARKA
2.0000 g., Aluminum, 24.1 mm. **Obv:** National Arms, date below **Rev:** Value at center between wheat, inside beaded circle **Edge:** Plain

Date	Mintage	F	VF	XF	Unc	BU
1988	—	—	—	0.50	1.40	2.25

KM# 35 1/2 LEKU
Zinc **Obv:** National Arms inside 3/4 circle of stars **Rev:** Value inside circle of stars, date at bottom

Date	Mintage	F	VF	XF	Unc	BU
1947	—	0.40	0.80	2.00	5.00	7.00
1957	—	0.25	0.50	1.00	2.00	3.00

KM# 36 LEK
Zinc **Obv:** National Arms inside 3/4 circle of stars **Rev:** Value inside circle of stars, date at bottom

Date	Mintage	F	VF	XF	Unc	BU
1947	—	0.60	1.00	3.00	6.00	8.00
1957	—	0.35	0.75	1.50	3.00	4.00

KM# 43 LEK
2.3000 g., Aluminum, 26.5 mm. **Obv:** National Arms between stars, date at bottom **Rev:** Five stars across top, value at center of wheat

Date	Mintage	F	VF	XF	Unc	BU
1964	—	0.50	1.00	2.00	4.00	5.50

KM# 48 LEK
2.3000 g., Aluminum, 26.5 mm. **Subject:** 25th Anniversary of Liberation **Obv:** National Arms between stars, two dates at bottom **Rev:** Armed man with knee on man on ground, value below

Date	Mintage	F	VF	XF	Unc	BU
ND (1969)	—	0.35	0.75	1.25	3.00	5.00

KM# 66 LEK
Aluminum-Bronze **Obv:** National Arms inside legend, date below **Rev:** Large value above wheat inside beaded circle

Date	Mintage	F	VF	XF	Unc	BU
1988	—	—	—	0.50	1.80	2.25

KM# 74 LEK
2.0000 g., Aluminum, 24.2 mm. **Obv:** National Arms, date below **Rev:** Large value above wheat inside beaded circle

Date	Mintage	F	VF	XF	Unc	BU
1988	—	—	—	0.40	1.60	2.00

KM# 37 2 LEKE
Zinc **Obv:** National Arms within 3/4 circle of stars, beaded edge **Rev:** Large value at center of circle stars, date below, beaded edge

Date	Mintage	F	VF	XF	Unc	BU
1947	—	0.50	1.25	3.00	6.00	8.00
1957	—	0.35	0.75	1.50	3.00	4.00

KM# 67 2 LEKE
7.6000 g., Copper-Nickel, 26 mm. **Subject:** 45th Anniversary - WWII **Obv:** National Arms, date below **Rev:** Armed man standing inside star, right arm raised, value to right

Date	Mintage	F	VF	XF	Unc	BU
1989	—	—	—	1.20	4.00	6.00

KM# 73 2 LEKE
Copper-Nickel **Obv:** National Arms, date below **Rev:** Large value above wheat within beaded circle **Edge:** Plain

Date	Mintage	F	VF	XF	Unc	BU
1989	—	—	—	1.20	4.00	5.50

KM# 38 5 LEKE
Zinc **Obv:** National Arms within 3/4 circle of stars **Rev:** Large value within circle of stars, date below

Date	Mintage	F	VF	XF	Unc	BU
1947	—	1.00	1.75	4.50	8.00	10.00
1957	—	0.50	1.00	2.00	3.50	5.00

KM# 49.1 5 LEKE
16.6600 g., 0.9990 Silver 0.5351 oz. ASW **Subject:** 500th Anniversary - Liga Lissi Skanderbeg's Victory Over the Turks **Obv:** Arms on shield, swords behind, flanking sides, cap on top, two dates below shield **Rev:** Arms above denomination, without date below, oval fineness countermark punched in

Date	Mintage	F	VF	XF	Unc	BU
ND (1969) Proof	8,540				Value: 30.00	

Note: Countermarks for 1968 and 1969 coins were hand positioned, then punched. The result is a variety of countermark positions, to the left and right of LEKE

KM# 49.2 5 LEKE
16.6600 g., 0.9990 Silver 0.5351 oz. ASW **Obv:** Arms on shield, cap above shield, swords behind, flanking sides, two dates below shield **Rev:** Denomination and date below arms

Date	Mintage	F	VF	XF	Unc	BU
1969 Proof	1,500				Value: 30.00	

Note: Countermarks for 1968 and 1969 coins were hand positioned, then punched. The result is a variety of countermark positions, to the left and right of LEKE

KM# 49.3 5 LEKE
16.6600 g., 0.9990 Silver 0.5351 oz. ASW **Obv:** Arms on shield, cap above shield, swords behind flanking sides, two dates below **Rev:** Denomination and date below arms, oval fineness in relief

Date	Mintage	F	VF	XF	Unc	BU
1970 Proof	500				Value: 55.00	

Note: For the 1970 issue the fineness marking has been incorporated in the dies

KM# 57 5 LEKE
28.2000 g., Copper-Nickel, 38.7 mm. **Subject:** Seaport of Durazzo **Obv:** National Arms, date below **Rev:** Seaport left of sailing ship, denomination below

Date	Mintage	F	VF	XF	Unc	BU
1987	Est. 50,000	—	—	7.00	14.00	20.00

KM# 57a 5 LEKE
50.0000 g., 0.9000 Gold 1.4467 oz. AGW **Subject:** Seaport of Durazzo **Obv:** National arms, date below **Rev:** Seaport left of sailing ship, denomination below

Date	Mintage	F	VF	XF	Unc	BU
1987 Proof	5				Value: 2,600	

KM# 61   5 LEKE
28.2000 g., Copper-Nickel, 38.7 mm.   **Subject:** 42nd
Anniversary of First Railroad **Obv:** Steam locomotive and
passenger train emerging from tunnel at left, date at lower left,
denomination below **Rev:** Diesel locomotive and train emerging
from tunnel on right, dates below **Edge:** Reeded

Date	Mintage	F	VF	XF	Unc	BU
1988	20,000	—	—	7.00	18.00	28.00

KM# 50.1   10 LEKE
33.3300 g., 0.9990 Silver 1.0705 oz. ASW   **Subject:** 500th
Anniversary - Death of Prince Skanderbeg **Obv:** Figure on
horseback right, divides dates **Rev:** Oval fineness countermark
punched in, no date below; value below arms

Date	Mintage	F	VF	XF	Unc	BU
ND Proof	8,540	Value: 45.00				

Note: Countermark for 1968 and 1969 coins were hand
positioned, then punched. The result is a variety of
countermark positions, to the left and right of LEKE

KM# 50.2   10 LEKE
33.3300 g., 0.9990 Silver 1.0705 oz. ASW   **Obv:** Figure on
horseback right, divides dates **Rev:** Denomination and date
below arms

Date	Mintage	F	VF	XF	Unc	BU
1969 Proof	1,500	Value: 60.00				

Note: Countermark for 1968 and 1969 coins were hand
positioned, then punched. The result is a variety of
countermark positions, to the left and right of LEKE

KM# 50.3   10 LEKE
33.3300 g., 0.9990 Silver 1.0705 oz. ASW   **Obv:** Figure on
horseback right, divides dates **Rev:** Oval fineness is in relief, date
and value below arms

Date	Mintage	F	VF	XF	Unc	BU
1970 Proof	500	Value: 70.00				

Note: For the 1970 issues the fineness marking has been
incorporated in the dies

KM# 50.4   10 LEKE
33.3300 g., 0.9990 Silver 1.0705 oz. ASW   **Obv:** Figure on
horseback right, divides dates **Rev:** Hallmark countermark left of
LEKE, oval fineness countermark in relief, date and value below arms

Date	Mintage	F	VF	XF	Unc	BU
1970 Proof	Inc. above	Value: 65.00				

Note: For the 1970 issues the fineness marking has been
incorporated in the dies

KM# 51.1   20 LEKE
3.9500 g., 0.9000 Gold 0.1143 oz. AGW   **Subject:** 500th
Anniversary - Death of Prince Skanderbeg **Obv:** Skanderbeg
helmet within wreath, scythe at left of helmet **Rev:** Arms, value
below, oval fineness countermark punched in

Date	Mintage	F	VF	XF	Unc	BU
1968	2,920	Value: 130				

Note: Countermark for 1968 and 1969 coins were hand
positioned, then punched. The result is a variety of
countermark positions, to the left and right of LEKE

KM# 51.2   20 LEKE
3.9500 g., 0.9000 Gold 0.1143 oz. AGW   **Obv:** Skanderbeg
helmet within wreath, scythe at left of helmet **Rev:** Without
fineness countermark (error)

Date	Mintage	F	VF	XF	Unc	BU
1968 Proof	Inc. above	Value: 130				

KM# 51.3   20 LEKE
3.9500 g., 0.9000 Gold 0.1143 oz. AGW   **Obv:** Skanderbeg helmet
within wreath, scythe at left of helmet **Rev:** Cornucopia countermark
at right of LEKE **Note:** Variety of countermark positions.

Date	Mintage	F	VF	XF	Unc	BU
1968 Paris	24	—	—	350	420	460

KM# 51.4   20 LEKE
3.9500 g., 0.9000 Gold 0.1143 oz. AGW   **Obv:** Skanderbeg
helmet within wreath, scythe at left **Rev:** Date added below arms
Note: Variety of countermark positions.

Date	Mintage	F	VF	XF	Unc	BU
1969 Proof	650	Value: 160				

KM# 51.5   20 LEKE
3.9500 g., 0.9000 Gold 0.1143 oz. AGW   **Obv:** Skanderbeg
helmet within wreath, scythe to left of helmet **Rev:** Date below
arms, oval fineness in relief, incorporated in die

Date	Mintage	F	VF	XF	Unc	BU
1970 Proof	500	Value: 165				

KM# 51.6   20 LEKE
3.9500 g., 0.9000 Gold 0.1143 oz. AGW   **Obv:** Skanderbeg
helmet within wreath, scythe to left of helmet **Rev:** Sunken
countermark 1 AR left of LEKE and raised oval fineness
countermark on right incorporated into the dies

Date	Mintage	F	VF	XF	Unc	BU
1970 Proof		Value: 225				

KM# 52.1   25 LEKE
83.3300 g., 0.9990 Silver 2.6763 oz. ASW   **Obv:** Dance with
swords, date below **Rev:** Denomination below arms, oval
fineness countermark

Date	Mintage	F	VF	XF	Unc	BU
1968 Proof	8,540	Value: 75.00				

Note: Countermarks for 1968 and 1969 coins were hand
positioned, then punched; the result is a variety of
countermark positions, to the left and the right of LEKE

KM# 52.2   25 LEKE
83.3300 g., 0.9990 Silver 2.6763 oz. ASW   **Obv:** Dance with
swords, date below **Rev:** Denomination below arms, oval
fineness countermark

Date	Mintage	F	VF	XF	Unc	BU
1969 Proof	—	Value: 85.00				

KM# 54.1 100 LEKE
19.7500 g., 0.9000 Gold 0.5715 oz. AGW **Obv:** Peasant girl in national dress, date below **Rev:** Oval fineness countermark

Date	Mintage	F	VF	XF	Unc	BU
1968 Proof	3,470	Value: 575				

KM# 54.2 100 LEKE
19.7500 g., 0.9000 Gold 0.5715 oz. AGW **Obv:** Peasant girl in national dress, date below **Rev:** Date below arms, oval fineness countermark

Date	Mintage	F	VF	XF	Unc	BU
1969 Proof	450	Value: 625				

KM# 54.3 100 LEKE
19.7500 g., 0.9000 Gold 0.5715 oz. AGW **Obv:** Without date **Rev:** Oval fineness countermark in relief incorporated into the dies

Date	Mintage	F	VF	XF	Unc	BU
1970 Proof	Inc. above	Value: 650				

KM# 59 100 LEKE
6.4500 g., 0.9000 Gold 0.1866 oz. AGW **Subject:** Seaport of Durazzo **Obv:** National arms, date below **Rev:** Seaport left of sailing ship, denomination below

Date	Mintage	F	VF	XF	Unc	BU
1987 Proof	5,000	Value: 195				

KM# 63 100 LEKE
6.4500 g., 0.9000 Gold 0.1866 oz. AGW **Subject:** 42nd Anniversary - First Railroad **Obv:** Train engine emerging from tunnel **Rev:** Caboose entering tunnel **Note:** Without hole in coin

Date	Mintage	F	VF	XF	Unc	BU
1988 Proof	2,000	Value: 285				

KM# 52.3 25 LEKE
83.3300 g., 0.9990 Silver 2.6763 oz. ASW, 60 mm. **Obv:** Dance with swords, without date **Rev:** Oval fineness countermark in relief **Note:** Illustration reduced.

Date	Mintage	F	VF	XF	Unc	BU
1970 Proof	500	Value: 100				

Note: For the 1970 issue the fineness marking has been incorporated in the dies

KM# 53.1 50 LEKE
9.8700 g., 0.9000 Gold 0.2856 oz. AGW **Obv:** Argirocastrum Ruins, date below **Rev:** Oval fineness countermark

Date	Mintage	F	VF	XF	Unc	BU
1968 Proof	3,120	Value: 290				

KM# 58 50 LEKE
168.1500 g., 0.9250 Silver 5.0005 oz. ASW, 65 mm. **Subject:** Seaport of Durazzo **Obv:** National arms, date below **Rev:** Seaport left of sailing ship, denomination below **Note:** Illustration reduced.

Date	Mintage	F	VF	XF	Unc	BU
1987 Proof	Est. 15,000	Value: 150				

KM# 58a 50 LEKE
155.5000 g., 0.9990 Gold 4.9942 oz. AGW **Subject:** Seaport of Durazzo **Obv:** National arms, date below **Rev:** Seaport left of sailing ship, denomination below

Date	Mintage	F	VF	XF	Unc	BU
1987 Proof	5	Value: 6,500				

KM# 53.2 50 LEKE
9.8700 g., 0.9000 Gold 0.2856 oz. AGW **Obv:** Argirocastrum ruins, date below **Rev:** Date below arms, oval fineness countermark, value below date

Date	Mintage	F	VF	XF	Unc	BU
1969 Proof	500	Value: 300				

KM# 53.3 50 LEKE
9.8700 g., 0.9000 Gold 0.2856 oz. AGW **Obv:** Ruins, without date **Rev:** Oval fineness countermark in relief

Date	Mintage	F	VF	XF	Unc	BU
1970 Proof	100	Value: 450				

Note: For the 1970 issue the fineness marking has been incorporated in the dies

KM# 62 50 LEKE
168.1500 g., 0.9250 Silver 5.0005 oz. ASW, 65 mm. **Subject:** 42nd Anniversary - First Railroad **Obv:** Steam locomotive and passenger train emerging from tunnel at left, date at left, denomination below **Rev:** Diesel locomotive and passenger train emerging from tunnel at right, dates below **Note:** Illustration reduced. Tunnel is a hole in the coin.

Date	Mintage	F	VF	XF	Unc	BU
1988 Proof	7,500	Value: 350				

KM# 55.1 200 LEKE
39.4900 g., 0.9000 Gold 1.1426 oz. AGW **Subject:** Buthrotum Ruins **Obv:** Head right, date at left, ruins in background **Rev:** Arms above denomination

Date	Mintage	F	VF	XF	Unc	BU
1968 Proof	2,170	Value: 1,200				

KM# 55.2 200 LEKE
39.4900 g., 0.9000 Gold 1.1426 oz. AGW **Obv:** Head right, date at left, ruins in background **Rev:** Date below arms, oval fineness countermark in a variety of positions

Date	Mintage	F	VF	XF	Unc	BU
1969 Proof	200	Value: 1,300				

KM# 55.3 200 LEKE
39.4900 g., 0.9000 Gold 1.1426 oz. AGW **Obv:** Head right, ruins in background, without date **Rev:** Oval fineness countermark in relief incorporated into the die

Date	Mintage	F	VF	XF	Unc	BU
1970 Proof	Inc. above	Value: 1,350				

KM# 56.1   500 LEKE
98.7400 g., 0.9000 Gold 2.8570 oz. AGW **Subject:** 500th Anniversary - Death of Prince Skanderbeg **Rev:** National arms above denomination

Date	Mintage	F	VF	XF	Unc	BU
1968 Proof	1,520	Value: 2,800				

KM# 56.2   500 LEKE
98.7400 g., 0.9000 Gold 2.8570 oz. AGW **Rev:** Date below arms, oval fineness countermark in a variety of positions

Date	Mintage	F	VF	XF	Unc	BU
1969 Proof	200	Value: 2,950				

KM# 56.3   500 LEKE
98.7400 g., 0.9000 Gold 2.8570 oz. AGW **Obv:** Without date **Rev:** Oval fineness countermark in relief incorporated into the die

Date	Mintage	F	VF	XF	Unc	BU
1970 Proof	Inc. above	Value: 3,000				

KM# 64   7500 LEKE
483.7500 g., 0.9000 Gold 13.997 oz. AGW **Subject:** 42nd Anniversary - First Railroad **Obv:** Engine emerging from tunnel **Rev:** Caboose entering tunnel **Note:** Similar to 50 Leke, KM#62.

Date	Mintage	F	VF	XF	Unc	BU
1988 Proof	50	Value: 15,000				

REPUBLIC

STANDARD COINAGE

KM# 75   LEK
3.0000 g., Bronze, 18.1 mm. **Obv:** Dalmatian pelican **Rev:** Denomination **Edge:** Plain

Date	Mintage	F	VF	XF	Unc	BU
1996	—	—	—	0.40	1.50	2.00

KM# 76   5 LEKE
3.1000 g., Steel, 20 mm. **Obv:** Imperial eagle **Rev:** Olive branch, denomination

Date	Mintage	F	VF	XF	Unc	BU
1995	—	—	—	—	1.00	1.25
2000	—	—	—	—	1.00	1.25

KM# 68   10 LEKE
52.5000 g., 0.9250 Silver 1.5613 oz. ASW **Subject:** 1992 Summer Olympics - Equestrian **Rev:** Horse and rider right, incuse design

Date	Mintage	F	VF	XF	Unc	BU
1991	980	—	—	150	200	240

KM# 69   10 LEKE
52.5000 g., 0.9250 Silver 1.5613 oz. ASW **Subject:** 1992 Summer Olympics - Equestrian **Obv:** National arms, value and date below **Rev:** Horse and rider left, relief design

Date	Mintage	F	VF	XF	Unc	BU
1991	980	—	—	150	200	240

KM# 70   10 LEKE
28.4600 g., 0.9250 Silver 0.8463 oz. ASW **Subject:** 1992 Summer Olympics - Boxing **Obv:** National arms divide date **Rev:** Boxers left, value right center

Date	Mintage	F	VF	XF	Unc	BU
1992 Proof	20,000	Value: 50.00				

KM# 77   10 LEKE
3.6000 g., Brass, 21.1 mm. **Obv:** Fortress **Rev:** Denomination above sprig with berries

Date	Mintage	F	VF	XF	Unc	BU
1996	—	—	—	—	1.25	1.50
2000	—	—	—	—	1.25	1.50

KM# 78   20 LEKE
4.9000 g., Brass, 23.5 mm. **Obv:** Ancient sailing vessel **Rev:** Denomination

Date	Mintage	F	VF	XF	Unc	BU
1996	—	—	—	—	1.60	2.00
2000	—	—	—	—	1.60	2.00

KM# 79   50 LEKE
5.5000 g., Copper-Nickel, 24.5 mm. **Obv:** Ancient equestrian **Rev:** Denomination, tied oak sprigs

Date	Mintage	F	VF	XF	Unc	BU
1996	—	—	—	—	2.00	3.00
2000	—	—	—	—	2.00	3.00

KM# 80   100 LEKE
6.7000 g., Bi-Metallic Aluminum-Bronze center in Copper-Nickel ring, 24.7 mm. **Obv:** Teuta, Illyrian queen, stateswoman, reigned 231 BC **Rev:** Denomination in wreath. **Edge:** Reeded

Date	Mintage	F	VF	XF	Unc	BU
2000	—	—	—	—	4.00	5.00

TRIAL STRIKES

KM#	Date	Mintage	Identification	Issue Price	Mkt Val
TS1	1969	—	500 Leke. Goldine-Brass. 56.3200 g. 55 mm. Blank with MET countermark. Like KM56.2.	—	200

PATTERNS
Including off metal strikes

KM#	Date	Mintage	Identification	Mkt Val
Pn1	1927	—	Frang Ar. Silver. Plain edge. Prev. KM#Pn7.	500
Pn2	1927	—	5 Franga Ari. Copper. Prev. KM#Pn9.	—
Pn3	1928	—	2 Lek. Copper-Nickel. Prev. KM#Pn11.	—
Pn4	1968	—	10 Leke. 0.9990 Silver. 31.6000 g. Like 10 Leke, KM#50. Blank except for MET in rectangle at 6 o'clock. Reeded edge.	—

ESSAIS

KM#	Date	Mintage	Identification	Mkt Val
E1	1926	—	5 Qindar Leku. Bronze.	—
E2	1926	—	10 Qindar Ari. Bronze. Prev. KM#Pn2.	—
E3	1926	—	1/2 Lek. Nickel. Prev. KM#Pn3.	—
E4	1926	50	2 Franga Ari. Silver. Prev. KM#Pn4.	500
E5	1927	—	Lek. Nickel. Prev. KM#Pn5.	—
E6	1927	—	Frang Ar. Silver. Prev. KM#Pn6.	500
E7	1927	50	2 Franga Ari. Silver. Prev. KM#Pn8.	650
E8	1927	—	100 Franga Ari. Silver. Prev.KM#Pn10.	—
E9	1928	—	2 Lek. Nickel. Prev. KM#Pn12.	—
E10	1928	50	Frang Ar. Silver. Prev. KM#Pn13.	500
E11	1928	50	2 Franga Ari. Silver. Prev. KM#Pn14.	650
E12	1938	—	100 Franga Ari. Gold. Without signature. Prev. KM#Pn15.	—
E13	1986	10	5 Leke. Copper-Nickel. 27.7900 g.	200

PIEFORTS

KM#	Date	Mintage	Identification	Mkt Val
P1	1988	250	50 Leke. 0.9250 Silver. KM#62 without tunnel hole.	500

PROVAS
Standard metals unless otherwise stated

KM#	Date	Mintage	Identification	Mkt Val
Pr1	1926R	50	5 Qindar Leku. Bronze. KM#1.	400
Pr2	1926R	50	10 Qindar Leku. Bronze. KM#2.	400
Pr3	1926R	50	1/4 Leku. Nickel. Male lion left. Oak leaf across top, value below. KM#3.	500
Pr4	1926	—	1/2 Lek. Nickel.	400
Pr5	1926R	—	1/2 Lek. Nickel. KM#4.	400
Pr6	1926R	50	Lek. Nickel. KM#5.	500
Pr7	1926R	—	2 Franga Ari. Silver. KM#7.	500
Pr8	1926R	—	5 Franga Ari. Silver. KM#8. Modern copy of 5 Franga Ari exist in copper and bronze.	750
Pr9	1926R	—	5 Franga Ari. Copper. KM#8. Modern copy of 5 Franga Ari exist in copper and bronze.	450
Pr10	1926R	—	5 Franga Ari. Silver. KM#8. Modern copy of 5 Franga Ari exist in copper and bronze.	500
Pr11	1926R	—	5 Franga Ari. Copper. KM#8. Modern copy of 5 Franga Ari exist in copper and bronze.	450
Pr12	1926R	50	20 Franga Ari. Gold. KM#12.	750
Pr13	1926	—	20 Franga Ari. Gold. KM#12.	5,000
Pr14	1926R	—	100 Franga Ari. Gold. KM#11.1.	2,200
Pr15	1926R	—	100 Franga Ari. Gold. Head left, star below. Biga right, denomination below.	2,200
Pr16	1926R	—	100 Franga Ari. Gold. Head left, two stars below. Biga right, denomination below.	2,200
Pr17	1927R	—	1/4 Leku. Nickel. Lion advancing left, date below. Oak branch above value.	500
Pr18	1927R	—	Lek. Nickel. Head right. Figure on horseback right, denomination below.	500

| Pr19 | 1927R | 50 | Frang Ar. Silver. Helmeted head right. Prow of ancient ship, denomination above. | 300 |

KM#	Date	Mintage Identification	Mkt Val
Pr20	1927V	— Frang Ar. Silver. Helmeted head right. Prow of ancient ship, denomination above.	350
Pr21	1927R	— 2 Franga Ari. Silver. Standing eagle with wings spread divides denomination. Seed sower.	300
Pr22	1927V	— 5 Franga Ari. Silver.	450
Pr23	1927V	— 5 Franga Ari. Silver. Matte proof.	—
Pr24	1927	— 10 Franga Ari. Gold. Head left. Double eagle divides denomination below.	900
PrA25	1927R	— Frang Ar. Silver. Head right. Double eagle, date and denomination below.	—
Pr25	1927R	50 10 Franga Ari. Gold. Head left. Double eagle, date and denomination below.	750
Pr26	1927	— 20 Franga Ari. Gold. Head left. Double eagle, date and denomination below.	850
Pr27	1927V	— 20 Franga Ari. Gold. Lion divides denomination, date below. Bust right.	650
Pr28	1927R	50 20 Franga Ari. Gold. Head left. Double eagle, date and denomination below.	650
Pr29	1927R	— 100 Franga Ari. Head left. Biga right, denomination below.	2,300
Pr30	1927R	— 100 Franga Ari. Gold. Head left, star below. Biga right, denomination below.	2,300
Pr31	1927R	— 100 Franga Ari. Gold. Head left, two stars below. Biga right, denomination below.	2,300
PrA32	1927V	— 100 Franga Ari. Silver. Head right. Man with oxen pulling plow left, denomination below.	2,300
Pr32	1928R	— 2 Lek. Copper-Nickel. Head left. Olive branch above denomination.	200
Pr33	1928R	— 2 Lek. Nickel. Head left. Olive branch above denomination.	—
PrA34	1928R	— 2 Lek. Nickel. 9.7800 g. Head right. Double eagle, date and denomination below.	300
Pr34	1928R	— Frang Ar. Silver. Helmeted head right. Prow of ancient ship, denomination above.	200
Pr35	1928R	— 2 Franga Ari. Silver. Standing eagle with wings spread divides denomination. Seed sower.	250
PrA36	1928R	— 2 Franga Ari. Silver. 10.0400 g. Head right. Double eagle, denomination and date below.	350
Pr36	1928R	50 100 Franga Ari. Gold. Head left. Double eagle, cap on top, date bottom left. Bare head.	3,200
Pr37	1928R	50 100 Franga Ari. Gold. Head left within wreath left. Double eagle, cap on top, date at bottom left. Bare head, wreath.	3,200
Pr38	1928R	50 100 Franga Ari. Gold. Uniformed bust right. Double eagle, cap on top, date bottom left.	4,000
Pr39	1929R	50 100 Franga Ari. Gold. Head left within wreath. Double eagle, cap on top, date below tail. Bare head, wreath.	3,200
PrA40	1930	— 1/2 Leku.	—
Pr40	1935R	50 Qindar Ar. Bronze. Double eagle, date below. Value above oak leaves.	300
Pr41	1935R	50 2 Qindar Ari. Bronze. Double eagle, date below. Denomination above leaves.	300
Pr42	1935	50 Frang Ar. Silver.	400
Pr43	1935	50 2 Franga Ari. Silver.	500
Pr44	1935	— 5 Franga Ari. Silver. Pattern.	—
Pr45	1937R	50 Frang Ar. Silver. Head right. King's arms, denomination below.	450
Pr46	1937R	50 Frang Ar. Silver.	500
Pr47	1937R	50 2 Franga Ari. Silver.	525
Pr48	1937R	— 10 Franga Ari. Gold. Reported, not confirmed	—
Pr49	1937R	50 20 Franga Ari. Gold. Head right. King's arms, denomination below.	900
Pr50	1937R	50 100 Franga Ari. Gold. Head right, date below. King's arms, denomination below.	2,500
Pr51	1938R	50 20 Franga Ari. Gold. Head right, date below. King's arms, denomination below.	850
Pr52	1938R	50 20 Franga Ari. Gold. Head right, date below. King's arms, denomination below.	850
Pr53	1938R	50 100 Franga Ari. Gold. Head right, date below. King's arms, denomination below.	2,300
Pr54	1938R	50 100 Franga Ari. Gold. Head right, date below. King's arms, denomination below.	2,500
Pr55	1938R	50 100 Franga Ari. Gold. Head right, date below. King's arms, denomination below.	2,500
Pr56	1939	— 0.05 Lek. Proof.	400
Pr57	1939	— 0.10 Lek. Proof.	400
Pr58	1939	— 0.20 Lek. Proof	500
Pr59	1939	— 0.50 Lek. Proof.	500
Pr60	1939	— Lek. Proof.	500
Pr61	1939	— 2 Lek. Proof.	525
Pr62	1939	— 5 Lek. Proof.	500
Pr63	1939	— 10 Lek. Silver. Proof.	625
Pr64	1947	— 10 Qindar Leku. Aluminum.	—
Pr65	1947	— 5 Qindar Leku. Tombac.	—
Pr66	1947	— 10 Qindar Leku. Aluminum.	—
Pr67	1947	— 10 Qindar Leku. Tombac.	—
Pr68	1947	— 20 Qindar Leku. Aluminum.	—
Pr69	1947	— 20 Qindar Leku. Tombac.	—
Pr70	1947	— 50 Qindar Leku. Aluminum.	—
Pr71	1947	— 50 Qindar Leku. Tombac.	—

MINT SETS

KM#	Date	Mintage Identification	Issue Price	Mkt Val
MS1	1969 (5)	— KM#44-48	6.00	25.00

PROOF SETS

KM#	Date	Mintage Identification	Issue Price	Mkt Val
PS1	1968 (5)	1,500 KM#51.1, 53.1-56	470	4,250
PS2	1968 (8)	1,540 KM#49-56	—	4,400
PSA2	1968 (3)	8,540 KM#49, 50, 52	44.00	135
PS3	1969 (5)	— KM#51, 53-56	470	4,600
PS4	1969 (8)	— KM#49-56	—	4,750
PSA4	1969 (3)	1,500 KM#49, 50, 52	45.00	150
PS5	1970 (5)	— KM#51.5, 53-56	516	4,950
PS6	1970 (3)	500 KM#49-50, 52	45.00	200
PS7	1991 (2)	980 KM#68-69	—	445

ALDERNEY

Alderney, the northernmost and third largest of the Channel Islands, separated from the coast of France by the dangerous 8-mile-wide tidal channel, has an area of 3 sq. mi. (8 km.) and a population of 1,686. It is a dependency of the British island of Guernsey, to the southwest. Capital: St. Anne. Principal industries are agriculture and raising cattle.

There is evidence of settlement in prehistoric times and Roman coins have been discovered on the island along with evidence of their buildings. Toward the close of the reign of Henry VIII, France began making plans to seize the Island of Sark. The English, realizing its strategic importance, began to build a defensive fort, which was abandoned some years later when Edward VI died. France constructed a large naval base at its northern tip, which incited the English into making Alderney the "Gibraltar of the Channel." Most of the Islanders were evacuated before the German occupation in 1940 but returned in 1945 when the Germans surrendered.

The Channel Islands have never been subject to the British Parliament and are self-governing units under the direct rule of the Crown acting through the Privy Council. Alderney is one of the nine Channel Islands, the only part of the Duchy of Normandy still belonging to the British Crown, and has been a British possession since the Norman Conquest of 1066. Legislation was only recently introduced for the issue of its own coinage, a right it now shares with Jersey and Guernsey.

RULER
British

MONETARY SYSTEM
100 Pence = 1 Pound Sterling

DEPENDENCY
STANDARD COINAGE

KM# 4 POUND
9.5000 g., 0.9250 Silver 0.2825 oz. ASW, 22.5 mm.
Ruler: Elizabeth II **Subject:** 40th Anniversary - Coronation
Obv: Crowned bust, right, date below **Rev:** Royal carriage

Date	Mintage	F	VF	XF	Unc	BU
1993 Proof	Est. 20,000				Value: 30.00	

KM# 12 POUND
9.5000 g., 0.9250 Silver 0.2825 oz. ASW, 22.5 mm.
Ruler: Elizabeth II **Subject:** VE Day **Obv:** crowned bust, right
Rev: VE Monogram and dove

Date	Mintage	F	VF	XF	Unc	BU
ND(1995) Proof	Est. 20,000				Value: 30.00	

KM# 12a POUND
15.8000 g., 0.9160 Gold 0.4653 oz. AGW, 22.5 mm. **Ruler:** Elizabeth II **Subject:** VE Day **Rev:** VE Monogram and dove

Date	Mintage	F	VF	XF	Unc	BU
ND(1995) Proof	500				Value: 450	

KM# 1 2 POUNDS
28.2800 g., Copper-Nickel, 38.5 mm. **Ruler:** Elizabeth II
Subject: Royal Visit **Obv:** Crowned bust, right, date below
Rev: Arms surrounded by thrift plant

Date	Mintage	F	VF	XF	Unc	BU
1989	—	—	—	9.00	10.00	

KM# 1a 2 POUNDS
28.2800 g., 0.9250 Silver 0.8410 oz. ASW, 38.6 mm.
Ruler: Elizabeth II **Subject:** Royal Visit

Date	Mintage	F	VF	XF	Unc	BU
1989 Proof	5,000			Value: 50.00		

KM# 1b 2 POUNDS
47.5400 g., 0.9170 Gold 1.4015 oz. AGW **Ruler:** Elizabeth II
Subject: Royal Visit

Date	Mintage	F	VF	XF	Unc	BU
1989 Proof	100			Value: 1,400		

KM# 2 2 POUNDS
28.2800 g., Copper-Nickel, 38.5 mm. **Ruler:** Elizabeth II
Subject: Queen Mother's 90th Birthday **Rev:** Queen Mother in cameo facing left, Glamis rose sprays flanking

Date	Mintage	F	VF	XF	Unc	BU
1990	—	—	—	8.50	9.50	

KM# 2a 2 POUNDS
28.2800 g., 0.9250 Silver 0.8410 oz. ASW, 38.6 mm. **Ruler:** Elizabeth II **Subject:** Royal Visit

Date	Mintage	F	VF	XF	Unc	BU
1990 Proof	5,000			Value: 50.00		

KM# 2b 2 POUNDS
47.5400 g., 0.9170 Gold 1.4015 oz. AGW **Ruler:** Elizabeth II
Subject: Queen Mother's 90th Birthday

Date	Mintage	F	VF	XF	Unc	BU
1990 Proof	90			Value: 1,450		

KM# 3 2 POUNDS
28.2800 g., Copper-Nickel, 38.5 mm. **Ruler:** Elizabeth II
Subject: 40th Anniversary - Queen's Reign **Rev:** Sailing ship on water, Crowned initials below within wreath

Date	Mintage	F	VF	XF	Unc	BU
1992	—	—	—	8.50	9.50	

KM# 3a   2 POUNDS
28.2800 g., 0.9250 Silver 0.8410 oz. ASW, 38.6 mm.
Ruler: Elizabeth II **Subject:** 40th Anniversary - Queen's Reign

Date	Mintage	F	VF	XF	Unc	BU
1992 Proof	5,000	Value: 40.00				

KM# 3b   2 POUNDS
47.5400 g., 0.9170 Gold 1.4015 oz. AGW **Ruler:** Elizabeth II
Subject: 40th Anniversary - Queen's Reign

Date	Mintage	F	VF	XF	Unc	BU
1992 Proof	150	Value: 1,350				

KM# 5   2 POUNDS
28.2800 g., Copper-Nickel, 38.8 mm. **Ruler:** Elizabeth II
Subject: 40th Anniversary - Coronation **Rev:** Coronation coach, flags of the Union, Alderney of May 24 1989

Date	Mintage	F	VF	XF	Unc	BU
1993	—	—	—	—	8.00	9.00

KM# 5a   2 POUNDS
28.2800 g., 0.9250 Silver 0.8410 oz. ASW, 38.6 mm.
Ruler: Elizabeth II **Subject:** 40th Anniversary - Coronation

Date	Mintage	F	VF	XF	Unc	BU
1993 Proof	Est. 5,000	Value: 45.00				

KM# 7   2 POUNDS
28.2800 g., Copper-Nickel, 38.5 mm. **Ruler:** Elizabeth II **Subject:** Normandy Invasion **Rev:** Normandy beach landing scene

Date	Mintage	F	VF	XF	Unc	BU
1994	Est. 5,000,000	—	—	—	9.00	10.00

KM# 7a   2 POUNDS
28.2800 g., 0.9250 Silver 0.8410 oz. ASW, 38.6 mm.
Ruler: Elizabeth II **Subject:** Normandy Invasion **Rev:** Normandy beach landing scene

Date	Mintage	F	VF	XF	Unc	BU
1994 Proof	—	Value: 45.00				

KM# 13   2 POUNDS
28.2800 g., Copper-Nickel, 38.5 mm. **Ruler:** Elizabeth II
Subject: Islander's Return **Rev:** Steamship Autocarrier

Date	Mintage	F	VF	XF	Unc	BU
ND(1995)	—	—	—	—	10.00	12.00

KM# 13a   2 POUNDS
28.2800 g., 0.9250 Silver 0.8410 oz. ASW, 38.6 mm.
Ruler: Elizabeth II **Subject:** Islander's Return **Rev:** Steamship

Date	Mintage	F	VF	XF	Unc	BU
ND(1995) Proof	10,000	Value: 45.00				

KM# 13b   2 POUNDS
47.5400 g., 0.9160 Gold 1.4000 oz. AGW **Ruler:** Elizabeth II
Subject: Islander's Return **Rev:** Steamship

Date	Mintage	F	VF	XF	Unc	BU
ND(1995) Proof	250	Value: 1,350				

KM# 16   2 POUNDS
28.2800 g., Copper-Nickel, 38.5 mm. **Ruler:** Elizabeth II
Subject: World Wildlife Fund **Obv:** Queen's portrait **Rev:** 2 Atlantic Puffin birds

Date	Mintage	F	VF	XF	Unc	BU
1997	—	—	—	—	12.00	15.00

KM# 16a   2 POUNDS
28.2800 g., 0.9250 Silver 0.8410 oz. ASW, 38.6 mm. **Ruler:** Elizabeth II **Subject:** World Wildlife Fund **Rev:** 2 Puffin birds

Date	Mintage	F	VF	XF	Unc	BU
1997 Proof	—	Value: 47.50				

KM# 17   2 POUNDS
28.2800 g., Silver, 38.5 mm. **Ruler:** Elizabeth II **Subject:** Queen's Golden Wedding Anniversary **Obv:** Queen's portrait **Rev:** Queen crowning Prince Charles

Date	Mintage	F	VF	XF	Unc	BU
ND(1997)	—	—	—	—	8.50	9.50

KM# 18   2 POUNDS
28.2800 g., Copper Nickel, 38.5 mm. **Ruler:** Elizabeth II
Subject: Total Eclipse of the Sun **Obv:** Queen's portrait **Rev:** 2 Northern Gannets and church

Date	Mintage	F	VF	XF	Unc	BU
1999	—	—	—	—	14.00	16.00

KM# 18a   2 POUNDS
28.2800 g., 0.9250 Silver 0.8410 oz. ASW, 38.6 mm.
Ruler: Elizabeth II **Subject:** Total Eclipse of the Sun
Obv: Queen's portrait **Rev:** 2 sea birds and church

Date	Mintage	F	VF	XF	Unc	BU
1999 Proof	Est. 10,000	Value: 45.00				

KM# 18b   2 POUNDS
47.5400 g., 0.9170 Gold 1.4015 oz. AGW **Ruler:** Elizabeth II
Subject: Total Eclipse of the Sun **Obv:** Queen's portrait **Rev:** 2 sea birds and church

Date	Mintage	F	VF	XF	Unc	BU
1999 Proof	Est. 100	Value: 1,500				

KM# 14   5 POUNDS
28.2800 g., Copper-Nickel, 38.5 mm. **Ruler:** Elizabeth II

Subject: Queen Mother - Children **Rev:** Queen Mother with children within circle

Date	Mintage	F	VF	XF	Unc	BU
1995	—	—	—	—	15.00	16.50

KM# 14a   5 POUNDS
28.2800 g., 0.9250 Silver 0.8410 oz. ASW, 38.6 mm.
Ruler: Elizabeth II **Subject:** Queen Mother - Children

Date	Mintage	F	VF	XF	Unc	BU
1995 Proof	10,000	Value: 50.00				

KM# 14b   5 POUNDS
47.5400 g., 0.9160 Gold 1.4000 oz. AGW **Ruler:** Elizabeth II
Subject: Queen Mother - Children

Date	Mintage	F	VF	XF	Unc	BU
1995 Proof	150	Value: 1,350				

KM# 56   5 POUNDS
28.2800 g., Copper-Nickel, 38.5 mm. **Ruler:** Elizabeth II
Subject: Queen Mother - Children

Date	Mintage	F	VF	XF	Unc	BU
1995	—	—	—	—	15.00	16.50

KM# 15   5 POUNDS
28.2800 g., Copper-Nickel, 38.5 mm. **Ruler:** Elizabeth II **Subject:** Queen Elizabeth's 70th Birthday - Flowers **Obv:** Crowned bust, right **Rev:** Rose, thistle, daffodil, clover representing the UK

Date	Mintage	F	VF	XF	Unc	BU
1996	—	—	—	—	16.00	17.50

KM# 15a   5 POUNDS
28.2800 g., 0.9250 Silver 0.8410 oz. ASW, 38.6 mm. **Ruler:** Elizabeth II **Subject:** Queen Elizabeth's 70th Birthday - Flowers

Date	Mintage	F	VF	XF	Unc	BU
1996 Proof	Est. 10,000	Value: 50.00				

KM# 15b   5 POUNDS
47.5400 g., 0.9170 Gold 1.4015 oz. AGW **Ruler:** Elizabeth II
Subject: Queen Elizabeth's 70th Birthday - Flowers

Date	Mintage	F	VF	XF	Unc	BU
1996 Proof	250	Value: 1,350				

KM# 19   5 POUNDS
Copper-Nickel **Ruler:** Elizabeth II **Subject:** Total Eclipse of the Sun **Obv:** Portrait of Queen **Rev:** Map of Alderney, pre, post and actual phases of eclipse

Date	Mintage	F	VF	XF	Unc	BU
1999	—	—	—	—	18.00	20.00

KM# 19a   5 POUNDS
28.2800 g., 0.9250 Silver 0.8410 oz. ASW, 38.6 mm. **Ruler:** Elizabeth II

Date	Mintage	F	VF	XF	Unc	BU
1999 Proof	Est. 10,000	Value: 55.00				

KM# 20   5 POUNDS
28.2800 g., 0.9250 Silver 0.8410 oz. ASW **Ruler:** Elizabeth II
Subject: Winston Churchill **Obv:** Queen's portrait **Rev:** Winston Churchill wearing hat, And our dear Channel Islands are also to be freed today

Date	Mintage	F	VF	XF	Unc	BU
1999	—	—	—	—	15.00	17.50

KM# 20a   5 POUNDS
47.5400 g., 0.9166 Gold 1.4009 oz. AGW **Ruler:** Elizabeth II
Subject: Winston Churchill **Obv:** Queen's portrait **Rev:** Winston Churchill wearing hat, And our dear Channel Islands are also to be freed today

Date	Mintage	F	VF	XF	Unc	BU
1999 Proof	125	Value: 1,350				

KM# 21   5 POUNDS
28.2800 g., Copper-Nickel **Ruler:** Elizabeth II **Subject:** 60th Anniversary - Battle of Britain **Obv:** Queen Elizabeth's head right **Rev:** Spitfires and Hurricane, pilot at bottom center **Edge:** Reeded

Date	Mintage	F	VF	XF	Unc	BU
2000	—	—	—	—	18.00	20.00

KM# 52   5 POUNDS
28.2800 g., 0.9250 Silver 0.8410 oz. ASW, 38.6 mm. **Ruler:** Elizabeth II **Subject:** Queen Mother's 100th Birthday **Obv:** Queen Elizabeth II **Rev:** Queen Mother above value **Edge:** Reeded

Date	Mintage	F	VF	XF	Unc	BU
2000	—	Value: 55.00				

KM# 26   5 POUNDS
28.0300 g., 0.9250 Silver 0.8336 oz. ASW, 38.5 mm. **Ruler:** Elizabeth II **Subject:** Millennium **Obv:** Queen's portrait **Rev:** Radiant light house and birds **Edge:** Reeded

Date	Mintage	F	VF	XF	Unc	BU
ND(2000) Proof	20,000	Value: 45.00				

KM# 21a   5 POUNDS
28.2800 g., 0.9250 Silver 0.8410 oz. ASW, 38.6 mm. **Ruler:** Elizabeth II **Subject:** 60th Anniversary - Battle of Britain **Obv:** Queen Elizabeth's head right **Rev:** Two spitfires in flight, pilot at bottom center **Edge:** Reeded

Date	Mintage	F	VF	XF	Unc	BU
2000 Proof	—	Value: 55.00				

KM# 8   10 POUNDS
3.1300 g., 0.9990 Gold 0.1005 oz. AGW **Ruler:** Elizabeth II **Subject:** Normandy Invasion **Rev:** Paratroopers and Transport Plane

Date	Mintage	F	VF	XF	Unc	BU
1994 Proof	Est. 1,000	Value: 120				

KM# 6   25 POUNDS
8.5130 g., 0.9170 Gold 0.2510 oz. AGW **Ruler:** Elizabeth II **Subject:** 40th Anniversary - Coronation **Rev:** Royal carriage

Date	Mintage	F	VF	XF	Unc	BU
1993 Proof	Est. 1,000	Value: 250				

KM# 9   25 POUNDS
7.8100 g., 0.9990 Gold 0.2508 oz. AGW **Ruler:** Elizabeth II **Subject:** Normandy Invasion **Rev:** Fighter planes and tank

Date	Mintage	F	VF	XF	Unc	BU
1994 Proof	Est. 1,000	Value: 250				

KM# 57   25 POUNDS
7.8100 g., 0.9990 Gold 0.2508 oz. AGW **Ruler:** Elizabeth II **Subject:** Normandy Invasion **Rev:** Fighter planes and tank

Date	Mintage	F	VF	XF	Unc	BU
1994 Proof	—	Value: 250				

KM# 23   25 POUNDS
28.0000 g., Copper-Nickel **Ruler:** Elizabeth II **Subject:** Golden Wedding Anniversary - Elizabeth and Philip **Obv:** Queen Elizabeth's head right **Rev:** Queen Elizabeth crowning Charles as Prince of Wales, date (1947-1997) in legend

Date	Mintage	F	VF	XF	Unc	BU
ND(1997)	—	—	—	—	18.00	20.00

KM# 23a   25 POUNDS
28.2800 g., 0.9250 Silver 0.8410 oz. ASW **Ruler:** Elizabeth II **Subject:** Golden Wedding Anniversary - Elizabeth and Philip **Obv:** Queen Elizabeth's head right **Rev:** Queen Elizabeth crowning Charles as Prince of Wales, date (1947-1997) in legend

Date	Mintage	F	VF	XF	Unc	BU
ND(1997) Proof	—	Value: 22.50				

KM# 23b   25 POUNDS
8.4300 g., 0.9160 Gold 0.2483 oz. AGW **Ruler:** Elizabeth II **Subject:** Golden Wedding Anniversary - Elizabeth and Philip **Obv:** Queen Elizabeth's head right **Rev:** Queen Elizabeth crowning Charles as Prince of Wales, date (1947-1997) in legend

Date	Mintage	F	VF	XF	Unc	BU
ND(1997) Proof	—	Value: 250				

KM# 71   25 POUNDS
7.8100 g., 0.9990 Gold 0.2508 oz. AGW **Ruler:** Elizabeth II **Subject:** Winston Churchill **Obv:** Crowned head right **Rev:** Churchill wearing hat

Date	Mintage	F	VF	XF	Unc	BU
1999 Proof	2,500	Value: 300				

KM# 72   25 POUNDS
7.8100 g., 0.9990 Gold 0.2508 oz. AGW **Ruler:** Elizabeth II **Subject:** Queen Mother's 100th Birthday **Obv:** Crowned head right **Rev:** Bust of Queen Mother 3/4 left

Date	Mintage	F	VF	XF	Unc	BU
2000 Proof	—	Value: 300				

KM# 22   25 POUNDS
7.8100 g., 0.9160 Gold 0.2300 oz. AGW **Ruler:** Elizabeth II **Subject:** 60th Anniversary - Battle of Britain **Obv:** Queen Elizabeth's head right **Rev:** Two spitfires in flight, pilot at bottom center **Edge:** Reeded

Date	Mintage	F	VF	XF	Unc	BU
2000	—	Value: 275				

KM# 10   50 POUNDS
15.6000 g., 0.9990 Gold 0.5010 oz. AGW **Ruler:** Elizabeth II **Subject:** Normandy Invasion **Rev:** British gliders

Date	Mintage	F	VF	XF	Unc	BU
1994	Est. 1,000	Value: 500				

Note: In Proof sets only

KM# 11   100 POUNDS
31.2100 g., 0.9990 Gold 1.0024 oz. AGW **Ruler:** Elizabeth II **Subject:** Normandy Invasion **Obv:** Crowned bust, right, date below **Rev:** Normandy beach landing scene

Date	Mintage	F	VF	XF	Unc	BU
1994 Proof	Est. 500	Value: 975				

PIEFORTS

KM#	Date	Mintage	Identification	Mkt Val
P1	1989	500	2 Pounds. 0.9250 Silver. KM#1a.	100
P2	1990	500	2 Pounds. 0.9250 Silver. KM#2a.	100
P3	1992	750	2 Pounds. 0.9250 Silver. KM#3a.	70.00
P4	1993	500	2 Pounds. 0.9250 Silver. KM#5a.	80.00
P5	1994	500	2 Pounds. 0.9250 Silver. KM#7a.	80.00
P6	ND(1995)	500	2 Pounds. 0.9250 Silver. KM#13a.	90.00
P7	1995	500	2 Pounds. 0.9250 Silver. KM#14a.	85.00
P8	1996	500	5 Pounds. 0.9250 Silver. KM#15a.	90.00

PROOF SETS

KM#	Date	Mintage	Identification	Issue Price	Mkt Val
PS1	1994 (5)	500	KM#7a, 8-11	—	1,700
PS2	1994 (4)	I.A.	KM#8-11	—	1,650
PS3	1994 (4)	500	KM#7a, 8-10	—	835
PS4	1994 (3)	I.A.	KM#8-10	—	800

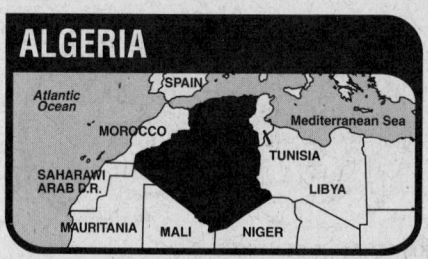

ALGERIA

The Democratic and Popular Republic of Algeria, a North African country fronting on the Mediterranean Sea between Tunisia and Morocco, has an area of 919,595 sq. mi. (2,381,740 sq. km.) and a population of 31.6 million. Capital: Algiers (Alger). Most of the country's working population is engaged in agriculture although a recent industrial diversification, financed by oil revenues, is making steady progress. Wines, fruits, iron and zinc ores, phosphates, tobacco products, liquified natural gas, and petroleum are exported.

Following the armistice signed by France and Nazi Germany on June 22, 1940, Algeria fell under Vichy Government control until liberated by the Allied invasion forces under the command of Gen. D. D. Eisenhower on Nov. 8, 1942. The inability to obtain equal rights with Frenchmen led to an organized revolt which began on Nov. 1, 1954 and lasted until a ceasefire was signed on July I, 1962. Independence was proclaimed on July 5, 1962, following a self-determination referendum, and the Republic was declared on September 25, 1962.

MINT MARK
(a) – Paris, privy marks only

MONETARY SYSTEM
100 Centimes = 1 Franc

FRENCH OCCUPATION
COLONIAL COINAGE

KM# 91   20 FRANCS
Copper-Nickel **Obv:** Head with laureled hood, right **Rev:** Value between columns of wheat, date at center

Date	Mintage	F	VF	XF	Unc	BU
1949	25,556,000	1.00	2.00	5.00	10.00	—
1956	7,500,000	1.00	2.50	6.00	12.50	—

KM# 92 50 FRANCS
Copper-Nickel **Obv:** Man with laureled hood, right **Rev:** Value between columns of wheat, date below

Date	Mintage	F	VF	XF	Unc	BU
1949	18,000,000	1.50	3.00	9.00	18.00	—

KM# 93 100 FRANCS
Copper-Nickel, 29.8 mm. **Obv:** Man with laureled hood, right **Rev:** Value between wheat columns, date below **Edge:** Reeded **Note:** During World War II homeland coins were struck at the Paris Mint and the French 2 Francs, Y#89 were struck at the Philadelphia Mint for use in French African Territories.

Date	Mintage	F	VF	XF	Unc	BU
1950	22,189,000	1.50	3.00	10.00	20.00	—
1952	12,000,000	2.00	4.00	12.00	25.00	—

TOKEN COINAGE
Alger

KM# TnA1 5 CENTIMES
Aluminum **Issuer:** Alger Chamber of Commerce **Obv:** Symbol between palm trees, beaded circle surrounding all **Rev:** Value above sprigs, with J. Bory

Date	Mintage	F	VF	XF	Unc	BU
1916	—	5.00	10.00	20.00	35.00	—
1917	—	—	175	250	500	—

Note: The year 1917 is not a regular issue

| 1919 | — | 4.00 | 6.00 | 12.00 | 18.00 | 35.00 |
| 1921 | — | 5.00 | 10.00 | 20.00 | 35.00 | — |

KM# TnA2 5 CENTIMES
Iron **Issuer:** Alger Chamber of Commerce

Date	Mintage	F	VF	XF	Unc	BU
1916	—	30.00	50.00	100	200	—

KM# TnA3 5 CENTIMES
Zinc **Issuer:** Alger Chamber of Commerce

Date	Mintage	F	VF	XF	Unc	BU
1917	—	3.50	10.00	20.00	40.00	—
1919	—	—	35.00	70.00	150	—

Note: The year 1919 is not a regular issue

KM# TnA4 5 CENTIMES
Brass **Issuer:** Alger Chamber of Commerce

Date	Mintage	F	VF	XF	Unc	BU
1921	—	—	35.00	70.00	150	—

Note: Not a regular issue

KM# TnA5 10 CENTIMES
Aluminum **Issuer:** Alger Chamber of Commerce **Obv:** Symbol between palm trees, beaded circle surrounding all **Rev:** Value above sprigs, without J. Bory

Date	Mintage	F	VF	XF	Unc	BU
1916 Without J. Bory	—	6.00	10.00	20.00	45.00	85.00
1918 with J. Bory	—	6.00	10.00	20.00	45.00	85.00
1918 Without J. Bory	—	6.00	10.00	15.00	32.00	85.00
1919 With J. Bory	—	4.00	6.00	12.00	25.00	75.00

Date	Mintage	F	VF	XF	Unc	BU
1921 With J. Bory	—	3.00	6.00	12.00	25.00	75.00
1921 Without J. Bory	—	6.00	10.00	20.00	45.00	85.00

KM# TnA6 10 CENTIMES
Iron **Issuer:** Alger Chamber of Commerce **Rev:** Without J. Bory

Date	Mintage	F	VF	XF	Unc	BU
1916	—	10.00	22.00	50.00	100	—

KM# TnA7 10 CENTIMES
Zinc **Issuer:** Alger Chamber of Commerce

Date	Mintage	F	VF	XF	Unc	BU
1917	—	5.00	12.50	30.00	60.00	—
1918	—	—	40.00	100	160	—

Note: 1918 is not a regular issue

| 1919 | — | — | 40.00 | 100 | 160 | — |

Note: 1919 is not a regular issue

KM# TnA8 10 CENTIMES
Brass **Issuer:** Alger Chamber of Commerce **Note:** Not a regular issue.

Date	Mintage	F	VF	XF	Unc	BU
1919	—	—	50.00	110	225	375
1921	—	—	65.00	125	245	—

Bone

KM# TnB1 5 CENTIMES
Aluminum **Issuer:** Bone Chamber of Commerce

Date	Mintage	F	VF	XF	Unc	BU
1915	—	6.00	10.00	15.00	30.00	75.00
ND(1915)	—	5.00	9.00	13.00	25.00	65.00

KM# TnB2 5 CENTIMES
Brass **Issuer:** Bone Chamber of Commerce **Note:** Not a regular issue.

Date	Mintage	F	VF	XF	Unc	BU
ND(1915)	—	—	30.00	80.00	120	—

KM# TnB3 10 CENTIMES
Aluminum **Issuer:** Bone Chamber of Commerce

Date	Mintage	F	VF	XF	Unc	BU
1915	—	4.00	10.00	22.00	40.00	90.00
ND(1915)	—	4.00	9.00	20.00	35.00	85.00

KM# TnB4 10 CENTIMES
Brass **Issuer:** Bone Chamber of Commerce **Note:** Not a regular issue.

Date	Mintage	F	VF	XF	Unc	BU
ND(1915)	—	—	32.50	65.00	130	—

KM# TnB5 50 CENTIMES
Brass **Issuer:** Bone Chamber of Commerce **Obv:** Head left, within wreath **Rev:** Value at center

Date	Mintage	F	VF	XF	Unc	BU
ND(1915)	—	15.00	30.00	50.00	75.00	150

KM# TnB6 50 CENTIMES
Copper-Nickel **Issuer:** Bone Chamber of Commerce **Note:** Not a regular issue.

Date	Mintage	F	VF	XF	Unc	BU
ND(1915)	—	—	40.00	90.00	185	350

KM# TnB7 FRANC
Brass **Issuer:** Bone Chamber of Commerce **Obv:** Head left, within wreath **Rev:** Value at center

Date	Mintage	F	VF	XF	Unc	BU
ND(1915)	—	25.00	40.00	65.00	120	—

KM# TnB8 FRANC
Copper-Nickel **Issuer:** Bone Chamber of Commerce **Note:** Not a regular issue.

Date	Mintage	F	VF	XF	Unc	BU
ND(1915)	—	—	60.00	120	225	—

KM# TnB9 FRANC
Copper **Issuer:** Bone Chamber of Commerce **Note:** Not a regular issue.

Date	Mintage	F	VF	XF	Unc	BU
ND(1915)	—	—	90.00	150	300	—

Bougie

KM# TnC1 5 CENTIMES
Aluminum **Issuer:** Bougie Chamber of Commerce **Obv:** Name of issuer, dots flank date **Rev:** Large value at center

Date	Mintage	F	VF	XF	Unc	BU
1915	—	5.00	10.00	25.00	50.00	100

KM# TnC2.1 10 CENTIMES
Aluminum **Issuer:** Bougie Chamber of Commerce **Obv:** Name of issuer, dots flank date **Rev:** Large value at center

Date	Mintage	F	VF	XF	Unc	BU
1915	—	6.00	12.00	28.00	60.00	120

KM# TnC2.2 10 CENTIMES
Aluminum **Issuer:** Bougie Chamber of Commerce **Obv:** Dot and triangle at right of date

Date	Mintage	F	VF	XF	Unc	BU
1915	—	5.00	10.00	20.00	45.00	—

KM# TnC2a 10 CENTIMES
Zinc **Issuer:** Bougie Chamber of Commerce

Date	Mintage	F	VF	XF	Unc	BU
1915	—	30.00	50.00	120	250	—

Constantine

KM# TnD1 5 CENTIMES
Aluminum **Issuer:** Constantine Chamber of Commerce

Date	Mintage	F	VF	XF	Unc	BU
1922	—	25.00	35.00	60.00	120	—

KM# TnD2 10 CENTIMES
Aluminum **Issuer:** Constantine Chamber of Commerce

Date	Mintage	F	VF	XF	Unc	BU
1922	—	20.00	30.00	50.00	100	200

Oran

KM# TnE1 5 CENTIMES
Aluminum **Issuer:** Oran Chamber of Commerce **Obv:** Small crowned shield, date below flanked by dots **Rev:** Large value left of spray

Date	Mintage	F	VF	XF	Unc	BU
1921	—	4.50	9.00	25.00	50.00	100

KM# TnE2 10 CENTIMES
Aluminum **Issuer:** Oran Chamber of Commerce **Obv:** Small crowned shield, date below flanked by dots **Rev:** Large value left of tree

Date	Mintage	F	VF	XF	Unc	BU
1921	—	3.00	7.00	25.00	45.00	—

KM# TnE2a 10 CENTIMES
Brass **Issuer:** Oran Chamber of Commerce

Date	Mintage	F	VF	XF	Unc	BU
1921	—	—	75.00	150	300	—

KM# TnE3 25 CENTIMES
Aluminum **Issuer:** Oran Chamber of Commerce **Obv:** Similar to 10 Centimes, KM#TnE2 **Rev:** Similar to 25 Centimes, KM#TnE4

Date	Mintage	F	VF	XF	Unc	BU
1921	—	4.00	8.50	25.00	50.00	

KM# TnE4 25 CENTIMES
Aluminum **Issuer:** Oran Chamber of Commerce **Obv:** Small crowned shield, chains **Rev:** Large value within wreath

Date	Mintage	F	VF	XF	Unc	BU
1921	—	5.00	10.00	30.00	60.00	—

KM# TnE5 25 CENTIMES
Aluminum **Issuer:** Oran Chamber of Commerce **Note:** For further listings of private token issues refer to the catalogue of "French Emergency Tokens of 1914-1922" by Robert Lamb.

Date	Mintage	F	VF	XF	Unc	BU
1922	—	5.00	10.00	30.00	60.00	115

REPUBLIC

MONETARY SYSTEM
100 Centimes = 1 Dinar

STANDARD COINAGE

KM# 94 CENTIME
Aluminum, 11.5 mm. **Obv:** Small arms within wreath **Rev:** Value at center of scalloped circle **Edge:** Plain

Date	Mintage	F	VF	XF	Unc	BU
AH1383-1964	35,000,000	—	0.20	0.40	1.00	2.00

KM# 95 2 CENTIMES
0.6000 g., Aluminum, 18.3 mm. **Obv:** Arms within wreath **Rev:** Value at center of scalloped circle **Edge:** Plain

Date	Mintage	F	VF	XF	Unc	BU
AH1383-1964	50,000,000	—	0.20	0.40	1.00	2.00

KM# 96 5 CENTIMES
0.8500 g., Aluminum, 21.1 mm. **Obv:** Arms within wreath **Rev:** Value at center of scalloped circle

Date	Mintage	F	VF	XF	Unc	BU
AH1383-1964	40,000,000	—	0.25	0.45	1.25	2.50

KM# 101 5 CENTIMES
Aluminum **Series:** F.A.O. **Subject:** 1st Four Year Plan **Obv:** Value at center **Rev:** Two dates center of circle, circle consists of gear teeth on left, sprays of grain on right **Note:** Varieties exist.

Date	Mintage	F	VF	XF	Unc	BU
ND(1970)	50,000,000	—	0.15	0.30	0.75	—

KM# 106 5 CENTIMES
Aluminum **Series:** F.A.O. **Subject:** 2nd Four Year Plan **Obv:** Large value at center **Rev:** Two dates at center of circle, circle consists of gear teeth on left, sprays of grain on right

Date	Mintage	F	VF	XF	Unc	BU
ND(1974)	10,000,000	—	0.15	0.30	0.75	1.50

KM# 113 5 CENTIMES
Aluminum **Series:** F.A.O. **Subject:** 1st Five Year Plan **Obv:** Inscription within circle of gear teeth on left, grain spray on right

Date	Mintage	F	VF	XF	Unc	BU
ND(1980)	—	2.00	5.00	12.00	25.00	—

KM# 116 5 CENTIMES
Aluminum **Series:** F.A.O. **Subject:** 2nd Five Year Plan **Obv:** Large value at center **Rev:** Two dates center of circle, circle consists of geared teeth on right, sprays of grain on left **Note:** Varieties exist in planchet thickness.

Date	Mintage	F	VF	XF	Unc	BU
ND(1985)	—	—	0.10	0.25	0.70	1.50

KM# 97 10 CENTIMES
Aluminum-Bronze **Obv:** Small arms within wreath **Rev:** Value in circle

Date	Mintage	F	VF	XF	Unc	BU
AH1383-1964	—	—	0.25	0.75	2.00	3.00

KM# 115 10 CENTIMES
Aluminum **Obv:** Large value in circle **Rev:** Palm tree flanked by rosettes, date below tree **Note:** Varieties exist.

Date	Mintage	F	VF	XF	Unc	BU
1984	—	0.15	0.25	0.75	3.00	4.00
1989 Rare	—	—	—	—	—	—

KM# 98 20 CENTIMES
Aluminum-Bronze **Obv:** Arms within wreath **Rev:** Value in circle

Date	Mintage	F	VF	XF	Unc	BU
AH1383-1964	—	—	0.25	0.75	2.00	3.00

KM# 103 20 CENTIMES
Brass **Series:** F.A.O. **Subject:** Agricultural Revolution **Obv:** Value in circle **Rev:** Cornucopeia, date above

Date	Mintage	F	VF	XF	Unc	BU
1972	20,000,000	—	0.10	0.25	0.75	1.25

KM# 107.1 20 CENTIMES
Aluminum-Bronze **Series:** F.A.O. **Obv:** Value at center of circle **Rev:** Rams head left, date below

Date	Mintage	F	VF	XF	Unc	BU
1975	50,000,000	—	0.20	0.45	1.75	2.00

KM# 107.2 20 CENTIMES
Aluminum-Bronze **Series:** F.A.O. **Obv:** Small flower above 20 **Rev:** Rams head left, date below

Date	Mintage	F	VF	XF	Unc	BU
1975	Inc. above	—	0.15	0.30	1.50	2.00

KM# 118 20 CENTIMES
Aluminum-Bronze **Series:** F.A.O. **Obv:** Value in circle **Rev:** Rams head left, date below

Date	Mintage	F	VF	XF	Unc	BU
1987	60,000,000	0.50	1.00	2.00	8.00	12.00

KM# 99 50 CENTIMES
Aluminum-Bronze **Obv:** Arms within wreath **Rev:** Value in circle

Date	Mintage	F	VF	XF	Unc	BU
AH1383-1964	—	—	0.25	0.75	2.00	3.50

KM# 102 50 CENTIMES
Copper-Nickel-Zinc **Obv:** Book, divider on top, bottle at bottom **Rev:** Value in circle **Edge:** Reeded

Date	Mintage	F	VF	XF	Unc	BU
AH1391-1971	10,000,000	0.25	0.50	1.50	6.00	—
AH1393-1973	10,000,000	0.25	0.50	1.50	6.00	—

KM# 109 50 CENTIMES
5.0000 g., Brass, 24 mm. **Subject:** 30th Anniversary French-Algerian Clash **Obv:** Value in circle **Rev:** Inscription

Date	Mintage	F	VF	XF	Unc	BU
ND(1975)	18,000,000	—	0.20	0.50	2.00	—

KM# 111 50 CENTIMES
Aluminum-Bronze **Subject:** 1400th Anniversary of Mohammad's Flight **Obv:** Value in circle **Rev:** Value, outline of Mosque

Date	Mintage	F	VF	XF	Unc	BU
AH1400-1980	—	0.15	0.25	0.50	2.50	4.50

KM# 119   50 CENTIMES
Aluminum-Bronze   **Subject:** 25th Anniversary of Constitution
Obv: Value in circle **Rev:** Stylized design

Date	Mintage	F	VF	XF	Unc	BU
1988	40,000,000	0.15	0.25	0.75	3.00	6.00

KM# 127   1/4 DINAR
1.1500 g., Aluminum   **Subject:** Fennec Fox **Obv:** Value in small circle **Rev:** Head facing

Date	Mintage	F	VF	XF	Unc	BU
1992-AH1413	—	—	0.65	1.25	2.50	3.00
1992-AH1413 Proof	—	Value: 12.00				
1998-AH1418	—	—	0.65	1.25	2.50	3.00

KM# 128   1/2 DINAR
Steel   **Subject:** Barbary Horse **Obv:** Value in small circle **Rev:** Encirled Barbary horse head dividing date at top, facing 3/4 left

Date	Mintage	F	VF	XF	Unc	BU
AH1413-1992	—	—	0.65	1.25	3.00	3.50
AH1413-1992 Proof	—	Value: 12.00				

KM# 100   DINAR
Copper-Nickel   **Obv:** Large arms within wreath **Rev:** Large value in circle

Date	Mintage	F	VF	XF	Unc	BU
AH1383-1964	15,000,000	0.25	0.50	1.00	4.00	
AH1383-1964 Proof	—	Value: 40.00				

KM# 104.1   DINAR
Copper-Nickel   **Series:** F.A.O. **Obv:** Large value in circle **Rev:** Hands grasped at top, man on tractor facing flanked by sprigs, date below

Date	Mintage	F	VF	XF	Unc	BU
1972	20,000,000	0.25	0.50	1.00	2.50	3.50

KM# 104.2   DINAR
Copper-Nickel   **Obv:** Legend touches inner circle

Date	Mintage	F	VF	XF	Unc	BU
1972	Inc. above	0.20	0.45	0.85	2.00	3.00

KM# 112   DINAR
Copper-Nickel   **Subject:** 20th Anniversary of Independence
Obv: Large value in circle **Rev:** Circle of hands

Date	Mintage	F	VF	XF	Unc	BU
ND(1983)	—	0.35	0.75	1.50	4.50	6.50

KM# 117   DINAR
Copper-Nickel   **Subject:** 25th Anniversary of Independence - Monument **Obv:** Large value in circle **Rev:** Monument within grain wreath

Date	Mintage	F	VF	XF	Unc	BU
1987	—	0.35	0.75	1.50	4.00	6.00

KM# 120   DINAR
3.2200 g., 0.9200 Gold 0.0952 oz. AGW   **Subject:** Historical Coin - 5 Aspers of Abd-el-Kader **Obv:** Old Islamic coin at center **Rev:** Old Islamic coin

Date	Mintage	F	VF	XF	Unc	BU
AH1411	—	—	—	—	135	150

KM# 129   DINAR
4.2400 g., Steel, 20.48 mm.   **Obv:** Value on silhouette of country, within circle **Rev:** African buffalo's head 3/4 left, ancient drawings above **Edge:** Plain

Date	Mintage	F	VF	XF	Unc	BU
AH1413-1992	—	—	1.00	2.00	4.00	6.00
AH1413-1992 Proof	—	Value: 15.00				
AH1417-1997	—	—	—	2.00	4.00	6.00
AH1420-1999	—	—	1.00	2.00	4.00	6.00
AH1421-2000	—	—	1.00	2.00	4.00	6.00

KM# 121   2 DINARS
6.4500 g., 0.9200 Gold 0.1908 oz. AGW   **Subject:** Historical Coin - Dinar of 762 A.D. Rostomiden Dynasty

Date	Mintage	F	VF	XF	Unc	BU
AH1411	—	—	—	—	265	300

KM# 130   2 DINARS
5.1300 g., Steel, 22.5 mm.   **Obv:** Value on silhouette of country **Rev:** Dromedary camel's head right **Edge:** Plain

Date	Mintage	F	VF	XF	Unc	BU
AH1413-1992	—	—	1.00	2.50	5.00	6.50
AH1413-1992 Proof	—	Value: 18.00				
AH1414-1993	—	—	1.00	2.50	5.00	6.50
AH1417-1996	—	—	—	—	—	
AH1417-1997	—	—	1.00	2.50	5.00	6.50

Date	Mintage	F	VF	XF	Unc	BU
AH1419-1999	—	—	1.00	2.50	5.00	6.50
AH1420-1999	—	—	1.00	2.00	4.00	6.00

KM# 133   2 DINARS
Gold   **Subject:** Historical Coin - 2 Dinar of Abd Al-Qadir, AH1222-1300

Date	Mintage	F	VF	XF	Unc	BU
AH1417	—	—	—	—	285	325

KM# 105   5 DINARS
12.0000 g., 0.7500 Silver 0.2893 oz. ASW, 31 mm.   **Series:** F.A.O. **Subject:** 10th Anniversary **Obv:** Large value flanked by small flowers within circle **Rev:** Tower with grain head at base dividing dates at bottom, Five stars flanking **Note:** Privy mark: owl.

Date	Mintage	F	VF	XF	Unc	BU
ND(1972)	5,000,000	—	6.00	10.00	16.50	

KM# 105a.1   5 DINARS
Nickel, 31 mm.   **Edge:** Reeded

Date	Mintage	F	VF	XF	Unc	BU
ND(1972)	10,000,000	—	4.00	8.00	14.50	

KM# 105a.2   5 DINARS
Nickel, 31 mm.   **Note:** Privy mark: dolphin.

Date	Mintage	F	VF	XF	Unc	BU
ND(1972)	10,000,000	—	4.00	8.00	14.50	

KM# 108   5 DINARS
Nickel, 31 mm.   **Subject:** 20th Anniversary of Revolution **Obv:** Large value in circle flanked by rosettes **Rev:** Armed revolutionary man leaning, right, two dates lower right

Date	Mintage	F	VF	XF	Unc	BU
ND(1974)	—	—	3.50	7.00	12.50	

KM# 114   5 DINARS
Nickel   **Subject:** 30th Anniversary of Revolution **Obv:** Value flanked by small rosettes in circle **Rev:** Hands holding symbol, flanked by dates divided by stars

Date	Mintage	F	VF	XF	Unc	BU
ND(1984)	—	—	2.50	5.00	10.00	

KM# 122   5 DINARS
16.1200 g., 0.9200 Gold 0.4768 oz. AGW   **Subject:** Historical Coin - Denar of Numidian King Massinissa, 238-148 B.C.
Obv: Standing elephant left, within circle flanked by value **Rev:** King, left within beaded circle

Date	Mintage	F	VF	XF	Unc	BU
AH1411-1991	—	—	—	—	550	650

KM# 123   5 DINARS
6.2000 g., Steel, 24.43 mm. **Obv:** Denomination within circle
Rev: Forepart of African elephant right **Edge:** Plain

Date	Mintage	F	VF	XF	Unc	BU
AH1413-1992	—	—	1.50	3.50	7.00	10.00
AH1413-1992 Proof	—	Value: 20.00				
AH1414-1993	—	—	1.50	3.50	7.00	10.00
AH1417-1997	—	—	1.50	3.50	7.00	10.00
AH1418-1997	—	—	1.50	3.50	7.00	10.00
AH1418-1998	—	—	1.50	3.50	7.00	10.00
AH1419-1998	—	—	1.50	3.50	7.00	10.00
AH1420-1999	—	—	1.50	3.50	7.00	10.00
AH1420-2000	—	—	1.50	3.50	7.00	10.00

KM# 110   10 DINARS
11.3700 g., Aluminum-Bronze **Obv:** Inscription within circle,
wreath surrounds **Rev:** Large value within circle, date above

Date	Mintage	F	VF	XF	Unc	BU
1979	25,001,000	—	2.00	4.00	8.00	—
1981	40,000,000	—	2.00	4.00	8.00	—

KM# 110a   10 DINARS
14.6000 g., 0.9250 Silver 0.4342 oz. ASW

Date	Mintage	F	VF	XF	Unc	BU
1979	1,000	—	—	—	35.00	—

KM# 110b   10 DINARS
24.5000 g., 0.9000 Gold 0.7089 oz. AGW

Date	Mintage	F	VF	XF	Unc	BU
1979	100	—	—	—	1,000	1,250

KM# 124   10 DINARS
4.9500 g., Bi-Metallic Aluminum center in Steel ring, 26.5 mm.
Obv: Denomination **Rev:** Barbary falcon's head right **Edge:** Plain

Date	Mintage	F	VF	XF	Unc	BU
AH1413-1992	—	—	2.00	4.50	10.00	—
AH1413-1992 Proof	—	—	—	—	—	—
AH1414-1993	—	—	2.00	4.50	10.00	—
AH1417-1997	—	—	1.75	4.00	9.00	—
AH1418-1997	—	—	2.00	4.50	10.00	—
AH1421-2000	—	—	1.75	4.00	9.00	—

KM# 134   10 DINARS
14.6000 g., 0.8350 Silver 0.3919 oz. ASW.
Subject: Jugurtha, King of Numidia (154-104BC)
Obv: Denomination **Rev:** Head of Jugurtha left **Edge:** Reeded

Date	Mintage	F	VF	XF	Unc	BU
AH1415 (1994)	—	—	—	—	75.00	—

KM# 135   10 DINARS
14.6000 g., 0.8350 Silver 0.3919 oz. ASW.
Subject: Abdelhamid Benbadis (1889-1940) **Obv:** Denomination
Rev: 1/2 bust of Benbadis half left **Edge:** Reeded

Date	Mintage	F	VF	XF	Unc	BU
AH1415 (1994)	—	—	—	—	75.00	—

KM# 136   10 DINARS
14.6000 g., 0.8350 Silver 0.3919 oz. ASW.
Subject: Houari Boumediene (1922-1978) **Obv:** Denomination
Rev: Bust of Boumediene half left **Edge:** Reeded

Date	Mintage	F	VF	XF	Unc	BU
AH1415 (1994)	—	—	—	—	75.00	—

KM# 125   20 DINARS
8.6200 g., Bi-Metallic Brass center in Steel ring, 27.5 mm.
Subject: Lion **Obv:** Denomination **Rev:** Head left

Date	Mintage	F	VF	XF	Unc	BU
AH1413-1992	—	—	3.00	6.00	12.50	—
AH1413-1992 Proof	—	—	—	—	—	—
AH1414-1993	—	—	3.00	6.00	12.50	—
AH1416-1996	—	—	3.00	6.00	12.50	—
AH1417-1996	—	—	3.00	6.00	12.50	—
AH1417-1997	—	—	3.00	6.00	12.50	—
AH1418-1997	—	—	3.00	6.00	12.50	—
AH1420-1999	—	—	3.00	6.00	12.50	—
AH1421-2000	—	—	3.00	6.00	12.50	—

KM# 126   50 DINARS
9.2700 g., Bi-Metallic Steel center in Brass ring, 28.5 mm.
Obv: Denomination **Rev:** Dama gazelle with head left

Date	Mintage	F	VF	XF	Unc	BU
AH1413-1992	—	—	4.00	—	15.00	—
AH1413-1992 Proof	—	Value: 35.00				
AH1414-1993	—	—	4.00	8.00	15.00	—
AH1414-1996	—	—	4.00	8.00	15.00	—
AH1416-1996	—	—	4.00	8.00	15.00	—
AH1417-1996	—	—	4.00	8.00	15.00	—
AH1417-1997	—	—	4.00	8.00	15.00	—
AH1418-1998	—	—	4.00	8.00	15.00	—
AH1419-1999	—	—	4.00	8.00	15.00	—
AH1420-1999	—	—	4.00	8.00	15.00	—
AH1421-2000	—	—	4.00	8.00	16.50	—

KM# 131   50 DINARS
9.2600 g., Bi-Metallic Steel center in Brass ring, 28.5 mm.
Subject: 40th Anniversary - Start of the Revolution **Obv:** Large
value in circle **Rev:** Star dividing dates at right in circle

Date	Mintage	F	VF	XF	Unc	BU
ND(1994)	—	—	6.00	10.00	17.50	—
ND(1994) Proof	—	Value: 37.50				

KM# 132   100 DINARS
11.0000 g., Bi-Metallic Aluminum-Bronze center in Stainless
Steel ring, 29.5 mm.   **Obv:** Denomination stylized with reverse
design **Rev:** Horse head right

Date	Mintage	F	VF	XF	Unc	BU
AH1413-1992	—	—	6.00	12.00	20.00	24.00
AH1414-1993	—	—	6.00	12.00	20.00	24.00
AH1415-1994	—	—	6.00	12.00	20.00	24.00
AH1417-1997	—	—	6.00	12.00	20.00	24.00
AH1418-1998	—	—	6.00	12.00	20.00	24.00
AH1421-2000	—	—	6.00	12.00	20.00	24.00

ESSAIS
Standard metals unless otherwise noted

KM#	Date	Mintage	Identification	Issue Price	Mkt Val
E1	1949	1,500	20 Francs. Copper-Nickel. KM#91.	—	35.00
E2	1949	1,500	50 Francs. Copper-Nickel. KM#92.	—	45.00
E3	1950	1,500	100 Francs. Copper-Nickel. KM#93.	—	50.00
E4	ND(1972)	2,250	5 Dinars. Silver. Value flanked by rosettes within circle. Tower with grain head at base dividing dates below, five stars flanking tower. KM#105.	—	28.00
E5	ND(1972)	1,000	5 Dinars. Nickel. KM#105a.	—	35.00
E6	ND(1974)	3,300	5 Dinars. Nickel. Large value flanked by rosettes within circle. Armed revolutionary man leaning, right, two dates bottom right. KM#108.	—	20.00
E7	1981	2,670	10 Dinars. Aluminum-Bronze. KM#110.	—	25.00

PIEFORTS WITH ESSAI
Double thickness - Standard metals unless otherwise noted

KM#	Date	Mintage	Identification	Issue Price	Mkt Val
PE1	1949	104	20 Francs. Copper-Nickel. Head with laureated hood, right. Value, with date below, between columns of grain. KM#91.	—	90.00
PE2	1949	104	50 Francs. Copper-Nickel. Head with laureated hood, right. Value, with date below, between columns of grain. KM#92.	—	95.00
PE3	1950	104	100 Francs. Copper-Nickel. Head with laureated hood, right. Value, with date below, between columns of grain. KM#93.	—	100

PROOF SETS

KM#	Date	Mintage	Identification	Issue Price	Mkt Val
PS1	AH1413 (1992) (8)	—	KM#123-130	—	160

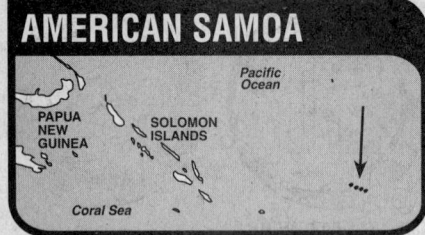

AMERICAN SAMOA

The Territory of American Samoa, with a population of 41,000, consists of seven major islands with a total land area of 76 sq. mi. (199 sq. km.) which are located about 2300 miles south-southwest of Hawaii. American Samoa was settled by the Polynesians around 600 BC. The capital is Pago Pago.

By 1900 the Samoan islands were being claimed by both Germany and the United States. Germany annexed several islands, which now comprise Western Samoa; the U.S. took Tutuila to use Pago Pago Bay as a coaling station for naval ships.

As Japan began emerging as an international power in the mid-1930's, the U.S. Naval station on Tutuila began to acquire new strategic importance; and in 1940 the Samoan Islands became a training and staging area for the U.S. Marine Corps.

A. P. Lutali, Governor of American Samoa, signed a historic proclamation on May 23, 1988 that authorized the minting of the first numismatic issue for this unincorporated territory administered by the United States Department of the Interior.

MONETARY SYSTEM
100 Cents = 1 Dollar

U.S. TERRITORY

MILLED COINAGE

KM# 1.1 DOLLAR
31.1000 g., Bronze 3mm Thick **Subject:** America's Cup **Obv:** Americas Cup **Rev:** Rope ornamentation at sides in legend gaps **Edge:** Reeded

Date	Mintage	F	VF	XF	Unc	BU
1988 Proof	100,000				Value: 30.00	

Note: Mintage limit of 100,000.

KM# 1.2 DOLLAR
31.1000 g., Bronze 3mm Thick, Lighter in color than KM-1.1, 39 mm. **Obv:** Americas Cup **Rev:** 2 sailboats with crossed sails; Rope-like ornamentation at sides in legend gaps **Edge:** Plain **Note:** Currently being minted under the 100,000 mintage limit authorization of KM-1.1

Date	Mintage	F	VF	XF	Unc	BU
1988 Proof	Inc. above				Value: 28.00	

KM# 2 5 DOLLARS
31.1000 g., 0.9990 Silver 0.9988 oz. ASW **Subject:** America's Cup **Obv:** Americas Cup

Date	Mintage	F	VF	XF	Unc	BU
1988 Proof	1,000				Value: 60.00	

KM# 6.1 5 DOLLARS
31.1000 g., 0.9990 Silver 0.9988 oz. ASW **Subject:** XXIV Olympics **Obv:** Olympic logo above crossed symbol within circle, date below circle **Rev:** Olympic rings above Chamshil Stadium, value below **Note:** Coin die alignment.

Date	Mintage	F	VF	XF	Unc	BU
1988 Proof	1,000				Value: 65.00	

KM# 6.2 5 DOLLARS
31.1000 g., 0.9990 Silver 0.9988 oz. ASW **Note:** Medallic die alignment.

Date	Mintage	F	VF	XF	Unc	BU
1988 Proof	—				Value: 225	

KM# 3 25 DOLLARS
155.5150 g., 0.9990 Silver 4.9947 oz. ASW, 63 mm. **Subject:** America's Cup '88 **Obv:** America's Cup **Rev:** Sailboat **Note:** Illustration reduced.

Date	Mintage	F	VF	XF	Unc	BU
1988 Proof	100				Value: 245	

KM# 7 25 DOLLARS
155.5150 g., 0.9990 Silver 4.9947 oz. ASW, 63 mm. **Subject:** XXIV Olympics **Obv:** Bust of Gov. Lutali left **Rev:** Chamshil Stadium, large value below, five olympic rings above **Note:** Illustration reduced.

Date	Mintage	F	VF	XF	Unc	BU
ND(1988) Proof	100				Value: 475	

KM# 9 25 DOLLARS
155.5150 g., 0.9990 Silver 4.9947 oz. ASW, 63 mm. **Subject:** Olympics **Obv:** Olympic logo above symbol within circle, date below circle **Rev:** Olympic logo above Chamshil Stadium, value at bottom **Note:** Illustration reduced.

Date	Mintage	F	VF	XF	Unc	BU
1988 Proof	100				Value: 245	

KM# 10 25 DOLLARS
155.5150 g., 0.9990 Silver 4.9947 oz. ASW, 63 mm. **Subject:** XXIV Olympics **Rev:** Chamshil Stadium **Note:** Similar to KM#7 but denomination: TWENTY-FIVE.

Date	Mintage	F	VF	XF	Unc	BU
1988 Proof	—				Value: 550	

KM# 4   50 DOLLARS
8.6397 g., 0.9000 Gold 0.2500 oz. AGW **Subject:** America's Cup **Obv:** Olympic symbols **Rev:** Americas Cup

Date	Mintage	F	VF	XF	Unc	BU
1988 Proof	100	Value: 300				

KM# 5   100 DOLLARS
31.1000 g., 0.9990 Gold 0.9988 oz. AGW **Subject:** America's Cup **Obv:** State seal **Rev:** USA's yacht passing New Zealand's yacht

Date	Mintage	F	VF	XF	Unc	BU
1988 Proof	50	Value: 985				

KM# 8   100 DOLLARS
31.1000 g., 0.9990 Gold 0.9988 oz. AGW **Subject:** XXIV Olympics **Obv:** State seal **Rev:** Olympic rings and Chamshil Stadium above denomination

Date	Mintage	F	VF	XF	Unc	BU
1988 Proof	50	Value: 1,250				

KM# 11   100 DOLLARS
31.1000 g., 0.9990 Gold 0.9988 oz. AGW **Obv:** USA's yacht passing New Zealand's yacht **Rev:** Olympic rings and Chamshil Stadium above denomination **Note:** Mule.

Date	Mintage	F	VF	XF	Unc	BU
1988 Proof	5	Value: 2,250				

PROOF SETS

KM#	Date	Mintage	Identification	Issue Price	Mkt Val
PS1	1988 (3)	—	KM#2-4	315	575

ANDORRA

Bay of Biscay FRANCE

SPAIN *Mediterranean Sea*

Principality of Andorra (Principat d'Andorra), situated on the southern slopes of the Pyrenees Mountains between France and Spain, has an area of 181 sq. mi. (453 sq. km.) and a population of 80,000. Capital: Andorra la Vella. Tourism is the chief source of income. Timber, cattle and derivatives, and furniture are exported.

According to tradition, the independence of Andorra derives from a charter Charlemagne granted the people of Andorra in 806 in recognition of their help in battling the Moors. An agreement between the Count of Foix (France) and the Bishop of Seo de Urgel (Spanish) in 1278 to recognize each other as Co-Princes of Andorra gave the state what has been its political form and territorial extent continuously to the present day. Over the years, the title on the French side passed to the Kings of Navarre, then to the Kings of France, and is now held by the President of France.

RULER
Joan D.M. Bisbe D'Urgell I

MONETARY SYSTEM
100 Centims = 1 Diner
NOTE: The Diners have been struck for collectors while the Euro is used in everyday commerce.

MINT MARK
Crowned M = Madrid

PRINCIPALITY
DECIMAL COINAGE

KM# 171   CENTIM
1.2900 g., Aluminum, 20.27 mm. **Subject:** F.A.O. **Obv:** Denomination **Rev:** Winged figure carrying wheat **Edge:** Plain

Date	Mintage	F	VF	XF	Unc	BU
1999	—	—	—	—	1.75	2.50

KM# 164   10 CENTIMS
6.8100 g., Brass **Obv:** National arms **Rev:** Building and arms **Edge:** Plain

Date	Mintage	F	VF	XF	Unc	BU
1997	—	—	—	—	4.00	5.00

KM# 33   25 CENTIMS
2.7000 g., Bronze, 22 mm. **Obv:** Joan D. M. Bisbe D'Urgell I **Rev:** Crowned value within wreath **Edge:** Plain

Date	Mintage	F	VF	XF	Unc	BU
1986	10,000	—	—	—	5.00	5.50

KM# 109   25 CENTIMS
Copper-Nickel, 30 mm. **Subject:** 50th Anniversary - F.A.O. **Obv:** Crowned arms to left of five line inscription, value below, date at bottom **Rev:** People on globe adoring F.A.O. logo

Date	Mintage	F	VF	XF	Unc	BU
1995	50,000	—	—	—	7.00	8.00

KM# 134   50 CENTIMS
0.6221 g., 0.9990 Gold 0.0200 oz. AGW **Obv:** Fleury cross **Rev:** Portrait of Queen Isabella I **Note:** Similar to 20 Diners, KM#137.

Date	Mintage	F	VF	XF	Unc	BU
1997 Proof	Est. 50,000	Value: 35.00				

KM# 14   DINER
Brass, 25 mm. **Obv:** Joan D.M. Bisbe D'Urgell I **Rev:** Arms within circle, lower circle divides value, date at bottom

Date	Mintage	F	VF	XF	Unc	BU
1983	28,000	—	—	—	8.50	11.50

KM# 15   DINER
Cast Copper-Zinc, 25 mm. **Obv:** Joan D.M.Bisbe D'Urgell I, left **Rev:** Crowned oval arms flanked by cherubs, value below

Date	Mintage	F	VF	XF	Unc	BU
1984	7,500	—	—	—	9.00	12.00

KM# 35   DINER
6.2000 g., Brass, 25 mm. **Obv:** Bust of Joan D.M.Bisbe D'Urgell I, right **Rev:** Crowned value within wreath

Date	Mintage	F	VF	XF	Unc	BU
1986	10,000	—	—	—	8.50	11.50

KM# 49   DINER
6.8500 g., Copper-Nickel, 25 mm. **Subject:** Pont de la Margineda **Obv:** Bridge **Rev:** Large value, date to left

Date	Mintage	F	VF	XF	Unc	BU
1988	5,000	—	—	—	10.00	12.00

KM# 66   DINER
10.3000 g., 0.9990 Silver 0.3308 oz. ASW, 29.3 mm. **Obv:** Golden Eagle with wings open, value below **Rev:** Arms within circle

Date	Mintage	F	VF	XF	Unc	BU
1990	6,000	—	—	—	25.00	27.50

KM# 127   DINER
10.0000 g., 0.5000 Silver 0.1607 oz. ASW **Subject:** Treaty of Rome **Obv:** Crowned arms **Rev:** Seated Europa placing laurel wreath on her head

Date	Mintage	F	VF	XF	Unc	BU
1997 Proof	30,000	Value: 20.00				

KM# 135   DINER
1.2441 g., 0.9990 Gold 0.0400 oz. AGW **Obv:** Fleury cross **Rev:** Portrait of Queen Isabella I **Note:** Similar to 20 Diners, KM#137.

Date	Mintage	F	VF	XF	Unc	BU
1997 Proof	Est. 10,000	Value: 55.00				

KM# 19   2 DINERS
15.0000 g., Bi-Metallic Bronze center in Copper-Nickel ring, 32 mm. **Subject:** Wildlife **Obv:** Crowned shield divide value **Rev:** Brown bear left

Date	Mintage	F	VF	XF	Unc	BU
1984	5,000	—	—	—	27.50	30.00

KM# 20   2 DINERS
15.0000 g., Bi-Metallic Bronze center in Copper-Nickel ring, 32 mm. **Subject:** Wildlife **Obv:** Crowned shield divide value **Rev:** Red squirrel, facing

Date	Mintage	F	VF	XF	Unc	BU
1984	5,000	—	—	—	27.50	30.00

KM# 21   2 DINERS
15.0000 g., Bi-Metallic Bronze center in Copper-Nickel ring, 32 mm. **Subject:** Wildlife **Obv:** Crowned shield divide value **Rev:** Chamois facing

Date	Mintage	F	VF	XF	Unc	BU
1984	5,000	—	—	—	27.50	30.00

KM# 27 2 DINERS
Bi-Metallic Bronze center in Copper-Nickel ring **Subject:** 1988
Winter Olympics **Obv:** Arms in circle **Rev:** Skier, facing

Date	Mintage	F	VF	XF	Unc	BU
1985	11,000	—	—	—	22.50	25.00

KM# 28 2 DINERS
15.0000 g., Bi-Metallic Bronze center in Copper-Nickel ring,
32 mm. **Subject:** 1988 Summer Olympics **Obv:** Arms within
circle **Rev:** High jumper

Date	Mintage	F	VF	XF	Unc	BU
1985	11,000	—	—	—	22.50	25.00

KM# 36 2 DINERS
7.8000 g., Brass, 28 mm. **Obv:** Joan D.M. Bisbe D'Urgell I, right
Rev: Crowned value, date below within wreath

Date	Mintage	F	VF	XF	Unc	BU
1986	10,000	—	—	—	12.50	14.50

KM# 40 2 DINERS
Copper-Nickel, 31.8 mm. **Subject:** 1988 Summer Olympics
Obv: Arms on ornate shield divide value **Rev:** Tennis player
facing, date bottom right

Date	Mintage	F	VF	XF	Unc	BU
1987	20,000	—	—	—	14.50	16.50

KM# 46.1 2 DINERS
12.0000 g., Copper-Nickel, 32 mm. **Subject:** 1992 Winter &
Summer Olympics **Obv:** Small arms on shield, upper right, value
at center, left **Rev:** Kayaker and skier **Note:** Prev. KM#46. Coin
die rotation.

Date	Mintage	F	VF	XF	Unc	BU
1987	20,000	—	—	—	13.50	15.00

KM# 46.2 2 DINERS
12.0000 g., Copper-Nickel, 32 mm. **Subject:** 1992 Winter &
Summer Olympics **Rev:** Kayaker and skier **Note:** Medallic die
rotation.

Date	Mintage	F	VF	XF	Unc	BU
1987	Inc. above	—	—	—	13.50	15.00

KM# 50 2 DINERS
9.5000 g., Copper-Nickel, 28 mm. **Obv:** Church of Santa
Coloma **Rev:** Large value, date to bottom right

Date	Mintage	F	VF	XF	Unc	BU
1988	5,000	—	—	—	15.00	17.50

KM# 140 2 DINERS
20.0000 g., 0.9250 Silver 0.5948 oz. ASW **Subject:** 1998 Winter
Olympics **Obv:** Crowned arms to left of five line inscription, value
below, date at bottom **Rev:** Bobsled

Date	Mintage	F	VF	XF	Unc	BU
1997 (1998) Proof	30,000	Value: 22.50				

KM# 16 5 DINERS
10.0000 g., Cast Copper, 30 mm. **Obv:** Joan D.M. Bisbe D'Urgell
I, left **Rev:** Crowned arms in oval flanked by cherubs, value below,
date at bottom

Date	Mintage	F	VF	XF	Unc	BU
1984	7,500	—	—	—	13.50	15.00

KM# 29 5 DINERS
16.0000 g., Cast Copper, 35 mm. **Subject:** 2nd Congress of the
Catalan Language **Obv:** Ornate arms **Rev:** Standing armored
figure holding shield, rose stem below shield, figure divides value,
date in legend

Date	Mintage	F	VF	XF	Unc	BU
1986	6,000	—	—	—	15.00	16.50

KM# 37 5 DINERS
9.8000 g., Bronze, 30 mm. **Obv:** Bust of Joan D.M. Bisbe
D'Urgell I, right **Rev:** Crowned value, date below within wreath

Date	Mintage	F	VF	XF	Unc	BU
1986	10,000	—	—	—	17.50	20.00

KM# 51 5 DINERS
13.7500 g., Copper-Nickel, 31.5 mm. **Obv:** Church of St. Climent
de Pal **Rev:** Large value, date

Date	Mintage	F	VF	XF	Unc	BU
1988	5,000	—	—	—	17.50	20.00

KM# 80 5 DINERS
10.0000 g., 0.5000 Silver 0.1607 oz. ASW **Subject:** 1994 Winter
Olympics **Obv:** Crowned arms to left of five line inscription, value
below, date at bottom **Rev:** Cross-country skier

Date	Mintage	F	VF	XF	Unc	BU
1993 Proof	50,000	Value: 13.50				

KM# 102 5 DINERS
15.0000 g., 0.9250 Silver 0.4461 oz. ASW **Subject:** Andorran
Circle of the Arts - 25th Anniversary **Obv:** Crowned arms to left
of five line inscription, value below, date at bottom **Rev:** 3/4 Statue
standing, left, tablet with quill on left of statue, figures in doorway
on right

Date	Mintage	F	VF	XF	Unc	BU
1993 Proof	3,000	Value: 25.00				

KM# 111 5 DINERS
1.2500 g., 0.9990 Gold 0.0401 oz. AGW **Subject:** Wildlife
Obv: Crowned arms to left of five line inscription, value below,
date at bottom **Rev:** Red squirrel, left

Date	Mintage	F	VF	XF	Unc	BU
1994 Proof	—	Value: 70.00				

KM# 112 5 DINERS
1.5552 g., 0.9999 Gold 0.0500 oz. AGW **Obv:** Defiant Golden
Eagle **Rev:** Crowned denomination within wreath

Date	Mintage	F	VF	XF	Unc	BU
1995 Proof	—	Value: 60.00				

KM# 116 5 DINERS
15.0000 g., 0.9250 Silver 0.4461 oz. ASW **Subject:** XXIII
Photographers Federation Congress **Rev:** Hand on camera

Date	Mintage	F	VF	XF	Unc	BU
1995 Proof	3,000	Value: 25.00				

KM# 117 5 DINERS
1.2441 g., 0.9990 Gold 0.0400 oz. AGW **Subject:** Wildlife
Obv: Crowned arms to left of five line inscription, value below, date at bottom **Rev:** Chamois, left

Date	Mintage	F	VF	XF	Unc	BU
1996 Proof	Est. 100,000				Value: 55.00	

KM# 118 5 DINERS
1.2441 g., 0.9990 Gold 0.0400 oz. AGW **Subject:** Wildlife
Rev: Brown bear and cub

Date	Mintage	F	VF	XF	Unc	BU
1996 Proof	Est. 100,000				Value: 55.00	

KM# 141 5 DINERS
3.1103 g., 0.5850 Gold 0.0585 oz. AGW **Subject:** 1998 Winter Olympics **Obv:** Crowned arms to left of five line inscription, value below, date at bottom **Rev:** Downhill skier

Date	Mintage	F	VF	XF	Unc	BU
1997 (1998) Proof	5,000				Value: 65.00	

KM# 155 5 DINERS
27.0000 g., Bi-Metallic Silver center in Brass ring, 38.3 mm.
Obv: World globe amid stars **Rev:** World globe with sun, planets and stars **Note:** Silver center and brass ring are within a silver ring.

Date	Mintage	F	VF	XF	Unc	BU
1999 Proof	—				Value: 30.00	

KM# 187 5 DINERS
15.5500 g., 0.9250 Silver 0.4624 oz. ASW **Obv:** National arms in wreath **Rev:** Nativity scene

Date	Mintage	F	VF	XF	Unc	BU
2000 Proof	25,000				Value: 22.50	

KM# 17 10 DINERS
8.0000 g., 0.9000 Cast Silver 0.2315 oz., 26 mm. **Obv:** Joan D.M. Bisbe D'Urgell I, left **Rev:** Crowned arms on oval shield flanked by cherubs, value below, date at bottom

Date	Mintage	F	VF	XF	Unc	BU
1984	7,500	—	—	—	22.50	25.00

KM# 34 10 DINERS
8.0000 g., 0.9000 Cast Silver 0.2315 oz., 30 mm. **Subject:** 1988 World Cup Soccer Games **Obv:** Arms on shield within legend **Rev:** Soccer ball below, world globe above, ball and globe divide value, date in legend, bottom

Date	Mintage	F	VF	XF	Unc	BU
1986 Prooflike	10,000	—	—	—	22.50	24.00

KM# 38 10 DINERS
8.0000 g., 0.9250 Silver 0.2379 oz. ASW, 28 mm. **Obv:** Joan D.M. Bisbe D'Urgell I, right **Rev:** Crowned value, date below within wreath

Date	Mintage	F	VF	XF	Unc	BU
1986	10,000	—	—	—	22.50	25.00

KM# 52 10 DINERS
8.0000 g., 0.9250 Silver 0.2379 oz. ASW, 28 mm. **Obv:** Church of St. Joan de Caselles **Rev:** Large value, small vertical date to left

Date	Mintage	F	VF	XF	Unc	BU
1988	5,000	—	—	—	22.50	25.00

KM# 53 10 DINERS
12.0000 g., 0.9250 Silver 0.3569 oz. ASW, 32 mm.
Subject: 1990 World Cup Soccer Games **Obv:** Crowned arms to left of five line inscription, value below, date at bottom **Rev:** Figures on soccer field

Date	Mintage	F	VF	XF	Unc	BU
1989 Proof	20,000				Value: 13.50	

KM# 55 10 DINERS
12.0000 g., 0.9250 Silver 0.3569 oz. ASW, 32 mm. **Subject:** 1992 Winter Olympics **Obv:** Crowned arms to left of five line inscription, value below, date at bottom **Rev:** Downhill skier

Date	Mintage	F	VF	XF	Unc	BU
1989 Proof	15,000				Value: 13.50	

KM# 56 10 DINERS
12.0000 g., 0.9250 Silver 0.3569 oz. ASW, 32 mm.
Subject: 1992 Summer Olympics **Obv:** Crowned arms to left of five line inscription, value below, date at bottom **Rev:** Soccer

Date	Mintage	F	VF	XF	Unc	BU
1989 Proof	15,000				Value: 13.50	

KM# 60 10 DINERS
12.0000 g., 0.9250 Silver 0.3569 oz. ASW, 32 mm.
Subject: 1990 World Cup Soccer Games **Obv:** Crowned arms to left of five line inscription, value below, date at bottom **Rev:** Map of Italy and soccer ball

Date	Mintage	F	VF	XF	Unc	BU
1989 Proof	20,000				Value: 13.50	

KM# 71 10 DINERS
31.4700 g., 0.9250 Silver 0.9359 oz. ASW, 38.61 mm.
Subject: ECU Customs Union **Obv:** Arms above "ECU", within circle of stars/beads **Rev:** Charlemagne

Date	Mintage	F	VF	XF	Unc	BU
ND(1992) Proof	15,000				Value: 35.00	

KM# 74 10 DINERS
31.1035 g., 0.9250 Silver 0.9250 oz. ASW, 38.7 mm.
Subject: Wildlife **Obv:** Crowned arms to left of five line inscription, value below, date at bottom **Rev:** Red squirrel, left

Date	Mintage	F	VF	XF	Unc	BU
1992 Proof	15,000				Value: 40.00	

KM# 75   10 DINERS
31.1035 g., 0.9250 Silver 0.9250 oz. ASW, 38.7 mm.
Subject: Wildlife **Obv:** Crowned arms to left of five line inscription, value below, date at bottom **Rev:** Chamois

Date	Mintage	F	VF	XF	Unc	BU
1992 Proof	15,000	Value: 40.00				

KM# 76   10 DINERS
31.1035 g., 0.9250 Silver 0.9250 oz. ASW, 38.7 mm.
Subject: Wildlife **Obv:** Crowned arms to left of five line inscription, value below, date at bottom **Rev:** Brown bear and cub

Date	Mintage	F	VF	XF	Unc	BU
1992 Proof	15,000	Value: 40.00				

KM# 78   10 DINERS
31.1035 g., 0.9250 Silver 0.9250 oz. ASW, 38.7 mm.
Subject: Discovery of the New World **Obv:** Crowned arms to left of five line inscription, value below, date at bottom **Rev:** Stylized ship on globe

Date	Mintage	F	VF	XF	Unc	BU
1992 Proof	15,000	Value: 28.00				

KM# 84   10 DINERS
31.4700 g., 0.9250 Silver 0.9359 oz. ASW **Obv:** Crowned arms above denomination and date **Rev:** Stylized tree and birds

Date	Mintage	F	VF	XF	Unc	BU
1993 Proof	15,000	Value: 30.00				

KM# 85   10 DINERS
31.4700 g., 0.9250 Silver 0.9359 oz. ASW **Subject:** Space Exploration **Obv:** Crowned arms to left of five line inscription, value below, date at bottom **Rev:** Tethered space walker Edward White

Date	Mintage	F	VF	XF	Unc	BU
1993 Proof	15,000	Value: 50.00				

KM# 86   10 DINERS
31.4700 g., 0.9250 Silver 0.9359 oz. ASW **Subject:** 1994 World Cup Soccer **Obv:** Crowned arms to left of five line inscription, value below, date at bottom **Rev:** Player before world map

Date	Mintage	F	VF	XF	Unc	BU
1993 Proof	20,000	Value: 28.00				

KM# 89   10 DINERS
31.4700 g., 0.9250 Silver 0.9359 oz. ASW **Subject:** ECU Customs Union **Obv:** Arms within circle of stars/beads **Rev:** St. George divides value, rose stem below feet

Date	Mintage	F	VF	XF	Unc	BU
1993 Proof	25,000	Value: 30.00				

KM# 95   10 DINERS
31.4700 g., 0.9250 Silver 0.9359 oz. ASW **Subject:** 1996 Summer Olympic Games **Rev:** Cyclists

Date	Mintage	F	VF	XF	Unc	BU
1994 Proof	50,000	Value: 27.50				

KM# 97   10 DINERS
31.4700 g., 0.9250 Silver 0.9359 oz. ASW **Subject:** Andorra U.N. Membership **Obv:** Crowned arms above "ECU" **Rev:** Woman kneeling, left hand on globe, globe symbol in wreath behind

Date	Mintage	F	VF	XF	Unc	BU
1994 Proof	25,000	Value: 37.50				

KM# 98   10 DINERS
31.4700 g., 0.9250 Silver 0.9359 oz. ASW **Subject:** Discovery of the New World **Obv:** Crowned arms to left of five line legend, value below, date at bottom **Rev:** Sailing ship, small bust of cherub, top left, eight pointed star to right of ship

Date	Mintage	F	VF	XF	Unc	BU
1994 Proof	20,000	Value: 42.50				

KM# 99   10 DINERS
31.4700 g., 0.9250 Silver 0.9359 oz. ASW **Subject:** ECU Customs Union **Obv:** Arms above "ECU", within circle of stars/beads **Rev:** Peter III of Catalonia and Aragon divides date, cross flanked by dots below feet

Date	Mintage	F	VF	XF	Unc	BU
1994 Proof	25,000	Value: 40.00				

KM# 105   10 DINERS
31.4700 g., 0.9250 Silver 0.9359 oz. ASW **Subject:** ECU
Customs Union **Rev:** Ramon Berenguer III

Date	Mintage	F	VF	XF	Unc	BU
1995 Proof	30,000	Value: 42.50				

KM# 108   10 DINERS
31.6000 g., 0.9250 Silver 0.9397 oz. ASW **Subject:** Admission to
the Council of Europe **Obv:** Arms above "ECU" **Rev:** Woman, left,
walking through starred arch, arms forward, container in right hand

Date	Mintage	F	VF	XF	Unc	BU
1995 Proof	35,000	Value: 37.50				

KM# 110   10 DINERS
31.1035 g., 0.9250 Silver 0.9250 oz. ASW **Subject:** 50th
Anniversary - F.A.O. **Obv:** Crowned arms to left of five line
inscription, value below, date at bottom **Rev:** Ceres holding grain

Date	Mintage	F	VF	XF	Unc	BU
1995 Proof	10,000	Value: 35.00				

KM# 113   10 DINERS
31.1035 g., 0.9250 Silver 0.9250 oz. ASW **Subject:** Wildlife
Obv: Crowned arms to left of five line inscription, value below,
date at bottom **Rev:** Wolf, facing

Date	Mintage	F	VF	XF	Unc	BU
1995 Proof	20,000	Value: 55.00				

KM# 114   10 DINERS
31.1035 g., 0.9250 Silver 0.9250 oz. ASW **Subject:** Agnus Dei
Obv: Crowned arms above "ECU" **Rev:** Lamb of God within circle,
circle of stars surrounding

Date	Mintage	F	VF	XF	Unc	BU
1995 Proof	Est. 35,000	Value: 35.00				

KM# 119   10 DINERS
31.4700 g., 0.9250 Silver 0.9359 oz. ASW **Obv:** Arms above
"ECU" **Rev:** Frederic II on throne

Date	Mintage	F	VF	XF	Unc	BU
1996 Proof	Est. 30,000	Value: 35.00				

KM# A127   10 DINERS
31.4700 g., 0.9250 Silver 0.9359 oz. ASW **Subject:** Wildlife
Protection **Obv:** Crowned arms **Rev:** Diving European Otter

Date	Mintage	F	VF	XF	Unc	BU
1996 Proof	15,000	Value: 50.00				

KM# 120   10 DINERS
31.4700 g., 0.9250 Silver 0.9359 oz. ASW **Obv:** Crowned Arms,
date below **Rev:** Sailing ship

Date	Mintage	F	VF	XF	Unc	BU
1996 Proof	Est. 20,000	Value: 40.00				

KM# 121   10 DINERS
31.4700 g., 0.9250 Silver 0.9359 oz. ASW **Obv:** Crowned Arms
above date **Rev:** Pope crowning Charlemagne

Date	Mintage	F	VF	XF	Unc	BU
1996 Proof	Est. 30,000	Value: 32.50				

KM# 131   10 DINERS
31.4700 g., 0.9250 Silver 0.9359 oz. ASW **Subject:** Wildlife **Obv:** Crowned arms, date below **Rev:** Red Fox vixen with kit

Date	Mintage	F	VF	XF	Unc	BU
1997 Proof	15,000	Value: 60.00				

KM# 143   10 DINERS
31.4700 g., 0.9250 Silver 0.9359 oz. ASW **Subject:** Human Rights **Obv:** Crowned arms above "EURO" **Rev:** Allegorical figure of Justice

Date	Mintage	F	VF	XF	Unc	BU
1998 Proof	25,000	Value: 42.50				

KM# 125   10 DINERS
31.4700 g., 0.9250 Silver 0.9359 oz. ASW **Subject:** 25th Anniversary - Msgr. Alanis, Co-prince and Bishop of Andorra **Obv:** Crowned arms above "EURO" **Rev:** Enthroned prince, date

Date	Mintage	F	VF	XF	Unc	BU
1996 Proof	30,000	Value: 32.50				

KM# 132   10 DINERS
31.4700 g., 0.9250 Silver 0.9359 oz. ASW **Obv:** Crowned arms above "ECU" **Rev:** Johan Sebastian Bach portrait, facing 3/4 right, dates

Date	Mintage	F	VF	XF	Unc	BU
1997 Proof	Est. 25,000	Value: 27.50				

KM# 130   10 DINERS
31.4700 g., 0.9250 Silver 0.9359 oz. ASW **Subject:** Treaty of Rome **Obv:** Crowned arms above "EURO" **Rev:** Seated Europa with olive branch and "EURO" shield, dates

Date	Mintage	F	VF	XF	Unc	BU
1997 Proof	25,000	Value: 40.00				

KM# 133   10 DINERS
31.4700 g., 0.9250 Silver 0.9359 oz. ASW **Obv:** Crowned arms above "ECU" **Rev:** Antonio Vivaldi portrait, 3/4 left, dates

Date	Mintage	F	VF	XF	Unc	BU
1997 Proof	Est. 25,000	Value: 27.50				

KM# 136   10 DINERS
3.1103 g., 0.9990 Gold 0.0999 oz. AGW **Obv:** Fleury cross **Rev:** Bust of Queen Isabella I right **Note:** Similar to 20 Diners, KM#137.

Date	Mintage	F	VF	XF	Unc	BU
1997 Proof	Est. 5,000	Value: 110				

KM# 165   10 DINERS
31.1100 g., 0.9990 Silver 0.9992 oz. ASW **Subject:** Year of the Tiger **Obv:** Multicolored cartoon tiger and Chinese legend **Rev:** Crowned value within wreath **Edge:** Reeded

Date	Mintage	F	VF	XF	Unc	BU
1998 Proof	—	Value: 50.00				

KM# 142   10 DINERS
31.4700 g., 0.9250 Silver 0.9359 oz. ASW **Subject:** 1998 World Cup Soccer **Obv:** Crowned arms and denomination **Rev:** Eiffel Tower and soccer ball

Date	Mintage	F	VF	XF	Unc	BU
1997 Proof	15,000	Value: 45.00				

KM# 166   10 DINERS
31.5500 g., 0.9250 Silver 0.9382 oz. ASW **Subject:** Palau del Princep **Obv:** Crowned arms above "EURO" **Rev:** Crowned arms on house corner **Edge:** Reeded

Date	Mintage	F	VF	XF	Unc	BU
1997 Proof	—	Value: 35.00				

KM# 146   10 DINERS
31.4700 g., 0.9250 Silver 0.9359 oz. ASW **Obv:** Crowned arms above "ECU" **Rev:** Portrait of Claudio Monteverdi, 3/4 right, dates

Date	Mintage	F	VF	XF	Unc	BU
1998 Proof	25,000	Value: 27.50				

KM# 147 10 DINERS
31.4700 g., 0.9250 Silver 0.9359 oz. ASW **Subject:** George
Friedrich Handel **Obv:** Crowned arms above "ECU" **Rev:** Portrait,
dates

Date	Mintage	F	VF	XF	Unc	BU
1998 Proof	25,000				Value: 27.50	

KM# 150 10 DINERS
31.4700 g., 0.9250 Silver 0.9359 oz. ASW **Subject:** Europa
Obv: Crowned arms above "EURO" **Rev:** Seated Europa

Date	Mintage	F	VF	XF	Unc	BU
1998 Proof	25,000				Value: 35.00	

KM# 151 10 DINERS
31.4700 g., 0.9250 Silver 0.9359 oz. ASW **Subject:** Europa
Obv: Crowned arms above "EURO" **Rev:** Europa driving quadriga

Date	Mintage	F	VF	XF	Unc	BU
1998 Proof	25,000				Value: 35.00	

KM# 153 10 DINERS
31.4700 g., 0.9250 Silver 0.9359 oz. ASW **Subject:** 50th
Anniversary - European Council **Obv:** Crowned arms above
"EURO" **Rev:** Statue of Democracy

Date	Mintage	F	VF	XF	Unc	BU
1999 Proof	15,000				Value: 37.50	

KM# 156 10 DINERS
31.4700 g., 0.9250 Silver 0.9359 oz. ASW, 38.6 mm.
Subject: Jubilee 2000 **Obv:** National arms **Rev:** Birth of Jesus
Edge: Reeded

Date	Mintage	F	VF	XF	Unc	BU
1999 Proof	15,000				Value: 40.00	

KM# 157 10 DINERS
31.4700 g., 0.9250 Silver 0.9359 oz. ASW **Subject:** Jubilee
2000 **Obv:** National arms **Rev:** Slaughter of the Innocents - Man
with sword killing children

Date	Mintage	F	VF	XF	Unc	BU
1999 Proof	15,000				Value: 40.00	

KM# 158 10 DINERS
31.4700 g., 0.9250 Silver 0.9359 oz. ASW **Subject:** Jubilee
2000 **Obv:** National arms **Rev:** John the Baptist baptizing Jesus

Date	Mintage	F	VF	XF	Unc	BU
1999 Proof	15,000				Value: 40.00	

KM# 154 10 DINERS
31.4700 g., 0.9250 Silver 0.9359 oz. ASW **Subject:** 50th
Anniversary - European Council **Obv:** Crowned arms above
"EURO" **Rev:** Statue of Human Rights

Date	Mintage	F	VF	XF	Unc	BU
1999 Proof	15,000				Value: 37.50	

KM# 159 10 DINERS
31.4700 g., 0.9250 Silver 0.9359 oz. ASW **Subject:** Jubilee
2000 **Obv:** National arms **Rev:** Prodigal Son - Son kneeling
before his father

Date	Mintage	F	VF	XF	Unc	BU
1999 Proof	15,000				Value: 40.00	

KM# 160 10 DINERS
31.4700 g., 0.9250 Silver 0.9359 oz. ASW **Subject:** Jubilee
2000 **Obv:** National arms **Rev:** Jesus' entry into Jerusalem

Date	Mintage	F	VF	XF	Unc	BU
1999 Proof	15,000				Value: 40.00	

KM# 161 10 DINERS
31.4700 g., 0.9250 Silver 0.9359 oz. ASW **Subject:** Jubilee
2000 **Obv:** National arms **Rev:** Last Supper scene

Date	Mintage	F	VF	XF	Unc	BU
1999 Proof	15,000				Value: 40.00	

KM# 162 10 DINERS
31.4700 g., 0.9250 Silver 0.9359 oz. ASW **Subject:** Jubilee
2000 **Obv:** National arms **Rev:** Jesus on the cross

Date	Mintage	F	VF	XF	Unc	BU
1999 Proof	15,000				Value: 40.00	

KM# 163   10 DINERS
31.4700 g., 0.9250 Silver 0.9359 oz. ASW **Subject:** Jubilee
2000 **Obv:** National arms **Rev:** Jesus standing in boat

Date	Mintage	F	VF	XF	Unc	BU
1999 Proof	15,000	Value: 40.00				

KM# 22   20 DINERS
16.0000 g., 0.8350 Silver 0.4295 oz. ASW, 35 mm.
Subject: Wildlife **Obv:** Crowned arms **Rev:** Bear with cub

Date	Mintage	F	VF	XF	Unc	BU
1984 Proof	5,000	Value: 37.50				

KM# 23   20 DINERS
16.0000 g., 0.8350 Silver 0.4295 oz. ASW, 35 mm.
Subject: Wildlife **Obv:** Crowned arms **Rev:** Red squirrel

Date	Mintage	F	VF	XF	Unc	BU
1984 Proof	5,000	Value: 40.00				

KM# 24   20 DINERS
16.0000 g., 0.8350 Silver 0.4295 oz. ASW, 35 mm.
Subject: Wildlife **Obv:** Crowned arms **Rev:** Chamois

Date	Mintage	F	VF	XF	Unc	BU
1984 Proof	5,000	Value: 40.00				

KM# 25   20 DINERS
16.0000 g., 0.9000 Silver 0.4630 oz. ASW, 35 mm.
Subject: 1984 Summer Olympics **Obv:** Crowned arms
Rev: Shooter

Date	Mintage	F	VF	XF	Unc	BU
1984 Proof	10,000	Value: 25.00				

KM# 26   20 DINERS
16.0000 g., 0.9000 Silver 0.4630 oz. ASW, 35 mm. **Subject:**
Christmas **Obv:** Ornate arms **Rev:** Madonna and child

Date	Mintage	F	VF	XF	Unc	BU
1985 Proof	7,000	Value: 27.50				

KM# 39   20 DINERS
16.0000 g., 0.9000 Silver 0.4630 oz. ASW, 35 mm.
Subject: Olympic Tennis **Rev:** Tennis player, date lower right

Date	Mintage	F	VF	XF	Unc	BU
1987	10,000	—	—	—	50.00	55.00

KM# 43   20 DINERS
16.0000 g., 0.9000 Silver 0.4630 oz. ASW, 35 mm. **Subject:** 1988
Summer Olympics **Obv:** Crowned arms **Rev:** Chamshil Stadium

Date	Mintage	F	VF	XF	Unc	BU
1988	12,000	—	—	—	50.00	55.00

KM# 47   20 DINERS
16.0000 g., 0.9250 Silver 0.4758 oz. ASW, 35 mm. **Subject:** 1992
Winter Olympics, Albertville **Obv:** Crowned arms to left of five line
inscription, value below, date at bottom **Rev:** Pair of figure skaters

Date	Mintage	F	VF	XF	Unc	BU
1988 Proof	15,000	Value: 25.00				

KM# 48   20 DINERS
16.0000 g., 0.9250 Silver 0.4758 oz. ASW, 35 mm. **Subject:**
1992 Summer Olympics **Obv:** Crowned arms to left of five line
inscription, value below, date at bottom **Rev:** Gymnast on rings

Date	Mintage	F	VF	XF	Unc	BU
1988 Proof	15,000	Value: 28.00				

KM# 54   20 DINERS
16.0000 g., 0.9250 Silver 0.4758 oz. ASW, 35 mm. **Subject:**
1992 Summer Olympics **Obv:** Crowned arms to left of five line
inscription, value below, date at bottom **Rev:** Wind surfer

Date	Mintage	F	VF	XF	Unc	BU
1989 Proof	15,000	Value: 35.00				

KM# 57   20 DINERS
16.0000 g., 0.9250 Silver 0.4758 oz. ASW, 35 mm. **Subject:**
1992 Summer Olympics **Obv:** Crowned arms to left of five line
inscription, value below, date at bottom **Rev:** Kayaker

Date	Mintage	F	VF	XF	Unc	BU
1989 Proof	15,000	Value: 35.00				

KM# 58   20 DINERS
16.0000 g., 0.9250 Silver 0.4758 oz. ASW, 35 mm. **Subject:**
1992 Summer Olympics, Barcelona **Obv:** Crowned arms to left
of five line inscription, value below, date at bottom **Rev:** Hurdler

Date	Mintage	F	VF	XF	Unc	BU
1990 Proof	15,000	Value: 35.00				

KM# 59   20 DINERS
16.0000 g., 0.9250 Silver 0.4758 oz. ASW, 35 mm. **Subject:**
1992 Summer Olympics **Obv:** Crowned arms to left of five line
inscription, value below, date at bottom **Rev:** Equestrian

Date	Mintage	F	VF	XF	Unc	BU
1990 Proof	15,000	Value: 35.00				

KM# 67   20 DINERS
21.0000 g., 0.9250 Silver 0.6245 oz. ASW, 34 mm.
Subject: European Small States Games **Obv:** Crowned arms to
left of five line inscription, value below, date at bottom **Rev:** Cyclist

Date	Mintage	F	VF	XF	Unc	BU
1991 Proof	5,000	Value: 40.00				

KM# 72 20 DINERS
26.5000 g., 0.9250 Silver With 1.5 g. 0.917 gold inlay, 0.0442 oz. AGW. 0.7881 oz. ASW, 38 mm. **Subject:** ECU Customs Union **Obv:** Similar to 10 Diners, KM#71 **Rev:** Charlemagne

Date	Mintage	F	VF	XF	Unc	BU
ND(1992)	5,000	—	—	—	110	115

KM# 90 20 DINERS
26.5000 g., 0.9250 Silver With 1.5 g. 0.917 gold inlay, 0.0442 oz. AGW. 0.7881 oz. ASW **Subject:** ECU Customs Union **Rev:** St. George

Date	Mintage	F	VF	XF	Unc	BU
1993 Matte	5,000	—	—	—	120	125

KM# 100 20 DINERS
26.5000 g., 0.9250 Silver With 1.5 g. 0.917 gold inlay, 0.0442 oz. AGW. 0.7881 oz. ASW **Subject:** ECU Customs Union **Obv:** Arms above "ECU",within wreath of stars on rope **Rev:** Peter III of Catalonia and Aragon

Date	Mintage	F	VF	XF	Unc	BU
1994	5,000	—	—	—	85.00	90.00

KM# 106 20 DINERS
25.0000 g., 0.9250 Silver With 1.6 g. 0.917 gold inlay, 0.0442 oz. AGW. 0.7435 oz. ASW **Subject:** ECU Customs Union **Obv:** Arms above "ECU", within wreath of stars on rope **Rev:** Ramon Berenger III, three pointed crown flanked by dots below horse hooves

Date	Mintage	F	VF	XF	Unc	BU
1995	6,000	—	—	—	85.00	90.00

KM# 122 20 DINERS
25.0000 g., 0.9250 Silver With 1.6 g. 0.917 gold inlay, 0.0442 oz. AGW. 0.7435 oz. ASW **Obv:** Crowned arms and "ECU", date below arms **Rev:** Charlemagne being crowned

Date	Mintage	F	VF	XF	Unc	BU
1996	Est. 5,000	—	—	—	170	175

KM# 128 20 DINERS
25.0000 g., 0.9250 Silver With 1.6 g. 0.917 gold inlay, 0.0442 oz. AGW. 0.7435 oz. ASW **Subject:** Treaty at Rome **Obv:** Crowned arms above "EURO" **Rev:** Seated Europa with child holding "EURO" shield

Date	Mintage	F	VF	XF	Unc	BU
1997	5,000	—	—	—	85.00	90.00

KM# 137 20 DINERS
6.2207 g., 0.9990 Gold 0.1998 oz. AGW **Obv:** Fleury cross **Rev:** Bust of Queen Isabella I right

Date	Mintage	F	VF	XF	Unc	BU
1997 Proof	Est. 3,500	Value: 210				

KM# 144 20 DINERS
25.0000 g., 0.9250 Silver with 1.5g, .917 gold inlay, .0442 oz. AGW. 0.7435 oz. ASW **Subject:** Human Rights **Obv:** Crowned arms above "EURO" **Rev:** Young family and broken chain

Date	Mintage	F	VF	XF	Unc	BU
1998	5,000	—	—	—	80.00	85.00

KM# 225 20 DINERS
25.0000 g., 0.9250 Silver with 1.5g, .917 gold inlay, .0442 oz. AGW 0.7435 oz. ASW **Subject:** XXVII Summer Olympics - Sydney 2000 **Obv:** Crowned arms **Rev:** 1500 meter runner in gold inlay

Date	Mintage	F	VF	XF	Unc	BU
1998	5,000	—	—	—	70.00	75.00

KM# 148 20 DINERS
25.0000 g., 0.9250 Silver With 1.5 g. 0.917 gold inlay, 0.0442 oz. AGW. 0.7435 oz. ASW **Subject:** XXVII Summer Olympics - Sydney 2000 **Obv:** Crowned arms above date **Rev:** Javelin thrower in gold inlay

Date	Mintage	F	VF	XF	Unc	BU
1998	5,000	—	—	—	70.00	75.00

KM# 149 20 DINERS
25.0000 g., 0.9250 Silver With 1.5g 0.917 gold inlay, 0.0442 oz. AGW. 0.7435 oz. ASW **Subject:** XXVII Summer Olympics - Sydney 2000 **Obv:** Crowned arms above date **Rev:** Discus thrower in gold inlay

Date	Mintage	F	VF	XF	Unc	BU
1998	5,000	—	—	—	70.00	75.00

KM# 226 20 DINERS
25.0000 g., 0.9250 Silver With 1.5g 0.917 gold inlay, 0.0442 oz. AGW. 0.7435 oz. ASW **Subject:** XXVII Summer Olympics - Sydney 2000 **Obv:** Crowned arms **Rev:** Shot putter in gold inlay

Date	Mintage	F	VF	XF	Unc	BU
1999	5,000	—	—	—	70.00	75.00

KM# 227 20 DINERS
25.0000 g., 0.9250 Silver With 1.5g 0.917 gold inlay, 0.0442 oz. AGW. 0.7435 oz. ASW **Subject:** XXVII Summer Olympics - Sydney 2000 **Obv:** Crowned arms **Rev:** 100 meter runner in gold inlay

Date	Mintage	F	VF	XF	Unc	BU
1999	5,000	—	—	—	70.00	75.00

KM# 228 20 DINERS
25.0000 g., 0.9250 Silver With 1.5g 0.917 gold inlay, 0.0442 oz. AGW. 0.7435 oz. ASW **Subject:** XXVII Summer Olympics - Sydney 2000 **Obv:** Crowned arms **Rev:** Pole vaulter in gold inlay

Date	Mintage	F	VF	XF	Unc	BU
1999	5,000	—	—	—	70.00	75.00

KM# 167 20 DINERS
25.0000 g., 0.9250 Silver 0.7435 oz. ASW **Subject:** XXVII Summer Olympics - Sydney 2000 **Obv:** Crowned arms, date and denomination **Rev:** Hurdler on gold inlay **Edge:** Plain

Date	Mintage	F	VF	XF	Unc	BU
2000	6,000	—	—	—	70.00	75.00

KM# 168 20 DINERS
25.0000 g., 0.9250 Silver 0.7435 oz. ASW **Subject:** XXVII JOCS 2000 Olympics **Obv:** Crowned arms, date and denomination **Rev:** Runner on gold inlay **Edge:** Plain

Date	Mintage	F	VF	XF	Unc	BU
2000	6,000	—	—	—	70.00	75.00

KM# 169 20 DINERS
25.0000 g., 0.9250 Silver 0.7435 oz. ASW **Subject:** XXVII JOCS 2000 Olympics **Obv:** Crowned arms, date and denomination **Rev:** Long jumper on gold inlay **Edge:** Plain

Date	Mintage	F	VF	XF	Unc	BU
2000	6,000	—	—	—	70.00	75.00

KM# 170 20 DINERS
25.0000 g., 0.9250 Silver 0.7435 oz. ASW **Subject:** XXVII JOCS 2000 Olympics **Obv:** Crowned arms, date and denomination **Rev:** Pole vaulter on gold inlay **Edge:** Plain

Date	Mintage	F	VF	XF	Unc	BU
2000	6,000	—	—	—	70.00	75.00

KM# 220 20 DINERS
26.5000 g., Bi-Metallic .925 Silver 25g planchet with .917 Gold 1.5 g inlay, 38 mm. **Subject:** XXVII JOCS Olympics **Obv:** Crowned arms, value and date **Rev:** High jumper on gold inlay **Edge:** Plain

Date	Mintage	F	VF	XF	Unc	BU
2000	6,000	—	—	—	70.00	75.00

KM# 18 25 DINERS
20.0000 g., 0.9000 Silver 0.5787 oz. ASW, 38 mm. **Obv:** Joan D.M. Bisbe D'Urgell I, left **Rev:** Crowned oval arms flanked by cherubs, value below, date at bottom

Date	Mintage	F	VF	XF	Unc	BU
1984	4,450	—	—	—	35.00	45.00
1984 Proof	550	Value: 120				

KM# 44.1 25 DINERS
20.0000 g., 0.9000 Silver 0.5787 oz. ASW, 38.5 mm. **Subject:** 700th Anniversary - Andorra's Governing Charter **Obv:** Fleury cross **Rev:** Grasped hands, right hand armored, left hand marked on back **Note:** Medallic die rotation.

Date	Mintage	F	VF	XF	Unc	BU
ND(1988)	20,000	—	—	—	32.50	40.00

KM# 44.2 25 DINERS
20.0000 g., 0.9000 Silver 0.5787 oz. ASW, 38.5 mm. **Subject:** 700th Anniversary - Andorra's Governing Charter **Note:** Medallic die rotation.

Date	Mintage	F	VF	XF	Unc	BU
ND(1988) Proof	10,000	Value: 45.00				

KM# 61 25 DINERS
20.0000 g., 0.9000 Silver 0.5787 oz. ASW, 37 mm. **Subject:** Millenary of the Bishop of Sala **Obv:** Building within circle **Rev:** Bishop on horseback, value below

Date	Mintage	F	VF	XF	Unc	BU
1989	Est. 5,000	—	—	—	50.00	60.00

KM# 65 25 DINERS
28.2800 g., 0.9250 Silver 0.8410 oz. ASW, 38.6 mm. **Subject:** Red Cross **Obv:** Crowned arms to left of five line inscription, value below **Rev:** Cross on dove, date below

Date	Mintage	F	VF	XF	Unc	BU
1991 Proof	3,000	Value: 57.50				

KM# 69 25 DINERS
25.0000 g., 0.9250 Silver 0.7435 oz. ASW, 38 mm. **Subject:** 20th Anniversary - Episcopal Co-prince **Note:** With 0.917 gold inlay, 0.0442 oz. AGW.

Date	Mintage	F	VF	XF	Unc	BU
1991	2,500	—	—	—	85.00	95.00

KM# 73 25 DINERS
7.7700 g., 0.5830 Gold 0.1456 oz. AGW, 25 mm. **Subject:** ECU Customs Union **Obv:** Arms with "ECU" below within circle of stars/beads **Rev:** St. Ermengol

Date	Mintage	F	VF	XF	Unc	BU
1992 Proof	3,000	Value: 150				

KM# 81 25 DINERS
7.7700 g., 0.5830 Gold 0.1456 oz. AGW **Subject:** 1994 Winter Olympic Games, Lillehammer **Obv:** Crowned arms to left of five line inscription, value below, date at bottom **Rev:** Downhill skier

Date	Mintage	F	VF	XF	Unc	BU
1993 Proof	6,000	Value: 150				

KM# 91 25 DINERS
7.7700 g., 0.5830 Gold 0.1456 oz. AGW **Subject:** ECU Customs Union **Obv:** Arms above "ECU" within circle of stars/beads **Rev:** Bishop riding a horse

Date	Mintage	F	VF	XF	Unc	BU
1993 Proof	5,000	Value: 145				

KM# 92 25 DINERS
7.7700 g., 0.5830 Gold 0.1456 oz. AGW **Subject:** 1994 World Cup Soccer **Obv:** Crowned arms to left of five line inscription, value below, date at bottom **Rev:** Soccer player on right, outline of bird on top left

Date	Mintage	F	VF	XF	Unc	BU
1993 Proof	5,000	Value: 150				

KM# 96 25 DINERS
7.7700 g., 0.5830 Gold 0.1456 oz. AGW **Subject:** 1994 Summer Olympic Games **Rev:** Tennis

Date	Mintage	F	VF	XF	Unc	BU
1994 Proof	5,000	Value: 150				

KM# 101 25 DINERS
7.7700 g., 0.5830 Gold 0.1456 oz. AGW **Subject:** ECU Customs Union **Obv:** Coat of arms **Rev:** Bishop Pere D'Urg standing

Date	Mintage	F	VF	XF	Unc	BU
1994 Proof	5,000	Value: 150				

KM# 107 25 DINERS
7.7700 g., 0.5830 Gold 0.1456 oz. AGW **Subject:** ECU Customs Union **Obv:** Coat of arms **Rev:** Bishop Pere D'Urg seated

Date	Mintage	F	VF	XF	Unc	BU
1995 Proof	5,000	Value: 150				

KM# 123 25 DINERS
7.7700 g., 0.5830 Gold 0.1456 oz. AGW **Obv:** Arms and "ECU" **Rev:** Seated Europa

Date	Mintage	F	VF	XF	Unc	BU
1996 Proof	Est. 5,000	Value: 150				

KM# 129 25 DINERS
7.7700 g., 0.5830 Gold 0.1456 oz. AGW **Subject:** Treaty of Rome **Obv:** Crowned arms **Rev:** Europa on knee, holding large "EURO" shield

Date	Mintage	F	VF	XF	Unc	BU
1997 Proof	5,000	Value: 150				

KM# 139 25 DINERS
Bi-Metallic Gold center in Platinum ring **Obv:** Fleury cross **Rev:** Swan in water

Date	Mintage	F	VF	XF	Unc	BU
1997 Proof	10,000	Value: 275				

KM# 145 25 DINERS
7.7700 g., 0.5850 Gold 0.1461 oz. AGW **Subject:** Human Rights **Obv:** Crowned arms **Rev:** Seated woman with quill

Date	Mintage	F	VF	XF	Unc	BU
1998 Proof	5,000	Value: 150				

KM# 63 50 DINERS
15.5500 g., 0.9990 Gold 0.4994 oz. AGW, 30 mm. **Obv:** Defiant Golden Eagle **Rev:** Arms within circle **Note:** There is a similar 1988 half-ounce without the denomination.

Date	Mintage	F	VF	XF	Unc	BU
1989	3,000	—	—	—		500
1989 Proof	—	Value: 550				

KM# 62 50 DINERS
17.0250 g., 0.9170 Gold 0.5019 oz. AGW, 29 mm. **Obv:** Arms within circle outlined with dots, value below **Rev:** Castle, Antoni Gaudi to left, two dates to right

Date	Mintage	F	VF	XF	Unc	BU
1990 Proof	3,000	Value: 500				

KM# 64 50 DINERS
15.5500 g., 0.9990 Gold 0.4994 oz. AGW, 27 mm.
Subject: Wildlife **Rev:** Red squirrel

Date	Mintage	F	VF	XF	Unc	BU
1990 Proof	2,500	Value: 500				

KM# 68 50 DINERS
15.5500 g., 0.9990 Gold 0.4994 oz. AGW, 27 mm.
Subject: Wildlife **Obv:** Crowned arms to left of five line inscription, value below, date below **Rev:** Chamois

Date	Mintage	F	VF	XF	Unc	BU
1991 Proof	Est. 2,500	Value: 500				

KM# 70 50 DINERS
13.3400 g., 0.5850 Gold 0.2509 oz. AGW, 27.5 mm. **Subject:** 1992 Summer Olympic Games **Obv:** Crowned arms to left of five line inscription, value below, date at bottom **Rev:** Gymnast on rings

Date	Mintage	F	VF	XF	Unc	BU
1991 Proof	3,000	Value: 275				

KM# 77 50 DINERS
15.5520 g., 0.9999 Gold 0.4999 oz. AGW, 27 mm.
Subject: Wildlife **Obv:** Crowned arms to left of five line inscription, value below, date at bottom **Rev:** Brown Bears

Date	Mintage	F	VF	XF	Unc	BU
1992 Proof	2,500	Value: 500				

KM# 82 50 DINERS
16.9650 g., 0.9160 Gold 0.4996 oz. AGW **Obv:** Crowned arms to left of five line inscription, value below, date at bottom **Rev:** Musician Pau Casals

Date	Mintage	F	VF	XF	Unc	BU
1993 Proof	5,000	Value: 500				

KM# 104 50 DINERS
155.5100 g., 0.9250 Silver 4.6246 oz. ASW, 65 mm. **Subject:** 1st Anniversary - Andorran Constitution **Obv:** Arms above "ECU" **Rev:** Seated woman with open scroll, within large letter "C", date below, value to right **Note:** Illustration reduced.

Date	Mintage	F	VF	XF	Unc	BU
1994	5,000	—	—	—	150	165

KM# 115 50 DINERS
155.5100 g., 0.9250 Silver 4.6246 oz. ASW, 65.8 mm.
Subject: 1996 Olympic Games **Obv:** Arms above date **Rev:** Angel lighting Olympic flame **Note:** Illustration reduced.

Date	Mintage	F	VF	XF	Unc	BU
1995	5,000	—	—	—	185	200

KM# 124 50 DINERS
155.5100 g., 0.9250 Silver 4.6246 oz. ASW, 65 mm.
Subject: Our Lady of Maritxell - Patroness of Andorra
Obv: Crowned arms in inner circle **Rev:** Enthroned Madonna and child **Note:** With insert of 2.5 g. 0.917 gold, 0.0737 AGW.
Illustration reduced.

Date	Mintage	F	VF	XF	Unc	BU
1996	5,000	—	—	—	225	240

KM# 224 50 DINERS
15.5500 g., 0.9999 Gold 0.4999 oz. AGW **Obv:** Fleury cross
Rev: Bust of Queen Isabella right

Date	Mintage	F	VF	XF	Unc	BU
1997 Proof	2,000	Value: 600				

KM# 152 50 DINERS
15.5520 g., 0.9160 Gold 0.4580 oz. AGW **Subject:** 250th Anniversary - Synod Constitution **Obv:** Clerical arms
Rev: Madonna and child

Date	Mintage	F	VF	XF	Unc	BU
1998 Proof	1,998	Value: 465				

KM# 41 100 DINERS
5.0000 g., 0.9990 Gold 0.1606 oz. AGW, 22 mm. **Obv:** Joan D.M. Bisbe D'Urgell I, left **Rev:** Value, date below, within crowned wreath

Date	Mintage	F	VF	XF	Unc	BU
1987	2,000	—	—	—	175	195

KM# 42 100 DINERS
5.0000 g., 0.9990 Gold 0.1606 oz. AGW **Obv:** Arms within circle **Rev:** Golden Eagle, mountains in background, date below

Date	Mintage	F	VF	XF	Unc	BU
1988	2,000	—	—	—	250	275

KM# 79 100 DINERS
31.1035 g., 0.9990 Gold 0.9990 oz. AGW, 35 mm. **Obv:** Defiant eagle above value **Note:** There is a similar 1988 one-ounce without the denomination.

Date	Mintage	F	VF	XF	Unc	BU
1989	3,000	—	—	—	875	1,000

KM# 94 100 DINERS
31.1035 g., 0.9990 Gold 0.9990 oz. AGW **Obv:** Defiant Golden Eagle, date below **Rev:** Value within crowned wreath

Date	Mintage	F	VF	XF	Unc	BU
1992		—	—	—	875	1,000

KM# 45 250 DINERS
12.0000 g., 0.9990 Gold 0.3854 oz. AGW, 28.1 mm.
Subject: 700th Anniversary - Andorra's Governing Charter
Obv: Fleury cross, value at bottom **Rev:** Grasped hands, right hand armored, left hand has mark on back

Date	Mintage	F	VF	XF	Unc	BU
ND(1988)	3,000	—	—	—	345	375

KM# 30 SOVEREIGN
8.0000 g., 0.9180 Gold 0.2361 oz. AGW **Obv:** Joan D.M. Bisbe D'Urgell I, left **Rev:** Divided arms, value at top **Note:** Latin legend.

Date	Mintage	F	VF	XF	Unc	BU
1982	1,500	—	—	—	220	250

KM# 31 SOVEREIGN
8.0000 g., 0.9180 Gold 0.2361 oz. AGW **Obv:** Joan D.M. Bisbe D'Urgell I, left **Rev:** Divided arms, value at top **Note:** Catalan legend.

Date	Mintage	F	VF	XF	Unc	BU
1982	1,500	—	—	—	220	250

KM# 32 SOVEREIGN
8.0000 g., 0.9180 Gold 0.2361 oz. AGW **Obv:** Joan D.M. Bisbe D'Urgell I, right **Rev:** Crowned arms flanked by cherubs, value below **Note:** Latin legends.

Date	Mintage	F	VF	XF	Unc	BU
1983	1,500	—	—	—	220	250

PATTERNS

KM#	Date	Mintage	Identification	Mkt Val
Pn1	1987	—	2 Diners. Nickel Plated Bronze. KM#46.	140
Pn2	1992	2	50 Diners. 0.9999 Gold. 15.5500 g. Defiant eagle. Prev. KM#93.	—
Pn3	1994	2	5 Diners. 0.9999 Gold. 1.5600 g. Defiant eagle. KM# 112.	—
Pn4	1994	2	10 Diners. 0.9999 Gold. 3.1100 g. Defiant eagle.	—
Pn5	1994	2	25 Diners. 0.9999 Gold. 7.7800 g. Defiant eagle.	—
Pn6	1994	2	50 Diners. 0.9999 Gold. 15.5500 g. Defiant eagle.	—

MINT SETS

KM#	Date	Mintage	Identification	Issue Price	Mkt Val
MS1	1986 (5)	—	KM#33, 35-38	31.00	75.00

PROOF SETS

KM#	Date	Mintage	Identification	Issue Price	Mkt Val
PS1	1963 (2)	1,000	KM#M3, M4	51.00	60.00
PS2	1964 (2)	—	M5, M6	51.00	60.00
PS4	1965 (2)	—	M7, M8	80.00	65.00

ANGOLA

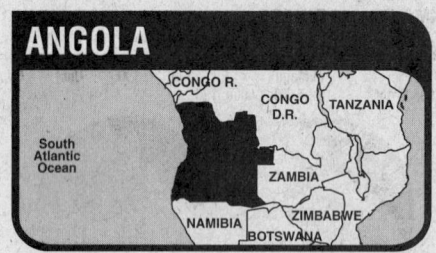

The Republic of Angola, a country on the west coast of southern Africa bounded by Congo Democratic Republic, Zambia, and Namibia (Southwest Africa), has an area of 481,351 sq. mi. (1,246,700 sq. km.) and a population of 12.78 million, predominantly Bantu in origin. Capital: Luanda. Most of the people are engaged in subsistence agriculture. However, important oil and mineral deposits make Angola potentially one of the richest countries in Africa. Iron and diamonds are exported.

The Portuguese navigator, Diogo Cao, discovered Angola in 1482 Angola. Portuguese settlers arrived in 1491, and established Angola as a major slaving center, which sent about 3 million slaves to the New World.

A revolt, characterized by guerrilla warfare, against Portuguese rule began in 1961 and continued until 1974, when a new regime in Portugal offered independence. The independence movement was actively supported by three groups; the National Front, based in Zaire, the Soviet-backed Popular Movement, and the moderate National Union. Independence was proclaimed on Nov. 11, 1975, and the Portuguese departed, leaving the Angolan people to work out their own political destiny. Within hours, each of the independence groups proclaimed itself Angola's sole ruler. A bloody intertribal civil war erupted in which the Communist Popular Movement, assisted by Soviet arms and Cuban mercenaries, was the eventual victor.

RULER
Portuguese until 1975

MINT MARK
KN - King's Norton

PORTUGUESE COLONY

DECIMAL COINAGE
Commencing 1910

100 Centavos = 20 Macutas = 1 Escudo

100 Centavos = 1 Escudo

KM# 60   CENTAVO
Bronze   **Obv:** Value **Rev:** Arms, date below

Date	Mintage	F	VF	XF	Unc	BU
1921	1,360,000	7.50	20.00	60.00	125	170

KM# 61   2 CENTAVOS
Bronze   **Obv:** Value **Rev:** Arms, date below

Date	Mintage	F	VF	XF	Unc	BU
1921	530,000	10.00	15.00	60.00	135	—

KM# 62   5 CENTAVOS
Bronze   **Obv:** Value **Rev:** Arms, date below

Date	Mintage	F	VF	XF	Unc	BU
1921	720,000	5.00	18.00	45.00	80.00	—
1922	5,680,000	4.00	14.00	30.00	55.00	90.00
1923	5,840,000	4.00	14.00	30.00	55.00	90.00
1924	—	12.00	35.00	70.00	140	—

KM# 66   5 CENTAVOS (1 Macuta)
Nickel-Bronze   **Obv:** Head left **Rev:** Arms, value below

Date	Mintage	F	VF	XF	Unc	BU
1927	2,001,999	2.50	6.00	15.00	27.50	—

KM# 63   10 CENTAVOS
Copper-Nickel   **Obv:** Value **Rev:** Head, left

Date	Mintage	F	VF	XF	Unc	BU
1921	160,000	10.00	30.00	65.00	120	—
1922	340,000	7.50	15.00	45.00	85.00	175
1923	2,960,000	3.50	8.00	20.00	45.00	115

KM# 70   10 CENTAVOS
Bronze, 17.8 mm.   **Subject:** 300th Anniversary - Revolution of 1648 **Obv:** Value **Rev:** Five crowns above arms, date below **Edge:** Plain

Date	Mintage	F	VF	XF	Unc	BU
1948	10,000,000	0.50	1.00	3.50	7.50	10.00
1949	10,000,000	0.35	0.75	3.00	6.50	9.00

KM# 82   10 CENTAVOS
Aluminum   **Obv:** Value **Rev:** Five crowns above arms, date below

Date	Mintage	F	VF	XF	Unc	BU
1974	4,000,000	—	—	—	17.50	22.00

Note: Not released for circulation, but relatively available

KM# 67   10 CENTAVOS (2 Macutas)
Copper-Nickel   **Obv:** Head, left **Rev:** Arms, value below

Date	Mintage	F	VF	XF	Unc	BU
1927	2,003,000	2.00	4.00	16.00	32.00	—
1928	1,000,000	2.00	4.00	16.00	32.00	45.00

KM# 64   20 CENTAVOS
Copper-Nickel   **Obv:** Value **Rev:** Head left

Date	Mintage	F	VF	XF	Unc	BU
1921	2,115,000	4.00	9.00	22.00	40.00	100
1922	1,730,000	6.50	14.50	35.00	65.00	—

KM# 71   20 CENTAVOS
2.8400 g., Bronze, 20.5 mm.   **Subject:** 300th Anniversary - Revolution of 1648 **Obv:** Value **Rev:** Five crowns above arms, date below **Edge:** Plain

Date	Mintage	F	VF	XF	Unc	BU
1948	7,850,000	0.50	1.00	2.00	4.50	25.00
1949	2,150,000	10.00	30.00	60.00	100	140

KM# 78   20 CENTAVOS
Bronze, 18.2 mm.   **Obv:** Value **Rev:** Five crowns above arms, date below **Edge:** Plain

Date	Mintage	F	VF	XF	Unc	BU
1962	3,000,000	—	0.25	0.65	1.75	—

KM# 68   20 CENTAVOS (4 Macutas)
Copper-Nickel   **Obv:** Laureled head, left **Rev:** Arms, value below

Date	Mintage	F	VF	XF	Unc	BU
1927	2,001,000	2.50	4.00	12.00	25.00	—
1928	500,000	3.50	6.00	20.00	35.00	50.00

KM# 65   50 CENTAVOS
Nickel   **Obv:** Head left, date below **Rev:** Arms, value in legend

Date	Mintage	F	VF	XF	Unc	BU
1922	6,000,000	3.00	10.00	25.00	40.00	—
1923	6,000,000	3.00	10.00	25.00	40.00	—
1923 KN	Inc. above	—	—	225	375	—

Note: Not released for circulation

KM# 69   50 CENTAVOS
Nickel-Bronze   **Obv:** Laureled, hooded bust with long hair, left **Rev:** Arms, value below

Date	Mintage	F	VF	XF	Unc	BU
1927	1,608,000	5.00	18.00	35.00	70.00	—
1928/7	1,600,000	5.00	18.00	40.00	75.00	—
1928	Inc. above	3.50	12.50	30.00	65.00	—

KM# 72   50 CENTAVOS
Nickel-Bronze   **Subject:** 300th Anniversary - Revolution of 1648 **Obv:** Value **Rev:** Five crowns above arms, date below

Date	Mintage	F	VF	XF	Unc	BU
1948	4,000,000	0.50	1.00	5.00	12.00	27.50
1950	4,000,000	0.50	1.00	5.00	12.00	27.50

KM# 75   50 CENTAVOS
4.0700 g., Bronze, 20 mm.   **Obv:** Value **Rev:** Five crowns above arms, date below **Edge:** Plain

Date	Mintage	F	VF	XF	Unc	BU
1953	5,000,000	—	0.25	0.65	2.50	6.00
1954	11,731,000	—	0.20	0.40	1.75	4.50
1955 Rare	1,126,000	—	3.00	10.00	40.00	85.00
1957	8,873,000	—	0.20	0.45	2.00	4.50
1958	17,520,000	—	0.15	0.35	1.50	4.00
1961	8,750,000	—	0.20	0.45	2.00	4.50

KM# 75a   50 CENTAVOS
Copper-Nickel

Date	Mintage	F	VF	XF	Unc	BU
1974	150	—	—	125	250	—

Note: Not released for circulation

KM# 76   ESCUDO
8.0200 g., Bronze, 26 mm.   **Obv:** Value **Rev:** Five crowns above arms, date below

Date	Mintage	F	VF	XF	Unc	BU
1953	2,001,000	—	1.50	6.00	15.00	—
1956	2,989,000	—	1.00	4.00	10.00	—
1963	5,000,000	—	1.00	2.00	7.00	18.00
1965	5,000,000	—	1.00	2.00	7.00	18.00
1972	10,000,000	—	0.75	1.50	4.50	10.00
1974	6,214,000	—	0.75	1.50	4.50	15.00

KM# 76a   ESCUDO
Copper-Nickel   **Note:** Not released for circulation.

Date	Mintage	F	VF	XF	Unc	BU
1972 Rare	—	—	—	—	—	—
1974 Rare	—	—	—	—	—	—

KM# 77   2-1/2 ESCUDOS
3.5300 g., Copper-Nickel, 20 mm.   **Obv:** Arms, date below **Rev:** Five crowns above arms, value below **Edge:** Reeded

Date	Mintage	F	VF	XF	Unc	BU
1953	6,008,000	—	1.00	7.00	15.00	27.50
1956	9,992,000	—	0.35	2.00	4.00	9.50

Date	Mintage	F	VF	XF	Unc	BU
1967	6,000,000	—	0.35	2.00	4.00	9.50
1968	5,000,000	—	0.35	2.00	4.00	9.50
1969	5,000,000	—	0.35	2.00	4.00	9.50
1974	19,999,000	—	0.25	1.00	3.00	9.00

KM# 81   5 ESCUDOS
Copper-Nickel   **Obv:** Arms, date below **Rev:** Five crowns above arms, value below

Date	Mintage	F	VF	XF	Unc	BU
1972	8,000,000	—	10.00	20.00	45.00	80.00
1974	Est. 3,343,000	—	—	250	450	

Note: Not released for circulation

KM# 73   10 ESCUDOS
5.0000 g., 0.7200 Silver 0.1157 oz. ASW, 24.0 mm.   **Obv:** Arms, date below **Rev:** Five crowns above arms, value below

Date	Mintage	F	VF	XF	Unc	BU
1952	2,023,000	—	2.50	5.00	10.00	20.00
1955	1,977,000	—	2.50	5.00	10.00	20.00

KM# 79   10 ESCUDOS
Copper-Nickel   **Obv:** Arms, date below **Rev:** Five crowns above arms, value below

Date	Mintage	F	VF	XF	Unc	BU
1969	3,022,000	—	1.50	3.00	6.00	14.50
1970	978,000	—	2.00	4.00	7.00	18.00

KM# 74   20 ESCUDOS
10.0000 g., 0.7200 Silver 0.2315 oz. ASW   **Obv:** Arms, date below **Rev:** Five crowns above arms, value below

Date	Mintage	F	VF	XF	Unc	BU
1952	1,002,999	—	4.75	7.00	14.00	32.50
1955	997,000	—	4.75	6.00	12.00	28.00

KM# 80   20 ESCUDOS
12.0600 g., Nickel   **Obv:** Arms on ornate shield, date below **Rev:** Arms, value below

Date	Mintage	F	VF	XF	Unc	BU
1971	1,572,000	—	0.75	2.00	4.00	7.50
1972	428,000	—	2.50	5.00	10.00	30.00

PEOPLES REPUBLIC
DECIMAL COINAGE
1975 - 1998

100 Lwei = 1 Kwanza

KM# 90   50 LWEI
Copper-Nickel   **Obv:** National arms **Rev:** Large value, dots near rim

Date	Mintage	F	VF	XF	Unc	BU
ND(1977)	—	—	0.15	0.35	1.25	2.50
1979	—	—	0.10	0.30	1.00	1.50

KM# 83   KWANZA
3.9100 g., Copper-Nickel, 20.9 mm.   **Obv:** National arms **Rev:** Large value, dots near rim

Date	Mintage	F	VF	XF	Unc	BU
ND(1977)	—	—	0.30	0.50	1.50	—
1978	—	—	0.25	0.40	1.50	—
1979	—	—	0.25	0.40	1.50	—

KM# 84   2 KWANZAS
5.0000 g., Copper-Nickel, 23.2 mm.   **Obv:** National arms **Rev:** Large value, dots near rim

Date	Mintage	F	VF	XF	Unc	BU
ND(1977)	—	—	0.40	0.60	1.75	—

KM# 85   5 KWANZAS
6.9000 g., Copper-Nickel, 25.5 mm.   **Obv:** National arms **Rev:** Large value, dots near rim

Date	Mintage	F	VF	XF	Unc	BU
ND(1977)	—	—	0.65	1.25	3.00	—

KM# 86.1   10 KWANZAS
Copper-Nickel   **Obv:** National arms **Rev:** Small date, dots near rim, Large value

Date	Mintage	F	VF	XF	Unc	BU
ND(1977)	—	—	1.25	2.00	3.50	—
1978	—	—	1.50	2.50	4.50	—

KM# 86.2   10 KWANZAS
Copper-Nickel   **Rev:** Large date, dots away from rim

Date	Mintage	F	VF	XF	Unc	BU
1978	—	—	1.50	2.50	4.50	—

KM# 87   20 KWANZAS
10.0000 g., Copper-Nickel   **Obv:** National arms **Rev:** Large value, dots near rim

Date	Mintage	F	VF	XF	Unc	BU
1978	—	—	2.00	3.00	6.00	—

KM# 91   50 KWANZAS
Copper   **Obv:** National arms **Rev:** Large value, dots near rim

Date	Mintage	F	VF	XF	Unc	BU
ND(1991)	—	—	2.50	4.50	9.00	—

KM# 101   50 KWANZAS
Copper Clad Steel, 23.3 mm.   **Subject:** 15th Anniversary of the Angolan Kwanza Currency **Obv:** National arms within legend **Rev:** Value above anniversary date "8 Jan. 92" **Edge:** Reeded

Date	Mintage	F	VF	XF	Unc	BU
ND(1992)	—	—	55.00	90.00	—	—

KM# 92   100 KWANZAS
Copper   **Obv:** National arms **Rev:** Large value, dots near rim

Date	Mintage	F	VF	XF	Unc	BU
ND(1991)	—	—	3.50	6.50	14.00	—

REFORM COINAGE
1999 -

KM# 95   10 CENTIMOS
1.5000 g., Copper Plated Steel, 15 mm.   **Obv:** National arms, country name and date **Rev:** Denomination **Edge:** Plain

Date	Mintage	F	VF	XF	Unc	BU
1999	—	—	—	—	0.50	—

KM# 96   50 CENTIMOS
3.0000 g., Copper Plated Steel, 18 mm.   **Obv:** National arms, country name and date **Rev:** Denomination **Edge:** Plain

Date	Mintage	F	VF	XF	Unc	BU
1999	—	—	—	—	1.00	—

KM# 97   KWANZA
4.5000 g., Nickel Plated Steel, 21 mm.   **Obv:** National arms, country name and date **Rev:** Denomination **Edge:** Reeded

Date	Mintage	F	VF	XF	Unc	BU
1999	—	—	—	—	1.50	—

KM# 98   2 KWANZAS
5.0000 g., Nickel Plated Steel, 22 mm.   **Obv:** National arms, country name and date **Rev:** Denomination **Edge:** Reeded

Date	Mintage	F	VF	XF	Unc	BU
1999	—	—	—	—	2.00	—

KM# 99   5 KWANZAS
7.0000 g., Nickel Plated Steel, 26 mm.   **Obv:** National arms, country name and date **Rev:** Denomination **Edge:** Reeded

Date	Mintage	F	VF	XF	Unc	BU
1999	—	—	—	—	3.50	—

KM# 93 10 KWANZAS
24.2250 g., Copper-Nickel **Subject:** Olympics **Obv:** National arms **Rev:** Olympic logo and allegory **Edge:** Reeded

Date	Mintage	F	VF	XF	Unc	BU
1999 Proof	— Value: 13.50					

KM# 100 10 KWANZAS
23.0500 g., Nickel Plated Steel **Subject:** Prince Henry the Navigator **Obv:** National arms **Rev:** Prince Henry in armor 3/4 left **Edge:** Reeded

Date	Mintage	F	VF	XF	Unc	BU
1999 Proof	10,000	Value: 15.00				

KM# 94 100 KWANZAS
25.0000 g., 0.9250 Silver 0.7435 oz. ASW **Subject:** Olympics **Obv:** National arms **Rev:** Olympic logo and Allegory

Date	Mintage	F	VF	XF	Unc	BU
1999 Proof	— Value: 30.00					

KM# 102 100 KWANZAS
25.0000 g., 0.9250 Silver 0.7435 oz. ASW **Subject:** Prince Henry the Navigator **Obv:** National arms **Rev:** Bust of Prince Henry in armor 3/4 left **Edge:** Reeded

Date	Mintage	F	VF	XF	Unc	BU
1999 Proof	10,000	Value: 60.00				

PATTERNS
Including off metal strikes

KM#	Date	Mintage Identification	Mkt Val
Pn7	1972	— 50 Escudos. Silver. Shield within circle. Cross with winged arms and waves on top.	1,500

PROVAS
Raised or stamped "PROVA" in field

KM#	Date	Mintage Identification	Issue Price	Mkt Val
Pr1	1921	— Centavo. Bronze. KM#60.	—	95.00
Pr2	1921	— 2 Centavos. Bronze center. KM#61.	—	135
Pr2	1921	— 2 Centavos. Bronze center. KM#61.	—	135
Pr3	1921	— 5 Centavos. Bronze. KM#62.	—	80.00
Pr4	1921	— 10 Centavos. Copper-Nickel. KM#63.	—	110
Pr5	1921	— 20 Centavos. Copper-Nickel. KM#64.	—	40.00
Pr6	1922	— 5 Centavos. Bronze. KM#62.	—	55.00
Pr7	1922	— 10 Centavos. Copper-Nickel. KM#63.	—	80.00
Pr8	1922	— 20 Centavos. Copper-Nickel. KM#64.	—	65.00
Pr9	1923	— 5 Centavos. Bronze. KM#62.	—	55.00
Pr10	1923	— 10 Centavos. Copper-Nickel. KM#63.	—	45.00
Pr12	1924	— 5 Centavos. Bronze. KM#62.	—	135
Pr13	1927	— 5 Centavos. Nickel-Bronze. KM#66.	—	35.00
Pr14	1927	— 10 Centavos. Copper-Nickel. KM#67.	—	35.00
Pr15	1927	— 20 Centavos. Copper-Nickel. KM#68.	—	30.00
Pr16	1927	— 50 Centavos. Nickel-Bronze. KM#69.	—	65.00
Pr17	1928	— 10 Centavos. Copper-Nickel. KM#67.	—	40.00
Pr18	1928	— 20 Centavos. Copper-Nickel. KM#68.	—	40.00
Pr19	1928	— 50 Centavos. Nickel-Bronze. KM#69.	—	65.00
Pr20	1948	— 10 Centavos. Bronze. KM#70.	—	22.50
Pr21	1948	— 20 Centavos. Bronze. KM#71.	—	22.50
Pr22	1948	— 50 Centavos. Nickel-Bronze. KM#72.	—	22.50
Pr23	1949	— 10 Centavos. Bronze. KM#70.	—	22.50
Pr24	1949	— 20 Centavos. Bronze. KM#71.	—	22.50
Pr25	1949	— 50 Centavos. Nickel-Bronze. KM#72.	—	22.50
Pr26	1950	— 50 Centavos. Nickel-Bronze. KM#72.	—	20.00
Pr27	1952	— 10 Escudos. Silver. KM#73.	—	30.00
Pr28	1952	— 20 Escudos. Silver. KM#74.	—	45.00
Pr29	1953	— 50 Centavos. Bronze. KM#75.	—	20.00
Pr30	1953	— Escudo. Bronze. KM#76.	—	22.50
Pr31	1953	— 2-1/2 Escudos. Copper-Nickel. KM#77.	—	32.00
Pr32	1954	— 50 Centavos. Bronze. KM#75.	—	20.00
Pr33	1954	— Escudo. Bronze. KM#76.	—	22.50
Pr34	1954	— 2-1/2 Escudos. Copper-Nickel. KM#77.	—	32.00
Pr35	1955	— 50 Centavos. Bronze. KM#75.	—	20.00
Pr36	1955	— Escudo. Bronze. KM#76.	—	22.50
Pr37	1955	— 2-1/2 Escudos. Copper-Nickel. KM#77.	—	32.00
Pr38	1955	— 10 Escudos. Silver. KM#73.	—	32.00
Pr39	1955	— 20 Escudos. Silver. KM#74.	—	45.00
Pr40	1956	— 50 Centavos. Bronze. KM#75.	—	15.00
Pr41	1956	— Escudo. Bronze. KM#76.	—	15.00
Pr42	1956	— 2-1/2 Escudos. Copper-Nickel. KM#77.	—	15.00
Pr43	1957	— 50 Centavos. Bronze. KM#75.	—	15.00
Pr44	1957	— Escudo. Bronze center. KM#76.	—	15.00
Pr45	1957	— 2-1/2 Escudos. Copper-Nickel. KM#77.	—	15.00
Pr46	1958	— 50 Centavos. Bronze center. KM#75.	—	15.00
Pr47	1958	— Escudo. Bronze. KM#76.	—	15.00
Pr48	1958	— 2-1/2 Escudos. Copper-Nickel. KM#77.	—	15.00
Pr49	1959	— 50 Centavos. Bronze. KM#75.	—	15.00
Pr50	1959	— Escudo. Bronze. KM#76.	—	15.00
Pr51	1959	— 2-1/2 Escudos. Copper-Nickel. KM#77.	—	15.00
Pr52	1960	— 50 Centavos. Bronze. KM#75.	—	15.00
Pr53	1960	— Escudo. Bronze. KM#76.	—	15.00
Pr54	1960	— 2-1/2 Escudos. Copper-Nickel. KM#77.	—	15.00
Pr55	1961	— 50 Centavos. Bronze. KM#75.	—	15.00
Pr56	1961	— Escudo. Bronze. KM#76.	—	15.00
Pr57	1961	— 2-1/2 Escudos. Copper-Nickel. KM#77.	—	15.00
Pr58	1962	— 20 Centavos. Bronze. KM#78.	—	15.00
Pr59	1962	— Escudo. Bronze. KM#76.	—	15.00
Pr60	1962	— 2-1/2 Escudos. Copper-Nickel. KM#77.	—	15.00
Pr61	1963	— Escudo. Bronze. KM#76.	—	15.00
Pr62	1963	— 2-1/2 Escudos. Copper-Nickel. KM#77.	—	15.00
Pr63	1964	— Escudo. Bronze. KM#76.	—	15.00
Pr64	1964	— 2-1/2 Escudos. Copper-Nickel. KM#77.	—	15.00
Pr65	1965	— Escudo. Bronze. KM#76.	—	15.00
Pr66	1965	— 2-1/2 Escudos. Copper-Nickel. KM#77.	—	15.00
Pr67	1966	— Escudo. Bronze. KM#76.	—	15.00
Pr68	1966	— 2-1/2 Escudos. Copper-Nickel. KM#77.	—	15.00
Pr69	1967	— Escudo. Bronze. KM#76.	—	15.00
Pr70	1967	— 2-1/2 Escudos. Copper-Nickel. KM#77.	—	15.00
Pr71	1968	— Escudo. Bronze. KM#76.	—	15.00
Pr72	1968	— 2-1/2 Escudos. Copper-Nickel. KM#77.	—	15.00
Pr73	1969	— Escudo. Bronze. KM#76.	—	15.00
Pr74	1969	— 2-1/2 Escudos. Copper-Nickel. KM#77.	—	15.00
Pr75	1969	— 10 Escudos. Copper-Nickel. KM#79.	—	15.00
Pr76	1970	— Escudo. Bronze. KM#76.	—	15.00
Pr77	1970	— 2-1/2 Escudos. Copper-Nickel. KM#77.	—	15.00
Pr78	1970	— 10 Escudos. Copper-Nickel. KM#79.	—	15.00
Pr79	1971	— Escudo. Bronze. KM#76.	—	15.00
Pr80	1971	— 2-1/2 Escudos. Copper-Nickel. KM#77.	—	15.00
Pr81	1971	— 20 Escudos. Nickel. KM#80.	—	15.00
Pr82	1972	— Escudo. Bronze. KM#76.	—	15.00
Pr83	1972	— 2-1/2 Escudos. Copper-Nickel. KM#77.	—	15.00
Pr84	1972	— 5 Escudos. Copper-Nickel. KM#81.	—	15.00
Pr85	1972	— 20 Escudos. Nickel. KM#80.	—	15.00
Pr86	1974	— Escudo. Bronze. KM#76.	—	15.00

MINT SETS

KM#	Date	Mintage Identification	Issue Price	Mkt Val
MS1	ND (1979) (6)	— KM#83, 84, 85, 86.2, 87, 90 This set was assembled by the National Bank of Angola in a folder which presents a brief monetary history of Angola including some banknote pictures.	20.00	20.00

ANGUILLA

The British dependency of Anguilla, a self-governing British territory situated in the east Caribbean Sea about 60 miles (100 km.) northwest of St. Kitts, has an area of 35 sq. mi. (91 sq. km.) and an approximate population of 12,000. Capital: The Valley. In recent years, tourism has replaced the traditional fishing, stock raising and salt production as the main industry.

Anguilla was discovered by Columbus in 1493 and became a British colony in 1650. As the other British areas in the West Indies did, Anguilla officially adapted to sterling beginning in 1825. From 1950 to 1965, Anguilla was a member of the British Caribbean Territories (Eastern Group) Currency Board, whose coinage it used. In March 1967, Anguilla was joined politically with St. Christopher (St. Kitts), as it had been for much of its colonial history, and Nevis to form a British associated state.

On June 16, 1967, the Provisional Government of Anguilla unilaterally declared its independence and seceded from the Federation. Later, on July 11, 1967, a vote of confidence was taken and the results favored independence. Britain refused to accept the declaration (nor did any other country recognize it) and appointed a British administrator whom Anguilla accepted. However, in Feb. 1969 Anguilla ousted the British emissary, voted to sever all ties with Britain, and established the Republic of Anguilla. The following month Britain landed a force of paratroopers and policemen. This bloodless counteraction ended the self-proclaimed republic and resulted in the installation of a governing commissioner. The troops were withdrawn in Sept. 1969, and the Anguilla Act of July 1971 placed Anguilla directly under British control. A new constitution in 1976 established Anguilla as a self-governing British dependant territory. Britain retains power over defense, police and civil service, and foreign affairs. Since 1981, Anguilla has employed the coinage of the East Caribbean States.

NOTE: There is no evidence that the issues of the self-proclaimed Provisional Government ever actually circulated. The c/s series most likely served as souvenirs of the "revolution".

RULER
British

BRITISH DEPENDANT TERRITORY
DECIMAL COINAGE

KM# 15 1/2 DOLLAR
3.6100 g., 0.9990 Silver 0.1159 oz. ASW **Obv:** St. Mary's Church **Rev:** State arms

Date	Mintage	F	VF	XF	Unc	BU
ND Proof	4,200	Value: 25.00				
1969 Proof	—	Value: 25.00				
1970 Proof	Inc. above	Value: 25.00				

KM# 16 DOLLAR
7.1800 g., 0.9990 Silver 0.2306 oz. ASW **Obv:** Map - Seahorse, Caribbean Silver Lobster, Shell **Rev:** State arms

Date	Mintage	F	VF	XF	Unc	BU
ND Proof	4,450	Value: 30.00				
1969 Proof	—	Value: 30.00				
1970 Proof	Inc. above	Value: 30.00				

KM# 17 2 DOLLARS
14.1400 g., 0.9990 Silver 0.4541 oz. ASW **Obv:** National flag and map **Rev:** State arms

Date	Mintage	F	VF	XF	Unc	BU
ND Proof	4,150	Value: 40.00				
1969 Proof	—	Value: 40.00				
1970 Proof	Inc. above	Value: 40.00				

KM# 18.1 4 DOLLARS
28.4800 g., 0.9990 Silver 0.9147 oz. ASW, 40 mm. **Obv:** Ship - Atlantic Star **Rev:** State arms, value at bottom

Date	Mintage	F	VF	XF	Unc	BU
ND Proof	5,100	Value: 70.00				
1969 Proof	—	Value: 70.00				
1970 Proof	Inc. above	Value: 70.00				

KM# 18.2 4 DOLLARS
28.4800 g., 0.9990 Silver 0.9147 oz. ASW, 40 mm. **Obv:** Ship- Atlantic Star **Rev:** 2 hallmarks at 4 o'clock, state arms, value at bottom

Date	Mintage	F	VF	XF	Unc	BU
1970 Proof	—	Value: 100				

KM# 20 5 DOLLARS
2.4600 g., 0.9000 Gold 0.0712 oz. AGW **Obv:** Methodist Church of West End

Date	Mintage	F	VF	XF	Unc	BU
ND Proof	1,925	Value: 85.00				
1969 Proof	Inc. above	Value: 85.00				
1970 Proof	Inc. above	Value: 85.00				

KM# 21 10 DOLLARS
4.9300 g., 0.9000 Gold 0.1426 oz. AGW **Obv:** Dolphin, Caribbean Silver Lobster, Starfish

Date	Mintage	F	VF	XF	Unc	BU
ND Proof	1,615	Value: 150				
1969 Proof	Inc. above	Value: 150				
1970 Proof	Inc. above	Value: 150				

KM# 22 20 DOLLARS
9.8700 g., 0.9000 Gold 0.2856 oz. AGW **Obv:** Mermaids

Date	Mintage	F	VF	XF	Unc	BU
ND Proof	1,395	Value: 300				
1969 Proof	Inc. above	Value: 300				
1970 Proof	Inc. above	Value: 300				

KM# 26 25 DOLLARS
31.0000 g., 0.9990 Silver 0.9956 oz. ASW **Subject:** 1st Year of Independence **Obv:** Three intertwined dolphins form circle **Rev:** President Ronald Webster bust left

Date	Mintage	F	VF	XF	Unc	BU
1968 Proof	—	Value: 70.00				

KM# 23 100 DOLLARS
49.3700 g., 0.9000 Gold 1.4285 oz. AGW **Subject:** Demonstrating Population **Obv:** People of Anguilla within beaded circle, grain spray below circle

Date	Mintage	F	VF	XF	Unc	BU
ND Proof	710	Value: 1,400				
1969 Proof	—	Value: 1,400				
1970 Proof	Inc. above	Value: 1,400				

KM# 27 200 DOLLARS
38.0000 g., 0.9170 Gold 1.1203 oz. AGW **Subject:** 1st Year of Independence **Obv:** Three intertwined dolphins form circle **Rev:** President Ronald Webster bust left

Date	Mintage	F	VF	XF	Unc	BU
1968 Proof	—	Value: 1,150				

KM# 28 1500 DOLLARS
62.0000 g., 0.9990 Platinum 1.9913 oz. APW **Subject:** 1st Year of Independence **Obv:** Three intertwined dolphins form circle **Rev:** President Ronald Wester bust facing left

Date	Mintage	F	VF	XF	Unc	BU
1968 Proof	—	Value: 4,000				

TRIAL STRIKES

KM#	Date	Mintage	Identification	Mkt Val
TS1	ND (1969)	—	5 Dollars. Goldine-Brass. 1.5100 g. 50 mm. Design of KM-20. Blank with MET countermark. Reeded edge. Uniface.	75.00
TS2	1969	—	100 Dollars. Goldine. 50 mm.	—
	1969	—	100 Dollars. Goldine. 50 mm.	—
TS3	ND (1969)	—	5 Dollars. Goldine-Brass. 29.2100 g. 14 mm. Design of KM-23. Blank with MET countermark. Reeded edge.	200

PROOF SETS

KM#	Date	Mintage	Identification	Issue Price	Mkt Val
PS1	1969 (8)	—	KM#15-18.1, 20-23	226	1,650
PS2	1969 (4)	—	KM#15-18.1	25.50	165
PS3	1969 (4)	—	KM#20-23	200	1,500
PS4	1970 (8)	—	KM#15-18.1, 20-23	226	1,650
PS5	1970 (4)	—	KM#15-18.1	25.50	165
PS6	1970 (4)	—	KM#20-23	200	1,500

ANTIGUA & BARBUDA

Antigua and Barbuda are located on the eastern edge of the Leeward Islands in the Caribbean Sea, have an area of 170 sq. mi. (440 sq. km.) and an estimated population of 68,000. Capital: St. John's. Prior to 1967, Antigua and its dependencies Barbuda and Redonda, comprised a presidency of the Leeward Islands. The mountainous island produces sugar, molasses, rum, cotton and fruit. Tourism is making an increasingly valuable contribution to the economy.

Antigua was discovered by Columbus in 1493, settled by British colonists from St. Kitts in 1632, occupied by the French in 1666, and ceded to Britain in 1667. It became an associated state with internal self-government on February 27, 1967. On November 1, 1981 it became independent as Antigua and Barbuda. As a constitutional monarchy, Elizabeth II is Queen of Antigua and Barbuda and Head of State.

Spanish silver coinage and French colonial "Black Dogs" were used throughout the islands' early history; however, late in the seventeenth century the introduction of British tin farthings was attempted with complete lack of success. In 1822, British colonial Anchor Money was introduced.

From 1825 to 1955, Antigua was on the sterling standard and used British coins. Coins of the British Caribbean Territories (Eastern Group) and East Caribbean States circulated from 1955, and banknotes of East Caribbean Currency Authority are now used on the island. The early coinage was augmented by that of the East Caribbean States in 1981.

RULER
British

ANTIGUA
BRITISH ADMINISTRATION
DECIMAL COINAGE

100 Cents = 1 Dollar

KM# 1   4 DOLLARS
28.3000 g., Copper-Nickel, 38.5 mm.   **Ruler:** Elizabeth II
Series: F.A.O. **Obv:** Helmeted arms with supporters, date below
Rev: Value at bottom divides sugar cane and banana tree branch
Edge: Reeded

Date	Mintage	F	VF	XF	Unc	BU
1970	14,000	—	6.00	10.00	20.00	30.00
1970 Proof	2,000	Value: 35.00				

Note: For similar issues see Barbados, Dominica, Grenada, Montserrat, St. Kitts, St. Lucia and St. Vincent.

ANTIGUA & BARBUDA
BRITISH ADMINISTRATION
DECIMAL COINAGE

KM# 5   10 DOLLARS
Copper-Nickel, 38.8 mm.   **Ruler:** Elizabeth II **Subject:** Royal Visit **Obv:** Crowned bust right **Rev:** Arms

Date	Mintage	F	VF	XF	Unc	BU
1985	100,000	—	—	—	25.00	35.00

KM# 5a   10 DOLLARS
28.2800 g., 0.9250 Silver 0.8410 oz. ASW **Ruler:** Elizabeth II
Subject: Royal Visit **Obv:** Crowned bust right **Rev:** Arms

Date	Mintage	F	VF	XF	Unc	BU
1985 Proof	5,000	Value: 50.00				

KM# 2   30 DOLLARS
31.1000 g., 0.5000 Silver 0.4999 oz. ASW **Ruler:** Elizabeth II
Subject: George Washington - Yorktown, 1781 **Obv:** Helmeted arms, date below, value at bottom **Rev:** George Washington between two figures, lighting cannon

Date	Mintage	F	VF	XF	Unc	BU
1982 Proof	1,200	Value: 60.00				

KM# 3   30 DOLLARS
31.1000 g., 0.5000 Silver 0.4999 oz. ASW **Ruler:** Elizabeth II
Subject: George Washington - Inauguration, 1789
Obv: Helmeted arms, date below, value at bottom **Rev:** George Washington and men rowing across the Delaware

Date	Mintage	F	VF	XF	Unc	BU
1982 Proof	1,125	Value: 60.00				

KM# 4   30 DOLLARS
31.3000 g., 0.5000 Silver 0.5031 oz. ASW **Ruler:** Elizabeth II
Subject: George Washington - Verplanck's Point, 1790
Obv: Helmeted arms, date below, value at bottom **Rev:** George Washington standing next to horse, left

Date	Mintage	F	VF	XF	Unc	BU
1982 Proof	675	Value: 70.00				

KM# 6   100 DOLLARS
129.6000 g., 0.9250 Silver 3.8541 oz. ASW **Ruler:** Elizabeth II
Subject: Tropical Birds **Obv:** Arms **Rev:** Cattle Egret

Date	Mintage	F	VF	XF	Unc	BU
1988 Proof	10,000	Value: 125				

KM# 7   500 DOLLARS
47.5400 g., 0.9170 Gold 1.4015 oz. AGW **Ruler:** Elizabeth II
Subject: Royal Visit **Obv:** Crowned bust right **Rev:** Arms

Date	Mintage	F	VF	XF	Unc	BU
1985 Proof	250	Value: 1,375				

ARGENTINA

The Argentine Republic, located in southern South America, has an area of 1,073,518 sq. mi. (3,761,274 sq. km.) and an estimated population of 37.03 million. Capital: Buenos Aires. Its varied topography ranges from the subtropical lowlands of the north to the towering Andean Mountains in the west and the wind-swept Patagonian steppe in the south. The rolling, fertile pampas of central Argentina are ideal for agriculture and grazing, and support most of the republic's population. Meatpacking, flour milling, textiles, sugar refining and dairy products are the principal industries. Oil is found in Patagonia, but most mineral requirements must be imported.

Argentina was discovered in 1516 by the Spanish navigator Juan de Solis. A permanent Spanish colony was established at Buenos Aires in 1580, but the colony developed slowly. When Napoleon conquered Spain, the Argentines set up their own government on May 25, 1810. Independence was formally declared on July 9, 1816. A strong tendency toward local autonomy, fostered by difficult transportation, resulted in a federalized union with much authority left to the states or provinces, which resulted in the coinage of 1817-1867.

Internal conflict through the first half century of Argentine independence resulted in a provisional national coinage, chiefly of crown-sized silver. Provincial issues mainly of minor denominations supplemented this.

MINT MARKS
A = Korea
B = Great Britain
BA = Buenos Aires
C = France

MONETARY SYSTEM
100 Centavos = 1 Peso
10 Pesos = 1 Argentino
      (Commencing 1970)
100 Old Pesos = 1 New Peso
      (Commencing June 1983)
10,000 New Pesos = 1 Peso Argentino
1,000 Pesos Argentino = 1 Austral
      (Commencing 1985)
1,000 Pesos Argentinos = 1 Austral
100 Centavos = 1 Austral
      (Commencing 1992)
100 Centavos = 1 Peso

REPUBLIC
DECIMAL COINAGE

KM# 37 CENTAVO
2.0200 g., Bronze **Obv:** Argentine arms **Rev:** Value within wreath **Note:** Prev. KM#12.

Date	Mintage	F	VF	XF	Unc	BU
1939	3,488,000	0.25	0.50	1.50	4.00	—
1940	3,140,000	0.15	0.35	1.00	2.00	—
1941	4,572,000	0.15	0.35	1.00	2.00	—
1942	495,000	0.30	0.75	1.50	7.50	—
1943	1,293,500	0.10	0.25	0.55	1.50	—
1944	3,102,743	0.20	0.50	1.00	2.75	—

KM# 37a CENTAVO
Copper **Obv:** Argentine arms **Rev:** Value within wreath **Note:** Cruder diework. Prev. KM#12a.

Date	Mintage	F	VF	XF	Unc	BU
1945	420,000	0.20	0.50	1.00	4.00	—
1946/6	4,450,000	0.15	0.35	0.50	2.00	3.00
1947	5,630,000	0.15	0.35	0.50	2.00	3.00
1948	4,419,545	0.15	0.35	0.50	2.00	3.00

KM# 38 2 CENTAVOS
3.4400 g., Bronze **Obv:** Argentine arms **Rev:** Value within wreath **Note:** Prev. KM#13.

Date	Mintage	F	VF	XF	Unc	BU
1939	5,490,000	0.15	0.35	1.00	4.50	—
1940	4,625,000	0.15	0.35	1.00	5.00	—
1941	4,566,805	0.15	0.35	1.00	5.00	—
1942	2,082,492	0.15	0.35	1.00	5.50	—
1944	387,072	0.25	0.50	1.25	7.50	—
1945	4,585,000	0.15	0.35	1.00	5.00	—
1946/1946	3,395,000	0.15	0.35	1.00	5.00	—
1947	4,395,000	0.15	0.35	1.00	5.00	—

KM# 38a 2 CENTAVOS
Copper **Obv:** Argentine arms **Rev:** Value within wreath **Note:** Cruder diework. Prev. KM#13a.

Date	Mintage	F	VF	XF	Unc	BU
1947	Inc. above	0.15	0.35	1.00	5.50	—
1948	3,645,000	0.15	0.35	1.00	5.50	—
1949/9	7,290,000	0.15	0.35	1.00	3.50	5.00
1950	903,070	0.25	0.65	1.25	6.50	—

KM# 34 5 CENTAVOS
2.0000 g., Copper-Nickel, 17.3 mm. **Obv:** Capped liberty head left **Rev:** Denomination within wreath **Note:** Prev. KM#9.

Date	Mintage	F	VF	XF	Unc	BU
1903	2,502,000	0.25	0.50	3.00	18.00	—
1904	2,518,000	0.25	0.50	3.00	18.00	—
1905	4,359,000	0.25	0.50	3.00	18.00	—
1906	3,939,000	0.25	0.50	3.00	18.00	—
1907	1,682,000	0.50	1.00	5.00	20.00	—
1908	1,693,000	0.50	1.00	5.00	20.00	—
1909	4,650,000	0.25	0.50	3.50	20.00	—
1910	1,469,000	0.75	2.00	6.00	24.00	—
1911	1,431,000	0.25	0.75	4.00	20.00	—
1912	2,377,000	0.25	0.75	4.00	20.00	—
1913	1,477,000	0.25	0.75	4.00	20.00	—
1914	1,097,000	0.50	1.00	5.00	22.00	—
1915	1,310,000	0.30	0.75	3.50	20.00	—
1916	1,310,000	0.30	0.75	3.50	18.00	—
1917	1,009,000	0.75	1.50	4.00	20.00	—
1918	2,287,000	0.25	0.50	3.00	15.00	—
1919	2,476,000	0.25	0.50	3.00	10.00	—
1920	5,235,000	0.25	0.50	3.00	10.00	—
1921	7,040,000	0.20	0.35	2.00	8.00	—
1922	9,427,000	0.20	0.35	2.00	10.00	—
1923	6,256,000	0.20	0.35	2.00	10.00	—
1924	6,355,000	0.20	0.35	2.00	10.00	—
1925	3,955,000	0.20	0.35	2.00	10.00	—
1926	3,560,000	0.20	0.35	2.00	10.00	—
1927	5,650,000	0.20	0.35	2.00	10.00	—
1928	6,380,000	0.20	0.35	2.00	10.00	—
1929	11,831,000	0.20	0.35	2.00	10.00	—
1930 round top 3	7,110,000	0.20	0.35	2.00	10.00	—
1931 flat top 3	506,000	2.00	4.00	9.00	25.00	—
1933 round top 3	5,537,000	0.10	0.25	1.00	4.00	—
1934 round top 3	1,288,000	0.25	0.50	3.00	8.00	—
1935	3,052,000	0.10	0.25	1.00	4.00	—
1936	7,175,000	0.10	0.25	1.00	4.00	—
1937	7,063,000	0.10	0.25	1.00	4.00	—
1938	10,252,000	0.10	0.25	1.00	3.50	—
1939	7,171,000	0.10	0.25	1.00	4.00	—
1940	10,191,000	0.10	0.25	1.00	3.50	—
1941	951,000	0.50	1.00	3.00	12.00	—
1942	8,692,000	0.10	0.25	1.00	3.50	—

KM# 40 5 CENTAVOS
2.0600 g., Aluminum-Bronze **Obv:** Value at center, grain spray on left, head of cow on right **Rev:** Grain sprig behind capped head, right **Note:** Prev. KM#15.

Date	Mintage	F	VF	XF	Unc	BU
1942	2,130,000	0.25	0.50	1.50	5.00	—
1943	15,778,000	0.10	0.25	0.75	3.00	4.00
1944	21,081,000	0.10	0.25	0.75	3.00	4.00
1945	21,600,000	0.10	0.25	0.75	3.00	4.00
1946	20,460,000	0.10	0.25	0.75	3.00	4.00
1947	22,520,000	0.10	0.25	0.75	3.00	4.00
1948	42,790,000	0.10	0.25	0.50	2.00	3.00
1949	35,470,000	0.10	0.25	0.75	3.00	4.00
1950	13,500,000	0.10	0.25	0.75	3.00	4.00

KM# 43 5 CENTAVOS
Copper-Nickel, 17 mm. **Obv:** Value **Rev:** Jose de San Martin bust facing right **Edge:** Reeded **Note:** Prev. KM#18.

Date	Mintage	F	VF	XF	Unc	BU
1950	3,460,000	0.20	0.40	0.60	2.00	3.00

KM# 46 5 CENTAVOS
1.9500 g., Copper-Nickel, 17 mm. **Obv:** Value **Rev:** Jose de San Martin bust facing right **Edge:** Reeded **Note:** Prev. KM#21.

Date	Mintage	F	VF	XF	Unc	BU
1951	34,994,000	—	0.20	0.30	0.50	0.75
1952	33,110,000	—	0.20	0.30	0.50	0.75
1953	20,129,000	—	0.20	0.30	0.50	0.75

KM# 46a 5 CENTAVOS
Copper-Nickel Clad Steel, 17 mm. **Rev:** Jose de San Martin bust facing right **Edge:** Plain **Note:** Prev. KM#21a.

Date	Mintage	F	VF	XF	Unc	BU
1953	36,300,000	—	0.15	0.20	0.35	0.50

KM# 50 5 CENTAVOS
Copper-Nickel Clad Steel, 17.2 mm. **Obv:** Value **Rev:** Jose de San Martin bust facing right **Edge:** Plain **Note:** Bust slightly smaller than KM# 46a. Prev. KM#25.

Date	Mintage	F	VF	XF	Unc	BU
1954	50,640,000	—	0.15	0.20	0.35	0.50
1955	42,200,000	—	0.15	0.20	0.35	0.50
1956	36,870,000	—	0.15	0.20	0.35	0.50

KM# 53 5 CENTAVOS
Copper-Nickel Clad Steel **Obv:** Capped liberty head, left **Rev:** Value within wreath **Edge:** Plain **Note:** Prev. KM#28.

Date	Mintage	F	VF	XF	Unc	BU
1957	26,930,000	—	0.15	0.20	0.35	0.50
1958	13,108,000	—	0.15	0.20	0.35	0.50
1959	14,971,000	—	0.15	0.20	0.35	0.50

KM# 35 10 CENTAVOS
3.0000 g., Copper-Nickel **Obv:** Capped liberty head **Rev:** Denomination **Edge:** Reeded **Note:** Prev. KM#10.

Date	Mintage	F	VF	XF	Unc	BU
1905	3,785,000	0.50	1.00	3.50	20.00	—
1906	3,854,000	0.50	1.00	3.50	20.00	—
1907	2,355,000	0.50	1.00	4.50	22.00	—
1908	2,280,000	0.50	1.00	4.50	22.00	—
1909	3,738,000	0.50	1.00	3.50	20.00	—
1910	3,026,000	0.50	1.00	3.50	20.00	—
1911	2,142,000	0.75	2.00	5.00	24.00	—
1912	2,993,000	0.75	2.00	5.00	24.00	—
1913 round top 3	1,828,000	1.00	2.50	5.50	25.00	—
1914	751,000	1.00	2.50	5.50	25.00	—
1915	2,607,000	0.50	1.00	3.50	20.00	—
1916	835,000	1.00	2.50	5.50	25.00	—
1918	3,897,000	0.50	1.00	3.50	20.00	—
1919	2,517,000	0.50	1.00	3.50	25.00	—
1920	7,509,000	0.25	0.75	2.50	20.00	—
1921	11,564,000	0.25	0.60	2.00	15.00	—
1922	6,542,000	0.20	0.50	2.00	20.00	—
1923	5,301,000	0.20	0.50	2.00	15.00	—
1924	3,489,000	0.20	0.50	1.75	10.00	—
1925	5,415,000	0.20	0.50	1.75	10.00	—
1926	5,055,000	0.15	0.35	1.50	9.00	—
1927	5,205,000	0.15	0.35	1.50	9.00	—
1928	8,255,000	0.15	0.35	1.50	9.00	—
1929	2,501,000	0.15	0.35	1.50	9.00	—
1930 round top 3	14,586,000	0.15	0.35	1.50	8.00	—
1931 flat top 3	893,000	0.50	1.00	2.50	20.00	—
1933	5,394,000	0.15	0.35	1.50	8.00	—
1934	3,319,000	0.15	0.35	1.50	8.00	—
1935	1,018,000	0.30	0.75	2.00	15.00	—
1936	3,000,000	0.15	0.35	1.50	12.00	—
1937	11,766,000	0.15	0.35	1.00	4.00	—
1938	10,494,000	0.15	0.35	1.00	4.00	—
1939	5,585,000	0.15	0.35	1.00	5.00	—
1940	3,955,000	0.15	0.35	1.00	5.00	—
1941	4,101,000	0.15	0.35	1.00	5.00	—
1942	2,962,000	0.15	0.25	1.00	5.00	—

KM# 41   10 CENTAVOS
Aluminum-Bronze **Obv:** Value center, grain sprig on left, head of cow on right **Rev:** Grain sprig behind capped head facing right **Note:** Prev. KM#16.

Date	Mintage	F	VF	XF	Unc	BU
1942	15,541,000	0.15	0.25	1.00	4.00	—
1943	13,916,000	0.15	0.35	1.25	6.00	—
1944	16,411,000	0.15	0.25	1.00	4.00	—
1945	12,500,000	0.25	0.50	2.00	7.00	—
1946	15,790,000	0.15	0.25	1.00	4.00	—
1947	36,430,000	0.15	0.25	1.00	2.50	3.50
1948	54,685,000	0.15	0.25	1.00	2.50	3.50
1949	57,740,000	0.15	0.25	1.00	2.50	3.50
1950	42,825,000	0.15	0.25	1.00	2.50	3.50

KM# 44   10 CENTAVOS
Copper-Nickel, 19 mm.   **Obv:** Value **Rev:** Jose de San Martin bust facing right **Edge:** Reeded **Note:** Prev. KM#19.

Date	Mintage	F	VF	XF	Unc	BU
1950	17,505,000	0.20	0.40	0.60	1.75	2.50

KM# 47   10 CENTAVOS
Copper-Nickel, 19 mm. **Obv:** Value **Rev:** Jose de San Martín bust right **Edge:** Reeded **Note:** Prev. KM#22.

Date	Mintage	F	VF	XF	Unc	BU
1951	98,521,000	—	0.20	0.30	0.50	0.75
1952	67,328,000	—	0.20	0.30	0.50	0.75

KM# 47a   10 CENTAVOS
Nickel Clad Steel, 19 mm. **Edge:** Plain **Note:** Prev. KM#22a.

Date	Mintage	F	VF	XF	Unc	BU
1952	33,240,000	—	0.10	0.15	0.25	0.50
1953	106,685,000	—	0.10	0.15	0.25	0.50

KM# 51   10 CENTAVOS
3.0500 g., Nickel Clad Steel, 19 mm. **Obv:** Value **Rev:** Jose de San Martin facing right **Edge:** Plain **Note:** Bust slightly smaller than KM# 47a. Prev. KM#26.

Date	Mintage	F	VF	XF	Unc	BU
1954	117,200,000	—	0.10	0.15	0.25	0.50
1955	97,045,000	—	0.10	0.15	0.25	0.50
1956	122,630,000	—	0.10	0.15	0.25	0.50

KM# 54   10 CENTAVOS
2.9500 g., Nickel Clad Steel, 19.24 mm. **Obv:** Capped liberty head facing left **Rev:** Value within wreath **Edge:** Plain **Note:** Prev. KM#29.

Date	Mintage	F	VF	XF	Unc	BU
1957	52,810,000	—	0.10	0.15	0.25	0.50
1958	41,916,000	—	0.10	0.15	0.25	0.50
1959	29,183,000	—	0.10	0.15	0.25	0.50

KM# 36   20 CENTAVOS
4.0000 g., Copper-Nickel **Obv:** Capped liberty head left **Rev:** Denomination within wreath **Note:** Prev. KM#11.

Date	Mintage	F	VF	XF	Unc	BU
1905	4,455,000	0.75	2.00	5.00	38.00	—
1906	4,331,000	0.75	2.00	5.00	38.00	—
1907	3,730,000	1.00	3.00	7.00	40.00	—
1908	719,000	2.25	5.00	10.00	45.00	—
1909	1,329,000	0.50	1.50	4.00	35.00	—
1910	1,845,000	0.50	1.50	4.00	35.00	—
1911	1,110,000	0.50	1.50	4.00	35.00	—
1912	2,402,000	0.50	1.50	4.00	35.00	—
1913	1,579,000	0.50	1.00	3.00	30.00	—
1914	527,000	2.25	5.00	12.00	50.00	—
1915	1,921,000	0.50	1.00	3.00	30.00	—
1916	985,000	0.50	1.25	4.00	35.00	—
1918	1,638,000	0.40	0.75	3.00	30.00	—
1919	2,280,000	0.40	0.75	3.00	30.00	—
1920	7,572,000	0.40	0.75	2.50	20.00	—
1921	5,286,000	0.25	0.60	2.50	30.00	—
1922	2,324,000	0.25	0.60	2.50	30.00	—
1923	4,416,000	0.25	0.60	2.50	30.00	—
1924	3,676,000	0.25	0.60	2.00	30.00	—
1925	3,799,000	0.25	0.60	2.00	30.00	—
1926	3,250,000	0.25	0.50	2.00	25.00	—
1927	2,880,000	0.25	0.50	2.00	25.00	—
1928	2,886,000	0.25	0.50	2.00	25.00	—
1929	8,361,000	0.25	0.50	1.25	12.00	—
1930	8,281,000	0.25	0.50	1.25	12.00	—
1931	315,000	2.25	5.00	10.00	35.00	—
1935	1,127,000	0.25	0.60	1.75	12.50	—
1936	855,000	0.50	1.25	2.50	15.00	—
1937	3,314,000	0.25	0.50	1.50	9.00	—
1938	6,449,000	0.25	0.50	1.25	9.00	—
1939	3,555,000	0.25	0.50	1.25	9.00	—
1940	4,465,000	0.25	0.50	1.25	9.00	—
1941	600,000	0.50	1.00	2.00	12.50	—
1942	4,844,000	0.25	0.50	1.25	9.00	—

KM# 42   20 CENTAVOS
4.2000 g., Aluminum-Bronze, 21.2 mm. **Obv:** Value at center, grain sprig to left, head of cow to right **Rev:** Grain sprig behind capped head right **Note:** Prev. KM#17.

Date	Mintage	F	VF	XF	Unc	BU
1942	10,255,000	0.25	0.50	2.00	10.00	—
1943	13,775,000	0.15	0.35	1.50	7.00	—
1944	12,225,000	0.15	0.35	1.75	8.00	—
1945	13,340,000	0.15	0.35	1.50	7.00	—
1946	14,625,000	0.15	0.35	1.50	7.00	—
1947	23,165,000	0.15	0.25	1.25	6.00	7.50
1948	32,245,000	0.15	0.25	1.25	6.00	7.50
1949	67,115,000	0.15	0.25	1.25	6.00	7.50
1950	40,071,000	0.15	0.25	1.25	6.00	7.50

KM# 45   20 CENTAVOS
4.0200 g., Copper-Nickel, 21 mm. **Obv:** Value **Rev:** Jose de San Martín portrait right **Edge:** Reeded **Note:** Prev. KM#20.

Date	Mintage	F	VF	XF	Unc	BU
1950	86,770,000	0.15	0.25	0.60	1.50	2.00

KM# 48   20 CENTAVOS
Copper-Nickel, 21 mm. **Obv:** Value **Rev:** Jose de San Martín bust right **Edge:** Reeded **Note:** Prev. KM#23.

Date	Mintage	F	VF	XF	Unc	BU
1951	85,782,000	0.10	0.20	0.30	0.50	0.75
1952	69,796,000	0.10	0.20	0.30	0.50	0.75

KM# 48a   20 CENTAVOS
4.0000 g., Nickel Clad Steel, 21 mm. **Rev:** Jose de San Martín portrait right **Edge:** Plain **Note:** Prev. KM#23a.

Date	Mintage	F	VF	XF	Unc	BU
1952	12,863,000	—	0.15	0.25	0.50	0.75
1953	36,893,000	—	0.15	0.40	1.00	1.50

KM# 52   20 CENTAVOS
3.9100 g., Nickel Clad Steel, 21 mm. **Obv:** Value **Rev:** Jose de San Martin bust facing right **Note:** Head size reduced slightly. Prev. KM#27.

Date	Mintage	F	VF	XF	Unc	BU
1954	52,563,000	—	0.15	0.20	0.25	0.50
1955	46,952,000	—	0.15	0.20	0.25	0.50
1956	35,995,000	—	0.15	0.20	0.25	0.50

KM# 55   20 CENTAVOS
4.0000 g., Nickel Clad Steel, 19.59 mm. **Obv:** Capped liberty head left **Rev:** Value within wreath **Edge:** Plain **Note:** Prev. KM#30.

Date	Mintage	F	VF	XF	Unc	BU
1957	89,365,000	—	0.15	0.20	0.25	0.50
1958	52,710,000	—	0.15	0.20	0.25	0.50
1959	56,585,000	—	0.15	0.20	0.25	0.50
1960	21,254,000	—	0.15	0.20	0.25	0.50
1961	2,083,000	—	0.25	0.50	1.50	2.00

KM# 39   50 CENTAVOS
6.0000 g., Nickel, 24.50 mm. **Obv:** Capped liberty head, left **Rev:** Value within wreath **Edge:** Reeded **Note:** Prev. KM#14.

Date	Mintage	F	VF	XF	Unc	BU
1941	1,000,000	0.40	1.00	2.00	6.00	—

KM# 49   50 CENTAVOS
Nickel Clad Steel **Obv:** Value **Rev:** Jose de San Martín bust right **Edge:** Plain **Note:** Prev. KM#24.

Date	Mintage	F	VF	XF	Unc	BU
1952	29,736,000	0.10	0.20	0.35	1.25	2.00
1953	62,814,000	0.10	0.20	0.35	1.25	2.00
1954	132,224,000	0.10	0.20	0.35	1.00	1.50
1955	75,490,000	0.10	0.20	0.35	1.25	2.00
1956	19,120,000	0.10	0.20	0.50	2.00	3.00

KM# 56   50 CENTAVOS
5.0500 g., Nickel Clad Steel, 23.2 mm. **Obv:** Capped liberty head left **Rev:** Value within wreath **Edge:** Plain **Note:** Prev. KM#31.

Date	Mintage	F	VF	XF	Unc	BU
1957	18,139,000	0.10	0.20	0.45	1.25	2.00
1958	51,750,000	0.10	0.20	0.35	1.00	1.50
1959	13,997,000	0.10	0.20	0.45	1.25	2.00
1960	26,038,000	0.10	0.20	0.35	1.00	1.50
1961	11,106,000	0.10	0.20	0.45	1.25	2.00

KM# 57 PESO
6.4100 g., Nickel Clad Steel **Obv:** Capped liberty head left **Rev:** Value within wreath **Note:** Prev. KM#32.

Date	Mintage	F	VF	XF	Unc	BU
1957	118,118,000	0.10	0.20	0.40	2.00	3.00
1958	118,151,000	0.10	0.20	0.40	2.00	3.00
1959	237,733,000	0.10	0.20	0.30	1.50	2.50
1960	75,048,000	0.10	0.30	0.50	2.50	3.50
1961	76,897,000	0.10	0.30	0.50	2.50	3.50
1962	30,006,000	0.10	0.30	0.50	3.00	4.00

KM# 58 PESO
6.6200 g., Nickel Clad Steel, 25.5 mm. **Subject:** 150th Anniversary - Removal of Spanish Viceroy **Obv:** Argentine arms, value at bottom **Rev:** Building, two dates below **Edge:** Reeded **Note:** Prev. KM#33.

Date	Mintage	F	VF	XF	Unc	BU
ND(1960)	98,751,000	0.20	0.50	0.75	2.00	3.00

KM# 59 5 PESOS
4.0000 g., Nickel Clad Steel, 21.5 mm. **Obv:** Sailing ship-Fragata Sarmiento **Rev:** Value above date flanked by sprays **Edge:** Plain **Note:** Prev. KM#34.

Date	Mintage	F	VF	XF	Unc	BU
1961	37,423,000	0.15	0.25	0.50	3.00	3.50
1962	42,362,000	0.15	0.25	0.50	3.00	3.50
1963	71,769,000	0.15	0.25	0.40	2.00	2.50
1964	12,302,000	0.20	0.35	0.60	3.50	4.00
1965	19,450,000	0.15	0.25	0.50	3.00	3.50
1966	17,259,000	0.15	0.25	0.50	3.00	3.50
1967	17,806,000	0.15	0.25	0.50	3.00	3.50
1968	12,634,000	0.20	0.35	0.60	3.50	4.00

KM# 60 10 PESOS
Nickel Clad Steel, 23.6 mm. **Obv:** Gaucho **Edge:** Plain **Note:** Prev. KM#35.

Date	Mintage	F	VF	XF	Unc	BU
1962	57,401,000	0.15	0.25	0.50	3.00	3.50
1963	136,792,000	0.15	0.20	0.35	2.00	2.50
1964	46,576,000	0.15	0.25	0.50	3.00	3.50
1965	40,640,000	0.15	0.25	0.50	3.00	3.50
1966	50,733,000	0.15	0.20	0.40	2.50	3.00
1967	43,050,000	0.15	0.25	0.50	3.00	3.50
1968	36,588,000	0.15	0.25	0.50	3.00	3.50

KM# 62 10 PESOS
Nickel Clad Steel **Subject:** 150th Anniversary - Declaration of Independence. **Rev:** Building facing right, two dates below **Note:** Prev. KM#37.

Date	Mintage	F	VF	XF	Unc	BU
ND(1966)	29,336,000	0.15	0.25	0.50	3.00	3.50

KM# 61 25 PESOS
6.4500 g., Nickel Clad Steel, 26 mm. **Subject:** 1st issue of National Coinage in 1813. **Obv:** Radiant sunface within circle **Rev:** Argentine arms within circle **Edge:** Plain **Note:** Prev. KM#36.

Date	Mintage	F	VF	XF	Unc	BU
1964	20,485,000	0.15	0.25	0.50	3.00	3.75
1965	14,884,000	0.15	0.25	0.50	3.00	3.75
1966	16,426,000	0.15	0.25	0.50	3.00	3.75
1967	15,734,000	0.15	0.25	0.50	3.00	3.75
1968	4,446,000	0.15	0.25	0.75	3.50	4.50

KM# 63 25 PESOS
Nickel Clad Steel, 26 mm. **Subject:** 80th Anniversary - Death of D. Faustino Sarmiento **Rev:** Head of Domingo Faustino Samiento, left, date below **Note:** Prev. KM#38.

Date	Mintage	F	VF	XF	Unc	BU
1968	15,804,000	0.25	0.60	0.85	1.65	2.00

REFORM COINAGE
1970-1983; 100 Old Pesos = 1 New Peso

KM# 64 CENTAVO
0.6200 g., Aluminum, 15.62 mm. **Obv:** Capped Liberty head, left **Rev:** Value to left of grain sprig, date below **Edge:** Plain **Note:** Prev. KM#39.

Date	Mintage	F	VF	XF	Unc	BU
1970	54,568,115	—	—	0.10	0.30	0.50
1971	44,644,000	—	—	0.10	0.30	0.50
1972	92,430,000	—	—	0.10	0.30	0.50
1973	29,515,000	—	—	0.10	0.30	0.50
1974	5,162,000	—	—	0.15	0.35	0.60
1975	3,840,000	—	0.10	0.20	0.50	0.75

KM# 65 5 CENTAVOS
0.9800 g., Aluminum, 16.63 mm. **Obv:** Capped liberty head left **Rev:** Value with grain sprig to left **Edge:** Plain **Note:** Prev. KM#40.

Date	Mintage	F	VF	XF	Unc	BU
1970	56,174,000	—	0.10	0.15	0.40	0.60
1971	3,798,000	0.10	0.20	0.35	0.65	0.90
1972	84,250,000	—	0.10	0.15	0.40	0.60
1973	113,912,000	—	0.10	0.15	0.40	0.60
1974	18,150,000	—	0.10	0.15	0.40	0.60
1975	6,940,000	0.10	0.20	0.35	0.65	0.90

KM# 66 10 CENTAVOS
Brass **Obv:** Capped liberty head, left **Rev:** Value with grain sprig to left **Note:** Prev. KM#41.

Date	Mintage	F	VF	XF	Unc	BU
1970	64,585,300	—	0.10	0.15	0.35	0.55
1971	135,623,000	—	0.10	0.15	0.35	0.55
1973	19,930,000	—	0.10	0.15	0.35	0.55
1974	79,156,000	—	0.10	0.15	0.35	0.55
1975	31,270,000	—	0.10	0.15	0.35	0.55
1976	730,000	0.10	0.20	0.35	1.00	1.75

KM# 67 20 CENTAVOS
3.0700 g., Brass, 18.75 mm. **Obv:** Capped liberty head, left **Rev:** Value with grain sprig to left **Edge:** Reeded **Note:** Prev. KM#42.

Date	Mintage	F	VF	XF	Unc	BU
1970	27,029,000	—	0.10	0.15	0.35	0.55
1971	33,211,000	—	0.10	0.15	0.35	0.55
1972	220,000	1.00	2.00	4.00	8.00	10.00
1973	9,676,000	—	0.10	0.15	0.35	0.55
1974	41,024,000	—	0.10	0.15	0.35	0.55
1975	26,540,000	—	0.10	0.15	0.35	0.55
1976	960,000	—	0.10	0.15	0.35	0.55

KM# 68 50 CENTAVOS
4.3500 g., Brass **Obv:** Capped liberty head left **Rev:** Value with grain sprig to left **Note:** Prev. KM#43.

Date	Mintage	F	VF	XF	Unc	BU
1970	56,103,729	0.10	0.15	0.30	0.60	0.80
1971	34,947,000	0.10	0.15	0.30	0.60	0.80
1972	40,960,000	0.10	0.15	0.30	0.60	0.80
1973	59,472,124	0.10	0.15	0.30	0.60	0.80
1974	64,063,000	0.10	0.15	0.30	0.60	0.80
1975	64,859,000	0.10	0.15	0.30	0.60	0.80
1976	9,768,000	0.10	0.15	0.30	0.60	0.80

KM# 69 PESO
5.0000 g., Aluminum-Brass, 22 mm. **Obv:** Radiant sunface, grain sprays below **Rev:** Value with grain sprig to left **Edge:** Reeded **Note:** Wide rim variety on 1974-75 issues; narrow rim variety on 1975-76 issues. Prev. KM#44.

Date	Mintage	F	VF	XF	Unc	BU
1974	77,292,000	—	0.10	0.25	0.75	1.00
1975 wide rim	423,000,000	—	0.10	0.20	0.50	0.75
1975 narrow rim	Inc. above	—	0.10	0.20	0.50	0.75
1976	100,075,000	—	0.10	0.20	0.50	0.75

KM# 71 5 PESOS
Aluminum-Bronze **Obv:** Radiant sunface, grain sprays below **Rev:** Value with grain sprig to left **Note:** Prev. KM#46.

Date	Mintage	F	VF	XF	Unc	BU
1976	118,353,000	—	0.10	0.20	0.65	1.00
1977	66,765,684	—	0.10	0.20	0.65	1.00

KM# 73 5 PESOS
Aluminum-Bronze **Subject:** Admiral G. Brown Bicentennial **Note:** Prev. KM#48.

Date	Mintage	F	VF	XF	Unc	BU
1977	11,297,808	0.10	0.15	0.30	0.75	1.00

KM# 72 10 PESOS
Aluminum-Bronze **Obv:** Radiant sunface, grain sprays below **Rev:** Value with grain sprig to left **Note:** Prev. KM#47.

Date	Mintage	F	VF	XF	Unc	BU
1976	130,216,724	0.10	0.15	0.35	1.00	1.50
1977	191,520,382	0.10	0.15	0.35	1.00	1.50
1978	259,424,310	0.10	0.15	0.35	1.00	1.50

KM# 74   10 PESOS
Aluminum-Bronze   **Subject:** Admiral G. Brown Bicentennial
Obv: Armored bust of Admiral G. Brown right dividing dates **Rev:** Value with grain sprigs to left, date below **Note:** Prev. KM#49.

Date	Mintage	F	VF	XF	Unc	BU
1977	60,008,179	0.10	0.20	0.50	1.25	1.50

KM# 75   20 PESOS
Aluminum-Bronze   **Subject:** 1978 World Soccer Championship
Obv: Two soccer players, country above with two numbered year below country to right **Rev:** Soccer ball within symbol, top right, small mark to left, value below, date at bottom **Note:** Prev. KM#50.

Date	Mintage	F	VF	XF	Unc	BU
1977	1,506,000	0.10	0.20	0.40	1.00	1.25
1978	2,000,000	0.10	0.20	0.40	1.00	1.25

KM# 76   50 PESOS
Aluminum-Bronze   **Subject:** 1978 World Soccer Championship
Obv: Soccer player on lined globe, country name above with two numbered year below at right **Rev:** Soccer ball within symbol, top right, value below, date at bottom, small mark to left of symbol **Note:** Prev. KM#51.

Date	Mintage	F	VF	XF	Unc	BU
1977	1,506,000	0.10	0.20	0.40	1.00	1.25
1978	2,000,000	0.10	0.20	0.40	1.00	1.25

KM# 81   50 PESOS
Aluminum-Bronze   **Subject:** 200th Anniversary - Birth of Jose de San Martín **Obv:** Value, date below flanked by stars **Rev:** Armored bust of Jose de San Martin left, two dates at right **Note:** Prev. KM#56.

Date	Mintage	F	VF	XF	Unc	BU
1978	40,601,000	0.20	0.50	1.00	2.00	2.50

KM# 83   50 PESOS
Aluminum-Bronze   **Obv:** Value, date below **Rev:** Bust of Jose de San Martin left **Note:** Prev. KM#58.

Date	Mintage	F	VF	XF	Unc	BU
1979	21,728,900	0.10	0.25	0.65	1.50	2.00
1980		0.10	0.25	0.65	1.50	2.00

Note: Mintage included with 1980 date of KM#83a.

KM# 83a   50 PESOS
7.3900 g., Brass Clad Steel, 26.14 mm.   **Rev:** Jose de San Martín portrait right **Edge:** Reeded **Note:** Prev. KM#58a.

Date	Mintage	F	VF	XF	Unc	BU
1980	94,730,000	0.10	0.25	0.65	1.25	1.50
1981	26,507,500	0.10	0.25	0.65	1.25	1.50

KM# 84   50 PESOS
Aluminum-Bronze   **Subject:** Conquest of Patagonia Centennial
Obv: Value, date below **Rev:** Man on horse, lance in right hand, facing left **Note:** Prev. KM#59.

Date	Mintage	F	VF	XF	Unc	BU
1979	34,761,829	0.10	0.25	0.65	2.50	3.50

KM# 77   100 PESOS
Aluminum-Bronze   **Subject:** 1978 World Soccer Championship
Obv: Stadium on lined globe, country name above with two numbered year below at right **Rev:** Soccer ball within symbol, top right, value below, date at bottom, small mark at left of symbol **Note:** Prev. KM#52.

Date	Mintage	F	VF	XF	Unc	BU
1977	1,506,000	0.15	0.30	0.75	1.50	2.00
1978	2,000,000	0.15	0.30	0.75	1.50	2.00

KM# 82   100 PESOS
Aluminum-Bronze   **Subject:** 200th Anniversary - Birth of Jose de San Martín **Obv:** Value at center, small mark at top, date at bottom **Rev:** Armored bust of Jose de San Martin, left **Note:** Prev. KM#57.

Date	Mintage	F	VF	XF	Unc	BU
1978	113,826,000	—	0.50	1.00	2.00	2.50
1979	—	—	—	—	—	800

KM# 85   100 PESOS
Aluminum-Bronze, 27.4 mm.   **Obv:** Value at center, small mark at top, date at bottom **Rev:** Jose de San Martín portrait left **Note:** Prev. KM#60.

Date	Mintage	F	VF	XF	Unc	BU
1978	—	—	—	—	—	300
1979	43,389,383	0.15	0.30	0.75	1.25	1.50
1980	154,260,000	0.15	0.30	0.75	1.25	1.50

KM# 85a   100 PESOS
7.9100 g., Brass Clad Steel   **Rev:** Jose de San Martín portrait left **Note:** Prev. KM#60a.

Date	Mintage	F	VF	XF	Unc	BU
1980	Inc. above	0.15	0.30	0.75	1.50	1.75
1981	99,512,000	0.15	0.30	0.75	1.25	1.50

KM# 86   100 PESOS
Aluminum-Bronze   **Subject:** Conquest of Patagonia Centennial
Obv: Value center, small mark at top, date below **Rev:** Man on horse holding lance in right, facing left **Note:** Prev. KM#61.

Date	Mintage	F	VF	XF	Unc	BU
1979	34,132,135	0.15	0.30	0.75	2.50	3.50

KM# 78   1000 PESOS
10.0000 g., 0.9000 Silver 0.2893 oz. ASW   **Subject:** 1978 World Soccer Championship **Obv:** Country name at top with two numbered year, below right, small radiant sunface to left of five line inscription **Note:** Prev. KM#53.

Date	Mintage	F	VF	XF	Unc	BU
1977	98,837	—	—	6.00	7.00	8.50
1977 Proof	1,000	Value: 17.50				
1978	187,383	—	—	6.00	7.00	8.50
1978 Proof	1,750	Value: 17.50				

KM# 79   2000 PESOS
15.0000 g., 0.9000 Silver 0.4340 oz. ASW   **Subject:** 1978 World Soccer Championship **Obv:** Argentine arms beneath five sets of small arms, country name, year at bottom **Rev:** Soccer ball within symbol, top right, value below, date at bottom **Note:** Prev. KM#54.

Date	Mintage	F	VF	XF	Unc	BU
1977	98,837	—	—	9.00	10.00	12.50
1977 Proof	1,000	Value: 22.50				
1978	187,383	—	—	9.00	10.00	12.00
1978 Proof	1,750	Value: 22.50				

KM# 80   3000 PESOS
25.0000 g., 0.9000 Silver 0.7234 oz. ASW   **Subject:** 1978 World Soccer Championship **Obv:** Map of country on lined globe, grain sprigs below, country at top **Rev:** Soccer ball within symbol, top right, value below, date at bottom **Note:** Prev. KM#55.

Date	Mintage	F	VF	XF	Unc	BU
1977	98,837	—	—	14.50	16.00	18.00
1977 Proof	1,000	Value: 35.00				
1978	187,383	—	—	14.50	15.00	18.00
1978 Proof	1,750	Value: 35.00				

REFORM COINAGE
1983-1985; 10,000 Pesos = 1 Peso Argentino;
100 Centavos = 1 Peso Argentino

KM# 87   CENTAVO
Aluminum **Obv:** Capped liberty head, left **Rev:** Value, date below
Note: Prev. KM#62.

Date	Mintage	F	VF	XF	Unc	BU
1983	19,959,000	—	—	—	0.20	0.35

KM# 88   5 CENTAVOS
1.2400 g., Aluminum **Obv:** Capped liberty head left **Rev:** Value, date below **Note:** Prev. KM#63.

Date	Mintage	F	VF	XF	Unc	BU
1983	59,870,000	—	—	—	0.25	0.40

KM# 89   10 CENTAVOS
1.5500 g., Aluminum, 20.08 mm. **Obv:** Capped liberty head, left **Rev:** Value, date below **Edge:** Plain **Note:** Prev. KM#64. Struck at the British Royal Mint.

Date	Mintage	F	VF	XF	Unc	BU
1983	307,513,000	—	—	—	0.25	0.40

KM# 90   50 CENTAVOS
Aluminum **Obv:** Capped liberty head, left **Rev:** Value, date below **Note:** Prev. KM#65.

Date	Mintage	F	VF	XF	Unc	BU
1983	243,909,000	—	—	—	0.45	0.60

KM# 91   PESO
Aluminum **Obv:** Capitol building **Rev:** Value, date below **Note:** National Congress. Prev. KM#66.

Date	Mintage	F	VF	XF	Unc	BU
1984	184,691,379	—	—	—	0.50	0.65

KM# 92   5 PESOS
Brass **Obv:** Buenos Aires City Hall **Rev:** Value, date at bottom **Note:** Prev. KM#67.

Date	Mintage	F	VF	XF	Unc	BU
1984	11,206,000	—	—	—	0.65	0.80
1985	14,168,000	—	—	—	0.65	0.80

KM# 93   10 PESOS
Brass **Obv:** Independence Hall at Tucuman **Rev:** Value, date at bottom **Note:** Prev. KM#68.

Date	Mintage	F	VF	XF	Unc	BU
1984	16,528,000	—	—	—	0.85	1.00
1985	9,898,717	—	—	—	0.85	1.00

KM# 94   50 PESOS
4.8300 g., Aluminum-Bronze **Subject:** 50th Anniversary of Central Bank **Obv:** Value, date at bottom **Rev:** Small capped liberty head within wreath, circle surrounding **Note:** Prev. KM#69.

Date	Mintage	F	VF	XF	Unc	BU
1985	3,300,000	—	—	—	1.25	1.50

REFORM COINAGE
1985-1992; 1,000 Pesos Argentinos = 1 Austral;
100 Centavos = 1 Austral

KM# 95   1/2 CENTAVO
Brass **Obv:** Rufous Hornero Bird **Rev:** Value, date below **Note:** Prev. KM#70.

Date	Mintage	F	VF	XF	Unc	BU
1985	7,490,000	—	—	—	0.75	1.50

KM# 96.1   CENTAVO
Brass, 20 mm. **Obv:** Common Rhea **Rev:** Value, date below **Note:** Thick flan. Prev. KM#71.1.

Date	Mintage	F	VF	XF	Unc	BU
1985	76,082,000	—	—	—	0.75	2.00

KM# 96.2   CENTAVO
3.1900 g., Brass, 20.56 mm. **Obv:** Common Rhea **Edge:** Plain **Note:** Thin flan. Prev. KM#71.2.

Date	Mintage	F	VF	XF	Unc	BU
1986	118,934,000	—	—	—	0.75	2.00
1987	87,315,000	—	—	—	0.75	2.00

KM# 97.1   5 CENTAVOS
Brass, 23 mm. **Obv:** Pampas Cat **Rev:** Value, date below **Edge:** Plain **Note:** Thick flan. Prev. KM#72.1.

Date	Mintage	F	VF	XF	Unc	BU
1985	36,924,000	—	—	—	1.60	3.00

KM# 97.2   5 CENTAVOS
4.9000 g., Brass, 23 mm. **Obv:** Pampas Cat **Edge:** Plain **Note:** Thin flan. Prev. KM#72.2.

Date	Mintage	F	VF	XF	Unc	BU
1986	66,414,000	—	—	—	1.50	3.00
1987	56,181,000	—	—	—	1.50	3.00
1988	23,895,000	—	—	—	1.50	3.00

KM# 98   10 CENTAVOS
4.4500 g., Brass, 21.5 mm. **Obv:** Argentine arms **Rev:** Value, date below **Note:** Prev. KM#73.

Date	Mintage	F	VF	XF	Unc	BU
1985	23,268,000	—	—	—	0.65	0.85
1986	158,427,000	—	—	—	0.65	0.85
1987	184,330,000	—	—	—	0.65	0.85
1988	174,003,000	—	—	—	0.65	0.85

KM# 99   50 CENTAVOS
5.4000 g., Brass, 24.5 mm. **Obv:** Capped liberty head, left **Rev:** Value, date below **Note:** Varieties exist. Previous KM#74.

Date	Mintage	F	VF	XF	Unc	BU
1985	13,884,000	—	—	—	1.50	2.00
1986	59,074,000	—	—	—	1.45	1.85
1987	64,525,000	—	—	—	1.45	1.85
1988	62,388,000	—	—	—	1.45	1.85

KM# 100   AUSTRAL
1.5500 g., Aluminum, 20.11 mm. **Obv:** Buenos Aires City Hall **Rev:** Large value in box at right, double lined "A" at top left, date below "A" **Edge:** Plain **Note:** Prev. KM#75.

Date	Mintage	F	VF	XF	Unc	BU
1989	57,400,000	—	—	—	0.15	0.30

KM# 101   5 AUSTRALES
Aluminum, 21.6 mm. **Obv:** Independence Hall at Tucuman **Rev:** Large value in box at right, double lined "A" at left top, date below "A" **Edge:** Plain **Note:** Prev. KM#76.

Date	Mintage	F	VF	XF	Unc	BU
1989	46,894,977	—	—	—	0.25	0.40

KM# 102   10 AUSTRALES
2.0000 g., Aluminum, 23.2 mm. **Obv:** Casa del Acuerdo **Rev:** Large value in box at right, double lined "A" at top left, date below "A" **Edge:** Plain **Note:** Prev. KM#77.

Date	Mintage	F	VF	XF	Unc	BU
1989	99,600,000	—	—	—	0.35	0.50

KM# 103   100 AUSTRALES
1.5000 g., Aluminum, 19.52 mm. **Obv:** Argentine arms **Rev:** Large value in box, small double lined "A" at top, date below box **Edge:** Plain **Note:** Prev. KM#78.

Date	Mintage	F	VF	XF	Unc	BU
1990	18,003,500	—	—	—	0.25	0.40
1991	31,996,500	—	—	—	0.25	0.40

KM# 104   500 AUSTRALES
Aluminum **Obv:** Argentine arms **Rev:** Large value in box, small double lined "A" at top, date below box **Note:** Prev. KM#79.

Date	Mintage	F	VF	XF	Unc	BU
1990	29,312,000	—	—	—	0.35	0.50
1991	50,087,100	—	—	—	0.35	0.50

KM# 105 1000 AUSTRALES
Aluminum, 24.5 mm. **Obv:** Argentine arms **Rev:** Large value in box, small double lined "A" at top, date below box **Edge:** Plain **Note:** Prev. KM#80.

Date	Mintage	F	VF	XF	Unc	BU
1990	8,282,000	—	—	—	0.60	0.75
1991	41,618,000	—	—	—	0.60	0.75

KM# 106 1000 AUSTRALES
27.0000 g., 0.9250 Silver 0.8029 oz. ASW **Subject:** Ibero - American Series **Obv:** Argentine arms within legend and circle of arms **Rev:** Two globes, rising radiant sun above with four crowns above, flanked by columns within inner circle surrounded by legend **Note:** Prev. KM#81.

Date	Mintage	F	VF	XF	Unc	BU
1991 Proof	5,000	Value: 50.00				

REFORM COINAGE
1992; 100 Centavos = 1 Peso

KM# 108 CENTAVO
Brass **Obv:** Four line inscription within wreath **Rev:** Large value, date below **Edge:** Plain **Note:** Prev. KM#83.

Date	Mintage	F	VF	XF	Unc	BU
1992	30,000,000	—	—	—	0.25	0.40

KM# 113 CENTAVO
Brass **Edge:** Reeded **Note:** Round flan. Prev. KM#88.

Date	Mintage	F	VF	XF	Unc	BU
1992	30,000,000	—	—	—	0.25	0.40
1993	79,000,000	—	—	—	0.25	0.40

KM# 113a CENTAVO
2.0200 g., Bronze, 16.2 mm. **Edge:** Reeded **Note:** Prev. KM#88a.

Date	Mintage	F	VF	XF	Unc	BU
1993	48,000,000	—	—	—	0.25	0.40
1997	50,000,000	—	—	—	0.25	0.40
1998	50,000,000	—	—	—	0.25	0.40
1999	70,000,000	—	—	—	0.25	0.40
2000	37,000,000	—	—	—	0.25	0.40

KM# 109 5 CENTAVOS
Brass **Obv:** Radiant sunface **Rev:** Large value, date below **Note:** Prev. KM#84.

Date	Mintage	F	VF	XF	Unc	BU
1992	230,000,000	—	—	—	0.45	0.60
1993	20,000,000	—	—	—	0.45	0.60

KM# 109a.1 5 CENTAVOS
Copper-Nickel **Obv:** Radiant sunface, Fine lettering **Rev:** Value, date below **Note:** Prev. KM#84a.1.

Date	Mintage	F	VF	XF	Unc	BU
1993	245,500,000	—	—	—	0.45	0.65

KM# 109a.2 5 CENTAVOS
Copper-Nickel **Obv:** Radiant sunface. Bold lettering **Note:** Prev. KM#84a.2.

Date	Mintage	F	VF	XF	Unc	BU
1994	5,000,000	—	—	—	0.45	0.65
1995	25,000,000	—	—	—	0.45	0.60

KM# 107 10 CENTAVOS
Aluminum-Bronze **Obv:** Argentine arms **Rev:** Value, date below **Edge:** Reeded **Note:** Prev. KM#82.

Date	Mintage	F	VF	XF	Unc	BU
1992	805,000,000	—	—	—	0.65	0.85
1993	500,000,000	—	—	—	0.65	0.85
1994	80,000,000	—	—	—	0.65	0.85

KM# 110.1 25 CENTAVOS
Brass **Obv:** Towered building, fine lettering **Rev:** Large value, date below **Note:** Prev. KM#85.1.

Date	Mintage	F	VF	XF	Unc	BU
1992	150,000,000	—	—	—	1.25	1.50

KM# 110.2 25 CENTAVOS
Brass **Obv:** Towered building, bold lettering **Note:** Prev. KM#85.2.

Date	Mintage	F	VF	XF	Unc	BU
1993	80,000,000	—	—	—	1.25	1.50

KM# 110a 25 CENTAVOS
Copper-Nickel **Obv:** Towered building, bold lettering **Note:** Prev. KM#85a.

Date	Mintage	F	VF	XF	Unc	BU
1993	390,000,000	—	—	—	1.25	1.50
1994	200,000,000	—	—	—	1.25	1.50
1996	96,000,000	—	—	—	1.25	1.50

KM# 111.1 50 CENTAVOS
Brass **Obv:** Tucuman Province Capital Building; fine lettering **Rev:** Large value, date below **Note:** Prev. KM#86.1.

Date	Mintage	F	VF	XF	Unc	BU
1992	290,000,000	—	—	—	1.75	2.00
1993	—	—	—	—	1.75	2.00
1994	—	—	—	—	1.75	2.00

KM# 111.2 50 CENTAVOS
Copper-Nickel **Obv:** Tucuman Province Capital Building; bold lettering. **Note:** Prev. KM#86.2.

Date	Mintage	F	VF	XF	Unc	BU
1993	120,000,000	—	—	—	1.75	2.00
1994	304,000,000	—	—	—	1.75	2.00

KM# 119 50 CENTAVOS
Copper-Aluminum **Subject:** 50th Anniversary - UNICEF **Obv:** Girl with rag doll **Rev:** UNICEF logo above denomination **Note:** Prev. KM#94.

Date	Mintage	F	VF	XF	Unc	BU
1996	1,000,000	—	—	—	2.00	2.25

KM# 121 50 CENTAVOS
Copper-Aluminum **Subject:** 50th Anniversary - Women's Right to Vote **Obv:** Bust of Eva Peron right **Rev:** Value with two dates above in circle, legend across top, date at bottom divides wreath **Note:** Prev. KM#96.

Date	Mintage	F	VF	XF	Unc	BU
1997	2,000,000	—	—	—	2.25	2.50

KM# 124 50 CENTAVOS
Copper-Aluminum **Subject:** Mercosur **Obv:** Southern Cross constellation **Rev:** Value in circle, date below circle **Note:** Prev. KM#99.

Date	Mintage	F	VF	XF	Unc	BU
1998	1,000,000	—	—	—	2.25	2.50

KM# 129.1 50 CENTAVOS
5.9200 g., Brass, 25.1 mm. **Subject:** General Guemes **Obv:** Bearded portrait, right **Rev:** Value in circle **Edge:** Plain **Note:** Prev. KM#129

Date	Mintage	F	VF	XF	Unc	BU
2000	1,695,000	—	—	—	2.25	2.50

KM# 129.2 50 CENTAVOS
5.9200 g., Brass, 25.1 mm. **Subject:** General Guemes **Obv:** Bearded portrait **Rev:** Denomination **Edge:** Reeded

Date	Mintage	F	VF	XF	Unc	BU
2000	5,000	—	—	—	4.50	6.00

KM# 130.1 50 CENTAVOS
5.9200 g., Brass, 25.1 mm. **Subject:** 150th Anniversary Death of General San Martin **Obv:** Bust facing **Rev:** Value to right of building **Edge:** Reeded **Note:** Previous KM#130

Date	Mintage	F	VF	XF	Unc	BU
2000	995,000	—	—	—	2.25	2.50

KM# 130.2 50 CENTAVOS
5.9200 g., Brass, 25.1 mm. **Subject:** 150th Anniversary Death of General San Martin **Obv:** Bust facing **Rev:** Denomination and building **Edge:** Plain

Date	Mintage	F	VF	XF	Unc	BU
2000	5,000	—	—	—	4.50	6.00

KM# 112.1   PESO
6.3700 g., Bi-Metallic Brass center in Copper-Nickel ring, 22.94 mm.   **Obv:** Argentine arms in circle **Rev:** Design of first Argentine coin in center **Edge:** Plain **Note:** Prev. KM#87.1.

Date	Mintage	F	VF	XF	Unc	BU
1994A	75,000,000	—	0.50	1.20	3.00	4.00
Note: Medal rotation						
1995B	14,000,000	—	0.50	1.20	3.00	4.00
1995A	185,000,000	—	0.50	1.20	3.00	4.00
Note: Medal rotation						
1996A	30,000,000	—	0.50	1.20	3.00	4.00

KM# 112.2   PESO
Bi-Metallic Brass center in Copper-Nickel ring   **Obv:** Smaller Argentine arms in circle **Rev:** Design of first Argentine coin in center **Note:** Prev. KM#87.2.

Date	Mintage	F	VF	XF	Unc	BU
1995C	90,000,000	—	—	—	4.50	5.00

KM# 112.3   PESO
Bi-Metallic Brass center in Copper-Nickel ring   **Obv:** Argentine arms in circle **Rev:** Design of first Argentine coin in center, with error PROVINGIAS in legend **Note:** Prev. KM#87.3.

Date	Mintage	F	VF	XF	Unc	BU
1995B	56,000,000	—	—	—	7.50	8.00

KM# 126   PESO
25.0000 g., 0.9000 Silver 0.7234 oz. ASW   **Subject:** 50th Anniversary - United Nations **Obv:** Stylized dove, national arms below **Rev. Leg.:** ARGENTINA POR LA PAZ EN EL MUNDO **Note:** Prev. KM#101.

Date	Mintage	F	VF	XF	Unc	BU
ND(1995) Proof	500	Value: 45.00				

KM# 120   PESO
Bi-Metallic Brass center in Copper-Nickel ring, 23 mm.   **Subject:** 50th Anniversary - UNICEF **Obv:** Girl with rag doll **Rev:** UNICEF logo above denomination **Note:** Prev. KM#95. Medal rotation.

Date	Mintage	F	VF	XF	Unc	BU
1996	1,000,000	—	—	—	4.50	5.00

KM# 122   PESO
Bi-Metallic Brass center in Copper-Nickel ring, 23 mm.   **Subject:** 50th Anniversary - Women's Suffrage Law **Obv:** Bust of Eva Duarte de Peron right (social reformer) **Rev:** Denomination **Edge:** Reeded **Note:** Prev. KM#97. Medal rotation.

Date	Mintage	F	VF	XF	Unc	BU
1997	1,000,000	—	—	—	5.00	5.50

KM# 125   PESO
Bi-Metallic Brass center in Copper-Nickel ring, 23 mm.   **Subject:** Mercosur **Obv:** Southern Cross constellation **Rev:** Denomination **Note:** Prev. KM#100. Medal rotation.

Date	Mintage	F	VF	XF	Unc	BU
1998	496,715	—	—	—	4.00	5.00

KM# 127   PESO
25.0000 g., 0.9000 Silver 0.7234 oz. ASW   **Subject:** 100th Anniversary - Birth of Jorge Luis Borges **Obv:** Profile of Borges left, dates **Rev:** Labyrinth, sundial, denomination and date **Note:** Prev. KM#102.

Date	Mintage	F	VF	XF	Unc	BU
1999 Proof	5,000	Value: 37.50				

KM# 114   2 PESOS
Nickel   **Subject:** National Constitution Convention **Obv:** Argentine arms above two small arms **Rev:** Open book, ribbon across left page, five line inscription on right page, value below book **Note:** Prev. KM#89.

Date	Mintage	F	VF	XF	Unc	BU
ND(1994)	1,000,000	—	—	—	8.00	9.00
ND(1994) Proof	1,000	Value: 16.00				

KM# 114a   2 PESOS
12.4800 g., 0.9000 Silver 0.3611 oz. ASW   **Subject:** National Constitution Convention **Note:** Prev. KM#89a.

Date	Mintage	F	VF	XF	Unc	BU
ND (1994)	5,000	—	—	—	12.50	14.50
ND (1994) Proof	1,500	Value: 25.00				

KM# 128   2 PESOS
Copper-Nickel   **Subject:** 100th Anniversary - Birth of Jorge Luis Borges **Obv:** Profile head of Borges left **Rev:** Labyrinth, sundial, denomination and date **Note:** Prev. KM#103.

Date	Mintage	F	VF	XF	Unc	BU
1999	1,000,000	—	—	—	8.00	9.00

KM# 115   5 PESOS
Nickel   **Subject:** National Constitution Convention **Obv:** Argentine arms above two smaller arms **Rev:** Open book, ribbon across left page, five line inscription on right page, value below **Note:** Prev. KM#90.

Date	Mintage	F	VF	XF	Unc	BU
ND (1994)	1,000,000	—	—	—	15.00	16.50
ND (1994) Proof	1,000	Value: 25.00				

KM# 115a   5 PESOS
24.8000 g., 0.9000 Silver 0.7176 oz. ASW   **Subject:** National Constitution Convention **Note:** Prev. KM#90a.

Date	Mintage	F	VF	XF	Unc	BU
ND(1994)	5,000	—	—	—	25.00	30.00
ND(1994) Proof	1,500	Value: 60.00				

KM# 152   5 PESOS
8.6040 g., 0.9000 Gold 0.2490 oz. AGW   **Subject:** 50th Anniversary - United Nations **Obv:** Stylized dove, national arms below **Rev:** UN logo, denomination **Rev. Leg.:** ARGENTINA POR LA PAZ EN EL MUNDO

Date	Mintage	F	VF	XF	Unc	BU
ND(1995) Proof	—	Value: 400				

KM# 136   5 PESOS
8.0640 g., 0.9000 Gold 0.2333 oz. AGW   **Subject:** 50th Anniversary O.N.U.

Date	Mintage	F	VF	XF	Unc	BU
1995 Proof	—	Value: 250				

KM# 134   5 PESOS
8.0640 g., 0.9000 Gold 0.2333 oz. AGW, 22 mm.   **Obv:** Writer Jorge Luis Borges, left, (1899-1986) **Rev:** Sundial within labyrinth **Edge:** Reeded

Date	Mintage	F	VF	XF	Unc	BU
1999 Proof	2,000	Value: 235				

KM# 148   5 PESOS
8.0640 g., 0.9000 Gold 0.2333 oz. AGW   **Subject:** General Martin Miguel de Güemes **Obv:** Head right **Rev:** Value **Rev. Leg.:** 17 de JUNIO de 1821

Date	Mintage	F	VF	XF	Unc	BU
2000 Proof	1,000	—	—	—	—	300

KM# 137   5 PESOS
8.0640 g., 0.9000 Gold 0.2333 oz. AGW, 22 mm.   **Subject:** 150th Anniversary Death of San Martin **Obv:** Bust facing **Rev:** Building and value **Edge:** Reeded

Date	Mintage	F	VF	XF	Unc	BU
2000 Proof	1,000	Value: 300				

KM# 116   25 PESOS
4.0320 g., 0.9000 Gold 0.1167 oz. AGW   **Subject:** National Constitution Convention **Obv:** Argentine arms above two small

arms **Rev:** Open book, ribbon across left page, five line inscription on right page **Note:** Prev. KM#91.

Date	Mintage	F	VF	XF	Unc	BU
ND(1994)	5,000	—	—	—	115	125
ND(1994) Proof	1,000	Value: 145				

KM# 118 25 PESOS
27.0000 g., 0.9250 Silver 0.8029 oz. ASW **Subject:** Environmental Protection **Rev:** Giant Armadillo **Note:** Prev. KM#93.

Date	Mintage	F	VF	XF	Unc	BU
1997 Proof	5,000	Value: 50.00				

KM# 123 25 PESOS
27.0000 g., 0.9250 Silver 0.8029 oz. ASW, 40 mm. **Subject:** Ibero-American Series - LaZamba **Obv:** Argentine arms within legend and circle of arms **Rev:** Zamba dancers **Note:** Prev. KM#98.

Date	Mintage	F	VF	XF	Unc	BU
1997 Proof	5,000	Value: 55.00				

KM# 131 25 PESOS
26.9000 g., 0.9250 Silver 0.8000 oz. ASW, 40 mm. **Subject:** Ibero-America Series **Obv:** Argentine arms within legend and circle of arms **Rev:** Bronco busting scene **Edge:** Reeded

Date	Mintage	F	VF	XF	Unc	BU
2000 Proof	5,000	Value: 60.00				

KM# 117 50 PESOS
8.0640 g., 0.9000 Gold 0.2333 oz. AGW **Subject:** National Constitution Convention **Obv:** Argentine arms above two small arms **Rev:** Open book, ribbon across left page, five line inscription on right page **Note:** Prev. KM#92.

Date	Mintage	F	VF	XF	Unc	BU
ND (1994)	5,000	—	—	—	225	235
ND (1994) Proof	1,000	Value: 250				

PATTERNS
Including off metal strikes

KM#	Date	Mintage	Identification	Mkt Val
Pn37	1925	—	2 Centavos. Copper.	—
Pn38	1925	—	2 Centavos. Bronze.	—
Pn39	1932	—	Argentino. Copper.	—
Pn40	1932	—	Argentino. Bronze.	—
Pn41	1933	—	Argentino. Bronze.	—
Pn42	1934	—	Argentino. Copper.	—
Pn43	1935	—	Centavo. Copper.	400
Pn44	1935	—	2 Centavos. Copper.	400
Pn45	1936	—	50 Centavos. Bronze.	—
Pn46	1936	—	50 Centavos. Copper-Nickel.	700
Pn47	1936	—	Peso. Bronze.	—
Pn48	1936	—	Peso. Copper-Nickel.	475
Pn49	1937	—	Centavo. Copper. Argentine arms within wreath. Blank, post horn mint mark.	—
Pn50	1938	—	Centavo. Copper.	250
Pn51	1938	—	2 Centavos. Copper.	275
Pn52	1940	—	50 Centavos. Bronze.	225
Pn53	1940	—	50 Centavos. Copper-Nickel. Head by Oudine.	375
Pn54	1940	—	50 Centavos. Nickel. Head by L. Bazor.	—
Pn55	1941	—	50 Centavos. Nickel.	—
Pn56	1943	—	Peso. Bronze.	—
Pn57	1943	—	Peso. Nickel.	—
Pn58	1943	—	Peso. Bronze. Condor.	—
Pn59	1945	—	Peso. Bronze.	—
Pn60	1945	—	Peso. Copper-Nickel.	—
Pn61	1946	—	Peso. Bronze.	—
Pn62	1946	—	Peso. Copper-Nickel.	550
Pn63	1971	—	50 Centavos. Silverish Aluminum. KM#43	75.00
Pn64	1975	—	Peso. Aluminum-Brass. KM#45	125
Pn65	1976	—	5 Pesos. Silverish Aluminum. KM#46	—
Pn66	1977	—	10 Pesos. Silverish Aluminum-Brass. KM#47	—

MINT SETS

KM#	Date	Mintage	Identification	Issue Price	Mkt Val
MS2	1970 (5)	—	KM#64-68	—	2.00
MS3	1977 (6)	—	KM#75-80	—	32.00
MS4	1977 (3)	—	KM#75-77	—	4.00
MS5	1978 (6)	—	KM#75-80	—	30.00
MS6	1978 (3)	—	KM#75-77.	—	4.00
MS7	1983 (4)	—	KM#87-90	—	2.00

PROOF SETS

KM#	Date	Mintage	Identification	Issue Price	Mkt Val
PS1	1977 (3)	1,000	KM#78-80	—	75.00
PS2	1978 (3)	1,750	KM#78-80	153	75.00
PS3	ND(1994) (2)	5,500	KM#114, 115	—	40.00
PS4	ND(1994) (2)	1,000	KM#114a, 115a	79.50	85.00
PS5	ND(1994) (2)	1,000	KM#116, 117	375	400
PS6	2007 (2)	300	KM#153 & 154	475	475

CATAMARCA

A province located in northwest Argentina having an area of 38,540 sq. mi. and a population of 309,130. Capital: Catamarca. Agriculture and mining are the main industries.

PROVINCE

TOKEN COINAGE
Stabilization Currency Unit

KM# Tn1 100000 AUSTRALES
15.0000 g., 0.9000 Silver 0.4340 oz. ASW **Subject:** Fray Mamerto Esquiu **Obv:** Double-headed figure **Rev:** Head, 3/4 left, date below

Date	Mintage	F	VF	XF	Unc	BU
1990	200,000	—	—	—	28.50	32.50

KM# Tn3 100000 AUSTRALES
14.8500 g., 0.9000 Silver 0.4297 oz. ASW **Subject:** 100th Anniversary - Coronation of Our Lady of the Valley **Obv:** Double-headed figure **Rev:** Imperial crown with cross on top dividing dates

Date	Mintage	F	VF	XF	Unc	BU
1991	—	—	—	—	28.50	32.50

KM# Tn2 4000000 AUSTRALES
20.0000 g., 0.7500 Gold 0.4822 oz. AGW **Subject:** Fray Mamerto Esquiu **Note:** Denomination determined upon release.

Date	Mintage	F	VF	XF	Unc	BU
1990	200	—	—	—	925	945

LA RIOJA

La Rioja (Rioxa), a city and province in northwest Argentina, directly to the south of Catamarca. More than one third of its population of 270,702 resides in the capital city of La Rioja. Total area of the province is 35,649 sq. mi. and the main industries are centered around agriculture and include olive trees, grapes and wine production.

PROVINCE

TOKEN COINAGE
Stabilization Currency Unit

KM# Tn1 100000 AUSTRALES
15.0000 g., 0.9000 Silver 0.4340 oz. ASW **Subject:** 400th Anniversary - Foundation of La Rioja **Obv:** Mountains in oval within wreath, 1/2 radiant sunface at top **Rev:** Statue standing, divides dates

Date	Mintage	F	VF	XF	Unc	BU
1991	200,000	—	—	—	28.50	32.50

KM# Tn2 4000000 AUSTRALES
20.0000 g., 0.7500 Gold 0.4822 oz. AGW **Subject:** 400th Anniversary - Foundation of La Rioja

Date	Mintage	F	VF	XF	Unc	BU
1991	1,000	—	—	—	900	925

ARMENIA

The Republic of Armenia, formerly Armenian S.S.R., is bordered to the north by Georgia, the east by Azerbaijan and the south and west by Turkey and Iran. It has an area of 11,506 sq. mi. (29,800 sq. km) and an estimated population of 3.66 million. Capital: Yerevan. Agriculture including cotton, vineyards and orchards, hydroelectricity, chemicals - primarily synthetic rubber and fertilizers, vast mineral deposits of copper, zinc and aluminum, and production of steel and paper are major industries.

Russia occupied Armenia in 1801 until the Russo-Turkish war of 1878. British intervention excluded either side from remaining although the Armenians remained more loyal to the Ottoman Turks, but in 1894 the Ottoman Turks sent in an expeditionary force of Kurds fearing a revolutionary movement. Large massacres were followed by retaliations, then amnesty was proclaimed which led right into WW I and once again occupation by Russian forces in 1916. After the Russian revolution the Georgians, Armenians and Azerbaijanis formed the short-lived Transcaucasian Federal Republic on Sept. 20, 1917, which broke up into three independent republics on May 26, 1918. Communism developed and in Sept. 1920 the Turks attacked the Armenian Republic; the Russians soon followed suit from Azerbaijan routing the Turks. On Nov. 29, 1920 Armenia was proclaimed a Soviet Socialist Republic. On March 12, 1922, Armenia, Georgia and Azerbaijan were combined to form the Transcaucasian Soviet Federated Socialist Republic, which on Dec. 30, 1922, became a part of U.S.S.R. On Dec. 5, 1936, the Transcaucasian federation was dissolved and Armenia became a constituent Republic of the U.S.S.R. A new constitution was adopted in April 1978. Elections took place on May 20, 1990. The Supreme Soviet adopted a declaration of sovereignty in Aug. 1991, voting to unite Armenia with Nagorno - Karabakh. This newly constituted "Republic of Armenia" became fully independent by popular vote in Sept. 1991. It became a member of the CIS in Dec. 1991.

Fighting between Christians in Armenia and Muslim forces of Azerbaijan escalated in 1992 and continued through early 1994. Each country claimed the Nagorno-Karabakh, an Armenian ethnic enclave, in Azerbaijan. A temporary cease-fire was announced in May 1994.

MONETARY SYSTEM
100 Luma = 1 Dram

MINT NAME
Revan, (Erevan, now Yerevan)

REPUBLIC

STANDARD COINAGE

KM# 51   10 LUMA
0.6000 g., Aluminum, 16 mm. **Obv:** National arms **Rev:** Value over date **Edge:** Plain

Date	Mintage	F	VF	XF	Unc	BU
1994	—	—	—	—	0.40	0.50

KM# 52   20 LUMA
0.7500 g., Aluminum, 18 mm. **Obv:** National arms **Rev:** Value over date **Edge:** Plain

Date	Mintage	F	VF	XF	Unc	BU
1994	—	—	—	—	0.50	0.65

KM# 53   50 LUMA
0.9500 g., Aluminum, 20 mm. **Obv:** National arms **Rev:** Value over date **Edge:** Plain

Date	Mintage	F	VF	XF	Unc	BU
1994	—	—	—	—	0.60	0.75

KM# 54   DRAM
1.4000 g., Aluminum, 20.29 mm. **Obv:** National arms **Rev:** Value over date in sprays **Edge:** Reeded

Date	Mintage	F	VF	XF	Unc	BU
1994	—	—	—	—	0.75	1.00

KM# 55   3 DRAM
1.6500 g., Aluminum, 24 mm. **Obv:** National arms **Rev:** Value over date within sprays **Edge:** Reeded

Date	Mintage	F	VF	XF	Unc	BU
1994	—	—	—	—	1.00	1.25

KM# 56   5 DRAM
2.0000 g., Aluminum, 26 mm. **Obv:** National arms **Rev:** Value over date within sprays **Edge:** Plain

Date	Mintage	F	VF	XF	Unc	BU
1994	—	—	—	—	1.50	1.75

KM# 81   5 DRAM
31.3700 g., 0.9990 Silver 1.0075 oz. ASW, 38 mm. **Subject:** 5th Anniversary - Dram Currency, introduced on November 22, 1993 **Obv:** National arms **Rev:** 6 banknote designs

Date	Mintage	F	VF	XF	Unc	BU
1998 Proof	500	Value: 70.00				

KM# 58   10 DRAM
2.3000 g., Aluminum, 26.3 mm. **Obv:** National arms **Rev:** Value over date within sprays **Edge:** Plain

Date	Mintage	F	VF	XF	Unc	BU
1994	—	—	—	—	2.00	2.50

KM# 82   10 DRAM
31.0000 g., 0.9990 Silver 0.9956 oz. ASW, 38 mm. **Subject:** 10th Anniversary - Earthquake, December 7, 1988 **Obv:** National arms **Rev:** Map and building

Date	Mintage	F	VF	XF	Unc	BU
1998 Proof	1,000	Value: 70.00				

KM# 57   25 DRAM
31.1035 g., 0.9990 Silver 0.9990 oz. ASW, 38 mm. **Subject:** 1918 Battle of Sardarapat **Obv:** National arms **Rev:** Symbolic design **Edge:** Numbered

Date	Mintage	F	VF	XF	Unc	BU
1994 Proof	3,000	Value: 60.00				

KM# 59   25 DRAM
28.2800 g., 0.9250 Silver 0.8410 oz. ASW, 38.61 mm. **Obv:** National arms above value **Rev:** Apricot

Date	Mintage	F	VF	XF	Unc	BU
1994 Proof	10,000	Value: 60.00				

KM# 60   25 DRAM
31.1035 g., 0.9990 Silver 0.9990 oz. ASW **Subject:** David of Sasun **Obv:** National arms above denomination **Rev:** Monument of David mounted on rearing horse with sword held with two hands **Edge:** Numbered

Date	Mintage	F	VF	XF	Unc	BU
1994 Proof	5,000	Value: 50.00				

KM# 61 25 DRAM
31.1035 g., 0.9990 Silver 0.9990 oz. ASW, 38 mm.
Subject: Temple of Garni **Obv:** National arms over value and date **Rev:** Temple building **Edge:** Numbered

Date	Mintage	F	VF	XF	Unc	BU
1994 Proof	5,000	Value: 50.00				

KM# 63 25 DRAM
31.1035 g., 0.9990 Silver 0.9990 oz. ASW **Subject:** Artsakh
Obv: National arms above denomination **Rev:** Symbolic artifacts, sword, eagle, church....

Date	Mintage	F	VF	XF	Unc	BU
1994 Proof	5,000	Value: 50.00				

KM# 72 100 DRAM
28.2800 g., 0.9250 Silver 0.8410 oz. ASW, 38.6 mm.
Subject: 50th Anniversary - United Nations **Obv:** National arms **Rev:** Seated Madonna and child

Date	Mintage	F	VF	XF	Unc	BU
1995 Proof	100,000	Value: 50.00				

KM# 64 100 DRAM
31.1035 g., 0.9990 Silver 0.9990 oz. ASW, 38 mm.
Subject: Chess Olympics in Yerevan **Obv:** National arms above value **Rev:** Symbolic chess board

Date	Mintage	F	VF	XF	Unc	BU
1996 Proof	2,000	Value: 50.00				

KM# 69 100 DRAM
10.8000 g., Copper-Nickel, 29.5 mm. **Subject:** XXXII Chess Olympiad in Yerevan **Obv:** Eagle and lion support arms **Rev:** Stylized stork and chessboard in inner circle

Date	Mintage	F	VF	XF	Unc	BU
1996	—				7.00	9.00
1996 Proof	2,000	Value: 12.50				

KM# 70 100 DRAM
28.2800 g., 0.9250 Silver 0.8410 oz. ASW, 38.61 mm.
Subject: XXXII Chess Olympiad **Obv:** Eagle and lion support arms **Rev:** Stylized stork and chessboard

Date	Mintage	F	VF	XF	Unc	BU
1996 Proof	10,000	Value: 55.00				

KM# 77 100 DRAM
31.1500 g., 0.9990 Silver 1.0005 oz. ASW, 38 mm.
Subject: Marshal Bagramian, Centennial **Obv:** National arms **Rev:** Uniformed portrait

Date	Mintage	F	VF	XF	Unc	BU
1996 Proof	—	Value: 300				
1997 Proof	1,200	Value: 50.00				

KM# 71 100 DRAM
28.2800 g., Copper-Nickel, 38.61 mm. **Subject:** WWF Conserving Nature 1997 **Obv:** National emblem **Rev:** Caucasian otter

Date	Mintage	F	VF	XF	Unc	BU
1997	—			—	12.00	15.00

KM# 71a 100 DRAM
28.2800 g., 0.9250 Silver 0.8410 oz. ASW, 38.61 mm.
Subject: WWF Conserving Nature **Obv:** National emblem **Rev:** Caucasian otter

Date	Mintage	F	VF	XF	Unc	BU
1997 Proof	15,000	Value: 80.00				

KM# 76 100 DRAM
10.8000 g., Copper-Nickel, 28.5 mm. **Subject:** Charents **Obv:** National emblem **Rev:** Facial portrait of poet, Yogishe Charents, Centennial

Date	Mintage	F	VF	XF	Unc	BU
1997	—				6.00	8.00

KM# 78 100 DRAM
Copper-Nickel, 38.61 mm. **Subject:** WWF Conserving Nature **Obv:** National arms **Rev:** Armenian silver seagull

Date	Mintage	F	VF	XF	Unc	BU
1998	—				12.00	15.00

KM# 78a 100 DRAM
28.2800 g., 0.9250 Silver 0.8410 oz. ASW, 38.61 mm.
Subject: WWF Conserving Nature **Obv:** National arms **Rev:** Armenian silver seagull

Date	Mintage	F	VF	XF	Unc	BU
1998 Proof	15,000	Value: 80.00				

KM# 79 100 DRAM
28.2800 g., 0.9250 Silver 0.8410 oz. ASW, 38.61 mm.
Subject: XVIII Olympic Winter Games **Obv:** Arms **Rev:** Downhill skiers

Date	Mintage	F	VF	XF	Unc	BU
1998 Proof	10,000	Value: 110				

KM# 80 100 DRAM
28.2800 g., 0.9250 Silver 0.8410 oz. ASW, 38.61 mm.
Subject: 1998 World Cup Soccer **Obv:** Arms **Rev:** Soccer players, map of France

Date	Mintage	F	VF	XF	Unc	BU
1998 Proof	10,000	Value: 110				

KM# 100   200 DRAM
31.1000 g., 0.9990 Silver 0.9988 oz. ASW, 38 mm.
Obv: National arms **Rev:** A.S. Pushkin left, 200th Anniversary of
birth June 6, 1799

Date	Mintage	F	VF	XF	Unc	BU
1999 Proof	500	Value: 65.00				

KM# 65   500 DRAM
155.5175 g., 0.9990 Silver 4.9948 oz. ASW, 63 mm. **Subject:**
National Assembly Building **Obv:** National arms above value
Rev: View of building **Edge:** 5TO .999 AG and serial number

Date	Mintage	F	VF	XF	Unc	BU
1995 Proof	300	Value: 400				

KM# 66   500 DRAM
155.5175 g., 0.9990 Silver 4.9948 oz. ASW, 63 mm. **Subject:**
Historical Armenian Coat of Arms Series **Obv:** National arms
Rev: Arms of the Kingdom of Cilicia **Note:** Illustration reduced.

Date	Mintage	F	VF	XF	Unc	BU
1995 Proof	300	Value: 400				

KM# 67   500 DRAM
155.5175 g., 0.9990 Silver 4.9948 oz. ASW, 63 mm. **Subject:**
Historical Armenian Coat of Arms Series **Obv:** National arms **Rev:**
Arms of Arshakonni dynasty 66-428 AD **Note:** Illustration reduced.

Date	Mintage	F	VF	XF	Unc	BU
1995 Proof	300	Value: 400				

KM# 74   500 DRAM
155.5175 g., 0.9990 Silver 4.9948 oz. ASW, 63 mm.
Subject: Historical Armenian Coat of Arms - Double Eagle
Obv: National arms **Rev:** Arms of the Artashesyan Dynasty 189
BC to 1 AD **Note:** Illustration reduced.

Date	Mintage	F	VF	XF	Unc	BU
1995 Proof	300	Value: 400				

KM# 73   500 DRAM
155.5175 g., 0.9990 Silver 4.9948 oz. ASW, 63 mm.
Subject: Historical Armenian Coat of Arms - Lion **Obv:** National
arms **Rev:** Arms of the Bagratourni dynasty **Edge:** With 5T0 .999
AG and serial number **Note:** Photo reduced.

Date	Mintage	F	VF	XF	Unc	BU
1995 Proof	300	Value: 400				

KM# 68   1000 DRAM
31.1035 g., 0.9990 Silver 0.9990 oz. ASW **Subject:** Early
Armenian Currency - Vignette from 100 Rouble Note **Obv:**
National arms above value **Rev:** Vignette from 100 Rouble note

Date	Mintage	F	VF	XF	Unc	BU
1994 Proof	5,000	Value: 50.00				

KM# 83   1000 DRAM
31.3100 g., 0.9990 Silver 1.0056 oz. ASW, 38 mm.
Subject: 1700th Anniversary of the Adoption of Christianity in
Armenia **Obv:** National arms **Rev:** Etchmiadzin church

Date	Mintage	F	VF	XF	Unc	BU
1998 Proof	1,700	Value: 200				

KM# 84   1000 DRAM
31.3100 g., 0.9990 Silver 1.0056 oz. ASW, 38 mm.
Subject: 1700th Anniversary of the Adoption of Christianity in
Armenia **Obv:** National arms **Rev:** Ani church tower

Date	Mintage	F	VF	XF	Unc	BU
1998 Proof	1,700	Value: 200				

KM# 85   1000 DRAM
31.3100 g., 0.9990 Silver 1.0056 oz. ASW, 38 mm. **Subject:**
1700th Anniversary of the Adoption of Christianity in Armenia
Obv: National arms **Rev:** Haghpat carved stone cross, khachkar

Date	Mintage	F	VF	XF	Unc	BU
1998 Proof	1,700	Value: 200				

KM# 88   2000 DRAM
28.2800 g., 0.9250 Silver 0.8410 oz. ASW, 38.6 mm.
Subject: Millennium **Obv:** National arms **Rev:** Mounted St.
George slaying a dragon **Edge:** Plain

Date	Mintage	F	VF	XF	Unc	BU
2000 Proof	30,000	Value: 60.00				

KM# 89   5000 DRAM
31.1000 g., 0.9990 Silver 0.9988 oz. ASW, 38 mm.
Subject: 1700th Anniversary of the adoption of Christianity in
Armenia **Obv:** National arms **Rev:** Holy Cross Church (915)
Aghtamar Island in Lake Van **Edge:** Plain with serial number

Date	Mintage	F	VF	XF	Unc	BU
1999 Proof	1,700	Value: 200				

KM# 101   5000 DRAM
31.1000 g., 0.9990 Silver 0.9988 oz. ASW, 38 mm.
Obv: National arms **Rev:** Chess Grand Master Tigran Petrosyan

Date	Mintage	F	VF	XF	Unc	BU
1999 Proof	500	Value: 100				

KM# 103   5000 DRAM
31.1000 g., 0.9990 Silver 0.9988 oz. ASW, 38 mm.
Obv: National arms **Rev:** First Pan-Armenian Games logo in
Yerevan August 28 to September 15 1999

Date	Mintage	F	VF	XF	Unc	BU
1999 Proof	500	Value: 100				

KM# 104   5000 DRAM
31.1000 g., 0.9990 Silver 0.9988 oz. ASW, 38 mm.
Obv: National arms **Rev:** Large tree logo of the First
Pan-Armenian Congress of the Armenian Diaspora September
22-23, 1999

Date	Mintage	F	VF	XF	Unc	BU
1999 Proof	500	Value: 65.00				

KM# 90   10000 DRAM
8.6400 g., 0.9000 Gold 0.2500 oz. AGW, 22 mm.
Subject: Christian Armenia - Ani **Obv:** National arms
Rev: Church tower **Edge:** Plain with serial number

Date	Mintage	F	VF	XF	Unc	BU
1998 Proof	1,700	Value: 400				

KM# 91   10000 DRAM
8.6400 g., 0.9000 Gold 0.2500 oz. AGW, 22 mm. **Subject:** 1700th
Anniversary of the adoption of Christianity in Armenia **Obv:** National
arms **Rev:** Multi-towered church **Edge:** Plain with serial number

Date	Mintage	F	VF	XF	Unc	BU
1998 Proof	1,700	Value: 400				

KM# 75.1   25000 DRAM
4.3000 g., 0.9000 Gold 0.1244 oz. AGW, 18 mm. **Obv:** National
arms **Rev:** Portrait of goddess Anahit **Edge:** Reeded

Date	Mintage	F	VF	XF	Unc	BU
1997 Proof	—	Value: 200				

KM# 75.2   25000 DRAM
4.3000 g., 0.9000 Gold 0.1244 oz. AGW, 18 mm. **Obv:** National
arms **Rev:** Portrait of goddess Anahit left **Edge:** Plain

Date	Mintage	F	VF	XF	Unc	BU
1997 Proof	—	Value: 200				

KM# 92   50000 DRAM
8.6400 g., 0.9000 Gold 0.2500 oz. AGW, 22 mm.
Subject: 1700th Anniversary of the Adoption of Christianity in
Armenia **Obv:** National arms **Rev:** Holy Cross Church (915)
Aghtamer Island in Lake Van **Edge:** Plain with serial number

Date	Mintage	F	VF	XF	Unc	BU
1999 Proof	1,700	Value: 400				

KM# 105   50000 DRAM
8.6000 g., 0.9000 Gold 0.2488 oz. AGW, 22 mm. **Obv:** National
arms on an ancient coin design **Rev:** Ancient Armenian King
Tigran the Great 95-55 BC

Date	Mintage	F	VF	XF	Unc	BU
1999 Proof	500	Value: 400				

KM# 102   100000 DRAM
17.2000 g., 0.9000 Gold 0.4977 oz. AGW, 30 mm.
Obv: National arms **Rev:** Noah's descent from Mt. Ararat

Date	Mintage	F	VF	XF	Unc	BU
1999 Proof	1,000	Value: 850				

MINT SETS

KM#	Date	Mintage	Identification	Issue Price	Mkt Val
MS1	1994 (7)	—	KM#51-56, 58	30.00	20.00

ARUBA

Aruba, formerly a part of the Netherlands Antilles, achieved
on Jan. 1, 1986 a special status, "status aparte" as the third state
under the Dutch crown, together with the Netherlands and the
remaining five islands of the Netherlands Antilles. On Dec. 15,
1954 the Netherlands Antilles were given complete domestic
autonomy and granted equality within the Kingdom of the Netherlands. The separate constitution put in place for Aruba in 1986
established it as an autonomous government within the Kingdom
of the Netherlands. In 1990 Aruba opted to remain a part of the
Kingdom without the promise of future independence.

The second largest island of the Netherlands Antilles, Aruba
is situated near the Venezuelan coast. The island has an area of
74-1/2 sq. mi. (193 sq. km.) and a population of 65,974. Capital:
Oranjestad, named after the Dutch royal family. Aruba was important in the processing and transportation of petroleum products in
the first part of the twentieth century, but today the chief industry
is tourism.

For earlier issues see Curacao and the Netherlands Antilles.

RULER
Dutch

MINT MARKS
(u) Utrecht - Privy marks only
　Anvil, 1986-1988
　Bow and Arrow, 1989-1999
　Bow and Arrow w/star, 2000-

MONETARY SYSTEM
100 Cents = 1 Florin

DUTCH STATE
"Status Aparte"

REGULAR COINAGE

KM# 1   5 CENTS
2.0000 g., Nickel Bonded Steel, 16 mm. **Ruler:** Beatrix **Obv:**
National arms **Rev:** Geometric design with value **Edge:** Plain

Date	Mintage	F	VF	XF	Unc	BU
1986(u)	776,000	—	0.10	0.15	0.30	0.50
1987(u)	461,651	—	0.10	0.15	0.30	0.50

Date	Mintage	F	VF	XF	Unc	BU
1988(u)	656,500	—	—	0.20	0.40	0.60
1989(u)	770,000	—	—	0.20	0.40	0.60
1990(u)	612,000	—	—	0.20	0.40	0.60
1991(u)	412,000	—	—	0.20	0.50	1.00
1992(u)	810,500	—	—	—	0.20	0.50
1993(u)	709,100	—	—	—	0.20	0.50
1994(u)	709,100	—	—	—	0.20	0.50
1995(u)	808,500	—	—	—	0.20	0.50
1996(u)	587,500	—	—	—	0.20	0.50
1997(u)	535,500	—	—	—	0.20	0.50
1998(u)	920,000	—	—	—	0.20	0.50
1999(u)	823,000	—	—	—	0.20	0.50
2000(u)	886,500	—	—	—	0.20	0.50

KM# 2   10 CENTS
3.0000 g., Nickel Bonded Steel, 18 mm. **Ruler:** Beatrix
Obv: National arms **Rev:** Geometric design with value
Edge: Reeded

Date	Mintage	F	VF	XF	Unc	BU
1986(u)	856,200	—	0.20	0.35	0.60	0.75
1987(u)	371,651	—	0.20	0.35	0.60	0.75
1988(u)	986,500	—	—	0.15	0.35	0.50
1989(u)	610,000	—	—	0.15	0.35	0.50
1990(u)	762,000	—	0.20	0.35	0.60	0.75
1991(u)	512,000	—	0.20	0.35	0.60	0.75
1992(u)	610,500	—	0.20	0.35	0.60	0.75
1993(u)	1,009,100	—	—	—	0.30	0.50
1994(u)	409,100	—	0.20	0.35	0.60	0.75
1995(u)	918,500	—	—	—	0.30	0.50
1996(u)	457,500	—	0.20	0.35	0.60	0.75
1997(u)	423,500	—	0.20	0.35	0.60	0.75
1998(u)	954,000	—	—	—	0.30	0.50
1999(u)	1,004,000	—	—	—	0.30	0.50
2000(u)	759,500	—	—	—	0.30	0.50

KM# 3   25 CENTS
3.5000 g., Nickel Bonded Steel, 20 mm. **Ruler:** Beatrix
Obv: National arms **Rev:** Geometric design with value
Edge: Plain

Date	Mintage	F	VF	XF	Unc	BU
1986(u)	856,200	—	0.20	0.40	0.75	1.50
1987(u)	331,651	—	0.20	0.40	0.75	1.50
1988(u)	116,500	—	0.20	0.40	0.75	1.50
1989(u)	360,000	—	0.20	0.40	0.75	1.50
1990(u)	512,000	—	—	—	0.45	0.80
1991(u)	612,000	—	—	—	0.45	0.80
1992(u)	460,500	—	—	—	0.45	0.80
1993(u)	609,100	—	—	—	0.45	0.80
1994(u)	109,100	—	0.20	0.40	0.75	1.50
1995(u)	608,500	—	—	—	0.35	0.80
1996(u)	287,500	—	—	—	0.60	1.00
1997(u)	467,500	—	—	—	0.50	0.90
1998(u)	641,000	—	—	—	0.35	0.80
1999(u)	332,000	—	—	—	0.40	0.80
2000(u)	330,500	—	—	—	0.40	0.80

KM# 4   50 CENTS
5.0000 g., Nickel Bonded Steel, 20 mm. **Ruler:** Beatrix
Obv: National arms **Rev:** Geometric design with value
Edge: Plain

Date	Mintage	F	VF	XF	Unc	BU
1986(u)	486,200	—	0.30	0.50	1.00	1.50
1987(u)	121,651	F	0.30	0.50	1.00	1.50
1988(u)	216,500	—	0.25	0.45	1.00	1.50
1989(u)	110,000	—	0.30	0.50	1.25	2.25
1990(u)	262,000	—	0.25	0.45	1.00	1.50
1991(u)	312,000	—	—	0.40	0.90	1.10
1992(u)	310,500	—	—	0.40	0.90	1.10
1993(u)	459,100	—	—	0.35	0.65	0.80
1994(u)	309,100	—	—	0.35	0.65	0.80
1995(u)	258,500	—	—	0.40	0.90	1.10
1996(u)	392,500	—	—	0.35	0.65	0.80
1997(u)	27,500	—	—	1.00	2.00	3.00
1998(u)	197,000	—	—	0.35	0.65	0.80
1999(u)	445,000	—	—	0.35	0.65	0.80
2000(u)	54,500	—	—	0.50	1.00	1.20

KM# 5   FLORIN
8.5000 g., Nickel Bonded Steel, 26 mm. **Ruler:** Beatrix **Obv:** Head
left **Rev:** National arms **Edge:** Lettered, GOD * ZiJ * MET * ONS

Date	Mintage	F	VF	XF	Unc	BU
1986(u)	586,200	—	0.60	1.00	2.00	3.00
1987(u)	271,651	—	0.60	1.00	2.00	3.00
1988(u)	566,500	—	—	0.65	1.25	2.25
1989(u)	410,000	—	—	0.65	1.25	2.25
1990(u)	412,000	—	—	0.65	1.25	2.25
1991(u)	162,000	—	—	0.75	1.75	3.00
1992(u)	510,500	—	—	0.65	1.25	2.25
1993(u)	409,100	—	—	0.65	1.25	2.25
1994(u)	109,100	—	—	0.65	1.25	2.25
1995(u)	208,500	—	—	0.65	1.25	2.25
1996(u)	132,500	—	—	0.75	1.75	3.00
1997(u)	415,500	—	—	0.65	1.25	2.25
1998(u)	300,000	—	—	0.65	1.25	2.25
1999(u)	430,000	—	—	0.65	1.25	2.25
2000(u)	295,500	—	—	0.65	1.25	2.25

KM# 6   2-1/2 FLORIN
10.3000 g., Nickel Bonded Steel, 30 mm. **Ruler:** Beatrix **Obv:** Head
left **Rev:** National arms **Edge:** Lettered, GOD * ZiJ * MET * ONS

Date	Mintage	F	VF	XF	Unc	BU
1986(u)	106,200	—	—	1.75	2.50	3.75
1987(u)	31,651	—	—	2.00	2.75	4.00
1988(u)	26,500	—	—	2.00	2.75	4.00
1989(u)	15,000	—	—	2.00	3.00	4.50
1990(u)	17,000	—	—	2.00	3.00	4.50
1991(u)	17,000	—	—	2.00	3.00	4.50
1992(u)	12,500	—	—	2.00	3.00	4.75
1993(u)	11,100	—	—	2.00	3.00	4.75
1994(u)	11,100	—	—	2.00	3.00	4.75
1995(u)	10,500	—	—	2.00	3.00	4.75
1996(u)	7,500	—	—	2.00	3.50	5.00
Note: In sets only						
1997(u)	7,500	—	—	1.75	3.50	5.00
Note: In sets only						
1998(u)	8,000	—	—	1.75	3.50	5.00
Note: In sets only						
1999(u)	7,500	—	—	1.75	3.50	5.00
Note: In sets only						
2000(u)	7,500	—	—	1.75	3.50	5.00
Note: In sets only						

KM# 12   5 FLORIN
8.6400 g., Nickel Bonded Steel, 26 mm. **Ruler:** Beatrix
Obv: Head left **Rev:** National arms **Edge:** Plain

Date	Mintage	F	VF	XF	Unc	BU
1995(u)	200,500	—	—	2.00	4.50	6.00
1996(u)	357,500	—	—	2.00	4.50	6.00
1997(u)	27,500	—	—	2.25	5.50	7.00
1998(u)	162,000	—	—	2.00	4.50	6.00
1999(u)	86,200	—	—	2.25	5.50	7.00
2000(u)	7,500	—	—	3.00	6.00	7.50

Note: In sets only

KM# 7   25 FLORIN
25.0000 g., 0.9250 Silver 0.7435 oz. ASW, 38 mm.
Subject: Independence **Obv:** Head of Queen Beatrix left **Rev:**
Arms, treaty name, date, and value, GOD * ZiJ * MET * ONS

Date	Mintage	F	VF	XF	Unc	BU
ND(1986)(u)	5,000	—	—	—	30.00	—
ND(1986)(u) Proof	10,250	Value: 30.00				

KM# 8   25 FLORIN
25.0000 g., 0.9250 Silver 0.7435 oz. ASW, 38 mm. **Subject:**
Independence **Obv:** Head of Queen Beatrix left **Rev:** Triangular
portion of flag, treaty name, date, value, GOD * ZiJ * MET * ONS

Date	Mintage	F	VF	XF	Unc	BU
ND(1991)(u)	2,500	—	—	—	30.00	—
ND(1991)(u) Proof	4,600	Value: 40.00				

KM# 10   25 FLORIN
25.0000 g., 0.9250 Silver 0.7435 oz. ASW, 38 mm. **Series:** 1992
Olympics **Subject:** Windsurfing **Obv:** Head of Queen Beatrix left
Rev: Windsurfer **Edge:** Plain

Date	Mintage	F	VF	XF	Unc	BU
1992(u)	2,000	—	—	—	32.50	—
1992(u) Proof	16,000	Value: 40.00				

KM# 11   25 FLORIN
25.0000 g., 0.9250 Silver 0.7435 oz. ASW, 38 mm.
Subject: Oil for Peace (WWII) **Obv:** Head of Queen Beatrix left
Rev: Freighter, tankers and refinery **Edge:** Plain

Date	Mintage	F	VF	XF	Unc	BU
1994(u)	1,500	—	—	—	35.00	—
1994(u) Proof	4,000	Value: 40.00				

KM# 13 25 FLORIN
25.0000 g., 0.9250 Silver 0.7435 oz. ASW, 38 mm.
Subject: 100th Anniversary of the Olympics **Obv:** Head of Queen Beatrix left **Rev:** Cyclist and logo **Edge:** Plain

Date	Mintage	F	VF	XF	Unc	BU
1995(u)	1,000	—	—	—	40.00	—
1995(u) Proof	2,100	Value: 50.00				

KM# 14 25 FLORIN
25.0000 g., 0.9250 Silver 0.7435 oz. ASW, 38 mm.
Subject: 100th Anniversary of the Olympics **Obv:** Head of Queen Beatrix left **Rev:** Cyclist, without logo **Edge:** Plain

Date	Mintage	F	VF	XF	Unc	BU
1995(u) Proof	1,700	Value: 65.00				

KM# 15 25 FLORIN
25.0000 g., 0.9250 Silver 0.7435 oz. ASW, 38 mm. **Obv:** Head of Queen Beatrix left **Rev:** Sea turtles with pre-Columbian design **Edge:** Plain

Date	Mintage	F	VF	XF	Unc	BU
1995(u)	3,500	—	—	—	—	50.00
1995(u) Proof	2,000	Value: 55.00				

KM# 18 25 FLORIN
25.0000 g., 0.9250 Silver 0.7435 oz. ASW, 38 mm.
Subject: Tradition With Vision - Discovery 1499 **Obv:** Portrait of Vespucci, sailing vessel, map **Rev:** Spanish fan and aboriginal design, dates **Edge:** Plain

Date	Mintage	F	VF	XF	Unc	BU
ND(1999)(u) Proof	1,850	Value: 60.00				

KM# 21 25 FLORIN
25.0000 g., 0.9250 Silver 0.7435 oz. ASW, 38 mm.
Subject: Olympics **Obv:** Head of Queen Beatrix left **Rev:** Catamaran sailboat **Edge:** Plain

Date	Mintage	F	VF	XF	Unc	BU
2000(u) Proof	3,500	Value: 40.00				

KM# 9 50 FLORIN
6.7200 g., 0.9000 Gold 0.1944 oz. AGW, 22.5 mm.
Subject: Independence **Obv:** Head of Queen Beatrix left **Rev:** Triangular portion of flag, treaty name and date **Edge:** Grained

Date	Mintage	F	VF	XF	Unc	BU
ND(1991)(u) Proof	2,600	Value: 200				

KM# 16 50 FLORIN
25.0000 g., 0.9250 Silver 0.7435 oz. ASW, 38 mm.
Subject: 10th Anniversary of Autonomy **Obv:** Head of Queen Beatrix left **Rev:** Portions of national flag and anthem score **Note:** Similar to 100 Florin, KM#17

Date	Mintage	F	VF	XF	Unc	BU
ND(1996)(u)	500	—	—	—	45.00	—
ND(1996)(u) Proof	2,000	Value: 40.00				

KM# 17 100 FLORIN
6.7200 g., 0.9000 Gold 0.1944 oz. AGW, 22.5 mm.
Subject: 10th Anniversary of Autonomy **Obv:** Head of Queen Beatrix left **Rev:** Portions of national flag and anthem score **Edge:** Grained

Date	Mintage	F	VF	XF	Unc	BU
ND(1996)(u) Proof	535	Value: 250				

KM# 19 100 FLORIN
6.7200 g., 0.9000 Gold 0.1944 oz. AGW, 22.5 mm.
Subject: Tradition With Vision - Discovery 1499 **Obv:** Portrait of Vespucci, sailing vessel, map **Rev:** Spanish fan and aboriginal design, dates **Edge:** Grained **Note:** Similar to 25 Florin, KM#18.

Date	Mintage	F	VF	XF	Unc	BU
ND(1999)(u) Proof	1,100	Value: 240				

MINT SETS

KM#	Date	Mintage	Identification	Issue Price	Mkt Val
MS1	1986 (6)	36,200	KM#1-6, with medal	8.95	10.00
MS2	1987 (6)	21,650	KM#1-6, with medal	9.95	10.00
MS3	1988 (6)	16,500	KM#1-6, with medal	12.95	10.00
MS4	1989 (6)	10,000	KM#1-6, with medal	12.00	12.50
MS5	1990 (6)	12,000	KM#1-6, with medal	—	15.00
MS6	1991 (6)	12,000	KM#1-6, with medal	14.50	15.00
MS7	1992 (6)	10,500	KM#1-6, with medal	—	17.50
MS8	1993 (6)	9,100	KM#1-6, with medal	—	17.50
MS9	1994 (6)	9,100	KM#1-6, with medal	14.50	17.50
MS10	1995 (1)	1,000	KM#12	—	20.00
MS11	1995 (6)	8,500	KM#1-6, with medal	17.50	17.50
MS12	1995 (2)	2,500	KM#15, 5 Florin banknote, with medal	56.50	50.00
MS13	1996 (7)	7,500	KM#1-6, 12, with medal	17.50	12.50
MS14	1997 (7)	7,500	KM#1-6, 12, with medal	17.50	12.50
MS15	1998 (7)	8,000	KM#1-6, 12, with medal	17.50	12.50
MS16	1999 (7)	7,000	KM#1-6, 12, with medal	17.50	12.50
MS17	2000 (7)	7,500	KM#1-6, 12	15.00	12.50

PROOF SETS

KM#	Date	Mintage	Identification	Issue Price	Mkt Val
PS1	1999 (5)	—	KM#18-19, with Netherlands Antilles KM#45-47 Tradition with Vision 1499-1999	580	850

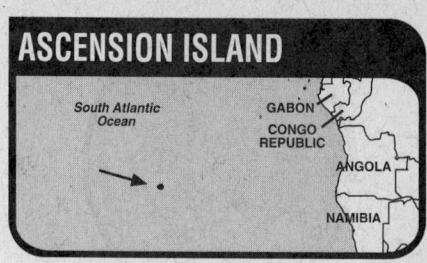

ASCENSION ISLAND

South Atlantic Ocean · GABON · CONGO REPUBLIC · ANGOLA · NAMIBIA

An island of volcanic origin, Ascension Island lies in the South Atlantic, 700 miles (1,100 km.) northwest of St. Helena. It has an area of 34 sq. mi. (88 sq. km.) on an island 9 miles (14 km.) long and 6 miles (10 km.) wide. Approximate population: 1,146. Although having little vegetation and scant rainfall, the island has a very healthy climate. The island is the nesting place for a large number of sea turtles and sooty terns. Phosphates and guano are the chief natural sources of income.

The island was discovered on Ascension Day, 1501, by Joao da Nova, a Portuguese navigator. It lay unoccupied until 1815, when occupied by the British. It was under Admiralty rule until 1922 when it was annexed as a dependency of St. Helena. During World War II an airfield was built that has been used as a fueling stop for Transatlantic flights to Southern Europe, North Africa and the Near-East.

RULER
British

MINT MARK
PM - Pobjoy Mint

BRITISH ADMINISTRATION
STANDARD COINAGE

KM# 1 25 PENCE (Crown)
Copper-Nickel, 38.5 mm. **Subject:** 25th Anniversary of Coronation **Obv:** Young bust of Queen Elizabeth right **Rev:** Lion left above sea turtle

Date	Mintage	F	VF	XF	Unc	BU
1978PM	—	—	—	—	7.50	10.00

KM# 1a 25 PENCE (Crown)
28.2800 g., 0.9250 Silver 0.8410 oz. ASW, 38.5 mm.
Subject: 25th Anniversary of Coronation **Obv:** Young bust of Queen Elizabeth II right **Rev:** Lion left above sea turtle

Date	Mintage	F	VF	XF	Unc	BU
1978PM	70,000	—	—	—	—	17.50
1978PM Proof	25,000	Value: 22.50				

KM# 2 25 PENCE (Crown)
28.2800 g., 0.9250 Silver 0.8410 oz. ASW, 38.5 mm.
Subject: 25th Anniversary of the Coronation **Obv:** Isle of Man,bust of young Elizabeth wearing crown, right **Rev:** Lion left above sea turtle **Note:** Error; mule.

Date	Mintage	F	VF	XF	Unc	BU
ND(1978)PM	367	—	—	150	200	—

KM# 3   25 PENCE (Crown)
Copper-Nickel, 38.5 mm.   **Subject:** Wedding of Prince Charles and Lady Diana **Obv:** Young bust of Queen Elizabeth II right **Rev:** 2 coats of arms

Date	Mintage	F	VF	XF	Unc	BU
1981PM	50,000	—	—	—	4.50	6.00

KM# 3a   25 PENCE (Crown)
28.2800 g., 0.5000 Silver 0.4546 oz. ASW, 38.5 mm.
Subject: Wedding of Prince Charles and Lady Diana **Obv:** Young bust of Queen Elizabeth II right **Rev:** 2 coats of arms

Date	Mintage	F	VF	XF	Unc	BU
1981	500	—	—	—	50.00	55.00

KM# 3b   25 PENCE (Crown)
28.2800 g., 0.9250 Silver 0.8410 oz. ASW, 38.5 mm.
Subject: Wedding of Prince Charles and Lady Diana **Obv:** Young bust of Queen Elizabeth II right **Rev:** 2 coats of arms

Date	Mintage	F	VF	XF	Unc	BU
1981 Proof	30,000	Value: 22.50				

KM# 4   25 PENCE (Crown)
28.2800 g., 0.9250 Silver 0.8410 oz. ASW, 38.5 mm.
Subject: International Year of the Scout **Obv:** Bust of Queen Elizabeth II right **Rev:** Sir. Robert S. S. Baden-Powell, 3/4 left

Date	Mintage	F	VF	XF	Unc	BU
ND(1983)	10,000	—	—	—	30.00	32.50
ND(1983) Proof	10,000	Value: 42.50				

KM# 6   50 PENCE
Copper-Nickel, 38.5 mm.   **Subject:** Royal Visit of Prince Andrew **Obv:** Young bust of Queen Elizabeth II, right **Rev:** Bust of Prince Andrew left

Date	Mintage	F	VF	XF	Unc	BU
1984	125,000	—	—	—	4.00	5.50

KM# 6a   50 PENCE
28.2800 g., 0.9250 Silver 0.8410 oz. ASW, 38.5 mm.
Subject: Royal Visit of Prince Andrew **Obv:** Bust of young Queen Elizabeth II right **Rev:** Bust of Prince Andrew left

Date	Mintage	F	VF	XF	Unc	BU
1984 Proof	5,000	Value: 22.50				

KM# 7   50 PENCE
Copper-Nickel, 38.5 mm.   **Obv:** Bust of crowned Queen Elizabeth II, right **Rev:** Queen Mother fishing with waders and hat

Date	Mintage	F	VF	XF	Unc	BU
1995	—	—	—	—	4.00	5.50

KM# 7a   50 PENCE
28.2800 g., 0.9250 Silver 0.8410 oz. ASW, 38.5 mm.
Obv: Crowned bust of Queen Elizabeth II right **Rev:** Queen Mother fishing in waders and hat

Date	Mintage	F	VF	XF	Unc	BU
1995 Proof	—	Value: 32.50				

KM# 7b   50 PENCE
47.5400 g., 0.9160 Gold 1.4000 oz. AGW **Obv:** Crowned bust of Queen Elizabeth II right **Rev:** Queen Mother fishing with waders and hat

Date	Mintage	F	VF	XF	Unc	BU
1995 Proof	150	Value: 1,400				

KM# 8   50 PENCE
Copper-Nickel, 38.5 mm.   **Subject:** 70th Birthday - Queen Elizabeth II **Obv:** Crowned bust of Queen Elizabeth II, right **Rev:** 2 soldiers with standard

Date	Mintage	F	VF	XF	Unc	BU
1996	—	—	—	—	6.50	8.00

KM# 8a   50 PENCE
28.2800 g., 0.9250 Silver 0.8410 oz. ASW, 38.5 mm.
Subject: 70th Birthday - Queen Elizabeth II **Obv:** Crowned bust of Queen Elizabeth II right **Rev:** 2 soldiers holding the standard

Date	Mintage	F	VF	XF	Unc	BU
1996 Proof	5,000	Value: 50.00				

KM# 11   50 PENCE
Copper-Nickel, 38.5 mm.   **Series:** Montreal Olympics
Subject: Queen's portrait **Obv:** Bust of Queen Elizabeth II right **Rev:** Royal couple behind horse and rider jumping British arms

Date	Mintage	F	VF	XF	Unc	BU
1997	—	—	—	—	8.00	10.00

KM# 9   50 PENCE
Copper-Nickel, 38.5 mm.   **Subject:** World Wildlife Fund - Conserving Nature **Obv:** Crowned bust of Queen Elizabeth I, right **Rev:** Frigate birds

Date	Mintage	F	VF	XF	Unc	BU
1998	—	—	—	—	10.00	15.00

KM# 9a   50 PENCE
28.2800 g., 0.9250 Silver 0.8410 oz. ASW, 38.5 mm.
Subject: World Wildlife Fund - Conserving Nature **Obv:** Crowned bust of Queen Elizabeth II right **Rev:** Frigate birds

Date	Mintage	F	VF	XF	Unc	BU
1998 Proof	—	Value: 45.00				

KM# 10   50 PENCE
Copper-Nickel   **Subject:** World Wildlife Fund - Conserving Nature **Obv:** Crowned bust of Queen Elizabeth II, right **Rev:** White-tailed tropicbird

Date	Mintage	F	VF	XF	Unc	BU
1998	—	—	—	—	10.00	15.00

KM# 10a   50 PENCE
28.2800 g., 0.9250 Silver 0.8410 oz. ASW   **Subject:** World Wildlife Fund - Conserving Nature **Obv:** Crowned bust of Queen Elizabeth II right **Rev:** Long-tailed birds

Date	Mintage	F	VF	XF	Unc	BU
1998 Proof	—	Value: 45.00				

KM# 12   50 PENCE
28.7600 g., Copper-Nickel, 38.5 mm.   **Subject:** 100th Birthday of the Queen Mother **Obv:** Crowned bust of Queen Elizabeth II, right **Rev:** Queen Mother's bust 3/4 facing half left **Edge:** Reeded

Date	Mintage	F	VF	XF	Unc	BU
ND(2000)	—	—	—	—	8.50	10.00

KM# 12a   50 PENCE
28.2800 g., 0.9250 Silver 0.8410 oz. ASW, 38.6 mm.
Subject: Queen Mother's 100th Birthday **Obv:** Crowned bust of Queen Elizabeth II right **Rev:** Queen Mother above dates 1900-2000 **Edge:** Reeded

Date	Mintage	F	VF	XF	Unc	BU
ND(2000) Proof	10,000	Value: 40.00				

KM# 12b   50 PENCE
47.5400 g., 0.9166 Gold 1.4009 oz. AGW, 38.6 mm.
Subject: Queen Mother's 100th Birthday **Obv:** Crowned bust of Queen Elizabeth II, right **Rev:** Queen Mother above dates 1900-2000 **Edge:** Reeded

Date	Mintage	F	VF	XF	Unc	BU
ND(2000) Proof	100	Value: 1,450				

KM# 5   2 POUNDS
15.9800 g., 0.9170 Gold 0.4711 oz. AGW **Series:** International Year of the Scout **Rev:** Boy Scout

Date	Mintage	F	VF	XF	Unc	BU
1983	2,000	—	—	—	—	475
1983 Proof	2,000	Value: 500				

PIEFORTS

KM#	Date	Mintage	Identification	Mkt Val
P1	1995	500	50 Pence. Silver. KM7a.	55.00

The Commonwealth of Australia, the smallest continent in the world, is located south of Indonesia between the Indian and Pacific oceans. It has an area of 2,967,893 sq. mi. (7,686,850 sq. km.) and an estimated population of 18.84 million. Capital: Canberra. Due to its early and sustained isolation, Australia is the habitat of such curious and unique fauna as the kangaroo, koala, platypus, wombat, echidna and frilled-necked lizard. The continent possesses extensive mineral deposits, the most important of which are iron ore, coal, gold, silver, nickel, uranium, lead and zinc. Raising livestock, mining and manufacturing are the principal industries. Chief exports are wool, meat, wheat, iron ore, coal and nonferrous metals.

The first Caucasians to see Australia probably were Portuguese and Spanish navigators of the late 16th century. In 1770, Captain James Cook explored the east coast and annexed it for Great Britain. New South Wales was founded as a penal colony, following the loss of British North America, by Captain Arthur Phillip on January 26, 1788, a date now celebrated as Australia Day. Dates of creation of the six colonies that now comprise the states of the Australian Commonwealth are: New South Wales, 1823; Tasmania, 1825; Western Australia, 1838; South Australia, 1842; Victoria, 1851; Queensland, 1859. The British Parliament approved a constitution providing for the federation of the colonies in 1900. The Commonwealth of Australia came into being in 1901. Australia passed the Statute of Westminster Adoption Act on October 9, 1942, which officially established Australia's complete autonomy in external and internal affairs, thereby formalizing a situation that had existed for years. Australia is a member of the Commonwealth of Nations. Elizabeth II is Head of State as Queen of Australia.

Australia's currency system was changed from Pounds-Shillings-Pence to a decimal system of Dollars and Cents on Feb. 14, 1966.

RULER
British until 1942

MINT MARKS

Abbr.	Mint	Marks
A	Adelaide	-
(b)	Bombay	I below bust; dots before and after HALF PENNY, 1942-43
(b)	Bombay	I below bust dots before and after PENNY, 1942-43
B	Brisbane	-
(c)	Calcutta	I above date, 1916-18
(c)	Canberra	None, 1966 to date
C	Canberra	-
D	Denver	D above date 1/-& 2/-, below date on 3d
D	Denver	D below date on 6d
H	Heaton	H below date on silver coins, 1914-15
H	Heaton	H above date on bronze coins
(L)	London	1910-1915 (no marks), 1966
M	Melbourne	M below date on silver coins, 1916-20
M	Melbourne	M above date on the ground on gold coins w/St. George
M	Melbourne	-
(m)	Melbourne	Dot below scroll on penny, 1919-20
(m)	Melbourne	Two dots; below lower scroll and above upper, 1919-20
(m)	Melbourne	None, 1921-1964, 1966
P	Perth	P above date on the ground on gold coins w/St. George
(p)	Perth	Dot between KG (designer's initials), 1940-41
(p)	Perth	Dot after PENNY, 1941-51, 1954-64
(p)	Perth	Dot after AUSTRALIA, 1952-53
(p)	Perth	Dot before SHILLING, 1946
(p)	Perth	None, 1922 penny, 1966
P	Perth	Nuggets, 1986
PL	London	PL after PENNY in 1951
PL	London	PL on bottom folds of ribbon, 1951 threepence
PL	London	PL above date on sixpence
PL	London	1951
S	San Francisco	S above or below date, 1942-44, mm exists w/ and w/o bulbous serifs
S	Sydney	S above date on the ground on gold coins w/St. George
S	Sydney	-
(sy)	Sydney	Dot above bottom scroll on penny 1920
(sy)	Sydney	None, 1919-1926

Mint designations are shown in ( ). Ex. 1978(m).
Mint marks are shown after date. Ex. 1978M.

PRIVY MARKS

(ae) - American Eagle

(aa) - Adelaide Assay

(ba) - Basler Stab

(bg) - Brandenburg Gate

(d) – Ducat

(dp) – Dump

(e) – Emu

(ev) - Edward V

(f) – Fok

(f1) - Rev. 1 Florin, KM#31

(f3) - Rev. 1 Florin, KM#33

(f7) - Rev. 1 Florin, KM#47

(ge) - Golden Eagle

(gv) - George V, small head

(gV) - George V, large head

(h) – Hague

(hd) - Holey Dollar

(j) – Johanna

(jw) - Japanese Royal Wedding

(l) – Luk

(lh) - Liberty Head

(p) – Prospector

(qv) - Queen Victoria

(rv) - Royal Visit Florin, Rev. 1 Florin, KM#55

(s) – Shu

(sg) - Spade Guinea

(sm) - Sydney Mint Sovereign

(so) - Sydney Opera House

(sp) - Star Pagoda

(sq) - State Quarter

(sr) - Swan River/Rottnest Island Tercentenary

(ta) - Team Australia (Commonwealth Games)

(hd) - Holey Dollar

(w) – Whales

(ww) - 50 Years Beyond WWII

MONETARY SYSTEM

Sterling Coinage (Until 1966)
12 Pence = 1 Shilling
2 Shillings = 1 Florin
5 Shillings = 1 Crown
20 Shillings = 1 Pound
1 Sovereign = 1 Pound

Decimal Coinage (Commencing 1966)
100 Cents = 1 Dollar

BRITISH COLONY

TRADE COINAGE

KM# 12 1/2 SOVEREIGN
3.9940 g., 0.9170 Gold 0.1177 oz. AGW **Ruler:** Victoria
Obv: Veiled head left **Rev:** St. George slaying dragon, mint mark above date

Date	Mintage	F	VF	XF	Unc	BU
1901M Proof	—	Value: 60,000				
1901P Proof	—	Value: 80,000				

Note: Imperfect proofs worth substantially less.

KM# 13 SOVEREIGN
7.9881 g., 0.9170 Gold 0.2355 oz. AGW **Ruler:** Victoria
Obv: Older veiled head left **Rev:** St. George slaying the dragon

Date	Mintage	F	VF	XF	Unc	BU
1901S	3,012,000	—	BV	235	265	500
1901M	3,987,000	—	BV	235	265	500
1901M Proof	—	Value: 47,000				
1901P	2,889,000	—	BV	230	275	650
1901P Proof	—	Value: 55,000				

COMMONWEALTH OF AUSTRALIA

MINT MARKS
M – Melbourne
P – Perth
S – Sydney
(sy) - Sydney

STERLING COINAGE

KM# 22 1/2 PENNY
Bronze **Ruler:** George V **Obv:** Crowned bust left
Rev: Denomination within circle **Edge:** Plain

Date	Mintage	F	VF	XF	Unc	BU
1911(L)	2,832,000	1.00	4.00	17.50	225	350
1911(L) Proof	—	Value: 15,000				
1912H	2,400,000	1.50	5.00	21.00	320	500
1912H Proof	—	Value: 15,000				
1913(L) Wide date	2,160,000	2.00	5.50	38.00	625	900

Date	Mintage	F	VF	XF	Unc	BU
1913(L) Narrow date	Inc. above	1.50	5.00	36.00	600	875
1914(L)	1,440,000	3.00	15.00	70.00	925	1,500
1914H	1,200,000	3.50	15.00	65.00	800	1,200
1915H	720,000	25.00	75.00	350	3,250	—
1916(c) I	3,600,000	0.50	1.50	17.50	230	350
1916(c) I Proof	—	Value: 15,000				
1917(c) I	5,760,000	0.50	1.50	17.00	230	330
1918(c) I	1,440,000	6.00	22.00	185	2,350	—
1919(sy)	3,326,000	0.25	1.00	15.00	230	325
1919(sy) Proof	—	Value: 17,000				
1920(sy)	4,114,000	1.00	5.00	30.00	350	520
1920(m) Proof	—	Value: 21,000				
1921(sy)	5,280,000	0.25	1.00	16.00	230	320
1922(sy)	6,924,000	0.25	1.00	17.00	235	350
1923(m)	Est. 1,113,000	1,300	3,500	14,000	60,000	

Note: Dies dated 1922 were used for the majority of the calendar year 1923, leaving only a small portion of this mintage figure as 1923 dated coins.

1923(m) Proof; Rare						

Note: Noble Numismatics sale No. 62, 11-99, nearly FDC proof realized $56,745.

Date	Mintage	F	VF	XF	Unc	BU
1924(m)	682,000	3.50	12.50	70.00	1,000	1,500
1924(m) Proof	—	Value: 20,000				
1925(m)	1,147,000	1.00	5.00	30.00	825	—
1925(m) Proof	—	Value: 32,000				
1926(m & sy)	4,139,000	0.25	1.00	17.00	400	800
1926(m) Proof	—	Value: 15,000				
1927(m)	3,072,000	0.25	1.00	15.00	250	400
1927(m) Proof	50	Value: 15,500				
1928(m)	2,318,000	1.00	5.00	25.00	625	1,000
1928(m) Proof	—	Value: 15,500				
1929(m)	2,635,000	0.25	1.00	15.00	275	450
1929(m) Proof	—	Value: 15,000				
1930(m)	638,000	1.50	6.00	35.00	900	1,250
1930(m) Proof	—	Value: 40,000				
1931(m)	370,000	1.50	6.00	35.00	900	1,250
1931(m) Proof	—	Value: 16,000				
1932(m)	2,554,000	0.25	1.00	10.00	175	285
1932(m) Proof	—	Value: 16,000				
1933(m)	4,608,000	0.20	0.50	9.00	125	200
1933(m) Proof	—	Value: 15,500				
1934(m)	3,816,000	0.20	0.50	9.00	125	200
1934(m) Proof	100	Value: 11,500				
1935(m)	2,916,000	0.20	0.50	9.00	125	200
1935(m) Proof	100	Value: 11,000				
1936(m)	2,562,000	0.20	0.40	5.00	75.00	125
1936(m) Proof	—	Value: 15,000				

KM# 30 1/2 PENNY
Bronze **Ruler:** George V **Obv:** India 1/4 Anna, KM#511
Rev: Value in inner circle **Note:** Mule.

Date	Mintage	F	VF	XF	Unc	BU
1916(c) I	Est. 10	55,000	85,000			

KM# 35 1/2 PENNY
Bronze **Ruler:** George VI **Obv:** Head left **Rev:** Value in inner circle **Edge:** Plain

Date	Mintage	F	VF	XF	Unc	BU
1938(m)	3,014,000	0.20	0.40	3.00	35.00	60.00
1938(m) Proof	250	Value: 6,500				
1939(m)	4,382,000	0.20	0.40	3.50	60.00	100
1939(m) Proof	—	Value: 14,000				

KM# 41 1/2 PENNY
5.7000 g., Bronze **Ruler:** George VI **Obv:** Head left
Rev: Kangaroo leaping right above value

Date	Mintage	F	VF	XF	Unc	BU
1939(m)	504,000	9.50	15.00	60.00	650	1,100
1939(m) Proof	100	Value: 11,000				
1940(m)	2,294,000	0.25	1.00	6.50	125	170
1940(m) Proof	—	Value: 15,500				
1941(m)	5,011,000	0.20	0.75	4.00	70.00	100
1941(m) Proof	—	Value: 15,500				
1941(p)	720,000	1.00	3.75	20.00	175	300
1942(m) Proof	—	Value: 11,000				
1942(p)	4,334,000	0.20	0.50	6.00	90.00	120
1942(p) Proof	—	Value: 10,500				
1942(b) I Wide date	6,000,000	0.20	0.50	3.00	40.00	60.00
1942(b) I Narrow date	Inc. above	0.20	0.50	3.00	40.00	60.00
1942(b) I Proof	—	Value: 10,500				
1943(m)	33,989,000	0.10	0.25	2.00	17.50	28.00

Date	Mintage	F	VF	XF	Unc	BU
1943(p) Proof	—	Value: 12,000				
1943(b) I	6,000,000	0.10	0.30	2.75	30.00	42.00
1943(b) I Proof	—	Value: 10,500				
1944(m)	720,000	1.00	3.75	27.50	185	375
1945(p)	3,033,000	0.75	2.00	13.50	85.00	150
1945(p) Proof	—	Value: 11,500				
1945(p) Without dot	Inc. above	1.00	2.25	13.50	85.00	150
1946(p)	13,747,000	0.10	0.25	2.00	20.00	30.00
1946(p) Proof	—	Value: 11,500				
1947(p)	9,293,000	0.10	0.25	2.50	25.00	37.50
1947(p) Proof	—	Value: 12,000				
1948(m)	4,608,000	0.25	0.50	3.50	32.50	42.00
1948(m) Proof	—	Value: 12,000				
1948(p)	25,553,000	0.10	0.25	2.00	21.50	30.00
1948(p) Proof	—	Value: 11,500				

KM# 42 1/2 PENNY
5.6000 g., Bronze **Ruler:** George VI **Obv:** Head left
Obv. Leg.: IND: IMP: dropped **Rev:** Kangaroo leaping right

Date	Mintage	F	VF	XF	Unc	BU
1949(m) Proof	—	Value: 13,500				

Note: Some consider this a pattern

Date	Mintage	F	VF	XF	Unc	BU
1949(p)	22,310,000	0.10	0.25	2.00	21.50	27.50
1949(p) Proof	—	Value: 11,500				
1950(p)	12,014,000	0.10	0.25	2.00	32.50	40.00
1950(p) Proof	—	Value: 11,500				
1951(p) With dot	—	0.10	0.25	2.00	21.50	27.50
1951(p) With dot, Proof	—	Value: 12,000				
1951(p) Without dot	29,422,000	0.10	0.50	3.50	23.50	32.50
1951(p) Without dot; Proof	—	Value: 12,000				
1951PL	17,040,000	0.10	0.15	0.75	6.25	10.00

Note: 5,040,000 struck at the Birmingham Mint.

Date	Mintage	F	VF	XF	Unc	BU
1951PL Proof	—	Value: 7,250				
1952(p)	1,832,000	0.50	1.50	4.00	55.00	85.00
1952(p) Proof	—	Value: 7,500				

KM# 49 1/2 PENNY
5.6700 g., Bronze **Ruler:** Elizabeth II **Obv:** Laureate bust right
Obv. Leg.: DEI • GRATIA • REGINA + ELIZABETH • II •
Rev: Kangaroo leaping right

Date	Mintage	F	VF	XF	Unc	BU
1953(p)	23,967,000	0.10	0.15	0.50	10.00	15.00
1953(p) Proof	16	Value: 7,500				
1954(p)	21,963,000	0.10	0.15	0.50	10.00	15.00
1954(p) Proof	—	Value: 7,500				
1955(p) Without dot	9,343,000	0.10	0.15	0.50	10.00	14.00
1955(p) Without dot; Proof	301	Value: 4,500				

KM# 61 1/2 PENNY
5.9000 g., Bronze **Ruler:** Elizabeth II **Obv:** Laureate bust right
Obv. Leg.: DEI • GRATIA • REGINA • F:D: + ELIZABETH • II •
Rev: Kangaroo leaping right

Date	Mintage	F	VF	XF	Unc	BU
1959(m)	10,166,000	0.10	0.15	0.25	1.50	3.00
1959(m) Proof	1,506	Value: 350				
1960(p)	17,812,000	0.10	0.15	0.25	1.00	1.50
1960(p) Proof	1,030	Value: 300				
1961(p)	20,183,000	0.10	0.15	0.25	1.00	1.50
1961(p) Proof	1,040	Value: 300				
1962(p)	10,259,000	0.10	0.15	0.25	1.00	1.50
1962(p) Proof	1,064	Value: 300				
1963(p)	16,410,000	0.10	0.15	0.25	0.75	1.00
1963(p) Proof	1,060	Value: 300				
1964(p)	18,230,000	0.10	0.15	0.25	0.75	1.00
1964(p) Proof; 1 known	—	Value: 16,500				

KM# 23 PENNY

9.4000 g., Bronze, 30.5 mm. **Ruler:** George V **Obv:** Crowned bust left **Obv. Leg.:** GEORGIVS V D.G. BRITT: OMN: REX F.D: IND: IMP **Rev:** Value in inner circle **Edge:** Plain

Date	Mintage	F	VF	XF	Unc	BU
1911(L)	3,768,000	1.00	4.00	22.50	200	400
1911(L) Proof	—	Value: 21,000				
1912H	3,600,000	1.25	4.50	27.50	350	775
1912H Proof	—	Value: 21,000				
1913(L) Narrow date	2,520,000	1.25	5.00	32.50	650	1,100
1913(L) Wide date	Inc. above	1.25	5.00	32.50	675	1,125
1914(L)	720,000	3.00	12.50	200	1,500	2,500
1915(L)	960,000	2.00	10.00	220	1,750	2,650
1915H	1,320,000	1.75	8.50	160	1,400	2,000
1916(c) I	3,324,000	0.50	1.50	20.00	250	650
1916(c) I Proof	—	Value: 36,500				
1917(c) I	6,240,000	0.50	1.50	20.00	200	650
1918(c) I	1,200,000	1.75	10.00	220	1,850	2,300
1919(m)	5,810,000	0.50	1.50	25.00	250	650
Note: Without dots						
1919(m)	Inc. above	0.50	1.50	25.00	250	650
Note: Dot below bottom scroll						
1919(m)	—	40.00	125	800	2,750	4,000
Note: Dots below bottom scroll and above upper						
1919(m) Proof	—	Value: 37,500				
1920(m & sy)	9,041,000	20.00	150	850	7,500	12,500
Note: Without dots						
1920(m)	Inc. above	1.75	10.00	145	1,350	1,750
Note: Dot below bottom scroll						
1920(m) Proof	—	Value: 35,000				
1920(sy)	Inc. above	1.75	10.00	145	1,350	1,750
Note: Dot above bottom scroll						
1920	Inc. above	20.00	125	725	5,000	—
Note: Dots below bottom scroll and above upper						
1921(m & sy)	7,438,000	0.50	6.00	35.00	600	1,050
1922(m & p)	12,697,000	0.50	6.00	40.00	650	1,100
1923(m)	5,654,000	0.50	6.00	35.00	575	1,000
1923(m) Proof	—	Value: 30,000				
1924(m & sy)	4,656,000	0.50	5.00	35.00	550	900
1924(m) Proof	—	Value: 19,500				
1925(m)	1,639,000	85.00	210	1,100	9,000	13,500
1925(m) Proof	—	Value: 95,000				
1926(m & sy)	1,859,000	1.50	8.00	160	1,250	2,000
1926(m) Proof	—	Value: 19,000				
1927(m)	4,922,000	0.50	2.25	35.00	275	450
1927(m) Proof	50	Value: 21,500				
1928(m)	3,038,000	0.50	3.00	50.00	950	1,500
1928(m) Proof	—	Value: 18,500				
1929(m)	2,599,000	0.50	3.00	55.00	1,100	1,900
1929(m) Proof	—	Value: 18,500				
1930(m)	Est. 3,000	8,500	13,000	33,000	65,000	100,000
1930(m) Proof; Rare	Est. 6	Value: 300,000				
Note: Noble Numismatics sale No. 52, 7-97, nearly FDC proof realized $126,500. Noble Numismatics sale No. 62, 11-99, FDC proof realized $162,665.						
1931(m) Normal date alignment	494,000	2.00	7.50	100	1,200	2,000
1931(m) Fallen 1 in date	Inc. above	2.00	7.50	100	1,200	2,000
1931(m) Proof	—	Value: 35,000				
1932(m)	2,117,000	0.50	3.00	50.00	275	500
1933/2(m)	5,818,000	15.00	30.00	150	1,100	1,800
1933(m)	Inc. above	0.25	1.50	20.00	125	200
1933(m) Proof	—	Value: 21,500				
1934(m)	5,808,000	0.25	1.50	20.00	125	200
1934(m) Proof	100	Value: 12,000				
1935(m)	3,725,000	0.25	1.50	20.00	120	200
1935(m) Proof	160	Value: 8,500				
1936(m)	9,890,000	0.25	0.75	10.00	80.00	140
1936(m) Proof	—	Value: 19,500				

KM# 36 PENNY

9.4100 g., Bronze, 30.5 mm. **Ruler:** George VI **Obv:** Head left **Obv. Leg.:** GEORGIVS VI D:G:BR: OMN: REX F.D: IND: IMP **Rev:** Kangaroo leaping left **Edge:** Plain

Date	Mintage	F	VF	XF	Unc	BU
1938(m)	5,552,000	0.25	0.75	8.00	45.00	80.00
1938(m) Proof	250	Value: 8,500				

Date	Mintage	F	VF	XF	Unc	BU
1939(m)	6,240,000	0.25	0.75	8.00	50.00	85.00
1939(m) Proof	—	Value: 15,000				
1940(m)	4,075,000	0.50	1.50	20.00	100	180
1940(p) K.G.	1,114,000	1.50	5.00	50.00	500	1,000
1941(m)	1,588,000	0.25	1.50	12.00	80.00	150
1941(p) K.G.	12,794,000	1.00	2.00	30.00	180	275
1941(p) Proof	—	Value: 15,000				
1941(p)	Inc. above	0.25	0.75	12.00	75.00	140
1941(p) K.G. high dot after Y	Inc. above	2.00	7.50	100	1,000	—
1942(p)	12,245,000	0.15	0.50	7.00	35.00	80.00
1942(b) I	9,000,000	0.15	0.50	5.00	22.50	60.00
1942(b) Without I	Inc. above	2.00	5.00	40.00	275	—
1942(b) Proof	—	Value: 9,500				
1943(m)	11,112,000	0.20	0.50	10.00	35.00	60.00
1943(b)	33,086,000	0.15	0.50	9.00	35.00	60.00
1943(p) Proof	—	Value: 12,500				
1943(p) I	9,000,000	0.15	0.50	8.00	35.00	60.00
Note: Small and large denticle varieties exist.						
1943(b) I Without I	Inc. above	2.00	4.00	25.00	125	—
1943(b) Proof	—	Value: 11,500				
1944(m)	2,112,000	0.50	3.00	25.00	145	260
1944(p)	27,830,000	0.15	0.50	7.00	35.00	50.00
1944(p) Proof	—	Value: 12,500				
1945(p)	15,173,000	0.20	0.75	9.00	60.00	100
Note: With and without a large dot after the KG.						
1945(p) Proof	—	Value: 12,500				
1945(b) I Rare	6	—	—	—	—	—
1945(m) Rare	—	Value: 100,000				
Note: Considered by many to be a pattern						
1946(m)	240,000	42.50	75.00	275	1,650	2,500
1947(m)	6,864,000	0.15	0.40	4.50	25.00	40.00
1947(p)	4,490,000	0.50	2.00	35.00	275	550
1947(p) Proof	—	Value: 12,500				
1948(m)	26,616,000	0.15	0.40	3.50	20.00	30.00
1948(p)	1,534,000	0.75	4.00	60.00	400	900
1948(p) Proof	—	Value: 15,000				

KM# 43 PENNY

Bronze, 30.5 mm. **Ruler:** George VI **Obv:** Head left **Obv. Leg.:** IND: IMP. dropped **Rev:** Kangaroo leaping left **Edge:** Plain

Date	Mintage	F	VF	XF	Unc	BU
1949(m)	27,065,000	0.15	0.25	2.50	16.00	28.00
1949(m) Proof	—	Value: 16,000				
1950(m)	36,359,000	0.15	0.25	2.50	18.00	28.00
1950(m) Proof	—	Value: 16,000				
1950(p)	21,488,000	0.20	0.75	12.50	60.00	100
1950(p) Proof	—	Value: 16,000				
1951(m)	21,240,000	0.15	0.20	1.00	15.00	25.00
1951(p)	12,888,000	0.20	0.75	10.00	50.00	85.00
1951(p) Proof	—	Value: 15,000				
1951PL	18,000,000	0.15	0.25	0.85	10.00	15.00
1951PL Proof	—	Value: 14,500				
1952(m)	12,408,000	0.15	0.30	1.00	12.00	17.50
1952(m) Proof	—	Value: 12,000				
1952(p)	45,514,000	0.15	0.25	0.85	9.00	15.00
Note: Two varieties of the 2 in the date.						
1952(p) Proof	—	Value: 12,000				

KM# 50 PENNY

Bronze, 30.5 mm. **Ruler:** Elizabeth II **Obv:** Laureate bust, right **Obv. Leg.:** DEI • GRATIA • REGINA + ELIZABETH • II • **Rev:** Kangaroo leaping left **Edge:** Plain

Date	Mintage	F	VF	XF	Unc	BU
1953(m)	6,936,000	0.20	0.50	2.00	20.00	35.00
Note: Two varieties to the numeral 5.						
1953(m) Proof	—	Value: 10,500				
1953(p)	6,203,000	0.20	0.65	2.50	20.00	35.00
1953(p) Proof	16	Value: 10,500				

KM# 56 PENNY

9.4500 g., Bronze, 30.5 mm. **Ruler:** Elizabeth II **Obv:** Laureate bust right **Obv. Leg.:** F:D: added **Rev:** Kangaroo leaping left **Edge:** Plain

Date	Mintage	F	VF	XF	Unc	BU
1955(m)	6,336,000	0.20	0.50	2.00	12.00	20.00
1955(m) Proof	1,200	Value: 400				
1955(p)	11,110,000	0.25	0.75	2.00	15.00	27.50
1955(p) Proof	301	Value: 3,150				
1956(m)	13,872,000	0.10	0.20	0.50	8.00	17.50
1956(m) Proof	1,500	Value: 400				
1956(p)	12,121,000	0.10	0.20	0.50	8.00	18.50
1956(p) Proof	417	Value: 2,900				
1957(p)	15,978,000	0.10	0.20	0.50	5.00	9.00
1957(p) Proof	1,112	Value: 550				
1958(m)	10,012,000	0.10	0.20	0.50	5.00	9.00
1958(m) Proof	1,506	Value: 400				
1958(p)	14,428,000	0.10	0.20	0.50	6.00	9.00
1958(p) Proof	1,028	Value: 500				
1959(p)	1,617,000	0.50	1.25	8.00	50.00	90.00
1959(m) Proof	1,506	Value: 500				
1959(p)	14,428,000	0.10	0.20	0.50	3.00	6.00
1959(p) Proof	1,030	Value: 500				
1960(p)	20,515,000	0.10	0.50	1.50	2.00	
1960(p) Proof	1,030	Value: 475				
1961(p)	30,607,000	0.10	0.20	0.40	1.00	1.75
1961(p) Proof	1,040	Value: 475				
1962(p)	34,851,000	0.10	0.20	0.30	0.75	1.25
1962(p) Proof	1,064	Value: 475				
1963(p)	10,258,000	0.10	0.20	0.30	0.75	1.25
1963(p) Proof	1,100	Value: 475				
1964(p)	49,130,000	0.10	0.15	0.20	0.75	1.00
1964(p)	54,590,000	0.10	0.15	0.30	0.75	1.00
1964(p) Proof; 1 known	—	Value: 12,500				

KM# 18 THREEPENCE

1.4100 g., 0.9250 Silver 0.0419 oz. ASW, 16 mm. **Ruler:** Edward VII **Obv:** Bust right **Rev:** Arms **Edge:** Plain

Date	Mintage	F	VF	XF	Unc	BU
1910(L)	4,000,000	1.75	7.00	20.00	65.00	100
1910(L) Proof	—	Value: 7,500				

KM# 24 THREEPENCE

1.4100 g., 0.9250 Silver 0.0419 oz. ASW, 16 mm. **Ruler:** George V **Obv:** Crowned bust left **Rev:** Arms **Edge:** Plain

Date	Mintage	F	VF	XF	Unc	BU
1911(L)	2,000,000	5.00	17.50	80.00	325	600
1911(L) Proof	—	Value: 14,500				
1911(L) Proof	—	Value: 45,000				
Note: Reeded edge						
1912(L)	2,400,000	10.00	50.00	200	1,250	2,400
1914(L)	1,600,000	11.00	40.00	190	800	1,600
1915(L)	800,000	25.00	90.00	325	1,650	2,750
1916M	1,913,000	5.00	17.50	110	600	1,100
1916M Proof	25	Value: 8,000				
1917M	3,808,000	1.75	7.00	35.00	200	375
M Proof	—	Value: 1,500				
1918M	3,119,000	1.75	7.00	35.00	200	375
1918M Proof	—	Value: 35,000				
1919M	3,201,000	1.75	7.00	40.00	220	395
1919M Proof	—	Value: 13,500				
1920M	4,196,000	5.00	35.00	100	675	1,150
1920M Proof	—	Value: 14,000				
1921M	7,378,000	1.25	3.50	35.00	145	250
1921(m)	Inc. above	5.00	35.00	175	725	1,150
1921M Proof	—	Value: 14,000				
1922(m)	5,531,000	1.75	7.00	50.00	260	500
1922(m) Proof	—	Value: 14,000				
1922/1(m)	900	8,500	22,500	42,000	—	—
1923(m)	815,000	14.00	60.00	215	1,300	2,450
1924(m & sy)	2,013,999	5.00	17.50	90.00	575	475
1924(m) Proof	—	Value: 11,000				
1925(m) Proof	—	Value: 12,500				

Date	Mintage	F	VF	XF	Unc	BU
1925(m & sy)	4,347,000	1.00	4.00	45.00	200	375
Proof						
1926(m & sy)	6,158,000	1.00	3.00	27.50	150	250
1926(m) Proof	—	Value: 11,500				
1927(m)	6,720,000	0.85	2.25	27.00	145	245
1927(m) Proof	50	Value: 11,500				
1928(m)	5,000,000	0.85	3.00	30.00	170	300
1928(m) Proof	—	Value: 11,500				
1934(m)	Inc. above	0.85	2.25	27.00	140	240
1934(m) Proof	100	Value: 6,000				
1934/3(m)	1,616,000	25.00	90.00	300	1,250	2,400
1935(m)	2,800,000	0.85	2.25	21.50	140	240
1935(m) Proof	—	Value: 6,000				
1936(m)	3,600,000	BV	1.00	12.50	75.00	135
1936(m) Proof	—	Value: 6,000				

KM# 37 THREEPENCE
1.4100 g., 0.9250 Silver 0.0419 oz. ASW, 16 mm. **Ruler:** George VI **Obv:** Head left **Rev:** Three wheat stalks divide date

Date	Mintage	F	VF	XF	Unc	BU
1938(m)	4,560,000	BV	1.00	6.50	27.50	45.00
1938(m) Proof	250	Value: 5,000				
1939(m)	3,856,000	BV	1.00	10.00	50.00	100
1939(m) Proof	—	—	—	—	—	—
1940(m)	3,840,000	BV	1.00	10.00	55.00	110
1941(m)	7,584,000	BV	0.75	6.50	30.00	55.00
1942(m)	528,000	12.50	35.00	250	1,300	2,500
1942D	16,000,000	—	BV	1.00	11.50	18.50
1942S	8,000,000	—	BV	1.00	11.50	18.50
1943(m)	24,912,000	—	BV	1.00	11.50	18.50
1943D	16,000,000	—	BV	1.00	11.50	18.50
1943S	8,000,000	—	BV	1.00	12.00	18.50
1944S	32,000,000	—	BV	0.85	5.00	9.50

Note: Two varieties to the "S" mintmark.

KM# 37a THREEPENCE
1.4100 g., 0.5000 Silver 0.0227 oz. ASW, 16 mm. **Ruler:** George VI **Obv:** Head left **Rev:** 3 wheat stalks divide date

Date	Mintage	F	VF	XF	Unc	BU
1947(m)	4,176,000	0.85	1.50	10.00	55.00	110
1948(m)	26,208,000	—	BV	0.85	7.00	14.00

KM# 44 THREEPENCE
1.4100 g., 0.5000 Silver 0.0227 oz. ASW, 16 mm. **Ruler:** George VI **Obv:** Head left **Obv. Leg.:** IND: IMP. dropped **Rev:** Three wheat stalks divide date

Date	Mintage	F	VF	XF	Unc	BU
1949(m)	26,400,000	—	BV	0.85	6.50	16.00
1949(m) Proof	—					
1950(m)	35,456,000	—	BV	0.85	6.50	14.00
1951(m)	15,856,000	—	0.50	1.50	11.50	23.50
1951PL	40,000,000	—	BV	0.50	4.00	7.00
1951PL Proof	—	Value: 7,500				
1952(m)	21,560,000	—	BV	1.00	8.00	15.00

KM# 51 THREEPENCE
1.4100 g., 0.5000 Silver 0.0227 oz. ASW, 16 mm. **Ruler:** Elizabeth II **Obv:** Laureate bust, right **Rev:** Three wheat stalks divide date **Edge:** Plain

Date	Mintage	F	VF	XF	Unc	BU
1953(m)	7,664,000	BV	1.50	4.00	20.00	40.00
1953(m) Proof	—	Value: 7,500				
1954(m)	2,672,000	0.85	2.50	5.00	32.50	55.00
1954(m) Proof	—	Value: 7,500				

KM# 57 THREEPENCE
1.4100 g., 0.5000 Silver 0.0227 oz. ASW, 16 mm. **Ruler:** Elizabeth II **Obv:** Laureate bust right **Obv. Leg.:** F:D: added **Rev:** Three wheat stalks divide date **Edge:** Plain

Date	Mintage	F	VF	XF	Unc	BU
1955(m)	27,088,000	—	BV	1.00	6.00	11.50
1955(m) Proof	1,040	Value: 250				
1956(m)	14,088,000	—	BV	1.00	6.00	11.50
1956(m) Proof	1,500	Value: 70.00				
1957(m)	26,704,000	—	BV	0.75	4.00	7.50
1957(m) Proof	1,256	Value: 70.00				
1958(m)	11,248,000	—	BV	0.75	6.00	11.50
1958(m) Proof	1,506	Value: 70.00				
1959(m)	19,888,000	—	BV	0.75	4.00	7.50
1959(m) Proof	1,506	Value: 70.00				
1960(m)	19,600,000	—	BV	0.50	1.50	3.00
1960(m) Proof	1,509	Value: 70.00				
1961(m)	33,840,000	—	BV	0.50	1.50	3.00
1961(m) Proof	1,506	Value: 70.00				
1962(m)	15,968,000	—	BV	0.50	1.50	3.00
1962(m) Proof	2,016	Value: 65.00				
1963(m)	44,016,000	—	BV	0.50	1.50	3.00
1963(m) Proof	5,042	Value: 55.00				
1964(m)	20,320,000	—	BV	0.50	1.00	2.00

KM# 19 SIXPENCE
2.8200 g., 0.9250 Silver 0.0839 oz. ASW, 19.5 mm. **Ruler:** Edward VII **Obv:** Crowned bust right **Rev:** Arms **Edge:** Reeded

Date	Mintage	F	VF	XF	Unc	BU
1910(L)	3,046,000	6.00	17.00	60.00	200	325
1910(L) Proof	—	Value: 10,500				

KM# 25 SIXPENCE
2.8200 g., 0.9250 Silver 0.0839 oz. ASW, 19.5 mm. **Ruler:** George V **Obv:** Crowned bust left **Rev:** Arms **Edge:** Reeded

Date	Mintage	F	VF	XF	Unc	BU
1911(L)	1,000,000	9.00	30.00	145	950	2,250
1911(L) Proof	—	Value: 20,000				
1912(L)	1,600,000	30.00	85.00	400	1,500	3,250
1914(L)	1,800,000	9.00	25.00	140	875	1,800
1916M	1,769,000	22.00	75.00	275	1,250	2,500
1916M Proof	25	Value: 12,500				
1917M	1,632,000	20.00	60.00	220	950	1,900
1917M Proof	—	Value: 20,000				
1918M	915,000	50.00	170	700	2,700	6,000
1918M Proof	—	Value: 60,000				
1919M	1,521,000	10.00	30.00	140	875	1,500
1919M Proof	—	Value: 20,000				
1920M	1,476,000	15.00	60.00	220	1,100	2,700
1920M Proof	—	Value: 20,000				
1921(m) Proof	—	Value: 20,000				
1921(m & sy)	3,795,000	5.00	16.50	75.00	400	700
1922(sy)	1,488,000	20.00	100	450	1,900	2,850
1922(sy) Proof	—	Value: 30,000				
1923(m & sy)	1,458,000	10.00	35.00	220	1,000	1,850
1924(m) Proof	—	Value: 16,500				
1924(m & sy)	1,038,000	15.00	60.00	275	1,500	2,750
1925(m) Proof	—	Value: 15,000				
1925(m & sy)	3,266,000	5.00	20.00	90.00	425	1,000
1926(m) Proof	—	Value: 15,000				
1926(m & sy)	3,609,000	2.50	9.00	30.00	190	350
1927(m)	3,592,000	2.50	8.00	25.00	180	350
1927(m) Proof	50	Value: 15,000				
1928(m)	2,721,000	2.50	8.00	25.00	185	400
1928(m) Proof	—	Value: 15,000				
1934(m)	1,024,000	2.50	9.00	55.00	400	1,000
1934(m) Proof	100	Value: 6,500				
1935(m)	392,000	5.00	18.00	100	675	1,300
1935(m) Proof	—	Value: 15,000				
1936(m)	1,800,000	1.50	3.00	10.00	130	295
1936(m) Proof	—	Value: 15,000				

KM# 38 SIXPENCE
2.8200 g., 0.9250 Silver 0.0839 oz. ASW, 19.5 mm. **Ruler:** George VI **Obv:** Head left **Rev:** Arms **Edge:** Reeded

Date	Mintage	F	VF	XF	Unc	BU
1938(m)	2,864,000	BV	2.25	6.00	40.00	70.00
1938(m) Proof	250	Value: 5,000				
1939(m)	1,600,000	BV	2.50	15.00	160	500
1940(m)	1,600,000	BV	2.25	10.00	80.00	150
1941(m)	2,912,000	BV	2.25	6.50	45.00	75.00
1942(m)	8,968,000	BV	1.75	3.00	30.00	50.00
1942D	12,000,000	BV	1.75	2.25	16.00	25.00
1942S	4,000,000	BV	1.75	2.25	20.00	30.00
1943D	8,000,000	BV	1.75	2.25	16.00	25.00
1943S	4,000,000	BV	1.75	2.25	20.00	30.00
1944S	4,000,000	BV	1.75	2.25	16.00	25.00
1945(m)	10,096,000	BV	1.75	2.50	20.00	30.00

KM# 38a SIXPENCE
2.8200 g., 0.5000 Silver 0.0453 oz. ASW, 19.5 mm. **Ruler:** George VI **Obv:** Head left **Rev:** Arms **Edge:** Reeded

Date	Mintage	F	VF	XF	Unc	BU
1946(m)	10,024,000	—	BV	3.00	30.00	50.00
1946(m) Proof	—	Value: 10,000				
1948(m)	1,584,000	—	BV	3.00	37.50	60.00

KM# 45 SIXPENCE
2.8200 g., 0.5000 Silver 0.0453 oz. ASW, 19.5 mm. **Ruler:** George VI **Obv:** Head left **Obv. Leg.:** IND: IMP. dropped **Rev:** Arms **Edge:** Plain

Date	Mintage	F	VF	XF	Unc	BU
1950(m)	10,272,000	BV	BV	3.00	37.50	55.00
1951(m)	13,760,000	BV	BV	2.50	25.00	47.50
1951PL	20,024,000	—	BV	2.00	7.50	12.50
1951PL Proof	—	Value: 9,000				
1952(m)	2,112,000	1.25	5.00	35.00	210	400

KM# 52 SIXPENCE
2.8200 g., 0.5000 Silver 0.0453 oz. ASW, 19.5 mm. **Ruler:** Elizabeth II **Obv:** Laureate bust right **Rev:** Arms **Edge:** Reeded

Date	Mintage	F	VF	XF	Unc	BU
1953(m)	1,152,000	1.25	4.00	25.00	150	295
1953(m) Proof	—	Value: 7,500				
1954(m)	7,672,000	—	BV	1.75	5.00	8.00
1954(m) Proof	—	Value: 8,000				

KM# 58 SIXPENCE
2.8200 g., 0.5000 Silver 0.0453 oz. ASW, 19.5 mm. **Ruler:** Elizabeth II **Obv:** Laureate bust right **Obv. Leg.:** F:D: added **Rev:** Arms **Edge:** Reeded

Date	Mintage	F	VF	XF	Unc	BU
1955(m)	14,248,000	—	BV	2.00	12.50	20.00
1955(m) Proof	1,200	Value: 150				
1956(m)	7,904,000	—	2.00	5.00	30.00	60.00
1956(m) Proof	1,500	Value: 90.00				
1957(m)	13,752,000	—	BV	1.25	4.00	6.50
1957(m) Proof	1,256	Value: 100				
1958(m)	17,944,000	—	BV	1.25	4.00	6.50
1958(m) Proof	1,506	Value: 95.00				
1959(m)	11,728,000	—	BV	1.25	6.00	9.00
1959(m) Proof	1,506	Value: 85.00				
1960(m)	18,592,000	—	BV	1.25	7.00	11.00
1960(m) Proof	1,509	Value: 85.00				
1961(m)	9,152,000	—	BV	1.25	3.00	5.00
1961(m) Proof	1,506	Value: 85.00				
1962(m)	44,816,000	—	BV	BV	1.50	3.00
1962(m) Proof	2,016	Value: 75.00				
1963(m)	25,056,000	—	BV	BV	1.50	3.00
1963(m) Proof	5,042	Value: 65.00				

KM# 20 SHILLING
5.6500 g., 0.9250 Silver 0.1680 oz. ASW, 23.5 mm. **Ruler:** Edward VII **Obv:** Crowned bust right **Rev:** Arms **Edge:** Reeded

Date	Mintage	F	VF	XF	Unc	BU
1910(L)	2,536,000	5.00	20.00	70.00	175	325
1910(L) Proof	—	Value: 21,000				

KM# 26 SHILLING
5.6500 g., 0.9250 Silver 0.1680 oz. ASW, 23.5 mm.
Ruler: George V **Obv:** Crowned bust left **Rev:** Arms
Edge: Reeded

Date	Mintage	F	VF	XF	Unc	BU
1911(L)	1,700,000	10.00	35.00	180	1,000	1,850
1911(L) Proof	—	Value: 36,000				
1912(L)	1,000,000	20.00	65.00	300	3,000	5,500
1913(L)	1,200,000	16.00	50.00	250	2,750	5,000
1914(L)	3,300,000	6.50	20.00	90.00	600	1,400
1915(L)	800,000	40.00	125	600	4,000	7,500
1915H	500,000	60.00	175	900	7,000	13,500
1915H Proof	—	Value: 55,000				
1916M	5,141,000	3.50	10.00	35.00	200	350
1916M Proof	25	Value: 13,000				
1917M	5,274,000	3.50	9.00	30.00	175	325
1918M	3,761,000	4.00	17.50	65.00	325	600
1919M	—	Value: 100,000				

Note: Some consider this a pattern.

Date	Mintage	F	VF	XF	Unc	BU
1920M	520,000	7.00	35.00	225	1,700	3,000
1920M	—	Value: 60,000				

Note: Some consider this to be a pattern

Date	Mintage	F	VF	XF	Unc	BU
1921(sy) Star	1,641,000	25.00	80.00	500	3,500	6,750
1921(sy) Star; Proof	—	Value: 40,000				
1922(m)	2,040,000	7.50	22.50	150	700	1,850
1922(m) Proof	—	Value: 22,000				
1924(m & sy)	674,000	10.00	45.00	250	2,000	3,850
1924(m) Proof	—	Value: 27,000				
1925/3(m & sy)	1,448,000	3.50	10.00	60.00	325	600
1925(m) Proof	—	Value: 22,000				
1926(m & sy)	2,352,000	3.50	10.00	70.00	350	700
1926(m) Proof	—	Value: 22,000				
1927(m)	1,146,000	3.50	50.00	300	550	—
1927(m) Proof	50	Value: 16,000				
1928(m)	664,000	12.00	35.00	235	1,700	2,850
1928(m) Proof	—	Value: 24,000				
1931(m)	1,000,000	3.50	7.50	50.00	300	550
1931(m) Proof	—	Value: 19,000				
1933(m)	220,000	65.00	190	900	4,500	8,000
1933(m) Proof	—	Value: 50,000				
1934(m)	480,000	7.50	22.50	110	500	900
1934(m) Proof	100	Value: 7,250				
1935(m)	500,000	3.50	9.00	45.00	325	600
1935(m) Proof	—	Value: 9,000				
1936(m)	2,000,000	BV	5.00	27.50	250	450
1936(m) Proof	—	Value: 15,000				

KM# 39 SHILLING
5.6500 g., 0.9250 Silver 0.1680 oz. ASW, 23.5 mm.
Ruler: George VI **Obv:** Head left **Rev:** Rams head left above value and date **Edge:** Reeded

Date	Mintage	F	VF	XF	Unc	BU
1938(m)	1,484,000	2.00	4.00	11.00	60.00	100
1938(m) Proof	250	Value: 5,100				
1939(m)	1,520,000	2.00	5.00	25.00	130	210
1939(m) Proof	—	Value: 19,000				
1940(m)	760,000	4.00	11.50	40.00	275	500
1941(m)	3,040,000	BV	3.00	7.00	50.00	90.00
1942(m)	1,380,000	BV	3.00	6.00	40.00	70.00
1942S	4,000,000	BV	2.00	3.50	25.00	40.00
1943(m)	2,720,000	2.50	5.00	20.00	100	180
1943S	16,000,000	BV	2.00	3.00	15.00	25.00
1944(m)	14,576,000	BV	2.75	8.00	52.50	95.00
1944S	8,000,000	BV	2.00	3.00	15.00	25.00

KM# 39a SHILLING
5.6500 g., 0.5000 Silver 0.0908 oz. ASW, 23.5 mm.
Ruler: George VI **Obv:** Head left **Rev:** Ram's head left above value **Edge:** Reeded

Date	Mintage	F	VF	XF	Unc	BU
1946(m)	10,072,000	BV	2.00	4.00	25.00	40.00
1946(p)	1,316,000	3.00	10.00	30.00	160	240
1948(m)	4,131,999	BV	2.00	5.00	28.00	45.00

KM# 46 SHILLING
5.6500 g., 0.5000 Silver 0.0908 oz. ASW, 23.5 mm.
Ruler: George VI **Obv:** Head left **Obv. Leg.:** IND: IMP. dropped **Rev:** Ram's head left above value, date **Edge:** Reeded

Date	Mintage	F	VF	XF	Unc	BU
1950(m)	7,188,000	BV	2.00	4.00	22.50	40.00
1952(m)	19,644,000	BV	2.00	3.50	15.00	25.00

KM# 53 SHILLING
5.5600 g., 0.5000 Silver 0.0894 oz. ASW, 23.5 mm.
Ruler: Elizabeth II **Obv:** Laureate bust right **Rev:** Ram's head left above value, date **Edge:** Reeded

Date	Mintage	F	VF	XF	Unc	BU
1953(m)	12,204,000	BV	2.00	3.00	13.00	20.00
1953(m) Proof	—	Value: 7,500				
1954(m)	16,187,999	BV	2.00	3.00	13.00	20.00
1954(m) Proof	—	Value: 8,000				

KM# 59 SHILLING
5.5600 g., 0.5000 Silver 0.0894 oz. ASW, 23.5 mm.
Ruler: Elizabeth II **Obv:** Laureate bust right **Obv. Leg.:** F:D: added **Rev:** Ram's head left above value, date **Edge:** Reeded

Date	Mintage	F	VF	XF	Unc	BU
1955(m)	7,492,000	BV	BV	3.50	22.50	37.50
1955(m) Proof	1,200	Value: 150				
1956(m)	6,064,000	BV	2.00	4.50	40.00	75.00
1956(m) Proof	1,500	Value: 110				
1957(m)	12,668,000	—	BV	2.00	6.00	10.00
1957(m) Proof	1,256	Value: 130				
1958(m)	7,412,000	—	BV	2.00	6.00	10.00
1958(m) Proof	1,506	Value: 110				
1959(m)	10,876,000	—	BV	2.00	5.00	8.50
1959(m) Proof	1,506	Value: 95.00				
1960(m)	14,512,000	—	—	BV	4.50	8.00
1960(m) Proof	1,509	Value: 95.00				
1961(m)	31,864,000	—	—	BV	2.00	3.00
1961(m) Proof	1,506	Value: 95.00				
1962(m)	6,592,000	—	—	BV	2.00	3.00
1962(m) Proof	2,016	Value: 90.00				
1963(m)	10,072,000	—	—	BV	2.00	3.00
1963(m) Proof	5,042	Value: 80.00				

KM# 21 FLORIN
11.3100 g., 0.9250 Silver 0.3363 oz. ASW, 28.5 mm.
Ruler: Edward VII **Obv:** Crowned bust right **Rev:** Arms **Edge:** Reeded

Date	Mintage	F	VF	XF	Unc	BU
1910(L)	1,259,000	27.00	150	375	1,400	2,500
1910(L) Proof	—	Value: 32,500				

KM# 27 FLORIN
11.3100 g., 0.9250 Silver 0.3363 oz. ASW, 28.5 mm. **Ruler:** George V **Obv:** Crowned bust left **Rev:** Arms **Edge:** Reeded

Date	Mintage	F	VF	XF	Unc	BU
1911(L)	950,000	27.00	200	800	4,200	8,250
1911(L) Proof	—	Value: 45,000				
1912(L)	1,000,000	25.00	225	1,050	6,000	12,000
1913(L)	1,200,000	22.50	200	1,050	5,750	11,500
1913(L) Proof	—	Value: 45,000				
1914(L)	2,300,000	8.00	40.00	350	1,450	2,800
1914H	500,000	45.00	300	1,200	6,800	13,000
1914H Proof	—	Value: 60,000				

Note: Noble Numismatics Sale Apr. 2008 Lot 2053 US $112,000

Date	Mintage	F	VF	XF	Unc	BU
1915(L)	500,000	50.00	310	1,300	7,500	13,750
1915H Proof	—	Value: 50,000				
1915H	750,000	27.00	210	700	3,250	6,000
1916M	2,752,000	7.50	30.00	275	1,000	1,800
1916M Proof	25	Value: 15,000				
1917M	4,305,000	7.50	28.00	275	900	1,600
1917M Proof	—	Value: 37,500				
1918M	2,095,000	10.00	30.00	300	1,050	2,000
1918M Proof	—	Value: 37,500				
1919M	1,677,000	20.00	200	700	2,500	4,500
1919M Proof	—	Value: 40,000				
1920M Star; Proof	—	Value: 100,000				
1921(m)	1,247,000	17.50	175	700	3,000	6,000
1921(m) Proof	—	Value: 40,000				
1922(m)	2,057,999	17.50	125	550	2,250	4,250
1922(m) Proof	—	Value: 40,000				
1923(m)	1,038,000	15.00	125	350	1,800	3,400
1923(m) Proof	—	Value: 37,500				
1924(m & sy)	1,582,000	10.00	60.00	315	1,250	2,200
1924(m) Proof	—	Value: 45,000				
1925(m & sy)	2,960,000	7.00	25.00	250	1,050	1,750
1925(m) Proof	—	Value: 30,000				
1926(m & sy)	2,487,000	7.00	25.00	300	1,200	2,500
1926(m) Proof	—	Value: 30,000				
1927(m)	3,420,000	7.00	15.00	70.00	425	800
1927(m) Proof	50	Value: 26,000				
1928(m)	1,962,000	7.00	15.00	75.00	550	850
1928(m) Proof	—	Value: 30,000				
1931(m)	3,129,000	7.00	9.00	27.50	160	295
1931(m) Proof	—	Value: 26,000				
1932(m)	188,000	100	425	1,500	6,600	12,500
1933(m)	488,000	22.50	200	750	6,000	12,000
1934(m)	1,674,000	7.00	12.50	55.00	350	600
1934(m) Proof	100	Value: 10,000				
1935(m)	915,000	7.00	12.50	65.00	425	800
1935(m) Proof	—	Value: 30,000				
1936(m)	2,382,000	BV	7.00	20.00	180	310
1936(m) Proof	—	Value: 23,500				

KM# 31 FLORIN
11.3100 g., 0.9250 Silver 0.3363 oz. ASW, 28.5 mm.
Ruler: George V **Subject:** Opening of Parliament House, Canberra **Obv:** Crowned head left **Edge:** Reeded

Date	Mintage	F	VF	XF	Unc	BU
1927(m)	2,000,000	BV	7.00	15.00	85.00	150
1927(m) Proof	400	Value: 15,000				

KM# 33 FLORIN
11.3100 g., 0.9250 Silver 0.3363 oz. ASW, 28.5 mm.
Ruler: George V **Subject:** Centennial of Victoria and Melbourne **Obv:** Crowned bust left **Rev:** Horse prancing left with rider holding torch

Date	Mintage	F	VF	XF	Unc	BU
ND(1934)	Est. 54,000	100	130	175	300	550

Date	Mintage	F	VF	XF	Unc	BU
Note: 21,000 pieces were melted						
ND(1934) Proof	—	Value: 16,500				

KM# 40 FLORIN
11.3100 g., 0.9250 Silver 0.3363 oz. ASW, 28.5 mm.
Ruler: George VI **Obv:** Head left **Rev:** Arms **Edge:** Reeded

Date	Mintage	F	VF	XF	Unc	BU
1938(m)	2,990,000	BV	4.50	15.00	45.00	80.00
1938(m) Proof	—	Value: 6,000				
1939(m)	630,000	10.00	30.00	250	1,000	1,700
1940(m)	8,410,000	—	BV	8.50	35.00	50.00
1941(m)	7,614,000	—	BV	7.50	30.00	40.00
1942(m)	17,986,000	—	BV	7.00	25.00	35.00
1942S	6,000,000	—	BV	7.00	20.00	30.00
1943(m)	12,762,000	—	BV	7.00	18.00	27.00
1943S	11,000,000	—	BV	7.00	18.00	27.00
1944(m)	22,440,000	—	BV	7.00	18.00	27.00
1944S	11,000,000	—	BV	7.00	18.00	25.00
1945(m)	11,970,000	—	BV	15.00	50.00	80.00

KM# 40a FLORIN
11.3100 g., 0.5000 Silver 0.1818 oz. ASW, 28.5 mm.
Ruler: George VI **Obv:** Head left **Rev:** Arms

Date	Mintage	F	VF	XF	Unc	BU
1946(m)	22,154,000	—	BV	4.00	16.50	23.00
1946(m) Proof	—	Value: 13,000				
1947(m)	39,292,000	—	BV	4.00	16.50	23.00
1947(m) Proof	—	Value: 13,000				

KM# 47 FLORIN
11.3100 g., 0.5000 Silver 0.1818 oz. ASW, 28.5 mm.
Ruler: George VI **Subject:** 50th Year Jubilee **Obv:** Head left
Rev: Crowned crossed scepter and sword divide Jubilee dates
Edge: Reeded

Date	Mintage	F	VF	XF	Unc	BU
1951(m)	2,000,000	—	BV	4.00	15.00	22.00

KM# 47a FLORIN
Copper-Nickel, 28.5 mm. **Ruler:** George VI **Subject:** 50th Year
Jubilee **Obv:** Head left **Rev:** Crowned crossed scepter and sword
divide Jubilee dates **Edge:** Reeded

Date	Mintage	F	VF	XF	Unc	BU
1951(L) Proof	—	Value: 17,500				
Note: Thought by many to be a trial strike or pattern						

KM# 48 FLORIN
11.3100 g., 0.5000 Silver 0.1818 oz. ASW, 28.5 mm.
Ruler: George VI **Obv:** Head left **Obv. Leg.:** IND: IMP. dropped
Rev: Arms **Edge:** Reeded

Date	Mintage	F	VF	XF	Unc	BU
1951(m)	10,068,000	—	—	10.00	45.00	90.00
1952(m)	10,044,000	—	—	10.00	45.00	90.00

KM# 54 FLORIN
11.3100 g., 0.5000 Silver 0.1818 oz. ASW, 28.5 mm. **Ruler:**
Elizabeth II **Obv:** Laureate bust right **Rev:** Arms **Edge:** Reeded

Date	Mintage	F	VF	XF	Unc	BU
1953(m)	12,658,000	—	BV	4.00	16.50	25.00
Note: Normal and large beads on the reverse.						
1953(m) Proof	—	Value: 8,000				
1954(m)	15,366,000	—	BV	5.00	25.00	50.00
1954(m) Proof	—	Value: 27,500				

KM# 55 FLORIN
11.3100 g., 0.5000 Silver 0.1818 oz. ASW, 28.5 mm.
Ruler: Elizabeth II **Subject:** Royal Visit **Obv:** Laureate bust right
Rev: Lion and kangaroo facing right

Date	Mintage	F	VF	XF	Unc	BU
1954(m)	4,000,000	—	—	4.00	15.00	20.00
1954(m) Proof	—	Value: 15,000				

KM# 60 FLORIN
11.3100 g., 0.5000 Silver 0.1818 oz. ASW, 28.5 mm.
Ruler: Elizabeth II **Obv:** Laureate bust right **Obv. Leg.:** F:D:
added **Rev:** Arms **Edge:** Reeded

Date	Mintage	F	VF	XF	Unc	BU
1956(m)	8,090,000	BV	4.00	8.00	55.00	110
1956(m) Proof	1,500	Value: 140				
1957(m)	9,278,000	—	BV	3.75	8.00	13.00
1957(m) Proof	1,256	Value: 150				
1958(m)	8,972,000	—	BV	3.75	7.00	12.00
1958(m) Proof	1,506	Value: 140				
1959(m)	3,500,000	—	BV	3.75	6.00	11.00
1959(m) Proof	1,506	Value: 150				
1960(m)	15,760,000	—	BV	3.75	5.00	10.00
1960(m) Proof	1,509	Value: 140				
1961(m)	9,452,000	—	BV	3.75	5.00	10.00
1961(m) Proof	1,506	Value: 140				
1962(m)	13,748,000	—	BV	3.75	5.00	9.00
1962(m) Proof	2,016	Value: 110				
1963(m)	12,002,000	—	BV	3.75	5.00	9.00
1963(m) Proof	5,042	Value: 100				

KM# 34 CROWN
28.2800 g., 0.9250 Silver 0.8410 oz. ASW, 38 mm.
Ruler: George VI **Obv:** Head left **Rev:** Crown above date and
value **Edge:** Reeded

Date	Mintage	F	VF	XF	Unc	BU
1937(m)	1,008,000	BV	17.50	22.50	75.00	150
1937(m) Proof	100	Value: 15,000				
1938(m)	102,000	40.00	60.00	90.00	375	800
1938(m) Proof	250	Value: 35,000				

TRADE COINAGE

KM# 14 1/2 SOVEREIGN
3.9940 g., 0.9170 Gold 0.1177 oz. AGW **Ruler:** Edward VII
Obv: Head right **Rev:** St. George slaying dragon

Date	Mintage	F	VF	XF	Unc	BU
1902S	84,000	BV	115	125	550	750
1902S Proof	—	Value: 50,000				

Date	Mintage	F	VF	XF	Unc	BU
1902S Frosted, Proof	—	Value: 50,000				
1903S	231,000	BV	115	125	700	1,500
1904P	60,000	115	230	1,300	5,000	—
1906S	308,000	BV	115	125	550	750
1906M	82,000	115	150	900	3,000	5,000
1907M	400,000	BV	115	125	950	1,550
1908S	538,000	BV	110	125	450	600
1908M	—	BV	115	125	750	1,200
1908	25,000	120	250	1,500	5,000	—
1909M	186,000	BV	115	125	1,000	1,500
1909P	44,000	115	175	600	3,000	5,000
1910S	474,000	BV	115	125	400	600

KM# 28 1/2 SOVEREIGN
3.9940 g., 0.9170 Gold 0.1177 oz. AGW **Ruler:** George V
Obv: Head left **Rev:** St. George slaying dragon

Date	Mintage	F	VF	XF	Unc	BU
1911S	252,000	BV	115	125	150	175
1911S Matte Proof	—	Value: 50,000				
1911P	130,000	BV	120	150	275	325
1912S	278,000	BV	115	125	125	150
1914S	322,000	BV	115	125	130	145
1915P	138,000	BV	115	140	255	300
1915S	892,000	—	BV	110	120	145
1915M	125,000	BV	115	125	150	175
1916S	448,000	—	BV	110	120	145
1918P	—	275	500	1,900	3,100	4,000
Note: Estimated 200-250 pieces minted						

KM# 15 SOVEREIGN
7.9881 g., 0.9170 Gold 0.2355 oz. AGW **Ruler:** Edward VII
Obv: Head right **Rev:** St. George on horseback with sword slaying
the dragon

Date	Mintage	F	VF	XF	Unc	BU
1902S	2,813,000	—	—	BV	235	350
1902S Proof	—	Value: 55,000				
1902S Frosted proof	—	Value: 55,000				
1902M	4,267,000	—	—	BV	235	350
1902P	4,289,000	—	—	BV	235	400
1903S	2,806,000	—	—	BV	235	400
1903M	3,521,000	—	—	BV	235	325
1903P	4,674,000	—	—	BV	235	300
1904S	2,986,000	—	—	BV	235	300
1904M	3,743,000	—	—	BV	235	350
1904M Proof	—	Value: 50,000				
1904P	4,506,000	—	—	BV	235	400
1905S	2,778,000	—	—	BV	235	325
1905M	3,633,000	—	—	BV	235	325
1905P	4,876,000	—	—	BV	235	325
1906S	2,792,000	—	—	BV	235	300
1906M	3,657,000	—	—	BV	235	300
1906P	4,829,000	—	—	BV	235	400
1907S	2,539,000	—	—	BV	235	265
1907M	3,332,000	—	—	BV	235	265
1907P	4,972,000	—	—	BV	235	325
1908S	2,017,000	—	—	BV	235	265
1908M	3,080,000	—	—	BV	235	265
1908P	4,875,000	—	—	BV	235	265
1909S	2,057,000	—	—	BV	235	265
1909M	3,029,000	—	—	BV	235	265
1909P	4,524,000	—	—	BV	235	265
1910S	2,135,000	—	—	BV	235	265
1910M	3,054,000	—	—	BV	235	265
1910M Proof	—	Value: 45,000				
1910P	4,690,000	—	—	BV	235	265

KM# 29 SOVEREIGN
7.9881 g., 0.9170 Gold 0.2355 oz. AGW **Ruler:** George V
Obv: Head left **Rev:** St. George on horseback with sword slaying
the dragon

Date	Mintage	F	VF	XF	Unc	BU
1911S	2,519,000	—	—	BV	235	250
1911S Proof	—	Value: 50,000				

Date	Mintage	F	VF	XF	Unc	BU
1911M	2,851,000	—	—	BV	235	250
1911M Proof	—	Value: 50,000				
1911P	4,373,000	—	—	BV	235	250
1912S	2,227,000	—	—	BV	235	250
1912M	2,467,000	—	—	BV	235	250
1912P	4,278,000	—	—	BV	235	250
1913S	2,249,000	—	—	BV	235	250
1913M	2,323,000	—	—	BV	235	250
1913P	4,635,000	—	—	BV	235	250
1914S	1,774,000	—	—	BV	235	250
1914S Proof	—	Value: 50,000				
1914M	2,012,000	—	—	BV	235	250
1914P	4,815,000	—	—	BV	235	250
1915S	1,346,000	—	—	BV	235	250
1915M	1,637,000	—	—	BV	235	250
1915P	4,373,000	—	—	BV	235	250
1916S	1,242,000	—	—	BV	235	250
1916M	1,277,000	—	—	BV	235	250
1916P	4,906,000	—	—	BV	235	250
1917S	1,666,000	—	—	BV	235	250
1917M	934,000	—	—	BV	235	250
1917P	4,110,000	—	—	BV	235	250
1918S	3,716,000	—	—	BV	235	250
1918M	4,969,000	—	—	BV	235	250
1918P	3,812,000	—	—	BV	235	250
1919S	1,835,000	—	—	BV	235	250
1919M	514,000	—	—	BV	235	300
1919P	2,995,000	—	—	BV	235	250
1920S	360,000	40,000	75,000	150,000	275,000	—
1920M	530,000	1,200	2,700	3,900	5,000	6,500
1920P	2,421,000	—	—	BV	235	250
1921S	839,000	500	750	1,200	1,700	2,200
1921M	240,000	4,500	8,000	12,000	16,000	18,500
1921P	2,314,000	—	—	BV	235	250
1922S	578,000	5,000	8,500	12,500	17,000	19,500
1922S Proof	—	Value: 50,000				
1922M	608,000	3,000	5,000	7,500	10,000	12,500
1922P	2,298,000	—	—	BV	235	250
1923S	416,000	3,000	5,200	8,000	12,500	14,000
1923S Proof	—	Value: 50,000				
1923M	510,000	Value: 300				
1923P	2,124,000	—	—	BV	235	250
1924S	394,000	500	750	1,200	1,700	2,200
1924M	278,000	—	—	BV	235	300
1924P	1,464,000	—	BV	235	250	350
1925S	5,632,000	—	—	BV	235	250
1925M	3,311,000	—	—	BV	235	250
1925P	1,837,000	—	—	BV	250	350
1926S	1,030,999	5,250	10,000	15,000	20,000	22,500
1926S Proof	—	Value: 60,000				
1926M	211,000	—	—	BV	235	300
1926P	1,131,000	500	750	1,250	2,500	2,800
1927M	310,000					
	Note: None known.					
1927P	1,383,000	—	BV	235	350	500
1928P	413,000	900	1,400	2,750	3,150	—
1928P	1,333,000	—	BV	235	245	265

KM# 32 SOVEREIGN

7.9881 g., 0.9170 Gold 0.2355 oz. AGW **Ruler:** George V
Obv: Head left **Rev:** St. George on horseback with sword slaying the dragon

Date	Mintage	F	VF	XF	Unc	BU
1929M	436,000	600	1,000	1,750	2,500	3,000
1929M Proof	—	Value: 50,000				
1929P	1,606,000	—	—	BV	235	250
1930M	77,000	BV	235	250	275	300
1930M Proof	—	Value: 50,000				
1930P	1,915,000	—	—	BV	235	250
1931M	57,000	235	260	350	550	700
1931M Proof	—	Value: 50,000				
1931P	1,173,000	—	—	BV	235	250

KM# 16 2 POUNDS

15.9761 g., 0.9170 Gold 0.4710 oz. AGW **Ruler:** Edward VII
Obv: Head right **Rev:** St. George on horseback with sword slaying the dragon **Note:** Gilt lead electrotypes exist.

Date	Mintage	F	VF	XF	Unc	BU
1902S Matte Proof Rare	4	Value: 60,000				

KM# 17 5 POUNDS

39.9403 g., 0.9170 Gold 1.1775 oz. AGW **Ruler:** Edward VII
Obv: Head right **Rev:** St. George on horseback with sword slaying the dragon **Note:** Gilt lead electrotypes exist.

Date	Mintage	F	VF	XF	Unc	BU
1902S Proof; Rare	Est. 3	Value: 110,000				
1902S Matte Proof; Rare	Inc. above	Value: 110,000				

Note: Spink Australia Sale #30 11-89 nearly FDC realized $38,500

DECIMAL COINAGE

KM# 62 CENT

2.6000 g., Bronze, 17.51 mm. **Ruler:** Elizabeth II **Obv:** Young bust right **Rev:** Feather-tailed Glider **Edge:** Plain

Date	Mintage	F	VF	XF	Unc	BU
1966(c)	146,457,000	—	—	—	0.65	1.00
1966(c) Proof	18,000	Value: 5.00				
1966(m)	238,990,000	—	—	—	1.00	2.50
	Note: Blunted whisker on right					
1966(p)	26,620,000	—	—	1.25	5.00	10.00
	Note: Blunted 2nd whisker from right					
1967	110,055,000	—	—	—	1.50	3.00
1968	19,930,000	0.15	0.30	1.25	9.00	18.00
1969	87,680,000	—	—	—	0.65	1.50
1969 Proof	13,000	Value: 3.00				
1970	72,560,000	—	—	—	0.50	0.85
1970 Proof	15,000	Value: 2.50				
1971	102,455,000	—	—	—	0.50	0.85
1971 Proof	10,000	Value: 2.50				
1972	82,400,000	—	—	—	0.50	0.85
1972 Proof	10,000	Value: 2.50				
1973	140,710,000	—	—	—	0.50	0.85
1973 Proof	10,000	Value: 2.50				
1974	131,720,000	—	—	—	0.40	0.60
1974 Proof	11,000	Value: 2.50				
1975	134,775,000	—	—	—	0.20	0.40
1975 Proof	23,000	Value: 1.00				
1976	172,935,000	—	—	—	0.20	0.40
1976 Proof	21,000	Value: 1.25				
1977	153,430,000	—	—	—	0.20	0.40
1977 Proof	55,000	Value: 1.25				
1978	97,253,000	—	—	—	0.20	0.40
1978 Proof	39,000	Value: 1.00				
1979	130,339,000	—	—	—	0.20	0.40
1979 Proof	36,000	Value: 1.00				
1980	137,892,000	—	—	—	0.20	0.40
1980 Proof	68,000	Value: 1.00				
1981	223,900,000	—	—	—	—	0.40
1981 Proof	86,000	Value: 1.00				
1982	134,290,000	—	—	—	0.20	0.40
1982 Proof	100,000	Value: 1.00				
1983	205,625,000	—	—	—	0.20	0.40
1983 Proof	80,000	Value: 1.00				
1984	74,735,000	—	—	—	0.20	0.40
1984 Proof	61,000	Value: 1.00				

KM# 78 CENT

2.6000 g., Bronze, 17.51 mm. **Ruler:** Elizabeth II **Obv:** Crowned head right **Rev:** Feather-tailed Glider

Date	Mintage	F	VF	XF	Unc	BU
1985	38,300,000	—	—	—	0.20	0.40
1985 Proof	75,000	Value: 1.00				
1986 In sets only	180,000	—	—	—	2.25	3.00
1986 Proof	67,000	Value: 3.00				
1987	127,000,000	—	—	—	0.20	0.40
1987 Proof	70,000	Value: 1.00				
1988	105,900,000	—	—	—	0.20	0.40
1988 Proof	106,000	Value: 1.00				
1989	150,000,000	—	—	—	0.20	0.40

Date	Mintage	F	VF	XF	Unc	BU
1989 Proof	67,000	Value: 1.00				
1990	51,900,000	—	—	—	0.20	0.40
1990 Proof	53,000	Value: 2.00				
1991 In sets only	148,000	—	—	—	2.25	3.00
1991 Proof	41,000	Value: 3.00				

KM# 78a CENT

3.0100 g., 0.9250 Silver 0.0895 oz. ASW, 17.51 mm. **Ruler:** Elizabeth II **Obv:** Crowned head right **Rev:** Feather-tailed Glider

Date	Mintage	F	VF	XF	Unc	BU
1991 Proof	25,000	Value: 10.00				

Note: In Proof sets only

KM# 63 2 CENTS

5.2000 g., Bronze, 21.6 mm. **Ruler:** Elizabeth II **Obv:** Young bust right **Rev:** Frill-necked Lizard

Date	Mintage	F	VF	XF	Unc	BU
1966(c)	145,226,000	—	—	—	0.65	1.00
1966(c) Proof	18,000	Value: 6.00				
1966(m)	66,575,000	—	—	—	2.25	4.00
	Note: Blunted 3rd left claw					
1966(p)	217,735,000	—	—	—	1.25	2.00
	Note: Blunted 1st right claw					
1967	73,250,000	—	—	—	3.50	6.00
1967	Inc. above	—	—	—	50.00	60.00
	Note: Without designer's initials on reverse					
1968	17,000,000	—	0.25	0.85	10.00	20.00
1969	12,940,000	—	—	—	2.25	4.00
1969 Proof	13,000	Value: 4.75				
1970	39,872,000	—	—	—	0.60	0.75
1970 Proof	15,000	Value: 4.00				
1971	60,735,000	—	—	—	0.60	0.75
1971 Proof	10,000	Value: 4.00				
1972	77,570,000	—	—	—	0.60	0.75
1972 Proof	10,000	Value: 4.00				
1973	94,058,000	—	—	—	0.60	0.75
1973 Proof	10,000	Value: 4.00				
1974	177,723,000	—	—	—	0.50	0.75
1974 Proof	11,000	Value: 3.00				
1975	100,045,000	—	—	—	0.50	0.75
1975 Proof	23,000	Value: 1.25				
1976	121,882,000	—	—	—	0.35	0.50
1976 Proof	21,000	Value: 2.00				
1977	102,000,000	—	—	—	0.35	0.50
1977 Proof	55,000	Value: 1.25				
1978	128,700,000	—	—	—	0.35	0.50
1978 Proof	39,000	Value: 1.25				
1979	69,705,000	—	—	—	0.35	0.50
1979 Proof	36,000	Value: 1.25				
1980	145,603,000	—	—	—	0.35	0.50
1980 Proof	68,000	Value: 1.25				
1981	247,300,000	—	—	—	0.35	0.50
1981 Proof	86,000	Value: 1.25				
1982	121,770,000	—	—	—	0.35	0.50
1982 Proof	121,770,000	Value: 1.25				
1983	177,227,000	—	—	—	0.35	0.50
1983 Proof	80,000	Value: 1.25				
1984	57,963,000	—	—	—	0.35	0.50
1984 Proof	61,000	Value: 1.25				

KM# 79 2 CENTS

5.2000 g., Bronze, 21.6 mm. **Ruler:** Elizabeth II **Obv:** Crowned head right **Rev:** Frill-necked Lizard **Edge:** Plain

Date	Mintage	F	VF	XF	Unc	BU
1985	34,700,000	—	—	—	0.35	0.50
1985 Proof	75,000	Value: 1.25				
1986 In sets only	180,000	—	—	—	2.50	3.50
1986 Proof	67,000	Value: 3.50				
1987 In sets only	200,000	—	—	—	2.50	3.50
1987 Proof	70,000	Value: 3.50				
1988	28,905,000	—	—	—	0.35	0.50
1988 Proof	106,000	Value: 1.25				
1989	110,000,000	—	—	—	0.35	0.50
1989 Proof	67,000	Value: 2.00				
1990 In sets only	103,000	—	—	—	25.00	30.00
1990 Proof	53,000	Value: 25.00				
1991 In sets only	148,000	—	—	—	5.00	7.00
1991 Proof	41,000	Value: 5.00				

KM# 79a 2 CENTS

6.0600 g., 0.9250 Silver 0.1802 oz. ASW, 21.6 mm. **Ruler:** Elizabeth II **Obv:** Crowned head right **Rev:** Frill-necked Lizard

Date	Mintage	F	VF	XF	Unc	BU
1991 Proof	25,000	Value: 10.00				

Note: In Proof sets only

KM# 64   5 CENTS
2.8000 g., Copper-Nickel, 19.4 mm. **Ruler:** Elizabeth II
Obv: Young bust right **Rev:** Echidna **Note:** For 1966 dated examples, the length of the whisker on top of the forward-most claw at left will indicate the mint: Canberra (less than .5mm) or London (greater than .6mm).

Date	Mintage	F	VF	XF	Unc	BU
1966(c)	45,427,000	—	—	—	0.85	1.50
1966(c) Proof	18,000	Value: 7.50				
1966(L)	30,000,000	—	—	—	1.00	1.75
1967	62,144,000	—	—	—	0.85	1.50
1968	67,336,000	—	—	—	0.85	1.50
1969	38,170,000	—	—	—	0.85	1.50
1969 Proof	13,000	Value: 7.50				
1970	46,058,000	—	—	—	0.60	0.80
1970 Proof	15,000	Value: 5.00				
1971	39,516,000	—	—	—	0.60	0.80
1971 Proof	10,000	Value: 5.00				
1972	8,256,000	0.15	0.30	1.50	12.50	20.00
1972 Proof	10,000	Value: 5.00				
1973	48,816,000	—	—	—	0.60	0.80
1973 Proof	10,000	Value: 5.00				
1974	64,248,000	—	—	—	0.60	0.80
1974 Proof	11,000	Value: 5.00				
1975	44,256,000	—	—	—	0.50	0.60
1975 Proof	23,000	Value: 2.00				
1976	113,180,000	—	—	—	0.50	0.60
1976 Proof	21,000	Value: 3.00				
1977	108,800,000	—	—	—	0.50	0.60
1977 Proof	55,000	Value: 2.00				
1978	25,210,000	—	—	—	0.50	0.60
1978 Proof	39,000	Value: 2.00				
1979	44,533,000	—	—	—	0.50	0.60
1979 Proof	36,000	Value: 2.00				
1980	115,042,000	—	—	—	0.50	0.60
1980 Proof	68,000	Value: 2.00				
1981	162,264,000	—	—	—	0.50	0.60
1981 Proof	86,000	Value: 2.00				
1982	139,468,000	—	—	—	0.50	0.60
1982 Proof	100,000	Value: 2.00				
1983	131,568,000	—	—	—	0.50	0.60
1983 Proof	80,000	Value: 2.00				
1984	35,436,000	—	—	—	0.50	0.60
1984 Proof	61,000	Value: 2.00				

KM# 80   5 CENTS
2.8000 g., Copper-Nickel, 19.25 mm. **Ruler:** Elizabeth II
Obv: Crowned head right **Rev:** Echidna **Edge:** Reeded

Date	Mintage	F	VF	XF	Unc	BU
1985	170,000	—	—	—	10.00	15.00
	Note: In Mint sets only					
1985 Proof	75,000	Value: 15.00				
1986	180,000	—	—	—	2.50	3.50
	Note: In Mint sets only					
1986 Proof	67,000	Value: 3.50				
1987	73,500,000	—	—	—	0.50	0.60
1987 Proof	70,000	Value: 2.00				
1988	106,100,000	—	—	—	0.50	0.60
1988 Proof	106,000	Value: 2.00				
1989	75,000,000	—	—	—	0.50	0.60
1989 Proof	67,000	Value: 2.00				
1990	33,200,000	—	—	—	0.50	0.60
1990 Proof	53,000	Value: 2.00				
1991	18,400,000	—	—	—	0.50	0.60
1991 Proof	41,000	Value: 2.00				
1992	36,200,000	—	—	—	0.50	0.60
1992 Proof	56,000	Value: 2.00				
1993	93,840,000	—	—	—	0.50	0.60
1993 Proof	46,000	Value: 2.00				
1994	146,669,000	—	—	—	0.50	0.60
1994 Proof	39,000	Value: 2.00				
1995	84,987,000	—	—	—	0.50	0.60
1995 Proof	48,000	Value: 2.00				
1996	79,210,000	—	—	—	0.50	0.60
1996 Proof	41,000	Value: 2.00				
1997	100,680,000	—	—	—	0.50	0.60
1997 Proof	32,000	Value: 3.00				
1998	88,532,000	—	—	—	0.40	0.50
1998 Proof	32,000	Value: 3.00				

KM# 80a   5 CENTS
3.2700 g., 0.9250 Silver 0.0972 oz. ASW, 19.4 mm.
Ruler: Elizabeth II **Obv:** Crowned head right **Rev:** Echidna

Date	Mintage	F	VF	XF	Unc	BU
1991 Proof	25,000	Value: 10.00				
	Note: In Proof sets only					

KM# 401   5 CENTS
2.8300 g., Copper-Nickel, 19.4 mm. **Ruler:** Elizabeth II
Obv: Head with tiara right **Rev:** Echidna **Edge:** Reeded

Date	Mintage	F	VF	XF	Unc	BU
1999	179,016,000	—	—	—	—	0.20
1999 Proof	28,000	Value: 3.00				
2000	97,422,000	—	—	—	—	0.20
2000 Proof	64,000	Value: 4.00				

KM# 481   5 CENTS
5.5300 g., 0.9990 Silver 0.1776 oz. ASW, 25 mm.
Ruler: Elizabeth II **Series:** Masterpieces in Silver **Rev:** Half penny reverse design of KM#41 **Edge:** Reeded

Date	Mintage	F	VF	XF	Unc	BU
1999 Proof	15,000	Value: 10.00				

KM# 65   10 CENTS
5.6500 g., Copper-Nickel, 23.6 mm. **Ruler:** Elizabeth II
Obv: Young bust right **Rev:** Lyrebird **Note:** For 1966 dated examples, 11 spikes on the left Lyrebird indicates a strike from Canberra, 12 spikes indicate a London strike.

Date	Mintage	F	VF	XF	Unc	BU
1966(c)	10,984,000	—	—	—	2.00	3.00
1966(c) Proof	18,000	Value: 8.00				
1966(L)	30,000,000	—	—	—	2.00	3.00
1967	51,032,000	—	—	—	4.00	6.00
1968	57,194,000	—	—	—	4.50	6.50
1969	22,146,000	—	—	—	2.75	3.50
1969 Proof	13,000	Value: 8.50				
1970	22,306,000	—	—	—	2.00	3.00
1970 Proof	15,000	Value: 6.50				
1971	20,726,000	—	—	—	5.00	7.50
1971 Proof	10,000	Value: 6.50				
1972	12,502,000	—	—	—	8.00	11.00
1972 Proof	10,000	Value: 6.50				
1973	27,320,000	—	—	—	2.00	3.00
1973 Proof	10,000	Value: 6.50				
1974	46,550,000	—	—	—	2.00	3.00
1974 Proof	11,000	Value: 6.50				
1975	50,900,000	—	—	—	0.75	1.00
1975 Proof	23,000	Value: 2.00				
1976	57,060,000	—	—	—	0.75	1.00
1976 Proof	21,000	Value: 3.75				
1977	10,940,000	—	—	—	0.75	1.00
1977 Proof	55,000	Value: 2.00				
1978	48,400,000	—	—	—	0.50	0.75
1978 Proof	39,000	Value: 2.00				
1979	36,950,000	—	—	—	0.50	0.75
1979 Proof	36,000	Value: 2.00				
1980	55,084,000	—	—	—	0.50	0.75
1980 Proof	68,000	Value: 2.00				
1981	116,060,000	—	—	—	0.50	0.75

Note: One 1981 coin was struck on a Sri Lanka 50 cents planchet, KM#135.1. It carries an approximate value of $600

Date	Mintage	F	VF	XF	Unc	BU
1981 Proof	86,000	Value: 2.00				
1982	61,492,000	—	—	—	0.50	0.75
1982 Proof	100,000	Value: 2.00				
1983	82,318,000	—	—	—	0.50	0.75
1983 Proof	80,000	Value: 2.00				
1984	25,728,000	—	—	—	0.50	0.75
1984 Proof	61,000	Value: 2.00				

KM# 81   10 CENTS
5.6500 g., Copper-Nickel, 23.6 mm. **Ruler:** Elizabeth II
Obv: Crowned head right **Rev:** Lyrebird

Date	Mintage	F	VF	XF	Unc	BU
1985	2,100,000	—	—	—	0.50	0.75
1985 Proof	75,000	Value: 3.00				
1986	180,000	—	—	—	2.50	3.50
	Note: In mint sets only					
1986 Proof	67,000	Value: 3.50				
1987	200,000	—	—	—	2.50	3.50
	Note: In mint sets only					

Date	Mintage	F	VF	XF	Unc	BU
1987 Proof	70,000	Value: 3.50				
1988	46,900,000	—	—	—	0.50	0.75
1988 Proof	106,000	Value: 2.50				
1989	45,000,000	—	—	—	0.50	0.75
1989 Proof	67,000	Value: 2.50				
1990	17,000,000	—	—	—	0.50	0.75
1990 Proof	53,000	Value: 2.50				
1991	3,174,000	—	—	—	0.50	0.75
1991 Proof	41,000	Value: 2.50				
1992	29,800,000	—	—	—	0.50	0.75
1992 Proof	56,000	Value: 2.50				
1993	23,100,000	—	—	—	0.50	0.75
1993 Proof	46,000	Value: 2.50				
1994	43,726,000	—	—	—	0.50	0.75
1994 Proof	39,000	Value: 2.50				
1995 Mint sets only	96,000	—	—	—	10.00	15.00
1995 Proof	41,000	Value: 15.00				
1996	108,000	—	—	—	10.00	15.00
1996 Proof	41,000	Value: 15.00				
1997	5,700,000	—	—	—	20.00	30.00
1997 Proof	32,000	Value: 30.00				
1998	47,989,000	—	—	—	0.50	0.75
1998 Proof	32,000	Value: 3.50				

KM# 81a   10 CENTS
6.5200 g., 0.9250 Silver 0.1939 oz. ASW, 23.6 mm.
Ruler: Elizabeth II **Obv:** Crowned head right **Rev:** Lyrebird

Date	Mintage	F	VF	XF	Unc	BU
1991 Proof	25,000	Value: 12.50				
	Note: In Proof sets only					

KM# 402   10 CENTS
5.6600 g., Copper-Nickel, 23.6 mm. **Ruler:** Elizabeth II
Obv: Head with tiara right **Rev:** Lyrebird **Edge:** Reeded

Date	Mintage	F	VF	XF	Unc	BU
1999	94,889,000	—	—	—	—	0.50
1999 Proof	28,000	Value: 3.00				
2000	51,117,000	—	—	—	—	0.50
2000 Proof	64,000	Value: 4.00				

KM# 482   10 CENTS
8.3600 g., 0.9990 Silver 0.2685 oz. ASW, 30 mm.
Ruler: Elizabeth II **Series:** Masterpieces in Silver **Obv:** Head right **Rev:** Penny reverse design of KM#23 **Edge:** Reeded

Date	Mintage	F	VF	XF	Unc	BU
1999 Proof	15,000	Value: 12.00				

KM# 66   20 CENTS
11.3000 g., Copper-Nickel, 28.5 mm. **Ruler:** Elizabeth II
Obv: Young bust right **Rev:** Duckbill Platypus **Note:** For 1966 dated examples, strikes from Canberra show a gap between sea line and right face of platypus.

Date	Mintage	F	VF	XF	Unc	BU
1966(c)	28,223,000	—	—	—	10.00	16.00
1966(c) Proof	18,000	Value: 12.00				
1966(L)		—	—	—	500	850
	Note: Wave on base of 2					
1966(L) Proof	—	Value: 12.50				
1967	83,848,000	—	—	1.00	15.00	22.00
1968	40,537,000	—	1.00	5.00	30.00	40.00
1969	16,501,999	—	—	—	15.00	22.00
1969 Proof	13,000	Value: 13.50				
1970	23,271,000	—	—	—	7.00	10.00
1970 Proof	15,000	Value: 11.50				
1971	8,947,000	—	—	5.00	25.00	32.00
1971 Proof	10,000	Value: 11.50				
1972	16,643,000	—	—	—	8.00	11.00
1972 Proof	10,000	Value: 10.00				
1973	23,356,000	—	—	—	8.00	11.00
1973 Proof	10,000	Value: 10.00				
1974	33,548,000	—	—	—	8.00	11.00
1974 Proof	11,000	Value: 10.00				
1975	53,300,000	—	—	—	1.75	2.50
1975 Proof	23,000	Value: 2.25				
1976	59,774,000	—	—	—	1.00	1.50
1976 Proof	21,000	Value: 3.75				
1977	41,272,000	—	—	—	1.00	1.50
1977 Proof	55,000	Value: 2.25				
1978	37,400,000	—	—	—	1.00	1.50
1978 Proof	39,000	Value: 2.25				

Date	Mintage	F	VF	XF	Unc	BU
1979	22,300,000	—	—	—	1.00	1.50
1979 Proof	36,000	Value: 2.25				
1980	84,400,000	—	—	—	0.70	1.00
1980 Proof	68,000	Value: 2.25				
1981	165,500,000	—	—	—	0.60	0.80

Note: Some 1981 dated coins were struck on a Hong Kong 2 Dollar planchet, KM#37. 6 pieces are reported. Each carries an approximate value of $800

Date	Mintage	F	VF	XF	Unc	BU
1981 Proof	86,000	Value: 2.25				
1982	76,600,000	—	—	—	0.60	0.80
1982 Proof	100,000	Value: 2.25				
1983	55,113,000	—	—	—	10.00	15.00
1983 Proof	80,000	Value: 10.00				
1984	27,820,000	—	—	—	12.00	17.00
1984 Proof	61,000	Value: 10.00				

KM# 82 20 CENTS
11.3000 g., Copper-Nickel, 28.5 mm. **Ruler:** Elizabeth II **Obv:** Crowned head right **Rev:** Duckbill Platypus

Date	Mintage	F	VF	XF	Unc	BU
1985	2,700,000	—	—	—	6.00	10.00
1985 Proof	75,000	Value: 10.00				
1986	180,000	—	—	—	6.00	10.00
Note: In mint sets only						
1986 Proof	67,000	Value: 10.00				
1987	200,000	—	—	—	6.00	10.00
Note: In mint sets only						
1987 Proof	70,000	Value: 10.00				
1988	240,000	—	—	—	6.00	10.00
Note: In mint sets only						
1988 Proof	106,000	Value: 10.00				
1989	150,000	—	—	—	6.00	10.00
1989 Proof	67,000	Value: 10.00				
1990	103,000	—	—	—	6.00	10.00
1990 Proof	53,000	Value: 10.00				
1991	148,000	—	—	—	6.00	10.00
1991 Proof	41,000	Value: 10.00				
1992	118,000	—	—	—	6.00	10.00
1992 Proof	56,000	Value: 10.00				
1993	84,000	—	—	—	6.00	10.00
1993 Proof	46,000	Value: 10.00				
1994	14,330,000	—	—	—	1.00	2.00
1994 Proof	39,000	Value: 3.50				
1995	4,840,000	—	—	—	15.00	25.00
1995 Proof	41,000	Value: 25.00				
1996	20,596,000	—	—	—	1.00	2.00
1996 Proof	41,000	Value: 10.00				
1997	16,730,000	—	—	—	1.00	2.00
1997 Proof	32,000	Value: 15.00				
1998	28,830,000	—	—	—	1.00	2.00
1998 Proof	32,000	Value: 10.00				

KM# 82a 20 CENTS
13.0900 g., 0.9250 Silver 0.3893 oz. ASW, 28.5 mm.
Ruler: Elizabeth II **Obv:** Head right **Rev:** Duckbill Platypus

Date	Mintage	F	VF	XF	Unc	BU
1991 Proof	25,000	Value: 20.00				
Note: In Proof sets only						

KM# 295 20 CENTS
11.3000 g., Copper-Nickel, 28.5 mm. **Ruler:** Elizabeth II **Subject:** 50th Anniversary - United Nations **Obv:** Crowned head right **Rev:** UN logo over value **Rev. Leg.:** UNITED NATIONS FIFTIETH ANNIVERSARY

Date	Mintage	F	VF	XF	Unc	BU
1995	4,800,000	—	—	—	2.00	4.00

KM# 410 20 CENTS
13.3600 g., 0.9990 Silver 0.4291 oz. ASW **Ruler:** Elizabeth II **Subject:** Masterpieces in Silver **Obv:** Queens head right **Rev:** 1927 Florin design

Date	Mintage	F	VF	XF	Unc	BU
1998 Proof	15,000	Value: 20.00				

KM# 403 20 CENTS
11.3000 g., Copper-Nickel, 26.87 mm. **Ruler:** Elizabeth II **Obv:** Head with tiara right **Rev:** Duckbill Platypus **Edge:** Reeded

Date	Mintage	F	VF	XF	Unc	BU
1999	64,181,000	—	—	—	—	0.80
1999 Proof	28,000	Value: 10.00				
2000	35,584,000	—	—	—	—	0.80
2000 Proof	64,000	Value: 15.00				

KM# 483 20 CENTS
2.9900 g., 0.9990 Silver 0.0960 oz. ASW, 17.5 mm.
Ruler: Elizabeth II **Series:** Masterpieces in Silver **Obv:** Head right **Rev:** Threepence reverse design of KM#37 **Edge:** Reeded

Date	Mintage	F	VF	XF	Unc	BU
1999 Proof	15,000	Value: 20.00				

KM# 496 20 CENTS
13.3600 g., 0.9990 Silver 0.4291 oz. ASW, 28.5 mm.
Ruler: Elizabeth II **Series:** Masterpieces in Silver - 2000 Set **Obv:** Head with tiara right **Rev:** Crowned bust right **Edge:** Reeded

Date	Mintage	F	VF	XF	Unc	BU
2000 Proof	15,000	Value: 20.00				

KM# 497 20 CENTS
13.3600 g., 0.9990 Silver 0.4291 oz. ASW, 28.5 mm.
Ruler: Elizabeth II **Series:** Masterpieces in Silver - 2000 Set **Obv:** Head with tiara right **Rev:** Crowned bust left **Edge:** Reeded

Date	Mintage	F	VF	XF	Unc	BU
2000 Proof	15,000	Value: 20.00				

KM# 498 20 CENTS
13.3600 g., 0.9990 Silver 0.4291 oz. ASW, 28.5 mm.
Ruler: Elizabeth II **Series:** Masterpieces in Silver - 2000 Set **Obv:** Rank-Broadley head with tiara right **Rev:** Laureate bust right **Edge:** Reeded

Date	Mintage	F	VF	XF	Unc	BU
2000 Proof	15,000	Value: 20.00				

KM# 113 25 CENTS (The Dump)
7.7750 g., 0.9990 Silver 0.2497 oz. ASW **Ruler:** Elizabeth II **Obv:** Crowned head right **Rev:** Aboriginal Culture **Note:** The center "plug" coin issued with 1 Dollar, KM#112.

Date	Mintage	F	VF	XF	Unc	BU
1988 Proof	100,000	Value: 10.00				

KM# 132 25 CENTS (The Dump)
7.7750 g., 0.9990 Silver 0.2497 oz. ASW **Ruler:** Elizabeth II **Obv:** Crowned head right **Rev:** Wandjina of Aboriginal Mythology **Note:** The center "plug" coin issued with 1 Dollar, KM#131.

Date	Mintage	F	VF	XF	Unc	BU
1989 Proof	45,000	Value: 15.00				

KM# 155 25 CENTS (The Dump)
7.7750 g., 0.9990 Silver 0.2497 oz. ASW **Ruler:** Elizabeth II **Obv:** Crowned head right **Rev:** 3 Mythological Creatures **Note:** The center "plug" coin issued with 1 Dollar, KM#154.

Date	Mintage	F	VF	XF	Unc	BU
1990 Proof	30,000	Value: 17.50				

KM# 67 50 CENTS
13.2800 g., 0.8000 Silver 0.3416 oz. ASW, 31.5 mm.
Ruler: Elizabeth II **Obv:** Young bust right **Rev:** Coat of arms with kangaroo and emu supporters

Date	Mintage	F	VF	XF	Unc	BU
1966	36,454,000	—	—	BV	6.00	8.50
Note: On reverse, two parallel horizontal bars behind Emu's head.						
1966 Proof	18,000	Value: 75.00				

KM# 68 50 CENTS
15.5500 g., Copper-Nickel, 31.5 mm. **Ruler:** Elizabeth II **Obv:** Young bust right **Rev:** Coat of arms with kangaroo and emu supporters **Edge:** 12-sided

Date	Mintage	F	VF	XF	Unc	BU
1969	14,015,000	—	—	—	10.00	16.50
1969 Proof	13,000	Value: 55.00				
1971	21,056,000	—	—	—	13.50	16.50
1971 Proof	10,000	Value: 35.00				
1972	5,586,000	—	—	2.50	20.00	30.00
1972 Proof	10,000	Value: 35.00				
1973	4,009,000	—	—	3.00	25.00	35.00
1973 Proof	10,000	Value: 35.00				
1974	8,962,000	—	—	—	15.00	20.00
1974 Proof	11,000	Value: 30.00				
1975	19,025,000	—	—	—	3.00	5.00
1975 Proof	23,000	Value: 10.00				
1976	27,280,000	—	—	—	3.00	5.00
1976 Proof	21,000	Value: 15.00				
1978	25,765,000	—	—	—	2.00	3.00
1978 Proof	39,000	Value: 4.00				
1979	24,886,000	—	—	—	2.00	3.00
1979 Proof	36,000	Value: 4.00				
1979	Inc. above	—	—	—	6.00	8.50
Note: On reverse, two parallel horizontal bars behind Emu's head.						
1980	38,681,000	—	—	—	2.00	3.00
1980	Inc. above	—	—	—	5.00	7.00
Note: On reverse, two parallel horizontal bars behind Emu's head.						
1980 Proof	68,000	Value: 3.50				
1981	24,168,000	—	—	—	1.00	1.50
1981 Proof	86,000	Value: 3.50				
1983	48,923,000	—	—	—	1.00	1.50
1983 Proof	80,000	Value: 3.75				
1984	26,281,000	—	—	—	1.00	1.50
1984 Proof	61,000	Value: 4.00				

KM# 69   50 CENTS
15.5500 g., Copper-Nickel, 31.5 mm. **Ruler:** Elizabeth II
Subject: 200th Anniversary - Cook's Australian Voyage
Obv: Young bust right **Rev:** Bust of Captain Cook at left, map of
Australia at right

Date	Mintage	F	VF	XF	Unc	BU
1970	16,540,000	—	0.50	2.00	3.50
1970 Proof	15,000	Value: 40.00				

KM# 70   50 CENTS
15.5500 g., Copper-Nickel, 31.5 mm. **Ruler:** Elizabeth II
Subject: Queen's Silver Jubilee **Obv:** Young bust right
Rev: Circular geometric design

Date	Mintage	F	VF	XF	Unc	BU
1977	25,076,000	—			1.00	1.75
1977 Proof	55,000	Value: 4.00				

KM# A72   50 CENTS
Copper-Nickel, 31.5 mm. **Ruler:** Elizabeth II **Subject:** Mule **Obv:**
Young bust right **Rev:** Sailing canoe-Takia, denomination below

Date	Mintage	F	VF	XF	Unc	BU
1978 Proof	—	Value: 750				

KM# 72   50 CENTS
15.5500 g., Copper-Nickel, 31.5 mm. **Ruler:** Elizabeth II
Subject: Wedding of Prince Charles and Lady Diana **Rev:**
Conjoined heads of Prince Charles and Lady Diana, left

Date	Mintage	F	VF	XF	Unc	BU
1981	44,100,000	—	0.40	0.50	1.00	1.50

KM# 74   50 CENTS
15.5500 g., Copper-Nickel, 31.5 mm. **Ruler:** Elizabeth II
Subject: XII Commonwealth Games - Brisbane **Obv:** Young bust
right **Rev:** Circle of images representing different sporting events

Date	Mintage	F	VF	XF	Unc	BU
1982	49,500,000	—			1.00	1.25
1982 Proof	100,000	Value: 4.00				

KM# 83   50 CENTS
15.5500 g., Copper-Nickel, 31.5 mm. **Ruler:** Elizabeth II
Obv: Young bust with tiara right **Rev:** Coat of arms with kangaroo
and emu supporters

Date	Mintage	F	VF	XF	Unc	BU
1985	1,000,000	—	—	2.00	6.00	10.00
1985 Proof	75,000	Value: 10.00				
1986 In sets only	180,000				6.00	10.00
1986 Proof	67,000	Value: 10.00				
1987 In sets only	200,000				6.00	10.00
1987 Proof	70,000	Value: 10.00				
1989 In sets only	—				6.00	10.00
1989 Proof	—	Value: 10.00				
1990 In sets only	—				6.00	10.00
1990 Proof	—	Value: 10.00				
1992 In sets only	—				6.00	10.00
1992 Proof	47,000	Value: 10.00				
1993	980,000				6.00	10.00
1993 Proof	—	Value: 10.00				
1996	19,297,000				1.50	2.25
1996 Proof	—	Value: 6.00				
1997	4,340,000				6.00	10.00
1997 Proof	—	Value: 16.00				

KM# 99   50 CENTS
15.5500 g., Copper-Nickel, 31.5 mm. **Ruler:** Elizabeth II
Subject: Australian Bicentennial **Obv:** Crowned head right
Rev: Ship sailing towards gridmarked map of Australia, compass
at upper center **Rev. Leg.:** AUSTRALIA - 1788-1988

Date	Mintage	F	VF	XF	Unc	BU
1988	8,100,000	—	—	—	2.25	3.00
1988 Proof	106,000	Value: 4.00				

KM# 99a   50 CENTS
18.0000 g., 0.9250 Silver 0.5353 oz. ASW, 31.5 mm.
Ruler: Elizabeth II **Subject:** Australian Bicentennial
Obv: Crowned head right **Rev:** Ship sailing towards gridmarked
map of Australia, compass at upper center

Date	Mintage	F	VF	XF	Unc	BU
1988 Proof	25,000	Value: 16.00				
1989 Proof	25,000	Value: 16.00				

KM# 127   50 CENTS
18.0000 g., 0.9250 Silver 0.5353 oz. ASW, 31.5 mm. **Ruler:**
Elizabeth II **Subject:** Cook Commemorative **Obv:** Crowned head
right **Rev:** Bust of Captain Cook at left, map of Australia at right

Date	Mintage	F	VF	XF	Unc	BU
1989 Proof	25,000	Value: 16.00				

KM# 128   50 CENTS
18.0000 g., 0.9250 Silver 0.5353 oz. ASW, 31.5 mm.
Ruler: Elizabeth II **Subject:** Queen's Silver Jubilee
Obv: Crowned head right **Rev:** Circular geometric design

Date	Mintage	F	VF	XF	Unc	BU
1989 Proof	25,000	Value: 16.00				

KM# 129   50 CENTS
18.0000 g., 0.9250 Silver 0.5353 oz. ASW, 31.5 mm.
Ruler: Elizabeth II **Subject:** Wedding of Prince Charles and Lady
Diana **Obv:** Crowned head right **Rev:** Conjoined heads of Prince
Charles and Lady Diana left

Date	Mintage	F	VF	XF	Unc	BU
1989 Proof	25,000	Value: 16.00				

KM# 130   50 CENTS
18.0000 g., 0.9250 Silver 0.5353 oz. ASW, 31.5 mm.
Ruler: Elizabeth II **Subject:** XII Commonwealth Games -
Brisbane **Obv:** Crowned head right **Rev:** Circle of images
representing different sporting events

Date	Mintage	F	VF	XF	Unc	BU
1989 Proof	25,000	Value: 16.00				

KM# 139   50 CENTS
15.5500 g., Copper-Nickel, 31.5 mm. **Ruler:** Elizabeth II
Subject: 25th Anniversary of Decimal Currency **Obv:** Crowned
head right **Rev:** Head of Merino ram

Date	Mintage	F	VF	XF	Unc	BU
1991	4,364,000	—	1.00	5.00	10.00
1991 Proof	—	Value: 12.50				

KM# 139a   50 CENTS
18.0000 g., 0.9250 Silver 0.5353 oz. ASW **Ruler:** Elizabeth II
Subject: 25th Anniversary of Decimal Currency **Obv:** Crowned
head right **Rev:** Head of Merino ram

Date	Mintage	F	VF	XF	Unc	BU
1991 Proof	25,000	Value: 20.00				

  Note: In Proof sets only

KM# 257   50 CENTS
15.5000 g., Copper-Nickel, 31.5 mm. **Ruler:** Elizabeth II
Subject: International Year of the Family **Obv:** Crowned head
right **Rev:** Crude drawings depicting a family

Date	Mintage	F	VF	XF	Unc	BU
1994	21,200,000	—	1.00	3.00	5.00
1994 Proof	39,000	Value: 11.50				

KM# 294   50 CENTS
15.5000 g., Copper-Nickel, 31.5 mm. **Ruler:** Elizabeth II
Subject: Weary Dunlop **Obv:** Crowned head right **Rev:** Bust of
Dunlop at center, value below

Date	Mintage	F	VF	XF	Unc	BU
1995	15,860,000	—	—	1.50	2.50
1995 Proof	48,000	Value: 11.50				

KM# 364   50 CENTS
15.5500 g., Copper-Nickel, 31.5 mm. **Ruler:** Elizabeth II
Subject: Discovery of Bass Strait **Obv:** Crowned head right
Rev: Busts of Bass and Flinders, map of mainland Australia and
Tasmania at left

Date	Mintage	F	VF	XF	Unc	BU
1998	22,390,000	—	—	1.50	2.50
1998 Proof	32,000	Value: 11.50				

KM# 411   50 CENTS
36.3100 g., 0.9990 Silver 1.1662 oz. ASW **Ruler:** Elizabeth II
Subject: Masterpieces in Silver **Obv:** Crowned head right
Rev: 1937 crown design

Date	Mintage	F	VF	XF	Unc	BU
1998 Proof	15,000	Value: 28.00				

KM# 404 50 CENTS
15.5500 g., Copper-Nickel, 31.51 mm. **Ruler:** Elizabeth II **Obv:** Head with tiara right **Rev:** Australian coat of arms with kangaroo and emu supporters **Edge:** Plain

Date	Mintage	F	VF	XF	Unc	BU
1999	20,318,000	—	—	1.50	2.50	
1999 Proof	28,000	Value: 12.50				

KM# 484 50 CENTS
3.2400 g., 0.9990 Silver 0.1041 oz. ASW, 19.4 mm. **Ruler:** Elizabeth II **Series:** Masterpieces in Silver **Obv:** Bust right **Rev:** Coat of arms with kangaroo and emu supporters **Edge:** Reeded

Date	Mintage	F	VF	XF	Unc	BU
1999 Proof	15,000	Value: 20.00				

KM# 437 50 CENTS
15.5500 g., Copper-Nickel, 31.5 mm. **Ruler:** Elizabeth II **Subject:** Royal Visit **Obv:** Head with tiara right **Rev:** Australian flag above Canberra Parliament House, British crown at right **Edge:** Plain

Date	Mintage	F	VF	XF	Unc	BU
2000	5,000	—	—	—	1.50	2.50

KM# 437a 50 CENTS
18.2400 g., 0.9990 Silver 0.5858 oz. ASW, 31.5 mm. **Ruler:** Elizabeth II **Subject:** Royal Visit **Obv:** Head with tiara right **Rev:** Australian flag above Canberra Parliament House, British crown at right

Date	Mintage	F	VF	XF	Unc	BU
2000 Proof	25,000	Value: 27.50				

KM# 488.1 50 CENTS
15.5500 g., Copper-Nickel, 31.5 mm. **Ruler:** Elizabeth II **Subject:** Millennium **Obv:** Head with tiara right **Rev:** Australian flag **Edge:** Plain **Note:** Prev. KM#488.

Date	Mintage	F	VF	XF	Unc	BU
2000	16,600,000	—	—	—	2.00	3.00

KM# 488.2 50 CENTS
15.5500 g., Copper-Nickel, 31.5 mm. **Ruler:** Elizabeth II **Subject:** Millennium **Obv:** Head with tiara right **Rev:** Multicolor Australian flag **Edge:** Plain **Note:** Prev. KM#488.1.

Date	Mintage	F	VF	XF	Unc	BU
2000 Proof	65,000	Value: 35.00				

KM# 522 50 CENTS
16.8860 g., 0.9990 Silver 0.5423 oz. ASW, 32.1 mm. **Ruler:** Elizabeth II **Series:** Dragons **Obv:** Head with tiara right **Rev:** Dragon **Edge:** Reeded

Date	Mintage	F	VF	XF	Unc	BU
2000 Proof	5,000	Value: 30.00				

KM# 499 50 CENTS
36.3100 g., 0.9990 Silver 1.1662 oz. ASW, 38.7 mm. **Ruler:** Elizabeth II **Series:** Masterpieces in Silver - 2000 Set **Obv:** Rank-Broadley head with tiara right **Rev:** Head left **Edge:** Reeded

Date	Mintage	F	VF	XF	Unc	BU
2000 Proof	15,000	Value: 28.00				

KM# 112 DOLLAR (Holey Dollar)
31.1000 g., 0.9990 Silver 0.9988 oz. ASW **Ruler:** Elizabeth II **Subject:** Aboriginal Culture **Obv:** Holey dollar with legend around **Rev:** Holey dollar with snake around eating its tail **Note:** The "outer ring" coin issued with the center "plug" 25 cents, KM#113.

Date	Mintage	F	VF	XF	Unc	BU
1988 Proof	100,000	Value: 35.00				

KM# 131 DOLLAR (Holey Dollar)
31.1000 g., 0.9990 Silver 0.9988 oz. ASW **Ruler:** Elizabeth II **Obv:** Holey dollar with small silhouette of crowned Queen at top dividing legend, value at bottom **Rev:** 2 crocodiles around hole **Note:** The "outer ring" coin issued with the center "plug" 25 cents, KM#132.

Date	Mintage	F	VF	XF	Unc	BU
1989 Proof	45,000	Value: 35.00				

KM# 154 DOLLAR (Holey Dollar)
31.1000 g., 0.9990 Silver 0.9988 oz. ASW **Ruler:** Elizabeth II **Rev:** Stylized Natives and Jungle **Note:** The "outer ring" coin issued with the center "plug" 25 cents, KM#155.

Date	Mintage	F	VF	XF	Unc	BU
1990 Proof	30,000	Value: 40.00				

KM# 77 DOLLAR
9.0000 g., Nickel-Aluminum-Copper, 25 mm. **Ruler:** Elizabeth II **Obv:** Young bust right **Rev:** 5 kangaroos, denomination **Edge:** Smooth, reeded alternating edge

Date	Mintage	F	VF	XF	Unc	BU
1984	185,985,000	—	—	1.00	2.00	5.00
1984 Proof	159,000	Value: 9.00				

KM# 84 DOLLAR
9.0000 g., Nickel-Aluminum-Copper, 25 mm. **Ruler:** Elizabeth II **Obv:** Crowned head right **Rev:** 5 kangaroos, value **Edge:** Smooth, reeded alternating edge

Date	Mintage	F	VF	XF	Unc	BU
1985	91,400,000	—	—	1.00	4.00	5.00
1985 Proof	75,000	Value: 9.00				
1987 In sets only	200,000	—	—	—	5.00	6.00
1987 Proof	70,000	Value: 9.00				
1989	—	—	—	1.00	4.00	5.00
1989 Proof	—	Value: 9.00				
1990	—	—	—	1.00	9.00	11.00
1990 Proof	—	Value: 9.00				
1991	—	—	—	1.00	4.00	5.00
1991 Proof	—	Value: 9.00				
1994	47,639,000	—	—	1.00	6.00	9.00
1994 Proof	—	Value: 9.00				
1995	21,412,000	—	—	1.00	4.00	6.00
1995 Proof	—	Value: 9.00				
1998	16,248,000	—	—	1.00	4.00	6.00
1998 Proof	—	Value: 9.00				

KM# 84a DOLLAR
11.4900 g., 0.9250 Silver 0.3417 oz. ASW, 25 mm. **Ruler:** Elizabeth II **Subject:** Masterpieces in Silver **Obv:** Crowned head right **Rev:** 5 kangaroos, value

Date	Mintage	F	VF	XF	Unc	BU
1990 Proof	25,000	Value: 35.00				
1991 Proof	23,000	Value: 35.00				

Note: In Proof sets only

KM# 87 DOLLAR
9.0000 g., Nickel-Aluminum-Copper, 25 mm. **Ruler:** Elizabeth II **Subject:** International Year of Peace **Obv:** Crowned head right **Rev:** Dove above hands within wreath, value and legend below **Rev. Leg.:** INTERNATIONAL YEAR OF PEACE **Edge:** Smooth, reeded alternating edge

Date	Mintage	F	VF	XF	Unc	BU
1986	25,100,000	—	—	—	4.00	6.00
1986 Proof	67,000	Value: 20.00				

KM# 87a DOLLAR
11.4900 g., 0.9250 Silver 0.3417 oz. ASW, 25 mm. **Ruler:** Elizabeth II **Subject:** Masterpieces in Silver **Obv:** Crowned head right

Date	Mintage	F	VF	XF	Unc	BU
1990 Proof	25,000	Value: 35.00				

KM# 100 DOLLAR
9.0000 g., Aluminum-Bronze, 25 mm. **Ruler:** Elizabeth II **Subject:** First Fleet Bicentenary **Obv:** Crowned head right **Rev:** Kangaroo on aboriginal art patterned background, denomination below **Edge:** Reeded, smooth alternating edge

Date	Mintage	F	VF	XF	Unc	BU
1988	20,294,000	—	—	—	4.00	6.00
1988 Proof	106,000	Value: 20.00				

KM# 100a DOLLAR
11.4900 g., 0.9250 Silver 0.3417 oz. ASW, 25 mm.
Ruler: Elizabeth II **Subject:** First Fleet Bicentenary
Obv: Crowned head right **Rev:** Kangaroo on aboriginal art
patterned background, denomination below

Date	Mintage	F	VF	XF	Unc	BU
1988 Proof	25,000	Value: 35.00				
1990 Proof	25,000	Value: 35.00				

KM# 175 DOLLAR
9.0000 g., Nickel-Aluminum-Copper, 25.12 mm.
Ruler: Elizabeth II **Subject:** Barcelona - 25th Olympics
Obv: Crowned head right **Rev:** Female javelin thrower
Edge: Alternating reeded and plain sections

Date	Mintage	F	VF	XF	Unc	BU
1992	13,996	—	—	—	65.00	
Note: RAM wallet						
1992	Inc. above	—	—	—	55.00	
Note: Olympic wallet						
1992 Proof	2,940	Value: 165				
1992	23,500	—	—	—	70.00	
Note: Olympic card						

KM# 175a.1 DOLLAR
11.4900 g., 0.9250 Silver 0.3417 oz. ASW, 25 mm.
Ruler: Elizabeth II **Subject:** Barcelona - 25th Olympiad
Obv: Crowned head right **Rev:** Female javelin thrower

Date	Mintage	F	VF	XF	Unc	BU
1992 Proof	12,500	Value: 145				
Note: In Proof sets only						

KM# 175a.2 DOLLAR
11.4900 g., 0.9250 Silver 0.3417 oz. ASW, 25 mm.
Ruler: Elizabeth II **Subject:** XXV Olympiad - Barcelona
Obv: Crowned head right **Rev:** Female javelin thrower
Edge: Reeded

Date	Mintage	F	VF	XF	Unc	BU
1992 Proof	2,500	Value: 300				

KM# 208 DOLLAR
9.0000 g., Nickel-Aluminum-Copper, 25 mm. **Ruler:** Elizabeth II
Obv: Crowned head right **Rev:** Stylized tree above value, 2 hands
above Landcare Australia **Edge:** Reeded, smooth alternating
edge **Note:** Visitors at mints and coin show were allowed to
strike a coin for a fee at the following C - Canberra, M - Royal
Melbourne Show and S - Sydney Royal Easter Show.

Date	Mintage	F	VF	XF	Unc	BU
1993	17,917,000	—	—	—	3.00	4.50
1993 Proof	—	Value: 16.50				
1993C	91,993	—	—	—	6.00	8.00
1993M	60,104	—	—	—	7.50	10.00
1993S	87,939	—	—	—	6.00	8.00

KM# 208a.1 DOLLAR
Silver, 25 mm. **Ruler:** Elizabeth II **Obv:** Crowned head right
Rev: Stylized tree, value below, hands above Landcare Australia
Edge: Alternating reeded and plain sections

Date	Mintage	F	VF	XF	Unc	BU
1993 Proof	20,000	Value: 42.50				

KM# 208a.2 DOLLAR
Silver, 25 mm. **Ruler:** Elizabeth II **Obv:** Crowned head right
Rev: Stylized tree, value below, hands above Landcare Australia
Edge: Reeded

Date	Mintage	F	VF	XF	Unc	BU
1993 Proof	5,000	Value: 115				

KM# 258a.1 DOLLAR
14.4900 g., 0.9250 Silver 0.4309 oz. ASW, 25 mm.
Ruler: Elizabeth II **Subject:** 10th Anniversary - Introduction of
Dollar Coin **Rev:** Paper money with coin design at left divides
dates **Edge:** Reeded and plain sections

Date	Mintage	F	VF	XF	Unc	BU
1994 Proof	20,000	Value: 52.50				

KM# 258a.2 DOLLAR
14.4900 g., 0.9250 Silver 0.4309 oz. ASW, 25 mm.
Ruler: Elizabeth II **Subject:** 10th Anniversary - Introduction of
Dollar Coin **Rev:** Paper money with coin design at left divides
dates **Edge:** Reeded

Date	Mintage	F	VF	XF	Unc	BU
1994 Proof	5,000	Value: 125				

KM# 258 DOLLAR
9.0000 g., Nickel-Aluminum-Copper, 25 mm. **Ruler:** Elizabeth II
Subject: 10th Anniversary - Introduction of Dollar Coin **Rev:**
Paper money with coin design at left divides dates **Edge:** Reeded,
smooth alternating edge **Note:** Visitors at mints and coin shows
were allowed to strike a coin for a fee at the following C - Canberra,
M - Royal Melbourne Show and S - Sydney Royal Easter Show.

Date	Mintage	F	VF	XF	Unc	BU
1994C	123,318	—	—	—	15.00	17.50
1994M	65,440	—	—	—	17.50	20.00
1994S	74,426	—	—	—	17.50	20.00

KM# 269 DOLLAR
9.0000 g., Nickel-Aluminum-Copper, 25 mm. **Ruler:** Elizabeth II
Subject: A.B. Banjo Paterson - Waltzing Matilda **Obv:** Crowned
head right **Rev:** 3/4-length figure of Banjo Paterson on a walkabout
with walking stick **Edge:** Reeded, smooth alternating edge **Note:**
Visitors at mints and coin shows were allowed to strike a coin for a
fee at the following C - Canberra, M - Royal Melbourne Show, S -
Sydney Royal Easter Show and B - Brisbane Agricultural Show.

Date	Mintage	F	VF	XF	Unc	BU
1995B	74,353	—	—	—	35.00	45.00
1995C	156,453	—	—	—	28.00	30.00
1995M	74,255	—	—	—	35.00	40.00
1995S	82,810	—	—	—	30.00	35.00

KM# 269a.1 DOLLAR
14.4900 g., 0.9250 Silver 0.4309 oz. ASW, 25 mm.
Ruler: Elizabeth II **Subject:** A.B. Banjo Paterson - Waltzing
Matilda **Obv:** Crowned head right **Rev:** 3/4-length figure of Banjo
Paterson on a walkabout with walking stick **Edge:** Alternating
reeded and plain sections

Date	Mintage	F	VF	XF	Unc	BU
1995 Proof	20,000	Value: 75.00				

KM# 269a.2 DOLLAR
14.4900 g., 0.9250 Silver 0.4309 oz. ASW, 25 mm.
Ruler: Elizabeth II **Subject:** A.B. Banjo Paterson - Waltzing
Matilda **Obv:** Crowned head right **Rev:** 3/4-length figure of Banjo
Paterson on a walkabout with walking stick **Edge:** Reeded

Date	Mintage	F	VF	XF	Unc	BU
1995 Proof	2,500	Value: 125				

KM# 310a DOLLAR
11.4900 g., 0.9250 Silver 0.3417 oz. ASW, 25 mm.
Ruler: Elizabeth II **Subject:** Sir Henry Parkes **Obv:** Crowned
head right **Rev:** Large head of Sir Henry Parkes half facing right,
legend around **Rev. Leg.:** SIR HENRY PARKES 1815-1896,
FATHER OF FEDERATION

Date	Mintage	F	VF	XF	Unc	BU
1996 Proof	20,000	Value: 50.00				

KM# 326 DOLLAR
31.1035 g., 0.9990 Silver 0.9990 oz. ASW **Ruler:** Elizabeth II
Subject: 30th Anniversary - Decimal Coinage **Obv:** Crowned
head right **Rev:** Map and seven different coin designs

Date	Mintage	F	VF	XF	Unc	BU
1996 Proof	19,927	Value: 100				

KM# 310 DOLLAR
9.0000 g., Nickel-Aluminum-Copper, 25 mm. **Ruler:** Elizabeth II
Subject: Sir Henry Parkes **Obv:** Crowned head right **Rev:** Large
head of Sir Henry Parkes half facing right, legend around
Rev. Leg. SIR HENRY PARKES 1815-1896, FATHER OF
FEDERATION **Edge:** Reeded, smooth alternating edge
Note: Visitors at mints and coin shows were allowed to strike a
coin for a fee at the following C - Canberra, M - Royal Melbourne
Show, S - Sydney Royal Easter Show, B - Brisbane Agricultural
Show and A - Adelaid Show.

Date	Mintage	F	VF	XF	Unc	BU
1996	26,200,000	—	—	—	5.00	6.00
1996 Proof	—	—	—	—	—	—
1996A	29,127	—	—	—	11.50	13.50
1996B	41,128	—	—	—	7.50	10.00
1996C	272,980	—	—	—	6.00	8.00
1996M	38,030	—	—	—	11.50	13.50
1996S	72,186	—	—	—	7.50	10.00

KM# 721 DOLLAR
31.6300 g., 0.9990 Silver 1.0159 oz. ASW, 39.9 mm. **Ruler:**
Elizabeth II **Obv:** Crowned head right **Rev:** Old Parliament
building above 1927 one florin KM #31 coin design **Edge:** Reeded

Date	Mintage	F	VF	XF	Unc	BU
1997 Proof	—	Value: 65.00				

KM# 327 DOLLAR
9.0000 g., Nickel-Aluminum-Copper, 25 mm. **Ruler:** Elizabeth II
Subject: Sir Charles Kingsford Smith **Obv:** Crowned head right
Rev: Pilot above airplane, dates

Date	Mintage	F	VF	XF	Unc	BU
1997	24,381,000	—	—	—	20.00	22.50

KM# 355a DOLLAR
11.6600 g., 0.9990 Silver 0.3745 oz. ASW, 25 mm.
Ruler: Elizabeth II **Subject:** Sir Charles Kingsford Smith
Obv: Crowned head right **Rev:** Head of Sir C. Kingsford Smith
over airplane over world map

Date	Mintage	F	VF	XF	Unc	BU
1997 Proof	20,000	Value: 55.00				

KM# 355 DOLLAR
9.0000 g., Nickel-Aluminum-Copper, 25 mm. **Ruler:** Elizabeth II
Subject: Sir Charles Kingsford Smith **Obv:** Crowned head right
Rev: Head of Sir kC. Kingsford Smith over airplane over world
map **Note:** Visitors at mints and coin shows were allowed to strike
a coin for a fee at the following C - Canberra, M - Royal Melbourne
Show, S - Sydney Royal Easter Show, B - Brisbane Agricultural
Show and A - Adelaide Show.

Date	Mintage	F	VF	XF	Unc	BU
1997A	33,060	—	—	—	22.50	25.00
1997B	40,800	—	—	—	22.50	25.00
1997C	244,450	—	—	—	18.50	20.00
1997M	48,120	—	—	—	22.50	25.00
1997S	89,800	—	—	—	20.00	22.50

KM# 722 DOLLAR
31.5100 g., 0.9990 Silver 1.0120 oz. ASW, 39.9 mm.
Ruler: Elizabeth II **Obv:** Crowned head right **Rev:** Old Parliament
building above 1988 5 dollar KM #102 coin design **Edge:** Reeded

Date	Mintage	F	VF	XF	Unc	BU
1998 Proof	21,791	Value: 50.00				

KM# 366 DOLLAR
9.0000 g., Nickel-Aluminum-Copper Visitors at mints and coin shows were allowed to strike a coin for a fee at the following C - Canberra, M - Royal Melbourne Show, S - Sydney Royal Easter Show, B - Brisbane Agricultural Show and A - Adelaide Show., 25 mm. **Ruler:** Elizabeth II **Obv:** Crowned head right **Rev:** Bust of Howard Florey facing

Date	Mintage	F	VF	XF	Unc	BU
1998A	21,120	—	—	—	11.50	13.50
1998B	29,914	—	—	—	11.50	13.50
1998C	82,035	—	—	—	9.00	11.50
1998M	21,309	—	—	—	11.50	13.50
1998S	58,514	—	—	—	9.00	11.50

KM# 366a DOLLAR
11.6600 g., 0.9990 Silver 0.3745 oz. ASW, 25 mm. **Ruler:** Elizabeth II **Obv:** Crowned head right **Rev:** Bust of Howard Florey facing

Date	Mintage	F	VF	XF	Unc	BU
1998 Proof	20,000	Value: 55.00				

KM# 412 DOLLAR
31.1035 g., 0.9990 Silver 0.9990 oz. ASW **Ruler:** Elizabeth II **Subject:** 10th Anniversary - New Parliament House **Obv:** Crowned head right **Rev:** Parliament building

Date	Mintage	F	VF	XF	Unc	BU
1998 Proof	17,096	Value: 50.00				

KM# 400a DOLLAR
11.6600 g., 0.9990 Silver 0.3745 oz. ASW, 25 mm. **Ruler:** Elizabeth II **Subject:** The Last of the Anzacs **Obv:** Rank-Broadley head with tiara right **Rev:** Anzac soldier wearing slouch hat **Edge:** Reeded and plain sections on edge

Date	Mintage	F	VF	XF	Unc	BU
1999 Proof	25,000	Value: 70.00				

KM# 405 DOLLAR
9.0000 g., Nickel-Aluminum-Copper, 25 mm. **Ruler:** Elizabeth II **Subject:** International Year of Older People **Obv:** Crowned head right **Rev:** IYOP logo **Rev. Leg.:** TOWARDS A SOCIETY FOR ALL AGES - INTERNATIONAL YEAR OF OLDER PERSONS

Date	Mintage	F	VF	XF	Unc	BU
1999	29,218,000	—	—	—	4.50	5.50
1999 Proof	—	Value: 18.50				

KM# 476 DOLLAR
31.1035 g., 0.9990 Silver 0.9990 oz. ASW **Ruler:** Elizabeth II **Subject:** Majestic Images **Obv:** Head with tiara right **Rev:** Conjoined busts of Queen Elizabeth II **Edge:** Reeded

Date	Mintage	F	VF	XF	Unc	BU
1999 Proof	17,000	Value: 55.00				

KM# 400 DOLLAR
9.0000 g., Nickel-Aluminum-Copper, 25 mm. **Ruler:** Elizabeth II **Obv:** Rank-Broadley head with tiara right **Rev:** Anzac soldier wearing slouch hat, 3/4 left **Note:** Visitors at mints and coin shows were allowed to strike a coin for a fee at the following C - Canberra, M - Royal Melbourne Show, S - Sydney Royal Easter Show, B - Brisbane Agricultural Show and A - Adelaide Show.

Date	Mintage	F	VF	XF	Unc	BU
1999A	28,681	—	—	—	25.00	28.00
1999C	126,161	—	—	—	22.50	25.00
1999M	49,841	—	—	—	22.50	25.00
1999S	53,286	—	—	—	22.50	25.00
1999B	33,634	—	—	—	25.00	28.00
2000	47,830	—	—	—	85.00	95.00

KM# 485 DOLLAR
6.5700 g., 0.9990 Silver 0.2110 oz. ASW, 23.6 mm. **Ruler:** Elizabeth II **Series:** Masterpieces in Silver **Obv:** Head right **Rev:** Ram left above denomination and date **Edge:** Reeded

Date	Mintage	F	VF	XF	Unc	BU
1999 Proof	15,000	Value: 18.00				

KM# 422 DOLLAR
9.0000 g., Nickel-Aluminum-Copper, 25 mm. **Ruler:** Elizabeth II **Subject:** HMAS Sydney II **Obv:** Head with tiara right **Rev:** Ship above denomination **Edge:** Reeded

Date	Mintage	F	VF	XF	Unc	BU
2000C	71,367	—	—	—	18.00	20.00
2000S	34,277	—	—	—	18.00	20.00

KM# 422a DOLLAR
11.6600 g., 0.9990 Silver 0.3745 oz. ASW, 25 mm. **Ruler:** Elizabeth II **Obv:** Head with tiara right **Rev:** HMAS Sydney II above value

Date	Mintage	F	VF	XF	Unc	BU
2000 Proof	20,000	Value: 55.00				

KM# 489 DOLLAR
9.0000 g., Aluminum-Bronze, 25 mm. **Ruler:** Elizabeth II **Obv:** Head with tiara right **Rev:** Circle of 5 kangaroos **Edge:** Reeded and plain sections

Date	Mintage	F	VF	XF	Unc	BU
2000	7,592,000	—	—	—	18.00	20.00

KM# 493 DOLLAR
9.0000 g., Nickel-Aluminum-Copper, 24.9 mm. **Ruler:** Elizabeth II **Subject:** Victoria Cross **Obv:** Head with tiara right **Rev:** The Victoria Cross **Edge:** Reeded and plain sections

Date	Mintage	F	VF	XF	Unc	BU
2000	49,877	—	—	—	165	175

KM# 509 DOLLAR
31.1035 g., 0.9990 Silver 0.9990 oz. ASW, 40 mm. **Ruler:** Elizabeth II **Subject:** Proclamation Coins of Australia **Obv:** Head with tiara right **Rev:** The Cartwell Penny of 1797 **Edge:** Reeded

Date	Mintage	F	VF	XF	Unc	BU
2000 Proof	—	Value: 45.00				

KM# 514 DOLLAR
31.1035 g., 0.9990 Silver 0.9990 oz. ASW, 40.4 mm. **Ruler:** Elizabeth II **Subject:** Millennium **Obv:** Head with tiara right **Rev:** Gold inlay earth and radiant sun as seen from the moon's surface **Edge:** Reeded

Date	Mintage	F	VF	XF	Unc	BU
2000 Prooflike	30,000	—	—	—	—	37.50

KM# 529.1 DOLLAR
9.0000 g., Nickel-Aluminum-Copper, 24.9 mm. **Ruler:** Elizabeth II **Subject:** Olymphilex Exhibition **Obv:** Head with tiara right **Rev:** Denomination and Olympic logo **Edge:** Plain, incuse SYDNEY

Date	Mintage	F	VF	XF	Unc	BU
2000S	98,567	—	—	—	15.00	17.50

KM# 529.2 DOLLAR
9.0000 g., Nickel-Aluminum-Copper, 24.9 mm. **Ruler:** Elizabeth II **Obv:** Head with tiara right **Rev:** Denomination and Olympic logo **Edge:** Plain, incuse CANBERRA

Date	Mintage	F	VF	XF	Unc	BU
2000C	72,573	—	—	—	15.00	17.50

KM# 101 2 DOLLARS
6.6000 g., Aluminum-Bronze, 20.62 mm. **Ruler:** Elizabeth II **Subject:** Aboriginal Elder **Obv:** Crowned head right **Rev:** 1/2-length figure of Aboriginal man at left, 5 stars above value at right **Edge:** Reeded, smooth alternating edge

Date	Mintage	F	VF	XF	Unc	BU
1988	160,700,000	—	—	—	4.25	5.00
1988 Proof	106,000	Value: 7.50				
1989	30,000,000	—	—	—	4.25	5.00
1989 Proof	—	Value: 7.50				
1990	8,700,000	—	—	—	4.25	5.00
1990 Proof	—	Value: 7.50				
1991	—	—	—	—	4.25	5.00
1991 Proof	—	Value: 7.50				
1992	11,500,000	—	—	—	4.25	5.00
1992 Proof	47,000	Value: 7.50				
1993	4,870,000	—	—	—	6.00	9.00
1993 Proof	—	Value: 7.50				
1994	22,143,000	—	—	—	4.50	6.00
1994 Proof	—	Value: 10.00				
1995	13,929,000	—	—	—	4.25	5.00
1995 Proof	—	Value: 10.00				
1996	13,909,000	—	—	—	4.50	6.00
1996 Proof	—	Value: 10.00				
1997	19,039,000	—	—	—	4.50	6.00
1997 Proof	—	Value: 10.00				
1998	8,719,000	—	—	—	4.25	5.00
1998 Proof	—	Value: 10.00				

KM# 101a 2 DOLLARS

8.4300 g., 0.9250 Silver 0.2507 oz. ASW, 20.62 mm.
Ruler: Elizabeth II **Obv:** Crowned head right **Rev:** Aboriginal
Elder at left, 5 stars above value at right

Date	Mintage	F	VF	XF	Unc	BU
1988 Proof	25,000	Value: 14.50				
1991 Proof	23,000	Value: 14.50				

Note: In Proof sets only

KM# 406 2 DOLLARS

6.6000 g., Aluminum-Bronze, 20.62 mm. **Ruler:** Elizabeth II
Obv: Head right **Rev:** Aboriginal Elder at left, stars above at right
Edge: Reeded, smooth alternating edge

Date	Mintage	F	VF	XF	Unc	BU
1999	10,494,000	—	—	—	6.00	10.00
1999 Proof		Value: 11.50				
2000	5,706,000	—	—	—	7.50	12.50
2000 Proof		Value: 20.00				

KM# 486 2 DOLLARS

13.3600 g., 0.9990 Silver 0.4291 oz. ASW, 28.5 mm. **Ruler:**
Elizabeth II **Series:** Masterpieces in Silver **Obv:** Crowned head right
Rev: St. George on horseback slaying the dragon **Edge:** Reeded

Date	Mintage	F	VF	XF	Unc	BU
1999 Proof	15,000	Value: 22.00				

KM# 500 2 DOLLARS

8.5500 g., 0.9990 Silver 0.2746 oz. ASW, 20.5 mm.
Ruler: Elizabeth II **Series:** Masterpieces in Silver - 2000 Set
Obv: Head with tiara right **Rev:** Queen Victoria's bust, older with
veiled head, left **Edge:** Reeded

Date	Mintage	F	VF	XF	Unc	BU
2000 Proof	15,000	Value: 27.50				

KM# 102 5 DOLLARS

Aluminum-Bronze, 38.74 mm. **Ruler:** Elizabeth II
Obv: Crowned head right **Rev:** Parliament House, Value below

Date	Mintage	F	VF	XF	Unc	BU
1988	3,000,000	—	—	—	5.00	6.50
1988 Proof	80,000	Value: 15.00				

KM# 102a 5 DOLLARS

35.7900 g., 0.9250 Silver 1.0643 oz. ASW, 38.74 mm. **Ruler:**
Elizabeth II **Obv:** Crowned head right **Rev:** Parliament House

Date	Mintage	F	VF	XF	Unc	BU
1988 Proof	25,000	Value: 18.50				

KM# 134 5 DOLLARS

Aluminum-Bronze, 38.74 mm. **Ruler:** Elizabeth II
Subject: ANZAC Memorial **Obv:** Crowned head right
Rev: Simpson and his donkey, value at top left

Date	Mintage	F	VF	XF	Unc	BU
1990	774,349	—	—	—	5.50	7.00
1990 Proof	33,752	Value: 37.50				

KM# 190 5 DOLLARS

Aluminum-Bronze, 38.74 mm. **Ruler:** Elizabeth II
Subject: Australian Role in Space Industry, value at bottom
Obv: Crowned head right

Date	Mintage	F	VF	XF	Unc	BU
1992	238,979	—	—	—	6.00	7.50
1992 Proof	25,006	Value: 20.00				

KM# 213 5 DOLLARS

35.7900 g., 0.9250 Silver 1.0643 oz. ASW **Ruler:** Elizabeth II
Subject: Aboriginal Exploration, value bottom left **Obv:** Crowned
head right **Rev:** Aborigine with spear in front of Australian
geophysical map

Date	Mintage	F	VF	XF	Unc	BU
1993 Proof	20,000	Value: 25.00				

KM# 214 5 DOLLARS

35.7900 g., 0.9250 Silver 1.0643 oz. ASW **Ruler:** Elizabeth II
Obv: Crowned head right **Rev:** Bust of Abel Tasman in front of
Australian map, value at top right

Date	Mintage	F	VF	XF	Unc	BU
1993 Proof	20,000	Value: 25.00				

KM# 215 5 DOLLARS

35.7900 g., 0.9250 Silver 1.0643 oz. ASW **Ruler:** Elizabeth II
Obv: Crowned head right **Rev:** Bust left in front of Australian
map, large value to right of head

Date	Mintage	F	VF	XF	Unc	BU
1993 Proof	20,000	Value: 25.00				

KM# 216 5 DOLLARS

35.7900 g., 0.9250 Silver 1.0643 oz. ASW **Ruler:** Elizabeth II
Obv: Crowned head right **Rev:** Bust left in front of Australian map
with value upper right

Date	Mintage	F	VF	XF	Unc	BU
1993 Proof	20,000	Value: 25.00				

KM# 217 5 DOLLARS

35.7900 g., 0.9250 Silver 1.0643 oz. ASW **Ruler:** Elizabeth II
Obv: Crowned head right **Rev:** Heads at left in front of Australian
map with value upper right

Date	Mintage	F	VF	XF	Unc	BU
1993 Proof	20,000	Value: 24.00				

KM# 224 5 DOLLARS

Bi-Metallic Aluminum-Bronze center in Stainless Steel ring,
28.12 mm. **Ruler:** Elizabeth II **Subject:** Women's
Enfranchisement - 100-Year Anniversary of Women's Vote in
South Australia **Obv:** Crowned head right within inner circle
Rev: Head of Irish-born suffragist Mary Lee facing, within inner
circle, value below circle **Note:** Non-magnetic.

Date	Mintage	F	VF	XF	Unc	BU
1994 Proof	22,500	Value: 25.00				
1994	250,121	—	—	—	11.00	12.50

KM# 224a 5 DOLLARS
Aluminum-Bronze **Ruler:** Elizabeth II **Subject:** Women's Enfranchisement - 100 Year Anniversary of Women's Vote in South Australia **Obv:** Crowned head right within inner circle **Rev:** Head of Mary Lee facing, Irish-born suffragist

Date	Mintage	F	VF	XF	Unc	BU
1994 Proof	2,500	Value: 35.00				

KM# 264 5 DOLLARS
31.1040 g., 0.9250 Silver 0.9250 oz. ASW **Ruler:** Elizabeth II **Subject:** Australian Explorers **Obv:** Crowned head right **Rev:** Bust of Ludwig Leichhardt in front of route he explored, value bottom right

Date	Mintage	F	VF	XF	Unc	BU
1994 Proof	Est. 20,000	Value: 22.00				

KM# 265 5 DOLLARS
31.1040 g., 0.9250 Silver 0.9250 oz. ASW **Ruler:** Elizabeth II **Subject:** Australian Explorers **Obv:** Crowned head right **Rev:** Bust 3/4 left, in front of route he explored on Australian map, value left of bust

Date	Mintage	F	VF	XF	Unc	BU
1994 Proof	Est. 20,000	Value: 22.00				

KM# 266 5 DOLLARS
31.1040 g., 0.9250 Silver 0.9250 oz. ASW **Ruler:** Elizabeth II **Subject:** Australian Explorers **Obv:** Crowned head right **Rev:** Bust 3/4 right, to right of route he explored on map, value above map

Date	Mintage	F	VF	XF	Unc	BU
1994 Proof	Est. 20,000	Value: 22.00				

KM# 267 5 DOLLARS
31.1040 g., 0.9250 Silver 0.9250 oz. ASW **Ruler:** Elizabeth II **Subject:** Australian Explorers **Obv:** Crowned head right **Rev:** Head 3/4 right, to right of map of exploration route at left, value right of beard

Date	Mintage	F	VF	XF	Unc	BU
1994 Proof	Est. 20,000	Value: 22.00				

KM# 268 5 DOLLARS
31.1040 g., 0.9250 Silver 0.9250 oz. ASW **Ruler:** Elizabeth II **Subject:** Australian Explorers **Obv:** Crowned head right **Rev:** Bust left of route explored on map at right, value above map

Date	Mintage	F	VF	XF	Unc	BU
1994 Proof	Est. 20,000	Value: 22.00				

KM# 303 5 DOLLARS
35.7900 g., 0.9250 Silver 1.0643 oz. ASW **Ruler:** Elizabeth II **Subject:** The Gold Rush Era **Obv:** Crowned head right **Rev:** Two miners with supplies in front of mine, value at right

Date	Mintage	F	VF	XF	Unc	BU
1995 Proof	20,000	Value: 22.00				

KM# 304 5 DOLLARS
35.7900 g., 0.9250 Silver 1.0643 oz. ASW **Ruler:** Elizabeth II **Subject:** Cobb and Co. 1853 **Obv:** Crowned head right **Rev:** Cobb & Co. Company stagecoach, value above

Date	Mintage	F	VF	XF	Unc	BU
1995 Proof	20,000	Value: 22.00				

KM# 305 5 DOLLARS
35.7900 g., 0.9250 Silver 1.0643 oz. ASW **Ruler:** Elizabeth II **Subject:** Elizabeth MacArthur, 1766-1850 - Wool Merchant **Obv:** Crowned head right **Rev:** Head facing at lower right, flock of sheep above left, value below

Date	Mintage	F	VF	XF	Unc	BU
1995 Proof	20,000	Value: 22.00				

KM# 306 5 DOLLARS
35.7900 g., 0.9250 Silver 1.0643 oz. ASW **Ruler:** Elizabeth II **Subject:** Col. William Light, 1786-1839 - City Plan **Obv:** Crowned head right **Rev:** Head of Col. Light at lower right half right, city plan at left, value below

Date	Mintage	F	VF	XF	Unc	BU
1995 Proof	20,000	Value: 22.00				

KM# 307 5 DOLLARS
35.7900 g., 0.9250 Silver 1.0643 oz. ASW **Ruler:** Elizabeth II **Subject:** Charles Todd, 1827-1910 - Telegraph Line **Obv:** Crowned head right **Rev:** Head of Todd at lower right, telegraph line in background, value at lower left

Date	Mintage	F	VF	XF	Unc	BU
1995 Proof	20,000	Value: 22.00				

KM# 311 5 DOLLARS
Bi-Metallic Aluminum-Bronze center in Stainless Steel ring, 28.12 mm. **Ruler:** Elizabeth II **Subject:** Sir Donald Bradman - Cricket Player **Obv:** Crowned head right **Rev:** 1/2-length figure holding bat within inner circle, value below, subject name above **Edge:** Smooth **Note:** Non-magnetic.

Date	Mintage	F	VF	XF	Unc	BU
1996	500,000	—	—	—	11.00	12.50
1997	—	—	—	—	11.00	12.50

KM# 312 5 DOLLARS
Aluminum-Bronze, 38.74 mm. **Ruler:** Elizabeth II **Subject:** Sir Donald Bradman, Cricket player, **Obv:** Crowned head right **Rev:** Standing figure in uniform within inner circle, value below

Date	Mintage	F	VF	XF	Unc	BU
1996 Proof	22,500	Value: 40.00				

KM# 328   5 DOLLARS
35.7900 g., 0.9250 Silver 1.0643 oz. ASW **Ruler:** Elizabeth II
Subject: Stockman **Obv:** Crowned head right **Rev:** Cowboy with whip, value top left

Date	Mintage	F	VF	XF	Unc	BU
1996 Proof	20,000	Value: 22.50				

KM# 329   5 DOLLARS
35.7900 g., 0.9250 Silver 1.0643 oz. ASW **Ruler:** Elizabeth II
Subject: Horse Racing **Obv:** Crowned head right **Rev:** Horse racing scene, denomination below

Date	Mintage	F	VF	XF	Unc	BU
1996 Proof	20,000	Value: 22.50				

KM# 330   5 DOLLARS
35.7900 g., 0.9250 Silver 1.0643 oz. ASW **Ruler:** Elizabeth II
Obv: Crowned head right **Rev:** Bust of soprano Dame Nellie Melba, with large hat, 3/4 facing, at right, drape, inscription and value at left

Date	Mintage	F	VF	XF	Unc	BU
1996 Proof	20,000	Value: 22.50				

KM# 331   5 DOLLARS
35.7900 g., 0.9250 Silver 1.0643 oz. ASW **Ruler:** Elizabeth II
Subject: Tom Roberts **Obv:** Crowned head right **Rev:** Half-length figure 3/4 facing, in front of painting, value at lower right

Date	Mintage	F	VF	XF	Unc	BU
1996 Proof	20,000	Value: 22.50				

KM# 332   5 DOLLARS
35.7900 g., 0.9250 Silver 1.0643 oz. ASW **Ruler:** Elizabeth II
Subject: Henry Lawson **Obv:** Crowned head right **Rev:** Author's portrait and letter to friends, value bottom left

Date	Mintage	F	VF	XF	Unc	BU
1996 Proof	20,000	Value: 22.50				

KM# 356   5 DOLLARS
20.0000 g., Aluminum-Bronze, 38.74 mm. **Ruler:** Elizabeth II
Subject: Sydney 2000 **Obv:** Crowned head right **Rev:** Runner, left, Olympic logo below right elbow, value lower left

Date	Mintage	F	VF	XF	Unc	BU
2000 (1997)	—	—	—	—	9.00	10.00

KM# 357   5 DOLLARS
20.0000 g., Aluminum-Bronze, 38.74 mm. **Ruler:** Elizabeth II
Series: Sydney 2000 Olympics **Obv:** Bust right **Rev:** Gymnast, value at right, Olympic logo bottom right

Date	Mintage	F	VF	XF	Unc	BU
2000 (1997)	—	—	—	—	8.00	9.00

KM# 358   5 DOLLARS
20.0000 g., Aluminum-Bronze, 38.74 mm. **Ruler:** Elizabeth II
Series: Sydney 2000 Olympics **Obv:** Crowned head right
Rev: Sailors, Olympic logo, upper right, value above rings

Date	Mintage	F	VF	XF	Unc	BU
2000 (1997)	—	—	—	—	9.00	10.00

KM# 359   5 DOLLARS
20.0000 g., Aluminum-Bronze **Ruler:** Elizabeth II
Subject: Sydney 2000 **Obv:** Crowned head right **Rev:** Archer on left, Olympic logo at right, value above head

Date	Mintage	F	VF	XF	Unc	BU
2000 (1997)	—	—	—	—	9.00	10.00

KM# 360   5 DOLLARS
20.0000 g., Aluminum-Bronze, 38.74 mm. **Ruler:** Elizabeth II
Series: Sydney 2000 Olympics **Obv:** Crowned head right
Rev: Field hockey player Olympic logo lower right, value at upper right

Date	Mintage	F	VF	XF	Unc	BU
2000 (1997)	—	—	—	—	8.00	9.00

KM# 361   5 DOLLARS
20.0000 g., Aluminum-Bronze, 38.74 mm. **Ruler:** Elizabeth II
Series: Sydney 2000 Olympics **Obv:** Crowned head right
Rev: Power lifter, Olympic logo at lower right, value upper right

Date	Mintage	F	VF	XF	Unc	BU
2000 (1997)	—	—	—	—	8.00	9.00

KM# 544   5 DOLLARS
35.7900 g., 0.9250 Silver 1.0643 oz. ASW, 38.9 mm.
Ruler: Elizabeth II **Series:** Masterpieces of Transportation
Obv: Crowned head right **Rev:** Camel pack train, value upper right
Edge: Reeded

Date	Mintage	F	VF	XF	Unc	BU
1997 Proof	10,000	Value: 30.00				

KM# 545 5 DOLLARS

35.7900 g., 0.9250 Silver 1.0643 oz. ASW, 38.9 mm.
Ruler: Elizabeth II **Series:** Masterpieces of Transportation
Obv: Crowned head right **Rev:** Riverboat, value below
Edge: Reeded

Date	Mintage	F	VF	XF	Unc	BU
1997 Proof	10,000	Value: 25.00				

KM# 546 5 DOLLARS

35.7900 g., 0.9250 Silver 1.0643 oz. ASW, 38.9 mm. **Ruler:**
Elizabeth II **Series:** Masterpieces of Transportation **Obv:** Crowned
head right **Rev:** Steam locomotive, value at top **Edge:** Reeded

Date	Mintage	F	VF	XF	Unc	BU
1997 Proof	10,000	Value: 25.00				

KM# 547 5 DOLLARS

35.7900 g., 0.9250 Silver 1.0643 oz. ASW, 38.9 mm.
Ruler: Elizabeth II **Series:** Masterpieces of Transportation
Obv: Crowned head right **Rev:** Ox-drawn wagons, value below
Edge: Reeded

Date	Mintage	F	VF	XF	Unc	BU
1997 Proof	10,000	Value: 25.00				

KM# 548 5 DOLLARS

35.7900 g., 0.9250 Silver 1.0643 oz. ASW, 38.9 mm.
Ruler: Elizabeth II **Series:** Masterpieces of Transportation
Obv: Crowned head right **Rev:** Steam tractor, value below
Edge: Reeded

Date	Mintage	F	VF	XF	Unc	BU
1997 Proof	10,000	Value: 25.00				

KM# 386 5 DOLLARS

20.0000 g., Aluminum-Bronze, 38.74 mm. **Ruler:** Elizabeth II
Subject: 70th Anniversary - Royal Flying Doctor **Obv:** Crowned
head right **Rev:** Radio dispatcher and airplane divides legend,
value at right

Date	Mintage	F	VF	XF	Unc	BU
1998 Proof	Est. 20,000	Value: 18.50				

KM# 368 5 DOLLARS

20.0000 g., Aluminum-Bronze, 38.74 mm. **Ruler:** Elizabeth II
Series: Sydney 2000 Olympics **Obv:** Crowned head right
Rev: Cyclist, Olympic logo to right of head, value behind cyclist

Date	Mintage	F	VF	XF	Unc	BU
2000 (1998)	—	—	—	—	9.00	10.00

KM# 369 5 DOLLARS

20.0000 g., Aluminum-Bronze, 38.74 mm. **Ruler:** Elizabeth II
Series: Sydney 2000 Olympics **Obv:** Crowned head right
Rev: Soccer player, Olympic logo on right, value at left

Date	Mintage	F	VF	XF	Unc	BU
2000 (1998)	—	—	—	—	9.00	10.00

KM# 370 5 DOLLARS

20.0000 g., Aluminum-Bronze, 38.74 mm. **Ruler:** Elizabeth II
Series: Sydney 2000 Olympics **Obv:** Crowned head right
Rev: Triathlon swimmer, Olympic logo on right, value upper left

Date	Mintage	F	VF	XF	Unc	BU
2000 (1998)	—	—	—	—	9.00	10.00

KM# 371 5 DOLLARS

31.6350 g., 0.9990 Silver 1.0160 oz. ASW **Ruler:** Elizabeth II
Series: Sydney 2000 Olympics **Obv:** Crowned head right
Rev: Australian map above multicolor logo, Olympic logo at
bottom

Date	Mintage	F	VF	XF	Unc	BU
2000 (1998) Proof	Est. 100,000	Value: 45.00				

KM# 372 5 DOLLARS

31.6350 g., 0.9990 Silver 1.0160 oz. ASW **Ruler:** Elizabeth II
Series: Sydney 2000 Olympics **Obv:** Crowned head right
Rev: Two Great White sharks within wreath, Olympic logo at
bottom

Date	Mintage	F	VF	XF	Unc	BU
2000 (1998) Proof	Est. 100,000	Value: 55.00				

KM# 374 5 DOLLARS

Bi-Metallic Aluminum-Bronze center in Stainless Steel ring,
28.12 mm. **Ruler:** Elizabeth II **Subject:** 70 Years - Royal Flying
Doctor Service **Obv:** Head with tiara right within inner circle
Rev: Insignia above bi-plane, two dates below, within circle, value
below circle

Date	Mintage	F	VF	XF	Unc	BU
1998	—	—	—	—	10.00	12.00

KM# 375 5 DOLLARS

20.0000 g., Aluminum-Bronze, 38.74 mm. **Ruler:** Elizabeth II
Series: Sydney 2000 Summer Olympics **Obv:** Crowned head
right **Rev:** Two netball players, Olympic logo at right, value on left

Date	Mintage	F	VF	XF	Unc	BU
2000 (1998)	—	—	—	—	9.00	10.00

KM# 376   5 DOLLARS
20.0000 g., Aluminum-Bronze, 38.74 mm.   **Ruler:** Elizabeth II
Series: Sydney 2000 Olympics **Obv:** Crowned head right
Rev: Two wrestlers, Olympic logo to left, value at upper right

Date	Mintage	F	VF	XF	Unc	BU
2000 (1998)	—	—	—	—	9.00	10.00

KM# 377   5 DOLLARS
20.0000 g., Aluminum-Bronze, 38.74 mm.   **Ruler:** Elizabeth II
Series: Sydney 2000 Summer Olympics **Obv:** Crowned head
right **Rev:** Canoeing event, Olympic logo at left, value at top

Date	Mintage	F	VF	XF	Unc	BU
2000 (1998)	—	—	—	—	9.00	10.00

KM# 378   5 DOLLARS
20.0000 g., Aluminum-Bronze, 38.74 mm.   **Ruler:** Elizabeth II
Series: Sydney 2000 Olympics **Obv:** Crowned head right
Rev: Softball player swinging bat, Olympic logo at right, value
at left

Date	Mintage	F	VF	XF	Unc	BU
2000 (1998)	—	—	—	—	9.00	10.00

KM# 379   5 DOLLARS
31.6350 g., 0.9990 Silver 1.0160 oz. ASW   **Ruler:** Elizabeth II
Series: Sydney 2000 Olympics **Obv:** Crowned head right
Rev: Frill-necked lizard within wreath, Olympic logo below

Date	Mintage	F	VF	XF	Unc	BU
2000 (1998) Proof Est. 100,000 Value: 55.00						

KM# 380   5 DOLLARS
31.6350 g., 0.9990 Silver 1.0160 oz. ASW   **Ruler:** Elizabeth II
Series: Sydney 2000 Olympics **Obv:** Crowned head right
Rev: 9 Australian faces of different races, Olympic logo at bottom

Date	Mintage	F	VF	XF	Unc	BU
2000 (1998) Proof Est. 100,000 Value: 40.00						

KM# 381   5 DOLLARS
31.6350 g., 0.9990 Silver 1.0160 oz. ASW   **Ruler:** Elizabeth II
Series: Sydney 2000 Olympics **Obv:** Crowned head right
Rev: Two dancing figures in dream circle, within circle of aquatic
life, wreath encircling all, Olympic logo at bottom

Date	Mintage	F	VF	XF	Unc	BU
2000 (1998) Proof Est. 100,000 Value: 45.00						

KM# 382   5 DOLLARS
31.6350 g., 0.9990 Silver 1.0160 oz. ASW   **Ruler:** Elizabeth II
Series: Sydney 2000 Olympics **Obv:** Crowned head right
Rev: Kangaroo in circle of grass trees, Olympic logo below,
legend encircling all **Rev. Insc.:** Stuart Devlin

Date	Mintage	F	VF	XF	Unc	BU
2000 (1998) Proof Est. 100,000 Value: 55.00						

KM# 407   5 DOLLARS
20.0000 g., Brass, 38.74 mm.   **Ruler:** Elizabeth II
Series: Sydney 2000 Olympics **Obv:** Crowned head right
Rev: Two basketball players, value upper right, Olympic logo
lower left

Date	Mintage	F	VF	XF	Unc	BU
2000 (1999)	—	—	—	—	8.00	9.00

KM# 408   5 DOLLARS
20.0000 g., Brass, 38.74 mm.   **Ruler:** Elizabeth II
Series: Sydney 2000 Summer Olympics **Obv:** Crowned head
right **Rev:** Tae Kwon Do competitor, Olympic logo at top, value
on right

Date	Mintage	F	VF	XF	Unc	BU
2000 (1999)	—	—	—	—	8.00	9.00

KM# 409   5 DOLLARS
20.0000 g., Brass, 38.74 mm.   **Ruler:** Elizabeth II
Series: Sydney 2000 Olympics **Obv:** Crowned head right
Rev: Tennis player, value at left, Olympic logo below tennis ball

Date	Mintage	F	VF	XF	Unc	BU
2000 (1999)	—	—	—	—	8.00	9.00

KM# 418 5 DOLLARS
20.0000 g., Brass, 38.74 mm. **Ruler:** Elizabeth II
Series: Sydney 2000 Olympics **Obv:** Crowned head right
Rev: Shooter with shotgun, Olympic logo above, value on right

Date	Mintage	F	VF	XF	Unc	BU
2000 (1999)	—	—	—	—	8.00	9.00

KM# 419 5 DOLLARS
20.0000 g., Brass, 38.74 mm. **Ruler:** Elizabeth II
Series: Sydney 2000 Olympics **Obv:** Crowned head right
Rev: Table tennis player, Olympic logo upper left, value at top

Date	Mintage	F	VF	XF	Unc	BU
2000 (1999)	—	—	—	—	8.00	9.00

KM# 420 5 DOLLARS
20.0000 g., Brass, 38.74 mm. **Ruler:** Elizabeth II
Series: Sydney 2000 Olympics **Obv:** Crowned head right
Rev: Fencer in action, Olympic logo below right arm, value at left

Date	Mintage	F	VF	XF	Unc	BU
2000 (1999)	—	—	—	—	8.00	9.00

KM# 421 5 DOLLARS
20.0000 g., Brass, 38.74 mm. **Ruler:** Elizabeth II
Series: Sydney 2000 Olympics **Obv:** Crowned head right
Rev: Badminton player, Olympic logo above, value top right

Date	Mintage	F	VF	XF	Unc	BU
2000 (1999)	—	—	—	—	9.00	10.00

KM# 438 5 DOLLARS
31.6350 g., 0.9990 Silver 1.0160 oz. ASW **Ruler:** Elizabeth II
Series: Sydney 2000 Olympics **Obv:** Crowned head right
Rev: Two emus with eggs and chicks within wreath, Olympic logo at bottom **Edge:** Reeded

Date	Mintage	F	VF	XF	Unc	BU
2000 (1999) Proof	100,000		Value: 50.00			

KM# 439 5 DOLLARS
31.6350 g., 0.9990 Silver 1.0160 oz. ASW **Ruler:** Elizabeth II
Series: Sydney 2000 Olympics **Obv:** Crowned head right
Rev: Koala in tree within wreath, Olympic logo below

Date	Mintage	F	VF	XF	Unc	BU
2000 (1999) Proof	100,000		Value: 45.00			

KM# 440 5 DOLLARS
31.6350 g., 0.9990 Silver 1.0160 oz. ASW **Ruler:** Elizabeth II
Series: Sydney 2000 Olympics **Obv:** Crowned head right
Rev: Three radiant circular views within circle of round maps Olympic logo at bottom

Date	Mintage	F	VF	XF	Unc	BU
2000 Proof	100,000		Value: 37.50			

KM# 441 5 DOLLARS
31.6350 g., 0.9990 Silver 1.0160 oz. ASW **Ruler:** Elizabeth II
Series: Sydney 2000 Olympics **Obv:** Crowned head right
Rev: 7 figures positioned like spokes in a wheel, Olympic logo at bottom

Date	Mintage	F	VF	XF	Unc	BU
2000 Proof	100,000		Value: 37.50			

KM# 478 5 DOLLARS
10.5200 g., Bi-Metallic Aluminum-Bronze center in Stainless Steel ring, 28.12 mm. **Ruler:** Elizabeth II **Subject:** Phar Lap **Obv:** Head with tiara right within inner circle **Rev:** Jockey atop Phar Lap racing, right, within circle, divides date, value below circle **Edge:** Plain

Date	Mintage	F	VF	XF	Unc	BU
2000	—	—	—	—	10.00	12.00

KM# 510 5 DOLLARS
28.0000 g., Aluminum-Bronze, 38.7 mm. **Ruler:** Elizabeth II
Subject: Phar Lap **Obv:** Head with tiara right within inner circle
Rev: Phar Lap and jockey facing right within horseshoe turned to left, value on bottom of shoe, subject name and date on top of shoe **Edge:** Reeded

Date	Mintage	F	VF	XF	Unc	BU
2000 Proof	20,000		Value: 25.00			

KM# 515 5 DOLLARS
31.6350 g., 0.9990 Silver 1.0160 oz. ASW, 40.5 mm.
Ruler: Elizabeth II **Series:** Olympics - Sydney Harbor Bridge
Obv: Crowned head right **Rev:** Sydney suspension bridge within harbor wreath, Olympic logo at bottom, GAMES OF THE XXVII OLYMPIAD twice

Date	Mintage	F	VF	XF	Unc	BU
2000 Prooflike	100,000	—	—	—	40.00	45.00

KM# 516 5 DOLLARS
31.6350 g., 0.9990 Silver 1.0160 oz. ASW, 40.5 mm.
Ruler: Elizabeth II **Series:** Olympics - Kookaburra
Obv: Crowned head right **Rev:** Kookaburra with Waratah leaves, within wreath, Olympic logo at bottom

Date	Mintage	F	VF	XF	Unc	BU
2000 Prooflike	100,000	—	—	—	45.00	45.00

KM# 517   5 DOLLARS
Aluminum-Bronze, 38.6 mm. **Ruler:** Elizabeth II **Subject:** Paralympics **Obv:** Crowned head right **Rev:** Wheelchair racer and multicolor logo, small value to right of chair **Edge:** Reeded

Date	Mintage	F	VF	XF	Unc	BU
2000	Est. 30,000	—	—	—	12.50	15.00

KM# 815   5 DOLLARS
31.6350 g., 0.9990 Silver 1.0160 oz. ASW, 40 mm.
Ruler: Elizabeth II **Obv:** Queen's portrait **Rev:** Sydney Opera House

Date	Mintage	F	VF	XF	Unc	BU
2000 Proof	100,000	Value: 40.00				

KM# 816   5 DOLLARS
31.6350 g., 0.9990 Silver 1.0160 oz. ASW, 40 mm.
Ruler: Elizabeth II **Obv:** Queen's portrait **Rev:** Platypus duckbill in water

Date	Mintage	F	VF	XF	Unc	BU
2000 Proof	100,000	Value: 40.00				

KM# 817   5 DOLLARS
31.6350 g., 0.9990 Silver 1.0160 oz. ASW, 40 mm.
Ruler: Elizabeth II **Obv:** Queen's portrait **Rev:** Echidna

Date	Mintage	F	VF	XF	Unc	BU
2000 Proof	100,000	Value: 40.00				

KM# 818   5 DOLLARS
31.6350 g., 0.9990 Silver 1.0160 oz. ASW, 40 mm.
Ruler: Elizabeth II **Obv:** Queen's portrait **Rev:** Birds flying above Sydney Harbor

Date	Mintage	F	VF	XF	Unc	BU
2000 Proof	100,000	Value: 40.00				

KM# 429   5 DOLLARS
20.0000 g., Brass, 38.74 mm. **Ruler:** Elizabeth II
Series: Sydney 2000 Olympics **Obv:** Crowned head right
Rev: Pentathlon events portrayed by 5 participants, Olympic logo at lower left, value at bottom

Date	Mintage	F	VF	XF	Unc	BU
2000	—	—	—	—	9.00	10.00

KM# 430   5 DOLLARS
20.0000 g., Brass, 38.74 mm. **Ruler:** Elizabeth II **Obv:** Crowned head right **Rev:** Judo match, Olympic logo lower right, value at top

Date	Mintage	F	VF	XF	Unc	BU
2000	—	—	—	—	8.00	9.00

KM# 431   5 DOLLARS
20.0000 g., Brass, 38.74 mm. **Ruler:** Elizabeth II
Series: Sydney 2000 Olympics **Obv:** Crowned head right
Rev: Rower, Olympic logo upper left, value upper right

Date	Mintage	F	VF	XF	Unc	BU
2000	—	—	—	—	9.00	10.00

KM# 432   5 DOLLARS
20.0000 g., Brass, 38.74 mm. **Ruler:** Elizabeth II **Series:** Sydney 2000 Olympics **Obv:** Crowned head right **Rev:** Two men boxing, value upper left, Olympic logo divides boxers at bottom

Date	Mintage	F	VF	XF	Unc	BU
2000	—	—	—	—	9.00	10.00

KM# 433   5 DOLLARS
20.0000 g., Brass, 38.74 mm. **Ruler:** Elizabeth II
Series: Sydney 2000 Olympics **Obv:** Crowned head right
Rev: Volleyball player, Olympic logo below ball, value at left

Date	Mintage	F	VF	XF	Unc	BU
2000	—	—	—	—	9.00	10.00

KM# 434   5 DOLLARS
20.0000 g., Brass, 38.74 mm. **Ruler:** Elizabeth II
Series: Sydney 2000 Olympics **Obv:** Crowned head right
Rev: Equestrian putting horse through jumps

Date	Mintage	F	VF	XF	Unc	BU
2000	—	—	—	—	9.00	10.00

KM# 435   5 DOLLARS
20.0000 g., Brass, 38.74 mm. **Ruler:** Elizabeth II
Series: Sydney 2000 Olympics **Obv:** Crowned head right
Rev: Pitcher winding up

Date	Mintage	F	VF	XF	Unc	BU
2000	—	—	—	—	9.00	10.00

KM# 436   5 DOLLARS
20.0000 g., Brass, 38.74 mm. **Ruler:** Elizabeth II
Series: Sydney 2000 Olympics **Obv:** Crowned head right
Rev: Swimmer, Olympic logo below, value above

Date	Mintage	F	VF	XF	Unc	BU
2000	—	—	—	—	9.00	10.00

KM# 75   10 DOLLARS
20.0000 g., 0.9250 Silver 0.5948 oz. ASW **Ruler:** Elizabeth II
Subject: XII Commonwealth Games - Brisbane **Obv:** Young bust right **Rev:** Outline of country with hurdles on top at center of shield of athletes, legend surrounds all

Date	Mintage	F	VF	XF	Unc	BU
1982	125,700	—	—	—	12.50	13.50
1982 Proof	85,142	Value: 16.50				

KM# 85   10 DOLLARS
20.0000 g., 0.9250 Silver 0.5948 oz. ASW **Ruler:** Elizabeth II
Subject: 150th Anniversary - State of Victoria **Obv:** Crowned head right **Rev:** Arms of Victoria, value at bottom, state name divides dates at top

Date	Mintage	F	VF	XF	Unc	BU
1985	81,751	—	—	—	12.50	14.00
1985 Proof	55,806	Value: 17.50				

KM# 88   10 DOLLARS
20.0000 g., 0.9250 Silver 0.5948 oz. ASW **Ruler:** Elizabeth II
Subject: 150th Anniversary - South Australia **Obv:** Crowned head right **Rev:** Arms of South Australia, value below, name divides dates at top

Date	Mintage	F	VF	XF	Unc	BU
1986	78,100	—	—	—	12.50	14.00
1986 Proof	52,150	Value: 17.50				

KM# 93   10 DOLLARS
20.0000 g., 0.9250 Silver 0.5948 oz. ASW **Ruler:** Elizabeth II
Subject: New South Wales **Obv:** Crowned head right **Rev:** Arms of New South Wales, value below

Date	Mintage	F	VF	XF	Unc	BU
1987	55,000	—	—	—	12.50	14.00
1987 Proof	50,500	Value: 17.50				

KM# 103 10 DOLLARS
20.0000 g., 0.9250 Silver 0.5948 oz. ASW **Ruler:** Elizabeth II
Subject: Landing of Governor Philip **Obv:** Crowned head right
Rev: Large sailing ship to right, smaller ships behind and left,
canoe with rowers in foreground, value at top left

Date	Mintage	F	VF	XF	Unc	BU
1988	111,497	—	—	—	13.50	15.00
1988 Proof	80,099	Value: 20.00				

KM# 114 10 DOLLARS
20.0000 g., 0.9250 Silver 0.5948 oz. ASW **Ruler:** Elizabeth II
Subject: Queensland **Obv:** Crowned head right **Rev:** Arms of
Queensland, name of subject at top, value below arms

Date	Mintage	F	VF	XF	Unc	BU
1989	48,929	—	—	—	12.50	14.00
1989 Proof	48,573	Value: 17.50				

KM# 133 10 DOLLARS
20.0000 g., 0.9250 Silver 0.5948 oz. ASW **Ruler:** Elizabeth II
Obv: Crowned head right **Rev:** Kookaburras, value above

Date	Mintage	F	VF	XF	Unc	BU
1989 Proof	50,000	Value: 45.00				

KM# 137 10 DOLLARS
20.0000 g., 0.9250 Silver 0.5948 oz. ASW **Ruler:** Elizabeth II
Subject: Western Australia **Obv:** Crowned head right
Rev: Western Australia coat of arms, value below

Date	Mintage	F	VF	XF	Unc	BU
1990	28,133	—	—	—	13.50	15.00
1990 Proof	29,089	Value: 25.00				

KM# 136 10 DOLLARS
20.0000 g., 0.9250 Silver 0.5948 oz. ASW **Ruler:** Elizabeth II **Obv:**
Crowned head right **Rev:** Sulpher-crested cockatoo, value above

Date	Mintage	F	VF	XF	Unc	BU
1990 Proof	49,801	Value: 50.00				

KM# 153 10 DOLLARS
20.0000 g., 0.9250 Silver 0.5948 oz. ASW **Ruler:** Elizabeth II
Subject: Tasmania **Obv:** Crowned head right **Rev:** Arms of
Tasmania, value below, subject name above

Date	Mintage	F	VF	XF	Unc	BU
1991	26,150	—	—	—	13.50	15.00
1991 Proof	27,664	Value: 30.00				

KM# 156 10 DOLLARS
20.0000 g., 0.9250 Silver 0.5948 oz. ASW **Ruler:** Elizabeth II
Obv: Crowned head right **Rev:** Jabiru Stork,right, value above

Date	Mintage	F	VF	XF	Unc	BU
1991 Proof	32,446	Value: 35.00				

KM# 188 10 DOLLARS
20.0000 g., 0.9250 Silver 0.5948 oz. ASW **Ruler:** Elizabeth II
Obv: Crowned head right **Rev:** Northern Territory state arms,
value below, subject name above

Date	Mintage	F	VF	XF	Unc	BU
1992	24,164	—	—	—	12.50	14.00
1992 Proof	24,404	Value: 20.00				

KM# 199 10 DOLLARS
20.0000 g., 0.9250 Silver 0.5948 oz. ASW **Ruler:** Elizabeth II
Obv: Crowned head right **Rev:** Emperor Penguins with chicks,
value above

Date	Mintage	F	VF	XF	Unc	BU
1992 Proof	Est. 25,319	Value: 55.00				

KM# 210 10 DOLLARS
20.0000 g., 0.9250 Silver 0.5948 oz. ASW **Ruler:** Elizabeth II
Obv: Crowned head right **Rev:** Australian Capital Territory state
arms, value below

Date	Mintage	F	VF	XF	Unc	BU
1993	19,288	—	—	—	13.50	15.00
1993 Proof	21,183	Value: 22.50				

KM# 317 10 DOLLARS
20.0000 g., 0.9250 Silver 0.5948 oz. ASW **Ruler:** Elizabeth II
Subject: UNEP - Palm Cockatoo **Obv:** Crowned head right
Rev: Palm cockatoo with UNEP logo at left, value at right

Date	Mintage	F	VF	XF	Unc	BU
1993 Proof	Est. 55,000	Value: 45.00				

KM# 221 10 DOLLARS
20.0000 g., 0.9250 Silver 0.5948 oz. ASW **Ruler:** Elizabeth II
Obv: Crowned head right **Rev:** Palm cockatoo, value at right

Date	Mintage	F	VF	XF	Unc	BU
1993 Proof	22,172	Value: 45.00				

KM# 225 10 DOLLARS
20.7700 g., 0.9990 Silver 0.6671 oz. ASW **Ruler:** Elizabeth II
Series: Olympic Gold Medalists - Edwin Flack 1896 **Obv:**
Crowned head right within circle **Rev:** Edwin Flack with Olympic
Flame above wreath within circle, legend above, value below

Date	Mintage	F	VF	XF	Unc	BU
1994 Matte Proof	21,484	Value: 18.50				

KM# 226   10 DOLLARS
20.7700 g., 0.9990 Silver 0.6671 oz. ASW   **Ruler:** Elizabeth II
Series: Olympic Gold Medalists - Sarah Durack 1912
Obv: Crowned head right within circle   **Rev:** Circle surrounds
swimmer within wreath above gold medal, denomination below

Date	Mintage	F	VF	XF	Unc	BU
1994 Matte Proof	21,484	Value: 18.50				

KM# 223   10 DOLLARS
20.0000 g., 0.9250 Silver 0.5948 oz. ASW   **Ruler:** Elizabeth II
Obv: Crowned head right **Rev:** Wedge-tailed eagle, left, value at left

Date	Mintage	F	VF	XF	Unc	BU
1994 Proof	23,326	Value: 45.00				

KM# 296   10 DOLLARS
20.7700 g., 0.9990 Silver 0.6671 oz. ASW   **Ruler:** Elizabeth II
Obv: Crowned head right **Rev:** Numbat right, value at left

Date	Mintage	F	VF	XF	Unc	BU
1995 Proof	25,000	Value: 40.00				

KM# 301   10 DOLLARS
20.7700 g., 0.9990 Silver 0.6671 oz. ASW   **Ruler:** Elizabeth II
Series: Olympic Gold Medalists - Dawn Fraser **Obv:** Crowned
head right **Rev:** Half-length portrait

Date	Mintage	F	VF	XF	Unc	BU
1995 Matte Proof	Est. 30,000	Value: 27.50				

KM# 302   10 DOLLARS
20.7700 g., 0.9990 Silver 0.6671 oz. ASW   **Ruler:** Elizabeth II
Series: Olympic Gold Medalists - Murray Rose **Obv:** Crowned
head right **Rev:** Murray Rose

Date	Mintage	F	VF	XF	Unc	BU
1995 Matte Proof	Est. 30,000	Value: 27.50				

KM# 314   10 DOLLARS
20.0000 g., 0.9250 Silver 0.5948 oz. ASW   **Ruler:** Elizabeth II
Rev: Southern right whale with baby, value below

Date	Mintage	F	VF	XF	Unc	BU
1996 Proof	24,000	Value: 50.00				

KM# 315   10 DOLLARS
20.7700 g., 0.9990 Silver 0.6671 oz. ASW   **Ruler:** Elizabeth II
Series: Australia's Greatest Olympics - 1956 **Obv:** Crowned
head right **Rev:** Betty Cuthbert, sprint champion 1956, born 1938
within circle, value below circle

Date	Mintage	F	VF	XF	Unc	BU
1996 Matte Unc	15,300	—	—	—	60.00	65.00

KM# 316   10 DOLLARS
20.7700 g., 0.9990 Silver 0.6671 oz. ASW   **Ruler:** Elizabeth II
Series: Australia's Greatest Olympics - 1956 **Obv:** Crowned
head right **Rev:** Shirley Strickland, hurdling champion, 1952 and
1956 within circle, value below circle

Date	Mintage	F	VF	XF	Unc	BU
1996 Matte Unc	15,300	—	—	—	60.00	65.00

KM# 353   10 DOLLARS
20.7700 g., 0.9990 Silver 0.6671 oz. ASW   **Ruler:** Elizabeth II
Subject: Sydney Opera House **Obv:** Crowned head right
Rev: Opera house and Sydney shoreline within circle, legend
above circle, value below

Date	Mintage	F	VF	XF	Unc	BU
1997 Matte Proof	20,000	Value: 32.50				

KM# 354   10 DOLLARS
20.7700 g., 0.9990 Silver 0.6671 oz. ASW   **Ruler:** Elizabeth II
Subject: Sydney Harbour Bridge **Obv:** Crowned head right
Rev: Bridge over harbour within circle, value below circle,
legend above

Date	Mintage	F	VF	XF	Unc	BU
1997 Matte Proof	20,000	Value: 32.50				

KM# 367.1   10 DOLLARS
20.0000 g., 0.9990 Silver 0.6423 oz. ASW   **Ruler:** Elizabeth II
Subject: Red-tailed Black Cockatoo **Obv:** Crowned head right
Rev: Cockatoo perched in dead tree, left, value to left

Date	Mintage	F	VF	XF	Unc	BU
1997 Proof	24,000	Value: 40.00				

KM# 367.2   10 DOLLARS
40.0000 g., 0.9250 Silver 1.1895 oz. ASW   **Ruler:** Elizabeth II
Subject: Red-tailed Black Cockatoo **Obv:** Crowned head right
Rev: Cockatoo perched in dead tree

Date	Mintage	F	VF	XF	Unc	BU
1997 Proof	14,000	Value: 50.00				

KM# 387   10 DOLLARS
20.7700 g., 0.9990 Silver 0.6671 oz. ASW   **Ruler:** Elizabeth II
Subject: Melbourne **Obv:** Crowned head right **Rev:** Melbourne
cricket grounds

Date	Mintage	F	VF	XF	Unc	BU
1998 Matte Proof	20,000	Value: 32.50				

KM# 388   10 DOLLARS
20.7700 g., 0.9990 Silver 0.6671 oz. ASW   **Ruler:** Elizabeth II
Subject: Melbourne **Obv:** Crowned head right **Rev:** Street car

Date	Mintage	F	VF	XF	Unc	BU
1998 Matte Proof	20,000	Value: 32.50				

KM# 397   10 DOLLARS
20.0000 g., 0.9250 Silver 0.5948 oz. ASW   **Ruler:** Elizabeth II
Subject: Northern Hairy-nosed Wombat **Obv:** Head with tiara
right **Rev:** Wombat above denomination

Date	Mintage	F	VF	XF	Unc	BU
1998 Proof	24,000	Value: 40.00				

KM# 414   10 DOLLARS
20.7700 g., 0.9990 Silver 0.6671 oz. ASW   **Ruler:** Elizabeth II
Subject: The Snowy Mountains Scheme **Obv:** Head with tiara
right within inner circle **Rev:** Tunnel building scene within circle,
value below, legend above

Date	Mintage	F	VF	XF	Unc	BU
1999	20,000	—	—	—	27.50	30.00

KM# 415   10 DOLLARS
20.7700 g., 0.9990 Silver 0.6671 oz. ASW   **Ruler:** Elizabeth II
Subject: The Snowy Mountains Scheme **Obv:** Head with tiara
right within inner circle **Rev:** Dam building scene within circle,
value below, legend above

Date	Mintage	F	VF	XF	Unc	BU
1999	20,000	—	—	—	27.50	30.00

KM# 423 10 DOLLARS
33.5300 g., Bi-Metallic Copper center in .999 Silver ring
Ruler: Elizabeth II **Subject:** Millennium Series, The Past
Obv: Head with tiara right within circle **Rev:** Seedling on
Australian map above denomination with rising sun background
Edge: Reeded

Date	Mintage	F	VF	XF	Unc	BU
1999 Proof	20,000	Value: 650				

KM# 511 10 DOLLARS
36.0100 g., 0.9990 Silver 1.1565 oz. ASW, 38.7 mm.
Ruler: Elizabeth II **Series:** Millennium - The Present **Obv:** Head
with tiara right within circle **Rev:** Australian map behind young
tree, value at base of tree, all within circle, surrounded by circle
of stick figures and ovals **Edge:** Reeded

Date	Mintage	F	VF	XF	Unc	BU
2000 Proof	20,000	Value: 225				

KM# 518 10 DOLLARS
311.0350 g., 0.9990 Silver 9.9896 oz. ASW, 75 mm.
Ruler: Elizabeth II **Subject:** Paralympics **Obv:** Head with tiara
right, denomination below **Rev:** Sydney Opera House and harbor
bridge **Edge:** Lettering with logo, GAMES OF THE XI
PARALYMPIAD **Note:** Illustration reduced.

Date	Mintage	F	VF	XF	Unc	BU
2000 Prooflike	3,000	—	—	—	—	400

KM# 218 20 DOLLARS
33.6200 g., 0.9250 Silver 0.9998 oz. ASW **Ruler:** Elizabeth II
Series: Olympics **Subject:** Track Winners **Obv:** Crowned head
right, denomination below **Rev:** Three athletes on podium, Olympic
logo uppper right with two dates below, CITIUS ALTIUS FORTIUS

Date	Mintage	F	VF	XF	Unc	BU
1993 Proof	100,000	Value: 35.00				

KM# 219 20 DOLLARS
33.6200 g., 0.9250 Silver 0.9998 oz. ASW **Ruler:** Elizabeth II
Series: Olympics **Subject:** Swimmers **Obv:** Crowned bust right,
denomination below **Rev:** Four swimmers, Olympic logo upper
right with two dates below, CITIUS ALTIUS FORTIUS

Date	Mintage	F	VF	XF	Unc	BU
1993 Proof	100,000	Value: 35.00				

KM# 519 20 DOLLARS
Bi-Metallic Gold center in Silver ring, 32 mm. **Ruler:** Elizabeth II
Subject: Millennium **Obv:** Head with tiara right within circle,
denomination below **Rev:** Earth view from space **Edge:** Reeded

Date	Mintage	F	VF	XF	Unc	BU
2000 Prooflike	Est. 7,500	—	—	—	—	550

KM# 200 25 DOLLARS
33.6300 g., 0.9250 Silver 1.0000 oz. ASW **Ruler:** Elizabeth II
Subject: 40th Anniversary - Reign of Queen Elizabeth II - Queen
Mother **Obv:** Queens portrait **Rev:** Bust of Queen Mother with
tiara right, value below, within wreath of crowns

Date	Mintage	F	VF	XF	Unc	BU
1992 Proof	—	Value: 30.00				

KM# 201 25 DOLLARS
33.6300 g., 0.9250 Silver 1.0000 oz. ASW **Ruler:** Elizabeth II
Subject: 40th Anniversary - Reign of Queen Elizabeth II -
Princess Diana **Obv:** Queens portrait **Rev:** Bust of Princess
Diana with tiara right, value below, within wreath of crowns

Date	Mintage	F	VF	XF	Unc	BU
1992 Proof	—	Value: 30.00				

KM# 202 25 DOLLARS
33.6300 g., 0.9250 Silver 1.0000 oz. ASW **Ruler:** Elizabeth II
Subject: 40th Anniversary - Reign of Queen Elizabeth II -
Princess Anne **Obv:** Queens portrait **Rev:** Bust of Princess Anne
with tiara right, value below, within wreath of crowns

Date	Mintage	F	VF	XF	Unc	BU
1992 Proof	—	Value: 30.00				

KM# 203 25 DOLLARS
33.6300 g., 0.9250 Silver 1.0000 oz. ASW **Ruler:** Elizabeth II
Subject: 40th Anniversary - Reign of Queen Elizabeth II -
Princess Margaret **Obv:** Queens portrait **Rev:** Bust of Princess
Margaret with tiara left, value below, within wreath of crowns

Date	Mintage	F	VF	XF	Unc	BU
1992 Proof	—	Value: 30.00				

KM# 520 30 DOLLARS
1002.5020 g., 0.9990 Silver 32.197 oz. ASW, 100 mm.
Ruler: Elizabeth II **Series:** Olympics **Obv:** Head with tiara right,
denomination below **Rev:** Multicolor logo in center, GAMES OF
THE XXVII OLYMPIAD (logo) 1 KILO .999 SILVER
Note: Illustration reduced.

Date	Mintage	F	VF	XF	Unc	BU
2000 Proof	20,000	Value: 675				

KM# 313   40 DOLLARS
31.1850 g., 0.9995 Palladium 1.0021 oz. **Ruler:** Elizabeth II **Obv:** Crowned head right, denomination below **Rev:** The Australian emu, left, date below

Date	Mintage	F	VF	XF	Unc	BU
1995	—	—	—	475	—	
1995 Proof	Est. 2,500	Value: 500				

KM# 343   40 DOLLARS
31.1850 g., 0.9995 Palladium 1.0021 oz. **Ruler:** Elizabeth II **Obv:** Crowned head right, denomination below **Rev:** Emu and chicks

Date	Mintage	F	VF	XF	Unc	BU
1996 Proof	Est. 2,500	Value: 500				

KM# 308   100 DOLLARS
10.3678 g., 0.9160 Gold 0.3053 oz. AGW **Ruler:** Elizabeth II **Obv:** Queens portrait **Rev:** The Waratah Flower, value below

Date	Mintage	F	VF	XF	Unc	BU
1995	3,000	—	—	—	—	300

KM# 308a   100 DOLLARS
10.3678 g., 0.9999 Gold 0.3333 oz. AGW **Ruler:** Elizabeth II **Obv:** Queens portrait **Rev:** The Waratah flower

Date	Mintage	F	VF	XF	Unc	BU
1995 Proof	2,500	Value: 320				

KM# 333   100 DOLLARS
10.3678 g., 0.9160 Gold 0.3053 oz. AGW **Ruler:** Elizabeth II **Subject:** Tasmanial Blue Gum Flower **Obv:** Queens portrait **Rev:** Flowering plant with long, droopy leaves

Date	Mintage	F	VF	XF	Unc	BU
1996	—	—	—	—	—	300

KM# 333a   100 DOLLARS
10.3678 g., 0.9999 Gold 0.3333 oz. AGW **Ruler:** Elizabeth II **Subject:** Tasmanial Blue Gum flower **Obv:** Queens portrait **Rev:** Flowering plant with long, droopy leaves

Date	Mintage	F	VF	XF	Unc	BU
1996 Proof	—	Value: 320				

KM# 384   100 DOLLARS
10.3678 g., 0.9167 Gold 0.3056 oz. AGW **Ruler:** Elizabeth II **Subject:** Mangles' Kangaroo Paw Flower, value below **Obv:** Queens portrait **Rev:** Flower

Date	Mintage	F	VF	XF	Unc	BU
1997	3,000	—	—	—	—	300

KM# 373   100 DOLLARS
10.0210 g., 0.9999 Gold 0.3221 oz. AGW **Ruler:** Elizabeth II **Series:** Sydney Olympics 2000 **Obv:** Crowned head right, denomination below **Rev:** Runner training in rain, Olympic logo above right foot

Date	Mintage	F	VF	XF	Unc	BU
2000 (1998) Proof	—	Value: 320				

KM# 383   100 DOLLARS
10.0210 g., 0.9999 Gold 0.3221 oz. AGW **Ruler:** Elizabeth II **Series:** Sydney Olympics 2000 **Obv:** Crowned head right, denomination below **Rev:** Multicolor games logo within wreath

Date	Mintage	F	VF	XF	Unc	BU
2000 (1998) Proof	Est. 30,000	Value: 320				

KM# 480   100 DOLLARS
10.3678 g., 0.9160 Gold 0.3053 oz. AGW, 25 mm. **Ruler:** Elizabeth II **Subject:** Stuart's Desert Pea **Obv:** Queens portrait **Rev:** Plant with pods **Edge:** Reeded

Date	Mintage	F	VF	XF	Unc	BU
1998	—	—	—	—	—	300

KM# 480a   100 DOLLARS
10.3678 g., 0.9990 Gold 0.3330 oz. AGW, 25 mm. **Ruler:** Elizabeth II **Subject:** Stuart's Desert Pea **Obv:** Queens portrait **Rev:** Plant with pods **Edge:** Reeded

Date	Mintage	F	VF	XF	Unc	BU
1998 Proof	2,500	Value: 320				

KM# 487   100 DOLLARS
10.3678 g., 0.9160 Gold 0.3053 oz. AGW, 25 mm. **Ruler:** Elizabeth II **Obv:** Queens portrait **Rev:** Common Heath flowers, value below **Edge:** Reeded

Date	Mintage	F	VF	XF	Unc	BU
1999	3,000	—	—	—	—	300

KM# 487a   100 DOLLARS
10.3678 g., 0.9990 Gold 0.3330 oz. AGW, 25 mm. **Ruler:** Elizabeth II **Obv:** Queens portrait **Rev:** Common Heath flowers **Edge:** Reeded

Date	Mintage	F	VF	XF	Unc	BU
1999 Proof	2,500	Value: 320				

KM# 442   100 DOLLARS
10.0000 g., 0.9990 Gold 0.3212 oz. AGW **Ruler:** Elizabeth II **Series:** Sydney Olympics 2000 **Obv:** Crowned head right **Rev:** 3 athletic workout scenes, Olympic logo at bottom **Edge:** Reeded

Date	Mintage	F	VF	XF	Unc	BU
2000 (1999) Proof	30,000	Value: 315				

KM# 443   100 DOLLARS
10.0000 g., 0.9990 Gold 0.3212 oz. AGW **Ruler:** Elizabeth II **Series:** Sydney Olympics 2000 **Obv:** Crowned head right **Rev:** Shot putter teaching seated children, Olympic logo below **Edge:** Reeded

Date	Mintage	F	VF	XF	Unc	BU
2000 (1999) Proof	30,000	Value: 315				

KM# 444   100 DOLLARS
10.0000 g., 0.9990 Gold 0.3212 oz. AGW **Ruler:** Elizabeth II **Series:** Sydney Olympics 2000 **Obv:** Crowned head right **Rev:** Sprinter being coached, Olympic logo at bottom **Edge:** Reeded

Date	Mintage	F	VF	XF	Unc	BU
2000 (1999) Proof	30,000	Value: 315				

KM# 474   100 DOLLARS
Bi-Metallic Gold center in Silver ring **Ruler:** Elizabeth II **Subject:** Perth Mint Centennial Sovereign **Obv:** Head with tiara right within inner circle **Rev:** St. George with sword on horseback slaying dragon, circle surrounds all, dates below **Edge:** Reeded

Date	Mintage	F	VF	XF	Unc	BU
ND(1999) Proof	7,500	Value: 500				

KM# 512   100 DOLLARS
10.3678 g., 0.9160 Gold 0.3053 oz. AGW, 25 mm. **Ruler:** Elizabeth II **Subject:** Cooktown Orchid **Obv:** Queens portrait **Rev:** Orchid and denomination **Edge:** Reeded

Date	Mintage	F	VF	XF	Unc	BU
2000	3,000	—	—	—	—	300

KM# 512a   100 DOLLARS
10.3678 g., 0.9990 Gold 0.3330 oz. AGW, 25 mm. **Ruler:** Elizabeth II **Subject:** Cooktown Orchid **Obv:** Queens portrait **Rev:** Orchid and denomination **Edge:** Reeded

Date	Mintage	F	VF	XF	Unc	BU
2000 Proof	2,500	Value: 320				

KM# 521   100 DOLLARS
10.0000 g., 0.9990 Gold 0.3212 oz. AGW, 25 mm. **Ruler:** Elizabeth II **Series:** Olympics **Obv:** Head with tiara right, denomination below **Rev:** Multicolor torch flames within circle of figures **Edge:** Reeded

Date	Mintage	F	VF	XF	Unc	BU
2000 Proof	20,000	Value: 385				

KM# 309   150 DOLLARS
15.5517 g., 0.9999 Gold 0.4999 oz. AGW **Ruler:** Elizabeth II **Obv:** Queens portrait **Rev:** The Waratah Flower above value

Date	Mintage	F	VF	XF	Unc	BU
1995 Proof	1,500	Value: 600				

KM# 334   150 DOLLARS
15.5517 g., 0.9999 Gold 0.4999 oz. AGW **Ruler:** Elizabeth II **Subject:** Tasmanian Blue Gum Flower **Obv:** Queens portrait **Rev:** Tasmanian Blue Gum Flower above value

Date	Mintage	F	VF	XF	Unc	BU
1996 Proof	—	Value: 520				

KM# 413   150 DOLLARS
15.5517 g., 0.9999 Gold 0.4999 oz. AGW **Ruler:** Elizabeth II **Obv:** Queens portrait **Rev:** Stuart's desert pea

Date	Mintage	F	VF	XF	Unc	BU
1998 Proof	1,500	Value: 520				

KM# 475 150 DOLLARS
15.5517 g., 0.9999 Gold 0.4999 oz. AGW **Ruler:** Elizabeth II
Subject: Common Heath Flower **Obv:** Queens portrait
Rev: Heath flowers above value **Edge:** Reeded

Date	Mintage	F	VF	XF	Unc	BU
1999 Proof	1,500	Value: 520				

KM# 513 150 DOLLARS
15.5518 g., 0.9990 Gold 0.4995 oz. AGW, 30 mm.
Ruler: Elizabeth II **Subject:** Cooktown Orchid **Obv:** Queens
portrait **Rev:** Orchid above value **Edge:** Reeded

Date	Mintage	F	VF	XF	Unc	BU
2000 Proof	1,500	Value: 520				

KM# 71 200 DOLLARS
10.0000 g., 0.9170 Gold 0.2948 oz. AGW **Ruler:** Elizabeth II
Obv: Young bust right **Rev:** Koala in tree, value below

Date	Mintage	F	VF	XF	Unc	BU
1980	207,500	—	—	—	285	—
1980 Proof	50,077	Value: 300				
1983	88,000	—	—	—	285	—
1983 Proof	15,889	Value: 300				
1984	49,200	—	—	—	285	—
1984 Proof	12,559	Value: 300				

KM# 73 200 DOLLARS
10.0000 g., 0.9170 Gold 0.2948 oz. AGW **Ruler:** Elizabeth II
Subject: Wedding of Prince Charles and Lady Diana **Obv:** Young
bust right **Rev:** Conjoined heads of Prince Charles and Lady
Diana left

Date	Mintage	F	VF	XF	Unc	BU
1981	77,890	—	—	—	285	—

KM# 76 200 DOLLARS
10.0000 g., 0.9170 Gold 0.2948 oz. AGW **Ruler:** Elizabeth II
Subject: XII Commonwealth Games - Brisbane **Obv:** Young bust
right **Rev:** Athlete running over hurdles, value below hurdler

Date	Mintage	F	VF	XF	Unc	BU
1982	77,206	—	—	—	285	—
1982 Proof	30,032	Value: 300				

KM# 86 200 DOLLARS
10.0000 g., 0.9170 Gold 0.2948 oz. AGW **Ruler:** Elizabeth II
Obv: Crowned head right **Rev:** Koala in tree, value below

Date	Mintage	F	VF	XF	Unc	BU
1985	29,186	—	—	—	285	—
1985 Proof	16,691	Value: 300				
1986	15,298	—	—	—	285	—
1986 Proof	16,654	Value: 300				

KM# 94 200 DOLLARS
10.0000 g., 0.9170 Gold 0.2948 oz. AGW **Ruler:** Elizabeth II
Obv: Crowned head right **Rev:** 1/2-length bust right, value below,
1787 above right shoulder

Date	Mintage	F	VF	XF	Unc	BU
1987	20,800	—	—	—	285	—
1987 Proof	20,000	Value: 300				

KM# 115 200 DOLLARS
10.0000 g., 0.9170 Gold 0.2948 oz. AGW **Ruler:** Elizabeth II
Subject: Bicentennial of Australia **Obv:** Crowned head right
Rev: Early colonist standing in front of water in Sydney Cove,
ship in background at right, value below

Date	Mintage	F	VF	XF	Unc	BU
1988	11,000	—	—	—	285	—
1988 Proof	20,000	Value: 300				

KM# 116 200 DOLLARS
10.0000 g., 0.9170 Gold 0.2948 oz. AGW **Ruler:** Elizabeth II
Subject: Pride of Australia **Obv:** Crowned head right **Rev:** Frilled-
neck lizard, value below

Date	Mintage	F	VF	XF	Unc	BU
1989	10,020	—	—	—	285	—
1989 Proof	24,736	Value: 300				

KM# 135 200 DOLLARS
10.0000 g., 0.9170 Gold 0.2948 oz. AGW **Ruler:** Elizabeth II
Subject: Pride of Australia **Obv:** Crowned head right
Rev: Platypus above value

Date	Mintage	F	VF	XF	Unc	BU
1990	8,340	—	—	—	285	—
1990 Proof	14,616	Value: 300				

KM# 160 200 DOLLARS
10.0000 g., 0.9170 Gold 0.2948 oz. AGW **Ruler:** Elizabeth II
Subject: Pride of Australia **Obv:** Crowned head right
Rev: Standing emu between tall grass, value below

Date	Mintage	F	VF	XF	Unc	BU
1991	6,879	—	—	—	285	—
1991 Proof	9,560	Value: 300				

KM# 259 200 DOLLARS
10.0000 g., 0.9170 Gold 0.2948 oz. AGW **Ruler:** Elizabeth II
Subject: Pride of Australia **Obv:** Crowned head right
Rev: Echidna above value

Date	Mintage	F	VF	XF	Unc	BU
1992	3,935	—	—	—	285	—
1992 Proof	5,921	Value: 300				

KM# 220 200 DOLLARS
16.8200 g., 0.9170 Gold 0.4959 oz. AGW **Ruler:** Elizabeth II
Series: Olympic Centenary - 1896-1996 **Obv:** Crowned head
right **Rev:** Gymnast in flight, Olympic logo top right, CITIUS
ALTIUS FORTIUS

Date	Mintage	F	VF	XF	Unc	BU
1993 Proof	60,000	Value: 475				

KM# 222 200 DOLLARS
10.0000 g., 0.9170 Gold 0.2948 oz. AGW **Ruler:** Elizabeth II
Subject: Pride of Australia **Obv:** Crowned head right
Rev: Squirrel glider possum, value below

Date	Mintage	F	VF	XF	Unc	BU
1993	3,014	—	—	—	285	—
1993 Proof	5,000	Value: 300				

KM# 262 200 DOLLARS
10.0000 g., 0.9170 Gold 0.2948 oz. AGW **Ruler:** Elizabeth II
Subject: Pride of Australia **Obv:** Crowned head right
Rev: Tasmanian devil, value below

Date	Mintage	F	VF	XF	Unc	BU
1994	4,000	—	—	—	285	—
1994 Proof	5,000	Value: 300				

KM# 385 200 DOLLARS
15.5517 g., 0.9999 Gold 0.4999 oz. AGW **Ruler:** Elizabeth II
Subject: Mangles' Kangaroo Paw Flower **Obv:** Queens portrait
Rev: Flower

Date	Mintage	F	VF	XF	Unc	BU
1997 Proof	—	Value: 500				

KM# 204 250 DOLLARS
16.9500 g., 0.9170 Gold 0.4997 oz. AGW **Ruler:** Elizabeth II
Subject: 40th Anniversary - Reign of Queen Elizabeth II - Queen
Mother **Obv:** Queens portrait **Rev:** Portrait of Queen Mother right,
within circle of crowns

Date	Mintage	F	VF	XF	Unc	BU
1992 Proof	Est. 5,000				Value: 500	

KM# 205 250 DOLLARS
16.9500 g., 0.9170 Gold 0.4997 oz. AGW **Ruler:** Elizabeth II
Subject: 40th Anniversary - Reign of Queen Elizabeth II -
Princess Diana **Obv:** Queens portrait **Rev:** Portrait of Princess
Diana right, within circle of crowns

Date	Mintage	F	VF	XF	Unc	BU
1992 Proof	Est. 5,000				Value: 500	

KM# 206 250 DOLLARS
16.9500 g., 0.9170 Gold 0.4997 oz. AGW **Ruler:** Elizabeth II
Subject: 40th Anniversary - Reign of Queen Elizabeth II -
Princess Anne **Obv:** Queens portrait **Rev:** Portrait of Princess
Anne right, within circle of crowns

Date	Mintage	F	VF	XF	Unc	BU
1992 Proof	Est. 5,000				Value: 500	

KM# 207 250 DOLLARS
16.9500 g., 0.9170 Gold 0.4997 oz. AGW **Ruler:** Elizabeth II
Subject: 40th Anniversary - Reign of Queen Elizabeth II -
Princess Margaret **Obv:** Queens portrait **Rev:** Bust of Princess
Margaret left, within circle of crowns

Date	Mintage	F	VF	XF	Unc	BU
1992 Proof	Est. 5,000				Value: 500	

SILVER BULLION - KANGAROO

KM# 211.1 DOLLAR
31.5700 g., 0.9990 Silver 1.0139 oz. ASW **Ruler:** Elizabeth II
Obv: Crowned head right **Rev:** Kangaroo leaping right, value
above **Edge:** Reeded

Date	Mintage	F	VF	XF	Unc	BU
1993C	73,000				23.50	

KM# 211.2 DOLLAR
31.5700 g., 0.9990 Silver 1.0139 oz. ASW **Ruler:** Elizabeth II
Obv: Crowned head right **Rev:** Kangaroo leaping right
Edge: Reeded and plain sections

Date	Mintage	F	VF	XF	Unc	BU
1993C	5,000				50.00	

KM# 263.1 DOLLAR
31.6350 g., 0.9990 Silver 1.0160 oz. ASW **Ruler:** Elizabeth II
Obv: Crowned head right **Rev:** Kangaroo leaping right, value
above **Edge:** Reeded

Date	Mintage	F	VF	XF	Unc	BU
1994C	45,000				30.00	

KM# 263.2 DOLLAR
31.6350 g., 0.9990 Silver 1.0160 oz. ASW **Ruler:** Elizabeth II
Obv: Crowned head right **Rev:** Kangaroo leaping right
Edge: Reeded and plain sections

Date	Mintage	F	VF	XF	Unc	BU
1994C	2,500				120	

KM# 293.1 DOLLAR
31.6350 g., 0.9990 Silver 1.0160 oz. ASW **Ruler:** Elizabeth II
Obv: Crowned head right **Rev:** Kangaroo head facing half left,
value above **Edge:** Reeded

Date	Mintage	F	VF	XF	Unc	BU
1995C	73,000				27.50	

KM# 293.2 DOLLAR
31.6350 g., 0.9990 Silver 1.0160 oz. ASW **Ruler:** Elizabeth II
Obv: Crowned head right **Rev:** Kangaroo head facing half left
Edge: Reeded and plain sections

Date	Mintage	F	VF	XF	Unc	BU
1995C	2,500				110	

KM# 297 DOLLAR
31.6350 g., 0.9990 Silver 1.0160 oz. ASW **Ruler:** Elizabeth II **Obv:**
Crowned head right **Rev:** Mother and baby kangaroo, value above

Date	Mintage	F	VF	XF	Unc	BU
1996					25.00	

KM# 325 DOLLAR
31.5600 g., 0.9990 Silver 1.0136 oz. ASW **Ruler:** Elizabeth II
Obv: Crowned head right **Rev:** Kangaroo drinking water,
reflection, value at bottom

Date	Mintage	F	VF	XF	Unc	BU
1997C					23.50	

KM# 365 DOLLAR
32.0000 g., 0.9990 Silver 1.0278 oz. ASW **Ruler:** Elizabeth II **Obv:**
Crowned head right **Rev:** Kangaroo bounding left, value above

Date	Mintage	F	VF	XF	Unc	BU
1998C					23.50	

KM# 398 DOLLAR
32.2500 g., 0.9990 Silver 1.0358 oz. ASW **Ruler:** Elizabeth II
Obv: Crowned head right **Rev:** Pair of kangaroos, value at right

Date	Mintage	F	VF	XF	Unc	BU
1999					25.00	
1999 Proof		Value: 75.00				

Date	Mintage	F	VF	XF	Unc	BU
1992 (ae) Proof	750	Value: 185				
1993	Est. 300,000	—	—	—	25.00	—

KM# 490.2 DOLLAR
32.1500 g., 0.9990 Silver 1.0326 oz. ASW, 39.9 mm.
Ruler: Elizabeth II **Obv:** Crowned head right **Rev:** Multicolor kangaroo on dark red map and green value **Edge:** Reeded

Date	Mintage	F	VF	XF	Unc	BU
2000	—	—	—	—	27.50	32.50

KM# 490.1 DOLLAR
31.1035 g., 0.9990 Silver 0.9990 oz. ASW, 40 mm.
Ruler: Elizabeth II **Obv:** Crowned head right **Rev:** Kangaroo with Australian map background, value top right **Edge:** Reeded

Date	Mintage	F	VF	XF	Unc	BU
2000 Proof	—	Value: 65.00				
2000	—	—	—	—	25.00	—

SILVER BULLION - KOOKABURRA

KM# 164 DOLLAR
31.1000 g., 0.9990 Silver 0.9988 oz. ASW **Ruler:** Elizabeth II
Obv: Crowned head right, denomination below **Rev:** Australian Kookaburra in tree left, date below

Date	Mintage	F	VF	XF	Unc	BU
1992	300,000	—	—	—	25.00	—

KM# 209 DOLLAR
31.1000 g., 0.9990 Silver 0.9988 oz. ASW **Ruler:** Elizabeth II
Obv: Crowned head right **Rev:** Australian kookaburra feeding nestlings in tree, date below

Date	Mintage	F	VF	XF	Unc	BU
1992 Proof	—	Value: 40.00				

KM# 212.1 DOLLAR
31.1035 g., 0.9990 Silver 0.9990 oz. ASW **Ruler:** Elizabeth II
Obv: Crowned head right, denomination below **Rev:** Pair of Kookaburras, date below

Date	Mintage	F	VF	XF	Unc	BU
1993 AE Proof	—	Value: 30.00				
1993 AE Proof	—	Value: 30.00				
1993 (ge) Proof	500	Value: 75.00				
1993 (so) Proof	13,000	Value: 45.00				
1994(p) BU	—	—	—	—	25.00	—
1994 Proof	2,500	Value: 32.10				
1994 (ta) Specimen	15,000	—	—	—	27.50	—

KM# 212.2 DOLLAR
31.1035 g., 0.9990 Silver 0.9990 oz. ASW **Ruler:** Elizabeth II
Obv: Crowned head right, denomination below **Rev:** American Eagle privy mark above date below 2 kookaburras on tree branch

Date	Mintage	F	VF	XF	Unc	BU
1993 AE Proof	500	Value: 65.00				
1993 AE Proof	500	Value: 75.00				

KM# 260 DOLLAR
31.1035 g., 0.9990 Silver 0.9990 oz. ASW **Ruler:** Elizabeth II
Obv: Crowned head right, denomination below **Rev:** Kookaburra on branch left, denmination below

Date	Mintage	F	VF	XF	Unc	BU
1994 Proof	2,500	Value: 45.00				
1995	300,000	—	—	—	27.50	—

KM# 289.1 DOLLAR
31.6350 g., 0.9990 Silver 1.0160 oz. ASW **Ruler:** Elizabeth II
Obv: Crowned head right **Rev:** Kookaburra in flight, date below

Date	Mintage	F	VF	XF	Unc	BU
1995P Proof	4,900	Value: 30.00				
1996	300,000	—	—	—	27.50	—
1996 (bg)	5,000	—	—	—	40.00	—
1996 (ba)	2,500	—	—	—	42.00	—
1996 (sr)	5,000	—	—	—	40.00	—

KM# 289.2 DOLLAR
31.1035 g., 0.9990 Silver 0.9990 oz. ASW **Ruler:** Elizabeth II
Obv: Crowned head right **Rev:** Kookaburra in flight, date below
Edge: Reeded and inscribed with date and serial

Date	Mintage	F	VF	XF	Unc	BU
1996	1,500	—	—	—	45.00	—

KM# 701 DOLLAR
31.1035 g., 0.9990 Silver 0.9990 oz. ASW **Ruler:** Elizabeth II
Obv: Crowned head right **Rev:** Kookaburra

Date	Mintage	F	VF	XF	Unc	BU
1996 Proof	—	Value: 35.00				
1997	—	—	—	—	—	—

KM# 318 DOLLAR
31.1035 g., 0.9990 Silver 0.9990 oz. ASW **Ruler:** Elizabeth II
Obv: Crowned head right within circle, denomination below
Rev: Kookaburra and nestlings, mark at right of bird, date below
Note: With Utrecht Coat of Arms privy mark.

Date	Mintage	F	VF	XF	Unc	BU
1997	—	—	—	—	27.50	—
1997 (u)	300,000	—	—	—	27.50	—

KM# 362 DOLLAR
31.1035 g., 0.9990 Silver 0.9990 oz. ASW **Ruler:** Elizabeth II
Obv: Crowned head right, denomination below **Rev:** Kookaburra on fence right, date below

Date	Mintage	F	VF	XF	Unc	BU
1997 Proof	2,000	Value: 35.00				
1998 (1997)	—	—	—	—	27.50	—

KM# 399 DOLLAR

32.2500 g., 0.9990 Silver 1.0358 oz. ASW **Ruler:** Elizabeth II
Obv: Head with tiara right within circle, denomination below **Rev:** Adult and chick kookaburras on branch left, date below

Date	Mintage	F	VF	XF	Unc	BU
1999	—	—	—	—	30.00	—
1999	5,000	—	—	—	27.50	—

Note: Austrian 20 schilling coin design privy mark

1999	5,000	—	—	—	27.50	—

Note: Belgian 50 frank coin design privy mark

| 1999 | 5,000 | — | — | — | 27.50 | — |

Note: Finnish 1 markka coin design privy mark

| 1999 | 5,000 | — | — | — | 27.50 | — |

Note: French 5 francs coin design privy mark

| 1999 | 5,000 | — | — | — | 27.50 | — |

Note: German 1 mark coin design privy mark

| 1999 | 5,000 | — | — | — | 27.50 | — |

Note: Irish 1 punt coin design privy mark

| 1999 | 5,000 | — | — | — | 27.50 | — |

Note: Italian 1000 lire coin design privy mark

| 1999 | 5,000 | — | — | — | 27.50 | — |

Note: Luxembourg 50 francs coin design privy mark

| 1999 | 5,000 | — | — | — | 27.50 | — |

Note: Netherlands 1 gulden coin design privy mark

| 1999 | 5,000 | — | — | — | 27.50 | — |

Note: Portuguese 50 escudo coin design privy mark

| 1999 | 5,000 | — | — | — | 27.50 | — |

Note: Spanish 100 pesetas coin design privy mark

KM# 604 DOLLAR

31.1035 g., 0.9990 Silver 0.9990 oz. ASW, 40.4 mm.
Ruler: Elizabeth II **Subject:** U.S. State Quarter - Delaware

Date	Mintage	F	VF	XF	Unc	BU
1999	75,000	—	—	—	27.50	—

KM# 605 DOLLAR

31.1035 g., 0.9990 Silver 0.9990 oz. ASW, 40.4 mm.
Ruler: Elizabeth II **Subject:** U.S. State Quarter - Pennsylvania

Date	Mintage	F	VF	XF	Unc	BU
1999	75,000	—	—	—	27.50	—

KM# 606 DOLLAR

31.1035 g., 0.9990 Silver 0.9990 oz. ASW, 40.4 mm.
Ruler: Elizabeth II **Subject:** U.S. State Quarter - New Jersey

Date	Mintage	F	VF	XF	Unc	BU
1999	75,000	—	—	—	27.50	—

KM# 607 DOLLAR

31.1035 g., 0.9990 Silver 0.9990 oz. ASW, 40.4 mm.
Ruler: Elizabeth II **Subject:** U.S. State Quarter - Georgia

Date	Mintage	F	VF	XF	Unc	BU
1999	75,000	—	—	—	27.50	—

KM# 608 DOLLAR

31.1035 g., 0.9990 Silver 0.9990 oz. ASW, 40.4 mm.
Ruler: Elizabeth II **Subject:** U.S. State Quarter - Connecticut

Date	Mintage	F	VF	XF	Unc	BU
1999	75,000	—	—	—	27.50	—

KM# 416 DOLLAR

31.7700 g., 0.9990 Silver 1.0204 oz. ASW **Obv:** Queen's head with tiara, right, within circle, value below circle **Rev:** Kookaburra on branch, left, silver weight and date in legend

Date	Mintage	F	VF	XF	Unc	BU
2000 (1999)	—	—	—	—	27.50	—

KM# 611 DOLLAR

31.1035 g., 0.9990 Silver 0.9990 oz. ASW, 40.4 mm.
Ruler: Elizabeth II **Subject:** U.S. State Quarter - Massachusetts

Date	Mintage	F	VF	XF	Unc	BU
2000	75,000	—	—	—	27.50	—

KM# 612 DOLLAR

31.1035 g., 0.9990 Silver 0.9990 oz. ASW, 40.4 mm.
Ruler: Elizabeth II **Subject:** U.S. State Quarter - Maryland

Date	Mintage	F	VF	XF	Unc	BU
2000	75,000	—	—	—	27.50	—

KM# 613 DOLLAR

31.1035 g., 0.9990 Silver 0.9990 oz. ASW, 40.4 mm.
Ruler: Elizabeth II **Subject:** U.S. State Quarter - South Carolina

Date	Mintage	F	VF	XF	Unc	BU
2000	75,000	—	—	—	27.50	—

KM# 614 DOLLAR

31.1035 g., 0.9990 Silver 0.9990 oz. ASW, 40.4 mm.
Ruler: Elizabeth II **Subject:** U.S. State Quarter - New Hampshire

Date	Mintage	F	VF	XF	Unc	BU
2000	75,000	—	—	—	27.50	—

KM# 615 DOLLAR

31.1035 g., 0.9990 Silver 0.9990 oz. ASW, 40.4 mm.
Ruler: Elizabeth II **Subject:** U.S. State Quarter - Virginia

Date	Mintage	F	VF	XF	Unc	BU
2000	75,000	—	—	—	27.50	—

KM# 179 2 DOLLARS

62.2070 g., 0.9990 Silver 1.9979 oz. ASW **Ruler:** Elizabeth II
Obv: Crowned head right within inner circle, denomination below
Rev: Australian Kookaburra on stump right within circle, date below

Date	Mintage	F	VF	XF	Unc	BU
1992	—	—	—	—	—	45.00
1992 Proof	5,000	Value: 85.00				
1992 (gv) Proof	500	Value: 165				
1992 (hd) Specimen	1,000	—	—	—	125	—
1993	—	—	—	—	115	—
1993 (dp) Specimen	1,000	—	—	—	125	—
1993 (w) Specimen	1,000	—	—	—	135	—
1993 (e) Specimen	1,000	—	—	—	115	—
1993 (ta) Specimen	1,000	—	—	—	115	—

KM# 227 2 DOLLARS

62.2070 g., 0.9990 Silver 1.9979 oz. ASW **Ruler:** Elizabeth II
Obv: Crowned head right, denomination below **Rev:** Kookaburra feeding nestling right, date below

Date	Mintage	F	VF	XF	Unc	BU
1992 Proof	—	Value: 85.00				
1992 (aa) Proof	500	Value: 375				
1993	—	—	—	—	—	45.00
1993 Proof	—	Value: 85.00				

KM# 176 2 DOLLARS

62.2070 g., 0.9990 Silver 1.9979 oz. ASW, 50 mm.
Subject: Kookaburra **Obv:** Elizabeth II **Rev:** Kookaburra on branch next to tree trunk **Edge:** Segmented reeding

Date	Mintage	F	VF	XF	Unc	BU
1992P	—	—	—	—	—	45.00

KM# 230 2 DOLLARS

62.2070 g., 0.9990 Silver 1.9979 oz. ASW **Ruler:** Elizabeth II
Obv: Crowned head right, denomination below **Rev:** Pair of Kookaburras on branch, date below

Date	Mintage	F	VF	XF	Unc	BU
1993	—	—	—	—	—	45.00
1993 Proof	—	Value: 85.00				
1993 (sm) Proof	750	Value: 200				
1993 (ae) Proof	500	Value: 300				
1994	—	—	—	—	—	45.00
1994 Proof	—	Value: 85.00				
1994 (ev) Proof	1,500	Value: 200				
1994 (gv) Specimen	1,500	—	—	—	180	—
1994 (gv) Specimen	1,000	—	—	—	275	—

KM# 261 2 DOLLARS

62.2070 g., 0.9990 Silver 1.9979 oz. ASW **Ruler:** Elizabeth II
Obv: Crowned head right, denomination below **Rev:** Kookaburra on branch right, within circle, date below

Date	Mintage	F	VF	XF	Unc	BU
1994P Proof	—	Value: 100				
1995	—	—	—	—	—	45.00
1995 (f1) Proof	1,500	Value: 120				
1995 (f3) Proof	1,500	Value: 135				

Date	Mintage	F	VF	XF	Unc	BU
1995 (f7) Proof	1,500	Value: 100				
1995 (rv) Proof	1,500	Value: 90.00				

KM# 290   2 DOLLARS
62.2070 g., 0.9990 Silver 1.9979 oz. ASW **Ruler:** Elizabeth II
Obv: Crowned head right, denomination below **Rev:** Kookaburra
in flight, date below

Date	Mintage	F	VF	XF	Unc	BU
1995P Proof	650	Value: 65.00				
1995P (ww) Proof	1,300	Value: 135				
1995 (ge) Proof	800	Value: 135				
Note: Privy marks on gold insert						
1996	—	—	—	—	—	45.00
1996 (h) Proof	1,500	Value: 70.00				
1996 (d) Proof	1,500	Value: 115				
Note: Privy marks on gold insert						
1996 (j) Proof	1,500	Value: 120				
1996 (sg) Proof	1,500	Value: 130				
Note: Privy marks on gold insert						
1996 (sp) Proof	1,500	Value: 135				
Note: Privy marks on gold insert						

KM# 319   2 DOLLARS
62.2070 g., 0.9990 Silver 1.9979 oz. ASW **Ruler:** Elizabeth II
Obv: Crowned head right, denomination below **Rev:** Kookaburra
and nestling within circle, date below

Date	Mintage	F	VF	XF	Unc	BU
1997	—	—	—	—	—	45.00

KM# 363   2 DOLLARS
62.2070 g., 0.9990 Silver 1.9979 oz. ASW **Ruler:** Elizabeth II
Obv: Crowned head right, denomination below **Rev:** Kookaburra
on fence, right, within circle, date below

Date	Mintage	F	VF	XF	Unc	BU
1998 (1997)	—	—	—	—	—	45.00
1997 Proof	2,000	Value: 110				

KM# 445   2 DOLLARS
62.7700 g., 0.9990 Silver 2.0160 oz. ASW **Ruler:** Elizabeth II
Obv: Crowned head right, denomination below **Rev:** Two
kookaburras on branch **Edge:** Interrupted reeding on edge

Date	Mintage	F	VF	XF	Unc	BU
1999	—	—	—	—	—	45.00
2000 Proof	—	Value: 100				

KM# 417.1   2 DOLLARS
62.8500 g., 0.9990 Silver 2.0186 oz. ASW, 49.83 mm.
Ruler: Elizabeth II **Obv:** Crowned head right **Rev:** Kookaburra
on branch left, within circle **Edge:** Segmented reeding

Date	Mintage	F	VF	XF	Unc	BU
1999 Proof	—	—	—	—	—	
2000(1999)	—	—	—	—	—	45.00

KM# 417.3   2 DOLLARS
62.8500 g., 0.9990 Silver 2.0186 oz. ASW, 49.83 mm.
Ruler: Elizabeth II **Obv:** Crowned head right **Rev:** Kookaburra
on branch **Edge:** Segmented reeding **Note:** Rev. with 1933
Shilling obv. & rev. design copper inserts.

Date	Mintage	F	VF	XF	Unc	BU
1999	1,500	—	—	—	—	70.00

KM# 417.4   2 DOLLARS
62.8500 g., 0.9999 Silver 2.0204 oz. ASW, 49.83 mm.
Ruler: Elizabeth II **Obv:** Crowned head right **Rev:** Kookaburra
perched on branch left **Edge:** Segmented reeding **Note:** Reverse
with 1930 Penny obverse and reverse design copper inserts.

Date	Mintage	F	VF	XF	Unc	BU
1999 Proof	—	Value: 95.00				

KM# 417.5   2 DOLLARS
62.8500 g., 0.9990 Silver 2.0186 oz. ASW, 49.83 mm.
Ruler: Elizabeth II **Obv:** Crowned head right **Rev:** Kookaburra
perched on branch left **Edge:** Segmented reeding **Note:** Reverse
with 1932 Florin obverse and reverse design copper inserts.

Date	Mintage	F	VF	XF	Unc	BU
1999 Proof	—	Value: 95.00				

KM# 609   2 DOLLARS
62.2070 g., 0.9990 Silver 1.9979 oz. ASW **Ruler:** Elizabeth II
Subject: USA State Quarters - 1999 **Obv:** Crowned head right,
denomination below **Rev:** Kookaburra on branch with five state
quarter designs added below **Edge:** Reeded and plain sections

Date	Mintage	F	VF	XF	Unc	BU
1999	10,000	—	—	—	—	50.00

KM# 616   2 DOLLARS
62.2070 g., 0.9990 Silver 1.9979 oz. ASW, 49.83 mm.
Ruler: Elizabeth II **Subject:** USA State Quarters - 2000
Obv: Crowned head right **Rev:** Kookaburra perched on branch
left with five state quarter designs added below **Edge:** Segmented
reeding **Note:** Prev. KM#417.2.

Date	Mintage	F	VF	XF	Unc	BU
2000	10,000	—	—	—	—	50.00

KM# 189   5 DOLLARS
31.1030 g., 0.9990 Silver 0.9989 oz. ASW **Ruler:** Elizabeth II
Obv: Crowned head right, denomination below **Rev:** Australian
Kookaburra sitting on stump right, date below

Date	Mintage	F	VF	XF	Unc	BU
1990	300,000	—	—	—	—	27.50

KM# 138   5 DOLLARS
31.1030 g., 0.9990 Silver 0.9989 oz. ASW **Ruler:** Elizabeth II
Obv: Crowned head right, denomination below **Rev:** Australian
Kookaburra sitting on branch facing right, date below
Note: Special coin fair issues exist.

Date	Mintage	F	VF	XF	Unc	BU
1990 Proof	22,000	Value: 30.00				
1991	300,000	—	—	—	—	27.50
1991 Proof	—	Value: 30.00				

KM# 161   10 DOLLARS

62.2140 g., 0.9990 Silver 1.9981 oz. ASW **Ruler:** Elizabeth II
Obv: Crowned head right, denomination below **Rev:** Australian
Kookaburra sitting on stump facing right, date below **Note:** Photo
reduced.

Date	Mintage	F	VF	XF	Unc	BU
1991	—	—	—	—	—	45.00
1991 Proof	5,000	Value: 60.00				
1992	—	—	—	—	—	45.00
1993	—	—	—	—	—	45.00

KM# 177   10 DOLLARS

311.0350 g., 0.9990 Silver 9.9896 oz. ASW, 75 mm.
Subject: Kookaburra **Obv:** Elizabeth II **Rev:** Kookaburra on
branch next to tree **Edge:** Segmented reeding **Note:** Photo
reduced.

Date	Mintage	F	VF	XF	Unc	BU
1992P	—	—	—	—	—	225
1992P Proof	—	Value: 325				

KM# 180   10 DOLLARS

311.0670 g., 0.9990 Silver 9.9906 oz. ASW **Ruler:** Elizabeth II
Obv: Crowned head right, denomination below **Rev:** Australian
kookaburra sitting on branch facing right, date below

Date	Mintage	F	VF	XF	Unc	BU
1992	—	—	—	—	—	220
1992 Proof	2,500	Value: 325				

KM# 228   10 DOLLARS

311.0670 g., 0.9990 Silver 9.9906 oz. ASW **Ruler:** Elizabeth II
Obv: Crowned head right, denomination below **Rev:** Kookaburra
feeding nestling

Date	Mintage	F	VF	XF	Unc	BU
1993	—	—	—	—	—	220
1993 Proof	—	Value: 245				

KM# 231   10 DOLLARS

311.0350 g., 0.9990 Silver 9.9896 oz. ASW, 75 mm. **Ruler:**
Elizabeth II **Subject:** The Australian Kookaburra **Obv:** Crowned
head right, denomination below **Rev:** Pair of Kookaburras on
branch, square mark above date below **Note:** Illustration reduced.

Date	Mintage	F	VF	XF	Unc	BU
1993 (ae) Proof	500	Value: 550				
1994	—	—	—	—	—	235
1994 Proof	—	Value: 250				

KM# 270   10 DOLLARS

311.0670 g., 0.9990 Silver 9.9906 oz. ASW **Ruler:** Elizabeth II
Obv: Crowned head right, denomination below **Rev:** Kookaburra
on branch looking left, date below **Note:** Photo reduced.

Date	Mintage	F	VF	XF	Unc	BU
1994P Proof	—	Value: 300				
1995	—	—	—	—	—	225
1995 Proof	—	Value: 300				

KM# 291   10 DOLLARS

311.0670 g., 0.9990 Silver 9.9906 oz. ASW, 75.5 mm.
Ruler: Elizabeth II **Obv:** Crowned head right, denomination
below **Rev:** Kookaburra in flight right, date below, small "p" above
bird's tail **Note:** Illustration reduced.

Date	Mintage	F	VF	XF	Unc	BU
1995P Proof	1,300	Value: 275				
1995 (ge) Proof	800	Value: 300				
Note: Privy mark on gold insert						
1996	—	—	—	—	—	225

KM# 351   10 DOLLARS

311.0670 g., 0.9990 Silver 9.9906 oz. ASW **Ruler:** Elizabeth II
Subject: Kookaburra and Nestling **Obv:** Crowned head right,
denomination below **Rev:** Kookaburra looking right, nestling

Date	Mintage	F	VF	XF	Unc	BU
1997	—	—	—	—	—	225

KM# 494   10 DOLLARS

311.0350 g., 0.9990 Silver 9.9896 oz. ASW, 75 mm. **Ruler:**
Elizabeth II **Subject:** Kookaburra Bullion **Obv:** Crowned head
right, denomination below **Rev:** Kookaburra on fence right, date
below **Edge:** Reeded and plain sections **Note:** Photo reduced.

Date	Mintage	F	VF	XF	Unc	BU
1997P Proof	—	Value: 325				

KM# 446   10 DOLLARS

312.3470 g., 0.9990 Silver 10.031 oz. ASW **Ruler:** Elizabeth II
Obv: Crowned head right, denomination below **Rev:** Two
kookaburras on branch **Edge:** Interrupted reeding **Note:** Photo
reduced.

Date	Mintage	F	VF	XF	Unc	BU
2000	—	—	—	—	—	225

KM# 178   30 DOLLARS

1000.0000 g., 0.9990 Silver 32.117 oz. ASW, 100 mm. **Subject:**
Kookaburra **Obv:** Elizabeth II **Rev:** Kookaburra on branch next
to tree trunk **Edge:** Segmented reeding

Date	Mintage	F	VF	XF	Unc	BU
1992P	—				650	—
1992P Proof	—	Value: 700				

KM# 181 30 DOLLARS
1100.1000 g., 0.9990 Silver 35.332 oz. ASW, 100 mm.
Ruler: Elizabeth II **Obv:** Crowned head right within inner circle, denomination below **Rev:** Australian Kookaburra on stump facing right within circle, date below **Note:** Illustration reduced.

Date	Mintage	F	VF	XF	Unc	BU
1992	—				650	—
1992 Proof	1,000	Value: 700				
1993	—				650	—
1993 (jw) Proof	210	Value: 720				

KM# 229 30 DOLLARS
1000.2108 g., 0.9990 Silver 32.124 oz. ASW **Ruler:** Elizabeth II **Obv:** Crowned head right, denomination below **Rev:** Kookaburra feeding nestling **Note:** Similar to 1 Dollar, KM#209.

Date	Mintage	F	VF	XF	Unc	BU
1993	—				650	—
1993 Proof	—	Value: 700				

KM# 232 30 DOLLARS
1000.2108 g., 0.9990 Silver 32.124 oz. ASW, 100 mm.
Obv: Bust of Queen Elizabeth II, right **Rev:** Pair of kookaburras on branch within circle, silver weight and date in legend **Note:** Illustration reduced.

Date	Mintage	F	VF	XF	Unc	BU
1994	—				700	—
1994 Proof	—	Value: 650				

KM# 271 30 DOLLARS
1000.2108 g., 0.9990 Silver 32.124 oz. ASW **Ruler:** Elizabeth II **Obv:** Crowned head right, denomination below **Rev:** Kookaburra on branch looking left, date below **Note:** Illustration reduced.

Date	Mintage	F	VF	XF	Unc	BU
1994P Proof	—	Value: 675				

Date	Mintage	F	VF	XF	Unc	BU
1995	—				650	—
1995 Proof	—	Value: 675				

KM# 292 30 DOLLARS
1000.2108 g., 0.9990 Silver 32.124 oz. ASW, 101 mm. **Ruler:** Elizabeth II **Obv:** Crowned head right, denomination below **Rev:** Kookaburra in flight, date below **Note:** Illustration reduced.

Date	Mintage	F	VF	XF	Unc	BU
1995 (lh) Proof	500	Value: 675				
1995P Proof	1,000	Value: 700				
1996	—				650	

KM# 495 30 DOLLARS
1100.1000 g., 0.9990 Silver 35.332 oz. ASW, 100 mm.
Ruler: Elizabeth II **Subject:** Kookaburra Bullion **Obv:** Crowned head right, denomination below **Rev:** Kookaburra on fence facing right, date below **Edge:** Reeded and plain sections with serial number **Note:** Photo reduced.

Date	Mintage	F	VF	XF	Unc	BU
1997P Proof	—	Value: 700				
1998P	—					650

KM# 610 30 DOLLARS
1002.5020 g., 0.9990 Silver 32.197 oz. ASW **Ruler:** Elizabeth II **Subject:** USA State Quarters - 1999 **Obv:** Crowned head right, denomination below **Rev:** Kookaburra on branch with five state quarter designs added below **Edge:** Reeded and plain sections

Date	Mintage	F	VF	XF	Unc	BU
1999	1,000					650

KM# 447 30 DOLLARS
1002.5020 g., 0.9990 Silver 32.197 oz. ASW **Ruler:** Elizabeth II **Obv:** Crowned head right, denomination below **Rev:** Two kookaburras on branch, date below **Edge:** Reeded **Note:** Photo reduced.

Date	Mintage	F	VF	XF	Unc	BU
1999	—					650
2000 Proof	—	Value: 700				

KM# 617 30 DOLLARS
1002.5020 g., 0.9990 Silver 32.197 oz. ASW **Ruler:** Elizabeth II **Subject:** USA State Quarters - 2000 **Obv:** Crowned head right, denomination below **Rev:** Kookaburra on branch with five state quarter designs added below **Edge:** Reeded and plain sections **Note:** Photo reduced.

Date	Mintage	F	VF	XF	Unc	BU
2000	1,000	—				650

KM# 162 50 DOLLARS
311.0670 g., 0.9990 Silver 9.9906 oz. ASW **Ruler:** Elizabeth II **Subject:** Australian Kookaburra **Obv:** Crowned head right, denomination below **Rev:** Kookaburra bird

Date	Mintage	F	VF	XF	Unc	BU
1991	—				—	285
1991 Proof	2,500	Value: 250				

KM# 163 150 DOLLARS
1000.1000 g., 0.9990 Silver 32.120 oz. ASW **Ruler:** Elizabeth II **Subject:** Australian Kookaburra **Obv:** Crowned head right, denomination below **Rev:** Kookaburra bird **Note:** Kilo

Date	Mintage	F	VF	XF	Unc	BU
1991	—					650
1991 Proof	1,000	Value: 700				

BULLION - LUNAR YEAR

KM# 501 50 CENTS
16.8860 g., 0.9990 Silver 0.5423 oz. ASW, 32.1 mm.
Ruler: Elizabeth II **Subject:** Year of the Rabbit **Obv:** Head with tiara right, denomination below **Rev:** Rabbit right, date at left **Edge:** Reeded

Date	Mintage	F	VF	XF	Unc	BU
1999	—			—	15.00	17.50
1999 Proof	5,000	Value: 28.00				

KM# 502 DOLLAR
31.6350 g., 0.9990 Silver 1.0160 oz. ASW, 40.6 mm.
Ruler: Elizabeth II **Subject:** Year of the Rabbit **Obv:** Head with tiara right, denomination below **Rev:** Rabbit right, date at left **Edge:** Reeded

Date	Mintage	F	VF	XF	Unc	BU
1999	50,000	—	—	—	25.00	27.50
1999 Proof	2,500	Value: 45.00				

KM# 502a DOLLAR
31.6350 g., 0.9990 Silver 1.0160 oz. ASW, 40.6 mm.
Ruler: Elizabeth II **Subject:** Year of the Rabbit **Obv:** Head with tiara right, denomination below **Rev:** Rabbit right, date at left **Edge:** Reeded

Date	Mintage	F	VF	XF	Unc	BU
1999	50,000	—	—	—	50.00	55.00

KM# 424a DOLLAR
31.6350 g., 0.9990 Silver 1.0160 oz. ASW, 40.6 mm.
Ruler: Elizabeth II **Subject:** Year of the Dragon **Obv:** Head with tiara right, denomination below **Rev:** Gold-plated dragon, date at left **Edge:** Reeded

Date	Mintage	F	VF	XF	Unc	BU
2000	50,000	—	—	—	50.00	55.00

KM# 424   DOLLAR
31.1035 g., 0.9990 Silver 0.9990 oz. ASW   **Ruler:** Elizabeth II
Subject: Year of the Dragon **Obv:** Head with tiara right within
circle, denomination below **Rev:** Dragon, date at left

Date	Mintage	F	VF	XF	Unc	BU
2000	—	—	—	—	25.00	27.50
2000 Proof	—	Value: 45.00				

KM# 503   2 DOLLARS
62.7700 g., 0.9990 Silver 2.0160 oz. ASW, 49.9 mm.
Ruler: Elizabeth II **Subject:** Year of the Rabbit **Obv:** Head with
tiara right, denomination below **Rev:** Rabbit right, date at left
Edge: Reeded and plain sections

Date	Mintage	F	VF	XF	Unc	BU
1999	—	—	—	—	35.00	—
1999 Proof	2,500	Value: 95.00				

KM# 523   2 DOLLARS
62.2070 g., 0.9990 Silver 1.9979 oz. ASW, 50.3 mm.
Ruler: Elizabeth II **Series:** Dragons **Subject:** Year of the Dragon
Obv: Head with tiara right, denomination below **Rev:** Dragon,
date at left **Edge:** Segmented reeding

Date	Mintage	F	VF	XF	Unc	BU
2000 Proof	—	Value: 110				

KM# 566   5 DOLLARS
1.5552 g., 0.9990 Gold 0.0499 oz. AGW, 14.1 mm.
Ruler: Elizabeth II **Subject:** Year of the Rat **Obv:** Crowned head
right, denomination below **Rev:** Rat, right **Edge:** Reeded

Date	Mintage	F	VF	XF	Unc	BU
1996P	100,000	—	—	—	—	55.00

KM# 567   5 DOLLARS
1.5552 g., 0.9990 Gold 0.0499 oz. AGW, 14.1 mm.
Ruler: Elizabeth II **Subject:** Year of the Ox **Obv:** Crowned head
right, denomination below **Rev:** Ox, left **Edge:** Reeded

Date	Mintage	F	VF	XF	Unc	BU
1997P	100,000	—	—	—	—	55.00

KM# 568   5 DOLLARS
1.5552 g., 0.9990 Gold 0.0499 oz. AGW, 14.1 mm.
Ruler: Elizabeth II **Subject:** Year of the Tiger **Obv:** Crowned
head right, denomination below **Rev:** Tiger springing right
Edge: Reeded

Date	Mintage	F	VF	XF	Unc	BU
1998P	100,000	—	—	—	—	55.00

KM# 425   5 DOLLARS
1.5710 g., 0.9999 Gold 0.0505 oz. AGW   **Ruler:** Elizabeth II
Subject: Year of the Rabbit **Obv:** Crowned head right,
denomination below **Rev:** Rabbit

Date	Mintage	F	VF	XF	Unc	BU
1999	Est. 100,000	—	—	—	—	55.00

KM# 569   5 DOLLARS
1.5552 g., 0.9990 Gold 0.0499 oz. AGW, 14.1 mm.
Ruler: Elizabeth II **Subject:** Year of the Dragon **Obv:** Crowned
head right, denomination below **Rev:** Dragon **Edge:** Reeded

Date	Mintage	F	VF	XF	Unc	BU
2000P	100,000	—	—	—	—	55.00

KM# 504   10 DOLLARS
312.3470 g., 0.9990 Silver 10.031 oz. ASW, 75.5 mm.
Ruler: Elizabeth II **Subject:** Year of the Rabbit **Obv:** Head with
tiara right, denomination below **Rev:** Rabbit right, date at left
Edge: Reeded and plain sections **Note:** Illustration reduced.

Date	Mintage	F	VF	XF	Unc	BU
1999	—	—	—	—	—	225
1999 Proof	2,500	Value: 350				

KM# 524   10 DOLLARS
311.0350 g., 0.9990 Silver 9.9896 oz. ASW, 75.5 mm.
Ruler: Elizabeth II **Series:** Dragons **Subject:** Year of the Dragon
Obv: Head with tiara right, denomination below **Rev:** Dragon
Edge: Segmented reeding

Date	Mintage	F	VF	XF	Unc	BU
2000	—	—	—	—	—	215
2000 Proof	—	Value: 285				

KM# 298   15 DOLLARS
3.1103 g., 0.9990 Gold 0.0999 oz. AGW   **Ruler:** Elizabeth II
Subject: Year of the Rat **Obv:** Crowned head right, denomination
below **Rev:** Rat facing right

Date	Mintage	F	VF	XF	Unc	BU
1996	—	—	—	—	—	110
1996 Proof	—	Value: 120				

KM# 335   15 DOLLARS
3.1103 g., 0.9990 Gold 0.0999 oz. AGW   **Ruler:** Elizabeth II
Subject: Year of the Ox **Obv:** Crowned head right, denomination
below **Rev:** Bull ox looking right

Date	Mintage	F	VF	XF	Unc	BU
1997	—	—	—	—	—	110
1997 Proof	—	Value: 120				

KM# 506   15 DOLLARS
3.1103 g., 0.9990 Gold 0.0999 oz. AGW, 16.1 mm.   **Ruler:**
Elizabeth II **Subject:** Year of the Tiger **Obv:** Crowned head right,
denomination below **Rev:** Tiger springing right **Edge:** Reeded

Date	Mintage	F	VF	XF	Unc	BU
1998	—	—	—	—	—	110
1998P Proof	—	Value: 120				

KM# 426   15 DOLLARS
3.1130 g., 0.9999 Gold 0.1001 oz. AGW   **Ruler:** Elizabeth II
Subject: Year of the Rabbit **Obv:** Crowned head right,
denomination below **Rev:** Rabbit facing right

Date	Mintage	F	VF	XF	Unc	BU
1999	Est. 80,000	—	—	—	—	110
1999 Proof	—	Value: 120				

KM# 526   15 DOLLARS
3.1103 g., 0.9990 Gold 0.0999 oz. AGW, 16.1 mm.
Ruler: Elizabeth II **Subject:** Year of the Dragon **Obv:** Crowned
head right, denomination below **Rev:** Dragon **Edge:** Reeded

Date	Mintage	F	VF	XF	Unc	BU
2000	—	—	—	—	—	110
2000 Proof	—	Value: 120				

KM# 299   25 DOLLARS
7.7508 g., 0.9990 Gold 0.2489 oz. AGW   **Ruler:** Elizabeth II
Subject: Year of the Rat **Obv:** Crowned head right, denomination
below **Rev:** Rat facing right

Date	Mintage	F	VF	XF	Unc	BU
1996	—	—	—	—	—	240
1996 Proof	—	Value: 250				

KM# 336   25 DOLLARS
7.7508 g., 0.9990 Gold 0.2489 oz. AGW   **Ruler:** Elizabeth II
Subject: Year of the Ox **Obv:** Crowned head right, denomination
below **Rev:** Bull ox looking right

Date	Mintage	F	VF	XF	Unc	BU
1997	—	—	—	—	—	240
1997 Proof	8,888	Value: 250				

KM# 507   25 DOLLARS
7.7759 g., 0.9990 Gold 0.2497 oz. AGW, 20.1 mm.
Ruler: Elizabeth II **Subject:** Year of the Tiger **Obv:** Crowned
head right, denomination below **Rev:** Tiger springing right
Edge: Reeded

Date	Mintage	F	VF	XF	Unc	BU
1998P	—	—	—	—	—	240
1998P Proof	—	Value: 250				

KM# 427   25 DOLLARS
7.8070 g., 0.9999 Gold 0.2510 oz. AGW   **Ruler:** Elizabeth II
Subject: Year of the Rabbit **Obv:** Crowned head right,
denomination below **Rev:** Rabbit facing right **Edge:** Reeded

Date	Mintage	F	VF	XF	Unc	BU
1999	Est. 60,000	—	—	—	—	240
1999 Proof	—	Value: 250				

KM# 527   25 DOLLARS
7.7508 g., 0.9990 Gold 0.2489 oz. AGW, 20.1 mm.
Ruler: Elizabeth II **Subject:** Year of the Dragon **Obv:** Crowned
head with tiara right, denomination below **Rev:** Dragon **Edge:** Reeded

Date	Mintage	F	VF	XF	Unc	BU
2000	—	—	—	—	—	250
2000 Proof	—	Value: 260				

KM# 505   30 DOLLARS
1002.5020 g., 0.9990 Silver 32.197 oz. ASW, 101 mm.
Ruler: Elizabeth II **Subject:** Year of the Rabbit **Obv:** Head with
tiara right, denomination below **Rev:** Rabbit right, date at left
Edge: Reeded and plain sections **Note:** Illustration reduced.

Date	Mintage	F	VF	XF	Unc	BU
1999	—	—	—	—	—	650
1999 Proof	2,500	Value: 675				

KM# 525.1   30 DOLLARS
1002.5020 g., 0.9990 Silver 32.197 oz. ASW, 101 mm.
Ruler: Elizabeth II **Subject:** Year of the Dragon **Obv:** Head with
tiara right, denomination below **Rev:** Dragon **Edge:** Segmented
reeding **Note:** Prev. KM#525.

Date	Mintage	F	VF	XF	Unc	BU
2000	—	—	—	—	—	670
2000 Proof	—	Value: 700				

KM# 525.2   30 DOLLARS
0.9990 Silver   **Ruler:** Elizabeth II **Subject:** Year of the Dragon
Obv: Head with tiara right, denomination below **Rev:** Dragon with
diamonds for eyes and multicolor ornamentation

Date	Mintage	F	VF	XF	Unc	BU
2000 Proof	5,000	Value: 650				

KM# 300   100 DOLLARS
31.1035 g., 0.9990 Gold 0.9990 oz. AGW **Ruler:** Elizabeth II
Subject: Year of the Rat **Obv:** Crowned head right, denomination
below **Rev:** Rat facing right, date at left

Date	Mintage	F	VF	XF	Unc	BU
1996	—	—	—	—	—	975
1996 Proof	—	Value: 1,000				

KM# 337   100 DOLLARS
31.1035 g., 0.9990 Gold 0.9990 oz. AGW **Ruler:** Elizabeth II
Subject: Year of the Ox **Obv:** Crowned head right, denomination
below **Rev:** Ox left, looking right, date at left

Date	Mintage	F	VF	XF	Unc	BU
1997	—	—	—	—	—	975
1997 Proof	8,888	Value: 1,000				

KM# 508   100 DOLLARS
31.1035 g., 0.9990 Gold 0.9990 oz. AGW, 32.1 mm.
Ruler: Elizabeth II **Subject:** Year of the Tiger **Obv:** Crowned
head right, denomination below **Rev:** Tiger springing right, date
at left **Edge:** Reeded

Date	Mintage	F	VF	XF	Unc	BU
1998	—	—	—	—	—	975
1998P Proof	—	Value: 1,000				

KM# 428   100 DOLLARS
31.1620 g., 0.9999 Gold 1.0017 oz. AGW **Ruler:** Elizabeth II
Subject: Year of the Rabbit **Obv:** Crowned head right, denomination
below **Rev:** Seated rabbit left, date at left **Edge:** Reeded

Date	Mintage	F	VF	XF	Unc	BU
1999	Est. 30,000	—	—	—	—	1,000
1999 Proof	—	Value: 1,050				

KM# 528   100 DOLLARS
31.1035 g., 0.9990 Gold 0.9990 oz. AGW, 32.1 mm.
Ruler: Elizabeth II **Subject:** Year of the Dragon **Obv:** Crowned
head right, denomination below **Rev:** Dragon **Edge:** Reeded

Date	Mintage	F	VF	XF	Unc	BU
2000	—	—	—	—	—	1,050
2000 Proof	—	Value: 1,100				

KM# 667   200 DOLLARS
62.2140 g., 0.9990 Gold 1.9981 oz. AGW, 40.6 mm.
Ruler: Elizabeth II **Subject:** Year of the Dragon **Obv:** Crowned
head right, denomination below **Rev:** Dragon **Edge:** Reeded

Date	Mintage	F	VF	XF	Unc	BU
2000	—	—	—	—	—	2,000

KM# 702   1000 DOLLARS
311.0480 g., 0.9999 Gold 9.9990 oz. AGW **Ruler:** Elizabeth II
Subject: Year of the Dragon **Obv:** Crowned head right,
denomination below **Rev:** Dragon

Date	Mintage	F	VF	XF	Unc	BU
2000	—	—	—	—	—	10,000

KM# 703   3000 DOLLARS
1000.0000 g., 0.9999 Gold 32.146 oz. AGW **Ruler:** Elizabeth II
Subject: Year of the Dragon **Obv:** Crowned head right,
denomination below **Rev:** Dragon

Date	Mintage	F	VF	XF	Unc	BU
2000	—	—	—	—	—	BV+3%

GOLD BULLION - KANGAROO

KM# 117   5 DOLLARS
1.5710 g., 0.9990 Gold 0.0505 oz. AGW **Ruler:** Elizabeth II
Subject: Red Kangaroo **Obv:** Crowned head right, denomination
below **Rev:** Kangaroo leaping left, date below

Date	Mintage	F	VF	XF	Unc	BU
1989 Proof	2,200	Value: 60.00				
1990	Est. 200,000	—	—	—	BV+ 35%	

KM# 140   5 DOLLARS
1.5710 g., 0.9990 Gold 0.0505 oz. AGW **Ruler:** Elizabeth II
Obv: Crowned head right, denomination below **Rev:** Gray
Kangaroo right, date below

Date	Mintage	F	VF	XF	Unc	BU
1990 Proof	7,000	Value: 60.00				
1991	200,000	—	—	—	BV+35%	

KM# 165   5 DOLLARS
1.5710 g., 0.9990 Gold 0.0505 oz. AGW **Ruler:** Elizabeth II
Subject: Common Wallaroo **Obv:** Crowned head right,
denomination below **Rev:** Kangaroo bounding left, date below
Note: 1992 (ae) previously listed here is now KM#389.

Date	Mintage	F	VF	XF	Unc	BU
1991 Proof	3,525	Value: 60.00				
1992	200,000	—	—	—	BV+ 35%	

KM# 389   5 DOLLARS
1.5710 g., 0.9990 Gold 0.0505 oz. AGW **Ruler:** Elizabeth II
Obv: Crowned head right, denomination below **Rev:** Nail-tailed
Wallaby

Date	Mintage	F	VF	XF	Unc	BU
1992 (ae) Proof	500	Value: 60.00				

KM# 233   5 DOLLARS
1.5710 g., 0.9990 Gold 0.0505 oz. AGW **Ruler:** Elizabeth II
Obv: Crowned head right, denomination below **Rev:** Whiptail
Wallaby

Date	Mintage	F	VF	XF	Unc	BU
1993 Proof	—	Value: 60.00				
1994	—	—	—	—	BV+ 35%	

KM# 241   5 DOLLARS
1.5710 g., 0.9990 Gold 0.0505 oz. AGW **Ruler:** Elizabeth II
Obv. Leg.: Crowned head right, denomination below **Rev:** Red
Kangaroo facing front, date below

Date	Mintage	F	VF	XF	Unc	BU
1994 Proof	—	Value: 60.00				
1995	200,000	—	—	—	BV+35%	

KM# 272   5 DOLLARS
1.5710 g., 0.9990 Gold 0.0505 oz. AGW **Ruler:** Elizabeth II
Obv: Crowned head right, denomination below **Rev:** Two
kangaroos standing, date below

Date	Mintage	F	VF	XF	Unc	BU
1995 Proof	300	Value: 60.00				
1996	200,000	—	—	—	—BV+35%	

KM# 320   5 DOLLARS
1.5710 g., 0.9990 Gold 0.0505 oz. AGW **Ruler:** Elizabeth II
Obv: Crowned head right, denomination below **Rev:** Kangaroo
bounding right

Date	Mintage	F	VF	XF	Unc	BU
1996P Proof	—	Value: 60.00				

Note: In proof sets only

KM# 338   5 DOLLARS
1.5710 g., 0.9999 Gold 0.0505 oz. AGW **Ruler:** Elizabeth II
Obv: Crowned head right, denomination below **Rev:** Kangaroo
bounding right

Date	Mintage	F	VF	XF	Unc	BU
1997	200,000	—	—	—	BV+ 35%	—
1997 Proof	—	Value: 60.00				

KM# 448   5 DOLLARS
1.5710 g., 0.9990 Gold 0.0505 oz. AGW **Ruler:** Elizabeth II
Obv: Crowned head right, denomination below **Rev:** Kangaroo
facing left **Edge:** Reeded

Date	Mintage	F	VF	XF	Unc	BU
1999	200,000	—	—	—	—	60.00

KM# 464   5 DOLLARS
1.5710 g., 0.9990 Gold 0.0505 oz. AGW **Ruler:** Elizabeth II
Obv: Crowned head right, denomination below **Rev:** Two
kangaroos bounding left

Date	Mintage	F	VF	XF	Unc	BU
2000	—	—	—	—	—	60.00

KM# 118   15 DOLLARS
3.1103 g., 0.9990 Gold 0.0999 oz. AGW **Ruler:** Elizabeth II
Obv: Crowned head right, denomination below **Rev:** Red
kangaroo leaping left, date below

Date	Mintage	F	VF	XF	Unc	BU
1989 Proof	2,200	Value: 100				
1990	200,000	—	—	—	BV+12%	

KM# 141   15 DOLLARS
3.1103 g., 0.9990 Gold 0.0999 oz. AGW **Ruler:** Elizabeth II
Obv: Crowned head right, denomination below **Rev:** Gray
kangaroo standing facing left, date below

Date	Mintage	F	VF	XF	Unc	BU
1990 Proof	7,000	Value: 100				
1991	150,000	—	—	—	BV+12%	

KM# 166   15 DOLLARS
3.1103 g., 0.9990 Gold 0.0999 oz. AGW **Ruler:** Elizabeth II
Subject: Common Wallaroo **Obv:** Crowned head right,
denomination below **Rev:** Radiant common walleroo facing right

Date	Mintage	F	VF	XF	Unc	BU
1991 Proof	1,975	Value: 100				
1992	150,000	—	—	—	BV+12%	

KM# 390   15 DOLLARS
3.1103 g., 0.9990 Gold 0.0999 oz. AGW **Ruler:** Elizabeth II
Obv: Crowned head right, denomination below **Rev:** Nail-tailed
wallaby

Date	Mintage	F	VF	XF	Unc	BU
1992 (ae) Proof	500	Value: 110				

KM# 234   15 DOLLARS
3.1103 g., 0.9990 Gold 0.0999 oz. AGW **Ruler:** Elizabeth II
Obv: Crowned head right, denomination below **Rev:** Whiptail
wallaby

Date	Mintage	F	VF	XF	Unc	BU
1993 Proof	—	Value: 100				
1994	—	—	—	—	BV+12%	

KM# 242   15 DOLLARS
3.1103 g., 0.9990 Gold 0.0999 oz. AGW **Ruler:** Elizabeth II
Obv: Crowned head right, denomination below **Rev:** Red
kangaroo standing facing forward, date below

Date	Mintage	F	VF	XF	Unc	BU
1994 Proof	—	Value: 100				
1995	200,000	—	—	—	BV+12%	—

KM# 273   15 DOLLARS
3.1103 g., 0.9990 Gold 0.0999 oz. AGW **Ruler:** Elizabeth II
Obv: Crowned head right, denomination below **Rev:** Two
kangaroos, date below

Date	Mintage	F	VF	XF	Unc	BU
1995 Proof	900	Value: 100				
1996	200,000	—	—	—	BV+12%	—

KM# 321   15 DOLLARS
3.1103 g., 0.9990 Gold 0.0999 oz. AGW **Ruler:** Elizabeth II
Obv: Crowned head right, denomination below **Rev:** Kangaroo
bounding right

Date	Mintage	F	VF	XF	Unc	BU
1996P Proof	400	Value: 200				

KM# 339   15 DOLLARS
3.1103 g., 0.9990 Gold 0.0999 oz. AGW **Ruler:** Elizabeth II
Obv: Crowned head right, denomination below **Rev:** Kangaroo
bounding right

Date	Mintage	F	VF	XF	Unc	BU
1997	200,000	—	—	—	BV+12%	—
1997 Proof	—	Value: 100				

KM# 449   15 DOLLARS
3.1330 g., 0.9990 Gold 0.1006 oz. AGW **Ruler:** Elizabeth II
Obv: Crowned head right, denomination below **Rev:** Kangaroo
facing left **Edge:** Reeded

Date	Mintage	F	VF	XF	Unc	BU
1999	200,000	—	—	—	100	—

KM# 465   15 DOLLARS
3.1330 g., 0.9990 Gold 0.1006 oz. AGW **Ruler:** Elizabeth II
Obv: Crowned head right, denomination below **Rev:** Two
kangaroos bounding left **Edge:** Reeded

Date	Mintage	F	VF	XF	Unc	BU
2000	—	—	—	—	100	—

KM# 119   25 DOLLARS
7.7508 g., 0.9990 Gold 0.2489 oz. AGW **Ruler:** Elizabeth II
Obv: Crowned head right, denomination below **Rev:** Red kangaroo

Date	Mintage	F	VF	XF	Unc	BU
1989 Proof	2,200	Value: 250				
1990	Est. 200,000	—	—	—	BV+10%	—

KM# 142   25 DOLLARS
7.7508 g., 0.9990 Gold 0.2489 oz. AGW **Ruler:** Elizabeth II
Obv: Crowned head right, denomination below **Rev:** Gray
kangaroo standing facing, date below

Date	Mintage	F	VF	XF	Unc	BU
1990 Proof	7,000	Value: 250				
1991	100,000	—	—	—	BV+10%	—

KM# 167   25 DOLLARS
7.7508 g., 0.9990 Gold 0.2489 oz. AGW **Ruler:** Elizabeth II
Subject: Common Wallaroo **Obv:** Crowned head right,
denomination below **Rev:** Radiant walleroo facing right

Date	Mintage	F	VF	XF	Unc	BU
1991 Proof	1,991	Value: 250				
1992	100,000	—	—	—	BV+10%	—

KM# 391   25 DOLLARS
7.7508 g., 0.9990 Gold 0.2489 oz. AGW **Ruler:** Elizabeth II
Obv: Crowned head right, denomination below **Rev:** Nail-tailed
wallaby standing right, date below

Date	Mintage	F	VF	XF	Unc	BU
1992 (ae) Proof	500	Value: 265				

KM# 235   25 DOLLARS
7.7508 g., 0.9990 Gold 0.2489 oz. AGW **Ruler:** Elizabeth II
Obv: Crowned head right, denomination below **Rev:** Whiptail
wallaby

Date	Mintage	F	VF	XF	Unc	BU
1993 (f) Proof	200	—	—	—	—	—
1993 Proof	—	Value: 250				
1994	—	—	—	—	BV+10%	—

KM# 243   25 DOLLARS
7.7508 g., 0.9990 Gold 0.2489 oz. AGW **Ruler:** Elizabeth II
Obv: Crowned head right, denomination below **Rev:** Red
kangaroo standing facing, date below

Date	Mintage	F	VF	XF	Unc	BU
1994 Proof	—	Value: 250				
1995	150,000	—	—	—	BV+10%	—

KM# 274   25 DOLLARS
7.7508 g., 0.9990 Gold 0.2489 oz. AGW **Ruler:** Elizabeth II
Obv: Crowned head right, denomination below **Rev:** Two
kangaroos, date below

Date	Mintage	F	VF	XF	Unc	BU
1995 Proof	650	Value: 225				
1996	150,000	250	—	—	BV+10%	—

KM# 322   25 DOLLARS
7.7508 g., 0.9990 Gold 0.2489 oz. AGW **Ruler:** Elizabeth II
Obv: Crowned head right, denomination below **Rev:** Kangaroo
bounding right

Date	Mintage	F	VF	XF	Unc	BU
1996(p) Proof	400	Value: 350				

Note: In sets only

KM# 340   25 DOLLARS
7.7508 g., 0.9990 Gold 0.2489 oz. AGW **Ruler:** Elizabeth II
Obv: Crowned head right, denomination below **Rev:** Kangaroo
bounding right

Date	Mintage	F	VF	XF	Unc	BU
1997	200,000	—	—	—	BV+10%	—
1997 Proof	—	Value: 250				

KM# 450   25 DOLLARS
7.8070 g., 0.9990 Gold 0.2507 oz. AGW **Ruler:** Elizabeth II
Obv: Crowned head right, denomination below **Rev:** Kangaroo
facing left **Edge:** Reeded

Date	Mintage	F	VF	XF	Unc	BU
1999	150,000	—	—	—	BV+10%	—

KM# 466   25 DOLLARS
7.8070 g., 0.9990 Gold 0.2507 oz. AGW **Ruler:** Elizabeth II
Obv: Crowned head right, denomination below **Rev:** Two
kangaroos bounding left **Edge:** Reeded

Date	Mintage	F	VF	XF	Unc	BU
2000	—	—	—	—	BV+10%	—

KM# 120   50 DOLLARS
15.5017 g., 0.9990 Gold 0.4979 oz. AGW **Ruler:** Elizabeth II
Obv: Crowned head right, denomination below **Rev:** Red
kangaroo leaping left, date below

Date	Mintage	F	VF	XF	Unc	BU
1989 Proof	2,200	Value: 485				
1990	Est. 240,000	—	—	—	BV+7%	—

KM# 143   50 DOLLARS
15.5017 g., 0.9990 Gold 0.4979 oz. AGW **Ruler:** Elizabeth II
Obv: Crowned head right, denomination below **Rev:** Gray
kangaroo facing right looking left, date below

Date	Mintage	F	VF	XF	Unc	BU
1990 Proof	5,000	Value: 485				
1991	100,000	—	—	—	BV+7%	—

KM# 168   50 DOLLARS
15.5017 g., 0.9990 Gold 0.4979 oz. AGW **Ruler:** Elizabeth II
Subject: Common wallaroo **Obv:** Crowned head right,
denomination below **Rev:** Radiant common wallaroo facing right

Date	Mintage	F	VF	XF	Unc	BU
1991 Proof	1,096	Value: 500				
1992	100,000	—	—	—	BV+7%	—

KM# 392   50 DOLLARS
15.5017 g., 0.9990 Gold 0.4979 oz. AGW **Ruler:** Elizabeth II
Obv: Crowned head right, denomination below **Rev:** Nail-tailed
wallaby

Date	Mintage	F	VF	XF	Unc	BU
1992 (ae) Proof	500	Value: 520				

KM# 236   50 DOLLARS
15.5017 g., 0.9990 Gold 0.4979 oz. AGW **Ruler:** Elizabeth II
Obv: Crowned head right, denomination below **Rev:** Whiptail
wallaby

Date	Mintage	F	VF	XF	Unc	BU
1993 Proof	—	Value: 500				
1994	—	—	—	—	BV+7%	—

KM# 244   50 DOLLARS
15.5017 g., 0.9990 Gold 0.4979 oz. AGW **Ruler:** Elizabeth II
Obv: Crowned head right, denomination below **Rev:** Red
kangaroo standing facing front, date below

Date	Mintage	F	VF	XF	Unc	BU
1994 Proof	—	Value: 500				
1995	30,000	—	—	—	BV+10%	—
1995 (f) Proof	10,000	Value: 485				

KM# 275.1   50 DOLLARS
15.5017 g., 0.9990 Gold 0.4979 oz. AGW **Ruler:** Elizabeth II
Obv: Crowned head right, denomination below **Rev:** Two
kangaroos, date below

Date	Mintage	F	VF	XF	Unc	BU
1995 Proof	300	Value: 500				
1996	100,000	—	—	—	BV+7%	—
1996 (s) Proof	13,000	Value: 485				
1996 (l) Proof	3,000	Value: 485				
	Note: In Proof sets only					
1996 (f) Proof	13,000	Value: 485				

KM# 275.2 50 DOLLARS
15.5017 g., 0.9990 Gold 0.4979 oz. AGW **Ruler:** Elizabeth II
Obv: Crowned head right, denomination below **Rev:** Two kangaroos, date below **Edge:** Reeded and inscribed with date and serial number

Date	Mintage	F	VF	XF	Unc	BU
1996 Proof	500	Value: 485				

KM# 341 50 DOLLARS
15.5017 g., 0.9990 Gold 0.4979 oz. AGW **Ruler:** Elizabeth II
Obv: Crowned head right, denomination below **Rev:** Kangaroo bounding right

Date	Mintage	F	VF	XF	Unc	BU
1996 (p) Proof	400	Value: 600				
Note: In Proof sets only						
1997	100,000	—	—	—	—	450
1997 Proof	—	Value: 485				
1997 (f) Proof	13,000	Value: 485				
1997 (I) Proof	10,000	Value: 485				
Note: In Proof sets only						
1997 (s) Proof	13,000	Value: 485				

KM# 451 50 DOLLARS
15.5940 g., 0.9990 Gold 0.5008 oz. AGW **Ruler:** Elizabeth II
Obv: Crowned head right, denomination below **Rev:** Kangaroo facing left **Edge:** Reeded

Date	Mintage	F	VF	XF	Unc	BU
1999	100,000	—	—	—	—	485

KM# 467 50 DOLLARS
15.5940 g., 0.9990 Gold 0.5008 oz. AGW **Ruler:** Elizabeth II
Obv: Crowned head right, denomination below **Rev:** Two kangaroos bounding left **Edge:** Reeded

Date	Mintage	F	VF	XF	Unc	BU
2000	—	—	—	—	—	485

KM# 121 100 DOLLARS
31.1035 g., 0.9990 Gold 0.9990 oz. AGW **Ruler:** Elizabeth II
Obv: Crowned head right, denomination below **Rev:** Red kangaroo bounding left, date below

Date	Mintage	F	VF	XF	Unc	BU
1989 Proof	2,200	Value: 975				
1990	—	—	—	—	BV+4%	—

KM# 144 100 DOLLARS
31.1035 g., 0.9990 Gold 0.9990 oz. AGW **Ruler:** Elizabeth II
Rev: Gray kangaroo standing looking left, date below

Date	Mintage	F	VF	XF	Unc	BU
1990 Proof	8,000	Value: 975				
1991	250,000	—	—	—	BV+4%	—

KM# 169 100 DOLLARS
31.1035 g., 0.9990 Gold 0.9990 oz. AGW **Ruler:** Elizabeth II
Obv: Crowned head right, denomination below **Rev:** Common wallaroo on all fours facing right, date below

---

Date	Mintage	F	VF	XF	Unc	BU
1991 Proof	3,000	Value: 975				
1992	250,000	—	—	—	BV+4%	—

KM# 393 100 DOLLARS
31.1035 g., 0.9990 Gold 0.9990 oz. AGW **Ruler:** Elizabeth II
Obv: Crowned head right, denomination below **Rev:** Nail-tailed wallaby

Date	Mintage	F	VF	XF	Unc	BU
1992 Proof	784	Value: 975				
1993	—	—	—	—	BV+4%	—

KM# 237 100 DOLLARS
31.1035 g., 0.9990 Gold 0.9990 oz. AGW **Ruler:** Elizabeth II
Obv: Crowned head right, denomination below **Rev:** Whiptail wallaby

Date	Mintage	F	VF	XF	Unc	BU
1993 Proof	—	Value: 985				
1993 (f) Proof	150	Value: 1,000				
1994	—	—	—	—	BV+4%	—

KM# 245 100 DOLLARS
31.1035 g., 0.9990 Gold 0.9990 oz. AGW **Ruler:** Elizabeth II
Obv: Crowned head right, denomination below **Rev:** Red kangaroo facing forward, date below

Date	Mintage	F	VF	XF	Unc	BU
1994 Proof	—	Value: 975				
1995	350,000	—	—	—	BV+4%	—

KM# 276 100 DOLLARS
31.1035 g., 0.9990 Gold 0.9990 oz. AGW **Ruler:** Elizabeth II **Obv:** Crowned head right, denomination below **Rev:** Two kangaroos

Date	Mintage	F	VF	XF	Unc	BU
1995 (ww) Proof	600	Value: 985				
1995 Proof	300	Value: 1,000				
1996	350,000	—	—	—	BV+4%	—

KM# 342 100 DOLLARS
31.1035 g., 0.9990 Gold 0.9990 oz. AGW **Ruler:** Elizabeth II
Obv: Crowned head right, denomination below **Rev:** Kangaroo bounding right

Date	Mintage	F	VF	XF	Unc	BU
1996 (p) Proof	—	Value: 975				
Note: In Proof sets only						
1997	350,000	—	—	—	BV+4%	—
1997 Proof	—	Value: 975				

KM# 452 100 DOLLARS
31.1035 g., 0.9990 Gold 0.9990 oz. AGW **Ruler:** Elizabeth II
Obv: Crowned head right, denomination below **Rev:** Kangaroo facing left **Edge:** Reeded

Date	Mintage	F	VF	XF	Unc	BU
1999	350,000	—	—	—	BV+4%	—

KM# 468 100 DOLLARS
31.1035 g., 0.9990 Gold 0.9990 oz. AGW **Ruler:** Elizabeth II
Obv: Crowned head right, denomination below **Rev:** Two kangaroos bounding left, date below **Edge:** Reeded

Date	Mintage	F	VF	XF	Unc	BU
2000	—	—	—	—	—	BV+4%

KM# 182 200 DOLLARS
62.2140 g., 0.9990 Gold 1.9981 oz. AGW **Ruler:** Elizabeth II
Obv: Crowned head right, denomination below **Rev:** Red kangaroo leaping left, date below

---

Date	Mintage	F	VF	XF	Unc	BU
1992	—	—	—	—	BV+4%	—
1994 Prooflike	—	—	—	—	BV+4%	—
1995	—	—	—	—	BV+4%	—
1996	—	—	—	—	BV+4%	—
1997	—	—	—	—	BV+4%	—

KM# 394 200 DOLLARS
62.2140 g., 0.9999 Gold 1.9999 oz. AGW **Ruler:** Elizabeth II **Obv:** Crowned head right, denomination below **Rev:** Nail-tailed wallaby

Date	Mintage	F	VF	XF	Unc	BU
1992 Proof	152	Value: 1,950				

KM# 238 200 DOLLARS
62.2140 g., 0.9999 Gold 1.9999 oz. AGW **Ruler:** Elizabeth II **Obv:** Crowned head right, denomination below **Rev:** Whiptail wallaby

Date	Mintage	F	VF	XF	Unc	BU
1993 Proof	—	Value: 2,150				

KM# 246 200 DOLLARS
62.2140 g., 0.9999 Gold 1.9999 oz. AGW **Ruler:** Elizabeth II **Obv:** Crowned head right, denomination below **Rev:** Red kangaroo

Date	Mintage	F	VF	XF	Unc	BU
1994 Proof	325	Value: 2,200				

KM# 277 200 DOLLARS
62.2140 g., 0.9999 Gold 1.9999 oz. AGW **Ruler:** Elizabeth II
Obv: Crowned head right, denomination below **Rev:** Two kangaroos, date below

Date	Mintage	F	VF	XF	Unc	BU
1995 Proof	100	Value: 2,250				

KM# 150 500 DOLLARS
62.2140 g., 0.9990 Gold 1.9981 oz. AGW **Ruler:** Elizabeth II
Obv: Crowned head right, denomination below **Rev:** Red kangaroo facing left

Date	Mintage	F	VF	XF	Unc	BU
1991	—	—	—	—	BV+4%	—
1991 Proof	491	Value: 2,150				

KM# 395 1000 DOLLARS
311.0670 g., 0.9990 Gold 9.9906 oz. AGW **Ruler:** Elizabeth II
Obv: Crowned head right, denomination below **Rev:** Nail-tailed wallaby

Date	Mintage	F	VF	XF	Unc	BU
1992 Proof	40	Value: 10,000				

KM# 239 1000 DOLLARS
311.0670 g., 0.9999 Gold 9.9996 oz. AGW **Ruler:** Elizabeth II
Obv: Crowned head right, denomination below **Rev:** Red kangaroo

Date	Mintage	F	VF	XF	Unc	BU
1993 Proof	—	Value: 10,000				

KM# 247 1000 DOLLARS
311.0670 g., 0.9999 Gold 9.9996 oz. AGW **Ruler:** Elizabeth II
Obv: Crowned head right, denomination below **Rev:** Kangaroo in diamond shape

Date	Mintage	F	VF	XF	Unc	BU
1994 Proof	—	Value: 8,500				

KM# 183 1000 DOLLARS
311.0670 g., 0.9999 Gold 9.9996 oz. AGW **Ruler:** Elizabeth II
Obv: Crowned head right, denomination below **Rev:** Red kangaroo

Date	Mintage	F	VF	XF	Unc	BU
1995	—	—	—	—	BV+3%	—
1996	—	—	—	—	BV+3%	—
1997	—	—	—	—	BV+3%	—

KM# 454 1000 DOLLARS
311.3170 g., 0.9990 Gold 9.9986 oz. AGW **Ruler:** Elizabeth II
Obv: Crowned head right, denomination below **Rev:** Red kangaroo bounding left **Edge:** Reeded

Date	Mintage	F	VF	XF	Unc	BU
1999	—	—	—	—	—	10,000

KM# 151 2500 DOLLARS
311.0670 g., 0.9990 Gold 9.9906 oz. AGW **Ruler:** Elizabeth II
Obv: Crowned head right, denomination below **Rev:** Red kangaroo

Date	Mintage	F	VF	XF	Unc	BU
1991	—	—	—	—	BV+3%	—
1991 Proof	124	Value: 10,000				

KM# 184 3000 DOLLARS
1000.1000 g., 0.9999 Gold 32.149 oz. AGW **Ruler:** Elizabeth II
Obv: Crowned head right, denomination below **Rev:** Red kangaroo

Date	Mintage	F	VF	XF	Unc	BU
1992	—	—	—	—	BV+3%	—
1992 Proof	25	Value: 32,000				
1995	—	—	—	—	BV+4%	—
1996	—	—	—	—	BV+3%	—
1997	—	—	—	—	BV+3%	—

KM# 396 3000 DOLLARS
1000.1000 g., 0.9999 Platinum 32.149 oz. APW
Ruler: Elizabeth II **Obv:** Crowned head right, denomination below **Rev:** Nail-tailed wallaby

Date	Mintage	F	VF	XF	Unc	BU
1992 Proof	25	Value: 65,000				

KM# 240 3000 DOLLARS
1000.1000 g., 0.9999 Gold 32.149 oz. AGW **Ruler:** Elizabeth II **Obv:** Crowned head right, denomination below **Rev:** Whiptail wallaby

Date	Mintage	F	VF	XF	Unc	BU
1993 Proof	—	Value: 32,000				

KM# 248 3000 DOLLARS
1000.1000 g., 0.9999 Gold 32.149 oz. AGW **Ruler:** Elizabeth II **Obv:** Crowned head right, denomination below **Rev:** Kangaroo in diamond shape

Date	Mintage	F	VF	XF	Unc	BU
1994 Proof	—	Value: 32,000				

KM# 455 3000 DOLLARS
1000.3500 g., 0.9990 Gold 32.128 oz. AGW **Ruler:** Elizabeth II **Obv:** Crowned head right, denomination below **Rev:** Red kangaroo bounding left **Edge:** Reeded

Date	Mintage	F	VF	XF	Unc	BU
1999	—	—	—	—	—	31,500
2000	—	—	—	—	—	31,500

KM# 152 10000 DOLLARS
1000.1000 g., 0.9990 Gold 32.120 oz. AGW **Ruler:** Elizabeth II **Obv:** Crowned head right, denomination below **Rev:** Red kangaroo leaping left, date below

Date	Mintage	F	VF	XF	Unc	BU
1991	—	—	—	—	BV+3%	—
1991 Proof	95	Value: 32,500				

GOLD BULLION - NUGGET

KM# 89 15 DOLLARS
3.1103 g., 0.9990 Gold 0.0999 oz. AGW **Ruler:** Elizabeth II **Obv:** Crowned head right, denomination below **Rev:** Little Hero, date below

Date	Mintage	F	VF	XF	Unc	BU
1986P Proof	15,000	Value: 100				
1987	266,000	—	—	—	BV+12%	—
1988	104,000	—	—	—	BV+12%	—
1989	—	—	—	—	BV+12%	—

KM# 95 15 DOLLARS
3.1103 g., 0.9990 Gold 0.0999 oz. AGW **Ruler:** Elizabeth II **Obv:** Crowned head right, denomination below **Rev:** Golden Aussie, date below

Date	Mintage	F	VF	XF	Unc	BU
1987P Proof	15,000	Value: 100				

KM# 104 15 DOLLARS
3.1103 g., 0.9990 Gold 0.0999 oz. AGW **Ruler:** Elizabeth II **Obv:** Crowned head right, denomination below **Rev:** Jubilee Nugget, date below

Date	Mintage	F	VF	XF	Unc	BU
1988P Proof	Est. 10,000	Value: 100				

KM# 90 25 DOLLARS
7.7508 g., 0.9990 Gold 0.2489 oz. AGW **Ruler:** Elizabeth II **Obv:** Crowned head right, denomination below **Rev:** Golden Eagle, date below

Date	Mintage	F	VF	XF	Unc	BU
1986P Proof	15,000	Value: 250				
1987	233,000	—	—	—	BV+10%	—
1988	75,000	—	—	—	BV+10%	—
1989	—	—	—	—	BV+10%	—

KM# 96 25 DOLLARS
7.7508 g., 0.9990 Gold 0.2489 oz. AGW **Ruler:** Elizabeth II **Obv:** Crowned head right, denomination below **Rev:** Father's Day, date below

Date	Mintage	F	VF	XF	Unc	BU
1987P Proof	15,000	Value: 250				

KM# 105 25 DOLLARS
7.7508 g., 0.9990 Gold 0.2489 oz. AGW **Ruler:** Elizabeth II **Obv:** Crowned head right, denomination below **Rev:** Ruby Well Nugget, date below

Date	Mintage	F	VF	XF	Unc	BU
1988P Proof	Est. 10,000	Value: 250				

KM# 91 50 DOLLARS
15.5017 g., 0.9990 Gold 0.4979 oz. AGW **Ruler:** Elizabeth II **Obv:** Crowned head right, denomination below **Rev:** Hand of Faith, date below

Date	Mintage	F	VF	XF	Unc	BU
1986P Proof	15,000	Value: 500				
1987	188,000	—	—	—	BV+7%	—
1988	75,000	—	—	—	BV+7%	—
1989	100,000	—	—	—	BV+7%	—

KM# 97 50 DOLLARS
15.5017 g., 0.9990 Gold 0.4979 oz. AGW **Ruler:** Elizabeth II **Obv:** Crowned head right, denomination below **Rev:** Bobby Dazzler, date below

Date	Mintage	F	VF	XF	Unc	BU
1987P Proof	15,000	Value: 500				

KM# 106 50 DOLLARS
15.5017 g., 0.9990 Gold 0.4979 oz. AGW **Ruler:** Elizabeth II **Obv:** Crowned head right, denomination below **Rev:** Welcome nugget, date below

Date	Mintage	F	VF	XF	Unc	BU
1988P Proof	Est. 10,000	Value: 500				

KM# 92 100 DOLLARS
31.1035 g., 0.9990 Gold 0.9990 oz. AGW **Ruler:** Elizabeth II **Obv:** Crowned head right, denomination below **Rev:** Welcome Stranger, date below

Date	Mintage	F	VF	XF	Unc	BU
1986P Proof	15,000	Value: 975				
1987	259,000	—	—	—	BV+4%	—
1988	116,000	—	—	—	BV+4%	—
1989	—	—	—	—	BV+4%	—

KM# 98 100 DOLLARS
31.1035 g., 0.9990 Gold 0.9990 oz. AGW **Ruler:** Elizabeth II **Obv:** Crowned head right, denomination below **Rev:** Poseidon, date below

Date	Mintage	F	VF	XF	Unc	BU
1987P Proof	15,000	Value: 975				

KM# 107 100 DOLLARS
31.1035 g., 0.9990 Gold 0.9990 oz. AGW **Ruler:** Elizabeth II **Obv:** Crowned head right, denomination below **Rev:** Pride of Australia nugget

Date	Mintage	F	VF	XF	Unc	BU
1988P Proof	Est. 10,000	Value: 975				

PLATINUM BULLION - KOALA

KM# 122 5 DOLLARS
1.5710 g., 0.9990 Platinum 0.0505 oz. APW **Ruler:** Elizabeth II **Obv:** Crowned head right, denomination below **Rev:** Koala

Date	Mintage	F	VF	XF	Unc	BU
1989 Proof	2,400	Value: 100				
1990 Proof	—	Value: 100				

KM# 145 5 DOLLARS
1.5710 g., 0.9990 Platinum 0.0505 oz. APW **Ruler:** Elizabeth II **Obv:** Crowned head right, denomination below **Rev:** Koala on tree limb facing right, date below

Date	Mintage	F	VF	XF	Unc	BU
1990 Proof	2,500	Value: 110				
1991	20,000	—	—	—	BV+ 35%	—
1991 Proof	1,000	Value: 110				

KM# 170 5 DOLLARS
1.5710 g., 0.9990 Platinum 0.0505 oz. APW **Ruler:** Elizabeth II **Subject:** Koala **Obv:** Crowned head right, denomination below **Rev:** Koala sitting facing in crook of tree

Date	Mintage	F	VF	XF	Unc	BU
1992	20,000	—	—	—	BV+ 35%	—

KM# 191 5 DOLLARS
1.5710 g., 0.9990 Platinum 0.0505 oz. APW **Ruler:** Elizabeth II **Obv:** Crowned head right, denomination below **Rev:** Koala facing left, sitting on branch, date below

Date	Mintage	F	VF	XF	Unc	BU
1993	Est. 20,000	—	—	—	BV+ 35%	—

KM# 249 5 DOLLARS
1.5710 g., 0.9990 Platinum 0.0505 oz. APW **Ruler:** Elizabeth II
Obv: Crowned head right, denomination below **Rev:** Koala mother and baby on branch facing, date below

Date	Mintage	F	VF	XF	Unc	BU
1994	20,000	—	—	—	BV+35%	—

KM# 278 5 DOLLARS
1.5710 g., 0.9990 Platinum 0.0505 oz. APW **Ruler:** Elizabeth II
Obv: Crowned head right, denomination below **Rev:** Koala in fork of tree facing, date below

Date	Mintage	F	VF	XF	Unc	BU
1994 Proof	—	Value: 110				
1995	—	—	—	—	BV+35%	—

KM# 283 5 DOLLARS
1.5710 g., 0.9990 Platinum 0.0505 oz. APW **Ruler:** Elizabeth II
Obv: Crowned head right, denomination below **Rev:** Baby koala on branch right, facing, date below

Date	Mintage	F	VF	XF	Unc	BU
1995 Proof	200	Value: 110				
1996	20,000	—	—	—	BV+35%	—

KM# 344 5 DOLLARS
1.5710 g., 0.9995 Platinum 0.0505 oz. APW **Ruler:** Elizabeth II
Subject: Koala Bullion **Obv:** Crowned head right, denomination below **Rev:** Cuddling koalas

Date	Mintage	F	VF	XF	Unc	BU
1997	20,000	—	—	—	BV+ 35%	—
1997 Proof	—	Value: 110				

KM# 456 5 DOLLARS
1.5710 g., 0.9990 Platinum 0.0505 oz. APW **Ruler:** Elizabeth II
Obv: Crowned head right, denomination below **Rev:** Koala on log

Date	Mintage	F	VF	XF	Unc	BU
1999	20,000	—	—	—	BV+35%	—

KM# 469 5 DOLLARS
1.5710 g., 0.9990 Platinum 0.0505 oz. APW **Ruler:** Elizabeth II
Obv: Crowned head right, denomination below **Rev:** Seated koala

Date	Mintage	F	VF	XF	Unc	BU
2000	—	—	—	—	BV+35%	—

KM# 108 15 DOLLARS
3.1370 g., 0.9990 Platinum 0.1008 oz. APW **Ruler:** Elizabeth II
Obv: Crowned head right, denomination below **Rev:** Koala sitting facing

Date	Mintage	F	VF	XF	Unc	BU
1988	—	—	—	—	BV+15%	—
1989 Proof	—	Value: 140				

KM# 123 15 DOLLARS
3.1370 g., 0.9990 Platinum 0.1008 oz. APW **Ruler:** Elizabeth II
Obv: Crowned head right, denomination below **Rev:** Koala on tree branch with cub on her back

Date	Mintage	F	VF	XF	Unc	BU
1989 Proof	2,400	Value: 200				
1990 Proof	—	Value: 200				

KM# 146 15 DOLLARS
3.1370 g., 0.9990 Platinum 0.1008 oz. APW **Ruler:** Elizabeth II
Subject: Koala **Obv:** Crowned head right, denomination below **Rev:** Koala on branch facing left, looking right, date below

Date	Mintage	F	VF	XF	Unc	BU
1990 Proof	2,500	Value: 200				
1991	20,000	—	—	—	BV+15%	—
1991 Proof	1,000	Value: 200				

KM# 171 15 DOLLARS
3.1370 g., 0.9990 Platinum 0.1008 oz. APW **Ruler:** Elizabeth II
Subject: Koala Bullion **Obv:** Crowned head right, denomination below **Rev:** Koala in crook of tree facing

Date	Mintage	F	VF	XF	Unc	BU
1992	20,000	—	—	—	BV+ 15%	—

KM# 192 15 DOLLARS
3.1370 g., 0.9990 Platinum 0.1008 oz. APW **Ruler:** Elizabeth II
Obv: Crowned head right, denomination below **Rev:** Koala climbing tree

Date	Mintage	F	VF	XF	Unc	BU
1993	Est. 20,000	—	—	—	BV+15%	—

KM# 250 15 DOLLARS
3.1370 g., 0.9990 Platinum 0.1008 oz. APW **Ruler:** Elizabeth II
Obv: Crowned head right, denomination below **Rev:** Koala mother and baby facing forward, date below

Date	Mintage	F	VF	XF	Unc	BU
1994	20,000	—	—	—	BV+15%	—

KM# 279 15 DOLLARS
3.1370 g., 0.9990 Platinum 0.1008 oz. APW **Ruler:** Elizabeth II
Obv: Crowned head right, denomination below **Rev:** Koala in fork of tree facing forward, date below

Date	Mintage	F	VF	XF	Unc	BU
1994 Proof	—	Value: 200				
1995	—	—	—	—	BV+15%	—

KM# 284 15 DOLLARS
3.1370 g., 0.9990 Platinum 0.1008 oz. APW **Ruler:** Elizabeth II
Obv: Crowned head right, denomination below **Rev:** Baby koala on branch, right facing forward, date below

Date	Mintage	F	VF	XF	Unc	BU
1995 Proof	800	Value: 200				
1996	—	—	—	—	BV+15%	—

KM# 345 15 DOLLARS
3.1103 g., 0.9995 Platinum 0.0999 oz. APW **Ruler:** Elizabeth II
Subject: Koalas **Obv:** Crowned head right, denomination below **Rev:** Cuddling koalas

Date	Mintage	F	VF	XF	Unc	BU
1997	20,000	—	—	—	BV+15%	—
1997 Proof	—	Value: 200				

KM# 457 15 DOLLARS
3.1370 g., 0.9990 Platinum 0.1008 oz. APW **Ruler:** Elizabeth II
Obv: Crowned head right, denomination below **Rev:** Koala on log facing forward, date below **Edge:** Reeded

Date	Mintage	F	VF	XF	Unc	BU
1999	20,000	—	—	—	BV+15%	—

KM# 470 15 DOLLARS
3.1370 g., 0.9990 Platinum 0.1008 oz. APW **Ruler:** Elizabeth II
Obv: Crowned head right, denomination below **Rev:** Seated koala **Edge:** Reeded

Date	Mintage	F	VF	XF	Unc	BU
2000	—	—	—	—	BV+15%	—

KM# 109 25 DOLLARS
7.8150 g., 0.9990 Platinum 0.2510 oz. APW **Ruler:** Elizabeth II
Obv: Crowned head right, denomination below **Rev:** Seated koala facing

Date	Mintage	F	VF	XF	Unc	BU
1988	—	—	—	—	BV+10%	—
1989 Proof	—	Value: 500				

KM# 124 25 DOLLARS
7.7508 g., 0.9990 Platinum 0.2489 oz. APW **Ruler:** Elizabeth II
Obv: Crowned head right, denomination below **Rev:** Koala bear with cub on its back sitting on branch

Date	Mintage	F	VF	XF	Unc	BU
1989 Proof	2,400	Value: 375				
1990 Proof	—	Value: 375				

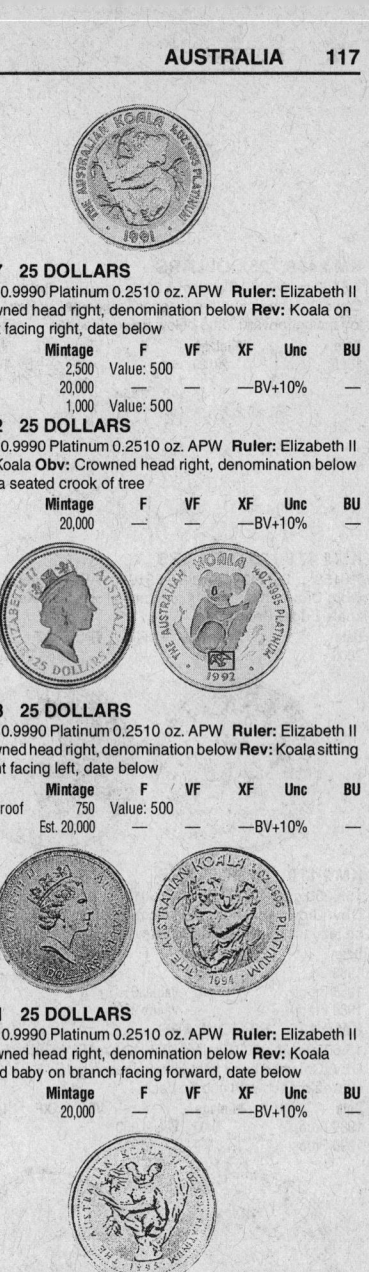

KM# 147 25 DOLLARS
7.8150 g., 0.9990 Platinum 0.2510 oz. APW **Ruler:** Elizabeth II
Obv: Crowned head right, denomination below **Rev:** Koala on branch left facing right, date below

Date	Mintage	F	VF	XF	Unc	BU
1990 Proof	2,500	Value: 500				
1991	20,000	—	—	—	BV+10%	—
1991 Proof	1,000	Value: 500				

KM# 172 25 DOLLARS
7.8150 g., 0.9990 Platinum 0.2510 oz. APW **Ruler:** Elizabeth II
Subject: Koala **Obv:** Crowned head right, denomination below **Rev:** Koala seated crook of tree

Date	Mintage	F	VF	XF	Unc	BU
1992	20,000	—	—	—	BV+10%	—

KM# 193 25 DOLLARS
7.8150 g., 0.9990 Platinum 0.2510 oz. APW **Ruler:** Elizabeth II
Obv: Crowned head right, denomination below **Rev:** Koala sitting in tree right facing left, date below

Date	Mintage	F	VF	XF	Unc	BU
1992 (ae) Proof	750	Value: 500				
1993	Est. 20,000	—	—	—	BV+10%	—

KM# 251 25 DOLLARS
7.8150 g., 0.9990 Platinum 0.2510 oz. APW **Ruler:** Elizabeth II
Obv: Crowned head right, denomination below **Rev:** Koala mother and baby on branch facing forward, date below

Date	Mintage	F	VF	XF	Unc	BU
1994	20,000	—	—	—	BV+10%	—

KM# 280 25 DOLLARS
7.8150 g., 0.9990 Platinum 0.2510 oz. APW **Ruler:** Elizabeth II
Obv: Crowned head right, denomination below **Rev:** Koala in fork of tree facing forward, date below

Date	Mintage	F	VF	XF	Unc	BU
1994 Proof	—	Value: 500				
1995	—	—	—	—	BV+10%	—

KM# 285 25 DOLLARS
7.8150 g., 0.9990 Platinum 0.2510 oz. APW **Ruler:** Elizabeth II
Obv: Crowned head right, denomination below **Rev:** Baby koala on branch right facing forward, date below

Date	Mintage	F	VF	XF	Unc	BU
1995 Proof	200	Value: 500				
1996	20,000	—	—	—	BV+10%	—

KM# 346 25 DOLLARS
7.7508 g., 0.9995 Platinum 0.2491 oz. APW **Ruler:** Elizabeth II
Subject: Koala Bullion **Obv:** Crowned head right, denomination below **Rev:** Cuddling koalas

Date	Mintage	F	VF	XF	Unc	BU
1997	20,000	—	—	—	BV+10%	—
1997 Proof	—	Value: 500				

KM# 458   25 DOLLARS
7.8150 g., 0.9990 Platinum 0.2510 oz. APW **Ruler:** Elizabeth II
Obv: Crowned head right, denomination below **Rev:** Koala on
log facing forward, date below **Edge:** Reeded

Date	Mintage	F	VF	XF	Unc	BU
1999	20,000	—	—	—	BV+10%	—

KM# 471   25 DOLLARS
7.8150 g., 0.9990 Platinum 0.2510 oz. APW **Ruler:** Elizabeth II
Obv: Crowned head right, denomination below **Rev:** Seated
koala **Edge:** Reeded

Date	Mintage	F	VF	XF	Unc	BU
2000	—	—	—	—	BV+10%	—

KM# 110   50 DOLLARS
15.6050 g., 0.9990 Platinum 0.5012 oz. APW **Ruler:** Elizabeth II
Obv: Crowned head right, denomination below **Rev:** Koala bear
on log facing forward, date below

Date	Mintage	F	VF	XF	Unc	BU
1988	—	—	—	—	BV+7%	—
1988 Proof	12,000	Value: 950				
1989 Proof	—	Value: 950				

KM# 125   50 DOLLARS
15.6050 g., 0.9990 Platinum 0.5012 oz. APW **Ruler:** Elizabeth II
Obv: Crowned head right, denomination below **Rev:** Koala bear
on tree branch with cub on back

Date	Mintage	F	VF	XF	Unc	BU
1989 Proof	2,400	Value: 950				
1990 Proof	8,000	Value: 950				

KM# 148   50 DOLLARS
15.6050 g., 0.9990 Platinum 0.5012 oz. APW **Ruler:** Elizabeth II
Obv: Crowned head right, denomination below **Rev:** Koala bear
in tree left facing right, date below

Date	Mintage	F	VF	XF	Unc	BU
1990 Proof	5,500	Value: 950				
1991	20,000	—	—	—	BV+7%	—
1991 Proof	2,000	Value: 950				

KM# 173   50 DOLLARS
15.6050 g., 0.9990 Platinum 0.5012 oz. APW **Ruler:** Elizabeth II
Subject: Koala **Obv:** Crowned head right, denomination below
Rev: Koala in crook of tree facing

Date	Mintage	F	VF	XF	Unc	BU
1992	20,000	—	—	—	BV+7%	—

KM# 194   50 DOLLARS
15.6050 g., 0.9990 Platinum 0.5012 oz. APW **Ruler:** Elizabeth II
Obv: Crowned head right, denomination below **Rev:** Koala sitting
in tree right, facing left, date below

Date	Mintage	F	VF	XF	Unc	BU
1993	Est. 20,000	—	—	—	BV+7%	—

KM# 252   50 DOLLARS
15.6050 g., 0.9990 Platinum 0.5012 oz. APW **Ruler:** Elizabeth II
Obv: Crowned head right, denomination below **Rev:** Koala
mother and baby in tree facing forward, date below

Date	Mintage	F	VF	XF	Unc	BU
1994	5,000	—	—	—	BV+7%	—

KM# 281   50 DOLLARS
15.6050 g., 0.9990 Platinum 0.5012 oz. APW **Ruler:** Elizabeth II
Obv: Crowned head right, denomination below **Rev:** Koala in
fork of tree left, facing forward

Date	Mintage	F	VF	XF	Unc	BU
1994 Proof	—	Value: 950				
1995	—	—	—	—	BV+7%	—

KM# 286   50 DOLLARS
15.6050 g., 0.9990 Platinum 0.5012 oz. APW **Ruler:** Elizabeth II
Obv: Crowned head right, denomination below **Rev:** Baby koala
on branch right, facing forward, date below

Date	Mintage	F	VF	XF	Unc	BU
1995 (ww) Proof	300	Value: 950				
Note: In Proof sets only						
1995 Proof	450	Value: 950				
1996	5,000	—	—	—	BV+7%	—

KM# 347   50 DOLLARS
15.5518 g., 0.9995 Platinum 0.4997 oz. APW **Ruler:** Elizabeth II
Subject: Koala Bullion **Obv:** Crowned head right, denomination
below **Rev:** Cuddling koalas

Date	Mintage	F	VF	XF	Unc	BU
1997	5,000	—	—	—	BV+7%	—
1997 Proof	—	Value: 950				

KM# 459   50 DOLLARS
15.6050 g., 0.9990 Platinum 0.5012 oz. APW **Ruler:** Elizabeth II
Obv: Crowned head right, denomination below **Rev:** Koala on
log left, facing forward **Edge:** Reeded

Date	Mintage	F	VF	XF	Unc	BU
1999	5,000	—	—	—	BV+7%	—

KM# 472   50 DOLLARS
15.6050 g., 0.9990 Platinum 0.5012 oz. APW **Ruler:** Elizabeth II
Obv: Crowned head right, denomination below **Rev:** Seated
koala **Edge:** Reeded

Date	Mintage	F	VF	XF	Unc	BU
2000	—	—	—	—	BV+7%	—

KM# 111   100 DOLLARS
31.1850 g., 0.9990 Platinum 1.0016 oz. APW **Ruler:** Elizabeth II
Obv: Crowned head right, denomination below **Rev:** Seated
Koala facing forward, date below

Date	Mintage	F	VF	XF	Unc	BU
1988	—	—	—	—	BV+4%	—
1989 Proof	—	Value: 1,850				

KM# 126   100 DOLLARS
31.1850 g., 0.9990 Platinum 1.0016 oz. APW **Ruler:** Elizabeth II
Obv: Crowned head right, denomination below **Rev:** Koala with
baby on branch left, facing right

Date	Mintage	F	VF	XF	Unc	BU
1989 Proof	2,400	Value: 1,850				
1990 Proof	—	Value: 1,850				

KM# 149   100 DOLLARS
31.1850 g., 0.9990 Platinum 1.0016 oz. APW **Ruler:** Elizabeth II
Obv: Crowned head right, denomination below **Rev:** Koala bear
in tree left, facing right

Date	Mintage	F	VF	XF	Unc	BU
1990 Proof	3,500	Value: 1,850				
1991	75,000	—	—	—	BV+4%	—
1991 Proof	1,000	Value: 1,850				

KM# 174   100 DOLLARS
31.1850 g., 0.9990 Platinum 1.0016 oz. APW **Ruler:** Elizabeth II
Obv: Crowned head right, denomination below **Rev:** Koala in
fork of tree facing, date below

Date	Mintage	F	VF	XF	Unc	BU
1992	75,000	—	—	—	BV+4%	—

KM# 195   100 DOLLARS
31.1850 g., 0.9990 Platinum 1.0016 oz. APW **Ruler:** Elizabeth II
Obv: Crowned head right, denomination below **Rev:** Koala in
fork of tree right, facing left, date below

Date	Mintage	F	VF	XF	Unc	BU
1993	Est. 80,000	—	—	—	BV+4%	—

KM# 253 100 DOLLARS
31.1850 g., 0.9990 Platinum 1.0016 oz. APW **Ruler:** Elizabeth II
Obv: Crowned head right, denomination below **Rev:** Koala
mother and baby on branch facing forward. date below

Date	Mintage	F	VF	XF	Unc	BU
1994 Prooflike	100,000	—	—	—	BV+4%	—

KM# 282 100 DOLLARS
31.1850 g., 0.9990 Platinum 1.0016 oz. APW **Ruler:** Elizabeth II
Obv: Crowned head of Queen Elizabeth II, right **Rev:** Koala in
fork of tree left, facing forward, date below

Date	Mintage	F	VF	XF	Unc	BU
1994 Proof	—	Value: 1,850				
1995	—	—	—	—	BV+4%	—

KM# 287 100 DOLLARS
31.1850 g., 0.9990 Platinum 1.0016 oz. APW **Ruler:** Elizabeth II
Obv: Crowned head right, denomination below **Rev:** Baby koala
on branch right, date below

Date	Mintage	F	VF	XF	Unc	BU
1995 Proof	200	Value: 1,850				
1996	100,000	—	—	—	BV+4%	—

KM# 348 100 DOLLARS
31.1850 g., 0.9990 Platinum 1.0016 oz. APW **Ruler:** Elizabeth II
Subject: Koala Bullion **Obv:** Crowned head right, denomination
below **Rev:** Cuddling koalas

Date	Mintage	F	VF	XF	Unc	BU
1997	100,000	—	—	—	BV+4%	—
1997 Proof	—	Value: 1,850				

KM# 460 100 DOLLARS
31.1850 g., 0.9990 Platinum 1.0016 oz. APW **Ruler:** Elizabeth II
Obv: Crowned head right, denomination below **Rev:** Koala on
log left, date below **Edge:** Reeded

Date	Mintage	F	VF	XF	Unc	BU
1999	100,000	—	—	—	BV+4%	—

KM# 473 100 DOLLARS
31.1850 g., 0.9990 Platinum 1.0016 oz. APW **Ruler:** Elizabeth II
Obv: Crowned head right, denomination below **Rev:** Seated
koala with branches left, date below **Edge:** Reeded

Date	Mintage	F	VF	XF	Unc	BU
2000	—	—	—	—	BV+4%	—

KM# 185 200 DOLLARS
62.2140 g., 0.9995 Platinum 1.9991 oz. APW **Ruler:** Elizabeth II
Obv: Crowned head right, denomination below **Rev:** Koala bear
in tree left, looking right, date below

Date	Mintage	F	VF	XF	Unc	BU
1992	—	—	—	—	BV+4%	—
1992 Proof	—	Value: 3,850				
1996	—	—	—	—	BV+4%	—

KM# 196 200 DOLLARS
62.2140 g., 0.9995 Platinum 1.9991 oz. APW **Ruler:** Elizabeth II
Obv: Crowned head right, denomination below **Rev:** Koala bear
in tree left, looking right, date below

Date	Mintage	F	VF	XF	Unc	BU
1993	—	—	—	—	BV+4%	—
1994	—	—	—	—	BV+4%	—
1995	—	—	—	—	BV+4%	—
1997	—	—	—	—	BV+4%	—

KM# 254 200 DOLLARS
62.2140 g., 0.9995 Platinum 1.9991 oz. APW **Ruler:** Elizabeth II
Obv: Crowned head right, denomination below **Rev:** Koala with cub

Date	Mintage	F	VF	XF	Unc	BU
1994 Proof	—	Value: 3,850				

KM# 288 200 DOLLARS
62.2140 g., 0.9995 Platinum 1.9991 oz. APW **Ruler:** Elizabeth II
Obv: Crowned head right, denomination below **Rev:** Baby koala
on branch right, date below

Date	Mintage	F	VF	XF	Unc	BU
1995 Proof	100	Value: 3,850				

KM# 461 200 DOLLARS
62.3130 g., 0.9990 Platinum 2.0013 oz. APW **Ruler:** Elizabeth II
Obv: Crowned head right, denomination below **Rev:** Koala in
tree left, looking right, date below **Edge:** Reeded

Date	Mintage	F	VF	XF	Unc	BU
1999	—	—	—	—	BV+4%	—

KM# 157 500 DOLLARS
62.2140 g., 0.9990 Platinum 1.9981 oz. APW **Ruler:** Elizabeth II
Subject: Koala Bullion **Obv:** Crowned head right, denomination
below **Rev:** Koala in tree

Date	Mintage	F	VF	XF	Unc	BU
1991	—	—	—	—	BV+4%	—
1991 Proof	250	Value: 3,850				

KM# 186 1000 DOLLARS
311.0670 g., 0.9995 Platinum 9.9956 oz. APW **Ruler:** Elizabeth II
Obv: Crowned head right, denomination below **Rev:** Koala

Date	Mintage	F	VF	XF	Unc	BU
1992	—	—	—	—	BV+4%	—
1992 Proof	—	Value: 20,000				
1996	—	—	—	—	BV+4%	—

KM# 197 1000 DOLLARS
311.0670 g., 0.9995 Platinum 9.9956 oz. APW, 60.3 mm.
Ruler: Elizabeth II **Obv:** Crowned head right, denomination
below **Rev:** Koala on branch left, looking right, date below
Note: Illustration reduced.

Date	Mintage	F	VF	XF	Unc	BU
1993	—	—	—	—	BV+4%	—
1994	—	—	—	—	BV+4%	—
1995	—	—	—	—	BV+4%	—
1997	—	—	—	—	BV+4%	—

KM# 255 1000 DOLLARS
311.0670 g., 0.9995 Platinum 9.9956 oz. APW
Ruler: Elizabeth II **Obv:** Crowned head right, denomination
below **Rev:** Koala with cub

Date	Mintage	F	VF	XF	Unc	BU
1994	—	—	—	—	BV+4%	—

KM# 462 1000 DOLLARS
311.6910 g., 0.9990 Platinum 10.010 oz. APW
Ruler: Elizabeth II **Obv:** Crowned head right, denomination
below **Rev:** Koala in tree **Edge:** Reeded **Note:** Photo reduced.

Date	Mintage	F	VF	XF	Unc	BU
1999	—	—	—	—	BV+4%	—

KM# 158 2500 DOLLARS
311.0670 g., 0.9990 Platinum 9.9906 oz. APW
Ruler: Elizabeth II **Subject:** Koala Bullion **Obv:** Crowned head
right, denomination below **Rev:** Koala in tree

Date	Mintage	F	VF	XF	Unc	BU
1991	—	—	—	—	BV+4%	—
1991 Proof	100	Value: 20,000				

KM# 187 3000 DOLLARS
1000.1000 g., 0.9999 Platinum 32.149 oz. APW
Ruler: Elizabeth II **Obv:** Crowned head right, denomination
below **Rev:** Koala in tree, date below

Date	Mintage	F	VF	XF	Unc	BU
1992	—	—	—	—	BV+3.5%	—
1992 Proof	—	Value: 65,000				
1996	—	—	—	—	BV+3.5%	—

KM# 198 3000 DOLLARS
1000.1000 g., 0.9999 Platinum 32.149 oz. APW, 75.3 mm.
Ruler: Elizabeth II **Obv:** Crowned head right, denomination below **Rev:** Koala on tree branch left, looking right, date below **Note:** Illustration reduced.

Date	Mintage	F	VF	XF	Unc	BU
1993	—	—	—	—	BV+3.5%	
1994	—	—	—	—	BV+3.5%	
1995	—	—	—	—	BV+3.5%	
1997	—	—	—	—	BV+3.5%	

KM# 256 3000 DOLLARS
1000.1000 g., 0.9995 Platinum 32.136 oz. APW **Ruler:** Elizabeth II **Obv:** Crowned head right, denomination below **Rev:** Koala with cub

Date	Mintage	F	VF	XF	Unc	BU
1994	—	—	—	—	BV+3.5%	

KM# 463 3000 DOLLARS
1001.0000 g., 0.9990 Platinum 32.149 oz. APW **Ruler:** Elizabeth II **Obv:** Crowned head right, denomination below **Rev:** Koala in tree **Edge:** Reeded **Note:** Photo reduced.

Date	Mintage	F	VF	XF	Unc	BU
1999	—	—	—	—	BV+3.5%	

KM# 159 10000 DOLLARS
1000.1000 g., 0.9990 Platinum 32.120 oz. APW **Ruler:** Elizabeth II **Subject:** Koala Bullion **Obv:** Crowned head right, denomination below **Rev:** Koala

Date	Mintage	F	VF	XF	Unc	BU
1991	—	—	—	—	BV+3.5%	
1991 Proof	50	Value: 65,000				

TOKEN COINAGE
P.O.W.

WWI Liverpool (NSW)

KM# Tn-A1 THREEPENCE
Aluminum **Issuer:** WWI Liverpool (NSW) **Obv:** Double-headed eagle **Rev:** Large 3d

Date	Mintage	F	VF	XF	Unc	BU
ND	—	—	350	550	1,250	—

KM# Tn-B1 THREEPENCE
Aluminum **Issuer:** WWI Liverpool (NSW) **Obv:** Crown divides D - K **Rev:** Small 3d

Date	Mintage	F	VF	XF	Unc	BU
ND	—	—	450	750	1,500	—

TOKEN COINAGE
P.O.W.

WWII Internment Camp

KM# Tn1.1 PENNY
Brass **Issuer:** WWII Internment Camp **Obv:** Center hole with beads and wreath around, legend above and below **Obv. Leg.:** INTERNMENT / CAMPS **Rev:** Center hole with beads and wreath around, legend above and below **Rev. Leg.:** ONE / PENNY

Date	Mintage	F	VF	XF	Unc	BU
ND(1943)	—	40.00	50.00	75.00	125	—

KM# Tn1.1a PENNY
Copper-Nickel **Issuer:** WWII Internment Camp **Obv:** Center hole with beads and wreath around, legend above and below **Obv. Leg.:** INTERNMENT / CAMPS **Rev:** Center hole with beads and wreath around, legend above and below **Rev. Leg.:** ONE / PENNY **Note:** Spink Australia Sale Nov. 1981. Lot 666A $600.

Date	Mintage	F	VF	XF	Unc	BU
ND(1943)	—	—	—	—	4,500	—

KM# Tn1.2 PENNY
Brass **Issuer:** WWII Internment Camp **Note:** Center hole misplaced (error).

Date	Mintage	F	VF	XF	Unc	BU
ND(1943)	—	75.00	90.00	120	—	—

KM# Tn1.3 PENNY
Brass **Issuer:** WWII Internment Camp **Note:** No hole (error).

Date	Mintage	F	VF	XF	Unc	BU
ND(1943)	—	—	—	175	200	—

KM# Tn2.1 THREEPENCE
Bronze **Issuer:** WWII Internment Camp **Obv:** Center hole with wreath around **Obv. Leg.:** INTERNMENT CAMPS **Rev:** Center hole with wreath around **Rev. Leg.:** THREE PENCE

Date	Mintage	F	VF	XF	Unc	BU
ND(1943)	—	40.00	55.00	80.00	135	—

KM# Tn2.2 THREEPENCE
Bronze **Issuer:** WWII Internment Camp **Obv:** Center hole with wreath around **Obv. Leg.:** INTERNMENT CAMP **Rev. Leg.:** THREE PENCE

Date	Mintage	F	VF	XF	Unc	BU
ND(1943) Rare						

KM# Tn3 SHILLING
Bronze **Issuer:** WWII Internment Camp **Obv:** Center hole with wreath around **Obv. Leg.:** INTERNMENT CAMPS **Rev:** Center hole with wreath around **Rev. Leg.:** ONE SHILLING

Date	Mintage	F	VF	XF	Unc	BU
ND(1943)	—	150	175	250	350	—

KM# Tn4.1 2 SHILLING
Bronze **Issuer:** WWII Internment Camp **Obv:** Center hole with beads and wreath around **Obv. Leg.:** INTERNMENT CAMPS **Rev:** Center hole with beads and wreath around **Rev. Leg.:** TWO SHILLINGS

Date	Mintage	F	VF	XF	Unc	BU
ND(1943)	—	200	300	500	750	—

KM# Tn4.2 2 SHILLING
Bronze **Issuer:** WWII Internment Camp **Obv:** Beaded circle at center, wreath around **Obv. Leg.:** INTERNMENT CAMPS **Rev:** Beaded circle at center, wreath around **Rev. Leg.:** TWO SHILLINGS **Note:** Without center hole.

Date	Mintage	F	VF	XF	Unc	BU
ND(1943)	—	325	450	650	—	—

KM# Tn4.3 2 SHILLING
Bronze **Issuer:** WWII Internment Camp **Obv:** Off center hole partially within beaded circle, wreath surrounding **Obv. Leg.:** Internment Camps **Rev:** Off center hole partially within beaded circle, wreath surrounding **Rev. Leg.:** Two shillings **Note:** Center hole misplaced.

Date	Mintage	F	VF	XF	Unc	BU
ND(1943)	—	275	400	600	900	—

KM# Tn5.1 5 SHILLING
Bronze **Obv:** Center hole with beads and wreath around **Obv. Leg.:** INTERNMENT CAMPS **Rev:** Center hole with beads and wreath around **Rev. Leg.:** FIVE SHILLINGS

Date	Mintage	F	VF	XF	Unc	BU
ND(1943)	—	—	600	750	1,000	—

KM# Tn5.2 5 SHILLING
Bronze **Obv:** Center circle with beads and wreath around **Obv. Leg.:** INTERNMENT CAMPS **Rev:** Center circle with beads and wreath around **Rev. Leg.:** FIVE SHILLINGS **Note:** Without center hole.

Date	Mintage	F	VF	XF	Unc	BU
ND(1943)	—	—	750	1,000	1,750	—

KM# Tn5.3 5 SHILLING
Bronze **Obv:** Center circle with beads and wreath around **Obv. Leg.:** INTERNMENT CAMPS **Rev:** Center circle with beads and wreath around **Rev. Leg.:** FIVE SHILLINGS **Note:** Center hole misplaced,(hole at top of coin)

Date	Mintage	F	VF	XF	Unc	BU
ND(1943)	—	—	650	850	1,350	—

PATTERNS
Including off metal strikes

KM#	Date	Mintage	Identification	Mkt Val
Pn7	1909	—	Florin.	
Pn8	1919	—	Penny. Copper-Nickel. 3.8900 g. T.3.	45,000
Pn8a	1919	—	Penny. Copper-Nickel. 4.2100 g. T.3.	45,000

KM#	Date	Mintage	Identification	Mkt Val
Pn8b	1919	—	Penny. Copper-Nickel. 4.5400 g. T.3.	45,000
Pn9	1919	—	Penny. Copper-Nickel. 3.8900 g. T.4.	50,000
Pn9a	1919	—	Penny. 0.9170 Silver. 4.6700 g. T.4.	90,000
Pn10	1919	—	Penny. Copper-Nickel. 3.8900 g. T.5.	50,000
Pn10a	1919	—	Penny. 0.9170 Silver. 4.6700 g. T.5.	90,000
Pn11	1919	—	Penny. Copper-Nickel. 3.8900 g. T.6.	45,000
Pn11a	1919	—	Penny. 0.9170 Silver. 4.4100 g. T.6.	90,000
Pn12	1919	—	Shilling. 0.6250 Silver. KM#26.	100,000
Pn13	1920	—	1/2 Penny. Copper-Nickel. 1.8100 g. T.1.	—
Pn13a	1920	—	1/2 Penny. 0.9170 Silver. T.1.	—
Pn14a	1920	—	Penny. Lead. T.7.	—
Pn14	1920	—	Penny. Copper-Nickel. 3.8900 g. T.7.	50,000
Pn15	1920	—	Penny. Copper-Nickel. 3.8900 g. T.8.	65,000
Pn16	1920	—	Penny. Copper-Nickel. 3.8900 g. T.9.	70,000
Pn17	1920	—	Penny. Copper-Nickel. 3.8900 g. T.10.	80,000
PnA18	1920	—	Shilling. Silver. KM#26, star above date.	60,000
Pn18	1920	—	Florin. Silver. KM#27, star above date.	100,000
Pn19	1921	—	1/2 Penny. Copper-Nickel. 1.8100 g. T.2.	75,000
Pn20	1921	—	Penny. Copper-Nickel. 3.8900 g. T.11.	35,000
Pn20a	1921	—	Penny. Copper-Nickel. 4.2100 g. T.11.	35,000
Pn20b	1921	—	Penny. Copper-Nickel. 4.5400 g. T.11.	35,000
Pn20c	1921	—	Penny. Nickel. T.11.	35,000
Pn21	1921	—	Penny. Copper-Nickel. 3.8900 g. T.12.	35,000
Pn21a	1921	—	Penny. Copper-Nickel. 4.2100 g. T.12.	35,000
Pn21b	1921	—	Penny. Copper-Nickel. 4.5400 g. T.12.	35,000
Pn22	1921	—	Penny. T.13.	37,500
Pn24	1937	12	Penny. Bronze. Head left. Kangaroo hopping, left, date below tail, value at bottom.	125,000
Pn25	1937	7	Threepence. Silver.	100,000
Pn26	1937	6	Shilling. Silver.	45,000
Pn28	1951	—	2 Shilling. Copper-Nickel. Jubilee.	25,000
Pn29	1967	—	50 Cents. Silver. KM#67.	—
Pn30	1968	—	50 Cents. Copper-Nickel. KM#68.	—

PIEFORTS

KM#	Date	Mintage	Identification	Mkt Val
P1	1989	15,000	10 Dollars. 0.9250 Silver. Kookaburra, KM#133.	100
P2	1990	15,000	10 Dollars. 0.9250 Silver. Cockatoo, KM#136.	115
P3	1991	17,000	10 Dollars. 0.9250 Silver. Jabiru Stork, Proof, KM#156.	70.00
P4	1992	15,000	10 Dollars. 0.9250 Silver. Penguins.	85.00
P5	1993	—	10 Dollars. 0.9250 Silver. Palm cockatoo, KM#221.	100
P6	1994	15,000	10 Dollars. 0.9250 Silver. Wedge tailed eagle, Proof, KM#223.	75.00
P7	1995	15,000	10 Dollars. 0.9250 Silver. Numbat, KM#296.	75.00
P8	1996	14,000	10 Dollars. Silver. Whales, Proof, KM#314.	75.00
P9	1997	14,000	10 Dollars. Silver. Cockatoo, Proof, KM#367.	75.00
P10	1998	14,000	10 Dollars. Silver. Wombat, Proof, KM#397.	75.00

TRIAL STRIKES

KM#	Date	Mintage	Identification	Mkt Val
TS1	ND(1927)	—	Shilling. Silver. Crowned head left. Uniface.	65,000
TS2	ND(1927)	—	Florin. Silver. Crowned head left. Uniface. KM7.	—
TS3	1937	8	Penny. Bronze. Kangaroo hopping, left, date below tail, value at bottom. Uniface, reverse.	75,000
TS4	1937	15	Threepence. Silver. Uniface, reverse.	72,500
TSA5	1937	—	Sixpence. Silver. Uniface, reverse.	—
TS5	1937	20	Shilling. Silver. Uniface, reverse.	65,000
TS6	1937	15	Florin. Uniface, reverse. Spink Remick Sale 9-06.	60,000
TS7	1937(L)	—	Crown. Uniface, reverse. Spink Remick Sale 9-06.	—

BABY MINT SETS

KM#	Date	Mintage	Identification	Issue Price	Mkt Val
BMS1	1993 (6)	17,000	KM#80-83, 101, 208	—	60.00
BMS2	1994 (6)	37,348	KM#80-82, 84, 101, 257	—	35.00
BMS3	1995 (6)	33,357	KM#80-82, 84, 101, 294 plus bronze medal	—	55.00
BMS4	1996 (6)	25,727	KM#80-83, 101, 310 plus bronze medal	—	135
BMS5	1997 (6)	27,421	KM#80-83, 101, 327 plus bronze medal	—	215
BMS6	1998 (6)	31,810	KM#80-82, 84, 101, 364 plus bronze medal	—	110
BMS7	1999 (6)	35,718	KM#401-406 Copper medal	—	50.00
BMS8	2000 (6)	39,120	KM#401-403, 406, 488.1, 489 plus bronze medal	—	75.00

BABY PROOF SETS

KM#	Date	Mintage	Identification	Issue Price	Mkt Val
BPS1	1995 (6)	3,624	KM#80-82, 84, 101, 294 plus silver medal	—	130
BPS2	1996 (6)	3,985	KM#80-83, 101, 310 plus silver medal	—	283
BPS3	1997 (6)	3,617	KM#80-83, 101, 327 plus silver medal	—	430
BPS4	1998 (6)	5,269	KM#80-82, 84, 101, 364 plus silver medal	—	265
BPS5	1999 (6)	6,707	KM#401-406 plus silver medal	—	230
BPS6	2000 (6)	15,287	KM#401-403, 406, 488.1, 489 plus silver medal	—	200

MINT SETS

KM#	Date	Mintage	Identification	Issue Price	Mkt Val
MS1	1966 (6)	16,359	KM62-67 (Card)	2.00	18.00
MS2	1969 (6)	31,176	KM62-66,68	2.50	25.00
MS3	1970 (6)	40,230	KM62-66, 69	2.50	10.00
MS4	1971 (6)	28,572	KM62-66,68	2.50	20.00
MS5	1972 (6)	39,068	KM62-66,68	2.75	20.00
MS6	1973 (6)	30,928	KM62-66,68	3.40	20.00
MS7	1974 (6)	25,948	KM62-66,68	3.60	18.00
MS8	1975 (6)	30,121	KM62-66,68	3.30	8.00
MS9	1976 (6)	40,004	KM62-66,68	3.80	8.00
MS10	1977 (6)	128,000	KM62-66, 70	4.20	5.00
MS11	1978 (6)	70,000	KM62-66,68	4.20	5.00
MS12	1979 (6)	70,000	KM62-66,68	4.50	4.50
MS13	1980 (6)	100,000	KM62-66,68	5.75	4.00
MS14	1981 (6)	120,010	KM62-66,68	6.50	4.50
MS15	1982 (6)	195,950	KM62-66,74	6.50	4.00
MS16	1983 (6)	155,700	KM62-66,68	5.00	7.50
MS17	1984 (6)	150,014	KM62-66,68	7.00	7.50
MS18	1985 (7)	170,000	KM78-84	4.00	8.50
MS19	1986 (7)	180,000	KM78-83,87	5.50	5.00
MS20	1987 (7)	200,000	KM78-84	8.00	4.00
MS21	1988 (8)	240,000	KM78-82,99-101	12.00	4.00
MS22	1989 (8)	—	KM78-84,101	12.00	4.00
MS23	1990 (8)	—	KM78-84, 101	12.00	45.00
MS24	1991 (8)	25,000	KM78-82,84,101,139	13.00	7.50
MS25	1992 (6)	104,000	KM80-83,101,175a.1	10.00	15.00
MS26	1993 (6)	—	KM80-83,101,208	10.00	5.00
MS27	1994 (6)	90,000	KM80-82,84,101,257	11.25	5.00
MS29	1995 (6)	—	KM80-82,84,101,294	—	16.00
MS30	1996 (6)	—	KM80-83,101,310	14.80	15.00
MS32	1997 (6)	—	KM80-83,101,327	—	17.50
MSA32	1997 (2)	—	KM327, 355	—	7.00
MS33	1998 (6)	—	KM80-82,83,101,364	12.75	12.75
MS34	1998 (6)	—	KM80-82,84,101,364	16.60	17.50
MS35	1999 (6)	—	KM401-406	16.95	16.95
MSB36	1999 (5)	500	KM501-505	—	1,050
MSC36	1999 (3)	—	KM#426-428	—	875
MS36	1999 (3)	—	KM#426-428	—	875
MS37	1999 (2)	—	KM400,405	—	10.00
MS38	2000 (6)	—	KM401-403, 406, 488-489	10.60	18.00

PROOF SETS

KM#	Date	Mintage	Identification	Issue Price	Mkt Val
PSA1	1887 (4)	2	KM#8-11 Rare	—	—
PS1	1902S (4)	—	KM14-17 Rare	—	—
PS2	1911(L) (4)	—	KM24-27	—	25,000
PS3	1916M (4)	25	KM24-27	—	7,000
PS4	1925(m) (5)	—	KM22-26	—	13,650
PS5	1926(m) (6)	—	KM22-27	—	9,400
PS6	1927(m) (6)	50	KM22-27	—	7,150
PS7	1928(m) (6)	—	KM22-27	—	9,550
PS8	1929(m) (2)	—	KM22-23	—	3,250
PSA9	1930(m) (2)	—	KM22-23	—	85.00
PS9	1931(m) (4)	—	KM22-27	—	7,000
PS10	1933(m) (2)	—	KM22-23	—	2,000
PS11	1934(m) (6)	100	KM22-27	—	7,500
PS12	1935(m) (6)	100	KM22-27	—	4,800
PS13	1936(m) (6)	—	KM22-27	—	6,350
PS14	1938(m) (6)	250	KM35-40	—	5,500
PS15	1953(p) (2)	—	KM49-50	—	3,500
PS16	1955(m) (4)	1,200	KM56-59	—	250
PS17	1955(p) (3)	301	KM49,56	—	2,000
PS18	1956(m) (5)	1,500	KM56-60	—	325
PS19	1957(m) (4)	1,256	KM57-60	—	225
PS20	1958(m) (5)	1,506	KM56-60	—	250
PS21	1959(m) (6)	1,506	KM56-61	—	325
PS22	1960(m) (4)	1,509	KM56-60	—	175
PS23	1960(p) (2)	1,030	KM56,61	—	225
PS24	1961(m) (4)	1,506	KM57-60	—	175
PS25	1961(p) (2)	1,040	KM56,61	—	225
PS25a	1961(p) (2)	1,040	KM56,61	—	225
PS26	1962(m) (4)	2,016	KM57-60	—	150
PS27	1962(p) (2)	1,064	KM56,61	—	200
PS28	1963(m) (4)	5,042	KM57-60	—	125
PS29	1963(p) (2)	1,064	KM56,61	—	225
PS30	1966 (6)	18,110	KM62-67	15.70	120
PS31	1969 (6)	12,696	KM62-66,68	11.25	110
PS32	1970 (6)	15,112	KM62-66,69	11.30	55.00
PS33	1971 (6)	10,066	KM62-66,68	11.30	50.00
PS34	1972 (6)	10,272	KM62-66,68	14.00	55.00
PS35	1973 (6)	10,090	KM62-66,68	15.50	70.00
PS36	1974 (6)	11,103	KM62-66,68	18.00	45.00
PS37	1975 (6)	23,021	KM62-66,68	17.00	15.00
PS38	1976 (6)	21,200	KM62-66,68	20.20	20.00
PS39	1977 (6)	55,000	KM62-66,70	20.20	12.00
PS40	1978 (6)	38,513	KM62-66,68	—	10.00
PS41	1979 (6)	36,000	KM62-66,68	—	10.00
PS42	1980 (6)	68,000	KM62-66,68	—	8.00
PS43	1981 (6)	86,008	KM62-66,68	48.00	8.00
PS44	1982 (6)	100,000	KM62-66,74	50.00	8.00
PS45	1983 (6)	80,000	KM62-66,68	39.00	10.00
PS46	1984 (6)	61,398	62-66,68	39.00	10.00
PS47	1985 (7)	74,809	KM78-84	27.50	20.00
PS48	1986 (7)	67,000	KM78-83,87	40.00	15.00
PS49	1986P (4)	12,000	KM89-92	1,445	1,350
PS50	1986P (2)	3,000	KM89,90	305	325
PS51	1987 (7)	69,684	KM78-84	40.00	12.00
PS52	1987 (4)	12,000	KM95-98	1,440	1,300
PS53	1987 (2)	3,000	KM95, 96	305	350
PS54	1988 (8)	101,000	KM78-82, 99-101	—	15.00
PS55	1988 (8)	5,000	KM78-82, 99-101, Coin Fair	—	80.00
PS56	1988 (4)	25,000	KM99a-102a	85.00	130
PS57	1988P (4)	9,000	KM104-107	—	1,300
PS58	1988 (2)	1,000	KM104-105	—	235
PS59	1988 (2)	—	KM112-113	50.00	42.50
PS60	1989 (8)	2,500	KM78-84,101	—	15.00
PS61	1989 (8)	—	KM78-84, 101 Coin Fair	—	70.00
PS62	1989 (5)	2,200	KM117-121	1,595	1,300
PS63	1989 (5)	2,400	KM122-126	1,995	1,300
PS64	1989 (5)	25,000	KM99a,127-130	—	130
PS65	1989 (2)	—	KM131-132	—	42.50
PS66	1990 (5)	—	KM78-84,101	55.00	20.00
PS67	1990 (5)	—	KM78-84, 101 Coin Fair	—	80.00
PS68	1990 (5)	5,000	KM140-144	—	1,300
PS69	1990 (5)	2,500	KM145-149	—	1,300
PS70	1990 (3)	2,000	KM140-142	464	300
PS71	1990 (3)	1,000	KM138,144,149	1,900	1,800
PS72	1990 (2)	—	KM154-155	—	42.50
PS73	1990 (3)	25,000	KM84a, 87a, 100a. Sydney Coin Fair.	135	110
PS74	1991 (3)	1,000	KM140-142	—	300
PS75	1991 (8)	24,000	KM78-82,84,101,139	55.00	30.00
PS76	1991 (8)	1,000	KM78-82,84,101a,139	—	70.00
PS77	1991 (8)	23,000	KM78a 82a,84a,101a, 139a	—	140
PS78	1991 (5)	2,000	KM140-144	—	1,100
PS79	1991 (5)	1,000	PS145-149	—	2,750
PS80	1992 (5)	47,000	KM80-83, 101, 175.1	40.00	25.00
PS81	1992 (4)	500	KM165-168	—	750
PS82	1992 (4)	—	KM200-203, plus medal	120	120
PS83	1992 (4)	5,000	KM204-207 plus medal	1,520	1,600
PSA84	1992 (3)	264	KM389-391	252	375
PSB84	1992 (3)	628	KM389-393	1,058	1,600
PSC84	1992 (4)	500	KM389-392 plus medal	759	1,000
PSD84	1992(ae) (3)	750	KM193, 209, 391	—	800
PSE84	1992 (ae) (3)	500	KM212.2, 230, 231 plus silver bar	310	975
PS84	1993 (6)	—	KM80-83, 101, 208	—	20.00
PS85	1993 (6)	20,000	KM213-217	94.50	100
PS86	1994 (6)	45,000	KM80-82, 84, 101, 257	—	20.00
PS87	1994 (5)	20,000	KM264-268	101	125
PS88	1994 (4)	20,000	KM182, 232 (2), 253	—	2,000
PSA89	1994 (4)	—	KM#260, 261, 270, 271	—	850
PS89	1994 (3)	25	KM241, 260, 278	304	350
PS90	1995 (5)	300	KM272-276	—	1,300
PSA91	1995 (3)	600	KM#289, 272, 283	—	350
PS91	1995 (5)	200	KM283-287	—	1,300
PSA92	1995 (3)	300	KM276, 286, 290	—	1,300
PS92	1995 (4)	1,000	KM289-292	—	1,290
PS93	1995 (3)	300	KM289-291	—	390
PS94	1995 (2)	600	KM289-290	—	42.00
PSA95	1995 (2)	800	KM290-291	—	395
PS95	1996 (3)	3,000	KM, (f), (l), (s) privy marks	—	800
PS97	1996 (7)	—	KM80-83, 101, 310, plus silver gumnut baby medal	59.25	75.00
PSA98	1996 (3)	400	KM321-322, 341	1,500	1,350
PSB98	1996 (6)	—	KM80-83, 101, 310	—	20.00
PS98	1997 (3)	3,888	KM335-337	914	975
PSA99	1997 (2)	20,000	KM#353, 354	—	56.00
PS99	1997 (3)	3,000	KM341 (f), (l), (s) privy marks	782	900
PS100	1998 (6)	—	KM80-82, 84, 101, 364	40.60	30.00
PS101	1998 (6)	—	KM80-82, 84, 101, 364. Baby set.	50.75	52.50
PS103	1999 (6)	1,000	KM501-503	—	170
PS104	1999 (6)	15,000	KM481-486	66.25	75.00
PS102	1999 (6)	—	KM401-406	—	35.00
PS105	2000 (5)	—	KM496-500 plus 20.5-gram silver ingot	—	135
PS106	2000 (6)	—	KM401-403, 406, 488.1, 489	34.35	40.00

AUSTRIA

The Republic of Austria, a parliamentary democracy located in mountainous central Europe, has an area of 32,374 sq. mi. (83,850 sq. km.) and a population of 8.08 million. Capital: Wien (Vienna). Austria is primarily an industrial country. Machinery, iron, steel, textiles, yarns and timber are exported.

The territories later to be known as Austria were overrun in pre-Roman times by various tribes, including the Celts. Upon the fall of the Roman Empire, the country became a margravate of Charlemagne's Empire. Premysl II of Otakar, King of Bohemia, gained possession in 1252, only to lose the territory to Rudolf of Habsburg in 1276. Thereafter, until World War I, the story of Austria was conducted by the ruling Habsburgs.

During the 17th century, Austrian coinage reflected the geopolitical strife of three wars. From 1618-1648, the Thirty Years' War between northern Protestants and southern Catholics produced low quality, "kipperwhipper" strikes of 12, 24, 30, 60, 75 and 150 Kreuzer. Later, during the Austrian-Turkish War, 1660-1664, coinages used to maintain soldier's salaries also reported the steady division of Hungarian territories. Finally, between 1683 and 1699, during the second Austrian-Turkish conflict, new issues of 3, 6 and 15 Kreuzers were struck, being necessary to help defray mounting expenses of the war effort.

During World War I, the Austro-Hungarian Empire was one of the Central Powers with Germany, Bulgaria and Turkey. At the end of the war, the Empire was dismembered and Austria established as an independent republic. In March 1938, Austria was incorporated into Hitler's short-lived Greater German Reich. Allied forces of both East and West occupied Austria in April 1945, and subsequently divided it into 4 zones of military occupation. On May 15, 1955, the 4 powers formally recognized Austria as a sovereign independent democratic state.

NOTE: During the **GERMAN OCCUPATION** (1938-1945), the German Reichsmark coins and banknotes were circulated.

MONETARY SYSTEM
150 Schillings = 100 Reichsmark

RULERS
Franz Joseph I, 1848-1916
Karl I, 1916-1918

EMPIRE

REFORM COINAGE
100 Heller = 1 Corona

KM# 2800 HELLER
1.6700 g., Bronze **Ruler:** Franz Joseph I

Date	Mintage	F	VF	XF	Unc	BU
1901	52,096,000	0.20	0.35	1.00	3.00	—
1902	20,553,000	0.20	0.50	1.25	3.00	—
1903	13,779,000	0.20	0.35	0.50	2.50	—
1909	12,668,000	0.20	0.35	0.50	2.50	—
1910	21,941,000	0.20	0.35	0.50	2.50	—
1911	18,387,000	0.20	0.35	0.50	2.50	—
1912	27,053,000	0.20	0.35	0.50	2.50	—
1913	8,782,000	0.20	0.35	0.50	2.50	—
1914	9,906,000	0.20	0.35	0.50	2.50	—
1915	5,673,000	0.20	0.35	0.75	2.50	—
1916	12,484,000	0.35	0.75	1.50	4.00	—

KM# 2823 HELLER
Bronze, 17 mm. **Ruler:** Franz Joseph I **Obv:** Austrian shield on crowned double eagle's breast **Rev:** Value above sprays, date below, within shield

Date	Mintage	F	VF	XF	Unc	BU
1916	Inc. above	4.00	6.00	14.00	20.00	—

KM# 2801 2 HELLER
3.3500 g., Bronze, 19 mm. **Ruler:** Franz Joseph I **Obv:** Crowned imperial double eagle **Rev:** Value above sprays, date below within shield **Edge:** Smooth

Date	Mintage	F	VF	XF	Unc	BU
1901	12,157,000	2.50	5.00	15.00	35.00	—
1902	18,760,000	0.15	0.50	1.50	3.00	—

Date	Mintage	F	VF	XF	Unc	BU
1903	26,983,000	0.50	1.50	3.00	8.00	—
1904	12,863,000	0.15	0.50	4.00	14.00	—
1905	6,679,000	0.75	2.75	5.50	15.00	—
1906	20,104,000	0.50	1.50	3.00	8.00	—
1907	23,804,000	0.15	0.25	0.75	3.00	—
1908	21,984,000	0.15	0.25	0.75	3.00	—
1909	25,975,000	0.15	0.25	0.75	3.00	—
1910	28,406,000	0.50	1.50	3.00	8.00	—
1911	50,007,058	0.15	0.25	0.50	2.00	—
1912	74,234,000	0.15	0.20	0.35	2.00	—
1913	27,432,000	0.35	0.75	2.25	6.00	—
1914	60,674,000	0.15	0.20	0.35	2.00	—
1915	7,871,000	0.15	0.20	0.35	2.00	—

KM# 2824 2 HELLER
Iron **Ruler:** Karl I **Obv:** Austrian shield on crowned double eagle's breast **Rev:** Value above date, within wreath

Date	Mintage	F	VF	XF	Unc	BU
1916	61,909,000	0.50	1.00	2.00	7.50	—
1917	81,186,000	0.25	0.50	1.00	5.00	—
1918	66,352,999	0.25	0.50	1.00	4.00	—

KM# 2802 10 HELLER
Nickel **Ruler:** Franz Joseph I **Obv:** Crowned imperial double eagle **Rev:** Value above date at center of ornate shield

Date	Mintage	F	VF	XF	Unc	BU
1907	8,662,000	0.25	0.50	1.00	4.00	—
1908	7,772,000	0.75	1.50	2.50	6.00	—
1909	20,462,000	0.15	0.25	0.75	2.50	—
1910	10,164,000	0.15	0.25	0.75	2.50	—
1911	3,634,000	1.00	2.00	3.50	8.00	—

KM# 2822 10 HELLER
Copper-Nickel-Zinc **Ruler:** Franz Joseph I **Obv:** Shield on crowned double eagle's breast **Rev:** Value within wreath, date below

Date	Mintage	F	VF	XF	Unc	BU
1915	18,366,000	0.15	0.25	0.50	2.00	—
1916	27,487,000	0.15	0.25	0.50	2.00	—

KM# 2825 10 HELLER
Copper-Nickel-Zinc **Ruler:** Franz Joseph I **Obv:** Austrian shield on crowned double eagle's breast **Rev:** Value within wreath, date below

Date	Mintage	F	VF	XF	Unc	BU
1916	14,804,000	0.75	1.50	3.00	5.00	—

KM# 2803 20 HELLER
Nickel, 21 mm. **Ruler:** Franz Joseph I **Obv:** Crowned imperial double eagle **Rev:** Value above date at center of ornate shield

Date	Mintage	F	VF	XF	Unc	BU
1907	7,650,000	0.75	1.50	3.00	12.00	—
1908	7,469,000	0.75	1.25	2.50	9.00	—
1909	7,592,000	3.00	6.00	12.00	20.00	—
1911	19,560,000	0.25	0.35	1.00	5.00	—
1914	2,342,000	5.00	10.00	15.00	25.00	—

KM# 2826 20 HELLER
Iron **Ruler:** Karl I **Obv:** Austrian shield on crowned double eagle's breast **Rev:** Value within wreath, date below

Date	Mintage	F	VF	XF	Unc	BU
1916	130,770,000	0.50	1.25	2.00	6.50	—
1917	127,420,000	0.50	1.25	2.00	5.50	—
1918	48,985,000	0.25	0.65	1.25	4.50	—

KM# 2804 CORONA
5.0000 g., 0.8350 Silver 0.1342 oz. ASW **Ruler:** Franz Joseph I **Obv:** Laureate head

Date	Mintage	F	VF	XF	Unc	BU
1901	10,387,000	2.00	3.00	5.00	10.00	—
1902	2,947,000	2.00	4.25	7.50	15.00	—
1903	2,198,000	2.00	4.25	8.00	29.00	—
1904	993,000	4.00	8.50	17.50	50.00	—
1905	505,000	1.00	25.00	45.00	70.00	—
1906	164,500	80.00	125	200	450	—
1907	244,000	30.00	60.00	100	300	—

KM# 2808 CORONA
5.0000 g., 0.8350 Silver 0.1342 oz. ASW **Ruler:** Franz Joseph I **Subject:** 60th Anniversary of Reign **Obv:** Crown at top divides dates, FII on spray at center, value at bottom

Date	Mintage	F	VF	XF	Unc	BU
ND(1908)	4,784,992	2.50	3.50	6.00	12.00	—

KM# 2820 CORONA
5.0000 g., 0.8350 Silver 0.1342 oz. ASW **Ruler:** Franz Joseph I **Obv:** Head right **Rev:** Crown above value, date at bottom, sprays flanking

Date	Mintage	F	VF	XF	Unc	BU
1912	8,457,000	BV	2.25	3.50	8.00	—
1913	9,345,000	BV	2.25	3.50	7.00	—
1914	37,897,000	BV	2.25	3.00	6.00	—
1915	23,000,134	BV	2.25	3.00	6.00	—
1916	12,415,404	BV	2.25	3.00	6.00	—

KM# 2821 2 CORONA
10.0000 g., 0.8350 Silver 0.2684 oz. ASW **Ruler:** Franz Joseph I **Obv:** Head right **Rev:** Crowned double eagle above date

Date	Mintage	F	VF	XF	Unc	BU
1912	10,244,500	BV	5.00	7.00	10.00	—
1913	7,256,002	BV	5.00	7.00	10.00	—

KM# 2807 5 CORONA
24.0000 g., 0.9000 Silver 0.6944 oz. ASW **Ruler:** Franz Joseph I **Obv:** Laureate, bearded head right **Rev:** Crowned imperial double eagle within circle surrounded by wreath of circled crowns and leaves

Date	Mintage	F	VF	XF	Unc	BU
1907	1,539,000	16.00	20.00	45.00	145	—
1907 Proof	—	Value: 650				

KM# 2809   5 CORONA
24.0000 g., 0.9000 Silver 0.6944 oz. ASW, 35 mm. **Ruler:** Franz Joseph I **Subject:** 60th Anniversary of Reign **Obv:** Head right **Rev:** Running figure of Fame

Date	Mintage	F	VF	XF	Unc	BU
ND(1908)	5,089,700	14.00	16.00	28.00	65.00	—
ND(1908) Proof	—	Value: 650				

KM# 2813   5 CORONA
24.0000 g., 0.9000 Silver 0.6944 oz. ASW **Ruler:** Franz Joseph I **Obv:** Large head, right, continuous legend **Rev:** Crowned double eagle with shield on breast within circle, five crowns in circles and leaf sprays surrounding, date divides value at bottom

Date	Mintage	F	VF	XF	Unc	BU
1909	1,708,800	15.00	18.00	40.00	125	—

KM# 2814   5 CORONA
24.0000 g., 0.9000 Silver 0.6944 oz. ASW **Ruler:** Franz Joseph I **Obv:** Head right **Rev:** National arms, date below divides denomination

Date	Mintage	F	VF	XF	Unc	BU
1909	1,775,787	15.00	17.00	35.00	90.00	—

KM# 2805   10 CORONA
3.3875 g., 0.9000 Gold 0.0980 oz. AGW, 19 mm. **Ruler:** Franz Joseph I **Obv:** Laureate, bearded head right **Rev:** Crowned imperial double eagle

Date	Mintage	F	VF	XF	Unc	BU
1905 - MDCCCCV	1,933,230	—	BV	100	120	—
1906 - MDCCCCVI	1,081,161	—	BV	100	120	—

KM# 2810   10 CORONA
3.3875 g., 0.9000 Gold 0.0980 oz. AGW, 19 mm. **Ruler:** Franz Joseph I **Subject:** 60th Anniversary of Reign **Obv:** Small plain head right **Rev:** Crowned double eagle, tail divides two dates, value at bottom

Date	Mintage	F	VF	XF	Unc	BU
ND(1908)	654,022	—	BV	90.00	100	110

KM# 2815   10 CORONA
3.3875 g., 0.9000 Gold 0.0980 oz. AGW, 19 mm. **Ruler:** Franz Joseph I **Obv:** Head right **Rev:** Crowned double eagle, date and value at bottom

Date	Mintage	F	VF	XF	Unc	BU
1909 - MDCCCCIX	2,319,872	—	BV	90.00	100	110

KM# 2816   10 CORONA
3.3875 g., 0.9000 Gold 0.0980 oz. AGW, 19 mm. **Ruler:** Franz Joseph I **Obv:** Large right **Rev:** Crowned double eagle, date and value at bottom

Date	Mintage	F	VF	XF	Unc	BU
1909 - MDCCCCIX	192,135	—	BV	95.00	110	120
1910 - MDCCCCX	1,055,387	—	BV	90.00	100	110
1911 - MDCCCCXI	1,285,667	—	BV	90.00	100	110
1912 - MDCCCCXII Restrike						BV

KM# 2806   20 CORONA
6.7751 g., 0.9000 Gold 0.1960 oz. AGW, 21 mm. **Ruler:** Franz Joseph I **Obv:** Laureate, bearded head right **Rev:** Crowned imperial double eagle

Date	Mintage	F	VF	XF	Unc	BU
1901 - MDCCCCI	48,677	200	400	600	800	950
1902 - MDCCCCII	440,751	—	BV	185	195	200
1903 - MDCCCCIII	322,679	—	BV	185	195	200
1904 - MDCCCCIV	494,356	—	BV	185	195	200
1905 - MDCCCCV	146,097	—	BV	185	195	210

KM# 2811   20 CORONA
6.7751 g., 0.9000 Gold 0.1960 oz. AGW, 21 mm. **Ruler:** Franz Joseph I **Subject:** 60th Anniversary of Reign **Obv:** Head right **Rev:** Crowned double eagle, crown divides two dates, value at bottom

Date	Mintage	F	VF	XF	Unc	BU
1908	188,000	BV	195	285	380	425

KM# 2817   20 CORONA
6.7751 g., 0.9000 Gold 0.1960 oz. AGW, 21 mm. **Ruler:** Franz Joseph I **Rev:** Crowned double eagle, value and date at bottom

Date	Mintage	F	VF	XF	Unc	BU
1909 - MDCCCCIX	227,754	450	750	1,400	1,800	2,100

KM# 2818   20 CORONA
6.7751 g., 0.9000 Gold 0.1960 oz. AGW, 21 mm. **Ruler:** Franz Joseph I **Obv:** Head of Franz Joseph I, right

Date	Mintage	F	VF	XF	Unc	BU
MDCCCCIX (1909)	102,404	575	1,150	2,000	2,800	—
MDCCCCX (1910)	386,031	BV	195	250	350	—
MDCCCCXI (1911)	59,313	185	550	800	975	—
MDCCCCXII (1912)	4,460	250	550	1,350	2,000	—
MDCCCCXIII (1913)	28,058	350	900	1,800	3,000	—

Date	Mintage	F	VF	XF	Unc	BU
MDCCCCXIV (1914)	82,104	185	550	800	1,000	—
MDCCCCXV (1915) Restrike	—	—	—	—	BV+ 5%	—
MDCCCCXVI (1916)	71,763	2,500	3,500	5,500	7,500	—

KM# 2827   20 CORONA
6.7751 g., 0.9000 Gold 0.1960 oz. AGW, 21 mm. **Ruler:** Franz Joseph I **Obv:** Head right **Rev:** Austrian shield on crowned double eagle, value and date at bottom

Date	Mintage	F	VF	XF	Unc	BU
1916 - MDCCCCXVI	Inc. above	450	750	900	1,200	—

KM# 2828   20 CORONA
6.7751 g., 0.9000 Gold 0.1960 oz. AGW, 21 mm. **Ruler:** Karl I **Obv:** Head right **Rev:** Crowned national arms, date below divides denomination **Note:** 2000 pieces struck, all but one specimen were remelted.

Date	Mintage	F	VF	XF	Unc	BU
1918 - MDCCCCXVIII Unique	Est. 2,000					

KM# 2812   100 CORONA
33.8753 g., 0.9000 Gold 0.9802 oz. AGW, 37 mm. **Ruler:** Franz Joseph I **Subject:** 60th Anniversary of Reign **Obv:** Head right **Rev:** Resting figure of Fame

Date	Mintage	F	VF	XF	Unc	BU
ND(1908)	16,000	BV	1,000	1,250	1,750	—
ND(1908) Proof	—	Value: 2,000				

KM# 2819   100 CORONA
33.8753 g., 0.9000 Gold 0.9802 oz. AGW, 37 mm. **Ruler:** Franz Joseph I **Obv:** Head right **Rev:** Crowned double eagle, tail dividing value, date at bottom

Date	Mintage	F	VF	XF	Unc	BU
1909	3,203	BV	950	1,000	1,500	—
1910	3,074	BV	950	1,000	1,500	—
1911	11,165	BV	950	1,000	1,500	—
1912	3,591	950	1,000	1,150	2,000	—
1913	2,696	BV	1,000	1,200	1,700	—
1914	1,195	BV	950	1,000	1,600	—
1915 Restrike	—	—	—	—	BV+ 2%	—
1915 Restrike, Proof	—	—	—	—	—	—

TRADE COINAGE

KM# 2267   DUCAT
3.4909 g., 0.9860 Gold 0.1107 oz. AGW **Ruler:** Franz Joseph I **Obv:** Laureate head right, heavy whiskers **Rev:** Crowned imperial double eagle **Note:** 996,721 pieces were struck from 1920-1936.

Date	Mintage	F	VF	XF	Unc	BU
1901	348,621	BV	115	125	175	185
1902	311,471	BV	115	125	175	185
1903	380,014	BV	115	125	175	185
1904	517,118	BV	115	125	175	185

Date	Mintage	F	VF	XF	Unc	BU
1905	391,534	BV	125	150	200	210
1906	491,574	BV	125	150	200	210
1907	554,205	BV	110	175	250	260
1908	408,832	BV	110	125	175	187
1909	366,318	BV	110	120	150	160
1910	440,424	BV	110	120	150	160
1911	590,826	BV	110	115	125	135
1912	494,991	BV	110	115	125	135
1913	319,926	BV	110	115	125	135
1914	378,241	BV	110	115	125	135
1915 Restrike	—	—	—	—	—	BV+10%
1915 Restrike, Proof	—	BV+5%				
1951 Error for 1915	—	BV	125	150	225	235

KM# 2276   4 DUCAT
13.9636 g., 0.9860 Gold 0.4426 oz. AGW **Ruler:** Franz Joseph I **Obv:** Laureate, armored bust right **Rev:** Crowned imperial double eagle **Note:** without mint

Date	Mintage	F	VF	XF	Unc	BU
1901	51,597	BV	450	800	1,100	1,200
1902	69,380	BV	450	800	1,100	1,200
1903	72,658	BV	450	800	1,100	1,200
1904	80,086	BV	450	800	1,100	1,200
1905	90,906	BV	450	800	1,100	1,200
1906	123,443	BV	425	500	800	850
1907	104,295	BV	425	500	800	850
1908	80,428	BV	425	550	870	900
1909	83,852	BV	400	450	680	710
1910	101,000	BV	400	425	580	600
1911	141,857	BV	400	425	450	500
1912	150,691	BV	400	425	450	500
1913	119,133	BV	400	425	450	500
1914	102,712	BV	400	425	450	500
1915 (- 1936) Restrike	—	—	—	—	BV+ 8%	

Note: 496,501 pieces were struck from 1920-1936.

TRADE COINAGE
Restrikes

KM# T1   THALER
28.0668 g., 0.8330 Silver 0.7516 oz. ASW, 41 mm.
Ruler: Joseph II **Obv:** Bust right **Rev:** Crowned imperial double eagle, heads in haloes **Note:** Many varieties exist. This type has been stuck by many different mints over the years, with some varieties commanding high premiums.

Date	Mintage	F	VF	XF	Unc	BU
1780 SF	—	—	—	—	17.50	—

Note: Restrike; 1853 to present

Date	Mintage	F	VF	XF	Unc	BU
1780 SF Proof			—	Value: 20.00		

Note: Restrike - 1853 to present

KM# T2   20 DUCAT
72.7500 g., Gold **Obv:** Bust of Maria Theresa, right **Rev:** Imperial Eagle **Note:** Struck for Haile Selassie.

Date	Mintage	F	VF	XF	Unc	BU
1780 SF			—	—	1,750	—

Note: Restrike - 1950s

REPUBLIC

REFORM COINAGE
10,000 Kronen = 1 Schilling

KM# 2830   20 KRONEN
6.7751 g., 0.9000 Gold 0.1960 oz. AGW **Obv:** Imperial Eagle, date below **Rev:** Value within wreath

Date	Mintage	F	VF	XF	Unc	BU
1923	6,988	650	1,400	1,850	2,500	—
1924	10,337	650	1,400	1,850	2,500	—

KM# 2831   100 KRONEN
33.8753 g., 0.9000 Gold 0.9802 oz. AGW **Obv:** Imperial Eagle, date below **Rev:** Value within wreath

Date	Mintage	F	VF	XF	Unc	BU
1923	617	950	1,550	2,250	3,500	—
1923 Proof			Value: 4,000			
1924	2,851	950	1,550	2,250	3,500	—

KM# 2832   100 KRONEN
Bronze **Obv:** Eagle's head, right **Rev:** Value to right of leaf, date below

Date	Mintage	F	VF	XF	Unc	BU
1923	6,403,680	4.00	8.00	15.00	30.00	—
1924	43,013,920	0.25	0.50	1.50	4.50	—

KM# 2833   200 KRONEN
Bronze **Obv:** Thick cross, date below **Rev:** Large value

Date	Mintage	F	VF	XF	Unc	BU
1924	57,160,000	0.50	1.00	2.00	6.50	—

KM# 2834   1000 KRONEN
Copper-Nickel **Obv:** Woman of Tyrol, right **Rev:** Value within wreath

Date	Mintage	F	VF	XF	Unc	BU
1924	72,353,000	0.75	1.50	3.00	8.00	—

PRE WWII DECIMAL COINAGE
100 Groschen - 1 Schilling

KM# 2836   GROSCHEN
Bronze **Obv:** Eagle's head, right **Rev:** Large value, date below

Date	Mintage	F	VF	XF	Unc	BU
1925	30,465,000	0.10	0.20	0.50	2.00	—
1926	15,487,000	0.10	0.30	0.75	2.00	—
1927	9,318,000	0.10	0.30	0.75	2.50	—
1928	17,189,000	0.10	0.30	0.75	2.50	—
1929	11,400,000	0.10	0.30	0.75	2.50	—
1930	8,893,000	0.10	0.30	0.75	2.50	—
1931	971,000	10.00	20.00	30.00	60.00	—
1932	3,040,000	1.00	2.50	5.00	7.50	—
1933	3,940,000	0.50	1.00	2.00	6.00	—
1934	4,232,000	0.15	0.50	1.00	4.00	—
1935	3,740,000	0.15	0.50	1.00	4.00	—
1936	6,020,000	0.50	1.00	3.00	9.00	—
1937	5,830,000	0.50	1.00	2.00	7.50	—
1938	1,650,000	2.00	3.00	6.00	15.00	—

KM# 2837   2 GROSCHEN
Bronze **Obv:** Thick cross, date below **Rev:** Large value

Date	Mintage	F	VF	XF	Unc	BU
1925	29,892,000	0.10	0.25	0.50	1.50	—
1926	17,700,000	0.10	0.30	0.75	2.00	—
1927	7,757,000	0.20	0.75	2.00	5.00	—
1928	19,478,000	0.10	0.30	0.75	2.00	—
1929	16,184,000	0.10	0.30	0.75	2.00	—
1930	5,709,000	0.20	0.60	1.50	4.00	—
1934	812,000	7.00	12.00	15.00	25.00	—
1935	3,148,000	0.20	0.60	1.50	4.00	—
1936	4,410,000	0.15	0.30	1.00	3.00	—
1937	3,790,000	0.20	0.40	1.25	3.50	—
1938	860,000	2.50	4.00	6.50	12.50	—

KM# 2846   5 GROSCHEN
Copper-Nickel **Obv:** Thick cross, date below **Rev:** Large value

Date	Mintage	F	VF	XF	Unc	BU
1931	16,631,000	0.15	0.40	0.80	2.00	—
1932	4,700,000	0.25	1.00	2.00	5.00	—
1934	3,210,000	0.30	1.00	2.50	6.00	—
1936	1,240,000	2.00	4.00	7.50	15.00	—
1937	1,540,000	20.00	30.00	45.00	80.00	—
1938	870,000	125	175	250	425	—

KM# 2838 10 GROSCHEN
Copper-Nickel, 22 mm. **Obv:** Woman of Tyrol, right **Rev:** Value above date within wreath

Date	Mintage	F	VF	XF	Unc	BU
1925	66,199,000	0.10	0.25	0.50	3.00	—
1928	11,468,000	0.50	1.00	4.00	12.00	—
1929	12,000,000	0.40	0.75	1.50	4.50	—

KM# 2850 50 GROSCHEN
Copper-Nickel **Obv:** Numeric value in box within circle, value at bottom **Rev:** Austrian shield on haloed double eagle's breast, tail dividing date

Date	Mintage	F	VF	XF	Unc	BU
1934	8,224,822	20.00	35.00	50.00	90.00	—
1934 Proof	Inc. above	Value: 125				

KM# 2854 50 GROSCHEN
5.5100 g., Copper-Nickel **Obv:** Austrian shield on haloed double eagle's breast, value at bottom **Rev:** Large value above date

Date	Mintage	F	VF	XF	Unc	BU
1935	11,435,000	0.75	1.25	2.50	5.00	—
1935 Proof	Inc. above	Value: 80.00				
1936	1,000,000	30.00	40.00	60.00	115	—
1936 Proof	Inc. above	Value: 140				

KM# 2839 1/2 SCHILLING
3.0000 g., 0.6400 Silver 0.0617 oz. ASW **Obv:** Austrian shield at center **Rev:** Numeric value in diamond at center

Date	Mintage	F	VF	XF	Unc	BU
1925	18,370,000	1.25	2.50	4.00	8.00	—
1926	12,943,000	2.00	4.00	7.00	12.50	—

KM# 2835 SCHILLING
7.0000 g., 0.8000 Silver 0.1800 oz. ASW **Obv:** Parliament building in Vienna, date below **Rev:** Coat of arms on spray of edelweiss, value

Date	Mintage	F	VF	XF	Unc	BU
1924	11,086,000	BV	3.50	6.00	10.00	—

KM# 2840 SCHILLING
6.0000 g., 0.6400 Silver 0.1235 oz. ASW **Obv:** Parliament building in Vienna, date below **Rev:** Coat of arms on spray of edelweiss, value

Date	Mintage	F	VF	XF	Unc	BU
1925	38,209,000	BV	2.25	3.50	7.00	—
1926	20,157,000	BV	2.50	4.00	8.00	—
1932	700,000	30.00	65.00	90.00	150	—

KM# 2851 SCHILLING
Copper-Nickel **Obv:** Two sprigs of grain in center with large numeric value on top **Rev:** Austrian shield on haloed double eagles breast, tail dividing date

Date	Mintage	F	VF	XF	Unc	BU
1934	30,641,000	1.00	2.00	3.50	7.50	—
1934 Proof		Value: 150				
1935	11,987,000	3.00	6.00	12.50	30.00	—

KM# 2843 2 SCHILLING
12.0000 g., 0.6400 Silver 0.2469 oz. ASW **Subject:** Centennial - Death of Franz Schubert **Obv:** Value within circle of shields **Rev:** Head of Franz Schubert, left, date at bottom left

Date	Mintage	F	VF	XF	Unc	BU
1928	6,900,000	BV	5.00	8.00	16.00	—

KM# 2844 2 SCHILLING
12.0000 g., 0.6400 Silver 0.2469 oz. ASW **Subject:** 100th Anniversary - Birth of Dr. Theodor Billroth, Surgeon **Obv:** Value within circle of shields **Rev:** Head of Dr. Theodor Billroth, left, date below

Date	Mintage	F	VF	XF	Unc	BU
1929	2,000,000	6.00	9.00	18.00	32.50	—

KM# 2845 2 SCHILLING
12.0000 g., 0.6400 Silver 0.2469 oz. ASW **Subject:** 7th Centennial - Death of Walther von der Vogelweide, Minstrel **Obv:** Value within circle of shields **Rev:** Figure of Walther von der Vogelweide sitting, left, with doves, harp on lower left. date at bottom

Date	Mintage	F	VF	XF	Unc	BU
1930	500,000	5.00	6.00	9.00	18.00	—
1930 Proof	Inc. above	Value: 125				

KM# 2847 2 SCHILLING
12.0000 g., 0.6400 Silver 0.2469 oz. ASW **Subject:** 175th Anniversary - Birth of Wolfgang Mozart, Composer **Obv:** Value within circle of shields **Rev:** Head of Wolfgang Mozart, right, two dates at bottom

Date	Mintage	F	VF	XF	Unc	BU
1931	500,000	9.00	18.00	28.00	50.00	—
1931 Proof	Inc. above	Value: 300				

KM# 2848 2 SCHILLING
12.0000 g., 0.6400 Silver 0.2469 oz. ASW **Subject:** 200th Anniversary - Birth of Joseph Haydn, Composer **Obv:** Value within circle of shields **Rev:** Head of Joseph Haydn, left, date below

Date	Mintage	F	VF	XF	Unc	BU
1932	300,000	25.00	50.00	100	175	—
1932 Proof	Inc. above	Value: 550				

KM# 2849 2 SCHILLING
12.0000 g., 0.6400 Silver 0.2469 oz. ASW **Subject:** Death of Dr. Ignaz Seipel, Chancellor **Obv:** Value within circle of shields **Rev:** Head of Dr. Ignaz Seipel, right, two dates at bottom

Date	Mintage	F	VF	XF	Unc	BU
ND(1933)	400,000	10.00	20.00	35.00	60.00	—
ND(1933) Proof	Inc. above	Value: 400				

KM# 2852 2 SCHILLING
12.0000 g., 0.6400 Silver 0.2469 oz. ASW **Subject:** Death of Dr. Engelbert Dollfuss, Chancellor **Obv:** Value within circle of shields **Rev:** Head of Dr. Engelbert Dollfuss, right, two dates at bottom

Date	Mintage	F	VF	XF	Unc	BU
1934	1,500,000	7.00	12.00	20.00	32.50	—
1934 Proof	Inc. above	Value: 275				

KM# 2855 2 SCHILLING
12.0000 g., 0.6400 Silver 0.2469 oz. ASW **Subject:** 25th Anniversary - Death of Dr. Karl Lueger, Politician, Social reformer **Obv:** Haloed double eagle with Austrian shield, date divides value at bottom **Rev:** Head of Dr. Karl Lueger, right

Date	Mintage	F	VF	XF	Unc	BU
1935	500,000	8.00	16.00	25.00	45.00	—
1935 Proof	Inc. above	Value: 285				

KM# 2858 2 SCHILLING
12.0000 g., 0.6400 Silver 0.2469 oz. ASW **Subject:** Bicentennial - Death of Prince Eugen of Savoy, Imperial Austrian Field Marshal **Obv:** Haloed double eagle with Austrian shield, date divides value below **Rev:** Head of Prince Eugen of Savoy, left

Date	Mintage	F	VF	XF	Unc	BU
1936	500,000	6.00	9.00	18.00	30.00	—
1936 Proof	Inc. above	Value: 225				

KM# 2859 2 SCHILLING
12.0000 g., 0.6400 Silver 0.2469 oz. ASW **Subject:** Bicentennial - Completion of St. Charles Church 1737 **Obv:** Haloed double eagle with Austrian shield, date divides value below **Rev:** St. Charles Church, date at bottom

Date	Mintage	F	VF	XF	Unc	BU
1937	500,000	6.00	9.00	18.00	30.00	—
1937 Proof	Inc. above	Value: 185				

KM# 2853 5 SCHILLING
15.0000 g., 0.8350 Silver 0.4027 oz. ASW **Obv:** Haloed double eagle with Austrian shield, value **Rev:** Standing figure of Madonna of Mariazell, date below

Date	Mintage	F	VF	XF	Unc	BU
1934	3,066,000	11.50	17.50	32.50	60.00	—
1934 Proof	—	Value: 220				
1935	5,377,000	11.50	17.50	32.50	60.00	—
1936	1,557,000	45.00	85.00	125	185	—

KM# 2841 25 SCHILLING
5.8810 g., 0.9000 Gold 0.1702 oz. AGW **Obv:** Imperial Eagle with Austrian shield on breast, holding hammer and sickle, **Rev:** Value at top flanked by edelweiss sprays, date divided by sprigs at bottom

Date	Mintage	F	VF	XF	Unc	BU
1926 Prooflike	276,705	—	—	—	175	—
1927 Prooflike	72,672	—	—	—	185	—
1928 Prooflike	134,041	—	—	—	175	—
1929 Prooflike	243,269	—	—	—	175	—
1930 Prooflike	129,535	—	—	—	185	—
1931 Prooflike	169,002	—	—	—	175	—
1933 Prooflike	4,944	—	—	—	1,850	—
1934 Prooflike	11,000	—	—	—	600	—

KM# 2856 25 SCHILLING
5.8810 g., 0.9000 Gold 0.1702 oz. AGW **Obv:** Haloed double eagle with Austrian shield on breast, value below **Rev:** Half figure of St. Leopold, facing 3/4 forward, date at bottom

Date	Mintage	F	VF	XF	Unc	BU
1935 Prooflike	2,880	—	—	—	1,000	—
1936 Prooflike	7,260	—	—	—	850	—
1937 Prooflike	7,660	—	—	—	850	—
1938 Prooflike	1,360	—	—	—	25,000	—

KM# 2842 100 SCHILLING
23.5245 g., 0.9000 Gold 0.6807 oz. AGW **Obv:** Imperial Eagle with Austrian shield on breast holding hammer and sickle **Rev:** Value at top flanked by edelweiss sprays, date below, one star on either side

Date	Mintage	F	VF	XF	Unc	BU
1926 Prooflike	63,795	—	—	—	675	—
1927 Prooflike	68,746	—	—	—	675	—
1928 Prooflike	40,188	—	—	—	750	—
1929 Prooflike	74,849	—	—	—	675	—
1930 Prooflike	24,849	—	—	—	675	—
1931 Prooflike	101,935	—	—	—	675	—
1933 Prooflike	4,727	—	—	—	1,550	—
1934 Prooflike	9,383	—	—	—	800	—

KM# 2857 100 SCHILLING
23.5245 g., 0.9000 Gold 0.6807 oz. AGW **Obv:** Haloed eagle with Austrian shield on breast, value below **Rev:** Standing figure of Madonna of Mariazell, facing, date below

Date	Mintage	F	VF	XF	Unc	BU
1935 Prooflike	951	—	—	—	5,500	—
1936 Prooflike	12,000	—	—	—	1,650	—
1937 Prooflike	2,900	—	—	—	2,250	—
1938 Prooflike	1,400	—	—	—	25,000	—

POST WWII DECIMAL COINAGE
100 Groschen - 1 Schilling

KM# 2873 GROSCHEN
Zinc **Obv:** Imperial Eagle with Austrian shield on breast **Rev:** Large value above date, spray of leaves below

Date	Mintage	F	VF	XF	Unc	BU
1947	23,758,000	0.15	0.25	0.75	2.50	—

KM# 2876 2 GROSCHEN
0.9000 g., Aluminum, 18 mm. **Obv:** Imperial Eagle with Austrian shield on breast, holding hammer and sickle **Rev:** Large value in circle, date below circle **Edge:** Plain

Date	Mintage	F	VF	XF	Unc	BU
1950	21,652,000	—	0.15	0.60	4.00	—
1950 Proof	—	Value: 28.00				
1951	7,377,000	—	0.25	1.00	4.50	—
1951 Proof	—	Value: 300				
1952	37,851,000	—	0.15	0.50	2.50	—
1952 Proof	—	Value: 25.00				
1954	46,167,000	—	0.15	0.50	2.50	—
1954 Proof	—	Value: 50.00				
1957	26,923,000	—	0.15	0.50	3.00	—
1957 Proof	—	Value: 45.00				
1962	6,692,000	—	0.15	0.50	1.50	—
1962 Proof	—	Value: 28.00				
1964	173,000	Value: 6.50				
1965	14,475,000	—	0.10	0.30	1.50	—
1965 Proof	—	Value: 2.50				
1966	7,454,000	—	0.10	0.30	1.50	—
1966 Proof	—	Value: 7.50				
1967 Proof	13,000	Value: 100				
1968	1,803,400	—	0.10	0.30	1.50	—
1968 Proof	21,600	Value: 10.00				
1969 Proof	57,000	Value: 6.00				
1970 Proof	260,000	Value: 2.50				
1971 Proof	145,000	Value: 2.50				
1972	2,763,000	—	—	0.20	0.50	—
1972 Proof	132,000	Value: 1.00				
1973	5,883,000	—	—	0.20	0.50	—
1973 Proof	149,000	Value: 1.00				
1974	1,387,000	—	—	0.20	0.50	—
1974 Proof	93,000	Value: 1.00				
1975	1,096,000	—	—	0.20	0.50	—
1975 Proof	52,000	Value: 1.00				
1976	2,755,000	—	—	0.20	0.50	—
1976 Proof	45,000	Value: 1.00				
1977	1,837,000	—	—	0.20	0.50	—
1977 Proof	47,000	Value: 1.00				
1978	1,527,000	—	—	0.20	0.50	—
1978 Proof	44,000	Value: 1.00				
1979	2,434,000	—	—	0.20	0.50	—
1979 Proof	44,000	Value: 1.00				
1980	1,893,000	—	—	0.20	0.50	—
1980 Proof	48,000	Value: 10.00				
1981	950,000	—	—	0.20	0.50	—
1981 Proof	49,000	Value: 8.00				
1982	3,950,000	—	—	0.20	0.50	—
1982 Proof	50,000	Value: 3.00				
1983	2,665,000	—	—	0.20	0.50	—
1983 Proof	65,000	Value: 2.00				
1984	500,000	—	—	0.20	0.50	—
1984 Proof	65,000	Value: 2.00				
1985	1,060,000	—	—	0.20	0.50	—

Date	Mintage	F	VF	XF	Unc	BU
1985 Proof	45,000	Value: 5.00				
1986	1,798,000	—	—	0.20	0.50	—
1986 Proof	42,000	Value: 10.00				
1987	958,000	—	—	0.20	0.50	—
1987 Proof	42,000	Value: 6.00				
1988	1,061,000	—	—	0.20	0.50	—
1988 Proof	39,000	Value: 2.00				
1989	950,000	—	—	0.20	0.50	—
1989 Proof	38,000	Value: 2.00				
1990 Proof	35,000	Value: 22.00				
1991	2,600,000	—	—	0.20	0.50	—
1991 Proof	27,000	Value: 5.00				
1992	25,000	—	—	—	20.00	—
Note: In sets only						
1992 Proof	25,000	Value: 15.00				
1993	35,000	—	—	—	20.00	—
Note: In sets only						
1993 Proof	28,000	Value: 7.00				
1994	25,000	—	—	—	25.00	—
Note: In sets only						
1994 Proof	25,000	Value: 30.00				

KM# 2875 5 GROSCHEN
2.5000 g., Zinc, 18.86 mm. **Obv:** Imperial Eagle with Austrian shield on breast, holding hammer and sickle **Edge:** Reeded

Date	Mintage	F	VF	XF	Unc	BU
1948	17,269,000	—	0.20	0.75	12.00	—
1950	19,426,431	—	0.20	0.75	8.00	—
1950 Proof	—	Value: 200				
1951	12,454,569	—	0.20	0.75	12.00	—
1951 Proof	—	Value: 35.00				
1953	14,931,000	—	0.15	0.75	8.00	—
1955	12,288,000	—	0.15	0.75	12.00	—
1957	26,809,000	—	0.15	0.75	6.00	—
1957 Proof	—	Value: 50.00				
1961	3,429,000	—	0.20	0.75	8.00	—
1961 Proof	—	Value: 25.00				
1962	5,999,000	—	0.20	0.75	8.00	—
1963	13,293,000	—	0.15	0.75	8.00	—
1963 Proof	—	Value: 40.00				
1964	4,659,000	—	0.15	0.75	8.00	—
1964 Proof	—	Value: 2.50				
1965	13,704,000	—	0.10	0.50	3.00	—
1965 Proof	—	Value: 2.50				
1966	9,348,000	—	0.10	0.50	3.00	—
1966 Proof	—	Value: 8.00				
1967	4,404,000	—	0.10	0.50	3.00	—
1967 Proof	—	Value: 10.00				
1968	31,418,400	—	0.10	0.50	3.00	—
1968 Proof	15,600	Value: 10.00				
1969 Proof	44,000	Value: 10.00				
1970 Proof	144,000	Value: 2.50				
1971 Proof	125,000	Value: 2.50				
1972	10,979,000	—	—	0.20	0.75	—
1972 Proof	116,000	Value: 1.00				
1973	10,336,000	—	—	0.20	0.75	—
1973 Proof	120,000	Value: 1.00				
1974	2,911,000	—	—	0.20	0.75	—
1974 Proof	87,000	Value: 1.00				
1975	7,102,000	—	—	0.20	0.75	—
1975 Proof	51,000	Value: 1.00				
1976	8,079,000	—	—	0.20	0.75	—
1976 Proof	45,000	Value: 1.00				
1977	1,600,000	—	—	0.20	0.75	—
1977 Proof	45,000	Value: 1.00				
1978	2,657,000	—	—	0.20	0.75	—
1978 Proof	44,000	Value: 1.00				
1979	4,927,000	—	—	0.20	0.75	—
1979 Proof	44,000	Value: 1.00				
1980	3,100,000	—	—	0.20	0.75	—
1980 Proof	48,000	Value: 8.00				
1981	450,000	—	—	0.20	0.75	—
1981 Proof	49,000	Value: 8.00				
1982	3,950,000	—	—	0.20	0.75	—
1982 Proof	50,000	Value: 2.50				
1983	501,000	—	—	0.20	0.75	—
1983 Proof	65,000	Value: 2.50				
1984	988,000	—	—	0.20	0.75	—
1984 Proof	65,000	Value: 2.50				
1985	1,914,000	—	—	0.20	0.75	—
1985 Proof	45,000	Value: 4.00				
1986	1,008,000	—	—	0.20	0.75	—
1986 Proof	42,000	Value: 7.00				
1987	1,458,000	—	—	0.20	0.75	—
1987 Proof	42,000	Value: 4.00				
1988	1,261,000	—	—	0.20	0.75	—
1988 Proof	39,000	Value: 3.00				
1989	2,604,000	—	—	0.20	0.75	—
1989 Proof	38,000	Value: 3.00				
1990	2,608,000	—	—	0.20	0.75	—
1990 Proof	35,000	Value: 6.00				
1991	2,400,000	—	—	0.20	0.75	—
1991 Proof	27,000	Value: 6.00				

Date	Mintage	F	VF	XF	Unc	BU
1992	671,000			0.20	0.75	—
1992 Proof	25,000	Value: 10.00				
1993	35,000				12.00	—
Note: In sets only						
1993 Proof	28,000	Value: 7.00				
1994	25,000				15.00	—
Note: In sets only						
1994 Proof	25,000	Value: 20.00				

KM# 2874   10 GROSCHEN
3.5000 g., Zinc, 21 mm. **Obv:** Imperial Eagle with Austrian shield on breast, holding hammer and sickle **Rev:** Large value above date, trumpet flower spray below **Edge:** Plain

Date	Mintage	F	VF	XF	Unc	BU
1947	6,845,000	0.75	2.00	4.00	22.00	—
1947 Proof	—	Value: 55.00				
1948	66,205,000	0.20	0.50	1.00	3.50	—
1948 Proof	—	Value: 65.00				
1949	51,202,000	0.20	0.50	1.00	3.50	—
1949 Proof	—	Value: 75.00				

KM# 2878   10 GROSCHEN
1.1000 g., Aluminum, 20 mm. **Obv:** Small Imperial Eagle with Austrian shield on breast, at top between numbers, scalloped rim, stylized inscription below **Rev:** Large value above date, scalloped rim **Edge:** Plain

Date	Mintage	F	VF	XF	Unc	BU
1951	9,573,000	—	0.20	0.75	8.00	—
1951 Proof	—	Value: 85.00				
1952	45,911,400	—	0.10	0.50	4.00	—
1952 Proof	—	Value: 50.00				
1953	22,577,600	—	0.10	0.50	4.00	—
1953 Proof	—	Value: 175				
1955	51,707,000	—	0.10	0.50	4.00	—
1955 Proof	—	Value: 28.00				
1957	33,509,000	—	0.10	0.50	4.00	—
1957 Proof	—	Value: 150				
1959	80,719,000	—	0.10	0.35	3.50	—
1959 Proof	—	Value: 45.00				
1961	11,283,000	—	0.20	0.75	8.00	—
1961 Proof	—					
1962	24,635,000	—	0.10	0.35	3.50	—
1962 Proof	—	Value: 40.00				
1963	38,062,000	—	0.10	0.35	3.50	—
1963 Proof	—	Value: 45.00				
1964	34,928,000	—	0.10	0.20	2.00	—
1964 Proof	—	Value: 1.50				
1965	40,615,000	—	0.10	0.20	2.00	—
1965 Proof	—	Value: 1.50				
1966	24,991,000	—	0.10	0.20	2.00	—
1966 Proof	—	Value: 6.00				
1967	32,552,999	—	0.10	0.20	2.00	—
1967 Proof	—	Value: 12.00				
1968	42,395,800	—	0.10	0.20	2.00	—
1968 Proof	16,000	Value: 8.00				
1969	19,953,000	—	0.10	0.20	2.00	—
1969 Proof	27,000	Value: 5.00				
1970	36,997,500	—		0.10	0.45	—
1970 Proof	102,000	Value: 1.00				
1971	57,450,000	—		0.10	0.45	—
1971 Proof	82,000	Value: 1.00				
1972	75,661,000	—		0.10	0.45	—
1972 Proof	81,000	Value: 1.00				
1973	60,244,000	—		0.10	0.45	—
1973 Proof	97,000	Value: 0.75				
1974	55,924,000	—		0.10	0.45	—
1974 Proof	78,000	Value: 0.75				
1975	60,576,000	—		0.10	0.45	—
1975 Proof	49,000	Value: 0.75				
1976	39,357,000	—		0.10	0.45	—
1976 Proof	44,000	Value: 0.75				
1977	53,610,000	—		0.10	0.45	—
1977 Proof	44,000	Value: 0.75				
1978	57,857,000	—		0.10	0.45	—
1978 Proof	43,000	Value: 0.75				
1979	103,686,000	—			0.45	—
1979 Proof	44,000	Value: 0.75				
1980	79,848,000	—			0.45	—
1980 Proof	48,000	Value: 2.00				
1981	92,268,000	—			0.45	—
1981 Proof	49,000	Value: 2.00				
1982	99,950,000	—			0.45	—
1982 Proof	50,000	Value: 0.75				
1983	93,768,000	—			0.45	—

Date	Mintage	F	VF	XF	Unc	BU
1983 Proof	65,000	Value: 0.75				
1984	86,603,000	—			0.45	—
1984 Proof	65,000	Value: 0.75				
1985	86,304,000	—			0.45	—
1985 Proof	45,000	Value: 0.75				
1986	108,912,000	—			0.45	—
1986 Proof	42,000	Value: 1.50				
1987	114,058,000	—			0.45	—
1987 Proof	42,000	Value: 0.75				
1988	114,461,000	—			0.45	—
1988 Proof	39,000	Value: 0.75				
1989	127,784,000	—			0.45	—
1989 Proof	38,000	Value: 0.75				
1990	182,050,000	—			0.45	—
1990 Proof	35,000	Value: 1.50				
1991	145,000,000	—			0.45	—
1991 Proof	27,000	Value: 1.50				
1992	125,000,000	—			0.45	—
1992 Proof	25,000	Value: 1.50				
1993	120,000,000	—			0.45	—
1993 Proof	28,000	Value: 1.50				
1994	110,000,000	—			0.45	—
1994 Proof	25,000	Value: 2.00				
1995	80,000,000	—			0.45	—
1995 Proof	27,000	Value: 2.00				
1996	100,000,000	—			0.45	—
1996 Proof	25,000	Value: 2.50				
1997	—	—			0.45	—
1997 Proof	25,000	Value: 2.50				
1998	32,000,000	—			0.45	—
1998 Proof	25,000	Value: 3.00				
1999	—	—			0.45	—
1999 Proof	50,000	Value: 1.50				
2000	—	—			0.45	—
2000 Proof	75,000	Value: 1.50				

KM# 2877   20 GROSCHEN
Aluminum-Bronze **Obv:** Imperial Eagle with Austrian shield on breast, holding hammer and sickle **Rev:** Value at center above date

Date	Mintage	F	VF	XF	Unc	BU
1950	1,610,000	0.20	0.50	2.00	13.50	—
1950 Proof	—	Value: 40.00				
1951	7,781,000	0.10	0.25	0.75	2.75	—
1951 Proof	—	Value: 25.00				
1954	5,343,000	0.10	0.25	0.75	2.75	—
1954 Proof	—	Value: 275				

KM# 2870   50 GROSCHEN
1.3400 g., Aluminum, 21.9 mm. **Obv:** Imperial Eagle with Austrian shield on breast holding hammer and sickle **Rev:** Numeric value on Austrian shield at center, date divided below shield

Date	Mintage	F	VF	XF	Unc	BU
1946	13,058,000	0.20	0.50	1.75	10.00	—
1946 Proof	—	Value: 75.00				
1947	26,990,000	0.15	0.35	1.25	6.50	—
1947 Proof	—	Value: 35.00				
1952	7,455,000	0.40	1.00	2.50	8.50	—
1952 Proof	—	Value: 55.00				
1955	16,919,000	0.20	0.40	1.25	4.50	—
1955 Proof	—	Value: 55.00				

KM# 2885   50 GROSCHEN
2.9700 g., Aluminum-Bronze, 19.44 mm. **Obv:** Austrian shield **Rev:** Large value above date **Edge:** Reeded

Date	Mintage	F	VF	XF	Unc	BU
1959	14,122,000	—	0.50	2.00	15.00	—
1959 Proof	—	Value: 25.00				
1960	22,404,000	—	0.20	1.50	12.00	—
1960 Proof	—	Value: 100				
1961	19,891,000	—	0.50	2.00	15.00	—
1961 Proof	—	Value: 75.00				
1962	10,008,000	—	0.40	1.75	15.00	—
1962 Proof	—	Value: 40.00				
1963	9,483,000	—	0.50	2.00	18.00	—
1963 Proof	—	Value: 40.00				

Date	Mintage	F	VF	XF	Unc	BU
1964	5,331,000	—	0.15	0.75	3.00	—
1964 Proof	—	Value: 1.50				
1965	1,500,700	—	0.15	0.75	3.00	—
1965 Proof	—	Value: 1.50				
1966	7,322,000	—	0.15	0.75	3.00	—
1966 Proof	—	Value: 10.00				
1967	8,237,000	—	0.15	0.75	3.00	—
1967 Proof	—	Value: 15.00				
1968	7,741,600	—	0.15	0.75	3.00	—
1968 Proof	15,400	Value: 10.00				
1969	7,070,000	—	0.15	0.75	3.00	—
1969 Proof	26,000	Value: 5.00				
1970	29,941,000	—	0.10	0.50	2.00	—
1970 Proof	128,000	Value: 3.00				
1971	14,217,000	—		0.25	1.50	—
1971 Proof	84,000	Value: 2.50				
1972	17,367,000	—		0.25	1.50	—
1972 Proof	80,000	Value: 2.00				
1973	17,902,000	—		0.25	1.50	—
1973 Proof	90,000	Value: 2.00				
1974	15,852,000	—		0.25	1.50	—
1974 Proof	76,000	Value: 2.00				
1975	7,726,000	—		0.15	1.00	—
1975 Proof	49,000	Value: 1.50				
1976	11,150,000	—		0.15	1.00	—
1976 Proof	44,000	Value: 1.50				
1977	7,258,000	—		0.15	1.00	—
1977 Proof	44,000	Value: 1.50				
1978	12,407,000	—		0.15	1.00	—
1978 Proof	43,000	Value: 1.50				
1979	16,351,000	—		0.15	1.00	—
1979 Proof	44,000	Value: 1.50				
1980	29,884,000	—		0.15	1.25	—
1980 Proof	48,000	Value: 3.50				
1981	12,993,000	—		0.15	1.25	—
1981 Proof	49,000	Value: 3.50				
1982	9,950,000	—		0.15	1.00	—
1982 Proof	50,000	Value: 1.50				
1983	15,182,000	—		0.15	1.00	—
1983 Proof	65,000	Value: 1.50				
1984	20,742,000	—		0.15	1.00	—
1984 Proof	65,000	Value: 2.00				
1985	15,654,000	—		0.15	1.00	—
1985 Proof	45,000	Value: 2.00				
1986	17,016,000	—		0.15	0.75	—
1986 Proof	42,000	Value: 2.00				
1987	7,258,000	—		0.15	0.75	—
1987 Proof	42,000	Value: 2.00				
1988	16,267,000	—		0.15	0.75	—
1988 Proof	39,000	Value: 2.00				
1989	17,353,000	—		0.15	0.75	—
1989 Proof	38,000	Value: 2.00				
1990	29,653,000	—		0.15	0.75	—
1990 Proof	35,000	Value: 2.00				
1991	44,990,000	—		0.15	0.75	—
1991 Proof	27,000	Value: 2.00				
1992	20,000,000	—			0.45	—
1992 Proof	25,000	Value: 2.00				
1993	15,000,000	—			0.45	—
1993 Proof	28,000	Value: 2.00				
1994	10,000,000	—			0.45	—
1994 Proof	25,000	Value: 2.50				
1995	20,000,000	—			0.45	—
1995 Proof	27,000	Value: 2.00				
1996	15,000,000	—			0.45	—
1996 Proof	25,000	Value: 2.00				
1997	10,000,000	—			0.45	—
1997 Proof	25,000	Value: 2.50				
1998	—	—			0.45	—
1998 Proof	25,000	Value: 3.00				
Note: In sets only						
1999	—	—			0.45	—
1999 Proof	50,000	Value: 2.00				
Note: In sets only						
2000	4,300,000	—			0.45	—
2000 Proof	75,000	Value: 2.00				
Note: In sets only						

KM# 2871   SCHILLING
Aluminum **Obv:** Full figure with seedbag on left hip, dropping seed from right hand, divides value **Rev:** Imperial Eagle with Austrian shield, tail dividing date

Date	Mintage	F	VF	XF	Unc	BU
1946	27,336,000	0.30	1.00	2.50	20.00	—
1946 Proof	—	Value: 500				
1947	35,838,000	0.20	0.50	1.50	6.00	—
1947 Proof	—	Value: 35.00				
1952	23,231,000	0.25	0.75	1.65	7.00	—
1952 Proof	—	Value: 50.00				
1957	28,649,000	0.25	0.75	1.65	7.00	—
1957 Proof	—	Value: 145				

KM# 2886 SCHILLING
4.2000 g., Aluminum-Bronze, 22.5 mm. **Obv:** Large value above date **Rev:** Edelweiss flower **Edge:** Plain

Date	Mintage	F	VF	XF	Unc	BU
1959	46,726,000	—	0.25	0.75	12.00	—
1959 Proof	—	Value: 15.00				
1960	46,111,000	—	0.25	1.50	20.00	—
1960 Proof	—	Value: 200				
1961	51,115,000	—	0.25	1.50	15.00	—
1961 Proof	—	Value: 400				
1962	9,303,000	—	0.25	1.50	15.00	—
1962 Proof	—	Value: 65.00				
1963	24,845,000	—	0.25	1.50	20.00	—
1963 Proof	—	Value: 45.00				
1964	11,709,000	—	0.25	1.25	3.50	—
1964 Proof	—	Value: 2.00				
1965	9,155,100	—	0.25	0.75	3.50	—
1965 Proof	27,900	Value: 8.00				
1966	18,688,000	—	0.25	0.75	3.50	—
1966 Proof	—	Value: 8.00				
1967	22,214,000	—	0.25	0.75	3.50	—
1967 Proof	—	Value: 12.00				
1968	30,860,000	—	0.25	0.75	3.50	—
1968 Proof	17,000	Value: 8.00				
1969	10,285,000	—	0.25	0.75	3.50	—
1969 Proof	28,000	Value: 4.00				
1970	10,678,600	—	0.20	0.50	2.50	—
1970 Proof	100,400	Value: 1.75				
1971	27,974,000	—	0.20	0.50	2.50	—
1971 Proof	82,000	Value: 1.75				
1972	54,577,000	—	0.15	0.30	1.50	—
1972 Proof	78,000	Value: 1.25				
1973	41,332,000	—	0.15	0.30	1.50	—
1973 Proof	90,000	Value: 1.25				
1974	43,712,000	—	0.15	0.30	1.50	—
1974 Proof	77,000	Value: 1.25				
1975	13,989,000	—	0.15	0.30	1.50	—
1975 Proof	49,000	Value: 1.25				
1976	28,748,000	—	0.15	0.30	1.50	—
1976 Proof	44,000	Value: 1.25				
1977	19,584,000	—	0.15	0.30	1.50	—
1977 Proof	44,000	Value: 1.25				
1978	35,632,000	—	0.15	0.30	1.50	—
1978 Proof	43,000	Value: 1.25				
1979	64,802,000	—	0.15	0.30	1.50	—
1979 Proof	44,000	Value: 1.25				
1980	49,855,000	—	—	0.15	0.75	—
1980 Proof	48,000	Value: 2.50				
1981	37,502,000	—	—	0.15	0.75	—
1981 Proof	49,000	Value: 2.50				
1982	29,950,000	—	—	0.15	0.75	—
1982 Proof	50,000	Value: 1.50				
1983	38,186,000	—	—	0.15	0.75	—

Note: Also exists with higher date

Date	Mintage	F	VF	XF	Unc	BU
1983 Proof	65,000	Value: 1.50				
1984	31,891,000	—	—	0.15	0.75	—
1984 Proof	65,000	Value: 1.50				
1985	49,154,000	—	—	0.15	0.75	—
1985 Proof	45,000	Value: 1.50				
1986	57,618,000	—	—	—	0.65	—
1986 Proof	42,000	Value: 1.50				
1987	44,158,000	—	—	—	0.65	—
1987 Proof	42,000	Value: 1.50				
1988	51,561,000	—	—	—	0.65	—
1988 Proof	39,000	Value: 1.50				
1989	62,821,000	—	—	—	0.65	—
1989 Proof	38,000	Value: 1.50				
1990	103,710,000	—	—	—	0.50	—
1990 Proof	35,000	Value: 1.50				
1991	117,700,000	—	—	—	0.50	—
1991 Proof	27,000	Value: 1.50				
1992	55,000,000	—	—	—	1.25	—
1992 Proof	25,000	Value: 2.00				
1993	60,000,000	—	—	—	1.25	—
1993 Proof	28,000	Value: 2.00				
1994	50,000,000	—	—	—	1.25	—
1994 Proof	25,000	Value: 3.00				
1995	70,000,000	—	—	—	1.25	—
1995 Proof	27,000	Value: 2.50				
1996	65,000,000	—	—	—	1.25	—
1996 Proof	25,000	Value: 3.50				
1997	50,000,000	—	—	—	1.25	—
1997 Proof	25,000	Value: 4.00				
1998	60,000,000	—	—	—	1.25	—
1998 Proof	25,000	Value: 4.50				
1999	—	—	—	—	1.25	—
1999 Proof	50,000	Value: 2.00				

Note: In sets only

Date	Mintage	F	VF	XF	Unc	BU
2000	42,200,000	—	—	—	1.25	—
2000 Proof	75,000	Value: 2.00				

Note: In sets only

KM# 2872 2 SCHILLING
Aluminum **Obv:** Imperial Eagle with Austrian shield on breast, holding hammer and sickle **Rev:** Thick value above spray of leaves and berries, grain sprigs at top

Date	Mintage	F	VF	XF	Unc	BU
1946	10,082,000	0.45	1.25	2.75	25.00	—
1946 Proof	—	Value: 700				
1947	20,140,000	0.45	1.25	2.50	20.00	—
1947 Proof	—	Value: 40.00				
1952	149,000	55.00	100	200	350	—
1952 Proof	—	Value: 900				

KM# 2879 5 SCHILLING
4.0000 g., Aluminum, 30.94 mm. **Obv:** Large value at center, geared rim **Rev:** Imperial Eagle with Austrian shield on breast, holding hammer and sickle

Date	Mintage	F	VF	XF	Unc	BU
1952	29,873,000	1.00	2.00	5.00	12.50	—
1952 Proof	—	Value: 45.00				
1957	240,000	100	380	540	900	—
1957 Proof	—	Value: 700				

KM# 2889 5 SCHILLING
5.2000 g., 0.6400 Silver 0.1070 oz. ASW, 23.5 mm. **Obv:** Lippizaner stallion with rider, rearing, left **Rev:** Austrian shield divides date, value above, sprays below **Edge:** Reeded

Date	Mintage	F	VF	XF	Unc	BU
1960	12,618,000	—	BV	2.50	5.50	—
1960 Proof	1,000	Value: 65.00				
1961	17,902,000	—	BV	2.50	4.50	—
1961 Proof	—	Value: 25.00				
1962	6,771,000	—	BV	2.50	4.50	—
1962 Proof	—	Value: 50.00				
1963	1,811,000	BV	2.00	4.00	14.50	—
1963 Proof	—	Value: 120				
1964	4,030,000	—	BV	2.00	3.50	—
1964 Proof	—	Value: 3.50				
1965	4,759,000	—	BV	2.00	3.50	—
1965 Proof	—	Value: 3.50				
1966	4,481,000	—	BV	2.00	3.50	—
1966 Proof	—	Value: 8.00				
1967	1,900,000	BV	2.00	4.00	6.00	—
1967 Proof	—	Value: 15.00				
1968	4,792,300	—	BV	2.00	3.50	—
1968 Proof	19,700	Value: 8.00				

KM# 2889a 5 SCHILLING
4.8000 g., Copper-Nickel, 23.5 mm. **Obv:** Lippizaner stallion with rider, rearing left **Rev:** Austrian shield divides date, value above, sprays below **Edge:** Plain

Date	Mintage	F	VF	XF	Unc	BU
1968	2,075,000	—	1.00	2.50	5.00	—
1969	41,222,000	—	0.75	1.50	4.00	—
1969 Proof	21,000	Value: 6.00				
1970	15,770,700	—	—	1.00	4.00	—
1970 Proof	92,300	Value: 2.50				
1971	21,422,000	—	—	1.00	4.00	—

Date	Mintage	F	VF	XF	Unc	BU
1971 Proof	84,000	Value: 2.50				
1972	5,430,000	—	—	1.00	4.00	—
1972 Proof	75,000	Value: 2.50				
1973	8,259,000	—	—	1.00	4.00	—
1973 Proof	87,000	Value: 2.50				
1974	17,956,000	—	—	1.00	4.00	—
1974 Proof	76,000	Value: 2.50				
1975	6,849,000	—	—	0.75	4.00	—
1975 Proof	49,000	Value: 2.50				
1976	1,458,000	—	—	1.00	5.00	—
1976 Proof	44,000	Value: 4.00				
1977	6,423,000	—	—	0.65	2.50	—
1977 Proof	44,000	Value: 2.75				
1978	9,907,000	—	—	0.65	2.50	—
1978 Proof	43,000	Value: 2.75				
1979	11,607,000	—	—	0.65	2.50	—
1979 Proof	44,000	Value: 2.75				
1980	14,898,000	—	—	0.65	2.50	—
1980 Proof	48,000	Value: 3.50				
1981	13,837,000	—	—	0.65	2.50	—
1981 Proof	49,000	Value: 3.50				
1982	4,950,000	—	—	0.65	2.00	—
1982 Proof	50,000	Value: 2.50				
1983	9,268,000	—	—	0.65	2.00	—
1983 Proof	65,000	Value: 2.50				
1984	13,763,000	—	—	0.65	2.00	—
1984 Proof	65,000	Value: 2.50				
1985	12,754,000	—	—	0.60	2.00	—
1985 Proof	45,000	Value: 3.00				
1986	16,558,000	—	—	0.60	2.00	—
1986 Proof	42,000	Value: 3.00				
1987	9,758,000	—	—	0.60	2.00	—
1987 Proof	42,000	Value: 3.00				
1988	10,161,000	—	—	0.60	2.00	—
1988 Proof	39,000	Value: 3.00				
1989	24,043,000	—	—	0.60	2.00	—
1989 Proof	38,000	Value: 3.00				
1990	36,512,000	—	—	0.60	2.00	—
1990 Proof	35,000	Value: 2.50				
1991	24,000,000	—	—	0.60	2.00	—
1991 Proof	27,000	Value: 2.50				
1992	20,000,000	—	—	—	2.00	—
1992 Proof	25,000	Value: 2.50				
1993	20,000,000	—	—	—	2.00	—
1993 Proof	28,000	Value: 2.50				
1994	10,000,000	—	—	—	2.00	—
1994 Proof	25,000	Value: 3.50				
1995	20,000,000	—	—	—	2.00	—
1995 Proof	27,000	Value: 2.50				
1996	10,000,000	—	—	—	2.00	—
1996 Proof	25,000	Value: 3.50				
1997	10,000,000	—	—	—	2.00	—
1997 Proof	25,000	Value: 4.00				
1998	10,000,000	—	—	—	2.00	—
1998 Proof	25,000	Value: 4.50				
1999	—	—	—	—	2.00	—
1999 Proof	50,000	Value: 2.50				

Note: In sets only

Date	Mintage	F	VF	XF	Unc	BU
2000	*1,500,000	—	—	—	2.00	—
2000 Proof	75,000	Value: 2.50				

Note: In sets only

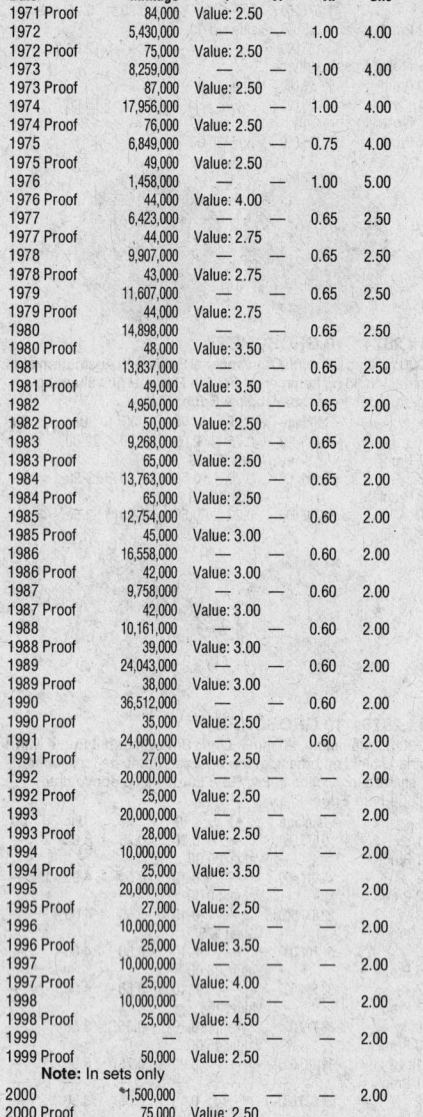

KM# 2882 10 SCHILLING
7.5000 g., 0.6400 Silver 0.1543 oz. ASW **Obv:** Austrian shield **Rev:** Woman of Wachau, left, value at lower right, date to right of hat

Date	Mintage	F	VF	XF	Unc	BU
1957	15,635,500	BV	2.25	3.00	7.50	—
1957 Proof	—	Value: 80.00				
1958	27,280,000	BV	2.25	3.00	7.50	—
1958 Proof	—	Value: 700				
1959	4,739,500	BV	2.25	3.50	11.50	—
1959 Proof	—	Value: 40.00				
1964	187,000	7.00	10.00	25.00	45.00	—
1964 Proof	27,000	Value: 15.00				
1965	1,721,000	BV	2.25	3.50	11.50	—
1965 Proof	—	Value: 8.00				
1966	3,430,500	BV	2.25	3.50	9.00	—
1966 Proof	—	Value: 12.00				
1967	1,393,500	BV	2.25	3.50	11.50	—
1967 Proof	—	Value: 15.00				
1968	1,525,000	BV	2.25	3.50	10.00	—
1968 Proof	15,000	Value: 9.00				
1969	1,317,500	BV	2.25	3.50	11.50	—
1969 Proof	20,000	Value: 12.00				
1970	4,493,900	—	—	BV	2.75	6.50	—
1970 Proof	89,100	Value: 5.00				
1971	7,320,500	—	—	BV	2.75	5.50	—
1971 Proof	80,000	Value: 5.00				
1972	14,210,500	—	—	BV	2.75	4.50	—
1972 Proof	75,000	Value: 5.00				

Date	Mintage	F	VF	XF	Unc	BU
1973	14,559,000	—	BV	2.75	4.50	—
1973 Proof	80,000	Value: 5.00				

KM# 2918   10 SCHILLING
6.2000 g., Copper-Nickel Plated Nickel, 26 mm. **Obv:** Imperial Eagle with Austrian shield on breast, holding hammer and sickle **Rev:** Woman of Wachau left, value and date right of hat

Date	Mintage	F	VF	XF	Unc	BU
1974	59,877,000	—	—	2.00	6.00	—
1974 Proof	75,500	Value: 4.00				
1975	16,869,500	—	—	2.00	6.00	—
1975 Proof	49,000	Value: 3.00				
1976	13,459,500	—	—	2.00	6.00	—
1976 Proof	44,000	Value: 3.00				
1977	3,804,000	—	—	2.00	6.00	—
1977 Proof	44,000	Value: 3.00				
1978	6,813,000	—	—	2.00	6.00	—
1978 Proof	43,000	Value: 3.00				
1979	11,702,000	—	—	2.00	6.00	—
1979 Proof	44,000	Value: 2.50				
1980	10,884,000	—	—	2.00	6.00	—
1980 Proof	48,000	Value: 6.50				
1981	9,470,000	—	—	2.00	6.00	—
1981 Proof	49,000	Value: 6.50				
1982	4,950,000	—	—	2.00	6.00	—
1982 Proof	50,000	Value: 2.50				
1983	8,993,000	—	—	1.50	4.00	—
1983 Proof	65,000	Value: 2.50				
1984	7,936,000	—	—	1.50	4.00	—
1984 Proof	65,000	Value: 2.50				
1985	9,009,000	—	—	1.50	4.00	—
1985 Proof	45,000	Value: 2.50				
1986	8,189,000	—	—	1.50	4.00	—
1986 Proof	42,000	Value: 2.50				
1987	9,258,000	—	—	1.50	4.00	—
1987 Proof	42,000	Value: 2.50				
1988	9,011,000	—	—	1.50	4.00	—
1988 Proof	39,000	Value: 4.50				
1989	16,233,000	—	—	1.25	3.00	—
1989 Proof	38,000	Value: 2.50				
1990	27,150,000	—	—	1.25	3.00	—
1990 Proof	35,000	Value: 2.50				
1991	18,000,000	—	—	1.25	3.00	—
1991 Proof	27,000	Value: 2.50				
1992	10,952,000	—	—	—	2.00	—
1992 Proof	25,000	Value: 2.50				
1993	12,500,000	—	—	—	2.00	—
1993 Proof	28,000	Value: 2.50				
1994	15,000,000	—	—	—	2.00	—
1994 Proof	25,000	Value: 3.50				
1995	12,500,000	—	—	—	2.00	—
1995 Proof	27,000	Value: 2.50				
1996	12,500,000	—	—	—	2.00	—
1996 Proof	25,000	Value: 4.00				
1997	11,000,000	—	—	—	2.00	—
1997 Proof	25,000	Value: 4.50				
1998	5,000,000	—	—	—	2.00	—
1998 Proof	25,000	Value: 5.00				
1999		—	—	—	2.00	—
1999 Proof	50,000	Value: 2.50				
	Note: In sets only					
2000	1,175,000	—	—	—	2.00	—
2000 Proof	75,000	Value: 2.50				
	Note: In sets only					

KM# 2946.1   20 SCHILLING
8.0000 g., Copper-Aluminum-Nickel, 27.8 mm. **Obv:** Nine people standing (representing the nine Austrian provinces), center figure holding Austrian shield aloft **Rev:** Numeric value within shaded box within circle, date below box **Edge:** Edge with incuse dots

Date	Mintage	F	VF	XF	Unc	BU
1980	9,851,500	—	—	2.50	3.50	—
1980 Proof	48,000	Value: 20.00				
1981	450,500	—	—	4.50	7.50	—
1981 Proof	49,000	Value: 22.50				
1991	140,000	—	—	2.25	5.00	—

KM# 2955.1   20 SCHILLING
8.0000 g., Copper-Aluminum-Nickel, 27.8 mm. **Subject:** 250th Anniversary - Birth of Joseph Haydn **Obv:** Value within box, small Austrian shield divides date below **Rev:** Bust of Joseph Haydn, 3/4 right, two dates to his left, his name to his right **Edge:** With incuse dots

Date	Mintage	F	VF	XF	Unc	BU
1982	3,100,000	—	—	2.25	3.50	—
1982 Proof	50,000	Value: 9.00				
1991	140,000	—	—	2.25	5.00	—

KM# 2955.2   20 SCHILLING
8.0000 g., Copper-Aluminum-Nickel, 27.8 mm. **Edge:** Plain

Date	Mintage	F	VF	XF	Unc	BU
1992	100,000	—	—	2.25	6.00	—
1993	180,000	—	—	2.25	5.00	—

KM# 2960.1   20 SCHILLING
8.0000 g., Copper-Aluminum-Nickel, 27.8 mm. **Obv:** Value within box, Austrian shield divides date below **Rev:** Hochosterwitz Castle **Edge:** With incuse dots

Date	Mintage	F	VF	XF	Unc	BU
1983	1,002,000	—	—	2.25	3.50	—
1983 Proof	65,000	Value: 7.50				
1991	140,000	—	—	2.25	4.50	—

KM# 2965.1   20 SCHILLING
8.0000 g., Copper-Aluminum-Nickel, 27.8 mm. **Obv:** Value within box, Austrian shield divides date below **Rev:** Grafenegg Palace, date at upper left **Edge:** With incuse dots

Date	Mintage	F	VF	XF	Unc	BU
1984	1,203,000	—	—	2.25	3.50	—
1984 Proof	65,000	Value: 7.50				
1991	140,000	—	—	2.25	4.50	—

KM# 2970.1   20 SCHILLING
8.0000 g., Copper-Aluminum-Nickel, 27.8 mm. **Subject:** 200th Anniversary - Diocese of Linz **Obv:** Value within box, Austrian shield divides date below **Rev:** Two shields on decorative background within circle, two dates below circle **Edge:** With incuse dots

Date	Mintage	F	VF	XF	Unc	BU
1985	814,000	—	—	2.25	4.50	—
1985 Proof	45,000	Value: 11.50				
1991	140,000	—	—	2.25	4.50	—

KM# 2975.1   20 SCHILLING
8.0000 g., Copper-Aluminum-Nickel, 27.8 mm. **Subject:** 800th Anniversary - Georgenberger Treaty **Obv:** Value within box, Austrian shield divides date below **Rev:** Ottakar IV of Steyr and Leopold V of Austria holding the secret treaty **Edge:** With incuse dots

Date	Mintage	F	VF	XF	Unc	BU
1986	801,000	—	—	2.25	4.50	—
1986 Proof	42,000	Value: 16.50				

KM# 2975.2   20 SCHILLING
8.0000 g., Copper-Aluminum-Nickel, 27.8 mm. **Edge:** Plain

Date	Mintage	F	VF	XF	Unc	BU
1992	100,000	—	—	2.25	5.00	—
1993	180,000	—	—	2.25	5.00	—

KM# 2980.1   20 SCHILLING
8.0000 g., Copper-Aluminum-Nickel, 27.8 mm. **Subject:** 300th Anniversary - Birth of Salzburg's Archbishop Thun **Obv:** Value within box, Austrian shield divides date below **Rev:** Bishop's hat above supported arms, dates below supporters, subject name at bottom wth date below **Edge:** With incuse dots

Date	Mintage	F	VF	XF	Unc	BU
1987	508,000	—	—	2.25	4.50	—
1987 Proof	42,000	Value: 11.50				
1991	140,000	—	—	2.25	4.50	—

KM# 2980.2   20 SCHILLING
8.0000 g., Copper-Aluminum-Nickel, 27.8 mm. **Edge:** Plain

Date	Mintage	F	VF	XF	Unc	BU
1992	100,000	—	—	2.25	5.00	—
1993	180,000	—	—	2.25	4.50	—

KM# 2988.1   20 SCHILLING
8.0000 g., Copper-Aluminum-Nickel, 27.8 mm. **Obv:** Value within box, Austrian shield divides date below **Rev:** Crowned eagle - Tyrol **Edge:** With incuse dots

Date	Mintage	F	VF	XF	Unc	BU
1989	252,000	—	—	2.25	4.50	—
1989 Proof	38,000	Value: 8.00				
1991	140,000	—	—	2.25	4.50	—

KM# 2988.2   20 SCHILLING
8.0000 g., Copper-Aluminum-Nickel, 27.8 mm. **Edge:** Plain

Date	Mintage	F	VF	XF	Unc	BU
1992	100,000	—	—	2.25	5.00	—
1993	180,000	—	—	2.25	4.50	—

KM# 2993.1   20 SCHILLING
8.0000 g., Copper-Aluminum-Nickel, 27.8 mm. **Obv:** Value within box, Austrian shield divides date below **Rev:** Martinsturm in Bregenz, small shield at upper left **Edge:** With incuse dots

Date	Mintage	F	VF	XF	Unc	BU
1990	250,000	—	—	2.25	4.50	—
1990 Proof	35,000	Value: 10.00				
1991		—	—	—	—	—
1991	140,000	—	—	2.25	4.50	—

KM# 2993.2   20 SCHILLING
8.0000 g., Copper-Aluminum-Nickel, 27.8 mm. **Edge:** Plain

Date	Mintage	F	VF	XF	Unc	BU
1992	100,000	—	—	2.25	5.00	—
1993	180,000	—	—	2.25	4.50	—

KM# 2995.1   20 SCHILLING
8.0000 g., Copper-Aluminum-Nickel, 27.8 mm. **Subject:** 200th Anniversary - Birth of Franz Grillparzer **Obv:** Value within shield, Austrian shield divides date below **Rev:** Bust of Franz Grillparzer on left, looking right, theater building on the right **Edge:** With incuse dots

Date	Mintage	F	VF	XF	Unc	BU
1991	1,860,000	—	—	2.25	4.50	—
1991 Proof	27,000	Value: 10.00				

KM# 2995.2   20 SCHILLING
8.0000 g., Copper-Aluminum-Nickel, 27.8 mm. **Edge:** Plain

Date	Mintage	F	VF	XF	Unc	BU
1992	1,000,000	—	—	2.25	5.00	—
1992 Proof	25,000	Value: 12.50				
1993	1,800,000	—	—	2.25	4.50	—
1993 Proof	28,000	Value: 10.00				

KM# 2965.2   20 SCHILLING
8.0000 g., Copper-Aluminum-Nickel, 27.8 mm. **Edge:** Plain

Date	Mintage	F	VF	XF	Unc	BU
1992	100,000	—	—	2.25	5.00	—
1993	180,000	—	—	2.25	4.50	—

KM# 2960.2   20 SCHILLING
8.0000 g., Copper-Aluminum-Nickel, 27.8 mm. **Edge:** Plain

Date	Mintage	F	VF	XF	Unc	BU
1992	100,000	—	—	2.25	5.00	—
1993	180,000	—	—	2.25	4.50	—

KM# 2946.2   20 SCHILLING
8.0000 g., Copper-Aluminum-Nickel, 27.8 mm. **Edge:** Plain

Date	Mintage	F	VF	XF	Unc	BU
1992	100,000	—	—	2.25	6.00	—
1992 Proof	25,000	Value: 10.00				
1993	180,000	—	—	2.25	5.00	—
1993 Proof	28,000	Value: 10.00				

KM# 2970.2   20 SCHILLING
8.0000 g., Copper-Aluminum-Nickel, 27.8 mm. **Edge:** Plain

Date	Mintage	F	VF	XF	Unc	BU
1992	100,000	—	—	2.25	5.00	—
1993	180,000	—	—	2.25	4.50	—

KM# 3016   20 SCHILLING
8.0000 g., Copper-Aluminum-Nickel, 27.8 mm. **Subject:** 800th Anniversary - Vienna Mint **Obv:** Value within box, Austrian shield divides date below **Rev:** Vienna Mint, two dates below

Date	Mintage	F	VF	XF	Unc	BU
1994	2,000,000	—	—	—	4.50	—
1994 Proof	25,000	Value: 12.50				

KM# 3022   20 SCHILLING
8.0000 g., Copper-Aluminum-Nickel, 27.8 mm. **Subject:** 1000th Anniversary - Krems **Obv:** Value within box, Austrian shield below **Rev:** Krems within box, dates flanking, legend at top

Date	Mintage	F	VF	XF	Unc	BU
1995	2,000,000	—	—	—	4.50	—
1995 Proof	27,000	Value: 10.00				

KM# 3033   20 SCHILLING
8.0000 g., Copper-Aluminum-Nickel, 27.8 mm. **Obv:** Value within box, Austrian shield divides date at bottom **Rev:** Bust of Anton Bruckner, 3/4 facing, two dates below, name on the left, building on the right

Date	Mintage	F	VF	XF	Unc	BU
1996		—	—	—	4.50	—
1996 Proof	25,000	Value: 15.00				

KM# 3041   20 SCHILLING
8.0000 g., Copper-Aluminum-Nickel, 27.8 mm. **Subject:** 850th Anniversary of St. Stephen's Cathedral **Obv:** Value within box, Austrian shield divides date below **Rev:** St. Stephen's Cathedral, two dates above

Date	Mintage	F	VF	XF	Unc	BU
1997	700,000	—	—	—	4.50	—
1997 Proof	25,000	Value: 16.50				

KM# 3048   20 SCHILLING
8.0000 g., Copper-Aluminum-Nickel, 27.8 mm. **Subject:** 500th Anniversary of Michael Pacher's Death **Obv:** Value within box, Austrian shield divides date below **Rev:** Pacher's altar at St. Wolfgang

Date	Mintage	F	VF	XF	Unc	BU
1998	200,000	—	—	—	5.00	—
1998 Proof	25,000	Value: 17.50				

KM# 3056   20 SCHILLING
8.0000 g., Copper-Aluminum-Nickel, 27.8 mm. **Obv:** Value within box, Austrian shield divides date below **Rev:** Hugo Von Hofmannsthal

Date	Mintage	F	VF	XF	Unc	BU
1999	400,000	—	—	—	4.50	—
1999 Proof	50,000	Value: 12.50				

KM# 3064   20 SCHILLING
8.0000 g., Brass, 27.8 mm. **Subject:** 150th Anniversary - First Austrian Postage Stamp **Obv:** Value within box, Austrian shield divides date below **Rev:** Canceled stamp design **Edge:** Plain

Date	Mintage	F	VF	XF	Unc	BU
2000	400,000	—	—	—	4.50	—
2000 Proof	75,000	Value: 12.50				

KM# 2880   25 SCHILLING
13.0000 g., 0.8000 Silver 0.3344 oz. ASW, 30.5 mm. **Subject:** Reopening of the National Theater in Vienna **Obv:** Dragon within 3/4 circle of shields, larger Austrian shield at lower left, value to right of this **Rev:** Muse with mask and lyre

Date	Mintage	F	VF	XF	Unc	BU
1955	1,499,000	BV	7.50	10.00	20.00	—
1955 Proof	Est. 5,000	Value: 100				

KM# 2881   25 SCHILLING
13.0000 g., 0.8000 Silver 0.3344 oz. ASW, 30.5 mm. **Subject:** 200th Anniversary - Birth of Wolfgang Mozart **Obv:** Value within beaded circle, small spray of leaves below, surrounded by 3/4 circle of shields, **Rev:** Full length statue of Wolfgang Mozart, two dates below

Date	Mintage	F	VF	XF	Unc	BU
1956	4,999,000	—	—	7.00	8.00	—
1956 Proof	Est. 1,500	Value: 350				

KM# 2883   25 SCHILLING
13.0000 g., 0.8000 Silver 0.3344 oz. ASW, 30.5 mm. **Subject:** 8th Centennial - Mariazell Basilica **Obv:** Value within beaded circle, small spray of leaves below, 3/4 circle of shields surrounding **Rev:** Mariazell Basilica, name below, two dates at bottom

Date	Mintage	F	VF	XF	Unc	BU
1957	4,999,000	—	—	7.00	8.00	—
1957 Proof	Est. 1,500	Value: 300				

KM# 2884   25 SCHILLING
13.0000 g., 0.8000 Silver 0.3344 oz. ASW, 30.5 mm. **Subject:** 100th Anniversary - Birth of Auer von Welsbach, Chemist **Obv:** Value within beaded circle, small spray below, 3/4 circle of shields surrounds **Rev:** Head of Auer von Welsbach, right, date below

Date	Mintage	F	VF	XF	Unc	BU
1958	4,999,000	—	—	7.00	8.00	—
1958 Proof	Est. 500	Value: 1,500				

KM# 2887   25 SCHILLING
13.0000 g., 0.8000 Silver 0.3344 oz. ASW, 30.5 mm.
Subject: Centennial - Death of Archduke Johann, military leader in the trench wars **Obv:** Dragon within 3/4 circle of shields, larger Austrian shield lower left, value to right of this **Rev:** Collared head of Archduke Johann, right, collar divides date

Date	Mintage	F	VF	XF	Unc	BU
1959	1,899,000	—	—	7.00	8.00	—
1959 Proof	Est. 1,000	Value: 300				

KM# 2890   25 SCHILLING
13.0000 g., 0.8000 Silver 0.3344 oz. ASW, 30.5 mm.
Subject: 40th Anniversary - Carinthian Plebescite **Obv:** Value within beaded circle above small spray of leaves, 3/4 circle of shields surrounds **Rev:** Large urn dividing two standing figures, shield below urn divides date

Date	Mintage	F	VF	XF	Unc	BU
1960	1,599,000	—	—	7.00	8.00	—
1960 Proof	Est. 900	Value: 350				

KM# 2891   25 SCHILLING
13.0000 g., 0.8000 Silver 0.3344 oz. ASW, 30.5 mm.
Subject: 40th Anniversary - Burgenland, Haydenkirche in Eisenstadt **Obv:** Value within beaded circle, small sprays below, 3/4 circle of shields surrounding **Rev:** Building, two dates lower left

Date	Mintage	F	VF	XF	Unc	BU
1961	1,399,000	—	—	7.00	8.00	—
1961 Proof	Est. 1,200	Value: 175				

KM# 2892   25 SCHILLING
13.0000 g., 0.8000 Silver 0.3344 oz. ASW, 30.5 mm.
Obv: Value within beaded circle, small spray of leaves below, 3/4 circle of shields surrounding **Rev:** Head of Anton Bruckner, right, Composer, date below

Date	Mintage	F	VF	XF	Unc	BU
1962	2,399,000	—	—	7.00	8.00	—
1962 Proof	Est. 3,000	Value: 150				

KM# 2893   25 SCHILLING
13.0000 g., 0.8000 Silver 0.3344 oz. ASW, 30.5 mm.
Subject: 300th Anniversary - Birth of Prince Eugen **Obv:** Value within beaded circle, small spray of leaves below, 3/4 circle of shields surrounding **Rev:** Half-length figure of Prince Eugen pointing, left, facing right, date below

Date	Mintage	F	VF	XF	Unc	BU
1963	1,994,000	—	—	7.00	8.00	—
1963 Proof	5,931	Value: 80.00				

KM# 2895.1   25 SCHILLING
13.0000 g., 0.8000 Silver 0.3344 oz. ASW, 30.5 mm.
Obv: Value within circle of shields **Rev:** Head of Franz Grillparzer, Poet, right, date below

Date	Mintage	F	VF	XF	Unc	BU
1964	1,664,000	—	—	7.00	8.00	—
1964 Proof	36,000	Value: 8.00				

KM# 2895.2   25 SCHILLING
13.0000 g., 0.8000 Silver 0.3344 oz. ASW, 30.5 mm.
Obv: Value within beaded circle, small spray of leaves below, surrounded by 3/4 circle of shields **Rev:** Head of Franz Grillparzer, right, date below **Note:** Obverse; Nine shields, (error)

Date	Mintage	F	VF	XF	Unc	BU
1964 Proof	3,660	Value: 300				

KM# 2897   25 SCHILLING
13.0000 g., 0.8000 Silver 0.3344 oz. ASW, 30.5 mm.
Subject: 150th Anniversary - Vienna Technical High School **Obv:** Value within circle of shields **Rev:** J.J. Ritter von Prechtl, technologist, director

Date	Mintage	F	VF	XF	Unc	BU
1965	1,563,000	—	—	7.00	8.00	—
1965 Proof	37,000	Value: 15.00				

KM# 2899   25 SCHILLING
13.0000 g., 0.8000 Silver 0.3344 oz. ASW, 30.5 mm.
Subject: 130th Anniversary - Death of Ferdinand Raimund **Obv:** Value within circle of shields **Rev:** 1/2-length figure of Ferdinand Raimund, arms crossed, 3/4 right, date on right

Date	Mintage	F	VF	XF	Unc	BU
1966	1,388,000	—	—	7.00	8.00	—
1966 Proof	11,800	Value: 50.00				

KM# 2901   25 SCHILLING
13.0000 g., 0.8000 Silver 0.3344 oz. ASW, 30.5 mm.
Subject: 250th Anniversary - Birth of Maria Theresa, Empress **Obv:** Value within circle of shields **Rev:** Bust of Maria Theresa, right, divides dates, date below right shoulder

Date	Mintage	F	VF	XF	Unc	BU
1967	2,472,000	—	—	7.00	8.00	—
1967 Proof	28,000	Value: 25.00				

KM# 2903   25 SCHILLING
13.0000 g., 0.8000 Silver 0.3344 oz. ASW, 30.5 mm.
Subject: 300th Anniversary - Birth of Von Hildebrandt **Obv:** Value within circle of shields **Rev:** Main gateway to Belvedere Castle

Date	Mintage	F	VF	XF	Unc	BU
1968	1,258,000	—	—	8.00	9.00	—
1968 Proof	42,000	Value: 18.00				

KM# 2905   25 SCHILLING
13.0000 g., 0.8000 Silver 0.3344 oz. ASW, 30.5 mm.
Obv: Value within circle of shields **Rev:** Head of Peter Rosegger, poet, writer left, date below

Date	Mintage	F	VF	XF	Unc	BU
1969	1,356,000	—	—	7.00	8.00	—
1969 Proof	44,000	Value: 18.00				

KM# 2907   25 SCHILLING
13.0000 g., 0.8000 Silver 0.3344 oz. ASW, 30.5 mm.
Subject: 100th Anniversary - Birth of Franz Lehar, Composer **Obv:** Value within circle of shields **Rev:** Head of Franz Lehar, 3/4 left, date to the left, two dates below

Date	Mintage	F	VF	XF	Unc	BU
1970	1,661,000	—	—	7.00	8.00	—
1970 Proof	139,000	Value: 7.50				

KM# 2910   25 SCHILLING
13.0000 g., 0.8000 Silver 0.3344 oz. ASW, 30.5 mm. **Subject:** 200th Anniversary - Vienna Bourse **Obv:** Value within circle of shields **Rev:** City building, two dates below, Austrian shield lower right

Date	Mintage	F	VF	XF	Unc	BU
1971	1,804,000	—	—	7.00	8.00	—
1971 Proof	196,000	Value: 6.00				

KM# 2912   25 SCHILLING
13.0000 g., 0.8000 Silver 0.3344 oz. ASW, 30.5 mm. **Subject:** 50th Anniversary - Death of Carl M. Ziehrer, Composer **Obv:** Value within circle of shields **Rev:** Head of Carl M. Ziehrer, facing, three dates below

Date	Mintage	F	VF	XF	Unc	BU
ND(1972)	1,955,000	—	—	7.00	8.00	—
ND(1972) Proof	145,000	Value: 6.00				

KM# 2915   25 SCHILLING
13.0000 g., 0.8000 Silver 0.3344 oz. ASW, 30.5 mm. **Subject:** 100th Anniversary - Birth of Max Reinhardt, Producer, Theatrical manager **Obv:** Value within circle of shields **Rev:** Head of Max Reinhardt, left, three dates below

Date	Mintage	F	VF	XF	Unc	BU
ND(1973)	2,323,000	—	—	7.00	8.00	—
ND(1973) Proof	177,000	Value: 6.00				

KM# 2888   50 SCHILLING
20.0000 g., 0.9000 Silver 0.5787 oz. ASW, 34 mm. **Subject:** 150th Anniversary - Liberation of Tyrol **Obv:** Imperial Eagle within 3/4 circle of shields, wreath encircling head **Rev:** Andreas Hofer facing forward, two dates below

Date	Mintage	F	VF	XF	Unc	BU
ND(1959)	2,999,000	—	—	BV	12.00	14.00
ND(1959) Proof	Est. 800	Value: 425				

KM# 2894   50 SCHILLING
20.0000 g., 0.9000 Silver 0.5787 oz. ASW, 34 mm. **Subject:** 600th Anniversary - Union with Tirol **Obv:** Value within beaded circle, small spray below, 3/4 circle of shields surrounding **Rev:** Arms of Tyrol and Austria above two dates

Date	Mintage	F	VF	XF	Unc	BU
ND(1963)	2,989,600	—	—	BV	12.00	14.00
ND(1963) Proof	10,400	Value: 75.00				

KM# 2896   50 SCHILLING
20.0000 g., 0.9000 Silver 0.5787 oz. ASW, 34 mm. **Series:** Winter Olympics **Obv:** Value within beaded circle, small spray of leaves below, 3/4 circle of shields surrounding **Rev:** Innsbruck - Ski jumper, left, Olympic logo above

Date	Mintage	F	VF	XF	Unc	BU
1964	2,832,050	—	—	BV	12.00	14.00
1964 Proof	67,950	Value: 20.00				

KM# 2898   50 SCHILLING
20.0000 g., 0.9000 Silver 0.5787 oz. ASW, 34 mm. **Subject:** 600th Anniversary - Vienna University **Obv:** Value within circle of shields **Rev:** Crowned head, 3/4 right

Date	Mintage	F	VF	XF	Unc	BU
ND(1965)	2,163,000	—	—	BV	12.00	14.00
ND(1965) Proof	37,000	Value: 30.00				

KM# 2900   50 SCHILLING
20.0000 g., 0.9000 Silver 0.5787 oz. ASW, 34 mm. **Subject:** 150th Anniversary - National Bank **Obv:** Value within circle of shields **Rev:** National Bank building above two line inscription, two dates below

Date	Mintage	F	VF	XF	Unc	BU
ND(1966)	1,782,600	—	—	BV	12.00	14.00
ND(1966) Proof	17,400	Value: 60.00				

KM# 2902   50 SCHILLING
20.0000 g., 0.9000 Silver 0.5787 oz. ASW, 34 mm. **Subject:** Centennial of the Blue Danube Waltz **Rev:** Johann Strauss the Younger, playing the violin, date below

Date	Mintage	F	VF	XF	Unc	BU
1967	2,973,900	—	—	BV	12.00	14.00
1967 Proof	26,100	Value: 60.00				

KM# 2904.1   50 SCHILLING
20.0000 g., 0.9000 Silver 0.5787 oz. ASW, 34 mm. **Subject:** 50th Anniversary - The Republic **Obv:** Value within circle of shields **Rev:** Parliament building in Vienna, matte surface between pillars, dates divided at bottom

Date	Mintage	F	VF	XF	Unc	BU
ND(1968)	1,660,200	—	—	BV	12.00	14.00
ND(1968) Proof	39,800	Value: 22.50				

KM# 2904.2   50 SCHILLING
20.0000 g., 0.9000 Silver 0.5787 oz. ASW, 34 mm. **Rev:** Parliament building in Vienna, proof surface between pillars

Date	Mintage	F	VF	XF	Unc	BU
1968 Proof	—	Value: 150				

KM# 2906   50 SCHILLING
20.0000 g., 0.9000 Silver 0.5787 oz. ASW, 34 mm. **Subject:** 450th Anniversary - Death of Maximilian I **Obv:** Value within circle of shields **Rev:** Bust of Maximillian I with hat, right, dates in legend

Date	Mintage	F	VF	XF	Unc	BU
1969	2,045,000	—	—	BV	12.00	14.00
1969 Proof	55,000	Value: 22.50				

KM# 2908   50 SCHILLING
20.0000 g., 0.9000 Silver 0.5787 oz. ASW, 34 mm. **Subject:** 300th Anniversary - Innsbruck University **Obv:** Value within circle of shields **Rev:** 1673 University seal, date at bottom

Date	Mintage	F	VF	XF	Unc	BU
1970	2,087,300	—	—	BV	12.00	14.00
1970 Proof	11,700	Value: 9.00				

KM# 2909 50 SCHILLING
20.0000 g., 0.9000 Silver 0.5787 oz. ASW, 34 mm.
Subject: 100th Anniversary - Birth of Dr. Karl Renner, president
Obv: Value within circle of shields **Rev:** Head of Dr. Karl Renner, right, date on left collar, two dates at left

Date	Mintage	F	VF	XF	Unc	BU
1970	2,213,800	—	BV	12.00	14.00	—
1970 Proof	286,200	Value: 8.00				

KM# 2911 50 SCHILLING
20.0000 g., 0.9000 Silver 0.5787 oz. ASW, 34 mm.
Subject: 80th Anniversary - Birth of Julius Raab, chancellor
Obv: Value within circle of shields **Rev:** Head of Julius Raab, right, date below, two dates at left

Date	Mintage	F	VF	XF	Unc	BU
1971	2,317,000	—	BV	12.00	14.00	—
1971 Proof	183,000	Value: 8.00				

KM# 2913 50 SCHILLING
20.0000 g., 0.9000 Silver 0.5787 oz. ASW, 34 mm. **Subject:** 350th Anniversary - Salzburg University **Obv:** Value within circle of shields **Rev:** Great seal of the University within circle, three dates below

Date	Mintage	F	VF	XF	Unc	BU
ND(1972)	2,864,000	—	BV	12.00	14.00	—
ND(1972) Proof	136,000	Value: 8.00				

KM# 2914 50 SCHILLING
20.0000 g., 0.9000 Silver 0.5787 oz. ASW, 34 mm.
Subject: 100th Anniversary - Institute of Agriculture **Obv:** Value within circle of shields **Rev:** Institute of Agriculture, shields flank inscription and dates below

Date	Mintage	F	VF	XF	Unc	BU
ND(1972)	1,891,000	—	BV	12.00	14.00	—
ND(1972) Proof	109,000	Value: 8.00				

KM# 2916 50 SCHILLING
20.0000 g., 0.9000 Silver 0.5787 oz. ASW, 34 mm. **Subject:** 500th Anniversary - Bummerl House **Obv:** Value within circle of shields **Rev:** Bummerl House within circle, two shields flank date at top

Date	Mintage	F	VF	XF	Unc	BU
1973	2,841,800	—	BV	12.00	14.00	—
1973 Proof	158,200	Value: 8.00				

KM# 2917 50 SCHILLING
20.0000 g., 0.9000 Silver 0.5787 oz. ASW, 34 mm.
Subject: 100th Anniversary - Birth of Dr. Theodor Korner, President **Obv:** Value within circle of shields **Rev:** Head of Dr. Theodor Korner, right, three dates below

Date	Mintage	F	VF	XF	Unc	BU
ND(1973)	2,868,000	—	BV	12.00	14.00	—
ND(1973) Proof	131,600	Value: 8.00				

KM# 2919 50 SCHILLING
20.0000 g., 0.6400 Silver 0.4115 oz. ASW **Subject:** Vienna International Flower show **Obv:** Value within circle of shields **Rev:** International Flower Show, date at bottom

Date	Mintage	F	VF	XF	Unc	BU
1974	2,279,000	—	—	9.00	10.00	—
1974 Proof	221,000	Value: 7.50				

KM# 2920 50 SCHILLING
20.0000 g., 0.6400 Silver 0.4115 oz. ASW **Subject:** 125th Anniversary - Austrian Police Force **Obv:** Value within circle of shields **Rev:** Imperial Eagle on shield, within wreath, within circle

Date	Mintage	F	VF	XF	Unc	BU
ND(1974)	2,258,600	—	—	9.00	10.00	—
ND(1974) Proof	241,400	Value: 7.50				

KM# 2921 50 SCHILLING
20.0000 g., 0.6400 Silver 0.4115 oz. ASW **Subject:** 1200th Anniversary - Salzburg Cathedral **Obv:** Value within circle of shields **Rev:** St. Rupert and St. Vincent holding cathedral, date below

Date	Mintage	F	VF	XF	Unc	BU
1974	2,292,600	—	—	9.00	10.00	—
1974 Proof	207,400	Value: 7.50				

KM# 2922 50 SCHILLING
20.0000 g., 0.6400 Silver 0.4115 oz. ASW **Subject:** 50th Anniversary - Austrian Broadcasting **Obv:** Value within circle of shields **Rev:** Broadcasting symbol, two dates at top

Date	Mintage	F	VF	XF	Unc	BU
1974	2,290,000	—	—	9.00	10.00	—
1974 Proof	210,000	Value: 7.50				

KM# 2937 50 SCHILLING
20.0000 g., 0.6400 Silver 0.4115 oz. ASW **Subject:** 150th Anniversary - Death of Franz Schubert, Composer **Obv:** Value within circle of shields **Rev:** Bust of Franz Schubert, looking left, date below

Date	Mintage	F	VF	XF	Unc	BU
1978	1,868,000	—	—	9.00	10.00	—
1978 Proof	132,000	Value: 7.50				

KM# 3038 50 SCHILLING
Bi-Metallic Copper-Nickel Clad Nickel center in Aluminum-Bronze ring, 26.5 mm. **Subject:** Austrian Millennium **Obv:** Circle of provincial arms around denomination **Rev:** Arms below Heinrich I as knight on horse back, within circle, two dates at right

Date	Mintage	F	VF	XF	Unc	BU
ND(1996)	900,000	—	—	—	14.00	—
ND(1996) BU	100,000	—	—	—	25.00	—

KM# 3044 50 SCHILLING
Bi-Metallic Copper-Nickel Clad Nickel center in Aluminum-Bronze ring, 26.5 mm. **Subject:** 100th Anniversary - Wiener Secession **Obv:** Value within circle of provincial arms **Rev:** Vienna Secession building portal within circle, two dates at bottom, divided

Date	Mintage	F	VF	XF	Unc	BU
ND(1997)	1,500,000	—	—	—	8.00	—
ND(1997) BU	100,000	—	—	—	—	11.50

KM# 3050   50 SCHILLING
Bi-Metallic Copper-Nickel Clad Nickel center in Aluminum-Bronze ring, 26.5 mm.   **Subject:** Austrian Presidency of the European Union **Obv:** Value within circle of provincial arms **Rev:** New Hofburg palace with logo, within circle, date at bottom

Date	Mintage	F	VF	XF	Unc	BU
1998	1,200,000	—	—	—	8.00	—
1998 BU	100,000	—	—	—	—	11.50

KM# 3053   50 SCHILLING
Bi-Metallic Copper-Nickel Clad Nickel center in Aluminum-Bronze ring, 26.5 mm.   **Obv:** Value within circle of provincial arms **Rev:** Head of Konrad Lorenz, looking right, with three Greylag geese on the right, within circle, two dates below circle

Date	Mintage	F	VF	XF	Unc	BU
1998	1,200,000	—	—	—	7.00	—
1998 Special Unc	100,000	—	—	—	9.00	—

KM# 3057   50 SCHILLING
Bi-Metallic Copper-Nickel Clad Nickel center in Aluminum-Bronze ring, 26.5 mm.   **Subject:** Euro Currency **Obv:** Value within circle of provincial arms **Rev:** Euro currency designs within circle, date below

Date	Mintage	F	VF	XF	Unc	BU
1999	1,200,000	—	—	—	7.00	—
1999 Special Unc	100,000	—	—	—	9.00	—

KM# 3061   50 SCHILLING
Bi-Metallic Copper-Nickel clad Nickel center in Aluminum-Bronze ring, 26.5 mm.   **Subject:** Centenary - Death of Johann Strauss **Obv:** Value within circle of provincial arms **Rev:** Bust of Johann Strauss, facing right, two dates to his right, two figures to his left, all within circle, music notes below circle

Date	Mintage	F	VF	XF	Unc	BU
ND(1999)	600,000	—	—	—	7.00	—
ND(1999) Special Unc	100,000	—	—	—	9.00	—

KM# 3066   50 SCHILLING
Bi-Metallic Copper-Nickel Clad Nickel center in Aluminum-Bronze ring, 26.5 mm.   **Obv:** Value within circle of provincial arms **Rev:** Bust of Sigmund Freud facing 1/4 left, two dates at upper right, all within circle **Edge:** Plain

Date	Mintage	F	VF	XF	Unc	BU
ND(2000)	600,000	—	—	—	7.00	—
ND(2000) Special Unc	90,000	—	—	—	9.00	—

KM# 3070   50 SCHILLING
Bi-Metallic Copper-Nickel clad Nickel center in Aluminum-Bronze ring, 26.5 mm.   **Obv:** Value within circle of provincial arms **Rev:** Antique automobile on left and portrait of Ferdinand Porsche, facing, on right within circle, two dates lower right of circle **Edge:** Plain **Note:** 100,000 of the Unc. coins are in blister-packs, with a value of $8.00 each.

Date	Mintage	F	VF	XF	Unc	BU
2000	700,000	—	—	—	7.00	—

KM# 2926   100 SCHILLING
23.9300 g., 0.6400 Silver 0.4924 oz. ASW **Series:** Winter Olympics - Innsbruck **Obv:** Value within circle of shields **Rev:** Emblem, Olympic logo above

Date	Mintage	F	VF	XF	Unc	BU
ND(1974)	2,826,000	—	—	—	11.00	—
ND(1974) Proof	374,000	Value: 12.00				

KM# 2927   100 SCHILLING
23.9300 g., 0.6400 Silver 0.4924 oz. ASW **Series:** Winter Olympics - Innsbruck **Obv:** Box surrounds stylized Imperial Eagle, Austrian shield on breast, holding hammer and sickle above value, small shield below box **Rev:** Buildings and Olympic logo

Date	Mintage	F	VF	XF	Unc	BU
ND(1974)(h)	2,692,000	—	—	—	11.00	—
ND(1974)(v) Select	Inc. above	—	—	—	12.50	—
ND(1974)(h) Proof	223,000	Value: 12.00				
ND(1974)(v)	2,718,000	—	—	—	11.00	—
ND(1974)(h) Select	Inc. above	—	—	—	12.50	—
ND(1974)(v) Proof	232,000	Value: 12.00				

KM# 2928   100 SCHILLING
23.9300 g., 0.6400 Silver 0.4924 oz. ASW **Series:** Winter Olympics - Innsbruck **Obv:** Box surrounds stylized Imperial Eagle, Austrian shield on breast, holding hammer and sickle above value, small shield below box **Rev:** Skier

Date	Mintage	F	VF	XF	Unc	BU
ND(1974)(h)	2,636,000	—	—	—	11.00	—
ND(1974)(v) Select	Inc. above	—	—	—	12.50	—
ND(1974)(h) Proof	179,000	Value: 12.00				
ND(1974)(v)	2,641,000	—	—	—	11.00	—
ND(1974)(h) Select	Inc. above	—	—	—	12.50	—
ND(1974)(v) Proof	184,000	Value: 12.00				

KM# 2929   100 SCHILLING
23.9300 g., 0.6400 Silver 0.4924 oz. ASW **Series:** Winter Olympics - Innsbruck **Obv:** Box surrounds stylized Imperial Eagle, Austrian shield on breast, above value, Olympic logo upper left, circle surrounds, date lower right

Date	Mintage	F	VF	XF	Unc	BU
ND(1974)(h)	2,611,000	—	—	—	11.00	—
ND(1974)(h) Select	Inc. above	—	—	—	12.50	—
ND(1974)(h) Proof	179,000	Value: 12.00				
ND(1974)(v)	2,627,000	—	—	—	11.00	—
ND(1974)(v) Select	Inc. above	—	—	—	12.50	—
ND(1974)(v) Proof	188,000	Value: 12.00				

KM# 2923   100 SCHILLING
23.9300 g., 0.6400 Silver 0.4924 oz. ASW **Subject:** 150th Anniversary - Birth of Johann Strauss the Younger, Composer **Obv:** Value within circle of shields **Rev:** Monument with standing statue of Strauss with violin, date below

Date	Mintage	F	VF	XF	Unc	BU
1975	2,646,000	—	—	—	11.00	—
1975 Select	Inc. above	—	—	—	12.50	—
1975 Proof	209,000	Value: 12.00				

KM# 2924   100 SCHILLING
23.9300 g., 0.6400 Silver 0.4924 oz. ASW **Subject:** 20th Anniversary - State Treaty **Obv:** Box surrounds stylized Imperial Eagle, Austrian shield on breast, holding hammer and sickle, value below **Rev:** Round Austrian shield at center, date below

Date	Mintage	F	VF	XF	Unc	BU
1975	3,215,000	—	—	—	11.00	—
1975 Select	Inc. above	—	—	—	12.50	—
1975 Proof	225,000	Value: 12.00				

KM# 2925   100 SCHILLING
23.9300 g., 0.6400 Silver 0.4924 oz. ASW **Subject:** 50th Anniversary - Schilling **Obv:** Box surrounds stylized Imperial Eagle, Austrian shield on breast, holding hammer and sickle, value below **Rev:** Sower, a plowed field

Date	Mintage	F	VF	XF	Unc	BU
1975	3,234,000	—	—	—	11.00	—
1975 Select	Inc. above	—	—	—	13.50	—
1975 Proof	201,000	Value: 12.00				

KM# 2930   100 SCHILLING
23.9300 g., 0.6400 Silver 0.4924 oz. ASW **Subject:** 200th Anniversary - Burgtheater **Obv:** Value within circle of shields **Rev:** Burgtheater, small crowned double eagle divides dates at top

Date	Mintage	F	VF	XF	Unc	BU
ND(1976)	1,630,000	—	—	—	11.50	—
ND(1976) Select	Inc. above	—	—	—	13.00	—
ND(1976) Proof	220,000	Value: 12.50				

KM# 2931   100 SCHILLING
23.9300 g., 0.6400 Silver 0.4924 oz. ASW **Subject:** 1000th Anniversary - Carinthia **Obv:** Box surrounds stylized Imperial Eagle, Austrian shield on breast, value below **Rev:** Monument, shield at lower right, two dates at bottom

Date	Mintage	F	VF	XF	Unc	BU
ND(1976)	1,632,000	—	—	—	11.50	—
ND(1976) Select	Inc. above	—	—	—	13.00	—
ND(1976) Proof	168,000	Value: 12.50				

KM# 2932   100 SCHILLING
23.9300 g., 0.6400 Silver 0.4924 oz. ASW **Subject:** 175th Anniversary - Birth of Johann Nestroy, Singer **Obv:** Value surrounds Imperial Eagle with Austrian shield on breast **Rev:** Head of Johann Nestroy, 3/4 left, two dates on the right, one date on left

Date	Mintage	F	VF	XF	Unc	BU
1976	1,761,000	—	—	—	11.50	—
1976 Select	—	—	—	—	13.00	—
1976 Proof	139,000	Value: 12.50				

KM# 2934   100 SCHILLING
23.9300 g., 0.6400 Silver 0.4924 oz. ASW **Subject:** 1200th Anniversary - Kremsmunster Monastery **Obv:** Value within circle of shields **Rev:** Chalice, divides dates at top

Date	Mintage	F	VF	XF	Unc	BU
ND(1977)	1,865,000	—	—	—	11.50	—
ND(1977) Select	Inc. above	—	—	—	13.00	—
ND(1977) Proof	135,000	Value: 14.00				

KM# 2935   100 SCHILLING
23.9300 g., 0.6400 Silver 0.4924 oz. ASW **Subject:** 900th Anniversary - Hohensalzburg Fortress **Obv:** Box surrounds stylized Imperial Eagle, Austrian shield on breast, value below **Rev:** Hohensalzburg Fortress on right, dates divided by four line inscription on left

Date	Mintage	F	VF	XF	Unc	BU
1977	1,878,000	—	—	—	11.50	—
1977 Select	Inc. above	—	—	—	13.00	—
1977 Proof	122,000	Value: 14.00				

KM# 2936   100 SCHILLING
23.9300 g., 0.6400 Silver 0.4924 oz. ASW **Subject:** 500th Anniversary - Hall Mint **Obv:** Value and three rows of shields within circle, two dates below circle **Rev:** Knight in full armor on armored horseback, right, and four shields, within circle, date in legend, two shields below circle

Date	Mintage	F	VF	XF	Unc	BU
1977	1,868,000	—	—	—	11.50	—
1977 Select	Inc. above	—	—	—	13.00	—
1977 Proof	132,000	Value: 16.50				

KM# 2938   100 SCHILLING
23.9300 g., 0.6400 Silver 0.4924 oz. ASW **Subject:** 700th Anniversary - Gmunden **Obv:** Box surrounds stylized Imperial Eagle, Austrian shield on breast, holding hammer and sickle, value below **Rev:** Gmunden, building within circle, two dates at upper left

Date	Mintage	F	VF	XF	Unc	BU
1978	1,870,000	—	—	—	11.50	—
1978 Select	Inc. above	—	—	—	13.00	—
1978 Proof	130,000	Value: 14.00				

KM# 2939   100 SCHILLING
23.9300 g., 0.6400 Silver 0.4924 oz. ASW **Subject:** 700th Anniversary - Battle of Durnkrut and Jedenspeigen **Obv:** Standing figures holding hands form a circle with an Austrian shield at center, value below, beaded circle surrounds all **Rev:** Bust of Rudolf I

Date	Mintage	F	VF	XF	Unc	BU
1978	1,677,000	—	—	—	11.50	—
1978 Select	Inc. above	—	—	—	13.00	—
1978 Proof	123,000	Value: 14.00				

KM# 2940   100 SCHILLING
23.9300 g., 0.6400 Silver 0.4924 oz. ASW **Subject:** 1100th Anniversary - Founding of Villach **Obv:** Box surrounds stylized Imperial Eagle, Austrian shield on breast, holding hammer and sickle, value below **Rev:** Village divides shields with dates above

Date	Mintage	F	VF	XF	Unc	BU
ND(1978)	1,569,000	—	—	—	11.50	—
ND(1978) Select	Inc. above	—	—	—	13.00	—
ND(1978) Proof	131,000	Value: 14.00				

KM# 2941   100 SCHILLING
23.9300 g., 0.6400 Silver 0.4924 oz. ASW **Subject:** Opening of Arlberg Tunnel **Obv:** Value and three rows of shields within circle, date below circle divided by small hammer and sickle **Rev:** Sun above banner, mountains below, hands in front of mountains, circle surrounds all, two dates in legend, two shields below circle

Date	Mintage	F	VF	XF	Unc	BU
1978	1,764,000	—	—	—	11.50	—
1978 Select	80,000	—	—	—	13.00	—
1978 Proof	156,000	Value: 14.00				

KM# 2942   100 SCHILLING
23.9300 g., 0.6400 Silver 0.4924 oz. ASW **Subject:** 700th Anniversary - Cathedral of Wiener Neustadt **Obv:** Imperial Eagle with Austrian shield on breast, holding hammer and sickle, value below **Rev:** Cathedral, date at bottom

Date	Mintage	F	VF	XF	Unc	BU
1979	1,796,000	—	—	—	11.50	—
1979 Select	70,000	—	—	—	13.00	—
1979 Proof	134,000	Value: 14.00				

KM# 2943   100 SCHILLING
23.9300 g., 0.6400 Silver 0.4924 oz. ASW **Subject:** 200th Anniversary - Inn District

Date	Mintage	F	VF	XF	Unc	BU
1979	1,795,000	—	—	—	11.50	—
1979 Select	75,000	—	—	—	13.00	—
1979 Proof	130,000	Value: 14.00				

KM# 2944   100 SCHILLING
23.9300 g., 0.6400 Silver 0.4924 oz. ASW **Obv:** Value within circle
of shields **Rev:** Vienna International center, date bottom right

Date	Mintage	F	VF	XF	Unc	BU
1979	1,780,000	—	—	—	11.50	—
1979 Select	75,000	—	—	—	13.00	—
1979 Proof	145,000	Value: 14.00				

KM# 2945   100 SCHILLING
23.9300 g., 0.6400 Silver 0.4924 oz. ASW **Obv:** Value within
circle of shields **Rev:** Festival and Congress Hall at Bregenz, date
lower right

Date	Mintage	F	VF	XF	Unc	BU
1979	1,498,000	—	—	—	11.50	—
1979 Select	75,000	—	—	—	13.00	—
1979 Proof	161,000	Value: 14.00				

KM# 2996   100 SCHILLING
20.0000 g., 0.9000 Silver 0.5787 oz. ASW, 34 mm. **Obv:**
Mozart-Salzburg, value below **Rev:** Mozart with violin and piano,
right, two dates at left

Date	Mintage	F	VF	XF	Unc	BU
1991 Proof	100,000	Value: 32.50				

KM# 2998   100 SCHILLING
20.0000 g., 0.9000 Silver 0.5787 oz. ASW, 34 mm.
Obv: Mozart's Vienna Years- Burgtheater, value below
Rev: Mozart seated at piano, left, two dates at right

Date	Mintage	F	VF	XF	Unc	BU
1991 Proof	100,000	Value: 32.50				

KM# 3001   100 SCHILLING
20.0000 g., 0.9000 Silver 0.5787 oz. ASW, 34 mm.
Obv: Rudolph I seated on throne flanked by figures kneeling,
value at bottom **Rev:** Half-length figure of Rudolph I, facing

Date	Mintage	F	VF	XF	Unc	BU
1991 Proof	75,000	Value: 135				

KM# 3003   100 SCHILLING
20.0000 g., 0.9000 Silver 0.5787 oz. ASW, 34 mm. **Obv:** Two
seated figures facing each other, ribbon between heads, value
at bottom **Rev:** Half-length figure of Maximillian I, with crown and
armor, right

Date	Mintage	F	VF	XF	Unc	BU
1992 Proof	75,000	Value: 75.00				

KM# 3005   100 SCHILLING
20.0000 g., 0.9000 Silver 0.5787 oz. ASW, 34 mm. **Obv:**
Theater building, value below **Rev:** Bust of Otto Nicolai, 3/4 right

Date	Mintage	F	VF	XF	Unc	BU
1992 Proof	75,000	Value: 35.00				

KM# 3007   100 SCHILLING
18.0000 g., 0.9000 Silver 0.5208 oz. ASW, 34 mm. **Obv:** Two
half-length figures, 3/4 left, above inscription, value at bottom
Rev: 3/4 length figure of Karl V in armor, facing 1/4 left, shield
above each shoulder

Date	Mintage	F	VF	XF	Unc	BU
1992 Proof	75,000	Value: 50.00				

KM# 3009   100 SCHILLING
20.0000 g., 0.9000 Silver 0.5787 oz. ASW, 34 mm. **Obv:** Armed
figures on kneeling horses outside of city, value at bottom
Rev: Kaiser Leopold I, in armor and robe, facing 1/4 right

Date	Mintage	F	VF	XF	Unc	BU
1993 Proof	75,000	Value: 35.00				

KM# 3019   100 SCHILLING
20.0000 g., 0.9000 Silver 0.5787 oz. ASW, 34 mm. **Obv:** City
buildings with water in foreground, date below, value at bottom
Rev: Half-length figure of Franz Joseph I in uniform, 3/4 facing,
two small crowns at left

Date	Mintage	F	VF	XF	Unc	BU
1994 Proof	75,000	Value: 35.00				

KM# 3020   100 SCHILLING
20.0000 g., 0.9000 Silver 0.5787 oz. ASW, 34 mm. **Subject:** 1848
Revolution **Obv:** Armed figures and Bishop in front of church, value
at bottom **Rev:** Seated half-length figure of Archduke Johann, 3/4
facing, looking right, two dates to right of left hand

Date	Mintage	F	VF	XF	Unc	BU
1994 Proof	75,000	Value: 35.00				

KM# 3034   100 SCHILLING
20.0000 g., 0.9000 Silver 0.5787 oz. ASW, 34 mm.
Subject: First Republic **Obv:** Columned buildings, statue at right,
people in foreground, date below, value at bottom **Rev:** Coin,
buildings and symbols, two dates lower right

Date	Mintage	F	VF	XF	Unc	BU
1995 Proof	75,000	Value: 35.00				

KM# 3036   100 SCHILLING
20.0000 g., 0.9000 Silver 0.5787 oz. ASW, 34 mm. **Obv:** Four
armored figures divide date, value at bottom **Rev:** Crowned half-
length figure of Leopold III, facing, Austrian shield in left hand

Date	Mintage	F	VF	XF	Unc	BU
1996 Proof	75,000	Value: 35.00				

KM# 3046   100 SCHILLING
20.0000 g., 0.9000 Silver 0.5787 oz. ASW, 34 mm. **Series:** Habsburg Tragedies **Obv:** Standing portrait in uniform of Emperor Maximilian of Mexico **Rev:** Miramar palace and the SMS Novard

Date	Mintage	F	VF	XF	Unc	BU
1997 Proof	45,000				Value: 40.00	

KM# 3051   100 SCHILLING
20.0000 g., 0.9000 Silver 0.5787 oz. ASW, 34 mm. **Series:** Habsburg Tragedies **Obv:** Standing portrait in uniform of Crown Prince Rudolf, 3/4 left **Rev:** Hearse with military honor guard

Date	Mintage	F	VF	XF	Unc	BU
1998 Proof	Est. 40,000				Value: 40.00	

KM# 3059   100 SCHILLING
20.0000 g., 0.9000 Silver 0.5787 oz. ASW, 34 mm. **Series:** Habsburg Tragedies **Obv:** Archduke Franz Ferdinand and Sophie, 3/4 right **Rev:** The Royal couple getting into the car

Date	Mintage	F	VF	XF	Unc	BU
1999 Proof	50,000				Value: 40.00	

KM# 3063   100 SCHILLING
Bi-Metallic Titanium center in Silver ring, 34 mm.
Subject: Communications **Obv:** Computer chip design **Rev:** World map at center in ring **Edge:** Plain

Date	Mintage	F	VF	XF	Unc	BU
2000 Proof	50,000				Value: 45.00	

KM# 3068   100 SCHILLING
20.0000 g., 0.9000 Silver 0.5787 oz. ASW, 34 mm. **Obv:** Celtic salt miner **Rev:** Celtic coin design with mounted warrior **Edge:** Reeded

Date	Mintage	F	VF	XF	Unc	BU
2000 Proof	30,000				Value: 40.00	

KM# 3069   100 SCHILLING
20.0000 g., 0.9000 Silver 0.5787 oz. ASW, 34 mm. **Obv:** Ancient Roman troops crossing pontoon bridge **Rev:** Bust of Marcus Aurelius right **Edge:** Reeded

Date	Mintage	F	VF	XF	Unc	BU
2000 Proof	30,000				Value: 40.00	

KM# 3026   200 SCHILLING
33.6300 g., 0.9250 Silver 1.0000 oz. ASW **Series:** Olympic Centenary, 1896-1996 **Obv:** Male and Female figures standing with outstretched arms joined form a circle around Austrian shield, value and date at bottom **Rev:** Ribbon dancer on knees, left, looking up, Olympic logo upper right, CITIUS ALTIUS FORTIUS

Date	Mintage	F	VF	XF	Unc	BU
1995 Proof	Est. 100,000				Value: 32.50	

KM# 3027   200 SCHILLING
33.6300 g., 0.9250 Silver 1.0000 oz. ASW **Series:** Olympics **Rev:** Skier, CITIUS ALTIUS FORTIUS

Date	Mintage	F	VF	XF	Unc	BU
1995 Proof	Est. 100,000				Value: 32.50	

KM# 2947   500 SCHILLING
24.0000 g., 0.6400 Silver 0.4938 oz. ASW **Subject:** Millennium **Obv:** Value within circle of shields **Rev:** City of Steyr

Date	Mintage	F	VF	XF	Unc	BU
1980	825,800				50.00	—
1980 Select	63,000				52.00	—
1980 Proof	111,200				Value: 58.00	

KM# 2948   500 SCHILLING
24.0000 g., 0.6400 Silver 0.4938 oz. ASW **Subject:** 25th Anniversary - State Treaty **Obv:** Value within circle of shields **Rev:** Belvedere Castle, two dates below

Date	Mintage	F	VF	XF	Unc	BU
ND(1980)	787,000	—	—	—	50.00	—
ND(1980) Select	79,000				52.00	—
ND(1980) Proof	134,000				Value: 58.00	

KM# 2949   500 SCHILLING
24.0000 g., 0.6400 Silver 0.4938 oz. ASW **Subject:** Bicentennial - Death of Maria Theresa **Obv:** Value within circle of shields **Rev:** Bust of Maria Theresa, right, date at right

Date	Mintage	F	VF	XF	Unc	BU
1980	842,000				50.00	—
1980 Select	86,400				50.00	—
1980 Proof	171,600				Value: 55.00	

KM# 2950   500 SCHILLING
24.0000 g., 0.6400 Silver 0.4938 oz. ASW **Subject:** Centennial - Austrian Red Cross **Obv:** Value within circle of shields **Rev:** Henri Dunant, Philanthropist, two dates at right

Date	Mintage	F	VF	XF	Unc	BU
ND(1980)	860,000	—	—	—	50.00	—
ND(1980) Select	90,000				50.00	—
ND(1980) Proof	200,000				Value: 55.00	

KM# 2951   500 SCHILLING
24.0000 g., 0.6400 Silver 0.4938 oz. ASW **Subject:** 800th Anniversary - Verdun Altar **Obv:** Value within circle of shields **Rev:** Man fighting lion in doorway divides dates, within circle

Date	Mintage	F	VF	XF	Unc	BU
ND(1981)	865,000	—	—	—	50.00	—
ND(1981) Select	85,000				50.00	—
ND(1981) Proof	200,000				Value: 58.00	

KM# 2952   500 SCHILLING
24.0000 g., 0.6400 Silver 0.4938 oz. ASW **Subject:** 100th
Anniversary - Birth of Anton Wildgans, Writer **Obv:** Value within
circle of shields **Rev:** Head of Anton Wildgans, left, within circle,
three dates outside circle

Date	Mintage	F	VF	XF	Unc	BU
1981	911,200	—	—	—	50.00	—
1981 Select	72,000	—	—	—	50.00	—
1981 Proof	166,800	Value: 55.00				

KM# 2953   500 SCHILLING
24.0000 g., 0.6400 Silver 0.4938 oz. ASW **Subject:** 100th
Anniversary - Birth of Otto Bauer, Politician **Obv:** Value within circle
of shields **Rev:** Head of Otto Bauer, 3/4 left, two dates at right

Date	Mintage	F	VF	XF	Unc	BU
ND(1981)	929,000	—	—	—	50.00	—
ND(1981) Select	65,000	—	—	—	50.00	—
ND(1981) Proof	156,000	Value: 55.00				

KM# 2954   500 SCHILLING
24.0000 g., 0.6400 Silver 0.4938 oz. ASW **Subject:** 200th
Anniversary - Religious Tolerance **Obv:** Value within circle of shields
Rev: Cross with religious symbols below, dates above, within circle

Date	Mintage	F	VF	XF	Unc	BU
ND(1981)	792,000	—	—	—	50.00	—
ND(1981) Select	60,000	—	—	—	50.00	—
ND(1981) Proof	148,000	Value: 55.00				

KM# 2956   500 SCHILLING
24.0000 g., 0.6400 Silver 0.4938 oz. ASW **Subject:** 1500th
Anniversary - Death of St. Severin **Obv:** Value within circle of
shields **Rev:** Standing figure of St. Severin divides dates, urns
lower left, pillars at lower right

Date	Mintage	F	VF	XF	Unc	BU
ND(1982)	837,400	—	—	—	50.00	—
ND(1982) Select	42,600	—	—	—	50.00	—
ND(1982) Proof	120,000	Value: 55.00				

KM# 2957   500 SCHILLING
24.0000 g., 0.6400 Silver 0.4938 oz. ASW **Subject:** 500 Years
of Austrian Printing **Obv:** Value within circle of shields
Rev: Ancient printing system, date at bottom

Date	Mintage	F	VF	XF	Unc	BU
1982	589,600	—	—	—	50.00	—
1982 Select	42,200	—	—	—	50.00	—
1982 Proof	118,200	Value: 55.00				

KM# 2958   500 SCHILLING
24.0000 g., 0.6400 Silver 0.4938 oz. ASW **Subject:** 825 Years
of the Mariazell Shrine **Obv:** Value within circle of shields
Rev: Standing figure of enshrined Madonna of Mariazell holding
child, date below in leaves

Date	Mintage	F	VF	XF	Unc	BU
1982	589,600	—	—	—	50.00	—
1982 Select	41,600	—	—	—	50.00	—
1982 Proof	118,800	Value: 55.00				

KM# 2959   500 SCHILLING
24.0000 g., 0.6400 Silver 0.4938 oz. ASW **Subject:** 80th
Anniversary - Birth of Leopold Figl **Obv:** Value within circle of
shields **Rev:** Bust of Leopold Figl, left

Date	Mintage	F	VF	XF	Unc	BU
1982	344,000	—	—	—	50.00	—
1982 Select	39,600	—	—	—	50.00	—
1982 Proof	116,400	Value: 60.00				

KM# 2961   500 SCHILLING
24.0000 g., 0.9250 Silver 0.7137 oz. ASW **Subject:** World Cup
Horse Jumping Championship **Obv:** Value within circle of shields
Rev: Horse Jumper

Date	Mintage	F	VF	XF	Unc	BU
1983	367,600	—	—	—	50.00	—
1983 Proof	132,400	Value: 55.00				

KM# 2962   500 SCHILLING
24.0000 g., 0.9250 Silver 0.7137 oz. ASW **Subject:** Centennial
- Vienna City Hall **Obv:** Value within circle of shields **Rev:** Vienna
City Hall, dates below

Date	Mintage	F	VF	XF	Unc	BU
ND(1983)	466,200	—	—	—	50.00	—
ND(1973) Proof	133,800	Value: 55.00				

KM# 2963   500 SCHILLING
24.0000 g., 0.9250 Silver 0.7137 oz. ASW **Subject:** Catholic
Day - Pope's Visit **Obv:** Value within circle of shields **Rev:** Pope
Johannes Paul II, left, arms raised, cross with Jesus in left hand,
cross dividing date behind head

Date	Mintage	F	VF	XF	Unc	BU
1983	600,000	—	—	—	50.00	—
1983 Select	60,000	—	—	—	50.00	—
1983 Proof	140,000	Value: 55.00				

KM# 2964   500 SCHILLING
24.0000 g., 0.9250 Silver 0.7137 oz. ASW **Subject:** Centennial
- Parliament Building **Obv:** Value within circle of shields
Rev: Parliament Building, date upper left

Date	Mintage	F	VF	XF	Unc	BU
1983	522,600	—	—	—	50.00	—
1983 Proof	137,000	Value: 55.00				

KM# 2966   500 SCHILLING
24.0000 g., 0.9250 Silver 0.7137 oz. ASW **Subject:** 175th
Anniversary - Tirolean Revolution **Obv:** Value within circle of
shields **Rev:** Atatue of Tirolean Man standing, two dates lower left

Date	Mintage	F	VF	XF	Unc	BU
ND(1984)	455,400	—	—	—	50.00	—
ND(1984) Proof	144,600	Value: 55.00				

KM# 2967   500 SCHILLING
24.0000 g., 0.9250 Silver 0.7137 oz. ASW **Subject:** 100th Anniversary - Commercial Shipping on Lake Constance **Obv:** Value within circle of shields **Rev:** Commercial ship on water, within 3/4 circle, date below, left of small shield

Date	Mintage	F	VF	XF	Unc	BU
1984	457,800	—	—	—	50.00	
1984 Proof	142,200	Value: 55.00				

KM# 2968   500 SCHILLING
24.0000 g., 0.9250 Silver 0.7137 oz. ASW **Subject:** 700th Anniversary - Stams Stift in Tirol **Obv:** Value within circle of shields **Rev:** Building, small shield below

Date	Mintage	F	VF	XF	Unc	BU
1984	462,000	—	—	—	50.00	
1984 Proof	138,000	Value: 55.00				

KM# 2969   500 SCHILLING
24.0000 g., 0.9250 Silver 0.7137 oz. ASW **Subject:** Centennial - Death of Fanny Elssler **Obv:** Value within circle of shields **Rev:** Full-length view of Fanny Elssler, 1810-1884, in inner circle

Date	Mintage	F	VF	XF	Unc	BU
1984	464,800	—	—	—	50.00	
1984 Proof	135,200	Value: 55.00				

KM# 2971   500 SCHILLING
24.0000 g., 0.9250 Silver 0.7137 oz. ASW **Subject:** 400th Anniversary - Graz University **Obv:** Value within circle of shields **Rev:** Bust of Archduke with ruffled collar, right, date below, within circle

Date	Mintage	F	VF	XF	Unc	BU
1985	481,000	—	—	—	50.00	
1985 Proof	119,000	Value: 55.00				

KM# 2972   500 SCHILLING
24.0000 g., 0.9250 Silver 0.7137 oz. ASW **Subject:** 40 Years of Peace in Austria **Obv:** Value within circle of shields **Rev:** Woman standing in front of Austrian map holding branch of leaves

Date	Mintage	F	VF	XF	Unc	BU
ND(1985)	384,000	—	—	—	50.00	
ND(1985) Proof	116,000	Value: 55.00				

KM# 2973   500 SCHILLING
24.0000 g., 0.9250 Silver 0.7137 oz. ASW **Subject:** 500th Anniversary - Canonization of Leopold III **Obv:** Value within circle of shields **Rev:** Crowned standing figure of Leopold III, facing, holding model of church in left hand, divides dates

Date	Mintage	F	VF	XF	Unc	BU
ND(1985)	388,000	—	—	—	50.00	
ND(1985) Proof	112,000	Value: 55.00				

KM# 2974   500 SCHILLING
24.0000 g., 0.9250 Silver 0.7137 oz. ASW **Subject:** 2000th Anniversary - Bregenz **Obv:** Value within circle of shields **Rev:** Two coins on coin, left one with laureate head right, right one with shield of arms, date at bottom

Date	Mintage	F	VF	XF	Unc	BU
1985	387,800	—	—	—	50.00	
1985 Proof	112,200	Value: 55.00				

KM# 2976   500 SCHILLING
24.0000 g., 0.9250 Silver 0.7137 oz. ASW **Subject:** 300th Anniversary - St. Florian's Abbey **Obv:** Value within circle of shields **Rev:** St. Florian's Abbey, two dates below, small shield lower left

Date	Mintage	F	VF	XF	Unc	BU
ND(1986)	303,200	—	—	—	50.00	
ND(1986) Proof	96,800	Value: 55.00				

KM# 2977   500 SCHILLING
24.0000 g., 0.9250 Silver 0.7137 oz. ASW **Subject:** 500th Anniversary - First Thaler Coin Struck at Hall Mint **Obv:** Value within circle of shields **Rev:** Crowned figure with scepter, center, small eagle with shield at left, within inner circle, two dates below circle

Date	Mintage	F	VF	XF	Unc	BU
ND(1986)	302,000	—	—	—	50.00	
ND(1986) Proof	99,000	Value: 58.00				

KM# 2978   500 SCHILLING
24.0000 g., 0.9250 Silver 0.7137 oz. ASW **Subject:** 250th Anniversary - Birth of Prince Eugene of Savoy **Obv:** Value within circle of shields **Rev:** Man on rearing horse, three dates at bottom

Date	Mintage	F	VF	XF	Unc	BU
1986	300,400	—	—	—	50.00	
1986 Proof	99,600	Value: 55.00				

KM# 2979   500 SCHILLING
24.0000 g., 0.9250 Silver 0.7137 oz. ASW **Subject:** European Conference on Security and Cooperation **Obv:** Value within circle of shields **Rev:** Globe with map at top, inscription below, small shield at bottom with date to right

Date	Mintage	F	VF	XF	Unc	BU
1986	202,600	—	—	—	50.00	
1986 Proof	97,400	Value: 55.00				

KM# 2981   500 SCHILLING
24.0000 g., 0.9250 Silver 0.7137 oz. ASW **Subject:** 150th Anniversary - Austrian Railroad **Obv:** Value within circle of shields **Rev:** Trains, two dates to lower right

Date	Mintage	F	VF	XF	Unc	BU
ND(1987)	206,000	—	—	—	50.00	
ND(1987) Proof	94,800	Value: 60.00				

KM# 2982   500 SCHILLING

24.0000 g., 0.9250 Silver 0.7137 oz. ASW **Subject:** 400th Anniversary - Birth of Salzburg's Archbishop von Raitenau **Obv:** Value within circle of shields **Rev:** Bust of Archbishop von Raitenau, 3/4 left, two dates at left

Date	Mintage	F	VF	XF	Unc	BU
ND(1987)	206,400	—	—	—	50.00	—
ND(1987) Proof	93,600	Value: 55.00				

KM# 2983   500 SCHILLING

24.0000 g., 0.9250 Silver 0.7137 oz. ASW **Subject:** 800th Anniversary - Holy Cross Church **Obv:** Value within circle of shields **Rev:** Holy Cross Church, date at upper left

Date	Mintage	F	VF	XF	Unc	BU
1987	205,200	—	—	—	50.00	—
1987 Proof	94,800	Value: 55.00				

KM# 2984   500 SCHILLING

24.0000 g., 0.9250 Silver 0.7137 oz. ASW **Subject:** 850th Anniversary - St. Georgenberg Abbey **Obv:** Value within circle of shields **Rev:** St. Georgenberg Abbey, two dates at bottom

Date	Mintage	F	VF	XF	Unc	BU
ND(1988)	211,800	—	—	—	50.00	—
ND(1988) Proof	88,200	Value: 58.00				

KM# 2985   500 SCHILLING

24.0000 g., 0.9250 Silver 0.7137 oz. ASW **Subject:** Pope's Visit to Austria **Obv:** Value within circle of shields **Rev:** Pope Johannes Paul II, with high collar, right, date at bottom

Date	Mintage	F	VF	XF	Unc	BU
1988	211,200	—	—	—	50.00	—
1988 Proof	88,800	Value: 58.00				

KM# 2986   500 SCHILLING

24.0000 g., 0.9250 Silver 0.7137 oz. ASW **Subject:** 100th Anniversary - Victor Adler and Christian Social Party **Obv:** Value within circle of shields **Rev:** Head of Victor Adler, facing, date below name at lower right

Date	Mintage	F	VF	XF	Unc	BU
1988	213,200	—	—	—	50.00	—
1988 Proof	86,800	Value: 58.00				

KM# 2987   500 SCHILLING

24.0000 g., 0.9250 Silver 0.7137 oz. ASW **Obv:** Bust of Gustav Klimt, facing, value below **Rev:** Art Nouveau bust of woman facing forward

Date	Mintage	F	VF	XF	Unc	BU
1989	236,600	—	—	—	50.00	—
1989 Proof	88,000	Value: 58.00				

KM# 2991   500 SCHILLING

24.0000 g., 0.9250 Silver 0.7137 oz. ASW **Obv:** Head of Koloman Moser, facing 3/4 left, value below **Rev:** Stained glass, winged figure standing at center

Date	Mintage	F	VF	XF	Unc	BU
1989	228,000	—	—	—	50.00	—
1989 Proof	83,200	Value: 55.00				

KM# 2992   500 SCHILLING

24.0000 g., 0.9250 Silver 0.7137 oz. ASW **Obv:** Bust of Egon Schiele, 3/4 facing, value below **Rev:** Expressionism, mother with two children

Date	Mintage	F	VF	XF	Unc	BU
1990	246,600	—	—	—	50.00	—
1990 Proof	81,800	Value: 55.00				

KM# 2994   500 SCHILLING

24.0000 g., 0.9250 Silver 0.7137 oz. ASW **Obv:** Head of Oskar Kokoschka, 3/4 left, value below **Rev:** Expressionism, woman figure facing right

Date	Mintage	F	VF	XF	Unc	BU
1990	245,200	—	—	—	50.00	—
1990 Proof	81,000	Value: 55.00				

KM# 2997   500 SCHILLING

8.1130 g., 0.9860 Gold 0.2572 oz. AGW **Obv:** Bust of Mozart, 3/4 right, value at lower right **Rev:** Half-length figure of Don Giovanni playing instrument, facing, looking right

Date	Mintage	F	VF	XF	Unc	BU
1991 Proof	50,000	Value: 265				

KM# 3000   500 SCHILLING

24.0000 g., 0.9250 Silver 0.7137 oz. ASW **Obv:** Head of Herbert von Karajan facing left, right of artistic inscription **Rev:** Salzburg Festspielhaus

Date	Mintage	F	VF	XF	Unc	BU
1991	240,000	—	—	—	47.50	—
1991 Proof	74,400	Value: 55.00				

KM# 3002   500 SCHILLING

24.0000 g., 0.9250 Silver 0.7137 oz. ASW **Obv:** Head of Karl Bohm facing at right, inscription at left **Rev:** Building, inscription below

Date	Mintage	F	VF	XF	Unc	BU
1991	240,000	—	—	—	47.50	—
1991 Proof	72,400	Value: 55.00				

KM# 3006   500 SCHILLING

8.1130 g., 0.9860 Gold 0.2572 oz. AGW **Subject:** 150th Anniversary - Vienna Philharmonic **Obv:** Vienna Philharmonic Hall, date below, value at bottom **Rev:** Orchestra instruments, three violins and two horns

Date	Mintage	F	VF	XF	Unc	BU
1992 Proof	43,000	Value: 250				

KM# 3010 500 SCHILLING

24.0000 g., 0.9250 Silver 0.7137 oz. ASW **Obv:** Head of Gustav Mahler facing left at right, inscription at left **Rev:** Nude figure standing in center with harp at top, inscription below feet

Date	Mintage	F	VF	XF	Unc	BU
1992	237,000	—	—	—	,47.50	—
1992 Proof	64,000	Value: 60.00				

KM# 3021 500 SCHILLING

24.0000 g., 0.9250 Silver 0.7137 oz. ASW **Obv:** Head of Richard Strauss facing forward at right, inscription at left **Rev:** Man and woman standing, man slightly bent at waist

Date	Mintage	F	VF	XF	Unc	BU
1992	236,000	—	—	—	47.50	—
1992 Proof	62,900	Value: 60.00				

KM# 3011 500 SCHILLING

24.0000 g., 0.9250 Silver 0.7137 oz. ASW **Obv:** Hallstatt and the Lakes Region, value below **Rev:** Boats on water

Date	Mintage	F	VF	XF	Unc	BU
1993	211,200	—	—	—	47.50	—
1993 Proof	60,000	Value: 60.00				

KM# 3012 500 SCHILLING

8.1130 g., 0.9860 Gold 0.2572 oz. AGW **Obv:** City building, date at right, value at bottom **Rev:** Aligned heads of Emperors Rudolf II, Ferdinand II, and Archduke Leopold Wilhelm, right

Date	Mintage	F	VF	XF	Unc	BU
1993 Proof	50,000	Value: 650				

KM# 3014 500 SCHILLING

24.0000 g., 0.9250 Silver 0.7137 oz. ASW **Obv:** Alpine Region, value at bottom **Rev:** Two Alpine dancers

---

Date	Mintage	F	VF	XF	Unc	BU
1993	211,600	—	—	—	47.50	—
1993 Proof	60,000	Value: 60.00				

KM# 3015 500 SCHILLING

8.1130 g., 0.9860 Gold 0.2572 oz. AGW **Obv:** Congress of Vienna, value below **Rev:** Armored bust of Franz I, facing, looking left, small crown at left, two dates on right

Date	Mintage	F	VF	XF	Unc	BU
1994 Proof	50,000	Value: 250				

KM# 3017 500 SCHILLING

24.0000 g., 0.9250 Silver 0.7137 oz. ASW **Obv:** Pannonian Region, value below **Rev:** Dancers

Date	Mintage	F	VF	XF	Unc	BU
1994	188,800	—	—	—	47.50	—
1994 Proof	55,000	Value: 60.00				

KM# 3024 500 SCHILLING

24.0000 g., 0.9250 Silver 0.7137 oz. ASW **Obv:** River Region, value below, date at bottom **Rev:** Folk paraders

Date	Mintage	F	VF	XF	Unc	BU
1994	187,800	—	—	—	47.50	—
1994 Proof	55,000	Value: 60.00				

KM# 3025 500 SCHILLING

24.0000 g., 0.9250 Silver 0.7137 oz. ASW **Obv:** Austrian Hill Country, value below, date at bottom **Rev:** Farm couple

Date	Mintage	F	VF	XF	Unc	BU
1995	185,000	—	—	—	47.50	—
1995 Proof	55,000	Value: 60.00				

Date	Mintage	F	VF	XF	Unc	BU
1995	Est. 184,000	—	—	—	47.50	—
1995 Proof	Est. 50,000	Value: 60.00				

KM# 3023 500 SCHILLING

Bi-Metallic Silver center in Gold ring **Subject:** European Union - Austrian Membership **Obv:** Symbol with Austrian shield at right, value below, within circle **Rev:** Scene of city within circle **Note:** Stars in outer ring are completely punched through.

Date	Mintage	F	VF	XF	Unc	BU
1995 Proof	40,000	Value: 200				

KM# 3032 500 SCHILLING

8.1130 g., 0.9860 Gold 0.2572 oz. AGW **Obv:** Men on horseback, value below, date at lower right **Rev:** Half-length figure of Heinrich II Jasomirgott, sword in right hand, 3/4 facing

Date	Mintage	F	VF	XF	Unc	BU
1996 Proof	Est. 50,000	Value: 265				

KM# 3035 500 SCHILLING

24.0000 g., 0.9250 Silver 0.7137 oz. ASW **Obv:** The Mill Region, value below, date at bottom **Rev:** Man and woman with grain

Date	Mintage	F	VF	XF	Unc	BU
1996	185,000	—	—	—	47.50	—
1996 Proof	50,000	Value: 60.00				

KM# 3039 500 SCHILLING

24.0000 g., 0.9250 Silver 0.7137 oz. ASW **Series:** Town Series - Innsbruck Square **Obv:** View of town square, value below, date at bottom **Rev:** Outdoor market scene

Date	Mintage	F	VF	XF	Unc	BU
1996	160,000	—	—	—	47.50	—
1996 BU	25,000	—	—	—	50.00	—
1996 Proof	50,000	Value: 60.00				

KM# 3040 500 SCHILLING

8.0400 g., 0.9950 Gold 0.2572 oz. AGW **Obv:** Franz Schubert at piano, S. M. Vogl in foreground, form a sepia sketch by Moritz von Schwind **Rev:** Bust of Franz Schubert, facing, two dates at left, line of musical score

Date	Mintage	F	VF	XF	Unc	BU
1997 Proof	Est. 50,000	Value: 260				

KM# 3042   500 SCHILLING
24.0000 g., 0.9250 Silver 0.7137 oz. ASW **Series:** Town Series - Bruck an der Mur **Obv:** Ornate pavilion on cobblestone street, value below, date at bottom **Rev:** Ironsmith at work

Date	Mintage	F	VF	XF	Unc	BU
1997	125,000	—	—	—	42.00	—
1997 Special Unc	25,000	—	—	—	50.00	—
1997 Proof	45,000	Value: 60.00				

KM# 3045   500 SCHILLING
24.0000 g., 0.9250 Silver 0.7137 oz. ASW **Obv:** Stone pulpit of St. Stephen's cathedral, value below **Rev:** Stone mason at work

Date	Mintage	F	VF	XF	Unc	BU
1997	125,000	—	—	—	42.00	—
1997 Special Unc	25,000	—	—	—	50.00	—
1997 Proof	45,000	Value: 60.00				

KM# 3047   500 SCHILLING
8.0400 g., 0.9950 Gold 0.2572 oz. AGW, 22 mm. **Obv:** New York and Kyoto views, value at bottom **Rev:** Vienna Boy's Choir

Date	Mintage	F	VF	XF	Unc	BU
ND(1998) Proof	Est. 50,000	Value: 260				

KM# 3049   500 SCHILLING
22.2000 g., 0.9250 Silver 0.6602 oz. ASW, 37 mm. **Obv:** Interior view of Adimont Abbey Library, value below legend, date at bottom **Rev:** Printers at work **Note:** Book printing.

Date	Mintage	F	VF	XF	Unc	BU
1998	125,000	—	—	—	42.00	—
1998 BU	25,000	—	—	—	50.00	—
1998 Proof	50,000	Value: 60.00				

KM# 3054   500 SCHILLING
22.2000 g., 0.9250 Silver 0.6602 oz. ASW, 37 mm. **Obv:** Gold chalice and church, value left of chalice, date at bottom **Rev:** Goldsmith at work

Date	Mintage	F	VF	XF	Unc	BU
1998	125,000	—	—	—	42.00	—
1998 Special Unc	17,000	—	—	—	50.00	—
1998 Proof	35,000	Value: 60.00				

KM# 3055   500 SCHILLING
8.0400 g., 0.9250 Gold 0.2391 oz. AGW, 22 mm. **Obv:** Waltzing couple and Strauss monument, value below **Rev:** Busts of Johann Strauss and son, Johann, 3/4 left, dates to left and right of busts

Date	Mintage	F	VF	XF	Unc	BU
1999 Proof	Est. 50,000	Value: 260				

KM# 3058   500 SCHILLING
24.0000 g., 0.9250 Silver 0.7137 oz. ASW **Obv:** Rosenburg Castle, falcon on perch in castle jousting court, value and date at bottom **Rev:** Jousting knights

Date	Mintage	F	VF	XF	Unc	BU
1999	Est. 125,000	—	—	—	42.00	—
1999 Special Unc	25,000	—	—	—	50.00	—
1999 Proof	50,000	Value: 60.00				

KM# 3060   500 SCHILLING
24.0000 g., 0.9250 Silver 0.7137 oz. ASW **Obv:** Burg Lockenhaus, value and date at bottom **Rev:** Two Templar knights on horseback, left

Date	Mintage	F	VF	XF	Unc	BU
1999	Est. 125,000	—	—	—	42.00	—
1999 Special Unc	25,000	—	—	—	50.00	—
1999 Proof	50,000	Value: 60.00				

KM# 3065   500 SCHILLING
10.1400 g., 0.9860 Gold 0.3214 oz. AGW, 22 mm. **Subject:** 2000th Birthday of Jesus Christ **Obv:** Three wise men presenting gifts within circle, value below circle **Rev:** Portrait of Jesus, facing

Date	Mintage	F	VF	XF	Unc	BU
2000 Proof	Est. 50,000	Value: 320				

KM# 3067   500 SCHILLING
24.0000 g., 0.9250 Silver 0.7137 oz. ASW, 37 mm. **Obv:** Hochosterwitz Castle, value lower left **Rev:** Walter von der Vogelweide and royal couple **Edge:** Lettered

Date	Mintage	F	VF	XF	Unc	BU
2000	95,000	—	—	—	42.00	—
2000 Special Unc	50,000	—	—	—	50.00	—
2000 Proof	25,000	Value: 55.00				

KM# 3071   500 SCHILLING
24.0000 g., 0.9250 Silver 0.7137 oz. ASW, 37 mm. **Obv:** Burg Hohenwerfen Castle, value at bottom **Rev:** Medieval falcon training scene **Edge:** Lettered

Date	Mintage	F	VF	XF	Unc	BU
2000	600,000	—	—	—	42.00	—
2000 Special Unc	100,000	—	—	—	50.00	—
2000 Proof	30,000	Value: 55.00				

KM# 2933   1000 SCHILLING
13.5000 g., 0.9000 Gold 0.3906 oz. AGW **Subject:** Babenberg Dynasty Millennium **Obv:** Imperial Eagle with Austrian shield on breast, holding hammer and sickle, value below **Rev:** Seal of Duke Friedrich II within circle, dates above circle **Note:** Exists in shades of red to yellow gold.

Date	Mintage	F	VF	XF	Unc	BU
ND(1976)	1,800,000	—	—	—	—	375

KM# 2999   1000 SCHILLING
16.2250 g., 0.9860 Gold 0.5143 oz. AGW **Obv:** Head of Mozart with high collar, left, date below collar, violin on right **Rev:** The Magic Flute Opera from a 1789 drawing by Dora Stode

Date	Mintage	F	VF	XF	Unc	BU
1991 Proof	30,000	Value: 520				

KM# 3008   1000 SCHILLING
16.2250 g., 0.9860 Gold 0.5143 oz. AGW **Obv:** City building, value below, date upper right **Rev:** 1/2-length figure of Johann Strauss playing violin looking forward

Date	Mintage	F	VF	XF	Unc	BU
1992 Proof	42,000	Value: 500				

KM# 3013   1000 SCHILLING
16.2250 g., 0.9860 Gold 0.5143 oz. AGW **Obv:** Buildings, date below, value at bottom **Rev:** 3/4 length torso of Maria Theresa holding scepter in right hand, half facing right

Date	Mintage	F	VF	XF	Unc	BU
1993 Proof	50,000	Value: 500				

KM# 3018   1000 SCHILLING
Bi-Metallic Gold center in Silver ring **Subject:** 800th Anniversary of the Vienna Mint **Obv:** Symbol at center of three circles, two dates above **Rev:** Crowned figure on horseback in center of three circles surrounded by circle of laborers

Date	Mintage	F	VF	XF	Unc	BU
ND(1994) Proof	50,000	Value: 350				

KM# 3028   1000 SCHILLING
16.9700 g., 0.9170 Gold 0.5003 oz. AGW **Series:** Olympics **Obv:** Building, statue on right, date at base, shield on left, value above **Rev:** Head of Zeus on left, facing, Olympic logo, flame to the right, CITIUS ALTIUS FORTIUS

Date	Mintage	F	VF	XF	Unc	BU
1995 Proof	Est. 60,000	Value: 485				

KM# 3030   1000 SCHILLING
16.2250 g., 0.9860 Gold 0.5143 oz. AGW **Subject:** 50th Anniversary - Second Republic **Obv:** Five men aligned behind railing, center man holding book, date below railing, value at bottom **Rev:** Stylized design

Date	Mintage	F	VF	XF	Unc	BU
1995 Proof	49,000	Value: 500				

KM# 3037   1000 SCHILLING
16.2250 g., 0.9860 Gold 0.5143 oz. AGW **Subject:** Millennium of the Name Osterreich **Obv:** Land grant within circle, dates at bottom, value below circle **Rev:** Seated, crowned figure of Otto III, facing

Date	Mintage	F	VF	XF	Unc	BU
ND(1996) Proof	50,000	Value: 450				

KM# 3043   1000 SCHILLING
16.0800 g., 0.9950 Gold 0.5144 oz. AGW **Subject:** Habsburg Tragedies - Marie Antoinette **Obv:** Half-length figure of Marie holding flowers, 3/4 right, value and date lower left **Rev:** Marie on trial

Date	Mintage	F	VF	XF	Unc	BU
1997 Proof	Est. 50,000	Value: 500				

KM# 3052   1000 SCHILLING
16.0800 g., 0.9950 Gold 0.5144 oz. AGW, 30 mm. **Subject:** 100th Anniversary of Queen Elisabeth's Assassination by Luigi Luccheni in Geneva **Obv:** Bust of Empress Elisabeth, Queen of Hungary, 3/4 right **Rev:** Scene of Elisabeth's final moment

Date	Mintage	F	VF	XF	Unc	BU
1998 Proof	Est. 50,000	Value: 500				

KM# 3062   1000 SCHILLING
16.0800 g., 0.9950 Gold 0.5144 oz. AGW, 30 mm. **Obv:** Emperor Karl I bust facing **Rev:** Interior view Habsburg crypt

Date	Mintage	F	VF	XF	Unc	BU
1999 Proof	Est. 50,000	Value: 500				

KM# 3072   1000 SCHILLING
16.2200 g., 0.9860 Gold 0.5142 oz. AGW **Obv:** Heidentor ancient gate and statue **Rev:** Constantius II portrait **Edge:** Reeded

Date	Mintage	F	VF	XF	Unc	BU
2000	30,000	—	—	—	—	500

BULLION COINAGE
Philharmonic Issues

KM# 3004   200 SCHILLING
3.1100 g., 0.9999 Gold 0.1000 oz. AGW **Series:** Vienna Philharmonic Orchestra **Obv:** The Golden Hall organ **Rev:** Wind and string instruments

Date	Mintage	F	VF	XF	Unc	BU
1991	93,000	—	—	—	BV+13%	—
1992	102,000	—	—	—	BV+13%	—
1993	107,500	—	—	—	BV+13%	—
1994	94,500	—	—	—	BV+13%	—
1995	169,500	—	—	—	BV+13%	—
1996	170,000	—	—	—	BV+13%	—
1997	59,000	—	—	—	BV+13%	—
1998	88,500	—	—	—	BV+13%	—
1999	101,500	—	—	—	BV+13%	—
2000	85,500	—	—	—	BV+13%	—

KM# 2989   500 SCHILLING
7.7760 g., 0.9999 Gold 0.2500 oz. AGW **Series:** Vienna Philharmonic Orchestra **Obv:** The Golden Hall organ **Rev:** Wind and string instruments

Date	Mintage	F	VF	XF	Unc	BU
1989	586,000	—	—	—	BV+10%	—
1990	46,000	—	—	—	BV+10%	—
1991	24,000	—	—	—	BV+10%	—
1992	186,000	—	—	—	BV+10%	—
1993	166,000	—	—	—	BV+10%	—
1994	12,000	—	—	—	BV+10%	—
1995	174,000	—	—	—	BV+10%	—
1996	184,000	—	—	—	BV+10%	—
1997	66,000	—	—	—	BV+10%	—
1998	38,000	—	—	—	BV+10%	—
1999	81,600	—	—	—	BV+10%	—
2000	38,000	—	—	—	BV+10%	—

KM# 3031   1000 SCHILLING
15.5500 g., 0.9999 Gold 0.4999 oz. AGW **Series:** Vienna Philharmonic Orchestra **Obv:** The Golden Hall organ **Rev:** Wind and string instruments

Date	Mintage	F	VF	XF	Unc	BU
1994	79,000	—	—	—	BV+8%	—
1995	105,500	—	—	—	BV+8%	—
1996	82,500	—	—	—	BV+8%	—
1997	65,500	—	—	—	BV+8%	—
1998	34,000	—	—	—	BV+8%	—
1999	10,000	—	—	—	BV+8%	—
2000	38,500	—	—	—	BV+8%	—

KM# 2990   2000 SCHILLING
31.1035 g., 0.9999 Gold 0.9999 oz. AGW **Series:** Vienna Philharmonic Orchestra **Obv:** The Golden Hall organ **Rev:** Wind and string instruments

Date	Mintage	F	VF	XF	Unc	BU
1989	484,000	—	—	—	BV+4%	—
1990	406,500	—	—	—	BV+4%	—
1991	341,000	—	—	—	BV+4%	—
1992	444,500	—	—	—	BV+4%	—
1993	339,500	—	—	—	BV+4%	—
1994	68,000	—	—	—	BV+4%	—
1995	650,000	—	—	—	BV+4%	—
1996	400,500	—	—	—	BV+4%	—
1997	381,500	—	—	—	BV+4%	—
1998	294,000	—	—	—	BV+4%	—
1999	275,000	—	—	—	BV+4%	—
2000	125,500	—	—	—	BV+4%	—

PATTERNS
Including off metal strikes

KM#	Date	Mintage	Identification	Mkt Val
Pn68	1908	— 100 Kronen. Without mint mark.		—
Pn69	1909	— 100 Kronen. Without mint mark.		—
Pn70	1910	— 2 Kronen. Silver. Similar to KM#2821.		2,350
Pn72	1913	— 2 Corona. Aluminum. KM#2821.		200
Pn71	1913	— Krone. Aluminum. KM#2820.		—
Pn73	ND	— 50 Heller. Iron.		235
Pn74	1914	— Heller. Copper. Privately produced by Karl Goetz in Munich, Germany.		150
Pn75	1914	— Heller. Silver. Privately produced by Karl Goetz in Munich, Germany.		275
Pn76	1915	— 2 Heller. Bronze. KM#2801.		—
Pn77	1915	— 2 Heller. Iron. KM#2801.		—
Pn78	1915	— 20 Heller. Iron. KM#2826.		450
Pn79	1915	— 1/2 Krone. Silver. 2.5200 g.		—
Pn80	1915	— Ducat. Aluminum. Plain edge.		100
Pn81	1915	— Ducat. Copper. Reeded edge.		400
Pn82	1916	— Heller. Iron. KM#2823.		275
Pn83	1916	— 2 Heller. Iron.		—
Pn84	1916	— 10 Heller. Aluminum. KM#2825.		275
Pn85	1916	— Krone. Aluminum. KM#2820.		145
Pn86	1917	— 10 Heller. Steel. Plain edge. 10 in square, thick planchet.		—
Pn87	1917	— 10 Heller. Steel. Plain edge. 10 in square, thin planchet.		250
Pn88	1917	— 10 Heller. Steel. Milled edge.		—
Pn89	1918	— 20 Heller. Aluminum. 20 in square.		—
Pn90	1918	— 20 Heller. Aluminum. KM#2826.		250
Pn91	1918	— 5 Kronen. Brass.		—
Pn92	1918	— 20 Kronen. Copper.		—
Pn93	1918	— 20 Kronen. Gold.		—
Pn94	ND	— 10 Schilling. Nickel.		180
Pn95	ND	— 20 Schilling. Nickel.		400
Pn96	1924	— 1/2 Schilling. Silver. KM#2839.		1,250
Pn97	1924	— Schilling. Silver. KM#2835.		825
Pn98	1924	— Schilling. Silver. KM#2835. KM#2835. Octagonal planchets, 1 pair.		700
Pn99	1924	— 20 Kronen. Copper. Reeded edge. KM#2830.		1,500
Pn100	1924	— 20 Kronen. Silver. Reeded edge. Uniface, KM#2830.		700
Pn101	1930	— 100 Schilling. Silver. Plain edge. KM#2842.		2,000
Pn102	1931	— 5 Groschen. Copper-Nickel.		—
Pn103	1931	— 5 Groschen. Gold. KM#2846.		1,200
Pn104	1931	— 100 Schilling. Copper. KM#2842.		1,000
Pn105	1934	— 50 Groschen. Copper-Nickel. Uniface.		—
Pn106	1934	— 50 Groschen. Copper-Nickel. Uniface.		—
Pn107	1934	— Schilling. Copper-Nickel.		1,750
Pn108	1934	— Schilling. Copper-Nickel. Uniface.		1,750
Pn109	1934	— 2 Schilling. Zinc. KM#2852.		1,000
Pn110	1934	— 2 Schilling. Zinc. One side struck on octagonal planchet. KM#2852.		600
Pn111	1935	— 25 Schilling. Gold. J. Prinz.		—
Pn112	1935	— 100 Schilling. Gold. J. Prinz.		—
Pn113	1937	— 2 Schilling. Copper. KM#2859.		200
Pn114	1938	— 5 Groschen. Gold. KM#2846.		1,200
Pn115	1947	— Schilling. Copper-Nickel. KM#2871.		500
Pn116	1959	— Schilling. Aluminum-Bronze. Similar to KM#2886.		850

TRIAL STRIKES

KM#	Date	Mintage	Identification	Mkt Val
TS1	1934	— 50 Groschen. Uniface.		—
TS2	1934	— 50 Groschen. Uniface.		—
TS3	ND(1973)	— 5 Schilling. Nickel.		275
TS4	ND(1973)	— 10 Schilling. Nickel.		200

KM#	Date	Mintage	Identification	Mkt Val
TS5	ND(1973)	— 20 Schilling. Nickel.		350
TS6	ND(1984)	— 5 Groschen. Aluminum. Plain edge.		175

MINT SETS

KM#	Date	Mintage	Identification	Issue Price	Mkt Val
MS1	1992 (8)	25,000	KM#2875-2876, 2878, 2885-2886, 2889a, 2918	—	50.00
MS2	1993 (8)	35,000	KM#2875-2876, 2878, 2885-2886, 2889a, 2918, 2946.2	—	40.00
MS3	1994 (8)	25,000	KM#2875-2876, 2878, 2885-2886, 2889a, 2918, 3016	—	70.00
MS4	1995 (6)	27,000	KM#2878, 2885-2886, 2889a, 2918, 3022	—	50.00
MS5	1996 (6)	25,000	KM#2878, 2885-2886, 2889a, 2918, 3033	—	35.00
MS6	1997 (6)	25,000	KM#2878, 2885-2886, 2889a, 2918, 3041	—	30.00
MS7	1998 (6)	—	KM#2878, 2885-2886, 2889a, 2918, 3048	—	22.50
MS8	1999 (6)	—	KM#2878, 2885-2886, 2889a, 2918, 3056	22.00	22.50
MS9	2000 (6)	—	KM#2878, 2885-2886, 2889a, 2918, 3064	—	22.50

PROOF SETS

KM#	Date	Mintage	Identification	Issue Price	Mkt Val
PS1	1959 (2)	1,000	KM#2887-2888	—	725
PS2	1964 (9)	69,731	KM#2875-2876, 2878, 2882, 2885-2886, 2889, 2895.1, 2896	—	55.00
PS3	1964 (9)	2,700	KM#2875-2876, 2878, 2882, 2885-2886, 2889, 2895.2, 2896 (error set)		365
PS4	1964 (7)	—	KM#2875-2876, 2878, 2882, 2885-2886, 2889		22.50
PS5	1965 (7)	83,000	KM#2875-2876, 2878, 2882, 2885-2886, 2889		10.00
PS6	1965 (4)	38,000	KM#2882, 2889, 2897-2898	5.00	42.50
PS7	1966 (9)	1,765	KM#2875-2876, 2878, 2882, 2885-2886, 2889, 2899-2900	—	180
PS8	1966 (7)	—	KM#2875-2876, 2878, 2882, 2885-2886, 2889	—	60.00
PS9	1967 (9)	1,163	KM#2875-2876, 2878, 2882, 2885-2886, 2889, 2901-2902	5.50	300
PS10	1967 (7)	—	KM#2875-2876, 2878, 2882, 2885-2886, 2889	—	200
PS11	1968 (9)	15,200	KM#2875-2876, 2878, 2882, 2885-2886, 2889, 2903, 2904.1	5.75	110
PS12	1968 (7)	20,000	KM#2875-2876, 2878, 2882, 2885-2886, 2889	—	65.00
PS13	1969 (9)	20,000	KM#2875-2876, 2878, 2882, 2885-2886, 2889a, 2905-2906	7.50	90.00
PS14	1969 (7)	21,000	KM#2875-2876, 2878, 2882, 2885-2886, 2889a	—	50.00
PS15	1970 (9)	—	KM#2875-2876, 2878, 2882, 2885-2886, 2889a, 2907-2908	8.25	35.00
PS16	1970 (9)	—	KM#2875-2876, 2878, 2882, 2885-2886, 2889a, 2907, 2909	8.25	35.00
PS17	1970 (7)	92,000	KM#2875-2876, 2878, 2882, 2885-2886, 2889a	—	8.50
PS18	1970 (3)	—	KM#2907-2909	7.00	25.00
PS19	1971 (9)	—	KM#2875-2876, 2878, 2882, 2885-2886, 2889a, 2910-2911	8.25	28.00
PS20	1971 (7)	84,000	KM#2875-2876, 2878, 2882, 2885-2886, 2889a	—	8.50
PS21	1972 (9)	—	KM#2875-2876, 2878, 2882, 2885-2886, 2889a, 2912-2913	8.50	25.00
PS22	1972 (9)	—	KM#2875-2876, 2878, 2882, 2885-2886, 2889a, 2912, 2914	8.50	25.00
PS23	1972 (7)	75,000	KM#2875-2876, 2878, 2882, 2885-2886, 2889a	—	8.50
PS24	1972 (3)	—	KM#2912-2914	7.50	22.50
PS25	1972 (3)	—	KM#2912-2914	—	22.50
PS26	1973 (9)	—	KM#2875-2876, 2878, 2882, 2885-2886, 289a, 2915-2916	—	25.00
PS27	1973 (7)	87,000	KM#2875-2876, 2878, 2882, 2885-2886, 2889a	—	10.00
PS28	1974 (12)	—	KM#2875-2876, 2878, 2885-2886, 2889a, 2918-2922, 2926	29.70	55.00
PS29	1974 (8)	—	KM#2875-2876, 2878, 2885-2886, 2889a, 2918, 2921	—	20.00
PS30	1974 (7)	76,000	KM#2875-2876, 2878, 2885-2886, 2889a, 2918	—	8.50
PS31	1974 (5)	—	KM#2919-2922, 2926	27.00	42.00
PS32	1975 (10)	—	KM#2875-2876, 2878, 2885-2886, 289a, 2918, 2923-2925	30.00	45.00
PS33	1975 (7)	49,000	KM#2875-2876, 2878, 2885-2886, 2889a, 2918	—	8.50
PS34	1975 (3)	—	KM#2923-2925	27.00	35.00
PS36	1976-77 (6)	—	KM#2930-2932, 2934-2936	27.00	85.00
PS35	1976 (7)	44,000	KM#2875-2876, 2878, 2885-2886, 2889a, 2918	3.00	9.50

KM#	Date	Mintage	Identification	Issue Price	Mkt Val
PS37	1977 (7)	44,000	KM#2875-2876, 2878, 2885-2886, 2889a, 2918	3.15	8.50
PS38	1978 (7)	43,000	KM#2875-2876, 2878, 2885-2886, 2889a, 2918	—	9.50
PS39	1979 (7)	44,000	KM#2875-2876, 2878, 2885-2886, 2889a, 2918	—	9.50
PS40	1980 (8)	48,000	KM#2875-2876, 2878, 2885-2886, 2889a, 2918, 2946	—	28.00
PS42	1981 (8)	49,000	KM#2875-2876, 2878, 2885-2886, 2889a, 2918, 2946.1	—	28.00
PS43	1982 (8)	50,000	KM#2875-2876, 2878, 2885-2886, 2889a, 2918, 2955.1	—	14.00
PS44	1983 (8)	65,000	KM#2875-2876, 2878, 2885-2886, 2889a, 2918, 2960.1	—	12.50
PS45	1984 (8)	65,000	KM#2875-2876, 2878, 2885-2886, 2889a, 2918, 2965.1	—	12.50
PS46	1985 (8)	45,000	KM#2875-2876, 2878, 2885-2886, 2889a, 2918, 2970.1	—	20.00
PS47	1986 (8)	42,000	KM#2875-2876, 2878, 2885-2886, 2889a, 2918, 2975.1	—	30.00
PS48	1987 (8)	42,000	KM#2875-2876, 2878, 2885-2886, 2889a, 2918, 2980.1	—	22.00
PS49	1988 (7)	39,000	KM#2875-2876, 2878, 2885-2886, 2889a, 2918	—	12.50
PS50	1989 (8)	38,000	KM#2875-2876, 2878, 2885-2886, 2889a, 2918, 2988.1	—	17.50
PS51	1990 (8)	35,000	KM#2875-2876, 2878, 2885-2886, 2889a, 2918, 2993.1	—	42.50
PS52	1991 (8)	27,000	KM#2875-2876, 2878, 2885-2886, 2889a, 2918, 2995.1	—	22.00
PS53	1992 (8)	25,000	KM#2875-2876, 2878, 2885-2886, 2889a, 2918	—	45.00
PS54	1993 (8)	28,000	KM#2875-2876, 2878, 2885-2886, 2889a, 2918, 2946.2	—	35.00
PS55	1994 (8)	25,000	KM#2875-2876, 2878, 2885-2886, 2889a, 2918, 3016	—	75.00
PS56	1995 (6)	27,000	KM#2878, 2885, 2886, 2889a, 2918, 3022	—	37.50
PS57	1996 (6)	25,000	KM#2878, 2885, 2886, 2889a, 2918, 3033	—	45.00
PS58	1997 (6)	25,000	KM#2878, 2885, 2886, 2889a, 2918, 3041	—	50.00
PS59	1998 (6)	25,000	KM#2878, 2885, 2886, 2889a, 2918, 3048	—	60.00
PS60	1999 (6)	25,000	KM#2878, 2885, 2886, 2889a, 2918, 3056	—	27.50
PS61	2000 (6)	—	KM#2878, 2885, 2886, 2889a, 2918, 3064	—	27.50

AZERBAIJAN

The Republic of Azerbaijan (formerly Azerbaijan S.S.R.) includes the Nakhichevan Autonomous Republic. Situated in the eastern area of Transcaucasia, it is bordered in the west by Armenia, in the north by Georgia and Dagestan, to the east by the Caspian Sea and to the south by Iran. It has an area of 33,430 sq. mi. (86,600 sq. km.) and a population of 7.8 million. Capital: Baku. The area is rich in mineral deposits of aluminum, copper, iron, lead, salt and zinc, with oil as its leading industry. Agriculture and livestock follow in importance.

Until the Russian Revolution of 1905, there was no political life in Azerbaijan. A Mussavat (Equality) party was formed in 1911 by Mohammed Emin Rasulzade, a former Social Democrat. After the Russian Revolution of March 1917, the party started a campaign for independence. Baku, however, the capital with its mixed population, constituted an alien enclave in the country. While a national Azerbaijani government was established at Gandzha (Elizavetpol), a Communist controlled council assumed power at Baku with Stepan Shaumian, an Armenian, at its head. The Gandzha government joined first, on Sept. 20, 1917, a Transcaucasian federal republic, but on May 28, 1918, proclaimed the independence of Azerbaijan. On June 4, 1918, at Batum, a peace treaty was signed with Turkey. Turko-Azerbaijani forces started an offensive against Baku, occupied since Aug. 17, 1918 by 1,400 British troops coming by sea from Anzali, Persia. On Sept. 14 the British evacuated Baku, returning to Anzali, and three days later the Azerbaijan government, headed by Fath Khoysky, established itself at Baku.

After the collapse of the Ottoman Empire, the British returned to Baku, at first ignoring the Azerbaijan government. A general election with universal suffrage for the Azerbaijan constituent assembly took place on Dec. 7, 1918 and out of 120 members there were 84 Mussavat supporters. On Jan. 15, 1920, the Allied powers recognized Azerbaijan de facto, but on April 27 of the same year the Red army invaded the country, and a Soviet republic of Azerbaijan was proclaimed the next day. Later it became a member of the Transcaucasian Federation joining the U.S.S.R. on Dec. 30, 1922, it became a self-constituent republic in 1936.

The Azerbaijan Communist party held its first congress at Baku in Feb. 1920. From 1921 to 1925 its first secretary was a Russian, S.M. Kirov, who directed a mass deportation to Siberia of about 120,000 Azerbaijani "nationalist deviationists," among them the country's first two premiers.

In 1990 it adopted a declaration of republican sovereignty and in Aug. 1991 declared itself formally independent. This action was approved by a vote of referendum in Jan. 1992. It announced its intention of joining the CIS in Dec. 1991, but a parliamentary resolution of Oct. 1992 declined to confirm its involvement. On Sept. 20, 1993, Azerbaijan became a member of the CIS. Communist President Mutaibov was relieved of his office in May 1992. On June 7, in the first democratic election in the country's history, a National Council replaced Mutaibov with Abulfez Elchibey. Surat Huseynov led a military coup against Elchibey and seized power on June 30, 1993. Huseynov became prime minister with former communist Geidar Aliyev, president.

Fighting commenced between Muslim forces of Azerbaijan and Christian forces of Armenia in 1992 and continued through early 1994. Each faction claimed the Nagorno-Karabakh, an Armenian ethnic enclave, in Azerbaijan. A cease-fire was declared in May 1994.

MONETARY SYSTEM
100 Qapik = 1 Manat

REPUBLIC
DECIMAL COINAGE

KM# 1 5 QAPIK
Brass **Obv:** Value **Rev:** Three symbols above date at center of sun

Date	Mintage	F	VF	XF	Unc	BU
1992	—	—	—	2.00	4.00	5.00

KM# 1a 5 QAPIK
0.8500 g., Aluminum, 17.1 mm. **Obv:** Value **Rev:** Three symbols above date at center of sun **Edge:** Plain

Date	Mintage	F	VF	XF	Unc	BU
1993	—	—	—	—	1.00	1.50

KM# 2 10 QAPIK
1.0500 g., Aluminum, 18.6 mm. **Obv:** Denomination **Rev:** Star with date **Edge:** Plain

Date	Mintage	F	VF	XF	Unc	BU
1992	—	—	—	1.00	2.00	2.50

KM# 3 20 QAPIK
Brass **Obv:** Moon and star at center **Rev:** Value above date within star **Edge:** Plain

Date	Mintage	F	VF	XF	Unc	BU
1992	—	—	—	1.00	2.00	2.50
1993	—	—	—	1.00	2.00	2.50

KM# 3a 20 QAPIK
1.1500 g., Aluminum, 20.1 mm. **Edge:** Plain **Note:** Varieties in spelling of Respublikas exist.

Date	Mintage	F	VF	XF	Unc	BU
1992	—	—	—	—	0.75	1.00
1993	—	—	—	—	0.75	1.00

Note: Two die varieties exist

KM# 4 50 QAPIK
Copper-Nickel **Obv:** Maiden tower ruins **Rev:** Value above date within ornate circle **Edge:** Plain

Date	Mintage	F	VF	XF	Unc	BU
1992	—	—	—	1.50	3.50	4.50
1994	—	—	—	1.50	3.50	4.50

KM# 4a 50 QAPIK
1.4500 g., Aluminum, 23 mm. **Edge:** Plain

Date	Mintage	F	VF	XF	Unc	BU
1992	—	—	—	—	1.25	1.50
1993	—	—	—	—	0.75	1.00

KM# 5 50 MANAT
28.2800 g., 0.9250 Silver 0.8410 oz. ASW **Subject:** 500th Anniversary Mehemmed Fuzuli **Obv:** Deer by man comforting fallen comrade within circle, date below circle **Rev:** Portrait of Fuzuli bust, looking left

Date	Mintage	F	VF	XF	Unc	BU
1996	—	—	—	—	45.00	50.00
1996 Proof	5,000	Value: 70.00				

KM# 38 50 MANAT
33.9200 g., 0.9250 Silver 1.0087 oz. ASW, 38.6 mm. **Subject:** 1300 Years of National Epic **Obv:** Musician riding horse within circle, date below circle **Rev:** Book title **Rev. Insc.:** KITABI / DÆDÆ / QORQUD / 1300 **Edge:** Reeded

Date	Mintage	F	VF	XF	Unc	BU
1999 Proof	1,000	Value: 70.00				

KM# 6 100 MANAT
7.9800 g., 0.9167 Gold 0.2352 oz. AGW **Subject:** 500th Anniversary Mehemmed Fuzuli **Obv:** Deer by man comforting fallen comrade **Rev:** Portrait of Fuzuli

Date	Mintage	F	VF	XF	Unc	BU
1996 Proof	500	Value: 325				

KM# 45 100 MANAT
17.2800 g., 0.9000 Gold 0.5000 oz. AGW **Subject:** 1300 Years of National Epic **Obv:** Musician riding horse right **Rev:** Book title **Rev. Insc.:** KITABI / DÆDÆ / QORQUD / 1300

Date	Mintage	F	VF	XF	Unc	BU
1999 Proof	150	Value: 750				

AZORES

The Azores, an archipelago of nine islands of volcanic origin, are located in the Atlantic Ocean 740 miles (1,190 km.) west of Cape de Roca, Portugal. They are the westernmost region of Europe under the administration of Portugal and have an area of 902 sq. mi. (2,305 sq. km.) and a population of 236,000. Principal city: Ponta Delgada. The natives are mainly of Portuguese descent and earn their livelihood by fishing, wine making, basket weaving and the growing of fruit, grains and sugar cane. Pineapples are the chief item of export. The climate is particularly temperate, making the islands a favorite winter resort.

The Azores were discovered about 1427 by the Portuguese navigator Diogo de Sevill. Portugal secured the islands in the 15th century and established the first settlement on Santa Maria about 1439. From 1580 to 1640 the Azores were subject to Spain.

The Azores' first provincial coinage was ordered by law of August 19, 1750. Copper coins were struck for circulation in both the Azores and Madeira Islands, keeping the same technical specifications but with different designs. In 1795 a second provincial coinage was introduced but the weight was reduced by 50 percent.

Angra on Terceira Island became the capital of the captaincy-general of the Azores in 1766 and it was here in 1826 that the constitutionalists set up a pro-Pedro government in opposition to King Miguel in Lisbon. The whole Portuguese fleet attacked Terceira and was repelled at Praia, after which Azoreans, Brazilians and British mercenaries defeated Miguel in Portugal. Maria de Gloria, Pedro's daughter, was proclaimed queen of Portugal on Terceira in 1828.

A U.S. naval base was established at Ponta Delgada in 1917. After World War II, the islands acquired a renewed importance as a refueling stop for transatlantic air transport. The United States maintains defense bases in the Azores as part of the collective security program of NATO.

In 1976 the archipelago became the Autonomous Region of Azores.

Note: Portuguese 50 Centavos and 1 Escudo pieces dated 1935 were issued for circulation in Azores. These are found under the appropriate listing in Portugal.

RULER
Portuguese

MONETARY SYSTEM
1000 Reis (Insulanos) = 1 Milreis

PORTUGUESE ADMINISTRATION
PROVINCIAL COINAGE

KM# 16 5 REIS
Copper **Subject:** Carlos I **Obv:** Crowned arms **Rev:** Value within wreath, date below

Date	Mintage	F	VF	XF	Unc	BU
1901	800,000	1.75	3.50	9.00	25.00	—

KM# 17   10 REIS
Copper **Subject:** Carlos I **Obv:** Crowned arms **Rev:** Value within wreath, date below

Date	Mintage	F	VF	XF	Unc	BU
1901	600,000	2.00	4.00	10.00	28.00	

REPUBLIC

DECIMAL COINAGE

KM# 43   25 ESCUDOS
11.0500 g., Copper-Nickel, 28.5 mm. **Subject:** Regional Autonomy **Obv:** Shields above denomination, stars below **Rev:** Supported arms **Edge:** Reeded

Date	Mintage	F	VF	XF	Unc	BU
1980	770,000	—	—	2.50	5.00	7.50

KM# 43a   25 ESCUDOS
11.0000 g., 0.9250 Silver 0.3271 oz. ASW **Subject:** Regional Autonomy **Obv:** Shields above denomination, stars below **Rev:** Supported arms

Date	Mintage	F	VF	XF	Unc	BU
1980 Proof	12,000	Value: 22.00				

KM# 44   100 ESCUDOS
Copper-Nickel **Subject:** Regional Autonomy **Obv:** Shields above denomination, stars below **Rev:** Supported arms

Date	Mintage	F	VF	XF	Unc	BU
1980	270,000	—	—	4.50	10.00	12.50

KM# 44a   100 ESCUDOS
16.5000 g., 0.9250 Silver 0.4907 oz. ASW **Subject:** Regional Autonomy **Obv:** Shields above denomination, stars below **Rev:** Supported arms

Date	Mintage	F	VF	XF	Unc	BU
1980 Proof	12,000	Value: 42.50				

KM# 45   100 ESCUDOS
16.5000 g., Copper-Nickel **Subject:** 10th Anniversary of Regional Autonomy **Obv:** Supported arms, value below **Rev:** Hydrangea plant, date below

Date	Mintage	F	VF	XF	Unc	BU
1986	750,000	—	—	—	6.50	8.50

KM# 45a   100 ESCUDOS
16.5000 g., 0.9250 Silver 0.4907 oz. ASW **Subject:** 10th Anniversary of Regional Autonomy **Rev:** Flower

Date	Mintage	F	VF	XF	Unc	BU
1986	20,000	—	—	—	25.00	28.00
1986 Proof	10,000	Value: 35.00				

KM# 46   100 ESCUDOS
Copper-Nickel **Subject:** 100th Anniversary - Death of Poet Antero de Quental **Obv:** Offered hand with radiant sun behind, shield of arms below left, value at right **Rev:** Bust of Antero de Quental, facing, two dates at left

Date	Mintage	F	VF	XF	Unc	BU
1991	750,000	—	—	—	5.00	7.50

KM# 46a   100 ESCUDOS
18.5000 g., 0.9250 Silver 0.5502 oz. ASW, 36 mm. **Subject:** 100th Anniversary - Death of Poet Antero de Quental **Obv:** Offered hand with radiant sun behind, shield of arms below left **Rev:** Bust of Antero de Quental facing

Date	Mintage	F	VF	XF	Unc	BU
1991	20,000	—	—	—	30.00	32.50
1991 Proof	30,000	Value: 40.00				

KM# 47   100 ESCUDOS
Copper-Nickel **Subject:** Centennial of Azorean Autonomy **Obv:** Sun with star at center, over water, shield of arms below, value at bottom **Rev:** Goshawk with wings spread below dates, 1895 above 1995

Date	Mintage	F	VF	XF	Unc	BU
ND(1995)	500,000	—	—	—	7.50	10.00

KM# 47a   100 ESCUDOS
18.5000 g., 0.9250 Silver 0.5502 oz. ASW **Subject:** Centennial of Azorean Autonomy **Rev:** Goshawk with wings spread below dates, 1895 over 1995

Date	Mintage	F	VF	XF	Unc	BU
ND(1995)	5,000	—	—	—	35.00	40.00
ND(1995) Proof	10,000	Value: 50.00				

PATTERNS
Including off metal strikes

KM#	Date	Mintage	Identification	Mkt Val
Pn4	ND	—	5 Reis. Copper. Crowned arms on ornate shield. Denomination within wreath. Similar to KM#16 but without obverse legend.	
Pn5	1901	—	5 Reis. Aluminum.	725
Pn6	1901	—	10 Reis. Aluminum.	725

PROVAS

KM#	Date	Mintage	Identification	Mkt Val
Pr1	1980	—	25 Escudos. Copper-Nickel. Incuse PROVA.	150
Pr2	1980	—	100 Escudos. Copper-Nickel. Shields above value, stars below. Supported arms. Incuse PROVA.	175
Pr3	1986	—	100 Escudos. Copper-Nickel. Incuse PROVA.	175

PROOF SETS

KM#	Date	Mintage	Identification	Issue Price	Mkt Val
PS1	1980 (2)	12,000	KM43a-44a	40.00	70.00

BAHAMAS

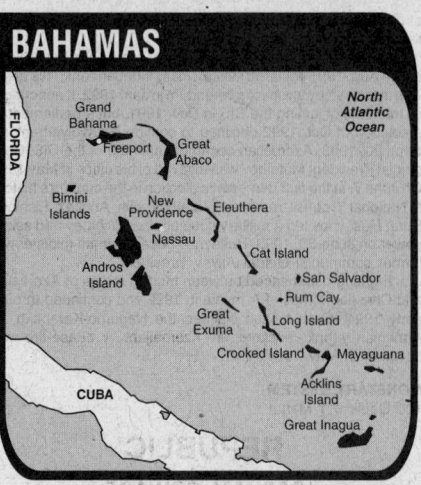

The Commonwealth of the Bahamas is an archipelago of about 3,000 islands, cays and rocks located in the Atlantic Ocean east of Florida and north of Cuba. The total land area of the 800 mile (1,287 km.) long chain of islands is 5,382 sq. mi. (13,935 sq. km.). They have a population of 302,000. Capital: Nassau. The Bahamas import most of their food and manufactured products and export cement, refined oil, pulpwood and lobsters. Tourism is the principal industry.

The Bahamas were discovered by Columbus October, 1492, upon his sighting of the island of San Salvador, but Spain made no attempt to settle them. British influence began in 1626 when Charles I granted them to the lord proprietors of Carolina, with settlements in 1629 at New Providence by colonists from the northern territory. Although the Bahamas were temporarily under Spanish control in 1641 and 1703, they continued under British proprietors until 1717, when, as the result of political and economic mismanagement, the civil and military governments were surrendered to the King and the islands designated a British Crown Colony. Full international agreement on British possession of the islands resulted from the Treaty of Versailles in 1783. The Bahamas obtained complete internal self-government under the constitution of Jan. 7, 1964. Full independence was achieved on July 10, 1973. The Bahamas is a member of the Commonwealth of Nations. Elizabeth II is Head of State as Queen of The Bahamas.

The coinage of Great Britain was legal tender in the Bahamas from 1825 to the issuing of a definitive coinage in 1966.

RULER
British

MINT MARKS
Through 1969 all decimal coinage of the Bahamas was executed at the Royal Mint in England. Since that time issues have been struck at both the Royal Mint and at the Franklin Mint (FM) in the U.S.A. While the mint mark of the latter appears on coins dated 1971 and subsequently, it is missing from the 1970 issues.
JP – John Pinches, London
None - Royal Mint
(t) - Tower of London
FM - Franklin Mint, U.S.A.
*NOTE: From 1975-1985 the Franklin Mint produced coinage in up to 3 different qualities. Qualities of issue are designated in ( ) after each date and are defined as follows:
(M) MATTE - Normal circulation strike or a dull finish produced by sandblasting special uncirculated (polish finish) or proof quality dies.
(U) SPECIAL UNCIRCULATED - Polished or proof-like in appearance without any frosted features.
(P) PROOF - The highest quality obtainable having mirror-like fields and frosted features.

MONETARY SYSTEM
12 Pence = 1 Shilling

COMMONWEALTH

DECIMAL COINAGE
100 Cents = 1 Dollar

KM# 2   CENT
4.1600 g., Nickel-Brass, 23 mm. **Ruler:** Elizabeth II **Obv:** Queen Elizabeth II right **Rev:** Starfish above date, value at top **Edge:** Smooth

Date	Mintage	F	VF	XF	Unc	BU
1966	7,312,000	—	—	0.10	0.50	2.00
1968	800,000	—	—	0.25	0.75	2.25
1969	4,036,000	—	—	0.10	0.50	2.00
1969 Proof	10,000	Value: 1.50				

KM# 15 CENT

Bronze, 19 mm. **Ruler:** Elizabeth II **Obv:** Bust of Queen Elizabeth II right with tiara **Rev:** Starfish above date, value at top **Edge:** Smooth **Note:** Proof specimens of this date are struck in "special brass" which looks like a pale bronze.

Date	Mintage	F	VF	XF	Unc	BU
1970	125,000	—	0.10	0.25	0.50	1.50
1970 Proof	23,000	Value: 1.00				

KM# 16 CENT

3.1300 g., Brass, 19 mm. **Ruler:** Elizabeth II **Obv:** Bust of Queen Elizabeth II right with tiara **Rev:** Starfish above date, value at top **Edge:** Smooth

Date	Mintage	F	VF	XF	Unc	BU
1971FM	1,007,000	—	—	0.10	0.50	2.00
1971FM (P)	31,000	Value: 1.50				
1972FM	1,037,000	—	—	0.10	0.50	2.00
1972FM (P)	35,000	Value: 1.50				
1973	7,000,000	—	—	0.20	0.50	2.00
1973FM	1,040,000	—	—	0.10	0.50	2.00
1973FM (P)	35,000	Value: 1.50				

KM# 59 CENT

3.1600 g., Brass, 19 mm. **Ruler:** Elizabeth II **Obv:** National arms above date **Rev:** Starfish, value at top **Edge:** Smooth

Date	Mintage	F	VF	XF	Unc	BU
1974	11,000	—	—	0.20	0.50	1.50
1974FM	71,000	—	—	0.10	0.25	1.00
1974FM (P)	94,000	Value: 1.50				
1975FM (M)	60,000	—	—	0.10	0.25	1.00
1975FM (U)	3,845	—	—	0.10	0.50	1.50
1975FM (P)	29,000	Value: 1.50				
1976FM (M)	60,000	—	—	0.10	0.25	1.00
1976FM (U)	1,453	—	—	0.10	0.50	1.50
1976FM (P)	23,000	Value: 1.50				
1977	3,000,000	—	—	0.10	0.25	1.00
1977FM (M)	60,000	—	—	0.10	0.25	1.00
1977FM (U)	713	—	—	0.50	1.50	4.50
1977FM (P)	11,000	Value: 1.50				
1978FM (M)	60,000	—	—	0.10	0.25	1.00
1978FM (U)	767	—	—	0.50	1.50	4.50
1978FM (P)	6,931	Value: 1.50				
1979	—	—	—	0.10	0.25	1.00
1979FM (P)	2,053	Value: 2.00				
1980	4,000,000	—	—	0.10	0.25	1.00
1980FM (P)	2,084	Value: 2.00				
1981	5,000,000	—	—	0.10	0.25	1.00
1981FM (M)	—	—	—	0.10	0.25	1.00
1981FM (P)	1,980	Value: 2.00				
1982	5,000,000	—	—	0.10	0.25	1.00
1982FM (M)	—	—	—	0.10	0.25	1.00
1982FM (P)	1,217	Value: 2.00				
1983	8,000,000	—	—	0.10	0.25	1.00
1983FM (P)	1,020	Value: 2.00				
1984	—	—	—	0.10	0.25	1.00
1984FM (P)	7,500	Value: 1.50				
1985	12,000,000	—	—	0.10	0.25	1.00
1985FM (P)	7,500	Value: 1.50				

KM# 59a CENT

2.5800 g., Copper Plated Zinc, 19.02 mm. **Ruler:** Elizabeth II **Obv:** National arms above date **Obv. Leg.:** COMMONWEALTH OF THE BAHAMAS **Rev:** Starfish, value at top **Edge:** Plain

Date	Mintage	F	VF	XF	Unc	BU
1985	—	—	—	0.10	0.25	0.75
1987	12,000,000	—	—	0.10	0.25	0.75
1989	12,000,000	—	—	0.10	0.25	0.75
1989 Proof	—	Value: 2.00				
1990	—	—	—	0.10	0.25	0.75
1991	—	—	—	0.10	0.25	0.75

Date	Mintage	F	VF	XF	Unc	BU
1992	—	—	—	0.10	0.25	0.75
1995	—	—	—	0.10	0.25	0.75
1997	—	—	—	0.10	0.25	0.75
1998	—	—	—	0.10	0.25	0.75
1999	—	—	—	0.10	0.25	0.75

KM# 3 5 CENTS

3.8700 g., Copper-Nickel, 21 mm. **Ruler:** Elizabeth II **Obv:** Bust of Queen Elizabeth II right with tiara **Rev:** Pineapple above garland divides date and value **Edge:** Smooth **Note:** The obverse of this coin also comes muled with the reverse of a New Zealand 2-cent piece, KM#32. The undated 1967 error is listed as New Zealand KM#33.

Date	Mintage	F	VF	XF	Unc	BU
1966	2,571,000	—	—	0.10	0.25	0.75
1968	600,000	—	—	0.30	1.25	3.00
1969	2,026,000	—	—	0.10	0.25	0.75
1969 Proof	75,000	Value: 1.00				
1970	26,000	—	—	0.30	0.60	1.80
1970 Proof	23,000	Value: 1.50				

KM# 17 5 CENTS

Copper-Nickel, 21 mm. **Ruler:** Elizabeth II **Obv:** Bust of Queen Elizabeth II right with tiara **Rev:** Pineapple above garland divides date and value **Edge:** Smooth

Date	Mintage	F	VF	XF	Unc	BU
1971FM	13,000	—	—	0.15	0.40	1.20
1971FM (P)	31,000	Value: 1.00				
1972FM	11,000	—	—	0.15	0.40	1.20
1972FM (P)	35,000	Value: 1.00				
1973FM	21,000	—	—	0.15	0.40	1.20
1973FM (P)	35,000	Value: 1.00				

KM# 38 5 CENTS

3.9000 g., Copper-Nickel, 21 mm. **Ruler:** Elizabeth II **Obv. Leg.:** THE COMMONWEALTH OF THE BAHAMAS **Edge:** Smooth

Date	Mintage	F	VF	XF	Unc	BU
1973	1,000,000	—	—	—	0.65	1.75

KM# 60 5 CENTS

3.9400 g., Copper-Nickel, 21 mm. **Ruler:** Elizabeth II **Obv:** National arms above date **Obv. Leg.:** COMMONWEALTH OF THE BAHAMAS **Rev:** Pineapple above garland divides value at top **Edge:** Smooth

Date	Mintage	F	VF	XF	Unc	BU
1974FM	23,000	—	—	0.10	0.50	1.50
1974FM (P)	94,000	Value: 1.00				
1975	—	—	—	0.10	0.30	0.90
1975FM (M)	12,000	—	—	0.10	0.50	1.50
1975FM (U)	3,845	—	—	0.15	0.75	2.25
1975FM (P)	29,000	Value: 1.00				
1976FM (M)	12,000	—	—	0.10	0.25	0.75
1976FM (U)	1,453	—	—	0.50	1.00	3.00
1976FM (P)	23,000	Value: 1.00				
1977FM (M)	12,000	—	—	0.10	0.35	1.00
1977FM (U)	713	—	—	0.50	1.50	4.50
1977FM (P)	11,000	Value: 1.00				
1978FM (M)	12,000	—	—	0.10	0.35	1.00
1978FM (U)	767	—	—	0.50	1.50	4.50
1978FM (P)	6,931	Value: 1.50				
1979FM (P)	2,053	Value: 1.50				
1980FM (P)	2,084	Value: 1.50				
1981	—	—	—	0.10	0.25	0.75
1981FM (P)	1,980	Value: 1.50				
1982FM (P)	1,217	Value: 1.50				
1983	2,000,000	—	—	0.10	0.25	0.75
1983FM (P)	1,020	Value: 1.50				
1984	—	—	—	0.10	0.25	0.75
1984FM (P)	1,036	Value: 1.50				
1985FM (P)	7,500	Value: 1.50				
1987	4,000,000	—	—	0.10	0.25	0.75
1989	—	—	—	0.10	0.25	0.75
1989 (P)	—	Value: 1.50				
1991	—	—	—	0.10	0.25	0.75
1992	—	—	—	0.10	0.25	0.75
1998	—	—	—	0.10	0.25	0.75

Date	Mintage	F	VF	XF	Unc	BU
1999	—	—	—	0.10	0.25	0.75
2000	—	—	—	0.10	0.25	0.75

KM# 4 10 CENTS

6.5500 g., Copper-Nickel, 23.5 mm. **Ruler:** Elizabeth II **Obv:** Bust of Queen Elizabeth II right with tiara, within beaded circle **Rev:** Bone Fish, value below, date above **Edge:** Smooth

Date	Mintage	F	VF	XF	Unc	BU
1966	2,198,000	—	—	0.10	0.50	1.50
1968	550,000	—	—	2.00	4.00	8.00
1969	2,026,000	—	—	0.10	0.50	1.50
1969 Proof	10,000	Value: 1.00				
1970	27,000	—	—	0.15	0.60	1.80
1970 Proof	23,000	Value: 1.00				

KM# 18 10 CENTS

Copper-Nickel, 23.5 mm. **Ruler:** Elizabeth II **Obv:** Bust of Queen Elizabeth II right with tiara, within beaded circle **Rev:** Bone Fish, value below, date above **Edge:** Smooth

Date	Mintage	F	VF	XF	Unc	BU
1971FM	13,000	—	—	0.15	0.50	1.50
1971FM (P)	31,000	Value: 1.00				
1972FM	11,000	—	—	0.15	0.50	1.50
1972FM (P)	35,000	Value: 1.00				
1973FM	15,000	—	—	0.15	0.50	1.50
1973FM (P)	35,000	Value: 1.00				

KM# 39 10 CENTS

Copper-Nickel, 23.5 mm. **Ruler:** Elizabeth II **Obv. Leg.:** THE COMMONWEALTH OF THE BAHAMAS **Edge:** Smooth

Date	Mintage	F	VF	XF	Unc	BU
1973	1,000,000	—	—	0.15	1.00	2.00

KM# 61 10 CENTS

5.5400 g., Copper-Nickel, 23.5 mm. **Ruler:** Elizabeth II **Obv:** National arms, date below, within beaded circle **Rev:** Arnold Machin **Edge:** Smooth

Date	Mintage	F	VF	XF	Unc	BU
1974FM	17,000	—	—	0.10	0.50	1.50
1974FM (P)	94,000	Value: 1.50				
1975	3,000,000	—	—	0.10	0.50	1.50
1975FM (M)	6,000	—	—	0.15	0.50	1.50
1975FM (U)	3,845	—	—	0.15	0.50	1.50
1975FM (P)	29,000	Value: 1.50				
1976FM (M)	6,000	—	—	0.15	0.50	1.50
1976FM (U)	1,453	—	—	0.25	1.00	3.00
1976FM (P)	23,000	Value: 1.50				
1977FM (M)	6,000	—	—	0.15	0.50	1.50
1977FM (U)	713	—	—	0.50	1.50	3.00
1977FM (P)	11,000	Value: 1.50				
1978FM (M)	6,000	—	—	0.15	0.50	1.50
1978FM (U)	767	—	—	0.50	1.50	3.00
1978FM (P)	6,931	Value: 2.00				
1979FM (P)	2,053	Value: 2.50				
1980	2,500,000	—	—	0.10	0.50	1.50
1980FM (P)	2,084	Value: 2.50				
1981FM (P)	1,980	Value: 2.50				
1982	2,000,000	—	—	0.10	0.50	1.50
1982FM (P)	1,217	Value: 2.50				
1983FM (P)	1,020	Value: 2.50				
1984FM (P)	1,036	Value: 2.50				
1985	2,000,000	—	—	0.10	0.50	1.50
1985FM (M)	—	—	—	0.15	0.50	1.50
1985FM (P)	7,500	Value: 2.00				
1987	3,000,000	—	—	0.15	0.50	1.50
1989	—	—	—	0.15	0.50	1.50
1989	—	Value: 2.00				
1991	—	—	—	0.15	0.50	1.50
1992	—	—	—	0.15	0.50	1.50
1998	—	—	—	0.15	0.50	1.50
2000	—	—	—	0.15	0.50	1.00

KM# 5 15 CENTS
Copper-Nickel, 25 mm. **Ruler:** Elizabeth II **Obv:** Bust of Queen Elizabeth II right with tiara **Rev:** Hibiscus, date divides value at bottom **Edge:** Smooth

Date	Mintage	F	VF	XF	Unc	BU
1966	930,000	—		1.00	2.00	3.00
1969	1,026,000	—		0.20	0.75	2.25
1969 Proof	10,000	Value: 2.00				
1970	28,000	—		0.25	0.75	2.25
1970 Proof	23,000	Value: 1.50				

KM# 19 15 CENTS
Copper-Nickel, 25 mm. **Ruler:** Elizabeth II **Obv:** Bust of Queen Elizabeth II right with tiara **Rev:** Hibiscus, date divides value below **Edge:** Smooth

Date	Mintage	F	VF	XF	Unc	BU
1971FM	13,000	—		0.20	0.50	1.50
1971FM Proof	31,000	Value: 1.50				
1972FM	11,000	—		0.20	0.50	1.50
1972FM Proof	35,000	Value: 1.50				
1973FM	14,000	—		0.20	0.50	1.50
1973FM Proof	35,000	Value: 1.50				

KM# 62 15 CENTS
Copper-Nickel, 25 mm. **Ruler:** Elizabeth II **Obv:** National arms above date **Rev:** Hibiscus, value divided at bottom **Edge:** Smooth

Date	Mintage	F	VF	XF	Unc	BU
1974FM	15,000	—		0.20	0.50	1.50
1974FM (P)	94,000	Value: 1.50				
1975FM (M)	3,500	—	—	0.25	1.00	3.00
1975FM (U)	3,845	—	—	0.25	1.00	3.00
1975FM (P)	29,000	Value: 1.50				
1976FM (M)	3,500	—	—	0.25	1.00	3.00
1976FM (U)	1,453	—	—	0.30	1.50	4.50
1976FM (P)	23,000	Value: 1.50				
1977FM (M)	3,500	—	—	0.25	1.00	3.00
1977FM (U)	713	—	—	0.50	2.00	6.00
1977FM (P)	11,000	Value: 1.00				
1978FM (M)	3,500	—	—	0.25	1.00	3.00
1978FM (U)	767	—	—	0.50	2.00	6.00
1978FM (P)	6,931	Value: 1.50				
1979FM (P)	2,053	Value: 2.00				
1980FM (P)	2,084	Value: 2.00				
1981FM (P)	1,980	Value: 2.00				
1982FM (P)	1,217	Value: 2.50				
1983FM (P)	1,020	Value: 3.00				
1984FM (P)	1,036	Value: 3.00				
1985FM (P)	7,500	Value: 2.25				
1989	—	—		0.20	0.50	1.50
1989 (P)	—	Value: 3.00				
1991	—	—		0.20	0.50	1.50
1992	—	—		0.20	0.50	1.50

KM# 6 25 CENTS
Nickel, 24 mm. **Ruler:** Elizabeth II **Obv:** Bust of Queen Elizabeth II right with tiara **Rev:** Bahaminian sloop, value, date **Edge:** Reeded

Date	Mintage	F	VF	XF	Unc	BU
1966	3,685,000	—	—	0.30	0.50	1.50
1969	1,026,000	—	—	0.30	0.50	1.50
1969	10,000	Value: 1.50				
1970	26,000	—	—	0.35	0.75	2.25

Date	Mintage	F	VF	XF	Unc	BU
1970FM (P)	23,000	Value: 2.00				
1970FM (M)	—	—				

KM# 20 25 CENTS
Nickel, 24 mm. **Ruler:** Elizabeth II **Obv:** Bust of Queen Elizabeth II right with tiara **Rev:** Bahaminian Sloop, value, date **Edge:** Reeded

Date	Mintage	F	VF	XF	Unc	BU
1971FM	13,000	—	—	0.30	0.50	1.50
1971FM (P)	31,000	Value: 1.50				
1972FM	11,000	—	—	0.30	0.50	1.50
1972FM (M)	—	—	—	0.30	0.50	1.50
1972FM (P)	35,000	Value: 1.50				
1973FM	12,000	—	—	0.30	0.50	1.50
1973FM (P)	35,000	Value: 1.50				

KM# 63.1 25 CENTS
6.9000 g., Nickel, 24 mm. **Ruler:** Elizabeth II **Obv:** National arms above date, beaded rim **Rev:** Bahaminian Sloop, value above **Edge:** Reeded

Date	Mintage	F	VF	XF	Unc	BU
1974FM	13,000	—	—	0.30	0.50	1.50
1974FM (P)	94,000	Value: 1.50				
1975FM (M)	2,400	—	—	0.35	1.00	3.00
1975FM (U)	3,845	—	—	0.35	1.00	3.00
1975FM (P)	29,000	Value: 1.50				
1976FM (M)	2,400	—	—	0.35	1.00	3.00
1976FM (U)	1,453	—	—	0.35	1.25	3.75
1976FM (P)	23,000	Value: 1.50				
1977	—	—		0.30	0.50	1.50
1977FM (M)	2,400	—	—	0.35	1.00	3.00
1977FM (U)	713	—	—	0.50	3.00	9.00
1977FM (P)	11,000	Value: 1.50				
1978FM	2,400	—	—	0.35	1.00	3.00
1978FM (U)	767	—	—	0.50	3.00	9.00
1978FM (P)	6,931	Value: 2.00				
1979	—	—		0.30	0.50	1.50
1979FM (P)	2,053	Value: 3.00				
1980FM (P)	2,084	Value: 3.00				
1981	1,600,000	—	—	0.30	0.50	1.50
1981FM (P)	1,980	Value: 3.00				
1982FM (P)	1,217	Value: 4.00				
1983FM (P)	1,020	Value: 4.00				
1984FM (P)	1,036	Value: 4.00				
1985	2,000,000	—	—	0.30	0.50	1.50
1985FM (P)	7,500	Value: 2.00				
1987	—	—		0.30	0.50	1.50
1989	—	—		0.30	0.50	1.50
1989 (P)	—	Value: 3.00				

KM# 63.2 25 CENTS
5.7000 g., Copper-Nickel, 24 mm. **Ruler:** Elizabeth II **Edge:** Reeded

Date	Mintage	F	VF	XF	Unc	BU
1991	—	—	—	0.30	0.50	1.50
1992	—	—	—	0.30	0.50	1.50
1998	—	—	—	0.30	0.50	1.50
2000	—	—	—	0.30	0.50	1.50

KM# 7 50 CENTS
10.3700 g., 0.8000 Silver 0.2667 oz. ASW, 29 mm. **Ruler:** Elizabeth II **Obv:** Bust of Queen Elizabeth II right with tiara **Rev:** Blue Marlin, value and date at right

Date	Mintage	F	VF	XF	Unc	BU
1966	701,000	—	—	BV	5.25	6.50
1969	26,000	—	—	BV	5.25	6.50
1969 Proof	10,000	Value: 7.00				
1970	25,000	—	—	BV	5.25	6.50
1970 Proof	23,000	Value: 7.00				

KM# 21 50 CENTS
10.3700 g., 0.8000 Silver 0.2667 oz. ASW, 29 mm. **Ruler:** Elizabeth II **Obv:** Bust of Queen Elizabeth II right with tiara **Rev:** Blue Marlin, value and date at right

Date	Mintage	F	VF	XF	Unc	BU
1971FM	14,000	—	—	BV	5.25	6.50
1971FM (P)	31,000	Value: 7.00				
1972FM	12,000	—	—	BV	5.25	6.50
1972FM (P)	35,000	Value: 7.00				
1973FM	11,000	—	—	BV	5.25	6.50
1973FM (P)	35,000	Value: 7.00				

KM# 64 50 CENTS
Copper-Nickel, 29 mm. **Ruler:** Elizabeth II **Obv:** National arms, date below **Rev:** Blue Marlin, value at right

Date	Mintage	F	VF	XF	Unc	BU
1974FM	12,000	—	—	0.60	2.00	4.00
1975FM (M)	1,200	—	—	1.00	6.00	12.00
1975FM (U)	3,828	—	—	0.65	4.00	8.00
1976FM (M)	1,200	—	—	0.75	5.00	10.00
1976FM (U)	1,453	—	—	0.65	4.00	8.00
1977FM (M)	1,200	—	—	0.75	5.00	10.00
1977FM (U)	713	—	—	1.25	10.00	15.00
1978FM (M)	1,200	—	—	1.00	8.00	12.00
1978FM (U)	767	—	—	1.25	10.00	15.00
1981FM (P)	1,980	Value: 6.00				
1982FM (P)	1,217	Value: 7.00				
1983FM (P)	1,020	Value: 7.00				
1984FM (P)	1,036	Value: 7.00				
1985FM (P)	7,500	Value: 5.00				
1989	—	—		0.75	2.25	3.00
1989 Proof	—	Value: 5.00				
1991	—	—		0.75	2.25	3.00
1992	—	—		0.75	2.25	3.00

KM# 64a 50 CENTS
10.3700 g., 0.8000 Silver 0.2667 oz. ASW, 29 mm. **Ruler:** Elizabeth II

Date	Mintage	F	VF	XF	Unc	BU
1974FM (P)	94,000	Value: 8.00				
1975FM (P)	29,000	Value: 8.00				
1976FM (P)	23,000	Value: 8.00				
1977FM (P)	11,000	Value: 8.00				
1978FM (P)	6,931	Value: 8.00				
1979FM (P)	2,053	Value: 15.00				
1980FM (P)	2,084	Value: 15.00				

KM# 8 DOLLAR
18.1400 g., 0.8000 Silver 0.4666 oz. ASW, 34 mm. **Ruler:** Elizabeth II **Obv:** Bust of Queen Elizabeth II right with tiara **Rev:** Conch shell above garland, within 3/4 beaded circle, value and date above circle

Date	Mintage	F	VF	XF	Unc	BU
1966	406,000	—	—	BV	9.50	11.00
1969	26,000	—	—	BV	7.50	11.00
1969 Proof	10,000	Value: 10.00				
1970	27,000	—	—	BV	9.50	11.00
1970 Proof	23,000	Value: 10.00				

KM# 22 DOLLAR
18.1400 g., 0.8000 Silver 0.4666 oz. ASW, 34 mm.
Ruler: Elizabeth II **Obv:** Bust of Queen Elizabeth II right with tiara
Rev: Conch shell above garland within 3/4 beaded circle, value and date above

Date	Mintage	F	VF	XF	Unc	BU
1971FM	15,000	—	—	BV	9.50	11.00
1971FM (P)	31,000	Value: 10.00				
1972FM	18,000	—	—	BV	9.50	11.00
1972FM (P)	35,000	Value: 10.00				
1973FM	10,000	—	—	BV	9.50	11.00
1973FM (P)	35,000	Value: 10.00				

KM# 65 DOLLAR
Copper-Nickel, 34 mm. **Ruler:** Elizabeth II **Obv:** National arms above daate **Rev:** Conch shell above garland within 3/4 beaded circle, value at top

Date	Mintage	F	VF	XF	Unc	BU
1974FM	12,000	—	—	1.25	4.00	6.00
1975FM (M)	600	—	—	7.50	25.00	—
1975FM (U)	3,845	—	—	1.50	9.00	12.00
1976FM (M)	600	—	—	7.50	25.00	—
1976FM (U)	1,453	—	—	1.75	10.00	13.50
1977FM (M)	600	—	—	7.50	25.00	—
1977FM (U)	713	—	—	5.00	25.00	—
1978FM (U)	1,367	—	—	2.00	10.00	13.50

KM# 65a DOLLAR
18.1400 g., 0.8000 Silver 0.4666 oz. ASW, 34 mm. **Ruler:**
Elizabeth II

Date	Mintage	F	VF	XF	Unc	BU
1974FM (P)	94,000	Value: 9.50				
1975FM (P)	29,000	Value: 9.50				
1976FM (P)	23,000	Value: 10.00				
1977FM (P)	11,000	Value: 10.00				
1978FM (P)	6,931	Value: 12.00				
1979FM (P)	2,053	Value: 17.00				
1980FM (P)	2,084	Value: 17.00				

KM# 65b DOLLAR
Copper-Nickel, 32 mm. **Ruler:** Elizabeth II

Date	Mintage	F	VF	XF	Unc	BU
1981FM (P)	1,980	Value: 17.00				
1989	—	—	—	1.50	4.00	6.00
1989 (P)	Est. 2,000	Value: 17.00				
1991	—	—	—	1.50	4.00	6.00
1992	—	—	—	1.50	4.00	6.00

KM# 89 DOLLAR
Copper-Nickel **Ruler:** Elizabeth II **Obv:** National arms, date below **Rev:** Poinciana flower, value above

Date	Mintage	F	VF	XF	Unc	BU
1982FM (P)	1,217	Value: 20.00				

KM# 93 DOLLAR
Copper-Nickel **Ruler:** Elizabeth II **Subject:** 10th Anniversary of Independence **Rev:** Allamanda flower, value above

Date	Mintage	F	VF	XF	Unc	BU
1983FM (P)	1,020	Value: 20.00				

KM# 104 DOLLAR
Copper-Nickel **Ruler:** Elizabeth II **Rev:** Bougainvillea flower, value above

Date	Mintage	F	VF	XF	Unc	BU
1984FM (P)	1,036	Value: 20.00				
1985FM (P)	7,500	Value: 10.00				

KM# 154 DOLLAR
Copper-Nickel **Ruler:** Elizabeth II **Note:** Golf - Hole in One. Similar to 5 Dollars, KM#155.

Date	Mintage	F	VF	XF	Unc	BU
1994	20,000	—	—	—	15.00	

KM# 186 DOLLAR
1.2442 g., 0.9999 Gold 0.0400 oz. AGW **Ruler:** Elizabeth II **Rev:** Two flamingos **Note:** Similar to 5 Dollars, KM#188.

Date	Mintage	F	VF	XF	Unc	BU
1995 Proof	—	Value: 50.00				

KM# 176 DOLLAR
31.1800 g., 0.9990 Silver 1.0014 oz. ASW **Ruler:** Elizabeth II **Subject:** Third Millennium - Year 2000 **Obv:** Crowned bust of Queen Elizabeth II right, date below **Rev:** Artistic map, value below

Date	Mintage	F	VF	XF	Unc	BU
1996 Proof	50,000	Value: 35.00				

KM# 214 DOLLAR
Copper-Nickel **Ruler:** Elizabeth II **Subject:** 2000 Years of Christianity **Obv:** Crowned bust right

Date	Mintage	F	VF	XF	Unc	BU
2000	—	—	—	—	9.00	12.00

KM# 9 2 DOLLARS
29.8000 g., 0.9250 Silver 0.8862 oz. ASW, 40 mm.
Ruler: Elizabeth II **Obv:** Bust of Queen Elizabeth II right with tiara
Rev: National bird - two flamingos, value and date at top

Date	Mintage	F	VF	XF	Unc	BU
1966	104,000	—	—	BV	17.50	20.00
1969	26,000	—	—	BV	17.50	20.00
1969 Proof	10,000	Value: 18.50				
1970	32,000	—	—	BV	17.50	20.00
1970 Proof	23,000	Value: 18.50				

KM# 23 2 DOLLARS
29.8000 g., 0.9250 Silver 0.8862 oz. ASW, 40 mm. **Ruler:** Elizabeth II **Obv:** Bust of Queen Elizabeth II right with tiara **Rev:** National bird-two flamingos, value and date at top

Date	Mintage	F	VF	XF	Unc	BU
1971FM	88,000	—	—	BV	17.50	20.00
1971FM (P)	60,000	Value: 18.50				
1972FM	65,000	—	—	BV	17.50	20.00
1972FM (P)	59,000	Value: 18.50				
1973FM	43,000	—	—	BV	17.50	20.00
1973FM (P)	50,000	Value: 18.50				

KM# 66 2 DOLLARS
Copper-Nickel, 40 mm. **Ruler:** Elizabeth II **Obv:** National arms, date below **Rev:** National bird-two flamingos, value above
Edge: Reeded

Date	Mintage	F	VF	XF	Unc	BU
1974FM	37,000	—	—	2.25	6.00	8.00
1975FM (M)	300	—	—	9.00	25.00	—

Date	Mintage	F	VF	XF	Unc	BU
1975FM (U)	8,810	—	—	2.25	7.00	9.00
1976FM (M)	300	—	—	9.00	25.00	—
1976FM (U)	4,381	—	—	2.50	10.00	12.00
1977FM (M)	300	—	—	9.00	25.00	—
1977FM (U)	946	—	—	3.00	20.00	—
1978FM (U)	1,067	—	—	3.00	15.00	—
1979FM (U)	300	—	—	7.50	25.00	—
1980FM (U)	—	—	—	—	75.00	—

KM# 66a 2 DOLLARS
29.8000 g., 0.9250 Silver 0.8862 oz. ASW, 40 mm,
Ruler: Elizabeth II

Date	Mintage	F	VF	XF	Unc	BU
1974FM (P)	129,000	Value: 18.50				
1975FM (P)	45,000	Value: 18.50				
1976FM (P)	35,000	Value: 18.50				
1977FM (P)	15,000	Value: 20.00				
1978FM (P)	11,000	Value: 22.50				
1979FM (P)	2,053	Value: 27.50				
1980FM (P)	2,084	Value: 27.50				

KM# 66b 2 DOLLARS
Copper-Nickel, 40 mm. **Ruler:** Elizabeth II

Date	Mintage	F	VF	XF	Unc	BU
1981FM (P)	1,980	Value: 25.00				
1989	—	—	—	2.25	6.00	8.00

KM# 66c 2 DOLLARS
16.8500 g., 0.9250 Silver 0.5011 oz. ASW **Ruler:** Elizabeth II
Obv: National arms, date below **Rev:** National bird-two
flamingos, value above

Date	Mintage	F	VF	XF	Unc	BU
1989	Est. 4,000	Value: 35.00				
1991	600	—	—	—	80.00	—

KM# 90 2 DOLLARS
Copper-Nickel **Ruler:** Elizabeth II **Obv:** National arms, date
below **Rev:** Bahama swallows, value at top

Date	Mintage	F	VF	XF	Unc	BU
1982FM (P)	1,217	Value: 30.00				

KM# 94 2 DOLLARS
Copper-Nickel **Ruler:** Elizabeth II **Subject:** 10th Anniversary of
Independence **Rev:** Honeycreepers, value at top

Date	Mintage	F	VF	XF	Unc	BU
1983FM (P)	1,020	Value: 30.00				

KM# 105 2 DOLLARS
Copper-Nickel **Ruler:** Elizabeth II **Rev:** Flamingos in flight, value
at top

Date	Mintage	F	VF	XF	Unc	BU
1984FM (P)	1,036	Value: 30.00				
1985FM (P)	7,500	Value: 25.00				

KM# 158 2 DOLLARS
28.2800 g., 0.9250 Silver 0.8410 oz. ASW **Ruler:** Elizabeth II
Subject: Royal Visit **Rev:** Portraits and yacht, date at right

Date	Mintage	F	VF	XF	Unc	BU
1994 Proof	10,000	Value: 40.00				

KM# 164 2 DOLLARS
31.1035 g., 0.9990 Silver 0.9990 oz. ASW **Ruler:** Elizabeth II
Series: Flora and Fauna **Obv:** National arms, date below
Rev: Hibiscus flower and value within square, coin value below
Note: Multicolor applique.

Date	Mintage	F	VF	XF	Unc	BU
1995 Proof	25,000	Value: 40.00				

KM# 165 2 DOLLARS
28.2800 g., 0.9990 Silver 0.9083 oz. ASW, 38.61 mm.
Ruler: Elizabeth II **Series:** Flora and Fauna **Rev:** Bahama
Amazon Parrot on branch, value below **Note:** Multicolor applique.

Date	Mintage	F	VF	XF	Unc	BU
1995 Proof	10,000	Value: 45.00				

KM# 166 2 DOLLARS
28.2800 g., 0.9990 Silver 0.9083 oz. ASW **Ruler:** Elizabeth II
Series: Flora and Fauna **Rev:** Caribbean Monk Seal, value below
Note: Multicolor applique.

Date	Mintage	F	VF	XF	Unc	BU
1995 Proof	10,000	Value: 45.00				

KM# 183.1 2 DOLLARS
23.3300 g., 0.9250 Silver 0.6938 oz. ASW **Ruler:** Elizabeth II
Series: Olympics **Subject:** Catamaran Sailing **Obv:** Crowned
bust of Queen Elizabeth II right, date below **Rev:** Two figures on
catamaran, sailing, value below **Rev. Leg.:** OLIMPIC GAMES...

Date	Mintage	F	VF	XF	Unc	BU
1995 Proof	30,000	Value: 35.00				

KM# 183.2 2 DOLLARS
23.3300 g., 0.9250 Silver 0.6938 oz. ASW **Ruler:** Elizabeth II
Series: Olympics **Subject:** Catamaran Sailing **Rev:** Two figures
on catamaran, sailing, value below **Rev. Leg.:** OLIMPIC GAMES...

Date	Mintage	F	VF	XF	Unc	BU
1995	—	—	—	—	150	165

KM# 187 2 DOLLARS
3.1103 g., 0.9999 Gold 0.1000 oz. AGW **Ruler:** Elizabeth II
Obv: Crowned bust right, date below **Rev:** Two flamingos

Date	Mintage	F	VF	XF	Unc	BU
1995 Proof	—	Value: 95.00				

KM# 203 2 DOLLARS
23.3300 g., 0.9250 Silver 0.6938 oz. ASW, 38.6 mm.
Ruler: Elizabeth II **Subject:** Protect Our World **Obv:** Queen's
head right **Rev:** Flamingo and map, value below **Edge:** Reeded

Date	Mintage	F	VF	XF	Unc	BU
1996 Proof	—	Value: 50.00				

KM# 177 2 DOLLARS
3.1103 g., 0.9999 Gold 0.1000 oz. AGW **Ruler:** Elizabeth II
Subject: Third Millennium - Year 2000 **Obv:** Queen's portrait
Rev: Sea shell shaped map **Note:** Similar to 1 Dollar, KM#176.

Date	Mintage	F	VF	XF	Unc	BU
1996 Proof	10,000	Value: 100				

KM# 206 2 DOLLARS
23.2300 g., 0.9250 Silver 0.6908 oz. ASW, 38.6 mm. **Ruler:**
Elizabeth II **Subject:** UNICEF **Obv:** Bust of Queen Elizabeth II,
right **Rev:** Two boys and a dolphin, value below **Edge:** Reeded

Date	Mintage	F	VF	XF	Unc	BU
1997 Proof	25,000	Value: 40.00				

KM# 204 2 DOLLARS
23.3200 g., 0.9250 Silver 0.6935 oz. ASW, 38.5 mm. **Ruler:**
Elizabeth II **Subject:** Queen Mother **Obv:** Crowned bust of
Queen Elizabeth II right, date below **Rev:** Queen Mother's portrait
circa 1908, within beaded circle, value below circle **Edge:** Reeded

Date	Mintage	F	VF	XF	Unc	BU
1997 Proof	—	Value: 50.00				

KM# 198 2 DOLLARS
28.2800 g., 0.9250 Silver 0.8410 oz. ASW **Ruler:** Elizabeth II
Subject: WWF Conserving Nature **Obv:** Queen's portrait
Rev: Spotfin Butterfly Fish and a Queen Angelfish, value below

Date	Mintage	F	VF	XF	Unc	BU
1997 Proof	Est. 15,000	Value: 45.00				

KM# 208 2 DOLLARS
23.3276 g., 0.9250 Silver 0.6937 oz. ASW **Ruler:** Elizabeth II
Subject: FIFA - XVI World Championship Football - France 1998
Obv: Crowned bust right **Rev:** Ball being played

Date	Mintage	F	VF	XF	Unc	BU
1997 Proof	—	Value: 50.00				

KM# 215 2 DOLLARS
Silver **Ruler:** Elizabeth II **Subject:** 2000 Years of Christianity
Obv: Crowned bust right

Date	Mintage	F	VF	XF	Unc	BU
2000 Proof	—	Value: 30.00				

KM# 207 2 DOLLARS
28.2000 g., 0.9250 Silver with gilt outer ring 0.8386 oz. ASW,
38.5 mm. **Ruler:** Elizabeth II **Subject:** Queen Mother **Obv:**
Queen's portrait **Rev:** Queen Mother with dog **Edge:** Reeded

Date	Mintage	F	VF	XF	Unc	BU
2000 Proof	—	Value: 50.00				

KM# 10 5 DOLLARS
42.1200 g., 0.9250 Silver 1.2526 oz. ASW, 45 mm. **Ruler:**
Elizabeth II **Obv:** Bust right with tiara **Rev:** Shield with crown at
top, sailing ships below, banner below shield, garland above, date
at right, value above

Date	Mintage	F	VF	XF	Unc	BU
1966	100,000	—	—	BV	25.00	28.00
1969	36,000	—	—	BV	25.00	28.00
1969 Proof	10,000	Value: 25.00				
1970	43,000	—	—	BV	25.00	28.00
1970 Proof	23,000	Value: 25.00				

KM# 24 5 DOLLARS
42.1200 g., 0.9250 Silver 1.2526 oz. ASW, 45 mm.
Ruler: Elizabeth II **Obv:** Young bust of Queen Elizabeth II right
Rev: National arms, date and value

Date	Mintage	F	VF	XF	Unc	BU
1971FM	29,000	—	—	BV	25.00	28.00
1971FM (P)	31,000	Value: 25.00				

KM# 33 5 DOLLARS
42.1200 g., 0.9250 Silver 1.2526 oz. ASW, 45 mm.
Ruler: Elizabeth II **Obv:** Young Queen Elizabeth II right
Rev: National arms, value, date

Date	Mintage	F	VF	XF	Unc	BU
1972FM	32,000	—	—	BV	25.00	28.00
1972FM (P)	35,000	Value: 25.00				
1973FM	32,000	—	—	BV	25.00	28.00
1973FM (P)	35,000	Value: 25.00				

KM# 67 5 DOLLARS
Copper-Nickel, 45 mm. **Ruler:** Elizabeth II **Obv:** National arms
Rev: National flag, value above **Edge:** Reeded

Date	Mintage	F	VF	XF	Unc	BU
1974FM	32,000	—	—	—	8.00	—
1975FM (M)	200	—	—	—	40.00	—
1975FM (U)	7,058	—	—	—	10.00	—
1976FM (M)	200	—	—	—	40.00	—
1976FM (U)	2,591	—	—	—	15.00	—
1977FM (M)	200	—	—	—	40.00	—
1977FM (U)	801	—	—	—	20.00	—
1978FM (U)	1,244	—	—	—	15.00	—

KM# 67a 5 DOLLARS
42.1200 g., 0.9250 Silver 1.2526 oz. ASW **Ruler:** Elizabeth II

Date	Mintage	F	VF	XF	Unc	BU
1974FM (P)	94,000	Value: 25.00				
1975FM (P)	29,000	Value: 27.50				
1976FM (P)	23,000	Value: 27.50				
1977FM (P)	11,000	Value: 30.00				
1978FM (P)	6,931	Value: 32.50				
1979FM (P)	2,053	Value: 35.00				
1980FM (P)	2,084	Value: 35.00				

KM# 67b 5 DOLLARS
42.1200 g., 0.5000 Silver 0.6771 oz. ASW **Ruler:** Elizabeth II
Note: Reduced diameter.

Date	Mintage	F	VF	XF	Unc	BU
1981FM (P)	1,980	Value: 35.00				

KM# 91 5 DOLLARS
42.1200 g., 0.5000 Silver 0.6771 oz. ASW **Ruler:** Elizabeth II
Obv: National arms **Rev:** Flag below globe, value at bottom

Date	Mintage	F	VF	XF	Unc	BU
1982FM (P)	1,217	Value: 40.00				

KM# 95 5 DOLLARS
42.1200 g., 0.5000 Silver 0.6771 oz. ASW **Ruler:** Elizabeth II
Subject: 10th Anniversary of Independence **Rev:** Flamingo

Date	Mintage	F	VF	XF	Unc	BU
1983FM (P)	1,020	Value: 40.00				

KM# 106 5 DOLLARS
42.1200 g., 0.5000 Silver 0.6771 oz. ASW **Ruler:** Elizabeth II
Rev: Historical map, value above

Date	Mintage	F	VF	XF	Unc	BU
1984FM (P)	1,036	Value: 40.00				

KM# 107   5 DOLLARS
42.1200 g., 0.5000 Silver 0.6771 oz. ASW **Ruler:** Elizabeth II **Obv:** National arms, date below **Rev:** Half-length Christopher Columbus looking left, value above

Date	Mintage	F	VF	XF	Unc	BU
1985FM (P)	7,847	Value: 25.00				

KM# 132   5 DOLLARS
19.4400 g., 0.9250 Silver 0.5781 oz. ASW **Ruler:** Elizabeth II **Obv:** National arms, date below **Rev:** Standing Christopher Columbus with sword and flag before radiant sun, value lower left, date below

Date	Mintage	F	VF	XF	Unc	BU
1989 Proof	Est. 4,000	Value: 35.00				
1991	750	—	—	—	—	85.00
1991 Proof	7,000	Value: 40.00				

KM# 139   5 DOLLARS
19.4400 g., 0.9250 Silver 0.5781 oz. ASW **Ruler:** Elizabeth II **Series:** 500th Anniversary of the Americas **Rev:** Bust of Columbus at left, standing Ferdinand and Isabella at right, value below

Date	Mintage	F	VF	XF	Unc	BU
1991 Proof	Est. 25,000	Value: 25.00				

KM# 140   5 DOLLARS
19.4400 g., 0.9250 Silver 0.5781 oz. ASW **Ruler:** Elizabeth II **Series:** 500th Anniversary of the Americas **Subject:** Columbus sighting land **Rev:** Columbus on ship, inset of picture at right, "1492" below inset, value at bottom

Date	Mintage	F	VF	XF	Unc	BU
1991 Proof	Est. 25,000	Value: 25.00				

KM# 141   5 DOLLARS
19.4400 g., 0.9250 Silver 0.5781 oz. ASW **Ruler:** Elizabeth II **Series:** 500th Anniversary of the Americas **Subject:** Columbus claiming the land **Rev:** Columbus claiming the land, value at bottom

Date	Mintage	F	VF	XF	Unc	BU
1991 Proof	Est. 25,000	Value: 25.00				

KM# 142   5 DOLLARS
19.4400 g., 0.9250 Silver 0.5781 oz. ASW **Ruler:** Elizabeth II **Series:** 500th Anniversary of the Americas **Rev:** Bust of Jacques Cartier, 3/4 right, and map, value at bottom

Date	Mintage	F	VF	XF	Unc	BU
1991 Proof	Est. 25,000	Value: 25.00				

KM# 143   5 DOLLARS
19.4400 g., 0.9250 Silver 0.5781 oz. ASW **Ruler:** Elizabeth II **Series:** 500th Anniversary of the Americas **Rev:** Bust of President Thomas Jefferson, facing, looking left, Independence Hall at left with date below, value at bottom

Date	Mintage	F	VF	XF	Unc	BU
1991 Proof	Est. 25,000	Value: 25.00				

KM# 138   5 DOLLARS
19.4400 g., 0.9250 Silver 0.5781 oz. ASW **Ruler:** Elizabeth II **Series:** Discovery of the New World **Obv:** Coat of arms **Rev:** Columbus' ships within circle, value below circle

Date	Mintage	F	VF	XF	Unc	BU
1992 Proof	Est. 25,000	Value: 25.00				

KM# 192   5 DOLLARS
1.5550 g., 0.5000 Gold 0.0250 oz. AGW **Ruler:** Elizabeth II **Obv:** Crowned bust of Queen Elizabeth II right, date below **Rev:** Facing pair of flamingos, value above

Date	Mintage	F	VF	XF	Unc	BU
1992 Proof	Est. 750	Value: 70.00				

KM# 144   5 DOLLARS
19.4400 g., 0.9250 Silver 0.5781 oz. ASW **Ruler:** Elizabeth II **Series:** 500th Anniversary of the Americas **Rev:** Heads of Simon Bolivar and Jose San Martin on right, looking left, small statue of man on horseback at left, names at left, value at bottom

Date	Mintage	F	VF	XF	Unc	BU
1992 Proof	Est. 25,000	Value: 25.00				

KM# 145   5 DOLLARS
19.4400 g., 0.9250 Silver 0.5781 oz. ASW **Ruler:** Elizabeth II **Series:** 500th Anniversary of the Americas **Subject:** Abolition of slavery **Rev:** Bust of President Abraham Lincoln, 3/4 right, two figures at right, date at left, value at bottom

Date	Mintage	F	VF	XF	Unc	BU
1992 Proof	Est. 25,000	Value: 25.00				

KM# 146   5 DOLLARS
19.4400 g., 0.9250 Silver 0.5781 oz. ASW **Ruler:** Elizabeth II **Series:** 500th Anniversary of the Americas **Subject:** Electric light demonstration **Rev:** Bust of Thomas Edison with arms crossed, facing, light bulbs and inscription over left shoulder, people and name at right shoulder, value at bottom

Date	Mintage	F	VF	XF	Unc	BU
1992 Proof	Est. 25,000	Value: 25.00				

KM# 147   5 DOLLARS
19.4400 g., 0.9250 Silver 0.5781 oz. ASW **Ruler:** Elizabeth II **Series:** 500th Anniversary of the Americas **Subject:** Wright brothers' first airplane flight **Rev:** Two standing figures below plane, small date at right, words on lower left, value at bottom

Date	Mintage	F	VF	XF	Unc	BU
1992 Proof	Est. 25,000	Value: 25.00				

Date	Mintage	F	VF	XF	Unc	BU
1994 Proof	250,000	Value: 120				

KM# 148   5 DOLLARS
19.4400 g., 0.9250 Silver 0.5781 oz. ASW **Ruler:** Elizabeth II
Series: 500th Anniversary of the Americas **Rev:** Bust of Henry
Ford on left facing right, automobiles at right with date and
inscription, value at bottom

Date	Mintage	F	VF	XF	Unc	BU
1992 Proof	Est. 25,000	Value: 25.00				

KM# 149   5 DOLLARS
19.4400 g., 0.9250 Silver 0.5781 oz. ASW **Ruler:** Elizabeth II
Series: 500th Anniversary of the Americas **Rev:** Bust of President
Roosevelt on right looking left, Panama Canal on left, value at bottom

Date	Mintage	F	VF	XF	Unc	BU
1992 Proof	Est. 25,000	Value: 25.00				

KM# 150   5 DOLLARS
19.4400 g., 0.9250 Silver 0.5781 oz. ASW **Ruler:** Elizabeth II
Series: 500th Anniversary of the Americas **Subject:** First
manned moonlanding **Rev:** Astronaut on moon on left, planets
in orbit and inscription on right, value at bottom

Date	Mintage	F	VF	XF	Unc	BU
1992 Proof	Est. 25,000	Value: 25.00				

KM# 159   5 DOLLARS
23.3300 g., 0.9250 Silver 0.6938 oz. ASW **Ruler:** Elizabeth II
Obv: Crowned bust of Queen Elizabeth II right, date below **Rev:**
Pirate Captain Howell Davis, value below, within circle

Date	Mintage	F	VF	XF	Unc	BU
1993 Proof	Est. 5,000	Value: 35.00				

KM# 160   5 DOLLARS
23.3300 g., 0.9250 Silver 0.6938 oz. ASW **Ruler:** Elizabeth II
Obv: Crowned bust of Queen Elizabeth II right, date below
Rev: Pirate Captain Charles Vane, value at left foot, within circle

Date	Mintage	F	VF	XF	Unc	BU
1993 Proof	Est. 5,000	Value: 35.00				

KM# 161   5 DOLLARS
23.3300 g., 0.9250 Silver 0.6938 oz. ASW **Ruler:** Elizabeth II
Rev: Pirate Captain Edward Teach, value lower left, within circle

Date	Mintage	F	VF	XF	Unc	BU
1993 Proof	Est. 5,000	Value: 35.00				

KM# 169   5 DOLLARS
23.3300 g., 0.9250 Silver 0.6938 oz. ASW **Ruler:** Elizabeth II
Subject: World Soccer Championship **Rev:** Soccer player
kicking soccer ball value at lower left

Date	Mintage	F	VF	XF	Unc	BU
1993 Proof	Est. 15,000	Value: 35.00				

KM# 170   5 DOLLARS
23.3300 g., 0.9250 Silver 0.6938 oz. ASW **Ruler:** Elizabeth II
Rev: Sailing ship, flamingo on right, Marlin on left, value at bottom

Date	Mintage	F	VF	XF	Unc	BU
1993 Proof	Est. 20,000	Value: 35.00				

KM# 201   5 DOLLARS
3.1103 g., 0.9990 Gold 0.0999 oz. AGW **Ruler:** Elizabeth II
Subject: Golf - Hole in One **Obv:** National arms within 3/4 circle,
legend around, date below **Obv. Leg.:** COMMONWEALTH OF THE
BAHAMAS **Rev:** Golf ball rolling towards cup, value lower right

KM# 171   5 DOLLARS
31.1035 g., 0.9990 Silver 0.9990 oz. ASW **Ruler:** Elizabeth II
Rev: Space shuttle and satellite, value at upper left

Date	Mintage	F	VF	XF	Unc	BU
1994 Proof	Est. 10,000	Value: 60.00				

KM# 172   5 DOLLARS
31.1035 g., 0.9990 Silver 0.9990 oz. ASW **Ruler:** Elizabeth II
Obv: Crowned bust of Queen Elizabeth II right, date below
Rev: Two Whistling Swans in flight, value at bottom

Date	Mintage	F	VF	XF	Unc	BU
1994 Proof	Est. 15,000	Value: 55.00				

KM# 173   5 DOLLARS
31.4700 g., 0.9250 Silver 0.9359 oz. ASW **Ruler:** Elizabeth II
Obv: Crowned bust of Queen Elizabeth II right, date below
Rev: Ponce De Leon on horseback at right, small building at left,
value below

Date	Mintage	F	VF	XF	Unc	BU
1994 Proof	Est. 10,000	Value: 40.00				

KM# 155   5 DOLLARS
31.1035 g., 0.9990 Silver 0.9990 oz. ASW **Ruler:** Elizabeth II
Subject: Golf - Hole in One **Obv:** National arms within 3/4 circle,
legend around, date below **Obv. Leg.:** COMMONWEALTH OF
THE BAHAMAS **Rev:** Golf ball rolling towards cup **Note:** The cup
is an actual hole in the coin.

Date	Mintage	F	VF	XF	Unc	BU
1994 Proof	Est. 50,000	Value: 45.00				

KM# 188   5 DOLLARS
6.2207 g., 0.9999 Gold 0.2000 oz. AGW **Ruler:** Elizabeth II
Obv: Crowned bust of Queen Elizabeth II right, date below
Rev: Two flamingos facing, value below

Date	Mintage	F	VF	XF	Unc	BU
1995 Proof	—	Value: 200				

KM# 178   5 DOLLARS
7.7758 g., 0.9999 Gold 0.2500 oz. AGW **Ruler:** Elizabeth II
Subject: Third Millennium - Year 2000 **Obv:** Bust of Queen
Elizabeth II right **Rev:** Seashell-shaped world map

Date	Mintage	F	VF	XF	Unc	BU
1996 Proof	5,000	Value: 245				

KM# 11   10 DOLLARS
3.9943 g., 0.9170 Gold 0.1178 oz. AGW **Ruler:** Elizabeth II
Subject: Adoption of New Constitution **Obv:** Bust of Queen
Elizabeth II right with tiara **Rev:** Fortress, date below, value above

Date	Mintage	F	VF	XF	Unc	BU
1967	6,200	—	—	—	120	—
1967 Proof	850	Value: 140				

KM# 25   10 DOLLARS
3.9943 g., 0.9170 Gold 0.1178 oz. AGW **Ruler:** Elizabeth II
Obv: Bust of Queen Elizabeth II right with tiara **Rev:** Fortress,
date below, value above

Date	Mintage	F	VF	XF	Unc	BU
1971	23,000	—	—	—	120	—
1971(t) Proof	1,250	Value: 130				

KM# 26.1   10 DOLLARS
3.9943 g., 0.9170 Gold 0.1178 oz. AGW **Ruler:** Elizabeth II
Obv: Bust of Queen Elizabeth II right with tiara **Rev:** Fortress,
date below, value above, hallmark and fineness stamped right of
date **Note:** Struck by the Gori and Zucchi Mint, Italy. Prev. KM#26.

Date	Mintage	F	VF	XF	Unc	BU
1971	—	—	—	—	120	—

KM# 26.2   10 DOLLARS
3.9943 g., 0.9170 Gold 0.1178 oz. AGW **Ruler:** Elizabeth II **Rev:**
Hallmark and finess stamped left of date **Note:** Struck by the Gori
and Zucchi Mint, Italy.

Date	Mintage	F	VF	XF	Unc	BU
1971	—	—	—	—	120	—

KM# 34   10 DOLLARS
3.1950 g., 0.9170 Gold 0.0942 oz. AGW **Ruler:** Elizabeth II
Obv: Bust of Queen Elizabeth II right **Rev:** Fortress, date below,
value above

Date	Mintage	F	VF	XF	Unc	BU
1972	11,000	—	—	—	95.00	—
1972 Proof	1,250	Value: 110				

KM# 40.1   10 DOLLARS
1.4500 g., 0.7500 Gold 0.0350 oz. AGW, 15 mm.
Ruler: Elizabeth II **Subject:** Independence Day - July 10

Obv: Bust of Queen Elizabeth II right with tiara, date below
Rev: Tobacco Dove, value, without fineness and date

Date	Mintage	F	VF	XF	Unc	BU
1973	—	—	—	—	35.00	—
1973 Proof	—	Value: 37.50				

KM# 40.2   10 DOLLARS
1.4500 g., 0.7500 Gold 0.0350 oz. AGW, 15 mm.
Ruler: Elizabeth II **Obv:** Bust of Queen Elizabeth II right with
tiara, date below **Rev:** Tobacco Dove divides value, date at right,
date without fineness

Date	Mintage	F	VF	XF	Unc	BU
1973	—	—	—	—	35.00	—

KM# 41   10 DOLLARS
1.4500 g., 0.5850 Gold 0.0273 oz. AGW, 15 mm. **Ruler:** Elizabeth II
Obv: Bust of Queen Elizabeth II right with tiara, date below **Rev:**
Tobacco Dove divides value, date at right, .585 fineness and date

Date	Mintage	F	VF	XF	Unc	BU
1973	9,960	—	—	—	35.00	—
1973 Proof	1,260	Value: 37.50				

KM# 42   10 DOLLARS
49.7500 g., 0.9250 Silver 1.4795 oz. ASW, 50 mm. **Ruler:**
Elizabeth II **Subject:** Independence Day - July 10 **Obv:**
Legend around queen's portrait **Rev:** Santa Maria with full sails, value below

Date	Mintage	F	VF	XF	Unc	BU
1973FM	28,000	—	—	—	32.50	—
1973FM Proof	63,000	Value: 32.50				

KM# 68   10 DOLLARS
Copper-Nickel, 50 mm. **Ruler:** Elizabeth II **Subject:** 1st
Anniversary of Independence **Obv:** National arms, date below
Rev: Head of Sir Milo B. Butler, Governor-General right, value
above, legend below

Date	Mintage	F	VF	XF	Unc	BU
1974FM Proof	4,825	—	—	—	12.00	—

KM# 68a   10 DOLLARS
50.4200 g., 0.9250 Silver 1.4994 oz. ASW, 50 mm.
Ruler: Elizabeth II **Subject:** 1st Anniversary of Independence
Obv: National arms, date below **Rev:** Head of Sir Milo B. Butler,
Governor-General right, value above, legend below

Date	Mintage	F	VF	XF	Unc	BU
1974FM Proof	43,000	Value: 32.50				

KM# 76   10 DOLLARS
Copper-Nickel, 50 mm. **Ruler:** Elizabeth II **Subject:** Anniversary
of Independence **Obv:** National arms with supporters, date below
Rev: Yellow Elder, value at top

Date	Mintage	F	VF	XF	Unc	BU
1975FM (M)	100	—	—	—	90.00	—
1975FM (U)	5,325	—	—	—	12.50	—
1976FM (M)	100	—	—	—	90.00	—
1976FM (U)	100	—	—	—	90.00	—
1977FM (M)	100	—	—	—	90.00	—
1977FM (U)	369	—	—	—	60.00	—

KM# 76a   10 DOLLARS
49.1000 g., 0.9250 Silver 1.4601 oz. ASW **Ruler:** Elizabeth II

Date	Mintage	F	VF	XF	Unc	BU
1975FM (P)	63,000	Value: 30.00				
1976FM (P)	10,000	Value: 32.50				
1977FM (P)	4,424	Value: 35.00				

KM# 78.1   10 DOLLARS
45.3600 g., 0.5000 Silver 0.7291 oz. ASW, 50 mm. **Ruler:**
Elizabeth II **Subject:** 5th Anniversary of Independence **Obv:**
National arms, date below **Rev:** Head of Prince Charles, right,
value at bottom

Date	Mintage	F	VF	XF	Unc	BU
1978 Proof	50,000	Value: 25.00				

KM# 78.2   10 DOLLARS
45.3600 g., 0.5000 Silver 0.7291 oz. ASW, 50 mm.
Ruler: Elizabeth II **Obv:** National arms, date below
Obv. Leg.: COMMONWEALTH OF THE BAHAMAS **Rev:** Head
of Prince Charles, right, tower mint mark after DOLLARS
Rev. Leg.: FIFTH ANNIVERSARY OF INDEPENDENCE 10
JULY 1973 **Edge:** Reeded

Date	Mintage	F	VF	XF	Unc	BU
1978(t) Proof	—	Value: 65.00				

KM# 79   10 DOLLARS
45.3600 g., 0.5000 Silver 0.7291 oz. ASW, 50 mm.
Ruler: Elizabeth II **Subject:** 5th Anniversary of Independence
Obv: National arms, date below **Rev:** Head of Sir Milo B. Butler,
3/4 left, value at bottom

Date	Mintage	F	VF	XF	Unc	BU
1978 Proof	50,000	Value: 20.00				

KM# 84   10 DOLLARS
30.2800 g., 0.5000 Silver 0.4867 oz. ASW **Ruler:** Elizabeth II
Subject: 10th Anniversary Caribbean Development Bank
Obv: National arms **Rev:** Flag below globe, value at bottom

Date	Mintage	F	VF	XF	Unc	BU
1980FM Proof	1,001	Value: 25.00				

KM# 85   10 DOLLARS
28.2800 g., 0.9250 Silver 0.8410 oz. ASW **Ruler:** Elizabeth II
Subject: Wedding of Prince Charles and Lady Diana **Obv:** Bust
of Queen Elizabeth II right with tiara **Rev:** Conjoined busts of
royal couple left

Date	Mintage	F	VF	XF	Unc	BU
1981 Proof	39,000	Value: 30.00				

KM# 96   10 DOLLARS
30.2800 g., 0.5000 Silver 0.4867 oz. ASW **Ruler:** Elizabeth II
Subject: 30th Anniversary - Coronation of Queen Elizabeth **Obv:**
National arms, date below **Rev:** Royal symbols divided by
sceptres, dates at either side, value at bottom

Date	Mintage	F	VF	XF	Unc	BU
1983FM Proof	3,374	Value: 25.00				

KM# 97   10 DOLLARS
23.3300 g., 0.9250 Silver 0.6938 oz. ASW **Ruler:** Elizabeth II
Subject: 10th Anniversary of Independence **Rev:** Standing figure
in front of flag, value below

Date	Mintage	F	VF	XF	Unc	BU
1983 Proof	800	Value: 37.50				

KM# 114   10 DOLLARS
23.3300 g., 0.9250 Silver 0.6938 oz. ASW **Ruler:** Elizabeth II
Subject: Los Angeles Olympics **Obv:** National arms
Rev: Sprinter, symbol at right, value at bottom

Date	Mintage	F	VF	XF	Unc	BU
1984 Proof	2,100	Value: 40.00				

KM# 127   10 DOLLARS
29.1700 g., 0.5000 Silver 0.4689 oz. ASW **Ruler:** Elizabeth II
Subject: 10th Anniversary of Central Bank **Obv:** National arms
Rev: Sand dollar, value at top **Edge:** Reeded

Date	Mintage	F	VF	XF	Unc	BU
1984FM Proof	1,001	Value: 45.00				

KM# 109   10 DOLLARS
28.2800 g., 0.9250 Silver 0.8410 oz. ASW **Ruler:** Elizabeth II
Subject: Royal Visit **Obv:** Bust of Queen Elizabeth II right **Rev:**
National arms, value below

Date	Mintage	F	VF	XF	Unc	BU
1985 Proof	1,060	Value: 40.00				

KM# 109a   10 DOLLARS
47.5400 g., 0.9170 Gold 1.4015 oz. AGW **Ruler:** Elizabeth II
Subject: Royal Visit

Date	Mintage	F	VF	XF	Unc	BU
1985 Proof	Est. 250	Value: 1,350				

KM# 113   10 DOLLARS
28.2800 g., 0.5000 Silver 0.4546 oz. ASW **Ruler:** Elizabeth II
Subject: Commonwealth Games **Obv:** National arms, date
below **Rev:** Competitor running left, value at right

Date	Mintage	F	VF	XF	Unc	BU
1986	899	—	—	—	30.00	—

KM# 113a   10 DOLLARS
28.2800 g., 0.9250 Silver 0.8410 oz. ASW **Ruler:** Elizabeth II
Subject: Commonwealth Games **Obv:** National arms, date
below **Rev:** Competitor running left, value at right

Date	Mintage	F	VF	XF	Unc	BU
1986 Proof	1,343	Value: 32.00				

KM# 120   10 DOLLARS
28.2800 g., 0.9250 Silver 0.8410 oz. ASW **Ruler:** Elizabeth II
Rev: Queen Isabella receiving Columbus

Date	Mintage	F	VF	XF	Unc	BU
1987 Proof	1,800	Value: 32.00				

KM# 123   10 DOLLARS
28.2800 g., 0.9250 Silver 0.8410 oz. ASW **Ruler:** Elizabeth II
Subject: Columbus discovering America **Obv:** Queen Elizabeth
Rev: Columbus sighting America, date below

Date	Mintage	F	VF	XF	Unc	BU
1988 Proof	1,704	Value: 32.00				

KM# 128   10 DOLLARS
28.2800 g., 0.9250 Silver 0.8410 oz. ASW **Ruler:** Elizabeth II
Obv: Queen Elizabeth **Rev:** Columbus with flag and sword

Date	Mintage	F	VF	XF	Unc	BU
1989 Proof	Est. 10,000	Value: 25.00				

KM# 133   10 DOLLARS
28.2800 g., 0.9250 Silver 0.8410 oz. ASW **Ruler:** Elizabeth II
Series: Discovery of the New World **Obv:** Queen Elizabeth
Rev: Bust of Columbus, left, within circle, value below

Date	Mintage	F	VF	XF	Unc	BU
1990	550	—	—	—	110	—
1990 Proof	10,000	Value: 25.00				

KM# 196   10 DOLLARS
28.2800 g., 0.9250 Silver 0.8410 oz. ASW **Ruler:** Elizabeth II
Series: Discovery of the New World **Obv:** Queen's portrait
Rev: 5 men rowing boat, Columbus' ships in background, all in
inner circle, value below

Date	Mintage	F	VF	XF	Unc	BU
1991 Proof	—	Value: 25.00				

KM# 193   10 DOLLARS
3.1100 g., 0.5000 Gold 0.0500 oz. AGW **Ruler:** Elizabeth II
Obv: Bust of Queen Elizabeth II right, date below **Rev:** Two
flamingos facing, value above

Date	Mintage	F	VF	XF	Unc	BU
1992 Proof	Est. 750	Value: 100				

KM# 197   10 DOLLARS
28.2800 g., 0.9250 Silver 0.8410 oz. ASW **Ruler:** Elizabeth II
Series: Discovery of the New World **Obv:** Crowned bust of Queen
Elizabeth II right, date below **Rev:** Nina, Pinta, Santa Maria ships
within circle, value below

Date	Mintage	F	VF	XF	Unc	BU
1992 Proof	—	Value: 25.00				

KM# 162   10 DOLLARS
136.0800 g., 0.9250 Silver 4.0468 oz. ASW **Ruler:** Elizabeth II
Subject: Expulsion of pirates **Obv:** Queen's portrait, legend
around, date below **Obv. Leg.:** • COMMONWEALTH OF THE
BAHAMAS • **Rev:** Pirate ship, value below **Rev. Leg.:** •
EXPULSIS PIRATIS • RESTITUTA COMMERCIA •

Date	Mintage	F	VF	XF	Unc	BU
1993 Proof	Est. 2,000	Value: 120				

KM# 156   10 DOLLARS
7.7759 g., 0.9990 Gold 0.2497 oz. AGW **Ruler:** Elizabeth II
Subject: Golf - Hole-in-One **Obv:** National arms **Rev:** Golfer
making hole-in-one

Date	Mintage	F	VF	XF	Unc	BU
1994 Proof	2,500	Value: 245				

KM# 167   10 DOLLARS
155.5175 g., 0.9990 Silver 4.9948 oz. ASW **Ruler:** Elizabeth II
Obv: Multicolor National arms **Rev:** Multicolor Bahama parrot on
branch, value at bottom

Date	Mintage	F	VF	XF	Unc	BU
1995 Proof	2,500	Value: 175				

KM# 168   10 DOLLARS
15.5518 g., 0.9990 Gold 0.4995 oz. AGW. **Ruler:** Elizabeth II
Obv: Queen's portrait **Rev:** Bahama Parrot

Date	Mintage	F	VF	XF	Unc	BU
1995 Proof	2,000	Value: 500				

KM# 174   10 DOLLARS
28.2800 g., 0.9250 Silver 0.8410 oz. ASW **Ruler:** Elizabeth II
Subject: 25th Anniversary - Caribbean Development Bank
Obv: National arms **Rev:** Globe within inscription, butterflies
flanking, birds and flowers below

Date	Mintage	F	VF	XF	Unc	BU
ND(1995) Proof	1,000	Value: 40.00				

KM# 189   10 DOLLARS
15.5517 g., 0.9999 Gold 0.4999 oz. AGW **Ruler:** Elizabeth II
Obv: Queen's portrait **Rev:** Two flamingos facing

Date	Mintage	F	VF	XF	Unc	BU
1995 Proof	—	Value: 500				

KM# 179   10 DOLLARS
15.5517 g., 0.9999 Gold 0.4999 oz. AGW **Ruler:** Elizabeth II
Subject: Third Millennium - Year 2000 **Obv:** Queen's portrait
Rev: Seashell-shaped world map

Date	Mintage	F	VF	XF	Unc	BU
1996 Proof	5,000	Value: 500				

KM# 200   10 DOLLARS
31.1035 g., 0.9990 Silver 0.9990 oz. ASW **Ruler:** Elizabeth II
Subject: 50th Anniversary of the University of the West Indies
Obv: National arms **Rev:** University arms, dates

Date	Mintage	F	VF	XF	Unc	BU
1998 Proof	1,000	Value: 50.00				

KM# 212   10 DOLLARS
Silver **Ruler:** Elizabeth II **Subject:** XXVII Summer Olympics -
Sydney 2000 **Obv:** National arms **Rev:** "The Golden Girls" - five
relay runners, gilt

Date	Mintage	F	VF	XF	Unc	BU
2000 Proof	—	Value: 165				

KM# 12   20 DOLLARS
7.9880 g., 0.9170 Gold 0.2355 oz. AGW **Ruler:** Elizabeth II
Subject: Adoption of New Constitution **Obv:** Bust right
Rev: Lighthouse, date below

Date	Mintage	F	VF	XF	Unc	BU
1967	6,200	—	—	—	225	—
1967 Proof	850	Value: 245				

KM# 27   20 DOLLARS
7.9880 g., 0.9170 Gold 0.2355 oz. AGW **Ruler:** Elizabeth II
Obv: Bust of Queen Elizabeth II with tiara right **Rev:** Lighthouse,
value at top, date at bottom

Date	Mintage	F	VF	XF	Unc	BU
1971	22,000	—	—	—	225	—
1971(t) Proof	1,250	Value: 240				

KM# 28   20 DOLLARS
7.9880 g., 0.9170 Gold 0.2355 oz. AGW **Ruler:** Elizabeth II
Obv: Bust of Queen Elizabeth II right with tiara **Rev:** Lighthouse
above date, value at top, hallmark and fineness stamped at
bottom **Note:** Struck by the Gori and Zucchi Mint, Italy.

Date	Mintage	F	VF	XF	Unc	BU
1971 Proof	—	—	—	—	225	—

KM# 35   20 DOLLARS
6.4800 g., 0.9170 Gold 0.1910 oz. AGW **Ruler:** Elizabeth II
Obv: Bust of Queen Elizabeth II right **Rev:** Lighthouse above
date, value at top

Date	Mintage	F	VF	XF	Unc	BU
1972	10,000	—	—	—	185	—
1972 Proof	1,250	Value: 200				

KM# 43.1   20 DOLLARS
2.9000 g., 0.7500 Gold 0.0699 oz. AGW, 19 mm. **Ruler:**
Elizabeth II **Subject:** Independence Day - July 10 **Obv:** Bust of
Queen Elizabeth II right with tiara, date below **Rev:** Flamingos,
without fineness and date, value at bottom

Date	Mintage	F	VF	XF	Unc	BU
1973	—	—	—	—	70.00	—
1973 Proof	—	Value: 80.00				

KM# 43.2   20 DOLLARS
2.9000 g., 0.7500 Gold 0.0699 oz. AGW, 19 mm. **Ruler:**
Elizabeth II **Subject:** Independence Day - July 10 **Obv:** Bust of
Queen Elizabeth II right with tiara **Rev:** Flamingos, without
fineness, high date

Date	Mintage	F	VF	XF	Unc	BU
1973	—	—	—	—	70.00	—
1973 Proof	—	Value: 80.00				

KM# 44   20 DOLLARS
2.9000 g., 0.5850 Gold 0.0545 oz. AGW, 19 mm. **Ruler:**
Elizabeth II **Obv:** Bust of Queen Elizabeth II right with tiara, date
below **Rev:** Flamingos, .585 fineness, low date, value at bottom

Date	Mintage	F	VF	XF	Unc	BU
1973	8,660	—	—	—	55.00	—
1973 Proof	1,260	Value: 60.00				

KM# 157 20 DOLLARS
15.5517 g., 0.9990 Gold 0.4995 oz. AGW **Ruler:** Elizabeth II
Obv: Arms **Rev:** Golfer making hole-in-one

Date	Mintage	F	VF	XF	Unc	BU
1994 Proof	2,500	Value: 500				

KM# 82 25 DOLLARS
37.3800 g., 0.9250 Silver 1.1116 oz. ASW **Ruler:** Elizabeth II
Subject: 250th Anniversary of Parliament **Obv:** National arms, date below **Rev:** Royal sceptre divides dates, value at bottom

Date	Mintage	F	VF	XF	Unc	BU
1979 Proof	3,002	Value: 40.00				

KM# 110 25 DOLLARS
120.0000 g., 0.9250 Silver 3.5686 oz. ASW, 63 mm. **Ruler:** Elizabeth II **Subject:** Columbus' Discovery of America **Obv:** National arms **Rev:** Columbus claiming the land by planting flag, crew with clergy holding cross behind, value above, date below

Date	Mintage	F	VF	XF	Unc	BU
1985 Proof	1,950	Value: 80.00				

KM# 115 25 DOLLARS
129.6000 g., 0.9250 Silver 3.8541 oz. ASW, 63 mm. **Ruler:** Elizabeth II **Subject:** Bird Conservation **Obv:** National arms **Rev:** Flamingos, value at top

Date	Mintage	F	VF	XF	Unc	BU
1985 Proof	1,060	Value: 85.00				

KM# 118 25 DOLLARS
129.6000 g., 0.9250 Silver 3.8541 oz. ASW **Ruler:** Elizabeth II
Obv: Queen's portrait **Rev:** Queen Isabella receiving Columbus

Date	Mintage	F	VF	XF	Unc	BU
1987 Proof	1,750	Value: 80.00				

KM# 124 25 DOLLARS
136.0000 g., 0.9250 Silver 4.0444 oz. ASW **Ruler:** Elizabeth II
Subject: Columbus Discovering New World **Obv:** Queen's portrait
Rev: Columbus on deck pointing towards land, date at bottom

Date	Mintage	F	VF	XF	Unc	BU
1988 Proof	954	Value: 120				

KM# 129 25 DOLLARS
136.0000 g., 0.9250 Silver 4.0444 oz. ASW **Ruler:** Elizabeth II
Obv: Queen Elizabeth **Rev:** Christopher Columbus, radiant sun and ocean in background, value below right hand, circle surrounds, date below circle

Date	Mintage	F	VF	XF	Unc	BU
1989 Proof	1,572	Value: 100				

KM# 134 25 DOLLARS
136.0000 g., 0.9250 Silver 4.0444 oz. ASW **Ruler:** Elizabeth II
Series: Discovery of the New World **Obv:** Queen Elizabeth **Rev:** Aborigine looking right, within circle, value below circle

Date	Mintage	F	VF	XF	Unc	BU
1990 Proof	5,000	Value: 85.00				

KM# 153 25 DOLLARS
136.0000 g., 0.9250 Silver 4.0444 oz. ASW **Ruler:** Elizabeth II
Series: Discovery of the New World **Obv:** Queen Elizabeth
Rev: Facing half bust of Columbus holding map, ship at left, circle surrounds, value below circle

Date	Mintage	F	VF	XF	Unc	BU
1991 Proof	Est. 500	Value: 175				

KM# 194 25 DOLLARS
7.7700 g., 0.5000 Gold 0.1249 oz. AGW **Ruler:** Elizabeth II
Obv: Bust of Queen Elizabeth II right, date below **Rev:** Pair of flamingos, value above

Date	Mintage	F	VF	XF	Unc	BU
1992 Proof	Est. 750	Value: 175				

KM# 191 25 DOLLARS
136.0000 g., 0.9250 Silver 4.0444 oz. ASW, 63 mm.
Ruler: Elizabeth II **Series:** Discovery of the New World **Obv:** Bust of Queen Elizabeth II right, date below **Rev:** Columbus meeting native Americans, within circle, value below circle
Note: Illustration reduced.

Date	Mintage	F	VF	XF	Unc	BU
1992 Proof	—	Value: 175				

KM# 202 25 DOLLARS
31.1035 g., 0.9999 Gold 0.9999 oz. AGW **Ruler:** Elizabeth II
Subject: Golf - Hole-in-One **Obv:** National arms **Rev:** Golf ball rolling towards hole

Date	Mintage	F	VF	XF	Unc	BU
1994 Proof	—	Value: 975				

KM# 190 25 DOLLARS
31.1035 g., 0.9999 Gold 0.9999 oz. AGW **Ruler:** Elizabeth II
Obv: Bust of Queen Elizabeth II right, date below **Rev:** Two flamingos, value at bottom

Date	Mintage	F	VF	XF	Unc	BU
1995 Proof	—	Value: 950				

KM# 180 25 DOLLARS
31.1035 g., 0.9999 Gold 0.9999 oz. AGW **Ruler:** Elizabeth II
Subject: Third Millennium - Year 2000 **Obv:** Bust of Queen
Elizabeth II right **Rev:** Seashell-shaped world map

Date	Mintage	F	VF	XF	Unc	BU
1996 Proof	5,000	Value: 950				

KM# 209 25 DOLLARS
Silver **Ruler:** Elizabeth II **Subject:** 25th Anniversary College of
the Bahamas **Obv:** Crowned bust right **Rev:** College facade

Date	Mintage	F	VF	XF	Unc	BU
1998 Proof	—	Value: 120				

KM# 211 25 DOLLARS
Silver **Ruler:** Elizabeth II **Subject:** 25th Anniversary Central
Bank **Obv:** Crowned bust right

Date	Mintage	F	VF	XF	Unc	BU
1999 Proof	—	Value: 120				

KM# 13 50 DOLLARS
19.9710 g., 0.9170 Gold 0.5888 oz. AGW **Ruler:** Elizabeth II
Subject: Adoption of New Constitution **Obv:** Bust of Queen
Elizabeth II right with tiara **Rev:** Santa Maria in full sail, value and
date above

Date	Mintage	F	VF	XF	Unc	BU
1967	1,200	—	—	—	575	—
1967 Proof	850	Value: 600				

KM# 29 50 DOLLARS
19.9710 g., 0.9170 Gold 0.5888 oz. AGW **Ruler:** Elizabeth II
Obv: Bust of Queen Elizabeth II right with tiara **Rev:** Santa Maria
in full sail, value and date above

Date	Mintage	F	VF	XF	Unc	BU
1971	6,800	—	—	—	575	—
1971(t) Proof	1,250	Value: 600				

KM# 30 50 DOLLARS
19.9710 g., 0.9170 Gold 0.5888 oz. AGW **Ruler:** Elizabeth II
Obv: Bust of Queen Elizabeth II right with tiara **Rev:** Santa Maria
in full sail, value and above, hallmark and fineness stamped at
bottom **Note:** Struck by the Gori and Zucchi Mint, Italy.

Date	Mintage	F	VF	XF	Unc	BU
1971	—	—	—	—	575	—
1971 Proof	1,250	Value: 500				

KM# 36 50 DOLLARS
15.9700 g., 0.9170 Gold 0.4708 oz. AGW **Ruler:** Elizabeth II
Obv: Bust of Queen Elizabeth II right

Date	Mintage	F	VF	XF	Unc	BU
1972	2,250	—	—	—	475	—
1972 Proof	1,250	Value: 500				

KM# 45 50 DOLLARS
7.2700 g., 0.7500 Gold 0.1753 oz. AGW, 22 mm. **Ruler:**
Elizabeth II **Subject:** Independence Day - July 10 **Obv:** Bust of
Queen Elizabeth II right, date below **Rev:** Spiny lobster, date
below, value at bottom; without fineness

Date	Mintage	F	VF	XF	Unc	BU
1973	—	—	—	—	175	—
1973 Proof	—	Value: 185				

KM# 46 50 DOLLARS
7.2700 g., 0.5850 Gold 0.1367 oz. AGW, 22 mm. **Ruler:** Elizabeth II
Obv: Bust of Queen Elizabeth II right with tiara, date below **Rev:**
Spiny lobster, .585 fineness to left, date to right, value at bottom

Date	Mintage	F	VF	XF	Unc	BU
1973	5,160	—	—	—	150	—
1973 Proof	1,260	Value: 165				

KM# 47 50 DOLLARS
7.3000 g., 0.7500 Gold 0.1760 oz. AGW, 22 mm. **Ruler:** Elizabeth II
Obv: Bust of Queen Elizabeth II right with tiara, date below **Rev:**
Spiny lobster, without date or fineness, value at bottom

Date	Mintage	F	VF	XF	Unc	BU
1973	—	—	—	—	185	—

KM# 48 50 DOLLARS
15.6448 g., 0.5000 Gold 0.2515 oz. AGW, 29.2 mm. **Ruler:**
Elizabeth II **Subject:** Independence Day - July 10 **Obv:** Bust of
Queen Elizabeth II right with tiara **Rev:** Two flamingos, value below

Date	Mintage	F	VF	XF	Unc	BU
1973JP	23,000	—	—	—	250	—
1973JP	18,000	Value: 270				

KM# 69 50 DOLLARS
2.7300 g., 0.9170 Gold 0.0805 oz. AGW, 17 mm. **Ruler:**
Elizabeth II **Subject:** 1st Anniversary of Independence **Obv:** Bust
of Queen Elizabeth II right with tiara, date below **Rev:** Tobacco
Dove, value, date, without fineness

Date	Mintage	F	VF	XF	Unc	BU
1974	34,000	—	—	—	75.00	—
1974 Proof	20,000	Value: 80.00				
1975	26,000	—	—	—	80.00	—
1975 Proof	15,000	Value: 85.00				
1976	2,207	—	—	—	85.00	—
1976 Proof	Inc. above	Value: 85.00				
1977	1,090	—	—	—	85.00	—
1977 Proof	—	Value: 100				

KM# 70 50 DOLLARS
2.7300 g., 0.9170 Gold 0.0805 oz. AGW **Ruler:** Elizabeth II
Obv: Bust of Queen Elizabeth II right with tiara, date below **Rev:**
Tobacco Dove, value date, .917 fineness

Date	Mintage	F	VF	XF	Unc	BU
1974	—	—	—	—	80.00	—

KM# 86 50 DOLLARS
2.6800 g., 0.5000 Gold 0.0431 oz. AGW **Ruler:** Elizabeth II
Obv: National arms, date below **Rev:** Flamingos in flight

Date	Mintage	F	VF	XF	Unc	BU
1981FM Proof	2,050	Value: 65.00				

KM# 92 50 DOLLARS
2.6800 g., 0.5000 Gold 0.0431 oz. AGW **Ruler:** Elizabeth II **Obv:**
National arms, date below **Rev:** Marlin (Swordfish), value above

Date	Mintage	F	VF	XF	Unc	BU
1982FM Proof	841	Value: 125				

KM# 98 50 DOLLARS
2.6800 g., 0.5000 Gold 0.0431 oz. AGW **Ruler:** Elizabeth II
Subject: 10th Anniversary of Independence **Obv:** National arms,
date below **Rev:** Flamingo, value above

Date	Mintage	F	VF	XF	Unc	BU
1983FM Proof	962	Value: 100				

KM# 103 50 DOLLARS
2.6800 g., 0.5000 Gold 0.0431 oz. AGW **Ruler:** Elizabeth II **Obv:**
National arms, date below **Rev:** Golden Allamanda, value above

Date	Mintage	F	VF	XF	Unc	BU
1984FM Proof	3,716	Value: 50.00				

KM# 108 50 DOLLARS
2.6800 g., 0.5000 Gold 0.0431 oz. AGW **Ruler:** Elizabeth II
Obv: National arms, date below **Rev:** Santa Maria, value above

Date	Mintage	F	VF	XF	Unc	BU
1985FM Proof	1,575	Value: 70.00				

KM# 199 50 DOLLARS
6.4800 g., 0.9167 Gold 0.1910 oz. AGW **Ruler:** Elizabeth II
Subject: Junkanoo Festival **Obv:** Crowned bust of Queen
Elizabeth II right, date below **Rev:** Three costumed musicians,
value below

Date	Mintage	F	VF	XF	Unc	BU
1994 Proof	—	Value: 200				

KM# 181 50 DOLLARS
2000.0000 g., 0.9990 Silver 64.234 oz. ASW **Ruler:** Elizabeth II
Subject: Third Millennium - Year 2000 **Obv:** Bust of Queen
Elizabeth II right **Rev:** Seashell-shaped world map

Date	Mintage	F	VF	XF	Unc	BU
1996 Proof	2,000	Value: 1,350				

KM# 14 100 DOLLARS
39.9400 g., 0.9170 Gold 1.1775 oz. AGW **Ruler:** Elizabeth II
Subject: Adoption of New Constitution **Obv:** Bust of Queen
Elizabeth II right with tiara **Rev:** Columbus, date divides value at
bottom

Date	Mintage	F	VF	XF	Unc	BU
1967	1,200	—	—	—	1,150	—
1967 Proof	850	Value: 1,200				

KM# 31 100 DOLLARS
39.9400 g., 0.9170 Gold 1.1775 oz. AGW **Ruler:** Elizabeth II **Obv:** Bust of Queen Elizabeth II right with tiara **Rev:** Shield with crown at top, sailing ship at bottom, ribbon below shield, garland above, value, date

Date	Mintage	F	VF	XF	Unc	BU
1971	6,800	—	—	—	1,150	—
1971(t) Proof	1,250	Value: 1,200				

KM# 32.1 100 DOLLARS
39.9400 g., 0.9170 Gold 1.1775 oz. AGW **Ruler:** Elizabeth II **Obv:** Bust of Queen Elizabeth II right with tiara **Rev:** Shield with crown at top, sailing ship at bottom, ribbon below shield, garland above, value, date; hallmark and fineness at bottom right

Date	Mintage	F	VF	XF	Unc	BU
1971	—	—	—	—	1,150	—

KM# 32.2 100 DOLLARS
39.9400 g., 0.9170 Gold 1.1775 oz. AGW **Ruler:** Elizabeth II **Obv:** Bust of Queen Elizabeth II right with tiara **Rev:** Shield with crown at top, sailing ship at bottom, ribbon below shield, garland on top, value, date; hallmark at bottom right, without fineness

Date	Mintage	F	VF	XF	Unc	BU
1971	—	—	—	—	1,150	—

KM# 32.3 100 DOLLARS
39.9400 g., 0.9170 Gold 1.1775 oz. AGW **Ruler:** Elizabeth II **Obv:** Bust of Queen Elizabeth II right with tiara **Rev:** Shield with crown at top, sailing ship at bottom, ribbon below shield, garland above, value, date; fineness at bottom right without hallmark
Note: Struck by the Gori and Zucchi Mint, Italy.

Date	Mintage	F	VF	XF	Unc	BU
1971	—	—	—	—	1,150	—

KM# 37 100 DOLLARS
31.9500 g., 0.9170 Gold 0.9419 oz. AGW **Ruler:** Elizabeth II **Obv:** Bust of Queen Elizabeth II right **Note:** The 1972 proof $100 is serially numbered on the edge.

Date	Mintage	F	VF	XF	Unc	BU
1972	2,250	—	—	—	900	—
1972 Proof	1,250	Value: 925				

KM# 49.1 100 DOLLARS
14.5400 g., 0.7500 Gold 0.3506 oz. AGW, 28 mm. **Ruler:** Elizabeth II **Subject:** Independence Day - July 10 **Obv:** Bust of Queen Elizabeth II right with tiara, date below **Rev:** National arms, value above, date below; without fineness

Date	Mintage	F	VF	XF	Unc	BU
1973	—	—	—	—	350	—

KM# 49.2 100 DOLLARS
14.5400 g., 0.7500 Gold 0.3506 oz. AGW, 28 mm. **Ruler:** Elizabeth II **Subject:** Independence Day - July 10 **Obv:** Bust of Queen Elizabeth II right with tiara, date below **Rev:** National arms, value above; without date or fineness

Date	Mintage	F	VF	XF	Unc	BU
1973 Proof	—	Value: 350				

KM# 50.1 100 DOLLARS
14.5400 g., 0.5850 Gold 0.2735 oz. AGW, 28 mm. **Ruler:** Elizabeth II **Obv:** Bust of Queen Elizabeth II right with tiara, date below **Rev:** National arms, value above, .585 fineness to left, date to right

Date	Mintage	F	VF	XF	Unc	BU
1973	4,660	—	—	—	275	—
1973 Proof	1,260	Value: 285				

Note: Serial number on reverse

KM# 50.2 100 DOLLARS
14.5400 g., 0.5850 Gold 0.2735 oz. AGW, 28 mm. **Ruler:** Elizabeth II **Obv:** Bust of Queen Elizabeth II right, date below **Rev:** National arms, value above, date and fineness at right, serial number at left

Date	Mintage	F	VF	XF	Unc	BU
1973	—	—	—	—	275	—

KM# 50.3 100 DOLLARS
14.5400 g., 0.5850 Gold 0.2735 oz. AGW, 28 mm. **Ruler:** Elizabeth II **Obv:** Bust of Queen Elizabeth II right with tiara, date below **Rev:** National arms, value above, serial number at left, fineness below, date at right

Date	Mintage	F	VF	XF	Unc	BU
1973	—	—	—	—	275	—

KM# 71 100 DOLLARS
18.0145 g., 0.5000 Gold 0.2896 oz. AGW, 33 mm. **Ruler:** Elizabeth II **Subject:** 1st Anniversary of Independence **Obv:** National arms, date below **Rev:** Two flamingos, value at bottom, date at right

Date	Mintage	F	VF	XF	Unc	BU
1974	4,486	—	—	—	285	—
1974 Proof	4,153	Value: 300				

KM# 72 100 DOLLARS
5.4600 g., 0.9170 Gold 0.1610 oz. AGW, 21 mm. **Ruler:** Elizabeth II **Obv:** Bust of Queen Elizabeth II right with tiara, date below **Rev:** Broken waves behind flamingos' legs, value at bottom

Date	Mintage	F	VF	XF	Unc	BU
1974	29,000	—	—	—	160	—
1975	—	—	—	—	165	—

KM# 73 100 DOLLARS
5.4600 g., 0.9170 Gold 0.1610 oz. AGW, 21 mm. **Ruler:** Elizabeth II **Obv:** Bust of Queen Elizabeth II right with tiara, date below **Rev:** Unbroken waves behind flamingos' legs, value at bottom

Date	Mintage	F	VF	XF	Unc	BU
1974 Proof	17,000	Value: 160				
1975 Proof	—	Value: 165				
1976	—	—	—	—	160	—
1976 Proof	—	Value: 165				
1977	—	—	—	—	165	—
1977 Proof	—	Value: 160				

KM# 74 100 DOLLARS
5.4600 g., 0.9170 Gold 0.1610 oz. AGW, 21 mm. **Ruler:** Elizabeth II **Obv:** Bust of Queen Elizabeth II right with tiara, date below **Rev:** Unbroken waves behind flamingos legs, date at right, value at bottom; .917 fineness in oval

Date	Mintage	F	VF	XF	Unc	BU
1974	—	—	—	—	160	—

KM# 77 100 DOLLARS
18.0145 g., 0.5000 Gold 0.2896 oz. AGW **Ruler:** Elizabeth II **Subject:** 2nd Anniversary of Independence **Obv:** National arms, date below **Rev:** Bahama Amazon Parrot, value at bottom

Date	Mintage	F	VF	XF	Unc	BU
1975	3,694	—	—	—	285	—
1975 Proof	3,145	Value: 300				
1976 Proof	761	Value: 325				
1977 Proof	2,023	Value: 300				

KM# 80   100 DOLLARS
13.6000 g., 0.9630 Gold 0.4211 oz. AGW **Ruler:** Elizabeth II
Subject: 5th Anniversary of Independence **Obv:** National arms,
date below **Rev:** Bust of H.R.H Prince Charles, right, value below

Date	Mintage	F	VF	XF	Unc	BU
1978 Proof	3,275				Value: 420	

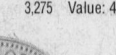

KM# 81   100 DOLLARS
13.6000 g., 0.9630 Gold 0.4211 oz. AGW **Ruler:** Elizabeth II
Subject: 5th Anniversary of Independence **Obv:** National arms,
date below **Rev:** Head of Sir Milo B. Butler, 1/2 left, value at bottom

Date	Mintage	F	VF	XF	Unc	BU
1978 Proof	25,000				Value: 420	

KM# 87   100 DOLLARS
6.4800 g., 0.9000 Gold 0.1875 oz. AGW **Ruler:** Elizabeth II
Subject: Wedding of Prince Charles and Lady Diana **Obv:** Bust
of Queen Elizabeth II right with tiara **Rev:** Conjoined busts of
royal couple left

Date	Mintage	F	VF	XF	Unc	BU
1981 Proof	10,000				Value: 195	

KM# 99   100 DOLLARS
6.4800 g., 0.9000 Gold 0.1875 oz. AGW **Ruler:** Elizabeth II
Subject: 10th Anniversary of Independence **Obv:** National arms,
date below **Rev:** Bust of soldier left within unfurled flag, value at
bottom

Date	Mintage	F	VF	XF	Unc	BU
1983 Proof	400				Value: 220	

KM# 111   100 DOLLARS
6.4800 g., 0.9000 Gold 0.1875 oz. AGW **Ruler:** Elizabeth II
Subject: Columbus' Discovery of America **Obv:** National arms
Rev: Columbus with group of people, date at bottom, value at top

Date	Mintage	F	VF	XF	Unc	BU
1985 Proof	450				Value: 220	

KM# 119   100 DOLLARS
6.4800 g., 0.9000 Gold 0.1875 oz. AGW **Ruler:** Elizabeth II
Obv: Crowned bust of Queen Elizabeth II right **Rev:** Queen
Isabella receiving Christopher Columbus, date below, value at top

Date	Mintage	F	VF	XF	Unc	BU
1987 Proof	849				Value: 200	

KM# 125   100 DOLLARS
6.4800 g., 0.9000 Gold 0.1875 oz. AGW **Ruler:** Elizabeth II
Subject: Columbus Discovering America **Obv:** Bust of Queen
Elizabeth II right **Rev:** Columbus sighting America

Date	Mintage	F	VF	XF	Unc	BU
1988 Proof	854				Value: 200	

KM# 130   100 DOLLARS
6.4800 g., 0.9000 Gold 0.1875 oz. AGW **Ruler:** Elizabeth II **Obv:**
Queen Elizabeth **Rev:** Christopher Columbus, radiant sun and
ocean in background within circle, date below, and at right of circle

Date	Mintage	F	VF	XF	Unc	BU
1989 Proof	Est. 5,000				Value: 195	

KM# 135   100 DOLLARS
6.4800 g., 0.9000 Gold 0.1875 oz. AGW **Ruler:** Elizabeth II
Subject: Discovery of New World **Obv:** Queen Elizabeth II, date
below **Rev:** Bust of Columbus left, value below circle

Date	Mintage	F	VF	XF	Unc	BU
1990	500				250	
1990 Proof	5,000				Value: 190	

KM# 151   100 DOLLARS
6.4800 g., 0.9000 Gold 0.1875 oz. AGW **Ruler:** Elizabeth II
Subject: Discovery of New World **Obv:** Crowned bust of Queen
Elizabeth II right, date below **Rev:** 5 men rowing boat, ships in
background within inner circle, legend above, value below

Date	Mintage	F	VF	XF	Unc	BU
1991	500				250	

KM# 152   100 DOLLARS
6.4800 g., 0.9000 Gold 0.1875 oz. AGW **Ruler:** Elizabeth II
Subject: Discovery of New World **Obv:** Crowned bust of Queen
Elizabeth II right, date below **Rev:** Columbus' ships within circle,
value below circle

Date	Mintage	F	VF	XF	Unc	BU
1992 Proof	Est. 5,000,000				Value: 190	
1992 Matte					Value: 250	

KM# 195   100 DOLLARS
1000.0000 g., 0.9990 Silver 32.117 oz. ASW **Ruler:** Elizabeth II
Subject: Discovery of New World **Obv:** Bust of Queen Elizabeth
II right, date below **Rev:** Columbus' three ships - the Niña, the
Pinta, the Santa Maria, within circle, value below circle

Date	Mintage	F	VF	XF	Unc	BU
1992 Proof	Est. 1,500				Value: 600	

KM# 163   100 DOLLARS
999.9775 g., 0.9990 Silver 32.116 oz. ASW **Ruler:** Elizabeth II
Series: Whales of the World **Obv:** Bust of Queen Elizabeth II
right, date below **Rev:** Blue Whale with baby, within circle, value
below circle

Date	Mintage	F	VF	XF	Unc	BU
1993	750	—	—	—	650	

KM# 184   100 DOLLARS
999.9775 g., 0.9990 Silver 32.116 oz. ASW **Ruler:** Elizabeth II
Series: Whales of the World **Obv:** Bust of Queen Elizabeth II
right, date below **Rev:** Killer Whales in inner circle, value below

Date	Mintage	F	VF	XF	Unc	BU
1994 Proof	750				Value: 650	

KM# 185   100 DOLLARS
999.9775 g., 0.9990 Silver 32.116 oz. ASW **Ruler:** Elizabeth II
Series: Whales of the World **Obv:** Bust of Queen Elizabeth II
right, date below **Rev:** Humpback Whales within inner circle,
value below

Date	Mintage	F	VF	XF	Unc	BU
1995 Proof	750				Value: 900	

KM# 51   150 DOLLARS
8.1900 g., 0.9170 Gold 0.2414 oz. AGW, 24 mm. **Ruler:**
Elizabeth II **Subject:** Independence Day - July 10 **Obv:** Bust of
Queen Elizabeth II right with tiara, date below **Rev:** Spiny Lobster,
value, small date at right

Date	Mintage	F	VF	XF	Unc	BU
1973		—	—	—	240	
1973 Proof	—				Value: 250	

Date	Mintage	F	VF	XF	Unc	BU
1974	7,128	—	—	—	240	—
1974 Proof	4,787	Value: 250				
1975	3,141	—	—	—	240	—
1975 Proof	2,770	Value: 260				
1976 Proof	168	Value: 320				
1977 Proof	327	Value: 275				

KM# 52 150 DOLLARS
8.1900 g., 0.9170 Gold 0.2414 oz. AGW **Ruler:** Elizabeth II
Obv: Bust of Queen Elizabeth II right with tiara, date below **Rev:** Spiny Lobster, value, small date at right

Date	Mintage	F	VF	XF	Unc	BU
1974 Proof	—	Value: 250				

KM# 53 150 DOLLARS
8.1900 g., 0.9170 Gold 0.2414 oz. AGW **Ruler:** Elizabeth II
Obv: Bust of Queen Elizabeth II right with tiara, date below **Rev:** Spiny Lobster, value, small date at right; .917 fineness in oval

Date	Mintage	F	VF	XF	Unc	BU
1974	—	—	—	—	250	—

KM# 54 200 DOLLARS
10.9200 g., 0.9170 Gold 0.3219 oz. AGW, 28 mm. **Ruler:** Elizabeth II **Subject:** Independence Day - July 10 **Obv:** Bust of Queen Elizabeth II right with tiara, date below **Rev:** National arms, value above small date at right

Date	Mintage	F	VF	XF	Unc	BU
1973	—	—	—	—	315	—
1973 Proof	—	Value: 325				
1974	5,528	—	—	—	315	—
1974 Proof	3,587	Value: 325				
1975	1,545	—	—	—	320	—
1975 Proof	1,570	Value: 335				
1976 Proof	168	Value: 375				
1977 Proof	321	Value: 350				

KM# 56 200 DOLLARS
10.9200 g., 0.9170 Gold 0.3219 oz. AGW **Ruler:** Elizabeth II **Obv:** Bust of Queen Elizabeth II right with tiara, date below **Rev:** National arms, value above, small date at right; .917 fineness in oval

Date	Mintage	F	VF	XF	Unc	BU
1974	—	—	—	—	315	—

KM# 57 200 DOLLARS
10.9200 g., 0.9170 Gold 0.3219 oz. AGW **Ruler:** Elizabeth II **Obv:** Bust of Queen Elizabeth II right **Rev:** .916 fineness at left, serial number stamped below arms

Date	Mintage	F	VF	XF	Unc	BU
1974	—	—	—	—	315	—

KM# 58 200 DOLLARS
Gold **Ruler:** Elizabeth II **Obv:** Bust right **Rev:** Without fineness, serial number to left

Date	Mintage	F	VF	XF	Unc	BU
1974	—	—	—	—	—	—
1974 Proof	—	Value: 345				

KM# 83 250 DOLLARS
10.5800 g., 0.9000 Gold 0.3061 oz. AGW **Ruler:** Elizabeth II **Subject:** 250th Anniversary of Parliament **Obv:** Princess Anne's bust 1/2 left in inner circle, value below **Rev:** National arms, date below

Date	Mintage	F	VF	XF	Unc	BU
1979 Proof	1,835	Value: 345				

KM# 117 250 DOLLARS
47.5400 g., 0.9170 Gold 1.4015 oz. AGW **Ruler:** Elizabeth II **Subject:** Commonwealth Games **Obv:** National arms **Rev:** Competitor running left, value at right, logo below

Date	Mintage	F	VF	XF	Unc	BU
1985 Proof	101	Value: 1,350				

KM# 137 250 DOLLARS
47.5400 g., 0.9170 Gold 1.4015 oz. AGW **Ruler:** Elizabeth II **Subject:** Royal Visit **Obv:** Crowned bust of Queen Elizabeth II, right **Rev:** National arms, value below

Date	Mintage	F	VF	XF	Unc	BU
1985 Proof	100	Value: 1,350				

KM# 121 250 DOLLARS
47.5400 g., 0.9170 Gold 1.4015 oz. AGW **Ruler:** Elizabeth II **Obv:** Bust of Queen Elizabeth II right **Rev:** Queen Isabella receiving Columbus, date at bottom, value at top

Date	Mintage	F	VF	XF	Unc	BU
1987 Proof	100	Value: 1,350				

KM# 126 250 DOLLARS
47.5400 g., 0.9170 Gold 1.4015 oz. AGW **Ruler:** Elizabeth II **Subject:** Columbus Discovers the New World **Obv:** Bust of Queen Elizabeth II right **Rev:** Columbus sighting land, date at bottom, value at top

Date	Mintage	F	VF	XF	Unc	BU
1988 Proof	53	Value: 1,450				

KM# 131 250 DOLLARS
47.5400 g., 0.9170 Gold 1.4015 oz. AGW **Ruler:** Elizabeth II **Obv:** Bust of Queen Elizabeth II right **Rev:** Christopher Columbus

Date	Mintage	F	VF	XF	Unc	BU
1989 Proof	Est. 250	Value: 1,350				

KM# 136 250 DOLLARS
47.5400 g., 0.9170 Gold 1.4015 oz. AGW **Ruler:** Elizabeth II **Subject:** Discovery of New World **Obv:** Bust of Queen Elizabeth II right **Rev:** Native American facing right, within circle, value at bottom

Date	Mintage	F	VF	XF	Unc	BU
1990 Proof	500	Value: 1,350				

KM# 175 250 DOLLARS
47.5400 g., 0.9170 Gold 1.4015 oz. AGW **Ruler:** Elizabeth II **Subject:** Discovery of the New World **Rev:** Columbus meeting native Americans, within circle, value below circle

Date	Mintage	F	VF	XF	Unc	BU
1992 Proof	Est. 500	Value: 1,350				

KM# 182 250 DOLLARS
47.5400 g., 0.9170 Gold 1.4015 oz. AGW **Ruler:** Elizabeth II **Subject:** Royal Visit **Note:** Similar to 2 Dollars, KM#158.

Date	Mintage	F	VF	XF	Unc	BU
1994 Proof	100	Value: 1,500				

KM# 210 250 DOLLARS
Gold **Ruler:** Elizabeth II **Subject:** 25th Anniversary College of the Bahamas **Obv:** Crowned bust right **Rev:** College facade

Date	Mintage	F	VF	XF	Unc	BU
1998 Proof	—	—	—	—	—	—

KM# 213 250 DOLLARS
31.1000 g., Gold, 38.61 mm. **Ruler:** Elizabeth II **Subject:** XXVII Summer Olympics - Sydney 2000 **Obv:** National arms **Rev:** "The Golden Girls" - five relay runners **Edge:** Reeded

Date	Mintage	F	VF	XF	Unc	BU
2000 Proof	—	Value: 1,500				

KM# 88 500 DOLLARS
25.9200 g., 0.9000 Gold 0.7500 oz. AGW **Ruler:** Elizabeth II **Subject:** Wedding of Prince Charles and Lady Diana **Obv:** Bust of Queen Elizabeth II right with tiara **Rev:** Conjoined busts of royal couple left

Date	Mintage	F	VF	XF	Unc	BU
1981 Proof	5,000	Value: 725				

KM# 100 1000 DOLLARS
41.4700 g., 0.9000 Gold 1.1999 oz. AGW **Ruler:** Elizabeth II
Subject: America's Cup Challenge **Obv:** Bust right with tiara,
date below **Rev:** Sailboat, value at left

Date	Mintage	F	VF	XF	Unc	BU
1983 Proof	300	Value: 1,200				

KM# 75 2500 DOLLARS
407.2600 g., 0.9170 Gold 12.006 oz. AGW, 72 mm. **Ruler:**
Elizabeth II **Obv:** National arms **Rev:** Two flamingos, value
above, date below **Note:** Illustration reduced.

Date	Mintage	F	VF	XF	Unc	BU
1974 Proof	204	Value: 11,500				
1977 Proof	168	Value: 12,000				

KM# 101 2500 DOLLARS
407.2600 g., 0.9170 Gold 12.006 oz. AGW, 72 mm. **Ruler:**
Elizabeth II **Subject:** 10th Anniversary of Independence **Obv:** Bust
right **Rev:** National arms, value below **Note:** Illustration reduced.

Date	Mintage	F	VF	XF	Unc	BU
1983 Proof	55	Value: 12,500				

KM# 112 2500 DOLLARS
407.2600 g., 0.9170 Gold 12.006 oz. AGW, 72 mm. **Ruler:**
Elizabeth II **Subject:** Columbus' Discovery of America **Obv:** Bust
of Queen Elizabeth II right **Rev:** Columbus with crew claiming land
for Spain, planting flag, date below **Note:** Illustration reduced.

Date	Mintage	F	VF	XF	Unc	BU
1985 Proof	37	Value: 13,000				

KM# 116 2500 DOLLARS
407.2600 g., 0.9170 Gold 12.006 oz. AGW, 72 mm. **Ruler:**
Elizabeth II **Rev:** Kneeling Columbus and Queen Isabella, date
at bottom

Date	Mintage	F	VF	XF	Unc	BU
1987 Proof	20	Value: 13,500				

KM# 122 2500 DOLLARS
407.2600 g., 0.9170 Gold 12.006 oz. AGW **Ruler:** Elizabeth II
Obv: Bust of Queen Elizabeth II right **Rev:** Columbus sighting
"New World"

Date	Mintage	F	VF	XF	Unc	BU
1988 Proof	32	Value: 13,000				

KM# 216 2500 DOLLARS
407.2680 g., 0.9167 Gold 12.002 oz. AGW **Ruler:** Elizabeth II
Subject: Millennium **Obv:** Crowned bust right **Rev:** Two
flamingos standing facing each other, sunrise in backgound

Date	Mintage	F	VF	XF	Unc	BU
2000 Proof	—	Value: 11,500				

MINT SETS

KM#	Date	Mintage	Identification	Issue Price	Mkt Val
MS1	1966 (9)	75,050	KM#2-10	16.00	18.00
MS2	1966 (8)	500,000	KM#2-8	5.25	9.00
MS3	1967 (4)	1,200	KM#11-14	180	1,950
MS4	1969	26,221	KM#2-10	20.25	20.00
MS5	1970 (9)	25,135	KM#3-10, 15	20.25	25.00
MS6	1971 (9)	12,895	KM#16-24	20.25	25.00
MS7	1971 (4)	6,800	KM#25, 27, 29, 31	185	1,950
MS8	1972 (9)	10,128	KM#16-23, 33	22.75	25.00
MS9	1972 (4)	2,250	KM#34-37	185	1,500
MS10	1973 (9)	9,853	KM#16-23, 33	23.75	30.00
MS11	1973 (4)	4,660	KM#40, 43, 47, 49.1	—	575
MS12	1973 (2)	—	KM#40, 43	—	100
MS13	1974 (9)	11,004	KM#59-67	22.50	32.00
MS14	1974 (4)	5,528	KM#51, 54, 69, 72	—	700
MS15	1974 (2)	—	KM#68, 71	—	275
MS16	1975 (9)	3,845	KM#59-67	27.00	35.00
MS17	1975 (4)	1,545	KM#51, 54, 69, 72	—	725
MS18	1976 (9)	1,453	KM#59-67	27.00	40.00
MS19	1977 (9)	731	KM#59-67	27.00	95.00
MS20	1978 (9)	767	KM#59-67	27.00	75.00
MS21	1989 (7)	—	KM#59a, 60-64, 65b	—	30.00
MS22	1991 (7)	5,000	KM#59a, 60-64, 65b	—	30.00
MS23	1992 (7)	—	KM#59a, 60-64, 65b	24.00	30.00

PROOF SETS

KM#	Date	Mintage	Identification	Issue Price	Mkt Val
PS1	1967 (4)	850	KM#11-14	252	2,000
PS2	1969 (9)	10,381	KM#2-10	35.00	30.00
PS3	1970 (9)	22,827	KM#3-10, 15	35.00	30.00
PS4	1971 (9)	30,507	KM#16-24	35.00	30.00
PS5A	1971 (4)	1,250	KM#25, 27, 29, 31	298	2,000
PS5B	1971 (4)	—	KM#26, 28, 30, 32.1	—	1,925
PS6	1972 (9)	34,789	KM#16-23, 33	35.00	30.00
PS7	1972 (4)	1,250	KM#34-37	565	1,575
PS8	1973 (9)	34,815	KM#16-23, 33	35.00	35.00
PS9	1973 (4)	1,260	KM#41, 44, 46, 50	402	500
PS10	1974 (9)	93,776	KM#59-63, 64a-67a	45.00	35.00
PS11	1974 (4)	3,587	KM#51, 54, 69, 73	1,000	750
PS12	1975 (9)	29,095	KM#59-63, 64a-67a	59.00	40.00
PS13	1975 (4)	1,570	KM#51, 54, 69, 73	1,000	775
PS14	1976 (9)	22,570	KM#59-63, 64a-67a	59.00	42.50
PS15	1976 (4)	—	KM#51, 54, 69, 73	1,000	925
PS16	1977 (9)	10,812	KM#59-63, 64a-67a	59.00	50.00
PS17	1977 (4)	—	KM#51, 54, 69, 73	—	875
PS18	1978 (9)	6,931	KM#59-63, 64a-67a	59.00	55.00
PS19	1979 (9)	2,053	KM#59-63, 64a-67a	115	75.00
PS20	1979 (2)	—	KM#82-83	445	325
PS21	1980 (9)	2,084	KM#59-63, 64a-67a	145	75.00
PS22	1981 (9)	1,980	KM#59-64, 65b-67b	62.00	60.00
PS23	1982 (9)	—	KM#59-64, 89-91	67.00	75.00
PS24	1983 (9)	1,009	KM#59-64, 93-95	67.00	75.00
PS25	1984 (9)	7,500	KM#59-64, 104-106	72.00	60.00
PS26	1985 (9)	1,576	KM#59-64, 104, 105, 107	—	65.00
PS27	1989 (9)	2,000	KM#59a, 60-64, 65b, 66c, 132	107	100
PS28	1991/92 (12)	25,000	KM#139-150	425	325
PS29	1992 (3)	750	KM#192-194 + gold-plated silver ingot	—	350

BAHRAIN

The State of Bahrain, a group of islands in the Persian Gulf
off Saudi Arabia, has an area of 268 sq. mi. (622 sq. km.) and a
population of 618,000. Capital: Manama. Prior to the depression
of the 1930's, the economy was based on pearl fishing. Petroleum
and aluminum industries and transit trade are the vital factors in
the economy today.

The Portuguese occupied the islands in 1507 but were driven
out in 1602 by Arab subjects of Persia. They in turn were ejected
by Arabs of the Ataiba tribe from the Arabian mainland who have
maintained possession up to the present time. The ruling sheikh
of Bahrain entered into relations with Great Britain in 1805 and
concluded a binding treaty of protection in 1861. In 1968 Great
Britain decided to terminate treaty relations with the Persian Gulf
sheikhdoms. Unable to agree on terms of union with the other
sheikhdoms, Bahrain decided to seek independence as a separate entity and became fully independent on August 14, 1971.

Bahrain took part in the Arab oil embargo against the U.S.
and other nations. The government bought controlling interest in
the oil industry in 1975.

The coinage of the State of Bahrain was struck at the Royal
Mint, London, England.

RULERS

Al Khalifa Dynasty
Isa Bin Ali, 1869-1932
Hamad Bin Isa, 1932-1942
Salman Bin Hamad, 1942-1961
Isa Bin Salman, 1961-1999
Hamed Bin Isa, 1999-

MINT MARKS

بحرين

Bahrain

البحرين

al-Bahrain = of the two seas

MONETARY SYSTEM

Falus, Fulus	Fals, Fils	Falsan

1000 Fils = 1 Dinar

KINGDOM

STANDARD COINAGE

KM# 1 FILS
Bronze, 1.5 mm. **Obv:** Palm tree within inner circle
Rev: Denomination

Date	Mintage	F	VF	XF	Unc	BU
AH1385-1965	1,500,000	—	0.10	0.20	0.40	0.60
AH1385-1965 Proof	12,000	Value: 1.00				
AH1386-1966	1,500,000	—	0.10	0.20	0.40	0.60
AH1386-1966 Proof	—	Value: 2.00				

KM# 1a FILS
1.5000 g., 0.9250 Silver 0.0446 oz. ASW, 1.5 mm. **Obv:** Palm tree within inner circle **Rev:** Denomination

Date	Mintage	F	VF	XF	Unc	BU
AH1403-1983 Proof	Est. 15,000	Value: 4.00				

KM# 2 5 FILS
2.0000 g., Bronze, 18.5 mm. **Obv:** Palm tree within inner circle **Rev:** Denomination

Date	Mintage	F	VF	XF	Unc	BU
AH1385-1965	8,000,000	—	0.10	0.20	0.40	0.60
AH1385-1965 Proof	12,000	Value: 1.00				

KM# 2a 5 FILS
2.0000 g., 0.9250 Silver 0.0595 oz. ASW, 18.5 mm. **Obv:** Palm tree within inner circle **Rev:** Denomination

Date	Mintage	F	VF	XF	Unc	BU
AH1403-1983 Proof	Est. 15,000	Value: 4.00				

KM# 16 5 FILS
2.5000 g., Brass, 18.98 mm. **Obv:** Palm tree within inner circle **Obv. Leg.:** STATE OF BAHRAIN **Rev:** Numeric denomination back of boxed denomination within circle, chain border

Date	Mintage	F	VF	XF	Unc	BU
AH1412-1991	—	—	—	—	0.50	0.75
AH1412-1992	—	—	—	—	0.50	0.75

KM# 3 10 FILS
4.7500 g., Bronze, 23.5 mm. **Obv:** Palm tree within inner circle **Rev:** Denomination

Date	Mintage	F	VF	XF	Unc	BU
AH1385-1965	8,500,000	—	0.10	0.25	0.50	0.75
AH1385-1965 Proof	12,000	Value: 1.50				

KM# 3a 10 FILS
4.7500 g., 0.9250 Silver 0.1413 oz. ASW, 23.5 mm. **Obv:** Palm tree within inner circle **Rev:** Denomination

Date	Mintage	F	VF	XF	Unc	BU
AH1403-1983 Proof	Est. 15,000	Value: 5.00				

KM# 17 10 FILS
3.4500 g., Brass, 19.22 mm. **Obv:** Palm tree within inner circle **Rev:** Numeric denomination back of boxed denomination within circle, chain surrounds **Edge:** Plain

Date	Mintage	F	VF	XF	Unc	BU
AH1412-1991	—	—	—	—	0.75	1.00
AH1412-1992	—	—	—	—	0.75	1.00
AH1420-2000	—	—	—	—	0.75	1.00

KM# 4 25 FILS
1.7500 g., Copper-Nickel, 16.5 mm. **Obv:** Palm tree within inner circle **Rev:** Denomination **Edge:** Reeded

Date	Mintage	F	VF	XF	Unc	BU
AH1385-1965	11,250,000	—	0.20	0.35	0.75	1.25
AH1385-1965 Proof	12,000	Value: 2.00				

KM# 4a 25 FILS
1.7500 g., 0.9250 Silver 0.0520 oz. ASW, 16.5 mm. **Obv:** Palm tree within inner circle **Rev:** Denomination **Edge:** Reeded

Date	Mintage	F	VF	XF	Unc	BU
AH1403-1983 Proof	Est. 15,000	Value: 5.00				

KM# 18 25 FILS
Copper-Nickel **Obv:** Ancient painting within circle **Rev:** Numeric denomination back of boxed denomination within circle, chain surrounds

Date	Mintage	F	VF	XF	Unc	BU
AH1412-1992	—	—	—	—	1.25	1.50
AH1420-2000	—	—	—	—	1.25	1.50

KM# 5 50 FILS
3.1000 g., Copper-Nickel, 20 mm. **Obv:** Palm tree within inner circle **Rev:** Denomination

Date	Mintage	F	VF	XF	Unc	BU
AH1385-1965	6,909,000	—	0.25	0.55	1.25	1.65
AH1385-1965 Proof	12,000	Value: 2.50				

KM# 5a 50 FILS
3.1000 g., 0.9250 Silver 0.0922 oz. ASW, 20 mm. **Obv:** Palm tree within inner circle **Rev:** Denomination

Date	Mintage	F	VF	XF	Unc	BU
AH1403-1983 Proof	Est. 15,000	Value: 6.00				

KM# 19 50 FILS
4.4600 g., Copper-Nickel **Obv:** Stylized sailboat **Rev:** Numeric denomination back of boxed denomination within circle, chain surrounds

Date	Mintage	F	VF	XF	Unc	BU
AH1412-1992	—	—	—	—	1.50	1.75
AH1420-2000	—	—	—	—	1.50	1.75

KM# 6 100 FILS
6.5000 g., Copper-Nickel, 25 mm. **Obv:** Palm tree within inner circle **Rev:** Denomination **Edge:** Reeded

Date	Mintage	F	VF	XF	Unc	BU
AH1385-1965	8,300,000	—	0.35	0.75	1.50	2.00
AH1385-1965 Proof	12,000	Value: 3.50				

KM# 6a 100 FILS
6.5000 g., 0.9250 Silver 0.1933 oz. ASW, 25 mm. **Obv:** Palm tree within inner circle **Rev:** Denomination **Edge:** Reeded

Date	Mintage	F	VF	XF	Unc	BU
AH1403-1983 Proof	Est. 15,000	Value: 7.00				

KM# 20 100 FILS
5.9600 g., Bi-Metallic Copper-Nickel center in Brass ring, 24 mm. **Obv:** Coat of arms within circle, dates at either side **Obv. Leg.:** STATE OF BAHRAIN **Rev:** Numeric denomination back of boxed denomination within circle, chain surrounds **Edge:** Reeded

Date	Mintage	F	VF	XF	Unc	BU
AH1412-1991	—	—	—	—	3.50	4.00
AH1412-1992	—	—	—	—	3.50	4.00
AH1415-1994	—	—	—	—	3.50	4.00
AH1416-1995	—	—	—	—	3.50	4.00
AH1417-1997	—	—	—	—	3.50	4.00
AH1420-2000	—	—	—	—	3.50	4.00

KM# 7 250 FILS
Copper-Nickel **Series:** F.A.O. **Obv:** Sailboat, palm tree at right **Rev:** F.A.O. logo divided by grain sprig

Date	Mintage	F	VF	XF	Unc	BU
AH1389-1969	50,000	—	1.50	2.50	5.00	6.50
AH1389-1969 Proof	—	Value: 8.00				
AH1403-1983	3,000	—	1.75	3.50	10.00	12.50

KM# 7a 250 FILS
15.0000 g., 0.9250 Silver 0.4461 oz. ASW **Series:** F.A.O. **Obv:** Sailboat, palm tree at left **Rev:** F.A.O. logo divided by grain sprig

Date	Mintage	F	VF	XF	Unc	BU
AH1403-1983 Proof	Est. 15,000	Value: 14.50				

KM# 8 500 FILS
18.3000 g., 0.8000 Silver 0.4707 oz. ASW **Ruler:** Isa Bin **Obv:** Bust left **Rev:** Opening of Isa Town, crowned arms at center of octagon, dates appear in western and arabic script: 1368-1968

Date	Mintage	F	VF	XF	Unc	BU
ND	50,000	—	9.00	10.00	15.00	18.00
ND Proof	—	Value: 20.00				

KM# 8a 500 FILS
18.0600 g., 0.9250 Silver 0.5371 oz. ASW **Ruler:** Isa Bin Salman **Obv:** Bust left **Rev:** Opening of Isa Town, crowned arms at center of octagon

Date	Mintage	F	VF	XF	Unc	BU
AH1403-1983 Proof	Est. 15,000	Value: 35.00				

KM# 22 500 FILS
Bi-Metallic Brass center in Copper-Nickel ring, 27 mm. **Ruler:** Hamed Bin Isa **Obv:** Monument and inscription **Obv. Insc.:** STATE OF BAHRAIN **Rev:** Denomination **Edge:** Reeded **Note:** Total weight: 9.05 grams.

Date	Mintage	F	VF	XF	Unc	BU
2000	—	—	—	—	6.00	7.50

KM# 13 5 DINARS
19.4400 g., 0.9250 Silver 0.5781 oz. ASW **Ruler:** Isa Bin Salman **Obv:** Bust left **Rev:** Goitered Gazelle running left, World Wildlife Fund

Date	Mintage	F	VF	XF	Unc	BU
AH1406-1986 Proof	Est. 25,000	Value: 40.00				

KM# 14 5 DINARS
19.4400 g., 0.9250 Silver 0.5781 oz. ASW **Ruler:** Isa Bin Salman **Subject:** Save The Children **Obv:** Bust left **Rev:** Children playing

Date	Mintage	F	VF	XF	Unc	BU
AH1410-1990 Proof	Est. 20,000	Value: 36.50				

KM# 21 5 DINARS
28.2300 g., 0.9250 Silver 0.8395 oz. ASW **Ruler:** Isa Bin Salman **Subject:** 50th Anniversary - United Nations **Obv:** Bust left **Rev:** UN building, logo

Date	Mintage	F	VF	XF	Unc	BU
ND(1995) Proof	—	Value: 32.50				

KM# 23 5 DINARS
19.4000 g., 0.9250 Silver 0.5769 oz. ASW, 35.9 mm. **Ruler:** Isa Bin Salman **Subject:** UNICEF **Obv:** Bust left **Rev:** Children within circle **Edge:** Reeded

Date	Mintage	F	VF	XF	Unc	BU
AH1419-1998 Proof	—	Value: 32.50				

KM# 11 50 DINARS
15.9800 g., 0.9170 Gold 0.4711 oz. AGW **Ruler:** Isa Bin Salman **Subject:** 50th Anniversary of Bahrain Monetary Agency

Date	Mintage	F	VF	XF	Unc	BU
AH1398-1978 Proof	5,000	Value: 500				

KM# 12 100 DINARS
31.9600 g., 0.9170 Gold 0.9422 oz. AGW **Ruler:** Isa Bin Salman **Subject:** 50th Anniversary of Bahrain Monetary Agency **Obv:** Bust left **Rev:** Coat of arms divides dates

Date	Mintage	F	VF	XF	Unc	BU
AH1398-1978 Proof	5,000	Value: 950				

MINT SETS

KM#	Date	Mintage	Identification	Issue Price	Mkt Val
MS1	1992 (5)	—	KM#16-20	—	10.00

PROOF SETS

KM#	Date	Mintage	Identification	Issue Price	Mkt Val
PS1	1965 (7)	12,000	KM#1-6, 8	—	30.00
PS2	1965, 1968, 1969 (8)	20,000	KM#1-6 1965; KM7 1969; KM8 1968	32.00	35.00
PS3	1983 (8)	15,000	KM#1a-8a	99.00	80.00

BANGLADESH

The Peoples Republic of Bangladesh (formerly East Pakistan), a parliamentary democracy located on the Bay of Bengal bordered by India and Burma, has an area of 55,598 sq. mi. (143,998 sq. km.) and a population of 128.1 million. Capital: Dhaka. The economy is predominantly agricultural. Jute products, jute and tea are exported.

British rule over the vast Indian sub-continent ended in 1947 when British India attained independence and was partitioned into the two successor states of India and Pakistan. Pakistan consisted of East and West Pakistan, two areas united by the Moslem religion but separated by culture and 1,000 miles of Indian territory. Restive under the de facto rule of the militant but fewer West Pakistanis, the East Pakistanis unsuccessfully demanded greater economic benefits and political reforms. The inability of the leaders of East and West Pakistan to resolve a political breakdown occasioned by the East Pakistan success in the general elections of 1970 precipitated massive civil disobedience in East Pakistan which West Pakistan sought to suppress militarily. East Pakistan seceded from Pakistan, March 26, 1971, and with the support of India declared an independent Peoples Republic of Bangladesh.

Bangladesh is a member of the Commonwealth of Nations. The president is the Head of State and the Government.

MONETARY SYSTEM
100 Poisha = 1 Taka

DATING
Christian era using Bengali numerals.

PEOPLES REPUBLIC
STANDARD COINAGE

KM# 5 POISHA
0.5300 g., Aluminum, 15.91 mm. **Obv:** National emblem, Shapla (water lily) **Rev:** Vallue within decorative circle **Edge:** Plain

Date	Mintage	F	VF	XF	Unc	BU
1974	300,000,000	—	—	0.10	0.15	—

KM# 1 5 POISHA
Aluminum **Obv:** National emblem, Shapla (water lily) **Rev:** Value and symbol within dentiled circle

Date	Mintage	F	VF	XF	Unc	BU
1973	Est. 47,088,000	—	—	0.10	0.20	—
1974	—	—	—	0.10	0.20	—

KM# 6 5 POISHA
1.4000 g., Aluminum **Series:** F.A.O. **Obv:** National emblem, Shapla (water lily) **Rev:** Value and sumbol within dentiled circle

Date	Mintage	F	VF	XF	Unc	BU
1974	5,000,000	—	—	0.10	0.20	—
1975	3,000,000	—	—	0.10	0.20	—
1976	3,000,000	—	—	0.10	0.20	—
1977	—	—	—	0.10	0.20	—

KM# 10 5 POISHA
1.4300 g., Aluminum **Series:** F.A.O. **Obv:** National emblem, Shapla (water lily) **Rev:** Value at right, 2/3 dentiled circle at left, symbol wihin **Edge:** Plain

Date	Mintage	F	VF	XF	Unc	BU
1977	90,000,000	—	—	0.10	0.15	—
1978	52,432,000	—	—	0.10	0.25	—
1979	120,096,000	—	—	0.10	0.15	—
1980	127,008,000	—	—	0.10	0.15	—
1981	72,992,000	—	—	0.10	0.15	—
1994	—	—	—	0.10	0.15	—

KM# 2 10 POISHA
1.9600 g., Aluminum, 24 mm. **Obv:** National emblem, Shapla (water lily) **Rev:** Large leaf at center, stem divides value

Date	Mintage	F	VF	XF	Unc	BU
1973	Est. 21,500,000	—	—	0.10	0.35	—
1974	—	—	—	0.10	0.35	—

KM# 7 10 POISHA
2.0000 g., Aluminum, 24 mm. **Series:** F.A.O. **Obv:** National emblem, Shapla (water lily) **Rev:** Value at bottom, vehicle and plant at center

Date	Mintage	F	VF	XF	Unc	BU
1974	5,000,000	—	—	0.15	0.35	—
1975	4,000,000	—	—	0.15	0.35	—
1976	4,000,000	—	—	0.15	0.35	—
1977	4,000,000	—	—	0.15	0.35	—
1978	141,744,000	—	—	0.15	0.30	—
1979	—	—	—	0.15	0.40	—

KM# 11.1   10 POISHA
1.9800 g., Aluminum, 24 mm.   **Series:** F.A.O. **Obv:** National emblem, Shapla (water lily) **Rev:** Family above value

Date	Mintage	F	VF	XF	Unc	BU
1977	48,000,000	—	—	0.15	0.30	—
1978	77,518,000	—	—	0.15	0.30	—
1979	170,112,000	—	—	0.15	0.30	—
1980	200,000,000	—	—	0.15	0.30	—

KM# 11.2   10 POISHA
1.3900 g., Aluminum, 22 mm.   **Series:** F.A.O. **Obv:** National emblem, Shapla (water lily) within wreath above water **Rev:** Family, value below **Note:** Reduced size.

Date	Mintage	F	VF	XF	Unc	BU
1981	—	—	—	0.25	0.50	—
1983	142,848,000	—	—	0.15	0.30	—
1984	57,152,000	—	—	0.15	0.30	—
1994	—	—	—	0.15	0.30	—

KM# 3   25 POISHA
2.6800 g., Steel, 19 mm.   **Obv:** National emblem, Shapla (water lily) **Rev:** Rohu, right, value below

Date	Mintage	F	VF	XF	Unc	BU
1973	Est. 25,072,000	—	—	0.25	0.75	1.00

KM# 8   25 POISHA
2.6600 g., Steel, 19 mm.   **Series:** F.A.O. **Obv:** National emblem, Shapla (water lily) **Rev:** Carp, egg, banana, squash, value at bottom

Date	Mintage	F	VF	XF	Unc	BU
1974	5,000,000	—	—	0.20	0.50	—
1975	6,000,000	—	—	0.20	0.50	—
1976	6,000,000	—	—	0.20	0.50	—
1977	51,300,000	—	—	0.15	0.50	—
1978	66,750,000	—	—	0.15	0.50	—
1979	—	—	—	0.15	0.50	—

KM# 12   25 POISHA
2.6400 g., Steel, 19 mm.   **Obv:** National emblem, Shapla (water lily) **Rev:** Tiger head left within inner circle **Edge:** Reeded

Date	Mintage	F	VF	XF	Unc	BU
1977	45,300,000	—	—	0.20	0.75	—
1978	66,750,000	—	—	0.20	0.75	—
1979	56,704,000	—	—	0.20	0.75	—
1980	228,992,000	—	—	0.20	0.75	—
1981	45,072,000	—	—	0.20	0.75	—
1983	96,128,000	—	—	0.20	0.75	—
1984	203,872,000	—	—	0.20	0.75	—
1991	50,002,000	—	—	0.20	0.75	—
1994	—	—	—	0.20	0.75	—

KM# 4   50 POISHA
Steel   **Obv:** National emblem, Shapla (water lily) **Rev:** Bird left, value below

Date	Mintage	F	VF	XF	Unc	BU
1973	18,000,000	—	0.25	0.75	2.50	3.50

KM# 13   50 POISHA
1.4500 g., Steel, 20.33 mm.   **Series:** F.A.O. **Obv:** National emblem, Shapla (water lily) **Rev:** Symbols within inner ring, value at bottom **Edge:** Plain

Date	Mintage	F	VF	XF	Unc	BU
1977	12,700,000	—	—	0.20	0.75	—
1978	37,300,000	—	—	0.20	0.75	—
1979	2,208,000	—	—	0.20	0.75	—
1980	124,512,000	—	—	0.20	0.50	—
1981	36,680,000	—	—	0.20	0.75	—
1983	31,392,000	—	—	0.20	0.75	—
1984	168,608,000	—	—	0.20	0.50	—
1994	—	—	—	0.20	0.50	—

KM# 9   TAKA
Copper-Nickel, 26 mm.   **Series:** F.A.O. **Obv:** National emblem, Shapla (water lily) **Rev:** Stylized family, value at right **Note:** Prev. KM # 9.1.

Date	Mintage	F	VF	XF	Unc	BU
1975	4,000,000	—	0.15	0.45	1.00	—
1976	—	—	0.15	0.45	1.00	—
1977	—	—	0.15	0.45	1.00	—

KM# 17   TAKA
31.3500 g., 0.9250 Silver 0.9323 oz. ASW   **Subject:** 20th Victory Day **Obv:** Seven portraits within circle **Rev:** National memorial, value divides date below

Date	Mintage	F	VF	XF	Unc	BU
1991 Proof	—	Value: 35.00				

KM# 9a   TAKA
6.1000 g., Steel, 25 mm.   **Obv:** National emblem, Shapla (water lily) **Rev:** Stylized family, value at right **Note:** Prev. KM # 9.2.

Date	Mintage	F	VF	XF	Unc	BU
1992	—	—	0.15	0.45	1.00	—
1993	—	—	0.15	0.45	1.00	—
1995	—	—	0.15	0.45	1.00	—

KM# 9b   TAKA
3.9800 g., Brass **Obv:** National emblem, Shapla (water lily) **Rev:** Stylized family, value at right **Edge:** Reeded **Note:** Prev. KM # 9.3.

Date	Mintage	F	VF	XF	Unc	BU
1996	—	—	0.20	0.55	1.35	1.80
1997	—	—	0.20	0.55	1.35	1.80
1998	—	—	0.20	0.50	1.35	1.80
1999	—	—	0.20	0.55	1.35	1.80

KM# 14   TAKA
31.3500 g., 0.9250 Silver 0.9323 oz. ASW   **Subject:** Barcelona 1992 - 25th Summer Olympics **Obv:** National emblem, Shapla (water lily) **Rev:** Torch runners

Date	Mintage	F	VF	XF	Unc	BU
1992 Proof	Est. 40,000	Value: 32.50				

KM# 15   TAKA
31.3500 g., 0.9250 Silver 0.9323 oz. ASW   **Subject:** Endangered Wildlife **Obv:** National emblem, Shapla (water lily) **Rev:** Deer

Date	Mintage	F	VF	XF	Unc	BU
1993 Proof	Est. 15,000	Value: 40.00				

KM# 16   TAKA
31.3500 g., 0.9250 Silver 0.9323 oz. ASW   **Subject:** World Cup Soccer, 1994 **Obv:** National emblem, Shapla (water lily)

Date	Mintage	F	VF	XF	Unc	BU
1993 Proof	40,000	Value: 35.00				

KM# 18.1   5 TAKA
7.8700 g., Steel, 27.7 mm.   **Obv:** Shapla flower on waves within wreath **Rev:** Bridge, value below

Date	Mintage	F	VF	XF	Unc	BU
1994	—	—	—	—	1.75	2.50
1996	—	—	—	—	1.75	2.50

KM# 18.2   5 TAKA
8.1700 g., Steel, 26.8 mm.   **Obv:** Shapla flower on waves within wreath, thicker design **Rev:** Bridge, value, denomination at bottom

Date	Mintage	F	VF	XF	Unc	BU
1996	—	—	—	—	1.50	3.00
1998	—	—	—	—	1.50	3.00

KM# 19   10 TAKA
31.4700 g., 0.9250 Silver 0.9359 oz. ASW   **Subject:** 25th Anniversary of Independence **Obv:** National monument in Savar **Rev:** Bust of Minister/President Mujibur Rahman, 1972-1975 left

Date	Mintage	F	VF	XF	Unc	BU
1996 Proof	—	Value: 75.00				

KM# 20 10 TAKA
31.4700 g., 0.9250 Silver 0.9359 oz. ASW **Subject:** 25th Anniversary Bangladesh Bank **Obv:** National arms **Rev:** Bangladesh Bank building in Dhaka

Date	Mintage	F	VF	XF	Unc	BU
ND(1996) Proof	— Value: 75.00					

KM# 21 10 TAKA
Silver **Subject:** Opening of Bangabandhu Jamuna bridge **Obv:** Statues of three liberation fighters **Rev:** Bridge

Date	Mintage	F	VF	XF	Unc	BU
1998 Proof	— Value: 65.00					

KM# 22 20 TAKA
25.0000 g., 0.9990 Silver 0.8029 oz. ASW **Subject:** Opening of Bangabandhu Lamuna bridge **Obv:** Bust of Mujibur Rahman facing **Rev:** Bridge

Date	Mintage	F	VF	XF	Unc	BU
1998 Proof	— Value: 90.00					

KM# 23 20 TAKA
10.0000 g., 0.9167 Gold 0.2947 oz. AGW **Subject:** International Mother Language **Obv:** Central bank logo **Rev:** Shaheed Minar memorial

Date	Mintage	F	VF	XF	Unc	BU
2000 Proof	— Value: 330					

BARBADOS

DOMINICA · MARTINIQUE · ST. LUCIA · ST. VINCENT AND THE GRENADINES · GRENADA

Barbados, a Constitutional Monarchy within the Commonwealth of Nations, is located in the Windward Islands of the West Indies east of St. Vincent. The coral island has an area of 166 sq. mi. (430 sq. km.) and a population of 269,000. Capital: Bridgetown. The economy is based on sugar and tourism. Sugar, petroleum products, molasses, and rum are exported.

Barbados was named by the Portuguese who achieved the first landing on the island in 1563. British sailors landed at the site of present-day Holetown in 1624. Barbados was under uninterrupted British control from the time of the first British settlement in 1627 until it obtained independence on Nov. 30, 1966. It is a member of the Commonwealth of Nations. Elizabeth II is Head of State as Queen of Barbados.

Unmarked side cut pieces of Spanish and Spanish Colonial 1, 2 and 8 reales were the principal coinage medium of 18th-century Barbados. The "Neptune" tokens issued by Sir Phillip Gibbs, a local plantation owner, circulated freely but were never established as legal coinage. The coinage and banknotes of the British Caribbean Territories (Eastern Group) were employed prior to 1973 when Barbados issued a decimal coinage.

RULER
British, until 1966

MINT MARKS
FM - Franklin Mint, U.S.A.*
None - Royal Mint
*NOTE: From 1973-1985 the Franklin Mint produced coinage in up to 3 different qualities. Qualities of issue are designated in ( ) after each date and are defined as follows:
(M) MATTE - Normal circulation strike or a dull finish produced by sandblasting special uncirculated (polish finish) or proof quality dies.
(U) SPECIAL UNCIRCULATED - Polished or proof-like in appearance without any frosted features.
(P) PROOF - The highest quality obtainable having mirror-like fields and frosted features.

MONETARY SYSTEM
100 Cents = 1 Dollar

COMMONWEALTH
DECIMAL COINAGE

KM# 10 CENT
3.1400 g., Bronze, 19 mm. **Obv:** National arms **Rev:** Trident above value **Edge:** Plain

Date	Mintage	F	VF	XF	Unc	BU
1973	5,000,000	—	—	0.10	0.25	0.75
1973FM (M)	7,500	—	—	0.50	1.00	3.00
1973FM (P)	97,000	Value: 1.00				
1974FM (M)	8,708	—	—	0.50	1.00	3.00
1974FM (P)	36,000	Value: 1.00				
1975FM (M)	5,000	—	—	0.35	0.75	2.25
1975FM (U)	1,360	—	—	0.50	1.00	3.00
1975FM (P)	20,000	Value: 1.00				
1977FM (M)	2,102	—	—	—	0.75	1.50
1977FM (U)	468	—	—	1.50	3.00	6.00
1977FM (P)	5,014	Value: 1.00				
1978	4,807,000	—	—	0.10	0.25	0.75
1978FM (M)	2,000	—	—	0.50	1.00	3.00
1978FM (U)	2,517	—	—	1.50	3.00	6.00
1978FM (P)	4,436	Value: 1.50				
1979	5,606,000	—	—	0.10	0.25	0.75
1979FM (M)	1,500	—	—	—	1.00	3.00
1979FM (U)	523	—	—	1.50	3.00	6.00
1979FM (P)	4,126	Value: 1.50				
1980	14,400,000	—	—	0.10	0.25	0.75
1980FM (M)	1,500	—	—	0.50	1.00	3.00
1980FM (U)	649	—	—	1.50	3.00	6.00
1980FM (P)	2,111	Value: 3.00				
1981	10,160,000	—	—	0.10	0.25	0.75
1981FM (M)	1,500	—	—	—	1.00	3.00
1981FM (U)	327	—	—	1.50	3.00	6.00
1981FM (P)	943	Value: 4.50				
1982	5,040,000	—	—	0.10	0.25	0.75
1982FM (M)	1,500	—	—	—	1.25	3.75
1982FM (P)	843	Value: 4.50				
1983FM (M)	1,500	—	—	—	1.00	4.50
1983FM (U)	—	—	—	—	1.25	3.75
1983FM (P)	459	Value: 4.50				
1984	5,008,000	—	—	0.10	0.25	0.75
1984FM (M)	868	—	—	—	1.25	4.50
1984FM (P)	—	Value: 3.00				
1985	—	—	—	0.10	0.25	0.75
1986	—	—	—	0.10	0.25	0.75
1987	10,000,000	—	—	0.10	0.25	0.75
1988	12,136,000	—	—	0.10	0.25	0.75
1989	—	—	—	0.10	0.25	0.75
1990	—	—	—	0.10	0.25	0.75
1991	—	—	—	0.10	0.25	0.75

KM# 10a CENT
2.5000 g., Copper Plated Zinc, 19 mm. **Obv:** National arms **Rev:** Broken trident above value **Edge:** Plain

Date	Mintage	F	VF	XF	Unc	BU
1992	—	—	—	0.10	0.25	0.75
1993	—	—	—	0.10	0.25	0.75
1995	—	—	—	0.10	0.25	0.75
1996	—	—	—	0.10	0.25	0.75
1997	—	—	—	0.10	0.25	0.75
1998	—	—	—	0.10	0.25	0.75
1999	—	—	—	0.10	0.25	0.75
2000	—	—	—	0.10	0.25	0.75

KM# 19 CENT
Bronze, 19 mm. **Subject:** 10th Anniversary of Independence **Obv:** National arms **Rev:** Trident above value **Edge:** Plain

Date	Mintage	F	VF	XF	Unc	BU
ND(1976)	6,406,000	—	—	0.10	0.20	0.60
ND(1976)FM (M)	5,000	—	—	—	0.50	1.50
ND(1976)FM (U)	996	—	—	—	1.00	3.00
ND(1976)FM (P)	12,000	Value: 1.00				

KM# 11 5 CENTS
3.8100 g., Brass, 19.21 mm. **Obv:** National arms **Rev:** South Point Lighthouse **Edge:** Plain

Date	Mintage	F	VF	XF	Unc	BU
1973FM (M)	7,500	—	—	—	1.25	3.75
1973	3,000,000	—	0.10	0.15	0.35	1.00
1973FM (P)	97,000	Value: 1.50				
1974FM (M)	8,708	—	—	—	1.25	3.75
1974FM (P)	36,000	Value: 1.50				
1975FM (M)	5,000	—	—	—	1.00	3.00
1975FM (U)	1,360	—	—	—	1.25	3.75
1975FM (P)	20,000	Value: 1.50				
1977FM (M)	2,100	—	—	1.00	2.00	5.00
1977FM (U)	468	—	—	1.50	3.00	6.00
1977FM (P)	5,014	Value: 1.50				
1978FM (M)	2,000	—	—	—	0.75	1.25
1978FM (U)	2,517	—	—	1.25	2.75	5.00
1978FM (P)	4,436	Value: 3.75				
1979	4,800,000	—	0.10	0.15	0.35	1.00
1979FM (M)	1,500	—	—	—	0.75	1.50
1979FM (U)	523	—	—	—	2.75	5.00
1979FM (P)	4,126	Value: 3.75				
1980FM (M)	1,500	—	—	—	1.00	3.00
1980FM (U)	649	—	—	1.00	2.25	6.75
1980FM (P)	2,111	Value: 4.25				
1981FM (M)	1,500	—	—	—	1.00	3.00
1981FM (U)	327	—	—	1.00	2.25	6.75
1981FM (P)	943	Value: 4.25				
1982	2,100,000	—	—	0.10	0.15	0.35
1982FM (U)	1,500	—	—	0.75	1.50	4.50
1982FM (P)	843	Value: 4.25				
1983FM (M)	1,500	—	—	0.75	1.50	4.50
1983FM (U)	—	—	—	0.75	1.50	4.50
1983FM (P)	459	Value: 4.25				
1984FM	1,737	—	—	0.75	1.50	4.50
1984FM (P)	—	Value: 4.25				
1985	—	—	—	0.10	0.25	0.75
1986	—	—	—	0.10	0.25	0.75
1988	4,200,000	—	—	0.10	0.25	0.75
1989	—	—	—	0.10	0.25	0.75
1991	—	—	—	0.10	0.25	0.75
1994	—	—	—	0.10	0.25	0.75
1995	—	—	—	0.10	0.25	0.75
1996	—	—	—	0.10	0.25	0.75
1997	—	—	—	0.10	0.25	0.75
1998	—	—	—	0.10	0.25	0.75
1999	—	—	—	0.10	0.25	0.75
2000	—	—	—	0.10	0.25	0.75

KM# 20 5 CENTS
Brass, 21 mm. **Subject:** 10th Anniversary of Independence **Obv:** National arms **Rev:** Lighthouse **Edge:** Plain

Date	Mintage	F	VF	XF	Unc	BU
ND(1976)FM (M)	5,000	—	—	—	1.00	3.00
ND(1976)FM (U)	12,000	—	—	—	1.00	2.00
ND(1976)FM (P)	—	Value: 1.50				

KM# 12 10 CENTS
2.2900 g., Copper-Nickel, 17.5 mm. **Obv:** National arms **Rev:** Laughing Gull left **Edge:** Reeded

Date	Mintage	F	VF	XF	Unc	BU
1973	4,000,000	—	0.10	0.15	0.50	1.50
1973FM (M)	5,000	—	—	—	1.50	3.00
1973FM (P)	97,000	Value: 2.00				
1974FM (M)	6,208	—	—	—	1.50	3.00
1974FM (P)	36,000	Value: 2.00				
1975FM (M)	2,500	—	—	—	1.00	3.00
1975FM (U)	1,360	—	—	—	1.50	3.00
1975FM (P)	20,000	Value: 2.00				
1977FM (M)	2,100	—	—	—	1.00	3.00
1977FM (U)	468	—	—	2.50	4.00	8.00
1977FM (P)	5,014	Value: 2.00				
1978FM (M)	2,000	—	—	—	1.00	3.00
1978FM (U)	2,517	—	—	—	3.00	6.00
1978FM (P)	4,436	Value: 3.00				
1979	2,500,000	—	0.10	0.20	0.60	1.25
1979FM (M)	1,500	—	—	—	1.00	2.50
1979FM (U)	523	—	—	1.50	3.00	8.00
1979FM (P)	4,126	Value: 3.00				
1980	3,500,000	—	0.10	0.15	0.50	1.25
1980FM (M)	1,500	—	—	—	1.00	3.00
1980FM (U)	649	—	—	1.00	2.50	7.00
1980FM (P)	2,111	Value: 4.00				
1981FM (M)	1,500	—	—	—	1.00	3.00
1981FM (U)	327	—	—	—	2.50	7.00
1981FM (P)	943	Value: 4.00				
1982FM (M)	1,500	—	—	—	1.00	3.00
1982FM (U)	1,500	—	—	—	1.75	4.25
1982FM (P)	843	Value: 4.00				
1983FM (M)	1,500	—	—	—	1.75	4.25
1983FM (U)	—	—	—	—	1.75	4.25
1983FM (P)	459	Value: 4.00				
1984	3,400,000	—	0.10	0.15	0.50	1.50
1984FM (P)	—	Value: 4.50				
1985	—	—	—	0.15	0.50	1.50
1986	—	—	—	0.15	0.50	1.50
1987	3,500,000	—	—	0.15	0.50	1.50
1988	—	—	—	0.15	0.50	1.50
1989	—	—	—	0.15	0.50	1.50
1990	—	—	—	0.15	0.50	1.50
1992	—	—	—	0.15	0.50	1.50
1995	—	—	—	0.15	0.50	1.50

Date	Mintage	F	VF	XF	Unc	BU
1996	—	—	0.10	0.15	0.50	1.50
1998	—	—	0.10	0.15	0.50	1.50
2000	—	—	0.10	0.15	0.50	1.50

KM# 21 10 CENTS
Copper-Nickel, 17.5 mm. **Subject:** 10th Anniversary of Independence **Obv:** National arms **Rev:** Gull left **Edge:** Reeded

Date	Mintage	F	VF	XF	Unc	BU
ND(1976)FM (M)	2,500	—	—	—	0.75	2.25
ND(1976)FM (U)	996	—	—	—	1.75	5.00
ND(1976)FM (P)	12,000	Value: 3.00				

KM# 13 25 CENTS
5.6700 g., Copper-Nickel, 23.6 mm. **Obv:** National arms **Rev:** Morgan Lewis Sugar Mill **Edge:** Reeded

Date	Mintage	F	VF	XF	Unc	BU
1973	6,000,000	—	0.15	0.30	0.60	1.20
1973FM (M)	4,300	—	—	—	1.75	3.50
1973FM (P)	97,000	Value: 2.50				
1974FM (M)	5,508	—	—	—	1.75	3.50
1974FM (P)	36,000	Value: 2.50				
1975FM (M)	1,800	—	—	—	1.25	3.00
1975FM (U)	1,360	—	—	—	1.75	3.50
1975FM (P)	20,000	Value: 2.50				
1977FM (M)	2,100	—	—	—	1.00	3.00
1977FM (U)	468	—	—	—	4.25	10.00
1977FM (P)	5,014	Value: 2.50				
1978	2,407,000	—	0.20	0.40	0.80	1.60
1978FM (M)	2,000	—	—	—	1.00	3.00
1978FM (U)	2,517	—	—	—	3.25	9.00
1978FM (P)	4,436	Value: 3.50				
1979	1,200,000	—	0.20	0.40	0.80	1.60
1979FM (M)	1,500	—	—	—	1.00	3.00
1979FM (U)	523	—	—	—	3.00	9.00
1979FM (P)	4,126,000	Value: 3.50				
1980	2,700,000	—	0.15	0.30	0.60	1.60
1980FM (U)	649	—	—	—	2.75	10.00
1980FM (M)	1,500	—	—	0.75	3.00	8.00
1980FM (P)	2,111	Value: 3.50				
1981	4,365,000	—	0.15	0.30	0.60	1.60
1981FM (U)	327	—	—	—	2.75	10.00
1981FM (M)	1,500	—	—	0.75	3.00	8.00
1981FM (P)	943	Value: 4.50				
1982FM (U)	1,500	—	—	—	2.00	4.50
1982FM (P)	843	Value: 4.50				
1983FM (M)	1,500	—	—	—	2.00	4.50
1983FM (U)	—	—	—	—	2.00	4.50
1983FM (P)	459	Value: 4.50				
1984FM	868	—	—	—	2.00	4.50
1984FM (P)	—	Value: 5.00				
1985	—	—	0.15	0.30	0.60	1.60
1986	—	—	0.15	0.30	0.60	1.60
1987	3,150,000	—	—	—	2.00	3.00
1988	—	—	0.15	0.30	0.60	1.60
1989	—	—	0.15	0.30	0.60	1.60
1990	—	—	0.15	0.30	0.60	1.60
1994	—	—	0.15	0.30	0.60	1.60
1996	—	—	0.15	0.30	0.60	1.60
1998	—	—	0.15	0.30	0.60	1.60
2000	—	—	0.15	0.30	0.60	1.60

KM# 22 25 CENTS
Copper-Nickel, 23.6 mm. **Subject:** 10th Anniversary of Independence **Obv:** National arms **Rev:** Morgan Lewis Sugar Mill **Edge:** Reeded

Date	Mintage	F	VF	XF	Unc	BU
ND(1976)FM (M)	1,800	—	—	—	1.25	3.75
ND(1976)FM (U)	996	—	—	1.00	2.00	6.00
ND(1976)FM (P)	12,000	Value: 2.00				

KM# 14.1 DOLLAR
9.9000 g., Copper-Nickel, 28 mm. **Obv:** National arms **Rev:** Flying fish left **Edge:** Plain

Date	Mintage	F	VF	XF	Unc	BU
1973	3,955,000	—	0.60	0.75	1.50	3.00
1973FM (M)	3,000	—	—	—	2.00	6.00
1973FM (P)	97,000	Value: 2.00				
1974FM (M)	4,208	—	—	—	2.00	6.00
1974FM (P)	36,000	Value: 3.00				
1975FM (M)	500	—	—	1.25	3.50	9.00
1975FM (U)	1,360	—	—	—	2.00	6.00
1975FM (P)	20,000	Value: 3.00				
1977FM (M)	600	—	—	1.75	5.00	9.00
1977FM (U)	468	—	—	1.50	4.50	10.00
1977FM (P)	5,014	Value: 6.00				
1978FM (M)		**Note:** Reported, not confirmed				
1978FM (U)	1,017	—	—	1.25	3.50	6.00
1978FM (P)	4,436	Value: 6.00				
1979	2,000,000	—	0.75	1.25	1.75	2.50
1979FM (M)	600	—	—	1.50	3.00	9.00
1979FM (U)	523	—	—	1.25	3.50	9.00
1979FM (P)	4,126	Value: 6.00				
1980FM (M)	600	—	—	1.50	3.50	9.00
1980FM (U)	649	—	—	1.50	3.50	9.00
1980FM (P)	2,111	Value: 6.00				
1981FM (M)	600	—	—	1.25	3.00	9.00
1981FM (U)	327	—	—	1.50	3.50	9.00
1981FM (P)	943	Value: 6.00				
1982FM (U)	600	—	—	1.25	3.00	9.00
1982FM (P)	843	Value: 6.00				
1983FM (M)	600	—	—	1.25	3.00	9.00
1983FM (U)	—	—	—	1.25	3.00	9.00
1983FM (P)	459	Value: 7.50				
1984FM	469	—	—	—	3.50	9.00
1984FM (P)	—	Value: 4.50				
1985	—	—	—	—	1.50	3.00
1986	—	—	—	—	1.50	3.00
2000	—	—	—	—	1.50	3.00

KM# 14.2 DOLLAR
6.3000 g., Copper-Nickel, 28 mm. **Obv:** National arms **Rev:** Flying fish left **Note:** Thinner planchet.

Date	Mintage	F	VF	XF	Unc	BU
1988	3,145,000	—	—	0.75	2.25	3.00
1989	—	—	—	0.75	2.25	3.00
1994	—	—	—	0.75	2.25	3.00
1998	—	—	—	0.75	2.25	3.00

KM# 23 DOLLAR
Copper-Nickel, 28 mm. **Subject:** 10th Anniversary of Independence **Obv:** National arms **Rev:** Flying fish left **Edge:** Plain

Date	Mintage	F	VF	XF	Unc	BU
ND(1976)FM (M)	500	—	—	1.50	4.00	9.00
ND(1976)FM (U)	996	—	—	1.25	3.50	9.00
ND(1976)FM (P)	12,000	Value: 4.00				

KM# 57 DOLLAR
10.0000 g., 0.5000 Silver 0.1607 oz. ASW **Subject:** Queen Elizabeth the Queen Mother **Obv:** National arms, date at bottom **Rev:** Bust facing

Date	Mintage	F	VF	XF	Unc	BU
1994 Proof	Est. 50,000	Value: 28.00				

KM# 65 DOLLAR
9.9400 g., 0.9250 Silver 0.2956 oz. ASW **Subject:** Queen Mother's 95th Birthday **Obv:** National arms **Rev:** Bust facing

Date	Mintage	F	VF	XF	Unc	BU
1995 Proof	Est. 50,000	Value: 35.00				

KM# 64 DOLLAR
10.2400 g., 0.9250 Silver 0.3045 oz. ASW, 30 mm. **Obv:** National arms **Rev:** Royal couple below gold inset monogrammed shield **Edge:** Reeded

Date	Mintage	F	VF	XF	Unc	BU
1997 Proof	—	Value: 30.00				

KM# 15 2 DOLLARS
Copper-Nickel, 37 mm. **Obv:** National arms **Rev:** Staghorn coral **Edge:** Reeded

Date	Mintage	F	VF	XF	Unc	BU
1973FM (M)	3,000	—	—	1.25	5.00	9.00
1973FM (P)	97,000	Value: 6.00				
1974FM (M)	4,208	—	—	1.25	5.00	9.00
1974FM (P)	36,000	Value: 6.00				
1975FM (M)	500	—	—	1.25	5.00	9.00
1975FM (U)	1,360	—	—	1.25	5.00	9.00
1975FM (P)	20,000	Value: 6.00				
1977FM (M)	600	—	—	1.25	5.00	9.00
1977FM (U)	468	—	—	1.50	5.50	10.00
1977FM (P)	5,014	Value: 9.00				
1978FM (M)		**Note:** Reported, not confirmed				
1978FM (U)	1,017	—	—	1.25	5.00	9.00
1978FM (P)	4,436	Value: 9.00				
1979FM (M)	600	—	—	1.25	5.00	10.00
1979FM (U)	523	—	—	1.25	5.00	10.00
1979FM (P)	4,126	Value: 9.00				
1980FM (M)	600	—	—	1.25	5.00	10.00
1980FM (U)	649	—	—	1.25	5.00	10.00
1980FM (P)	2,111	Value: 9.00				
1981FM (M)	600	—	—	1.25	5.00	10.00
1981FM (U)	327	—	—	1.25	5.00	10.00
1981FM (P)	943	Value: 9.00				
1982FM (U)	600	—	—	1.25	5.00	10.00
1982FM (P)	843	Value: 9.00				
1983FM (U)	—	—	—	1.25	5.00	10.00
1983FM (P)	459	Value: 9.00				
1984FM (U)	473	—	—	1.25	5.00	10.00
1984FM (P)	—	Value: 9.00				

KM# 24 2 DOLLARS

Copper-Nickel, 37 mm. **Subject:** 10th Anniversary of Independence **Obv:** National arms **Rev:** Staghorn coral **Edge:** Reeded

Date	Mintage	F	VF	XF	Unc	BU
ND(1976)FM (M)	500	—	—	2.00	6.00	10.00
ND(1976)FM (U)	996	—	—	2.00	6.00	9.00
ND(1976)FM (P)	12,000	Value: 10.00				

KM# A9 4 DOLLARS

Copper-Nickel, 38.5 mm. **Series:** F.A.O. **Obv:** National arms **Rev:** Sugarcane and banana tree branch **Edge:** Reeded

Date	Mintage	F	VF	XF	Unc	BU
1970	30,000	—	4.00	7.00	15.00	20.00
1970 Proof	2,000	Value: 25.00				

KM# 16 5 DOLLARS

Copper-Nickel, 40 mm. **Obv:** National arms **Rev:** Shell Fountain in Bridgetown's Trafalgar Square **Edge:** Reeded

Date	Mintage	F	VF	XF	Unc	BU
1974FM (M)	3,958	—	—	1.25	5.00	7.50
1975FM (U)	1,360	—	—	1.25	5.00	7.50
1975FM (M)	250	—	—	1.25	8.00	9.50
1977FM (M)	600	—	—	1.25	5.00	7.50
1977FM (U)	468	—	—	1.25	5.00	7.50
1978FM (U)	1,017	—	—	1.25	5.00	7.50
1979FM (M)	600	—	—	1.25	5.00	7.50
1979FM (U)	523	—	—	1.25	5.00	7.50
1980FM (M)	600	—	—	1.25	5.00	7.50
1980FM (U)	649	—	—	1.25	5.00	7.50
1981FM (M)	600	—	—	1.25	5.00	7.50
1981FM (U)	1,156	—	—	1.25	5.00	7.50
1982FM (P)	843	—	—	1.25	5.00	7.50
1982FM (U)	600	—	—	1.25	5.00	7.50
1983FM (M)	600	—	—	1.25	5.00	7.50
1983FM (U)	261	—	—	1.25	5.00	7.50
1984FM	470	—	—	1.25	5.00	7.50

KM# 16a 5 DOLLARS

31.1000 g., 0.8000 Silver 0.7999 oz. ASW, 40 mm. **Obv:** National arms **Rev:** Shell Fountain in Bridgetown's Trafalgar Square **Edge:** Reeded

Date	Mintage	F	VF	XF	Unc	BU
1973FM (P)	97,000	Value: 16.00				
1973FM (M)	2,750	—	—	—	—	22.00
1974FM (P)	36,000	Value: 17.00				
1975FM (P)	20,000	Value: 18.00				
1977FM (P)	5,014	Value: 20.00				
1978FM (P)	4,436	Value: 20.00				
1979FM (P)	4,126	Value: 20.00				
1980FM (P)	2,111	Value: 22.50				
1981FM (P)	835	Value: 25.00				
1982FM (P)	658	Value: 25.00				
1983FM (P)	130	Value: 32.00				
1984FM (P)	—	Value: 32.00				

KM# 25 5 DOLLARS

Copper-Nickel, 40 mm. **Subject:** 10th Anniversary of Independence **Obv:** National arms **Rev:** Shell Fountain **Edge:** Reeded

Date	Mintage	F	VF	XF	Unc	BU
ND(1976)FM (M)	250	—	—	7.50	25.00	—
ND(1976)FM (U)	996	—	—	7.50	12.50	—

KM# 25a 5 DOLLARS

31.1000 g., 0.8000 Silver 0.7999 oz. ASW, 40 mm. **Subject:** 10th Anniversary of Independence **Obv:** National arms **Rev:** Shell Fountain **Edge:** Reeded

Date	Mintage	F	VF	XF	Unc	BU
ND(1976)FM (P)	12,000	Value: 22.00				

KM# 54 5 DOLLARS

28.5500 g., 0.9250 Silver 0.8490 oz. ASW **Subject:** World Cup Soccer **Obv:** National arms **Rev:** Head of Native American with headdress left, soccer player in foreground

Date	Mintage	F	VF	XF	Unc	BU
1994 Proof	Est. 10,000	Value: 37.50				

KM# 55 5 DOLLARS

28.2800 g., 0.9250 Silver 0.8410 oz. ASW **Subject:** UN Global SIDS Conference **Obv:** National arms **Rev:** Stylized tropical island view

Date	Mintage	F	VF	XF	Unc	BU
1994 Proof	2,000	Value: 40.00				

KM# 59 5 DOLLARS

28.2800 g., 0.9250 Silver 0.8410 oz. ASW **Subject:** Pedro A. Campo **Obv:** National arms **Rev:** Seated figure at left facing right

Date	Mintage	F	VF	XF	Unc	BU
1994 Proof	Est. 10,000	Value: 50.00				

KM# 62 5 DOLLARS

Copper-Nickel **Subject:** 50th Anniversary - United Nations **Obv:** National arms **Rev:** Military figure raising flag, numbers at right signify years

Date	Mintage	F	VF	XF	Unc	BU
1995	—	—	—	—	8.00	—

KM# 62a 5 DOLLARS

28.2800 g., 0.9250 Silver 0.8410 oz. ASW **Subject:** 50th Anniversary - United Nations **Obv:** National arms **Rev:** Military figure raising flag, numbers at right signify years

Date	Mintage	F	VF	XF	Unc	BU
1995 Proof	Est. 105,000	Value: 32.50				

KM# 63 5 DOLLARS

28.2800 g., 0.9250 Silver 0.8410 oz. ASW **Obv:** National arms **Rev:** First European settlers, 1625

Date	Mintage	F	VF	XF	Unc	BU
1995 Proof	Est. 15,000	Value: 40.00				

KM# 68 5 DOLLARS

28.5000 g., 0.9250 Silver 0.8475 oz. ASW, 38.5 mm. **Subject:** Queen's 70th Birthday **Obv:** National arms **Rev:** Royal couple waving, two dates below **Edge:** Reeded

Date	Mintage	F	VF	XF	Unc	BU
1996 Proof	—	Value: 40.00				

KM# 58 5 DOLLARS

31.4700 g., 0.9250 Silver 0.9359 oz. ASW **Series:** Queen Elizabeth the Queen Mother **Subject:** Engagement **Obv:** National arms **Rev:** Bust right, spray below

Date	Mintage	F	VF	XF	Unc	BU
1994 Proof	Est. 20,000	Value: 50.00				

KM# 67   5 DOLLARS
28.1000 g., 0.9250 Silver 0.8356 oz. ASW, 38.6 mm.
Obv: National arms **Rev:** Eternal flame **Edge:** Reeded

Date	Mintage	F	VF	XF	Unc	BU
1999-2000 Proof	—	Value: 60.00				

KM# 17   10 DOLLARS
Copper-Nickel **Subject:** Neptune, God of the Sea **Obv:** National arms divide date **Rev:** Neptune at left looking right, whale under right hand **Edge:** Reeded

Date	Mintage	F	VF	XF	Unc	BU
1974FM (M)	3,958	—	—	3.00	10.00	12.00
1975FM (M)	250	—	—	3.00	20.00	25.00
1975FM (U)	1,360	—	—	3.00	12.50	14.00
1977FM (M)	600	—	—	3.00	12.50	14.50
1977FM (U)	468	—	—	3.00	12.50	14.50
1978FM (M)	1,017	—	—	3.00	12.50	14.00
1979FM (M)	600	—	—	3.00	12.50	14.50
1979FM (U)	523	—	—	3.00	12.50	14.50
1980FM (M)	600	—	—	3.00	12.50	14.50
1980FM (U)	649	—	—	3.00	12.50	14.50
1981FM (M)	600	—	—	3.00	12.50	14.50
1981FM (U)	1,156	—	—	3.00	12.50	14.00

KM# 17a   10 DOLLARS
37.9000 g., 0.9250 Silver 1.1271 oz. ASW **Subject:** Neptune, God of the Sea **Obv:** National arms **Rev:** Neptune at left looking right, whale under right hand **Edge:** Reeded

Date	Mintage	F	VF	XF	Unc	BU
1973FM (M)	2,750	—	—	—	—	25.00
1973FM (P)	97,000	Value: 22.50				
1974FM (P)	57,000	Value: 22.50				
1975FM (P)	29,000	Value: 22.50				
1977FM (P)	7,212	Value: 25.00				
1978FM (P)	7,079	Value: 25.00				
1979FM (P)	6,534	Value: 25.00				
1980FM (P)	3,618	Value: 27.50				
1981FM (P)	835	Value: 45.00				

KM# 26   10 DOLLARS
Copper-Nickel **Subject:** 10th Anniversary of Independence **Obv:** National arms **Rev:** Neptune at left looking right, dolphin fish under right hand **Edge:** Reeded

Date	Mintage	F	VF	XF	Unc	BU
ND(1976)FM (M)	250	—	—	10.00	30.00	35.00
ND(1976)FM (U)	996	—	—	7.50	15.00	17.50

KM# 26a   10 DOLLARS
37.9000 g., 0.9250 Silver 1.1271 oz. ASW **Subject:** 10th Anniversary of Independence **Obv:** National arms **Rev:** Neptune at left looking right, whale under right hand **Edge:** Reeded

Date	Mintage	F	VF	XF	Unc	BU
ND(1976)FM (P)	16,000	Value: 25.00				

KM# 34   10 DOLLARS
Copper-Nickel **Subject:** 10th Anniversary of the Central Bank of Barbados **Obv:** National arms **Rev:** Upright Blue Marlin divides date **Edge:** Reeded

Date	Mintage	F	VF	XF	Unc	BU
1982FM (U)	600	—	—	—	55.00	—

KM# 34a   10 DOLLARS
35.5200 g., 0.9250 Silver 1.0563 oz. ASW **Obv:** National arms **Rev:** Upright Blue Marlin divides date

Date	Mintage	F	VF	XF	Unc	BU
1982FM (P)	851	Value: 45.00				

KM# 36   10 DOLLARS
32.7000 g., Copper-Nickel, 41.5 mm. **Subject:** Summer Olympics **Obv:** National arms **Rev:** Pelican with wings raised right

Date	Mintage	F	VF	XF	Unc	BU
1983FM (M)	600	—	—	—	110	—
1983FM (U)	141	—	—	—	160	—

KM# 36a   10 DOLLARS
35.5200 g., 0.9250 Silver 1.0563 oz. ASW **Subject:** Summer Olympics **Obv:** National arms **Rev:** Pelican with wings raised right

Date	Mintage	F	VF	XF	Unc	BU
1983FM (P)	679	Value: 125				

KM# 40   10 DOLLARS
35.5200 g., 0.9250 Silver 1.0563 oz. ASW **Subject:** Dolphins **Obv:** National arms **Rev:** Three dolphins left

Date	Mintage	F	VF	XF	Unc	BU
1984FM (M)	—	—	—	—	—	—
1984FM (P)	469	Value: 185				

KM# 50   10 DOLLARS
28.2800 g., 0.9250 Silver 0.8410 oz. ASW **Subject:** International Cricket Belt Buckle **Obv:** National arms **Rev:** Belt buckle

Date	Mintage	F	VF	XF	Unc	BU
1991 Proof	5,000	Value: 55.00				

KM# 52   10 DOLLARS
23.3300 g., 0.9250 Silver 0.6938 oz. ASW **Subject:** Discovery of America **Obv:** Crowned bust right **Rev:** Columbus and Native American, ship and scroll

Date	Mintage	F	VF	XF	Unc	BU
1991 Matte	750	Value: 65.00				
1991 Proof	Est. 25,000	Value: 35.00				

KM# 53   10 DOLLARS
23.3300 g., 0.9250 Silver 0.6938 oz. ASW **Subject:** Discovery of America **Obv:** Crowned bust right **Rev:** Columbus and Tribal Chief with scroll

Date	Mintage	F	VF	XF	Unc	BU
1992 Matte	500	Value: 65.00				
1992 Proof	Est. 25,000	Value: 35.00				

KM# 61   10 DOLLARS
23.3300 g., 0.9250 Silver 0.6938 oz. ASW **Subject:** 1992 Summer Olympics **Obv:** Crowned bust right **Rev:** Sailboards

Date	Mintage	F	VF	XF	Unc	BU
1992 Proof	10,000	Value: 50.00				

KM# 60   10 DOLLARS
7.7800 g., 0.5830 Gold 0.1458 oz. AGW **Subject:** Queen Mother's Engagement **Obv:** National arms **Rev:** Bust right, spray below

Date   Mintage   F   VF   XF   Unc   BU
1995 Proof Est. 5,000   Value: 150

KM# 66   10 DOLLARS

28.2800 g., 0.9250 Silver 0.8410 oz. ASW **Subject:** 50th
Anniversary of the University of the West Indies **Obv:** National
arms **Rev:** University arms

Date	Mintage	F	VF	XF	Unc	BU
1998 Proof	1,000	Value: 55.00				

KM# 30   25 DOLLARS

30.2800 g., 0.5000 Silver 0.4867 oz. ASW **Subject:** 10th
Anniversary of Caribbean Development Bank **Obv:** National
arms **Rev:** Globe above flag

Date	Mintage	F	VF	XF	Unc	BU
ND(1980)FM (P)	2,345	Value: 25.00				
Proof						

KM# 31   25 DOLLARS

30.2800 g., 0.5000 Silver 0.4867 oz. ASW **Subject:** Caribbean
Festival of Arts **Obv:** National arms **Rev:** Artistic design

Date	Mintage	F	VF	XF	Unc	BU
1981FM (P)	1,008	Value: 30.00				

KM# 44   25 DOLLARS

28.2800 g., 0.5000 Silver 0.4546 oz. ASW **Subject:** Commonwealth Games **Obv:** National arms **Rev:** Discus thrower right

Date	Mintage	F	VF	XF	Unc	BU
1986	Est. 50,000	—	—	—	25.00	—

KM# 44a   25 DOLLARS

28.2800 g., 0.9250 Silver 0.8410 oz. ASW **Subject:** Commonwealth Games **Obv:** National arms **Rev:** Discus thrower right

Date	Mintage	F	VF	XF	Unc	BU
1986	Est. 20,000	Value: 30.00				

KM# 70   25 DOLLARS

31.4400 g., 0.9990 Silver 1.0098 oz. ASW, 37.85 mm.
Subject: 25th Anniversary of the Central Bank **Obv:** National
arms **Rev:** Upright Blue Marlin right divides dates **Edge:** Reeded

Date	Mintage	F	VF	XF	Unc	BU
ND (1997) Proof	—	Value: 75.00				

KM# 46   20 DOLLARS

23.3300 g., 0.9250 Silver 0.6938 oz. ASW **Subject:** Decade For
Women **Obv:** National arms **Rev:** Teacher and class

Date	Mintage	F	VF	XF	Unc	BU
1985 Proof	1,633	Value: 45.00				

KM# 49   20 DOLLARS

23.3300 g., 0.9250 Silver 0.6938 oz. ASW **Subject:** Summer
Olympics **Obv:** National arms **Rev:** Men running hurdles

Date	Mintage	F	VF	XF	Unc	BU
1988	15,000	—	—	—	28.00	—

KM# 27   25 DOLLARS

28.2800 g., 0.9250 Silver 0.8410 oz. ASW **Subject:** Coronation
Jubilee **Obv:** Young bust right **Rev:** Imperial Crown with supporters

Date	Mintage	F	VF	XF	Unc	BU
1978FM (M)	300	—	—	—	90.00	—
1978FM (U)	69	—	—	—	250	—
1978FM (P)	8,728	Value: 20.00				

KM# 37   25 DOLLARS

30.2800 g., 0.5000 Silver 0.4867 oz. ASW **Subject:** 30th
Anniversary Coronation of Queen Elizabeth II **Obv:** National arms
Rev: Crossed sceptres divide royal symbols

Date	Mintage	F	VF	XF	Unc	BU
1983FM (P)	2,951	Value: 22.50				

KM# 43   25 DOLLARS

28.2800 g., 0.9250 Silver 0.8410 oz. ASW **Subject:** Royal Visit
Obv: Crowned bust right **Rev:** National arms

Date	Mintage	F	VF	XF	Unc	BU
1985	Est. 5,000	—	—	—	32.50	—

KM# 32   50 DOLLARS

27.3500 g., 0.5000 Silver 0.4396 oz. ASW **Subject:** World Food
Day **Obv:** F.A.O. logo divided by grain sprig **Rev:** Black Belly
Sheep right

Date	Mintage	F	VF	XF	Unc	BU
1981FM (U)	6,012	—	—	—	50.00	—

KM# 42 50 DOLLARS
16.8500 g., 0.5000 Silver 0.2709 oz. ASW **Series:** F.A.O.
Obv: F.A.O. divided by grain sprig **Rev:** Fourwing flying fish
Edge: Reeded

Date	Mintage	F	VF	XF	Unc	BU
1984	3,600	—	—	—	40.00	45.00

KM# 47 50 DOLLARS
33.6250 g., 0.9250 Silver 0.9999 oz. ASW **Subject:** 350th
Anniversary of Parliament **Obv:** National arms **Rev:** Parliament
Building

Date	Mintage	F	VF	XF	Unc	BU
ND(1989) Proof	Est. 5,000	Value: 35.00				

KM# 51 50 DOLLARS
15.9800 g., 0.9170 Gold 0.4711 oz. AGW **Subject:** International
Cricket Belt Buckle **Obv:** National arms **Rev:** Belt buckle

Date	Mintage	F	VF	XF	Unc	BU
1991 Proof	500	Value: 530				

KM# 56 50 DOLLARS
15.9800 g., 0.9170 Gold 0.4711 oz. AGW **Subject:** UN Global
SIDS Conference **Obv:** National arms **Rev:** Small house and tree
within hand design

Date	Mintage	F	VF	XF	Unc	BU
1994 Proof	100	Value: 550				

KM# 18 100 DOLLARS
6.2100 g., 0.5000 Gold 0.0998 oz. AGW **Subject:** 350th
Anniversary - The English Ship **Obv:** National arms **Rev:** Olive
Blossom with full sails

Date	Mintage	F	VF	XF	Unc	BU
ND(1975)FM (M)	50	—	—	—	250	—
ND(1975)FM (U)	16,000	—	—	—	100	—
ND(1975)FM (P)	23,000	Value: 110				

KM# 28 100 DOLLARS
4.0600 g., 0.9000 Gold 0.1175 oz. AGW **Subject:** Human Rights
Obv: National arms **Rev:** Praying hands beneath rolled scroll

Date	Mintage	F	VF	XF	Unc	BU
1978	1,114	—	—	—	125	—

KM# 28a 100 DOLLARS
5.0500 g., 0.9000 Gold 0.1461 oz. AGW **Subject:** Human Rights
Obv: National arms **Rev:** Praying hands beneath rolled scroll

Date	Mintage	F	VF	XF	Unc	BU
1978 Proof	Inc. above	Value: 150				

KM# 38 100 DOLLARS
6.2100 g., 0.5000 Gold 0.0998 oz. AGW **Subject:** Neptune, God
of the Sea **Obv:** National arms **Rev:** Standing figure looking right

Date	Mintage	F	VF	XF	Unc	BU
1983FM (U)	3	—	—	—	—	—
1983FM (P)	484	Value: 225				

KM# 39 100 DOLLARS
6.2100 g., 0.5000 Gold 0.0998 oz. AGW **Subject:** Triton, Son
of Neptune **Obv:** National arms **Rev:** Full figure left blowing horn

Date	Mintage	F	VF	XF	Unc	BU
1984FM (P)	1,103	Value: 170				

KM# 41 100 DOLLARS
6.2100 g., 0.5000 Gold 0.0998 oz. AGW **Subject:** Amphitrite,
Wife of Neptune **Obv:** National arms **Rev:** Full figure facing
looking left

Date	Mintage	F	VF	XF	Unc	BU
1985FM (P)	1,276	Value: 185				

KM# 48 100 DOLLARS
15.9760 g., 0.9170 Gold 0.4710 oz. AGW **Subject:** 350th
Anniversary of Parliament **Obv:** Crowned bust right
Rev: Parliament Building

Date	Mintage	F	VF	XF	Unc	BU
ND(1989)FM	Est. 500	Value: 450				

KM# 33 150 DOLLARS
7.1300 g., 0.5000 Gold 0.1146 oz. AGW **Subject:** National
Flower - Poinciana **Obv:** National arms **Rev:** Flower and map

Date	Mintage	F	VF	XF	Unc	BU
1981FM (U)	7	—	—	—	—	—
1981FM (P)	1,140	Value: 135				

KM# 29 200 DOLLARS
8.1200 g., 0.9000 Gold 0.2349 oz. AGW **Subject:** Year of the
Child **Obv:** National arms **Rev:** Shaded circle above large shaded
letter "Y" depicts child figure

Date	Mintage	F	VF	XF	Unc	BU
1979	1,121	—	—	—	250	—

KM# 29a 200 DOLLARS
10.1000 g., 0.9000 Gold 0.2922 oz. AGW **Subject:** Year of the
Child **Obv:** National arms **Rev:** Shaded circle above large shaded
letter "Y" depicts child figure

Date	Mintage	F	VF	XF	Unc	BU
1979 Proof	Inc. above	Value: 300				

KM# 35 250 DOLLARS
6.6000 g., 0.9000 Gold 0.1910 oz. AGW **Subject:** 250th
Anniversary of Birth of George Washington **Obv:** National arms
Rev: Small head left below building

Date	Mintage	F	VF	XF	Unc	BU
1982FM (P)	802	Value: 200				

KM# 45 250 DOLLARS
47.5400 g., 0.9170 Gold 1.4015 oz. AGW **Subject:** Commonwealth Games **Obv:** National arms **Rev:** Discus thrower right

Date	Mintage	F	VF	XF	Unc	BU
1986 Proof	150	Value: 1,400				

KM# 71 500 DOLLARS
47.5400 g., 0.9170 Gold 1.4015 oz. AGW **Subject:** Royal Visit
Obv: Crowned bust right **Rev:** National arms

Date	Mintage	F	VF	XF	Unc	BU
1985	Est. 250	Value: 1,350				

MINT SETS

KM#	Date	Mintage	Identification	Issue Price	Mkt Val
MS1	1973 (8)	2,500	KM#10-15, 16a, 17a	25.00	25.00
MS2	1974 (8)	3,708	KM#10-17	25.00	20.00
MS3	1975 (8)	1,360	KM#10-17	27.50	22.50
MS4	1976 (8)	996	KM#19-26	27.50	30.00
MS5	1977 (8)	468	KM#10-17	27.50	30.00
MS6	1978 (8)	517	KM#10-17	29.00	30.00
MS7	1979 (8)	523	KM#10-17	29.00	30.00
MS8	1980 (8)	649	KM#10-17	30.00	30.00
MS9	1981 (8)	327	KM#10-17	30.00	35.00
MS10	1982 (8)	—	KM#10-16, 34	35.00	45.00
MS11	1983 (8)	141	KM#10-16, 36	35.50	185
MS12	1989 (5)	—	KM#10-13 & 14.2	17.00	17.00

PROOF SETS

KM#	Date	Mintage	Identification	Issue Price	Mkt Val
PS1	1973 (8)	97,454	KM#10-15, 16a, 17a	37.50	30.00
PS2	1974 (8)	35,600	KM#10-15, 16a, 17a	50.00	30.00
PS3	1975 (8)	20,458	KM#10-15, 16a, 17a	55.00	30.00
PS4	1976 (8)	11,929	KM#19-24, 25a, 26a	55.00	40.00
PS5	1977 (8)	5,014	KM#10-15, 16a, 17a	55.00	35.00
PS6	1978 (8)	4,436	KM#10-15, 16a, 17a	58.00	37.50
PS7	1979 (8)	4,126	KM#10-15, 16a, 17a	60.00	37.50
PS8	1980 (8)	2,011	KM#10-15, 16a, 17a	117	45.00
PS9	1980 (2)	—	KM#16a, 17a	115	32.50
PS10	1981 (8)	—	KM#10-15, 16a, 17a	117	95.00
PS11	1982 (8)	—	KM#10-15, 16a, 34a	117	95.00
PS12	1983 (8)	—	KM#10-15, 16a, 36a	—	190
PS13	1984 (8)	—	KM#10-15, 16a, 40	132	245

BELARUS

Belarus (Byelorussia, Belorussia, or White Russia- formerly the Belorussian S.S.R.) is situated along the western Dvina and Dnieper Rivers, bounded in the west by Poland, to the north by Latvia and Lithuania, to the east by Russia and the south by the Ukraine. It has an area of 80,154 sq. mi. (207,600 sq. km.) and a population of 4.8 million. Capital: Minsk. Chief products: peat, salt, and agricultural products including flax, fodder and grasses for cattle breeding and dairy products.

There never existed an independent state of Byelorussia. Until the partitions of Poland at the end of the 18th century, the history of Byelorussia is identical with that of Lithuania.

When Russia incorporated the whole of Byelorussia into its territories in 1795, it claimed to be recovering old Russian lands and denied that the Byelorussians were a separate nation. Significant efforts for independence did not occur until 1918 and were met by external antagonism from German, Polish, and Russian influences.

Soviet and anti-Communist sympathies continued to reflect the political and social unrest of the U.S.S.R. for Byelorussia. Finally, on August 25, 1991, following an unsuccessful coup, the Supreme Soviet adopted a declaration of independence, and the "Republic of Belarus" was proclaimed in September. In December, it became a founder member of the CIS.

MONETARY SYSTEM
100 Kapeek = 1 Rouble

REPUBLIC
STANDARD COINAGE

KM# 6   ROUBLE
Copper-Nickel, 38.61 mm.   **Subject:** 50th Anniversary - United Nations **Obv:** National arms, date at bottom **Rev:** Crane flying over map and UN logo

Date	Mintage	F	VF	XF	Unc	BU
1996	15,000	—	—	—	25.00	—

KM# 6a   ROUBLE
28.5100 g., 0.9250 Silver 0.8478 oz. ASW, 38.61 mm.
Obv: National arms **Rev:** Crane flying over map and UN logo

Date	Mintage	F	VF	XF	Unc	BU
1996 Proof	20,000	Value: 250				

KM# 7   ROUBLE
Copper-Nickel, 32 mm.   **Subject:** Olympics **Obv:** National arms and denomination **Rev:** Gymnast on the rings

Date	Mintage	F	VF	XF	Unc	BU
1996 Prooflike	5,000	—	—	—	20.00	—

KM# 8   ROUBLE
Copper-Nickel, 32 mm.   **Subject:** Olympics **Obv:** National arms **Rev:** Ribbon dancer

Date	Mintage	F	VF	XF	Unc	BU
1996 Prooflike	5,000	—	—	—	20.00	—

KM# 31   ROUBLE
7.9800 g., 0.9167 Gold 0.2352 oz. AGW, 22.85 mm.
Subject: United Nations 50th Anniversary **Obv:** National arms, date at bottom **Rev:** Crane flying over map and U.N. logo

Date	Mintage	F	VF	XF	Unc	BU
1996 Proof	5,000	Value: 4,500				

KM# 9   ROUBLE
Copper-Nickel, 33 mm.   **Subject:** Third Anniversary of Independence **Obv:** National arms, date below, circle surrounds **Rev:** Monument July 3

Date	Mintage	F	VF	XF	Unc	BU
1997 Prooflike	5,000	—	—	—	20.00	—

KM# 34   ROUBLE
Copper-Nickel, 32 mm.   **Subject:** Olympics **Obv:** National arms and denomination **Rev:** Biathalon skier with rifle

Date	Mintage	F	VF	XF	Unc	BU
1997 Prooflike	5,000	—	—	—	20.00	—

KM# 36   ROUBLE
Copper-Nickel, 32 mm.   **Subject:** Olympics **Obv:** National arms and denomination **Rev:** Two hockey players

Date	Mintage	F	VF	XF	Unc	BU
1997 Prooflike	5,000	—	—	—	20.00	—

KM# 18   ROUBLE
Copper-Nickel, 32 mm.   **Subject:** Architecture of Belarus **Obv:** National arms **Rev:** Castle at Mir

Date	Mintage	F	VF	XF	Unc	BU
1998 Proof	2,000	Value: 80.00				

KM# 19   ROUBLE
Copper-Nickel, 32 mm.   **Subject:** Cities of Belarus **Obv:** National arms **Rev:** Walled city of Polatsk with city arms

Date	Mintage	F	VF	XF	Unc	BU
1998 Proof	2,000	Value: 75.00				

KM# 20   ROUBLE
Copper-Nickel, 33 mm.   **Subject:** 200th Anniversary - Birth of A. Mitskevich - Poet **Obv:** National arms **Rev:** Head of Mitskevich, dates 1798-1855

Date	Mintage	F	VF	XF	Unc	BU
1998 Proof	2,000	Value: 180				

KM# 21   ROUBLE
Copper-Nickel   **Subject:** Olympics **Obv:** National arms and denomination **Rev:** Hurdlers, Olympic crest

Date	Mintage	F	VF	XF	Unc	BU
1998 Proof	5,000	Value: 15.00				

KM# 22   ROUBLE
Copper-Nickel, 33 mm.   **Subject:** Cities of Belarus **Obv:** National arms, date below, within circle **Rev:** Minsk view with city arms, within circle

Date	Mintage	F	VF	XF	Unc	BU
1999 Proof	2,000	Value: 80.00				

KM# 23 ROUBLE
Copper-Nickel, 33 mm. **Subject:** 100th Anniversary - Birth of
Mikhas Lynkou **Obv:** National arms **Rev:** Head of Lynkou facing right

Date	Mintage	F	VF	XF	Unc	BU
1999 Proof	1,000	Value: 325				

KM# 40 ROUBLE
14.5000 g., Copper-Nickel, 33 mm. **Subject:** G.P. Glebov
Obv: National arms **Rev:** Glebats portrait with two smaller
portraits, dates 1899-1967 **Edge:** Reeded

Date	Mintage	F	VF	XF	Unc	BU
1999 Proof	1,000	Value: 400				

KM# 41 ROUBLE
Copper-Nickel, 33 mm. **Subject:** 2000 Years **Obv:** National
arms **Rev:** Bethlehem view

Date	Mintage	F	VF	XF	Unc	BU
1999 Proof	10,000	Value: 40.00				

KM# 63 ROUBLE
14.3600 g., Copper-Nickel, 33 mm. **Subject:** Jubilee 2000
Obv: National arms **Rev:** Logo and three churches of Pinsk,
Grodna and Minsk **Edge:** Reeded

Date	Mintage	F	VF	XF	Unc	BU
1999 Proof	10,000	Value: 40.00				

KM# 65 ROUBLE
Copper-Nickel, 32 mm. **Subject:** Borisoglebsk Church **Obv:**
National arms **Rev:** Borisoglebsk Church, seal

Date	Mintage	F	VF	XF	Unc	BU
1999	2,000	—	—	—	—	60.00

KM# 108 ROUBLE
Copper-Nickel, 33 mm. **Subject:** City Of Vitebsk **Obv:** National
arms **Rev:** City coat of arms, Blagoveschenskaya Church, City
Hall

Date	Mintage	F	VF	XF	Unc	BU
2000	2,000	—	—	—	50.00	

KM# 48 ROUBLE
13.2000 g., Copper-Nickel, 31.9 mm. **Subject:** Architecture
Obv: National arms **Rev:** St. Boris and St. Gleb Church
Edge: Reeded

Date	Mintage	F	VF	XF	Unc	BU
2000 Proof	2,000	Value: 50.00				

KM# 24 10 ROUBLES
16.9600 g., 0.9250 Silver 0.5044 oz. ASW, 33 mm. **Subject:**
200th Anniversary - Birth of A. Mitskevich **Obv:** National arms
Rev: Portrait Mitskevich facing left, dates 1798-1855

Date	Mintage	F	VF	XF	Unc	BU
1998 Proof	2,000	Value: 200				

KM# 25 10 ROUBLES
16.9600 g., 0.9250 Silver 0.5044 oz. ASW, 33 mm. **Subject:**
G.P. Glebov - Theatre Artist **Obv:** National arms **Rev:** Glebats
portrait with two smaller portraits, dates 1899-1967

Date	Mintage	F	VF	XF	Unc	BU
1999 Proof	1,200	Value: 125				

KM# 26 10 ROUBLES
16.9600 g., 0.9250 Silver 0.5044 oz. ASW, 33 mm. **Subject:**
100th Anniversary - Birth of Mikhas Lynkou **Obv:** National arms
Rev: Head of Lynkou facing right, dates 1899-1975

Date	Mintage	F	VF	XF	Unc	BU
1999 Proof	1,200	Value: 125				

KM# 13 20 ROUBLES
33.8400 g., 0.9250 Silver 1.0063 oz. ASW, 39 mm. **Subject:**
Olympics **Obv:** National arms and denomination **Rev:** Olympic
crest, gymnast on rings

Date	Mintage	F	VF	XF	Unc	BU
1996 Proof	1,000	Value: 250				

KM# 14 20 ROUBLES
33.8400 g., 0.9250 Silver 1.0063 oz. ASW, 39 mm.
Subject: Olympics **Obv:** National arms and denomination
Rev: Ribbon dancer

Date	Mintage	F	VF	XF	Unc	BU
1996 Proof	1,000	Value: 250				

KM# 10 20 ROUBLES
34.7400 g., 0.9000 Silver 1.0052 oz. ASW, 39 mm.
Subject: Monument of Independence **Obv:** National arms and
denomination **Rev:** Date July 3

Date	Mintage	F	VF	XF	Unc	BU
1997 Proof	3,000	Value: 50.00				

KM# 11 20 ROUBLES
34.7400 g., 0.9000 Silver 1.0052 oz. ASW, 39 mm. **Subject:**
Russia-Belarus State Treaty **Obv:** National arms **Rev:** 2 city
views with respective national emblems and the date April 2 1996
at bottom

Date	Mintage	F	VF	XF	Unc	BU
1997 Proof	5,000	Value: 50.00				

KM# 12   20 ROUBLES
31.4800 g., 0.9990 Silver 1.0111 oz. ASW, 39 mm. **Subject:**
75th Anniversary - Banking System **Obv:** National arms **Rev:**
Bank building

Date	Mintage	F	VF	XF	Unc	BU
1997 Proof	2,000	Value: 175				

KM# 15   20 ROUBLES
31.0300 g., 0.9250 Silver 0.9228 oz. ASW, 39 mm. **Subject:**
Olympics **Obv:** National arms and denomination **Rev:** Biathlon skier

Date	Mintage	F	VF	XF	Unc	BU
1997 Proof	Est. 1,000	Value: 250				

KM# 16   20 ROUBLES
31.1500 g., 0.9250 Silver 0.9263 oz. ASW, 39 mm. **Subject:**
Olympics **Obv:** National arms **Rev:** Two hockey players

Date	Mintage	F	VF	XF	Unc	BU
1997 Proof	Est. 1,000	Value: 225				

KM# 27   20 ROUBLES
33.5200 g., 0.9250 Silver 0.9968 oz. ASW, 38.61 mm.
Subject: Architecture of Belarus **Obv:** National arms, date below,
within circle **Rev:** Castle and Mir and seal

Date	Mintage	F	VF	XF	Unc	BU
1998 Proof	2,000	Value: 200				

KM# 28   20 ROUBLES
33.5200 g., 0.9250 Silver 0.9968 oz. ASW **Subject:** Cities of
Belarus **Obv:** National arms **Rev:** Polatsk with city arms above

Date	Mintage	F	VF	XF	Unc	BU
1998 Proof	2,000	Value: 150				

KM# 29   20 ROUBLES
33.5200 g., 0.9250 Silver 0.9968 oz. ASW **Subject:** Olympics
Obv: National arms and denomination **Rev:** Hurdlers, Olympic crest

Date	Mintage	F	VF	XF	Unc	BU
1998 Proof	1,000	Value: 200				

KM# 17   20 ROUBLES
33.9000 g., 0.9250 Silver 1.0081 oz. ASW, 39 mm.
Subject: 80th Anniversary - Financial System **Obv:** National
arms, date below, within circle **Rev:** Anniversary logo

Date	Mintage	F	VF	XF	Unc	BU
1999 Proof	1,000	Value: 600				

KM# 30   20 ROUBLES
33.5200 g., 0.9250 Silver 0.9968 oz. ASW, 39 mm.
Subject: Cities of Belarus **Obv:** National arms, date below, within
circle **Rev:** Minsk view with city arms

Date	Mintage	F	VF	XF	Unc	BU
1999 Proof	2,000	Value: 180				

KM# 42   20 ROUBLES
33.8600 g., 0.9250 Silver 1.0069 oz. ASW **Subject:** 2000 Years
of Christianity **Obv:** National arms, date below, within circle
Rev: Bethlehem view **Edge:** Reeded

Date	Mintage	F	VF	XF	Unc	BU
1999 Proof	5,000	Value: 200				

KM# 43   20 ROUBLES
33.8600 g., 0.9250 Silver 1.0069 oz. ASW **Subject:** Jubilee
2000 **Obv:** National arms **Rev:** Three churches of Pinsk, Grodno
and Minsk

Date	Mintage	F	VF	XF	Unc	BU
1999 Proof	5,000	Value: 200				

KM# 66   20 ROUBLES
33.8500 g., 0.9250 Silver 1.0066 oz. ASW, 38.5 mm. **Obv:** National
arms **Rev:** Borisoglebsk church in Grodno **Edge:** Reeded

Date	Mintage	F	VF	XF	Unc	BU
1999 Proof	2,000	Value: 150				

KM# 68   20 ROUBLES
33.8500 g., 0.9250 Silver 1.0066 oz. ASW, 38.5 mm.
Obv: National arms **Rev:** Synkovichi church **Edge:** Reeded

Date	Mintage	F	VF	XF	Unc	BU
2000 Proof	2,000	Value: 100				

KM# 109   20 ROUBLES
31.1000 g., 0.9250 Silver 0.9249 oz. ASW, 39 mm.
Subject: City of Vitebsk **Obv:** National arms **Rev:** City coat of
arms, Blagoveschenskaya Church, City Hall

Date	Mintage	F	VF	XF	Unc	BU
2000 Proof	2,000	Value: 100				

KM# 52   20 ROUBLES
31.4500 g., 0.9250 Silver 0.9353 oz. ASW, 38.6 mm.
Subject: 2002 Winter Olympics **Obv:** National arms, date below,
within circle **Rev:** Discus thrower **Edge:** Reeded

Date	Mintage	F	VF	XF	Unc	BU
2000 Proof	20,000	Value: 175				

KM# 32   50 ROUBLES
7.7800 g., 0.9990 Gold 0.2499 oz. AGW, 22 mm.
Subject: Olympics **Obv:** National arms and denomination
Rev: Ribbon dancer

Date	Mintage	F	VF	XF	Unc	BU
1996 Proof	500	Value: 1,500				

KM# 33   50 ROUBLES
7.7800 g., 0.9990 Gold 0.2499 oz. AGW, 22 mm. **Obv:** National arms and denomination **Rev:** Gymnast on rings

Date	Mintage	F	VF	XF	Unc	BU
1996 Proof	500	Value: 1,500				

KM# 35   50 ROUBLES
7.7800 g., 0.9990 Gold 0.2499 oz. AGW, 22 mm. **Obv:** National arms and denomination **Rev:** Biathalow skier with rifle

Date	Mintage	F	VF	XF	Unc	BU
1997 Proof	500	Value: 1,500				

KM# 37   50 ROUBLES
7.7800 g., 0.9990 Gold 0.2499 oz. AGW, 22 mm. **Obv:** National arms and denomination **Rev:** Two hockey players

Date	Mintage	F	VF	XF	Unc	BU
1997 Proof	500	Value: 1,500				

KM# 38   50 ROUBLES
7.7800 g., 0.9990 Gold 0.2499 oz. AGW **Obv:** National arms and denomination **Rev:** Two hurdlers

Date	Mintage	F	VF	XF	Unc	BU
1997 Proof	500	Value: 1,250				

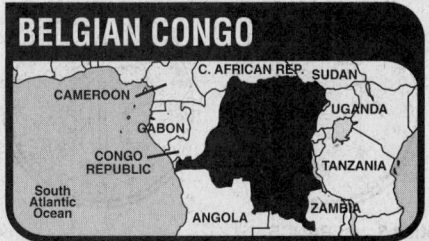

The Belgian Congo and Ruanda-Urundi were united administratively from 1925 to 1960. Ruanda-Urundi was made a U.N. Trust territory in 1946. Coins for these 2 areas were made jointly between 1952 and 1960. Ruanda-Urundi became the Republic of Rwanda on June 1, 1962.

MONETARY SYSTEM
100 Centimes = 1 Franc

RULER
Belgium

MINT MARK
(H) – Heaton, Birmingham – smaller, thicker "C" in denomination

COLONY
DECIMAL COINAGE

KM# 15   CENTIME
Copper **Obv:** Hole at center of crowned "A"s, circle surrounds **Rev:** Center hole within star, date below star, value above

Date	Mintage	F	VF	XF	Unc	BU
1910	2,000,000	1.00	2.00	3.00	10.00	25.00
1919	500,000	1.00	2.00	3.00	15.00	40.00

KM# 16   2 CENTIMES
Copper **Obv:** Hole at center of crowned "A"s, circle surrounds **Rev:** Hole at center of star, date below star, value above

Date	Mintage	F	VF	XF	Unc	BU
1910	1,500,000	1.00	3.00	7.00	30.00	60.00
1919	500,000	1.50	3.50	10.00	35.00	75.00

KM# 12   5 CENTIMES
Copper-Nickel **Obv:** Hole at cente of crowned "JL", circle surrounds **Rev:** Hole at center of star, date below star, value above

Date	Mintage	F	VF	XF	Unc	BU
1909	1,800,000	5.00	12.50	40.00	125	210

KM# 17   5 CENTIMES
2.3900 g., Copper-Nickel, 19 mm. **Obv:** Hole at center of crowned "A"s, within circle **Rev:** Hole at center of star, date below star, value above **Note:** Coins struck at Heaton mint (H) have smaller dates than those produced elsewhere.

Date	Mintage	F	VF	XF	Unc	BU
1910	6,000,000	0.75	1.50	3.50	16.00	60.00
1911	5,000,000	0.75	1.50	3.50	16.00	50.00
1917	1,000,000	3.00	7.00	18.00	55.00	200
1917 Proof	—	Value: 300				
1919	3,000,000	1.50	3.00	7.00	25.00	—
1919	6,850,000	0.50	1.00	2.50	16.00	—
1920	2,740,000	0.50	1.00	3.50	18.00	—
1920/10	—	—	—	—	—	—
1921	17,260,000	0.25	0.75	1.50	10.00	—
1921	3,000,000	1.00	2.00	6.00	20.00	—
1925	11,000,000	0.25	0.75	2.00	10.00	—
1926/5	5,770,000	2.25	4.50	—	—	—
1926	Inc. above	0.25	1.00	2.00	9.00	—
1927	2,000,000	0.50	1.00	2.50	10.00	—
1928/6	1,500,000	2.00	4.00	8.00	20.00	—
1928	Inc. above	0.75	1.00	3.00	10.00	—

KM# 10   10 CENTIMES
Copper-Nickel

Date	Mintage	F	VF	XF	Unc	BU
1906	100,000	4.00	10.00	25.00	60.00	—
1908	800,000	3.00	7.50	20.00	50.00	—

KM# 13   10 CENTIMES
Copper-Nickel **Obv:** Hole at center of crowned "L"s, backs touching, within circle **Rev:** Hole at center of star, date below star, value above

Date	Mintage	F	VF	XF	Unc	BU
1909	1,500,000	8.00	20.00	70.00	200	300

KM# 18   10 CENTIMES
Copper-Nickel **Obv:** Hole at center of crowned "A"s, within circle **Rev:** Hole at center of star, date below star, value above **Note:** Coins struck at Heaton mint (H) have smaller dates than those produced elsewhere.

Date	Mintage	F	VF	XF	Unc	BU
1910	5,000,000	0.50	1.00	3.00	15.00	50.00
1911	5,000,000	0.50	1.00	3.00	15.00	50.00
1917(H)	500,000	5.00	10.00	25.00	75.00	220
1919(H)	1,500,000	0.75	1.25	4.00	18.00	—
1919	3,430,000	0.50	1.00	3.50	16.50	—
1920	1,510,000	0.75	1.25	4.00	18.00	—
1921(H)	3,000,000	0.75	1.50	3.50	16.50	—
1921	13,540,000	0.25	0.75	2.00	10.00	—
1922	14,950,000	0.25	1.00	2.50	10.00	—
1924	3,600,000	0.50	1.50	3.00	15.00	—
1925/4	4,800,000	2.00	4.00	8.00	50.00	—
1925	Inc. above	0.25	1.00	3.00	15.00	—
1927	2,020,000	0.25	1.00	3.00	12.00	—
1928	Inc. above	0.25	1.00	3.00	12.00	—
1928/3	—	—	—	—	—	—
1928/5	—	—	—	—	60.00	—
1928/7	5,600,000	1.00	3.00	8.00	40.00	—

KM# 11   20 CENTIMES
Copper-Nickel

Date	Mintage	F	VF	XF	Unc	BU
1906	100,000	5.00	12.50	25.00	70.00	—
1908	400,000	4.00	7.50	15.00	50.00	—

KM# 14   20 CENTIMES
Copper-Nickel **Obv:** Hole at center of crowned "L"s, backs touching, within circle **Rev:** Hole at center of star, date below star, value above

Date	Mintage	F	VF	XF	Unc	BU
1909	300,000	10.00	25.00	65.00	185	300

KM# 19   20 CENTIMES
5.9200 g., Copper-Nickel, 25.1 mm. **Obv:** Hole at center of crowned "A"s, within circle **Rev:** Hole at center of star, date below star, value above

Date	Mintage	F	VF	XF	Unc	BU
1910	1,000,000	2.00	5.00	12.00	40.00	120
1911	1,250,000	1.50	4.00	10.00	35.00	120

KM# 22   50 CENTIMES
6.4300 g., Copper-Nickel, 24.2 mm. **Obv:** Laureate head left, French legend **Rev:** Oil palm divides denomination and date **Rev. Leg.:** CONGO BELGE **Edge:** Reeded

Date	Mintage	F	VF	XF	Unc	BU
1921	4,000,000	0.60	2.00	8.00	35.00	80.00
1922	6,000,000	0.60	2.00	8.00	30.00	80.00
1923	7,200,000	0.60	2.00	8.00	30.00	80.00
1924	1,096,000	0.75	3.00	10.00	45.00	—
1925	16,104,000	0.60	2.00	7.00	30.00	80.00
1926/5	16,000,000	1.00	4.00	12.00	50.00	—
1926	Inc. above	0.60	2.00	8.00	30.00	80.00
1927	10,000,000	0.60	2.00	8.00	30.00	80.00
1929/7	7,504,000	0.60	2.00	9.00	50.00	—

Date	Mintage	F	VF	XF	Unc	BU
1929/8	Inc. above	1.00	4.00	15.00	90.00	—
1929	Inc. above	0.60	2.00	7.00	30.00	80.00

Date	Mintage	F	VF	XF	Unc	BU
1946	15,000,000	0.75	1.50	3.50	11.00	13.50
1949	15,000,000	0.75	1.50	3.00	11.00	13.50

PATTERNS
Including off metal strikes

KM#	Date	Mintage	Identification	Mkt Val
Pn1	1930	—	Franc. Aluminum-Bronze. 6.9000 g. KM#20.	400
Pn2	1944	—	Franc. Brass. KM#26.	300
Pn3	1944	—	Franc. Steel. KM#26.	300

TRIAL STIRKES

KM#	Date	Mintage	Identification	Mkt Val
30	1949	—	Franc. Copper. KM#26; Uniface.	500

KM# 23   50 CENTIMES
6.5100 g., Copper-Nickel **Obv:** Laureate head left **Rev:** Oil palm divides denomination and date, Flemish legend **Rev. Leg.:** BELGISCH CONGO

Date	Mintage	F	VF	XF	Unc	BU
1921	4,000,000	0.60	2.00	8.00	32.00	—
1922	5,592,000	0.60	2.00	7.00	30.00	—
1923	7,208,000	0.60	2.00	7.00	30.00	—
1924	7,000,000	0.60	2.00	8.00	32.00	—
1925/4	10,600,000	1.50	7.00	20.00	90.00	—
1925	Inc. above	0.60	2.00	7.00	30.00	—
1926	25,200,000	0.60	2.00	7.00	27.50	—
1927	4,800,000	0.60	2.00	8.00	30.00	—
1928	7,484,000	0.60	2.00	7.00	30.00	—
1929/8	116,000	25.00	50.00	75.00	120	—
1929	Inc. above	20.00	40.00	70.00	100	—

KM# 20   FRANC
10.0000 g., Copper-Nickel **Obv:** Laureate head left **Rev:** Oil palm divides denomination and date, French legend **Rev. Leg.:** CONGO BELGE

Date	Mintage	F	VF	XF	Unc	BU
1920	4,000,000	0.85	2.75	10.00	37.50	—
1922	5,000,000	0.85	2.75	9.00	32.00	—
1923/2	5,000,000	2.00	7.00	16.00	45.00	—
1923	Inc. above	0.85	2.75	9.00	32.00	—
1924	6,030,000	0.85	2.75	9.00	35.00	—
1925	10,470,000	0.85	2.75	9.00	32.00	—
1926/5	12,500,000	2.00	7.00	16.50	50.00	—
1926	Inc. above	0.85	2.75	8.00	30.00	—
1927	15,250,000	0.85	2.75	8.00	30.00	—
1929	5,763,000	0.85	2.75	9.00	32.00	—
1930	5,000,000	0.85	2.75	10.00	40.00	—

KM# 21   FRANC
10.1500 g., Copper-Nickel, 29 mm. **Obv:** Laureate head left **Rev:** Oil palm divides denomination and date, Flemish legend **Rev. Leg.:** BELGISCH CONGO

Date	Mintage	F	VF	XF	Unc	BU
1920	475,000	2.00	5.00	16.50	50.00	—
1921	3,525,000	0.85	3.00	9.00	37.50	—
1922	5,000,000	0.85	3.00	9.00	37.50	—
1923/2	7,362,000	2.00	5.00	17.00	55.00	—
1923	Inc. above	0.85	2.75	9.00	32.00	—
1924	4,608,000	0.85	3.00	10.00	37.50	—
1925	9,530,000	0.85	2.75	9.00	32.00	—
1925/3	—	—	—	—	—	—
1926/5	17,000,000	2.00	5.00	17.00	55.00	—
1926	Inc. above	0.85	2.75	9.00	32.00	—
1928	9,250,000	0.85	2.75	9.00	32.00	—
1929	4,250,000	0.85	3.00	10.00	37.50	—

KM# 26   FRANC
2.4800 g., Brass, 19.20 mm. **Obv:** Denomination, legend at top and bottom **Rev:** African elephant, date below

Date	Mintage	F	VF	XF	Unc	BU
1944	25,000,000	0.50	1.00	3.00	10.00	12.50

KM# 25   2 FRANCS
5.8900 g., Brass **Obv:** Denomination, stars flanking **Rev:** African elephant left, date below

Date	Mintage	F	VF	XF	Unc	BU
1943	25,000,000	2.50	6.00	15.00	50.00	75.00

KM# 28   2 FRANCS
Brass **Obv:** Denomination, stars flanking, legend at top and bottom **Rev:** African elephant left, date below

Date	Mintage	F	VF	XF	Unc	BU
1946	13,000,000	1.00	2.00	3.50	22.00	—
1947	12,000,000	1.00	2.00	4.00	25.00	—

KM# 24   5 FRANCS
Nickel-Bronze **Obv:** Head of Leopold III, left **Rev:** Lion above denomination, star at left of denomination, legend surrounds

Date	Mintage	F	VF	XF	Unc	BU
1936	2,600,000	5.00	10.00	30.00	125	150
1937	11,400,000	4.00	12.00	35.00	140	170

KM# 29   5 FRANCS
Brass **Obv:** Denomination at center, stars flanking, legend at top and bottom **Rev:** Africian elephant left, date below

Date	Mintage	F	VF	XF	Unc	BU
1947	10,000,000	3.00	7.00	15.00	50.00	90.00

KM# 27   50 FRANCS
17.5000 g., 0.5000 Silver 0.2813 oz. ASW **Obv:** Denomination at center, stars flanking, legend at top and bottom **Rev:** Africian elephant left, date below

Date	Mintage	F	VF	XF	Unc	BU
1944	1,000,000	20.00	50.00	95.00	185	450

RUANDA-URUNDI
PROVINCE
DECIMAL COINAGE

KM# 2   50 CENTIMES
0.6700 g., Aluminum **Obv:** Crowned arms divide date **Rev:** Oil palm divides denomination

Date	Mintage	F	VF	XF	Unc	BU
1954 DB	4,700,000	—	0.35	0.75	2.00	4.00
1955 DB	20,300,000	—	0.15	0.60	1.50	3.00

KM# 4   FRANC
1.4000 g., Aluminum **Obv:** Crowned arms divide date **Rev:** Oil palm divides denomination

Date	Mintage	F	VF	XF	Unc	BU
1957	10,000,000	—	0.50	1.00	3.00	5.00
1958	20,000,000	—	0.50	1.00	3.00	4.00
1959	20,000,000	—	0.50	1.00	3.00	4.00
1960	20,000,000	—	0.50	1.00	3.00	4.00

KM# 1   5 FRANCS
7.3000 g., Brass

Date	Mintage	F	VF	XF	Unc	BU
1952	10,000,000	—	2.50	5.00	10.00	20.00

KM# 3   5 FRANCS
2.2000 g., Aluminum, 31 mm. **Obv:** Crowned arms divide date **Rev:** Oil palm divides denomination **Edge:** Reeded

Date	Mintage	F	VF	XF	Unc	BU
1956 DB	10,000,000	—	1.00	2.00	4.00	8.00
1958 DB	26,110,000	—	0.75	1.75	3.50	7.00
1959 DB	3,890,000	—	1.00	2.50	5.00	9.00

ESSAIS

KM#	Date	Mintage	Identification	Mkt Val
E1	1952	—	5 Francs. Value at center of star. Tree divides denomination and date.	50.00
E1a	1952	—	5 Francs.. Silver.	250
E2	1954	—	50 Centimes.	50.00
E3	1954	—	50 Centimes. Silver.	150
E4	1956 DB	—	5 Francs. Crowned arms divide date. Tree divides denomination.	50.00
E5	1957	—	Franc. Crowned arms divides date. Tree divides denomination.	50.00
E6	1960	—	Franc. Bronze.	175

BELGIUM

The Kingdom of Belgium, a constitutional monarchy in north-west Europe, has an area of 11,780 sq. mi. (30,519 sq. km.) and a population of 10.1 million, chiefly Dutch-speaking Flemish and French-speaking Walloons. Capital: Brussels. Agriculture, dairy farming, and the processing of raw materials for re-export are the principal industries. Beurs voor Diamant in Antwerp is the world's largest diamond trading center. Iron and steel, machinery motor vehicles, chemicals, textile yarns and fabrics comprise the principal exports.

At the Congress of Vienna in 1815 the area was reunited with the Netherlands, but in 1830 independence was gained and the constitutional monarchy of Belgium was established. A large part of the Duchy of Luxembourg was incorporated into Belgium and the first king was Leopold I of Saxe-Coburg-Gotha. It was invaded by the German Army in August, 1914 and the German forces carried on a devastating occupation of most of the territory until the Armistice. Belgium joined the League of Nations. On May 10, 1940 it was invaded again by the German army. The Belgian and Allied forces were quickly overwhelmed and were evacuated through Dunkirk. Allied troops reached Belgium again in Sept. 1944. Prince Charles, Count of Flanders, assumed King Leopold's responsibilities until liberation by the U.S. Army in Austria on May 8, 1945. As of January 1, 1989, Belgium became a federal kingdom.

RULERS
Leopold II, 1865-1909
Albert I, 1909-1934
Leopold III, 1934-1950
Baudouin I, 1951-1993
Albert II, 1993-

MINT MARK
Angel head - Brussels

MINTMASTERS' INITIALS & PRIVY MARKS
(b) - bird - Vogelier
Lamb head – Lambret
NOTE: Beginning in 1987, the letters "qp" appear on the coins - (quality proof)

MONETARY SYSTEM
100 Centimes = 1 Franc
1 Euro = 100 Cents

LEGENDS
Belgian coins are usually inscribed either in Dutch, French or both. However some modern coins are being inscribed in Latin or German. The language used is best told by noting the spelling of the name of the country.
(Fr) French: BELGIQUE or BELGES
(Du) Dutch: BELGIE or BELGEN
(La) Latin: BELGICA
(Ge) German: BELGIEN
Many Belgian coins are collected by what is known as Position A and Position B edges. Some dates command a premium depending on the position which are as follows:

Position A: Coins with portrait side down having upright edge lettering.
Position B: Coins with portrait side up having upright edge lettering.

KINGDOM
DECIMAL COINAGE

KM# 33.1   CENTIME
2.0001 g., Copper, 16.5 mm. **Ruler:** Leopold II **Obv:** Crowned monogram, legend in French **Obv. Leg.:** DES BELGES **Rev:** Seated lion with tablet **Rev. Leg.:** L'UNION FAIT LA FORCE

Date	Mintage	F	VF	XF	Unc	BU
1901/801 Near 1	3,743,000	0.50	2.50	5.00	18.00	—
1901/801 Far 1	Inc. above	0.50	2.50	5.00	18.00	—
1901	Inc. above	0.25	0.50	1.50	5.00	—
1902/802 Near 2	2,847,000	1.00	2.00	4.00	10.00	—
1902/802 Far 2	Inc. above	1.00	2.00	4.00	10.00	—
1902/801	Inc. above	1.00	2.00	4.00	10.00	—
1902/1	Inc. above	1.00	2.00	4.00	10.00	—
1902	Inc. above	0.20	0.50	1.50	5.00	—
1907	3,967,000	0.20	0.50	1.50	4.00	—

KM# 33.2   CENTIME
2.0080 g., Copper **Ruler:** Leopold II **Obv:** Crowned monogram, legend in French **Obv. Leg.:** DES BELGES **Rev:** Seated lion with tablet **Rev. Leg.:** L'UNION FAIT LA FORCE **Note:** Thin flan.

Date	Mintage	F	VF	XF	Unc	BU
1901	Inc. above	1.00	1.50	4.00	12.50	—
1902	Inc. above	1.00	1.50	6.00	15.00	—

KM# 33.3   CENTIME
2.0000 g., Copper, 16.5 mm. **Ruler:** Leopold II **Obv:** Crowned monogram, legend in French **Obv. Leg.:** DES BELGES **Rev:** Seated lion with tablet, additional stop in signature... BRAEMT.F. **Rev. Leg.:** L'UNION FAIT LA FORCE

Date	Mintage	F	VF	XF	Unc	BU
1902	Inc. above	1.00	2.00	10.00	30.00	—

KM# 34.1   CENTIME
2.0001 g., Copper, 16.5 mm. **Ruler:** Leopold II **Obv:** Crowned monogram, legend in Dutch **Obv. Leg.:** DER BELGEN **Rev:** Seated lion with tablet **Rev. Leg.:** EENDRACHT MAAKT MACHT

Date	Mintage	F	VF	XF	Unc	BU
1901/899	Inc. above	0.75	2.25	4.50	18.00	—
1901	Inc. above	0.25	0.50	1.50	5.00	—
1902/1	2,482,000	1.25	3.50	9.00	10.00	—
1902	Inc. above	0.25	0.50	1.50	5.00	—
1907	3,966,000	0.25	0.50	1.50	4.00	—

KM# 34.2   CENTIME
2.0001 g., Copper, 16.5 mm. **Ruler:** Leopold II **Obv:** Crowned monogram legend in Dutch **Obv. Leg.:** DER BELGEN **Rev:** Seated lion with tablet **Rev. Leg.:** EENDRACHT MAAKT MACHT **Note:** Thin flan.

Date	Mintage	F	VF	XF	Unc	BU
1901	Inc. above	1.00	1.50	8.00	25.00	—
1902	Inc. above	1.00	1.50	8.00	25.00	—

KM# 76   CENTIME
2.0008 g., Copper, 16.5 mm. **Obv:** Crowned letter "A", date below, legend in French **Obv. Leg.:** DES BELGES **Rev:** Tablet at left of seated lion looking right, denomination below **Edge:** Reeded

Date	Mintage	F	VF	XF	Unc	BU
1912	2,540,000	0.20	0.50	2.50	7.00	—
1914	870,000	0.25	0.75	3.50	10.00	—

KM# 77   CENTIME
2.0000 g., Copper, 16.5 mm. **Obv:** Crowned letter "A", date below, legend in Dutch **Obv. Leg.:** DER BELGEN **Rev:** Tablet to left of seated lion looking right, denomination below **Edge:** Reeded

Date	Mintage	F	VF	XF	Unc	BU
1912	2,542,000	0.20	0.50	1.50	4.00	—

KM# 35.1   2 CENTIMES
4.0000 g., Copper, 21.5 mm. **Ruler:** Leopold II **Obv:** Legend in French **Obv. Leg.:** DES BELGES

Date	Mintage	F	VF	XF	Unc	BU
1902	2,490,000	0.15	0.50	4.00	15.00	—
1905	4,981,000	0.15	0.50	4.00	10.00	—
1909	Inc. above	0.15	0.50	4.00	10.00	—
1909/5	4,983,000	0.75	3.00	15.00	50.00	—
1909/1809	Inc. above	1.00	5.00	30.00	85.00	—

KM# 35.2   2 CENTIMES
Copper **Note:** Thin flan.

Date	Mintage	F	VF	XF	Unc	BU
1902	Inc. above	3.00	5.00	35.00	75.00	125

KM# 36   2 CENTIMES
4.0000 g., Copper, 21.5 mm. **Obv:** Crowned design, date below, legend in Dutch **Obv. Leg.:** DER BELGEN **Rev:** Tablet to left of seated lion looking right, denomination below

Date	Mintage	F	VF	XF	Unc	BU
1902	2,488,000	0.15	1.50	4.00	15.00	—
1905/2	4,986,000	1.50	3.00	15.00	50.00	—
1905	Inc. above	0.15	1.00	4.00	10.00	—
1909	565,000	0.50	2.00	12.00	50.00	—

KM# 65   2 CENTIMES
4.0000 g., Copper, 21.6 mm. **Obv:** Crowned letter "A", date below, legend in Dutch **Obv. Leg.:** DER BELGEN **Rev:** Tablet to left of seated lion looking right, denomination below

Date	Mintage	F	VF	XF	Unc	BU
1910	1,248,000	0.25	0.50	3.00	10.00	—
1911 Large date	6,441,000	0.15	0.35	1.50	5.00	—
1911 Small date	Inc. above	0.15	0.35	1.50	5.00	—
1912	1,602,000	0.35	1.00	3.00	8.00	—
1919	4,998,000	0.15	0.35	0.75	3.00	—

KM# 64   2 CENTIMES
4.0000 g., Copper, 21.6 mm. **Obv:** Crowned letter "A", date below, legend in French **Obv. Leg.:** DES BELGES **Rev:** Tablet to left of seated lion looking right, denomination below

Date	Mintage	F	VF	XF	Unc	BU
1911	645,000	1.50	3.00	14.00	40.00	—
1912/1	4,928,000	1.00	3.00	10.00	25.00	—
1912	Inc. above	0.15	0.50	2.00	5.00	—
1914	491,000	1.00	2.50	12.00	30.00	—
1919/4	5,000,000	0.75	1.00	3.00	7.00	—
1919	Inc. above	0.15	0.25	1.00	3.00	—

KM# 40   5 CENTIMES
3.0000 g., Copper-Nickel, 19 mm. **Ruler:** Leopold II **Obv:** Legend in French **Obv. Leg.:** DES BELGES

Date	Mintage	F	VF	XF	Unc	BU
1901	—	10.00	30.00	65.00	140	—

KM# 44   5 CENTIMES
3.0000 g., Copper-Nickel, 19 mm. **Obv:** Denomination above star, circle surrounds **Rev:** Rampant lion left within circle, date below

Date	Mintage	F	VF	XF	Unc	BU
1901	2,494,000	3.00	20.00	35.00	70.00	—

KM# 45   5 CENTIMES
3.0000 g., Copper-Nickel, 19 mm. **Obv:** Denomination above star, circle surrounds, legend in Dutch **Obv. Leg.:** DER BELGEN **Rev:** Rampant lion left within circle, date below

Date	Mintage	F	VF	XF	Unc	BU
1901	2,491,000	3.00	20.00	35.00	70.00	—

KM# 46   5 CENTIMES
2.5000 g., Copper-Nickel, 19 mm. **Obv:** Hole at center of crowned monogram, small date below, legend in French **Obv. Leg.:** BELGIQUE **Rev:** Spray of leaves to left of center hole, denomination at right

Date	Mintage	F	VF	XF	Unc	BU
1901	202,000	15.00	50.00	90.00	175	—
1902/1	1,416,000	0.50	8.00	15.00	45.00	—
1902	Inc. above	0.25	3.00	7.00	22.00	—
1903	864,000	1.00	8.00	15.00	45.00	—

KM# 47 5 CENTIMES
2.5000 g., Copper-Nickel, 19 mm. **Obv:** Center hole within crowned monogram, small date below, legend in Dutch **Obv. Leg.:** BELGIE **Rev:** Spray of leaves to left of center hole, denomination to right

Date	Mintage	F	VF	XF	Unc	BU
1902/1	1,485,000	1.75	5.50	22.50	45.00	—
1902	Inc. above	0.15	3.00	7.00	22.00	—
1903	1,002,000	1.00	8.00	25.00	50.00	—

KM# 54 5 CENTIMES
2.5000 g., Copper-Nickel, 19 mm. **Obv:** Center hole within crowned monogram, large date below, legend in French **Obv. Leg.:** BELGIQUE **Rev:** Spray of leaves to left of center hole, denomination to right

Date	Mintage	F	VF	XF	Unc	BU
1904	5,814,000	0.15	0.35	2.00	7.00	—
1905/4	9,575,000	0.30	1.00	3.00	15.00	—
1905	Inc. above	0.15	0.35	2.00	7.00	—
1905 WICHAUX (error)	Inc. above	2.00	15.00	25.00	60.00	—
1905 A. MICHAUX	Inc. above	1.00	3.50	15.00	40.00	—
1906/5	8,463,000	0.30	1.50	3.00	12.00	—
1906	Inc. above	0.15	0.35	2.00	6.00	—
1907	993,000	1.00	6.00	12.00	30.00	—

KM# 55 5 CENTIMES
2.5000 g., Copper-Nickel, 19 mm. **Obv:** Center hole within crowned monogram, large date below, legend in Dutch **Obv. Leg.:** BELGIE **Rev:** Spray of leaves to left of center hole, denomination to right

Date	Mintage	F	VF	XF	Unc	BU
1904	5,812,000	0.15	0.35	2.00	7.00	—
1905/3	7,002,000	0.35	2.50	15.00	30.00	—
1905/4	Inc. above	0.30	1.50	4.00	15.00	—
1905	Inc. above	0.15	0.35	2.00	7.00	—
1905 Without cross	Inc. above	—	1.50	6.00	20.00	—
1906	11,016,000	0.15	0.35	2.00	7.00	—
1906 Without cross	Inc. above	0.30	1.50	4.00	15.00	—
1907	998,000	1.00	3.00	15.00	30.00	—

KM# 66 5 CENTIMES
2.5000 g., Copper-Nickel, 19 mm. **Obv:** Center hole within crowned monogram, date below, legend in French **Obv. Leg.:** BELGIQUE **Rev:** Spray of leaves to left of center hole, denomination to right

Date	Mintage	F	VF	XF	Unc	BU
1910	8,011,000	0.10	0.35	1.25	4.00	—
1913/0	5,005,000	0.20	0.75	2.25	10.00	—
1913	Inc. above	0.10	0.40	1.50	7.00	—
1914	1,004,000	1.00	3.00	8.00	25.00	—
1920/10	10,040,000	0.10	1.00	3.00	4.00	—
1920	Inc. above	0.10	0.35	1.25	4.00	—
1922/0	12,640,000	0.10	1.50	4.00	9.00	—
1922/1	Inc. above	0.10	1.50	3.50	9.00	—
1922	Inc. above	0.10	0.35	1.25	4.00	—
1923/13	9,000,000	0.10	0.75	2.50	8.00	—
1923	Inc. above	0.10	0.35	1.25	4.00	—
1925/13	15,860,000	0.10	0.50	2.00	8.00	—
1925/23	Inc. above	0.10	0.50	2.00	8.00	—
1925	Inc. above	0.10	0.35	1.25	4.00	—
1926/5	7,000,000	0.10	1.00	2.50	8.00	—
1926	Inc. above	0.10	0.35	1.25	4.00	—
1927	2,000,000	0.10	1.00	2.50	9.00	—
1927 5 Cen	—	10.00	20.00	50.00	100	

Note: Obverse of KM#66 in French paired with the reverse of KM#67 in Flemish.

1928	12,507,000	0.10	0.35	1.25	4.00	—

KM# 67 5 CENTIMES
2.5000 g., Copper-Nickel, 19 mm. **Obv:** Center hole within crowned monogram, date below, legend in Dutch **Obv. Leg.:** BELGIE **Rev:** Spray of leaves to left of center hole, denomination to right, plain field above 5

Date	Mintage	F	VF	XF	Unc	BU
1910	8,033,000	0.10	0.35	1.25	4.00	—
1914	6,040,000	0.10	0.35	1.25	4.00	—
1920/10	10,030,000	0.10	0.35	1.25	6.00	—
1920	Inc. above	0.10	0.50	3.00	12.00	—
1921/11	4,200,000	0.10	1.00	2.50	12.00	—
1921	Inc. above	0.10	1.00	2.00	9.00	—
1922/12	13,180,000	0.10	1.00	2.50	8.00	—
1922/0	Inc. above	0.10	1.00	3.00	9.00	—
1922	Inc. above	0.10	0.35	1.25	4.00	—
1923/13	3,530,000	0.10	1.00	3.00	10.00	—
1923	Inc. above	0.10	0.75	2.00	9.00	—
1924/11	5,260,000	0.10	1.00	2.50	9.00	—
1924/14	Inc. above	0.10	0.50	1.75	9.00	—
1924	Inc. above	0.10	0.35	1.25	4.00	—
1925/13	13,000,000	0.10	1.00	2.50	8.00	—
1925/15 High 2	Inc. above	0.10	1.00	2.00	9.00	—
1925/15 Level 2	Inc. above	0.10	1.00	2.00	9.00	—
1925/3	Inc. above	0.10	0.60	2.00	9.00	—
1925	Inc. above	0.10	0.35	1.25	4.00	—
1927	6,938,000	0.10	0.35	1.25	4.00	—
1928/3	6,252,000	0.10	0.75	2.50	9.00	—
1928	Inc. above	0.10	0.35	1.25	4.00	—

KM# 80 5 CENTIMES
2.5000 g., Zinc, 19 mm. **Obv:** Denomination within circle, date below circle, legend in French **Obv. Leg.:** BELGIQUE-BELGIE **Rev:** Rampant lion, left, within circle **Note:** German Occupation WW I

Date	Mintage	F	VF	XF	Unc	BU
1915	10,199,000	0.15	2.00	4.00	15.00	30.00
1916	45,464,000	0.10	0.60	2.00	7.00	15.00

KM# 94 5 CENTIMES
2.5000 g., Nickel-Brass, 19 mm. **Obv:** Center hole within crowned monogram, date below, legend in Dutch **Obv. Leg.:** BELGIE **Rev:** Spray of leaves to left of center hole, denomination at right, star added above 5

Date	Mintage	F	VF	XF	Unc	BU
1930	3,000,000	0.10	0.20	0.35	3.00	—
1931	7,430,000	0.10	0.20	0.35	3.00	—

KM# 93 5 CENTIMES
2.5000 g., Nickel-Brass, 19 mm. **Obv:** Legend in French **Obv. Leg.:** BELGIQUE **Rev:** Star added above 5

Date	Mintage	F	VF	XF	Unc	BU
1932	5,520,000	0.10	0.20	0.35	3.00	—

KM# 110.1 5 CENTIMES
2.5000 g., Nickel-Brass, 19 mm. **Obv:** Three shields above denomination, legend in French, hole at center **Obv. Leg.:** BELGIQUE-BELGIE **Rev:** Hole at center of crowned design, date below

Date	Mintage	F	VF	XF	Unc	BU
1938	4,970,000	0.10	0.20	0.75	2.00	—
1939	—	—	—	—	—	—

Note: Struck at a later date

KM# 110.2 5 CENTIMES
2.5000 g., Nickel-Brass, 19 mm. **Obv:** Three shields above denomination, legend in French, hole at center **Obv. Leg.:** BELGIQUE-BELGIE **Rev:** Hole at center of crowned design, date below **Note:** Medal alignment.

Date	Mintage	F	VF	XF	Unc	BU
1938	Inc. above	7.00	12.00	20.00	40.00	—

KM# 111 5 CENTIMES
2.5000 g., Nickel-Brass, 19 mm. **Obv:** Three shields above denomination, hole at center, legend in Dutch **Obv. Leg.:** BELGIE-BELGIQUE **Rev:** Crowned design above date, hole at center

Date	Mintage	F	VF	XF	Unc	BU
1939	3,000,000	0.10	0.20	0.75	3.00	—
1940	1,970,000	0.20	0.50	1.50	5.00	—

KM# 124 5 CENTIMES
2.5000 g., Zinc, 19 mm. **Obv:** Three shields above denomination, hole at center, legend in Dutch **Obv. Leg.:** BELGIE-BELGIQUE **Rev:** Crowned design above date, hole at center

Date	Mintage	F	VF	XF	Unc	BU
1941	4,000,000	0.15	0.75	2.50	15.00	—
1942	18,430,000	0.10	0.20	1.00	4.00	—

KM# 123 5 CENTIMES
2.5000 g., Zinc, 19 mm. **Obv:** Three shields above denomination, legend in French, hole at center **Obv. Leg.:** BELGIQUE-BELGIE **Rev:** Hole at center of crowned design, date below **Note:** German Occupation WW II

Date	Mintage	F	VF	XF	Unc	BU
1941	10,000,000	0.10	0.20	—	4.00	—
1943	7,606,000	0.10	0.20	1.50	6.00	—

KM# 42 10 CENTIMES
4.5000 g., Copper-Nickel, 21 mm. **Ruler:** Leopold II **Obv:** Denomination and star within circle **Obv. Leg.:** LEOPOLD II ROI DES BELGES **Rev:** Rampant lion left within circle **Rev. Leg.:** L'UNION FAIT LA FORCE

Date	Mintage	F	VF	XF	Unc	BU
1901	551,000	30.00	140	200	325	375

KM# 43 10 CENTIMES
4.5000 g., Copper-Nickel, 21 mm. **Ruler:** Leopold II **Obv:** Denomination above star, within circle, legend in Dutch **Obv. Leg.:** LEOPOLD II KONING DER BELGEN **Rev:** Rampant lion left within circle **Rev. Leg.:** EENDRACHT MAAKT MACHT

Date	Mintage	F	VF	XF	Unc	BU
1901	556,000	30.00	175	225	350	450

KM# 48 10 CENTIMES
4.0000 g., Copper-Nickel, 22 mm. **Obv:** Center hole within crowned monogram, small date below, legend in French **Obv. Leg.:** BELGIQUE **Rev:** Spray of leaves to left of center hole, denomination to right

Date	Mintage	F	VF	XF	Unc	BU
1901	582,000	6.00	15.00	40.00	130	—
1902/1	5,866,000	0.50	3.00	15.00	30.00	—
1902	Inc. above	0.15	1.00	3.00	7.00	—
1903	763,000	1.00	4.00	15.00	35.00	—

KM# 49 10 CENTIMES
4.0000 g., Copper-Nickel, 22 mm. **Obv:** Center hole within crowned monogram, date below, legend in Dutch, **Obv. Leg.:** BELGIE **Rev:** Spray of leaves to left of center hole, denomination to right

Date	Mintage	F	VF	XF	Unc	BU
1902	1,560,000	0.20	2.00	8.00	15.00	—
1903/2	—	0.50	1.25	7.00	20.00	—
1903	5,658,000	0.20	1.00	2.50	7.00	—

KM# 52 10 CENTIMES
4.0000 g., Copper-Nickel, 22 mm. **Obv:** Center hole within crowned monogram, large date below, legend in French **Obv. Leg.:** BELGIQUE **Rev:** Spray of leaves to left center hole, denomination to right

Date	Mintage	F	VF	XF	Unc	BU
1903	Inc. above	2.00	15.00	30.00	55.00	—
1904	16,354,000	0.15	1.00	3.00	7.00	—
1905/4	14,392,000	0.25	1.00	5.00	15.00	—
1905	Inc. above	0.15	0.60	2.00	7.00	—
1906/5	1,483,000	0.50	1.50	5.00	18.00	—
1906	Inc. above	0.25	0.75	5.00	15.00	—

KM# 53 10 CENTIMES
4.0000 g., Copper-Nickel, 22 mm. **Obv:** Center hole within crowned monogram, large date below, legend in Dutch **Obv. Leg.:** BELGIE **Rev:** Spray of leaves to left of center hole, denomination to right

Date	Mintage	F	VF	XF	Unc	BU
1903	Inc. above	1.00	4.00	15.00	35.00	—
1904	16,834,000	0.20	0.50	2.00	7.00	—
1905/3	13,758,000	0.35	1.00	3.00	15.00	—
1905/4	Inc. above	0.30	1.00	3.00	15.00	—
1905	Inc. above	0.20	0.50	2.00	7.00	—
1906/5	2,017,000	0.50	1.25	4.00	15.00	—
Note: Point above center of 6						
1906/5	Inc. above	0.50	1.25	4.00	15.00	—
Note: Point above right side of 6						
1906	Inc. above	0.10	0.75	5.00	18.00	—

KM# 81 10 CENTIMES
4.0000 g., Zinc, 22 mm. **Obv:** Denomination within circle, date below, legend in French **Obv. Leg.:** BELGIQUE-BELGIE **Rev:** Rampant lion, left, within circle **Note:** German Occupation. All of KM#81 have dots after the date. The 1916 is distinguished by a period after the date.

Date	Mintage	F	VF	XF	Unc	BU
1915	9,681,000	0.25	1.50	4.00	15.00	30.00
1916/15	37,382,000	20.00	30.00	100	175	225
.1916	Inc. above	0.15	0.75	3.00	10.00	20.00
Note: With dots before and after date						
.1916	Inc. above	7.00	15.00	50.00	100	—
Note: With dot before date only						
1916.	Inc. above	10.00	25.00	100	200	—
Note: With dot after date only						
1917	1,447,000	17.50	25.00	85.00	200	—

KM# 85.1 10 CENTIMES
4.0000 g., Copper-Nickel, 22 mm. **Obv:** Center hole within crowned monogram, date below, legend in French **Obv. Leg.:** BELGIQUE **Rev:** Spray of leaves to left of center hole, denomination to right

Date	Mintage	F	VF	XF	Unc	BU
1911	—					—
Note: Struck at a later date						
1920	6,520,000	0.15	0.40	1.50	4.50	—
1921	7,215,000	0.15	0.20	1.00	4.00	—
1923	20,625,000	0.10	0.20	1.00	4.00	—
1926	Inc. above	0.15	0.20	1.00	4.00	—
1926/3	6,916,000	0.20	0.75	3.00	12.00	—
1926/5	Inc. above	0.20	0.75	3.00	12.00	—
1927	8,125,000	0.15	0.20	1.00	4.00	—
1928/3	6,895,000	0.20	1.00	4.00	10.00	—
1928/5	Inc. above	0.20	1.00	4.00	10.00	—
1928	Inc. above	0.15	0.20	1.00	4.00	—
1929	12,260,000	0.15	0.20	1.00	4.00	—

KM# 85.2 10 CENTIMES
4.0000 g., Copper-Nickel, 22 mm. **Obv:** Center hole within crowned monogram, date below, legend in French **Obv. Leg.:** BELGIQUE **Rev:** Spray of leaves to left of center hole, denomination to right, center line below ES of CES

Date	Mintage	F	VF	XF	Unc	BU
1920	Inc. above	0.50	3.00	10.00	20.00	—
1921	Inc. above	1.50	10.00	18.00	45.00	—

KM# 86 10 CENTIMES
4.0000 g., Copper-Nickel, 22 mm. **Obv:** Center hole within crowned monogram, date below, legend in Dutch **Obv. Leg.:** BELGIE **Rev:** Spray of leaves to left of center hole, denomination to right, plain field above 10 **Edge:** Plain

Date	Mintage	F	VF	XF	Unc	BU
1920	5,050,000	0.15	0.20	1.00	5.00	—
1921	7,580,000	0.15	0.20	1.00	4.00	—
1922	6,250,000	0.15	0.20	1.00	4.00	—
1924	5,825,000	0.15	0.20	1.00	6.00	—
1925/3	Inc. above	0.20	0.40	2.00	10.00	—
1925/4	8,160,000	0.20	0.40	2.00	10.00	—
1925	Inc. above	0.10	0.20	1.00	4.00	—
1926/3	Inc. above	0.20	0.40	2.00	10.00	—
1926/5	6,250,000	0.20	0.40	2.00	10.00	—
1926	Inc. above	0.15	0.20	1.00	4.00	—
1927	10,625,000	0.15	0.20	1.00	4.00	—
1928/3	Inc. above	0.20	0.40	2.00	10.00	—
1928/5	6,750,000	0.20	0.40	2.00	10.00	—
1928	Inc. above	0.15	0.20	1.00	4.00	—
1929	4,668,000	0.15	0.20	1.00	4.00	—
1930	—	15.00	30.00	100	250	—

KM# 95.1 10 CENTIMES
4.0000 g., Nickel-Brass, 22 mm. **Obv:** Center hole within crowned monogram, date below, legend in French **Obv. Leg.:** BELGIQUE **Rev:** Spray of leaves to left of center hole, denomination to right, star added above 10 **Edge:** Plain

Date	Mintage	F	VF	XF	Unc	BU
1930/20	2,000,000	50.00	120	275	450	—
1930	Inc. above	20.00	100	250	400	—
1931	6,270,000	5.00	10.00	20.00	50.00	80.00
1932	1,270,000	35.00	200	300	450	—
1932	Inc. above	50.00	220	350	500	—
Note: A instead of signature						

KM# 95.2 10 CENTIMES
4.0000 g., Nickel-Brass, 22 mm. **Obv:** Legend in French **Obv. Leg.:** BELGIQUE **Rev:** Single line below ES of CES, star added above 10

Date	Mintage	F	VF	XF	Unc	BU
1931	Inc. above	2.00	8.00	20.00	50.00	—
1932	Inc. above	45.00	200	350	500	—

KM# 96 10 CENTIMES
4.0000 g., Nickel-Brass, 22 mm. **Obv:** Center hole within crowned monogram, date below, legend in Dutch **Obv. Leg.:** BELGIE **Rev:** Spray of leaves to left of center hole, denomination to right, star added above 10

Date	Mintage	F	VF	XF	Unc	BU
1930	1,581,000	0.30	0.75	3.00	10.00	—
1931	5,000,000	25.00	100	200	350	—

KM# 112 10 CENTIMES
4.0000 g., Nickel-Brass, 22 mm. **Obv:** Three shields above denomination, hole at center, legend in French **Obv. Leg.:** BELGIQUE-BELGIE **Rev:** Crowned design above date, hole at center

Date	Mintage	F	VF	XF	Unc	BU
1938	6,000,000	0.10	0.25	0.50	1.50	—
1939	7,000,000	0.50	1.00	3.00	15.00	—

KM# 113.1 10 CENTIMES
4.0000 g., Nickel-Brass, 22 mm. **Obv:** Three shields above denomination, hole at center, legend in Dutch **Obv. Leg.:** BELGIE-BELGIQUE **Rev:** Crowned design above date, hole at center

Date	Mintage	F	VF	XF	Unc	BU
1939	8,425,000	0.10	0.25	0.50	1.50	—

KM# 113.2 10 CENTIMES
Nickel-Brass, 22 mm. **Obv:** Three shields above denomination, hole at center, legend in Dutch **Obv. Leg.:** BELGIE-BELGIQUE **Rev:** Crowned design above date, hole at center **Note:** Thin flan.

Date	Mintage	F	VF	XF	Unc	BU
1939	Inc. above	1.25	3.00	10.00	35.00	—

KM# 126 10 CENTIMES
4.0000 g., Zinc, 22 mm. **Obv:** Three shields above denomination, hole at center, legend in Dutch **Obv. Leg.:** BELGIE-BELGIQUE **Rev:** Crowned design above date, hole at center **Edge:** Plain

Date	Mintage	F	VF	XF	Unc	BU
1941	7,000,000	0.15	2.00	5.00	10.00	—
1942	21,000,000	0.15	0.25	1.50	4.00	—
1943	22,000,000	0.15	0.25	1.50	4.00	—
1944	28,140,000	0.15	0.25	1.50	4.00	—
1945	8,000,000	0.15	2.00	5.00	10.00	—
1946	5,370,000	0.15	1.00	2.00	8.00	—

KM# 125 10 CENTIMES
4.0000 g., Zinc, 22 mm. **Obv:** Three shields above denomination, hole at center, legend in French **Obv. Leg.:** BELGIQUE-BELGIE **Rev:** Crowned design above date, hole at center **Edge:** Plain **Note:** German Occupation WW II.

Date	Mintage	F	VF	XF	Unc	BU
1941	10,000,000	0.15	0.25	1.50	4.00	—
1942	17,000,000	0.15	0.25	1.50	4.00	—
1943	22,500,000	0.15	0.25	1.50	4.00	—
1945	—	—	—	—	—	—
Note: Struck at a later date						
1946	Est. 10,370,000	—	—	—	—	—
Note: Not released for circulation						

KM# 146 20 CENTIMES
2.0000 g., Bronze, 17 mm. **Obv:** Crowned denomination divides date, legend in French **Obv. Leg.:** BELGIQUE **Rev:** Helmeted head, left, small miner's lamp at right **Edge:** Plain

Date	Mintage	F	VF	XF	Unc	BU
1953	14,150,000	—	0.10	0.20	0.50	—
1953	—	—	0.10	0.75	2.50	—

Date	Mintage	F	VF	XF	Unc	BU
Note: CENTIMES not touching rim						
1954	—	—	600	800	1,000	—
Note: Considered by some to be an Essai						
1957	13,300,000	—	—	0.10	0.50	—
1958	8,700,000	—	—	0.10	0.50	—
1959	19,670,000	—	—	0.10	0.50	—
1962	410,000	—	6.00	10.00	18.00	—
1963	2,550,000	0.10	0.20	0.50	1.00	—

KM# 147.1   20 CENTIMES
2.0000 g., Bronze, 17 mm. **Obv:** Crowned denomination divides date, legend in Dutch **Obv. Leg.:** BELGIE **Rev:** Helmeted head, left, small miner's lamp at right **Edge:** Plain

Date	Mintage	F	VF	XF	Unc	BU
1954	50,130,000	—	—	0.10	0.50	—
1960	7,530,000	—	—	0.10	0.50	—

KM# 147.2   20 CENTIMES
2.0000 g., Bronze, 17 mm. **Obv:** CENTIMES touching rim, crowned denomination divides date, legend in Dutch **Obv. Leg.:** BELGIE **Rev:** Helmeted head, left, small miner's lamp at right **Edge:** Plain

Date	Mintage	F	VF	XF	Unc	BU
1954	Inc. above	—	0.15	0.75	2.50	—
1960	Inc. above	—	0.15	0.75	2.50	—

KM# 62   25 CENTIMES
6.5000 g., Copper-Nickel **Obv:** Center hole within crowned monogram, date below, legend in French **Obv. Leg.:** BELGIQUE **Rev:** Spray of leaves to left of center hole, denomination to right

Date	Mintage	F	VF	XF	Unc	BU
1908	4,007,000	0.50	4.00	20.00	50.00	—
1909/8	1,998,000	4.00	40.00	150	275	—
1909	Inc. above	1.00	8.00	30.00	70.00	—

KM# 63   25 CENTIMES
6.5000 g., Copper-Nickel **Obv:** Center hole within crowned monogram, date below, legend in Dutch **Obv. Leg.:** BELGIE **Rev:** Spray of leaves to left of center hole, denomination to right

Date	Mintage	F	VF	XF	Unc	BU
1908	4,011,000	0.50	4.00	20.00	50.00	—

KM# 69   25 CENTIMES
6.5000 g., Copper-Nickel, 25.8 mm. **Obv:** Center hole within crowned monogram, date below, legend in Dutch **Obv. Leg.:** BELGIE **Rev:** Sprays to left of center hole, denomination to right

Date	Mintage	F	VF	XF	Unc	BU
1910	2,006,000	0.15	1.00	8.00	20.00	—
1911	—	—	—	—	—	—
Note: Struck at a later date						
1913	2,010,000	0.15	3.00	8.00	20.00	—
1921	11,173,000	0.15	0.25	2.00	6.00	—
1922/1	14,200,000	1.00	10.00	20.00	45.00	—
1922	Inc. above	0.15	0.25	2.00	6.00	—
1926/3	6,400,000	0.35	6.00	12.00	25.00	—
1926	Inc. above	0.10	0.40	2.00	6.00	—
1927/3	3,799,000	0.35	5.00	10.00	25.00	—
1927	Inc. above	0.10	0.25	2.00	6.00	—
1928	9,200,000	0.10	0.25	2.00	6.00	—
1929	8,980,000	0.10	0.25	2.00	6.00	—

KM# 68.1   25 CENTIMES
6.5000 g., Copper-Nickel, 26 mm. **Obv:** Center hole within crowned monogram, date below, legend in French **Obv. Leg.:** BELGIQUE **Rev:** Spray +f leaves to left of center hole, denomination to right

Date	Mintage	F	VF	XF	Unc	BU
1913	2,011,000	0.15	3.00	8.00	20.00	—
1920	2,844,000	0.15	2.00	7.00	18.00	—
1921	7,464,000	0.10	0.25	2.00	6.00	—
1922	7,600,000	0.10	0.25	2.00	6.00	—
1923	11,356,000	0.15	0.25	2.00	6.00	—
1926/3	1,300,000	1.00	5.00	12.00	30.00	—
1926	Inc. above	0.50	5.00	12.00	30.00	—
1927/3	8,800,000	1.00	10.00	20.00	45.00	—
1927	Inc. above	0.10	0.25	2.00	6.00	—
1928	4,351,000	0.10	1.00	2.00	8.00	—
1929	9,600,000	0.10	0.25	2.00	6.00	—

KM# 68.2   25 CENTIMES
6.5000 g., Copper-Nickel, 26 mm. **Obv:** Center hole within crowned monogram, date below, legend in French **Obv. Leg.:** BELIQUE **Rev:** Single line below ES of CES, spray of leaves to left of center hole, denomination to right

Date	Mintage	F	VF	XF	Unc	BU
1920	Inc. above	0.50	2.00	8.00	25.00	—
1921	Inc. above	0.35	1.50	6.00	15.00	—

KM# 82   25 CENTIMES
6.5000 g., Zinc, 26 mm. **Obv:** Denomination within beaded circle, stars flank date below, legend in French **Obv. Leg.:** BELGIQUE-BELGIE **Rev:** Rampant lion left within beaded circle **Note:** German Occupation WW I

Date	Mintage	F	VF	XF	Unc	BU
1915	8,080,000	0.50	4.00	9.00	22.00	—
1916	10,671,000	0.50	3.00	7.00	15.00	—
1917	3,555,000	2.00	10.00	18.00	40.00	—
1918	5,489,000	1.00	8.00	12.00	30.00	—

KM# 114.1   25 CENTIMES
6.5000 g., Nickel-Brass, 26 mm. **Obv:** Three shields above denomination, hole in center, legend in French **Obv. Leg.:** BELGIQUE-BELGIE **Rev:** Crowned design above date, hole in center

Date	Mintage	F	VF	XF	Unc	BU
1938	7,200,000	—	0.25	1.00	4.00	—
1939	7,732,000	—	0.25	1.00	4.00	—

KM# 114.2   25 CENTIMES
6.5000 g., Nickel-Brass, 26 mm. **Obv:** Three shields above denomination, hole in center, legend in French **Obv. Leg.:** BELGIQUE-BELGIE **Rev:** Crowned design above date, hole in center **Note:** Medal alignment.

Date	Mintage	F	VF	XF	Unc	BU
1939	Inc. above	5.00	10.00	20.00	35.00	—

KM# 115.1   25 CENTIMES
6.5000 g., Nickel-Brass, 26 mm. **Obv:** Three shields above denomination, hole at center, legend in Dutch **Obv. Leg.:** BELGIE-BELGIQUE **Rev:** Crowned design above date, hole at center

Date	Mintage	F	VF	XF	Unc	BU
1938	14,932,000	—	0.25	1.00	3.00	—

KM# 115.2   25 CENTIMES
6.5000 g., Nickel-Brass, 26 mm. **Obv:** Three shields above denomination, hole at center, legend in Dutch **Obv. Leg.:** BELGIQUE **Rev:** Crowned design above date, hole at center **Note:** Medal alignment.

Date	Mintage	F	VF	XF	Unc	BU
1938	Inc. above	5.00	10.00	20.00	30.00	—

KM# 131   25 CENTIMES
6.5000 g., Zinc, 26 mm. **Obv:** Three shields above denomination, hole at center, legend in French **Obv. Leg.:** BELGIQUE-BELGIE **Rev:** Crowned design above date, hole at center **Note:** German Occupation WW II.

Date	Mintage	F	VF	XF	Unc	BU
1941 Rare	—	—	—	—	—	—
1942	14,400,000	—	0.20	0.75	3.00	10.00
1943	21,600,000	—	0.20	0.75	3.00	10.00
1945	—	—	—	—	—	—
Note: Struck at a later date						
1946	21,428,000	—	0.20	0.75	3.00	10.00
1947	Est. 300,000	—	—	—	—	—
Note: Not released for circulation						

KM# 132   25 CENTIMES
6.5000 g., Zinc, 26 mm. **Obv:** Three shields above denomination, hole at center, legend in Dutch **Obv. Leg.:** BELGIE-BELGIQUE **Rev:** Crowned design above date, hole at center

Date	Mintage	F	VF	XF	Unc	BU
1942	14,400,000	—	1.00	2.00	6.00	18.00
1943	21,600,000	—	0.20	0.75	3.00	10.00
1944	25,960,000	—	0.20	0.75	3.00	10.00
1945	8,200,000	—	0.50	2.50	8.00	22.00
1946	11,652,000	—	0.50	2.50	10.00	30.00
1947	Est. 316,000	—	—	—	—	—
Note: Not released for circulation						

KM# 153.1   25 CENTIMES
2.0000 g., Copper-Nickel, 16 mm. **Obv:** Large denomination between mint marks, legend in French **Obv. Leg.:** BELGIQUE **Rev:** Crowned "B" divides date **Note:** Mint mark - Angel Head. Mintmaster Vogeleer's privy mark - Bird.

Date	Mintage	F	VF	XF	Unc	BU
1964	21,770,000	—	—	0.10	0.15	—
1965	11,440,000	—	—	0.10	0.15	—
1966	19,990,000	—	—	0.10	0.15	—
1967	6,820,000	—	—	0.10	0.50	—
1968	25,250,000	—	—	0.10	0.15	—
1969	7,670,000	—	—	0.10	0.30	—
1970	27,000,000	—	—	0.10	0.15	—
1971	16,000,000	—	—	0.10	0.15	—
1972	20,000,000	—	—	0.10	0.15	—
1973	12,500,000	—	—	0.10	0.15	—
1974	20,000,000	—	—	0.10	0.15	—
1975	12,000,000	—	—	0.10	0.15	—

KM# 153.2   25 CENTIMES
2.0000 g., Copper-Nickel, 16 mm. **Obv:** Large denomination between mint marks, legend in French **Obv. Leg.:** BELGIQUE **Rev:** Crowned "B" divides date **Note:** Medal alignment. Mint mark - Angel Head. Mintmaster Vogeleer's privy mark - Bird.

Date	Mintage	F	VF	XF	Unc	BU
1964	Inc. above	—	—	5.00	12.00	—
1965	Inc. above	—	—	10.00	25.00	—
1967	Inc. above	—	—	10.00	25.00	—
1970	Inc. above	—	—	5.00	12.00	—
1971	Inc. above	—	—	5.00	12.00	—
1974	Inc. above	—	—	10.00	25.00	—

KM# 154.1 25 CENTIMES

2.0000 g., Copper-Nickel, 16 mm. **Obv:** Large denomination between mint marks, legend in Dutch **Obv. Leg.:** BELGIE **Rev:** Crowned "B" divides date **Edge:** Plain **Note:** Mint mark - Angel Head. Mintmaster Vogeleer's privy mark - Bird.

Date	Mintage	F	VF	XF	Unc	BU
1964	21,300,000	—	—	0.10	0.15	—
1965	7,900,000	—	—	0.10	0.30	—
1966	23,420,000	—	—	0.10	0.15	—
1967	7,720,000	—	—	0.10	0.30	—
1968	22,750,000	—	—	0.10	0.15	—
1969	25,190,000	—	—	0.10	0.15	—
1970	12,000,000	—	—	0.10	0.15	—
1971	16,000,000	—	—	0.10	0.15	—
1972	20,000,000	—	—	0.10	0.15	—
1973	12,500,000	—	—	0.10	0.15	—
1974	20,000,000	—	—	0.10	0.15	—
1975	12,000,000	—	—	0.10	0.15	—

KM# 154.2 25 CENTIMES

2.0000 g., Copper-Nickel, 16 mm. **Obv:** Large denomination between mint marks, legend in Dutch **Obv. Leg.:** BELGIE **Rev:** Crowned "B" divides date **Edge:** Plain **Note:** Medal alignment. Mint mark - Angel Head. Mintmaster Vogeleer's privy mark - Bird.

Date	Mintage	F	VF	XF	Unc	BU
1964	Inc. above	—	—	5.00	12.00	—
1965	Inc. above	—	—	5.00	15.00	—
1966	Inc. above	—	—	5.00	12.00	—
1967	Inc. above	—	—	6.00	15.00	—
1969	Inc. above	—	—	5.00	12.00	—
1971	Inc. above	—	—	6.00	15.00	—
1972	Inc. above	—	—	5.00	12.00	—

KM# 50 50 CENTIMES

2.5000 g., 0.8350 Silver 0.0671 oz. ASW **Obv:** Bearded head of Leopold II, left, legend in French **Obv. Leg.:** DES BELGES **Rev:** Tablet to right of seated lion, looking left, denomination below, date to left of lion

Date	Mintage	F	VF	XF	Unc	BU
1901	3,000,000	2.00	8.00	30.00	75.00	160

KM# 51 50 CENTIMES

2.5000 g., 0.8350 Silver 0.0671 oz. ASW **Obv:** Legend in Dutch **Obv. Leg.:** DER BELGEN

Date	Mintage	F	VF	XF	Unc	BU
1901	3,000,000	2.00	8.00	30.00	75.00	150

KM# 60.1 50 CENTIMES

2.5000 g., 0.8350 Silver 0.0671 oz. ASW **Obv:** Bearded head of Leopold II, left, legend in French **Obv. Leg.:** DES BELGES **Rev:** Denomination above date within wreath

Date	Mintage	F	VF	XF	Unc	BU
1907	545,000	3.00	8.00	18.00	70.00	140
1909	2,503,000	2.00	4.00	12.00	35.00	—

KM# 60.2 50 CENTIMES

2.5000 g., 0.8350 Silver 0.0671 oz. ASW **Obv:** Bearded head of Leopold II, left, legend in French, without period in signature **Obv. Leg.:** DES BELGES **Rev:** Denomination above date within wreath

Date	Mintage	F	VF	XF	Unc	BU
1907	Inc. above	4.00	10.00	25.00	100	140
1909	Inc. above	—	5.00	12.00	35.00	—

KM# 61.1 50 CENTIMES

2.5000 g., 0.8350 Silver 0.0671 oz. ASW **Obv:** Bearded head of Leopold II, left, legend in Dutch **Obv. Leg.:** DER BELGEN **Rev:** Denomination above date within wreath

Date	Mintage	F	VF	XF	Unc	BU
1907	545,000	3.00	10.00	25.00	70.00	140
1909	2,510,000	2.00	5.00	12.00	35.00	—

KM# 61.2 50 CENTIMES

2.5000 g., 0.8350 Silver 0.0671 oz. ASW **Obv:** Bearded head of Leopold II, left, legend in Dutch **Obv. Leg.:** DER BELGEN **Rev:** Denomination above date within wreath **Note:** Medal alignment

Date	Mintage	F	VF	XF	Unc	BU
1909	Inc. above	12.50	15.00	45.00	135	180

KM# 70 50 CENTIMES

2.5000 g., 0.8350 Silver 0.0671 oz. ASW **Obv:** Head of Albert, left, legend in French **Obv. Leg.:** DES BELGES **Rev:** Denomination above date within wreath

Date	Mintage	F	VF	XF	Unc	BU
1910	1,900,000	2.00	5.00	12.00	30.00	—
1911	2,063,000	3.00	10.00	15.00	60.00	—
1912	1,000,000	BV	1.25	2.00	6.00	—
1914	240,000	2.50	9.00	15.00	40.00	—

KM# 71 50 CENTIMES

2.5000 g., 0.8350 Silver 0.0671 oz. ASW **Obv:** Head of Albert, left, legend in Dutch **Obv. Leg.:** DER BELGEN **Rev:** Denomination above date within wreath

Date	Mintage	F	VF	XF	Unc	BU
1910	1,900,000	3.00	10.00	15.00	60.00	—
1911	2,063,000	BV	1.25	2.00	6.00	—
1912	1,000,000	BV	1.25	2.00	6.00	—

KM# 83 50 CENTIMES

5.0000 g., Zinc, 24 mm. **Obv:** Hole at center of star, tiny stars flank date below, legend in Dutch **Obv. Leg.:** BELGIE-BELGIQUE **Rev:** Spray of leaves to left of center hole, denomination to right, small shield with rampant lion on spray **Note:** German Occupation WW I

Date	Mintage	F	VF	XF	Unc	BU
1918	7,394,000	0.50	6.00	10.00	25.00	50.00

KM# 87 50 CENTIMES

2.5000 g., Nickel, 18 mm. **Obv:** Allegorically female figure of Belgium kneeling, wounded but recovering **Obv. Leg.:** BELGIQUE **Rev:** Caduceus divides denomination and dates

Date	Mintage	F	VF	XF	Unc	BU
1922	6,180,000	0.15	0.25	0.50	3.00	—
1923	8,820,000	0.15	0.25	0.50	3.00	—
1927	1,750,000	0.15	0.30	0.50	3.00	—
1928	3,000,000	0.15	0.35	1.00	4.00	—
1929	1,000,000	0.25	0.50	3.00	12.00	—
1930	1,000,000	0.25	0.50	3.00	10.00	—
1932/23	2,530,000	1.00	3.00	10.00	25.00	—
1932	Inc. above	0.15	0.50	1.00	4.00	—
1933	2,861,000	0.15	0.25	0.75	4.00	—

KM# 88 50 CENTIMES

2.5000 g., Nickel, 18 mm. **Obv:** Allegorically female figure of Belgium kneeling, wounded but recovering **Obv. Leg.:** BELGIE **Rev:** Caduceus divides denomination and date

Date	Mintage	F	VF	XF	Unc	BU
1922	—	—	—	—	—	—
	Note: Struck at a later date					
1923	15,000,000	0.20	0.25	0.50	3.00	—
1928/3	10,000,000	0.25	0.50	3.00	10.00	—
1928	Inc. above	0.20	0.25	0.50	3.00	—
1930/20	2,252,000	0.50	2.00	3.50	16.00	—
1930	Inc. above	0.20	0.75	2.50	6.00	—
1932/22	—	0.25	3.00	3.00	15.00	—
1932	2,000,000	0.20	0.50	1.00	4.00	—
1933	1,189,000	1.00	5.00	9.00	16.50	—
1934	935,000	75.00	175	225	300	—

KM# 118 50 CENTIMES

2.5000 g., Nickel, 18 mm. **Obv:** Legend in French **Obv. Leg.:** BELGIQUE-BELGIE **Note:** Striking interrupted by the war. Very few coins have been officially released into circulation.

Date	Mintage	F	VF	XF	Unc	BU
1939	15,500,000	200	400	800	1,300	—

KM# 144 50 CENTIMES

2.7500 g., Bronze, 19 mm. **Obv:** Crowned denomination divides date, legend in French **Obv. Leg.:** BELGIQUE **Rev:** Helmeted mine worker, left, miner's lamp at r. Large head, tip of neck 1/2 mm from rim **Edge:** Plain

Date	Mintage	F	VF	XF	Unc	BU
1952	3,520,000	—	0.10	0.50	2.50	—
1953	22,620,000	—	—	0.10	0.35	—
1955	29,160,000	—	—	0.10	0.35	—

KM# 145 50 CENTIMES

2.7500 g., Bronze, 19 mm. **Obv:** Crowned denomination divides date, legend in Dutch **Obv. Leg.:** BELGIE **Rev:** Helmeted mine worker left, miner's lamp at right, large head **Edge:** Plain

Date	Mintage	F	VF	XF	Unc	BU
1952	5,830,000	—	0.10	0.50	2.00	—
1953	22,930,000	—	—	0.10	0.35	—
1954	15,730,000	—	—	0.10	0.35	—

KM# 149.1 50 CENTIMES

2.7500 g., Bronze, 19 mm. **Ruler:** Baudouin I **Obv:** Crowned denomination divides date, legend in Dutch **Obv. Leg.:** BELGIE **Rev:** Helmeted mine worker left, miner's lamp at right, large head **Edge:** Plain

Date	Mintage	F	VF	XF	Unc	BU
1956	5,640,000	—	—	0.10	0.75	—
1957	13,800,000	—	—	0.10	0.25	—
1958	19,480,000	—	—	0.10	0.20	—
1962	4,150,000	—	—	0.10	3.00	—
1963	1,110,000	—	—	0.10	3.00	—
1964	10,340,000	—	—	0.10	0.15	—
1965	9,590,000	—	—	0.10	0.15	—
1966	6,930,000	—	—	0.10	0.15	—
1967	6,970,000	—	—	0.10	0.15	—
1968	2,000,000	—	—	0.10	1.00	—
1969	10,000,000	—	—	0.10	0.15	—
1970	12,000,000	—	—	0.10	0.15	—
1971	1,250,000	—	—	0.10	1.00	—
1972	7,000,000	—	—	0.10	0.15	—
1973	3,000,000	—	—	0.10	0.15	—
1974	5,000,000	—	—	0.10	0.15	—
1975	7,000,000	—	—	0.10	0.15	—
1976	8,000,000	—	—	0.10	0.15	—
1977	13,000,000	—	—	0.10	0.15	—
1978	2,500,000	—	—	0.10	1.00	—
1979	40,000,000	—	—	0.10	0.15	—
1980	20,000,000	—	—	0.10	0.15	—
1981	2,000,000	—	—	0.10	1.00	—
1982	7,000,000	—	—	0.10	0.15	—
1983	14,100,000	—	—	0.10	0.15	—
1985	6,000,000	—	—	0.10	0.15	—
1987	9,000,000	—	—	0.10	0.15	—
1988	9,000,000	—	—	0.10	0.15	—
1989	60,000	—	—	—	3.00	—
	Note: In sets only					
1990	60,000	—	—	—	3.00	—
	Note: In sets only					
1991	6,000,000	—	—	—	0.50	—
1992	7,060,000	—	—	0.10	0.15	—
1993	10,000,000	—	—	0.10	0.15	—
1994	10,000,000	—	—	0.10	0.15	—
1995	60,000	—	—	—	2.00	—
	Note: In sets only					
1996	11,000,000	—	—	—	0.50	—
1997	60,000	—	—	—	2.00	—
	Note: In sets only					
1998	30,000,000	—	—	—	0.10	—
1999	60,000	—	—	—	2.00	—
	Note: In sets only					
2000	60,000	—	—	—	2.00	—
	Note: In sets only					

KM# 148.2   50 CENTIMES

2.7500 g., Bronze, 19 mm. **Ruler:** Baudouin I **Obv:** Crowned denomination divides date, legend in French **Obv. Leg.:** BELGIQUE **Rev:** Helmeted mine worker, left, miner's lamp at right large head, tip of neck 1/2 mm from rim **Edge:** Plain **Note:** Medal alignment.

Date	Mintage	F	VF	XF	Unc	BU
1953	Inc. above	—	—	15.00	30.00	—
1959	Inc. above	—	—	15.00	30.00	—
1965	Inc. above	—	—	15.00	30.00	—
1966	Inc. above	—	—	15.00	30.00	—
1969	Inc. above	—	—	15.00	30.00	—
1974	Inc. above	—	—	15.00	30.00	—
1976	Inc. above	—	—	15.00	30.00	—
1999 Proof	—	Value: 30.00				

Note: In sets only

| 2000 Proof | — | Value: 30.00 | | | | |

Note: In sets only

KM# 149.2   50 CENTIMES

2.7500 g., Bronze, 19 mm. **Ruler:** Baudouin I **Obv:** Crowned denomination divides date, legend in French **Obv. Leg.:** BELGIQUE **Rev:** Helmeted mine worker, left, miner's lamp at right large head, tip of neck 1/2 mm from rim **Edge:** Plain **Note:** Medal alignment.

Date	Mintage	F	VF	XF	Unc	BU
1953	Inc. above	—	—	15.00	30.00	—
1967	Inc. above	—	—	15.00	30.00	—
1969	Inc. above	—	—	15.00	30.00	—
1979	Inc. above	—	—	15.00	30.00	—
1988	Inc. above	—	—	15.00	30.00	—
1999 Proof	—	Value: 30.00				

Note: In sets only

| 2000 Proof | — | Value: 30.00 | | | | |

Note: In sets only

KM# 148.1   50 CENTIMES

2.7500 g., Bronze, 19 mm. **Ruler:** Baudouin I **Obv:** Crowned denomination divides date, legend in French **Obv. Leg.:** BELGIQUE **Rev:** Helmeted mine worker, left, miner's lamp at right large head, tip of neck 1/2 mm from rim **Edge:** Plain

Date	Mintage	F	VF	XF	Unc	BU
1958	9,750,000	—	—	0.10	0.25	—
1959	17,350,000	—	—	0.10	0.20	—
1962	6,160,000	—	—	0.10	2.00	—
1964	5,860,000	—	—	0.10	2.00	—
1965	10,320,000	—	—	0.10	0.15	—
1966	11,040,000	—	—	0.10	0.15	—
1967	7,200,000	—	—	0.10	0.15	—
1968	2,000,000	—	—	0.10	2.00	—
1969	10,000,000	—	—	0.10	0.15	—
1970	16,000,000	—	—	0.10	0.15	—
1971	1,250,000	—	—	0.10	2.00	—
1972	3,000,000	—	—	0.10	0.15	—
1973	3,000,000	—	—	0.10	0.15	—
1974	5,000,000	—	—	0.10	0.15	—
1974 Wide rim	Inc. above	—	—	0.10	0.15	—
1975	7,000,000	—	—	0.10	0.15	—
1976	8,000,000	—	—	0.10	0.15	—
1977	13,000,000	—	—	0.10	0.15	—
1978	2,500,000	—	—	0.10	1.00	—
1979	20,000,000	—	—	0.10	0.15	—
1980	20,000,000	—	—	0.10	0.15	—
1981	2,000,000	—	—	0.10	1.00	—
1982	7,000,000	—	—	0.10	0.15	—
1983	14,100,000	—	—	0.10	0.15	—
1985	6,000,000	—	—	0.10	0.15	—
1987	9,000,000	—	—	0.10	0.15	—
1988	4,500,000	—	—	0.10	0.15	—
1989	60,000	—	—	—	3.00	—
		Note: In sets only				
1990	60,000	—	—	—	3.00	—
		Note: In sets only				
1991	6,000,000	—	—	—	0.15	—
1992	7,060,000	—	—	0.10	0.15	—
1993	10,000,000	—	—	0.10	0.15	—
1994	10,000,000	—	—	0.10	0.15	—
1995	60,000	—	—	—	2.00	—
		Note: In sets only				
1996	11,000,000	—	—	0.10	0.15	—
1997	60,000	—	—	—	2.00	—
		Note: In sets only				
1998	30,000,000	—	—	—	0.10	—
1999	60,000	—	—	—	2.00	—
		Note: In sets only				
2000	60,000	—	—	—	2.00	—
		Note: In sets only				

KM# 56.1   FRANC

5.0000 g., 0.8350 Silver 0.1342 oz. ASW **Obv:** Legend in French **Obv. Leg.:** DES BELGES

Date	Mintage	F	VF	XF	Unc	BU
1904	803,000	4.00	14.00	40.00	75.00	160
1909	2,250,000	3.00	10.00	30.00	45.00	—

KM# 56.2   FRANC

5.0000 g., 0.8350 Silver 0.1342 oz. ASW **Obv:** Without period in signature

Date	Mintage	F	VF	XF	Unc	BU
1904	Inc. above	5.00	35.00	60.00	140	325
1909	Inc. above	3.00	10.00	30.00	45.00	—

KM# 57.1   FRANC

5.0000 g., 0.8350 Silver 0.1342 oz. ASW **Obv:** Bearded head of Leopold II, left, legend in Dutch **Obv. Leg.:** DER BELGEN **Rev:** Denomination above date within wreath

Date	Mintage	F	VF	XF	Unc	BU
1904	803,000	4.00	14.00	40.00	75.00	—
1909	2,250,000	3.00	10.00	30.00	50.00	—

KM# 57.2   FRANC

5.0000 g., 0.8350 Silver 0.1342 oz. ASW **Obv:** Bearded head of Leopold II, left, legend in Dutch, without period in signature **Obv. Leg.:** DER BELGEN **Rev:** Denomination above date within wreath

Date	Mintage	F	VF	XF	Unc	BU
1909	Inc. above	3.00	8.00	30.00	45.00	—

KM# 73.1   FRANC

5.0000 g., 0.8350 Silver 0.1342 oz. ASW, 23 mm. **Obv:** Head of Albert, left, legend in Dutch **Obv. Leg.:** DER BELGEN **Rev:** Denomination above date within wreath

Date	Mintage	F	VF	XF	Unc	BU
1910	2,750,000	3.00	15.00	35.00	65.00	145
1911	2,250,000	—	—	5.00	12.00	—
1912	3,250,000	—	—	2.50	5.00	—
1913	3,000,000	—	—	2.50	5.00	—
1914	10,222,000	—	—	2.50	5.00	—
1918	—	300	600	1,400	2,000	—

KM# 72   FRANC

5.0000 g., 0.8350 Silver 0.1342 oz. ASW **Obv:** Legend in French **Obv. Leg.:** DES BELGES **Note:** Prev. KM#72.1.

Date	Mintage	F	VF	XF	Unc	BU
1910	2,190,000	2.75	5.00	18.00	35.00	—
1911	2,810,000	BV	2.75	5.00	12.00	—
1912	3,250,000	—	—	2.50	5.00	—
1913	3,000,000	—	—	2.50	5.00	—
1914	10,563,000	—	—	2.50	5.00	—
1917	8,540,000	350	700	1,500	2,000	—
1918	1,469,000	300	600	1,400	2,000	—

KM# 73.2   FRANC

5.0000 g., 0.8350 Silver 0.1342 oz. ASW, 23 mm. **Obv:** Head of Albert, left, legend in Dutch **Obv. Leg.:** DER BELGEN **Rev:** Denomination above date within wreath **Note:** Medal alignment.

Date	Mintage	F	VF	XF	Unc	BU
1914	Inc. above	4.50	12.50	50.00	125	300

KM# 89   FRANC

5.0000 g., Nickel, 23 mm. **Obv:** Kneeling figure, legend in French **Obv. Leg.:** BELGIQUE **Rev:** Caduceus divides denomination and date **Edge:** Reeded

Date	Mintage	F	VF	XF	Unc	BU
1922	14,000,000	0.15	0.25	1.00	3.00	—
1923	22,500,000	0.15	0.25	1.00	3.00	—
1928/3	5,000,000	0.25	1.50	5.00	12.00	—
1928/7	Inc. above	0.25	1.50	5.00	12.00	—
1928	Inc. above	0.15	0.25	1.00	4.00	—
1929	7,415,000	0.15	0.25	1.00	3.50	—
1930	5,365,000	0.15	0.25	1.00	3.00	—
1931	—	250	700	1,000	1,800	—
1933	1,998,000	0.25	1.50	5.00	15.00	—
1934/24	10,263,000	0.25	1.50	6.00	12.00	—
1934	Inc. above	0.15	0.25	1.00	3.00	—

KM# 90   FRANC

5.0000 g., Nickel, 23 mm. **Obv:** Kneeling figure, legend in Dutch **Obv. Leg.:** BELGIE **Rev:** Caduceus divides denomination and date **Edge:** Reeded

Date	Mintage	F	VF	XF	Unc	BU
1922	19,000,000	0.15	0.25	1.00	3.00	—
1923/2	17,500,000	0.20	1.50	4.00	12.00	—
1923	Inc. above	0.15	0.25	1.00	3.00	—
1928/3	4,975,000	0.20	2.00	5.00	12.00	—
1928/7	Inc. above	0.20	2.00	5.00	12.00	—
1928	Inc. above	0.15	0.50	2.00	6.00	—
1929	10,365,000	0.15	0.25	1.00	3.00	—
1933	786,000	200	900	1,200	2,000	—
1934/24	8,025,000	0.35	2.50	7.00	15.00	—
1934	Inc. above	0.15	0.50	1.00	3.00	—
1935/23	2,238,000	1.50	4.00	12.00	35.00	—
1935	Inc. above	0.25	0.75	2.00	6.00	—

KM# 90.1   FRANC

5.0000 g., Nickel, 23 mm. **Obv:** Kneeling figure, legend in Dutch **Obv. Leg.:** BELGIE **Rev:** Caduceus divides denomination and date **Edge:** Reeded

Date	Mintage	F	VF	XF	Unc	BU
1934	Inc. above	25.00	40.00	60.00	100	—

KM# 119   FRANC

4.5000 g., Nickel, 21.5 mm. **Obv:** Three shields, legend in French **Obv. Leg.:** BELGIQUE-BELGIE **Rev:** Seated lion, right, facing left above date, denomination to right

Date	Mintage	F	VF	XF	Unc	BU
1939	46,865,000	0.15	0.25	0.50	1.50	—

KM# 120   FRANC

4.5000 g., Nickel, 21.5 mm. **Obv:** Three shields, legend in Dutch **Obv. Leg.:** BELGIE-BELGIQUE **Rev:** Seated lion, right, facing left above date, denomination at right

Date	Mintage	F	VF	XF	Unc	BU
1939	36,000,000	0.15	0.25	0.50	1.50	—
1940	10,865,000	0.20	0.40	0.75	2.50	—

KM# 127   FRANC

4.2500 g., Zinc, 21.5 mm. **Obv:** Rampant lion, left on shield, legend in French **Obv. Leg.:** BELGIQUE-BELGIE **Rev:** Crowned letter "L"s, backs touching, divide denomination, date below **Edge:** Reeded **Note:** German Occupation WW II.

Date	Mintage	F	VF	XF	Unc	BU
1941	16,000,000	0.20	0.75	1.50	12.00	25.00
1942	25,000,000	0.20	0.75	1.50	5.00	10.00
1943	28,000,000	0.20	0.75	1.50	5.00	10.00
1947	3,175,000	60.00	125	400	700	1,000

KM# 128   FRANC

4.2500 g., Zinc, 21.5 mm. **Obv:** Rampant lion, left, on shield, legend in Dutch **Obv. Leg.:** BELGIE-BELGIQUE **Rev:** Crowned "L"s, backs touching, divide denomination, date below **Edge:** Reeded

Date	Mintage	F	VF	XF	Unc	BU
1942	42,000,000	0.20	0.75	1.50	5.00	10.00
1943	28,000,000	0.20	0.75	1.50	5.00	10.00

Date	Mintage	F	VF	XF	Unc	BU
1944	24,190,000	0.20	0.75	1.50	5.00	10.00
1945	15,930,000	0.20	1.00	4.00	12.00	25.00
1946	36,000,000	0.20	0.75	1.50	6.00	18.00
1947	3,000,000	25.00	40.00	100	200	350

KM# 142.1 FRANC
4.0000 g., Copper-Nickel, 21 mm. **Obv:** Plant divides
denomination , crown at top, legend in French **Obv. Leg.:**
BELGIQUE **Rev:** Laureate bust, left, small symbol at right, date
at left **Edge:** Reeded

Date	Mintage	F	VF	XF	Unc	BU
1950	13,630,000	—	—	0.10	8.00	—
1951	51,025,000	—	—	0.10	3.00	—
1952	53,205,000	—	—	0.10	5.00	—
1954	4,980,000	—	0.10	0.25	4.00	—
1955	3,960,000	—	0.10	0.25	3.00	—
1956	10,000,000	—	—	0.10	1.00	—
1958	31,750,000	—	—	0.10	1.00	—
1959	9,000,000	—	—	0.10	1.00	—
1960	10,000,000	—	—	0.10	1.00	—
1961	5,030,000	—	—	0.10	2.00	—
1962	12,250,000	—	—	0.10	0.50	—
1963	18,700,000	—	—	0.10	0.50	—
1964	10,110,000	—	—	0.10	0.50	—
1965	10,185,000	—	—	0.10	0.50	—
1966	16,430,000	—	—	0.10	0.50	—
1967	32,945,000	—	—	0.10	0.50	—
1968	8,000,000	—	—	0.10	0.50	—
1969	21,950,000	—	—	0.10	0.50	—
1970	35,500,000	—	—	0.10	0.50	—
1971	10,000,000	—	—	0.10	0.30	—
1972	35,000,000	—	—	0.10	0.30	—
1973	42,500,000	—	—	0.10	0.30	—
1974	30,000,000	—	—	0.10	0.30	—
1975	80,000,000	—	—	0.10	0.30	—
1976	18,000,000	—	—	0.10	0.30	—
1977	68,500,000	—	—	0.10	0.30	—
1978	47,500,000	—	—	0.10	0.30	—
1979	25,000,000	—	—	0.10	0.30	—
1980	66,500,000	—	—	0.10	0.30	—
1981	2,000,000	0.10	0.20	0.50	3.00	—
1988	17,500,000	—	—	0.10	0.30	—

KM# 143.1 FRANC
4.0000 g., Copper-Nickel, 21 mm. **Obv:** Plant divides
denomination, crown at top, legend in Dutch **Obv. Leg.:** BELGIE
Rev: Laureate bust, left, date at left, small symbol at right
Edge: Reeded

Date	Mintage	F	VF	XF	Unc	BU
1950	10,000,000	—	—	0.10	8.00	—
1951	53,750,000	—	—	0.10	3.00	—
1952	49,145,000	—	—	0.10	5.00	—
1953	9,915,000	—	—	0.10	3.00	—
1954	4,940,000	—	0.10	0.25	4.00	—
1955	3,960,000	—	0.10	0.25	4.00	—
1956	10,040,000	—	—	0.10	1.00	—
1957	18,315,000	—	—	0.10	1.00	—
1958	17,365,000	—	—	0.10	1.00	—
1959	5,830,000	—	—	0.10	2.00	—
1960	5,555,000	—	—	0.10	2.00	—
1961	9,350,000	—	—	0.10	1.00	—
1962	10,720,000	—	—	0.10	0.50	—
1963	23,460,000	—	—	0.10	0.50	—
1964	7,430,000	—	—	0.10	0.50	—
1965	11,190,000	—	—	0.10	0.50	—
1966	20,990,000	—	—	0.10	0.50	—
1967	27,470,000	—	—	0.10	0.50	—
1968	8,170,000	—	—	0.10	0.30	—
1969	21,730,000	—	—	0.10	0.30	—
1970	35,730,000	—	—	0.10	0.30	—
1971	10,000,000	—	—	0.10	0.30	—
1972	35,000,000	—	—	0.10	0.30	—
1973	42,500,000	—	—	0.10	0.30	—
1974	30,000,000	—	—	0.10	0.30	—
1975	80,000,000	—	—	0.10	0.30	—
1976	18,000,000	—	—	0.10	0.30	—
1977	68,500,000	—	—	0.10	0.30	—
1978	47,500,000	—	—	0.10	0.30	—
1979	50,000,000	—	—	0.10	0.30	—
1980	66,500,000	—	—	0.10	0.30	—
1981	2,000,000	—	—	0.10	3.00	—
1988	17,500,000	—	—	0.10	0.30	—

KM# 142.2 FRANC
4.0000 g., Copper-Nickel, 21 mm. **Obv:** Plant divides
denomination, crown at top, legend in Dutch **Obv. Leg.:** BELGIE
Rev: Laureate bust, left, date at left, small symbol at right
Edge: Reeded **Note:** Medal alignment.

Date	Mintage	F	VF	XF	Unc	BU
1952	Inc. above	—	10.00	30.00	60.00	—
1959	Inc. above	—	10.00	30.00	60.00	—
1963	Inc. above	—	10.00	30.00	60.00	—
1965	Inc. above	—	10.00	30.00	60.00	—
1970	Inc. above	—	10.00	30.00	60.00	—
1974	Inc. above	—	10.00	30.00	60.00	—
1977	Inc. above	—	10.00	30.00	60.00	—
1978	Inc. above	—	10.00	30.00	60.00	—
1979	Inc. above	—	10.00	30.00	60.00	—

KM# 143.2 FRANC
4.0000 g., Copper-Nickel, 21 mm. **Obv:** Pland divides
denomination, crown at top, legend in Dutch **Obv. Leg.:** BELGIE
Rev: Laureate bust, left, date at left, small symbol at right
Edge: Reeded **Note:** Medal alignment.

Date	Mintage	F	VF	XF	Unc	BU
1952	Inc. above	—	10.00	30.00	60.00	—
1958	Inc. above	—	10.00	30.00	60.00	—
1970	Inc. above	—	10.00	30.00	60.00	—
1971	Inc. above	—	10.00	30.00	60.00	—
1973	Inc. above	—	10.00	30.00	60.00	—
1979	Inc. above	—	10.00	30.00	60.00	—

KM# 171 FRANC
2.7500 g., Nickel Plated Iron, 18 mm. **Obv:** Head, left, small
mark lower right, dutch legend **Obv. Leg.:** BOUDEWIJN I
Rev: Center symbol divides Crown at left from denomination at
right and dates, legend in Dutch **Rev. Leg.:** BELGIE

Date	Mintage	F	VF	XF	Unc	BU
1989	200,060,000	—	—	—	0.35	—
1989 medal alignment	—	—	10.00	30.00	60.00	—
1990	200,060,000	—	—	—	0.35	—
1990 medal alignment	—	—	10.00	30.00	60.00	—
1991	200,060,000	—	—	—	0.35	—
1991 medal alignment	—	—	10.00	30.00	60.00	—
1992 In sets only	60,000	—	—	—	18.00	—
1993	15,060,000	—	—	—	0.35	—

KM# 170 FRANC
2.7500 g., Nickel Plated Iron, 18 mm. **Obv:** Head left, French
legend **Obv. Leg.:** BAUDOUIN I **Rev:** Center symbol divides
Crown on left from denomination on right and dates, legend in
French **Rev. Leg.:** BELGIQUE

Date	Mintage	F	VF	XF	Unc	BU
1989	200,060,000	—	—	—	0.35	—
1989 medal alignment	—	—	10.00	30.00	60.00	—
1990	200,060,000	—	—	—	0.35	—
1991	200,060,000	—	—	—	0.35	—
1991 medal alignment	—	—	10.00	30.00	60.00	—
1992 In sets only	60,000	—	—	—	18.00	—
1993	15,060,000	—	—	—	0.35	—

KM# 188 FRANC
2.7500 g., Nickel Plated Iron, 18 mm. **Ruler:** Albert II **Obv:** Head
left, outline around back of head **Rev:** Vertical line divides date
and large denomination, legend in Dutch **Rev. Leg.:** BELGIE
Edge: Plain

Date	Mintage	F	VF	XF	Unc	BU
1994	75,060,000	—	—	—	0.30	—
1995	75,060,000	—	—	—	0.30	—
1996	95,060,000	—	—	—	0.30	—
1997	95,060,000	—	—	—	0.30	—
1998	75,060,000	—	—	—	0.30	—
1999	60,000	—	—	—	3.00	—

Note: In sets only
| 1999 Proof | 5,000 | Value: 25.00 |

Note: Medal alignment; in sets only
| 2000 | 60,000 | — | — | — | 3.00 | — |

Note: In sets only
| 2000 Proof | 5,000 | Value: 25.00 |

Note: Medal alignment; in sets only

KM# 187 FRANC
2.7500 g., Nickel Plated Iron, 18 mm. **Ruler:** Albert II **Obv:** Head
left, outline around back of head **Rev:** Vertical line divides date and
large denomination, legend in French **Rev. Leg.:** BELGIQUE **Note:**
Mint mark - Angel Head. Unknown mintmaster's privy mark - scales.

Date	Mintage	F	VF	XF	Unc	BU
1994	75,060,000	—	—	—	0.30	—
1995	75,060,000	—	—	—	0.30	—
1996	75,060,000	—	—	—	0.30	—
1997	95,060,000	—	—	—	0.30	—
1998	75,060,000	—	—	—	0.30	—
1999	60,000	—	—	—	3.00	—

Note: In sets only
| 1999 Proof | 5,000 | Value: 25.00 |

Note: Medal alignment; in sets only
| 2000 | 60,000 | — | — | — | 3.00 | — |

Note: In sets only
| 2000 Proof | 5,000 | Value: 25.00 |

Note: Medal alignment; in sets only

KM# 58.1 2 FRANCS (2 Frank)
10.0000 g., 0.8350 Silver 0.2684 oz. ASW **Obv:** Legend in
French **Obv. Leg.:** DES BELGES

Date	Mintage	F	VF	XF	Unc	BU
1904	400,000	6.00	20.00	55.00	100	250
1909	1,088,000	5.00	10.00	30.00	50.00	—

KM# 58.2 2 FRANCS (2 Frank)
10.0000 g., 0.8350 Silver 0.2684 oz. ASW **Obv:** Without period
in signature, Legend in French **Obv. Leg.:** DES BELGES

Date	Mintage	F	VF	XF	Unc	BU
1904	Inc. above	9.00	50.00	120	225	500

KM# 59 2 FRANCS (2 Frank)
10.0000 g., 0.8350 Silver 0.2684 oz. ASW **Obv:** Bearded head
of Leopold II, left, legend in Dutch **Obv. Leg.:** DER BELGEN
Rev: Denomination above date within wreath

Date	Mintage	F	VF	XF	Unc	BU
1904	400,000	6.00	20.00	55.00	100	—
1909	1,088,000	5.00	10.00	30.00	50.00	—

KM# 74 2 FRANCS (2 Frank)
10.0000 g., 0.8350 Silver 0.2684 oz. ASW **Obv:** Head of Albert,
left, legend in French **Obv. Leg.:** DES BELGES
Rev: Denomination above date within wreath

Date	Mintage	F	VF	XF	Unc	BU
1910	800,000	BV	10.00	25.00	50.00	—
1911	1,000,000	BV	7.00	15.00	30.00	—
1912	375,000	6.00	15.00	30.00	55.00	—

KM# 75 2 FRANCS (2 Frank)
10.0000 g., 0.8350 Silver 0.2684 oz. ASW **Obv:** Head of Albert,
left, legend in Dutch **Obv. Leg.:** DER BELGEN
Rev: Denomination above date within wreath

Date	Mintage	F	VF	XF	Unc	BU
1911	1,775,000	BV	5.00	10.00	25.00	—
1912	375,000	BV	10.00	20.00	50.00	—

KM# 91.1 2 FRANCS (2 Frank)
10.0000 g., Nickel, 27 mm. **Obv:** Kneeling figure, legend in French **Obv. Leg.:** BELGIQUE **Rev:** Caduceus divides denomination and date

Date	Mintage	F	VF	XF	Unc	BU
1923	7,500,000	0.50	2.00	8.00	20.00	—
1930/20	1,250,000	12.00	60.00	140	250	—
1930	Inc. above	10.00	50.00	100	200	—

KM# 92 2 FRANCS (2 Frank)
10.0000 g., Nickel, 27 mm. **Obv:** Kneeling figure, legend in Dutch **Obv. Leg.:** BELGIE **Rev:** Caduceus divides denomination and date

Date	Mintage	F	VF	XF	Unc	BU
1923	6,500,000	0.25	3.00	10.00	25.00	—
1924	1,000,000	5.00	20.00	45.00	100	—
1930/20	1,252,000	15.00	55.00	125	250	360
1930	Inc. above	8.00	45.00	100	200	300

KM# 91.2 2 FRANCS (2 Frank)
Nickel **Obv:** Kneeling figure, legend in French **Obv. Leg.:** BELGIQUE **Rev:** Caduceus divides denomination and date **Note:** Medal alignment

Date	Mintage	F	VF	XF	Unc	BU
1923	Inc. above	5.00	8.00	45.00	110	—

KM# 133 2 FRANCS (2 Frank)
2.7500 g., Zinc Coated Steel, 19 mm. **Obv:** Sprays below legend, small star at top, legend in French **Obv. Leg.:** BELGIQUE-BELGIE **Rev:** Denomination flanked by sprays, date below **Edge:** Plain **Note:** Allied Occupation issue. Made in U.S.A. on blanks for 1943 cents.

Date	Mintage	F	VF	XF	Unc	BU
1944	25,000,000	0.25	0.50	1.50	5.00	10.00

KM# 133a 2 FRANCS (2 Frank)
3.5750 g., Silver, 19 mm. **Note:** Made in error in U.S.A. on blanks for Netherlands 25 cents.

Date	Mintage	F	VF	XF	Unc	BU
1944	—	200	300	325	450	700

KM# 97.1 5 FRANCS (5 Frank)
14.0000 g., Nickel, 31 mm. **Obv:** Head of Albert, left **Obv. Leg.:** DES BELGES **Rev:** Wreath surrounds denomination and date, crown at top, value: UN BELGA **Note:** All dates exist in position A and B, values are the same.

Date	Mintage	F	VF	XF	Unc	BU
1930	1,600,000	1.50	6.00	12.00	25.00	—
1931	9,032,000	1.00	4.00	10.00	20.00	—
1932	3,600,000	1.50	7.00	14.00	30.00	—
1933	1,387,000	6.00	15.00	35.00	80.00	—
1934	1,000,000	30.00	75.00	160	350	—

KM# 98 5 FRANCS (5 Frank)
14.0000 g., Nickel, 31 mm. **Obv:** Head of Albert, legend in Dutch **Obv. Leg.:** DER BELGEN **Rev:** Denomination and date within wreath, Crown at top, value: UN BELGA **Note:** All dates exist in position A and B, values are the same.

Date	Mintage	F	VF	XF	Unc	BU
1930	5,086,000	2.00	8.00	16.00	40.00	—
1931	5,336,000	1.50	6.00	12.00	25.00	—
1932	3,683,000	1.50	7.00	14.00	30.00	—
1933	2,514,000	8.00	20.00	40.00	80.00	—

KM# 97.2 5 FRANCS (5 Frank)
14.0000 g., Nickel, 31 mm. **Obv:** Head of Albert, left **Obv. Leg.:** DES BELGES **Rev:** Wreath surrounds denomination and date, crown at top,k value: UN BELGA **Note:** Medal alignment. Edge varieties exist.

Date	Mintage	F	VF	XF	Unc	BU
1930	Inc. above	17.50	50.00	150	350	—

KM# 108 5 FRANCS (5 Frank)
Nickel, 31 mm. **Rev:** Crown above denomination, sprays below **Rev. Leg.:** BELGIQUE **Note:** Both dates exist in position A and B, values are the same. Prev. KM#108.1.

Date	Mintage	F	VF	XF	Unc	BU
1936	650,000	6.00	25.00	50.00	85.00	—
1937	1,848,000	6.00	20.00	40.00	70.00	—

KM# 109.1 5 FRANCS (5 Frank)
12.0000 g., Nickel, 31 mm. **Obv:** Head of Leopold III, left, small date, lower right **Rev:** Crown above denomination, sprays below, legend in Dutch **Rev. Leg.:** BELGIE **Note:** Both dates exist in position A and B, values are the same.

Date	Mintage	F	VF	XF	Unc	BU
1936	2,498,000	4.00	15.00	35.00	50.00	—

KM# 109.2 5 FRANCS (5 Frank)
21.0000 g., Nickel, 31 mm. **Obv:** Head of Leopold III, left, small date, lower right **Rev:** Crown above denomination, sprays below, legend in Dutch **Rev. Leg.:** BELGIE **Note:** Medal alignment. Edge varieties exist.

Date	Mintage	F	VF	XF	Unc	BU
1936	Inc. above	15.00	50.00	150	325	—

KM# 117.2 5 FRANCS (5 Frank)
9.0000 g., Nickel **Obv:** Three shields, legend in Dutch **Obv. Leg.:** BELGIE-BELGIQUE **Rev:** Seated lion, right, looking left, date below, denomination at right **Note:** Milled edge, lettering with star.

Date	Mintage	F	VF	XF	Unc	BU
1938 Position B	Inc. above	25.00	60.00	90.00	160	—
1938 Position A	Inc. above	25.00	60.00	90.00	160	—
1939 Position A	Inc. above	0.15	2.00	3.00	5.00	—
1939 Position B	Inc. above	0.15	2.00	3.00	5.00	—

KM# 117.1 5 FRANCS (5 Frank)
9.0000 g., Nickel, 25 mm. **Obv:** Three shields, legend in Dutch **Obv. Leg.:** BELGIE-BELGIQUE **Rev:** Seated lion, right, looking left, date below, denomination at right **Note:** Milled edge, lettering with crown.

Date	Mintage	F	VF	XF	Unc	BU
1938 Position A	3,200,000	20.00	50.00	80.00	125	—
1938 Position B	Inc. above	20.00	50.00	80.00	125	—
1939 Position A	8,219,000	20.00	50.00	80.00	125	—
1939 Position B	Inc. above	20.00	50.00	80.00	125	—

KM# 116.2 5 FRANCS (5 Frank)
9.0000 g., Nickel, 25 mm. **Obv:** Three shields, legend in French **Obv. Leg.:** BELGIQUE-BELGIE **Rev:** Seated lion, right, looking left, denomination at right, date below **Note:** Milled edge, lettering with star.

Date	Mintage	F	VF	XF	Unc	BU
1939 Position A	Inc. above	500	1,200	2,000	3,000	—
1939 Position B	Inc. above	500	1,200	2,000	3,000	—

KM# 116.1 5 FRANCS (5 Frank)
9.0000 g., Nickel, 25 mm. **Obv:** Three shields, legend in French **Obv. Leg.:** BELGIQUE-BELGIE **Rev:** Seated lion, right, looking left, denomination at right, date below **Note:** Milled edge, lettering with crown.

Date	Mintage	F	VF	XF	Unc	BU
1938 Position A	11,419,000	0.20	4.00	7.00	10.00	—
1938 Position B	Inc. above	0.30	4.00	7.00	10.00	—

KM# 116.3 5 FRANCS (5 Frank)
9.0000 g., Nickel, 25 mm. **Obv:** Three shields, legend in French **Obv. Leg.:** BELGIQUE-BELGIE **Rev:** Seated lion, right, looking left, denomination at right, date below **Note:** Milled edge, without lettering (error).

Date	Mintage	F	VF	XF	Unc	BU
1938	Inc. above	40.00	70.00	135	300	—

KM# 117.3 5 FRANCS (5 Frank)
9.0000 g., Nickel, 25 mm. **Obv:** Three shields, legend in Dutch **Obv. Leg.:** BELGIE-BELGIQUE **Rev:** Seated lion, right, looking left, date below, denomination at right **Note:** Milled edge, without lettering (error).

Date	Mintage	F	VF	XF	Unc	BU
1939	Inc. above	30.00	60.00	175	350	500

KM# 129.1 5 FRANCS (5 Frank)
6.0000 g., Zinc, 25 mm. **Obv:** Head of Leopold III, right, legend in French **Obv. Leg.:** DES BELGES **Rev:** Crown above large decorated denomination, flanked by symbols, date at bottom **Edge:** Reeded **Note:** German Occupation WW II.

Date	Mintage	F	VF	XF	Unc	BU
1941	15,200,000	1.00	2.50	5.00	12.00	—
1943	16,236,000	1.00	2.50	5.00	12.00	—
1944	1,868,000	6.00	17.00	35.00	65.00	—
1945	3,200,000	2.00	5.00	10.00	25.00	—

Date	Mintage	F	VF	XF	Unc	BU
1946	4,452,000	5.00	12.00	20.00	35.00	—
1947	3,100,000	30.00	80.00	150	240	—

KM# 130 5 FRANCS (5 Frank)
6.0000 g., Zinc, 25 mm. **Obv:** Head of Leopold III, right, legend in Dutch **Obv. Leg.:** DER BELGEN **Rev:** Crown above large decorated denomination flanked by symbols, date at bottom

Date	Mintage	F	VF	XF	Unc	BU
1941	27,544,000	0.75	2.00	4.00	10.00	—
1945	3,200,000	30.00	80.00	125	200	—
1946 Rare	4,000,000	—	—	—	—	—
1947	36,000	175	650	900	1,500	—

KM# 129.2 5 FRANCS (5 Frank)
6.0000 g., Zinc, 25 mm. **Obv:** Head of Leopold III, right, legend in Dutch **Obv. Leg.:** DER BELGEN **Rev:** Crown above large decorated denomination flanked by symbols, date at bottom **Note:** Medal alignment.

Date	Mintage	F	VF	XF	Unc	BU
1943	Inc. above	5.00	15.00	50.00	130	—

KM# 134.1 5 FRANCS (5 Frank)
6.0000 g., Copper-Nickel, 24 mm. **Obv:** Plant divides denomination, Crown at top, legend in French **Obv. Leg.:** BELGIQUE **Rev:** Laureate head, left, small diamonds flank date at left, symbol at right **Edge:** Reeded

Date	Mintage	F	VF	XF	Unc	BU
1948	5,304,000	—	4.00	10.00	25.00	—
1949	38,752,000	—	—	1.00	6.00	—
1950	23,948,000	—	—	1.00	6.00	—
1958	9,088,000	—	—	1.00	3.00	—
1961	6,000,000	—	—	1.00	3.00	—
1962	6,576,000	—	—	1.00	3.00	—
1963	11,144,000	—	—	1.00	3.00	—
1964	3,520,000	—	1.00	2.00	5.00	—
1965	11,988,000	—	—	1.00	3.00	—
1966	6,772,000	—	—	1.00	3.00	—
1967	13,268,000	—	—	1.00	3.00	—
1968	5,192,000	—	1.00	2.00	4.00	—
1969	22,235,000	—	—	1.00	3.00	—
1969	Inc. above	3.00	5.00	10.00	20.00	—

Note: Without engraver's name

Date	Mintage	F	VF	XF	Unc	BU
1970	2,000,000	—	1.00	2.00	5.00	—
1971	6,000,000	—	—	0.20	0.50	—
1972	17,500,000	—	—	0.20	0.50	—
1973	10,000,000	—	—	0.20	0.50	—
1974	25,000,000	—	—	0.20	0.50	—
1975	34,000,000	—	—	0.20	0.50	—
1975	—	1.00	5.00	8.00	15.00	—

Note: Without engraver's name

Date	Mintage	F	VF	XF	Unc	BU
1976	7,500,000	—	—	0.20	0.75	—
1977	22,500,000	—	—	0.20	0.50	—
1978	27,500,000	—	—	0.20	0.50	—
1979	5,000,000	—	—	0.50	1.00	—
1980	11,000,000	—	—	0.20	0.35	—
1981	2,000,000	—	—	1.00	2.00	—

KM# 135.1 5 FRANCS (5 Frank)
6.0000 g., Copper-Nickel, 24 mm. **Obv:** Plant divides denomination, Crown at top, legend in Dutch **Obv. Leg.:** BELGIE **Rev:** Laureate head, left, small diamonds flank date at left, symbol at right **Edge:** Reeded

Date	Mintage	F	VF	XF	Unc	BU
1948	4,800,000	—	4.00	10.00	25.00	—
1948	—	3.00	15.00	40.00	—	—

Note: Without engraver's name

Date	Mintage	F	VF	XF	Unc	BU
1949	31,500,000	—	—	1.00	6.00	—
1950	34,728,000	—	—	1.00	6.00	—
1958	2,672,000	—	1.00	2.00	6.00	—
1960	5,896,000	—	—	1.00	3.00	—
1961	4,120,000	—	1.00	2.00	5.00	—
1962	7,624,000	—	—	1.00	3.00	—
1963	6,136,000	—	—	1.00	3.00	—
1964	8,128,000	—	—	1.00	3.00	—
1965	9,956,000	—	—	1.00	3.00	—
1966	7,136,000	—	—	1.00	3.00	—
1966	—	3.00	5.00	10.00	20.00	—

Note: Without engraver's name

Date	Mintage	F	VF	XF	Unc	BU
1967	16,132,000	—	—	1.00	3.00	—
1968	3,200,000	—	1.00	2.00	5.00	—
1969	21,500,000	—	—	1.00	3.00	—
1970	2,000,000	—	1.00	2.00	5.00	—
1971	15,000,000	—	—	0.20	0.50	—
1972	17,500,000	—	—	0.20	0.50	—
1972	—	1.00	5.00	8.00	15.00	—

Note: Without engraver's name

Date	Mintage	F	VF	XF	Unc	BU
1973	10,000,000	—	—	0.20	0.50	—
1974	25,000,000	—	—	0.20	0.50	—
1974	—	1.00	5.00	8.00	15.00	—

Note: Without engraver's name

Date	Mintage	F	VF	XF	Unc	BU
1975	34,000,000	—	—	0.20	0.50	—
1976	7,500,000	—	—	0.20	0.75	—
1977	22,500,000	—	—	0.20	0.50	—
1978	27,500,000	—	—	0.20	0.50	—
1979	10,000,000	—	—	0.50	1.00	—
1980	11,000,000	—	—	0.20	0.50	—
1981	—	—	—	—	—	—

KM# 134.2 5 FRANCS (5 Frank)
6.0000 g., Copper-Nickel, 24 mm. **Obv:** Plant divides denomination, Crown at top, legend in French **Obv. Leg.:** BELGIQUE **Rev:** Laureate head, left, small diamonds flank date at left, symbol at right **Rev. Leg.:** Rau **Edge:** Reeded **Note:** Medal alignment.

Date	Mintage	F	VF	XF	Unc	BU
1949	Inc. above	—	4.00	10.00	30.00	—
1950	Inc. above	—	4.00	10.00	30.00	—

Date	Mintage	F	VF	XF	Unc	BU
1963	Inc. above	—	4.00	10.00	30.00	
1966	Inc. above	—	4.00	10.00	30.00	
1969	Inc. above	—	4.00	10.00	30.00	
1975	Inc. above	—	4.00	10.00	30.00	

KM# 135.2 5 FRANCS (5 Frank)
6.0000 g., Copper-Nickel, 24 mm. **Obv:** Plant divides denomination, Crown at top, legend in French **Obv. Leg.:** BELGIQUE **Rev:** Laureate head, left, small diamonds flank date at left, symbol at right **Edge:** Reeded **Note:** Medal alignment.

Date	Mintage	F	VF	XF	Unc	BU
1950	Inc. above	—	4.00	10.00	30.00	
1962	Inc. above	—	4.00	10.00	30.00	
1965	Inc. above	—	4.00	10.00	30.00	
1974	Inc. above	—	4.00	10.00	30.00	

KM# 163 5 FRANCS (5 Frank)
5.5000 g., Brass Or Aluminum-Bronze, 24 mm. **Obv:** Face, left, on divided coin **Rev:** Stylized denomination, date at bottom, legend in French **Rev. Leg.:** BELGIQUE

Date	Mintage	F	VF	XF	Unc	BU
1986	208,400,000	—	—	0.35	0.65	
1987	22,500,000	—	—	0.35	1.00	
1988	26,500,000	—	—	0.35	1.00	
1989	60,000	—	—	—	4.00	
	Note: In sets only					
1990	60,000	—	—	—	4.00	
	Note: In sets only					
1991	60,000	—	—	—	4.00	
	Note: In sets only					
1992	5,060,000	—	—	0.35	2.00	
1993	15,060,000	—	—	0.35	1.00	

KM# 164 5 FRANCS (5 Frank)
5.5000 g., Brass Or Aluminum-Bronze, 24 mm. **Obv:** Face, left, on divided coin **Rev:** Stylized denomination, date at bottom, legend in Dutch **Rev. Leg.:** BELGIE

Date	Mintage	F	VF	XF	Unc	BU
1986	208,400,000	—	—	0.35	0.65	
1987	22,500,000	—	—	0.35	1.00	
1988	26,500,000	—	—	0.35	1.00	
1989	60,000	—	—	—	4.00	
	Note: In sets only					
1990	60,000	—	—	—	4.00	
	Note: In sets only					
1991	60,000	—	—	—	4.00	
	Note: In sets only					
1992	5,060,000	—	—	0.35	2.00	
1993	15,060,000	—	—	0.35	1.00	

KM# 189 5 FRANCS (5 Frank)
5.5000 g., Aluminum-Bronze, 24 mm. **Ruler:** Albert II **Obv:** Head left, outline around back of head **Rev:** Vertical line divides date and denomination, legend in French **Rev. Leg.:** BELGIQUE **Note:** Mint mark - Angel head. Mintmaster R. Coenen's privy mark - Scale.

Date	Mintage	F	VF	XF	Unc	BU
1994	15,060,000	—	—	—	0.50	
1995	60,000	—	—	—	4.00	
	Note: In sets only					
1996	6,860,000	—	—	—	1.00	
1997	60,000	—	—	—	5.00	
	Note: In sets only					
1998	32,560,000	—	—	—	0.50	
1999	60,000	—	—	—	4.00	
	Note: In sets only					
1999 Proof	5,000	Value: 25.00				
	Note: Medal alignment; in sets only					
2000		—	—	—	4.00	
	Note: In sets only					
2000 Proof	5,000	Value: 25.00				
	Note: Medal alignment; in sets only					

KM# 190 5 FRANCS (5 Frank)
5.5000 g., Aluminum-Bronze, 24 mm. **Ruler:** Albert II **Obv:** Head left, outline around back of head **Rev:** Vertical line divides date and large denomination, legend in Dutch **Rev. Leg.:** BELGIE **Note:** Mint mark - Angel head. Mintmaster R. Coenen's privy mark - Scale.

Date	Mintage	F	VF	XF	Unc	BU
1994	30,060,000	—	—	—	0.50	
1995	60,000	—	—	—	2.00	
	Note: In sets only					
1996	3,133,000	—	—	—	1.00	
1997	60,000	—	—	—	5.00	
	Note: In sets only					
1998	6,500,000	—	—	—	0.50	
1999	60,000	—	—	—	4.00	
	Note: In sets only					
1999	5,000	—	—	—	20.00	
	Note: Medal alignment					
2000	60,000	—	—	—	4.00	
	Note: In sets only					
2000 Proof	5,000	Value: 25.00				
	Note: Medal alignment; in sets only					

KM# 99 10 FRANCS-10 FRANK (Deux / Twee Belgas)
17.5000 g., Nickel, 34 mm. **Subject:** Independence Centennial **Rev:** Legend in French **Rev. Leg.:** BELGIQUE **Note:** Exists in position A or B, values are the same.

Date	Mintage	F	VF	XF	Unc	BU
1930	2,699,000	25.00	70.00	130	200	—

KM# 100 10 FRANCS-10 FRANK (Deux / Twee Belgas)
17.5000 g., Nickel, 34 mm. **Obv:** Conjoined heads of Leopold I, Leopold II and Albert I, left, two dates at bottom **Rev:** Denomination flanked by sprays, legend in Dutch **Rev. Leg.:** BELGIE **Note:** Exists in position A or B, values are the same.

Date	Mintage	F	VF	XF	Unc	BU
1930	3,000,000	30.00	75.00	140	300	590

KM# 155.2 10 FRANCS (10 Frank)
8.0000 g., Nickel, 27 mm. **Obv:** Head, left **Rev:** Crowned arms divide denomination, date at bottom, legend in French **Rev. Leg.:** BELGIQUE **Edge:** Plain **Note:** Medal alignment. Mint mark - Angel head. Mintmaster Vogeleer's privy mark - Bird.

Date	Mintage	F	VF	XF	Unc	BU
1969	Inc. above	—	6.00	12.00	35.00	—
1974	Inc. above	—	6.00	12.00	35.00	—

KM# 155.1 10 FRANCS (10 Frank)
8.0000 g., Nickel, 27 mm. **Obv:** Head, left **Rev:** Crowned arms divide denomination, date at bottom, legend in French **Rev. Leg.:** BELGIQUE **Edge:** Plain **Note:** Mint mark - Angel head. Mintmaster Vogeleer's privy mark - Bird.

Date	Mintage	F	VF	XF	Unc	BU
1969	22,235,000	—	—	0.40	0.70	—
1970	9,500,000	—	—	0.40	0.70	—
1971	15,000,000	—	—	0.40	0.70	—
1972	10,000,000	—	—	0.40	0.70	—
1973	10,000,000	—	—	0.40	0.70	—
1974	5,000,000	—	—	0.50	1.00	—
1975	5,000,000	—	—	0.50	1.00	—
1976	7,500,000	—	—	0.50	1.00	—
1977	7,000,000	—	—	0.50	1.00	—
1978	2,500,000	—	—	1.00	2.50	—
1979	5,000,000	—	—	0.60	1.50	—

KM# 156.1 10 FRANCS (10 Frank)
8.0000 g., Nickel, 27 mm. **Obv:** Head, left **Rev:** Crowned arms divide denomination, date at bottom, legend in Dutch **Rev. Leg.:** BELGIE **Edge:** Plain **Note:** Mint mark - Angel head. Mintmaster Vogeleer's privy mark - Bird.

Date	Mintage	F	VF	XF	Unc	BU
1969	21,500,000	—	—	0.40	0.70	—
1970	10,000,000	—	—	0.40	0.70	—
1971	15,000,000	—	—	0.40	0.70	—
1972	10,000,000	—	—	0.40	0.70	—
1973	10,000,000	—	—	0.40	0.70	—
1974	5,000,000	—	—	0.50	1.00	—
1975	5,000,000	—	—	0.50	1.00	—
1976	7,500,000	—	—	0.50	1.00	—
1977	7,000,000	—	—	0.50	1.00	—
1978	2,500,000	—	—	1.00	2.50	—
1979	10,000,000	—	—	0.60	1.50	—

KM# 156.2 10 FRANCS (10 Frank)
8.0000 g., Nickel, 27 mm. **Obv:** Head, left **Rev:** Crowned arms divide denomination, date at bottom, legend in French **Edge:** Plain **Note:** Medal alignment. Struck at Brussels Mint. Mint mark - Angel head. Mintmaster Vogeleer's privy mark - Bird.

Date	Mintage	F	VF	XF	Unc	BU
1971	Inc. above	—	6.00	12.00	35.00	—
1976	Inc. above	—	6.00	12.00	35.00	—
1978	Inc. above	—	6.00	12.00	35.00	—

KM# 78 20 FRANCS (20 Frank)
6.4516 g., 0.9000 Gold 0.1867 oz. AGW **Obv:** Armored bust of Albert, left, legend in French **Obv. Leg.:** DES BELGES **Rev:** Crowned arms divide denomination and date

Date	Mintage	F	VF	XF	Unc	BU
1914 Position A	125,000	—	—	BV	185	250
1914 Position B	Inc. above	300	600	800	1,200	—

KM# 79 20 FRANCS (20 Frank)
6.4516 g., 0.9000 Gold 0.1867 oz. AGW **Obv:** Armored bust of Albert, left, legend in Dutch **Obv. Leg.:** DER BELGEN **Rev:** Crowned arms divide denomination and date

Date	Mintage	F	VF	XF	Unc	BU
1914 Position A	125,000	—	—	BV	175	200
1914 Position B	Inc. above	—	—	BV	175	190	220

KM# 101.1 20 FRANCS (20 Frank)
20.0000 g., Nickel, 37 mm. **Obv:** Head of Albert, left, legend in French **Obv. Leg.:** DES BELGES **Rev:** Crowned arms divide denomination and date **Note:** All dates exist in position A and B, values are the same.

Date	Mintage	F	VF	XF	Unc	BU
1931	3,957,000	20.00	50.00	110	160	175
1932	5,472,000	20.00	50.00	110	160	175

KM# 102 20 FRANCS (20 Frank)
20.0000 g., Nickel, 37 mm. **Obv:** Legend in Dutch **Obv. Leg.:** DER BELGEN **Note:** All dates exist in position A and B, values are the same.

Date	Mintage	F	VF	XF	Unc	BU
1931	2,600,000	25.00	55.00	120	175	200
1932	6,950,000	15.00	45.00	100	140	175

KM# 101.2 20 FRANCS (20 Frank)
20.0000 g., Nickel, 37 mm. **Obv:** Head of Albert, left, legend in French **Obv. Leg.:** DES BELGES **Rev:** Crowned arms divide denomination and date **Note:** Medal alignment. Edge varieties exist.

Date	Mintage	F	VF	XF	Unc	BU
1932	Inc. above	65.00	175	400	600	—

KM# 103.1 20 FRANCS (20 Frank)
11.0000 g., 0.6800 Silver 0.2405 oz. ASW **Obv:** Head of Albert, left, legend in French **Obv. Leg.:** DES BELGES **Rev:** Crowned arms divide denomination and date

Date	Mintage	F	VF	XF	Unc	BU
1933 Position A	200,000	20.00	60.00	100	150	180
1933 Position B	200,000	25.00	75.00	120	175	200
1934 Position A	12,300,000	—	5.00	8.00	12.00	—
1934 Position B	Inc. above	—	5.00	8.00	12.00	—

KM# 104.1 20 FRANCS (20 Frank)
11.0000 g., 0.6800 Silver 0.2405 oz. ASW **Obv:** Head of Albert, left, legend in Dutch **Obv. Leg.:** DER BELGEN **Rev:** Crowned arms divide denomination and date

Date	Mintage	F	VF	XF	Unc	BU
1933 Position B	Inc. above	16.00	40.00	65.00	125	—
1933 Position B	200,000	14.00	30.00	60.00	110	—
1934 Position A	12,300,000	—	BV	5.00	8.00	—
1934 Position B	Inc. above	—	BV	5.00	8.00	—

KM# 103.2 20 FRANCS (20 Frank)
11.0000 g., 0.6800 Silver 0.2405 oz. ASW **Obv:** Head of Albert, left, legend in French **Obv. Leg.:** DES BELGES **Rev:** Crowned arms divide denomination and date **Note:** Medal alignment.

Date	Mintage	F	VF	XF	Unc	BU
1934	Inc. above	35.00	80.00	190	400	600

KM# 104.2 20 FRANCS (20 Frank)
11.0000 g., 0.6800 Silver 0.2405 oz. ASW **Obv:** Head of Albert, left, legend in Dutch **Obv. Leg.:** DER BELGEN **Rev:** Crowned arms divide denomination and date **Note:** Medal alignment.

Date	Mintage	F	VF	XF	Unc	BU
1934	Inc. above	30.00	70.00	170	350	500

KM# 105 20 FRANCS (20 Frank)
11.0000 g., 0.6800 Silver 0.2405 oz. ASW **Obv:** Head of Leopold II left, neck divides date **Rev:** Crown above sprig divides denomination **Note:** Both dates exist in position A and B, values are the same. Coins dated 1934 exist with and without umlauts above E in BELGIE.

Date	Mintage	F	VF	XF	Unc	BU
1934	1,250,000	BV	8.00	12.00	20.00	—
1935	10,760,000	—	BV	5.50	8.00	—

KM# 140.2 20 FRANCS (20 Frank)
8.0000 g., 0.8350 Silver 0.2148 oz. ASW, 27 mm. **Obv:** Rampant lion left with shield, denomination below, legend in French **Obv. Leg.:** BELGIQUE **Rev:** Helmeted head right, small caduceus divides date at left **Edge:** Reeded **Note:** Medal alignment.

Date	Mintage	F	VF	XF	Unc	BU
1949	Inc. above	15.00	35.00	75.00	125	—
1950	Inc. above	15.00	35.00	75.00	125	—

KM# 141.2 20 FRANCS (20 Frank)
8.0000 g., 0.8350 Silver 0.2148 oz. ASW, 27 mm. **Obv:** Rampant lion left with shield, denomination below, legend in Dutch **Obv. Leg.:** BELGIE **Rev:** Helmeted head right, small caduceus divides date at left **Edge:** Reeded **Note:** Medal alignment.

Date	Mintage	F	VF	XF	Unc	BU
1949	Inc. above	20.00	35.00	85.00	135	—
1951	Inc. above	15.00	40.00	95.00	160	—

KM# 140.1† 20 FRANCS (20 Frank)
8.0000 g., 0.8350 Silver 0.2148 oz. ASW, 27 mm. **Obv:** Rampant lion left with shield, denomination below, legend in French **Obv. Leg.:** BELGIQUE **Rev:** Helmeted head right, small caduceus divides date at left **Edge:** Reeded

Date	Mintage	F	VF	XF	Unc	BU
1949	4,600,000	—	BV	6.00	10.00	—
1950	12,957,000	—	BV	5.00	8.00	—

Date	Mintage	F	VF	XF	Unc	BU
1953	3,953,000	—	6.00	9.00	15.00	—
1954	4,835,000	15.00	45.00	80.00	120	—
1955	1,730,000	200	650	900	1,400	—

KM# 141.1   20 FRANCS (20 Frank)
8.0000 g., 0.8350 Silver 0.2148 oz. ASW, 27 mm.
Obv: Rampant lion left with shield, denomination below, legend in Dutch **Obv. Leg.:** BELGIE **Rev:** Helmeted head right, small caduceus divides date at left **Edge:** Reeded

Date	Mintage	F	VF	XF	Unc	BU
1949	5,545,000	—	5.00	6.00	10.00	—
1950	—	150	500	800	1,200	—
1951	7,885,000	—	2.50	4.00	7.00	—
1953	6,625,000	—	2.50	4.50	8.00	—
1954	5,323,000	12.00	35.00	60.00	100	—
1955	3,760,000	50.00	125	200	275	—

KM# 159   20 FRANCS (20 Frank)
8.5000 g., Nickel-Bronze, 25.65 mm. **Obv:** Head, left **Rev:** Denomination at right above stylized spray, legend in French **Rev. Leg.:** BELGIQUE

Date	Mintage	F	VF	XF	Unc	BU
1980	60,000,000	—	—	0.70	2.00	—
1980	—	—	4.00	10.00	30.00	—
Note: Medal alignment						
1981	60,000,000	—	—	0.70	2.00	—
1982	54,000,000	—	—	0.70	2.00	—
1989	60,000	—	—	—	6.00	—
Note: In sets only						
1990	60,000	—	—	—	6.00	—
Note: In sets only						
1991	60,000	—	—	—	6.00	—
Note: In sets only						
1992	2,610,000	—	—	0.70	4.00	—
1993	7,540,000	—	—	0.70	3.00	—

KM# 160   20 FRANCS (20 Frank)
8.5000 g., Nickel-Bronze, 25.65 mm. **Obv:** Head, left **Rev:** Denomination at right above stylized spray, legend in Dutch **Rev. Leg.:** BELGIE

Date	Mintage	F	VF	XF	Unc	BU
1980	60,000,000	—	—	0.70	2.00	—
1980	—	—	4.00	10.00	30.00	—
Note: Medal alignment						
1981	60,000,000	—	—	0.70	2.00	—
1982	54,000,000	—	—	0.70	2.00	—
1989	60,000	—	—	—	6.00	—
Note: In sets only						
1990	60,000	—	—	—	6.00	—
Note: In sets only						
1991	60,000	—	—	—	6.00	—
Note: In sets only						
1992	2,610,000	—	—	0.70	4.00	—
1993	7,540,000	—	—	0.70	3.00	—

KM# 191   20 FRANCS (20 Frank)
8.5000 g., Nickel-Bronze, 25.65 mm. **Ruler:** Albert II **Obv:** Head left, outline around back of head **Rev:** Vertical line divides date and large denomination, legend in French **Rev. Leg.:** BELGIQUE **Note:** Mint mark - Angel head. Mintmaster R. Coenen's privy mark - Scale.

Date	Mintage	F	VF	XF	Unc	BU
1994	12,560,000	—	—	0.70	1.00	—
1995	60,000	—	—	—	5.00	—
Note: In sets only						
1996	14,485,000	—	—	—	1.00	—
1997	60,000	—	—	—	5.00	—
Note: In sets only						
1998	6,500,000	—	—	—	3.00	—
1999	60,000	—	—	—	5.00	—
Note: In sets only						
1999 Proof	5,000	Value: 25.00				
Note: Medal alignment; in sets only						
2000	60,000	—	—	—	5.00	—
Note: In sets only						
2000 Proof	5,000	Value: 25.00				
Note: Medal alignment; in sets only						

KM# 192   20 FRANCS (20 Frank)
8.5000 g., Nickel-Bronze, 25.65 mm. **Ruler:** Albert II **Obv:** Head left, outline around back of head **Rev:** Vertical line divides date and large denomination, legend in Dutch **Rev. Leg.:** BELGIE **Note:** Mint mark - Angel head. Mintmaster R. Coenen's privy mark - Scale.

Date	Mintage	F	VF	XF	Unc	BU
1994	12,560,000	—	—	0.70	1.00	—
1995	60,000	—	—	—	5.00	—
Note: In sets only						
1996	3,133,000	—	—	—	1.00	—
1997	60,000	—	—	—	5.00	—
Note: In sets only						
1998	6,500,000	—	—	—	3.00	—
1999	60,000	—	—	—	5.00	—
Note: In sets only						
1999 Proof	5,000	Value: 25.00				
Note: Medal alignment; in sets only						
2000	60,000	—	—	—	5.00	—
Note: In sets only						
2000 Proof	5,000	Value: 25.00				
Note: Medal alignment; in sets only						

KM# 106.1   50 FRANCS (50 Frank)
22.0000 g., 0.6800 Silver 0.4810 oz. ASW, 35 mm. **Subject:** Brussels Exposition and Railway Centennial **Obv:** St. Michael slaying dragon (Brussels' patron saint) **Obv. Leg.:** DE BELGIQUE **Rev:** Brussels train station, two dates above, legend in French **Rev. Leg.:** DE FER BELGES, SOUSLE REGNE DELEOPOLD III **Note:** Exists in positions A and B, values are the same.

Date	Mintage	F	VF	XF	Unc	BU
1935	140,000	50.00	90.00	125	300	540

KM# 106.2   50 FRANCS (50 Frank)
22.0000 g., 0.6800 Silver 0.4810 oz. ASW, 35 mm. **Subject:** Brussels Exposition and Railway Centenial **Obv:** St. Michael slaying dragon (Brussels' patron saint) **Obv. Leg.:** DE BELGIQUE **Rev:** Brussels train station, two dates above, legend in French **Rev. Leg.:** DE FER BELGES, SOUSLE REGNE DELEOPOLD III **Note:** Medal alignment. Exists in positions A and B, values are the same.

Date	Mintage	F	VF	XF	Unc	BU
1935	Inc. above	200	450	600	825	—

KM# 107.1   50 FRANCS (50 Frank)
22.0000 g., 0.6800 Silver 0.4810 oz. ASW, 35 mm.   **Obv:** St. Michael slaying dragon (Brussels' patron saint) **Obv. Leg.:** BELGIE **Rev:** Brussels railway station, two dates above, legend in Dutch **Rev. Leg.:** DER BELGISCHE, ONDER DE REGEERING VAN KONIG LEOPOLD III **Note:** Exists in positions A and B, values are the same.

Date	Mintage	F	VF	XF	Unc	BU
1935	140,000	60.00	125	150	225	450

KM# 107.2   50 FRANCS (50 Frank)
22.0000 g., 0.6800 Silver 0.4810 oz. ASW, 35 mm. **Obv:** St. Michael slaying dragon (Brussels' patron saint) **Obv. Leg.:** BELGIE **Rev:** Brussels railway station, two dates above, legend in Dutch **Rev. Leg.:** DER BELGISCHE, ONDER DE REGEERING VAN KONIG LEOPOLD III **Note:** Medal alignment. Exists in positions A and B, values are the same.

Date	Mintage	F	VF	XF	Unc	BU
1935	Inc. above	300	700	900	1,500	—

KM# 121   50 FRANCS (50 Frank)
20.0000 g., 0.8350 Silver 0.5369 oz. ASW, 33 mm. **Obv:** Head of Leopold III, left, date below **Rev:** Crown above nine shields dividing denomination, legend in French **Rev. Leg.:** BELGIQUE: BELGIE **Note:** Both dates exist in positions A and B, values are the same.

Date	Mintage	F	VF	XF	Unc	BU
1939	1,000,000	—	BV	12.00	18.00	—
1940	631,000	BV	15.00	25.00	35.00	—

KM# 122.1   50 FRANCS (50 Frank)
20.0000 g., 0.8350 Silver 0.5369 oz. ASW, 33 mm. **Obv:** Head of Leopold III left, date below **Rev:** Crown above nine shields dividing denomination, legend in Dutch **Rev. Leg.:** BELGIE: BELGIQUE **Note:** Both dates exist in positions A and B, values are the same.

Date	Mintage	F	VF	XF	Unc	BU
1939	1,000,000	—	BV	12.00	18.00	—
1940	631,000	BV	15.00	25.00	35.00	—

KM# 122.2   50 FRANCS (50 Frank)
20.0000 g., 0.8350 Silver 0.5369 oz. ASW, 33 mm. **Obv:** Head of Leopold III left, date below **Rev:** Crown above nine shields dividing denomination, legend in French, without cross on crown **Rev. Leg.:** BELGIE: BELGIQUE **Note:** Both dates exist in positions A and B, values are the same.

Date	Mintage	F	VF	XF	Unc	BU
1939	Inc. above	12.00	30.00	40.00	55.00	—
1940	Inc. above	12.00	30.00	40.00	55.00	—

KM# 122.3   50 FRANCS (50 Frank)
20.0000 g., 0.8350 Silver 0.5369 oz. ASW, 33 mm. **Obv:** Head of Leopold III left, date below **Rev:** Triangle in third arms from left, cross on crown **Rev. Leg.:** BELGIE: BELGIQUE **Note:** Both dates exist in positions A and B, values are the same.

Date	Mintage	F	VF	XF	Unc	BU
1940	—	15.00	30.00	60.00	85.00	—

KM# 122.4   50 FRANCS (50 Frank)
20.0000 g., 0.8350 Silver 0.5369 oz. ASW, 33 mm. **Obv:** Head of Leopold III, left, date below **Rev:** Without cross on crown and with triangle in third arms from left **Rev. Leg.:** BEGIE: BELGIQUE **Note:** Both dates exist in positions A and B, values are the same.

Date	Mintage	F	VF	XF	Unc	BU
1940	Inc. above	30.00	90.00	140	200	375

KM# 136.1   50 FRANCS (50 Frank)
12.5000 g., 0.8350 Silver 0.3356 oz. ASW, 30 mm. **Obv:** Rampant lion with shield, left, denomination below, legend in French **Obv. Leg.:** BELGIQUE **Rev:** Helmeted head, right, small caduceus divides date at left **Edge:** Reeded

Date	Mintage	F	VF	XF	Unc	BU
1948	2,000,000	—	—	BV	9.00	—
1949	4,354,000	—	—	BV	8.00	—
1950	—	200	600	1,000	1,750	—
1951	2,904,000	—	—	BV	8.50	—
1954	3,232,000	BV	12.00	20.00	30.00	—

KM# 137   50 FRANCS (50 Frank)
12.5000 g., 0.8350 Silver 0.3356 oz. ASW, 30 mm. **Obv:** Rampant lion with shield left, denomination below, legend in Dutch **Obv. Leg.:** BELGIE **Rev:** Helmeted head right, small caduceus divides date at left **Edge:** Reeded

Date	Mintage	F	VF	XF	Unc	BU
1948	3,000,000	—	—	BV	9.00	—
1950	4,110,000	—	—	BV	8.00	—
1951	1,698,000	—	—	BV	10.00	—
1954	2,978,000	—	—	BV	8.50	—

KM# 136.2   50 FRANCS (50 Frank)
12.5000 g., 0.8350 Silver 0.3356 oz. ASW, 30 mm. **Obv:** Rampant lion with shield, left, denomination below, legend in French **Obv. Leg.:** BELGIQUE **Rev:** Helmeted head, right, small caduceus divides date at left **Edge:** Reeded **Note:** Medal alignment.

Date	Mintage	F	VF	XF	Unc	BU
1949	Inc. above	10.00	30.00	90.00	175	250

KM# 150.1   50 FRANCS (50 Frank)
12.5000 g., 0.8350 Silver 0.3356 oz. ASW, 29 mm.
Subject: Brussels World Fair **Obv:** Head of Baudouin, left, within circle, legend in French **Obv. Leg.:** DES BELGES **Rev:** World's Fair, Steeple divides date from denomination

Date	Mintage	F	VF	XF	Unc	BU
1958	476,000	—	BV	6.50	10.00	—

KM# 150.2   50 FRANCS (50 Frank)
12.5000 g., 0.8350 Silver 0.3356 oz. ASW, 29 mm. **Note:** Medal alignment.

Date	Mintage	F	VF	XF	Unc	BU
1958	Inc. above	18.00	45.00	100	180	250

KM# 151.1   50 FRANCS (50 Frank)
12.5000 g., 0.8350 Silver 0.3356 oz. ASW, 29 mm. **Obv:** Head of Baudouin, left, within circle, legend in Dutch **Obv. Leg.:** DER BELGEN **Rev:** World's Fair, Steeple divides date from denomination **Edge:** Reeded

Date	Mintage	F	VF	XF	Unc	BU
1958	382,000	—	BV	7.50	10.00	—

KM# 151.2   50 FRANCS (50 Frank)
12.5000 g., 0.8350 Silver 0.3356 oz. ASW, 29 mm. **Obv:** Head of Baudouin, left, within circle, legend in Dutch **Obv. Leg.:** DER BELGEN **Rev:** World's Fair, Steeple divides date from denomination **Edge:** Reeded **Note:** Medal alignment.

Date	Mintage	F	VF	XF	Unc	BU
1958	Inc. above	15.00	35.00	75.00	125	—

KM# 152.1   50 FRANCS (50 Frank)
12.5000 g., 0.8350 Silver 0.3356 oz. ASW, 29 mm.
Subject: King Baudouin's marriage to Doña Fabiola de Mora y Aragon **Obv:** Conjoined heads of King Baudoin and Doña Fabiola de Mora y Aragon, left **Rev:** Arms flanked by sprays divide Crown and denomination

Date	Mintage	F	VF	XF	Unc	BU
1960	500,000	—	BV	7.00	9.00	15.00

KM# 152.2   50 FRANCS (50 Frank)
12.5000 g., 0.8350 Silver 0.3356 oz. ASW, 29 mm.
Subject: King Baudouin's marriage to Doña Fabiola de Mora y Aragon **Obv:** Conjoined heads of King Baudoin and Doña Fabiola de Mora y Aragon, left **Rev:** Arms flanked by sprays divide Crown and denomination **Note:** Medal alignment.

Date	Mintage	F	VF	XF	Unc	BU
1960	Inc. above	12.50	30.00	60.00	120	200

KM# 168   50 FRANCS (50 Frank)
7.0000 g., Nickel, 22.75 mm. **Obv:** Face left on divided coin **Rev:** Denomination, date at bottom, legend in French **Rev. Leg.:** BELGIQUE

Date	Mintage	F	VF	XF	Unc	BU
1987	30,000,000	—	—	2.00	3.00	—
1988	3,500,000	—	—	2.00	6.00	—
1989	15,060,000	—	—	2.00	4.00	—
1990	15,060,000	—	—	2.00	4.00	—

Date	Mintage	F	VF	XF	Unc	BU
1991	3,500,000	—	—	2.00	5.00	—
1992	15,060,000	—	—	2.00	4.00	—
1993	15,060,000	—	—	2.00	4.00	—

KM# 169   50 FRANCS (50 Frank)
7.0000 g., Nickel, 22.75 mm. **Obv:** Face, left, on divided coin **Rev:** Denomination, date at bottom **Rev. Leg.:** BELGIE

Date	Mintage	F	VF	XF	Unc	BU
1987	30,000,000	—	—	2.00	3.00	—
1988	3,500,000	—	—	2.00	6.00	—
1989	15,060,000	—	—	2.00	4.00	—
1990	15,060,000	—	—	2.00	4.00	—
1991	3,500,000	—	—	2.00	5.00	—
1992	15,060,000	—	—	2.00	4.00	—
1993	15,060,000	—	—	2.00	4.00	—

KM# 193   50 FRANCS (50 Frank)
7.0000 g., Nickel, 22.75 mm. **Ruler:** Albert II **Obv:** Head left, outline around back of head **Rev:** Vertical line divides large denomination and date, legend in French **Rev. Leg.:** BELGIQUE **Note:** Mint mark - Angel head. Mintmaster R. Coenen's privy mark - Scale.

Date	Mintage	F	VF	XF	Unc	BU
1994	5,060,000	—	—	2.00	3.00	—
1995	60,000	—	—	5.00	8.00	—
Note: In sets only						
1996	60,000	—	—	5.00	8.00	—
Note: In sets only						
1997	60,000	—	—	5.00	8.00	—
Note: In sets only						
1998	3,060,000	—	—	3.00	4.50	—
1999	60,000	—	—	5.00	8.00	—
Note: In sets only						
1999 Proof	5,000	Value: 20.00				
Note: Medal alignment; in sets only						
2000	60,000	—	—	5.00	8.00	—
Note: In sets only						
2000 Proof	5,000	Value: 20.00				
Note: Medal alignment; in sets only						

KM# 194   50 FRANCS (50 Frank)
7.0000 g., Nickel, 22.75 mm. **Ruler:** Albert II **Obv:** Head left, outline around back of head **Rev:** Vertical line divides large denomination and date, legend in Dutch **Rev. Leg.:** BELGIE **Note:** Mint mark - Angel head. Mintmaster R. Coenen's privy mark - Scale.

Date	Mintage	F	VF	XF	Unc	BU
1994	5,060,000	—	—	2.00	3.00	—
1995	60,000	—	—	5.00	8.00	—
Note: In sets only						
1996	60,000	—	—	5.00	8.00	—
Note: In sets only						
1997	60,000	—	—	5.00	8.00	—
Note: In sets only						
1998	3,060,000	—	—	3.00	4.50	—
1999	60,000	—	—	5.00	8.00	—
Note: In sets only						
1999 Proof	5,000	Value: 25.00				
Note: Medal alignment; in sets only						
2000	60,000	—	—	5.00	8.00	—
Note: In sets only						
2000 Proof	5,000	Value: 25.00				
Note: Medal alignment; in sets only						

KM# 213.2   50 FRANCS (50 Frank)
7.0000 g., Nickel, 22.75 mm. **Subject:** Eurpoean Soccer Championship **Obv:** Head of Albert II, left **Rev:** Soccer ball, legend in French **Rev. Leg.:** BELGIQUE **Edge:** Coarse reeding **Note:** Medal alignment.

Date	Mintage	F	VF	XF	Unc	BU
2000	20,000	Value: 22.00				
Note: In the "Euro 2000" sets only						

KM# 213.1   50 FRANCS (50 Frank)
7.0000 g., Nickel, 22.75 mm. **Subject:** European Soccer Championship **Obv:** Head of Albert II, left **Rev:** Soccer ball, legend in French **Rev. Leg.:** BELGIQUE **Edge:** Coarse reeding

Date	Mintage	F	VF	XF	Unc	BU
2000	500,000	—	—	—	6.00	—

KM# 214.1   50 FRANCS (50 Frank)
7.0000 g., Nickel, 22.75 mm. **Subject:** European Soccer Championship **Obv:** Head of Albert II, left, rear of head outlined **Rev:** Soccer ball, legend in Dutch **Rev. Leg.:** BELGIE **Edge:** Coarse reeding

Date	Mintage	F	VF	XF	Unc	BU
2000	500,000	—	—	4.00	6.00	—

KM# 214.2   50 FRANCS (50 Frank)
7.0000 g., Nickel, 22.75 mm. **Subject:** European Soccer Championship **Obv:** Head of Albert II, left rear of head outlined **Rev:** Soccer ball, legend in Dutch **Rev. Leg.:** BELGIE **Edge:** Coarse reeding **Note:** Medal alignment.

Date	Mintage	F	VF	XF	Unc	BU
2000	20,000	Value: 22.00				
Note: In the "Euro 2000" sets only						

KM# 138.1   100 FRANCS (100 Frank)
18.0000 g., 0.8350 Silver 0.4832 oz. ASW, 33 mm.
Obv: Crowned arms within wreath divide denomination, legend in French **Obv. Leg.:** BELGIQUE **Rev:** Conjoined heads left of Leopold I, Leopold II, Albert I and Leopold III, left, Crown divides date at top, star at bottom

Date	Mintage	F	VF	XF	Unc	BU
1948	1,000,000	—	BV	9.00	12.00	—
1949	106,000	10.00	15.00	40.00	60.00	75.00
1950	2,807,000	—	BV	9.00	10.00	—
1954	2,517,000	—	BV	9.00	12.00	—

KM# 139.1   100 FRANCS (100 Frank)
18.0000 g., 0.8350 Silver 0.4832 oz. ASW, 33 mm. **Obv:** Crowned arms within wreath divide denomination, legend in Dutch **Obv. Leg.:** BELGIE **Rev:** Conjoined heads left of Leopold I, Leopold II, Albert I and Leopold III, left, Crown divides date at top, star at bottom

Date	Mintage	F	VF	XF	Unc	BU
1948	1,000,000	—	BV	9.00	12.00	—
1949	2,271,000	—	BV	9.00	10.00	—
1950	—	300	500	850	1,200	—
1951	4,691,000	—	BV	9.00	10.00	—

KM# 138.2   100 FRANCS (100 Frank)
18.0000 g., 0.8350 Silver 0.4832 oz. ASW, 33 mm.
Obv: Crowned arms within wreath divide denomination, legend in French **Obv. Leg.:** BELGIQUE **Rev:** Conjoined heads left of Leopold I, Leopold II, Albert I and Leopold III, left, Crown divides date at top, star at bottom **Note:** Medal alignment.

Date	Mintage	F	VF	XF	Unc	BU
1948	Inc. above	10.00	40.00	90.00	220	—
1950	Inc. above	10.00	40.00	90.00	200	—

KM# 139.2 100 FRANCS (100 Frank)
18.0000 g., 0.8350 Silver 0.4832 oz. ASW, 33 mm.
Obv: Crowned arms within wreath divide denomination, legend in Dutch **Obv. Leg.:** BELGIE **Rev:** Conjoined heads left of Leopold I, Leopold II, Albert I and Leopold III, left, Crown divides date at top, star at bottom **Note:** Medal alignment.

Date	Mintage	F	VF	XF	Unc	BU
1948	Inc. above	15.00	40.00	90.00	200	—
1949	Inc. above	10.00	30.00	75.00	160	—

KM# 215 200 FRANCS (200 Frank)
18.7500 g., 0.9250 Silver 0.5576 oz. ASW, 33 mm. **Subject:** The Universe **Obv:** Legend in French **Obv. Leg.:** BELGIQUE

Date	Mintage	F	VF	XF	Unc	BU
2000	50,000	—	—	—	25.00	—
2000 (qp)	10,000		Value: 50.00			

KM# 216 200 FRANCS (200 Frank)
18.7500 g., 0.9250 Silver 0.5576 oz. ASW, 33 mm. **Subject:** The City **Obv:** Legend in Dutch **Obv. Leg.:** BELGIE

Date	Mintage	F	VF	XF	Unc	BU
2000	50,000	—	—	—	25.00	—
2000 (qp)	10,000		Value: 50.00			

KM# 217 200 FRANCS (200 Frank)
18.7500 g., 0.9250 Silver 0.5576 oz. ASW, 33. mm. **Subject:** The Nature **Obv:** Legend in German **Obv. Leg.:** BELGIEN

Date	Mintage	F	VF	XF	Unc	BU
2000	50,000	—	—	—	25.00	—
2000 (qp)	10,000		Value: 50.00			

KM# 157.1 250 FRANCS (250 Frank)
25.0000 g., 0.8350 Silver 0.6711 oz. ASW, 37 mm. **Subject:** Silver Jubilee of King Baudouin **Obv:** Head of Baudouin, left, legend in French **Obv. Leg.:** ROI DES BELGES **Rev:** Crowned large "B", denomination below **Edge:** Reeded **Note:** Mint mark - Angel head. Mintmaster Vogeleer's privy mark - Bird.

Date	Mintage	F	VF	XF	Unc	BU
ND(1976)	1,000,000	—	—	BV	15.00	—
Note: Large B, slant 5						
ND(1976)	Inc. above		BV	15.00	20.00	—
Note: Small B, upright 5						

KM# 157.2 250 FRANCS (250 Frank)
25.0000 g., 0.8350 Silver 0.6711 oz. ASW, 37 mm. **Subject:** Silver Jubilee of King Baudouin **Obv:** Head of Baudouin, left, legend in French **Obv. Leg.:** ROIDES BELGES **Rev:** Crowned large "B", denomination below **Edge:** Stars **Note:** Mint mark - Angel head. Mintmaster Vogeleer's privy mark - Bird.

Date	Mintage	F	VF	XF	Unc	BU
ND(1976) Prooflike	100,000	—	—	—	18.00	—

KM# 158.1 250 FRANCS (250 Frank)
25.0000 g., 0.8350 Silver 0.6711 oz. ASW, 37 mm. **Obv:** Head of Baudouin left, legend in Dutch **Obv. Leg.:** KONING DER BELGEN **Rev:** Crowned large "B", denomination below **Edge:** Reeded **Note:** Mint mark - Angel head. Mintmaster Vogeleer's privy mark - Bird.

Date	Mintage	F	VF	XF	Unc	BU
ND(1976)	1,000,000	—	—	BV	15.00	—
Note: Large B, slant 5						
ND(1976)	Inc. above		BV	15.00	20.00	30.00	—
Note: Small B, upright 5						

KM# 158.2 250 FRANCS (250 Frank)
25.0000 g., 0.8350 Silver 0.6711 oz. ASW, 37 mm. **Obv:** Head of Baudouin left, legend in Dutch **Obv. Leg.:** KONING DER BELGEN **Rev:** Crowned large "B", denomination below **Edge:** Stars **Note:** Mint mark - Angel head. Mintmaster Vogeleer's privy mark - Bird.

Date	Mintage	F	VF	XF	Unc	BU
ND(1976) Prooflike	100,000	—	—	—	18.00	—

KM# 195 250 FRANCS (250 Frank)
18.7500 g., 0.9250 Silver 0.5576 oz. ASW, 33 mm. **Subject:** BE-NE-LUX Treaty **Obv:** Head of Albert II, 3/4 facing **Rev:** Three buildings, three sets of arms below, divide denomination and dates, legend on left **Note:** Mint mark - Angel head. Mintmaster R. Coenen's privy mark - Scale.

Date	Mintage	F	VF	XF	Unc	BU
ND(1994)	90,000	—	—	—	20.00	—
ND(1994) Proof	31,800		Value: 65.00			

KM# 199 250 FRANCS (250 Frank)
18.7500 g., 0.9250 Silver 0.5576 oz. ASW, 33 mm. **Subject:** 60th Anniversary - Death of Queen Astrid (car death) **Obv:** Crown above two sets of arms, denomination at bottom **Rev:** Bust of crowned Queen Astrid 1/4 facing right **Note:** Mint mark - Angel head. Mintmaster R. Coenen's privy mark - Scale.

Date	Mintage	F	VF	XF	Unc	BU
ND(1995)	177,000	—	—	—	15.00	—
ND(1995) Proof	25,000		Value: 65.00			

KM# 202 250 FRANCS (250 Frank)
18.7500 g., 0.9250 Silver 0.5576 oz. ASW, 33 mm. **Subject:** 20th Anniversary - King Baudouin Foundation **Obv:** Royal couple and monogram **Rev:** Denomination, stylized design and royal monogram

Date	Mintage	F	VF	XF	Unc	BU
ND(1996)	100,000	—	—	—	15.00	—
ND(1996) Proof	25,000		Value: 35.00			

KM# 207 250 FRANCS (250 Frank)
18.7500 g., 0.9250 Silver 0.5576 oz. ASW, 33 mm. **Subject:** 60th Birthday - Queen Paola **Obv:** Denomination **Rev:** Portrait, left **Note:** Mint mark - Angel head. Mintmaster R. Coenen's privy mark - Scale.

Date	Mintage	F	VF	XF	Unc	BU
1997	100,000	—	—	—	15.00	—
1997 Proof	25,000		Value: 35.00			

KM# 208 250 FRANCS (250 Frank)
18.7500 g., 0.9250 Silver 0.5576 oz. ASW, 33 mm. **Subject:** 5th Anniversary Death of King Boudewijn - 70th Birthday of Queen Fabiola **Obv:** Heads of King and Queen, queen in profile facing left, king 1/4 facing **Rev:** Pelican with nestlings, above denomination, at right, "F" dividing dates at center

Date	Mintage	F	VF	XF	Unc	BU
ND(1998)	100,000	—	—	—	15.00	—
ND(1998) Proof	25,000		Value: 35.00			

KM# 209 250 FRANCS (250 Frank)
18.7500 g., 0.9250 Silver 0.5576 oz. ASW, 33 mm. **Subject:** 40th Wedding Anniversary - King Albert and Queen Paola **Obv:** King and Queen's conjoining busts left **Rev:** St. Gudule Cathedral and city hall, dates at right, denomination at bottom **Edge:** Reeded

Date	Mintage	F	VF	XF	Unc	BU
ND(1999)	100,000	—	—	—	15.00	—
ND(1999) Proof	25,000		Value: 35.00			

KM# 218 250 FRANCS (250 Frank)
18.7500 g., 0.9250 Silver 0.5576 oz. ASW, 33 mm. **Subject:** Marriage of Prince Philip and Princess Mathilde **Rev:** Two hands joined on a rose

Date	Mintage	F	VF	XF	Unc	BU
1999	200,000	—	—	—	15.00	—
1999 Proof	25,000		Value: 35.00			

KM# 161 500 FRANCS (500 Frank)
25.0000 g., Silver Clad Copper-Nickel, 37 mm. **Subject:** 150th Anniversary of Independence **Obv:** Five heads within circles, legend and crown divide dates, French legend **Rev:** Legend on map of country, denomination below, French legend **Note:** Mint mark - Angel head. Mintmaster Vogeleer's privy mark - Bird.

Date	Mintage	F	VF	XF	Unc	BU
ND(1980)	1,000,000	—	3.00	5.00	8.00	—

KM# 161a 500 FRANCS (500 Frank)
25.0000 g., 0.5100 Silver 0.4099 oz. ASW, 37 mm. **Subject:** 150th Anniversary of Independence **Obv:** Five heads within circles, legend and crown divide dates, French legend **Rev:** Legend on map of country, denomination below, French legend **Note:** Mint mark - Angel head. Mintmaster Vogeleer's privy mark - Bird.

Date	Mintage	F	VF	XF	Unc	BU
ND(1980) Proof	53,000		Value: 20.00			

KM# 162   500 FRANCS (500 Frank)
25.0000 g., Silver Clad Copper-Nickel, 37 mm. **Obv:** Five heads within circles, legend with crown divides dates, Dutch legend **Rev:** Legend on map of country, denomination below, Dutch legend **Note:** Mint mark - Angel head. Mintmaster Vogeleer's privy mark - Bird.

Date	Mintage	F	VF	XF	Unc	BU
ND(1980)	1,000,000	—	3.00	5.00	8.00	—

KM# 162a   500 FRANCS (500 Frank)
25.0000 g., 0.5100 Silver 0.4099 oz. ASW, 37 mm. **Obv:** Five heads within circles, legend with crown divides dates, Dutch legend **Rev:** Legend on map of country, denomination below, Dutch legend **Note:** Mint mark - Angel Head. Mintmaster Vogeleer's privy mark - Bird.

Date	Mintage	F	VF	XF	Unc	BU
ND(1980) Proof	52,000		Value: 20.00			

KM# 165   500 FRANCS (500 Frank)
25.0000 g., 0.5100 Silver 0.4099 oz. ASW **Obv:** Five heads within circles, legend with crown divides dates, French legend **Rev:** Legend on map of country, denomination below, Dutch legend **Note:** Mule. Mint mark - Angel head. Mintmaster Vogeleer's privy mark - Bird.

Date	Mintage	F	VF	XF	Unc	BU
1980	—	—	—	—	1,250	—

KM# 178   500 FRANCS (500 Frank)
22.8500 g., 0.8330 Silver 0.6119 oz. ASW, 37 mm. **Subject:** 60th Birthday of King Baudouin **Obv:** Head of King Baudouin, left, two dates below **Rev:** Denomination divides crown and date, Dutch legends

Date	Mintage	F	VF	XF	Unc	BU
1990	475,000	—	—	—	20.00	—
1990 Proof	10,000		Value: 45.00			

KM# 179   500 FRANCS (500 Frank)
22.8500 g., 0.8330 Silver 0.6119 oz. ASW, 37 mm. **Subject:** 60th Birthday of King Boudouin **Obv:** Head of King Boudouin, left, two dates below **Rev:** Denomination divides crown and date, French legends

Date	Mintage	F	VF	XF	Unc	BU
1990	475,000	—	—	—	20.00	—
1990 Proof	10,000		Value: 45.00			

KM# 180   500 FRANCS (500 Frank)
22.8500 g., 0.8330 Silver 0.6119 oz. ASW, 37 mm. **Subject:** 60th Birthday of King Baudouin **Obv:** Head of King Baudouin, left, two dates below **Rev:** Denomination divides crown and date, German legends

Date	Mintage	F	VF	XF	Unc	BU
1990	50,000	—	—	—	30.00	—
1990 Proof	10,000		Value: 45.00			

KM# 196   500 FRANCS (500 Frank)
22.8500 g., 0.8330 Silver 0.6119 oz. ASW, 37 mm. **Subject:** 40th Year of Reign **Obv:** Stylized design around **Rev:** Crown above, denomination, year below, Dutch legend

Date	Mintage	F	VF	XF	Unc	BU
1991	250,000	—	—	—	20.00	—
1991 Proof	10,000		Value: 30.00			

KM# 197   500 FRANCS (500 Frank)
22.8500 g., 0.8330 Silver 0.6119 oz. ASW, 37 mm. **Subject:** 40th Year of Reign **Obv:** Stylized design around **Rev:** Crown above, denomination, year below, French legend

Date	Mintage	F	VF	XF	Unc	BU
1991	250,000	—	—	—	20.00	—
1991 Proof	10,000		Value: 30.00			

KM# 198   500 FRANCS (500 Frank)
22.8500 g., 0.8330 Silver 0.6119 oz. ASW, 37 mm. **Subject:** 40th Year of Reign **Obv:** Stylized design around **Rev:** Crown above, denomination, year below, German legend

Date	Mintage	F	VF	XF	Unc	BU
1991	250,000	—	—	—	30.00	—
1991 Proof	10,000		Value: 30.00			

KM# 186   500 FRANCS (500 Frank)
22.8500 g., 0.8330 Silver 0.6119 oz. ASW, 37 mm. **Subject:** Europalaia - Mexico Exposition **Obv:** Design, legend and denomination within circle **Rev:** Mexico Exposition designs **Note:** Mint mark - Angel head. Mintmaster R. Coenen's privy mark - Scale.

Date	Mintage	F	VF	XF	Unc	BU
ND(1993)	52,000	—	—	—	30.00	—
ND(1993) Proof	8,000		Value: 40.00			

KM# 212   500 FRANCS (500 Frank)
22.8500 g., 0.9250 Silver 0.6795 oz. ASW, 37 mm. **Subject:** Brussels - European Culture Capital **Obv:** Denomination and European map **Rev:** Portraits of Albert and Elizabeth in ruffled collars **Edge:** Plain

Date	Mintage	F	VF	XF	Unc	BU
ND(1999)	200,000	—	—	—	45.00	—
ND(1999) (qp)	30,000		Value: 60.00			

KM# 219   500 FRANCS (500 Frank)
22.8500 g., 0.9250 Silver 0.6795 oz. ASW, 37 mm. **Subject:** Europe: Charles V **Obv:** Map and denomination **Rev:** Charles V of Spain and building **Edge:** Plain

Date	Mintage	F	VF	XF	Unc	BU
ND(2000)	100,000		Value: 45.00			
ND(2000) (qp)	20,000		Value: 60.00			

KM# 210   5000 FRANCS
15.5500 g., 0.9990 Gold 0.4994 oz. AGW, 29 mm. **Subject:** Brussels - European Culture Capital **Obv:** Denomination and European map **Rev:** Portraits of Albert and Elizabeth in ruffled collars **Edge:** Reeded

Date	Mintage	F	VF	XF	Unc	BU
ND(1999) (qp)	2,000		Value: 800			
ND(1999) (qp)	—		Value: 1,500			

Note: Plain edge

KM# 220   5000 FRANCS
15.5500 g., 0.9990 Gold 0.4994 oz. AGW, 29 mm. **Subject:** Europe: Charles V **Obv:** Map and denomination **Rev:** Charles V of Spain with building **Edge:** Reeded

Date	Mintage	F	VF	XF	Unc	BU
ND(2000) (qp)	2,000		Value: 800			
ND(2000) (qp)	—		Value: 1,500			

Note: Plain edge

TRADE COINAGE
European Currency Units

KM# 166   5 ECU
22.8500 g., 0.8330 Silver 0.6119 oz. ASW, 37 mm. **Subject:** 30th Anniversary - Treaties of Rome **Obv:** Denomination, date and stars within circle **Rev:** Bust of Charles V, right

Date	Mintage	F	VF	XF	Unc	BU
1987	985,000	—	—	—	14.50	—
1987 (qp)	15,000		Value: 70.00			
1988 (qp)	15,000		Value: 70.00			

KM# 183   5 ECU
22.8500 g., 0.8330 Silver 0.6119 oz. ASW, 37 mm. **Obv:** Denomination, date and stars within circle **Rev:** Laureate head of Charlemagne, right

Date	Mintage	F	VF	XF	Unc	BU
1991 (qp)	10,000		Value: 55.00			

KM# 185   5 ECU
22.8500 g., 0.9250 Silver 0.6795 oz. ASW, 37 mm. **Subject:** Belgian Presidency of the E.C. **Obv:** Head of King Baudouin, left **Rev:** Denomination, date and stars within circle

Date	Mintage	F	VF	XF	Unc	BU
1993 (qp)	25,000		Value: 45.00			

KM# 200   5 ECU
22.8500 g., 0.9250 Silver 0.6795 oz. ASW, 37 mm. **Subject:** 50th Anniversary - United Nations **Obv:** Head of King Albert II, facing right, denomination and date **Rev:** UN logos with "50"

Date	Mintage	F	VF	XF	Unc	BU
1995 (qp)	125,000		Value: 35.00			

KM# 203   5 ECU
22.8500 g., 0.9250 Silver 0.6795 oz. ASW, 37 mm. **Subject:** 50th Anniversary - UNICEF **Obv:** Royal couple, left **Rev:** UNICEF logo

Date	Mintage	F	VF	XF	Unc	BU
1996 (qp)	Est. 40,000		Value: 45.00			

KM# 205   5 ECU
22.8500 g., 0.9250 Silver 0.6795 oz. ASW, 37 mm. **Subject:** 40th Anniversary - Treaty of Rome **Obv:** Portraits of Albert II and Baudouin, left, date at bottom **Rev:** European Union map

Date	Mintage	F	VF	XF	Unc	BU
1997 (qp)	Est. 30,000		Value: 45.00			

KM# 221   5 ECU
22.8500 g., 0.9250 Silver 0.6795 oz. ASW, 37 mm. **Subject:** 50th Anniversary - Human Rights Declaration **Obv:** Head of King Albert II, facing left, denomination and date **Rev:** Symbolic representation with "50"

Date	Mintage	F	VF	XF	Unc	BU
1998 (qp)	30,000		Value: 45.00			

KM# 172   10 ECU
3.1100 g., 0.9990 Gold 0.0999 oz. AGW, 16 mm. **Rev:** Charles V bust right

Date	Mintage	F	VF	XF	Unc	BU
1989 (qp)	2,000		Value: 200			
1990 (qp)	5,000		Value: 140			

KM# 176   10 ECU
Bi-Metallic 5.30g .900 Gold center, .100 oz AGW, .833 Silver ring, 22 mm. **Subject:** 60th Birthday of King Baudouin **Rev:** Denomination, date and stars within circle

Date	Mintage	F	VF	XF	Unc	BU
1990 (qp)	42,000		Value: 85.00			

KM# 181   10 ECU
Bi-Metallic 5.30g .900 Gold center, .100 oz AGW, .833 Silver ring, 22 mm. **Subject:** 40th Year of Reign of King Baudouin **Obv:** Head of King Baudouin, left within circle, two dates below circle **Rev:** Denomination, date and stars within circle

Date	Mintage	F	VF	XF	Unc	BU
1991 (qp)	15,738		Value: 120			

KM# 177   20 ECU
Bi-Metallic 10.50g .900 Gold center, .200 oz AGW, .833 Silver ring, 29 mm. **Subject:** 60th Birthday of King Baudouin **Obv:** Head of King Baudouin, left, within circle, two dates below circle **Rev:** Denomination, date and stars within circle

Date	Mintage	F	VF	XF	Unc	BU
1990 (qp)	34,902		Value: 170			

KM# 182   20 ECU
10.5000 g., 0.9000 Bi-Metallic Gold center in 0.200 oz AGW, .833 Silver ring 0.3038 oz. **Subject:** 40th Year of Reign of King Baudouin **Obv:** Head of King Baudouin, left within circle, two dates below circle **Rev:** Denomination, date and stars within circle

Date	Mintage	F	VF	XF	Unc	BU
1991 (qp)	13,082		Value: 200			

KM# 173   25 ECU
7.7840 g., 0.9990 Gold 0.2500 oz. AGW, 21 mm. **Obv:** Denomination, date and stars within circle **Rev:** Laureate Diocletian bust, right

Date	Mintage	F	VF	XF	Unc	BU
1989	30,000	—	—	BV	240	—
1989 (qp)	2,000		Value: 275			
1990 (qp)	5,000		Value: 250			

KM# 167   50 ECU
17.2800 g., 0.9000 Gold 0.5000 oz. AGW, 23 mm. **Subject:** 30th Anniversary - Treaties of Rome **Obv:** Denomination, date and stars within circle **Rev:** Bust of Charles V, right

Date	Mintage	F	VF	XF	Unc	BU
1987	1,502,000	—	—	BV	500	—
1987 (qp)	15,000		Value: 520			
1988 (qp)	15,000		Value: 520			

KM# 174   50 ECU
15.5550 g., 0.9990 Gold 0.4996 oz. AGW, 29 mm. **Obv:** Denomination, date and stars within circle **Rev:** Charlemagne seated on dais, facing

Date	Mintage	F	VF	XF	Unc	BU
1989	60,000	—	—	BV	500	—
1989 (qp)	2,000		Value: 550			
1990 (qp)	5,000		Value: 520			

KM# 184   50 ECU
15.5550 g., 0.9990 Gold 0.4996 oz. AGW, 29 mm. **Obv:** Denomination, date and stars within circle **Rev:** Laureate head of Charlemagne, right

Date	Mintage	F	VF	XF	Unc	BU
1991 (qp)	4,000		Value: 600			

KM# 213   50 ECU
15.5550 g., 0.9990 Gold 0.4996 oz. AGW, 29 mm. **Subject:** Belgian Presidency of the E.C. **Obv:** Head of King Baudouin, left **Rev:** Denomination, date and stars within circle

Date	Mintage	F	VF	XF	Unc	BU
1993 (qp)	10,000		Value: 525			

KM# 201   50 ECU
15.5550 g., 0.9990 Gold 0.4996 oz. AGW, 29 mm. **Subject:** 50th Anniversary - United Nations **Obv:** Head of King Albert II, facing right, denomination and date **Rev:** UN logo with "50"

Date	Mintage	F	VF	XF	Unc	BU
1995 (qp)	2,500		Value: 550			

KM# 204   50 ECU
15.5550 g., 0.9990 Gold 0.4996 oz. AGW, 29 mm. **Subject:** 50th Anniversary - UNICEF **Obv:** Royal couple, left **Rev:** UNICEF logo

Date	Mintage	F	VF	XF	Unc	BU
1996 (qp)	2,500		Value: 600			

KM# 206   50 ECU
15.5550 g., 0.9990 Gold 0.4996 oz. AGW, 29 mm. **Subject:** 40th Anniversary - Treaty of Rome **Obv:** Portraits of Albert II and Baudouin, left, date at bottom **Rev:** European Union map

Date	Mintage	F	VF	XF	Unc	BU
1997 (qp)	2,500		Value: 600			

KM# 211   50 ECU
15.5550 g., 0.9990 Gold 0.4996 oz. AGW, 29 mm. **Subject:** 50th Anniversary - Human Rights Declaration **Obv:** Head of King Albert II, facing left, denomination and date **Rev:** Symbolic representation with "50"

Date	Mintage	F	VF	XF	Unc	BU
1998 (qp)	2,500		Value: 600			

KM# 175   100 ECU
31.1030 g., 0.9990 Gold 0.9989 oz. AGW, 37 mm. **Obv:** Denomination, date and stars within circle **Rev:** Bust of Maria Theresa, of Austria, right

Date	Mintage	F	VF	XF	Unc	BU
1989	50,000	—	—	BV	975	—
1989 (qp)	2,000		Value: 1,100			
1990 (qp)	5,000		Value: 1,000			

EURO COINAGE
European Union Issues

KM# 224   EURO CENT
2.2700 g., Copper Plated Steel, 16.2 mm. **Ruler:** Albert II **Obv:** Head left within inner circle, stars 3/4 surround, date below **Rev:** Denomination and globe **Edge:** Plain

Date	Mintage	F	VF	XF	Unc	BU
1999	235,240,000	—	—	0.30	0.75	1.00
1999 Proof	15,000		Value: 12.00			
2000	40,000	—	—	—	37.50	42.50
2000 Proof	15,000		Value: 15.00			

KM# 225   2 EURO CENT
3.0300 g., Copper Plated Steel, 18.7 mm. **Ruler:** Albert II **Obv:** Head left within circle, stars 3/4 surround, date below **Rev:** Denomination and globe **Edge:** Grooved

Date	Mintage	F	VF	XF	Unc	BU
1999	40,000	—	—	—	10.00	12.50
1999 Proof	15,000		Value: 15.00			

Date	Mintage	F	VF	XF	Unc	BU
2000	373,040,000	—	—	0.30	0.75	1.00
2000 Proof	15,000	Value: 12.00				

KM# 226 5 EURO CENT
3.8600 g., Copper Plated Steel, 21.2 mm. **Ruler:** Albert II
Obv: Head left within circle, stars 3/4 surround, date below
Rev: Denomination and globe **Edge:** Plain

Date	Mintage	F	VF	XF	Unc	BU
1999	300,040,000	—	—	0.50	1.20	1.60
1999 Proof	15,000	Value: 12.00				
2000	40,000	—	—	4.00	10.00	12.50
2000 Proof	15,000	Value: 15.00				

KM# 227 10 EURO CENT
4.0700 g., Brass, 19.7 mm. **Ruler:** Albert II **Obv:** Head left within inner circle, stars 3/4 surround, date below **Rev:** Denomination and map **Edge:** Reeded

Date	Mintage	F	VF	XF	Unc	BU
1999	180,990,000	—	—	—	0.75	1.25
1999 Proof	15,000	Value: 12.00				
2000	40,000	—	—	—	10.00	12.50
2000 Proof	15,000	Value: 15.00				

KM# 228 20 EURO CENT
5.7300 g., Brass, 22.1 mm. **Ruler:** Albert II **Obv:** Head left within circle, stars 3/4 surround, date below **Rev:** Denomination and map **Edge:** Notched

Date	Mintage	F	VF	XF	Unc	BU
1999	40,000	—	—	—	10.00	12.50
1999 Proof	15,000	Value: 15.00				
2000	181,040,000	—	—	—	0.75	1.25
2000 Proof	15,000	Value: 12.00				

KM# 229 50 EURO CENT
7.8100 g., Brass, 24.2 mm. **Ruler:** Albert II **Obv:** Head left within circle, stars 3/4 surround, date below **Rev:** Denomination and map **Edge:** Reeded

Date	Mintage	F	VF	XF	Unc	BU
1999	197,040,000	—	—	—	0.75	1.25
1999 Proof	15,000	Value: 12.00				
2000	40,000	—	—	—	10.00	12.50
2000 Proof	15,000	Value: 15.00				

KM# 230 EURO
7.5700 g., Bi-Metallic Copper-Nickel center in Brass ring, 23.2 mm. **Ruler:** Albert II **Obv:** Head left within circle, stars 3/4 surround, date below **Rev:** Denomination and map **Edge:** Reeded and plain sections

Date	Mintage	F	VF	XF	Unc	BU
1999	160,040,000	—	—	—	2.50	4.50
1999 Proof	15,000	Value: 15.00				
2000	40,000	—	—	—	12.50	15.00
2000 Proof	15,000	Value: 18.00				

KM# 231 2 EURO
8.5200 g., Bi-Metallic Brass center in Copper-Nickel ring, 25.7 mm. **Ruler:** Albert II **Obv:** Head left within circle, stars 3/4 surround, date below **Rev:** Denomination and map **Edge:** Reeded with 2's and stars

Date	Mintage	F	VF	XF	Unc	BU
1999	40,000	—	—	—	12.50	15.00
1999 Proof	15,000	Value: 20.00				
2000	120,040,000	—	—	—	3.50	5.50
2000 Proof	15,000	Value: 18.00				

PATTERNS
Including off metal strikes

KM#	Date	Mintage	Identification	Mkt Val
Pn90	19xx	—	Franc.	450
Pn91	1901	—	Centime. Copper. KM#33.3	260
Pn92	1901	—	5 Centimes. Pewter.	200
Pn93	1901	—	5 Centimes. Brass Plated Nickel.	260
Pn94	1901	—	5 Centimes. Copper-Iron Alloy. KM#45	250
Pn95	1901	—	5 Centimes. Copper. Designer's initials as A.M.; KM#46	300
Pn96	1901	—	5 Centimes. Copper. Thin flan, KM#46	250
Pn97	1901	—	10 Centimes. Nickel. KM#48	270
Pn98	1901	—	10 Centimes. Copper-Nickel.	275
Pn99	1901	—	50 Centimes. Copper. KM#50	250
Pn100	1901	—	50 Centimes. Silver.	525
Pn101	1901	—	Franc. Silver.	600
Pn102	1901	—	Franc. Silver. Head left. Lion with constitution.	650
Pn103	1901	—	2 Francs. Silver.	825
Pn104	1901	—	2 Francs. Silver. Head left. Lion with constitution. Reeded edge.	950
Pn105	1902	—	5 Centimes. Nickel.	100
Pn106	1902	—	5 Centimes. Copper-Nickel. Without center hole; KM#47.	200
Pn107	19xx	—	Franc. Nickel-Brass.	400
Pn108	1902	—	Franc. Silver. Reeded edge. Small portrait, KM#56.1	350
Pn109	1902	—	Franc. Silver. Plain edge. Small portrait, KM#56.1	350
Pn110	1903	—	Franc. Silver. Reeded edge. Small portrait, KM#56.1	350
Pn111	1903	—	Franc. Silver. Plain edge. Small portrait, KM#56.1	350
Pn112	1903	—	Franc. Silver.	—
Pn113	1903	—	Franc. Silver.	—
Pn114	1903	—	Franc. Silver.	—
Pn115	1903	—	Franc. Silver.	—
Pn116	1903	—	Franc. Silver.	—
Pn117	1903	—	Franc. Silver.	—
Pn118	1903	—	Franc. Silver.	—
Pn119	1903	—	Franc. Silver.	—
Pn136	1904	—	50 Centimes. Silver. Plain edge. KM#60.1	—
Pn137	1904	—	50 Centimes. Silver. Reeded edge. KM#60.1	—
Pn138	1904	—	50 Centimes. Silver. Smaller designs, KM#60.1	—
Pn139	1904	—	Franc. Silver. Reeded edge. Thin flan, KM#56.1.	—
Pn140	1904	—	Franc. Silver. Plain edge. Thick flan, KM#56.1.	500
Pn141	1904	—	2 Francs. Silver. Plain edge. KM#58.1.	—
Pn142	1904	—	2 Francs. Silver. Reeded edge. Thin flan, KM#58.1.	—
Pn143	1904	—	2 Francs. Silver. Plain edge. Thick flan, KM#58.1.	600
Pn144	1904	—	2 Francs. Silver. Plain edge. KM#59.1.	—
Pn145	1904	—	2 Francs. Silver. Reeded edge. Thin flan, KM#59.1.	—
Pn146	1904	—	2 Francs. Silver. Plain edge. Thick flan, KM#59.1.	600
Pn147	1906	—	5 Centimes. Nickel-Brass. Restrike, KM#93.	—
Pn148	1907	—	Centime. Copper. Reeded edge. Thick flan, KM#34.1.	—
Pn149	1907	—	25 Centimes. Copper-Nickel.	—
Pn150	1909	—	Franc. Silver. Reeded edge. KM#73.1	400
Pn151	1910	—	5 Centimes. Gold. Not holed, KM#67	1,000
Pn152	1910	—	5 Centimes. Silver. Not holed, KM#67	450
Pn153	1910	—	5 Centimes. Bronze. Not holed, KM#67	175
Pn154	1910	—	5 Centimes. Aluminum. Not holed, KM#67	150
Pn155	1910	—	Franc. Silver. Reeded edge. KM#72.	350
Pn156	1910	—	Franc. Silver. Reeded edge. Thick planchet, KM#72.	450
Pn157	1910	—	Franc. Silver. Reeded edge. Thin planchet, KM#72.	—
Pn158	1910	—	Franc. Silver. Designer's name as Devreese, KM#72.	—
Pn159	1910	—	Franc. Silver. Plain edge. KM#73.1	—
Pn160	1910	—	2 Francs. Silver. Plain edge. KM#74.	425
Pn161	1911	—	Centime. Copper. Restrike.	—
Pn162	1911	—	10 Centimes. Copper. Not holed.	—
Pn163	1911	—	10 Centimes. Brass. Holed.	—
Pn164	1911	—	10 Centimes. Copper-Nickel. Not holed.	—
Pn165	1911	—	10 Centimes. Gold. KM#85.1.	1,600
Pn166	1911	—	10 Centimes. Silver. KM#85.1.	490
Pn167	1911	—	10 Centimes. Bronze. KM#85.1.	—
Pn168	1911	—	10 Centimes. Copper. KM#85.1.	—
Pn169	1911	—	10 Centimes. Aluminum. KM#85.1.	—
Pn170	1911	—	10 Centimes. Gold. KM#86.	—
Pn171	1911	—	10 Centimes. Silver. KM#86.	—
Pn172	1911	—	10 Centimes. Bronze. KM#86.	—
Pn173	1911	—	10 Centimes. Copper. KM#86.	—
Pn174	1911	—	10 Centimes. Aluminum. KM#86.	—

KM#	Date	Mintage	Identification	Mkt Val
Pn175	1911	—	Franc. Silver. Reeded edge. Designer's name as Devreese, KM#73.	—
Pn176	1911	—	Franc. Silver. Plain edge. Designer's name as Devreese, KM#73.	—
Pn177	1911	—	2 Francs. Copper. KM#74.	350
Pn178	1911	—	2 Francs. Gold.	1,500
Pn179	1911	—	10 Francs. Gold. Dutch legend.	2,150
Pn180	1911	—	10 Francs. Gold. French legend.	2,000
Pn181	1911	—	20 Francs. Brass Plated Copper.	—
Pn182	1911	—	20 Francs. Nickel.	—
Pn183	1911	—	20 Francs. Gold. Dutch legend.	2,400
Pn184	1911	—	20 Francs. Gold. French legend.	2,500
Pn185	1911	—	20 Francs. Pewter.	—
Pn186	1911	—	100 Francs. Aluminum-Nickel. Dutch legend.	—
Pn187	1911	—	100 Francs. Aluminum-Nickel. French legend.	—
Pn188	1911	—	100 Francs. Silver. Reeded edge.	—
Pn189	1912/1	—	Centime. Copper. Restrike, ESSAI.	400
Pn190	1912	—	10 Francs. Gold. Dutch legend.	2,000
Pn191	1912	—	10 Francs. Gold. French legend.	2,000
Pn192	1912	—	10 Francs. Gold. Reeded edge.	—
Pn193	1912	3	100 Francs. Gold. Dutch legend.	16,000
Pn194	1912	6	100 Francs. Gold. French legend.	12,500
Pn195	1914	—	2 Francs. Silver. Unadopted portrait. ESSAI/MONETAIRE/1914.	4,000
Pn196	ND(1915)	—	Centime. Zinc.	—
Pn197	1915	—	5 Centimes. Copper-Iron Bi-Metal. Reeded edge. KM#66.	—
Pn198	1915	—	10 Centimes. Copper-Iron Bi-Metal. KM#681.	—
Pn199	1915	—	25 Centimes. Pot Metal.	—
Pn200	1916	—	10 Centimes. Copper-Iron Bi-Metal. KM#81.	—
Pn201	1917	—	10 Centimes. Silver. Plain edge. KM#81.	—
Pn202	1918	—	25 Centimes. Silver. Plain edge. KM#82.	—
Pn203	ND(1918)	—	25 Centimes. Copper-Iron Bi-Metal. 2 branches around legend. ESSAI MONETAIRE. Legend around 25 CES.	475
Pn204	ND(1918)	—	25 Centimes. Zinc. Legend around 25 CENT. Lion, ESSAI.	350
Pn205	ND(1918)	—	25 Centimes. Silver. 16 sided.	—
Pn206	1918	—	50 Centimes. Gold. KM#83.	1,500
Pn207	1918	—	50 Centimes. Silver. KM#83.	—
Pn208	1918	—	50 Centimes. Tan Bronze. KM#83.	—
Pn209	1918	—	50 Centimes. Red Bronze. KM#83.	—
Pn210	1918	—	50 Centimes. Aluminum. KM#83.	—
Pn211	1918	—	50 Centimes. Silver. Not holed.	—
Pn212	1918	—	50 Centimes. Nickel. Not holed.	—
Pn213	1918	—	50 Centimes. Copper-Nickel. Not holed.	—
PnA215	1920	—	20 Francs. Silver. Victory and Peace.	500
Pn214	1920	—	5 Centimes. Nickel. Reeded edge. Not holed, KM#66.	400
Pn215	1920	—	20 Francs. 0.6000 Silver. Victory.	400
Pn216	1921	—	5 Centimes. Nickel. KM#69	—
Pn218	1922	—	50 Centimes. Bronze.	—
Pn217	1922	—	5 Centimes. Nickel-Brass. Restrike, KM#94	—
Pn226	1922	—	50 Centimes. Bronze. Reeded edge. KM#87.	—
Pn219	1922	—	50 Centimes. Silver. Plain edge. KM#87	—
Pn220	1922	—	50 Centimes. Bronze. Plain edge. KM#87	—
Pn221	1922	—	50 Centimes. Aluminum. Plain edge. KM#87	—
Pn222	1922	—	50 Centimes. Nickel. Plain edge. KM#87	—
Pn223	1922	—	50 Centimes. Copper. Plain edge. KM#87	—
Pn224	1922	—	50 Centimes. Copper-Tin Alloy. Plain edge. KM#87	—
Pn225	1922	—	50 Centimes. Silver. Reeded edge. KM#87	—
Pn227	1922	—	50 Centimes. Aluminum. Reeded edge. KM#87	—
Pn228	1922	—	50 Centimes. Nickel. Reeded edge. KM#87	—
Pn229	1922	—	50 Centimes. Copper. Reeded edge. KM#87	•
Pn230	1922	—	50 Centimes. Copper-Tin Alloy. Reeded edge. KM#87	—
Pn231	1922	—	50 Centimes. Silver. Plain edge. KM#88	—
Pn232	1922	—	50 Centimes. Bronze. Plain edge. KM#88	—
Pn233	1922	—	50 Centimes. Aluminum. Plain edge. KM#88	—
Pn234	1922	—	50 Centimes. Copper. Plain edge. KM#88	—
Pn235	1922	—	50 Centimes. Copper-Tin Alloy. Plain edge. KM#88	—
Pn236	1922	—	50 Centimes. Silver. Reeded edge. KM#88	—
Pn237	1922	—	50 Centimes. Bronze. Reeded edge. KM#88	—
Pn238	1922	—	50 Centimes. Aluminum. Reeded edge. KM#88	—
Pn239	1922	—	50 Centimes. Copper. Reeded edge. KM#88	—

KM#	Date	Mintage	Identification	Mkt Val
Pn240	1922	—	50 Centimes. Copper-Tin Alloy. Reeded edge. KM#88	—
Pn241	1922	—	Franc. Silver. Plain edge. KM#89	800
Pn242	1922	—	Franc. Bronze. Plain edge. KM#89	—
Pn243	1922	—	Franc. Aluminum. Plain edge. KM#89	—
Pn244	1922	—	Franc. Copper. Plain edge. KM#89	—
Pn245	1922	—	Franc. Copper-Tin Alloy. Plain edge. KM#89	—
Pn246	1922	—	Franc. Silver. Reeded edge. KM#89	750
Pn247	1922	—	Franc. Bronze. Reeded edge. KM#89	—
Pn248	1922	—	Franc. Aluminum. Reeded edge. KM#89	—
Pn249	1922	—	Franc. Copper. Reeded edge. KM#89	—
Pn250	1922	—	Franc. Copper-Tin Alloy. Reeded edge. KM#89	—
Pn251	1922	—	Franc. Silver. Plain edge. KM#90	—
Pn252	1922	—	Franc. Bronze. Plain edge. KM#90	—
Pn253	1922	—	Franc. Aluminum. Plain edge. KM#90	—
Pn254	1922	—	Franc. Nickel. Plain edge. Irregular flan, KM#90.	—
Pn255	1922	—	Franc. Copper. Plain edge. KM#90.	—
Pn256	1922	—	Franc. Copper-Tin Alloy. Plain edge. KM#90.	—
Pn257	1922	—	Franc. Silver. Reeded edge. KM#90.	—
Pn258	1922	—	Franc. Bronze. Reeded edge. KM#90.	—
Pn259	1922	—	Franc. Aluminum. Reeded edge. KM#90.	—
Pn260	1922	—	Franc. Copper. Reeded edge. KM#90.	—
Pn261	1922	—	Franc. Copper-Tin Alloy. Reeded edge. KM#90.	—
Pn262	1922	—	Franc. Nickel. KM#89. KM#90.	—
Pn263	1923	—	2 Francs. Silver. ESSAI, KM#91.1.	—
Pn264	1923	—	2 Francs. Bronze. ESSAI, KM#91.1.	—
Pn265	1923	—	2 Francs. Aluminum. ESSAI, KM#91.1.	—
Pn266	1923	—	2 Francs. Copper-Tin Alloy. ESSAI, KM#91.1.	—
Pn267	1926	—	5 Francs. Red Bronze. ESSAI	—
Pn268	1926	—	5 Francs. Silver. Head left. Wreath with 5 FR within.	—
Pn269	1926	—	5 Francs. Bronze. Head left. Wreath with 5 FR within.	—
Pn270	1926	—	5 Francs. Nickel. Head left. Wreath with 5 FR within.	—
Pn271	1926	—	5 Francs. Copper-Tin Alloy. Head left. Wreath with 5 FR within.	—
Pn272	1926	—	5 Francs. Silver. Crown above 5 Francs.	—
Pn273	1926	—	5 Francs. Bronze. Crown above 5 Francs.	—
Pn274	1926	—	5 Francs. Nickel. Crown above 5 Francs.	—
Pn275	1926	—	5 Francs. Copper-Tin Alloy. Crown above 5 Francs.	—
Pn276	1926	—	5 Francs. Silver. Crown above oak wreath, 5 Francs within.	—
Pn277	1926	—	5 Francs. Bronze. Crown above oak wreath, 5 Francs within.	—
Pn278	1926	—	5 Francs. Copper-Tin Alloy. Crown above oak wreath, 5 Francs within.	—
Pn279	1926	—	5 Francs. Gold. Wreath, UN BELGA CINQ FRANCS.	1,750
Pn280	1926	—	5 Francs. Silver. Wreath, UN BELGA CINQ FRANCS.	—
Pn281	1926	—	5 Francs. Bronze. Wreath, UN BELGA CINQ FRANCS.	—
Pn282	1926	—	5 Francs. Nickel. Wreath, UN BELGA CINQ FRANCS.	—
Pn283	1926	—	5 Francs. Copper-Tin Alloy. Wreath, UN BELGA CINQ FRANCS.	—
Pn284	1926	—	5 Francs. Gold. Lion in shield, SF flanking.	1,750
Pn285	1926	—	5 Francs. Silver. Lion in shield, SF flanking.	—
Pn286	1926	—	5 Francs. Bronze. Lion in shield, SF flanking.	—
Pn287	1926	—	5 Francs. Nickel. Lion in shield, SF flanking.	—
Pn288	1926	—	5 Francs. Copper-Tin Alloy. Lion in shield, SF flanking.	—
Pn289	1927	—	5 Francs. Silver. Head by Bonnetain. 2 laurel branches, UN BELGA/OU/5 FRANCS/ESSAI.	450
Pn290	1927	—	5 Francs. Copper. Head by Bonnetain. 2 laurel branches, UN BELGA/OU/5 FRANCS/ESSAI.	450
Pn291	1927	—	5 Francs. Copper-Tin Alloy. Head by Bonnetain. 2 laurel branches, UN BELGA/OU/5 FRANCS/ESSAI.	450
Pn292	1927	—	5 Francs. Nickel.	—
Pn293	1929	—	5 Centimes. Copper-Nickel. Not holed, KM#67.	—
Pn294	1929	—	10 Centimes. Nickel. Not holed, ESSAI, KM#85.1.	—
Pn295	1929	—	10 Centimes. Gold. KM#85.1.	1,000
Pn296	1929	—	10 Centimes. Silver. KM#85.1.	—
Pn297	1929	—	10 Centimes. Bronze. KM#85.1.	—
Pn298	1929	—	10 Centimes. Copper. KM#85.1.	—
Pn299	1929	—	10 Centimes. Aluminum. KM#85.1.	—
Pn300	1929	—	25 Centimes. Gold. ESSAI, KM#68.1.	1,200
Pn301	1929	—	25 Centimes. Silver. ESSAI, KM#68.1.	—
Pn302	1929	—	25 Centimes. Bronze. ESSAI, KM#68.1.	—
Pn303	1929	—	25 Centimes. Copper. ESSAI, KM#68.1.	—
Pn304	1929	—	25 Centimes. Aluminum. ESSAI, KM#68.1.	—
Pn305	1929	—	25 Centimes. Gold. ESSAI, KM#69.	1,200
Pn306	1929	—	25 Centimes. Silver. ESSAI, KM#69.	—
Pn307	1929	—	25 Centimes. Bronze. ESSAI, KM#69.	—
Pn308	1929	—	25 Centimes. Copper. ESSAI, KM#69.	—
Pn309	1929	—	25 Centimes. Aluminum. ESSAI, KM#69.	—
Pn310	1929	—	5 Francs. Nickel.	—
Pn311	1929	—	5 Francs. Bronze.	—
Pn312	1930	—	2 Francs. Copper. KM#92.	—
Pn313	1930	—	2 Francs. Matte Bronze. KM#92.	—
Pn314	1930	—	10 Francs. Brass.	250
Pn315	1930	—	20 Francs. Silver.	—
Pn316	1931	—	Franc. Nickel.	—
Pn317	1931	—	20 Francs. Bronze. French legend.	250
Pn318	1931	—	20 Francs. Bronze. Dutch legend.	250
Pn319	1932	—	5 Centimes. Copper-Nickel.	—
Pn320	1932	—	5 Centimes. Dupriez's design.	—
Pn321	1932	—	5 Centimes. Copper. Not holed, KM#93.	—
Pn322	1932	—	50 Centimes. Nickel. KM#87. KM#88. Reeded edge.	—
Pn323	1932	—	50 Centimes. Nickel. KM#87. KM#88. Plain edge.	—
Pn324	1933	—	5 Francs. Silver.	—
Pn325	1933	—	10 Francs. Nickel.	—
Pn326	1933	—	10 Francs. Nickel. DEUX BELGAS/OU/10 FRANCS.	—
Pn327	1933	—	5 Francs. Silver. 10/BELGAS/50/FRANCS within 2 oak branches. Plain edge.	—
Pn328	1933	—	50 Francs. Silver. Cross ornaments on edge.	—
Pn329	1933	—	50 Francs. Silver. Reeded edge.	—
Pn330	1933	—	50 Francs. Silver. Small head of Albert within pellet circle. Value within 2 laurel branches.	—
Pn331	1933	—	50 Francs. Silver. Bust by Bonnetain. Value within laurel branches.	—
Pn332	1933	—	100 Francs. Silver. Bust by Bonnetain. 20/BELGAS/100/FRANCS within 2 laurel branches.	—
Pn333	1933	—	100 Francs. By Devreese	—
Pn334	1933	—	100 Francs. L'UNION FAIT LA FORCE/100 FRS. By Devreese	—
Pn335	1933	—	100 Francs. Bronze. 20/BELGAS/100 FRANCS between 2 branches.	—
Pn336	1933	—	500 Francs. Bronze. 20/BELGAS/500/FRANCS between laurel and oak branches.	250
Pn337	1933	—	500 Francs. Nickel.	—
Pn338	1934	—	5 Francs. Bronze.	100
Pn339	1934	—	20 Francs. Bronze.	125
Pn340	1935	—	Franc. Copper-Tin Alloy. Reeded edge.	—
Pn341	1935	—	Franc. Nickel. Reeded edge.	—
Pn342	1935	—	Franc. Silver. Allegory of Belgium kneeling left; BELGIQUE \ BELGIE at sides. Caduceus between IF and date. Plain edge.	—
Pn343	1935	—	Franc. Silver. Allegory of Belgium kneeling left. Plain edge.	—
Pn344	1935	—	Franc. Copper. Allegory of Belgium kneeling left. Plain edge.	—
Pn345	1935	—	Franc. Nickel. Allegory of Belgium kneeling left. Plain edge.	—
Pn346	1935	—	40 Francs. 0.6800 Silver. Lettered edge.	14,000
Pn347	1935	—	40 Francs. Silver. Plain edge. Restrike.	—
Pn348	1935	—	40 Francs. Copper-Tin Alloy. Lettered edge. Expo commemorative.	—
Pn349	1935	—	40 Francs. Gold. Reeded edge. Expo commemorative.	—
Pn350	1935	—	40 Francs. Silver. Reeded edge. Expo commemorative.	—
Pn351	1935	—	40 Francs. Bronze. Reeded edge. Expo commemorative.	—
Pn352	1935	—	40 Francs. Copper. Reeded edge. Expo commemorative.	—
Pn353	1935	—	40 Francs. Copper-Tin Alloy. Reeded edge. Expo commemorative.	—
Pn354	1935	—	40 Francs. Nickel. Reeded edge. Expo commemorative.	—
Pn355	1935	—	40 Francs. Aluminum. Reeded edge. Expo commemorative.	—
Pn356	1935	—	40 Francs. Gold. Expo commemorative, thin planchet.	2,000
Pn357	1935	—	40 Francs. Silver. Expo commemorative, thin planchet.	800
Pn358	1935	—	40 Francs. Bronze. Expo commemorative, thin planchet.	400
Pn359	1935	—	40 Francs. Copper. Expo commemorative, thin planchet.	400
Pn360	1935	—	40 Francs. Copper-Tin Alloy. Expo commemorative, thin planchet.	400
Pn361	1935	—	40 Francs. Nickel. Expo commemorative, thin planchet.	450
Pn362	1935	—	40 Francs. Aluminum. Expo commemorative, thin planchet	400
Pn363	1935	—	50 Francs. 0.6800 Silver. Plain edge.	600
Pn364	1935	—	50 Francs. Silver. Plain edge. KM#106.1.	—
Pn365	1935	—	50 Francs. Copper. Plain edge. KM#106.1.	—
Pn366	1935	—	50 Francs. Copper-Tin Alloy. Plain edge. KM#106.1.	—
Pn367	1935	—	50 Francs. Copper-Tin Alloy. Edge inscription. KM#106.1.	—
Pn368	1935	—	50 Francs. Gold. Reeded edge. KM#106.1.	—
Pn369	1935	—	50 Francs. Silver. Reeded edge. KM#106.1.	—
Pn370	1935	—	50 Francs. Bronze. Reeded edge. KM#106.1.	—
Pn371	1935	—	50 Francs. Copper. Reeded edge. KM#106.1.	—
Pn372	1935	—	50 Francs. Copper-Tin Alloy. Reeded edge. KM#106.1.	—
Pn373	1935	—	50 Francs. Aluminum. Reeded edge. KM#106.1.	—
Pn374	1935	—	50 Francs. Silver. Plain edge. KM#107.1.	—
Pn375	1935	—	50 Francs. Copper-Tin Alloy. Plain edge. KM#107.1.	—
Pn376	1935	—	50 Francs. Bronze. Edge inscription, KM#107.1.	—
Pn377	1935	—	50 Francs. Copper-Tin Alloy. Reeded edge. KM#107.1.	—
Pn378	1936	—	5 Francs. Nickel.	—
Pn379	1938	—	5 Centimes. Copper-Tin Alloy. KM#110.1	—
Pn380	1938	—	5 Centimes. Bronze. KM#110.1	—
Pn381	1938	—	5 Centimes. Tin. Not holed, KM#110.1	—
Pn382	1938	—	10 Centimes. Copper-Tin Alloy. Thin planchet, KM#112.	—
Pn383	1938	—	10 Centimes. Copper-Tin Alloy. Thick planchet, KM#112.	—
Pn384	1938	—	10 Centimes. Bronze. KM#112.	—
Pn385	1938	—	10 Centimes. Copper-Tin Alloy. Large letters, not holed.	—
Pn386	1938	—	25 Centimes. Nickel. Large shields.	—
Pn387	1938	—	25 Centimes. Copper-Tin Alloy. Not holed.	—
Pn388	1938	—	20 Francs. Silver.	—
Pn389	1938	—	20 Francs. Silver. Similar to KM#121.	—
Pn390	1938	—	20 Francs. Bronze. Similar to KM#121.	—
Pn391	1938	—	20 Francs. Copper. Similar to KM#121.	—
Pn392	1938	—	20 Francs. Copper-Tin Alloy. Similar to KM#121.	—
Pn393	1938	—	20 Francs. Nickel. Similar to KM#121.	—
Pn394	1938	—	20 Francs. Silver.	—
Pn395	1938	—	20 Francs. Copper-Tin Alloy.	—
Pn396	1938	—	20 Francs. Tin.	—
Pn397	1938	—	20 Francs. Silver. Thick planchet.	1,000
Pn398	1938	—	20 Francs. Copper-Tin Alloy. Thick planchet.	500
Pn399	1938	—	20 Francs. Tin. Thick planchet.	—
Pn400	1938	—	20 Francs. Silver. Small portrait.	—
Pn401	1938	—	20 Francs. Bronze. Small portrait.	—
Pn402	1938	—	20 Francs. Copper-Tin Alloy. Small portrait.	—
Pn403	1938	—	20 Francs. Tin. Small portrait.	—
Pn404	1938	—	50 Francs. Silver. Plain edge. KM#121.1.	—
Pn405	1938	—	50 Francs. Copper-Tin Alloy. Plain edge. KM#121.1.	—
Pn406	1938	—	50 Francs. Copper. Plain edge.	—
Pn407	1938	—	50 Francs. Copper. Plain edge. ESSAI	—
Pn408	1939	—	25 Centimes. Copper-Tin Alloy. Not holed, KM#114.1.	—
Pn409	1939	—	25 Centimes. Bronze. KM#114.1.	—
Pn410	1939	—	Franc. Nickel. KM#120.	—
Pn411	1939	—	Franc. Bronze. Reeded edge. KM#120.	—
Pn412	1939	—	Franc. Copper-Tin Alloy. Reeded edge. KM#120.	—
Pn413	1939	—	50 Francs. Silver. Lettered edge. KM#121.1.	—
Pn414	1939	—	50 Francs. Bronze. Lettered edge. KM#121.1.	—
Pn415	1940	—	Franc. Nickel. Restrike, KM#119.	—
Pn416	1940	—	5 Francs. Copper-Tin Alloy. Portrait by Rau, Leopold III ROI DE BELGES. 5/FRANCS/1940 between oak and laurel branches.	—
Pn417	1940	—	5 Francs. Copper-Tin Alloy. Portrait by Rau. Thick planchet.	400
Pn418	1940	—	5 Francs. Copper-Tin Alloy. Portrait by Rau. KM#108.1.	—
Pn419	1940	—	5 Francs. Copper-Tin Alloy. Portrait by Rau. KM#108.1. Thick planchet.	400
Pn420	1940	—	5 Francs. Copper-Tin Alloy. Leopold III.	—
Pn421	1940	—	5 Francs. Copper-Tin Alloy. Leopold III. Thick planchet.	400
Pn422	1940	—	5 Francs. Nickel. Leopold III. Reeded edge.	—

KM#	Date	Mintage	Identification	Mkt Val
Pn423	1940	—	5 Francs. Nickel. Leopold III. Reeded edge. Thick planchet.	400
Pn424	1940	—	5 Francs. Silver. Leopold III. KM#108.1.	—
Pn425	1940	—	5 Francs. Silver. Leopold III. KM#108.1. Thick planchet.	425
Pn426	1940	—	5 Francs. Copper-Tin Alloy. Leopold III, ROI DES BELGES. KM#108.1. Thick planchet.	400
Pn427	1941	—	10 Centimes. Silver. Reeded edge. KM#130.	—
Pn428	1941	—	5 Francs. Silver. Reeded edge. KM#130.	—
Pn429	1944	—	2 Francs. Silver. KM#133.	—
Pn430	1948	—	100 Francs. Copper. ESSAI, KM#138.	—
Pn431	1948	—	100 Francs. Copper. ESSAI, KM#139.1.	—
Pn432	1949	—	5 Francs. Copper. KM#134.1.	—
Pn433	1949	—	5 Francs. Copper. KM#135.1.	—
Pn434	1949	—	50 Francs. Bronze.	—
Pn435	1949	—	100 Francs. Silver.	—
Pn436	1949	—	100 Francs. Silver.	—
Pn437	1949	—	1000 Francs. Bronze. Plain edge.	—
Pn438	1949	—	1000 Francs. Silver.	900
Pn439	1949	—	1000 Francs. Gold. ESSAI	10,920
Pn440	ND	—	1000 Francs. Bronze.	—
Pn441	1949	—	1000 Francs. Bronze. Milled edge.	—
Pn442	1951	—	20 Francs. Copper. ESSAI, KM#140.1	—
Pn443	1951	—	20 Francs. Copper. ESSAI, KM#141.1	—
Pn444	1951	—	20 Francs. Copper. ESSAI, KM#136.1.	—
Pn445	1951	—	50 Francs. Copper. ESSAI, KM#137	—
Pn446	1952	—	Franc. Copper. KM#142.1	—
Pn447	1952	—	Franc. Copper. KM#143.1	—

PIEFORTS

KM#	Date	Mintage	Identification	Mkt Val
P4	1912	—	10 Francs. Gold. Plain edge.	2,500
P5	1912	—	10 Francs. Silver. Plain edge.	900
P6	1918	—	50 Centimes. Zinc. Plain edge. Not holed, KM#83.	900
P7	1920	—	25 Centimes. Nickel. Plain edge. KM#68.1.	—
P8	1926	—	5 Centimes. Copper. Plain edge. Not holed, KM#66.	—
P9	1935	—	Franc. Silver.	1,000
P10	1935	—	Franc. Copper.	400
P11	1935	—	Franc. Nickel.	250
P12	1989	—	100 Ecu. Gold. KM#175	1,400

TRIAL STRIKES

KM#	Date	Mintage	Identification	Mkt Val
TS5	1903	—	Franc. Pewter. Uniface. Rectangle planchet.	1,000
TS6	1904	—	Franc. Pewter. Uniface. Rectangle planchet.	1,000
TS7	ND(1904)	—	2 Francs. Lead. Uniface.	50.00
TS8	1910	—	2 Francs. Portrait, uniface.	—
TS9	1910	—	2 Francs. KM#74. Uniface.	—
TS10	1911	—	20 Francs. Gold. Error obverse.	1,250
TS11	1911	—	20 Francs. Aluminum. Error obverse.	600
TS12	1918	—	50 Centimes. Klippe.	1,000
TS13	1926	—	5 Francs. Nickel. Klippe.	1,000
TS14	1933	—	10 Francs. Silver. Legend within 2 branches.	—
TS15	1933	—	50 Francs. Silver. Irregular flan.	—
TS16	1949	—	1000 Francs. Red. Copper. Klippe.	450
TS17	1949	—	1000 Francs. Yellow Copper. Klippe.	450
TS18	1949	—	1000 Francs. Red. Copper. Klippe.	450
TS19	1949	—	1000 Francs. Yellow Copper. Klippe.	450
TS20	1949	—	1000 Francs. Silver. Klippe.	850

"FDC" SETS

KM#	Date	Mintage	Identification	Issue Price	Mkt Val
SS1	1970 (5)	5,000	KM#135.1, 143.1, 149.1, 154.1, 156.1 DU	0.60	225
SS2	1970 (5)	5,000	KM#134.1, 142.1, 148.1, 153.1, 155.1 FR	0.60	225
SS3	1971 (5)	10,000	KM#135.1, 143.1, 149.1, 154.1, 156.1 DU	0.63	75.00
SS4	1971 (5)	10,000	KM#134.1, 142.1, 148.1, 153.1, 155.1 FR	0.63	75.00
SS5	1972 (5)	10,000	KM#135.1, 143.1, 149.1, 154.1, 156.1 DU	0.70	85.00
SS6	1972 (5)	10,000	KM#134.1, 142.1, 148.1, 153.1, 155.1 FR	0.70	85.00
SS7	1973 (5)	16,778	KM#135.1, 143.1, 149.1, 154.1, 156.1 DU	0.80	40.00
SS8	1973 (5)	15,000	KM#134.1, 142.1, 148.1, 153.1, 155.1 FR	0.80	40.00
SS10	1974 (5)	19,000	KM#134.1, 142.1, 148.1, 153.1, 155.1 FR	1.10	22.00
SS9	1974 (5)	20,608	KM#135.1, 143.1, 149..1 154.1, 156.1 DU	1.10	22.00
SS11	1975 (10)	45,752	KM#135.1, 143.1, 149.1, 154.1, 156.1 DU, 134.1, 142.1, 148.1, 153.1, 155.1 FR	2.50	10.00
SS12	1976 (10)	15,000	KM#135, 143, 149, 156, 158.1 DU, 134, 142, 148, 155, 157.1 FR	20.75	60.00
SS13	1977 (8)	45,938	KM#135, 143, 149, 156 DU, 134, 142, 148, 155 FR	2.65	6.00
SS14	1978 (8)	46,237	KM#135, 143, 149, 156 DU, 134, 142, 148, 155 FR	4.00	8.00
SS15	1979 (8)	49,997	KM#135, 143, 149, 156 DU, 134, 142, 148, 155 FR	4.00	6.00
SS16	1980 (8)	60,000	KM#135, 143, 149, 160 DU, 134, 142, 148, 159 FR	4.00	5.00
SS17	1981 (8)	54,331	KM#135, 143, 149, 160 DU, 134, 142, 148, 159 FR	3.25	8.00

MINT SETS

KM#	Date	Mintage	Identification	Issue Price	Mkt Val
MS1	1989 (10)	60,000	KM#149, 160, 164, 169, 171 DU; 148, 159, 163, 168, 170 FR	11.00	35.00
MS2	1990 (10)	60,000	KM#149, 160, 164, 169, 171 DU; 148, 159, 163, 168, 170 FR	13.00	30.00
MS3	1991 (10)	60,000	KM#149, 160, 164, 169, 171 DU; 148, 159, 163, 168, 170 FR	13.00	25.00
MS4	1991 (3)	—	KM#196-198	—	30.00
MS5	1992 (10)	60,000	KM#149, 160, 164, 169, 171 DU; 148, 159,	15.00	40.00
MS6	1993 (10)	40,000	KM#149, 160, 164, 169, 171 DU; 148, 159, 163, 168, 170 FR	15.00	15.00
MS7	1994 (10)	60,000	KM#148.1, 149.1, 187-194, medal	15.00	15.00
MS8	1995 (10)	60,000	KM#148.1, 149.1, 187-194, medal	15.00	25.00
MS9	1996 (10)	60,000	KM#148.1, 149.1, 187-194, medal	15.00	17.00
MS10	1997 (10)	60,000	KM#148.1, 149.1, 187-194, medal	—	25.00
MS11	1998 (10)	60,000	KM#148.1, 149.1, 187-194	15.00	20.00
MS12	1999 (10)	60,000	KM#148.1, 149.1, 187-194	15.00	30.00
MS13	2000 (10)	60,000	KM#148.1, 149.1, 187-194	15.00	30.00

PROOF SETS

KM#	Date	Mintage	Identification	Issue Price	Mkt Val
PS1	1987 (2)	15,000	KM#166-167	395	520
PS2	1988 (2)	15,000	KM#166-167	395	520
PS3	1989 (4)	2,000	KM#172-175	1,300	1,950
PS4	1990 (4)	5,000	KM#172-175	1,300	1,700
PS5	1990 (3)	10,000	KM#178-180	100	120
PS6	1991 (3)	10,000	KM#196-198	100	85.00
PS8	1999 (8)	15,000	KM#224-231	80.00	85.00
PS7	2000 (3)	10,000	KM#215-217	75.00	150
PS9	2000 (8)	15,000	KM#224-231	80.00	85.00

GHENT
GERMAN OCCUPATION WWI

TOKEN COINAGE

KM# Tn1a   50 CENTIMES
Brass-Plated Iron   **Rev:** Thick "50"

Date	Mintage	F	VF	XF	Unc	BU
1915	Inc. above	7.00	15.00	25.00	40.00	140

KM# Tn1   50 CENTIMES
Brass-Plated Iron   **Obv:** Rampant lion, left, within inner circle
Rev: Denomination within inner circle, box surrounds
Note: Similar to KM#Tn1a, thin "50".

Date	Mintage	F	VF	XF	Unc	BU
1915	512,000	7.00	15.00	25.00	40.00	140

KM# Tn2   FRANKEN
Brass-Plated Iron   **Obv:** Rampant lion, left, within inner circle
Rev: Denomination within inner circle, box surrounds

Date	Mintage	F	VF	XF	Unc	BU
1915	370,000	7.00	15.00	25.00	40.00	140

KM# Tn2a   FRANKEN
Brass-Plated Iron   **Rev:** 11. 1919 instead of 1.1. 1919

Date	Mintage	F	VF	XF	Unc	BU
1915	Inc. above	8.00	17.00	26.00	45.00	160

KM# Tn3   FRANKEN
Gilt Copper   **Obv:** Lion in circle, STAD GENT VILLE DE GAND around   **Rev:** 1915 1 FR in circle, UIT BETAALBAAR 1 JANUARI 1918 REMBOURSABLE 1 JANVIER 1920 along sides of square   **Note:** This token was struck in 1920 for the benefit of charity.

Date	Mintage	F	VF	XF	Unc	BU
1915	—	50.00	200	350	600	1,100

KM# Tn4   2 FRANKEN
Brass-Plated Iron   **Obv:** Rampant lion, left, within inner circle
Rev: Denomination within inner circle, box surrounds

Date	Mintage	F	VF	XF	Unc	BU
1915	314,000	10.00	25.00	40.00	60.00	160

KM# Tn5   2 FRANKEN
Gilt Copper   **Obv:** Arms in circle, STAD GENT FIDES ET AMOR around   **Rev:** 1928 2 FRANK in circle, UIT BETAAL BAAR JANUARI 1922 PAX ET LABOR around   **Note:** This token was struck in 1920 for the benefit of charity.

Date	Mintage	F	VF	XF	Unc	BU
1918	—	45.00	175	300	550	900

KM# Tn6   5 FRANKEN
Brass-Plated Iron   **Obv:** Crowned shield within circle
Rev: Denomination within inner circle, box surrounds

Date	Mintage	F	VF	XF	Unc	BU
1917	108,000	17.50	30.00	45.00	100	225

KM# Tn7   5 FRANKEN
Brass-Plated Iron   **Obv:** Crowned arms within circle
Rev: Denomination below date, within circle

Date	Mintage	F	VF	XF	Unc	BU
1918	339,000	15.00	27.00	40.00	90.00	170

BELIZE

MEXICO

Caribbean Sea

GUATEMALA

HONDURAS

Belize, formerly British Honduras, but now a Constitutional Monarchy within the Commonwealth of Nations, is situated in Central America south of Mexico and east and north of Guatemala, with an area of 8,867 sq. mi. (22,960 sq. km.) and a population of *242,000. Capital: Belmopan. Tourism now augments Belize's economy, in addition to sugar, citrus fruits, chicle and hardwoods which are exported.

The area, site of the ancient Mayan civilization, was sighted by Columbus in 1502, and settled by shipwrecked English seamen in 1638. British buccaneers settled the former capital of Belize in the 17th century. Britain claimed administrative right over the area after the emancipation of Central America from Spain. In 1825, Imperial coins were introduced into the colony and were rated against the Spanish dollar and Honduran currency. It was declared a colony subordinate to Jamaica in 1862 and was established as the separate Crown Colony of British Honduras in 1884. In May, 1885 an order in Council authorized coins for the colony, with the first shipment arriving in July. While the Guatemalan peso was originally the standard of value, in 1894 the colony changed to the gold standard, based on the U.S. gold dollar. The anti-British Peoples United Party, which attained power in 1954, won a constitution, effective in 1964 which established self-government under a British appointed governor. British Honduras became Belize on June 1, 1973, following the passage of a surprise bill by the Peoples United Party, but the constitutional relationship with Britain remained unchanged.

In Dec. 1975, the U.N. General Assembly adopted a resolution supporting the right of the people of Belize to self-determination, and asking Britain and Guatemala to renew their negotiations on the future of Belize. Independence was obtained on Sept. 21, 1981. Elizabeth II is Head of State as Queen of Belize.

RULER
British, until 1981

MINT MARKS
H - Birmingham Mint
No mm - Royal Mint

*NOTE: From 1975-1985 the Franklin Mint produced coinage in up to 3 different qualities. Qualities of issue are designated in ( ) after each date and are defined as follows:

(M) MATTE - Normal circulation strike or a dull finish produced by sandblasting special uncirculated (polish finish) or proof quality dies.

(U) SPECIAL UNCIRCULATED - Polished or proof-like in appearance without any frosted features.

(P) PROOF - The highest quality obtainable having mirror-like fields and frosted features.

MONETARY SYSTEM
100 Cents = 1 Dollar

COMMONWEALTH
DECIMAL COINAGE

KM# 33   CENT
2.7000 g., Bronze, 19.5 mm.   **Obv:** Bust of Queen Elizabeth right **Rev:** Denomination within circle, date lower right of circle **Edge:** Smooth

Date	Mintage	F	VF	XF	Unc	BU
1973	400,000	—	—	0.10	0.25	0.60
1974	2,000,000	—	—	0.10	0.20	0.50
1975	Inc. above	—	—	0.10	0.15	0.45
1976	3,000,000	—	—	0.10	0.15	0.45

KM# 33a   CENT
0.8000 g., Aluminum, 19.5 mm.   **Obv:** Bust of Queen Elizabeth right **Rev:** Denomination within circle **Edge:** Smooth, scalloped

Date	Mintage	F	VF	XF	Unc	BU
1976	2,049,999	—	—	0.10	0.25	0.60
1979	2,505,000	—	—	0.10	0.25	0.60
1980	1,505,000	—	—	0.10	0.25	0.60

Date	Mintage	F	VF	XF	Unc	BU
1982	—	—	—	0.10	0.25	0.60
1983	—	—	—	0.10	0.25	0.60
1986	—	—	—	0.10	0.25	0.60
1987	—	—	—	0.10	0.25	0.60
1989	—	—	—	0.10	0.25	0.60
1991	—	—	—	0.10	0.25	0.60
1992	—	—	—	0.10	0.25	0.60
1994	—	—	—	0.10	0.25	0.60
1996	—	—	—	0.10	0.20	0.50
1998	—	—	—	0.10	0.25	0.60
2000	—	—	—	0.10	0.25	0.60

KM# 38   CENT
2.6700 g., Bronze   **Obv:** National arms, date below, within wreath **Rev:** Swallow-tailed kite right, denomination above **Edge:** Smooth

Date	Mintage	F	VF	XF	Unc	BU
1974FM (M)	225,000	—	—	0.40	0.75	1.50
1974FM (P)	21,000	Value: 1.25				

KM# 38a   CENT
3.0200 g., 0.9250 Silver 0.0898 oz. ASW   **Rev:** Swallow-tailed kite

Date	Mintage	F	VF	XF	Unc	BU
1974FM (P)	31,000	Value: 3.50				

KM# 46   CENT
Bronze   **Obv:** National arms, date below, within wreath **Rev:** Swallow-tailed kite, right, denomination above **Edge:** Smooth

Date	Mintage	F	VF	XF	Unc	BU
1975FM (M)	118,000	—	—	0.10	0.75	2.00
1975FM (U)	1,095	—	—	0.50	1.00	2.25
1975FM (P)	8,794	Value: 2.00				
1976FM (M)	126,000	—	—	0.10	0.75	2.00
1976FM (U)	759	—	—	0.50	1.00	2.25
1976FM (P)	4,893	Value: 2.00				

KM# 46a   CENT
3.0200 g., 0.9250 Silver 0.0898 oz. ASW   **Rev:** Swallow-tailed kite

Date	Mintage	F	VF	XF	Unc	BU
1975FM (P)	13,000	Value: 3.00				
1976FM (P)	5,897	Value: 3.00				
1977FM (P)	3,197	Value: 3.00				
1978FM (P)	3,342	Value: 3.00				
1979FM (P)	2,445	Value: 3.00				
1980FM (P)	1,826	Value: 3.00				
1981FM (P)	615	Value: 3.50				

KM# 46b   CENT
Aluminum   **Obv:** National arms, date below, within wreath **Rev:** Swallow-tailed kite, right, denomination above **Edge:** Smooth

Date	Mintage	F	VF	XF	Unc	BU
1977FM (U)	126,000	—	—	0.10	0.75	1.30
1977FM (P)	2,107	Value: 2.00				
1978FM (U)	125,000	—	—	0.10	0.75	1.30
1978FM (P)	1,671	Value: 2.00				
1979FM (U)	808	—	—	0.50	1.00	2.00
1979FM (P)	1,287	Value: 2.00				
1980FM (U)	761	—	—	0.15	0.75	1.00
1980FM (P)	920	Value: 2.00				
1981FM (U)	297	—	—	1.00	2.00	3.00
1981FM (P)	643	Value: 2.00				

KM# 83   CENT
Aluminum   **Rev:** Swallow-tailed kite **Edge:** Smooth

Date	Mintage	F	VF	XF	Unc	BU
1982FM (U)	—	—	0.15	0.25	1.50	1.75
1982FM (P)	—	Value: 3.00				
1983FM (U)	—	—	0.15	0.25	1.50	1.75
1983FM (P)	—	Value: 3.00				

KM# 83a   CENT
3.0200 g., 0.9250 Silver 0.0898 oz. ASW   **Rev:** Swallow-tailed kite

Date	Mintage	F	VF	XF	Unc	BU
1982FM (P)	381	Value: 7.50				
1983FM (P)	336	Value: 7.50				

KM# 90   CENT
Aluminum   **Rev:** Swallow-tailed kite, right, denomination above **Edge:** Smooth

Date	Mintage	F	VF	XF	Unc	BU
1984FM (U)	—	—	0.15	0.25	1.50	1.75
1984FM (P)	—	Value: 3.00				

KM# 90a   CENT
3.0200 g., 0.9250 Silver 0.0898 oz. ASW   **Rev:** Swallow-tailed kite

Date	Mintage	F	VF	XF	Unc	BU
1984FM (P)	—	Value: 7.50				
1985 Proof	212	Value: 10.00				

KM# 34   5 CENTS
3.6000 g., Nickel-Brass, 20.15 mm.   **Obv:** Crowned bust of Queen Elizabeth II right **Rev:** Denomination within circle, date below circle **Edge:** Smooth

Date	Mintage	F	VF	XF	Unc	BU
1973	210,000	—	—	0.50	1.00	2.00
1974	210,000	—	—	0.50	1.00	2.00
1975	420,000	—	—	0.15	0.40	1.00
1976	570,000	—	—	0.15	0.40	1.00
1979	—	—	—	0.15	0.40	1.00

KM# 34a   5 CENTS
1.0700 g., Aluminum, 20.15 mm.   **Obv:** Bust of Queen Elizabeth II right **Rev:** Denomination within circle **Edge:** Plain

Date	Mintage	F	VF	XF	Unc	BU
1976	1,000,000	—	—	0.10	0.25	0.60
1979	960,000	—	—	0.10	0.25	0.75
1980	1,040,000	—	—	0.10	0.25	0.60
1986	—	—	—	0.10	0.25	0.60
1987	—	—	—	0.10	0.25	0.60
1989	—	—	—	0.10	0.25	0.60
1991	—	—	—	0.10	0.25	0.60
1992	—	—	—	0.10	0.25	0.60
1993	—	—	—	0.10	0.25	0.60
1994	—	—	—	0.10	0.25	0.60
2000	—	—	—	0.10	0.25	0.60

KM# 39   5 CENTS
Nickel-Brass, 20 mm.   **Obv:** National arms, date below, within wreath **Rev:** Fork-tailed flycatchers, denomination above **Edge:** Smooth

Date	Mintage	F	VF	XF	Unc	BU
1974FM (M)	50,000	—	—	0.25	1.25	2.50
1974FM (P)	21,000	Value: 2.00				

KM# 39a   5 CENTS
4.3500 g., 0.9250 Silver 0.1294 oz. ASW, 20 mm.   **Rev:** Fork-tailed flycatcher

Date	Mintage	F	VF	XF	Unc	BU
1974FM (P)	31,000	Value: 3.50				

KM# 47   5 CENTS
3.6000 g., Nickel-Brass, 20 mm.   **Obv:** National arms, date below, within wreath **Rev:** Fork-tailed flycatchers, denomination above **Edge:** Smooth

Date	Mintage	F	VF	XF	Unc	BU
1975FM (M)	24,000	—	—	0.25	1.50	2.50
1975FM (U)	1,095	—	—	0.50	1.00	2.50

Date	Mintage	F	VF	XF	Unc	BU
1975FM (P)	8,794	Value: 1.25				
1976FM (M)	25,000	—	—	0.25	1.50	2.50
1976FM (U)	759	—	—	0.50	1.50	2.50
1976FM (P)	4,893	Value: 1.25				

KM# 47a 5 CENTS
4.3500 g., 0.9250 Silver 0.1294 oz. ASW, 20 mm. **Rev:** Fork-tailed flycatcher

Date	Mintage	F	VF	XF	Unc	BU
1975FM (P)	13,000	Value: 2.75				
1976FM (P)	5,897	Value: 2.75				
1977FM (P)	3,197	Value: 2.75				
1978FM (P)	3,342	Value: 2.75				
1979FM (P)	2,445	Value: 2.75				
1980FM (P)	1,826	Value: 2.75				
1981FM (P)	615	Value: 3.50				

KM# 47b 5 CENTS
Aluminum **Rev:** Fork-tailed flycatcher **Edge:** Smooth

Date	Mintage	F	VF	XF	Unc	BU
1977FM (U)	26,000	—	—	0.10	0.50	0.75
1977FM (P)	2,107	Value: 2.00				
1978FM (U)	25,000	—	—	0.10	0.50	0.75
1978FM (P)	1,671	Value: 2.00				
1979FM (U)	808	—	—	0.15	0.75	1.00
1979FM (P)	1,287	—	—	0.25	1.00	1.50
1980FM (U)	761	—	—	0.15	0.75	1.00
1980FM (P)	920	Value: 2.00				
1981FM (U)	297	—	—	0.15	0.75	1.00
1981FM (P)	643	Value: 2.00				

KM# 64 5 CENTS
1.0000 g., Aluminum, 20.15 mm. **Series:** World Food Day
Obv: Crowned bust of Queen Elizabeth, right
Rev: Denomination, date upper right **Edge:** Smooth

Date	Mintage	F	VF	XF	Unc	BU
1981	—	—	—	0.10	0.35	0.70

KM# 84 5 CENTS
Aluminum **Obv:** National arms within wreath, date below
Rev: Fork-tailed flycatchers, denomination above **Edge:** Smooth

Date	Mintage	F	VF	XF	Unc	BU
1982FM (U)	—	—	0.15	0.35	1.50	2.00
1982FM (P)	—	Value: 3.00				
1983FM (U)	—	—	0.15	0.35	1.50	2.00
1983FM (P)	—	Value: 3.00				

KM# 84a 5 CENTS
4.3500 g., 0.9250 Silver 0.1294 oz. ASW **Rev:** Fork-tailed flycatcher

Date	Mintage	F	VF	XF	Unc	BU
1982FM (P)	381	Value: 12.00				
1983FM (P)	479	Value: 12.00				

KM# 91 5 CENTS
Aluminum

Date	Mintage	F	VF	XF	Unc	BU
1984FM (U)	—	—	0.25	0.50	1.75	2.25
1984FM (P)	—	Value: 3.00				

KM# 91a 5 CENTS
4.3500 g., 0.9250 Silver 0.1294 oz. ASW **Obv:** National arms within wreath, date below **Rev:** Fork-tailed flycatchers, denomination above

Date	Mintage	F	VF	XF	Unc	BU
1984FM (P)	—	Value: 12.00				
1985 Proof	212	Value: 13.50				

KM# 115 5 CENTS
Aluminum

Date	Mintage	F	VF	XF	Unc	BU
1992	—	—	—	0.10	0.20	0.40
1993	—	—	—	0.10	0.20	0.40
1994	—	—	—	0.10	0.20	0.40
2000	—	—	—	0.10	0.20	0.40

KM# 35 10 CENTS
2.4000 g., Copper-Nickel, 16.95 mm. **Obv:** Crowned bust of Queen Elizabeth, right **Rev:** Denomination within circle, date below **Edge:** Reeded

Date	Mintage	F	VF	XF	Unc	BU
1974	100,000	—	0.15	0.35	0.60	1.25
1975	200,000	—	0.10	0.25	0.50	1.00
1976	700,000	—	0.10	0.20	0.45	0.75
1979	800,000	—	0.10	0.20	0.40	0.75
1980	—	—	0.10	0.20	0.40	0.75
1981	—	—	0.10	0.20	0.40	0.75
1992	—	—	0.10	0.20	0.40	0.75
2000	—	—	—	0.15	0.40	0.60

KM# 40 10 CENTS
2.4000 g., Copper-Nickel, 16.95 mm. **Obv:** National arms, date below, within wreath **Rev:** Long-tailed hermit, right, denomination above **Edge:** Reeded

Date	Mintage	F	VF	XF	Unc	BU
1974FM (M)	27,000	—	—	0.50	2.00	4.00
1974FM (P)	21,000	Value: 1.75				

KM# 40a 10 CENTS
2.7900 g., 0.9250 Silver 0.0830 oz. ASW, 16.95 mm. **Rev:** Long-tailed hermit

Date	Mintage	F	VF	XF	Unc	BU
1974FM (P)	31,000	Value: 3.50				

KM# 48 10 CENTS
2.4000 g., Copper-Nickel, 16.95 mm. **Obv:** National arms, date below, within wreath **Rev:** Long-tailed hermit, right, denomination above **Edge:** Reeded

Date	Mintage	F	VF	XF	Unc	BU
1975FM (M)	12,000	—	—	0.25	1.50	2.00
1975FM (U)	1,095	—	—	0.30	2.00	4.00
1975FM (P)	8,794	Value: 1.50				
1976FM (M)	13,000	—	—	0.25	1.50	2.00
1976FM (U)	759	—	—	1.00	2.00	4.00
1976FM (P)	4,893	Value: 1.50				
1977FM (U)	14,000	—	—	0.25	1.50	2.00
1977FM (P)	2,107	Value: 2.00				
1978FM (U)	13,000	—	—	0.25	1.50	1.75
1978FM (P)	1,671	Value: 3.00				
1979FM (U)	808	—	—	1.00	3.00	6.00
1979FM (P)	1,287	Value: 3.00				
1980FM (U)	761	—	—	1.00	3.00	6.00
1980FM (P)	920	Value: 3.00				
1981FM (U)	297	—	—	1.00	3.00	6.00
1981FM (P)	643	Value: 4.00				

KM# 48a 10 CENTS
2.7900 g., 0.9250 Silver 0.0830 oz. ASW, 16.95 mm. **Rev:** Long-tailed hermit

Date	Mintage	F	VF	XF	Unc	BU
1975FM (P)	13,000	Value: 3.00				
1976FM (P)	5,897	Value: 3.00				
1977FM (P)	3,197	Value: 3.00				
1978FM (P)	3,342	Value: 3.00				
1979FM (P)	2,445	Value: 3.00				
1980FM (P)	1,826	Value: 3.00				
1981FM (P)	615	Value: 4.00				

KM# 85 10 CENTS
2.4000 g., Copper-Nickel, 16.95 mm. **Rev:** Long-tailed hermit **Edge:** Reeded

Date	Mintage	F	VF	XF	Unc	BU
1982FM (U)	—	—	0.25	0.50	2.50	3.50
1982FM (P)	—	Value: 3.50				
1983FM (U)	—	—	0.25	0.50	2.50	3.50
1983FM (P)	—	Value: 3.50				

KM# 85a 10 CENTS
2.7900 g., 0.9250 Silver 0.0830 oz. ASW, 16.95 mm. **Rev:** Long-tailed hermit

Date	Mintage	F	VF	XF	Unc	BU
1982FM (P)	381	Value: 13.50				
1983FM (P)	312	Value: 13.50				

KM# 92 10 CENTS
2.4000 g., Copper-Nickel, 16.95 mm. **Obv:** National arms within wreath, date below **Rev:** Long-tailed hermit, right, denomination above **Edge:** Reeded

Date	Mintage	F	VF	XF	Unc	BU
1984FM (U)	—	—	0.25	0.50	2.50	3.50
1984FM (P)	—	Value: 3.50				

KM# 92a 10 CENTS
2.7900 g., 0.9250 Silver 0.0830 oz. ASW, 16.95 mm.
Obv: National arms within wreath, date below **Rev:** Long-tailed hermit, right, denomination above

Date	Mintage	F	VF	XF	Unc	BU
1984FM (P)	—	Value: 13.50				
1985 Proof	212	Value: 15.50				

KM# 36 25 CENTS
5.6500 g., Copper-Nickel, 23.6 mm. **Obv:** Crowned bust of Queen Elizabeth II right **Rev:** Denomination within circle, date below **Edge:** Reeded

Date	Mintage	F	VF	XF	Unc	BU
1974	100,000	—	0.35	0.65	1.25	2.50
1975	200,000	—	0.20	0.35	0.75	1.00
1976	790,000	—	0.20	0.35	0.75	1.00
1979	500,000	—	0.20	0.35	0.75	1.00
1980	—	—	0.20	0.35	0.75	1.00
1981	—	—	0.20	0.35	0.75	1.00
1986	—	—	0.20	0.35	0.75	1.00
1987	—	—	0.20	0.35	0.75	1.00
1988	—	—	0.20	0.35	0.75	1.00
1989	—	—	0.20	0.35	0.75	1.00
1991	—	—	0.20	0.35	0.75	1.00
1992	—	—	0.20	0.35	0.75	1.00
1993	—	—	0.20	0.35	0.75	1.00
1994	—	—	0.20	0.35	0.75	1.00
2000	—	—	0.20	0.35	0.75	1.50

KM# 41 25 CENTS
Copper-Nickel, 23.6 mm. **Obv:** National arms, date below, within wreath **Rev:** Blue-crowned motmot, left, denomination above **Edge:** Reeded

Date	Mintage	F	VF	XF	Unc	BU
1974FM (M)	13,000	—	—	1.00	3.50	5.00
1974FM (P)	21,000	Value: 3.00				

KM# 41a 25 CENTS
6.6000 g., 0.9250 Silver 0.1963 oz. ASW, 23.6 mm. **Rev:** Blue-crowned motmot

Date	Mintage	F	VF	XF	Unc	BU
1974FM (P)	31,000	Value: 5.00				

KM# 49 25 CENTS
Copper-Nickel, 23.6 mm. **Obv:** National arms above date within wreath **Rev:** Blue-crowned motmot left, denomination below **Edge:** Reeded

Date	Mintage	F	VF	XF	Unc	BU
1975FM (M)	4,716	—	—	0.40	3.00	4.00
1975FM (U)	1,095	—	—	1.00	3.00	4.00
1975FM (P)	8,794	Value: 2.50				

Date	Mintage	F	VF	XF	Unc	BU
1976FM (M)	5,000	—	—	0.50	4.00	5.00
1976FM (U)	759	—	—	2.00	4.00	6.00
1976FM (P)	4,893	Value: 2.50				
1977FM (U)	5,520	—	—	0.30	3.00	4.00
1977FM (P)	2,107	Value: 2.75				
1978FM (U)	5,458	—	—	0.30	3.00	4.50
1978FM (P)	1,671	Value: 2.75				
1979FM (U)	808	—	—	2.00	4.00	6.00
1979FM (P)	1,287	Value: 3.00				
1980FM (U)	761	—	—	0.40	3.00	4.50
1980FM (P)	920	Value: 3.00				
1981FM (U)	297	—	—	0.40	3.00	6.00
1981FM (P)	643	Value: 3.00				

KM# 49a 25 CENTS
6.6000 g., 0.9250 Silver 0.1963 oz. ASW, 23.6 mm. **Obv:** National arms above date within wreath **Rev:** Blue-crowned motmot

Date	Mintage	F	VF	XF	Unc	BU
1975FM (P)	13,000	Value: 4.75				
1976FM (P)	5,897	Value: 4.75				
1977FM (P)	3,197	Value: 4.75				
1978FM (P)	3,342	Value: 4.75				
1979FM (P)	2,445	Value: 4.75				
1980FM (P)	1,826	Value: 4.75				
1981FM (P)	615	Value: 6.50				

KM# 86 25 CENTS
Copper-Nickel, 23.6 mm. **Obv:** National arms within wreath, date below **Rev:** Blue-crowned motmot, right, denomination below

Date	Mintage	F	VF	XF	Unc	BU
1982FM (U)	—	—	0.50	1.00	4.00	5.00
1982FM (P)	—	Value: 5.00				
1983FM (U)	—	—	0.50	1.00	4.00	5.00
1983FM (P)	—	Value: 5.00				

KM# 86a 25 CENTS
6.6000 g., 0.9250 Silver 0.1963 oz. ASW, 23.6 mm. **Obv:** National arms within wreath, date below **Rev:** Blue-crowned motmot

Date	Mintage	F	VF	XF	Unc	BU
1982FM (P)	381	Value: 18.50				
1983FM (P)	314	Value: 18.50				

KM# 93 25 CENTS
Copper-Nickel, 23.6 mm. **Obv:** National arms within wreath, date below **Rev:** Blue-crowned motmot, right, denomination below **Edge:** Reeded

Date	Mintage	F	VF	XF	Unc	BU
1984FM (U)	—	—	0.50	1.00	4.00	5.00
1984FM (P)	—	Value: 5.00				

KM# 93a 25 CENTS
6.6000 g., 0.9250 Silver 0.1963 oz. ASW, 23.6 mm. **Obv:** National arms within wreath, date below **Rev:** Blue-crowned motmot

Date	Mintage	F	VF	XF	Unc	BU
1984FM (P)	—	Value: 18.50				
1985 Proof	212	Value: 22.50				

KM# 77 25 CENTS
5.6000 g., Copper-Nickel, 23.6 mm. **Subject:** World Forestry Congress **Obv:** Crowned bust of Queen Elizabeth right **Rev:** Denomination within circle, date below **Edge:** Reeded

Date	Mintage	F	VF	XF	Unc	BU
1985	—	—	0.25	0.40	0.85	1.10

KM# 37 50 CENTS
9.0000 g., Copper-Nickel, 27.7 mm. **Obv:** Crowned bust of Queen Elizabeth right **Rev:** Denomination within circle, date below **Edge:** Reeded

Date	Mintage	F	VF	XF	Unc	BU
1974	123,000	—	0.50	1.50	3.00	4.50
1975	Inc. above	—	0.40	0.75	2.00	3.00
1976	312,000	—	0.40	0.75	2.00	3.00
1979	125,000	—	0.50	1.50	3.00	4.50
1980	—	—	0.40	0.75	1.75	2.75
1989	—	—	0.40	0.75	1.75	2.75
1991	—	—	0.50	1.00	2.00	3.00
1992	—	—	0.50	1.00	2.00	3.00
1993	—	—	0.50	1.00	2.00	3.00

KM# 42 50 CENTS
Copper-Nickel, 27.7 mm. **Rev:** Frigate bird **Edge:** Reeded

Date	Mintage	F	VF	XF	Unc	BU
1974FM (M)	8,806	—	—	0.40	4.50	—
1974FM (P)	21,000	Value: 3.50				

KM# 42a 50 CENTS
9.9400 g., 0.9250 Silver 0.2956 oz. ASW, 27.7 mm. **Rev:** Frigate bird

Date	Mintage	F	VF	XF	Unc	BU
1974FM (P)	31,000	Value: 8.00				

KM# 50 50 CENTS
Copper-Nickel, 27.7 mm. **Obv:** National arms above date within wreath **Rev:** Frigate birds, denomination above **Edge:** Reeded

Date	Mintage	F	VF	XF	Unc	BU
1975FM (M)	2,358	—	—	0.65	6.00	7.00
1975FM (U)	1,095	—	—	0.45	4.50	6.00
1975FM (P)	8,794	Value: 4.00				
1976FM (M)	3,259	—	—	0.55	5.00	6.00
1976FM (U)	759	—	—	2.00	5.00	6.00
1976FM (P)	4,893	Value: 6.00				
1977FM (U)	3,540	—	—	0.45	4.50	6.00
1977FM (P)	2,107	Value: 6.00				
1978FM (U)	2,958	—	—	0.45	4.50	6.00
1978FM (P)	1,671	Value: 6.00				
1979FM (U)	808	—	—	0.55	5.00	7.50
1979FM (P)	1,287	Value: 6.00				
1980FM (U)	761	—	—	0.55	5.00	7.50
1980FM (P)	920	Value: 6.50				
1981FM (U)	297	—	—	0.55	5.00	7.50
1981FM (P)	643	Value: 6.50				

KM# 50a 50 CENTS
9.9400 g., 0.9250 Silver 0.2956 oz. ASW, 27.7 mm. **Obv:** National arms above date within wreath **Rev:** Frigate bird

Date	Mintage	F	VF	XF	Unc	BU
1975FM (P)	13,000	Value: 6.75				
1976FM (P)	5,897	Value: 6.75				
1977FM (P)	3,197	Value: 6.75				
1978FM (P)	3,342	Value: 6.75				
1979FM (P)	2,445	Value: 6.75				
1980FM (P)	1,826	Value: 6.75				
1981FM (P)	615	Value: 9.00				

KM# 87 50 CENTS
Copper-Nickel, 27.7 mm. **Obv:** National arms within wreath, date below **Rev:** Frigate birds, denomination above **Edge:** Reeded

Date	Mintage	F	VF	XF	Unc	BU
1982FM (U)	—	—	0.75	1.50	6.50	7.00
1982FM (P)	—	Value: 7.50				
1983FM (U)	—	—	0.75	1.50	6.50	7.00
1983FM (P)	—	Value: 7.50				

KM# 87a 50 CENTS
9.9400 g., 0.9250 Silver 0.2956 oz. ASW, 27.7 mm. **Obv:** National arms within wreath, date below **Rev:** Frigate bird

Date	Mintage	F	VF	XF	Unc	BU
1982FM (P)	381	Value: 27.50				
1983FM (P)	312	Value: 27.50				

KM# 94 50 CENTS
Copper-Nickel, 27.7 mm. **Obv:** National arms within wreath, date below **Rev:** Frigate birds, denomination above **Edge:** Reeded

Date	Mintage	F	VF	XF	Unc	BU
1984FM (U)	—	—	0.75	1.50	6.50	7.00
1984FM (P)	—	Value: 7.50				

KM# 94a 50 CENTS
9.9400 g., 0.9250 Silver 0.2956 oz. ASW, 27.7 mm. **Obv:** National arms within wreath, date below **Rev:** Frigate bird

Date	Mintage	F	VF	XF	Unc	BU
1984FM (P)	—	Value: 27.50				
1985 Proof	212	Value: 32.50				

KM# 118 50 CENTS
Copper-Nickel **Obv:** New portrait of Queen Elizabeth II **Rev:** Denomination within circle, date below

Date	Mintage	F	VF	XF	Unc	BU
1992	—	—	0.50	1.00	2.00	3.50
1993	—	—	0.50	1.00	2.00	3.50

KM# 43 DOLLAR
Copper-Nickel, 35 mm. **Obv:** National arms above date within wreath **Rev:** Scarlet macaws, denomination above **Edge:** Reeded

Date	Mintage	F	VF	XF	Unc	BU
1974FM (M)	6,656	—	—	1.00	9.00	12.00
1974FM (P)	21,000	Value: 6.00				
1975FM (M)	1,182	—	—	1.50	10.00	12.50
1975FM (U)	1,095	—	—	0.75	9.00	12.00
1975FM (P)	8,794	Value: 6.00				
1976FM (M)	1,250	—	—	1.50	10.00	12.50
1976FM (U)	759	—	—	1.25	9.00	12.50
1976FM (P)	4,893	Value: 6.00				
1977FM (U)	1,770	—	—	1.00	9.00	12.00
1977FM (P)	2,107	Value: 6.00				
1978FM (U)	1,708	—	—	1.00	9.00	12.00
1978FM (P)	1,671	Value: 6.00				
1979FM (U)	808	—	—	1.25	9.00	12.00
1979FM (P)	1,287	Value: 6.00				
1980FM (U)	761	—	—	1.25	9.00	12.00
1980FM (P)	920	Value: 6.00				
1981FM (U)	297	—	—	1.50	10.00	12.50
1981FM (P)	643	Value: 8.50				

KM# 43a DOLLAR
19.8900 g., 0.9250 Silver 0.5915 oz. ASW, 35 mm. **Obv:** National arms above date within wreath **Rev:** Scarlet macaw

Date	Mintage	F	VF	XF	Unc	BU
1974FM (P)	31,000	Value: 12.00				
1975FM (P)	13,000	Value: 13.50				
1976FM (P)	5,897	Value: 13.50				
1977FM (P)	3,197	Value: 13.50				
1978FM (P)	3,342	Value: 13.50				
1979FM (P)	2,445	Value: 13.50				
1980FM (P)	1,826	Value: 13.50				
1981FM (P)	615	Value: 15.00				

KM# 88 DOLLAR
Copper-Nickel, 35 mm. **Obv:** National arms within wreath, date
below **Rev:** Scarlet macaws, denomination above

Date	Mintage	F	VF	XF	Unc	BU
1982FM (U)	—	—	1.50	3.00	10.00	12.50
1982FM (P)	—	Value: 8.50				
1983FM (U)	—	—	1.50	3.00	10.00	12.50
1983FM (P)	—	Value: 8.50				

KM# 88a DOLLAR
19.8900 g., 0.9250 Silver 0.5915 oz. ASW, 35 mm.
Obv: National arms within wreath, date below **Rev:** Scarlet
macaw

Date	Mintage	F	VF	XF	Unc	BU
1982FM (P)	381	Value: 37.50				
1983FM (P)	1,589	Value: 37.50				

KM# 95 DOLLAR
Copper-Nickel, 35 mm. **Obv:** National arms within wreath, date
below **Rev:** Scarlet macaws, denomination above

Date	Mintage	F	VF	XF	Unc	BU
1984FM (U)	—	—	1.50	3.00	10.00	12.50
1984FM (P)	—	Value: 8.50				

KM# 95a DOLLAR
19.8900 g., 0.9250 Silver 0.5915 oz. ASW, 35 mm.
Obv: National arms within wreath, date below **Rev:** Scarlet
macaws, denomination above

Date	Mintage	F	VF	XF	Unc	BU
1984FM (P)	—	Value: 37.50				
1985 Proof	212	Value: 45.00				

KM# 99 DOLLAR
8.9000 g., Nickel-Brass, 27 mm. **Obv:** Crowned bust of Queen
Elizabeth II right **Rev:** Columbus' three ships, denomination
above, date below **Edge:** Alternating reeded and plain

Date	Mintage	F	VF	XF	Unc	BU
1990	—	—	—	—	2.25	3.00
1991	—	—	—	—	2.25	3.00
1992	—	—	—	—	2.25	3.00
2000	—	—	—	—	2.25	3.00

KM# 99a DOLLAR
9.0000 g., 0.9250 Silver 0.2676 oz. ASW, 27 mm.
Obv: Crowned Queen's portrait, right **Rev:** Columbus' three ships

Date	Mintage	F	VF	XF	Unc	BU
1990 Proof	Est. 5,000	Value: 32.50				

KM# 135 DOLLAR
15.9500 g., Silver, 28.2 mm. **Subject:** Queen Elizabeth II - The
Queen Mother - Summer in Balmoral Castle **Obv:** National arms
Rev: Balmoral Castle **Edge:** Reeded

Date	Mintage	F	VF	XF	Unc	BU
1997	—	—	—	—	—	30.00

KM# 100 2 DOLLARS
Copper-Nickel **Subject:** Queen Mother's 90th Birthday
Obv: Crowned bust of Queen Elizabeth II right **Rev:** Crowned
ornate "E"s, backs intertwined, sprays flanking, two dates below

Date	Mintage	F	VF	XF	Unc	BU
ND(1990)	—	—	—	—	6.00	7.50

KM# 100a 2 DOLLARS
28.2800 g., 0.9250 Silver 0.8410 oz. ASW **Subject:** Queen
Mother's 90th Birthday **Obv:** Crowned Queen's portrait, right
Rev: Crowned ornate "E"s, backs intertwined, sprays flanking,
two dates below

Date	Mintage	F	VF	XF	Unc	BU
ND(1990) Proof	Est. 10,000	Value: 45.00				

KM# 119 2 DOLLARS
28.2800 g., 0.9250 Silver 0.8410 oz. ASW **Subject:** 40th
Anniversary - Coronation of Queen Elizabeth II **Obv:** Crowned
Queen's portrait, right **Rev:** Facing Queen Elizabeth II on
horseback saluting, two dates at bottom

Date	Mintage	F	VF	XF	Unc	BU
ND(1993) Proof	Est. 10,000	Value: 45.00				

KM# 131 2 DOLLARS
Copper-Nickel, 28 mm. **Subject:** Battle of St. George's Caye
Obv: National arms within wreath, denomination below **Rev:** Oar-
powered landing craft shorebound, within circle, two dates below

Date	Mintage	F	VF	XF	Unc	BU
ND(1998)	—	—	—	—	7.00	10.00

KM# 132 2 DOLLARS
28.2800 g., 0.9250 Silver 0.8410 oz. ASW, 38.6 mm.
Subject: Heritage Protection **Obv:** National arms **Rev:** Large
building, people, jaguar and arms, denomination below
Edge: Reeded

Date	Mintage	F	VF	XF	Unc	BU
1998 Proof	5,000	Value: 55.00				

KM# 44 5 DOLLARS
Copper-Nickel, 37.8 mm. **Obv:** National arms above date within
wreath **Rev:** Keel-billed toucan, right, denomination above
Edge: Reeded

Date	Mintage	F	VF	XF	Unc	BU
1974FM (M)	4,936	—	—	2.75	7.50	—
1974FM (P)	21,000	Value: 6.50				
1975FM (M)	237	—	—	5.00	22.50	—
1975FM (U)	1,095	—	—	2.75	7.50	—
1975FM (P)	8,794	Value: 6.50				
1976FM (M)	250	—	—	5.00	20.00	—
1976FM (U)	759	—	—	2.75	7.50	—
1976FM (P)	4,893	Value: 6.50				
1977FM (U)	720	—	—	2.75	7.50	—
1977FM (P)	2,107	Value: 7.50				
1978FM (U)	708	—	—	2.75	7.50	—
1978FM (P)	1,671	Value: 7.50				
1979FM (U)	808	—	—	2.75	7.50	—
1979FM (P)	1,287	Value: 7.50				
1980FM (U)	761	—	—	2.75	7.50	—
1980FM (P)	920	Value: 7.50				
1981FM (U)	297	—	—	2.75	7.50	—
1981FM (P)	643	Value: 8.50				

KM# 44a 5 DOLLARS
26.4000 g., 0.9250 Silver 0.7851 oz. ASW, 37.8 mm.
Obv: National arms above date within wreath **Rev:** Keel-billed
toucan

Date	Mintage	F	VF	XF	Unc	BU
1974FM (P)	31,000	Value: 16.00				
1975FM (P)	13,000	Value: 16.50				
1976FM (P)	5,897	Value: 17.50				
1977FM (P)	3,197	Value: 17.50				
1978FM (P)	3,342	Value: 17.50				
1979FM (P)	2,445	Value: 18.00				
1980FM (P)	1,826	Value: 18.00				
1981FM (P)	615	Value: 20.00				

KM# 89 5 DOLLARS
Copper-Nickel, 37.8 mm. **Obv:** National arms above date within
wreath **Rev:** Keel-billed toucan

Date	Mintage	F	VF	XF	Unc	BU
1982FM (U)	—	—	2.00	4.00	12.00	15.00
1982FM (P)	—	Value: 15.00				
1983FM (U)	—	—	2.00	4.00	12.00	15.00
1983FM (P)	—	Value: 15.00				

KM# 89a 5 DOLLARS
26.4000 g., 0.9250 Silver 0.7851 oz. ASW, 37.8 mm.
Obv: National arms above date within wreath **Rev:** Keel-billed
toucan

Date	Mintage	F	VF	XF	Unc	BU
1982FM (P)	381	Value: 50.00				
1983FM (P)	311	Value: 50.00				

KM# 96   5 DOLLARS
Copper-Nickel, 37.8 mm.   **Obv:** National arms within wreath, date below **Rev:** Keel-billed toucan, right, denomination above

Date	Mintage	F	VF	XF	Unc	BU
1984FM (U)	—	.	2.00	4.00	12.00	15.00
1984FM (P)	—	Value: 17.50				

KM# 96a   5 DOLLARS
26.4000 g., 0.9250 Silver 0.7851 oz. ASW, 37.8 mm.
Obv: National arms within wreath, date below **Rev:** Keel-billed toucan, right, denomination above

Date	Mintage	F	VF	XF	Unc	BU
1984FM (P)	—	Value: 50.00				
1985 Proof	212	Value: 60.00				

KM# 107   5 DOLLARS
28.2800 g., 0.9250 Silver 0.8410 oz. ASW **Subject:** 50th Anniversary - Battle of El Alamein - Field Marshall Rommel **Obv:** Bust of Queen Elizabeth II right **Rev:** Field Marshall Rommel, right, in uniform, denomination lower right

Date	Mintage	F	VF	XF	Unc	BU
1992 Proof	Est. 5,000	Value: 45.00				

KM# 108   5 DOLLARS
28.2800 g., 0.9250 Silver 0.8410 oz. ASW **Subject:** 50th Anniversary - Battle of El Alamein - Lt. Gen. Montgomery **Obv:** Bust of Queen Elizabeth II right **Rev:** Lt. Gen. Montgomery, denomination at bottom

Date	Mintage	F	VF	XF	Unc	BU
1992 Proof	Est. 5,000	Value: 45.00				

KM# 126   5 DOLLARS
28.2800 g., 0.9250 Silver 0.8410 oz. ASW **Subject:** Queen Mother - Balmoral Castle **Obv:** National arms within wreath, date below **Rev:** Balmoral Castle above date, denomination at bottom

Date	Mintage	F	VF	XF	Unc	BU
1995 Proof	Est. 40,000	Value: 35.00				

KM# 133   5 DOLLARS
28.5000 g., 0.9250 Silver 0.8475 oz. ASW, 38.5 mm.
Subject: Queen Elizabeth II's Golden Wedding Anniversary **Obv:** National arms within wreath, date below gold inset shield, denomination at bottom **Rev:** Royal couple below gold inset shield, denomination at bottom **Edge:** Reeded

Date	Mintage	F	VF	XF	Unc	BU
1997 Proof	—	Value: 45.00				

KM# 45   10 DOLLARS
Copper-Nickel, 40 mm.   **Obv:** National arms above date within wreath **Rev:** Great curassow, right, denomination above **Edge:** Reeded

Date	Mintage	F	VF	XF	Unc	BU
1974FM (M)	4,726	—	—	3.50	9.00	12.00
1974FM (P)	21,000	Value: 8.00				
1975FM (M)	117	—	—	12.50	45.00	55.00
1975FM (U)	1,095	—	—	3.50	10.00	12.50
1975FM (P)	8,794	Value: 9.00				
1976FM (M)	125	—	—	10.00	35.00	55.00
1976FM (U)	759	—	—	3.50	10.00	12.50
1976FM (P)	4,893	Value: 10.00				
1977FM (U)	645	—	—	4.00	12.00	15.00
1977FM (P)	2,107	Value: 12.50				
1978FM (U)	583	—	—	5.00	12.00	15.00
1978FM (P)	1,671	Value: 12.50				

KM# 45a   10 DOLLARS
29.8000 g., 0.9250 Silver 0.8862 oz. ASW, 40 mm.   **Obv:** National arms above date within wreath **Rev:** Great curassow

Date	Mintage	F	VF	XF	Unc	BU
1974FM (P)	31,000	Value: 18.50				
1975FM (P)	13,000	Value: 20.00				
1976FM (P)	5,897	Value: 20.00				
1977FM (P)	3,197	Value: 22.00				
1978FM (P)	3,342	Value: 22.00				

KM# 57   10 DOLLARS
Copper-Nickel, 40 mm.   **Obv:** National arms above date within wreath **Rev:** Flying jabiru, denomination above

Date	Mintage	F	VF	XF	Unc	BU
1979FM (U)	808	—	—	5.00	25.00	35.00
1979FM (P)	1,287	Value: 30.00				

KM# 57a   10 DOLLARS
29.8000 g., 0.9250 Silver 0.8862 oz. ASW, 40 mm.
Obv: National arms above date within wreath **Rev:** Flying jabiru

Date	Mintage	F	VF	XF	Unc	BU
1979FM (P)	2,445	Value: 40.00				

KM# 60   10 DOLLARS
Copper-Nickel, 40 mm.   **Obv:** National arms above date within wreath **Rev:** Two Scarlet ibis, denomination above

Date	Mintage	F	VF	XF	Unc	BU
1980FM (U)	761	—	—	5.00	25.00	35.00
1980FM (P)	920	Value: 30.00				

KM# 60a   10 DOLLARS
25.5000 g., 0.9250 Silver 0.7583 oz. ASW, 40 mm.
Obv: National arms above date within wreath **Rev:** Scarlet ibis

Date	Mintage	F	VF	XF	Unc	BU
1980FM (P)	1,826	Value: 50.00				

KM# 65   10 DOLLARS
Copper-Nickel, 40 mm.   **Obv:** National arms above date within wreath **Rev:** Roseate spoonbill, left, denomination above

Date	Mintage	F	VF	XF	Unc	BU
1981FM (U)	297	—	7.50	15.00	40.00	50.00
1981FM (P)	643	Value: 50.00				

KM# 65a   10 DOLLARS
25.5000 g., 0.9250 Silver 0.7583 oz. ASW, 40 mm.
Obv: National arms above date within wreath **Rev:** Roseate spoonbill

Date	Mintage	F	VF	XF	Unc	BU
1981FM (P)	615	Value: 75.00				

KM# 69   10 DOLLARS
Copper-Nickel, 40 mm.   **Obv:** National arms above date within wreath **Rev:** Yellow-crowned Amazon parrot, right, denomination at bottom

Date	Mintage	F	VF	XF	Unc	BU
1982FM (U)	—	—	10.00	20.00	45.00	50.00
1982FM (P)	—	Value: 65.00				

KM# 69a   10 DOLLARS
25.5000 g., 0.9250 Silver 0.7583 oz. ASW, 40 mm.
Obv: National arms above date within wreath **Rev:** Yellow-crowned Amazon parrot

Date	Mintage	F	VF	XF	Unc	BU
1982FM (P)	381	Value: 120				

KM# 80 10 DOLLARS
Copper-Nickel, 40 mm. **Obv:** National arms within wreath, date below **Rev:** Great Curassow, right, denomination above **Note:** Mule.

Date	Mintage	F	VF	XF	Unc	BU
1982FM (U)	—	—	—	—	25.00	35.00

KM# 71 10 DOLLARS
Copper-Nickel, 40 mm. **Obv:** National arms above date within wreath **Rev:** Ringed Kingfisher, right, denomination above

Date	Mintage	F	VF	XF	Unc	BU
1983FM (U)	—	—	10.00	20.00	50.00	60.00
1983FM (P)	—	Value: 65.00				

KM# 71a 10 DOLLARS
25.5000 g., 0.9250 Silver 0.7583 oz. ASW, 40 mm. **Obv:** National arms above date within wreath **Rev:** Ringed kingfisher

Date	Mintage	F	VF	XF	Unc	BU
1983FM (P)	334	Value: 135				

KM# 75 10 DOLLARS
Copper-Nickel, 40 mm. **Obv:** National arms within wreath, date below **Rev:** Laughing falcon, left, head divides denomination at top

Date	Mintage	F	VF	XF	Unc	BU
1984FM (U)	—	—	—	—	50.00	55.00
1984FM (P)	—	Value: 60.00				

KM# 75a 10 DOLLARS
25.5000 g., 0.9250 Silver 0.7583 oz. ASW, 40 mm. **Obv:** National arms within wreath, date below **Rev:** Laughing falcon

Date	Mintage	F	VF	XF	Unc	BU
1984FM (P)	—	Value: 115				
1985 Proof	212	Value: 135				

KM# 102 10 DOLLARS
Copper-Nickel **Subject:** 10th Anniversary of Independence **Obv:** National arms within wreath, denomination below **Rev:** Building within circle, dates below

Date	Mintage	F	VF	XF	Unc	BU
ND(1991)	1,000,000	—	—	—	8.50	10.00

KM# 102a 10 DOLLARS
28.2800 g., 0.9250 Silver 0.8410 oz. ASW **Subject:** 10th Anniversary of Independence **Obv:** National arms within wreath, denomination below **Rev:** Building within circle, dates below

Date	Mintage	F	VF	XF	Unc	BU
ND(1991) Proof	Est. 1,000	Value: 37.50				

KM# 104 10 DOLLARS
28.2800 g., 0.9250 Silver 0.8410 oz. ASW **Subject:** 10th Anniversary of Central Bank **Obv:** National arms within wreath, denomination below **Rev:** Jabiru stork, left, within circle, two dates at bottom

Date	Mintage	F	VF	XF	Unc	BU
1992 Proof	Est. 1,000	Value: 40.00				

KM# 109 10 DOLLARS
155.6000 g., 0.9990 Silver 4.9974 oz. ASW **Subject:** 50th Anniversary - Battle of El Alamein - Lt. Gen. Montgomery **Obv:** Portrait of Queen Elizabeth II **Rev:** Similar to 250 Dollars, KM#113

Date	Mintage	F	VF	XF	Unc	BU
1992 Proof	Est. 2,500	Value: 165				

KM# 121 10 DOLLARS
28.2800 g., 0.9250 Silver 0.8410 oz. ASW **Subject:** Royal visit **Obv:** Queen's portrait **Rev:** Cameo portraits above flowers

Date	Mintage	F	VF	XF	Unc	BU
1994 Proof	—	Value: 42.50				

KM# 123 10 DOLLARS
28.2800 g., 0.9250 Silver 0.8410 oz. ASW **Subject:** World Cup Soccer **Obv:** National arms within wreath, date below **Rev:** Soccer net and ball, denomination at bottom

Date	Mintage	F	VF	XF	Unc	BU
1994 Proof	Est. 10,000	Value: 45.00				

KM# 124 10 DOLLARS
28.2800 g., 0.9250 Silver 0.8410 oz. ASW **Obv:** National arms within wreath, date at below **Rev:** Carrack sailing ship, denomination at bottom

Date	Mintage	F	VF	XF	Unc	BU
1995 Proof	Est. 15,000	Value: 40.00				

KM# 125 10 DOLLARS
28.2800 g., 0.9250 Silver 0.8410 oz. ASW **Series:** Endangered Wildlife **Obv:** National arms within wreath, date below **Rev:** Howler monkey on branch, left, denomination below

Date	Mintage	F	VF	XF	Unc	BU
1995 Proof	Est. 10,000	Value: 45.00				

KM# 127 10 DOLLARS
28.2800 g., 0.9250 Silver 0.8410 oz. ASW **Series:** Atlanta 1996 - 26th Summer Olympics **Obv:** National arms within wreath, date below **Rev:** Female softball player, denomination below

Date	Mintage	F	VF	XF	Unc	BU
1996 Proof	Est. 10,000	Value: 45.00				

KM# 128 10 DOLLARS
28.2800 g., 0.9250 Silver 0.8410 oz. ASW **Subject:** Battle of St. George's Caye **Obv:** National arms within wreath, denomination below **Rev:** Oar-powered gunboats within circle, two dates below

Date	Mintage	F	VF	XF	Unc	BU
ND(1998) Proof	—	Value: 55.00				

KM# 130 10 DOLLARS
28.2800 g., 0.9250 Silver 0.8410 oz. ASW **Subject:** 50th Anniversary - University of the West Indies **Obv:** National arms within wreath, denomination below **Rev:** University arms, two dates below

Date	Mintage	F	VF	XF	Unc	BU
ND(1999) Proof	1,000	Value: 55.00				

KM# 79   20 DOLLARS
23.3300 g., 0.9250 Silver 0.6938 oz. ASW   **Series:** Los Angeles Olympics   **Obv:** National arms within wreath, date below   **Rev:** Bicyclist, Olympic torch at right, denomination lower left

Date	Mintage	F	VF	XF	Unc	BU
1984 Proof	1,050			Value: 45.00		

KM# 82   20 DOLLARS
23.3300 g., 0.9250 Silver 0.6938 oz. ASW   **Series:** Decade for Women   **Obv:** National arms within wreath, date below   **Rev:** Figures of women and trees, 3/4 surround legend and symbol at center, denomination at bottom

Date	Mintage	F	VF	XF	Unc	BU
1985 Proof	Est. 20,000			Value: 27.50		

KM# 54   25 DOLLARS
27.8100 g., 0.9250 Silver 0.8270 oz. ASW   **Subject:** 25th Anniversary of Coronation   **Obv:** Bust of Queen Elizabeth II, right, date below   **Rev:** Crown with supporters, two dates below, denomination at bottom

Date	Mintage	F	VF	XF	Unc	BU
1978FM (U)	352	—	—	22.00	50.00	65.00
1978FM (P)	8,438			Value: 18.50		

KM# 61   25 DOLLARS
30.2800 g., 0.5000 Silver 0.4867 oz. ASW   **Subject:** 10th Anniversary - Caribbean Development Bank   **Obv:** National arms   **Rev:** Globe above flag, denomination below

Date	Mintage	F	VF	XF	Unc	BU
ND(1980)FM (P)	2,647			Value: 25.00		

KM# 72   25 DOLLARS
30.2800 g., 0.5000 Silver 0.4867 oz. ASW   **Subject:** 30th Anniversary of Coronation   **Obv:** National arms within wreath, date below   **Rev:** Crossed sceptres divide dates and royal symbols, denomination at bottom

Date	Mintage	F	VF	XF	Unc	BU
1983FM (P)	2,944			Value: 20.00		

KM# 78   25 DOLLARS
28.2800 g., 0.9250 Silver 0.8410 oz. ASW   **Subject:** Royal visit

Date	Mintage	F	VF	XF	Unc	BU
1985 Proof	Est. 5,000			Value: 25.00		

KM# 97   25 DOLLARS
28.2800 g., 0.9250 Silver 0.8410 oz. ASW   **Subject:** 500th Anniversary - Columbus Discovery of New World   **Obv:** Crowned bust of Queen Elizabeth II right   **Rev:** Ship in full sail, denomination at bottom

Date	Mintage	F	VF	XF	Unc	BU
1989 Proof	Est. 5,000			Value: 35.00		

KM# 106   25 DOLLARS
28.2800 g., 0.9250 Silver 0.8410 oz. ASW   **Series:** Barcelona 1992 - 25th Summer Olympics   **Obv:** National arms within wreath, denomination below   **Rev:** Hurdlers jumping large date

Date	Mintage	F	VF	XF	Unc	BU
1992 Proof	30,000			Value: 27.50		

KM# 110   25 DOLLARS
3.1300 g., 0.9990 Gold 0.1005 oz. AGW   **Subject:** 50th Anniversary - Battle of El Alamein   **Obv:** Bust of Queen Elizabeth II right   **Rev:** 4 tanks, denomination at bottom

Date	Mintage	F	VF	XF	Unc	BU
1992 Proof	Est. 500			Value: 110		

KM# 66   50 DOLLARS
1.5000 g., 0.5000 Gold 0.0241 oz. AGW   **Obv:** National arms, date below, 3/4 wreath surrounds   **Rev:** White-necked Jacobin hummingbird, right, drinking from flower, date below

Date	Mintage	F	VF	XF	Unc	BU
1981FM (U)	200	—	—	—	65.00	70.00
1981FM (P)	2,873			Value: 50.00		

KM# 81   50 DOLLARS
129.6000 g., 0.9250 Silver 3.8541 oz. ASW, 63 mm.   **Subject:** Bird conservation   **Obv:** National arms within wreath, date below   **Rev:** Red-footed booby, left, denomination above

Date	Mintage	F	VF	XF	Unc	BU
1985 Proof	Est. 10,000			Value: 125		

KM# 111   50 DOLLARS
7.8100 g., 0.9990 Gold 0.2508 oz. AGW   **Subject:** 50th Anniversary - Battle of El Alamein   **Obv:** Bust of Queen Elizabeth II right   **Rev:** Field Marshall Rommel, right, in uniform, denomination lower right

Date	Mintage	F	VF	XF	Unc	BU
1992 Proof	Est. 500			Value: 250		

KM# 51   100 DOLLARS
6.2100 g., 0.5000 Gold 0.0998 oz. AGW   **Subject:** 30th Anniversary of United Nations   **Obv:** National arms above date within wreath   **Rev:** Buildings, design above, denomination at top

Date	Mintage	F	VF	XF	Unc	BU
1975FM (M)	100	—	—	—	200	—
1975FM (U)	2,028	—	—	—	120	—
1975FM (P)	8,126			Value: 110		

KM# 52 100 DOLLARS
6.2100 g., 0.5000 Gold 0.0998 oz. AGW **Obv:** National arms above date, denomination below **Rev:** Ancient Mayan symbols representing numbers and days

Date	Mintage	F	VF	XF	Unc	BU
1976FM (M)	216	—	—	—	175	—
1976FM (P)	11,000	Value: 110				

KM# 53 100 DOLLARS
6.2100 g., 0.5000 Gold 0.0998 oz. AGW **Obv:** National arms above date, denomination at bottom **Rev:** Kinich Ahau, Mayan sun god

Date	Mintage	F	VF	XF	Unc	BU
1977FM (M)	200	—	—	—	135	—
1977FM (U)	51	—	—	—	350	—
1977FM (P)	7,859	Value: 110				

KM# 55 100 DOLLARS
6.2100 g., 0.5000 Gold 0.0998 oz. AGW **Obv:** National arms above date, denomination below **Rev:** Itzamna Lord of Heaven, Ruler of the Gods

Date	Mintage	F	VF	XF	Unc	BU
1978FM (U)	351	—	—	—	150	—
1978FM (P)	7,178	Value: 110				

KM# 58 100 DOLLARS
6.2100 g., 0.5000 Gold 0.0998 oz. AGW **Obv:** National arms, denomination below **Rev:** Queen angelfish, left, date above

Date	Mintage	F	VF	XF	Unc	BU
1979FM (U)	400	—	—	—	135	—
1979FM (P)	4,465	Value: 120				

KM# 59 100 DOLLARS
6.4700 g., 0.5000 Gold 0.1040 oz. AGW **Obv:** National arms, denomination below **Rev:** Star of Bethlehem, date below

Date	Mintage	F	VF	XF	Unc	BU
1979FM (U)	—	—	—	—	135	—
1979FM (P)	—	Value: 120				

KM# 62 100 DOLLARS
6.2100 g., 0.5000 Gold 0.0998 oz. AGW **Obv:** National arms, denomination below **Rev:** Moorish idol reef fish, date below

Date	Mintage	F	VF	XF	Unc	BU
1980FM (U)	400	—	—	—	150	—
1980FM (P)	3,993	Value: 130				

KM# 63 100 DOLLARS
6.2100 g., 0.5000 Gold 0.0998 oz. AGW **Obv:** National arms, denomination below **Rev:** Orchids, date below

Date	Mintage	F	VF	XF	Unc	BU
1980FM (U)	250	—	—	—	140	—
1980FM (P)	2,454	Value: 125				

KM# 67 100 DOLLARS
6.2100 g., 0.5000 Gold 0.0998 oz. AGW **Obv:** National arms above denomination within circle **Rev:** Yellow swallowtail butterfly within circle, date below

Date	Mintage	F	VF	XF	Unc	BU
1981FM (U)	200	—	—	—	250	—
1981FM (P)	1,658	Value: 250				

KM# 68 100 DOLLARS
6.2100 g., 0.5000 Gold 0.0998 oz. AGW **Subject:** National independence **Rev:** Vertical date to left of map

Date	Mintage	F	VF	XF	Unc	BU
1981FM (U)	50	—	—	—	325	—
1981FM (P)	1,401	Value: 145				

KM# 70 100 DOLLARS
6.2100 g., 0.5000 Gold 0.0998 oz. AGW **Obv:** National arms within wreath, denomination below **Rev:** Kinkajou, left, date below

Date	Mintage	F	VF	XF	Unc	BU
1982FM (U)	10	—	—	—	500	—
1982FM (P)	586	Value: 200				

KM# 73 100 DOLLARS
6.2100 g., 0.5000 Gold 0.0998 oz. AGW **Obv:** National arms within wreath, denomination below **Rev:** Margay jungle cat, right, date below

Date	Mintage	F	VF	XF	Unc	BU
1983FM (U)	20	—	—	—	400	—
1983FM (P)	494	Value: 250				

KM# 74 100 DOLLARS
6.2100 g., 0.5000 Gold 0.0998 oz. AGW **Obv:** National arms within wreath, denomination below **Rev:** White-tailed deer, facing, date lower right

Date	Mintage	F	VF	XF	Unc	BU
1984FM (P)	965	Value: 150				

KM# 76 100 DOLLARS
6.2100 g., 0.5000 Gold 0.0998 oz. AGW **Obv:** national arms within wreath, denomination below **Rev:** Ocelot, facing, date below

Date	Mintage	F	VF	XF	Unc	BU
1985FM (P) Proof	899	Value: 250				

KM# 103 100 DOLLARS
15.9760 g., 0.9170 Gold 0.4710 oz. AGW **Subject:** 10th Anniversary of Independence **Note:** Similar to 10 Dollars, KM#102.

Date	Mintage	F	VF	XF	Unc	BU
1991 Proof	Est. 500	Value: 550				

KM# 112 100 DOLLARS
15.6000 g., 0.9990 Gold 0.5010 oz. AGW **Subject:** 50th Anniversary - Battle of El Alamein **Obv:** Bust of Queen Elizabeth II right **Rev:** Infantry advancing, denomination below

Date	Mintage	F	VF	XF	Unc	BU
1992 Proof	Est. 500	Value: 500				

KM# 129 100 DOLLARS
15.9700 g., 0.9170 Gold 0.4708 oz. AGW **Subject:** Battle of St. George's Caye **Note:** Similar to KM#128.

Date	Mintage	F	VF	XF	Unc	BU
ND(1998) Proof	—	Value: 675				

KM# 56 250 DOLLARS
8.8100 g., 0.9000 Gold 0.2549 oz. AGW **Obv:** National arms above date, denomination below **Rev:** Jaguar, date at right

Date	Mintage	F	VF	XF	Unc	BU
1978FM (U)	200	—	—	—	250	275
1978FM (P)	Est. 3,399	Value: 275				

Note: 1,712 pieces were used in first-day covers

KM# 98   250 DOLLARS
15.9800 g., 0.9170 Gold 0.4711 oz. AGW **Subject:** 500th Anniversary of Columbus' Discovery of America

Date	Mintage	F	VF	XF	Unc	BU
1989 Proof	Est. 500			Value: 475		

KM# 105   250 DOLLARS
15.9800 g., 0.9170 Gold 0.4711 oz. AGW **Subject:** 10th Anniversary of Central Bank **Rev:** Jabiru stork **Note:** Similar to KM#104.

Date	Mintage	F	VF	XF	Unc	BU
1992	Est. 500			Value: 475		

KM# 113   250 DOLLARS
31.2100 g., 0.9990 Gold 1.0024 oz. AGW **Subject:** 50th Anniversary - Battle of El Alamein **Obv:** Bust of Queen Elizabeth II right **Rev:** Lt. Gen. Montgomery, denomination at bottom

Date	Mintage	F	VF	XF	Unc	BU
1992 Proof	Est. 500			Value: 1,000		

KM# 101   500 DOLLARS
47.5400 g., 0.9170 Gold 1.4015 oz. AGW **Subject:** Royal Visit **Note:** Similar to KM#78.

Date	Mintage	F	VF	XF	Unc	BU
1985 Proof	Est. 250			Value: 1,400		

KM# 120   500 DOLLARS
47.5400 g., 0.9170 Gold 1.4015 oz. AGW **Subject:** 40th Anniversary - Coronation of Queen Elizabeth II

Date	Mintage	F	VF	XF	Unc	BU
1993 Proof	Est. 100			Value: 1,500		

KM# 122   500 DOLLARS
47.5400 g., 0.9170 Gold 1.4015 oz. AGW **Subject:** Royal Visit **Rev:** Cameo portraits, flanked by roses, flowers above denomination

Date	Mintage	F	VF	XF	Unc	BU
1994 Proof	—			Value: 1,500		

PIEFORTS

KM#	Date	Mintage	Identification	Mkt Val
P1	1990	1,000	Dollar. 0.9250 Silver. KM99a.	60.00

MINT SETS

KM#	Date	Mintage	Identification	Issue Price	Mkt Val
MS1	1974 (8)	4,506	KM38-45	20.00	37.50
MS2	1975 (8)	1,095	KM43-50	27.50	30.00
MS4	1977 (8)	—	KM43-45, 46b -47b, 48-50	27.50	30.00
MS3	1976 (8)	759	KM43-50	27.50	32.00
MS5	1978 (8)	458	KM43-45, 46b-47b, 48-50	28.50	32.00
MS6	1979 (8)	808	KM43-44, 46b-47b, 48-50, 57	28.50	32.00
MS7	1980 (8)	761	KM43-44, 46b-47b, 48-50, 60	29.50	40.00
MS8	1981 (8)	297	KM43-44, 46b-47b, 48-50, 65	29.50	60.00
MS9	1982 (8)	—	KM69, 83-89	29.50	60.00
MS10	1983 (8)	—	KM71, 83-89	29.50	65.00
MS11	1984 (8)	—	KM75, 90-96	—	75.00
MS12	1992 (6)	—	KM33a, 34a, 35-37, 99	24.00	24.00

PROOF SETS

KM#	Date	Mintage	Identification	Issue Price	Mkt Val
PS2	1974 (8)	31,368	KM38a-45a	100	40.00
PS1	1974 (8)	21,470	KM38-45	35.00	18.00
PS4	1975 (8)	13,275	KM43-50a	110	40.00
PS3	1975 (8)	8,794	KM43-50	37.50	22.00
PS6	1976 (8)	5,897	KM43-50a	110	45.00
PS5	1976 (8)	4,893	KM43-50	37.50	25.00
PS8	1977 (8)	3,197	KM43a-50a	110	47.50
PS7	1977 (8)	2,107	KM43-45, 46b-47b, 48-50	37.50	30.00
PS10	1978 (8)	3,342	KM43a-50a	110	47.50
PS9	1978 (8)	1,671	KM43-45, 46b, 47b, 48-50	39.50	30.00
PS11	1979 (8)	1,287	KM43-44, 46b-47b, 48-50, 57	41.50	35.00
PS12	1979 (8)	2,445	KM43a-44a, 46a-50a, 57a	112	70.00
PS14	1980 (8)	1,826	KM43a-44a, 46a-50a, 60a	222	80.00
PS13	1980 (8)	920	KM43-44, 46b-47b, 48-50, 60	41.50	40.00

KM#	Date	Mintage	Identification	Issue Price	Mkt Val
PS15	1981 (8)	643	KM43-44, 46b-47b, 48-50, 65	41.50	60.00
PS16	1981 (8)	615	KM43a-44a, 46a-50a, 65a	—	115
PS18	1982 (8)	381	KM69a, 83a-89a	222	285
PS17	1982 (8)	—	KM69, 83-89	49.50	75.00
PS20	1983 (8)	241	KM71a, 83a-89a	197	300
PS19	1983 (8)	306	KM71, 83-89	37.00	70.00
PS21	1984 (8)	—	KM75, 90-96	37.00	65.00
PS22	1984 (8)	397	KM75a, 90a-96a	197	280
PS23	1985 (8)	212	KM75a, 90a-96a	—	325
PS24	1992 (4)	500	KM110-113	1,600	1,875
PS25	1992 (2)	—	KM107-108	100	95.00

BENIN

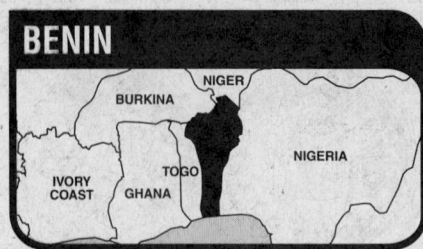

The Republic of Benin (formerly the Republic of Dahomey), located on the south side of the African bulge between Togo and Nigeria, has an area of 43,500 sq. mi. (112,620 sq. km.) and a population of 5.5 million. Capital: Porto-Novo. The principal industry of Benin, one of the poorest countries of West Africa, is the processing of palm oil products. Palm kernel oil, peanuts, cotton, and coffee are exported.

PEOPLES REPUBLIC

STANDARD COINAGE

KM# 52   1000 CFA FRANCS
19.9900 g., Silver, 24.10x42.26 mm. **Obv:** Arms **Obv. Leg.:** REPUBLIQUE **Rev:** German ocean liner Kaiser Wilhelm der Grosse **Edge:** Plain

Date	Mintage	VG	F	VF	XF	Unc
1998	—	—	—	—	—	—

KM# 10   200 FRANCS
Copper **Obv:** National arms, denomination below **Rev:** Sailing ship - Preussen, date below

Date	Mintage	F	VF	XF	Unc	BU
1993	—	—	—	—	7.50	—
1993 Proof	100			Value: 85.00		

KM# 8   200 FRANCS
Copper-Nickel **Series:** Prehistoric Animals **Obv:** National arms, denomination below **Rev:** Dinosaurs - Acanthopholis, right, date lower right

Date	Mintage	F	VF	XF	Unc	BU
1994	—	—	—	—	30.00	—

KM# 15   200 FRANCS
Copper **Series:** Prehistoric Animals **Obv:** National arms, denomination below **Rev:** Dinosaurs - Tyrannosaurus Rex, left, date lower right

Date	Mintage	F	VF	XF	Unc	BU
1994	—	—	—	—	25.00	—
1994 Proof	100			Value: 85.00		

KM# 16   200 FRANCS
Copper-Nickel **Subject:** United Nations - 50 Years **Obv:** National arms, denomination below **Rev:** Family in boat, building in background, two dates at bottom

Date	Mintage	F	VF	XF	Unc	BU
ND(1995)	—	—	—	—	8.50	—

KM# 17   200 FRANCS
Nickel-Bonded Steel And Enamel **Rev:** WWI Austrian Hansa - Brandenburg D. I

Date	Mintage	F	VF	XF	Unc	BU
1995	25,000	—	—	—	30.00	—

KM# 23   200 FRANCS
Copper **Series:** Prehistoric Animals **Obv:** National arms, denomination below **Rev:** Iguanodon, looking left, date at lower left

Date	Mintage	F	VF	XF	Unc	BU
1995 Proof	100			Value: 85.00		

KM# 25   200 FRANCS
Copper-Nickel **Series:** Sydney 2000 **Obv:** National arms, denomination below **Rev:** Classic sculpture and racing scullcraft, date below

Date	Mintage	F	VF	XF	Unc	BU
1999	10,000	—	—	—	7.50	—

KM# 3 500 FRANCS
12.0000 g., 0.9990 Silver 0.3854 oz. ASW **Subject:** 1992 World Cup Soccer **Obv:** National arms, denomination below **Rev:** Soccer goalie, large date in legend, small date at bottom

Date	Mintage	F	VF	XF	Unc	BU
1992	Est. 10,000	—	—	—	45.00	—

KM# 14 500 FRANCS
8.2500 g., 0.9990 Silver 0.2650 oz. ASW **Rev:** Soccer - Eifel Tower, flag and ball, date below, 1995 World Cup Soccer

Date	Mintage	F	VF	XF	Unc	BU
1995 Proof	30,000	Value: 22.50				

KM# 31 500 FRANCS
8.2500 g., 0.9990 Silver 0.2650 oz. ASW, 30.1 mm. **Obv:** National arms, denomination below **Rev:** Sailing ship, Gorch Fock **Edge:** Plain

Date	Mintage	F	VF	XF	Unc	BU
1996 Proof	10,000	Value: 22.50				

KM# 1 1000 FRANCS
19.9100 g., 0.9990 Silver 0.6395 oz. ASW **Obv:** National arms, denomination below **Rev:** Five hands holding jar **Note:** Five hands holding jar

Date	Mintage	F	VF	XF	Unc	BU
ND(1992) Proof	1,000	Value: 38.00				

KM# 2 1000 FRANCS
19.9100 g., 0.9990 Silver 0.6395 oz. ASW **Obv:** National arms, denomination below **Rev:** National map in radiant sun

Date	Mintage	F	VF	XF	Unc	BU
ND(1992) Proof	1,000	Value: 37.50				

KM# 4 1000 FRANCS
20.0000 g., 0.9990 Silver 0.6423 oz. ASW **Series:** Barcelona 1992 - 25th Summer Olympics **Rev:** Gymnast, date at right

Date	Mintage	F	VF	XF	Unc	BU
1992 Proof	Est. 5,000	Value: 28.00				

KM# 5 1000 FRANCS
20.0000 g., 0.9990 Silver 0.6423 oz. ASW **Subject:** 1992 World Cup Soccer **Obv:** National arms, denomination below **Rev:** Player kicking ball, date at rght

Date	Mintage	F	VF	XF	Unc	BU
1992 Proof	Est. 10,000	Value: 35.00				

KM# 6 1000 FRANCS
20.0000 g., 0.9990 Silver 0.6423 oz. ASW **Subject:** Protection of Nature **Rev:** Elephant, within inner circle, elephants, (trunk to tail), form outer circle

Date	Mintage	F	VF	XF	Unc	BU
1993 Proof	—	Value: 60.00				

KM# 7 1000 FRANCS
20.0000 g., 0.9990 Silver 0.6423 oz. ASW **Rev:** Sailing ship - Preussen, date below

Date	Mintage	F	VF	XF	Unc	BU
1993	100	—	—	—	150	—
1993 Proof	10,000	Value: 32.50				

KM# 27 1000 FRANCS
20.0000 g., 0.9990 Silver 0.6423 oz. ASW **Series:** Protection of Nature **Rev:** Elephant, people, tree, map

Date	Mintage	F	VF	XF	Unc	BU
1993 Proof	—	Value: 37.50				

KM# 9 1000 FRANCS
15.8600 g., 0.9940 Silver 0.5068 oz. ASW **Series:** Dinosaurs **Obv:** National arms, denomination below **Rev:** Tyrannosaurus Rex, left, date below tail

Date	Mintage	F	VF	XF	Unc	BU
1994 Proof	—	Value: 50.00				

KM# 12 1000 FRANCS
20.0000 g., 0.9990 Silver 0.6423 oz. ASW **Series:** 1996 Olympics **Rev:** Three runners, large date below, small date at left

Date	Mintage	F	VF	XF	Unc	BU
1995 Proof	15,000	Value: 28.00				

KM# 13 1000 FRANCS
20.0000 g., 0.9990 Silver 0.6423 oz. ASW **Subject:** 35 Years of Independence **Rev:** Woman stirring pot, hut at back left

Date	Mintage	F	VF	XF	Unc	BU
1995 Proof	2,000	Value: 35.00				

KM# 18 1000 FRANCS
20.0000 g., 0.9990 Silver 0.6423 oz. ASW **Rev:** WWI Austrian Hansa - Brandenburg D. I, date lower right

Date	Mintage	F	VF	XF	Unc	BU
1995 Proof	15,000	Value: 45.00				

KM# 28   1000 FRANCS
20.0000 g., 0.9990 Silver 0.6423 oz. ASW **Series:** Prehistoric Animals **Rev:** Iguanodon, looking left, date below tail **Edge:** Plain

Date	Mintage	F	VF	XF	Unc	BU
1995 Proof	—				Value: 40.00	

KM# 19   1000 FRANCS
20.0000 g., 0.9990 Silver 0.6423 oz. ASW **Rev:** Head of Multicolor panther, 3/4 facing, date above

Date	Mintage	F	VF	XF	Unc	BU
1996 Proof	—				Value: 60.00	

KM# 20   1000 FRANCS
15.0000 g., 0.9990 Silver 0.4818 oz. ASW **Subject:** 1996 World Cup Soccer **Obv:** National arms, denomination below **Rev:** Two multicolor soccer players, small date at left

Date	Mintage	F	VF	XF	Unc	BU
1996 Proof	—				Value: 45.00	

KM# 50   1000 FRANCS
Silver, 35 mm. **Subject:** Sports **Rev:** 16th World Series Soccer

Date	Mintage	F	VF	XF	Unc	BU
1996	—				Value: 35.00	

KM# 43   1000 FRANCS
15.0000 g., 0.9990 Silver 0.4818 oz. ASW, 35 mm. **Obv:** National arms, denomination below **Rev:** Multicolor zebra **Edge:** Plain

Date	Mintage	F	VF	XF	Unc	BU
1997 Proof	—				Value: 60.00	

KM# 48   1000 FRANCS
15.0000 g., 0.9990 Silver 0.4818 oz. ASW, 34 mm. **Subject:** Soccer **Obv:** National arms **Rev:** Multicolor Eiffel Tower and ball **Edge:** Plain

Date	Mintage	F	VF	XF	Unc	BU
1997 Proof	—				Value: 25.00	

KM# 21   1000 FRANCS
15.0000 g., 0.9990 Silver 0.4818 oz. ASW **Series:** 2000 Summer Olympics **Obv:** National arms, denomination below **Rev:** Multicolored shot-putter and Olympic torch, date at right

Date	Mintage	F	VF	XF	Unc	BU
1997	100	—	—	—	150	—
1997 Proof	—				Value: 40.00	

KM# 24   1000 FRANCS
20.0000 g., 0.9990 Silver 0.6423 oz. ASW **Series:** 2000 Summer Olympics **Obv:** National arms, denomination below **Rev:** Two runners and statue

Date	Mintage	F	VF	XF	Unc	BU
1997	100	—	—	—	100	—
1997 Proof	7,500				Value: 32.50	

KM# 26   1000 FRANCS
20.1300 g., 0.9990 Silver 0.6465 oz. ASW **Series:** 2000 Summer Olympics **Obv:** National arms, denomination below **Rev:** Classic statue and racing scullcraft, date below

Date	Mintage	F	VF	XF	Unc	BU
1999 Proof	5,000				Value: 35.00	

KM# 39   1000 FRANCS
14.9600 g., 0.9990 Silver 0.4805 oz. ASW, 34.9 mm. **Subject:** Gutenberg **Obv:** National arms, denomination below **Rev:** Portrait and printing press, two dates lower right **Edge:** Plain

Date	Mintage	F	VF	XF	Unc	BU
1999 Proof	7,000				Value: 30.00	

KM# 51   1000 FRANCS
Silver, 23 mm. **Subject:** Wildlife **Rev:** Elephant with calf

Date	Mintage	F	VF	XF	Unc	BU
1999	—				Value: 40.00	

KM# 47   1000 FRANCS
14.9600 g., 0.9990 Silver 0.4805 oz. ASW, 35 mm. **Obv:** National arms **Rev:** Calipers, radiant sun and grid **Edge:** Plain

Date	Mintage	F	VF	XF	Unc	BU
2000 Proof	—				Value: 35.00	

KM# 11   6000 FRANCS
20.1300 g., 0.9990 Silver 0.6465 oz. ASW **Series:** Protection of Nature **Obv:** National arms, denomination below **Rev:** Elephant within inner circle, elephants, (trunk to tail), form outer circle

Date	Mintage	F	VF	XF	Unc	BU
1993 Proof	5,000				Value: 60.00	

KM# 22   6000 FRANCS
28.3400 g., 0.9250 Silver 0.8428 oz. ASW **Subject:** 50th Anniversary U.N. **Obv:** National arms, denomination below **Rev:** Family in boat, two dates at bottom

Date	Mintage	F	VF	XF	Unc	BU
ND(1995) Proof	—				Value: 42.50	

KM# 34   15000 FRANCS
500.0000 g., 0.9990 Silver 16.058 oz. ASW, 84.8 mm. **Subject:** Wildlife Protection **Obv:** National arms, denomination below **Rev:** Multicolor crocodile, date at right **Edge:** Reeded **Note:** Illustration reduced.

Date	Mintage	F	VF	XF	Unc	BU
1996 Proof	300				Value: 375	
1997 Proof	—				Value: 350	

KM# 36   20000 FRANCS
846.0152 g., 0.9990 Silver 27.171 oz. ASW, 90.4 mm. **Subject:** African Fauna **Obv:** National arms, denomination below **Rev:** Multicolor zebra, date upper right **Edge:** Plain **Note:** Illustration reduced.

Date	Mintage	F	VF	XF	Unc	BU
1997 Proof	—				Value: 600	

KM# 29 30000 FRANCS
15.5500 g., 0.9990 Gold 0.4994 oz. AGW **Obv:** National arms **Rev:** Map in radiant sun **Edge:** Reeded

Date	Mintage	F	VF	XF	Unc	BU
ND(1992) Proof	Est. 100	Value: 650				

KM# 30 100000 FRANCS
31.1035 g., 0.9990 Gold 0.9990 oz. AGW **Obv:** National arms **Rev:** President **Edge:** Reeded

Date	Mintage	F	VF	XF	Unc	BU
1992 Rare	Est. 10	Value: 1,600				

PIEFORTS

KM#	Date	Mintage	Identification	Mkt Val
P1	1997	—	1000 Francs. Silver. KM#21.	200
P2	1997	—	1000 Francs. Silver. KM#24.	175
P3	1999	—	1000 Francs. Silver. KM#26.	135

BERMUDA

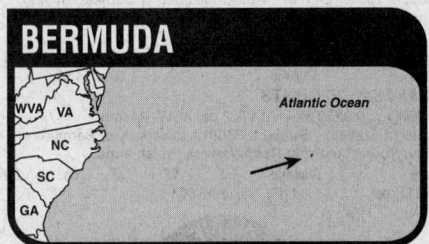

The Parliamentary British Colony of Bermuda, situated in the western Atlantic Ocean 660 miles (1,062 km.) east of North Carolina, has an area of 20.6 sq. mi. (53 sq. km.) and a population of 61,600. Capital: Hamilton. Concentrated essences, beauty preparations, and cut flowers are exported. Most Bermudians derive their livelihood from tourism. The British monarch is the head of state and is represented by a governor.

Bermuda was discovered by Juan de Bermudez, a Spanish navigator, in about 1503. British influence dates from 1609 when a group of Virginia-bound British colonists under the command of Sir George Somers was shipwrecked on the islands for 10 months. The islands were settled in 1612 by 60 British colonists from the Virginia Colony and became a crown colony in 1684. The earliest coins issued for the island were the "Hogge Money" series of 2, 3, 6 and 12 pence, the name derived from the pig in the obverse design, a recognition of the quantity of such animals then found there. The next issue for Bermuda was the Birmingham coppers of 1793; all locally circulating coinage was demonetized in 1842, when the currency of the United Kingdom became standard. Internal autonomy was obtained by the constitution of June 8, 1968.

In February, 1970, Bermuda converted from its former currency, which was sterling, to a decimal currency, the dollar unit which is equal to one U.S. dollar. On July 31, 1972, Bermuda severed its monetary link with the British pound sterling and pegged its dollar to be the same value as the U.S. dollar.

RULER
British

MINT MARKS
CHI - Valcambi, Switzerland
FM - Franklin Mint, U.S.A.*

*NOTE: From 1975-1985 the Franklin Mint produced coinage in up to 3 different qualities. Qualities of issue are designated in ( ) after each date and are defined as follows:

(M) MATTE - Normal circulation strike or a dull finish produced by sandblasting special uncirculated (polish finish) or proof quality dies.

(U) SPECIAL UNCIRCULATED - Polished or proof-like in appearance without any frosted features.

(P) PROOF - The highest quality obtainable having mirror-like fields and frosted features.

MONETARY SYSTEM
12 Pence = 1 Shilling
20 Shillings = 1 Pound

BRITISH COLONY
DECIMAL COINAGE

KM# 163 3 DOLLARS
1.5550 g., 0.9990 Gold 0.0499 oz. AGW, 15 mm. **Ruler:** Elizabeth II **Obv:** Crowned bust right **Rev:** 17th century galleon, map grids, islands **Edge:** Plain

Date	Mintage	F	VF	XF	Unc	BU
1998 Proof	—	Value: 55.00				

POUND STERLING COINAGE

KM# 13 CROWN
28.2800 g., 0.9250 Silver 0.8410 oz. ASW, 38 mm. **Ruler:** Elizabeth II **Subject:** 350th Anniversary - Colony Founding **Obv:** Crowned head right **Rev:** Depicts "Deliverance" and "Patience" ships

Date	Mintage	F	VF	XF	Unc	BU
1959	100,000	—	BV	17.50	20.00	25.00
1959 Matte proof	—	Value: 1,000				

Note: Mintage: 6-10

KM# 14 CROWN
22.6200 g., 0.5000 Silver 0.3636 oz. ASW, 36 mm. **Ruler:** Elizabeth II **Obv:** Crowned head right **Rev:** Lion holding shield divides date **Edge:** Reeded

Date	Mintage	F	VF	XF	Unc	BU
1964	470,000	—	—	BV	8.00	10.00
1964 Proof	30,000	Value: 12.00				

DECIMAL COINAGE
100 Cents = 1 Dollar

KM# 15 CENT
3.1100 g., Bronze, 19 mm. **Ruler:** Elizabeth II **Obv:** Young bust right **Rev:** Wild boar left **Edge:** Smooth

Date	Mintage	F	VF	XF	Unc	BU
1970	5,500,000	—	—	0.10	0.30	0.50
1970 Proof	11,000	Value: 0.50				
1971	4,256,000	—	—	0.10	0.30	0.50
1973	2,144,000	—	—	0.10	0.30	0.50
1974	856,000	—	—	0.10	0.35	0.60
1975	1,000,000	—	—	0.10	0.30	0.50
1976	1,000,000	—	—	0.10	0.30	0.50
1977	2,000,000	—	—	0.10	0.30	0.50
1978	3,160,000	—	—	0.10	0.30	0.50
1980	3,520,000	—	—	0.10	0.30	0.50
1981	3,200,000	—	—	0.10	0.30	0.50
1982	320,000	—	—	0.10	0.30	0.50
1983	800,000	—	—	0.10	0.30	0.50
1983 Proof	6,474	Value: 1.00				
1984	800,000	—	—	0.10	0.30	0.50
1985	800,000	—	—	0.10	0.30	0.50

KM# 44 CENT
Bronze, 19 mm. **Ruler:** Elizabeth II **Obv:** Crowned head right **Rev:** Wild boar left **Edge:** Smooth

Date	Mintage	F	VF	XF	Unc	BU
1986	1,360,000	—	—	0.10	0.30	0.50
1986 Proof	Inc. above	Value: 2.00				

Date	Mintage	F	VF	XF	Unc	BU
1987	2,048,000	—	—	0.10	0.30	0.50
1990	1,500,000	—	—	0.10	0.30	0.50

KM# 44a CENT
3.1300 g., Steel, 19 mm. **Ruler:** Elizabeth II **Obv:** Crowned head right **Rev:** Wild boar left **Edge:** Smooth **Note:** Copper coated.

Date	Mintage	F	VF	XF	Unc	BU
1988	2,500,000	—	—	—	2.50	3.50

KM# 44b CENT
Copper Plated Zinc, 19 mm. **Ruler:** Elizabeth II **Obv:** Crowned head right **Rev:** Wild boar left **Edge:** Smooth

Date	Mintage	F	VF	XF	Unc	BU
1991	2,400,000	—	—	0.10	0.25	0.50
1993	1,600,000	—	—	0.10	0.25	0.50
1994	1,440,000	—	—	0.10	0.25	0.50
1995	1,920,000	—	—	0.10	0.25	0.50
1996	3,200,000	—	—	0.10	0.25	0.50
1997	3,400,000	—	—	0.10	0.25	0.50

KM# 44c CENT
3.7000 g., 0.9250 Silver 0.1100 oz. ASW, 19 mm. **Ruler:** Elizabeth II **Obv:** Crowned head right **Rev:** Wild boar left **Note:** In sets only.

Date	Mintage	F	VF	XF	Unc	BU
1995 Proof	2,000	Value: 5.00				

KM# 44d CENT
6.2000 g., 0.9170 Gold 0.1828 oz. AGW, 19 mm. **Ruler:** Elizabeth II **Obv:** Crowned head right **Rev:** Wild boar left **Note:** In sets only.

Date	Mintage	F	VF	XF	Unc	BU
1995 Proof	500	Value: 185				

KM# 107 CENT
Copper Plated Zinc, 19 mm. **Ruler:** Elizabeth II **Obv:** Head with tiara right **Rev:** Wild boar left **Edge:** Smooth

Date	Mintage	F	VF	XF	Unc	BU
1999	2,400,000	—	—	—	0.50	0.75
1999 Proof	2,500	Value: 2.50				
2000	—	—	—	—	0.50	0.75
2000 Proof	—	Value: 2.50				

KM# 16 5 CENTS
5.0600 g., Copper-Nickel, 21 mm. **Ruler:** Elizabeth II **Obv:** Young bust right **Rev:** Queen angel fish left **Edge:** Smooth

Date	Mintage	F	VF	XF	Unc	BU
1970	2,190,000	—	0.10	0.15	0.50	0.75
1970 Proof	11,000	Value: 0.50				
1974	310,000	—	0.10	0.15	0.50	0.75
1975	500,000	—	0.10	0.15	0.50	0.75
1977	500,000	—	0.10	0.15	0.50	0.75
1979	500,000	—	0.10	0.15	0.50	0.75
1980	1,100,000	—	0.10	0.15	0.50	0.75
1981	900,000	—	0.10	0.15	0.50	0.75
1982	200,000	—	0.10	0.15	0.50	0.75
1983	800,000	—	0.10	0.15	0.50	0.75
1983 Proof	6,474	Value: 1.50				
1984	500,000	—	0.10	0.15	0.50	0.75
1985	—	—	0.10	0.15	0.50	0.75

KM# 45 5 CENTS
2.5400 g., Copper-Nickel, 19.59 mm. **Ruler:** Elizabeth II **Obv:** Crowned head right **Rev:** Queen angel fish left **Edge:** Plain

Date	Mintage	F	VF	XF	Unc	BU
1986	1,400,000	—	0.10	0.15	0.50	0.75
1986 Proof	Inc. above	Value: 2.50				
1987	1,050,000	—	0.10	0.15	0.50	0.75
1988	700,000	—	0.10	0.15	0.50	0.75
1990	700,000	—	0.10	0.15	0.50	0.75

Date	Mintage	F	VF	XF	Unc	BU
1993	600,000	—	0.10	0.15	0.50	0.75
1994	1,100,000	—	0.10	0.15	0.50	0.75
1995	700,000	—	0.10	0.15	0.50	0.75
1996	1,500,000	—	0.10	0.15	0.50	0.75
1997	300,000	—	0.10	0.15	0.50	0.75

KM# 45a 5 CENTS
5.7000 g., 0.9250 Silver 0.1695 oz. ASW, 21 mm.
Ruler: Elizabeth II **Obv:** Crowned head right **Rev:** Queen angel fish left **Note:** In sets only.

Date	Mintage	F	VF	XF	Unc	BU
1995 Proof	2,000	Value: 9.00				

KM# 45b 5 CENTS
5.7000 g., 0.9170 Gold 0.1680 oz. AGW, 21 mm.
Ruler: Elizabeth II **Obv:** Crowned head right **Rev:** Queen angel fish left **Note:** In sets only.

Date	Mintage	F	VF	XF	Unc	BU
1995 Proof	500	Value: 215				

KM# 108 5 CENTS
5.0600 g., Copper-Nickel, 21 mm. **Ruler:** Elizabeth II **Obv:** Head with tiara right **Rev:** Queen angel fish left **Edge:** Smooth

Date	Mintage	F	VF	XF	Unc	BU
1999	900,000	—	—	—	0.75	1.00
1999 Proof	2,500	Value: 3.50				
2000	1,000,000	—	—	—	0.75	1.00
2000 Proof	—	Value: 3.50				

KM# 17 10 CENTS
2.4500 g., Copper-Nickel, 17.8 mm. **Ruler:** Elizabeth II **Obv:** Young bust right **Rev:** Bermuda lily **Edge:** Reeded

Date	Mintage	F	VF	XF	Unc	BU
1970	2,500,000	—	0.10	0.15	0.35	0.50
1970 Proof	11,000	Value: 0.50				
1971	2,000,000	—	0.10	0.15	0.35	0.50
1978	500,000	—	0.10	0.15	0.40	0.60
1979	800,000	—	0.10	0.15	0.40	0.60
1980	1,100,000	—	0.10	0.15	0.35	0.50
1981	1,300,000	—	0.10	0.15	0.35	0.50
1982	400,000	—	0.10	0.15	0.40	0.60
1983	1,000,000	—	0.10	0.15	0.35	0.50
1983 Proof	6,474	Value: 2.00				
1984	500,000	—	0.10	0.15	0.40	0.60
1985	—	—	0.10	0.15	0.40	0.60

KM# 46 10 CENTS
Copper-Nickel, 17.8 mm. **Ruler:** Elizabeth II **Obv:** Crowned head right **Rev:** Bermuda lily **Edge:** Reeded

Date	Mintage	F	VF	XF	Unc	BU
1986	750,000	—	0.10	0.15	0.40	0.60
1986 Proof	Inc. above	Value: 3.50				
1987	2,000,000	—	0.10	0.15	0.40	0.60
1988	720,000	—	0.10	0.15	0.40	0.60
1990	1,500,000	—	0.10	0.15	0.40	0.60
1993	15,000	—	0.10	0.15	0.40	0.60
1994	1,400,000	—	0.10	0.15	0.40	0.60
1995	1,400,000	—	0.10	0.15	0.40	0.60
1996	1,000,000	—	0.10	0.15	0.40	0.60
1997	800,000	—	0.10	0.15	0.40	0.60

KM# 46a 10 CENTS
2.8000 g., 0.9250 Silver 0.0833 oz. ASW, 17.8 mm.
Ruler: Elizabeth II **Obv:** Crowned head right **Rev:** Bermuda lily **Note:** In sets only.

Date	Mintage	F	VF	XF	Unc	BU
1995 Proof	2,000	Value: 12.00				

KM# 46b 10 CENTS
4.7500 g., 0.9170 Gold 0.1400 oz. AGW, 17.8 mm.
Ruler: Elizabeth II **Obv:** Crowned head right **Rev:** Bermuda lily **Note:** In sets only.

Date	Mintage	F	VF	XF	Unc	BU
1995 Proof	500	Value: 150				

KM# 109 10 CENTS
2.4000 g., Copper-Nickel, 17.8 mm. **Ruler:** Elizabeth II **Obv:** Head with tiara right **Rev:** Bermuda lily **Edge:** Reeded

Date	Mintage	F	VF	XF	Unc	BU
1999	1,400,000				0.85	1.00
1999 Proof	2,500	Value: 6.00				
2000					0.85	1.00
2000 Proof	—	Value: 6.00				

KM# 18 25 CENTS
5.9200 g., Copper-Nickel, 24 mm. **Ruler:** Elizabeth II **Obv:** Young bust right **Rev:** Yellow-billed tropical bird **Edge:** Reeded

Date	Mintage	F	VF	XF	Unc	BU
1970	1,500,000	—	0.30	0.50	1.25	1.50
1970 Proof	11,000	Value: 2.00				
1973	1,000,000	—	0.30	0.50	1.25	1.50
1979	570,000	—	0.30	0.50	1.25	1.50
1980	1,120,000	—	0.30	0.50	1.25	1.50
1981	2,200,000	—	0.30	0.50	1.25	1.50
1982	160,000	—	0.30	0.50	1.50	1.75
1983	600,000	—	0.30	0.50	1.25	1.50
1983 Proof	6,474	Value: 2.50				
1984	400,000	—	0.30	0.50	1.25	1.50
1985	—	—	0.30	0.50	1.25	1.50

KM# 32 25 CENTS
Copper-Nickel, 24 mm. **Ruler:** Elizabeth II **Subject:** 375th Anniversary of Bermuda **Obv:** Young bust right **Rev:** Arms of the Bermudas **Edge:** Reeded

Date	Mintage	F	VF	XF	Unc	BU
1984	36,850	—	—	1.50	4.50	—

KM# 32a 25 CENTS
5.9600 g., 0.9250 Silver 0.1772 oz. ASW, 24 mm.
Ruler: Elizabeth II **Subject:** 375th Anniversary of Bermuda **Obv:** Young bust right **Rev:** Arms of the Bermudas

Date	Mintage	F	VF	XF	Unc	BU
1984 Proof	19,250	Value: 15.00				

KM# 33 25 CENTS
Copper-Nickel, 24 mm. **Ruler:** Elizabeth II **Subject:** 375th Anniversary of Bermuda **Obv:** Young bust right **Rev:** City of Hamilton arms **Edge:** Reeded

Date	Mintage	F	VF	XF	Unc	BU
1984	36,850	—	—	1.50	4.50	—

KM# 33a 25 CENTS
5.9600 g., 0.9250 Silver 0.1772 oz. ASW, 24 mm.
Ruler: Elizabeth II **Subject:** 375th Anniversary of Bermuda **Obv:** Young bust right **Rev:** City of Hamilton arms

Date	Mintage	F	VF	XF	Unc	BU
1984 Proof	19,250	Value: 15.00				

KM# 34 25 CENTS
Copper-Nickel, 24 mm. **Ruler:** Elizabeth II **Subject:** 375th Anniversary of Bermuda **Obv:** Young bust right **Rev:** Town of St. George arms **Edge:** Reeded

Date	Mintage	F	VF	XF	Unc	BU
1984	36,850	—	—	1.50	4.50	—

KM# 34a 25 CENTS
5.9600 g., 0.9250 Silver 0.1772 oz. ASW, 24 mm.
Ruler: Elizabeth II **Subject:** 375th Anniversary of Bermuda **Obv:** Young bust right **Rev:** Town of St. George arms

Date	Mintage	F	VF	XF	Unc	BU
1984 Proof	19,250	Value: 15.00				

KM# 35 25 CENTS
Copper-Nickel, 24 mm. **Ruler:** Elizabeth II **Subject:** 375th Anniversary of Bermuda **Obv:** Young bust right **Rev:** Warwick Parish arms **Edge:** Reeded

Date	Mintage	F	VF	XF	Unc	BU
1984	36,850	—	—	1.50	4.50	—

KM# 35a 25 CENTS
5.9600 g., 0.9250 Silver 0.1772 oz. ASW, 24 mm.
Ruler: Elizabeth II **Subject:** 375th Anniversary of Bermuda **Obv:** Young bust right **Rev:** Warwick Parish arms

Date	Mintage	F	VF	XF	Unc	BU
1984 Proof	19,250	Value: 15.00				

KM# 36 25 CENTS
Copper-Nickel, 24 mm. **Ruler:** Elizabeth II **Subject:** 375th Anniversary of Bermuda **Obv:** Young bust right **Rev:** Smith's Parish arms **Edge:** Reeded

Date	Mintage	F	VF	XF	Unc	BU
1984	36,850	—	—	1.50	4.50	—

KM# 36a 25 CENTS
5.9600 g., 0.9250 Silver 0.1772 oz. ASW, 24 mm.
Ruler: Elizabeth II **Subject:** 375th Anniversary of Bermuda **Obv:** Young bust right **Rev:** Smith's Parish arms

Date	Mintage	F	VF	XF	Unc	BU
1984 Proof	19,250	Value: 15.00				

KM# 37 25 CENTS
Copper-Nickel, 24 mm. **Ruler:** Elizabeth II **Subject:** 375th Anniversary of Bermuda **Obv:** Young bust right **Rev:** Devonshire Parish arms **Edge:** Reeded

Date	Mintage	F	VF	XF	Unc	BU
1984	36,850	—	—	1.50	4.50	—

KM# 37a 25 CENTS
5.9600 g., 0.9250 Silver 0.1772 oz. ASW, 24 mm.
Ruler: Elizabeth II **Subject:** 375th Anniversary of Bermuda **Obv:** Young bust right **Rev:** Devonshire Parish arms

Date	Mintage	F	VF	XF	Unc	BU
1984 Proof	19,250	Value: 15.00				

KM# 38 25 CENTS
Copper-Nickel, 24 mm. **Ruler:** Elizabeth II **Subject:** 375th Anniversary of Bermuda **Obv:** Young bust right **Rev:** Sandy's Parish arms **Edge:** Reeded

Date	Mintage	F	VF	XF	Unc	BU
1984	36,850	—	—	1.50	4.50	—

KM# 38a 25 CENTS
5.9600 g., 0.9250 Silver 0.1772 oz. ASW, 24 mm.
Ruler: Elizabeth II **Subject:** 375th Anniversary of Bermuda **Obv:** Young bust right **Rev:** Sandy's Parish arms

Date	Mintage	F	VF	XF	Unc	BU
1984 Proof	19,250	Value: 15.00				

KM# 39 25 CENTS
Copper-Nickel, 24 mm. **Ruler:** Elizabeth II **Subject:** 375th Anniversary of Bermuda **Obv:** Young bust right **Rev:** Hamilton Parish arms **Edge:** Reeded

Date	Mintage	F	VF	XF	Unc	BU
1984	36,850	—	—	1.50	4.50	—

KM# 39a 25 CENTS
5.9600 g., 0.9250 Silver 0.1772 oz. ASW, 24 mm. **Ruler:** Elizabeth II **Subject:** 375th Anniversary of Bermuda **Obv:** Young bust right **Rev:** Hamilton Parish arms

Date	Mintage	F	VF	XF	Unc	BU
1984 Proof	19,250	Value: 15.00				

KM# 40 25 CENTS
Copper-Nickel, 24 mm. **Ruler:** Elizabeth II **Subject:** 375th Anniversary of Bermuda **Obv:** Young bust right **Rev:** Southampton Parish arms **Edge:** Reeded

Date	Mintage	F	VF	XF	Unc	BU
1984	36,850	—	—	1.50	4.50	—

KM# 40a 25 CENTS
5.9600 g., 0.9250 Silver 0.1772 oz. ASW, 24 mm. **Ruler:** Elizabeth II **Subject:** 375th Anniversary of Bermuda **Obv:** Young bust right **Rev:** Southampton Parish arms

Date	Mintage	F	VF	XF	Unc	BU
1984 Proof	19,250	Value: 15.00				

KM# 41 25 CENTS
Copper-Nickel, 24 mm. **Ruler:** Elizabeth II **Subject:** 375th Anniversary of Bermuda **Obv:** Young bust right **Rev:** Pembroke Parish arms **Edge:** Reeded

Date	Mintage	F	VF	XF	Unc	BU
1984	36,850	—	—	1.50	4.50	—

KM# 41a 25 CENTS
5.9600 g., 0.9250 Silver 0.1772 oz. ASW, 24 mm. **Ruler:** Elizabeth II **Subject:** 375th Anniversary of Bermuda **Obv:** Young bust right **Rev:** Pembroke Parish arms

Date	Mintage	F	VF	XF	Unc	BU
1984 Proof	19,250	Value: 15.00				

KM# 42 25 CENTS
Copper-Nickel, 24 mm. **Ruler:** Elizabeth II **Subject:** 375th Anniversary of Bermuda **Obv:** Young bust right **Rev:** Paget Parish arms **Edge:** Reeded

Date	Mintage	F	VF	XF	Unc	BU
1984	36,850	—	—	1.50	4.50	—

KM# 42a 25 CENTS
5.9600 g., 0.9250 Silver 0.1772 oz. ASW, 24 mm. **Ruler:** Elizabeth II **Subject:** 375th Anniversary of Bermuda **Obv:** Young bust right **Rev:** Paget Parish arms

Date	Mintage	F	VF	XF	Unc	BU
1984 Proof	19,250	Value: 15.00				

KM# 47 25 CENTS
6.0000 g., Copper-Nickel, 24 mm. **Ruler:** Elizabeth II **Subject:** Yellow-billed tropical bird right **Obv:** Crowned head right **Edge:** Reeded

Date	Mintage	F	VF	XF	Unc	BU
1986	560,000	—	0.30	0.50	1.00	1.50
1986 Proof	2,500	Value: 6.00				
1987	600,000	—	0.30	0.50	1.00	1.50
1988	600,000	—	0.30	0.50	1.00	1.50
1993	480,000	—	0.30	0.50	1.00	1.50
1994	1,040,000	—	0.30	0.50	1.00	1.50
1995	960,000	—	0.30	0.50	1.00	1.50
1996	1,200,000	—	0.30	0.50	1.00	1.50
1997	—	—	0.30	0.50	1.00	1.50
1998	—	—	0.30	0.50	1.00	1.50

KM# 47a 25 CENTS
7.0000 g., 0.9250 Silver 0.2082 oz. ASW, 24 mm. **Ruler:** Elizabeth II **Subject:** Yellow-billed tropical bird right **Obv:** Crowned head right **Note:** In sets only.

Date	Mintage	F	VF	XF	Unc	BU
1995 Proof	2,000	Value: 18.00				

KM# 47b 25 CENTS
11.7000 g., 0.9170 Gold 0.3449 oz. AGW, 24 mm. **Ruler:** Elizabeth II **Subject:** Yellow-billed tropical bird right **Obv:** Crowned head right **Note:** In sets only.

Date	Mintage	F	VF	XF	Unc	BU
1995 Proof	500	Value: 350				

KM# 110 25 CENTS
Copper-Nickel, 24 mm. **Ruler:** Elizabeth II **Obv:** Head with tiara right **Rev:** Yellow-billed tropical bird right **Edge:** Reeded

Date	Mintage	F	VF	XF	Unc	BU
1999	800,000	—	—	—	1.50	2.00
1999 Proof	2,500	Value: 10.00				
2000	800,000	—	—	—	1.50	2.00
2000 Proof		Value: 9.00				

KM# 19 50 CENTS
12.4200 g., Copper-Nickel, 30.5 mm. **Ruler:** Elizabeth II **Obv:** Young bust right **Rev:** Arms **Edge:** Reeded

Date	Mintage	F	VF	XF	Unc	BU
1970	1,000,000	—	0.60	0.75	1.00	1.50
1970 Proof	11,000	Value: 2.00				
1978	200,000	—	0.60	0.85	1.25	1.75
1980	60,000	—	0.60	0.85	1.50	2.00
1981	100,000	—	0.60	0.85	1.25	1.75
1982	80,000	—	0.60	0.85	1.50	2.00
1983	60,000	—	0.60	0.85	1.50	2.00
1983 Proof	6,474	Value: 4.50				
1984	40,000	—	0.60	0.85	1.50	2.00
1985	40,000	—	0.60	0.85	1.50	2.00

KM# 48 50 CENTS
12.6000 g., Copper-Nickel, 30.5 mm. **Ruler:** Elizabeth II **Obv:** Crowned head right **Rev:** National arms **Edge:** Reeded

Date	Mintage	F	VF	XF	Unc	BU
1986	60,000	—	0.60	0.85	1.50	2.00

Date	Mintage	F	VF	XF	Unc	BU
1986 Proof	Inc. above	Value: 6.00				
1988	60,000	—	0.60	0.85	1.50	2.00

KM# 20 DOLLAR
28.2800 g., 0.8000 Silver 0.7273 oz. ASW **Ruler:** Elizabeth II **Obv:** Young bust right **Rev:** Jugate heads right

Date	Mintage	F	VF	XF	Unc	BU
1970 Proof	11,000	Value: 18.00				

KM# 22 DOLLAR
28.2800 g., 0.5000 Silver 0.4546 oz. ASW **Ruler:** Elizabeth II **Subject:** Silver Wedding Anniversary **Obv:** Young bust right **Rev:** Crowned monograms divided by map

Date	Mintage	F	VF	XF	Unc	BU
1972	65,074	—	—	—	12.00	14.00

KM# 22a DOLLAR
28.2800 g., 0.9250 Silver 0.8410 oz. ASW **Ruler:** Elizabeth II **Subject:** Silver Wedding Anniversary **Obv:** Young bust right **Rev:** Crowned monograms divided by map

Date	Mintage	F	VF	XF	Unc	BU
1972 Proof	14,708	Value: 18.50				

KM# 28 DOLLAR
Copper-Nickel, 38.5 mm. **Ruler:** Elizabeth II **Subject:** Wedding of Prince Charles and Lady Diana **Obv:** Young bust right **Rev:** Jugate heads right

Date	Mintage	F	VF	XF	Unc	BU
1981	65,004	—	—	—	7.00	9.00

KM# 28a DOLLAR
28.2800 g., 0.9250 Silver 0.8410 oz. ASW **Ruler:** Elizabeth II **Subject:** Wedding of Prince Charles and Lady Diana **Obv:** Young bust right **Rev:** Jugate heads right

Date	Mintage	F	VF	XF	Unc	BU
1981 Proof	16,296	Value: 18.00				

KM# 30 DOLLAR
Nickel-Brass **Ruler:** Elizabeth II **Subject:** Cahow over Bermuda **Obv:** Young bust right **Rev:** Bird flying over map

Date	Mintage	F	VF	XF	Unc	BU
1983	250,000	—	—	—	4.00	6.00
1983 Proof	6,474	Value: 7.50				

KM# 43 DOLLAR

Copper-Nickel, 38.5 mm. **Ruler:** Elizabeth II **Subject:** Cruise Ship Tourism **Obv:** Crowned bust right **Rev:** The Bermuda Buttery, an early refrigeration building and a cruise ship in the distance **Edge:** Reeded

Date	Mintage	F	VF	XF	Unc	BU
1985	11,000	—	—	—	5.00	6.50

KM# 43a DOLLAR

28.2800 g., 0.9250 Silver 0.8410 oz. ASW, 38.5 mm. **Ruler:** Elizabeth II **Subject:** Cruise Ship Tourism **Obv:** Young bust right **Rev:** The Bermuda Buttery, an early refrigeration building and a cruise ship in the distance **Edge:** Reeded

Date	Mintage	F	VF	XF	Unc	BU
1985	2,500	—	—	—	25.00	27.50
1985 Proof	4,000	Value: 25.00				

KM# 49 DOLLAR

Copper-Nickel, 38.5 mm. **Ruler:** Elizabeth II **Series:** World Wildlife Fund **Obv:** Crowned head right **Rev:** Sea turtle, chelonia mydas

Date	Mintage	F	VF	XF	Unc	BU
1986	33,320	—	—	—	17.50	20.00

KM# 49a DOLLAR

28.2800 g., 0.9250 Silver 0.8410 oz. ASW **Ruler:** Elizabeth II **Series:** World Wildlife Fund **Obv:** Crowned head right **Rev:** Sea turtle

Date	Mintage	F	VF	XF	Unc	BU
1986	10,000	—	—	—	30.00	32.50
1986 Proof	Est. 21,872	Value: 35.00				

KM# 50 DOLLAR

Nickel-Brass **Ruler:** Elizabeth II **Obv:** Crowned head right **Rev:** Cahow over Bermuda

Date	Mintage	F	VF	XF	Unc	BU
1986 Proof	—	Value: 12.50				

KM# 52 DOLLAR

Copper-Nickel, 38.5 mm. **Ruler:** Elizabeth II **Subject:** 50th Anniversary of Commercial Aviation **Obv:** Crowned head right **Rev:** Amphibious plane

Date	Mintage	F	VF	XF	Unc	BU
1987	9,000	—	—	—	7.00	9.00

KM# 52a DOLLAR

28.2800 g., 0.6250 Silver 0.5682 oz. ASW **Ruler:** Elizabeth II **Subject:** 50th Anniversary of Commercial Aviation **Obv:** Crowned head right **Rev:** Amphibious plane

Date	Mintage	F	VF	XF	Unc	BU
1987	5,000	—	—	—	20.00	22.50
1987 Proof	5,000	Value: 22.50				

KM# 56 DOLLAR

7.5600 g., Nickel-Brass, 26 mm. **Ruler:** Elizabeth II **Obv:** Crowned head right **Rev:** Boat with full sails **Edge:** Alternating reeded and plain **Note:** Circulation type.

Date	Mintage	F	VF	XF	Unc	BU
1988	2,000,000	—	—	—	3.00	4.00
1993	15,000	—	—	—	4.00	5.00
Note: In sets only.						
1996		—	—	—	3.00	4.00
1997		—	—	—	3.00	4.00

KM# 56a DOLLAR

9.2000 g., 0.9250 Silver 0.2736 oz. ASW **Ruler:** Elizabeth II **Obv:** Crowned head right **Rev:** Boat with full sails

Date	Mintage	F	VF	XF	Unc	BU
1988 Proof	Est. 3,000	Value: 25.00				
1995 Proof	2,000	Value: 32.00				
Note: In sets only.						

KM# 56b DOLLAR

15.5000 g., 0.9170 Gold 0.4570 oz. AGW **Ruler:** Elizabeth II **Obv:** Crowned head right **Rev:** Train

Date	Mintage	F	VF	XF	Unc	BU
1995 Proof	500	Value: 475				
Note: In sets only.						

KM# 55 DOLLAR

Copper-Nickel, 38.5 mm. **Ruler:** Elizabeth II **Subject:** Railroad **Obv:** Crowned head right **Rev:** Train **Edge:** Reeded

Date	Mintage	F	VF	XF	Unc	BU
1988	2,000,000	—	—	—	7.00	9.00

KM# 55a DOLLAR

28.2800 g., 0.9250 Silver 0.8410 oz. ASW **Ruler:** Elizabeth II **Subject:** Railroad **Obv:** Crowned head right **Rev:** Train

Date	Mintage	F	VF	XF	Unc	BU
1988	5,000	—	—	—	20.00	22.50
1988 Proof	5,000	Value: 25.00				

KM# 61 DOLLAR

Copper-Nickel, 38.5 mm. **Ruler:** Elizabeth II **Subject:** Monarch Conservation Project **Obv:** Crowned head right **Rev:** Monarch Butterflies within flower chain

Date	Mintage	F	VF	XF	Unc	BU
1989	5,000	—	—	—	20.00	22.50

KM# 61a DOLLAR

28.2800 g., 0.9250 Silver 0.8410 oz. ASW **Ruler:** Elizabeth II **Subject:** Monarch Conservation Project **Obv:** Crowned head right **Rev:** Monarch butterflies within flower chain

Date	Mintage	F	VF	XF	Unc	BU
1989	5,000	—	—	—	30.00	32.50
1989 Proof	5,000	Value: 35.00				

KM# 67 DOLLAR

Copper-Nickel, 38.5 mm. **Ruler:** Elizabeth II **Subject:** Queen Mother's 90th birthday **Obv:** Crowned head right **Rev:** Crowned monogram flanked by flowers

Date	Mintage	F	VF	XF	Unc	BU
1990	5,000	—	—	—	5.00	6.50

KM# 67a DOLLAR

28.2800 g., 0.9250 Silver 0.8410 oz. ASW **Ruler:** Elizabeth II **Subject:** Queen Mother's 90th birthday **Obv:** Crowned head right **Rev:** Crowned monogram flanked by flowers

Date	Mintage	F	VF	XF	Unc	BU
1990 Proof	5,000	Value: 45.00				

KM# 78 DOLLAR

Bronze **Ruler:** Elizabeth II **Series:** Olympics **Obv:** Crowned head right **Rev:** Olympic rings

Date	Mintage	F	VF	XF	Unc	BU
1992 Proof	Est. 250	Value: 100				

KM# 85 DOLLAR

31.4700 g., 0.9250 Silver 0.9359 oz. ASW **Ruler:** Elizabeth II **Series:** 1992 Olympics **Rev:** Sailboats

Date	Mintage	F	VF	XF	Unc	BU
ND(1993) Proof	25,000	Value: 30.00				

KM# 91 DOLLAR

Copper-Nickel, 38.5 mm. **Ruler:** Elizabeth II **Subject:** International Senior Games **Rev:** Map divides monograms

Date	Mintage	F	VF	XF	Unc	BU
1996	1,000	—	—	—	25.00	28.00

KM# 127 DOLLAR

28.2800 g., Copper-Nickel, 38.6 mm. **Ruler:** Elizabeth II **Obv:** Crowned head right **Rev:** 1937 Coronation portrait **Edge:** Reeded

Date	Mintage	F	VF	XF	Unc	BU
1996	10,000	—	—	—	10.00	12.00

KM# 127a DOLLAR

28.3700 g., 0.9250 Silver 0.8437 oz. ASW, 38.6 mm.
Ruler: Elizabeth II **Obv:** Crowned head right **Rev:** 1937
Coronation portrait **Edge:** Reeded

Date	Mintage	F	VF	XF	Unc	BU
1996 Proof	30,000	Value: 35.00				

KM# 135 DOLLAR

17.0300 g., Copper-Nickel, 35 mm. **Ruler:** Elizabeth II **Obv:**
Crowned head right **Rev:** Compass rose, map and ship **Edge:** Plain

Date	Mintage	F	VF	XF	Unc	BU
1996	500	—	—	—	12.00	15.00

KM# 94 DOLLAR

Copper-Nickel, 38.5 mm. **Ruler:** Elizabeth II **Subject:** Queen
Elizabeth II's 70th Birthday **Obv:** Crowned head right **Rev:** Horse-
drawn carriage

Date	Mintage	F	VF	XF	Unc	BU
ND(1996)	5,000	—	—	—	12.00	14.00

KM# 105 DOLLAR

28.2800 g., 0.9250 Silver 0.8410 oz. ASW **Ruler:** Elizabeth II
Series: Olympic Games **Obv:** Crowned head right **Rev:** Horse
with rider jumping right

Date	Mintage	F	VF	XF	Unc	BU
1996 Proof	30,000	Value: 30.00				

KM# 95 DOLLAR

Copper-Nickel, 35 mm. **Ruler:** Elizabeth II **Subject:** Wreck of
the Sea Venture **Obv:** Crowned head right **Rev:** Shipwreck from
Bermudan arms **Edge:** Smooth

Date	Mintage	F	VF	XF	Unc	BU
1997	—	—	—	—	12.00	15.00

KM# 119 DOLLAR

28.2800 g., 0.9250 Silver 0.8410 oz. ASW, 39 mm.
Ruler: Elizabeth II **Subject:** World Wildlife Fund - Conserving
Nature **Obv:** Crowned head right **Rev:** Bermuda Rock Skink
(Eumeces longirostris) on rock **Edge:** Reeded

Date	Mintage	F	VF	XF	Unc	BU
1997 Proof	—	Value: 35.00				

KM# 126 DOLLAR

16.0000 g., 0.9250 Silver 0.4758 oz. ASW, 28.3 mm. **Ruler:**
Elizabeth II **Subject:** Queen Mother **Obv:** Crowned head right
Rev: 1937 Coronation portrait **Edge:** Reeded

Date	Mintage	F	VF	XF	Unc	BU
1997 Proof	—	Value: 20.00				

KM# 104 DOLLAR

Copper-Nickel, 35 mm. **Ruler:** Elizabeth II **Obv:** Crowned head
right **Rev:** Sailing ship Deliverance and map

Date	Mintage	F	VF	XF	Unc	BU
1998	—	—	—	—	12.00	15.00

KM# 104a DOLLAR

20.0000 g., 0.9250 Silver 0.5948 oz. ASW, 35 mm.
Ruler: Elizabeth II **Obv:** Crowned head right **Rev:** Ship on map
Edge: Plain

Date	Mintage	F	VF	XF	Unc	BU
1998 Proof	6,500	Value: 50.00				

KM# 125 DOLLAR

28.2800 g., Copper-Nickel, 38.6 mm. **Ruler:** Elizabeth II
Subject: Millennium **Obv:** Crowned head right **Rev:** Radiant sun
behind sailing ship

Date	Mintage	F	VF	XF	Unc	BU
1999-2000	—	—	—	—	22.00	25.00

KM# 111 DOLLAR

Nickel-Brass, 26 mm. **Ruler:** Elizabeth II **Obv:** Head with tiara
right **Rev:** Sailboat

Date	Mintage	F	VF	XF	Unc	BU
1999	12,000	—	—	—	3.00	3.50
1999 Proof	2,500	Value: 22.00				

Date	Mintage	F	VF	XF	Unc	BU
2000	—	—	—	—	3.00	3.50
2000 Proof	—	Value: 22.00				

KM# 117 DOLLAR

28.2800 g., Copper-Nickel, 38.6 mm. **Ruler:** Elizabeth II
Subject: Tall Ships **Obv:** Head with tiara right **Rev:** Three-
masted sailing ship **Edge:** Reeded

Date	Mintage	F	VF	XF	Unc	BU
2000	10,000	—	—	—	12.00	14.00

KM# 117a DOLLAR

28.2800 g., 0.9250 Silver 0.8410 oz. ASW, 38.6 mm.
Ruler: Elizabeth II **Subject:** Tall Ships **Obv:** Head with tiara right
Rev: Three-masted sailing ship **Edge:** Reeded

Date	Mintage	F	VF	XF	Unc	BU
2000 Proof	10,000	Value: 100				

KM# 122 DOLLAR

28.3000 g., 0.9250 Silver 0.8416 oz. ASW, 38.5 mm.
Ruler: Elizabeth II **Subject:** Queen Mother **Obv:** Head with tiara
right **Rev:** 1937 Coronation portrait **Edge:** Reeded

Date	Mintage	F	VF	XF	Unc	BU
2000 Proof	—	Value: 40.00				

KM# 64 2 DOLLARS

28.2800 g., 0.9250 Silver 0.8410 oz. ASW **Ruler:** Elizabeth II
Obv: Crowned head right **Rev:** Cicada insects

Date	Mintage	F	VF	XF	Unc	BU
1990 Proof	3,000	Value: 35.00				

KM# 65   2 DOLLARS
28.2800 g., 0.9250 Silver 0.8410 oz. ASW **Ruler:** Elizabeth II
Subject: Wildlife **Obv:** Crowned head right **Rev:** Tree frog

Date	Mintage	F	VF	XF	Unc	BU
1990 Proof	3,000				Value: 35.00	

KM# 72   2 DOLLARS
28.2800 g., 0.9250 Silver 0.8410 oz. ASW **Ruler:** Elizabeth II
Obv: Crowned head right **Rev:** Cedar tree

Date	Mintage	F	VF	XF	Unc	BU
1992 Proof	2,500				Value: 30.00	

KM# 86   2 DOLLARS
27.2800 g., 0.9250 Silver 0.8113 oz. ASW **Ruler:** Elizabeth II
Subject: Royal visit **Obv:** Crowned head right **Rev:** Map divides
conjoined heads of royal couple and royal emblem

Date	Mintage	F	VF	XF	Unc	BU
1994 Proof	10,000				Value: 35.00	

KM# 81   2 DOLLARS
23.0000 g., 0.9250 Silver 0.6840 oz. ASW **Ruler:** Elizabeth II
Subject: 200 Years of Bermudan Coinage

Date	Mintage	F	VF	XF	Unc	BU
1993 Proof	5,000				Value: 28.00	

KM# 68   2 DOLLARS
28.2800 g., 0.9250 Silver 0.8410 oz. ASW **Ruler:** Elizabeth II
Obv: Crowned head right **Rev:** Yellow-crowned night heron

Date	Mintage	F	VF	XF	Unc	BU
1991 Proof	3,000				Value: 35.00	

KM# 83   2 DOLLARS
28.2800 g., 0.9250 Silver 0.8410 oz. ASW **Ruler:** Elizabeth II
Obv: Crowned head right **Rev:** Humpback whale leaping right

Date	Mintage	F	VF	XF	Unc	BU
1993 Proof	2,000				Value: 35.00	

KM# 87   2 DOLLARS
28.2800 g., 0.9250 Silver 0.8410 oz. ASW **Ruler:** Elizabeth II
Obv: Crowned head right **Rev:** Long-snouted seahorse

Date	Mintage	F	VF	XF	Unc	BU
1994 Proof	1,500				Value: 40.00	

KM# 69   2 DOLLARS
28.2800 g., 0.9250 Silver 0.8410 oz. ASW **Ruler:** Elizabeth II
Obv: Crowned head right **Rev:** Spiny lobster

Date	Mintage	F	VF	XF	Unc	BU
1991 Proof	3,000				Value: 30.00	

KM# 84   2 DOLLARS
28.2800 g., 0.9250 Silver 0.8410 oz. ASW **Ruler:** Elizabeth II
Obv: Crowned head right **Rev:** White-tailed tropicbird

Date	Mintage	F	VF	XF	Unc	BU
1993 Proof	2,000				Value: 30.00	

KM# 88   2 DOLLARS
28.2800 g., 0.9250 Silver 0.8410 oz. ASW **Ruler:** Elizabeth II
Obv: Crowned head right **Rev:** Lightbourn's fusinus (seashell)

Date	Mintage	F	VF	XF	Unc	BU
1994 Proof	1,500				Value: 40.00	

KM# 71   2 DOLLARS
28.2800 g., 0.9250 Silver 0.8410 oz. ASW **Ruler:** Elizabeth II
Obv: Crowned head right **Rev:** Eastern Bluebird feeding nestling

Date	Mintage	F	VF	XF	Unc	BU
1992 Proof	2,500				Value: 35.00	

KM# 89   2 DOLLARS
28.2800 g., 0.9250 Silver 0.8410 oz. ASW **Ruler:** Elizabeth II
Subject: City of Hamilton's 200th Anniversary **Obv:** Crowned
head right **Rev:** Ship at dock within circle

Date	Mintage	F	VF	XF	Unc	BU
1993 Proof	250				Value: 70.00	

KM# 123   2 DOLLARS
28.2000 g., 0.9250 Silver 0.8386 oz. ASW, 38.6 mm.
Ruler: Elizabeth II **Subject:** Queen's 70th Birthday
Obv: Crowned head right **Rev:** Carriage and tree **Edge:** Reeded

Date	Mintage	F	VF	XF	Unc	BU
1996 Proof	12,500				Value: 35.00	

KM# 136   2 DOLLARS
28.1400 g., 0.9250 Silver 0.8368 oz. ASW, 38.6 mm.
Ruler: Elizabeth II **Subject:** Town of St. George 200th
Anniversary **Obv:** Crowned head right **Rev:** St. George slaying
the dragon **Edge:** Reeded

Date	Mintage	F	VF	XF	Unc	BU
1997 Proof	250	Value: 150				

KM# 121   2 DOLLARS
28.1300 g., 0.9250 Silver 0.8365 oz. ASW, 38.5 mm.
Ruler: Elizabeth II **Subject:** Queen's Golden Wedding
Anniversary **Obv:** Crowned head right **Rev:** Royal couple
descending stairs with gold insert shield at right **Edge:** Reeded

Date	Mintage	F	VF	XF	Unc	BU
ND(1997) Proof	—	Value: 45.00				

KM# 116   2 DOLLARS
28.2800 g., 0.9250 Silver 0.8410 oz. ASW, 38.6 mm.
Ruler: Elizabeth II **Subject:** Millennium **Obv:** Crowned head right
Rev: Radiant gilt sun behind sailing ship dividing dates 1999-
2000 above map **Edge:** Plain

Date	Mintage	F	VF	XF	Unc	BU
ND(2000) Proof	30,000	Value: 55.00				

KM# 92   3 DOLLARS
20.0000 g., 0.9250 Silver 0.5948 oz. ASW **Ruler:** Elizabeth II
Subject: Bermuda Triangle **Obv:** Crowned head right **Rev:** Map,
compass, and capsizing ship

Date	Mintage	F	VF	XF	Unc	BU
1996 Proof	5,000	Value: 55.00				

KM# 99   3 DOLLARS
20.2500 g., 0.9250 Silver 0.6022 oz. ASW **Ruler:** Elizabeth II
Subject: Wreck of the Sea Venture **Obv:** Crowned head right
Rev: Shipwreck scene

Date	Mintage	F	VF	XF	Unc	BU
1997 Proof	6,000	Value: 50.00				

KM# 106   3 DOLLARS
20.0000 g., 0.9250 Silver 0.5948 oz. ASW **Ruler:** Elizabeth II
Obv: Crowned head right **Rev:** Sailing ship Deliverance and map

Date	Mintage	F	VF	XF	Unc	BU
1998 Proof	6,500	Value: 50.00				

KM# 106a   3 DOLLARS
31.4890 g., 0.9990 Gold 1.0113 oz. AGW, 35 mm.
Ruler: Elizabeth II **Obv:** Crowned head right **Rev:** Ship on map
Edge: Plain

Date	Mintage	F	VF	XF	Unc	BU
1998	—	—	—	—	—	1,400

KM# 31   5 DOLLARS
Nickel-Brass **Ruler:** Elizabeth II **Obv:** Young bust right
Rev: Onion superimposed over map

Date	Mintage	F	VF	XF	Unc	BU
1983	100,000	—	—	—	6.00	8.00
1983 Proof	6,474	Value: 10.00				

KM# 51   5 DOLLARS
Brass **Ruler:** Elizabeth II **Obv:** Young bust right **Rev:** Onion
superimposed over Bermuda map

Date	Mintage	F	VF	XF	Unc	BU
1986 Proof	2,500	Value: 12.50				

KM# 54   5 DOLLARS
155.5150 g., 0.9990 Silver 4.9947 oz. ASW, 65 mm.
Ruler: Elizabeth II **Subject:** Sea Venture Wreck **Obv:** Crowned
head right **Rev:** Sailing ship **Note:** Illustration reduced.

Date	Mintage	F	VF	XF	Unc	BU
1987 Proof	6,800	Value: 125				

KM# 62   5 DOLLARS
155.5150 g., 0.9990 Silver 4.9947 oz. ASW, 65 mm.
Ruler: Elizabeth II **Subject:** San Antonio **Obv:** Crowned head
right **Rev:** Sailing ship **Note:** Illustration reduced.

Date	Mintage	F	VF	XF	Unc	BU
1988 Proof	1,500	Value: 145				

KM# 79   5 DOLLARS
155.5150 g., 0.9990 Silver 4.9947 oz. ASW, 65 mm.
Ruler: Elizabeth II **Series:** Olympics **Obv:** Crowned head right
Rev: Various events depicted within Olympic rings
Note: Illustration reduced.

Date	Mintage	F	VF	XF	Unc	BU
1992 Proof	Est. 1,250	Value: 150				

KM# 90   5 DOLLARS
56.5600 g., 0.9250 Silver 1.6820 oz. ASW **Ruler:** Elizabeth II
Subject: 375th Anniversary of Bermudan Parliament

Date	Mintage	F	VF	XF	Unc	BU
1995 Proof	375	Value: 130				

KM# 96   9 DOLLARS
155.5175 g., 0.9990 Silver 4.9948 oz. ASW, 65.27 mm.
Ruler: Elizabeth II **Subject:** Bermuda Triangle **Obv:** Crowned
head right **Rev:** Map of island, compass, early sailing ship listing
Edge: Plain **Note:** Illustration reduced

Date	Mintage	F	VF	XF	Unc	BU
1996 Proof	Est. 1,000	Value: 200				

KM# 100   9 DOLLARS
155.5175 g., 0.9990 Silver 4.9948 oz. ASW, 65.27 mm.
Ruler: Elizabeth II **Subject:** Wreck of the Sea Venture
Obv: Crowned head right **Rev:** Shipwreck scene **Edge:** Plain

Date	Mintage	F	VF	XF	Unc	BU
1997 Proof	1,000	Value: 200				

KM# 112 9 DOLLARS
155.5200 g., 0.9990 Silver 4.9949 oz. ASW, 65.27 mm.
Ruler: Elizabeth II **Subject:** Bermuda Triangle **Obv:** Crowned head right **Rev:** Sailing ship Deliverance, map in background **Edge:** Plain **Note:** Illustration reduced.

Date	Mintage	F	VF	XF	Unc	BU
1998 Proof	1,000	Value: 200				

KM# 57 10 DOLLARS
3.1340 g., 0.9990 Gold 0.1007 oz. AGW **Ruler:** Elizabeth II **Subject:** Hogge money **Obv:** Crowned head right **Rev:** Wild pig

Date	Mintage	F	VF	XF	Unc	BU
1989 Proof	500	Value: 120				

KM# 74 10 DOLLARS
3.1340 g., 0.9990 Gold 0.1007 oz. AGW **Ruler:** Elizabeth II **Subject:** Hogge money **Obv:** Crowned head right **Rev:** Ship circle

Date	Mintage	F	VF	XF	Unc	BU
1990 Proof	500	Value: 120				

KM# 66 10 DOLLARS
3.1340 g., 0.9990 Gold 0.1007 oz. AGW **Ruler:** Elizabeth II **Subject:** Wildlife **Obv:** Crowned head right **Rev:** Tree frog

Date	Mintage	F	VF	XF	Unc	BU
1990 Proof	500	Value: 110				

KM# 70 10 DOLLARS
3.1340 g., 0.9990 Gold 0.1007 oz. AGW **Ruler:** Elizabeth II **Obv:** Crowned head right **Rev:** Yellow-crowned night heron

Date	Mintage	F	VF	XF	Unc	BU
1991	2,500	—	—	—	110	115

KM# 73 10 DOLLARS
3.1340 g., 0.9990 Gold 0.1007 oz. AGW **Ruler:** Elizabeth II **Obv:** Crowned head right **Rev:** Eastern Bluebird feeding nestling

Date	Mintage	F	VF	XF	Unc	BU
1992	2,500	—	—	—	110	115

KM# 132 10 DOLLARS
3.1340 g., 0.9990 Gold 0.1007 oz. AGW, 17 mm.
Ruler: Elizabeth II **Obv:** Crowned head right **Rev:** White-tailed Tropic Bird **Edge:** Reeded

Date	Mintage	F	VF	XF	Unc	BU
1993	1,501	—	—	—	110	115

KM# 133 10 DOLLARS
3.1340 g., 0.9990 Gold 0.1007 oz. AGW, 17 mm. **Ruler:** Elizabeth II **Obv:** Crowned head right **Rev:** Sea Horse **Edge:** Reeded

Date	Mintage	F	VF	XF	Unc	BU
1994	1,000	—	—	—	110	115

KM# 138 10 DOLLARS
7.7760 g., 0.5830 Gold Alloyed with .417 Silver 0.1457 oz. AGW, 25 mm. **Ruler:** Elizabeth II **Obv:** Crowned head right **Rev:** 1937 Coronation portrait **Edge:** Reeded

Date	Mintage	F	VF	XF	Unc	BU
1996 Proof	5,000	Value: 175				

KM# 118 15 DOLLARS
15.9700 g., 0.9990 Gold 0.5129 oz. AGW, 28.4 mm.
Ruler: Elizabeth II **Subject:** Tall Ships **Obv:** Head with tiara right **Rev:** Three-masted sailing ship **Edge:** Reeded

Date	Mintage	F	VF	XF	Unc	BU
2000 Proof	1,500	Value: 500				

KM# 21 20 DOLLARS
7.9881 g., 0.9170 Gold 0.2355 oz. AGW **Ruler:** Elizabeth II **Obv:** Young bust right **Rev:** Cahow in flight left

Date	Mintage	F	VF	XF	Unc	BU
1970 Proof	1,000	Value: 265				

KM# 137 20 DOLLARS
7.9800 g., 0.9990 Gold 0.2563 oz. AGW, 22 mm.
Ruler: Elizabeth II **Obv:** Head with tiara right **Rev:** New Millennium dawning over a ship at sea **Edge:** Plain

Date	Mintage	F	VF	XF	Unc	BU
2000 Proof	2,000	Value: 250				

KM# 23 25 DOLLARS
Copper-Nickel **Ruler:** Elizabeth II **Subject:** Royal Visit **Obv:** Young bust right **Rev:** Scepter divides royal monograms **Edge:** Reeded

Date	Mintage	F	VF	XF	Unc	BU
1975FM (M)	100	—	—	—	45.00	—
1975FM (U)	1,193	—	—	—	60.00	—

KM# 23a 25 DOLLARS
48.7000 g., 0.9250 Silver 1.4483 oz. ASW **Ruler:** Elizabeth II **Subject:** Royal Visit **Obv:** Young bust right **Rev:** Scepter divides royal monograms **Edge:** Reeded

Date	Mintage	F	VF	XF	Unc	BU
1975FM (P) Proof	14,708	Value: 82.50				

KM# 25 25 DOLLARS
54.7500 g., 0.9250 Silver 1.6282 oz. ASW **Ruler:** Elizabeth II **Subject:** Queen's Silver Jubilee **Obv:** Young bust right **Rev:** Sailing ship

Date	Mintage	F	VF	XF	Unc	BU
1977	6,225	—	—	—	40.00	—
1977 Proof	5,613	Value: 40.00				

Date	Mintage	F	VF	XF	Unc	BU
1977	Est. 2,312	—	—	—	80.00	—

Note: Struck at the Royal Canadian Mint

| 1977 Proof | Est. 1,887 | Value: 100 | | | | |

Note: Struck at the Royal Canadian Mint

KM# 53 25 DOLLARS
31.1000 g., 0.9990 Palladium 0.9988 oz. **Ruler:** Elizabeth II **Subject:** Sea Venture **Obv:** Crowned head right **Rev:** Ship

Date	Mintage	F	VF	XF	Unc	BU
1987 Proof	15,800	Value: 475				

KM# 63 25 DOLLARS
31.1000 g., 0.9990 Palladium 0.9988 oz. **Ruler:** Elizabeth II **Subject:** Shipwreck of San Antonio **Obv:** Crowned head right **Rev:** Capsizing ship

Date	Mintage	F	VF	XF	Unc	BU
1988 Proof	2,000	Value: 500				

KM# 58 25 DOLLARS
7.8140 g., 0.9990 Gold 0.2510 oz. AGW **Ruler:** Elizabeth II **Subject:** Hogge Money **Obv:** Crowned head right **Rev:** Ship

Date	Mintage	F	VF	XF	Unc	BU
1989 Proof	500	Value: 250				

KM# 75 25 DOLLARS
7.8140 g., 0.9990 Gold 0.2510 oz. AGW **Ruler:** Elizabeth II **Subject:** Hogge Money **Obv:** Crowned head right **Rev:** Wild pig

Date	Mintage	F	VF	XF	Unc	BU
1990 Proof	500	Value: 250				

KM# 97 30 DOLLARS
15.5518 g., 0.9990 Gold 0.4995 oz. AGW **Ruler:** Elizabeth II **Subject:** Bermuda Triangle **Obv:** Crowned head right **Rev:** Map, compass, capsizing ship

Date	Mintage	F	VF	XF	Unc	BU
1996 Proof	Est. 1,500	Value: 500				

KM# 101 30 DOLLARS
15.5518 g., 0.9990 Gold 0.4995 oz. AGW **Ruler:** Elizabeth II **Subject:** Wreck of the Sea Venture **Obv:** Crowned head right **Rev:** Shipwreck scene

Date	Mintage	F	VF	XF	Unc	BU
1997 Proof	1,500	Value: 500				

KM# 113 30 DOLLARS
15.5500 g., 0.9990 Gold 0.4994 oz. AGW **Ruler:** Elizabeth II **Obv:** Crowned head right **Rev:** Sailing ship Deliverance and map

Date	Mintage	F	VF	XF	Unc	BU
1998 Proof	1,500	Value: 500				

KM# 26 50 DOLLARS
4.0500 g., 0.9000 Gold 0.1172 oz. AGW **Ruler:** Elizabeth II **Subject:** Queen's Silver Jubilee **Obv:** Young bust right **Rev:** Sailboat

Date	Mintage	F	VF	XF	Unc	BU
1977Chi	3,950	—	—	—	120	—
1977Chi Proof	4,070	Value: 130				

Date	Mintage	F	VF	XF	Unc	BU
1977	Est. 520	—	—	—	235	—

Note: Struck at the Royal Canadian Mint

Date	Mintage					
1977 Proof	Est. 580	Value: 240				

Note: Struck at the Royal Canadian Mint

KM# 59 50 DOLLARS
15.6080 g., 0.9990 Gold 0.5013 oz. AGW **Ruler:** Elizabeth II
Subject: Hogge Money **Obv:** Crowned head right **Rev:** Wild pig

Date	Mintage	F	VF	XF	Unc	BU
1989 Proof	500	Value: 485				

KM# 76 50 DOLLARS
15.6080 g., 0.9990 Gold 0.5013 oz. AGW **Ruler:** Elizabeth II
Subject: Hogge Money **Obv:** Crowned head right **Rev:** Ship

Date	Mintage	F	VF	XF	Unc	BU
1990 Proof	500	Value: 485				

KM# 93 60 DOLLARS
31.4890 g., 0.9990 Gold 1.0113 oz. AGW **Ruler:** Elizabeth II
Subject: Bermuda Triangle **Obv:** Crowned head right **Rev:** Map, compass and capsizing ship

Date	Mintage	F	VF	XF	Unc	BU
1996 Proof	1,500	Value: 1,000				

KM# 102 60 DOLLARS
31.4890 g., 0.9990 Gold 1.0113 oz. AGW **Ruler:** Elizabeth II
Subject: Wreck of the Sea Venture **Obv:** Crowned head right
Rev: Shipwreck scene

Date	Mintage	F	VF	XF	Unc	BU
1997 Proof	1,500	Value: 1,000				

KM# 114 60 DOLLARS
31.4800 g., 0.9990 Gold 1.0111 oz. AGW **Ruler:** Elizabeth II
Obv: Crowned head right **Rev:** Sailing ship Deliverance and map

Date	Mintage	F	VF	XF	Unc	BU
1998 Proof	1,500	Value: 1,000				

KM# 24 100 DOLLARS
7.0300 g., 0.9000 Gold 0.2034 oz. AGW **Ruler:** Elizabeth II
Subject: Royal Visit **Obv:** Young bust right **Rev:** Sceptre divides royal emblems

Date	Mintage	F	VF	XF	Unc	BU
1975FM (M) Trial pieces	25	—	—	—	350	—
1975FM (M)	18,852	—	—	—	210	—
1975FM (M) Proof	27,270	Value: 220				

KM# 27 100 DOLLARS
8.1000 g., 0.9000 Gold 0.2344 oz. AGW **Ruler:** Elizabeth II
Subject: Queen's Silver Jubilee **Obv:** Young bust right
Rev: Sailing ship Deliverance

Date	Mintage	F	VF	XF	Unc	BU
1977Chi	6,225	—	—	—	220	—
1977Chi Proof	5,613	Value: 235				
1977	Est. 2,312	—	—	—	250	—

Note: Struck at the Royal Canadian Mint

Date	Mintage					
1977 Proof	Est. 1,887	Value: 275				

Note: Struck at the Royal Canadian Mint

KM# 60 100 DOLLARS
31.2100 g., 0.9990 Gold 1.0024 oz. AGW **Ruler:** Elizabeth II
Subject: Hogge Money **Obv:** Crowned head right **Rev:** Ship

Date	Mintage	F	VF	XF	Unc	BU
1989 Proof	500	Value: 975				

KM# 77 100 DOLLARS
31.2100 g., 0.9990 Gold 1.0024 oz. AGW **Ruler:** Elizabeth II
Subject: Hogge Money **Obv:** Crowned head right **Rev:** Wild pig

Date	Mintage	F	VF	XF	Unc	BU
1990 Proof	500	Value: 975				

KM# 80 100 DOLLARS
47.5400 g., 0.9170 Gold 1.4015 oz. AGW **Ruler:** Elizabeth II
Series: Olympics **Subject:** Crowned head right **Rev:** Olympic rings

Date	Mintage	F	VF	XF	Unc	BU
1992 Proof	Est. 250	Value: 1,350				

KM# 134 100 DOLLARS
47.5400 g., 0.9170 Gold 1.4015 oz. AGW, 38.6 mm.
Ruler: Elizabeth II **Subject:** Royal Visit **Obv:** Crowned head right
Rev: Royal couple above map **Edge:** Reeded

Date	Mintage	F	VF	XF	Unc	BU
1994 Proof	250	Value: 1,350				

KM# 98 180 DOLLARS
155.5175 g., 0.9990 Gold 4.9948 oz. AGW **Ruler:** Elizabeth II
Subject: Bermuda Triangle **Obv:** Crowned head right **Rev:** Map, compass, capsizing ship

Date	Mintage	F	VF	XF	Unc	BU
1996 Proof	Est. 1,500	Value: 5,000				

KM# 103 180 DOLLARS
155.5175 g., 0.9990 Gold 4.9948 oz. AGW **Ruler:** Elizabeth II
Subject: Wreck of the Sea Venture **Obv:** Crowned head right
Rev: Shipwreck scene

Date	Mintage	F	VF	XF	Unc	BU
1997 Proof	99	Value: 5,500				

KM# 115 180 DOLLARS
155.5200 g., 0.9990 Gold 4.9949 oz. AGW **Ruler:** Elizabeth II
Obv: Crowned head right **Rev:** Sailing ship Deliverance and map

Date	Mintage	F	VF	XF	Unc	BU
1998 Proof	99	Value: 5,500				

KM# 82 200 DOLLARS
28.5000 g., 0.9990 Gold 0.9153 oz. AGW **Ruler:** Elizabeth II
Subject: 200 Years - Bermudan Coinage **Obv:** Crowned head right **Rev:** Sailing ship

Date	Mintage	F	VF	XF	Unc	BU
1993 Proof	200	Value: 925				

KM# 29 250 DOLLARS
15.9760 g., 0.9170 Gold 0.4710 oz. AGW **Ruler:** Elizabeth II
Subject: Wedding of Prince Charles and Lady Diana
Obv: Crowned head right **Rev:** Jugate heads of the royal couple right

Date	Mintage	F	VF	XF	Unc	BU
1981	217	—	—	—	500	550
1981 Proof	790	Value: 450				

PIEFORTS

KM#	Date	Mintage	Identification	Mkt Val
P1	1981	690	250 Dollars. 31.9520 g. KM29.	850
P2	1988	500	Dollar 250 Sa. 16.00 g. KM59a	185

MINT SETS

KM#	Date	Mintage	Identification	Issue Price	Mkt Val
MS1	1970 (5)	360,000	KM15-19	3.25	4.00
MS2	1977Chi (3)	—	KM25-27	175	335
MSA2	1977 (3)	—	KM25-27	—	650
MS3	1977Chi (2)	—	KM26-27	150	300
MS4	1984 (11)	3,350	KM32-42	24.95	60.00
MS5	1993 (5)	15,000	KM44b, 45-47, 56	—	10.00
MS7	1999 (5)	5,000	KM107-111	15.00	20.00

PROOF SETS

KM#	Date	Mintage	Identification	Issue Price	Mkt Val
PS1	1970 (6)	10,000	KM15-20	24.00	20.00
PS2	1970 (5)	1,000	KM15-21	216	280
PS3	1977Chi (3)	—	KM25-27	245	350
PSA3	1977 (3)	—	KM25-27	—	675
PS4	1977Chi (2)	—	KM26-27	210	325
PS5	1981 (3)	500	KM28a, 29, (P1), numbered set	1,500	1,350
PS6	1983 (7)	6,474	KM15-19, 30, 31	30.00	30.00
PS7	1984 (11)	1,750	KM32a-42a	250	185
PS8	1986 (7)	2,500	KM44-48, 50-51	50.00	50.00
PS10	1989 (5)	500	KM57-60	1,495	1,700
PS11	1990 (4)	500	KM74-77	—	1,700
PS12	1992 (3)	250	KM78-80	1,075	1,500
PS13	1992 (2)	500	KM71-72	75.00	80.00
PS14	1995 (5)	500	KM44d, 45b-47b, 56b	1,100	1,350
PSA14	1995 (5)	2,000	KM#44c, 45a, 46a, 47a, 56a	—	75.00
PS15	1996 (2)	1,000	KM96-97	—	625
PS16	1999 (5)	2,500	KM107-111	50.00	45.00

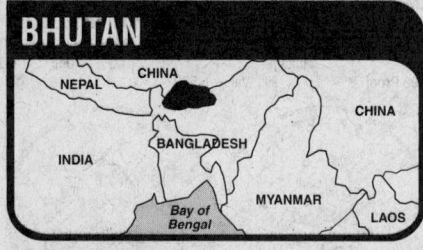

BHUTAN

The Kingdom of Bhutan, a landlocked Himalayan country bordered by Tibet and India, has an area of 18,150 sq. mi. (47,000 sq. km.) and a population of *2.03 million. Capital: Thimphu. Virtually the entire population is engaged in agricultural and pastoral activities. Rice, wheat, barley, and yak butter are produced in sufficient quantity to make the country self-sufficient in food. The economy of Bhutan is primitive and many transactions are conducted on a barter basis.

Bhutan's early history is obscure, but is thought to have resembled that of rural medieval Europe. The country was conquered by Tibet in the 9th century, and a dual temporal and spiritual rule developed which operated until the mid-19th century, when the southern part of the country was occupied by the British and annexed to British India. Bhutan was established as a hereditary monarchy in 1907, and in 1910 agreed to British control of its external affairs. In 1949, India and Bhutan concluded a treaty whereby India assumed Britain's role in subsidizing Bhutan and guiding its foreign affairs. In 1971 Bhutan became a full member of the United Nations.

RULERS
Ugyen Wangchuk, 1907-1926
Jigme Wangchuk, 1926-1952
Jigme Dorji Wangchuk, 1952-1972
Jigme Singye Wangchuk, 1972-

CYCLICAL DATES

Earth-Dragon	Iron-Tiger
KM# 23, 24, 25 (1928)	KM# 26, 28 (1950)

OBVERSE LEGENDS

Normal	Modified

KINGDOM

HAMMERED COINAGE
Period III, 1835-1910AD

'Sa' ཨ

KM# A7 1/2 RUPEE (Deb)
Copper Or Brass **Obv:** Small "Sa" at upper right
Date	Mintage	Good	VG	F	VF	XF
ND(1835-1910)	—	1.00	2.25	4.50	7.50	—

'Sa' ཨ

KM# 7.1 1/2 RUPEE (Deb)
Copper Or Brass **Obv:** "Sa" at lower left
Date	Mintage	Good	VG	F	VF	XF
ND(1835-1910)	—	1.00	1.50	3.00	6.00	—

KM# 7.1a 1/2 RUPEE (Deb)
1.8500 g., Copper Or Brass **Obv. Insc.:** "Sa" at lower left **Note:** Small flan.
Date	Mintage	Good	VG	F	VF	XF
ND(1835-1910)	—	1.00	1.50	3.00	6.00	—

KM# 7.2 1/2 RUPEE (Deb)
Copper Or Brass **Obv:** Dots added
Date	Mintage	Good	VG	F	VF	XF
ND(1835-1910)	—	1.00	1.50	3.00	6.00	—

KM# 7.3 1/2 RUPEE (Deb)
Copper Or Brass **Obv:** "Sa" at upper right
Date	Mintage	Good	VG	F	VF	XF
ND(1835-1910)	—	1.00	1.50	3.00	6.00	—

KM# 7.4 1/2 RUPEE (Deb)
Copper Or Brass **Obv:** Large "Sa" below 5 pellets
Date	Mintage	Good	VG	F	VF	XF
ND(1835-1910)	—	1.00	1.50	3.00	6.00	—

卐

KM# 7.5 1/2 RUPEE (Deb)
Copper Or Brass **Obv:** Large "Sa" below swastika
Date	Mintage	Good	VG	F	VF	XF
ND(1835-1910)	—	1.00	1.50	3.00	6.00	—

🌲

KM# 7.6 1/2 RUPEE (Deb)
Copper Or Brass **Obv:** Branch
Date	Mintage	Good	VG	F	VF	XF
ND(1835-1910)	—	1.00	1.50	3.00	6.00	—

KM# A8.1 1/2 RUPEE (Deb)
Copper Or Brass **Obv. Insc.:** Retrograde **Rev. Insc.:** Retrograde
Date	Mintage	Good	VG	F	VF	XF
ND(1835-1910)	—	1.00	2.00	3.50	7.00	—

KM# A8.2 1/2 RUPEE (Deb)
Copper Or Brass **Rev:** Dots added
Date	Mintage	Good	VG	F	VF	XF
ND(1835-1910)	—	1.00	1.50	3.00	6.00	—

KM# A8.3 1/2 RUPEE (Deb)
Copper Or Brass **Rev:** Four pellets
Date	Mintage	Good	VG	F	VF	XF
ND(1835-1910)	—	1.00	1.50	3.00	6.00	—

KM# A8.4 1/2 RUPEE (Deb)
Copper Or Brass **Obv:** Two dots above crescent
Date	Mintage	Good	VG	F	VF	XF
ND(1835-1910)	—	1.00	1.50	3.00	6.00	—

KM# 8.1 1/2 RUPEE (Deb)
Copper Or Brass **Obv:** X above crescent
Date	Mintage	Good	VG	F	VF	XF
ND(1835-1910)	—	1.00	1.50	3.00	6.00	—

KM# 8.2 1/2 RUPEE (Deb)
Copper Or Brass **Obv:** One or two dots in center inscription
Date	Mintage	Good	VG	F	VF	XF
ND(1835-1910)	—	0.50	1.00	2.00	4.00	—

☾

KM# 8.3 1/2 RUPEE (Deb)
Copper Or Brass **Obv:** Crescent above "+" at left
Date	Mintage	Good	VG	F	VF	XF
ND(1835-1910)	—	1.00	2.00	3.50	7.00	—

KM# 8.4 1/2 RUPEE (Deb)
Copper Or Brass **Obv:** "+" above crescent
Date	Mintage	Good	VG	F	VF	XF
ND(1835-1910)	—	1.00	2.00	3.50	7.00	—

☾
✕

KM# 8.6 1/2 RUPEE (Deb)
Copper Or Brass **Obv:** Low "x" at left
Date	Mintage	Good	VG	F	VF	XF
ND(1835-1910)	—	1.00	2.00	3.50	7.00	—

☾
✕

KM# 8.7 1/2 RUPEE (Deb)
Copper Or Brass **Obv:** Three pellets at left, low "x" at right
Date	Mintage	Good	VG	F	VF	XF
ND(1835-1910)	—	1.00	2.00	3.50	7.00	—

KM# 8.8 1/2 RUPEE (Deb)
Copper Or Brass **Obv:** "Hooks" added **Rev:** Four pellets
Date	Mintage	Good	VG	F	VF	XF
ND(1835-1910)	—	1.00	2.00	3.50	7.00	—

KM# 8.9 1/2 RUPEE (Deb)
Copper Or Brass **Obv:** Two rows of pellets, high "x" at right
Date	Mintage	Good	VG	F	VF	XF
ND(1835-1910)	—	1.00	2.00	3.50	7.00	—

KM# 9.1 1/2 RUPEE (Deb)
Copper Or Brass **Obv:** Swastika

Date	Mintage	Good	VG	F	VF	XF
ND(1835-1910)	—	2.00	3.00	5.00	9.00	—

KM# 9.2 1/2 RUPEE (Deb)
Copper Or Brass **Obv:** Swastika reversed

Date	Mintage	Good	VG	F	VF	XF
ND(1835-1910)	—	2.00	3.00	5.00	9.00	—

KM# 10 1/2 RUPEE (Deb)
Copper Or Brass **Obv:** "Wang"

Date	Mintage	Good	VG	F	VF	XF
ND(1835-1910)	—	3.00	5.00	8.00	12.00	—

KM# 11 1/2 RUPEE (Deb)
Copper Or Brass **Obv:** "Sa dar"

Date	Mintage	Good	VG	F	VF	XF
ND(1835-1910)	—	3.00	5.00	8.00	12.00	—

KM# 11a 1/2 RUPEE (Deb)
Copper Or Brass

Date	Mintage	Good	VG	F	VF	XF
ND(1835-1910)	—	3.00	5.00	8.00	12.00	—

KM# 11b 1/2 RUPEE (Deb)
Copper Or Brass

Date	Mintage	Good	VG	F	VF	XF
ND(1835-1910)	—	3.00	5.00	8.00	12.00	—

KM# 12 1/2 RUPEE (Deb)
Copper Or Brass **Obv:** Rosette **Rev:** Swastika

Date	Mintage	Good	VG	F	VF	XF
ND(1835-1910)	—	3.00	5.00	8.00	12.00	—

KM# 13 1/2 RUPEE (Deb)
Copper Or Brass **Obv:** Rosette **Rev:** Two fish

Date	Mintage	Good	VG	F	VF	XF
ND(1835-1910)	—	3.00	5.00	8.00	12.00	—

KM# 14 1/2 RUPEE (Deb)
Copper Or Brass **Rev:** Two fish **Note:** Varieties exist.

Date	Mintage	Good	VG	F	VF	XF
ND(1835-1910)	—	2.00	3.00	5.00	9.00	—

KM# 15 1/2 RUPEE (Deb)
Copper Or Brass **Obv:** Knot **Rev:** Conch shell

Date	Mintage	Good	VG	F	VF	XF
ND(1835-1910)	—	1.50	2.50	4.00	8.00	—

HAMMERED COINAGE
Period IV, 1910-1927AD

KM# 16 1/2 RUPEE (Deb)
Copper **Obv:** Buddh. symbols **Rev:** Buddh. symbols

Date	Mintage	Good	VG	F	VF	XF
ND(1910-27)	—	—	—	—	15.00	20.00

KM# 17 1/2 RUPEE (Deb)
Silver **Obv:** Syllable "ndra" and Buddh. symbols **Rev:** Buddh. symbols

Date	Mintage	Good	VG	F	VF	XF
ND(1910-27)	—	10.00	15.00	25.00	55.00	—

KM# 17a 1/2 RUPEE (Deb)
Copper **Obv:** Obverse is similar to KM#17 **Rev:** Symbols on reverse are arranged differently **Note:** Varieties exist with and without syllable "ndra".

Date	Mintage	Good	VG	F	VF	XF
ND(1910-1927)	—	2.00	3.50	15.00	20.00	—

KM# 18 1/2 RUPEE (Deb)
Silver **Obv:** Syllable "ndra" and Buddh. symbols **Rev:** Swastika in square buddh. symbols

Date	Mintage	Good	VG	F	VF	XF
ND(1910-27)	—	10.00	15.00	25.00	55.00	—

KM# 18a 1/2 RUPEE (Deb)
Copper **Note:** Obverse is similar to KM#18, but symbols on reverse are arranged differently.

Date	Mintage	Good	VG	F	VF	XF
ND(1910-1927)	—	2.00	3.50	5.00	9.00	—

KM# 18b 1/2 RUPEE (Deb)
Brass **Note:** Different obverse than KM#18, syllable "ndra" is retrograd

Date	Mintage	Good	VG	F	VF	XF
ND(1910-1927)	—	2.00	3.50	5.00	9.00	—

KM# 19 1/2 RUPEE (Deb)
Silver **Obv:** Buddh. symbols **Rev:** Buddh. symbols

Date	Mintage	Good	VG	F	VF	XF
ND(1910-27)	—	10.00	15.00	25.00	55.00	—

KM# 19a 1/2 RUPEE (Deb)
Copper **Note:** Obverse is similar to KM#19, but symbols on reverse are arranged differently.

Date	Mintage	Good	VG	F	VF	XF
ND(1910-1927)	—	2.00	3.50	5.00	9.00	—

KM# 20 1/2 RUPEE (Deb)
Silver **Obv:** Buddh. symbols **Rev:** Buddh. symbols

Date	Mintage	Good	VG	F	VF	XF
ND(1910-27)	—	10.00	15.00	25.00	55.00	—

KM# 20a 1/2 RUPEE (Deb)
Copper **Note:** Obverse is similar to KM#20, but symbols on reverse are arranged differently.

Date	Mintage	Good	VG	F	VF	XF
ND(1910-27)	—	3.00	4.50	6.00	10.00	—

KM# 21 1/2 RUPEE (Deb)
Copper **Obv:** Buddh. symbols **Rev:** Buddh. symbols **Note:** Many varieties.

Date	Mintage	Good	VG	F	VF	XF
ND(1910-27)	—	1.50	2.50	3.50	6.00	—

DECIMAL COINAGE

KM# 23.1 PICE
7.0000 g., Bronze, 26.5 mm. **Note:** Similar to KM#23.2.

Date	Mintage	F	VF	XF	Unc	BU
1928	—	22.50	40.00	65.00	100	—

KM# 23.2 PICE
4.9000 g., Bronze, 25.1 mm. **Obv:** Crowned bust, left **Rev:** Coin divided into nine sections, symbol on each section **Note:** Actually struck in 1931.

Date	Mintage	F	VF	XF	Unc	BU
1928	10,000	20.00	35.00	60.00	90.00	—
1928 Proof	—	Value: 100				

KM# A27 PICE
3.3000 g., Bronze **Rev:** Coin divided into nine sections, symbol in each section

Date	Mintage	F	VF	XF	Unc	BU
ND	—	—	—	—	—	—

KM# 27 PICE
2.9000 g., Bronze, 21.28 mm. **Obv:** Square at center, four sections, one symbol in each **Rev:** Coin divided into nine sections, one symbol in each section **Note:** Actually struck in 1951 and 1955. Later strikes of 1955 dates differ in detail because of recut dies.

Date	Mintage	F	VF	XF	Unc	BU
ND	Est. 1,260,000	0.75	1.00	1.50	2.25	—

KM# 29 25 NAYA PAISA
Copper-Nickel **Subject:** 40th Anniversary - Accession of Jigme Wangchuk **Obv:** Crowned bust, left, two dates below **Rev:** Emblem within circle, denomination below

Date	Mintage	F	VF	XF	Unc	BU
1966	10,000	—	0.25	0.50	1.00	2.00
1966 Proof	6,000	Value: 1.50				

KM# 30   50 NAYA PAISA
Copper-Nickel **Subject:** 40th Anniversary - Accession of Jigme Wangchuk **Obv:** Crowned bust, left, dates below **Rev:** Emblem withn circle, denomination below

Date	Mintage	F	VF	XF	Unc	BU
1966	10,000	—	0.35	0.75	1.50	3.00
1966 Proof	6,000	Value: 2.50				

KM# 26   1/2 RUPEE
5.7200 g., Nickel, 24.00 mm. **Obv:** Crowned bust, left, normal legend **Rev:** Coin divided into nine sections, one symbol in each section **Note:** Weight varies: 5.78-5.90 grams.

Date	Mintage	F	VF	XF	Unc	BU
ND(1928)	20,000	2.00	3.00	4.50	7.00	—
Note: Actually struck in 1951						
ND(1950)	202,000	1.50	2.50	3.00	4.50	—
Note: Actually struck in 1955						

KM# 24   1/2 RUPEE
Silver **Obv:** Crowned bust, left **Rev:** Coin divided into nine sections, one symbol in each section **Note:** Weight varies: 5.83-5.85 grams.

Date	Mintage	F	VF	XF	Unc	BU
ND(1928)	50,000	10.00	15.00	22.50	35.00	—
Note: Actually struck in 1929						
ND(1928) Proof	—	Value: 100				

KM# 25   1/2 RUPEE
Silver **Obv:** Legend modified

Date	Mintage	F	VF	XF	Unc	BU
ND(1928)	Inc. above	10.00	15.00	22.50	35.00	—
Note: Actually struck in 1930						

KM# 28   1/2 RUPEE
5.0800 g., Nickel **Obv:** Legend normal

Date	Mintage	F	VF	XF	Unc	BU
ND(1950)	10,000,000	0.75	1.00	1.50	2.25	—
Note: Actually struck in 1967-68						

KM# 31   RUPEE
Copper-Nickel **Subject:** 40th Anniversary - Accession of Jigme Wangchuk **Obv:** Crowned bust, left, dates below **Rev:** Emblem divides date, denomination below

Date	Mintage	F	VF	XF	Unc	BU
1966	10,000	—	0.50	1.00	2.00	4.00
1966 Proof	6,000	Value: 3.50				

KM# 32   3 RUPEE
Copper-Nickel **Subject:** 40th Anniversary - Accession of Jigme Wangchuk **Obv:** Crowned bust, left, dates below **Rev:** Emblem divides date, denomination below

Date	Mintage	F	VF	XF	Unc	BU
1966	5,826	—	—	—	6.00	9.00
1966 Proof	6,000	Value: 7.50				

KM# 32a   3 RUPEE
28.2800 g., 0.9250 Silver 0.8410 oz. ASW **Subject:** 40th Anniversary - Accession of Jigme Wangchuk

Date	Mintage	F	VF	XF	Unc	BU
1966	—	—	—	—	375	—
1966 Proof	2,000	Value: 25.00				
1966 Matte proof	—	Value: 375				

KM# 33   SERTUM
7.9800 g., 0.9170 Gold 0.2353 oz. AGW **Subject:** 40th Anniversary - Accession of Jigme Wangchuk **Obv:** Crowned bust left, dates below **Rev:** Emblem divides date, denomination below

Date	Mintage	F	VF	XF	Unc	BU
1966	2,300	—	—	—	245	—
1966 Proof	598	Value: 265				

KM# 33a   SERTUM
9.8400 g., 0.9500 Platinum 0.3005 oz. APW **Subject:** 40th Anniversary - Accession of Jigme Wangchuk

Date	Mintage	F	VF	XF	Unc	BU
1966 Proof	72	Value: 600				

KM# 36   SERTUM
7.9800 g., 0.9170 Gold 0.2353 oz. AGW **Obv:** Bust, right, date below

Date	Mintage	F	VF	XF	Unc	BU
1970	3,111	—	—	—	220	240

KM# 34   2 SERTUMS
15.9800 g., 0.9170 Gold 0.4711 oz. AGW **Subject:** 40th Anniversary - Accession of Jigme Wangchuk **Obv:** Crowned bust, left, dates below **Rev:** Emblem divides date, denomination below

Date	Mintage	F	VF	XF	Unc	BU
1966	800	—	—	—	450	—
1966 Proof	598	Value: 475				

KM# 34a   2 SERTUMS
19.6700 g., 0.9500 Platinum 0.6008 oz. APW **Subject:** 40th Anniversary - Accession of Jigme Wangchuk

Date	Mintage	F	VF	XF	Unc	BU
1966 Proof	72	Value: 1,200				

KM# 35   5 SERTUMS
39.9400 g., 0.9170 Gold 1.1775 oz. AGW **Subject:** 40th Anniversary - Accession of Jigme Wangchuk **Obv:** Crowned bust, left, dates below **Rev:** Emblem divides date, denomination below

Date	Mintage	F	VF	XF	Unc	BU
1966	800	—	—	—	1,150	—
1966 Proof	598	Value: 1,250				

KM# 35a   5 SERTUMS
49.1800 g., 0.9500 Platinum 1.5021 oz. APW **Subject:** 40th Anniversary - Accession of Jigme Wangchuk **Obv:** Crowned bust, left, dates below **Rev:** Emblem divides date, denomination below

Date	Mintage	F	VF	XF	Unc	BU
1966 Proof	72	Value: 3,000				

REFORM COINAGE

Commencing 1974; 100 Chetrums (Paisa) = 1 Ngultrum (Rupee); 100 Ngultrums = 1 Sertum

KM# 37   5 CHETRUMS
1.4800 g., Aluminum, 22 mm. **Obv:** Crowned bust left, date at left **Rev:** Emblem above denomination **Edge:** Plain

Date	Mintage	F	VF	XF	Unc	BU
1974	—	—	0.10	0.20	0.50	0.75
1974 Proof	1,000	Value: 1.25				
1975	—	—	0.10	0.15	0.20	0.50
1975 Proof	—	Value: 1.25				

KM# 45   5 CHETRUMS
1.9000 g., Bronze, 17.15 mm. **Obv:** Symbols within circle, date below **Rev:** Symbols within circle, denomination below

Date	Mintage	F	VF	XF	Unc	BU
1979	—	—	0.10	0.20	0.50	0.75
1979 Proof	—	Value: 1.00				

KM# 38   10 CHETRUMS
2.2700 g., Aluminum, 26 mm. **Obv:** Crowned bust left, date at left **Rev:** Denomination below design

Date	Mintage	F	VF	XF	Unc	BU
1974	—	—	0.15	0.25	0.50	1.00
1974 Proof	1,000	Value: 1.50				

KM# 43   10 CHETRUMS
2.3000 g., Aluminum, 26 mm. **Series:** F.A.O. and International Women's Year **Obv:** Emblem above denomination **Rev:** Half figure left, grain sprig on left, date below

Date	Mintage	F	VF	XF	Unc	BU
1975	4,000,000	—	0.15	0.25	0.65	1.25
1975 Proof	—	Value: 2.50				

KM# 46 10 CHHERTUM
3.6000 g., Bronze, 20.35 mm. **Obv:** Shell and design within circle, date below **Rev:** Coin divided into nine sections, within circle, symbol in each section, denomination below

Date	Mintage	F	VF	XF	Unc	BU
1979	—	—	0.15	0.30	1.00	1.50
1979 Proof	—	Value: 2.00				

KM# 39 20 CHETRUM
Aluminum-Bronze, 22 mm. **Series:** F.A.O. **Obv:** Emblem above denomination **Rev:** Rice cultivation **Edge:** Reeded

Date	Mintage	F	VF	XF	Unc	BU
1974	1,194,000	—	0.15	0.25	0.50	0.75
1974 Prooflike	—	—	—	—	1.50	
Note: In mint sets only						
1974 Proof	1,000	Value: 2.00				

KM# 40.1 25 CHETRUMS
Copper-Nickel **Obv:** Crowned bust, left, date at left **Rev:** Fish above denomination, type I

Date	Mintage	F	VF	XF	Unc	BU
1974	—	—	0.10	0.20	0.75	1.25

KM# 40.2 25 CHETRUMS
Copper-Nickel **Obv:** Crowned bust, left, date at left **Rev:** Fish above denomination, type II **Note:** Bottom of bust closer to rim; upper character at left revised.

Date	Mintage	F	VF	XF	Unc	BU
1974	—	—	0.10	0.20	0.75	1.25
1974 Proof	—	Value: 3.00				
1975	—	—	0.10	0.20	0.75	1.25
1975 Proof	—	Value: 3.00				

KM# 47 25 CHHERTUM
4.6000 g., Copper-Nickel, 21.95 mm. **Obv:** Fish within circle, date below **Rev:** Emblem within circle, denomination below

Date	Mintage	F	VF	XF	Unc	BU
1979	—	—	0.25	0.50	1.25	1.75
1979 Proof	—	Value: 4.00				

KM# 47a 25 CHHERTUM
4.4500 g., Steel, 22.2 mm. **Obv:** Fish within circle, date below **Rev:** Emblem within circle, denomination below **Note:** Aluminum-bronze clad.

Date	Mintage	F	VF	XF	Unc	BU
1979	—	—	—	—	2.50	3.00

KM# 48 50 CHHERTUM
6.9000 g., Copper-Nickel, 25.85 mm. **Obv:** Emblem within circle, date below **Rev:** Coin divided into nine sections within circle, symbol in each section, denomination below

Date	Mintage	F	VF	XF	Unc	BU
1979	—	—	0.25	0.65	1.50	2.00
1979 Proof	—	Value: 5.00				

KM# 41 NGULTRUM
Copper-Nickel, 28 mm. **Obv:** Crowned bust, left, date at left **Rev:** Emblem above denomination **Edge:** Reeded security edge

Date	Mintage	F	VF	XF	Unc	BU
1974	—	—	0.20	0.50	1.25	1.75
1974 Proof	1,000	Value: 5.00				
1975	—	—	0.20	0.50	1.25	1.75
1975 Proof	—	Value: 5.00				

KM# 49 NGULTRUM
8.2000 g., Copper-Nickel, 27.95 mm. **Obv:** Emblem within circle, date below **Rev:** Coin divided into nine sections within circle, each has symbol, denomination below

Date	Mintage	F	VF	XF	Unc	BU
1979	—	—	0.30	0.75	2.00	2.75
1979 Proof	—	Value: 5.50				

KM# 49a NGULTRUM
7.9000 g., Copper-Nickel Clad Steel, 27.8 mm. **Obv:** Emblem within circle, date below **Rev:** Coin divided into nine sections within circle, each has symbol, denomination below **Note:** Magnetic

Date	Mintage	F	VF	XF	Unc	BU
1979	—	—	—	—	3.00	3.50

KM# 50 3 NGULTRUMS
Copper-Nickel, 38.5 mm. **Obv:** Crowned head, left, date below **Rev:** National emblem within circle, denomination at right **Edge:** Reeded

Date	Mintage	F	VF	XF	Unc	BU
1979	—	—	1.25	2.50	5.50	—
1979 Proof	—	Value: 8.50				

KM# 50a 3 NGULTRUMS
28.2800 g., 0.9250 Silver 0.8410 oz. ASW **Obv:** Crowned head, left, date below **Rev:** National emblem within circle, denomination at right

Date	Mintage	F	VF	XF	Unc	BU
1979 Proof	Est. 10,000	Value: 32.50				

KM# 42 15 NGULTRUMS
22.3000 g., 0.5000 Silver 0.3585 oz. ASW **Series:** F.A.O. **Obv:** Emblem above denomination **Rev:** Rice cultivation

Date	Mintage	F	VF	XF	Unc	BU
1974	30,000	—	—	—	8.50	—
1974 Prooflike	—	—	—	—	10.00	
Note: In mint sets only						
1974 Proof	1,000	Value: 42.50				

KM# 44 30 NGULTRUMS
25.0000 g., 0.5000 Silver 0.4019 oz. ASW **Series:** F.A.O. and International Women's Year **Obv:** Emblem above denomination **Rev:** Half figure looking left, grain sprig on left, date at bottom

Date	Mintage	F	VF	XF	Unc	BU
1975	14,000	—	—	—	10.00	—
1975 Proof	—	Value: 20.00				

KM# 54 50 NGULTRUMS
28.2800 g., 0.9250 Silver 0.8410 oz. ASW **Series:** World Food Day **Obv:** Yak right, within circle, denomination below

Date	Mintage	F	VF	XF	Unc	BU
1981	15,000	—	—	—	40.00	—
1981 Proof	5,000	Value: 45.00				

KM# 83   50 NGULTRUMS
Copper-Nickel **Subject:** 50 Years - United Nations **Obv:** National emblem within circle divides dates **Rev:** Bust, 3/4 right, symbol and dates at right, denomination below

Date	Mintage	F	VF	XF	Unc	BU
1995	—	—	—	—	8.00	—

KM# 104   50 NGULTRUMS
16.0000 g., 0.9250 Silver 0.4758 oz. ASW, 28.3 mm. **Subject:** British Queen Mother **Obv:** National emblem within circle divides dates **Rev:** Home at St. Paul's Walden Bury, date and denomination below **Edge:** Reeded

Date	Mintage	F	VF	XF	Unc	BU
1997 Proof	—	Value: 20.00				
1997 Proof	—	Value: 20.00				

KM# 58   100 NGULTRUMS
23.3300 g., 0.9250 Silver 0.6938 oz. ASW **Series:** Decade for Women **Obv:** National emblem within circle, date above, denomination below **Rev:** Women working

Date	Mintage	F	VF	XF	Unc	BU
1984 Proof	1,050	Value: 28.00				

KM# 84   100 NGULTRUMS
Copper-Nickel **Subject:** St. Paul's Walden Bury Palace **Obv:** National emblem within circle divides dates **Rev:** Palace within circle, date and denomination below

Date	Mintage	F	VF	XF	Unc	BU
1995	Est. 35,000	—	—	—	12.50	15.00

KM# 103   100 NGULTRUMS
20.0000 g., 0.9250 Silver 0.5948 oz. ASW, 34 mm. **Subject:** Olympic Games 2000 **Obv:** National arms within circle divides dates **Rev:** Archer at left sighting in on target at right, denomination below **Edge:** Reeded

Date	Mintage	F	VF	XF	Unc	BU
1998 Proof	—	Value: 18.50				

KM# 57   200 NGULTRUMS
28.2800 g., 0.9250 Silver 0.8410 oz. ASW **Series:** International Year of Disabled Persons **Obv:** Elephant carrying animals, tree and hills, date and denomination below **Rev:** Typist

Date	Mintage	F	VF	XF	Unc	BU
1981	10,000	—	—	—	40.00	42.50
1981 Proof	10,000	Value: 45.00				

KM# 86   200 NGULTRUMS
10.0000 g., 0.5000 Silver 0.1607 oz. ASW **Series:** Olympics **Obv:** National emblem within circle divides dates **Rev:** Two basketball players, denomination below

Date	Mintage	F	VF	XF	Unc	BU
1996 Proof	Est. 10,000	—	—	—	20.00	22.50

KM# 87   200 NGULTRUMS
10.0000 g., 0.5000 Silver 0.1607 oz. ASW **Series:** Olympics **Obv:** National emblem divides dates **Rev:** Skiing scene, denomination at right

Date	Mintage	F	VF	XF	Unc	BU
1996 Proof	Est. 50,000	—	—	—	15.00	18.00

KM# 55   250 NGULTRUMS
28.2800 g., 0.9250 Silver 0.8410 oz. ASW **Subject:** 75th Anniversary of Monarchy **Obv:** Crowned bust, facing, date below **Rev:** National emblem within circle **Note:** Issued in 1983.

Date	Mintage	F	VF	XF	Unc	BU
1982	10,000	—	—	—	30.00	—
1982 Proof	5,000	Value: 40.00				

KM# 61   300 NGULTRUMS
28.2800 g., 0.9250 Silver 0.8410 oz. ASW **Subject:** World Championship Soccer, denomination below **Obv:** Crowned head, left, date below

Date	Mintage	F	VF	XF	Unc	BU
1990 Proof	20,000	Value: 35.00				

KM# 65   300 NGULTRUMS
31.4700 g., 0.9250 Silver 0.9359 oz. ASW **Series:** Endangered wildlife **Rev:** Snow leopard, denomination below

Date	Mintage	F	VF	XF	Unc	BU
1991 Proof	Est. 25,000	Value: 35.00				

KM# 63   300 NGULTRUMS
28.2800 g., 0.9250 Silver 0.8410 oz. ASW **Obv:** National emblem divides dates **Rev:** Solar system scene, denomination below

Date	Mintage	F	VF	XF	Unc	BU
1992 Proof	—	Value: 32.50				

KM# 72   300 NGULTRUMS
31.4700 g., 0.9250 Silver 0.9359 oz. ASW **Subject:** World Cup Soccer **Obv:** National emblem within circle divides dates **Rev:** Two soccer players, radiant sunset behind, denomination below

Date	Mintage	F	VF	XF	Unc	BU
1992 Proof	20,000	Value: 27.50				

KM# 74   300 NGULTRUMS
31.4700 g., 0.9250 Silver 0.9359 oz. ASW **Series:** Lillehammer
1994 - 17th Winter Olympic Games **Obv:** National emblem within
circle divides dates **Rev:** Speed skating, denomination below

Date	Mintage	F	VF	XF	Unc	BU
1992 Proof	40,000	Value: 22.50				

KM# 75   300 NGULTRUMS
31.4700 g., 0.9250 Silver 0.9359 oz. ASW **Series:** Endangered
Wildlife **Obv:** National emblem within circle divides dates
Rev: Golden langur monkey, denomination below

Date	Mintage	F	VF	XF	Unc	BU
1992 Proof	—	Value: 35.00				

KM# 76   300 NGULTRUMS
31.4700 g., 0.9250 Silver 0.9359 oz. ASW **Series:** Barcelona
1992 - 25th Summer Olympics **Obv:** National emblem within
circle divides dates **Rev:** Archery scene, denomination below

Date	Mintage	F	VF	XF	Unc	BU
1992 Proof	20,000	Value: 20.00				

KM# 77   300 NGULTRUMS
31.4700 g., 0.9250 Silver 0.9359 oz. ASW **Series:** 1992 Olympic
Games **Obv:** National emblem within circle divides dates
Rev: Boxer, denomination below

Date	Mintage	F	VF	XF	Unc	BU
1992 Proof	20,000	Value: 22.00				

KM# 66   300 NGULTRUMS
31.4700 g., 0.9250 Silver 0.9359 oz. ASW **Subject:** 40th
Anniversary - Coronation of Queen Elizabeth II **Obv:** National
emblem within circle divides dates **Rev:** Royal Guard, palace in
background, denomination and dates below

Date	Mintage	F	VF	XF	Unc	BU
1993 Proof	Est. 10,000	Value: 32.50				

KM# 67   300 NGULTRUMS
31.4700 g., 0.9250 Silver 0.9359 oz. ASW **Series:** Endangered
Wildlife **Obv:** National emblem within circle divides dates
Rev: Takin, denomination below

Date	Mintage	F	VF	XF	Unc	BU
1993 Proof	Est. 10,000	Value: 35.00				

KM# 68   300 NGULTRUMS
31.4700 g., 0.9250 Silver 0.9359 oz. ASW **Subject:** Protect Our
World **Obv:** National emblem within circle divides dates
Rev: Elephant, rhino, tree, and tiger, denomination below

Date	Mintage	F	VF	XF	Unc	BU
1993 Proof	Est. 10,000	Value: 50.00				

KM# 78   300 NGULTRUMS
31.3200 g., 0.9250 Silver 0.9314 oz. ASW **Subject:** World
Championship Soccer **Obv:** National emblem within circle divides
dates **Rev:** Ball in flight, denomination below

Date	Mintage	F	VF	XF	Unc	BU
1993 Proof	30,000	Value: 40.00				

KM# 79   300 NGULTRUMS
31.3200 g., 0.9250 Silver 0.9314 oz. ASW **Series:** Olympic
Games **Obv:** National emblem within inner circle **Rev:** Soccer,
denomination below

Date	Mintage	F	VF	XF	Unc	BU
1993 Proof	30,000	Value: 25.00				

KM# 89   300 NGULTRUMS
31.3200 g., 0.9250 Silver 0.9314 oz. ASW **Subject:** Maurice
Ravel **Obv:** National emblem **Rev:** Portrait, musician, dancer,
and dates, denomination below

Date	Mintage	F	VF	XF	Unc	BU
1993 Proof	—	Value: 42.50				

KM# 69   300 NGULTRUMS
31.3200 g., 0.9250 Silver 0.9314 oz. ASW **Subject:** Protect Our
World **Obv:** National emblem within inner circle **Rev:** Rain forest,
denomination below

Date	Mintage	F	VF	XF	Unc	BU
1994 Proof	Est. 10,000	Value: 45.00				

KM# 73   300 NGULTRUMS
31.3200 g., 0.9250 Silver 0.9314 oz. ASW **Series:** 1996 Olympic
Games **Obv:** National emblem within inner circle **Rev:** Basketball,
denomination below

Date	Mintage	F	VF	XF	Unc	BU
1994 Proof	30,000	Value: 25.00				

KM# 88   300 NGULTRUMS
31.4500 g., 0.9250 Silver 0.9353 oz. ASW **Series:** Endangered Wildlife **Obv:** National emblem within inner circle **Rev:** Kalij pheasant, denomination below

Date	Mintage	F	VF	XF	Unc	BU
1994 Proof	—				Value: 37.50	

KM# 81   300 NGULTRUMS
31.4500 g., 0.9250 Silver 0.9353 oz. ASW **Subject:** Joao Cabral **Obv:** National emblem **Rev:** Two explorers, denomination below

Date	Mintage	F	VF	XF	Unc	BU
1994 Proof	Est. 10,000				Value: 32.50	

KM# 80   300 NGULTRUMS
28.2800 g., 0.9250 Silver 0.8410 oz. ASW **Subject:** 50th Anniversary - United Nations **Obv:** National emblem within circle divides dates **Rev:** Bust, 3/4 right, symbol and dates at right, denomination below

Date	Mintage	F	VF	XF	Unc	BU
1995 Proof	Est. 100,000				Value: 32.50	

KM# 106   300 NGULTRUMS
31.7700 g., 0.9250 Silver 0.9448 oz. ASW, 38.55 mm. **Ruler:** Jigme Singye Wangchuck **Subject:** Queen Mother's parents home St. Paul's Walden Bury **Obv:** National arms **Rev. Leg.:** QUEEN ELIZABETH THE QUEEN MOTHER **Edge:** Reeded

Date	Mintage	F	VF	XF	Unc	BU
1995 Proof	25,000				Value: 40.00	

KM# 108   300 NGULTRUMS
1.2240 g., 1.0000 Gold 0.0394 oz. AGW, 13.92 mm. **Ruler:** Jigme Singye Wangchuck **Obv:** National arms **Rev:** Statue of Bodhisattvas seated in lotus blossom **Edge:** Reeded

Date	Mintage	F	VF	XF	Unc	BU
1996 Proof	50,000				Value: 55.00	

KM# 98   300 NGULTRUMS
31.5000 g., 0.9250 Silver 0.9368 oz. ASW **Subject:** Chinese Lunar Year **Obv:** National emblem **Rev:** Stylized dragon within circle, denomination below

Date	Mintage	F	VF	XF	Unc	BU
1996 Proof	—				Value: 30.00	

KM# 90   300 NGULTRUMS
31.5000 g., 0.9250 Silver 0.9368 oz. ASW **Subject:** Chinese Lunar Year **Obv:** National emblem within circle divides dates **Rev:** Seated monkey within circle, denomination below

Date	Mintage	F	VF	XF	Unc	BU
1996 Proof	—				Value: 30.00	

KM# 91   300 NGULTRUMS
31.5000 g., 0.9250 Silver 0.9368 oz. ASW **Subject:** Chinese Lunar Year **Obv:** National emblem **Rev:** Stylized rooster within circle, denomination below

Date	Mintage	F	VF	XF	Unc	BU
1996 Proof	—				Value: 30.00	

KM# 92   300 NGULTRUMS
31.5000 g., 0.9250 Silver 0.9368 oz. ASW **Subject:** Chinese Lunar Year **Obv:** National emblem **Rev:** Stylized dog within circle, denomination below

Date	Mintage	F	VF	XF	Unc	BU
1996 Proof	—				Value: 30.00	

KM# 93   300 NGULTRUMS
31.5000 g., 0.9250 Silver 0.9368 oz. ASW **Subject:** Chinese Lunar Year **Obv:** National emblem **Rev:** Stylized pig within circle, denomination below

Date	Mintage	F	VF	XF	Unc	BU
1996 Proof	—				Value: 30.00	

KM# 94   300 NGULTRUMS
31.5000 g., 0.9250 Silver 0.9368 oz. ASW **Subject:** Chinese Lunar Year **Obv:** National emblem **Rev:** Stylized rat within circle, denomination below

Date	Mintage	F	VF	XF	Unc	BU
1996 Proof	—				Value: 30.00	

KM# 95   300 NGULTRUMS
31.5000 g., 0.9250 Silver 0.9368 oz. ASW **Subject:** Chinese Lunar Year **Obv:** National emblem **Rev:** Stylized ox within circle, denomination below

Date	Mintage	F	VF	XF	Unc	BU
1996 Proof	—				Value: 30.00	

KM# 96   300 NGULTRUMS
31.5000 g., 0.9250 Silver 0.9368 oz. ASW **Subject:** Chinese Lunar Year **Obv:** National emblem within circle divides dates **Rev:** Stylized tiger within circle, denomination below

Date	Mintage	F	VF	XF	Unc	BU
1996 Proof	—				Value: 30.00	

KM# 97 300 NGULTRUMS

31.5000 g., 0.9250 Silver 0.9368 oz. ASW **Subject:** Chinese Lunar Year **Obv:** National emblem **Rev:** Stylized rabbit within circle, denomination below

Date	Mintage	F	VF	XF	Unc	BU
1996 Proof	—	Value: 30.00				

KM# 99 300 NGULTRUMS

31.5000 g., 0.9250 Silver 0.9368 oz. ASW **Subject:** Chinese Lunar Year **Obv:** National emblem **Rev:** Stylized snake within circle, denomination below

Date	Mintage	F	VF	XF	Unc	BU
1996 Proof	—	Value: 30.00				

KM# 100 300 NGULTRUMS

31.5000 g., 0.9250 Silver 0.9368 oz. ASW **Subject:** Chinese Lunar Year **Obv:** National emblem **Rev:** Stylized horse within circle, denomination below

Date	Mintage	F	VF	XF	Unc	BU
1996 Proof	—	Value: 30.00				

KM# 101 300 NGULTRUMS

31.5000 g., 0.9250 Silver 0.9368 oz. ASW **Subject:** Chinese Lunar Year **Obv:** National emblem **Rev:** Stylized ram within circle, denomination below

Date	Mintage	F	VF	XF	Unc	BU
1996 Proof	—	Value: 28.50				

KM# 102 300 NGULTRUMS

1.2441 g., 0.9990 Gold 0.0400 oz. AGW **Obv:** National emblem within circle divides dates **Rev:** Mask, facing, denomination at lower right

Date	Mintage	F	VF	XF	Unc	BU
1997 Proof	—	Value: 45.00				

KM# 51 SERTUM

7.9800 g., 0.9170 Gold 0.2353 oz. AGW **Obv:** Crowned bust, left, dates below **Rev:** Two dragons around inner circle

Date	Mintage	F	VF	XF	Unc	BU
1979	1,000	—	—	—	235	—
1979 Proof	1,000	Value: 250				

KM# 51a SERTUM

9.8500 g., 0.9500 Platinum 0.3008 oz. APW **Obv:** Crowned bust left, dates below **Rev:** Two dragons around inner circle

Date	Mintage	F	VF	XF	Unc	BU
1979 Proof	—	Value: 600				

KM# 56 SERTUM

7.9900 g., 0.9170 Gold 0.2356 oz. AGW **Subject:** 75th Anniversary of Monarchy

Date	Mintage	F	VF	XF	Unc	BU
1982(1983)	1,000	—	—	—	235	—
1982(1983) Proof	1,000	Value: 250				

KM# 85 SERTUM

1.2442 g., 0.9999 Gold 0.0400 oz. AGW **Subject:** 40th Anniversary - Queen Elizabeth II's Coronation **Obv:** National emblem within circle divides dates **Rev:** Royal Guard, palace in background, denomination and dates below

Date	Mintage	F	VF	XF	Unc	BU
1995	Est. 250,000	—	—	—	50.00	60.00

KM# 107 SERTUM

1.2200 g., 0.9990 Gold 0.0392 oz. AGW, 13.90 mm. **Ruler:** Jigme Singye Wangchuck **Obv:** National arms **Obv. Leg.:** KINGDOM OF BHUTAN **Rev:** Solar System **Edge:** Reeded

Date	Mintage	F	VF	XF	Unc	BU
1995 Proof	—	Value: 55.00				

KM# 52 2 SERTUMS

15.9800 g., 0.9170 Gold 0.4711 oz. AGW **Obv:** Crowned bust, left, dates below **Rev:** Two dragons around inner circle

Date	Mintage	F	VF	XF	Unc	BU
1979	1,000	—	—	—	450	—
1979 Proof	1,000	Value: 475				

KM# 52a 2 SERTUMS

19.7000 g., 0.9500 Platinum 0.6017 oz. APW **Obv:** Crowned bust, left, dates below **Rev:** Two dragons around inner circle

Date	Mintage	F	VF	XF	Unc	BU
1979 Proof	—	Value: 1,200				

KM# 60 2 SERTUMS

15.9800 g., 0.9170 Gold 0.4711 oz. AGW **Series:** International Year of Disabled Persons **Obv:** Dragon, date below, denomination at right **Rev:** Typist

Date	Mintage	F	VF	XF	Unc	BU
1981	—	—	—	—	700	—
1981 Proof	—	Value: 900				

KM# 53 5 SERTUMS

39.9400 g., 0.9170 Gold 1.1775 oz. AGW **Obv:** Crowned bust, left, dates below **Rev:** Two dragons around inner circle

Date	Mintage	F	VF	XF	Unc	BU
1979	1,000	—	—	—	1,150	—
1979 Proof	1,000	Value: 1,200				

KM# 53a 5 SERTUMS

49.2000 g., 0.9500 Platinum 1.5027 oz. APW **Obv:** Crowned bust, left, dates below **Rev:** Two dragons around inner circle

Date	Mintage	F	VF	XF	Unc	BU
1979 Proof	—	Value: 3,000				

KM# 64 5 SERTUMS

7.7760 g., 0.5833 Gold 0.1458 oz. AGW **Series:** Endangered Wildlife **Obv:** National emblem within circle divides dates **Rev:** Black-necked crane, denomination below

Date	Mintage	F	VF	XF	Unc	BU
1992 Proof	2,000	Value: 150				

KM# 70 5 SERTUMS

7.7760 g., 0.5833 Gold 0.1458 oz. AGW **Series:** 1992 Olympics **Obv:** National emblem within circle divides dates **Rev:** Archer, denomination below

Date	Mintage	F	VF	XF	Unc	BU
1993 Proof	Est. 3,000	Value: 165				

KM# 71 5 SERTUMS

7.7760 g., 0.5833 Gold 0.1458 oz. AGW **Subject:** World Cup '94 Soccer **Obv:** National emblem within circle divides dates **Rev:** Soccer players, denomination below

Date	Mintage	F	VF	XF	Unc	BU
1993 Proof	Est. 2,000	Value: 165				

KM# 82 5 SERTUMS

7.7760 g., 0.5833 Gold 0.1458 oz. AGW **Series:** Olympics **Subject:** Tae kwon do **Obv:** National emblem within circle divides dates **Rev:** Karate practitioner, denomination below

Date	Mintage	F	VF	XF	Unc	BU
1994 Proof	Est. 3,000	Value: 165				

PIEFORTS

KM#	Date	Mintage	Identification	Mkt Val
P1	1981	—	2 Sertums. Gold. KM60.	1,500
P2	1981	—	200 Ngultrums. Silver. KM57.	300

MINT SETS

KM#	Date	Mintage	Identification	Issue Price	Mkt Val
MS1	1966 (3)	300	KM33-35	175	1,750
MS2	1974 (2)	—	KM39, 42	4.00	11.50
MS3	1974 (4)	—	KM37-38, 40-41	6.00	3.00
MS4	1979 (3)	1,000	KM51-53	1,575	1,750

PROOF SETS

KM#	Date	Mintage	Identification	Issue Price	Mkt Val
PS1	1966 (4)	6,000	KM29-32	11.50	15.00
PS2	1966 (3)	598	KM33-35	300	1,875
PS3	1966 (3)	72	KM33a-35a	685	3,200
PS4	1974 (6)	1,000	KM37-42	18.00	65.00
PS5	1975 (5)	—	KM37, 40-41, 43-44; rare	—	—
PS6	1979 (5)	20,000	KM45-49	30.00	15.00
PS7	1979 (3)	1,000	KM51-53	2,100	1,850
PS8	1979 (3)	—	KM51a-53a	2,400	4,000

BIAFRA

On May 30, 1967, the Eastern Region of the Republic of Nigeria, an area occupied principally by the proud and resourceful Ibo tribe, seceded from Nigeria and proclaimed itself the independent Republic of Biafra with Odumegwu Ojukwu as Chief of State. Civil war erupted and raged for 31 months. Casualties, including civilian, were about two million, the majority succumbing to malnutrition and disease. Biafra surrendered to the federal government on January 15, 1970.

MONETARY SYSTEM
12 Pence = 1 Shilling
20 Shillings = 1 Pound

INDEPENDENT REPUBLIC OF BIAFRA

STANDARD COINAGE

KM# 1   3 PENCE
Aluminum

Date	Mintage	F	VF	XF	Unc	BU
1969	—		15.00	22.50	35.00	—

KM# 12   6 PENCE
Aluminum **Obv:** Denomination, date above **Rev:** Radiant sun rising behind tree, legend below horseshoe design

Date	Mintage	F	VF	XF	Unc	BU
1969 5-10 pieces known	—		500	1,000	2,000	—

KM# 2   SHILLING
Aluminum, 23.5 mm. **Obv:** Eagle divides denomination and date **Rev:** Radiant sun rising behind tree, legend below horseshoe design

Date	Mintage	F	VF	XF	Unc	BU
1969	—		8.00	14.00	25.00	—

KM# 3   SHILLING
Aluminum, 23.5 mm. **Obv:** Eagle divides date and denomination **Rev:** Radiant sun rising behind tree, legend below horseshoe design

Date	Mintage	F	VF	XF	Unc	BU
1969	—	—		350	550	—

KM# 4   2-1/2 SHILLING
Aluminum **Obv:** Date and denomination below large cat **Rev:** Rising radiant sun behind tree, legend below horseshoe design

Date	Mintage	F	VF	XF	Unc	BU
1969	—		8.00	18.00	40.00	—

KM# 5   CROWN
28.0000 g., Silver **Subject:** Independence and Liberty **Obv:** Head right within circle **Rev:** Tree within circle, denomination below **Edge:** Plain

Date	Mintage	F	VF	XF	Unc	BU
1969 Rare	—	—	—	—	—	—

KM# 6   POUND
19.7600 g., 0.7500 Silver 0.4765 oz. ASW **Obv:** National arms, date below **Rev:** Defiant eagle with scroll, wreathed shield at back, denomination below

Date	Mintage	F	VF	XF	Unc	BU
1969	—	—		75.00	125	—

KM# 7   POUND
3.9940 g., 0.9170 Gold 0.1177 oz. AGW **Subject:** 2nd Anniversary of Independence **Obv:** Similar to 25 Pounds, KM#11, (national arms) **Rev:** Defiant eagle with scroll, wreathed shield at back, denomination below

Date	Mintage	F	VF	XF	Unc	BU
1969 Proof	3,000	Value: 175				

KM# 8   2 POUNDS
7.9881 g., 0.9170 Gold 0.2355 oz. AGW **Subject:** 2nd Anniversary of Independence **Obv:** Similar to 25 Pounds, KM#11, (national arms) **Rev:** Defiant eagle with scroll, wreathed shield at back, denomination below

Date	Mintage	F	VF	XF	Unc	BU
1969 Proof	3,000	Value: 250				

KM# 9   5 POUNDS
15.9761 g., 0.9170 Gold 0.4710 oz. AGW **Subject:** 2nd Anniversary of Independence **Obv:** Similar to 25 Pounds, KM#11, (national arms) **Rev:** Defiant eagle with scroll, wreathed shield at back, denomination below

Date	Mintage	F	VF	XF	Unc	BU
1969 Proof	3,000	Value: 500				

KM# 10   10 POUNDS
39.9403 g., 0.9170 Gold 1.1775 oz. AGW **Subject:** 2nd Anniversary of Independence **Obv:** Similar to 25 Pounds, KM#11, (national arms) **Rev:** Defiant eagle with scroll, wreathed shield at back, denomination below

Date	Mintage	F	VF	XF	Unc	BU
1969 Proof	3,000	Value: 1,175				

KM# 11   25 POUNDS
79.8805 g., 0.9170 Gold 2.3550 oz. AGW **Subject:** 2nd Anniversary of Independence **Obv:** National arms **Rev:** Defiant eagle with scroll, wreathed shield at back, denomination below

Date	Mintage	F	VF	XF	Unc	BU
1969 Proof	3,000	Value: 2,250				

PATTERNS

KM#	Date	Mintage Identification	Mkt Val
Pn1	1968	— Shilling. Aluminum. 29 mm. Similar to KM#3, without rope between eagle and denomination. Similar to KM#3, with textured palm trunk. Plain edge. Similar to KM#3, without rope below eagle, with textured palm trunk	1,500

PROOF SETS

KM#	Date	Mintage Identification	Issue Price	Mkt Val
PS1	1969 (5)	3,000 KM7-11	464	4,350

BOHEMIA & MORAVIA

Bohemia, a western province in the Czech Republic, was combined with the majority of Moravia in central Czechoslovakia (excluding parts of north and south Moravia which were joined with Silesia in 1938) to form the German protectorate in March, 1939, after the German invasion. Toward the end of war in 1945 the protectorate was dissolved and Bohemia and Moravia once again became part of Czechoslovakia.

MONETARY SYSTEM
100 Haleru = 1 Koruna

GERMAN PROTECTORATE

STANDARD COINAGE

KM# 1   10 HALERU
1.8800 g., Zinc, 17 mm.   **Obv:** Czech lion crowned left **Rev:** Charles bridge in Prague, denomination below **Edge:** Plain

Date	Mintage	F	VF	XF	Unc	BU
1940	82,114,000	0.35	0.75	1.50	10.00	13.50
1941	Inc. above	0.25	0.50	1.25	9.00	12.00
1942	Inc. above	0.25	0.50	1.25	9.00	12.00
1943	Inc. above	0.35	0.75	1.50	10.00	13.50
1944	Inc. above	0.75	1.50	3.00	14.00	17.50

KM# 2   20 HALERU
2.6300 g., Zinc, 20 mm.   **Obv:** Czech lion crowned left **Rev:** Wheat ears with sickle, denomination on left **Edge:** Plain

Date	Mintage	F	VF	XF	Unc	BU
1940	106,526,000	0.25	0.50	1.25	9.00	12.00
1941	Inc. above	0.25	0.50	1.25	9.00	12.00
1942	Inc. above	0.25	0.50	1.25	9.00	12.00
1943	Inc. above	0.50	0.75	1.50	10.00	13.50
1944	Inc. above	0.50	1.00	2.00	12.00	16.50

KM# 3   50 HALERU
3.7000 g., Zinc, 22 mm.   **Obv:** Czech lion crowned **Rev:** Value within linden branches, wheat ears below **Edge:** Milled

Date	Mintage	F	VF	XF	Unc	BU
1940	53,270,000	0.35	0.75	1.50	10.00	13.50
1941	Inc. above	0.35	0.75	1.50	10.00	13.50
1942	Inc. above	0.35	0.75	1.50	10.00	13.50
1943	Inc. above	0.75	1.50	3.00	15.00	20.00
1944	Inc. above	0.75	1.50	3.00	15.00	20.00

KM# 4   KORUNA
4.5000 g., Zinc, 23 mm.   **Obv:** Czech lion crowned left **Rev:** Linden branches divide denomination and date **Edge:** Milled

Date	Mintage	F	VF	XF	Unc	BU
1941	102,817,000	0.50	0.75	1.75	12.50	16.50
1942	Inc. above	0.50	0.75	1.75	12.50	16.50
1943	Inc. above	0.50	0.75	1.75	12.50	16.50
1944	Inc. above	0.50	0.75	1.75	12.50	16.50

PATTERNS
Including off metal strikes

KM#	Date	Mintage	Identification	Mkt Val
Pn1	1940	—	20 Haleru. Zinc. 2.6600 g. 19 mm. KM#2.	—
Pn2	1940	—	20 Haleru. Aluminum. 1.7800 g. 20.03 mm. KM#2.	—
Pn3	1940	—	50 Haleru. Aluminum. KM#3.	—
Pn4	1940	—	Koruna. Aluminum. KM#4.	—

BOLIVIA

The Republic of Bolivia, a landlocked country in west central South America, has an area of 424,165 sq. mi. (1,098,580 sq. km.) and a population of *8.33 million. Its capitals are: La Paz (administrative) and Sucre (constitutional). Principal exports are tin, zinc, antimony, tungsten, petroleum, natural gas, cotton and coffee.

Much of present day Bolivia was first dominated by the Tiahuanaco Culture ca.400 BC. It had in turn been incorporated into the Inca Empire by 1440AD prior to the arrival of the Spanish, in 1535, who reduced the Indian population to virtual slavery. When Joseph Napoleon was placed upon the throne of occupied Spain in 1809, a fervor of revolutionary activity quickened throughout Alto Peru - culminating in the 1809 Proclamation of Liberty. Sixteen bloody years of struggle ensued before the republic, named for the famed liberator Simon Bolivar, was established on August 6, 1825. Since then Bolivia has survived more than 16 constitutions, 78 Presidents, 3 military juntas and over 160 revolutions.

MINT MARKS
A - Paris
(a) - Paris, privy marks only
CHI - Valcambia
H - Heaton
KN - Kings' Norton

REPUBLIC

REFORM COINAGE
1870 - 1951

KM# 173.1   5 CENTAVOS
Copper-Nickel   **Obv:** Arms without shield **Rev:** Caduceus above sprays divides denomination **Note:** Coins dated 1893, 1918 and 1919 medal rotation were struck at the Heaton Mint.

Date	Mintage	F	VF	XF	Unc	BU
1909	4,000,000	1.00	6.00	12.00	20.00	—
1918	530,000	6.00	15.00	40.00	75.00	—
1919	4,370,000	5.00	10.00	20.00	45.00	—

KM# 173.3   5 CENTAVOS
Copper-Nickel   **Obv:** State arms within circle, stars below **Rev:** Cornucopia and torch flank date

Date	Mintage	F	VF	XF	Unc	BU
1902	2,000,000	1.00	6.00	15.00	35.00	—
1907(a)	2,000,000	1.00	6.00	15.00	35.00	—
1908	3,000,000	2.00	8.00	20.00	35.00	—
1909	—	3.00	10.00	30.00	60.00	—

KM# 178   5 CENTAVOS
Copper-Nickel   **Obv:** State emblem within circle, stars below **Rev:** Caduceus divides denomination, sprays below, date at bottom

Date	Mintage	F	VF	XF	Unc	BU
1935	5,000,000	1.00	2.00	5.00	12.00	—

KM# 174.1   10 CENTAVOS
Copper-Nickel   **Obv:** State arms within circle, stars below **Obv. Leg.:** REPUBLICA DE BOLIVIA **Rev:** Without privy marks **Note:** Coins dated 1893, 1918 and 1919 medal rotation were struck at the Heaton Mint.

Date	Mintage	F	VF	XF	Unc	BU
1918	1,335,000	3.00	8.00	20.00	45.00	—
1919	6,165,000	2.00	6.00	15.00	35.00	—

KM# 174.3   10 CENTAVOS
Copper-Nickel   **Obv:** State emblem within circle, stars below **Rev:** Caduceus divides denomination, sprays below, date at bottom

Date	Mintage	F	VF	XF	Unc	BU
1901	—	20.00	30.00	60.00	100	—
1902	8,500,000	2.00	5.00	12.00	30.00	—
1907/2	4,000,000	6.00	10.00	25.00	50.00	—
1907	Inc. above	2.00	5.00	12.00	30.00	—
1908	6,000,000	2.00	5.00	12.00	30.00	—
1909	8,000,000	2.00	5.00	12.00	30.00	—

KM# 179.1   10 CENTAVOS
Copper-Nickel   **Obv:** State emblem within circle, stars below **Rev:** Caduceus divides denomination, sprays below, date at bottom

Date	Mintage	F	VF	XF	Unc	BU
1935	10,000,000	0.50	1.00	2.50	10.00	—
1936	10,000,000	0.50	1.00	2.50	10.00	—

KM# 179.2   10 CENTAVOS
4.5100 g., Copper-Nickel, 22.58 mm.   **Obv:** State emblem within circle, stars below **Rev:** Caduceus divides denomination, sprays below, date at bottom

Date	Mintage	F	VF	XF	Unc	BU
1939	—	0.50	1.00	2.50	10.00	—

KM# 179a   10 CENTAVOS
1.7500 g., Zinc, 17.90 mm.   **Obv:** State emblem within circle, stars below **Rev:** Caduceus divides denomination, sprays below, date at bottom

Date	Mintage	F	VF	XF	Unc	BU
1942 (p)	10,000,000	0.50	1.00	2.50	10.00	—

KM# 180   10 CENTAVOS
Copper-Nickel, 22.5 mm.   **Obv:** State emblem within circle, stars below **Rev:** Caduceus divides denomination, sprays below, date at bottom **Edge:** Reeded

Date	Mintage	F	VF	XF	Unc	BU
1937	20,000,000	0.50	1.00	2.50	10.00	—

KM# 159.2   20 CENTAVOS
4.6000 g., 0.9000 Silver 0.1331 oz. ASW   **Obv:** Crossed flags and weapons behind condor topped oval arms, stars below **Obv. Leg.:** REPUBLICA BOLIVIANA **Rev:** Denomination within wreath, date below **Note:** Reduced size dates and lettering, bar below CENTS. The small bar usually found below "S" in "9DS" is missing in the 1886-1888 and 1902 dates. Mint mark in monogram.

Date	Mintage	VG	F	VF	XF	Unc
1901PTS MM	40,000	3.00	5.00	13.50	28.00	60.00
1901PTS MM/.WM	—	3.00	5.00	16.50	35.00	75.00
1902PTS MM	—	6.50	10.00	20.00	50.00	100
1903PTS MM	10,000	10.00	15.00	30.00	75.00	125
1904PTS MM	—	7.00	12.00	20.00	75.00	150
1907PTS MM	—	45.00	90.00	150	275	475

KM# 176   20 CENTAVOS
4.0000 g., 0.8330 Silver 0.1071 oz. ASW Obv: National arms, stars below Rev: Denomination within wreath, date below

Date	Mintage	F	VF	XF	Unc	BU
1909H	1,500,000	2.50	5.00	15.00	30.00	—
1909H Proof	— Value: 500					

KM# 183   20 CENTAVOS
3.2500 g., Zinc, 21.7 mm. Obv: State emblem within circle, stars below Rev: Caduceus divides denomination, sprays below, date at bottom Note: Medal rotation strike.

Date	Mintage	F	VF	XF	Unc	BU
1942 (p)	10,000,000	1.00	2.00	6.00	20.00	—

KM# 175.1   50 CENTAVOS (1/2 Boliviano)
11.5000 g., 0.9000 Silver 0.3327 oz. ASW Obv: Crossed flags and weapons behind condor topped oval arms, stars below Obv. Leg.: REPUBLICA BOLICIANA Rev: Denomination within wreath, date below Note: Mint mark in monogram.

Date	Mintage	VG	F	VF	XF	Unc
1901/0PTS MM	—	BV	8.00	18.50	37.50	60.00
1901PTS MM	Inc. above	BV	6.00	8.00	20.00	45.00
1902PTS MM	1,530,000	BV	6.00	8.00	20.00	45.00
1903/2PTS MM	690,000	BV	7.00	16.00	37.50	60.00
1903PTS MM	Inc. above	BV	6.00	8.00	20.00	45.00
1904PTS MM	1,290,000	BV	6.00	8.00	20.00	45.00
1905PTS MM	1,690,000	BV	6.00	8.00	20.00	45.00
1905PTS AB	Inc. above	BV	6.00	8.00	20.00	45.00
1906PTS MM	630,000	BV	6.00	10.00	30.00	55.00
1906PTS AB	5,500,000	BV	6.00	8.00	20.00	45.00
1907PTS MM	50,000	BV	7.00	10.00	30.00	55.00
1908PTS MM	—	BV	6.00	8.00	20.00	45.00
1908PTS MM Inverted 8	—	BV	12.00	25.00	50.00	75.00

KM# 177   50 CENTAVOS (1/2 Boliviano)
10.0000 g., 0.8330 Silver 0.2678 oz. ASW Obv: National arms, stars below Rev: Denomination within wreath, date below

Date	Mintage	VG	F	VF	XF	Unc
1909H	1,400,000	BV	6.00	10.00	25.00	40.00
1909H	— Value: 350					

KM# 181   50 CENTAVOS (1/2 Boliviano)
Copper-Nickel Obv: State emblem within circle, stars below Rev: Hand holding torch divides date and denomination Note: Most melted upon receipt in Bolivia. Medal rotation strike.

Date	Mintage	F	VF	XF	Unc	BU
1937	8,000,000	10.00	25.00	45.00	75.00	—

KM# 182   50 CENTAVOS (1/2 Boliviano)
8.4500 g., Copper-Nickel, 29.05 mm. Obv: State emblem within circle, stars below Rev: Caduceus divides denomination, sprays below, date at bottom Note: Medal rotation strike.

Date	Mintage	F	VF	XF	Unc	BU
1939	—	0.25	0.50	1.00	5.00	—

KM# 182a.1   50 CENTAVOS (1/2 Boliviano)
Bronze, 24 mm. Obv: State emblem within circle, stars below Rev: Caduceus divides denomination, sprays below, date at bottom Note: Medal rotation strike.

Date	Mintage	F	VF	XF	Unc	BU
1942 (p)	10,000,000	0.35	0.60	1.25	5.00	—

KM# 182a.2   50 CENTAVOS (1/2 Boliviano)
5.0900 g., Bronze, 25 mm. Obv: State emblem within circle, stars below Rev: Caduceus divides denomination, sprays below, date at bottom Edge: Reeded Note: Restrike - poor detail. Medal rotation strike.

Date	Mintage	F	VF	XF	Unc	BU
1942	5,310,000	0.25	0.50	1.00	4.00	—

KM# 184   BOLIVIANO
Bronze Obv: State emblem within circle, stars below Rev: Denomination within wreath, date below Note: Medal rotation strike.

Date	Mintage	F	VF	XF	Unc	BU
1951	10,000,000	0.10	0.20	1.00	3.00	5.00
1951 Proof	10 Value: 200					
1951H	15,000,000	0.10	0.20	1.00	3.00	5.00
1951KN	15,000,000	0.25	0.50	1.50	4.00	6.00

KM# 185   5 BOLIVIANOS
Bronze Obv: National arms, stars below Rev: Denomination within wreath, date below Note: Medal rotation strike.

Date	Mintage	F	VF	XF	Unc	BU
1951	7,000,000	0.25	0.50	1.00	3.50	5.50
1951 Proof	— Value: 200					
1951 H	15,000,000	0.25	0.50	1.00	3.50	5.50
1951 KN	15,000,000	0.60	0.90	1.50	4.00	6.00

KM# 186   10 BOLIVIANOS (1 Bolivar)
Bronze Obv: Armored bust, right Rev: Denomination within wreath, date below Note: Medal rotation strike.

Date	Mintage	F	VF	XF	Unc	BU
1951	40,000,000	0.60	1.00	2.00	4.50	6.50
1951 Proof	— Value: 200					

REFORM COINAGE
1965-1979; 100 Centavos = 1 Peso Boliviano

KM# 187   5 CENTAVOS
Copper Clad Steel Obv: State emblem within circle, stars below Rev: Denomination, date below Note: Medal rotation.

Date	Mintage	F	VF	XF	Unc	BU
1965	10,000,000	0.20	0.30	0.65	1.50	2.00
1970	100,000	0.20	0.30	0.65	2.00	2.50

KM# 188   10 CENTAVOS
Copper Clad Steel Obv: State emblem within circle, stars below Rev: Denomination, date below Note: Medal rotation.

Date	Mintage	F	VF	XF	Unc	BU
1965	10,000,000	0.10	0.25	0.50	1.50	2.00
1967	—	0.10	0.20	0.40	1.00	1.50
1969	5,700,000	0.10	0.20	0.40	1.00	1.50
1971	200,000	0.15	0.25	0.50	1.00	1.50
1972	100,000	0.20	0.40	0.80	1.50	2.00
1973	6,000,000	0.10	0.20	0.40	1.00	1.50

KM# 189   20 CENTAVOS
Nickel Clad Steel Obv: State emblem within circle, stars below Rev: Denomination, date below Note: Medal rotation.

Date	Mintage	F	VF	XF	Unc	BU
1965	5,000,000	0.20	0.40	0.70	2.00	2.50
1967	—	0.20	0.40	0.65	1.75	2.25
1970	400,000	0.20	0.40	0.80	2.50	3.50
1971	400,000	0.20	0.40	0.80	2.50	3.50
1973	5,000,000	0.20	0.40	0.60	1.50	2.00

KM# 193   25 CENTAVOS
Nickel Clad Steel Obv: State emblem within circle, stars below Rev: Denomination, date below Note: Medal rotation.

Date	Mintage	F	VF	XF	Unc	BU
1971	—	0.15	0.30	0.60	1.00	1.50
1972	9,998,000	0.15	0.30	0.60	1.00	1.50

KM# 190   50 CENTAVOS
4.0000 g., Nickel Clad Steel, 24 mm. Obv: State emblem within circle, stars below Rev: Denomination, date at bottom Note: Medal rotation.

Date	Mintage	F	VF	XF	Unc	BU
1965	10,000,000	0.15	0.30	0.65	1.75	2.25
1967	—	0.15	0.30	0.65	1.25	1.75
1972	—	0.15	0.30	0.65	1.25	1.75
1973	5,000,000	0.15	0.30	0.65	1.25	1.75
1974	15,000,000	0.15	0.30	0.65	1.25	1.75
1978	5,000,000	0.15	0.30	0.65	1.25	1.75
1980	3,600,000	0.15	0.30	0.65	1.25	1.75

KM# 192   PESO BOLIVIANO
6.0000 g., Nickel Clad Steel, 27 mm. Series: F.A.O. Obv: State emblem within circle, stars below Rev: Denomination, date below Edge: Reeded Note: Medal rotation.

Date	Mintage	F	VF	XF	Unc	BU
1968	10,000,000	0.20	0.40	0.80	1.75	2.50
1969	—	0.20	0.40	0.80	1.75	2.50

Date	Mintage	F	VF	XF	Unc	BU
1970	10,000,000	0.20	0.40	0.80	1.75	2.50
1972	—	0.20	0.40	0.80	1.75	2.50
1973	5,000,000	0.20	0.40	0.80	1.75	2.50
1974	15,000,000	0.20	0.40	0.80	1.75	2.50
1978	10,000,000	0.20	0.40	0.80	1.75	2.50
1980	2,993,000	0.20	0.40	0.80	1.75	2.50

KM# 191 PESO BOLIVIANO
6.0000 g., Nickel Clad Steel, 27 mm. **Series:** F.A.O. **Obv:** State emblem within circle, stars below **Rev:** Denomination **Note:** Medal rotation.

Date	Mintage	F	VF	XF	Unc	BU
ND(1968)	40,000	1.50	2.50	3.50	6.50	9.00

KM# 197 5 PESOS BOLIVIANOS
8.5000 g., Nickel Clad Steel, 30 mm. **Obv:** State arms within circle, stars below **Rev:** Denomination, date below **Note:** Medal rotation.

Date	Mintage	F	VF	XF	Unc	BU
1976	20,000,000	0.65	1.25	2.50	5.00	6.50
1978	10,000,000	0.65	1.25	2.50	5.00	6.50
1980	5,231,000	0.65	1.25	2.50	5.00	6.50

KM# 194 100 PESOS BOLIVIANOS
10.0000 g., 0.9330 Silver 0.3000 oz. ASW **Subject:** 150th Anniversary of Independence **Obv:** National arms divide dates **Rev:** Simon Bolivar and Hugo Banzer Suarez left, denomination below **Note:** Medal rotation.

Date	Mintage	F	VF	XF	Unc	BU
ND(1975)	160,000	—	BV	7.00	12.00	

KM# 198 200 PESOS BOLIVIANOS
23.3300 g., 0.9250 Silver 0.6938 oz. ASW **Subject:** International Year of the Child **Obv:** State emblem within circle, eagle at top, stars below **Rev:** Children divide small symbols, date at bottom, denomination at top **Note:** Medal rotation.

Date	Mintage	F	VF	XF	Unc	BU
1979	15,000	Value: 17.50				

KM# 195 250 PESOS BOLIVIANOS
15.0000 g., 0.9330 Silver 0.4499 oz. ASW **Subject:** 150th Anniversary of Independence **Obv:** National arms divide dates **Rev:** Conjoined heads left with armored collars, denomination below **Note:** Medal rotation.

Date	Mintage	F	VF	XF	Unc	BU
ND(1975)	140,000	—	BV	10.00	15.00	

KM# 196 500 PESOS BOLIVIANOS
22.0000 g., 0.9330 Silver 0.6599 oz. ASW **Subject:** 150th Anniversary of Independence

Date	Mintage	F	VF	XF	Unc	BU
ND(1975)	100,000	—	BV	16.00	22.50	—

KM# 199 4000 PESOS BOLIVIANOS
17.1700 g., 0.9000 Gold 0.4968 oz. AGW **Subject:** International Year of the Child **Obv:** State emblem within circle, eagle at top, stars below **Rev:** Child playing flute divides symbols, date below, denomination above

Date	Mintage	F	VF	XF	Unc	BU
1979 Proof	6,315	Value: 485				

REFORM COINAGE
1987-; 1,000,000 Peso Bolivianos = 1 Boliviano;
100 Centavos = 1 Boliviano

KM# 200 2 CENTAVOS
1.0000 g., Stainless Steel, 14.01 mm. **Obv:** National arms, star below **Rev:** Denomination within circle, date below **Edge:** Plain

Date	Mintage	F	VF	XF	Unc	BU
1987	20,000,000				0.35	0.50

KM# 201 5 CENTAVOS
Stainless Steel **Obv:** National arms, star below **Rev:** Denomination within circle, date below

Date	Mintage	F	VF	XF	Unc	BU
1987	20,000,000				0.50	0.65

KM# 202 10 CENTAVOS
Stainless Steel **Obv:** National arms, star below **Rev:** Denomination within circle, date below

Date	Mintage	F	VF	XF	Unc	BU
1987	20,000,000			0.25	0.60	0.80
1991	23,000,000			0.20	0.50	0.70
1995	14,000,000			0.20	0.50	0.70
1997	33,000,000			0.20	0.50	0.70

KM# 202a 10 CENTAVOS
2.2300 g., Copper Clad Steel, 18.94 mm. **Obv:** National arms **Obv. Leg.:** REPUBLICA DE BOLIVIA **Rev:** Denomination. **Rev. Leg.:** LA UNION ES LA FUERZA **Edge:** Plain

Date	Mintage	F	VF	XF	Unc	BU
1997	—			0.20	0.50	0.65

KM# 203 20 CENTAVOS
3.6600 g., Stainless Steel, 22 mm. **Obv:** National arms, star below **Obv. Leg.:** REPUBLICA DE BOLIVIA **Rev:** Denomination within circle, date below **Rev. Leg.:** LA UNION ES LA FUERZA **Edge:** Plain

Date	Mintage	F	VF	XF	Unc	BU
1987	20,000,000	—	—	0.30	0.75	1.00
1991	20,000,000	—	—	0.25	0.60	0.80
1995	14,000,000	—	—	0.25	0.60	0.80
1997	19,000,000	—	—	0.25	0.60	0.80

KM# 204 50 CENTAVOS
3.8000 g., Stainless Steel, 23.96 mm. **Obv:** National arms, star below **Obv. Leg.:** REPUBLICA DE BOLIVIA **Rev:** Denomination within circle, date below **Rev. Leg.:** LA UNION ES LA FUERTZA **Edge:** Plain

Date	Mintage	F	VF	XF	Unc	BU
1987	15,000,000	—	—	0.40	1.00	1.25
1991	20,000,000	—	—	0.30	0.75	1.00
1995	14,000,000	—	—	0.30	0.75	1.00
1997	15,000,000	—	—	0.30	0.75	1.00

KM# 205 BOLIVIANO
5.0800 g., Stainless Steel, 26.92 mm. **Obv:** National arms, star below **Obv. Leg.:** REPUBLICA DE BOLIVIA **Rev:** Denomination within circle, date below sprays **Rev. Leg.:** LA UNION ES LA FUERZA **Edge:** Plain

Date	Mintage	F	VF	XF	Unc	BU
1987	10,000,000	—	—	0.60	1.50	2.00
1991	20,000,000	—	—	0.35	0.90	1.20
1995	9,000,000	—	—	0.35	0.90	1.20
1997	17,000,000	—	—	0.35	0.90	1.20

KM# 210 BOLIVIANO
27.0000 g., 0.9250 Silver 0.8029 oz. ASW **Subject:** 70th Anniversary - Bolivian Central Bank **Obv:** National arms above date, stars below **Rev:** Denomination above bank emblem, two dates below sprays

Date	Mintage	F	VF	XF	Unc	BU
1998 Proof	1,000	Value: 75.00				

KM# 206.1   2 BOLIVIANOS
Stainless Steel   **Obv:** National arms, star below
Rev: Denomination within circle, date below

Date	Mintage	F	VF	XF	Unc	BU
1991	18,000,000	—	—	—	2.00	3.00

KM# 206.2   2 BOLIVIANOS
Stainless Steel, 29 mm.   **Obv:** National arms, star below **Rev:**
Denomination within circle, date below **Note:** Increased size.

Date	Mintage	F	VF	XF	Unc	BU
1995	11,000,000	—	—	—	2.00	3.00
1997	—	—	—	—	2.00	3.00

KM# 207   10 BOLIVIANOS
27.0000 g., 0.9250 Silver 0.8029 oz. ASW   **Series:** Ibero -
American **Obv:** National arms within legend, arms surrounding
Rev: Radiant sun behind mountains, denomination, within circle,
two dates below

Date	Mintage	F	VF	XF	Unc	BU
1991 Proof	Est. 50,000	Value: 65.00				

KM# 209   10 BOLIVIANOS
27.1300 g., 0.9250 Silver 0.8068 oz. ASW   **Series:** Ibero -
American **Obv:** Bolivian arms within legend, arms surrounding
Rev: Folk dancer, denomination within circle, date below

Date	Mintage	F	VF	XF	Unc	BU
1997 Proof	33,000	Value: 65.00				

KM# 211   50 BOLIVIANOS
27.0000 g., 0.9250 Silver 0.8029 oz. ASW   **Subject:** 450th
Anniversary of La Paz **Obv:** National arms, date below, stars at
bottom **Rev:** City arms above church building, denomination,
within circle, two dates below

Date	Mintage	F	VF	XF	Unc	BU
1998 Proof	2,000	Value: 70.00				

PATTERNS
Including off metal strikes

KM#	Date	Mintage	Identification	Mkt Val
Pn54	1902 MM	—	20 Centavos. Brass. Struck at La Paz.	100
Pn55	1902 MM	—	20 Centavos. Brass. Struck at La Paz. 1/2 Medio Boliviano/20 Centavos error.	75.00
Pn56	1902 MM	—	50 Centavos. Brass.	100
Pn57	1942	—	50 Centavos. Silver. Struck at La Paz. KM#182a.1.	300
Pn58	1952	—	35 Gramos. Brass. Struck at La Paz. KM MB4.	—

PIEFORTS

KM#	Date	Mintage	Identification	Issue Price	Mkt Val
P9	1979	90	200 Pesos. Silver. KM#198.	—	200
P10	1979	47	4000 Pesos. Gold. KM#199.	—	1,000

TRIAL STRIKES

KM#	Date	Mintage	Identification	Issue Price	Mkt Val
TS1	ND(1909)	—	20 Centavos. Silver. 23.2 mm. Uniface.	—	—
TS2	1942	—	10 Centavos. Lead. KM179a, uniface	—	150

BOSNIA AND HERZEGOVINA

The Republic of Bosnia and Herzegovina borders Croatia to
the north and west, Serbia to the east and Montenegro in the
southeast with only 12.4 mi. of coastline. The total land area is
19,735 sq. mi. (51,129 sq. km.). They have a population of *4.34
million. Capital: Sarajevo. Electricity, mining and agriculture are
leading industries.

After the defeat of Germany in WWII, during which Bosnia
was under the control of Pavelic of Croatia, a new Socialist
Republic was formed under Marshall Tito having six constituent
republics, all subservient, quite similar to the constitution of the
U.S.S.R. Military and civil loyalty was with Tito, not with Moscow.
In Jan. 1990, the Yugoslav Government announced a rewriting
of the Constitution, abolishing the Communist Party's monopoly
of power. Opposition parties were legalized in July 1990. On Oct.
15, 1991 the National Assembly adopted a "Memorandum on
Sovereignty", the envisaged Bosnian autonomy within a Yugoslav federation. In March 1992, an agreement was reached under
EC auspices by Moslems, Serbs and Croats to set up 3 autonomous ethnic communities under a central Bosnian authority.
Independence was declared on April 5, 1992. The 2 Serbian
members of government resigned and fighting broke out
between all 3 ethnic communities. The Dayton (Ohio) Peace
Accord was signed in 1995, which recognized the Federation of
Bosnia and Herzegovina and the Srpska (Serbian) Republic.
Both governments maintain separate military forces, school systems, etc. The United Nations is currently providing humanitarian
aid while a recent peace treaty allowed NATO "Peace Keeping"
forces to be deployed in Dec. 1995 replacing the United Nations
troops previously acting in a similar role.

MINT MARK
PM - Pobjoy Mint

MONETARY SYSTEM
1 Dinara = 100 Para, 1992-1998
1 Convertible Marka = 100 Convertible Feniga =
1 Deutschemark 1998-
  NOTE: German Euros circulate freely.

REPUBLIC
DINARA COINAGE

KM# 1   500 DINARA
Copper-Nickel   **Series:** Preserve Planet Earth **Obv:** National
arms above bridge, date at bottom **Rev:** Brontosaurus, facing
back, looking left, denomination below

Date	Mintage	F	VF	XF	Unc	BU
1993 Prooflike	—	—	—	—	—	14.00

KM# 4   500 DINARA
Copper-Nickel   **Series:** Preserve Planet Earth **Obv:** National
arms above bridge, date below **Rev:** Tyrannosaurus Rex, facing
right, looking left, denomination below

Date	Mintage	F	VF	XF	Unc	BU
1993 Prooflike	—	—	—	—	—	14.00

KM# 20   500 DINARA
Copper-Nickel **Series:** Preserve Planet Earth **Obv:** National arms above bridge, date below **Rev:** Eohippus

Date	Mintage	F	VF	XF	Unc	BU
1994 Proof	—	—	—	—	10.00	15.00

KM# 23   500 DINARA
Copper-Nickel **Series:** Preserve Planet Earth **Obv:** National arms above bridge, date below **Rev:** Gray Wolf, right, above denomination

Date	Mintage	F	VF	XF	Unc	BU
1994 Prooflike	—	—	—	—	—	14.00

KM# 24   500 DINARA
Copper-Nickel **Series:** Preserve Planet Earth **Obv:** National arms above bridge, date below **Rev:** Black Bear, left, with cub facing, denomination below

Date	Mintage	F	VF	XF	Unc	BU
1994 Prooflike	—	—	—	—	—	14.00

KM# 25   500 DINARA
Copper-Nickel **Series:** Preserve Planet Earth **Obv:** National arms above bridge, date below **Rev:** River Kingfisher, left, fish in beak, denomination below

Date	Mintage	F	VF	XF	Unc	BU
1994	—	—	—	—	10.00	14.00

KM# 39   500 DINARA
Copper-Nickel **Series:** Preserve Planet Earth **Obv:** National arms above bridge, date below **Rev:** Przewalskii Horses

Date	Mintage	F	VF	XF	Unc	BU
1995	—	—	—	—	12.00	15.00

KM# 42   500 DINARA
Copper-Nickel **Series:** Preserve Planet Earth **Obv:** National arms above bridge, date below **Rev:** Hedgehogs

Date	Mintage	F	VF	XF	Unc	BU
1995	—	—	—	—	12.00	15.00

KM# 64   500 DINARA
Copper-Nickel **Series:** European Youth Olympics **Obv:** National arms above bridge, date below **Rev:** Flame

Date	Mintage	F	VF	XF	Unc	BU
1995	—	—	—	—	8.50	10.00

KM# 65   500 DINARA
Copper-Nickel **Series:** European Youth Olympics **Obv:** National arms above bridge, date below **Rev:** Rings

Date	Mintage	F	VF	XF	Unc	BU
1995	—	—	—	—	8.50	10.00

KM# 52   500 DINARA
Copper-Nickel **Series:** Olympics **Obv:** National arms above bridge, date below **Rev:** Long jumper

Date	Mintage	F	VF	XF	Unc	BU
1996	—	—	—	—	8.50	10.00

KM# 53   500 DINARA
Copper-Nickel **Series:** Olympics **Obv:** National arms above bridge, date below **Rev:** Sprinter

Date	Mintage	F	VF	XF	Unc	BU
1996	—	—	—	—	8.50	10.00

KM# 54   500 DINARA
Copper-Nickel **Series:** Olympics **Obv:** National arms above bridge, date below **Rev:** Wrestlers

Date	Mintage	F	VF	XF	Unc	BU
1996	—	—	—	—	8.50	10.00

KM# 55   500 DINARA
Copper-Nickel **Series:** Olympics **Obv:** National arms above bridge, date below **Rev:** Fencers

Date	Mintage	F	VF	XF	Unc	BU
1996	—	—	—	—	8.50	10.00

KM# 76   500 DINARA
Copper-Nickel **Series:** Preserve Planet Earth **Obv:** National arms above bridge, date below **Rev:** Hoopoe Birds

Date	Mintage	F	VF	XF	Unc	BU
1996	—	—	—	—	12.00	15.00

KM# 79   500 DINARA
Copper-Nickel **Series:** Preserve Planet Earth **Obv:** National arms above bridge, date below **Rev:** Goosander Birds

Date	Mintage	F	VF	XF	Unc	BU
1996	—	—	—	—	14.00	18.00

KM# 95   500 DINARA
Copper-Nickel **Subject:** Jurassic Park **Obv:** National arms above bridge, date below **Rev:** Tyrannosaurus Rex, Jurassic Park logo

Date	Mintage	F	VF	XF	Unc	BU
1997	—	—	—	—	14.00	18.00

KM# 2   750 DINARA
28.2800 g., 0.9250 Silver 0.8410 oz. ASW **Series:** Preserve Planet Earth **Obv:** National arms above bridge, date below **Rev:** Brontosaurus facing back, looking left, denomination below

Date	Mintage	F	VF	XF	Unc	BU
1993 Proof	Est. 30,000		Value: 37.50			

KM# 5   750 DINARA
28.2800 g., 0.9250 Silver 0.8410 oz. ASW **Series:** Preserve Planet Earth **Obv:** National arms above bridge, date below **Rev:** Tyrannosaurus Rex, facing right, looking left, denomination below

Date	Mintage	F	VF	XF	Unc	BU
1993 Proof	Est. 30,000		Value: 37.50			

KM# 7   750 DINARA
28.2800 g., 0.9250 Silver 0.8410 oz. ASW **Series:** Olympics **Obv:** National arms above bridge, date below **Rev:** 2 Bobsledders with sled, denomination below, within circle

Date	Mintage	F	VF	XF	Unc	BU
1993 Proof	Est. 30,000		Value: 45.00			

KM# 9   750 DINARA
28.2800 g., 0.9250 Silver 0.8410 oz. ASW **Series:** Olympics **Obv:** National arms above bridge, date below **Rev:** Downhill skier above denomination, within circle

Date	Mintage	F	VF	XF	Unc	BU
1993 Proof	Est. 30,000		Value: 45.00			

KM# 11   750 DINARA
28.2800 g., 0.9250 Silver 0.8410 oz. ASW **Series:** Olympics **Obv:** National arms above bridge, date below **Rev:** Cross-country skier above denomination, within circle

Date	Mintage	F	VF	XF	Unc	BU
1993 Proof	Est. 30,000		Value: 45.00			

KM# 13   750 DINARA
28.2800 g., 0.9250 Silver 0.8410 oz. ASW **Series:** Lillehammer 1994 - 17th Winter Olympic Games **Obv:** National arms above bridge, date below **Rev:** Pairs Figure Skating above denomination, within circle

Date	Mintage	F	VF	XF	Unc	BU
1993 Proof	Est. 30,000		Value: 45.00			

KM# 26   750 DINARA
28.2800 g., 0.9250 Silver 0.8410 oz. ASW **Series:** Preserve Planet Earth **Obv:** National arms above bridge, date below **Rev:** Wolf right, denomination below

Date	Mintage	F	VF	XF	Unc	BU
1994 Proof	Est. 30,000		Value: 40.00			

KM# 27   750 DINARA
28.2800 g., 0.9250 Silver 0.8410 oz. ASW **Series:** Preserve
Planet Earth **Obv:** National arms above bridge, date below
Rev: Black bear left with cub facing, denomination below

Date	Mintage	F	VF	XF	Unc	BU
1994 Proof	Est. 30,000			Value: 40.00		

KM# 28   750 DINARA
28.2800 g., 0.9250 Silver 0.8410 oz. ASW **Series:** Preserve
Planet Earth **Obv:** National arms above bridge, date below
Rev: River Kingfisher left, fish in beak, denomination below

Date	Mintage	F	VF	XF	Unc	BU
1994 Proof	Est. 30,000			Value: 35.00		

KM# 21   750 DINARA
28.2800 g., 0.9250 Silver 0.8410 oz. ASW **Series:** Preserve
Planet Earth **Obv:** National arms above bridge, date below
Rev: Eohippu **Note:** Similar to 10,000 Dinara, KM#22.

Date	Mintage	F	VF	XF	Unc	BU
1994 Proof	Est. 30,000			Value: 37,50		

KM# 40   750 DINARA
28.2800 g., 0.9250 Silver 0.8410 oz. ASW **Series:** Preserve
Planet Earth **Obv:** National arms above bridge, date below **Rev:**
Przewalskii horses right, denomination below

Date	Mintage	F	VF	XF	Unc	BU
1995 Proof	Est. 30,000			Value: 40.00		

KM# 43   750 DINARA
28.2800 g., 0.9250 Silver 0.8410 oz. ASW **Series:** Preserve
Planet Earth **Obv:** National arms above bridge, date below
Rev: Hedgehog left with babies, denomination below

Date	Mintage	F	VF	XF	Unc	BU
1995 Proof	Est. 30,000			Value: 40.00		

KM# 66   750 DINARA
28.2800 g., 0.9250 Silver 0.8410 oz. ASW **Series:** European
Youth Olympics **Obv:** National arms above bridge, date below
Rev: Figures within small circles on flame, denomination below

Date	Mintage	F	VF	XF	Unc	BU
1995 Proof	Est. 30,000			Value: 37.50		

KM# 67   750 DINARA
28.2800 g., 0.9250 Silver 0.8410 oz. ASW **Series:** European
Youth Olympics **Obv:** National arms above bridge, date below
Rev: Man on rings event, denomination below

Date	Mintage	F	VF	XF	Unc	BU
1995 Proof	Est. 30,000			Value: 37.50		

KM# 56   750 DINARA
28.2800 g., 0.9250 Silver 0.8410 oz. ASW **Series:** Atlanta 1996
- 26th Summer Olympics **Obv:** National arms above bridge, date
below **Rev:** Long jumper right, denomination below

Date	Mintage	F	VF	XF	Unc	BU
1996 Proof	Est. 30,000			Value: 35.00		

KM# 57   750 DINARA
28.2800 g., 0.9250 Silver 0.8410 oz. ASW **Series:** Olympics
Obv: National arms above bridge, date below **Rev:** Sprinter, right,
denomination below

Date	Mintage	F	VF	XF	Unc	BU
1996 Proof	Est. 30,000			Value: 35.00		

KM# 58   750 DINARA
28.2800 g., 0.9250 Silver 0.8410 oz. ASW **Series:** Olympics
Obv: National arms above bridge, date below **Rev:** Wrestlers,
denomination below

Date	Mintage	F	VF	XF	Unc	BU
1996 Proof	Est. 30,000			Value: 35.00		

KM# 59   750 DINARA
28.2800 g., 0.9250 Silver 0.8410 oz. ASW **Series:** Olympics
Obv: National arms above bridge, date below **Rev:** Fencers,
denomination below

Date	Mintage	F	VF	XF	Unc	BU
1996 Proof	Est. 30,000			Value: 35.00		

KM# 77   750 DINARA
28.2800 g., 0.9250 Silver 0.8410 oz. ASW **Series:** Preserve
Planet Earth **Obv:** National arms above bridge, date below
Rev: Hoopoe birds, denomination below

Date	Mintage	F	VF	XF	Unc	BU
1996 Proof	Est. 30,000			Value: 35.00		

KM# 80   750 DINARA
28.2800 g., 0.9250 Silver 0.8410 oz. ASW **Series:** Preserve
Planet Earth **Obv:** National arms above bridge, date below
Rev: Goosander birds, denomination below

Date	Mintage	F	VF	XF	Unc	BU
1996 Proof	Est. 30,000			Value: 35.00		

KM# 96   750 DINARA
28.2800 g., 0.9250 Silver 0.8410 oz. ASW **Subject:** Jurassic Park
Obv: National arms above bridge, date below **Rev:** Tyrannosaurus
Rex, left, Jurassic Park logo, denomination at bottom

Date	Mintage	F	VF	XF	Unc	BU
1997 Proof	Est. 10,000			Value: 45.00		

KM# 3 10000 DINARA
6.2200 g., 0.9990 Gold 0.1998 oz. AGW **Series:** Preserve
Planet Earth **Obv:** National arms above bridge, date below
Rev: Brontosaurus, facing back, looking left, denomination below

Date	Mintage	F	VF	XF	Unc	BU
1993 Proof	Est. 5,000		Value: 195			

KM# 6 10000 DINARA
6.2200 g., 0.9990 Gold 0.1998 oz. AGW **Series:** Preserve
Planet Earth **Obv:** National arms above bridge, date below **Rev:**
Tyrannosaurus Rex, facing right, looking left, denomination below

Date	Mintage	F	VF	XF	Unc	BU
1993 Proof	Est. 5,000		Value: 195			

KM# 8 10000 DINARA
6.2200 g., 0.9990 Gold 0.1998 oz. AGW **Series:** Olympics
Obv: National arms above bridge, date below **Rev:** Two
bobsledders starting race

Date	Mintage	F	VF	XF	Unc	BU
1993 Proof	Est. 5,000		Value: 200			

KM# 10 10000 DINARA
6.2200 g., 0.9990 Gold 0.1998 oz. AGW **Series:** Olympics
Obv: National arms above bridge, date below **Rev:** Downhill skier

Date	Mintage	F	VF	XF	Unc	BU
1993	Est. 5,000		Value: 200			

KM# 12 10000 DINARA
6.2200 g., 0.9990 Gold 0.1998 oz. AGW **Series:** Olympics **Obv:**
National arms above bridge, date below **Rev:** Cross-country skier

Date	Mintage	F	VF	XF	Unc	BU
1993 Proof	Est. 5,000		Value: 200			

KM# 14 10000 DINARA
6.2200 g., 0.9990 Gold 0.1998 oz. AGW **Series:** Olympics
Obv: National arms above bridge, date below **Rev:** Pair skating

Date	Mintage	F	VF	XF	Unc	BU
1993 Proof	Est. 5,000		Value: 200			

KM# 22 10000 DINARA
6.2200 g., 0.9990 Gold 0.1998 oz. AGW **Series:** Preserve
Planet Earth **Obv:** National arms above bridge, date below
Rev: Eohippu, right, denomination below

Date	Mintage	F	VF	XF	Unc	BU
1994 Proof	Est. 5,000		Value: 195			

KM# 29 10000 DINARA
6.2200 g., 0.9990 Gold 0.1998 oz. AGW **Series:** Preserve
Planet Earth **Obv:** National arms above bridge, date below
Rev: Wolf walking right

Date	Mintage	F	VF	XF	Unc	BU
1994 Proof	5,000		Value: 195			

KM# 30 10000 DINARA
6.2200 g., 0.9990 Gold 0.1998 oz. AGW **Series:** Preserve
Planet Earth **Obv:** National arms above bridge, date below
Rev: Black bear and cub walking right

Date	Mintage	F	VF	XF	Unc	BU
1994 Proof	5,000		Value: 195			

KM# 31 10000 DINARA
6.2200 g., 0.9990 Gold 0.1998 oz. AGW **Series:** Preserve
Planet Earth **Obv:** National arms above bridge, date below
Rev: Kingfisher left with fish in bill

Date	Mintage	F	VF	XF	Unc	BU
1994 Proof	5,000		Value: 195			

KM# 41 10000 DINARA
6.2200 g., 0.9990 Gold 0.1998 oz. AGW **Series:** Preserve
Planet Earth **Obv:** National arms above bridge, date below
Rev: Przewalskii horses

Date	Mintage	F	VF	XF	Unc	BU
1995 Proof	Est. 5,000		Value: 195			

KM# 44 10000 DINARA
6.2200 g., 0.9990 Gold 0.1998 oz. AGW **Series:** Preserve
Planet Earth **Obv:** National arms above bridge, date below
Rev: Hedgehogs

Date	Mintage	F	VF	XF	Unc	BU
1995 Proof	Est. 5,000		Value: 195			

KM# 60 10000 DINARA
6.2200 g., 0.9990 Gold 0.1998 oz. AGW **Series:** Olympics
Obv: National arms above bridge, date below **Rev:** Long jumper

Date	Mintage	F	VF	XF	Unc	BU
1996 Proof	Est. 5,000		Value: 200			

KM# 61 10000 DINARA
6.2200 g., 0.9990 Gold 0.1998 oz. AGW **Series:** Olympics
Obv: National arms above bridge, date below **Rev:** Sprinter

Date	Mintage	F	VF	XF	Unc	BU
1996 Proof	Est. 5,000		Value: 200			

KM# 62 10000 DINARA
6.2200 g., 0.9990 Gold 0.1998 oz. AGW **Series:** Olympics
Obv: National arms above bridge, date below **Rev:** Wrestlers

Date	Mintage	F	VF	XF	Unc	BU
1996 Proof	Est. 5,000		Value: 200			

KM# 63 10000 DINARA
6.2200 g., 0.9990 Gold 0.1998 oz. AGW **Series:** Olympics
Obv: National arms above bridge, date below **Rev:** Fencers

Date	Mintage	F	VF	XF	Unc	BU
1996 Proof	Est. 5,000		Value: 200			

KM# 78 10000 DINARA
6.2200 g., 0.9990 Gold 0.1998 oz. AGW **Series:** Preserve
Planet Earth **Obv:** National arms above bridge, date below
Rev: Hoopoe birds

Date	Mintage	F	VF	XF	Unc	BU
1996 Proof	Est. 5,000		Value: 195			

KM# 81 10000 DINARA
6.2200 g., 0.9990 Gold 0.1998 oz. AGW **Series:** Preserve
Planet Earth **Obv:** National arms above bridge, date below
Rev: Goosander birds

Date	Mintage	F	VF	XF	Unc	BU
1996 Proof	Est. 5,000		Value: 195			

KM# 97 10000 DINARA
6.2200 g., 0.9990 Gold 0.1998 oz. AGW **Subject:** Jurassic Park
Obv: National arms above bridge, date below **Rev:** Tyrannosaurus
Rex, left, Jurassic Park logo above, denomination below

Date	Mintage	F	VF	XF	Unc	BU
1997 Proof	Est. 2,500		Value: 195			

MARKA / MARAKA COINAGE

KM# 98 5 MARKA
Copper-Nickel **Subject:** Princess Diana **Obv:** National arms
above bridge, date below **Rev:** Portrait and map

Date	Mintage	F	VF	XF	Unc	BU
1998	—	—	—	—	9.50	12.00

KM# 111 5 MARKA
Copper-Nickel **Subject:** Sydney 2000 - 27th Summer Olympics
Obv: National arms above bridge, date below **Rev:** Javelin thrower

Date	Mintage	F	VF	XF	Unc	BU
1998	—	—	—	—	8.50	10.00

KM# 99 10 MARKA
28.2800 g., 0.9250 Silver 0.8410 oz. ASW **Subject:** Princess
Diana **Obv:** National arms above bridge, date below **Rev:** Portrait
and map divide dates, denomination at bottom

Date	Mintage	F	VF	XF	Unc	BU
1998 Proof	Est. 10,000		Value: 55.00			

KM# 112 10 MARKA
28.2800 g., 0.9250 Silver 0.8410 oz. ASW **Subject:** Sydney
2000 - 27th Summer Olympics **Obv:** National arms above bridge,
date below **Rev:** Javelin thrower, right, denomination lower left

Date	Mintage	F	VF	XF	Unc	BU
1998 Proof	Est. 10,00u		Value: 50.00			

KM# 100 20 MARKA
1.2441 g., 0.9999 Gold 0.0400 oz. AGW **Subject:** Princess Diana
Obv: National arms above bridge, date below **Rev:** Portrait and map

Date	Mintage	F	VF	XF	Unc	BU
1998 Proof	Est. 10,000		Value: 55.00			

KM# 101 50 MARKA
3.1103 g., 0.9999 Gold 0.1000 oz. AGW **Subject:** Princess Diana
Obv: National arms above bridge, date below **Rev:** Portrait and map

Date	Mintage	F	VF	XF	Unc	BU
1998 Proof	Est. 7,500		Value: 110			

KM# 102 100 MARKA
6.2206 g., 0.9999 Gold 0.2000 oz. AGW **Subject:** Princess Diana
Obv: National arms above bridge, date below **Rev:** Portrait and map

Date	Mintage	F	VF	XF	Unc	BU
1998 Proof	Est. 5,000		Value: 195			

KM# 113 100 MARKA
6.2206 g., 0.9999 Gold 0.2000 oz. AGW **Subject:** Sydney 2000
- 27th Summer Olympics **Obv:** National arms above bridge, date
below **Rev:** Javelin thrower

Date	Mintage	F	VF	XF	Unc	BU
1998 Proof	Est. 5,000		Value: 195			

KM# 103 250 MARKA
15.5517 g., 0.9999 Gold 0.4999 oz. AGW **Subject:** Princess Diana
Obv: National arms above bridge, date below **Rev:** Portrait and map

Date	Mintage	F	VF	XF	Unc	BU
1998 Proof	Est. 3,000		Value: 495			

TRADE COINAGE

KM# 15 1/25 DUKAT
1.2440 g., 0.9999 Gold 0.0400 oz. AGW **Subject:** Hajj - Kaaba
in Mecca **Obv:** National arms above bridge, date below
Rev: Building and denomination within circle

Date	Mintage	F	VF	XF	Unc	BU
1993 Proof	Est. 25,000		Value: 50.00			

KM# 16 1/10 DUKAT
3.1103 g., 0.9999 Gold 0.1000 oz. AGW **Subject:** Hajj - Kaaba
in Mecca **Obv:** National arms above bridge, date below
Rev: Building and denomination within circle

Date	Mintage	F	VF	XF	Unc	BU
1993 Proof	Est. 20,000		Value: 100			

KM# 17 1/5 DUKAT
6.2200 g., 0.9999 Gold 0.1999 oz. AGW **Subject:** Hajj - Kaaba
in Mecca **Obv:** National arms above bridge, date below
Rev: Building and denomination within circle

Date	Mintage	F	VF	XF	Unc	BU
1993 Proof	Est. 5,000		Value: 200			

KM# 18 1/2 DUKAT
15.5510 g., 0.9999 Gold 0.4999 oz. AGW **Subject:** Hajj - Kaaba
in Mecca **Obv:** National arms above bridge, date below **Rev:**
Building and denomination within circle

Date	Mintage	F	VF	XF	Unc	BU
1993 Proof	Est. 5,000		Value: 475			

KM# 19 DUKAT
31.1030 g., 0.9999 Gold 0.9998 oz. AGW **Subject:** Hajj - Kaaba
in Mecca **Obv:** National arms above bridge, date below
Rev: Building and denomination within circle

Date	Mintage	F	VF	XF	Unc	BU
1993 Proof	Est. 5,000		Value: 975			
1994 Proof	—		Value: 975			

KM# 32 1/25 SUVERENA
1.2441 g., 0.9999 Gold 0.0400 oz. AGW **Subject:** Lipizzaner
Stallion **Obv:** National arms above bridge, date below **Rev:** Horse
rearing right, denomination below

Date	Mintage	F	VF	XF	Unc	BU
1994 Proof	—		Value: 52.00			

KM# 45 1/25 SUVERENA
1.2441 g., 0.9999 Gold 0.0400 oz. AGW **Subject:** English Hack
Obv: National arms above bridge, date below **Rev:** Horse running
left, denomination below

Date	Mintage	F	VF	XF	Unc	BU
1995 Proof	Est. 15,000		Value: 52.00			

KM# 70 1/25 SUVERENA
1.2441 g., 0.9999 Gold 0.0400 oz. AGW **Subject:** Hanoverian
Stallion **Obv:** National arms above bridge, date below **Rev:** Horse
left, denomination below

Date	Mintage	F	VF	XF	Unc	BU
1996 Proof	Est. 15,000		Value: 52.00			

KM# 89 1/25 SUVERENA
1.2441 g., 0.9999 Gold 0.0400 oz. AGW **Subject:** The Arab
Obv: National arms above bridge, date below **Rev:** Horse right,
denomination below

Date	Mintage	F	VF	XF	Unc	BU
1997 Proof	Est. 15,000		Value: 52.00			

KM# 104   1/25 SUVERENA
1.2441 g., 0.9999 Gold 0.0400 oz. AGW **Subject:** Chinese Horse **Obv:** National arms above bridge, date below **Rev:** Horse, denomination below

Date	Mintage	F	VF	XF	Unc	BU
1998 Proof	Est. 15,000	Value: 52.00				

KM# 33   1/10 SUVERENA
3.1103 g., 0.9999 Gold 0.1000 oz. AGW **Subject:** Lipizzaner Stallion **Obv:** National arms above bridge, date below **Rev:** Horse rearing right, denomination below

Date	Mintage	F	VF	XF	Unc	BU
1994 Proof	—	Value: 100				

KM# 46   1/10 SUVERENA
3.1103 g., 0.9999 Gold 0.1000 oz. AGW **Subject:** English Hack **Obv:** National arms above bridge, date below **Rev:** Horse running left, denomination below

Date	Mintage	F	VF	XF	Unc	BU
1995 Proof	Est. 10,000	Value: 100				

KM# 71   1/10 SUVERENA
3.1103 g., 0.9999 Gold 0.1000 oz. AGW **Subject:** Hanoverian Stallion **Obv:** National arms above bridge, date below **Rev:** Horse left, denomination below

Date	Mintage	F	VF	XF	Unc	BU
1996 Proof	Est. 10,000	Value: 100				

KM# 90   1/10 SUVERENA
3.1103 g., 0.9999 Gold 0.1000 oz. AGW **Subject:** The Arab **Obv:** National arms above bridge, date below **Rev:** Horse right, denomination below

Date	Mintage	F	VF	XF	Unc	BU
1997 Proof	Est. 10,000	Value: 100				

KM# 105   1/10 SUVERENA
3.1103 g., 0.9999 Gold 0.1000 oz. AGW **Subject:** Chinese Horse **Obv:** National arms above bridge, date below **Rev:** Horse left, denomination below

Date	Mintage	F	VF	XF	Unc	BU
1998 Proof	Est. 10,000	Value: 100				

KM# 34   1/5 SUVERENA
6.2207 g., 0.9999 Gold 0.2000 oz. AGW **Subject:** Lipizzaner Stallion **Obv:** National arms above bridge, date below **Rev:** Horse rearing right, denomination below

Date	Mintage	F	VF	XF	Unc	BU
1994 Proof	—	Value: 195				

KM# 47   1/5 SUVERENA
6.2207 g., 0.9999 Gold 0.2000 oz. AGW **Subject:** English Hack **Obv:** National arms above bridge, date below **Rev:** Horse running left, denomination below

Date	Mintage	F	VF	XF	Unc	BU
1995 Proof	Est. 5,000	Value: 195				

KM# 72   1/5 SUVERENA
6.2207 g., 0.9999 Gold 0.2000 oz. AGW **Subject:** Hanoverian Stallion **Obv:** National arms above bridge, date below **Rev:** Horse left, denomination below

Date	Mintage	F	VF	XF	Unc	BU
1996 Proof	Est. 5,000	Value: 195				

KM# 91   1/5 SUVERENA
6.2207 g., 0.9999 Gold 0.2000 oz. AGW **Subject:** The Arab **Obv:** National arms above bridge, date below **Rev:** Horse right, denomination below

Date	Mintage	F	VF	XF	Unc	BU
1997 Proof	Est. 5,000	Value: 195				

KM# 106   1/5 SUVERENA
6.2207 g., 0.9999 Gold 0.2000 oz. AGW **Subject:** Chinese Horse **Obv:** National arms above bridge, date below **Rev:** Horse left, denomination below

Date	Mintage	F	VF	XF	Unc	BU
1998 Proof	Est. 5,000	Value: 195				

KM# 35   1/2 SUVERENA
15.5517 g., 0.9999 Gold 0.4999 oz. AGW **Subject:** Lipizzaner Stallion **Obv:** National arms above bridge, date below **Rev:** Horse rearing right, denomination below

Date	Mintage	F	VF	XF	Unc	BU
1994 Proof	—	Value: 475				

KM# 48   1/2 SUVERENA
15.5517 g., 0.9999 Gold 0.4999 oz. AGW **Subject:** English Hack **Obv:** National arms above bridge, date below **Rev:** Horse running left, denomination below

Date	Mintage	F	VF	XF	Unc	BU
1995 Proof	Est. 2,500	Value: 475				

KM# 73   1/2 SUVERENA
15.5517 g., 0.9999 Gold 0.4999 oz. AGW **Subject:** Hanoverian Stallion **Obv:** National arms above bridge, date below **Rev:** Horse left, denomination below

Date	Mintage	F	VF	XF	Unc	BU
1996 Proof	Est. 2,500	Value: 475				

KM# 92   1/2 SUVERENA
15.5517 g., 0.9999 Gold 0.4999 oz. AGW **Subject:** The Arab **Obv:** National arms above bridge, date below **Rev:** Horse right, denomination below

Date	Mintage	F	VF	XF	Unc	BU
1997 Proof	Est. 2,500	Value: 475				

KM# 107   1/2 SUVERENA
15.5517 g., 0.9999 Gold 0.4999 oz. AGW **Subject:** Chinese Horse **Obv:** National arms above bridge, date below **Rev:** Horse left, denomination below

Date	Mintage	F	VF	XF	Unc	BU
1998 Proof	Est. 2,500	Value: 475				

KM# 37   SUVERENA
31.1035 g., 0.9999 Silver 0.9999 oz. ASW **Subject:** Lipizzaner Stallion **Obv:** National arms above bridge, date below **Rev:** Horse rearing right, denomination below

Date	Mintage	F	VF	XF	Unc	BU
1994 Proof	—	Value: 50.00				

KM# 37a   SUVERENA
31.1035 g., 0.9999 Gold 0.9999 oz. AGW **Subject:** Lipizzaner Stallion **Obv:** National arms above bridge, date below **Rev:** Horse rearing right, denomination below

Date	Mintage	F	VF	XF	Unc	BU
1994 Proof	—	Value: 1,000				

KM# 36   SUVERENA
Copper-Nickel **Subject:** Lipizzaner Stallion **Obv:** National arms above bridge, date below **Rev:** Horse rearing right, denomination below

Date	Mintage	F	VF	XF	Unc	BU
1994	—	—	—	10.00	12.00	

KM# 49   SUVERENA
Copper-Nickel **Subject:** English Hack **Obv:** National arms above bridge, date below **Rev:** Horse running left, denomination below

Date	Mintage	F	VF	XF	Unc	BU
1995	—	—	—	10.00	12.00	

KM# 50   SUVERENA
31.1035 g., 0.9999 Silver 0.9999 oz. ASW **Subject:** English Hack **Obv:** National arms above bridge, date below **Rev:** Horse running left, denomination below

Date	Mintage	F	VF	XF	Unc	BU
1995 Proof	Est. 30,000	Value: 50.00				

KM# 51   SUVERENA
31.1035 g., 0.9999 Gold 0.9999 oz. AGW **Subject:** English Hack **Obv:** National arms above bridge, date below **Rev:** Horse running left, denomination below

Date	Mintage	F	VF	XF	Unc	BU
1995 Proof	Est. 850	Value: 1,000				

KM# 74   SUVERENA
Copper-Nickel **Subject:** Hanoverian Stallion **Obv:** National arms above bridge, date below **Rev:** Horse left, denomination below

Date	Mintage	F	VF	XF	Unc	BU
1996	—	—	—	10.00	12.00	

KM# 75   SUVERENA
31.1035 g., 0.9999 Silver 0.9999 oz. ASW **Subject:** Hanoverian Horse **Obv:** National arms above bridge, date below **Rev:** Horse left, denomination below

Date	Mintage	F	VF	XF	Unc	BU
1996 Proof	Est. 30,000	Value: 50.00				

KM# A76   SUVERENA
31.1035 g., 0.9999 Gold 0.9999 oz. AGW **Subject:** Hanoverian Horse **Obv:** National arms above bridge, date below **Rev:** Horse left, denomination below

Date	Mintage	F	VF	XF	Unc	BU
1996 Proof	850	Value: 1,000				

KM# 93   SUVERENA
Copper-Nickel **Subject:** The Arab **Obv:** National arms above bridge, date below **Rev:** Horse right, denomination below

Date	Mintage	F	VF	XF	Unc	BU
1997	—	—	—	12.00	15.00	

KM# 93a   SUVERENA
31.1035 g., 0.9999 Silver 0.9999 oz. ASW **Subject:** The Arab **Obv:** National arms above bridge, date below **Rev:** Horse right, denomination below

Date	Mintage	F	VF	XF	Unc	BU
1997 Proof	Est. 30,000	Value: 50.00				

KM# 93b   SUVERENA
31.1035 g., 0.9999 Gold 0.9999 oz. AGW **Subject:** The Arab **Obv:** National arms above bridge, date below **Rev:** Horse right, denomination below

Date	Mintage	F	VF	XF	Unc	BU
1997 Proof	850	Value: 1,000				

KM# 108   SUVERENA
Copper-Nickel **Subject:** Chinese Horse **Obv:** National arms above bridge, date below **Rev:** Horse left, denomination below

Date	Mintage	F	VF	XF	Unc	BU
1998	—	—	—	12.00	15.00	

KM# 108a   SUVERENA
31.1035 g., 0.9999 Silver 0.9999 oz. ASW **Subject:** Chinese Horse **Obv:** National arms above bridge, date below **Rev:** Horse left, denomination below

Date	Mintage	F	VF	XF	Unc	BU
1998 Proof	Est. 30,000	Value: 50.00				

KM# 109   SUVERENA
31.1035 g., 0.9999 Gold 0.9999 oz. AGW **Subject:** Chinese Horse **Obv:** National arms above bridge, date below **Rev:** Horse left, denomination below

Date	Mintage	F	VF	XF	Unc	BU
1998 Proof	—	Value: 1,000				

KM# 82   14 ECUS
10.0000 g., 0.9250 Silver 0.2974 oz. ASW **Subject:** International Day of Peace **Obv:** National arms above bridge, date below **Rev:** Hands releasing bird of peace, symbol at center, denomination below

Date	Mintage	F	VF	XF	Unc	BU
1993 Proof	Est. 20,000	Value: 45.00				

KM# 83   14 ECUS
10.0000 g., 0.9250 Silver 0.2974 oz. ASW **Subject:** Peace - Teddy Bear **Obv:** National arms above bridge, date below **Rev:** Teddy bear above denomination

Date	Mintage	F	VF	XF	Unc	BU
1994 Proof	20,000	Value: 40.00				

KM# 84 14 ECUS
10.1000 g., 0.9250 Silver 0.3004 oz. ASW **Subject:** Peace - Allegorical Europa **Obv:** National arms above bridge, date below **Rev:** Allegorical Europa, denomination below

Date	Mintage	F	VF	XF	Unc	BU
1995 Proof	Est. 20,000		Value: 27.50			

KM# 85 14 ECUS + 2
9.9700 g., 0.9990 Silver 0.3202 oz. ASW **Subject:** War Relief Funding - Sarajevo Mosque **Obv:** National arms above bridge, date below **Rev:** Sarajevo Mosque, denomination below

Date	Mintage	F	VF	XF	Unc	BU
1993 Proof	20,000		Value: 30.00			

KM# 86 21 ECUS + 3
15.5600 g., 0.9990 Silver 0.4997 oz. ASW **Subject:** War Relief Funding - Sarajevo Mosque

Date	Mintage	F	VF	XF	Unc	BU
1993 Proof	Est. 15,000		Value: 60.00			

KM# 87 70 ECUS + 10
6.2200 g., 0.9990 Gold 0.1998 oz. AGW **Subject:** War Relief Funding - Sarajevo Mosque **Obv:** National arms above bridge, date below **Rev:** Dove of Peace above Sarajevo Mosque

Date	Mintage	F	VF	XF	Unc	BU
1993 Proof	Est. 5,000		Value: 195			

KM# 88 14 EURO
10.0000 g., 0.9250 Silver 0.2974 oz. ASW **Subject:** Peace **Obv:** National arms above bridge, date below **Rev:** Rose and the word PEACE in many languages, denomination below

Date	Mintage	F	VF	XF	Unc	BU
1996PM Proof	Est. 20,000		Value: 35.00			

KM# 110 14 EURO
10.0000 g., 0.9250 Silver 0.2974 oz. ASW **Subject:** Peace II **Obv:** National arms above bridge, date below **Rev:** Dove in flight with PEACE written in many different languages, denomination below

Date	Mintage	F	VF	XF	Unc	BU
1998PM Proof	Est. 20,000		Value: 40.00			

KM# 114 14 EURO
10.0000 g., 0.9250 Silver 0.2974 oz. ASW **Subject:** The Tree of Stability **Obv:** National arms above bridge, date below **Rev:** Woman planting oak tree, denomination below

Date	Mintage	F	VF	XF	Unc	BU
1999PM Proof	Est. 20,000		Value: 40.00			

REFORM COINAGE
1998-

KM# 115 10 FENINGA
3.9000 g., Copper-Plated-Steel, 20 mm. **Obv:** Denomination on map within circle **Rev:** Triangle and stars, date at left, within circle **Edge:** Plain

Date	Mintage	F	VF	XF	Unc	BU
1998	—	—	—	—	0.50	0.75
2000 In mint sets only	—	—	—	—	—	1.00

KM# 116 20 FENINGA
4.5000 g., Copper-Plated-Steel, 22 mm. **Obv:** Denomination on map within circle **Rev:** Triangle and stars, date at left, within circle

Date	Mintage	F	VF	XF	Unc	BU
1998	—	—	—	—	1.00	1.25
2000 In mint sets only	—	—	—	—	—	1.50

KM# 117 50 FENINGA
Copper-Plated-Steel **Obv:** Denomination on map within circle **Rev:** Triangle and stars, date at left, within circle

Date	Mintage	F	VF	XF	Unc	BU
1998	—	—	—	—	2.25	2.50
2000 In mint sets only	—	—	—	—	—	3.00

KM# 118 KONVERTIBLE MARKA
4.9000 g., Nickel Plated Steel, 24 mm. **Obv:** Denomination **Rev:** Coat of arms above date **Edge:** Reeded and plain sections

Date	Mintage	F	VF	XF	Unc	BU
2000	—	—	—	—	5.50	6.00

KM# 119 2 KONVERTIBLE MARKA
6.9000 g., Bi-Metallic Copper-Nickel center in Nickel-Brass ring, 25.75 mm. **Obv:** Denomination within circle **Rev:** Dove of peace, date at right, within circle **Edge:** Reeded and plain sections

Date	Mintage	F	VF	XF	Unc	BU
2000	—	—	—	—	13.50	15.00

MINT SETS

KM#	Date	Mintage Identification	Issue Price	Mkt Val
MS1	2000 (5)	— KM#115, 116, 117, 118, 119	20.00	25.00

PROOF SETS

KM#	Date	Mintage Identification	Issue Price	Mkt Val
PS1	1996 (5)	500 KM#70-73, 76	—	1,675

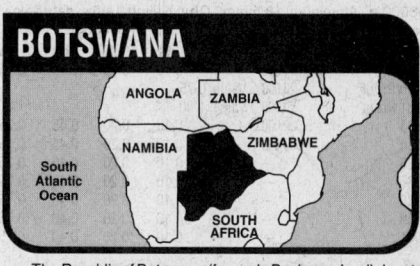

BOTSWANA

The Republic of Botswana (formerly Bechuanaland), located in south central Africa between Namibia and Zimbabwe, has an area of 224,607 sq. mi. (600,370 sq. km.) and a population of *1.62 million. Capital: Gaborone. Botswana is a member of a Customs Union with South Africa, Lesotho, and Swaziland. The economy is primarily pastoral with a rapidly developing mining industry, of which diamonds, copper and nickel are the chief elements. Meat products and diamonds comprise 85 percent of the exports.

Little is known of the origin of the peoples of Botswana. The early inhabitants, the Bushmen, did not develop a recorded history and are now dying out. The ancestors of the present Botswana residents probably arrived about 1600AD in Bantu migrations from the north and east. Bechuanaland was first united early in the 19th century under Chief Khama III to more effectively resist incursions by the Boer trekkers from Transvaal and by the neighboring Matabeles. As the Boer threat intensified, appeals for protection were made to the British Government, which proclaimed the whole of Bechuanaland a British protectorate in 1885. In 1895, the southern part of the protectorate was annexed to Cape Province. The northern part, known as the Bechuanaland Protectorate, remained under British administration until it became the independent Republic of Botswana on Sept. 30, 1966. Botswana is a member of the Commonwealth of Nations. The president is Chief of State and Head of government.

MINT MARK
B - Berne

MONETARY SYSTEM
100 Cents = 1 Thebe

REPUBLIC
STANDARD COINAGE

KM# 1 50 CENTS
10.0000 g., 0.8000 Silver 0.2572 oz. ASW **Subject:** Independence Commemorative **Obv:** National arms with supporters, denomination below **Rev:** Sir Seretse Khama left

Date	Mintage	F	VF	XF	Unc	BU
ND(1966)B	40,000	—	5.50	7.50	10.00	—
ND(1966)B Proof	10,000		Value: 12.00			

KM# 2   10 THEBE
11.2900 g., 0.9000 Gold 0.3267 oz. AGW **Subject:**
Independence Commemorative **Obv:** National arms with
supporters, denomination below **Rev:** Sir Seretse Khama left

Date	Mintage	F	VF	XF	Unc	BU
ND(1966)B	5,100	—	—	—	325	345

REFORM COINAGE
100 Thebe = 1 Pula

KM# 3   THEBE
0.8000 g., Aluminum, 18.5 mm. **Obv:** National arms, date below
Rev: Head of Turako, denomination upper right **Edge:** Reeded

Date	Mintage	F	VF	XF	Unc	BU
1976	15,000,000	—	0.10	0.15	0.40	0.75
1976 Proof	26,000	Value: 0.75				
1981 Proof	10,000	Value: 1.00				
1983	5,000,000	—	0.10	0.20	0.45	0.75
1984	5,000,000	—	0.10	0.20	0.45	0.75
1985	—	—	0.10	0.20	0.45	0.75
1987	—	—	0.10	0.20	0.40	0.75
1988	—	—	0.10	0.20	0.40	0.75
1989	—	—	0.10	0.20	0.40	0.75
1991	—	—	0.10	0.20	0.40	0.75

KM# 14   2 THEBE
1.8000 g., Bronze, 17.4 mm. **Subject:** World Food Day
Obv: National arms above date **Rev:** Millet, denomination at top

Date	Mintage	F	VF	XF	Unc	BU
1981	9,990,000	—	0.15	0.25	0.50	0.75
1981 Proof	10,000	Value: 1.00				
1985	—	—	0.15	0.25	0.50	0.75

KM# 4   5 THEBE
2.8000 g., Bronze, 19.5 mm. **Obv:** National arms above date
Rev: Toko left, denomination at top **Edge:** Reeded

Date	Mintage	F	VF	XF	Unc	BU
1976	3,000,000	—	0.15	0.25	0.50	1.00
1976 Proof	26,000	Value: 1.25				
1977	250,000	—	0.15	0.25	0.50	1.00
1979	200,000	—	0.15	0.25	0.50	1.00
1980	1,000,000	—	0.15	0.25	0.50	1.00
1981	4,990,000	—	0.15	0.25	0.50	1.00
1981 Proof	10,000	Value: 1.50				
1984	2,000,000	—	0.15	0.25	0.50	1.00
1985	—	—	0.15	0.25	0.50	1.00
1988	—	—	0.15	0.25	0.50	1.00
1989	—	—	0.15	0.25	0.50	1.00

KM# 4a.1   5 THEBE
Bronze Clad Steel, 19.5 mm. **Edge:** Plain

Date	Mintage	F	VF	XF	Unc	BU
1991	—	—	0.15	0.25	0.50	1.00

KM# 4a.2   5 THEBE
Bronze Clad Steel, 19.5 mm. **Edge:** Reeded **Note:** Modified design.

Date	Mintage	F	VF	XF	Unc	BU
1996	—	—	0.15	0.25	0.50	1.00

KM# 26   5 THEBE
2.4100 g., Bronze Clad Steel, 16.79 mm. **Obv:** National arms
Rev: Toko bird **Edge:** Plain

Date	Mintage	F	VF	XF	Unc	BU
1998	—	—	0.15	0.25	0.50	1.00

KM# 5   10 THEBE
4.0000 g., Copper-Nickel, 22 mm. **Rev:** South African Oryx right,
denomination above **Edge:** Reeded

Date	Mintage	F	VF	XF	Unc	BU
1976	1,500,000	—	0.25	0.40	0.75	1.25
1976 Proof	26,000	Value: 1.50				
1977	500,000	—	0.25	0.40	0.75	1.25
1979	750,000	—	0.25	0.40	0.75	1.25
1980	—	—	0.25	0.40	0.75	1.25
1981	2,590,000	—	0.25	0.40	0.75	1.25
1981 Proof	10,000	Value: 1.75				
1984	4,000,000	—	0.20	0.30	0.60	1.00
1985	—	—	0.20	0.30	0.60	1.00
1989	—	—	0.20	0.30	0.60	1.00

KM# 5a   10 THEBE
3.8000 g., Nickel Clad Steel, 22 mm. **Edge:** Reeded

Date	Mintage	F	VF	XF	Unc	BU
1991	—	—	0.20	0.30	0.60	1.00

KM# 27   10 THEBE
Nickel Clad Steel **Obv:** National arms, date below **Rev:** South
African Oryx right, denomination above

Date	Mintage	F	VF	XF	Unc	BU
1998	—	—	0.20	0.30	0.75	1.25

KM# 6   25 THEBE
5.8000 g., Copper-Nickel, 25 mm. **Obv:** National arms with
supporters, date below **Rev:** Zebu left, denomination above
Edge: Reeded

Date	Mintage	F	VF	XF	Unc	BU
1976	1,500,000	—	0.25	0.55	1.50	2.00
1976 Proof	26,000	Value: 2.50				
1977	265,000	—	0.25	0.60	1.75	2.25
1981	740,000	—	0.25	0.60	1.50	2.00
1981 Proof	10,000	Value: 2.50				
1982	400,000	—	0.25	0.60	1.75	2.25
1984	2,000,000	—	0.25	0.55	1.50	2.00
1985	—	—	0.30	0.60	1.50	2.00
1989	—	—	0.30	0.60	1.50	2.00

KM# 6a   25 THEBE
Nickel Clad Steel, 25 mm.

Date	Mintage	F	VF	XF	Unc	BU
1991	—	—	0.30	0.60	1.50	2.00

KM# 28   25 THEBE
3.5000 g., Nickel Clad Steel **Obv:** National arms with supporters,
date below **Rev:** Zebu bull, left, denomination above

Date	Mintage	F	VF	XF	Unc	BU
1998	—	—	0.30	0.60	1.50	2.00
1999	—	—	0.30	0.60	1.50	2.00

KM# 7   50 THEBE
11.4000 g., Copper-Nickel, 28.5 mm. **Obv:** National arms with
supporters, date below **Rev:** African Fish Eagle left, denomination
above

Date	Mintage	F	VF	XF	Unc	BU
1976	266,000	—	0.65	1.35	2.25	2.75
1976 Proof	26,000	Value: 3.00				
1977	250,000	—	0.65	1.35	2.25	2.75
1980	—	—	0.65	1.35	2.25	2.75
1981 Proof	10,000	Value: 3.50				
1984	2,000,000	—	0.65	1.35	2.25	2.75
1985	—	—	0.65	1.35	2.25	2.75

KM# 7a   50 THEBE
11.1700 g., Nickel Clad Steel, 28.5 mm.

Date	Mintage	F	VF	XF	Unc	BU
1991	—	—	0.65	1.35	2.25	2.75

KM# 29   50 THEBE
4.8200 g., Nickel Clad Steel **Obv:** National arms with supporters,
date below **Rev:** African Fish Eagle left, denomination above

Date	Mintage	F	VF	XF	Unc	BU
1996	—	—	0.50	1.00	2.00	2.50
1998	—	—	0.50	1.00	2.00	2.50

KM# 8   PULA
16.4000 g., Copper-Nickel, 29.5 mm. **Obv:** National arms with
supporters, date below **Rev:** Zebra left, denomination above

Date	Mintage	F	VF	XF	Unc	BU
1976	166,000	—	1.50	2.50	5.00	7.50
1976 Proof	26,000	Value: 7.00				
1977	500,000	—	1.50	2.50	5.00	7.50
1981	—	—	1.50	2.50	5.00	7.50
1981 Proof	10,000	Value: 7.50				
1985	—	—	1.50	2.50	5.00	7.50
1987	—	—	1.50	2.50	5.00	7.50

KM# 24   PULA
Nickel-Brass **Obv:** National arms with supporters, date below
Rev: Zebra left, denomination above

Date	Mintage	F	VF	XF	Unc	BU
1991	—	—	1.00	1.75	3.50	6.00
1997	—	—	1.00	1.75	3.50	6.00

KM# 17 2 PULA
28.2800 g., 0.5000 Silver 0.4546 oz. ASW, 38.61 mm. **Subject:** Commonwealth Games **Obv:** National arms with supporters, date below **Rev:** Sprinter with flag, denomination below

Date	Mintage	F	VF	XF	Unc	BU
1986	Est. 50,000	—	—	—	12.50	14.00

KM# 17a 2 PULA
28.2800 g., 0.9250 Silver 0.8410 oz. ASW **Obv:** National arms with supporters, date below **Rev:** Sprinter with flag, denomination below

Date	Mintage	F	VF	XF	Unc	BU
1986 Proof	Est. 20,000	Value: 25.00				

KM# 18 2 PULA
28.2800 g., 0.9250 Silver 0.8410 oz. ASW **Subject:** Wildlife **Rev:** Slaty Egret, egretta vinaceiguia

Date	Mintage	F	VF	XF	Unc	BU
1986 Proof	Est. 25,000	Value: 27.50				

KM# 22 2 PULA
28.2800 g., 0.9250 Silver 0.8410 oz. ASW **Subject:** Save The Children Fund **Obv:** National arms with supporters, date below **Rev:** Child milking goat, denomination below

Date	Mintage	F	VF	XF	Unc	BU
1989 Proof	Est. 20,000	Value: 32.00				

KM# 25 2 PULA
6.0300 g., Nickel-Brass **Subject:** Wildlife **Obv:** National arms with suppporters, date below **Rev:** Rhinoceros left, denomination above

Date	Mintage	F	VF	XF	Unc	BU
1994	—	—	1.75	2.75	5.50	10.00

KM# 9 5 PULA
28.2800 g., 0.5000 Silver 0.4546 oz. ASW **Subject:** 10th Anniversary of Independence **Obv:** Bust left **Rev:** National Assembly Building, denomination above

Date	Mintage	F	VF	XF	Unc	BU
ND(1976)	31,000	—	—	—	16.50	18.50

KM# 9a 5 PULA
28.2800 g., 0.9250 Silver 0.8410 oz. ASW **Obv:** Bust left **Rev:** Buildings and flag, denomination above

Date	Mintage	F	VF	XF	Unc	BU
ND(1976) Proof	22,000	Value: 22.50				

KM# 11 5 PULA
28.5000 g., 0.5000 Silver 0.4581 oz. ASW **Subject:** Wildlife **Obv:** National arms with supporters, date below **Rev:** Gemsbok left, denomination above

Date	Mintage	F	VF	XF	Unc	BU
1978	4,026	—	—	—	24.00	26.00

KM# 11a 5 PULA
28.5000 g., 0.9250 Silver 0.8475 oz. ASW **Obv:** National arms with supporters, date below **Rev:** Gemsbok left, denomination below

Date	Mintage	F	VF	XF	Unc	BU
1978 Proof	4,172	Value: 35.00				

KM# 15 5 PULA
28.5000 g., 0.9250 Silver 0.8475 oz. ASW **Subject:** International Year of Disabled Persons **Obv:** National arms with supporters, date below **Rev:** Figures at table, hut in background, denomination lower left

Date	Mintage	F	VF	XF	Unc	BU
1981	13,000	—	—	—	25.00	30.00
1981 Proof	11,000	Value: 35.00				

KM# 19 5 PULA
15.9800 g., 0.9170 Gold 0.4711 oz. AGW **Subject:** Wildlife **Obv:** National arms with supporters, date below **Rev:** Red Lechwes (kobus leche leche) right, denomination above left

Date	Mintage	F	VF	XF	Unc	BU
1986 Proof	Est. 5,000	Value: 450				

KM# 20 5 PULA
Copper-Nickel **Subject:** Pope's Visit **Obv:** National arms with supporters, date below **Rev:** Bust left, denomination below

Date	Mintage	F	VF	XF	Unc	BU
1988	Est. 50,000	—	—	—	9.50	12.00

KM# 20a 5 PULA
28.2800 g., 0.9250 Silver 0.8410 oz. ASW **Obv:** Bust left **Rev:** National arms with supporters, date below

Date	Mintage	F	VF	XF	Unc	BU
1988 Proof	Est. 5,000	Value: 45.00				

KM# 21 5 PULA
28.2800 g., 0.9250 Silver 0.8410 oz. ASW **Subject:** 1988 Summer Olympics **Obv:** National arms with supporters, date below **Rev:** Runners

Date	Mintage	F	VF	XF	Unc	BU
1988 Proof	25,000	Value: 25.00				

Note: A copper-nickel strike variety of this coin does not exist

KM# 23 5 PULA
10.0000 g., 0.9170 Gold 0.2948 oz. AGW **Subject:** Save the Children Fund **Obv:** National arms with supporters, date below **Rev:** Woman with child left, denomination on left

Date	Mintage	F	VF	XF	Unc	BU
1989 Proof	Est. 3,000	Value: 350				

KM# 30 5 PULA
6.2000 g., Bi-Metallic Copper-Nickel center in Brass ring, 23.4 mm. **Obv:** National arms with supporters, date below, within circle **Rev:** Mophane worm on a mophane leaf, denomination below, within circle **Edge:** Reeded

Date	Mintage	F	VF	XF	Unc	BU
2000	—	—	—	—	6.50	10.00

KM# 12 10 PULA
35.0000 g., 0.5000 Silver 0.5626 oz. ASW **Subject:** Wildlife **Obv:** National arms with supporters, date below **Rev:** Klipspringer left, denomination above

Date	Mintage	F	VF	XF	Unc	BU
1978	4,088	—	—	—	32.00	40.00

KM# 12a 10 PULA
35.0000 g., 0.9250 Silver 1.0408 oz. ASW **Obv:** National arms with supporters, date below **Rev:** Klipspringer left, denomination above

Date	Mintage	F	VF	XF	Unc	BU
1978 Proof	3,989	Value: 42.00				

KM# 10 150 PULA
15.9800 g., 0.9170 Gold 0.4711 oz. AGW **Subject:** 10th Anniversary of Independence **Obv:** National arms with supporters, denomination above **Rev:** Bust left

Date	Mintage	F	VF	XF	Unc	BU
ND(1976)	2,520	—	—	—	450	465
ND(1976) Proof	2,000	Value: 485				

KM# 13 150 PULA
33.4370 g., 0.9000 Gold 0.9675 oz. AGW **Subject:** Wildlife **Obv:** National arms with supporters, date below **Rev:** Brown Hyena facing, denomination above left

Date	Mintage	F	VF	XF	Unc	BU
1978	664	—	—	—	950	975
1978 Proof	219	Value: 1,000				

KM# 16 150 PULA
15.9800 g., 0.9170 Gold 0.4711 oz. AGW **Subject:** International Year of Disabled Persons **Obv:** National arms with supporters, date below **Rev:** Figures with box, denomination lower right

Date	Mintage	F	VF	XF	Unc	BU
1981	4,158	—	—	—	450	465
1981 Proof	4,155	Value: 475				

PIEFORTS

KM#	Date	Mintage	Identification	Issue Price	Mkt Val
P1	1981	1,000	5 Pula. Silver. KM#15.	—	65.00
P2	1981	510	150 Pula. Gold. KM#16.	—	950

MINT SETS

KM#	Date	Mintage	Identification	Issue Price	Mkt Val
MS1	1978 (2)	—	KM#11, 12	—	55.00

PROOF SETS

KM#	Date	Mintage	Identification	Issue Price	Mkt Val
PS1	1976 (6)	20,000	KM#3-8	18.00	14.50
PS2	1978 (6)	—	KM#11a, 12a	—	65.00
PS3	1981 (7)	10,000	KM#3-8, 14	33.00	17.50

BRAZIL

The Federative Republic of Brazil, which comprises half the continent of South America and is the only Latin American country deriving its culture and language from Portugal, has an area of 3,286,488 sq. mi. (8,511,965 sq. km.) and a population of *169.2 million. Capital: Brasilia. The economy of Brazil is as varied and complex as any in the developing world. Agriculture is a mainstay of the economy, while only 4 percent of the area is under cultivation. Known mineral resources are almost unlimited in variety and size of reserves. A large, relatively sophisticated industry ranges from basic steel and chemical production to finished consumer goods. Coffee, cotton, iron ore and cocoa are the chief exports.

Brazil was discovered and claimed for Portugal by Admiral Pedro Alvares Cabral in 1500. Portugal established a settlement in 1532 and proclaimed the area a royal colony in 1549. During the Napoleonic Wars, Dom Joao VI established the seat of Portuguese government in Rio de Janeiro. When he returned to Portugal, his son Dom Pedro I declared Brazil's independence on Sept. 7, 1822, and became emperor of Brazil. The Empire of Brazil was maintained until 1889 when the federal republic was established. The Federative Republic was established in 1946 by terms of a constitution drawn up by a constituent assembly. Following a coup in 1964 the armed forces retained overall control under a dictatorship until civilian government was restored on March 15, 1985. The current constitution was adopted in 1988.

MINT MARKS
(a) - Paris, privy marks only
A - Berlin 1913
B - Bahia

MONETARY SYSTEM
(1833-1942)
1000 Reis = 1 Mil Reis
(1942-1967)
100 Centavos = 1 Cruzeiro

REPUBLIC
FIRST COINAGE - REIS
1889-1942

KM# 490 20 REIS
7.4900 g., Bronze, 25 mm. **Obv:** Star with wreath in background **Rev:** Denomination

Date	Mintage	F	VF	XF	Unc	BU
1901	713,000	1.00	4.50	9.50	20.00	—
1904	850,000	1.00	4.50	9.50	20.00	—
1905	1,075,000	3.50	7.00	14.50	48.00	—
1906	215,000	2.00	5.00	12.00	30.00	—
1908	4,558,000	1.00	4.50	9.50	20.00	—
1909	1,215,000	5.00	10.00	22.00	95.00	—
1910	828,000	1.00	4.50	9.50	20.00	—
1911	1,545,000	1.00	4.50	9.50	20.00	—
1912	480,000	1.00	4.50	9.50	25.00	—

KM# 516.2 20 REIS
Copper-Nickel, 15 mm. **Obv:** Denomination at center, dot between "2" and "0" in denomination **Rev:** Bust with cap, right, within 3/4 circle of stars

Date	Mintage	F	VF	XF	Unc	BU
1918	—	0.25	0.50	1.00	4.00	—
1919	2,870,000	0.25	0.50	1.00	4.00	—
1920	825,000	0.25	0.50	1.25	5.00	—
1921	1,020,000	0.25	0.50	1.25	5.00	—
1927	53,000	5.00	10.00	30.00	80.00	—
1935	100	200	450	900	1,500	—

KM# 516.1 20 REIS
Copper-Nickel, 15 mm. **Rev:** No dot between "2" and "0" in denomination

Date	Mintage	F	VF	XF	Unc	BU
1918	—	0.25	0.50	2.00	5.00	—
1919	—	0.25	0.50	1.00	4.00	—
1920	—	0.25	0.50	1.25	5.00	—

KM# 491 40 REIS
Bronze, 30 mm. **Obv:** Stars at center surrounded by circle of stars **Rev:** Denomination within circle

Date	Mintage	F	VF	XF	Unc	BU
1901	525,000	0.75	2.00	3.00	15.00	—
1907	218,000	0.75	2.00	3.00	15.00	—
1908	4,639,000	0.75	2.00	3.00	15.00	—
1909	4,226,000	0.75	2.00	3.50	17.50	—
1910	848,000	0.75	2.00	4.00	20.00	—
1911	1,660,000	0.75	2.00	4.00	20.00	—
1912	819,000	1.00	2.50	4.50	22.50	—

KM# 517 50 REIS
Copper-Nickel, 17 mm. **Obv:** Denomination within circle, date flanked by stars below **Rev:** Liberty head right

Date	Mintage	F	VF	XF	Unc	BU
1918	558,000	0.15	0.35	1.00	6.00	—
1919	558,000	0.15	0.35	1.00	6.00	—
1920	72,000	0.40	1.00	3.50	16.00	—
1921	682,000	0.15	0.35	1.00	6.00	—
1922	176,000	0.40	1.00	3.50	16.00	—
1925	128,000	0.40	1.50	4.00	20.00	—
1926	194,000	0.40	1.50	4.00	20.00	—
1931	20,000	2.00	10.00	40.00	85.00	—
1935	100	125	300	800	1,500	—

KM# 503 100 REIS
5.0000 g., Copper-Nickel, 20.96 mm. **Obv:** National arms, denomination above **Rev:** Liberty bust right **Note:** Roman numeral date.

Date	Mintage	F	VF	XF	Unc	BU
1901	15,775,000	0.40	1.50	3.50	20.00	—

KM# 518 100 REIS
4.9400 g., Copper-Nickel, 21.3 mm. **Obv:** Denomination within circle, date below **Rev:** Liberty bust right

Date	Mintage	F	VF	XF	Unc	BU
1918	600,000	0.40	1.50	3.25	17.50	—
1919	1,219,000	0.40	1.50	3.25	17.50	—
1920	1,251,000	0.40	1.50	3.25	17.50	—
1921	853,000	0.40	1.50	3.25	17.50	—
1922	347,000	0.40	1.50	4.75	20.00	—
1923	956,000	0.40	1.50	4.75	20.00	—
1924	1,478,000	1.00	2.50	8.50	25.00	—
1925	2,502,000	0.30	1.25	2.75	17.00	—
1926	1,807,000	0.50	1.50	4.75	20.00	—
1927	1,451,000	0.30	1.25	2.75	17.00	—
1928	1,514,000	0.30	1.25	2.75	17.00	—
1929	2,503,000	0.30	1.25	2.75	17.00	—
1930	2,398,000	0.30	1.25	2.75	17.00	—
1931	2,500,000	0.25	1.00	2.25	17.00	—
1932	948,000	0.25	1.00	2.25	17.00	—
1933	1,314,000	0.25	1.00	2.25	17.00	—
1934	3,614,000	0.25	1.00	2.25	17.00	—
1935	3,442,000	0.25	1.00	2.25	17.00	—

KM# 527 100 REIS
Copper-Nickel, 21 mm. **Subject:** 400th Anniversary of Colonization **Obv:** Cazique Tibirica **Rev:** Denomination below design **Edge:** Reeded **Note:** Medal rotation.

Date	Mintage	F	VF	XF	Unc	BU
ND(1932)	1,012,000	0.50	1.00	2.25	6.50	—

KM# 536 100 REIS
4.6200 g., Copper-Nickel, 19 mm. **Obv:** Anchor divides denomination **Rev:** Admiral Marques Tamandare, founder of Brazilian Navy **Edge:** Plain **Note:** Medal rotation.

Date	Mintage	F	VF	XF	Unc	BU
1936	3,928,000	0.20	0.50	1.50	3.00	—
1937	7,905,000	0.10	0.35	1.00	2.50	—
1938	8,618,000	0.10	0.35	1.00	2.50	—

KM# 544 100 REIS
2.5300 g., Copper-Nickel, 16.87 mm. **Obv:** Denomination within wreath **Rev:** Dr. Getulio Vargas **Edge:** Fluted

Date	Mintage	F	VF	XF	Unc	BU
1938	8,106,000	0.10	0.20	0.50	1.50	—
1940	8,797,000	0.10	0.20	0.50	1.50	—
1942	1,285,000	0.10	0.20	0.50	1.50	—

Note: The 1942 issue has a deeper yellow cast due to higher copper content

KM# 504 200 REIS
Copper-Nickel, 25 mm. **Obv:** National arms, denomination above **Rev:** Liberty bust right **Edge:** Plain **Note:** Roman numeral date.

Date	Mintage	F	VF	XF	Unc	BU
1901	12,625,000	0.35	1.00	2.50	15.00	—

KM# 519 200 REIS
7.8200 g., Copper-Nickel, 25 mm. **Obv:** Denomination within circle, date below **Rev:** Liberty bust right

Date	Mintage	F	VF	XF	Unc	BU
1918	625,000	0.35	1.00	2.00	15.00	—
1919	882,000	0.35	1.00	2.00	15.00	—
1920	1,657,000	0.35	1.00	2.00	15.00	—
1921	1,135,000	0.35	1.00	2.00	15.00	—
1922	678,000	0.35	1.00	2.00	15.00	—
1923	1,655,000	0.35	1.00	2.00	15.00	—
1924	1,750,000	0.35	1.00	2.00	15.00	—
1925	2,081,999	0.35	1.00	2.00	15.00	—
1926	324,000	1.00	3.00	8.00	22.50	—
1927	1,806,000	0.35	1.00	2.00	15.00	—
1928	782,000	0.35	1.00	2.00	15.00	—
1929	2,440,000	0.25	1.00	2.00	15.00	—
1930	1,697,000	0.25	1.00	2.00	15.00	—
1931	1,830,000	0.25	1.00	2.00	15.00	—
1932	761,000	0.25	1.00	2.00	15.00	—
1933	173,000	0.35	1.00	2.00	15.00	—
1934	612,000	0.25	1.00	2.00	15.00	—
1935	1,329,000	0.25	1.00	2.00	15.00	—

KM# 528 200 REIS
7.9300 g., Copper-Nickel, 25 mm. **Subject:** 400th Anniversary of Colonization **Obv:** Globe with sash **Rev:** Ship, denomination below, two dates divided at top **Note:** Medal rotation.

Date	Mintage	F	VF	XF	Unc	BU
ND(1932)	596,000	0.75	1.75	3.50	16.50	—

KM# 537 200 REIS
6.0000 g., Copper-Nickel, 22 mm. **Obv:** Steam engine, date above, denomination below **Rev:** Viscount de Maua, railway builder facing **Edge:** Plain **Note:** Medal rotation.

Date	Mintage	F	VF	XF	Unc	BU
1936	2,256,000	0.30	0.75	2.00	8.50	—
1937	6,506,000	0.30	0.75	2.00	8.50	—
1938	5,787,000	0.30	0.75	2.00	8.50	—

KM# 545 200 REIS
3.4400 g., Copper-Nickel, 18.82 mm. **Obv:** Denomination, date below, within wreath **Rev:** Dr. Getulio Vargas left **Edge:** Fluted

Date	Mintage	F	VF	XF	Unc	BU
1938	7,666,000	0.20	0.50	0.85	2.75	—
1940	10,161,000	0.15	0.40	0.60	2.25	—
1942	1,966,000	0.15	0.40	0.60	2.25	—

Note: The 1942 issue has a yellow cast due to higher copper content

KM# 538 300 REIS
8.0800 g., Copper-Nickel, 25 mm. **Obv:** Harp divides denomination, date above **Rev:** Composer Antonio Carlos Gomes facing **Edge:** Plain **Note:** Medal rotation.

Date	Mintage	F	VF	XF	Unc	BU
1936	3,029,000	0.30	1.25	4.00	11.50	—
1937	4,507,000	0.30	1.25	4.00	11.50	—
1938	3,753,000	0.30	1.25	4.00	11.50	—

KM# 546 300 REIS
4.5400 g., Copper-Nickel, 20.83 mm. **Obv:** Denomination above date within wreath **Rev:** Dr. Getulio Vargas left **Edge:** Fluted

Date	Mintage	F	VF	XF	Unc	BU
1938	12,080,000	0.20	0.35	0.50	2.25	—
1940	8,124,000	0.20	0.35	0.50	2.25	—
1942	2,020,000	0.25	0.40	0.75	3.25	—

Note: The 1942 issue has a yellow cast due to higher copper content

KM# 505 400 REIS
11.7300 g., Copper-Nickel, 30 mm. **Obv:** National arms, denomination above **Rev:** Liberty bust right, circle of stars surround **Edge:** Plain

Date	Mintage	F	VF	XF	Unc	BU
MCMI (1901)	5,531,000	1.50	3.00	8.00	30.00	—

KM# 515 400 REIS
Copper-Nickel, 30 mm. **Obv:** National arms, denomination above within circle, date below **Rev:** Liberty bust left

Date	Mintage	F	VF	XF	Unc	BU
1914	646,000	15.00	35.00	75.00	150	—

Note: This is considered a pattern by many authorities

KM# 520 400 REIS
Copper-Nickel, 30 mm. **Obv:** Denomination within circle, date below **Rev:** Liberty bust right

Date	Mintage	F	VF	XF	Unc	BU
1918	491,000	0.75	2.00	5.50	18.00	—
1919	891,000	0.75	2.00	5.50	18.00	—
1920	1,521,000	0.75	2.00	5.50	18.00	—
1921	871,000	0.50	1.75	5.50	18.00	—
1922	1,275,000	0.50	1.75	5.50	18.00	—
1923	764,000	0.50	1.75	5.50	18.00	—
1925	2,048,000	0.50	1.75	5.50	18.00	—
1926	1,034,000	0.50	1.75	5.50	18.00	—
1927	738,000	0.50	1.75	5.50	18.00	—
1929	869,000	0.50	1.75	5.50	18.00	—
1930	1,030,999	0.50	1.75	5.50	18.00	—
1931	1,431,000	0.50	1.75	5.50	18.00	—
1932	588,000	0.50	1.75	5.50	18.00	—
1935	225,000	0.50	1.75	5.50	18.00	—

KM# 529 400 REIS
Copper-Nickel, 30 mm. **Subject:** 400th Anniversary of Colonization **Obv:** Map divides dates within circle **Rev:** Lusinian Cross **Note:** Medal rotation.

Date	Mintage	F	VF	XF	Unc	BU
ND(1932)	416,000	1.00	2.75	5.50	15.00	—

KM# 539 400 REIS
10.0800 g., Copper-Nickel, 27 mm. **Obv:** Oil lamp, date above, denomination below **Rev:** Bust of Oswaldo Cruz, Microbiologist, 3/4 left **Note:** Medal rotation.

Date	Mintage	F	VF	XF	Unc	BU
1936	2,079,000	0.50	1.00	2.75	8.50	—
1937	3,111,000	0.50	1.00	2.75	8.50	—
1938	2,681,000	0.50	1.00	2.75	8.50	—

KM# 547 400 REIS
5.4400 g., Copper-Nickel, 23 mm. **Obv:** Denomination above date within wreath **Rev:** Bust of Dr. Getulio Vargas left **Edge:** Fluted

Date	Mintage	F	VF	XF	Unc	BU
1938	10,620,000	0.25	0.50	1.00	2.25	—
1940	7,312,000	0.25	0.50	1.00	2.25	—
1942	1,496,000	0.25	0.50	1.50	3.25	—

Note: The 1942 issue has a yellow cast due to higher copper content

KM# 506 500 REIS
5.0000 g., 0.9000 Silver 0.1447 oz. ASW, 22 mm. **Obv:** Liberty bust left, date below **Rev:** Denomination at center

Date	Mintage	F	VF	XF	Unc	BU
1906	352,000	BV	2.75	4.75	16.50	—
1907	1,282,000	BV	2.75	4.75	16.50	—
1908	498,000	BV	2.75	4.75	16.50	—
1911	8,000	20.00	35.00	70.00	150	—
1912	Est. 222,000	20.00	40.00	80.00	200	—

KM# 509   500 REIS
5.0000 g., 0.9000 Silver 0.1447 oz. ASW, 22 mm. **Obv:** Liberty bust right within circle, date below **Rev:** Denomination within wreath, arms above

Date	Mintage	F	VF	XF	Unc	BU
1912	—	3.00	7.00	14.00	38.00	—

KM# 512   500 REIS
5.0000 g., 0.9000 Silver 0.1447 oz. ASW, 22 mm. **Obv:** Liberty bust right within circle of stars, date below **Rev:** Denomination within wreath, arms above

Date	Mintage	F	VF	XF	Unc	BU
1913 A	—	BV	2.50	4.50	16.00	—

KM# 521.1   500 REIS
3.8700 g., Aluminum-Bronze, 23 mm. **Subject:** Independence Centennial **Obv:** Dom Pedro and President Pessoa left **Rev:** Denomination at top, dates divided by centennial symbols

Date	Mintage	F	VF	XF	Unc	BU
ND(1922)	13,744,000	0.25	0.60	1.25	4.75	—

KM# 521.2   500 REIS
Aluminum-Bronze, 23 mm. **Obv:** Dom Pedro and President Pessoa left **Rev:** Denomination at top, dates divided by centennial symbols **Edge:** Reeded **Note:** Error: BBASIL instead of BRASIL.

Date	Mintage	F	VF	XF	Unc	BU
ND(1922)	Inc. above	17.50	35.00	55.00	120	—

KM# 524   500 REIS
3.9500 g., Aluminum-Bronze, 22.73 mm. **Obv:** Denomination within wreath, date below **Rev:** Kneeling liberty figure right

Date	Mintage	F	VF	XF	Unc	BU
1924	7,400,000	0.30	0.75	1.50	7.00	—
1927	2,725,000	0.30	0.75	1.50	7.00	—
1928	9,432,000	0.30	0.75	1.50	7.00	—
1930	146,000	1.00	2.00	3.75	9.00	—

KM# 530   500 REIS
Aluminum-Bronze, 23 mm. **Subject:** 400th Ann. of Colonization **Obv:** Joao Ramalho, colonist, 3/4 right **Rev:** Clothing divides denomination **Edge:** Reeded **Note:** Medal rotation.

Date	Mintage	F	VF	XF	Unc	BU
ND(1932)	34,000	1.50	4.00	11.50	20.00	—

KM# 533   500 REIS
4.0000 g., Aluminum-Bronze, 22 mm. **Obv:** Column divides denomination, date below **Rev:** Bust of Diego Antonio Feijo Regent of Brazil 1835-1837, 3/4 left **Note:** Medal rotation; wide rim.

Date	Mintage	F	VF	XF	Unc	BU
1935	14,000	2.00	9.00	20.00	40.00	—

KM# 540   500 REIS
5.0000 g., Aluminum-Bronze, 22 mm. **Obv:** Denomination divided by column, date below **Rev:** Bust of Diego Antonio Feijo 3/4 left **Note:** Medal rotation; thicker planchet.

Date	Mintage	F	VF	XF	Unc	BU
1936	1,326,000	0.60	1.25	4.75	9.00	—
1937	Inc. above	0.60	1.25	4.75	9.00	—
1938	—	0.60	1.25	4.75	9.00	—

KM# 549   500 REIS
5.0000 g., Aluminum-Bronze, 21 mm. **Obv:** Denomination above date within wreath **Rev:** Joaquim Machado de Assis, Author and Poet, 3/4 facing

Date	Mintage	F	VF	XF	Unc	BU
1939	5,928,000	0.50	1.00	3.00	8.00	—

KM# 507   1000 REIS
10.0000 g., 0.9000 Silver 0.2893 oz. ASW **Obv:** Laureate liberty head left, date below flanked by stars **Rev:** Denomination at center **Edge:** Reeded

Date	Mintage	F	VF	XF	Unc	BU
1906	420,000	BV	6.00	9.00	25.00	—
1907	1,282,000	BV	6.00	9.00	25.00	—
1908	1,624,000	BV	6.00	9.00	25.00	—
1909	816,000	BV	6.00	9.00	25.00	—
1910	2,354,000	BV	6.00	9.00	25.00	—
1911	2,810,000	BV	6.00	9.00	25.00	—
1912	Est. 1,570,000	BV	6.00	9.00	25.00	—

KM# 510   1000 REIS
10.0000 g., 0.9000 Silver 0.2893 oz. ASW **Obv:** Laureate head of Liberty right, circle surrounds, date below **Rev:** Denomination within wreath, arms above

Date	Mintage	F	VF	XF	Unc	BU
1912	Inc. above	BV	6.50	10.00	32.50	—
1913	2,525,000	BV	6.50	10.00	32.50	—

KM# 513   1000 REIS
10.0000 g., 0.9000 Silver 0.2893 oz. ASW, 26 mm. **Obv:** Laureate liberty head right, star circle surrounds, date below **Rev:** Denomination within wreath, arms above **Edge:** Reeded

Date	Mintage	F	VF	XF	Unc	BU
1913 A	—		BV	7.00	18.00	—

KM# 522.1   1000 REIS
7.8000 g., Aluminum-Bronze, 26.8 mm. **Subject:** Independence Centennial **Obv:** Dom Pedro and President Pessoa **Rev:** Denomination at top, dates divided by centennial symbols **Edge:** Reeded

Date	Mintage	F	VF	XF	Unc	BU
ND(1922)	16,698,000	0.40	0.60	2.00	6.50	—

KM# 522.2   1000 REIS
Aluminum-Bronze, 25 mm. **Obv:** Dom Pedro and President Pessoa left **Rev:** Denomination at top, dates divided by centennial symbols at center **Edge:** Reeded **Note:** Error: BBASIL instead of BRASIL.

Date	Mintage	F	VF	XF	Unc	BU
ND(1922)	Inc. above	2.50	5.00	10.00	20.00	—

KM# 525   1000 REIS
8.0600 g., Aluminum-Bronze, 26.57 mm. **Obv:** Denomination within wreath, date below, monogram left of knot **Rev:** Kneeling liberty figure right

Date	Mintage	F	VF	XF	Unc	BU
1924	9,354,000	0.50	1.00	2.25	7.50	—
1925	6,205,000	0.50	1.00	2.25	7.50	—
1927	35,817,000	0.50	1.00	2.25	7.50	—
1928	1,899,000	0.50	1.00	2.25	7.50	—
1929	83,000	3.50	14.00	45.00	100	—
1930	45,000	3.50	14.00	45.00	100	—
1931	200,000	1.00	4.50	8.00	16.00	—

KM# 531   1000 REIS
7.0000 g., Aluminum-Bronze, 32 mm. **Subject:** 400th Anniversary of Colonization **Obv:** 3/4 figure of Martin Affonso da Sousa looking left **Rev:** Denomination encircles arms **Edge:** Reeded **Note:** Medal rotation.

Date	Mintage	F	VF	XF	Unc	BU
ND(1932)	56,000	2.00	4.00	7.50	18.00	—

KM# 534   1000 REIS
8.0000 g., Aluminum-Bronze, 26 mm. **Obv:** Open bible, date above, denomination at top **Rev:** Head of Jose de Anchieta left **Note:** Medal rotation.

Date	Mintage	F	VF	XF	Unc	BU
1935	138,000	1.00	2.00	4.00	9.00	—

KM# 541   1000 REIS
7.1000 g., Aluminum-Bronze, 24.3 mm. **Obv:** Open bible, date above, denomination at top **Rev:** Head of Jose de Anchieta left **Edge:** Reeded **Note:** Size reduced. Medal rotation.

Date	Mintage	F	VF	XF	Unc	BU
1936	926,000	0.50	1.00	2.50	7.00	—
1937	Inc. above	0.50	1.00	2.50	7.00	—
1938 LGCB under chin	—	0.50	1.00	2.50	7.00	—

KM# 550   1000 REIS
6.6700 g., Aluminum-Bronze, 23 mm. **Obv:** Denomination above date within wreath **Rev:** Tobias Barreto de Menezes, Philosopher and Poet 3/4 right, BR monogram right of bust, two dates above right shoulder

Date	Mintage	F	VF	XF	Unc	BU
1939	9,586,000	0.25	0.75	2.00	6.50	—

KM# 508   2000 REIS
20.0000 g., 0.9000 Silver 0.5787 oz. ASW **Obv:** Liberty head left, date below flanked by stars **Rev:** Denomination at center

Date	Mintage	F	VF	XF	Unc	BU
1906	256,000	12.00	13.50	17.50	55.00	—
1907	2,863,000	BV	12.00	14.00	45.00	—
1908	1,707,000	BV	12.00	14.00	45.00	—
1910	585,000	12.00	13.50	17.50	55.00	—
1911	1,929,000	BV	12.00	14.00	45.00	—
1912	741,000	12.00	13.50	17.50	55.00	—

KM# 511   2000 REIS
20.0000 g., 0.9000 Silver 0.5787 oz. ASW, 32.5 mm.
Obv: Liberty head within circle, date below **Rev:** Denomination within wreath, national arms above

Date	Mintage	F	VF	XF	Unc	BU
1912	Inc. above	12.00	15.00	23.50	58.00	—
1913	395,000	12.00	15.00	25.00	62.00	—

KM# 514   2000 REIS
20.0000 g., 0.9000 Silver 0.5787 oz. ASW, 32.5 mm.
Obv: Laureate liberty head right within circle, date below **Rev:** Denomination within wreath, national arms above, continuous legend

Date	Mintage	F	VF	XF	Unc	BU
1913 A	—	12.00	14.00	16.50	42.50	—

KM# 523   2000 REIS
7.9000 g., 0.9000 Silver 0.2286 oz. ASW, 26 mm. **Subject:** Indep. Centennial **Obv:** Dom Pedro and President Pessoa left **Rev:** Two sets of arms, dates below, denom. at bottom **Edge:** Reeded

Date	Mintage	F	VF	XF	Unc	BU
ND(1922)	1,560,000	—	BV	4.75	9.00	—

KM# 523a   2000 REIS
7.9000 g., 0.5000 Silver 0.1270 oz. ASW, 26 mm. **Edge:** Reeded **Note:** Struck in both .900 and .500 fine silver, but can only be distinguished by analysis (and color), on worn specimens

Date	Mintage	F	VF	XF	Unc	BU
ND(1922)	Inc. above	BV	2.75	3.75	8.50	—

KM# 526   2000 REIS
7.9000 g., 0.5000 Silver 0.1270 oz. ASW **Obv:** Denomination within wreath, date below **Rev:** Laureate liberty head, right, within circle, stars surround

Date	Mintage	F	VF	XF	Unc	BU
1924	9,147,000	BV	2.75	3.75	13.50	—
1925	723,000	BV	2.75	3.75	13.50	—
1926	1,787,000	BV	2.75	3.75	13.50	—
1927	1,008,999	BV	3.00	4.75	16.00	—
1928	1,250,000	BV	2.75	3.75	13.50	—
1929	1,744,000	BV	2.75	3.75	13.50	—
1930	1,240,000	BV	2.75	3.75	13.50	—
1931	546,000	BV	2.75	3.75	13.50	—
1934	938,000	BV	2.75	3.75	13.50	—

KM# 532   2000 REIS
7.9000 g., 0.5000 Silver 0.1270 oz. ASW, 26 mm. **Subject:** 400th Anniversary of Colonization **Obv:** Bust of John III 3/4 right **Rev:** Arms, denomination above **Note:** Medal rotation.

Date	Mintage	F	VF	XF	Unc	BU
ND(1932)	695,000	2.75	3.75	7.00	16.50	—

KM# 535   2000 REIS
7.9000 g., 0.5000 Silver 0.1270 oz. ASW, 26 mm. **Obv:** Sword divides denomination, date lower right **Rev:** Armored head of Duke of Caxias; left, CB below chin **Edge:** Reeded **Note:** Medal rotation.

Date	Mintage	F	VF	XF	Unc	BU
1935	2,131,000	BV	2.75	3.75	12.50	—

KM# 542   2000 REIS
8.6200 g., Aluminum-Bronze, 26 mm. **Obv:** Hilt divides denomination, date upper right **Rev:** Armored bust of Duke of Caxias right, crown at left **Edge:** Plain **Note:** Medal rotation.

Date	Mintage	F	VF	XF	Unc	BU
1936	665,000	0.50	1.00	2.00	5.50	—
1937	Inc. above	0.50	1.00	2.00	5.50	—
1938	—	2.50	4.75	11.50	28.00	—

KM# 548   2000 REIS
Aluminum-Bronze, 26.3 mm. **Edge:** Plain **Note:** 24-sided planchet. Medal rotation.

Date	Mintage	F	VF	XF	Unc	BU
1937	—	25.00	50.00	125	300	—
1938	—	0.75	1.50	3.25	7.50	—

KM# 551   2000 REIS
Aluminum-Bronze, 26 mm. **Obv:** Denomination above date within wreath **Rev:** Bust of President Floriano Peixoto facing

Date	Mintage	F	VF	XF	Unc	BU
1939	5,048,000	0.50	1.00	2.00	5.50	—

KM# 543   5000 REIS
10.0000 g., 0.6000 Silver 0.1929 oz. ASW, 26 mm. **Obv:** Wing above denomination **Rev:** Head of aviation pioneer Alberto Santos Dumont left **Edge:** Reeded **Note:** Medal rotation.

Date	Mintage	F	VF	XF	Unc	BU
1936	1,986,000	BV	4.00	6.00	10.00	—
1937	414,000	BV	4.00	6.00	10.00	—
1938	994,000	BV	4.00	6.00	10.00	—

KM# 496   10000 REIS
8.9645 g., 0.9170 Gold 0.2643 oz. AGW **Obv:** Liberty head left within circle **Rev:** Star with wreath in background

Date	Mintage	F	VF	XF	Unc	BU
1901	111	BV	275	700	1,150	—
1902 Unique	—	—	—	—	—	—
1903	391	BV	275	700	1,150	—
1904	541	BV	275	700	1,150	—
1906	572	BV	275	700	1,150	—
1907	878	BV	265	600	1,100	—
1908	689	BV	265	600	1,100	1,500
1909	1,069	BV	265	600	1,100	1,750
1911	137	265	375	800	1,350	—
1914	969	265	500	1,500	2,400	—
1915	4,314	265	500	1,400	2,000	—
1916	4,720	BV	275	700	1,150	—
1919	526	BV	275	700	1,150	—
1921	2,435	BV	265	600	1,000	—
1922 Rare	6	—	—	—	—	—

KM# 497 20000 REIS
17.9290 g., 0.9170 Gold 0.5286 oz. AGW **Obv:** Liberty head left **Rev:** Stars at center surrounded by circle of stars

Date	Mintage	F	VF	XF	Unc	BU
1901	784	—	BV	700	1,350	1,850
1902	884	—	BV	700	1,350	—
1903	675	—	BV	700	1,350	—
1904	444	—	BV	700	1,350	—
1906	396	BV	550	900	1,600	—
1907	3,310	—	BV	600	1,100	—
1908	6,001,000	—	BV	600	1,100	—
1909	4,427	—	BV	600	1,100	—
1910	5,119	—	BV	600	1,100	1,350
1911	8,467	—	BV	600	1,100	—
1912	4,878	—	BV	600	1,100	—
1913	5,182	—	BV	650	1,200	—
1914	1,980	—	BV	700	1,400	—
1917	2,269	BV	550	800	1,550	—
1918	1,216	BV	550	800	1,550	—
1921	5,924	—	BV	650	1,200	—
1922	2,681	—	BV	800	1,550	—

REFORM COINAGE
1942-1967

100 Centavos = 1 Cruzeiro

KM# 555 10 CENTAVOS
2.8800 g., Copper-Nickel, 17.22 mm. **Obv:** Bust of Getulio Vargas 3/4 left **Rev:** Denomination above line, date below **Edge:** Plain **Note:** KM#555 has a very light yellowish appearance while KM#555a is a deeper yellow.

Date	Mintage	F	VF	XF	Unc	BU
1942	3,826,000	—	0.35	0.50	1.00	—
1943	13,565,000	—	0.25	0.35	0.75	—

KM# 555a.1 10 CENTAVOS
2.9700 g., Aluminum-Bronze, 17.2 mm. **Obv:** Bust left, initial after "Brasil" **Rev:** Denomination above line, date below, initial at end of line above date **Edge:** Plain **Note:** KM#555 has a very light yellowish appearance while KM#555a is a deeper yellow.

Date	Mintage	F	VF	XF	Unc	BU
1943	Inc. above	—	0.25	0.35	0.75	—
1944	12,617,000	—	0.25	0.60	1.00	—
1945	24,674,000	—	0.25	0.60	1.00	—

KM# 555a.2 10 CENTAVOS
2.8400 g., Aluminum-Bronze, 17.2 mm. **Obv:** Bust left **Rev:** Denomination above line, date below **Note:** Without initials.

Date	Mintage	F	VF	XF	Unc	BU
1944	—	—	0.25	0.60	1.00	—
1945	—	—	0.25	0.60	1.00	—
1946	35,159,000	—	0.25	0.60	1.00	—
1947	20,664,000	—	0.25	0.60	0.75	—

KM# 561 10 CENTAVOS
2.9600 g., Aluminum-Bronze, 17.04 mm. **Obv:** Jose Bonifacio de Andrada e Silva, Father of Independence left **Rev:** Denomination above line, date below

Date	Mintage	F	VF	XF	Unc	BU
1947	Inc. above	—	0.15	0.20	0.35	—
1948	45,041,000	—	0.15	0.20	0.35	—
1949	21,763,000	—	0.15	0.20	0.35	—
1950	16,329,999	—	0.15	0.20	0.35	—
1951	15,561,000	—	0.10	0.15	0.35	—
1952	10,966,000	—	0.10	0.20	0.50	—
1953	25,883,000	—	0.10	0.15	0.35	—

Date	Mintage	F	VF	XF	Unc	BU
1954	17,031,000	—	0.10	0.15	0.35	—
1955	25,172,000	—	0.10	0.15	0.35	—

KM# 564 10 CENTAVOS
1.0200 g., Aluminum, 17.41 mm. **Obv:** National Arms **Rev:** Denomination above line, date below

Date	Mintage	F	VF	XF	Unc	BU
1956	741,000	—	0.10	0.15	0.50	—
1957	25,311,000	—	0.10	0.15	0.25	—
1958	5,813,000	—	0.10	0.15	0.25	—
1959	2,611,000	—	0.10	0.15	0.25	—
1960	624,000	—	0.10	0.15	0.50	—
1961	951,000	—	0.10	0.15	0.50	—

KM# 556 20 CENTAVOS
Copper-Nickel, 20 mm. **Obv:** Bust of Getulio Vargas 3/4 left **Rev:** Denomination above line, date below **Edge:** Plain **Note:** KM#556 has a very light yellowish appearance while KM#556a is a deeper yellow.

Date	Mintage	F	VF	XF	Unc	BU
1942	3,007,000	—	0.25	0.50	1.00	—
1943	13,392,000	—	0.15	0.40	0.75	—

KM# 556a 20 CENTAVOS
4.0000 g., Aluminum-Bronze, 20 mm. **Obv:** Getulio Vargas bust left **Rev:** Denomination above line, date below **Edge:** Plain **Note:** KM#556 has a very light yellowish appearance while KM#556a is a deeper yellow.

Date	Mintage	F	VF	XF	Unc	BU
1943	Inc. above	—	0.15	0.35	0.75	—
1944	12,673,000	—	0.15	0.35	0.75	—

Note: Coins dated 1944 exist with and without designer's initials and straight or curved-back 9 in date

1945	61,632,000	—	0.15	0.35	0.60	—
1946	31,526,000	—	0.15	0.35	0.60	—
1947	36,422,000	—	0.15	0.35	0.75	—
1948	39,671,000	—	0.15	0.35	0.75	—

KM# 562 20 CENTAVOS
4.0000 g., Aluminum-Bronze, 19.26 mm. **Obv:** Bust of author and lawyer Ruy Barbosa left **Rev:** Denomination above line, date below

Date	Mintage	F	VF	XF	Unc	BU
1948	Inc. above	—	0.15	0.25	0.50	—
1949	24,805,000	—	0.15	0.25	0.50	—
1950	15,145,000	—	0.15	0.25	0.50	—
1951	14,964,000	—	0.15	0.25	0.50	—
1952	10,942,000	—	0.15	0.25	0.50	—
1953	25,585,000	—	0.15	0.25	0.50	—
1954	16,477,000	—	0.15	0.25	0.50	—
1955	25,122,000	—	0.15	0.25	0.50	—
1956	6,716,000	—	0.15	0.25	0.50	—

KM# 565 20 CENTAVOS
Aluminum **Obv:** National arms **Rev:** Denomination above line, date below **Note:** Varieties exist in the thickness of the planchet for year 1956.

Date	Mintage	F	VF	XF	Unc	BU
1956	Inc. above	—	0.10	0.25	0.50	—
1957	27,110,000	—	0.10	0.20	0.40	—
1958	8,552,000	—	0.10	0.20	0.40	—
1959	4,810,000	—	0.10	0.20	0.40	—
1960	510,000	—	0.10	0.25	0.50	—
1961	2,332,000	—	0.10	0.20	0.40	—

KM# 557 50 CENTAVOS
4.7500 g., Copper-Nickel, 21 mm. **Obv:** Bust of Getulio Vargas 3/4 left **Rev:** Denomination above line, date below **Note:** KM#557 has a very light yellowish appearance while KM#557a is a deeper yellow.

Date	Mintage	F	VF	XF	Unc	BU
1942	2,358,000	—	0.40	0.75	1.50	—
1943	13,392,000	—	0.35	0.50	1.00	—

KM# 557a 50 CENTAVOS
4.7500 g., Aluminum-Bronze, 21.3 mm. **Obv:** Getulio Vargas bust left **Rev:** Denomination above line, date below **Edge:** Plain **Note:** KM#557 has a very light yellowish appearance while KM#557a is a deeper yellow.

Date	Mintage	F	VF	XF	Unc	BU
1943	Inc. above	—	0.30	0.50	1.00	—
1944	12,102,000	—	0.30	0.50	1.00	—
1945	73,222,000	—	0.30	0.50	1.00	—
1946	13,941,000	—	0.30	0.50	1.00	—
1947	23,588,000	—	0.20	0.50	1.00	—

KM# 563 50 CENTAVOS
5.0000 g., Aluminum-Bronze, 21.40 mm. **Obv:** Bust of General Eurico Gaspar Dutra left **Rev:** Denomination above line, date below

Date	Mintage	F	VF	XF	Unc	BU
1948	32,023,000	—	0.15	0.25	0.50	—
1949	11,392,000	—	0.15	0.25	0.50	—
1950	7,804,000	—	0.15	0.35	0.75	—
1951	7,523,000	—	0.15	0.35	0.75	—
1952	6,863,000	—	0.15	0.35	0.75	—
1953	17,372,000	—	0.15	0.25	0.50	—
1954	11,353,000	—	0.15	0.25	0.50	—
1955	27,150,000	—	0.15	0.25	0.50	—
1956	32,130,000	—	0.15	0.25	0.50	—

KM# 566 50 CENTAVOS
3.0000 g., Aluminum-Bronze, 17.04 mm. **Obv:** National arms **Rev:** Denomination above line, date below

Date	Mintage	F	VF	XF	Unc	BU
1956	Inc. above	—	0.15	0.25	0.50	—

KM# 569 50 CENTAVOS
1.8300 g., Aluminum, 21.07 mm. **Obv:** National arms **Rev:** Denomination above line, date below

Date	Mintage	F	VF	XF	Unc	BU
1957	49,350,000	—	0.10	0.20	0.35	—
1958	59,815,000	—	0.10	0.20	0.35	—
1959	32,891,000	—	0.10	0.20	0.35	—
1960	15,997,000	—	0.10	0.20	0.35	—
1961	18,456,000	—	0.10	0.20	0.35	—

KM# 558 CRUZEIRO
6.9200 g., Aluminum-Bronze, 22.9 mm. **Obv:** Topographical map **Rev:** Denomination, date at left

Date	Mintage	F	VF	XF	Unc	BU
1942	381,000	—	0.50	1.00	3.50	—
1943	2,728,000	—	0.25	0.50	1.00	—
1944	3,820,000	—	0.25	0.50	1.00	—
1945	32,543,999	—	0.25	0.50	0.75	—
1946	49,794,000	—	0.25	0.50	1.00	—

Date	Mintage	F	VF	XF	Unc	BU
1947	15,391,000	—	0.25	0.50	1.00	—
1949	7,889,000	—	0.25	0.50	1.00	—
1950	5,163,000	—	0.25	0.50	1.00	—
1951	3,757,000	—	0.25	0.50	1.00	—
1952	1,769,000	—	0.50	1.00	3.50	—
1953	5,195,000	—	0.25	0.50	1.00	—
1954	1,145,000	—	0.25	0.50	1.50	—
1955	1,758,000	—	0.25	0.50	1.00	—
1956	668,000	—	6.00	12.00	20.00	—

KM# 567 CRUZEIRO
4.0300 g., Aluminum-Bronze, 19.03 mm. **Obv:** National arms
Rev: Denomination above line, date below

Date	Mintage	F	VF	XF	Unc	BU
1956	Inc. above	—	0.20	0.35	0.65	—

KM# 570 CRUZEIRO
2.3800 g., Aluminum, 23.23 mm. **Obv:** National arms
Rev: Denomination above line, date below

Date	Mintage	F	VF	XF	Unc	BU
1957	11,849,000	—	0.20	0.75	2.50	—
1958	15,443,000	—	0.20	1.00	3.00	—
1959	25,010,000	—	0.20	0.75	2.50	—
1960	35,267,000	—	0.20	0.75	2.50	—
1961	22,181,000	—	0.20	1.00	3.00	—

KM# 559 2 CRUZEIROS
8.3000 g., Aluminum-Bronze, 25 mm. **Obv:** Topographical map
Rev: Denomination, date at left **Edge:** Reeded

Date	Mintage	F	VF	XF	Unc	BU
1942	276,000	—	0.75	1.50	4.00	—
1943	1,929,000	—	0.25	0.50	1.00	—
1944	3,820,000	—	0.25	0.50	1.00	—
1945	32,543,999	—	0.20	0.40	1.00	—
1946	33,650,000	—	0.20	0.40	1.00	—
1947	9,908,000	—	0.20	0.40	1.00	—
1949	11,252,000	—	0.20	0.40	1.00	—
1950	7,754,000	—	0.25	0.50	1.00	—
1951	390,000	—	0.40	1.00	3.00	—
1952	1,456,000	—	1.00	2.00	5.00	—
1953	3,582,000	—	0.20	0.40	1.00	—
1954	1,197,000	—	0.25	1.00	2.00	—
1955	1,838,000	—	0.20	0.50	1.00	—
1956	253,000	—	2.00	4.00	10.00	—

KM# 568 2 CRUZEIROS
Aluminum-Bronze **Obv:** National arms **Rev:** Denomination
above line, date below

Date	Mintage	F	VF	XF	Unc	BU
1956	Inc. above	—	0.20	0.40	1.50	—

KM# 571 2 CRUZEIROS
2.7600 g., Aluminum, 25.26 mm. **Obv:** National arms
Rev: Denomination above line, date below

Date	Mintage	F	VF	XF	Unc	BU
1957	194,000	—	0.25	0.50	1.50	—
1958	13,687,000	—	0.20	0.30	1.00	—

Date	Mintage	F	VF	XF	Unc	BU
1959	20,894,000	—	0.20	0.30	1.00	—
1960	19,624,000	—	0.20	0.30	1.00	—
1961	24,924,000	—	0.20	0.30	1.00	—

KM# 560 5 CRUZEIROS
Aluminum-Bronze, 26 mm. **Obv:** Topographical map
Rev: Denomination, date at left

Date	Mintage	F	VF	XF	Unc	BU
1942	115,000	—	1.50	3.50	9.00	—
1943	222,000	—	1.00	2.50	7.00	—

KM# 572 10 CRUZEIROS
2.1500 g., Aluminum, 23 mm. **Obv:** Topographical map
Rev: Large denomination, date below

Date	Mintage	F	VF	XF	Unc	BU
1965	46,057,000	—	0.10	0.20	0.50	—

KM# 573 20 CRUZEIROS
2.4500 g., Aluminum, 25 mm. **Obv:** Topographical map
Rev: Large denomination, date below

Date	Mintage	F	VF	XF	Unc	BU
1965	52,026,000	—	0.15	0.25	0.75	—

KM# 574 50 CRUZEIROS
3.3000 g., Copper-Nickel, 18 mm. **Obv:** Liberty head left
Rev: Denomination above date

Date	Mintage	F	VF	XF	Unc	BU
1965	28,213,000	—	0.20	0.40	1.50	—

REFORM COINAGE
1967-1985

1000 Old Cruzeiros = 1 Cruzeiro Novo (New)
100 Centavos = 1 (New) Cruzeiro

KM# 575.1 CENTAVO
2.6300 g., Stainless Steel, 17 mm. **Obv:** Liberty head left
Rev: Denomination above date

Date	Mintage	F	VF	XF	Unc	BU
1967	100,246,000	—	—	—	0.15	0.25

KM# 575.2 CENTAVO
1.7500 g., Stainless Steel, 17 mm. **Obv:** Liberty head left
Rev: Denomination above date **Note:** Thinner planchet.

Date	Mintage	F	VF	XF	Unc	BU
1969	243,966,303	—	—	—	0.15	0.25
1975	50,043,000	—	—	0.15	0.30	0.50

KM# 585 CENTAVO
1.7700 g., Stainless Steel, 17 mm. **Series:** F.A.O.
Subject: Sugar Cane **Obv:** Liberty head left **Rev:** Sugar cane,
denomination and date to right **Edge:** Plain

Date	Mintage	F	VF	XF	Unc	BU
1975	Inc. above	—	—	0.15	0.25	0.45
1976	112,000	—	—	0.50	0.75	1.00
1977	100,000	—	—	0.50	0.75	1.00
1978	50,000	—	—	1.00	1.50	2.00

KM# 589 CENTAVO
1.5800 g., Stainless Steel, 14 mm. **Series:** F.A.O. **Subject:** Soja
Obv: Plants **Rev:** Denomination above date

Date	Mintage	F	VF	XF	Unc	BU
1979	100,000	—	0.50	0.75	1.00	1.25
1980	60,000	—	0.75	1.00	1.50	2.00
1981	100,000	—	0.50	0.75	1.00	1.25
1982	100,000	—	0.50	0.75	1.00	1.25
1983	100,000	—	0.50	0.75	1.00	1.25

KM# 576.1 2 CENTAVOS
3.2500 g., Stainless Steel, 19 mm. **Obv:** Liberty head left
Rev: Denomination above date

Date	Mintage	F	VF	XF	Unc	BU
1967	104,121,000	—	—	—	0.25	0.50

KM# 576.2 2 CENTAVOS
2.1600 g., Stainless Steel, 19 mm. **Obv:** Liberty head left
Edge: Plain **Note:** Thinner planchet.

Date	Mintage	F	VF	XF	Unc	BU
1969	252,839,303	—	—	—	0.50	0.75

Note: Mintage figure includes coins struck through 1974
dated 1969

Date	Mintage	F	VF	XF	Unc	BU
1975	5,015,000	—	—	0.25	0.75	1.00

KM# 586 2 CENTAVOS
2.2100 g., Stainless Steel, 19 mm. **Series:** F.A.O. **Subject:** Soja
Obv: Liberty head left **Rev:** Denomination above date, plant at left

Date	Mintage	F	VF	XF	Unc	BU
1975	Inc. above	—	—	0.15	0.25	0.45
1976	136,000	—	—	0.50	0.75	1.00
1977	100,000	—	—	0.50	0.75	1.00
1978	50,000	—	—	1.00	1.50	2.00

KM# 577.1 5 CENTAVOS
3.9700 g., Stainless Steel, 21 mm. **Obv:** Liberty head left
Rev: Denomination above date

Date	Mintage	F	VF	XF	Unc	BU
1967	98,532,000	—	—	0.20	0.50	0.75

KM# 577.2 5 CENTAVOS
2.6400 g., Stainless Steel, 21 mm. **Obv:** Liberty head left
Rev: Denomination above date **Note:** Thinner planchet.

Date	Mintage	F	VF	XF	Unc	BU
1969	548,716,303	—	—	0.20	0.50	0.75
	Note: Mintage figure includes coins struck through 1974 dated 1969					
1975	85,123,000	—	—	0.20	0.50	0.75

KM# 587.1 5 CENTAVOS
2.6900 g., Stainless Steel, 21 mm. **Series:** F.A.O.
Subject: Zebu **Obv:** Liberty head left **Rev:** Denomination and date to right of Zebu **Edge:** Plain

Date	Mintage	F	VF	XF	Unc	BU
1975	Inc. above	—	—	0.20	0.50	0.75
1976	93,644,000	—	—	0.20	0.50	0.75
1977	85,360,000	—	—	0.20	0.65	1.00
1978	34,090,000	—	—	0.20	0.65	1.00

KM# 587.2 5 CENTAVOS
2.6400 g., Stainless Steel, 21.21 mm. **Obv:** Liberty head left
Rev: Denomination and date to right of Zebu, "5" over wavy lines

Date	Mintage	F	VF	XF	Unc	BU
1975	Inc. above	—	—	0.20	0.50	0.75
1976	Inc. above	—	—	0.20	0.50	0.75
1977	Inc. above	—	—	0.20	0.50	0.75
1978	Inc. above	—	—	0.20	0.65	1.00

KM# 578.1 10 CENTAVOS
5.5200 g., Copper-Nickel, 23 mm. **Obv:** Liberty head left
Rev: Oil refinery, denomination and date at right

Date	Mintage	F	VF	XF	Unc	BU
1967	108,269,000	—	—	0.20	0.50	0.75

KM# 578.1a 10 CENTAVOS
4.2200 g., Stainless Steel **Obv:** Liberty head left **Rev:** Oil refinery, denomination and date at right

Date	Mintage	F	VF	XF	Unc	BU
1974	114,598,153	—	—	0.20	0.40	0.60
1975	142,783,000	—	—	0.20	0.40	0.60
1976	129,060,000	—	—	0.20	0.40	0.60
1977	225,213,000	—	—	0.20	0.40	0.60
1978	225,000,000	—	—	0.20	0.40	0.60
1979	100,000,000	—	—	0.20	0.50	0.75

KM# 578.2 10 CENTAVOS
4.7800 g., Copper-Nickel, 23 mm. **Obv:** Liberty head left **Rev:** Oil refinery, denomination and date at right **Note:** Thinner planchet.

Date	Mintage	F	VF	XF	Unc	BU
1970	498,927,200	—	—	—	0.40	0.60
	Note: Mintage figure includes coins struck through 1974 dated 1970					

KM# 579.1a 20 CENTAVOS
5.6700 g., Stainless Steel, 25 mm. **Obv:** Liberty head left
Rev: Denomination above date, oil derrick at left

Date	Mintage	F	VF	XF	Unc	BU
1975	102,386,000	—	—	0.20	0.50	0.75
1976	65,687,000	—	—	0.20	0.50	0.75

Date	Mintage	F	VF	XF	Unc	BU
1977	240,001,000	—	—	0.20	0.50	0.75
1978	225,000,000	—	—	0.20	0.50	0.75
1979	116,000,000	—	—	0.25	0.65	1.00

KM# 579.1 20 CENTAVOS
7.8600 g., Copper-Nickel, 25 mm. **Obv:** Liberty head left
Rev: Denomination above date, oil derrick at left **Note:** Thick planchet

Date	Mintage	F	VF	XF	Unc	BU
1967	125,814,000	—	—	0.20	0.50	0.75

KM# 579.2 20 CENTAVOS
6.5500 g., Copper-Nickel, 25 mm. **Obv:** Liberty head left
Rev: Denomination above date, oil derrick at left **Note:** Thinner planchet.

Date	Mintage	F	VF	XF	Unc	BU
1970	634,780,353	—	—	0.20	0.60	0.85
	Note: Mintage figure includes coins struck through 1974 dated 1970					

KM# 580 50 CENTAVOS
8.7400 g., Nickel, 27 mm. **Obv:** Liberty head left **Rev:** Freighter at pier divides date and denomination

Date	Mintage	F	VF	XF	Unc	BU
1967	13,089,000	—	0.25	0.50	1.25	1.50

KM# 580a 50 CENTAVOS
7.7100 g., Copper-Nickel, 27 mm. **Obv:** Liberty head left
Rev: Freighter at pier divides date and denomination
Edge: Reeded **Note:** Varieties of "7" in the date, with serif at top or bottom.

Date	Mintage	F	VF	XF	Unc	BU
1970	440,643,353	—	0.20	0.35	1.00	1.25
1975	134,454,000	—	0.20	0.35	1.00	1.25

KM# 580b 50 CENTAVOS
6.6500 g., Stainless Steel, 27 mm. **Obv:** Liberty head left **Rev:** Freighter at pier divides denomination and date **Edge:** Plain
Note: Varieties of "7" in the date, with serif at top or bottom.

Date	Mintage	F	VF	XF	Unc	BU
1975	Inc. above	—	0.20	0.35	1.00	1.25
1976	135,781,000	—	0.20	0.35	1.00	1.25
1977	160,019,000	—	0.20	0.35	1.00	1.25
1978	200,000,000	—	0.20	0.35	1.00	1.25
1979	104,000,000	—	0.25	0.45	1.25	1.50

KM# 581 CRUZEIRO
10.0800 g., Nickel, 29 mm. **Obv:** Liberty head left
Rev: Denomination above date, spray at left

Date	Mintage	F	VF	XF	Unc	BU
1970	53,271,000	—	0.25	0.50	1.00	1.25
	Note: Mintage figure includes coins struck through 1972 dated 1970					
1970 Proof	18,000	Value: 3.50				

KM# 581a CRUZEIRO
10.2500 g., Copper-Nickel, 28.8129 mm. **Obv:** Liberty head left
Rev: Denomination above date, spray at left

Date	Mintage	F	VF	XF	Unc	BU
1974	24,135,256	—	0.20	0.45	1.00	1.25
1975	21,613,000	—	0.20	0.45	1.00	1.25
1976	26,146,000	—	0.20	0.45	1.00	1.25
1977	98,000	—	1.00	2.00	3.00	5.00
1978	77,000	—	1.00	2.00	3.00	5.00

KM# 582 CRUZEIRO
10.0800 g., Nickel, 29 mm. **Subject:** 150th Anniversary of Independence **Obv:** Pedro I and General Emilio Garrastazu Medici heads left, date below **Rev:** Map above denomination, SESQUICENTENARIO DA INDEPENDENCIA

Date	Mintage	F	VF	XF	Unc	BU
1972	19,999,800	—	0.40	0.85	1.65	2.00
	Note: Lettered edge					
1972	Inc. above	—	0.40	0.85	1.65	2.00
	Note: Plain edge; Coins with plain edge are believed by some to be errors					
1972 Proof	—	Value: 3.50				
	Note: Lettered edge					
1972 Proof	—	Value: 3.50				
	Note: Plain edge; Coins with plain edge are believed by some to be errors					

KM# 590 CRUZEIRO
3.2300 g., Stainless Steel, 20 mm. **Obv:** Sugar cane
Rev: Denomination above date, linear design **Edge:** Plain

Date	Mintage	F	VF	XF	Unc	BU
1979	596,419,000	—	0.15	0.25	0.75	1.00
1980	690,497,000	—	0.15	0.25	0.65	0.85
1981	560,000,000	—	0.15	0.25	0.65	0.85
1982	300,000,000	—	0.15	0.25	0.65	0.85
1983	100,000	—	1.00	2.00	3.00	5.00
1984	62,100,000	—	0.15	0.25	0.65	0.85

KM# 598 CRUZEIRO
2.7900 g., Stainless Steel, 19.9 mm. **Series:** F.A.O. **Obv:** Sugar cane **Rev:** Denomination above date, linear design

Date	Mintage	F	VF	XF	Unc	BU
1985	10,000,000	—	—	0.20	0.50	0.75

KM# 591 5 CRUZEIROS
4.5000 g., Stainless Steel, 21.8 mm. **Obv:** Coffee plant
Rev: Denomination above date, linear design **Edge:** Plain

Date	Mintage	F	VF	XF	Unc	BU
1980	388,250,000	—	0.20	0.35	0.75	1.00
1981	82,000,000	—	0.20	0.35	0.75	1.00
1982	108,000,000	—	0.20	0.35	0.75	1.00
1983	113,400,000	—	0.20	0.35	0.75	1.00
1984	243,400,000	—	0.20	0.35	0.75	1.00

KM# 599 5 CRUZEIROS
4.0200 g., Stainless Steel, 22 mm. **Series:** F.A.O. **Obv:** Coffee plant **Rev:** Denomination above date, linear design

Date	Mintage	F	VF	XF	Unc	BU
1985	10,000,000	—	0.20	0.40	0.85	1.25

KM# 588 10 CRUZEIROS
11.3000 g., 0.8000 Silver 0.2906 oz. ASW, 28 mm.
Subject: 10th Anniversary of Central Bank **Obv:** Bust of
Humberto de Alencar Castelo Branco left **Rev:** Denomination,
design at upper right **Note:** Medal rotation.

Date	Mintage	F	VF	XF	Unc	BU
1975	20,000	—	—	—	55.00	65.00

KM# 592.1 10 CRUZEIROS
5.3500 g., Stainless Steel, 24 mm. **Obv:** Map of Brazil
Rev: Denomination, value, date, linear design

Date	Mintage	F	VF	XF	Unc	BU
1980	100,060,000	—	—	0.50	0.75	1.00
1981	200,000,000	—	—	0.50	0.75	1.00
1982	331,000,000	—	—	0.50	0.75	1.00
1983	390,000,000	—	—	0.50	0.75	1.00
1984	409,600,000	—	—	0.50	0.75	1.00

KM# 592.2 10 CRUZEIROS
4.7800 g., Stainless Steel, 24 mm. **Obv:** Map of Brazil
Rev: Value, date, linear design **Note:** Reduced weight.

Date	Mintage	F	VF	XF	Unc	BU
1985	201,000,000	—	—	0.50	0.75	1.00
1986	39,109,000	—	—	0.75	1.00	1.25

KM# 583 20 CRUZEIROS
18.0400 g., 0.9000 Silver 0.5220 oz. ASW, 34.1 mm. **Subject:**
150th Anniversary of Independence **Obv:** Pedro I and General
Emilio Garrastazu Medici heads left, date below **Rev:** Map above
denomination, SESQUICENTENARIO DA INDEPENDENCIA

Date	Mintage	F	VF	XF	Unc	BU
1972(a)	502,000	—	BV	11.50	13.50	15.00

KM# 593.1 20 CRUZEIROS
6.3300 g., Stainless Steel, 26 mm. **Obv:** Francis of Assisi Church
Rev: Denomination above date, linear design **Edge:** Plain

Date	Mintage	F	VF	XF	Unc	BU
1981	88,297,000	—	—	0.25	0.85	1.20
1982	158,200,000	—	—	0.20	0.65	0.85
1983	312,000,000	—	—	0.20	0.65	0.85
1984	226,000,000	—	—	0.20	0.65	0.85

KM# 593.2 20 CRUZEIROS
5.6000 g., Stainless Steel, 26 mm. **Obv:** Francis of Assisi Church
Rev: Denomination above date, linear design **Edge:** Plain
Note: Reduced weight.

Date	Mintage	F	VF	XF	Unc	BU
1985	205,000,000	—	—	0.20	0.65	0.85
1986	26,840,000	—	—	0.30	0.75	1.00

KM# 594.1 50 CRUZEIROS
7.3400 g., Stainless Steel, 28 mm. **Obv:** Map of Brasilia
Rev: Denomination above date, linear design **Edge:** Plain

Date	Mintage	F	VF	XF	Unc	BU
1981	57,000,000	—	—	0.35	1.00	1.50
1982	134,000,000	—	—	0.20	0.65	0.85
1983	181,800,000	—	—	0.20	0.65	0.85
1984	292,418,000	—	—	0.20	0.65	0.85

KM# 594.2 50 CRUZEIROS
6.9400 g., Stainless Steel, 28 mm. **Obv:** Map **Rev:**
Denomination above date, linear design **Note:** Reduced weight.

Date	Mintage	F	VF	XF	Unc	BU
1985	180,000,000	—	—	0.20	0.65	0.85
1986	52,580,000	—	—	0.20	0.65	0.85

KM# 595 100 CRUZEIROS
2.0500 g., Stainless Steel, 17 mm. **Obv:** National arms
Rev: Denomination above date

Date	Mintage	F	VF	XF	Unc	BU
1985	162,000,000	—	—	0.20	0.40	0.65
1986	97,169,000	—	—	0.20	0.40	0.65

KM# 596 200 CRUZEIROS
2.5500 g., Stainless Steel, 19 mm. **Obv:** National arms
Rev: Denomination above date

Date	Mintage	F	VF	XF	Unc	BU
1985	55,000,000	—	—	0.25	0.50	0.75
1986	54,830,000	—	—	0.25	0.50	0.75

KM# 584 300 CRUZEIROS
16.6500 g., 0.9200 Gold 0.4925 oz. AGW **Subject:** 150th
Anniversary of Independence **Obv:** Pedro I and general Emilio
Garrastazu Medici heads left, date below **Rev:** Denomination
below map, SESQUICENTENARIO DA INDEPENDENCIA

Date	Mintage	F	VF	XF	Unc	BU
1972(a)	50,000	—	—	—	500	525

KM# 597 500 CRUZEIROS
3.6500 g., Stainless Steel, 21 mm. **Obv:** National arms
Rev: Denomination above date

Date	Mintage	F	VF	XF	Unc	BU
1985	74,000,000	—	—	0.35	1.00	1.25
1986	95,740,000	—	—	0.35	1.00	1.25

REFORM COINAGE
1986-1989
1000 Cruzeiros Novos = 1 Cruzado;
100 Centavos = 1 Cruzado

KM# 600 CENTAVO
1.6000 g., Stainless Steel, 15 mm. **Obv:** National arms
Rev: Denomination above date **Edge:** Plain

Date	Mintage	F	VF	XF	Unc	BU
1986	100,000,000	—	—	—	0.15	0.25
1987	1,000,000	—	—	—	0.20	0.35
1988	1,000,000	—	—	—	0.20	0.35

KM# 601 5 CENTAVOS
1.8100 g., Stainless Steel, 16 mm. **Obv:** National arms
Rev: Denomination above date **Edge:** Plain

Date	Mintage	F	VF	XF	Unc	BU
1986	99,282,000	—	—	—	0.15	0.25
1987	1,000,000	—	—	—	0.20	0.35
1988	1,000,000	—	—	—	0.20	0.35

KM# 602 10 CENTAVOS
2.0500 g., Stainless Steel, 17 mm. **Obv:** National arms
Rev: Denomination above date **Edge:** Plain

Date	Mintage	F	VF	XF	Unc	BU
1986	200,000,000	—	—	—	0.15	0.25
1987	245,628,000	—	—	—	0.15	0.25
1988	21,293,000	—	—	—	0.20	0.35

KM# 603 20 CENTAVOS
2.5500 g., Stainless Steel, 19 mm. **Obv:** National arms
Rev: Denomination above date **Edge:** Plain

Date	Mintage	F	VF	XF	Unc	BU
1986	140,000,000	—	—	—	0.20	0.30
1987	157,500,000	—	—	—	0.20	0.30
1988	16,000,000	—	—	—	0.25	0.40

KM# 604 50 CENTAVOS
3.6500 g., Stainless Steel, 21 mm. **Obv:** National arms
Rev: Denomination above date

Date	Mintage	F	VF	XF	Unc	BU
1986	200,000,000	—	—	—	0.35	0.50
1987	201,884,000	—	—	—	0.35	0.50
1988	131,255,000	—	—	—	0.35	0.50

KM# 605 CRUZADO
4.3800 g., Stainless Steel, 23 mm. **Obv:** National arms
Rev: Date divides denomination **Edge:** Plain

Date	Mintage	F	VF	XF	Unc	BU
1986	235,500,000	—	—	—	1.00	1.25
1987	403,600,000	—	—	—	0.45	0.65
1988	321,216,000	—	—	—	0.45	0.65

KM# 606   5 CRUZADOS
5.2100 g., Stainless Steel, 25 mm. **Obv:** National arms
Rev: Date divides denomination **Edge:** Plain

Date	Mintage	F	VF	XF	Unc	BU
1986	97,263,000	—	—	—	1.50	1.75
1987	141,000,000	—	—	—	0.65	0.85
1988	291,906,000	—	—	—	0.65	0.85

KM# 607   10 CRUZADOS
6.0600 g., Stainless Steel, 27 mm. **Obv:** National arms
Rev: Date divides denomination **Edge:** Plain

Date	Mintage	F	VF	XF	Unc	BU
1987	131,500,000	—	—	—	1.75	2.00
1988	608,736,000	—	—	—	0.85	1.00

KM# 608   100 CRUZADOS
9.9500 g., Stainless Steel, 31 mm. **Subject:** Abolition of Slavery
Centennial - Male **Obv:** Denomination **Rev:** Outline divides dates
on left from head on right

Date	Mintage	F	VF	XF	Unc	BU
1988	200,000	—	—	1.50	3.50	4.00

KM# 609   100 CRUZADOS
9.9500 g., Stainless Steel, 31 mm. **Subject:** Abolition of Slavery
Centennial - Female **Obv:** Denomination **Rev:** Outline divides
dates on left from head on right

Date	Mintage	F	VF	XF	Unc	BU
1988	200,000	—	—	1.50	3.50	4.00

KM# 610   100 CRUZADOS
9.9500 g., Stainless Steel, 31 mm. **Subject:** Abolition of Slavery
Centennial - Child **Obv:** Denomination **Rev:** Outline divides dates
on left from head on right

Date	Mintage	F	VF	XF	Unc	BU
1988	200,000	—	—	1.50	3.50	4.00

REFORM COINAGE
1989-1990
1000 Old Cruzados = 1 Cruzado Novo

KM# 611   CENTAVO
2.0100 g., Stainless Steel, 16.5 mm. **Obv:** Outlined denomination
Rev: Farmer, date divides cows at bottom **Edge:** Plain

Date	Mintage	F	VF	XF	Unc	BU
1989	208,100,000	—	—	—	0.35	0.50
1990	1,000,000	—	—	—	1.00	1.50

KM# 612   5 CENTAVOS
2.2600 g., Stainless Steel, 17.5 mm. **Obv:** Outlined
denomination **Rev:** Fisherman, two fish above date at bottom
Edge: Plain

Date	Mintage	F	VF	XF	Unc	BU
1989	270,400,000	—	—	—	0.45	0.60
1990	934,000	—	—	—	1.00	1.50

KM# 613   10 CENTAVOS
2.5400 g., Stainless Steel, 18.5 mm. **Obv:** Outlined denomination
Rev: Miner, three diamonds above date at bottom **Edge:** Plain

Date	Mintage	F	VF	XF	Unc	BU
1989	362,900,000	—	—	—	0.60	0.75
1990	136,000,000	—	—	—	0.60	0.75

KM# 614   50 CENTAVOS
2.8300 g., Stainless Steel, 19.5 mm. **Obv:** Outlined denomination
Rev: Figure above design, date at bottom **Edge:** Plain

Date	Mintage	F	VF	XF	Unc	BU
1989	453,800,000	—	—	—	1.25	1.50
1990	216,644,000	—	—	—	1.25	1.50

KM# 615   NOVO CRUZADO
9.9500 g., Stainless Steel, 31 mm. **Subject:** Centennial of the
Republic **Obv:** Denomination **Rev:** Laureate liberty bust 3/4 left
divides dates

Date	Mintage	F	VF	XF	Unc	BU
ND(1989)	10,000,000	—	—	—	2.00	2.50

KM# 616   200 NOVOS CRUZADOS
13.4700 g., 0.9990 Silver 0.4326 oz. ASW, 31 mm. **Subject:**
Centennial of the Republic **Obv:** Denomination **Rev:** Laureate
liberty bust 3/4 left divides dates

Date	Mintage	F	VF	XF	Unc	BU
ND (1989) Proof	30,000	Value: 35.00				

REFORM COINAGE
1990-1993
100 Centavos = 1 Cruzeiro; 1 Cruzado Novo = 1 Cruzeiro

KM# 617   CRUZEIRO
3.6100 g., Stainless Steel, 20.5 mm. **Obv:** Outlined
denomination **Rev:** Date lower right of design

Date	Mintage	F	VF	XF	Unc	BU
1990	377,000,000	—	—	—	0.35	0.50

KM# 618.1   5 CRUZEIROS
3.9700 g., Stainless Steel, 21.5 mm. **Obv:** Outlined
denomination **Rev:** Laborer, date at bottom **Edge:** Plain

Date	Mintage	F	VF	XF	Unc	BU
1990	517,000,000	—	—	—	0.45	0.60
1991	510,000,000	—	—	—	0.45	0.60

KM# 618.2   5 CRUZEIROS
3.4000 g., Stainless Steel, 21.5 mm. **Obv:** Outlined
denomination **Rev:** Laborer at top, small village above date at
bottom **Edge:** Plain **Note:** Thinner planchet.

Date	Mintage	F	VF	XF	Unc	BU
1991	Inc. above	—	—	—	0.45	0.60
1992	19,881,000	—	—	—	0.60	0.75

KM# 619.1   10 CRUZEIROS
4.3600 g., Stainless Steel, 22.5 mm. **Obv:** Outlined denomination
Rev: Laborer at top, small village above date at bottom

Date	Mintage	F	VF	XF	Unc	BU
1990	413,000,000	—	—	—	0.50	0.75
1991	947,909,000	—	—	—	0.50	0.75

KM# 619.2   10 CRUZEIROS
3.7400 g., Stainless Steel, 22.5 mm. **Note:** Thinner planchet.

Date	Mintage	F	VF	XF	Unc	BU
1991	Inc. above	—	—	—	0.50	0.75
1992	25,000,000	—	—	—	0.75	1.00

KM# 620.1   50 CRUZEIROS
4.7800 g., Stainless Steel, 23.5 mm. **Obv:** Outlined
denomination **Rev:** Farmer, fish above date below

Date	Mintage	F	VF	XF	Unc	BU
1990	10,000,000	—	—	—	1.00	1.25
1991	74,945,000	—	—	—	0.65	0.80

KM# 620.2   50 CRUZEIROS
4.0900 g., Stainless Steel, 23.5 mm. **Obv:** Outlined
denomination **Rev:** Farmer, fish above date below **Edge:** Plain
Note: Thinner planchet.

Date	Mintage	F	VF	XF	Unc	BU
1991	Inc. above	—	—	—	0.60	0.80
1992	128,298,000	—	—	—	0.60	0.80

KM# 623   100 CRUZEIROS
2.3900 g., Stainless Steel, 18 mm. **Obv:** Date left of
denomination **Rev:** Manatee **Edge:** Plain

Date	Mintage	F	VF	XF	Unc	BU
1992	500,000,000	—	—	—	1.50	2.50
1993	70,000,000	—	—	—	1.50	2.50

KM# 621 500 CRUZEIROS
27.0000 g., 0.9250 Silver 0.8029 oz. ASW, 40 mm. **Obv:** National arms at center, denomination below, 13 sets of arms surround **Rev:** Ibero - American Series, two dates at bottom

Date	Mintage	F	VF	XF	Unc	BU
1991 Proof	40,000	Value: 60.00				

KM# 624 500 CRUZEIROS
2.6600 g., Stainless Steel, 19 mm. **Obv:** Date left of denomination **Rev:** Loggerhead Sea Turtle

Date	Mintage	F	VF	XF	Unc	BU
1992	250,000,000	—	—	—	1.50	2.50
1993	105,000,000	—	—	—	1.50	2.50

KM# 626 1000 CRUZEIROS
2.9600 g., Stainless Steel, 20 mm. **Obv:** Date to left of denomination **Rev:** Fish - Acara **Edge:** Plain

Date	Mintage	F	VF	XF	Unc	BU
1992	30,000,000	—	—	—	2.00	3.00
1993	435,000,000	—	—	—	1.50	2.50

KM# 622 2000 CRUZEIROS
27.0000 g., 0.9250 Silver 0.8029 oz. ASW, 40 mm. **Subject:** U.N. Conference on Environment and Development **Obv:** Hummingbird and flower, denomination above **Rev:** Ocean and mountains, date above

Date	Mintage	F	VF	XF	Unc	BU
1992 Proof	30,000	Value: 55.00				

KM# 625 5000 CRUZEIROS
9.9500 g., Stainless Steel, 31 mm. **Subject:** 200th Anniversary of Tiradentes' Death **Obv:** Denomination **Rev:** Bust left, two dates below

Date	Mintage	F	VF	XF	Unc	BU
1992	10,000,000	—	—	—	2.50	3.50

REFORM COINAGE
1993-1994
1000 Cruzeiros = 1 Cruzeiro Real

KM# 627 5 CRUZEIROS REAIS
3.2700 g., Stainless Steel, 21 mm. **Obv:** Date to left of denomination **Rev:** Macaw Parrots - Arara, left **Edge:** Plain

Date	Mintage	F	VF	XF	Unc	BU
1993	250,000,000	—	—	—	1.50	2.50
1994	70,000,000	—	—	—	1.50	2.50

KM# 628 10 CRUZEIROS REAIS
3.5900 g., Stainless Steel, 22 mm. **Obv:** Date to left of denomination **Rev:** Anteater - Tamandua, right **Edge:** Plain

Date	Mintage	F	VF	XF	Unc	BU
1993	300,000,000	—	—	—	1.50	2.50
1994	150,252,000	—	—	—	1.50	2.50

KM# 629 50 CRUZEIROS REAIS
3.9200 g., Stainless Steel, 23 mm. **Obv:** Date to left of denomination **Rev:** Mother jaguar and cub facing **Edge:** Plain

Date	Mintage	F	VF	XF	Unc	BU
1993	50,000,000	—	—	—	1.75	3.00
1994	30,000,000	—	—	—	1.75	3.00

KM# 630 100 CRUZEIROS REAIS
4.2700 g., Stainless Steel, 24 mm. **Obv:** Date to left of denomination **Rev:** Maned wolf right **Edge:** Plain

Date	Mintage	F	VF	XF	Unc	BU
1993	50,000,000	—	—	—	1.75	3.00
1994	40,000,000	—	—	—	1.75	3.00

REFORM COINAGE
1994-present
2750 Cruzeiros Reais = 1 Real; 100 Centavos = 1 Real

KM# 631 CENTAVO
2.9600 g., Stainless Steel, 20 mm. **Obv:** Laureate liberty head left, linear design **Rev:** Denomination above date **Edge:** Plain

Date	Mintage	F	VF	XF	Unc	BU
1994	887,100,000	—	—	—	0.35	0.50
1995	283,799,000	—	—	—	0.35	0.50
1996	320,000,000	—	—	—	0.35	0.50
1997	500,000,000	—	—	—	0.35	0.50

KM# 647 CENTAVO
2.4300 g., Copper Plated Steel, 17 mm. **Obv:** Cabral bust at right **Rev:** Denomination on linear design at left, 3/4 globe with sash on right, date below **Edge:** Plain

Date	Mintage	F	VF	XF	Unc	BU
1998	185,250,000	—	—	—	0.35	0.50
1999	104,874,000	—	—	—	0.10	0.20
2000	88,256,000	—	—	—	0.10	0.20

KM# 632 5 CENTAVOS
3.2700 g., Stainless Steel, 21 mm. **Obv:** Laureate liberty head left, linear design **Rev:** Denomination above date **Edge:** Plain

Date	Mintage	F	VF	XF	Unc	BU
1994	732,980,000	—	—	—	0.45	0.65
1995	240,000,000	—	—	—	0.45	0.65
1996	111,600,000	—	—	—	0.45	0.65
1997	235,000,000	—	—	—	0.45	0.65

KM# 648 5 CENTAVOS
4.1000 g., Copper Plated Steel, 22 mm. **Obv:** Tiradente bust at right, dove at left **Rev:** Denomination on linear design at left, 3/4 globe with sash on right, date below **Edge:** Plain

Date	Mintage	F	VF	XF	Unc	BU
1998	116,324,000	—	—	—	0.45	0.65
1999	11,264,000	—	—	—	0.70	1.00
2000	28,416,000	—	—	—	0.60	0.80

KM# 633 10 CENTAVOS
3.5900 g., Stainless Steel, 22 mm. **Obv:** Laureate liberty head, left, lined background **Rev:** Denomiation above date **Edge:** Plain

Date	Mintage	F	VF	XF	Unc	BU
1994	640,682,000	—	—	—	0.60	0.80
1995	239,000,000	—	—	—	0.60	0.80
1996	255,000,000	—	—	—	0.60	0.80
1997	265,000,000	—	—	—	0.60	0.80

KM# 641 10 CENTAVOS
3.5900 g., Stainless Steel, 22 mm. **Series:** F.A.O. **Obv:** Hands holding seedling **Rev:** Denomination above date

Date	Mintage	F	VF	XF	Unc	BU
1995	1,000,000	—	—	—	0.65	0.85

KM# 649.1 10 CENTAVOS
Brass Plated Steel, 20 mm. **Subject:** Pedro I **Obv:** Bust of Pedro, horseman with sword in left hand **Rev:** Denomination **Edge:** Plain **Note:** Majority of mintage recalled and melted.

Date	Mintage	F	VF	XF	Unc	BU
1997	—	—	—	—	—	—
1998	—	—	—	—	—	—

KM# 649.2 10 CENTAVOS
4.8000 g., Brass Plated Steel, 20 mm. **Obv:** Bust of Pedro at right, horseman with sword in right hand at left **Rev:** Denomination on linear design at left, 3/4 globe with sash on right, date below **Edge:** Plain **Note:** 1998-2000 dates have reeded edge.

Date	Mintage	F	VF	XF	Unc	BU
1998	141,540,000	—	—	—	0.60	0.80
1999	9,620,000	—	—	—	1.00	1.25
2000	26,880,000	—	—	—	0.80	1.00

KM# 634 25 CENTAVOS
4.7800 g., Stainless Steel, 23.5 mm. **Obv:** Stylized laureate liberty head left, date below **Rev:** Outlined denomination, linear design **Edge:** Plain

Date	Mintage	F	VF	XF	Unc	BU
1994	285,000,000	—	—	—	0.75	1.00
1995	140,000,000	—	—	—	0.75	1.00

KM# 642 25 CENTAVOS
4.7800 g., Stainless Steel, 23.5 mm. **Series:** F.A.O. **Obv:** Farmer working **Rev:** Outlined denomination, linear design

Date	Mintage	F	VF	XF	Unc	BU
1995	1,000,000	—	—	—	0.80	1.20

KM# 650 25 CENTAVOS
7.5500 g., Brass Plated Steel, 25 mm. **Obv:** Deodoro bust at right, national arms at left **Rev:** Denomination on linear design at left, 3/4 globe with sash on right, date below **Edge:** Reeded

Date	Mintage	F	VF	XF	Unc	BU
1998	43,238,000	—	—	—	0.80	1.10
1999	32,766,000	—	—	—	0.80	1.10
2000	25,312,000	—	—	—	0.80	1.10

KM# 635 50 CENTAVOS
3.9200 g., Stainless Steel, 23 mm. **Obv:** Laureate liberty head left, linear design **Rev:** Denomination above date **Edge:** Plain

Date	Mintage	F	VF	XF	Unc	BU
1994	421,898,000	—	—	—	1.25	1.50
1995	60,000,000	—	—	—	1.25	1.50

KM# 651 50 CENTAVOS
9.2500 g., Copper-Nickel, 23 mm. **Obv:** Rio Branco bust at right, map at left **Rev:** Denomination on linear design at left, 3/4 globe with sash on right, date below, BRASIL ORDEM E PROGRESSO

Date	Mintage	F	VF	XF	Unc	BU
1998	24,900,000	—	—	—	1.25	1.50
1999	—	—	—	—	1.25	1.50
1999 Proof	2,000	—	—	—		
2000	14,912,000	—	—	—	1.25	1.50

KM# 636 REAL
4.2700 g., Stainless Steel, 24 mm. **Obv:** Laureate liberty head left, linear design

Date	Mintage	F	VF	XF	Unc	BU
1994	215,000,000	—	—	—	2.50	2.75

KM# 652 REAL
7.8490 g., Bi-Metallic **Ring:** Brass **Center:** Copper-Nickel, 27 mm. **Obv:** Allegorical portrait left **Rev:** Denomination on linear design at left, 3/4 globe with sash on right, date below **Edge:** Segmented reeding **Note:** Total coin weight 7.8 grams.

Date	Mintage	F	VF	XF	Unc	BU
1998	18,000,000	—	—	—	2.75	3.50
1999	3,840,000	—	—	—	4.00	5.00

KM# 653 REAL
7.8400 g., Bi-Metallic Copper-Nickel center in Brass ring, 27 mm. **Subject:** Universal Declaration of Human Rights **Obv:** Globe **Rev:** Denomination left, globe with sash at right, date below, linear design

Date	Mintage	F	VF	XF	Unc	BU
1998	600,000	—	—	—	2.75	4.00

KM# 637 2 REAIS
27.0000 g., 0.9250 Silver 0.8029 oz. ASW, 40 mm. **Subject:** 300th Anniversary - First Brazilian Mint **Obv:** Denomination to right of date, design in background **Rev:** 300th Anniversary year below inscription

Date	Mintage	F	VF	XF	Unc	BU
1994 Proof	7,000		Value: 65.00			

KM# 643 2 REAIS
27.0000 g., 0.9250 Silver 0.8029 oz. ASW, 40 mm. **Subject:** Ayrton Senna - Race Driver

Date	Mintage	F	VF	XF	Unc	BU
1995 Proof	10,000		Value: 75.00			

KM# 640 3 REAIS
11.5000 g., 0.9250 Silver 0.3420 oz. ASW, 28 mm. **Subject:** 30th Anniversary - Central Bank **Obv:** Bank logo **Rev:** Denomination, linear design

Date	Mintage	F	VF	XF	Unc	BU
1995 Proof	5,000		Value: 42.50			

KM# 645 3 REAIS
11.5000 g., 0.9250 Silver 0.3420 oz. ASW, 28 mm. **Subject:** Centennial of Belo Horizonte **Obv:** Denomination, date lower right **Rev:** Collage, name, dates

Date	Mintage	F	VF	XF	Unc	BU
1997 Proof	20,000		Value: 42.50			

KM# 638 4 REAIS
27.0000 g., 0.9250 Silver 0.8029 oz. ASW, 40 mm. **Subject:** World Cup Soccer **Obv:** Hands lofting trophy divides date at bottom **Rev:** Denomination, background is soccer net

Date	Mintage	F	VF	XF	Unc	BU
1994 Proof	9,000		Value: 75.00			

KM# 654 5 REAIS
28.0000 g., 0.9990 Silver 0.8993 oz. ASW, 40 mm. **Subject:** 500 Years - Discovery of Brazil **Obv:** Partial compass face and feathers, anniversary inscription and dates at left **Rev:** Figure at left, ship at right, partial compass face and feathers at lower right **Edge:** Reeded

Date	Mintage	F	VF	XF	Unc	BU
ND(2000) Proof	15,385		Value: 65.00			

KM# 639 20 REAIS
8.0000 g., 0.9000 Gold 0.2315 oz. AGW, 22 mm. **Subject:** World Cup Soccer **Obv:** Hand held trophy **Rev:** Denomination in net

Date	Mintage	F	VF	XF	Unc	BU
1994 Proof	2,000		Value: 245			

KM# 644 20 REAIS
8.0000 g., 0.9000 Gold 0.2315 oz. AGW, 22 mm.
Subject: Ayrton Senna - Race Driver

Date	Mintage	F	VF	XF	Unc	BU
1995 Proof	5,000	Value: 245				

KM# 655 20 REAIS
8.0000 g., 0.9000 Gold 0.2315 oz. AGW, 22 mm. **Subject:** 500 Years - Discovery of Brazil **Obv:** Partial compass face and feathers at right, anniversary dates at left **Rev:** Ornamented map, denomination at left **Edge:** Reeded

Date	Mintage	F	VF	XF	Unc	BU
ND(2000) Proof	6,558	Value: 245				

LEPROSARIUM COINAGE

KM# L1 100 REIS
Brass **Issuer:** Colonia Santa Teresa **Obv:** Denomination **Rev:** C.S.I.

Date	Mintage	F	VF	XF	Unc	BU
ND(ca.1940)	—	—	150	250	350	

KM# L2 200 REIS
Brass **Issuer:** Colonia Santa Teresa **Obv:** Denomination **Rev:** C.S.I.

Date	Mintage	F	VF	XF	Unc	BU
ND(ca.1940)	—	—	200	300	400	

KM# L3 300 REIS
Brass **Issuer:** Colonia Santa Teresa **Obv:** Denomination **Rev:** C.S.I.

Date	Mintage	F	VF	XF	Unc	BU
ND(ca.1940)	—	—	250	350	450	

KM# L4 500 REIS
Brass **Issuer:** Colonia Santa Teresa **Obv:** Denomination **Rev:** C.S.I.

Date	Mintage	F	VF	XF	Unc	BU
ND(ca.1940)	—	—	300	400	500	

KM# L5 1000 REIS
Brass **Issuer:** Colonia Santa Teresa **Obv:** Denomination **Rev:** C.S.I.

Date	Mintage	F	VF	XF	Unc	BU
ND(ca.1940)	—	—	350	450	550	

KM# L6 1.00 REIS
Brass **Issuer:** Santa Casa de Misericordia

Date	Mintage	F	VF	XF	Unc	BU
ND(ca.1920) Rare						

KM# L7 2.00 REIS
Brass **Issuer:** Santa Casa de Misericordia **Obv:** Issuer name **Rev:** Denomination within circle

Date	Mintage	F	VF	XF	Unc	BU
ND(ca.1920)	—	—	250	450		

KM# L8 5.00 REIS
Brass **Issuer:** Santa Casa de Misericordia

Date	Mintage	F	VF	XF	Unc	BU
ND(ca.1920) Rare						

KM# L9 1.000 REIS
Brass **Issuer:** Santa Casa de Misericordia

Date	Mintage	F	VF	XF	Unc	BU
ND(ca.1920) Rare						

KM# L10 5.000 REIS
Brass **Issuer:** Santa Casa de Misericordia

Date	Mintage	F	VF	XF	Unc	BU
ND(ca.1920)	—	—	550	750	—	

PATTERNS
Including off metal strikes

KM#	Date	Mintage	Identification	Mkt Val
Pn179	1901	—	100 Reis. Nickel-Silver.	185
Pn180	1901	—	100 Reis. Nickel. Birmingham Mint	185
Pn181	1901	—	100 Reis. Nickel. Hamburg Mint	185
Pn182	1901	—	100 Reis. Silver.	285
Pn183	1901	—	100 Reis. Gold.	1,250
Pn184	1901	—	200 Reis. Nickel-Silver.	235
Pn185	1901	—	200 Reis. Nickel. Birmingham Mint	235
Pn186	1901	—	200 Reis. Nickel. Hamburg Mint	235
Pn187	1901	—	200 Reis. Silver.	300
Pn188	1901	—	200 Reis. Gold.	2,000
Pn189	1901	—	400 Reis. Nickel-Silver.	235
Pn190	1901	—	400 Reis. Nickel. Birmingham Mint	235
Pn192	1901	—	400 Reis. Silver.	600
Pn193	1901	—	400 Reis. Gold.	3,000
Pn191	1901	—	400 Reis. Nickel. Hamburg Mint	235
Pn194	1902	—	100 Reis. Nickel. MCMI. 1902.	375
Pn195	1907	—	100 Reis. Silver.	400
Pn196	1907	—	200 Reis. Silver.	600
Pn197	1907	—	500 Reis. Silver.	400
Pn198	1907	—	1000 Reis. Silver.	400
Pn199	1907	—	2000 Reis. Silver.	400
Pn200	1908	—	50 Reis. Silver.	400
Pn201	1908	—	500 Reis. Silver.	400
Pn202	1908	—	1000 Reis. Silver.	400
Pn203	1908	—	2000 Reis. Silver.	400
Pn204	1910	—	40 Reis. Silver.	400
Pn205	1910	—	1000 Reis. Silver.	400
Pn206	1910	—	2000 Reis. Silver.	450
Pn207	1912	—	2000 Reis. Copper.	325
Pn208	1913	—	1000 Reis. Copper.	325
Pn209	1914	—	50 Reis. Silver.	375
Pn210	1914	—	400 Reis. Nickel.	350
Pn211	1914	—	2000 Reis. Nickel.	800
Pn212	1916	—	20 Reis. Silver.	300
Pn213	1916	—	200 Reis. Nickel.	285
Pn214	1916	—	200 Reis. Silver.	500
Pn215	1916	—	2000 Reis. Silver.	800
Pn216	1917	—	50 Reis. Nickel.	325
Pn217	1917	—	100 Reis. Nickel.	325
Pn218	1917	—	200 Reis. Nickel.	325
Pn219	1917	—	400 Reis. Nickel.	325
Pn220	1917	—	500 Reis. Nickel.	375
Pn221	1917	—	1000 Reis. Nickel.	325
Pn222	1917	—	2000 Reis. Nickel.	325
Pn223	1918	—	20 Reis. Nickel.	235
Pn224	1918	—	20 Reis. Nickel. Large planchet.	185
Pn225	1918	—	20 Reis. Silver.	350
Pn226	1918	—	2000 Reis. Nickel. Center hole.	285
Pn227	1921	—	1000 Reis.	200
Pn228	1921	—	2000 Reis.	400
Pn229	1921	—	10000 Reis. Gold.	1,150
Pn230	1921	—	20000 Reis. Gold.	1,150
Pn231	1922	—	50 Reis. Copper-Nickel.	285
Pn232	1922	—	50 Reis. Nickel-Silver.	185
Pn233	1922	—	500 Reis. Aluminum-Bronze.	185
Pn234	1922	—	500 Reis. Silver. Large planchet.	200
Pn235	1922	—	1000 Reis. Aluminum-Bronze.	185
Pn236	1922	—	2000 Reis. Silver.	300
Pn237	1922	—	2000 Reis. Silver.	275
Pn238	ND	—	2000 Reis. Silver.	275
Pn239	1922	—	2000 Reis. Silver.	275
Pn240	1922	—	2000 Reis. 0.6500 Silver.	275
Pn241	1922	—	2000 Reis. 0.8350 Silver.	275
Pn242	1922	—	2000 Reis. 0.9000 Silver.	275
Pn243	1923	—	1000 Reis. Silver.	400
Pn244	1923	—	2000 Reis. Silver.	285
Pn245	1923	—	2000 Reis. Silver.	285
Pn246	1923	—	2000 Reis. Silver.	285
Pn247	1923	—	2000 Reis. Silver.	285
Pn248	1923	—	2000 Reis. Silver.	285
Pn249	1923	—	2000 Reis. Silver.	285
Pn250	1924	—	100 Reis. Nickel.	185
Pn251	1924	—	400 Reis. Nickel.	185
Pn252	1924	—	500 Reis. Nickel.	185
Pn253	1924	—	500 Reis. Silver.	200
Pn254	1924	—	1000 Reis. Silver.	200
Pn255	1924	—	1000 Reis. Silver.	200
Pn256	1924	—	1000 Reis. Silver.	100
Pn257	1924	—	1000 Reis. Silver.	100
Pn258	1927	—	Cruzeiro. Copper.	185
Pn259	1927	—	Cruzeiro. Silver.	250
Pn260	1927	—	Cruzeiro. Gold.	300
Pn261	1927	—	2 Cruzeiros. Gold.	325
Pn262	1928	—	Cruzeiro. Nickel.	235
Pn263	1928	—	2 Cruzeiros. Nickel.	235
Pn265	1928	—	5 Cruzeiros. Nickel.	235
Pn264	1928	—	4 Cruzeiros. Nickel.	235
Pn266	1928	—	10 Cruzeiros. Nickel.	400
Pn267	1931	—	10 Reis. Silver.	185
Pn268	1932	—	100 Reis. Nickel-Silver. St. Vincent.	185
Pn269	1932	—	100 Reis. Silver. St. Vincent.	400
Pn270	1932	—	200 Reis. Nickel-Silver.	235
Pn271	1932	—	200 Reis. Copper-Nickel. St. Vincent.	235
Pn272	1932	—	200 Reis. Silver. St. Vincent.	250
Pn273	1932	—	400 Reis. Nickel-Silver.	265
Pn274	1932	—	400 Reis. Silver. St. Vincent.	285
Pn275	1932	—	500 Reis. Copper. Large planchet.	265
Pn276	1932	—	1000 Reis. Copper. St. Vincent.	285
Pn277	1932	—	1000 Reis. Aluminum-Bronze. Arms.	285
Pn278	1932	—	1000 Reis. Silver.	300
Pn279	1932	—	1000 Reis. Silver. Large planchet.	400
Pn280	1932	—	2000 Reis. Silver. St. Vincent.	285
Pn281	1935	—	200 Reis. Nickel. Large planchet.	185
Pn282	1935	—	400 Reis. Silver.	200
Pn283	1935	—	500 Reis. Nickel. 3.8500 g.	375
Pn284	1935	—	500 Reis. Nickel-Silver. 6.0000 g.	375
Pn285	1935	—	1000 Reis. Copper.	185
Pn286	1935	—	1000 Reis. Nickel.	185
Pn287	1935	—	1000 Reis. Nickel-Silver.	375
Pn288	1935	—	1000 Reis. Silver.	400
Pn290	1935	—	2000 Reis. Bronze.	265
Pn291	1935	—	2000 Reis. Copper.	265
Pn292	1935	—	2000 Reis. Nickel-Silver.	375
Pn293	1935	—	2000 Reis. Silver.	350
Pn294	1936	—	100 Reis. Nickel-Silver.	185
Pn295	1936	—	100 Reis. Silver.	350
Pn296	1936	—	200 Reis. Nickel-Silver.	90.00
Pn297	1936	—	200 Reis. Silver.	100
Pn298	1936	—	300 Reis. Nickel-Silver.	90.00
Pn299	1936	—	400 Reis. Nickel-Silver.	90.00
Pn300	1936	—	400 Reis. Silver.	100
Pn301	1936	—	500 Reis. Nickel-Silver.	90.00
Pn302	1936	—	500 Reis. Silver.	100
Pn303	1936	—	1000 Reis. Nickel-Silver.	90.00
Pn304	1936	—	1000 Reis. Silver.	100
Pn305	1936	—	2000 Reis. Nickel-Silver.	90.00
Pn306	1936	—	5000 Reis. Zinc.	90.00
Pn307	1936	—	5000 Reis. Nickel-Silver.	90.00
Pn308	1936	—	5000 Reis. Silver.	100
Pn309	1937	—	100 Reis. Nickel.	90.00
Pn310	1937	—	300 Reis. Nickel-Silver.	90.00
Pn311	1937	—	300 Reis. Nickel.	90.00
Pn312	1938	—	200 Reis. Nickel.	90.00
Pn313	1938	—	2000 Reis. Copper.	90.00
Pn314	1939	—	500 Reis. Nickel.	90.00
Pn315	1939	—	1000 Reis.	90.00
Pn316	1939	—	2000 Reis. Aluminum-Bronze.	90.00
Pn317	1939	—	2000 Reis. Aluminum-Bronze. Peixoto.	90.00
Pn318	1940	—	10 Centavos. Silver.	90.00
Pn319	1940	—	100 Reis. Copper-Nickel.	90.00
Pn320	1940	—	100 Reis. Nickel.	90.00
Pn321	1940	—	200 Reis. Copper-Nickel.	90.00
Pn322	1940	—	200 Reis. Nickel.	90.00
Pn323	1940	—	300 Reis. Copper-Nickel.	90.00
Pn324	1940	—	300 Reis. Nickel.	90.00
Pn325	1940	—	400 Reis. Copper-Nickel.	90.00
Pn326	1940	—	400 Reis. Nickel.	90.00
Pn327	1941	—	10 Centavos. Nickel.	90.00
Pn328	1941	—	10 Centavos. Nickel-Silver.	90.00
Pn329	1941	—	50 Centavos. Brass.	90.00
Pn330	1941	—	50 Centavos. Nickel.	90.00
Pn331	1941	—	50 Centavos. Nickel-Silver.	90.00
Pn332	1941	—	50 Centavos. Nickel-Silver.	90.00
Pn333	1941	—	50 Centavos. Silver.	90.00
Pn334	1941	—	50 Centavos. Silver.	90.00
Pn335	1941	—	Cruzeiro. Nickel-Silver.	90.00
Pn336	1941	—	2 Cruzeiros. Nickel.	90.00
Pn337	1941	—	2 Cruzeiros. Nickel-Silver.	45.00
Pn338	1941	—	2 Cruzeiros. Silver.	75.00
Pn339	1942	—	100 Reis. Nickel.	45.00
Pn340	1942	—	200 Reis. Nickel.	45.00
Pn341	1942	—	300 Reis. Nickel.	45.00
Pn342	1942	—	400 Reis. Nickel.	45.00
Pn343	1942	—	2 Cruzeiros. Nickel.	45.00
Pn344	1942	—	2 Cruzeiros. Nickel-Silver.	45.00
Pn345	1943	—	10 Centavos. Nickel-Silver.	45.00
Pn346	1943	—	20 Centavos. Nickel-Silver.	45.00
Pn347	1943	—	20 Centavos. Silver.	45.00
Pn348	1943	—	50 Centavos. Nickel-Silver.	45.00
Pn349	1943	—	Cruzeiro. Silver.	50.00
Pn350	1945	—	10 Centavos. Nickel-Silver.	45.00
Pn351	1945	—	10 Centavos. Silver.	45.00
Pn352	1945	—	50 Centavos. Nickel-Silver.	45.00
Pn353	1945	—	50 Centavos. Silver.	45.00
Pn354	1945	—	Cruzeiro. Nickel.	45.00
Pn355	1945	—	Cruzeiro. Nickel-Silver.	45.00

KM#	Date	Mintage	Identification	Mkt Val
Pn356	1947	—	20 Centavos. Aluminum-Bronze.	150
Pn357	1947	—	50 Centavos. Aluminum-Bronze.	150
Pn358	1947	—	2 Cruzeiros. Aluminum-Bronze.	90.00
Pn360	1950	—	Cruzeiro. Silver.	60.00
Pn361	1950	—	Cruzeiro. Gold.	—
Pn362	1955	—	50 Centavos. Aluminum.	45.00
Pn363	1956	—	10 Centavos. Aluminum. Arms.	45.00
Pn364	1956	—	10 Centavos. Aluminum-Bronze. Arms.	45.00
Pn365	1956	—	10 Centavos. Aluminum-Bronze. Bonifacio.	45.00
Pn366	1956	—	20 Centavos. Aluminum-Bronze.	45.00
Pn367	1956	—	50 Centavos. Aluminum.	45.00
Pn368	1956	—	Cruzeiro. Aluminum.	45.00
Pn369	1961	—	2 Cruzeiros. Aluminum-Bronze.	90.00
Pn370	1962	—	5 Cruzeiros.	90.00
Pn371	1963	—	5 Cruzeiros. Aluminum. Map.	90.00
Pn372	1963	—	5 Cruzeiros. Aluminum. Arms.	90.00
Pn373	1963	—	5 Cruzeiros. Aluminum-Bronze. Arms.	90.00
Pn374	1964	—	5 Cruzeiros. Aluminum.	90.00
Pn375	1964	—	10 Cruzeiros. Aluminum.	90.00
Pn376	1964	—	20 Cruzeiros. Aluminum.	90.00
Pn377	1964	—	50 Cruzeiros. Nickel.	90.00
Pn378	1964	—	100 Cruzeiros. Nickel.	90.00
Pn379	1964	—	200 Cruzeiros. Nickel.	90.00
Pn380	1965	—	5 Cruzeiros. Aluminum. Map.	90.00
Pn381	1965	—	5 Cruzeiros. Aluminum. Arms.	90.00
Pn382	1966	—	Centavo. Stainless Steel.	90.00
Pn383	1966	—	2 Centavos. Stainless Steel.	90.00
Pn384	1966	—	5 Centavos. Stainless Steel.	90.00
Pn385	1966	—	5 Centavos. Nickel.	90.00
Pn386	1966	—	10 Centavos. Copper-Nickel.	90.00
Pn387	1966	—	20 Centavos. Copper-Nickel.	90.00
Pn388	1967	—	10 Centavos. Stainless Steel.	90.00
Pn389	1972	—	20 Cruzeiros. 0.9000 Silver. KM#583.	100

PROVAS

KM#	Date	Mintage	Identification	Mkt Val
Pr1	1967	—	Cruzeiro. Nickel. PROVA.	45.00
Pr2	1967	—	Cruzeiro. Nickel. PROVA.	45.00
Pr3	1970	—	20 Centavos. Stainless Steel. KM#579.1.	45.00
Pr5	1972	—	Cruzeiro. Nickel. Y#94.	150
Pr6	1972	—	20 Cruzeiros. Silver. Pedro I and General Emilio Garrastazu Medici heads, left, date below. Denomination below map. KM#583.	50.00
Pr7	1972	—	300 Cruzeiros. Brass. KM#584.	115
Pr8	1972	—	300 Cruzeiros. Gold. KM#584.	550
Pr9	1974	—	10 Centavos. Stainless Steel. KM#578.1a.	45.00
Pr10	1974	—	Cruzeiro. Nickel. KM#581.	45.00
Pr12	1975	—	2 Centavos. Stainless Steel. KM#586.	45.00
Pr13	1975	—	5 Centavos. Stainless Steel. KM#587.1.	45.00
Pr14	1975	—	10 Centavos. Stainless Steel. KM#578.1a.	45.00
Pr15	1975	—	50 Centavos. Stainless Steel. KM#580b.	45.00
Pr16	1975	—	10 Cruzeiros. Silver. KM#588.	75.00
Pr17	1976	—	Centavo. Silver. KM#585.	75.00
Pr18	1976	—	2 Centavos. Stainless Steel. KM#586.	28.00
Pr19	1976	—	5 Centavos. Stainless Steel. KM#587.1.	45.00
Pr20	1980	5,000	Centavo. Steel. KM#589.	28.00
Pr21	1980	5,000	10 Centavos. Steel.	28.00
Pr22	1980	5,000	50 Centavos. Steel.	28.00
Pr23	1980	5,000	Cruzeiro. Steel. KM#590.	28.00
Pr24	1980	5,000	5 Cruzeiros. Steel. KM#591.	28.00
Pr25	1980	5,000	10 Cruzeiros. Steel. KM#592.	28.00
PrA26	1988	—	100 Cruzados. Stainless Steel. KM#608.	45.00
PrB26	1988	—	100 Cruzados. Stainless Steel. KM#609.	45.00
PrC26	1988	—	100 Cruzados. Stainless Steel. KM#610.	45.00
Pr26	1989	—	Centavo. Steel. KM#611.	38.00
Pr27	1989	—	5 Centavos. Steel. KM#612.	38.00
Pr28	1989	—	10 Centavos. Steel. KM#613.	42.00
Pr29	1989	—	50 Centavos. Steel. KM#614.	45.00
Pr30	ND	—	200 Novos Cruzados. 0.9990 Silver. KM#616.	100
Pr31	1990	—	Cruzeiro. Steel. KM#617.	38.00
Pr32	1990	—	5 Cruzeiros. Steel. KM#618.	38.00
Pr33	1990	—	10 Cruzeiros. Steel. KM#619.	42.00
Pr34	1990	—	50 Cruzeiros. Steel. KM#620.	45.00
Pr35	1991	—	500 Cruzeiros. 0.9250 Silver. KM#621.	125
Pr36	1992	—	2000 Cruzeiros. Silver. KM#622.	175
Pr37	ND	—	5000 Cruzeiros. Steel. KM#625.	80.00
Pr38	1994	—	4 Reais. 0.9250 Silver. KM#638.	185

TRIAL STRIKES

KM#	Date	Mintage	Identification	Mkt Val
TS4	1948	—	1000 Cruzeiros. Uniface.	750

MINT SETS

KM#	Date	Mintage	Identification	Issue Price	Mkt Val
MS1	1972 (2)	—	KM#582-583	—	12.50

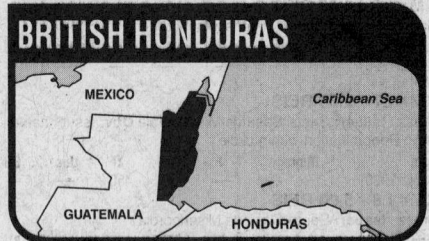

BRITISH HONDURAS

This area, site of the ancient Mayan civilization, was sighted by Columbus in 1502, and settled by shipwrecked English seamen in 1638. British buccaneers settled the former capital of Belize in the 17th century. Britain claimed administrative right over the area after the emancipation of Central America from Spain. In 1825, Imperial coins were introduced into the colony and were rated against the Spanish dollar and Honduran currency. It was declared a colony subordinate to Jamaica in 1862 and was established as the separate Crown Colony of British Honduras in 1884. In May, 1885 an order in Council authorized coins for the colony, with the first shipment arriving in July. While the Guatemalan peso was originally the standard of value, in 1894 the colony changed to the gold standard, based on the U.S. gold dollar. The anti-British Peoples United Party, which attained power in 1954, won a constitution, effective in 1964 which established self-government under a British appointed governor. British Honduras became Belize on June 1, 1973, following the passage of a surprise bill by the Peoples United Party, but the constitutional relationship with Britain remained unchanged. Full independence was achieved in 1981.

MONETARY SYSTEM
100 Cents = 1 Dollar

MINT MARKS
H - Heaton

BRITISH COLONY
DECIMAL COINAGE

KM# 11   CENT
Bronze **Ruler:** Edward VII **Obv:** Bust of King Edward VII right **Rev:** Numeric denomination within circle, denomination and date below

Date	Mintage	F	VF	XF	Unc	BU
1904	50,000	6.00	15.00	50.00	90.00	—
1904 Proof	—	Value: 200				
1904 Matte Proof	—	Value: 1,550				
1906	50,000	12.00	27.50	65.00	225	—
1906 Matte Proof	—	Value: 1,050				
1909	25,000	35.00	80.00	150	300	—

KM# 15   CENT
Bronze **Ruler:** George V **Obv:** Bust of King George V left **Rev:** Numeric denomination within circle, denomination and date below

Date	Mintage	F	VF	XF	Unc	BU
1911	50,000	60.00	100	200	500	—
1912H	50,000	85.00	160	250	600	—
1913	25,000	100	200	300	700	—

KM# 19   CENT
Bronze **Ruler:** George V **Obv:** Bust of King George V left **Rev:** Numeric denomination within scalloped circle, denomination and date below

Date	Mintage	F	VF	XF	Unc	BU
1914	175,000	3.00	7.50	25.00	120	—
1916H	125,000	3.50	8.50	27.50	125	—

Date	Mintage	F	VF	XF	Unc	BU
1918	40,000	7.00	15.00	40.00	150	—
1919	50,000	7.00	15.00	40.00	150	—
1924	50,000	7.00	15.00	40.00	125	—
1924 Proof	—	Value: 250				
1926	50,000	5.00	12.00	35.00	125	—
1926 Proof	—	Value: 225				
1936	40,000	2.00	5.00	20.00	65.00	—
1936 Proof	50	Value: 170				

KM# 21   CENT
Bronze **Ruler:** George VI **Obv:** Bust of King George VI left **Rev:** Numeric denomination within scalloped circle, denomination and date below

Date	Mintage	F	VF	XF	Unc	BU
1937	80,000	0.75	4.00	12.00	75.00	—
1937 Proof	—	Value: 170				
1939	50,000	2.00	7.00	20.00	150	—
1939 Proof	—	Value: 100				
1942	50,000	2.00	7.00	20.00	150	—
1942 Proof	—	Value: 125				
1943	100,000	1.00	5.00	15.00	125	—
1943 Proof	—	Value: 150				
1944	100,000	2.00	7.00	20.00	150	—
1944 Proof	—	Value: 200				
1945	130,000	0.75	2.00	7.50	50.00	—
1945 Proof	—	Value: 120				
1947	100,000	0.75	2.50	10.00	70.00	—
1947 Proof	—	Value: 150				

KM# 24   CENT
Bronze **Ruler:** George VI **Obv:** Bust of King George VI left **Obv. Leg.:** Without EMPEROR OF INDIA **Rev:** Numeric denomination within scalloped circle, denomination and date below

Date	Mintage	F	VF	XF	Unc	BU
1949	100,000	0.60	1.50	4.00	16.50	—
1949 Proof	—	Value: 135				
1950	100,000	0.40	1.00	2.50	6.50	—
1950 Proof	—	Value: 135				
1951	100,000	0.60	1.50	4.00	16.50	—
1951 Proof	—	Value: 135				

KM# 27   CENT
Bronze **Ruler:** Elizabeth II **Obv:** Head right **Rev:** Numeric denomination within scalloped circle, date and denomination below **Edge:** Plain

Date	Mintage	F	VF	XF	Unc	BU
1954	200,000	0.50	0.75	1.00	5.00	—
1954 Proof	—	Value: 150				

KM# 30   CENT
2.5000 g., Bronze, 19.5 mm. **Ruler:** Elizabeth II **Obv:** Bust of Queen Elizabeth II right **Rev:** Numeric denomination within scalloped circle, date and denomination below **Edge:** Plain

Date	Mintage	F	VF	XF	Unc	BU
1956	200,000	0.10	0.25	0.50	3.50	—
1956 Proof	—	Value: 80.00				
1958	400,000	1.00	2.00	9.00	80.00	—
1958 Proof	—	Value: 80.00				
1959	200,000	1.00	2.50	10.00	100	—
1959 Proof	—	Value: 100				
1961	800,000	—	0.15	0.25	0.50	—
1961 Proof	—	Value: 80.00				
1964	300,000	—	0.10	0.30	0.90	—
1965	400,000	—	—	0.10	0.50	—

Date	Mintage	F	VF	XF	Unc	BU
1966	100,000	—	—	0.10	0.50	—
1967	400,000	—	—	0.10	0.50	—
1968	200,000	—	—	0.10	0.50	—
1969	520,000	—	—	0.10	0.40	—
1970	120,000	—	—	0.10	0.40	—
1971	800,000	—	—	0.10	0.40	—
1972	800,000	—	—	0.10	0.40	—
1973	400,000	—	—	0.10	0.40	—

KM# 14   5 CENTS
Copper-Nickel **Ruler:** Edward VII **Obv:** Bust of King Edward VII right within circle, date below **Rev:** Denomination within circle **Edge:** Plain

Date	Mintage	F	VF	XF	Unc	BU
1907	10,000	25.00	50.00	100	250	—
1909	10,000	25.00	50.00	100	250	—

KM# 16   5 CENTS
Copper-Nickel **Ruler:** George V **Obv:** Bust of King George V left within circle, date below **Rev:** Denomination within circle **Edge:** Plain

Date	Mintage	F	VF	XF	Unc	BU
1911	10,000	25.00	50.00	100	250	—
1912H	20,000	10.00	25.00	55.00	175	—
1912H Proof	—	Value: 550				
1916H	20,000	10.00	25.00	55.00	175	—
1918	20,000	10.00	25.00	55.00	175	—
1919	20,000	8.00	20.00	50.00	160	—
1936	60,000	2.50	5.00	20.00	75.00	—
1936 Proof	50	Value: 450				

KM# 22   5 CENTS
Copper-Nickel **Ruler:** George VI **Obv:** Head of King George VI left **Rev:** Denomination within circle, date below **Edge:** Plain

Date	Mintage	F	VF	XF	Unc	BU
1939	20,000	3.00	6.00	25.00	75.00	—
1939 Proof	—	Value: 275				

KM# 22a   5 CENTS
Nickel-Brass **Ruler:** George VI **Obv:** Head of King George VI left **Rev:** Denomination within circle, date below

Date	Mintage	F	VF	XF	Unc	BU
1942	30,000	5.00	15.00	65.00	200	—
1942 Proof	—	Value: 300				
1943	40,000	2.00	12.00	60.00	190	—
1944	50,000	1.50	10.00	50.00	175	—
1944 Proof	—	Value: 275				
1945	65,000	1.00	5.00	15.00	75.00	—
1945 Proof	—	Value: 150				
1947	40,000	1.50	5.00	15.00	85.00	—
1947 Proof	—	Value: 185				

KM# 25   5 CENTS
Nickel-Brass, 20 mm. **Ruler:** George VI **Obv:** Head of King George VI left **Obv. Leg.:** Legend without EMPEROR OF INDIA **Rev:** Denomination within circle, date below **Edge:** Plain

Date	Mintage	F	VF	XF	Unc	BU
1949	40,000	1.50	3.00	10.00	50.00	—
1949 Proof	—	Value: 150				

Date	Mintage	F	VF	XF	Unc	BU
1950	225,000	0.40	1.00	4.00	30.00	—
1950 Proof	—	Value: 200				
1952	100,000	0.50	2.00	6.00	35.00	—
1952 Proof	—	Value: 250				

KM# 31   5 CENTS
3.6000 g., Nickel-Brass, 20.26 mm. **Ruler:** Elizabeth II **Obv:** Bust of Queen Elizabeth II right **Rev:** Denomination within circle, date below **Edge:** Plain

Date	Mintage	F	VF	XF	Unc	BU
1956	100,000	0.20	0.50	3.00	75.00	—
1956 Proof	—	Value: 125				
1957	100,000	0.30	0.75	1.50	10.00	—
1957 Proof	—	Value: 175				
1958	200,000	0.30	1.00	7.50	90.00	—
1958 Proof	—	Value: 125				
1959	100,000	0.40	2.00	10.00	100	—
1959 Proof	—	Value: 185				
1961	100,000	0.30	0.75	2.50	35.00	—
1961 Proof	—	Value: 120				
1962	200,000	0.15	0.35	0.65	2.00	—
1962 Proof	—	Value: 115				
1963	—	0.10	0.20	0.50	1.50	—
1963 Proof	—	Value: 175				
1964	100,000	0.10	0.15	0.35	1.00	—
1965	150,000	—	0.10	0.25	0.75	—
1966	150,000	—	0.10	0.20	0.60	—
1968	200,000	—	0.10	0.15	0.50	—
1969	540,000	—	0.10	0.15	0.50	—
1970	240,000	—	0.10	0.15	0.50	—
1971	450,000	—	0.10	0.15	0.50	—
1972	200,000	—	0.10	0.15	0.50	—
1973	210,000	—	0.10	0.15	0.75	—

KM# 20   10 CENTS
2.3240 g., 0.9250 Silver 0.0691 oz. ASW **Ruler:** George V **Obv:** Bust of King George V left **Rev:** Denomination within circle, date below **Edge:** Reeded

Date	Mintage	F	VF	XF	Unc	BU
1918	10,000	15.00	25.00	100	350	—
1919	10,000	15.00	25.00	100	350	—
1936	30,000	6.00	12.00	75.00	100	—
1936 Proof	50	Value: 325				

KM# 23   10 CENTS
2.3240 g., 0.9250 Silver 0.0691 oz. ASW **Ruler:** George VI **Obv:** Head of King George VI left **Rev:** Denomination within circle, date below **Edge:** Plain

Date	Mintage	F	VF	XF	Unc	BU
1939	20,000	3.00	7.00	20.00	60.00	—
1939 Proof	—	Value: 300				
1942	10,000	10.00	20.00	60.00	250	—
1943	20,000	3.00	6.00	45.00	250	—
1944	30,000	2.50	5.00	35.00	150	—
1944 Proof	—	Value: 250				
1946	10,000	5.00	12.00	45.00	200	—
1946 Proof	—	Value: 450				

KM# 32   10 CENTS
2.3400 g., Copper-Nickel, 18 mm. **Ruler:** Elizabeth II **Obv:** Bust of Queen Elizabeth II right **Rev:** Denomination within circle, date below **Edge:** Plain

Date	Mintage	F	VF	XF	Unc	BU
1956	100,000	0.45	1.00	2.00	7.50	—
1956 Proof	—	Value: 200				
1959	100,000	0.65	1.50	2.00	7.50	—
1959 Proof	—	Value: 135				
1961	50,000	0.35	0.75	1.25	3.00	—
1961 Proof	—	Value: 135				
1963	50,000	0.20	0.50	0.75	2.00	—
1963 Proof	—	Value: 135				

Date	Mintage	F	VF	XF	Unc	BU
1964	60,000	0.15	0.25	0.50	1.00	—
1965/6	200,000	5.00	10.00	20.00	40.00	—
1965	Inc. above	—	0.10	0.15	0.50	—
1970	—	—	0.10	0.15	0.75	—

KM# 9   25 CENTS
5.8100 g., 0.9250 Silver 0.1728 oz. ASW **Ruler:** Victoria **Obv:** Head of Queen Victoria left **Rev:** Denomination within circle, date below **Edge:** Plain

Date	Mintage	F	VF	XF	Unc	BU
1901	20,000	20.00	35.00	125	400	—
1901 Proof	30	Value: 650				

KM# 12   25 CENTS
5.8100 g., 0.9250 Silver 0.1728 oz. ASW **Ruler:** Edward VII **Obv:** Bust of King Edward VII right **Rev:** Denomination within circle, date below **Edge:** Reeded

Date	Mintage	F	VF	XF	Unc	BU
1906	30,000	15.00	30.00	110	375	—
1907	60,000	10.00	25.00	95.00	325	—

KM# 17   25 CENTS
5.8100 g., 0.9250 Silver 0.1728 oz. ASW **Ruler:** George V **Obv:** Bust of King George V left **Rev:** Denomination within circle, date below **Edge:** Reeded

Date	Mintage	F	VF	XF	Unc	BU
1911	14,000	25.00	60.00	150	400	—
1919	40,000	8.00	17.50	75.00	250	—

KM# 26   25 CENTS
Copper-Nickel **Ruler:** George VI **Obv:** Head of King George VI left **Rev:** Denomination within circle, date below **Edge:** Reeded

Date	Mintage	F	VF	XF	Unc	BU
1952	75,000	2.00	5.00	50.00	200	—
1952 Proof	—	Value: 250				

KM# 29   25 CENTS
5.6200 g., Copper-Nickel, 23.53 mm. **Ruler:** Elizabeth II **Obv:** Bust of Queen Elizabeth II right **Edge:** Reeded

Date	Mintage	F	VF	XF	Unc	BU
1955	75,000	0.45	1.00	3.50	15.00	—
1955 Proof	—	Value: 150				
1960	75,000	0.45	1.00	5.00	100	—
1960 Proof	—	Value: 250				
1962	50,000	0.30	0.50	1.00	2.50	—
1962 Proof	—	Value: 150				
1963	50,000	0.30	0.50	1.00	7.50	—
1963 Proof	—	Value: 150				
1964	100,000	0.30	0.50	0.75	1.50	—
1965	75,000	—	0.50	1.00	2.00	—
1966	75,000	0.45	1.00	2.00	8.00	—
1968	125,000	0.25	0.50	1.00	2.00	—
1970	—	—	0.20	0.35	0.75	1.50
1971	150,000	0.20	0.30	0.50	1.50	—

Date	Mintage	F	VF	XF	Unc	BU
1972	200,000	0.20	0.30	0.50	1.50	—
1973	100,000	0.20	0.30	0.60	1.75	—

KM# 10   50 CENTS
11.6200 g., 0.9250 Silver 0.3456 oz. ASW **Ruler:** Victoria
Obv: Head of Queen Victoria left **Rev:** Denomination within circle, date below

Date	Mintage	F	VF	XF	Unc	BU
1901	10,000	35.00	80.00	400	1,000	—
1901 Proof	30	Value: 1,000				

KM# 13   50 CENTS
11.6200 g., 0.9250 Silver 0.3456 oz. ASW **Ruler:** Edward VII
Obv: Bust of King Edward VII right **Rev:** Denomination within circle, date below

Date	Mintage	F	VF	XF	Unc	BU
1906	15,000	20.00	60.00	225	600	—
1907	19,000	18.00	55.00	170	500	—

KM# 18   50 CENTS
11.6200 g., 0.9250 Silver 0.3456 oz. ASW **Ruler:** George V
Obv: Bust of King George V left **Rev:** Denomination within circle, date below

Date	Mintage	F	VF	XF	Unc	BU
1911	12,000	30.00	75.00	250	850	—
1919	40,000	20.00	40.00	150	400	—
1919 Proof	—	Value: 1,250				

KM# 28   50 CENTS
Copper-Nickel **Ruler:** Elizabeth II **Obv:** Bust of Queen Elizabeth II right **Rev:** Denomination within circle, date below

Date	Mintage	F	VF	XF	Unc	BU
1954	75,000	0.30	0.50	1.00	4.00	—
1954 Proof	—	Value: 175				
1962	50,000	0.30	0.50	1.50	5.00	—
1962 Proof	—	Value: 200				
1964	50,000	0.30	0.50	1.50	3.50	—
1965	25,000	1.25	3.00	5.00	22.50	—
1966	25,000	1.00	2.00	4.00	15.00	—
1971	30,000	0.30	0.50	1.50	3.50	—

PROOF SETS

KM#	Date	Mintage	Identification	Issue Price	Mkt Val
PS2	1901 (2)	30	KM#9, 10	—	2,500
PS3	1936 (3)	50	KM#16, 19, 20	—	1,000
PS4	1939 (3)	—	KM#21-23	—	675
PS5	1949 (2)	—	KM#24, 25	—	300
PS6	1950 (2)	—	KM#24, 25	—	350
PS7	1954 (2)	—	KM#27, 28	—	300
PS8	1956 (3)	—	KM#30-32	—	400
PS9	1958 (2)	—	KM#30, 31	—	200

BRITISH NORTH BORNEO

British North Borneo (now known as *Sabah*), a former British protectorate and crown colony, occupies the northern tip of the island of Borneo. The island of Labuan, which lies 6 miles off the northwest coast of the island of Borneo, was attached to Singapore settlement in 1907. It became an independent settlement of the Straits Colony in 1912 and was incorporated with British North Borneo in 1946. In 1963 it became part of Malaysia.

RULER
British

MINT MARKS
H - Heaton, Birmingham

MONETARY SYSTEM
100 Cents = 1 Straits Dollar

BRITISH PROTECTORATE
STANDARD COINAGE

KM# 1   1/2 CENT
Bronze **Obv:** Denomination within wreath **Rev:** National arms, date below

Date	Mintage	F	VF	XF	Unc	BU
1907H	1,000,000	55.00	150	210	450	—
1907H Proof	—	Value: 800				

KM# 3   CENT
Copper-Nickel **Obv:** Denomination within circle, date below **Rev:** National arms with supporters

Date	Mintage	F	VF	XF	Unc	BU
1904H	2,000,000	3.50	10.00	20.00	60.00	—
1921H	1,000,000	3.50	10.00	20.00	60.00	—
1935H	1,000,000	2.70	6.00	16.00	45.00	—
1938H	1,000,000	2.70	6.00	16.00	45.00	—
1941H	1,000,000	2.70	6.00	16.00	45.00	—

KM# 2   CENT
Bronze **Obv:** Denomination within wreath **Rev:** National arms with supporters, date below

Date	Mintage	F	VF	XF	Unc	BU
1907H	1,000,000	55.00	130	250	460	—
1907H Proof	—	Value: 1,000				

KM# 4   2-1/2 CENT
Copper-Nickel **Obv:** Denomination within circle, date below **Rev:** National arms with supporters

Date	Mintage	F	VF	XF	Unc	BU
1903H	2,000,000	5.00	18.00	45.00	150	—

Date	Mintage	F	VF	XF	Unc	BU
1903H Proof	—	Value: 680				
1920H	280,000	13.00	40.00	90.00	280	—

KM# 5   5 CENTS
Copper-Nickel **Obv:** Denomination within circle, date below **Rev:** National arms with supporters

Date	Mintage	F	VF	XF	Unc	BU
1903H	1,000,000	8.00	16.00	30.00	75.00	—
1920H	100,000	12.00	30.00	70.00	140	—
1921H	500,000	6.00	12.00	25.00	75.00	—
1927H	150,000	6.00	12.00	25.00	75.00	—
1928H	150,000	4.00	8.00	18.00	70.00	—
1938H	500,000	3.00	5.00	12.00	32.00	—
1940H	500,000	3.00	5.00	12.00	32.00	—
1941H	1,000,000	3.00	5.00	12.00	32.00	—

KM# 6   25 CENTS
2.8300 g., 0.5000 Silver 0.0455 oz. ASW **Obv:** Denomination within circle, date below **Rev:** National arms with supporters

Date	Mintage	F	VF	XF	Unc	BU
1929H	400,000	40.00	60.00	130	250	—
1929H Proof	—	Value: 600				

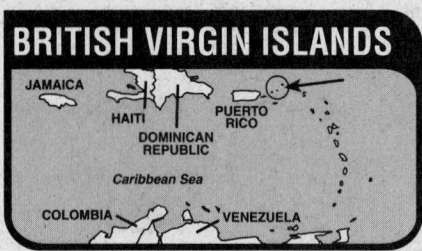

BRITISH VIRGIN ISLANDS

The Colony of the Virgin Islands, a British colony situated in the Caribbean Sea northeast of Puerto Rico and west of the Leeward Islands, has an area of 59 sq. mi. (155 sq. km.) and a population of 13,000. Capital: Road Town. The principal islands of the 36-island group are Tortola, Virgin Gorda, Anegada, and Jost Van Dyke. The chief industries are fishing and stock raising. Fish, livestock and bananas are exported.

The Virgin Islands were discovered by Columbus in 1493, and named by him, Las Virgienes, in honor of St. Ursula and her companions. The British Virgin Islands were formerly part of the administration of the Leeward Islands but received a separate administration as a Crown Colony in 1950. A new constitution promulgated in 1967 provided for a ministerial form of government headed by the Governor.

The Government of the British Virgin Islands issued the first official coinage in its history on June 30, 1973, in honor of 300 years of constitutional government in the islands. U.S. coins and currency continue to be the primary medium of exchange, though the coinage of the British Virgin Islands is legal tender.

*NOTE: From 1975-1985 the Franklin Mint produced coinage in up to 3 different qualities. Qualities of issue are designated in ( ) after each date and are defined as follows:

(M) MATTE - Normal circulation strike or a dull finish produced by sandblasting special uncirculated (polish finish) or proof quality dies.

(U) SPECIAL UNCIRCULATED - Polished or proof-like in appearance without any frosted features.

(P) PROOF - The highest quality obtainable having mirror-like fields and frosted features.

BRITISH COLONY
STANDARD COINAGE

KM# 1   CENT
Bronze **Ruler:** Elizabeth II **Obv:** Young bust right **Rev:** Green-throated Carib and Antillean Crested Hummingbird

Date	Mintage	F	VF	XF	Unc	BU
1973FM	53,000	—	—	0.10	0.50	1.00
1973FM (P)	181,000	Value: 1.00				
1974FM	22,000	—	—	0.10	0.50	1.00
1974FM (P)	94,000	Value: 1.00				
1975FM (M)	6,000	—	—	0.10	0.75	1.20
1975FM (U)	2,351	—	—	0.10	0.50	1.00
1975FM (P)	32,000	Value: 1.00				
1976FM (M)	12,000	—	—	0.10	0.50	1.00
1976FM (U)	996	—	—	0.10	0.50	1.00
1976FM (P)	15,000	Value: 1.00				
1977FM (M)	500	—	—	0.25	2.00	3.00
1977FM (U)	782	—	—	0.10	0.50	1.00
1977FM (P)	7,218	Value: 1.00				
1978FM (U)	1,443	—	—	0.10	0.50	1.00
1978FM (P)	7,059	Value: 1.00				
1979FM (U)	680	—	—	0.10	0.50	1.00
1979FM (P)	5,304	Value: 1.00				
1980FM (U)	1,007	—	—	0.10	0.50	1.00
1980FM (P)	3,421	Value: 1.00				
1981FM (U)	472	—	—	0.10	0.50	1.00
1981FM (P)	1,124	Value: 1.50				
1982FM (U)	—	—	—	0.10	0.50	1.00
1982FM (P)	—	Value: 1.50				
1983FM (U)	—	—	—	0.10	0.50	1.00
1983FM (P)	—	Value: 1.50				
1984FM (P)	—	Value: 1.50				

KM# 9 CENT
1.7500 g., 0.9250 Silver 0.0520 oz. ASW **Ruler:** Elizabeth II
Subject: Queen's Silver Jubilee **Obv:** Young bust right
Rev: Green-throated Carib and Antillean Crested Hummingbird

Date	Mintage	F	VF	XF	Unc	BU
1977FM (P)	17,000	Value: 2.50				

KM# 16 CENT
1.7500 g., 0.9250 Silver 0.0520 oz. ASW **Ruler:** Elizabeth II
Subject: Coronation Jubilee **Obv:** Young bust right
Rev: Hummingbird

Date	Mintage	F	VF	XF	Unc	BU
1978FM (P)	6,196	Value: 8.00				

KM# 42 CENT
Bronze **Ruler:** Elizabeth II **Obv:** Crowned head right
Rev: Hawksbill Turtle left

Date	Mintage	F	VF	XF	Unc	BU
1985FM (P)	—	Value: 5.00				

KM# 42a CENT
1.7500 g., 0.9250 Silver 0.0520 oz. ASW **Ruler:** Elizabeth II
Obv: Crowned head right **Rev:** Hawksbill turtle left

Date	Mintage	F	VF	XF	Unc	BU
1985FM (P)	1,474	Value: 7.50				

KM# 2 5 CENTS
Copper-Nickel, 19.5 mm. **Ruler:** Elizabeth II **Obv:** Young bust right **Rev:** Zenaida Doves

Date	Mintage	F	VF	XF	Unc	BU
1973FM	26,000	—	—	0.15	0.75	1.00
1973FM (P)	181,000	Value: 1.25				
1974FM	18,000	—	—	0.15	0.75	1.00
1974FM (P)	94,000	Value: 1.25				
1975FM (M)	3,800	—	—	0.20	1.00	1.25
1975FM (U)	2,351	—	—	0.15	0.75	1.00
1975FM (P)	32,000	Value: 1.25				
1976FM (M)	4,800	—	—	0.20	1.00	1.25
1976FM (U)	996	—	—	0.15	1.25	1.50
1976FM (P)	15,000	Value: 1.25				
1977FM (M)	500	—	—	0.35	3.50	5.00
1977FM (U)	782	—	—	0.15	1.00	1.25
1977FM (P)	7,218	Value: 1.25				
1978FM (U)	1,443	—	—	0.15	1.00	1.25
1978FM (P)	7,059	Value: 1.25				
1979FM (U)	680	—	—	0.15	1.00	1.25
1979FM (P)	5,304	Value: 1.25				
1980FM (U)	1,007	—	—	0.15	1.00	1.25
1980FM (P)	3,421	Value: 1.25				
1981FM (U)	472	—	—	0.15	1.00	1.25
1981FM (P)	1,124	Value: 1.25				
1982FM (U)	—	—	—	0.15	1.00	1.25
1982FM (P)	—	Value: 1.25				
1983FM (U)	—	—	—	0.15	1.00	1.25
1983FM (P)	—	Value: 1.25				
1984FM (P)	—	Value: 1.25				

KM# 10 5 CENTS
3.5500 g., 0.9250 Silver 0.1056 oz. ASW, 19.5 mm.
Ruler: Elizabeth II **Subject:** Queen's Silver Jubilee **Obv:** Young bust right **Rev:** Zenaida Doves

Date	Mintage	F	VF	XF	Unc	BU
1977FM (P)	17,000	Value: 3.00				

KM# 17 5 CENTS
3.5500 g., 0.9250 Silver 0.1056 oz. ASW, 19.5 mm.
Ruler: Elizabeth II **Subject:** Coronation Jubilee **Obv:** Young bust right divides dates **Rev:** Zenaida Doves

Date	Mintage	F	VF	XF	Unc	BU
ND(1978)FM (P)	6,196	Value: 4.50				

KM# 43 5 CENTS
Copper-Nickel **Ruler:** Elizabeth II **Obv:** Crowned head right **Rev:** Bonito Fish left

Date	Mintage	F	VF	XF	Unc	BU
1985FM (P)	—	Value: 6.00				

KM# 43a 5 CENTS
3.5550 g., 0.9250 Silver 0.1057 oz. ASW **Ruler:** Elizabeth II **Obv:** Crowned head right **Rev:** Bonito fish left

Date	Mintage	F	VF	XF	Unc	BU
1985FM (P)	1,471	Value: 6.00				

KM# 3 10 CENTS
Copper-Nickel **Ruler:** Elizabeth II **Obv:** Young bust right **Rev:** Ringed Kingfisher right

Date	Mintage	F	VF	XF	Unc	BU
1973FM (U)	23,000	—	—	0.20	1.00	1.25
1973FM (P)	181,000	Value: 1.50				
1974FM (U)	13,000	—	—	0.20	1.00	1.25
1974FM (P)	94,000	Value: 1.50				
1975FM (M)	2,000	—	—	0.20	1.25	1.50
1975FM (U)	2,351	—	—	0.20	1.00	1.25
1975FM (P)	32,000	Value: 1.50				
1976FM (U)	3,000	—	—	0.20	1.00	1.25
1976FM (U)	996	—	—	0.20	1.25	1.50
1976FM (P)	15,000	Value: 1.50				
1977FM (M)	500	—	—	0.45	4.00	6.00
1977FM (U)	782	—	—	0.20	1.50	2.00
1977FM (P)	7,218	Value: 1.50				
1978FM (U)	1,443	—	—	0.20	1.25	1.50
1978FM (P)	7,059	Value: 1.50				
1979FM (U)	680	—	—	0.20	1.50	2.00
1979FM (P)	5,304	Value: 1.50				
1980FM (U)	1,007	—	—	0.20	1.50	2.00
1980FM (P)	3,421	Value: 1.50				
1981FM (U)	472	—	—	0.20	2.00	2.50
1981FM (P)	1,124	Value: 1.50				
1982FM (U)	—	—	—	0.20	2.00	2.50
1982FM (P)	—	Value: 1.50				
1983FM (U)	—	—	—	0.20	2.00	2.50
1983FM (P)	—	Value: 1.50				
1984FM (P)	—	Value: 1.50				

KM# 11 10 CENTS
6.4000 g., 0.9250 Silver 0.1903 oz. ASW **Ruler:** Elizabeth II
Subject: Queen's Silver Jubilee **Obv:** Young bust right
Rev: Ringed Kingfisher left

Date	Mintage	F	VF	XF	Unc	BU
1977FM (P)	17,000	Value: 5.00				

KM# 18 10 CENTS
6.4000 g., 0.9250 Silver 0.1903 oz. ASW **Ruler:** Elizabeth II
Subject: Coronation Jubilee **Obv:** Young bust right divides dates
Rev: Ringed Kingfisher left

Date	Mintage	F	VF	XF	Unc	BU
ND(1978)FM (P)	6,196	Value: 6.50				

KM# 44 10 CENTS
Copper-Nickel **Ruler:** Elizabeth II **Obv:** Crowned head right **Rev:** Great Barracuda right

Date	Mintage	F	VF	XF	Unc	BU
1985FM (P)	—	Value: 7.50				

KM# 44a 10 CENTS
6.4000 g., 0.9250 Silver 0.1903 oz. ASW **Ruler:** Elizabeth II
Obv: Crowned head right **Rev:** Great Barracuda right

Date	Mintage	F	VF	XF	Unc	BU
1985FM (P)	1,474	Value: 10.00				

KM# 4 25 CENTS
Copper-Nickel **Ruler:** Elizabeth II **Obv:** Young bust right
Rev: Mangrove Cuckoo

Date	Mintage	F	VF	XF	Unc	BU
1973FM	21,000	—	—	0.30	1.50	1.75
1973FM (P)	181,000	Value: 1.50				
1974FM	12,000	—	—	0.30	1.50	1.75
1974FM (P)	94,000	Value: 2.00				
1975FM (M)	1,000	—	—	0.35	3.00	4.00
1975FM (U)	2,351	—	—	0.30	1.50	1.75
1975FM (P)	32,000	Value: 2.00				
1976FM (M)	2,000	—	—	0.30	2.00	3.00
1976FM (U)	996	—	—	0.30	2.50	3.50
1976FM (P)	15,000	Value: 2.00				
1977FM (M)	500	—	—	0.50	5.00	7.00
1977FM (U)	782	—	—	0.30	2.00	3.00
1977FM (P)	7,218	Value: 2.00				
1978FM (U)	1,443	—	—	0.30	1.75	2.25
1978FM (P)	7,059	Value: 2.00				
1979FM (U)	680	—	—	0.30	2.00	3.00
1979FM (P)	5,304	Value: 2.00				
1980FM (U)	1,007	—	—	0.30	2.00	3.00
1980FM (P)	3,421	Value: 2.00				
1981FM (U)	472	—	—	0.30	2.25	3.50
1981FM (P)	1,124	Value: 2.00				
1982FM (U)	—	—	—	0.30	2.00	2.50
1982FM (P)	—	Value: 2.00				
1983FM (U)	—	—	—	0.30	2.25	3.50
1983FM (P)	—	Value: 2.00				
1984FM (P)	—	Value: 2.00				

KM# 12 25 CENTS
8.8100 g., 0.9250 Silver 0.2620 oz. ASW **Ruler:** Elizabeth II
Subject: Queen's Silver Jubilee **Obv:** Young bust right

Date	Mintage	F	VF	XF	Unc	BU
1977FM (P)	17,000	Value: 7.00				

KM# 19   25 CENTS
8.8100 g., 0.9250 Silver 0.2620 oz. ASW **Ruler:** Elizabeth II
Subject: Coronation Jubilee **Obv:** Young bust right divides dates
Rev: Mangrove Cuckoo

Date	Mintage	F	VF	XF	Unc	BU
ND(1978)FM (P)	6,196			Value: 8.50		

KM# 45   25 CENTS
Copper-Nickel **Ruler:** Elizabeth II **Obv:** Crowned head right
Rev: Blue Marlin jumping

Date	Mintage	F	VF	XF	Unc	BU
1985FM (P)	—			Value: 12.00		

KM# 45a   25 CENTS
8.8100 g., 0.9250 Silver 0.2620 oz. ASW **Ruler:** Elizabeth II
Obv: Crowned head right **Rev:** Blue Marlin jumping

Date	Mintage	F	VF	XF	Unc	BU
1985FM (P)	1,480			Value: 15.00		

KM# 5   50 CENTS
Copper-Nickel **Ruler:** Elizabeth II **Obv:** Young bust right
Rev: Brown Pelican

Date	Mintage	F	VF	XF	Unc	BU
1973FM	20,000	—	—	0.75	2.00	3.00
1973FM (P)	181,000	Value: 2.50				
1974FM	12,000	—	—	0.75	2.00	3.00
1974FM (P)	94,000	Value: 2.50				
1975FM (M)	1,000	—	—	1.00	5.00	6.00
1975FM (U)	2,351	—	—	0.75	2.50	3.00
1975FM (P)	32,000	Value: 2.50				
1976FM (M)	2,000	—	—	0.75	3.00	4.00
1976FM (U)	996	—	—	0.75	3.50	4.50
1976FM (P)	15,000	Value: 2.50				
1977FM (M)	600	—	—	1.00	6.00	7.50
1977FM (U)	782	—	—	0.75	3.50	4.50
1977FM (P)	7,218	Value: 2.50				
1978FM (U)	1,543	—	—	0.75	2.50	3.00
1978FM (P)	7,059	Value: 2.50				
1979FM (U)	680	—	—	0.75	3.50	4.50
1979FM (P)	5,304	Value: 2.50				
1980FM (U)	1,007	—	—	0.75	3.00	4.00
1980FM (P)	3,421	Value: 2.50				
1981FM (U)	472	—	—	0.75	3.50	5.00
1981FM (P)	1,124	Value: 2.50				
1982FM (U)	—	—	—	0.75	3.50	5.00
1982FM (P)	—	Value: 2.50				
1983FM (U)	—	—	—	0.75	3.50	5.00
1983FM (P)	—	Value: 2.50				
1984FM (P)	—	Value: 2.50				

KM# 13   50 CENTS
16.7200 g., 0.9250 Silver 0.4972 oz. ASW **Ruler:** Elizabeth II
Subject: Queen's Silver Jubilee **Obv:** Young bust right
Rev: Brown Pelican

Date	Mintage	F	VF	XF	Unc	BU
1977FM (P)	17,000			Value: 11.50		

KM# 20   50 CENTS
16.7200 g., 0.9250 Silver 0.4972 oz. ASW **Ruler:** Elizabeth II
Subject: Coronation Jubilee **Obv:** Young bust right divides dates
Rev: Brown Pelican

Date	Mintage	F	VF	XF	Unc	BU
ND(1978)FM (P)	6,196			Value: 13.50		

KM# 46   50 CENTS
Copper-Nickel **Ruler:** Elizabeth II **Obv:** Crowned head right
Rev: Dolphin fish

Date	Mintage	F	VF	XF	Unc	BU
1985FM (P)	—			Value: 14.00		

KM# 46a   50 CENTS
16.7200 g., 0.9250 Silver 0.4972 oz. ASW **Ruler:** Elizabeth II
Obv: Crowned head right **Rev:** Dolphin fish

Date	Mintage	F	VF	XF	Unc	BU
1985FM (P)	1,406			Value: 25.00		

KM# 6   DOLLAR
Copper-Nickel **Ruler:** Elizabeth II **Obv:** Young bust right
Rev: Magnificent Frigate

Date	Mintage	F	VF	XF	Unc	BU
1974FM (M)	12,000	—	—	2.00	5.50	7.00
1974FM (U)	—	—	—	—	—	—
1975FM (M)	800	—	—	2.50	8.00	9.00
1975FM (U)	2,351	—	—	2.50	6.50	7.00
1976FM (M)	1,800	—	—	2.50	6.50	7.00
1976FM (U)	996	—	—	2.50	8.00	9.00
1977FM (M)	800	—	—	2.50	8.00	9.00
1977FM (U)	782	—	—	2.50	8.00	9.00
1978FM (U)	1,743	—	—	2.50	6.50	7.00
1979FM (U)	680	—	—	2.50	8.00	9.00
1980FM (U)	1,007	—	—	2.50	6.50	7.00
1981FM (U)	472	—	—	2.50	10.00	11.50
1982FM (U)	—	—	—	2.50	10.00	11.50
1983FM (U)	—	—	—	2.50	10.00	11.50

KM# 6a   DOLLAR
25.7000 g., 0.9250 Silver 0.7643 oz. ASW **Ruler:** Elizabeth II
Obv: Young bust right **Rev:** Magnificent Frigate

Date	Mintage	F	VF	XF	Unc	BU
1973FM (P)	181,000	Value: 16.00				
1973FM (M)	20,000	—	—	15.50	17.50	—
1974FM (P)	94,000	Value: 17.00				
1975FM (P)	32,000	Value: 18.00				
1976FM (P)	15,000	Value: 18.00				
1977FM (P)	7,218	Value: 20.00				
1978FM (P)	7,059	Value: 20.00				
1979FM (P)	5,304	Value: 20.00				
1980FM (P)	3,421	Value: 20.00				
1981FM (P)	1,124	Value: 22.00				
1982FM (P)	1,865	Value: 22.00				
1983FM (P)	478	Value: 25.00				
1984FM (P)	—	Value: 22.00				

KM# 14   DOLLAR
25.7000 g., 0.9250 Silver 0.7643 oz. ASW **Ruler:** Elizabeth II
Subject: Queen's Silver Jubilee **Obv:** Young bust right
Rev: Magnificent Frigate

Date	Mintage	F	VF	XF	Unc	BU
1977FM (P)	17,000			Value: 20.00		

KM# 21   DOLLAR
25.7000 g., 0.9250 Silver 0.7643 oz. ASW **Ruler:** Elizabeth II
Subject: Coronation Jubilee **Obv:** Young bust right
Rev: Magnificent Frigate

Date	Mintage	F	VF	XF	Unc	BU
ND(1978)FM (P)	6,196			Value: 22.00		

KM# 47   DOLLAR
Copper-Nickel **Ruler:** Elizabeth II **Obv:** Crowned head right
Rev: Butterfly Fish

Date	Mintage	F	VF	XF	Unc	BU
1985FM (P)	—			Value: 35.00		

KM# 47a   DOLLAR
24.7400 g., 0.9250 Silver 0.7357 oz. ASW **Ruler:** Elizabeth II
Obv: Crowned head right **Rev:** Butterfly fish

Date	Mintage	F	VF	XF	Unc	BU
1985FM (P)	1,372			Value: 40.00		

KM# 169   DOLLAR
Copper-Nickel **Ruler:** Elizabeth II **Subject:** 500th Anniversary -
Columbus' First Voyage to America **Obv:** Crowned head right
Rev: VIGILATE on banner below shield with woman and twelve
lamps

Date	Mintage	F	VF	XF	Unc	BU
ND(1992)	—			Value: 20.00		

KM# 172   DOLLAR
Copper-Nickel, 38.6 mm. **Ruler:** Elizabeth II **Subject:** Queen
Mother's 100th Birthday **Obv:** Crowned head right **Rev:** Bust
facing divides dates **Edge:** Reeded

Date	Mintage	F	VF	XF	Unc	BU
2000	100,000	—	—	—	6.50	8.50

KM# 175 DOLLAR
Copper-Nickel **Ruler:** Elizabeth II **Subject:** 1st Anniversary - Earl and Countess of Wessex **Obv:** Crowned head right **Rev:** Half figures facing, anniversary date below **Edge:** Reeded

Date	Mintage	F	VF	XF	Unc	BU
2000	—	—	—	—	6.50	8.50

KM# 24 5 DOLLARS
Copper-Nickel **Ruler:** Elizabeth II **Obv:** Young bust right **Rev:** Snowy Egret left

Date	Mintage	F	VF	XF	Unc	BU
1979FM (U)	680	—	—	—	50.00	—

KM# 24a 5 DOLLARS
40.5000 g., 0.9250 Silver 1.2044 oz. ASW **Ruler:** Elizabeth II **Obv:** Young bust right **Rev:** Snowy Egret left

Date	Mintage	F	VF	XF	Unc	BU
1979FM (P)	5,304		Value: 37.50			

KM# 26 5 DOLLARS
Copper-Nickel **Ruler:** Elizabeth II **Obv:** Young bust right **Rev:** Great Blue Heron right

Date	Mintage	F	VF	XF	Unc	BU
1980FM (U)	1,007	—	—	—	50.00	—

KM# 26a 5 DOLLARS
40.5000 g., 0.9250 Silver 1.2044 oz. ASW **Ruler:** Elizabeth II **Obv:** Young bust right **Rev:** Great Blue Heron right

Date	Mintage	F	VF	XF	Unc	BU
1980FM (P)	3,421		Value: 45.00			

KM# 30 5 DOLLARS
Copper-Nickel **Ruler:** Elizabeth II **Subject:** Royal Tern left **Obv:** Young bust right

Date	Mintage	F	VF	XF	Unc	BU
1981FM (U)	472	—	—	—	50.00	—

KM# 30a 5 DOLLARS
40.5000 g., 0.9250 Silver 1.2044 oz. ASW **Ruler:** Elizabeth II **Obv:** Young bust right **Rev:** Royal Tern left

Date	Mintage	F	VF	XF	Unc	BU
1981FM (P)	1,124		Value: 37.50			

KM# 33 5 DOLLARS
Copper-Nickel **Ruler:** Elizabeth II **Obv:** Young bust right **Rev:** White-tailed tropic birds

Date	Mintage	F	VF	XF	Unc	BU
1982FM (U)	—	—	—	—	50.00	—

KM# 33a 5 DOLLARS
40.5000 g., 0.9250 Silver 1.2044 oz. ASW **Ruler:** Elizabeth II **Obv:** Young bust right **Rev:** White-tailed tropic birds

Date	Mintage	F	VF	XF	Unc	BU
1982FM (P)	1,865		Value: 37.50			

KM# 35 5 DOLLARS
Copper-Nickel **Ruler:** Elizabeth II **Obv:** Young bust right **Rev:** Yellow Warblers

Date	Mintage	F	VF	XF	Unc	BU
1983FM (U)	—	—	—	—	50.00	—

KM# 35a 5 DOLLARS
40.5000 g., 0.9250 Silver 1.2044 oz. ASW **Ruler:** Elizabeth II **Obv:** Young bust right **Rev:** Yellow Warblers

Date	Mintage	F	VF	XF	Unc	BU
1983FM (P)	478		Value: 50.00			
1984FM (P)	—		Value: 50.00			

KM# 36 10 DOLLARS
30.2800 g., 0.5000 Silver 0.4867 oz. ASW **Ruler:** Elizabeth II **Subject:** 30th Anniversary - Coronation of Queen Elizabeth II **Obv:** Young bust right **Rev:** Sceptres divide dates and royal symbols

Date	Mintage	F	VF	XF	Unc	BU
1983FM (P)	2,957		Value: 17.50			

KM# 157 10 DOLLARS
Copper-Nickel **Ruler:** Elizabeth II **Subject:** Discovery of America **Obv:** Crowned head right **Rev:** Columbus landing

Date	Mintage	F	VF	XF	Unc	BU
ND(1992)FM (P)	—		Value: 12.50			

KM# 173.1 10 DOLLARS
28.2800 g., 0.9250 Silver 0.8410 oz. ASW, 38.6 mm. **Ruler:** Elizabeth II **Obv:** Crowned head right **Rev:** Bust facing divides dates **Edge:** Reeded

Date	Mintage	F	VF	XF	Unc	BU
2000 Proof	10,000		Value: 40.00			

KM# 173.2 10 DOLLARS
28.2800 g., 0.9250 Silver 0.8410 oz. ASW, 38.6 mm. **Ruler:** Elizabeth II **Subject:** Queen Mother **Obv:** Crowned head right **Rev:** Queen Mother's portrait with a tiny sapphire mounted on her broach **Edge:** Reeded

Date	Mintage	F	VF	XF	Unc	BU
2000 Proof	1,000		Value: 45.00			

KM# 176 10 DOLLARS
28.2800 g., 0.9250 Silver 0.8410 oz. ASW **Ruler:** Elizabeth II **Subject:** 1st Anniversary - Earl and Countess of Wessex **Obv:** Crowned head right **Rev:** Half figures facing, anniversary date below **Edge:** Reeded

Date	Mintage	F	VF	XF	Unc	BU
2000 Proof	10,000		Value: 40.00			

KM# 48 20 DOLLARS
19.0900 g., 0.9250 Silver 0.5677 oz. ASW, 38 mm. **Ruler:** Elizabeth II **Obv:** Crowned head right **Rev:** Crossed cannons

Date	Mintage	F	VF	XF	Unc	BU
1985FM (P)	—		Value: 15.00			

KM# 49 20 DOLLARS
19.0900 g., 0.9250 Silver 0.5677 oz. ASW, 38 mm. **Ruler:** Elizabeth II **Obv:** Crowned head right **Rev:** Porcelain cup

Date	Mintage	F	VF	XF	Unc	BU
1985FM (P)	—		Value: 15.00			

KM# 50   20 DOLLARS
19.0900 g., 0.9250 Silver 0.5677 oz. ASW, 38 mm.
Ruler: Elizabeth II **Obv:** Crowned head right **Rev:** Sextant

Date	Mintage	F	VF	XF	Unc	BU
1985FM (P)	—	Value: 15.00				

KM# 51   20 DOLLARS
19.0900 g., 0.9250 Silver 0.5677 oz. ASW, 38 mm.
Ruler: Elizabeth II **Obv:** Crowned head right **Rev:** Emerald and gold ring

Date	Mintage	F	VF	XF	Unc	BU
1985FM (P)	—	Value: 15.00				

KM# 52   20 DOLLARS
19.0900 g., 0.9250 Silver 0.5677 oz. ASW, 38 mm.
Ruler: Elizabeth II **Obv:** Crowned head right **Rev:** Gold doubloon of 1702

Date	Mintage	F	VF	XF	Unc	BU
1985FM (P)	—	Value: 15.00				

KM# 53   20 DOLLARS
19.0900 g., 0.9250 Silver 0.5677 oz. ASW, 38 mm.
Ruler: Elizabeth II **Obv:** Crowned head right **Rev:** Anchor

Date	Mintage	F	VF	XF	Unc	BU
1985FM (P)	—	Value: 15.00				

KM# 54   20 DOLLARS
19.0900 g., 0.9250 Silver 0.5677 oz. ASW, 38 mm.   **Ruler:** Elizabeth II **Obv:** Crowned head right **Rev:** Brass nocturnal

Date	Mintage	F	VF	XF	Unc	BU
1985FM (P)	—	Value: 15.00				

KM# 55   20 DOLLARS
19.0900 g., 0.9250 Silver 0.5677 oz. ASW, 38 mm.
Ruler: Elizabeth II **Obv:** Crowned head right **Rev:** Sword guillon

Date	Mintage	F	VF	XF	Unc	BU
1985FM (P)	—	Value: 15.00				

KM# 56   20 DOLLARS
19.0900 g., 0.9250 Silver 0.5677 oz. ASW, 38 mm.
Ruler: Elizabeth II **Obv:** Crowned head right **Rev:** Gold bar

Date	Mintage	F	VF	XF	Unc	BU
1985FM (P)	—	Value: 15.00				

KM# 57   20 DOLLARS
19.0900 g., 0.9250 Silver 0.5677 oz. ASW, 38 mm.
Ruler: Elizabeth II **Subject:** Gold Escudo **Obv:** Crowned head right **Rev:** Obverse and reverse of gold escudo of 1733

Date	Mintage	F	VF	XF	Unc	BU
1985FM (P)	—	Value: 15.00				

KM# 58   20 DOLLARS
19.0900 g., 0.9250 Silver 0.5677 oz. ASW, 38 mm.
Ruler: Elizabeth II **Obv:** Crowned head right **Rev:** Ivory sundial

Date	Mintage	F	VF	XF	Unc	BU
1985FM (P)	—	Value: 15.00				

KM# 59   20 DOLLARS
19.0900 g., 0.9250 Silver 0.5677 oz. ASW, 38 mm.
Ruler: Elizabeth II **Obv:** Crowned head right **Rev:** Gold monstrance, within square

Date	Mintage	F	VF	XF	Unc	BU
1985FM (P)	—	Value: 15.00				

KM# 60   20 DOLLARS
19.0900 g., 0.9250 Silver 0.5677 oz. ASW, 38 mm.
Ruler: Elizabeth II **Obv:** Crowned head right **Rev:** Teapot

Date	Mintage	F	VF	XF	Unc	BU
1985FM (P)	—	Value: 15.00				

KM# 61   20 DOLLARS
19.0900 g., 0.9250 Silver 0.5677 oz. ASW, 38 mm.
Ruler: Elizabeth II **Obv:** Crowned head right **Rev:** Brass religious medallion

Date	Mintage	F	VF	XF	Unc	BU
1985FM (P)	—	Value: 15.00				

KM# 62   20 DOLLARS
19.0900 g., 0.9250 Silver 0.5677 oz. ASW, 38 mm.
Ruler: Elizabeth II **Obv:** Crowned head right **Rev:** Astrolabe

Date	Mintage	F	VF	XF	Unc	BU
1985FM (P)	—				Value: 15.00	

KM# 64   20 DOLLARS
19.0900 g., 0.9250 Silver 0.5677 oz. ASW, 38 mm. **Ruler:**
Elizabeth II **Obv:** Crowned head right **Rev:** Porcelain bottle

Date	Mintage	F	VF	XF	Unc	BU
1985FM (P)	—				Value: 15.00	

KM# 65   20 DOLLARS
19.0900 g., 0.9250 Silver 0.5677 oz. ASW, 38 mm.
Ruler: Elizabeth II **Obv:** Crowned head right **Rev:** Ship and
Dutch cannons

Date	Mintage	F	VF	XF	Unc	BU
1985FM (P)	—				Value: 15.00	

KM# 67   20 DOLLARS
19.0900 g., 0.9250 Silver 0.5677 oz. ASW, 38 mm.
Ruler: Elizabeth II **Obv:** Crowned head right **Rev:** Ship's
stern lantern

Date	Mintage	F	VF	XF	Unc	BU
1985FM (P)	—				Value: 15.00	

KM# 68   20 DOLLARS
19.0900 g., 0.9250 Silver 0.5677 oz. ASW, 38 mm.
Ruler: Elizabeth II **Obv:** Crowned head right **Rev:** Brass dividers

Date	Mintage	F	VF	XF	Unc	BU
1985FM (P)	—				Value: 15.00	

KM# 69   20 DOLLARS
19.0900 g., 0.9250 Silver 0.5677 oz. ASW, 38 mm.
Ruler: Elizabeth II **Obv:** Crowned head right **Rev:** Gold cross

Date	Mintage	F	VF	XF	Unc	BU
1985FM (P)	—				Value: 15.00	

KM# 70   20 DOLLARS
19.0900 g., 0.9250 Silver 0.5677 oz. ASW, 38 mm.
Ruler: Elizabeth II **Obv:** Crowned head right **Rev:** Perfume bottle

Date	Mintage	F	VF	XF	Unc	BU
1985FM (P)	—				Value: 15.00	

KM# 71   20 DOLLARS
19.0900 g., 0.9250 Silver 0.5677 oz. ASW, 38 mm.
Ruler: Elizabeth II **Obv:** Crowned head right **Rev:** Pocket watch

Date	Mintage	F	VF	XF	Unc	BU
1985FM (P)	—				Value: 15.00	

KM# 72   20 DOLLARS
19.0900 g., 0.9250 Silver 0.5677 oz. ASW, 38 mm.
Ruler: Elizabeth II **Obv:** Crowned head right **Rev:** Gold bracelet
and button

Date	Mintage	F	VF	XF	Unc	BU
1985FM (P)	—				Value: 15.00	

KM# 63.1   20 DOLLARS
19.0900 g., 0.9250 Silver 0.5677 oz. ASW, 38 mm.
Ruler: Elizabeth II **Obv:** Crowned head right **Rev:** Bells
Note: FM mint mark at right.

Date	Mintage	F	VF	XF	Unc	BU
1985FM (P)	—				Value: 15.00	

KM# 63.2   20 DOLLARS
19.0900 g., 0.9250 Silver 0.5677 oz. ASW, 38 mm.
Ruler: Elizabeth II **Obv:** Crowned head right **Rev:** Bells
Note: FM mint mark in center.

Date	Mintage	F	VF	XF	Unc	BU
1985FM (P)	—				Value: 15.00	

KM# 66   20 DOLLARS
19.0900 g., 0.9250 Silver 0.5677 oz. ASW, 38 mm.
Ruler: Elizabeth II **Obv:** Crowned head right **Rev:** Ancient coin
Note: Spanish Colonial 8 Reales, Cob coin.

Date	Mintage	F	VF	XF	Unc	BU
1985FM (P)	—				Value: 15.00	

KM# 259 20 DOLLARS
19.1100 g., 0.9250 Silver 0.5683 oz. ASW, 37.9 mm.
Ruler: Elizabeth II **Obv:** Crowned head right **Rev:** Ancient
Egyptian reed sail boat **Edge:** Reeded

Date	Mintage	F	VF	XF	Unc	BU
2000FM Proof	—	Value: 22.50				

KM# 260 20 DOLLARS
19.6500 g., 0.9250 Silver 0.5844 oz. ASW, 37.9 mm.
Ruler: Elizabeth II **Obv:** Crowned head right **Rev:** Hansa Cog
trading ship, 14th Century **Edge:** Reeded

Date	Mintage	F	VF	XF	Unc	BU
2000FM Proof	—	Value: 22.50				

KM# 261 20 DOLLARS
18.9300 g., 0.9250 Silver 0.5629 oz. ASW, 37.9 mm.
Ruler: Elizabeth II **Obv:** Crowned head right **Rev:** Flag ship
Santa Maria, 1492 **Edge:** Reeded

Date	Mintage	F	VF	XF	Unc	BU
2000FM Proof	—	Value: 22.50				

KM# 262 20 DOLLARS
19.2400 g., 0.9250 Silver 0.5722 oz. ASW, 37.9 mm.
Ruler: Elizabeth II **Obv:** Crowned head right **Rev:** The Ark Royal,
1588 **Edge:** Reeded

Date	Mintage	F	VF	XF	Unc.	BU
2000FM Proof	—	Value: 22.50				

KM# 263 20 DOLLARS
18.8000 g., 0.9250 Silver 0.5591 oz. ASW, 37.9 mm.
Ruler: Elizabeth II **Obv:** Crowned head right **Rev:** Clipper ship
Cutty Sark, 1869 **Edge:** Reeded

Date	Mintage	F	VF	XF	Unc	BU
2000FM Proof	—	Value: 22.50				

KM# 264 20 DOLLARS
19.2000 g., 0.9250 Silver 0.5710 oz. ASW, 37.9 mm.
Ruler: Elizabeth II **Obv:** Crowned head right **Rev:** Training ship
SMS Preussen **Edge:** Reeded

Date	Mintage	F	VF	XF	Unc	BU
2000FM Proof	—	Value: 22.50				

KM# 22 25 DOLLARS
28.1000 g., 0.9250 Silver 0.8356 oz. ASW **Ruler:** Elizabeth II
Subject: Coronation Jubilee **Obv:** Young bust right **Rev:** Imperial
crown with supporters, dates below

Date	Mintage	F	VF	XF	Unc	BU
1978FM (P)	8,438	Value: 25.00				

KM# 27 25 DOLLARS
1.5000 g., 0.5000 Gold 0.0241 oz. AGW **Ruler:** Elizabeth II
Obv: Young bust right **Rev:** Diving Osprey left

Date	Mintage	F	VF	XF	Unc	BU
1980FM (P)	11,000	Value: 40.00				

KM# 31.1 25 DOLLARS
1.5000 g., 0.5000 Gold 0.0241 oz. AGW **Ruler:** Elizabeth II
Obv: Young bust right **Rev:** Caribbean Sparrow Hawk left

Date	Mintage	F	VF	XF	Unc	BU
1981FM (P)	2,513	Value: 50.00				

KM# 31.2 25 DOLLARS
1.5000 g., 0.5000 Gold 0.0241 oz. AGW **Ruler:** Elizabeth II
Obv: Young bust right, error, without FM mint mark
Rev: Caribbean Sparrow Hawk left

Date	Mintage	F	VF	XF	Unc	BU
1981 (P)	—	Value: 60.00				

KM# 41 25 DOLLARS
1.5000 g., 0.5000 Gold 0.0241 oz. AGW **Ruler:** Elizabeth II
Obv: Young bust right **Rev:** Hawk in flight

Date	Mintage	F	VF	XF	Unc	BU
1982FM (P)	3,819	Value: 55.00				

KM# 37 25 DOLLARS
1.5000 g., 0.5000 Gold 0.0241 oz. AGW **Ruler:** Elizabeth II
Obv: Young bust right **Rev:** Merlin Hawk left

Date	Mintage	F	VF	XF	Unc	BU
1983FM (P)	5,949	Value: 50.00				

KM# 40 25 DOLLARS
1.5000 g., 0.5000 Gold 0.0241 oz. AGW **Ruler:** Elizabeth II
Obv: Young bust right **Rev:** Peregrine Falcon

Date	Mintage	F	VF	XF	Unc	BU
1984FM (P)	97	Value: 115				

KM# 73 25 DOLLARS
1.5000 g., 0.5000 Gold 0.0241 oz. AGW **Ruler:** Elizabeth II
Obv: Crowned head right **Rev:** Marsh Hawk

Date	Mintage	F	VF	XF	Unc	BU
1985FM (P)	1,294	Value: 80.00				

KM# 90 25 DOLLARS
20.0900 g., 0.9250 Silver 0.5974 oz. ASW **Ruler:** Elizabeth II
Series: Sunken Ship Treasures **Obv:** Crowned head right
Rev: Ornamental lock plate

Date	Mintage	F	VF	XF	Unc	BU
1988FM (P)	—	Value: 26.00				

KM# 91 25 DOLLARS
20.0900 g., 0.9250 Silver 0.5974 oz. ASW **Ruler:** Elizabeth II
Series: Sunken Ship Treasures **Obv:** Crowned head right
Rev: Royal coat of arms on bottle

Date	Mintage	F	VF	XF	Unc	BU
1988FM (P)	—	Value: 26.00				

KM# 92 25 DOLLARS
20.0900 g., 0.9250 Silver 0.5974 oz. ASW **Ruler:** Elizabeth II
Series: Sunken Ship Treasures **Obv:** Crowned head right
Rev: Finger ring

Date	Mintage	F	VF	XF	Unc	BU
1988FM (P)	—	Value: 26.00				

KM# 93 25 DOLLARS
20.0900 g., 0.9250 Silver 0.5974 oz. ASW **Ruler:** Elizabeth II
Series: Sunken Ship Treasures **Obv:** Crowned head right
Rev: Hour glass

Date	Mintage	F	VF	XF	Unc	BU
1988FM (P)	—	Value: 26.00				

KM# 94 25 DOLLARS
20.0900 g., 0.9250 Silver 0.5974 oz. ASW **Ruler:** Elizabeth II
Series: Sunken Ship Treasures **Obv:** Crowned head right
Rev: Dagger and scabbard

Date	Mintage	F	VF	XF	Unc	BU
1988FM (P)	—	Value: 26.00				

KM# 95 25 DOLLARS
20.0900 g., 0.9250 Silver 0.5974 oz. ASW **Ruler:** Elizabeth II
Series: Sunken Ship Treasures **Obv:** Crowned head right
Rev: Jewel-encrusted cross

Date	Mintage	F	VF	XF	Unc	BU
1988FM (P)	—	Value: 26.00				

KM# 96   25 DOLLARS
20.0900 g., 0.9250 Silver 0.5974 oz. ASW   **Ruler:** Elizabeth II
Series: Sunken Ship Treasures **Obv:** Crowned head right
Rev: Crossed keys

Date	Mintage	F	VF	XF	Unc	BU
1988FM (P)	—				Value: 26.00	

KM# 97   25 DOLLARS
20.0900 g., 0.9250 Silver 0.5974 oz. ASW   **Ruler:** Elizabeth II
Series: Sunken Ship Treasures **Obv:** Crowned head right
Rev: Belt buckle

Date	Mintage	F	VF	XF	Unc	BU
1988FM (P)	—				Value: 26.00	

KM# 98   25 DOLLARS
20.0900 g., 0.9250 Silver 0.5974 oz. ASW   **Ruler:** Elizabeth II
Series: Sunken Ship Treasures **Obv:** Crowned head right
Rev: American bottle

Date	Mintage	F	VF	XF	Unc	BU
1988FM (P)	—				Value: 26.00	

KM# 99   25 DOLLARS
20.0900 g., 0.9250 Silver 0.5974 oz. ASW   **Ruler:** Elizabeth II
Series: Sunken Ship Treasures **Obv:** Crowned head right
Rev: Religious medallion

Date	Mintage	F	VF	XF	Unc	BU
1988FM (P)	—				Value: 26.00	

KM# 100   25 DOLLARS
20.0900 g., 0.9250 Silver 0.5974 oz. ASW   **Ruler:** Elizabeth II
Series: Sunken Ship Treasures **Obv:** Crowned head right
Rev: Baby figurines

Date	Mintage	F	VF	XF	Unc	BU
1988FM (P)	—				Value: 26.00	

KM# 101   25 DOLLARS
20.0900 g., 0.9250 Silver 0.5974 oz. ASW   **Ruler:** Elizabeth II
Series: Sunken Ship Treasures **Obv:** Crowned head right
Rev: Insignia of the Royal French Marines

Date	Mintage	F	VF	XF	Unc	BU
1988FM (P)	—				Value: 26.00	

KM# 102   25 DOLLARS
20.0900 g., 0.9250 Silver 0.5974 oz. ASW   **Ruler:** Elizabeth II
Series: Sunken Ship Treasures **Obv:** Crowned head right
Rev: Engraved printing block

Date	Mintage	F	VF	XF	Unc	BU
1988FM (P)	—				Value: 26.00	

KM# 103   25 DOLLARS
20.0900 g., 0.9250 Silver 0.5974 oz. ASW   **Ruler:** Elizabeth II
Series: Sunken Ship Treasures **Obv:** Crowned head right
Rev: Antique clock

Date	Mintage	F	VF	XF	Unc	BU
1988FM (P)	—				Value: 26.00	

KM# 132   25 DOLLARS
20.0900 g., 0.9250 Silver 0.5974 oz. ASW   **Ruler:** Elizabeth II
Obv: Crowned head right **Rev:** Flintlock pistol

Date	Mintage	F	VF	XF	Unc	BU
1988FM (P)	—				Value: 26.00	

KM# 133   25 DOLLARS
20.0900 g., 0.9250 Silver 0.5974 oz. ASW   **Ruler:** Elizabeth II
Obv: Crowned head right **Rev:** Stylized fish statue

Date	Mintage	F	VF	XF	Unc	BU
1988FM (P)	—				Value: 26.00	

KM# 134   25 DOLLARS
20.0900 g., 0.9250 Silver 0.5974 oz. ASW   **Ruler:** Elizabeth II
Obv: Crowned head right **Rev:** Mortar and pestle

Date	Mintage	F	VF	XF	Unc	BU
1988FM (P)	—				Value: 26.00	

KM# 135   25 DOLLARS
20.0900 g., 0.9250 Silver 0.5974 oz. ASW   **Ruler:** Elizabeth II
Obv: Crowned head right **Rev:** Open-mouthed dragon head
sculpture

Date	Mintage	F	VF	XF	Unc	BU
1988FM (P)	—				Value: 26.00	

KM# 136   25 DOLLARS
20.0900 g., 0.9250 Silver 0.5974 oz. ASW   **Ruler:** Elizabeth II
Obv: Crowned head right **Rev:** Military mortar

Date	Mintage	F	VF	XF	Unc	BU
1988FM (P)	—	Value: 26.00				

KM# 137   25 DOLLARS
20.0900 g., 0.9250 Silver 0.5974 oz. ASW   **Ruler:** Elizabeth II
Obv: Crowned head right **Rev:** Seated figure sculpture

Date	Mintage	F	VF	XF	Unc	BU
1988FM (P)	—	Value: 26.00				

KM# 138   25 DOLLARS
20.0900 g., 0.9250 Silver 0.5974 oz. ASW   **Ruler:** Elizabeth II
Obv: Crowned head right **Rev:** Lion sculpture

Date	Mintage	F	VF	XF	Unc	BU
1988FM (P)	—	Value: 26.00				

KM# 139   25 DOLLARS
20.0900 g., 0.9250 Silver 0.5974 oz. ASW   **Ruler:** Elizabeth II
Obv: Crowned head right **Rev:** Violin

Date	Mintage	F	VF	XF	Unc	BU
1988FM (P)	—	Value: 26.00				

KM# 140   25 DOLLARS
20.0900 g., 0.9250 Silver 0.5974 oz. ASW   **Ruler:** Elizabeth II
Obv: Crowned head right **Rev:** Chalice

Date	Mintage	F	VF	XF	Unc	BU
1988FM (P)	—	Value: 26.00				

KM# 141   25 DOLLARS
20.0900 g., 0.9250 Silver 0.5974 oz. ASW   **Ruler:** Elizabeth II
Obv: Crowned head right **Rev:** Pitcher

Date	Mintage	F	VF	XF	Unc	BU
1988FM (P)	—	Value: 26.00				

KM# 142   25 DOLLARS
20.0900 g., 0.9250 Silver 0.5974 oz. ASW   **Ruler:** Elizabeth II
Obv: Crowned head right **Rev:** Cannon

Date	Mintage	F	VF	XF	Unc	BU
1988FM (P)	—	Value: 26.00				

KM# 104   25 DOLLARS
21.5400 g., 0.9250 Silver 0.6406 oz. ASW   **Ruler:** Elizabeth II
Series: Discovery of America **Obv:** Crowned head right
Rev: Columbus planning voyage

Date	Mintage	F	VF	XF	Unc	BU
ND(1992)FM (P)	—	Value: 30.00				

KM# 105   25 DOLLARS
21.5400 g., 0.9250 Silver 0.6406 oz. ASW   **Ruler:** Elizabeth II
Series: Discovery of America **Obv:** Crowned head right
Rev: Columbus lecturing

Date	Mintage	F	VF	XF	Unc	BU
ND(1992)FM (P)	—	Value: 30.00				

KM# 106   25 DOLLARS
21.5400 g., 0.9250 Silver 0.6406 oz. ASW   **Ruler:** Elizabeth II
Series: Discovery of America **Obv:** Crowned head right
Rev: Queen Isabella offering jewels

Date	Mintage	F	VF	XF	Unc	BU
ND(1992)FM (P)	—	Value: 30.00				

KM# 107   25 DOLLARS
21.5400 g., 0.9250 Silver 0.6406 oz. ASW   **Ruler:** Elizabeth II
Series: Discovery of America **Obv:** Crowned head right
Rev: Columbus aboard ship

Date	Mintage	F	VF	XF	Unc	BU
ND(1992)FM (P)	—	Value: 30.00				

KM# 108   25 DOLLARS
21.5400 g., 0.9250 Silver 0.6406 oz. ASW   **Ruler:** Elizabeth II
Series: Discovery of America **Obv:** Crowned head right
Rev: Columbus on horseback

Date	Mintage	F	VF	XF	Unc	BU
ND(1992)FM (P)	—	Value: 30.00				

KM# 109   25 DOLLARS
21.5400 g., 0.9250 Silver 0.6406 oz. ASW   **Ruler:** Elizabeth II
Series: Discovery of America **Obv:** Crowned head right
Rev: Ship under full sail

Date	Mintage	F	VF	XF	Unc	BU
ND(1992)FM	—	Value: 30.00				

KM# 110   25 DOLLARS
21.5400 g., 0.9250 Silver 0.6406 oz. ASW   **Ruler:** Elizabeth II
Series: Discovery of America **Obv:** Crowned head right
Rev: Ship at anchor

Date	Mintage	F	VF	XF	Unc	BU
ND(1992)FM (P)	—	Value: 30.00				

KM# 111   25 DOLLARS
21.5400 g., 0.9250 Silver 0.6406 oz. ASW   **Ruler:** Elizabeth II
Series: Discovery of America **Obv:** Crowned head right
Rev: Natives offering gifts

Date	Mintage	F	VF	XF	Unc	BU
ND(1992)FM (P)	—	Value: 30.00				

KM# 112   25 DOLLARS
21.5400 g., 0.9250 Silver 0.6406 oz. ASW   **Ruler:** Elizabeth II
Series: Discovery of America **Obv:** Crowned head right
Rev: Shipwreck

Date	Mintage	F	VF	XF	Unc	BU
ND(1992)FM (P)	—	Value: 30.00				

KM# 113   25 DOLLARS
21.5400 g., 0.9250 Silver 0.6406 oz. ASW   **Ruler:** Elizabeth II
Series: Discovery of America **Obv:** Crowned head right
Rev: Royal banquet

Date	Mintage	F	VF	XF	Unc	BU
ND(1992)FM (P)	—	Value: 30.00				

KM# 114   25 DOLLARS
21.5400 g., 0.9250 Silver 0.6406 oz. ASW   **Ruler:** Elizabeth II
Series: Discovery of America **Obv:** Crowned head right
Rev: Columbus predicting lunar eclipse to natives

Date	Mintage	F	VF	XF	Unc	BU
ND(1992)FM (P)	—	Value: 30.00				

KM# 115   25 DOLLARS
21.5400 g., 0.9250 Silver 0.6406 oz. ASW   **Ruler:** Elizabeth II
Series: Discovery of America **Obv:** Crowned head right
Rev: Columbus on shore

Date	Mintage	F	VF	XF	Unc	BU
ND(1992)FM (P)	—	Value: 30.00				

KM# 116   25 DOLLARS
21.5400 g., 0.9250 Silver 0.6406 oz. ASW   **Ruler:** Elizabeth II
Series: Discovery of America **Obv:** Crowned head right
Rev: Spanish figures

Date	Mintage	F	VF	XF	Unc	BU
ND(1992)FM (P)	—	Value: 30.00				

KM# 117   25 DOLLARS
21.5400 g., 0.9250 Silver 0.6406 oz. ASW   **Ruler:** Elizabeth II
Series: Discovery of America **Obv:** Crowned head right
Rev: Columbus with shore party

Date	Mintage	F	VF	XF	Unc	BU
ND(1992)FM (P)	—	Value: 30.00				

KM# 118   25 DOLLARS
21.5400 g., 0.9250 Silver 0.6406 oz. ASW   **Ruler:** Elizabeth II
Series: Discovery of America **Obv:** Crowned head right
Rev: Columbus on death bed

Date	Mintage	F	VF	XF	Unc	BU
ND(1992)FM (P)	—	Value: 30.00				

KM# 122   25 DOLLARS
21.5400 g., 0.9250 Silver 0.6406 oz. ASW   **Ruler:** Elizabeth II
Series: Discovery of America **Obv:** Crowned head right
Rev: Columbus bowing before King Ferdinand

Date	Mintage	F	VF	XF	Unc	BU
ND(1992)FM (P)	—	Value: 30.00				

KM# 123   25 DOLLARS
21.5400 g., 0.9250 Silver 0.6406 oz. ASW   **Ruler:** Elizabeth II
Series: Discovery of America **Obv:** Crowned head right
Rev: Columbus before Queen Isabella

Date	Mintage	F	VF	XF	Unc	BU
ND(1992)FM (P)	—	Value: 30.00				

KM# 124 25 DOLLARS
21.5400 g., 0.9250 Silver 0.6406 oz. ASW **Ruler:** Elizabeth II **Series:** Discovery of America **Obv:** Crowned head right **Rev:** Columbus before King Ferdinand and Queen Isabella

Date	Mintage	F	VF	XF	Unc	BU
ND(1992)FM (P)	—	Value: 30.00				

KM# 125 25 DOLLARS
21.5400 g., 0.9250 Silver 0.6406 oz. ASW **Ruler:** Elizabeth II **Series:** Discovery of America **Obv:** Crowned head right **Rev:** Columbus getting provisions for his ships

Date	Mintage	F	VF	XF	Unc	BU
ND(1992)FM (P)	—	Value: 30.00				

KM# 126 25 DOLLARS
21.5400 g., 0.9250 Silver 0.6406 oz. ASW **Ruler:** Elizabeth II **Series:** Discovery of America **Obv:** Crowned head right **Rev:** Four sailing ships

Date	Mintage	F	VF	XF	Unc	BU
ND(1992)FM (P)	—	Value: 30.00				

KM# 127 25 DOLLARS
21.5400 g., 0.9250 Silver 0.6406 oz. ASW **Series:** Discovery of America **Obv:** Head right, two dates below **Rev:** Columbus navigating by stars

Date	Mintage	F	VF	XF	Unc	BU
ND(1992)FM (P)	—	Value: 30.00				

KM# 128 25 DOLLARS
21.5400 g., 0.9250 Silver 0.6406 oz. ASW **Series:** Discovery of America **Obv:** Head right, two dates below **Rev:** Sighting land, denomination upper left

Date	Mintage	F	VF	XF	Unc	BU
ND(1992)FM (P)	—	Value: 30.00				

KM# 129 25 DOLLARS
21.5400 g., 0.9250 Silver 0.6406 oz. ASW **Ruler:** Elizabeth II **Series:** Discovery of America **Obv:** Crowned head right **Rev:** Columbus claiming the newly discovered land

Date	Mintage	F	VF	XF	Unc	BU
ND(1992)FM (P)	—	Value: 30.00				

KM# 130 25 DOLLARS
21.5400 g., 0.9250 Silver 0.6406 oz. ASW **Ruler:** Elizabeth II **Series:** Discovery of America **Obv:** Crowned head right **Rev:** Columbus seated on shore with shipwreck offshore

Date	Mintage	F	VF	XF	Unc	BU
ND(1992)FM (P)	—	Value: 30.00				

KM# 131 25 DOLLARS
21.5400 g., 0.9250 Silver 0.6406 oz. ASW **Ruler:** Elizabeth II **Series:** Discovery of America **Obv:** Crowned head right **Rev:** Columbus as prisoner

Date	Mintage	F	VF	XF	Unc	BU
ND(1992)FM (P)	—	Value: 30.00				

KM# 186 25 DOLLARS
20.0900 g., 0.9250 Silver 0.5974 oz. ASW, 40 mm. **Ruler:** Elizabeth II **Obv:** Crowned head right, 1988 type of KM#90-103 **Rev:** Figure bowing to King, type of KM#122 originally minted in 1992 **Edge:** Reeded **Note:** Mint error; muled dies.

Date	Mintage	F	VF	XF	Unc	BU
1988	—	—	—	—	800	—

KM# 178 25 DOLLARS
21.6000 g., 0.9250 Silver 0.6423 oz. ASW, 40 mm. **Ruler:** Elizabeth II **Series:** Endangered Wildlife **Obv:** Crowned head right **Rev:** Three flamingos and four nests **Edge:** Reeded

Date	Mintage	F	VF	XF	Unc	BU
1993 Proof	—	Value: 40.00				

KM# 179 25 DOLLARS
20.9000 g., 0.9250 Silver 0.6215 oz. ASW, 40 mm. **Ruler:** Elizabeth II **Subject:** Endangered Wildlife **Obv:** Crowned head right **Rev:** Front half of tiger stalking left **Edge:** Reeded

Date	Mintage	F	VF	XF	Unc	BU
1993FM (P)	—	Value: 40.00				

KM# 143 25 DOLLARS
20.0900 g., 0.9250 Silver 0.5974 oz. ASW **Ruler:** Elizabeth II **Series:** Endangered Wildlife **Obv:** Crowned head right **Rev:** African elephants right, trunks raised

Date	Mintage	F	VF	XF	Unc	BU
1993FM (P)	—	Value: 40.00				

KM# 144   25 DOLLARS
20.0900 g., 0.9250 Silver 0.5974 oz. ASW   **Ruler:** Elizabeth II
Series: Endangered Wildlife **Obv:** Crowned head right
Rev: Mountain gorilla left

Date	Mintage	F	VF	XF	Unc	BU
1993FM (P)	—	Value: 40.00				

KM# 145   25 DOLLARS
20.0900 g., 0.9250 Silver 0.5974 oz. ASW   **Ruler:** Elizabeth II
Series: Endangered Wildlife **Obv:** Crowned head right
Rev: Cape mountain zebra right

Date	Mintage	F	VF	XF	Unc	BU
1993FM (P)	—	Value: 40.00				

KM# 146   25 DOLLARS
20.0900 g., 0.9250 Silver 0.5974 oz. ASW   **Ruler:** Elizabeth II
Series: Endangered Wildlife **Obv:** Crowned head right
Rev: Polar bear right

Date	Mintage	F	VF	XF	Unc	BU
1993FM (P)	—	Value: 40.00				

KM# 147   25 DOLLARS
20.0900 g., 0.9250 Silver 0.5974 oz. ASW   **Ruler:** Elizabeth II
Series: Endangered Wildlife **Obv:** Crowned head right **Rev:** Bald
Eagle, wings spread

Date	Mintage	F	VF	XF	Unc	BU
1993FM (P)	—	Value: 40.00				

KM# 148   25 DOLLARS
20.0900 g., 0.9250 Silver 0.5974 oz. ASW   **Ruler:** Elizabeth II
Series: Endangered Wildlife **Obv:** Crowned head right
Rev: Snow Leopard right

Date	Mintage	F	VF	XF	Unc	BU
1993FM (P)	—	Value: 40.00				

KM# 149   25 DOLLARS
20.0900 g., 0.9250 Silver 0.5974 oz. ASW   **Ruler:** Elizabeth II
Series: Endangered Wildlife **Obv:** Crowned head right
Rev: Javan Rhinoceros left

Date	Mintage	F	VF	XF	Unc	BU
1993FM (P)	—	Value: 40.00				

KM# 150   25 DOLLARS
20.0900 g., 0.9250 Silver 0.5974 oz. ASW   **Ruler:** Elizabeth II
Series: Endangered Wildlife **Obv:** Crowned head right
Rev: Asian Lion left

Date	Mintage	F	VF	XF	Unc	BU
1993FM (P)	—	Value: 40.00				

KM# 151   25 DOLLARS
20.0900 g., 0.9250 Silver 0.5974 oz. ASW   **Ruler:** Elizabeth II
Series: Endangered Wildlife **Obv:** Crowned head right
Rev: Seated Giant Panda right

Date	Mintage	F	VF	XF	Unc	BU
1993FM (P)	—	Value: 40.00				

KM# 152   25 DOLLARS
20.0900 g., 0.9250 Silver 0.5974 oz. ASW   **Ruler:** Elizabeth II
Series: Endangered Wildlife **Obv:** Crowned head right
Rev: Golden Lion Tamarin

Date	Mintage	F	VF	XF	Unc	BU
1993FM (P)	—	Value: 40.00				

KM# 153   25 DOLLARS
20.0900 g., 0.9250 Silver 0.5974 oz. ASW   **Ruler:** Elizabeth II
Series: Endangered Wildlife **Obv:** Crowned head right **Rev:** Pere
David's deer

Date	Mintage	F	VF	XF	Unc	BU
1993FM (P)	—	Value: 35.00				

KM# 154   25 DOLLARS
20.0900 g., 0.9250 Silver 0.5974 oz. ASW   **Ruler:** Elizabeth II
Series: Endangered Wildlife **Obv:** Crowned head right
Rev: Spectacled bear standing

Date	Mintage	F	VF	XF	Unc	BU
1993FM (P)	—	Value: 40.00				

KM# 155   25 DOLLARS
20.0900 g., 0.9250 Silver 0.5974 oz. ASW, 40 mm.
Ruler: Elizabeth II **Series:** Endangered Wildlife **Obv:** Crowned
head right **Rev:** Imperial Parrot on tree branch **Edge:** Reeded

Date	Mintage	F	VF	XF	Unc	BU
1993FM (P)	—	Value: 50.00				

KM# 158   25 DOLLARS
21.5900 g., 0.9250 Silver 0.6420 oz. ASW   **Ruler:** Elizabeth II
Series: Endangered Wildlife **Obv:** Crowned head right **Rev:** Pair
of black-footed ferrets, one standing

Date	Mintage	F	VF	XF	Unc	BU
1993FM Proof	—	Value: 50.00				

KM# 159 25 DOLLARS
21.5900 g., 0.9250 Silver 0.6420 oz. ASW **Ruler:** Elizabeth II
Series: Endangered Wildlife **Obv:** Crowned head right
Rev: Large Anegada rock iguana right

Date	Mintage	F	VF	XF	Unc	BU
1993FM Proof	—				Value: 60.00	

KM# 160 25 DOLLARS
21.5900 g., 0.9250 Silver 0.6420 oz. ASW **Ruler:** Elizabeth II
Series: Endangered Wildlife **Obv:** Crowned head right **Rev:** Two
Parma wallabies, one with offspring

Date	Mintage	F	VF	XF	Unc	BU
1993FM Proof	—				Value: 40.00	

KM# 161 25 DOLLARS
21.5900 g., 0.9250 Silver 0.6420 oz. ASW **Ruler:** Elizabeth II
Series: Endangered Wildlife **Obv:** Crowned head right **Rev:** Pair
of leatherback sea turtles and Portuguese Man-o-War jelly fish

Date	Mintage	F	VF	XF	Unc	BU
1993FM Proof	—				Value: 50.00	

KM# 170 25 DOLLARS
21.3500 g., 0.9250 Silver 0.6349 oz. ASW **Ruler:** Elizabeth II
Series: Endangered Wildlife **Obv:** Crowned head right
Rev: Cheetah running left

Date	Mintage	F	VF	XF	Unc	BU
1993FM (P)	—				Value: 40.00	

KM# 171 25 DOLLARS
21.3500 g., 0.9250 Silver 0.6349 oz. ASW **Ruler:** Elizabeth II
Series: Endangered Wildlife **Obv:** Crowned head right
Rev: European Bison in forest

Date	Mintage	F	VF	XF	Unc	BU
1993FM (P)	—				Value: 40.00	

KM# 165 25 DOLLARS
21.5900 g., 0.9250 Silver 0.6420 oz. ASW **Ruler:** Elizabeth II
Series: Endangered Wildlife **Obv:** Crowned head right **Rev:** Two
seals frolicking

Date	Mintage	F	VF	XF	Unc	BU
1997	—	—	—	—	—	40.00

KM# 166 25 DOLLARS
21.5900 g., 0.9250 Silver 0.6420 oz. ASW **Ruler:** Elizabeth II
Series: Endangered Wildlife **Obv:** Crowned head right **Rev:** Sea
otter holding a sea urchin

Date	Mintage	F	VF	XF	Unc	BU
1997	—	—	—	—	—	45.00

KM# 167 25 DOLLARS
21.5900 g., 0.9250 Silver 0.6420 oz. ASW **Ruler:** Elizabeth II
Series: Endangered Wildlife **Obv:** Crowned head right **Rev:** Pair
of sparring Arabian oryx

Date	Mintage	F	VF	XF	Unc	BU
1997	—	—	—	—	—	35.00

KM# 168 25 DOLLARS
21.5900 g., 0.9250 Silver 0.6420 oz. ASW **Ruler:** Elizabeth II
Series: Endangered Wildlife **Obv:** Crowned head right
Rev: Diving humpback whale

Date	Mintage	F	VF	XF	Unc	BU
1997	—	—	—	—	—	40.00

KM# 28 50 DOLLARS
2.6800 g., 0.5000 Gold 0.0431 oz. AGW **Ruler:** Elizabeth II
Obv: Young bust right **Rev:** Golden Dove of Christmas

Date	Mintage	F	VF	XF	Unc	BU
1980 Proof	6,379			Value: 60.00		

KM# 75 50 DOLLARS
2.0687 g., 0.5000 Gold 0.0333 oz. AGW **Ruler:** Elizabeth II
Obv: Crowned head right **Rev:** Flute player

Date	Mintage	F	VF	XF	Unc	BU
1988 Proof	—			Value: 55.00		

KM# 76 50 DOLLARS
2.0687 g., 0.5000 Gold 0.0333 oz. AGW **Ruler:** Elizabeth II
Obv: Crowned head right **Rev:** Bird's-head staff

Date	Mintage	F	VF	XF	Unc	BU
1988 Proof	—			Value: 55.00		

KM# 77 50 DOLLARS
2.0687 g., 0.5000 Gold 0.0333 oz. AGW **Ruler:** Elizabeth II
Obv: Crowned head right **Rev:** Double-spouted vessel

Date	Mintage	F	VF	XF	Unc	BU
1988 Proof	—			Value: 55.00		

KM# 78 50 DOLLARS
2.0687 g., 0.5000 Gold 0.0333 oz. AGW **Ruler:** Elizabeth II
Obv: Crowned head right **Rev:** Deer-top bell

Date	Mintage	F	VF	XF	Unc	BU
1988 Proof	—			Value: 55.00		

KM# 79 50 DOLLARS
2.0687 g., 0.5000 Gold 0.0333 oz. AGW **Ruler:** Elizabeth II
Obv: Crowned head right **Rev:** Two-headed animal

Date	Mintage	F	VF	XF	Unc	BU
1988 Proof	—			Value: 55.00		

KM# 80   50 DOLLARS
2.0687 g., 0.5000 Gold 0.0333 oz. AGW   **Ruler:** Elizabeth II
Obv: Crowned head right **Rev:** Turtle

Date	Mintage	F	VF	XF	Unc	BU
1988 Proof	—	Value: 55.00				

KM# 81   50 DOLLARS
2.0687 g., 0.5000 Gold 0.0333 oz. AGW   **Ruler:** Elizabeth II
Obv: Crowned head right **Rev:** Frog

Date	Mintage	F	VF	XF	Unc	BU
1988 Proof	—	Value: 55.00				

KM# 82   50 DOLLARS
2.0687 g., 0.5000 Gold 0.0333 oz. AGW   **Ruler:** Elizabeth II
Obv: Crowned head right **Rev:** Mixtec mask

Date	Mintage	F	VF	XF	Unc	BU
1988 Proof	—	Value: 55.00				

KM# 83   50 DOLLARS
2.0687 g., 0.5000 Gold 0.0333 oz. AGW   **Ruler:** Elizabeth II
Obv: Crowned head right **Rev:** Chimu gold beaker

Date	Mintage	F	VF	XF	Unc	BU
1988 Proof	—	Value: 55.00				

KM# 84   50 DOLLARS
2.0687 g., 0.5000 Gold 0.0333 oz. AGW   **Ruler:** Elizabeth II
Obv: Crowned head right **Rev:** Bird vessel

Date	Mintage	F	VF	XF	Unc	BU
1988 Proof	—	Value: 55.00				

KM# 85   50 DOLLARS
2.0687 g., 0.5000 Gold 0.0333 oz. AGW   **Ruler:** Elizabeth II
Obv: Crowned head right **Rev:** Ceremonial headdress

Date	Mintage	F	VF	XF	Unc	BU
1988 Proof	—	Value: 55.00				

KM# 86   50 DOLLARS
2.0687 g., 0.5000 Gold 0.0333 oz. AGW   **Ruler:** Elizabeth II
Obv: Crowned head right **Rev:** Sacrificial knife

Date	Mintage	F	VF	XF	Unc	BU
1988 Proof	—	Value: 55.00				

KM# 87   50 DOLLARS
2.0687 g., 0.5000 Gold 0.0333 oz. AGW   **Ruler:** Elizabeth II
Obv: Crowned head right **Rev:** Ceremonial dancer

Date	Mintage	F	VF	XF	Unc	BU
1988 Proof	—	Value: 55.00				

KM# 88   50 DOLLARS
2.0687 g., 0.5000 Gold 0.0333 oz. AGW   **Ruler:** Elizabeth II
Obv: Crowned head right **Rev:** Spanish Colonial gold coin

Date	Mintage	F	VF	XF	Unc	BU
1988 Proof	—	Value: 55.00				

KM# 89   50 DOLLARS
2.0687 g., 0.5000 Gold 0.0333 oz. AGW   **Ruler:** Elizabeth II
Obv: Crowned head right **Rev:** Crossed hands

Date	Mintage	F	VF	XF	Unc	BU
1988 Proof	—	Value: 55.00				

KM# 7   100 DOLLARS
7.1000 g., 0.9000 Gold 0.2054 oz. AGW   **Ruler:** Elizabeth II
Obv: Young bust right **Rev:** Royal Tern

Date	Mintage	F	VF	XF	Unc	BU
1975FM (M) Rare	10	—	—	—	—	—
1975FM (U)	13,000	—	—	—	195	—
1975FM (P)	Est. 23,000	Value: 200				

Note: Includes 8,754 in First Day Covers

KM# 8   100 DOLLARS
7.1000 g., 0.9000 Gold 0.2054 oz. AGW   **Ruler:** Elizabeth II
Subject: 50th Birthday of Queen Elizabeth II **Obv:** Young bust
right **Rev:** Crowned monogram above shield with woman and
twelve lamps, VIGILATE on banner below

Date	Mintage	F	VF	XF	Unc	BU
1976FM (M) Rare	10	—	—	—	—	—
1976FM (U)	1,752	—	—	—	195	—
1976FM (P)	12,000	Value: 200				

KM# 15   100 DOLLARS
7.1000 g., 0.9000 Gold 0.2054 oz. AGW   **Ruler:** Elizabeth II
Subject: Queen's Silver Jubilee **Obv:** Young bust right
Rev: Imperial crown above two dates

Date	Mintage	F	VF	XF	Unc	BU
1977FM (U) Rare	10	—	—	—	—	—
1977FM (P)	6,715	Value: 200				

KM# 23   100 DOLLARS
7.1000 g., 0.9000 Gold 0.2054 oz. AGW   **Ruler:** Elizabeth II
Subject: Coronation Jubilee **Obv:** Young bust right **Rev:** Crossed
sceptres with royal orb at center

Date	Mintage	F	VF	XF	Unc	BU
1978FM (P)	5,772	Value: 210				

KM# 25   100 DOLLARS
7.1000 g., 0.9000 Gold 0.2054 oz. AGW   **Ruler:** Elizabeth II **Obv:**
Young bust right **Rev:** Bust of Sir Francis Drake with ruffed collar right

Date	Mintage	F	VF	XF	Unc	BU
1979FM (P)	3,216	Value: 220				

KM# 29   100 DOLLARS
7.1000 g., 0.9000 Gold 0.2054 oz. AGW   **Ruler:** Elizabeth II
Subject: 400th Anniversary of Drake's Voyage **Obv:** Young bust
right **Rev:** The Golden Hind

Date	Mintage	F	VF	XF	Unc	BU
1980 Proof	5,412	Value: 210				

KM# 32   100 DOLLARS
7.1000 g., 0.9000 Gold 0.2054 oz. AGW   **Ruler:** Elizabeth II
Subject: Knighting of Sir Francis Drake **Obv:** Young bust right
Rev: Queen with kneeling figure

Date	Mintage	F	VF	XF	Unc	BU
1981FM (P)	1,321	Value: 230				

KM# 34   100 DOLLARS
7.1000 g., 0.9000 Gold 0.2054 oz. AGW   **Ruler:** Elizabeth II
Subject: 30th Anniversary - Reign of Queen Elizabeth II
Obv: Young bust right **Rev:** Crowned monogram

Date	Mintage	F	VF	XF	Unc	BU
1982FM (P)	620	Value: 250				

KM# 38   100 DOLLARS
7.1000 g., 0.9000 Gold 0.2054 oz. AGW   **Ruler:** Elizabeth II
Subject: 30th Anniversary - Coronation of Queen Elizabeth II **Obv:**
Young bust right **Rev:** Sceptres divide royal symbols and dates

Date	Mintage	F	VF	XF	Unc	BU
1983FM (P)	624	Value: 250				

KM# 39   100 DOLLARS
7.1000 g., 0.9000 Gold 0.2054 oz. AGW   **Ruler:** Elizabeth II
Subject: Flora - Ginger Thomas **Obv:** Young bust right **Rev:** Flower

Date	Mintage	F	VF	XF	Unc	BU
1984FM (P)	25	Value: 475				

KM# 74   100 DOLLARS
7.1000 g., 0.9000 Gold 0.2054 oz. AGW **Ruler:** Elizabeth II
Subject: Sir Francis Drake's West Indian Voyage **Obv:** Crowned head right **Rev:** Ship

Date	Mintage	F	VF	XF	Unc	BU
1985FM (P)	772	Value: 245				

KM# 119   100 DOLLARS
4.1180 g., 0.5000 Gold 0.0662 oz. AGW **Subject:** Discovery of America - King Ferdinand of Spain **Obv:** Crowned head right **Rev:** Bust facing

Date	Mintage	F	VF	XF	Unc	BU
ND(1991)FM (P)	—	Value: 100				

KM# 162   100 DOLLARS
4.1180 g., 0.5000 Gold 0.0662 oz. AGW **Ruler:** Elizabeth II **Obv:** Crowned head right **Rev:** The Pinta

Date	Mintage	F	VF	XF	Unc	BU
ND(1994) Proof	—	Value: 100				

KM# 256   100 DOLLARS
4.3100 g., 0.5000 Gold 0.0693 oz. AGW, 20.75 mm.
Ruler: Elizabeth II **Obv:** Crowned head right **Rev:** Columbus' landing scene **Edge:** Reeded

Date	Mintage	F	VF	XF	Unc	BU
ND(1996?)FM Proof	—	Value: 100				

KM# 174.1   100 DOLLARS
6.2200 g., 0.9990 Gold 0.1998 oz. AGW **Ruler:** Elizabeth II
Subject: Queen Mother's 100th Birthday **Obv:** Crowned head right **Rev:** Bust facing divides dates **Edge:** Reeded

Date	Mintage	F	VF	XF	Unc	BU
2000 Proof	5,000	Value: 200				

KM# 174.2   100 DOLLARS
6.2200 g., 0.9999 Gold 0.1999 oz. AGW, 22 mm.
Ruler: Elizabeth II **Subject:** Queen Mother's 100th Birthday **Obv:** Crowned head right **Rev:** Bust facing, tiny black sapphire mounted on her broach **Edge:** Reeded

Date	Mintage	F	VF	XF	Unc	BU
2000 Proof	1,000	Value: 235				

KM# 177   100 DOLLARS
6.2200 g., 0.9990 Gold 0.1998 oz. AGW **Ruler:** Elizabeth II
Subject: 1st Anniversary - Earl and Countess of Wessex
Obv: Crowned head right **Rev:** 1/2 figures facing, anniversary dates below **Edge:** Reeded

Date	Mintage	F	VF	XF	Unc	BU
2000 Proof	5,000	Value: 200				

KM# 120   250 DOLLARS
8.0494 g., 0.5000 Gold 0.1294 oz. AGW **Ruler:** Elizabeth II
Subject: Quincentennial - Discovery of America **Obv:** Crowned head right **Rev:** Bust of young Queen Isabella 3/4 left

Date	Mintage	F	VF	XF	Unc	BU
ND(1991)FM (P)	—	Value: 290				

KM# 163   250 DOLLARS
8.0494 g., 0.5000 Gold 0.1294 oz. AGW **Ruler:** Elizabeth II
Subject: The Nina **Obv:** Crowned head right **Rev:** Ship

Date	Mintage	F	VF	XF	Unc	BU
ND(1994) Proof	—	Value: 290				

KM# 257   250 DOLLARS
8.1700 g., 0.5000 Gold 0.1313 oz. AGW, 26 mm.
Ruler: Elizabeth II **Obv:** Crowned head right **Rev:** Columbus' personal coat of arms **Edge:** Reeded

Date	Mintage	F	VF	XF	Unc	BU
ND(1996?)FM Proof	—	Value: 250				

KM# 121   500 DOLLARS
19.8126 g., 0.5000 Gold 0.3185 oz. AGW **Ruler:** Elizabeth II
Subject: Discovery of America **Obv:** Crowned head right
Rev: Christopher Columbus 3/4 facing

Date	Mintage	F	VF	XF	Unc	BU
ND(1991)FM (P)	—	Value: 500				

KM# 164   500 DOLLARS
19.8126 g., 0.5000 Gold 0.3185 oz. AGW **Ruler:** Elizabeth II
Subject: The Santa Maria **Obv:** Crowned head right **Rev:** Ship sailing left, no gulls

Date	Mintage	F	VF	XF	Unc	BU
ND(1994) Proof	—	Value: 500				

KM# 258   500 DOLLARS
20.2200 g., 0.5000 Gold 0.3250 oz. AGW, 35.75 mm.
Ruler: Elizabeth II **Obv:** Crowned head right **Rev:** Columbus' three ships crossing the Atlantic to America **Edge:** Reeded

Date	Mintage	F	VF	XF	Unc	BU
ND(1996?)FM Proof	—	Value: 550				

KM# 156   1000 DOLLARS
14.8000 g., 0.9990 Platinum 0.4753 oz. APW **Ruler:** Elizabeth II
Subject: Discovery of America **Obv:** Crowned head right
Rev: Three ships sailing

Date	Mintage	F	VF	XF	Unc	BU
ND(1992) Proof	—	Value: 1,000				

MINT SETS

KM#	Date	Mintage	Identification	Issue Price	Mkt Val
MS1	1973 (6)	18,402	KM#1-5, 6a	11.50	8.00
MS2	1974 (6)	9,474	KM#1-6	10.00	8.00
MS3	1975 (6)	2,351	KM#1-6	12.50	10.00
MS4	1976 (6)	996	KM#1-6	13.50	12.00
MS5	1977 (6)	782	KM#1-6	12.50	12.00
MS6	1978 (6)	943	KM#1-6	13.00	12.00
MS7	1979 (7)	680	KM#1-6, 24	20.00	25.00
MS8	1980 (7)	1,007	KM#1-6, 26	21.00	25.00
MS9	1981 (9)	472	KM#1-6, 30	20.00	30.00
MS10	1982 (7)	—	KM#1-6, 33	28.50	35.00
MS11	1983 (7)	203	KM#1-6, 35	22.00	50.00

PROOF SETS

KM#	Date	Mintage	Identification	Issue Price	Mkt Val
PS1	1973 (6)	146,581	KM#1-5, 6a. Includes 34,418 proofs in First Day Covers	15.00	15.00
PS2	1974 (6)	93,555	KM#1-5, 6a	20.00	16.50
PS3	1975 (6)	32,244	KM#1-5, 6a	25.00	18.50
PS4	1976 (6)	15,003	KM#1-5, 6a	25.00	18.50
PS5	1977 (6)	7,218	KM#1-5, 6a	26.00	20.00
PS6	1977 (6)	17,366	KM#9-14	60.00	40.00
PS7	1978 (6)	7,059	KM#1-5, 6a	25.00	20.00
PS8	1978 (6)	6,196	KM#16-21	—	40.00
PS9	1979 (6)	5,304	KM#1-5, 6a, 24a	39.50	37.50
PS10	1980 (7)	3,421	KM#105, 6a, 26a	97.00	47.50
PS11	1981 (7)	1,124	KM#1-5, 6a, 30a	97.00	60.00
PS12	1982 (7)	—	KM#1-5, 6a, 33a	97.00	60.00
PS13	1983 (7)	478	KM#1-5, 6a, 35a	77.00	65.00
PS14	1984 (7)	5,000	KM#1-5, 6a, 35a	77.00	60.00
PS15	1985 (6)	—	KM#42-47	20.50	45.00
PS16	1985 (6)	—	KM#42a-47a	76.00	140
PS17	ND (1991) (3)	—	KM#119-121	975	900
PS18	ND (1994) (3)	—	KM#162-164	975	900
PS19	ND (1996) (3)	—	KM#256, 257, 258	—	900

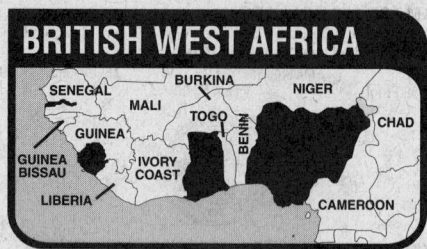

BRITISH WEST AFRICA

British West Africa was an administrative grouping of the four former British West African colonies of Gambia, Sierra Leone, Nigeria and Gold Coast (now Ghana). All are now independent republics and members of the British Commonwealth of Nations. See separate entries for individual statistics and history.

The Bank of British West Africa became the banker to the Colonial Government in 1894 and held this status until 1912. As such they were responsible for maintaining a proper supply of silver coinage for the colonies.

Through the subsidiary efforts of the Governor of Lagos, Nigeria a specific British West African coinage was put into use between 1907 and 1911. These coins bear the inscription, NIGERIA-BRITISH WEST AFRICA.

The four colonies were supplied with a common coinage and banknotes by the West African Currency Board from 1912 through 1958. This coinage bore the inscription BRITISH WEST AFRICA. The coinage, which includes three denominations of 1936 bearing the name of Edward VIII, is obsolete.

For later coinage see Gambia, Ghana, Sierra Leone and Nigeria.

RULER
British, until 1958

MINT MARKS
G-J.R. Gaunt & Sons, Birmingham
H - Heaton Mint, Birmingham
K, KN - King's Norton, Birmingham
SA - Pretoria, South Africa
No mm - Royal Mint, London

MONETARY SYSTEM
12 Pence = 1 Shilling
20 Shillings = 1 Pound

BRITISH COLONIES
POUND COINAGE

KM# 1   1/10 PENNY
Aluminum **Ruler:** Edward VII **Obv:** Crown above center hole, denomination around hole in English, in Arabic beneath **Obv. Leg.:** EDWARD VII KING & EMPEROR **Rev:** Hexagram divides date at bottom **Rev. Leg.:** NIGERIA BRITISH WEST AFRICA

Date	Mintage	F	VF	XF	Unc	BU
1907	1,254,000	2.00	4.00	10.00	20.00	35.00
1908	8,363,000	1.00	3.00	6.00	15.00	25.00
1908 Proof	—	Value: 300				

KM# 3 1/10 PENNY
Copper-Nickel **Ruler:** Edward VII **Obv:** Crown above center hole, denomination around hole in English, in Arabic beneath **Obv. Leg.:** EDWARD VII KING & EMPEROR **Rev:** Hexagram divides date at bottom **Rev. Leg.:** NIGERIA BRITISH WEST AFRICA

Date	Mintage	F	VF	XF	Unc	BU
1908	9,600,000	0.30	0.50	1.00	2.00	3.50
1909	4,800,000	0.40	0.75	1.50	5.00	9.00
1910	7,200,000	0.50	1.00	2.00	7.50	12.50

KM# 4 1/10 PENNY
Copper-Nickel **Ruler:** George V **Obv:** Crown above center hole, denomination around hole in English, in Arabic beneath **Obv. Leg.:** GEORGIVS V REX ET IND: IMP: **Rev:** Hexagram divides date at bottom **Rev. Leg.:** NIGERIA BRITISH WEST AFRICA

Date	Mintage	F	VF	XF	Unc	BU
1911H	7,200,000	1.50	3.50	7.50	15.00	28.00

KM# 7 1/10 PENNY
1.7200 g., Copper-Nickel, 20.5 mm. **Ruler:** George V **Obv:** Crown above center hole, denomination around hole in English, in Arabic beneath **Obv. Leg.:** GEORGIVS V REX ET IND: IMP: **Rev:** Hexagram divides date at bottom **Rev. Leg.:** BRITISH WEST AFRICA **Edge:** Plain

Date	Mintage	F	VF	XF	Unc	BU
1912H	10,800,000	0.30	0.75	1.50	3.50	7.00
1913H	1,080,000	0.30	0.75	1.50	3.50	7.00
1913	4,632,000	1.00	2.00	3.50	6.50	11.50
1914H	20,088,000	0.50	1.25	2.00	5.00	9.00
1914	1,200,000	3.00	5.00	10.00	22.50	40.00
1915H	10,032,000	0.30	0.75	1.50	5.00	9.00
1916H	480,000	25.00	50.00	75.00	150	175
1917H	9,384,000	2.00	3.00	5.00	15.00	25.00
1919H	912,000	1.25	2.00	4.00	7.50	13.50
1919KN	480,000	10.00	25.00	50.00	75.00	—
1920KN	12,996,000	0.40	1.00	3.00	5.00	9.00
1920H	1,560,000	2.00	3.00	5.00	10.00	18.00
1920KN Proof	—	Value: 125				
1922KN	7,265,000	1.00	1.75	4.50	12.00	20.00
1923KN	12,000,000	0.30	0.75	1.50	5.00	9.00
1925KN	12,000,000	0.75	1.50	3.00	8.00	15.00
1925H	12,000,000	2.00	3.00	5.00	12.00	20.00
1925	2,400,000	5.00	10.00	20.00	40.00	70.00
1926	12,000,000	0.75	1.50	2.50	6.00	10.00
1927	3,984,000	0.20	0.50	1.50	3.00	6.00
1927 Proof	—	Value: 150				
1928	11,760,000	0.20	0.50	1.50	3.00	6.00
1928 Proof	—	Value: 150				
1928H	2,964,000	0.20	0.50	1.50	3.00	6.00
1928KN	3,151,000	2.00	3.00	6.00	15.00	25.00
1930	9,600,000	2.00	3.00	6.00	15.00	25.00
1930 Proof	—	Value: 150				
1931	9,840,000	0.20	0.50	1.00	3.00	6.00
1931 Proof	—	Value: 150				
1932	3,600,000	0.20	0.50	1.50	5.00	9.00
1932 Proof	—	Value: 150				
1933	7,200,000	0.20	0.50	1.50	3.50	7.00
1933 Proof	—	Value: 150				
1934	4,800,000	0.75	1.50	3.00	6.00	10.00
1934 Proof	—	Value: 150				
1935	13,200,000	0.75	1.50	3.00	7.50	12.50
1935 Proof	—	Value: 150				
1936	9,720,000	0.20	0.50	1.00	3.00	6.00
1936 Proof	—	Value: 150				

KM# 14 1/10 PENNY
1.9000 g., Copper-Nickel **Ruler:** Edward VIII **Obv:** Crown above center hole, denomination around hole in English, in Arabic beneath **Obv. Leg.:** EDWARDVS VIII REX ET IND: IMP: **Rev:** Hexagram divides date at bottom **Rev. Leg.:** BRITISH WEST AFRICA

Date	Mintage	F	VF	XF	Unc	BU
1936	5,880,000	0.25	0.50	1.00	2.50	4.50
1936 Proof	—	Value: 200				
1936H	1,404,000	50.00	75.00	125	250	—
1936H Proof	—	Value: 300				
1936KN	3,000,000	1.00	2.00	3.50	9.00	15.00
1936KN Proof	—	Value: 200				

KM# 20 1/10 PENNY
1.8900 g., Copper-Nickel, 20 mm. **Ruler:** George VI **Obv:** Crown above center hole, denomination around hole in English, in Arabic beneath **Obv. Leg.:** GEORGIVS VI REX ET IND: IMP: **Rev:** Hexagram divides date at bottom **Rev. Leg.:** BRITISH WEST AFRICA

Date	Mintage	F	VF	XF	Unc	BU
1938	12,000,000	0.10	0.25	0.50	1.50	2.50
1938 Proof	—	Value: 125				
1938H	1,596,000	5.00	8.00	12.00	22.50	40.00
1938H Proof	—	Value: 100				
1939	9,840,000	0.25	0.50	1.00	3.50	6.00
1939 Proof	—	Value: 200				
1940	13,920,000	0.25	0.50	1.00	2.00	3.50
1940 Proof	—	Value: 125				
1941	16,560,000	1.00	2.00	4.00	8.00	14.00
1941 Proof	—	Value: 125				
1942	12,360,000	1.00	2.50	4.50	10.00	18.00
1942 Proof	—	Value: 125				
1943	22,560,000	1.00	2.50	5.00	10.00	18.00
1944	10,440,000	1.00	2.50	5.00	10.00	18.00
1944 Proof	—	Value: 150				
1945	25,706,000	0.50	1.00	1.75	6.00	10.00
1945 Proof	—	Value: 125				
1946	2,803,000	1.00	2.00	4.00	9.00	15.00
1946 Proof	—	Value: 125				
1946H	5,004,000	1.00	2.00	4.00	9.00	15.00
1946KN	1,152,000	0.25	0.50	1.00	3.00	5.50
1946KN Proof	—	Value: 125				
1947	4,202,000	0.50	1.00	2.00	5.00	9.00
1947 Proof	—	Value: 125				
1947KN	3,900,000	200	300	500	600	—

KM# 26 1/10 PENNY
Copper-Nickel, 20 mm. **Obv:** Crown above center hole, denomination around hole in English, in Arabic beneath **Obv. Leg.:** GEORGIVS SEXTVS REX **Rev:** Hexagram divides date at bottom **Rev. Leg.:** BRITISH WEST AFRICA

Date	Mintage	F	VF	XF	Unc	BU
1949H	3,700,000	1.00	2.00	3.00	6.00	10.00
1949KN	3,036,000	1.00	2.00	3.00	5.00	9.00
1950KN	13,200,000	0.25	0.50	1.00	2.50	4.50
1950KN Proof	—	Value: 150				

KM# 26a 1/10 PENNY
Bronze, 20 mm. **Obv:** Crown above center hole, denomination around hole in English, in Arabic beneath **Obv. Leg.:** GEORGIVS SEXTVS REX **Rev:** Hexagram divides date at bottom **Rev. Leg.:** BRITISH WEST AFRICA

Date	Mintage	F	VF	XF	Unc	BU
1952	15,060,000	0.50	1.00	2.00	6.00	10.00
1952 Proof	—	Value: 150				

KM# 32 1/10 PENNY
Bronze, 20 mm. **Ruler:** Elizabeth II **Obv:** Crown above center hole, denomination around hole in English, in Arabic beneath **Obv. Leg.:** QUEEN ELIZABETH THE SECOND **Rev:** Hexagram divides date at bottom **Rev. Leg.:** BRITISH WEST AFRICA

Date	Mintage	F	VF	XF	Unc	BU
1954	4,800,000	0.50	1.00	2.00	4.00	8.00
1954 Proof	—	Value: 150				

Date	Mintage	F	VF	XF	Unc	BU
1956	2,400,000	100	200	400	700	—
1956 Proof	—	Value: 750				
1957	7,200,000	60.00	120	220	325	—
1957 Proof	—	Value: 600				

KM# 5 1/2 PENNY
Copper-Nickel **Ruler:** George V **Obv:** Crown above center hole, denomination around hole in English, in Arabic beneath **Obv. Leg.:** GEORGIVS V REX ET IND: IMP: **Rev:** Hexagram divides date at bottom **Rev. Leg.:** NIGERIA BRITISH WEST AFRICA

Date	Mintage	F	VF	XF	Unc	BU
1911H	3,360,000	4.50	12.00	25.00	40.00	75.00

KM# 8 1/2 PENNY
Copper-Nickel, 25.2 mm. **Ruler:** George V **Obv:** Crown above center hole, denomination around hole in English, in Arabic beneath **Obv. Leg.:** GEORGIVS V REX ET IND: IMP: **Rev:** Hexagram divides date at bottom **Rev. Leg.:** BRITISH WEST AFRICA **Edge:** Plain

Date	Mintage	F	VF	XF	Unc	BU
1912H	3,120,000	2.00	5.00	7.00	20.00	35.00
1913	1,382,000	150	250	325	500	—
1913H	216,000	5.00	10.00	17.50	30.00	55.00
1914	240,000	10.00	20.00	35.00	60.00	110
1914H	586,000	20.00	30.00	50.00	75.00	135
1914K	3,360,000	3.00	6.00	17.50	30.00	55.00
1914K Proof	—	Value: 225				

Note: Issued with East Africa KM#11 in a double (4 pc.) specimen set

Date	Mintage	F	VF	XF	Unc	BU
1915H	3,577,000	1.00	2.00	4.00	15.00	25.00
1916H	4,046,000	1.00	3.00	5.00	15.00	25.00
1917H	214,000	6.00	12.00	28.00	50.00	90.00
1918H	490,000	2.50	5.00	10.00	30.00	55.00
1919H	4,950,000	1.25	2.50	6.00	20.00	35.00
1919KN	3,861,000	1.25	2.50	7.50	25.00	45.00
1920H	26,285,000	1.50	3.00	7.50	15.00	25.00
1920KN	13,844,000	0.50	3.00	8.50	16.50	30.00
1922KN	5,817,000	300	500	750	1,200	—
1927	528,000	20.00	30.00	65.00	135	250
1927 Proof	—	Value: 225				
1929	336,000	6.00	22.00	47.50	95.00	165
1929 Proof	—	Value: 225				
1931	96,000	500	800	1,200	1,500	—
1931 Proof	—	Value: 225				
1932	960,000	2.50	15.00	35.00	55.00	100
1932 Proof	—	Value: 225				
1933	2,122,000	12.00	23.50	55.00	110	200
1933 Proof	—	Value: 225				
1934	1,694,000	2.50	15.00	35.00	75.00	135
1934 Proof	—	Value: 225				
1935	3,271,000	1.00	3.00	18.00	35.00	60.00
1935 Proof	—	Value: 225				
1936	5,400,000	2.50	5.00	18.00	32.00	55.00
1936 Proof	—	Value: 225				

KM# 15 1/2 PENNY
Copper-Nickel, 25.2 mm. **Ruler:** Edward VIII **Obv:** Crown above center hole, denomination around hole in English, in Arabic beneath **Obv. Leg.:** EDWARDVS VIII REX • ET IND: IMP: **Rev:** Hexagram divides date at bottom **Rev. Leg.:** BRITISH WEST AFRICA **Edge:** Plain

Date	Mintage	F	VF	XF	Unc	BU
1936	14,760,000	0.25	0.50	1.00	2.50	4.50
1936 Proof	—	Value: 200				
1936H	2,400,000	1.00	2.00	5.00	12.50	20.00
1936H Proof	—	Value: 200				
1936KN	2,298,000	0.65	1.25	2.25	4.00	7.00
1936KN Proof	—	Value: 200				

KM# 18 1/2 PENNY

5.6600 g., Copper-Nickel, 25.9 mm. **Ruler:** George VI **Obv:** Crown above center hole, denomination around hole in English, in Arabic beneath **Obv. Leg.:** GEORGIVS VI REX • ET IND: IMP: **Rev:** Hexagram divides date at bottom **Rev. Leg.:** BRITISH WEST AFRICA

Date	Mintage	F	VF	XF	Unc	BU
1937H	4,800,000	0.40	0.85	1.50	4.00	7.00
1937H Proof	—	Value: 125				
1937KN	5,577,000	0.40	0.85	3.00	5.00	9.00
1940KN	2,410,000	2.00	4.00	6.00	15.00	25.00
1940KN Proof	—	Value: 125				
1941	2,400,000	0.40	2.00	6.00	12.00	20.00
1942	4,800,000	0.40	0.85	4.00	8.50	15.00
1943	3,360,000	0.50	1.00	5.00	10.00	18.00
1944	3,600,000	1.00	3.00	7.00	20.00	35.00
1944 Proof	—	Value: 125				
1946	3,600,000	0.25	1.00	3.00	7.00	12.50
1946 Proof	—	Value: 125				
1947H	15,218,000	0.35	0.75	1.25	5.00	9.00
1947KN	12,000,000	0.40	0.85	2.00	6.00	10.00

KM# 6 PENNY

Copper-Nickel, 30.5 mm. **Ruler:** George V **Obv:** Crown above center hole, denomination around hole in English, in Arabic beneath **Obv. Leg.:** GEORGIVS V REX ET IND: IMP: **Rev:** Hexagram, date beneath **Rev. Leg.:** NIGERIA BRITISH WEST AFRICA

Date	Mintage	F	VF	XF	Unc	BU
1911H	1,920,000	18.00	50.00	100	150	—

KM# 17 PENNY

Copper-Nickel, 30.5 mm. **Ruler:** Edward VIII **Obv:** Crown above center hole, denomination in English beneath **Obv. Leg.:** EDWARDVS VIII REX ET IND: IMP: **Rev:** Hexagram, date beneath **Rev. Leg.:** BRITISH WEST AFRICA

Date	Mintage	F	VF	XF	Unc	BU
1936H	—	125	165	225	350	—

KM# 27 1/2 PENNY

Copper-Nickel **Ruler:** Edward VII **Obv:** Crown above center hole, denomination around hole in English, in Arabic beneath **Obv. Leg.:** GEORGIVS SEXTVS REX **Rev:** Hexagram divides date at bottom **Rev. Leg.:** BRITISH WEST AFRICA

Date	Mintage	F	VF	XF	Unc	BU
1949H	5,909,000	1.50	3.50	12.00	22.00	40.00
1949KN	3,413,000	1.50	3.50	12.00	25.00	45.00
1951	3,468,000	1.50	3.50	12.00	25.00	45.00
1951 Proof	—	Value: 250				

KM# 9 PENNY

Copper-Nickel, 30.5 mm. **Ruler:** George V **Obv:** Crown above center hole, denomination around hole in English, in Arabic beneath **Obv. Leg.:** GEORGIVS V REX ET IND: IMP: **Rev:** Hexagram, date beneath **Rev. Leg.:** BRITISH WEST AFRICA

Date	Mintage	F	VF	XF	Unc	BU
1912H	1,560,000	1.50	10.00	22.50	40.00	
1913	1,680,000	7.50	25.00	45.00	75.00	135
1913H	144,000	5.00	10.00	17.50	35.00	60.00
1914	3,000,000	2.50	5.00	10.00	22.50	40.00
1914H	72,000	35.00	50.00	120	200	—
1915H	3,295,000	1.25	2.00	7.00	15.00	25.00
1916H	3,461,000	1.25	2.00	10.00	20.00	35.00
1917H	444,000	5.00	7.00	24.00	45.00	80.00
1918H	994,000	7.50	15.00	45.00	75.00	135
1919H	21,864,000	1.25	2.50	7.00	15.00	25.00
1919KN	264,000	7.50	25.00	35.00	50.00	90.00
1920H	37,870,000	1.00	1.75	5.50	12.50	22.50
1920KN	20,685,000	1.00	2.00	8.00	17.50	30.00
1922KN	3,971,000	400	750	1,000	1,500	—
1926	8,039,999	2.00	4.00	15.00	30.00	55.00
1927	792,000	25.00	45.00	125	200	—
1927 Proof	—	Value: 225				
1928	6,672,000	2.00	4.00	12.00	25.00	45.00
1928 Proof	—	Value: 225				
1929	636,000	20.00	35.00	65.00	100	—
1929 Proof	—	Value: 225				
1933	2,806,000	2.00	14.00	32.50	65.00	120
1933 Proof	—	Value: 225				
1934	2,640,000	3.50	15.00	35.00	75.00	135
1934 Proof	—	Value: 225				
1935	8,551,000	1.25	12.50	27.50	45.00	80.00
1935 Proof	—	Value: 225				
1936	7,368,000	1.25	3.50	12.00	25.00	45.00
1936 Proof	—	Value: 225				

KM# 19 PENNY

9.6500 g., Copper-Nickel, 30.5 mm. **Ruler:** George VI **Obv:** Crown above center hole, denomination around hole in English, in Arabic beneath **Obv. Leg.:** GEORGIVS VI REX • ET IND: IMP: **Rev:** Hexagram, date beneath **Rev. Leg.:** BRITISH WEST AFRICA **Edge:** Plain

Date	Mintage	F	VF	XF	Unc	BU
1937H	11,999,000	0.50	0.75	1.25	2.00	3.50
1937H Proof	—	Value: 200				
1937KN	11,999,000	0.50	0.75	1.25	2.00	3.50
1937KN Proof	—	Value: 200				
1940	3,840,000	0.50	0.75	1.25	2.00	3.50
1940 Proof	—	—	—	—	—	—
1940H	2,400,000	0.50	0.75	3.00	8.00	14.00
1940KN	2,400,000	0.75	1.50	4.50	10.00	18.00
1941	6,960,000	0.35	0.75	1.25	3.50	6.00
1941 Proof	—	—	—	—	—	—
1942	18,840,000	0.30	0.60	1.00	—	5.00
1943	28,920,000	0.30	0.60*	1.00	3.00	5.00
1943H	7,140,000	2.00	5.00	10.00	20.00	35.00
1944	19,440,000	0.30	0.60	1.00	4.00	7.00
1945	6,072,000	0.45	0.90	1.75	5.00	9.00
1945 Proof	—	Value: 150				
1945H	9,000,000	1.00	2.00	4.50	10.00	18.00
1945KN	9,557,000	0.75	1.50	3.00	7.00	12.00
1946H	10,446,000	0.85	1.75	3.75	8.00	14.00
1946KN	11,976,000	0.30	0.60	1.00	5.00	9.00
1946SA	1,020,000	250	500	750	1,150	—
1947H	12,443,000	0.30	0.60	1.00	5.00	9.00
1947KN	9,829,000	0.30	0.60	1.00	5.00	9.00
1947SA	58,980,000	0.30	0.60	1.00	4.50	7.50

KM# 27a 1/2 PENNY

5.6000 g., Bronze, 25.9 mm. **Obv:** Crown above center hole, denomination around hole in English, in Arabic beneath **Obv. Leg.:** GEORGIVS SEXTVS REX **Rev:** Denomination around hole in English, in Arabic beneath **Rev. Leg.:** BRITISH WEST AFRICA

Date	Mintage	F	VF	XF	Unc	BU
1952	11,332,000	0.25	0.50	2.50	5.50	9.50
1952 Proof	—	Value: 150				
1952H	27,603,000	0.20	0.35	0.75	2.00	3.50
1952KN	4,800,000	0.50	2.00	5.00	10.00	18.00

KM# 2 PENNY

Copper-Nickel, 30.5 mm. **Ruler:** Edward VII **Obv:** Crown above center hole, denomination around hole in English, in Arabic beneath **Obv. Leg.:** EDWARD VII KING & EMPEROR **Rev:** Hexagram, date beneath **Rev. Leg.:** NIGERIA BRITISH WEST AFRICA

Date	Mintage	F	VF	XF	Unc	BU
1907	863,000	2.00	5.00	9.00	20.00	35.00
1908	3,217,000	2.00	4.00	8.00	17.50	30.00
1909	960,000	3.50	9.00	28.00	45.00	80.00
1910	2,520,000	2.75	7.00	12.00	25.00	45.00

KM# 16 PENNY

Copper-Nickel, 30.5 mm. **Ruler:** Edward VIII **Obv:** Crown above center hole, denomination around hole in English, in Arabic beneath **Obv. Leg.:** EDWARDVS VIII REX ET IND: IMP: **Rev:** Hexagram, date beneath **Rev. Leg.:** BRITISH WEST AFRICA **Edge:** Plain

Date	Mintage	F	VF	XF	Unc	BU
1936	7,992,000	0.50	1.00	3.50	7.00	12.50
1936 Proof	—	Value: 250				
1936H	12,600,000	0.35	0.75	1.00	2.25	4.00
1936H Proof	—	Value: 250				
1936KN	12,512,000	0.35	0.75	1.00	2.25	4.00
1936KN Proof	—	Value: 250				

KM# 25 PENNY

Copper-Nickel, 30.5 mm. **Ruler:** George VI **Obv:** Crown above center hole, denomination around hole in English, in Arabic beneath **Obv. Leg.:** GEORGIVS VI REX • ET IND: IMP: **Rev:** Hexagram, date beneath **Rev. Leg.:** BRITISH WEST AFRICA **Note:** Mule, obverse KM#16, reverse KM#19.

Date	Mintage	F	VF	XF	Unc	BU
1945H	—	2,000	3,000	4,000	6,000	

KM# 30 PENNY

Copper-Nickel, 30.5 mm. **Obv:** Crown above center hole, denomination around hole in English, in Arabic beneath **Obv. Leg.:** GEORGIVS SEXTVS REX **Rev:** Hexagram, date beneath **Rev. Leg.:** BRITISH WEST AFRICA

Date	Mintage	F	VF	XF	Unc	BU
1951	1,258,000	7.50	12.50	27.50	45.00	80.00
1951 Proof	—	Value: 250				
1951KN	2,692,000	6.00	10.00	20.00	35.00	60.00

KM# 30a PENNY
Bronze, 30.5 mm. **Obv:** Crown above center hole, denomination around hole in English, in Arabic beneath **Obv. Leg:** GEORGIVS SEXTVS REX **Rev:** Hexagram, date beneath **Rev. Leg.:** BRITISH WEST AFRICA

Date	Mintage	F	VF	XF	Unc	BU
1952	10,542,000	0.75	1.50	3.00	8.50	15.00
1952 Proof	—	Value: 175				
1952H	30,794,000	0.20	0.40	0.60	3.00	5.00
1952KN	45,398,000	0.20	0.40	0.60	3.00	5.00
1952KN Proof	—	Value: 175				

KM# 33 PENNY
Bronze, 30.5 mm. **Ruler:** Elizabeth II **Obv:** Crown above center hole, denomination around hole in English, in Arabic beneath **Obv. Leg.:** QUEEN ELIZABETH THE SECOND **Rev:** Hexagram, date beneath **Rev. Leg.:** BRITISH WEST AFRICA

Date	Mintage	F	VF	XF	Unc	BU
1956H	13,503,000	0.75	1.50	3.50	9.00	16.00
1956KN	13,500,000	0.30	0.60	2.50	8.00	14.00
1957	9,000,000	0.75	1.50	6.00	13.50	25.00
1957 Proof	—	Value: 150				
1957H	5,340,000	1.00	2.50	10.00	20.00	35.00
1957KN	5,600,000	1.00	2.50	8.00	16.00	28.00
1957 N	Inc. above	125	175	250	—	—

Note: Error strike missing the K

Date	Mintage	F	VF	XF	Unc	BU
1958	12,200,000	0.75	1.50	6.00	13.50	25.00
1958 Proof	—	Value: 125				
1958KN	Inc. above	0.75	1.50	5.00	10.00	18.00

KM# 34 PENNY
Bronze, 30.5 mm. **Obv:** Crown above center hole, denomination around hole in English, in Arabic beneath **Obv. Leg.:** GEORGIVS SEXTVS REX **Rev:** Hexagram, date beneath **Rev. Leg.:** BRITISH WEST AFRICA **Note:** Mule, obverse KM#30, reverse KM#33.

Date	Mintage	F	VF	XF	Unc	BU
1956H	—	50.00	100	175	250	—

KM# 10 3 PENCE
1.1438 g., 0.9250 Silver 0.0340 oz. ASW **Ruler:** George V **Obv:** Bust of King George V left **Obv. Leg.:** GEORGIVS D.G.BRITT: OMN:REX F.D.IND:IMP: **Rev:** Denomination in wreath, date beneath **Rev. Leg.:** BRITISH WEST AFRICA

Date	Mintage	F	VF	XF	Unc	BU
1913	240,000	3.50	7.50	45.00	90.00	
1913 Proof	—	Value: 250				
1913H	496,000	2.00	4.00	15.00	30.00	65.00
1914H	1,560,000	1.00	2.00	12.50	25.00	45.00
1915H	270,000	18.00	25.00	60.00	100	—
1916H	820,000	10.00	15.00	35.00	65.00	—
1917H	3,600,000	1.50	2.50	12.50	25.00	45.00
1918H	1,722,000	1.75	3.50	10.00	20.00	35.00
1919H	19,826,000	1.00	2.00	6.00	15.00	25.00
1919H Proof	—	Value: 200				

KM# 10a 3 PENCE
1.1438 g., 0.5000 Silver 0.0184 oz. ASW **Ruler:** George V **Obv:** Bust of George V facing left **Obv. Leg.:** GEORGIVS D.G.BRITT: OMN:REX F.D.IND:IMP: **Rev:** Denomination in wreath, date beneath **Rev. Leg.:** BRITISH WEST AFRICA

Date	Mintage	F	VF	XF	Unc	BU
1920H	3,616,000	25.00	50.00	125	185	—

KM# 10b 3 PENCE
Tin-Brass **Ruler:** George V **Obv:** Bust of George V facing left **Obv. Leg.:** GEORGIVS V D.G.BRITT: OMN:REX F.D.IND:IMP: **Rev:** Denomination in wreath, date beneath **Rev. Leg.:** BRITISH WEST AFRICA

Date	Mintage	F	VF	XF	Unc	BU
1920KN	19,000,000	1.00	5.00	12.50	25.00	45.00
1920KN Proof	—	Value: 75.00				
1920KN Unique	—	—	—	—	—	—

Note: Mint mark on obverse below bust

Date	Mintage	F	VF	XF	Unc	BU
1925	8,800,000	1.50	5.00	20.00	40.00	70.00
1926	1,600,000	.10.00	25.00	50.00	85.00	—
1927	800,000	20.00	40.00	100	200	—
1928	1,760,000	10.00	35.00	70.00	125	—
1928 Proof	—	Value: 175				
1933	2,800,000	2.00	4.50	28.00	50.00	70.00
1933 Proof	—	Value: 200				
1934	6,400,000	1.00	12.50	20.00	35.00	60.00
1934 Proof	—	Value: 200				
1935	11,560,000	1.00	12.50	20.00	35.00	60.00
1935 Proof	—	Value: 200				
1936	17,160,000	1.00	3.50	15.00	28.00	50.00
1936 Proof	—	Value: 200				
1936H	1,000,000	15.00	15.00	55.00	85.00	—
1936H Proof	—	Value: 200				
1936KN	2,037,999	10.00	15.00	35.00	65.00	110

KM# 21 3 PENCE
5.2000 g., Copper-Nickel, 21.45 mm. **Ruler:** George VI **Obv:** Bust of George VI left **Obv. Leg.:** GEORGIVS VI D.G.BRITT: OMN:REX F.D.IND:IMP: **Rev:** Denomination in wreath, date beneath **Rev. Leg.:** BRITISH WEST AFRICA

Date	Mintage	F	VF	XF	Unc	BU
1938H	7,000,000	0.30	0.60	2.50	7.50	12.50
1938H Proof	—	Value: 200				
1938KN	9,056,000	0.35	0.75	2.50	8.00	14.00
1938KN Proof	—	Value: 250				
1939H	16,500,000	0.30	0.60	2.00	9.00	—
1939H Proof	—	Value: 300				
1939KN	15,500,000	0.30	0.60	2.00	8.00	14.00
1939KN Proof	—	Value: 200				
1940H	3,862,000	0.50	1.00	2.50	7.50	13.50
1940KN	10,000,000	0.30	0.60	2.00	5.00	9.00
1941H	5,032,000	0.40	0.85	3.50	9.00	16.00
1943H	5,106,000	0.40	0.85	6.00	15.00	25.00
1943KN	9,502,000	0.40	0.85	3.50	9.00	16.00
1944KN	2,536,000	0.40	0.85	6.50	15.00	25.00
1945H	998,000	3.00	5.00	12.00	20.00	35.00
1945KN	3,000,000	0.40	0.85	5.00	12.50	22.00
1946KN	7,488,000	0.40	0.85	3.50	9.00	16.00
1947H	10,000,000	0.35	0.75	3.50	8.00	14.00
1947KN	11,248,000	0.40	0.85	3.50	8.00	14.00

KM# 35 3 PENCE
Copper-Nickel **Ruler:** Elizabeth II **Obv:** Bust of Queen Elizabeth II facing right **Obv. Leg.:** QUEEN ELIZABETH THE SECOND **Rev:** Denomination in wreath, date beneath **Rev. Leg.:** BRITISH WEST AFRICA

Date	Mintage	F	VF	XF	Unc	BU
1957H	800,000	35.00	60.00	180	300	—

KM# 11 6 PENCE
2.8276 g., 0.9250 Silver 0.0841 oz. ASW **Ruler:** George V **Obv:** Bust of King George V facing left **Obv. Leg.:** GEORGIVS V D.G.BRITT: OMN:REX F.D.IND:IMP: **Rev:** Denomination in wreath, date beneath **Rev. Leg.:** BRITISH WEST AFRICA

Date	Mintage	F	VF	XF	Unc	BU
1913	560,000	3.00	5.00	20.00	35.00	60.00
1913 Proof	—	Value: 350				

Date	Mintage	F	VF	XF	Unc	BU
1913H	400,000	3.00	5.00	20.00	37.50	65.00
1914H	952,000	2.75	5.00	25.00	40.00	70.00
1916H	400,000	5.00	10.00	40.00	60.00	—
1917H	2,400,000	3.00	5.00	20.00	37.50	65.00
1918H	1,160,000	2.00	5.00	20.00	37.50	65.00
1919H	8,676,000	2.00	3.50	11.50	22.00	40.00
1919H Proof	—	Value: 200				

KM# 11a 6 PENCE
2.8276 g., 0.5000 Silver 0.0455 oz. ASW **Ruler:** George V **Obv:** Bust of George V facing left **Obv. Leg.:** GEORGIVS V D.G.BRITT: OMN:REX F.D.IND:IMP: **Rev:** Denomination in wreath, date beneath **Rev. Leg.:** BRITISH WEST AFRICA

Date	Mintage	F	VF	XF	Unc	BU
1920H	2,948,000	12.50	30.00	100	185	—
1920H Proof	—	Value: 275				

KM# 11b 6 PENCE
Tin-Brass **Ruler:** George V **Obv:** Bust of George V facing left **Obv. Leg.:** GEORGIVS V D.G.BRITT: OMN:REX F.D.IND:IMP: **Rev:** Denomination in wreath, date beneath **Rev. Leg.:** BRITISH WEST AFRICA

Date	Mintage	F	VF	XF	Unc	BU
1920KN	12,000,000	1.00	5.00	20.00	37.50	65.00
1920KN Proof	—	Value: 125				
1923H	2,000,000	5.00	22.50	60.00	95.00	—
1924	1,000,000	15.00	30.00	100	165	—
1924H	1,000,000	15.00	30.00	100	165	—
1924KN	1,000,000	15.00	30.00	100	165	—
1925	2,800,000	3.50	7.00	35.00	60.00	100
1928	400,000	25.00	50.00	175	250	—
1928 Proof	—	Value: 200				
1933	1,000,000	20.00	40.00	125	185	—
1933 Proof	—	Value: 225				
1935	4,000,000	5.00	12.50	25.00	50.00	90.00
1935 Proof	—	Value: 225				
1936	10,400,000	7.50	15.00	25.00	50.00	90.00
1936 Proof	—	Value: 225				
1936H	480,000	25.00	50.00	125	200	—
1936H Proof	—	Value: 225				
1936KN	2,696,000	15.00	25.00	35.00	70.00	125
1936KN Proof	—	Value: 225				

KM# 22 6 PENCE
3.4900 g., Nickel-Brass **Ruler:** George VI **Obv:** Bust of King George VI left **Obv. Leg.:** GEORGIVS VI D.G.BRITT: OMN:REX F.D.IND:IMP: **Rev:** Denomination in wreath, date beneath **Rev. Leg.:** BRITISH WEST AFRICA

Date	Mintage	F	VF	XF	Unc	BU
1938	12,114,000	0.50	1.00	2.00	8.00	14.00
1938 Proof	—	Value: 200				
1940	17,829,000	0.75	1.50	3.00	10.00	18.00
1940 Proof	—	Value: 200				
1942	1,600,000	2.50	4.00	10.00	20.00	35.00
1943	10,586,000	0.75	1.75	5.00	11.00	20.00
1944	1,814,000	2.00	3.00	15.00	30.00	55.00
1945	4,000,000	1.00	2.00	12.50	25.00	45.00
1945 Proof	—	Value: 200				
1946	4,000,000	2.50	5.00	25.00	50.00	90.00
1946 Proof	—	Value: 225				
1947	6,120,000	0.50	1.50	5.00	15.00	25.00
1947 Proof	—	Value: 175				

KM# 31 6 PENCE
Nickel-Brass **Ruler:** George VI **Obv:** Bust of King George VI facing left **Obv. Leg.:** GEORGIVS VI DIE GRA. BRITT. OMN: REX FID: DEF: **Rev:** Denomination in wreath, date beneath **Rev. Leg.:** BRITISH WEST AFRICA

Date	Mintage	F	VF	XF	Unc	BU
1952	2,544,000				325	425
1952 Proof	—	Value: 500				

Note: This type was never released into circulation and the majority of the mintage was melted down at Riverside Metal Company in New Jersey; Approximately 167 pieces avoided the furnace and found their way into the numismatic market

KM# 12 SHILLING
5.6552 g., 0.9250 Silver 0.1682 oz. ASW **Ruler:** George V
Obv: Bust of King George V facing left **Obv. Leg.:** GEORGIVS
V D.G.BRITT: OMN:REX F.D.IND:IMP: **Rev:** Palm tree divides
date in circular frame **Rev. Leg.:** BRITISH WEST AFRICA

Date	Mintage	F	VF	XF	Unc	BU
1913	8,800,000	3.50	5.00	12.50	22.50	45.00
1913 Proof	—	Value: 400				
1913H	3,540,000	10.00	20.00	55.00	100	—
1914	3,000,000	3.50	5.00	15.00	35.00	65.00
1914H	11,292,000	3.50	5.00	12.50	30.00	55.00
1915H	254,000	20.00	40.00	100	165	—
1916H	11,838,000	3.75	6.00	18.50	35.00	65.00
1917H	15,018,000	8.75	6.00	18.50	35.00	65.00
1918H	9,486,000	3.75	6.50	20.00	40.00	70.00
1918H Proof	—	Value: 200				
1919	2,000,000	10.00	15.00	30.00	55.00	95.00
1919H	992,000	15.00	30.00	65.00	100	—
1919H Proof	—	Value: 200				
1920	828,000	22.50	40.00	100	165	—

KM# 12a SHILLING
Tin-Brass **Ruler:** George V **Obv:** Bust of George V facing left
Obv. Leg.: GEORGIVS V D.G.BRITT: OMN:REX F.D.IND:IMP:
Rev: Palm tree divides date in circular frame **Rev. Leg.:** BRITISH
WEST AFRICA

Date	Mintage	F	VF	XF	Unc	BU
1920G	16,000	1,000	2,000	2,500	3,000	—
1920KN	38,800,000	1.50	5.00	12.50	32.50	55.00
1920KN Proof	—	Value: 200				
1920KN Unique	—	—	—	—	—	—
Note: Mint mark on obverse below bust						
1922KN	32,324,000	2.00	6.50	35.00	70.00	—
1923H	24,384,000	4.00	7.50	25.00	45.00	80.00
1923KN	5,000,000	8.00	15.00	50.00	90.00	—
1924	17,000,000	2.00	6.50	35.00	60.00	110
1924H	9,567,000	10.00	20.00	70.00	125	—
1924KN	7,000,000	7.50	15.00	45.00	80.00	—
1925	19,800,000	4.00	8.00	22.00	45.00	80.00
1926	19,952,000	2.00	5.00	20.00	40.00	70.00
1927	22,248,000	1.50	4.00	18.50	35.00	60.00
1927 Proof	—	Value: 250				
1928	10,000,000	20.00	35.00	75.00	225	—
1928 Proof	—	Value: 300				
1936	70,200,000	3.00	6.50	18.00	32.50	55.00
1936 Proof	—	Value: 225				
1936H	10,920,000	12.50	22.50	45.00	75.00	—
1936KN	14,962,000	2.00	5.00	25.00	42.50	75.00
1936KN Proof	—	Value: 200				

KM# 23 SHILLING
5.6300 g., Nickel-Brass, 23.5 mm. **Ruler:** George VI **Obv:** Bust
of King George VI left **Obv. Leg.:** GEORGIVS VI D.G.BRITT:
OMN:REX F.D.IND:IMP: **Rev:** Palm tree divides date in circular
frame **Rev. Leg.:** BRITISH WEST AFRICA

Date	Mintage	F	VF	XF	Unc	BU
1938	57,806,000	0.50	1.25	4.50	12.00	20.00
1938 Proof	—	Value: 200				
1939	55,472,000	0.50	1.25	6.50	18.00	30.00
1939 Proof	—	Value: 200				
1940	40,311,000	0.50	1.25	5.50	15.00	25.00
1940 Proof	—	Value: 200				
1942	42,000,000	0.50	1.25	6.50	18.00	30.00
1943	133,600,000	0.50	1.25	5.50	15.00	25.00
1945	8,010,000	1.00	1.50	12.00	25.00	42.00
1945 Proof	—	Value: 200				
1945H	12,864,000	2.00	3.50	18.00	35.00	60.00
1945KN	11,120,000	1.00	2.00	12.00	25.00	42.00
1946	37,350,000	1.00	2.00	18.00	35.00	60.00
1946 Proof	—	Value: 200				
1946H	—	750	1,000	2,000	4,000	—
1947	99,200,000	0.50	1.00	4.50	12.00	20.00
1947 Proof	—	Value: 200				

Date	Mintage	F	VF	XF	Unc	BU
1947H	10,000,000	1.50	3.00	17.50	30.00	50.00
1947KN	10,384,000	0.50	1.00	6.50	16.50	28.00

KM# 28 SHILLING
Tin-Brass **Ruler:** George VI **Obv:** Bust of King George VI facing
left **Obv. Leg.:** GEORGIVS VI DIE GRA. BRITT. OMN: REX FID:
DEF: **Rev:** Palm tree divides date in circular frame
Rev. Leg.: BRITISH WEST AFRICA

Date	Mintage	F	VF	XF	Unc	BU
1949	70,000,000	0.50	2.50	12.00	25.00	42.00
1949 Proof	—	Value: 175				
1949H	10,000,000	1.25	4.00	12.50	27.50	47.50
1949KN	10,016,000	1.25	4.00	12.50	27.50	47.50
1949KN Proof	—	Value: 200				
1951	35,346,000	1.25	5.00	15.00	30.00	50.00
1951 Proof	—	Value: 175				
1951H	10,000,000	1.25	5.00	15.00	30.00	50.00
1951KN	16,832,000	1.25	5.00	15.00	30.00	50.00
1952	98,654,000	0.50	1.00	3.00	9.00	15.00
1952 Proof	—	Value: 200				
1952KN	41,653,000	0.50	1.00	2.00	5.00	10.00
1952H	44,096,000	0.50	1.00	2.00	7.50	12.50
1952KN Proof	—	Value: 175				

KM# 13 2 SHILLINGS
11.3104 g., 0.9250 Silver 0.3364 oz. ASW **Ruler:** George V
Obv: Bust of King George V facing left **Obv. Leg.:** GEORGIVS
V D.G.BRITT: OMN:REX F.D.IND:IMP: **Rev:** Palm tree divides
date in circular frame **Rev. Leg.:** BRITISH WEST AFRICA

Date	Mintage	F	VF	XF	Unc	BU
1913	2,100,000	7.00	10.00	17.50	45.00	80.00
1913 Proof	—	Value: 500				
1913H	1,176,000	8.00	15.00	27.50	55.00	95.00
1914	330,000	15.00	50.00	125	200	—
1914H	637,000	10.00	25.00	45.00	75.00	135
1915H	66,000	25.00	60.00	125	185	—
1916H	9,824,000	7.00	15.00	30.00	60.00	110
1917H	1,059,000	15.00	40.00	100	165	—
1917H Proof	—	Value: 300				
1918H	7,294,000	7.00	12.00	30.00	55.00	95.00
1919	2,000,000	8.00	12.00	50.00	85.00	150
1919H	10,866,000	7.00	10.00	40.00	65.00	115
1919H Proof	—	Value: 200				
1920	683,000	30.00	60.00	175	250	—

KM# 13a 2 SHILLINGS
11.3104 g., 0.5000 Silver 0.1818 oz. ASW **Ruler:** George V
Obv: Bust of George V facing left **Obv. Leg.:** GEORGIVS V
D.G.BRITT: OMN:REX F.D.IND:IMP: **Rev:** Palm tree divides
date in circular frame **Rev. Leg.:** BRITISH WEST AFRICA

Date	Mintage	F	VF	XF	Unc	BU
1920H	1,926,000	30.00	55.00	175	275	—

KM# 13b 2 SHILLINGS
Tin-Brass **Ruler:** George V **Obv:** Bust of George V facing left
Obv. Leg.: GEORGIVS V D.G.BRITT: OMN:REX F.D.IND:IMP:
Rev: Palm tree divides date in circular frame **Rev. Leg.:** BRITISH
WEST AFRICA

Date	Mintage	F	VF	XF	Unc	BU
1920KN	15,856,000	2.50	5.00	20.00	40.00	70.00
1920KN Proof	—	Value: 250				
1922	10,000,000	3.00	9.00	27.50	55.00	95.00
1922KN	5,500,000	6.00	15.00	45.00	75.00	135
1922KN Proof	—	Value: 250				
1923H	12,696,000	4.00	12.00	37.50	65.00	115
1924	1,500,000	8.00	20.00	55.00	90.00	160
1925	3,700,000	4.00	12.00	40.00	70.00	125
1926	11,500,000	4.50	15.00	50.00	80.00	140
1927	11,100,000	6.00	20.00	65.00	100	185
1927 Proof	—	Value: 250				
1928	7,900,000	1,500	2,000	3,000	5,000	—
1928 Proof	—	Value: 3,000				
1936	32,939,999	5.00	12.00	30.00	60.00	100
1936 Proof	—	Value: 250				
1936H	8,703,000	6.00	18.00	45.00	75.00	130
1936KN	8,794,000	8.00	18.00	45.00	75.00	130

KM# 24 2 SHILLINGS
11.3700 g., Nickel-Brass, 28.51 mm. **Ruler:** George VI
Obv: Bust of King George VI left **Obv. Leg.:** GEORGIVS VI
D.G.BRITT: OMN:REX F.D.IND:IMP: **Rev:** Palm tree divides
date in circular frame **Rev. Leg.:** BRITISH WEST AFRICA

Date	Mintage	F	VF	XF	Unc	BU
1938H	32,000,000	1.00	2.00	6.50	15.00	28.00
1938KN	27,852,000	1.00	2.00	6.50	15.00	28.00
Note: Grained edge variety exists, valued at $325						
1939H	5,750,000	2.00	5.00	20.00	35.00	65.00
1939KN	6,250,000	1.00	4.00	16.50	30.00	55.00
1939KN Proof	—	Value: 200				
1942KN	10,000,000	1.25	4.50	17.00	30.00	55.00
1946H	10,500,000	1.25	4.00	12.00	27.50	50.00
1946KN	4,800,000	1.25	7.00	27.00	42.50	80.00
1947H	5,055,000	1.00	6.00	25.00	40.00	75.00
1947KN	4,200,000	1.25	7.00	27.00	42.50	80.00

KM# 29 2 SHILLINGS
Nickel-Brass **Ruler:** George VI **Obv:** Bust of King George VI
facing left **Obv. Leg.:** GEORGIVS VI DIE GRA. BRITT. OMN:
REX FID: DEF: **Rev:** Palm tree divides date in circular frame
Rev. Leg.: BRITISH WEST AFRICA

Date	Mintage	F	VF	XF	Unc	BU
1949H	7,500,000	1.25	7.00	22.00	40.00	75.00
1949KN	7,576,000	1.25	6.00	20.00	35.00	65.00
1951H	6,566,000	1.75	7.00	22.00	40.00	75.00
1951H Proof	—	Value: 250				
1952H	4,410,000	2.00	8.00	22.50	42.00	80.00
1952KN	1,236,000	8.00	20.00	50.00	75.00	145

PATTERNS
Including off metal strikes

KM#	Date	Mintage	Identification	Mkt Val
Pn1	1906	4	1/10 Penny. Aluminum. Crown above center hole, denomination around hole in English, in Arabic beneath. EDWARD VII KING & EMPEROR. Hexagram divides date at bottom. NIGERIA BRITISH WEST AFRICA.	3,000
Pn2	1906	—	Penny. Copper-Nickel. Two varieties known, thick and thin flan.	3,000
Pn3	1920G	—	Shilling. Silver. 6.2700 g.	1,500
PnA4	1920	—	Penny. Brass. #KM9.	1,800
Pn4	1920KN	—	2 Shillings. Silver. Uniface.	250
Pn5	1925	—	Shilling. Nickel-Brass. Bare headed. ROYAL MINT 1925 edge.	2,000
Pn6	1936H	—	Shilling. Nickel-Brass. King's bust, left. Palm tree divides date in circular frame. Security edge. Raised word SPECIMEN in field above date.	600
Pn7	1936KN	—	Shilling. Nickel-Brass. Fine reeded edge. Word SPECIMEN in field above date.	450
Pn8	1936KN	—	Shilling. Nickel-Brass. Security edge. Raised word SPECIMEN in field above date.	550
Pn9	1936KN	—	Shilling. Nickel-Brass. Coarser reeded edge. Without word SPECIMEN.	1,500
PnA6	1936	—	Shilling. Nickel-Brass. Security edge. Raised word SPECIMEN in field above date.	—
PnA10	1937H	—	Penny. Bronze. KM#19.	1,000
Pn10	1938KN	—	2 Shillings. Nickel-Brass. Security edge. Raised word SPECIMEN in field.	800
PnA11	1949KN	—	2 Shillings. Copper Nickel.	140
Pn11	1952KN	—	2 Shillings. Nickel-Brass. Raised word SPECIMEN in field below date.	450
Pn12	ND	—	Shilling. Nickel-Brass. KM#13b. Raised word MODEL.	1,000

TRIAL STRIKES

KM#	Date	Mintage	Identification	Mkt Val
TS1	1952	—	Shilling. Steel. King's head, left. Palm tree divides date within circular frame. Raised word TRIAL vertical in field on both sides.	175
TS2	1952	—	Shilling. Nickel. Raised word TRIAL vertical in field on both sides.	125
TS3	1952	—	Shilling. Steel. Palm tree divides date, raised word TRIAL vertical. King's head, raised word TRIAL horizontal.	185
TS4	1952	—	Shilling. Nickel. Raised word TRIAL vertical. Raised word TRIAL horizontal.	100

SPECIMEN SETS (SS)

KM#	Date	Mintage	Identification	Issue Price	Mkt Val
SS1	1913 (8)	14	KM10-13 Double set	—	1,250
SS2	1913 (4)	200	KM10-13	—	550
SS3	1919H (8)	2	KM10-13 Double set	—	1,500
SS4	1920KN (8)	36	KM10b-11b, 12a, 13b Double set	—	1,150
SSA5	1920KN (4)	4	KM10b-11b, 12a, 13b	—	—
SS5	1928 (4)	—	KM10b-11b, 12a, 13b	—	1,000
SS6	1936H (3)	—	KM14-16	—	450
SS7	1952 (4)	—	KM26a-27a, 30a, 31	—	750

BRUNEI

Negara Brunei Darussalam (State of Brunei), an independent sultanate on the northwest coast of the island of Borneo, has an area of 2,226 sq. mi. (5,765 sq. km.) and a population of *326,000. Capital: Bandar Seri Begawan. Crude oil and rubber are exported.

Magellan was the first European to visit Brunei in 1521. It was a powerful state, ruling over northern Borneo and adjacent islands from the 16th to the 19th century. Brunei became a British protectorate in 1888 and a British dependency in 1905. The Constitution of 1959 restored control over internal affairs to the sultan, while delegating responsibility for defense and foreign affairs to Britain. On January 1, 1984 it became independent and is a member of the Commonwealth of Nations.

TITLES

نكري بروني

Negri Brunei

RULERS
Sultan Hashim Jalal, 1885-1906
British 1906-1950
Sultan Sir Omar Ali Saifuddin III, 1950-1967
Sultan Hassanal Bolkiah I, 1967-

MONETARY SYSTEM
100 Sen = 1 Dollar

SULTANATE

DECIMAL COINAGE
100 Sen = 1 Dollar (Ringgit)

KM# 4 SEN
Bronze **Ruler:** Sultan Sir Omar Ali Saifuddin III **Obv:** Uniformed head left **Rev:** Native design, denomination below, date at right

Date	Mintage	F	VF	XF	Unc	BU
1967	1,000,000	—	0.20	1.00	1.40	2.00

KM# 9 SEN
Bronze **Ruler:** Sultan Hassanal Bolkiah **Obv:** Head right **Rev:** Native design, denomination below, date at right

Date	Mintage	F	VF	XF	Unc	BU
1968	60,000	—	0.30	1.70	3.50	4.00
1970	140,000	—	0.20	0.60	1.00	1.50
1970 Proof	4,000	Value: 4.00				
1971	400,000	—	0.10	0.25	0.80	1.25
1973	120,000	—	0.20	0.80	2.50	3.00
1974	640,000	—	—	0.25	0.80	1.25
1976	140,000	—	—	0.25	0.80	1.25
1977	140,000	—	—	0.25	0.80	1.25

KM# 15 SEN
Bronze **Ruler:** Sultan Hassanal Bolkiah **Obv:** Head right **Rev:** Native design, denomination below, date at right, legend without numeral 'I' in title

Date	Mintage	F	VF	XF	Unc	BU
1977	280,000	—	—	0.25	0.70	1.00
1978	269,000	—	—	0.25	0.70	1.00
1979	250,000	—	0.10	0.50	1.00	1.50
1979 Proof	10,000	Value: 2.00				
1980	260,000	—	—	0.25	0.70	1.00
1981	540,000	—	—	0.25	0.70	1.00
1982	100,000	—	—	2.00	3.00	3.50
1983	500,000	—	—	0.25	0.50	0.75
1984	400,000	—	—	0.25	0.50	0.75

Date	Mintage	F	VF	XF	Unc	BU
1984 Proof	3,000	Value: 2.00				
1985	200,000	—	—	0.20	0.50	0.75
1985 Proof	—	Value: 2.00				
1986	101,000	—	—	—	0.50	0.75
1986 Proof	7,000	Value: 2.00				

KM# 15a SEN
Copper Clad Steel **Ruler:** Sultan Hassanal Bolkiah **Obv:** Head right **Rev:** Native design, denomination below, date at right, legend without numeral 'I' in title

Date	Mintage	F	VF	XF	Unc	BU
1986	102,000	—	—	—	0.40	0.65
1987	390,000	—	—	—	0.40	0.65
1988	500,000	—	—	—	0.40	0.65
1989	601,000	—	—	—	0.40	0.65
1990	680,000	—	—	—	0.40	0.65
1991	680,000	—	—	—	0.40	0.65
1992	887,000	—	—	—	0.40	0.65
1993	948,000	—	—	—	0.40	0.65

KM# 15b SEN
2.9200 g., 0.9250 Silver 0.0868 oz. ASW **Ruler:** Sultan Hassanal Bolkiah **Obv:** Head right **Rev:** Native design, denomination below, date at right, legend without numeral 'I' in title

Date	Mintage	F	VF	XF	Unc	BU
1987 Proof	2,000	Value: 3.00				
1988 Proof	2,000	Value: 3.00				
1989 Proof	2,000	Value: 3.00				
1990 Proof	2,000	Value: 3.00				
1991 Proof	2,000	Value: 3.00				
1992 Proof	2,000	Value: 3.00				
1993 Proof	2,000	Value: 3.00				

KM# 42 SEN
3.1000 g., 0.9250 Silver 0.0922 oz. ASW **Subject:** 25 Years - Currency Board **Obv:** Sultan's portrait **Rev:** Mosque **Edge:** Reeded

Date	Mintage	F	VF	XF	Unc	BU
1992 Proof	2,000	—	—	—	5.00	—

KM# 34a SEN
2.9200 g., 0.9250 Silver 0.0868 oz. ASW, 17.7 mm.
Ruler: Sultan Hassanal Bolkiah **Obv:** Uniformed bust facing **Rev:** Native design denomination below, date at right **Edge:** Plain

Date	Mintage	F	VF	XF	Unc	BU
1993 Proof	—	Value: 4.00				
1994 Proof	—	Value: 4.00				

KM# 34 SEN
1.7500 g., Copper Clad Steel, 17.74 mm. **Ruler:** Sultan Hassanal Bolkiah **Obv:** Uniformed bust facing **Rev:** Native design denomination below, date at right **Edge:** Plain

Date	Mintage	F	VF	XF	Unc	BU
1993	680,000	—	—	0.15	0.40	0.50
1994	1,900,000	—	—	0.15	0.40	0.50
1995	—	—	—	0.15	0.40	0.50
1996	3,044,000	—	—	0.15	0.40	0.50

KM# 54 SEN
Copper Clad Steel **Ruler:** Sultan Hassanal Bolkiah **Subject:** 10 Years of Independence **Obv:** Sultan's portrait **Rev:** National arms

Date	Mintage	F	VF	XF	Unc	BU
ND(1994)	—	—	—	—	1.00	1.50

KM# 54a SEN
3.1000 g., 0.9250 Silver 0.0922 oz. ASW **Ruler:** Sultan Hassanal Bolkiah **Subject:** 10 Years of Independence **Obv:** Sultan's portrait **Rev:** National arms

Date	Mintage	F	VF	XF	Unc	BU
ND(1994) Proof	1,980	Value: 7.00				

KM# 5 5 SEN
Copper-Nickel **Ruler:** Sultan Sir Omar Ali Saifuddin III **Obv:** Uniformed head left **Rev:** Native design, denomination below, date at right

Date	Mintage	F	VF	XF	Unc	BU
1967	1,500,000	—	0.20	1.20	2.00	2.50

KM# 10 5 SEN
Copper-Nickel **Ruler:** Sultan Hassanal Bolkiah **Obv:** Head right **Rev:** Native design, denomination below, date at right

Date	Mintage	F	VF	XF	Unc	BU
1968	320,000	—	0.15	0.75	1.50	2.00
1970	760,000	—	0.15	0.75	1.50	2.00
1970 Proof	4,000	Value: 4.00				
1971	320,000	—	0.15	0.75	1.50	2.00

Date	Mintage	F	VF	XF	Unc	BU
1973	128,000	—	0.25	1.50	2.50	3.00
1974	576,000	—	0.15	0.50	1.25	2.00
1976	384,000	—	0.15	0.75	1.50	2.00
1977	384,000	—	0.15	0.75	1.50	2.00

KM# 16 5 SEN
Copper-Nickel **Ruler:** Sultan Hassanal Bolkiah **Obv:** Head right, legend without numeral 'I' in title **Rev:** Native design denomination below, date at right

Date	Mintage	F	VF	XF	Unc	BU
1977	920,000	—	0.10	0.30	0.60	1.00
1978	640,000	—	0.10	0.30	0.60	1.00
1979	650,000	—	0.15	0.45	0.80	1.25
1979 Proof	10,000	Value: 3.00				
1980	640,000	—	0.10	0.30	0.50	0.75
1981	960,000	—	0.10	0.30	0.50	0.75
1982	240,000	—	0.50	1.25	2.25	3.00
1983	1,280,000	—	—	0.10	0.30	0.50
1984	800,000	—	—	0.10	0.30	0.50
1984 Proof	3,000	Value: 3.00				
1985	800,000	—	—	0.10	0.30	0.50
1985 Proof	—	Value: 3.00				
1986	189,000	—	—	—	0.30	0.50
1986 Proof	7,000	Value: 3.00				
1987	960,000	—	—	—	0.30	0.50
1988	820,000	—	—	—	0.30	0.50
1989	1,504,000	—	—	—	0.30	0.50
1990	1,340,000	—	—	—	0.30	0.50
1991	1,340,000	—	—	—	0.30	0.50
1992	1,900,000	—	—	—	0.30	0.50
1993	1,951,000	—	—	—	0.30	0.50

KM# 16a 5 SEN
1.6500 g., 0.9250 Silver 0.0491 oz. ASW **Ruler:** Sultan Hassanal Bolkiah **Obv:** Head right, legend without numeral "1" in title **Rev:** Native design denomination below, date at right

Date	Mintage	F	VF	XF	Unc	BU
1987 Proof	2,000	Value: 3.00				
1988 Proof	2,000	Value: 3.00				
1989 Proof	2,000	Value: 3.00				
1990 Proof	2,000	Value: 3.00				
1991 Proof	2,000	Value: 3.00				
1992 Proof	2,000	Value: 3.00				
1993 Proof	2,000	Value: 3.00				

KM# 43 5 SEN
1.9000 g., 0.9250 Silver 0.0565 oz. ASW **Subject:** 25 Years - Currency Board **Obv:** Sultan's portrait **Rev:** Mosque **Edge:** Reeded

Date	Mintage	F	VF	XF	Unc	BU
1992 Proof	2,000	Value: 7.00				

KM# 35 5 SEN
1.2500 g., Copper-Nickel, 16.19 mm. **Ruler:** Sultan Hassanal Bolkiah **Obv:** Uniformed bust facing **Rev:** Native design, denomination below, date at right **Edge:** Reeded

Date	Mintage	F	VF	XF	Unc	BU
1993	1,340,000	—	—	0.20	0.50	0.75
1994	2,600,000	—	—	0.20	0.50	0.75
1996	3,571,000	—	—	0.20	0.50	0.75
2000	—	—	—	0.20	0.50	0.75

KM# 35a 5 SEN
1.6500 g., 0.9250 Silver 0.0491 oz. ASW, 16.26 mm.
Ruler: Sultan Hassanal Bolkiah **Obv:** Uniformed bust facing **Rev:** Native design **Edge:** Reeded

Date	Mintage	F	VF	XF	Unc	BU
1993 Proof	—	Value: 4.00				
1994 Proof	—	Value: 4.00				

KM# 55 5 SEN
Copper-Nickel **Ruler:** Sultan Hassanal Bolkiah **Subject:** 10 Years of Independence **Obv:** Sultan's portrait **Rev:** National arms

Date	Mintage	F	VF	XF	Unc	BU
ND(1994)	3,000	—	—	—	1.50	2.00

KM# 55a 5 SEN
1.9000 g., 0.9250 Silver 0.0565 oz. ASW **Ruler:** Sultan Hassanal Bolkiah **Subject:** 10 Years of Independence **Obv:** Sultan's portrait **Rev:** National arms

Date	Mintage	F	VF	XF	Unc	BU
ND(1994) Proof	1,980	Value: 9.00				

KM# 6 10 SEN
2.7700 g., Copper-Nickel **Ruler:** Sultan Sir Omar Ali Saifuddin III **Obv:** Military head left **Rev:** Native design, denomination below, date at right

Date	Mintage	F	VF	XF	Unc	BU
1967	3,510,000	—	0.25	1.00	2.00	3.00

KM# 11   10 SEN
Copper-Nickel

Date	Mintage	F	VF	XF	Unc	BU
1968	580,000	—	0.25	0.75	1.50	2.00
1970	1,360,000	—	0.25	0.75	1.50	2.00
1970 Proof	4,000	Value: 4.00				
1971	420,000	—	0.25	0.75	1.30	2.00
1973	300,000	—	0.25	0.75	1.30	2.00
1974	1,410,000	—	0.15	0.55	1.00	1.50
1976	920,000	—	0.15	0.55	1.00	1.50
1977	920,000	—	0.15	0.55	1.00	1.50

KM# 17   10 SEN
Copper-Nickel **Ruler:** Sultan Hassanal Bolkiah **Obv:** Head right, legend without numeral 'I' in title **Rev:** Native design, denomination below, date at right **Edge:** Reeded

Date	Mintage	F	VF	XF	Unc	BU
1977	1,800,000	—	0.10	0.30	0.80	1.25
1978	1,080,000	—	0.10	0.30	0.80	1.25
1979	2,050,000	—	0.10	0.30	0.80	1.25
1979 Proof	10,000	Value: 4.00				
1980	2,840,000	—	—	0.10	0.40	0.65
1981	976,000	—	—	0.10	0.40	0.65
1983	1,080,000	—	—	0.10	0.40	0.65
1984	1,400,000	—	—	0.10	0.40	0.65
1984 Proof	3,000	Value: 4.25				
1985	1,540,000	—	—	0.10	0.30	0.50
1985 Proof	—	Value: 4.25				
1986	2,181,000	—	—	—	0.30	0.50
1986 Proof	7,000	Value: 4.25				
1987	2,560,000	—	—	—	0.30	0.50
1988	960,000	—	—	—	0.30	0.50
1989	1,000,000	—	—	—	0.30	0.50
1990	1,800,000	—	—	—	0.30	0.50
1991	1,800,000	—	—	—	0.30	0.50
1992	3,839,000	—	—	—	0.30	0.50
1993	3,973,000	—	—	—	0.30	0.50

KM# 17a   10 SEN
3.3500 g., 0.9250 Silver 0.0996 oz. ASW **Ruler:** Sultan Hassanal Bolkiah **Obv:** Head right, legend without numeral 'I' in title **Rev:** Native design, denomination below, date at right

Date	Mintage	F	VF	XF	Unc	BU
1987 Proof	2,000	Value: 6.00				
1988 Proof	2,000	Value: 6.00				
1989 Proof	2,000	Value: 6.00				
1990 Proof	2,000	Value: 6.00				
1991 Proof	2,000	Value: 6.00				
1992 Proof	2,000	Value: 6.00				
1993 Proof	2,000	Value: 6.00				

KM# 44   10 SEN
3.5000 g., 0.9250 Silver 0.1041 oz. ASW **Obv:** Sultan's portrait **Rev:** Mosque **Edge:** Reeded

Date	Mintage	F	VF	XF	Unc	BU
1992 Proof	2,000	Value: 10.00				

KM# 36a   10 SEN
3.3500 g., 0.9250 Silver 0.0996 oz. ASW, 19.4 mm. **Ruler:** Sultan Hassanal Bolkiah **Obv:** Uniformed portrait **Rev:** Native design **Edge:** Reeded

Date	Mintage	F	VF	XF	Unc	BU
1993 Proof	—	Value: 6.00				
1994 Proof	—	Value: 6.00				

KM# 36   10 SEN
2.8200 g., Copper-Nickel, 19.41 mm. **Ruler:** Sultan Hassanal Bolkiah **Obv:** Uniformed bust facing **Rev:** Native design, denomination below, date at right **Edge:** Reeded

Date	Mintage	F	VF	XF	Unc	BU
1993	1,800,000	—	—	0.25	0.60	0.80
1994	2,200,000	—	—	0.25	0.60	0.80
1996	3,618,000	—	—	0.25	0.60	0.80

KM# 56   10 SEN
Copper-Nickel **Subject:** 10 Years of Independence **Obv:** Sultan's portrait **Rev:** National arms

Date	Mintage	F	VF	XF	Unc	BU
ND(1994)	3,000	—	—	—	2.00	3.00

KM# 56a   10 SEN
3.5000 g., 0.9250 Silver 0.1041 oz. ASW **Subject:** 10 Years of Independence **Obv:** Sultan's portrait **Rev:** National arms

Date	Mintage	F	VF	XF	Unc	BU
ND(1994) Proof	1,980	Value: 12.00				

KM# 7   20 SEN
Copper-Lead Alloy **Ruler:** Sultan Sir Omar Ali Saifuddin III **Obv:** Uniformed head left **Rev:** Native design, denomination below, date at right

Date	Mintage	F	VF	XF	Unc	BU
1967	2,130,000	—	0.35	1.50	4.00	6.00

KM# 12   20 SEN
5.6500 g., Copper-Nickel, 23.62 mm. **Ruler:** Sultan Hassanal Bolkiah **Obv:** Head right **Rev:** Native design, denomination below, date at right

Date	Mintage	F	VF	XF	Unc	BU
1968	510,000	—	0.20	1.00	3.00	3.50
1970	850,000	—	0.15	0.85	3.00	3.50
1970 Proof	4,000	Value: 4.00				
1971	450,000	—	0.20	1.00	2.00	2.50
1973	450,000	—	0.20	2.00	4.00	4.50
1974	700,000	—	0.15	1.00	2.00	2.50
1976	640,000	—	0.15	1.00	2.00	2.50
1977	640,000	—	0.15	1.00	2.00	2.50

KM# 18   20 SEN
5.4400 g., Copper-Nickel, 23.58 mm. **Ruler:** Sultan Hassanal Bolkiah **Obv:** Head right, legend without numeral 'I' in title **Rev:** Native design, denomination below, date at right

Date	Mintage	F	VF	XF	Unc	BU
1977	1,200,000	—	0.15	0.65	2.00	2.50
1978	720,000	—	0.20	0.75	2.00	2.50
1979	1,060,000	—	0.20	0.75	2.00	2.50
1979 Proof	10,000	Value: 4.50				
1980	1,540,000	—	0.15	0.65	2.00	2.50
1981	2,140,000	—	0.10	0.60	2.00	2.50
1982	120,000	—	2.00	6.00	12.00	15.00
1983	1,350,000	—	0.10	0.35	1.00	1.50
1984	750,000	—	0.10	0.35	1.00	1.50
1984 Proof	3,000	Value: 4.75				
1985	1,000,000	—	—	0.10	0.35	1.00	1.50
1985 Proof	—	Value: 4.75				
1986	2,639,000	—	—	—	1.00	1.50
1986 Proof	7,000	Value: 4.75				
1987	2,400,000	—	—	—	1.00	1.50
1988	560,000	—	—	—	1.00	1.50
1989	500,000	—	—	—	1.00	1.50
1990	720,000	—	—	—	1.00	1.50
1991	725,000	—	—	—	1.00	1.50
1992	2,432,000	—	—	—	1.00	1.50
1993	2,521,000	—	—	—	1.00	1.50

KM# 18a   20 SEN
6.5100 g., 0.9250 Silver 0.1936 oz. ASW **Ruler:** Sultan Hassanal Bolkiah **Obv:** Head right, legend without numeral 'I' in title **Rev:** Native design, denomination below, date at right

Date	Mintage	F	VF	XF	Unc	BU
1987 Proof	2,000	Value: 10.00				
1988 Proof	2,000	Value: 10.00				
1989 Proof	2,000	Value: 10.00				
1990 Proof	2,000	Value: 10.00				
1991 Proof	2,000	Value: 10.00				
1992 Proof	2,000	Value: 10.00				
1993 Proof	2,000	Value: 10.00				

KM# 45   20 SEN
6.7000 g., 0.9250 Silver 0.1992 oz. ASW **Subject:** 25 Years - Currency Board **Obv:** Sultan's portrait **Rev:** Mosque **Edge:** Reeded

Date	Mintage	F	VF	XF	Unc	BU
1992 Proof	2,000	Value: 12.00				

KM# 37a   20 SEN
6.5100 g., 0.9250 Silver 0.1936 oz. ASW, 23.5 mm. **Ruler:** Sultan Hassanal Bolkiah **Obv:** Uniformed portrait **Rev:** Native design **Edge:** Reeded

Date	Mintage	F	VF	XF	Unc	BU
1993 Proof	—	Value: 10.00				
1994 Proof	—	Value: 10.00				

KM# 37   20 SEN
5.6700 g., Copper-Nickel, 23.62 mm. **Ruler:** Sultan Hassanal Bolkiah **Obv:** Uniformed bust facing **Rev:** Native design, denomination below, date at right **Edge:** Reeded

Date	Mintage	F	VF	XF	Unc	BU
1993	720,000	—	—	0.45	1.10	1.50
1994	2,000,000	—	—	0.45	1.10	1.50
1996	2,767,000	—	—	0.45	1.10	1.50
2000		—	—	0.45	1.10	1.50

KM# 57   20 SEN
Copper-Nickel **Subject:** 10 Years of Independence **Obv:** Sultan's portrait **Rev:** National arms

Date	Mintage	F	VF	XF	Unc	BU
ND(1994)	3,000	—	—	—	2.50	3.50

KM# 57a   20 SEN
6.7000 g., 0.9250 Silver 0.1992 oz. ASW **Subject:** 10 Years of Independence **Obv:** Sultan's portrait **Rev:** National arms

Date	Mintage	F	VF	XF	Unc	BU
ND(1994) Proof	1,980	Value: 15.00				

KM# 8   50 SEN
Copper-Nickel **Ruler:** Sultan Sir Omar Ali Saifuddin III **Obv:** Uniformed head left within circle **Rev:** National arms, denomination below, date at right

Date	Mintage	F	VF	XF	Unc	BU
1967	788,000	—	0.75	2.00	5.00	7.00

KM# 13   50 SEN
Copper-Nickel **Ruler:** Sultan Hassanal Bolkiah **Obv:** Head right **Rev:** National arms within circle, denomination below, date at right

Date	Mintage	F	VF	XF	Unc	BU
1968	212,000	—	0.50	2.00	3.00	3.50
1970	300,000	—	0.50	2.00	3.00	3.50
1970 Proof	4,000	Value: 6.50				
1971	320,000	—	0.45	2.00	3.00	3.50
1973	140,000	—	2.00	4.00	6.00	8.00
1974	244,000	—	0.45	2.00	3.00	3.50
1976	240,000	—	0.45	2.00	3.00	3.50
1977	240,000	—	0.45	2.00	3.00	3.50

KM# 19   50 SEN
Copper-Nickel **Ruler:** Sultan Hassanal Bolkiah **Obv:** Head right, legend without numeral 'I' in title **Rev:** National arms within circle, denomination below, date at right

Date	Mintage	F	VF	XF	Unc	BU
1977	499,000	—	0.30	1.10	2.00	2.50
1978	264,000	—	0.30	1.10	2.00	2.50
1979	730,000	—	0.30	1.10	2.00	2.50
1979 Proof	10,000	Value: 6.50				
1980	536,000	—	0.30	1.00	2.00	2.50
1981	960,000	—	0.30	1.00	1.50	2.00
1982	136,000	—	2.00	5.00	12.00	14.00
1983	408,000	—	0.30	0.80	1.50	2.00
1984	320,000	—	0.30	0.80	1.50	2.00
1984 Proof	3,000	Value: 6.75				
1985	450,000	—	0.30	0.80	1.50	2.00
1985 Proof	—	—	—	—	—	—
1986	1,067,000	—	—	—	1.50	2.00

Date	Mintage	F	VF	XF	Unc	BU
1986 Proof	7,000	Value: 6.75				
1987	1,120,000	—	—	—	1.50	2.00
1988	250,000	—	—	—	1.50	2.00
1989	500,000	—	—	—	1.50	2.00
1990	472,000	—	—	—	1.50	2.00
1991	508,000	—	—	—	1.50	2.00
1992	1,072,000	—	—	—	1.50	2.00
1993	1,102,000	—	—	—	1.50	2.00

KM# 19a 50 SEN
10.8200 g., 0.9250 Silver 0.3218 oz. ASW **Ruler:** Sultan Hassanal Bolkiah **Obv:** Head right, legend without numeral 'I' in title **Rev:** National arms within circle, denomination below, date at right

Date	Mintage	F	VF	XF	Unc	BU
1987 Proof	2,000	Value: 15.00				
1988 Proof	2,000	Value: 15.00				
1989 Proof	2,000	Value: 15.00				
1990 Proof	2,000	Value: 15.00				
1991 Proof	2,000	Value: 15.00				
1992 Proof	2,000	Value: 15.00				
1993 Proof	2,000	Value: 15.00				

KM# 46 50 SEN
11.1000 g., 0.9250 Silver 0.3301 oz. ASW **Subject:** 25 Years - Currency Board **Obv:** Sultan's portrait **Rev:** Mosque

Date	Mintage	F	VF	XF	Unc	BU
1992 Proof	2,000	Value: 20.00				

KM# 38 50 SEN
9.3000 g., Copper-Nickel, 27.75 mm. **Ruler:** Sultan Hassanal Bolkiah **Obv:** Uniformed bust facing **Rev:** National arms within circle, denomination below, date at right **Edge:** Reeded and security edge

Date	Mintage	F	VF	XF	Unc	BU
1993	472,000	—	—	0.60	1.50	2.00
1994	600,000	—	—	0.60	1.50	2.00
1996	458,000	—	—	0.60	1.50	2.00

KM# 38a 50 SEN
10.8200 g., 0.9250 Silver 0.3218 oz. ASW, 27.7 mm. **Ruler:** Sultan Hassanal Bolkiah **Obv:** Uniformed bust facing **Rev:** National arms within circle, denomination below, date at right **Edge:** Reeded

Date	Mintage	F	VF	XF	Unc	BU
1993 Proof	—	Value: 15.00				
1994 Proof	—	Value: 15.00				

KM# 58 50 SEN
Copper-Nickel **Subject:** 10 Years of Independence **Obv:** Sultan's portrait **Rev:** National arms

Date	Mintage	F	VF	XF	Unc	BU
ND(1994)	3,000	—	—	—	4.50	6.00

KM# 58a 50 SEN
11.1000 g., 0.9250 Silver 0.3301 oz. ASW **Subject:** 10 Years of Independence **Obv:** Sultan's portrait **Rev:** National arms

Date	Mintage	F	VF	XF	Unc	BU
ND(1994) Proof	1,980	Value: 20.00				

KM# 64 50 SEN
Copper-Nickel **Subject:** Sultan's 50th Birthday **Obv:** Sultan's portrait **Rev:** Waterfront building

Date	Mintage	F	VF	XF	Unc	BU
ND(1996) Proof	500	Value: 25.00				

KM# 14 DOLLAR
Copper-Nickel **Ruler:** Sultan Hassanal Bolkiah **Obv:** Head right **Rev:** Antique cannon, date above, denomination below

Date	Mintage	F	VF	XF	Unc	BU
1970 Proof	5,000	Value: 80.00				

KM# 20 DOLLAR
Copper-Nickel **Obv:** Legend without numeral 'I' in title

Date	Mintage	F	VF	XF	Unc	BU
1979 Proof	10,000	Value: 20.00				
1984	5,000	—	—	—	10.00	12.00
1984 Proof	3,000	Value: 22.00				
1985	15,000	—	—	—	8.00	10.00
1985 Proof	10,000	Value: 20.00				
1986	10,000	—	—	—	8.00	10.00
1986 Proof	7,000	Value: 22.00				

Date	Mintage	F	VF	XF	Unc	BU
1987	2,000	—	—	—	10.00	12.50
1988	2,000	—	—	—	10.00	12.50
1989	2,000	—	—	—	10.00	12.50
1990	3,000	—	—	—	10.00	12.50
1991	3,000	—	—	—	10.00	12.50
1992	—	—	—	—	10.00	12.50

KM# 20a DOLLAR
18.0500 g., 0.9250 Silver 0.5368 oz. ASW **Obv:** Legend without numeral 'I' in title

Date	Mintage	F	VF	XF	Unc	BU
1987 Proof	2,000	Value: 40.00				
1988 Proof	2,000	Value: 40.00				
1989 Proof	2,000	Value: 40.00				
1990 Proof	2,000	Value: 40.00				
1991 Proof	2,000	Value: 40.00				
1992 Proof	2,000	Value: 40.00				
1993 Proof	2,000	Value: 40.00				

KM# 47 DOLLAR
18.2000 g., 0.9250 Silver 0.5412 oz. ASW **Ruler:** Sultan Hassanal Bolkiah **Subject:** 25th Anniversary of Brunei Currency Board **Obv:** Sultan Hassanal Bolkiah **Rev:** Mosque

Date	Mintage	F	VF	XF	Unc	BU
1992 Proof	2,000	Value: 40.00				

KM# 47a DOLLAR
0.9170 Gold **Ruler:** Sultan Hassanal Bolkiah **Subject:** 25th Anniversary of Brunei Currency Board **Obv:** Sultan Hassanal Bolkiah **Rev:** Mosque

Date	Mintage	F	VF	XF	Unc	BU
1992 Proof	1,000	Value: 550				

KM# 76 DOLLAR
16.8000 g., Copper-Nickel, 33.3 mm. **Ruler:** Sultan Hassanal Bolkiah **Obv:** Uniformed bust facing **Rev:** Antique cannon **Edge:** Reeded

Date	Mintage	F	VF	XF	Unc	BU
1993	—	—	—	—	10.00	12.50

KM# 76a DOLLAR
18.0500 g., 0.9250 Silver 0.5368 oz. ASW, 33.3 mm. **Ruler:** Sultan Hassanal Bolkiah **Obv:** Uniformed bust facing **Rev:** Antique cannon **Edge:** Reeded

Date	Mintage	F	VF	XF	Unc	BU
1993 Proof	2,000	Value: 40.00				

KM# 59 DOLLAR
Copper-Nickel **Subject:** 10 Years of Independence **Obv:** Sultan's portrait **Rev:** National arms

Date	Mintage	F	VF	XF	Unc	BU
ND(1994)	3,000	—	—	—	8.00	10.00

KM# 59a DOLLAR
18.2000 g., 0.9250 Silver 0.5412 oz. ASW **Subject:** 10 Years of Independence **Obv:** Sultan's portrait **Rev:** National arms

Date	Mintage	F	VF	XF	Unc	BU
ND(1994) Proof	1,980	—	—	—	—	—

KM# 71 2 DOLLARS
9.3000 g., Copper-Nickel **Subject:** 20th SEA Games **Obv:** Sultan's multicolor portrait **Rev:** Multicolor logo above stadium **Edge:** Reeded

Date	Mintage	F	VF	XF	Unc	BU
1999 Proof	1,350	Value: 25.00				

KM# 74 2 DOLLARS
9.8000 g., Copper-Nickel, 27.3 mm. **Ruler:** Sultan Hassanal Bolkiah **Subject:** APEC **Obv:** Multicolor bust of Sultan 3/4 left, facing **Obv. Leg.:** SULTAN HAJI HASSANAL BOLKIAH **Rev:** Multicolor flower and APEC initials above date below world map, denomination at bottom **Rev. Leg.:** ASIA PACIFIC ECONOMIC COOPERATION NEGARA BRUNEI DARUSSALAM **Edge:** Reeded

Date	Mintage	F	VF	XF	Unc	BU
2000 Proof	3,000	Value: 50.00				

KM# 68 3 DOLLARS
10.0000 g., Copper-Nickel **Subject:** 30 Years ASEAN **Obv:** Sultan's portrait **Rev:** Map and sailboat **Edge:** Reeded

Date	Mintage	F	VF	XF	Unc	BU
1997 Proof	750	Value: 35.00				

KM# 23 5 DOLLARS
Copper-Nickel **Ruler:** Sultan Hassanal Bolkiah **Subject:** Year of Hejira 1400 **Obv:** Head right, legend without numeral 'I' in title **Rev:** Denomination below design

Date	Mintage	F	VF	XF	Unc	BU
AH1400 (1980)	10,000	—	5.00	15.00	30.00	35.00

KM# 48 5 DOLLARS
0.9170 Gold **Ruler:** Sultan Hassanal Bolkiah **Subject:** 25th Anniversary of Brunei Currency Board **Obv:** Sultan Hassanal Bolkiah **Rev:** Mosque

Date	Mintage	F	VF	XF	Unc	BU
1992 Proof	1,000	Value: 600				

KM# 60 5 DOLLARS
Copper-Nickel **Subject:** 10 Years of Independence **Obv:** Sultan's portrait **Rev:** National arms

Date	Mintage	F	VF	XF	Unc	BU
ND(1994)	3,000	—	—	—	16.00	18.00

KM# 60a 5 DOLLARS
28.2800 g., 0.9250 Silver 0.8410 oz. ASW **Subject:** 10 Years of Independence **Obv:** Sultan's portrait **Rev:** National arms

Date	Mintage	F	VF	XF	Unc	BU
ND(1994) Proof	1,980	Value: 35.00				

KM# 21 10 DOLLARS
28.2800 g., 0.9250 Silver 0.8410 oz. ASW **Ruler:** Sultan Hassanal Bolkiah **Subject:** 10th Anniversary of Brunei Currency Board **Obv:** Head right, legend without numeral 'I' in title **Rev:** Mosque above denomination

Date	Mintage	F	VF	XF	Unc	BU
1977 Proof	10,000	Value: 100				

KM# 26 10 DOLLARS
Copper-Nickel **Ruler:** Sultan Hassanal Bolkiah **Subject:** Independence Day **Obv:** Uniformed bust 3/4 right **Rev:** Building within circle, denomination below

Date	Mintage	F	VF	XF	Unc	BU
1984	15,000	—	—	—	25.00	30.00
1984 Proof	5,000	Value: 50.00				

KM# 49 10 DOLLARS
0.9170 Gold **Ruler:** Sultan Hassanal Bolkiah **Subject:** 25th Anniversary of Brunei Currency Board **Obv:** Bust right **Rev:** Mosque

Date	Mintage	F	VF	XF	Unc	BU
1992 Proof	1,000	Value: 600				

KM# 61a 10 DOLLARS
30.7000 g., 0.9250 Silver 0.9130 oz. ASW **Subject:** 10 Years of Independence **Obv:** Sultan's portrait **Rev:** National arms

Date	Mintage	F	VF	XF	Unc	BU
ND(1994)	2,500	—	—	—	40.00	45.00
ND(1994) Proof	2,480	Value: 60.00				

KM# 61 10 DOLLARS
Copper-Nickel **Subject:** 10 Years of Independence **Obv:** Sultan's portrait **Rev:** National arms

Date	Mintage	F	VF	XF	Unc	BU
ND	3,000	—	—	—	18.00	20.00

KM# 32   20 DOLLARS
28.2800 g., 0.9250 Silver 0.8410 oz. ASW **Ruler:** Sultan
Hassanal Bolkiah **Subject:** 20th Anniversary of Brunei Currency
Board **Obv:** Uniformed bust 3/4 right **Rev:** Mosque above
denomination

Date	Mintage	F	VF	XF	Unc	BU
1987 Proof	3,000	Value: 70.00				

KM# 29   20 DOLLARS
28.2800 g., 0.9250 Silver 0.8410 oz. ASW **Ruler:** Sultan
Hassanal Bolkiah **Subject:** 20th Anniversary of Coronation **Obv:**
Uniformed bust 3/4 right **Rev:** Arms within wreath divides dates
at top, denomination below wreath

Date	Mintage	F	VF	XF	Unc	BU
ND(1988)	5,000	—	—	—	30.00	35.00
ND(1988) Proof	1,000	Value: 85.00				

KM# 72   20 DOLLARS
62.2000 g., 0.9990 Silver 1.9977 oz. ASW **Subject:** 20th SEA
Games **Obv:** Sultan's multicolor portrait **Rev:** Multicolor logo
above stadium **Edge:** Reeded

Date	Mintage	F	VF	XF	Unc	BU
1999 Proof	500	Value: 150				

KM# 79   20 DOLLARS
62.2000 g., 0.9990 Silver 1.9977 oz. ASW **Ruler:** Sultan
Hassanal Bolkiah **Subject:** APEC **Obv:** Multicolor flower at left,
bust of Sultan 3/4 left, facing at right **Obv. Leg.:** Sultan Haji
Hassanal Bolkiah **Rev:** Eliptical globe at center **Rev. Leg.:** ASIA
PACIFIC ECONOMIC COOPERATION

Date	Mintage	F	VF	XF	Unc	BU
2000 Proof	400	Value: 220				

KM# 39   25 DOLLARS
Copper-Nickel **Subject:** 25th Anniversary of Accession

Date	Mintage	F	VF	XF	Unc	BU
ND(1992) Proof	7,500	Value: 50.00				

KM# 39a   25 DOLLARS
0.9170 Gold **Subject:** 25th Anniversary of Accession

Date	Mintage	F	VF	XF	Unc	BU
ND(1992) Proof	—	Value: 900				

KM# 50a   25 DOLLARS
Gold **Ruler:** Sultan Hassanal Bolkiah **Subject:** 25th Anniversary
of Brunei Currency Board **Obv:** Sultan Hassanal Bolkiah **Rev:**
Mosque

Date	Mintage	F	VF	XF	Unc	BU
1992 Proof	1,000	—	—	—	—	—

KM# 50   25 DOLLARS
31.1000 g., 0.9250 Silver 0.9249 oz. ASW, 38.7 mm. **Ruler:**
Sultan Hassanal Bolkiah **Subject:** 25th Anniversary of Brunei
Currency Board **Obv:** Sultan Hassanal Bolkiah **Rev:** Mosque

Date	Mintage	F	VF	XF	Unc	BU
1992 Proof	2,000	Value: 75.00				

KM# 70   30 DOLLARS
31.1000 g., 0.9170 Gold 0.9169 oz. AGW **Subject:** 30 Years -
ASEAN **Obv:** Sultan Hassanal Bolkiah **Rev:** ASEAN logo

Date	Mintage	F	VF	XF	Unc	BU
1997 Proof	300	Value: 950				

KM# 69   30 DOLLARS
62.2070 g., 0.9990 Silver 1.9979 oz. ASW **Ruler:** Sultan
Hassanal Bolkiah **Subject:** 30 Years - ASEAN **Obv:** Sultan
Hassanal Bolkiah **Rev:** Seven multicolor flags

Date	Mintage	F	VF	XF	Unc	BU
1997 Proof	500	Value: 150				

KM# 24   50 DOLLARS
28.2800 g., 0.9250 Silver 0.8410 oz. ASW **Ruler:** Sultan
Hassanal Bolkiah **Subject:** Year of Hejira 1400 **Obv:** Head right,
legend without numeral 'I' in title **Rev:** Design above
denomination

Date	Mintage	F	VF	XF	Unc	BU
AH1400 (1980) Proof	3,000	Value: 145				

KM# 40   50 DOLLARS
30.7000 g., 0.9250 Silver 0.9130 oz. ASW, 42 mm. **Ruler:** Sultan
Hassanal Bolkiah **Subject:** 25th Anniversary of Accession **Obv:**
Sultan Hassanal Bolkiah **Rev:** Royal procession **Edge:** Reeded

Date	Mintage	F	VF	XF	Unc	BU
ND(1992) Proof	3,500	Value: 140				

KM# 40a   50 DOLLARS
0.9170 Gold **Ruler:** Sultan Hassanal Bolkiah **Subject:** 25th
Anniversary of Accession **Obv:** Sultan Hassanal Bolkiah
Rev: Royal procession

Date	Mintage	F	VF	XF	Unc	BU
ND(1992)	—	—	—	—	—	—

KM# 51   50 DOLLARS
0.9170 Gold **Ruler:** Sultan Hassanal Bolkiah **Subject:** 25th
Anniversary of Brunei Currency Board **Obv:** Sultan Hassanal
Bolkiah **Rev:** Mosque

Date	Mintage	F	VF	XF	Unc	BU
1992 Proof	1,000	Value: 750				

KM# 65   50 DOLLARS
62.2070 g., 0.9990 Silver 1.9979 oz. ASW **Ruler:** Sultan
Hassanal Bolkiah **Subject:** 50th Birthday - Sultan Hassanal
Bolkiah **Obv:** Sultan Hassanal Bolkiah's multicolor portrait
Rev: Buildings on waterfront

Date	Mintage	F	VF	XF	Unc	BU
ND(1996) Proof	1,100	Value: 230				

KM# 66   50 DOLLARS
62.2070 g., 0.9990 Silver 1.9979 oz. ASW **Ruler:** Sultan
Hassanal Bolkiah **Subject:** 50th Birthday - Sultan Hassanal
Bolkiah **Obv:** Sultan Bolkiah arms **Rev:** Building

Date	Mintage	F	VF	XF	Unc	BU
ND(1996) Proof	1,000	Value: 230				

KM# 67   50 DOLLARS
31.1035 g., 0.9170 Gold 0.9170 oz. AGW **Ruler:** Sultan
Hassanal Bolkiah **Subject:** 50th Birthday - Sultan Hassanal
Bolkiah **Obv:** Sultan Hassanal Bolkiah **Rev:** Mosque

Date	Mintage	F	VF	XF	Unc	BU
ND(1996) Proof	500	Value: 950				

KM# 27   100 DOLLARS
28.2800 g., 0.9250 Silver 0.8410 oz. ASW **Ruler:** Sultan
Hassanal Bolkiah **Subject:** Independence Day **Obv:** Uniformed
bust 3/4 right **Rev:** Mosque within circle, denomination below

Date	Mintage	F	VF	XF	Unc	BU
1984	5,000	—	—	—	140	150
1984 Proof	2,000	Value: 185				

KM# 33   100 DOLLARS
13.5000 g., 0.9170 Gold 0.3980 oz. AGW **Ruler:** Sultan
Hassanal Bolkiah **Subject:** 20th Anniversary of Brunei Currency
Board **Obv:** Uniformed bust 3/4 right **Rev:** Mosque above
denomination

Date	Mintage	F	VF	XF	Unc	BU
1987 Proof	1,000	Value: 500				

KM# 30   100 DOLLARS
31.1000 g., 0.9250 Silver 0.9249 oz. ASW **Ruler:** Sultan
Hassanal Bolkiah **Subject:** 20th Anniversary of Coronation
Obv: Uniformed bust 3/4 right **Rev:** Arms within wreath divides
dates at top, denomination below wreath

Date	Mintage	F	VF	XF	Unc	BU
ND(1988) Proof	2,000	Value: 175				

KM# 52   100 DOLLARS
0.9170 Gold **Ruler:** Sultan Hassanal Bolkiah **Subject:** 25th
Anniversary of Brunei Currency Board **Obv:** Sultan Hassanal
Bolkiah **Rev:** Mosque

Date	Mintage	F	VF	XF	Unc	BU
1992 Proof	1,000	Value: 900				

KM# 62   100 DOLLARS
0.9170 White Gold **Ruler:** Sultan Hassanal Bolkiah **Subject:**
10th Year of Independence **Obv:** Sultan Hassanal Bolkiah I **Rev:**
National arms

Date	Mintage	F	VF	XF	Unc	BU
ND(1994)	1,480	—	—	—	750	775
ND(1994) Proof	1,500	Value: 800				

KM# 73   200 DOLLARS
31.1000 g., 0.9170 Gold 0.9169 oz. AGW **Ruler:** Sultan
Hassanal Bolkiah **Subject:** 20th SEA Games **Obv:** Sultan
Hassanal Bolkiah I **Rev:** Multicolor logo above stadium

Date	Mintage	F	VF	XF	Unc	BU
1999 Proof	100	Value: 950				

KM# 53   250 DOLLARS
0.9170 Gold **Ruler:** Sultan Hassanal Bolkiah **Subject:** 25th
Anniversary of Brunei Currency Board **Obv:** Sultan Hassanal
Bolkiah I **Rev:** Mosque

Date	Mintage	F	VF	XF	Unc	BU
1992 Proof	1,000	Value: 950				

KM# 41   500 DOLLARS
50.0000 g., 0.9170 Gold 1.4740 oz. AGW **Ruler:** Sultan
Hassanal Bolkiah **Subject:** 25th Anniversary of Accession
Obv: Sultan's portrait **Rev:** Other portrait

Date	Mintage	F	VF	XF	Unc	BU
MS(1992) Proof	1,500	Value: 1,450				

KM# 25   750 DOLLARS
15.9800 g., 0.9170 Gold 0.4711 oz. AGW **Ruler:** Sultan
Hassanal Bolkiah **Subject:** Year of Hejira 1400 **Obv:** Head right
Rev: Design above denomination

Date	Mintage	F	VF	XF	Unc	BU
AH1400 (1980) Proof	1,000	Value: 650				

KM# 22 1000 DOLLARS
50.0000 g., 0.9170 Gold 1.4740 oz. AGW **Ruler:** Sultan Hassanal Bolkiah **Subject:** 10th Anniversary of Sultan's Coronation **Obv:** Head right **Rev:** Coronation design above denomination, date at right

Date	Mintage	F	VF	XF	Unc	BU
ND(1978) Proof	1,000	Value: 1,650				

KM# 28 1000 DOLLARS
50.0000 g., 0.9170 Gold 1.4740 oz. AGW **Ruler:** Sultan Hassanal Bolkiah **Subject:** Independence Day **Obv:** Bust half right **Rev:** Off-shore oil rig, denomination below

Date	Mintage	F	VF	XF	Unc	BU
1984	4,000				1,350	1,450
1984 Proof	1,000	Value: 1,600				

KM# 31 1000 DOLLARS
50.0000 g., 0.9170 Gold 1.4740 oz. AGW **Ruler:** Sultan Hassanal Bolkiah **Subject:** 20th Anniversary of Coronation **Obv:** Uniformed bust 3/4 right **Rev:** Arms within wreath divide dates at top, denomination below

Date	Mintage	F	VF	XF	Unc	BU
ND(1988) Proof	1,000	Value: 1,600				

KM# 63 1000 DOLLARS
0.9990 Gold **Ruler:** Sultan Hassanal Bolkiah **Subject:** 10 Years of Independence **Obv:** Sultan Hassanal Bolkiah I **Rev:** National arms

Date	Mintage	F	VF	XF	Unc	BU
ND(1994)	500	—	—		1,400	1,500
ND(1994) Proof	480	Value: 1,700				

PROOF SETS

KM#	Date	Mintage	Identification	Issue Price	Mkt Val
PSA1	1970 (5)	—	KM9-13	—	30.00
PS1	1979 (6)	10,000	KM15-20	30.00	90.00
PS2	1984 (6)	3,000	MS15-20	—	80.00
PS3	1984 (3)	500	KM26-28	—	1,500
PS4	1985 (6)	10,000	KM15-20	30.00	80.00
PS5	1986 (6)	5,000	KM15-20	30.00	80.00
PS6	1987 (6)	2,000	KM15b, 16a-20a	52.00	80.00
PS7	1988 (6)	2,000	KM15b, 16a-20a	—	80.00
PS8	1989 (6)	2,000	KM15b, 16a-20a	—	80.00
PS9	1990 (6)	2,000	KM15b, 16a-20a	—	80.00
PS10	1991 (6)	2,000	KM15b, 16a-20a	—	80.00
PS11	1992 (6)	2,000	KM15b, 16a-20a	—	80.00
PS12	1992 (7)	2,000	KM42-47, 50	—	190
PS13	1992 (7)	1,000	KM47a, 48-53	—	3,000
PS14	1993 (6)	2,000	KM15b, 16a-20a	—	80.00
PS15	1994 (8)	1,980	KM54a-61a	—	200
PS16	1996 (4)	500	KM64-67	—	1,075
PS17	1997 (3)	500	KM68-70	—	740
PS18	1999 (3)	350	KM71-73	—	765
PS19	2000 (2)	400	KM#74, 79	—	250

SPECIMEN SETS (SS)

KM#	Date	Mintage	Identification	Issue Price	Mkt Val
MS2	1984 (6)	5,000	KM15-20	—	15.00
MS3	1984 (3)	500	KM26-28	—	1,250
MS4	1985 (6)	15,000	KM15-20	10.00	30.00
MS5	1986 (6)	10,000	KM15-20	10.00	30.00
MS6	1987 (6)	3,000	KM15a, 16-20	15.60	30.00
MS7	1988 (6)	2,000	KM15a, 16-20	15.60	30.00
MS8	1989 (6)	2,000	KM15a, 16-20	—	30.00
MS9	1990 (6)	3,000	KM15a, 16-20	—	30.00
MS10	1991 (6)	3,000	KM15a, 16-20	—	30.00
MS11	1994 (8)	—	KM54-61	—	50.00

BULGARIA

[Map: BOSNIA, SERBIA, MONTENEGRO, MACEDONIA, ROMANIA, Black Sea, GREECE, TURKEY, Adriatic Sea]

The Republic of Bulgaria, formerly the Peoples Republic of Bulgaria, a Balkan country on the Black Sea in southeastern Europe, has an area of 42,855 sq. mi. (110,910 sq. km.) and a population of *8.31 million. Capital: Sofia. Agriculture remains a key component of the economy but industrialization, particularly heavy industry, has been emphasized since the late 1940s. Machinery, tobacco and cigarettes, wines and spirits, clothing and metals are the chief exports.

The area now occupied by Bulgaria was conquered by the Bulgars, an Asiatic tribe, in the 7th century. Bulgarian kingdoms continued to exist on the Bulgarian peninsula until it came under Turkish rule in 1395. In 1878, after nearly 500 years of Turkish rule, Bulgaria was made a principality under Turkish suzerainty. Union seven years later with Eastern Rumelia created a Balkan state with borders approximating those of present-day Bulgaria. A Bulgarian kingdom, fully independent of Turkey, was proclaimed Sept. 22, 1908. During WWI Bulgaria had been aligned with Germany. After the Armistice certain land concessions were given to Greece and Romania. In 1934 King Boris III suspended all political parties and established a dictatorial monarchy. In 1938 the military began rearming through the aide of the Anglo-French loan. As WW II developed, Bulgaria again supported the Germans but protected their Jewish community. Boris died mysteriously in 1943 and Simeon II became King at the age of six. The country was then ruled by a pro-Nazi regency until it was liberated by Soviet forces in 1944.

The monarchy was abolished and Simeon was ousted by plebiscite in 1946 and Bulgaria became a Peoples Republic on the Soviet pattern. After democratic reforms in 1989 the name was changed to the Republic of Bulgaria.

Coinage of the Peoples Republic features a number of politically oriented commemoratives.

RULERS
Ferdinand I, as Prince, 1887-1908
  As King, 1908-1918
Boris III, 1918-1943

MINT MARKS
A - Berlin
(a) Cornucopia & torch - Paris
BP - Budapest
H - Heaton Mint, Birmingham
KB - Kormoczbanya
(p) Poissy - Thunderbolt

MONETARY SYSTEM
100 Stotinki = 1 Lev

PRINCIPALITY
Under Turkish Suzerainty
STANDARD COINAGE

KM# 22.1 STOTINKA
Bronze **Ruler:** Ferdinand I as Prince **Obv:** Crowned arms within circle **Rev:** Denomination above date, within wreath, privy marks and design name below denomination

Date	Mintage	F	VF	XF	Unc	BU
1901	20,000,000	1.25	2.50	8.00	20.00	—

KM# 22.2 STOTINKA
Bronze **Ruler:** Ferdinand I as Prince **Obv:** Crowned arms within circle **Rev:** Denomination above date within wreath, without privy marks and designer name

Date	Mintage	F	VF	XF	Unc	BU
1912	20,000,000	0.75	1.75	6.00	14.00	—

KM# 23.1 2 STOTINKI
2.0100 g., Bronze, 20.14 mm. **Ruler:** Ferdinand I **Obv:** Crowned arms within circle **Rev:** Denomination above date within wreath, privy marks and designer name below denomination

Date	Mintage	F	VF	XF	Unc	BU
1901(a)	40,000,000	1.00	2.00	5.00	12.00	—

KM# 23.2 2 STOTINKI
Bronze **Obv:** Crowned arms within circle **Rev:** Denomination above date within wreath, without privy marks and designer name

Date	Mintage	F	VF	XF	Unc	BU
1912	40,000,000	0.50	1.00	2.00	5.00	—

KM# 24 5 STOTINKI
3.0400 g., Copper-Nickel, 17 mm. **Obv:** Crowned arms within circle **Rev:** Denomination above date within wreath

Date	Mintage	F	VF	XF	Unc	BU
1906	14,000,000	0.20	0.60	2.50	8.00	—
1912	14,000,000	0.20	0.40	1.40	4.50	—
1913	20,000,000	0.20	0.40	1.50	4.00	—
1913 Proof	—	Value: 120				

KM# 24a 5 STOTINKI
Zinc **Obv:** Crowned arms within circle **Rev:** Denomination above date within wreath

Date	Mintage	F	VF	XF	Unc	BU
1917	53,200,000	0.60	1.00	2.50	7.00	—

KM# 25 10 STOTINKI
Copper-Nickel **Obv:** Crowned arms within circle **Rev:** Denomination above date within wreath

Date	Mintage	F	VF	XF	Unc	BU
1906	13,000,000	0.50	1.00	3.00	9.00	—
1912	13,000,000	0.20	0.40	1.75	4.50	—
1912 Proof	—	Value: 110				
1913	20,000,000	0.20	0.40	1.00	2.50	—

KM# 25a 10 STOTINKI
Zinc **Obv:** Crowned arms within circle **Rev:** Denomination above date within wreath

Date	Mintage	F	VF	XF	Unc	BU
1917	59,100,000	0.40	1.00	2.50	6.00	—
1917 Proof	—	Value: 135				

KM# 26 20 STOTINKI
Copper-Nickel **Obv:** Crowned arms within circle
Rev: Denomination above date within wreath

Date	Mintage	F	VF	XF	Unc	BU
1906	10,000,000	0.50	1.50	4.00	12.00	—
1912	10,000,000	0.20	0.50	1.50	5.50	—
1913	5,000,000	0.20	1.00	2.00	6.00	—
1913	—	—				

KM# 26a 20 STOTINKI
3.9000 g., Zinc **Obv:** Crowned arms within circle
Rev: Denomination above date within wreath

Date	Mintage	F	VF	XF	Unc	BU
1917	40,000,000	0.50	1.75	5.00	10.00	—
1917 Proof	—	Value: 130				

KINGDOM
STANDARD COINAGE

KM# 27 50 STOTINKI
2.5000 g., 0.8350 Silver 0.0671 oz. ASW **Obv:** Head right
Rev: Denomination above date within wreath

Date	Mintage	F	VF	XF	Unc	BU
1910	400,000	1.75	4.00	12.00	24.00	—

KM# 30 50 STOTINKI
2.5000 g., 0.8350 Silver 0.0671 oz. ASW, 18.06 mm. **Obv:** Head
left **Rev:** Denomination above date within wreath

Date	Mintage	F	VF	XF	Unc	BU
1912	2,000,000	1.50	3.00	6.00	15.00	—
1913	3,000,000	1.50	2.50	4.00	12.00	—
1916	4,562,000	—	—	275	450	—

Note: Withdrawn from circulation and destroyed possibly
only 100 pieces remain; Beware possible counterfeits

KM# 46 50 STOTINKI
Aluminum-Bronze **Obv:** Crowned arms with supporters
Rev: Denomination above date within wreath

Date	Mintage	F	VF	XF	Unc	BU
1937	60,200,000	0.25	0.50	1.25	4.00	—

KM# 28 LEV
5.0000 g., 0.8350 Silver 0.1342 oz. ASW, 23 mm. **Obv:** Head
right **Rev:** Denomination above date within wreath

Date	Mintage	F	VF	XF	Unc	BU
1910	3,000,000	2.75	4.50	9.00	19.00	—

KM# 31 LEV
5.0000 g., 0.8350 Silver 0.1342 oz. ASW **Obv:** Head left **Rev:**
Denomination above date within wreath

Date	Mintage	F	VF	XF	Unc	BU
1912	2,000,000	2.75	4.00	7.50	16.00	—
1913	3,500,000	2.75	4.00	6.00	19.00	—

Date	Mintage	F	VF	XF	Unc	BU
1916	4,569,000	—	—	600	950	—

Note: Withdrawn from circulation and destroyed possibly
only 50 pieces remain; Beware possible counterfeits

KM# 35 LEV
Aluminum **Obv:** Crowned arms with supporters on ornate shield
Rev: Denomination above date within wreath

Date	Mintage	F	VF	XF	Unc	BU
1923	40,000,000	3.00	7.50	16.00	45.00	—

KM# 37 LEV
2.9900 g., Copper-Nickel, 19.7 mm. **Obv:** Crowned arms with
supporters on ornate shield **Rev:** Denomination above date within
wreath **Edge:** Reeded

Date	Mintage	F	VF	XF	Unc	BU
1925	35,000,000	0.30	0.60	1.50	4.00	—
1925(p)	34,982,000	0.25	0.60	1.50	3.50	—

Note: The Poissy issue bears the thunderbolt mint mark

KM# 37a LEV
Iron **Obv:** Crowned arms with supporters on ornate shield
Rev: Denomination above date within wreath

Date	Mintage	F	VF	XF	Unc	BU
1941	10,000,000	3.00	8.00	20.00	52.00	—

KM# 29 2 LEVA
10.0000 g., 0.8350 Silver 0.2684 oz. ASW **Obv:** Head right
Rev: Denomination above date within wreath

Date	Mintage	F	VF	XF	Unc	BU
1910	400,000	6.00	12.00	22.00	54.00	—

KM# 32 2 LEVA
10.0000 g., 0.8350 Silver 0.2684 oz. ASW **Obv:** Head left
Rev: Denomination above date within wreath

Date	Mintage	F	VF	XF	Unc	BU
1912	1,000,000	5.50	8.00	14.00	24.00	—
1913	500,000	5.50	8.50	16.00	26.00	—
1916	2,286,000	—	—	1,200	2,000	—

Note: Withdrawn from circulation and destroyed possibly
only 30 pieces remain; Beware possible counterfeits

KM# 36 2 LEVA
Aluminum **Obv:** Crowned arms with supporters on ornate shield
Rev: Denomination above date within wreath

Date	Mintage	F	VF	XF	Unc	BU
1923	20,000,000	3.50	8.50	22.00	65.00	—

KM# 38 2 LEVA
4.9700 g., Copper-Nickel, 22.95 mm. **Obv:** Crowned arms with
supporters on ornate shield **Rev:** Denomination above date
within wreath

Date	Mintage	F	VF	XF	Unc	BU
1925	20,000,000	0.60	1.00	2.00	6.00	—

Date	Mintage	F	VF	XF	Unc	BU
1925(p)	20,000,000	0.50	1.00	2.25	5.50	—

Note: The Poissy issue bears the thunderbolt privy mark

KM# 38a 2 LEVA
Iron **Obv:** Crowned arms with supporters on ornate shield
Rev: Denomination above date within wreath

Date	Mintage	F	VF	XF	Unc	BU
1941	15,000,000	0.75	1.50	8.00	20.00	—

KM# 49 2 LEVA
Iron **Obv:** Crowned arms with supporters **Rev:** Denomination
above date within wreath

Date	Mintage	F	VF	XF	Unc	BU
1943	35,000,000	0.75	2.00	14.00	36.00	—

KM# 39 5 LEVA
7.7500 g., Copper-Nickel, 26.13 mm. **Obv:** Denomination above
date within wreath **Rev:** Figure on horseback, animals below

Date	Mintage	F	VF	XF	Unc	BU
1930	20,001,000	0.60	1.50	4.50	12.00	—

KM# 39a 5 LEVA
Iron **Obv:** Denomination above date within wreath **Rev:** Figure
on horseback, animals below

Date	Mintage	F	VF	XF	Unc	BU
1941	15,000,000	1.00	3.00	8.50	26.00	—

KM# 39b 5 LEVA
Nickel Clad Steel **Obv:** Denomination above date within wreath
Rev: Figure on horseback, animals below

Date	Mintage	F	VF	XF	Unc	BU
1943	36,000,000	0.50	1.00	3.50	10.00	—

KM# 40 10 LEVA
Copper-Nickel, 30 mm. **Obv:** Denomination above date within
wreath **Rev:** Figure on horseback, animals below **Edge:** Reeded

Date	Mintage	F	VF	XF	Unc	BU
1930	15,001,000	0.75	2.20	5.00	12.00	—

KM# 40a 10 LEVA
Iron **Obv:** Denomination above date within wreath **Rev:** Figure
on horseback, animals below

Date	Mintage	F	VF	XF	Unc	BU
1941	2,200,000	6.00	12.00	26.00	68.00	—

KM# 40b 10 LEVA
Nickel Clad Steel **Obv:** Denomination above date within wreath
Rev: Figure on horseback, animals below

Date	Mintage	F	VF	XF	Unc	BU
1943	25,000,000	0.60	1.25	3.00	9.00	—

KM# 33 20 LEVA
6.4516 g., 0.9000 Gold 0.1867 oz. AGW, 21 mm.
Subject: Declaration of Independence **Obv:** Head left
Rev: Crowned arms, denomination and date below

Date	Mintage	F	VF	XF	Unc	BU
1912	75,000	BV	165	285	465	—
1912 Proof	Inc. above	Value: 3,000				
1912 Proof; restrike	2,950	Value: 300				

Note: Official restrikes of this type were produced at the
Bulgarian Mint in Sophia from 1967-68 and released
prior to 2002; These pieces can be distinguished by
their thicker more widely spaced edge legends

KM# 41   20 LEVA
4.0000 g., 0.5000 Silver 0.0643 oz. ASW   **Obv:** Head left
Rev: Denomination above date within wreath

Date	Mintage	F	VF	XF	Unc	BU
1930BP	10,016,000	1.50	2.75	5.00	10.00	—

KM# 47   20 LEVA
Copper-Nickel   **Obv:** Head left   **Rev:** Denomination above date within wreath

Date	Mintage	F	VF	XF	Unc	BU
1940A	6,650,000	0.50	1.00	2.50	8.00	—

KM# 42   50 LEVA
10.0000 g., 0.5000 Silver 0.1607 oz. ASW   **Obv:** Head left
Rev: Denomination above date within wreath

Date	Mintage	F	VF	XF	Unc	BU
1930BP	9,028,000	3.50	5.50	12.00	24.00	—

KM# 44   50 LEVA
10.0000 g., 0.5000 Silver 0.1607 oz. ASW   **Obv:** Head left
Rev: Denomination at top, date below, flower at bottom, grain sprigs flank

Date	Mintage	F	VF	XF	Unc	BU
1934	3,001,000	3.50	6.00	11.00	24.00	—
1934 Proof	—	—	—	—	—	—

KM# 48   50 LEVA
10.0000 g., Copper-Nickel   **Obv:** Head left   **Rev:** Denomination above date within wreath

Date	Mintage	F	VF	XF	Unc	BU
1940A	12,340,000	0.75	1.75	3.50	9.50	—

KM# 48a   50 LEVA
9.8700 g., Nickel Clad Steel   **Obv:** Head left **Rev:** Denomination above date within wreath

Date	Mintage	F	VF	XF	Unc	BU
1943A	15,000,000	1.00	2.50	5.00	12.00	—

KM# 34   100 LEVA
32.2580 g., 0.9000 Gold 0.9334 oz. AGW, 35 mm.
Subject: Declaration of Independence **Obv:** Head left
Rev: Crowned arms divide denomination, date below

Date	Mintage	F	VF	XF	Unc	BU
1912	5,000	900	1,000	1,850	3,200	—
1912 Proof	Inc. above	Value: 6,000				
1912 Proof; restrike	1,000	Value: 1,150				

Note: Official restrikes of this type were produced at the Bulgarian Mint in Sophia from 1967-68 and released prior to 2002; These pieces can be distinguished by their thicker more widely spaced edge legends

KM# 43   100 LEVA
20.0000 g., 0.5000 Silver 0.3215 oz. ASW   **Obv:** Head, left
Rev: Denomination above date within wreath

Date	Mintage	F	VF	XF	Unc	BU
1930BP	1,556,000	BV	8.00	14.00	38.00	—

KM# 45   100 LEVA
20.0000 g., 0.5000 Silver 0.3215 oz. ASW   **Obv:** Head left
Rev: Denomination at top, date below, flower at bottom, grain sprigs flank

Date	Mintage	F	VF	XF	Unc	BU
1934	2,506,000	BV	7.00	12.00	18.00	—
1934 Proof	—	—	—	—	—	—
1937	2,207,000	BV	6.75	9.00	16.00	—

PEOPLES REPUBLIC
STANDARD COINAGE

KM# 50   STOTINKA
0.9900 g., Brass, 15.18 mm.   **Obv:** National arms within circle
Rev: Denomination above date at right, grain sprig at left
Edge: Reeded

Date	Mintage	F	VF	XF	Unc	BU
1951	—	—	—	0.10	0.25	—

KM# 59   STOTINKA
1.0300 g., Brass, 15.20 mm.   **Obv:** National arms within circle, date 9 / IX / 1944 on ribbon **Rev:** Denomination above date, grain sprigs flank **Edge:** Reeded

Date	Mintage	F	VF	XF	Unc	BU
1962	—	—	—	0.10	0.25	—
1970	—	—	0.30	0.80	3.00	—

KM# 84   STOTINKA
1.0000 g., Brass, 15.2 mm.   **Obv:** National arms within circle, two dates on ribbon, '681-1944 **Rev:** Denomination above date, grain sprigs flank **Edge:** Reeded **Note:** Reeded and security edge varieties exist.

Date	Mintage	F	VF	XF	Unc	BU
1974	—	—	—	0.10	0.15	—
1979 Proof	2,000	Value: 1.50				
1980 Proof	2,000	Value: 1.50				
1981	137	—	—	—	22.00	—
1988	—	—	—	0.10	0.15	—
1989	—	—	—	0.10	0.15	—
1990	—	—	—	0.10	0.15	—

KM# 111   STOTINKA
Brass   **Subject:** 1300th Anniversary of Bulgaria

Date	Mintage	F	VF	XF	Unc	BU
1981	—	—	0.10	0.20	0.50	—
1981 Proof	—	Value: 2.00				

KM# 60   2 STOTINKI
2.0000 g., Brass, 18.16 mm.   **Obv:** National arms within circle, date 9*IX*1944 on ribbon **Rev:** Denomination above date, grain sprigs flank **Edge:** Reeded

Date	Mintage	F	VF	XF	Unc	BU
1962	—	—	—	0.10	0.25	—

KM# 85   2 STOTINKI
1.9700 g., Brass, 18.1 mm.   **Obv:** National arms within circle, two dates on ribbon, '681-1944 **Rev:** Denomination above date at right, grain sprig at left **Edge:** Plain

Date	Mintage	F	VF	XF	Unc	BU
1974	—	—	—	0.10	0.25	—
1979 Proof	2,000	Value: 2.00				
1980 Proof	2,000	Value: 2.00				
1981 Rare	20	—	—	—	—	—
1988	—	—	—	0.10	0.25	—
1989	—	—	—	0.10	0.25	—
1990	—	—	—	0.10	0.25	—

KM# 112   2 STOTINKI
Brass   **Subject:** 1300th Anniversary of Bulgaria **Obv:** National arms within circle **Rev:** Denomination above date at right, grain sprig at left

Date	Mintage	F	VF	XF	Unc	BU
1981	—	—	0.10	0.20	0.60	—
1981 Proof	—	Value: 2.50				

KM# 51   3 STOTINKI
2.2400 g., Brass, 19.66 mm.   **Obv:** National arms within circle **Rev:** Denomination above date at right, grain sprig at left **Edge:** Reeded

Date	Mintage	F	VF	XF	Unc	BU
1951	—	—	0.10	0.25	0.75	—

KM# 52   5 STOTINKI
2.9700 g., Brass, 22.16 mm.   **Obv:** National arms within circle **Rev:** Denomination above date at right, grain sprig at left **Edge:** Reeded

Date	Mintage	F	VF	XF	Unc	BU
1951	—	0.10	0.15	0.25	0.75	—

KM# 61   5 STOTINKI
Brass   **Obv:** National arms within circle, date 9 • IX • 1944 on ribbon **Rev:** Denomination above date, grain sprigs flank

Date	Mintage	F	VF	XF	Unc	BU
1962	—	0.10	0.20	0.50	—	

KM# 86   5 STOTINKI
3.1000 g., Brass, 22.18 mm.   **Obv:** National arms within circle, two dates on ribbon '681-1944' **Rev:** Denomination above date, grain sprigs flank **Edge:** Reeded

Date	Mintage	F	VF	XF	Unc	BU
1974	—		0.10	0.15	0.25	—
1979 Proof	2,000	Value: 2.00				
1980 Proof	2,000	Value: 2.00				
1988	—			0.15	0.25	—
1989	—			0.15	0.25	—
1990	—			0.15	0.25	—

KM# 113   5 STOTINKI
Brass   **Subject:** 1300th Anniversary of Bulgaria **Obv:** National arms within circle **Rev:** Denomination above date within wreath

Date	Mintage	F	VF	XF	Unc	BU
1981	—		0.10	0.25	0.75	—
1981 Proof	—	Value: 2.50				

KM# 53   10 STOTINKI
1.8000 g., Copper-Nickel, 16.59 mm.   **Obv:** National arms within circle **Rev:** Denomination above date at right, grain sprig at left **Edge:** Reeded

Date	Mintage	F	VF	XF	Unc	BU
1951	—	0.10	0.20	0.40	—	

KM# 62   10 STOTINKI
1.5900 g., Nickel-Brass, 16.11 mm.   **Obv:** National arms within circle, date 9 • IX • 1944 on ribbon **Rev:** Denomination above date within wreath **Edge:** Reeded

Date	Mintage	F	VF	XF	Unc	BU
1962	—	—	0.10	0.20	0.40	—

KM# 87   10 STOTINKI
1.7000 g., Nickel-Brass, 16.10 mm.   **Obv:** National arms within circle, two dates on arms, '681-1944' **Rev:** Denomination above date within wreath **Edge:** Reeded

Date	Mintage	F	VF	XF	Unc	BU
1974	—		0.10	0.15	0.25	—
1979 Proof	2,000	Value: 3.50				
1980 Proof	2,000	Value: 3.50				
1988	—			0.15	0.25	—
1989	—			0.15	0.25	—
1990	—			0.15	0.25	—

KM# 114   10 STOTINKI
Copper-Nickel   **Subject:** 1300th Anniversary of Bulgaria **Obv:** National arms within circle **Rev:** Denomination above date within wreath

Date	Mintage	F	VF	XF	Unc	BU
1981	—		0.20	0.50	1.50	—
1981 Proof	—	Value: 3.50				

KM# 55   20 STOTINKI
2.8000 g., Copper-Nickel, 19.49 mm.   **Obv:** National arms within circle **Rev:** Denomination above date at right, grain sprig at left **Edge:** Reeded

Date	Mintage	F	VF	XF	Unc	BU
1952	—	1.00	2.50	7.50	20.00	—
1954	—	0.10	0.25	0.75	1.50	—

KM# 63   20 STOTINKI
2.8500 g., Nickel-Brass, 19.62 mm.   **Obv:** Date 9 • IX • 1944 on ribbon **Edge:** Reeded

Date	Mintage	F	VF	XF	Unc	BU
1962	—	0.10	0.20	0.30	0.75	—

KM# 88   20 STOTINKI
3.1000 g., Nickel-Brass, 19.59 mm.   **Obv:** National arms within circle, two dates on ribbon, '681-1944' **Rev:** Denomination above date within wreath **Edge:** Reeded

Date	Mintage	F	VF	XF	Unc	BU
1974	—	0.10	0.20	0.30	0.60	—
1979 Proof	2,000	Value: 3.50				
1980 Proof	2,000	Value: 3.50				
1988	—			0.30	0.60	—

Note: Large date (7mm) and small date (5mm) exist

1989	—			0.30	0.60	—
1990	—			0.30	0.60	—

KM# 115   20 STOTINKI
Copper-Nickel   **Subject:** 1300th Anniversary of Bulgaria **Obv:** National arms within circle **Rev:** Denomination above date within wreath

Date	Mintage	F	VF	XF	Unc	BU
1981	—		0.25	0.65	2.00	—
1981 Proof	—	Value: 4.00				

KM# 54   25 STOTINKI
Copper-Nickel   **Obv:** National arms within circle **Rev:** Denomination above date at right, grain sprig at left

Date	Mintage	F	VF	XF	Unc	BU
1951	—	0.10	0.20	0.50	1.20	—

KM# 56   50 STOTINKI
4.0400 g., Copper-Nickel, 22.62 mm.   **Obv:** National arms within circle **Rev:** Denomination above date at right, grain sprig at left

Date	Mintage	F	VF	XF	Unc	BU
1959	—	0.10	0.20	0.40	0.80	—

KM# 64   50 STOTINKI
4.1000 g., Nickel-Brass, 23.22 mm.   **Obv:** National arms within circle, date 9 • IX • 1944 on ribbon **Rev:** Denomination above date within wreath **Edge:** Reeded

Date	Mintage	F	VF	XF	Unc	BU
1962	—	0.10	0.40	0.65	1.00	—

KM# 89   50 STOTINKI
4.2000 g., Nickel-Brass, 23.3 mm.   **Obv:** Two dates on ribbon, '681-1944'

Date	Mintage	F	VF	XF	Unc	BU
1974	—	0.10	0.40	0.65	1.50	—
1979 Proof	2,000	Value: 4.00				
1980 Proof	2,000	Value: 4.00				
1988	—			0.50	1.00	—
1989	—			0.50	1.00	—
1990	—			0.50	1.00	—

KM# 98   50 STOTINKI
Copper-Nickel   **Subject:** University Games at Sofia **Obv:** Runner with torch, left, date at lower left **Rev:** Denomination divides arms and date

Date	Mintage	F	VF	XF	Unc	BU
1977	2,000,000	0.25	0.50	1.00	2.00	—

KM# 116   50 STOTINKI
4.0000 g., Copper-Nickel   **Subject:** 1300th Anniversary of Bulgaria **Obv:** National arms within circle **Rev:** Denomination above date within wreath

Date	Mintage	F	VF	XF	Unc	BU
1981	—	—	0.30	0.60	1.80	—
1981 Proof	—	Value: 4.00				

KM# 57   LEV
Copper-Nickel   **Obv:** National arms within circle, date 9 • IX • 1944 on ribbon **Rev:** Denomination above date within wreath

Date	Mintage	F	VF	XF	Unc	BU
1960	—	0.10	0.25	0.60	1.00	—

KM# 58 LEV
Nickel-Brass **Obv:** National arms within circle
Rev: Denomination above date, grain sprigs flank

Date	Mintage	F	VF	XF	Unc	BU
1962	—	—	0.50	1.20	2.00	—

KM# 74 LEV
7.7000 g., Nickel-Brass, 27 mm. **Subject:** 25th Anniversary of
Socialist Revolution **Obv:** Wide denomination above date, grain
sprigs flanking **Rev:** Monumont to the fighters of the resistance

Date	Mintage	F	VF	XF	Unc	BU
1969	2,410,196	0.35	0.60	1.25	2.75	—

KM# 76 LEV
Nickel-Brass, 27 mm. **Subject:** 90th Anniversary Liberation
From Turks **Obv:** Denomination within wreath, date below
Rev: Equestrian statue of Alexander II, Czar of Russia, dates
flank

Date	Mintage	F	VF	XF	Unc	BU
1969	1,290,373	0.35	0.65	1.75	3.50	—

KM# 90 LEV
Nickel-Brass, 27 mm. **Obv:** Two dates '681-1944' on ribbon

Date	Mintage	F	VF	XF	Unc	BU
1974	—	—	0.50	1.00	2.00	—
1979 Proof	2,000	Value: 6.00				
1980 Proof	2,000	Value: 6.00				
1988	—	—	—	0.75	2.00	—
1989	—	—	—	0.75	2.00	—
1990	—	—	—	0.75	2.00	—

KM# 94 LEV
Bronze, 27 mm. **Subject:** 100th Anniversary of the "April
Uprising" Against the Turks **Obv:** Lion above denomination, date
at left, circle surrounds **Rev:** Weapons above date within circle

Date	Mintage	F	VF	XF	Unc	BU
1976	300,000	0.35	0.60	1.50	3.00	—
1976 Proof	—	Value: 4.00				

KM# 107 LEV
Copper-Nickel, 27 mm. **Subject:** World Cup Soccer Games in
Spain **Obv:** Arms divide date above denomination **Rev:** World
Cup trophy **Edge:** Plain

Date	Mintage	F	VF	XF	Unc	BU
1980	220,000	—	0.60	1.50	3.00	—
1980 Proof	30,000	Value: 4.00				

KM# 117 LEV
Copper-Nickel **Subject:** 1300th Anniversary of Bulgaria
Obv: National arms within circle **Rev:** Denomination above date,
grain sprigs flank

Date	Mintage	F	VF	XF	Unc	BU
1981	—	—	0.50	1.00	2.50	—
1981 Proof	—	—	—	—	—	—

KM# 118 LEV
Copper-Nickel, 27 mm. **Subject:** International Hunting
Exposition **Obv:** Arms above denomination, grain sprigs flank,
date at bottom left **Rev:** Antlered deer head, left, inscription at right

Date	Mintage	F	VF	XF	Unc	BU
1981	250,000	—	0.60	1.50	3.00	—
1981 Proof	50,000	Value: 4.00				

KM# 119 LEV
Copper-Nickel, 31 mm. **Subject:** Russo-Bulgarian Friendship
Obv: Arms above denomination **Rev:** Flags at top, hands grasped
at center, date at bottom **Note:** The same reverse die was used for
both Bulgaria 1 Lev, KM#119 and Russia 1 Rouble, KM#189.

Date	Mintage	F	VF	XF	Unc	BU
1981	220,800	—	0.60	1.50	3.00	—
1981 Proof	50,000	Value: 4.00				

KM# 175 LEV
Copper-Nickel, 27 mm. **Series:** 1980 Winter Olympics
Obv: National arms **Rev:** Hockey player, denomination and date
at bottom **Edge:** Reeded

Date	Mintage	F	VF	XF	Unc	BU
1987	—	—	—	1.50	3.00	—
1987 Proof	300,000	Value: 4.00				

KM# 176 LEV
Copper-Nickel, 27 mm. **Series:** Summer Olympics **Obv:** National
arms **Rev:** Sprinters, denomination and date below **Edge:** Reeded

Date	Mintage	F	VF	XF	Unc	BU
1988	—	—	—	—	3.00	—
1988 Proof	300,000	Value: 4.00				

KM# 65 2 LEVA
8.8889 g., 0.9000 Silver 0.2572 oz. ASW **Subject:** 1100th
Anniversary - Slovanic Alphabet **Obv:** Denomination above
shield **Rev:** St. Cyril and St. Methodias, dates at bottom

Date	Mintage	F	VF	XF	Unc	BU
ND(1963) Proof	10,000	Value: 16.00				

KM# 69 2 LEVA
8.8889 g., 0.9000 Silver 0.2572 oz. ASW **Subject:** 20th
Anniversary Peoples Republic **Obv:** Flag above denomination,
two dates at bottom **Rev:** Head left, two dates below

Date	Mintage	F	VF	XF	Unc	BU
ND(1964) Proof	20,000	Value: 16.00				

KM# 73 2 LEVA
Copper-Nickel, 30 mm. **Subject:** 1050th Anniversary - Death of
Ochridsky, Founder of the First European University
Obv: Denomination between columns **Rev:** Figure divides dates

Date	Mintage	F	VF	XF	Unc	BU
ND(1966)	506,000	—	1.50	2.50	5.00	—

KM# 75 2 LEVA
10.8000 g., Copper-Nickel, 30 mm. **Subject:** 25th Anniversary
of Socialist Revolution, September 9, 1944 **Obv:** Large
denomination between grain sprigs, date at bottom
Rev: Monument to the Soviet Soldiers in Plovdiv

Date	Mintage	F	VF	XF	Unc	BU
1969	1,082,210	—	0.75	2.00	4.00	—

KM# 77 2 LEVA
Copper-Nickel, 30 mm. **Subject:** 90th Anniversary - Liberation
from Turks **Obv:** Denomination within wreath, date below
Rev: The Battle on the Orlovo Enesdo (Eagle's nest) by the
Russian painter Popov, two dates below

Date	Mintage	F	VF	XF	Unc	BU
1969	756,759	—	0.75	2.00	4.00	—

KM# 80   2 LEVA
Nickel-Brass, 30 mm. **Subject:** 150th Anniversary - Birth of Dobri Chintulov **Obv:** Denomination above date **Rev:** Head facing, two dates below

Date	Mintage	F	VF	XF	Unc	BU
1972	100,000	—	1.25	3.00	5.25	—

KM# 95.1   2 LEVA
Copper-Nickel, 30 mm. **Subject:** 100th Anniversary of the "April Uprising" Against the Turks **Obv:** Wreath above denomination, date at left, circle surrounds **Rev:** Figure with cannon, date at left, within circle

Date	Mintage	F	VF	XF	Unc	BU
1976	224,800	—	0.75	1.75	3.50	—
1976 Proof	—	Value: 5.00				

KM# 95.2   2 LEVA
Copper-Nickel, 30 mm. **Obv:** Wreath above denomination, date at left, circle surrounds **Rev:** Figure with cannon, date at left, within circle **Edge:** Lettered

Date	Mintage	F	VF	XF	Unc	BU
1976	138	—	—	—	—	—

KM# 108   2 LEVA
Copper-Nickel, 30 mm. **Subject:** World Cup Soccer Games in Spain **Obv:** Soccer logo **Rev:** National arms within circle divides dates above denomination, grain sprigs flank **Edge:** Plain

Date	Mintage	F	VF	XF	Unc	BU
1980	220,000	—	0.60	1.50	3.25	—
1980 Proof	30,000	Value: 4.50				

KM# 110   2 LEVA
Copper-Nickel, 30 mm. **Subject:** 100th Anniversary - Birth of Yordan Yovkov, Writer **Obv:** Denomination above date **Rev:** Head facing, two dates below **Edge:** Plain

Date	Mintage	F	VF	XF	Unc	BU
1980	200,000	—	1.20	3.00	5.00	—

KM# 120   2 LEVA
Copper-Nickel, 30 mm. **Subject:** International Hunting Exposition **Obv:** National arms above denomination, date bottom left **Rev:** Half figure of hunter with hawk, left

---

Date	Mintage	F	VF	XF	Unc	BU
1981	250,000	—	0.75	2.00	3.50	—
1981 Proof	50,000	Value: 5.00				

KM# 121   2 LEVA
Copper-Nickel, 30 mm. **Subject:** 1300th Anniversary of Nationhood **Obv:** Line divides anniversary years and denomination, circle surrounds **Rev:** Equestrian figure, right, animal below **Edge:** Reeded

Date	Mintage	F	VF	XF	Unc	BU
1981	—	—	—	—	3.00	—
1981 Proof	—	Value: 4.50				

KM# 122   2 LEVA
Copper-Nickel, 30 mm. **Subject:** 1300th Anniversary of Nationhood **Obv:** Wreath divides arms and denomination, date at bottom left **Rev:** Mother and child, radiant sun in background **Edge:** Reeded

Date	Mintage	F	VF	XF	Unc	BU
1981 Proof	—	Value: 4.50				

KM# 123   2 LEVA
Copper-Nickel, 30 mm. **Subject:** 1300th Anniversary of Nationhood **Obv:** Line divides left facing head, date at right and denomination, circle surrounds **Rev:** Dimitrov **Edge:** Reeded

Date	Mintage	F	VF	XF	Unc	BU
1981	—	—	—	—	4.00	—
1981 Proof	—	Value: 5.50				

KM# 124   2 LEVA
Copper-Nickel, 30 mm. **Subject:** 1300th Anniversary of Nationhood **Obv:** Buildings above denomination, date lower right **Rev:** King and saint **Edge:** Reeded

Date	Mintage	F	VF	XF	Unc	BU
1981	—	—	—	—	3.00	—
1981 Proof	—	Value: 4.50				

KM# 125   2 LEVA
Copper-Nickel, 30 mm. **Subject:** 1300th Anniversary of Nationhood **Obv:** Line divides weapons on oak leaf, date at right and denomination within circle **Rev:** Soldier **Edge:** Reeded

---

Date	Mintage	F	VF	XF	Unc	BU
1981	—	—	—	—	3.00	—
1981 Proof	—	Value: 4.50				

KM# 126   2 LEVA
Copper-Nickel, 30 mm. **Subject:** 1300th Anniversary of Nationhood **Obv:** Line divides flower, date at right and denomination within circle **Rev:** Clandestine meeting **Edge:** Reeded

Date	Mintage	F	VF	XF	Unc	BU
1981 Proof	—	Value: 5.00				

KM# 127   2 LEVA
Copper-Nickel, 30 mm. **Subject:** 1300th Anniversary of Nationhood **Obv:** Decorative arms with supporters above denomination, date at left **Rev:** Cyrillic alphabet **Edge:** Reeded

Date	Mintage	F	VF	XF	Unc	BU
1981	—	—	—	—	3.00	—
1981 Proof	—	Value: 4.50				

KM# 128   2 LEVA
Copper-Nickel, 30 mm. **Subject:** 1300th Anniversary of Nationhood **Obv:** Arms within circle, denomination below flanked by symbols, date at lower left **Rev:** Rila Monastary **Edge:** Reeded

Date	Mintage	F	VF	XF	Unc	BU
1981	—	—	—	—	3.00	—
1981 Proof	—	Value: 4.50				

KM# 129   2 LEVA
Copper-Nickel, 30 mm. **Subject:** 1300th Anniversary of Nationhood **Obv:** Line divides weapons on shield flanked by flags, date at right and denomination below **Rev:** Russky monument **Edge:** Reeded

Date	Mintage	F	VF	XF	Unc	BU
1981 Proof	—	Value: 5.00				

KM# 130   2 LEVA
Copper-Nickel, 30 mm. **Subject:** 1300th Anniversary of Nationhood **Obv:** Sevastokratoritza Desislava - Founder of Bojana Church. denomination, date below **Rev:** Bojana church **Edge:** Reeded

Date	Mintage	F	VF	XF	Unc	BU
1981 Proof	300,000	Value: 5.00				

KM# 161   2 LEVA
Copper-Nickel, 30 mm. **Subject:** 1300th Anniversary of
Nationhood - Oboriste Assembly **Obv:** National arms within circle
at top, denomination below flanked by weapons, date at bottom
left **Rev:** Inscription on monument within wreath **Edge:** Reeded

Date	Mintage	F	VF	XF	Unc	BU
1981 Proof	300,000		Value: 5.00			

KM# 162   2 LEVA
Copper-Nickel, 30 mm. **Subject:** 1300th Anniversary of Nationhood
- Uprising of Assen and Peter **Obv:** Building above denomination
and date **Rev:** Soldiers with weapons on horseback **Edge:** Reeded

Date	Mintage	F	VF	XF	Unc	BU
1981 Proof	300,000		Value: 5.00			

KM# 163   2 LEVA
Copper-Nickel, 30 mm. **Subject:** 1300th Anniversary of Nationhood
- 100th Anniversary of Serbo-Bulgarian War **Obv:** Inscription within
wreath above denomination and date **Rev:** Warrior women, facing,
with shields and swords, rampant lion at left **Edge:** Reeded

Date	Mintage	F	VF	XF	Unc	BU
1981 Proof	—		Value: 5.00			

KM# 155   2 LEVA
Copper-Nickel, 30 mm. **Subject:** Soccer **Obv:** National arms
Rev: Outstretched soccer figure, date at right, denomination
below **Edge:** Reeded

Date	Mintage	F	VF	XF	Unc	BU
1986 Proof	100,000		Value: 5.00			

KM# 158   2 LEVA
Copper-Nickel, 30 mm. **Subject:** 13th World Eurythmic
Championships - Varna 1987 **Obv:** Arena below map, denomination
at bottom, date lower left **Rev:** Ribbon Dancer, left **Edge:** Reeded

Date	Mintage	F	VF	XF	Unc	BU
1987 Proof	300,000		Value: 4.00			

KM# 159   2 LEVA
Copper-Nickel, 30 mm. **Series:** Winter Olympics **Obv:** National
arms **Rev:** Skier, denomination and date below **Edge:** Reeded

Date	Mintage	F	VF	XF	Unc	BU
1987	300,000		Value: 5.00			

KM# 165   2 LEVA
Copper-Nickel, 30 mm. **Subject:** 100th Anniversary of Sophia
University **Obv:** University building, denomination and date at
bottom **Rev:** Half figure with open book, two dates over left
shoulder **Edge:** Reeded

Date	Mintage	F	VF	XF	Unc	BU
1988 Proof	—		Value: 5.00			

KM# 166   2 LEVA
Copper-Nickel, 30 mm. **Subject:** Soviet-Bulgarian Space Flight
Obv: Denomination and date within wreath, arms above
Rev: Space flight within diamond **Edge:** Reeded

Date	Mintage	F	VF	XF	Unc	BU
1988 Proof	300,000		Value: 4.00			

KM# 177   2 LEVA
Copper-Nickel, 30 mm. **Series:** Seoul 1988 - 24th Summer
Olympic Games **Obv:** National arms **Rev:** High jumper,
denomination and date below **Edge:** Reeded

Date	Mintage	F	VF	XF	Unc	BU
1988 Proof	300,000		Value: 4.00			

KM# 178   2 LEVA
Copper-Nickel, 30 mm. **Subject:** Sports **Obv:** National arms
above denomination and date **Rev:** Rowers **Edge:** Reeded

Date	Mintage	F	VF	XF	Unc	BU
1989 Proof	300,000		Value: 4.00			

KM# 66   5 LEVA
16.6667 g., 0.9000 Silver 0.4822 oz. ASW **Subject:** 1100th
Anniversary Slavic Alphabet **Obv:** Denomination above shield
Rev: St. Cyril and St. Medhodius standing, two dates below

Date	Mintage	F	VF	XF	Unc	BU
ND(1963) Proof	5,000		Value: 30.00			

KM# 70   5 LEVA
16.6667 g., 0.9000 Silver 0.4822 oz. ASW **Subject:** 20th
Anniversary Peoples Republic, Georgi Dimstrov **Obv:** Flag above
denomination, two dates below **Rev:** Head left, two dates below

Date	Mintage	F	VF	XF	Unc	BU
ND(1964) Proof	10,000		Value: 28.00			

KM# 78   5 LEVA
20.5000 g., 0.9000 Silver 0.5932 oz. ASW **Subject:** 120th
Anniversary - Birth of Ivan Vazov, Poet **Obv:** National above date
and denomination **Rev:** Head right, two dates at bottom

Date	Mintage	F	VF	XF	Unc	BU
1970	370,000	—		12.00	13.50	15.00
1970 Proof	109,700		Value: 17.50			

KM# 79   5 LEVA
20.5000 g., 0.9000 Silver 0.5932 oz. ASW **Subject:** 150th
Anniversary - Birth of Georgi S. Rakovski, Constitution Author
Obv: National arms above date, denomination below **Rev:** Bust
3/4 left, two dates below

Date	Mintage	F	VF	XF	Unc	BU
1971 Prooflike	300,000	—	—	—	13.50	15.00

KM# 81   5 LEVA
20.5000 g., 0.9000 Silver 0.5932 oz. ASW **Subject:** 250th
Anniversary - Birth of Paisi Hilendarski, Historian **Obv:** National
arms above denomination, date at left **Rev:** Figure with open
book looking left, two dates below

Date	Mintage	F	VF	XF	Unc	BU
1972 Proof	200,000		Value: 15.00			

KM# 82   5 LEVA
20.5000 g., 0.9000 Silver 0.5932 oz. ASW **Subject:** Centennial - Death of Vasil Levski, Revolutionary **Obv:** National arms above denomination, date at left **Rev:** Head facing, divides dates

Date	Mintage	F	VF	XF	Unc	BU
1973 Proof	200,000	Value: 15.00				

KM# 83   5 LEVA
20.5000 g., 0.9000 Silver 0.5932 oz. ASW **Subject:** 50th Anniversary - Anti-fascist Uprising of September 9, 1923 **Obv:** National arms, date below **Rev:** Soldiers with flag, date below

Date	Mintage	F	VF	XF	Unc	BU
1973 Proof	200,000	Value: 15.00				

KM# 91   5 LEVA
20.5000 g., 0.9000 Silver 0.5932 oz. ASW **Subject:** 50th Anniversary - Death of Alexander Stamboliiski, Politician **Obv:** National arms, date and denomination below **Rev:** Head left, two dates below

Date	Mintage	F	VF	XF	Unc	BU
1974 Proof	200,000	Value: 15.00				

KM# 92   5 LEVA
20.5000 g., 0.9000 Silver 0.5932 oz. ASW **Subject:** 30th Anniversary - Liberation from Fascism September 9, 1944 **Obv:** National arms above denomination, date at left **Rev:** 2 soldiers and factory, two dates at right

Date	Mintage	F	VF	XF	Unc	BU
1974 Proof	200,000	Value: 13.50				

KM# 96   5 LEVA
20.5000 g., 0.9000 Silver 0.5932 oz. ASW **Subject:** Centennial - Death of Khristo Botev **Obv:** National arms above date and denomination **Rev:** Head 3/4 left, two dates upper right

Date	Mintage	F	VF	XF	Unc	BU
1976 Proof	196,660	Value: 15.00				

KM# 97   5 LEVA
20.5000 g., 0.5000 Silver 0.3295 oz. ASW **Subject:** 100th Anniversary of the "April Uprising" against the Turks **Obv:** Woman with sword divides dates, circle surrounds **Rev:** National arms above denomination, date at left

Date	Mintage	F	VF	XF	Unc	BU
1976 Proof	200,000	Value: 10.00				

KM# 99   5 LEVA
20.5000 g., 0.5000 Silver 0.3295 oz. ASW **Subject:** 150th Anniversary - Birth of Petko Slaveykov, Poet **Obv:** National arms above denomination, date at left **Rev:** Bust 3/4 left, two dates below

Date	Mintage	F	VF	XF	Unc	BU
1977 Proof	200,000	Value: 10.00				

KM# 100   5 LEVA
20.5000 g., 0.5000 Silver 0.3295 oz. ASW **Subject:** 100th Anniversary - Birth of Peio Javoroff, Poet and Actor **Obv:** National arms above denomination, date bottom left **Rev:** Bust left, looking forward, two dates at right

Date	Mintage	F	VF	XF	Unc	BU
1978 Proof	200,000	Value: 10.00				

KM# 101   5 LEVA
20.5000 g., 0.5000 Silver 0.3295 oz. ASW **Subject:** 100th Anniversary - National Library **Obv:** National arms, denomination below **Rev:** Statue in front of library, two dates above

Date	Mintage	F	VF	XF	Unc	BU
ND(1978) Proof	200,000	Value: 10.00				

KM# 103   5 LEVA
20.5000 g., 0.5000 Silver 0.3295 oz. ASW **Subject:** 100th Anniversary - Communication Systems **Obv:** National arms above denomination, date at left **Rev:** Radio tower within soundwaves, horn below divides dates

Date	Mintage	F	VF	XF	Unc	BU
1979	35,000	—	—	—	12.00	13.00
1979 Proof	15,000	Value: 15.00				

KM# 109   5 LEVA
Copper-Nickel, 34 mm. **Subject:** World Cup Soccer Games in Spain **Obv:** National arms divides date above denomination flanked by grain sprigs **Rev:** Soccer players, date at bottom right **Edge:** Plain

Date	Mintage	F	VF	XF	Unc	BU
1980	220,000	—	—	—	5.00	6.00
1980 Proof	30,000	Value: 8.00				

KM# 131   5 LEVA
Copper-Nickel **Subject:** International Hunting Exposition **Obv:** National arms above denomination, date at bottom left **Rev:** Antlered deer head, facing, date between antlers

Date	Mintage	F	VF	XF	Unc	BU
1981	250,000	—	—	—	5.00	5.50
1981 Proof	50,000	Value: 8.00				

KM# 132 5 LEVA
Copper-Nickel **Subject:** 1300th Ann. of Nationhood - Friendship with Hungary **Obv:** National arms above denomination, date below, grain sprigs flank **Rev:** Quill and sword handle divide heads

Date	Mintage	F	VF	XF	Unc	BU
1981	140,000	—	—	—	5.00	6.50
1981 Proof	47,000	Value: 9.00				

KM# 140 5 LEVA
Copper-Nickel **Subject:** 100th Anniversary - Birth of Vladimir Dimitrov **Obv:** Denomination, date below **Rev:** Bust 3/4 left

Date	Mintage	F	VF	XF	Unc	BU
1982 Proof	283,050	Value: 7.50				

KM# 141 5 LEVA
Copper-Nickel, 34 mm. **Subject:** 40th Anniversary - Birth of Lyudmila Zhivkova **Obv:** Arms above denomination, date at lower left **Rev:** Head left, two dates at right

Date	Mintage	F	VF	XF	Unc	BU
1982 Proof	20,000	Value: 8.00				

KM# 142 5 LEVA
Copper-Nickel **Subject:** 2nd International Children's Assembly **Obv:** Assembly logo above denomination, bells encircle outer edge **Rev:** Tower within circle, bells encircle edge

Date	Mintage	F	VF	XF	Unc	BU
1982 Proof	200,000	Value: 5.00				

KM# 151 5 LEVA
Copper-Nickel, 34.5 mm. **Subject:** 3rd International Children's Assembly **Obv:** Assembly logo at top, denomination devides bells below, date lower left, child figures encircle edge **Rev:** Mosaic girl and boy with flowers, child figures encircle edge

Date	Mintage	F	VF	XF	Unc	BU
1985 Proof	100,000	Value: 6.00				

KM# 152 5 LEVA
Copper-Nickel **Subject:** 90th Anniversary of Tourism Movement - Konstantinov **Obv:** National arms above denomination, date lower left **Rev:** Head left within circle, two dates below

Date	Mintage	F	VF	XF	Unc	BU
1985 Proof	100,000	Value: 6.00				

KM# 153 5 LEVA
Copper-Nickel **Subject:** 4th Anniversary of UNESCO **Obv:** National arms above, bigas flank, denomination below, date lower left **Rev:** Logo above building

Date	Mintage	F	VF	XF	Unc	BU
1985 Proof	100,000	Value: 6.00				

KM# 154 5 LEVA
Copper-Nickel **Subject:** Young Inventors' Exposition **Obv:** Rose on globe, denomination and date below **Rev:** Expo design

Date	Mintage	F	VF	XF	Unc	BU
1985 Proof	100,000	Value: 6.00				

KM# 167.1 5 LEVA
Copper-Nickel **Subject:** Chiprovo Uprising **Obv:** National arms, date and denomination below **Rev:** Activists **Edge:** Plain

Date	Mintage	F	VF	XF	Unc	BU
1988 Proof	100,000	Value: 6.00				

KM# 167.2 5 LEVA
Copper-Nickel **Edge:** Reeded

Date	Mintage	F	VF	XF	Unc	BU
1988 Proof	—	Value: 6.00				

KM# 168 5 LEVA
Copper-Nickel **Subject:** 120th Anniversary - Dimitar and Karadzha **Obv:** National arms above denomination and date, oak leaves flank **Rev:** Conjoined busts above dates

Date	Mintage	F	VF	XF	Unc	BU
1988 Proof	100,000	Value: 6.00				

KM# 170 5 LEVA
Copper-Nickel, 34 mm. **Subject:** Childrens' Assembly **Obv:** Denomination and date divides bell and logo within inner circle **Rev:** Child with birds within circle

Date	Mintage	F	VF	XF	Unc	BU
1988 Proof	100,000	Value: 6.00				

KM# 169 5 LEVA
Copper-Nickel **Obv:** National arms above denomination, date to left **Rev:** Bust of Kremikovski facing **Note:** Kremikovski

Date	Mintage	F	VF	XF	Unc	BU
1988 Proof	148,000	Value: 5.50				

KM# 179 5 LEVA
Copper-Nickel **Subject:** 200th Birthday of Aprilov **Obv:** Building above denomination and date **Rev:** Bust 3/4 left, two dates below

Date	Mintage	F	VF	XF	Unc	BU
1989 Proof	100,000	Value: 6.00				

KM# 180 5 LEVA
Copper-Nickel **Subject:** 250th Anniversary - Birth of Vrachanski **Obv:** National arms within wreath, denomination below, date at bottom **Rev:** Half figure facing divides dates

Date	Mintage	F	VF	XF	Unc	BU
1989 Proof	100,000	Value: 6.00				

KM# 67   10 LEVA
8.4444 g., 0.9000 Gold 0.2443 oz. AGW **Subject:** 1100th Anniversary - Slavic Alphabet **Obv:** Denomination above shield **Rev:** Two figures above dates

Date	Mintage	F	VF	XF	Unc	BU
ND(1963) Proof	7,000	Value: 275				

KM# 71   10 LEVA
8.4444 g., 0.9000 Gold 0.2443 oz. AGW **Subject:** 20th Anniversary - Peoples Republic **Obv:** Flag above denomination, two dates below **Rev:** Head of Georgi Dimitrov, left, two dates below

Date	Mintage	F	VF	XF	Unc	BU
ND(1964) Proof	10,000	Value: 275				

KM# 93.1   10 LEVA
29.9500 g., 0.9000 Silver 0.8666 oz. ASW **Subject:** 10th Olympic Congress **Obv:** National arms above date and denomination **Rev:** Old coin above Olympic rings **Edge:** Inscription in Latin

Date	Mintage	F	VF	XF	Unc	BU
1975 Proof	50,000	Value: 20.00				

KM# 93.2   10 LEVA
29.9500 g., 0.9000 Silver 0.8666 oz. ASW **Obv:** National arms above date and denomination **Rev:** Old coin above Olympic rings **Edge:** Inscription in Cyrillic

Date	Mintage	F	VF	XF	Unc	BU
1975 Proof	50,000	Value: 20.00				

KM# 102   10 LEVA
29.8500 g., 0.5000 Silver 0.4798 oz. ASW **Subject:** 100th Anniversary - Liberation from Turks **Obv:** National arms **Rev:** Monument above dates

Date	Mintage	F	VF	XF	Unc	BU
ND(1978) Proof	200,000	Value: 16.00				

KM# 104   10 LEVA
23.3280 g., 0.9250 Silver 0.6937 oz. ASW **Series:** International Year of the Child **Obv:** Arms divide date above denomination **Rev:** Children divide symbols, date below

Date	Mintage	F	VF	XF	Unc	BU
1979 Proof	16,906	Value: 25.00				

KM# 105   10 LEVA
14.0000 g., 0.5000 Silver 0.2250 oz. ASW **Subject:** Bulgarian-Soviet Cosmonaut Flight **Obv:** National arms above denomination and date **Rev:** Cosmonaut flight; space shuttle

Date	Mintage	F	VF	XF	Unc	BU
1979 Proof	35,000	Value: 25.00				

KM# 105a   10 LEVA
23.8500 g., 0.9000 Silver 0.6901 oz. ASW **Obv:** National arms above denomination and date **Rev:** Cosmonaut flight; space shuttle

Date	Mintage	F	VF	XF	Unc	BU
1979 Proof	15,000	Value: 30.00				

KM# 143   10 LEVA
18.8800 g., 0.5000 Silver 0.3035 oz. ASW **Subject:** Soccer Games **Obv:** National arms divide date above denomination **Rev:** Ball and net

Date	Mintage	F	VF	XF	Unc	BU
1982 Proof	7,800	Value: 25.00				

KM# 144   10 LEVA
18.8800 g., 0.5000 Silver 0.3035 oz. ASW **Subject:** Soccer Games **Obv:** National arms within circle divide date, wreathed denomination below **Rev:** Soccer players

Date	Mintage	F	VF	XF	Unc	BU
1982 Proof	7,200	Value: 25.00				

KM# 146   10 LEVA
23.3300 g., 0.9250 Silver 0.6938 oz. ASW **Series:** Winter Olympics **Obv:** National arms above denomination, date at bottom left **Rev:** Downhill skier

Date	Mintage	F	VF	XF	Unc	BU
1984 Proof	8,464	Value: 20.00				

KM# 147   10 LEVA
Copper-Nickel **Subject:** Summer Olympics **Obv:** Arms over value **Rev:** Gymnast executing ribbon dance

Date	Mintage	F	VF	XF	Unc	BU
1984 Proof	2,000	Value: 16.00				

KM# 147a   10 LEVA
23.3300 g., 0.9250 Silver 0.6938 oz. ASW **Subject:** Summer Olympics **Obv:** Arms over value **Rev:** Gymnast executing the ribbon dance event

Date	Mintage	F	VF	XF	Unc	BU
1984 Proof	300	Value: 18.00				

KM# 149   10 LEVA
23.3300 g., 0.9250 Silver 0.6938 oz. ASW **Subject:** International Decade for Women **Obv:** National arms within wreath of roses, denomination and date below **Rev:** Woman carrying baskets of flowers, dates above

Date	Mintage	F	VF	XF	Unc	BU
1984 Proof	5,572	Value: 35.00				

KM# 157   10 LEVA
18.7500 g., 0.6400 Silver 0.3858 oz. ASW **Obv:** Design above denomination, date at left **Rev:** Cosmonauts

Date	Mintage	F	VF	XF	Unc	BU
1985 Proof	7,501	Value: 32.00				

KM# 184   10 LEVA
18.7500 g., 0.6400 Silver 0.3858 oz. ASW **Series:** 1988 Winter Olympics **Obv:** National arms **Rev:** Hockey player, denomination and date below

Date	Mintage	F	VF	XF	Unc	BU
1987 Proof	15,000	Value: 22.00				

KM# 185   10 LEVA
18.7500 g., 0.6400 Silver 0.3858 oz. ASW **Series:** Summer Olympics **Obv:** National arms **Rev:** Sprinters, denomination and date below

Date	Mintage	F	VF	XF	Unc	BU
1988 Proof	22,650	Value: 17.50				

KM# 68   20 LEVA

16.8889 g., 0.9000 Gold 0.4887 oz. AGW **Subject:** 100th Anniversary - Slavic Alphabet **Obv:** Denomination above shield **Rev:** Two figures above dates

Date	Mintage	F	VF	XF	Unc	BU
ND(1963) Proof	3,000	Value: 520				

KM# 72   20 LEVA

16.8889 g., 0.9000 Gold 0.4887 oz. AGW **Subject:** 20th Anniversary - Peoples Republic **Obv:** Flag above denomination, dates at bottom **Rev:** Head of Georgi Dimitrov, left, two dates below

Date	Mintage	F	VF	XF	Unc	BU
ND(1964) Proof	5,000	Value: 490				

KM# 106   20 LEVA

21.8000 g., 0.5000 Silver 0.3504 oz. ASW **Subject:** Centennial of Sofia as Capital **Obv:** National arms above ribbon, denomination and date at bottom **Rev:** Crowned head left, two dates bottom right

Date	Mintage	F	VF	XF	Unc	BU
1979	35,000	—	—	—	25.00	27.50

KM# 106a   20 LEVA

32.0000 g., 0.9000 Silver 0.9259 oz. ASW **Subject:** Centennial of Sofia as Capital **Obv:** National arms above ribbon, denomination and date at bottom **Rev:** Crowned head left, two dates lower right

Date	Mintage	F	VF	XF	Unc	BU
1979 Proof	15,000	Value: 35.00				

KM# 133.1   20 LEVA

14.0000 g., 0.5000 Silver 0.2250 oz. ASW **Subject:** 40th Anniversary - Birth of Lyudmila Zhivkova **Obv:** Denomination with date to left **Rev:** Head of Lyudmila Zhivkova left

Date	Mintage	F	VF	XF	Unc	BU
1982 Proof	10,000	Value: 25.00				

KM# 133.2   20 LEVA

14.0000 g., 0.5000 Silver 0.2250 oz. ASW **Obv:** Denomination between emblems of Children's Assembly and Year of the Child **Rev:** Head of Lyudmila Zhivkova, left, two dates at right

Date	Mintage	F	VF	XF	Unc	BU
1982 Proof	—	Value: 300				

KM# 164   20 LEVA

11.2200 g., 0.5000 Silver 0.1804 oz. ASW **Obv:** National arms, date and denomination below **Rev:** Bust of Vasil Levsky facing

Date	Mintage	F	VF	XF	Unc	BU
1987 Proof	100,000	Value: 15.00				

KM# 171   20 LEVA

11.3900 g., 0.5000 Silver 0.1831 oz. ASW **Subject:** Bulgarian Railways **Obv:** National arms within circle, denomination and date below **Rev:** Train engines, old and new, within circle

Date	Mintage	F	VF	XF	Unc	BU
1988 Proof	93,000	Value: 16.00				

KM# 172   20 LEVA

11.2200 g., 0.5000 Silver 0.1804 oz. ASW **Subject:** 110th Anniversary of Liberation **Obv:** Monument above denomination, date at right **Rev:** Liberation celebration, date below

Date	Mintage	F	VF	XF	Unc	BU
1988 Proof	100,000	Value: 15.00				

KM# 173   20 LEVA

11.5500 g., 0.5000 Silver 0.1857 oz. ASW **Subject:** 100th Anniversary of Sophia University **Obv:** University above spray, denomination and date below **Rev:** Man, moth and kite, dates at left

Date	Mintage	F	VF	XF	Unc	BU
1988 Proof	100,000	Value: 15.00				

KM# 174   20 LEVA

11.1900 g., 0.5000 Silver 0.1799 oz. ASW **Subject:** Soviet-Bulgarian Space Flight **Obv:** National arms above denomination, date at left **Rev:** Astronauts

Date	Mintage	F	VF	XF	Unc	BU
1988 Proof	100,000	Value: 15.00				

KM# 181   20 LEVA

Copper-Nickel-Zinc **Obv:** National arms within circle **Rev:** Denomination above date, grain sprigs flank

Date	Mintage	F	VF	XF	Unc	BU
1989 Proof	—	Value: 9.00				

KM# 183   20 LEVA

12.1300 g., 0.5000 Silver 0.1950 oz. ASW **Subject:** Academy of Science **Obv:** National arms within pegged circle **Rev:** Academy building, two dates above, denomination and date below within pegged circle

Date	Mintage	F	VF	XF	Unc	BU
1989 Proof	58,000	Value: 16.00				

KM# 134   25 LEVA

14.0000 g., 0.5000 Silver 0.2250 oz. ASW **Subject:** 1300th Anniversary of Nationhood **Obv:** National arms within wreath above denomination and date **Rev:** Woman and child, radiant sun in background

Date	Mintage	F	VF	XF	Unc	BU
1981 Proof	Est. 100,000	Value: 25.00				

KM# 145   25 LEVA

14.0000 g., 0.5000 Silver 0.2250 oz. ASW **Subject:** 100th Anniversary - Birth of Georgi Dimitrov **Obv:** National arms, denomination below, date at right **Rev:** Head left, two dates lower right

Date	Mintage	F	VF	XF	Unc	BU
1982 Proof	15,000	Value: 15.00				

KM# 148   25 LEVA

14.0000 g., 0.5000 Silver 0.2250 oz. ASW **Subject:** 40th Anniversary of Peoples Republic **Obv:** National arms at top, denomination below divides dates **Rev:** Flowers on design

Date	Mintage	F	VF	XF	Unc	BU
ND(1984) Proof	91,000	Value: 14.00				

KM# 156.1   25 LEVA
23.3300 g., 0.9250 Silver 0.6938 oz. ASW   **Subject:** Soccer
Obv: National arms **Rev:** Stylized eagle with soccer ball,
denomination and date at left

Date	Mintage	F	VF	XF	Unc	BU
1986 Proof	12,902			Value: 26.00		

KM# 156.2   25 LEVA
23.3300 g., 0.9250 Silver 0.6938 oz. ASW   **Obv:** National arms
Rev: Stylized eagle with soccer ball, denomination at left, without
date in field above eagle's head

Date	Mintage	F	VF	XF	Unc	BU
1986 Proof	Inc. above			Value: 32.00		

KM# 194   25 LEVA
23.3300 g., 0.9250 Silver 0.6938 oz. ASW   **Subject:** Soccer
Obv: National arms **Rev:** Soccer player, vertical date above,
denomination at right

Date	Mintage	F	VF	XF	Unc	BU
1986 Proof	12,250			Value: 25.00		

KM# 160   25 LEVA
23.3300 g., 0.9250 Silver 0.6938 oz. ASW   **Series:** Winter Olympics
Obv: National arms **Rev:** Skier, date and denomination below

Date	Mintage	F	VF	XF	Unc	BU
1987 Proof	15,000			Value: 25.00		

KM# 186   25 LEVA
23.3300 g., 0.9250 Silver 0.6938 oz. ASW   **Series:** Seoul 1988
- Summer Olympic Games **Subject:** High Jump **Obv:** National
arms **Rev:** High jumper, date and denomination below

Date	Mintage	F	VF	XF	Unc	BU
1988 Proof	20,000			Value: 24.00		

KM# 187   25 LEVA
23.3300 g., 0.9250 Silver 0.6938 oz. ASW   **Subject:** Soccer
Obv: Denomination above date **Rev:** Two players, date below

Date	Mintage	F	VF	XF	Unc	BU
1989 Proof	17,600			Value: 25.00		

KM# 189   25 LEVA
23.3800 g., 0.9250 Silver 0.6953 oz. ASW   **Series:** 1992
Summer Olympics **Obv:** National arms, date and denomination
below **Rev:** Two rowers, date upper left

Date	Mintage	F	VF	XF	Unc	BU
1989 Proof	57,560			Value: 20.00		

KM# 190   25 LEVA
23.3800 g., 0.9250 Silver 0.6953 oz. ASW   **Series:** Albertville
1992 - 16th Winter Olympic Games **Obv:** National arms, date
and denomination below **Rev:** Figure skating pairs competition,
date at right

Date	Mintage	F	VF	XF	Unc	BU
1989 Proof	48,449			Value: 20.00		

KM# 193   25 LEVA
23.3800 g., 0.9250 Silver 0.6953 oz. ASW   **Subject:** Wildlife
Obv: National arms, denomination and date below **Rev:** Mother
bear and cubs

Date	Mintage	F	VF	XF	Unc	BU
1989 Proof	15,000			Value: 38.00		

KM# 191   25 LEVA
23.3800 g., 0.9250 Silver 0.6953 oz. ASW   **Subject:** Soccer
Obv: National arms, denomination and date below **Rev:** Globe,
net, and shoe

Date	Mintage	F	VF	XF	Unc	BU
1990 Proof	15,600			Value: 26.00		

KM# 192   25 LEVA
23.3800 g., 0.9250 Silver 0.6953 oz. ASW   **Subject:** Soccer
Obv: National arms, date and denomination below **Rev:** Ball design,
date

Date	Mintage	F	VF	XF	Unc	BU
1990 Proof	14,900			Value: 26.00		

KM# 195   25 LEVA
23.3800 g., 0.9250 Silver 0.6953 oz. ASW   **Series:** Winter
Olympics **Obv:** National arms, date and denomination below
Rev: Cross-country skiers, date at right

Date	Mintage	F	VF	XF	Unc	BU
1990 Proof	46,400			Value: 20.00		

KM# 196 25 LEVA
23.3800 g., 0.9250 Silver 0.6953 oz. ASW **Series:** Summer Olympics **Obv:** National arms, date and denomination below **Rev:** Runners, date below

Date	Mintage	F	VF	XF	Unc	BU
1990 Proof	50,235	Value: 18.00				

KM# 197 25 LEVA
23.3800 g., 0.9250 Silver 0.6953 oz. ASW **Subject:** Wildlife **Obv:** National arms, date and denomination below **Rev:** Two lynx

Date	Mintage	F	VF	XF	Unc	BU
1990 Proof	14,840	Value: 36.00				

KM# 135 50 LEVA
20.5000 g., 0.9000 Silver 0.5932 oz. ASW **Subject:** 1300th Anniversary of Nationhood **Obv:** Dates above denomination **Rev:** Equestrian figure right, animal below

Date	Mintage	F	VF	XF	Unc	BU
1981 Proof	Est. 10,000	Value: 32.00				

KM# 136 50 LEVA
20.5000 g., 0.9000 Silver 0.5932 oz. ASW **Subject:** 1300th Anniversary of Nationhood **Obv:** Head of Georgi Dimitrov left, denomination below line **Rev:** Woman striding left

Date	Mintage	F	VF	XF	Unc	BU
1981 Proof	1,000	Value: 30.00				

KM# 137 50 LEVA
20.5000 g., 0.9000 Silver 0.5932 oz. ASW **Subject:** 1300th Anniversary of Nationhood **Obv:** National arms above sprays, date and denomination below **Rev:** Mother and child in front of radiant sun

Date	Mintage	F	VF	XF	Unc	BU
1981 Proof	1,000	Value: 32.00				

KM# 138 50 LEVA
20.5000 g., 0.9000 Silver 0.5932 oz. ASW **Subject:** 1300th Anniversary of Nationhood **Obv:** Buildings above date and denomination **Rev:** Warrior figures

Date	Mintage	F	VF	XF	Unc	BU
1981 Proof	Est. 10,000	Value: 25.00				

KM# 182 50 LEVA
Copper-Nickel-Zinc **Obv:** National arms within circle **Rev:** Denomination above date, grain sprays flank

Date	Mintage	F	VF	XF	Unc	BU
1989 Proof	—	Value: 13.00				

KM# 150 100 LEVA
8.4444 g., 0.9000 Gold 0.2443 oz. AGW **Subject:** International Womens Decade **Obv:** National arms within wreath, date and denomination below **Rev:** Woman with child divides dates **Note:** .076 Silver, .024 Copper

Date	Mintage	F	VF	XF	Unc	BU
1984 Proof	500	Value: 360				

KM# 150a 100 LEVA
8.4444 g., 0.9000 Gold 0.2443 oz. AGW **Subject:** International Womens Decade **Obv:** National arms within wreath, date and denomination below **Rev:** Woman with child divides date **Note:** .100 Copper

Date	Mintage	F	VF	XF	Unc	BU
1984	2,032	Value: 280				

KM# 139 1000 LEVA
16.8800 g., 0.9000 Gold 0.4884 oz. AGW **Subject:** 1300th Anniversary of Nationhood **Obv:** National arms above denomination and date **Rev:** Mother and child in front of radiant sun

Date	Mintage	F	VF	XF	Unc	BU
1981 Proof	2,000	Value: 500				

REPUBLIC

STANDARD COINAGE

KM# 199 10 STOTINKI
1.6500 g., Nickel-Brass, 16.16 mm. **Obv:** Ancient lion sculpture left within circle **Rev:** Denomination divides date **Edge:** Reeded

Date	Mintage	F	VF	XF	Unc	BU
1992	—	—	—	—	0.25	0.35

KM# 200 20 STOTINKI
Nickel-Brass **Obv:** Ancient lion sculpture left within circle **Rev:** Denomination divides date

Date	Mintage	F	VF	XF	Unc	BU
1992	—	—	—	—	0.35	0.50

KM# 201 50 STOTINKI
3.0200 g., Nickel-Brass, 19.55 mm. **Obv:** Ancient lion sculpture left within circle **Rev:** Denomination divides date **Edge:** Reeded

Date	Mintage	F	VF	XF	Unc	BU
1992	—	—	—	—	0.50	0.75

KM# 202 LEV
4.1200 g., Nickel-Brass, 23.19 mm. **Obv:** Madara horseman right within circle **Rev:** Denomination divides symbols, date below **Edge:** Reeded

Date	Mintage	F	VF	XF	Unc	BU
1992	—	—	—	—	0.75	1.00

KM# 203 2 LEVA
5.0800 g., Nickel-Brass, 25.14 mm. **Obv:** Madara horseman right within circle **Rev:** Denomination divides symbols, date below **Edge:** Reeded

Date	Mintage	F	VF	XF	Unc	BU
1992	—	—	—	—	1.25	1.50

KM# 204   5 LEVA
6.0000 g., Nickel-Brass, 27.13 mm. **Obv:** Madara horseman right within circle **Rev:** Denomination divides symbols, date below **Edge:** Reeded

Date	Mintage	F	VF	XF	Unc	BU
1992	—	—	—	—	1.75	2.00

KM# 205   10 LEVA
Copper-Nickel **Obv:** Madara horseman right within circle **Rev:** Denomination divides symbols, date below

Date	Mintage	F	VF	XF	Unc	BU
1992	—	—	—	—	2.50	3.00

KM# 224   10 LEVA
Brass **Obv:** Madara horseman right within circle **Rev:** Denomination divides symbols, date below **Note:** Reduced size and metal change.

Date	Mintage	F	VF	XF	Unc	BU
1997	—	—	—	—	1.25	1.50

KM# 228   20 LEVA
Brass **Obv:** Madara horseman right within circle **Rev:** Denomination divides symbols, date below

Date	Mintage	F	VF	XF	Unc	BU
1997	—	—	—	—	1.50	1.75

KM# 198   50 LEVA
10.0700 g., 0.9250 Silver 0.2995 oz. ASW **Series:** Olympics **Obv:** Denomination above date within wreath **Rev:** Downhill skier, date below

Date	Mintage	F	VF	XF	Unc	BU
1992 Proof	52,390	Value: 12.00				

KM# 225   50 LEVA
Brass **Obv:** Madara horseman right within circle **Rev:** Denomination divides symbols, date below

Date	Mintage	F	VF	XF	Unc	BU
1997	—	—	—	—	1.75	2.00

KM# 212   100 LEVA
23.2300 g., 0.9250 Silver 0.6908 oz. ASW **Obv:** Denomination above date within wreath **Rev:** Old Ship Radetsky, date at right

Date	Mintage	F	VF	XF	Unc	BU
1992 Proof	28,765	Value: 26.00				

KM# 226   100 LEVA
23.2300 g., 0.9250 Silver 0.6908 oz. ASW **Obv:** Denomination above date within wreath **Rev:** Eagle descending on prey

Date	Mintage	F	VF	XF	Unc	BU
1992 Proof	27,651	Value: 35.00				

KM# 209   100 LEVA
23.3300 g., 0.9250 Silver 0.6938 oz. ASW **Series:** 1994 Olympics **Obv:** Denomination above date within wreath **Rev:** Bobsled, date upper right

Date	Mintage	F	VF	XF	Unc	BU
1993 Proof	33,690	Value: 24.00				

KM# 227   100 LEVA
23.3300 g., 0.9250 Silver 0.6938 oz. ASW **Obv:** Denomination above date within wreath **Rev:** Chamois left

Date	Mintage	F	VF	XF	Unc	BU
1993 Proof	20,000	Value: 36.00				

KM# 231   100 LEVA
23.3300 g., 0.9250 Silver 0.6938 oz. ASW **Obv:** Denomination above date within wreath **Rev:** Parliament building

Date	Mintage	F	VF	XF	Unc	BU
1993 Proof	15,000	Value: 32.00				

KM# 206   500 LEVA
33.6250 g., 0.9250 Silver 0.9999 oz. ASW **Subject:** European Community - St. Theodor Stratilat **Obv:** ECU monogram and date in circle of stars **Rev:** Face within design, denomination at right

Date	Mintage	F	VF	XF	Unc	BU
1993 Proof	51,031	Value: 30.00				

KM# 213   50 LEVA
Copper-Nickel **Subject:** Centennial of Olympics in Bulgaria **Obv:** Denomination above date within wreath **Rev:** Gymnasts divide dates

Date	Mintage	F	VF	XF	Unc	BU
1994 Proof	19,210	Value: 6.00				

KM# 210   100 LEVA
23.3300 g., 0.9250 Silver 0.6938 oz. ASW **Subject:** 1994 World Cup Soccer **Obv:** Denomination above date within circle **Rev:** Soccer player and buildings, within circle

Date	Mintage	F	VF	XF	Unc	BU
1993 Proof	27,840	Value: 30.00				

KM# 211   500 LEVA
23.0000 g., 0.9250 Silver 0.6840 oz. ASW **Subject:** World Cup Soccer **Obv:** Denomination above date within wreath **Rev:** Soccer ball and net, date below

Date	Mintage	F	VF	XF	Unc	BU
1994 Proof	24,351	Value: 34.00				

KM# 219 500 LEVA
10.0000 g., 0.9250 Silver 0.2974 oz. ASW **Subject:** Soccer
Obv: Denomination above date within wreath **Rev:** Two soccer
players

Date	Mintage	F	VF	XF	Unc	BU
1996 Proof	60,000	Value: 26.00				

KM# 223 500 LEVA
10.0000 g., 0.9250 Silver 0.2974 oz. ASW, 30 mm. **Subject:** 100th
Anniversary - National Art Academy **Obv:** Denomination above date
within wreath **Rev:** Academy on paint palette **Edge:** Plain

Date	Mintage	F	VF	XF	Unc	BU
1996 Proof	30,000	Value: 52.00				

KM# 229 500 LEVA
Copper-Nickel-Zinc **Subject:** NATO **Obv:** Denomination above
date within wreath **Rev:** City arms and NATO flag

Date	Mintage	F	VF	XF	Unc	BU
1997	30,000	—	—	—	6.00	

KM# 214 1000 LEVA
23.3300 g., 0.9250 Silver 0.6938 oz. ASW **Series:** 50 Years -
F.A.O. **Obv:** Denomination above date within wreath **Rev:** Wheat
and globe within circle, two dates below

Date	Mintage	F	VF	XF	Unc	BU
1995 Proof	12,000	Value: 34.00				

KM# 215 1000 LEVA
23.3300 g., 0.9250 Silver 0.6938 oz. ASW **Subject:** 100 Years
of Olympic Games **Obv:** Denomination above date within wreath
Rev: Equestrian, left

Date	Mintage	F	VF	XF	Unc	BU
1995 Proof	28,713	Value: 32.00				

KM# 216 1000 LEVA
23.3300 g., 0.9250 Silver 0.6938 oz. ASW **Subject:** 110 Years
- Union of Eastern Rumelia with the Bulgarian Principality
Obv: Denomination above date within wreath **Rev:** Map behind
figure with flag, two dates upper left

Date	Mintage	F	VF	XF	Unc	BU
1995 Proof	15,000	Value: 35.00				

KM# 217 1000 LEVA
33.6250 g., 0.9250 Silver 0.9999 oz. ASW **Subject:** Rozhen
Peak Astronomical Observatory **Obv:** ECU monogram and date
within circle of stars **Rev:** Observatory, circle of stars above,
denomination below

Date	Mintage	F	VF	XF	Unc	BU
1995 Proof	32,796	Value: 34.00				

KM# 220 1000 LEVA
23.3300 g., 0.9250 Silver 0.6938 oz. ASW **Obv:** Denomination
above date within wreath **Rev:** Sailing Ship Kaliakra

Date	Mintage	F	VF	XF	Unc	BU
1996 Proof	23,052	Value: 36.00				

KM# 221 1000 LEVA
23.3300 g., 0.9250 Silver 0.6938 oz. ASW **Series:** Olympics
Obv: Denomination above date within wreath **Rev:** Speed skater

Date	Mintage	F	VF	XF	Unc	BU
1996 Proof	22,602	Value: 32.00				

KM# 222 1000 LEVA
33.6250 g., 0.9250 Silver 0.9999 oz. ASW **Subject:** St. Ivan of
Rila **Obv:** ECU monogram and date within circle of stars
Rev: Standing saint, church, and denomination

Date	Mintage	F	VF	XF	Unc	BU
1996 Proof	42,445	Value: 34.00				

KM# 232 1000 LEVA
23.3300 g., 0.9250 Silver 0.6938 oz. ASW **Subject:** UNICEF
Obv: Denomination above date within wreath **Rev:** Singing child,
UNICEF logo

Date	Mintage	F	VF	XF	Unc	BU
1997 Proof	6,001	Value: 35.00				

KM# 233 1000 LEVA
23.3300 g., 0.9250 Silver 0.6938 oz. ASW **Subject:** World Cup Soccer - France 1998 **Obv:** Denomination above date within wreath **Rev:** Three soccer players

Date	Mintage	F	VF	XF	Unc	BU
1997 Proof	22,606	Value: 36.00				

KM# 230 1000 LEVA
Copper-Nickel-Zinc **Subject:** Bulgarian Telegraphic Agency Centennial **Obv:** Crowned arms **Rev:** World map and logo **Note:** Prev. KM#239.

Date	Mintage	F	VF	XF	Unc	BU
1998 Proof	—	Value: 6.00				

KM# 207 5000 LEVA
8.6400 g., 0.9000 Gold 0.2500 oz. AGW **Subject:** European Community - Slavonic Alphabet **Obv:** ECU monogram and date within circle of stars **Rev:** Denomination to left of design

Date	Mintage	F	VF	XF	Unc	BU
1993 Proof	Est. 2,500	Value: 260				

KM# 243 5000 LEVA
10.0000 g., 0.9250 Silver 0.2974 oz. ASW **Obv:** National arms, date and denomination below **Rev:** Building above "EURO"

Date	Mintage	F	VF	XF	Unc	BU
1998 Proof	—	Value: 20.00				

KM# 208 10000 LEVA
15.5670 g., 0.9990 Platinum 0.5000 oz. APW **Rev:** Bust of Sevastokratoritza Desislava 1/2 right, founder of Boyana church, denomination at right

Date	Mintage	F	VF	XF	Unc	BU
1993 Proof	Est. 2,500	Value: 1,200				

KM# 218 10000 LEVA
8.6400 g., 0.9000 Gold 0.2500 oz. AGW **Obv:** Denomination above date within wreath **Rev:** St. Alexander Nevski Cathedral

Date	Mintage	F	VF	XF	Unc	BU
1994 Proof	30,000	Value: 260				

KM# 234 10000 LEVA
23.3300 g., 0.9250 Silver 0.6938 oz. ASW **Subject:** 120th Anniversary of Liberation **Obv:** National arms above date, denomination below. **Rev:** Decorated soldier with flag

Date	Mintage	F	VF	XF	Unc	BU
1998 Proof	15,000	Value: 42.00				

KM# 235 10000 LEVA
23.3300 g., 0.9250 Silver 0.6938 oz. ASW **Subject:** United Europe **Obv:** Rider of Madara over dead lion **Rev:** Ancient cup and map

Date	Mintage	F	VF	XF	Unc	BU
1998 Proof	18,152	Value: 41.00				

KM# 236 20000 LEVA
1.5552 g., 0.9990 Gold 0.0499 oz. AGW **Subject:** Czar Ivan Alexander **Obv:** Stylized lion, left, date and denomination below **Rev:** Four human figure sculptures

Date	Mintage	F	VF	XF	Unc	BU
1998 Proof	—	Value: 80.00				

REFORM COINAGE

KM# 237 STOTINKA
Brass, 16 mm. **Obv:** Madara horseman right, animal below **Rev:** Denomination above date **Edge:** Plain

Date	Mintage	F	VF	XF	Unc	BU
1999	1,277,500	—	—	—	0.25	0.35
2000	—	—	—	—	0.25	0.35

KM# 238 2 STOTINKI
Brass, 18 mm. **Obv:** Madara horseman right, animal below **Rev:** Denomination above date **Edge:** Plain

Date	Mintage	F	VF	XF	Unc	BU
1999	2,048,900	—	—	—	0.35	0.50
2000	—	—	—	—	0.35	0.50

KM# 239 5 STOTINKI
Brass, 20 mm. **Obv:** Madara horseman right, animal below **Rev:** Denomination above date **Edge:** Plain **Note:** Prev. KM#A239.

Date	Mintage	F	VF	XF	Unc	BU
1999	3,453,025	—	—	—	0.50	0.65
2000	—	—	—	—	0.50	0.65

KM# 240 10 STOTINKI
Copper-Nickel, 18.5 mm. **Obv:** Madara horseman right, animal below **Rev:** Denomination above date **Edge:** Reeded

Date	Mintage	F	VF	XF	Unc	BU
1999	8,231,400	—	—	—	0.65	0.85

KM# 241 20 STOTINKI
Copper-Nickel, 20.5 mm. **Obv:** Madara horseman right, animal below **Rev:** Denomination above date **Edge:** Reeded

Date	Mintage	F	VF	XF	Unc	BU
1999	11,967,500	—	—	—	0.85	1.00

KM# 242 50 STOTINKI
Copper-Nickel, 22.5 mm. **Obv:** Madara horseman right, animal below **Rev:** Denomination above date **Edge:** Reeded

Date	Mintage	F	VF	XF	Unc	BU
1999	15,607,000	—	—	—	1.25	1.50

KM# 245 10 LEVA
23.3500 g., 0.9250 Silver 0.6944 oz. ASW, 38.5 mm. **Obv:** National arms **Rev:** Mediterranean Monk Seal, denomination above, date at left **Edge:** Plain

Date	Mintage	F	VF	XF	Unc	BU
1999 Proof	15,000	—	—	—	30.00	35.00

KM# 248 10 LEVA
23.3300 g., 0.9250 Silver 0.6938 oz. ASW, 38.5 mm. **Obv:** Bust of Theodor Burmov 3/4 left, denomination and date below **Rev:** "EURO" map in circle of stars **Edge:** Plain

Date	Mintage	F	VF	XF	Unc	BU
1999 Proof	20,000	Value: 35.00				

KM# 249 10 LEVA

23.3300 g., 0.9250 Silver 0.6938 oz. ASW, 38.5 mm.
Subject: Euro Integration **Obv:** National arms, date and denomination below **Rev:** Plovdiv old town street view **Edge:** Plain

Date	Mintage	F	VF	XF	Unc	BU
1999 Proof	20,000	Value: 35.00				

KM# 250 10 LEVA

23.3300 g., 0.9250 Silver 0.6938 oz. ASW, 38.5 mm.
Subject: Summer Olympic Games **Obv:** National arms **Rev:** High jumper divides date and denomination **Edge:** Plain

Date	Mintage	F	VF	XF	Unc	BU
1999 Proof	20,000	Value: 35.00				

KM# 251 10 LEVA

23.3300 g., 0.9250 Silver 0.6938 oz. ASW, 38.5 mm.
Subject: Summer Olympics **Obv:** National arms, date and denomination below **Rev:** Weight lifter **Edge:** Plain

Date	Mintage	F	VF	XF	Unc	BU
2000 Proof	20,000	Value: 35.00				

KM# 252 10 LEVA

23.3300 g., 0.9250 Silver 0.6938 oz. ASW, 38.5 mm.
Subject: Christianity **Obv:** National arms **Rev:** Church patriarch **Edge:** Plain

Date	Mintage	F	VF	XF	Unc	BU
2000 Proof	—	Value: 40.00				

KM# 253 10 LEVA

23.3300 g., 0.9250 Silver 0.6938 oz. ASW, 38.5 mm.
Subject: Bulgarian Association with the European Union **Obv:** National arms, date and denomination below **Rev:** Bulgarian coin design of the Middle Ages featuring Czar Theodor Svetoslav **Edge:** Plain

Date	Mintage	F	VF	XF	Unc	BU
2000 Proof	20,000	Value: 40.00				

KM# 244 10 LEVA

10.3500 g., 0.8000 Silver 0.2662 oz. ASW, 33.9 mm.
Subject: The Year 2000 **Obv:** National arms above date with pierced zeros, denomination below **Rev:** Bell above date with pierced zeros **Edge:** Plain

Date	Mintage	F	VF	XF	Unc	BU
2000 Proof	—	Value: 65.00				

KM# 278 20 LEVA

1.5500 g., Gold, 13.93 mm. **Obv:** National arms **Rev:** Busts of Mother Mary and Jesus at left **Edge:** Reeded

Date	Mintage	F	VF	XF	Unc	BU
1999 Proof	—	Value: 50.00				

KM# 255 100 LEVA

16.0000 g., 0.9000 Gold 0.4630 oz. AGW, 30 mm.
Subject: Todor Burmov **Obv:** Bust 3/4 facing, date and denomination below **Rev:** "EURO" and map **Edge:** Plain

Date	Mintage	F	VF	XF	Unc	BU
1999 Proof	5,000	Value: 465				

KM# 256 20000 LEVA

1.5500 g., 0.9990 Gold 0.0498 oz. AGW **Obv:** National arms **Rev:** National Bank building, date and denomination below **Edge:** Plain

Date	Mintage	F	VF	XF	Unc	BU
1999 Proof	30,000	Value: 65.00				

ESSAIS

KM#	Date	Mintage	Identification	Mkt Val
E9	1925(a)	—	2 Leva. Copper-Nickel.	150

PIEFORTS

KM#	Date	Mintage	Identification	Mkt Val
P3	1979	2,000	10 Leva. Silver. KM#104	75.00

TRIAL STRIKES

KM#	Date	Mintage	Identification	Mkt Val
TS1	1901	—	2 Stotinki. Bronze. Uniface.	—
TS2	1901	—	2 Stotinki. Bronze. Uniface.	—

PATTERNS

Including off metal strikes

KM#	Date	Mintage	Identification	Mkt Val
PnA6	1923H	—	Lev. Aluminum. Similar to KM#35.	—
Pn6	1923H	—	Lev. Aluminum-Bronze.	—
Pn7	1923H	—	2 Leva. Aluminum.	275
PnA8	1923H	—	2 Leva. Aluminum. Similar to KM#36.	—
Pn8	1923H	—	2 Leva. Aluminum-Bronze.	—
Pn9	1928	2	5 Leva.	—
Pn10	1930	2	5 Leva.	—
Pn11	1930	2	10 Leva.	—
Pn12	1950	—	2 Leva. Nickel Alloy. 1.0800 g. 20.17 mm.	—
Pn13	1950	—	5 Leva. Nickel Alloy. 1.2400 g. 21.45 mm.	—
Pn14	1952	—	2 Stotinki. Copper-Nickel. 1.0000 g. 16mm.	—
Pn15	1952	—	20 Stotinki. Copper-Nickel. 3.0000 g. 21mm.	—
Pn16	1960	—	Lev. Copper-Nickel. 6.0000 g. 24mm.	—

KM#	Date	Mintage	Identification	Mkt Val
Pn17	1960	—	Lev. Copper-Nickel. 5.0000 g. 24mm.	—
Pn18	1960	—	Lev. Aluminum. 2.3000 g. 25mm.	—
Pn19	1960	—	Lev. Aluminum. 1.3000 g. 20mm.	—
Pn20	1960	—	Lev. Copper. 3.6000 g. 20mm.	—
Pn21	1962	—	Lev. Copper-Nickel. 5.0000 g. 24mm.	—
Pn22	1962	—	Lev. Copper-Nickel. 5.0000 g. 24mm.	—
Pn23	1964	—	20 Leva. Copper. 8.6000 g. KM#72, 27mm.	—
Pn24	1966	—	Lev. Copper-Nickel. 4.8000 g. 24mm.	—
Pn25	1984	1,500	10 Leva. Copper-Nickel. Reeded edge. PROBA I; KM#146.	50.00
Pn26	1984	250	10 Leva. 0.6400 Silver. Plain edge. PROBA II; KM#146a.	120
Pn27	1984	50	10 Leva. 0.9250 Silver. Lettered edge. SPECIMEN; KM#146a.	200
Pn28	1984	2,000	10 Leva. Copper-Nickel. Reeded edge. PROBA I; KM#147.	65.00
Pn29	1984	300	10 Leva. 0.6400 Silver. Plain edge. PROBA II; KM#147a.	150
Pn30	1984	50	10 Leva. 0.9250 Silver. Lettered edge. SPECIMEN; KM#147a.	275

MINT SETS

KM#	Date	Mintage	Identification	Issue Price	Mkt Val
MSA1	1962 (7)	—	KM#58-64, either restrikes or leftovers marketed post 2000	—	—
MS1	1981 (3)	—	KM#118, 120, 131	—	20.00
MS2	1992 (7)	—	KM#199-205	—	10.00
MS3	1999 (6)	—	KM#237-242, plus medal	—	12.00

PROOF SETS

KM#	Date	Mintage	Identification	Issue Price	Mkt Val
PS1	1912 (2)	—	KM#33-34. Official restrikes of these types were made in the 1960's.	—	7,500
PS2	1962/66 (9)	—	KM#58-64 (1962), 73 (1966) Issued after these types were demonetized in 1995 and 1997.	—	—
PS3	1963 (2)	5,000	KM#65-66	—	27.50
PS4	1963/73 (8)	—	KM#65-66, 69-70, 78-79, 80-81 mixed date set, REPUBLIQUE DE BULGARIE	—	155
PS5	1964 (2)	10,000	KM#69-70	—	27.50
PS6	1979 (7)	2,000	KM#84-90	—	22.50
PS7	1980 (7)	2,000	KM#84-90	—	22.50

BURUNDI

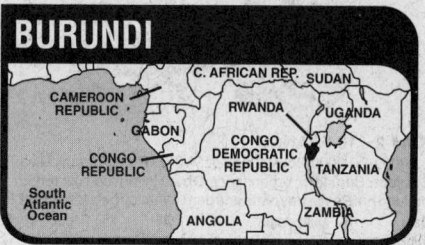

The Republic of Burundi, a landlocked country in central Africa, was a kingdom with a feudalistic society, caste system and Mwami (king) for more than 400 years before independence. It has an area of 10,740 sq. mi. (27,830 sq. km.) and a population of 6.3 million. Capital: Bujumbura. Plagued by poor soil, irregular rainfall and a single-crop economy, coffee, Burundi is barely able to feed itself. Coffee and tea are exported.

Although the area was visited by European explorers and missionaries in the latter half of the 19th century, it wasn't until the 1890s that it, together with Rwanda, fell under European domination as part of German East Africa. Following World War I, the territory was mandated to Belgium by the League of Nations and administered with the Belgian Congo. After World War II it became a U.N. Trust Territory. Limited self-government was established by U.N.-supervised elections in 1961. Burundi gained independence as a kingdom under Mwami Mwambutsa IV on July 1, 1962. The republic was established by military coup in 1966.

NOTE: For earlier coinage see Belgian Congo, and Rwanda and Burundi. For previously listed coinage dated 1966, coins of Mwambutsa IV and Ntare V, refer to *UNUSUAL WORLD COINS*, 3rd edition, Krause Publications, 1992.

RULERS

Mwambutsa IV, 1962-1966
Ntare V, 1966

MINT MARKS

PM - Pobjoy Mint
(b) - Privy Marks, Brussels

MONETARY SYSTEM

100 Centimes = 1 Franc

KINGDOM
STANDARD COINAGE

KM# 6   FRANC
Brass, 23 mm. **Obv:** Denomination within circle, circle with monogram below **Rev:** Arms above date **Edge:** Reeded

Date	Mintage	F	VF	XF	Unc	BU
1965	10,000,000	—	0.75	1.50	3.00	—

KM# 1   5 FRANCS
Copper Nickel **Ruler:** Mwambutsa IV **Subject:** Burundi Independence **Obv:** Uniformed bust left **Rev:** Arms, date and denomination below

Date	Mintage	F	VF	XF	Unc	BU
1962	—	—	—	—	—	—
1962 Proof	—	—	—	—	—	—

KM# 1a   5 FRANCS
24.1100 g., 0.9000 Silver 0.6976 oz. ASW **Ruler:** Mwambutsa IV **Subject:** Burundi Independence **Obv:** Uniformed bust left **Rev:** Arms, date and denomination below

Date	Mintage	F	VF	XF	Unc	BU
1962 Proof	—	—	—	—	—	—

KM# 2   10 FRANCS
3.2000 g., 0.9000 Gold 0.0926 oz. AGW **Ruler:** Mwambutsa IV **Subject:** Burundi Independence **Obv:** Uniformed bust left, beaded rim **Rev:** Arms, date and denomination below, beaded rim

Date	Mintage	F	VF	XF	Unc	BU
1962 Proof	7,500		Value: 100			

KM# 7   10 FRANCS
3.0000 g., 0.9000 Gold 0.0868 oz. AGW **Ruler:** Mwambutsa IV **Subject:** 50th Anniversary - Reign of Mwambutsa IV **Obv:** Uniformed bust 3/4 facing divides dates, beaded rim **Rev:** Arms, denomination below, beaded rim

Date	Mintage	F	VF	XF	Unc	BU
ND(1965)	—	—	—	—	90.00	—
ND(1965) Proof	5,000		Value: 100			

KM# 3   25 FRANCS
8.0000 g., 0.9000 Gold 0.2315 oz. AGW **Ruler:** Mwambutsa IV **Subject:** Burundi Independence **Obv:** Uniformed bust left, beaded rim **Rev:** Arms, denomination and date below, beaded rim

Date	Mintage	F	VF	XF	Unc	BU
1962 Proof	15,000		Value: 220			

KM# 8   25 FRANCS
7.5000 g., 0.9000 Gold 0.2170 oz. AGW **Ruler:** Mwambutsa IV **Subject:** 50th Anniversary - Reign of Mwambutsa IV **Obv:** Uniformed bust 3/4 facing divides dates, beaded rim **Rev:** Arms, denomination below, beaded rim

Date	Mintage	F	VF	XF	Unc	BU
ND(1965)	—	—	—	—	210	—
ND(1965) Proof	5,000		Value: 220			

KM# 4   50 FRANCS
16.0000 g., 0.9000 Gold 0.4630 oz. AGW **Ruler:** Mwambutsa IV **Subject:** Burundi Independence **Obv:** Uniformed bust left, beaded rim **Rev:** Arms, denomination and date below, beaded rim

Date	Mintage	F	VF	XF	Unc	BU
1962 Proof	3,500		Value: 450			

KM# 9   50 FRANCS
15.0000 g., 0.9000 Gold 0.4340 oz. AGW **Ruler:** Mwambutsa IV **Subject:** 50th Anniversary - Reign of Mwambutsa IV **Obv:** Uniformed bust 3/4 facing divides dates, beaded rim **Rev:** Arms, denomination below, beaded rim

Date	Mintage	F	VF	XF	Unc	BU
ND(1965)	—	—	—	—	425	—
ND(1965) Proof	5,000		Value: 450			

KM# 5   100 FRANCS
32.0000 g., 0.9000 Gold 0.9259 oz. AGW **Ruler:** Mwambutsa IV **Subject:** Burundi Independence **Obv:** Uniformed bust left, beaded rim **Rev:** Arms, denomination and date below, beaded rim

Date	Mintage	F	VF	XF	Unc	BU
1962 Proof	2,500		Value: 900			

KM# 10   100 FRANCS
30.0000 g., 0.9000 Gold 0.8680 oz. AGW **Ruler:** Mwambutsa IV **Subject:** 50th Anniversary - Reign of Mwambutsa IV **Obv:** Uniformed bust 3/4 facing divides dates, beaded rim **Rev:** Arms, denomination below, beaded rim

Date	Mintage	F	VF	XF	Unc	BU
ND(1965)	—	—	—	—	850	—
ND(1965) Proof	5,000		Value: 900			

REPUBLIC
1966-
STANDARD COINAGE

KM# 18   FRANC
0.8400 g., Aluminum, 19.2 mm. **Obv:** Rising sun above date **Rev:** Denomination

Date	Mintage	F	VF	XF	Unc	BU
1970	10,000,000	2.00	4.50	7.50	17.50	20.00

KM# 19   FRANC
0.8700 g., Aluminum, 18.91 mm. **Obv:** Denomination **Rev:** Arms above date **Edge:** Reeded

Date	Mintage	F	VF	XF	Unc	BU
1976	5,000,000	—	0.30	0.75	1.75	2.50
1980	—	—	0.20	0.65	1.75	2.50
1990PM	—	—	0.15	0.50	1.50	2.00
1993PM	—	—	0.15	0.50	1.50	2.00

KM# 16   5 FRANCS
Aluminum **Obv:** Three stars at center, date below leaves **Rev:** Denomination within wreath

Date	Mintage	F	VF	XF	Unc	BU
1968(b)	2,000,000	—	0.25	0.85	2.00	2.75
1969(b)	2,000,000	—	0.25	0.85	2.00	2.75
1971(b)	2,000,000	—	0.25	0.85	2.00	2.75

KM# 20   5 FRANCS
2.2000 g., Aluminum, 25 mm. **Obv:** Arms above date **Rev:** Denomination

Date	Mintage	F	VF	XF	Unc	BU
1976	2,000,000	—	0.25	0.65	1.75	2.50
1980	—	—	0.25	0.65	1.75	2.50

KM# 11   10 FRANCS
3.2000 g., 0.9000 Gold 0.0926 oz. AGW **Subject:** First Anniversary of Republic

Date	Mintage	F	VF	XF	Unc	BU
1967 Proof	—		Value: 95.00			

KM# 17   10 FRANCS
7.8500 g., Copper-Nickel, 28 mm. **Series:** F.A.O. **Subject:** First Anniversary of Republic **Obv:** Date at center **Rev:** Denomination at center **Edge:** Reeded

Date	Mintage	F	VF	XF	Unc	BU
1968	2,000,000	—	0.75	1.50	3.50	4.00
1971	2,000,000	—	0.75	1.50	3.50	4.00

KM# 12   20 FRANCS
6.4000 g., 0.9000 Gold 0.1852 oz. AGW **Subject:** First Anniversary of Republic

Date	Mintage	F	VF	XF	Unc	BU
ND(1967) Proof	—		Value: 175			

KM# 13 25 FRANCS
8.0000 g., 0.9000 Gold 0.2315 oz. AGW **Subject:** First
Anniversary of Republic

Date	Mintage	F	VF	XF	Unc	BU
ND(1967) Proof	—	Value: 225				

KM# 14 50 FRANCS
16.0000 g., 0.9000 Gold 0.4630 oz. AGW **Subject:** First
Anniversary of Republic **Obv:** Bust, facing **Rev:** Arms above
denomination

Date	Mintage	F	VF	XF	Unc	BU
ND(1967) Proof	—	Value: 450				

KM# 15 100 FRANCS
32.0000 g., 0.9000 Gold 0.9259 oz. AGW **Subject:** First
Anniversary of Republic

Date	Mintage	F	VF	XF	Unc	BU
ND(1967) Proof	—	Value: 900				

PROOF SETS

KM#	Date	Mintage	Identification	Issue Price	Mkt Val
PS1	1962 (4)	2,500	KM2-5	—	1,675
PS2	1965 (4)	5,000	KM7-10	—	1,675
PS3	1967 (5)	—	KM11-15	—	1,850

CAMBODIA

The State of Cambodia, formerly Democratic Kampuchea
and the Khmer Republic, a land of paddy fields and forest-clad
hills located on the Indo-Chinese peninsula, fronting on the Gulf
of Thailand, has an area of 70,238 sq. mi. (181,040 sq. km.) and
a population of *11.21 million. Capital: Phnom Penh. Agriculture
is the basis of the economy, with rice the chief crop. Native industries include cattle breeding, weaving and rice milling. Rubber,
cattle, corn, and timber are exported.

The region was the nucleus of the Khmer empire which flourished from the 5th to the 12th century and attained an excellence
in art and architecture still evident in the magnificent ruins at
Angkor. The Khmer empire once ruled over much of Southeast
Asia, but began to decline in the 13th century as the Thai and Vietnamese invaded the region and attached its territories. At the
request of the Cambodian king, a French protectorate attached
to Cochin-China was established over the country in 1863, saving
it from dissolution, and in 1885, Cambodia was included in the
French Union of Indo-China.

France established a constitutional monarchy for Cambodia
within the French Union in 1949. The 1954 Geneva Convention
resulted in full independence for the Kingdom of Cambodia. King Sihanouk abdicated to his father and won the office of Prime Minister.

Prince Sihanouk was toppled by a bloodless coup led by Lon
Nol in March of 1970. Sihanouk moved to Peking to head a government-in-exile. On Oct. 9, 1970, Cambodia became the Khmer
Republic, and Lon Nol its President. The government of Lon Nol
was in turn toppled, April 17, 1975, by the Khmer Rouge insur-
gents who took control of the government and renamed the country Democratic Kampuchea.

The Khmer Rouge completely eliminated the economy and
created a state without money, exchange or barter while exter-
minating about 2 million Cambodians. These atrocities were
finally halted at the beginning of 1979 when the Vietnamese reg-
ulars and Cambodian rebels launched an offensive that drove the
Khmer Rouge out of Phnom Penh and the country acquired
another new title - The Peoples Republic of Kampuchea.

In 1993 Prince Norodom Sihanouk returned to Kampuchea
to lead the Supreme National Council.

RULERS

Kings of Cambodia
Norodom I, 1859-1904
Sisowath, 1904-1927
Sisowath Monivong, 1927-1941
Norodom Sihanouk, 1941-1955
Norodom Suramarit, 1955-1960
Heng Samrin, 1979-1985
Hun Sen, 1985-1991
Norodom Sihanouk, 1991-1993
 Chairman, Supreme National Council
 King, 1993-

MINT MARKS
(a) - Paris, privy marks only
(k) - Key, Havana, Cuba

MONETARY SYSTEM
(Commencing 1860)
100 Centimes = 1 Franc

INDEPENDENT KINGDOM
DECIMAL COINAGE

KM# 51 10 CENTIMES
Aluminum **Obv:** Bird statue left **Rev:** Denomination within wreath

Date	Mintage	F	VF	XF	Unc	BU
1953(a)	4,000,000	0.25	0.45	0.85	2.00	6.00

KM# 52 20 CENTIMES
Aluminum **Obv:** Two ceremonial bowls **Rev:** Denomination
within wreath

Date	Mintage	F	VF	XF	Unc	BU
1953(a)	3,000,000	0.25	0.65	1.50	3.00	5.50

KM# 53 50 CENTIMES
Aluminum **Obv:** Royal emblem **Rev:** Denomination within wreath

Date	Mintage	F	VF	XF	Unc	BU
1953(a)	4,200,000	0.45	0.85	2.00	4.00	6.00

KM# 54 10 SEN
Aluminum, 23 mm. **Obv:** Bird statue left **Rev:** Denomination
within wreath

Date	Mintage	F	VF	XF	Unc	BU
1959(a)	1,000,000	0.10	0.20	0.35	1.00	2.00

KM# 55 20 SEN
Aluminum, 27 mm. **Obv:** Two ceremonial bowls
Rev: Denomination within wreath

Date	Mintage	F	VF	XF	Unc	BU
1959(a)	1,004,000	0.15	0.25	0.60	1.00	1.50

KM# 56 50 SEN
Aluminum **Obv:** Royal emblem **Rev:** Denomination within wreath

Date	Mintage	F	VF	XF	Unc	BU
1959(a)	3,399,000	0.20	0.35	0.75	1.50	2.50

KHMER REPUBLIC
1970 - 1975
DECIMAL COINAGE

KM# 59 RIEL
2.8500 g., Copper-Nickel, 19.42 mm. **Series:** F.A.O.
Obv: Temple of Angkor Wat **Rev:** Grain bouquet, denomination
Edge: Reeded

Date	Mintage	F	VF	XF	Unc	BU
1970	5,000,000	—	—	7.50	16.50	22.50

Note: According to the Royal Mint of Great Britain, this coin
was minted at the Llantrissant Branch Mint in 1972 but
dated 1969. According to the FAO, the coin was to
have been dated 1971, but was "not minted" due to the
fall of the Cambodian government in 1970. However,
this coin was released in limited numbers in 1983. The
photograph of the coin, supplied by the FAO, is dated
1970. This type is currently available from many sources in the numismatic market.

KM# 60 5000 RIELS
19.0100 g., 0.9250 Silver 0.5653 oz. ASW **Obv:** Temple of
Angkor Wat **Rev:** Royal emblem above denomination

Date	Mintage	F	VF	XF	Unc	BU
1974	500	—	—	65.00	70.00	
1974 Proof	800	Value: 70.00				

KM# 61 5000 RIELS
19.0100 g., 0.9250 Silver 0.5653 oz. ASW **Obv:** Cambodian
dancers **Rev:** Similar to KM#60, (royal emblem above denomination)

Date	Mintage	F	VF	XF	Unc	BU
1974	500	—	—	85.00	90.00	
1974 Proof	800	Value: 90.00				

KM# 62   10000 RIELS
38.0300 g., 0.9250 Silver 1.1309 oz. ASW **Obv:** Bust of President Lon Nol left **Rev:** Royal emblem above denomination

Date	Mintage	F	VF	XF	Unc	BU
1974	500	—	—	—	110	115
1974 Proof	800	Value: 115				

KM# 63   10000 RIELS
38.0300 g., 0.9250 Silver 1.1309 oz. ASW **Obv:** Celestial dancer **Rev:** Royal emblem above denomination

Date	Mintage	F	VF	XF	Unc	BU
1974	500	—	—	—	140	150
1974 Proof	800	Value: 150				

KM# 64   50000 RIELS
6.7100 g., 0.9000 Gold 0.1942 oz. AGW **Obv:** Cambodian dancers **Rev:** Royal emblem above denomination

Date	Mintage	F	VF	XF	Unc	BU
1974	3,250	—	—	—	200	220
1974 Proof	2,300	Value: 245				

KM# 65   50000 RIELS
6.7100 g., 0.9000 Gold 0.1942 oz. AGW **Obv:** Celestial dancer **Rev:** Royal emblem above denomination

Date	Mintage	F	VF	XF	Unc	BU
1974	450	—	—	—	250	275
1974 Proof	300	Value: 375				

KM# 66   100000 RIELS
13.4200 g., 0.9000 Gold 0.3883 oz. AGW **Obv:** Bust of President Lon Nol left **Rev:** Royal emblem above denomination

Date	Mintage	F	VF	XF	Unc	BU
1974	250	—	—	—	400	425
1974 Proof	100	Value: 725				

PEOPLE'S REPUBLIC
OF KAMPUCHEA
1979 - 1990
DECIMAL COINAGE

KM# 69   5 SEN
2.4900 g., Aluminum, 20.39 mm. **Obv:** Royal emblem **Rev:** Denomination, date at bottom **Edge:** Plain

Date	Mintage	F	VF	XF	Unc	BU
1979	—	—	0.60	1.25	3.00	4.00

KM# 71   4 RIELS
Copper-Nickel **Subject:** Cambodian Transportation **Obv:** Royal emblem above denomination **Rev:** Old sailing ship, date at right

Date	Mintage	F	VF	XF	Unc	BU
1988(k)	1,500	—	—	—	12.50	14.50

KM# 91   4 RIELS
Copper   **Rev:** Angkor Wat Temples

Date	Mintage	F	VF	XF	Unc	BU
ND(1988)	—	—	—	—	7.50	10.00

KM# 75   4 RIELS
Copper   **Subject:** 700th Anniversary of Swiss Unity **Obv:** Royal emblem above denomination **Rev:** Standing figures of man and boy **Note:** Size varies 38-39mm.

Date	Mintage	F	VF	XF	Unc	BU
ND(1988)	15,000	—	—	—	10.00	12.00

KM# 74   4 RIELS
Copper-Nickel **Subject:** World Championship Soccer - Italy **Obv:** Royal emblem above denomination **Rev:** Soccer ball with country names and dates, Italy at center

Date	Mintage	F	VF	XF	Unc	BU
1989	2,000	—	—	—	7.00	9.00

KM# 90   4 RIELS
Copper **Obv:** Royal emblem above denomination **Rev:** Angkor Wat Temples

Date	Mintage	F	VF	XF	Unc	BU
1989	—	—	—	—	8.50	11.50

KM# 70   20 RIELS
12.0600 g., 0.9990 Silver 0.3873 oz. ASW **Subject:** Cambodian Transportation **Obv:** Royal emblem above denomination **Rev:** Old sailing ship

Date	Mintage	F	VF	XF	Unc	BU
1988(k)	3,000	—	—	—	30.00	32.50

KM# 72   20 RIELS
12.0600 g., 0.9990 Silver 0.3873 oz. ASW **Subject:** World Championship Soccer - Mexico **Obv:** Royal emblem above denomination **Rev:** Soccer goalie, country name and date below

Date	Mintage	F	VF	XF	Unc	BU
1988	5,000	—	—	—	30.00	32.50

KM# 73   20 RIELS
16.0000 g., 0.9990 Silver 0.5139 oz. ASW **Subject:** 700th Anniversary of Swiss Unity - 1991 **Obv:** Royal emblem above denomination **Rev:** Standing figures of man and boy

Date	Mintage	F	VF	XF	Unc	BU
ND(1988) Proof	2,000	Value: 45.00				

KM# 78   20 RIELS
12.0000 g., 0.9990 Silver 0.3854 oz. ASW   **Subject:** European Soccer Championship - Germany **Obv:** Royal emblem above denomination **Rev:** Soccer players, date below

Date	Mintage	F	VF	XF	Unc	BU
1988(k)	5,000	—	—	—	40.00	42.50

KM# 76   20 RIELS
16.0000 g., 0.9990 Silver 0.5139 oz. ASW   **Obv:** Royal emblem above denomination **Rev:** Angkor Wat Temples

Date	Mintage	F	VF	XF	Unc	BU
1989 Proof	2,000	Value: 40.00				

KM# 79   20 RIELS
16.0000 g., 0.9990 Silver 0.5139 oz. ASW   **Subject:** World Championship Soccer - Italy **Obv:** Royal emblem above denomination **Rev:** Soccer ball with country names and dates, Italy at center

Date	Mintage	F	VF	XF	Unc	BU
1989 Proof	10,000	Value: 28.00				

KM# 80   20 RIELS
16.0000 g., 0.9990 Silver 0.5139 oz. ASW   **Subject:** Summer Olympics **Obv:** Royal emblem above denomination **Rev:** Fencers, date at right

Date	Mintage	F	VF	XF	Unc	BU
1989 Proof	10,000	Value: 32.50				

KM# 81   20 RIELS
16.0000 g., 0.9990 Silver 0.5139 oz. ASW   **Subject:** Winter Olympics **Obv:** Royal emblem above denomination **Rev:** Skier, date at lower left

Date	Mintage	F	VF	XF	Unc	BU
1989 Proof	5,000	Value: 35.00				

KM# 77   40 RIELS
3.1500 g., 0.9990 Gold 0.1012 oz. AGW   **Obv:** Royal emblem above denomination **Rev:** Angkor Wat Temples

Date	Mintage	F	VF	XF	Unc	BU
1989	500	—	—	—	145	160

KM# 82   40 RIELS
3.1500 g., 0.9990 Gold 0.1012 oz. AGW   **Obv:** Royal emblem above denomination **Rev:** Folklore dance, date lower left

Date	Mintage	F	VF	XF	Unc	BU
1990	500	Value: 175				

STATE OF CAMBODIA
1990 - 1993
DECIMAL COINAGE

KM# 83   4 RIELS
Nickel Plated Steel   **Subject:** Barcelona 1992 - 25th Summer Olympic Games **Obv:** National flag above denomination **Rev:** Tennis player, date below

Date	Mintage	F	VF	XF	Unc	BU
1991	5,000	—	—	—	13.50	15.00

KM# 86   4 RIELS
Copper-Nickel   **Series:** Prehistoric animals, date at left **Obv:** National flag above denomination **Rev:** Cryptocleidus

Date	Mintage	F	VF	XF	Unc	BU
1993	—	—	—	—	25.00	30.00

KM# 89   4 RIELS
Copper-Nickel   **Series:** Prehistoric Animals **Obv:** National flag above denomination **Rev:** Anatosaurus, date at right

Date	Mintage	F	VF	XF	Unc	BU
1994	—	—	—	—	25.00	30.00

KM# 84   20 RIELS
11.9600 g., 0.9990 Silver 0.3841 oz. ASW   **Subject:** World Cup Soccer - 1994 **Obv:** National flag above denomination **Rev:** Player kicking ball, date at left

Date	Mintage	F	VF	XF	Unc	BU
1991	30,000	—	—	—	30.00	32.50

KM# 88   20 RIELS
11.9600 g., 0.9990 Silver 0.3841 oz. ASW   **Subject:** World Cup Soccer - 1994 **Obv:** National flag above denomination **Rev:** 2 players kicking ball, date below

Date	Mintage	F	VF	XF	Unc	BU
1992 Proof	—	Value: 42.50				

KM# 85   20 RIELS
19.9500 g., 0.9990 Silver 0.6407 oz. ASW   **Subject:** Protection of Nature **Obv:** National flag above denomination **Rev:** Asian elephants, date at right

Date	Mintage	F	VF	XF	Unc	BU
1993 Proof	—	Value: 50.00				

KM# 87   20 RIELS
16.0600 g., 0.9990 Silver 0.5158 oz. ASW **Series:** Prehistoric Animals **Obv:** National flag above denomination **Rev:** Indricotherium, date lower right

Date	Mintage	F	VF	XF	Unc	BU
1993	—	Value: 40.00				

KM# 96   20 RIELS
16.1000 g., 0.9990 Silver 0.5171 oz. ASW **Series:** Prehistoric Animals **Obv:** National flag above denomination **Rev:** Nothosaurus at water's edge, date lower right **Edge:** Plain

Date	Mintage	F	VF	XF	Unc	BU
1994 Proof	—	Value: 50.00				

KM# 97   20 RIELS
16.1000 g., 0.9990 Silver 0.5171 oz. ASW, 37.9 mm. **Subject:** Prehistoric Animals **Obv:** National flag above denomination **Rev:** Monoclonius, date lower left **Edge:** Plain

Date	Mintage	F	VF	XF	Unc	BU
1994 Proof	—	Value: 55.00				

KINGDOM
1993 -
DECIMAL COINAGE

KM# 92   50 RIELS
1.6000 g., Steel, 15.9 mm. **Obv:** Single towered building **Rev:** Denomination within wreath **Edge:** Plain

Date	Mintage	F	VF	XF	Unc	BU
BE2538-1994	—	—	—	—	0.25	0.45

KM# 93   100 RIELS
2.0000 g., Steel, 17.9 mm. **Obv:** Three-towered building **Rev:** Denomination within wreath

Date	Mintage	F	VF	XF	Unc	BU
BE2538-1994	—	—	—	—	0.50	0.85

KM# 94   200 RIELS
2.4000 g., Steel, 19.9 mm. **Obv:** 2 Ceremonial bowls **Rev:** Denomination within wreath

Date	Mintage	F	VF	XF	Unc	BU
BE2538-1994	—	—	—	—	1.00	1.50

KM# 95   500 RIELS
6.5000 g., Bi-Metallic Steel center in Brass ring, 25.8 mm. **Obv:** Royal emblem **Rev:** Denomination within wreath **Edge:** Plain and reeded sections

Date	Mintage	F	VF	XF	Unc	BU
BE2538-1994	—	—	—	—	4.50	6.00

ESSAIS

KM#	Date	Mintage	Identification	Issue Price	Mkt Val
E9	1953	1,200	10 Centimes.	—	20.00
E10	1953	1,200	20 Centimes.	—	22.00
E11	1953	1,200	50 Centimes.	—	25.00

PATTERNS
Including off metal strikes

KM#	Date	Mintage	Identification	Mkt Val
Pn15	1902	—	4 Francs. Silver. Palace at Phnom Penh	275
Pn16	1970	—	Riel. Copper-Nickel. KM59.	—

PIEFORTS WITH ESSAI
Double thickness
Standard metals unless otherwise noted

KM#	Date	Mintage	Identification	Issue Price	Mkt Val
PE9	1953	104	10 Centimes.	—	80.00
PE10	1953	104	20 Centimes.	—	80.00
PE11	1953	104	50 Centimes.	—	100

PIEFORTS

KM#	Date	Mintage	Identification	Mkt Val
P12	1989	110	20 Riels. 0.9990 Silver. KM80.	125
P13	1989	110	20 Riels. 0.9990 Silver. KM76.	125

MINT SETS

KM#	Date	Mintage	Identification	Issue Price	Mkt Val
MS1	1953 (3)	—	KM51,-53	—	12.00
MS2	1974 (7)	250	KM60-66	—	1,500
MS3	1974 (4)	500	KM60-63	—	425
MS4	BE2538 (1994) (4)	—	KM92-95 with 7 laminated banknotes	0.38	9.50

PROOF SETS

KM#	Date	Mintage	Identification	Issue Price	Mkt Val
PS1	1974 (7)	100	KM60-66	—	1,775
PS2	1974 (4)	800	KM60-63	—	425

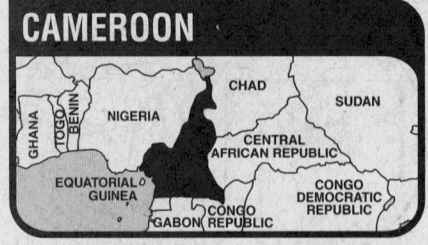

CAMEROON

The Republic of Cameroon, located in west-central Africa on the Gulf of Guinea, has an area of 183,569 sq. mi. (475,445 sq. km.) and a population of *15.13 million. Capital: Yaounde. About 90 percent of the labor force is employed on the land; cash crops account for 80 percent of the country's export revenue. Cocoa, coffee, aluminum, cotton, rubber, and timber are exported.

European contact with what is now the United Republic of Cameroon began in the 16th century with the voyage of Portuguese navigator Fernando Po. The following three centuries saw continuous activity by Spanish, Dutch, and British traders and missionaries. The land was spared colonial rule until 1884, when treaties with tribal chiefs brought German domination. In 1919, the League of Nations divided the Cameroons between Great Britain and France, with the larger eastern area going to France. The French and British mandates were converted into United Nations trusteeships in 1946. French Cameroon became the independent Cameroon Republic on Jan. 1, 1960. The federation of East (French) and West (British) Cameroon was established in 1961 when the southern part of British Cameroon voted for reunification with the Cameroon Republic, and the northern part for union with Nigeria Cameroon joined the Commonwealth of Nations in November 1995.

Coins of French Equatorial Africa and of the monetary unions identified as the Equatorial African States and Central African States are also current in Cameroon.

MINT MARKS
(a) - Paris, privy marks only
SA - Pretoria, 1943

MONETARY SYSTEM
100 Centimes = 1 Franc

FRENCH MANDATE
STANDARD COINAGE

KM# 1   50 CENTIMES
2.5300 g., Aluminum-Bronze, 17.5 mm. **Obv:** Laureate head left, date below **Rev:** Spray of branches below denomination

Date	Mintage	F	VF	XF	Unc	BU
1924(a)	4,000,000	1.50	3.50	45.00	100	250
1925(a)	2,500,000	2.00	5.00	50.00	110	275
1926(a)	7,800,000	1.00	2.00	30.00	85.00	200

KM# 4   50 CENTIMES
Bronze, 20.2 mm. **Obv:** Rooster left, monogramed shield top right **Rev:** Cross of Lorraine divides denomination below, date at bottom

Date	Mintage	F	VF	XF	Unc	BU
1943SA	4,000,000	2.00	3.50	12.00	28.00	38.00

KM# 6   50 CENTIMES
Bronze **Obv:** Rooster left, monogramed shield at top right, LIBRE added to legend **Rev:** Cross of Lorraine divides denomination below, date at bottom

Date	Mintage	F	VF	XF	Unc	BU
1943SA	4,000,000	2.50	5.50	12.00	22.00	32.00

KM# 2   FRANC
Aluminum-Bronze, 23 mm. **Obv:** Laureate head left, date below **Rev:** Denomination above three branched spray **Edge:** Reeded

Date	Mintage	F	VF	XF	Unc	BU
1924(a)	3,000,000	2.00	4.00	45.00	100	260
1925(a)	1,722,000	3.00	6.00	60.00	125	285
1926(a)	12,928,000	1.00	2.00	25.00	60.00	150

KM# 5   FRANC
Bronze, 25 mm. **Obv:** Rooster left, monogrammed shield top right **Rev:** Cross of Lorraine divides denomination below, date at bottom

Date	Mintage	F	VF	XF	Unc	BU
1943SA	3,000,000	2.50	4.50	17.50	32.00	42.00

KM# 7 FRANC
Bronze, 25 mm. **Obv:** Rooster left, monogrammed shield at top right, LIBRE added to legend **Rev:** Cross of Lorraine divides denomination below, date at bottom

Date	Mintage	F	VF	XF	Unc	BU
1943SA	3,000,000	3.50	6.50	20.00	38.00	48.00

KM# 8 FRANC
Aluminum, 23 mm. **Obv:** Winged bust left, date below **Rev:** Gazelle (gazella Leptoceros), antlers divide denomination

Date	Mintage	F	VF	XF	Unc	BU
1948(a)	8,000,000	0.15	0.35	0.85	1.50	2.50

KM# 3 2 FRANCS
Aluminum-Bronze, 27 mm. **Obv:** Laureate head left, date below **Rev:** Denomination above three branch spray

Date	Mintage	F	VF	XF	Unc	BU
1924(a)	500,000	5.00	15.00	100	185	300
1925(a)	100,000	8.00	25.00	160	300	500

KM# 9 2 FRANCS
2.2100 g., Aluminum, 27 mm. **Obv:** Winged bust left, date below **Rev:** Gazelle (gazella leptoceros), antlers divide denomination

Date	Mintage	F	VF	XF	Unc	BU
1948(a)	5,000,000	0.65	1.25	2.00	4.00	6.00

FRENCH EQUATORIAL AFRICA - CAMEROON
STANDARD COINAGE

KM# 10 5 FRANCS
Aluminum-Bronze **Obv:** Three giant eland **Rev:** Denomination

Date	Mintage	F	VF	XF	Unc	BU
1958(a)	30,000,000	0.25	0.50	1.00	3.00	5.00

KM# 11 10 FRANCS
Aluminum-Bronze **Obv:** Three giant eland left, date below **Rev:** Denomination within wreath

Date	Mintage	F	VF	XF	Unc	BU
1958(a)	25,000,000	0.25	0.50	1.50	4.00	6.00

KM# 12 25 FRANCS
Aluminum-Bronze **Obv:** Three giant eland left, date below **Rev:** Denomination within wreath

Date	Mintage	F	VF	XF	Unc	BU
1958(a)	12,000,000	0.50	1.00	2.00	6.00	8.00

REPUBLIC
STANDARD COINAGE

KM# 13 50 FRANCS
Copper-Nickel, 30 mm. **Subject:** Independence Commemorative **Obv:** Three giant eland left, date above **Rev:** Denomination within wreath

Date	Mintage	F	VF	XF	Unc	BU
1960(a)	9,000,000	2.00	3.50	5.50	10.00	12.50

KM# 14 100 FRANCS
12.0000 g., Nickel **Obv:** Three giant eland left **Rev:** Denomination, date above **Note:** KM#14 was issued double thick and should not be considered a piefort.

Date	Mintage	F	VF	XF	Unc	BU
1966(a)	4,000,000	1.00	2.00	4.50	10.00	12.50
1967(a)	4,000,000	1.00	2.00	4.50	10.00	12.50
1968(a)	5,000,000	1.00	2.00	4.50	10.00	12.50

KM# 15 100 FRANCS
Nickel **Obv:** Three giant eland left **Rev:** Denomination within circle, date below **Note:** Refer also to Equatorial African States and Central African States.

Date	Mintage	F	VF	XF	Unc	BU
1971(a)	9,000,000	2.00	3.00	6.00	12.50	—
1972(a)	3,000,000	2.00	3.00	6.00	12.50	—

KM# 16 100 FRANCS
Nickel **Obv:** Three giant eland left **Rev:** Denomination within circle, date below **Note:** Mule

Date	Mintage	F	VF	XF	Unc	BU
1972(a)	4,000,000	6.50	12.50	22.50	45.00	—

KM# 17 100 FRANCS
Nickel **Obv:** Three giant eland left **Rev:** Denomination above date, within circle

Date	Mintage	F	VF	XF	Unc	BU
1975(a)	—	1.00	2.00	3.00	5.50	7.00
1980(a)	—	1.00	2.00	3.00	5.50	7.00
1982(a)	—	0.75	1.50	2.50	4.50	6.00
1983(a)	—	0.75	1.50	2.50	4.50	6.00
1984(a)	—	0.75	1.50	2.50	4.50	6.00
1986(a)	—	0.75	1.50	2.50	4.50	6.00

KM# 23 500 FRANCS
10.8900 g., Copper-Nickel, 30.04 mm. **Obv:** Plants divide denomination and date **Rev:** Head 3/4 left

Date	Mintage	F	VF	XF	Unc	BU
1985(a)	—	2.00	3.50	5.50	10.00	12.50
1986(a)	—	2.00	3.50	5.50	10.00	12.50
1988	—	2.00	3.50	5.50	10.00	12.50

KM# 18 1000 FRANCS
3.5000 g., 0.9000 Gold 0.1013 oz. AGW **Subject:** 10th Anniversary of Independence **Obv:** Head of President El Hajj Ahmadou Ahidjo left **Rev:** Design at center, denomination below, arms above

Date	Mintage	F	VF	XF	Unc	BU
1970 Proof	4,000	Value: 110				

KM# 19 3000 FRANCS
10.5000 g., 0.9000 Gold 0.3038 oz. AGW **Subject:** 10th Anniversary of Independence **Obv:** Head of President El Hajj Ahmadou Ahidjo left **Rev:** Design at center, denomination below, arms above

Date	Mintage	F	VF	XF	Unc	BU
1970 Proof	4,000	Value: 310				

Note: With or without cornucopia mint mark on reverse

KM# 20 5000 FRANCS
17.5000 g., 0.9000 Gold 0.5064 oz. AGW **Subject:** 10th Anniversary of Independence **Obv:** Head of President El Hajj Ahmadou Ahidjo left **Rev:** Head, left, within center circle, denomination below, arms above

Date	Mintage	F	VF	XF	Unc	BU
1970 Proof	4,000	Value: 500				

KM# 21   10000 FRANCS
35.0000 g., 0.9000 Gold 1.0127 oz. AGW **Subject:** 10th
Anniversary of Independence **Obv:** President El Hajj Ahmadou
Ahidjo left **Rev:** Elands facing center, denomination below, arms
above

Date	Mintage	F	VF	XF	Unc	BU
1970 Proof	4,000	Value: 1,000				

KM# 22   20000 FRANCS
70.0000 g., 0.9000 Gold 2.0254 oz. AGW **Subject:** 10th
Anniversary of Independence **Obv:** Head of President El Hajj
Ahmadou Ahidjo left **Rev:** Arms, denomination below

Date	Mintage	F	VF	XF	Unc	BU
1970 Proof	4,000	Value: 2,150				

ESSAIS
Standard metals unless otherwise noted

KM#	Date	Mintage	Identification	Issue Price	Mkt Val
E1	1924(a)	—	50 Centimes. Aluminum-Bronze. KM1.	—	100
E2	1924(a)	—	Franc. Aluminum-Bronze. KM2.	—	110
E3	1924(a)	—	2 Francs. Aluminum-Bronze. Laureate head left, date below. Denomination above three branch spray. KM3.	—	140
E4	1943	—	1/2 Franc.	—	600
E5	1948(a)	2,000	Franc. Copper-Nickel. KM8.	—	25.00
E6	1948(a)	2,000	2 Francs. Copper-Nickel. KM9.	—	35.00
E7	1958(a)	2,030	5 Francs. Bi-Metallic. Copper-Nickel center. Brass ring. KM24.	—	15.00
E8	1958(a)	2,030	10 Francs. Iron-Blued. KM25.	—	17.50
E9	1958(a)	2,030	25 Francs. Nickel Plated Iron. KM26.	—	20.00
E10	1960(a)	1,500	50 Francs. Copper-Nickel. Three giant eland left, date above. Denomination within wreath. KM13.	—	27.50
E11	1966(a)	1,200	100 Francs. Nickel. KM14.	—	35.00
E12	1970(a)	—	1000 Francs. Bronze. KM18.	—	95.00
E12	1970(a)	—	1000 Francs. Bronze. KM18.	—	95.00
E13	1971(a)	1,550	100 Francs. Nickel. KM15.	—	22.50
E14	1971	6	100 Francs. Gold. KM15.	—	1,300
E14	1971	6	100 Francs. Gold. KM15.	—	1,300
E15	1972(a)	1,550	100 Francs. Nickel. KM16.	—	30.00
E16	1975(a)	1,700	100 Francs. Nickel. KM17.	—	22.50
E17	1985(a)	—	500 Francs. Copper-Nickel. Plants divide denomination and date. KM23.	—	30.00

PIEFORTS WITH ESSAI
Double thickness - Standard metals unless otherwise noted

KM#	Date	Mintage	Identification	Issue Price	Mkt Val
PE1	1948(a)	104	Franc. Aluminum. KM8.	—	70.00
PE2	1948(a)	104	2 Francs. Aluminum. KM9.	—	80.00
PE3	1948(a)	—	2 Francs. Aluminum. KM9, double piefort.	—	500
PE4	1948(a)	—	2 Francs. Copper-Nickel. KM9.	—	250

PROOF SETS

KM#	Date	Mintage	Identification	Issue Price	Mkt Val
PS1	1970 (5)	4,000	KM18-22	—	4,075

CANADA

CONFEDERATION

Canada is located to the north of the United States, and spans the full breadth of the northern portion of North America from Atlantic to Pacific oceans, except for the State of Alaska. It has a total area of 3,850,000 sq. mi. (9,971,550 sq. km.) and a population of 30.29 million. Capital: Ottawa.

Jacques Cartier, a French explorer, took possession of Canada for France in 1534, and for more than a century the history of Canada was that of a French colony. Samuel de Champlain helped to establish the first permanent colony in North America, in 1604 at Port Royal, Acadia – now Annapolis Royal, Nova Scotia. Four years later he founded the settlement in Quebec.

The British settled along the coast to the south while the French, motivated by a grand design, pushed into the interior. France's plan for a great American empire was to occupy the Mississippi heartland of the country, and from there to press in upon the narrow strip of English coastal settlements from the west. Inevitably, armed conflict erupted between the French and the British; consequently, Britain acquired Hudson Bay, Newfoundland and Nova Scotia from the French in 1713. British control of the rest of New France was secured in 1763, largely because of James Wolfe's great victory over Montcalm near Quebec in 1759.

During the American Revolution, Canada became a refuge for great numbers of American Royalists, most of whom settled in Ontario, thereby creating an English majority west of the Ottawa River. The ethnic imbalance contravened the effectiveness of the prevailing French type of government, and in 1791 the Constitutional act was passed by the British parliament, dividing Canada at the Ottawa River into two parts, each with its own government: Upper Canada, chiefly English and consisting of the southern section of what is now Ontario; and Lower Canada, chiefly French and consisting principally of the southern section of Quebec. Subsequent revolt by dissidents in both sections caused the British government to pass the Union Act, July 23, 1840, which united Lower and Upper Canada (as Canada East and Canada West) to form the Province of Canada, with one council and one assembly in which the two sections had equal numbers.

The union of the two provinces did not encourage political stability; the equal strength of the French and British made the task of government all but impossible. A further change was made with the passage of the British North American Act, which took effect on July 1, 1867, and established Canada as the first federal union in the British Empire. Four provinces entered the union at first: Upper Canada as Ontario, Lower Canada as Quebec, Nova Scotia and New Brunswick. The Hudson Bay Company's territories were acquired in 1869 out of which were formed the provinces of Manitoba, Saskatchewan and Alberta. British Columbia joined in 1871 and Prince Edward Island in 1873. Canada took over the Arctic Archipelago in 1895. In 1949 Newfoundland came into the confederation.

In the early years, Canada's coins were struck in England at the Royal Mint in London or at the Heaton Mint in Birmingham. Issues struck at the Royal Mint do not bear a mint mark, but those produced by Heaton carry an "H". All Canadian coins have been struck since January 2, 1908, at the Royal Canadian Mints at Ottawa and recently at Winnipeg except for some 1968 pure nickel dimes struck at the U.S. Mint in Philadelphia, and do not bear mint marks. Ottawa's mint mark (C) does not appear on some 20th Century Newfoundland issues, however, as it does on English type sovereigns struck there from 1908 through 1918.

Canada is a member of the Commonwealth of Nations. Elizabeth II is Head of State as Queen of Canada.

RULER
British 1763-

MONETARY SYSTEM
1 Dollar = 100 Cents

CIRCULATION COINAGE

KM# 7 CENT 4.5400 g. Bronze **Ruler:** Victoria **Obv.:** Crowned head left within beaded circle **Obv. Leg.:** VICTORIA DEI GRATIA REGINA. CANADA **Obv. Des.:** Leonard C. Wyon **Rev.:** Denomination and date within beaded circle, chain of leaves surrounds **Edge:** Plain **Size:** 25.5 mm.

Date	Mintage	VG-8	F-12	VF-20	XF-40	MS-60	MS-63	Proof
1901	4,100,000	2.25	3.00	4.50	8.50	35.00	85.00	—

KM# 8 CENT 4.5400 g. Bronze **Ruler:** Edward VII **Obv.:** Kings bust right within beaded circle **Obv. Des.:** G. W. DeSaulles **Rev.:** Denomination above date within circle, chain of leaves surrounds **Edge:** Plain **Size:** 25.5 mm.

Date	Mintage	VG-8	F-12	VF-20	XF-40	MS-60	MS-63	Proof
1902	3,000,000	1.75	2.25	3.50	6.00	25.00	75.00	—
1903	4,000,000	1.75	2.25	3.00	6.00	30.00	80.00	—
1904	2,500,000	2.00	3.50	5.00	8.00	35.00	85.00	—
1905	2,000,000	3.50	6.00	7.50	12.00	45.00	150	—
1906	4,100,000	1.75	2.25	3.00	6.00	35.00	175	—
1907	2,400,000	2.00	3.50	4.50	9.00	35.00	200	—
1907H	800,000	12.00	24.00	30.00	50.00	175	550	—
1908	2,401,506	3.00	3.50	5.00	8.00	30.00	90.00	150
1909	3,973,339	1.75	2.50	3.00	6.00	30.00	100	—
1910	5,146,487	1.75	2.50	3.00	5.00	26.00	70.00	—

KM# 15 CENT 4.5400 g. Bronze **Ruler:** George V **Obv.:** King's bust left **Obv. Des.:** E. B. MacKennal **Rev.:** Denomination above date within beaded circle, chain of leaves surrounds **Edge:** Plain **Size:** 25.5 mm.

Date	Mintage	VG-8	F-12	VF-20	XF-40	MS-60	MS-63	Proof
1911	4,663,486	0.80	1.30	1.75	3.50	25.00	75.00	250

KM# 21 CENT 4.5400 g. Bronze **Ruler:** George V **Obv.:** King's bust left **Obv. Des.:** E. B. MacKennal **Rev.:** Denomination above date within beaded circle, chain of leaves surrounds **Edge:** Plain **Size:** 25.5 mm.

Date	Mintage	VG-8	F-12	VF-20	XF-40	MS-60	MS-63	Proof
1912	5,107,642	0.75	1.50	2.25	3.50	25.00	80.00	—
1913	5,735,405	0.75	1.50	2.25	4.00	23.00	80.00	—
1914	3,405,958	1.00	1.50	2.50	4.00	35.00	125	—
1915	4,932,134	0.75	2.25	3.00	4.00	30.00	100	—
1916	11,022,367	0.50	0.65	1.25	3.00	16.00	50.00	—
1917	11,899,254	0.50	0.65	0.90	2.25	13.00	45.00	—
1918	12,970,798	0.50	0.65	0.90	2.25	12.00	45.00	—
1919	11,279,634	0.50	0.65	0.90	2.25	12.00	45.00	—
1920	6,762,247	0.60	0.75	1.00	2.25	20.00	100	—

Dot below date

KM# 28 CENT 3.2400 g. Bronze **Ruler:** George V **Obv.:** King's bust left **Obv. Des.:** E. B. MacKennal **Rev.:** Denomination above date, leaves flank **Rev. Des.:** Fred Lewis **Edge:** Plain **Size:** 19.10 mm.

Date	Mintage	VG-8	F-12	VF-20	XF-40	MS-60	MS-63	Proof
1920	15,483,923	0.20	0.50	1.00	2.00	15.00	50.00	—
1921	7,601,627	0.50	0.70	1.75	5.00	35.00	200	—
1922	1,243,635	13.00	16.00	21.00	35.00	200	1,200	—
1923	1,019,002	29.00	35.00	40.00	50.00	300	2,000	—
1924	1,593,195	5.00	6.50	8.50	15.00	125	850	—
1925	1,000,622	18.00	21.00	27.00	40.00	200	1,600	—
1926	2,143,372	3.50	4.50	7.00	11.00	100	650	—
1927	3,553,928	1.25	2.00	3.50	6.00	40.00	225	—
1928	9,144,860	0.15	0.30	0.65	1.50	20.00	90.00	—
1929	12,159,840	0.15	0.30	0.65	1.50	20.00	80.00	—
1930	2,538,613	2.00	2.50	4.50	8.50	50.00	225	—
1931	3,842,776	0.65	1.00	2.50	5.50	40.00	200	—
1932	21,316,190	0.15	0.20	0.50	1.50	14.00	45.00	—
1933	12,079,310	0.15	0.30	0.50	1.50	15.00	65.00	—
1934	7,042,358	0.20	0.30	0.75	1.50	14.00	45.00	—
1935	7,526,400	0.20	0.30	0.75	1.50	14.00	45.00	—
1936	8,768,769	0.15	0.30	0.75	1.50	14.00	45.00	—
1936 dot below date; Rare	678,823							—

Note: Only one possible business strike is known to exist. No other examples (or possible business strikes) have ever surfaced.

1936 dot below date, specimen, 3 known		—	—	—	—	—	—	—

Date	Mintage	VG-8	F-12	VF-20	XF-40	MS-60	MS-63	Proof
1975	642,318,000	—	—	—	—	0.10	0.15	
1976	701,122,890	—	—	—	—	0.10	0.15	
1977	453,762,670	—	—	—	—	0.10	0.15	
1978	911,170,647	—	—	—	—	0.10	0.15	

Note: At the David Akers auction of the John Jay Pittman collection (Part 1, 10-97), a gem specimen realized $121,000. At the David Akers auction of the John Jay Pittman collection (Part 3, 10-99), a near choice specimen realized $115,000.

Maple leaf

KM#32 CENT 3.2400 g. Bronze **Ruler:** George VI **Obv.:** Head left **Obv. Des.:** T. H. Paget **Rev.:** Maple leaf divides date and denomination **Rev. Des.:** George E. Kruger-Gray **Edge:** Plain **Size:** 19.10 mm.

Date	Mintage	VG-8	F-12	VF-20	XF-40	MS-60	MS-63	Proof
1937	10,040,231	0.35	0.50	1.00	2.00	3.00	9.00	—
1938	18,365,608	0.15	0.20	0.35	0.75	3.00	13.00	—
1939	21,600,319	0.10	0.20	0.35	0.70	1.75	5.00	—
1940	85,740,532	0.10	0.15	0.25	0.50	2.25	5.50	—
1941	56,336,011	0.10	0.15	0.25	0.50	8.00	60.00	—
1942	76,113,708	0.10	0.15	0.25	0.50	8.00	60.00	—
1943	89,111,969	0.10	0.15	0.25	0.45	3.50	25.00	—
1944	44,131,216	0.10	0.15	0.30	0.60	12.00	100	—
1945	77,268,591	0.10	0.15	0.20	0.35	3.00	22.00	—
1946	56,662,071	0.10	0.15	0.20	0.35	3.00	7.50	—
1947	31,093,901	0.10	0.15	0.20	0.35	3.00	7.50	—
1947 maple leaf	47,855,448	0.10	0.15	0.20	0.35	3.00	5.00	—

KM# 41 CENT 3.2400 g. Bronze **Ruler:** George VI **Obv.:** Modified legend **Obv. Des.:** T. H. Paget **Rev. Des.:** George E. Kruger-Gray **Edge:** Plain **Size:** 19.10 mm.

Date	Mintage	VG-8	F-12	VF-20	XF-40	MS-60	MS-63	Proof
1948	25,767,779	—	0.15	0.25	0.70	4.00	35.00	—
1949	33,128,933	—	0.10	0.15	0.35	3.00	9.00	—
1950	60,444,992	—	0.10	0.15	0.25	2.00	9.00	—
1951	80,430,379	—	0.10	0.15	0.20	2.00	13.00	—
1952	67,631,736	—	0.10	0.15	0.20	2.00	7.00	—

No strap   With strap

KM# 49 CENT 3.2400 g. Bronze **Ruler:** Elizabeth II **Obv.:** Laureate bust right **Obv. Des.:** Mary Gillick **Rev.:** Maple leaf divides date and denomination **Rev. Des.:** George E. Kruger-Gray **Size:** 19.10 mm.

Date	Mintage	VG-8	F-12	VF-20	XF-40	MS-60	MS-63	Proof
1953	67,806,016	0.10	0.10	0.10	0.35	0.65	1.50	—
Note: Without strap								
1953	Inc. above	0.50	1.00	1.50	2.50	12.00	55.00	—
Note: With strap								
1954	22,181,760	0.10	0.10	0.10	0.40	2.00	6.00	—
Note: With strap								
1954 Prooflike only	Inc. above	—	—	—	—	250	500	—
Note: Without strap								
1955	56,403,193	—	0.10	0.10	0.20	0.55	1.50	—
Note: With strap								
1955	Inc. above	85.00	125	150	250	600	1,800	—
Note: Without strap								
1956	78,658,535	—	—	—	0.15	0.50	0.90	—
1957	100,601,792	—	—	—	0.10	0.30	0.60	—
1958	59,385,679	—	—	—	0.10	0.30	0.60	—
1959	83,615,343	—	—	—	0.10	0.15	0.30	—
1960	75,772,775	—	—	—	0.10	0.15	0.30	—
1961	139,598,404	—	—	—	—	0.15	0.30	—
1962	227,244,069	—	—	—	—	0.15	0.30	—
1963	279,076,334	—	—	—	—	0.15	0.30	—
1964	484,655,322	—	—	—	—	0.15	0.30	—

KM# 59.1 CENT 3.2400 g. Bronze **Ruler:** Elizabeth II **Obv.:** Queens bust right **Obv. Des.:** Arnold Machin **Rev.:** Maple leaf divides date and denomination **Rev. Des.:** George E. Kruger-Gray **Edge:** Plain **Size:** 19.10 mm.

Date	Mintage	VG-8	F-12	VF-20	XF-40	MS-60	MS-63	Proof
1965	304,441,082	—	—	—	0.40	1.00	4.00	—
Note: Small beads, pointed 5								
1965	Inc. above	—	—	—	—	0.10	0.20	—
Note: Small beads, blunt 5								
1965	Inc. above	—	—	4.50	7.50	18.00	35.00	—
Note: Large beads, pointed 5								
1965	Inc. above	—	—	—	0.10	0.10	0.20	—
Note: Large beads, blunt 5								
1966	184,151,087	—	—	—	—	0.10	0.20	—
1968	329,695,772	—	—	—	—	0.10	0.15	—
1969	335,240,929	—	—	—	—	0.10	0.15	—
1970	311,145,010	—	—	—	—	0.10	0.15	—
1971	298,228,936	—	—	—	—	0.10	0.15	—
1972	451,304,591	—	—	—	—	0.10	0.15	—
1973	457,059,852	—	—	—	—	0.10	0.15	—
1974	692,058,489	—	—	—	—	0.10	0.15	—

KM# 65 CENT Bronze **Ruler:** Elizabeth II **Subject:** Confederation Centennial **Obv.:** Queen's bust right **Obv. Des.:** Arnold Machin **Rev.:** Dove with wings spread, denomination above, two dates below **Rev. Des.:** Alex Coville **Size:** 19.10 mm.

Date	Mintage	VG-8	F-12	VF-20	XF-40	MS-60	MS-63	Proof
ND(1967)	345,140,645	—	—	—	—	0.10	0.20	1.00

KM# 59.2 CENT 3.2400 g. Bronze **Ruler:** Elizabeth II **Obv.:** Queen's bust right **Rev.:** Dove with wings spread, denomination above, dates below **Rev. Des.:** George E. Kruger-Gray **Edge:** Plain **Size:** 19.10 mm.

Date	Mintage	VG-8	F-12	VF-20	XF-40	MS-60	MS-63	Proof
1979	754,394,064	—	—	—	—	0.10	0.15	—

KM# 127 CENT 2.8000 g. Bronze **Ruler:** Elizabeth II **Obv.:** Queen's bust right **Obv. Des.:** Arnold Machin **Rev. Des.:** George E. Kruger-Gray **Edge:** Plain **Size:** 19.10 mm. **Note:** Reduced weight.

Date	Mintage	VG-8	F-12	VF-20	XF-40	MS-60	MS-63	Proof
1980	912,052,318	—	—	—	—	0.10	0.15	—
1981	1,209,468,500	—	—	—	—	0.10	0.15	—
1981 Proof	199,000	—	—	—	—	—	—	1.50

KM# 132 CENT 2.5000 g. Bronze **Ruler:** Elizabeth II **Obv.:** Queen's bust right **Obv. Des.:** Arnold Machin **Rev.:** Maple leaf divides date and denomination **Rev. Des.:** George E. Kruger-Gray **Edge:** Plain **Size:** 19.10 mm. **Note:** Reduced weight.

Date	Mintage	VG-8	F-12	VF-20	XF-40	MS-60	MS-63	Proof
1982	911,001,000	—	—	—	—	0.10	0.15	—
1982 Proof	180,908	—	—	—	—	—	—	1.50
1983	975,510,000	—	—	—	—	0.10	0.15	—
1983 Proof	168,000	—	—	—	—	—	—	1.50
1984	838,225,000	—	—	—	—	0.10	0.15	—
1984 Proof	161,602	—	—	—	—	—	—	1.50
1985	771,772,500	—	—	—	3.00	10.00	19.00	—
Note: Pointed 5								
1985	Inc. above	—	—	—	—	0.10	0.15	—
Note: Blunt 5								
1985 Proof	157,037	—	—	—	—	—	—	1.50
Note: Blunt 5								
1986	740,335,000	—	—	—	—	0.10	0.15	—
1986 Proof	175,745	—	—	—	—	—	—	1.50
1987	774,549,000	—	—	—	—	0.10	0.15	—
1987 Proof	179,004	—	—	—	—	—	—	1.50
1988	482,676,752	—	—	—	—	0.10	0.15	—
1988 Proof	175,259	—	—	—	—	—	—	1.50
1989	1,077,347,200	—	—	—	—	0.10	0.15	—
1989 Proof	170,928	—	—	—	—	—	—	1.50

KM# 181 CENT 2.5000 g. Bronze **Ruler:** Elizabeth II **Obv.:** Crowned Queen's head right **Obv. Des.:** Dora dePedery-Hunt **Rev.:** Maple leaf divides date and denomination **Rev. Des.:** George E. Kruger-Gray **Edge:** Plain **Size:** 19.10 mm.

Date	Mintage	VG-8	F-12	VF-20	XF-40	MS-60	MS-63	Proof
1990	218,035,000	—	—	—	—	0.10	0.15	—
1990 Proof	140,649	—	—	—	—	—	—	2.50
1991	831,001,000	—	—	—	—	0.10	0.15	—
1991 Proof	131,888	—	—	—	—	—	—	3.50
1993	752,034,000	—	—	—	—	0.10	0.15	—
1993 Proof	145,065	—	—	—	—	—	—	2.00
1994	639,516,000	—	—	—	—	0.10	0.15	—
1994 Proof	146,424	—	—	—	—	—	—	2.50
1995	624,983,000	—	—	—	—	0.10	0.15	—
1995 Proof		—	—	—	—	—	—	2.50
1996	445,746,000	—	—	—	—	0.10	0.15	—
1996 Proof		—	—	—	—	—	—	2.50

KM# 204 CENT Bronze **Ruler:** Elizabeth II **Subject:** Confederation 125 **Obv.:** Crowned Queen's head right **Obv. Des.:** Dora dePedery-Hunt **Rev.:** Maple leaf divides date and denomination **Rev. Des.:** George E. Kruger-Gray **Size:** 19.10 mm.

Date	Mintage	VG-8	F-12	VF-20	XF-40	MS-60	MS-63	Proof
ND(1992)	673,512,000	—	—	—	—	0.10	0.15	—
ND(1992) Proof	147,061	—	—	—	—	—	—	2.50

KM# 289 CENT Copper Plated Steel **Ruler:** Elizabeth II **Obv.:** Crowned head right **Obv. Des.:** Dora dePédery-Hunt **Rev.:** Maple twig design **Rev. Des.:** George E. Kruger-Gray **Edge:** Round and plain **Size:** 19.1 mm.

Date	Mintage	MS-63	Proof
1997	549,868,000	0.15	—
1997 Proof	—	—	2.75
1998	999,578,000	0.15	—
1998 Proof	—	—	3.00
1998W	—	1.75	—
1999P	—	6.00	—
Note: Plated planchet, set only			
1999	1,089,625,000	0.15	—
1999W	—	—	—
1999 Proof	—	—	4.00
2000	771,908,206	0.15	—
2000 Proof	—	—	4.00
2000W	—	1.75	—

KM# 289a CENT Bronze **Size:** 19.10 mm.

Date	Mintage	VG-8	F-12	VF-20	XF-40	MS-60	MS-63	Proof
1998		—	—	—	—	—	0.75	—
Note: In Specimen sets only								

KM# 309 CENT 5.6700 g. 0.9250 Copper-Plated Silver 0.1686 oz. **Subject:** 90th Anniversary Royal Canadian Mint - 1908-1998 **Obv. Des.:** Dora dePédery-Hunt **Rev. Des.:** G. W. DeSaulles

Date	Mintage	VG-8	F-12	VF-20	XF-40	MS-60	MS-63	Proof
ND(1998)	25,000	—	—	—	—	—	16.00	—
Note: Antique finish								
ND(1998) Proof	—	—	—	—	—	—	—	—

KM# 332 CENT 5.6700 g. 0.9250 Silver 0.1686 oz. ASW **Ruler:** Elizabeth II **Subject:** 90th Anniversary Royal Canadian Mint - 1908-1998 **Obv.:** Crowned Queen's head right, with "Canada" added to head **Obv. Des.:** Dora dePedery-Hunt **Rev.:** Denomination above dates withn beaded circle, chain of leaves surrounds **Rev. Des.:** G. W. DeSaulles

Date	Mintage	VG-8	F-12	VF-20	XF-40	MS-60	MS-63	Proof
ND(2000) Proof	25,000	—	—	—	—	—	—	16.00
Note: Mirror finish								

Oval O's   Round O's

KM# 2 5 CENTS 1.1620 g. 0.9250 Silver 0.0346 oz. ASW **Ruler:** Victoria **Obv.:** Head left **Obv. Leg.:** VICTORIA DEI GRATIA REGINA.

CANADA **Rev.:** Denomination and date within wreath, crown above

Date	Mintage	VG-8	F-12	VF-20	XF-40	MS-60	MS-63	Proof
1901	2,000,000	4.50	6.50	12.00	35.00	150	400	—

KM# 9 5 CENTS 1.1620 g. 0.9250 Silver 0.0346 oz. ASW **Ruler:** Edward VII **Obv. Des.:** G. W. DeSaulles **Rev. Des.:** Leonard C. Wyon

Date	Mintage	VG-8	F-12	VF-20	XF-40	MS-60	MS-63	Proof
1902	2,120,000	2.25	3.00	4.00	7.00	35.00	55.00	—
1902	2,200,000	2.25	3.25	5.50	11.00	35.00	60.00	—
Note: Large broad H								
1902	Inc. above	7.50	13.00	24.00	40.00	100	175	—
Note: Small narrow H								

KM# 13 5 CENTS 1.1620 g. 0.9250 Silver 0.0346 oz. ASW **Ruler:** Edward VII **Obv.:** King's bust right **Rev.:** Denomination and date within wreath, crown at top

Date	Mintage	VG-8	F-12	VF-20	XF-40	MS-60	MS-63	Proof
1903	1,000,000	4.00	7.00	17.00	35.00	150	350	—
Note: 22 leaves								
1903H	2,640,000	1.75	3.00	7.00	16.00	100	300	—
Note: 21 leaves								
1904	2,400,000	2.75	4.50	7.00	23.00	175	500	—
1905	2,600,000	1.75	3.00	9.00	16.00	100	225	—
1906	3,100,000	2.25	3.00	6.00	13.00	85.00	225	—
1907	5,200,000	2.25	3.00	4.00	10.00	55.00	150	—
1908	1,220,524	6.00	10.00	23.00	35.00	100	175	—
1909	1,983,725	3.00	6.50	10.00	30.00	175	500	—
Note: Round leaves								
1909	Inc. above	12.00	18.00	35.00	95.00	550	1,300	—
Note: Pointed leaves								
1910	3,850,325	2.25	2.75	5.00	11.00	50.00	95.00	—
Note: Pointed leaves								
1910	Inc. above	15.00	17.00	30.00	85.00	400	1,300	—
Note: Round leaves								

KM# 16 5 CENTS 1.1620 g. 0.9250 Silver 0.0346 oz. ASW **Ruler:** George V **Obv.:** King's bust left **Obv. Des.:** E. B. MacKennal **Rev.:** Denomination and date within wreath, crown above **Rev. Des.:** Leonard C. Wyon

Date	Mintage	VG-8	F-12	VF-20	XF-40	MS-60	MS-63	Proof
1911	3,692,350	2.00	3.00	6.00	9.00	60.00	100	—

KM# 22 5 CENTS 1.1620 g. 0.9250 Silver 0.0346 oz. ASW **Ruler:** George V **Obv.:** King's bust left **Obv. Des.:** E. B. MacKennal **Rev.:** Denomination and date within wreath, crown above **Rev. Des.:** Leonard C. Wyon

Date	Mintage	VG-8	F-12	VF-20	XF-40	MS-60	MS-63	Proof
1912	5,863,170	2.00	3.00	5.00	9.00	50.00	150	—
1913	5,488,048	2.00	2.75	4.25	7.50	26.00	50.00	—
1914	4,202,179	2.00	3.00	5.00	9.00	50.00	125	—
1915	1,172,258	11.00	15.00	26.00	50.00	325	600	—
1916	2,481,675	2.75	7.50	13.00	22.00	100	250	—
1917	5,521,373	1.75	2.50	3.00	7.00	30.00	80.00	—
1918	6,052,298	1.75	2.50	3.00	6.50	30.00	65.00	—
1919	7,835,400	1.75	2.50	3.00	6.50	30.00	65.00	—

KM# 22a 5 CENTS 1.1664 g. 0.8000 Silver 0.0300 oz. ASW **Ruler:** George V **Obv. Des.:** E. B. MacKennal **Rev. Des.:** Leonard C. Wyon **Size:** 15.48 mm.

Date	Mintage	VG-8	F-12	VF-20	XF-40	MS-60	MS-63	Proof
1920	10,649,851	1.75	2.50	3.00	6.50	26.00	50.00	—
1921	2,582,495	2,700	3,000	4,500	6,750	9,500	16,500	—
Note: Approximately 460 known; balance remelted. Stack's A.G. Carter Jr. Sale (12-89) choice BU, finest known, realized $57,200								

Near 6   Far 6

KM# 29 5 CENTS 4.5200 g. Nickel **Ruler:** George V **Obv.:** King's bust left **Obv. Des.:** E. B. MacKennal **Rev.:** Maple leaves divide denomination and date **Rev. Des.:** W. H. J. Blakemore **Size:** 21.2 mm.

Date	Mintage	VG-8	F-12	VF-20	XF-40	MS-60	MS-63	Proof
1922	4,794,119	0.35	1.00	1.75	7.00	45.00	95.00	—
1923	2,502,279	0.40	1.25	5.50	16.00	100	275	—
1924	3,105,839	0.50	1.00	3.75	10.00	85.00	200	—
1925	201,921	55.00	70.00	100	350	1,200	3,600	—
1926 Near 6	938,162	3.00	7.00	16.00	60.00	375	1,300	—
1926 Far 6	Inc. above	100	150	300	600	1,500	4,300	—
1927	5,285,627	0.35	0.65	2.75	15.00	60.00	125	—
1928	4,577,712	0.35	0.65	2.75	15.00	55.00	100	—
1929	5,611,911	0.35	0.65	2.75	15.00	60.00	150	—
1930	3,704,673	0.35	1.50	2.75	15.00	90.00	200	—
1931	5,100,830	0.35	1.50	3.25	18.00	175	475	—
1932	3,198,566	0.35	1.00	3.25	16.00	150	350	—
1933	2,597,867	0.40	1.50	6.00	18.00	175	650	—
1934	3,827,304	0.35	1.00	3.00	16.00	150	375	—
1935	3,900,000	0.35	1.00	2.75	11.00	95.00	250	—
1936	4,400,450	0.35	0.65	1.75	9.00	50.00	100	—

KM# 33 5 CENTS 4.5000 g. Nickel **Ruler:** George VI **Obv.:** Head left **Obv. Des.:** T. H. Paget **Rev.:** Beaver on rock divides denomination and date **Rev. Des.:** George E. Kruger-Gray **Size:** 21.2 mm.

Date	Mintage	VG-8	F-12	VF-20	XF-40	MS-60	MS-63	Proof
1937 Dot	4,593,263	0.25	0.35	1.25	2.50	9.00	22.00	—
1938	3,898,974	0.30	0.90	2.00	7.00	75.00	150	—
1939	5,661,123	0.25	0.35	1.25	3.00	45.00	80.00	—
1940	13,920,197	0.20	0.30	0.75	2.25	18.00	55.00	—
1941	8,681,785	0.20	0.30	0.75	2.25	23.00	70.00	—
1942 Round	6,847,544	0.20	0.30	0.75	1.75	18.00	35.00	—

KM# 39   5 CENTS   Tombac Brass **Ruler:** George VI **Obv.:** Head left **Obv. Des.:** T. H. Paget **Rev.:** Beaver on rock divides denomination and date **Rev. Des.:** George E. Kruger-Gray **Shape:** 12-sided **Size:** 21.2 mm.

Date	Mintage	VG-8	F-12	VF-20	XF-40	MS-60	MS-63	Proof
1942	3,396,234	0.40	0.65	1.25	1.75	3.00	14.00	—

KM# 40   5 CENTS   Tombac Brass **Ruler:** George VI **Subject:** Victory **Obv.:** Head left **Obv. Des.:** T. H. Paget **Rev.:** Torch on "V" divides date **Rev. Des.:** Thomas Shingles **Size:** 21.2 mm.

Date	Mintage	VG-8	F-12	VF-20	XF-40	MS-60	MS-63	Proof
1943	24,760,256	0.20	0.30	0.40	0.80	3.00	9.00	—
1944	8,000	—	—	—	—	—	—	—

Note: 1 known

KM# 40a   5 CENTS   4.4000 g. Chrome Plated Steel **Ruler:** George VI **Obv.:** Head left **Rev.:** Torch on "V" divides date **Size:** 21.2 mm.

Date	Mintage	VG-8	F-12	VF-20	XF-40	MS-60	MS-63	Proof
1944	11,532,784	0.10	0.35	0.50	0.90	2.00	7.00	—
1945	18,893,216	0.10	0.20	0.40	0.80	2.00	7.00	—

Dot   Maple leaf

KM# 39a   5 CENTS   4.5000 g. Nickel **Ruler:** George VI **Obv.:** Head left **Obv. Des.:** T. H. Paget **Rev.:** Beaver on rock divides denomination and date **Rev. Des.:** George E. Kruger-Gray **Size:** 21.2 mm.

Date	Mintage	VG-8	F-12	VF-20	XF-40	MS-60	MS-63	Proof
1946	6,952,684	0.10	0.30	0.50	2.00	14.00	32.00	—
1947	7,603,724	0.20	0.30	0.50	1.25	10.00	25.00	—
1947 Dot	Inc. above	12.00	20.00	27.00	60.00	175	300	—
1947 Maple leaf	9,595,124	0.20	0.30	0.45	1.25	10.00	25.00	—

KM# 42   5 CENTS   4.5400 g. Nickel **Ruler:** George VI **Obv.:** Head left, modified legend **Obv. Des.:** T. H. Paget **Rev.:** Beaver on rock divides date and denomination **Rev. Des.:** George E. Kruger-Gray **Size:** 21.2 mm.

Date	Mintage	VG-8	F-12	VF-20	XF-40	MS-60	MS-63	Proof
1948	1,810,789	0.40	0.50	1.00	3.00	18.00	35.00	—
1949	13,037,090	0.20	0.30	0.50	0.75	6.00	12.00	—
1950	11,970,521	0.20	0.30	0.50	0.75	6.00	12.00	—

KM# 42a   5 CENTS   Chromium And Nickel-Plated Steel **Ruler:** George VI **Obv.:** Head left **Obv. Des.:** T. H. Paget **Rev.:** Beaver on rock divides date and denomination **Rev. Des.:** George E. Kruger-Gray **Size:** 21.2 mm.

Date	Mintage	VG-8	F-12	VF-20	XF-40	MS-60	MS-63	Proof
1951	4,313,410	0.10	0.25	0.50	—	3.50	11.00	—

Note: Low relief; Second "A" in GRATIA points between denticles

| 1951 | Inc. above | 350 | 525 | 700 | 1,000 | 1,900 | 3,100 | — |

Note: High relief; Second "A" in GRATIA points to a denticle

| 1952 | 10,891,148 | 0.10 | 0.20 | 0.45 | 0.80 | 3.00 | 7.50 | — |

KM# 48   5 CENTS   4.5500 g. Nickel **Ruler:** George VI **Subject:** Nickel Bicentennial **Obv.:** Head left **Obv. Des.:** T. H. Paget **Rev.:** Buildings with center tower divide dates and denomination **Rev. Des.:** Stephen Trenka **Shape:** 12-sided **Size:** 21.2 mm.

Date	Mintage	VG-8	F-12	VF-20	XF-40	MS-60	MS-63	Proof
ND(1951)	9,028,507	0.20	0.30	0.35	0.45	1.75	5.50	—

KM# 50   5 CENTS   Chromium And Nickel-Plated Steel **Ruler:** Elizabeth II **Obv.:** Laureate queen's bust, right **Obv. Des.:** Mary Gillick **Rev.:** Beaver on rock divides date and denomination **Rev. Des.:** George E. Kruger-Gray **Size:** 21.2 mm.

Date	Mintage	VG-8	F-12	VF-20	XF-40	MS-60	MS-63	Proof
1953	Inc. above	150	225	300	475	1,100	2,300	—

Note: With strap, far leaf

| 1953 | 16,635,552 | 0.10 | 0.20 | 0.40 | 0.90 | 3.00 | 7.00 | — |

Note: Without strap

| 1953 | Inc. above | 300 | 500 | 750 | 900 | 1,300 | 2,300 | — |

Note: Without strap, near leaf

| 1953 | Inc. above | 0.10 | 0.20 | 0.40 | 0.90 | 3.50 | 7.00 | — |

Note: With strap

| 1954 | 6,998,662 | 0.10 | 0.25 | 0.50 | 1.00 | 4.00 | 8.00 | — |

KM# 50a   5 CENTS   4.5900 g. Nickel **Ruler:** Elizabeth II **Obv.:** Laureate queen's bust right **Obv. Des.:** Mary Gillick **Rev.:** Beaver on rock divides date and denomination **Rev. Des.:** George E. Kruger-Gray **Size:** 21.2 mm.

Date	Mintage	VG-8	F-12	VF-20	XF-40	MS-60	MS-63	Proof
1955	5,355,028	0.20	0.25	0.40	0.75	3.50	4.50	—
1956	9,399,854	—	0.20	0.30	0.45	2.25	5.00	—
1957	7,387,703	—	—	0.25	0.30	2.00	3.00	—
1958	7,607,521	—	—	0.25	0.30	2.00	3.00	—
1959	11,552,523	—	—	—	0.20	0.70	1.50	—
1960	37,157,433	—	—	—	0.20	0.75	1.50	—
1961	47,889,051	—	—	—	—	0.30	0.80	—
1962	46,307,305	—	—	—	—	0.30	0.80	—

KM# 57   5 CENTS   Nickel **Ruler:** Elizabeth II **Obv.:** Laureate queen's bust right **Obv. Des.:** Mary Gillick **Rev.:** Beaver on rock divides date and denomination **Rev. Des.:** George E. Kruger-Gray **Shape:** Round **Size:** 21.2 mm.

Date	Mintage	VG-8	F-12	VF-20	XF-40	MS-60	MS-63	Proof
1963	43,970,320	—	—	—	—	0.20	0.75	—
1964	78,075,068	—	—	—	—	0.20	0.75	—
1964		8.00	10.00	12.00	17.00	35.00	100	—

Note: Extra water line

KM# 60.1   5 CENTS   4.5400 g. Nickel **Ruler:** Elizabeth II **Obv.:** Queen's bust right **Obv. Des.:** Arnold Machin **Rev.:** Beaver on rock divides date and denomination **Rev. Des.:** George E. Kruger-Gray **Size:** 21.2 mm.

Date	Mintage	VG-8	F-12	VF-20	XF-40	MS-60	MS-63	Proof
1965	84,876,018	—	—	—	—	0.20	0.30	—
1966	27,976,648	—	—	—	—	0.20	0.30	—
1968	101,930,379	—	—	—	—	0.20	0.30	—
1969	27,830,229	—	—	—	—	0.20	0.30	—
1970	5,726,010	—	—	—	0.20	0.35	0.75	—
1971	27,312,609	—	—	—	—	0.20	0.30	—
1972	62,417,387	—	—	—	—	0.20	0.30	—
1973	53,507,435	—	—	—	—	0.20	0.30	—
1974	94,704,645	—	—	—	—	0.20	0.30	—
1975	138,882,000	—	—	—	—	0.20	0.30	—
1976	55,140,213	—	—	—	—	0.20	0.30	—
1977	89,120,791	—	—	—	—	0.20	0.30	—
1978	137,079,273	—	—	—	—	0.20	0.30	—

KM# 66   5 CENTS   Nickel **Ruler:** Elizabeth II **Subject:** Confederation Centennial **Obv.:** Queen's bust right **Obv. Des.:** Arnold Machin **Rev.:** Snowshoe rabbit bounding left divides dates and denomination **Rev. Des.:** Alex Coville **Size:** 21.2 mm.

Date	Mintage	VG-8	F-12	VF-20	XF-40	MS-60	MS-63	Proof
ND(1967)	36,876,574	—	—	—	—	0.20	0.40	1.00

KM# 60.2   5 CENTS   Nickel **Ruler:** Elizabeth II **Obv.:** Queen's bust right **Obv. Des.:** Arnold Machin **Rev.:** Beaver on rock divides date and denomination **Rev. Des.:** George E. Kruger-Gray **Size:** 21.2 mm.

Date	Mintage	VG-8	F-12	VF-20	XF-40	MS-60	MS-63	Proof
1979	186,295,825	—	—	—	—	0.20	0.30	—
1980	134,878,000	—	—	—	—	0.20	0.30	—
1981	99,107,900	—	—	—	—	0.20	0.30	—
1981 Proof	199,000	—	—	—	—	—	—	1.50

KM# 60.2a 5 CENTS 4.6000 g. Copper-Nickel **Ruler:** Elizabeth II **Obv.:** Queen's bust right **Obv. Des.:** Arnold Machin **Rev.:** Beaver on rock divides date and denomination **Rev. Des.:** George E. Kruger-Gray **Size:** 21.2 mm.

Date	Mintage	VG-8	F-12	VF-20	XF-40	MS-60	MS-63	Proof
1982	64,924,400	—	—	—	—	0.20	0.30	—
1982 Proof	180,908	—	—	—	—	—	—	1.50
1983	72,596,000	—	—	—	—	0.20	0.30	—
1983 Proof	168,000	—	—	—	—	—	—	1.50
1984	84,088,000	—	—	—	—	0.20	0.30	—
1984 Proof	161,602	—	—	—	—	—	—	1.50
1985	126,618,000	—	—	—	—	0.20	0.30	—
1985 Proof	157,037	—	—	—	—	—	—	1.50
1986	156,104,000	—	—	—	—	0.20	0.30	—
1986 Proof	175,745	—	—	—	—	—	—	1.50
1987	106,299,000	—	—	—	—	0.15	0.30	—
1987 Proof	179,004	—	—	—	—	—	—	1.50
1988	75,025,000	—	—	—	—	0.15	0.30	—
1988 Proof	175,259	—	—	—	—	—	—	1.50
1989	141,570,538	—	—	—	—	0.15	0.30	—
1989 Proof	170,928	—	—	—	—	—	—	1.50

KM# 182 5 CENTS 4.6000 g. Copper-Nickel **Ruler:** Elizabeth II **Obv.:** Crowned head right **Obv. Des.:** Dora dePedery-Hunt **Rev.:** Beaver on rock divides dates and denomination **Rev. Des.:** George E. Kruger-Gray **Edge:** Plain **Size:** 19.55 mm.

Date	Mintage	VG-8	F-12	VF-20	XF-40	MS-60	MS-63	Proof
1990	42,537,000	—	—	—	—	0.15	0.30	—
1990 Proof	140,649	—	—	—	—	—	—	2.50
1991	10,931,000	—	—	—	—	0.30	0.55	—
1991 Proof	131,888	—	—	—	—	—	—	7.00
1993	86,877,000	—	—	—	—	0.15	0.30	—
1993 Proof	143,065	—	—	—	—	—	—	2.50
1994	99,352,000	—	—	—	—	0.15	0.30	—
1994 Proof	146,424	—	—	—	—	—	—	3.00
1995	78,528,000	—	—	—	—	0.15	0.30	—
1995 Proof	50,000	—	—	—	—	—	—	2.50
1996 Far 6	36,686,000	—	—	—	—	0.75	2.25	—
1996 Near 6	Inc. above	—	—	—	—	0.70	2.25	—
1996 Proof	—	—	—	—	—	—	—	6.00
1997	27,354,000	—	—	—	—	0.15	0.30	—
1997 Proof	—	—	—	—	—	—	—	5.00
1998	156,873,000	—	—	—	—	0.15	0.30	—
1998W	—	—	—	—	—	—	1.50	—
1998 Proof	—	—	—	—	—	—	—	5.00
1999	124,861,000	—	—	—	—	0.15	0.30	—
1999W	—	—	—	—	—	—	—	—
1999 Proof	—	—	—	—	—	—	—	5.00
2000	108,514,000	—	—	—	—	0.15	0.30	—
2000W	—	—	—	—	—	—	1.50	—
2000 Proof	—	—	—	—	—	—	—	5.00

KM# 205 5 CENTS Copper-Nickel **Ruler:** Elizabeth II **Subject:** Confederation 125 **Obv.:** Crowned head right **Obv. Des.:** Dora dePedery-Hunt **Rev.:** Beaver on rock divides date and denomination **Rev. Des.:** George E. Kruger-Gray **Size:** 21.2 mm.

Date	Mintage	VG-8	F-12	VF-20	XF-40	MS-60	MS-63	Proof
ND(1992)	53,732,000	—	—	—	—	0.15	0.30	—
ND(1992) Proof	147,061	—	—	—	—	—	—	4.00

KM# 182b 5 CENTS 3.9000 g. Nickel Plated Steel **Ruler:** Elizabeth II **Obv.:** Crowned head right **Obv. Des.:** Dora dePedery-Hunt **Rev.:** Beaver on rock divides date and denomination **Rev. Des.:** George E. Kruger-Gray **Edge:** Plain **Size:** 21.2 mm.

Date	Mintage	MS-63	Proof
1999 P	Est. 20,000	15.00	—
2000 P	Est. 2,300,000	3.50	—

KM# 182a 5 CENTS 5.3500 g. 0.9250 Silver 0.1591 oz. ASW **Ruler:** Elizabeth II **Obv.:** Crowned head right **Obv. Des.:** Dora dePedery-Hunt **Rev.:** Beaver on rock divides date and denomination **Rev. Des.:** George E. Kruger-Gray **Size:** 21.2 mm.

Date	Mintage	MS-63	Proof
1996 Proof	—	—	5.00
1997 Proof	—	—	5.00
1998 Proof	—	—	5.00
1998O Proof	—	—	5.00
1999 Proof	—	—	5.00
2000 Proof	—	—	5.00

KM# 310 5 CENTS 1.1670 g. 0.9250 Silver 0.0347 oz. ASW **Ruler:** Elizabeth II **Subject:** 90th Anniversary Royal Canadian Mint **Obv.:** Crowned head right **Obv. Des.:** Dora dePedery-Hunt **Rev.:** Denomination and date within wreath, crown above **Rev. Des.:** W. H. J. Blackmore

Date	Mintage	MS-63	Proof
ND(1998)	25,000	12.00	—
ND(1998) Proof	25,000	—	12.00

KM# 400 5 CENTS 0.9250 Silver **Ruler:** Elizabeth II **Subject:** First French-Canadian Regiment **Obv.:** Crowned head right **Obv. Des.:** Dora dePedery-Hunt **Rev.:** Regimental drums, sash and baton, denomination above, date at right **Rev. Des.:** R. C. M. Staff **Edge:** Plain **Size:** 21.2 mm.

Date	Mintage	MS-63	Proof
2000 Proof	—	—	9.00

KM# 3 10 CENTS 2.3240 g. 0.9250 Silver 0.0691 oz. ASW **Ruler:** Victoria **Obv.:** Head left **Obv. Leg.:** VICTORIA DEI GRATIA REGINA. CANADA **Rev.:** Denomination and date within wreath, crown above **Edge:** Reeded **Size:** 18.03 mm.

Date	Mintage	VG-8	F-12	VF-20	XF-40	MS-60	MS-63	Proof
1901	1,200,000	8.50	18.00	40.00	85.00	225	650	—

KM# 10 10 CENTS 2.3240 g. 0.9250 Silver 0.0691 oz. ASW **Ruler:** Edward VII **Obv.:** Crowned bust right **Obv. Des.:** G. W. DeSaulles **Rev.:** Denomination and date within wreath, crown above **Rev. Des.:** Leonard C. Wyon **Edge:** Reeded **Size:** 18.03 mm.

Date	Mintage	VG-8	F-12	VF-20	XF-40	MS-60	MS-63	Proof
1902	720,000	8.00	16.00	30.00	80.00	325	1,100	—
1902H	1,100,000	4.00	8.00	18.00	40.00	100	250	—
1903	500,000	14.00	30.00	75.00	200	1,000	2,100	—
1903H	1,320,000	7.00	16.00	30.00	65.00	250	550	—
1904	1,000,000	11.00	24.00	45.00	100	325	700	—
1905	1,000,000	6.50	24.00	55.00	100	475	1,100	—
1906	1,700,000	6.50	12.00	30.00	60.00	275	750	—
1907	2,620,000	4.25	11.00	23.00	40.00	200	425	—
1908	776,666	8.00	24.00	55.00	95.00	200	400	—
1909	1,697,200	6.00	18.00	40.00	95.00	375	1,000	—

Note: "Victorian" leaves, similar to 1902-08 coins

1909	Inc. above	10.00	27.00	55.00	125	500	1,300	—

Note: Broad leaves, similar to 1910-12 coins

1910	4,468,331	4.00	8.00	18.00	35.00	125	300	—

KM# 17 10 CENTS 2.3240 g. 0.9250 Silver 0.0691 oz. ASW **Ruler:** George V **Obv.:** Crowned bust left **Obv. Des.:** E. B. MacKennal **Rev.:** Denomination and date within wreath, crown above **Rev. Des.:** Leonard C. Wyon **Edge:** Reeded **Size:** 18.03 mm.

Date	Mintage	VG-8	F-12	VF-20	XF-40	MS-60	MS-63	Proof
1911	2,737,584	4.50	11.00	18.00	40.00	100	200	—

Small leaves   Large leaves

KM# 23 10 CENTS 2.3240 g. 0.9250 Silver 0.0691 oz. ASW **Ruler:** George V **Obv.:** Crowned bust left **Obv. Des.:** E. B. MacKennal **Rev.:** Denomination and date within wreath, crown above **Rev. Des.:** Leonard C. Wyon **Edge:** Reeded **Size:** 18.03 mm.

Date	Mintage	VG-8	F-12	VF-20	XF-40	MS-60	MS-63	Proof
1912	3,235,557	1.75	4.25	9.00	30.00	175	500	—
1913	3,613,937	1.50	2.25	8.50	23.00	125	325	—

Note: Small leaves

1913	Inc. above	95.00	175	350	900	5,750	20,000	—

Note: Large leaves

1914	2,549,811	1.50	2.50	8.50	25.00	125	375	—
1915	688,057	6.00	15.00	30.00	100	325	650	—

Date	Mintage	VG-8	F-12	VF-20	XF-40	MS-60	MS-63	Proof
1916	4,218,114	1.25	2.25	4.00	17.00	75.00	225	—
1917	5,011,988	1.25	1.50	3.00	10.00	50.00	95.00	—
1918	5,133,602	1.25	1.50	3.00	9.00	45.00	80.00	—
1919	7,877,722	1.25	1.50	3.00	9.00	45.00	80.00	—

KM# 23a 10 CENTS
2.3328 g. 0.8000 Silver 0.0600 oz. ASW **Ruler:** George V
Obv.: Crowned bust left **Obv. Des.:** E. B. MacKennal **Rev.:** Denomination and date within wreath, crown above **Edge:** Reeded **Size:** 18.03 mm.

Date	Mintage	VG-8	F-12	VF-20	XF-40	MS-60	MS-63	Proof
1920	6,305,345	1.00	1.50	3.00	12.00	75.00	125	—
1921	2,469,562	1.25	2.00	6.00	20.00	80.00	225	—
1928	2,458,602	1.00	1.75	4.00	12.00	55.00	125	—
1929	3,253,888	1.00	2.00	3.50	12.00	55.00	100	—
1930	1,831,043	1.00	2.50	4.50	14.00	60.00	125	—
1931	2,067,421	1.00	1.75	4.00	12.00	55.00	100	—
1932	1,154,317	1.50	2.50	9.00	23.00	90.00	225	—
1933	672,368	2.00	4.50	12.00	35.00	175	350	—
1934	409,067	3.00	6.00	22.00	60.00	250	500	—
1935	384,056	3.50	6.00	19.00	60.00	250	500	—
1936	2,460,871	1.00	1.25	3.00	9.00	45.00	80.00	—
1936	—	—	—	—	—	—	—	—

Note: Dot on reverse. Specimen, 4 known; David Akers sale of John Jay Pittman collection, Part 1, 10-97, a gem specimen realized $120,000

Maple leaf

KM# 34 10 CENTS
2.3328 g. 0.8000 Silver 0.0600 oz. ASW **Ruler:** George VI
Obv.: Head left **Obv. Des.:** T. H. Paget **Rev.:** Bluenose sailing left, date at right, denomination below **Rev. Des.:** Emanuel Hahn **Edge:** Reeded **Size:** 18.03 mm.

Date	Mintage	VG-8	F-12	VF-20	XF-40	MS-60	MS-63	Proof
1937	2,500,095	BV	1.00	2.00	3.75	12.00	18.00	—
1938	4,197,323	0.85	1.75	3.25	6.50	40.00	90.00	—
1939	5,501,748	BV	1.25	2.50	5.00	45.00	90.00	—
1940	16,526,470	—	BV	1.50	3.00	15.00	30.00	—
1941	8,716,386	BV	1.25	2.50	6.00	35.00	90.00	—
1942	10,214,011	—	BV	1.25	4.00	20.00	50.00	—
1943	21,143,229	—	BV	1.25	4.00	18.00	35.00	—
1944	9,383,582	—	BV	1.50	4.50	25.00	45.00	—
1945	10,979,570	—	BV	1.25	4.00	18.00	27.00	—
1946	6,300,066	BV	1.00	2.00	4.50	30.00	50.00	—
1947	4,431,926	BV	1.25	2.50	6.00	30.00	50.00	—
1947	9,638,793	—	BV	1.50	3.00	10.00	15.00	—

Note: Maple leaf

KM# 43 10 CENTS
2.3328 g. 0.8000 Silver 0.0600 oz. ASW **Ruler:** George VI
Obv.: Head left, modified legend **Obv. Des.:** T. H. Paget **Rev.:** Bluenose sailing left, date at right, denomination below **Rev. Des.:** Emanuel Hahn **Size:** 18.03 mm.

Date	Mintage	VG-8	F-12	VF-20	XF-40	MS-60	MS-63	Proof
1948	422,741	2.00	3.50	7.50	13.00	45.00	70.00	—
1949	11,336,172	—	BV	1.00	2.00	9.00	13.00	—
1950	17,823,075	—	—	BV	1.50	8.00	12.00	—
1951	15,079,265	—	—	BV	1.50	6.00	11.00	—
1951	—	—	1.50	2.50	7.00	35.00	60.00	—

Note: Doubled die

| 1952 | 10,474,455 | — | — | BV | 1.50 | 5.00 | 9.00 | — |

KM# 51 10 CENTS
2.3328 g. 0.8000 Silver 0.0600 oz. ASW **Ruler:** Elizabeth II
Obv.: Laureate bust right **Obv. Des.:** Mary Gillick **Rev.:** Bluenose sailing left, date at right, denomination below **Rev. Des.:** Emanuel Hahn **Size:** 18.03 mm.

Date	Mintage	VG-8	F-12	VF-20	XF-40	MS-60	MS-63	Proof
1953	Inc. above	—	BV	1.00	1.25	5.00	8.00	—

Note: With straps

| 1953 | 17,706,395 | — | BV | 1.00 | 1.25 | 3.00 | 6.00 | — |

Note: Without straps

1954	4,493,150	—	BV	1.00	2.25	10.00	17.00	—
1955	12,237,294	—	—	BV	1.00	4.50	7.00	—
1956	16,732,844	—	—	BV	1.00	3.00	6.00	—
1956	Inc. above	—	—	2.25	3.00	4.50	13.00	22.00

Note: Dot below date

1957	16,110,229	—	—	—	BV	2.25	3.00	—
1958	10,621,236	—	—	—	BV	2.25	3.00	—
1959	19,691,433	—	—	—	BV	2.25	3.00	—
1960	45,446,835	—	—	—	BV	1.50	2.25	—
1961	26,850,859	—	—	—	BV	1.00	2.25	—
1962	41,864,335	—	—	—	—	1.00	1.50	—

Date	Mintage	VG-8	F-12	VF-20	XF-40	MS-60	MS-63	Proof
1963	41,916,208	—	—	—	BV	1.00	1.50	—
1964	49,518,549	—	—	—	BV	1.00	1.50	—

KM# 61 10 CENTS
2.3328 g. 0.8000 Silver 0.0600 oz. ASW **Ruler:** Elizabeth II
Obv.: Young bust right **Obv. Des.:** Arnold Machin **Rev.:** Bluenose sailing left, date at right, denomination below **Size:** 18.03 mm.

Date	Mintage	VG-8	F-12	VF-20	XF-40	MS-60	MS-63	Proof
1965	56,965,392	—	—	—	BV	1.00	1.50	—
1966	34,567,898	—	—	—	BV	1.00	1.50	—

KM# 67 10 CENTS
2.3328 g. 0.8000 Silver 0.0600 oz. ASW **Ruler:** Elizabeth II
Subject: Confederation Centennial **Obv.:** Bust right **Rev.:** Atlantic mackerel left, denomination above, dates below **Rev. Des.:** Alex Colville **Size:** 18.03 mm.

Date	Mintage	VG-8	F-12	VF-20	XF-40	MS-60	MS-63	Proof
ND(1967)	62,998,215	—	—	—	BV	1.00	1.50	2.00

KM# 67a 10 CENTS
2.3328 g. 0.5000 Silver 0.0375 oz. ASW **Ruler:** Elizabeth II
Subject: Confederation Centennial **Obv.:** Young bust right **Rev.:** Fish left, denomination above dates below **Size:** 18.03 mm.

Date	Mintage	VG-8	F-12	VF-20	XF-40	MS-60	MS-63	Proof
ND(1967)	Inc. above	—	—	—	BV	0.60	1.50	—

Ottawa

KM# 72 10 CENTS
2.3328 g. 0.5000 Silver 0.0375 oz. ASW **Ruler:** Elizabeth II
Obv.: Young bust right **Obv. Des.:** Arnold Machin **Rev.:** Bluenose sailing left, date at right, denomination below **Rev. Des.:** Emanuel Hahn **Size:** 18.03 mm. **Note:** Ottawa Mint reeding has pointed deep areas in the edge reeding.

Date	Mintage	VG-8	F-12	VF-20	XF-40	MS-60	MS-63	Proof
1968	70,460,000	—	—	—	BV	0.60	1.25	—

Ottawa

KM# 72a 10 CENTS
Nickel **Ruler:** Elizabeth II **Obv.:** Young bust right **Obv. Des.:** Arnold Machin **Rev.:** Bluenose sailing left, date at right, denomination below **Rev. Des.:** Emanuel Hahn **Size:** 18.03 mm. **Note:** Ottawa Mint reeding has pointed deep areas in the edge reeding.

Date	Mintage	VG-8	F-12	VF-20	XF-40	MS-60	MS-63	Proof
1968	87,412,930	—	—	—	0.15	0.20	0.35	—

Philadelphia

KM# 73 10 CENTS
2.3300 g. Nickel **Ruler:** Elizabeth II **Obv.:** Young bust right **Obv. Des.:** Arnold Machin **Rev.:** Bluenose sailing left, date at right, denomination below **Rev. Des.:** Emanuel Hahn **Size:** 18.03 mm. **Note:** Philadelphia Mint reeding has pointed deep areas in the edge reeding.

Date	Mintage	VG-8	F-12	VF-20	XF-40	MS-60	MS-63	Proof
1968	85,170,000	—	—	—	0.15	0.25	0.35	—
1969	—	—	6,200	8,400	11,500	19,500	—	—

Note: Large date, large ship, 10-20 known

KM# 77.1 10 CENTS
2.0700 g. Nickel **Ruler:** Elizabeth II **Obv.:** Young bust right **Obv. Des.:** Arnold Machin **Rev.:** Redesigned smaller Bluenose sailing left, date at right, denomination below **Rev. Des.:** Emanuel Hahn **Size:** 18.03 mm.

Date	Mintage	VG-8	F-12	VF-20	XF-40	MS-60	MS-63	Proof
1969	55,833,929	—	—	—	0.15	0.25	0.35	—
1970	5,249,296	—	—	—	0.25	0.40	0.90	—
1971	41,016,968	—	—	—	0.15	0.20	0.35	—
1972	60,169,387	—	—	—	0.15	0.20	0.35	—
1973	167,715,435	—	—	—	0.15	0.20	0.35	—
1974	201,566,565	—	—	—	0.15	0.20	0.35	—
1975	207,680,000	—	—	—	0.15	0.20	0.35	—
1976	95,018,533	—	—	—	0.15	0.20	0.35	—
1977	128,452,206	—	—	—	0.15	0.20	0.35	—
1978	170,366,431	—	—	—	0.15	0.20	0.35	—

KM# 77.2 10 CENTS
2.0700 g. Nickel **Ruler:** Elizabeth II **Obv.:** Smaller young bust right **Obv. Des.:** Arnold Machin **Rev.:** Redesigned smaller Bluenose sailing left, denomination below, date at right **Rev. Des.:** Emanuel Hahn **Size:** 18.03 mm.

Date	Mintage	VG-8	F-12	VF-20	XF-40	MS-60	MS-63	Proof
1979	237,321,321	—	—	—	0.15	0.20	0.35	—
1980	170,111,533	—	—	—	0.15	0.20	0.35	—
1981	123,912,900	—	—	—	0.15	0.20	0.35	—
1981 Proof	199,000	—	—	—	—	—	—	1.50
1982	93,475,000	—	—	—	0.15	0.20	0.35	—
1982 Proof	180,908	—	—	—	—	—	—	1.50

Date	Mintage	VG-8	F-12	VF-20	XF-40	MS-60	MS-63	Proof
1983	111,065,000	—	—	—	0.15	0.20	0.35	—
1983 Proof	168,000	—	—	—	—	—	—	1.50
1984	121,690,000	—	—	—	0.15	0.20	0.35	—
1984 Proof	161,602	—	—	—	—	—	—	1.50
1985	143,025,000	—	—	—	0.15	0.20	0.35	—
1985 Proof	157,037	—	*	—	—	—	—	1.50
1986	168,620,000	—	—	—	0.15	0.20	0.35	—
1986 Proof	175,745	—	—	—	—	—	—	1.50
1987	147,309,000	—	—	—	0.15	0.20	0.35	—
1987 Proof	179,004	—	—	—	—	—	—	1.50
1988	162,998,558	—	—	—	0.15	0.20	0.35	—
1988 Proof	175,259	—	—	—	—	—	—	1.50
1989	199,104,414	—	—	—	0.15	0.20	0.35	—
1989 Proof	170,528	—	—	—	—	—	—	1.50

KM# 183 10 CENTS   2.1400 g. Nickel **Ruler:** Elizabeth II **Obv.:** Crowned head right **Obv. Des.:** Dora dePedery-Hunt **Rev.:** Bluenose sailing left, date at right, denomination below **Rev. Des.:** Emanuel Hahn **Edge:** Reeded **Size:** 18.03 mm.

Date	Mintage	VG-8	F-12	VF-20	XF-40	MS-60	MS-63	Proof
1990	65,023,000	—	—	—	0.15	0.20	0.35	—
1990 Proof	140,649	—	—	—	—	—	—	2.50
1991	50,397,000	—	—	—	0.15	0.30	0.45	—
1991 Proof	131,888	—	—	—	—	—	—	4.00
1993	135,569,000	—	—	—	0.15	0.20	0.35	—
1993 Proof	143,065	—	—	—	—	—	—	2.00
1994	145,800,000	—	—	—	0.15	0.20	0.35	—
1994 Proof	146,424	—	—	—	—	—	—	2.50
1995	123,875,000	—	—	—	0.15	0.20	0.35	—
1995 Proof	50,000	—	—	—	—	—	—	2.50
1996	51,814,000	—	—	—	0.15	0.20	0.35	—
1996 Proof	—	—	—	—	—	—	—	2.50
1997	43,126,000	—	—	—	0.15	0.20	0.35	—
1997 Proof	—	—	—	—	—	—	—	2.50
1998	203,514,000	—	—	—	0.15	0.20	0.35	—
1998W	—	—	—	—	—	—	1.50	—
1998 Proof	—	—	—	—	—	—	—	2.50
1999	258,462,000	—	—	—	0.15	0.20	0.35	—
1999 Proof	—	—	—	—	—	—	—	2.50
2000	159,125,000	—	—	—	0.15	0.20	0.35	—
2000 Proof	—	—	—	—	—	—	—	2.50
2000W	—	—	—	—	—	—	1.50	—

KM# 206 10 CENTS   Nickel **Ruler:** Elizabeth II **Subject:** Confederation 125 **Obv.:** Crowned head right **Rev.:** Bluenose sailing left, date at right, denomination below **Size:** 18.03 mm.

Date	Mintage	VG-8	F-12	VF-20	XF-40	MS-60	MS-63	Proof
ND(1992)	174,476,000	—	—	—	—	0.25	0.35	—
ND(1992) Proof	147,061	—	—	—	—	—	—	3.00

KM#183a 10 CENTS   2.4000 g. 0.9250 Silver 0.0714 oz. ASW **Ruler:** Elizabeth II **Obv.:** Crowned head right **Rev.:** Bluenose sailing left, date at right, denomination below **Size:** 18.03 mm.

Date	Mintage	MS-63	Proof
1996 Proof	—	—	5.50
1997 Proof	—	—	5.50
1998 Proof	—	—	4.00
1998O Proof	—	—	4.00
1999 Proof	—	—	5.00
2000 Proof	—	—	5.00

KM# 299 10 CENTS   2.4000 g. 0.9250 Silver 0.0714 oz. ASW **Ruler:** Elizabeth II **Subject:** John Cabot **Obv.:** Crowned head right **Rev.:** Ship with full sails divides dates, denomination below **Rev. Des.:** Donald H. Curley **Size:** 18.03 mm.

Date	Mintage	MS-63	Proof
ND(1997) Proof	49,848	—	17.50

KM#311 10 CENTS   2.3200 g. 0.9250 Silver 0.0690 oz. ASW **Ruler:** Elizabeth II **Subject:** 90th Anniversary Royal Canadian Mint **Obv.:** Crowned head right **Rev.:** Denomination and date within wreath, crown above **Size:** 18.03 mm.

Date	Mintage	MS-63	Proof
ND(1998) Matte	25,000	—	10.00
ND(1998) Proof	25,000	—	10.00

KM# 183b 10 CENTS   Nickel Plated Steel **Ruler:** Elizabeth II **Obv.:** Crowned head right **Obv. Des.:** Dora dePedery-Hunt **Rev.:** Bluenose sailing left, date at right, denomination below **Rev. Des.:** Emanuel Hahn **Edge:** Reeded **Size:** 18.03 mm.

Date	Mintage	MS-63	Proof
1999 P	Est. 20,000	15.00	—
2000 P	Est. 200	1,000	—

KM# 409 10 CENTS   2.4000 g. 0.9250 Silver 0.0714 oz. ASW **Ruler:** Elizabeth II **Subject:** First Canadian Credit Union **Obv.:** Crowned head right **Rev.:** Alphonse Desjardins' house (founder of the first credit union in Canada), dates at right, denomination below **Edge:** Reeded **Size:** 18.03 mm.

Date	Mintage	MS-63	Proof
ND(2000) Proof	66,336	—	8.00

KM# 5 25 CENTS   5.8100 g. 0.9250 Silver 0.1728 oz. ASW **Ruler:** Victoria **Obv.:** Crowned head left **Obv. Leg.:** VICTORIA DEI GRATIA REGINA. CANADA **Obv. Des.:** Leonard C. Wyon **Rev.:** Denomination and date within wreath, crown above **Size:** 23.88 mm.

Date	Mintage	VG-8	F-12	VF-20	XF-40	MS-60	MS-63	Proof
1901	640,000	12.00	22.00	50.00	150	550	1,200	—

KM# 11 25 CENTS   5.8100 g. 0.9250 Silver 0.1728 oz. ASW **Ruler:** Edward VII **Obv.:** Crowned bust right **Obv. Des.:** G. W. DeSaulles **Rev.:** Denomination and date within wreath, crown above **Size:** 23.4 mm.

Date	Mintage	VG-8	F-12	VF-20	XF-40	MS-60	MS-63	Proof
1902	464,000	10.00	27.00	65.00	175	750	1,900	—
1902H	800,000	6.50	16.00	45.00	100	250	500	—
1903	846,150	15.00	29.00	75.00	200	800	1,900	—
1904	400,000	20.00	55.00	150	350	1,600	5,000	—
1905	800,000	15.00	30.00	100	300	1,400	4,600	—
1906	1,237,843	8.00	21.00	55.00	225	750	1,700	—
	Note: Large crown							
1906 Rare	Inc. above	2,500	3,900	6,000	7,500	10,000	16,000	—
	Note: Small crown							
1907	2,088,000	6.50	16.00	55.00	125	425	1,200	—
1908	495,016	15.00	35.00	95.00	200	400	750	—
1909	1,335,929	12.00	26.00	70.00	175	600	1,700	—

KM# 11a 25 CENTS   5.8319 g. 0.9250 Silver 0.1734 oz. ASW **Ruler:** Edward VII **Obv.:** Crowned bust right **Rev.:** Denomination and date within wreath, crown above

Date	Mintage	VG-8	F-12	VF-20	XF-40	MS-60	MS-63	Proof
1910	3,577,569	5.50	16.00	40.00	85.00	275	600	—

KM# 18 25 CENTS   5.8319 g. 0.9250 Silver 0.1734 oz. ASW **Ruler:** George V **Obv.:** Crowned bust left **Obv. Des.:** E. B. MacKennal **Rev.:** Denomination and date within wreath, crown above

Date	Mintage	VG-8	F-12	VF-20	XF-40	MS-60	MS-63	Proof
1911	1,721,341	6.50	18.00	35.00	85.00	250	425	—

KM# 24 25 CENTS   5.8319 g. 0.9250 Silver 0.1734 oz. ASW **Ruler:** George V **Obv.:** Crowned bust left **Obv. Des.:** E. B. MacKennal **Rev.:** Denomination and date within wreath, crown above **Size:** 23.5 mm.

Date	Mintage	VG-8	F-12	VF-20	XF-40	MS-60	MS-63	Proof
1912	2,544,199	5.50	9.00	20.00	55.00	350	1,200	—
1913	2,213,595	3.25	8.50	17.00	50.00	300	950	—
1914	1,215,397	5.00	10.00	23.00	60.00	500	1,600	—
1915	242,382	16.00	45.00	150	425	2,200	6,250	—
1916	1,462,566	3.00	7.50	18.00	40.00	225	700	—
1917	3,365,644	3.00	6.00	12.00	30.00	125	225	—
1918	4,175,649	3.00	5.00	12.00	26.00	95.00	175	—
1919	5,852,262	3.00	5.00	9.50	25.00	95.00	175	—

Dot below wreath

KM# 24a 25 CENTS 5.8319 g. 0.8000 Silver 0.1500 oz. ASW **Ruler:** George V
Obv.: Crowned bust left **Obv. Des.:** E. B. MacKennal **Rev.:** Denomination and date within wreath, crown below

Date	Mintage	VG-8	F-12	VF-20	XF-40	MS-60	MS-63	Proof
1920	1,975,278	3.00	6.00	12.00	30.00	150	400	—
1921	597,337	11.00	24.00	80.00	225	1,100	2,700	—
1927	468,096	27.00	50.00	100	225	750	1,600	—
1928	2,114,178	3.00	6.00	13.00	35.00	125	325	—
1929	2,690,562	3.00	6.00	13.00	35.00	125	325	—
1930	968,748	3.00	6.00	18.00	40.00	200	500	—
1931	537,815	3.00	6.00	20.00	50.00	200	500	—
1932	537,994	3.00	6.00	25.00	50.00	200	500	—
1933	421,282	3.00	6.50	28.00	65.00	175	325	—
1934	384,350	3.50	9.00	30.00	70.00	225	500	—
1935	537,772	3.50	7.50	22.00	50.00	150	325	—
1936	972,094	3.00	6.00	12.00	21.00	95.00	175	—
1936	153,322	26.00	65.00	150	300	800	1,800	—

Note: Dot below wreath. David Akers John Jay Pittman sale Part Three, 10-99, nearly Choice Unc. realized $6,900; considered a possible specimen example

Maple leaf after date

KM# 35 25 CENTS 5.8319 g. 0.8000 Silver 0.1500 oz. ASW **Ruler:** George VI
Obv.: Head left **Obv. Des.:** T. H. Paget **Rev.:** Caribou left, denomination above, date at right **Rev. Des.:** Emanuel Hahn **Size:** 23.5 mm.

Date	Mintage	VG-8	F-12	VF-20	XF-40	MS-60	MS-63	Proof
1937	2,690,176	2.50	3.00	4.00	6.00	16.00	35.00	—
1938	3,149,245	2.50	3.00	5.00	10.00	65.00	125	—
1939	3,532,495	2.50	3.50	5.00	7.00	50.00	100	—
1940	9,583,650	—	BV	2.50	3.00	15.00	30.00	—
1941	6,654,672	—	BV	2.50	3.00	16.00	30.00	—
1942	6,935,871	—	BV	2.50	3.00	17.00	45.00	—
1943	13,559,575	—	BV	2.50	3.00	16.00	30.00	—
1944	7,216,237	—	BV	2.50	3.00	26.00	50.00	—
1945	5,296,495	—	BV	2.50	3.00	16.00	45.00	—
1946	2,210,810	BV	2.50	4.00	8.00	45.00	75.00	—
1947	1,524,554	—	BV	4.00	8.00	50.00	95.00	—
1947	Inc. above	30.00	40.00	70.00	150	250	500	—
Note: Dot after 7								
1947	4,393,938	—	BV	2.50	3.00	16.00	32.00	—
Note: Maple leaf								

KM# 44 25 CENTS 5.8319 g. 0.8000 Silver 0.1500 oz. ASW **Ruler:** George VI **Obv.:** Head left, modified legend **Obv. Des.:** T. H. Paget **Rev.:** Caribou left, denomination above, date at right **Rev. Des.:** Emanuel Hahn **Size:** 23.5 mm.

Date	Mintage	VG-8	F-12	VF-20	XF-40	MS-60	MS-63	Proof
1948	2,564,424	BV	2.50	3.00	13.00	55.00	75.00	—
1949	7,988,830	—	BV	2.50	3.00	10.00	20.00	—
1950	9,673,335	—	—	BV	2.50	8.00	15.00	—
1951	8,290,719	—	—	BV	2.50	7.00	12.00	—
1952	8,859,642	—	—	BV	2.50	6.00	11.00	—

KM# 52 25 CENTS 5.8319 g. 0.8000 Silver 0.1500 oz. ASW **Ruler:** Elizabeth II
Obv.: Laureate bust right **Obv. Des.:** Mary Gillick **Rev.:** Caribou left, denomination above, date at right **Rev. Des.:** Emanuel Hahn **Size:** 23.8 mm.

Date	Mintage	VG-8	F-12	VF-20	XF-40	MS-60	MS-63	Proof
1953	10,546,769	—	—	BV	2.75	5.00	10.00	—

Date	Mintage	VG-8	F-12	VF-20	XF-40	MS-60	MS-63	Proof
Note: Without strap								
1953	Inc. above	—	—	BV	2.75	6.50	18.00	—
Note: With strap								
1954	2,318,891	—	BV	2.50	7.00	25.00	40.00	—
1955	9,552,505	—	—	BV	2.75	6.00	15.00	—
1956	11,269,353	—	—	BV	2.75	3.25	6.50	—
1957	12,770,190	—	—	—	BV	2.75	5.00	—
1958	9,336,910	—	—	—	BV	2.75	5.00	—
1959	13,503,461	—	—	—	BV	2.75	3.50	—
1960	22,835,327	—	—	—	BV	2.75	3.50	—
1961	18,164,368	—	—	—	BV	2.75	3.50	—
1962	29,559,266	—	—	—	BV	2.75	3.50	—
1963	21,180,652	—	—	—	BV	2.75	3.00	—
1964	36,479,343	—	—	—	BV	2.75	3.00	—

KM# 62 25 CENTS 5.8319 g. 0.8000 Silver 0.1500 oz. ASW **Ruler:** Elizabeth II
Obv.: Young bust right **Obv. Des.:** Arnold Machin **Rev.:** Caribou left, denomination above, date at right **Rev. Des.:** Emanuel Hahn **Size:** 23.8 mm.

Date	Mintage	VG-8	F-12	VF-20	XF-40	MS-60	MS-63	Proof
1965	44,708,869	—	—	—	BV	2.75	3.00	—
1966	25,626,315	—	—	—	BV	2.75	3.00	—

KM# 68 25 CENTS 5.8319 g. 0.8000 Silver 0.1500 oz. ASW **Ruler:** Elizabeth II
Subject: Confederation Centennial **Obv.:** Young bust right **Rev.:** Lynx striding left divides dates and denomination **Rev. Des.:** Alex Colville **Size:** 23.8 mm.

Date	Mintage	VG-8	F-12	VF-20	XF-40	MS-60	MS-63	Proof
ND(1967)	48,855,500	—	—	—	BV	2.75	3.00	—

KM# 68a 25 CENTS 5.8319 g. 0.5000 Silver 0.0937 oz. ASW **Ruler:** Elizabeth II
Subject: Confederation Centennial **Obv.:** Young bust right **Rev.:** Lynx striding left divides dates and denomination **Size:** 23.8 mm.

Date	Mintage	VG-8	F-12	VF-20	XF-40	MS-60	MS-63	Proof
ND(1967)	Inc. above	—	—	—	BV	2.00	3.00	—

KM# 62a 25 CENTS 5.8319 g. 0.5000 Silver 0.0937 oz. ASW **Ruler:** Elizabeth II
Obv.: Young bust right **Obv. Des.:** Machin **Rev.:** Caribou left, denomination above, date at right **Size:** 23.8 mm.

Date	Mintage	VG-8	F-12	VF-20	XF-40	MS-60	MS-63	Proof
1968	71,464,000	—	—	—	BV	2.00	3.00	—

KM# 62b 25 CENTS 5.0600 g. Nickel **Ruler:** Elizabeth II **Obv.:** Young bust right **Obv. Des.:** Machin **Rev.:** Caribou left, denomination above, date at right **Size:** 23.8 mm.

Date	Mintage	VG-8	F-12	VF-20	XF-40	MS-60	MS-63	Proof
1968	88,686,931	—	—	—	0.30	0.45	0.75	—
1969	133,037,929	—	—	—	0.30	0.45	0.75	—
1970	10,302,010	—	—	—	0.30	1.00	2.00	—
1971	48,170,428	—	—	—	0.30	0.45	0.75	—
1972	43,743,387	—	—	—	0.30	0.45	0.75	—
1973	135,958,589	—	—	—	0.30	0.50	1.00	—
Note: Small bust								
1973	Inc. above	—	60.00	70.00	100	150	500	—
Note: Large bust								
1974	192,360,598	—	—	—	0.30	0.45	0.75	—
1975	141,148,000	—	—	—	0.30	0.45	0.75	—
1976	86,898,261	—	—	—	0.30	0.45	0.75	—
1977	99,634,555	—	—	—	0.30	0.45	0.75	—
1978	176,475,408	—	—	—	0.30	0.45	0.75	—

KM# 81.1 25 CENTS Nickel **Ruler:** Elizabeth II **Subject:** Royal Canadian Mounted Police Centennial **Obv.:** Young bust right **Rev.:** Mountie divides dates, denomination above **Rev. Des.:** Paul Cedarberg **Size:** 23.8 mm. **Note:** 120 beads.

Date	Mintage	VG-8	F-12	VF-20	XF-40	MS-60	MS-63	Proof
ND(1973)	134,958,587	—	—	—	0.30	0.55	1.00	—

KM# 81.2 25 CENTS Nickel **Ruler:** Elizabeth II **Subject:** RCMP Centennial **Obv.:** Young bust right **Rev.:** Mountie divides dates, denomination above **Size:** 23.8 mm. **Note:** 132 beads.

Date	Mintage	VG-8	F-12	VF-20	XF-40	MS-60	MS-63	Proof
ND(1973)	Inc. above	40.00	55.00	70.00	85.00	100	200	—

KM# 74 25 CENTS 5.0700 g. Nickel **Ruler:** Elizabeth II **Obv.:** Small young bust right **Obv. Des.:** Machin **Rev. Des.:** Emanuel Hahn **Size:** 23.88 mm.

Date	Mintage	VG-8	F-12	VF-20	XF-40	MS-60	MS-63	Proof
1979	131,042,905	—	—	—	0.30	0.45	0.75	—
1980	76,178,000	—	—	—	0.30	0.45	0.75	—
1981	131,580,272	—	—	—	0.30	0.45	0.75	—
1981 Proof	199,000	—	—	—	—	—	—	2.00
1982	171,926,000	—	—	—	0.30	0.45	0.75	—
1982 Proof	180,908	—	—	—	—	—	—	2.00
1983	13,162,000	—	—	—	0.30	0.75	1.50	—
1983 Proof	168,000	—	—	—	—	—	—	3.00
1984	121,668,000	—	—	—	0.30	0.45	0.75	—
1984 Proof	161,602	—	—	—	—	—	—	2.00
1985	158,734,000	—	—	—	0.30	0.45	0.75	—
1985 Proof	157,037	—	—	—	—	—	—	2.00
1986	132,220,000	—	—	—	0.30	0.45	0.75	—
1986 Proof	175,745	—	—	—	—	—	—	2.00
1987	53,408,000	—	—	—	0.30	0.60	1.25	—
1987 Proof	179,004	—	—	—	—	—	—	2.00
1988	80,368,473	—	—	—	0.30	0.45	1.00	—
1988 Proof	175,259	—	—	—	—	—	—	2.00
1989	119,796,307	—	—	—	0.30	0.45	0.75	—
1989 Proof	170,928	—	—	—	—	—	—	2.00

KM# 184 25 CENTS 5.0700 g. Nickel **Ruler:** Elizabeth II **Obv.:** Crowned head right **Obv. Des.:** Dora dePedery-Hunt **Rev.:** Caribou left, denomination above, date at right **Rev. Des.:** Emanuel Hahn **Size:** 23.88 mm.

Date	Mintage	MS-63	Proof
1990	31,258,000	0.90	—
1990 Proof	140,649	—	2.50
1991	459,000	12.00	—
1991 Proof	131,888	—	20.00
1993	73,758,000	0.70	—
1993 Proof	143,065	—	2.00
1994	77,670,000	0.70	—
1994 Proof	146,424	—	3.00
1995	89,210,000	0.70	—
1995 Proof	50,000	—	3.00
1996	28,106,000	0.70	—
1996 Proof	—	—	6.00
1997	—	0.70	—
1997 Proof	—	—	6.00
1998W	—	5.00	—
1999	258,888,000	0.75	—
1999 Proof	—	—	6.00
2000	434,087,000	0.75	—
2000 Proof	—	—	6.00
2000W	—	5.00	—

KM# 184a 25 CENTS 5.9000 g. 0.9250 Silver 0.1755 oz. ASW **Ruler:** Elizabeth II **Obv.:** Crowned head right **Rev.:** Caribou left, denomination above, date at right **Size:** 23.88 mm.

Date	Mintage	MS-63	Proof
1996 Proof	—	—	6.50
1997 Proof	—	—	6.50
1998 Proof	—	—	5.50
1998O Proof	—	—	5.50
1999 Proof	—	—	5.50

KM# 184b 25 CENTS Nickel Plated Steel **Ruler:** Elizabeth II **Obv.:** Crowned head right **Rev.:** Caribou left, denomination above, date at right **Size:** 23.88 mm.

Date	Mintage	MS-63	Proof
1999 P	Est. 20,000	20.00	—
2000 P	—	5,500	—

Note: 3-5 known

KM# 213 25 CENTS Nickel **Series:** 125th Anniversary of Confederation **Subject:** Newfoundland **Rev.:** Fisherman rowing a dory, denomination below **Rev. Des.:** Christopher Newhook **Size:** 23.8 mm.

Date	Mintage	VG-8	F-12	VF-20	XF-40	MS-60	MS-63	Proof
ND(1992)	11,405,000	—	—	—	—	0.35	0.70	—

KM#213a 25CENTS 5.8319 g. 0.9250 Silver 0.1734 oz. ASW **Series:** 125th Anniversary of Confederation **Subject:** Newfoundland **Rev.:** Fisherman rowing a dory, denomination below **Size:** 23.8 mm.

Date	Mintage	VG-8	F-12	VF-20	XF-40	MS-60	MS-63	Proof
ND(1992) Proof	149,579	—	—	—	—	—	—	5.50

KM# 207 25 CENTS Nickel **Ruler:** Elizabeth II **Subject:** Confederation 125 **Obv.:** Crowned head right **Obv. Des.:** Dora dePedery-Hunt **Rev.:** Caribou left, denomination above, date at right **Rev. Des.:** Emanuel Hahn **Size:** 23.8 mm.

Date	Mintage	VG-8	F-12	VF-20	XF-40	MS-60	MS-63	Proof
ND(1992)	442,986	—	—	—	—	—	12.50	—
ND(1992) Proof	147,061	—	—	—	—	—	—	20.00

KM# 203 25 CENTS Nickel **Ruler:** Elizabeth II **Series:** 125th Anniversary of Confederation **Subject:** New Brunswick **Obv.:** Crowned head right **Rev.:** Covered bridge in Newton, denomination below **Rev. Des.:** Ronald Lambert **Size:** 23.8 mm.

Date	Mintage	VG-8	F-12	VF-20	XF-40	MS-60	MS-63	Proof
ND(1992)	12,174,000	—	—	—	—	0.35	0.70	—

KM# 203a 25 CENTS 5.8319 g. 0.9250 Silver 0.1734 oz. ASW **Ruler:** Elizabeth II **Series:** 125th Anniversary of Confederation **Subject:** New Brunswick **Obv.:** Crowned head right **Rev.:** Covered bridge in Newton, denomination below **Size:** 23.8 mm.

Date	Mintage	VG-8	F-12	VF-20	XF-40	MS-60	MS-63	Proof
ND(1992) Proof	149,579	—	—	—	—	—	—	5.50

KM# 212 25 CENTS Nickel **Ruler:** Elizabeth II **Series:** 125th Anniversary of Confederation **Subject:** Northwest Territories **Obv.:** Crowned head right **Rev. Des.:** Beth McEachen **Size:** 23.8 mm.

Date	Mintage	VG-8	F-12	VF-20	XF-40	MS-60	MS-63	Proof
ND(1992)	12,582,000	—	—	—	—	0.35	0.70	—

KM# 212a 25 CENTS 5.8319 g. 0.9250 Silver 0.1734 oz. ASW **Ruler:** Elizabeth II **Series:** 125th Anniversary of Confederation **Subject:** Northwest Territories **Obv.:** Crowned head right **Size:** 23.8 mm.

Date	Mintage	VG-8	F-12	VF-20	XF-40	MS-60	MS-63	Proof
ND(1992) Proof	149,579	—	—	—	—	—	—	5.50

KM# 214 25 CENTS Nickel **Ruler:** Elizabeth II **Series:** 125th Anniversary of Confederation **Subject:** Manitoba **Obv.:** Crowned head right **Rev. Des.:** Muriel Hope **Size:** 23.8 mm.

Date	Mintage	VG-8	F-12	VF-20	XF-40	MS-60	MS-63	Proof
ND(1992)	11,349,000	—	—	—	—	0.35	0.70	—

KM# 214a 25 CENTS 5.8319 g. 0.9250 Silver 0.1734 oz. ASW **Ruler:** Elizabeth II **Series:** 125th Anniversary of Confederation **Subject:** Manitoba **Obv.:** Crowned head right **Size:** 23.8 mm.

Date	Mintage	VG-8	F-12	VF-20	XF-40	MS-60	MS-63	Proof
ND(1992) Proof	149,579	—	—	—	—	—	—	5.50

KM# 220 25 CENTS Nickel **Ruler:** Elizabeth II **Series:** 125th Anniversary of Confederation **Subject:** Yukon **Obv.:** Crowned head right **Rev. Des.:** Libby Dulac **Size:** 23.8 mm.

Date	Mintage	VG-8	F-12	VF-20	XF-40	MS-60	MS-63	Proof
ND(1992)	10,388,000	—	—	—	—	0.35	0.70	—

KM# 220a 25 CENTS 5.8319 g. 0.9250 Silver 0.1734 oz. ASW **Ruler:** Elizabeth II **Series:** 125th Anniversary of Confederation **Subject:** Yukon **Obv.:** Crowned head right **Size:** 23.8 mm.

Date	Mintage	VG-8	F-12	VF-20	XF-40	MS-60	MS-63	Proof
ND(1992) Proof	149,579	—	—	—	—	—	—	5.50

KM# 221 25 CENTS Nickel **Ruler:** Elizabeth II **Series:** 125th Anniversary of Confederation **Subject:** Alberta **Obv.:** Crowned head right **Rev.:** Rock formations in the badlands near Drumhelter, denomination below **Rev. Des.:** Mel Heath **Size:** 23.8 mm.

Date	Mintage	VG-8	F-12	VF-20	XF-40	MS-60	MS-63	Proof
ND(1992)	12,133,000	—	—	—	—	0.35	0.70	—

KM# 221a 25 CENTS 5.8319 g. 0.9250 Silver 0.1734 oz. ASW **Ruler:** Elizabeth II **Series:** 125th Anniversary of Confederation **Subject:** Alberta **Obv.:** Crowned head right **Rev.:** Rock formations in the badlands near Drumhelter, denomination below **Rev. Des.:** Mel Heath **Size:** 23.8 mm.

Date	Mintage	VG-8	F-12	VF-20	XF-40	MS-60	MS-63	Proof
ND(1992) Proof	—	—	—	—	—	—	—	5.50

KM# 222 25 CENTS Nickel **Ruler:** Elizabeth II **Series:** 125th Anniversary of Confederation **Subject:** Prince Edward Island **Obv.:** Crowned head right **Rev. Des.:** Nigel Roe **Size:** 23.8 mm.

Date	Mintage	VG-8	F-12	VF-20	XF-40	MS-60	MS-63	Proof
ND(1992)	13,001,000	—	—	—	—	0.35	0.70	—

KM# 222a 25 CENTS 5.8319 g. 0.9250 Silver 0.1734 oz. ASW **Ruler:** Elizabeth II **Series:** 125th Anniversary of Confederation **Subject:** Prince Edward Island **Obv.:** Crowned head right **Rev. Des.:** Nigel Roe **Size:** 23.8 mm.

Date	Mintage	VG-8	F-12	VF-20	XF-40	MS-60	MS-63	Proof
ND(1992) Proof	149,579	—	—	—	—	—	—	5.50

KM# 223 25 CENTS   Nickel **Ruler:** Elizabeth II **Series:** 125th Anniversary of Confederation **Subject:** Ontario **Obv.:** Crowned head right **Rev.:** Jack pine, denomination below **Rev. Des.:** Greg Salmela **Size:** 23.8 mm.

Date	Mintage	VG-8	F-12	VF-20	XF-40	MS-60	MS-63	Proof
ND(1992)	14,263,000	—	—	—	—	0.35	0.70	—

KM# 223a 25 CENTS   5.8319 g. 0.9250 Silver 0.1734 oz. ASW **Ruler:** Elizabeth II **Series:** 125th Anniversary of Confederation **Subject:** Ontario **Obv.:** Crowned head right **Rev.:** Jack pine, denomination below **Rev. Des.:** Greg Salmela **Size:** 23.8 mm.

Date	Mintage	VG-8	F-12	VF-20	XF-40	MS-60	MS-63	Proof
ND(1992) Proof	149,579	—	—	—	—	—	—	5.50

KM# 231 25 CENTS   5.0300 g. Nickel **Ruler:** Elizabeth II **Series:** 125th Anniversary of Confederation **Subject:** Nova Scotia **Obv.:** Crowned head right **Rev.:** Lighthouse, denomination below **Rev. Des.:** Bruce Wood **Size:** 23.8 mm.

Date	Mintage	VG-8	F-12	VF-20	XF-40	MS-60	MS-63	Proof
ND(1992)	13,600,000	—	—	—	—	0.35	0.70	—

KM# 231a 25 CENTS   5.8319 g. 0.9250 Silver 0.1734 oz. ASW **Ruler:** Elizabeth II **Series:** 125th Anniversary of Confederation **Subject:** Nova Scotia **Obv.:** Crowned head right **Rev.:** Lighthouse, denomination below **Rev. Des.:** Bruce Wood **Size:** 23.8 mm.

Date	Mintage	VG-8	F-12	VF-20	XF-40	MS-60	MS-63	Proof
ND(1992) Proof	149,579	—	—	—	—	—	—	5.50

KM# 232 25 CENTS   Nickel **Ruler:** Elizabeth II **Series:** 125th Anniversary of Confederation **Subject:** British Columbia **Obv.:** Crowned head right, dates below **Rev.:** Large rock, whales, denomination below **Rev. Des.:** Carla Herrera Egan **Size:** 23.8 mm.

Date	Mintage	VG-8	F-12	VF-20	XF-40	MS-60	MS-63	Proof
ND(1992)	14,001,000	—	—	—	—	0.35	0.70	—

KM# 232a 25 CENTS   5.8319 g. 0.9250 Silver 0.1734 oz. ASW **Ruler:** Elizabeth II **Series:** 125th Anniversary of Confederation **Subject:** British Columbia **Obv.:** Crowned head right, dates below **Rev.:** Large rock, whales, denomination below **Rev. Des.:** Carla Herrera Egan **Size:** 23.8 mm.

Date	Mintage	VG-8	F-12	VF-20	XF-40	MS-60	MS-63	Proof
ND(1992) Proof	149,579	—	—	—	—	—	—	5.50

KM# 233 25 CENTS   Nickel **Ruler:** Elizabeth II **Series:** 125th Anniversary of Confederation **Subject:** Saskatchewan **Obv.:** Crowned head right **Rev.:** Buildings behind wall, grain stalks on right, denomination below **Rev. Des.:** Brian Cobb **Size:** 23.8 mm.

Date	Mintage	VG-8	F-12	VF-20	XF-40	MS-60	MS-63	Proof
ND(1992)	14,165,000	—	—	—	—	0.35	0.70	—

KM# 233a 25 CENTS   5.8319 g. 0.9250 Silver 0.1734 oz. ASW **Ruler:** Elizabeth II **Series:** 125th Anniversary of Confederation **Subject:** Saskatchewan **Obv.:** Crowned head right **Rev.:** Buildings behind wall, grain stalks on right, denomination below **Rev. Des.:** Brian Cobb **Size:** 23.8 mm.

Date	Mintage	VG-8	F-12	VF-20	XF-40	MS-60	MS-63	Proof
ND(1992) Proof	149,579	—	—	—	—	—	—	5.50

KM# 234 25 CENTS   Nickel **Ruler:** Elizabeth II **Series:** 125th Anniversary of Confederation **Subject:** Quebec **Obv.:** Crowned head right **Rev.:** Boats on water, large rocks in background, denomination below **Rev. Des.:** Romualdas Bukauskas **Size:** 23.8 mm.

Date	Mintage	VG-8	F-12	VF-20	XF-40	MS-60	MS-63	Proof
ND(1992)	13,607,000	—	—	—	—	0.35	0.70	—

KM# 234a 25 CENTS   5.8319 g. 0.9250 Silver 0.1734 oz. ASW **Ruler:** Elizabeth II **Series:** 125th Anniversary of Confederation **Subject:** Quebec **Obv.:** Crowned head right **Rev.:** Boats on water, large rocks in background, denomination below **Rev. Des.:** Romualdas Bukauskas **Size:** 23.8 mm.

Date	Mintage	VG-8	F-12	VF-20	XF-40	MS-60	MS-63	Proof
ND(1992) Proof	149,579	—	—	—	—	—	—	5.50

KM# 312 25 CENTS   **Ruler:** Elizabeth II **Subject:** 90th Anniversary Royal Canadian Mint **Obv.:** Crowned head right **Rev.:** Denomination and date within wreath, crown above **Size:** 23.8 mm.

Date	Mintage	VG-8	F-12	VF-20	XF-40	MS-60	MS-63	Proof
ND(1998) Matte	25,000	—	—	—	—	—	—	15.00
ND(1998) Proof	—	—	—	—	—	—	—	15.00

KM# 342 25 CENTS   Nickel **Ruler:** Elizabeth II **Series:** Millennium **Subject:** January - A Country Unfolds **Obv.:** Crowned head right **Rev.:** Totem pole, portraits **Rev. Des.:** P. Ka-Kin Poon **Size:** 23.8 mm.

Date	Mintage	VG-8	F-12	VF-20	XF-40	MS-60	MS-63	Proof
1999	12,181,200	—	—	—	—	0.50	0.65	—

KM# 342a 25 CENTS   5.8319 g. 0.9250 Silver 0.1734 oz. ASW **Ruler:** Elizabeth II **Series:** Millennium **Subject:** January **Obv.:** Crowned head right **Rev.:** Totem pole, portraits **Rev. Des.:** P. Ka-kin Poon **Size:** 23.8 mm.

Date	Mintage	VG-8	F-12	VF-20	XF-40	MS-60	MS-63	Proof
1999 Proof	113,645	—	—	—	—	—	—	8.00

KM# 343 25 CENTS   5.0900 g. Nickel **Ruler:** Elizabeth II **Series:** Millennium **Subject:** February - Etched in Stone **Obv.:** Crowned head right **Rev.:** Native petroglyphs **Rev. Des.:** L. Springer **Size:** 23.8 mm.

Date	Mintage	VG-8	F-12	VF-20	XF-40	MS-60	MS-63	Proof
1999	14,469,250	—	—	—	—	0.50	0.65	—

KM# 343a 25 CENTS   5.8319 g. 0.9250 Silver 0.1734 oz. ASW **Ruler:** Elizabeth II **Series:** Millennium **Subject:** February **Obv.:** Crowned head right **Rev.:** Native petroglyphs **Rev. Des.:** L. Springer **Size:** 23.8 mm.

Date	Mintage	VG-8	F-12	VF-20	XF-40	MS-60	MS-63	Proof
1999 Proof	113,645	—	—	—	—	—	—	8.00

KM# 344 25 CENTS   Nickel **Ruler:** Elizabeth II **Series:** Millennium **Subject:** March - The Log Drive **Obv.:** Crowned head right **Rev.:** Lumberjack **Rev. Des.:** M. Lavoie **Size:** 23.8 mm.

Date	Mintage	VG-8	F-12	VF-20	XF-40	MS-60	MS-63	Proof
1999	15,033,500	—	—	—	—	0.50	0.65	—

KM# 344a 25 CENTS   5.8319 g. 0.9250 Silver 0.1734 oz. ASW **Ruler:** Elizabeth II **Series:** Millennium **Subject:** March **Obv.:** Crowned head right **Rev.:** Lumberjack **Rev. Des.:** M. Lavoie **Size:** 23.8 mm.

Date	Mintage	VG-8	F-12	VF-20	XF-40	MS-60	MS-63	Proof
1999 Proof	113,645	—	—	—	—	—	—	8.00

KM# 345 25 CENTS   5.0500 g. Nickel **Ruler:** Elizabeth II **Series:** Millennium **Subject:** April - Our Northern Heritage **Obv.:** Crowned head right **Rev.:** Owl, polar bear **Rev. Des.:** Ken Ojnak Ashevac **Size:** 23.8 mm.

Date	Mintage	VG-8	F-12	VF-20	XF-40	MS-60	MS-63	Proof
1999	15,446,000	—	—	—	—	0.50	0.65	—

KM# 345a 25 CENTS   5.8319 g. 0.9250 Silver 0.1734 oz. ASW **Ruler:** Elizabeth II **Series:** Millennium **Subject:** April **Obv.:** Crowned head right **Rev.:** Owl, polar bear **Rev. Des.:** Ken Ojnak Ashevac **Size:** 23.8 mm.

Date	Mintage	VG-8	F-12	VF-20	XF-40	MS-60	MS-63	Proof
1999 Proof	113,645	—	—	—	—	—	—	8.00

KM# 346 25 CENTS   Nickel **Ruler:** Elizabeth II **Series:** Millennium **Subject:** May - The Voyageures **Obv.:** Crowned head right **Rev.:** Voyageurs in canoe **Rev. Des.:** S. Mineok **Size:** 23.8 mm.

Date	Mintage	VG-8	F-12	VF-20	XF-40	MS-60	MS-63	Proof
1999	15,566,100	—	—	—	—	0.50	0.65	—

KM# 346a 25 CENTS   5.8319 g. 0.9250 Silver 0.1734 oz. ASW **Ruler:** Elizabeth II **Series:** Millennium **Subject:** May **Obv.:** Crowned head right **Rev.:** Voyageurs in canoe **Rev. Des.:** S. Mineok **Size:** 23.8 mm.

Date	Mintage	VG-8	F-12	VF-20	XF-40	MS-60	MS-63	Proof
1999 Proof	113,645	—	—	—	—	—	—	8.00

KM# 347 25 CENTS   5.0300 g. Nickel **Ruler:** Elizabeth II **Series:** Millennium **Subject:** June - From Coast to Coast **Obv.:** Crowned head right **Rev.:** 19th-century locomotive **Rev. Des.:** G. Ho **Edge:** Reeded **Size:** 23.8 mm.

Date	Mintage	VG-8	F-12	VF-20	XF-40	MS-60	MS-63	Proof
1999	20,432,750	—	—	—	—	0.50	0.65	—

KM# 347a 25 CENTS   5.8319 g. 0.9250 Silver 0.1734 oz. ASW **Ruler:** Elizabeth II **Series:** Millennium **Subject:** June **Obv.:** Crowned head right **Rev.:** 19th-century locomotive **Rev. Des.:** G. Ho **Edge:** Reeded **Size:** 23.8 mm.

Date	Mintage	VG-8	F-12	VF-20	XF-40	MS-60	MS-63	Proof
1999 Proof	113,645	—	—	—	—	—	—	8.00

KM# 348 25 CENTS   Nickel **Ruler:** Elizabeth II **Series:** Millennium **Subject:** July - A Nation of People **Obv.:** Crowned head right **Rev.:** 6 stylized portraits **Rev. Des.:** M. H. Sarkany **Size:** 23.8 mm.

Date	Mintage	VG-8	F-12	VF-20	XF-40	MS-60	MS-63	Proof
1999	17,321,000	—	—	—	—	0.50	0.65	—

KM# 348a 25 CENTS   5.8319 g. 0.9250 Silver 0.1734 oz. ASW **Ruler:** Elizabeth II **Series:** Millennium **Subject:** July **Obv.:** Crowned head right **Rev.:** 6 stylized portraits **Rev. Des.:** M.H. Sarkany **Size:** 23.8 mm.

Date	Mintage	VG-8	F-12	VF-20	XF-40	MS-60	MS-63	Proof
1999 Proof	113,645	—	—	—	—	—	—	8.00

KM# 349 25 CENTS   5.1000 g. Nickel **Ruler:** Elizabeth II **Series:** Millennium **Subject:** August - The Pioneer Spirit **Obv.:** Crowned head right **Rev.:** Hay harvesting **Rev. Des.:** A. Botelho **Size:** 23.8 mm.

Date	Mintage	VG-8	F-12	VF-20	XF-40	MS-60	MS-63	Proof
1999	18,153,700	—	—	—	—	0.50	0.65	—

KM# 349a 25 CENTS   5.8319 g. 0.9250 Silver 0.1734 oz. ASW **Ruler:** Elizabeth II **Series:** Millennium **Subject:** August **Obv.:** Crowned head right **Rev.:** Hay harvesting **Rev. Des.:** A. Botelho **Size:** 23.8 mm.

Date	Mintage	VG-8	F-12	VF-20	XF-40	MS-60	MS-63	Proof
1999 Proof	113,645	—	—	—	—	—	—	8.00

KM# 350 25 CENTS Nickel **Ruler:** Elizabeth II **Series:** Millennium **Subject:** September - Canada Through a Child's Eye **Obv.:** Crowned head right **Rev.:** Childlike artwork **Rev. Des.:** Claudia Bertrand **Size:** 23.8 mm.

Date	Mintage	VG-8	F-12	VF-20	XF-40	MS-60	MS-63	Proof
1999	31,539,350	—	—	—	—	0.50	0.65	—

KM# 350a 25 CENTS 5.8319 g. 0.9250 Silver 0.1734 oz. ASW **Ruler:** Elizabeth II **Series:** Millennium **Subject:** September **Obv.:** Crowned head right **Rev.:** Childlike artwork **Rev. Des.:** Claudia Bertrand **Size:** 23.8 mm.

Date	Mintage	VG-8	F-12	VF-20	XF-40	MS-60	MS-63	Proof
1999 Proof	113,645	—	—	—	—	—	—	8.00

KM# 351 25 CENTS 5.1000 g. Nickel **Ruler:** Elizabeth II **Series:** Millennium **Subject:** October - Tribute to the First Nations **Obv.:** Crowned head right **Rev.:** Aboriginal artwork **Rev. Des.:** J. E. Read **Size:** 23.8 mm.

Date	Mintage	VG-8	F-12	VF-20	XF-40	MS-60	MS-63	Proof
1999	32,136,650	—	—	—	—	0.50	0.65	—

KM# 351a 25 CENTS 5.8319 g. 0.9250 Silver 0.1734 oz. ASW **Ruler:** Elizabeth II **Series:** Millennium **Subject:** October **Obv.:** Crowned head right **Rev.:** Aboriginal artwork **Rev. Des.:** J.E. Read **Size:** 23.8 mm.

Date	Mintage	VG-8	F-12	VF-20	XF-40	MS-60	MS-63	Proof
1999 Proof	113,645	—	—	—	—	—	—	8.00

KM# 352 25 CENTS Nickel **Ruler:** Elizabeth II **Series:** Millennium **Subject:** November - The Airplane Opens the North **Obv.:** Crowned head right **Rev.:** Bush plane with landing skis **Rev. Des.:** B. R. Brown **Size:** 23.8 mm.

Date	Mintage	VG-8	F-12	VF-20	XF-40	MS-60	MS-63	Proof
1999	27,162,800	—	—	—	—	0.50	0.65	—

KM# 352a 25 CENTS 5.8319 g. 0.9250 Silver 0.1734 oz. ASW **Ruler:** Elizabeth II **Series:** Millennium **Subject:** November **Obv.:** Crowned head right **Rev.:** Bush plane with landing skis **Rev. Des.:** B.R. Brown **Size:** 23.8 mm.

Date	Mintage	VG-8	F-12	VF-20	XF-40	MS-60	MS-63	Proof
1999 Proof	113,645	—	—	—	—	—	—	8.00

KM# 353 25 CENTS 5.0900 g. Nickel **Ruler:** Elizabeth II **Series:** Millennium **Subject:** December - This is Canada **Obv.:** Crowned head right **Rev.:** Eclectic geometric design **Rev. Des.:** J. L. P. Provencher **Size:** 23.8 mm.

Date	Mintage	VG-8	F-12	VF-20	XF-40	MS-60	MS-63	Proof
1999	43,339,200	—	—	—	—	0.50	0.70	—

KM# 353a 25 CENTS 5.8319 g. 0.9250 Silver 0.1734 oz. ASW **Ruler:** Elizabeth II **Series:** Millennium **Subject:** December **Obv.:** Crowned head right **Rev.:** Eclectic geometric design **Rev. Des.:** J.L.P. Provencher **Size:** 23.8 mm.

Date	Mintage	VG-8	F-12	VF-20	XF-40	MS-60	MS-63	Proof
1999 Proof	113,645	—	—	—	—	—	—	8.00

KM# 373 25 CENTS Nickel **Ruler:** Elizabeth II **Subject:** Health **Obv.:** Crowned head right, denomination below **Rev.:** Ribbon and caduceus, date above **Rev. Des.:** Anny Wassef **Size:** 23.8 mm.

Date	Mintage	VG-8	F-12	VF-20	XF-40	MS-60	MS-63	Proof
2000	35,470,900	—	—	—	—	0.50	0.65	—

KM# 373a 25 CENTS 0.9250 Silver **Ruler:** Elizabeth II **Subject:** Health **Obv.:** Crowned head right, denomination below **Rev.:** Ribbon and caduceus, date above **Rev. Des.:** Anny Wassef **Size:** 23.8 mm.

Date	Mintage	VG-8	F-12	VF-20	XF-40	MS-60	MS-63	Proof
2000 Proof	76,956	—	—	—	—	—	—	8.00

KM# 374 25 CENTS 5.1000 g. Nickel **Ruler:** Elizabeth II **Subject:** Freedom **Obv.:** Crowned head right, denomination below **Rev.:** 2 children on maple leaf and rising sun, date above **Rev. Des.:** Kathy Vinish **Size:** 23.8 mm.

Date	Mintage	VG-8	F-12	VF-20	XF-40	MS-60	MS-63	Proof
2000	35,188,900	—	—	—	—	0.50	0.65	—

KM#374a 25 CENTS 0.9250 Silver **Ruler:** Elizabeth II **Subject:** Freedom **Obv.:** Crowned head right, denomination below **Rev.:** 2 children on maple leaf and rising sun, date above **Rev. Des.:** Kathy Vinish **Size:** 23.8 mm.

Date	Mintage	VG-8	F-12	VF-20	XF-40	MS-60	MS-63	Proof
2000 Proof	76,956	—	—	—	—	—	—	6.00

KM# 375 25 CENTS Nickel **Ruler:** Elizabeth II **Subject:** Family **Obv.:** Crowned head right, denomination below **Rev.:** Wreath of native carvings, date above **Rev. Des.:** Wade Stephen Baker **Size:** 23.8 mm.

Date	Mintage	VG-8	F-12	VF-20	XF-40	MS-60	MS-63	Proof
2000	35,107,700	—	—	—	—	0.50	0.65	—

KM# 375a 25 CENTS 0.9250 Silver **Ruler:** Elizabeth II **Subject:** Family **Obv.:** Crowned head right **Rev.:** Wreath of native carvings, date above **Rev. Des.:** Wade Stephen Baker **Size:** 23.8 mm.

Date	Mintage	VG-8	F-12	VF-20	XF-40	MS-60	MS-63	Proof
2000 Proof	76,956	—	—	—	—	—	—	6.00

KM# 376 25 CENTS 5.0800 g. Nickel **Ruler:** Elizabeth II **Subject:** Community **Obv.:** Crowned head right, denomination below **Rev.:** Map on globe, symbols surround, date above **Rev. Des.:** Michelle Thibodeau **Size:** 23.8 mm.

Date	Mintage	VG-8	F-12	VF-20	XF-40	MS-60	MS-63	Proof
2000	35,155,400	—	—	—	—	0.50	0.65	—

KM# 376a 25 CENTS 0.9250 Silver **Ruler:** Elizabeth II **Subject:** Community **Obv.:** Crowned head right, denomination below **Rev.:** Map on globe, symbols surround, date above **Rev. Des.:** Michelle Thibodeau **Size:** 23.8 mm.

Date	Mintage	VG-8	F-12	VF-20	XF-40	MS-60	MS-63	Proof
2000 Proof	76,956	—	—	—	—	—	—	6.00

KM# 377 25 CENTS Nickel **Ruler:** Elizabeth II **Subject:** Harmony **Obv.:** Crowned head right, denomination below **Rev.:** Maple leaf, date above **Rev. Des.:** Haver Demirer **Size:** 23.8 mm.

Date	Mintage	VG-8	F-12	VF-20	XF-40	MS-60	MS-63	Proof
2000	35,184,200	—	—	—	—	0.50	0.65	—

KM# 377a 25 CENTS 0.9250 Silver **Ruler:** Elizabeth II **Subject:** Harmony **Obv.:** Crowned head right, denomination below **Rev.:** Maple leaf **Rev. Des.:** Haver Demirer **Size:** 23.8 mm.

Date	Mintage	VG-8	F-12	VF-20	XF-40	MS-60	MS-63	Proof
2000 Proof	76,956	—	—	—	—	—	—	6.00

KM# 378 25 CENTS Nickel **Ruler:** Elizabeth II **Subject:** Wisdom **Obv.:** Crowned head right, denomination below **Rev.:** Man with young child, date above **Rev. Des.:** Cezar Serbanescu **Size:** 23.8 mm.

Date	Mintage	VG-8	F-12	VF-20	XF-40	MS-60	MS-63	Proof
2000	35,123,950	—	—	—	—	0.50	0.65	—

KM# 378a 25 CENTS 0.9250 Silver **Ruler:** Elizabeth II **Subject:** Wisdom **Obv.:** Crowned head right, denomination below **Rev.:** Man with young child **Rev. Des.:** Cezar Serbanescu **Size:** 23.8 mm.

Date	Mintage	VG-8	F-12	VF-20	XF-40	MS-60	MS-63	Proof
2000 Proof	76,956	—	—	—	—	—	—	6.00

KM# 379 25 CENTS Nickel **Ruler:** Elizabeth II **Subject:** Creativity **Obv.:** Crowned head right, denomination below **Rev.:** Canoe full of children, date above **Rev. Des.:** Kong Tat Hui **Size:** 23.8 mm.

Date	Mintage	VG-8	F-12	VF-20	XF-40	MS-60	MS-63	Proof
2000	35,316,770	—	—	—	—	0.50	0.65	—

KM# 379a 25 CENTS 0.9250 Silver **Ruler:** Elizabeth II **Subject:** Creativity **Obv.:** Crowned head right, denomination below **Rev.:** Canoe full of children **Rev. Des.:** Kong Tat Hui **Size:** 23.8 mm.

Date	Mintage	VG-8	F-12	VF-20	XF-40	MS-60	MS-63	Proof
2000 Proof	76,956	—	—	—	—	—	—	6.00

KM# 380 25 CENTS Nickel **Ruler:** Elizabeth II **Subject:** Ingenuity **Obv.:** Crowned head right, denomination below **Rev.:** Crescent-shaped city views, date above **Rev. Des.:** John Jaciw **Size:** 23.8 mm.

Date	Mintage	VG-8	F-12	VF-20	XF-40	MS-60	MS-63	Proof
2000	36,078,360	—	—	—	—	0.50	0.65	—

KM# 380a 25 CENTS 0.9250 Silver **Ruler:** Elizabeth II **Subject:** Ingenuity **Obv.:** Crowned head right, denomination below **Rev.:** Crescent-shaped city views **Rev. Des.:** John Jaciw **Size:** 23.8 mm.

Date	Mintage	VG-8	F-12	VF-20	XF-40	MS-60	MS-63	Proof
2000 Proof	76,956	—	—	—	—	—	—	6.00

KM# 381 25 CENTS Nickel **Ruler:** Elizabeth II **Subject:** Achievement **Obv.:** Crowned head right, denomination below **Rev.:** Rocket above jagged design, date above **Rev. Des.:** Daryl Dorosz **Size:** 23.8 mm.

Date	Mintage	VG-8	F-12	VF-20	XF-40	MS-60	MS-63	Proof
2000	35,312,750	—	—	—	—	0.50	0.65	—

KM# 381a 25 CENTS 0.9250 Silver **Ruler:** Elizabeth II **Subject:** Achievement **Obv.:** Crowned head right, denomination below **Rev.:** Rocket above jagged design **Rev. Des.:** Daryl Dorosz **Size:** 23.8 mm.

Date	Mintage	VG-8	F-12	VF-20	XF-40	MS-60	MS-63	Proof
2000 Proof	76,956	—	—	—	—	—	—	6.00

KM# 382 25 CENTS Nickel **Ruler:** Elizabeth II **Subject:** Natural legacy **Obv.:** Crowned head right, denomination below **Rev.:** Environmental elements, date above **Rev. Des.:** Randy Trantau **Size:** 23.8 mm.

Date	Mintage	VG-8	F-12	VF-20	XF-40	MS-60	MS-63	Proof
2000	36,236,900	—	—	—	—	0.50	0.65	—

KM# 382a 25 CENTS 0.9250 Silver **Ruler:** Elizabeth II **Subject:** Natural legacy **Obv.:** Crowned head right, denomination below **Rev.:** Environmental elements **Rev. Des.:** Randy Trantau **Size:** 23.8 mm.

Date	Mintage	VG-8	F-12	VF-20	XF-40	MS-60	MS-63	Proof
2000 Proof	76,956	—	—	—	—	—	—	6.00

KM# 383 25 CENTS Nickel **Ruler:** Elizabeth II **Subject:** Celebration **Obv.:** Crowned head right, denomination below **Rev.:** Fireworks, children behind flag, date above **Rev. Des.:** Laura Paxton **Size:** 23.8 mm.

Date	Mintage	VG-8	F-12	VF-20	XF-40	MS-60	MS-63	Proof
2000	35,144,100	—	—	—	—	0.50	0.65	—

KM# 383a 25 CENTS 0.9250 Silver **Ruler:** Elizabeth II **Subject:** Celebration **Obv.:** Crowned head right, denomination below **Rev.:** Fireworks, children behind flag **Rev. Des.:** Laura Paxton **Size:** 23.8 mm.

Date	Mintage	VG-8	F-12	VF-20	XF-40	MS-60	MS-63	Proof
2000 Proof	76,956	—	—	—	—	—	—	6.00

KM# 384.1 25 CENTS Nickel **Ruler:** Elizabeth II **Subject:** Pride **Obv.:** Crowned head right, denomination below **Rev.:** Large ribbon 2 in red with 3 small red maple leaves on large maple leaf, date above **Rev. Des.:** Donald F. Warkentin **Edge:** Reeded **Size:** 23.8 mm. **Note:** Colorized version.

Date	Mintage	VG-8	F-12	VF-20	XF-40	MS-60	MS-63	Proof
2000	49,399	—	—	—	—	—	6.50	—

KM# 384.2 25 CENTS Nickel **Ruler:** Elizabeth II **Subject:** Pride **Obv.:** Crowned head right, denomination below **Rev.:** Large ribbon 2 with three small maple leaves on large maple leaf, date above **Rev. Des.:** Donald F. Warkentin **Size:** 23.8 mm.

Date	Mintage	VG-8	F-12	VF-20	XF-40	MS-60	MS-63	Proof
2000	50,666,800	—	—	—	—	0.50	0.65	—

KM# 384.2a 25 CENTS 0.9250 Silver **Ruler:** Elizabeth II **Subject:** Pride **Obv.:** Crowned head right, denomination below **Rev.:** Ribbon 2 with 3 small maple leaves on large maple leaf **Rev. Des.:** Donald F. Warkentin **Size:** 23.8 mm.

Date	Mintage	VG-8	F-12	VF-20	XF-40	MS-60	MS-63	Proof
2000 Proof	76,956	—	—	—	—	—	—	6.00

KM# 6 50 CENTS 11.6200 g. 0.9250 Silver 0.3456 oz. ASW **Ruler:** Victoria **Obv.:** VICTORIA DEI GRATIA REGINA. CANADA **Obv. Des.:** Leonard C. Wyon **Rev.:** Denomination and date within wreath, crown above

Date	Mintage	VG-8	F-12	VF-20	XF-40	MS-60	MS-63	Proof
1901	80,000	55.00	150	225	550	5,700	15,000	—

Victorian leaves

KM# 12 50 CENTS 11.6200 g. 0.9250 Silver 0.3456 oz. ASW **Ruler:** Edward VII **Obv.:** Crowned bust right **Obv. Des.:** G. W. DeSaulles **Rev.:** Denomination and date within wreath, crown above

Date	Mintage	VG-8	F-12	VF-20	XF-40	MS-60	MS-63	Proof
1902	120,000	15.00	35.00	100	250	1,300	3,500	—
1903H	140,000	22.00	45.00	175	450	1,500	3,700	—
1904	60,000	150	200	600	1,000	3,300	9,500	—
1905	40,000	150	275	600	1,400	6,000	15,000	—
1906	350,000	12.00	35.00	95.00	250	1,300	3,500	—
1907	300,000	12.00	35.00	95.00	250	1,400	3,900	—
1908	128,119	21.00	65.00	175	375	1,000	2,000	—
1909	302,118	17.00	60.00	175	475	2,400	7,600	—
1910	649,521	22.00	45.00	175	400	1,600	6,000	—

Note: Victorian leaves

Edwardian leaves

KM# 12a 50 CENTS 11.6638 g. 0.9250 Silver 0.3469 oz. ASW **Ruler:** Edward VII **Obv.:** Crowned bust right **Obv. Des.:** G. W. DeSaulles **Rev.:** Denomination and date within wreath

Date	Mintage	VG-8	F-12	VF-20	XF-40	MS-60	MS-63	Proof
1910	Inc. above	8.00	29.00	85.00	250	1,200	3,300	—

Note: Edwardian leaves

KM# 19 50 CENTS 11.6638 g. 0.9250 Silver 0.3469 oz. ASW **Ruler:** George V **Obv.:** Crowned bust left **Obv. Des.:** E. B. MacKennal **Rev.:** Denomination and date within wreath, crown above

Date	Mintage	VG-8	F-12	VF-20	XF-40	MS-60	MS-63	Proof
1911	209,972	18.00	70.00	250	550	1,400	3,200	—

KM# 25 50 CENTS 11.6638 g. 0.9250 Silver 0.3469 oz. ASW **Ruler:** George V **Obv.:** Crowned bust left, modified legend **Obv. Des.:** E. B. MacKennal **Rev.:** Denomination and date within wreath, crown above

Date	Mintage	VG-8	F-12	VF-20	XF-40	MS-60	MS-63	Proof
1912	285,867	9.00	24.00	100	225	1,100	2,900	—
1913	265,889	9.00	24.00	150	300	1,400	4,800	—
1914	160,128	22.00	55.00	225	550	2,800	7,800	—
1916	459,070	7.00	14.00	55.00	175	650	2,100	—
1917	752,213	6.50	11.00	40.00	100	475	1,100	—
1918	754,989	6.50	10.00	30.00	90.00	400	1,000	—

Date	Mintage	VG-8	F-12	VF-20	XF-40	MS-60	MS-63	Proof
1919	1,113,429	6.50	10.00	30.00	90.00	375	1,200	—

KM# 25a 50 CENTS 11.6638 g. 0.8000 Silver 0.3000 oz. ASW Ruler: George V
Obv.: Crowned bust left Obv. Des.: E. B. MacKennal Rev.: Denomination and date within wreath, crown below

Date	Mintage	VG-8	F-12	VF-20	XF-40	MS-60	MS-63	Proof
1920	584,691	6.00	13.00	35.00	125	500	1,800	—
1921	—	22,000	24,000	28,000	32,000	50,000	90,000	—
	Note: 75 to 100 known; David Akers John Jay Pittman sale, Part Three, 10-99, Gem Unc. realized $63,250							
1929	228,328	6.00	13.00	35.00	100	475	1,100	—
1931	57,581	11.00	29.00	80.00	225	800	1,800	—
1932	19,213	150	185	375	800	3,600	8,300	—
1934	39,539	15.00	30.00	100	225	650	1,300	—
1936	38,550	15.00	29.00	100	175	500	1,000	—

KM# 36 50 CENTS 11.6638 g. 0.8000 Silver 0.3000 oz. ASW Ruler: George VI
Obv.: Head left Obv. Des.: T. H. Paget Rev.: Crowned arms with supporters, denomination above, date below Rev. Des.: George E. Kruger-Gray Size: 30 mm.

Date	Mintage	VG-8	F-12	VF-20	XF-40	MS-60	MS-63	Proof
1937	192,016	BV	6.00	7.00	10.00	30.00	85.00	—
1938	192,018	BV	6.50	10.00	25.00	90.00	400	—
1939	287,976	BV	6.00	8.00	17.00	60.00	250	—
1940	1,996,566	—	—	BV	6.00	27.00	60.00	—
1941	1,714,874	—	—	BV	6.00	27.00	60.00	—
1942	1,974,164	—	—	BV	6.00	27.00	60.00	—
1943	3,109,583	—	—	BV	6.00	27.00	60.00	—
1944	2,460,205	—	—	BV	6.00	27.00	60.00	—
1945	1,959,528	—	—	BV	6.00	30.00	90.00	—
1946	950,235	—	BV	6.00	8.00	60.00	175	—
1946	Inc. above	15.00	28.00	45.00	150	1,100	2,800	—
	Note: hoof in 6							
1947	424,885	—	6.00	8.00	12.00	65.00	175	—
	Note: straight 7							
1947	Inc. above	—	6.00	9.00	22.00	100	300	—
	Note: curved 7							
1947	38,433	18.00	23.00	45.00	70.00	160	275	—
	Note: maple leaf, straight 7							
1947	Inc. above	1,000	1,300	1,700	2,200	3,900	7,000	—
	Note: maple leaf, curved 7							

KM# 45 50 CENTS 11.6638 g. 0.8000 Silver 0.3000 oz. ASW Ruler: George VI
Obv.: Head left, modified legend Obv. Des.: T. H. Paget Rev.: Crowned arms with supporters, denomination above, date below Rev. Des.: George E. Kruger-Gray

Date	Mintage	VG-8	F-12	VF-20	XF-40	MS-60	MS-63	Proof
1948	37,784	65.00	85.00	100	150	250	350	—
1949	858,991	—	—	BV	7.00	35.00	150	—
1949	Inc. above	10.00	18.00	35.00	60.00	325	750	—
	Note: hoof over 9							
1950	2,384,179	6.00	10.00	11.00	35.00	125	225	—
	Note: no lines							
1950	Inc. above	—	—	BV	6.00	9.00	30.00	—
	Note: lines in 0							
1951	2,421,730	—	—	—	BV	9.00	26.00	—
1952	2,596,465	—	—	—	BV	7.00	18.00	—

KM# 53 50 CENTS 11.6638 g. 0.8000 Silver 0.3000 oz. ASW Ruler: Elizabeth II
Obv.: Laureate bust right Obv. Des.: Mary Gillick Rev.: Crowned arms with supporters, denomination above, date below

Date	Mintage	VG-8	F-12	VF-20	XF-40	MS-60	MS-63	Proof
1953	1,630,429	—	—	—	BV	7.00	15.00	—
1953	Note: small date							
1953	Inc. above	—	—	BV	6.00	22.00	35.00	—
	Note: large date, straps							
1953	Inc. above	—	6.00	7.50	14.00	75.00	150	—
	Note: large date without straps							
1954	506,305	—	BV	6.00	7.00	18.00	35.00	—
1955	753,511	—	BV	6.00	15.00	30.00	—	—
1956	1,379,499	—	—	—	BV	7.00	14.00	—
1957	2,171,689	—	—	—	BV	6.00	10.00	—
1958	2,957,266	—	—	—	BV	6.00	8.50	—

KM# 56 50 CENTS 11.6638 g. 0.8000 Silver 0.3000 oz. ASW Ruler: Elizabeth II
Obv.: Luareate bust right Obv. Des.: Mary Gillick Rev.: Crown divides date above arms with supporters, denomination at right Rev. Des.: Thomas Shingles Size: 30 mm.

Date	Mintage	VG-8	F-12	VF-20	XF-40	MS-60	MS-63	Proof
1959	3,095,535	—	—	—	BV	6.50	7.50	—
	Note: horizontal shading							
1960	3,488,897	—	—	—	BV	6.00	7.00	—
1961	3,584,417	—	—	—	BV	6.00	7.00	—
1962	5,208,030	—	—	—	BV	6.00	7.00	—
1963	8,348,871	—	—	—	BV	6.00	7.00	—
1964	9,377,676	—	—	—	BV	6.00	7.00	—

KM# 63 50 CENTS 11.6638 g. 0.8000 Silver 0.3000 oz. ASW Ruler: Elizabeth II
Obv.: Young bust right Obv. Des.: Arnold Machin Rev.: Crown divides date above arms with supporters, denomination at right Rev. Des.: Thomas Shingles

Date	Mintage	VG-8	F-12	VF-20	XF-40	MS-60	MS-63	Proof
1965	12,629,974	—	—	—	BV	6.00	7.00	—
1966	7,920,496	—	—	—	BV	6.00	7.00	—

KM# 69 50 CENTS 11.6638 g. 0.8000 Silver 0.3000 oz. ASW Ruler: Elizabeth II
Subject: Confederation Centennial Obv.: Young bust right Rev.: Seated wolf howling divides denomination at top, dates at bottom Rev. Des.: Alex Colville Size: 29.5 mm.

Date	Mintage	VG-8	F-12	VF-20	XF-40	MS-60	MS-63	Proof
ND(1967)	4,211,392	—	—	—	—	—	—	9.00

KM# 75.1 50 CENTS Nickel Ruler: Elizabeth II Obv.: Young bust right Obv. Des.: Arnold Machin Rev.: Crown divides date above arms with supporters, denomination at right Rev. Des.: Thomas Shingles Size: 27.1 mm.

Date	Mintage	VG-8	F-12	VF-20	XF-40	MS-60	MS-63	Proof
1968	3,966,932	—	—	—	0.50	0.65	1.00	—
1969	7,113,929	—	—	—	0.50	0.65	1.00	—
1970	2,429,526	—	—	—	0.50	0.65	1.00	—
1971	2,166,444	—	—	—	0.50	0.65	1.00	—
1972	2,515,632	—	—	—	0.50	0.65	1.00	—
1973	2,546,096	—	—	—	0.50	0.65	1.00	—
1974	3,436,650	—	—	—	0.50	0.65	1.00	—
1975	3,710,000	—	—	—	0.50	0.65	1.00	—
1976	2,940,719	—	—	—	0.50	0.65	1.00	—

KM# 75.2 50 CENTS
8.1000 g. Nickel **Ruler:** Elizabeth II **Obv.:** Small young bust right **Obv. Des.:** Arnold Machin **Rev.:** Crown divides date above arms with supporters, denomination at right **Rev. Des.:** Thomas Shingles **Size:** 27 mm.

Date	Mintage	VG-8	F-12	VF-20	XF-40	MS-60	MS-63	Proof
1977	709,839	—	—	0.50	0.75	1.35	2.00	—

KM# 75.3 50 CENTS
8.1000 g. Nickel **Ruler:** Elizabeth II **Obv.:** Young bust right **Obv. Des.:** Arnold Machin **Rev.:** Crown divides date above arms with supporters, denomination at right, redesigned arms **Rev. Des.:** Thomas Shingles **Size:** 27 mm.

Date	Mintage	VG-8	F-12	VF-20	XF-40	MS-60	MS-63	Proof
1978	3,341,892	—	—	—	0.50	0.65	1.00	—
Note: square jewels								
1978	Inc. above	—	—	1.00	2.50	4.50	6.00	—
Note: round jewels								
1979	3,425,000	—	—	—	0.50	0.65	1.00	—
1980	1,574,000	—	—	—	0.50	0.65	1.00	—
1981	2,690,272	—	—	—	0.50	0.65	1.00	—
1981 Proof	199,000	—	—	—	—	—	—	3.00
1982	2,236,674	—	—	—	30.00	65.00	100	—
Note: small beads								
1982 Proof	180,908	—	—	—	—	—	—	3.00
Note: small beads								
1982	Inc. above	—	—	—	0.50	0.65	1.00	—
Note: large beads								
1983	1,177,000	—	—	—	0.50	0.65	1.00	—
1983 Proof	168,000	—	—	—	—	—	—	3.00
1984	1,502,989	—	—	—	0.50	0.65	1.00	—
1984 Proof	161,602	—	—	—	—	—	—	3.00
1985	2,188,374	—	—	—	0.50	0.65	1.00	—
1985 Proof	157,037	—	—	—	—	—	—	3.00
1986	781,400	—	—	—	0.50	1.00	1.25	—
1986 Proof	175,745	—	—	—	—	—	—	3.00
1987	373,000	—	—	—	0.50	1.00	1.25	—
1987 Proof	179,004	—	—	—	—	—	—	3.50
1988	220,000	—	—	—	0.50	1.00	1.25	—
1988 Proof	175,259	—	—	—	—	—	—	3.00
1989	266,419	—	—	—	0.50	1.00	1.25	—
1989 Proof	170,928	—	—	—	—	—	—	3.00

KM# 185 50 CENTS
Nickel **Ruler:** Elizabeth II **Obv.:** Crowned head right **Obv. Des.:** Dora dePedery-Hunt **Rev.:** Crown divides date above arms with supporters, denomination at right **Rev. Des.:** Thomas Shingles **Size:** 27 mm.

Date	Mintage	VG-8	F-12	VF-20	XF-40	MS-60	MS-63	Proof
1990	207,000	—	—	—	0.50	1.00	1.25	—
1990 Proof	140,649	—	—	—	—	—	—	5.00
1991	490,000	—	—	—	0.50	0.85	1.00	—
1991 Proof	131,888	—	—	—	—	—	—	7.00
1993	393,000	—	—	—	0.50	0.85	1.00	—
1993 Proof	143,065	—	—	—	—	—	—	3.00
1994	987,000	—	—	—	0.50	0.75	1.00	—
1994 Proof	146,424	—	—	—	—	—	—	4.00
1995	626,000	—	—	—	0.50	0.75	1.00	—
1995 Proof	50,000	—	—	—	—	—	—	4.00
1996	458,000	—	—	—	0.50	0.65	1.00	—
1996 Proof	—	—	—	—	—	—	—	4.00

KM# 185a 50 CENTS
11.6380 g. 0.9250 Silver 0.3461 oz. ASW **Ruler:** Elizabeth II **Obv.:** Crowned head right **Obv. Des.:** Dora dePedery-Hunt **Rev.:** Crown divides date above arms with supporters, denomination at right **Rev. Des.:** Thomas Shingles

Date	Mintage	MS-63	Proof
1996 Proof	—	—	9.00

KM# 208 50 CENTS
Nickel **Ruler:** Elizabeth II **Subject:** Confederation 125 **Obv.:** Crowned head right **Obv. Des.:** Dora dePedery-Hunt **Rev.:** Crown divides date above arms with supporters, denomination at right **Rev. Des.:** Thomas Shingles **Size:** 27 mm.

Date	Mintage	VG-8	F-12	VF-20	XF-40	MS-60	MS-63	Proof
ND(1992)	445,000	—	—	—	0.50	0.75	1.00	—
ND(1992) Proof	147,061	—	—	—	—	—	—	5.00

KM# 261 50 CENTS
11.6638 g. 0.9250 Silver 0.3469 oz. ASW **Ruler:** Elizabeth II **Obv.:** Crowned head right **Rev.:** Atlantic Puffin, denomination and date at right **Rev. Des.:** Sheldon Beveridge

Date	Mintage	MS-63	Proof
1995 Proof	—	—	24.00

KM# 262 50 CENTS
11.6638 g. 0.9250 Silver 0.3469 oz. ASW **Ruler:** Elizabeth II **Obv.:** Crowned head right **Rev.:** Whooping crane left, denomination and date at right **Rev. Des.:** Stan Witten

Date	Mintage	MS-63	Proof
1995 Proof	—	—	24.00

KM# 263 50 CENTS
11.6638 g. 0.9250 Silver 0.3469 oz. ASW **Ruler:** Elizabeth II **Obv.:** Crowned head right **Rev.:** Gray Jays, denomination and date at right **Rev. Des.:** Sheldon Beveridge

Date	Mintage	MS-63	Proof
1995 Proof	—	—	24.00

KM# 264 50 CENTS
11.6638 g. 0.9250 Silver 0.3469 oz. ASW **Ruler:** Elizabeth II **Obv.:** Crowned head right **Rev.:** White-tailed ptarmigans, date and denomination at right **Rev. Des.:** Cosme Saffioti

Date	Mintage	MS-63	Proof
1995 Proof	—	—	22.00

KM# 283 50 CENTS
11.6638 g. 0.9250 Silver 0.3469 oz. ASW **Ruler:** Elizabeth II **Obv.:** Crowned head right **Rev.:** Moose calf left, denomination and date at right **Rev. Des.:** Ago Aarand

Date	Mintage	MS-63	Proof
1996 Proof	—	—	20.00

KM# 284 50 CENTS
11.6638 g. 0.9250 Silver 0.3469 oz. ASW **Ruler:** Elizabeth II **Obv.:** Crowned head right **Rev.:** Wood ducklings, date and denomination at right **Rev. Des.:** Sheldon Beveridge

Date	Mintage	MS-63	Proof
1996 Proof	—	—	20.00

KM# 285 50 CENTS
11.6638 g. 0.9250 Silver 0.3469 oz. ASW **Ruler:** Elizabeth II **Obv.:** Crowned head right **Rev.:** Cougar kittens, date and denomination at right **Rev. Des.:** Stan Witten

Date	Mintage	MS-63	Proof
1996 Proof	—	—	20.00

KM# 286 50 CENTS
11.6638 g. 0.9250 Silver 0.3469 oz. ASW **Ruler:** Elizabeth II **Obv.:** Crowned head right **Rev.:** Bear cubs standing, date and denomination at right **Rev. Des.:** Sheldon Beveridge

Date	Mintage	MS-63	Proof
1996 Proof	—	—	20.00

KM# 290 50 CENTS
6.9000 g. Nickel **Ruler:** Elizabeth II **Obv.:** Crowned head right **Obv. Des.:** Dora dePedery-Hunt **Rev.:** Redesigned arms **Rev. Des.:** Cathy Bursey-Sabourin **Size:** 27.13 mm.

Date	Mintage	F-12	VF-20	XF-40	AU-50	MS-60	MS-63	Proof
1997	387,000	—	—	0.50	—	0.70	1.00	—
1997 Proof	—	—	—	—	—	—	—	5.00
1998	308,000	—	—	0.50	—	0.70	1.00	—

Date	Mintage	F-12	VF-20	XF-40	AU-50	MS-60	MS-63	Proof
1998 Proof	—	—	—	—	—	—	—	—
1998W	—	—	—	—	—	—	2.00	—
1999	496,000	—	—	0.50	—	0.70	1.00	—
1999 Proof	—	—	—	—	—	—	—	5.00
2000	559,000	—	—	0.50	—	0.70	1.00	—
2000 Proof	—	—	—	—	—	—	—	5.00
2000W	—	—	—	—	—	—	1.50	—

KM# 290a 50 CENTS 11.6380 g. 0.9250 Silver 0.3461 oz. ASW **Ruler:** Elizabeth II **Obv.:** Crowned head right **Obv. Des.:** Dora dePedery-Hunt **Rev.:** Redesigned arms **Rev. Des.:** Cathy Bursey-Sabourin **Size:** 27.13 mm.

Date	Mintage	MS-63	Proof
1997 Proof	—	—	10.00
1998 Proof	—	—	10.00
1999 Proof	—	—	10.00
2000 Proof	—	—	10.00

KM# 290b 50 CENTS 6.9000 g. Nickel Plated Steel **Ruler:** Elizabeth II **Obv.:** Crowned head right **Obv. Des.:** Dora dePedery-Hunt **Rev.:** Redesigned arms **Rev. Des.:** Cathy Bursey-Sabourin **Size:** 27.13 mm.

Date	Mintage	MS-63	Proof
1999 P	Est. 20,000	15.00	—
2000 P	Est. 50	3,500	—

Note: Available only in RCM presentation coin clocks

KM# 292 50 CENTS 11.6638 g. 0.9250 Silver 0.3469 oz. ASW **Ruler:** Elizabeth II **Obv.:** Crowned head right **Rev.:** Duck Toling Retriever, date and denomination at right **Rev. Des.:** Stan Witten

Date	Mintage	MS-63	Proof
1997 Proof	—	—	17.00

KM# 293 50 CENTS 11.6638 g. 0.9250 Silver 0.3469 oz. ASW **Ruler:** Elizabeth II **Obv.:** Crowned head right **Rev.:** Labrador leaping left, date and denomination at right **Rev. Des.:** Sheldon Beveridge

Date	Mintage	MS-63	Proof
1997 Proof	—	—	17.00

KM# 294 50 CENTS 11.6638 g. 0.9250 Silver 0.3469 oz. ASW **Ruler:** Elizabeth II **Obv.:** Crowned head right **Rev.:** Newfoundland right, date and denomination at right **Rev. Des.:** William Woodruff

Date	Mintage	MS-63	Proof
1997 Proof	—	—	17.00

KM# 295 50 CENTS 11.6638 g. 0.9250 Silver 0.3469 oz. ASW **Ruler:** Elizabeth II **Obv.:** Crowned head right **Rev.:** Eskimo dog leaping forward, date and denomination at right **Rev. Des.:** Cosme Saffioti

Date	Mintage	MS-63	Proof
1997 Proof	—	—	17.00

KM# 313 50 CENTS 11.6638 g. 0.9250 Silver 0.3469 oz. ASW **Ruler:** Elizabeth II **Subject:** 90th Anniversary Royal Canadian Mint **Obv.:** Crowned head right **Rev.:** Denomination and date within wreath, crown above **Rev. Des.:** W. H. J. Blakemore

Date	Mintage	MS-63	Proof
ND(1998) Matte	25,000	—	15.00
ND(1998) Proof	25,000	—	15.00

KM# 314 50 CENTS 11.6638 g. 0.9250 Silver 0.3469 oz. ASW **Ruler:** Elizabeth II **Subject:** 110 Years Canadian Speed and Figure Skating **Obv.:** Crowned head right **Rev.:** Speed skaters, dates below, denomination above **Rev. Des.:** Sheldon Beveridge

Date	Mintage	MS-63	Proof
ND(1998) Proof	—	—	10.00

KM# 315 50 CENTS 11.6638 g. 0.9250 Silver 0.3469 oz. ASW **Ruler:** Elizabeth II **Subject:** 100 Years Canadian Ski Racing **Obv.:** Crowned head right **Rev.:** Skiers, dates below, denomination upper left **Rev. Des.:** Ago Aarand

Date	Mintage	MS-63	Proof
ND(1998) Proof	—	—	10.00

KM# 318 50 CENTS 11.6638 g. 0.9250 Silver 0.3469 oz. ASW **Ruler:** Elizabeth II **Obv.:** Crowned head right **Rev.:** Killer Whales, date and denomination at right **Rev. Des.:** William Woodruff

Date	Mintage	MS-63	Proof
1998 Proof	—	—	17.00

KM# 319 50 CENTS 11.6638 g. 0.9250 Silver 0.3469 oz. ASW **Ruler:** Elizabeth II **Obv.:** Crowned head right **Rev.:** Humpback whale, date and denomination at right **Rev. Des.:** Sheldon Beveridge

Date	Mintage	MS-63	Proof
1998 Proof	—	—	17.00

KM# 320 50 CENTS 11.6638 g. 0.9250 Silver 0.3469 oz. ASW **Ruler:** Elizabeth II **Obv.:** Crowned head right **Rev.:** Beluga whales, date and denomination at right **Rev. Des.:** Cosme Saffioti

Date	Mintage	MS-63	Proof
1998 Proof	—	—	17.00

KM# 321 50 CENTS 11.6638 g. 0.9250 Silver 0.3469 oz. ASW **Ruler:** Elizabeth II **Obv.:** Crowned head right **Rev.:** Blue whale, date and denomination at right **Rev. Des.:** Stan Witten

Date	Mintage	MS-63	Proof
1998 Proof	—	—	17.00

KM# 327 50 CENTS 11.6638 g. 0.9250 Silver 0.3469 oz. ASW **Ruler:** Elizabeth II **Subject:** 110 Years Canadian Soccer **Obv.:** Crowned head right **Rev.:** Soccer players, dates above, denomination at right **Rev. Des.:** Stan Witten

Date	Mintage	MS-63	Proof
ND(1998) Proof	—	—	10.00

KM# 328 50 CENTS 11.6638 g. 0.9250 Silver 0.3469 oz. ASW **Ruler:** Elizabeth II **Subject:** 20 Years Canadian Auto Racing **Obv.:** Crowned head right **Rev.:** Race car divides date and denomination **Rev. Des.:** Cosme Saffioti

Date	Mintage	MS-63	Proof
ND(1998) Proof	—	—	10.00

KM# 333 50 CENTS 11.6638 g. 0.9250 Silver 0.3469 oz. ASW **Ruler:** Elizabeth II **Subject:** 1904 Canadian Open **Obv.:** Crowned head right **Rev.:** Golfers, date at right, denomination below **Rev. Des.:** William Woodruff

Date	Mintage	MS-63	Proof
ND(1999) Proof	—	—	13.50

KM# 334 50 CENTS 11.6638 g. 0.9250 Silver 0.3469 oz. ASW **Ruler:** Elizabeth II **Subject:** First U.S.-Canadian Yacht Race **Obv.:** Crowned head right **Rev.:** Yachts, dates at left, denomination below **Rev. Des.:** Stan Witten

Date	Mintage	MS-63	Proof
ND(1999) Proof	—	—	10.00

KM# 335 50 CENTS 11.6638 g. 0.9250 Silver 0.3469 oz. ASW **Ruler:** Elizabeth II **Series:** Canadian Cats **Obv.:** Crowned head right **Rev.:** Cymric cat, date below, denomination at bottom **Rev. Des.:** Susan Taylor

Date	Mintage	MS-63	Proof
1999 Proof	—	—	20.00

KM# 336   50 CENTS   11.6638 g. 0.9250 Silver 0.3469 oz. ASW **Ruler:** Elizabeth II
Series: Canadian Cats **Obv.:** Crowned head right **Rev.:** Tonkinese cat, date below, denomination at bottom **Rev. Des.:** Susan Taylor

Date	Mintage	MS-63	Proof
1999 Proof	—	—	20.00

KM# 337   50 CENTS   11.6638 g. 0.9250 Silver 0.3469 oz. ASW **Ruler:** Elizabeth II
Series: Canadian Cats **Obv.:** Crowned head right **Rev.:** Cougar, date and denomination below **Rev. Des.:** Susan Taylor

Date	Mintage	MS-63	Proof
1999 Proof	—	—	20.00

KM# 338   50 CENTS   11.6638 g. 0.9250 Silver 0.3469 oz. ASW **Ruler:** Elizabeth II
Series: Canadian Cats **Obv.:** Crowned head right **Rev.:** Lynx, date and denomination below **Rev. Des.:** Susan Taylor

Date	Mintage	MS-63	Proof
1999 Proof	—	—	20.00

KM# 371   50 CENTS   9.3600 g. 0.9250 Silver 0.2783 oz. ASW **Ruler:** Elizabeth II
Subject: Basketball **Obv.:** Crowned head right **Rev.:** Basketball players **Rev. Des.:** Sheldon Beveridge **Edge:** Reeded **Size:** 27.1 mm.

Date	Mintage	MS-63	Proof
ND(1999) Proof	—	—	9.00

KM# 372   50 CENTS   9.3600 g. 0.9250 Silver 0.2783 oz. ASW **Ruler:** Elizabeth II
Obv.: Crowned head right **Rev.:** Football players **Rev. Des.:** Cosme Saffioti **Edge:** Reeded **Size:** 27.1 mm.

Date	Mintage	MS-63	Proof
ND(1999) Proof	—	—	10.00

KM#385   50 CENTS   0.9250 Silver **Ruler:** Elizabeth II **Subject:** Ice Hockey **Obv.:** Crowned head right **Rev.:** 4 hockey players **Rev. Des.:** Stanley Witten

Date	Mintage	MS-63	Proof
ND(2000) Proof	—	—	12.00

KM# 386   50 CENTS   0.9250 Silver **Ruler:** Elizabeth II **Subject:** Curling **Obv.:** Crowned head right **Rev.:** Motion study of curlers, dates and denomination below **Rev. Des.:** Cosme Saffioti

Date	Mintage	MS-63	Proof
ND(2000) Proof	—	—	10.00

KM# 389   50 CENTS   9.3500 g. 0.9250 Silver 0.2781 oz. ASW **Ruler:** Elizabeth II
Obv.: Crowned head right **Rev.:** Great horned owl, facing, date and denomination at right **Rev. Des.:** Susan Taylor

Date	Mintage	MS-63	Proof
2000 Proof	—	—	20.00

KM# 390   50 CENTS   9.3500 g. 0.9250 Silver 0.2781 oz. ASW **Ruler:** Elizabeth II
Obv.: Crowned head right **Rev.:** Red-tailed hawk, dates and denomination at right

Date	Mintage	MS-63	Proof
2000 Proof	—	—	20.00

KM# 391   50 CENTS   9.3500 g. 0.9250 Silver 0.2781 oz. ASW **Ruler:** Elizabeth II
Obv.: Crowned head right **Rev.:** Osprey, dates and denomination at right **Rev. Des.:** Susan Taylor

Date	Mintage	MS-63	Proof
2000 Proof	—	—	20.00

KM# 392   50 CENTS   9.3500 g. 0.9250 Silver 0.2781 oz. ASW **Ruler:** Elizabeth II **Obv.:** Crowned head right **Rev.:** Bald eagle, dates and denomination at right **Rev. Des.:** William Woodruff

Date	Mintage	MS-63	Proof
2000 Proof	—	—	20.00

KM# 393   50 CENTS   0.9250 Silver **Ruler:** Elizabeth II **Subject:** Steeplechase **Obv.:** Crowned head right **Rev.:** Steeplechase, dates and denomination below **Rev. Des.:** Susan Taylor

Date	Mintage	MS-63	Proof
2000 Proof	—	—	10.00

KM# 394   50 CENTS   0.9250 Silver **Ruler:** Elizabeth II **Subject:** Bowling **Obv.:** Crowned head right **Rev. Des.:** William Woodruff

Date	Mintage	MS-63	Proof
2000 Proof	—	—	10.00

KM# 30   DOLLAR   23.3276 g. 0.8000 Silver 0.6000 oz. ASW **Ruler:** George V
Subject: Silver Jubilee **Obv.:** Bust left **Obv. Des.:** Percy Metcalfe **Rev.:** Voyager, date and denomination below **Rev. Des.:** Emanuel Hahn

Date	Mintage	F-12	VF-20	XF-40	AU-50	MS-60	MS-63	Proof
1935	428,707	13.00	18.00	28.00	32.00	37.50	60.00	4,500

KM# 31   DOLLAR   23.3276 g. 0.8000 Silver 0.6000 oz. ASW **Ruler:** George V
Obv.: Crowned bust left **Obv. Des.:** E. B. MacKennal **Rev.:** Voyageur, date and denomination below **Rev. Des.:** Emanuel Hahn

Date	Mintage	F-12	VF-20	XF-40	AU-50	MS-60	MS-63	Proof
1936	339,600	13.00	15.00	26.00	30.00	35.00	75.00	5,000

Pointed 7	Blunt 7	Maple leaf

KM# 37   DOLLAR   23.3276 g. 0.8000 Silver 0.6000 oz. ASW **Ruler:** George VI
Obv.: Head left **Obv. Des.:** T. H. Paget **Rev.:** Voyageur, date and denomination below **Rev. Des.:** Emanuel Hahn

Date	Mintage	F-12	VF-20	XF-40	AU-50	MS-60	MS-63	Proof
1937	207,406	10.00	11.00	12.00	22.00	25.00	100	—
1937 Mirror Proof	1,295	—	—	—	—	—	—	650
1937 Matte Proof	Inc. above	—	—	—	—	—	—	250
1938	90,304	25.00	35.00	65.00	80.00	100	175	6,000
1945	38,391	75.00	150	175	225	300	475	2,000
1946	93,055	15.00	25.00	35.00	45.00	95.00	300	1,800
1947	—	60.00	80.00	150	125	265	1,400	3,500
Note: Pointed 7								
1947	65,595	45.00	60.00	80.00	95.00	125	250	4,500
Note: Blunt 7								
1947	21,135	125	150	175	200	250	475	1,800
Note: Maple leaf								

KM# 38 DOLLAR
23.3276 g. 0.8000 Silver 0.6000 oz. ASW **Ruler:** George VI
Subject: Royal Visit **Obv.:** Head left **Obv. Des.:** T. H. Paget **Rev.:** Tower at center of building, date and denomination below **Rev. Des.:** Emanuel Hahn

Date	Mintage	F-12	VF-20	XF-40	AU-50	MS-60	MS-63	Proof
1939	1,363,816	—	BV	10.00	11.00	12.00	30.00	—
1939								475
Note: Matte specimen								
1939 Proof								750
Note: Mirror specimen								

KM# 46 DOLLAR
23.3276 g. 0.8000 Silver 0.6000 oz. ASW **Ruler:** George VI
Obv.: Head left, modified left legend **Obv. Des.:** T. H. Paget **Rev.:** Voyageur, date and denomination below **Rev. Des.:** Emanuel Hahn

Date	Mintage	F-12	VF-20	XF-40	AU-50	MS-60	MS-63	Proof
1948	18,780	500	600	1,000	1,100	1,300	1,950	3,000
1950	261,002	BV	10.00	11.00	12.00	16.00	50.00	800
Note: With 3 water lines								
1950 Matte Proof								
Note: With 4 water lines, 1 known								
1950	Inc. above	11.00	14.00	21.00	28.00	40.00	90.00	1,500
Note: Arnprior with 2-1/2 water lines								
1951	416,395	BV	10.00	11.00	12.00	14.00	23.00	650
Note: With 3 water lines								
1951	Inc. above	35.00	50.00	60.00	100	175	400	2,000
Note: Arnprior with 1-1/2 water lines								
1952	406,148	BV	10.00	11.00	12.00	14.00	25.00	1,000
Note: With 3 water lines								
1952	Inc. above	11.00	12.00	22.00	30.00	40.00	100	1,250
Note: Arnprior type								
1952	Inc. above	BV	10.00	11.00	12.00	16.50	45.00	—
Note: Without water lines								

KM# 47 DOLLAR
23.3276 g. 0.8000 Silver 0.6000 oz. ASW **Ruler:** George VI
Subject: Newfoundland **Obv.:** Head left **Obv. Des.:** T. H. Paget **Rev.:** The "Matthew", John Cabot's ship, date and denomination below **Rev. Des.:** Thomas Shingles

Date	Mintage	F-12	VF-20	XF-40	AU-50	MS-60	MS-63	Proof
1949	672,218	11.00	13.00	16.50	18.50	22.50	27.50	—
1949 Specimen proof								1,200

KM# 54 DOLLAR
23.3276 g. 0.8000 Silver 0.6000 oz. ASW **Ruler:** Elizabeth II
Obv.: Laureate bust right **Obv. Des.:** Mary Gillick **Rev.:** Voyageur, date and denomination below **Rev. Des.:** Emanuel Hahn **Note:** All genuine circulation strike 1955 Arnprior dollars have a die break running along the top of TI in the word GRATIA on the obverse.

Date	Mintage	F-12	VF-20	XF-40	AU-50	MS-60	MS-63	Proof
1953	1,074,578	—	—	BV	10.00	12.00	25.00	400
Note: Without strap, wire rim								
1953	Inc. above	—	—	BV	10.00	12.00	25.00	—
Note: With strap, flat rim								
1954	246,606	BV	10.00	11.00	12.00	16.00	35.00	—
1955	268,105	BV	10.00	11.00	12.00	15.00	30.00	—
Note: With 3 water lines								
1955	Inc. above	45.00	65.00	90.00	100	125	175	—
Note: Arnprior with 1-1/2 water lines* and die break								
1956	209,092	BV	10.00	13.00	16.00	20.00	50.00	—
1957	496,389	—	—	—	BV	10.00	16.00	—
Note: With 3 water lines								
1957	Inc. above	—	BV	10.00	11.00	15.00	35.00	—
Note: With 1 water line								
1959	1,443,502	—	—	—	—	BV	12.00	—
1960	1,420,486	—	—	—	—	BV	12.00	—
1961	1,262,231	—	—	—	—	BV	12.00	—
1962	1,884,789	—	—	—	—	BV	12.00	—
1963	4,179,981	—	—	—	—	BV	10.00	—

KM# 55 DOLLAR
23.3276 g. 0.8000 Silver 0.6000 oz. ASW **Ruler:** Elizabeth II
Subject: British Columbia **Obv.:** Laureate bust right **Obv. Des.:** Mary Gillick **Rev.:** Totem Pole, dates at left, denomination below **Rev. Des.:** Stephan Trenka

Date	Mintage	F-12	VF-20	XF-40	AU-50	MS-60	MS-63	Proof
ND(1958)	3,039,630	—	—	BV	10.00	12.00	15.00	—

KM# 58 DOLLAR
23.3276 g. 0.8000 Silver 0.6000 oz. ASW **Ruler:** Elizabeth II
Subject: Charlottetown **Obv.:** Laureate bust right **Rev.:** Design at center, dates at outer edges, denomination below **Rev. Des.:** Dinko Voldanovic **Size:** 36 mm.

Date	Mintage	F-12	VF-20	XF-40	AU-50	MS-60	MS-63	Proof
ND(1964)	7,296,832	—	—	—	—	BV	10.00	—
ND(1964) Specimen proof	Inc. above	—	—	—	—	—	—	250

Small beads   Medium beads

Large beads

KM# 64.1 DOLLAR
23.3276 g. 0.8000 Silver 0.6000 oz. ASW **Ruler:** Elizabeth II
Obv.: Young bust right **Obv. Des.:** Arnold Machin **Rev.:** Voyageur, date and denomination below **Rev. Des.:** Emanual Hahn **Size:** 36 mm.

Date	Mintage	F-12	VF-20	XF-40	AU-50	MS-60	MS-63	Proof
1965	10,768,569	—	—	—	—	BV	10.00	—

Date	Mintage	F-12	VF-20	XF-40	AU-50	MS-60	MS-63	Proof
Note: Small beads, pointed 5								
1965	Inc. above	—	—	—	—	BV	10.00	—
Note: Small beads, blunt 5								
1965	Inc. above	—	—	—	—	BV	10.00	—
Note: Large beads, blunt 5								
1965	Inc. above	—	—	—	—	BV	12.00	—
Note: Large beads, pointed 5								
1965	Inc. above	BV	10.00	12.00	14.00	35.00		
Note: Medium beads, pointed 5								
1966	9,912,178	—	—	—	—	BV	11.00	—
Note: Large beads								
1966	485	—	1,200	1,500	1,800	3,300		
Note: Small beads								

KM# 64.2a DOLLAR   23.3276 g. 0.5000 Silver 0.3750 oz. ASW **Ruler:** Elizabeth II **Obv.:** Smaller young bust right **Obv. Des.:** Arnold Machin **Rev.:** Voyageur **Rev. Des.:** Emanuel Hahn **Size:** 36 mm.

Date	Mintage	MS-63	P/L	Proof
1972	341,598	—	—	8.50
Note: Specimen $5.50.				

KM# 70 DOLLAR   23.3276 g. 0.8000 Silver 0.6000 oz. ASW **Ruler:** Elizabeth II **Subject:** Confederation Centennial **Obv.:** Young bust right **Obv. Des.:** Arnold Machin **Rev.:** Goose left, dates below, denomination above **Rev. Des.:** Alex Colville **Size:** 36 mm.

Date	Mintage	MS-63	Proof
ND(1967)	6,767,496	12.00	13.00

KM# 76.1 DOLLAR   Nickel **Ruler:** Elizabeth II **Obv.:** Young bust right **Obv. Des.:** Arnold Machin **Rev.:** Voyageur, date and denomination below **Rev. Des.:** Emanuel Hahn **Size:** 32 mm.

Date	Mintage	MS-63	P/L	Proof
1968	5,579,714	1.25	—	—
1968	1,408,143	—	1.75	—
1968	—	8.50	—	—
Note: Small island				
1968	—	—	4.00	—
Note: No island				
1968	—	—	25.00	—
Note: Doubled die; exhibits extra water lines				
1969	4,809,313	1.25	—	—
1969	594,258	—	2.00	—
1972	2,676,041	1.50	—	—
1972	405,865	—	2.50	—

KM# 76.2 DOLLAR   15.6200 g. Nickel **Ruler:** Elizabeth II **Obv.:** Smaller young bust right **Obv. Des.:** Arnold Machin **Rev.:** Voyageur **Rev. Des.:** Emanuel Hahn **Size:** 32 mm.

Date	Mintage	MS-63	P/L	Proof
1975	322,325	—	2.50	—
1975	3,256,000	1.50	—	—
1976	2,498,204	1.50	—	—
1976	274,106	—	2.50	—

KM# 76.3 DOLLAR   Nickel **Ruler:** Elizabeth II **Obv.:** Young bust right **Obv. Des.:** Arnold Machin **Rev.:** Voyageur **Rev. Des.:** Emanuel Hahn **Size:** 32 mm. **Note:** Only known in prooflike sets with 1976 obverse slightly modified.

Date	Mintage	MS-63	P/L	Proof
1975	Inc. above	—	3.00	—
Note: mule with 1976 obv.				

KM# 78 DOLLAR   Nickel **Ruler:** Elizabeth II **Subject:** Manitoba **Obv.:** Young bust right **Rev.:** Pasque flower divides dates and denomination **Rev. Des.:** Raymond Taylor **Size:** 32 mm.

Date	Mintage	MS-63	P/L	Proof
1970	4,140,058	2.00	—	—
1970	645,869	—	2.50	—

KM# 79 DOLLAR   Nickel **Ruler:** Elizabeth II **Subject:** British Columbia **Obv.:** Young bust right **Rev.:** Shield divides dates, denomination below, flowers above **Rev. Des.:** Thomas Shingles **Size:** 32 mm.

Date	Mintage	MS-63	P/L	Proof
1971	4,260,781	2.00	—	—
1971	468,729	—	2.25	—

KM# 80 DOLLAR   23.3276 g. 0.5000 Silver 0.3750 oz. ASW **Ruler:** Elizabeth II **Subject:** British Columbia **Obv.:** Young bust right **Rev.:** Crowned arms with supporters divide dates, maple at top divides denomination, crowned lion atop crown on shield **Rev. Des.:** Patrick Brindley **Size:** 36 mm.

Date	Mintage	MS-63	Spec	Proof
1971	585,674	—	7.00	—

KM# 82 DOLLAR   Nickel **Ruler:** Elizabeth II **Subject:** Prince Edward Island **Obv.:** Young bust right **Rev.:** Building, inscription below divides dates, denomination above **Rev. Des.:** Terry Manning **Size:** 32 mm.

Date	Mintage	MS-63	P/L	Proof
1973	3,196,452	2.00	—	—
1973 (c)	466,881	—	2.50	—

KM# 83 DOLLAR   23.3276 g. 0.5000 Silver 0.3750 oz. ASW **Ruler:** Elizabeth II **Obv.:** Young bust right **Rev.:** Mountie left, dates below, denomination at right **Rev. Des.:** Paul Cedarberg **Size:** 36 mm.

Date	Mintage	MS-63	Spec	Proof
1973	1,031,271	—	7.00	—
1973		—	7.00	—
Note: Doller housed in special blue case with RCMP crest.				

KM# 88 DOLLAR Nickel **Ruler:** Elizabeth II **Subject:** Winnipeg Centennial **Obv.:** Young bust right **Rev.:** Zeros frame pictures, dates below, denomination at bottom **Rev. Des.:** Paul Pederson and Patrick Brindley **Size:** 32 mm.

Date	Mintage	MS-63	P/L	Proof
1974	2,799,363	2.00	—	—
1974 (c)	363,786	—	2.50	—

KM# 88a DOLLAR 0.5000 Silver **Ruler:** Elizabeth II **Subject:** Winnipeg Centennial **Obv.:** Young bust right **Rev.:** Zeros frame pictures, dates below, denomination at bottom **Rev. Des.:** Paul Pederson and Patrick Brindley **Size:** 36 mm.

Date	Mintage	MS-63	P/L	Proof
1974	728,947	—	7.00	—

KM# 97 DOLLAR 23.3276 g. 0.5000 Silver 0.3750 oz. ASW **Ruler:** Elizabeth II **Subject:** Calgary **Obv.:** Youmg bust right **Rev.:** Figure on bucking horse, dates divided below, denomination above **Rev. Des.:** Donald D. Paterson **Size:** 36 mm.

Date	Mintage	MS-63	P/L	Proof
1975	930,956	—	7.00	—

KM#106 DOLLAR 23.3276 g. 0.5000 Silver 0.3750 oz. ASW **Ruler:** Elizabeth II **Subject:** Parliament Library **Obv.:** Young bust right **Rev.:** Library building, dates below, denomination above **Rev. Des.:** Walter Ott and Patrick Brindley **Size:** 36 mm.

Date	Mintage	MS-63	P/L	Proof
1976	578,708	—	7.00	—
1976	Inc. above	—	15.00	—
Note: Blue case VIP				

KM# 118 DOLLAR 23.3276 g. 0.5000 Silver 0.3750 oz. ASW **Ruler:** Elizabeth II **Subject:** Silver Jubilee **Obv.:** Young bust right, dates below **Rev.:** Throne, denomination below **Rev. Des.:** Raymond Lee **Size:** 36 mm.

Date	Mintage	MS-63	P/L	Proof
1977	744,848	—	7.00	—
1977	Inc. above	—	25.00	—
Note: red case VIP				

KM# 117 DOLLAR Nickel **Ruler:** Elizabeth II **Obv.:** Young bust right **Obv. Des.:** Arnold Machin **Rev.:** Voyageur modified **Rev. Des.:** Emanuel Hahn **Size:** 32 mm.

Date	Mintage	MS-63	P/L	Proof
1977	1,393,745	2.25	—	—
1977		—	2.50	—

KM# 120.1 DOLLAR 15.6200 g. Nickel **Ruler:** Elizabeth II **Obv.:** Young bust right **Obv. Des.:** Arnold Machin **Rev.:** Voyageur, date and denomination below **Rev. Des.:** Emanuel Hahn **Size:** 32.13 mm. **Note:** Modified design.

Date	Mintage	MS-63	Proof
1978	2,948,488	1.50	—
1979	2,954,842	1.50	—
1980	3,291,221	1.50	—
1981	2,778,900	1.50	—
1981 Proof	—	—	—
1982	1,098,500	1.50	—
1982 Proof	180,908	—	5.25
1983	2,267,525	1.50	—
1983 Proof	166,779	—	5.25
1984	1,223,486	1.50	—
1984 Proof	161,602	—	6.00
1985	3,104,092	1.50	—
1985 Proof	153,950	—	7.00
1986	3,089,225	2.00	—
1986 Proof	176,224	—	7.50
1987	287,330	3.50	—
1987 Proof	175,686	—	7.50

KM# 120.2 DOLLAR Nickel **Ruler:** Elizabeth II **Obv.:** Young bust right **Rev.:** Voyageur **Size:** 32.13 mm. **Note:** Modified design.

Date	Mintage	VG-8	F-12	VF-20	XF-40	MS-60	MS-63	Proof
1985	—	—	—	—	—	1,000	1,900	—
Note: Mule with New Zealand 50 cent, KM-37 obverse								

KM# 121 DOLLAR 23.3276 g. 0.5000 Silver 0.3750 oz. ASW **Ruler:** Elizabeth II **Subject:** XI Commonwealth Games **Obv.:** Young bust right **Rev.:** Commonwealth games, logo at center **Rev. Des.:** Raymond Taylor **Size:** 36 mm.

Date	Mintage	MS-63	P/L	Proof
1978	709,602	—	7.00	—

KM# 124 DOLLAR 23.3276 g. 0.5000 Silver 0.3750 oz. ASW **Ruler:** Elizabeth II **Subject:** Griffon **Obv.:** Young bust right **Rev.:** Ship, dates below, denomination above **Rev. Des.:** Walter Schluep **Size:** 36 mm.

Date	Mintage	MS-63	P/L	Proof
1979	826,695	—	8.50	—

KM# 128 DOLLAR   23.3276 g. 0.5000 Silver 0.3750 oz. ASW **Ruler:** Elizabeth II
Subject: Arctic Territories **Obv.:** Young bust right **Rev.:** Bear right, date below, denomination
above **Rev. Des.:** Donald D. Paterson **Size:** 36 mm.

Date	Mintage	MS-63	P/L	Proof
1980	539,617		22.00	—

KM#130 DOLLAR   23.3276 g. 0.5000 Silver 0.3750 oz. ASW **Ruler:** Elizabeth II **Subject:**
Transcontinental Railroad **Obv.:** Young bust right **Rev.:** Train engine and map, date below,
denomination above **Rev. Des.:** Christopher Gorey **Size:** 36 mm.

Date	Mintage	MS-63	P/L	Proof
1981	699,494	8.50	—	—
1981 Proof	—	—	—	13.50

KM# 133 DOLLAR   23.3276 g. 0.5000 Silver 0.3750 oz. ASW **Ruler:** Elizabeth II
Subject: Regina **Obv.:** Young bust right **Rev.:** Cattle skull divides dates and denomination below
Rev. Des.: Huntley Brown **Size:** 36 mm.

Date	Mintage	MS-63	P/L	Proof
1982	144,930	8.50	—	—
1982 Proof	758,958	—	—	8.50

KM# 134 DOLLAR   15.4200 g. Nickel **Ruler:** Elizabeth II **Subject:** Constitution **Obv.:**
Young bust right **Rev.:** Meeting of Government **Rev. Des.:** Ago Aarand **Size:** 32 mm.

Date	Mintage	MS-63	P/L	Proof
1982	9,709,422	3.00	6.00	—

KM# 138 DOLLAR   23.3276 g. 0.5000 Silver 0.3750 oz. ASW **Ruler:** Elizabeth II
Subject: Edmonton University Games **Obv.:** Young bust right **Rev.:** Athlete within game logo,
date and denomination below **Rev. Des.:** Carola Tietz **Size:** 36 mm.

Date	Mintage	MS-63	P/L	Proof
1983	159,450	8.50	—	—
1983 Proof	506,847	—	—	8.50

KM# 140 DOLLAR   23.3276 g. 0.5000 Silver 0.3750 oz. ASW **Ruler:** Elizabeth II
Subject: Toronto Sesquicentennial **Obv.:** Young bust right **Rev. Des.:** D. J. Craig **Size:** 36 mm.

Date	Mintage	MS-63	P/L	Proof
1984	133,610	8.50	—	—
1984 Proof	732,542	—	—	8.50

KM# 141 DOLLAR   15.6400 g. Nickel **Ruler:** Elizabeth II **Subject:** Jacques Cartier **Obv.:**
Young bust right **Rev.:** Cross with shield above figures **Rev. Des.:** Hector Greville **Size:** 32 mm.

Date	Mintage	MS-63	P/L	Proof
1984	7,009,323	2.25	—	—
1984 Proof	87,760	—	—	6.00

KM# 143 DOLLAR   23.3276 g. 0.5000 Silver 0.3750 oz. ASW **Ruler:** Elizabeth II
Subject: National Parks **Obv.:** Young bust right **Rev.:** Moose right, dates above, denomination
below **Rev. Des.:** Karel Rohlicek **Size:** 36 mm.

Date	Mintage	MS-63	P/L	Proof
1985	163,314	8.50	—	—
1985 Proof	733,354	—	—	10.00

KM# 149 DOLLAR   23.3276 g. 0.5000 Silver 0.3750 oz. ASW **Ruler:** Elizabeth II
Subject: Vancouver **Obv.:** Young bust right **Rev.:** Train left, dates divided below, denomination
above **Rev. Des.:** Elliot John Morrison **Size:** 36 mm.

Date	Mintage	MS-63	P/L	Proof
1986	125,949	8.50	—	—
1986 Proof	680,004	—	—	8.50

KM# 154 DOLLAR   23.3276 g. 0.5000 Silver 0.3750 oz. ASW **Ruler:** Elizabeth II
Subject: John Davis **Obv.:** Young bust right **Rev.:** Ship "John Davis" with masts, rock in
background, dates below, denomination at bottom **Rev. Des.:** Christopher Gorey **Size:** 36 mm.

Date	Mintage	MS-63	P/L	Proof
1987	118,722	8.50	—	—
1987 Proof	602,374	—	—	9.00

Date	Mintage	MS-63	Proof
1990	68,402,000	1.75	—
1990 Proof	140,649	—	7.00
1991	23,156,000	1.75	—
1991 Proof	131,888	—	13.00
1993	33,662,000	2.00	—
1993 Proof	143,065	—	6.00
1994	16,232,530	2.00	—
1994 Proof	104,485	—	7.00
1995	27,492,630	3.00	—
1995 Proof	101,560	—	7.00
1996	17,101,000	2.00	—
1996 Proof	112,835	—	7.50
1997	—	5.00	—
1997 Proof	113,647	—	8.00
1998	—	2.50	—
1998 Proof	93,632	—	10.00
1998W	—	—	—
1999	—	2.00	—
1999 Proof	95,113	—	8.00
2000	—	2.00	—
2000 Proof	90,921	—	8.00

KM# 157 DOLLAR 7.0000 g. Aureate-Bronze Plated Nickel **Ruler:** Elizabeth II
Obv.: Young bust right **Obv. Des.:** Arnold Machin **Rev.:** Loon right, date and denomination below
Rev. Des.: Robert R. Carmichael **Shape:** 11-sided **Size:** 26.5 mm.

Date	Mintage	MS-63	Proof
1987	205,405,000	2.25	—
1987 Proof	178,120	—	8.00
1988	138,893,539	2.25	—
1988 Proof	175,259	—	6.75
1989	184,773,902	3.00	—
1989 Proof	170,928	—	6.75

KM# 161 DOLLAR 23.3276 g. 0.5000 Silver 0.3750 oz. ASW **Ruler:** Elizabeth II
Subject: Ironworks **Obv.:** Young bust right **Rev.:** Ironworkers, date and denomination below
Rev. Des.: Robert R. Carmichael **Size:** 36 mm.

Date	Mintage	MS-63	P/L	Proof
1988	106,872	8.50	—	—
1988 Proof	255,013	—	—	16.00

KM# 168 DOLLAR 23.3276 g. 0.5000 Silver 0.3750 oz. ASW **Ruler:** Elizabeth II
Subject: MacKenzie River **Obv.:** Young bust right **Rev.:** People in canoe, date above, denomination below **Rev. Des.:** John Mardon **Size:** 36 mm.

Date	Mintage	MS-63	P/L	Proof
1989	99,774	14.00	—	—
1989 Proof	244,062	—	—	16.00

KM# 170 DOLLAR 23.3276 g. 0.5000 Silver 0.3750 oz. ASW **Ruler:** Elizabeth II
Subject: Henry Kelsey **Obv.:** Crowned head right **Rev.:** Kelsey with natives, dates below, denomination above **Rev. Des.:** D. J. Craig **Size:** 36 mm.

Date	Mintage	MS-63	P/L	Proof
1990	99,455	8.50	—	—
1990 Proof	254,959	—	—	18.00

KM# 186 DOLLAR 7.0000 g. Aureate-Bronze Plated Nickel **Ruler:** Elizabeth II
Obv.: Crowned head right **Obv. Des.:** Dora dePedery-Hunt **Rev.:** Loon right, date and denomination **Rev. Des.:** Robert R. Carmichael **Shape:** 11-sided **Size:** 26.5 mm.

KM# 179 DOLLAR 23.3276 g. 0.5000 Silver 0.3750 oz. ASW **Ruler:** Elizabeth II
Subject: S.S. Frontenac **Obv.:** Crowned head right **Rev.:** Ship, "Frontenac", date and denomination below **Rev. Des.:** D. J. Craig **Size:** 36 mm.

Date	Mintage	MS-63	P/L	Proof
1991	73,843	8.50	—	—
1991 Proof	195,424	—	—	24.00

KM# 210 DOLLAR 25.1750 g. 0.9250 Silver 0.7487 oz. ASW **Ruler:** Elizabeth II
Subject: Stagecoach service **Obv.:** Crowned head right **Rev.:** Stagecoach, date and denomination below **Rev. Des.:** Karsten Smith **Size:** 36 mm.

Date	Mintage	MS-63	P/L	Proof
1992	78,160	16.50	—	—
1992 Proof	187,612	—	—	16.50

KM# 209 DOLLAR Aureate **Ruler:** Elizabeth II **Subject:** Loon right, dates and denomination **Obv.:** Crowned head right **Rev. Des.:** Robert R. Carmichael **Size:** 26.5 mm.

Date	Mintage	MS-63	Proof
ND(1992)	4,242,085	2.00	—
ND(1992),Proof	147,061	—	8.00

KM# 218 DOLLAR Aureate **Ruler:** Elizabeth II **Subject:** Parliament **Obv.:** Crowned head right, dates below **Rev.:** Backs of three seated figures in front of building, denomination below **Rev. Des.:** Rita Swanson **Size:** 26 mm.

Date	Mintage	MS-63	Proof
ND(1992)	23,915,000	2.25	—
ND(1992) Proof	24,227	—	9.00

KM# 235 DOLLAR   25.1750 g. 0.9250 Silver 0.7487 oz. ASW **Ruler:** Elizabeth II
Subject: Stanley Cup hockey **Obv.:** Crowned head right **Rev.:** Hockey players between cups, dates below, denomination above **Rev. Des.:** Stewart Sherwood **Size:** 36 mm.

Date	Mintage	MS-63	P/L	Proof
1993	88,150	16.50	—	—
1993 Proof	294,314	—	—	16.50

KM# 274 DOLLAR   25.1750 g. 0.9250 Silver 0.7487 oz. ASW **Ruler:** Elizabeth II
Subject: McIntosh Apple **Obv.:** Crowned head right **Rev.:** Apple, dates and denomination below **Rev. Des.:** Roger Hill **Size:** 36 mm.

Date	Mintage	MS-63	P/L	Proof
1996	58,834	16.50	—	—
1996 Proof	133,779	—	—	24.00

KM# 251 DOLLAR   25.1750 g. 0.9250 Silver 0.7487 oz. ASW **Ruler:** Elizabeth II
Subject: Last RCMP sled-dog patrol **Obv.:** Crowned head right **Rev.:** Dogsled, denomination divides dates below **Rev. Des.:** Ian Sparks **Size:** 36 mm.

Date	Mintage	MS-63	P/L	Proof
1994	61,561	16.50	—	—
1994 Proof	170,374	—	—	25.00

KM# 282 DOLLAR   25.1750 g. 0.9250 Silver 0.7487 oz. ASW **Ruler:** Elizabeth II
Subject: 25th Anniversary Hockey Victory **Obv.:** Crowned head right **Rev.:** The winning goal by Paul Aenderson. Based on a painting by Andre l'Archeveque, dates at right, denomination at bottom **Rev. Des.:** Walter Burden **Size:** 36 mm.

Date	Mintage	MS-63	P/L	Proof
ND(1997)	155,252	16.50	—	—
ND(1997) Proof	184,965	—	—	24.00

KM# 248 DOLLAR   Aureate **Ruler:** Elizabeth II **Subject:** War Memorial **Obv.:** Crowned head right, date below **Rev.:** Memorial, denomination at right **Rev. Des.:** R. C. M. Staff **Size:** 26 mm.

Date	Mintage	MS-63	Proof
1994	20,004,830	2.25	—
1994 Proof	54,524	—	7.50

KM# 291 DOLLAR   Aureate **Ruler:** Elizabeth II **Subject:** Loon Dollar 10th Anniversary **Obv.:** Crowned head right **Rev.:** Loon in flight left, dates above, denomination below **Rev. Des.:** Jean-Luc Grondin **Size:** 26 mm.

Date	Mintage	MS-63	P/L	Proof
1997	—	—	22.00	—

KM# 258 DOLLAR   7.0000 g. Aureate **Ruler:** Elizabeth II **Subject:** Peacekeeping Monument in Ottawa **Obv.:** Crowned head right, date below **Rev.:** Monument, denomination above right **Rev. Des.:** J. K. Harmon, R. G. Henriquez and C. H. Oberlander **Size:** 26 mm.
Note: Mintage included with KM#186.

Date	Mintage	MS-63	Proof
1995	18,502,750	2.25	—
1995 Proof	43,293	—	7.50

KM# 296 DOLLAR   25.1750 g. 0.9250 Silver 0.7487 oz. ASW **Ruler:** Elizabeth II
Subject: Loon Dollar 10th Anniversary **Obv.:** Crowned head right **Rev.:** Loon in flight left, dates above, denomination below **Rev. Des.:** Jean-Luc Grondin **Size:** 36 mm.

Date	Mintage	MS-63	P/L	Proof
1997 Proof	24,995	—	—	75.00

KM#259 DOLLAR   25.1750 g. 0.9250 Silver 0.7487 oz. ASW **Ruler:** Elizabeth II **Subject:** Hudson Bay Co. **Obv.:** Crowned head right **Rev.:** Explorers and ship, date and denomination below **Rev. Des.:** Vincent McIndoe **Size:** 36 mm.

Date	Mintage	MS-63	P/L	Proof
1995	61,819	16.50	—	—
1995 Proof	166,259	—	—	30.00

KM# 306 DOLLAR   25.1750 g. 0.9250 Silver 0.7487 oz. ASW **Ruler:** Elizabeth II
Subject: 120th Anniversary Royal Canadian Mounted Police **Obv.:** Crowned head right **Rev.:** Mountie on horseback, dates at left, denomination above **Rev. Des.:** Adeline Halvorson **Size:** 36 mm. **Note:** Individually cased prooflikes, proofs or specimens are from broken-up prooflike or specimen sets. .

Date	Mintage	MS-63	P/L	Proof
1998	79,777	—	16.50	
1998 Proof	120,172			20.00

KM# 355 DOLLAR 25.1750 g. 0.9250 Silver 0.7487 oz. ASW **Ruler:** Elizabeth II **Subject:** International Year of Old Persons **Obv.:** Crowned head right **Rev.:** Figures amid trees, date and denomination below **Rev. Des.:** S. Armstrong-Hodgson **Size:** 36 mm.

Date	Mintage	MS-63	P/L	Proof
1999 Proof	24,976	—		40.00

KM# 356 DOLLAR 25.1750 g. 0.9250 Silver 0.7487 oz. ASW **Ruler:** Elizabeth II **Subject:** Discovery of Queen Charlotte Isle **Obv.:** Crowned head right **Rev.:** Ship and three boats, dates at right, denomination below **Rev. Des.:** D. J. Craig **Size:** 36 mm.

Date	Mintage	MS-63	P/L	Proof
ND(1999)	67,655	—	16.50	
ND(1999) Proof	126,435	—		22.50

KM# 401 DOLLAR 25.1750 g. 0.9250 Silver 0.7487 oz. ASW **Ruler:** Elizabeth II **Subject:** Voyage of Discovery **Obv.:** Crowned head right **Rev.:** Human and space shuttle, date above, denomination below **Rev. Des.:** D. F. Warkentine **Size:** 36 mm.

Date	Mintage	MS-63	P/L	Proof
2000	60,100	—	16.50	
2000 Proof	114,130	—		22.50

KM# 443 DOLLAR 25.1750 g. 0.9250 Silver 0.7487 oz. ASW **Ruler:** Elizabeth II **Subject:** Queen's Golden Jubilee **Obv.:** Crowned head right, with anniversary date at left **Obv. Des.:** Dora dePédery-Hunt **Rev.:** Queen in her coach and a view of the coach, denomination below **Edge:** Reeded **Size:** 36 mm.

Date	Mintage	MS-63	P/L	Proof
ND(2000) Proof	—	—		20.00

KM# 270 2 DOLLARS 7.3000 g. Bi-Metallic Aluminumn-Bronze center in Nickel ring **Ruler:** Elizabeth II **Obv.:** Crowned head right within circle, date below **Obv. Des.:** Dora dePedery-

Hunt **Rev.:** Polar bear right within circle, denomination below **Rev. Des.:** Brent Townsend **Size:** 28 mm.

Date	Mintage	MS-63	Proof
1996	375,483,000	3.25	—
1996 Proof	—	—	10.00
1997	16,942,000	3.25	—
1998	4,926,000	3.25	—
1998W	Inc. above	3.25	—
1999	25,130,000	3.25	—
2000	29,847,000	3.25	—
2000W	Inc. above	3.25	—

KM# 270c 2 DOLLARS 8.8300 g. 0.9250 Silver gold plated center 0.2626 oz. ASW **Ruler:** Elizabeth II **Obv.:** Crowned head right within circle, date below **Rev.:** Polar bear right within circle, denomination below **Size:** 28 mm. **Note:** 1.9mm thick.

Date	Mintage	MS-63	Proof
1996 Proof	10,000	—	12.00
1997 Proof	—	—	10.00
1998O Proof	—	—	12.00
1999 Proof	—	—	12.00
2000 Proof	—	—	12.00

KM# 270b 2 DOLLARS 25.0000 g. 0.9250 Bi-Metallic Gold plated silver center on Silver planchet 0.7435 oz. **Ruler:** Elizabeth II **Obv.:** Crowned head right within circle, date below **Rev.:** Polar bear right within circle, denomination below **Edge:** 4.5mm thick **Size:** 28 mm.

Date	Mintage	MS-63	P/L	Proof
1996 Proof	10,000	—		55.00
1998 Proof	—	—		

KM# 270a 2 DOLLARS 10.8414 g. Bi-Metallic .999 Gold 5.7456g center in .999 Silver 5.0958g ring **Ruler:** Elizabeth II **Obv.:** Crowned head right within circle, date below **Rev.:** Polar bear right within circle, denomination below **Size:** 28 mm.

Date	Mintage	MS-63	P/L	Proof
1996 Proof	5,000	—		165

KM# 357 2 DOLLARS 7.3000 g. Bi-Metallic Aluminumn-Bronze center in Nickel ring **Ruler:** Elizabeth II **Subject:** Nunavut **Obv.:** Crowned head right **Rev.:** Inuit person with drum, denomination below **Rev. Des.:** G. Arnaktavyok **Edge:** Segmented reeding **Size:** 28 mm.

Date	Mintage	MS-63	Proof
1999	—	4.00	—

KM# 357a 2 DOLLARS 8.5200 g. 0.9250 Silver gold plated center. 0.2534 oz. ASW **Ruler:** Elizabeth II **Subject:** Nunavut **Obv.:** Crowned head right **Rev.:** Drum dancer **Edge:** Interrupted reeding **Size:** 28 mm.

Date	Mintage	MS-63	P/L	Proof
1999 Proof	39,873	—		15.00

KM# 357b 2 DOLLARS Gold Yellow gold center in White Gold ring **Ruler:** Elizabeth II **Subject:** Nunavut **Obv.:** Crowned head right **Rev.:** Drum dancer

Date	Mintage	MS-63	P/L	Proof
1999 Proof	4,298	—		200

KM# 399 2 DOLLARS 7.3000 g. Bi-Metallic Aluminumn-Bronze center in Nickel ring **Ruler:** Elizabeth II **Subject:** Knowledge **Obv.:** Crowned head right within circle, denomination below **Rev.:** Polar bear and 2 cubs right within circle, date above **Rev. Des.:** Tony Bianco **Edge:** Reeded and plain sections **Size:** 28 mm.

Date	Mintage	MS-63	Proof
2000	—	3.50	—

KM# 399a 2 DOLLARS 8.5200 g. 0.9250 Silver gold plated center. 0.2534 oz. ASW **Ruler:** Elizabeth II **Subject:** Knowledge **Obv.:** Crowned head right within circle, denomination below **Rev.:** Polar bear and 2 cubs within circle, date above

Date	Mintage	MS-63	P/L	Proof
2000 Proof	39,768	—		15.00

KM# 399b 2 DOLLARS 6.3100 g. 0.9160 Gold Yellow gold center in White Gold ring 0.1858 oz. AGW **Ruler:** Elizabeth II **Subject:** Knowledge **Obv.:** Crowned head right within circle, denomination below **Rev.:** Polar bear and two cubs right within circle, date above

Date	Mintage	MS-63	P/L	Proof
2000 Proof	5,881	—		200

KM# 14 SOVEREIGN 7.9881 g. 0.9170 Gold 0.2355 oz. AGW **Ruler:** Edward VII **Rev.:** St. George slaying dragon, mint mark below horse's rear hooves

Date	Mintage	F-12	VF-20	XF-40	AU-50	MS-60	MS-63
1908C	636	1,250	1,850	2,350	2,600	2,850	4,000
1909C	16,273	225	235	250	285	500	1,600
1910C	28,012	BV	225	225	265	500	3,000

KM# 20 SOVEREIGN   7.9881 g. 0.9170 Gold 0.2355 oz. AGW **Ruler:** George V
Rev.: St. George slaying dragon, mint mark below horse's rear hooves

Date	Mintage	F-12	VF-20	XF-40	AU-50	MS-60	MS-63
1911C	256,946	—	—	—	BV	225	250
1911C Specimen	—	—	—	—	—	—	—
1913C	3,715	550	700	950	1,200	1,500	3,000
1914C	14,871	225	240	350	450	600	950
1916C About 20 known	—	8,000	12,500	15,750	17,750	20,000	27,500

Note: Stacks' A.G. Carter Jr. Sale 12-89 Gem BU realized $82,500

Date	Mintage	F-12	VF-20	XF-40	AU-50	MS-60	MS-63
1917C	58,845	—	—	—	BV	225	750
1918C	106,514	—	—	—	BV	225	1,100
1919C	135,889	—	—	—	BV	225	750

KM# 26 5 DOLLARS   8.3592 g. 0.9000 Gold 0.2419 oz. AGW **Ruler:** George V
Obv.: Crowned bust left **Obv. Des.:** E. B. MacKennal **Rev.:** Arms within wreath, date and denomination below **Rev. Des.:** W. H. J. Blakemore

Date	Mintage	F-12	VF-20	XF-40	AU-50	MS-60	MS-63
1912	165,680	BV	230	250	275	325	800
1913	98,832	BV	230	250	275	325	900
1914	31,122	230	—	350	425	650	3,000

KM# 84 5 DOLLARS   24.3000 g. 0.9250 Silver 0.7226 oz. ASW **Ruler:** Elizabeth II
Subject: 1976 Montreal Olympics **Obv.:** Young bust right, small maple below, date at right
Rev.: Sailboat "Kingston", date at left, denomination below **Rev. Des.:** Georges Huel **Size:** 38 mm.
Note: Series I.

Date	Mintage	MS-63	Proof
1973	—	13.50	—
1973 Proof	165,203	—	13.50

KM# 85 5 DOLLARS   0.9250 Silver **Ruler:** Elizabeth II **Subject:** 1976 Montreal Olympics
Obv.: Young bust right, small maple leaf below, date at right **Rev.:** North American map,
denominaton below **Rev. Des.:** Georges Huel **Note:** Series I.

Date	Mintage	MS-63	Proof
1973	—	13.50	—
1973 Proof	165,203	—	13.50

KM# 89 5 DOLLARS   24.3000 g. 0.9250 Silver 0.7226 oz. ASW **Ruler:** Elizabeth II
Subject: 1976 Montreal Olympics **Obv.:** Young bust right, small maple leaf below, date at right
Rev.: Olympic rings, denomination below **Rev. Des.:** Anthony Mann **Size:** 38 mm. **Note:** Series II.

Date	Mintage	MS-63	Proof
1974	—	13.50	—
1974 Proof	97,431	—	13.50

KM# 90 5 DOLLARS   24.3000 g. 0.9250 Silver 0.7226 oz. ASW **Ruler:** Elizabeth II
Subject: 1976 Montreal Olympics **Obv.:** Young bust right, small maple leaf below, date at right
Rev.: Athlete with torch, denomination below **Rev. Des.:** Anthony Mann **Size:** 38 mm. **Note:** Series II.

Date	Mintage	MS-63	Proof
1974	—	13.50	—
1974 Proof	97,431	—	13.50

KM# 91 5 DOLLARS   24.3000 g. 0.9250 Silver 0.7226 oz. ASW **Ruler:** Elizabeth II
Subject: 1976 Montreal Olympics **Obv.:** Young bust right, small maple leaf below, date at right
Rev.: Rower, denomination below **Rev. Des.:** Ken Danby **Size:** 38 mm. **Note:** Series III.

Date	Mintage	MS-63	Proof
1974	—	13.50	—
1974 Proof	104,684	—	13.50

KM# 92 5 DOLLARS   24.3000 g. 0.9250 Silver 0.7226 oz. ASW **Ruler:** Elizabeth II
Subject: 1976 Montreal Olympics **Obv.:** Young bust right, small maple leaf below, date at right
Rev.: Canoeing, denomination below **Rev. Des.:** Ken Danby **Size:** 38 mm. **Note:** Series III.

Date	Mintage	MS-63	Proof
1974	—	13.50	—
1974 Proof	104,684	—	13.50

KM# 98 5 DOLLARS 24.3000 g. 0.9250 Silver 0.7226 oz. ASW **Ruler:** Elizabeth II
Subject: 1976 Montreal Olympics **Obv.:** Young bust right, small maple leaf below, date at right
Rev.: Marathon, denomination below **Rev. Des.:** Leo Yerxa **Size:** 38 mm. **Note:** Series IV.

Date	Mintage	MS-63	Proof
1975	—	13.50	—
1975 Proof	89,155	—	13.50

KM# 107 5 DOLLARS 24.3000 g. 0.9250 Silver 0.7226 oz. ASW **Ruler:** Elizabeth II
Subject: 1976 Montreal Olympics **Obv.:** Young bust right, small maple leaf below, date at right
Rev.: Fencing, denomination below **Rev. Des.:** Shigeo Fukada **Size:** 38 mm. **Note:** Series VI.

Date	Mintage	MS-63	Proof
1976	—	13.50	—
1976 Proof	82,302	—	13.50

KM# 99 5 DOLLARS 24.3000 g. 0.9250 Silver 0.7226 oz. ASW **Ruler:** Elizabeth II
Subject: Montreal 1976 - 21st Summer Olympic Games **Obv.:** Young bust right, small maple leaf below, date at right **Rev.:** Women's javelin event, denomination below **Rev. Des.:** Leo Yerxa **Size:** 38 mm. **Note:** Series IV.

Date	Mintage	MS-63	Proof
1975	—	13.50	—
1975 Proof	89,155	—	13.50

KM# 108 5 DOLLARS 24.3000 g. 0.9250 Silver 0.7226 oz. ASW **Ruler:** Elizabeth II
Subject: 1976 Montreal Olympics **Obv.:** Young bust right, small maple leaf below, date at right **Obv. Leg.:** Boxing **Rev.:** Boxers, denomination below **Rev. Des.:** Shigeo Fukada **Size:** 38 mm. **Note:** Series VI.

Date	Mintage	MS-63	Proof
1976	—	13.50	—
1976 Proof	82,302	—	13.50

KM# 100 5 DOLLARS 24.3000 g. 0.9250 Silver 0.7226 oz. ASW **Ruler:** Elizabeth II
Subject: 1976 Montreal Olympics **Obv.:** Young bust right, small maple leaf below, date at right
Rev.: Swimmer, denomination below **Rev. Des.:** Lynda Cooper **Size:** 38 mm. **Note:** Series V.

Date	Mintage	MS-63	Proof
1975	—	13.50	—
1975 Proof	89,155	—	13.50

KM# 109 5 DOLLARS 24.3000 g. 0.9250 Silver 0.7226 oz. ASW **Ruler:** Elizabeth II
Subject: 1976 Montreal Olympics **Obv.:** Young bust right, small maple leaf below, date at right
Rev.: Olympic village, denomination below **Rev. Des.:** Elliot John Morrison **Size:** 38 mm. **Note:** Series VII.

Date	Mintage	MS-63	Proof
1976	—	13.50	—
1976 Proof	76,908	—	13.50

KM# 101 5 DOLLARS 24.3000 g. 0.9250 Silver 0.7226 oz. ASW **Ruler:** Elizabeth II
Subject: Montreal 1976 - 21st Summer Olympic Games **Obv.:** Young bust right, small maple leaf below, date at right **Rev.:** Platform Diver, denomination below **Rev. Des.:** Lynda Cooper **Size:** 38 mm. **Note:** Series V.

Date	Mintage	MS-63	Proof
1975	—	13.50	—
1975 Proof	89,155	—	13.50

KM# 110 5 DOLLARS 24.3000 g. 0.9250 Silver 0.7226 oz. ASW **Ruler:** Elizabeth II
Subject: 1976 Montreal Olympics **Obv.:** Young bust right, maple leaf below, date at right **Rev.:** Olympic flame, denomination below **Rev. Des.:** Elliot John Morrison **Size:** 38 mm. **Note:** Series VII.

Date	Mintage	MS-63	Proof
1976	—	13.50	—
1976 Proof	79,102	—	13.50

KM# 316   5 DOLLARS   31.3900 g. 0.9999 Silver 1.0091 oz. ASW **Ruler:** Elizabeth II
Subject: Dr. Norman Bethune **Obv.:** Young bust right **Rev.:** Bethune and party, date at upper right **Rev. Des.:** Harvey Chan

Date	Mintage	MS-63	Proof
1998 Proof	61,000	—	30.00

KM# 398   5 DOLLARS   Copper-Zinc-Nickel **Ruler:** Elizabeth II **Obv.:** Young bust right **Rev.:** Viking ship under sail **Rev. Des.:** Donald Curley **Note:** Sold in sets with Norway 20 kroner, KM#465.

Date	Mintage	MS-63	Proof
1999 Proof	—	—	18.50

KM# 27   10 DOLLARS   16.7185 g. 0.9000 Gold 0.4837 oz. AGW **Ruler:** George V
Obv.: Crowned bust left **Obv. Des.:** E. B. MacKennal **Rev.:** Arms within wreath, date and denomination below **Rev. Des.:** W. H. J. Blakemore

Date	Mintage	F-12	VF-20	XF-40	AU-50	MS-60	MS-63
1912	74,759	—	BV	465	500	800	3,000
1913	149,232	—	BV	465	500	800	3,000
1914	140,068	BV	465	500	550	1,000	4,000

KM# 86.1   10 DOLLARS   48.6000 g. 0.9250 Silver 1.4453 oz. ASW **Ruler:** Elizabeth II
Subject: 1976 Montreal Olympics **Obv.:** Young bust right, maple leaf below, date at right **Rev.:** World map, denomination below **Rev. Des.:** Georges Huel **Size:** 45 mm. **Note:** Series I.

Date	Mintage	MS-63	Proof
1973	103,426	26.00	—
1973 Proof	165,203	—	26.00

KM# 86.2   10 DOLLARS   48.6000 g. 0.9250 Silver 1.4453 oz. ASW **Ruler:** Elizabeth II
Subject: 1976 Montreal Olympics **Obv.:** Young bust right, small maple leaf below, date at right **Rev.:** World map **Rev. Des.:** Georges Huel **Size:** 45 mm. **Note:** Series I.

Date	Mintage	MS-63	Proof
1974	320	285	—

Note: Error: mule

KM# 87   10 DOLLARS   48.6000 g. 0.9250 Silver 1.4453 oz. ASW **Ruler:** Elizabeth II
Subject: 1976 Montreal Olympics **Obv.:** Young bust right, small maple leaf below, date at right **Rev.:** Montreal skyline, denomination below **Rev. Des.:** Georges Huel **Size:** 45 mm. **Note:** Series I.

Date	Mintage	MS-63	Proof
1973	—	26.00	—
1973 Proof	165,203	—	26.00

KM# 93   10 DOLLARS   48.6000 g. 0.9250 Silver 1.4453 oz. ASW **Ruler:** Elizabeth II
Subject: 1976 Montreal Olympics **Obv.:** Young bust right, small maple leaf below, date at right **Rev.:** Head of Zeus, denomination below **Rev. Des.:** Anthony Mann **Size:** 45 mm. **Note:** Series II.

Date	Mintage	MS-63	Proof
1974	—	26.00	—
1974 Proof	104,684	—	26.00

KM# 94   10 DOLLARS   48.6000 g. 0.9250 Silver 1.4453 oz. ASW **Ruler:** Elizabeth II
Subject: 1976 Montreal Olympics **Obv.:** Young bust right, small maple leaf below, date at right **Rev.:** Temple of Zeus, denomination below **Rev. Des.:** Anthony Mann **Size:** 45 mm. **Note:** Series II.

Date	Mintage	MS-63	Proof
1974	—	26.00	—
1974 Proof	104,684	—	26.00

KM# 95   10 DOLLARS   48.6000 g. 0.9250 Silver 1.4453 oz. ASW **Ruler:** Elizabeth II
Subject: 1976 Montreal Olympics **Obv.:** Young bust right, small maple leaf below, date at right **Rev.:** Cycling, denomination below **Rev. Des.:** Ken Danby **Size:** 45 mm. **Note:** Series III.

Date	Mintage	MS-63	Proof
1974	—	26.00	—
1974 Proof	97,431	—	26.00

KM# 96   10 DOLLARS   48.6000 g. 0.9250 Silver 1.4453 oz. ASW **Ruler:** Elizabeth II
Subject: 1976 Montreal Olympics **Obv.:** Young bust right, small maple leaf below, date at right **Rev.:** Lacrosse, denomination below **Rev. Des.:** Ken Danby **Size:** 45 mm. **Note:** Series III.

Date	Mintage	MS-63	Proof
1974	—	26.00	—
1974 Proof	97,431	—	26.00

KM# 102 10 DOLLARS 48.6000 g. 0.9250 Silver 1.4453 oz. ASW **Ruler:** Elizabeth II
Subject: 1976 Montreal Olympics **Obv.:** Young bust right, small maple leaf below, date at right
Rev.: Men's hurdles, denomination below **Rev. Des.:** Leo Yerxa **Size:** 45 mm. **Note:** Series IV.

Date	Mintage	MS-63	Proof
1975	—	26.00	—
1975 Proof	82,302	—	26.00

KM# 103 10 DOLLARS 48.6000 g. 0.9250 Silver 1.4453 oz. ASW **Ruler:** Elizabeth II
Subject: Montreal 1976 - 21st Summer Olympic Games **Obv.:** Young bust right, small maple
leaf below, date at right **Rev.:** Women's shot put, denomination below **Rev. Des.:** Leo Yerxa
Size: 45 mm. **Note:** Series IV.

Date	Mintage	MS-63	Proof
1975	—	26.00	—
1975 Proof	82,302	—	26.00

KM# 104 10 DOLLARS 48.6000 g. 0.9250 Silver 1.4453 oz. ASW **Ruler:** Elizabeth II
Subject: 1976 Montreal Olympics **Obv.:** Young bust right, small maple leaf below, date at right
Rev.: Sailing, denomination below **Rev. Des.:** Lynda Cooper **Size:** 45 mm. **Note:** Series V.

Date	Mintage	MS-63	Proof
1975	—	26.00	—
1975 Proof	89,155	—	26.00

KM# 105 10 DOLLARS 48.6000 g. 0.9250 Silver 1.4453 oz. ASW **Ruler:** Elizabeth II
Subject: 1976 Montreal Olympics **Obv.:** Young bust right, small maple leaf below, date at right
Rev.: Canoeing, denomination below **Rev. Des.:** Lynda Cooper **Size:** 45 mm. **Note:** Series V.

Date	Mintage	MS-63	Proof
1975	—	26.00	—
1975 Proof	89,155	—	26.00

KM# 111 10 DOLLARS 48.6000 g. 0.9250 Silver 1.4453 oz. ASW **Ruler:** Elizabeth II
Subject: 1976 Montreal Olympics **Obv.:** Young bust right, small maple leaf below, date at right
Rev.: Football, denomination below **Rev. Des.:** Shigeo Fukada **Size:** 45 mm. **Note:** Series VI.

Date	Mintage	MS-63	Proof
1976	—	26.00	—
1976 Proof	76,908	—	26.00

KM# 112 10 DOLLARS 48.6000 g. 0.9250 Silver 1.4453 oz. ASW **Ruler:** Elizabeth II
Subject: 1976 Montreal Olympics **Obv.:** Young bust right, small maple leaf below, date at right
Rev.: Field hockey **Rev. Des.:** Shigeo Fukada **Size:** 45 mm. **Note:** Series VI.

Date	Mintage	MS-63	Proof
1976	—	26.00	—
1976 Proof	76,908	—	26.00

KM# 113 10 DOLLARS 48.6000 g. 0.9250 Silver 1.4453 oz. ASW **Ruler:** Elizabeth II
Subject: 1976 Montreal Olympics **Obv.:** Young bust right, small maple leaf below, date at right
Rev.: Olympic Stadium, denomination below **Rev. Des.:** Elliot John Morrison **Size:** 45 mm.
Note: Series VII.

Date	Mintage	MS-63	Proof
1976	—	26.00	—
1976 Proof	79,102	—	26.00

KM# 114 10 DOLLARS 48.6000 g. 0.9250 Silver 1.4453 oz. ASW **Ruler:** Elizabeth II
Subject: 1976 Montreal Olympics **Obv.:** Young bust right, small maple leaf below, date at right
Rev.: Olympic Velodrome, denomination below **Rev. Des.:** Elliot John Morrison **Size:** 45 mm.
Note: Series VII.

Date	Mintage	MS-63	Proof
1976	—	26.00	—
1976 Proof	79,102	—	26.00

KM# 215   15 DOLLARS   33.6300 g. 0.9250 Silver 1.0000 oz. ASW   **Ruler:** Elizabeth II
Subject: 1992 Olympics **Obv.:** Crowned head right, date at left, denomination below **Rev.:** Coaching track **Rev. Des.:** Stewart Sherwood **Size:** 39 mm.

Date	Mintage	MS-63	Proof
1992 Proof	275,000	—	28.00

KM# 145   20 DOLLARS   33.6300 g. 0.9250 Silver 1.0000 oz. ASW   **Ruler:** Elizabeth II
Subject: 1988 Calgary Olympics **Obv.:** Young bust right, maple leaf below, date at right **Rev.:** Downhill skier, denomination below **Rev. Des.:** Ian Stewart **Edge:** Lettered **Size:** 40 mm.

Date	Mintage	MS-63	Proof
1985 Proof	406,360	—	21.50
1985 Proof	Inc. above	—	175
Note: Plain edge			

KM# 216   15 DOLLARS   33.6300 g. 0.9250 Silver 1.0000 oz. ASW   **Ruler:** Elizabeth II
Subject: 1992 Olympics **Obv.:** Crowned head right, date at left, denomination below **Rev.:** High jump, rings, speed skating **Rev. Des.:** David Craig

Date	Mintage	MS-63	Proof
1992 Proof	275,000	—	28.00

KM# 146   20 DOLLARS   33.6300 g. 0.9250 Silver 1.0000 oz. ASW   **Ruler:** Elizabeth II
Subject: 1988 Calgary Olympics **Obv.:** Young bust right, small maple leaf below, date at right **Rev.:** Speed skater, denomination below **Rev. Des.:** Friedrich Peter **Edge:** Lettered **Size:** 40 mm.

Date	Mintage	MS-63	Proof
1985 Proof	354,222	—	21.50
1985 Proof	Inc. above	—	175
Note: Plain edge			

KM# 147   20 DOLLARS   33.6300 g. 0.9250 Silver 1.0000 oz. ASW   **Ruler:** Elizabeth II
Subject: 1988 Calgary Olympics **Obv.:** Young bust right, small maple leaf below, date at right **Rev.:** Biathlon, denomination below **Rev. Des.:** John Mardon **Edge:** Lettered **Size:** 40 mm.

Date	Mintage	MS-63	Proof
1986 Proof	308,086	—	21.50
1986 Proof	Inc. above	—	175
Note: Plain edge			

KM# 304   15 DOLLARS   Bi-Metallic 0.999 gold center in 0.925 silver ring **Ruler:** Elizabeth II **Subject:** Year of the Tiger **Obv.:** Crowned head right **Rev.:** Tiger within octagon at center, animal figures surround **Rev. Des.:** Harvey Chan **Size:** 40 mm.

Date	Mintage	MS-63	Proof
1998 Proof	68,888	—	275

KM# 331   15 DOLLARS   Bi-Metallic 0.999 Gold center in 0.925 Silver ring **Ruler:** Elizabeth II **Subject:** Year of the Rabbitt **Obv.:** Crowned head right **Rev.:** Rabbit within octagon at center, animal figures surround **Rev. Des.:** Harvey Chan

Date	Mintage	MS-63	Proof
1999 Proof	77,791	—	100

KM# 387   15 DOLLARS   Bi-Metallic 0.999 Gold center in 0.925 Silver ring **Ruler:** Elizabeth II **Subject:** Year of the Dragon **Obv.:** Crowned head right **Rev. Des.:** Harvey Chan

Date	Mintage	MS-63	Proof
2000 Proof	88,634	—	125

KM# 148   20 DOLLARS   33.6300 g. 0.9250 Silver 1.0000 oz. ASW   **Ruler:** Elizabeth II
Subject: 1988 Calgary Olympics **Obv.:** Young bust right, small maple leaf below, date at right **Rev.:** Hockey, denomination below **Rev. Des.:** Ian Stewart **Edge:** Lettered **Size:** 40 mm.

Date	Mintage	MS-63	Proof
1986 Proof	396,602	—	21.50
1986 Proof	Inc. above	—	175
Note: Plain edge			

KM# 150   20 DOLLARS   33.6300 g. 0.9250 Silver 1.0000 oz. ASW   **Ruler:** Elizabeth II
Subject: Calgary 1988 - 15th Winter Olympic Games **Obv.:** Young bust right, small maple leaf below, date at right **Rev.:** Cross-country skier, denomination below **Rev. Des.:** Ian Stewart **Edge:** Lettered **Size:** 40 mm.

Date	Mintage	MS-63	Proof
1986 Proof	303,199	—	21.50

KM# 71   20 DOLLARS   18.2733 g. 0.9000 Gold 0.5287 oz. AGW   **Ruler:** Elizabeth II
Subject: Centennial **Obv.:** Crowned head right **Rev.:** Crowned and supported arms
Edge: Reeded **Size:** 27.05 mm.

Date	Mintage	MS-63	Proof
1967 Proof	337,688	—	525

Date	Mintage	MS-63	Proof
1990 Proof	43,596	—	100

KM# 151 20 DOLLARS 33.6300 g. 0.9250 Silver 1.0000 oz. ASW **Ruler:** Elizabeth II **Subject:** 1988 Calgary Olympics **Obv.:** Young bust right, small maple leaf below, date at right **Rev.:** Free-style skier, denomination below **Rev. Des.:** Walter Ott **Edge:** Lettered **Size:** 40 mm.

Date	Mintage	MS-63	Proof
1986 Proof	294,322	—	21.50
1986 Proof	Inc. above	—	175

Note: Plain edge

KM# 155 20 DOLLARS 34.1070 g. 0.9250 Silver 1.0143 oz. ASW **Ruler:** Elizabeth II **Subject:** Calgary 1988 - 15th Winter Olympic Games **Obv.:** Young bust right, small maple leaf below, date at right **Rev.:** Figure skating pairs event, denomination below **Rev. Des.:** Raymond Taylor **Edge:** Lettered **Size:** 40 mm.

Date	Mintage	MS-63	Proof
1987 Proof	334,875	—	21.50

KM# 173 20 DOLLARS 31.1030 g. 0.9250 Silver 0.9249 oz. ASW **Ruler:** Elizabeth II **Subject:** Aviation **Obv.:** Crowned head right, date below **Rev.:** Anson and Harvard, Air Marshal Robert Leckie in cameo, denomination below **Rev. Des.:** Geoff Bennett **Size:** 38 mm.

Date	Mintage	MS-63	Proof
1990 Proof	41,844	—	35.00

KM# 196 20 DOLLARS 31.1030 g. 0.9250 Silver 0.9249 oz. ASW **Ruler:** Elizabeth II **Subject:** Aviation **Obv.:** Crowned head right, date below **Rev.:** Silver Dart, John A. D. McCurdy and F. W. "Casey" Baldwin in cameo, denomination below **Rev. Des.:** George Velinger **Size:** 38 mm.

Date	Mintage	MS-63	Proof
1991 Proof	28,791	—	30.00

KM# 156 20 DOLLARS 34.1070 g. 0.9250 Silver 1.0143 oz. ASW **Ruler:** Elizabeth II **Subject:** 1988 Calgary Olympics **Obv.:** Young bust right, small maple leaf below, date at right **Rev.:** Curling, denomination below **Rev. Des.:** Ian Stewart **Edge:** Lettered **Size:** 40 mm.

Date	Mintage	MS-63	Proof
1987 Proof	286,457	—	21.50

KM# 159 20 DOLLARS 34.1070 g. 0.9250 Silver 1.0143 oz. ASW **Ruler:** Elizabeth II **Subject:** 1988 Calgary Olympics **Obv.:** Young bust right, small maple leaf below, date at right **Rev.:** Ski jumper, denomination below **Rev. Des.:** Raymond Taylor **Edge:** Lettered **Size:** 40 mm.

Date	Mintage	MS-63	Proof
1987 Proof	290,954	—	21.50

KM# 197 20 DOLLARS 31.1030 g. 0.9250 Silver 0.9249 oz. ASW **Ruler:** Elizabeth II **Subject:** Aviation **Obv.:** Crowned head right, date below **Rev.:** de Haviland Beaver, Philip C. Garratt in cameo, denomination below **Rev. Des.:** Peter Massman **Size:** 38 mm.

Date	Mintage	MS-63	Proof
1991 Proof	29,399	—	30.00

KM# 224 20 DOLLARS 31.1030 g. 0.9250 Silver 0.9249 oz. ASW **Ruler:** Elizabeth II **Subject:** Aviation **Obv.:** Crowned head right, date below **Rev.:** Curtiss JN-4 Canick ("Jenny"), Sir Frank W. Baillie in cameo, denomination below **Rev. Des.:** George Velinger **Size:** 38 mm.

Date	Mintage	MS-63	Proof
1992 Proof	33,105	—	30.00

KM# 160 20 DOLLARS 34.1070 g. 0.9250 Silver 1.0143 oz. ASW **Ruler:** Elizabeth II **Subject:** 1988 Calgary Olympics **Obv.:** Young bust right, maple leaf below, date at right **Rev.:** Bobsled, denomination below **Rev. Des.:** John Mardon **Edge:** Lettered **Size:** 40 mm.

Date	Mintage	MS-63	Proof
1987 Proof	274,326	—	21.50

KM# 225 20 DOLLARS 31.1030 g. 0.9250 Silver 0.9249 oz. ASW **Ruler:** Elizabeth II **Subject:** Aviation **Obv.:** Crowned head right, date below **Rev.:** de Haviland Gypsy Moth, Murton A. Seymour in cameo, denomination below **Rev. Des.:** John Mardon **Size:** 38 mm.

Date	Mintage	MS-63	Proof
1992 Proof	32,537	—	30.00

KM# 236 20 DOLLARS 31.1030 g. 0.9250 Silver 0.9249 oz. ASW **Ruler:** Elizabeth II **Subject:** Aviation **Obv.:** Crowned head right, date below **Rev.:** Fairchild 71C float plane, James A. Richardson, Sr. in cameo, denomination below **Rev. Des.:** Robert R. Carmichael **Size:** 38 mm.

Date	Mintage	MS-63	Proof
1993 Proof	32,199	—	30.00

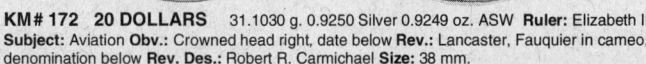

KM# 172 20 DOLLARS 31.1030 g. 0.9250 Silver 0.9249 oz. ASW **Ruler:** Elizabeth II **Subject:** Aviation **Obv.:** Crowned head right, date below **Rev.:** Lancaster, Fauquier in cameo, denomination below **Rev. Des.:** Robert R. Carmichael **Size:** 38 mm.

KM# 237 20 DOLLARS 31.1030 g. 0.9250 Silver 0.9249 oz. ASW **Ruler:** Elizabeth II **Subject:** Aviation **Obv.:** Crowned head right, date below **Rev.:** Lockheed 14, Zebulon Lewis Leigh in cameo, denomination below **Rev. Des.:** Robert R. Carmichael **Size:** 38 mm.

Date	Mintage	MS-63	Proof
1993 Proof	32,550		30.00

KM# 246   20 DOLLARS   31.1030 g. 0.9250 Silver 0.9249 oz. ASW **Ruler:** Elizabeth II
Subject: Aviation **Obv.:** Crowned head right, date below **Rev.:** Curtiss HS-2L seaplane, Stewart Graham in cameo, denomination below **Rev. Des.:** John Mardon **Size:** 38 mm.

Date	Mintage	MS-63	Proof
1994 Proof	31,242		30.00

KM# 247   20 DOLLARS   31.1030 g. 0.9250 Silver 0.9249 oz. ASW **Ruler:** Elizabeth II
Subject: Aviation **Obv.:** Crowned head right, date below **Rev.:** Vickers Vedette, Wilfred T. Reid in cameo, denomination below **Rev. Des.:** Robert R. Carmichael **Size:** 38 mm.

Date	Mintage	MS-63	Proof
1994 Proof	30,880		30.00

KM# 271   20 DOLLARS   31.1030 g. 0.9250 Silver 0.9249 oz. ASW **Ruler:** Elizabeth II
Subject: Aviation **Obv.:** Crowned head right, date below **Rev.:** C-FEA1 Fleet Cannuck, denomination below **Rev. Des.:** Robert Bradford **Size:** 38 mm.

Date	Mintage	MS-63	Proof
1995 Proof	17,438		30.00

KM# 272   20 DOLLARS   31.1030 g. 0.9250 Silver 0.9249 oz. ASW **Ruler:** Elizabeth II
Subject: Aviation **Obv.:** Crowned head right, date below **Rev.:** DHC-1 Chipmunk, denomination below **Rev. Des.:** Robert Bradford **Size:** 38 mm.

Date	Mintage	MS-63	Proof
1995 Proof	17,722		30.00

KM# 276   20 DOLLARS   31.1030 g. 0.9250 Silver 0.9249 oz. ASW **Ruler:** Elizabeth II
Subject: Aviation **Obv.:** Crowned head right, date below **Rev.:** CF-100 Cannuck, denomination below **Rev. Des.:** Jim Bruce **Size:** 38 mm.

Date	Mintage	MS-63	Proof
1996 Proof	18,508		32.50

KM# 277   20 DOLLARS   31.1030 g. 0.9250 Silver 0.9249 oz. ASW **Ruler:** Elizabeth II
Subject: Aviation **Obv.:** Crowned head right, date below **Obv. Leg.:** CF-105 Arrow, denomination below **Rev. Des.:** Jim Bruce **Size:** 38 mm.

Date	Mintage	MS-63	Proof
1996 Proof	27,163		65.00

KM# 297   20 DOLLARS   31.1030 g. 0.9250 Silver 0.9249 oz. ASW **Ruler:** Elizabeth II
Subject: Aviation **Obv.:** Crowned head right, date below **Rev.:** Canadair F-86 Sabre, denomination below **Rev. Des.:** Ross Buckland **Size:** 38 mm.

Date	Mintage	MS-63	Proof
1997 Proof	14,389		30.00

KM# 298   20 DOLLARS   31.1030 g. 0.9250 Silver 0.9249 oz. ASW **Ruler:** Elizabeth II
Subject: Aviation **Obv.:** Crowned head right, date below **Rev.:** Canadair CT-114 Tutor, denomination below **Rev. Des.:** Ross Buckland **Size:** 38 mm.

Date	Mintage	MS-63	Proof
1997 Proof	15,669		30.00

KM# 329   20 DOLLARS   31.1030 g. 0.9250 Silver 0.9249 oz. ASW **Ruler:** Elizabeth II
Subject: Aviation **Obv.:** Crowned head, right, date below **Rev.:** CP-107 Argus, denomination below **Size:** 38 mm.

Date	Mintage	MS-63	Proof
1998 Proof	Est. 50,000		37.50

KM# 330   20 DOLLARS   31.1030 g. 0.9250 Silver 0.9249 oz. ASW **Ruler:** Elizabeth II
Subject: Aviation **Obv.:** Crowned head right, date below **Rev.:** CP-215 Waterbomber, denomination below **Rev. Des.:** Peter Mossman **Size:** 38 mm.

Date	Mintage	MS-63	Proof
1998 Proof	Est. 50,000		37.50

KM# 339   20 DOLLARS   31.1030 g. 0.9250 Silver 0.9249 oz. ASW **Ruler:** Elizabeth II
Subject: Aviation **Obv.:** Crowned head right, date below **Rev.:** DHC-6 Twin Otter, denomination below **Rev. Des.:** Neil Aird **Size:** 38 mm.

Date	Mintage	MS-63	Proof
1999 Proof	Est. 50,000		37.50

KM# 340 20 DOLLARS   31.1030 g. 0.9250 Silver 0.9249 oz. ASW **Ruler:** Elizabeth II
Subject: Aviation **Obv.:** Crowned head right, date below **Rev.:** DHC-8 Dash 8, denomination
below **Size:** 38 mm.

Date	Mintage	MS-63	Proof
1999 Proof	50,000,000	—	37.50

KM# 395 20 DOLLARS   0.9250 Silver **Ruler:** Elizabeth II **Subject:** First Canadian
locomotive **Obv.:** Crowned head right, date below **Rev.:** Locomotive below multicolored cameo,
denomination below **Size:** 38 mm.

Date	Mintage	MS-63	Proof
2000 Proof	—	—	40.00

KM# 396 20 DOLLARS   0.9250 Silver **Ruler:** Elizabeth II **Subject:** First Canadian self-
propelled car **Obv.:** Crowned head right, date below **Rev.:** Car below multicolored cameo,
denomination below **Size:** 38 mm.

Date	Mintage	MS-63	Proof
2000 Proof	—	—	40.00

KM# 397 20 DOLLARS   0.9250 Silver **Ruler:** Elizabeth II **Subject:** Bluenose sailboat
Obv.: Crowned head right, date below **Rev.:** Bluenose sailing left below multicolored cameo,
denomination below **Size:** 38 mm.

Date	Mintage	MS-63	Proof
2000 Proof	—	—	150

KM# 115 100 DOLLARS   13.3375 g. 0.5830 Gold 0.2500 oz. AGW **Ruler:** Elizabeth II
Subject: 1976 Montreal Olympics **Obv.:** Young bust right, maple leaf below, date at right, beaded
borders **Rev.:** Past and present Olympic figures, denomination at right **Rev. Des.:** Dora dePedery-
Hunt **Size:** 27 mm.

Date	Mintage	MS-63	Proof
1976	650,000	235	—

KM# 116 100 DOLLARS   16.9655 g. 0.9170 Gold 0.5002 oz. AGW **Ruler:** Elizabeth II
Subject: 1976 Montreal Olympics **Obv.:** Young bust right, maple leaf below, date at right, plain
borders **Rev.:** Past and present Olympic figures, denomination at right **Rev. Des.:** Dora
dePedery-Hunt **Size:** 25 mm.

Date	Mintage	MS-63	Proof
1976 Proof	337,342	—	475

KM# 119 100 DOLLARS   16.9655 g. 0.9170 Gold 0.5002 oz. AGW **Ruler:** Elizabeth II
Subject: Queen's silver jubilee **Obv.:** Young bust right **Rev.:** Bouquet of provincial flowers,
denomination below **Rev. Des.:** Raymond Lee

Date	Mintage	MS-63	Proof
ND(1977) Proof	180,396	—	475

KM# 122 100 DOLLARS   16.9655 g. 0.9170 Gold 0.5002 oz. AGW **Ruler:** Elizabeth II
Subject: Canadian unification **Obv.:** Young bust right, denomination at left, date upper right
Rev.: Geese (representing the provinces) in flight formation **Rev. Des.:** Roger Savage

Date	Mintage	MS-63	Proof
1978 Proof	200,000	—	475

KM# 126 100 DOLLARS   16.9655 g. 0.9170 Gold 0.5002 oz. AGW **Ruler:** Elizabeth II
Subject: International Year of the Child **Obv.:** Young bust right **Rev.:** Children with hands joined
divide denomination and date **Rev. Des.:** Carola Tietz

Date	Mintage	MS-63	Proof
1979 Proof	250,000	—	475

KM# 129 100 DOLLARS   16.9655 g. 0.9170 Gold 0.5002 oz. AGW **Ruler:** Elizabeth II
Subject: Arctic Territories **Obv.:** Young bust right, denomination at left, date above right **Rev.:**
Kayaker **Rev. Des.:** Arnaldo Marchetti

Date	Mintage	MS-63	Proof
1980 Proof	300,000	—	475

KM# 131 100 DOLLARS   16.9655 g. 0.9170 Gold 0.5002 oz. AGW **Ruler:** Elizabeth II
Subject: National anthem **Obv.:** Young bust right, denomination at left, date above right
Rev.: Music score on map **Rev. Des.:** Roger Savage

Date	Mintage	MS-63	Proof
1981 Proof	102,000	—	475

KM# 137   100 DOLLARS   16.9655 g. 0.9170 Gold 0.5002 oz. AGW **Ruler:** Elizabeth II
Subject: New Constitution **Obv.:** Young bust right, denomination at left **Rev.:** Open book, maple leaf on right page, date below **Rev. Des.:** Friedrich Peter

Date	Mintage	MS-63	Proof
1982 Proof	121,708	—	475

KM# 139   100 DOLLARS   16.9655 g. 0.9170 Gold 0.5002 oz. AGW **Ruler:** Elizabeth II
Subject: 400th Anniversary of St. John's, Newfoundland **Obv.:** Young bust right **Rev.:** Anchor divides building and ship, denomination below, dates above **Rev. Des.:** John Jaciw

Date	Mintage	MS-63	Proof
ND(1983) Proof	83,128	—	475

KM# 142   100 DOLLARS   16.9655 g. 0.9170 Gold 0.5002 oz. AGW **Ruler:** Elizabeth II
Subject: Jacques Cartier **Obv.:** Young bust right **Rev.:** Cartier head on right facing left, ship on left, date lower right, denomination above **Rev. Des.:** Carola Tietz

Date	Mintage	MS-63	Proof
ND(1984) Proof	67,662	—	475

KM# 144   100 DOLLARS   16.9655 g. 0.9170 Gold 0.5002 oz. AGW **Ruler:** Elizabeth II
Subject: National Parks **Obv.:** Young bust right **Rev.:** Bighorn sheep, denomination divides dates below **Rev. Des.:** Hector Greville

Date	Mintage	MS-63	Proof
ND(1985) Proof	61,332	—	475

KM# 152   100 DOLLARS   16.9655 g. 0.9170 Gold 0.5002 oz. AGW **Ruler:** Elizabeth II
Subject: Peace **Obv.:** Young bust right **Rev.:** Maple leaves and letters intertwined, date at right, denomination below **Rev. Des.:** Dora dePedery-Hunt

Date	Mintage	MS-63	Proof
1986 Proof	76,409	—	475

KM# 158   100 DOLLARS   13.3375 g. 0.5830 Gold 0.2500 oz. AGW **Ruler:** Elizabeth II
Subject: 1988 Calgary Olympics **Obv.:** Young bust right, maple leaf below, date at right **Rev.:** Torch and logo, denomination below **Rev. Des.:** Friedrich Peter **Edge:** Lettered in English and French

Date	Mintage	MS-63	Proof
1987 Proof	142,750	—	235
Note: lettered edge			

Date	Mintage	MS-63	Proof
1987 Proof	Inc. above	—	350
Note: plain edge			

KM# 162   100 DOLLARS   13.3375 g. 0.5830 Gold 0.2500 oz. AGW **Ruler:** Elizabeth II
Subject: Bowhead Whales, balaera mysticetus **Rev.:** Whales left, date below, within circle, denomination below **Rev. Des.:** Robert R. Carmichael

Date	Mintage	MS-63	Proof
1988 Proof	52,594	—	235

KM# 169   100 DOLLARS   13.3375 g. 0.5830 Gold 0.2500 oz. AGW **Ruler:** Elizabeth II
Subject: Sainte-Marie **Obv.:** Young bust right **Rev.:** Huron Indian, Missionary and Mission building, denomination below, dates above **Rev. Des.:** D. J. Craig

Date	Mintage	MS-63	Proof
ND(1989) Proof	59,657	—	235

KM# 171   100 DOLLARS   13.3375 g. 0.5830 Gold 0.2500 oz. AGW **Ruler:** Elizabeth II
Subject: International Literacy Year **Obv.:** Crowned head right, date below **Rev.:** Woman with children, denomination below **Rev. Des.:** John Mardon

Date	Mintage	MS-63	Proof
1990 Proof	49,940	—	235

KM# 180   100 DOLLARS   13.3375 g. 0.5830 Gold 0.2500 oz. AGW **Ruler:** Elizabeth II
Subject: S.S. Empress of India **Obv.:** Crowned head right, date below **Rev.:** Ship, "SS Empress", denomination below **Rev. Des.:** Karsten Smith

Date	Mintage	MS-63	Proof
1991 Proof	33,966	—	235

KM# 211   100 DOLLARS   13.3375 g. 0.5830 Gold 0.2500 oz. AGW **Ruler:** Elizabeth II
Subject: Montreal **Obv.:** Crowned head right, date below **Rev.:** Half figure in foreground with paper, buildings in back, denomination below **Rev. Des.:** Stewart Sherwood

Date	Mintage	MS-63	Proof
1992 Proof	28,162	—	235

KM# 245   100 DOLLARS   13.3375 g. 0.5830 Gold 0.2500 oz. AGW **Ruler:** Elizabeth II
Subject: Antique Automobiles **Obv.:** Crowned head right, date below **Rev.:** German Bene Victoria; Simmonds Steam Carriage; French Panhard-Levassor's Daimler; American Duryea; Canadian Featherston Haugh in center, denomination below **Rev. Des.:** John Mardon

Date	Mintage	MS-63	Proof
1993 Proof	25,971	—	235

KM# 249   100 DOLLARS   13.3375 g. 0.5830 Gold 0.2500 oz. AGW **Ruler:** Elizabeth II
Subject: World War II Home Front **Obv.:** Crowned head right, date below **Rev.:** Kneeling figure working on plane, denomination below **Rev. Des.:** Paraskeva Clark

Date	Mintage	MS-63	Proof
1994 Proof	16,201	—	235

KM# 260   100 DOLLARS   13.3375 g. 0.5830 Gold 0.2500 oz. AGW **Ruler:** Elizabeth II
Subject: Louisbourg **Obv.:** Crowned head right, date below **Rev.:** Ship and buildings, dates and denomination above **Rev. Des.:** Lewis Parker

Date	Mintage	MS-63	Proof
1995 Proof	16,916	—	235

KM# 273 100 DOLLARS   13.3375 g. 0.5830 Gold 0.2500 oz. AGW **Ruler:** Elizabeth II
Subject: Klondike Gold Rush Centennial **Obv.:** Crowned head right, date below **Rev.:** Scene of Kate Carmack panning for gold, dates above, denomination lower left **Rev. Des.:** John Mantha

Date	Mintage	MS-63	Proof
ND(1996) Proof	17,973	—	235

KM# 287 100 DOLLARS   13.3375 g. 0.5830 Gold 0.2500 oz. AGW **Ruler:** Elizabeth II
Subject: Alexander Graham Bell **Obv.:** Crowned head right, date below **Rev.:** A. G. Bell head right, globe and telephone, denomination upper right **Rev. Des.:** Donald H. Carley

Date	Mintage	MS-63	Proof
1997 Proof	14,775	—	235

KM# 307 100 DOLLARS   13.3375 g. 0.5830 Gold 0.2500 oz. AGW **Ruler:** Elizabeth II
Subject: Discovery of Insulin **Obv.:** Crowned head right, date below **Rev.:** Nobel prize award figurine, dates at left, denomination at right **Rev. Des.:** Robert R. Carmichael

Date	Mintage	MS-63	Proof
1998 Proof	11,220	—	235

KM# 341 100 DOLLARS   13.3375 g. 0.5830 Gold 0.2500 oz. AGW **Ruler:** Elizabeth II
Subject: 50th Anniversary Newfoundland Unity With Canada **Obv.:** Crowned head right, date below **Rev.:** Two designs at front, mountains in back, denomination below **Rev. Des.:** Jackie Gale-Vaillancourt

Date	Mintage	MS-63	Proof
1999 Proof	10,242	—	235

KM# 402 100 DOLLARS   13.3375 g. 0.5830 Gold 0.2500 oz. AGW **Ruler:** Elizabeth II
Subject: McClure's Arctic expedition **Obv.:** Crowned head right, date below **Rev.:** Six men pulling supply sled to an icebound ship, denomination below **Rev. Des.:** John Mardon **Edge:** Reeded **Size:** 27 mm.

Date	Mintage	MS-63	Proof
2000 Proof	9,767	—	235

KM# 388 150 DOLLARS   13.6100 g. 0.7500 Gold 0.3282 oz. AGW **Ruler:** Elizabeth II
Subject: Year of the Dragon **Obv.:** Crowned head right **Rev. Des.:** Harvey Chan

Date	Mintage	MS-63	Proof
2000 Proof	8,851	—	650

KM# 217 175 DOLLARS   16.9700 g. 0.9170 Gold 0.5003 oz. AGW **Ruler:** Elizabeth II
Subject: 1992 Olympics **Obv.:** Crowned head right, date at left, denomination below **Rev.:** Passing the torch **Rev. Des.:** Stewart Sherwood **Edge:** Lettered

Date	Mintage	MS-63	Proof
1992 Proof	22,092	—	475

KM# 178 200 DOLLARS   17.1350 g. 0.9166 Gold 0.5049 oz. AGW **Ruler:** Elizabeth II
Subject: Canadian flag silver jubilee **Obv.:** Crowned head right, date below **Rev.:** People with flag, denomination above **Rev. Des.:** Stewart Sherwood **Size:** 29 mm.

Date	Mintage	MS-63	Proof
1990 Proof	20,980	—	475

KM# 202 200 DOLLARS   17.1350 g. 0.9166 Gold 0.5049 oz. AGW **Ruler:** Elizabeth II
Subject: Hockey **Obv.:** Crowned head right **Rev.:** Hockey players, denomination above **Rev. Des.:** Stewart Sherwood **Size:** 29 mm.

Date	Mintage	MS-63	Proof
1991 Proof	10,215	—	475

KM# 230 200 DOLLARS   17.1350 g. 0.9166 Gold 0.5049 oz. AGW **Ruler:** Elizabeth II
Subject: Niagara Falls **Obv.:** Crowned head right **Rev.:** Niagara Falls, denomination above **Rev. Des.:** John Mardon **Size:** 29 mm.

Date	Mintage	MS-63	Proof
1992 Proof	9,465	—	475

KM# 244 200 DOLLARS   17.1350 g. 0.9166 Gold 0.5049 oz. AGW **Ruler:** Elizabeth II
Subject: Mounted police **Obv.:** Crowned head right, date below **Rev.:** Mountie with children, denomination above **Rev. Des.:** Stewart Sherwood **Size:** 29 mm.

Date	Mintage	MS-63	Proof
1993 Proof	10,807	—	475

KM# 250 200 DOLLARS   17.1350 g. 0.9166 Gold 0.5049 oz. AGW **Ruler:** Elizabeth II
Subject: Interpretation of 1908 novel by Lucy Maud Montgomery, 1874-1942, Anne of Green Gables **Obv.:** Crowned head right **Rev.:** Figure sitting in window, denomination above **Rev. Des.:** Phoebe Gilman **Size:** 29 mm.

Date	Mintage	MS-63	Proof
1994 Proof	10,655	—	475

KM# 265 200 DOLLARS   17.1350 g. 0.9166 Gold 0.5049 oz. AGW **Ruler:** Elizabeth II
Subject: Maple-syrup production **Obv.:** Crowned head right, date below **Rev.:** Maple syrup making, denomination at right **Rev. Des.:** J. D. Mantha **Size:** 29 mm.

Date	Mintage	MS-63	Proof
1995 Proof	6,579	—	475

KM# 275 200 DOLLARS   17.1350 g. 0.9166 Gold 0.5049 oz. AGW **Ruler:** Elizabeth II
Subject: Transcontinental Canadian Railway **Obv.:** Crowned head right, date below **Rev.:** Train going through mountains, denomination below **Rev. Des.:** Suzanne Duranceau **Size:** 29 mm.

Date	Mintage	MS-63	Proof
1996 Proof	8,047	—	475

KM# 288 200 DOLLARS   17.1350 g. 0.9166 Gold 0.5049 oz. AGW **Ruler:** Elizabeth II
Subject: Haida mask **Obv.:** Crowned head right, date below **Rev.:** Haida mask **Rev. Des.:** Robert Davidson **Size:** 29 mm.

Date	Mintage	MS-63	Proof
1997 Proof	11,610	—	485

KM# 317 200 DOLLARS 17.1350 g. 0.9166 Gold 0.5049 oz. AGW **Ruler:** Elizabeth II
Subject: Legendary white buffalo **Obv.:** Crowned head right, date below **Rev.:** Buffalo
Rev. Des.: Alex Janvier **Size:** 29 mm.

Date	Mintage	MS-63	Proof
1998 Proof	7,149	—	475

KM# 358 200 DOLLARS 17.1350 g. 0.9166 Gold 0.5049 oz. AGW **Ruler:** Elizabeth II
Subject: Mikmaq butterfly **Obv.:** Crowned head right **Rev.:** Butterfly within design
Rev. Des.: Alan Syliboy **Size:** 29 mm.

Date	Mintage	MS-63	Proof
1999 Proof	6,510	—	475

KM# 403 200 DOLLARS 17.1350 g. 0.9166 Gold 0.5049 oz. AGW **Ruler:** Elizabeth II
Subject: Motherhood **Obv.:** Crowned head right, date above, denomination at right **Rev.:** Inuit
mother with infant **Rev. Des.:** Germaine Arnaktauyak **Edge:** Reeded **Size:** 29 mm.

Date	Mintage	MS-63	Proof
2000 Proof	6,284	—	475

KM# 308 350 DOLLARS 38.0500 g. 0.9999 Gold 1.2232 oz. AGW **Ruler:** Elizabeth II
Subject: Flowers of Canada's Coat of Arms **Obv.:** Crowned head right, date behind, denomination
at bottom **Rev.:** Flowers **Rev. Des.:** Pierre Leduc

Date	Mintage	MS-63	Proof
1998 Proof	664	—	1,150

KM# 370 350 DOLLARS 38.0500 g. 0.9999 Gold 1.2232 oz. AGW **Ruler:** Elizabeth II
Rev.: Lady's slipper **Rev. Des.:** Henry Purdy

Date	Mintage	MS-63	Proof
1999 Proof	1,990	—	1,150

KM# 404 350 DOLLARS 38.0500 g. 0.9999 Gold 1.2232 oz. AGW **Ruler:** Elizabeth II
Obv.: Crowned head right **Rev.:** Three Pacific Dogwood flowers **Rev. Des.:** Caren Heine
Edge: Reeded **Size:** 34 mm.

Date	Mintage	MS-63	Proof
2000 Proof	1,506	—	1,150

SILVER BULLION COINAGE

KM# 163 5 DOLLARS 31.1000 g. 0.9999 Silver 0.9997 oz. ASW **Ruler:** Elizabeth II
Obv.: Young bust right, denomination and date below **Obv. Des.:** Arnold Machin **Rev.:** Maple
leaf flanked by 9999

Date	Mintage	MS-63	Proof
1988	1,155,931	20.00	—
1989	3,332,200	20.00	—
1989 Proof	29,999	—	30.00

KM# 187 5 DOLLARS 31.1000 g. 0.9999 Silver 0.9997 oz. ASW **Ruler:** Elizabeth II
Obv.: Crowned head right, date and denomination below **Obv. Des.:** Dora de Pedery-Hunt
Rev.: Maple leaf flanked by 9999

Date	Mintage	MS-63	Proof
1990	1,708,800	20.00	—
1991	644,300	20.00	—
1992	343,800	20.00	—
1993	889,946	20.00	—
1994	1,133,900	20.00	—
1995	326,244	20.00	—
1996	250,445	32.50	—
1997	100,970	22.00	—
1998	591,359	20.00	—
1998 90th Anniversary R.C.M. privy mark	13,025	20.00	—
1998 R.C.M.P. privy mark	25,000	32.50	—
1998 Tiger privy mark	25,000	22.00	—
1998 Titanic privy mark	26,000	75.00	—
1999	1,229,442	20.00	—
1999 Rabbit privy mark	25,000	22.50	—
1999 "Y2K" privy mark	9,999	27.50	—
2000	403,652	20.00	—
2000 Dragon privy mark	25,000	25.00	—
2000 Expo Hanover privy mark	—	35.00	—

KM# 363 5 DOLLARS 31.1000 g. 0.9999 Silver 0.9997 oz. ASW **Ruler:** Elizabeth II
Obv.: Crowned head right, date and denomination below **Rev.:** Maple leaf flanked by 9999

Date	Mintage	MS-63	Proof
1999/2000 Fireworks privy mark	298,775	22.00	—

KM# 326 50 DOLLARS 311.0350 g. 0.9999 Silver 9.9986 oz. ASW **Ruler:** Elizabeth II
Subject: 10th Anniversary Silver Maple Leaf **Obv.:** Crowned head right **Rev.:** Maple leaf flanked
by 9999 **Edge:** 10th ANNIVERSARY 10e ANNIVERSAIRE

Date	Mintage	MS-63	Proof
1998 Proof	25,000	—	200

GOLD BULLION COINAGE

KM# 238 DOLLAR   1.5551 g. 0.9999 Gold 0.0500 oz. AGW **Ruler:** Elizabeth II
Obv.: Crowned head right, denomination and date below **Rev.:** Maple leaf flanked by 9999

Date	Mintage	MS-63	Proof
1993	37,080	BV+37%	—
1994	78,860	BV+37%	—
1995	85,920	BV+37%	—
1996	56,520	BV+37%	—
1997	59,720	BV+37%	—
1998	44,260	BV+37%	—
1999 oval "20 YEARS ANS" privy mark	—	BV+46%	—
2000 oval "2000" privy mark	—	BV+46%	—

KM# 365 DOLLAR   1.5551 g. 0.9999 Gold 0.0500 oz. AGW **Ruler:** Elizabeth II
Obv.: Crowned head right **Rev.:** Maple leaf hologram

Date	Mintage	MS-63	Proof
1999	500	90.00	—

KM# 256 2 DOLLARS   2.0735 g. 0.9999 Gold 0.0667 oz. AGW **Ruler:** Elizabeth II
Obv.: Crowned head right, denomination and date below **Rev.:** Maple leaf flanked by 9999

Date	Mintage	MS-63	Proof
1994	5,493	85.00	—

KM# 135 5 DOLLARS   3.1200 g. 0.9999 Gold 0.1003 oz. AGW **Ruler:** Elizabeth II
Obv.: Young bust right, date and denomination below **Obv. Des.:** Arnold Machin **Rev.:** Maple leaf flanked by 9999

Date	Mintage	MS-63	Proof
1982	246,000	BV+14%	—
1983	304,000	BV+14%	—
1984	262,000	BV+14%	—
1985	398,000	BV+14%	—
1986	529,516	BV+14%	—
1987	459,000	BV+14%	—
1988	506,500	BV+14%	—
1989	539,000	BV+14%	—
1989 Proof	16,992	—	180

KM# 188 5 DOLLARS   3.1200 g. 0.9999 Gold 0.1003 oz. AGW **Ruler:** Elizabeth II
Obv.: Elizabeth II effigy **Obv. Des.:** Dora dePedery-Hunt **Rev.:** Maple leaf

Date	Mintage	MS-63	Proof
1990	476,000	BV+14%	—
1991	322,000	BV+14%	—
1992	384,000	BV+14%	—
1993	248,630	BV+14%	—
1994	313,150	BV+14%	—
1995	294,890	BV+14%	—
1996	179,220	BV+14%	—
1997	188,540	BV+14%	—
1998	301,940	BV+14%	—
1999 oval "20 Years ANS" privy mark	—	BV+19%	—
2000 oval "2000" privy mark	—	BV+19%	—

KM# 366 5 DOLLARS   3.1200 g. 0.9999 Gold 0.1003 oz. AGW **Ruler:** Elizabeth II
Rev.: Maple leaf hologram

Date	Mintage	MS-63	Proof
1999	500	160	—

KM# 136 10 DOLLARS   7.7850 g. 0.9999 Gold 0.2503 oz. AGW **Ruler:** Elizabeth II
Obv.: Young bust right, date and denomination below **Obv. Des.:** Arnold Machin **Rev.:** Maple leaf flanked by 9999

Date	Mintage	MS-63	Proof
1982	184,000	BV+10%	—
1983	308,600	BV+10%	—
1984	242,400	BV+10%	—
1985	620,000	BV+10%	—
1986	915,200	BV+10%	—
1987	376,000	BV+10%	—
1988	436,000	BV+10%	—
1989	328,800	BV+10%	—
1989 Proof	6,998	—	265

KM# 189 10 DOLLARS   7.7850 g. 0.9999 Gold 0.2503 oz. AGW **Ruler:** Elizabeth II
Obv.: Crowned head right, date and denomination below **Obv. Des.:** Dora dePedery-Hunt **Rev.:** Maple leaf flanked by 9999

Date	Mintage	MS-63	Proof
1990	253,600	BV+10%	—
1991	166,400	BV+10%	—
1992	179,600	BV+10%	—
1993	158,452	BV+10%	—
1994	148,792	BV+10%	—
1995	127,596	BV+10%	—
1996	89,148	BV+10%	—
1997	98,104	BV+10%	—
1998	85,472	BV+10%	—
1999 oval "20 Years ANS" privy mark	—	BV+15%	—
2000 oval "2000" privy mark	—	BV+15%	—

KM# 367 10 DOLLARS   7.7850 g. 0.9999 Gold 0.2503 oz. AGW **Ruler:** Elizabeth II
Rev.: Maple leaf hologram

Date	Mintage	MS-63	Proof
1999	—	325	—

KM# 153 20 DOLLARS   15.5515 g. 0.9999 Gold 0.4999 oz. AGW **Ruler:** Elizabeth II
Obv.: Young bust right, date and denomination below **Obv. Des.:** Arnold Machin **Rev.:** Maple leaf flanked by 9999 **Size:** 32 mm.

Date	Mintage	MS-63	Proof
1986	529,200	BV+7%	—
1987	332,800	BV+7%	—
1988	538,400	BV+7%	—
1989	259,200	BV+7%	—
1989 Proof	6,998	—	525

KM# 190 20 DOLLARS   15.5515 g. 0.9999 Gold 0.4999 oz. AGW **Ruler:** Elizabeth II
Obv.: Crowned head right, date and denomination below **Obv. Des.:** Dora dePedery-Hunt **Rev.:** Maple leaf flanked by 9999

Date	Mintage	MS-63	Proof
1990	174,400	BV+7%	—
1991	96,200	BV+7%	—
1992	108,000	BV+7%	—
1993	99,492	BV+7%	—
1994	104,766	BV+7%	—
1995	103,162	BV+7%	—
1996	66,246	BV+7%	—
1997	63,354	BV+7%	—
1998	65,366	BV+7%	—
1999 oval "20 Years ANS" privy mark	—	BV+12%	—
2000 oval "2000" privy mark	—	BV+12%	—

KM# 368 20 DOLLARS   15.5515 g. 0.9999 Gold 0.4999 oz. AGW **Ruler:** Elizabeth II
Rev.: Maple leaf hologram

Date	Mintage	MS-63	Proof
1999	500	700	—

KM# 125.1 50 DOLLARS   31.1030 g. 0.9990 Gold 0.9989 oz. AGW **Ruler:** Elizabeth II **Obv.:** Young bust right, denomination and date below **Rev.:** Maple leaf flanked by .999

Date	Mintage	MS-63	Proof
1979	1,000,000	BV+4%	—
1980	1,251,500	BV+4%	—
1981	863,000	BV+4%	—
1982	883,000	BV+4%	—

KM# 125.2 50 DOLLARS   31.1030 g. 0.9999 Gold 0.9998 oz. AGW **Ruler:** Elizabeth II
Obv.: Young bust right, date and denomination below **Rev.:** Maple leaf flanked by .9999

Date	Mintage	MS-63	Proof
1983	843,000	BV+4%	—
1984	1,067,500	BV+4%	—
1985	1,908,000	BV+4%	—
1986	779,115	BV+4%	—
1987	978,000	BV+4%	—
1988	826,500	BV+4%	—
1989	856,000	BV+4%	—
1989 Proof	17,781	—	1,000

KM# 191 50 DOLLARS   31.1030 g. 0.9999 Gold 0.9998 oz. AGW **Ruler:** Elizabeth II
Obv.: Crowned head right, date and denomination below **Obv. Des.:** Dora dePedery-Hunt **Rev.:** Maple leaf flanked by .9999

Date	Mintage	MS-63	Proof
1990	815,000	BV+4%	—
1991	290,000	BV+4%	—
1992	368,900	BV+4%	—
1993	321,413	BV+4%	—
1994	180,357	BV+4%	—
1995	208,729	BV+4%	—
1996	143,682	BV+4%	—
1997	478,211	BV+4%	—
1998	593,704	BV+4%	—
1999 oval "20 Years ANS" privy mark	—	BV+7%	—
2000 oval "2000" privy mark	—	BV+7%	—
2000 oval fireworks privy mark	—	BV+7%	—

KM# 305 50 DOLLARS   31.1030 g. 0.9999 Gold 0.9998 oz. AGW **Ruler:** Elizabeth II
Obv.: Crowned head denomination below, within circle, dates below **Rev.:** Mountie at gallop right, within circle **Rev. Des.:** Ago Aarand **Shape:** 10-sided

Date	Mintage	MS-63	Proof
1997	12,913	1,000	—

KM# 369 50 DOLLARS   31.1030 g. 0.9999 Gold 0.9998 oz. AGW **Ruler:** Elizabeth II
Obv.: Crowned head right, date and denomination below **Rev.:** Maple leaf hologram flanked by 9999, with fireworks privy mark

Date	Mintage	MS-63	Proof
2000	500	1,400	—

PLATINUM BULLION COINAGE

KM# 239 DOLLAR   1.5552 g. 0.9995 Platinum 0.0500 oz. APW **Ruler:** Elizabeth II
Obv.: Crowned head right, date and denomination below **Rev.:** Maple leaf flanked by 9995

Date	Mintage	MS-63	Proof
1993	2,120	BV+35%	—

Date	Mintage	MS-63	Proof
1994	4,260	BV+35%	—
1995	460	135	—
1996	1,640	BV+35%	—
1997	1,340	BV+35%	—
1998	2,000	BV+35%	—
1999	2,000	BV+35%	—

KM# 257 2 DOLLARS   2.0735 g. 0.9995 Platinum 0.0666 oz. APW **Ruler:** Elizabeth II
Obv.: Crowned head right, date and denomination below **Rev.:** Maple leaf flanked by 9995

Date	Mintage	MS-63	Proof
1994	1,470	235	—

KM# 164 5 DOLLARS   3.1203 g. 0.9995 Platinum 0.1003 oz. APW **Ruler:** Elizabeth II
Obv.: Young bust right, date and denomination below **Obv. Des.:** Arnold Machin **Rev.:** Maple leaf flanked by 9995

Date	Mintage	MS-63	Proof
1988	74,000	BV+18%	—
1989	18,000	BV+18%	—
1989 Proof	11,999	—	250

KM# 192 5 DOLLARS   3.1203 g. 0.9995 Platinum 0.1003 oz. APW **Ruler:** Elizabeth II
Obv. Des.: dePedery-Hunt **Rev.:** Maple leaf

Date	Mintage	MS-63	Proof
1990	9,000	BV+18%	—
1991	13,000	BV+18%	—
1992	16,000	BV+18%	—
1993	14,020	BV+18%	—
1994	19,190	BV+18%	—
1995	8,940	BV+18%	—
1996	8,820	BV+18%	—
1997	7,050	BV+18%	—
1998	5,710	BV+18%	—
1999	2,000	BV+18%	—

KM# 165 10 DOLLARS   7.7857 g. 0.9995 Platinum 0.2502 oz. APW **Ruler:** Elizabeth II **Obv.:** Young bust right, date and denomination below **Obv. Des.:** Machin **Rev.:** Maple leaf flanked by 9995

Date	Mintage	MS-63	Proof
1988	93,600	BV+13%	—
1989	3,200	BV+13%	—
1989 Proof	1,999	—	575

KM# 193 10 DOLLARS   7.7857 g. 0.9995 Platinum 0.2502 oz. APW **Ruler:** Elizabeth II **Obv. Des.:** dePedery-Hunt **Rev.:** Maple leaf

Date	Mintage	MS-63	Proof
1990	1,600	BV+13%	—
1991	7,200	BV+13%	—
1992	11,600	BV+13%	—
1993	8,048	BV+13%	—
1994	9,456	BV+13%	—
1995	6,524	BV+13%	—
1996	6,160	BV+13%	—
1997	4,552	BV+13%	—
1998	3,816	BV+13%	—
1999	2,000	BV+13%	—

KM# 166 20 DOLLARS   15.5519 g. 0.9995 Platinum 0.4997 oz. APW **Ruler:** Elizabeth II **Obv.:** Young bust right, denomination and date below **Obv. Des.:** Machin **Rev.:** Maple leaf flanked by 9995

Date	Mintage	MS-63	Proof
1988	23,600	BV+9%	—
1989	4,800	BV+9%	—
1989 Proof	1,999	—	1,150

KM# 194 20 DOLLARS   15.5519 g. 0.9995 Platinum 0.4997 oz. APW **Ruler:** Elizabeth II **Obv. Des.:** dePedery-Hunt **Rev.:** Maple leaf

Date	Mintage	MS-63	Proof
1990	2,600	BV+9%	—
1991	5,600	BV+9%	—
1992	12,800	BV+9%	—
1993	6,022	BV+9%	—
1994	6,710	BV+9%	—

Date	Mintage	MS-63	Proof
1995	6,308	BV+9%	—
1996	5,490	BV+9%	—
1997	3,990	BV+9%	—
1998	5,486	BV+9%	—
1999	500	BV+15%	—

KM# 174 30 DOLLARS 3.1100 g. 0.9990 Platinum 0.0999 oz. APW **Ruler:** Elizabeth II **Obv.:** Crowned head right **Rev.:** Polar bear swimming, denomination below **Rev. Des.:** Robert Bateman

Date	Mintage	MS-63	Proof
1990 Proof	2,629	—	220

KM# 167 50 DOLLARS 31.1030 g. 0.9995 Platinum 0.9994 oz. APW **Ruler:** Elizabeth II **Obv.:** Young bust right, denomination and date below **Obv. Des.:** Machin **Rev.:** Maple leaf flanked by 9995

Date	Mintage	MS-63	Proof
1988	37,500	BV+4%	—
1989	10,000	BV+4%	—
1989 Proof	5,965		1,850

KM# 198 30 DOLLARS 3.1100 g. 0.9990 Platinum 0.0999 oz. APW **Ruler:** Elizabeth II **Obv.:** Crowned head right **Rev.:** Snowy owl, denomination below **Rev. Des.:** Glen Loates

Date	Mintage	MS-63	Proof
1991 Proof	3,500	—	220

KM# 195 50 DOLLARS 31.1030 g. 0.9995 Platinum 0.9994 oz. APW **Ruler:** Elizabeth II **Obv. Des.:** dePedery-Hunt **Rev.:** Maple leaf

Date	Mintage	MS-63	Proof
1990	15,100	BV+4%	—
1991	31,900	BV+4%	—
1992	40,500	BV+4%	—
1993	17,666	BV+4%	—
1994	36,245	BV+4%	—
1995	25,829	BV+4%	—
1996	62,273	BV+4%	—
1997	25,480	BV+4%	—
1998	10,403	BV+4%	—
1999	1,300	BV+10%	—

KM# 226 30 DOLLARS 3.1100 g. 0.9990 Platinum 0.0999 oz. APW **Ruler:** Elizabeth II **Obv.:** Crowned head right **Rev.:** Cougar head and shoulders, denomination below **Rev. Des.:** George McLean

Date	Mintage	MS-63	Proof
1992 Proof	3,500	—	220

KM# 240 30 DOLLARS 3.1100 g. 0.9990 Platinum 0.0999 oz. APW **Ruler:** Elizabeth II **Obv.:** Crowned head right **Rev.:** Arctic fox, denomination below **Rev. Des.:** Claude D'Angelo

Date	Mintage	MS-63	Proof
1993 Proof	3,500	—	220

KM# 175 75 DOLLARS 7.7760 g. 0.9990 Platinum 0.2497 oz. APW **Ruler:** Elizabeth II **Obv.:** Crowned head right **Rev.:** Polar bear resting, denomination below **Rev. Des.:** Robert Bateman

Date	Mintage	MS-63	Proof
1990 Proof	2,629	—	550

KM# 252 30 DOLLARS 3.1100 g. 0.9990 Platinum 0.0999 oz. APW **Ruler:** Elizabeth II **Obv.:** Crowned head right, date below **Rev.:** Sea otter, denomination below **Rev. Des.:** Ron S. Parker

Date	Mintage	MS-63	Proof
1994 Proof	1,500	—	220

KM# 266 30 DOLLARS 3.1100 g. 0.9990 Platinum 0.0999 oz. APW **Ruler:** Elizabeth II **Obv.:** Crowned head right, date below **Rev.:** Canadian lynx, denomination below **Rev. Des.:** Michael Dumas

Date	Mintage	MS-63	Proof
1995 Proof	620	—	220

KM# 278 30 DOLLARS 3.1100 g. 0.9990 Platinum 0.0999 oz. APW **Ruler:** Elizabeth II **Obv.:** Crowned head right, date below **Rev.:** Falcon portrait, denomination below **Rev. Des.:** Dwayne Harty

Date	Mintage	MS-63	Proof
1996 Proof	489	—	220

KM# 300 30 DOLLARS 3.1100 g. 0.9995 Platinum 0.0999 oz. APW **Ruler:** Elizabeth II **Obv.:** Crowned head right, date below **Rev.:** Bison head, denomination below **Rev. Des.:** Chris Bacon

Date	Mintage	MS-63	Proof
1997 Proof	5,000	—	220

KM# 322 30 DOLLARS 3.1100 g. 0.9990 Platinum 0.0999 oz. APW **Ruler:** Elizabeth II **Obv.:** Crowned head right, date below **Rev.:** Grey wolf **Rev. Des.:** Kerr Burnett

Date	Mintage	MS-63	Proof
ND(1998) Proof	2,000	—	220

KM# 359 30 DOLLARS 3.1100 g. 0.9995 Platinum 0.0999 oz. APW **Ruler:** Elizabeth II **Obv.:** Crowned head right, date below **Rev.:** Musk ox **Rev. Des.:** Mark Hobson

Date	Mintage	MS-63	Proof
1999 Proof	1,500	—	220

KM# 199 75 DOLLARS 7.7760 g. 0.9990 Platinum 0.2497 oz. APW **Ruler:** Elizabeth II **Obv.:** Crowned head right **Rev.:** Snowy owls perched on branch, denomination below **Rev. Des.:** Glen Loates

Date	Mintage	MS-63	Proof
1991 Proof	3,500	—	550

KM# 227 75 DOLLARS 7.7760 g. 0.9990 Platinum 0.2497 oz. APW **Ruler:** Elizabeth II **Obv.:** Crowned head right **Rev.:** Cougar prowling, denomination below **Rev. Des.:** George McLean

Date	Mintage	MS-63	Proof
1992 Proof	3,500	—	550

KM# 241 75 DOLLARS 7.7760 g. 0.9990 Platinum 0.2497 oz. APW **Ruler:** Elizabeth II **Obv.:** Crowned head right **Rev.:** Two Arctic foxes, denomination below **Rev. Des.:** Claude D'Angelo

Date	Mintage	MS-63	Proof
1993 Proof	3,500	—	550

KM# 253 75 DOLLARS 7.7760 g. 0.9990 Platinum 0.2497 oz. APW **Ruler:** Elizabeth II **Obv.:** Crowned head right, date below **Rev.:** Sea otter eating urchin, denomination below **Rev. Des.:** Ron S. Parker

Date	Mintage	MS-63	Proof
1994 Proof	1,500	—	550

KM# 405 30 DOLLARS 3.1100 g. 0.9995 Platinum 0.0999 oz. APW **Ruler:** Elizabeth II **Obv.:** Crowned head right, date below **Rev.:** Pronghorn antelope head, denomination below **Rev. Des.:** Mark Hobson **Edge:** Reeded **Size:** 16 mm.

Date	Mintage	MS-63	Proof
2000 Proof	600	—	220

KM# 267   75 DOLLARS   7.7760 g. 0.9990 Platinum 0.2497 oz. APW **Ruler:** Elizabeth II
Obv.: Crowned head right, date below **Rev.:** Two lynx kittens, denomination below
Rev. Des.: Michael Dumas

Date	Mintage	MS-63	Proof
1995 Proof	1,500	—	550

KM# 279   75 DOLLARS   7.7760 g. 0.9990 Platinum 0.2497 oz. APW **Ruler:** Elizabeth II
Obv.: Crowned head right, date below **Rev.:** Peregrine falcon, denomination below
Rev. Des.: Dwayne Harty

Date	Mintage	MS-63	Proof
1996 Proof	1,500	—	550

KM# 301   75 DOLLARS   7.7760 g. 0.9990 Platinum 0.2497 oz. APW **Ruler:** Elizabeth II
Obv.: Crowned head right, date below **Rev.:** Two bison calves, denomination below
Rev. Des.: Chris Bacon

Date	Mintage	MS-63	Proof
1997 Proof	1,500	—	550

KM# 323   75 DOLLARS   7.7760 g. 0.9990 Platinum 0.2497 oz. APW **Ruler:** Elizabeth II
Obv.: Crowned head right, date below **Rev.:** Gray wolf **Rev. Des.:** Kerr Burnett

Date	Mintage	MS-63	Proof
1998 Proof	1,000	—	550

KM# 360   75 DOLLARS   7.7760 g. 0.9990 Platinum 0.2497 oz. APW **Ruler:** Elizabeth II
Obv.: Crowned head right, date below **Rev.:** Musk ox **Rev. Des.:** Mark Hobson

Date	Mintage	MS-63	Proof
1999 Proof	500	—	550

KM# 406   75 DOLLARS   7.7760 g. 0.9990 Platinum 0.2497 oz. APW **Ruler:** Elizabeth II
Obv.: Crowned head right **Rev.:** Standing pronghorn antelope, denomination below
Rev. Des.: Mark Hobson **Edge:** Reeded **Size:** 20 mm.

Date	Mintage	MS-63	Proof
2000 Proof	600	—	550

KM# 176   150 DOLLARS   15.5520 g. 0.9990 Platinum 0.4995 oz. APW **Ruler:** Elizabeth II
Obv.: Crowned head right **Rev.:** Polar bear walking, denomination below **Rev. Des.:** Robert Bateman

Date	Mintage	MS-63	Proof
1990 Proof	2,629	—	1,100

KM# 200   150 DOLLARS   15.5520 g. 0.9990 Platinum 0.4995 oz. APW **Ruler:** Elizabeth II
Obv.: Crowned head right **Rev.:** Snowy owl flying, denomination below **Rev. Des.:** Glen Loates

Date	Mintage	MS-63	Proof
1991 Proof	3,500	—	1,100

KM# 228   150 DOLLARS   15.5520 g. 0.9990 Platinum 0.4995 oz. APW **Ruler:** Elizabeth II
Obv.: Crowned head right **Rev.:** Cougar mother and cub, denomination below
Rev. Des.: George McLean

Date	Mintage	MS-63	Proof
1992 Proof	3,500	—	1,100

KM# 242   150 DOLLARS   15.5520 g. 0.9990 Platinum 0.4995 oz. APW **Ruler:** Elizabeth II
Obv.: Crowned head right **Rev.:** Arctic fox by lake, denomination below **Rev. Des.:** Claude D'Angelo

Date	Mintage	MS-63	Proof
1993 Proof	3,500	—	1,100

KM# 254   150 DOLLARS   15.5520 g. 0.9990 Platinum 0.4995 oz. APW **Ruler:** Elizabeth II **Obv.:** Crowned head right, date below **Rev.:** Sea otter mother carrying pup, denomination below **Rev. Des.:** Ron S. Parker

Date	Mintage	MS-63	Proof
1994 Proof	—	—	1,100

KM# 268   150 DOLLARS   15.5520 g. 0.9990 Platinum 0.4995 oz. APW **Ruler:** Elizabeth II **Obv.:** Crowned head right, date below **Rev.:** Prowling lynx, denomination below
Rev. Des.: Michael Dumas

Date	Mintage	MS-63	Proof
1995 Proof	226	—	1,100

KM# 280   150 DOLLARS   15.5520 g. 0.9990 Platinum 0.4995 oz. APW **Ruler:** Elizabeth II **Obv.:** Crowned head right, date below **Rev.:** Peregrine falcon on branch, denomination below
Rev. Des.: Dwayne Harty

Date	Mintage	MS-63	Proof
1996 Proof	100	—	1,100

KM# 302   150 DOLLARS   15.5520 g. 0.9990 Platinum 0.4995 oz. APW **Ruler:** Elizabeth II **Obv.:** Crowned head right, date below **Rev.:** Bison bull, denomination below **Rev. Des.:** Chris Bacon

Date	Mintage	MS-63	Proof
1997 Proof	4,000	—	1,100

KM# 324   150 DOLLARS   15.5520 g. 0.9990 Platinum 0.4995 oz. APW **Ruler:** Elizabeth II **Obv.:** Crowned head right, date below **Rev.:** Two gray wolf cubs, denomination below
Rev. Des.: Kerr Burnett

Date	Mintage	MS-63	Proof
1998 Proof	2,000	—	1,100

KM# 361   150 DOLLARS   15.5520 g. 0.9990 Platinum 0.4995 oz. APW **Ruler:** Elizabeth II **Obv.:** Crowned head right **Rev.:** Musk ox, denomination below **Rev. Des.:** Mark Hobson

Date	Mintage	MS-63	Proof
1999 Proof	500	—	1,100

KM# 407   150 DOLLARS   15.5500 g. 0.9990 Platinum 0.4994 oz. APW **Ruler:** Elizabeth II **Obv.:** Crowned head right **Rev.:** Two pronghorn antelope, denomination below **Rev. Des.:** Mark Hobson **Edge:** Reeded **Size:** 25 mm.

Date	Mintage	MS-63	Proof
2000 Proof	600	—	1,100

KM# 177   300 DOLLARS   31.1035 g. 0.9990 Platinum 0.9990 oz. APW **Ruler:** Elizabeth II **Obv.:** Crowned head right **Rev.:** Polar bear mother and cub, denomination below **Rev. Des.:** Robert Bateman

Date	Mintage	MS-63	Proof
1990 Proof	2,629	—	2,000

KM# 201   300 DOLLARS   31.1035 g. 0.9990 Platinum 0.9990 oz. APW **Ruler:** Elizabeth II **Obv.:** Crowned head right **Rev.:** Snowy owl with chicks, denomination below **Rev. Des.:** Glen Loates

Date	Mintage	MS-63	Proof
1991 Proof	3,500	—	2,000

KM# 325   300 DOLLARS   31.1035 g. 0.9990 Platinum 0.9990 oz. APW **Ruler:** Elizabeth II **Obv.:** Crowned head right, date below **Rev.:** Gray wolf and two cubs, denomination below **Rev. Des.:** Kerr Burnett

Date	Mintage	MS-63	Proof
1998 Proof	—	—	2,000

KM# 362   300 DOLLARS   31.1035 g. 0.9990 Platinum 0.9990 oz. APW **Ruler:** Elizabeth II **Obv.:** Crowned head right, date below **Rev.:** Musk ox **Rev. Des.:** Mark Hobson

Date	Mintage	MS-63	Proof
1999 Proof	500	—	2,000

KM# 408   300 DOLLARS   31.1035 g. 0.9990 Platinum 0.9990 oz. APW **Ruler:** Elizabeth II **Obv.:** Crowned head right, date below **Rev.:** Four pronghorn antelope, denomination below **Rev. Des.:** Mark Hobson **Edge:** Reeded **Size:** 30 mm.

Date	Mintage	MS-63	Proof
2000 Proof	600	—	2,000

KM# 229   300 DOLLARS   31.1035 g. 0.9990 Platinum 0.9990 oz. APW **Ruler:** Elizabeth II **Obv.:** Crowned head right **Rev.:** Cougar resting in tree, denomination below **Rev. Des.:** George McLean

Date	Mintage	MS-63	Proof
1992 Proof	3,500	—	2,000

PATTERNS

Including off metal strikes

KM	Date	Mintage	Identification	Mkt Val
Pn14	1911	—	Cent. Bronze. Similar to 1912-1920.	10,000
Pn15	1911	—	Dollar. Silver.	650,000
Pn16	1911	—	Dollar. Lead.	—
Pn17	1911	—	5 Dollars. Gold.	—
Pn18	1911	—	10 Dollars. Gold.	—
Pn19	1928	—	5 Dollars. Bronze.	—
Pn20	1928	—	10 Dollars. Bronze.	—
Pn23	1964	—	Dollar. Tin. Piefort.	—
Pn24	1967	—	Dollar. Silver. Unique.	—

KM# 243   300 DOLLARS   31.1035 g. 0.9990 Platinum 0.9990 oz. APW **Ruler:** Elizabeth II **Obv.:** Crowned head right **Rev.:** Mother fox and three kits, denomination below **Rev. Des.:** Claude D'Angelo

Date	Mintage	MS-63	Proof
1993 Proof	3,500	—	2,000

TRIAL STRIKES

KM	Date	Mintage	Identification	Mkt Val
TS3	1928	—	5 Dollars. Bronze.	—
TS4	1928	—	10 Dollars. Bronze.	—
TS5	1937	—	Cent. Brass. Thick planchet.	2,500
TS6	1937	—	5 Cents. Brass. Thick planchet.	2,500
TS7	1937	—	10 Cents. Brass. Thick planchet.	2,500
TS8	1937	—	25 Cents. Brass. Thick planchet.	3,500
TS9	1937	—	25 Cents. Bronze.	3,500
TS10	1937	—	50 Cents. Brass. Thick planchet.	5,000
TS11	1942	—	5 Cents. Nickel. 12 sided.	—
TS12	1943	—	Cent. Copper Plated Steel.	—
TS13	1943	—	5 Cents. Steel.	—
TS14	1944	—	5 Cents. Tombac.	—
TS15	1951	—	5 Cents. Chrome Plated Steel.	—
TS16	1952	—	5 Cents.	—
TS17	1959	—	50 Cents. Tin.	—
TS18	1964	—	Dollar. Tin. Piefort, unique.	—

KM# 255   300 DOLLARS   31.1035 g. 0.9990 Platinum 0.9990 oz. APW **Ruler:** Elizabeth II **Obv.:** Crowned head right, date below **Rev.:** Two otters swimming, denomination below **Rev. Des.:** Ron S. Parker

Date	Mintage	MS-63	Proof
1994 Proof	—	—	2,000

KM# 269   300 DOLLARS   31.1035 g. 0.9990 Platinum 0.9990 oz. APW **Ruler:** Elizabeth II **Obv.:** Crowned head right, date below **Rev.:** Female lynx and three kittens, denomination below **Rev. Des.:** Michael Dumas

Date	Mintage	MS-63	Proof
1995 Proof	1,500	—	2,000

CUSTOM PROOF-LIKE SETS (CPL)

KM	Date	Mintage	Identification	Issue Price	Mkt Val
CPL1	1971	33,517	KM59.1 (2 pcs.), 60.1, 62b-75.1, 77.1 ,79	6.50	5.00
CPL2	1971	38,198	KM59.1 (2 pcs.), 60.1, 62b, 75.1-77.1	6.50	5.00
CPL3	1973	35,676	KM59.1 (2 pcs.), 60.1, 75.1, 77.1, 81.1 obv. 120 beads, 82	6.50	6.50
CPL4	1973	I.A.	KM59.1 (2 pcs.), 60.1, 75.1, 77.1, 81.1 obv. 132 beads, 82	6.50	200
CPL5	1974	44,296	KM59.1 (2 pcs.), 60.1, 62b-75.1, 88	8.00	5.00
CPL6	1975	36,851	KM59.1 (2 pcs.), 60.1, 62b-75.1, 76.2, 77.1	8.00	5.00
CPL7	1976	28,162	KM59.1 (2 pcs.), 60.1, 62b-75.1, 76.2, 77.1	8.00	5.50
CPL8	1977	44,198	KM59.1 (2 pcs.), 60.1, 62b-75.2, 77.1, 117	8.15	5.00
CPL9	1978	41,000	KM59.1 (2 pcs.), 60.1, 62b-75.3, 77.1, 120.1		5.00
CPL10	1979	31,174	KM59.2 (2 pcs.), 60.2, 74, 75.3, 77.2, 120.1	10.75	5.00
CPL11	1980	41,447	KM60.2, 74, 75.3, 77.2, 120.1, 127 (2 pcs.)	10.75	6.00

KM# 281   300 DOLLARS   31.1035 g. 0.9990 Platinum 0.9990 oz. APW **Ruler:** Elizabeth II **Obv.:** Crowned head right, date below **Rev.:** Peregrine falcon feeding nestlings, denomination below **Rev. Des.:** Dwayne Harty

Date	Mintage	MS-63	Proof
1996 Proof	1,500	—	2,000

KM# 303   300 DOLLARS   31.1035 g. 0.9990 Platinum 0.9990 oz. APW **Ruler:** Elizabeth II **Obv.:** Crowned head right, date below **Rev.:** Bison family, denomination below **Rev. Des.:** Chris Bacon

Date	Mintage	MS-63	Proof
1997 Proof	1,500	—	2,000

MINT SETS

KM	Date	Mintage	Identification	Issue Price	Mkt Val
MS1	1973	I.A.	KM84-85, 86.1, 87; Olympic Commemoratives, Series I	45.00	70.00
MS2	1974	I.A.	KM89-90, 93-94; Olympic Commemoratives, Series II	48.00	70.00
MS3	1974	I.A.	KM91-92, 95-96; Olympic Commemoratives, Series III	48.00	70.00
MS4	1975	I.A.	KM98-99, 102-103; Olympic Commemoratives, Series IV	48.00	70.00
MS5	1975	I.A.	KM100-101, 104-105; Olympic Commemoratives, Series V	60.00	70.00
MS6	1976	I.A.	KM107-108, 111-112; Olympic Commemoratives, Series VI	60.00	70.00
MS7	1976	I.A.	KM109-110, 113-114; Olympic Commemoratives, Series VII	60.00	70.00

OLYMPIC COMMEMORATIVES (OCP)

KM	Date	Mintage	Identification	Issue Price	Mkt Val
OCP1	1973	I.A.	KM84-87, Series I	78.50	70.00
OCP2	1974	I.A.	KM89-90, 93-94, Series II	88.50	70.00
OCP3	1974	I.A.	KM91-92, 95-96, Series III	88.50	70.00
OCP4	1975	I.A.	KM98-99, 102-103, Series IV	88.50	70.00
OCP5	1975	I.A.	KM100-101, 104-105, Series V	88.50	70.00
OCP6	1976	I.A.	KM107-108, 111-112, Series VI	88.50	70.00
OCP7	1976	I.A.	KM109-110, 113-114, Series VII	88.50	70.00

PROOF SETS

KM	Date	Mintage	Identification	Issue Price	Mkt Val
PS1	1981	199,000	KM60.2, 74, 75.3, 77.2, 120.1, 127, 130	36.00	17.50

KM	Date	Mintage Identification	Issue Price	Mkt Val
PS2	1982	180,908 KM60.2a, 74, 75.3, 77.2, 120.1, 132-133	36.00	14.00
PS3	1983	166,779 KM60.2a, 74, 75.3, 77.2, 120.1, 132, 138	36.00	14.00
PS4	1984	161,602 KM60.2a, 74, 75.3, 77.2, 120.1, 132, 140	30.00	17.00
PS5	1985	157,037 KM60.2a, 74, 75.3, 77.2, 120.1, 132, 143	30.00	18.00
PS6	1986	175,745 KM60.2a, 74, 75.3, 77.2, 120.1, 132, 149	30.00	18.00
PS7	1987	179,004 KM60.2a, 74, 75.3, 77.2, 120.1, 132, 154	34.00	18.00
PS8	1988	175,259 KM60.2a, 74, 75.3, 77.2, 132, 157, 161	37.50	23.00
PS9	1989	170,928 KM60.2a, 74, 75.3, 77.2, 132, 157, 168	40.00	24.00
PS10	1989	6,823 KM125.2, 135-136, 153	1,190	1,100
PS11	1989	1,995 KM164-167	1,700	2,100
PS12	1989	2,550 KM125.2, 163, 167	1,530	1,775
PS13	1989	9,979 KM135, 163-164	165	225
PS14	1990	158,068 KM170, 181, 182, 183, 184, 185, 186	41.00	24.00
PS15	1990	2,629 KM174-177	1,720	2,475
PS16	1991	14,629 KM179, 181, 182, 183, 184, 185, 186	—	45.00
PS17	1991	873 KM198-201	1,760	2,475
PS18	1992	84,397 KM203a, 212a-214a, 218, 220a-223a, 231a-234a	—	90.00
PS19	1992	147,061 KM204-210	42.75	30.00
PS20	1992	3,500 KM226-229	1,680	2,500
PS21	1993	143,065 KM181, 182, 183, 184, 185, 186, 235	42.75	20.00
PS22	1993	3,500 KM240-243	1,329	2,500
PS23	1994	47,303 KM181-186, 248	47.50	28.00
PS24	1994	99,121 KM181, 182, 183, 184, 185, 186, 251	43.00	28.00
PS25	1994	1,500 KM252-255	915	2,520
PS26	1995	I.A. KM181, 182, 183, 184, 185, 186, 259	37.45	25.00
PS27	1995	50,000 KM181, 182, 183, 184, 185, 258-259	49.45	22.00
PS28	1995	I.A. KM261-264	42.00	60.00
PS29	1995	682 KM266-269	1,555	2,500
PS30	1995	I.A. KM261-262	22.00	21.00
PS31	1995	I.A. KM263-264	22.00	30.00
PS32	1996	423 KM278-281	1,555	2,500
PS33	1996	I.A. KM181a, 182a, 183a, 184a, 185a, 186, 274	49.00	35.00
PS34	1996	I.A. KM283-286	44.45	45.00
PS35	1997	I.A. KM182a, 183a, 184a, 209, 270c, 282, 289	60.00	45.00
PS36	1997	I.A. KM292-295	44.45	35.00
PS37	1997	I.A. KM300-303	1,530	2,485
PS38	1998	I.A. KM182a, 183a, 184a, 186, 270b, 289, 290a, 306	59.45	50.00
PS39	1998	25,000 KM309-313	73.50	55.00
PS40	1998	61,000 KM316 w/China Y-727	72.50	30.00
PS41	1998	I.A. KM318-321	44.45	38.00
PS42	1998	1,000 KM322-325	1,552	2,500
PS43	1998	25,000 KM310-313, 332	73.50	30.00
PS44	1999	I.A. KM182a-184a, 186, 270c, 289, 290a,	59.45	90.00
PS45	1999	I.A. KM335-338	39.95	40.00
PS46	1999	I.A. KM342a-353a	99.45	75.00
PS47	1999	I.A. KM359-362	1,425	2,520
PS49	2000	— KM389-392	44.00	40.00
PS50	2000	600 KM405-408	1,416	2,520
PS48	2000	— KM373a, 374a, 375a, 376a, 377a, 378a, 379a, 380a, 381a, 382a, 383a, 384.2a	101	90.00

PROOF-LIKE DOLLARS

KM	Date	Mintage Identification	Issue Price	Mkt Val
D1.1	1951	I.A. KM46, Canoe		250
D1.2	1951	I.A. KM46, Arnprior		700
D2.1	1952	I.A. KM46, water lines		1,100
D2.2	1952	I.A. KM46, without water lines		350
D3	1953	1,200 KM54, Canoe w/shoulder fold	—	325
D4	1954	5,300 KM54, Canoe	1.25	150
D5	1955	7,950 KM54, Canoe	1.25	125
D5a	1955	KM54, Arnprior	1.25	175
D6	1956	10,212 KM54, Canoe	1.25	70.00
D7	1957	16,241 KM54, Canoe	1.25	40.00
D8	1958	33,237 KM55, British Columbia	1.25	25.00
D9	1959	45,160 KM54, Canoe	1.25	15.00
D10	1960	82,728 KM54, Canoe	1.25	10.00
D11	1961	120,928 KM54, Canoe	1.25	9.50
D12	1962	248,901 KM54, Canoe	1.25	9.50
D13	1963	963,525 KM54, Canoe	1.25	9.50
D14	1964	2,862,441 KM58, Charlottetown	1.25	9.50
D15	1965	2,904,352 KM64.1, Canoe	—	9.50
D16	1966	672,514 KM64.1, Canoe	—	9.50
D17	1967	1,036,176 KM70, Confederation	—	9.50

PROOF-LIKE SETS (PL)

KM	Date	Mintage Identification	Issue Price	Mkt Val
PL1	1953	1,200 KM49 w/o shoulder fold, 50-54	2.20	1,250
PL2	1953	I.A. KM49-54	2.20	760
PL3	1954	3,000 KM49-54	2.50	450
PL4	1954	KM49 w/o shoulder fold, 50-54	2.50	1,100
PL5	1955	6,300 KM49, 50a, 51-54	2.50	375
PL6	1955	I.A. KM49, 50a, 51-54, Arnprior	2.50	500
PL7	1956	6,500 KM49, 50a, 51-54	2.50	225
PL8	1957	11,862 KM49, 50a, 51-54	2.50	150
PL9	1958	18,259 KM49, 50a, 51-53, 55	2.50	100
PL10	1959	31,577 KM49, 50a, 51, 52, 54, 56	2.50	45.00
PL11	1960	64,097 KM49, 50a, 51, 52, 54, 56	3.00	35.00
PL12	1961	98,373 KM49, 50a, 51, 52, 54, 56	3.00	30.00
PL13	1962	200,950 KM49, 50a, 51, 52, 54, 56	3.00	17.50
PL14	1963	673,006 KM49, 51, 52, 54, 56, 57	3.00	17.00
PL15	1964	1,653,162 KM49, 51, 52, 56-58	3.00	17.00
PL16	1965	2,904,352 KM59.1-60.1, 61-63, 64.1	4.00	17.00
PL17	1966	672,514 KM59.1-60.1, 61-63, 64.1	4.00	17.00
PL18	1967	961,887 KM65-70 (pliofilm flat pack)	4.00	17.00
PL18A	1967	70,583 KM65-70 and Silver Medal (red box)	12.00	29.00
PL18B	1967	337,688 KM65-71 (black box)	40.00	475
PL19	1968	521,641 KM59.1-60.1, 62b, 72a, 75.1-76.1	4.00	2.25
PL20	1969	326,203 KM59.1-60.1, 62b, 75.1-77.1	4.00	2.75
PL21	1970	349,120 KM59.1-60.1, 62b, 75.1, 77.1, 78	4.00	3.25

KM	Date	Mintage Identification	Issue Price	Mkt Val
PL22	1971	253,311 KM59.1-60.1, 62b, 75.1, 77.1, 79	4.00	2.75
PL23	1972	224,275 KM59.1-60.1, 62b-77.1	4.00	2.75
PL24	1973	243,695 KM59.1-60.1, 62b-75.1 obv. 120 beads, 77.1, 81.1, 82	4.00	4.00
PL25	1973	I.A. KM59.1-60.1, 62b-75.1 obv. 132 beads, 77.1, 81.2, 82	4.00	250
PL26	1974	213,589 KM59.1-60.1, 62b-75.1, 77.1, 88	5.00	3.00
PL27.1	1975	197,372 KM59.1, 60.1, 62b-75.1, 76.2, 77.1	5.00	3.50
PL27.2	1975	I.A. KM59.1, 60.1, 62b-75.1, 76.3, 77.1	5.00	5.00
PL28	1976	171,737 KM59.1, 60.1, 62b-75.1, 76.2, 77.1	5.15	2.75
PL29	1977	225,307 KM59.1, 60.1, 62b, 75.2, 77.1, 117.1	5.15	2.75
PL30	1978	260,000 KM59.1, 60.1, 62b, 75.3, 77.1, 120.1	5.25	2.75
PL31	1979	187,624 KM59.2-60.2, 74, 75.3, 77.2, 120.1	6.25	2.75
PL32	1980	410,842 KM60.2, 74, 75.3, 77.2, 120.1, 127	6.50	4.50
PL33	1981	186,250 KM60.2, 74, 75.3, 77.2, 120.1, 123	5.00	3.25
PL34	1982	203,287 KM60.2, 74, 75.3, 77.2, 120.1, 123	6.00	3.50
PL36	1983	190,838 KM60.2a, 74, 75.3, 77.2, 120.1, 132	5.00	5.00
PL36.1	1983	I.A. KM60.2a, 74, 75.3, 77.2, 120.1, 132; set in folder packaged by British Royal Mint Coin Club	—	—
PL37	1984	181,249 KM60.2a, 74, 75.3, 77.2, 120.1, 132	5.25	5.00
PL38	1985	173,924 KM60.2a, 74, 75.3, 77.2, 120.1, 132	5.25	6.00
PL39	1986	167,338 KM60.2a, 74, 75.3, 77.2, 120.1, 132	5.25	6.50
PL40	1987	212,136 KM60.2a, 74, 75.3, 77.2, 120.1, 132	5.25	5.00
PL41	1988	182,048 KM60.2a, 74, 75.3, 77.2, 132, 157	6.05	5.00
PL42	1989	173,622 KM60.2a, 74, 75.3, 77.2, 132, 157	6.60	8.00
PL43	1990	170,791 KM181-186	7.40	8.00
PL44	1991	147,814 KM181-186	7.40	25.00
PL45	1992	217,597 KM204-209	8.25	11.00
PL46	1993	171,680 KM181-186	8.25	4.00
PL47	1994	141,676 KM181-185, 258	8.50	5.50
PL48	1994	18,794 KM181-185, 258 (Oh Canada holder)	—	8.50
PL49	1995	143,892 KM181-186	6.95	6.00
PL50	1995	50,927 KM181-186 (Oh Canada holder)	14.65	8.50
PL51	1995	36,443 KM181-186 (Baby Gift holder)	—	9.00
PL52	1996	116,736 KM181-186	—	27.00
PL53	1996	29,747 KM181-186 (Baby Gift holder)	—	14.00
PL54	1996	I.A. KM181a-185a, 186	8.95	16.00
PL55	1996	I.A. KM181a-185a, 186 (Oh Canada holder)	14.65	12.00
PL56	1996	I.A. KM181a-185a, 186 (Baby Gift holder)	—	12.00
PL57	1997	I.A. KM182a-184a, 209, 270, 289-290	10.45	8.00
PL58	1997	I.A. KM182a-184a, 270, 289-291 (Oh Canada holder)	16.45	30.00
PL59	1997	I.A. KM182a-184a, 209, 270, 289-290 (Baby Gift holder)	18.50	9.50
PL60	1998	I.A. KM182a-184, 186, 270, 289-290	10.45	15.00
PL61	1998	I.A. KM182a-184, 186, 270, 289-290 (Oh Canada holder)	16.45	17.00
PL62	1998	I.A. KM182a-184, 186, 270, 289-290 (Tiny Treasures holder)	16.45	17.00
PL63	1999	I.A. KM342-353	16.95	10.00
PL64	2000	— KM373-384	16.95	10.00

SPECIMEN SETS (SS)

KM	Date	Mintage Identification	Issue Price	Mkt Val
SS12	1902	100 KM8-12	—	25,000
SS13	1902	I.A. KM9 (Large H), 10, 11	—	6,500
SS14	1903	I.A. KM10, 12, 13	—	7,000
SS15	1908	1,000 KM8, 10-13	—	2,200
SS16	1911	1,000 KM15-19	—	5,500
SS17	1911/12	5 KM15-20, 26-27	—	52,250
SS18	1921	I.A. KM22-25, 28	—	120,000
SS19	1922	I.A. KM28, 29	—	2,500
SS20	1923	I.A. KM28, 29	—	5,000
SS21	1924	I.A. KM28, 29	—	4,000
SS22	1925	I.A. KM28, 29	—	7,000
SS23	1926	I.A. KM28, 29 (Near 6)	—	5,000
SS24	1927	I.A. KM24a, 28, 29	—	8,000
SS25	1928	I.A. KM23a, 24a, 28, 29	—	12,000
SS26	1929	I.A. KM23a,-25a, 28, 29	—	22,500
SS27	1930	I.A. KM23a, 24a, 28, 29	—	16,000
SS28	1931	I.A. KM23a-25a, 28, 29	—	26,500
SS29	1932	I.A. KM23a-25a, 28, 29	—	20,000
SS30	1934	I.A. KM23-25, 28, 29	—	23,000
SS31	1936	I.A. KM23-25, 28, 29	—	12,000
SS32	1936	I.A. KM23a(dot), 24a(dot), 25a, 28(dot), 29, 30	—	400,000
SS33	1937	1,025 KM32-37, Matte Finish	—	750
SS34	1937	I.A. KM32-35, Mirror Fields	—	1,350
SS35	1937	75 KM32-37, Mirror Fields	—	3,900
SS36	1938	I.A. KM32-37	—	18,250
SS-A36	1939	I.A. KM32-35, 38, Matte Finish	—	1,000
SS-B36	1939	I.A. KM32-35, 38, Mirror Fields	—	1,000
SS-C36	1942	I.A. KM32, 33	—	1,000
SS-D36	1943	I.A. KM32, 40	—	1,000
SS-A37	1944	I.A. KM32, 40a	—	1,000
SS37	1944	3 KM32, 34-37, 40a	—	11,300
SS-A38	1945	I.A. KM32, 40a	—	1,000
SS38	1945	6 KM32, 34-37, 40a	—	4,650
SS39	1946	15 KM32, 34-37, 39a	—	4,000
SS40	1947	I.A. KM32, 34-37(7 curved), 37(7 pointed),	—	8,500
SS41	1947	I.A. KM32, 34-36(7 curved), 37(blunt 7), 39a	—	6,200
SS42	1947	I.A. KM32, 34-36(7 curved right), 37, 39a	—	4,250
SS43	1948	30 KM41-46	—	6,000
SS44	1949	20 KM41-45, 47	—	6,400
SS44A	1949	I.A. KM47	—	1,550
SS45	1950	12 KM41-46	—	1,650
SS46	1950	I.A. KM41-45, 46 (Arnprior)	—	3,175
SS47	1951	12 KM41, 48, 42a, 43-46 (w/water lines)	—	2,725
SS48	1952	2,317 KM41, 42a, 43-46 (water lines)	—	3,175
SS48A	1952	I.A. KM41, 42a, 43-46 (w/o water lines)	—	3,175
SS49	1953	28 KM49 w/o straps, 50-54	—	1,850
SS50	1953	I.A. KM49 w/ straps, 50-54	—	875
SS51	1964	I.A. KM49, 51, 52, 56-58	—	850
SS52	1965	I.A. KM59.1-60.1, 61-63, 64.1	—	850
SS56	1971	66,860 KM59.1-60.1, 62b-75.1, 77.1, 79 (2 pcs.); Double Dollar Prestige Sets	12.00	14.50

KM	Date	Mintage	Identification	Issue Price	Mkt Val
SS57	1972	36,349	KM59.1,-60.1, 62b-75.1, 76.1 (2 pcs.)	12.00	18.00
SS58	1973	119,819	KM59.1-60.1, 75.1, 77.1, 81.1, 82, 83	12.00	16.00
SS59	1973	—	I.A. KM59.1-60.1, 75.1, 77.1, 81.2, 82, 83	—	225
SS60	1974	85,230	KM59.1-60.1, 62b-75.1, 76.2, 77.1, 97	15.00	10.00
SS61	1975	97,263	KM59.1-60.1, 62b-75.1, 76.2, 77.1, 97	15.00	10.00
SS62	1976	87,744	KM59.1-60, 62b-75.1, 76.2, 77.1, 106	16.00	10.00
SS63	1977	142,577	KM59.1-60.1, 62b, 75.2, 77.1, 117.1, 118	16.50	10.00
SS64	1978	147,000	KM59.1-60.1, 62b, 75.3, 77.1, 120.1, 121	16.50	10.00
SS65	1979	155,698	KM59.2-60.2, 74, 75.3, 77.2, 120, 124	18.50	11.50
SS66	1980	162,875	KM60.2, 74-75.3, 77.2, 120, 127, 128	30.50	22.50
SS67	1981	71,300	KM60.2, 74, 75.3, 77.2, 120.1, 127	10.00	5.50
SS68	1982	62,298	KM60.2a, 74, 75.3, 77.2, 120.1, 132	11.50	5.50
SS69	1983	60,329	KM60.2a, 74, 75.3, 77.2, 120.1, 132	12.75	5.50
SS70	1984	60,400	KM60.2a, 74, 75.3, 77.2, 120.1, 132	—	5.50
SS71	1985	61,553	KM60.2a, 74, 75.3, 77.2, 120.1, 132	10.00	6.00
SS72	1986	67,152	KM60.2a, 74, 75.3, 77.2, 120.1, 132	10.00	9.00
SS72A	1987	75,194	KM60.2a, 74, 75.3, 77.2, 120.1, 132	11.00	6.50
SS73	1988	70,205	KM60.2a, 74, 75.3, 77.2, 132, 157	12.30	6.50
SS74	1989	75,306	KM60.2a, 74, 75.3, 77.2, 132, 157	14.50	8.50
SS75	1990	76,611	KM181-186	15.50	8.50
SS76	1991	68,552	KM181-186	15.50	30.00
SS77	1992	78,328	KM204-209	16.25	13.00
SS78	1993	77,351	KM181-186	16.25	13.00
SS79	1994	77,349	KM181-186	16.50	9.50
SS80	1995	—	I.A. KM181-186	13.95	9.50
SS82	1996	—	I.A. KM181a-185a, 186	18.95	19.00
SS83	1997	—	I.A. KM182a-184a, 270, 289-291	19.95	25.00
SS84	1998	—	I.A. KM182-184, 186, 270, 289, 290	19.95	18.00
SS85	1999	—	I.A. KM182-184, 186, 270, 289a, 290	19.95	11.00

V.I.P. SPECIMEN SETS (VS)

KM	Date	Mintage	Identification	Issue Price	Mkt Val
VS1	1969	4		—	2,000
VS2	1970	100	KM59.1-60.1, 74.1-75.1, 77.1, 78	—	525
VS3	1971	69	KM59.1-60.1, 74.1-75.1, 77.1, 79(2 pcs.)	—	525
VS4	1972	25	KM59.1-60.1, 74.1-75.1, 76.1, (2 pcs.), 77.1	—	650
VS5	1973	26	KM59.1-60.1, 75.1, 77.1, 81.1, 82, 83	—	650
VS6	1974	72	KM59.1-60.1, 74.1-75.1, 77.1, 88, 88a	—	525
VS7	1975	94	KM59.1-60.1, 74.1-75.1, 76.2, 77.1, 97	—	525
VS8	1976	—	I.A. KM59.1-60.1, 74.1-75.1, 76.2, 77.1, 106	—	525

NEWFOUNDLAND

PROVINCE

Island which along with Labrador became a province of Canada. Prehistoric inhabitants left evidence of an early presence on the island. Norsemen briefly settled on the island but officially discovered in 1497 by Italian explorer John Cabot. English settlements were sporadic and disputed by France. The English settled along the east coast and the French along the west coast of the island. With the treaty of Utrecht in 1713, it officially became English, but the fishing rights went to France. Controversies continued through the 19th century.

CIRCULATION COINAGE

KM# 9 LARGE CENT Bronze **Obv.:** Crowned bust right **Obv. Des.:** G.W. DeSaulles **Rev.:** Crown and date within center circle, wreath surrounds, denomination above **Rev. Des.:** Horace Morehen

Date	Mintage	VG-8	F-12	VF-20	XF-40	MS-60	MS-63	Proof
1904H	100,000	7.00	14.00	20.00	55.00	300	700	—
1904H Proof	—							4,000
1907	200,000	2.00	4.00	8.00	30.00	220	650	—
1909	200,000	2.00	4.00	7.00	19.00	100	150	—
1909 Proof	—							400

KM# 16 LARGE CENT Bronze **Obv.:** Crowned bust left **Obv. Des.:** E.B. MacKennal **Rev.:** Crown and date within center circle, wreath surrounds, denomination above **Rev. Des.:** Horace Morehen

Date	Mintage	VG-8	F-12	VF-20	XF-40	MS-60	MS-63	Proof
1913	400,000	1.00	1.50	3.00	7.00	40.00	75.00	—
1917C	702,350	1.00	1.50	3.00	6.00	75.00	200	—
1917C Proof	—							800

Date	Mintage	VG-8	F-12	VF-20	XF-40	MS-60	MS-63	Proof
1919C	300,000	1.00	2.00	3.00	10.00	175	300	—
1919C Proof	—							1,000
1920C	302,184	1.00	2.00	5.00	18.00	300	1,000	—
1929	300,000	1.00	1.50	3.00	6.00	55.00	100	—
1929C Proof	—							1,000
1936	300,000	1.00	1.25	1.75	4.00	28.00	75.00	—

KM# 18 SMALL CENT 3.2000 g. Bronze **Obv.:** Crowned head left **Obv. Des.:** Percy Metcalfe **Rev.:** Pitcher plant divides date, denomination below **Rev. Des.:** Walter J. Newman **Size:** 19 mm.

Date	Mintage	VG-8	F-12	VF-20	XF-40	MS-60	MS-63	Proof
1938	500,000	0.50	0.75	1.50	2.50	16.00	40.00	—
1938 Proof	—							1,000
1940	300,000	1.25	2.00	3.00	10.00	75.00	250	—
1940 Proof	—							1,000
1940 Re-engraved date	—	30.00	40.00	125	70.00	500	900	—
1941C	827,662	0.35	0.45	0.70	2.00	20.00	120	—
1941C Re-engraved date	—	9.00	13.00	30.00	65.00	250	700	—
1942	1,996,889	0.35	0.45	0.70	2.00	30.00	125	—
1943C	1,239,732	0.35	0.45	0.70	2.00	13.50	70.00	—
1944C	1,328,776	1.00	2.00	10.00	30.00	250	550	—
1947C	313,772	0.90	1.65	5.00	12.00	80.00	200	—
1947C Proof	—							2,000

KM# 7 5 CENTS 1.1782 g. 0.9250 Silver 0.0350 oz. ASW **Obv.:** Crowned bust right **Rev.:** Denomination and date within circle

Date	Mintage	VG-8	F-12	VF-20	XF-40	MS-60	MS-63	Proof
1903	100,000	4.00	9.00	18.00	45.00	435	1,350	—
1903 Proof	—							2,000
1904H	100,000	3.00	5.00	14.00	35.00	160	285	—
1904H Proof	—							1,200
1908	400,000	3.00	6.00	11.50	30.00	260	750	—

KM# 13 5 CENTS 1.1782 g. 0.9250 Silver 0.0350 oz. ASW **Obv.:** Crowned bust left **Obv. Des.:** E.B. MacKennal **Rev.:** Denomination and date within circle **Rev. Des.:** G.W. DeSaulles

Date	Mintage	VG-8	F-12	VF-20	XF-40	MS-60	MS-63	Proof
1912	300,000	1.50	2.00	5.00	20.00	125	275	—
1912 Proof	—							2,000
1917C	300,319	1.50	3.00	7.00	25.00	250	650	—
1917C Proof	—							2,000
1919C	100,844	5.00	9.00	25.00	100	950	2,800	—
1919C Proof	—							2,000
1929	300,000	1.50	2.50	3.25	12.00	165	350	—

KM# 19 5 CENTS 1.1782 g. 0.9250 Silver 0.0350 oz. ASW **Obv.:** Crowned head left **Obv. Des.:** Percy Metcalfe **Rev.:** Denomination and date within circle **Rev. Des.:** G.W. DeSaulles

Date	Mintage	VG-8	F-12	VF-20	XF-40	MS-60	MS-63	Proof
1938	100,000	0.85	1.50	2.00	7.00	70.00	225	—
1938 Proof	—							1,000
1940C	200,000	0.85	1.50	2.00	7.00	85.00	300	—
1940C Proof	—							2,000
1941C	621,641	0.65	1.50	2.00	4.00	15.00	35.00	—
1942C	298,348	0.85	1.50	2.00	4.00	17.50	40.00	—
1943C	351,666	0.65	1.00	2.00	4.00	15.00	30.00	—

KM# 19a 5 CENTS 1.1664 g. 0.8000 Silver 0.0300 oz. ASW **Obv.:** Crowned head left **Obv. Des.:** Percy Metcalfe **Rev.:** Denomination and date within circle **Rev. Des.:** G.W. DeSaulles **Edge:** Reeded **Size:** 15.67 mm.

Date	Mintage	VG-8	F-12	VF-20	XF-40	MS-60	MS-63	Proof
1944C	286,504	1.25	1.75	3.00	7.00	50.00	120	—
1945C	203,828	0.65	1.00	2.00	4.00	14.00	32.00	—
1946C	2,041	200	300	350	400	1,200	1,900	—
1946C Prooflike	—							2,500
1947C	38,400	2.00	3.00	5.00	17.00	65.00	200	—
1947C Prooflike	—							375

KM# 8 10 CENTS   2.3564 g. 0.9250 Silver 0.0701 oz. ASW **Obv.:** Crowned bust right
Rev.: Denomination and date within circle

Date	Mintage	VG-8	F-12	VF-20	XF-40	MS-60	MS-63	Proof
1903	100,000	8.00	25.00	70.00	200	1,200	4,400	—
1903 Proof	—	—	—	—	—	—	—	2,500
1904H	100,000	4.00	10.00	30.00	90.00	200	350	—
1904H Proof	—	—	—	—	—	—	—	1,500

KM# 14 10 CENTS   2.3564 g. 0.9250 Silver 0.0701 oz. ASW **Obv.:** Crowned bust left
Obv. Des.: E.B. MacKennal **Rev. Des.:** G.W. DeSaulles

Date	Mintage	VG-8	F-12	VF-20	XF-40	MS-60	MS-63	Proof
1912	150,000	1.20	3.00	10.00	40.00	165	300	—
1917C	250,805	1.20	3.00	11.00	40.00	400	1,500	—
1919C	54,342	2.00	6.00	18.00	55.00	175	350	—

KM# 20 10 CENTS   2.3564 g. 0.9250 Silver 0.0701 oz. ASW **Obv.:** Crowned head left
Obv. Des.: Percy Metcalfe **Rev.:** Denomination and date within circle **Rev. Des.:** G.W. DeSaulles

Date	Mintage	VG-8	F-12	VF-20	XF-40	MS-60	MS-63	Proof
1938	100,000	1.10	1.75	3.00	11.00	80.00	300	—
1938 Proof	—	—	—	—	—	—	—	2,000
1940	100,000	1.10	1.50	3.00	10.00	80.00	300	—
1940 Proof	—	—	—	—	—	—	—	2,500
1941C	483,630	1.10	1.50	2.20	5.00	40.00	125	—
1942C	293,736	1.10	1.50	2.20	5.00	50.00	130	—
1943C	104,706	1.10	1.50	2.50	6.00	60.00	200	—
1944C	151,471	2.50	3.50	10.00	20.00	200	800	—

KM# 20a 10 CENTS   2.3328 g. 0.8000 Silver 0.0600 oz. ASW **Obv.:** Crowned head left
Obv. Des.: Percy Metcalfe **Rev. Des.:** G.W. DeSaulles

Date	Mintage	VG-8	F-12	VF-20	XF-40	MS-60	MS-63	Proof
1945C	175,833	1.00	1.35	2.25	4.50	45.00	225	—
1946C	38,400	2.00	4.00	10.00	25.00	100	275	—
1946C Proof	—	—	—	—	—	—	—	750
1947C	61,988	1.50	3.00	4.50	14.00	65.00	275	—

KM# 10 20 CENTS   4.7127 g. 0.9250 Silver 0.1401 oz. ASW **Obv.:** Crowned bust right
Obv. Des.: G.W. DeSaulles **Rev.:** Denomination and date within circle **Rev. Des.:** W.H.J. Blakemore

Date	Mintage	VG-8	F-12	VF-20	XF-40	MS-60	MS-63	Proof
1904H	75,000	10.00	30.00	55.00	275	2,500	6,000	—
1904H Proof	—	—	—	—	—	—	—	1,850

KM# 15 20 CENTS   4.7127 g. 0.9250 Silver 0.1401 oz. ASW **Obv.:** Crowned bust left
Obv. Des.: E.B. MacKennal **Rev.:** Denomination and date within circle **Rev. Des.:** W.H.J. Blakemore

Date	Mintage	VG-8	F-12	VF-20	XF-40	MS-60	MS-63	Proof
1912	350,000	2.50	5.00	14.00	55.00	325	850	—
1912 Proof	—	—	—	—	—	—	—	2,500

KM# 17 25 CENTS   5.8319 g. 0.9250 Silver 0.1734 oz. ASW **Obv.:** Crowned bust left
Obv. Des.: E.B. MacKennal **Rev.:** Denomination and date within circle **Rev. Des.:** W.H.J. Blakemore

Date	Mintage	VG-8	F-12	VF-20	XF-40	MS-60	MS-63	Proof
1917C	464,779	3.00	4.00	7.00	17.00	145	300	—
1917C Proof	—	—	—	—	—	—	—	2,500
1919C	163,939	3.00	5.00	14.00	25.00	350	1,250	—
1919C Proof	—	—	—	—	—	—	—	2,500

KM# 11 50 CENTS   11.7800 g. 0.9250 Silver 0.3503 oz. ASW **Obv.:** Crowned bust right
Obv. Des.: G.W. DeSaulles **Rev. Des.:** W.H.J. Blakemore **Size:** 30 mm.

Date	Mintage	VG-8	F-12	VF-20	XF-40	MS-60	MS-63	Proof
1904H	140,000	5.00	6.00	14.00	55.00	275	850	—
1904H Proof	—	—	—	—	—	—	—	5,000
1907	100,000	5.00	6.00	22.00	65.00	350	1,000	—
1908	160,000	5.00	6.00	13.50	50.00	225	700	—
1909	200,000	5.00	12.00	21.00	55.00	300	800	—

KM# 12 50 CENTS   11.7800 g. 0.9250 Silver 0.3503 oz. ASW **Obv.:** Crowned bust left
Obv. Des.: E.B. MacKennal **Rev.:** Denomination and date within circle **Rev. Des.:** W.H.J. Blakemore **Size:** 30 mm.

Date	Mintage	VG-8	F-12	VF-20	XF-40	MS-60	MS-63	Proof
1911	200,000	5.00	6.00	11.00	35.00	200	550	—
1917C	375,560	5.00	6.00	11.00	28.00	145	350	—
1917C Proof	—	—	—	—	—	—	—	2,500
1918C	294,824	5.00	6.00	11.00	28.00	145	350	—
1919C	306,267	5.00	6.00	11.00	30.00	325	1,150	—
1919C Proof	—	—	—	—	—	—	—	2,500

TRIAL STRIKES

KM	Date	Mintage	Identification	Mkt Val
TS3	1945	—	10 Cents. Nickel.	—

CAPE VERDE

MAURITANIA
GAMBIA
SENEGAL
GUINEA BISSAU
GUINEA

The Republic of Cape Verde, Africa's smallest republic, is located in the Atlantic Ocean, about 370 miles (595 km.) west of Dakar, Senegal, off the coast of Africa. The 14-island republic has an area of 1,557 sq. mi. (4,033 sq. km.) and a population of 435,983. Capital: Praia. The refueling of ships and aircraft is the chief economic function of the country. Fishing is important and agriculture is widely practiced, but the Cape Verdes are not self-sufficient in food. Fish products, salt, bananas, and shellfish are exported.

The date of discovery of the islands is uncertain. Possibly they were visited by Venetian captain Alvise Cadamosto in 1456. Portuguese navigator Diogo Gomes claimed them for Portugal in May of 1460. Settlement began two years later. The early importance and wealth of the islands, which caused them to be attacked by Sir Francis Drake and the Dutch, resulted from the monopoly of the Guinea slave trade granted the inhabitants in 1466. Poverty and famine occasioned by frequent periods of severe drought have marked the history of the country since abolition of the slave trade in 1876.

After 500 years of Portuguese rule, the Cape Verdes became independent on July 5, 1975. At the first general election, all seats of the new national assembly were won by the Party for the Independence of Guinea-Bissau and Cape Verde (PAIGC). The PAIGC linked the two former colonies into one state. Antonio Mascarenhas Monteiro won the first free presidential election in 1991.

RULER
Portuguese, until 1975

MONETARY SYSTEM
100 Centavos = 1 Escudo

PORTUGUESE COLONY

COLONIAL COINAGE

KM# 1   5 CENTAVOS
Bronze   Obv: Liberty head left Rev: Denomination at center, date below

Date	Mintage	F	VF	XF	Unc	BU
1930	1,000,000	0.75	1.50	3.50	10.00	—

KM# 2   10 CENTAVOS
Bronze   Obv: Denomination at center, date below Rev: Liberty head left

Date	Mintage	F	VF	XF	Unc	BU
1930	1,500,000	0.75	1.50	4.00	12.00	—

KM# 3   20 CENTAVOS
Bronze   Obv: Denomination at center, date below Rev: Liberty head left

Date	Mintage	F	VF	XF	Unc	BU
1930	1,500,000	1.00	2.00	5.00	15.00	—

KM# 4   50 CENTAVOS
Nickel-Bronze   Obv: Liberty head right, long loose hair Rev: Encircled arms within wreath, denomination below

Date	Mintage	F	VF	XF	Unc	BU
1930	1,000,000	7.00	30.00	95.00	275.	—

KM# 6   50 CENTAVOS
Nickel-Bronze   Obv: Denomination Rev: Miniature crowns above encircled arms, date below

Date	Mintage	F	VF	XF	Unc	BU
1949	1,000,000	0.50	1.00	2.50	6.00	—

KM# 11   50 CENTAVOS
3.4000 g., Bronze, 20 mm.   Obv: Denomination Rev: Miniature crowns above arms, date below

Date	Mintage	F	VF	XF	Unc	BU
1968	1,000,000	0.25	0.50	1.00	2.50	—

KM# 5   ESCUDO
Nickel-Bronze, 26 mm.   Obv: Liberty head right, long loose hair Rev: Encircled arms within wreath, denomination below

Date	Mintage	F	VF	XF	Unc	BU
1930	50,000	15.00	65.00	125	350	—

KM# 7   ESCUDO
Nickel-Bronze, 26 mm.   Obv: Denomination Rev: Miniature crowns above encircled arms, date below

Date	Mintage	F	VF	XF	Unc	BU
1949	500,000	1.25	2.50	5.50	12.50	—

KM# 8   ESCUDO
8.0000 g., Bronze, 26 mm.   Obv: Denomination Rev: Miniature crowns above encircled arms, date below

Date	Mintage	F	VF	XF	Unc	BU
1953	250,000	1.00	5.00	18.00	35.00	—
1968	500,000	0.50	1.00	2.00	5.00	—

KM# 9   2-1/2 ESCUDOS
3.5000 g., Nickel-Bronze, 20 mm.   Obv: Arms on cross, date below Rev: Miniature crowns above arms, denomination below

Date	Mintage	F	VF	XF	Unc	BU
1953	500,000	1.50	8.00	35.00	85.00	—
1967	400,000	0.50	1.00	2.50	8.00	—

KM# 12   5 ESCUDOS
4.4100 g., Nickel-Bronze, 21 mm.   Obv: Miniature crowns above arms, denomination below Rev: Arms on cross, date below

Date	Mintage	F	VF	XF	Unc	BU
1968	200,000	0.75	1.50	3.50	10.00	—

KM# 10   10 ESCUDOS
5.0000 g., 0.7200 Silver 0.1157 oz. ASW   Obv: Arms on cross, date below Rev: Miniature crowns above arms, denomination below

Date	Mintage	F	VF	XF	Unc	BU
1953	400,000	2.00	3.50	6.50	18.00	—

REPUBLIC

DECIMAL COINAGE

KM# 15   20 CENTAVOS
1.3000 g., Aluminum, 21 mm.   Obv: Emblem within wreath, date below Rev: Denomination above fish

Date	Mintage	F	VF	XF	Unc	BU
1977	—	0.10	0.20	0.30	0.65	—
1980	—	0.10	0.20	0.30	0.65	—

KM# 16   50 CENTAVOS
2.1000 g., Aluminum, 24.5 mm.   Obv: Emblem within wreath, date below Rev: Denomination above fish

Date	Mintage	F	VF	XF	Unc	BU
1977	—	0.15	0.25	0.40	0.85	—
1980	—	0.15	0.25	0.40	0.85	—

KM# 17   ESCUDO
4.1000 g., Nickel-Bronze, 23.5 mm.   Series: F.A.O. Subject: Education Obv: Emblem within wreath, denomination below, date at bottom Rev: Student at desk Edge: Reeded

Date	Mintage	F	VF	XF	Unc	BU
1977	1,000,000	0.25	0.50	0.85	1.75	3.00
1980	—	0.25	0.50	0.85	1.75	3.00

KM# 23   ESCUDO
3.9500 g., Brass Plated Steel, 23.5 mm. **Subject:** 10th Anniversary of Independence **Obv:** Emblem within wreath below denomination and date **Rev:** Inscription below building **Edge:** Reeded

Date	Mintage	F	VF	XF	Unc	BU
1985	—			0.75	1.50	2.50
1985 Proof	—	Value: 350				

KM# 23a   ESCUDO
4.0000 g., 0.9250 Silver 0.1190 oz. ASW, 23.5 mm. **Subject:** 10th Anniversary of Independence **Obv:** Emblem within wreath below denomination and date **Rev:** Inscription below building

Date	Mintage	F	VF	XF	Unc	BU
1985 Proof	—	Value: 350				

KM# 23b   ESCUDO
6.0000 g., 0.7500 Gold 0.1447 oz. AGW **Subject:** 10th Anniversary of Independence **Obv:** Emblem within wreath below denomination and date **Rev:** Inscription below building

Date	Mintage	F	VF	XF	Unc	BU
1985 Proof	50	Value: 250				

KM# 27   ESCUDO
2.5500 g., Brass Plated Steel, 18 mm. **Obv:** Denomination on National emblem, date below **Rev:** Tartaruga Sea Turtle **Edge:** Plain

Date	Mintage	F	VF	XF	Unc	BU
1994	—				1.00	1.25

KM# 18   2-1/2 ESCUDOS
7.0000 g., Nickel-Bronze, 26 mm. **Series:** F.A.O. **Obv:** Emblem within wreath above denomination and date **Rev:** Coffee tree planting

Date	Mintage	F	VF	XF	Unc	BU
1977	1,200,000	0.25	0.50	0.85	1.75	—
1980	—	0.25	0.50	0.85	1.75	3.00
1982	—	0.25	0.50	0.85	1.75	—

KM# 28   5 ESCUDOS
3.9200 g., Copper Plated Steel, 20.97 mm. **Obv:** National emblem to right of denomination, date below **Rev:** Osprey

Date	Mintage	F	VF	XF	Unc	BU
1994	—				2.50	3.00

KM# 31   5 ESCUDOS
3.9600 g., Copper Plated Steel, 20.99 mm. **Obv:** National emblem to right of denomination, date below **Rev:** Flowers - Contra Bruxas

Date	Mintage	F	VF	XF	Unc	BU
1994	—				1.00	1.50

KM# 36   5 ESCUDOS
4.0000 g., Copper Plated Steel, 20.98 mm. **Obv:** National emblem to right of denomination, date below **Rev:** Sailboat - Belmira

Date	Mintage	F	VF	XF	Unc	BU
1994	—			1.00	1.50	

KM# 19   10 ESCUDOS
9.0000 g., Copper-Nickel, 28.1 mm. **Obv:** Emblem within wreath above denomination and date **Rev:** Eduardo Mondlane

Date	Mintage	F	VF	XF	Unc	BU
1977	—	0.25	0.50	1.00	2.25	—
1980	—	0.25	0.50	1.00	2.25	—
1982	—	0.20	0.40	0.75	2.00	—

KM# 24   10 ESCUDOS
Copper-Nickel **Subject:** 10th Anniversary of Independence **Obv:** Emblem within wreath below denomination and date **Rev:** Letter design at center, star above

Date	Mintage	F	VF	XF	Unc	BU
1985	—			2.00	3.00	
1985 Proof	—	Value: 350				

KM# 24a   10 ESCUDOS
9.0000 g., 0.9250 Silver 0.2676 oz. ASW **Subject:** 10th Anniversary of Independence **Obv:** Emblem within wreath below denomination and date **Rev:** Letter design at center, star above

Date	Mintage	F	VF	XF	Unc	BU
1985 Proof	—	Value: 145				

KM# 24b   10 ESCUDOS
9.0000 g., 0.7500 Gold 0.2170 oz. AGW **Subject:** 10th Anniversary of Independence **Obv:** Emblem within wreath below denomination and date **Rev:** Letter design at center, star above

Date	Mintage	F	VF	XF	Unc	BU
1985 Proof	50	Value: 400				

KM# 29   10 ESCUDOS
4.5100 g., Nickel Plated Steel **Obv:** National emblem, date at left, denomination upper left **Rev:** Brown-headed Kingfisher

Date	Mintage	F	VF	XF	Unc	BU
1994	—				4.00	5.00

KM# 32   10 ESCUDOS
4.5400 g., Nickel Plated Steel, 21.95 mm. **Obv:** National emblem, date at left, denomination upper left **Rev:** Flowers - Lingua De Vaca

Date	Mintage	F	VF	XF	Unc	BU
1994	—				1.50	2.00

KM# 41   10 ESCUDOS
4.5100 g., Nickel Plated Steel **Obv:** National emblem, date at left, denomination upper left **Rev:** Sailship "Carvalho"

Date	Mintage	F	VF	XF	Unc	BU
1994	—				1.50	2.00

KM# 20   20 ESCUDOS
12.0000 g., Copper-Nickel, 31.1 mm. **Obv:** Emblem within wreath above denomination and date **Rev:** Domingos Ramos

Date	Mintage	F	VF	XF	Unc	BU
1977	—	0.35	0.65	1.25	2.75	—
1980	—	0.35	0.65	1.25	2.75	—
1982	—	0.25	0.50	1.00	2.50	—

KM# 30   20 ESCUDOS
5.8000 g., Nickel Plated Steel, 24.94 mm. **Obv:** National emblem, date divided below, denomination at bottom **Rev:** Brown Booby

Date	Mintage	F	VF	XF	Unc	BU
1994	—				4.00	5.00

KM# 33   20 ESCUDOS
5.8000 g., Nickel Plated Steel, 24.93 mm. **Obv:** National emblem, date divided below, denomination at bottom **Rev:** Flowers - Carqueja

Date	Mintage	F	VF	XF	Unc	BU
1994	—				2.00	3.00

KM# 42   20 ESCUDOS
5.8100 g., Nickel Plated Steel, 24.90 mm. **Obv:** National emblem, date divided below, denomination at bottom **Rev:** Sailship "Novas de Alegria"

Date	Mintage	F	VF	XF	Unc	BU
1994	—				2.00	3.00

KM# 21   50 ESCUDOS
16.3000 g., Copper-Nickel, 34.1 mm. **Obv:** Emblem within wreath above denomination and date **Rev:** Head of Amilcar Lopes Cabral left, two dates on right

Date	Mintage	F	VF	XF	Unc	BU
1977	—	1.00	1.50	2.50	4.50	—
1980	—	1.00	1.50	2.50	4.50	—

KM# 22   50 ESCUDOS
16.0000 g., Copper-Nickel, 34 mm. **Series:** F.A.O.
Subject: World Fisheries Conference **Rev:** White sea bream fish left, two dates below

Date	Mintage	F	VF	XF	Unc	BU
1984	Est. 115,000	—	—	—	—	17.50

KM# 22a   50 ESCUDOS
16.0000 g., 0.9250 Silver 0.4758 oz. ASW, 34 mm.
Series: F.A.O. **Subject:** World Fisheries Conference **Rev:** White sea bream fish left, two dates below

Date	Mintage	F	VF	XF	Unc	BU
1984 Proof	Est. 20,000	Value: 50.00				

KM# 22b   50 ESCUDOS
27.0000 g., 0.9170 Gold 0.7960 oz. AGW **Series:** F.A.O.
Subject: World Fisheries Conference **Rev:** White sea bream fish left, two dates below

Date	Mintage	F	VF	XF	Unc	BU
1984 Proof	Est. 100,000	Value: 1,500				

KM# 37   50 ESCUDOS
7.4000 g., Copper Nickel, 27.89 mm. **Obv:** National emblem divides date, denomination above **Rev:** Cape Verde Sparrow left

Date	Mintage	F	VF	XF	Unc	BU
1994	—	—	—	—	12.00	15.00

KM# 43   50 ESCUDOS
Nickel Plated Steel, 27.99 mm. **Obv:** National emblem divides date, denomination above **Rev:** Sailship "Senhor das Areias"

Date	Mintage	F	VF	XF	Unc	BU
1994	—	—	—	—	5.00	6.00

KM# 44   50 ESCUDOS
5.0000 g., Nickel Plated Steel, 27.89 mm. **Obv:** National emblem **Rev:** Macelina flowers

Date	Mintage	F	VF	XF	Unc	BU
1994	—	—	—	—	5.00	6.00

KM# 25   100 ESCUDOS
Copper-Nickel **Subject:** Papal Visit **Obv:** Emblem within wreath above denomination and date **Rev:** Half figure of Pope

Date	Mintage	F	VF	XF	Unc	BU
1990	—	—	—	—	7.50	9.50

KM# 25b   100 ESCUDOS
33.4000 g., 0.9000 Gold 0.9664 oz. AGW **Subject:** Papal Visit **Obv:** Emblem within wreath above denomination and date **Rev:** Half figure of Pope

Date	Mintage	F	VF	XF	Unc	BU
1990 Proof	—	—				

KM# 25a   100 ESCUDOS
Silver **Subject:** Papal Visit **Obv:** Emblem within wreath above denomination and date **Rev:** Half figure of Pope

Date	Mintage	F	VF	XF	Unc	BU
1990 Proof	—	Value: 35.00				

KM# 38   100 ESCUDOS
Bi-Metallic Copper-Nickel center in Bronze ring **Obv:** National emblem divides date, denomination at top, value at bottom **Rev:** Saiao flowers

Date	Mintage	F	VF	XF	Unc	BU
1994	—	—	—	—	8.00	9.00

KM# 38a   100 ESCUDOS
Bi-Metallic Copper-Nickel center in Brass ring **Obv:** National emblem divides date, denomination at top, value at bottom **Rev:** Saiao flowers

Date	Mintage	F	VF	XF	Unc	BU
1994	—	—	—	—	8.00	9.00

KM# 39   100 ESCUDOS
Bi-Metallic Copper-Nickel center in Bronze ring **Obv:** National emblem divides date, denomination at top, value at bottom **Rev:** Raza Lark left within circle

Date	Mintage	F	VF	XF	Unc	BU
1994	—	—	—	—	12.50	13.50

KM# 39a   100 ESCUDOS
10.7100 g., Bi-Metallic Copper-Nickel center in Brass ring, 26 mm. **Obv:** National emblem divides date, denomination at top, value at bottom **Rev:** Calhandra do Ilheu Raso bird

Date	Mintage	F	VF	XF	Unc	BU
1994	—	—	—	—	12.50	13.50

KM# 40   100 ESCUDOS
Bi-Metallic Copper-Nickel center in Bronze ring **Obv:** National emblem divides date, denomination at top, value at bottom **Rev:** Sailship "Madalan"

Date	Mintage	F	VF	XF	Unc	BU
1994	—	—	—	—	9.00	10.00

KM# 40a   100 ESCUDOS
10.9200 g., Bi-Metallic Copper-Nickel center in Brass ring, 27 mm. **Obv:** National emblem divides date, denomination at top, value at bottom

Date	Mintage	F	VF	XF	Unc	BU
1994	—	—	—	—	9.00	10.00

KM# 34   200 ESCUDOS
Copper-Nickel **Series:** F.A.O. **Obv:** National emblem above denomination **Rev:** Globe on water, date at right

Date	Mintage	F	VF	XF	Unc	BU
1995	—	—	—	—	8.00	9.50

KM# 35   200 ESCUDOS
Copper-Nickel **Subject:** 20th Year of Independence **Obv:** National emblem above denomination **Rev:** Two figures back to back, two dates below

Date	Mintage	F	VF	XF	Unc	BU
ND(1995)	—	—	—	—	8.00	9.50

KM# 13   250 ESCUDOS
16.4000 g., 0.9000 Silver 0.4745 oz. ASW, 33.5 mm. **Subject:** 1st Anniversary of Independence **Obv:** Denomination at right above fish, date below **Rev:** Date in center, star divides chain at bottom

Date	Mintage	F	VF	XF	Unc	BU
1976	13,000	—	—	—	16.50	18.50
1976 Proof	3,525	Value: 32.50				

KM# 26   1000 ESCUDOS
28.1100 g., 0.9250 Silver 0.8359 oz. ASW **Subject:** Tordesilhas Treaty **Obv:** National emblem at center, denomination below **Rev:** Ship between maps, two dates above

Date	Mintage	F	VF	XF	Unc	BU
ND(1994)	—	—	—	—	25.00	27.50
ND(1994) Proof	Est. 10,000	Value: 45.00				

KM# 14   2500 ESCUDOS
8.0000 g., 0.9000 Gold 0.2315 oz. AGW **Subject:** 1st Anniversary of Independence **Obv:** Emblem within wreath above denomination **Rev:** Head left, date below

Date	Mintage	F	VF	XF	Unc	BU
1976 Proof	3,409	Value: 250				

PIEFORTS

KM#	Date	Mintage	Identification	Issue Price	Mkt Val
P1	1984	520	50 Escudos. 0.9250 Silver. KM22a.	—	75.00

PROVAS

KM#	Date	Mintage	Identification	Issue Price	Mkt Val
Pr1	1930	—	5 Centavos. Bronze. Stamped "PROVA" in field. KM1.	—	35.00
Pr2	1930	—	10 Centavos. Bronze. Stamped "PROVA" in field. KM2.	—	35.00
Pr3	1930	—	20 Centavos. Bronze. Stamped "PROVA" in field. KM3.	—	35.00
Pr4	1930	—	50 Centavos. Nickel-Bronze. Stamped "PROVA" in field. KM4.	—	75.00
Pr5	1930	—	Escudo. Nickel-Bronze. Stamped "PROVA" in field. KM5.	—	100
Pr6	1949	—	50 Centavos. Nickel-Bronze. Stamped "PROVA" in field. KM6.	—	30.00
Pr7	1949	—	Escudo. Nickel-Bronze. Stamped "PROVA" in field. KM7.	—	35.00
Pr8	1953	—	Escudo. Bronze. Stamped "PROVA" in field. KM8.	—	35.00
Pr9	1953	—	2-1/2 Escudos. Nickel-Bronze. Stamped "PROVA" in field. KM9.	—	30.00
Pr10	1953	—	10 Escudos. Silver. Stamped "PROVA" in field. KM10.	—	35.00
Pr11	1954	—	Escudo. Stamped "PROVA" in field.	—	22.50
Pr12	1954	—	2-1/2 Escudos. Stamped "PROVA" in field.	—	30.00
Pr13	1955	—	Escudo. Stamped "PROVA" in field.	—	22.50
Pr14	1955	—	2-1/2 Escudos. Stamped "PROVA" in field.	—	30.00
Pr15	1956	—	Escudo. Stamped "PROVA" in field.	—	22.50
Pr16	1956	—	2-1/2 Escudos. Stamped "PROVA" in field.	—	30.00
Pr17	1957	—	Escudo. Stamped "PROVA" in field.	—	22.50
Pr18	1957	—	2-1/2 Escudos. Stamped "PROVA" in field.	—	30.00
Pr19	1958	—	Escudo. Stamped "PROVA" in field.	—	22.50
Pr20	1958	—	2-1/2 Escudos. Stamped "PROVA" in field.	—	30.00
Pr21	1959	—	Escudo. Stamped "PROVA" in field.	—	22.50
Pr22	1959	—	2-1/2 Escudos. Stamped "PROVA" in field.	—	30.00
Pr23	1960	—	Escudo. Stamped "PROVA" in field.	—	22.50
Pr24	1960	—	2-1/2 Escudos. Stamped "PROVA" in field.	—	30.00
Pr25	1961	—	Escudo. Stamped "PROVA" in field.	—	22.50
Pr26	1961	—	2-1/2 Escudos. Stamped "PROVA" in field.	—	30.00
Pr27	1962	—	Escudo. Stamped "PROVA" in field.	—	22.50
Pr28	1962	—	2-1/2 Escudos. Stamped "PROVA" in field.	—	30.00
Pr29	1963	—	Escudo. Stamped "PROVA" in field.	—	22.50
Pr30	1963	—	2-1/2 Escudos. Stamped "PROVA" in field.	—	30.00
Pr31	1964	—	Escudo. Stamped "PROVA" in field.	—	22.50
Pr32	1964	—	2-1/2 Escudos. Stamped "PROVA" in field.	—	30.00
Pr33	1965	—	Escudo. Stamped "PROVA" in field.	—	22.50
Pr34	1965	—	2-1/2 Escudos. Stamped "PROVA" in field.	—	30.00
Pr35	1966	—	Escudo. Stamped "PROVA" in field.	—	22.50
Pr36	1966	—	2-1/2 Escudos. Stamped "PROVA" in field.	—	30.00
Pr37	1967	—	Escudo. Stamped "PROVA" in field.	—	17.50
Pr38	1967	—	2-1/2 Escudos. Nickel-Bronze. Stamped "PROVA" in field. KM9.	—	22.50
Pr39	1968	—	50 Centavos. Bronze. Stamped "PROVA" in field. KM11.	—	17.50
Pr40	1968	—	Escudo. Bronze center. Stamped "PROVA" in field. KM8.	—	22.50
Pr41	1968	—	5 Escudos. Nickel-Bronze. Stamped "PROVA" in field. KM12.	—	25.00

PROOF SETS

KM#	Date	Mintage	Identification	Issue Price	Mkt Val
PS1	1976-77 (4)	—	KM13-14 1976, KM17-18 1977	—	300
PS2	1985 (2)	—	KM23a, 24a	—	265
PSA2	1985 (2)	—	KM23 & 24	—	—

CAYMAN ISLANDS

The Cayman Islands is a British Crown Colony situated about 180 miles (280 km) northwest of Jamaica. It consists of three islands: Grand Cayman, Little Cayman, and Cayman Brac. The islands have an area of 102 sq. mi. (259 sq. km.) and a population of 33,200. Capital: George Town. Seafaring, commerce, banking, and tourism are the principal industries. Rope, turtle shells, and sharkskins are exported.

The islands were discovered by Columbus in 1503, and named by him Tortugas (Spanish for turtles') because of the great number of turtles in the nearby waters. Ceded to Britain in 1670, they were colonized from Jamaica by the British and remained dependencies of Jamaica until 1959, when they became a unit ter-

ritory within the Federation of the West Indies. They became a separate colony when the Federation was dissolved in 1962. Since 1972 a form of self-government has existed, with the Governor responsible for defense and certain other affairs.

While the islands used Jamaican currency for much of their history, the Caymans issued its first national coinage in 1972. The $25 gold and silver commemorative coins issued in 1972 to celebrate the silver wedding anniversary of Queen Elizabeth II and Prince Philip are the first coins in 300 years of Commonwealth coinage to portray a member of the British royal family other than the reigning monarch.

RULER
British

MINT MARKS
CHI - Valcambi
FM - Franklin Mint, U.S.A.*

MONETARY SYSTEM
100 Cents = 1 Dollar

BRITISH COLONY
DECIMAL COINAGE

KM# 1 CENT
2.8700 g., Bronze, 17 mm. **Ruler:** Elizabeth II **Obv:** Young bust right **Rev:** Great Caiman Thrush

Date	Mintage	F	VF	XF	Unc	BU
1972	2,155,000	—	—	0.10	0.25	0.75
1972 Proof	11,000	Value: 0.50				
1973 Proof	9,988	Value: 0.50				
1974 Proof	30,000	Value: 0.50				
1975 Proof	7,175	Value: 0.50				
1976 Proof	3,044	Value: 0.50				
1977	1,800,000	—	—	0.20	0.35	0.90
1977 Proof	1,970	Value: 1.00				
1979FM Proof	4,247	Value: 0.50				
1980FM	—	—	—	0.10	0.25	0.75
1980FM Proof	1,215	Value: 1.25				
1981 Proof	865	Value: 1.50				
1982	—	—	—	0.10	0.25	0.75
1982 Proof	589	Value: 1.50				
1983 Proof	—	Value: 1.50				
1984 Proof	—	Value: 1.50				
1986	1,000	Value: 1.50				

KM# 26 CENT
Bronze, 17 mm. **Ruler:** Elizabeth II **Subject:** 25th Anniversary of Coronation **Obv:** Young bust right **Rev:** Great Caiman Thrush

Date	Mintage	F	VF	XF	Unc	BU
1978 Proof	1,303	Value: 2.00				

KM# 87 CENT
2.9500 g., Bronze, 16 mm. **Ruler:** Elizabeth II **Obv:** Crowned bust right **Rev:** Great Caiman Thrush **Edge:** Plain

Date	Mintage	F	VF	XF	Unc	BU
1987	—	—	—	0.10	0.25	0.75
1987 Proof	317	Value: 3.00				
1988 Proof	318	Value: 3.00				
1990	—	—	—	0.10	0.25	0.75

KM# 87a CENT
2.5500 g., Bronze Clad Steel, 17 mm. **Ruler:** Elizabeth II **Obv:** Crowned bust right **Rev:** Great Caiman Thrush

Date	Mintage	F	VF	XF	Unc	BU
1992	—	—	—	0.20	0.50	1.00
1996	—	—	—	0.15	0.35	0.75

KM# 131 CENT
2.5300 g., Bronze Plated Steel, 17 mm. **Ruler:** Elizabeth II **Obv:** Crowned head right **Rev:** Grand Caiman thrush

Date	Mintage	F	VF	XF	Unc	BU
1999	—	—	—	0.20	0.50	1.00

KM# 2 5 CENTS
Copper-Nickel, 18 mm. **Ruler:** Elizabeth II **Obv:** Young bust right **Rev:** Pink-spotted shrimp

Date	Mintage	F	VF	XF	Unc	BU
1972	300,000	—	—	0.10	0.50	1.00
1972 Proof	12,000	Value: 0.75				
1973	200,000	—	—	0.30	0.65	1.00
Note: 1973 Business strikes were not released to circulation						
1973 Proof	9,988	Value: 0.75				
1974 Proof	30,000	Value: 0.75				
1975 Proof	7,175	Value: 0.75				
1976 Proof	3,044	Value: 0.75				
1977	600,000	—	—	0.10	0.50	1.00
1977 Proof	1,980	Value: 0.75				
1979 Proof	4,247	Value: 0.75				
1980 Proof	—	Value: 2.00				
1981 Proof	—	Value: 2.50				
1982	—	—	—	0.10	0.50	1.00
1982 Proof	—	Value: 2.50				
1983 Proof	—	Value: 2.50				
1984 Proof	—	Value: 2.50				
1986	1,000	Value: 2.50				

KM# 27 5 CENTS
Copper-Nickel, 18 mm. **Ruler:** Elizabeth II **Subject:** 25th Anniversary of Coronation **Obv:** Young bust right **Rev:** Pink-spotted shrimp

Date	Mintage	F	VF	XF	Unc	BU
1978 Proof	1,303	Value: 3.00				

KM# 88 5 CENTS
Copper-Nickel, 18 mm. **Ruler:** Elizabeth II **Obv:** Crowned bust right **Rev:** Pink-spotted shrimp

Date	Mintage	F	VF	XF	Unc	BU
1987	—	—	—	0.10	0.35	1.00
1987 Proof	317	Value: 5.00				
1988 Proof	318	Value: 5.00				
1990	—	—	—	0.10	0.35	1.00

KM# 88a 5 CENTS
2.0000 g., Nickel Clad Steel, 18 mm. **Ruler:** Elizabeth II **Obv:** Crowned bust right **Rev:** Pink-spotted shrimp **Edge:** Plain

Date	Mintage	F	VF	XF	Unc	BU
1992	—	—	—	0.20	0.50	1.00
1996	—	—	—	0.10	0.35	1.00

KM# 132 5 CENTS
2.0000 g., Nickel Clad Steel, 18 mm. **Ruler:** Elizabeth II **Obv:** Crowned head right **Rev:** Pink-spotted shrimp **Edge:** Plain

Date	Mintage	F	VF	XF	Unc	BU
1999	—	—	—	—	0.50	1.00

KM# 3 10 CENTS
3.9200 g., Copper-Nickel, 21 mm. **Ruler:** Elizabeth II **Obv:** Young bust right **Rev:** Green Turtle surfacing

Date	Mintage	F	VF	XF	Unc	BU
1972	550,000	—	0.15	0.20	0.50	1.00
1972 Proof	11,000	Value: 1.00				
1973	200,000	—	0.25	0.50	1.00	1.25
Note: 1973 Business strikes were not released to circulation						
1973 Proof	9,988	Value: 1.00				
1974 Proof	30,000	Value: 1.00				
1975 Proof	7,175	Value: 1.00				

Date	Mintage	F	VF	XF	Unc	BU
1976 Proof	3,044	Value: 1.00				
1977	960,000	—	0.15	0.20	0.50	1.00
1977 Proof	1,980	Value: 1.00				
1979FM Proof	4,247	Value: 1.00				
1980FM Proof	1,215	Value: 3.00				
1981FM Proof	865	Value: 3.00				
1982	—	—	0.15	0.20	0.50	1.00
1982FM Proof	589	Value: 3.00				
1983FM Proof	—	Value: 3.00				
1984FM Proof	—	Value: 3.00				
1986	1,000	Value: 3.00				

KM# 28 10 CENTS
Copper-Nickel, 21 mm. **Ruler:** Elizabeth II **Subject:** 25th Anniversary of Coronation **Rev:** Green Turtle surfacing

Date	Mintage	F	VF	XF	Unc	BU
1978 Proof	1,304	Value: 3.50				

KM# 89 10 CENTS
3.8800 g., Copper-Nickel, 21 mm. **Ruler:** Elizabeth II **Obv:** Crowned bust right **Rev:** Green turtle surfacing

Date	Mintage	F	VF	XF	Unc	BU
1987	—	—	0.15	0.20	0.50	1.00
1987 Proof	317	Value: 6.00				
1988 Proof	318	Value: 6.00				
1990	—	—	0.15	0.20	0.50	1.00

KM# 89a 10 CENTS
3.4500 g., Nickel Clad Steel, 21 mm. **Ruler:** Elizabeth II **Obv:** Crowned bust right **Rev:** Green turtle surfacing

Date	Mintage	F	VF	XF	Unc	BU
1992	—	—	0.25	0.40	1.00	1.25
1996	—	—	0.20	0.30	0.75	1.00

KM# 133 10 CENTS
3.4300 g., Nickel Clad Steel, 21 mm. **Ruler:** Elizabeth II **Obv:** Head with tiara right **Rev:** Green turtle surfacing **Edge:** Reeded

Date	Mintage	F	VF	XF	Unc	BU
1999	—	—	0.25	0.40	1.00	1.25

KM# 4 25 CENTS
5.6700 g., Copper-Nickel, 24.2 mm. **Ruler:** Elizabeth II **Obv:** Young bust right **Rev:** Schooner sailing right

Date	Mintage	F	VF	XF	Unc	BU
1972	350,000	—	0.35	0.50	1.00	1.25
1972 Proof	11,000	Value: 1.00				
1973	100,000	—	1.00	1.50	2.00	2.50

Note: 1973 Business strikes were not released to circulation

1973 Proof	9,988	Value: 1.00				
1974 Proof	30,000	Value: 1.00				
1975 Proof	7,175	Value: 1.00				
1976 Proof	3,044	Value: 1.00				
1977	520,000	—	0.35	0.50	1.00	1.25
1977 Proof	1,980	Value: 1.00				
1979FM Proof	4,247	Value: 1.00				
1980FM Proof	1,215	Value: 3.50				
1981FM Proof	865	Value: 4.00				
1982	—	—	0.35	0.50	1.00	1.25
1982FM Proof	589	Value: 4.00				
1983FM Proof	—	Value: 4.00				
1984FM Proof	—	Value: 4.00				
1986 Proof	1,000	Value: 4.00				

KM# 29 25 CENTS
Copper-Nickel, 24.2 mm. **Ruler:** Elizabeth II **Subject:** 25th Anniversary of Coronation **Obv:** Young bust right **Rev:** Schooner sailing right

Date	Mintage	F	VF	XF	Unc	BU
1978 Proof	1,303	Value: 4.00				

KM# 90 25 CENTS
5.7200 g., Copper-Nickel, 24.2 mm. **Ruler:** Elizabeth II **Obv:** Crowned head right **Rev:** Schooner sailing right

Date	Mintage	F	VF	XF	Unc	BU
1987	—	—	0.35	0.50	1.00	1.25
1987 Proof	317	Value: 8.00				
1988 Proof	318	Value: 8.00				
1990	—	—	0.35	0.50	1.00	1.25

KM# 90a 25 CENTS
5.1000 g., Nickel Clad Steel, 24.2 mm. **Ruler:** Elizabeth II **Obv:** Crowned head right **Rev:** Schooner sailing right

Date	Mintage	F	VF	XF	Unc	BU
1992	—	—	0.45	0.75	1.50	1.75
1996	—	—	0.35	0.60	1.25	1.50

KM# 134 25 CENTS
5.0400 g., Nickel-Clad Steel, 24.2 mm. **Ruler:** Elizabeth II **Obv:** Head with tiara right **Rev:** Schooner sailing right **Edge:** Reeded

Date	Mintage	F	VF	XF	Unc	BU
1999	—	—	—	0.75	1.50	1.75

KM# 5 50 CENTS
10.3000 g., 0.9250 Silver 0.3063 oz. ASW, 28.2 mm. **Ruler:** Elizabeth II **Obv:** Young bust right **Rev:** Caribbean Emperor Fish

Date	Mintage	F	VF	XF	Unc	BU
1972	500	—	—	7.50	12.50	15.00
1972 Proof	11,000	Value: 10.00				
1973 Proof	9,988	Value: 10.00				
1974 Proof	30,000	Value: 10.00				
1975 Proof	7,175	Value: 10.00				
1976 Proof	3,044	Value: 10.00				
1977 Proof	1,980	Value: 10.00				
1979FM Proof	4,247	Value: 10.00				
1980FM Proof	1,215	Value: 10.00				
1981FM Proof	865	Value: 10.00				
1982FM Proof	589	Value: 10.00				

KM# 30 50 CENTS
10.3000 g., 0.9250 Silver 0.3063 oz. ASW, 28.2 mm. **Ruler:** Elizabeth II **Subject:** 25th Anniversary of Coronation **Obv:** Young bust right **Rev:** Caribbean Emperor Fish

Date	Mintage	F	VF	XF	Unc	BU
1978 Proof	2,169	Value: 12.50				

KM# 73 50 CENTS
10.3000 g., 9.2500 Silver 3.0630 oz. ASW, 28.2 mm. **Ruler:** Elizabeth II **Obv:** Young bust right **Rev:** Morning Glory

Date	Mintage	F	VF	XF	Unc	BU
1983FM Proof	—	Value: 15.00				
1984FM Proof	411	Value: 15.00				
1986 Proof	1,000	Value: 15.00				

KM# 91 50 CENTS
10.3000 g., 0.9250 Silver 0.3063 oz. ASW, 28.2 mm. **Ruler:** Elizabeth II **Obv:** Crowned head right **Rev:** Map of the Islands

Date	Mintage	F	VF	XF	Unc	BU
1987 Proof	317	Value: 20.00				
1988 Proof	318	Value: 20.00				

KM# 6 DOLLAR
18.0000 g., 0.9250 Silver 0.5353 oz. ASW **Ruler:** Elizabeth II **Obv:** Young bust right **Rev:** Poinciana flower

Date	Mintage	F	VF	XF	Unc	BU
1972	500	—	—	11.00	15.00	—
1972 Proof	11,000	Value: 10.00				
1973 Proof	9,988	Value: 10.00				
1974 Proof	30,000	Value: 10.00				
1975 Proof	7,175	Value: 10.00				
1976 Proof	3,044	Value: 11.00				
1977 Proof	1,980	Value: 11.00				
1979FM Proof	4,247	Value: 11.00				
1980FM Proof	1,215	Value: 11.00				
1981FM Proof	865	Value: 12.00				
1982FM Proof	589	Value: 12.00				

KM# 31 DOLLAR
18.0000 g., 0.9250 Silver 0.5353 oz. ASW **Ruler:** Elizabeth II **Subject:** 25th Anniversary of Coronation **Obv:** Young bust right **Rev:** Poinciana flower

Date	Mintage	F	VF	XF	Unc	BU
1978 Proof	2,168	Value: 12.00				

KM# 74 DOLLAR
18.0000 g., 0.9250 Silver 0.5353 oz. ASW **Ruler:** Elizabeth II **Obv:** Young bust right **Rev:** Pineapple

Date	Mintage	F	VF	XF	Unc	BU
1983FM Proof	1,686	Value: 16.00				
1984FM Proof	456	Value: 16.00				
1986 Proof	1,000	Value: 16.00				

KM# 92 DOLLAR
18.0000 g., 0.9250 Silver 0.5353 oz. ASW **Ruler:** Elizabeth II **Obv:** Crowned bust right **Rev:** Map of the Islands

Date	Mintage	F	VF	XF	Unc	BU
1987 Proof	317	Value: 22.00				
1988 Proof	318	Value: 22.00				

KM# 103 DOLLAR
18.1400 g., 0.9250 Silver 0.5395 oz. ASW **Ruler:** Elizabeth II
Obv: Crowned bust right **Rev:** Green Turtle

Date	Mintage	F	VF	XF	Unc	BU
1990 Proof	Est. 5,000	Value: 75.00				

KM# 111 DOLLAR
18.1400 g., 0.9250 Silver 0.5395 oz. ASW **Ruler:** Elizabeth II
Obv: Crowned bust right **Rev:** Lesser Caymans' Rock Iquana

Date	Mintage	F	VF	XF	Unc	BU
1992 Proof	Est. 5,000	Value: 50.00				

KM# 116 DOLLAR
18.1400 g., 0.9250 Silver 0.5395 oz. ASW **Ruler:** Elizabeth II
Obv: Crowned bust right **Rev:** Cayman Ironwood Tree

Date	Mintage	F	VF	XF	Unc	BU
1994 Proof	Est. 10,000	Value: 37.50				

KM# 118 DOLLAR
28.2800 g., 0.9250 Silver 0.8410 oz. ASW **Ruler:** Elizabeth II
Subject: Royal Visit **Obv:** Crowned bust right **Rev:** Royal couple
in cameo above yacht "Britannia"

Date	Mintage	F	VF	XF	Unc	BU
1994 Proof	Est. 10,000	Value: 50.00				

KM# 120 DOLLAR
28.2800 g., 0.9250 Silver 0.8410 oz. ASW **Ruler:** Elizabeth II
Obv: Crowned bust right **Rev:** Queen Mother's arms

Date	Mintage	F	VF	XF	Unc	BU
1994 Proof	Est. 20,000	Value: 28.50				

KM# 121 DOLLAR
28.2800 g., 0.9250 Silver 0.8410 oz. ASW **Ruler:** Elizabeth II
Obv: Crowned bust right **Rev:** Sir Francis Drake at left looking
right, arms at right

Date	Mintage	F	VF	XF	Unc	BU
1994 Proof	Est. 10,000	Value: 30.00				

KM# 125 DOLLAR
28.2800 g., 0.9250 Silver 0.8410 oz. ASW **Ruler:** Elizabeth II
Obv: Crowned bust right **Rev:** Blue Rock Iguana left

Date	Mintage	F	VF	XF	Unc	BU
1995 Proof	Est. 10,000	Value: 55.00				

KM# 122 DOLLAR
18.1400 g., 0.9250 Silver 0.5395 oz. ASW **Ruler:** Elizabeth II
Obv: Crowned bust right **Rev:** Amazona Leucocephala
Caymanesis - Parrot right

Date	Mintage	F	VF	XF	Unc	BU
1996 Proof	Est. 10,000	Value: 50.00				

KM# 124 DOLLAR
28.2800 g., 0.9250 Silver 0.8410 oz. ASW **Ruler:** Elizabeth II
Subject: Olympics **Obv:** Crowned bust right **Rev:** Two sailboats

Date	Mintage	F	VF	XF	Unc	BU
1996 Proof	Est. 30,000	Value: 30.00				

KM# 7 2 DOLLARS
29.4500 g., 0.9250 Silver 0.8758 oz. ASW **Ruler:** Elizabeth II
Obv: Young bust right **Rev:** Great Blue Heron

Date	Mintage	F	VF	XF	Unc	BU
1972	500	—	—	—	20.00	25.00
1972 Proof	11,000	Value: 16.50				
1973 Proof	9,988	Value: 16.50				
1974 Proof	30,000	Value: 16.50				
1975 Proof	5,390	Value: 16.50				
1976 Proof	3,044	Value: 16.50				
1977 Proof	1,980	Value: 16.50				
1979FM Proof	4,247	Value: 16.50				
1980FM Proof	1,215	Value: 18.00				
1981FM Proof	865	Value: 25.00				
1982FM Proof	589	Value: 25.00				
1986 Proof	1,000	Value: 18.00				

KM# 32 2 DOLLARS
29.4500 g., 0.9250 Silver 0.8758 oz. ASW **Ruler:** Elizabeth II
Subject: 25th Anniversary of Coronation **Rev:** Great Blue Heron
right

Date	Mintage	F	VF	XF	Unc	BU
1978 Proof	2,169	Value: 22.50				

KM# 75 2 DOLLARS
29.4500 g., 0.9250 Silver 0.8758 oz. ASW **Ruler:** Elizabeth II
Rev: Parrot looking right

Date	Mintage	F	VF	XF	Unc	BU
1983FM Proof	409	Value: 45.00				
1984FM Proof	200	Value: 55.00				

KM# 93 2 DOLLARS
29.4500 g., 0.9250 Silver 0.8758 oz. ASW **Ruler:** Elizabeth II
Obv: Crowned bust right **Rev:** Great Blue Heron

Date	Mintage	F	VF	XF	Unc	BU
1987 Proof	317	Value: 45.00				
1988 Proof	318	Value: 45.00				

KM# 114 2 DOLLARS
28.2800 g., 0.9250 Silver 0.8410 oz. ASW **Ruler:** Elizabeth II
Obv: Crowned bust right **Rev:** Wreck of the "Ten Sails"

Date	Mintage	F	VF	XF	Unc	BU
1994 Proof	15,000	Value: 30.00				

KM# 130 2 DOLLARS
15.5520 g., 0.9990 Silver 0.4995 oz. ASW **Ruler:** Elizabeth II
Subject: Millennium **Obv:** Crowned bust right **Rev:** Ornate clock

Date	Mintage	F	VF	XF	Unc	BU
2000 Proof	30,000	Value: 47.50				

KM# 81 5 DOLLARS
28.2800 g., 0.9250 Silver 0.8410 oz. ASW, 38.61 mm.
Ruler: Elizabeth II **Subject:** 250th Anniversary of Royal Land
Grant **Obv:** Crowned bust right **Rev:** Map of islands

Date	Mintage	F	VF	XF	Unc	BU
1985 Proof	Est. 1,000	Value: 31.50				

KM# 127 2 DOLLARS
28.2800 g., 0.9250 Silver 0.8410 oz. ASW **Ruler:** Elizabeth II
Subject: 25th Anniversary - Currency Board **Obv:** Crowned bust
right **Rev:** Coins and arms within circle

Date	Mintage	F	VF	XF	Unc	BU
ND Proof	Est. 2,000	Value: 55.00				

KM# 8 5 DOLLARS
35.5000 g., 0.9250 Silver 1.0557 oz. ASW **Ruler:** Elizabeth II
Obv: Young bust right **Rev:** Island arms

Date	Mintage	F	VF	XF	Unc	BU
1972	500	—	—	—	35.00	—
1972 Proof	11,000	Value: 22.00				
1973 Proof	17,000	Value: 22.00				
1974 Proof	26,000	Value: 22.00				
1975 Proof	7,753	Value: 22.00				
1976 Proof	5,177	Value: 22.00				
1977 Proof	3,525	Value: 22.50				
1979FM Proof	—	Value: 24.00				
1980FM Proof	—	Value: 25.00				
1981FM Proof	—	Value: 27.50				
1984FM Proof	—	Value: 27.50				
1986 Proof	1,000	Value: 27.50				

KM# 33 5 DOLLARS
35.5000 g., 0.9250 Silver 1.0557 oz. ASW **Ruler:** Elizabeth II
Subject: 25th Anniversary of Coronation **Obv:** Young bust right

Date	Mintage	F	VF	XF	Unc	BU
1978 Proof	2,168	Value: 28.50				

KM# 80 5 DOLLARS
28.2800 g., 0.5000 Silver 0.4546 oz. ASW **Ruler:** Elizabeth II
Subject: Commonwealth Games **Obv:** Crowned bust right
Rev: Long Jumper

Date	Mintage	F	VF	XF	Unc	BU
1986	50,000	—	—	—	12.50	—

KM# 80a 5 DOLLARS
28.2800 g., 0.9250 Silver 0.8410 oz. ASW **Ruler:** Elizabeth II
Subject: Commonwealth Games **Obv:** Crowned bust right
Rev: Long Jumper

Date	Mintage	F	VF	XF	Unc	BU
1986 Proof	Est. 20,000	Value: 25.00				

KM# 128 2 DOLLARS
28.2800 g., 0.9250 Silver 0.8410 oz. ASW, 38.6 mm.
Ruler: Elizabeth II **Subject:** Queen's Golden Wedding
Anniversary **Obv:** Crowned bust right **Rev:** Royal couple in
carriage above gold-plated shield

Date	Mintage	F	VF	XF	Unc	BU
1997 Proof	Est. 30,000	Value: 57.00				

KM# 70 5 DOLLARS
35.5000 g., 0.9250 Silver 1.0557 oz. ASW **Ruler:** Elizabeth II
Subject: 150th Anniversary of Parliamentary Government
Obv: Young bust right **Rev:** Island arms

Date	Mintage	F	VF	XF	Unc	BU
1982FM Proof	1,105	Value: 40.00				

KM# 76 5 DOLLARS
35.5000 g., 0.9250 Silver 1.0557 oz. ASW **Ruler:** Elizabeth II
Subject: Royal Visit

Date	Mintage	F	VF	XF	Unc	BU
1983FM Proof	419	Value: 38.50				

KM# 85 5 DOLLARS
28.2800 g., 0.9250 Silver 0.8410 oz. ASW **Ruler:** Elizabeth II
Subject: Queen Elizabeth II and Philip's 40th Wedding
Anniversary **Obv:** Crowned bust right **Rev:** Monogram above
dates within wreath

Date	Mintage	F	VF	XF	Unc	BU
ND(1987) Proof	Est. 2,000	Value: 30.00				

KM# 85a 5 DOLLARS
35.6400 g., 0.9250 Silver 1.0599 oz. ASW **Ruler:** Elizabeth II
Subject: Queen Elizabeth II and Philip's 40th Wedding
Anniversary **Obv:** Crowned bust right **Rev:** Monogram above
dates within wreath

Date	Mintage	F	VF	XF	Unc	BU
ND(1987) Proof	317	Value: 90.00				

KM# 129 2 DOLLARS
28.2800 g., 0.9250 Silver 0.8410 oz. ASW, 38.6 mm.
Ruler: Elizabeth II **Obv:** Crowned bust right **Rev:** Schooners
Arbutus I and *Goldfield* under sail

Date	Mintage	F	VF	XF	Unc	BU
1997 Proof	Est. 5,000	Value: 60.00				

KM# 95 5 DOLLARS
28.2800 g., 0.9250 Silver 0.8410 oz. ASW **Ruler:** Elizabeth II
Subject: World Wildlife Fund **Obv:** Crowned bust right
Rev: Cuban Amazon

Date	Mintage	F	VF	XF	Unc	BU
1987 Proof	—	Value: 35.00				

KM# 96   5 DOLLARS
28.2800 g., 0.9250 Silver 0.8410 oz. ASW **Ruler:** Elizabeth II
Subject: 500th Anniversary of Columbus' Discovery of America
Obv: Crowned bust right **Rev:** Columbus in cameo above ships

Date	Mintage	F	VF	XF	Unc	BU
1988 Proof	10,000				Value: 27.50	

KM# 98   5 DOLLARS
28.2800 g., 0.9250 Silver 0.8410 oz. ASW **Ruler:** Elizabeth II
Subject: Visit of Princess Alexandra **Obv:** Crowned bust right
Rev: Arms of Princess Alexandria

Date	Mintage	F	VF	XF	Unc	BU
1988 Proof	Est. 5,000				Value: 37.50	

KM# 94.1   5 DOLLARS
28.2800 g., 0.9250 Silver 0.8410 oz. ASW **Ruler:** Elizabeth II
Subject: Seoul Olympics **Obv:** Crowned bust right **Rev:** Sailboards

Date	Mintage	F	VF	XF	Unc	BU
1988 Proof	20,000				Value: 27.50	

KM# 94.2   5 DOLLARS
35.6400 g., 0.9250 Silver 1.0599 oz. ASW **Ruler:** Elizabeth II
Subject: Seoul Olympics **Obv:** Crowned bust right **Rev:**
Sailboards, denomination at left

Date	Mintage	F	VF	XF	Unc	BU
1988 Proof	318				Value: 200	

KM# 100   5 DOLLARS
28.2800 g., 0.9250 Silver 0.8410 oz. ASW **Ruler:** Elizabeth II
Subject: 100 Years of Postal Service **Rev:** Ship with small shield
above

Date	Mintage	F	VF	XF	Unc	BU
ND(1989) Proof	10,000				Value: 40.00	

KM# 102   5 DOLLARS
28.2800 g., 0.9250 Silver 0.8410 oz. ASW **Ruler:** Elizabeth II
Subject: Save the Children Fund **Obv:** Crowned bust right
Rev: Two children sailing boats in water

Date	Mintage	F	VF	XF	Unc	BU
1989 Proof	Est. 20,000				Value: 20.00	

KM# 108   5 DOLLARS
28.2800 g., 0.9250 Silver 0.8410 oz. ASW **Ruler:** Elizabeth II
Subject: Queen Mother's Birth Centennial **Obv:** Crowned bust
right **Rev:** Crowned monogram within flowers

Date	Mintage	F	VF	XF	Unc	BU
ND(1990) Proof	Est. 10,000				Value: 25.00	

KM# 109   5 DOLLARS
28.2800 g., 0.9250 Silver 0.8410 oz. ASW **Ruler:** Elizabeth II
Subject: 20th Anniversary of the Currency Board **Obv:** Crowned
bust right **Rev:** Islands and compass above ship within circle

Date	Mintage	F	VF	XF	Unc	BU
ND(1991) Proof	Est. 2,500				Value: 40.00	

KM# 110   5 DOLLARS
28.2800 g., 0.9250 Silver 0.8410 oz. ASW **Ruler:** Elizabeth II
Subject: 1992 Olympics - Barcelona **Obv:** Crowned bust right
Rev: Cyclists

Date	Mintage	F	VF	XF	Unc	BU
1992 Proof	Est. 50,000				Value: 27.50	

KM# 112   5 DOLLARS
28.2800 g., 0.9250 Silver 0.8410 oz. ASW **Ruler:** Elizabeth II
Subject: 40th Anniversary - Coronation of Queen Elizabeth
Obv: Crowned bust right **Rev:** Royal symbols

Date	Mintage	F	VF	XF	Unc	BU
ND(1993) Proof	Est. 13,000				Value: 45.00	

KM# 126   5 DOLLARS
28.2800 g., 0.9250 Silver 0.8410 oz. ASW **Ruler:** Elizabeth II
Subject: 70th Birthday of Queen Elizabeth II **Obv:** Crowned bust
right **Rev:** The Queen on horseback divides monogram

Date	Mintage	F	VF	XF	Unc	BU
ND(1996) Proof	13,000				Value: 45.00	

KM# 68   10 DOLLARS
Copper-Nickel **Ruler:** Elizabeth II **Subject:** Wedding of Prince
Charles and Lady Diana **Obv:** Young bust right **Rev:** Facing
busts, small island arms above

Date	Mintage	F	VF	XF	Unc	BU
1981	—	—	—	—	7.50	—

KM# 68a 10 DOLLARS
28.2800 g., 0.9250 Silver 0.8410 oz. ASW **Ruler:** Elizabeth II
Subject: Wedding of Prince Charles and Lady Diana **Obv:** Young
bust right **Rev:** Facing busts, small arms above

Date	Mintage	F	VF	XF	Unc	BU
1981 Proof	40,000	Value: 20.00				

KM# 72 10 DOLLARS
27.8900 g., 0.9250 Silver 0.8294 oz. ASW **Ruler:** Elizabeth II
Subject: International Year of the Child **Obv:** Young bust right
Rev: Two children following sea turtle

Date	Mintage	F	VF	XF	Unc	BU
1982 Proof	6,616	Value: 22.50				

KM# 77 10 DOLLARS
23.4500 g., 0.9250 Silver 0.6974 oz. ASW **Ruler:** Elizabeth II
Subject: Royal Visit **Obv:** Young bust right **Rev:** Royal couple
facing each other above small island arms

Date	Mintage	F	VF	XF	Unc	BU
1983FM Proof	10,000	Value: 30.00				

KM# 9 25 DOLLARS
51.3500 g., 0.9250 Silver 1.5271 oz. ASW, 45 mm.
Ruler: Elizabeth II **Subject:** Queen Elizabeth II and Philip's 25th
Wedding Anniversary **Obv:** Young bust right **Rev:** Jugate heads
right

Date	Mintage	F	VF	XF	Unc	BU
1972	186,000	—	—	—	27.50	—
1972 Proof	26,000	Value: 32.50				

KM# 9a 25 DOLLARS
13.8200 g., 0.5000 Gold 0.2222 oz. AGW, 27 mm.
Ruler: Elizabeth II **Subject:** Queen Elizabeth II and Philip's 25th
Wedding Anniversary **Obv:** Young bust right **Rev:** Jugate heads
right

Date	Mintage	F	VF	XF	Unc	BU
1972	7,706	—	—	—	—	225
1972 Proof	21,000	Value: 215				

KM# 10 25 DOLLARS
51.3500 g., 0.9250 Silver 1.5271 oz. ASW, 45 mm.
Ruler: Elizabeth II **Subject:** Churchill Centenary **Obv:** Island
arms **Rev:** Bust facing

Date	Mintage	F	VF	XF	Unc	BU
1974	1,200	—	—	—	35.00	—
1974 Proof	12,000	Value: 32.50				

Note: 4300 sets were issued in proof containing KM#10 and
Turks & Caicos Islands 20 Crowns KM#2 with an issue
price of $80.00

KM# 14 25 DOLLARS
51.3500 g., 0.9250 Silver 1.5271 oz. ASW, 45 mm.
Ruler: Elizabeth II **Subject:** Queen's Silver Jubilee **Obv:** Young
bust right **Rev:** Crowned arms with supporters

Date	Mintage	F	VF	XF	Unc	BU
1977	3,600	—	—	—	45.00	—
1977 Proof	7,854	Value: 45.00				

KM# 16 25 DOLLARS
51.3500 g., 0.9250 Silver 1.5271 oz. ASW, 45 mm.
Ruler: Elizabeth II **Subject:** Queen Mary I, 1553-1558
Obv: Young bust right **Rev:** Bust 3/4 facing

Date	Mintage	F	VF	XF	Unc	BU
1977 Proof	2,720	Value: 55.00				

KM# 17 25 DOLLARS
51.3500 g., 0.9250 Silver 1.5271 oz. ASW, 45 mm.
Ruler: Elizabeth II **Subject:** Elizabeth I, 1558-1603 **Obv:** Young
bust right **Rev:** Bust with high ruffled collar 3/4 right

Date	Mintage	F	VF	XF	Unc	BU
1977 Proof	2,677	Value: 55.00				

KM# 18 25 DOLLARS
51.3500 g., 0.9250 Silver 1.5271 oz. ASW, 45 mm.
Ruler: Elizabeth II **Subject:** Queen Mary II, 1688-1694
Obv: Young bust right **Rev:** Bust 3/4 right

Date	Mintage	F	VF	XF	Unc	BU
1977 Proof	2,653	Value: 55.00				

KM# 19 25 DOLLARS
51.3500 g., 0.9250 Silver 1.5271 oz. ASW, 45 mm.
Ruler: Elizabeth II **Subject:** Queen Anne, 1702-1714
Obv: Young bust right **Rev:** Bust 3/4 facing

Date	Mintage	F	VF	XF	Unc	BU
1977 Proof	2,630	Value: 55.00				

KM# 20 25 DOLLARS
51.3500 g., 0.9250 Silver 1.5271 oz. ASW, 45 mm.
Ruler: Elizabeth II **Subject:** Queen Victoria, 1837-1901
Obv: Young bust right **Rev:** Crowned bust left

Date	Mintage	F	VF	XF	Unc	BU
1977 Proof	2,623	Value: 55.00				

KM# 36   25 DOLLARS
51.3500 g., 0.9250 Silver 1.5271 oz. ASW, 45 mm.
Ruler: Elizabeth II **Subject:** 25th Anniversary of Coronation
Obv: Young bust right **Rev:** Ampulla

Date	Mintage	F	VF	XF	Unc	BU
1978 Proof	5,000	Value: 47.50				

KM# 37   25 DOLLARS
51.3500 g., 0.9250 Silver 1.5271 oz. ASW, 45 mm.
Ruler: Elizabeth II **Subject:** 25th Anniversary of Coronation
Obv: Young bust right **Rev:** Royal orb

Date	Mintage	F	VF	XF	Unc	BU
1978 Proof	5,000	Value: 47.50				

KM# 38   25 DOLLARS
51.3500 g., 0.9250 Silver 1.5271 oz. ASW, 45 mm.
Ruler: Elizabeth II **Subject:** 25th Anniversary of Coronation **Obv:** Young bust right **Rev:** St. Edward's crown

Date	Mintage	F	VF	XF	Unc	BU
1978 Proof	5,000	Value: 47.50				

KM# 39   25 DOLLARS
51.3500 g., 0.9250 Silver 1.5271 oz. ASW, 45 mm.
Ruler: Elizabeth II **Subject:** 25th Anniversary of Coronation
Obv: Young bust right **Rev:** Coronation chair

Date	Mintage	F	VF	XF	Unc	BU
1978 Proof	5,000	Value: 47.50				

KM# 40   25 DOLLARS
51.3500 g., 0.9250 Silver 1.5271 oz. ASW, 45 mm.
Ruler: Elizabeth II **Subject:** 25th Anniversary of Coronation
Obv: Young bust right **Rev:** Royal sceptre

Date	Mintage	F	VF	XF	Unc	BU
1978 Proof	5,000	Value: 47.50				

KM# 41   25 DOLLARS
51.3500 g., 0.9250 Silver 1.5271 oz. ASW, 45 mm.
Ruler: Elizabeth II **Subject:** 25th Anniversary of Coronation
Obv: Young bust right **Rev:** Spoon

Date	Mintage	F	VF	XF	Unc	BU
1978 Proof	5,000	Value: 47.50				

KM# 48   25 DOLLARS
35.6400 g., 0.5000 Silver 0.5729 oz. ASW **Ruler:** Elizabeth II
Obv: Young bust right **Rev:** Saxon Kings

Date	Mintage	F	VF	XF	Unc	BU
1980CHI Proof	12,000	Value: 35.00				

KM# 49   25 DOLLARS
35.6400 g., 0.5000 Silver 0.5729 oz. ASW **Ruler:** Elizabeth II
Obv: Young bust right **Rev:** Norman kings

Date	Mintage	F	VF	XF	Unc	BU
1980CHI Proof	12,000	Value: 35.00				

KM# 50   25 DOLLARS
35.6400 g., 0.5000 Silver 0.5729 oz. ASW **Ruler:** Elizabeth II
Obv: Young bust right **Rev:** House of Plantagenet - I

Date	Mintage	F	VF	XF	Unc	BU
1980CHI Proof	12,000	Value: 35.00				

KM# 51   25 DOLLARS
35.6400 g., 0.5000 Silver 0.5729 oz. ASW **Ruler:** Elizabeth II
Obv: Young bust right **Rev:** House of Plantagenet - II

Date	Mintage	F	VF	XF	Unc	BU
1980CHI Proof	12,000	Value: 35.00				

KM# 52   25 DOLLARS
35.6400 g., 0.5000 Silver 0.5729 oz. ASW **Ruler:** Elizabeth II
Obv: Young bust right **Rev:** House of Lancaster

Date	Mintage	F	VF	XF	Unc	BU
1980CHI Proof	12,000	Value: 35.00				

KM# 53   25 DOLLARS
35.6400 g., 0.5000 Silver 0.5729 oz. ASW **Ruler:** Elizabeth II
Obv: Young bust right **Rev:** House of York

Date	Mintage	F	VF	XF	Unc	BU
1980CHI Proof	12,000	Value: 35.00				

KM# 54   25 DOLLARS
35.6400 g., 0.5000 Silver 0.5729 oz. ASW **Ruler:** Elizabeth II
Obv: Young bust right **Rev:** House of Tudor

Date	Mintage	F	VF	XF	Unc	BU
1980CHI Proof	12,000	Value: 35.00				

KM# 55   25 DOLLARS
35.6400 g., 0.5000 Silver 0.5729 oz. ASW **Ruler:** Elizabeth II
Obv: Young bust right **Rev:** House of Stuart & Orange

Date	Mintage	F	VF	XF	Unc	BU
1980CHI Proof	12,000	Value: 35.00				

KM# 56   25 DOLLARS
35.6400 g., 0.5000 Silver 0.5729 oz. ASW **Ruler:** Elizabeth II
Obv: Young bust right **Rev:** House of Hanover

Date	Mintage	F	VF	XF	Unc	BU
1980CHI Proof	12,000	Value: 35.00				

KM# 57   25 DOLLARS
35.6400 g., 0.5000 Silver 0.5729 oz. ASW **Ruler:** Elizabeth II
Obv: Young bust right **Rev:** House of Saxe-Coburg and Windsor

Date	Mintage	F	VF	XF	Unc	BU
1980CHI Proof	12,000	Value: 35.00				

KM# 78   25 DOLLARS
64.8000 g., 0.9250 Silver 1.9270 oz. ASW **Ruler:** Elizabeth II
Subject: Royal Visit **Obv:** Young bust right **Rev:** Royal couple
facing each other above small island arms

Date	Mintage	F	VF	XF	Unc	BU
1983FM Proof	5,000	Value: 50.00				

KM# 104   25 DOLLARS
3.1340 g., 0.9990 Gold 0.1007 oz. AGW **Ruler:** Elizabeth II
Subject: Winston Churchill **Obv:** Young bust right
Rev: Evacuation of Dunkirk

Date	Mintage	F	VF	XF	Unc	BU
1990 Proof	Est. 500	Value: 100				

KM# 12   50 DOLLARS
64.9400 g., 0.9250 Silver 1.9312 oz. ASW **Ruler:** Elizabeth II
Subject: Sovereign Queens of England **Obv:** Young bust right
Rev: Portraits of sovereign queens in circle with names and dates

Date	Mintage	F	VF	XF	Unc	BU
1975	33,000	—	—	—	50.00	
1975 Proof	7,800	Value: 55.00				
1976	1,292	—	—	—	60.00	
1976 Proof	2,843	Value: 60.00				
1977	2,400	—	—	—	60.00	
1977 Proof	Inc. above	Value: 60.00				

KM# 21   50 DOLLARS
11.3400 g., 0.5000 Gold 0.1823 oz. AGW **Ruler:** Elizabeth II
Subject: Queen Mary I, 1553-1558 **Obv:** Young bust right
Rev: Bust 3/4 facing

Date	Mintage	F	VF	XF	Unc	BU
1977 Proof	1,999	Value: 185				

KM# 22   50 DOLLARS
11.3400 g., 0.5000 Gold 0.1823 oz. AGW **Ruler:** Elizabeth II
Subject: Queen Elizabeth I, 1558-1603 **Obv:** Young bust right
Rev: Bust with high ruffled collar 3/4 right

Date	Mintage	F	VF	XF	Unc	BU
1977 Proof	1,969	Value: 185				

KM# 23   50 DOLLARS
11.3400 g., 0.5000 Gold 0.1823 oz. AGW **Ruler:** Elizabeth II
Subject: Queen Mary II, 1688-1694 **Obv:** Young bust right
Rev: Bust 3/4 right

Date	Mintage	F	VF	XF	Unc	BU
1977 Proof	1,961	Value: 185				

KM# 24   50 DOLLARS
11.3400 g., 0.5000 Gold 0.1823 oz. AGW **Ruler:** Elizabeth II
Subject: Queen Anne, 1702-1714 **Obv:** Young bust right
Rev: Bust 3/4 left

Date	Mintage	F	VF	XF	Unc	BU
1977 Proof	1,938	Value: 185				

KM# 25   50 DOLLARS
11.3400 g., 0.5000 Gold 0.1823 oz. AGW **Ruler:** Elizabeth II
Subject: Queen Victoria, 1837-1901 **Obv:** Young bust right
Rev: Crowned bust left

Date	Mintage	F	VF	XF	Unc	BU
1977 Proof	1,932	Value: 185				

KM# 34   50 DOLLARS
64.9400 g., 0.9250 Silver 1.9312 oz. ASW **Ruler:** Elizabeth II
Obv: Young bust right **Rev:** Coronation Anniversary legend
added to KM#12

Date	Mintage	F	VF	XF	Unc	BU
1978 Proof	5,775	Value: 65.00				

KM# 42   50 DOLLARS
11.3400 g., 0.5000 Gold 0.1823 oz. AGW **Ruler:** Elizabeth II
Subject: 25th Anniversary of Coronation **Obv:** Young bust right
Rev: The Ampulla

Date	Mintage	F	VF	XF	Unc	BU
1978 Proof	771	Value: 195				

KM# 43   50 DOLLARS
11.3400 g., 0.5000 Gold 0.1823 oz. AGW **Ruler:** Elizabeth II
Subject: 25th Anniversary of Coronation **Obv:** Young bust right
Rev: Royal orb

Date	Mintage	F	VF	XF	Unc	BU
1978 Proof	771	Value: 195				

KM# 44   50 DOLLARS
11.3400 g., 0.5000 Gold 0.1823 oz. AGW **Ruler:** Elizabeth II
Subject: 25th Anniversary of Coronation **Obv:** Young bust right
Rev: St. Edward's Crown

Date	Mintage	F	VF	XF	Unc	BU
1978 Proof	771	Value: 195				

KM# 45   50 DOLLARS
11.3400 g., 0.5000 Gold 0.1823 oz. AGW **Ruler:** Elizabeth II
Subject: 25th Anniversary of Coronation **Obv:** Young bust right
Rev: Coronation chair

Date	Mintage	F	VF	XF	Unc	BU
1978 Proof	771	Value: 195				

KM# 46   50 DOLLARS
11.3400 g., 0.5000 Gold 0.1823 oz. AGW **Ruler:** Elizabeth II
Subject: 25th Anniversary of Coronation **Obv:** Young bust right
Rev: Scepter

Date	Mintage	F	VF	XF	Unc	BU
1978 Proof	771	Value: 195				

KM# 47   50 DOLLARS
11.3400 g., 0.5000 Gold 0.1823 oz. AGW **Ruler:** Elizabeth II
Subject: 25th Anniversary of Coronation **Obv:** Young bust right
Rev: Spoon

Date	Mintage	F	VF	XF	Unc	BU
1978 Proof	771	Value: 195				

KM# 58   50 DOLLARS
11.3400 g., 0.5000 Gold 0.1823 oz. AGW **Ruler:** Elizabeth II
Obv: Young bust right **Rev:** Saxon Kings

Date	Mintage	F	VF	XF	Unc	BU
1980 Proof	10,000	Value: 195				

KM# 59   50 DOLLARS
11.3400 g., 0.5000 Gold 0.1823 oz. AGW **Ruler:** Elizabeth II
Obv: Young bust right **Rev:** Norman Kings

Date	Mintage	F	VF	XF	Unc	BU
1980 Proof	10,000	Value: 195				

KM# 60   50 DOLLARS
11.3400 g., 0.5000 Gold 0.1823 oz. AGW **Ruler:** Elizabeth II
Obv: Young bust right **Rev:** House of Plantagenet - I

Date	Mintage	F	VF	XF	Unc	BU
1980 Proof	11,000	Value: 195				

KM# 61   50 DOLLARS
11.3400 g., 0.5000 Gold 0.1823 oz. AGW **Ruler:** Elizabeth II
Obv: Young bust right **Rev:** House of Plantagenet - II

Date	Mintage	F	VF	XF	Unc	BU
1980 Proof	11,000	Value: 195				

KM# 62   50 DOLLARS
11.3400 g., 0.5000 Gold 0.1823 oz. AGW **Ruler:** Elizabeth II
Obv: Young bust right **Rev:** House of Lancaster

Date	Mintage	F	VF	XF	Unc	BU
1980 Proof	11,000	Value: 195				

KM# 63   50 DOLLARS
11.3400 g., 0.5000 Gold 0.1823 oz. AGW **Ruler:** Elizabeth II
Obv: Young bust right **Rev:** House of York

Date	Mintage	F	VF	XF	Unc	BU
1980 Proof	11,000	Value: 195				

KM# 64   50 DOLLARS
11.3400 g., 0.5000 Gold 0.1823 oz. AGW **Ruler:** Elizabeth II
Obv: Young bust right **Rev:** House of Tudor

Date	Mintage	F	VF	XF	Unc	BU
1980 Proof	11,000	Value: 195				

KM# 65   50 DOLLARS
11.3400 g., 0.5000 Gold 0.1823 oz. AGW **Ruler:** Elizabeth II
Obv: Young bust right **Rev:** House of Stuart and Orange

Date	Mintage	F	VF	XF	Unc	BU
1980 Proof	11,000	Value: 195				

KM# 66   50 DOLLARS
11.3400 g., 0.5000 Gold 0.1823 oz. AGW   **Ruler:** Elizabeth II
Obv: Young bust right **Rev:** House of Hanover

Date	Mintage	F	VF	XF	Unc	BU
1980 Proof	11,000	Value: 195				

KM# 67   50 DOLLARS
11.3400 g., 0.5000 Gold 0.1823 oz. AGW   **Ruler:** Elizabeth II
Obv: Young bust right **Rev:** House of Saxe-Coburg and Windsor

Date	Mintage	F	VF	XF	Unc	BU
1980 Proof	11,000	Value: 195				

KM# 71   50 DOLLARS
5.0000 g., 0.9000 Gold 0.1447 oz. AGW   **Ruler:** Elizabeth II
Subject: 150th Anniversary of Parliamentary Government
Obv: Young bust right **Rev:** Island arms

Date	Mintage	F	VF	XF	Unc	BU
1982 Proof	585	Value: 160				

KM# 79   50 DOLLARS
5.1900 g., 0.9170 Gold 0.1530 oz. AGW   **Ruler:** Elizabeth II
Subject: Royal Visit **Obv:** Young bust right **Rev:** Royal couple
facing each other above small arms

Date	Mintage	F	VF	XF	Unc	BU
1983	5,000	—	—	—	150	—

KM# 83   50 DOLLARS
129.6000 g., 0.9250 Silver 3.8541 oz. ASW, 63 mm.
Ruler: Elizabeth II **Subject:** Bird Conservation **Obv:** Crowned
bust right **Rev:** Snowy Egret left

Date	Mintage	F	VF	XF	Unc	BU
1985 Proof	10,000	Value: 100				

KM# 105   50 DOLLARS
7.8140 g., 0.9990 Gold 0.2510 oz. AGW   **Ruler:** Elizabeth II
Obv: Crowned bust right **Rev:** Cameo Winston Churchill above
Spitfires over Dover

Date	Mintage	F	VF	XF	Unc	BU
1990 Proof	Est. 500	Value: 250				

KM# 115   50 DOLLARS
15.9800 g., 0.9170 Gold 0.4711 oz. AGW   **Ruler:** Elizabeth II
Obv: Crowned bust right **Rev:** Wreck of the "Ten Sails"

Date	Mintage	F	VF	XF	Unc	BU
1994 Proof	Est. 200	Value: 500				

KM# 11   100 DOLLARS
22.6801 g., 0.5000 Gold 0.3646 oz. AGW   **Ruler:** Elizabeth II
Subject: Winston Churchill Centenary **Obv:** Island arms
Rev: Bust facing

Date	Mintage	F	VF	XF	Unc	BU
1974	1,400	—	—	—	365	—
1974 Proof	6,300	Value: 350				

KM# 13   100 DOLLARS
22.6801 g., 0.5000 Gold 0.3646 oz. AGW   **Ruler:** Elizabeth II
Obv: Young bust right **Rev:** Sovereign Queens of England in circle

Date	Mintage	F	VF	XF	Unc	BU
1975	8,053	—	—	—	360	—
1975 Proof	4,950	Value: 375				
1976	2,028	—	—	—	360	—
1976 Proof	3,560	Value: 375				
1977	—	—	—	—	360	—
1977 Proof	2,845	Value: 375				

KM# 69   100 DOLLARS
8.0352 g., 0.9170 Gold 0.2369 oz. AGW   **Ruler:** Elizabeth II
Subject: Wedding of Prince Charles and Lady Diana **Obv:** Young
bust right **Rev:** Busts facing, small island arms above

Date	Mintage	F	VF	XF	Unc	BU
1981 Proof	11,000	Value: 225				

KM# 97   100 DOLLARS
15.9800 g., 0.9170 Gold 0.4711 oz. AGW   **Ruler:** Elizabeth II
Subject: 500th Anniversary of Columbus' Discovery of America

Date	Mintage	F	VF	XF	Unc	BU
1988 Proof	380	Value: 450				

KM# 101   100 DOLLARS
15.9800 g., 0.9170 Gold 0.4711 oz. AGW   **Ruler:** Elizabeth II
Subject: 100 Years of Postal Service **Obv:** Crowned bust right
Rev: Ship with small shield above

Date	Mintage	F	VF	XF	Unc	BU
1989 Proof	93	Value: 500				

KM# 106   100 DOLLARS
15.6080 g., 0.9990 Gold 0.5013 oz. AGW   **Ruler:** Elizabeth II
Subject: Winston Churchill **Obv:** Crowned bust right
Rev: Evacuation of Dunkirk

Date	Mintage	F	VF	XF	Unc	BU
1990 Proof	500	Value: 475				

KM# 117   100 DOLLARS
30.5000 g., 0.9170 Gold 0.8992 oz. AGW   **Ruler:** Elizabeth II
Obv: Crowned bust right **Rev:** Cayman Ironwood Tree

Date	Mintage	F	VF	XF	Unc	BU
1994 Proof	Est. 15,000	Value: 875				

KM# 123   100 DOLLARS
15.9800 g., 0.9170 Gold 0.4711 oz. AGW   **Ruler:** Elizabeth II
Obv: Crowned bust right **Rev:** Amazona Leucocephala
Caymanesis - Parrot

Date	Mintage	F	VF	XF	Unc	BU
1996 Proof	Est. 150	Value: 475				

KM# 82   250 DOLLARS
47.5400 g., 0.9170 Gold 1.4015 oz. AGW, 38.61 mm.
Ruler: Elizabeth II **Subject:** 250th Anniversary of Royal Land
Grant **Obv:** Crowned bust right **Rev:** Map of islands

Date	Mintage	F	VF	XF	Unc	BU
1985 Proof	Est. 250	Value: 1,350				

KM# 15   100 DOLLARS
22.6801 g., 0.5000 Gold 0.3646 oz. AGW   **Ruler:** Elizabeth II
Subject: Queen's Silver Jubilee **Obv:** Young bust right
Rev: Crowned arms with supporters

Date	Mintage	F	VF	XF	Unc	BU
1977	562	—	—	—	360	—
1977 Proof	4,386	Value: 375				

KM# 35   100 DOLLARS
22.6801 g., 0.5000 Gold 0.3646 oz. AGW   **Ruler:** Elizabeth II
Obv: Young bust right **Rev:** Sovereign Queens of England in circle

Date	Mintage	F	VF	XF	Unc	BU
1978 Proof	1,973	Value: 385				

KM# 84 250 DOLLARS
47.5400 g., 0.9170 Gold 1.4015 oz. AGW **Ruler:** Elizabeth II
Subject: Commonwealth Games **Obv:** Crowned bust right
Rev: Long jumper

Date	Mintage	F	VF	XF	Unc	BU
1986 Proof	64	Value: 1,400				

KM# 86 250 DOLLARS
47.5400 g., 0.9170 Gold 1.4015 oz. AGW **Ruler:** Elizabeth II
Subject: Queen Elizabeth II and Philip's 40th Wedding
Anniversary **Obv:** Crowned bust right **Rev:** E & P monogram

Date	Mintage	F	VF	XF	Unc	BU
ND Proof	75	Value: 1,400				

KM# 99 250 DOLLARS
47.5400 g., 0.9170 Gold 1.4015 oz. AGW **Ruler:** Elizabeth II
Subject: Visit of Princess Alexandra **Obv:** Crowned bust right
Rev: Royal Arms of Princess Alexandra

Date	Mintage	F	VF	XF	Unc	BU
1988 Proof	86	Value: 1,400				

KM# 107 250 DOLLARS
31.2100 g., 0.9990 Gold 1.0024 oz. AGW **Ruler:** Elizabeth II
Obv: Crowned bust right **Rev:** Cameo Winston Churchill above
Spitfires over Dover

Date	Mintage	F	VF	XF	Unc	BU
1990 Proof	Est. 500	Value: 975				

KM# 113 250 DOLLARS
47.5400 g., 0.9170 Gold 1.4015 oz. AGW **Ruler:** Elizabeth II
Subject: 40th Anniversary - Coronation of Queen Elizabeth II

Date	Mintage	F	VF	XF	Unc	BU
1993 Proof	Est. 100	Value: 1,375				

KM# 119 250 DOLLARS
47.5400 g., 0.9170 Gold 1.4015 oz. AGW **Ruler:** Elizabeth II
Subject: Royal Visit **Obv:** Crowned bust right **Rev:** Royal couple
above yacht "Britannia"

Date	Mintage	F	VF	XF	Unc	BU
1994 Proof	200	Value: 1,375				

PIEFORTS

KM#	Date	Mintage	Identification	Issue Price	Mkt Val
P1	1982	74	10 Dollars. Silver. KM72.	250	120

MINT SETS

KM#	Date	Mintage	Identification	Issue Price	Mkt Val
MS1	1987 (4)	—	KM87-90	—	5.00
MS2	1992 (4)	—	KM87a-90a	8.00	8.00
MS3	1996 (4)	—	KM87a-90a	—	12.00
MS4	1999 (4)	—	KM131-134	—	15.00

PROOF SETS

KM#	Date	Mintage	Identification	Issue Price	Mkt Val
PS1	1972 (8)	10,757	KM1-8	40.00	25.00
PS2	1973 (8)	9,988	KM1-8	40.00	25.00
PS3	1974 (8)	15,387	KM1-8	40.00	25.00
PS4	1974 (2)	2,400	KM10-11	245	255
PS5	1975 (8)	5,390	KM1-8	54.50	28.00
PS6	1975 (6)	1,785	KM1-6	31.50	10.00
PS7	1975 (2)	3,650	KM12-13	293	295
PS8	1976 (8)	3,044	KM1-8	54.50	30.00
PS9	1976 (2)	1,531	KM12-13	293	295
PS11	1977 (8)	1,970	KM1-8	52.50	35.00
PS12	1977 (6)	2,445	KM12, 16-20	315	310
PS13	1977 (6)	1,932	KM13, 21-25	651	775
PS14	1977 (2)	223	KM14-15	290	275
PS15	1978 (8)	1,303	KM26-33	79.50	60.00
PS16	1978 (6)	5,000	KM36-41	306	270
PS17	1978 (6)	771	KM42-47	600	850
PS18	1979 (8)	4,427	KM1-8	117	50.00
PS19	1980 (8)	1,215	KM1-8	147	45.00
PS20	1980 (10)	—	KM48-57	—	350
PS21	1981 (8)	865	KM1-8	147	50.00
PS22	1982 (8)	589	KM1-7, 70	147	65.00
PS23	1983 (8)	348	KM1-4, 73-76	157	125
PS24	1984 (8)	—	KM1-4, 8, 73-75	159	120
PS25	1986 (8)	330	KM1-4, 7-8, 73-74	150	85.00
PS26	1987 (8)	317	KM85a, 87-93	160	200
PS27	1988 (8)	318	KM87-93, 94.2	170	300
PS28	1990 (4)	500	KM104-107	1,650	1,625

CENTRAL AFRICAN REPUBLIC

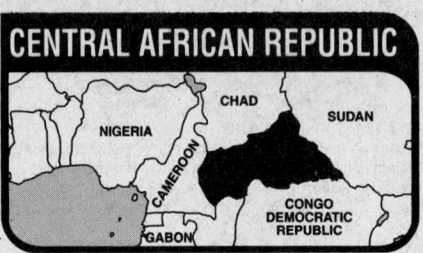

The Central African Republic, a landlocked country in Central Africa, bounded by Chad on the north, Cameroon on the west, Congo (Brazzaville) and Congo Democratic Republic, (formerly Zaire) on the south and the Sudan on the east, has an area of 240,324 sq. mi. (622,984 sq. km.) and a population of 3.2 million. Capital: Bangui. Deposits of uranium, iron ore, manganese and copper remain to be developed. Diamonds, cotton, timber and coffee are exported.

The area that is now the Central African Republic was constituted as the French territory of Ubangi-Shari in 1894. It was united with Chad in 1905 and joined with Middle Congo and Gabon in 1910, becoming one of the four territories of French Equatorial Africa. Upon dissolution of the federation on Dec. 1, 1958, the constituent territories became fully autonomous members of the French Community. Ubangi-Shari proclaimed its complete independence as the Central African Republic on Aug. 13, 1960.

On Jan. 1, 1966, Col. Jean-Bedel Bokassa, Chief of Staff of the Armed Forces, overthrew the government of President David Dacko and assumed power as president of the republic. President Bokassa abolished the constitution of 1959 and dissolved the National Assembly. In 1975 the Congress of the sole political party appointed Bokassa president for life. The republic became a constitutional monarchy on Dec. 4, 1976; President Bokassa was named Emperor Bokassa I. Bokassa was ousted as Central African emperor in a bloodless takeover of the government led by former president David Dacko on Sept. 20, 1979, and the African nation proclaimed once again a republic.

NOTE: For earlier coinage see French Equatorial Africa and Equatorial African States including later coinage as listed in Central African States.

RULERS
French, until 1960
Marshal Jean-Bedel Bokassa, 1976-1979

MINT MARKS
(a) - Paris, privy marks only

MONETARY SYSTEM
100 Centimes = 1 Franc

REPUBLIC
DECIMAL COINAGE

KM# 6 100 FRANCS
7.0000 g., Nickel, 25.5 mm. **Obv:** Three giant eland left
Rev: Denomination within circle

Date	Mintage	F	VF	XF	Unc	BU
1971(a)	2,500,000	5.00	8.00	13.50	28.00	—
1972(a)	3,500,000	5.00	8.00	13.50	28.00	—

KM# 7 100 FRANCS
7.0000 g., Nickel, 25.5 mm. **Obv:** Three giant eland left
Rev: Denomination, date below, within circle

Date	Mintage	F	VF	XF	Unc	BU
1975(a)	—	4.50	7.50	12.50	22.50	—
1976(a)	—	2.00	3.50	6.00	10.00	—
1979(a)	—	6.00	13.50	20.00	35.00	—
1982(a)	—	2.75	4.50	8.00	15.00	—
1983(a)	—	2.75	4.50	9.00	20.00	—
1984(a)	—	2.50	4.00	7.00	11.50	—
1985(a)	—	2.50	4.00	7.00	11.50	—
1988(a)	—	2.50	4.00	7.00	11.50	—
1990(a)	—	2.00	3.50	6.00	10.00	—
1996(a)	—	2.00	3.50	6.00	10.00	—
1998(a)	—	2.00	3.50	6.00	10.00	—

KM# 8 100 FRANCS
7.0000 g., Nickel, 25.5 mm. **Obv:** Three giant eland left
Rev: Denomination and date within circle **Rev. Leg.:** EMPIRE
CENTRAFRICAIN

Date	Mintage	F	VF	XF	Unc	BU
1978(a)	—	40.00	70.00	165	500	850

Note: These were produced during the short-lived reign of dictator Jean-Bedel Bokassa as Emperor, but not released for circulation

KM# 1 1000 FRANCS
3.5000 g., 0.9000 Gold 0.1013 oz. AGW **Subject:** 10th Anniversary of Independence **Obv:** Bust of President Jean Bedel Bokassa facing **Rev:** Three joined shields, radiant sun above center shield, denomination below

Date	Mintage	F	VF	XF	Unc	BU
1970 Proof	4,000	Value: 120				

KM# 2 3000 FRANCS
10.5000 g., 0.9000 Gold 0.3038 oz. AGW **Subject:** 10th Anniversary of Independence **Rev:** Bust with mortarboard facing, denomination below

Date	Mintage	F	VF	XF	Unc	BU
1970 Proof	4,000	Value: 325				

KM# 3 5000 FRANCS
17.5000 g., 0.9000 Gold 0.5064 oz. AGW **Subject:** 10th Anniversary of Independence; 1972 Munich Olympics **Obv:** Head left divides dates **Rev:** Wrestlers, date and denomination below

Date	Mintage	F	VF	XF	Unc	BU
1970 Proof	4,000	Value: 500				

KM# 4 10000 FRANCS
35.0000 g., 0.9000 Gold 1.0127 oz. AGW **Subject:** 10th Anniversary of Independence; ONU 24th Anniversary **Obv:** Head left divides dates **Rev:** Map at center, heads above, denomination below

Date	Mintage	F	VF	XF	Unc	BU
1970 Proof	4,000	Value: 1,000				

KM# 5 20000 FRANCS
70.0000 g., 0.9000 Gold 2.0254 oz. AGW **Subject:** 10th Anniversary of Independence; Operation Bokassa **Obv:** Head of Bokassa left, divides dates **Rev:** Symbols of independence, denomination below

Date	Mintage	F	VF	XF	Unc	BU
1970 Proof	4,000	Value: 2,100				

SECOND REPUBLIC

DECIMAL COINAGE

KM# 11 500 FRANCS
Copper-Nickel

Date	Mintage	F	VF	XF	Unc	BU
1985	—	7.50	15.00	30.00	55.00	—
1986	—	7.50	15.00	30.00	55.00	—

ESSAIS

KM#	Date	Mintage	Identification	Issue Price	Mkt Val
E1	1970	—	1000 Francs. Bronze. KM1.	—	125
E1a	1970	—	1000 Francs. Nickel.	—	125
E2	1971	1,450	100 Francs. Nickel. KM6.	—	25.00
E3	1971	4	100 Francs. Gold. KM6.	—	1,400
E4	1975	1,700	100 Francs. Nickel center. KM7.	—	22.00
E5	1978	1,900	100 Francs. Nickel. KM8.	—	300
E6	1985	1,700	500 Francs. Copper-Nickel. Plants divide date and denomination. Woman's head, 3/4 left. KM11.	—	45.00

PROOF SETS

KM#	Date	Mintage	Identification	Issue Price	Mkt Val
PS1	1970 (5)	40,000	KM1-5	375	3,000

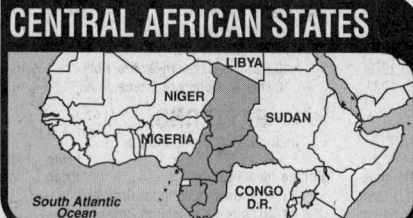

CENTRAL AFRICAN STATES

The Central African States, a monetary union comprised of Equatorial Guinea (a former Spanish possession), the former French possessions and now independent states of the Republic of Congo (Brazzaville), Gabon, Central African Republic, Chad and Cameroon, issues a common currency for the member states from a common central bank. The monetary unit, the African Financial Community franc, is tied to and supported by the French franc.

In 1960, an attempt was made to form a union of the newly independent republics of Chad, Congo, Central Africa and Gabon. The proposal was discarded when Chad refused to become a constituent member. The four countries then linked into an Equatorial Customs Unit, to which Cameroon became an associate member in 1961. A more extensive cooperation of the five republics, identified as the Central African Customs and Economic Union, was entered into force at the beginning of 1966.

In 1974 the Central Bank of the Equatorial African States, which had issued coins and paper currency in its own name and with the names of the constituent member nations, changed its name to the Bank of the Central African States. Equatorial Guinea converted to the CFA currency system issuing its first 100 Franc in 1985.

For earlier coinage see French Equatorial Africa.

Country Code Letters

To observe the movement of coinage throughout the states, the country of origin in which the coin is intended to circulate is designated by the following additional code letters:

A = Chad
B = Central African Republic
C = Congo
D = Gabon
E = Cameroon

By 1996 this practice was discontinued as the strategy had proved to be inconclusive.

MONETARY UNION

STANDARD COINAGE

KM# 8 FRANC
1.3000 g., Aluminum, 23 mm. **Obv:** Three giant eland left, date below **Rev:** Denomination within wreath

Date	Mintage	F	VF	XF	Unc	BU
1974	3,000,000	0.30	0.60	1.00	2.50	—
1976	4,000,000	0.30	0.60	1.00	2.50	—
1978	1,100,000	0.20	0.40	0.80	2.00	—
1979	250,000	0.20	0.40	0.80	2.00	—
1982	400,000	0.20	0.40	0.80	2.00	—
1985	300,000	0.20	0.40	0.80	2.00	—
1986	300,000	0.20	0.40	0.80	2.00	—
1988	100,000	0.20	0.40	0.80	2.00	—
1990	900,000	0.20	0.40	0.80	2.00	—
1992	300,000	0.20	0.40	0.80	2.00	—
1998(a)	10,000,000	0.20	0.40	0.80	2.00	—

KM# 7 5 FRANCS
3.0000 g., Aluminum-Bronze, 20 mm. **Obv:** Three giant eland left, date below **Rev:** Denomination within wreath

Date	Mintage	F	VF	XF	Unc	BU
1973	26,000,000	0.15	0.30	0.60	1.65	—
1975	—	0.15	0.30	0.60	1.65	—
1976	—	0.15	0.30	0.60	1.65	—
1977	—	0.15	0.30	0.60	1.65	—
1978	—	0.15	0.30	0.60	1.65	—
1979	—	0.15	0.30	0.60	1.65	—
1980	—	0.15	0.30	0.60	1.35	—
1981	—	0.15	0.30	0.60	1.35	—
1982	—	0.15	0.30	0.60	1.35	—
1983	—	0.15	0.30	0.60	1.35	—
1984	—	0.15	0.30	0.60	1.35	—
1985	—	0.15	0.30	0.60	1.35	—
1992	—	0.15	0.30	0.60	1.35	—

Date	Mintage	F	VF	XF	Unc	BU
1996(a)	—	0.15	0.30	0.60	1.25	—
1998(a)	—	0.15	0.30	0.60	1.25	—

KM# 9 10 FRANCS
4.0000 g., Aluminum-Bronze, 23 mm. **Obv:** Three giant eland left, date below **Rev:** Denomination within wreath

Date	Mintage	F	VF	XF	Unc	BU
1974	18,500,000	0.20	0.35	0.75	2.00	—
1975	—	0.20	0.35	0.75	2.00	—
1976	—	0.20	0.35	0.75	2.00	—
1977	—	0.20	0.35	0.75	2.00	—
1978	—	0.20	0.35	0.75	2.00	—
1979	—	0.20	0.35	0.75	2.00	—
1980	—	0.20	0.35	0.65	1.35	—
1981	—	0.20	0.35	0.65	1.35	—
1982	—	0.20	0.35	0.65	1.35	—
1983	—	0.20	0.35	0.65	1.35	—
1984	—	0.20	0.35	0.65	1.35	—
1985	—	0.20	0.35	0.65	1.35	—
1992	—	0.20	0.35	0.65	1.35	—
1996	—	0.20	0.35	0.75	1.65	—
1998(a)	—	0.20	0.35	0.75	1.50	—

KM# 10 25 FRANCS
8.0000 g., Aluminum-Bronze, 27.1 mm. **Obv:** Three giant eland left, date below **Rev:** Denomination within wreath

Date	Mintage	F	VF	XF	Unc	BU
1975(a)	—	0.50	1.00	1.75	3.00	—
1976(a)	—	0.50	1.00	1.50	2.75	—
1978(a)	—	0.50	1.00	1.50	2.75	—
1982(a)	—	0.35	0.75	1.25	2.50	—
1983(a)	—	0.35	0.75	1.25	2.50	—
1984(a)	—	0.35	0.75	1.25	2.50	—
1985(a)	—	0.35	0.75	1.25	2.50	—
1986(a)	—	0.35	0.75	1.25	2.50	—
1988(a)	—	0.35	0.75	1.25	2.50	—
1990(a)	—	0.35	0.75	1.25	2.50	—
1991(a)	—	0.35	0.75	1.25	2.50	—
1992(a)	—	0.35	0.75	1.25	2.50	—
1996(a)	—	0.35	0.75	1.25	2.50	—
1998(a)	—	0.25	0.50	1.00	2.00	—

KM# 11 50 FRANCS
4.7000 g., Nickel, 21.5 mm. **Obv:** Three giant eland left, date below **Rev:** Denomination within flower design **Note:** Starting in 1996 an extra flora item was added where the mintmark was formerly located.

Date	Mintage	F	VF	XF	Unc	BU
1976(a) A	10,000,000	2.00	3.50	7.50	12.00	—
1976(a) B	Inc. above	2.00	3.50	7.50	12.00	—
1976(a) C	Inc. above	1.00	2.00	4.00	7.00	—
1976(a) D	Inc. above	1.00	2.00	4.00	7.00	—
1976(a) E	Inc. above	1.00	2.00	4.00	7.50	—
1977(a) A	—	2.00	3.50	7.50	12.00	—
1977(a) B	—	2.00	3.50	7.50	12.00	—
1977(a) C	—	1.00	2.00	4.00	7.00	—
1977(a) D	—	1.00	2.00	4.00	7.00	—
1977(a) E	—	1.00	2.00	4.00	7.50	—
1978(a) A	—	2.00	3.50	7.50	12.00	—
1978(a) B	—	2.00	3.50	7.50	12.00	—
1978(a) C	—	1.00	2.00	4.00	7.00	—
1978(a) D	—	1.00	2.00	4.00	7.00	—
1979(a) E	—	1.00	2.00	4.00	7.00	—
1979(a) B	—	1.00	2.00	4.00	7.50	—
1980(a) A	—	1.50	2.75	5.50	11.50	—
1980(a) C	—	0.75	1.50	3.50	6.00	—
1981(a) C	—	0.75	1.50	3.50	6.00	—
1981(a) D	—	0.85	1.75	3.75	6.50	—
1982(a) A	—	1.50	2.75	5.50	11.50	—
1983(a) B	—	0.75	1.50	3.50	6.00	—
1983(a) D	—	0.75	1.50	3.50	6.00	—
1983(a) E	—	0.75	1.50	3.50	6.00	—

Date	Mintage	F	VF	XF	Unc	BU
1984(a) A	—	1.50	2.75	5.50	11.50	—
1984(a) B	—	1.50	2.75	5.50	11.50	—
1984(a) C	—	0.75	1.50	3.50	6.00	—
1984(a) D	—	0.75	1.50	3.50	6.00	—
1985(a) A	—	1.50	2.75	5.50	11.50	—
1985(a) B	—	1.50	2.75	5.50	11.50	—
1985(a) D	—	0.75	1.50	3.50	6.00	—
1986(a) A	—	1.50	2.75	5.50	11.50	—
1986(a) E	—	0.85	1.75	3.75	6.50	—
1988(a) B	—	1.50	2.75	5.50	11.50	—
1989(a) A	—	1.50	2.75	5.50	11.50	—
1990(a) B	—	1.50	2.75	5.50	11.50	—
1990 A	—	1.50	2.75	5.50	11.50	—
1991(a) A	—	1.50	2.75	5.50	11.50	—
1996(a) Cocoa bean	—	0.75	1.50	3.50	6.00	—
1998(a) Cocoa bean	—	0.75	1.50	3.50	6.00	—

KM# 13   100 FRANCS
7.0500 g., Nickel, 25.5 mm. **Obv:** Three giant eland
Rev: Denomination

Date	Mintage	F	VF	XF	Unc	BU
1992(a)	—	—	—	—	4.50	6.00
1996(a)	—	—	—	—	4.50	6.00
1998(a)	—	—	—	—	4.50	6.00

KM# 12   500 FRANCS
9.0000 g., Nickel, 28 mm. **Obv:** Half figure of woman within circle,
date lower right **Rev:** Eland head left divides denomination above

Date	Mintage	F	VF	XF	Unc	BU
1976 A	4,000,000	5.50	8.50	13.50	22.00	—
1976 B	Inc. above	5.50	8.50	13.50	22.00	—
1976 C	Inc. above	4.50	8.00	12.50	20.00	—
1976 D	Inc. above	4.50	8.00	12.50	20.00	—
1976 E	Inc. above	4.50	8.00	12.50	20.00	—
1977 A	—	5.50	8.50	15.00	25.00	—
1977 B	—	5.50	8.50	15.00	25.00	—
1977 C	—	4.50	8.00	12.50	25.00	—
1977 D	—	4.50	8.00	12.50	20.00	—
1977 E	—	3.00	6.00	10.00	16.50	—
1979 D	—	3.50	7.00	12.00	18.50	—
1979(a) B	—	3.50	7.00	12.00	18.50	—
1979(a) E	—	3.50	7.00	12.00	18.50	—
1982 D	—	3.50	7.00	12.00	18.50	—
1984 A	—	3.50	7.00	12.00	18.50	—
1984 B	—	3.50	7.00	12.00	18.50	—
1984 C	—	3.50	7.00	12.00	18.50	—
1984 E	—	3.50	7.00	12.00	18.50	—

KM# 14   500 FRANCS
11.0000 g., Copper-Nickel, 30 mm. **Obv:** Native woman's head
half left **Rev:** Plant divides denomination and date **Edge:** Plain

Date	Mintage	F	VF	XF	Unc	BU
1998(a)	—	—	—	—	16.00	18.00

ESSAIS
Standard metals unless otherwise noted

KM#	Date	Mintage	Identification	Issue Price	Mkt Val
E1	1973	1,550	5 Francs. Aluminum-Bronze. KM7.	—	11.50
E2	1974	1,550	Franc. Aluminum. KM8.	—	10.00
E3	1974	1,550	10 Francs. Aluminum-Bronze. KM9.	—	10.00
EA4	1975	—	10 Francs. Aluminum-Bronze. KM9.	—	10.00
E4	1975	1,700	25 Francs. Aluminum-Bronze. KM10.	—	10.00
E5	1976	—	Franc. KM6.	—	10.00
E6	1976	—	5 Francs. Aluminum-Bronze. KM7.	—	10.00
E7	1976	—	10 Francs. Aluminum-Bronze. KM9.	—	11.50

KM#	Date	Mintage	Identification	Issue Price	Mkt Val
E8	1976	—	50 Francs. Nickel. KM11.	—	12.50
E9	1976(a)	—	500 Francs. Nickel. KM12.	—	30.00
E10	1979	—	10 Francs. Aluminum-Bronze. KM9.	—	10.00
E11	1983	—	10 Francs. Aluminum-Bronze. KM9.	—	10.00

PATTERNS
Including off metal strikes

KM#	Date	Mintage	Identification	Issue Price	Mkt Val
Pn1	1956	33	40 Francs. Aluminum-Bronze.	—	375
Pn2	1956	33	40 Francs. Aluminum-Bronze.	—	375
Pn3	1956	33	40 Francs. Aluminum-Bronze.	—	375
Pn4	1956	33	40 Francs. Aluminum-Bronze.	—	375
Pn5	1956	33	40 Francs. Aluminum-Bronze.	—	375
Pn6	1956	33	40 Francs. Aluminum-Bronze.	—	375

CENTRAL ASIA

In the several centuries prior to 1500 which witnessed the breakup of the Mongol Empire and the subsequent rise of smaller successor states, no single power or dynasty was able to control the vast expanses of Western and Central Asia. The region known previously as Transoxiana, the land beyond the Oxus River (modern Amu Darya), became the domain of the Shaybanids, then the Janids. The territory ruled by these dynasties had no set borders, which rather expanded and contracted as the fortunes of the rulers ebbed and flowed. At their greatest extent, the khanate took in parts of what are now northern Iran and Afghanistan, as well as part or all of modern Turkmenistan, Uzbekistan, Kazakhstan, Tadzhikistan and Kyrgyzstan. Coins are known to have been struck by virtually every ruler, but some are quite scarce owing to short reigns or the ever-changing political and economic situation.

MINTS
Abivard
Akhshi/Akhshikath
Andigan/Andijan
Asfarayin/Isfarayin
Astarabad
Awbah
Badakhshan
Balkh
Bistam
Bukhara
Damghan
Herat
Hisar
Karmin
Kish
Kufan/Kufin
Langar
Marw
Mashhad
Nasaf
Nimruz
Nisa
Qarshi (copper only)
Qayin
Qunduz
Sabzavar
Samarqand
Tashkand (Tashkent)
Termez
Tun
Turbat
Urdu (camp mint)
Yazur

BUKHARA

Bukhara, a city and former emirate in southern Russian Turkestan, formed part (Sogdiana) of the Seleucid Empire after the conquest of Alexander the Great and incessantly remained an important region throughout the middle ages, often serving as the capital center for a succession of ruling dynasties of Iranian and Turkish origin until the 19th century. It became virtually a Russian vassal in 1868 as a consequence of the Czarist invasion of 1866, following which it gradually became a part of Russian Turkestan and then part of Uzbekistan S.S.R., now Uzbekistan.

RULERS
Russian Vassal,
  (since AH1284/1868AD)
Emir Abd al-Ahad,
  AH1303-1328 / 1886-1910AD
Emir Sayyid Alim Khan,
  AH1329-1339 / 1911-1920AD

MINT NAME

بخاراي شريف بخارا

Bukhara   Bukhara-yi Sharif

MONETARY SYSTEM

Until AH1322/1905AD: 45 to 64 Pul (Fulus) = 4 Miri = 1 silver Tenga
19 to 21 Tenga = 1 Tilla (gold 4.55 g.)
Until AH1336-1338/1918-1920AD: copper Tenga or Tenga-fulus

Within the protectorate period, Russian currency of Roubles and Kopeks were officially in circulation: 1 silver Tenga = 20 Kopeks

Note: All copper, bronze and brass issues of Bukhara in the 20th century are anonymous. Some silver and gold issues traditionally bear the names of Emirs long since deceased.

Note: Denominations of 1/32 Tenga & Tilla are of very similar design under various rulers, but can be distinguished by date.

Note: Tilla coins are known with a date appearing as "134-", which is actually 1316 with the "1" and "6" stuck close together, appearing as a Persian "4".

Note: Most copper, bronze and brass AH1336-1338 dated coins of 2, 3, 10 and especially 20 Tenga exhibit considerable flat spots, die shifts and other defects. Well-struck specimens with fully struck design demand a considerable premium.

Note: The numerals "0" and "5" have variant forms in Bukhara, including an open "J"–type symbol for "5" instead of a closed symbol:

0   ０   and   ♦

5   ﻝ   or   ﻝ   instead of   ٥   ٥

KHANATE

Abd Al-Ahad
AH1303-1329/1886-1910AD

HAMMERED COINAGE

KM# 67.2   PUL (Fulus)
Copper **Obv:** Inscription and date **Obv. Insc.:** "Bukhara"
Rev: Denomination and date

Date	Mintage	Good	VG	F	VF	XF
AH1319	—	—	—	—	—	—

KM# 87   1/32 TENGA (2 Fulus)
Copper **Obv:** Inscription and date **Obv. Insc.:** "zarb Bukhara-yi sharif" **Rev:** Inscription and date **Rev. Insc.:** "Fulus 32"
Note: Large "32" above Fulus indicates the denomination (1/32 Tenga). Varieties exist. Prev. Y#1.

Date	Mintage	Good	VG	F	VF	XF
AH1322	—	10.00	15.00	20.00	30.00	40.00
AH1324	—	10.00	15.00	20.00	30.00	40.00

KM# 86   1/32 TENGA (2 Fulus)
Copper **Obv:** Inscription and date **Obv. Insc.:** "Fulus Bukhara"
Rev: "32" in 6-petal ornate cartouche **Note:** Varieties exist on round or irregular flans. Size varies 14-17 mm. Large "32" above Fulus indicates the denomination (1/32 Tenga). Prev. #Y4.1.

Date	Mintage	Good	VG	F	VF	XF
AH1322	—	—	5.00	8.50	16.50	25.00
AH1323	—	—	4.00	7.00	12.00	20.00

Note: Coins exist with denomination error "23"

Date	Mintage	Good	VG	F	VF	XF
AH1324	—	—	4.00	7.00	12.00	20.00
AH1327	—	—	6.00	10.00	18.00	20.00
AH1328	—	—	6.00	10.00	18.00	30.00

KM# 75   TENGA
Silver **Rev:** Mint and date **Mint:** Bukhara **Note:** Previous KM#63.

Date	Mintage	Good	VG	F	VF	XF
AH1319//1308	—	30.00	50.00	75.00	100	
AH1319//1311	—	30.00	50.00	75.00	100	
AH1319 Recut 1311	—	10.00	20.00	35.00	60.00	
AH1319	—	10.00	15.00	25.00	60.00	
AH1320//1319	—	10.00	20.00	35.00	60.00	
AH1320//1320	—	17.50	30.00	50.00	80.00	
AH1321//1320 1321 recut from 1320	—	10.00	20.00	35.00	60.00	
AH1322	—	7.50	15.00	27.50	45.00	

Note: Doubled flan errors dated AH1322/1322 consisting of two strikes forged together exist, weighing approximately 6.25 grams

KM# 65 TILLA
4.5500 g., Gold **Note:** Struck in the name of late Ma'sum Ghazi (Emir Shah Murad). Die varieties exist with and without date on reverse. Prev. #Y3.

Date	Mintage	Good	VG	F	VF	XF
AH1319	—	—	115	120	140	185
AH1321	—	—	125	165	250	350
AH1322//1322	—	—	115	120	140	185
AH1324/1324	—	—	115	120	140	185
AH1324//1316	—	—	125	165	250	350
AH1324//1321	—	—	125	165	250	350
AH1325//1325	—	—	115	120	140	185
AH1325//1325	—	—	120	155	225	320

Note: Reverse date recut from 1324

Date	Mintage	Good	VG	F	VF	XF
AH1327	—	—	115	135	200	300
AH1328	—	—	115	135	200	300
AH1328//1292	—	—	175	250	350	500
AH1328//1304	—	—	125	165	250	350
AH1328//1321	—	—	175	250	350	500

Alim Khan
AH1329-1339/1910-1920AD
HAMMERED COINAGE

KM# A63 1/32 TENGA (2 Fulus)
Copper **Obv. Insc.:** "Fulus Bukhara" **Rev:** "32" in a 6-petal ornate cartouche **Note:** Size varies 12-14 mm. Similar to KM#86. "32" indicates denomination (1/32 Tenga). Numerous die varieties exist including placement of date for 1332 with date inside or below Fulus.

Date	Mintage	Good	VG	F	VF	XF
AH1329	—	—	6.00	12.00	20.00	35.00
AH1330	—	—	4.00	7.00	15.00	22.50

Note: Date appearing as "1335" is actually "1330" with small circle instead of dot for zero

Date	Mintage	Good	VG	F	VF	XF
AH1331	—	—	5.00	8.50	16.50	25.00
AH1332	—	—	4.00	7.00	15.00	22.50
AH1333	—	—	6.00	12.00	20.00	35.00

Note: Exists with denomination errors 21, 201, 22, 31, etc.

Date	Mintage	Good	VG	F	VF	XF
AH13-33 Divided date	—	—	8.00	15.00	25.00	40.00
ND	—	—	12.50	20.00	40.00	75.00

KM# 42 2 FULUS
Copper **Obv:** Inscription and date **Obv. Insc.:** "Fulus Bukhara" **Rev:** "2" in 6-petal ornate cartouche **Note:** Many varieties exist, including placement of date for 1332 and 1333 with date inside or below Fulu. Size varies: 11-14mm. Prev. #Y4.

Date	Mintage	Good	VG	F	VF	XF
AH1330	—	—	15.00	27.50	45.00	70.00
AH1332	—	—	7.50	14.00	22.50	35.00

Note: This date exists with denomination error "6" and with "2" engraved above "32"

Date	Mintage	Good	VG	F	VF	XF
AH1333	—	—	15.00	20.00	45.00	70.00
AH13-33 Divided date	—	—	20.00	35.00	50.00	75.00
ND	—	—	20.00	35.00	50.00	75.00

Note: With 2 above crescent in circle resembling an Arabic "4"

KM# 44 4 FULUS
Copper **Obv:** Sanah and date, inscription below **Obv. Insc.:** "Bukhara" **Rev. Insc.:** "Chahar Fulus" **Note:** Size varies: 14-16 mm. Die varieties exist. Prev. #Y5.

Date	Mintage	Good	VG	F	VF	XF
AH1334	—	—	5.00	8.50	16.50	25.00
AH1335	—	—	30.00	50.00	80.00	125

KM# 45 8 FULUS
Copper **Obv:** Inscription, date below double line **Obv. Insc.:** "Bukhara" **Rev. Insc.:** "Hasht Fulus" **Note:** Size varies: 15-18mm. Die varieties exist. Prev. #YA5.

Date	Mintage	Good	VG	F	VF	XF
AH1335	—	—	5.00	8.50	16.50	25.00

KM# A6 1/2 TENGA
Copper, 14 mm. **Obv. Insc.:** Inscription and date in hextagonal frame **Rev:** "zarb Buhkhara" **Rev. Insc.:** "fulus nim tangah" **Note:** Prev. #Y6.

Date	Mintage	Good	VG	F	VF	XF
AH1336	—	—	15.00	30.00	50.00	100

KM# 46.1 TENGA
Copper **Obv:** Inscription and date in dotted circle **Obv. Insc.:** "zarb Bukhara" **Rev. Insc.:** "fulus yak tangah" **Note:** Size varies 13-16mm. Small round or irregular flans, no border. Die varieties exist.

Date	Mintage	Good	VG	F	VF	XF
AH1336	—	—	20.00	35.00	55.00	80.00

KM# 46.2 TENGA
Copper **Obv:** Inscription and date in beaded circle **Obv. Insc.:** "zarb Bukhara" **Rev. Insc.:** "fulus yak tangah" **Note:** Size varies 17-20mm. Large round or irregular flans, irregular flans are scarcer than round flans. Many varieties exist. Prev. #Y6a.

Date	Mintage	Good	VG	F	VF	XF
AH1336	—	—	6.00	12.00	20.00	35.00
AH1337	—	—	6.00	12.00	20.00	35.00

Note: This date exists with 5-rayed (outlined and full), and 6-rayed (outlined) star on obverse

	—	—	10.00	17.50	30.00	50.00

Note: Overstruck on 4 or 8 Fulus, KM#44 and 45

AH1337	—	—	10.00	17.50	30.00	50.00

Note: Overstruck on 8 Fulus KM#45

AH1338	—	—	75.00	100	135	185

KM# 47 2 TENGA
Bronze **Obv:** Inscription and date in dotted circle **Obv. Insc.:** "zarb bukhara" **Rev. Insc.:** "fulus du tangah" **Note:** Size varies 22-23mm. Varieties with upright and oblique milled edge exist, both years exist with 5-rayed (outlined and full), and 6-rayed (outlined) star on obverse. Prev. #Y7.

Date	Mintage	Good	VG	F	VF	XF
AH1336	—	—	6.00	12.00	25.00	55.00
AH1337	—	—	6.00	12.00	25.00	55.00

Note: Also exists without star (rare)

KM# 48 3 TENGA
Bronze **Obv:** Inscription and date **Obv. Insc.:** "zarb Bukhara" **Rev. Insc.:** "fulus se tangah" **Note:** Greek meander circle both sides. Varieties with upright and oblique milled edge exist. Size varies 24-26mm. Prev. #Y8.

Date	Mintage	Good	VG	F	VF	XF
AH1336	—	—	6.00	12.00	25.00	50.00
AH1337	—	—	6.00	12.00	25.00	50.00

Note: Exists with 5-rayed outlined and full (whole or broken) star on obverse

AH1337						

Note: Struck on small 23 mm and thin 2 Tenga flan

KM# 49 4 TENGA
Bronze, 30 mm. **Obv:** Inscription and date **Obv. Insc.:** "zarb Bukhara" **Rev. Insc.:** "fulus chahar tangah" **Note:** Floral design circle on both sides. Prev. #Y9.

Date	Mintage	Good	VG	F	VF	XF
AH1336 Rare						

Note: This denomination was officially announced for circulation, but its production in quantity was reduced as it was considered excessive and economically senseless

KM# 50 5 TENGA
Bronze **Obv:** Inscription and date in almond-shaped inner border **Obv. Insc.:** "zarb Bukhara" **Rev. Insc.:** "fulus panj tangah" **Note:** Greek meander circle on both sides. Varieties exist with upright and oblique milled edge. Size varies 28-30mm. Prev. #Y10.

Date	Mintage	Good	VG	F	VF	XF
AH1336	—	—	25.00	40.00	65.00	100
AH1337	—	—	25.00	40.00	65.00	100

KM# 53 10 TENGA
Brass, 29 mm. **Obv:** Inscription and date **Obv. Insc.:** "zarb Bukhara" **Rev. Insc.:** "fulus yakdah tangah" **Note:** Square frames on both sides vary in size, varieties exist with upright and oblique milled edge. Reverse date varies in position and arrangement (full or divided dates with different combinations). Prev. #Y11.

Date	Mintage	Good	VG	F	VF	XF
AH1337//1337	—	—	8.00	15.00	25.00	40.00

Note: With chain border on both sides

AH1337//1337	—	—	12.50	22.50	40.00	60.00

Note: With branch border (similar to 20 Tenga) on obverse

AH1337//1338	—	—	10.00	17.50	32.50	50.00
AH1338//1338	—	—	30.00	45.00	80.00	125

KM# 51.1 20 TENGA
Bronze Or Brass **Obv:** Inscription and date in crescent, 6-pointed circled star above **Obv. Insc.:** "zarb Bukharayi sharif" **Rev:** Inscription and date within 6-pointed star **Rev. Insc.:** "bist tangah" **Note:** Varieties exist with upright and oblique milled edge, obverse date varies in position and arrangement (full or divided dates with different combinations). Prev. KM#51 and #Y12.

Date	Mintage	Good	VG	F	VF	XF
AH1337	—	—	22.50	35.00	50.00	85.00

Note: Dated on both sides

AH1337	—	—	27.50	45.00	75.00	110

Note: Dated reverse only

KM# 51.2 20 TENGA
Brass, 33 mm. **Obv:** Inscription (mintname in error without second alif) and date in crescent, 6-pointed circled star above **Obv. Insc.:** "zarb Bukhari sharif" **Rev:** Inscription and date within 6-pointed star **Rev. Insc.:** "bist tangah"

Date	Mintage	Good	VG	F	VF	XF
AH1337	—	—	40.00	55.00	80.00	120

Note: Dated on both sides

KM# A65 TILLA
4.5500 g., Gold **Note:** Struck in the name of late Ma'sum Ghazi (Emir Shah Murad).

Date	Mintage	Good	VG	F	VF	XF
AH1329	—	—	95.00	110	135	185
AH1330	—	—	150	250	350	500
AH1331	—	—	120	180	250	350

KHIVA

Khiva (Khwarezm), a present town but once a great kingdom under the names of Chorasmia, Khwarezm and Urgenj. Khiva is located in Central Asia east of the Caspian Sea and south of the Aral Sea. It was the westernmost successor of the former Janid state, now divided between Uzbekistan and Turkmenistan.

Almost all coins bear the mint name Khwarizm (Khorezm), sometimes paired with the epithet *dar al-islam*. A few have the mint name Khivaq (for Khiva). The gold coins are rare, but generally well-struck, as are the early silver coins, until about AH1280/1863AD. The later silver is often weakly struck, and is usually found worn, as is the copper of all periods.

Russia established relations with Khwarezm (Khiva) in the 17th century, occupied it in AH1290/1873AD, and annexed it in 1875. Revolution concentrated Russia's preoccupation elsewhere during 1917 and Khwarezm (Khiva) seized this opportunity to declare its independence. It was able to sustain this status for a scant two years. By 1919 the Soviet regime had reestablished control over the region and extinguished the independent state. In AH1338/1920AD it became Khwarezm Soviet People's Republic and later became part of the Uzbekistan S.S.R., now Uzbekistan.

RULERS

Sayyid Abdullah Khan and Junaid Khan,

AH1337-1338/1918-1920AD

MINT NAMES

خوارزم

Khwarezm

دار الاسلام خوارزم

Dar al-Islam Khwarezm

Note: All copper, bronze and brass issues of Khiva (Khorezm, Khwarezm) in the 20th century are anonymous, except the silver Tenga Y#8, which bears the name of a Khan, long since deceased.

KHANATE

Sayyid Muhammad Rahim
AH1282-1328 / 1865-1910 AD
HAMMERED COINAGE

Y# 3.1 PUL (Fulus)
Copper **Obv:** Inscription in circle **Obv. Insc.:** "Khwarezm" **Rev:** Inscription, date appears as "3" above "1" or "2" above "2" **Rev. Insc.:** "fulus" **Note:** Oblong or irregular flans.

Date	Mintage	Good	VG	F	VF	XF
AH1322	—	5.00	8.00	20.00	35.00	
AH1323	—	5.00	8.00	20.00	35.00	
AH1324	—	5.00	8.00	20.00	35.00	
AH1325	—	5.00	8.00	20.00	35.00	
AH1326	—	5.00	8.00	20.00	35.00	

Isfandiyar
AH1328-1336 / 1910-1918 AD
HAMMERED COINAGE

Y# 3.2 PUL (Fulus)
Copper **Obv:** Inscription in circle **Obv. Insc.:** "Khwarezm" **Rev:** Inscription, date appears as "3" above "1" or "2" above "2" **Rev. Insc.:** "fulus" **Note:** Oblong or irregular flans, similar to Y#3.1.

Date	Mintage	Good	VG	F	VF	XF
AH1328	—	5.00	8.00	20.00	35.00	
AH1329	—	5.00	8.00	20.00	35.00	

Sayyid Abdullah and Junaid Khan
AH1337-1338 / 1919-1920 AD
HAMMERED COINAGE

Y# A9.1   TENGA
Copper **Obv:** Inscription and date in dotted or reeded circle **Obv. Insc.:** "zarb Khwarezm" **Rev:** Rising sun and crescent, inscription below **Rev. Insc.:** "fulus bir tangah" **Note:** Size varies: 17-19 mm.

Date	Mintage	Good	VG	F	VF	XF
AH1337	—	75.00	120	200	400

Y# A9.2   TENGA
Copper **Obv:** Inscription and date in dotted or reeded circle **Obv. Insc.:** "zarb Khwarezm" **Rev:** No crescent above rising sun **Rev. Insc.:** "fulus bir tangah" **Note:** Die varieties exist with different border patterns and date above or below mint name. Crudely struck specimens with Tajik inscription "fulus yak tangah" (instead of the Uzbek "bir tangah") are modern forgeries. Size varies: 17-19mm.

Date	Mintage	Good	VG	F	VF	XF
AH1337	—	60.00	100	150	250

Y# 8   TENGA
2.2800 g., Silver **Note:** Struck in the name of Sayyid Muhammad Rahim; die varieties exist.

Date	Mintage	Good	VG	F	VF	XF
AH1337//1337	—	—	250	400	600	850

Note: The estimated number known to exist does not exceed 20 pieces

Y# 9.1   2-1/2 TENGA
Copper Or Bronze **Obv:** Inscription and date **Obv. Insc.:** "zarb Dar al-Islam Khwarezm" **Rev:** Rising sun and crescent, inscription below **Rev. Insc.:** "fulus iki yarim tangah" **Note:** Die varieties exist. Number of sun rays vary from 7 to 13. Date above mint name and strikes with additional date on reverse exist.

Date	Mintage	Good	VG	F	VF	XF
AH1337	—	30.00	45.00	75.00	120

Y# 9.2   2-1/2 TENGA
Bronze Or Brass **Obv:** Inscription and date **Obv. Insc.:** "zarb Dar al-Islam Khwarezm" **Rev:** Full sun and crescent, inscription below **Rev. Insc.:** "fulus iki yarim tangah" **Note:** Many die varieties exist. Number of sun rays vary from 8 to 18, date above or below mintname. Strikes with additional date on reverse exist. Size varies 20-22mm.

Date	Mintage	Good	VG	F	VF	XF
AH1337	—	30.00	45.00	75.00	120

Note: Rare 1337 strikes over Russian Kopek Y#9.2 are known

Y# 9.3   2-1/2 TENGA
Bronze Or Brass **Obv:** Inscription and date **Obv. Insc.:** "zarb Dar al-Islam Khwarezm" **Rev:** Full sun and crescent, modified inscription below **Rev. Insc.:** "iki yarim tangah fulus" **Note:** Many die varieties exist. Number of sun rays vary from 10-13. Size varies 20-22mm.

Date	Mintage	Good	VG	F	VF	XF
AH1337	—	25.00	40.00	70.00	

Note: Date above or below mint name

| AH1338 | — | 150 | 250 | 400 | |

Note: Date below mint name

Y# 10.1   5 TENGA
Copper Or Bronze, 30 mm. **Obv:** Inscription and date **Obv. Insc.:** "zarb Dar al-Islam Khwarezm" **Rev:** Rising sun and crescent, inscription below **Rev. Insc.:** "fulus besh tangah"

Date	Mintage	Good	VG	F	VF	XF
AH1337 Rare	—	—	—	—	—	—

Y# 10.2   5 TENGA
Copper Or Bronze **Obv:** Inscription and date **Obv. Insc.:** "zarb Dar al-Islam Khwarezm" **Rev:** Full sun and crescent, inscription below **Rev. Insc.:** "fulus besh tangah" **Note:** Many die varieties exist. Number of sun rays vary from 9-20, date above or below mint name. Strikes with additional date on reverse exist. Size varies 29-32mm.

Date	Mintage	Good	VG	F	VF	XF
AH1337	—	25.00	40.00	125	

Y# 10.3   5 TENGA
Bronze Or Brass **Obv:** Inscription and date **Obv. Insc.:** "zarb Dar al-Islam Khwarezm" **Rev:** Full sun and crescent, modified inscription below **Rev. Insc.:** "besh tangah fulus" **Note:** Many die varieties exist. Number of sun rays vary from 9-18, date appears above or below mint name. Strikes with additional date on reverse exist. Size varies 29-32mm.

Date	Mintage	Good	VG	F	VF	XF
AH1337	—	20.00	35.00	60.00	90.00

Date	Mintage	Good	VG	F	VF	XF

Note: Rare 1337 strikes over Russian 3 Kopek Y#11.2 are known

| AH1338 | — | 35.00 | 55.00 | 80.00 | 120 |

Y# 11.1   15 TENGA
Bronze **Obv:** Inscription and date **Obv. Insc.:** "zarb Dar al-Islam Khwarezm" **Rev:** Inscription and date in crescent, 6-pointed circled star above **Rev. Insc.:** "on besh tangah fulus" **Note:** Size varies 28-31mm.

Date	Mintage	Good	VG	F	VF	XF
AH1338	—	120	200	350	600

Note: Struck on flans of 5 Tenga with obverse of 5 Tenga; In an attempt to replace 5 Tenga by 15 Tenga due to inflation, flans of 5 Tenga with obverse dies of 5 Tenga were used first; Confusion due to the similar size led to production and usage of special broader flans (see Y#11.2)

Y# 11.2   15 TENGA
Bronze **Obv. Insc.:** "zarb Dar al-Islam Khwarezm" **Rev:** Inscription and date in crescent, 6-pointed circled star above **Rev. Insc.:** "on besh tangah fulus" **Note:** Struck on broad flans. Strikes with or without date above mint name on obverse exist. Die varieties with different rim patterns on reverse exist. Size varies 32-34mm.

Date	Mintage	Good	VG	F	VF	XF
AH1338	—	100	175	250	400

KHOREZM PEOPLE'S SOVIET REPUBLIC
AH1338-1343 / 1920-1924 AD
HAMMERED COINAGE

Y# 15.1   20 ROUBLES
Copper Or Bronze **Obv:** Inscription and date, star above, legend around **Obv. Leg.:** "zarb fulus Khwarezm shuralar qarari ilan" **Obv. Insc.:** "yigirma manat" **Rev:** Divided arms above, inscription (in Russian) below **Note:** Die varieties exist. Both dates have 6 points in obverse star. Size varies 25-26mm.

Date	Mintage	Good	VG	F	VF	XF
AH1338	—	—	25.00	40.00	70.00	100
AH1339	—	—	40.00	70.00	100	150

Y# 15.2   20 ROUBLES
Copper Or Bronze **Obv:** Inscription and date, star above, legend around **Obv. Leg.:** "zarb fulus Khwarezm shuralar qarari ilan" **Obv. Insc.:** "yigirma manat" **Rev:** Crossed arms above, denomination "20 / RUB" (in Russian) below **Note:** Die varieties exist. Size varies 25-26mm.

Date	Mintage	Good	VG	F	VF	XF
AH1338	—	—	30.00	50.00	80.00	120

Note: 6 points in obverse star

Date	Mintage	Good	VG	F	VF	XF
AH1339	—	—	20.00	35.00	50.00	80.00

Note: Varieties exist with 6 or 8 points in obverse star, with 8 stars much scarcer

Y# 16.1   25 ROUBLES

Bronze Or Brass Obv: Inscription and date above, legend below (starting on the right with "Khwarezm") Obv. Leg.: "zarb fulus Khwarezm shuralar qarari ilan" Obv. Insc.: "yigirma besh manat" Rev: Arms in center, crescent and star above, denomination "25 RUBLES" (in Russian) around Note: Many die varieties exist with different arms design. Varieties exist with 8, 12, 16 or 18 points in reverse star. The strike with inverted "R" has 12 points in star. Size varies 24-26mm.

Date	Mintage	Good	VG	F	VF	XF
AH1339	—	—	17.50	30.00	40.00	75.00
AH1339	—	—	50.00	70.00	100	175

Note: With inverted Russian "R" in "Rubles"

Y# 16.2   25 ROUBLES

Bronze Or Brass Obv: Inscription and date above, legend below (starting on the right with "shuralar") Obv. Leg.: "zarb fulus Khwarezm shuralar qarari ilan" Obv. Insc.: "yigirma besh manat" Rev: Arms in center, crescent and star above, denomination "25 Rubles" (in Russian) around Note: Many die varieties exist with different arms design. Varieties exist with 8, 12, 16 or 18 points in reverse star. The strike with inverted "R" has 12 points in star. Size varies 24-26mm.

Date	Mintage	Good	VG	F	VF	XF
AH1339	—	—	17.50	25.00	40.00	70.00
AH1339	—	—	50.00	70.00	100	175

Note: With inverted Russian "R" in "Rubles"

Y# 17   100 ROUBLES

Bronze Obv: Crescent and star in center, inscription and date above, legend below Obv. Leg.: "zarb fulus Khwarezm shuralar qarari ilan" Obv. Insc.: "yuz manat" Rev: Denomination "100 Rubles" (in Russian), arms below Note: Die varieties exist. Varieties exist with 6 or 8 points in obverse star. Size varies 20-22.

Date	Mintage	Good	VG	F	VF	XF
AH1339	—	—	22.50	40.00	60.00	90.00

Y# 18   500 ROUBLES

Bronze, 24 mm. Obv: Inscription in center, 12-pointed star and date above, legend around Obv. Leg.: "zarb fulus Khwarezm jumhuriyeti" Obv. Insc.: "500 / besh yuz manat / 500" Rev: Arms with two stars above, "Rubles" (in Russian) / "500" below Note: Genuine specimens appear like the pictured coin, no die varieties exist.

Date	Mintage	Good	VG	F	VF	XF
AH1339	—	—	100	175	250	350

Y# 19.1   500 ROUBLES

Bronze Or Brass Obv: Inscription (in one word) in center, star and divided date above, legend around Obv. Leg.: "zarb fulus jumhuriyeti Khwarezm" Obv. Insc.: "beshyuz manat" Rev: Arms with two stars above, "Rubles" (in Russian) / "500" below Note: Die varieties exist. Varieties exist with 8 or 17 points in obverse star, the later is much scarcer. Size varies 18-20mm.

Date	Mintage	Good	VG	F	VF	XF
AH1339	—	—	20.00	35.00	50.00	80.00

Y# 19.2   500 ROUBLES

Bronze Or Brass Obv: Inscription (in 2 words) in center, star and divided date above, legend around Obv. Leg.: "zarb fulus jumhuriyeti Khwarezm" Obv. Insc.: "besh yuz manat" Rev: Arms with two stars above, "Rubles" (in Russian) / "500" below Note: Die varieties exist. Two varieties of the arms design exist. Size varies 18-20mm.

Date	Mintage	Good	VG	F	VF	XF
AH1339	—	—	17.50	25.00	40.00	70.00

Note: Varieties exist with 5, 6, 8, 12 or 16 points in obverse star

Date	Mintage	Good	VG	F	VF	XF
AH1340	—	—	22.50	40.00	60.00	90.00

Note: Varieties exist with 5 or 6 points in obverse star

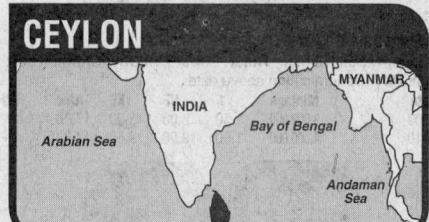

CEYLON

INDIA
Arabian Sea
Bay of Bengal
MYANMAR
Andaman Sea

The earliest known inhabitants of Ceylon, the Veddahs, were subjugated by the Sinhalese from northern India in the 6th century B.C. Sinhalese rule was maintained until 1408, after which the island was controlled by China for 30 years. The Portuguese came to Ceylon in 1505 and maintained control of the coastal area for 150 years. The Dutch supplanted them in 1658, which were in turn supplanted by the British who seized the Dutch colonies in 1796, and made them a Crown Colony in 1802. In 1815, the British conquered the independent Kingdom of Kandy in the central part of the island. Constitutional changes in 1931 and 1946 granted the Ceylonese a measure of autonomy and a parliamentary form of government. Britain granted Ceylon independence as a self-governing state within the British Commonwealth on Feb. 4, 1948. On May 22, 1972, the Ceylonese adopted a new Constitution, which declared Ceylon to be the Republic of Sri Lanka –'Resplendent Island'

RULER
British, 1796-1948

BRITISH COLONY
DECIMAL COINAGE
100 Cents = 1 Rupee

KM# 90   1/4 CENT

Copper Ruler: Victoria Obv: Head left within circle Obv. Leg.: QUEEN VICTORIA Rev: Tree within circle

Date	Mintage	F	VF	XF	Unc	BU
1901	216,000	1.50	3.00	5.00	12.00	—
1901 Proof	—	Value: 125				

KM# 100   1/4 CENT

Copper Ruler: Edward VII Obv: Crowned bust right Rev: Tree within circle, date below, denomination above

Date	Mintage	F	VF	XF	Unc	BU
1904	103,000	2.50	5.00	10.00	22.00	—
1904 Proof	—	Value: 150				

KM# 100a   1/4 CENT

Gold Ruler: Edward VII Obv: Crowned bust right Rev: Tree within circle, date below, denomination above

Date	Mintage	F	VF	XF	Unc	BU
1904	—	Value: 1,000				

KM# 91   1/2 CENT

2.3600 g., Copper, 18.3 mm. Ruler: Victoria Obv: Head left within circle Obv. Leg.: QUEEN VICTORIA Rev: Tree within circle

Date	Mintage	F	VF	XF	Unc	BU
1901	2,020,000	1.25	2.50	4.00	10.00	—

KM# 101   1/2 CENT

Copper Ruler: Edward VII Obv: Crowned bust right Rev: Tree within circle, date below, denomination above

Date	Mintage	F	VF	XF	Unc	BU
1904	2,012,000	1.00	2.00	5.00	12.00	—
1904 Proof	—	Value: 120				
1905	1,000,000	1.50	3.00	6.00	15.00	—
1905 Proof	—	Value: 120				
1906	3,056,000	1.00	2.00	5.00	12.00	—
1906 Proof	—	Value: 120				
1908	1,000,000	1.50	3.00	6.00	15.00	—
1908 Proof	—	Value: 200				
1909	3,000,000	1.00	2.00	5.00	12.00	—
1909 Proof	—	Value: 120				

KM# 106   1/2 CENT

Copper Ruler: George V Obv: Crowned bust left Rev: Tree within circle, date below, denomination above

Date	Mintage	F	VF	XF	Unc	BU
1912	5,008,000	1.25	2.75	4.00	10.00	—
1912 Proof	—	Value: 120				
1914	2,000,000	1.25	2.75	6.00	12.00	—
1914 Proof	—	Value: 120				
1917	2,000,000	1.50	3.00	6.00	12.00	—
1917 Proof	—	Value: 120				
1926	5,000,000	0.50	1.00	2.00	5.00	—
1926 Proof	—	Value: 120				

KM# 110   1/2 CENT

Copper Ruler: George VI Obv: Crowned head left Rev: Tree within circle, date below, denomination above

Date	Mintage	F	VF	XF	Unc	BU
1937	3,026,000	0.30	0.85	1.50	3.50	—
1937 Proof	—	Value: 175				
1940	5,080,000	0.25	0.65	1.25	3.00	—

KM# 92   CENT

Copper Ruler: Victoria Obv: Head left within circle Obv. Leg.: QUEEN VICTORIA Rev: Tree within circle

Date	Mintage	F	VF	XF	Unc	BU
1901	1,014,000	2.50	5.00	10.00	22.00	—

KM# 102   CENT

Copper Ruler: Edward VII Obv: Crowned bust right Rev: Tree within circle, date below, denomination above

Date	Mintage	F	VF	XF	Unc	BU
1904	2,529,000	1.00	2.00	4.00	8.00	—
1904 Proof	—	Value: 125				
1905	1,509,000	1.25	2.25	5.00	10.00	—
1905 Proof	—	Value: 125				
1906	1,751,000	1.25	2.25	5.00	10.00	—
1906 Proof	—	Value: 125				
1908	—	1.00	2.00	4.00	8.00	—
1908 Proof	—	Value: 225				
1909	2,500,000	1.00	2.00	4.00	8.00	—
1909 Proof	—	Value: 125				
1910	8,236,000	0.50	1.00	2.50	5.00	—
1910 Proof	—	Value: 125				

KM# 107   CENT
4.5700 g., Copper, 23 mm. **Ruler:** George V **Obv:** Crowned bust left **Rev:** Tree within circle, date below, denomination above

Date	Mintage	F	VF	XF	Unc	BU
1912	5,855,000	0.50	1.00	2.00	4.00	—
1912 Proof	—	Value: 115				
1914	6,000,000	0.50	1.00	2.25	5.00	—
1914 Proof	—	Value: 115				
1917	1,000,000	1.00	1.75	3.00	8.00	—
1917 Proof	—	Value: 115				
1920	2,000,000	0.50	1.00	2.25	5.00	—
1920 Proof	—	Value: 115				
1922	2,930,000	0.50	1.00	2.25	5.00	—
1922 Proof	—	Value: 115				
1923	2,500,000	0.50	1.00	2.25	5.00	—
1923 Proof	—	Value: 115				
1925	7,490,000	0.35	0.75	1.50	3.50	—
1925 Proof	—	Value: 115				
1926	3,750,000	0.35	0.75	1.50	3.50	—
1926 Proof	—	Value: 115				
1928	2,500,000	0.35	0.75	1.50	4.00	—
1928 Proof	—	Value: 115				
1929	5,000,000	0.35	0.75	1.50	3.50	—
1929 Proof	—	Value: 115				

KM# 111   CENT
4.6400 g., Copper, 22 mm. **Ruler:** George VI **Obv:** Crowned head left, PM below neck at right **Rev:** Tree within circle, date below, denomination above **Note:** High relief. Thickness: 1.73mm.

Date	Mintage	F	VF	XF	Unc	BU
1937	4,538,000	0.25	0.50	1.25	3.00	—
1937 Proof	—	Value: 100				
1940	10,190,000	0.15	0.30	1.00	2.00	—
1940 Proof	—	Value: 75.00				
1942	20,780,000	0.15	0.30	1.00	2.00	—

KM# 111a   CENT
2.3600 g., Bronze, 22.35 mm. **Ruler:** George VI **Obv:** Crowned head left **Rev:** Tree within circle, date below, denomination above **Note:** Low relief. Thin planchet. .87mm.

Date	Mintage	F	VF	XF	Unc	BU
1942	Inc. above	0.15	0.30	0.75	1.75	—
1942 Proof	—	Value: 75.00				
1943	43,705,000	0.15	0.30	0.50	1.00	—
1945	34,100,000	0.15	0.35	0.60	1.20	—
1945 Proof	—	Value: 20.00				
Note: Frozen year 1945, restruck until 1962

KM# 117   2 CENTS
2.5400 g., Nickel-Brass, 18 mm. **Ruler:** George VI **Obv:** Crowned head left **Rev:** Denomination above date

Date	Mintage	F	VF	XF	Unc	BU
1944	30,165,000	0.10	0.25	0.50	1.25	—

KM# 119   2 CENTS
2.5500 g., Brass, 18 mm. **Ruler:** George VI **Obv:** Crowned head left, legend without EMPEROR OF INDIA **Rev:** Denomination above date

Date	Mintage	F	VF	XF	Unc	BU
1951	15,000,000	0.10	0.25	0.75	1.75	—
1951 Proof	150	Value: 20.00				

KM# 124   2 CENTS
Brass **Ruler:** Elizabeth II **Obv:** Laureate bust right **Rev:** Denomination above date

Date	Mintage	F	VF	XF	Unc	BU
1955	37,131,000	0.10	0.15	0.25	0.65	—
1957	38,200,000	0.10	0.15	0.25	0.65	—
1957 Proof	—	Value: 75.00				

KM# 103   5 CENTS
Copper-Nickel, 18 mm. **Ruler:** Edward VII **Obv:** Crowned bust right **Rev:** Denomination above date

Date	Mintage	F	VF	XF	Unc	BU
1909	2,000,000	1.50	3.00	5.00	17.00	—
1910	4,000,000	1.00	2.00	3.50	12.00	—

KM# 108   5 CENTS
3.6600 g., Copper-Nickel, 18 mm. **Ruler:** George V **Obv:** Crowned bust left **Rev:** Denomination above date

Date	Mintage	F	VF	XF	Unc	BU
1912 H	4,000,000	0.75	1.50	3.00	10.00	—
1920	6,000,000	0.50	1.00	2.00	7.00	—
1926	3,000,000	0.75	1.50	4.00	12.50	—

KM# 113.1   5 CENTS
Nickel-Brass, 18 mm. **Ruler:** George VI **Obv:** Crowned head left **Rev:** Denomination above date

Date	Mintage	F	VF	XF	Unc	BU
1942	12,752,000	0.35	0.75	1.50	4.50	—
1942 Proof	—	Value: 50.00				
1943	Inc. above	0.35	0.75	1.50	4.50	—
1943 Proof	—	Value: 50.00				

KM# 113.2   5 CENTS
Nickel-Brass, 18 mm. **Ruler:** George VI **Obv:** Crowned head left **Rev:** Denomination above date **Note:** Thin planchet.

Date	Mintage	F	VF	XF	Unc	BU
1944	18,064,000	0.20	0.35	0.70	2.00	—
1945	31,192,000	0.15	0.30	0.60	1.75	—
1945 Proof	—	Value: 60.00				
Note: Varieties exist in bust, denomination and legend placement for 1945; The date was frozen at 1945 and these coins were struck until 1962

KM# 120   5 CENTS
Nickel-Brass, 18 mm. **Ruler:** George VI **Obv:** Crowned head left, legend without EMPEROR OF INDIA **Rev:** Denomination above date

Date	Mintage	F	VF	XF	Unc	BU
1951 Proof	150	Value: 20.00				
1951 Proof, restrike	—	Value: 12.00				

KM# 97   10 CENTS
1.1664 g., 0.8000 Silver 0.0300 oz. ASW **Ruler:** Edward VII **Obv:** Crowned bust right **Rev:** Plant divides denomination above date

Date	Mintage	F	VF	XF	Unc	BU
1902	1,000,000	1.00	2.75	6.00	20.00	—
1902 Proof	—	Value: 150				

Date	Mintage	F	VF	XF	Unc	BU
1903	1,000,000	1.00	2.75	6.00	20.00	—
1903 Proof	—	Value: 150				
1907	500,000	2.50	5.00	15.00	25.00	—
1908	1,500,000	1.00	2.75	6.00	15.00	—
1909	1,000,000	1.00	2.75	6.00	15.00	—
1910	2,000,000	1.00	2.75	6.00	15.00	—

KM# 104   10 CENTS
1.1664 g., 0.8000 Silver 0.0300 oz. ASW **Ruler:** George V **Obv:** Crowned bust left **Rev:** Plant divides denomination, date below

Date	Mintage	F	VF	XF	Unc	BU
1911	1,000,000	1.00	1.75	5.00	12.00	—
1912	1,000,000	1.25	2.00	6.00	15.00	—
1913	2,000,000	1.00	1.50	4.00	10.00	—
1914	2,000,000	1.00	1.50	4.00	10.00	—
1914 Proof	—	Value: 150				
1917	879,000	1.00	2.50	7.50	17.50	—
1917 Proof	—	Value: 150				

KM# 104a   10 CENTS
1.1664 g., 0.5500 Silver 0.0206 oz. ASW **Ruler:** George V **Obv:** Crowned bust left **Rev:** Plant divides denomination, date below

Date	Mintage	F	VF	XF	Unc	BU
1919 B	750,000	1.50	3.50	10.00	20.00	—
1919 B Proof	—	Value: 150				
1920 B	3,059,000	1.00	2.50	6.00	15.00	—
1920 B Proof	—	Value: 150				
1921 B	1,583,000	0.75	1.75	5.00	10.00	—
1921 Proof	—	Value: 150				
1922	282,000	1.75	3.50	10.00	25.00	—
1922 Proof	—	Value: 150				
1924	1,508,000	0.75	1.75	4.00	10.00	—
1924 Proof	—	Value: 150				
1925	1,500,000	0.75	1.75	4.00	10.00	—
1925 Proof	—	Value: 150				
1926	1,500,000	0.75	1.75	4.00	10.00	—
1926 Proof	—	Value: 150				
1927	1,500,000	0.75	1.75	4.00	10.00	—
1927 Proof	—	Value: 150				
1928	1,500,000	0.75	1.75	4.00	10.00	—
1928 Proof	—	Value: 150				

KM# 112   10 CENTS
1.1664 g., 0.8000 Silver 0.0300 oz. ASW, 15.5 mm. **Ruler:** George VI **Obv:** Crowned head left **Rev:** Plant divides denomination, date below **Edge:** Reeded

Date	Mintage	F	VF	XF	Unc	BU
1941	16,271,000	0.65	1.00	2.50	6.00	—

KM# 118   10 CENTS
Nickel-Brass, 23 mm. **Ruler:** George VI **Obv:** Crowned head left **Rev:** Denomination above date

Date	Mintage	F	VF	XF	Unc	BU
1944	30,500,000	0.25	0.50	1.00	3.00	—
1944 Proof	—	Value: 90.00				

KM# 121   10 CENTS
4.1400 g., Nickel-Brass, 23 mm. **Ruler:** George VI **Obv:** Crowned head left, legend without EMPEROR OF INDIA **Rev:** Denomination above date

Date	Mintage	F	VF	XF	Unc	BU
1951	34,760,000	0.10	0.20	0.40	1.25	—
1951 Proof	150	Value: 15.00				

Date	Mintage	F	VF	XF	Unc	BU
1951 Proof, restrike	—	Value: 4.00				

Note: Frozen year 1951; restruck until 1962. Royal Mint strikes (1959-62) differ slightly in the formation of native inscriptions

KM# 98   25 CENTS
2.9160 g., 0.8000 Silver 0.0750 oz. ASW **Ruler:** Edward VII **Obv:** Crowned bust right **Rev:** Plant divides denomination, date below

Date	Mintage	F	VF	XF	Unc	BU
1902	400,000	4.00	8.00	20.00	40.00	—
1902 Proof	—	Value: 150				
1903	400,000	4.00	8.00	20.00	40.00	—
1903 Proof	—	Value: 150				
1907	120,000	7.50	20.00	30.00	50.00	—
1908	400,000	4.00	8.00	15.00	35.00	—
1909	400,000	4.00	8.00	15.00	35.00	—
1910	800,000	2.00	5.00	10.00	20.00	—

KM# 105   25 CENTS
2.9160 g., 0.8000 Silver 0.0750 oz. ASW **Ruler:** George V **Obv:** Crowned bust left **Rev:** Plant divides denomination, date below

Date	Mintage	F	VF	XF	Unc	BU
1911	400,000	3.00	6.00	12.00	30.00	—
1911 Proof	—	Value: 175				
1913	1,200,000	1.50	2.50	7.50	17.50	—
1913 Proof	—	Value: 175				
1914	400,000	3.00	6.00	12.00	25.00	—
1914 Proof	—	Value: 175				
1917	300,000	4.00	8.00	15.00	35.00	—
1917 Proof	—	Value: 175				

KM# 105a   25 CENTS
2.9160 g., 0.5500 Silver 0.0516 oz. ASW **Ruler:** George V **Obv:** Crowned bust left **Rev:** Plant divides denomination, date below

Date	Mintage	F	VF	XF	Unc	BU
1919 B	1,400,000	1.25	3.00	7.50	15.00	—
1919 B Proof	—	Value: 150				
1920 B	1,600,000	1.25	3.00	7.50	15.00	—
1920 B Proof	—	Value: 150				
1921 B	600,000	3.50	7.50	15.00	30.00	—
1921 B Proof	—	Value: 150				
1922	1,211,000	1.25	3.25	7.50	15.00	—
1922 Proof	—	Value: 150				
1925	1,004,000	1.25	3.50	7.50	15.00	—
1925 Proof	—	Value: 150				
1926	1,000,000	1.25	3.50	7.50	15.00	—
1926 Proof	—	Value: 150				

KM# 115   25 CENTS
2.7400 g., Nickel-Brass, 19.3 mm. **Ruler:** George VI **Obv:** Crowned head left **Rev:** Crown at top divides date, denomination below **Note:** Frozen date 1943, restruck until 1951.

Date	Mintage	F	VF	XF	Unc	BU
1943	13,920,000	0.25	0.50	1.00	2.50	—

KM# 122   25 CENTS
Nickel-Brass **Ruler:** George VI **Obv:** Legend without EMPEROR OF INDIA **Rev:** Crown divides date at top, denomination below

Date	Mintage	F	VF	XF	Unc	BU
1951	25,940,000	0.10	0.30	0.60	1.75	—
1951 Proof	150	Value: 20.00				

Date	Mintage	F	VF	XF	Unc	BU
1951 Proof, restrike	—	Value: 4.00				

Note: Frozen year 1951; restruck until 1962. Royal Mint strikes (1959-62) differ in numerals 9 and 5

KM# 99   50 CENTS
5.8319 g., 0.8000 Silver 0.1500 oz. ASW **Ruler:** Edward VII **Obv:** Crowned bust right **Rev:** Plant divides denomination, date below

Date	Mintage	F	VF	XF	Unc	BU
1902	200,000	5.00	10.00	30.00	70.00	—
1902 Proof	—	Value: 175				
1903	800,000	3.00	8.00	18.00	35.00	—
1903 Proof	—	Value: 175				
1910	200,000	7.00	13.00	30.00	60.00	—

KM# 109   50 CENTS
5.8319 g., 0.8000 Silver 0.1500 oz. ASW **Ruler:** George V **Obv:** Crowned bust left **Rev:** Plant divides denomination, date below

Date	Mintage	F	VF	XF	Unc	BU
1913	400,000	7.00	13.00	30.00	60.00	—
1913 Proof	—	Value: 175				
1914	200,000	5.00	15.00	30.00	60.00	—
1914 Proof	—	Value: 175				
1917	1,073,000	2.50	5.00	10.00	20.00	—
1917 Proof	—	Value: 175				

KM# 109a   50 CENTS
5.8319 g., 0.5500 Silver 0.1031 oz. ASW **Ruler:** George V **Obv:** Crowned bust left **Rev:** Plant divides denomination, date below

Date	Mintage	F	VF	XF	Unc	BU
1919 B	750,000	1.65	3.50	7.00	16.00	—
1919 B Proof	—	Value: 120				
1920 B	800,000	1.65	3.50	7.00	16.00	—
1920 B Proof	—	Value: 120				
1921 B	800,000	1.65	3.50	7.00	16.00	—
1921 B Proof	—	Value: 120				
1922	1,040,000	1.65	3.50	7.00	16.00	—
1922 Proof	—	Value: 120				
1924	1,010,000	1.65	3.50	7.00	16.00	—
1924 Proof	—	Value: 120				
1925	500,000	2.00	5.00	10.00	20.00	—
1925 Proof	—	Value: 120				
1926	500,000	2.00	5.00	10.00	20.00	—
1926 Proof	—	Value: 120				
1927	500,000	2.00	5.00	10.00	20.00	—
1927 Proof	—	Value: 120				
1928	500,000	2.00	5.00	10.00	20.00	—
1928 Proof	—	Value: 120				
1929	500,000	2.00	5.00	10.00	20.00	—
1929 Proof	—	Value: 120				

KM# 114   50 CENTS
5.8319 g., 0.8000 Silver 0.1500 oz. ASW **Ruler:** George VI **Obv:** Crowned head left **Rev:** Plant divides denomination, date below

Date	Mintage	F	VF	XF	Unc	BU
1942	662,000	2.50	4.50	9.00	18.50	—

KM# 116   50 CENTS
5.5400 g., Nickel-Brass **Ruler:** George VI **Obv:** Crowned head left **Rev:** Crown divides date above denomination **Note:** Frozen date 1943, restruck until 1951.

Date	Mintage	F	VF	XF	Unc	BU
1943	8,600,000	0.35	0.75	1.50	3.50	—

KM# 123   50 CENTS
5.4900 g., Nickel-Brass **Ruler:** George VI **Obv:** Crowned head left, legend without EMPEROR OF INDIA **Rev:** Crown divides date above denomination

Date	Mintage	F	VF	XF	Unc	BU
1951	19,980,000	0.20	0.35	0.75	1.75	—
1951 Proof	150	Value: 20.00				
1951 Proof, restrike	—	Value: 5.00				

Note: Frozen year 1951; restruck until 1962. Royal Mint strikes (1959-62) differ slightly in the formation of native inscriptions

BRITISH COMMONWEALTH

DECIMAL COINAGE
100 Cents = 1 Rupee

KM# 125   RUPEE
Copper-Nickel, 28 mm. **Ruler:** Elizabeth II **Subject:** 2,500 Years of Buddhism **Obv:** Date and design at center, denomination at left **Rev:** Temple above 2500, design in background

Date	Mintage	F	VF	XF	Unc	BU
1957	2,000,000	0.50	1.00	2.00	3.00	—
1957 Proof	1,800	Value: 12.00				

KM# 126   5 RUPEES
28.2757 g., 0.9250 Silver 0.8409 oz. ASW, 39 mm.
Ruler: Elizabeth II **Subject:** 2,500 Years of Buddhism
Obv: Flowers and date at center, denomination at left **Rev:** 2500 within inner circle of flower, circle of animals surround, ducks encircle them

Date	Mintage	F	VF	XF	Unc	BU
1957	500,000	15.00	16.00	18.00	30.00	50.00

Note: 258,000 returned in 1962 to be melted at The Royal Mint

1957 Proof	1,800	Value: 75.00				

DECIMAL COINAGE

KM# 127 CENT
0.7000 g., Aluminum, 16 mm. **Ruler:** Elizabeth II
Obv: Denomination at center, date below **Rev:** Crowned arms

Date	Mintage	F	VF	XF	Unc	BU
1963	33,000,000	—	—	—	0.10	0.20
1965	12,000,000	—	—	0.10	0.15	0.25
1967	10,000,000	—	—	0.10	0.15	0.25
1968	22,505,000	—	—	—	0.10	0.20
1969	10,000,000	—	—	—	0.10	0.20
1970	15,000,000	—	—	—	0.10	0.20
1971	55,000,000	—	—	—	0.10	0.20
1971 Proof	20,000	Value: 0.50				

KM# 128 2 CENTS
0.7600 g., Aluminum, 18.3 mm. **Ruler:** Elizabeth II
Obv: Denomination at center, date below **Rev:** Crowned arms

Date	Mintage	F	VF	XF	Unc	BU
1963	26,000,000	—	—	0.10	0.15	0.25
1965	7,000,000	—	—	0.10	0.15	0.25
1967	15,000,000	—	—	0.10	0.15	0.25
1968	15,000,000	—	—	0.10	0.15	0.25
1970	13,000,000	—	—	0.10	0.15	0.25
1971	45,000,000	—	—	0.10	0.15	0.25
1971 Proof	20,000	Value: 1.00				

KM# 129 5 CENTS
3.2000 g., Nickel-Brass, 18 mm. **Ruler:** Elizabeth II
Obv: Denomination at center, date below **Rev:** Crowned arms

Date	Mintage	F	VF	XF	Unc	BU
1963	16,000,000	—	0.10	0.15	0.25	0.35
1965	9,000,000	—	0.10	0.15	0.25	0.35
1968	12,000,000	—	0.10	0.15	0.25	0.35
1969	2,500,000	—	0.10	0.20	0.40	0.60
1970	7,000,000	—	0.10	0.15	0.25	0.35
1971	32,000,000	—	0.10	0.15	0.25	0.35
1971 Proof	20,000	Value: 1.50				

KM# 130 10 CENTS
4.1200 g., Nickel-Brass, 23 mm. **Ruler:** Elizabeth II
Obv: Denomination at center, date below **Rev:** Crowned arms

Date	Mintage	F	VF	XF	Unc	BU
1963	14,000,000	—	0.10	0.15	0.25	0.50
1965	3,000,000	—	0.10	0.15	0.35	0.50
1969	6,000,000	—	0.10	0.15	0.25	0.35
1971	29,000,000	—	0.10	0.15	0.25	0.30
1971 Proof	20,000	Value: 1.25				

KM# 131 25 CENTS
Copper-Nickel, 18 mm. **Ruler:** Elizabeth II **Obv:** Denomination at center, date below **Rev:** Crowned arms

Date	Mintage	F	VF	XF	Unc	BU
1963	30,000,000	—	0.10	0.20	0.40	0.55
1965	8,000,000	—	0.10	0.25	0.50	0.65
1971	24,000,000	—	0.10	0.15	0.30	0.45
1971 Proof	20,000	Value: 1.50				

KM# 132 50 CENTS
Copper-Nickel, 21.5 mm. **Ruler:** Elizabeth II
Obv: Denomination at center, date below **Rev:** Crowned arms

Date	Mintage	F	VF	XF	Unc	BU
1963	15,000,000	0.10	0.20	0.35	0.75	1.00
1965	7,000,000	0.10	0.20	0.35	0.75	1.00
1971	4,000,000	0.25	0.50	0.75	1.50	1.75
1971 Proof	20,000	Value: 2.50				
1972		0.25	0.50	0.75	1.50	1.75

KM# 133 RUPEE
7.1000 g., Copper-Nickel, 25.3 mm. **Ruler:** Elizabeth II
Obv: Denomination above date **Rev:** Crowned arms

Date	Mintage	F	VF	XF	Unc	BU
1963	20,000,000	0.10	0.20	0.40	1.00	1.25
1965	5,000,000	0.15	0.25	0.50	1.25	1.50
1969	2,500,000	0.15	0.25	0.50	1.75	2.00
1971	5,000,000	0.15	0.25	0.50	1.50	1.75
1971 Proof	20,000	Value: 4.50				

KM# 134 2 RUPEES
Copper-Nickel **Ruler:** Elizabeth II **Series:** F.A.O. **Obv:** Large denomination above date **Rev:** King Parakramabahu I (1153-1186) between wheat stalks

Date	Mintage	F	VF	XF	Unc	BU
1968	500,000	0.50	1.50	2.25	3.50	5.00

PATTERNS
Including off metal strikes

KM#	Date	Mintage	Identification	Mkt Val
Pn8	1904	—	5 Cents. Copper.	3,500
Pn9	1942	—	Cent. Copper center. 22.4 mm. plain edge. KM#111 struck in Black Bakelite.	500
Pn10	1943	—	50 Cents.	—
Pn11	1965	—	10 Cents. Nickel-Brass. Similar to KM#130, with "TRIAL" in raised letters on obverse and reverse, struck at Birmingham Mint.	—
Pn12	1968	—	5 Cents. Nickel-Brass. Similar to KM#129, with "TRIAL" in raised letters on obverse and reverse, struck at Birmingham Mint.	—

PROOF SETS

KM#	Date	Mintage	Identification	Issue Price	Mkt Val
PS1	1951 (6)	150	KM111a (1945), 119-123 (1951). Restrikes exist.	—	40.00
PS2	1957 (2)	400	KM125-126	—	90.00
PS3	1957 (4)	700	KM125-126, 2 each	—	160
PS4	1971 (7)	20,000	KM127-133	—	12.50

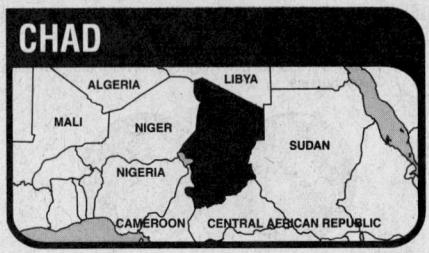

CHAD

The Republic of Chad, a landlocked country of central Africa, is the largest country of former French Equatorial Africa. It has an area of 495,755 sq. mi. (1,284,000 sq. km.) and a population of *7.27 million. Capital: N'Djamena. An expanding livestock industry produces camels, cattle and sheep. Cotton (the chief product), ivory and palm oil are important exports.

Although supposedly known to Ptolemy, the Chad area was first visited by white men in 1823. Exaggerated estimates of its economic importance led to a race for its possession (1890-93), which resulted in the territory being divided by treaty between Great Britain, France and Germany. As a consequence of World War I, the German area was mandated to France in 1919. Chad was absorbed into the colony of French Equatorial Africa, as part of Ubangi-Shari, in 1910 and became a separate colony in 1920. Upon dissolution of French Equatorial Africa in 1959, the component states became autonomous members of the French Union. Chad became an independent republic on Aug. 11, 1960.

NOTE: For earlier and related coinage see French Equatorial Africa and the Equatorial African States. For later coinage see Central African States.

MINT MARKS
(a) - Paris, privy marks only
(b) = Brussels
NI - Numismatica Italiana, Arezzo, Italy

COMMEMORATIVE EDGE INSCRIPTIONS
1960 LIBERTE PROGRES SOLIDARITE
1970/REPUBLIQUE DU TCHAD

REPUBLIC

DECIMAL COINAGE

KM# 1 100 FRANCS
5.0000 g., 0.9250 Silver 0.1487 oz. ASW **Subject:** 10th Anniversary of Independence **Obv:** Map of African continent **Rev:** Robert Francis Kennedy 3/4 right, denomination below

Date	Mintage	F	VF	XF	Unc	BU
1970(b) Proof	975	Value: 75.00				

KM# 2 100 FRANCS
7.0000 g., Nickel, 25.5 mm. **Obv:** Three Giant Eland left **Rev:** Denomination within circle, date below

Date	Mintage	F	VF	XF	Unc	BU
1971(a)	5,000,000	10.00	17.50	27.50	45.00	—
1972(a)	5,000,000	10.00	17.50	27.50	45.00	—

KM# 3 100 FRANCS
7.0000 g., Nickel, 25.5 mm. **Obv:** Three Giant Eland **Rev:** Denomination and date within circle

Date	Mintage	F	VF	XF	Unc	BU
1975(a)	—	10.00	15.00	22.00	35.00	—
1978(a)	—	12.00	20.00	28.00	45.00	—
1980(a)	—	10.00	17.50	25.00	40.00	—
1982(a)	—	10.00	15.00	22.00	35.00	—
1984(a)	—	10.00	15.00	22.00	35.00	—
1985(a)	—	10.00	14.00	20.00	30.00	—
1988(a)	—	10.00	14.00	20.00	30.00	—

Date	Mintage	F	VF	XF	Unc	BU
1990(a)	—	10.00	14.00	20.00	30.00	
1991(a)	—	—	—	—	—	

KM# 4 200 FRANCS
15.0000 g., 0.9250 Silver 0.4461 oz. ASW **Subject:** 10th Anniversary of Independence **Obv:** Map of African continent **Rev:** Martin Luther King Jr. facing divides dates, denomination below

Date	Mintage	F	VF	XF	Unc	BU
1970(b) Proof	952	Value: 150				

KM# 5 200 FRANCS
15.0000 g., 0.8000 Silver 0.3858 oz. ASW **Subject:** 10th Anniversary of Independence **Obv:** Map of African continent, denomination at left **Rev:** Charles de Gaulle 3/4 right divides dates

Date	Mintage	F	VF	XF	Unc	BU
1970(b) Proof	442	Value: 185				

KM# 6 200 FRANCS
15.0000 g., 0.8000 Silver 0.3858 oz. ASW **Subject:** 10th Anniversary of Independence **Rev:** Egypt's President Nasser 3/4 facing

Date	Mintage	F	VF	XF	Unc	BU
1970(b) Proof	435	Value: 150				

KM# 7 300 FRANCS
25.0000 g., 0.9250 Silver 0.7435 oz. ASW **Subject:** 10th Anniversary of Independence **Obv:** Map of African continent **Rev:** John Fitzgerald Kennedy left, Space Shuttle at left, denomination below

Date	Mintage	F	VF	XF	Unc	BU
1970(b) Proof	504	Value: 600				

KM# 13 500 FRANCS
Copper-Nickel **Obv:** Plants divide date and denomination **Rev:** Woman's head 3/4 left

Date	Mintage	F	VF	XF	Unc	BU
1985(a)	—	15.00	22.00	35.00	50.00	—

KM# 17 500 FRANCS
12.0000 g., Silver, 30 mm. **Subject:** Millennium **Obv:** Native portrait right within circle, denomination below **Rev:** Date atop radiant map of Africa

Date	Mintage	F	VF	XF	Unc	BU
2000 Proof	—	Value: 30.00				

KM# 8 1000 FRANCS
3.5000 g., 0.9000 Gold 0.1013 oz. AGW **Subject:** 10th Anniversary of Independence **Obv:** Nude half figure of woman right, shield of arms above, denomination at right **Rev:** Commandant Lamy 3/4 facing, date below

Date	Mintage	F	VF	XF	Unc	BU
ND(1970)(a)NI Proof	4,000	Value: 185				
ND(1970)NI Proof	Inc. above	Value: 185				

KM# 24 1000 FRANCS
15.0000 g., 0.9850 Silver 0.4750 oz. ASW, 34 mm. **Rev:** Okapi Johnston

Date	Mintage	F	VF	XF	Unc	BU
1999 Proof	—	Value: 45.00				

KM# 25 1000 FRANCS
15.0000 g., 0.9850 Silver 0.4750 oz. ASW, 34 mm. **Rev:** Bird of Paradise

Date	Mintage	F	VF	XF	Unc	BU
1999 Proof	—	Value: 45.00				

KM# 26 1000 FRANCS
15.0000 g., 0.9850 Silver 0.4750 oz. ASW, 34 mm. **Rev:** Giraffe

Date	Mintage	F	VF	XF	Unc	BU
1999 Proof	—	Value: 45.00				

KM# 27 1000 FRANCS
15.0000 g., 0.9850 Silver 0.4750 oz. ASW, 34 mm. **Rev:** Hippopotamus

Date	Mintage	F	VF	XF	Unc	BU
ND Proof	—	Value: 55.00				

KM# 16 1000 FRANCS
14.9700 g., 0.9850 Silver 0.4741 oz. ASW, 34 mm. **Obv:** Native portrait right within circle, denomination below **Rev:** Portrait of Galileo **Edge:** Plain

Date	Mintage	F	VF	XF	Unc	BU
1999 Proof	—	Value: 30.00				

KM# 9 3000 FRANCS
10.5000 g., 0.9000 Gold 0.3038 oz. AGW **Subject:** 10th Anniversary of Independence **Obv:** Shield of arms above map, denomination below, right **Rev:** Governor Eboue 3/4 left, date below

Date	Mintage	F	VF	XF	Unc	BU
ND(1970)(a)NI	4,000	Value: 300				
ND(1970)NI	Inc. above	Value: 300				

KM# 10 5000 FRANCS
17.5000 g., 0.9000 Gold 0.5064 oz. AGW **Subject:** 10th Anniversary of Independence **Obv:** Trees divide arch and arms, denomination below **Rev:** General Leclerc 3/4 facing, date below

Date	Mintage	F	VF	XF	Unc	BU
ND(1970)(a)NI Proof	4,000	Value: 500				
ND(1970)NI Proof	Inc. above	Value: 500				

KM# 11 10000 FRANCS
36.0000 g., 0.9000 Gold 1.0416 oz. AGW **Subject:** 10th Anniversary of Independence **Obv:** Arms above double cross, denomination below **Rev:** General Charles de Gaulle right, date below

Date	Mintage	F	VF	XF	Unc	BU
ND(1970)(a)NI Proof	4,000	Value: 1,000				
ND (1970)NI Proof	Inc. above	Value: 1,000				

KM# 14   10000 FRANCS
36.0000 g., 0.9000 Gold 1.0416 oz. AGW **Subject:** 10th Anniversary of Independence **Obv:** Map of African continent, denomination at left **Rev:** Egypt's President Nasser facing

Date	Mintage	F	VF	XF	Unc	BU
1970(b) Proof	205	Value: 1,175				

KM# 15   10000 FRANCS
36.0000 g., 0.9000 Gold 1.0416 oz. AGW **Subject:** 10th Anniversary of Independence **Obv:** Map of Africa **Rev:** Charles de Gaulle facing

Date	Mintage	F	VF	XF	Unc	BU
1970 Proof	90	Value: 1,350				

KM# 12   20000 FRANCS
70.0000 g., 0.9000 Gold 2.0254 oz. AGW **Subject:** 10th Anniversary of Independence **Obv:** Arms with supporters, denomination below

Date	Mintage	F	VF	XF	Unc	BU
ND (1970)(a)NI Proof	Est. 4,000	Value: 2,000				
ND (1970)NI Proof	Inc. above	Value: 2,000				

ESSAIS
Standard metals unless otherwise noted

KM#	Date	Mintage	Identification	Issue Price	Mkt Val
E1	1970(a)	—	10000 Francs. Copper-Nickel-Aluminum. Arms above double cross, denomination below. Head of de Gaulle right, date below. KM#11.	—	200
E1	1970(a)	—	10000 Francs. Copper-Nickel-Aluminum. Arms above double cross, denomination below. Head of de Gaulle right, date below. KM#11.	—	200
E3	1971(a)	1,400	100 Francs. Nickel. Three Giant Eland left. Denomination within circle, date below. KM#2.	—	23.50
E4	1971	4	100 Francs. Gold. KM#2.	—	1,600
E4	1971	4	100 Francs. Gold. KM#2.	—	1,600
E5	1975(a)	1,700	100 Francs. Nickel. KM#3.	—	22.50
E6	1985(a)	1,700	500 Francs. Copper-Nickel. Plants divide denomination and date. Woman's head 3/4 left. KM#13.	—	85.00

PROOF SETS

KM#	Date	Mintage	Identification	Issue Price	Mkt Val
PS1	1970 (5)	4,000	KM8-12	413	3,900
PS2	1970 (3)	—	KM1, 4, 7	33.00	775

CHILE

The Republic of Chile, a ribbon-like country on the Pacific coast of southern South America, has an area of 292,135 sq. mi. (756,950 sq. km.) and a population of *15.21 million. Capital: Santiago. Historically, the economic base of Chile has been the rich mineral deposits of its northern provinces. Copper has accounted for more than 75 percent of Chile's export earnings in recent years. Other important mineral exports are iron ore, iodine and nitrate of soda. Fresh fruits and vegetables, as well as wine are increasingly significant in inter-hemispheric trade.

Chile had developed a strong democracy. This was displaced when rampant inflation characterized chaotic and subsequently repressive governments in the mid to late 20th century.

MINT MARK
So - Santiago

MONETARY SYSTEM
100 Centavos = 1 Peso

REPUBLIC
DECIMAL COINAGE

KM# 161   CENTAVO
Copper, 20 mm. **Obv:** Liberty head left **Rev:** Denomination within wreath, date below

Date	Mintage	F	VF	XF	Unc	BU
1904	970,000	0.75	1.50	3.00	8.00	—
1908	174,000	1.50	3.00	9.00	16.00	—
1919	173,000	1.25	2.50	8.50	15.00	—
1991 Rare	Inc. above	—	—	—	—	—
Note: Error for 1919						

KM# 164   2 CENTAVOS
Copper, 21 mm. **Obv:** Liberty head left **Rev:** Denomination within wreath, date below

Date	Mintage	F	VF	XF	Unc	BU
1919	147,000	1.50	3.00	6.00	17.50	—

KM# 162   2-1/2 CENTAVOS
Copper, 25 mm. **Obv:** Liberty head left **Rev:** Denomination within wreath

Date	Mintage	F	VF	XF	Unc	BU
1904	277,000	3.50	7.50	20.00	50.00	—
1906	161,000	4.50	10.00	22.00	55.00	—
1907	262,000	3.50	7.50	20.00	45.00	—
Note: Varieties exist for 1907 dated coins						
1908	201,000	3.00	7.00	19.00	45.00	—

KM# 155.2   5 CENTAVOS
1.0000 g., 0.5000 Silver 0.0161 oz. ASW, 14 mm. **Obv:** Defiant Condor on rock left, 0.5 below condor **Rev:** Denomination above date within wreath **Note:** Varieties exist with 0.5, 0.5., 0/5.5., 0,5 or 05. below condor.

Date	Mintage	F	VF	XF	Unc	BU
1901/801	2,109,000	3.00	6.00	15.00	32.50	—
Note: With 05.						
1901/891	Inc. above	3.00	6.00	15.00	32.50	—
1901/896	Inc. above	3.00	6.00	15.00	32.50	—
1904/891/9	2,527,000	3.50	7.50	15.00	37.50	—
1904/894	Inc. above	3.50	7.50	15.00	37.50	—
1904/1	Inc. above	3.50	7.00	15.00	37.50	—
Note: With 0.5						
1904	Inc. above	2.00	5.00	10.00	27.50	—
Note: With 05.						
1906/4	713,000	5.00	10.00	25.00	45.00	—
1906	Inc. above	2.00	5.00	10.00	27.50	—
1907	2,791,000	2.00	3.00	8.00	22.50	—
Note: Exists with both 0.5 and 0.5. obverse varieties						
1907.	Inc. above	2.00	3.00	8.00	22.50	—
1909/899	Inc. below	2.50	5.00	12.00	27.50	—

KM# 155.2a   5 CENTAVOS
1.0000 g., 0.4000 Silver 0.0129 oz. ASW **Obv:** Defiant Condor on rock left **Rev:** Denomination above date within wreath **Note:** Without fineness below condor.

Date	Mintage	F	VF	XF	Unc	BU
1908/1	3,642,000	2.50	5.00	10.00	22.50	—
1908/2	Inc. above	2.50	5.00	10.00	22.50	—
1908	Inc. above	2.00	3.00	7.00	18.00	—
1909/1	1,177,000	2.00	4.00	9.00	20.00	—
1909/2	Inc. above	2.00	4.00	9.00	20.00	—
1909/8	Inc. above	2.00	5.00	9.00	20.00	—
1909	Inc. above	2.00	5.00	9.00	20.00	—
1910/01	1,587,000	2.00	3.00	7.00	18.00	—
1910	Inc. above	2.00	3.00	7.00	18.00	—
1911	847,000	2.00	4.00	9.00	20.00	—
1913/1	2,573,000	2.50	5.00	10.00	22.50	—
1913/2	Inc. above	3.00	7.00	15.00	35.00	—
Note: Varieties exist with a dot below 1 in date for 1913						
1913	Inc. above	2.00	3.00	7.00	18.00	—
Note: Varieties exist with a dot below 1 in date for 1913						
1919	Inc. below	1.50	3.00	7.00	18.00	—
Note: With and without dash below second 9 in date						

KM# 155.3   5 CENTAVOS
1.0000 g., 0.4500 Silver 0.0145 oz. ASW **Obv:** Defiant Condor on rock left, 0.45 below condor **Rev:** Denomination above date within wreath

Date	Mintage	F	VF	XF	Unc	BU
1915/1	2,250,000	1.50	3.50	6.00	16.50	—
1915	Inc. above	1.50	3.00	5.00	15.00	—
Note: 1915 exists with flat and curved top on 5						
1916/1	4,337,000	1.50	3.50	6.00	16.50	—
1916/5	Inc. above	1.50	3.50	6.00	16.50	—
1916	Inc. above	1.50	3.00	5.00	15.00	—
1919/1	1,494,000	3.00	7.00	15.00	35.00	—
Note: With dash below second 9 in date						
1919/2	Inc. above	2.00	4.00	8.00	22.50	—
1919/5	Inc. above	2.00	4.00	8.00	22.50	—
1919	Inc. above	3.00	5.00	10.00	22.50	—

KM# 165   5 CENTAVOS
Copper-Nickel, 16.5 mm. **Obv:** Defiant Condor on rock left, without designer's name O. ROTY at bottom **Rev:** Denomination above date within wreath **Note:** Varieties exist.

Date	Mintage	F	VF	XF	Unc	BU
1920	718,000	1.00	1.50	3.00	12.00	—
1921	2,406,000	0.60	1.25	2.00	7.00	—
1922	3,872,000	0.60	1.25	2.00	7.00	—
1923	2,150,000	0.60	1.25	2.00	7.00	—
1925	994,000	0.60	1.25	2.00	7.00	—
Note: Obverse variety known with dot to left of right wing tip.						
1926	594,000	1.50	2.50	3.00	9.00	—
1927	1,276,000	0.50	1.00	2.00	6.00	—

Date	Mintage	F	VF	XF	Unc	BU
1928	5,197,000	0.50	1.00	2.00	6.00	—
1933	3,000,000	5.00	10.00	25.00	55.00	—
1934	Inc. above	0.25	0.50	1.00	3.00	—
1936	2,000,000	0.25	0.50	1.00	3.00	—
1937	2,000,000	0.25	0.50	1.00	3.00	—
1938	2,000,000	0.25	0.50	1.00	3.00	—

KM# 156.2 10 CENTAVOS
2.0000 g., 0.5000 Silver 0.0321 oz. ASW, 17 mm. **Obv:** Defiant Condor on rock left, 0.5 below condor **Rev:** Denomination above date within wreath **Note:** Obverse varieties exist with 0.5, 0,5, 0.5. or 0.5/9 below condor. Struck by law of January 19, 1899.

Date	Mintage	F	VF	XF	Unc	BU
1901/891	Inc. above	17.50	30.00	55.00	150	—
1901/896	Inc. above	17.50	30.00	55.00	150	—
1904/896	779,000	2.00	3.50	7.00	16.50	—
1904/899	Inc. above	2.00	3.50	7.00	16.50	—
1906	139,000	2.50	4.50	8.50	18.00	—
1907/2	Inc. above	2.50	4.50	8.50	18.00	—
1907/807	3,151,000	2.50	4.50	8.50	18.00	—
1907	Inc. above	2.00	3.50	7.00	16.50	—

Note: Exists with both 0.5 and 0.5. obverse varieties

KM# 156.2a 10 CENTAVOS
1.5000 g., 0.4000 Silver 0.0193 oz. ASW, 17 mm. **Obv:** Defiant Condor on rock left **Rev:** Denomination above date within wreath **Note:** Varieties exist.

Date	Mintage	F	VF	XF	Unc	BU
1908/1	4,149,000	1.50	3.00	6.00	15.00	—
1908	Inc. above	1.00	2.00	4.50	12.00	—
1908/inverted 6	Inc. above	1.50	3.00	6.00	15.00	—
1909/8	2,964,000	1.50	3.00	6.00	15.00	—
1909	Inc. above	1.00	2.00	4.50	12.00	—
1913	1,269,000	1.50	3.00	6.00	15.00	—
1919/8	883,000	3.00	6.00	12.00	25.00	—
1919	Inc. above	2.50	5.00	10.00	20.00	—
1920/5	2,109,000	1.50	3.00	6.00	18.00	—
1920	Inc. above	1.00	2.00	4.50	12.00	—

KM# 156.3 10 CENTAVOS
1.5000 g., 0.4500 Silver 0.0217 oz. ASW, 17 mm. **Obv:** Defiant Condor on rock left, 0.45 below condor **Rev:** Denomination above date within wreath

Date	Mintage	F	VF	XF	Unc	BU
1915	1,620,000	1.00	1.50	3.00	7.50	—
1916	2,855,000	1.00	1.50	3.00	7.50	—
1917/1	736,000	2.00	3.50	7.00	18.00	—
1917	Inc. above	1.50	2.50	5.00	14.00	—
1918/5	—	2.00	3.50	7.00	18.00	—
1918	—	1.50	2.50	5.00	14.00	—
1919/3	—	2.00	3.50	7.00	18.00	—

KM# 166 10 CENTAVOS
3.0800 g., Copper-Nickel, 19.7 mm. **Obv:** Defiant Condor on rock left, without designer's name O. ROTY at bottom **Rev:** Denomination above date within wreath **Edge:** Plain

Date	Mintage	F	VF	XF	Unc	BU
1920	451,000	1.50	3.50	7.00	15.00	—
1921	2,654,000	0.50	0.75	1.50	3.00	—
1922	4,017,000	0.50	0.75	1.50	3.00	—
1923	3,356,000	0.50	0.75	1.50	7.00	—
1924	1,445,000	0.50	0.75	1.50	3.00	—
1925	2,665,000	0.50	0.75	1.50	3.00	—
1927	523,000	1.00	2.00	3.50	7.00	—
1928	3,052,000	0.50	0.75	1.50	3.00	—
1932	1,500,000	1.00	2.00	3.50	7.00	—
1933/2	5,800,000	0.75	1.00	2.00	4.00	—
1933	Inc. above	0.25	0.50	1.00	2.00	—
1933 Over reversed 3	Inc. above	0.50	1.00	2.00	5.00	—
1934	900,000	0.50	0.75	1.50	3.00	—
1935	1,500,000	0.50	0.75	1.50	3.00	—

Date	Mintage	F	VF	XF	Unc	BU
1936	3,300,000	0.25	0.50	1.00	2.00	—
1937	2,000,000	0.25	0.50	1.00	2.00	—
1937 Over reversed 3	Inc. above	0.50	1.00	2.00	4.00	—
1938	5,000,000	0.25	0.50	1.00	2.00	—
1938 Over reversed 3	Inc. above	0.50	1.00	2.00	5.00	—
1939	1,200,000	0.25	0.50	1.00	2.00	—
1939 Over reversed 3	Inc. above	0.50	1.00	2.00	5.00	—
1940	6,100,000	0.25	0.50	1.00	2.00	—
1941	900,000	1.00	2.00	3.00	6.00	—

KM# 151.2 20 CENTAVOS
4.0000 g., 0.5000 Silver 0.0643 oz. ASW, 21.5 mm. **Obv:** Defiant Condor on rock left, 0.5 below condor **Rev:** Denomination above date within wreath **Note:** Obverse varieties with 0.5 or 0.5. exist. Issued by law of January 19, 1899.

Date	Mintage	F	VF	XF	Unc	BU
1906/806	866,000	2.50	6.00	12.00	25.00	—
1906/896	Inc. above	2.50	6.00	12.00	25.00	—
1906	Inc. above	2.00	5.00	10.00	20.00	—
1907/807	7,625,000	2.00	5.00	10.00	20.00	—
1907/895	Inc. above	2.00	5.00	10.00	20.00	—
1907	Inc. above	1.50	4.00	10.00	20.00	—

KM# 151.3 20 CENTAVOS
3.0000 g., 0.4000 Silver 0.0386 oz. ASW, 21.5 mm. **Obv:** Defiant Condor on rock left, without 0.5 below condor **Rev:** Denomination above date within wreath

Date	Mintage	F	VF	XF	Unc	BU
1907/807	1,201,000	1.50	3.50	8.00	16.50	—
1907	Inc. above	1.00	3.00	7.00	15.00	—
1908/808	5,869,000	1.50	3.50	8.00	16.50	—
1908	Inc. above	0.85	3.00	6.00	12.50	—
1909	1,080,000	0.85	3.00	6.00	12.50	—
1913/1	3,507,000	1.00	4.00	8.00	20.00	—
1913/50	Inc. above	1.00	4.00	8.00	20.00	—
1913	Inc. above	1.50	4.00	8.00	20.00	—
1919	3,749,000	0.85	3.00	6.00	12.50	—
1920	4,189,000	0.85	3.00	6.00	12.50	—

KM# 151.4 20 CENTAVOS
3.0000 g., 0.4500 Silver 0.0434 oz. ASW, 21.5 mm. **Obv:** Defiant Condor on rock left, 0.45 below condor's wing, O'Roty at bottom **Rev:** Denomination above date within wreath

Date	Mintage	F	VF	XF	Unc	BU
1916	3,377,000	2.00	4.00	8.00	20.00	—

KM# 167.1 20 CENTAVOS
4.5000 g., Copper-Nickel, 22.68 mm. **Obv:** Without designer's name O. ROTY at bottom **Rev:** Denomination and date within wreath, large numeral **Edge:** Plain

Date	Mintage	F	VF	XF	Unc	BU
1920	499,000	1.00	2.50	5.50	15.00	—
1921	6,547,000	0.35	1.00	3.00	7.00	—
1922	8,261,000	0.35	1.00	3.00	7.00	—
1923	5,439,000	0.35	1.00	3.00	7.00	—
1924	16,096,000	0.35	1.00	3.00	7.00	—
1925	9,830,000	0.35	1.00	3.00	7.00	—

Note: Varieties exist with dot under 5 in date for 1925

Date	Mintage	F	VF	XF	Unc	BU
1929	9,685,000	0.35	1.00	3.00	7.00	—

KM# 167.3 20 CENTAVOS
4.2700 g., Copper-Nickel, 22.5 mm. **Obv:** Defiant Condor on rock left, with designer's name O. ROTY at bottom **Rev:** Denomination above date within wreath

Date	Mintage	F	VF	XF	Unc	BU
1932 Over reversed 3	—	0.50	1.00	2.00	6.50	—
1932	—	0.35	0.75	1.25	5.00	—

Date	Mintage	F	VF	XF	Unc	BU
1933	1,000,000	0.35	0.75	1.25	5.00	—
1933 Over reversed 3X	Inc. above	1.00	1.50	2.50	7.00	—
1933 Over reversed 33	Inc. above	1.00	1.50	2.50	7.00	—
1937	—	0.35	0.75	1.25	5.00	—
1937 Over reversed 3	—	1.00	1.50	2.50	7.00	—
1938	3,043,000	0.35	0.75	1.25	5.00	—
1938 3 over reversed 3	Inc. above	1.00	1.50	2.50	7.00	—
1939	5,283,000	0.35	0.75	1.25	3.50	—
1939 3 over reversed 3	Inc. above	1.00	1.50	2.50	7.00	—
1940	9,300,000	0.35	0.75	1.25	3.00	—
1941	3,000,000	0.35	0.75	1.25	3.50	—

KM# 167.4 20 CENTAVOS
Copper-Nickel **Obv:** With designer's name O. ROTY at bottom **Rev:** Denomination and date within wreath

Date	Mintage	F	VF	XF	Unc	BU
1929	Inc. above	1.00	2.50	5.00	10.00	—

KM# 167.2 20 CENTAVOS
4.4900 g., Copper-Nickel **Obv:** Without designer's name **Rev:** Denomination and date within wreath, small numeral

Date	Mintage	F	VF	XF	Unc	BU
1932	—	0.50	1.00	2.00	6.00	—
1932 Over reversed 3	—	0.75	1.50	3.00	8.00	—
1933 Over reversed 3X	—	0.50	1.00	2.00	5.00	—
1933/ Reversed 33	59,000,000	0.50	1.00	2.00	5.00	—
1933	Inc. above	0.35	0.75	1.25	3.50	—

KM# 177 20 CENTAVOS
2.9200 g., Copper, 18 mm. **Obv:** Armored bust of General Bernardo O'Higgins right, Thenot on truncation **Rev:** Denomination above date

Date	Mintage	F	VF	XF	Unc	BU
1942	30,000,000	0.15	0.25	1.00	4.00	—
1943	396,000,000	0.15	0.25	1.00	4.00	—
1944	29,100,000	0.15	0.25	1.00	4.00	—
1945	11,400,000	0.15	0.25	1.00	4.00	—
1946	13,800,000	0.15	0.25	1.00	4.00	—
1947	15,700,000	0.15	0.25	1.00	4.00	—
1948	15,200,000	0.15	0.25	1.00	4.00	—
1949	14,700,000	0.15	0.25	1.00	4.00	—
1950	15,200,000	0.15	0.25	1.00	4.00	—
1951	14,700,000	0.15	0.25	1.00	4.00	—
1952	15,500,000	0.15	0.25	1.00	4.00	—
1953	7,800,000	0.15	0.25	1.00	4.00	—

KM# 163 40 CENTAVOS
6.0000 g., 0.4000 Silver 0.0772 oz. ASW, 25 mm. **Obv:** Defiant Condor on rock, left **Rev:** Denomination above date within wreath

Date	Mintage	F	VF	XF	Unc	BU
1907	56,000	20.00	40.00	80.00	195	—
1908/6	1,452,000	7.00	14.00	28.00	55.00	—
1908	Inc. above	6.00	12.00	25.00	50.00	—

KM# 160 50 CENTAVOS
10.0000 g., 0.7000 Silver 0.2250 oz. ASW, 28 mm. **Obv:** Defiant Condor on rock left **Rev:** Denomination above date within wreath **Note:** Varieties with 0.7 or 0.7. exist.

Date	Mintage	F	VF	XF	Unc	BU
1902	2,022,000	6.00	12.00	22.50	50.00	—
1903	1,111,000	6.00	12.00	22.50	50.00	—
1905	1,075,000	6.00	12.00	22.50	50.00	—

KM# 178 50 CENTAVOS
Copper, 20.5 mm. **Obv:** Bust of General Bernardo O'Higgins right, Thenot on truncation **Rev:** Denomination above date **Edge:** Plain

Date	Mintage	F	VF	XF	Unc	BU
1942	4,715,000	1.00	2.00	5.00	10.00	—

KM# 152.2 PESO
20.0000 g., 0.7000 Silver 0.4501 oz. ASW, 35 mm. **Obv:** Defiant Condor on rock, left, 0.7 below right wing **Rev:** Denomination above date within wreath

Date	Mintage	F	VF	XF	Unc	BU
1902	178,000	12.00	25.00	60.00	125	—
1903	372,000	9.00	18.00	38.00	80.00	—
1905	429,000	9.00	18.00	38.00	80.00	—

KM# 152.3 PESO
12.0000 g., 0.9000 Silver 0.3472 oz. ASW, 31.5 mm. **Obv:** Defiant Condor on rock, left, 0.9 below right wing **Rev:** Denomination above date within wreath

Date	Mintage	F	VF	XF	Unc	BU
1910	2,166,000	6.50	8.50	12.50	28.00	—

KM# 152.4 PESO
9.0000 g., 0.7200 Silver 0.2083 oz. ASW, 27.5 mm. **Obv:** Defiant Condor on rock, left, 0.72 below right wing **Rev:** Denomination above date within wreath

Date	Mintage	F	VF	XF	Unc	BU
1915	6,032,000	3.75	5.50	8.00	18.00	—
1917	3,033,000	4.00	6.50	12.00	25.00	—

KM# 152.5 PESO
9.0000 g., 0.5000 Silver 0.1447 oz. ASW, 29 mm. **Obv:** Defiant Condor on rock, left, 0.5 below right wing **Rev:** Denomination above date within wreath

Date	Mintage	F	VF	XF	Unc	BU
1921	2,287,000	2.75	3.75	7.50	16.00	—
1922	2,718,000	2.75	3.75	7.50	16.00	—

KM# 152.6 PESO
9.0000 g., 0.5000 Silver 0.1447 oz. ASW, 29 mm. **Obv:** Defiant Condor on rock left, 0.5 below right wing **Rev:** Date and denomination within wreath **Note:** Struck with medal rotation.

Date	Mintage	F	VF	XF	Unc	BU
1924	1,748,000	2.75	3.75	7.50	16.00	—
1925	2,037,000	2.75	3.75	7.50	16.00	—

Note: Varieties of 1925 dated coins exist with flat and curved tops

KM# 142.2 PESO
25.0000 g., 0.9000 Silver 0.7234 oz. ASW **Obv:** Plumed arms within wreath **Rev:** Defiant Condor above date, shield in right talon, flat top 3 **Note:** Medal alignment.

Date	Mintage	F	VF	XF	Unc	BU
1883(1925)	712,000	—	150	350	1,400	2,000

KM# 142.3 PESO
25.0000 g., 0.9000 Silver 0.7234 oz. ASW **Obv:** Three plumes above shield within wreath, denomination below **Rev:** Defiant Condor above date, shield in right talon, flat-top 3 **Note:** Coin alignment. Minted in 1925-26 and most coins were melted down in 1927.

Date	Mintage	F	VF	XF	Unc	BU
1883(1926)	149,000	—	150	300	850	1,250

KM# A171.1 PESO
9.0000 g., 0.5000 Silver 0.1447 oz. ASW, 29 mm. **Obv:** Defiant Condor on rock left, 0.5 below right wing **Rev:** Date and denomination within wreath **Note:** A mule, with 0.5 and without mint mark on obverse.

Date	Mintage	F	VF	XF	Unc	BU
1927	—	15.00	30.00	45.00	90.00	—

KM# 171.1 PESO
9.0000 g., 0.5000 Silver 0.1447 oz. ASW, 29 mm. **Obv:** Defiant Condor on rock left, 0.5 below right wing **Rev:** Denomination above date within wreath

Date	Mintage	F	VF	XF	Unc	BU
1927So	3,890,000	4.00	6.00	10.00	20.00	—

KM# 171.2 PESO
9.0000 g., 0.5000 Silver 0.1447 oz. ASW, 29 mm. **Obv:** Defiant Condor on rock left, 0.5 below right wing **Rev:** Date and denomination within wreath, thick numeral **Note:** Varieties 0.5 and 0,5 exist. Total of 2,431,608 pieces dated 1921-1927 were melted down in 1932.

Date	Mintage	F	VF	XF	Unc	BU
1927So	—	4.00	6.00	10.00	20.00	—

KM# 174 PESO
6.0000 g., 0.4000 Silver 0.0772 oz. ASW, 26 mm. **Obv:** Defiant Condor on rock left **Rev:** Denomination above date within wreath

Date	Mintage	F	VF	XF	Unc	BU
1932	4,000,000	1.75	2.75	5.00	10.00	—

KM# 176.1 PESO
Copper-Nickel, 29 mm. **Obv:** Defiant Condor on rock left **Rev:** Denomination above date within wreath

Date	Mintage	F	VF	XF	Unc	BU
1933	29,976,000	0.35	0.75	1.75	3.50	—

KM# 176.2 PESO
Copper-Nickel, 29 mm. **Obv:** Defiant Condor on rock left, O ROTY incuse on rock base **Rev:** Denomination above date within wreath

Date	Mintage	F	VF	XF	Unc	BU
1940	150,000	2.00	3.00	6.00	12.00	—

KM# 179 PESO
7.3900 g., Copper, 25 mm. **Obv:** Armored bust of General Bernardo O'Higgins right **Rev:** Denomination above date

Date	Mintage	F	VF	XF	Unc	BU
1942	15,150,000	0.10	0.35	2.00	9.00	—
1943	16,900,000	0.10	0.35	2.00	9.00	—
1944	12,050,000	0.10	0.35	2.00	9.00	—
1945	7,600,000	0.10	0.35	2.00	9.00	—
1946	2,050,000	0.10	0.35	5.00	15.00	—
1947	2,200,000	0.10	0.35	5.00	15.00	—
1948	5,900,000	0.10	0.25	2.00	5.00	—
1949	7,100,000	0.10	0.20	1.00	4.00	—
1950	7,250,000	0.10	0.20	1.00	4.00	—
1951	8,150,000	0.10	0.20	1.00	4.00	—
1952	10,400,000	0.10	0.20	1.00	4.00	—
1953 Short top 5	17,200,000	0.10	0.20	1.00	3.00	—
1953 Long top 5	Inc. above	0.10	0.20	1.00	3.00	—
1954	7,566,000	0.10	0.20	1.00	3.00	—

KM# 179a PESO
2.0000 g., Aluminum, 25 mm. **Obv:** Armored bust, right **Rev:** Denomination above date

Date	Mintage	F	VF	XF	Unc	BU
1954	43,550,000	0.10	0.15	0.50	1.50	—
1954 Proof		Value: 25.00				
1955	69,050,000	0.10	0.15	0.50	1.50	—
1956	58,250,000	0.10	0.15	0.50	1.50	—
1956 Proof		Value: 25.00				
1957	49,250,000	0.10	0.15	0.50	1.50	—
1958	29,900	0.10	0.15	0.50	1.50	—

KM# 172 2 PESOS
18.0000 g., 0.5000 Silver 0.2893 oz. ASW, 33 mm. **Obv:** Defiant Condor on rock left **Rev:** Denomination above date within wreath **Note:** Obverse varieties 0.5 and 0,5 with curved top and flat top 5 exist. 459,510 pieces were melted down in 1932.

Date	Mintage	F	VF	XF	Unc	BU
1927	1,060,000	BV	5.50	10.00	20.00	—

KM# 159 5 PESOS
2.9955 g., 0.9170 Gold 0.0883 oz. AGW, 16.5 mm. **Obv:** Head left **Rev:** Plumed arms with supporters

Date	Mintage	F	VF	XF	Unc	BU
1911	1,399	—	—	200	350	

KM# 173.1 5 PESOS
25.0000 g., 0.9000 Silver 0.7234 oz. ASW **Obv:** Defiant Condor on rock, left, 0.9 below right wing **Rev:** Denomination above date within wreath, narrow 5, width = 2.5mm

Date	Mintage	F	VF	XF	Unc	BU
1927	965,000	14.00	16.00	22.50	50.00	250

KM# 173.2 5 PESOS
25.0000 g., 0.9000 Silver 0.7234 oz. ASW **Obv:** Defiant Condor on rock left, 0.9 below right wing **Rev:** Denomination and date within wreath, wide numeral, width = 3mm **Note:** Varieties 0.9 and 0.9 exist. 436,510 pieces of KM#173.1 and #173.2 were melted down in 1932.

Date	Mintage	F	VF	XF	Unc	BU
1927	Inc. above	14.00	16.00	22.50	50.00	—

KM# 180 5 PESOS
Aluminum, 23.5 mm. **Obv:** Condor in flight **Rev:** Denomination above date flanked by grain sprigs

Date	Mintage	F	VF	XF	Unc	BU
1956	1,600,000	0.15	0.35	0.50	1.25	—

KM# 182 5 PESOS
22.5000 g., 0.9990 Silver 0.7226 oz. ASW **Subject:** 150th Anniversary of Naval Academy **Obv:** Arms with supporters, date at left, denomination below **Rev:** Bust of Admiral Arturo Prat Chacon, 3/4 facing

Date	Mintage	F	VF	XF	Unc	BU
1968 Proof	1,200	Value: 28.50				

KM# 157 10 PESOS
5.9910 g., 0.9170 Gold 0.1766 oz. AGW, 21 mm. **Obv:** Head left **Rev:** Plumed arms with supporters

Date	Mintage	F	VF	XF	Unc	BU
1901	1,651,000	—	BV	170	200	—

KM# 181 10 PESOS
2.9600 g., Aluminum, 28 mm. **Obv:** Condor in flight **Rev:** Denomination above date, grain sprigs flank

Date	Mintage	F	VF	XF	Unc	BU
1956	13,100,000	0.15	0.35	0.50	0.75	1.50
1957	28,800,000	0.15	0.35	0.50	0.75	1.50

Date	Mintage	F	VF	XF	Unc	BU
1958	44,500,000	0.15	0.35	0.50	0.75	1.50
1959	10,220,000	0.25	0.50	1.00	1.50	2.50

KM# 183 10 PESOS
45.0000 g., 0.9990 Silver 1.4453 oz. ASW **Subject:** Arrival of Liberation Fleet in 1820 under command of Lord Cochrane **Rev:** Liberation fleet, dates below

Date	Mintage	F	VF	XF	Unc	BU
1968 Proof	1,215	Value: 85.00				

KM# 158 20 PESOS
11.9821 g., 0.9170 Gold 0.3532 oz. AGW, 27 mm. **Obv:** Head left **Rev:** Plumed arms with supporters

Date	Mintage	F	VF	XF	Unc	BU
1906	41,000	—	—	BV	345	—
1907	12,000	—	—	BV	345	—
1908	26,000	—	—	BV	345	—
1910	28,000	—	—	BV	345	365
1911	17,000	—	—	BV	345	365
1913/11	18,000	—	—	BV	345	365
1913	Inc. above	—	—	BV	345	365
1914	22,000	—	—	BV	345	365
1915	65,000	—	—	BV	345	365
1916	36,000	—	—	BV	345	365
1917	717,000	—	—	BV	345	365

KM# 168 20 PESOS
4.0679 g., 0.9000 Gold 0.1177 oz. AGW **Obv:** Head left, date below **Rev:** Arms with supporters, denomination above

Date	Mintage	F	VF	XF	Unc	BU
1926	85,000	—	—	BV	125	—
1958	500	BV	120	140	220	—
1959	25,000	—	—	BV	120	—
1961	20,000	—	—	BV	120	—
1964		—	—	BV	120	—
1976	99,000	—	—	BV	120	—
1977	38,000	—	—	BV	120	—
1979	30,000	—	—	BV	120	—
1980	30,000	—	—	BV	120	—

KM# 188 20 PESOS
4.0679 g., 0.9000 Gold 0.1177 oz. AGW **Obv:** Head left, date below **Rev:** Coat of arms on ornamental vines, denomination above

Date	Mintage	F	VF	XF	Unc	BU
1976	Inc. above	—	—	BV	120	—

KM# 169 50 PESOS
10.1698 g., 0.9000 Gold 0.2943 oz. AGW **Obv:** Head left, date below **Rev:** Coat of arms, denomination above

Date	Mintage	F	VF	XF	Unc	BU
1926	126,000	—	—	BV	285	300
1958	10,000	—	—	BV	285	300
1961	20,000	—	—	BV	285	300
1962	30,000	—	—	BV	285	300
1965		—	—	BV	285	300
1966		—	—	BV	285	300
1967		—	—	BV	285	300
1968		—	—	BV	285	300
1969		—	—	BV	285	300
1970		—	—	—	650	
1974		—	—	BV	285	300

KM# 184 50 PESOS
10.1698 g., 0.9000 Gold 0.2943 oz. AGW **Subject:** 150th Anniversary of Military Academy **Obv:** Coat of arms above denomination **Rev:** Armored bust right of Bernardo O'Higgins, two dates below

Date	Mintage	F	VF	XF	Unc	BU
1968 Proof	2,515	Value: 300				

KM# 170 100 PESOS
20.3397 g., 0.9000 Gold 0.5885 oz. AGW **Obv:** Head left, date below **Rev:** Coat of arms, denomination above

Date	Mintage	F	VF	XF	Unc	BU
1926	678,000	—	—	BV	575	600

KM# 175 100 PESOS
20.3397 g., 0.9000 Gold 0.5885 oz. AGW **Obv:** Head left, date below, revised bust and legend style **Rev:** Coat of arms, denomination above, revised legend style

Date	Mintage	F	VF	XF	Unc	BU
1932	9,315	—	BV	575	620	—
1946	260,000	—	—	BV	575	600
1947	540,000	—	—	BV	575	600
1948	420,000	—	—	BV	575	600
1949	310,000	—	—	BV	575	600
1950	20,000	—	—	BV	575	600
1951	145,000	—	—	BV	575	600
1952	245,000	—	—	BV	575	600
1953	175,000	—	—	BV	575	600
1954	190,000	—	—	BV	575	600
1955	150,000	—	—	BV	575	600
1956	60,000	—	—	BV	575	600
1957	40,000	—	—	BV	575	600
1958	157,000	—	—	BV	575	600
1959	90,000	—	—	BV	575	600
1960	200,000	—	—	BV	575	600
1961	295,000	—	—	BV	575	600
1962	260,000	—	—	BV	575	600
1963	210,000	—	—	BV	575	600
1964		—	—	BV	575	600
1968		—	—	BV	575	600
1969		—	—	BV	575	600
1970		—	—	BV	575	600
1971		—	—	BV	575	600
1972		—	—	BV	575	600
1973		—	—	BV	575	600
1974		—	—	BV	575	600
1976	172,000	—	—	BV	575	600
1977	25,000	—	—	BV	575	600
1979	100,000	—	—	BV	575	600
1980	50,000	—	—	BV	575	600

KM# 185   100 PESOS
20.3397 g., 0.9000 Gold 0.5885 oz. AGW **Subject:** 150th Anniversary of National Coinage **Obv:** Coat of arms, date at left, denomination below **Rev:** Coinage press, liberty bust left

Date	Mintage	F	VF	XF	Unc	BU
1968 Proof	1,815	Value: 600				

KM# 186   200 PESOS
40.6794 g., 0.9000 Gold 1.1770 oz. AGW **Subject:** 150th Anniversary of San Martin's passage through Andes Mountains, from a painting by Vila Prades **Obv:** Coat of arms, date at left, denomination below **Rev:** Riders passing through mountains, two dates below

Date	Mintage	F	VF	XF	Unc	BU
1968 Proof	965	Value: 1,150				

KM# 187   500 PESOS
101.6985 g., 0.9000 Gold 2.9426 oz. AGW **Subject:** 150th Anniversary of National Flag **Rev:** Liberty bust left, waving flag in background, two dates below

Date	Mintage	F	VF	XF	Unc	BU
1968 Proof	—	Value: 3,000				

REFORM COINAGE
10 Pesos = 1 Centesimo; 100 Centesimos = 1 Escudo

KM# 192   1/2 CENTESIMO
Aluminum, 25 mm. **Obv:** Condor in flight **Rev:** Denomination above date, grain sprigs flank

Date	Mintage	F	VF	XF	Unc	BU
1962	3,750,000	—	0.10	0.30	0.50	1.50
1962 Proof	—	Value: 10.00				
1963	8,100,000	—	0.10	0.30	0.50	1.50

KM# 189   CENTESIMO
Aluminum, 29 mm. **Obv:** Condor in flight **Rev:** Denomination above date, grain sprigs flank

Date	Mintage	F	VF	XF	Unc	BU
1960	20,160,000	—	0.50	1.00	2.00	3.00
1960 Proof	—	Value: 45.00				
1961	Inc. above	—	0.50	1.00	2.00	3.00
1962	26,320,000	—	0.50	1.00	2.00	3.00
1963	27,100,000	—	0.50	1.00	2.00	3.00
1963 Proof	—	Value: 45.00				

KM# 193   2 CENTESIMOS
3.0700 g., Aluminum-Bronze, 20 mm. **Obv:** Condor in flight **Rev:** Denomination above date, grain sprigs flank **Edge:** Plain

Date	Mintage	F	VF	XF	Unc	BU
1960	2,050,000	—	—	—	50.00	—
Note: Not released for circulation						
1960 Proof	—	Value: 50.00				
1964	2,050,000	—	—	0.10	2.00	3.00
1965	32,550,000	—	—	0.10	2.00	3.00
1966	31,800,000	—	—	0.10	2.00	3.00
1967	34,750,000	—	—	0.10	2.00	3.00
1967 Proof	—	Value: 50.00				
1968	29,400,000	—	—	0.10	2.00	3.00
1969	—	—	—	—	3.00	5.00
1969 Proof	—	Value: 50.00				
1970	20,250,000	—	—	0.10	2.00	3.00

KM# 190   5 CENTESIMOS
4.1200 g., Aluminum-Bronze, 23.14 mm. **Obv:** Condor in flight **Rev:** Denomination above date, grain sprigs flank

Date	Mintage	F	VF	XF	Unc	BU
1960	—	—	—	—	75.00	—
Note: Not released for circulation						
1960 Proof	—	Value: 100				
1961	12,000	—	2.50	5.00	10.00	15.00
1962	—	—	2.00	4.00	10.00	15.00
1964	16,628,000	—	—	0.10	0.15	2.00	3.00
1965	27,680,000	—	—	0.10	0.15	2.00	3.00
1966	32,360,000	—	—	0.10	0.15	2.00	3.00
1966 Proof	—	Value: 50.00				
1967	19,680,000	—	—	0.10	0.15	2.00	3.00
1968	4,400,000	—	—	0.10	0.15	2.00	3.00
1968 Proof	—	Value: 50.00				
1969	13,200,000	—	—	—	5.00	7.00
1969 Proof	—	Value: 50.00				
1970	30,680,000	—	—	0.10	0.15	2.00	3.00
1971	16,080,000	—	—	0.10	0.15	2.00	3.00

KM# 191   10 CENTESIMOS
8.1000 g., Aluminum-Bronze, 27.17 mm. **Obv:** Condor in flight **Rev:** Denomination above date, grain sprigs flank

Date	Mintage	F	VF	XF	Unc	BU
1960	—	—	2.00	4.00	10.00	15.00
1960 Proof	—	Value: 70.00				
1961	1,915,000	—	0.10	1.00	4.00	6.00
1962	1,480,000	—	0.10	0.20	2.00	3.00
1963 Small date	10,980,000	—	0.10	0.20	2.00	3.00
1964	27,070,000	—	0.10	0.20	2.00	3.00
1965	49,480,000	—	0.10	0.20	2.00	3.00

Date	Mintage	F	VF	XF	Unc	BU
1966	60,680,000	—	0.10	0.20	2.00	3.00
1967	27,520,000	—	0.10	0.25	2.00	3.00
1967 Proof	—	Value: 50.00				
1968	8,040,000	—	0.10	0.20	2.00	3.00
1969	15,660,000	—	—	—	5.00	7.00
1970 Large date	42,080,000	—	0.10	0.20	1.00	2.00

KM# 194   10 CENTESIMOS
2.5400 g., Aluminum-Bronze, 18.10 mm. **Obv:** Armored bust of Bernardo O'Higgins, right **Rev:** Arms above denomination, date at left **Edge:** Plain

Date	Mintage	F	VF	XF	Unc	BU
1971	99,700,000	—	—	0.10	0.15	0.25

KM# 195   20 CENTESIMOS
3.0000 g., Aluminum-Bronze, 19.97 mm. **Obv:** Bust of Jose Manuel Balmaceda left **Rev:** Arms above denomination, date at left **Edge:** Plain

Date	Mintage	F	VF	XF	Unc	BU
1971	89,200,000	—	—	0.10	0.20	0.35
1972	—	—	0.10	0.20	1.00	1.50

KM# 196   50 CENTESIMOS
Aluminum-Bronze **Obv:** Bust of Manuel Rodriguez right **Rev:** Arms above denomination, date at left

Date	Mintage	F	VF	XF	Unc	BU
1971	58,300,000	—	0.10	0.15	0.25	0.45

KM# 197   ESCUDO
2.7400 g., Copper-Nickel, 18.90 mm. **Obv:** Bust of Jose Miguel Carrera 3/4 facing **Rev:** Arms above denomination, date at left **Edge:** Reeded

Date	Mintage	F	VF	XF	Unc	BU
1971	160,900,000	—	0.10	0.20	0.40	0.60
1972	Inc. above	—	0.10	0.20	0.40	0.60
1972 Proof	—	Value: 50.00				

KM# 198   2 ESCUDOS
Copper-Nickel **Obv:** Caupolican, Chief of Araucanian Indians **Rev:** Arms above denomination, date at left

Date	Mintage	F	VF	XF	Unc	BU
1971	106	—	—	—	150	—
Note: Not released for circulation						
1971 Proof	—	Value: 65.00				

KM# 199   5 ESCUDOS
4.5100 g., Copper-Nickel, 23.03 mm. **Obv:** Lautaro, Araucanian Indian, upriser against Spain **Rev:** Arms above denomination, date at left

Date	Mintage	F	VF	XF	Unc	BU
1971	—	—	0.10	0.25	0.75	1.25

Date	Mintage	F	VF	XF	Unc	BU
1972	—		0.10	0.25	0.75	1.25
1972 Proof	—	Value: 50.00				

KM# 199a 5 ESCUDOS
Aluminum Obv: Lautaro, Araucanian Indian, upriser against Spain Rev: Arms above denomination, date at left

Date	Mintage	F	VF	XF	Unc	BU
1972	—		0.10	0.15	0.20	0.50

KM# 200 10 ESCUDOS
2.1000 g., Aluminum, 24.93 mm. Obv: Defiant Condor on rock left Rev: Denomination above date within wreath Edge: Plain

Date	Mintage	F	VF	XF	Unc	BU
1974	33,750,000		0.10	0.15	0.35	0.50
1974 Proof	—	Value: 50.00				
1975	31,600,000					

Note: Although recorded with mintage, no examples are known with this date

KM# 201 50 ESCUDOS
4.0000 g., Nickel-Brass, 21.48 mm. Obv: Defiant Condor on rock left Rev: Denomination above date within wreath

Date	Mintage	F	VF	XF	Unc	BU
1974	5,700,000	—	0.15	0.25	0.60	0.85
1975	20,300,000	—	0.15	0.20	0.50	0.75

KM# 202 100 ESCUDOS
5.0100 g., Nickel-Brass, 23.5 mm. Obv: Defiant Condor on rock left Rev: Denomination above date within wreath

Date	Mintage	F	VF	XF	Unc	BU
1974	32,100,000	—	0.20	0.35	0.75	1.00
1975	65,600,000	—	0.20	0.35	0.75	1.00

REFORM COINAGE
100 Centavos = 1 Peso; 1000 Old Escudos = 1 Peso

KM# 203 CENTAVO
2.0000 g., Aluminum, 24.93 mm. Obv: Defiant Condor on rock left Rev: Denomination above date within wreath Edge: Plain

Date	Mintage	F	VF	XF	Unc	BU
1975	2,000,000	—	0.10	0.15	0.50	0.75

KM# 204 5 CENTAVOS
Aluminum-Bronze Obv: Defiant Condor on rock left Rev: Denomination above date within wreath

---

Date	Mintage	F	VF	XF	Unc	BU
1975	5,400,000	—	—	0.10	0.25	0.75
1976	6,600,000					

Note: Although recorded with mintage, no examples are known with this date

KM# 204a 5 CENTAVOS
Aluminum Obv: Defiant Condor on rock left Rev: Date and denomination within wreath

Date	Mintage	F	VF	XF	Unc	BU
1976	5,000,000	—	—	0.10	0.25	0.75

KM# 205 10 CENTAVOS
Aluminum-Bronze Obv: Defiant Condor on rock left Rev: Denomination above date within wreath

Date	Mintage	F	VF	XF	Unc	BU
1975	8,600,000	—	—	0.10	0.25	0.75
1976	9,000,000					

Note: Although recorded with mintage, no examples are known with this date

KM# 205a 10 CENTAVOS
2.0200 g., Aluminum, 23.75 mm. Obv: Defiant Condor on rock left Rev: Denomination above date within wreath

Date	Mintage	F	VF	XF	Unc	BU
1976	6,600,000	—	—	0.10	0.25	0.50
1977	57,800,000	—	—	0.10	0.25	0.50
1978	58,050,000	—	—	0.10	0.25	0.50
1979	101,950,000	—	—	0.10	0.25	0.50

KM# 206 50 CENTAVOS
4.1300 g., Copper-Nickel, 22.17 mm. Obv: Defiant Condor on rock left Rev: Denomination above date within wreath

Date	Mintage	F	VF	XF	Unc	BU
1975	38,000,000	—	—	0.10	0.25	0.50
1976	1,000,000	—	0.50	1.00	2.00	3.00
1977	10,000,000	—	—	0.10	0.25	0.50

KM# 206a 50 CENTAVOS
3.9500 g., Aluminum-Bronze, 22.06 mm. Obv: Defiant Condor on rock left Rev: Denomination above date within wreath

Date	Mintage	F	VF	XF	Unc	BU
1978	19,250,000	—	—	0.10	0.25	0.60
1979	28,000,000	—	—	0.10	0.25	0.60

KM# 207 PESO
Copper-Nickel, 24 mm. Obv: Armored bust of Bernardo O'Higgins right Obv. Leg.: BERNARDO O'HIGGINS Rev: Denomination above date within wreath

Date	Mintage	F	VF	XF	Unc	BU
1975	51,000,000	—	0.10	0.15	0.25	0.35

KM# 208 PESO
5.1100 g., Copper-Nickel, 24 mm. Obv: Armored bust of Bernardo O'Higgins right Obv. Leg.: LIBERTADOR. B. O'HIGGINS Rev: Denomination above date within wreath

Date	Mintage	F	VF	XF	Unc	BU
1976	30,000,000	—	—	0.10	0.25	0.35
1977	20,000,000	—	—	0.10	0.25	0.35

KM# 208a PESO
Aluminum-Bronze, 24 mm. Obv: Armored bust of Bernardo O'Higgins right Rev: Denomination above date within wreath

Date	Mintage	F	VF	XF	Unc	BU
1978	39,706,000	—	—	0.10	0.25	0.35
1979	63,000,000	—	—	0.10	0.25	0.35

KM# 216.1 PESO
2.0000 g., Aluminum-Bronze, 17 mm. Obv: Armored bust right Rev: Denomination above date within wreath Note: Reduced size. Wide date.

Date	Mintage	F	VF	XF	Unc	BU
1981	40,000,000	—	—	0.10	0.20	0.30
1984	60,000,000	—	—	0.10	0.20	0.30
1985	20,000,000	—	—	0.10	0.20	0.30
1986	45,000,000	—	—	0.10	0.20	0.30
1987	80,000,000	—	—	0.10	0.20	0.30

KM# 216.2 PESO
2.0100 g., Aluminum-Bronze, 16.98 mm. Obv: Armored bust, right Rev: Denomination above date within wreath Edge: Plain Note: Narrow date.

Date	Mintage	F	VF	XF	Unc	BU
1988	105,000,000	—	—	0.10	0.20	0.30
1989	205,000,000	—	—	0.10	0.20	0.30
1990	140,000,000	—	—	0.10	0.20	0.30
1991	140,000,000	—	—	0.10	0.20	0.30
1992		—	—	0.10	0.20	0.30

KM# 231 PESO
0.7000 g., Aluminum, 16.32 mm. Obv: Gen. Bernardo O'Higgins bust right Obv. Leg.: REPUBLICA - DE CHILE Rev: Denomination above date within wreath Edge: Plain Note: Varieties exist.

Date	Mintage	F	VF	XF	Unc	BU
1992So Narrow date	—	—	—	—	0.10	0.20
1992So Wide date	—	—	—	—	0.10	0.20
1993So	—	—	—	—	0.10	0.20
1994So	—	—	—	—	0.10	0.20
1995So	—	—	—	—	0.10	0.20
1996So	—	—	—	—	0.10	0.20
1997So	—	—	—	—	0.10	0.20
1998So	—	—	—	—	0.10	0.20
1999So	—	—	—	—	0.10	0.20
2000So	—	—	—	—	0.10	0.20

KM# 204 5 CENTAVOS
Aluminum-Bronze Obv: Defiant Condor on rock left Rev: Denomination above date within wreath

KM# 209 5 PESOS
6.9400 g., Copper-Nickel, 25.8 mm. **Subject:** 3rd Anniversary of New Government **Obv:** Winged figure with upraised arms, broken chain on wrists **Rev:** Denomination above date within wreath

Date	Mintage	F	VF	XF	Unc	BU
1976	2,100,000	—	0.15	0.25	2.00	3.50
1977	28,300,000	—	0.15	0.25	2.00	3.00
1978	11,704,000	—	0.15	0.25	2.00	3.00
1980	8,200,000	—	0.15	0.25	2.00	3.00

KM# 217.1 5 PESOS
2.7000 g., Nickel-Brass, 19 mm. **Obv:** Winged figure with arms upraised, broken chain on wrists **Rev:** Denomination above date within wreath **Note:** Wide date.

Date	Mintage	F	VF	XF	Unc	BU
1981	17,000,000	—	—	0.10	0.50	0.75
1982	20,000,000	—	—	0.10	0.50	0.75
1984	12,000,000	—	—	0.10	0.50	0.75
1985	16,000,000	—	—	0.10	0.50	0.75
1986	16,000,000	—	—	0.10	0.50	0.75
1987	8,000,000	—	—	0.10	0.50	0.75

KM# 217.2 5 PESOS
2.7800 g., Nickel-Brass **Obv:** Winged figure with arms upraised, broken chain on wrists **Rev:** Denomination above date within wreath **Note:** Narrow date.

Date	Mintage	F	VF	XF	Unc	BU
1988	27,000,000	—	—	0.10	0.50	0.75
1989	32,000,000	—	—	0.10	0.50	0.75
1990	23,000,000	—	—	0.10	0.50	0.75

KM# 229 5 PESOS
2.7500 g., Nickel-Brass **Obv:** Armored bust of Bernardo O'Higgins right **Rev:** Denomination above date within wreath

Date	Mintage	F	VF	XF	Unc	BU
1990	8,000,000	—	—	0.10	0.50	0.75
1991	2,000,000	—	—	0.10	0.50	0.75
1992	—	—	—	0.10	0.50	0.75

KM# 232 5 PESOS
2.1600 g., Aluminum-Bronze, 16.43 mm. **Obv:** Gen. Bernardo O'Higgins bust right **Obv. Leg.:** REPUBLICA - DE CHILE **Rev:** Denomination above date within wreath **Edge:** Plain **Note:** Varieties exist.

Date	Mintage	F	VF	XF	Unc	BU
1992So	—	—	—	0.10	0.35	0.60
1993So	—	—	—	0.10	0.35	0.60
1994So	—	—	—	0.10	0.35	0.60
1995So	—	—	—	0.10	0.35	0.60
1996So	—	—	—	0.10	0.35	0.60
1997So	—	—	—	0.10	0.35	0.60
1998So	—	—	—	0.10	0.35	0.60
1999So	—	—	—	0.10	0.35	0.60
2000So	—	—	—	0.10	0.35	0.60

KM# 210 10 PESOS
9.0000 g., Copper-Nickel, 28 mm. **Subject:** 3rd Anniversary of New Government **Obv:** Winged figure with arms upraised, broken chains on wrists **Rev:** Denomination above date within wreath

Date	Mintage	F	VF	XF	Unc	BU
1976	2,100,000	—	0.10	0.20	1.25	1.50
1977	30,000,000	—	0.10	0.20	1.00	1.25
1978	20,004,000	—	0.10	0.20	1.00	1.25
1979	7,000,000	—	0.10	0.20	1.00	1.25
1980	20,000,000	—	0.10	0.20	1.00	1.25

KM# 211 10 PESOS
44.8000 g., 0.9990 Silver 1.4389 oz. ASW **Subject:** 3rd Anniversary of New Government **Obv:** Coat of arms above denomination **Rev:** Winged figure with arms upraised, two dates above

Date	Mintage	F	VF	XF	Unc	BU
ND(1976) Proof	1,000	Value: 115				

KM# 218.1 10 PESOS
3.5000 g., Nickel-Brass, 21 mm. **Obv:** Winged figure with arms upraised, broken chain on wrists **Rev:** Denomination above date within wreath **Note:** Wide date, narrow rim.

Date	Mintage	F	VF	XF	Unc	BU
1981	55,000,000	—	0.10	0.20	0.50	0.75
1982	45,000,000	—	0.10	0.20	0.50	0.75
1984	30,000,000	—	0.10	0.20	0.50	0.75
1985	400,000	—	0.50	1.50	3.50	5.00
1986 Narrow date	25,000,000	—	0.10	0.20	0.50	0.75
1986 Wide date	Inc. above	—	0.10	0.20	0.50	0.75
1987	8,000,000	—	0.10	0.20	0.50	0.75

KM# 218.2 10 PESOS
Nickel-Brass **Obv:** Winged figure with arms upraised, broken chain on wrists **Rev:** Denomination above date within wreath **Note:** Narrow date.

Date	Mintage	F	VF	XF	Unc	BU
1988	45,000,000	—	0.10	0.20	0.50	0.75
1989	73,000,000	—	0.10	0.20	0.50	0.75

KM# 218.3 10 PESOS
Nickel-Brass **Obv:** Winged figure with arms upraised, broken chain on wrists **Rev:** Denomination above date within wreath **Note:** Wide rim.

Date	Mintage	F	VF	XF	Unc	BU
1990	10,000,000	—	0.10	0.20	0.50	0.75

KM# 228.1 10 PESOS
Nickel-Brass **Obv:** Small bust of Bernardo O'Higgins right, wide rim **Rev:** Denomination above date within wreath

Date	Mintage	F	VF	XF	Unc	BU
1990	5,000,000	—	0.10	0.20	0.50	0.75

KM# 228.2 10 PESOS
3.5500 g., Nickel-Brass, 20.92 mm. **Obv:** Bust of Gen. Bernardo O'Higgins right **Obv. Leg.:** REPUBLICA - DE CHILE **Rev:** Denomination above date within sprays **Edge:** Reeded **Note:** All 9's are curl tail 9's except for the 1999 date, these are straight tail 9's. Normal rim.

Date	Mintage	F	VF	XF	Unc	BU
1990So	25,000,000	—	0.10	0.20	0.50	0.65
1991So	—	—	0.10	0.20	0.50	0.65
1992So	—	—	0.10	0.20	0.50	0.65
1993So	—	—	0.10	0.20	0.50	0.65
1994So	—	—	0.10	0.20	0.50	0.65
1995So	—	—	0.10	0.20	0.50	0.65
1996So	—	—	0.10	0.20	0.50	0.65
1997So	—	—	0.10	0.20	0.50	0.65
1998So	—	—	0.10	0.20	0.50	0.65
1999So	—	—	0.10	0.20	0.50	0.65
2000So	—	—	0.10	0.20	0.50	0.65

KM# 212 50 PESOS
10.1500 g., 0.9000 Gold 0.2937 oz. AGW **Subject:** 3rd Anniversary of New Government **Obv:** Coat of arms above denomination **Rev:** Winged figure with arms upraised, two dates above

Date	Mintage	F	VF	XF	Unc	BU
ND(1976)	1,900	—	—	—	285	300
ND(1976) Proof	Inc. above	Value: 325				

KM# 219.1 50 PESOS
7.0000 g., Aluminum-Bronze, 25.71 mm. **Obv:** Armored bust right **Rev:** Denomination above date within wreath **Note:** Wide date.

Date	Mintage	F	VF	XF	Unc	BU
1981	12,000,000	—	0.25	0.50	1.25	1.50
1982	14,000,000	—	0.25	0.50	1.25	1.50
1985	400,000	—	0.60	1.50	3.50	5.00
1986	1,000,000	—	0.25	0.50	1.25	1.50
1987	4,000,000	—	0.25	0.50	1.25	1.50

KM# 219.2 50 PESOS
7.0000 g., Aluminum-Bronze, 25.40 mm. **Obv:** Bust of Gen. Bernardo O'Higgins right **Obv. Leg.:** REPUBLICA - DE CHILE **Rev:** Denomination above date within sprays **Edge:** Plain **Note:** Narrow date.

Date	Mintage	F	VF	XF	Unc	BU
1988So	4,800,000	—	0.25	0.50	1.25	1.50
1989So	4,000,000	—	0.25	0.50	1.25	1.50
1991So	10,845,000	—	0.25	0.50	1.25	1.50
1992So	—	—	0.25	0.50	1.25	1.50
1993So	—	—	0.25	0.50	1.25	1.50
1994So	—	—	0.25	0.50	1.25	1.50
1995So	—	—	0.25	0.50	1.25	1.50
1996So	—	—	0.25	0.50	1.25	1.50
1997So	—	—	0.25	0.50	1.25	1.50
1998So	—	—	0.25	0.50	1.25	1.50
1999So	—	—	0.25	0.50	1.25	1.50
2000So	—	—	0.25	0.50	1.25	1.50

KM# 213 100 PESOS
20.3000 g., 0.9000 Gold 0.5874 oz. AGW **Subject:** 3rd Anniversary of New Government **Obv:** Coat of arms above date and denomination **Rev:** Winged figure with upraised arms, two dates above

Date	Mintage	F	VF	XF	Unc	BU
1976	2,900	—	—	—	575	600
1976 Proof	100	Value: 775				

KM# 226.1 100 PESOS

Aluminum-Bronze, 26.8 mm. **Obv:** Coat of arms **Rev:** Denomination above date within wreath **Edge:** POR LA RAZON O LA FUERZA **Note:** Wide date with pointed 9.

Date	Mintage	F	VF	XF	Unc	BU
1981	10,000,000	—	0.50	0.75	2.50	3.00
1984	8,000,000	—	0.50	0.75	2.50	3.00
1985	15,000,000	—	0.50	0.75	2.50	3.00
1986	11,000,000	—	0.50	0.75	2.50	3.00
1987	15,000,000	—	0.50	0.75	2.50	3.00

KM# 226.2 100 PESOS

Aluminum-Bronze, 26.8 mm. **Obv:** Coat of arms **Rev:** Denomination above date within wreath **Edge:** POR LA RAZON O LA FUERZA **Note:** Narrow date with curved 9.

Date	Mintage	F	VF	XF	Unc	BU
1989	20,000,000	—	0.50	0.75	2.50	3.00
1991	4,320,000	—	0.50	0.75	2.50	3.00
1992	—	—	0.50	0.75	2.50	3.00
1993	—	—	0.50	0.75	2.50	3.00
1994	—	—	0.50	0.75	2.50	3.00
1995	—	—	0.50	0.75	2.50	3.00
1996	—	—	0.50	0.75	2.50	3.00
1997	—	—	0.50	0.75	2.50	3.00
1998	—	—	0.50	0.75	2.50	3.00
1999	—	—	0.50	0.75	2.50	3.00
2000	—	—	0.50	0.75	2.50	3.00

KM# 214 500 PESOS

102.2700 g., 0.9000 Gold 2.9591 oz. AGW **Subject:** 3rd Anniversary of New Government **Obv:** Coat of arms, denomination below **Rev:** Winged figure with upraised arms, two dates above **Note:** Similar to 100 Pesos, KM#213.

Date	Mintage	F	VF	XF	Unc	BU
1976	500	—	—	—	2,850	3,000
1976 Proof	700	Value: 3,200				

KM# 235 500 PESOS

6.6000 g., Bi-Metallic Aluminum-Bronze center in Copper-Nickel ring, 25.9 mm. **Subject:** Cardinal Raul Silva Henriquez **Obv:** Bust of Henriquez within inner ring facing left **Rev:** Denomination above date within wreath **Edge:** Reeded

Date	Mintage	F	VF	XF	Unc	BU
2000So	—	—	—	—	6.00	6.50
2000So Proof	—	—	—	—	—	—

KM# 233 2000 PESOS

8.2000 g., 0.5000 Silver 0.1318 oz. ASW **Subject:** 250th Anniversary of the Mint **Obv:** Building divides date and denomination **Rev:** Metal workers, two dates below

Date	Mintage	F	VF	XF	Unc	BU
1993	50,000	—	—	—	16.50	18.00

KM# 230 10000 PESOS

27.0000 g., 0.9250 Silver 0.8029 oz. ASW **Series:** Ibero - American **Obv:** Inner circle holds Coat of Arms, denomination within outer circle, 13 shields surround **Rev:** Three dates below three ships, globe in background

Date	Mintage	F	VF	XF	Unc	BU
1991 Proof	75,000	Value: 45.00				

PATTERNS

Including off metal strikes

KM#	Date	Mintage	Identification	Mkt Val
PnA26	1908	—	5 Centavos. Copper-Nickel.	250
PnB26	1908	—	10 Centavos. Brass.	
PnC26	1914	—	50 Centavos. Silver.	—
Pn26	1914	—	Peso. Silver.	600
PnA27	1914	—	2 Pesos. Silver. Piefort, large flan.	500
Pn27	1914	—	2 Pesos. Silver. Piefort, small flan.	500
Pn28	1916	—	20 Centavos. Silver. 4.0000 g.	—
Pn29	1916	—	20 Centavos. Silver. 4.0400 g.	—
Pn30	1917	—	10 Centavos. Silver. 1.9000 g.	—
Pn31	1917	—	10 Centavos. Silver. 2.5200 g.	—
Pn32	1919	—	5 Centavos. Copper-Nickel.	—
Pn33	1919	—	5 Centavos. Silver. 1.4900 g.	—
Pn34	1919	—	5 Centavos. Silver. 1.5300 g.	—
Pn35	1919	—	10 Centavos. Copper-Nickel.	—
Pn36	1919	—	20 Centavos. Copper-Nickel.	—
Pn37	ND19xx	—	10 Centavos. Copper-Nickel. Center hole.	—
Pn38	1926	—	Peso. Silver. Indian, date below chin. Star within wreath divides denomination.	550
Pn39	1926	—	Peso. Silver. Fineness added.	550
	1926	—	Peso. Silver. Fineness added.	550
Pn40	1926	—	Peso. Silver. Coat of arms. Without fineness.	600
Pn41	1926	—	2 Pesos. Silver. Condor. Coat of arms. Without fineness.	1,000
Pn42	1926	—	2 Pesos. Silver. Indian. Star in wreath. "5" fineness, Pn43.	600
Pn43	1926	—	2 Pesos. Silver. Indian. Star in wreath. "72" fineness, Pn44.	600
Pn44	1926	—	5 Pesos.	1,500
Pn45	1926	—	5 Pesos. Silver. Weak or no fineness (effaced from die).	1,500
Pn46	1926	—	5 Pesos. Silver.	1,250
Pn47	1927	—	Peso. Copper-Nickel.	250
Pn48	1927	—	Peso. Silver.	500
Pn49	1927	—	5 Pesos. Silver.	300
Pn50	1929	—	20 Centavos. Copper-Nickel. Center hole.	150
Pn51	1929	—	20 Centavos. Copper-Nickel. Pn49 but "CHILE" on reverse instead of "20".	125
Pn52	1929	—	Peso. Silver.	250
Pn53	ND(1929)	—	Peso. Silver. Without country, date or fineness.	250
Pn54	ND(1929)	—	Peso. Silver. Similar to Pn52, without mountains on obverse.	250
Pn55	1930	—	20 Centavos. Copper-Nickel. Center hole.	200
Pn56	1930	—	20 Centavos. Copper-Nickel. Pn54 but "20" instead of "CHILE" on obverse, with center hole.	200
Pn57	1930	—	Peso. Silver. Worker and factory. Value.	350
Pn58	1930	—	2 Pesos. Copper-Nickel. Condor. Value and date in wreath.	375
PnA59	1933	—	Peso. Nickel. KM#176.1.	—
Pn59	1933	—	Peso. Copper-Nickel. Condor. Value and date in wreath.	275
PnA60	1933	—	Peso. Copper-Nickel. Condor. Value and date in wreath. Mint punched cancelled.	275
Pn60	1938	—	5 Pesos. Brass.	500
Pn61	1938	—	5 Pesos. Copper-Nickel.	—
PnA62	ND(1938)	—	5 Pesos. Plain edge. Aluminum-Bronze or Silver.	400
Pn62	ND(1938)	—	5 Pesos. Silver. Without date.	300
PnA63	1941	—	20 Centavos. Bronze.	100
Pn63	1942	—	Peso. Copper. Like KM#179, but smaller diameter.	100
Pn64	1947	—	100 Pesos. Copper.	—
Pn65	1948	—	Onza. Silver.	75.00
Pn65a	1948	—	Onza. Copper.	25.00
PnA66	1951	—	10 Pesos. Aluminum-Bronze. Thick flan.	100
Pn66	1953	—	20 Centavos. Aluminum.	125
Pn67	1956	—	5 Pesos. Brass. KM#180.	—

KM#	Date	Mintage	Identification	Mkt Val
Pn68	1959	—	10 Pesos. Brass. KM#181.	—
Pn69	1960	—	2 Centesimos. Brass. Uniface.	100
PnA70	1960	—	2 Centesimos. Aluminum-Bronze.	75.00
Pn70	1960	—	2 Centesimos. Copper-Nickel.	60.00
Pn71	1960	—	5 Centesimos. Copper. KM#190.	100
Pn72	1960	—	5 Centesimos. Copper-Nickel. Plain edge. KM#190.	90.00
Pn73	1960	—	5 Centesimos. Copper-Nickel. Milled edge. KM#190.	75.00
Pn74	1960	—	10 Centesimos. Copper. KM#191.	100
Pn75	1960	—	10 Centesimos. Copper-Nickel. KM#191.	40.00
Pn76	1960	—	10 Centesimos. Brass. KM#191.	—
Pn77	1960	—	10 Centesimos. Brass.	—
Pn78	1960	—	10 Centesimos. Aluminum-Bronze. Legend. Arms flanked by C-M.	65.00
Pn79	1960	—	10 Centesimos. Copper-Nickel. Legend. Arms flanked by C-M.	65.00
Pn80	1964	—	2 Centesimos. Copper-Nickel. KM#193.	75.00
Pn81	1968	—	100 Pesos. Copper. Center hole.	125
Pn82	1969	—	Peso. Copper-Nickel. Ten sided. Ten sided, arms with "C.M." below.	100
Pn84	ND	—	50 Pesos. Aluminum-Bronze. Equestrian statue of O'Higgins, left. Arms above denomination within wreath.	—
Pn83	1971	—	Peso. Nickel.	—
Pn85	1971	—	2 Escudos. Silver. KM#198.	—
Pn86	1972	—	5 Escudos. Silver. KM#199.	—
Pn87	1972	—	Escudo. Silver. KM197.	—
Pn88	1974	—	10 Escudos. Aluminum.	—
Pn89	1979	5	100 Pesos. 0.5000 Silver. Equestrian statue of O'Higgins.	—

PIEFORTS

KM#	Date	Mintage	Identification	Mkt Val
P4	1951	—	10 Pesos. Aluminum-Bronze. KM#181.	125

TRIAL STRIKES

KM#	Date	Mintage	Identification	Mkt Val
TS7	ND(1960)	—	10 Centesimos. Copper-Nickel. Coat of arms flanked by C-M. Coat of arms flanked by C-M.	60.00
TS8	ND(1960)	—	10 Centesimos. Aluminum-Bronze. Coat of arms flanked by C-M. Coat of arms flanked by C-M.	50.00

PROOF SETS

KM#	Date	Mintage	Identification	Issue Price	Mkt Val
PS1	1968 (6)	—	KM#182-187. Total of 12,000 coins struck for each denomination including those available singly.	560	4,400
PS2	1968 (4)	—	KM#184-187. Total of 12,000 coins struck for each denomination including those available singly.	528	4,300
PS3	1968 (2)	—	KM#182, 183. Total of 12,000 coins struck for each denomination including those available singly.	31.50	100
PS4	1971/2 (3)	—	KM#197 (1972), KM#198 (1971), KM#199 (1972). Total of 12,000 coins struck for each denomination including those available singly.	—	150

VALDIVIA

Emergency coinage issued by Don Antonio Adriazola by order of the Governor during a shortage of coin with which to pay the local garrison.

REPUBLIC

SILVER BULLION COINAGE

KM# 223 1/4 ONZA

7.7770 g., 0.9990 Silver 0.2498 oz. ASW **Subject:** 10th Anniversary of National Liberation

Date	Mintage	F	VF	XF	Unc	BU
ND(1983) Proof	1,000	Value: 12.50				

KM# 225 ONZA

31.1070 g., 0.9990 Silver 0.9991 oz. ASW **Subject:** 10th Anniversary of National Liberation

Date	Mintage	F	VF	XF	Unc	BU
ND(1983) Proof	1,000	Value: 45.00				

KM# 234 ONZA

31.1035 g., 0.9990 Silver 0.9990 oz. ASW **Subject:** Numismatic Association of Chile **Obv:** Similar to 4 Escudos, KM#2 **Rev:** Similar to 1/2 Real, KM#90 obverse

Date	Mintage	F	VF	XF	Unc	BU
ND(1999) Proof	75	Value: 55.00				

PROOF SETS

KM#	Date	Mintage	Identification	Issue Price	Mkt Val
PS1	1968 (6)	—	KM#182-187	560	3,350
PS2	1968 (4)	—	KM#184-187	528	3,250
PS3	1968 (2)	—	KM#182, 183	31.50	100
PS4	1971/2 (3)	—	KM#197 (1972), KM#198 (1971), KM#199 (1972)	—	150

a map of the
CHINESE PROVINCES

CHINA

EMPIRE

Before 1912, China was ruled by an imperial government. The republican administration which replaced it was itself supplanted on the Chinese mainland by a communist government in 1949, but it has remained in control of Taiwan and other offshore islands in the China Sea with a land area of approximately 14,000 square miles and a population of more than 14 million. The People's Republic of China administers some 3.7 million square miles and an estimated 1.19 billion people. This communist government, officially established on October 1, 1949, was admitted to the United Nations, replacing its nationalist predecessor, the Republic of China, in 1971.

Cast coins in base metals were used in China many centuries before the Christian era, but locally struck coinages of the western type in gold, silver, copper and other metals did not appear until 1888. In spite of the relatively short time that modern coins have been in use, the number of varieties is exceptionally large.

Both Nationalist and Communist China, as well as the pre-revolutionary Imperial government and numerous provincial or other agencies, including some foreign-administered agencies and governments, have issued coins in China. Most of these have been in dollar (yuan) or dollar-fraction denominations, based on the internationally used dollar system, but coins in tael denominations were issued in the 1920's and earlier. The striking of coins nearly ceased in the late 1930's through the 1940's due to the war effort and a period of uncontrollable inflation while vast amounts of paper currency were issued by the Nationalist, Communist and Japanese occupation institutions.

EMPERORS
Obverse Types

光 緒
KUANG-HSÜ
德 宗

Te Tsung 1875-1908

Type A

光 緒 通 寶
Kuang-hsü T'ung-pao (Guangxu)

Type B

光 緒 重 寶
Kuang-hsü Chung-pao

Kuang-hsü - When the previous emperor died, his mother, the Empress Dowager Tz'u-hsi, chose her four-year-old nephew, born August 14, 1871, as emperor. She adopted the boy so that she could act as regent and on February 25, 1875, the young prince ascended the throne, taking the reign title of Kuang-hsü. In 1898 he tried to assert himself and collected a group of progressive officials around him. He issued a series of edicts for revamping of the military, abolition of civil service examinations, improvement of agriculture and restructuring of administrative procedures. During Kuang-hsü's reign (1875-1908) the Empress Dowager totally dominated the government. She confined the emperor to his palace and spread rumors that he was deathly ill. Foreign powers let it be known they would not take kindly to the Emperor's death. This saved his life but thereafter he had no power over the government. On November 15, 1908, Tz'u-hsi died under highly suspicious circumstances and the usually healthy emperor was announced as having died the previous day.

宣 統
HSÜAN-T'UNG 1908-1911

Type A

宣 統

Hsüan-t'ung T'ung-pao (Xuantong)

Hsuan-t'ung - The last emperor of the Ch'ing dynasty in China and Japan's puppet emperor, under the assumed name of K'ang-te, in Manchoukuo from 1934 to 1945, was born on February 7, 1906. He succeeded to the throne at the age of three on November 14, 1908. He reigned under a regency for three years but on February 12, 1912, was forced to abdicate the throne. He was permitted to continue living in the palace in Peking until he left secretly in 1924. On March 9, 1932, he was installed as president, and from 1934 to 1945 was emperor of Manchoukuo under the reign title of K'ang-te. He was taken prisoner by the Russians in August of 1945 and returned to China as a war criminal in 1950. He was pardoned in 1959 and went to live in Peking where he worked in the repair shop of a botanical garden. He died peacefully in Peking in 1967.

Although Hsüan-t'ung became Emperor in 1908, all the coins of his reign are based on an Accession year of 1909.

憲 洪
HUNG-HSIEN

宣 統 通
(Yuan Shih-k'ai)
Dec. 15, 1915 - March 21, 1916

憲 洪 通 寶
Hung-hsien T'ung-pao

Hung-hsien (more popularly known as Yuan Shih-K'ai). Born in 1859 in Honan Province, he was the first Han Chinese to hold a vice-royalty and become a grand councillor without any academic qualifications. In 1885 he was made Chinese commissioner at Seoul. During the Boxer Rebellion of 1900, the division under his command was the only remnant of China's army to survive. He enjoyed the trust and support of the dowager empress, Tz'u-hsi, and at her death he was stripped of all his offices. However, when the tide of the revolution threatened to engulf the Manchus Yuan appeared as the only man who could lead the country to peace and unity. Both the Emperor and the provisional president recommended that Yuan be the first president of China. He contrived to make himself president for life and boldly tried to create a new imperial dynasty in 1915-1916. He died of uremia on June 6, 1916.

NOTE: For other legend types refer to Rebel Issues listed after Yunnan-Szechuan.

PROVINCIAL MINT NAMES
(and other source indicators)

Provincial names throughout the catalog are based on the Wade-Giles transliteration of the Chinese word. Current spellings, known as the "Pinyin" form, are widely adopted by the printed media. Example: Sinkiang = Xinjiang.

The column at left illustrates the full name as used on most provincial coinage while the column at right illustrates the abbreviated name that appears in the center of the obverse of the Tai-Ch'ing-Ti-Kuo copper coinage.

Full Name Right to Left reading	Single Character (1)
徽安 ANHWEI	皖 Huan
	Also An-hwi, Anhui, now Anhui
江浙 CHEKIANG	浙 Che
	Also Cheh-kiang, now Zhejiang
隸直 CHIHLI	直 Chih
	Also Hopei (after 1928) now Hebei
清大 CH'ING DYNASTY	
	Tai Ch'ing, also Tsing Dynasty now Qing Dynasty
江清 CHING-KIANG	淮 Huai
	Also Tsing-kiang now Qingjiang
天奉 FENGTIEN	奉 Feng
	Also Fung-tien, Fun-tien Shengching Manchurian Provinces, now Liaoning
建福 FUKIEN	閩 Min
	Also Foo-kien, F.K., now Fujian
江龍黑 HEILUNGKIANG	黑 Hei
	Also Hei Lung Kiang, now Heilongjiang
南河 HONAN	豫 Yu
	Also Ho-nan, now Henan
北河 HOPEH	冀 Chi
	Also Chihli, Hopei, now Hebei
南湖 HUNAN	湘 Hsiang
	Also Hu-nan
北湖 HUPEH	鄂 O
	Also Hupei, Hu-peh, now Hubei
部戶 HU PU (Board of Revenue)	戶 Hu
	Also Hu Poo, Hoo Poo
肅甘 KANSU	甘 Kan
	Now Gansu
南江 KIANGNAN	寧 Ning
	Also Kiang Nan, now Jiangnan

KIANGNAN — Also Kiang Nan, now Jiangnan

Ning

T'ien   Li   Kung   Fen

MINT MARK IDENTIFIER

西江 顚 or 贛
KIANGSI   Kan
Also Kiang-si, Kiang-see, now Jiangxi

蘇江 蘇
KIANGSU   Su
Also Kiang-soo, now Jiangsu

省三東
TUNG SAN SHENG
Manchuria

滇川
YUNNAN-SZECHUAN

GOVERNMENTAL NAMES
(and other source indicators)
Full Names (Right to left reading)

Boo-Clowan (Peking)
Hu-PU BOARD OF REVENUE

Boo-Yuwan (Peking)
Kung-Pu BOARD OF PUBLIC WORKS

林吉 吉
KIRIN   Chi
Also Chi-lin, now Jilin

府 政 東 冀
CHITUNG (Japanese puppet)

西廣 桂
KWANGSI, KWANGSEA   Kuei
Also Kwang-si, now Guangxi

國和共埃維蘇華中
CHINESE SOVIET REPUBLIC

Boo-an
An Mint
ANHWEI

東廣 粤
KWANGTUNG   Yüeh
Also Kwang-tung, now Guangdong

國洲滿大
MANCHOUKUO (Japanese puppet) (2)

州貴 黔
KWEICHOW   Ch'ien
Also Kweichou, now Guizhou

行銀疆蒙
MENGCHIANG (Japanese puppet)

Boo-Je
Chê Mint
Hangchow
CHEKIANG

Boo-Ji
Chih Mint
Paoting
CHIHLI

洋北
PEIYANG MINT (Tientsin)
Also Pei Yang

中華人民共和國
PEOPLES REPUBLIC OF CHINA (Communist) (3)

國民華中
REPUBLIC OF CHINA (Nationalist)

Boo-Gi
Chi Mint
Chichow
CHIHLI

Boo-Jiyen
Ching Mint
Tientsin
CHIHLI

(Through Hsien-Feng era)

西山 山
SHANSI   Shan
Now Shanxi (Chin)

西陝 陝
SHENSI   Shan
Also Shen-si, now Shaanxi

行銀備準合聯國中
NORTH CHINA (Japanese puppet)

(1) Single-character designators for provincial or regional mints are used primarily on copper coins of the Tai Ching Ti Kuo series.
(2) Vertical readings predominate.
(3) Reads left to right.
(4) For lists of mints in Sinkiang, see that section.

ADDITIONAL CHARACTERS
The additional characters illustrated and defined below are found on the reverse of cast bronze cash coins, usually above the square center hole. In the period covered by this catalog the following mints produced cash coins with these additional marks: Board of Revenue and Board of Works in Peking, Kweichow, Aksu and Ili in Sinkiang, Shantung, Szechuan, and all three mints listed in Yunnan.

東山 東
SHANTUNG   TUNG
Also Shang-tung, Shan-tung, now Shandong (Lu)

魯
SIKANG

Boo-Fung
Fung Mint
FENGTIEN

Boo-Fu
Fu Mint
Fuchou
FUKIEN

疆新 新
SINKIANG   Hsin
(Chinese Turkestan)
Also Sin-kiang, Hsin-kiang Sungarei, now Xinjiang

CHARACTERS

一	I, YI	十	Shih I	心	Hsin
二	Erh	合	Ho	字	Yu
三	San	工	Kung	宙	Chou
四	Szu	主	Chu	來	Lai
五	Wu	川	Ch'uan	往	Wang
六	Liu	之	Chih	晋	Chin
七	Ch'i	正	Cheng	村	Ts'un
八	Pa	又	Yu	日	Jih
九	Chiu	山	Shan	列	Lieh
十	Shih	大	Ta	仁	Jen
主	Chung	中	Feng	手	Shang
順	Shun	云	Yun	手	Shou

川四 川 蜀
SZECHUAN   Ch'uan
Also Szechwan Szechuen, now Sichuan (Shu)

灣臺 臺
TAIWAN   T'ai
Also Tai-wan, now Taiwan

Boo-Ho
Ho Mint
K'aifeng
HONAN

灣台 台
TAIWAN   T'ai
(Alternate)

南雲 雲 滇
YÜNNAN   Yün   (Alternate) (Tien)
Also Yun-nan, now Yunnan

Boo-Nan
Nan Mint
Ch'ang-sha
HUNAN

Boo-Ji
Chi Mint
Chinan
SHANTUNG

Boo-Cuwan
Chuan Mint
Chengtu
SZECHUAN

Yarkand (Soche)
SINKIANG

Boo-Tai
Tai Mint
TAIWAN

Boo-De
Teh Mint
Chengte
CHIHLI

Boo-U
Wu Mint
Wuch'ang
HUPEH

Boo-San
Shan Mint
Sian
SHENSI

Boo-Yôn
Yûn Mint
Yûnnan Fu
YUNNAN

Boo-Dong
Tung Mint
Tungch'uan
YUNNAN

Boo-Gung
Kung Mint
Kungchang
KANSU

Boo-ch'ang
Ch'ang Mint
Nanchang
KIANGSI

Aksu (Hocheng)
SINKIANG

Boo-Yi
Ili (Hweiyuan)
SINKIANG

Boo-Gu
Ku Mint
Taku Arsenal
TIENTSIN, CHIHLI

Boo-Fu
Fu Mint
Fuchow
YUNNAN

Boo-Su
Su Mint
Soohow
KIANGSU

Boo-Gi
Chi Mint
KIRIN

(Kuang-hsu Era)

Kotsha (Kuche)
SINKIANG

Boo-Jing
Ching Mint
Chingchow Fu
HUPEH

NON-CIRCULATING ISSUES:

Along with regular circulation coinage produced by the various mints certain cash types were cast in various sizes with the emperor's reign title on the obverse but with various characters and/or symbols not found in our mint identifiers. This listing is not complete but it will benefit the collector as an aid to proper identification.

PALACE ISSUES

(Palace Cash)

Usually 1-6 mace in weight, made of 60" copper and 40" zinc. Made for distribution in the palace during new year. Usually given to eunuchs and guards. Recipients hanged them under lamps - "lamp 'hanging' money."

Obv. ins: Kuang-hsŭ T'ung-pao
Rev. ins: T'ien-hsia T'ai-p'ing
"Peace under Heaven."

Note: The market value is about $60.00-100.00 in VF condition.

Boo-Gui
Kue Mint
Kuelin
KWANGSI

Boo-Guwang
Kuang Mint
Canton
KWANGTUNG

Kashgar (Shufu)
SINKIANG

Khotan (Hotien)
SINKIANG

Boo-Giyan
Kwei Mint
Kweiyang
KWEICHOW

Boo-Jin
Chin Mint
Taiyuan
SHANSI

Boo-Di
Di Mint
Urumchi (Tihwa)
SINKIANG

Ushi (Wushih)
SINKIANG

BIRTHDAY CASH

壽 福

These issues have the normal reign title on the obverse but the reverse has two Chinese characters *Fu* in normal or seal script (happiness), at right and *Shou* (birthday) at left. The market value is about $60.00-100.00 in F/VF condition. Some are palace issues, but most are made by private sources as good luck amulets.

Kuang-hsü

NUMERALS

NUMBER	CONVENTIONAL	FORMAL	COMMERCIAL
1	一 元	壹 弌	〡
2	二	弍 貳	〢
3	三	叁 弎	〣
4	四	肆	乄
5	五	伍	〤
6	六	陸	〦
7	七	柒	〧
8	八	捌	〨
9	九	玖	〩
10	十	拾 什	十
20	十二 or 廿	拾貳	〢十
25	五十二 or 五廿	伍拾貳	〢十〤
30	十三 or 卅	拾叁	〣十
100	百一	佰壹	〡百
1,000	千一	仟壹	〡千
10,000	萬一	萬壹	〡万
100,000	萬十 億一	萬拾 億壹	十万
1,000,000	萬百一	萬佰壹	〡万/百

NOTE: This table has been adapted from *Chinese Bank Notes* by Ward Smith and Brian Matravers.

MONETARY UNITS

Dollar Amounts		
DOLLAR (Yuan)	元 or 員	圓 or 圆
HALF DOLLAR (Pan Yuan)	圓半	元中
50¢ (Chiao/Hao)	角伍	毫伍
10¢ (Chiao/Hao)	角壹	毫壹
1¢ (Fen/Hsien)	分壹	仙壹

COPPER AND CASH COIN AMOUNTS

COPPER (Mei)	枚	CASH (Wen)	文

Tael Amounts	
1 TAEL (Liang)	兩
HALF TAEL (Pan Liang)	兩半
5 MACE (Wu Ch'ien)	錢伍
1 MACE (I Ch'ien)	錢壹
1 CANDAREEN (I Fen)	分壹

COMMON PREFIXES

COPPER (T'ung)	銅	GOLD (Chin)	金
SILVER (Yin)	銀	Ku Ping (Tael)*	平庫

NOTE: This table has been adapted from *Chinese Bank Notes* by Ward Smith and Brian Matravers.

MONETARY SYSTEM
Cash Coin System

800-1600 Cash = 1 Tael
400 Sinkiang 'red' cash = 1 Tael

In theory, 1000 cash were equal to a tael of silver, but in actuality the rate varied from time to time and place to place.

Dollar System

10 Cash (Wen, Ch'ien) = 1 Cent (Fen, Hsien)
10 Cents = 1 Chiao (Hao)
100 Cents = 1 Dollar (Yuan)
1 Dollar = 0.72 Tael

Imperial silver coins normally bore no denomination, but were inscribed with their weights as follows:
1 Dollar = 7 Mace and 2 Candareens
50 Cents = 3 Mace and 6 Candareens
20 Cents = 1 Mace and 4.4 Candareens
10 Cents = 7.2 Candareens
5 Cents = 3.6 Candareens

NOTE: *Candareen* is spelled *Candarin* and misspelled as *Caindarin* on Kirin Province Imperial coinage.

Tael System

10 Li = 1 Fen (Candareen)
10 Fen (Candareen) = 1 Ch'ien (Mace)
10 Ch'ien (Mace) = 1 Liang (Tael)

DATING

Yuan: (first)
Nien (year)
Chung Hua Min Kuo (Republic of China)

Most struck Chinese coins are dated by year within a given period, such as the regnal eras or the republican periods. A 1907 issue, for example, would be dated in the 33rd year of the Kuang Hsu era (1875 + 33 - 1 = 1907) or a 1926 issue is dated in the 15th year of the Republic (1912 + 15 - 1 = 1926). The mathematical discrepancy in both instances is accounted for by the fact that the first year is included in the elapsed time. Modern Chinese Communist coins are dated in western numerals using the western calendar, but earlier issues use conventional Chinese numerals. The coins of the Republic of China (Taiwan) are also dated in the year of the Republic, which is added to equal the calendar year. Still another method is a 60-year, repeating cycle, outlined in the table below.

The date is shown by the combination of two characters, the first from the top row and the second from the column at left. In this catalog, when a cyclical date is used, the abbreviation CD appears before the AD date.

Dates not in parentheses are those which appear on the coins. For undated coins, dates appearing in parentheses are the years in which the coin was actually minted. Undated coins for which the year of minting is unknown are listed with ND (No Date) in the date or year column.

CYCLICAL DATES

	庚	辛	壬	癸	甲	乙	丙	丁	戊	己
戌	1850 1910		1862 1922		1874 1934		1886 1946		1838 1898	
亥		1851 1911		1863 1923		1875 1935		1887 1947		1839 1899
子	1840 1900		1852 1912		1864 1924		1876 1936		1888 1948	
丑		1841 1901		1853 1913		1865 1925		1877 1937		1889 1949
寅	1830 1890		1842 1902		1854 1914		1866 1926		1878 1938	
卯		1831 1891		1843 1903		1855 1915		1867 1927		1879 1939
辰	1880 1940		1832 1892		1844 1904		1856 1916		1868 1928	
巳		1881 1941		1833 1893		1845 1905		1857 1917		1869 1929
午	1870 1930		1882 1942		1834 1894		1846 1906		1858 1918	
未		1871 1931		1883 1943		1835 1895		1847 1907		1859 1919
申	1860 1920		1872 1932		1884 1944		1836 1896		1848 1908	
酉		1861 1921		1873 1933		1885 1945		1837 1897		1849 1909

NOTE: This table has been adapted from *Chinese Bank Notes* by Ward Smith and Brian Matravers.

GRADING

Chinese coins should not be graded entirely by western standards. In addition to Fine, Very Fine, Extremely Fine (XF), and Uncirculated, the type of strike should be considered weak, medium or sharp strike. China had no rigid minting rules as we know them. For instance, Kirin (Jilin) and Sinkiang (Xinjiang) Provinces used some dies made of iron - hence, they wore out rapidly. Some communist army issues were apparently struck by crude hand methods on soft dies (it is hard to find two coins of the same die!). In general, especially for some minor coins, dies were used until they were worn well beyond western standards. Subsequently, one could have an uncirculated coin struck from worn dies with little of the design or letters still visible, but still uncirculated! All prices quoted are for well-struck (sharp struck), well-centered specimens. Most silver coins can be found from very fine to uncirculated. Some copper coins are difficult to find except in poorer grades.

REFERENCES

The following references have been used for this section:
K - Edward Kann - Illustrated Catalog of Chinese Coins.
Hsu - T.K. Hsu - Illustrated Catalog of Chinese Coins, 1981 edition.
W - A.M. Tracey Woodward - The Minted Ten-Cash Coins of China.

NOTE: The die struck 10 and 20 Cash coins are often found silver plated. This was not done at the mint. They were apparently plated to be passed to the unwary as silver coins.

IDENTIFICATION

Board of Revenue
Cyclical Date (1905)
Cash 10
Standard Coin
Equal To
Province Indicator (Mintmark)

DRAGON TYPES
(Chinese Imperial Coins)

Side View Dragon-left (Silver Coins)

First used by the Kwangtung Mint in 1889. This was the standard (though not the only) dragon used on silver coins. Normally there is no circle around the dragon. Note the fireball beneath the dragon's chin. Normally there are seven flames on the fireball.

Side View Dragon-left (Copper Coins)

First used on copper coins in 1901 or 1902. The dragon may be circled or uncircled. Many varieties exist, with three to seven flames on the fireball.

Side View Dragon-right (Silver Coins)

First appears on the second series of Fukien. The dragon is redesigned with the dragon's body reversed.

Flying Dragon

Introduced in 1901. Copied from the dragon on Japanese coins. China used this dragon only on copper coins (with one rare exception). Note that the clouds around the dragon's body are curly and snake-like instead of puffy like those around the side view dragon. The fireball now appears as a pearl which the dragon is about to grasp, and normally has no flames. This dragon is normally circled.

Front View Dragon

Introduced about 1904, this type of dragon was not used by many mints. The dragon is usually uncircled and has few clouds around its body. Note the tiny mountain under the cloud beneath the fireball.

Tai Ch'ing Ti Kuo Dragon

In 1905 China carried out a coinage reform which standardized the designs of copper coins. All mints were ordered to use the same obverse and reverse designs, but to place a mint mark in the center of the obverse.

SYCEE (INGOTS)

Prior to 1889 the general coinage issued by the Chinese government was the copper-alloy cash coin. Despite occasional short-lived experiments with silver and gold coinage, and disregarding paper money which tended to be unreliable, the government expected the people to get by solely with cash coins. This system worked well for individuals making purchases for themselves, but was unsatisfactory for trade and large business transactions, since a dollar's worth of cash coins weighed about four pounds. As a result, a private currency consisting of silver ingots, usually stamped by the firm which made them, came into use. These were the sycee ingots.

It is not known when these ingots first came into use. Some sources date them to the Yuan (Mongol) dynasty but they are certainly much older. Examples are known from as far back as the Han dynasty (206 BC - 220 AD) but prior to the Sung era (960 - 1280AD) they were used mainly for hoarding wealth. The development of commerce by the Sung dynasty, however, required the use of silver or gold to pay for large purchases. By the Mongol period (1280-1368) silver ingots and paper money had become the dominant currencies, especially for trade. The western explorers who traveled to China during this period (such as Marco Polo) mention both paper money and sycee but not a single one refers to cash coins.

During the Ming dynasty (1368-1644) trade fell off and the use of silver decreased. But toward the end of that dynasty, Dutch and British ships began a new China trade and sycee once again became common. During the 19th and early 20th centuries, the trade in sycee became enormous. Most of the sycee around today are from this period. In 1935 the Chinese government and in 1939 Sinkiang banned the use of sycee and it soon disappeared.

The word sycee (pronounced "sigh - see") is a western corruption of the Chinese word hsi-szu ("fine silk") or hsi yin ("fine silver") and is first known to have appeared in the English language in the late 1600's. By the early 1700's the word appeared regularly in the records of the British East India Company. Westerners also called these ingots "boat money" or "shoe money" owing to the fact that the most common type of ingot resembles a Chinese shoe. The Chinese, however, called the ingots by a variety of names, the most common of which were yuan pao, wen-yin (fine silver) and yin-ting (silver ingot).

While the ingots were cast in molds (giving them their characteristic shapes) and while the metal was still semi-liquid, the inscription was impressed. It was due to this procedure that the sides of some sycee are higher than the center. The manufacturers were usually silver firms, often referred to as lu fang's, and after the sycee was finished it was occasionally tested and marked by the kung ku (public assayer).

Sycee were not circulated as we understand it. One didn't usually carry a sycee to market and spend it. Usually the ingots were used as a means of carrying a large amount of money on trips (as we would carry $100 bills instead of $5 bills) or for storing wealth. Large transactions between merchants or banks were paid by means of crates of sycee - each containing 60 fifty tael ingots.

Sycee are known in a variety of shapes the most common of which are the shoe or boat shaped, drum shaped, and loaf shaped (rectangular or hourglass-shaped, with a generally flat surface). Other shapes include one that resembles a double headed axe (this is the oldest type known), one that is square and flat, and others that are "fancy" (in the form of fish, butterflies, leaves, etc.).

Sycee have no denominations as they were simply ingots that passed by weight. Most are in more or less standard weights, however, the most common being 1, 5, 10 and 50 taels. Other weights known include 1/10, 1/5, 1/4, 1/3, 1/2, 2/3, 72/100 (this is the weight of a dollar), 3/4, 2, 3, 4, 6, 7, 8 and 25 taels. Most of the pieces weighing less than 5 taels were used as gifts or souvenirs.

The actual weight of any given value of sycee varied considerably due to the fact that the tael was not a single weight but a general term for a wide range of local weight standards. The weight of the tael varied depending upon location and type of tael in question. For example in one town, the weight of a tael of rice, of silver and of stones may each be different. In addition, the fineness of silver also varied depending upon location and type of tael in question. It was not true, as westerners often wrote, that sycee were made of pure silver. For most purposes, a weight of 37 grams may be used for the tael.

Weights and Current Market Value of Sycee

(Weights are approximate)

1/2 Tael	17-19 grams	26
72/100 Tael	25-27 grams	36
1 Tael	35-38 grams	46
2 Taels	70-75 grams	70
3 Taels	100-140 grams	85
5 Taels	175-190 grams	110
7 Taels	240-260 grams	125
10 Taels	350-380 grams	250
25 Taels	895-925 grams	3500
50 Taels	1790-1850 grams	2000
50 Taels, square	1790-1850 grams	1600

SZECHUAN WARLORD ISSUE
200-Cash

Obv: Mirror image of normal coin, Y#459.

NOTE: Certain coins found with degenerate or reversed English legends are usually considered to be local warlord issues while some authorities insist on referring to them as contemporary counterfeits.

CH'ING DYNASTY
Manchu, 1644 - 1911
GENERAL CAST COINAGE

C# 1-16 CASH
Cast Brass **Ruler:** Kuang-hsü **Obv. Insc.:** Kuang-hsü T'ung-pao **Rev. Insc.:** Boo-ciowan

Date	Mintage	Good	VG	F	VF	XF
ND(1875-1908)	—	1.50	2.00	2.75	4.00	—

Note: For crude cast, red copper issues, see Sinkiang General coinage.

C# 1-16.1 CASH
Cast Brass **Ruler:** Kuang-hsü **Series:** Thousand Character Classic **Obv. Insc.:** Kuang-hsü T'ung-pao **Rev:** Manchu inscription with "Chin" above **Rev. Insc.:** Boo-ciowan

Date	Mintage	Good	VG	F	VF	XF
ND(1875-1908)	—	6.00	9.00	13.50	20.00	—

C# 1-16.2 CASH
Cast Brass **Ruler:** Kuang-hsü **Series:** Thousand Character Classic **Obv. Insc.:** Kuang-hsü T'ung-pao **Rev:** Manchu inscription with "Chou" above **Rev. Insc.:** Boo-ciowan

Date	Mintage	Good	VG	F	VF	XF
ND(1875-1908)	—	6.00	9.00	13.50	20.00	—

C# 1-16.3 CASH
Cast Brass **Ruler:** Kuang-hsü **Series:** Thousand Character Classic **Obv. Insc.:** Kuang-hsü T'ung-pao **Rev:** Manchu inscription with "Jih" above **Rev. Insc.:** Boo-ciowan

Date	Mintage	Good	VG	F	VF	XF
ND(1875-1908)	—	6.00	9.00	13.50	20.00	—

C# 1-16.4 CASH
Cast Brass **Ruler:** Kuang-hsü **Series:** Thousand Character Classic **Obv. Insc.:** Kuang-hsü T'ung-pao **Rev:** Manchu inscription with "Lai" above **Rev. Insc.:** Boo-ciowan

Date	Mintage	Good	VG	F	VF	XF
ND(1875-1908)	—	6.00	9.00	13.50	20.00	—

C# 1-16.5 CASH
Cast Brass **Ruler:** Kuang-hsü **Series:** Thousand Character Classic **Obv. Insc.:** Kuang-hsü T'ung-pao **Rev:** Manchu inscription with "Lieh" above **Rev. Insc.:** Boo-ciowan

Date	Mintage	Good	VG	F	VF	XF
ND(1875-1908)	—	6.00	9.00	13.50	20.00	—

C# 1-16.6 CASH
Cast Brass **Ruler:** Kuang-hsü **Series:** Thousand Character Classic **Obv. Insc.:** Kuang-hsü T'ung-pao **Rev:** Manchu inscription with "Wang" above **Rev. Insc.:** Boo-ciowan

Date	Mintage	Good	VG	F	VF	XF
ND(1875-1908)	—	6.00	9.00	13.50	20.00	—

C# 1-16.7 CASH
Cast Brass **Ruler:** Kuang-hsü **Series:** Thousand Character Classic **Obv. Insc.:** Kuang-hsü T'ung-pao **Rev:** Manchu inscription with "Yu" above **Rev. Insc.:** Boo-ciowan

Date	Mintage	Good	VG	F	VF	XF
ND(1875-1908)	—	6.00	9.00	13.50	20.00	—

C# 1-16.10 CASH
Cast Brass **Ruler:** Kuang-hsü **Series:** Thousand Character Classic **Obv. Insc.:** Kuang-hsü T'ung-pao **Rev:** Manchu inscription with "Shou" above **Rev. Insc.:** Boo-ciowan

Date	Mintage	Good	VG	F	VF	XF
ND(1875-1908)	—	6.00	9.00	13.50	20.00	—

C# 2-15 CASH
Cast Brass **Ruler:** Kuang-hsü **Obv. Insc.:** Kuang-hsü T'ung-pao **Rev:** Manchu inscription **Rev. Insc.:** Boo-yuwan **Note:** Size varies: 25-26mm.

Date	Mintage	Good	VG	F	VF	XF
ND(1875-1908)	—	1.50	3.00	6.00	7.00	—

Note: For crude cast copper strikes, see Sinkiang General Coinage

C# 1-16.8 CASH
Cast Brass **Ruler:** Kuang-hsü **Obv. Insc.:** Kuang-hsü T'ung-pao **Rev:** Manchu inscription with dot below **Rev. Insc.:** Boo-ciowan

Date	Mintage	Good	VG	F	VF	XF
ND(1899-1901)	—	1.75	3.00	4.00	6.00	—

C# 1-16.9 CASH
Cast Brass **Ruler:** Kuang-hsü **Obv. Insc.:** Kuang-hsü T'ung-pao **Rev:** Manchu inscription with dot above **Rev. Insc.:** Boo-ciowan

Date	Mintage	Good	VG	F	VF	XF
ND(1899-1901)	—	1.75	3.00	4.00	6.00	—

C# 2-15.2 CASH
Cast Brass **Ruler:** Kuang-hsü **Series:** Thousand Character Classic **Obv. Insc.:** Kuang-hsü T'ung-pao **Rev:** Manchu inscription with "Lai" above **Rev. Insc.:** Boo-yuwan

Date	Mintage	Good	VG	F	VF	XF
ND(1899-1901)	—	6.00	10.00	15.00	20.00	—

C# 2-15.3 CASH
Cast Brass **Ruler:** Kuang-hsü **Series:** Thousand Character Classic **Obv. Insc.:** Kuang-hsü T'ung-pao **Rev:** Manchu inscription with "Lieh" above **Rev. Insc.:** Boo-yuwan

Date	Mintage	Good	VG	F	VF	XF
ND(1899-1901)	—	6.00	10.00	15.00	20.00	—

C# 2-15.4 CASH
Cast Brass **Ruler:** Kuang-hsü **Series:** Thousand Character Classic **Obv. Insc.:** Kuang-hsü T'ung-pao **Rev:** Manchu inscription with "Yu" above **Rev. Insc.:** Boo-yuwan

Date	Mintage	Good	VG	F	VF	XF
ND(1899-1901)	—	6.00	10.00	15.00	20.00	—

C# 2-15.5 CASH
Cast Brass, 20 mm. **Ruler:** Kuang-hsü **Series:** Thousand Character Classic **Obv. Insc.:** Kuang-hsü T'ung-pao **Rev:** Manchu inscription with "Jih" above **Rev. Insc.:** Boo-yuwan

Date	Mintage	Good	VG	F	VF	XF
ND(1899-1901)	—	6.00	10.00	15.00	20.00	—

C# 2-15.6 CASH
Cast Brass **Ruler:** Kuang-hsü **Series:** Thousand Character Classic **Obv. Insc.:** Kuang-hsü T'ung-pao **Rev:** Manchu inscription with "Wang" above **Rev. Insc.:** Boo-yuwan

Date	Mintage	Good	VG	F	VF	XF
ND(1899-1901)	—	6.00	10.00	15.00	20.00	—

C# 2-15.7 CASH
Cast Brass **Ruler:** Kuang-hsü **Series:** Thousand Character Classic **Obv. Insc.:** Kuang-hsü T'ung-pao **Rev:** Manchu inscription with "Jih" above, dot below **Rev. Insc.:** Boo-yuwan

Date	Mintage	Good	VG	F	VF	XF
ND(1899-1901)	—	6.00	10.00	15.00	20.00	—

C# 2-15.1 CASH
Cast Brass **Ruler:** Kuang-hsü **Series:** Thousand Character Classic **Obv. Insc.:** Kuang-hsü T'ung-pao **Rev:** Manchu inscription with "Chou" above **Rev. Insc.:** Boo-yuwan **Note:** Size varies: 19-20mm.

Date	Mintage	Good	VG	F	VF	XF
ND(1899-1901)	—	6.00	10.00	15.00	20.00	—

C# 1-19.1 CASH
Cast Brass, 19 mm. **Ruler:** Hsüan-t'ung **Obv. Insc.:** Hsüan-t'ung T'ung-pao **Rev:** Manchu inscription **Rev. Insc.:** Boo-ciowan

Date	Mintage	Good	VG	F	VF	XF
ND(1909-11)	—	5.50	7.00	10.00	15.00	—

C# 1-19.2 CASH
Cast Brass, 24 mm. **Ruler:** Hsüan-t'ung **Obv. Insc.:** Hsüan-t'ung T'ung-pao **Rev:** Manchu inscription **Rev. Insc.:** Boo-ciowan

Date	Mintage	Good	VG	F	VF	XF
ND(1909-11)	—	10.00	15.00	25.00	30.00	—

C# 1-19a CASH
Iron, 23 mm. **Ruler:** Hsüan-t'ung **Obv. Insc.:** Hsüan-t'ung T'ung-pao **Rev:** Manchu inscription **Rev. Insc.:** Boo-ciowan

Date	Mintage	Good	VG	F	VF	XF
ND(1909-11)	—	12.00	20.00	30.00	50.00	—

C# 2-16 5 CASH
Cast Brass **Ruler:** Kuang-hsü **Obv. Insc.:** Kuang-hsü T'ung-pao **Rev:** Manchu inscription **Rev. Insc.:** Boo-yuwan

Date	Mintage	Good	VG	F	VF	XF
ND(1875-1908)	—	200	350	500	700	—

C# 1-17 10 CASH
Cast Brass, 30 mm. **Ruler:** Kuang-hsü **Obv. Insc.:** Kuang-hsü Chung-pao **Rev:** Manchu inscription with normal "Shih" for 10 below **Rev. Insc.:** Boo-ciowan

Date	Mintage	Good	VG	F	VF	XF
ND(1875-1908)	—	3.00	5.00	8.00	10.00	—

C# 1-18   10 CASH
Cast Brass, 28 mm. **Ruler:** Kuang-hsü **Obv. Insc.:** Kuang-hsü Chung-pao **Rev:** Manchu inscription with official "Shih" for 10 below **Rev. Insc.:** Boo-ciowan

Date	Mintage	Good	VG	F	VF	XF
ND(1875-1908)	—	4.50	7.50	10.00	15.00	—

C# 1-18.1   10 CASH
Cast Brass, 22 mm. **Ruler:** Kuang-hsü **Obv. Insc.:** Kuang-hsü Chung-pao **Rev:** Manchu inscription with official "Shih" for 10 below **Rev. Insc.:** Boo-ciowan

Date	Mintage	Good	VG	F	VF	XF
ND(1875-1908)	—	6.00	9.00	15.00	20.00	—

C# 2-17   10 CASH
Cast Brass **Ruler:** Kuang-hsü **Obv. Insc.:** Kuang-hsü Chung-pao **Rev:** Manchu inscription with normal Shih (10) below **Rev. Insc.:** Boo-yuwan **Note:** Size varies: 31-32mm.

Date	Mintage	Good	VG	F	VF	XF
ND(1875-1908)	—	4.50	7.50	10.00	25.00	—

C# 2-18   10 CASH
Cast Brass **Ruler:** Kuang-hsü **Obv. Insc.:** Kuang-hsü T'ung-pao **Rev:** Manchu inscription with official Shih (10) below **Rev. Insc.:** Boo-yuwan

Date	Mintage	Good	VG	F	VF	XF
ND(1880-1908)	—	6.00	10.00	15.00	35.00	—

STANDARD UNIFIED GENERAL COINAGE

A Central mint opened at Tientsin in 1905, was made responsible for producing most of the dies for the Tai Ch'ing Hu Poo coinage and for the 1910 and 1911 unified coinage. The mint was burned down in 1912 but resumed operations in 1914 with Yuan Shih-k'ai dollar issues. It continued producing dies for selected branch mints until 1921. It was superseded as the Central mint of China by Nanking in 1927 and by the new Nationalist Government mint at Shanghai in 1933.

Y# 7   CASH
Brass **Ruler:** Kuang-hsü **Obv. Leg.:** "Kuang-hsü" **Rev:** Dragon **Note:** Struck.

Date	Mintage	VG	F	VF	XF	Unc
CD1908	—	1.00	3.00	6.00	12.00	—

Y# 18   CASH
Brass **Ruler:** Hsüan-t'ung **Obv. Leg.:** "Hsüan-t'ung" **Rev:** Dragon **Note:** Struck.

Date	Mintage	VG	F	VF	XF	Unc
CD1909	—	25.00	50.00	85.00	135	—

Note: Inc. Y25

Y# 25   CASH
Brass **Obv. Insc.:** Tai-ch'ing T'ung-pi

Date	Mintage	VG	F	VF	XF	Unc
ND(1909)	92,126,000	1.00	1.50	2.00	3.00	—

Y# 8   2 CASH
Copper **Ruler:** Kuang-hsü **Obv. Insc.:** Tai-ch'ing T'ung-pi **Rev:** Dragon

Date	Mintage	VG	F	VF	XF	Unc
CD1905 Hu-pu	—	2.50	4.50	10.00	17.50	—
CD1906 Hu-pu	—	3.00	6.00	10.00	25.00	—

Y# 8.1   2 CASH
Copper **Ruler:** Kuang-hsü **Obv:** Four dots divide legend **Obv. Insc.:** Tai-ch'ing T'ung-pi **Rev:** Dragon

Date	Mintage	VG	F	VF	XF	Unc
CD1907	—	7.00	18.00	25.00	40.00	—

Y# A18   2 CASH
Copper **Ruler:** Hsüan-t'ung **Obv. Insc.:** Hsüan-t'ung

Date	Mintage	VG	F	VF	XF	Unc
CD1909 Rare	13,353,000	—	—	—	—	—

Y# 3   5 CASH
Copper **Ruler:** Kuang-hsü **Obv. Insc.:** Kuang-hsü Yüan-pao **Rev:** Dragon **Rev. Leg.:** HU POO

Date	Mintage	VG	F	VF	XF	Unc
ND(1903-05) Hu-pu	3,671,000	7.00	14.00	21.00	35.00	—

Y# 9   5 CASH
Copper **Ruler:** Kuang-hsü **Obv. Insc.:** Tai-ch'ing T'ung-pi **Rev:** Dragon; smaller legend **Rev. Leg.:** Kuang-hsü

Date	Mintage	VG	F	VF	XF	Unc
CD1905	—	5.00	10.00	20.00	35.00	—
CD1906 Rare	—	—	—	—	—	—

Y# 9.1   5 CASH
Copper **Ruler:** Kuang-hsü **Obv:** Four dots divide legend **Obv. Leg.:** Kuang-hsü **Obv. Insc.:** Tai-ch'ing T'ung-pi **Rev:** Dragon

Date	Mintage	VG	F	VF	XF	Unc
CD1907	—	16.50	40.00	75.00	125	—

Y# 19   5 CASH
Copper **Ruler:** Hsüan-t'ung **Obv. Leg.:** Hsüan-t'ung

Date	Mintage	VG	F	VF	XF	Unc
CD1909	2,170,000	—	—	850	1,200	—

Y# 4   10 CASH
Copper **Ruler:** Kuang-hsü **Obv. Insc.:** Kuang-hsü Yüan-pao **Rev:** Side view dragon **Rev. Leg.:** HU POO

Date	Mintage	VG	F	VF	XF	Unc
ND(1903-05)	281,171,000	0.65	2.00	3.50	6.00	25.00

Y# 4.1   10 CASH
Copper **Ruler:** Kuang-hsü **Rev:** Side view dragon; different rosettes; smaller legend **Rev. Leg.:** HU POO

Date	Mintage	VG	F	VF	XF	Unc
ND(1903-05)	Inc. above	0.35	1.00	2.00	5.00	20.00

Y# 10   10 CASH
Copper **Ruler:** Kuang-hsü **Obv. Insc.:** Tai-ch'ing T'ung-pi **Rev:** Side view dragon **Rev. Leg.:** Kuang-hsü Nien-tsao TAI-CHING-TI-KUO...

Date	Mintage	VG	F	VF	XF	Unc
CD1905	Inc. above	0.50	1.50	3.00	5.00	25.00

Y# 10.1   10 CASH
Copper **Ruler:** Kuang-hsü **Obv. Insc.:** Tai-ch'ing T'ung-pi **Rev:** Different dragon; larger legend **Rev. Leg.:** TAI-CHING-TI-KUO...

Date	Mintage	VG	F	VF	XF	Unc
CD1905	—	10.00	25.00	65.00	110	200

Y# 10.2   10 CASH
Copper **Ruler:** Kuang-hsü **Obv. Insc.:** Tai-ch'ing T'ung-pi **Rev:** Dragon **Rev. Leg.:** Kuang-hsü Nien-tsao TAI-CHING-TI-KUO

Date	Mintage	VG	F	VF	XF	Unc
CD1906	—	0.25	0.75	1.50	3.00	20.00

Y# 10.3   10 CASH
Copper **Ruler:** Kuang-hsü **Obv:** Without dots **Obv. Insc.:** Tai-ch'ing T'ung-pi **Rev:** Dragon; legend without dot after "KUO" **Rev. Leg.:** Kuang-hsü Nien-tsao TAI-CHING-TI-KUO

Date	Mintage	VG	F	VF	XF	Unc
CD1907	—	0.35	1.00	2.00	4.50	18.00

Y# 10.4 10 CASH
Copper **Ruler:** Kuang-hsü **Obv. Insc.:** Tai-ch'ing T'ung-pi **Rev:** Dragon; legend with dot after "KUO" **Rev. Leg.:** Kuang-hsü Nien-tsao TAI-CHING-TI-KUO.

Date	Mintage	VG	F	VF	XF	Unc
CD1907	—	0.35	1.00	2.00	4.50	18.00

Y# 10.4a 10 CASH
Brass **Ruler:** Kuang-hsü **Obv:** Without dots **Obv. Insc.:** Tai-ch'ing T'ung-pi **Rev:** Dragon **Rev. Leg.:** Kuang-hsü Nien-tsao TAI-CHING-TI-KUO.

Date	Mintage	VG	F	VF	XF	Unc
CD1907	—	1.85	5.50	20.00	35.00	80.00

Y# 10.5 10 CASH
Copper **Ruler:** Kuang-hsü **Obv:** Four dots divide legend **Obv. Insc.:** Tai-ch'ing T'ung-pi **Rev:** Dragon **Rev. Leg.:** Kuang-hsü Nien-tsao TAI-CHING-TI-KUO.

Date	Mintage	VG	F	VF	XF	Unc
CD1907	—	0.35	1.00	2.00	4.50	18.00

Y# 10.5a 10 CASH
Brass **Ruler:** Kuang-hsü **Obv. Insc.:** Tai-ch'ing T'ung-pi **Rev:** Dragon **Rev. Leg.:** Kuang-hsü Nien-tsao TAI-CHING-TI-KUO.

Date	Mintage	VG	F	VF	XF	Unc
CD1907	—	1.85	5.50	15.00	30.00	85.00

Y# 20 10 CASH
Copper **Ruler:** Hsüan-t'ung **Obv. Insc.:** Tai-ch'ing T'ung-pi **Rev:** Waves below dragon **Rev. Leg.:** Hsüan-t'ung Nien-tsao TAI-CHING-TI-KUO.

Date	Mintage	VG	F	VF	XF	Unc
CD1909	—	0.35	1.00	2.00	4.00	22.50

Y# 20.1 10 CASH
Copper **Ruler:** Hsüan-t'ung **Obv. Insc.:** Tai-ch'ing T'ung-pi **Rev:** Rosette below dragon, "U" of "KUO" inverted "A" **Rev. Leg.:** Hsüan-t'ung Nien-tsao TAI-CHING-TI-KUO.

Date	Mintage	VG	F	VF	XF	Unc
CD1909	—	1.85	5.50	12.00	25.00	60.00

Note: Although this coin bears no indication of its origin, it was minted in the Manchurian Provinces ca.1922

Y# 20x 10 CASH
Copper **Ruler:** Hsüan-t'ung **Obv:** Rosette in center **Obv. Insc.:** Tai-ch'ing T'ung-pi **Rev:** Dragon **Rev. Leg.:** Hsüan-t'ung Nien-tsao TAI-CHING-TI-KUO.

Date	Mintage	VG	F	VF	XF	Unc
CD1909	—	3.50	10.00	20.00	30.00	80.00

Note: Although this coin bears no indication of its origin, it was minted in Kirin Province

Y# 27 10 CASH
Bronze **Ruler:** Hsüan-t'ung **Obv:** Dragon **Obv. Insc.:** Tai-ch'ing T'ung-pi **Rev. Leg.:** Hsüan-t'ung...

Date	Mintage	VG	F	VF	XF	Unc
3(1911)	95,585,000	0.85	2.50	4.00	8.00	90.00
3(1911) Proof; Rare						

Y# 27a 10 CASH
Brass **Ruler:** Hsüan-t'ung **Obv:** Dragon **Obv. Insc.:** Tai-ch'ing T'ung-pi **Rev. Leg.:** Hsüan-t'ung...

Date	Mintage	VG	F	VF	XF	Unc
3(1911)	—	12.00	30.00	45.00	95.00	150

Y# 5 20 CASH
Copper, 32 mm. **Ruler:** Kuang-hsü **Obv. Insc.:** Kuang-hsü Yüan-pao **Rev:** Dragon **Rev. Leg.:** HU POO

Date	Mintage	VG	F	VF	XF	Unc
ND(1903)	—	0.50	1.00	2.00	3.00	—

Y# 5.1 20 CASH
Copper, 32 mm. **Ruler:** Kuang-hsü **Obv:** Four-point rosette in center **Obv. Insc.:** Kuang-hsü Yüan-pao **Rev:** Dragon **Rev. Leg.:** HU POO

Date	Mintage	VG	F	VF	XF	Unc
ND(1903)	—	2.50	6.00	12.00	25.00	—

Y# 5.2 20 CASH
Copper, 32 mm. **Ruler:** Kuang-hsü **Obv. Insc.:** Kuang-hsü Yüan-pao **Rev:** Head of dragon and clouds redesigned **Rev. Leg.:** HU POO

Date	Mintage	VG	F	VF	XF	Unc
ND(1903) Restrike	—	2.50	6.00	12.00	25.00	

Note: Y#5-5.2 were struck at the Wuchang Mint in 1917 from unused dies prepared in 1903

Y# 5a 20 CASH
Copper, 32 mm. **Ruler:** Kuang-hsü **Obv. Insc.:** Kuang-hsü Yüan-pao **Rev:** Dragon in circle of dots **Rev. Leg.:** HU POO

Date	Mintage	VG	F	VF	XF	Unc
ND(1903-05)	—	30.00	50.00	85.00	125	—

Y# 11 20 CASH
Copper, 32 mm. **Ruler:** Kuang-hsü **Obv. Insc.:** Tai-ch'ing T'ung-pi **Rev:** Dragon **Rev. Leg.:** Kuang-hsü Nien-tsao, TAI-CHING-TI-KUO

Date	Mintage	VG	F	VF	XF	Unc
CD1905	—	12.50	30.00	50.00	75.00	

Y# 11.1 20 CASH
Copper, 32 mm. **Ruler:** Kuang-hsü **Obv. Insc.:** Tai-ch'ing T'ung-pi **Rev:** Dragon **Rev. Leg.:** Kuang-hsü Nien-tsao, TAI-CHING-TI-KUO

Date	Mintage	VG	F	VF	XF	Unc
CD1906	—	12.50	30.00	50.00	75.00	

Y# 11.3a 20 CASH
Brass, 32 mm. **Ruler:** Kuang-hsü **Obv. Insc.:** Tai-ch'ing T'ung-pi **Rev:** Dragon **Rev. Leg.:** Kuang-hsü Nien-tsao, TAI-CHING-TI-KUO

Date	Mintage	VG	F	VF	XF	Unc
CD1907	—	3.50	8.00	15.00	30.00	

Y# 11.2 20 CASH
Copper, 32 mm. **Ruler:** Kuang-hsü **Obv:** Dots around date **Obv. Insc.:** Tai-ch'ing T'ung-pi **Rev:** Dragon **Rev. Leg.:** Kuang-hsü Nien-tsao, TAI-CHING-TI-KUO **Note:** 1.2-1.7 mm. thick.

Date	Mintage	VG	F	VF	XF	Unc
CD1907	—	0.60	1.50	2.00	4.00	

Y# 11.3 20 CASH
Copper, 32 mm. **Ruler:** Kuang-hsü **Obv. Insc.:** Tai-ch'ing T'ung-pi **Rev:** Dragon **Rev. Leg.:** Kuang-hsü Nien-tsao, TAI-CHING-TI-KUO **Note:** 2.0-2.3 mm. thick.

Date	Mintage	VG	F	VF	XF	Unc
CD1907	—	2.50	6.00	12.00	25.00	

Y# 21 20 CASH
Brass, 32 mm. **Ruler:** Hsüan-t'ung **Obv. Insc.:** Tai-ch'ing T'ung-pi **Rev:** With dot between "KUO" and COPPER; six waves beneath dragon **Rev. Leg.:** Hsüan-t'ung Nien-tsao, TAI-CHING-TI-KUO...

Date	Mintage	VG	F	VF	XF	Unc
CD1909	—	1.00	2.50	5.00	10.00	—

Y# 21.1   20 CASH
Copper, 32 mm. **Ruler:** Hsüan-t'ung **Obv. Insc.:** Tai-ch'ing T'ung-pi **Rev:** With dot between "KUO" and "COPPER"; six waves beneath dragon **Rev. Leg.:** Hsüan-t'ung Nien-tsao, TAI-CHING-TI-KUO... **Note:** 1.2-1.7 mm. thick.

Date	Mintage	VG	F	VF	XF	Unc
CD1909	—	1.25	3.00	6.00	10.00	—

Y# 21.2   20 CASH
Copper, 32 mm. **Ruler:** Hsüan-t'ung **Obv. Insc.:** Tai-ch'ing T'ung-pi **Rev:** Without dot between "KUO" and "COPPER"; six waves beneath dragon **Rev. Leg.:** Hsüan-t'ung Nien-tsao, TAI-CHING-TI-KUO... **Note:** 2.0-2.3 mm. thick.

Date	Mintage	VG	F	VF	XF	Unc
CD1909	—	1.25	3.00	6.00	10.00	—

Y# 21.3   20 CASH
Copper, 32 mm. **Ruler:** Hsüan-t'ung **Obv. Insc.:** Tai-ch'ing T'ung-pi **Rev:** Without dot between "KUO" and "COPPER"; rosette beneath dragon **Rev. Leg.:** Hsüan-t'ung Nien-tsao, TAI-CHING-TI-KUO...

Date	Mintage	VG	F	VF	XF	Unc
CD1909 Restrike	—	6.00	15.00	40.00	70.00	—

Note: Although this coin bears no indication of its origin, it was minted in the Manchurian Provinces ca.1922

Y# 21.4   20 CASH
Copper, 32 mm. **Ruler:** Hsüan-t'ung **Obv. Insc.:** Tai-ch'ing T'ung-pi **Rev:** Without dot between "KUO" and "COPPER"; dot below dragon's chin **Rev. Leg.:** Hsüan-t'ung Nien-tsao, TAI-CHING-TI-KUO...

Date	Mintage	VG	F	VF	XF	Unc
CD1909 Restrike	—	3.50	8.50	16.00	30.00	—

Note: Although this coin bears no indication of its origin, it was minted in the Manchurian Provinces ca.1922

Y# 21.5   20 CASH
Copper, 32 mm. **Ruler:** Hsüan-t'ung **Obv:** Inner circle of large dots **Obv. Insc.:** Tai-ch'ing T'ung-pi **Rev:** Without dot between "KUO" and "COPPER"; five crude waves beneath dragon with redesigned forehead; inner circle of large dots **Rev. Leg.:** Hsüan-t'ung Nien-tsao, TAI-CHING-TI-KUO...

Date	Mintage	VG	F	VF	XF	Unc
CD1909	—	1.25	3.00	6.00	30.00	100

K# 215   10 CENTS
2.7000 g., 0.8200 Silver 0.0712 oz. ASW **Ruler:** Kuang-hsü **Obv. Insc.:** Tai-ch'ing T'ung-pi **Rev:** Dragon **Rev. Leg.:** Kuang-hsü Nien-tsao, TAI-CHING-TI-KUO...

Date	Mintage	VG	F	VF	XF	Unc
CD1907	—	150	250	500	850	2,000

Y# 12   10 CENTS
2.7000 g., 0.8200 Silver 0.0712 oz. ASW **Ruler:** Kuang-hsü **Obv. Insc.:** Kuang-hsü Yüan-pao **Rev:** Dragon **Rev. Leg.:** Kuang-hsü Nien-tsao, TAI-CHING-TI-KUO...

Date	Mintage	VG	F	VF	XF	Unc
ND(1908)	—	12.00	30.00	40.00	120	300

K# 222   10 CENTS
3.2000 g., 0.6500 Silver 0.0669 oz. ASW **Ruler:** Hsüan-t'ung **Obv. Insc.:** Tai-ch'ing Yin-pi **Rev:** Dragon **Rev. Leg.:** Hsüan-t'ung Nien-tsao

Date	Mintage	VG	F	VF	XF	Unc
ND(1910)	—	80.00	120	250	500	1,000
ND(1910) Proof	—	Value: 1,500				

Y# 28   10 CENTS
2.7000 g., Silver **Ruler:** Hsüan-t'ung **Obv. Leg.:** Hsüan-t'ung Yin-pi **Rev:** Dragon **Rev. Leg.:** Hsüan-t'ung Nien-tsao

Date	Mintage	VG	F	VF	XF	Unc
3(1911)	—	10.00	20.00	40.00	85.00	250

Note: Refer to Hunan Republic 10 Cents, K#762

K# 214   20 CENTS
5.5000 g., 0.8200 Silver 0.1450 oz. ASW **Ruler:** Kuang-hsü **Obv. Insc.:** Tai-ch'ing Yin-pi **Rev:** Dragon **Rev. Leg.:** Kuang-hsü Nien-tsao, TAI-CHING-TI-KUO...

Date	Mintage	VG	F	VF	XF	Unc
CD1907	—	200	400	650	1,100	2,500

Y# 13   20 CENTS
5.3000 g., 0.8200 Silver 0.1397 oz. ASW **Ruler:** Kuang-hsü **Obv. Insc.:** Kuang-hsü Yüan-pao **Rev:** Dragon **Rev. Leg.:** Kuang-hsü Nien-tsao, TAI-CHING-TI-KUO...

Date	Mintage	VG	F	VF	XF	Unc
ND(1908)	—	20.00	60.00	100	150	400

K# 217w   20 CENTS
5.3000 g., 0.8200 Silver 0.1397 oz. ASW **Ruler:** Kuang-hsü **Obv. Insc.:** Kuang-hsü Yüan-pao **Rev:** Dragon **Rev. Leg.:** Kuang-hsü Nien-tsao, TAI-CHING-TI-KUO... with "COPPER COIN" (error)

Date	Mintage	VG	F	VF	XF	Unc
ND(1908) Rare	—	—	—	—	—	—

Y# 29   20 CENTS
5.4000 g., 0.8200 Silver 0.1424 oz. ASW **Ruler:** Hsüan-t'ung **Obv. Leg.:** Hsüan-t'ung **Obv. Insc.:** Tai-ch'ing Yin-pi **Rev:** Dragon

Date	Mintage	VG	F	VF	XF	Unc
3(1911)	—	45.00	100	200	350	600

K# 221   25 CENTS
6.7000 g., 0.8000 Silver 0.1723 oz. ASW **Ruler:** Hsüan-t'ung **Obv. Leg.:** Hsüan-t'ung Nien-tsao **Obv. Insc.:** Tai-ch'ing Yin-pi **Rev:** Dragon

Date	Mintage	VG	F	VF	XF	Unc
ND(1910)	1,410,000	65.00	200	400	750	1,200
ND(1910) Proof	—	Value: 3,000				

K# 213   50 CENTS
13.6000 g., 0.8600 Silver 0.3760 oz. ASW **Ruler:** Kuang-hsü **Obv. Insc.:** Tai-ch'ing Yin-pi **Rev:** Dragon **Rev. Leg.:** Kuang-hsü Nien-tsao, TAI-CHING-TI-KUO...

Date	Mintage	VG	F	VF	XF	Unc
CD1907	—	500	800	1,200	2,000	4,500

Y# 23   50 CENTS
13.4000 g., 0.8000 Silver 0.3446 oz. ASW **Ruler:** Hsüan-t'ung **Obv. Insc.:** Tai-ch'ing Yin-pi **Rev:** Dragon **Rev. Leg.:** Hsüan-t'ung Nien-tsao

Date	Mintage	VG	F	VF	XF	Unc
ND(1910)	1,571,000	65.00	100	200	350	900
ND(1910) Proof	—	Value: 2,000				

Y# 30   50 CENTS
13.4000 g., 0.8000 Silver 0.3446 oz. ASW **Ruler:** Hsüan-t'ung **Obv. Leg.:** Hsüan-t'ung **Obv. Insc.:** Tai-ch'ing Yin-pi **Rev:** Dragon

Date	Mintage	VG	F	VF	XF	Unc
3(1911)	Inc. above	500	900	1,500	2,500	6,000
3(1911) Proof	—	Value: 8,000				

K# 212 DOLLAR

26.9000 g., 0.9000 Silver 0.7783 oz. ASW **Ruler:** Kuang-hsü
Obv. Insc.: Tai-ch'ing Yin-pi **Rev:** Dragon **Rev. Leg.:** Kuang-hsü
Nien-tsao, TAI-CHING-TI-KOU...

Date	Mintage	VG	F	VF	XF	Unc
CD1907	—	1,000	1,500	2,500	5,000	10,000

Y# 14 DOLLAR

26.9000 g., 0.9000 Silver 0.7783 oz. ASW **Ruler:** Kuang-hsü
Obv. Insc.: Kuang-hsü Yüan-pao **Rev:** Dragon **Rev. Leg.:**
Kuang-hsü Nien-tsao, TAI-CHING-TI-KOU...

Date	Mintage	VG	F	VF	XF	Unc
ND(1908)	—	20.00	50.00	100	150	900

K# 219 DOLLAR

26.9000 g., 0.9000 Silver 0.7783 oz. ASW **Ruler:** Hsüan-t'ung
Obv. Insc.: Tai-ch'ing Yin-pi **Rev:** Dragon **Rev. Leg.:** Hsüan-
t'ung Nien-tsao

Date	Mintage	VG	F	VF	XF	Unc
ND(1910)	—	400	800	1,500	2,500	5,000
ND(1910) Proof	—	Value: 7,000				

Y# 31 DOLLAR

26.9000 g., 0.9000 Silver 0.7783 oz. ASW **Ruler:** Hsüan-t'ung
Obv. Leg.: Hsüan-t'ung **Obv. Insc.:** Tai-ch'ing Yin-pi **Rev:** Dragon

Date	Mintage	VG	F	VF	XF	Unc
3(1911)	77,153,000	15.00	30.00	45.00	75.00	450

Note: Struck at the Tientsin, Nanking, and Wuchang Mints
without distinctive marks

Y# 31.1 DOLLAR

26.9000 g., 0.9000 Silver 0.7783 oz. ASW **Ruler:** Hsüan-t'ung
Obv. Leg.: Hsüan-t'ung **Obv. Insc.:** Tai-ch'ing Yin-pi
Rev: Dragon; "dot" after "DOLLAR"

Date	Mintage	VG	F	VF	XF	Unc
3(1911)	Inc. above	20.00	40.00	80.00	200	1,000

PATTERNS
Standard Unified General

KM#	Date	Mintage	Identification	Mkt Val
Pn264	ND	—	Cash. Brass. Hsu4a, square hole.	400
Pn265	ND	—	Cash. Brass. Hsu4b, without hole.	400
Pn266	ND	—	Cash. Copper. Y#7.	400
Pn267	ND	—	Cash. Brass. Y#25; without hole.	400
Pn268	CD1907	—	Dollar. Copper. K212.	—
Pn269	ND(1908)	—	20 Cents. Nickel. Milled edge. K217w.	—
Pn310	ND(1908)	—	20 Cents. Nickel. K217y.	—
Pn272	ND(1910)	—	Li. Copper. Hsu33.	400
Pn273	ND(1910)	—	5 Li. Copper. Hsu34.	550
Pn274	ND(1910)	—	5 Li. Bronze.	550
Pn275	ND(1910)	—	2 Cash. Copper. Hsu13.	400
Pn276	ND(1910)	—	2 Cash. Brass. With hole, Hsu13.	400
Pn277	ND(1910)	—	Fen. Copper. Hsu35.	600
Pn278	ND(1910)	—	Fen. Bronze.	600
Pn279	ND(1910)	—	2 Fen. Copper. Hsu36.	1,000
Pn280	ND(1910)	—	2 Fen. Bronze.	1,000
Pn250	ND(1910)	—	10 Cents. Nickel. K222.	—
Pn251	ND(1910)	—	1/4 Dollar. Silver center. Plain edge. K221.	—
Pn311	ND(1910)	—	10 Cents. Nickel. K222y.	125
Pn306	3(1911)	—	Dollar. Silver. K223b.	—
Pn281	3(1911)	—	5 Cash. Copper. Y26; Hsu30.	600
Pn282	3(1911)	—	5 Cash. Bronze. Y26a.	600
Pn283	3(1911)	—	20 Cash. Copper. Hsu32.	700
Pn284	3(1911)	—	20 Cash. Bronze.	700
Pn304	3(1911)	—	Dollar. Silver. K223.	25,000
Pn305	3(1911)	—	Dollar. Silver. K223a.	25,000
Pn307	3(1911)	—	Dollar. Silver. K224.	35,000
Pn308	3(1911)	—	Dollar. Silver. K225.	25,000
Pn309	3(1911)	—	Dollar. Silver. K226.	20,000

PATTERNS
Peking Tael Series

KM#	Date	Mintage	Identification	Mkt Val
Pn290	29(1903)	—	5 Fen. Silver. K931.	2,500
Pn291	29(1903)	—	Ch'ien. Silver. K930.	2,800
Pn292	29(1903)	—	2 Ch'ien. Silver. K929.	3,800
Pn293	29(1903)	—	2 Ch'ien. Gold. K929v.	30,000
Pn294	29(1903)	—	5 Ch'ien. Silver. K928.	12,000
Pn295	29(1903)	—	Liang. Silver. K927.	48,000
Pn296	29(1903)	—	Liang. Gold. K927v.	80,000
Pn297	CD1906	—	Ch'ien. Silver. K937.	1,500
Pn298	CD1906	—	2 Ch'ien. Silver. 7.4800 g. K936.	1,800
Pn299	CD1906	—	5 Ch'ien. Silver. K935.	3,000
Pn300	CD1906	—	Liang. Silver. K934.	12,000
Pn301	CD1906	—	Liang. Gold. K1540. Tientsin Mint. 39.5mm, 37g. Large clouds, plain edge.	50,000
PnA302	CD1906	—	Liang. Gold. Tientsin Mint. 39.5mm, 37g. Small clouds, reeded edge. Rare.	—
PnA303	CD1907	—	Liang. Gold. K1541a. Tientsin Mint. 39.5mm, 37g. Large clouds, plain edge. Rare.	—
Pn302	CD1907	—	Liang. Gold. K1541. Tientsin Mint. 39.5mm, 37g. Small clouds, reeded edge.	50,000
Pn303	CD1907	—	Liang. Silver. K1541v.	13,000

TRIAL STRIKES

KM#	Date	Mintage	Identification	Mkt Val
TS3	1(1910)	—	Fen. White Metal. Hsu35, KM#Pn275. Uniface obverse.	125

PROOF SETS

KM#	Date	Mintage	Identification	Issue Price	Mkt Val
PS1	ND(1910) (4)	—	Y#23, K#219, 221, 222	—	—

ANHWEI PROVINCE

Anhui

A province located in eastern China. Made a separate province
during the Manchu dynasty in the 17th century. Principally agricultural
with some mining of coal and iron ore. Spanish-American 8 Reales
saw wide circulation in this province until the end of World War I. The
provincial mint at Anking began operations in 1897, closed in 1899,
and later reopened in 1902. The primary production of the mint was
cash coins but included a series of silver coinage.

EMPIRE
MILLED COINAGE

Y# 35 5 CASH

Copper **Ruler:** Kuang-hsü **Obv. Leg.:** An-hui Sheng Tsao **Obv.
Insc.:** Kuang-hsü Yüan-pao **Rev:** Circled dragon **Rev. Leg.:** AN-
HWEI

Date	Mintage	VG	F	VF	XF	Unc
ND(1902)	—	150	200	300	680	—

Y# 35.1 5 CASH

Copper **Ruler:** Kuang-hsü **Obv. Leg.:** An-hui Sheng Tsao
Obv. Insc.: Kuang-hsü Yüan-pao **Rev:** Uncircled dragon
Rev. Leg.: AN-HUI

Date	Mintage	VG	F	VF	XF	Unc
ND(c. 1902) Rare						

Y# 36 10 CASH

Copper **Ruler:** Kuang-hsü **Obv. Leg.:** An-hui Sheng Tsao
Obv. Insc.: Kuang-hsü Yüan-pao **Rev:** Letter "N" backwards in
"AN-HWEI" and in "TEN"

Date	Mintage	VG	F	VF	XF	Unc
ND(1902-06)	—	6.00	12.00	20.00	65.00	—

Y# 34a 10 CASH

Copper **Ruler:** Kuang-hsü **Obv. Leg.:** An-hui Sheng Tsao
Obv. Insc.: Kuang-hsü Yüan-pao **Rev:** Letter "A" inverted,
denomination "ONE SEN"

Date	Mintage	VG	F	VF	XF	Unc
ND(1902)	—	50.00	80.00	125	350	—

Y# 34a.1   10 CASH
Copper   **Ruler:** Kuang-hsü **Obv. Leg.:** An-hui Sheng Tsao
Rev: Letter "A" corrected, denomination "ONE SEN"

Date	Mintage	VG	F	VF	XF	Unc
ND(1902)	—	40.00	65.00	100	250	—

Y# 36.1   10 CASH
Copper   **Ruler:** Kuang-hsü **Obv:** Small Manchu in center
Obv. Leg.: An-hui Sheng Tsao **Obv. Insc.:** Kuang-hsü Yüan-pao
Rev: Rosettes close together, letter "N" corrected in "AN-HWEI"
and in "TEN" **Edge:** Plain

Date	Mintage	VG	F	VF	XF	Unc
ND(1902-06)	—	1.00	2.50	5.00	20.00	—

Y# 36.1a   10 CASH
Copper   **Ruler:** Kuang-hsü **Obv:** Small Manchu in center
Obv. Leg.: An-hui Sheng Tsao **Obv. Insc.:** Kuang-hsü Yüan-pao
Rev: Rosettes close together, letter "N" corrected in AN-HWEI
and in TEN **Edge:** Milled

Date	Mintage	VG	F	VF	XF	Unc
ND(1902-06) Rare	—	—	—	—	—	—

Y# 34   10 CASH
Copper   **Ruler:** Kuang-hsü **Obv. Leg.:** An-hui Sheng Tsao
Obv. Insc.: Kuang-hsü Yüan-pao **Rev:** Denomination: "ONE
CEN" **Note:** May show various stages of recutting of "C" in "CEN."

Date	Mintage	VG	F	VF	XF	Unc
ND1902	—	35.00	50.00	85.00	150	—

Y# 36.2   10 CASH
Copper   **Ruler:** Kuang-hsü **Obv:** Smaller, redesigned rosettes,
larger Manchu words in center **Obv. Leg.:** An-hui Sheng Tsao
Obv. Insc.: Kuang-hsü Yüan-pao **Rev:** Rosettes close together,
larger clouds around redesigned dragon

Date	Mintage	VG	F	VF	XF	Unc
ND(1902-06)	—	1.50	4.00	6.00	20.00	—

Y# 36.3   10 CASH
Copper   **Ruler:** Kuang-hsü **Obv:** Rosettes crude and heavy
Obv. Leg.: An-hui Sheng Tsao **Obv. Insc.:** Kuang-hsü Yüan-pao
Rev: Rosettes close together, dragon's head redesigned

Date	Mintage	VG	F	VF	XF	Unc
ND(1902-08)	—	5.00	12.00	17.50	50.00	—

Y# 36.4   10 CASH
Copper   **Ruler:** Kuang-hsü **Obv. Leg.:** An-hui Sheng Tsao
Obv. Insc.: Kuang-hsü Yüan-pao **Rev:** Rosettes far apart

Date	Mintage	VG	F	VF	XF	Unc
ND(1902-06)	—	1.00	2.50	5.00	20.00	—

Y# 36a   10 CASH
Copper   **Ruler:** Kuang-hsü **Obv:** Small rosette at center, legend
with 5 characters at bottom **Obv. Leg.:** An-hui Sheng Tsao
Obv. Insc.: Kuang-hsü Yüan-pao **Rev:** Large English legend
above dragon, without "TEN CASH"

Date	Mintage	VG	F	VF	XF	Unc
ND(1902-06)	—	1.00	2.50	5.00	18.00	—

Y# 36a.1   10 CASH
Copper   **Ruler:** Kuang-hsü **Obv:** Small rosette **Obv. Leg.:** An-
hui Sheng Tsao **Obv. Insc.:** Kuang-hsu Yüan-pao **Rev:** Small
English legend above dragon

Date	Mintage	VG	F	VF	XF	Unc
ND(1902-06)	—	1.50	3.00	6.00	15.00	—

Y# 36a.2   10 CASH
Copper   **Ruler:** Kuang-hsü **Obv. Leg.:** An-hui Sheng Tsao
Obv. Insc.: Kuang-hsü Yüan-pao **Rev:** Small English legend with
larger clouds around dragon and only one cloud below dragon's tail

Date	Mintage	VG	F	VF	XF	Unc
ND(1902-06)	—	2.00	5.00	8.00	18.00	—

Y# 36a.3   10 CASH
Copper   **Ruler:** Kuang-hsü **Obv:** Large rosette at center, legend
with 2 characters at bottom **Obv. Leg.:** An-hui Sheng Tsao
Obv. Insc.: Kuang-hsü Yüan-pao

Date	Mintage	VG	F	VF	XF	Unc
ND(1902-06)	—	1.00	2.50	5.00	15.00	—

Y# 36a.4   10 CASH
Copper   **Ruler:** Kuang-hsü **Obv:** Large rosette at center, legend
with 5 characters at bottom **Obv. Leg.:** An-hui Sheng Tsao
Obv. Insc.: Kuang-hsü Yüan-pao

Date	Mintage	VG	F	VF	XF	Unc
ND(1902-06)	—	1.25	2.50	5.00	20.00	—

Y# 36a.5   10 CASH
Copper   **Ruler:** Kuang-hsü **Obv:** Legend with 2 characters at
bottom **Obv. Leg.:** An-hui Sheng Tsao **Obv. Insc.:** Kuang-hsü
Yüan-pao **Rev:** Small English legend above dragon

Date	Mintage	VG	F	VF	XF	Unc
ND(1902-06)	—	3.50	7.50	15.00	30.00	—

Y# 36a.6   10 CASH
Copper   **Ruler:** Kuang-hsü **Obv:** Slightly smaller rosette at center
with right Manchu word slightly higher than on Y#36a.5
Obv. Leg.: An-hui Sheng Tsao **Obv. Insc.:** Kuang-hsü Yüan-pao
Rev: Small English legend above dragon

Date	Mintage	VG	F	VF	XF	Unc
ND(1902-06)	—	1.00	2.50	5.00	20.00	—

Y# 38a   10 CASH
Copper   **Ruler:** Kuang-hsü **Obv:** Legend with 2 characters at
bottom **Obv. Leg.:** An-hui Sheng Tsao **Obv. Insc.:** Kuang-hsü
Yüan-pao **Rev:** "Ten" spelled "TOEN"

Date	Mintage	VG	F	VF	XF	Unc
ND(1902-06)	—	8.00	15.00	30.00	50.00	—

Y# 38a.1   10 CASH
Copper   **Ruler:** Kuang-hsü **Obv:** Legend with 5 characters at
bottom **Obv. Leg.:** An-hui Sheng Tsao **Obv. Insc.:** Kuang-hsü
Yüan-pao **Rev:** "Ten" spelled "TOEN"

Date	Mintage	VG	F	VF	XF	Unc
ND(1902-06)	—	35.00	70.00	150	250	—

Y# 38b   10 CASH
Copper   **Ruler:** Kuang-hsü **Obv:** Legend with 2 characters at
bottom **Obv. Leg.:** An-hui Sheng Tsao **Obv. Insc.:** Kuang-hsü
Yüan-pao **Rev:** Without "TEN CASH"

Date	Mintage	VG	F	VF	XF	Unc
ND(1902-06)	—	5.00	12.00	25.00	65.00	—

Y# 38b.1   10 CASH
Copper **Ruler:** Kuang-hsü **Obv:** Legend with 5 characters at bottom **Obv. Leg.:** An-hui Sheng Tsao **Obv. Insc.:** Kuang-hsü Yüan-pao

Date	Mintage	VG	F	VF	XF	Unc
ND(1902-06)	—	15.00	35.00	50.00	140	

Y# 39   10 CASH
Copper **Ruler:** Kuang-hsü **Obv:** Legend with 7 characters at bottom **Obv. Leg.:** An-hui Sheng Tsao **Obv. Insc.:** Kuang-hsü Yüan-pao **Rev:** Rosettes at side and "AN-HUI" above dragon

Date	Mintage	VG	F	VF	XF	Unc
ND(1902-06) Rare	—					

Y# 39.1   10 CASH
Copper **Ruler:** Kuang-hsü **Obv. Leg.:** An-hui Sheng Tsao **Obv. Insc.:** Kuang-hsü Yüan-pao **Rev:** Stars at sides and "AN-HUI" above dragon

Date	Mintage	VG	F	VF	XF	Unc
ND(1902-06) Rare	—					

Y# 39.2   10 CASH
Copper **Ruler:** Kuang-hsü **Obv. Leg.:** An-hui Sheng Tsao **Obv. Insc.:** Kuang-hsü Yüan-pao **Rev:** "AN-HUI", upright dragon **Note:** Square-holed center.

Date	Mintage	VG	F	VF	XF	Unc
ND(1902-06) Rare	—					

Y# 10a   10 CASH
Copper **Ruler:** Kuang-hsü **Obv:** Large mint mark at center **Obv. Insc.:** Tai-ch'ing T'ung-pi **Rev. Leg.:** Kuang-hsü Nien-tsao, TAI-CHING-TI-KUO ...

Date	Mintage	VG	F	VF	XF	Unc
CD(1906)	—	1.00	2.50	5.00	18.00	

Y# 10a.1   10 CASH
Copper **Ruler:** Kuang-hsü **Obv:** Small mint mark at center **Obv. Insc.:** Tai-ch'ing T'ung-pi **Rev. Leg.:** Kuang-hsü Nien-tsao, TAI-CHING-TI-KUO ...

Date	Mintage	VG	F	VF	XF	Unc
CD(1906)	—	1.50	3.00	6.00	18.00	

Y# 10a.2   10 CASH
Copper **Ruler:** Kuang-hsü **Obv:** More finely engraved, cloud near dragon's lower foot shaped like a 3 **Obv. Insc.:** Tai-ch'ing T'ung-pi **Rev:** More finely engraved **Rev. Leg.:** Kuang-hsü Nien-tsao, TAI-CHING-TI-KUO ...

Date	Mintage	VG	F	VF	XF	Unc
CD1906	—	1.00	2.50	5.00	18.00	

Y# 20a   10 CASH
Copper **Ruler:** Hsüan-t'ung **Obv. Insc.:** Tai-ch'ing T'ung-pi **Rev. Leg.:** Hsüan-t'ung Nien-tsao, TAI-CHING-TI-KUO ...

Date	Mintage	VG	F	VF	XF	Unc
CD1909	—	12.50	25.00	50.00	125	

Y# 20a.1   10 CASH
Copper **Ruler:** Hsüan-t'ung **Obv. Insc.:** Tai-ch'ing T'ung-pi **Rev:** Dot after "COIN" **Rev. Leg.:** Hsüan-t'ung Nien-tsao, TAI-CHING-TI-KUO ...

Date	Mintage	VG	F	VF	XF	Unc
CD1909	—	35.00	65.00	130	225	

Y# 37   20 CASH
Copper **Ruler:** Kuang-hsü **Obv. Leg.:** An-hui Sheng Tsao **Obv. Insc.:** Kuang-hsü Yüan-pao

Date	Mintage	VG	F	VF	XF	Unc
ND(1902)	—	375	750	1,100	1,500	

Y# 11a   20 CASH
Copper **Ruler:** Kuang-hsü **Obv. Insc.:** Tai-ch'ing T'ung-pi **Rev:** TAI-CHING-TI-KUO ... **Rev. Insc.:** Kuang-hsü Nien-tsao

Date	Mintage	VG	F	VF	XF	Unc
CD1906	—	80.00	150	300	600	

Y# 43.5   20 CENTS
5.3000 g., 0.9200 Silver 0.1568 oz. ASW **Ruler:** Kuang-hsü **Obv. Insc.:** Kuang-hsü Yüan-pao **Rev:** Dragon

Date	Mintage	VG	F	VF	XF	Unc
27(1901) 1 known	—	—	—	—	—	

Note: D.K.E. Ching Sale 6-91 VF++ realized $2,420

MILITARY TOKEN COINAGE

Given to An-hui Imperial troops by the Military Bureau for faithful and/or meritorious service.

KM# W45   10 CASH
Copper **Ruler:** Kuang-hsü **Issuer:** Anhwei Military Bureau **Obv:** Large central Chinese character "Cheang" (reward) **Obv. Leg.:** An-hui Wu Dih Buh Yuen **Rev:** Legend around dragon **Rev. Leg.:** AN-HWEI***TEN CASH***

Date	Mintage	VG	F	VF	XF	Unc
ND	—	125	225	375	550	

KM# W46   10 CASH
Copper **Ruler:** Kuang-hsü **Issuer:** Anhwei Military Bureau **Obv. Leg.:** An-hui Wu Dih Buh Yuen **Rev:** Legend around Dragon **Rev. Leg.:** AN-HWEI***TEN CASH***

Date	Mintage	VG	F	VF	XF	Unc
ND	—	125	225	375	550	

KM# W47   10 CASH
Copper **Ruler:** Kuang-hsü **Issuer:** Anhwei Military Bureau **Obv. Leg.:** An-hui Wu Dih Buh Yuen **Rev:** Legend without "TEN CASH"

Date	Mintage	VG	F	VF	XF	Unc
ND	—	200	350	600	900	

CHEKIANG PROVINCE

Zhejiang
A province located along the east coast of China. Although the smallest of the Chinese mainland provinces, it is one of the most densely populated. Economic interests are mostly agricultural with iron and coal mining and some fishing. A small mint opened in 1897. This was replaced by a larger mint which operated briefly 1898-99. Other mints opened in 1903 and 1905. These were merged with the Fukien Mint in 1906-07.

EMPIRE

PROVINCIAL CAST COINAGE

C# 4-19   CASH
Cast Brass **Ruler:** Kuang-hsü **Obv:** Type A **Obv. Insc.:** Kuang-hsü T'ung-pao **Rev. Insc.:** Boo-je **Note:** Size varies: 21-22mm.

Date	Mintage	Good	VG	F	VF	XF
ND(1875-1908)	—	3.00	4.50	6.50	10.00	12.00

C# 4-19.1   CASH
Cast Brass **Ruler:** Kuang-hsü **Obv. Insc.:** Kuang-hsü T'ung-pao **Rev:** More angular mint mark

Date	Mintage	Good	VG	F	VF	XF
ND(1875-1908)	—	2.00	3.00	4.00	6.00	8.00

MILLED COINAGE

Y# 8b   2 CASH
Copper **Ruler:** Kuang-hsü **Obv. Insc.:** Tai-ch'ing T'ung-pi
Rev: Dragon

Date	Mintage	VG	F	VF	XF	Unc
CD1906	—	5.00	10.00	16.00	30.00	—

Y# 9b   5 CASH
Copper **Ruler:** Kuang-hsü **Obv. Insc.:** Tai-ch'ing T'ung-pi
Rev. Leg.: Kuang-hsü Nien-tsao, TAI-CHING-TI-KUO ...

Date	Mintage	VG	F	VF	XF	Unc
CD1906	—	5.00	10.00	16.00	30.00	—

Y# 49   10 CASH
Copper **Ruler:** Kuang-hsü **Obv:** Ball in circle in center
Obv. Leg.: Che-kiang Sheng Tsao **Obv. Insc.:** Kuang-hsü Yüan-pao **Rev:** Dragon

Date	Mintage	VG	F	VF	XF	Unc
ND(1903-06)	—	0.50	1.50	2.50	4.50	—

Y# 49.1   10 CASH
Copper **Ruler:** Kuang-hsü **Obv:** Rosette at center and large Manchu "Boo" at left **Obv. Leg.:** Che-kiang Sheng Tsao
Obv. Insc.: Kuang-hsü Yüan-pao **Rev:** Dragon

Date	Mintage	VG	F	VF	XF	Unc
ND(1903-06)	—	0.50	1.50	2.50	4.50	—

Y# 49.1a   10 CASH
Brass **Ruler:** Kuang-hsü **Obv:** Rosette at center and large Manchu "Boo" at left **Obv. Leg.:** Che-kiang Sheng Tsao
Obv. Insc.: Kuang-hsü Yüan-pao **Rev:** Dragon

Date	Mintage	VG	F	VF	XF	Unc
ND(1903-06)	—	2.00	4.00	8.00	15.00	—

Y# 49.2   10 CASH
Copper **Ruler:** Kuang-hsü **Obv:** Small Manchu "Boo" at left **Obv. Leg.:** Che-kiang Sheng Tsao **Obv. Insc.:** Kuang-hsü Yüan-pao **Rev:** Dragon **Note:** Similar to Y#49.1 but with coin die alignment

Date	Mintage	VG	F	VF	XF	Unc
ND(1903-06)	—	0.75	1.50	3.00	6.00	—

Y# 49.3   10 CASH
Copper **Ruler:** Kuang-hsü **Obv:** Rosette at center and small Manchu word at left **Obv. Leg.:** Che-kiang Sheng Tsao
Obv. Insc.: Kuang-hsü Yüan-pao **Rev:** Small, cramped dragon with few clouds around body

Date	Mintage	VG	F	VF	XF	Unc
ND(1903-06)	—	0.75	1.50	3.00	6.00	—

Y# 49.4   10 CASH
Copper **Ruler:** Kuang-hsü **Obv. Leg.:** Che-kiang Sheng Tsao
Obv. Insc.: Kuang-hsü Yüan-pao **Rev:** Dragon without ball in center circle

Date	Mintage	VG	F	VF	XF	Unc
ND(1903-06)	—	1.25	2.50	5.00	10.00	—

Y# 49a   10 CASH
Brass **Ruler:** Kuang-hsü **Obv:** Legend has 4 characters at bottom **Obv. Leg.:** Che-kiang Sheng Tsao **Obv. Insc.:** Kuang-hsü Yüan-pao **Rev:** Dragon

Date	Mintage	VG	F	VF	XF	Unc
ND(1903-06)	—	3.00	6.00	11.00	20.00	—

Y# 49b   10 CASH
Copper **Ruler:** Kuang-hsü **Obv. Leg.:** Che-kiang Sheng Tsao
Obv. Insc.: Kuang-hsü Yüan-pao **Rev:** Dragon

Date	Mintage	VG	F	VF	XF	Unc
ND(1903-06)	—	6.00	12.00	25.00	45.00	—

Y# 10b   10 CASH
Copper **Ruler:** Kuang-hsü **Obv. Insc.:** Tai-ch'ing T'ung-pi
Rev: Dragon **Rev. Leg.:** Kuang hsü Nien-tsao, TAI-CHING-TI-KUO with KUO spelled KIIO

Date	Mintage	VG	F	VF	XF	Unc
CD1906	—	1.00	2.00	4.00	8.00	—

Y# 10b.1   10 CASH
Copper **Ruler:** Kuang-hsü **Obv. Insc.:** Tai-ch'ing T'ung-pi
Rev: Dragon **Rev. Leg.:** Kuang hsü Nien-tsao, TAI-CHING-TI-KUO with KUO spelled KUO

Date	Mintage	VG	F	VF	XF	Unc
CD1906	—	2.50	5.00	10.00	20.00	—

    Note: Chekiang and other 10 Cash coin types found struck over Korean 5 Fun coins are known; Why they were overstruck in China is unknown

Y# 50   20 CASH
Copper **Ruler:** Kuang-hsü **Obv. Leg.:** Che-kiang Sheng Tsao
Obv. Insc.: Kuang-hsü Yüan-pao **Rev:** Dragon **Note:** Two planchet sizes exist.

Date	Mintage	VG	F	VF	XF	Unc
ND(1903-04)	—	100	200	350	600	—

Y# 11b   20 CASH
Copper **Ruler:** Kuang-hsü **Obv. Insc.:** Tai-ch'ing T'ung-Pi
Rev. Leg.: Kuang-hsü Nien-tsao, TAI-CHING-TI-KUO ...

Date	Mintage	VG	F	VF	XF	Unc
CD1906	—	60.00	100	200	350	—

REPUBLIC

MILLED COINAGE

Y# 371   10 CENTS
2.6500 g., 0.6500 Silver 0.0554 oz. ASW **Obv:** Crossed flags
Rev. Leg.: CHE-KIANG PROVINCE

Date	Mintage	VG	F	VF	XF	Unc
13(1924)	4,464,000	1.50	4.00	7.00	10.00	25.00

Y# 373   20 CENTS
5.3000 g., Silver **Rev:** Large value "20" **Rev. Leg.:** CHE-KIANG PROVINCE.

Date	Mintage	VG	F	VF	XF	Unc
13(1924)	—	100	300	500	850	1,500

PATTERNS
Including off metal strikes

KM#	Date	Mintage	Identification	Mkt Val
Pn4	ND(1902)	—	5 Cents. Silver. CHE-KIANG. K123-I.	2,100
Pn5	ND(1902)	—	10 Cents. Silver. CHE-KIANG K122-I.	1,500
Pn6	ND(1902)	—	20 Cents. Silver. CHE-KIANG. K121-I.	1,500
Pn7	ND(1902)	—	Dollar. Silver. CHE-KIANG. K119-I.	35,000
Pn8	ND(1902)	—	Dollar. Copper. CHE-KIANG. K 119-I.	10,000
Pn9	ND(1903)	—	10 Cash. Copper. Y.49.3a.	1,000
Pn10	ND(1903)	—	10 Cash. White Copper. Y.49.3a. W132.	—
Pn11	13(1924)	—	20 Cents. Silver. Crossed flags. Y372.	2,000

CHIHLI PROVINCE

Hebei, Hopei

A province located in northeastern China which contains the eastern end of the Great Wall. An important producer of coal and some iron ore. In 1928 the provincial name was changed from Chihli to Hopei. The Paoting mint was established in 1745 and only produced cast cash coins.

A mint for struck cash was established in 1888 and the mint for the Peiyang silver coinage was added in 1896. This was destroyed during the Boxer Rebellion. A replacement mint was built in 1902 for the provincial coinage and merged with the Tientsin (Tianjin) Central mint in 1910.

EMPIRE

PROVINCIAL CAST COINAGE

C# 8-1.10   CASH
Brass, 22.1 mm. **Ruler:** Kuang-hsü **Obv. Insc.:** Kuang-hsü T'ung-pao **Rev:** Dot at upper left **Rev. Insc.:** Boo-jiyen

Date	Mintage	Good	VG	F	VF	XF
ND(1875-1908)	—	2.75	4.50	7.50	15.00	—

C# 8-1.9   CASH
Brass, 22.3 mm. **Ruler:** Kuang-hsü **Obv. Insc.:** Kuang-hsü T'ung-pao **Rev:** Dash above **Rev. Insc.:** Boo-jiyen

Date	Mintage	Good	VG	F	VF	XF
ND(1875-1908)	—	2.00	3.75	7.50	15.00	—

C# 3-1.1   CASH

Cast Brass, 23 mm. **Ruler:** Kuang-hsü **Obv. Insc.:** Kuang-hsü T'ung-pao **Rev:** Type 1 mint mark, Manchu inscription **Rev. Insc.:** Boo-gu

Date	Mintage	Good	VG	F	VF	XF
ND(1875-1908)	—	90.00	125	200	300	—

C# 3-1.2   CASH

Cast Brass, 22 mm. **Ruler:** Kuang-hsü **Obv. Insc.:** Kuang-hsü T'ung-pao **Rev:** Type 2 mint mark, Manchu inscription **Rev. Insc.:** Boo-gu

Date	Mintage	Good	VG	F	VF	XF
ND(1875-1908)	—	20.00	30.00	50.00	75.00	—

C# 5-10   CASH

Cast Brass **Ruler:** Kuang-hsü **Obv:** Type A **Obv. Insc.:** Kuang-hsü T'ung-pao **Note:** Schjöth #1572.

Date	Mintage	Good	VG	F	VF	XF
ND(1875-86)	—	3.50	6.00	10.00	16.50	—

C# 5-10.1   CASH

Cast Brass **Ruler:** Kuang-hsü **Obv. Insc.:** Kuang-hsü T'ung-pao **Rev:** Dot above **Note:** Schjöth #1568.

Date	Mintage	Good	VG	F	VF	XF
ND(1875-86)	—	4.50	7.50	12.50	25.00	—

C# 5-10.2   CASH

Cast Brass **Ruler:** Kuang-hsü **Obv. Insc.:** Kuang-hsü T'ung-pao **Rev:** Crescent above

Date	Mintage	Good	VG	F	VF	XF
ND(1875-86)	—	4.50	7.50	12.00	20.00	—

Note: The crescent is known in various positions above the center hole

C# 5-10.3   CASH

Cast Brass **Ruler:** Kuang-hsü **Obv. Insc.:** Kuang-hsü T'ung-pao **Rev:** Circle above

Date	Mintage	Good	VG	F	VF	XF
ND(1875-86)	—	4.50	7.50	12.50	25.00	—

C# 5-10.4   CASH

Cast Brass **Ruler:** Kuang-hsü **Obv. Insc.:** Kuang-hsü T'ung-pao **Rev:** Dot below

Date	Mintage	Good	VG	F	VF	XF
ND(1875-86)	—	3.50	6.00	10.00	16.00	—

C# 5-10.5   CASH

Cast Brass **Ruler:** Kuang-hsü **Obv. Insc.:** Kuang-hsü T'ung-pao **Rev:** Circle below

Date	Mintage	Good	VG	F	VF	XF
ND(1875-86)	—	4.50	7.50	12.00	20.00	—

C# 5-10.6   CASH

Cast Brass **Ruler:** Kuang-hsü **Obv. Insc.:** Kuang-hsü T'ung-pao **Rev:** Dash above

Date	Mintage	Good	VG	F	VF	XF
ND(1875-86)	—	4.50	7.50	12.00	20.00	—

C# 5-10.7   CASH

Cast Brass **Ruler:** Kuang-hsü **Obv. Insc.:** Kuang-hsü T'ung-pao **Rev:** Dash below

Date	Mintage	Good	VG	F	VF	XF
ND(1875-86)	—	4.50	7.50	12.00	20.00	—

C# 5-10.8   CASH

Cast Brass **Ruler:** Kuang-hsü **Obv. Insc.:** Kuang-hsü T'ung-pao **Rev:** Dot upper left

Date	Mintage	Good	VG	F	VF	XF
ND(1875-86)	—	4.50	7.50	12.50	25.00	—

C# 5-10.9   CASH

Cast Brass **Ruler:** Kuang-hsü **Obv. Insc.:** Kuang-hsü T'ung-pao **Rev:** Dot upper right

Date	Mintage	Good	VG	F	VF	XF
ND(1875-86)	—	4.50	7.50	12.50	25.00	—

C# 8-1   CASH

Cast Brass, 23 mm. **Ruler:** Kuang-hsü **Obv. Insc.:** Kuang-hsü T'ung-pao **Rev:** Manchu inscription

Date	Mintage	Good	VG	F	VF	XF
ND(1875-1908)	—	2.50	4.50	7.50	12.00	—

C# 8-1.1   CASH

Cast Brass **Ruler:** Kuang-hsü **Obv. Insc.:** Kuang-hsü T'ung-pao **Rev:** Dot above, Manchu inscription **Rev. Insc.:** Boo-jiyen

Date	Mintage	Good	VG	F	VF	XF
ND(1875-1908)	—	2.75	4.50	7.50	15.00	—

C# 8-1.2   CASH

Cast Brass **Ruler:** Kuang-hsü **Obv. Insc.:** Kuang-hsü T'ung-pao **Rev:** Dot below, Manchu inscription **Rev. Insc.:** Boo-jiyen

Date	Mintage	Good	VG	F	VF	XF
ND(1875-1908)	—	2.00	3.50	6.00	10.00	—

C# 8-1.3   CASH

Cast Brass **Ruler:** Kuang-hsü **Obv. Insc.:** Kuang-hsü T'ung-pao **Rev:** 2 dots below, Manchu inscription **Rev. Insc.:** Boo-jiyen

Date	Mintage	Good	VG	F	VF	XF
ND(1875-1908)	—	3.50	5.50	9.00	15.00	—

C# 8-1.4   CASH

Cast Brass **Ruler:** Kuang-hsü **Obv. Insc.:** Kuang-hsü T'ung-pao **Rev:** Circle above Manchu inscription **Rev. Insc.:** Boo-jiyen

Date	Mintage	Good	VG	F	VF	XF
ND(1875-1908)	—	3.50	5.50	9.00	18.00	—

C# 8-1.5   CASH

Cast Brass **Ruler:** Kuang-hsü **Obv. Insc.:** Kuang-hsü T'ung-pao **Rev:** Circle below Manchu inscription **Rev. Insc.:** Boo-jiyen

Date	Mintage	Good	VG	F	VF	XF
ND(1875-1908)	—	3.50	5.50	9.00	18.00	—

C# 8-1.6   CASH

Cast Brass **Ruler:** Kuang-hsü **Obv. Insc.:** Kuang-hsü T'ung-pao **Rev:** Crescent above Manchu inscription **Rev. Insc.:** Boo-jiyen

Date	Mintage	Good	VG	F	VF	XF
ND(1875-1908)	—	3.50	5.50	9.00	18.00	—

C# 8-1.7   CASH

Cast Brass **Ruler:** Kuang-hsü **Obv. Insc.:** Kuang-hsü T'ung-pao **Rev:** Crescent below Manchu inscription **Rev. Insc.:** Boo-jiyen

Date	Mintage	Good	VG	F	VF	XF
ND(1875-1908)	—	2.00	3.75	7.50	17.00	—

C# 8-1.8   CASH

Cast Brass **Ruler:** Kuang-hsü **Obv. Insc.:** Kuang-hsü T'ung-pao **Rev:** Dash below Manchu inscription **Rev. Insc.:** Boo-jiyen

Date	Mintage	Good	VG	F	VF	XF
ND(1875-1908)	—	2.00	3.75	7.50	15.00	—

Note: Varieties exist with dots and crescents in different corners on reverse and also with incuse dots.

MILLED COINAGE

Y# 66   CASH

Brass **Ruler:** Kuang-hsü **Obv. Insc.:** Kuang-hsü T'ung-pao **Note:** Struck at Chin Mint, Tientsin.

Date	Mintage	Good	VG	F	VF	XF
ND(1904-07)	—	1.50	4.00	6.00	12.00	25.00

Y# 7c   CASH

Brass **Ruler:** Kuang-hsü **Obv. Leg.:** Kuang-hsü **Rev:** Dragon **Note:** Struck at Chin Mint(Peiyang Arsenal), Tientsin.

Date	Mintage	Good	VG	F	VF	XF
CD1908	—	1.00	2.50	4.50	7.50	13.50

Y# 8c   2 CASH

Copper **Ruler:** Kuang-hsü **Note:** Struck at Chin Mint(Peiyang Arsenal), Tientsin.

Date	Mintage	VG	F	VF	XF	Unc
CD1906 Rare	—					

Y# 9c   5 CASH

Copper **Ruler:** Kuang-hsü **Obv. Insc.:** Tai-ch'ing T'ung-pi **Rev:** Kuang-hsü Nien-tsao, TAI-CHING-TI-KUO ... **Note:** Struck at Chin Mint (Peiyang Arsenal), Tientsin.

Date	Mintage	Good	VG	F	VF	XF
CD1906	—	4.00	10.00	20.00	35.00	48.00

Y# 67   10 CASH

Copper **Ruler:** Kuang-hsü **Obv. Insc.:** Kuang-hsü Yüan-pao **Rev:** Side-view square-mouth dragon, hole in center of rosette **Rev. Leg.:** PEI YANG **Note:** Struck at Chin Mint(Peiyang Arsenal), Tientsin.

Date	Mintage	Good	VG	F	VF	XF
ND(c.1906)	—	0.40	1.00	2.00	2.50	4.00

Note: Mulings exist with obverse of Kwangtung (Guangdong) Y#192 and reverse of Chihli Y#67; Refer to Kwangtung listings

Y# 67.1   10 CASH

Copper **Ruler:** Kuang-hsü **Obv. Insc.:** Kuang-hsü Yüan-pao **Rev:** Dragon with round mouth **Note:** Struck at Chin Mint (Peiyang Arsenal), Tientsin.

Date	Mintage	Good	VG	F	VF	XF
ND(c.1906)	—	0.40	1.00	2.00	2.50	4.00

Y# 67.2   10 CASH

Copper **Ruler:** Kuang-hsü **Obv. Insc.:** Kuang-hsü Yüan-pao **Rev:** Dot in center of rosettes, dragon with square mouth **Note:** Struck at Chin Mint (Peiyang Arsenal), Tientsin.

Date	Mintage	Good	VG	F	VF	XF
ND(c.1906)	—	0.40	1.00	2.00	2.50	4.00

Y# 67.3   10 CASH
Copper **Ruler:** Kuang-hsü **Obv. Insc.:** Kuang-hsü Yüan-pao
Rev: Dot in center of rosettes, dragon with round mouth
Note: Struck at Chin Mint (Peiyang Arsenal), Tientsin.

Date	Mintage	Good	VG	F	VF	XF
ND(c.1906)	—	0.40	1.00	2.00	2.50	4.00

Y# 67.4   10 CASH
Copper **Ruler:** Kuang-hsü **Obv. Insc.:** Kuang-hsü Yüan-pao
Rev: Redesigned dragon with smaller body and smaller English
legends **Note:** Struck at Chin Mint (Peiyang Arsenal), Tientsin.

Date	Mintage	Good	VG	F	VF	XF
ND(c.1906)	—	0.60	1.50	3.50	7.00	15.00

Y# 10c   10 CASH
Copper **Ruler:** Kuang-hsü **Obv. Insc.:** Tai-ch'ing T'ung-pi
Rev. Leg.: Kuang-hsü Nien-tsao, TAI-CHING-TI-KUO ...
Note: Struck at Chin Mint (Peiyang Arsenal), Tientsin.

Date	Mintage	Good	VG	F	VF	XF
CD1906	—	0.40	1.00	2.00	3.00	5.00

Y# 68   20 CASH
Copper **Ruler:** Kuang-hsü **Note:** Struck at Chin Mint (Peiyang
Arsenal), Tientsin.

Date	Mintage	Good	VG	F	VF	XF
ND(c. 1906)	—	10.00	20.00	30.00	40.00	100

Y# 68a   20 CASH
Brass **Ruler:** Kuang-hsü **Obv. Insc.:** Kuang-hsü Yüan-pao
Rev: Side view dragon **Rev. Leg.:** PEI YANG **Note:** Struck at
Chin Mint (Peiyang Arsenal), Tientsin.

Date	Mintage	VG	F	VF	XF	Unc
ND(c.1906) Rare	—	—	—	—	—	—

Y# 68.1   20 CASH
Copper **Ruler:** Kuang-hsü **Obv. Insc.:** Kuang-hsü Yüan-pao
Rev: Smaller lettering **Note:** Struck at Chin Mint (Peiyang
Arsenal), Tientsin.

Date	Mintage	VG	F	VF	XF	Unc
ND(c.1906)	—	25.00	35.00	50.00	120	—

Y# 11c   20 CASH
Copper **Ruler:** Kuang-hsü **Obv. Insc.:** Tai-ch'ing T'ung-pi
Rev. Leg.: Kuang-hsü Nien-tsao, TAI-CHING-TI-KUO ...
Note: Struck at Chin Mint (Peiyang Arsenal), Tientsin.

Date	Mintage	VG	F	VF	XF	Unc
CD1906	—	15.00	30.00	60.00	120	—

Y# 71a   20 CENTS
5.3000 g., 0.8200 Silver 0.1397 oz. ASW **Ruler:** Kuang-hsü
Obv. Insc.: Kuang-hsü Yüan-pao **Rev:** Side view dragon, legend
at bottom **Rev. Leg.:** PEI YANG **Note:** Struck at Chin Mint
(Peiyang Arsenal), Tientsin.

Date	Mintage	VG	F	VF	XF	Unc
31(1905)	161,000	40.00	75.00	150	250	600

Y# 73   DOLLAR
26.7000 g., 0.9000 Silver 0.7726 oz. ASW **Ruler:** Kuang-hsü
Obv. Insc.: Kuang-hsü Yüan-pao **Rev:** Side view dragon, legend
at bottom **Rev. Leg.:** PEI YANG

Date	Mintage	VG	F	VF	XF	Unc
25(1899)	1,566,000	17.00	35.00	50.00	125	1,200
26(1900)	—	20.00	40.00	80.00	175	1,500
29(1903)	22,018,000	20.00	30.00	45.00	100	900

Y# 73.1   DOLLAR
26.7000 g., 0.9000 Silver 0.7726 oz. ASW **Ruler:** Kuang-hsü
Obv. Insc.: Kuang-hsü Yüan-pao **Rev:** Side view dragon, legend
at bottom, period after legend **Rev. Leg.:** PEI YANG **Note:** Struck
at Chin Mint (Peiyang Arsenal), Tientsin.

Date	Mintage	VG	F	VF	XF	Unc
29(1903)	Inc. above	20.00	30.00	45.00	100	900

Y# 73.2   DOLLAR
26.7000 g., 0.9000 Silver 0.7726 oz. ASW **Ruler:** Kuang-hsü
Obv. Insc.: Kuang-hsü Yüan-pao **Rev:** Thinner side-view
dragon, legend at bottom, year as "33rd" **Rev. Leg.:** PEI YANG
Note: Struck at Chin Mint (Peiyang Arsenal), Tientsin.

Date	Mintage	VG	F	VF	XF	Unc
33(1907)	2,341,000	20.00	358	60.00	120	1,100
34(1908)	—	15.00	25.00	35.00	60.00	500

Y# 73.3   DOLLAR
26.7000 g., 0.9000 Silver 0.7726 oz. ASW **Ruler:** Kuang-hsü
Obv. Insc.: Kuang-hsü Yüan-pao **Rev:** Side view dragon, legend
at bottom, short center spine to tail **Rev. Leg.:** PEI YANG
Note: Struck at Chin Mint (Peiyang Arsenal), Tientsin. Restruck
during Republican times.

Date	Mintage	VG	F	VF	XF	Unc
34(1908)	—	15.00	25.00	35.00	60.00	500

Y# 73.4   DOLLAR
26.7000 g., 0.9000 Silver 0.7726 oz. ASW **Ruler:** Kuang-hsü
Obv. Insc.: Kuang-hsü Yüan-pao **Rev:** Side view dragon, legend
at bottom, crosslet 4 in date **Rev. Leg.:** PEI YANG **Note:** Struck
at Chin Mint (Peiyang Arsenal), Tientsin. Restruck during
Republican times.

Date	Mintage	VG	F	VF	XF	Unc
34(1908)	—	30.00	50.00	125	250	1,500

Y# 74   TAEL
51.2000 g., Silver **Ruler:** Kuang-hsü **Obv. Insc.:** Kuang-hsü
Yüan-pao **Rev:** Side view dragon, legend at bottom **Rev. Leg.:**
PEI YANG **Note:** Struck at Chin Mint (Peiyang Arsenal), Tientsin.

Date	Mintage	VG	F	VF	XF	Unc
33(1907)	—	—	15,000	25,000	50,000	

Y# 74.1   TAEL
51.2000 g., Silver **Ruler:** Kuang-hsü **Obv. Insc.:** Kuang-hsü
Yüan-pao **Rev:** Side view dragon, legend at bottom, 3 dots on
pearl arranged horizontally **Rev. Leg.:** PEI YANG **Note:** Struck
at Chin Mint (Peiyang Arsenal), Tientsin.

Date	Mintage	VG	F	VF	XF	Unc
33(1907)	—	—	15,000	25,000	50,000	

Y# 74.2   TAEL
51.2000 g., Silver **Ruler:** Kuang-hsü **Obv. Insc.:** Kuang-hsü
Yüan-pao **Rev:** Side view dragon, legend at bottom, 3 dots on
pearl arranged in arc **Rev. Leg.:** PEI YANG **Note:** Struck at Chin
Mint (Peiyang Arsenal), Tientsin.

Date	Mintage	VG	F	VF	XF	Unc
33(1907)	—	—	10,000	22,000	45,000	

PATTERNS
Including off metal strikes

KM#	Date	Mintage	Identification	Mkt Val
Pn6	29(1903)	—	Dollar. Brass. Y73.	—
Pn7	33(1907)	—	Tael. Gold. Y74.	—

FENGTIEN PROVINCE

(Fungtien)
Liaoning

The southernmost province of the Three Eastern Provinces was known by a variety of names including Fengtien, Shengching, and Liaoning. The modern Mukden (Fengtien Province) Mint operated from 1897 to 1931.

EMPIRE

PROVINCIAL CAST COINAGE

C# 9-1 CASH
Cast Brass **Ruler:** Kuang-hsü **Obv:** Type A **Obv. Insc.:** Kuang-hsü T'ung-pao **Rev:** Manchu inscription **Rev. Insc.:** Boo-fung

Date	Mintage	Good	VG	F	VF	XF
ND(1875-1908)	—	20.00	30.00	40.00	60.00	80.00

MILLED COINAGE

Y# 19e 5 CASH
Copper **Ruler:** Hsüan-t'ung **Obv. Insc.:** Tai-ching T'ung-pi **Rev. Leg.:** Hsüan-t'ung Nien-tsao, TAI-CHING-TI-KUO ...

Date	Mintage	VG	F	VF	XF	Unc
CD1909	—	37.50	75.00	125	200	—

Y# 88 10 CASH
Brass **Ruler:** Kuang-hsü **Obv. Insc.:** Kuang-hsü Yüan-pao **Rev:** Province name spelled "FEN-TIEN"

Date	Mintage	VG	F	VF	XF	Unc
CD1903	—	50.00	90.00	135	225	—

Y# 89 10 CASH
Brass **Ruler:** Kuang-hsü **Obv. Insc.:** Kuang-hsü Yüan-pao **Rev. Leg.:** FUNG-TIEN PROVINCE

Date	Mintage	VG	F	VF	XF	Unc
CD1903	—	3.75	7.50	25.00	40.00	—
CD1904	—	1.25	3.00	5.00	8.00	—
CD1905	—	1.50	4.50	10.00	12.00	—
CD1906	35,036,000	3.00	6.00	25.00	35.00	—

Y# 89.1 10 CASH
Brass **Ruler:** Kuang-hsü **Obv:** Manchu words in center reversed **Obv. Insc.:** Kuang-hsü Yüan-pao **Rev. Leg.:** FUNG-TIEN PROVINCE

Date	Mintage	VG	F	VF	XF	Unc
CD1903	—	28.00	85.00	150	250	—

Y# 89.2 10 CASH
Brass **Ruler:** Kuang-hsü **Obv. Insc.:** Kuang-hsü Yüan-pao **Rev:** Large pearl **Rev. Leg.:** FUNG-TIEN PROVINCE

Date	Mintage	VG	F	VF	XF	Unc
CD1905	—	1.25	4.00	8.00	15.00	—

Y# 10e 10 CASH
Copper **Ruler:** Kuang-hsü **Obv. Insc.:** Tai-ch'ing T'ung-pi **Rev:** Dragon, small pearl **Rev. Leg.:** Kuang-hsü Nien-tsao, TAI-CHING TI KUO ...

Date	Mintage	VG	F	VF	XF	Unc
CD1905	—	1.25	4.00	8.00	15.00	—

Y# 10e.1 10 CASH
Copper **Ruler:** Kuang-hsü **Obv. Insc.:** Tai-ch'ing T'ung-pi **Rev:** Large pearl **Rev. Leg.:** Kuang-hsü Nien-tsao, TAI-CHING-TI-KUO...

Date	Mintage	VG	F	VF	XF	Unc
CD1905	—	1.25	4.00	8.00	15.00	—

Y# 10e.2 10 CASH
Copper **Ruler:** Kuang-hsü **Obv:** Mint mark on spherical disc in center **Obv. Insc.:** Tai-ch'ing T'ung-pi **Rev:** Large pearl **Rev. Leg.:** Kuang-hsü Nien-tsao, TAI-CHING-TI-KUO ...

Date	Mintage	VG	F	VF	XF	Unc
CD1907	130,000	1.00	3.00	6.00	20.00	—

Y# 10e.3 10 CASH
Copper **Ruler:** Kuang-hsü **Obv:** Mint mark on flat disc in center **Obv. Insc.:** Tai-ch'ing T'ung-pi **Rev. Leg.:** Kuang-hsü Nien-tsao, TAI CHING TI KUO ...

Date	Mintage	VG	F	VF	XF	Unc
CD1907	Inc. above	0.50	1.50	3.00	6.00	—

Y# 20e 10 CASH
Copper **Ruler:** Hsüan-t'ung **Obv:** Mint mark on flat disc in center **Obv. Insc.:** Tai-ch'ing T'ung-pi **Rev. Leg.:** Hsüan-T'ung Nien-tsao, TAI-CHING-TI-KUO ...

Date	Mintage	VG	F	VF	XF	Unc
CD1909	—	2.75	8.00	17.50	30.00	—

Y# 20e.1 10 CASH
Copper **Ruler:** Kuang-hsü **Obv. Insc.:** Tai-ch'ing T'ung-pi **Rev. Leg.:** Kuang-hsü Nien-tsao, TAI CHING TI KUO ... **Note:** Mule, obverse Y#20e, reverse Y#10e. Prev. #W286.

Date	Mintage	VG	F	VF	XF	Unc
CD1909 6 known	—	—	—	—	—	—

Y# 90 20 CASH
Brass **Ruler:** Kuang-hsü **Obv. Leg.:** Feng-tien Sheng Tsao **Obv. Insc.:** Kuang-hsü Yüan-pao **Rev. Leg.:** FUNG TIEN PROVINCE

Date	Mintage	VG	F	VF	XF	Unc
CD1903	—	75.00	100	125	175	—
CD1904	—	5.50	11.00	22.50	55.00	—
CD1905	—	9.00	18.00	25.00	60.00	—

Y# 11e 20 CASH
Brass **Ruler:** Kuang-hsü **Obv. Insc.:** Tai-ching T'ung-pi **Rev. Leg.:** Kuang-hsü Nien-tsao, TAI-CHING-TI-KUO ...

Date	Mintage	VG	F	VF	XF	Unc
CD1905	—	4.00	7.00	20.00	40.00	—
CD1907	—	6.00	12.00	25.00	50.00	—

Y# 11g 20 CASH
Copper **Ruler:** Kuang-hsü **Obv:** Inscription with Hu at right, Pu at left **Obv. Insc.:** Tai-ch'ing T'ung-pi **Rev:** Dragon **Rev. Leg.:** Kuang-hsü Nien-tsao, TAI-CHING-TI-KUO...

Date	Mintage	VG	F	VF	XF	Unc
CD1905	—	—	—	—	—	—

Y# 11f 20 CASH
Copper **Ruler:** Kuang-hsü **Obv:** Inscription with "CD" at left and right **Obv. Insc.:** Tai-ch'ing T'ung-pi **Rev. Leg.:** Kuang-hsü Nien-tsao, TAI-CHING-TI-KUO...

Date	Mintage	VG	F	VF	XF	Unc
CD1907	—	—	—	—	—	—

Y# 21e 20 CASH
Brass **Ruler:** Hsüan-t'ung **Obv. Insc.:** Tai-ching T'ung-pi **Rev. Leg.:** Hsüan-t'ung Nien-tsao, TAI-CHING-TI-KUO ...

Date	Mintage	VG	F	VF	XF	Unc
CD1909	—	25.00	60.00	110	175	—

Y# 91 20 CENTS
Silver, 24 mm. **Ruler:** Kuang-hsü **Obv. Leg.:** Feng-tien Sheng Tsao **Obv. Insc.:** Kuang-hsü Yüan-pao **Rev:** Side view dragon, 8 rows of scales on dragon **Rev. Leg.:** FUNG-TIEN PROVINCE

Date	Mintage	VG	F	VF	XF	Unc
CD1904	—	4.00	9.00	15.00	30.00	70.00

Y# 91.1 20 CENTS
Silver **Ruler:** Kuang-hsü **Obv. Leg.:** Feng-tien Sheng Tsao
Obv. Insc.: Kuang-hsü Yüan-pao **Rev:** Side view dragon, 5 rows
of scales on dragon **Rev. Leg.:** FUNG-TIEN PROVINCE

Date	Mintage	VG	F	VF	XF	Unc
CD1904	—	5.00	10.00	18.00	35.00	80.00

Y# 92 DOLLAR
26.4000 g., 0.8500 Silver 0.7214 oz. ASW **Ruler:** Kuang-hsü
Obv. Leg.: Feng-tien Sheng Tsao **Obv. Insc.:** Kuang-hsü Yüan-
pao **Rev:** Side view dragon **Rev. Leg.:** FUNG-TIEN PROVINCE

Date	Mintage	VG	F	VF	XF	Unc
CD1903	262,000	100	200	450	1,000	4,000

Y# 92.1 DOLLAR
26.4000 g., 0.8500 Silver 0.7214 oz. ASW **Ruler:** Kuang-hsü
Obv: Manchu "Boo-funs" in center are reversed **Obv. Leg.:** Feng-
tien Sheng Tsao **Obv. Insc.:** Kuang-hsü Yüan-pao **Rev:** Side
view dragon **Rev. Leg.:** FUNG-TIEN PROVINCE

Date	Mintage	VG	F	VF	XF	Unc
CD1903	Inc. above	100	250	500	1,200	4,000

TOKEN COINAGE

KM# TnA1 10 CENTS
Copper **Ruler:** Kuang-hsü **Obv:** Dragon **Rev:** Tang-shih (10)

Date	Mintage	VG	F	VF	XF	Unc
ND(c.1904)	—	—	—	900	1,500	2,500

KM# Tn1 DOLLAR
Copper **Ruler:** Kuang-hsü **Obv:** Reverse of 10 Cash, Y#10e,
small spiral on pearl **Rev. Insc.:** Tang-yüan(1 Dollar)
Note: Woodward #242.

Date	Mintage	VG	F	VF	XF	Unc
ND(c.1904)	—	—	—	550	900	1,500

KM# Tn1a DOLLAR
Brass **Ruler:** Kuang-hsü **Obv:** Reverse of 10 Cash, Y#10e,
small spiral on pearl **Rev. Insc.:** Tang-yüan(1 Dollar)

Date	Mintage	VG	F	VF	XF	Unc
ND(c.1904)	—	—	—	550	900	1,500

KM# Tn2 100 CENTS
Copper **Ruler:** Kuang-hsü **Obv:** Dragon, large spiral on pearl
Obv. Leg.: FUNG TIEN PROVINCE **Rev. Insc.:** Tang Pai
Note: Silver forgeries exist. Woodward #243.

Date	Mintage	VG	F	VF	XF	Unc
ND(c.1904)	—	—	—	550	900	1,500

KM# Tn3 100 CENTS
Brass **Ruler:** Kuang-hsü **Obv. Leg.:** FUNG-TIEN PROVINCE
Rev. Insc.: Tang Pai **Note:** Silver forgeries exist.

Date	Mintage	VG	F	VF	XF	Unc
ND(c.1904)	—	—	—	—	—	—

PATTERNS
Including off metal strikes

KM#	Date	Mintage	Identification	Mkt Val
Pn2A	ND(c.1902)	—	10 Cents. Brass. Regular provincial design.	—
Pn3	ND(c.1902)	—	20 Cents. Brass. Regular provincial design.	—
Pn4	ND(c.1902)	—	20 Cents. Brass. Error, TENG-TIEN.	—
Pn5	ND(c.1902)	—	20 Cents. Silver. FENG-TIEN.	—
Pn6	ND(c.1902)	—	50 Cents. Brass. Error, TENG-TIEN.	—
Pn7	ND(c.1902)	—	Dollar. Aluminum. Error, TENG-TIEN.	55,000
Pn8	ND(c.1902)	—	Dollar. Silver. Error, TENG-TIEN.	—
Pn9	ND(c.1902)	—	Dollar. Brass. Error, TENG-TIEN.	—
Pn10	ND(c.1902)	—	10 Cash. Copper.	—
Pn11	CD1903	—	10 Cash. Copper. Y88.	—
Pn12	CD1903	—	10 Cash. Copper. Y89.	—
Pn13	CD1903	—	10 Cash. Copper. Y89.1.	—
Pn14	CD1903	—	20 Cash. Copper. Y90.	—
PnA15	CD1903	—	Tael. Silver. K931-l.	—
	Note: Superior Goodman sale 6-91 about XF realized $187,000.			
Pn15	CD1904	—	10 Cash. Copper. Y89.	—
Pn16	CD1905	—	10 Cash. Copper. Y89.	—
Pn17	CD1905	—	20 Cash. Copper. Y90.	—

FUKIEN PROVINCE
Fujian

A province located on the southeastern coast of China, including the island of Taiwan until it became its own separate province in
1885. Although known mainly as an agricultural area, forestry and
some mining, particularly iron ore and coal, are also important to the
economy. The Foochow Mint operated throughout the Manchu
dynasty. The Viceroy's or City mint was opened in 1896 for struck
coinage. Two other mints were established in 1905, the Mamoi Arsenal Mint which struck the Custom-House issues until it closed in
1906, and the West Mint which later became the main Fukien
(Fujian) Mint. It closed between 1914 and 1920. Various subsidiary
mints were in operation from 1924 to 1925.

EMPIRE
MILLED COINAGE

Y# 95 CASH
Brass **Ruler:** Kuang-hsü **Obv. Insc.:** Kuang hsü T'ung-pao
Rev. Insc.: Manchu Boo-fu

Date	Mintage	VG	F	VF	XF	Unc
ND(1908)	—	6.00	10.00	15.00	30.00	100

Y# 7f CASH
Brass **Ruler:** Kuang-hsü **Obv. Insc.:** Kuang hsü **Rev:** Dragon

Date	Mintage	VG	F	VF	XF	Unc
CD1908	—	35.00	75.00	110	175	—

Y# 106 CASH
Brass **Ruler:** Hsüan-T'ung **Obv. Insc.:** Hsüan-t'ung T'ung-pao
Rev: Manchu inscription **Rev. Insc.:** Manchu Boo-fu

Date	Mintage	VG	F	VF	XF	Unc
ND(1909)	—	15.00	25.00	50.00	80.00	300

Y# 8f 2 CASH
Brass **Obv. Insc.:** Tai-ching T'ung-pi **Rev:** Dragon

Date	Mintage	VG	F	VF	XF	Unc
CD1906	—	3.00	8.00	14.00	25.00	—

Y# 99 5 CASH
Copper **Ruler:** Kuang-hsü **Obv. Leg.:** Fu-kien Kuan Chü Tsao
Obv. Insc.: Kuang-hsü Yüan-pao **Rev:** Dragon **Rev. Leg.:** FOO-
KIEN

Date	Mintage	VG	F	VF	XF	Unc
ND(1901-03)	590,000	18.00	25.00	37.50	60.00	—

Y# 99a 5 CASH
Brass **Ruler:** Kuang-hsü **Obv. Leg.:** Fu-kien Kuan Chü Tsao
Obv. Insc.: Kuang-hsü Yüan-pao **Rev:** Dragon **Rev. Leg.:** FOO-
KIEN

Date	Mintage	VG	F	VF	XF	Unc
ND(1901-03)	—	12.00	25.00	50.00	75.00	—

Y# 97 10 CASH
Copper **Ruler:** Kuang-hsü **Obv:** Large characters at left and
right **Obv. Leg.:** Fu-kien Kuan Chü Tsao **Obv. Insc.:** Kuang-hsü
Yüan-pao **Rev:** Dragon **Rev. Leg.:** F.K. CUSTOM-HOUSE

Date	Mintage	VG	F	VF	XF	Unc
ND(1901-05)	417,031,000	0.50	2.00	4.00	10.00	65.00

Y# 97.1 10 CASH
Copper **Ruler:** Kuang-hsü **Obv:** Small characters at left and
right sides **Obv. Leg.:** Fu-kien Kuan Chü Tsao
Obv. Insc.: Kuang-hsü Yüan-pao **Rev:** Dragon **Rev. Leg.:** F.K.
CUSTOM-HOUSE

Date	Mintage	VG	F	VF	XF	Unc
ND(1901-05)	Inc. above	0.65	2.00	4.00	10.00	65.00

Y# 98 10 CASH
Copper **Ruler:** Kuang-hsü **Obv. Leg.:** Fu-kien Kuan Chü Tsao
Obv. Insc.: Kuang-hsü Yüan-pao **Rev:** Dragon **Rev. Leg.:** FOO-
KIEN CUSTOM

Date	Mintage	VG	F	VF	XF	Unc
ND(1901-05)	Inc. above	35.00	100	150	250	—

Y# 100 10 CASH
Copper **Ruler:** Kuang-hsü **Obv. Leg.:** Fu-kien Kuan Chü Tsao
Obv. Insc.: Kuang-hsü Yüan-pao **Rev:** 1 cloud left of pearl,
dragon **Rev. Leg.:** FOO-KIEN

Date	Mintage	VG	F	VF	XF	Unc
ND(1901-05)	Inc. above	1.00	3.00	6.00	9.00	65.00

Y# 100.1   10 CASH
Copper **Ruler:** Kuang-hsü **Obv. Leg.:** Fu-kien Kuan Chü Tsao **Obv. Insc.:** Kuang-hsü Yüan-pao **Rev:** 3 clouds left of pearl and without cloud above tip of dragon's tail, dragon **Rev. Leg.:** FOO-KIEN

Date	Mintage	VG	F	VF	XF	Unc
ND(1901-05)	Inc. above	0.65	2.00	4.00	7.00	65.00

Y# 100.2   10 CASH
Copper **Ruler:** Kuang-hsü **Obv. Leg.:** Fu-kien Kuan Chü Tsao **Obv. Insc.:** Kuang-hsü Yüan-pao **Rev:** 3 clouds left of pearl and a cloud above tip of dragon's tail, dragon **Rev. Leg.:** FOO-KIEN

Date	Mintage	VG	F	VF	XF	Unc
ND(1901-05)	Inc. above	0.35	1.00	2.00	4.00	65.00

Y# 100.3   10 CASH
Copper **Ruler:** Kuang-hsü **Obv. Leg.:** Fu-kien Kuan Chü Tsao **Obv. Insc.:** Kuang-hsü Yüan-pao **Rev:** Dragon, denomination: 10 CASHES **Rev. Leg.:** FOO-KIEN

Date	Mintage	VG	F	VF	XF	Unc
ND(1901-05)	Inc. above	4.00	12.00	20.00	45.00	—

Y# 100.2a   10 CASH
Brass **Ruler:** Kuang-hsü **Obv. Leg.:** Fu-kien Kuan Chü Tsao **Obv. Insc.:** Kuang-hsü Yüan-pao **Rev:** Dragon **Rev. Leg.:** FOO-KIEN

Date	Mintage	VG	F	VF	XF	Unc
ND(1901-05)	Inc. above	—	—	—	—	—

Y# 10f   10 CASH
Copper **Ruler:** Kuang-hsü **Obv. Insc.:** Tai-ch'ing T'ung-pi **Rev:** Dragon, inscription, denomination 10 CASHES **Rev. Leg.:** Kuang-hsü Nien-tsao, TAI-CHING-TI-KUO ...

Date	Mintage	VG	F	VF	XF	Unc
CD1906	—	0.25	0.75	1.50	3.00	20.00

Y# 20f   10 CASH
Copper **Ruler:** Hsüan-T'ung **Obv. Insc.:** Tai-ch'ing T'ung-pi **Rev:** Dragon **Rev. Leg.:** Hsüan-tung Nien-tsao, TAI-CHING-TI-KUO ...

Date	Mintage	VG	F	VF	XF	Unc
CD1909	—	16.50	50.00	85.00	125	—

Y# 101   20 CASH
Copper **Ruler:** Kuang-hsü **Obv. Leg.:** Fu-kien Kuan Chü Tsao **Obv. Insc.:** Kuang-hsü Yüan-pao **Rev:** Dragon **Rev. Leg.:** FOO-KIEN

Date	Mintage	VG	F	VF	XF	Unc
ND(1901-02)	18,000	12.00	30.00	45.00	75.00	—

Y# 101.1   20 CASH
Copper **Ruler:** Kuang-hsü **Obv. Leg.:** Fu-kien Kuan Chü Tsao **Obv. Insc.:** Kuang-hsü Yüan-pao **Rev:** Dragon **Rev. Leg.:** FOO-KIEN

Date	Mintage	VG	F	VF	XF	Unc
ND(1901-02)	Inc. above	25.00	60.00	90.00	150	—

Y# 102.1   5 CENTS
1.3500 g., 0.8200 Silver 0.0356 oz. ASW **Ruler:** Kuang-hsü **Obv:** Legend with four characters at top **Obv. Leg.:** Fu-kien Kuan Chü Tsao **Obv. Insc.:** Kuang-hsü Yüan-pao **Rev:** Rosette at either side of side view dragon right

Date	Mintage	VG	F	VF	XF	Unc
ND(1903-08)	—	3.00	6.00	10.00	20.00	40.00

Y# 102.2   5 CENTS
1.3500 g., 0.8200 Silver 0.0356 oz. ASW **Ruler:** Kuang-hsü **Obv. Leg.:** Fu-kien Kuan Chü Tsao **Obv. Insc.:** Kuang-hsü Yüan-pao **Rev:** Rosette above dragon's head

Date	Mintage	VG	F	VF	XF	Unc
ND(1903-08)	—	3.50	6.50	12.50	25.00	50.00

Y# 102.3   5 CENTS
1.3500 g., 0.8200 Silver 0.0356 oz. ASW **Ruler:** Kuang-hsü **Obv. Leg.:** Fu-kien Kuan Chü Tsao **Obv. Insc.:** Kuang-hsü Yüan-pao **Rev. Leg.:** PROVINCE FOO-KIEN

Date	Mintage	VG	F	VF	XF	Unc
ND(1903-08)	—	—	—	—	—	—

Y# 103.2   10 CENTS
2.7000 g., 0.8200 Silver 0.0712 oz. ASW **Ruler:** Kuang-hsü **Obv:** Legend has 4 characters at top **Obv. Leg.:** Fu-kien Kuan Chü Tsao **Obv. Insc.:** Kuang-hsü Yüan-pao **Rev:** Small side view dragon right

Date	Mintage	VG	F	VF	XF	Unc
ND(1903-08)	Inc. above	1.50	3.00	6.00	12.00	30.00

Y# 103.3   10 CENTS
2.7000 g., 0.8200 Silver 0.0712 oz. ASW **Ruler:** Kuang-hsü **Obv:** Legend has 4 characters at top **Obv. Leg.:** Fu-kien Kuan Chü Tsao **Obv. Insc.:** Kuang-hsü Yüan-pao **Rev:** Large side view dragon right

Date	Mintage	VG	F	VF	XF	Unc
ND(1903-08)	Inc. above	2.50	6.00	12.00	24.00	50.00

Y# 104.2   20 CENTS
5.4000 g., 0.8200 Silver 0.1424 oz. ASW **Ruler:** Kuang-hsü **Obv:** Legend has 4 characters at top **Obv. Leg.:** Fu-kien Kuan Chü Tsao **Obv. Insc.:** Kuang-hsü Yüan-pao **Rev:** Side view dragon right **Note:** Variety with large side view dragon right on reverse exists.

Date	Mintage	VG	F	VF	XF	Unc
ND(1903-08)	Inc. above	2.25	4.50	7.00	12.50	30.00

REPUBLIC

PROVINCIAL CAST COINAGE

Y# 374   CASH
Cast Brass **Obv. Insc.:** Fu-chien T'ung-pao **Rev:** 6 stripes on right flag

Date	Mintage	VG	F	VF	XF	Unc
ND(c.1912)	—	50.00	80.00	125	165	—

Y# 375   2 CASH
Cast Brass **Obv. Insc.:** Fu-chien T'ung-pao **Rev:** 5 stripes on right flag

Date	Mintage	VG	F	VF	XF	Unc
ND(c.1912)	—	12.50	17.50	22.50	30.00	—

Y# 375.1   2 CASH
Cast Brass **Obv. Insc.:** Fu-chien T'ung-pao **Rev:** 6 stripes on right flag

Date	Mintage	VG	F	VF	XF	Unc
ND(c.1912)	—	30.00	50.00	80.00	125	—

MILLED COINAGE

Y# 379   10 CASH
Copper **Obv. Leg.:** Fu-Kien Túng Pien Tsang Tsao **Obv. Insc.:** Chung-hua Yüan-pao **Rev. Leg.:** FOO-KIEN COPPER COIN

Date	Mintage	VG	F	VF	XF	Unc
ND(c.1912)	—	1.25	4.00	8.00	15.00	35.00

Y# 379a   10 CASH
Brass **Obv. Leg.:** Fu-Kien Túng Pien Tsang Tsao **Obv. Insc.:** Chung-hua Yüan-pao **Rev. Leg.:** FOO-KIEN COPPER COIN

Date	Mintage	VG	F	VF	XF	Unc
ND(c.1912)	—	18.50	37.50	50.00	87.50	125

Y# 380   10 CENTS
2.6000 g., Silver **Obv. Insc.:** Chung-hua Yüan-pao

Date	Mintage	VG	F	VF	XF	Unc
ND(c.1912)	—	25.00	40.00	100	200	350

Y# 382   10 CENTS
2.6000 g., Silver **Obv. Insc.:** Chung-hua Yüan-pao

Date	Mintage	VG	F	VF	XF	Unc
ND(c.1913)	—	1.25	2.50	5.00	9.00	20.00

Y# 380a   10 CENTS
2.6000 g., Silver **Obv:** Different legend in center
Obv. Insc.: Chung-hua Yüan-pao **Note:** Similar to Y#380.

Date	Mintage	VG	F	VF	XF	Unc
CD1924	—	25.00	50.00	120	200	300

Y# 388   10 CENTS
2.6000 g., Silver, 18 mm. **Subject:** Canton martyrs

Date	Mintage	VG	F	VF	XF	Unc
17(1928)	—	4.00	10.00	15.00	30.00	50.00
20(1931)	—	5.00	12.00	25.00	50.00	75.00

Y# 390   10 CENTS
2.6000 g., Silver, 18 mm. **Subject:** Canton martyrs

Date	Mintage	VG	F	VF	XF	Unc
Yr. 21(1932)	—	40.00	100	150	200	400

Y# 377   20 CENTS
5.0000 g., Silver **Obv. Insc.:** Chung-hua Yüan-pao

Date	Mintage	VG	F	VF	XF	Unc
CD1911	—	4.00	10.00	20.00	35.00	100

Y# A381   20 CENTS
5.4000 g., Silver **Obv. Insc.:** Chung-hua Yüan-pao

Date	Mintage	VG	F	VF	XF	Unc
ND(1912)	—	2.25	4.50	8.00	15.00	25.00

Y# 383   20 CENTS
5.2000 g., Silver

Date	Mintage	VG	F	VF	XF	Unc
ND(1923)	—	2.00	3.50	6.00	10.00	20.00

Note: Kann dates this coin 1913, but evidence suggests that it was struck in 1923

Y# 381   20 CENTS
5.3000 g., Silver **Obv:** Rosettes at sides, dot in middle of rosette center **Rev:** Rosettes at sides

Date	Mintage	VG	F	VF	XF	Unc
CD1923	—	2.25	4.00	7.50	12.00	28.00

Y# 381.1   20 CENTS
5.3000 g., Silver **Rev:** "MADE" spelled "MAIE" in legend

Date	Mintage	VG	F	VF	XF	Unc
CD1923	—	2.25	4.00	7.50	12.50	30.00

Y# 381.2   20 CENTS
5.3000 g., Silver **Rev. Leg.:** MADEIN FOO-KIENMINT

Date	Mintage	VG	F	VF	XF	Unc
CD1923	—	2.25	4.00	7.50	12.50	30.00

Y# 381.3   20 CENTS
5.3000 g., Silver **Obv:** Without dot in middle of center rosette, 5-pointed star at sides in place of rosette

Date	Mintage	VG	F	VF	XF	Unc
CD1923	—	4.00	10.00	15.00	20.00	40.00

Y# 381.4   20 CENTS
5.0000 g., Silver **Obv:** Different legend in center

Date	Mintage	VG	F	VF	XF	Unc
CD1924	—	2.50	5.00	8.00	15.00	35.00

Y# 383a   20 CENTS
5.7000 g., Silver

Date	Mintage	VG	F	VF	XF	Unc
13(1924)	—	11.50	35.00	50.00	70.00	90.00

Y# 384   20 CENTS
5.0000 g., Silver **Subject:** Northern Expedition **Obv:** Crossed flags

Date	Mintage	VG	F	VF	XF	Unc
16(1927)	—	75.00	200	350	500	1,000

Y# 385   20 CENTS
5.3000 g., Silver **Subject:** Northern Expedition **Obv:** Crossed flags

Date	Mintage	VG	F	VF	XF	Unc
16(1927)	—	200	650	1,000	1,350	2,000

Y# 389.1   20 CENTS
5.3000 g., Silver, 23 mm. **Subject:** Canton martyrs **Obv:** Two rows of bricks at right of gate

Date	Mintage	VG	F	VF	XF	Unc
17(1928)	—	2.50	5.00	7.50	12.50	30.00
20(1931)	—	3.00	7.50	12.00	20.00	60.00

Y# 389.2   20 CENTS
5.5000 g., Silver, 23 mm. **Subject:** Canton martyrs **Obv:** Half brick in 3rd row of bricks at right of gate

Date	Mintage	VG	F	VF	XF	Unc
17(1928)	—	2.25	4.00	6.50	10.00	30.00
20(1931)	—	2.75	6.00	10.00	16.50	50.00

Y# 389.3   20 CENTS
5.5000 g., Silver, 23 mm. **Subject:** Canton martyrs
Rev: 6-pointed star in legend

Date	Mintage	VG	F	VF	XF	Unc
20(1931)	—	—	—	—	—	—

Y# 391   20 CENTS
5.3000 g., Silver, 23 mm. **Subject:** Canton martyrs
Rev: Crossed flags

Date	Mintage	VG	F	VF	XF	Unc
21(1932)	—	20.00	45.00	75.00	125	250

PATTERNS
Including off metal strikes

KM#	Date	Mintage	Identification	Mkt Val
Pn3	ND(c.1912)	—	2 Wen. Cast Brass. Obv. Ins: Fu-chien Sheng-tsao.	500
Pn4	ND(c.1912)	—	2 Wen. Cast Brass. Obv. Ins: Fu-chien T'ung-pao.	500
Pn5	ND(c.1912)	—	2 Wen. Cast Brass. Obv. Ins: Min-sheng T'ung-pao.	500
Pn6	16(1927)	—	20 Cents. Silver. 5.0000 g. Sun Yat-sen Memorial. K712.	1,500
Pn7	17(1928)	—	20 Cents. Brass. Y389.1.	—
Pn8	21(1932)	—	20 Cents. Brass. Y391.	—

HEILUNGKIANG PROVINCE
Heilongjiang

The northwesternmost of the former Three Eastern Provinces, bordering on Siberia. Though very large in extent, it is only sparsely populated, for wide areas are desert land. Economically the district was always backward. Heilungkiang (Heilongjiang) Province had no mint of its own, and seemingly no silver money bearing its name was ever placed in circulation although Imperial patterns in the standard dragon design exist for at least the dollar and 50 cent denominations. During the beginning of the 20th century it was suggested to contract for silver coins from the Berlin Mint.

PATTERNS
Including off metal strikes

KM#	Date	Mintage	Identification	Mkt Val
Pn1	ND(1903)	—	50 Cents. Brass. KM584x.	25,000
Pn2	ND(1903)	—	Dollar. Silver. Rare.	
Pn3	ND(1903)	—	Dollar. Brass.	60,000
Pn4	ND(1903)	—	Dollar. Silver Plated Brass.	—

HONAN PROVINCE
Henan

A province in east-central China. As well as being one of the most densely populated provinces it is also one of the most important agriculturally. It is the area of earliest settlement in China and has housed the capital during various dynasties. The Kaifeng Mint issued coins from its opening in 1647 through most of the rulers of the Manchu dynasty. In 1905 a modern mint opened at Kaifeng but closed in 1914. A mint in Loyang opened in 1924.

EMPIRE

PROVINCIAL CAST COINAGE

C# 3-1.1a   CASH
Cast Zinc **Ruler:** Kuang-hsü **Obv. Insc.:** Kuang-hsü T'ung-pao
Rev: Dot at upper left, Manchu inscription **Rev. Insc.:** Boo-ho

Date	Mintage	Good	VG	F	VF	XF
ND(1875-1908)	—	—	—	—	—	—
Rare						

C# 11-9   CASH
Cast Brass **Ruler:** Kuang-hsü **Obv. Insc.:** Kuang-hsü T'ung-pao **Rev:** Manchu inscription **Rev. Insc.:** Boo-ho

Date	Mintage	Good	VG	F	VF	XF
ND(1875-1908)	—	4.00	8.00	10.00	12.00	—

C# 11-9.1   CASH
Cast Brass **Ruler:** Kuang-hsü **Obv. Insc.:** Kuang-hsü T'ung-pao **Rev:** Circle above, Manchu inscription **Rev. Insc.:** Boo-ho

Date	Mintage	Good	VG	F	VF	XF
ND(1875-1908)	—	5.00	9.00	13.50	35.00	—

C# 11-9.2   CASH
Cast Brass **Ruler:** Kuang-hsü **Obv. Insc.:** Kuang-hsü T'ung-pao **Rev:** Circle below, Manchu inscription **Rev. Insc.:** Boo-ho

Date	Mintage	Good	VG	F	VF	XF
ND(1875-1908)	—	5.00	9.00	13.50	25.00	—

C# 11-9.3   CASH
Cast Brass **Ruler:** Kuang-hsü **Obv. Insc.:** Kuang-hsü T'ung-pao **Rev:** Crescent above, Manchu inscription **Rev. Insc.:** Boo-ho

Date	Mintage	Good	VG	F	VF	XF
ND(1875-1908)	—	5.00	9.00	13.50	25.00	—

C# 11-9.4   CASH
Cast Brass **Ruler:** Kuang-hsü **Obv. Insc.:** Kuang-hsü T'ung-pao **Rev:** Crescent below, Manchu inscription **Rev. Insc.:** Boo-ho

Date	Mintage	Good	VG	F	VF	XF
ND(1875-1908)	—	5.00	9.00	13.50	25.00	—

C# 11-9.5   CASH
Cast Brass **Ruler:** Kuang-hsü **Obv. Insc.:** Kuang-hsü T'ung-pao **Rev:** Crescent above, dot below, Manchu inscription **Rev. Insc.:** Boo-ho **Note:** Schjöth #1571.

Date	Mintage	Good	VG	F	VF	XF
ND(1875-1908)	—	5.00	9.00	13.50	25.00	—

C# 11-9.6   CASH
Cast Brass **Ruler:** Kuang-hsü **Obv. Insc.:** Kuang-hsü T'ung-pao **Rev:** Dot above, Manchu inscription **Rev. Insc.:** Boo-ho

Date	Mintage	Good	VG	F	VF	XF
ND(1875-1908)	—	5.00	9.00	13.50	20.00	—

C# 11-9.7   CASH
Cast Brass **Ruler:** Kuang-hsü **Obv. Insc.:** Kuang-hsü T'ung-pao **Rev:** Dot below, Manchu inscription **Rev. Insc.:** Boo-ho

Date	Mintage	Good	VG	F	VF	XF
ND(1875-1908)	—	5.00	9.00	13.50	20.00	—

C# 11-9.8   CASH
Cast Brass **Ruler:** Kuang-hsü **Obv. Insc.:** Kuang-hsü T'ung-pao **Rev:** Dot at upper left, Manchu inscription **Rev. Insc.:** Boo-ho **Note:** Crescent and dot varieties exist.

Date	Mintage	Good	VG	F	VF	XF
ND(1875-1908)	—	5.00	9.00	13.50	20.00	—

C# 11-9.9   CASH
Cast Brass **Ruler:** Kuang-hsü **Obv. Insc.:** Kuang-hsü T'ung-pao **Rev:** Crescent above, circle below

Date	Mintage	Good	VG	F	VF	XF
ND(1875-1908)	—	10.00	17.50	25.00	35.00	—

C# 11-9.10   CASH
Cast Brass **Ruler:** Kuang-hsü **Obv. Insc.:** Kuang-hsü T'ung-pao **Rev:** Dot in circle below

Date	Mintage	Good	VG	F	VF	XF
ND(1875-1908)	—	15.00	25.00	35.00	50.00	—

MILLED COINAGE

Y# 7g   CASH
Brass **Ruler:** Kuang-hsü **Obv. Leg.:** Kuang-hsü **Rev:** Side view dragon

Date	Mintage	VG	F	VF	XF	Unc
CD1908	—	10.00	25.00	42.50	75.00	—

Y# 7ga   CASH
Copper **Ruler:** Kuang-hsü **Obv. Leg.:** Kuang-hsü **Rev:** Side view dragon

Date	Mintage	VG	F	VF	XF	Unc
CD1908	—	20.00	50.00	85.00	150	—

Y# 108   10 CASH
Copper **Ruler:** Kuang-hsü **Obv. Leg.:** Ho-nan Sheng Tsao **Obv. Insc.:** Kuang-hsü Yüan-pao **Rev:** Circled dragon without mountain below pearl with 3 flames

Date	Mintage	VG	F	VF	XF	Unc
ND(1905)	—	4.00	10.00	20.00	45.00	—

Y# 108.1   10 CASH
Copper **Ruler:** Kuang-hsü **Obv. Leg.:** Ho-nan Sheng Tsao **Obv. Insc.:** Kuang-hsü Yüan-pao **Rev:** Circled dragon without mountain below pearl with 5 flames

Date	Mintage	VG	F	VF	XF	Unc
ND(1905)	—	1.00	3.00	5.00	10.00	—

Y# 108.2   10 CASH
Copper **Ruler:** Kuang-hsü **Obv. Leg.:** Ho-nan Sheng Tsao **Obv. Insc.:** Kuang-hsü Yüan-pao **Rev:** Circled dragon, mountain below pearl, very small English lettering

Date	Mintage	VG	F	VF	XF	Unc
ND(1905)	—	6.00	15.00	30.00	50.00	—

Y# 108.3   10 CASH
Copper **Ruler:** Kuang-hsü **Obv. Leg.:** Ho-nan Sheng Tsao **Obv. Insc.:** Kuang-hsü Yüan-pao **Rev:** Circled dragon, large English legend

Date	Mintage	VG	F	VF	XF	Unc
ND(1905)	—	5.00	10.00	15.00	30.00	—

Y# 108a   10 CASH
Brass **Ruler:** Kuang-hsü **Obv:** Raised circled yin-yang in center **Obv. Leg.:** Ho-nan Sheng Tsao **Obv. Insc.:** Kuang-hsü Yüan-pao **Rev:** Uncircled dragon, Honan spelled HOU-NAN **Note:** Dies made in Japan.

Date	Mintage	VG	F	VF	XF	Unc
ND(1905) Rare	—	—	—	—	—	—

Y# 108a.1   10 CASH
Copper **Ruler:** Kuang-hsü **Obv:** Flat circled yin-yang **Obv. Leg.:** Ho-nan Sheng Tsao **Obv. Insc.:** Kuang-hsü Yüan-pao **Rev:** Uncircled dragon

Date	Mintage	VG	F	VF	XF	Unc
ND(1905)	—	1.00	3.00	5.00	10.00	—

Y# 108a.2   10 CASH
Copper **Ruler:** Kuang-hsü **Obv:** Curved line on raised yin-yang slanted more **Obv. Leg.:** Ho-nan Sheng Tsao **Obv. Insc.:** Kuang-hsü Yüan-pao **Rev:** Uncircled dragon

Date	Mintage	VG	F	VF	XF	Unc
ND(1905)	—	1.00	3.00	5.00	10.00	—

Y# 108a.3   10 CASH
Copper **Ruler:** Kuang-hsü **Obv:** Flat yin-yang slanted more **Obv. Leg.:** Ho-nan Sheng Tsao **Obv. Insc.:** Kuang-hsü Yüan-pao **Rev:** Circled dragon, plain pearl

Date	Mintage	VG	F	VF	XF	Unc
ND(1905)	—	0.75	2.50	4.00	8.00	—

Note: Dies made in United States

Y# 108a.3a   10 CASH
Brass **Ruler:** Kuang-hsü **Obv. Leg.:** Ho-nan Sheng Tsao **Obv. Insc.:** Kuang-hsü Yüan-pao **Rev:** Dragon

Date	Mintage	VG	F	VF	XF	Unc
ND(1905)	—	2.50	5.00	10.00	20.00	—

Y# 108a.4   10 CASH
Copper **Ruler:** Kuang-hsü **Obv. Leg.:** Ho-nan Sheng Tsao **Obv. Insc.:** Kuang-hsü Yüan-pao **Rev:** Dragon, incuse swirl in pearl

Date	Mintage	VG	F	VF	XF	Unc
ND(1905)	—	1.00	3.00	5.00	12.00	—

Note: Dies made in United States

Y# 10g   10 CASH
Copper   **Ruler:** Kuang-hsü **Obv. Insc.:** Tai-ch'ing T'ung-pi
Rev: Dragon, period after COIN in legend **Rev. Leg.:** Kuang-hsü
Nien-tsao, TAI-CHING-TI-KUO ...

Date	Mintage	VG	F	VF	XF	Unc
CD1906	132,000,000	0.85	2.00	5.00	10.00	—

Y# 10g.1   10 CASH
Copper   **Ruler:** Kuang-hsü **Obv. Insc.:** Tai-ch'ing T'ung-pi
Rev: Dragon, period after COPPER in legend **Rev. Leg.:** Kuang-
hsü Nien-tsao, TAI-CHING-TI-KUO ...

Date	Mintage	VG	F	VF	XF	Unc
CD1906	—	1.25	3.00	6.00	10.00	—

Y# 10g.2   10 CASH
Copper   **Ruler:** Kuang-hsü **Obv. Insc.:** Tai-ch'ing T'ung-pi
Rev: Dragon **Rev. Leg.:** Kuang-hsü Nien-tsao, TAI-CHING-
TI-KUO ... **Note:** Cyclical dates at sides.

Date	Mintage	VG	F	VF	XF	Unc
CD1907 Rare						

Y# 20g   10 CASH
Copper   **Ruler:** Hsüan-t'ung **Obv. Insc.:** Tai-ch'ing T'ung-pi
Rev: Dragon **Rev. Leg.:** Hsüan-t'ung Nien-tsao, TAI-CHING-
TI-KUO ... **Note:** Normally encountered with weak legends.

Date	Mintage	VG	F	VF	XF	Unc
CD1909	—	20.00	40.00	60.00	125	—
CD1911	—	5.00	15.00	25.00	50.00	—

REPUBLIC

MILLED COINAGE

Y# A392   10 CASH
Copper   **Obv:** With lines above and below rosettes
Obv. Leg.: Chung Hua Min Kuo **Rev:** Crossed flags, florals at
left and right **Rev. Leg.:** HO-NAN

Date	Mintage	VG	F	VF	XF	Unc
ND(1913-14)	—	0.35	1.00	2.00	6.00	20.00

Y# A392.1   10 CASH
Copper   **Obv:** Without lines above and below rosettes
Obv. Leg.: Chung Hua Min Kuo **Rev:** Crossed flags, florals at
left and right **Rev. Leg.:** HO-NAN

Date	Mintage	VG	F	VF	XF	Unc
ND(1913-14)	—	0.35	1.00	2.00	6.00	20.00

Y# A392.2   10 CASH
Copper   **Obv. Leg.:** Chung Hua Min Kuo **Rev:** Crossed flags,
florals at left and right, letter "S" in "CASH" backwards
Rev. Leg.: HO-NAN

Date	Mintage	VG	F	VF	XF	Unc
ND(c.1920)	—	6.00	17.50	30.00	60.00	—

Y# 392.2   10 CASH
Copper   **Obv:** Yüan at lower left with 3 horizontal strokes.
Obv. Leg.: Chung Hua Min Kuo **Rev:** Crossed flags, florals at
left and right **Rev. Leg.:** HO-NAN

Date	Mintage	VG	F	VF	XF	Unc
ND(ca.1920)	—	0.65	2.00	3.50	6.00	20.00

Y# 392   10 CASH
Copper   **Obv:** Yüan at lower left with 2 horizontal strokes
Obv. Leg.: Chung Hua Min Kuo **Rev:** Value "TEN CASH" in larger
letters at bottom **Rev. Leg.:** HO-NAN

Date	Mintage	VG	F	VF	XF	Unc
ND(c.1920)	—	0.25	0.75	1.50	4.00	18.00

Y# 392.1   10 CASH
Copper   **Obv:** Rosette in center higher in relation to heart-shaped
leaves below, Yuan at lower left with 2 horizontal strokes
Obv. Leg.: Chung Hua Min Kuo **Rev:** Crossed flags, florals at
left and right **Rev. Leg.:** HO-NAN

Date	Mintage	VG	F	VF	XF	Unc
ND(c.1920)	—	0.65	2.00	3.50	6.00	20.00

Y# 393   20 CASH
Copper, 32 mm.   **Obv:** Value in 6 characters at bottom
Obv. Leg.: Chung Hua Min Kuo **Rev:** Crossed flags, florals at
left and right **Rev. Leg.:** HO-NAN

Date	Mintage	Good	VG	F	VF	XF
ND(c.1920)	—	1.25	2.50	5.00	10.00	30.00

Y# 393.1   20 CASH
Copper, 32 mm.   **Obv:** Value in 5 characters at bottom
Obv. Leg.: Chung Hua Min Kuo **Rev:** Crossed flags, florals at
left and right **Rev. Leg.:** HO-NAN

Date	Mintage	Good	VG	F	VF	XF
ND(c.1920)	—	1.00	2.00	4.00	6.00	20.00

Y# 393.2   20 CASH
Copper, 32 mm.   **Obv:** Value in 6 characters below
Obv. Leg.: Chung Hua Min Kuo **Rev:** Crossed flags, florals at
left and right **Rev. Leg.:** CHINA

Date	Mintage	Good	VG	F	VF	XF
ND(c.1921)	—	12.50	25.00	45.00	175	—

Y# A397   20 CASH
Copper, 38 mm.   **Obv:** Value in 6 characters below
Obv. Leg.: Chung Hua Min Kuo (year) Nien **Rev:** Star above
crossed flags, florals at left and right

Date	Mintage	Good	F	VF	XF
20(1931)	—	500	1,500	3,000	—

Y# 394   50 CASH
Copper, 38 mm.   **Obv. Leg.:** Chung Hua Min Kuo **Rev:** Crossed
flags, florals at left and right, short flagpoles **Rev. Leg.:** HO-NAN

Date	Mintage	Good	VG	F	VF	XF
ND(c.1920)	—	2.00	5.00	10.00	20.00	60.00

Y# 394.1   50 CASH
Copper, 38 mm.   **Obv. Leg.:** Chung Hua Min Kuo **Rev:** Crossed
flags, florals at left and right, long flagpoles **Rev. Leg.:** HO-NAN

Date	Mintage	Good	VG	F	VF	XF
ND(c.1920)	—	2.00	5.00	10.00	20.00	60.00

Y# 394b   50 CASH
Brass, 38 mm.   **Obv. Leg.:** Chung Hua Min Kuo **Rev:** Crossed
flags, florals at left and right **Rev. Leg.:** HO-NAN

Date	Mintage	Good	VG	F	VF	XF
ND(c.1920)	—	10.00	20.00	40.00	80.00	225

Y# 394a   50 CASH
Copper, 38 mm.   **Obv. Leg.:** Chung Hua Min Kuo **Rev:** Crossed
flags, florals at left and right **Rev. Leg.:** CHINA

Date	Mintage	Good	VG	F	VF	XF
ND(c.1921)	—	6.50	12.50	25.00	60.00	175

Y# 397   50 CASH
Copper **Obv:** National star at center **Obv. Leg.:** Chung Hua Min Kuo (year) Nien **Rev:** Star above value in grain sprays

Date	Mintage	VG	F	VF	XF	Unc
20(1931)	—	120	200	330	—	—

Y# 397a   50 CASH
Brass **Obv:** National star at center **Obv. Leg.:** CHUNG HUA MIN KUO (year) NIEN **Rev:** Star above value in grain sprays

Date	Mintage	VG	F	VF	XF	Unc
20 (1931)	—	120	200	330	—	—

Y# 395   100 CASH
Copper, 40 mm. **Obv. Leg.:** Chung Hua Min Kuo **Rev:** Crossed flags, florals at left and right, small star in right flag, tassels 4mm long **Rev. Leg.:** HO-NAN

Date	Mintage	Good	VG	F	VF	XF
ND(c. 1928)	—	3.00	5.00	10.00	25.00	75.00

Y# 395.1   100 CASH
Copper, 40 mm. **Rev:** Tassels 5mm long

Date	Mintage	Good	VG	F	VF	XF
ND(c. 1928)	—	3.75	6.50	12.50	30.00	90.00

Y# 395.2   100 CASH
Copper, 40 mm. **Obv. Leg.:** Chung Hua Min Kuo **Rev:** Crossed flags, florals at left and right, large star in right flag **Rev. Leg.:** HO-NAN

Date	Mintage	Good	VG	F	VF	XF
ND(c. 1928)	—	—	—	—	—	—

Y# 398   100 CASH
Copper, 40 mm. **Obv:** National star at center **Obv. Leg.:** Chung Hua Min Kuo (year) Nien **Rev:** Star above value in grain sprays

Date	Mintage	VG	F	VF	XF	Unc
20(1931)	—	35.00	60.00	100	—	—

Y# 396   200 CASH
Copper, 42 mm. **Obv. Leg.:** Chung Hua Min Kuo **Rev:** Crossed flags, florals at left and right, large square inside right flag **Rev. Leg.:** HO-NAN

Date	Mintage	Good	VG	F	VF	XF
ND(c.1928)	—	3.00	5.00	10.00	25.00	100

Y# 396.1   200 CASH
Copper, 42 mm. **Obv. Leg.:** Chung Hua Min Kuo **Rev:** Crossed flags, small panel with small star inside right flag, florals at left and right **Rev. Leg.:** HO-NAN

Date	Mintage	Good	VG	F	VF	XF
ND(c.1928)	—	2.50	4.50	9.00	25.00	100

Y# 396.2   200 CASH
Copper, 42 mm. **Obv. Leg.:** Chung Hua Min Kuo **Rev:** Crossed flags, small panel with large star inside right flag, florals at left and right **Rev. Leg.:** HO-NAN

Date	Mintage	Good	VG	F	VF	XF
ND(c.1928)	—	2.50	4.50	9.00	25.00	100

Y# 396a   200 CASH
Brass, 42 mm. **Obv. Leg.:** Chung Hua Min Kuo **Rev:** Crossed flags, small panel with large star inside right flag, florals at left and right **Rev. Leg.:** HO-NAN

Date	Mintage	Good	VG	F	VF	XF
ND(c.1928)	—	6.00	15.00	22.50	45.00	135

PATTERNS
Including off metal strikes

KM#	Date	Mintage	Identification	Mkt Val
Pn1	CD1909	—	2 Cash. Brass.	—
Pn2	CD1909	—	5 Cash. Copper. Y19g.	—
Pn3	CD1909	—	20 Cash. Copper. Y21g.	—

HUNAN PROVINCE

A province in south-central China. Mining of coal, antimony, tungsten and tin is important as well as raising varied agricultural products. The Changsha Mint produced Cash coins from early in the Manchu dynasty. Its facility for struck coinage opened in 1897, and two further copper mints were added in 1905. All three mints were closed down in 1907, but one mint was reopened at a later date and produced vast quantities of republican copper coinage until 1926.

EMPIRE
MILLED COINAGE

Y# 112   10 CASH
Copper **Ruler:** Kuang-hsü **Obv:** Rosette in center with center of petals depressed; Manchu words at sides, "Tang Shih" at bottom **Obv. Leg.:** Hu-nan Sheng Tsao **Obv. Insc.:** Kuang-hsü Yüan-pao **Rev:** Narrow spacing in HU-NAN above dragon **Rev. Leg.:** HU-NAN

Date	Mintage	VG	F	VF	XF	Unc
ND(1902-06)	—	0.35	1.00	2.00	5.00	65.00

Y# 112.1   10 CASH
Copper **Ruler:** Kuang-hsü **Obv. Leg.:** Hu-nan Sheng Tsao **Obv. Insc.:** Kuang-hsü Yüan-pao **Rev:** Dragon; wide spacing in HU-NAN **Rev. Leg.:** HU-NAN

Date	Mintage	VG	F	VF	XF	Unc
ND(1902-06)	—	0.75	2.25	4.00	9.00	65.00

Y# 112.2   10 CASH
Copper **Ruler:** Kuang-hsü **Obv:** Petals of rosettes not depressed **Obv. Leg.:** Hu-nan Sheng Tsao **Obv. Insc.:** Kuang-hsü Yüan-pao **Rev:** Dragon **Rev. Leg.:** HU-NAN

Date	Mintage	VG	F	VF	XF	Unc
ND(1902-06)	—	0.50	1.50	2.50	6.00	65.00

Y# 112.3   10 CASH
Copper **Ruler:** Kuang-hsü **Obv:** Two Manchu words in center, "T'ung Yüan" at bottom **Obv. Leg.:** Hu-nan Sheng Tsao **Obv. Insc.:** Kuang-hsü Yüan-pao **Rev:** Dragon **Rev. Leg.:** HU-NAN

Date	Mintage	VG	F	VF	XF	Unc
ND(1902-06)	—	1.00	3.00	6.00	10.00	65.00

Y# 112.4   10 CASH
Copper **Ruler:** Kuang-hsü **Obv. Leg.:** Hu-nan Sheng Tsao **Obv. Insc.:** Kuang-hsü Yüan-pao **Rev:** Dragon; narrow spacing in "HU-NAN" **Rev. Leg.:** HU-NAN

Date	Mintage	VG	F	VF	XF	Unc
ND(1902-06)	—	0.50	1.50	2.50	6.00	65.00

Y# 112.5   10 CASH
Copper **Ruler:** Kuang-hsü **Obv:** Rosette in center, "Tang Shih" at bottom **Obv. Leg.:** Hu-nan Sheng Tsao **Obv. Insc.:** Kuang-hsü Yüan-pao **Rev:** Dragon; ring around pearl **Rev. Leg.:** HU-NAN

Date	Mintage	VG	F	VF	XF	Unc
ND(1902-06)	—	0.40	1.25	2.00	4.00	65.00

Y# 112.6   10 CASH
Copper **Ruler:** Kuang-hsü **Obv:** Centers of petals on rosette depressed **Obv. Leg.:** Hu-nan Sheng Tsao **Obv. Insc.:** Kuang-hsü Yüan-pao **Rev:** Dragon **Rev. Leg.:** HU-NAN

Date	Mintage	VG	F	VF	XF	Unc
ND(1902-06)	—	0.50	1.50	2.50	6.00	65.00

Y# 112.7   10 CASH
Copper **Ruler:** Kuang-hsü **Obv:** two Manchu words in center, "T'ung Yüan" at bottom **Obv. Leg.:** Hu-nan Sheng Tsao **Obv. Insc.:** Kuang-hsü Yüan-pao **Rev:** Dragon; ring around pearl **Rev. Leg.:** HU-NAN

Date	Mintage	VG	F	VF	XF	Unc
ND(1902-06)	—	0.50	1.50	2.50	6.00	65.00

Y# 112.8 10 CASH
Copper **Ruler:** Kuang-hsü **Obv:** Larger characters at left and right, and different characters below **Obv. Leg.:** Hu-nan Sheng Tsao **Obv. Insc.:** Kuang-hsü Yüan-pao **Rev:** Dragon redesigned and small star at either side **Rev. Leg.:** HU-NAN

Date	Mintage	VG	F	VF	XF	Unc
ND(1902-06)	—	1.75	5.00	10.00	17.50	80.00

Y# 112.9 10 CASH
Copper **Ruler:** Kuang-hsü **Obv:** Rosette in center; legend: four characters at bottom **Obv. Leg.:** Hu-nan Sheng Tsao **Obv. Insc.:** Kuang-hsü Yüan-pao **Rev:** Redesigned dragon without pearl; rosette at either side **Rev. Leg.:** HU-NAN

Date	Mintage	VG	F	VF	XF	Unc
ND(1902-06)	—	2.50	7.50	15.00	30.00	100

Y# 112.10 10 CASH
Copper **Ruler:** Kuang-hsü **Obv:** Two Manchu words in center with dot between; "T'ung Yüan" at bottom **Obv. Leg.:** Hu-nan Sheng Tsao **Obv. Insc.:** Kuang-hsü Yüan-pao **Rev:** Dragon **Rev. Leg.:** HU-NAN

Date	Mintage	VG	F	VF	XF	Unc
ND(1902-06)	—	0.35	1.00	2.00	4.00	65.00

Y# 112.11 10 CASH
Copper **Ruler:** Kuang-hsü **Obv:** Without dot between Manchu words, "T'ung Yüan" at bottom **Obv. Leg.:** Hu-nan Sheng Tsao **Obv. Insc.:** Kuang-hsü Yüan-pao **Rev:** Dragon **Rev. Leg.:** HU-NAN

Date	Mintage	VG	F	VF	XF	Unc
ND(1902-06)	—	0.35	1.00	2.00	4.00	65.00

Y# 112.12 10 CASH
Copper **Ruler:** Kuang-hsü **Obv:** Smaller 15.5 millimeter inner circle, with larger beads, "T'ung Yüan" at bottom **Obv. Leg.:** Hu-nan Sheng Tsao **Obv. Insc.:** Kuang-hsü Yüan-pao **Rev:** Dragon **Rev. Leg.:** HU-NAN

Date	Mintage	VG	F	VF	XF	Unc
ND(1902-06)	—	0.35	1.00	2.00	4.00	65.00

Y# 112.13 10 CASH
Copper **Ruler:** Kuang-hsü **Obv:** Two Manchu words in center, 18.4mm inner circle; "Huang T'ung" at bottom **Obv. Leg.:** Hu-nan Sheng Tsao **Obv. Insc.:** Kuang-hsü Yüan-pao **Rev:** Dragon **Rev. Leg.:** HU-NAN

Date	Mintage	VG	F	VF	XF	Unc
ND(1902-06)	—	8.50	25.00	45.00	80.00	—

Y# 112.14 10 CASH
Copper **Ruler:** Kuang-hsü **Obv:** Smaller 17.5mm inner circle; "Huang T'ung Yüan" at bottom **Obv. Leg.:** Hu-nan Sheng Tsao **Obv. Insc.:** Kuang-hsü Yüan-pao **Rev:** Dragon **Rev. Leg.:** HU-NAN

Date	Mintage	VG	F	VF	XF	Unc
ND(1902-06)	—	8.50	25.00	45.00	80.00	—

Y# 113 10 CASH
Copper **Ruler:** Kuang-hsü **Obv. Leg.:** Hu-nan Sheng Tsao, six characters at bottom **Obv. Insc.:** Kuang-hsü Yüan-pao **Rev:** Flying dragon **Rev. Leg.:** HU-NAN **Edge:** Reeded

Date	Mintage	VG	F	VF	XF	Unc
ND(1902-06)	—	1.25	4.00	8.00	15.00	80.00

Y# 113.1 10 CASH
Copper **Ruler:** Kuang-hsü **Obv. Leg.:** Hu-nan Sheng Tsao **Obv. Insc.:** Kuang-hsü Yüan-pao **Rev:** Dragon **Rev. Leg.:** Inverted U in HU-NAN **Edge:** Reeded

Date	Mintage	VG	F	VF	XF	Unc
ND(1902-06)	—	4.50	12.50	25.00	45.00	—

Y# 113a 10 CASH
Brass, 28 mm. **Ruler:** Kuang-hsü **Obv. Leg.:** Hu-nan Sheng Tsao, three characters at bottom **Obv. Insc.:** Kuang-hsü Yüan-pao **Rev:** Dragon **Rev. Leg.:** HU-NAN

Date	Mintage	VG	F	VF	XF	Unc
ND(1902-06)	—	1.25	3.50	6.00	12.50	80.00

Y# 10h 10 CASH
Copper **Ruler:** Kuang-hsü **Obv:** Upper and lower parts of character "Hu" connected **Obv. Insc.:** Tai-ch'ing T'ung-pi **Rev:** Dragon; dot between Chinese characters above dragon **Rev. Leg.:** Kuang-hsü Nien-tsao, TAI-CHING-TI-KUO...

Date	Mintage	VG	F	VF	XF	Unc
CD1906	—	6.00	17.50	35.00	70.00	—

Y# 10h.1 10 CASH
Copper **Ruler:** Kuang-hsü **Obv:** Upper and lower parts of character "Hu" not connected **Obv. Insc.:** Tai-ch'ing T'ung-pi **Rev:** Dragon; dot between Chinese characters at top **Rev. Leg.:** Kuang-hsü Nien-tsao, TAI-CHING-TI-KUO...

Date	Mintage	VG	F	VF	XF	Unc
CD1906	—	6.00	17.50	35.00	70.00	—

Y# 10h.2 10 CASH
Copper **Ruler:** Kuang-hsü **Obv. Insc.:** Tai-ch'ing T'ung-pi **Rev:** Dragon; seven flames on pearl **Rev. Leg.:** Kuang-hsü Nien-tsao, TAI-CHING-TI-KUO...

Date	Mintage	VG	F	VF	XF	Unc
CD1906	—	0.65	2.00	4.00	8.00	65.00

Y# 10h.3 10 CASH
Copper **Ruler:** Kuang-hsü **Obv. Insc.:** Tai-ch'ing T'ung-pi **Rev:** Dragon; seven-flame pearl ornamented with toothlike projections **Rev. Leg.:** Kuang-hsü Nien-tsao, TAI-CHING-TI-KUO...

Date	Mintage	VG	F	VF	XF	Unc
CD1906	—	0.65	2.00	3.50	6.00	65.00

Y# 10h.4 10 CASH
Copper **Ruler:** Kuang-hsü **Obv. Insc.:** Tai-ch'ing T'ung-pi **Rev:** Dragon; four flames on pearl **Rev. Leg.:** Kuang-hsü Nien-tsao, TAI-CHING-TI-KUO...

Date	Mintage	VG	F	VF	XF	Unc
CD1906	—	1.00	3.00	6.00	10.00	65.00

Y# 10h.5 10 CASH
Copper **Ruler:** Kuang-hsü **Obv. Insc.:** Tai-ch'ing T'ung-pi **Rev:** Redesigned dragon with high waves beneath **Rev. Leg.:** Kuang-hsü Nien-tsao, TAI-CHING-TI-KUO...

Date	Mintage	VG	F	VF	XF	Unc
CD1906	—	13.50	40.00	80.00	150	—

Y# 10h.6 10 CASH
Copper **Ruler:** Kuang-hsü **Obv:** Character "Hu" connected **Obv. Insc.:** Tai-ch'ing T'ung-pi **Rev:** Redesigned dragon, dot between COPPER COIN **Rev. Leg.:** Kuang-hsü Nien-tsao, TAI-CHING-TI-KUO...

Date	Mintage	VG	F	VF	XF	Unc
CD1906	—	4.50	12.50	20.00	40.00	—

Y# 10h.7 10 CASH
Copper **Ruler:** Kuang-hsü **Obv:** Character "Hu" connected **Obv. Insc.:** Tai-ch'ing T'ung-pi **Rev:** Redesigned dragon with five flames on pearl **Rev. Leg.:** Kuang-hsü Nien-tsao, TAI-CHING-TI-KUO... **Note:** Woodward #342 and #343

Date	Mintage	VG	F	VF	XF	Unc
CD1906	—	10.00	30.00	45.00	75.00	—

Y# 114 5 CENTS
1.3000 g., 0.8200 Silver 0.0343 oz. ASW **Ruler:** Kuang-hsü
Obv. Insc.: Kuang-hsü Yüan-pao **Note:** Kann #164.

Date	Mintage	F	VF	XF	Unc	BU
ND(c.1902) Rare	—					

Y# 115 10 CENTS
2.5000 g., 0.8200 Silver 0.0659 oz. ASW **Ruler:** Kuang-hsü
Obv: Two rosettes at both sides **Obv. Insc.:** Kuang-hsü Yüan-pao

Date	Mintage	F	VF	XF	Unc	BU
ND(c.1902)	—	7.00	15.00	25.00	100	—

Y# 116 20 CENTS
5.3000 g., 0.8200 Silver 0.1397 oz. ASW **Ruler:** Kuang-hsü
Obv. Insc.: Kuang-hsü Yüan-pao

Date	Mintage	F	VF	XF	Unc	BU
ND(c.1902)	—	50.00	100	200	350	—

BULLION COINAGE
Mace/Tael Series

K# 951 CH'IEN (MACE)
3.7000 g., Silver **Issuer:** Fo-nau Official Bureau **Obv:** Two lines
of two characters each **Rev:** Two lines of one character each

Date	Mintage	VG	F	VF	XF	Unc
ND(1906)	—	75.00	150	200	300	600

K# 961 CH'IEN (MACE)
3.6000 g., Silver **Obv:** Three lines of two characters each
Rev: Two lines of two characters each

Date	Mintage	VG	F	VF	XF	Unc
ND(ca. 1906)	—	—	—	—	—	—

K# 971 CH'IEN (MACE)
3.7000 g., Silver **Issuer:** Ta Ching Gov't. Bank **Obv:** Two lines
of two characters each **Rev:** Two lines of two characters each

Date	Mintage	VG	F	VF	XF	Unc
ND(ca.1908)	—	50.00	500	700	900	1,200

K# 984/5 CH'IEN (MACE)
3.7000 g., Silver **Issuer:** Chien-I, Changsha **Obv:** Two lines of
three characters each **Rev:** Two lines of one character each

Date	Mintage	VG	F	VF	XF	Unc
ND(1908)	—	75.00	150	200	300	500

K# 950 2 CH'IEN (MACE)
7.3000 g., Silver **Issuer:** Fo-nan Official Bureau **Obv:** Two lines
of two characters each **Rev:** Two lines of two characters each

Date	Mintage	VG	F	VF	XF	Unc
ND(1906)	—	75.00	150	200	300	600

K# 960 2 CH'IEN (MACE)
7.3000 g., Silver **Obv:** Three lines of two characters each
Rev: Two lines of two characters each

Date	Mintage	VG	F	VF	XF	Unc
ND(1906)	—	—	—	—	—	—

K# 970 2 CH'IEN (MACE)
7.3000 g., Silver **Issuer:** Ta Ch'ing Gov't. Bank **Obv:** Three lines
of two characters each **Rev:** Two lines of three characters each

Date	Mintage	VG	F	VF	XF	Unc
ND(1908)	—	250	500	700	900	1,200

K# 982/3 2 CH'IEN (MACE)
7.3000 g., Silver **Issuer:** Chien-I, Changsha **Obv:** Two lines of
three characters each **Rev:** Two lines of two characters each

Date	Mintage	VG	F	VF	XF	Unc
ND(ca.1908)	—	75.00	150	200	300	500

K# 949 3 CH'IEN (MACE)
10.7000 g., Silver **Issuer:** Fo-nan Official Bureau **Obv:** Two lines
of three characters each **Rev:** Two lines of three characters each

Date	Mintage	VG	F	VF	XF	Unc
ND(1906)	—	85.00	175	250	350	700

K# 959 3 CH'IEN (MACE)
10.7000 g., Silver **Obv:** Three lines of two characters each
Rev: Two lines of three characters each

Date	Mintage	VG	F	VF	XF	Unc
ND(ca.1906)	—	85.00	175	250	350	700

K# 969 3 CH'IEN (MACE)
10.7000 g., Silver **Issuer:** Ta Ch'ing Gov't. Bank **Obv:** Three lines
of two characters each **Rev:** Two lines of three characters each

Date	Mintage	VG	F	VF	XF	Unc
ND(ca.1908)	—	250	500	700	900	1,200

K# 981 3 CH'IEN (MACE)
10.7000 g., Silver **Issuer:** Chien-I, Changsha **Obv:** Two lines
of three characters each **Rev:** Two lines of three characters each

Date	Mintage	VG	F	VF	XF	Unc
ND(ca.1908)	—	85.00	175	250	350	600

K# 981a 3 CH'IEN (MACE)
10.7000 g., Silver **Issuer:** Chien-I, Changsha **Obv:** Two lines
of three characters each **Rev:** Two lines of three characters each
Note: "official" character for three

Date	Mintage	VG	F	VF	XF	Unc
ND(ca.1908)	—	85.00	175	250	350	600

K# 948 4 CH'IEN (MACE)
14.3000 g., Silver **Issuer:** Fo-nan Official Bureau **Obv:** Two lines
of three characters each **Rev:** Two lines of three characters each

Date	Mintage	VG	F	VF	XF	Unc
ND(1906)	—	85.00	175	250	350	700

K# 958 4 CH'IEN (MACE)
14.3000 g., Silver **Obv:** Three lines of two characters each
Rev: Two lines of three characters each

Date	Mintage	VG	F	VF	XF	Unc
ND(ca.1906)	—	—	—	—	—	—

K# 968 4 CH'IEN (MACE)
14.3000 g., Silver **Issuer:** Ta Ch'ing Gov't. Bank **Obv:** Three lines
of two characters each **Rev:** Two lines of three characters each

Date	Mintage	VG	F	VF	XF	Unc
ND(ca.1908)	—	300	600	800	1,000	1,200

K# 980 4 CH'IEN (MACE)
14.3000 g., Silver **Issuer:** Chien-I, Changsha **Obv:** Two lines
of three characters each **Rev:** Two lines of three characters each

Date	Mintage	VG	F	VF	XF	Unc
ND(ca.1908)	—	85.00	175	250	350	600

K# 947 5 CH'IEN (MACE)
18.3000 g., Silver **Issuer:** Fo-nan Official Bureau **Obv:** Two lines
of three characters each **Rev:** Two lines of three characters each

Date	Mintage	VG	F	VF	XF	Unc
ND(1906)	—	85.00	175	250	350	700

K# 957 5 CH'IEN (MACE)
18.3000 g., Silver **Obv:** Three lines of two characters each
Rev: Two lines of three characters each

Date	Mintage	VG	F	VF	XF	Unc
ND(ca.1906)	—	70.00				

K# 967 5 CH'IEN (MACE)
18.3000 g., Silver **Issuer:** Ta Ch'ing Gov't. Bank **Obv:** Three lines
of two characters each **Rev:** Two lines of three characters each

Date	Mintage	VG	F	VF	XF	Unc
ND(ca.1908)	—	300	600	800	1,000	1,200

K# 979 5 CH'IEN (MACE)
18.3000 g., Silver **Issuer:** Chien-I, Changsha **Obv:** Two lines
of three characters each **Rev:** Two lines of three characters each

Date	Mintage	VG	F	VF	XF	Unc
ND(ca.1908)	—	85.00	175	250	350	600

K# 946 6 CH'IEN (MACE)
21.4000 g., Silver **Issuer:** Fo-nan Official Bureau **Obv:** Two lines
of three characters each **Rev:** Two lines of three characters each

Date	Mintage	VG	F	VF	XF	Unc
ND(1906)	—	175	350	425	550	800

K# 956 6 CH'IEN (MACE)
21.4000 g., Silver **Obv:** Three lines of two characters each
Rev: Two lines of three characters each

Date	Mintage	VG	F	VF	XF	Unc
ND(ca.1906)	—	—	—	—	—	—

K# 966 6 CH'IEN (MACE)
21.4000 g., Silver **Issuer:** Ta Ch'ing Gov't. Bank **Obv:** Three lines
of two characters each **Rev:** Two lines of three characters each

Date	Mintage	VG	F	VF	XF	Unc
ND(ca.1908)	—	300	600	800	1,000	1,200

K# 978 6 CH'IEN (MACE)
21.4000 g., Silver **Issuer:** Chien-I, Changsha **Obv:** Two lines
of three characters each **Rev:** Two lines of three characters each

Date	Mintage	VG	F	VF	XF	Unc
ND(ca.1908)	—	110	225	300	400	700

K# 945 7 CH'IEN (MACE)
25.9000 g., Silver **Issuer:** Fo-nan Official Bureau **Obv:** Two lines
of three characters each **Rev:** Two lines of three characters each

Date	Mintage	VG	F	VF	XF	Unc
ND(1906)	—	150	300	400	550	900

K# 955 7 CH'IEN (MACE)
25.9000 g., Silver **Obv:** Three lines of two characters each
Rev: Two lines of three characters each

Date	Mintage	VG	F	VF	XF	Unc
ND(ca.1906)	—	—	—	—	—	—

K# 965   7 CH'IEN (MACE)
25.9000 g., Silver **Issuer:** Ta Ch'ing Gov't. Bank **Obv:** Three lines of two characters each **Rev:** Two lines of three characters each

Date	Mintage	VG	F	VF	XF	Unc
ND(ca.1908)	—	350	700	900	1,100	1,300

K# 977   7 CH'IEN (MACE)
25.9000 g., Silver **Issuer:** Chien-I, Changsha **Obv:** Two lines of three characters each **Rev:** Two lines of three characters each

Date	Mintage	VG	F	VF	XF	Unc
ND(ca.1908)	—	85.00	175	250	350	600

K# 944   8 CH'IEN (MACE)
29.2000 g., Silver **Issuer:** Fo-nan Official Bureau **Obv:** Two lines of three characters each **Rev:** Two lines of three characters each

Date	Mintage	VG	F	VF	XF	Unc
ND(1906)	—	150	300	400	550	900

K# 954   8 CH'IEN (MACE)
29.2000 g., Silver **Obv:** Three lines of two characters each **Rev:** Two lines of three characters each

Date	Mintage	VG	F	VF	XF	Unc
ND(ca.1906)	—	—	—	—	—	—

K# 964   8 CH'IEN (MACE)
29.2000 g., Silver **Issuer:** Ta Ch'ing Gov't. Bank **Obv:** Three lines of two characters each **Rev:** Two lines of three characters each

Date	Mintage	VG	F	VF	XF	Unc
ND(ca.1908)	—	275	700	900	1,100	1,300

K# 976   8 CH'IEN (MACE)
29.2000 g., Silver **Issuer:** Chien-I, Changsha **Obv:** Two lines of three characters each **Rev:** Two lines of three characters each

Date	Mintage	VG	F	VF	XF	Unc
ND(ca.1908)	—	175	350	425	550	900

K# 943   9 CH'IEN (MACE)
29.2000 g., Silver **Issuer:** Fo-nan Official Bureau **Obv:** Two lines of three characters each **Rev:** Two lines of three characters each

Date	Mintage	VG	F	VF	XF	Unc
ND(1906)	—	150	300	400	550	900

K# 953   9 CH'IEN (MACE)
29.2000 g., Silver **Obv:** Three lines of two characters each **Rev:** Two lines of three characters each

Date	Mintage	VG	F	VF	XF	Unc
ND(ca.1906)	—	—	—	—	—	—

K# 963   9 CH'IEN (MACE)
29.2000 g., Silver **Issuer:** Ta Ch'ing Gov't. Bank **Obv:** Three lines of two characters each **Rev:** Two lines of three characters each

Date	Mintage	VG	F	VF	XF	Unc
ND(ca.1908)	—	275	700	900	1,100	1,300

K# 975   9 CH'IEN (MACE)
29.2000 g., Silver **Issuer:** Chien-I, Changsha **Obv:** Two lines of three characters each **Rev:** Two lines of three characters each

Date	Mintage	VG	F	VF	XF	Unc
ND(ca.1908)	—	175	350	425	550	900

K# 942   LIANG (Tael)
35.9000 g., Silver **Issuer:** Fo-nan Official Bureau **Obv:** Two lines of three characters each **Rev:** Two lines of three characters each

Date	Mintage	VG	F	VF	XF	Unc
ND(1906)	—	110	225	300	450	800

K# 952   LIANG (Tael)
35.9000 g., Silver **Obv:** Three lines of two characters each **Rev:** Two lines of three characters each

Date	Mintage	VG	F	VF	XF	Unc
ND(ca.1906)	—	100	200	250	300	600

K# 962   LIANG (Tael)
35.9000 g., Silver **Issuer:** Ta Ch'ing Gov't. Bank **Obv:** Three lines of two characters each **Rev:** Two lines of three characters each

Date	Mintage	VG	F	VF	XF	Unc
ND(ca.1908)	—	250	600	800	1,000	1,200

K# 974   LIANG (Tael)
35.9000 g., Silver **Issuer:** Chien-I, Changsha **Obv:** Two lines of three characters each **Rev:** Two lines of three characters each

Date	Mintage	VG	F	VF	XF	Unc
ND(ca.1908)	—	125	250	325	450	700

K# 942r   LIANG (Tael)
35.9000 g., Silver **Obv:** Three lines of four characters each

Date	Mintage	VG	F	VF	XF	Unc
ND(1908) Rare Uniface	—	200	400	500	600	1,000

TRANSITIONAL COINAGE

Y# 401.1   10 CASH
Copper **Ruler:** Hung-hsien **Obv. Leg.:** THE FIRST YEAR OF HUNG SHUAN **Rev. Leg.:** Hung-hsien Yüan-nien

Date	Mintage	Good	VG	F	VF	XF
1(1915)	—	17.50	35.00	60.00	100	150

Y# 401.2   10 CASH
Copper **Ruler:** Hung-hsien **Obv:** Wider space in legend

Date	Mintage	VG	F	VF	XF	Unc
1(1915)	—	10.00	20.00	30.00	45.00	—

REPUBLIC

MILLED COINAGE

Y# 399   10 CASH
Copper **Obv. Leg.:** Chung Hua Min Kuo **Obv. Insc.:** Hu-nan Tung-Yuan **Rev:** Center of star convex

Date	Mintage	VG	F	VF	XF	Unc
ND(1912)	—	0.65	2.00	4.00	7.50	24.00

Y# 399a   10 CASH
Brass **Obv. Leg.:** Chung Hua Min Kuo **Obv. Insc.:** Hu-nan T'ung-Tüan

Date	Mintage	VG	F	VF	XF	Unc
ND(1912)	—	1.75	5.00	10.00	17.50	45.00

Y# 399.1   10 CASH
Copper **Obv:** Small rosette **Obv. Leg.:** Chung Hua Min Kuo **Obv. Insc.:** Hu-nan Tung-Yuan **Rev:** Center of star convex

Date	Mintage	VG	F	VF	XF	Unc
ND(1912)	—	0.67	2.00	4.00	7.00	24.00

Y# 399.2   10 CASH
Copper **Obv. Leg.:** Chung Hua Min Kuo **Obv. Insc.:** Hu-nan Tung-Yuan **Rev:** Center of star concave; star outlined

Date	Mintage	VG	F	VF	XF	Unc
ND(1912)	—	0.75	2.25	4.50	8.50	26.00

Y# 399.3   10 CASH
Copper **Obv. Leg.:** Chung Hua Min Kuo **Obv. Insc.:** Hu-nan Tung-Yuan **Rev:** Star not outlined

Date	Mintage	VG	F	VF	XF	Unc
ND(1912)	—	0.75	2.25	4.50	8.50	26.00

Y# 399.4   10 CASH
Copper **Obv:** Large rosette **Obv. Leg.:** Chung Hua Min Kuo **Obv. Insc.:** Hu-nan Tung-Yuan **Rev:** Center of star concave

Date	Mintage	VG	F	VF	XF	Unc
ND(1912)	—	0.75	2.25	4.50	8.50	26.00

Y# 399.5   10 CASH
Copper **Note:** Mule. General Issue, Y#306.

Date	Mintage	VG	F	VF	XF	Unc
ND(1912)	—	—	—	—	—	—

Y# 402   10 CASH
Copper   **Subject:** Provincial Constitution **Obv:** Rosette above crossed flags **Obv. Leg.:** THE REPUBLIC OF CHINA **Rev:** Trigram of the Pah Kwah in grain sprays

Date	Mintage	VG	F	VF	XF	Unc
11(1922)	—	15.00	25.00	38.00	60.00	—

Y# 400.3   20 CASH
Copper   **Obv:** 25 small curls in ribbon at base of plant **Obv. Leg.:** THE REPUBLIC OF CHINA **Rev. Leg.:** Hu-Nan Shan Tsoh

Date	Mintage	VG	F	VF	XF	Unc
ND(1919)	—	0.60	1.00	3.00	6.00	—

Y# 400.8   20 CASH
Copper   **Obv:** Larger star-shaped rosette above flags **Obv. Leg.:** THE REPUBLIC OF CHINA **Rev. Leg.:** Hu-Nan Shan Tsoh

Date	Mintage	VG	F	VF	XF	Unc
ND(1919)	—	1.00	2.50	4.00	7.00	—

Y# 402.1   10 CASH
Copper   **Obv:** Star above crossed flags **Obv. Leg.:** THE REPUBLIC OF CHINA **Rev:** Trigram of the Pah Kwah in grain sprays

Date	Mintage	VG	F	VF	XF	Unc
11(1922)	—	18.50	26.00	40.00	65.00	—

Y# 400.4   20 CASH
Copper   **Obv:** Smaller rice grains **Obv. Leg.:** THE REPUBLIC OF CHINA **Rev:** Crossed flags, floral ornament at left smaller **Rev. Leg.:** Hu-Nan Shan Tsoh

Date	Mintage	VG	F	VF	XF	Unc
ND(1919)	—	0.60	1.00	3.00	6.00	—

Y# 400.9   20 CASH
Copper   **Obv. Leg.:** THE REPUBLIC OF CHINA **Rev:** Sharp pointed star above crossed flags, long inner ribbons **Rev. Leg.:** Hu-Nan Shan Tsoh

Date	Mintage	VG	F	VF	XF	Unc
ND(1919)	—	1.00	2.50	4.00	7.00	—

Y# 400   20 CASH
Copper   **Obv. Leg.:** THE REPUBLIC OF CHINA **Rev:** Rosette above crossed flags, florals at left and right, five characters at bottom in legend **Rev. Leg.:** Hu Nan Shan Tsoh

Date	Mintage	VG	F	VF	XF	Unc
ND(1919)	—	1.25	3.00	7.50	15.00	—

Y# 400.5   20 CASH
Copper   **Obv:** Thin ribbon at base of plant **Obv. Leg.:** THE REPUBLIC OF CHINA **Rev. Leg.:** Hu-Nan Shan Tsoh

Date	Mintage	VG	F	VF	XF	Unc
ND(1919)	—	0.60	1.00	3.00	6.00	—

Y# 400.10   20 CASH
Copper   **Obv. Leg.:** THE REPUBLIC OF CHINA **Rev:** Sharp 5-pointed star over crossed flags, short inner ribbons **Rev. Leg.:** Hu-nan Sheng Tsao

Date	Mintage	VG	F	VF	XF	Unc
ND(1919)	—	20.00	25.00	30.00	35.00	—

Y# 400a   20 CASH
9.4700 g., Copper   **Obv:** Denomination: "20 CASH" **Obv. Leg.:** THE REPUBLIC OF CHINA **Rev. Leg.:** Hu-Nan Shan Tsoh

Date	Mintage	VG	F	VF	XF	Unc
ND(1919)	—	50.00	75.00	100	150	—

Y# 400b   20 CASH
Brass   **Obv:** Denomination: "20 CASH" **Obv. Leg.:** THE REPUBLIC OF CHINA **Rev. Leg.:** Hu-Nan Shan Tsoh

Date	Mintage	VG	F	VF	XF	Unc
ND(1919)	—	1.65	4.00	10.00	20.00	—

Y# 400.6   20 CASH
Copper   **Obv. Leg.:** THE REPUBLIC OF CHINA **Rev:** Small pentagonal rosette above crossed flags **Rev. Leg.:** Hu-Nan Shan Tsoh

Date	Mintage	VG	F	VF	XF	Unc
ND(1919)	—.	0.60	1.00	3.00	6.00	—

Y# 400.11   20 CASH
Copper   **Obv. Leg.:** THE REPUBLIC OF CHINA **Rev:** Similar to Y#400.2; no dot in rosette above flags **Rev. Leg.:** Hu-nan Sheng Tsao

Date	Mintage	VG	F	VF	XF	Unc
ND(1919)	—	—	—	—	—	—

Y# 400.7   20 CASH
Copper   **Obv. Leg.:** THE REPUBLIC OF CHINA **Rev:** Larger star-shaped rosette above crossed flags **Rev. Leg.:** Hu-Nan Shan Tsoh

Date	Mintage	VG	F	VF	XF	Unc
ND(1919)	—	1.00	2.50	4.00	7.00	—

Y# 400.7b   20 CASH
Brass   **Obv. Leg.:** THE REPUBLIC OF CHINA **Rev. Leg.:** Hu-Nan Shan Tsoh

Date	Mintage	VG	F	VF	XF	Unc
ND(1919)	—	1.65	4.00	8.00	15.00	—

Y# 400.2   20 CASH
Copper   **Rev. Leg.:** Hu-Nan Shan Tsoh

Date	Mintage	VG	F	VF	XF	Unc
ND(1919)	—	0.60	1.00	3.00	6.00	—

Y# 403.1   20 CASH
Copper   **Subject:** Provincial Constitution **Obv:** Rosette above crossed flags **Obv. Leg.:** THE REPUBLIC OF CHINA **Rev:** Trigram of the Pah Kwah in large grain sprays

Date	Mintage	VG	F	VF	XF	Unc
11(1922)	—	22.50	35.00	65.00	90.00	—

Y# 403.2 20 CASH
Copper **Subject:** Provincial Constitution **Obv:** Rosette above crossed flags **Obv. Leg.:** THE REPUBLIC OF CHINA **Rev:** Trigram of the Pah Kwah in smaller grain sprays

Date	Mintage	VG	F	VF	XF	Unc
11(1922)	—	35.00	75.00	100	150	—

Y# 404 DOLLAR
27.4000 g., Silver **Subject:** Provincial Constitution
Obv. Leg.: THE REPUBLIC OF CHINA **Rev:** Trigram of the Pah Kwah in grain sprays

Date	Mintage	VG	F	VF	XF	Unc
11(1922)	—	225	450	900	1,200	2,800

TRANSITIONAL COINAGE

K# 762 10 CENTS
Silver **Ruler:** Hung-hsien **Obv. Leg.:** Hung-hsien Yüan-nien **Obv. Insc.:** Chung-hua Yin-pi **Rev:** "Flying" dragon

Date	Mintage	VG	F	VF	XF	Unc
ND(1915)	—	200	350	800	1,500	2,500

Note: Though Kann calls this coin as Essai, contemporary reports indicate that the coin actually circulated briefly in 1915. Not to be confused with Y#28, the obverse of which has a different legend in Chinese. (See General Issues - Empire.)

PATTERNS
Including off metal strikes

KM#	Date	Mintage	Identification	Mkt Val
Pn4	ND(1902)	—	10 Cash. Copper. Three characters at bottom, Y#112.10.	850
Pn5	ND(1902)	—	10 Cash. Copper. Three characters at bottom, Y#112.12.	350

Note: Two Heaton (Birmingham) proof patterns for a proposed brass coinage which wasn't adopted. Dies were recut with only 2 characters for issue.

Pn6	ND(1915)	—	10 Cents. Nickel. Plain edge. K#762x	—
Pn7	ND(1915)	—	10 Cents. Copper. Plain edge. K#762y	450
Pn9	11(1922)	—	Dollar. Silver. General Chao Heng-ti	—
Pn10	11(1922)	—	Dollar. Copper. General Chao Heng-ti	—

HUPEH PROVINCE

Hubei

A province located in east-central China. Hilly, with some lakes and swamps, it has rich coal and iron deposits plus a varied agricultural program. The Wuchang Mint had been active from early in the Manchu dynasty and its modern equipment began operations in 1895. It probably closed in 1929.

EMPIRE

PROVINCIAL CAST COINAGE

C# 13-11 CASH
Cast Brass **Ruler:** Kuang-hsü **Obv. Insc.:** Kuang-hsü T'ung-pao **Rev. Insc.:** Manchu Boo-ching

Date	Mintage	Good	VG	F	VF	XF
ND(1875-1908)	—	12.50	20.00	30.00	45.00	—

C# 13-11.1 CASH
Cast Brass **Ruler:** Kuang-hsü **Obv. Insc.:** Kuang-hsü T'ung-pao **Rev. Insc.:** Manchu Boo-ching **Note:** Attribution of this mint mark to Chingchow is uncertain. Some authorities claim the Taku (Dagu) Mint in Tientsin struck this coin.

Date	Mintage	Good	VG	F	VF	XF
ND(1875-1908)	—	12.00	15.00	22.50	30.00	—

MILLED COINAGE

Y# 121 CASH
Brass **Ruler:** Kuang-hsü **Obv. Insc.:** Kuang-hsü Yüan-pao **Rev:** Dragon

Date	Mintage	VG	F	VF	XF	Unc
ND(1906)	66,474,000	8.00	12.00	18.00	30.00	50.00

Y# 7j CASH
Brass **Ruler:** Kuang-hsü **Obv:** Small mint mark on small disc in center **Obv. Leg.:** Kuang-hsü **Rev:** Dragon

Date	Mintage	VG	F	VF	XF	Unc
CD1908	Inc. above	3.50	8.00	15.00	25.00	45.00

Y# 7j.1 CASH
Brass **Ruler:** Kuang-hsü **Obv:** Large mint mark on small disc in center **Obv. Leg.:** Kuang-hsü **Rev:** Dragon

Date	Mintage	VG	F	VF	XF	Unc
CD1908	Inc. above	3.50	8.00	15.00	25.00	45.00

Y# 8j 2 CASH
Copper **Ruler:** Kuang-hsü **Obv. Insc.:** Tai-ch'ing T'ung-pi **Rev:** Dragon

Date	Mintage	VG	F	VF	XF	Unc
CD(1906)	844,000	50.00	80.00	125	200	—

Y# 9j 5 CASH
Copper, 24 mm. **Ruler:** Kuang-hsü **Obv. Insc.:** Tai-ch'ing T'ung-pi **Rev. Leg.:** Kuang-hsü Nien-tsao, TAI-CHING-TI-KUO ...

Date	Mintage	VG	F	VF	XF	Unc
CD1906	9,846,000	5.00	9.00	15.00	30.00	—

Y# 9j.1 5 CASH
Copper, 23 mm. **Ruler:** Kuang-hsü **Obv. Insc.:** Tai-ch'ing T'ung-pi **Rev:** Dragon redesigned **Rev. Leg.:** Kuang-hsü Nien-tsao, TAI-CHING-TI-KUO ...

Date	Mintage	VG	F	VF	XF	Unc
CD1906	Inc. above	6.00	11.00	17.50	35.00	—

Y# 120 10 CASH
Copper **Ruler:** Kuang-hsü **Obv:** 8-petaled rosette **Obv. Leg.:** Hu Peh Sheng Tsao **Obv. Insc.:** Kuang-hsü Yüan-pao **Rev:** Dragon surrounded by clouds

Date	Mintage	VG	F	VF	XF	Unc
ND(1902-05)	4,475,000	1.75	5.00	8.00	15.00	60.00

Y# 120a 10 CASH
Copper **Ruler:** Kuang-hsü **Obv. Leg.:** Hu Peh Sheng Tsao **Obv. Insc.:** Kuang-hsü Yüan-pao **Rev:** Uncircled large dragon

Date	Mintage	VG	F	VF	XF	Unc
ND(1902-05)	Inc. above	1.00	3.50	7.00	13.50	60.00

Y# 120a.1 10 CASH
Copper **Ruler:** Kuang-hsü **Obv. Leg.:** Hu Peh Sheng Tsao **Obv. Insc.:** Kuang-hsü Yüan-pao **Rev:** Slightly larger English letters, wide face on dragon

Date	Mintage	VG	F	VF	XF	Unc
ND(1902-05)	Inc. above	0.35	1.00	2.00	3.00	60.00

Y# 120a.2 10 CASH
Copper **Ruler:** Kuang-hsü **Obv. Leg.:** Hu Peh Sheng Tsao **Obv. Insc.:** Kuang-hsü Yüan-pao **Rev:** Large pearl with many spines, narrower face on dragon

Date	Mintage	VG	F	VF	XF	Unc
ND(1902-05)	Inc. above	0.25	0.75	1.50	2.75	60.00

Y# 120a.3 10 CASH
Copper **Ruler:** Kuang-hsü **Obv. Leg.:** Hu Peh Sheng Tsao **Obv. Insc.:** Kuang-hsü Yüan-pao **Rev:** Smaller pearl with fewer spines on dragon **Note:** Commonly found with medal alignment but also exists with coin alignment.

Date	Mintage	VG	F	VF	XF	Unc
ND(1902-05)	Inc. above	0.25	0.75	1.50	2.75	60.00

Y# 120a.3a 10 CASH
Brass **Ruler:** Kuang-hsü **Obv. Leg.:** Hu Peh Sheng Tsao **Obv. Insc.:** Kuang-hsü Yüan-pao **Rev:** Dragon

Date	Mintage	VG	F	VF	XF	Unc
ND(1902-05)	Inc. above	—	—	—	—	—

Y# 120a.4 10 CASH
Copper **Ruler:** Kuang-hsü **Obv:** 5-petaled rosette, small Manchu word at right **Obv. Leg.:** Hu Peh Sheng Tsao **Obv. Insc.:** Kuang-hsü Yüan-pao **Rev:** 4 dots in shape of cross at either side of dragon, PROVINCE spelled PHOVINCE, with "V" an inverted "A"

Date	Mintage	VG	F	VF	XF	Unc
ND(1902-05)	Inc. above	0.35	1.00	2.00	3.00	60.00

Y# 120a.5 10 CASH
Copper **Ruler:** Kuang-hsü **Obv:** Large Manchu at right **Obv. Leg.:** Hu Peh Sheng Tsao **Obv. Insc.:** Kuang-hsü Yüan-pao **Rev:** "R" in PROVINCE inverted, "V" an inverted "A", dragon

Date	Mintage	VG	F	VF	XF	Unc
ND(1902-05)	Inc. above	0.35	1.00	2.00	3.00	60.00

Y# 120a.6 10 CASH
Copper **Ruler:** Kuang-hsü **Obv. Leg.:** Hu Peh Sheng Tsao **Obv. Insc.:** Kuang-hsü Yüan-pao **Rev:** 6-pointed star at either side of dragon, hyphen in HU-PEH

Date	Mintage	VG	F	VF	XF	Unc
ND(1902-05)	Inc. above	0.35	1.00	2.00	3.00	60.00

Y# 120a.7 10 CASH
Copper **Ruler:** Kuang-hsü **Obv. Leg.:** Hu Peh Sheng Tsao **Obv. Insc.:** Kuang-hsü Yüan-pao **Rev:** 6-pointed star at either side of dragon, without hyphen in HU-PEH

Date	Mintage	VG	F	VF	XF	Unc
ND(1902-05)	Inc. above	0.50	1.50	3.00	6.00	60.00

Y# 120a.8 10 CASH
Copper **Ruler:** Kuang-hsü **Obv:** 5-petaled rosette and small Manchu **Obv. Leg.:** Hu Peh Sheng Tsao **Obv. Insc.:** Kuang-hsü Yüan-pao **Rev:** Dragon, very small pearl

Date	Mintage	VG	F	VF	XF	Unc
ND(1902-05)	Inc. above	1.00	3.50	6.00	12.00	60.00

Y# 120a.9 10 CASH
Copper **Ruler:** Kuang-hsü **Obv:** Square in circle **Obv. Leg.:** Hu Peh Sheng Tsao **Obv. Insc.:** Kuang-hsü Yüan-pao **Rev:** Dragon, hyphen in HU-PEH

Date	Mintage	VG	F	VF	XF	Unc
ND(1902-05)	Inc. above	1.25	4.00	7.50	15.00	70.00

Y# 120a.10 10 CASH
Copper **Ruler:** Kuang-hsü **Obv:** Square in circle **Obv. Leg.:** Hu Peh Sheng Tsao **Obv. Insc.:** Kuang-hsü Yüan-pao **Rev:** Dragon, without hyphen in HU-PEH

Date	Mintage	VG	F	VF	XF	Unc
ND(1902-05)	Inc. above	0.50	1.50	2.50	5.00	60.00

Y# 122 10 CASH
7.1800 g., Copper **Ruler:** Kuang-hsü **Obv:** Second character from right at top is larger, 6-petalled rosette **Obv. Leg.:** Hu-peh Sheng Tsao **Obv. Insc.:** Kuang-hsü Yüan-pao **Rev:** Front view dragon

Date	Mintage	VG	F	VF	XF	Unc
ND(1902-05)	Inc. above	0.20	0.60	1.50	3.00	60.00

Y# 122.1 10 CASH
Copper **Ruler:** Kuang-hsü **Obv:** Second character from right "Pei" smaller **Obv. Leg.:** Hu-peh Sheng Tsao **Obv. Insc.:** Kuang-hsü Yüan-pao **Rev:** Dragon

Date	Mintage	VG	F	VF	XF	Unc
ND(1902-05)	Inc. above	0.20	0.50	1.50	3.00	60.00

Y# 122.3 10 CASH
Copper **Ruler:** Kuang-hsü **Obv. Leg.:** Hu-peh Sheng Tsao **Obv. Insc.:** Kuang-hsü Yüan-pao **Rev:** Clouds above dragon's head, 2 clouds below pearl instead of 1

Date	Mintage	VG	F	VF	XF	Unc
ND(1902-05)	Inc. above	0.65	2.00	5.00	10.00	70.00

Y# 122.4 10 CASH
Copper **Ruler:** Kuang-hsü **Obv. Leg.:** Hu-peh Sheng Tsao **Obv. Insc.:** Kuang-hsü Yüan-pao **Rev:** Dragon, small circle around lower part of pearl, without dots on either side of mountain

Date	Mintage	VG	F	VF	XF	Unc
ND(1902-05)	Inc. above	0.65	2.00	5.00	10.00	70.00

Y# 122.5 10 CASH
Copper **Ruler:** Kuang-hsü **Obv. Leg.:** Hu-peh Sheng Tsao **Obv. Insc.:** Kuang-hsü Yüan-pao **Rev:** Dragon, larger circle around larger pearl, larger English letters

Date	Mintage	VG	F	VF	XF	Unc
ND(1902-05)	Inc. above	0.65	2.00	5.00	10.00	65.00

Y# 122a 10 CASH
Copper **Ruler:** Kuang-hsü **Obv. Leg.:** Hu-peh Sheng Tsao **Obv. Insc.:** Kuang-hsü Yüan-pao **Rev:** Circled front view of dragon

Date	Mintage	VG	F	VF	XF	Unc
ND(1902-05)	—	45.00	125	175	225	—

Y# 10j 10 CASH
Copper **Ruler:** Kuang-hsü **Obv. Insc.:** Tai-ch'ing T'ung-pi **Rev:** Dragon, 7 flames on pearl **Rev. Leg.:** Kuang hsü Nien-tsao, TAI-CHING-TI-KUO ...

Date	Mintage	VG	F	VF	XF	Unc
CD1906	1,865,558,000	0.25	0.75	1.00	2.00	70.00

Y# 10j.1 10 CASH
Copper, 28-29 mm. **Ruler:** Kuang-hsü **Obv. Insc.:** Tai-ch'ing T'ung-pi **Rev:** Redesigned dragon with wide lips, cloud-shaped bar below pearl with 5 flames **Rev. Leg.:** Kuang hsü Nien-tsao, TAI-CHING-TI-KUO ...

Date	Mintage	VG	F	VF	XF	Unc
CD1906	Inc. above	0.65	2.00	5.00	10.00	60.00

Y# 10j.2 10 CASH
Copper, 30 mm. **Ruler:** Kuang-hsü **Obv. Insc.:** Tai-ch'ing T'ung-pi **Rev:** Dragon **Rev. Leg.:** Kuang hsü Nien-tsao, TAI-CHING-TI-KUO ...

Date	Mintage	VG	F	VF	XF	Unc
CD1906	Inc. above	0.65	2.00	5.00	10.00	60.00

Y# 10j.3 10 CASH
Copper **Ruler:** Kuang-hsü **Obv. Insc.:** Tai-ch'ing T'ung-pi **Rev:** Different dragon with hook-shaped cloud beneath, pearl with 4 flames, large incuse swirl on pearl **Rev. Leg.:** Kuang hsü Nien-tsao, TAI-CHING-TI-KUO ...

Date	Mintage	VG	F	VF	XF	Unc
CD1906	Inc. above	0.35	1.00	2.00	3.00	60.00

Y# 10j.4   10 CASH
Copper **Ruler:** Kuang-hsü **Obv. Insc.:** Tai-ch'ing T'ung-pi
Rev: Dragon, small incuse swirl on pearl with 4 flames
Rev. Leg.: Kuang hsü Nien-tsao, TAI-CHING-TI-KUO ...

Date	Mintage	VG	F	VF	XF	Unc
CD1906	Inc. above	0.20	0.50	1.00	2.00	60.00

Y# 10j.5   10 CASH
Copper **Ruler:** Kuang-hsü **Obv. Insc.:** Tai-ch'ing T'ung-pi
Rev: Dragon, swirl on pearl in relief with 4 flames
Rev. Leg.: Kuang hsü Nien-tsao, TAI-CHING-TI-KUO ...

Date	Mintage	VG	F	VF	XF	Unc
CD1906	Inc. above	0.25	0.75	1.00	2.00	60.00

Y# 20j   10 CASH
Copper **Ruler:** Hsüan-t'ung **Obv. Insc.:** Tai-ch'ing T'ung-pi
Rev: Dragon, large incuse swirl on pearl **Rev. Leg.:** Hsüan-t'ung
Nien-tsao, TAI-CHING-TI-KUO ...

Date	Mintage	VG	F	VF	XF	Unc
CD1909	371,577,000	0.50	1.50	3.00	6.00	60.00

Y# 20j.1   10 CASH
Copper **Ruler:** Hsüan-t'ung **Obv. Insc.:** Tai-ch'ing T'ung-pi **Rev:**
Dragon, small swirl in relief on pearl **Rev. Leg.:** Hsüan-t'ung Nien-
tsao, TAI-CHING-TI-KUO ...

Date	Mintage	VG	F	VF	XF	Unc
CD1909	Inc. above	0.50	1.50	3.00	6.00	60.00

Y# 20j.2   10 CASH
Copper **Ruler:** Hsüan-t'ung **Obv:** CD1909 over CD1906 **Obv.
Insc.:** Tai-ch'ing T'ung-pi **Rev:** Dragon **Rev. Leg.:** Hsüan-t'ung
Nien-tsao, TAI-CHING-TI-KUO ...

Date	Mintage	VG	F	VF	XF	Unc
CD1909/1906	—	—	—	—	—	—

Y# 20j.3   10 CASH
Copper **Ruler:** Hsüan-t'ung **Obv:** Characters "Hsuan T'ung" re-
engraved over characters "Kuang Hsu" **Obv. Insc.:** Tai-ch'ing
T'ung-pi **Rev:** Dragon **Rev. Leg.:** Hsüan-t'ung Nien-tsao, TAI-
CHING-TI-KUO ...

Date	Mintage	VG	F	VF	XF	Unc
CD1909 Rare	—	—	—	—	—	—

Y# 11j   20 CASH
Copper **Ruler:** Kuang-hsü **Obv. Insc.:** Tai-ch'ing T'ung-pi
Rev: Dragon **Rev. Leg.:** Kuang-hsü Nien-tsao, TAI-CHING-
TI-KUO ...

Date	Mintage	VG	F	VF	XF	Unc
CD1906	3,710,000	150	250	480	900	—

Y# 123   5 CENTS
1.3500 g., 0.8200 Silver 0.0356 oz. ASW **Ruler:** Kuang-hsü
Obv. Leg.: Hu-peh Sheng Tsao **Obv. Insc.:** Kuang-hsü Yüan-pao
Rev: Dragon **Rev. Leg.:** HU-PEH PROVINCE **Edge:** Reeded

Date	Mintage	VG	F	VF	XF	Unc
ND(1895-1905)	4,278,000	17.50	50.00	100	150	250

Y# 124   10 CENTS
2.7000 g., 0.8200 Silver 0.0712 oz. ASW **Ruler:** Kuang-hsü
Obv. Insc.: Kuang-hsü Yüan-pao **Rev:** Character at either side
of dragon "Pen Sheng" indicating coin was for provincial use

Date	Mintage	F	VF	XF	Unc	BU
ND(1894)	—	300	700	1,300	2,000	—

Y# 124.1   10 CENTS
2.7000 g., 0.8200 Silver 0.0712 oz. ASW, 18.6 mm.
Ruler: Kuang-hsü **Obv. Leg.:** Hu-peh Sheng Tsao
Obv. Insc.: Kuang-hsü Yüan-pao **Rev:** Without characters
beside dragon **Rev. Leg.:** HU-PEH PROVINCE **Edge:** Reeded

Date	Mintage	VG	F	VF	XF	Unc
ND(1895-1907)	—	1.50	2.50	4.50	8.00	20.00

Note: 2 varieties of edge milling exist

Y# 129   10 CENTS
Silver **Ruler:** Hsüan-t'ung **Obv. Leg.:** Hu-peh Sheng Tsao
Obv. Insc.: Hsüan-t'ung Yüan-pao **Rev:** Dragon **Rev. Leg.:** HU-
PEH PROVINCE

Date	Mintage	VG	F	VF	XF	Unc
ND(1909)	—	150	300	750	1,200	2,000

Y# 125   20 CENTS
5.3000 g., 0.8200 Silver 0.1397 oz. ASW, 23.6 mm.
Ruler: Kuang-hsü **Obv. Insc.:** Kuang-hsü Yüan-pao
Rev: Character at either side of dragon "Pen Sheng" indicating
coin was for provincial use **Edge:** Reeded

Date	Mintage	F	VF	XF	Unc	BU
ND(1894)	—	1,500	3,500	4,000	5,000	—

Y# 125.1   20 CENTS
5.3000 g., 0.8200 Silver 0.1397 oz. ASW **Ruler:** Kuang-hsü
Obv. Leg.: Hu-peh Sheng Tsao **Obv. Insc.:** Kuang-hsü Yüan-pao **Rev. Leg.:** HU-PEH
PROVINCE

Date	Mintage	VG	F	VF	XF	Unc
ND(1895-1907)	—	2.50	5.00	10.00	15.00	30.00

Y# 130   20 CENTS
Silver **Ruler:** Hsüan-t'ung **Obv. Leg.:** Hu-peh Sheng Tsao
Obv. Insc.: Hsüan-t'ung Yüan-pao **Rev:** Dragon **Rev. Leg.:** HU-
PEH PROVINCE

Date	Mintage	VG	F	VF	XF	Unc
ND(1909-11)	—	200	400	1,000	1,500	2,500

Y# 126   50 CENTS
13.5000 g., 0.8600 Silver 0.3733 oz. ASW **Ruler:** Kuang-hsü
Obv. Leg.: Hu-peh Sheng Tsao **Obv. Insc.:** Kuang-hsü Yüan-
pao **Rev:** Dragon **Rev. Leg.:** HU-PEH PROVINCE

Date	Mintage	VG	F	VF	XF	Unc
ND(1895-1905)	—	15.00	40.00	80.00	120	250

Y# 127   DOLLAR
26.7000 g., 0.9000 Silver 0.7726 oz. ASW **Ruler:** Kuang-hsü
Obv. Insc.: "Kuang-hsü Yüan-pao" **Rev:** Characters "Pen Sheng"
at either side of dragon indicating coin was for provincial use

Date	Mintage	F	VF	XF	Unc	BU
ND(1894)	—	7,500	10,000	15,000	25,000	—

Y# 127.1   DOLLAR

26.7000 g., 0.9000 Silver 0.7726 oz. ASW   **Ruler:** Kuang-hsü
Obv. Leg.: Hu-peh Sheng Tsao **Obv. Insc.:** Kuang-hsü Yüan-pao **Rev:** Without "Pen Sheng" at either side of dragon
Rev. Leg.: HU-PEH PROVINCE **Edge:** Reeded

Date	Mintage	VG	F	VF	XF	Unc
ND(1895-1907)	19,935,000	15.00	25.00	45.00	85.00	500

Y# 131   DOLLAR

27.0000 g., 0.9000 Silver 0.7812 oz. ASW   **Ruler:** Hsüan-t'ung
Obv. Leg.: Hu-peh Sheng Tsao **Obv. Insc.:** Hsüan-t'ung Yüan-pao **Rev:** Dragon

Date	Mintage	VG	F	VF	XF	Unc
ND(1909-11)	2,703,000	20.00	35.00	60.00	125	550

BULLION COINAGE/TAEL SYSTEM

Y# 128.1   TAEL

37.7000 g., 0.8770 Silver 1.0630 oz. ASW   **Ruler:** Kuang-hsü
Obv: Large inscription **Obv. Insc.:** Kuang-hsü Yin-pi **Rev:** Two dragons forming circle **Rev. Leg.:** HU-PEH PROVINCE

Date	Mintage	VG	F	VF	XF	Unc
30(1904)	648,000	165	525	1,000	3,000	4,500

Y# 128.2   TAEL

37.7000 g., 0.8770 Silver 1.0630 oz. ASW   **Ruler:** Kuang-hsü
Obv: Smaller inscription **Obv. Insc.:** Kuang-hsü Yin-pi **Rev:** Two dragons forming circle **Rev. Leg.:** HU-PEH PROVINCE

Date	Mintage	VG	F	VF	XF	Unc
30(1904)	Inc. above	200	400	900	1,750	3,000

REPUBLIC

MILLED COINAGE

Y# A405   20 CASH

Brass   **Note:** Attribution is uncertain. Probably minted in Szechuan (Sichuan).

Date	Mintage	VG	F	VF	XF	Unc
ND(c.1914)	—	40.00	85.00	115	165	—

Y# 405   50 CASH

Copper Or Brass   **Obv. Leg.:** Chung Hua Min Kuo (year) Nien
Note: Crude strike. Similar coins dated Yr. 1 and Yr. 8 are known, but their status is uncertain.

Date	Mintage	VG	F	VF	XF	Unc
3(1914)	—	575	850	1,100	—	—
7(1918)	—	400	600	850	—	—

Y# 405.1   50 CASH

Copper Or Brass   **Obv. Leg.:** Chung Hua Min Kuo (year) Nien
Note: Machine strike. Not to be confused with Szechuan (Sichuan) Y#449.

Date	Mintage	VG	F	VF	XF	Unc
7(1918)	—	575	850	1,100	—	—

Y# 406   20 CENTS

5.2000 g., Silver   **Obv:** Characters "Tsao" at left and "Hu" at right of military bust of Yuan Shih-k'ai left **Note:** Do not confuse with Y#327 (see Republic-general issues).

Date	Mintage	VG	F	VF	XF	Unc
9(1920)	—	30.00	80.00	150	220	800

PATTERNS

Including off metal strikes

KM#	Date	Mintage	Identification	Mkt Val
PnA6	ND(1902)	—	10 Cash. White Copper. Y122.5. W518.	—
Pn6	ND(1902)	—	10 Cash. Brass. W480.	—
PnA7	3(1911)	—	10 Cents. Pewter. K48y.	—
Pn7	1(1916)	—	10 Cents. White Metal. K764x.	—

KANSU PROVINCE

Gansu

A province located in north-central China with a contrast of mountains and sandy plains. The west end of the Great Wall with its branches lies in Kansu (Gansu). Kansu (Gansu) was the eastern end of the "Silk Road" that led to central and western Asia. Two mints issued Cash coins. It has been reported, but not confirmed, that the Lanchow Mint operated as late as 1949.

REPUBLIC

CAST COINAGE

Y# C407   20 CASH

Brass **Obv:** Crossed flags, striped flag at right **Obv. Leg.:** Chung Hua Min Kuo **Rev:** Value in grain sprays **Rev. Leg.:** THE REPUBELIC OF CHINA **Edge:** Plain

Date	Mintage	Good	VG	F	VF	XF
ND(1920)	—	16.00	40.00	90.00	150	—

Y# E407   20 CASH

6.4000 g., Brass, 31.85 mm.   **Obv:** Crossed flags, striped flag at left **Obv. Leg.:** Chung Hua Min Kuo **Rev:** Value in grain sprays **Rev. Leg.:** TJ REPUBLIC OF CHINA + TEVC + **Edge:** Plain

Date	Mintage	Good	VG	F	VF	XF
ND(1920)	—	22.00	55.00	120	200	—

Y# D407   50 CASH

Brass **Obv:** Crossed flags in floral sprays, striped flag at right **Obv. Leg.:** Chung Hua Min Kuo **Rev:** Value in grain sprays **Rev. Leg.:** THE REPUBLIC OE CHINA **Edge:** Plain

Date	Mintage	Good	VG	F	VF	XF
ND(1920)	—	38.00	70.00	150	250	—

MILLED COINAGE

Y# 408   50 CASH
Copper **Obv. Leg.:** Chung Hua Min Kuo (year) Nien

Date	Mintage	VG	F	VF	XF	Unc
15(1926)	2,564,000	85.00	175	275	450	—

Y# A408   50 CASH
Copper **Obv:** National star **Obv. Leg.:** Chung Hua Min Kuo (year) Nien **Rev:** Crossed flags

Date	Mintage	VG	F	VF	XF	Unc
ND(1927)	—	500	900	1,500	—	—

Y# 409   100 CASH
Copper **Obv. Leg.:** Chung Hua Min Kuo (year) Nien **Rev:** Crossed flags

Date	Mintage	VG	F	VF	XF	Unc
15(1926)	—	35.00	50.00	100	150	—

Y# 407   DOLLAR
26.6000 g., Silver **Obv:** Military bust of Yüan Shih-kai left, "Su" at left, "Kan" at right **Obv. Leg.:** Chung Hua Min Kuo (year) Nien **Rev:** Value in sprays

Date	Mintage	VG	F	VF	XF	Unc
3(1914)	—	270	450	900	1,500	—

Y# 410   DOLLAR
26.6000 g., Silver **Obv:** Facing bust of Sun Yat-sen **Obv. Leg.:** Chung Hua Min Kuo (year) Nien **Rev:** National star

Date	Mintage	VG	F	VF	XF	Unc
17(1928)	—	450	1,050	1,800	3,000	—

PATTERNS
Including off metal strikes

KM#	Date	Mintage	Identification	Mkt Val
Pn1	ND(ca.1928)	—	5 Cash. Copper. Hsu#385.	650
Pn2	ND(ca.1928)	—	10 Cash. Copper.	
Pn3	ND(1928)	—	5 Fen. Copper. Hsu#383.	300
Pn4	17(1928)	—	50 Cash. Copper.	
Pn5	ND(ca.1928)	—	10 Fen. Copper. Hsu#384.	400

KIANGNAN

A district in eastern China made up of Anhwei (Anhui) and Kiangsu (Jiangsu) provinces. In 1667 the province of Kiangnan was divided into the present provinces of Anhwei (Anhui) and Kiangsu (Jiangsu). In 1723 Nanking, formerly the capital of Kiangnan, was made the capital of Liang-Chiang Chiang (an administrative area consisting of Anhwei (Anhui), Kiangsu (Jiangsu), and Kiangsi (Jiangxi) provinces.

Always highly regarded because of location, agriculture and manufacturing, Kiangnan has frequently been sought after by contending forces.

The Nanking Mint had been active during imperial times. Modern minting facilities began operations in 1897. A second mint was planned for the Kiangnan Arsenal in Shanghai in 1905. Mints for copper coins also operated in Chingkiang (Qingjiang) in central Kiangsu and at Soochow which is further south. A silver mint was planned for Shanghai in 1921. The Nanking Mint, the most important of the group, burned down in 1929. The Nationalist Government Central Mint was completed in Shanghai in 1930 and opened in 1933.

EMPIRE

MILLED COINAGE

The initials HAH, SY, CH and TH are those of mint officials and were placed on the coins as a guarantee of the coin's fineness. The 5-, 10-, and 20-cent coins are often found without a decimal point between the numbers on the reverse. The 1904 dated dollar was restruck during Republican times.

Y# 7k   CASH
Brass **Ruler:** Kuang-hsü **Obv:** Bottom horizontal stroke in mint mark extends beyond outside vertical strokes **Obv. Leg.:** Kuanghsü **Rev:** Dragon

Date	Mintage	VG	F	VF	XF	Unc
CD(1908)	25,450,000	2.50	4.50	8.50	16.00	—

Y# 7k.1   CASH
Brass **Ruler:** Kuang-hsü **Obv:** Bottom horizontal stroke in mint mark does not extend beyond outside vertical strokes **Obv. Leg.:** Kuang-hsü **Rev:** Dragon

Date	Mintage	VG	F	VF	XF	Unc
CD1908	Inc. above	3.50	6.50	12.50	21.50	—

Y# 9k.1   5 CASH
Copper **Ruler:** Kuang-hsü **Obv:** Mint mark incused on raised disk **Obv. Insc.:** Tai-ch'ing T'ung-pi **Rev:** Dragon **Rev. Leg.:** Kuang-hsü Nien-tsao, TAI-CHING-TI-KUO...

Date	Mintage	VG	F	VF	XF	Unc
CD1906	—	35.00	65.00	100	150	—

Y# 9k.1a   5 CASH
Brass **Ruler:** Kuang-hsü **Obv. Insc.:** Tai-ch'ing T'ung-pi **Rev:** Dragon **Rev. Leg.:** Kuang-hsü Nien-tsao, TAI-CHING-TI-KUO...

Date	Mintage	VG	F	VF	XF	Unc
CD1906	—	45.00	90.00	125	200	—

Y# 9k.2   5 CASH
Copper **Ruler:** Kuang-hsü **Obv:** Mint mark in relief at center without disk **Obv. Insc.:** Tai-ch'ing T'ung-pi **Rev:** Dragon **Rev. Leg.:** Kuang-hsü Nien-tsao, TAI-CHING-TI-KUO...

Date	Mintage	VG	F	VF	XF	Unc
CD1906	—	45.00	90.00	125	200	—

Y# 135.2   10 CASH
Copper **Ruler:** Kuang-hsü **Obv:** Small Manchu words in center **Obv. Leg.:** Chiang-nan Sheng Tsao **Obv. Insc.:** Kuang-hsü Yüan-pao **Rev:** Dragon

Date	Mintage	F	VF	XF	Unc	BU
CD1902	—	1.50	3.00	5.00	20.00	—

Y# 135   10 CASH
Copper **Ruler:** Kuang-hsü **Obv. Leg.:** Chiang-nan Sheng Tsao **Obv. Insc.:** Kuang-hsü Yüan-pao **Rev:** Dragon **Edge:** Reeded

Date	Mintage	VG	F	VF	XF	Unc
ND(ca.1902)	—	10.00	30.00	60.00	100	—

Y# 135.1   10 CASH
Copper **Ruler:** Kuang-hsü **Obv. Leg.:** Chiang-nan Sheng Tsao **Obv. Insc.:** Kuang-hsü Yüan-pao **Rev:** Dragon **Edge:** Plain

Date	Mintage	VG	F	VF	XF	Unc
ND(ca.1902)	—	10.00	30.00	60.00	100	—

Y# 135.3   10 CASH
Copper **Ruler:** Kuang-hsü **Obv:** Large Manchu words in center **Obv. Leg.:** Chiang-nan Sheng Tsao **Obv. Insc.:** Kuang-hsü Yüan-pao **Rev:** Dragon

Date	Mintage	VG	F	VF	XF	Unc
CD1902	—	2.00	6.50	12.50	25.00	45.00

Y# C140   10 CASH
Copper **Ruler:** Kuang-hsü **Obv:** Kiang-nan **Obv. Leg.:** Chiang-nan Sheng Tsao **Obv. Insc.:** Kuang-hsü Yüan-pao **Rev:** Dragon **Rev. Leg.:** KIANG-SOO **Note:** Mule; often confused with Y#162.

Date	Mintage	VG	F	VF	XF	Unc
CD1902	—	—	—	—	—	—
ND(ca.1902)	—	50.00	150	200	250	—

Y# 135.4   10 CASH
Copper **Ruler:** Kuang-hsü **Obv. Leg.:** Chiang-nan Sheng Tsao **Obv. Insc.:** Kuang-hsü Yüan-pao **Rev:** Dragon

Date	Mintage	VG	F	VF	XF	Unc
CD1903	—	1.25	4.00	5.00	7.00	65.00

Y# 135.5   10 CASH
Copper **Ruler:** Kuang-hsü **Obv. Leg.:** Chiang-nan Sheng Tsao **Obv. Insc.:** Kuang-hsü Yüan-pao **Rev:** Dragon; cloud above letter "T" looks like number "3"

Date	Mintage	VG	F	VF	XF	Unc
CD1904	351,974,000	0.35	1.00	2.00	5.00	65.00

Y# 135.6   10 CASH
Copper **Ruler:** Kuang-hsü **Obv. Leg.:** Chiang-nan Sheng Tsao **Obv. Insc.:** Kuang-hsü Yüan-pao **Rev:** Dragon; cloud above "T" redesigned; "CASH" spelled "GASH"

Date	Mintage	VG	F	VF	XF	Unc
CD1904	Inc. above	1.50	4.50	9.00	17.50	90.00

Y# 135.7   10 CASH
Copper **Ruler:** Kuang-hsü **Obv. Leg.:** Chiang-nan Sheng Tsao **Obv. Insc.:** Kuang-hsü Yüan-pao **Rev:** Thin-tailed dragon; third design of cloud above letter "T"

Date	Mintage	VG	F	VF	XF	Unc
CD1904	Inc. above	0.50	1.50	3.00	5.00	65.00

Y# 135.8   10 CASH
Copper **Ruler:** Kuang-hsü **Obv. Leg.:** Chiang-nan Sheng Tsao **Obv. Insc.:** Kuang-hsü Yüan-pao **Rev:** Fewer clouds around dragon; scales on dragon's body different, pearl smaller

Date	Mintage	VG	F	VF	XF	Unc
CD1904	Inc. above	1.50	4.50	9.00	17.50	90.00

Note: This coin is believed to be counterfeit

Y# 135.9   10 CASH
Copper **Ruler:** Kuang-hsü **Obv. Leg.:** Chiang-nan Sheng Tsao **Obv. Insc.:** Kuang-hsü Yüan-pao **Rev:** Small rosette at either side of dragon

Date	Mintage	VG	F	VF	XF	Unc
CD1905	496,020,000	0.35	1.00	2.00	5.00	60.00

Y# 135.10   10 CASH
Copper **Ruler:** Kuang-hsü **Obv. Leg.:** Chiang-nan Sheng Tsao **Obv. Insc.:** Kuang-hsü Yüan-pao **Rev:** Large oblong rosettes at either side of dragon

Date	Mintage	VG	F	VF	XF	Unc
CD1905	Inc. above	0.50	1.50	3.00	5.00	60.00

Y# 138   10 CASH
Copper **Ruler:** Kuang-hsü **Obv. Leg.:** Chiang-nan Sheng Tsao **Obv. Insc.:** Kuang-hsü Yüan-pao **Rev:** Dragon; denomination: "TEN-CASH"

Date	Mintage	VG	F	VF	XF	Unc
CD1905	Inc. above	1.25	3.50	6.00	12.00	65.00

Y# 138.1   10 CASH
Copper **Ruler:** Kuang-hsü **Obv:** Rosette in center **Obv. Leg.:** Chiang-nan Sheng Tsao **Obv. Insc.:** Kuang-hsü Yüan-pao **Rev:** Dragon; without hyphen in "TEN CASH"

Date	Mintage	VG	F	VF	XF	Unc
CD1905	Inc. above	0.25	0.75	1.50	5.00	60.00

Y# 10k   10 CASH
Copper **Ruler:** Kuang-hsü **Obv:** Mint mark in relief on raised disc **Obv. Insc.:** Tai-ch'ing T'ung-pi **Rev:** Dragon with wide face and incuse eyes **Rev. Leg.:** Kuang-hsü Nien-tsao, TAI-CHING-TI-KUO...

Date	Mintage	VG	F	VF	XF	Unc
CD1906	504,800,000	0.45	1.25	2.50	5.00	60.00

Y# 10k.1   10 CASH
Copper **Ruler:** Kuang-hsü **Obv. Insc.:** Tai-ch'ing T'ung-pi **Rev:** Dragon with narrower face and raised dots for eyes **Rev. Leg.:** Kuang-hsü Nien-tsao, TAI-CHING-TI-KUO...

Date	Mintage	VG	F	VF	XF	Unc
CD1906	Inc. above	0.45	1.25	2.50	5.00	60.00

Y# 10k.2   10 CASH
Copper **Ruler:** Kuang-hsü **Obv:** Mint mark in relief without raised disc **Obv. Insc.:** Tai-ch'ing T'ung-pi **Rev:** Dragon with wide face and incuse eyes **Rev. Leg.:** Kuang-hsü Nien-tsao, TAI-CHING-TI-KUO...

Date	Mintage	VG	F	VF	XF	Unc
CD1906	Inc. above	0.35	1.00	2.50	5.00	60.00

Y# 10k.3   10 CASH
Copper **Ruler:** Kuang-hsü **Obv. Insc.:** Tai-ch'ing T'ung-pi **Rev:** Dragon with narrow face and raised dots for eyes **Rev. Leg.:** Kuang-hsü Nien-tsao, TAI-CHING-TI-KUO...

Date	Mintage	VG	F	VF	XF	Unc
CD1906	Inc. above	0.35	1.00	2.50	5.00	60.00

Y# 10k.4   10 CASH
Copper **Ruler:** Kuang-hsü **Obv:** Mint mark incuse on raised disc **Obv. Insc.:** Tai-ch'ing T'ung-pi **Rev:** Dragon **Rev. Leg.:** Kuang-hsü Nien-tsao, TAI-CHING-TI-KUO...

Date	Mintage	VG	F	VF	XF	Unc
CD1906	Inc. above	4.50	12.50	25.00	45.00	—

Y# 10k.4a   10 CASH
Brass **Ruler:** Kuang-hsü **Obv. Insc.:** Tai-ch'ing T'ung-pi **Rev:** Dragon **Rev. Leg.:** Kuang-hsü Nien-tsao, TAI-CHING-TI-KUO...

Date	Mintage	VG	F	VF	XF	Unc
CD1906	—					

Y# A140   10 CASH
Copper **Ruler:** Kuang-hsü **Obv:** Y#10k.2 **Obv. Insc.:** Tai-ch'ing T'ung-Pi **Rev:** Dragon; Y#138 **Note:** Mule.

Date	Mintage	VG	F	VF	XF	Unc
CD1906	Inc. above	8.50	25.00	40.00	60.00	—

Y# B140   10 CASH
Copper **Ruler:** Kuang-hsü **Obv:** Y#138 **Obv. Leg.:** Chiang-nan Sheng Tsao **Obv. Insc.:** Kuang-hsü Yüan-pao **Rev:** Dragon; Y#10k **Note:** Mule.

Date	Mintage	VG	F	VF	XF	Unc
CD1905	Inc. above	10.00	30.00	50.00	70.00	—

Y# D140   10 CASH
Copper **Ruler:** Kuang-hsü **Obv:** Y#138.1 **Obv. Leg.:** Chiang-nan Sheng Tsao **Obv. Insc.:** Kuang-hsü Yüan-pao **Rev:** Dragon; Y#135 **Note:** Mule.

Date	Mintage	VG	F	VF	XF	Unc
CD1905	Inc. above	35.00	100	150	200	—

Note: Other Kiangnan mules exist, dated 1902 and 1903

Y# E140   10 CASH
Copper **Ruler:** Kuang-hsü **Obv:** Y#10.5 **Obv. Insc.:** Tai-ch'ing T'ung-pi **Rev:** Dragon; Kiangnan Y#138.1 **Note:** Mule.

Date	Mintage	VG	F	VF	XF	Unc
CD1907	—	35.00	100	225	300	—

Y# 140.1   10 CASH
7.1200 g., Copper, 28.6 mm. **Ruler:** Kuang-hsü **Obv:** Y#10k **Obv. Insc.:** Tai-ch'ing T'ung-Pi **Rev:** Dragon; Y#138 **Note:** Mule; raised or incused mint mark.

Date	Mintage	VG	F	VF	XF	Unc
CD1906	Inc. above	1.00	3.00	5.00	12.00	70.00

Y# 140.2   10 CASH
Copper **Ruler:** Kuang-hsü **Obv:** Y#10k **Obv. Insc.:** Tai-ch'ing T'ung-pi **Rev:** Dragon, Y#138 **Note:** Mule; mint mark incuse on raised disk.

Date	Mintage	VG	F	VF	XF	Unc
CD1906	Inc. above	1.00	3.00	5.00	12.00	70.00

Y# 10k.5   10 CASH
Copper **Ruler:** Kuang-hsü **Obv:** Mint mark incuse on raised disc **Obv. Insc.:** Tai-ch'ing T'ung-pi **Rev:** Dragon with wide face; seven flames on pearl **Rev. Leg.:** Kuang-hsü Nien-tsao, TAI-CHING-TI-KUO...

Date	Mintage	VG	F	VF	XF	Unc
CD1907	552,000,000	0.50	1.50	3.00	5.00	60.00

Y# 10k.6   10 CASH
Copper **Ruler:** Kuang-hsü **Obv. Insc.:** Tai-ch'ing T'ung-pi **Rev:** Different dragon with narrow face and small mouth; five flames on pearl; dot after "COIN" **Rev. Leg.:** Kuang-hsü Nien-tsao, TAI-CHING-TI-KUO...

Date	Mintage	VG	F	VF	XF	Unc
CD1907	Inc. above	0.35	1.00	2.00	4.50	60.00

Y# 10k.6a   10 CASH
Brass **Ruler:** Kuang-hsü **Obv. Insc.:** Tai-ch'ing T'ung-pi **Rev:** Dragon **Rev. Leg.:** Kuang-hsü Nien-tsao, TAI-CHING-TI-KUO...

Date	Mintage	VG	F	VF	XF	Unc
CD1907	Inc. above	3.00	9.00	17.50	30.00	

Y# 10k.7   10 CASH
Copper **Ruler:** Kuang-hsü **Obv. Insc.:** Tai-ch'ing T'ung-pi **Rev:** Dragon with large mouth and redesigned head; flame below pearl has long tail which touches dragon's body; "KUO" spelled "KIIO" **Rev. Leg.:** Kuang-hsü Nien-tsao, TAI-CHING-TI-KUO...

Date	Mintage	VG	F	VF	XF	Unc
CD1907	Inc. above	0.35	1.00	2.50	5.00	60.00

Y# 10k.8   10 CASH
Copper **Ruler:** Kuang-hsü **Obv. Insc.:** Tai-ch'ing T'ung-pi **Rev:** Tail of flame below pearl does not touch dragon's body; dash after word "COIN"; "KUO" spelled "KUO" **Rev. Leg.:** Kuang-hsü Nien-tsao, TAI-CHING-TI-KUO...

Date	Mintage	VG	F	VF	XF	Unc
CD1907	Inc. above	0.35	1.00	2.50	5.00	60.00

Y# 10k.9   10 CASH
Copper **Ruler:** Kuang-hsü **Obv. Insc.:** Tai-ch'ing T'ung-pi **Rev:** Dragon with square mouth; letter "K" in "KUO" larger than other letters; without dot or dash after "COIN" **Rev. Leg.:** Kuang-hsü Nien-tsao, TAI-CHING-TI-KUO...

Date	Mintage	VG	F	VF	XF	Unc
CD1907	Inc. above	0.35	1.00	2.25	4.50	60.00

Y# 10k.9a   10 CASH
Copper **Ruler:** Kuang-hsü **Obv. Insc.:** Tai-ch'ing T'ung-pi **Rev:** Large flat-faced dragon **Rev. Leg.:** Kuang-hsü Nien-tsao, TAI-CHING-TI-KUO...

Date	Mintage	VG	F	VF	XF	Unc
CD1907	—	—	—	—	—	—

Y# 10k.10   10 CASH
Copper **Ruler:** Kuang-hsü **Obv:** Mint mark incuse on raised disc **Obv. Insc.:** Tai-ch'ing T'ung-pi **Rev:** Dragon with small mouth; five-flame pearl; dot after "COIN"; "KUO" spelled "KUO" **Rev. Leg.:** Kuang-hsü Nien-tsao, TAI-CHING-TI-KUO...

Date	Mintage	VG	F	VF	XF	Unc
CD1908	442,750,000	0.35	1.00	2.50	5.00	20.00

Y# 10k.15   10 CASH
Copper, 28.54 mm. **Ruler:** Kuang-hsü **Obv. Insc.:** Tai-ch'ing T'ung-pi **Rev:** Dragon has large mouth and redesigned head; tail on cloud beneath pearl touches dragon's body. **Rev. Leg.:** Kuang-hs? Nien-tsao, TAI-CHING-TI-KUO... **Edge:** Plain

Date	Mintage	VG	F	VF	XF	Unc
CD1908	Inc. above	0.35	1.00	2.00	4.00	20.00

Y# 10k.12   10 CASH
Copper **Ruler:** Kuang-hsü **Obv. Insc.:** Tai-ch'ing T'ung-pi **Rev:** Dragon; dash after "COIN"; "KUO" spelled "KUO" **Rev. Leg.:** Kuang-hsü Nien-tsao, TAI-CHING-TI-KUO...

Date	Mintage	VG	F	VF	XF	Unc
CD1908	Inc. above	0.50	1.50	3.00	5.00	20.00

Y# 10k.13   10 CASH
Copper **Ruler:** Kuang-hsü **Obv. Insc.:** Tai-ch'ing T'ung-pi **Rev:** Dragon's head redesigned; without dot or dash after "COIN"; "KUO" spelled "KIIO" **Rev. Leg.:** Kuang-hsü Nien-tsao, TAI-CHING-TI-KUO...

Date	Mintage	VG	F	VF	XF	Unc
CD1908	Inc. above	0.35	1.00	2.00	4.00	20.00

Note: Most of the 1907 and 1908 ten cash above have copper spelled GOPPER

Y# 10k.14   10 CASH
Copper **Ruler:** Kuang-hsü **Obv. Insc.:** Tai-ch'ing T'ung-pi **Rev:** Dragon's right mustache without hook **Rev. Leg.:** TAI-GIIING-TI-KIIO GOPPER COIN

Date	Mintage	VG	F	VF	XF	Unc
CD1908	Inc. above	0.35	1.00	2.50	5.00	

Y# 141a   5 CENTS
13.0000 g., 0.8200 Silver 0.3427 oz. ASW **Ruler:** Kuang-hsü **Obv. Leg.:** Chiang-nan Sheng Tsao **Obv. Insc.:** Kuang-hsü Yüan-pao **Rev:** Without circle around dragon

Date	Mintage	VG	F	VF	XF	Unc
ND(1898)	Inc. above	2.50	10.00	15.00	30.00	50.00
CD1899	3,812	17.50	50.00	100	150	300
CD1900	618,000	3.00	10.00	15.00	30.00	50.00
CD1901	—	30.00	70.00	150	250	600

Y# 142a.5   10 CENTS
2.6000 g., 0.8200 Silver 0.0685 oz. ASW **Ruler:** Kuang-hsü **Obv:** Without initials **Obv. Leg.:** Chiang-nan Sheng Tsao **Obv. Insc.:** Kuang-hsü Yüan-pao **Rev:** Large English letters

Date	Mintage	VG	F	VF	XF	Unc
CD1901	7,794,000	2.50	4.00	7.50	12.50	50.00

Y# 142a.6   10 CENTS
2.6000 g., 0.8200 Silver 0.0685 oz. ASW **Ruler:** Kuang-hsü **Obv:** Without initials **Obv. Leg.:** Chiang-nan Sheng Tsao **Obv. Insc.:** Kuang-hsü Yüan-pao **Rev:** Small English letters

Date	Mintage	VG	F	VF	XF	Unc
CD1901	Inc. above	2.50	4.00	7.50	12.50	50.00

Y# 142a.7   10 CENTS
2.6000 g., 0.8200 Silver 0.0685 oz. ASW **Ruler:** Kuang-hsü **Obv:** Initials "HAH" **Obv. Leg.:** Chiang-nan Sheng Tsao **Obv. Insc.:** Kuang-hsü Yüan-pao **Rev:** Large rosettes beside dragon

Date	Mintage	VG	F	VF	XF	Unc
CD1901	Inc. above	2.50	5.00	8.50	15.00	55.00

Y# 142a.8   10 CENTS
2.6000 g., 0.8200 Silver 0.0685 oz. ASW **Ruler:** Kuang-hsü **Obv. Leg.:** Chiang-nan Sheng Tsao **Obv. Insc.:** Kuang-hsü Yüan-pao **Rev:** Small rosettes beside dragon

Date	Mintage	VG	F	VF	XF	Unc
CD1901	Inc. above	2.50	5.00	8.50	15.00	55.00

Y# 142a.9   10 CENTS
2.6000 g., 0.8200 Silver 0.0685 oz. ASW **Ruler:** Kuang-hsü **Obv. Leg.:** Chiang-nan Sheng Tsao **Obv. Insc.:** Kuang-hsü Yüan-pao **Rev:** Large stars beside dragon

Date	Mintage	VG	F	VF	XF	Unc
CD1902	3,778,000	2.50	4.50	8.00	15.00	50.00

Y# 142a.10   10 CENTS
2.6000 g., 0.8200 Silver 0.0685 oz. ASW **Ruler:** Kuang-hsü
Obv. Leg.: Chiang-nan Sheng Tsao **Obv. Insc.:** Kuang-hsü
Yüan-pao **Rev:** Small stars beside dragon

Date	Mintage	VG	F	VF	XF	Unc
CD1902	Inc. above	2.75	6.00	10.00	17.50	75.00

Y# 142a.11   10 CENTS
2.6000 g., 0.8200 Silver 0.0685 oz. ASW **Ruler:** Kuang-hsü
Obv: Large rosette **Obv. Leg.:** Chiang-nan Sheng Tsao
Obv. Insc.: Kuang-hsü Yüan-pao

Date	Mintage	VG	F	VF	XF	Unc
CD1903	1,161,000	4.50	12.50	30.00	60.00	200

Y# 142a.12   10 CENTS
2.6000 g., 0.8200 Silver 0.0685 oz. ASW **Ruler:** Kuang-hsü
Obv: Small rosette **Obv. Leg.:** Chiang-nan Sheng Tsao
Obv. Insc.: Kuang-hsü Yüan-pao

Date	Mintage	VG	F	VF	XF	Unc
CD1903	Inc. above	4.50	12.50	30.00	60.00	200

Y# 142a.13   10 CENTS
2.6000 g., 0.8200 Silver 0.0685 oz. ASW **Ruler:** Kuang-hsü
Obv: Initials "HAH TH" **Obv. Leg.:** Chiang-nan Sheng Tsao
Obv. Insc.: Kuang-hsü Yüan-pao

Date	Mintage	VG	F	VF	XF	Unc
CD1904	897,000	3.25	6.00	12.50	30.00	250

Y# 142a.14   10 CENTS
2.6000 g., 0.8200 Silver 0.0685 oz. ASW **Ruler:** Kuang-hsü
Obv: Initials "SY" upside down **Obv. Leg.:** Chiang-nan Sheng
Tsao **Obv. Insc.:** Kuang-hsü Yüan-pao

Date	Mintage	VG	F	VF	XF	Unc
CD1905	681,000	4.00	7.00	20.00	37.50	200

Y# 142a.15   10 CENTS
2.6000 g., 0.8200 Silver 0.0685 oz. ASW **Ruler:** Kuang-hsü
Obv: Without SY initials

Date	Mintage	VG	F	VF	XF	Unc
CD(1905)	Inc. above	2.50	5.00	10.00	25.00	200

Y# 146   10 CENTS
2.6000 g., 0.8200 Silver 0.0685 oz. ASW **Ruler:** Hsüan-T'ung
Obv. Leg.: Chiang-nan Sheng Tsao **Obv. Insc.:** Hsüan-t'ung
Yüan-pao **Rev:** Dragon

Date	Mintage	VG	F	VF	XF	Unc
ND(1911)	Est. 820,000	4.50	15.00	30.00	65.00	300

Note: Includes 590,000 pieces struck in debased silver in 1916

Y# 143a.6   20 CENTS
5.3000 g., 0.8200 Silver 0.1397 oz. ASW **Ruler:** Kuang-hsü
Obv: Without initials **Obv. Leg.:** Chiang-nan Sheng Tsao
Obv. Insc.: Kuang-hsü Yüan-pao

Date	Mintage	VG	F	VF	XF	Unc
CD1901	47,114,000	4.00	6.50	10.00	16.50	100

Y# 143a.7   20 CENTS
5.3000 g., 0.8200 Silver 0.1397 oz. ASW **Ruler:** Kuang-hsü
Obv: Initials "HAH" **Obv. Leg.:** Chiang-nan Sheng Tsao
Obv. Insc.: Kuang-hsü Yüan-pao

Date	Mintage	VG	F	VF	XF	Unc
CD1901	Inc. above	2.50	5.00	7.50	13.50	150

Y# 143a.8   20 CENTS
5.3000 g., 0.8200 Silver 0.1397 oz. ASW **Ruler:** Kuang-hsü **Obv.
Leg.:** Chiang-nan Sheng Tsao **Obv. Insc.:** Kuang-hsü Yüan-pao

Date	Mintage	VG	F	VF	XF	Unc
CD1902	15,754,000	2.75	5.00	7.50	13.50	150

Y# 143a.9   20 CENTS
5.3000 g., 0.8200 Silver 0.1397 oz. ASW **Ruler:** Kuang-hsü
Obv: Rosette in outer legend **Obv. Leg.:** Chiang-nan Sheng Tsao
Obv. Insc.: Kuang-hsü Yüan-pao

Date	Mintage	VG	F	VF	XF	Unc
CD1903	2,432,000	4.00	12.50	25.00	55.00	250

Y# 143a.10   20 CENTS
5.3000 g., 0.8200 Silver 0.1397 oz. ASW **Ruler:** Kuang-hsü
Obv: Without rosette **Obv. Leg.:** Chiang-nan Sheng Tsao
Obv. Insc.: Kuang-hsü Yüan-pao

Date	Mintage	VG	F	VF	XF	Unc
CD1903	Inc. above	10.00	20.00	50.00	100	400

Y# 143a.11   20 CENTS
5.3000 g., 0.8200 Silver 0.1397 oz. ASW **Ruler:** Kuang-hsü
Obv: Initials "HAH TH" **Obv. Leg.:** Chiang-nan Sheng Tsao
Obv. Insc.: Kuang-hsü Yüan-pao

Date	Mintage	VG	F	VF	XF	Unc
CD1904	1,172,000	5.00	15.00	35.00	60.00	300

Y# 143a.12   20 CENTS
5.3000 g., 0.8200 Silver 0.1397 oz. ASW **Ruler:** Kuang-hsü
Obv: Without initials **Obv. Leg.:** Chiang-nan Sheng Tsao
Obv. Insc.: Kuang-hsü Yüan-pao

Date	Mintage	VG	F	VF	XF	Unc
CD1905	828,000	4.00	12.50	30.00	50.00	200

Y# 143a.13   20 CENTS
5.3000 g., 0.8200 Silver 0.1397 oz. ASW **Ruler:** Kuang-hsü
Obv: Initials "SY" **Obv. Leg.:** Chiang-nan Sheng Tsao
Obv. Insc.: Kuang-hsü Yüan-pao

Date	Mintage	VG	F	VF	XF	Unc
CD1905	Inc. above	4.00	12.50	25.00	40.00	200

Y# 143a.14   20 CENTS
5.3000 g., 0.8200 Silver 0.1397 oz. ASW **Ruler:** Kuang-hsü
Obv. Leg.: Chiang-nan Sheng Tsao **Obv. Insc.:** Kuang-hsü
Yüan-pao **Rev. Leg.:** ...MACl...

Date	Mintage	VG	F	VF	XF	Unc
CD1901	Inc. above	3.50	6.50	12.50	30.00	150

Y# 147   20 CENTS
5.3000 g., 0.8200 Silver 0.1397 oz. ASW **Ruler:** Hsüan-T'ung
Obv. Leg.: Chiang-nan Sheng Tsao **Obv. Insc.:** Hsüan-T'ung
Yüan-pao **Rev:** Dragon

Date	Mintage	VG	F	VF	XF	Unc
ND(1911)	2,320,000	10.00	25.00	50.00	100	300

Note: Includes 2,005,000 pieces struck in debased silver in
1916

Y# 145a.6   DOLLAR
26.7000 g., 0.9000 Silver 0.7726 oz. ASW **Ruler:** Kuang-hsü
Obv: Bold initials "HAH" without rosette **Obv. Leg.:** Chiang-nan
Sheng Tsao **Obv. Insc.:** Kuang-hsü Yüan-pao **Rev:** Petals of
rosettes separated from each other

Date	Mintage	VG	F	VF	XF	Unc
CD1901	Inc. above	32.00	95.00	185	300	2,000

Y# 145a.7   DOLLAR
26.7000 g., 0.9000 Silver 0.7726 oz. ASW **Ruler:** Kuang-hsü
Obv: Initials "HAH" and rosette **Obv. Leg.:** Chiang-nan Sheng
Tsao **Obv. Insc.:** Kuang-hsü Yüan-pao **Rev:** Petals of rosettes
run together

Date	Mintage	VG	F	VF	XF	Unc
CD1901	Inc. above	17.00	30.00	50.00	125	1,500

Y# 145a.5   DOLLAR
26.7000 g., 0.9000 Silver 0.7726 oz. ASW **Ruler:** Kuang-hsü
Obv: Without initials **Obv. Leg.:** Chiang-nan Sheng Tsao
Obv. Insc.: Kuang-hsü Yüan-pao **Note:** Kann#86.

Date	Mintage	VG	F	VF	XF	Unc
CD1901	2,377,000	75.00	225	300	500	2,500

Y# 145a.21   DOLLAR
26.7000 g., 0.9000 Silver 0.7726 oz. ASW **Ruler:** Kuang-hsü
Obv: Fine initials "HAH" without rosette **Obv. Leg.:** Chiang-nan
Sheng Tsao **Obv. Insc.:** Kuang-hsü Yüan-pao **Rev:** Similar to
Y#145a.6 **Note:** Kann#90.

Date	Mintage	VG	F	VF	XF	Unc
CD1901	Inc. above	32.00	95.00	185	300	1,500

Y# 145a.22   DOLLAR
26.7000 g., 0.9000 Silver 0.7726 oz. ASW **Ruler:** Kuang-hsü
Obv: Cross of six dots at upper right **Obv. Leg.:** Chiang-nan
Sheng Tsao **Obv. Insc.:** Kuang-hsü Yüan-pao **Rev:** Similar to
Y#145a.6 **Note:** Kann#90b.

Date	Mintage	VG	F	VF	XF	Unc
CD1901	Inc. above	50.00	150	300	550	2,000

Y# 145a.8   DOLLAR
25.7000 g., 0.9000 Silver 0.7436 oz. ASW **Ruler:** Kuang-hsü
Obv: Small date, small "HAH" **Obv. Leg.:** Chiang-nan Sheng
Tsao **Obv. Insc.:** Kuang-hsü Yüan-pao **Rev:** Similar to Y#145a.4
Note: Kann#94.

Date	Mintage	VG	F	VF	XF	Unc
CD1902	3,562,000	20.00	35.00	75.00	150	1,000

Y# 145a.9   DOLLAR
27.0000 g., 0.9000 Silver 0.7812 oz. ASW **Ruler:** Kuang-hsü
Obv: Larger date, larger "HAH" **Obv. Leg.:** Chiang-nan Sheng
Tsao **Obv. Insc.:** Kuang-hsü Yüan-pao

Date	Mintage	VG	F	VF	XF	Unc
CD1902	Inc. above	20.00	35.00	75.00	150	1,000

Y# 149.2 10 CASH
Copper **Ruler:** Kuang-hsü **Obv:** Different Manchu word at right
Obv. Leg.: Chiang-hsi Sheng Tsao **Obv. Insc.:** Kuang-hsü Yüan-
pao **Rev:** Circled dragon **Note:** May be a pattern.

Date	Mintage	VG	F	VF	XF	Unc
ND(c.1902) Rare	—	—	—	—	—	—

Y# 145a.10 DOLLAR
26.9000 g., 0.9000 Silver 0.7783 oz. ASW **Ruler:** Kuang-hsü
Obv: "HAH" and rosettes in outer ring **Obv. Leg.:** Chiang-nan
Sheng Tsao **Obv. Insc.:** Kuang-hsü Yüan-pao **Note:** Kann#96.

Date	Mintage	VG	F	VF	XF	Unc
CD1903	1,489,000	20.00	60.00	125	275	2,000

Y# 145a.11 DOLLAR
27.0000 g., 0.9000 Silver 0.7812 oz. ASW **Ruler:** Kuang-hsü
Obv: Without rosette in outer ring **Obv. Leg.:** Chiang-nan Sheng
Tsao **Obv. Insc.:** Kuang-hsü Yüan-pao **Note:** Kann#96c.

Date	Mintage	VG	F	VF	XF	Unc
CD1903	Inc. above	250	700	1,000	1,500	6,000

Y# 145a.17 DOLLAR
27.1000 g., 0.9000 Silver 0.7841 oz. ASW **Ruler:** Kuang-hsü
Obv: Initials "SY" **Obv. Leg.:** Chiang-nan Sheng Tsao
Obv. Insc.: Kuang-hsü Yüan-pao **Rev:** Similar to Y#145a.10

Date	Mintage	VG	F	VF	XF	Unc
CD1905	634,000	25.00	55.00	110	325	2,000

PATTERNS
Including off metal strikes

KM#	Date	Mintage	Identification	Mkt Val
Pn5	CD1906	—	2 Cash. Copper. Y#8k	2,000
Pn6	CD1906	—	20 Cash. Copper. Y#11k	—

Y# 150 10 CASH
Copper **Ruler:** Kuang-hsü **Obv:** Manchu "Pao Yuan" at 3 and
9 o'clock **Obv. Leg.:** Chiang-hsi Sheng Tsao **Obv. Insc.:** Kuang-
hsü Yüan-pao **Rev:** Province name spelled "KIANG-SI", 2 stars
at either side of dragon

Date	Mintage	VG	F	VF	XF	Unc
ND(c.1902)	—	2.00	6.00	11.00	17.50	70.00

KIANGSI PROVINCE

Jiangxi, Kiangsee
   A province located in southeastern China. Mostly hilly with
some mountains on the borders that produce coal and tungsten.
Some of China's finest porcelain comes from this province.
Kiangsi was visited by Marco Polo. A mint was opened in Nanchang in 1729, closed in 1733, reopened in 1736 and operated
with reasonable continuity from that time. Modern machinery was
introduced in 1901 although it only produced copper coins. The
mint closed amidst internal problems in the 1920's.

EMPIRE
MILLED COINAGE

Horizontal rosette   Vertical rosette

   Many Kiangsi (Jiangxi) coins have a six-petalled rosette in
the center of the obverse, arranged so that two sides of the rosette
are formed by two petals in line with each other. The remaining
two sides have a single petal, standing out from the rest. The
direction that these single petals point, determines whether the
rosette is horizontal or vertical. A horizontal rosette has the single
petals pointing left and right, while the single petals of the vertical
rosette point up and down.

Y# 150.1 10 CASH
Copper **Ruler:** Kuang-hsü **Obv:** Manchu "Pao Ch'ang" at center
and Chinese reading "Ku P'ing" at 3 and 9 o'clock **Obv. Leg.:**
Chiang-hsi Sheng Tsao **Obv. Insc.:** Kuang-hsü Yüan-pao

Date	Mintage	VG	F	VF	XF	Unc
ND(c.1902)	—	1.00	3.00	6.00	12.00	60.00

Y# 150.2 10 CASH
Copper **Ruler:** Kuang-hsü **Obv:** Manchu "Pao Ch'ang" at 3 and
9 o'clock, horizontal rosette in center **Obv. Leg.:** Chiang-hsi
Sheng Tsao **Obv. Insc.:** Kuang-hsü Yüan-pao

Date	Mintage	VG	F	VF	XF	Unc
ND(c.1902)	—	0.35	1.00	2.00	5.00	60.00

Y# 150.2a 10 CASH
Brass **Ruler:** Kuang-hsü **Obv. Leg.:** Chiang-hsi Sheng Tsao
Obv. Insc.: Kuang-hsü Yüan-pao

Date	Mintage	VG	F	VF	XF	Unc
ND(c.1902)	—	1.75	5.00	10.00	20.00	80.00

Y# 150.3 10 CASH
Copper **Ruler:** Kuang-hsü **Obv:** Vertical rosette in center
Obv. Leg.: Chiang-hsi Sheng Tsao **Obv. Insc.:** Kuang-hsü
Yüan-pao

Date	Mintage	VG	F	VF	XF	Unc
ND(c.1902)	—	0.35	1.00	2.00	5.00	60.00

Y# 145a.12 DOLLAR
26.7000 g., 0.9000 Silver 0.7726 oz. ASW **Ruler:** Kuang-hsü
Obv: Initials "HAH" and "CH" without dots or rosettes
Obv. Leg.: Chiang-nan Sheng Tsao **Obv. Insc.:** Kuang-hsü
Yüan-pao **Rev:** Similar to Y#145a.4 **Note:** Kann#99.

Date	Mintage	VG	F	VF	XF	Unc
CD1904	44,725,000	25.00	40.00	65.00	100	800

Y# 145a.13 DOLLAR
27.0000 g., 0.9000 Silver 0.7812 oz. ASW **Ruler:** Kuang-hsü
Obv: Dot at either side **Obv. Leg.:** Chiang-nan Sheng Tsao
Obv. Insc.: Kuang-hsü Yüan-pao

Date	Mintage	VG	F	VF	XF	Unc
CD1904	Inc. above	25.00	40.00	65.00	100	700

Y# 145a.19 DOLLAR
27.0000 g., 0.9000 Silver 0.7812 oz. ASW **Ruler:** Kuang-hsü
Obv: Dot at either side, without four central characters **Obv. Leg.:**
Chiang-nan Sheng Tsao **Obv. Insc.:** Kuang-hsü Yüan-pao

Date	Mintage	VG	F	VF	XF	Unc
CD1904	—	—	—	—	—	—

Y# 145a.14 DOLLAR
27.0000 g., 0.9000 Silver 0.7812 oz. ASW **Ruler:** Kuang-hsü
Obv. Insc.: Kuang-hsü Yüan-pao **Rev:** Dot to left of numeral 7

Date	Mintage	VG	F	VF	XF	Unc
CD1904	Inc. above	25.00	40.00	65.00	100	750

Y# 145a.15 DOLLAR
27.0000 g., 0.9000 Silver 0.7812 oz. ASW **Ruler:** Kuang-hsü
Obv: Four-petalled rosette at either side "HAH" and "CH" **Obv.
Leg.:** Chiang-nan Sheng Tsao **Obv. Insc.:** Kuang-hsü Yüan-pao

Date	Mintage	VG	F	VF	XF	Unc
CD1904	Inc. above	40.00	75.00	200	325	900

Y# 145a.16 DOLLAR
27.0000 g., 0.9000 Silver 0.7812 oz. ASW **Ruler:** Kuang-hsü
Obv: Initials "HAH" and "TH" **Obv. Leg.:** Chiang-nan Sheng Tsao
Obv. Insc.: Kuang-hsü Yüan-pao

Date	Mintage	VG	F	VF	XF	Unc
CD1904	Inc. above	40.00	75.00	250	375	2,000

Y# 149 10 CASH
Copper **Ruler:** Kuang-hsü **Obv:** Vertical rosette at center
Obv. Leg.: Chiang-hsi Sheng Tsao **Obv. Insc.:** Kuang-hsü Yüan-
pao **Rev:** Province name spelled "KIANG-SEE"

Date	Mintage	VG	F	VF	XF	Unc
ND(c. 1902)	—	5.00	10.00	15.00	30.00	—

Y# 149.1 10 CASH
Copper **Ruler:** Kuang-hsü **Obv:** Horizontal rosette at center
Obv. Leg.: Chiang-hsi Sheng Tsao **Obv. Insc.:** Kuang-hsü
Yüan-pao

Date	Mintage	VG	F	VF	XF	Unc
ND(c.1902)	—	5.00	10.00	15.00	30.00	—

Y# 150.4 10 CASH
Copper **Ruler:** Kuang-hsü **Obv:** Horizontal rosette
Obv. Leg.: Chiang-hsi Sheng Tsao **Obv. Insc.:** Kuang-hsü Yüan-
pao **Rev:** 1 star at either side of dragon, large English lettering

Date	Mintage	VG	F	VF	XF	Unc
ND(c.1902)	—	0.35	1.00	2.00	5.00	60.00

Y# 150.4a 10 CASH
Brass **Ruler:** Kuang-hsü **Obv:** Horizontal rosette
Obv. Leg.: Chiang-hsi Sheng Tsao **Obv. Insc.:** Kuang-hsü Yüan-
pao **Rev:** 1 star at either side of dragon, large English lettering

Date	Mintage	VG	F	VF	XF	Unc
ND(c.1902)	—	1.25	5.00	9.00	17.50	70.00

Y# 150.5   10 CASH
Copper   **Ruler:** Kuang-hsü **Obv:** Vertical rosette **Obv. Leg.:** Chiang-hsi Sheng Tsao **Obv. Insc.:** Kuang-hsü Yüan-pao

Date	Mintage	VG	F	VF	XF	Unc
ND(c.1902)	—	0.35	1.00	2.00	5.00	60.00

Y# 150.6   10 CASH
Copper   **Ruler:** Kuang-hsü **Obv. Leg.:** Chiang-hsi Sheng Tsao **Obv. Insc.:** Kuang-hsü Yüan-pao **Rev:** Smaller English lettering, 1 star at either side of dragon

Date	Mintage	VG	F	VF	XF	Unc
ND(c.1902)	—	0.35	1.00	2.00	5.00	60.00

Y# 150.7   10 CASH
Copper   **Ruler:** Kuang-hsü **Obv:** Small rosette center **Obv. Leg.:** Chiang-hsi Sheng Tsao **Obv. Insc.:** Kuang-hsü Yüan-pao **Rev:** 1 star at either side of dragon

Date	Mintage	VG	F	VF	XF	Unc
ND(c.1902)	—	2.00	6.00	11.00	17.50	70.00

Y# 150.8   10 CASH
Copper   **Ruler:** Kuang-hsü **Obv. Leg.:** Chiang-hsi Sheng Tsao **Obv. Insc.:** Kuang-hsü Yüan-pao **Rev:** 3 stars at either side of dragon

Date	Mintage	VG	F	VF	XF	Unc
ND(c.1902)	. —	4.50	12.50	20.00	30.00	120

Y# 152   10 CASH
Copper   **Ruler:** Kuang-hsü **Obv:** Manchu "Pao Ch'ang" at 3 and 9 o'clock **Obv. Leg.:** Chiang-hsi Sheng Tsao **Obv. Insc.:** Kuang-hsü Yüan-pao **Rev:** Province name spelled "KIANG-SI", front view dragon, mountain below pearl

Date	Mintage	VG	F	VF	XF	Unc
ND(c.1902)	—	2.50	4.00	6.00	12.00	—

Y# 152.1   10 CASH
Copper   **Ruler:** Kuang-hsü **Obv:** Horizontal rosette in center, Manchu "Pao Ch'ang" at 3 and 9 o'clock **Obv. Leg.:** Chiang-hsi Sheng Tsao **Obv. Insc.:** Kuang-hsü Yüan-pao

Date	Mintage	VG	F	VF	XF	Unc
ND(c.1902)	—	2.50	4.00	6.00	12.00	—

Y# 152.2   10 CASH
Copper   **Ruler:** Kuang-hsü **Obv:** Horizontal rosette in center, Manchu "Pao Ch'ang" at 3 and 9 o'clock, small character "10" **Obv. Leg.:** Chiang-hsi Sheng Tsao **Obv. Insc.:** Kuang-hsü Yüan-pao

Date	Mintage	VG	F	VF	XF	Unc
ND(c.1902)	—	5.00	12.00	17.50	27.50	—

Y# 152.3   10 CASH
Copper   **Ruler:** Kuang-hsü **Obv:** Horizontal rosette in center, Manchu "Pao Ch'ang" at 3 and 9 o'clock, large character "10" **Obv. Leg.:** Chiang-hsi Sheng Tsao **Obv. Insc.:** Kuang-hsü Yüan-pao **Rev:** Without mountain below dragon

Date	Mintage	VG	F	VF	XF	Unc
ND(c.1902)	—	3.50	8.00	12.00	17.50	—

Y# 152.7   10 CASH
Copper   **Ruler:** Kuang-hsü **Obv:** Vertical rosette in center **Obv. Leg.:** Chiang-hsi Sheng Tsao **Obv. Insc.:** Kuang-hsü Yüan-pao

Date	Mintage	VG	F	VF	XF	Unc
ND(c.1902)	—	—	—	—	—	—

Y# 152.4   10 CASH
Copper   **Ruler:** Kuang-hsü **Obv:** Horizontal rosette in center, small character "10" **Obv. Leg.:** Chiang-hsi Sheng Tsao **Obv. Insc.:** Kuang-hsü Yüan-pao

Date	Mintage	VG	F	VF	XF	Unc
ND(c.1902)	—	3.50	8.00	12.00	17.50	—

Y# 152.5   10 CASH
Copper   **Ruler:** Kuang-hsü **Obv:** Manchu "Pao Ch'ang" in center, Chinese "K'u P'ing" at 3 and 9 o'clock **Obv. Leg.:** Chiang-hsi Sheng Tsao **Obv. Insc.:** Kuang-hsü Yüan-pao **Rev:** Without mountain below pearl, dragon's body repositioned

Date	Mintage	VG	F	VF	XF	Unc
ND(c.1902)	—	3.50	8.50	12.50	17.50	—

Y# 152.6   10 CASH
Copper   **Ruler:** Kuang-hsü **Obv. Leg.:** Chiang-hsi Sheng Tsao **Obv. Insc.:** Kuang-hsü Yüan-pao **Rev:** Mountain below dragon

Date	Mintage	VG	F	VF	XF	Unc
ND(c.1902)	—	3.25	7.50	11.00	16.00	—

Y# 153   10 CASH
Copper   **Ruler:** Kuang-hsü **Obv. Leg.:** Chiang-hsi Sheng Tsao **Obv. Insc.:** Kuang-hsü Yüan-pao **Rev:** Legend above front view dragon **Rev. Leg.:** KIANG-SEE PROVINCE **Note:** Found with and without a swirl on the pearl below dragon's mouth.

Date	Mintage	VG	F	VF	XF	Unc
ND(c.1902)	—	2.00	4.50	7.00	11.00	—

Y# 153.1   10 CASH
Copper   **Ruler:** Kuang-hsü **Obv:** Manchu "Pao Ch'ang" at center and Chinese "K'u P'ing" at 3 and 9 o'clock **Obv. Leg.:** Chiang-hsi Sheng Tsao **Obv. Insc.:** Kuang-hsü Yüan-pao **Note:** Found with and without a swirl on the pearl below dragon's mouth.

Date	Mintage	VG	F	VF	XF	Unc
ND(c.1902)	—	0.80	2.00	3.50	7.00	—

Y# 153.2   10 CASH
Copper   **Ruler:** Kuang-hsü **Obv:** Small Manchu "Pao Ch'ang" at 3 and 9 o'clock, small horizontal rosette in center **Obv. Leg.:** Chiang-hsi Sheng Tsao **Obv. Insc.:** Kuang-hsü Yüan-pao **Note:** Found with and without a swirl on the pearl below dragon's mouth.

Date	Mintage	VG	F	VF	XF	Unc
ND(c. 1902)	—	0.80	2.00	3.50	7.00	—

Y# 153.3   10 CASH
Copper   **Ruler:** Kuang-hsü **Obv:** Small vertical rosette in center **Obv. Leg.:** Chiang-hsi Sheng Tsao **Obv. Insc.:** Kuang-hsü Yüan-pao **Note:** Found with and without a swirl on the pearl below dragon's mouth.

Date	Mintage	VG	F	VF	XF	Unc
ND(c.1902)	—	2.00	5.00	10.00	17.50	—

Y# 154   10 CASH
Copper   **Ruler:** Kuang-hsü **Obv. Leg.:** Chiang-hsi Sheng Tsao **Obv. Insc.:** Kuang-hsü Yüan-pao **Rev:** Legend above flying dragon **Rev. Leg.:** KIANG SI

Date	Mintage	VG	F	VF	XF	Unc
ND(c.1902)	—	40.00	60.00	80.00	100	—

Y# 10m   10 CASH
Copper   **Ruler:** Kuang-hsü **Obv. Insc.:** Tai-ch'ing T'ung-pi **Rev:** Dragon's eyes in relief **Rev. Leg.:** Kuang-hsü Nien-tsao, TAI-CHING-TI-KUO ...

Date	Mintage	VG	F	VF	XF	Unc
CD1906	—	1.25	3.00	6.00	12.00	—

Y# 10m.1   10 CASH
Copper   **Ruler:** Kuang-hsü **Obv. Insc.:** Tai-ch'ing T'ung-pi **Rev:** Dragon's eyes incuse **Rev. Leg.:** Kuang-hsü Nien-tsao, TAI-CHING-TI-KUO ...

Date	Mintage	VG	F	VF	XF	Unc
CD1906	—	1.25	3.00	6.00	12.00	—

Y# 10m.2   10 CASH
Copper   **Ruler:** Kuang-hsü **Obv. Insc.:** Tai-ch'ing T'ung-pi **Rev:** Dragon redesigned, small faint cloud beneath pearl **Rev. Leg.:** Kuang-hsü Nien-tsao, TAI-CHING-TI-KUO ...

Date	Mintage	VG	F	VF	XF	Unc
CD1906	—	5.00	12.00	17.50	30.00	

REPUBLIC
MILLED COINAGE

Y# 412   10 CASH
5.9000 g., Copper **Obv:** Date appears at 3 and 9 o'clock, value in 5 characters in legend **Obv. Leg.:** Chiang-hsi Sheng-tsao **Rev:** 9-pointed star inside circle and 5-petalled rosette at 3 and 9 o'clock, value in 5 characters below

Date	Mintage	VG	F	VF	XF	Unc
CD1912	—	200	300	450	650	—

Y# 412a   10 CASH
6.7000 g., Copper, 28.46 mm. **Obv:** Horizontal rosette in center with Chinese characters "Chiang Hsi" above and below; Value in 2 characters in legend **Obv. Leg.:** Chung Hua Min Kuo **Rev:** 6-petalled rosette at either side, value in 2 characters below

Date	Mintage	VG	F	VF	XF	Unc
CD1912	—	1.25	3.00	5.00	9.00	—

Y# 412a.1   10 CASH
Copper   **Obv:** Small, vertical rosette in center **Obv. Leg.:** Chung Hua Min Kuo

Date	Mintage	VG	F	VF	XF	Unc
CD1912	—	1.25	3.00	5.00	9.00	—

Y# 412a.2   10 CASH
Copper   **Obv:** Large, vertical rosette in center; thick, large-center characters **Obv. Leg.:** Chung Hua Min Kuo **Rev:** Small, 5-petalled rosettes at either side

Date	Mintage	VG	F	VF	XF	Unc
CD1912	—	6.00	12.00	17.50	27.50	—

Y# 412a.3   10 CASH
Copper   **Obv:** Large, vertical rosette in center; thin-center characters **Obv. Leg.:** Chung Hua Min Kuo

Date	Mintage	VG	F	VF	XF	Unc
CD1912	—	1.25	3.00	5.00	10.00	—

REBEL COINAGE

"Ta Han" was a rebel issue made before the revolution. Not only a symbol of defiance, this coin indicated secret membership. Ching law subjected those carrying these coins to execution.

Y# 411   10 CASH
Copper   **Obv:** Mint mark incused on raised-disc center with Chinese characters on 4 sides, "Ta-Han T'ung-pi" character value in outer ring at bottom **Rev:** Ring of 9 balls without inscription

Date	Mintage	VG	F	VF	XF	Unc
CD1911 Rare	—	—	—	—	—	—

KIANGSU-CHINGKIANG
PROVINCE
MILLED COINAGE

Y# 77.7   10 CASH
Copper   **Ruler:** Kuang-hsü **Obv:** Without rosette **Obv. Insc.:** Kuang-hsü Yüan-pao **Rev. Leg.:** * CHING * KIANG **Edge:** Plain

Date	Mintage	VG	F	VF	XF	Unc
ND(1905)	—	2.75	8.00	10.00	15.00	100

Y# 78.3   10 CASH
Copper   **Ruler:** Kuang-hsü **Obv:** Small character at 3 o'clock **Obv. Insc.:** Kuang-hsü Yüan-pao **Rev. Leg.:** TSING-KIANG **Edge:** Plain

Date	Mintage	VG	F	VF	XF	Unc
ND(1905)	—	0.35	1.00	2.00	5.00	20.00

Y# 77   10 CASH
Copper   **Ruler:** Kuang-hsü **Obv:** Large character at 3 o'clock **Obv. Insc.:** Kuang-hsü Yüan-pao **Rev. Leg.:** * CHING * KIANG **Edge:** Reeded

Date	Mintage	VG	F	VF	XF	Unc
ND(1905)	—	0.85	2.50	4.00	7.50	65.00

Y# 77.1   10 CASH
Copper   **Ruler:** Kuang-hsü **Obv:** Large character at 3 o'clock **Obv. Insc.:** Kuang-hsü Yüan-pao **Rev. Leg.:** * CHING * KIANG **Edge:** Plain

Date	Mintage	VG	F	VF	XF	Unc
ND(1905)	—	0.85	2.50	4.00	7.50	60.00

Y# 77.2   10 CASH
Copper   **Ruler:** Kuang-hsü **Obv:** Ring around center dot in rosette **Obv. Insc.:** Kuang-hsü Yüan-pao **Rev. Leg.:** * CHING * KIANG **Edge:** Reeded.

Date	Mintage	VG	F	VF	XF	Unc
ND(1905)	—	1.00	3.00	5.00	10.00	70.00

Y# 77.3   10 CASH
Copper   **Ruler:** Kuang-hsü **Obv:** Ring around center dot in rosette **Obv. Insc.:** Kuang-hsü Yüan-pao **Rev. Leg.:** * CHING * KIANG **Edge:** Plain

Date	Mintage	VG	F	VF	XF	Unc
ND(1905)	—	3.00	9.00	12.00	15.00	80.00

Y# 77.4   10 CASH
Copper   **Ruler:** Kuang-hsü **Obv:** Smaller character at 3 o'clock **Obv. Insc.:** Kuang-hsü Yüan-pao **Rev. Leg.:** * CHING * KIANG **Edge:** Reeded

Date	Mintage	VG	F	VF	XF	Unc
ND(1905)	—	1.25	3.50	6.00	12.00	70.00

Y# 77.5   10 CASH
Copper   **Ruler:** Kuang-hsü **Obv:** Smaller character at 3 o'clock **Obv. Insc.:** Kuang-hsü Yüan-pao **Rev. Leg.:** * Ching * Kiang **Edge:** Plain

Date	Mintage	VG	F	VF	XF	Unc
ND(1905)	—	1.25	3.50	6.00	12.00	70.00

Y# 77.6   10 CASH
Copper   **Ruler:** Kuang-hsü **Obv:** Without rosette **Obv. Insc.:** Kuang-hsü Yüan-pao **Rev. Leg.:** * CHING * KIANG **Edge:** Reeded

Date	Mintage	VG	F	VF	XF	Unc
ND(1905)	—	1.00	3.00	5.00	10.00	70.00

Y# 78   10 CASH
Copper   **Ruler:** Kuang-hsü **Obv:** Large character at 3 o'clock **Obv. Insc.:** Kuang-hsü Yüan-pao **Rev. Leg.:** TSING-KIANG **Edge:** Reeded

Date	Mintage	VG	F	VF	XF	Unc
ND(1905)	—	0.50	1.50	3.00	5.00	60.00

Y# 78.1   10 CASH
Copper   **Ruler:** Kuang-hsü **Obv:** Large character at 3 o'clock **Obv. Insc.:** Kuang-hsü Yüan-pao **Rev. Leg.:** TSING-KIANG **Edge:** Plain

Date	Mintage	VG	F	VF	XF	Unc
ND(1905)	—	1.00	3.00	5.00	10.00	70.00

Y# 78.2   10 CASH
Copper   **Ruler:** Kuang-hsü **Obv:** Small character at 3 o'clock **Obv. Insc.:** Kuang-hsü Yüan-pao **Rev. Leg.:** TSING-KIANG **Edge:** Reeded

Date	Mintage	VG	F	VF	XF	Unc
ND(1905)	—	0.35	1.00	2.00	5.00	60.00

Y# 78.4   10 CASH
Copper   **Ruler:** Kuang-hsü **Obv:** Without rosette **Obv. Insc.:** Kuang-hsü Yüan-pao **Rev. Leg.:** TSING-KIANG **Edge:** Reeded

Date	Mintage	VG	F	VF	XF	Unc
ND(1905)	—	1.25	3.50	6.00	15.00	70.00

Y# 10d   10 CASH
Copper   **Ruler:** Kuang-hsü **Obv:** Small mint mark in center, without center raised disc **Obv. Insc.:** Tai-ch'ing T'ung-pi **Rev:** 5 flames on pearl **Rev. Leg.:** Kuang-hsü Nien-tsao, TAI-CHING TI-KUO

Date	Mintage	VG	F	VF	XF	Unc
CD1906	—	8.50	25.00	50.00	100	—

Y# 10d.1 10 CASH
Copper **Ruler:** Kuang-hsü **Obv:** Small mint mark
Obv. Insc.: Tai-ch'ing T'ung-pi **Rev:** 7 flames on pearl
Rev. Leg.: Kuang-hsü Nien-tsao, TAI-CHING-TI-KUO

Date	Mintage	VG	F	VF	XF	Unc
CD1906	—	0.50	1.50	2.50	5.00	60.00

Y# 10d.2 10 CASH
Copper **Ruler:** Kuang-hsü **Obv. Insc.:** Tai-ch'ing T'ung-pi
Rev: 9 flames on pearl **Rev. Leg.:** Kuang-hsü Nien-tsao, TAI-CHING- TI-KUO

Date	Mintage	VG	F	VF	XF	Unc
CD1906	—	0.35	1.00	2.00	5.00	65.00

Y# 10d.3 10 CASH
Copper **Ruler:** Kuang-hsü **Obv:** Large mint mark
Obv. Insc.: Tai-ch'ing T'ung-pi **Rev:** 5 flames on pearl
Rev. Leg.: Kuang-hsü Nien-tsao, TAI-CHING TI-KUO

Date	Mintage	VG	F	VF	XF	Unc
CD1906	—	0.50	1.50	2.50	5.00	65.00

Y# 10d.4 10 CASH
Copper **Ruler:** Kuang-hsü **Obv. Insc.:** Tai-ch'ing T'ung-pi
Rev: 7 flames on pearl **Rev. Leg.:** Kuang-hsü Nien-tsao, TAI-CHING TI-KUO

Date	Mintage	VG	F	VF	XF	Unc
CD1906	—	0.50	1.50	2.50	5.00	65.00

Y# 10d.5 10 CASH
Copper **Ruler:** Kuang-hsü **Obv. Insc.:** Tai-ch'ing T'ung-pi
Rev: 9 flames on pearl **Rev. Leg.:** Kuang-hsü Nien-tsao, TAI-CHING TI-KUO

Date	Mintage	VG	F	VF	XF	Unc
CD1906	—	0.50	1.50	2.50	5.00	65.00

Y# 10d.6 10 CASH
Copper **Ruler:** Kuang-hsü **Obv:** Mint mark incused on raised disc **Obv. Insc.:** Tai-ch'ing T'ung-pi **Rev. Leg.:** Kuang-hsü Nien-tsao, TAI-CHING TI-KUO... **Note:** Trial piece.

Date	Mintage	VG	F	VF	XF	Unc
CD1906	—	—	—	—	—	—

Note: 10 cash coins of Kiangsu (Jiangsu) and Chingkiang are often found plated with a silvery material. This was not done at the mint. Apparently they were plated so they could be passed to the unwary as silver coins.

KIANGSU-KIANGSOO PROVINCE
Jiangsu
A province located on the east coast of China. One of the smallest and most densely populated of all Chinese provinces. A mint opened in Soochow in 1667, but closed shortly after in 1670.

A new mint opened in 1734 for producing cast coins and had continuous operation until about 1870. Modern equipment was introduced in 1898 and a second mint was opened in 1904. Both mints closed down production in 1906. Taels were produced in Shanghai by local silversmiths as early as 1856. These saw limited circulation in the immediate area.

EMPIRE
PROVINCIAL CAST COINAGE
C# 16-12 CASH
Cast Brass **Ruler:** Kuang-hsü **Obv. Insc.:** Kuang-hsü T'ung-pao **Rev:** Manchu inscription **Rev. Insc.:** Boo-su

Date	Mintage	Good	VG	F	VF	XF
ND(1875-1908)	—	2.25	4.50	8.00	13.00	—

C# 16-12.1 CASH
Cast Brass **Ruler:** Kuang-hsü **Obv. Insc.:** Kuang-hsü T'ung-pao **Rev:** Manchu inscription, circle above **Rev. Insc.:** Boo-su

Date	Mintage	Good	VG	F	VF	XF
ND(1875-1908)	—	3.00	6.00	10.00	16.00	—

C# 16-12.2 CASH
Cast Brass **Ruler:** Kuang-hsü **Obv. Insc.:** Kuang-hsü T'ung-pao **Rev:** Manchu inscription, crescent above **Rev. Insc.:** Boo-su

Date	Mintage	Good	VG	F	VF	XF
ND(1875-1908)	—	3.00	6.00	10.00	16.00	—

C# 16-13 5 CASH
Cast Brass **Ruler:** Kuang-hsü **Obv. Insc.:** Kuang-hsü Chung-pao **Rev:** Manchu inscription **Rev. Insc.:** Boo-su

Date	Mintage	Good	VG	F	VF	XF
ND(1875-86)	—	25.00	40.00	55.00	75.00	—

MILLED COINAGE

Y# 158 5 CASH
Copper **Ruler:** Kuang-hsü **Obv. Leg.:** Chiang-hsü Sheng Tsao **Obv. Insc.:** Kuang-hsü Yüan-pao **Rev:** Side view dragon, "EIVE" for "FIVE"

Date	Mintage	VG	F	VF	XF	Unc
ND(1901)	—	12.00	32.50	55.00	100	—

Y# 9n 5 CASH
Brass **Ruler:** Kuang-hsü **Obv. Insc.:** Tai-ching T'ung-pi **Rev. Leg.:** Kuang-hsü Nien-tsao, TAI-CHING-TI-KUO ...

Date	Mintage	VG	F	VF	XF	Unc
CD(1906)	—	25.00	75.00	125	200	—

Y# 162 10 CASH
Brass **Ruler:** Kuang-hsü **Obv:** Manchu words at center, without rosettes **Obv. Insc.:** Kuang-hsü Yüan-pao **Edge:** Reeded

Date	Mintage	VG	F	VF	XF	Unc
ND(c.1902)	—	1.25	3.75	6.00	12.00	70.00

Y# 162.1 10 CASH
Brass **Ruler:** Kuang-hsü **Obv:** Manchu in center, rosettes at 2 and 10 o'clock **Obv. Leg.:** Chiang-hsü Sheng Tsao **Obv. Insc.:** Kuang-hsü Yüan-pao

Date	Mintage	VG	F	VF	XF	Unc
ND(c.1902)	—	0.35	1.00	2.00	5.00	60.00

Y# 162.2 10 CASH
Brass **Ruler:** Kuang-hsü **Obv. Leg.:** Chiang-hsü Sheng Tsao **Obv. Insc.:** Kuang-hsü Yüan-pao **Edge:** Plain

Date	Mintage	VG	F	VF	XF	Unc
ND(c.1902)	—	0.35	1.00	2.00	5.00	65.00

Y# 162.3 10 CASH
Brass **Ruler:** Kuang-hsü **Obv:** Tiny rosettes **Obv. Leg.:** Chiang-hsü Sheng Tsao **Obv. Insc.:** Kuang-hsü Yüan-pao **Rev:** Tiny rosettes **Edge:** Reeded

Date	Mintage	VG	F	VF	XF	Unc
ND(c.1902)	—	0.45	1.25	2.50	5.00	65.00

Y# 162.4 10 CASH
Brass **Ruler:** Kuang-hsü **Obv:** Rosette center, Manchu at 3 and 9 o'clock **Obv. Leg.:** Chiang-hsü Sheng Tsao **Obv. Insc.:** Kuang-hsü Yüan-pao

Date	Mintage	VG	F	VF	XF	Unc
ND(c.1902)	—	0.35	1.00	2.00	5.00	65.00

Y# 162.5 10 CASH
Brass **Ruler:** Kuang-hsü **Obv. Leg.:** Chiang-hsü Sheng Tsao **Obv. Insc.:** Kuang-hsü Yüan-pao **Edge:** Plain

Date	Mintage	VG	F	VF	XF	Unc
ND(c.1902)	—	0.35	1.00	2.00	5.00	65.00

Y# 162.6 10 CASH
Brass **Ruler:** Kuang-hsü **Obv:** Rosette center, large Manchu at 3 and 9 o'clock, higher than on Y#162.4 **Obv. Leg.:** Chiang-hsü Sheng Tsao **Obv. Insc.:** Kuang-hsü Yüan-pao **Edge:** Reeded

Date	Mintage	VG	F	VF	XF	Unc
ND(c.1902)	—	0.50	1.50	2.50	5.00	65.00

Y# 162.7 10 CASH
Copper **Ruler:** Kuang-hsü **Obv. Leg.:** Chiang-hsü Sheng Tsao **Obv. Insc.:** Kuang-hsü Yüan-pao **Edge:** Plain

Date	Mintage	VG	F	VF	XF	Unc
ND(c.1902)	—	0.50	1.50	2.50	5.00	65.00

Y# 162.7a 10 CASH
Brass **Ruler:** Kuang-hsü **Obv. Leg.:** Chiang-hsü Sheng Tsao **Obv. Insc.:** Kuang-hsü Yüan-pao

Date	Mintage	VG	F	VF	XF	Unc
ND(c.1902) Rare	—	—	—	—	—	—

Y# 162.8 10 CASH
Copper **Ruler:** Kuang-hsü **Obv:** Manchu "Boo-su" at center **Obv. Leg.:** Chiang-hsü Sheng Tsao **Obv. Insc.:** Kuang-hsü Yüan-pao **Edge:** Reeded

Date	Mintage	VG	F	VF	XF	Unc
CD(1902)	—	0.65	2.00	4.00	7.50	65.00

Y# 162.13 10 CASH
Copper **Ruler:** Kuang-hsü **Obv. Leg.:** Chiang-hsü Sheng Tsao **Obv. Insc.:** Kuang-hsü Yüan-pao **Edge:** Plain

Date	Mintage	VG	F	VF	XF	Unc
CD(1902)	—	—	—	—	—	—

Y# B162 10 CASH
Copper **Ruler:** Kuang-hsü **Obv:** Kiangsu Y#162.8
Obv. Leg.: Chiang-hsü Sheng Tsao **Obv. Insc.:** Kuang-hsü Yüan-pao **Rev:** Kiangnan Y#135 **Note:** Mule.

Date	Mintage	VG	F	VF	XF	Unc
CD(1902)	—	30.00	90.00	150	250	—

Y# 162.11 10 CASH
Copper **Ruler:** Kuang-hsü **Obv:** Larger Manchu "Boo-su"
Obv. Leg.: Chiang-hsü Sheng Tsao **Obv. Insc.:** Kuang-hsü Yüan-pao

Date	Mintage	VG	F	VF	XF	Unc
CD1905	—	0.85	2.50	5.00	8.00	65.00

Y# 11n.1 20 CASH
Copper **Ruler:** Kuang-hsü **Obv. Insc.:** Tai-ch'ing T'ung-pi
Rev. Leg.: Kuang-hsü Nien-tsao, TAI-CHING-TI-KUO ...

Date	Mintage	VG	F	VF	XF	Unc
CD1906	—	25.00	40.00	60.00	90.00	—

Y# 11n.1a 20 CASH
Brass **Ruler:** Kuang-hsü **Obv. Insc.:** Tai-ch'ing T'ung-pi
Rev. Leg.: Kuang-hsü Nien-tsao, TAI-CHING-TI-KUO ...

Date	Mintage	VG	F	VF	XF	Unc
CD1906	—	35.00	60.00	90.00	150	—

Y# 162.9 10 CASH
Copper **Ruler:** Kuang-hsü **Obv:** Manchu "Boo-su" at center
Obv. Leg.: Chiang-hsü Sheng Tsao **Obv. Insc.:** Kuang-hsü Yüan-pao **Edge:** Reeded

Date	Mintage	VG	F	VF	XF	Unc
CD(1903)	—	1.75	5.00	7.50	12.00	90.00

Y# C162 10 CASH
Copper **Ruler:** Kuang-hsü **Obv:** Kiangsu Y#162.9
Obv. Leg.: Chiang-hsü Sheng Tsao **Obv. Insc.:** Kuang-hsü Yüan-pao **Rev:** Kiangnan Y#135 **Note:** Mule.

Date	Mintage	VG	F	VF	XF	Unc
CD(1903)	—	30.00	90.00	150	250	—

Y# 162.12 10 CASH
Copper **Ruler:** Kuang-hsü **Obv. Leg.:** Chiang-hsü Sheng Tsao
Obv. Insc.: Kuang-hsü Yüan-pao **Rev:** Kiangsu spelled "KIANG-COO"

Date	Mintage	VG	F	VF	XF	Unc
CD1905	—	100	250	500	750	—

Note: Considered a contemporary counterfeit by some authorities.

PATTERNS
Including off metal strikes

KM#	Date	Mintage	Identification	Mkt Val
Pn2	ND(c. 1901)	—	2 Cash. Brass. Y159.	350
Pn3	CD1906	—	2 Cash. Brass. Y8n.	350
Pn4	ND(c. 1906)	—	5 Cash. Brass. EIVE for FIVE. Y161.1.	400
Pn5	ND(c. 1906)	—	5 Cash. Copper. EIVE for FIVE. Y161.1a.	400
Pn6	ND(c. 1906)	—	10 Cash. White Copper. Y162.5, W826.	
Pn7	CD(1906)	—	20 Cash. Copper. Character "Huai" in center. Y11d.	

KIRIN PROVINCE

Jilin

A province of northeast China that was formed in 1945. Before that it was one of the three original provinces of Manchuria. Besides growing corn, wheat and tobacco, there is also coal mining. An arsenal in Kirin (Jilin) opened in 1881 and was chosen as a source for coinage attempts. In 1884 Tael trials were struck and regular coinage began in 1895. Modern equipment was installed in a new mint in Kirin (Jilin) in 1901. The issues of this mint were very prolific and many varieties exist due to the use of hand cut dies for the earlier issues. The mint burned down in 1911.

EMPIRE

MILLED COINAGE

Errors in the English legends are very common in the Kirin coinage. It has been estimated there are over 2500 die varieties of Kirin (Jilin) silver coins and more than 1000 varieties of copper 10 Cash. Listed here are basic types and major varieties only.

Y# 160 10 CASH
Brass **Ruler:** Kuang-hsü **Obv. Leg.:** Chiang-hsü Sheng Tsao **Obv. Insc.:** Kuang-hsü Yüan-pao **Rev:** Cloud below all 3 letters of "SOO"

Date	Mintage	VG	F	VF	XF	Unc
ND(1904-05)	—	0.85	2.50	4.00	8.00	65.00

Y# 10n 10 CASH
Copper **Ruler:** Kuang-hsü **Obv:** Mint mark incused on raised disc **Obv. Insc.:** Tai-ch'ing T'ung-pi **Rev. Leg.:** Kuang-hsü Nien-tsao, TAI-CHING-TI-KUO ... **Edge:** Plain

Date	Mintage	VG	F	VF	XF	Unc
CD1906	—	0.85	2.50	5.00	10.00	90.00

Y# 10n.1 10 CASH
Copper **Ruler:** Kuang-hsü **Obv:** Mint mark incused on raised disc **Obv. Insc.:** Tai-ch'ing T'ung-pi **Rev. Leg.:** Kuang-hsü Nien-tsao, TAI-CHING-TI-KUO ... **Edge:** Reeded

Date	Mintage	VG	F	VF	XF	Unc
CD1906	—	2.00	6.00	11.00	17.50	100

Y# 175 2 CASH
Bronze **Ruler:** Kuang-hsü **Obv. Insc.:** Kuang-hsü T'ung-pao
Note: Mint mark: Manchu "Boo-gi".

Date	Mintage	VG	F	VF	XF	Unc
ND(ca.1905)	—	80.00	120	160	250	—

Y# 10n.2 10 CASH
Copper **Ruler:** Kuang-hsü **Obv:** Mint mark in relief in field at center without raised disc **Obv. Insc.:** Tai-ch'ing T'ung-pi **Rev. Leg.:** Kuang-hsü Nien-tsao, TAI-CHING-TI-KUO ... **Edge:** Plain

Date	Mintage	VG	F	VF	XF	Unc
CD1906	—	2.00	6.00	11.00	17.50	100

Y# 160.1 10 CASH
Brass **Ruler:** Kuang-hsü **Obv. Leg.:** Chiang-hsü Sheng Tsao
Obv. Insc.: Kuang-hsü Yüan-pao **Rev:** Cloud below first 2 letters of "SOO", Manchu "Boo" at 9 o'clock higher, dragon's body thinner

Date	Mintage	VG	F	VF	XF	Unc
ND(1904-05)	—	0.85	2.50	4.00	8.00	65.00

Y# 162.10 10 CASH
Copper **Ruler:** Kuang-hsü **Obv:** Rosette center, small Manchu "Boo-su" at 3 and 9 o'clock **Obv. Leg.:** Chiang-hsü Sheng Tsao **Obv. Insc.:** Kuang-hsü Yüan-pao **Edge:** Plain

Date	Mintage	VG	F	VF	XF	Unc
CD(1905)	—	0.35	1.00	2.00	5.00	65.00

Y# 163 20 CASH
Copper **Ruler:** Kuang-hsü **Obv. Leg.:** Chiang-hsü Sheng Tsao
Obv. Insc.: Kuang-hsü Yüan-pao **Rev:** Dragon

Date	Mintage	VG	F	VF	XF	Unc
ND(c.1902)	—	17.50	32.50	45.00	65.00	—

Y# 163a 20 CASH
Brass **Ruler:** Kuang-hsü **Obv. Leg.:** Chiang-hsü Sheng Tsao
Obv. Insc.: Kuang-hsü Yüan-pao **Rev:** Dragon

Date	Mintage	VG	F	VF	XF	Unc
ND(c.1902)	—	30.00	45.00	70.00	110	—

Y# 174 10 CASH
Bronze **Ruler:** Kuang-hsü **Obv. Insc.:** Kuang-hsü Yüan-pao
Note: Mint mark: Manchu "Chi".

Date	Mintage	VG	F	VF	XF	Unc
ND(1901) Rare	—	—	—	—	—	—

Y# A162 10 CASH
Copper **Ruler:** Kuang-hsü **Obv:** Kiangsu Y#162
Obv. Leg.: Chiang-hsü Sheng Tsao **Obv. Insc.:** Kuang-hsü Yüan-pao **Rev:** Kiangnan Y#135 **Note:** Mule.

Date	Mintage	VG	F	VF	XF	Unc
ND(c.1905)	—	30.00	90.00	150	250	—

Y# 176   10 CASH(ES)
Copper   **Ruler:** Kuang-hsü **Obv. Leg.:** Chi-lin Sheng Tsao
Obv. Insc.: Kuang-hsü Yüan-pao **Rev:** Dragon

Date	Mintage	VG	F	VF	XF	Unc
ND(ca.1901)	—	35.00	60.00	90.00	125	

Y# 176.1   10 CASH(ES)
Copper   **Ruler:** Kuang-hsü **Obv. Leg.:** Chi-lin Sheng Tsao
Obv. Insc.: Kuang-hsü Yüan-pao **Rev:** Thinner dragon

Date	Mintage	VG	F	VF	XF	Unc
ND(ca.1901)	—	35.00	60.00	90.00	125	

Y# 177   10 CASH(ES)
Copper   **Ruler:** Kuang-hsü **Obv:** Small rosettes **Obv. Leg.:** Chi-lin Sheng Tsao **Obv. Insc.:** Kuang-hsü Yüan-pao **Rev:** Dragon; large rosettes

Date	Mintage	VG	F	VF	XF	Unc
ND(ca.1903)	—	5.00	10.00	15.00	25.00	—

Y# 177.1   10 CASH(ES)
Copper   **Ruler:** Kuang-hsü **Obv. Leg.:** Chi-lin Sheng Tsao **Obv. Insc.:** Kuang-hsü Yüan-pao **Rev:** Dragon; small stars

Date	Mintage	VG	F	VF	XF	Unc
ND(ca.1903)	—	5.00	10.00	15.00	25.00	—

Y# 177.2   10 CASH(ES)
Copper   **Ruler:** Kuang-hsü **Obv:** Small stars **Obv. Leg.:** Chi-lin Sheng Tsao **Obv. Insc.:** Kuang-hsü Yüan-pao **Rev:** Dragon; large rosettes

Date	Mintage	VG	F	VF	XF	Unc
ND(ca.1903)	—	5.00	10.00	17.50	30.00	—

Y# 177.3   10 CASH(ES)
Copper   **Ruler:** Kuang-hsü **Obv:** Small stars **Obv. Leg.:** Chi-lin Sheng Tsao **Obv. Insc.:** Kuang-hsü Yüan-pao **Rev:** Dragon; small stars

Date	Mintage	VG	F	VF	XF	Unc
ND(ca.1903)	—	5.00	10.00	15.00	25.00	—

Y# 177.3a   10 CASH(ES)
Brass   **Ruler:** Kuang-hsü **Obv. Leg.:** Chi-lin Sheng Tsao
Obv. Insc.: Kuang-hsü Yüan-pao **Rev:** Dragon

Date	Mintage	VG	F	VF	XF	Unc
ND(ca.1903)	—	5.00	10.00	17.50	30.00	—

Y# 177.4   10 CASH(ES)
Brass   **Ruler:** Kuang-hsü **Obv:** Large stars **Obv. Leg.:** Chi-lin Sheng Tsao **Obv. Insc.:** Kuang-hsü Yüan-pao **Rev:** Dragon; large stars

Date	Mintage	VG	F	VF	XF	Unc
ND(ca.1903)	—	4.00	7.00	12.00	17.50	—

Y# 177.5   10 CASH(ES)
Brass   **Ruler:** Kuang-hsü **Obv:** Large stars **Obv. Leg.:** Chi-lin Sheng Tsao **Obv. Insc.:** Kuang-hsü Yüan-pao **Rev:** Dragon; large rosettes

Date	Mintage	VG	F	VF	XF	Unc
ND(ca.1903)	—	4.00	7.00	12.00	17.50	—

Y# 177.6   10 CASH(ES)
Brass   **Ruler:** Kuang-hsü **Obv:** Medium rosettes **Obv. Leg.:** Chi-lin Sheng Tsao **Obv. Insc.:** Kuang-hsü Yüan-pao **Rev:** Dragon

Date	Mintage	VG	F	VF	XF	Unc
ND(ca.1903)	—	4.00	7.00	12.00	17.50	—

Y# 177.7   10 CASH(ES)
Brass   **Ruler:** Kuang-hsü **Obv. Leg.:** Chi-lin Sheng Tsao **Obv. Insc.:** Kuang-hsü Yüan-pao **Rev:** Dragon; "CASHES" spelled "CASHIS"

Date	Mintage	VG	F	VF	XF	Unc
ND(ca.1903)	—	60.00	100	160	250	—

Note: It is difficult to differentiate the stars and rosettes on worn coins; the rosettes have a raised dot in the center while the stars have a hole in the center; it has been estimated that 1000 varieties of Y#177 exist

Y# 20p   10 CASH(ES)
Copper   **Ruler:** Hsüan-t'ung **Obv:** Very small mint mark **Obv. Insc.:** Tai-ch'ing T'ung-pi **Rev. Leg.:** Hsüan-t'ung Nien-tsao, TAI-CHING-TI-KUO...

Date	Mintage	VG	F	VF	XF	Unc
CD1909	—	8.00	15.00	25.00	40.00	—

Y# 20p.1   10 CASH(ES)
Copper   **Ruler:** Hsüan-t'ung **Obv:** Larger mint mark **Obv. Insc.:** Tai-ch'ing T'ung-pi **Rev:** Head of dragon, redesigned with more whiskers **Rev. Leg.:** Hsüan-t'ung Nien-tsao, TAI-CHING-TI-KUO...

Date	Mintage	VG	F	VF	XF	Unc
CD1909	—	10.00	17.50	30.00	45.00	—

Y# 20p.2   10 CASH(ES)
Copper   **Ruler:** Hsüan-t'ung **Obv:** Larger mint mark **Obv. Insc.:** Tai-ch'ing T'ung-pi **Rev:** Dragon similar to Y#20p **Rev. Leg.:** Hsüan-t'ung Nien-tsao, TAI-CHING-TI-KUO...

Date	Mintage	VG	F	VF	XF	Unc
CD1909	—	10.00	17.50	30.00	45.00	—

Note: For Y#20x refer to General Issues-Empire

Y# 20p.3   10 CASH(ES)
Copper   **Ruler:** Hsüan-t'ung **Obv:** Y#20p **Obv. Insc.:** Tai-ch'ing T'ung-pi **Rev:** General Issue - Empire Y#20.1 **Rev. Leg.:** Hsüan-t'ung Nien-tsao, TAI-CHING-TI-KUO... **Note:** Mule.

Date	Mintage	VG	F	VF	XF	Unc
CD1909 2 known	—				3,500	

Note: Though dated 1909, minted at Mukden ca.1922

Y# 178   20 CASH(ES)
Copper   **Ruler:** Kuang-hsü **Obv. Leg.:** Chi-lin Sheng Tsao **Obv. Insc.:** Kuang-hsü Yüan-pao **Rev:** Dragon

Date	Mintage	VG	F	VF	XF	Unc
ND(1903)	—	35.00	65.00	100	175	—

Y# A176   20 CASH(ES)
Copper   **Ruler:** Kuang-hsü **Obv:** Manchu in center, eight characters below **Obv. Leg.:** Chi-lin Sheng Tsao **Obv. Insc.:** Kuang-hsü Yüan-pao **Rev:** Dragon

Date	Mintage	VG	F	VF	XF	Unc
ND(1903)	—	80.00	200	400	700	—

Y# A176.1   20 CASH(ES)
Copper   **Ruler:** Kuang-hsü **Obv:** Rosette in center, three characters below **Obv. Leg.:** Chi-lin Sheng Tsao **Obv. Insc.:** Kuang-hsü Yüan-pao **Rev:** Dragon

Date	Mintage	VG	F	VF	XF	Unc
ND(1903)	—	80.00	225	425	725	—

Y# 178.1   20 CASH(ES)
Copper   **Ruler:** Kuang-hsü **Obv. Insc.:** Kuang-hsü Yüan-pao **Rev:** Dragon, "CASHES" spelled "CASHIS"

Date	Mintage	VG	F	VF	XF	Unc
ND(1903)	—	35.00	65.00	100	175	—

Y# 21p   20 CASH(ES)
Copper   Ruler: Kuang-hsü Obv. Insc.: Tai-ch'ing T'ung-pi Rev:
Dragon Rev. Leg.: Hsüan-t'ung Nien-tsao, TAI-CHING-TI-KUO...

Date	Mintage	VG	F	VF	XF	Unc
CD1909	—	120	250	450	750	—

Y# E176   30 CASHES
Brass   Ruler: Kuang-hsü Obv. Insc.: Kuang-hsü Yüan-pao
Rev: Side view dragon

Date	Mintage	VG	F	VF	XF	Unc
CD1901 Rare	—	—	—	—	—	—

Y# B176   50 CASHES
Brass   Ruler: Kuang-hsü Obv: Chi-lin Sheng Tsao
Obv. Insc.: Kuang-hsü Yüan-pao Rev: Side view dragon

Date	Mintage	Good	VG	F	VF	XF
CD1901 3 known	—	—	—	—	—	—

Note: D.K.E. Ching Sale 6-91 VG-F realized $3,410; a similar 20 Cashes and silver 50 Cent have been reported and are believed to be fantasies by some authorities

Y# F176   100 CASHES
Brass   Ruler: Kuang-hsü Obv. Insc.: Kuang-hsü Yüan-pao
Rev: Side view dragon

Date	Mintage	VG	F	VF	XF	Unc
CD1901	—	—	—	—	—	—

Y# C176   10 COPPERS
Brass   Ruler: Kuang-hsü Obv. Insc.: Kuang-hsü Yüan-pao
Rev: Dragon Note: Similar to 50 Cashes, Y#B176

Date	Mintage	VG	F	VF	XF	Unc
CD1901	—	—	—	—	—	—

Y# 179a   5 CENTS
1.2700 g., Silver   Ruler: Kuang-hsü Obv: Yin-yang in center
Obv. Insc.: Kuang-hsü Yüan-pao Rev: Side view dragon
Note: Kann #444,465, 481, 510, 533.

Date	Mintage	VG	F	VF	XF	Unc
CD1900	—	2.50	7.50	15.00	30.00	100
CD1901	—	2.50	5.50	11.50	30.00	120
CD1902	—	3.00	6.50	12.50	30.00	150
CD1903	—	5.00	12.50	25.00	60.00	250
CD1904	—	4.00	10.00	15.00	40.00	130
CD1905	—	3.50	7.50	15.00	35.00	120

Y# 179.1   5 CENTS
1.2700 g., Silver   Ruler: Kuang-hsü Obv. Insc.: Kuang-hsü
Yüan-pao Rev: Side view dragon; without crosses flanking weight
Note: Kann #394, 416, 549

Date	Mintage	VG	F	VF	XF	Unc
ND(ca.1898)	—	1.75	5.00	10.00	20.00	90.00
CD1899	—	2.25	6.50	12.50	25.00	100
CD1900	—	3.50	10.00	20.00	35.00	120
CD1906	—	2.75	6.50	12.50	30.00	130
CD1907	—	3.50	8.00	15.00	30.00	130
CD1908 Rare	—	—	—	—	—	—

Y# 180a   10 CENTS
2.5500 g., Silver   Ruler: Kuang-hsü Obv: Yin-yang in center
Obv. Leg.: Chi-lin Sheng Tsao Obv. Insc.: Kuang-hsü Yüan-pao
Rev: Side view dragon Note: Kann #440, 464, 484.

Date	Mintage	VG	F	VF	XF	Unc
CD1900	—	2.50	7.50	15.00	30.00	120
CD1901	—	2.50	5.50	11.50	25.00	100

Date	Mintage	VG	F	VF	XF	Unc
CD1902	—	3.00	7.50	15.00	35.00	120
CD1903	—	4.00	9.00	18.50	40.00	200
CD1904	—	15.00	35.00	60.00	150	500
CD1905	—	3.00	6.50	11.50	25.00	100

Y# 180.1   10 CENTS
2.5500 g., Silver   Ruler: Kuang-hsü Obv: Large flower vase
center Obv. Leg.: Chi-lin Sheng Tsao Obv. Insc.: Kuang-hsü
Yüan-pao Rev: Side view dragon; without crosses flanking weight
Note: Kann #393, 416, 546.

Date	Mintage	VG	F	VF	XF	Unc
ND(ca.1898)	—	1.85	5.50	11.50	22.50	85.00
CD1899	—	2.25	6.50	12.50	25.00	90.00
CD1900	—	2.25	6.50	12.50	25.00	90.00
CD1906	—	3.00	6.50	12.50	30.00	100
CD1907	—	20.00	50.00	100	200	450

Y# 180c   10 CENTS
2.5500 g., Silver   Ruler: Kuang-hsü Obv: Numeral 1 in center
Obv. Leg.: Chi-lin Tsao Obv. Insc.: Kuang-hsü Yüan-pao
Rev: Side view dragon

Date	Mintage	VG	F	VF	XF	Unc
CD1908	—	30.00	80.00	150	225	500

Y# 181a   20 CENTS
5.1000 g., Silver   Ruler: Kuang-hsü Obv: Yin-yang in center
Obv. Leg.: Chi-lin Sheng Tsao Obv. Insc.: Kuang-hsü Yüan-pao
Rev: Side view dragon

Date	Mintage	VG	F	VF	XF	Unc
CD1900	—	2.75	7.50	15.00	30.00	120
CD1901	22,508,000	3.50	6.50	15.00	25.00	120
CD1902	Inc. above	3.50	6.50	15.00	25.00	120
CD1903	Inc. above	3.50	6.50	15.00	25.00	120
CD1904	Inc. above	3.50	6.50	15.00	25.00	120
CD1905	Inc. above	3.50	6.50	15.00	25.00	120

Y# 181   20 CENTS
5.1000 g., Silver   Ruler: Kuang-hsü Obv: Flower vase center
Obv. Leg.: Chi-lin Sheng Tsao Obv. Insc.: Kuang-hsü Yüan-pao
Rev: Side view dragon

Date	Mintage	VG	F	VF	XF	Unc
ND(ca.1898)	—	2.75	7.50	15.00	30.00	120
CD1899	—	2.50	6.50	12.50	25.00	110
CD1900	—	2.75	7.50	15.00	30.00	120
CD1906	Inc. below	3.50	6.50	12.50	25.00	120
CD1907	Inc. below	3.50	6.50	12.50	25.00	120
CD1908	Inc. below	30.00	90.00	175	300	700

Y# 181b   20 CENTS
5.1000 g., Silver   Ruler: Kuang-hsü Obv: Manchu words in
center Obv. Leg.: Chi-lin Tsao Obv. Insc.: Kuang-hsü Yüan-pao
Rev: Side view dragon

Date	Mintage	VG	F	VF	XF	Unc
CD1908	Inc. above	17.50	50.00	100	150	400

Y# 181c   20 CENTS
5.1000 g., Silver   Ruler: Kuang-hsü Obv: Numeral 2 center
Obv. Leg.: Chi-lin Tsao Obv. Insc.: Kuang-hsü Yüan-pao
Rev: Side view dragon

Date	Mintage	VG	F	VF	XF	Unc
CD1908	Inc. above	8.50	25.00	50.00	85.00	300

Y# 22   20 CENTS
5.1000 g., Silver   Ruler: Hsüan-t'ung Obv: Mint mark in relief on
raised disc at center Obv. Leg.: Chi-lin Sheng Tsao
Obv. Insc.: Hsüan-t'ung Yüan-pao Rev: Side view dragon

Date	Mintage	VG	F	VF	XF	Unc
ND(1909)	—	12.00	35.00	70.00	125	300

Y# 22.2   20 CENTS
5.1000 g., Silver   Ruler: Hsüan-t'ung Obv: Mint mark in circle at
center Obv. Insc.: Hsüan-t'ung Yüan-pao Rev: Side view dragon

Date	Mintage	VG	F	VF	XF	Unc
ND(1909)	—	12.00	35.00	70.00	125	300

Y# 182a.1   50 CENTS
13.1000 g., Silver   Ruler: Kuang-hsü Obv: Redesigned yin-yang
in center Obv. Leg.: Chi-lin Sheng Tsao Obv. Insc.: Kuang-hsü
Yüan-pao Rev: Side view dragon

Date	Mintage	VG	F	VF	XF	Unc
CD1901	—	10.00	20.00	35.00	60.00	300
CD1902	—	10.00	20.00	35.00	60.00	300
CD1903	—	12.00	25.00	40.00	65.00	310
CD1904	—	10.00	20.00	35.00	60.00	300
CD1905	—	9.00	15.00	30.00	50.00	300

Y# 182.3   50 CENTS
13.1000 g., Silver   Ruler: Kuang-hsü Obv. Leg.: Chi-lin Sheng
Tsao Obv. Insc.: Kuang-hsü Yüan-pao Rev: Side view dragon

Date	Mintage	VG	F	VF	XF	Unc
CD1898	—	10.00	25.00	45.00	80.00	350
CD1899	—	10.00	25.00	45.00	80.00	350
CD1900	—	10.00	20.00	35.00	60.00	300
CD1906	—	10.00	20.00	35.00	60.00	300
CD1907	—	10.00	20.00	35.00	60.00	300
CD1908	—	20.00	50.00	80.00	125	500

Y# 182b   50 CENTS
13.1000 g., Silver   Ruler: Kuang-hsü Obv: Manchu words in
center Obv. Leg.: Chi-lin Tsao Obv. Insc.: Kuang-hsü Yüan-pao
Rev: Side view dragon

Date	Mintage	VG	F	VF	XF	Unc
CD1908	—	25.00	75.00	150	275	600

Y# 183a.1 DOLLAR
26.1000 g., Silver **Ruler:** Kuang-hsü **Obv:** Redesigned Yin-yang in center **Obv. Leg.:** Chi-lin Sheng Tsao **Obv. Insc.:** "Kuang-hsü Yüan-pao" **Rev:** Coarse-scaled, beady-eyed dragon

Date	Mintage	VG	F	VF	XF	Unc
CD1901	—	30.00	90.00	190	350	2,400
CD1902	—	30.00	90.00	190	350	2,400

Y# 183a.2 DOLLAR
26.1000 g., Silver **Ruler:** Kuang-hsü **Obv. Leg.:** Chi-lin Sheng Tsao **Obv. Insc.:** "Kuang-hsü Yüan-pao" **Rev:** Fine dot-scaled, beady-eyed dragon

Date	Mintage	VG	F	VF	XF	Unc
CD1902	—	25.00	70.00	190	350	2,400
CD1903	—	30.00	90.00	190	350	1,900
CD1904	—	30.00	90.00	190	325	1,800
CD1905	—	30.00	90.00	190	325	1,800

Y# 183a.3 DOLLAR
26.1000 g., Silver **Ruler:** Kuang-hsü **Obv. Leg.:** Chi-lin Sheng Tsao **Obv. Insc.:** "Kuang-hsü Yüan-pao" **Rev:** Fine oval-scaled, round-eyed dragon

Date	Mintage	VG	F	VF	XF	Unc
CD1905	—	25.00	60.00	190	325	1,700

Y# 183.1 DOLLAR
26.1000 g., Silver **Ruler:** Kuang-hsü **Obv:** Large rosettes **Obv. Insc.:** Kuang-hsü Yüan-pao **Rev:** Side view dragon; without rosettes flanking weight

Date	Mintage	VG	F	VF	XF	Unc
ND(ca.1905)	—	450	1,450	2,700	4,800	9,000

Y# 183.2 DOLLAR
26.1000 g., Silver **Ruler:** Kuang-hsü **Obv. Insc.:** Kuang-hsü Yüan-pao **Rev:** Side view dragon **Rev. Leg.:** 3.2 CAINDARINS 2 (error)

Date	Mintage	VG	F	VF	XF	Unc
CD1906	—	180	425	600	950	2,100

Y# 183.3 DOLLAR
26.1000 g., Silver **Ruler:** Kuang-hsü **Obv:** Small rosettes **Obv. Insc.:** "Kuang-hsü Yüan-pao" **Rev:** Side view dragon; small rosettes before and after weight "7 CANDARINS 2"

Date	Mintage	VG	F	VF	XF	Unc
ND(ca.1906)	—	90.00	190	300	475	1,900

Y# 183.4 DOLLAR
26.1000 g., Silver **Ruler:** Kuang-hsü **Obv:** Small leaves out of left basket **Obv. Leg.:** Chi-lin Sheng Tsao **Obv. Insc.:** "Kuang-hsü Yüan-pao" **Rev:** Side view dragon; similar to Y#183.2

Date	Mintage	VG	F	VF	XF	Unc
ND(ca.1906)	—	36.00	110	240	350	1,800

Y# 183 DOLLAR
26.1000 g., Silver **Ruler:** Kuang-hsü **Obv:** Flower vase center **Obv. Leg.:** Chi-lin Sheng Tsao **Obv. Insc.:** Kuang-hsü Yüan-pao **Rev:** Side view dragon; small rosettes before and after weight: "7 CANDARINS 2" or "7 CAINDARINS 2"

Date	Mintage	VG	F	VF	XF	Unc
ND(ca.1898)	—	25.00	70.00	120	300	2,500
CD1899	—	25.00	70.00	120	300	2,500
CD1900	—	25.00	70.00	120	350	3,000
CD1906	—	25.00	70.00	170	350	2,500
CD1907	—	55.00	150	240	475	3,000
CD1908	—	450	1,450	2,400	6,000	10,000

Y# 183b DOLLAR
26.1000 g., Silver **Ruler:** Kuang-hsü **Obv:** Manchu words in center **Obv. Leg.:** Chi-lin Tsao **Obv. Insc.:** "Kuang-hsü Yüan-pao" **Rev:** Side view dragon

Date	Mintage	VG	F	VF	XF	Unc
CD1908	—	300	1,000	2,400	5,100	12,000

Y# 183c DOLLAR
26.1000 g., Silver **Ruler:** Kuang-hsü **Obv:** Numeral 11 in center **Obv. Leg.:** Chi-lin Tsao **Obv. Insc.:** "Kuang-hsü Yüan-pao" **Rev:** Side view dragon

Date	Mintage	VG	F	VF	XF	Unc
CD1908	—	325	1,050	2,600	5,400	14,500

Note: The numeral 11 in center reflects the discount in subsidiary coinage; it took 11 dimes to equal the dollar

PATTERNS
Including off metal strikes

KM#	Date	Mintage	Identification	Mkt Val
Pn10	CD1902	—	50 Cents. Brass. Y#182a.1	—
Pn11	CD1908	—	20 Cents. Zinc. Y#181c	—
Pn12	ND(1909)	—	20 Cents. Silver. K#583, formerly Y#22.1	—

KWANGSI-KWANGSEA
Guangxi
A hilly region in southeast China with many forests. Large amounts of rice are grown adjacent to the many rivers. A mint opened in Kweilin in 1667, closed in 1670, reopened in 1679, closed again in 1681. It reopened in the mid-1700's and was a rather prolific issuer of Cash coins. In 1905 the government allowed modern mints to be established in Kwangsi (Guangxi) at Nanning (1905) and Kweilin (1905). The Nanning Mint began operation in 1919 and closed in 1923. In 1920 a new mint was opened at Wuchow and operated sporadically until 1929. In 1938 part of the Shanghai Central Mint was moved to Kweilin where it operated until at least 1945 and perhaps as late as 1949.

REPUBLIC
PROVINCIAL CAST COINAGE

C# 18-9 CASH
Cast Brass **Ruler:** Kuang-hsü **Obv. Insc.:** Kuang-hsü T'ung-pao **Rev:** Manchu inscription **Rev. Insc.:** Boo-gui

Date	Mintage	Good	VG	F	VF	XF
ND(1875-1908)	—	5.50	8.50	13.50	25.00	—

MILLED COINAGE

Y# 413 CENT
Brass **Obv. Leg.:** KWANG-SEA PROVINCE

Date	Mintage	VG	F	VF	XF	Unc
8(1919)	—	50.00	150	250	400	—

Y# 413a CENT
Brass **Obv. Leg.:** Chung Hua Min Kuo (year) Nien

Date	Mintage	VG	F	VF	XF	Unc
8(1919)	—	15.00	40.00	75.00	150	—

Y# A415 5 CENTS
Copper-Nickel **Obv. Leg.:** Chung Hua Min Kuo (year) Nien **Rev:** Large "5" in sprays

Date	Mintage	VG	F	VF	XF	Unc
12(1923)	—	50.00	150	250	400	600

Y# 414 10 CENTS
2.7000 g., Silver **Obv. Leg.:** Chung Hua Min Kuo (year) Nien

Date	Mintage	VG	F	VF	XF	Unc
9(1920)	—	25.00	75.00	125	175	300

Y# 415 20 CENTS
5.3000 g., Silver **Obv. Leg.:** Chung Hua Min Kuo (year) Nien **Rev. Leg.:** KWANG-SEA PROVINCE

Date	Mintage	VG	F	VF	XF	Unc
8(1919)	—	25.00	60.00	85.00	135	200
9(1920)	—	30.00	80.00	125	175	300

Y# 415a 20 CENTS
5.3000 g., Silver **Obv. Leg.:** Chung Hua Min Kuo (year) Nien **Rev. Leg.:** KWANG-SI PROVINCE

Date	Mintage	VG	F	VF	XF	Unc
8(1919)	—	5.00	10.00	25.00	50.00	125
9(1920)	—	5.00	10.00	25.00	50.00	125
11(1922)	—	5.00	10.00	25.00	50.00	125
12(1923)	—	5.00	10.00	25.00	50.00	125
13(1924)	—	5.00	10.00	25.00	50.00	125
14(1925)	—	5.00	10.00	25.00	50.00	125

Y# 415a.1 20 CENTS
5.3000 g., Silver **Obv:** Character "Kuei" in center instead of dot **Obv. Leg.:** Chung Hua Min Kuo (year) Nien

Date	Mintage	VG	F	VF	XF	Unc
13(1924)	—	35.00	80.00	100	150	250

Y# 415b 20 CENTS
5.3000 g., Silver **Obv:** Tiny character "Hsi" on dot center **Obv. Leg.:** Chung Hua Min Kuo (year) Nien **Rev:** Wreath added around "20"

Date	Mintage	VG	F	VF	XF	Unc
15(1926)	—	2.00	3.50	6.50	10.00	20.00
15(1926)	—	2.00	3.50	6.50	10.00	20.00
Note: Without HSI						
16(1927)	—	2.00	3.50	6.50	10.00	20.00

Y# 416 20 CENTS
5.3000 g., Silver **Obv. Leg.:** Chung Hua Min Kuo (year) Nien **Rev:** Elephant nose rock at Kueilin

Date	Mintage	VG	F	VF	XF	Unc
38(1949)	—	40.00	100	175	250	375

PIEFORTS

KM#	Date	Mintage	Identification	Mkt Val
P1	19(1921)	—	10 Cents. Bronze. Y414c. KM#Pn5.	250
P2	10(1921)	—	10 Cents. Brass. 3.2900 g. Y414b. KM#Pn4.	150

PATTERNS
Including off metal strikes

KM#	Date	Mintage	Identification	Mkt Val
Pn1	ND(1905)	—	10 Cash. Copper.	
Pn2	CD1906	—	10 Cash. Copper.	
Pn3	10(1921)	—	10 Cents. Copper. 2.11-2.22 grams. Y414a, K746-llx.	110
Pn4	10(1921)	—	10 Cents. Brass. Y414b.	
Pn5	10(1921)	—	10 Cents. Bronze. Y414c.	140
Pn6	10(1921)	—	10 Cents. Silver. Y414f.	—
Pn7	10(1921)	—	20 Cents. Copper. 4.68-4.97 grams. Y415c, K746-lx.	100
Pn8	10(1921)	—	20 Cents. Bronze. Y415d.	—
Pn9	10(1921)	—	20 Cents. Brass. Y415e.	—
Pn10	10(1921)	—	20 Cents. Silver. 4.8700 g. Y415f.	750

KWANGTUNG PROVINCE
Guangdong

A province located on the southeast coast of China. Kwangtung (Guangdong) lies mostly in the tropics and has both mountains and plains. Its coastline is nearly 800 miles long and provides many good harbors. Because of the location of Guangzhou (Canton) in the province, Kwangtung (Guangdong) was the first to be visited by seaborne foreign traders. Hong Kong was ceded to Great Britain after the First Opium War in 1841. Kowloon was later ceded to Britain in 1860 and the New Territories (100 year lease) in 1898 and Macao to Portugal in 1887, Kwangchowwan was leased to France in 1898 (a property was restored in 1946). A modern mint opened in Guangzhou (Canton) in 1889 with Edward Wyon as superintendent. The mint was a large issuer of coins until it closed in 1931. The Nationalists reopened the mint briefly in 1949, striking a few silver dollars, before abandoning the mainland for their retreat to Taiwan.

The large island of Hainan was split off from Kwangtung (Guangdong) Province in 1988 and established as a separate province.

Hong Kong was returned to China by Britain on July 1, 1997 and established as a special administrative region, retaining its own coinage.

EMPIRE
PROVINCIAL CAST COINAGE

C# 19-7 CASH
Cast Brass **Ruler:** Kuang-hsü **Obv. Insc.:** Kuang-hsü T'ung-pao **Rev:** Manchu inscription **Rev. Insc.:** Boo-guwang

Date	Mintage	Good	VG	F	VF	XF
ND(1875-1908)	—	12.00	22.00	32.00	45.00	—

MILLED COINAGE

Y# 190 CASH
2.7000 g., Brass, 24 mm. **Ruler:** Kuang-hsü **Obv:** "Kuang" in a different style **Obv. Insc.:** Kuang-hsü T'ung-pao **Rev:** Manchu inscription **Rev. Insc.:** Boo-guwang

Date	Mintage	VG	F	VF	XF	Unc
ND(1890-1908)	1,059,253,000	—	0.10	0.25	1.00	2.00

Y# 191 CASH
Brass **Ruler:** Kuang-hsü **Obv. Insc.:** Kuang-hsü T'ung-pao **Rev:** Manchu inscription **Rev. Insc.:** Boo-guwang

Date	Mintage	VG	F	VF	XF	Unc
ND(1906-08)	—	—	0.10	0.25	1.00	20.00

Y# 204 CASH
Brass **Obv. Insc.:** Hsüan-t'ung T'uang pao **Rev:** Manchu inscription **Rev. Insc.:** Boo-guwang

Date	Mintage	VG	F	VF	XF	Unc
ND(1909-11)	—	0.20	0.50	1.00	2.00	25.00

Y# 20r 10 CASH
Copper **Ruler:** Hsuan-T'ung **Obv. Insc.:** Tai-ch'ing T'ung-pi **Rev:** Dragon **Rev. Leg.:** Hsüan-t'ung Nien-tsao, TAI-CHING-TI KUO ...

Date	Mintage	VG	F	VF	XF	Unc
CD1909	—	0.50	1.50	3.00	5.00	80.00

Y# 10r CENT (10 Cash)
Copper **Ruler:** Kuang-hsü **Obv. Insc.:** Tai-ch'ing T'ung-pi **Rev:** Dragon **Rev. Leg.:** Kuang-hsü Nien-tsao, TAI-CHING-TI KUO ...

Date	Mintage	VG	F	VF	XF	Unc
CD1906	79,000,000	0.35	1.00	2.00	4.00	70.00
CD1907	46,000,000	—	1.00	2.00	4.00	70.00
CD1908	62,736,000	0.35	1.00	2.00	4.00	70.00

Y# A193 CENT (10 Cash)
Copper **Ruler:** Kuang-hsü **Obv:** Y#192 **Obv. Leg.:** Kuang-tung Sheng Tsao **Obv. Insc.:** Kuang-hsü Yuan-pao **Rev:** Y#193, dragon, "TEN CASH" **Note:** Mule.

Date	Mintage	VG	F	VF	XF	Unc
ND(c.1906)	—	6.50	20.00	28.50	40.00	100

Y# B193 CENT (10 Cash)
Copper **Ruler:** Kuang-hsü **Obv:** Y#193 **Obv. Leg.:** Kuang-tung Sheng Tsao **Obv. Insc.:** Kuang-hsü Yuan-pao **Rev:** Y#192, dragon **Note:** Mule.

Date	Mintage	VG	F	VF	XF	Unc
ND(c.1906)	—	6.50	20.00	28.50	40.00	100

KM# B192 CENT
Copper **Ruler:** Kuang-hsü **Obv. Leg.:** Kuang-hsü Yüan-pao **Obv. Insc.:** Kuang-hsü Yüan-pao **Note:** Prev. W#896.

Date	Mintage	VG	F	VF	XF	Unc
ND(ca.1906)	—	22.50	65.00	100	150	225

Y# 205 20 CENTS
5.5000 g., 0.8000 Silver 0.1415 oz. ASW **Ruler:** Hsuan-T'ung **Obv. Insc.:** Hsüan-t'ung Yüan-pao **Rev:** Dragon **Note:** Two varieties of edge reeding known.

Date	Mintage	VG	F	VF	XF	Unc
ND(1909-11)	94,774,000	3.00	5.00	7.00	11.00	25.00

Y# 206 DOLLAR
27.0000 g., 0.9000 Silver 0.7812 oz. ASW **Obv. Leg.:** Kuang-tung Sheng Tsao **Obv. Insc.:** Hsüan-t'ung Yüan-pao **Rev:** Dragon

Date	Mintage	VG	F	VF	XF	Unc
ND(1909-11)	—	15.00	20.00	45.00	75.00	1,000

REPUBLIC
MILLED COINAGE

Y# 417 CENT
Bronze **Obv. Leg.:** Chung Hua Min Kuo (year) Nien **Rev. Leg.:** KWANG-TUNG PROVINCE

Date	Mintage	VG	F	VF	XF	Unc
1(1912)	18,836,000	0.50	1.50	2.25	5.00	22.00
3(1914)	14,750,000	0.50	1.50	2.25	5.00	22.00
4(1915)	6,350,000	1.25	4.00	6.00	15.00	35.00
5(1916)	18,388,000	0.65	2.00	3.00	7.50	30.00
7(1918)	—	2.50	7.50	12.50	20.00	45.00

Y# 417a CENT
Brass **Obv. Leg.:** Chung Hua Min Kuo (year) Nien **Rev. Leg.:** KWANG-TUNG PROVINCE

Date	Mintage	VG	F	VF	XF	Unc
1(1912)	Inc. above	—	—	—	—	—
3(1914)	Inc. above	0.65	2.00	5.00	10.00	25.00
4(1915)	Inc. above	1.00	3.00	7.50	15.00	30.00
5(1916)	Inc. above	0.45	1.25	3.00	6.00	20.00

Y# 418 2 CENTS
Brass **Obv. Leg.:** Chung Hua Min Kuo (year) Nien **Rev. Leg.:** KWANG-TUNG PROVINCE

Date	Mintage	VG	F	VF	XF	Unc
7(1918)	—	10.00	30.00	50.00	90.00	175

Y# 418a   2 CENTS
Copper   **Obv. Leg.:** Chung Hua Min Kuo (year) Nien
Rev. Leg.: KWANG-TUNG PROVINCE

Date	Mintage	VG	F	VF	XF	Unc
7(1918) Rare	—	—	—	—	—	—

Y# 420   5 CENTS
Copper-Nickel   **Obv. Leg.:** Chung Hua Min Kuo (year) Nien
Rev: Large "5" in sprays **Rev. Leg.:** KWANG-TUNG PROVINCE

Date	Mintage	VG	F	VF	XF	Unc
8(1919)	916,000	0.35	1.00	2.00	3.00	5.00

Y# 421   5 CENTS
Copper-Nickel   **Obv. Leg.:** Chung Hua Min Kuo (year) Nien
Rev: Flag **Rev. Leg.:** KWANG-TUNG PROVINCE

Date	Mintage	VG	F	VF	XF	Unc
10(1921)	666,000	0.45	1.25	3.00	6.50	12.50

Y# 420a   5 CENTS
Copper-Nickel   **Obv. Leg.:** Chung Hua Min Kuo (year) Nien
Rev: Large "5" in sprays **Rev. Leg.:** KWANG-TUNG PROVINCE

Date	Mintage	F	VF	XF	Unc	BU
12(1923)	480,000	1.00	2.00	3.00	5.00	—

Y# 422   10 CENTS
2.7000 g., Silver   **Obv. Leg.:** Chung Hua Min Kuo (year) Nien
Rev: Large "10" **Rev. Leg.:** KWANG-TUNG PROVINCE

Date	Mintage	VG	F	VF	XF	Unc
2(1913)	8,798,000	1.50	2.50	4.00	5.00	10.00
3(1914)	Inc. above	1.75	2.75	4.50	6.00	12.00
11(1922)	—	2.25	4.00	7.00	10.00	25.00

Y# 425   10 CENTS
2.5000 g., Silver   **Obv. Leg.:** Chung Hua Min Kuo (year) Nien
Rev: Bust of Sun Yat-sen **Rev. Leg.:** KWANG-TUNG PROVINCE

Date	Mintage	VG	F	VF	XF	Unc
18(1929)	48,960,000	1.25	2.00	3.50	5.50	9.00

Y# 423   20 CENTS
5.4000 g., Silver   **Obv. Leg.:** Chung Hua Min Kuo (year) Nien
Rev. Leg.: KWANG-TUNG PROVINCE **Note:** The fineness of many of these 20-cent pieces, especially those dated Yr. 13 (1924), is as low as .500. In 1924 the Anhwei (Anhui) Mint secretly produced quantities of Kwangtung (Guangdong) 20-cent pieces that were only .400 fine. Standard issues were struck with a small dot in the center, 2 small rosettes at 4 and 8 o'clock; varieties exist with a large dot and large rosettes.

Date	Mintage	VG	F	VF	XF	Unc
1(1912)	88,000,000	2.25	2.75	3.75	6.50	12.00
2(1913)	109,974,000	2.25	2.75	3.75	6.50	12.00
3(1914)	41,691,000	2.25	2.75	3.75	6.50	12.00
4(1915)	22,332,000	3.00	6.00	12.00	25.00	100
7(1918)	—	2.25	2.75	3.75	6.00	10.00
8(1919)	195,000,000	2.00	2.50	3.50	4.50	7.00

Date	Mintage	VG	F	VF	XF	Unc
9(1920)	197,000,000	2.00	2.50	3.50	4.50	7.00
10(1921)	402,250,000	2.00	2.50	3.50	4.50	7.00
11(1922)	350,000,000	2.00	2.50	3.50	4.50	7.00
12(1923)	4,400,000	2.50	3.50	5.50	8.50	20.00
13(1924)	55,109,000	2.50	3.50	5.50	8.50	20.00

Y# 424   20 CENTS
5.3000 g., Silver   **Obv. Leg.:** Chung Hua Min Kuo (year) Nien
Rev: Bust of Sun Yat-sen **Rev. Leg.:** KWANG-TUNG PROVINCE

Date	Mintage	VG	F	VF	XF	Unc
13(1924)	—	8.50	25.00	45.00	70.00	175

Y# 426   20 CENTS
5.3000 g., Silver   **Obv:** Value in sprays **Obv. Leg.:** Chung Hua Min Kuo (year) Nien **Rev:** Bust of Sun Yat-sen
Rev. Leg.: KWANG-TUNG PROVINCE

Date	Mintage	VG	F	VF	XF	Unc
17(1928)	28,530,000	8.50	25.00	60.00	100	200
18(1929)	779,738,000	2.50	3.50	5.50	7.00	12.50
19(1930) 1 known	—	—	—	—	—	3,500

PATTERNS
Including off metal strikes

KM#	Date	Mintage Identification	Mkt Val
Pn16	ND(c. 1902)	— 1/2 Cent. Copper. Circled "flying" dragon.	—
Pn17	ND(1904)	— Tael. Silver. K932.	—
		Note: Superior Goodman sale 6-91 proof realized $41,800.	
PnA18	ND(1904)	— Tael. Pewter. 6mm thick. K932x.	—
Pn18	ND(1904)	— Tael. White Metal. K932y.	—
PnA19	ND(1906)	— 20 Cash. Copper. TCTK.	—
Pn19	3(1914)	— 10 Cents. Copper. Y422.	—
PnA20	4(1915)	— Cent. Red Copper. Y417.	—
PnB20	5(1916)	— Cent. Red Copper. Y417.	—
PnC20	7(1918)	— Cent. Red Copper. Y417.	—
Pn20	8(1919)	— 20 Cents. Copper. Y423.	150
Pn21	9(1920)	— 20 Cents. Copper. Y423.	150
Pn22	10(1921)	— 20 Cents. Copper. Y423.	150
PnA23	11(1922)	— 20 Cents. Copper. Y423.	150
Pn23	13(1924)	— 20 Cents. Gold. Y424.	—
Pn24	17(1928)	— 20 Cents. Copper. Y426.	—
Pn25	18(1929)	— 20 Cents. Copper. Y426.	—
Pn26	ND(ca. 1929)	— 20 Cents. Gold. Y426.	850
Pn27	25(1936)	— Cent. Bronze. Sun Yat Sen.	3,000
Pn28	25(1936)	— Cent. Copper.	700

KWEICHOW PROVINCE

Guizhou
A province located in southern China. It is basically a plateau region that is somewhat remote from the general traffic of China. The Kweichow Mint opened in 1730 and produced Cash coins until the end of the reign of Kuang Hsu. The Republic issues for this province are enigmatic as to their origin, as a mint supposedly did not exist in Kweichow (Guizhou) at this time.

REPUBLIC

PROVINCIAL CAST COINAGE

C# 20-9   CASH
Cast Brass   **Ruler:** Kuang-hsü **Obv. Insc.:** Kuang-hsü T'ung-pao **Rev:** Manchu inscription **Rev. Insc.:** Boo-jiyan

Date	Mintage	Good	VG	F	VF	XF
ND(1875-1908)	—	4.00	7.50	10.00	15.00	

C# 20-9.1   CASH
Cast Brass   **Ruler:** Kuang-hsü **Obv. Insc.:** Kuang-hsü T'ung-pao **Rev:** Manchu inscription **Rev. Insc.:** Boo-jiyan

Date	Mintage	Good	VG	F	VF	XF
ND(1875-1908)	—	5.00	9.00	12.50	18.50	

C# 20-9.2   CASH
Cast Brass   **Ruler:** Kuang-hsü **Obv. Insc.:** Kuang-hsü T'ung-pao **Rev:** Chinese "Kung" above **Rev. Insc.:** Boo-jiyan

Date	Mintage	Good	VG	F	VF	XF
ND(1875-1905)	—	8.50	11.50	16.50	25.00	—

MILLED COINAGE

Y# 428   DOLLAR
25.8000 g., Silver, 39 mm.   **Subject:** First Road in Kweichow
Obv. Leg.: Chung Hua Min Kuo (year) Nien

Date	Mintage	VG	F	VF	XF	Unc
17(1928)	648,000	350	750	2,000	4,500	10,000

Note: This coin is known as the "Auto Dollar" as it purports to portray the governor's automobile; minor varieties exist in Chinese legends and various automobile designs

Y# 433a   DOLLAR
26.4000 g., Silver   **Obv:** Square window in pavilion
Obv. Leg.: Chung Hua Min Kuo (year) Nien **Note:** Many conterfeits exist.

Date	Mintage	VG	F	VF	XF	Unc
38(1949) Rare	—	500	1,000	2,750	5,500	15,000

Note: This coin is known as the "Bamboo Dollar".

Y# 433   DOLLAR
26.4000 g., Silver   **Obv:** Round window in pavilion
Obv. Leg.: Chung Hua Min Kuo (year) Nien **Rev:** Bamboo

Date	Mintage	VG	F	VF	XF	Unc
38(1949)	—	450	900	2,250	4,750	10,000

Note: This coin is known as the "Bamboo Dollar".

Y# A429 1/2 CENT
Copper **Obv. Leg.:** Chung Hua Min Kuo (year) Nien

Date	Mintage	VG	F	VF	XF	Unc
38(1949)	—	450	750	—	—	—

Y# A429a 1/2 CENT
Brass **Obv. Leg.:** Chung Hua Min Kuo (year) Nien

Date	Mintage	VG	F	VF	XF	Unc
38(1949)	—	300	450	—	—	—

Y# A429a.2 1/2 CENT
Brass **Obv.** Narrow, thick characters **Obv. Leg.:** Chung Hua Min Kuo (year) Nien

Date	Mintage	VG	F	VF	XF	Unc
38(1949)	—	450	650	—	—	—

Y# 429 10 CENTS
Antimony **Obv. Leg.:** Chung Hua Min Kuo (year) Nien

Date	Mintage	VG	F	VF	XF	Unc
20(1931)	—	250	450	650	1,000	—

Y# 430 20 CENTS
Silver **Obv. Leg.:** Chung Hua Min Kuo (year) Nien

Date	Mintage	VG	F	VF	XF	Unc
38(1949)	—	60.00	150	300	450	750

Y# 431 20 CENTS
Silver **Obv. Leg.:** Chung Hua Min Kuo (year) Nien

Date	Mintage	VG	F	VF	XF	Unc
38(1949)	—	—	—	—	6,500	8,500

Y# 432 50 CENTS
Silver **Obv. Leg.:** Chung Hua Min Kuo (year) Nien

Date	Mintage	VG	F	VF	XF	Unc
38(1949)	—	—	—	5,500	12,500	16,000

MANCHURIAN PROVINCES

Since the 17th century, Manchuria has been divided into three provinces. The two northern provinces were called Heilungkiang and Kirin. Together the three provinces of Manchuria were known as the Manchurian Provinces in English or the Three Eastern Provinces in Chinese. Since the communist takeover in 1949, western Mongol-populated areas of Manchuria have been included in the Inner Mongolia Autonomous Region.

EMPIRE
MILLED COINAGE

Y# 209 10 CENTS
2.6000 g., 0.8900 Silver 0.0744 oz. ASW **Ruler:** Kuang-Hsü **Obv. Leg.:** Tung-san Sheng Tsao **Obv. Insc.:** Kuang-hsü Yüan-pao **Rev:** Legend at bottom **Rev. Leg.:** MANCHURIAN PROVINCES

Date	Mintage	VG	F	VF	XF	Unc
33(1907)	1,079,000	3.50	10.00	25.00	40.00	100

Y# 210 20 CENTS
5.2000 g., 0.8900 Silver 0.1488 oz. ASW **Ruler:** Kuang-Hsü **Obv.** One dot at either side **Obv. Leg.:** Tung-san Sheng Tsao **Obv. Insc.:** Kuang-hsü Yüan-pao **Rev:** Legend at bottom **Rev. Leg.:** MANCHURIAN PROVINCES

Date	Mintage	VG	F	VF	XF	Unc
33(1907)	—	6.50	20.00	30.00	60.00	120

Y# 210a.1 20 CENTS
5.2000 g., 0.8900 Silver 0.1488 oz. ASW **Ruler:** Kuang-Hsü **Obv.** Three rosettes at either side **Obv. Leg.:** Tung-san Sheng Tsao **Obv. Insc.:** Kuang-hsü Yüan-pao **Rev:** Legend at bottom **Rev. Leg.:** MANCHURIAN PROVINCES

Date	Mintage	VG	F	VF	XF	Unc
33(ca.1908)	249,219,000	3.50	9.00	17.50	35.00	70.00

Y# 210a.2 20 CENTS
5.2000 g., 0.8900 Silver 0.1488 oz. ASW **Ruler:** Kuang-Hsü **Obv.** One rosette at either side **Obv. Leg.:** Tung-san Sheng Tsao **Obv. Insc.:** Kuang-hsü Yüan-pao **Rev:** Legend at bottom **Rev. Leg.:** MANCHURIAN PROVINCES

Date	Mintage	VG	F	VF	XF	Unc
33(ca.1908)	Inc. above	2.75	6.00	12.00	20.00	60.00

Y# 213.2 20 CENTS
5.2000 g., 0.8900 Silver 0.1488 oz. ASW **Ruler:** Hsüan-t'ung **Obv:** One large-petaled rosette at either side **Obv. Leg.:** Tung-san Sheng Tsao **Obv. Insc.:** Hsüan-t'ung Yüan-pao **Rev:** Legend at bottom; date as 1ST YEAR **Rev. Leg.:** MANCHURIAN PROVINCES

Date	Mintage	VG	F	VF	XF	Unc
1(1909)	Inc. above	2.50	4.00	8.50	15.00	40.00

Y# 213 20 CENTS
5.2000 g., 0.8900 Silver 0.1488 oz. ASW **Ruler:** Hsüan-t'ung **Obv:** Two small stars flanking one large star at either side **Obv. Leg.:** Tung-san Sheng Tsao **Obv. Insc.:** Hsüan-t'ung Yüan-pao **Rev:** Legend at bottom; date given as FIRST YEAR **Rev. Leg.:** MANCHURIAN PROVINCES

Date	Mintage	VG	F	VF	XF	Unc
1(ca.1910)	Inc. above	2.50	4.00	7.50	12.50	30.00

Y# 213.1 20 CENTS
5.2000 g., 0.8900 Silver 0.1488 oz. ASW **Ruler:** Hsüan-t'ung **Obv:** One small star at either side **Obv. Leg.:** Tung-san Sheng Tsao **Obv. Insc.:** Hsüan-t'ung Yüan-pao **Rev:** Legend at bottom **Rev. Leg.:** MANCHURIAN PROVINCES

Date	Mintage	VG	F	VF	XF	Unc
1(ca.1910)	Inc. above	2.50	4.00	8.50	15.00	35.00

Y# 213.3 20 CENTS
5.2000 g., 0.8900 Silver 0.1488 oz. ASW **Ruler:** Hsüan-t'ung **Obv:** One large star between two dots **Obv. Leg.:** Tung-san Sheng Tsao **Obv. Insc.:** Hsüan-t'ung Yüan-pao **Rev:** Legend at bottom **Rev. Leg.:** MANCHURIAN PROVINCES

Date	Mintage	VG	F	VF	XF	Unc
1(ca.1910)	Inc. above	2.50	4.00	8.50	15.00	35.00

Y# 213a 20 CENTS
5.2000 g., 0.8900 Silver 0.1488 oz. ASW **Ruler:** Hsüan-t'ung **Obv:** Manchu "Boo-fu" at center **Obv. Leg.:** Tung-san Sheng Tsao **Obv. Insc.:** Hsüan-t'ung Yüan-pao **Rev:** Error in legend **Rev. Leg.:** MANCHURIAN PROVIENCES

Date	Mintage	VG	F	VF	XF	Unc
ND(ca.1911)	Inc. above	2.50	4.00	8.50	15.00	35.00

Y# 213a.6 20 CENTS
5.2000 g., 0.8900 Silver 0.1488 oz. ASW **Ruler:** Hsüan-t'ung **Obv:** Without Manchu "Boo-fu" at center **Obv. Leg.:** Tung-san Sheng Tsao **Obv. Insc.:** Hsüan-t'ung Yüan-pao **Rev:** Error in legend **Rev. Leg.:** MANCHURIAN PROVIENCES

Date	Mintage	VG	F	VF	XF	Unc
ND(ca.1912)	Inc. above	2.75	5.00	10.00	20.00	40.00

Y# 213a.4 20 CENTS
5.2000 g., 0.7000 Silver 0.1170 oz. ASW **Ruler:** Hsüan-t'ung **Obv:** Without Manchu "Boo-fu" at center **Obv. Leg.:** Tung-san Sheng Tsao **Obv. Insc.:** Hsüan-t'ung Yüan-pao **Rev:** Legend at top **Rev. Leg.:** MANCHURIAN PROVINCES

Date	Mintage	VG	F	VF	XF	Unc
ND(ca.1913)	Inc. above	2.50	5.00	10.00	20.00	40.00

Y# 213a.1 20 CENTS
5.2000 g., 0.7000 Silver 0.1170 oz. ASW **Ruler:** Hsüan-t'ung **Obv:** 5-petaled rosette in center with dot in center of rosette; dot below side rosettes **Obv. Leg.:** Tung-san Sheng Tsao **Obv. Insc.:** Hsüan-t'ung Yüan-pao **Rev:** Legend at top **Rev. Leg.:** MANCHURIAN PROVINCES

Date	Mintage	VG	F	VF	XF	Unc
ND(ca.1914-15)	Inc. above	2.25	4.00	8.50	15.00	30.00

Y# 213a.2 20 CENTS
5.2000 g., 0.7000 Silver 0.1170 oz. ASW **Ruler:** Hsüan-t'ung **Obv:** With dot below side rosettes **Obv. Leg.:** Tung-san Sheng Tsao **Obv. Insc.:** Hsüan-t'ung Yüan-pao **Rev:** Legend at top **Rev. Leg.:** MANCHURIAN PROVINCES

Date	Mintage	VG	F	VF	XF	Unc
ND(ca.1914-15)	Inc. above	2.25	4.00	8.50	15.00	30.00

Y# 213a.3 20 CENTS
5.2000 g., 0.7000 Silver 0.1170 oz. ASW **Ruler:** Hsüan-t'ung **Obv:** Without dot in center of 5-petaled rosette **Obv. Insc.:** Hsüan-t'ung Yüan-pao **Rev:** Legend at top **Rev. Leg.:** MANCHURIAN PROVINCES

Date	Mintage	VG	F	VF	XF	Unc
ND(ca.1914-15)	Inc. above	2.25	4.00	8.50	15.00	30.00

Y# 211   50 CENTS
13.1000 g., 0.8900 Silver 0.3748 oz. ASW **Ruler:** Kuang-Hsü **Obv. Leg.:** Tung-san Sheng Tsao **Obv. Insc.:** Kuang-Hsü Yüan-pao **Rev:** Legend at bottom **Rev. Leg.:** MANCHURIAN PROVINCES

Date	Mintage	VG	F	VF	XF	Unc
33(1907)	—	65.00	175	350	650	2,000

Y# 212   DOLLAR
26.4000 g., 0.8900 Silver 0.7554 oz. ASW **Ruler:** Kuang-Hsü **Obv. Leg.:** Tung-san Sheng Tsao **Obv. Insc.:** Kuang-Hsü Yüan-pao **Rev:** Legend at bottom **Rev. Leg.:** MANCHURIAN PROVINCES

Date	Mintage	VG	F	VF	XF	Unc
33(1907)	—	150	400	800	1,500	6,000

REPUBLIC
MILLED COINAGE

Y# 434   CENT
Copper **Obv. Leg.:** Chung Hua Min Kuo... **Rev:** Sunburst in floral sprays

Date	Mintage	VG	F	VF	XF	Unc
18(1929)	—	0.65	2.00	3.00	5.00	25.00

Y# 434a   CENT
Brass **Obv. Leg.:** Chung Hua Min Kuo... **Rev:** Sunburst in floral sprays

Date	Mintage	VG	F	VF	XF	Unc
18(1929)	—					

PATTERNS
Including off metal strikes

KM#	Date	Mintage	Identification	Mkt Val
Pn1	18(1929)	—	Dollar. Silver.	—

Note: Superior Goodman sale 6-91 choice AU realized, $22,000.

| Pn2 | 18(1929) | — | Fen. Copper. Y#434 with formal Chinese "One Fen" | — |

SHANSI PROVINCE
Shanxi
A province located in northeastern China that has some of the richest coal deposits in the world. Parts of the Great Wall cross the province. Extensive agriculture of early China started here. Cited as a "model province" in the new Chinese Republic. Intermittently active mints from 1645. The modern mint was established in 1919. It operated until the mid-1920's and closed because of the public's resistance against the coins that were being produced.

REPUBLIC
PROVINCIAL CAST COINAGE

C# 21-8   CASH
Cast Brass **Ruler:** Kuang-hsü **Obv:** Manchu inscription **Obv. Insc.:** Kuang-hsü T'ung-pao **Rev. Insc.:** Boo-Jin

Date	Mintage	Good	VG	F	VF	XF
ND(1875-1908)	—	6.50	11.50	17.50	35.00	

MILLED COINAGE

Y# A435   10 CASH (1 Cent)
Copper **Obv:** Crossed flags **Obv. Leg.:** Chung Hua Min Kuo **Rev:** Value in wheat sprays

Date	Mintage	VG	F	VF	XF	Unc
ND(ca.1912)	—	35.00	100	150	220	

Y# 217   20 CENTS
4.8000 g., Silver **Ruler:** Hsuan-Tung **Obv. Leg.:** Shan-hsi Sheng Tsao **Obv. Insc.:** Hsuan-t'ung Yuan-pao **Rev:** Side view dragon

Date	Mintage	VG	F	VF	XF	Unc
ND(ca.1911)	—	100	200	350	500	—

Note: Several varieties exist similar to Y#217, but struck more crudely in base metal and with different Chinese legends at the top of the obverse. English legends are usually blundered. These were struck about 1913 and thought to be warlord issues. Do not confuse these with coins of Fengtien (Liaoning), from which this was copied.

PATTERNS
Including off metal strikes

KM#	Date	Mintage	Identification	Mkt Val
Pn2	14(1925)	—	5 Cents. Nickel. K823.	

SHANTUNG PROVINCE
Shandong
A province located on the northeastern coast of China. Confucius was born in this province. Parts of the province were leased to Great Britain and to Germany. Farming, fishing and mining are the chief occupations. A mint was opened at Tsinan in 1647 and was an intermittent producer for the empire. A modern mint was opened at Tsinan in 1905, but closed in 1906. Patterns were prepared between 1926-1933 in anticipation of a new coinage, but none were struck for circulation.

EMPIRE
PROVINCIAL CAST COINAGE

C# 22-6   CASH
Cast Brass **Ruler:** Kuang-hsü **Obv. Insc.:** Kuang-hsü T'ung-pao **Rev:** Type 1 mint mark **Rev. Insc.:** Boo-ji

Date	Mintage	Good	VG	F	VF	XF
ND(1875-1908)	—	10.00	18.50	27.50	40.00	

Note: Refer to Tungch'uan, Yünnan Province, for one-cash C#27 series coins previously listed here.

MILLED COINAGE

Y# 8a   2 CASH
Copper **Ruler:** Kuang-hsü **Obv. Insc.:** Kuang-hsü T'ung-pao **Rev:** Dragon

Date	Mintage	VG	F	VF	XF	Unc
CD1906	—	12.00	25.00	35.00	70.00	—

Y# 220   10 CASH
Copper **Ruler:** Kuang-hsü **Obv. Insc.:** Kuang-hsü Yüan-pao **Rev:** Side view dragon

Date	Mintage	VG	F	VF	XF	Unc
ND(1904-05)	—	8.00	15.00	30.00	40.00	60.00

Y# 221   10 CASH
Copper **Ruler:** Kuang-hsü **Obv:** Thin Manchu words in center, flying dragon **Obv. Leg.:** Shen-tung Sheng Tsao **Obv. Insc.:** Kuang-hsü Yüan-pao **Rev:** SHANTUNG

Date	Mintage	VG	F	VF	XF	Unc
ND(1904-05)	—	2.75	7.00	11.00	17.50	90.00

Y# 221.1   10 CASH
Copper **Ruler:** Kuang-hsü **Obv:** Thick Manchu in center, flying dragon **Obv. Leg.:** Shen-tung Sheng Tsao **Obv. Insc.:** Kuang-hsü Yüan-pao

Date	Mintage	VG	F	VF	XF	Unc
ND(1904-05)	—	1.50	3.50	7.00	14.00	80.00

Y# 221.2   10 CASH
Copper **Ruler:** Kuang-hsü **Obv:** Smaller stars, flying dragon **Obv. Leg.:** Shen-tung Sheng Tsao **Obv. Insc.:** Kuang-hsü Yüan-pao

Date	Mintage	VG	F	VF	XF	Unc
ND(1904-05)	—	1.50	3.50	7.00	14.00	80.00

Y# 221.3   10 CASH
Copper **Ruler:** Kuang-hsü **Obv:** Similar to Y#220, flying dragon **Obv. Leg.:** Shen-tung Sheng Tsao **Obv. Insc.:** Kuang-hsü Yüan-pao **Rev:** Similar to Y#221

Date	Mintage	VG	F	VF	XF	Unc
ND(1904-05)	—	62.50	125	200	300	—

Y# 221a   10 CASH
Copper **Ruler:** Kuang-hsü **Obv:** Thick Manchu in center, flying dragon **Obv. Leg.:** Shen-tung Sheng Tsao **Obv. Insc.:** Kuang-hsü Yüan-pao **Rev:** SHANG-TUNG

Date	Mintage	VG	F	VF	XF	Unc
ND(1904-05)	—	1.00	2.50	4.00	7.50	20.00

Y# 221a.1 10 CASH

Copper **Ruler:** Kuang-hsü **Obv:** Thin Manchu in center, flying dragon **Obv. Leg.:** Shen-tung Sheng Tsao **Obv. Insc.:** Kuang-hsü Yüan-pao

Date	Mintage	VG	F	VF	XF	Unc
ND(1904-05)	—	2.00	5.00	10.00	17.50	40.00

Y# 10s 10 CASH

Brass **Ruler:** Kuang-hsü **Obv. Insc.:** Tai-ch'ing T'ung-pi **Rev:** 6 large waves below dragon **Rev. Leg.:** Kuang-hsü Nien-tsao, TAI-CHING-TI-KUO ...

Date	Mintage	VG	F	VF	XF	Unc
CD1906	—	2.00	6.00	10.00	17.50	40.00

Y# 10s.1 10 CASH

Copper **Ruler:** Kuang-hsü **Obv. Insc.:** Tai-ch'ing T'ung-pi **Rev. Leg.:** Kuang-hsü Nien-tsao, TAI-CHING-TI-KUO ...

Date	Mintage	VG	F	VF	XF	Unc
CD1906	—	2.50	7.50	12.50	25.00	50.00

Y# 10s.1a 10 CASH

Copper **Ruler:** Kuang-hsü **Obv. Insc.:** Tai-ch'ing T'ung-pi **Rev:** 5 small waves below dragon **Rev. Leg.:** Kuang-hsü Nien-tsao, TAI-CHING-TI-KUO ...

Date	Mintage	VG	F	VF	XF	Unc
CD1906	—	1.75	5.00	10.00	17.50	40.00

Y# 10s.2a 10 CASH

Copper **Ruler:** Kuang-hsü **Obv. Insc.:** Tai-ch'ing T'ung-pi **Rev:** Dragon with larger forehead and narrower face, pearl redesigned **Rev. Leg.:** Kuang-hsü Nien-tsao, TAI-CHING-TI-KUO ...

Date	Mintage	VG	F	VF	XF	Unc
CD1906	—	2.75	8.00	15.00	30.00	60.00

PATTERNS
Including off metal strikes

KM#	Date	Mintage	Identification	Mkt Val
Pn7	15(1926)	—	10 Dollars. Gold. K1536.	2,500
Pn8	15(1926)	—	10 Dollars. Pewter. K1536y.	—
Pn9	15(1926)	—	20 Dollars. Gold. K1535.	3,000
Pn10	15(1926)	—	20 Dollars. Pewter. K1535y.	—
Pn11	21(1932)	—	20 Cash. Copper. Wide flan.	—
Pn12	22(1933)	—	2 Cents. Nickel. K827.	—
Pn13	22(1933)	—	20 Cash. Copper.	—

SHENSI PROVINCE

Shaanxi

A province located in central China that is a rich agricultural area. A very important province in the early development of China. An active imperial mint was located at Sian (Xi'an).

REPUBLIC

PROVINCIAL CAST COINAGE

C# 23-13 CASH

Cast Brass **Ruler:** Kuang-hsü **Obv:** Type A **Obv. Insc.:** Kuang-hsü T'ung-pao **Rev:** Manchu inscription **Rev. Insc.:** Boo-san

Date	Mintage	Good	VG	F	VF	XF
ND(1875-1908)	—	20.00	35.00	50.00	75.00	

MILLED COINAGE

Y# 435 CENT

Copper **Obv:** Crossed flags **Obv. Leg.:** IMTYPIF: "I Mei Ta Yuan Pi I (1) Fen" (One is 1/100 of Large Dollar Coin = 1 Cent) **Obv. Insc.:** Chung Hua Min Kuo **Rev:** Value above wheat sprays

Date	Mintage	VG	F	VF	XF	Unc
ND(c.1928)	—	25.00	40.00	70.00	150	—

Y# 436 2 CENTS

Copper **Obv:** Crossed flags, star between flags **Obv. Leg.:** IMTYPEF: "I Mei Ta Yüan Pi Erh (2) Fen" **Obv. Insc.:** Chung Hua Min Kuo **Rev:** Value above wheat sprays **Note:** Dentilated borders.

Date	Mintage	VG	F	VF	XF	Unc
ND(c.1928)	—	35.00	60.00	90.00	150	—

Y# 436.1 2 CENTS

Copper **Obv:** Crossed flags, without star between flags **Obv. Leg.:** IMTYPEF: "I Mei Ta Yüan Pi Erh (2) Fen" **Obv. Insc.:** Chung Hua Min Kuo **Rev:** Value above wheat sprays **Note:** Large Chinese legends.

Date	Mintage	VG	F	VF	XF	Unc
ND(c.1928)	—	15.00	25.00	40.00	75.00	—

Y# 436.2 2 CENTS

Copper **Obv:** Crossed flags, star in center **Obv. Leg.:** IMTYPEF: "I Mei Ta Yüan Pi Erh (2) Fen" **Obv. Insc.:** Chung Hua Min Kuo **Rev:** Value above wheat sprays, star in center

Date	Mintage	VG	F	VF	XF	Unc
ND(c.1928)	—	40.00	75.00	120	225	—

Y# 436.3 2 CENTS

Copper **Obv:** Crossed flags, without star between flags **Obv. Leg.:** IMTYPEF: "I Mei Ta Yüan Pi Erh (2) Fen" **Obv. Insc.:** Chung Hua Min Kuo **Rev:** Value above wheat sprays **Note:** Small Chinese legends.

Date	Mintage	VG	F	VF	XF	Unc
ND(c.1928)	—	25.00	50.00	80.00	125	—

Y# 436.4 2 CENTS

Copper **Obv:** Crossed flags **Obv. Leg.:** IMTYPEF: "I Mei Ta Yüan Pi Erh (2) Fen" **Obv. Insc.:** Chung Hua Min Kuo **Rev:** Value above wheat sprays **Note:** Pearled borders.

Date	Mintage	VG	F	VF	XF	Unc
ND(c.1928)	—	50.00	80.00	120	200	—

Y# 436.5 2 CENTS

Copper **Obv:** Crossed flags, similar to Y#436.2 but with star between flags **Obv. Leg.:** IMTYPEF: "I Mei Ta Yüan Pi Erh (2) Fen" **Obv. Insc.:** Chung Hua Min Kuo **Rev:** Value above wheat sprays **Note:** Large Chinese legends.

Date	Mintage	VG	F	VF	XF	Unc
ND(c.1928)	—	40.00	75.00	120	225	—

SINKIANG PROVINCE

Hsinkiang, Xinjiang
"New Dominion"

An autonomous region in western China, often referred to as Chinese Turkestan. High mountains surround 2000 ft. tableland on three sides with a large desert in center of this province. Many salt lakes, mining and some farming and oil. Inhabited by early man and was referred to as the "Silk Route" to the West. Sinkiang (Xinjiang) has been historically under the control of many factions, including Genghis Khan. It became a province in 1884. China has made claim to Sinkiang (Xinjiang) for many, many years. This rule has been more nominal than actual. Sinkiang (Xinjiang) had eight imperial mints, only three of which were in operation toward the end of the reign of Kuang Hsu. Only two mints operated during the early years of the republic. In 1949, due to a drastic coin shortage and lack of confidence in the inflated paper money, it was planned to mint some dollars in Sinkiang (Xinjiang). These did not see much circulation, however, due to the defeat of the nationalists, though they have recently appeared in considerable numbers in today's market.

PATTERNS

NOTE: A number of previously listed cast coins of Sinkiang Province are now known to be patterns - "mother" cash or "seed" cash for which no circulating issues are known. The following coins are, therefore, no longer listed. Most were probably manufactured in Beijing. They are generally made of brass rather than the purer copper usual to Sinkiang. The following coins are, therefore, no longer listed here: Craig #30-9, 30-11a, 30-12a, 30-14, 30-15a, 30-16, 30-17, 28-4.1, 28-8a, 28-9a,28-9c, 28-10, 31-1a, 31-1v, 31-2, 32-4, 32-5, 33-12, 33-21, 34-2, 34-3, 35-5a and 35-6.

MONETARY SYSTEM

2 Pul = 1 Cash
2 Cash = 5 Li
4 Cash = 10 Li = 1 Fen
25 Cash = 10 Fen = 1 Miscal = 1 Ch'ien, Mace, Tanga
10 Miscals (Mace) = 1 Liang (Tael or Sar)
20 Miscals (Tangas) = 1 Tilla

LOCAL MINT NAMES AND MARKS

Mint	Chinese	Uyghur	Manchu
Aksu	城阿	اقصو	
Ili, now Yining	犁伊	الي	
Kashgar, now Kashi	什喀	كشقر	

Khotan, now Hotan	闐和	ختن	
Kuche, now Kuqa	車庫	كوچا	
Urumchi, now Urumqi (Tihwa)		اورمچي اوش	
Ushi, now Wushi (Uqturpan)	化廸	اوش	
Yangihissar, now Yengisar		ينگى حصار	
Yarkand, now Shache (Yarkant)	羌爾葉	ياركند	

EMPIRE
LOCAL CAST COINAGE

C# 30-18   10 CASH
Cast Copper   **Ruler:** Kuang-hsü **Obv. Insc.:** Kuang-hsü Chung-pao **Rev:** Character "A" (for Aksu) above center hole, "Aksu" in Turki at right, in Manchu at left

Date	Mintage	Good	VG	F	VF	XF
ND(1875-1908)	—	2.75	4.00	7.00	14.00	—

C# 30-18.1   10 CASH
Cast Copper   **Ruler:** Kuang-hsü **Rev:** "Asku" in Manchu at right, in Turki at left

Date	Mintage	Good	VG	F	VF	XF
ND(1875-1908)	—	7.50	12.50	19.00	35.00	—

C# 30-19   10 CASH
Cast Copper   **Ruler:** Kuang-hsü **Obv. Insc.:** Kuang-hsü T'ung-pao **Rev:** Character "K'a" (for Kashgar) above

Date	Mintage	Good	VG	F	VF	XF
ND(1886-1908)	—	4.00	8.00	11.00	22.50	—

Note: Cast in the Aksu Mint for the Kashgar Mint, beginning in 1886 during the reign of Kuang-Hsü

PROVINCIAL CAST COINAGE

KM# 10   CASH
Cast Copper   **Ruler:** Kuang-hsü **Obv. Insc.:** Kuang-hsü T'ung-pao **Rev:** Manchu inscription for Hu-pu Board of Revenue **Rev. Insc.:** Boo Ciowan

Date	Mintage	Good	VG	F	VF	XF
ND(1875-1908)	—	2.75	6.00	11.00	17.00	—

KM# 11   CASH
Cast Copper   **Ruler:** Kuang-hsü **Rev:** Similar to KM#10 but entire reverse is in inverted mirror image

Date	Mintage	Good	VG	F	VF	XF
ND(1875-1908)	—	6.00	11.00	16.00	22.50	—

KM# 12   CASH
Cast Copper   **Ruler:** Kuang-hsü **Obv. Insc.:** Kuang-hsü T'ung-pao **Rev:** Similar to KM#11

Date	Mintage	Good	VG	F	VF	XF
ND(1875-1908)	—	2.75	6.00	11.00	17.00	—

KM# 13   CASH
Cast Copper   **Ruler:** Kuang-hsü **Obv. Insc.:** Kuang-hsü T'ung-pao **Rev:** Illiterate Manchu inscription **Rev. Insc.:** Boo Chuan or Yuan

Date	Mintage	Good	VG	F	VF	XF
ND(1875-1908)	—	2.75	6.00	11.00	17.00	—

KM# 14   CASH
Cast Copper   **Ruler:** Kuang-hsü **Obv. Insc.:** Kuang-hsü T'ung-pao **Rev:** Illiterate Manchu inscription **Rev. Insc.:** Boo-Chuan

Date	Mintage	Good	VG	F	VF	XF
ND(1875-1908)	—	2.75	5.00	9.00	15.00	—

Note: The five one-cash varieties listed above could be confused with Beijing issues C1-16 or C2-15, but they are much more crudely cast, and are made of red copper rather than brass; see Landon Ross, 1986, Numismatics International Bulletin 20(3) for a more detailed review

C# 33-23   CASH
Cast Copper   **Ruler:** Kuang-hsü **Obv. Insc.:** Kuang-hsü T'ung-pao

Date	Mintage	Good	VG	F	VF	XF
ND(1875-1908)	—	6.00	8.00	12.00	20.00	—

C# 33-18.1   10 CASH
Cast Copper   **Ruler:** Kuang-hsü **Rev:** Semi-circle at lower right

Date	Mintage	Good	VG	F	VF	XF
ND(1875-1908)	—	7.50	13.50	22.50	35.00	—

KM# 7.1   10 CASH
Cast Copper   **Ruler:** Kuang-hsü **Obv. Insc.:** Kuang-hsü T'ung-pao **Rev:** "Pao Ku" with "K'u" (for Kuche) above

Date	Mintage	Good	VG	F	VF	XF
ND(1875-1908)	—	2.75	5.00	9.00	18.00	—

KM# 7.2   10 CASH
Cast Copper   **Ruler:** Kuang-hsü **Obv. Insc.:** Kuang-hsü T'ung-pao **Rev:** "Pao" (for Kuche) at left reversed

Date	Mintage	Good	VG	F	VF	XF
ND(1875-1908)	—	9.00	17.00	27.50	45.00	—

KM# 8   10 CASH
Cast Copper   **Ruler:** Kuang-hsü **Obv. Insc.:** Kuang-hsü T'ung-pao **Rev:** "Manchu Boo Hsin" with "Hsin" (new, but here standing for the Tihwa (now Urumqi) Mint) above

Date	Mintage	Good	VG	F	VF	XF
ND(1875-1908)	—	4.00	6.00	9.00	19.00	—

KM# 9   10 CASH
Cast Copper   **Ruler:** Kuang-hsü **Obv. Insc.:** Kuang-hsü T'ung-pao **Rev:** "Manchu Boo Hsin" (for Tihwa Mint) with "Hsin" (new) above

Date	Mintage	Good	VG	F	VF	XF
ND(1875-1908)	—	4.00	6.00	9.00	19.00	—

C# 32-6   10 CASH
Cast Copper   **Ruler:** Kuang-hsü **Obv. Insc.:** Kuang-hsü T'ung-pao **Rev:** "Kashgar" in Turki at left, in Manchu at right, "K'a" (Kashgar) above

Date	Mintage	Good	VG	F	VF	XF
ND(1875-1908)	—	6.00	12.00	20.00	32.00	—

C# 32-6.1   10 CASH
Cast Copper   **Ruler:** Kuang-hsü **Obv. Insc.:** Kuang-hsü T'ung-pao **Rev:** Turki-Manchu inscription (right-left) **Rev. Insc.:** Boo-Kashgar

Date	Mintage	Good	VG	F	VF	XF
ND(1875-1908)	—	6.00	12.00	20.00	32.00	—

C# 33-16   10 CASH
Cast Copper   **Ruler:** Kuang-hsü **Obv. Insc.:** Kuang-hsü T'ung-pao

Date	Mintage	Good	VG	F	VF	XF
ND(1875-1908)	—	10.00	20.00	30.00	50.00	—

C# 33-18   10 CASH
Cast Copper **Ruler:** Kuang-hsü **Obv. Insc.:** Kuang-hsü T'ung-pao **Rev:** Character "K'u" above

Date	Mintage	Good	VG	F	VF	XF
ND1875-1908)	—	9.00	15.00	22.50	45.00	—

C# 33-19   10 CASH
Cast Copper **Ruler:** Kuang-hsü **Obv. Insc.:** Kuang-hsü T'ung-pao **Rev:** Manchu inscription, "kuce" in simple style **Rev. Insc.:** Boo-kuce

Date	Mintage	Good	VG	F	VF	XF
ND(1875-1908)	—	4.00	5.00	18.00	32.00	—

C# 34-4   10 CASH
Cast Copper **Ruler:** Hsüan-t'ung **Rev:** "K'u" (Kuche) above, "Ushi" in Manchu and Turki right and left

Date	Mintage	Good	VG	F	VF	XF
ND(1909-1911)	—	50.00	80.00	150	—	—

Note: Cast in Ushi to the order of the Kuche Mint; it is the last of the "red" copper cash

GENERAL CAST COINAGE

KM# 16   10 CASH
Cast Copper **Ruler:** Kuang-hsü **Obv. Insc.:** Kuang-hsü Ting Wei **Rev:** "Boo-yuan?" with "Hsin" (new) above

Date	Mintage	Good	VG	F	VF	XF
CD1907	—	7.50	17.50	30.00	—	—

KM# 17   10 CASH
Cast Copper **Ruler:** Kuang-hsü **Obv. Insc.:** "Kuang-hsü Wu-shen"

Date	Mintage	Good	VG	F	VF	XF
CD1908	—	11.50	25.00	45.00	—	—

MILLED COINAGE

Y# 1a   FEN, 5 LI
Copper **Ruler:** Kuang-hsü **Obv:** Small dots in circle, dotted rims **Obv. Insc.:** Kuang-hsü Yüan-pao **Rev:** Front view dragon **Note:** Modern copy.

Date	Mintage	F	VF	XF	Unc	BU
ND(ca.1906)	—	—	—	50.00	100	—

Note: The legend on this coin states that it is valued at 1 Fen 5 Li of silver (about 15 Cash); the coin is the size of a normal 10 Cash piece of Sinkiang (Xinjiang), but these pieces are usually larger than those of the other provinces; for this reason, it is assumed the coin was overvalued to benefit the government

Y# 1   FEN, 5 LI
Copper **Ruler:** Kuang-hsü **Obv:** Large dots in circle, dentilated rims **Obv. Insc.:** Kuang-hsü Yüan-pao **Rev:** Front view dragon **Note:** Two varieties are reported.

Date	Mintage	Good	VG	F	VF	XF
ND(ca.1906)	—	150	200	350	550	—

Y# A1   2 FEN 5 LI
Copper **Ruler:** Kuang-hsü **Obv. Insc.:** Kuang-hsü Yüan-pao **Rev:** Front view dragon

Date	Mintage	Good	VG	F	VF	XF
ND(ca.1906) Rare	—	—	—	—	—	—

Note: This denomination was recalled shortly after issue and the dies re-engraved 1 Fen and 5 Li to produce Y#1; do not confuse poorly re-engraved Chinese numeral "172" examples of Y#1 for Y#A1; note the difference in spacing of the Chinese characters below the rosettes between Y#1 and Y#A1

Y# B1   2 FEN 5 LI
Copper **Ruler:** Kuang-hsü **Obv. Insc.:** Kuang-hsü Yüan-pao **Rev:** Side view dragon

Date	Mintage	Good	VG	F	VF	XF
ND(ca.1906) Rare	—	—	—	—	—	—

Note: Status unknown

Y# 2.1   10 CASH
Copper **Ruler:** Hsüan-t'ung **Obv. Insc.:** Hsüan-t'ung Yüan-pao **Rev:** Without Chinese legend above side-view dragon

Date	Mintage	Good	VG	F	VF	XF
ND(ca.1909)	—	25.00	42.50	75.00	175	—

Y# 2.2   10 CASH
Copper **Ruler:** Hsüan-t'ung **Obv. Insc.:** Hsüan-t'ung Yüan-pao **Rev:** Chinese legend with "Nien" (year) added above dragon

Date	Mintage	Good	VG	F	VF	XF
CD1910	—	25.00	42.50	75.00	175	—
CD1911	—	30.00	50.00	100	200	—

Y# 2.3   10 CASH
Copper **Ruler:** Hsüan-t'ung **Obv:** Double ring around star in center of inscription **Obv. Insc.:** Hsüan-t'ung Yüan-pao

Date	Mintage	Good	VG	F	VF	XF
CD1911	—	30.00	50.00	100	200	—

Y# 2a   10 CASH
Copper **Ruler:** Hsüan-t'ung **Obv:** Large characters within center circle **Obv. Insc.:** Hsüan-t'ung Yüan-pao

Date	Mintage	VG	F	VF	XF	Unc
CD1910	—	—	—	—	25.00	35.00

Note: Modern copy

Y# A38.1   10 CASH
Copper **Ruler:** Hung-hsien **Obv:** Chinese legend in inner dotted circle **Obv. Leg.:** Hung-hsien T'ung-pi

Date	Mintage	Good	VG	F	VF	XF
AH1334	—	120	180	250	—	—

Y# A38.2   10 CASH
Copper **Ruler:** Hung-hsien

Date	Mintage	Good	VG	F	VF	XF
AH1334	—	120	180	250	—	—

Note: Y#A38.1 and A38.2 were issued for the brief reign of Yuan Shih-kai as Emperor Hung-hsien (1916)

Y# B16   MISCAL (Mace)
3.5000 g., Silver **Ruler:** Kuang-hsü **Obv:** "Kashgar" at right, value at left **Obv. Insc.:** Kuang-hsü Yin-yüan

Date	Mintage	VG	F	VF	XF	Unc
AH1331 Error for 1321	—	50.00	85.00	175	250	—
AH1322	—	50.00	85.00	175	250	—

Y# C16　MISCAL (Mace)
3.5000 g., Silver　**Ruler:** Kuang-hsü **Obv:** "Kashgar" in Chinese at right and left of value **Rev:** Turki inscription in sprays

Date	Mintage	VG	F	VF	XF	Unc
AH1322	—	45.00	70.00	125	200	—

Y# 3　MISCAL (Mace)
3.5000 g., Silver　**Ruler:** Kuang-hsü **Obv:** Outer legend: Turki without dot in center **Rev:** Without Turki legend

Date	Mintage	VG	F	VF	XF	Unc
ND(1905)	—	75.00	125	200	325	—

Y# 3.1　MISCAL (Mace)
3.5000 g., Silver　**Ruler:** Kuang-hsü **Obv. Leg.:** Turki with dot in center **Rev:** Without Turki legend

Date	Mintage	VG	F	VF	XF	Unc
ND(1905)	—	75.00	125	200	325	—

Y# 3.2　MISCAL (Mace)
3.5000 g., Silver　**Ruler:** Kuang-hsü **Obv:** Without outer Turki legend **Rev:** Turki legend

Date	Mintage	VG	F	VF	XF	Unc
ND(1905)	—	325	550	900	1,500	—

Y# 3.3　MISCAL (Mace)
3.5000 g., Silver　**Ruler:** Kuang-hsü **Obv:** Without outer Turki legend **Rev:** Without Turki legend

Date	Mintage	VG	F	VF	XF	Unc
ND(1905)	—	90.00	150	250	400	—

Y# A20.1　MISCAL (Mace)
3.5000 g., Silver　**Ruler:** Kuang-hsü **Obv:** Turki at right and left of value, date at lower left **Rev:** Side view dragon

Date	Mintage	VG	F	VF	XF	Unc
AH1323	—	200	350	600	1,000	—

Y# A20.2　MISCAL (Mace)
3.5000 g., Silver　**Ruler:** Kuang-hsü **Obv:** Turki at right and left of value, date at lower right **Rev:** Side view dragon

Date	Mintage	VG	F	VF	XF	Unc
AH1323	—	200	350	600	1,000	—

Y# A20.3　MISCAL (Mace)
3.5000 g., Silver　**Ruler:** Kuang-hsü **Obv:** Inverted Turki legends at right and left of value

Date	Mintage	VG	F	VF	XF	Unc
AH1323	—	200	350	600	1,000	—

Y# 10　MISCAL (Mace)
3.5000 g., Silver　**Ruler:** Kuang-hsü **Obv:** Without outer Turki legend **Rev:** Legend above dragon, 1 MACE below **Rev. Leg.:** SUNGAREI

Date	Mintage	VG	F	VF	XF	Unc
ND(1906)	—	110	225	400	650	—

Y# A12　GOLD MISCAL (Mace)
7.8000 g., Gold　**Ruler:** Kuang-hsü **Rev:** Legend above dragon, "2 MACE" below **Rev. Leg.:** SUNGAREI **Note:** Similar to 2 Miscals (Silver) Y#11.

Date	Mintage	VG	F	VF	XF	Unc
ND(ca.1906)	—					

Note: Reported, not confirmed

Y# 8　GOLD MISCAL (Mace)
3.9000 g., Gold　**Ruler:** Kuang-hsü **Rev:** Turki legend around uncircled dragon

Date	Mintage	VG	F	VF	XF	Unc
ND(ca.1907)	—	150	400	650	950	1,450

Y# 8.1　GOLD MISCAL (Mace)
3.9000 g., Gold　**Ruler:** Kuang-hsü **Rev:** Without Turki legend around uncircled dragon

Date	Mintage	VG	F	VF	XF	Unc
ND(ca.1907)	—	250	750	1,250	1,850	2,750

Y# 8.2　GOLD MISCAL (Mace)
3.9000 g., Gold　**Ruler:** Kuang-hsü **Rev:** Turki legend at left differs

Date	Mintage	VG	F	VF	XF	Unc
ND(ca.1907)	—	175	450	750	1,150	1,750

Y# 8.3　GOLD MISCAL (Mace)
3.9000 g., Gold　**Ruler:** Kuang-hsü **Rev:** Turki legend in outer circle

Date	Mintage	VG	F	VF	XF	Unc
ND(ca.1907)	—	200	550	950	1,350	2,150

Y# 9　GOLD 2 MISCALS
7.8000 g., Gold　**Ruler:** Kuang-hsü **Obv:** Narrow-spaced Chinese "2" **Rev:** Turki legend around uncircled dragon

Date	Mintage	VG	F	VF	XF	Unc
ND(ca.1906)	—	275	775	1,350	2,000	3,000

Y# 9.1　GOLD 2 MISCALS
7.8000 g., Gold　**Ruler:** Kuang-hsü **Obv:** Wide-spaced Chinese "2" **Rev:** Redesigned dragon

Date	Mintage	VG	F	VF	XF	Unc
ND(ca.1906)	—	275	775	1,350	2,000	3,000

Y# 17a　2 MISCALS (2 Mace)
7.2000 g., Silver, 23 mm.　**Ruler:** Kuang-hsü **Obv:** Inscription between Kashgar and value **Obv. Insc.:** Kuang-hsü Yin-yüan

Date	Mintage	VG	F	VF	XF	Unc
AH1311	—					
Note: Error						
AH1312	—	12.50	22.50	32.50	50.00	—
AH1313	—	12.50	22.50	32.50	50.00	—
AH1314	—	12.50	22.50	32.50	50.00	—
AH1315	—	12.50	22.50	32.50	50.00	—
AH1317	—	12.50	22.50	32.50	50.00	—
AH1319	—	12.50	22.50	32.50	50.00	—
AH1320	—	17.50	30.00	45.00	75.00	—

Y# 17a.1　2 MISCALS (2 Mace)
7.2000 g., Silver, 23 mm.　**Ruler:** Kuang-hsü **Obv:** Inscription between "K'a Tsao" at right, value at left **Obv. Insc.:** Kuang-hsü Yin-yüan

Date	Mintage	VG	F	VF	XF	Unc
AH1320 Rare						
AH1321	—	17.50	30.00	45.00	75.00	—
AH1322	—	20.00	35.00	55.00	100	—

Y# 33　2 MISCALS (2 Mace)
Silver, 24 mm.　**Ruler:** Kuang-hsü **Obv:** Inscription between "Tihwa" and value with normal Êrh (2) at left **Obv. Insc.:** "Kuang-hsü Yin-yüan" **Rev:** Turki inscription in floral wreath **Rev. Insc.:** Urumchi

Date	Mintage	VG	F	VF	XF	Unc
AH1321	—	15.00	22.00	55.00	90.00	—
AH1322	—	15.00	22.00	55.00	90.00	—
AH1323	—	17.50	30.00	55.00	90.00	—

Y# 33.1　2 MISCALS (2 Mace)
Silver, 24 mm.　**Ruler:** Kuang-hsü **Obv:** Inscription between "Tihwa" and value with official Êrh (2) at left **Obv. Insc.:** "Kuang-hsü Yin-yüan" **Rev:** Turki inscription in floral wreath **Rev. Insc.:** Urumchi

Date	Mintage	VG	F	VF	XF	Unc
AH1323	—	15.00	22.00	55.00	90.00	—
AH1324	—	15.00	22.00	55.00	90.00	—
AH1325	—	15.00	22.00	55.00	90.00	—

Y# B20.1　2 MISCALS (2 Mace)
7.3200 g., Silver, 23.5 mm.　**Obv. Leg.:** Chinese and Turki around inscription Kuang-hsü Yüan-pao **Rev:** Dragon, lowest coil points right **Edge:** Reeded

Date	Mintage	VG	F	VF	XF	Unc
AH1323	—	800	1,500	2,500		—

Y# B20.2　2 MISCALS (2 Mace)
7.3200 g., Silver, 23.5 mm.　**Obv. Leg.:** Chinese and Turki around inscription Kuang-hsü Yüan-pao **Rev:** Dragon, lowest coil points left

Date	Mintage	VG	F	VF	XF	Unc
AH1323	—	800	1,500	2,500		—

Y# 4　2 MISCALS (2 Mace)
7.2000 g., Silver　**Ruler:** Kuang-hsü **Obv:** Turki outer legend **Rev:** Without Turki legend

Date	Mintage	VG	F	VF	XF	Unc
ND(1905)	—	50.00	75.00	150	400	—

Y# 4.1　2 MISCALS (2 Mace)
7.2000 g., Silver　**Ruler:** Kuang-hsü **Obv:** Continuous Turki outer legend **Rev:** Without Turki legend

Date	Mintage	VG	F	VF	XF	Unc
ND(1905)	—	100	150	250	325	—

Y# 4.2　2 MISCALS (2 Mace)
7.2000 g., Silver　**Ruler:** Kuang-hsü **Obv:** Without outer Turki legend **Rev:** Turki legend

Date	Mintage	VG	F	VF	XF	Unc
ND(1905)	—	150	250	400	650	—

Date	Mintage	VG	F	VF	XF	Unc
AH1311 Error	—	—	—	—	—	—
AH1313	—	13.00	20.00	32.50	65.00	—
AH1314	—	13.00	20.00	32.50	65.00	—
AH1315	—	13.00	20.00	32.50	65.00	—
AH1316	—	13.00	20.00	32.50	65.00	—
AH1317	—	13.00	20.00	32.50	65.00	—
AH1319	—	13.00	20.00	32.50	65.00	—
AH1320	—	13.00	20.00	32.50	65.00	—

Y# 4.3   2 MISCALS (2 Mace)
7.2000 g., Silver **Ruler:** Kuang-hsü **Rev:** Redesigned dragon without Turki legends

Date	Mintage	VG	F	VF	XF	Unc
ND(1905)	—	150	250	400	650	—

Y# 4.4   2 MISCALS (2 Mace)
7.2000 g., Silver **Ruler:** Kuang-hsü **Obv:** Turki outer legend **Rev:** Circled dragon without Turki legend

Date	Mintage	VG	F	VF	XF	Unc
ND(1905) Rare	—	—	—	—	—	—

Y# 11   2 MISCALS (2 Mace)
7.2000 g., Silver **Ruler:** Kuang-hsü **Rev:** Legend above dragon, "2 MACE" below **Rev. Leg.:** SUNGAREI

Date	Mintage	VG	F	VF	XF	Unc
ND(1906)	—	200	425	850	1,350	—

Y# 18a.1   3 MISCALS
10.5000 g., Silver **Ruler:** Kuang-hsü **Obv:** Inscription between "K'a Tsao" and value **Obv. Insc.:** "Kuang-hsü Yin-yüan" **Rev:** Turki in floral wreath

Date	Mintage	VG	F	VF	XF	Unc
AH1320	—	10.00	20.00	32.50	65.00	—
AH1321	—	10.00	20.00	32.50	65.00	—
AH1322	—	10.00	20.00	32.50	65.00	—

Y# 20.1   3 MISCALS
10.5000 g., Silver, 27 mm. **Ruler:** Kuang-hsü **Obv. Leg.:** Turki and Chinese around inscription with official "San"; (3) in Chinese at bottom **Obv. Insc.:** "Ta-ch'ing Yüan-pao"

Date	Mintage	VG	F	VF	XF	Unc
AH1323	—	100	200	325	550	—

Y# 20.2   3 MISCALS
10.5000 g., Silver, 27 mm. **Ruler:** Kuang-hsü **Obv. Leg.:** Turki and Chinese around inscription with official "San", (3) in Chinese at bottom, date at lower right **Obv. Insc.:** "Ta-ch'ing Yüan-pao"

Date	Mintage	VG	F	VF	XF	Unc
AH1323	—	100	200	365	600	—

Y# 23   2 MISCALS (2 Mace)
7.2000 g., Silver, 24 mm. **Obv:** Chinese and Turki legend around inscription **Obv. Insc.:** Ta-Ch'ing Yin-pi **Rev:** Dragon in circle surrounded by sprays

Date	Mintage	VG	F	VF	XF	Unc
AH1324 Rare	—	—	—	—	—	—
AH1325	—	20.00	40.00	65.00	110	—
AH1326	—	20.00	40.00	65.00	110	—
AH1327	—	25.00	50.00	80.00	150	—
AH1329	—	35.00	65.00	110	175	—

Y# 34   3 MISCALS
10.3000 g., Silver **Ruler:** Kuang-hsü **Obv:** Inscription between "Tihwa" and value with normal "San" (3) at left **Obv. Insc.:** "Kuang-hs? Yin-y?an" **Rev:** Turki inscription in floral wreath **Rev. Insc.:** Urumchi **Edge:** Reeded

Date	Mintage	VG	F	VF	XF	Unc
AH1321	—	17.50	30.00	75.00	110	—
AH1322	—	17.50	30.00	75.00	110	—
AH1323	—	17.50	30.00	75.00	110	—

Y# 30   3 MISCALS
10.5000 g., Silver **Obv. Insc.:** "Yin-yüan San-ch'ien" **Rev:** Turki legend below small, side view dragon in circle

Date	Mintage	VG	F	VF	XF	Unc
AH1329	—	200	350	600	1,000	—

Y# 14   3 MISCALS (3 Mace)
10.5000 g., Silver

Date	Mintage	VG	F	VF	XF	Unc
AH1310	—	40.00	80.00	140	225	—
AH1311	—	32.50	65.00	110	200	—
AH1312	—	32.50	65.00	110	200	—

Y# 29   2 MISCALS (2 Mace)
7.2000 g., Silver **Obv:** Turki legend around Yin-Yüan Êrh-ch'ien within a beaded circle **Rev:** Double ring around small dragon, floral pattern outside without legend

Date	Mintage	VG	F	VF	XF	Unc
AH1329	—	55.00	90.00	150	250	—

Y# 34a   3 MISCALS
10.3000 g., Silver **Ruler:** Kuang-hsü **Obv:** Inscription between "Tihwa" and value with official "San" (3) at left **Obv. Insc.:** Kuang-hsü Yin-yüan **Rev:** Turki inscription in floral wreath **Rev. Insc.:** Urumchi

Date	Mintage	VG	F	VF	XF	Unc
AH1322	—	10.00	20.00	32.50	65.00	—
AH1323	—	10.00	20.00	32.50	65.00	—
AH1324	—	10.00	20.00	32.50	65.00	—
AH1325	—	10.00	20.00	32.50	65.00	—

Y# 5   4 MISCALS (4 Mace)
14.2000 g., Silver **Ruler:** Kuang-hsü

Date	Mintage	VG	F	VF	XF	Unc
ND(1905)	—	85.00	125	200	400	—

K# 1040   5 MISCALS
10.5000 g., Silver **Ruler:** Kuang-hsü **Obv:** Inscription above value between Turki and Manchu **Obv. Insc.:** Kuang-hsü Yin-yüan **Rev:** Dragon

Date	Mintage	VG	F	VF	XF	Unc
AH1307	—	1,250	2,000	3,500	5,000	—

Y# 19   5 MISCALS
10.5000 g., Silver **Ruler:** Kuang-hsü **Obv:** Inscription between value **Obv. Insc.:** Kuang-hsü Yin-yüan **Rev. Insc.:** Turki within sprays

Date	Mintage	VG	F	VF	XF	Unc
AH1310	—	17.50	30.00	55.00	100	—
AH1311	—	10.00	20.00	35.00	70.00	—
AH1312	—	15.00	27.50	45.00	90.00	—
AH1313	—	15.00	27.50	45.00	90.00	—
AH1315	—	15.00	27.50	45.00	90.00	—

Y# 29.1   2 MISCALS (2 Mace)
7.2000 g., Silver **Obv:** Yin-yüan Êrh-ch'ien **Rev:** Turki legend below larger dragon within single circle

Date	Mintage	VG	F	VF	XF	Unc
AH1329	—	75.00	125	200	325	—

Y# A18   3 MISCALS
10.5000 g., Silver **Ruler:** Kuang-hsü **Obv:** Inscription between Turki and Manchu **Obv. Insc.:** Kuang-hsü Yin-yüan **Rev:** Dragon

Date	Mintage	Good	VG	F	VF	XF
AH1307	—	750	1,250	2,250	3,750	5,500

Y# 20   3 MISCALS
10.5000 g., Silver, 27 mm. **Ruler:** Kuang-hsü **Obv. Leg.:** Turki and Chinese around inscription with normal "San"; (3) in Chinese at bottom **Obv. Insc.:** "Ta-ch'ing Yüan-pao"

Date	Mintage	VG	F	VF	XF	Unc
AH1323	—	85.00	175	275	450	—

Y# 19a   5 MISCALS
17.2000 g., Silver **Ruler:** Kuang-hsü **Obv:** Inscription between "Kashgar" and value; Chinese characters "K'a Shih" at right **Obv. Insc.:** Kuang-hsü Yin-yüan **Rev:** Turki inscription within sprays

Y# 18a   3 MISCALS
10.5000 g., Silver **Ruler:** Kuang-hsü **Obv:** Inscription between Kashgar and value **Obv. Insc.:** Kuang-hsü Yin-yüan **Rev:** Turki in floral wreath

Date	Mintage	VG	F	VF	XF	Unc
AH1311 Error	—	—	—	—	—	—
AH1313	—	17.50	25.00	40.00	70.00	—
AH1314	—	17.50	25.00	40.00	70.00	—
AH1315	—	17.50	25.00	40.00	70.00	—
AH1316	—	17.50	25.00	40.00	70.00	—
AH1317	—	17.50	25.00	40.00	70.00	—
AH1319	—	17.50	25.00	40.00	70.00	—
AH1320	—	17.50	25.00	40.00	70.00	—

Y# 19a.1 5 MISCALS
17.2000 g., Silver **Ruler:** Kuang-hsü **Obv:** Inscription between "K'a Tsao" at right, value at left **Obv. Insc.:** Kuang-hsü Yin-yüan

Date	Mintage	VG	F	VF	XF	Unc
AH1321	—	12.50	20.00	30.00	60.00	—
AH1322	—	12.50	20.00	30.00	60.00	—

Y# 35 5 MISCALS
17.9000 g., Silver **Ruler:** Kuang-hsü **Obv:** Inscription between "Tihwa" and value with normal "Wu" (5) at left **Obv. Insc.:** "Kuang-hsü Yin-yüan" **Rev:** Turki inscription in floral wreath **Rev. Insc.:** Urumchi

Date	Mintage	VG	F	VF	XF	Unc
AH1321	—	20.00	35.00	70.00	125	—
AH1322	—	20.00	35.00	70.00	125	—
AH1323	—	20.00	35.00	70.00	125	—

Y# 35a 5 MISCALS
17.9000 g., Silver **Ruler:** Kuang-hsü **Obv:** Inscription between "Tihwa" and value with official "Wu" (5) at left **Obv. Insc.:** "Kuang-hsü Yin-yüan" **Rev:** Turki inscription in floral wreath **Rev. Insc.:** Urumchi

Date	Mintage	VG	F	VF	XF	Unc
AH1323	—	20.00	40.00	70.00	125	—
AH1324	—	15.00	30.00	60.00	100	—
AH1325	—	15.00	30.00	60.00	100	—

Y# 21 5 MISCALS
17.2000 g., Silver, 32 mm. **Ruler:** Kuang-hsü **Obv:** Chinese and Turki around inscription; date at upper left **Obv. Insc.:** "Ta-ch'ing Yüan-pao" **Rev:** Side view dragon's tail points to right **Note:** K#1110.

Date	Mintage	VG	F	VF	XF	Unc
AH1323	—	20.00	30.00	45.00	75.00	—

Y# 21.1 5 MISCALS
17.2000 g., Silver, 32 mm. **Obv:** Simple 5 in Chinese, date at lower right **Rev:** Dragon's tail points to right

Date	Mintage	VG	F	VF	XF	Unc
AH1323	—	20.00	30.00	45.00	75.00	—

Y# 21.2 5 MISCALS
17.2000 g., Silver, 32 mm. **Ruler:** Kuang-hsü **Obv:** Inverted Turki legend, date at lower right **Rev:** Dragon

Date	Mintage	VG	F	VF	XF	Unc
AH1323	—	22.50	35.00	60.00	100	—

Y# 21.3 5 MISCALS
17.2000 g., Silver, 32 mm. **Ruler:** Kuang-hsü **Obv:** Normal "Wu" (5) at bottom, date at lower right **Rev:** Dragon

Date	Mintage	VG	F	VF	XF	Unc
AH1323 Rare						

Y# 21.4 5 MISCALS
17.2000 g., Silver, 32 mm. **Ruler:** Kuang-hsü **Obv:** Date at upper left **Rev:** Side view dragon's tail points to left

Date	Mintage	VG	F	VF	XF	Unc
AH1323	—	15.00	25.00	50.00	90.00	—

Y# 21.5 5 MISCALS
17.2000 g., Silver, 32 mm. **Ruler:** Kuang-hsü **Obv:** Date at lower right **Rev:** Dragon

Date	Mintage	VG	F	VF	XF	Unc
AH1323	—	15.00	25.00	50.00	90.00	—

Y# 21.6 5 MISCALS
17.2000 g., Silver, 32 mm. **Ruler:** Kuang-hsü **Obv:** Inverted Turki legend, date at lower right **Rev:** Dragon

Date	Mintage	VG	F	VF	XF	Unc
AH1323	—	20.00	35.00	80.00	135	—

Y# 21.7 5 MISCALS
17.2000 g., Silver, 32 mm. **Ruler:** Kuang-hsü **Obv:** Date at upper right **Rev:** Dragon

Date	Mintage	VG	F	VF	XF	Unc
AH1323	—	20.00	30.00	45.00	75.00	—

Y# 25 5 MISCALS
17.2000 g., Silver **Ruler:** Kuang-hsü **Obv:** "Kashgar Tsao" at top between standard Turki legend; inscription: "Ta-ch'ing Yin-pi" **Rev:** Dragon

Date	Mintage	VG	F	VF	XF	Unc
ND(ca.1906)	—	22.50	40.00	85.00	150	—

Y# 25.1 5 MISCALS
17.2000 g., Silver **Obv:** Date at left or upper left **Rev:** Dragon

Date	Mintage	VG	F	VF	XF	Unc
AH1325	—	22.50	40.00	85.00	150	—
AH1326	—	22.50	40.00	85.00	150	—
AH1327	—	22.50	40.00	85.00	150	—

Y# 25.3 5 MISCALS
17.2000 g., Silver **Obv:** Inverted Turki legend, date at upper right, right, or lower right **Obv. Leg.:** Dragon

Date	Mintage	VG	F	VF	XF	Unc
AH1325	—	17.50	25.00	75.00	110	—
AH1326	—	17.50	25.00	75.00	110	—
AH1328	—	17.50	25.00	75.00	110	—

Note: Error for 1326

Y# 25.2 5 MISCALS
17.2000 g., Silver **Rev:** Dragon **Note:** Similar to Y#25.1. Varieties exist in date placement.

Date	Mintage	VG	F	VF	XF	Unc
AH1325	—	22.50	40.00	85.00	150	—
AH1326	—	22.50	40.00	85.00	150	—
AH1327	—	22.50	40.00	85.00	150	—

Y# 25.4 5 MISCALS
17.2000 g., Silver **Obv:** "Kashgar" at top between standard Turki legend with date at upper right **Rev:** Dragon

Date	Mintage	VG	F	VF	XF	Unc
AH1325	—	20.00	35.00	100	150	—

Y# 25.8 5 MISCALS
17.2000 g., Silver **Obv:** Date at upper left or left **Rev:** Dragon **Note:** Varieties exist.

Date	Mintage	VG	F	VF	XF	Unc
AH1325	—	17.50	25.00	75.00	110	—

Y# 25.9 5 MISCALS
17.2000 g., Silver **Obv:** Similar to Y#25.4 **Rev:** Dragon, floral sprays reversed

Date	Mintage	VG	F	VF	XF	Unc
AH1325	—	50.00	100	165	275	—

Y# 25.10   5 MISCALS
17.2000 g., Silver Obv: Date at upper left **Rev:** Dragon, standard florals

Date	Mintage	VG	F	VF	XF	Unc
AH1325	—	50.00	100	165	275	—

Y# 25.11   5 MISCALS
17.2000 g., Silver **Obv:** Date at upper left **Rev:** Dragon, three rosettes at top

Date	Mintage	VG	F	VF	XF	Unc
AH1325	—	600	800	1,000	1,200	—

Y# 27   5 MISCALS
17.2000 g., Silver **Ruler:** Hsüan-t'ung **Obv:** "Kashgar" at top, Turki below; star in center **Obv. Insc.:** "Hsüan-t'ung Yin-pi" **Rev:** Dragon

Date	Mintage	VG	F	VF	XF	Unc
AH1327	—	20.00	30.00	65.00	110	—
AH1328	—	25.00	50.00	90.00	150	—

Y# 27.1   5 MISCALS
17.2000 g., Silver **Ruler:** Hsüan-t'ung **Obv:** Official "Wu" (5) at right, dot in center **Rev:** Dragon

Date	Mintage	VG	F	VF	XF	Unc
AH1328	—	35.00	65.00	150	225	—

Y# 31   5 MISCALS
17.2000 g., Silver **Ruler:** Kuang-hsü **Obv. Leg.:** Legend "Kashgar" at top, Turki below around side view dragon, star at center and at right **Rev:** Inscription between value
Rev. Insc.: "Hsiang-yin" (soldier's pay) **Note:** Varieties with two and three tail spines on dragon exist.

Date	Mintage	VG	F	VF	XF	Unc
AH1329	—	20.00	40.00	100	150	—
AH1330	—	20.00	40.00	100	150	—
AH1321	—	20.00	40.00	100	150	—
Note: Error for 1331						
AH1331	—	20.00	40.00	100	150	—

Y# 27.2   5 MISCALS
17.2000 g., Silver **Ruler:** Hsüan-t'ung **Obv:** Rosette in center

Date	Mintage	VG	F	VF	XF	Unc
AH1329	—	50.00	100	200	275	—

Y# A28   5 MISCALS
17.2000 g., Silver **Ruler:** Hsüan-t'ung **Obv:** "Kashgar" at top, normal "Wu" (5) at right, star in center **Obv. Insc.:** "Hsüan-t'ung Yüan-pao" **Rev:** Side view dragon **Note:** Prev. Y#27.3.

Date	Mintage	VG	F	VF	XF	Unc
AH1329	—	17.50	25.00	75.00	110	—

Y# A28.1   5 MISCALS
17.2000 g., Silver **Ruler:** Hsüan-t'ung **Obv:** Dot in center **Rev:** Side view dragon **Note:** Prev. Y#27.4.

Date	Mintage	VG	F	VF	XF	Unc
AH1329	—	17.50	25.00	75.00	110	—

Y# A28.2   5 MISCALS
17.2000 g., Silver **Ruler:** Hsüan-t'ung **Obv:** Rosette in center **Rev:** Side view dragon **Note:** Prev. Y#27.5.

Date	Mintage	VG	F	VF	XF	Unc
AH1329	—	17.50	25.00	75.00	110	—

Y# A28.3   5 MISCALS
17.2000 g., Silver **Ruler:** Hsüan-t'ung **Obv:** Official "Wu" (5) at right, star in center **Rev:** Side view dragon **Note:** Prev. Y#27.6.

Date	Mintage	VG	F	VF	XF	Unc
AH1329	—	17.50	25.00	75.00	110	—

Y# 31.2   5 MISCALS
17.2000 g., Silver **Ruler:** Kuang-hsü **Obv:** Rosettes in outer field

Date	Mintage	VG	F	VF	XF	Unc
AH1329	—	50.00	100	165	275	—

Y# 31.3   5 MISCALS
17.2000 g., Silver **Ruler:** Kuang-hsü **Rev:** Rosettes in center

Date	Mintage	VG	F	VF	XF	Unc
AH1329	—	22.50	75.00	100	150	—

Y# 6   5 MISCALS (5 Mace)
17.9000 g., Silver **Ruler:** Kuang-hsü **Obv:** Without dot or rosette in center **Rev:** Uncircled dragon

Date	Mintage	VG	F	VF	XF	Unc
ND(1905)	—	15.00	25.00	60.00	175	—

Y# 6.1   5 MISCALS (5 Mace)
17.9000 g., Silver **Ruler:** Kuang-hsü **Rev:** Circled dragon, without rosettes

Date	Mintage	VG	F	VF	XF	Unc
ND(1905)	—	15.00	25.00	50.00	90.00	—

Y# 6.2   5 MISCALS (5 Mace)
17.9000 g., Silver **Ruler:** Kuang-hsü **Rev:** Large rosettes at sides of dragon

Date	Mintage	VG	F	VF	XF	Unc
ND(1905)	—	15.00	25.00	50.00	90.00	—

Y# 6.3   5 MISCALS (5 Mace)
17.9000 g., Silver **Ruler:** Kuang-hsü **Obv:** Dot in center **Rev:** Without rosettes, circled dragon

Date	Mintage	VG	F	VF	XF	Unc
ND(1905)	—	15.00	25.00	50.00	90.00	—

Y# 6.4   5 MISCALS (5 Mace)
17.9000 g., Silver **Ruler:** Kuang-hsü **Obv:** Cross in center

Date	Mintage	VG	F	VF	XF	Unc
ND(1905)	—	15.00	25.00	50.00	90.00	—

Y# 6.5   5 MISCALS (5 Mace)
17.9000 g., Silver **Ruler:** Kuang-hsü **Obv:** Large rosette in center, middle of which is depressed

Date	Mintage	VG	F	VF	XF	Unc
ND(1905)	—	15.00	25.00	50.00	90.00	—

Y# 6.6   5 MISCALS (5 Mace)
17.9000 g., Silver **Ruler:** Kuang-hsü **Obv:** Eight-petalled rosette in center, middle of which is raised **Rev:** Small rosettes at sides of dragon

Date	Mintage	VG	F	VF	XF	Unc
ND(1905)	—	15.00	25.00	50.00	90.00	—

Y# 6.7   5 MISCALS (5 Mace)
17.9000 g., Silver **Ruler:** Kuang-hsü **Rev:** Bat above uncircled dragon's head

Date	Mintage	VG	F	VF	XF	Unc
ND(1905)	—	175	300	450	700	—

Y# 6.8   5 MISCALS (5 Mace)
17.9000 g., Silver **Ruler:** Kuang-hsü **Rev:** Turki legend around uncircled dragon

Date	Mintage	VG	F	VF	XF	Unc
ND(1905)	—	400	600	—	—	—

Y# 6.9   5 MISCALS (5 Mace)
17.9000 g., Silver **Ruler:** Kuang-hsü **Rev:** Legend above uncircled dragon, "5 MACE" below **Rev. Leg.:** SUNGAREI

Date	Mintage	VG	F	VF	XF	Unc
ND(1906) Rare	—	—	—	—	—	—
Note: Some authorities consider this coin a fantasy						

Y# 6.10   5 MISCALS (5 Mace)
17.9000 g., Silver **Ruler:** Kuang-hsü **Rev:** Without SUNGREI, with four bats and many clouds around dragon

Date	Mintage	VG	F	VF	XF	Unc
ND(1906) Rare	—	—	—	—	—	—

Y# 6.11 5 MISCALS (5 Mace)
17.9000 g., Silver **Ruler:** Kuang-hsü **Obv:** Turki legend rotated
Rev: Bat above dragon's head

Date	Mintage	VG	F	VF	XF	Unc
ND(1906) Rare	—	—	—	—	—	—

Y# 7 SAR (Tael)
35.5000 g., Silver **Ruler:** Kuang-hsü **Obv:** Without Turki legend
Rev: Without Turki legend, rosettes at sides of uncircled dragon

Date	Mintage	VG	F	VF	XF	Unc
ND(1905)	—	25.00	40.00	60.00	200	800

Y# 7.1 SAR (Tael)
35.5000 g., Silver **Ruler:** Kuang-hsü **Rev:** Turki legend around
circled dragon, without rosettes

Date	Mintage	VG	F	VF	XF	Unc
ND(1905)	—	40.00	65.00	100	300	900

Y# 7.2 SAR (Tael)
35.5000 g., Silver **Ruler:** Kuang-hsü **Rev:** Turki legend around
uncircled dragon

Date	Mintage	VG	F	VF	XF	Unc
ND(1905)	—	500	850	1,250	1,600	—

Y# 7.3 SAR (Tael)
35.5000 g., Silver **Ruler:** Kuang-hsü **Obv:** Outer Turki legend,
rosette in center **Rev:** Without Turki legend, with rosettes at sides
of uncircled dragon

Date	Mintage	VG	F	VF	XF	Unc
ND(1905)	—	100	300	500	1,500	—

Y# 26 SAR (Tael)
35.2000 g., Silver, 40 mm. **Obv:** Chinese "Kashgar" at top wtih
Turki "Kashgar" to left **Obv. Insc.:** "Ta-ch'ing Yin-pi" **Rev:** Side
view dragon in sprays

Date	Mintage	VG	F	VF	XF	Unc
AH1325	—	200	300	500	850	—

Y# 26.1 SAR (Tael)
35.2000 g., Silver, 40 mm. **Obv:** "Kashgar Tsao" at top

Date	Mintage	VG	F	VF	XF	Unc
AH1325	—	1,200	2,750	5,000	7,000	—

Y# 26.2 SAR (Tael)
35.2000 g., Silver, 40 mm. **Obv:** Chinese "Kashgar" at top wtih
Turki "Kashgar" to right

Date	Mintage	VG	F	VF	XF	Unc
AH1325	—	300	500	700	1,200	—

REPUBLIC
PROVINCIAL CAST COINAGE

Y# 37.1 10 CASH
Cast Copper, 32 mm. **Obv. Insc.:** Chung Hua Min Kuo
Rev: Crossed flags

Date	Mintage	Good	VG	F	VF	XF
ND(ca.1912)	—	35.00	55.00	80.00	—	—

Y# 37.2 10 CASH
Cast Copper, 29 mm. **Obv. Insc.:** Chung Hua Min Kuo
Rev: Crossed flags

Date	Mintage	Good	VG	F	VF	XF
ND(ca.1912)	—	35.00	55.00	80.00	—	—

MILLED COINAGE

Y# A36.1 5 CASH
Copper **Obv:** Large Chinese inscription **Obv. Insc.:** "Chung-
hua Min-kuo" between "T'ung-pi" **Rev:** Flag **Rev. Leg.:** Chinese
outer, Turki inner, around flag

Date	Mintage	Good	VG	F	VF	XF
ND(ca.1912)	—	275	375	500	700	—

Y# A36.2 5 CASH
Copper **Obv:** Small Chinese inscription **Obv. Insc.:** "Chung-hua
Min-kuo" between "T'ung-pi" **Rev:** Flag **Rev. Leg.:** Chinese outer,
Turki inner, around flag

Date	Mintage	Good	VG	F	VF	XF
ND(ca.1912)	—	275	375	500	700	—

Y# 36 5 CASH
Copper **Obv. Leg.:** Chinese around inscription "Chung-hua Min-
kuo" **Rev:** Crossed flags **Rev. Insc.:** Turki above and below
crossed flags

Date	Mintage	Good	VG	F	VF	XF
AH1331	—	100	135	225	350	—

Y# B39.1   10 CASH
Copper **Obv:** Large character "Shih" (ten), normal "Pao"
Obv. Leg.: Chung Hua Min Kuo **Rev:** Crossed flags

Date	Mintage	Good	VG	F	VF	XF
ND	—	8.50	15.00	25.00	37.50	65.00

Y# B39.2   10 CASH
Copper **Obv:** Small character "Shih" (ten) **Obv. Leg.:** Chung Hua Min Kuo **Rev:** Small crossed flags

Date	Mintage	Good	VG	F	VF	XF
ND	—	12.50	25.00	35.00	50.00	85.00

Y# A39.1   10 CASH
Copper **Obv. Leg.:** Chung Hua Min Kuo **Rev:** Large crossed flags with vertical stripes

Date	Mintage	Good	VG	F	VF	XF
CD1	—	7.50	13.50	18.50	28.50	49.50
1 (1912)	—	7.50	13.50	18.50	28.50	49.50

Y# B36.1   10 CASH
Copper **Obv. Insc.:** "Chung-hua Min-kuo" between "T'ung-pi" **Rev:** Flag **Rev. Leg.:** Chinese outer, Turki inner, around flag

Date	Mintage	Good	VG	F	VF	XF
ND(ca.1912)	—	25.00	37.50	50.00	85.00	—

Y# B36.2   10 CASH
Copper **Obv:** Small Chinese inscription **Obv. Insc.:** "Chung-hua Min-kuo" between "T'ung-pi" **Rev:** Flag **Rev. Leg.:** Chinese outer, Turki inner, around flag

Date	Mintage	Good	VG	F	VF	XF
ND(ca.1912)	—	25.00	37.50	50.00	85.00	—

Y# A39.2   10 CASH
Copper **Rev:** Small crossed flags with vertical stripes

Date	Mintage	Good	VG	F	VF	XF
CD1 (1912)	—	7.00	12.00	16.50	25.50	47.50

Note: This type exists with a great variety of the "Shih" (ten), and "Pao" characters

Date	Mintage	Good	VG	F	VF	XF
CD1 (1912)	—	7.00	12.00	16.50	25.50	47.50

Y# 38.2   10 CASH
Copper **Rev:** Crossed flags, modified Turki legend with date at bottom

Date	Mintage	Good	VG	F	VF	XF
AH1331 (1912)	—	8.50	12.50	17.50	30.00	—
AH1332 (1913)	—	8.50	12.50	17.50	30.00	—
AH1334 (1915)	—	8.50	12.50	17.50	30.00	—
AH1335 (1916)	—	8.50	12.50	17.50	30.00	—

Y# F38   10 CASH
Copper **Ruler:** Kuang-hsü **Obv:** Chinese characters "Shih Wen" (10 Wen) at lower left **Rev:** Crossed flags, upper Turki legend inverted

Date	Mintage	Good	VG	F	VF	XF
AH1332 (1913)	—	35.00	65.00	85.00	125	—

Y# 38.1   10 CASH
Copper **Obv:** Chinese legend: "Shih Wen" (10 Cash) at upper left **Rev:** Crossed flags, date at upper center

Date	Mintage	Good	VG	F	VF	XF
ND (1913)	—	7.50	15.00	20.00	35.00	—
AH1332 (1913)	—	7.50	15.00	20.00	35.00	—
AH1333 (1914)	—	7.50	15.00	20.00	35.00	—
AH1334 (1915)	—	7.50	15.00	20.00	35.00	—

Y# 38.3   10 CASH
Copper **Obv:** Two lower right Chinese characters different **Obv. Insc.:** Chung Hua Min Kuo **Rev:** Crossed flags, AH date at top

Date	Mintage	Good	VG	F	VF	XF
AH133-4 (1915)	—	50.00	75.00	125	200	—

Y# 38.5   10 CASH
Copper **Obv:** Outer Chinese legend wtihout "Shih" of "Kashgar" at lower left **Obv. Insc.:** Chung Hua Min Kuo **Rev:** Crossed flags, Turki legend in florals with "Zarb Kashgar" at top **Note:** Rev: similar to Y#A38.2

Date	Mintage	Good	VG	F	VF	XF
AH1334 (1915)	—	37.50	60.00	100	150	—

Y# 38.6   10 CASH
Copper **Obv. Insc.:** Chung Hua Min Kuo **Rev:** Single flower in lower Turki legend

Date	Mintage	Good	VG	F	VF	XF
AH1334	—	—	—	—	—	—

Y# 38.7   10 CASH
Copper **Obv. Insc.:** Chung Hua Min Kuo **Rev:** Without flowers or florals in Turki legends

Date	Mintage	Good	VG	F	VF	XF
AH1334 (1915)	—	—	—	—	—	—

Y# C39   10 CASH
Copper **Obv. Insc.:** Chung Hua Min Kuo **Rev:** Turki legend around crossed flags

Date	Mintage	Good	VG	F	VF	XF
CD1921 Rare	—	—	—	—	—	—

Note: Status unknown

Y# 38a.1   10 CASH
Copper **Obv:** Chinese date at upper right with rosette **Obv. Insc.:** Chung Hua Min Kuo

Date	Mintage	Good	VG	F	VF	XF
AH1340 (1921)	—	6.00	10.00	15.00	25.00	—
AH1339 (1921)	—	6.00	10.00	15.00	25.00	—

Y# 38a.3 10 CASH
Copper **Obv. Insc.:** Chung Hua Min Kuo **Rev:** Crossed flags, Turki legend rearranged

Date	Mintage	Good	VG	F	VF	XF
AH1340 (1921)	—	6.00	10.00	15.00	25.00	—
AH1339 (1921)	—	6.00	10.00	15.00	25.00	—

Y# 38a.2 10 CASH
Copper **Obv:** Outer Chinese legend without "Shih" of "Kashgar" at upper left **Obv. Insc.:** Chung Hua Min Kuo **Rev:** Crossed flags

Date	Mintage	Good	VG	F	VF	XF
AH134x (1921)	—	6.00	10.00	15.00	25.00	—

Y# 38a.5 10 CASH
Copper **Obv:** Crowded Chinese year "11" **Obv. Insc.:** Chung Hua Min Kuo **Rev:** Crossed flags

Date	Mintage	Good	VG	F	VF	XF
AH1340 (1921)	—	25.00	40.00	65.00	100	—

Y# 38b.1 10 CASH
Copper **Obv:** Chinese legend "Min-kuo T'ung-yüan" in inner circle with "Kashgar" at right **Obv. Insc.:** Min Kuo T'ung Yüan **Rev:** Crossed flags

Date	Mintage	Good	VG	F	VF	XF
AH1340 (1921)	—	15.00	30.00	40.00	65.00	—

Y# 38b.2 10 CASH
Copper **Obv:** Outer Chinese legend rotated **Obv. Insc.:** Min Kuo T'ung Yüan **Rev:** Crossed flags

Date	Mintage	Good	VG	F	VF	XF
AH134x (1921)	—	15.00	30.00	40.00	65.00	—

Y# A44.1 10 CASH
Copper **Obv. Insc.:** Chung Hua Min Kuo **Rev:** Crossed flags

Date	Mintage	Good	VG	F	VF	XF
11(1922)	—	50.00	75.00	100	125	—

Y# A44.2 10 CASH
Copper **Obv. Insc.:** Chung Hua Min Kuo **Rev:** Crossed flags reversed

Date	Mintage	Good	VG	F	VF	XF
11(1922)	—	50.00	75.00	100	125	—

Y# B38.4 10 CASH
Copper **Obv:** Chinese date at left and right **Obv. Insc.:** Chung Hua Min Kuo **Rev:** Outlined sunburst **Rev. Insc.:** T'ung Yüan

Date	Mintage	Good	VG	F	VF	XF
CD1928	—	5.00	8.00	12.00	25.00	—
CD1929	—	8.00	11.00	22.50	37.50	—

Y# B38.1 10 CASH
Copper **Obv:** Chinese legend in inner circle; Chinese date at left and right of upper legend **Obv. Insc.:** Min Kuo T'ung Yüan **Rev:** Chinese characters "T'ung Yüan" in solid sunburst

Date	Mintage	Good	VG	F	VF	XF
CD1928	—	40.00	80.00	120	200	—

Y# B38.2 10 CASH
Copper **Obv:** Upper legend **Obv. Leg.:** "Hsinchiang Kashgar Tsao" **Obv. Insc.:** Min Kuo T'ung Yüan **Rev:** Outlined sunburst **Rev. Insc.:** Small T'ung Yüan

Date	Mintage	Good	VG	F	VF	XF
CD1928	—	30.00	70.00	100	180	—

Note: A similar coin with same upper legend and cyclical date 1929 at sides is reported

Y# B38.3 10 CASH
Copper **Obv:** Upper legend **Obv. Leg.:** "Hsinchiang K'a Tsao" **Obv. Insc.:** Min Kuo T'ung Yüan **Rev:** Outlined sunburst **Rev. Insc.:** Large T'ung Yüan

Date	Mintage	Good	VG	F	VF	XF
CD1928	—	15.00	23.00	30.00	50.00	—

Y# B38.5 10 CASH
Copper **Obv. Insc.:** Chung Hua Min Kuo **Rev:** Outlined finely rayed sunburst **Rev. Insc.:** T'ung Yüan

Date	Mintage	Good	VG	F	VF	XF
CD1928	—	60.00	90.00	140	200	—

Y# B38.7 10 CASH
Copper **Obv. Leg.:** HSINCHIANG KASHGAR TSAO **Obv. Insc.:** Chung Hua Min Kuo **Rev:** Outlined sunburst (as Y#B38.3) **Rev. Insc.:** Large T'ung Yüan

Date	Mintage	Good	VG	F	VF	XF
CD1928	—	15.00	23.00	50.00	—	—

Y# B38b.1 10 CASH
Copper **Obv. Insc.:** Chung Hua Min Kuo **Rev:** Turki legend in solid sunburst

Date	Mintage	Good	VG	F	VF	XF
AH1346	—	125	175	300	400	—

Y# B38b.2 10 CASH
Copper **Obv:** Similar to Y#B838d **Obv. Insc.:** Chung Hua Min Kuo **Rev:** Turki legend in solid sunburst

Date	Mintage	Good	VG	F	VF	XF
AH1346	—	150	200	350	500	—

Y# B38c.1 10 CASH
Copper **Obv. Insc.:** Min Kuo T'ung Yüan **Rev:** Chinese character "Jih" in solid sunburst

Date	Mintage	Good	VG	F	VF	XF
CD1928	—	175	275	425	600	—

Y# B38c.2 10 CASH
Copper **Obv:** Like B38c.1 **Obv. Insc.:** Min Kuo T'ung Yüan **Rev:** Chinese character "Jih" in rayed sunburst

Date	Mintage	Good	VG	F	VF	XF
CD1928	—	175	275	425	600	—

Y# B38c.3 10 CASH
Copper **Obv:** Like Y#B38b.1 **Obv. Insc.:** Min Kuo T'ung Yüan **Rev:** Like Y#B38c.1

Date	Mintage	Good	VG	F	VF	XF
CD1928	—	175	275	425	600	—

Y# B38c.4 10 CASH
Copper **Obv. Leg.:** Cyclic date at left and right like Y#B38.4
Obv. Insc.: Min Kuo T'ung Yüan

Date	Mintage	Good	VG	F	VF	XF
CD1928	—	175	275	425	600	—

Y# B38d 10 CASH
Copper **Obv:** Chinese legend in inner circle **Obv. Insc.:** Min Kuo T'ung Yüan **Rev:** Chinese characters "T'ung Yüan" in solid sunburst

Date	Mintage	Good	VG	F	VF	XF
CD1928	—	125	175	300	400	—

Y# 40.1 10 CASH
Copper **Obv:** Chinese legend in inner circle with "Hsin Chiang" at upper right **Obv. Insc.:** Chung Hua Min Kuo **Rev:** Flags with solid sunbursts with inner circles

Date	Mintage	Good	VG	F	VF	XF
CD1929	—	7.00	12.00	16.50	25.00	40.00
CD1930 Rare	—	—	—	—	—	—

Note: The cyclical date character at left exists closed, which is rare, and open for CD1929

Y# 44.2 10 CASH
Copper **Obv:** Small eight-petaled rosette in center **Obv. Insc.:** Chung Hua Min Kuo **Rev:** Flag at right without inner circle

Date	Mintage	Good	VG	F	VF	XF
CD1929	—	7.00	11.00	18.00	25.00	—
CD1930	—	7.00	11.00	18.00	25.00	—

Y# 44.6 10 CASH
Copper **Obv. Insc.:** Chung Hua Min Kuo **Rev:** Reversed flags with large solid sunbursts

Date	Mintage	Good	VG	F	VF	XF
CD1929	—	5.00	11.00	20.00	27.50	—
CD1930	—	6.00	12.00	22.50	30.00	—

Y# 40.2 10 CASH
Copper **Obv:** Large starburst in center **Obv. Insc.:** Chung Hua Min Kuo **Rev:** Long streamers

Date	Mintage	Good	VG	F	VF	XF
CD1929 Rare	—	7.00	12.00	16.50	25.00	40.00

Note: Y#40 inscribed "Sheng Ch'eng" (provincial capital) in upper legend refers to Tihwa (Urumchi, now Urümqi)

Y# 40.3 10 CASH
Copper **Obv:** Cyclical date at upper right in legend **Obv. Insc.:** Chung Hua Min Kuo

Date	Mintage	Good	VG	F	VF	XF
CD1930 Rare	—	—	—	—	—	—

Y# 44.1 10 CASH
Copper **Obv. Leg.:** "Hsinchiang K'ashih Tsao" **Obv. Insc.:** Chung Hua Min Kuo **Rev:** Crossed flags with wide outlined sunbursts; flags at right with inner circle

Date	Mintage	Good	VG	F	VF	XF
CD1929	—	5.00	8.50	17.50	32.50	—

Y# 44.3 10 CASH
Copper **Obv:** Star with rays in center **Obv. Insc.:** Chung Hua Min Kuo **Rev:** Crossed flags

Date	Mintage	Good	VG	F	VF	XF
CD1930	—	8.50	17.50	22.50	37.50	—

Y# 44.4 10 CASH
Copper **Obv:** Eight-petaled rosette in center **Obv. Insc.:** Chung Hua Min Kuo **Rev:** Crossed flags with narrow outlined sunbursts

Date	Mintage	Good	VG	F	VF	XF
CD1930	—	10.00	20.00	35.00	55.00	—

Y# 44.5 10 CASH
Copper **Obv. Insc.:** Chung Hua Min Kuo **Rev:** Crossed flags with solid sunbursts

Date	Mintage	Good	VG	F	VF	XF
CD1933	—	6.00	12.00	22.50	30.00	—

Y# 44.7 10 CASH
Copper **Obv. Insc.:** Chung Hua Min Kuo **Rev:** Reversed crossed flags with small solid sunbursts

Date	Mintage	Good	VG	F	VF	XF
CD1930	—	25.00	50.00	100	165	—

Y# 44.8 10 CASH
Copper **Obv:** Upper legend **Obv. Leg.:** "Hsinchiang K'ashih Tsao" **Obv. Insc.:** Chung Hua Min Kuo **Rev:** Crossed flags

Date	Mintage	Good	VG	F	VF	XF
CD1929	—	75.00	100	125	150	—

Y# 44.9 10 CASH
Copper **Obv. Insc.:** Chung Hua Min Kuo **Rev:** Reversed crossed flags with large "flower petal" outlined sunbursts

Date	Mintage	Good	VG	F	VF	XF
CD1930	—	6.00	12.00	22.50	30.00	—

Y# 44.10 10 CASH
Copper **Obv. Insc.:** Chung Hua Min Kuo **Rev:** Crossed flags reversed

Date	Mintage	Good	VG	F	VF	XF
CD1930	—	—	—	—	—	—

Y# B38.6 10 CASH
Copper **Obv. Insc.:** Chung Hua Min Kuo **Rev:** Sunburst **Rev. Insc.:** T'ung Yüan

Date	Mintage	Good	VG	F	VF	XF
CD1929	—	40.00	60.00	100	170	—

Y# B38a.1 10 CASH
Copper **Obv:** Chinese characters for date to left and right of "Chung Hua Min Kuo" in inner circle **Obv. Insc.:** Chung Hua Min Kuo **Rev:** Turki legend in oulined sunburst

Date	Mintage	Good	VG	F	VF	XF
CD1929	—	100	165	250	350	—

Y# B38a.2 10 CASH
Copper **Obv. Leg.:** "Hsinchiang K'ashih Tsao"
Obv. Insc.: Chung Hua Min Kuo **Rev:** Sunburst

Date	Mintage	Good	VG	F	VF	XF
CD1929	—	75.00	100	125	150	—

Y# 48 20 CASH
Copper **Obv. Insc.:** Chung Hua Min Kuo **Rev:** Crossed flags

Date	Mintage	Good	VG	F	VF	XF
AH133x (1921) Rare	—	—	—	—	—	—

Y# A41.1 20 CASH
Copper **Obv:** Chinese legend in inner circle with "Hsin Chiang" at upper right **Obv. Insc.:** Chung Hua Min Kuo **Rev:** Crossed flags

Date	Mintage	Good	VG	F	VF	XF
CD1929	—	75.00	125	200	300	—
CD1930	—	85.00	140	225	335	—

Note: Y#A41.1 inscribed "Sheng Ch'eng" (provincial capital) in upper legend refers to Tihwa (Urumchi now Urumqi)

Y# A41.2 20 CASH
Copper **Obv:** Cyclical date at upper right **Obv. Insc.:** Chung Hua Min Kuo **Rev:** Crossed flags

Date	Mintage	Good	VG	F	VF	XF
CD1930 Rare	—	—	—	—	—	—

Y# 39.1 20 CASH
Copper **Obv:** 8-petaled rosette in center **Obv. Insc.:** Hsin Chiang T'ung Pao **Rev:** Two stripes in crossed flags have arabesques

Date	Mintage	VG	F	VF	XF	Unc
ND	—	10.00	16.50	20.00	27.50	—

Y# 39.2 20 CASH
Copper **Obv:** 5-petaled rosette in center **Obv. Insc.:** Hsin Chiang T'ung Pao **Rev:** Crossed flags

Date	Mintage	VG	F	VF	XF	Unc
ND	—	50.00	100	150	225	—

Y# 39.3 20 CASH
Copper **Obv. Insc.:** Hsin Chiang T'ung Pao **Rev:** Crossed flags without arabesques

Date	Mintage	VG	F	VF	XF	Unc
ND Restrike	—	—	—	—	50.00	75.00

Y# 43 5 MISCALS
17.3000 g., Silver **Obv:** Stars dividing Chinese legends **Obv. Insc.:** Chung Hua Min Kuo **Rev:** Crossed flags dividing Turki legend

Date	Mintage	VG	F	VF	XF	Unc
AH1331	—	40.00	75.00	160	275	—
AH1332	—	40.00	75.00	160	275	—

Y# 43.1 5 MISCALS
17.3000 g., Silver **Obv:** Rosettes dividing Chinese legend **Obv. Insc.:** Chung Hua Min Kuo **Rev:** Crossed flags **Note:** Varieties exist.

Date	Mintage	VG	F	VF	XF	Unc
AH1330	—	35.00	65.00	135	225	—
AH1331	—	35.00	65.00	135	225	—
AH1332	—	35.00	65.00	135	225	—
AH13-32	—	35.00	65.00	135	225	—

Y# 43.3 5 MISCALS
17.3000 g., Silver **Obv:** Rosette in center, floral arrangements dividing Chinese legend **Obv. Insc.:** Chung Hua Min Kuo **Rev:** Crossed flags **Note:** Varieties exist.

Date	Mintage	VG	F	VF	XF	Unc
AH13-32	—	40.00	75.00	160	275	—
AH133-2	—	40.00	75.00	160	275	—
AH133-4	—	45.00	85.00	185	325	—

Y# 43.2   5 MISCALS
17.3000 g., Silver   **Obv:** Rosettes dividing Chinese legend
Obv. Insc.: Chung Hua Min Kuo   **Rev:** Crossed flags

Date	Mintage	VG	F	VF	XF	Unc
AH1334	—	45.00	85.00	185	325	—
AH133-4	—	45.00	85.00	185	325	—

Note: Varieties exist

Y# 43.4   5 MISCALS
17.3000 g., Silver   **Obv:** Stars divide rotated outer Chinese legend **Obv. Insc.:** Chung Hua Min Kuo   **Rev:** Crossed flags

Date	Mintage	VG	F	VF	XF	Unc
AHx13x(ca.1916)	—	—	—	—	—	—

Note: Considered contemporary forgeries by some experts

Y# 41   5 MISCALS (5 Mace)
17.9000 g., Silver   **Obv. Leg.:** Chung Hua Min Kuo (year) Nien
Rev: Two stripes in crossed flags have arabesques

Date	Mintage	VG	F	VF	XF	Unc
1(1912)	—	40.00	65.00	150	200	—

Y# 41a   5 MISCALS (5 Mace)
17.9000 g., Silver   **Obv. Leg.:** Chung Hua Min Kuo (year) Nien
Rev: Four stripes in crossed flags have arabesques

Date	Mintage	VG	F	VF	XF	Unc
1(1912)	—	40.00	65.00	150	200	—

Y# 42   SAR (Tael)
35.9000 g., Silver   **Obv. Leg.:** Chung Hua Min Kuo (year) Nien
Rev: Two stripes in crossed flags have arabesques

Date	Mintage	VG	F	VF	XF	Unc
1(1912)	—	60.00	100	200	350	—

Y# 42a   SAR (Tael)
35.9000 g., Silver   **Obv:** Similar to Y#42 **Obv. Leg.:** Chung Hua Min Kuo (year) Nien **Rev:** Four stripes in crossed flags havez arabesques

Date	Mintage	VG	F	VF	XF	Unc
1(1912)	—	60.00	100	200	350	—

Y# 45   SAR (Tael)
35.0000 g., Silver   **Obv:** Large characters **Rev:** Rosette at top between wheat ears

Date	Mintage	VG	F	VF	XF	Unc
6(1917)	—	17.50	25.00	40.00	200	—

Y# 45.1   SAR (Tael)
35.0000 g., Silver   **Obv:** Similar to Y#45 but with small characters
Rev: Without rosette at top

Date	Mintage	VG	F	VF	XF	Unc
6(1917)	—	17.50	5.00	40.00	75.00	—

Y# 45.2   SAR (Tael)
35.0000 g., Silver   **Rev:** Rosette at top between more ornate branches

Date	Mintage	VG	F	VF	XF	Unc
7(1918)	—	20.00	30.00	50.00	200	—

Y# 46   DOLLAR (Yuan)
Silver   **Obv:** Similar to Y#46.2 but with larger Chinese characters
Rev: Think pointed base "1" **Note:** Kann #1267a reports a variety in the character "Kuo".

Date	Mintage	VG	F	VF	XF	Unc
38//1949	—	16.00	25.00	35.00	175	500

Y# 46.1   DOLLAR (Yuan)
Silver   **Obv:** Similar to Y#46.2 but with larger Chinese characters
Rev: Think pointed base "1" with large serif

Date	Mintage	VG	F	VF	XF	Unc
38//1949	—	16.00	25.00	35.00	175	500

Y# 46.2   DOLLAR (Yuan)
Silver   **Obv:** Smaller Chinese characters **Rev:** Thin pointed base "1"

Date	Mintage	VG	F	VF	XF	Unc
38//1949	—	16.00	22.50	37.50	175	—

Y# 46.3   DOLLAR (Yuan)
Silver   **Rev:** Square-based "1"

Date	Mintage	VG	F	VF	XF	Unc
38//1949	—	20.00	30.00	50.00	200	—

Y# 46.4   DOLLAR (Yuan)
Silver   Obv: Outlined Chinese characters "Yüan" in center

Date	Mintage	VG	F	VF	XF	Unc
38//1949	—	60.00	100	150	300	—

Y# 46.5   DOLLAR (Yuan)
Silver   Note: 9-4-9-1 (1949) at bottom.

Date	Mintage	VG	F	VF	XF	Unc
38//1949	—	150	300	500	1,000	—

ISLAMIC REPUBLIC OF EASTERN TURKESTAN

MILLED COINAGE

Y# E38.1   20 CASH
Copper, 32-34 mm.   Rev: Crossed flags

Date	Mintage	Good	VG	F	VF	XF
AH1352	—	50.00	100	200	350	—

Y# E38.2   20 CASH
Copper   Rev: Crossed flags reversed

Date	Mintage	Good	VG	F	VF	XF
AH1352	—	50.00	100	200	350	—

Y# E38.3   20 CASH
Copper, 32-34 mm.   Rev: Crossed flags, sun in partial frame in left flag, denomination given as two wen (sic)

Date	Mintage	Good	VG	F	VF	XF
AH1352	—	60.00	150	300	450	—

Y# E38.4   20 CASH
Copper   Rev: Crossed flags, large sun in national flag at left
Note: Varieties exist.

Date	Mintage	Good	VG	F	VF	XF
AH1352	—	50.00	150	300	450	—

Note: Crudely cut Chinese denomination appears as 2 instead of 20; also encountered overstruck on 10 Cash, Y#44 varieties

Y# G38   20 CASH
Copper   Obv: Similar to 20 Cash, Y#E38.3   Rev: Crossed flags, small flag at left

Date	Mintage	Good	VG	F	VF	XF
AH1352	—	50.00	150	300	450	—

Y# E39   MISCAL
Silver   Obv: Turki legend around central Turki legend Obv. Leg.: "Sharket Turkhestan Cumhuriyet Islamiyesi" around "Muskuk, sanah 1252"   Rev: Turki legend Rev. Leg.: "Zarb Kashgar"

Date	Mintage	Good	VG	F	VF	XF
AH1352 Rare	—	—	—	—	—	—

Note: Varieties of sun with eight and nine rays exist

UIGHURISTAN REPUBLIC
Uighuristan was a rebel Islamic republic that sought independence from China. The rebellion was quickly crushed. Coins of the Republic were all made by over-striking on Kashgar Republic 10 Cash coins.

MILLED COINAGE

Y# D38.1   10 CASH
Copper   Rev: Crossed flags, flag at right without fringe

Date	Mintage	Good	VG	F	VF	XF
AH1352	—	50.00	100	160	250	—

Y# D38.2   10 CASH
Copper   Rev: Crossed flags, flag at right with partial fringe

Date	Mintage	Good	VG	F	VF	XF
AH1352	—	50.00	100	160	250	—

Y# D38.3   10 CASH
Copper   Rev: Crossed flags, flag at right with full fringe

Date	Mintage	Good	VG	F	VF	XF
AH1352	—	50.00	100	160	250	—

Note: Encountered overstruck on various earlier Republican Series 10 Cash

PATTERNS
Including off metal strikes

KM#	Date	Mintage	Identification	Mkt Val
Pn41	ND(ca.1906)	—	Mace. Copper. SUNGAREI. Y#10; Kann#1034.	1,600
Pn42	ND(ca.1906)	—	2 Mace. Silver. SUNGAREI. Y#11; Kann #1033.	3,000
Pn43	ND(ca.1906)	—	2 Mace. Copper. SUNGAREI. Kann #1033x.	1,200
Pn44	ND(ca.1906)	—	4 Mace. Silver. SUNGAREI.	8,000
Pn45	ND(ca.1906)	—	4 Mace. Brass. SUNGAREI.	1,250
Pn46	ND(ca.1906)	—	5 Mace. Silver. Kann #1032.	—
Pn47	ND(ca.1906)	—	7 Mace. Silver. SUNGAREI. 2 Candareens, Y#12. Kann #1031.	—
Pn40	AH1324	—	Tael. Silver.	—

SUIYUAN PROVINCE
In November 1913, the central government grouped together 19 Mongolian and 12 Shansi districts to form the Suiyuan Special Administrative Zone. In 1928, the name was changed to Suiyuan Province. The province was joined with other Mongolian provinces to form Inner Mongolia after the communist takeover in 1949.

REPUBLIC

MILLED COINAGE

KM# 3   FEN
Shell Casing Brass   Obv: White Tower Rev: Ancient spade coin between Yi and Fen

Date	Mintage	VG	F	VF	XF	Unc
38(1949)	—	175	250	350	550	—

KM# 5   5 FEN
Shell Casing Brass   Obv: White Tower Rev: Ancient spade coin between Wu(5) and Fen

Date	Mintage	VG	F	VF	XF	Unc
38(1949)	—	600	750	1,000	1,350	—

SZECHUAN PROVINCE
Sichuan

A province located in south-central China. The largest of the traditional Chinese provinces, Szechuan (Sichuan) is a plateau region watered by many rivers. These rivers carry much trading traffic. Agriculture or mining are the occupational choices of most of the populace. In World War II the national capital was moved to Chungking in Szechuan (Sichuan). Chengtu was an active imperial mint that opened in 1732 and was in practically continuous operation until the advent of modern equipment. Modern minting was introduced in the province when Chengtu began milled coinage in 1898. A mint was authorized for Chungking in 1905 but it did not begin operations until 1913. The Chengtu Mint was looted by soldiers in 1925. The last republic issues from Szechuan (Sichuan) were dated 1932.

The machinery for the first Szechuan (Sichuan) Mint was produced in New Jersey and the dies were engraved in Philadelphia. The mint was opened in 1898, but closed within a few months and did not reopen until 1901. There is no doubt now that Y#234-238 (K#145-149) were the first issues of this mint, contrary to the Kann listings.

EMPIRE
PROVINCIAL CAST COINAGE

C# 24-9   CASH
Cast Brass   **Ruler:** Kuang-hsü **Obv. Insc.:** Kuang-hsü T'ung-pao **Rev:** Manchu inscription **Rev. Insc.:** Boo-Cuwan

Date	Mintage	Good	VG	F	VF	XF
ND(1875-1908)	—	4.50	7.50	11.50	22.50	—

C# 24-10   10 CASH
Cast Brass   **Ruler:** Kuang-hsü **Obv. Insc.:** Kuang-hsü Chung-pao **Rev:** Type I mint mark

Date	Mintage	Good	VG	F	VF	XF
ND(1875-80) Rare						

MILLED COINAGE

Y# 225   5 CASH
Copper   **Ruler:** Kuang-hsü **Obv:** Manchu at center **Obv. Leg.:** Szu-ch'uan Kuan Chü Tsao **Obv. Insc.:** Kuang-hsü Yüan-pao **Rev:** Side view dragon

Date	Mintage	VG	F	VF	XF	Unc
ND(1903-04)	85,000	50.00	70.00	100	150	—

Y# 225a   5 CASH
Brass   **Ruler:** Kuang-hsü **Obv. Leg.:** Szu-ch'uan Kuan Chü Tsao **Obv. Insc.:** Kuang-hsü Yüan-pao

Date	Mintage	VG	F	VF	XF	Unc
ND(1903-04) Rare Inc. above						

Y# 228   5 CASH
Brass   **Ruler:** Kuang-hsü **Obv:** Flower at center **Obv. Leg.:** Szu-ch'uan Sheng Tsao **Obv. Insc.:** Kuang-hsü Yüan-pao **Rev:** Flying dragon

Date	Mintage	VG	F	VF	XF	Unc
ND(1903-04)		350	500	750	—	—

Y# A229   5 CASH
Brass   **Ruler:** Kuang-hsü **Obv:** Flower at center **Obv. Leg.:** Szu-ch'uan Sheng Tsao **Obv. Insc.:** Kuang-hsü Yüan-pao **Rev:** Side view dragon **Note:** Prev. Y#A228.

Date	Mintage	VG	F	VF	XF	Unc
ND(1903-04)	Inc. above	100	140	200	300	—

Y# 226   10 CASH
Copper   **Ruler:** Kuang-hsü **Obv:** Thick Manchu in center, large rosettes **Obv. Leg.:** Szu-ch'uan Kuan Chü Tsao **Obv. Insc.:** Kuang-hsü Yüan-pao

Date	Mintage	VG	F	VF	XF	Unc
ND(1903-05)	95,960,000	12.50	25.00	35.00	60.00	—

Y# 226.1   10 CASH
Copper   **Ruler:** Kuang-hsü **Obv:** Thin Manchu in center, small rosettes **Obv. Leg.:** Szu-ch'uan Kuan Chü Tsao **Obv. Insc.:** Kuang-hsü Yüan-pao

Date	Mintage	VG	F	VF	XF	Unc
ND(1903-05)	Inc. above	22.50	45.00	70.00	125	—

Y# 226.2   10 CASH
Copper   **Ruler:** Kuang-hsü **Obv:** Large rosettes **Obv. Leg.:** Szu-ch'uan Kuan Chü Tsao **Obv. Insc.:** Kuang-hsü Yüan-pao

Date	Mintage	VG	F	VF	XF	Unc
ND(1903-05)	Inc. above	20.00	40.00	60.00	100	—

Y# 229   10 CASH
Copper   **Ruler:** Kuang-hsü **Obv:** Legend with two characters at bottom, 6-9mm apart **Obv. Leg.:** Szu-ch'uan Sheng Tsao **Obv. Insc.:** Kuang-hsü Yüan-pao **Rev:** Trident-shaped flame on dragon's body below letters CHU

Date	Mintage	VG	F	VF	XF	Unc
ND(1903-05)	Inc. above	4.00	6.50	10.00	17.50	—

Y# 229.1   10 CASH
Copper   **Ruler:** Kuang-hsü **Obv:** Legend with characters at bottom, 4-5mm apart **Obv. Leg.:** Szu-ch'uan Sheng Tsao **Obv. Insc.:** Kuang-hsü Yüan-pao

Date	Mintage	VG	F	VF	XF	Unc
ND(1903-05)	Inc. above	4.00	6.50	10.00	17.50	—

Y# 229.2   10 CASH
Copper   **Ruler:** Kuang-hsü **Obv:** Manchu at 3 o'clock is lower in relation to center characters **Obv. Leg.:** Szu-ch'uan Sheng Tsao **Obv. Insc.:** Kuang-hsü Yüan-pao

Date	Mintage	VG	F	VF	XF	Unc
ND(1903-05)	Inc. above	4.00	6.50	10.00	17.50	—

Y# 229.3   10 CASH
Copper   **Ruler:** Kuang-hsü **Obv:** Characters 6-9mm apart **Obv. Leg.:** Szu-ch'uan Sheng Tsao **Obv. Insc.:** Kuang-hsü Yüan-pao **Rev:** Trident-shaped flame below letters HUE

Date	Mintage	VG	F	VF	XF	Unc
ND(1903-05)	Inc. above	4.00	6.50	10.00	17.50	—

Y# 229.3a   10 CASH
Brass   **Ruler:** Kuang-hsü **Obv. Leg.:** Szu-ch'uan Sheng Tsao **Obv. Insc.:** Kuang-hsü Yüan-pao

Date	Mintage	VG	F	VF	XF	Unc
ND(1903-05)	Inc. above	4.00	6.50	10.00	17.50	—

Y# 229.4   10 CASH
Brass   **Ruler:** Kuang-hsü **Obv:** Characters 4-5mm apart **Obv. Leg.:** Szu-ch'uan Sheng Tsao **Obv. Insc.:** Kuang-hsü Yüan-pao

Date	Mintage	VG	F	VF	XF	Unc
ND(1903-05)	Inc. above	4.00	6.50	10.00	17.50	—

Y# 229.5   10 CASH
Brass   **Ruler:** Kuang-hsü **Obv:** Bottom characters 6-9mm apart **Obv. Leg.:** Szu-ch'uan Sheng Tsao **Obv. Insc.:** Kuang-hsü Yüan-pao **Rev:** Without trident-shaped flame, instead a cloud pointing to the letter U

Date	Mintage	VG	F	VF	XF	Unc
ND(1903-05)	Inc. above	2.50	4.00	7.50	12.00	—

Y# 229.5a   10 CASH
Copper   **Ruler:** Kuang-hsü **Obv. Leg.:** Szu-ch'uan Sheng Tsao **Obv. Insc.:** Kuang-hsü Yüan-pao

Date	Mintage	VG	F	VF	XF	Unc
ND(1903-05)	Inc. above	3.00	5.00	10.00	15.00	—

Y# 229.6   10 CASH
Brass   **Ruler:** Kuang-hsü **Obv:** Characters 4-5mm apart **Obv. Leg.:** Szu-ch'uan Sheng Tsao **Obv. Insc.:** Kuang-hsü Yüan-pao

Date	Mintage	VG	F	VF	XF	Unc
ND(1903-05)	Inc. above	4.00	6.00	10.00	17.50	—

Y# 229.6a   10 CASH
Copper   **Ruler:** Kuang-hsü **Obv. Leg.:** Szu-ch'uan Sheng Tsao **Obv. Insc.:** Kuang-hsü Yüan-pao

Date	Mintage	VG	F	VF	XF	Unc
ND(1903-05)	Inc. above	2.00	3.00	5.50	10.00	—

Y# 229.7   10 CASH
Brass   **Ruler:** Kuang-hsü **Obv:** Manchu at 3 o'clock is lower **Obv. Leg.:** Szu-ch'uan Sheng Tsao **Obv. Insc.:** Kuang-hsü Yüan-pao

Date	Mintage	VG	F	VF	XF	Unc
ND(1903-05)	Inc. above	3.75	6.00	10.00	17.50	—

Y# 229.7a   10 CASH
Copper   **Ruler:** Kuang-hsü **Obv. Leg.:** Szu-ch'uan Sheng Tsao **Obv. Insc.:** Kuang-hsü Yüan-pao

Date	Mintage	VG	F	VF	XF	Unc
ND(1903-05)	Inc. above	2.00	3.50	6.00	9.00	—

Y# 229.8   10 CASH
Brass   **Ruler:** Kuang-hsü **Obv:** Characters 4-5mm apart **Obv. Leg.:** Szu-ch'uan Sheng Tsao **Obv. Insc.:** Kuang-hsü Yüan-pao **Rev:** Without cloud below CHU, high point of dragon's body below letter "C", tail joins body above "S" in "CASH"

Date	Mintage	VG	F	VF	XF	Unc
ND(1903-05)	Inc. above	4.00	6.00	9.00	17.50	—

Y# 229.8a   10 CASH
Copper   **Ruler:** Kuang-hsü **Obv. Leg.:** Szu-ch'uan Sheng Tsao **Obv. Insc.:** Kuang-hsü Yüan-pao

Date	Mintage	VG	F	VF	XF	Unc
ND(1903-05)	Inc. above	2.00	3.50	6.00	9.00	—

Y# 229.9   10 CASH
Copper   **Ruler:** Kuang-hsü **Obv. Leg.:** Szu-ch'uan Sheng Tsao **Obv. Insc.:** Kuang-hsü Yüan-pao **Rev:** High point of dragon's body below letter H, tail joins body above letter "C" in "CASH"

Date	Mintage	VG	F	VF	XF	Unc
ND(1903-05)	Inc. above	2.00	3.50	6.00	9.00	—

Y# 231   10 CASH
Copper   **Ruler:** Kuang-hsü **Obv. Leg.:** Szu-ch'uan Sheng Tsao **Obv. Insc.:** Kuang-hsü Yüan-pao

Date	Mintage	VG	F	VF	XF	Unc
ND(1903-05)	Inc. above	150	200	225	275	—

Y# 10t 10 CASH
Copper **Ruler:** Kuang-hsü **Obv. Insc.:** Ta-ch'ing T'ung-pi
Rev. Leg.: Kuang-hsü Nien-tsao, TAI-CHING-TI-KUO...

Date	Mintage	VG	F	VF	XF	Unc
CD(1906)	337,748,000	1.00	1.50	3.00	6.00	

Y# 20t.1 10 CASH
Copper **Ruler:** Hsüan-t'ung **Obv:** Bottom of Manchu word at 11 o'clock curls to left **Obv. Insc.:** Ta-ch'ing T'ung-pi
Rev. Leg.: Hsüan-t'ung Nien-tsao, TAI-CHING-TI-KUO...

Date	Mintage	VG	F	VF	XF	Unc
CD(1909)	231,930,000	1.00	1.50	3.00	6.00	

Y# 20t.1a 10 CASH
Brass **Ruler:** Hsüan-t'ung **Obv. Insc.:** Ta-ch'ing T'ung-pi
Rev. Leg.: Hsüan-t'ung Nien-tsao, TAI-CHING-TI-KUO...

Date	Mintage	VG	F	VF	XF	Unc
CD(1909)	Inc. above	3.00	5.00	10.00	15.00	

Y# 20t.2 10 CASH
Copper **Ruler:** Hsüan-t'ung **Obv:** Bottom of Manchu word at 11 o'clock curls to right **Obv. Insc.:** Ta-ch'ing T'ung-pi
Rev. Leg.: Hsüan-t'ung Nien-tsao, TAI-CHING-TI-KUO...

Date	Mintage	VG	F	VF	XF	Unc
CD1909	Inc. above	5.00	9.00	12.00	17.50	

Y# 227 20 CASH
Copper **Ruler:** Kuang-hsü **Obv. Insc.:** Kuang-hsü Yüan-pao

Date	Mintage	VG	F	VF	XF	Unc
ND(1903-05)	25,319,000	100	125	175	250	

Y# 230 20 CASH
Copper **Ruler:** Kuang-hsü **Obv:** Small Manchu at 3 and 9 o'clock **Obv. Leg.:** Szu-ch'uan Sheng Tsao **Obv. Insc.:** Kuang-hsü Yüan-pao **Rev:** Trident flame points to "E" of "SZE"

Date	Mintage	VG	F	VF	XF	Unc
ND(1903-05)	Inc. above	10.00	15.00	30.00	50.00	

Y# 230.1 20 CASH
Copper **Ruler:** Kuang-hsü **Obv:** Large Manchu at 3 and 9 o'clock **Obv. Leg.:** Szu-ch'uan Sheng Tsao **Obv. Insc.:** Kuang-hsü Yüan-pao **Rev:** Large trident flame points to "C" of "CHUEN"
Note: Varieties exist.

Date	Mintage	VG	F	VF	XF	Unc
ND(1903-05)	Inc. above	30.00	50.00	80.00	150	—

Y# 230.3 20 CASH
Copper **Ruler:** Kuang-hsü **Obv:** Large Manchu **Obv. Leg.:** Szu-ch'uan Sheng Tsao **Obv. Insc.:** Kuang-hsü Yüan-pao **Rev:** Trident flame below "ZE"

Date	Mintage	VG	F	VF	XF	Unc
ND(1903-05)	Inc. above	15.00	30.00	50.00	80.00	—

Y# 230.4 20 CASH
Copper **Ruler:** Kuang-hsü **Obv. Leg.:** Szu-ch'uan Sheng Tsao **Obv. Insc.:** Kuang-hsü Yüan-pao **Rev:** Trident flame below "CHU" of "CHUEN", large letters

Date	Mintage	VG	F	VF	XF	Unc
ND(1903-05)	—	30.00	60.00	100	160	—

Y# 230.5 20 CASH
Copper **Ruler:** Kuang-hsü **Obv. Leg.:** Szu-ch'uan Sheng Tsao **Obv. Insc.:** Kuang-hsü Yüan-pao **Rev:** Trident flame points to "E" of "CHUEN", small letters

Date	Mintage	VG	F	VF	XF	Unc
ND(1903-05)	Inc. above					

Y# 230.6 20 CASH
Copper **Ruler:** Kuang-hsü **Obv:** Different small Manchu **Obv. Leg.:** Szu-ch'uan Sheng Tsao **Obv. Insc.:** Kuang-hsü Yüan-pao **Rev:** Large 5-petaled rosettes, dragon differs

Date	Mintage	VG	F	VF	XF	Unc
ND(1903-05)	Inc. above	12.50	20.00	35.00	60.00	—

Y# 230.7a 20 CASH
Brass **Ruler:** Kuang-hsü **Obv:** Small Manchu **Obv. Leg.:** Szu-ch'uan Sheng Tsao **Obv. Insc.:** Kuang-hsü Yüan-pao **Rev:** Larger cloud below "CHUEN"

Date	Mintage	VG	F	VF	XF	Unc
ND(1903-05)	Inc. above	15.00	25.00	40.00	70.00	—

Y# 11t 20 CASH
Copper **Obv. Insc.:** Ta-ch'ing T'ung-pi

Date	Mintage	VG	F	VF	XF	Unc
CD1906	51,028,000	10.00	22.50	35.00	60.00	

Y# 21t.1 20 CASH
Copper **Obv:** Bottom of Manchu word at 11 o'clock curls right **Obv. Insc.:** Ta-ch'ing T'ung-pi

Date	Mintage	VG	F	VF	XF	Unc
CD1909	33,414,000	15.00	27.50	40.00	70.00	

Y# 21t.1a 20 CASH
Brass **Obv. Insc.:** Ta-ch'ing T'ung-pi

Date	Mintage	VG	F	VF	XF	Unc
CD1909	Inc. above	25.00	35.00	65.00	100	—

Y# 21t.2 20 CASH
Copper **Obv:** Bottom of Manchu word at 11 o'clock curls left **Obv. Insc.:** Ta-ch'ing T'ung-pi

Date	Mintage	VG	F	VF	XF	Unc
CD1909		15.00	27.50	40.00	70.00	

Y# 234.1 5 CENTS
1.3000 g., 0.8200 Silver 0.0343 oz. ASW, 15.82 mm. **Ruler:** Kuang-hsü **Obv. Leg.:** Szu-ch'uan Sheng Tsao **Obv. Insc.:** Kuang-hsü Yüan-pao **Rev:** With errors in the English legend **Rev. Leg.:** 8ZECHUEN PROVIN(D inverted) EI? (errors) **Edge:** Reeded

Date	Mintage	VG	F	VF	XF	Unc
ND(1901-08)	Inc. above	5.00	15.00	25.00	50.00	300

Y# 239 5 CENTS
1.3000 g., 0.8200 Silver 0.0343 oz. ASW **Ruler:** Hsüan-t'ung **Obv. Leg.:** Szu-ch'uan Sheng Tsao **Obv. Insc.:** Hsüan-t'ung Yüan-pao

Date	Mintage	VG	F	VF	XF	Unc
ND(1910)	566,000	10.00	25.00	40.00	100	400

Y# 240 10 CENTS
2.6000 g., 0.8200 Silver 0.0685 oz. ASW **Ruler:** Hsüan-t'ung **Obv. Leg.:** Szu-ch'uan Sheng Tsao **Obv. Insc.:** Hsüan-t'ung Yüan-pao

Date	Mintage	VG	F	VF	XF	Unc
ND(1909-11)	278,000	8.50	25.00	30.00	70.00	250

Y# 236.3   20 CENTS
5.3000 g., 0.8200 Silver 0.1397 oz. ASW   **Ruler:** Kuang-hsü
Obv. Leg.: Szu-ch'uan Sheng Tsao **Obv. Insc.:** Kuang-hsü
Yüan-pao **Rev:** Various errors in English legend

Date	Mintage	VG	F	VF	XF	Unc
ND(1901-08)	Inc. above	5.00	15.00	25.00	50.00	200

Y# 241   20 CENTS
5.3000 g., 0.8200 Silver 0.1397 oz. ASW   **Ruler:** Hsüan-t'ung
Obv. Leg.: Szu-ch'uan Sheng-Tsao **Obv. Insc.:** Hsüan-t'ung Yüan-pao

Date	Mintage	VG	F	VF	XF	Unc
ND(1909-11) Rare	41,000	—	—	—	—	—

Y# 237.1   50 CENTS
13.2000 g., 0.8600 Silver 0.3650 oz. ASW   **Ruler:** Kuang-hsü
Obv. Leg.: Szu-ch'uan Sheng Tsao **Obv. Insc.:** Kuang-hsü
Yüan-pao **Rev:** Various errors in English legend

Date	Mintage	VG	F	VF	XF	Unc
ND(1901-08)	Inc. above	15.00	30.00	75.00	150	700

Y# 237.2   50 CENTS
13.2000 g., 0.8600 Silver 0.3650 oz. ASW   **Ruler:** Kuang-hsü
Obv. Leg.: Szu-ch'uan Sheng Tsao **Obv. Insc.:** Kuang-hsü
Yüan-pao **Rev:** Dragon with tapering face and small chin, small
fireball, small cross at either side of dragon

Date	Mintage	VG	F	VF	XF	Unc
ND(1901-08)	Inc. above	12.50	25.00	50.00	135	600

Y# 237.3   50 CENTS
13.2000 g., 0.8600 Silver 0.3650 oz. ASW   **Ruler:** Kuang-hsü
Obv. Leg.: Szu-ch'uan Sheng Tsao **Obv. Insc.:** Kuang-hsü Yüan-
pao **Rev:** Dragon with wide face and smaller fireball, thicker spines
on top of dragon's head, small cross at either side of dragon

Date	Mintage	VG	F	VF	XF	Unc
ND(1901-08)	Inc. above	12.50	25.00	50.00	135	600

Y# 242   50 CENTS
13.2000 g., 0.8600 Silver 0.3650 oz. ASW   **Ruler:** Hsüan-t'ung
Obv. Leg.: Szu-ch'uan Sheng Tsao **Obv. Insc.:** Hsüan-t'ung
Yüan-pao

Date	Mintage	VG	F	VF	XF	Unc
ND(1909-11)	38,000	30.00	85.00	150	300	1,000

Y# 242.1   50 CENTS
13.2000 g., 0.8600 Silver 0.3650 oz. ASW   **Ruler:** Hsüan-t'ung
Obv. Leg.: Szu-ch'uan Sheng Tsao **Obv. Insc.:** Hsüan-t'ung Yüan-
pao **Rev:** Inverted "A" in place of "V" in "PROVINCE" in legend

Date	Mintage	VG	F	VF	XF	Unc
ND(1901-11)	Inc. above	30.00	85.00	150	300	1,000

Y# 238   DOLLAR
26.8000 g., 0.9000 Silver 0.7754 oz. ASW   **Ruler:** Kuang-hsü
Obv. Leg.: Szu-ch'uan Sheng Tsao **Obv. Insc.:** Kuang-hsü
Yüan-pao **Rev:** Dragon with narrow face and large fireball, small
cross at either side of dragon

Date	Mintage	VG	F	VF	XF	Unc
ND(1901-08)	6,487,000	15.00	25.00	37.50	85.00	2,000

Y# 238.1   DOLLAR
26.8000 g., 0.9000 Silver 0.7754 oz. ASW   **Ruler:** Kuang-hsü
Obv. Leg.: Szu-ch'uan Sheng Tsao **Obv. Insc.:** Kuang-hsü Yüan-
pao **Rev:** Inverted "A" instead of "V" in "PROVINCE" in legend

Date	Mintage	VG	F	VF	XF	Unc
ND(1901-08)	Inc. above	15.00	25.00	35.00	80.00	2,000

Y# 238.2   DOLLAR
26.8000 g., 0.9000 Silver 0.7754 oz. ASW   **Ruler:** Kuang-hsü
Obv. Insc.: Kuang-hsü Yüan-pao **Rev:** Dragon with wider face
and flatter pearl, small cross at either side of dragon

Date	Mintage	VG	F	VF	XF	Unc
ND(1901-08)	Inc. above	15.00	20.00	30.00	80.00	2,000

Y# 238.3   DOLLAR
26.8000 g., 0.9000 Silver 0.7754 oz. ASW   **Ruler:** Kuang-hsü
Obv. Leg.: Szu-ch'uan Sheng Tsao **Obv. Insc.:** Kuang-hsü
Yüan-pao **Rev:** "7 MACE" and "3 CANDAREENS" instead of "2
CANDAREENS"

Date	Mintage	VG	F	VF	XF	Unc
ND(1901-08)	Inc. above	20.00	40.00	80.00	175	3,000

Y# 243   DOLLAR
26.8000 g., 0.9000 Silver 0.7754 oz. ASW   **Ruler:** Hsüan-t'ung
Obv. Leg.: Szu-ch'uan Sheng Tsao **Obv. Insc.:** Hsüan-t'ung
Yüan-pao **Rev:** Large spines on dragon's body

Date	Mintage	VG	F	VF	XF	Unc
ND(1909-11)	2,846,000	15.00	25.00	45.00	100	2,500

Y# 243.1   DOLLAR
26.8000 g., 0.9000 Silver 0.7754 oz. ASW   **Ruler:** Hsüan-t'ung
Obv. Leg.: Szu-ch'uan Sheng Tsao **Obv. Insc.:** Hsüan-t'ung
Yüan-pao **Rev:** Inverted "A" instead of "V" in "PROVINCE"

Date	Mintage	VG	F	VF	XF	Unc
ND(1909-11)	Inc. above	15.00	25.00	50.00	120	2,200

Y# 243.2   DOLLAR
26.8000 g., 0.9000 Silver 0.7754 oz. ASW   **Ruler:** Hsüan-t'ung
Obv. Leg.: Szu-ch'uan Sheng Tsao **Obv. Insc.:** Hsüan-t'ung
Yüan-pao **Rev:** Small spines on dragon's body

Date	Mintage	VG	F	VF	XF	Unc
ND(1909-11)	Inc. above	25.00	65.00	100	200	2,500

REPUBLIC
CUT MILLED COINAGE

Y# 459y   50 CASH
Brass **Note:** 200 Cash, Y#459 cut into quarters.

Date	Mintage	VG	F	VF	XF	Unc
2(1913)	—	30.00	35.00	40.00	50.00	—

Y# 459x   100 CASH
Copper Or Brass **Note:** 200 Cash, Y#459 cut in half.

Date	Mintage	VG	F	VF	XF	Unc
2(1913)	—	3.50	9.50	17.00	45.00	—

MILLED COINAGE

Y# 466   100 CASH
Copper **Obv. Leg.:** "Chung Hua Min Kuo Nien" - (Years)
Obv. Insc.: Ch'uan **Note:** Beware of modern forgeries

Date	Mintage	VG	F	VF	XF	Unc
15 (1926)	—	150	225	300	400	—
19 (1930)	—	125	150	200	300	—

Y# 466a   100 CASH
Brass **Obv. Leg.:** CHUNG HUA MIN KUO NIEN (Years)
Obv. Insc.: Ch'uan **Rev:** Manchu "Boo-yuan" with Chinese "K'u"
(for Kuche) above **Note:** Beware of modern forgeries

Date	Mintage	VG	F	VF	XF	Unc
19 (1930)	—	125	150	225	375	—

DECIMAL COINAGE

Y# 441a   5 CASH
Brass **Obv:** Crossed flags **Obv. Leg.:** Chung Hua Min Kuo (year)
Nien **Rev:** Lion standing left

Date	Mintage	VG	F	VF	XF	Unc
1(1912)	Inc. above	—	—	—	—	—

Y# 441b   5 CASH
Silver **Obv:** Crossed flags **Obv. Leg.:** Chung Hua Min Kuo (year)
Nien **Rev:** Lion standing left

Date	Mintage	VG	F	VF	XF	Unc
1(1912)	—	—	—	1,000	1,500	—

Note: Modern forgeries of Y#441 in copper and of Y#441b
in silver exist

Y# 443   5 CASH
Copper **Obv. Leg.:** Chung Hua Min Kuo (year) Nien

Date	Mintage	VG	F	VF	XF	Unc
1(1912)	Inc. above	35.00	70.00	110	150	—

Y# 443a   5 CASH
Brass **Obv. Leg.:** Chung Hua Min Kuo (year) Nien

Date	Mintage	VG	F	VF	XF	Unc
1(1912) Rare	—	—	—	—	—	—

Y# 446   5 CASH
Copper   **Obv. Leg.:** Chung Hua Min Kuo (year) Nien

Date	Mintage	VG	F	VF	XF	Unc
1(1912) Rare	Inc. above	—	—	—	—	—

Y# 446a   5 CASH
Brass   **Obv:** Chung Hua Min Kuo (year) Nien

Date	Mintage	VG	F	VF	XF	Unc
1(1912) Rare	Inc. above	—	—	—	—	—

Y# 441   5 CASH
Copper   **Obv:** Crossed flags **Obv. Leg.:** Chung Hua Min Kuo (year) Nien **Rev:** Lion standing left **Note:** Varieties exist.

Date	Mintage	VG	F	VF	XF	Unc
1(1912)	471,000	40.00	80.00	130	250	—

Y# 447   10 CASH
Copper   **Obv:** Two rosettes **Obv. Leg.:** Chung Hua Min Kuo (year) Nien

Date	Mintage	VG	F	VF	XF	Unc
1(1912)	108,618,000	1.75	3.00	10.00	20.00	—
2(1913)	Inc. above	6.00	15.00	25.00	50.00	—

Y# 447a   10 CASH
Brass   **Obv. Leg.:** Chung Hua Min Kuo (year) Nien

Date	Mintage	VG	F	VF	XF	Unc
1(1912)	Inc. above	0.80	1.50	2.50	5.00	—
2(1913)	Inc. above	1.65	4.00	8.00	20.00	—

Y# 447.1a   10 CASH
Brass   **Obv:** Three rosettes **Obv. Leg.:** Chung Hua Min Kuo (year) Nien

Date	Mintage	VG	F	VF	XF	Unc
2(1913) Rare	Inc. above	—	—	—	—	—

Y# 475   10 CASH
Red Copper   **Obv:** Characters in five-petaled flower **Obv. Leg.:** Chung Hua Min Kuo (year) Nien **Rev:** Denomination above sun

Date	Mintage	VG	F	VF	XF	Unc
19(1930) Rare	—	—	—	—	—	—

Y# 448   20 CASH
Copper, 32 mm.   **Obv:** Two rosettes **Obv. Leg.:** Chung Hua Min Kuo (year) Nien

Date	Mintage	VG	F	VF	XF	Unc
1(1912)	115,061,000	1.00	2.50	5.00	15.00	—

Note: Character for "first" instead of number one in date

Y# 448a   20 CASH
Brass, 32 mm.   **Obv. Leg.:** Chung Hua Min Kuo (year) Nien

Date	Mintage	VG	F	VF	XF	Unc
1(1912)	Inc. above	0.75	1.50	2.50	6.00	—
2(1913)	Inc. above	1.00	2.00	3.50	7.00	—

Note: Character for "first" instead of number one in date

Y# 448.1   20 CASH
Copper, 32 mm.   **Obv:** Three rosettes

Date	Mintage	VG	F	VF	XF	Unc
2(1913)	Inc. above	250	350	450	800	—
3(1914)	Inc. above	250	350	450	800	—

Y# 448.1a   20 CASH
Brass, 32 mm.   **Obv. Leg.:** Chung Hua Min Kuo (year) Nien

Date	Mintage	VG	F	VF	XF	Unc
2(1913)	Inc. above	2.50	6.00	12.00	25.00	—
3(1914)	Inc. above	2.50	6.00	12.00	25.00	—

Note: There are many varieties of this 20 Cash; small and large rosettes; open and closed size characters and exaggerated size character with horns

Y# 449   50 CASH
Copper, 36 mm.   **Obv. Leg.:** Chung Hua Min Kuo (year) Nien **Rev:** Small flower in center

Date	Mintage	VG	F	VF	XF	Unc
1(1912)	489,382,000	2.00	4.00	7.00	15.00	—

Y# 449a   50 CASH
Brass, 36 mm.   **Obv. Leg.:** Chung Hua Min Kuo (year) Nien

Date	Mintage	VG	F	VF	XF	Unc
1(1912)	Inc. above	1.50	3.50	6.00	10.00	—

Y# 449.1   50 CASH
Copper, 36 mm.   **Obv. Leg.:** Chung Hua Min Kuo (year) Nien **Rev:** Larger flower in center

Date	Mintage	VG	F	VF	XF	Unc
1(1912)	Inc. above	2.00	5.00	10.00	20.00	—

Y# 449.1a   50 CASH
Brass, 36 mm.   **Obv. Leg.:** Chung Hua Min Kuo (year) Nien

Date	Mintage	VG	F	VF	XF	Unc
1(1912)	Inc. above	2.50	6.00	12.50	25.00	—

Note: A Yr. 7 is reported, but its authenticity is not verified

Y# 449.2   50 CASH
Copper, 36 mm.   **Obv:** Three rosettes **Obv. Leg.:** Chung Hua Min Kuo (year) Nien **Rev:** Small flower in center

Date	Mintage	VG	F	VF	XF	Unc
2(1913)	Inc. above	2.25	5.50	11.00	22.00	—

Y# 449.2a   50 CASH
Brass, 36 mm.   **Obv. Leg.:** Chung Hua Min Kuo (year) Nien

Date	Mintage	VG	F	VF	XF	Unc
2(1913)	Inc. above	2.25	5.50	11.00	22.00	—
3(1914)	Inc. above	2.25	5.50	11.00	22.00	—

Y# 462   50 CASH
Copper   **Obv. Leg.:** Chung Hua Min Kuo (year) Nien

Date	Mintage	VG	F	VF	XF	Unc
15(1926)	90,000	18.50	35.00	65.00	100	—

Y# 462a   50 CASH
Brass   **Obv. Leg.:** Chung Hua Min Kuo (year) Nien

Date	Mintage	VG	F	VF	XF	Unc
15(1926)	Inc. above	16.50	32.50	55.00	80.00	—

Y# 450   100 CASH
Copper, 39 mm.   **Obv:** Two rosettes **Obv. Leg.:** Chung Hua Min Kuo (year) Nien **Rev:** Large flower in center

Date	Mintage	VG	F	VF	XF	Unc
2(1913)	399,212,000	2.50	6.00	8.50	17.50	—
3(1914)	—	30.00	40.00	50.00	60.00	—

Y# 450a   100 CASH
Brass, 39 mm.   **Obv. Leg.:** Chung Hua Min Kuo (year) Nien

Date	Mintage	VG	F	VF	XF	Unc
2(1913)	Inc. above	1.50	3.00	6.00	10.00	—

Y# 450.1 100 CASH
Copper, 39 mm. **Obv:** Three rosettes **Obv. Leg.:** Chung Hua Min Kuo (year) Nien **Rev:** Small flower in center

Date	Mintage	VG	F	VF	XF	Unc
2(1913)	Inc. above	3.50	9.00	15.00	25.00	—
3(1914)						

Y# 463.1 100 CASH
Copper **Obv. Leg.:** Chung Hua Min Kuo (year) Nien **Rev:** Large value "100", large leaves

Date	Mintage	VG	F	VF	XF	Unc
15(1926)	7,055,000	3.50	9.00	15.00	25.00	—

Y# 463a.1 100 CASH
Brass **Obv. Leg.:** Chung Hua Min Kuo (year) Nien **Rev:** Large value "100", large leaves

Date	Mintage	VG	F	VF	XF	Unc
15(1926)	Inc. above	3.25	8.00	12.50	20.00	—

Y# 463.2 100 CASH
Copper **Obv. Leg.:** Chung Hua Min Kuo (year) Nien **Rev:** Small value "100", small leaves

Date	Mintage	VG	F	VF	XF	Unc
15(1926)	Inc. above	3.50	9.00	15.00	25.00	—

Y# 463a.2 100 CASH
Brass **Obv. Leg.:** Chung Hua Min Kuo (year) Nien **Rev:** Small value "100", small leaves

Date	Mintage	VG	F	VF	XF	Unc
15(1926)	Inc. above	3.25	8.00	12.50	20.00	—

Y# 459a 200 CASH
Brass **Obv:** Flowers **Obv. Leg.:** Chung Hua Min Kuo (year) Nien **Rev:** Crossed flags, short tassels **Rev. Leg.:** THE REPUBLIC OF CHINA

Date	Mintage	VG	F	VF	XF	Unc
2(1913)	—	20.00	40.00	80.00	125	—

Y# 459.1 200 CASH
Copper **Obv:** Flowers **Obv. Leg.:** Chung Hua Min Kuo (year) Nien **Rev:** Crossed flags, long tassels **Rev. Leg.:** THE REPUBLIC OF CHINA

Date	Mintage	VG	F	VF	XF	Unc
2(1913)	Inc. above	6.00	10.00	25.00	40.00	—

Y# 459.1a 200 CASH
Brass **Obv:** Flowers **Obv. Leg.:** Chung Hua Min Kuo (year) Nien **Rev:** Crossed flags, long tassels **Rev. Leg.:** THE REPUBLIC OF CHINA

Date	Mintage	VG	F	VF	XF	Unc
2(1913)	—	4.50	8.00	20.00	35.00	—

Y# 459.2 200 CASH
Copper **Obv:** Flowers **Obv. Leg.:** Chung Hua Min Kuo (year) Nien **Rev:** Crossed flags **Rev. Leg.:** THE REPUBLIC OF CHINA

Date	Mintage	VG	F	VF	XF	Unc
2(1913)	Inc. above	5.00	9.00	22.50	37.50	—

Note: For cut segments refer to 50 Cash, Y#459y and 100 Cash, Y#459x.

Y# 459 200 CASH
Copper **Obv:** Flowers **Obv. Leg.:** Chung Hua Min Kuo (year) Nien **Rev:** Crossed flags, short tassels **Rev. Leg.:** THE REPUBLIC OF CHINA

Date	Mintage	VG	F	VF	XF	Unc
2(1913) Rare	—	—	—	—	—	—

Y# 464.2 200 CASH
Brass **Obv:** Similar to Y#464 **Obv. Leg.:** Chung Hua Min Kuo (year) Nien **Obv. Insc:** Ch'uan **Rev:** Dot within first 0 of 200

Date	Mintage	VG	F	VF	XF	Unc
15(1926)	Inc. above					

Note: Many varieties: open and closed buds; overstruck on earlier pieces and on virgin flans; different sizes and thicknesses

Y# 464 200 CASH
Copper **Obv. Leg.:** Chung Hua Min Kuo (year) Nien **Obv. Insc.:** Ch'uan **Edge:** Plain

Date	Mintage	VG	F	VF	XF	Unc
15(1926)	404,644,000	4.00	12.00	17.00	35.00	—

Y# 464a 200 CASH
Brass **Obv. Leg.:** Chung Hua Min Kuo (year) Nien **Obv. Insc.:** Ch'uan **Edge:** Plain

Date	Mintage	VG	F	VF	XF	Unc
15(1926)	Inc. above	4.50	12.00	17.00	35.00	—

Y# 464.1 200 CASH
Copper **Obv. Leg.:** Chung Hua Min Kuo (year) Nien **Obv. Insc.:** Ch'uan **Edge:** Reeded

Date	Mintage	VG	F	VF	XF	Unc
15(1926)	Inc. above	6.00	15.00	25.00	45.00	—

Y# 464.1a 200 CASH
Brass **Obv. Leg.:** Chung Hua Min Kuo (year) Nien **Obv. Insc.:** Ch'uan **Edge:** Reeded

Date	Mintage	VG	F	VF	XF	Unc
15(1926)	Inc. above	—	—	—	—	—

Y# 476 2 CENTS
Copper **Obv. Leg.:** Chung Hua Min Kuo (year) Nien

Date	Mintage	VG	F	VF	XF	Unc
19(1930) Rare	—	—	—	—	—	—

Y# 476a 2 CENTS
Brass **Obv. Leg.:** Chung Hua Min Kuo (year) Nien

Date	Mintage	VG	F	VF	XF	Unc
19(1930)	—	—	—	—	—	—

Y# 453 10 CENTS
2.6000 g., Silver **Obv. Leg.:** Chung Hua Min Kuo (year) Nien

Date	Mintage	VG	F	VF	XF	Unc
1(1912)	370,000	8.50	25.00	40.00	100	200

Y# 468 10 CENTS
Copper-Nickel **Obv. Leg.:** Chung Hua Min Kuo (year) Nien

Date	Mintage	VG	F	VF	XF	Unc
ND(ca.1926)	—	4.50	12.50	20.00	45.00	70.00

Y# 468a 10 CENTS
Silver **Obv. Leg.:** Chung Hua Min Kuo (year) Nien

Date	Mintage	VG	F	VF	XF	Unc
ND(ca.1926)	—	12.00	35.00	75.00	125	200

Y# 468b 10 CENTS
Iron **Obv. Leg.:** Chung Hua Min Kuo (year) Nien

Date	Mintage	VG	F	VF	XF	Unc
ND(ca.1926)	—	6.50	20.00	50.00	70.00	125

Y# 454 20 CENTS
5.2000 g., Silver **Obv. Leg.:** Chung Hua Min Kuo (year) Nien

Date	Mintage	VG	F	VF	XF	Unc
1(1912)	95,000	17.00	50.00	100	250	500

K# 795 20 CENTS
5.2000 g., Silver, 25 mm. **Subject:** Sikang Szechuan Army in the Tibetan War **Obv:** Bust of governor Liu Wen-hwei of Szechuan facing **Obv. Leg.:** Chung Hua Min Kuo (year) Nien **Rev:** Crossed flags

Date	Mintage	VG	F	VF	XF	Unc
1932	—	3,000	5,000	6,000	7,500	18,000

Y# 455 50 CENTS
12.9000 g., Silver **Obv. Leg.:** Chung Hua Min Kuo (year) Nien

Date	Mintage	VG	F	VF	XF	Unc
1(1912)	37,942,000	7.50	15.00	25.00	50.00	125
2(1913) Rare	Inc. above	—	—	—	—	—

Y# 473   50 CENTS
10.5000 g., Silver **Subject:** Sun Yat-sen **Obv. Leg.:** Chung Hua
Min Kuo (year) Nien

Date	Mintage	VG	F	VF	XF	Unc
17(1928)	Inc. above	—	—	—	—	—

Y# 456   DOLLAR
25.6000 g., Silver **Obv. Leg.:** Chung Hua Min Kuo (year) Nien

Date	Mintage	VG	F	VF	XF	Unc
1(1912)	55,670,000	10.00	14.00	22.00	55.00	350
2(1913) Rare	Inc. above	—	—	—	—	—

Y# 456.1   DOLLAR
25.6000 g., Silver **Obv. Leg.:** Chung Hua Min Kuo (year) Nien
Rev: Right hand character with two dots instead of horizontal stroke

Date	Mintage	VG	F	VF	XF	Unc
1(1912)	Inc. above	12.00	25.00	50.00	100	550

Note: Silver content ranged from 0.880 to 0.500 fine

Y# 474   DOLLAR
25.5000 g., Silver **Subject:** Sun Yat-sen **Obv. Leg.:** Chung Hua
Min Kuo (year) Nien

Date	Mintage	VG	F	VF	XF	Unc
17(1928)	Inc. above	—	—	—	—	—

PATTERNS
Including off metal strikes

KM#	Date	Mintage	Identification	Mkt Val
Pn16	ND(ca.1901)	—	20 Cents. Aluminum. Dragon type.	—
Pn17	ND(1902)	—	5 Cents. Brass. K#149y	200
Pn18	ND(1902)	—	10 Cents. Brass. K#148y	250
Pn19	ND(1902)	—	20 Cents. Brass. K#147y	300
Pn20	ND(1902)	—	50 Cents. Brass. K#146y	400
Pn21	ND(1902)	—	Dollar. Brass. K#145y	800
Pn22	CD1906	—	2 Cash. Copper. Y#8t	—
Pn23	CD1906	—	5 Cash. Copper. Y#9t	—
Pn24	CD1908	—	Cash. Brass. Y#7t	200
Pn25	CD1908	—	5 Cash. Brass.	—
Pn26	ND(ca.1912)	—	10 Cents. Copper.	—
Pn27	1(1912)	—	50 Cents. Copper. Y#455	—
Pn28	ND(ca.1926)	—	10 Cents. Brass. Y#468	—
Pn29	17(1928)	—	Dollar. Copper. Y#474	—
Pn30	ND(1941)	—	50 Cents. Temple. Spade. World War II	—

YUNNAN PROVINCE

A province located in south China bordering Burma, Laos and
Vietnam. It is very mountainous with many lakes. Yunnan was the
home of various active imperial mints. A modern mint was established at Kunming in 1905 and the first struck copper coins were
issued in 1906 and the first struck silver coins in 1908. General Tang
Chi-yao issued coins in gold, silver and copper with his portrait in
1919. The last Republican coins were struck here in 1949.

EMPIRE

PROVINCIAL CAST COINAGE

C# 27-6   CASH
Cast Brass **Ruler:** Kuang-hsü **Obv. Insc.:** Kuang-hsü T'ung-
pao **Rev:** Manchu inscription **Rev. Insc.:** Boo-dong

Date	Mintage	Good	VG	F	VF	XF
ND(1875-1908)	—	4.00	6.50	9.00	15.00	—

C# 26-9   CASH
Cast Brass **Ruler:** Kuang-hsü **Obv. Insc.:** Kuang-hsü T'ung-
pao **Rev:** Manchu inscription **Rev. Insc.:** Boo-yôn

Date	Mintage	Good	VG	F	VF	XF
ND(1875-1908)	—	2.00	4.00	6.50	9.00	—

C# 26-9.1   CASH
Cast Brass **Ruler:** Kuang-hsü **Obv. Insc.:** Kuang-hsü T'ung-
pao **Rev:** Manchu inscription, "Kung" above **Rev. Insc.:** Boo-yôn

Date	Mintage	Good	VG	F	VF	XF
ND(1875-1908)	—	2.00	5.00	7.50	10.00	—

C# 26-9.2   CASH
Cast Brass **Ruler:** Kuang-hsü **Obv. Insc.:** Kuang-hsü T'ung-pao
Rev: Manchu inscription, "Szu" (four) above **Rev. Insc.:** Boo-yôn

Date	Mintage	Good	VG	F	VF	XF
ND(1875-1908)	—	2.50	5.00	7.50	10.00	—

C# 26-9.3   CASH
Cast Brass **Ruler:** Kuang-hsü **Obv. Insc.:** Kuang-hsü T'ung-
pao **Rev:** Manchu inscription, "Chin" above **Rev. Insc.:** Boo-yôn

Date	Mintage	Good	VG	F	VF	XF
ND(1875-1908)	—	2.50	5.00	7.50	10.00	—

C# 26-9.4   CASH
Cast Brass **Ruler:** Kuang-hsü **Obv. Insc.:** Kuang-hsü T'ung-
pao **Rev:** Manchu inscription, crescent above, dot below
Rev. Insc.: Boo-yôn

Date	Mintage	Good	VG	F	VF	XF
ND(1875-1908)	—	2.50	5.00	7.50	12.00	—

C# 26-9.5   CASH
Cast Brass **Ruler:** Kuang-hsü **Obv. Insc.:** Kuang-hsü T'ung-
pao **Rev:** Manchu inscription, dot above hole **Rev. Insc.:** Boo-yôn

Date	Mintage	Good	VG	F	VF	XF
ND(1875-1908)	—	2.50	5.00	7.50	12.00	—

C# 27-6.1   CASH
Cast Brass **Ruler:** Kuang-hsü **Obv. Insc.:** Kuang-hsü T'ung-
pao **Rev:** Manchu inscription, "Chin" above **Rev. Insc.:** Boo-dong

Date	Mintage	Good	VG	F	VF	XF
ND(1875-1908)	—	5.00	7.50	10.00	15.00	—

C# 27-6.2   CASH
Cast Brass **Ruler:** Kuang-hsü **Obv. Insc.:** Kuang-hsü T'ung-pao
Rev: Manchu inscription, "Ts'un" below **Rev. Insc.:** Boo-dong

Date	Mintage	Good	VG	F	VF	XF
ND(1875-1908)	—	5.00	7.50	10.00	15.00	—

C# 27-7   CASH
Cast Brass **Ruler:** Hsüan-t'ung **Obv. Insc.:** Hsuan-t'ung T'ung-
pao **Rev:** "Ts'un" below inscription **Rev. Insc.:** Manchu Boo-dong

Date	Mintage	Good	VG	F	VF	XF
ND(1909-11) Rare	—	—	—	—	—	—

C# 26-11   CASH
Cast Brass **Ruler:** Hsüan-t'ung **Obv. Insc.:** Hsuan-t'ung T'ung-
pao **Rev:** "Kung" above hole **Rev. Insc.:** Manchu Boo-yôn
Note: Struck at Yün Mint (Yünnanfu).

Date	Mintage	Good	VG	F	VF	XF
ND(1909-11)	—	75.00	100	150	220	—

C# 26-12   CASH
Cast Brass **Ruler:** Hsüan-t'ung **Obv. Insc.:** Hsuan-t'ung T'ung-
pao **Rev:** "Shan" above hole **Rev. Insc.:** Manchu Boo-yôn

Date	Mintage	Good	VG	F	VF	XF
ND(1909-11)	—	30.00	40.00	50.00	100	—

C# 26-13   CASH
Cast Brass **Ruler:** Hsüan-t'ung **Obv. Insc.:** Hsuan-t'ung T'ung-
pao **Rev:** Without character above hole **Rev. Insc.:** Manchu Boo-
yôn

Date	Mintage	Good	VG	F	VF	XF
ND(1909-11)	—	35.00	45.00	55.00	100	—

MILLED COINAGE

Y# 10u   10 CASH
Copper **Obv:** Inscription: Tai-ching T'ung-pi with large mint mark
"Yun" in center **Rev:** Side view dragon

Date	Mintage	VG	F	VF	XF	Unc
CD1906	36,701,000	10.00	22.00	35.00	60.00	—

Y# 10u.1   10 CASH
Copper **Obv:** Inscription with small mint mark "Yun" in center
Obv. Insc.: Tai-ching T'ung-pi **Rev:** Side view dragon

Date	Mintage	VG	F	VF	XF	Unc
CD1906	Inc. above	25.00	55.00	85.00	125	—

Y# 10v   10 CASH

Copper   **Obv:** Inscription with mint mark "Tien" in center
Obv. Insc.: Tai-ching T'ung-pi   **Rev:** Side view dragon

Date	Mintage	VG	F	VF	XF	Unc
CD1906	Inc. above	12.50	30.00	40.00	65.00	—

Y# 11u   20 CASH

Copper   **Obv:** Inscription with large mint mark "Yun" in center
Obv. Insc.: Tai-ching T'ung-pi   **Rev:** Side view dragon

Date	Mintage	VG	F	VF	XF	Unc
CD1906	645,000	125	175	225	275	—

Y# 11u.1   20 CASH

Copper   **Obv:** Inscription with small mint mark "Yun" in center
Obv. Insc.: Tai-ching T'ung-pi   **Rev:** Side view dragon

Date	Mintage	VG	F	VF	XF	Unc
CD1906	—	150	275	400	550	—

Y# 11v.1   20 CASH

Copper   **Obv:** Inscription with mint mark "Tien" in center
Obv. Insc.: Tai-ching T'ung-pi   **Rev:** Side view dragon

Date	Mintage	VG	F	VF	XF	Unc
CD1906	Inc. above	150	275	400	550	—

Y# 11v.1a   20 CASH

Brass   **Obv. Insc.:** Tai-ching T'ung-pi   **Rev:** Side view dragon

Date	Mintage	VG	F	VF	XF	Unc
CD1906	Inc. above	175	350	450	600	—

Y# 252   20 CENTS

Brass   **Ruler:** Kuang-hsü   **Obv. Leg.:** Yün-nan Sheng Tsao
Obv. Insc.: Kuang-hsü Yüan-pao   **Rev:** Side view dragon
Note: Many minor varieties.

Date	Mintage	VG	F	VF	XF	Unc
ND(1908)	532,000	6.00	18.50	35.00	60.00	125

Y# 253   50 CENTS

13.2000 g., 0.8000 Silver 0.3395 oz. ASW   **Ruler:** Kuang-hsü
Obv. Insc.: Kuang-hsü Yüan-pao   **Obv. Insc.:** Kuang-hsü Yüan-pao   **Rev:** Side view dragon

Date	Mintage	VG	F	VF	XF	Unc
ND(1908)	—	6.50	9.00	16.00	25.00	300

Y# 259   50 CENTS

13.2000 g., 0.8000 Silver 0.3395 oz. ASW   **Ruler:** Hsüan-t'ung
Obv. Leg.: Yün-nan Sheng Tsao   **Obv. Insc.:** Hsüan-t'ung-pao
Rev: Side view dragon; seven flames on pearl

Date	Mintage	VG	F	VF	XF	Unc
ND(1909-11)	—	6.50	9.00	16.50	27.50	300

Y# 259.1   50 CENTS

13.2000 g., 0.8000 Silver 0.3395 oz. ASW   **Ruler:** Hsüan-t'ung
Obv. Leg.: Yün-nan Sheng Tsao   **Obv. Insc.:** Hsüan-t'ung-pao
Rev: Side view dragon; nine flames on pearl

Date	Mintage	VG	F	VF	XF	Unc
ND(1909-11)	—	8.00	15.00	20.00	30.00	250

Y# 254   DOLLAR

26.8000 g., 0.9000 Silver 0.7754 oz. ASW   **Ruler:** Kuang-hsü
Obv. Leg.: Yün-nan Sheng Tsao   **Obv. Insc.:** Kuang-hsü Yüan-pao   **Rev:** Side view dragon

Date	Mintage	VG	F	VF	XF	Unc
ND(1908)	—	22.00	35.00	80.00	150	1,300

Y# 260   DOLLAR

26.8000 g., 0.9000 Silver 0.7754 oz. ASW   **Ruler:** Hsüan-t'ung
Obv. Leg.: Yün-nan Sheng Tsao   **Obv. Insc.:** Hsüan-t'ung T'ung-pao   **Rev:** Side view dragon

Date	Mintage	VG	F	VF	XF	Unc
ND(1909-11)	—	30.00	45.00	70.00	125	1,100

Y# 260.1   DOLLAR

26.8000 g., 0.9000 Silver 0.7754 oz. ASW   **Ruler:** Hsüan-t'ung
Obv. Leg.: Yün-nan Sheng Tsao   **Obv. Insc.:** Hsüan-t'ung T'ung-pao   **Rev:** Side view dragon

Date	Mintage	VG	F	VF	XF	Unc
CD1910 Rare	—	—	—	—	—	—

REPUBLIC

TRANSITIONAL COINAGE

In the name of the Republic

KM# 5   CASH

Cast Copper Or Brass   **Obv. Insc.:** Min-kuo T'ung-pao
Rev: Inscription **Rev. Insc.:** Tung-ch'uan

Date	Mintage	Good	VG	F	VF	XF
ND(1912)	—	10.00	20.00	50.00	100	—

KM# 5a   CASH

Cast Copper Or Brass   **Obv. Insc.:** Min-kuo T'ung-pao
Rev: Inscription **Rev. Insc.:** Boo-yôn

Date	Mintage	Good	VG	F	VF	XF
ND(1912)	—	100	125	180	—	—

KM# 4   10 CASH

Brass   **Obv. Insc.:** Min-kuo T'ung-pao

Date	Mintage	Good	VG	F	VF	XF
ND(1912)	—	15.00	25.00	55.00	100	—

RESTRUCK IMPERIAL COINAGE

The following imperial coins are reign-dated 1875-1908.
These coins were apparently restruck from previously unused dies at intervals from 1911 through to 1949, and with
a progressively reduced silver content. The dates and silver
content shown are approximate.

Y# 255   10 CENTS

2.6500 g., 0.6500 Silver 0.0554 oz. ASW   **Obv. Leg.:** Yün-nan
Sheng Tsao **Obv. Insc.:** Kuang-hsü Yüan-pao   **Rev:** Side view
dragon with two circles beneath pearl

Date	Mintage	VG	F	VF	XF	Unc
ND(1911-15)	902,000	5.00	15.00	30.00	45.00	120

Y# 256   20 CENTS

5.3000 g.; 0.8000 Silver 0.1363 oz. ASW **Obv. Leg.:** Yün-nan
Sheng Tsao **Obv. Insc.:** Kuang-hsü Yüan-pao **Rev:** Side view
dragon with two circles beneath pearl

Date	Mintage	VG	F	VF	XF	Unc
ND(1911-15)	—	4.50	12.50	17.50	32.50	75.00

Y# 256a   20 CENTS

5.3000 g.; 0.6500 Silver 0.1108 oz. ASW **Obv. Leg.:** Yün-nan
Sheng Tsao **Obv. Insc.:** Kuang-hsü Yüan-pao **Rev:** Side view
dragon with three circles beneath pearl

Date	Mintage	VG	F	VF	XF	Unc
ND(1911-15)	—	4.50	12.50	22.50	37.50	75.00

Y# 256b   20 CENTS

5.3000 g.; 0.4000 Silver 0.0682 oz. ASW **Obv. Leg.:** Yün-nan
Sheng Tsao **Obv. Insc.:** Kuang-hsü Yüan-pao **Rev:** Side view
dragon with two or three circles beneath pearl

Date	Mintage	VG	F	VF	XF	Unc
ND(1920-31)	—	—	—	—	—	—

Y# 257   50 CENTS

13.2000 g., 0.8000 Silver 0.3395 oz. ASW **Obv. Leg.:** Yün-nan
Sheng Tsao **Obv. Insc.:** Kuang-hsü Yüan-pao **Rev:** Side view
dragon with two circles below pearl

Date	Mintage	VG	F	VF	XF	Unc
ND(1911-15)	—	5.00	7.00	12.00	20.00	35.00

Note: There are more than 30 minor varieties of Y#257.

Y# 257.1   50 CENTS

13.2000 g., 0.8000 Silver 0.3395 oz. ASW **Obv. Leg.:** Yün-nan
Sheng Tsao **Obv. Insc.:** Kuang-hsü Yüan-pao **Rev:** Side view
dragon with three circles below pearl

Date	Mintage	VG	F	VF	XF	Unc
ND(1911-15)	—	4.75	6.50	10.00	16.00	28.00

Y# 257.2   50 CENTS

13.2000 g., 0.5000 Silver 0.2122 oz. ASW **Obv. Leg.:** Yün-nan
Sheng Tsao **Obv. Insc.:** Kuang-hsü Yüan-pao **Rev:** Side view
dragon with four circles below pearl

Date	Mintage	VG	F	VF	XF	Unc
ND(1920-31)	—	4.75	6.50	10.00	16.00	28.00

Y# 257.3   50 CENTS

13.2000 g., 0.5000 Silver-Billon 0.2122 oz. **Obv. Leg.:** Yün-nan
Sheng Tsao **Obv. Insc.:** Kuang-hsü Yuan-pao **Rev:** Side view
dragon with two circles beneath pearl, large circle around center
circle of rosettes

Date	Mintage	VG	F	VF	XF	Unc
ND(1949)	—	—	BV	5.00	8.00	14.00

Y# 258   DOLLAR

26.8000 g., 0.9000 Silver 0.7754 oz. ASW **Obv. Leg.:** Yün-nan
Sheng Tsao **Obv. Insc.:** Kuang-hsü Yüan-pao **Rev:** Side view
dragon with one circle below pearl

Date	Mintage	VG	F	VF	XF	Unc
ND(1911-15)	—	22.00	30.00	55.00	100	500

Y# 258.1   DOLLAR

26.8000 g., 0.9000 Silver 0.7754 oz. ASW **Obv. Leg.:** Yün-nan
Sheng Tsao **Obv. Insc.:** Kuang-hsü Yüan-pao **Rev:** Side view
dragon with four circles below pearl

Date	Mintage	VG	F	VF	XF	Unc
ND(1920-22)	—	15.00	22.50	40.00	65.00	500

STANDARD COINAGE

Y# 488   CENT

Brass **Obv:** Crossed flags **Obv. Leg.:** Chung Hua Min Kuo

Date	Mintage	VG	F	VF	XF	Unc
21 (1932) Rare						

Y# 489   2 CENTS

Brass **Obv:** Crossed flags **Obv. Leg.:** Chung Hua Min Kuo

Date	Mintage	VG	F	VF	XF	Unc
21 (1932)	—	175	325	500	750	—

Y# 478   50 CASH

Brass **Obv:** Crossed flags **Obv. Leg.:** Yün-nan Sheng Tsao
Rev: Bust of General T'ang Chi-yao facing

Date	Mintage	VG	F	VF	XF	Unc
ND(ca.1919)	—	10.00	20.00	40.00	70.00	—

Y# 478a   50 CASH

Copper **Obv:** Crossed flags **Obv. Leg.:** Yün-nan Sheng Tsao
Rev: Bust of General T'ang Chi-yao facing

Date	Mintage	VG	F	VF	XF	Unc
ND(ca.1919)	—	20.00	40.00	80.00	125	—

Y# 485   5 CENTS

Copper-Nickel **Obv. Leg.:** Chung Hua Min Kuo (year) Nien
Rev: Flag

Date	Mintage	VG	F	VF	XF	Unc
12(1923)	—	22.50	32.50	47.50	75.00	—

Y# 490   5 CENTS

Copper **Obv:** Crossed flags **Obv. Leg.:** Chung Hua Min Kuo

Date	Mintage	VG	F	VF	XF	Unc
21(1932)	—	125	175	250	350	—

Y# 486   10 CENTS

Copper-Nickel **Obv. Leg.:** Chung Hua Min Kuo (year) Nien
Rev: Flag **Edge:** Reeded

Date	Mintage	VG	F	VF	XF	Unc
12(1923)	—	1.75	2.50	3.75	7.50	—

Y# 486.1   10 CENTS

Copper-Nickel **Obv. Leg.:** Chung Hua Min Kuo (year) Nien
Rev: Flag **Edge:** Plain

Date	Mintage	VG	F	VF	XF	Unc
12(1923)	—	2.50	4.00	6.50	12.50	—

Y# 491   20 CENTS

5.6000 g., Silver **Obv:** Crossed flags **Obv. Leg.:** Chung Hua
Min Kuo (year) Nien

Date	Mintage	VG	F	VF	XF	Unc
21(1932)	—	2.50	4.00	6.00	9.00	20.00

Y# 493   20 CENTS

5.6000 g., Silver **Rev:** Provincial capitol

Date	Mintage	VG	F	VF	XF	Unc
38(1949)	—	2.75	5.00	7.50	12.50	40.00

Y# 480   50 CENTS

13.1000 g., 0.8500 Silver 0.3580 oz. ASW **Obv:** Bust of General
T'ang Chi-yao right **Rev:** Crossed flags

Date	Mintage	VG	F	VF	XF	Unc
ND(ca.1916)	—	7.00	12.00	22.00	50.00	250

Y# 479   50 CENTS

13.1000 g., 0.8500 Silver 0.3580 oz. ASW, 33 mm. **Obv:** Bust
of General T'ang Chi-yao facing **Rev:** Crossed flags

Date	Mintage	VG	F	VF	XF	Unc
ND(ca.1917)	—	6.50	9.00	18.00	30.00	95.00

Y# 479.1   50 CENTS

13.1000 g., 0.8500 Silver 0.3580 oz. ASW, 33 mm. **Obv:** Bust
of General T'ang Chi-yao facing **Rev:** Crossed flags with circle
in center of flag at left

Date	Mintage	VG	F	VF	XF	Unc
ND(ca.1917)	—	6.50	9.00	18.00	30.00	95.00

Y# 492   50 CENTS

13.1000 g., 0.5000 Silver 0.2106 oz. ASW **Obv:** Crossed flags
Obv. Leg.: Chung Hua Min Kuo (year) Nien

Date	Mintage	VG	F	VF	XF	Unc
21	—	4.50	6.50	10.00	18.00	50.00

K# 1521   5 DOLLARS
Gold **Obv. Insc.:** "Equal to 5 (silver) Dollars" **Note:** Uniface; Similar to 10 Dollars, K#1520.

Date	Mintage	VG	F	VF	XF	Unc
ND(1917) Rare	—	—	—	—	—	—

Y# 481.1   5 DOLLARS
4.5000 g., 0.7500 Gold 0.1085 oz. AGW, 18 mm. **Obv:** Bust of General T'ang Chi-yao facing **Rev:** Without numeral 2 below flag tassels

Date	Mintage	F	VF	XF	Unc	BU
ND(1919)	Inc. above	—	—	—	—	—

Note: Reported, not confirmed

Y# 481   5 DOLLARS
4.5000 g., 0.7500 Gold 0.1085 oz. AGW, 18 mm. **Obv:** Bust of General T'ang Chi-yao facing **Rev:** With numeral 2 below flag tassels

Date	Mintage	VG	F	VF	XF	Unc
ND(1919)	Est. 60,000	120	220	500	800	1,250

K# 1529   5 DOLLARS
4.5000 g., 0.7500 Gold 0.1085 oz. AGW **Obv. Insc.:** Wu(5)-Yüan Chin-pi **Rev:** Tien in wheat sprays **Edge:** Plain

Date	Mintage	VG	F	VF	XF	Unc
ND(1925)	—	—	1,500	2,200	3,000	—

K# 1520   10 DOLLARS
Gold **Obv. Insc.:** "Equal to 10 Silver Dollars" **Note:** Uniface.

Date	Mintage	VG	F	VF	XF	Unc
ND Rare	—	—	—	—	—	—

Y# 482   10 DOLLARS
8.5000 g., 0.7500 Gold 0.2050 oz. AGW, 23 mm. **Obv:** Bust of General T'ang Chi-yao facing **Rev:** With numeral 1 below flag tassels

Date	Mintage	VG	F	VF	XF	Unc
ND(1919)	900,000	200	300	650	1,000	1,500

Y# 482.1   10 DOLLARS
8.5000 g., 0.7500 Gold 0.2050 oz. AGW, 23 mm. **Obv:** Bust of General T'ang Chi-yao facing **Rev:** Without numeral 1 below flag tassels

Date	Mintage	VG	F	VF	XF	Unc
ND(1919)	Inc. above	220	350	900	1,200	1,850

K# 1528   10 DOLLARS
8.5000 g., 0.7500 Gold 0.2050 oz. AGW **Obv. Insc.:** Shih(10)-yüan Chin-pi **Rev:** Tien in wheat sprays **Edge:** Plain

Date	Mintage	VG	F	VF	XF	Unc
ND(1925)	—	—	1,500	2,200	3,000	—

PATTERNS
Including off metal strikes

KM#	Date	Mintage	Identification	Mkt Val
Pn1	ND(ca.1902)	—	Cash. Brass. Tungch'uwan	—
Pn2	ND(1908)	—	10 Cash. Copper.	250
Pn3	ND(1908)	—	50 Cents. Copper. Y#253.	200
Pn4	ND(1908)	—	50 Cents. Brass. Y#253.	250
Pn5	ND(1908)	—	50 Cents. Copper. Y#257.	200
Pn6	ND(1908)	—	Dollar. Copper. Y#254.	350
Pn7	ND(1925)	—	5 Dollars. Silver.	200

KM#	Date	Mintage	Identification	Mkt Val
Pn8	ND(1925)	—	10 Dollars. Silver.	300
Pn9	ND(1925)	—	10 Dollars. Pewter. K#1528y.	—

YUNNAN-SZECHUAN
Yunnan-Sichuan

These two coins have a 2-character mint mark in the center of the obverse, indicating the provinces of Yunnan and Szechuan (Sichuan).

EMPIRE
PROVINCIAL CAST COINAGE

Y# 10w   10 CASH
Copper **Ruler:** Kuang-hsü **Obv. Insc.:** Ta-ching T'ung-pi **Rev. Leg.:** Kuang-hsu Nien Tsao, TAI-CHING-TI-KUO...

Date	Mintage	VG	F	VF	XF	Unc
CD 1906	—	20.00	40.00	60.00	150	—

Y# 11w   20 CASH
Copper **Ruler:** Kuang-hsü **Obv. Insc.:** Ta-ch'ing T'ung-pi **Rev. Leg.:** Kuang-hsü Nien Tsao, TAI-CHING-TI-KUO...

Date	Mintage	VG	F	VF	XF	Unc
CD 1906	—	100	150	200	300	—

CHINA, REPUBLIC OF

On December 15, 1915 Yuan Shih-K'ai had himself formally chosen and proclaimed emperor. Opposition developed within China and among various foreign powers. A rebellion broke out in Yünnan and spread to other southern provinces. Opposition was so great that Yuan rescinded the monarchy on March 21, 1916. On June 6th he died.

EMPIRE
TRANSITIONAL COINAGE

KM# 1   5 CASH (5 Wen)
Copper **Ruler:** Hung-hsien **Obv:** Inscription: Hung-hsien T'ung-pao

Date	Mintage	VG	F	VF	XF	Unc
ND(1916) Rare	—	—	—	—	—	—

Note: Questionable, believed to be a fantasy by some authorities

REPUBLIC
STANDARD COINAGE

Y# 301   10 CASH (10 Wen)
Copper **Obv:** Crossed flags, florals at left and right **Rev:** Double circle with small rosettes separating legend **Mint:** Nanking

Date	Mintage	VG	F	VF	XF	Unc
ND(ca.1912)	—	0.20	0.50	0.75	1.50	15.00

Y# 301a   10 CASH (10 Wen)
Brass **Obv:** Crossed flags, florals at left and right **Rev:** Double circle with small rosettes separating legend

Date	Mintage	VG	F	VF	XF	Unc
ND(ca.1912)	—	—	—	—	—	—

Y# 301.1   10 CASH (10 Wen)
Copper **Obv:** Second character from right in bottom legend is rounded **Rev:** Double circle with three dots separating legend

Date	Mintage	VG	F	VF	XF	Unc
ND(ca.1912)	—	0.35	1.00	2.00	5.00	22.00

Y# 301.2   10 CASH (10 Wen)
Copper **Obv:** Second character from right in bottom legend is rounded **Rev:** Double circle with two dots separating legend

Date	Mintage	VG	F	VF	XF	Unc
ND(ca.1912)	—	0.20	0.50	1.00	2.50	16.00

Y# 301.3   10 CASH (10 Wen)
Copper **Obv:** Small star on flag **Rev:** Double circle with six-pointed stars separating legend **Mint:** Nanking

Date	Mintage	VG	F	VF	XF	Unc
ND(ca.1912)	—	0.25	0.75	1.50	3.00	18.00

Y# 301.4   10 CASH (10 Wen)
Copper **Obv:** Large star on flag extending to edges of flag **Rev:** Double circle with six-pointed stars separating legend

Date	Mintage	VG	F	VF	XF	Unc
ND(ca.1912)	—	3.50	10.00	15.00	25.00	65.00

Y# 301.4a   10 CASH (10 Wen)
Brass **Obv:** Large star on flag extending to edges of flag **Rev:** Double circle with six-pointed stars separating legend

Date	Mintage	VG	F	VF	XF	Unc
ND(ca.1912)	—	—	—	—	—	—

Y# 301.5   10 CASH (10 Wen)
Copper   **Obv:** Flower wtih many stems   **Rev:** Single circle

Date	Mintage	VG	F	VF	XF	Unc
ND(ca.1912)	—	0.25	0.75	1.50	3.00	20.00

Y# 301.6   10 CASH (10 Wen)
Copper   **Obv:** Flower wtih fewer stems   **Rev:** Single circle

Date	Mintage	VG	F	VF	XF	Unc
ND(ca.1912)	—	0.25	0.75	1.50	3.00	20.00

Y# 309   10 CASH (10 Wen)
Copper   **Mint:** Tientsin

Date	Mintage	VG	F	VF	XF	Unc
ND(1914-17)	—	3.50	10.00	20.00	40.00	120

Note: Pieces with L. GIORGI near rim are patterns

Y# 307   10 CASH (10 Wen)
Copper   **Obv:** One large rosette on either side   **Rev:** Slender leaves and short ribbon   **Mint:** Taiyüan

Date	Mintage	VG	F	VF	XF	Unc
ND(1919)	421,138,000	0.20	0.50	1.00	3.00	14.00

Y# 307a   10 CASH (10 Wen)
Copper   **Obv:** Crossed flags, three rosettes on either side, ornate right flag   **Rev:** Long ribbon

Date	Mintage	VG	F	VF	XF	Unc
ND(1919)	Inc. above	0.40	1.00	2.00	4.00	12.50

Y# 307a.1   10 CASH (10 Wen)
6.6400 g., Copper, 28.05 mm.   **Obv:** Crossed flags, three rosettes on either side, ornate right flag   **Rev:** Short ribbon and smaller wheat ears

Date	Mintage	VG	F	VF	XF	Unc
ND(1919)	Inc. above	3.50	10.00	20.00	40.00	100

Y# 307b   10 CASH (10 Wen)
Brass   **Obv:** Crossed flags, three rosettes at either side, ornate right flag   **Rev:** Long ribbon

Date	Mintage	VG	F	VF	XF	Unc
ND(1919)						

Y# 307.1   10 CASH (10 Wen)
Copper   **Rev:** Larger leaves and longer ribbon

Date	Mintage	VG	F	VF	XF	Unc
ND(1919)	Inc. above	3.50	10.00	20.00	40.00	100

Y# 302   10 CASH (10 Wen)
Copper   **Rev:** Vine above leaf at 12-o'clock; wreath tied at bottom; M-shaped leaves at base of wheat ears   **Mint:** Anhwei

Date	Mintage	VG	F	VF	XF	Unc
ND(ca.1920)	—	0.20	0.60	1.50	3.00	18.00

Y# 302a   10 CASH (10 Wen)
Brass   **Obv:** Crossed flags, florals at left and right   **Rev:** Vine above leaf at 12-o'clock; wreath tied at bottom; M-shaped leaves at base of wheat ears

Date	Mintage	VG	F	VF	XF	Unc
ND(ca.1920)	—	—	—	—	—	—

Y# 302.1   10 CASH (10 Wen)
Copper   **Obv:** Crossed flags, florals at left and right   **Rev:** Vine above leaf at 12-o'clock, wreath tied at bottom; M-shaped leaves at base of larger wheat ears

Date	Mintage	VG	F	VF	XF	Unc
ND(ca.1920)	—	0.35	1.00	3.50	6.50	20.00

Y# 302.2   10 CASH (10 Wen)
Copper   **Rev:** Vine beneath leaf at 12-o'clock; wreath not tied at bottom; without M-shaped leaves at base of wheat ears

Date	Mintage	VG	F	VF	XF	Unc
ND(ca.1920)	—	0.50	1.50	4.00	8.00	22.00

Y# 302.3   10 CASH (10 Wen)
Copper   **Rev:** Leaves pointing clockwise

Date	Mintage	VG	F	VF	XF	Unc
ND(ca.1920)	—	10.00	30.00	40.00	60.00	115

Y# 303   10 CASH (10 Wen)
Copper   **Obv:** Crossed flags, small star-shaped rosettes at left and right   **Rev:** Small 4-petaled rosettes separating legend

Date	Mintage	VG	F	VF	XF	Unc
ND(ca.1920)	—	0.20	0.50	1.00	2.00	15.00

Y# 303a   10 CASH (10 Wen)
Brass   **Obv:** Crossed flags, stars replace rosettes at left and right   **Rev:** Small 4-petaled rosettes separating legend

Date	Mintage	VG	F	VF	XF	Unc
ND(ca.1920)	—	0.50	1.50	4.00	10.00	22.50

Y# 303.1   10 CASH (10 Wen)
Copper   **Obv:** Crossed flags, left flag's star in relief, small star-shaped rosettes at left and right   **Rev:** Small 4-petaled rosettes separating legend

Date	Mintage	VG	F	VF	XF	Unc
ND(ca.1920)	—	0.20	0.50	1.00	2.00	15.00

Y# 303.3   10 CASH (10 Wen)
Copper   **Obv:** Large rosettes replace stars   **Rev:** Stars separating legend

Date	Mintage	VG	F	VF	XF	Unc
ND(ca.1920)	—	1.00	3.00	6.25	12.50	25.00

Y# 303.4   10 CASH (10 Wen)
Copper   **Obv:** Crossed flags, very small pentagonal rosettes at left and right

Date	Mintage	VG	F	VF	XF	Unc
ND(ca.1920)	—	0.25	0.75	1.50	3.00	15.00

Y# 303.4a   10 CASH (10 Wen)
Brass   **Obv:** Crossed flags, very small pentagonal rosettes at left and right   **Rev:** Stars separating legend

Date	Mintage	VG	F	VF	XF	Unc
ND(ca.1920)	—	3.00	6.25	12.50	25.00

Y# 303.5   10 CASH (10 Wen)
Brass   **Obv:** Crossed flags, three large rosettes at left and right   **Rev:** Stars separate legend

Date	Mintage	VG	F	VF	XF	Unc
ND(ca.1920)	—	—	—	—	—

Y# 304   10 CASH (10 Wen)
Copper   **Obv:** Circled flags flanked by pentagonal rosettes   **Mint:** Anhwei

Date	Mintage	VG	F	VF	XF	Unc
ND(ca.1920)	—	3.75	11.50	21.50	42.50	85.00

Y# 305   10 CASH (10 Wen)
Copper **Rev:** Chrysanthemum **Mint:** Changsha

Date	Mintage	VG	F	VF	XF	Unc
ND(ca.1920)	—	5.00	15.00	25.00	50.00	115

Y# 306a   10 CASH (10 Wen)
Copper **Obv:** Crossed flags, five characters in lower legend

Date	Mintage	VG	F	VF	XF	Unc
ND(ca.1920)	—	1.75	5.00	12.00	25.00	65.00

Y# 306b   10 CASH (10 Wen)
Brass **Obv:** Crossed flags, five characters in lower legend

Date	Mintage	VG	F	VF	XF	Unc
ND(ca.1920)	—	0.35	1.00	2.50	5.00	18.00

Y# 306.1   10 CASH (10 Wen)
Copper **Obv:** Crossed flags, florals at left and right **Rev:** Wheat ear design within circle **Mint:** Changsha

Date	Mintage	VG	F	VF	XF	Unc
ND(ca.1920)	—	0.20	0.50	1.25	3.00	14.00

Y# 306.1b   10 CASH (10 Wen)
Copper **Obv:** Crossed flags, florals at left and right **Rev:** Thin leaf blade between lower wheat ears

Date	Mintage	VG	F	VF	XF	Unc
ND(ca.1920)	—	1.75	5.00	7.50	14.00	30.00

Y# 306.2   10 CASH (10 Wen)
Copper **Obv:** Crossed flags, florals at left and right, dot on either side of upper legend **Rev:** Wheat ear design within circle

Date	Mintage	VG	F	VF	XF	Unc
ND(ca.1920)	—	0.35	1.00	2.00	3.50	15.00

Y# 306.2b   10 CASH (10 Wen)
Brass **Obv:** Crossed flags, florals at left and right, dot on either side of upper legend **Rev:** Thin leaf blade between lower wheat ears

Date	Mintage	VG	F	VF	XF	Unc
ND(ca.1920)	—	0.45	1.25	—	5.00	15.00

Y# 306.3   10 CASH (10 Wen)
Copper **Obv:** Star between flags **Rev:** Wheat ear design within circle

Date	Mintage	VG	F	VF	XF	Unc
ND(ca.1920)	—	6.50	20.00	40.00	75.00	—

Y# 306.4   10 CASH (10 Wen)
Copper **Obv:** Elongated rosettes, different characters in bottom legend **Rev:** Thin leaf blade between lower wheat ears

Date	Mintage	VG	F	VF	XF	Unc
ND(ca.1920)	—	9.00	27.50	55.00	85.00	215

Y# 311   10 CASH (10 Wen)
Copper **Mint:** Kalgan

Date	Mintage	VG	F	VF	XF	Unc
13 (1924)	—	65.00	175	350	500	850

Y# 308   20 CASH (20 Wen)
Copper, 32.3 mm. **Obv:** Crossed flags **Rev:** Value in sprays **Mint:** Taiyüan

Date	Mintage	VG	F	VF	XF	Unc
8 (1919)	200,861,000	0.50	1.50	1.50	7.50	30.00

Y# 308b   20 CASH (20 Wen)
Cast Brass **Obv:** Crossed flags **Rev:** Value in sprays

Date	Mintage	Good	VG	F	VF	XF
8(1919)	—	10.00	15.00	18.50	27.50	

Note: A "warlord" issue; refer to note under Szechuan - Republic

Y# 308a   20 CASH (20 Wen)
Copper **Obv:** Crossed flags **Rev:** Value in sprays

Date	Mintage	VG	F	VF	XF	Unc
10 (1921)	Inc. above	0.35	1.00	2.50	6.00	30.00

Y# 310   20 CASH (20 Wen)
Copper **Obv:** Crossed flags **Rev:** Value in sprays **Mint:** Tientsin

Date	Mintage	VG	F	VF	XF	Unc
ND(ca.1921)	—	5.00	15.00	30.00	70.00	135

Note: Some sources date these 20 Cash pieces bearing crossed flags ca.1912, but many were not struck until the 1920s; this coin is usually found weakly struck and lightweight

Y# 312   20 CASH (20 Wen)
Copper **Obv. Leg.:** REPUBLIC OF CHINA **Obv. Insc.:** Chunghua T'ung-pien **Rev:** Value in sprays; date above **Mint:** Kalgan

Date	Mintage	VG	F	VF	XF	Unc
13 (1924)	—	3.50	10.00	30.00	70.00	135

Note: This coin is usually found weakly struck

HSU# 9   20 CASH (20 Wen)
Copper **Obv:** Crossed flags **Rev:** Value in sprays
Note: Nationalist commemorative.

Date	Mintage	VG	F	VF	XF	Unc
ND(1927-28)	—	75.00	225	400	650	900

HSU# 445a   500 CASH (500 Wen)
Copper   **Subject:** Nationalist Commemorative   **Obv:** Crossed flags   **Rev:** Value in sprays

Date	Mintage	VG	F	VF	XF	Unc
ND(1927/8) Rare	12	—	—	—	—	—

Y# 323   1/2 CENT (1/2 Fen)
Bronze   **Mint:** Tientsin

Date	Mintage	VG	F	VF	XF	Unc
5 (1916)	1,789,000	1.75	5.00	10.00	20.00	45.00

Y# 346   1/2 CENT (1/2 Fen)
Bronze

Date	Mintage	VG	F	VF	XF	Unc
25 (1936)	64,720,000	0.25	0.75	1.50	3.00	7.50
28 (1939) Rare	—	—	—	—	—	—

Y# 324   CENT (1 Fen)
Bronze   **Mint:** Tientsin

Date	Mintage	VG	F	VF	XF	Unc
5 (1916)	—	1.75	5.00	10.00	20.00	50.00

Note: Pieces with "L. GIORGI" near rim are patterns

Y# 347   CENT (1 Fen)
Copper   **Obv. Leg.:** Chung Hua Min Kuo (year) Nien   **Rev:** Large "Kuel" mint mark below Pu

Date	Mintage	VG	F	VF	XF	Unc
25 (1936)	311,780,000	0.15	0.40	0.75	1.75	2.50
26 (1937)	307,198,000	0.15	0.45	1.00	1.50	3.00
27 (1938)	12,000,000	1.00	3.00	5.00	8.00	16.00
28 (1939)	75,000,000	0.65	2.00	4.00	7.00	15.00

KM# 347.1   CENT (1 Fen)
Copper   **Obv. Leg.:** Chung Hua Min Kuo (year) Nien   **Rev:** Small "Kuel" mint mark below Pu

Date	Mintage	VG	F	VF	XF	Unc
28 (1939) Rare	—	—	—	—	—	—

Y# 353   CENT (1 Fen)
Brass   **Note:** Shi Kwan Cent.

Date	Mintage	VG	F	VF	XF	Unc
28(1939)	—	13.50	40.00	60.00	120	200

Y# 355   CENT (1 Fen)
Aluminum

Date	Mintage	VG	F	VF	XF	Unc
29 (1940)	150,000,000	—	0.10	0.25	0.50	1.50

Y# 357   CENT (1 Fen)
Brass

Date	Mintage	VG	F	VF	XF	Unc
29 (1940)	50,000,000	0.25	0.75	1.00	2.00	4.00

Y# 363   CENT (1 Fen)
Bronze

Date	Mintage	VG	F	VF	XF	Unc
37 (1948)	—	1.50	4.00	10.00	15.00	20.00

Y# 325a   2 CENTS (2 Fen)
Bronze

Date	Mintage	VG	F	VF	XF	Unc
22(1933)	—	13.50	40.00	60.00	95.00	150

Y# 354   2 CENTS (2 Fen)
Brass

Date	Mintage	VG	F	VF	XF	Unc
28(1939)	300,000,000	3.50	10.00	15.00	25.00	50.00

Y# 358   2 CENTS (2 Fen)
Brass

Date	Mintage	VG	F	VF	XF	Unc
29(1940)	—	0.20	0.50	1.00	1.50	2.00
30(1941) Rare	—	—	—	—	—	—

Y# 348   5 CENTS (5 Fen)
3.0700 g., Nickel, 18.5 mm.

Date	Mintage	VG	F	VF	XF	Unc
25(1936)	72,844,000	0.35	1.00	1.50	3.00	6.00
27(1938)	34,325,000	0.75	2.50	4.50	8.00	15.00
28(1939)	6,000,000	3.50	10.00	15.00	25.00	50.00

Y# 348.1   5 CENTS (5 Fen)
Nickel   **Rev:** A mint mark below spade (Vienna)

Date	Mintage	VG	F	VF	XF	Unc
25(1936)	20,000,000	0.35	1.00	2.00	3.50	15.00

Y# 348.2   5 CENTS (5 Fen)
Nickel   **Obv:** Character "P'ing" on both sides of portrait

Date	Mintage	VG	F	VF	XF	Unc
25 (1936)	—	17.50	50.00	80.00	125	175

Y# 348.3   5 CENTS (5 Fen)
Nickel   **Obv:** Character "Ch'ing" on both sides of portrait

Date	Mintage	VG	F	VF	XF	Unc
25 (1936)	—	17.50	50.00	80.00	125	175

Y# 356   5 CENTS (5 Fen)
1.1000 g., Aluminum

Date	Mintage	VG	F	VF	XF	Unc
29(1940)	350,000,000	0.20	0.50	1.00	2.50	4.00

Y# 359   5 CENTS (5 Fen)
Copper-Nickel

Date	Mintage	VG	F	VF	XF	Unc
29(1940)	57,000,000	0.10	0.25	1.50	2.50	5.00
30(1941)	96,000,000	0.10	0.25	1.50	2.50	6.00

K# 602   10 CENTS (1 Chiao)
2.3000 g., Silver, 18 mm.   **Subject:** Sun Yat-sen Founding of the Republic   **Obv:** Bust left within circle   **Rev:** Two 5-pointed stars dividing legend at top   **Note:** vertical reeding

Date	Mintage	VG	F	VF	XF	Unc
ND(1912)	—	65.00	200	500	700	1,250

K# 602b   10 CENTS (1 Chiao)
2.3000 g., Silver, 18 mm.   **Subject:** Sun Yat-sen Founding of the Republic   **Obv:** Bust left within circle   **Rev:** Two 5-pointed stars dividing legend at top   **Edge:** Engrailed with circles

Date	Mintage	VG	F	VF	XF	Unc
ND(1912)	—	—	—	700	850	1,500

Y# 326   10 CENTS (1 Chiao)
2.7000 g., 0.7000 Silver 0.0608 oz. ASW

Date	Mintage	VG	F	VF	XF	Unc
3 (1914)	—	2.00	5.00	10.00	20.00	70.00
3 (1914) Specimen	—	Value: 500				
5 (1916)	—	6.50	20.00	35.00	60.00	150
5 (1916) Specimen	—	Value: 750				

Y# 334   10 CENTS (1 Chiao)
Silver   **Subject:** Unadopted design of national emblem

Date	Mintage	VG	F	VF	XF	Unc
15 (1926)	—	6.00	10.00	15.00	30.00	100

Y# 339   10 CENTS (1 Chiao)
2.5000 g., Silver, 18 mm. **Subject:** Death of Sun Yat-sen

Date	Mintage	VG	F	VF	XF	Unc
16 (1927)	—	10.00	25.00	40.00	70.00	150

Y# 349   10 CENTS (1 Chiao)
Nickel, 21 mm.

Date	Mintage	VG	F	VF	XF	Unc
25(1936)	73,866,000	0.20	0.60	1.00	3.00	7.50
27(1938)	110,203,000	0.65	2.00	4.25	8.00	20.00
28(1939)	68,000,000	0.50	1.50	3.50	10.00	27.50

Y# 349a   10 CENTS (1 Chiao)
Non-Magnetic Nickel Alloy

Date	Mintage	VG	F	VF	XF	Unc
25(1936)	1,000,000	6.00	18.00	30.00	40.00	65.00

Note: All of the Y#349 coins were supposed to have been minted in pure nickel at the Shanghai Mint; However, in 1936 a warlord had the Tientsin Mint produce about one million 10 Cent pieces of heavily alloyed nickel; The result is that the Shanghai pieces are attracted to a magnet while the Tientsin pieces are not

Y# 349.1   10 CENTS (1 Chiao)
Nickel **Rev:** Mint mark A below spade (Vienna Mint)

Date	Mintage	VG	F	VF	XF	Unc
25(1936)A	60,000,000	0.35	1.00	2.00	8.00	25.00

Y# 360   10 CENTS (1 Chiao)
Copper-Nickel, 21 mm. **Edge:** Reeded

Date	Mintage	VG	F	VF	XF	Unc
29(1940)	68,000,000	0.20	0.50	2.50	8.00	15.00
30(1941)	254,000,000	0.20	0.50	1.50	2.50	5.00
31(1942)	10,000,000	8.50	25.00	60.00	80.00	120

Y# 360.1   10 CENTS (1 Chiao)
Copper-Nickel **Edge:** Plain

Date	Mintage	VG	F	VF	XF	Unc
29(1940) Rare	Inc. above	—	—	—	—	—
30(1941)	Inc. above	0.65	2.00	7.50	10.00	15.00

Y# 317   20 CENTS (2 Chiao)
5.2000 g., Silver, 23 mm. **Subject:** Founding of the Republic

Date	Mintage	VG	F	VF	XF	Unc
ND(1912)	155,000	15.00	25.00	40.00	75.00	150

Y# 327   20 CENTS (2 Chiao)
5.4000 g., 0.7000 Silver 0.1215 oz. ASW, 22.88 mm.

Date	Mintage	VG	F	VF	XF	Unc
3 (1914)	—	2.25	3.50	6.00	12.00	70.00
3 (1914) Specimen	—	Value: 250				

Date	Mintage	VG	F	VF	XF	Unc
5 (1916)	—	2.25	3.50	6.00	15.00	90.00
5 (1916) Specimen	—	Value: 500				
9 (1920)	—	45.00	100	275	500	1,500

Y# 335   20 CENTS (2 Chiao)
5.2000 g., Silver **Subject:** Unadopted design of national emblem

Date	Mintage	VG	F	VF	XF	Unc
15 (1926)	—	10.00	15.00	20.00	30.00	120

Y# 340   20 CENTS (2 Chiao)
5.3000 g., Silver, 23 mm. **Subject:** Death of Sun Yat-sen

Date	Mintage	VG	F	VF	XF	Unc
16(1927)	—	6.50	15.00	25.00	40.00	100

Y# 350   20 CENTS (20 Fen)
6.0500 g., Nickel, 24.06 mm.

Date	Mintage	VG	F	VF	XF	Unc
25(1936)	49,620,000	0.20	0.50	2.50	6.00	10.00
27(1938)	61,248,000	0.35	1.00	2.00	7.00	12.00
28(1939)	38,000,000	0.65	2.00	5.00	10.00	15.00

Y# 350.1   20 CENTS (20 Fen)
Nickel **Rev:** Mint mark A below spade (Vienna Mint)

Date	Mintage	VG	F	VF	XF	Unc
25(1936)A	40,000,000	0.35	1.00	2.00	3.50	6.00

Y# 361   20 CENTS (20 Fen)
Copper-Nickel

Date	Mintage	VG	F	VF	XF	Unc
31(1942)	32,300,000	0.15	0.40	1.00	2.25	4.00

Y# 328   50 CENTS (1/2 Yuan)
13.6000 g., 0.7000 Silver 0.3061 oz. ASW

Date	Mintage	VG	F	VF	XF	Unc
3 (1914)	—	8.50	25.00	45.00	75.00	250
3 (1914) Specimen	—	Value: 1,000				

Y# 362   50 CENTS (1/2 Yuan)
9.0600 g., Copper-Nickel, 28 mm. **Edge:** Reeded

Date	Mintage	VG	F	VF	XF	Unc
31(1942)	57,000,000	0.50	1.50	3.00	7.50	15.00
32(1943)	4,000,000	2.00	4.00	10.00	20.00	40.00

Y# 318   DOLLAR (Yuan)
26.9000 g., 0.9000 Silver 0.7783 oz. ASW, 39 mm.
Subject: Sun Yat-sen Founding of the Republic **Obv:** Sun Yat-sen facing left **Rev:** Two five-pointed stars dividing legend at top

Date	Mintage	VG	F	VF	XF	Unc
ND(1912)	—	50.00	150	300	450	850

Y# 318.1   DOLLAR (Yuan)
26.9000 g., 0.9000 Silver 0.7783 oz. ASW, 39 mm. **Obv:** Dot below ear

Date	Mintage	VG	F	VF	XF	Unc
ND(1912)						

Note: For similar issue with rosettes see Y#318a.1 (1927)

Y# 319   DOLLAR (Yuan)
27.3000 g., 0.9000 Silver 0.7899 oz. ASW, 39 mm. **Obv:** Sun Yat-sen facing left

Date	Mintage	VG	F	VF	XF	Unc
ND(1912)	—	35.00	100	285	400	650

Y# 320 DOLLAR (Yuan)
26.5000 g., Silver, 39 mm. **Subject:** Li Yüan-hung Founding of Republic

Date	Mintage	VG	F	VF	XF	Unc
ND(1912)	—	150	450	900	1,500	2,000

Y# 320.1 DOLLAR (Yuan)
26.5000 g., Silver, 39 mm. **Rev. Leg.:** OE for OF

Date	Mintage	VG	F	VF	XF	Unc
ND(1912)	—	175	550	1,100	1,800	—

Y# 320.2 DOLLAR (Yuan)
26.5000 g., Silver **Rev. Leg.:** CIIINA for CHINA

Date	Mintage	VG	F	VF	XF	Unc
ND(1912)	—	175	550	1,100	1,800	—

Y# 321 DOLLAR (Yuan)
26.5000 g., Silver, 39 mm. **Subject:** Li Yüan-hung Founding of Republic

Date	Mintage	VG	F	VF	XF	Unc
ND(1912)	—	50.00	100	150	200	600

Y# 321.1 DOLLAR (Yuan)
26.5000 g., Silver, 39 mm. **Rev:** H of "THE" in legend engraved as I I

Date	Mintage	VG	F	VF	XF	Unc
ND(1912)	—	50.00	100	170	250	650

Y# 322 DOLLAR (Yuan)
26.7000 g., 0.9000 Silver 0.7726 oz. ASW, 39 mm. **Subject:** Yüan Shih-kai Founding of Republic **Note:** 2.8mm thickness.

Date	Mintage	VG	F	VF	XF	Unc
ND (1914)	20,000	100	175	300	450	600

Y# 322.1 DOLLAR (Yuan)
26.7000 g., 0.9000 Silver 0.7726 oz. ASW, 39 mm. **Subject:** Yüan Shih-kai Founding of Republic **Note:** 3.25mm thickness.

Date	Mintage	VG	F	VF	XF	Unc
ND(ca.1918)	—	100	175	300	450	600

Note: A restrike made about 1918 for collectors

Y# 329 DOLLAR (Yuan)
26.4000 g., 0.8900 Silver 0.7554 oz. ASW, 39 mm. **Subject:** Yüan Shih-kai **Obv:** Six characters above head **Note:** Vertical reeding.

Date	Mintage	VG	F	VF	XF	Unc
3 (1914)	—	13.50	15.00	18.00	25.00	50.00

Y# 329.1 DOLLAR (Yuan)
26.4000 g., 0.8900 Silver 0.7554 oz. ASW, 39 mm. **Note:** Edge engrailed with circles.

Date	Mintage	VG	F	VF	XF	Unc
3 (1914)	—	18.00	60.00	150	1,000	2,200

Y# 329.2 DOLLAR (Yuan)
26.4000 g., 0.8900 Silver 0.7554 oz. ASW, 39 mm. **Edge:** Ornamented with alternating T's

Date	Mintage	VG	F	VF	XF	Unc
3	—	18.00	60.00	150	1,000	2,200

Y# 329.3 DOLLAR (Yuan)
26.4000 g., 0.8900 Silver 0.7554 oz. ASW, 39 mm. **Edge:** Plain

Date	Mintage	VG	F	VF	XF	Unc
3 (1914)	—	16.00	40.00	75.00	500	800

Y# 329.4 DOLLAR (Yuan)
26.4000 g., 0.8900 Silver 0.7554 oz. ASW, 39 mm. **Note:** Tiny circle in ribbon bow. This is a mint mark, but it is not clear what mint is indicated.

Date	Mintage	VG	F	VF	XF	Unc
3 (1914)	—	15.00	20.00	40.00	85.00	200

Y# 332 DOLLAR (Yuan)
26.8000 g., Silver, 39 mm. **Ruler:** Hung-hsien **Subject:** Inauguration of Hung-hsien Regime **Obv:** Bust of Hung-hsien in military uniform with plumed hat facing **Rev:** Winged dragon left **Note:** K#663.

Date	Mintage	VG	F	VF	XF	Unc
ND (1916)	—	100	400	700	1,000	1,500

Y# 329.6 DOLLAR (Yuan)
26.4000 g., 0.8900 Silver 0.7554 oz. ASW **Obv:** Seven characters above head

Date	Mintage	VG	F	VF	XF	Unc
8 (1919)	—	13.50	15.00	18.50	45.00	150
9 (1920)	—	13.50	15.00	16.50	22.50	50.00
10 (1921)	—	13.50	15.00	16.50	22.50	50.00

Y# 329.5 DOLLAR (Yuan)
26.4000 g., 0.8900 Silver 0.7554 oz. ASW **Edge:** Oblique reeding

Date	Mintage	VG	F	VF	XF	Unc
10 (1921)	—	15.00	20.00	32.50	45.00	75.00

K# 676 DOLLAR (Yuan)
26.5000 g., Silver, 39 mm. **Subject:** President Hsu Shih-chang **Edge:** Reeded

Date	Mintage	VG	F	VF	XF	Unc
10 (1921)	—	125	250	500	900	1,650

K# 676.1 DOLLAR (Yuan)
26.5000 g., Silver, 39 mm. **Edge:** Plain

Date	Mintage	VG	F	VF	XF	Unc
10 (1921)	—	200	500	800	1,500	2,500

K# 677 DOLLAR (Yuan)
26.7000 g., Silver, 39 mm. **Obv:** Bust of President Tsao Kun facing

Date	Mintage	VG	F	VF	XF	Unc
ND (1923)	50,000	125	250	500	850	1,500

K# 678 DOLLAR (Yuan)
26.7000 g., Silver, 39 mm. **Obv:** Bust of President Tsao Kun in military uniform facing

Date	Mintage	VG	F	VF	XF	Unc
ND (1923)	—	—	—	500	850	1,500

Y# 336 DOLLAR (Yuan)
26.8000 g., Silver **Subject:** Unadopted design of national emblem **Rev:** Value in small characters

Date	Mintage	VG	F	VF	XF	Unc
12 (1923)	—	200	500	900	1,500	2,500

Y# 336.1   DOLLAR (Yuan)

26.8000 g., Silver   **Subject:** Unadopted design of national emblem **Rev:** Value in large characters

Date	Mintage	VG	F	VF	XF	Unc
12 (1923)	—	250	500	1,000	2,750	4,500

K# 683   DOLLAR (Yuan)

Silver, 39 mm.   **Obv:** Bust of President Tuan Chi-jui facing

Date	Mintage	VG	F	VF	XF	Unc
ND (1924)	—	125	200	450	800	1,500

K# 690   DOLLAR (Yuan)

26.5000 g., Silver, 39 mm.   **Obv:** Bust of General Chu Yu-pu facing

Date	Mintage	VG	F	VF	XF	Unc
ND (1927)	—	—	—	5,000	12,000	25,000

Y# 318a.1   DOLLAR (Yuan)

27.0000 g., 0.8900 Silver 0.7726 oz. ASW   **Obv:** Bust of Sun Yat-sen left **Rev:** Two rosettes dividing legend at top **Edge:** Incuse reeding

Date	Mintage	VG	F	VF	XF	Unc
ND(1927)	—	14.50	16.50	18.00	20.00	35.00

Y# 318a.2   DOLLAR (Yuan)

27.0000 g., 0.8900 Silver 0.7726 oz. ASW   **Edge:** Reeding in relief

Date	Mintage	VG	F	VF	XF	Unc
ND(1927)	—	14.50	16.50	18.00	20.00	35.00

Note: Varieties exist with errors in the English legend. For similar coins with 5-pointed stars dividing legends, see Y#318 (1912). In 1949 the Canton Mint restruck Memento dollars. There are modern restrikes in red copper and brass.

K# 609   DOLLAR (Yuan)

27.0000 g., Silver   **Obv:** Bust of Sun Yat-sen **Rev:** Sun Yat-sen Memorial

Date	Mintage	VG	F	VF	XF	Unc
16(1927)	480	750	1,500	3,000	5,000	9,500

Y# 344   DOLLAR (Yuan)

26.7000 g., 0.8800 Silver 0.7554 oz. ASW   **Obv:** Bust of Sun Yat-sen left **Rev:** 3 wild geese flying above junk, rising sun

Date	Mintage	VG	F	VF	XF	Unc
21(1932)	2,260,000	100	175	300	400	600

Y# 345   DOLLAR (Yuan)

26.7000 g., 0.8800 Silver 0.7554 oz. ASW   **Rev:** Without birds above junk or rising sun

Date	Mintage	VG	F	VF	XF	Unc
22(1933)	46,400,000	13.50	15.00	17.00	25.00	50.00
23(1934)	128,740,000	13.50	15.00	17.00	20.00	35.00

Note: In 1949, three U.S. mints restruck a total of 30 million "Junk Dollars" dated Year 23.

Y# 333   10 DOLLARS

7.0500 g., Red Gold   **Ruler:** Hung-hsien **Obv:** Bust of Hung-hsien left **Rev:** Winged dragon left **Note:** K#1515.

Date	Mintage	VG	F	VF	XF	Unc
1 (1916)	—	—	—	2,500	4,000	5,500

Y# 333a   10 DOLLARS

7.0500 g., Yellow Gold   **Ruler:** Hung-hsien

Date	Mintage	VG	F	VF	XF	Unc
1 (1916)	—	—	—	2,500	4,000	5,500

Y# 330   10 DOLLARS

8.1500 g., 0.8500 Gold 0.2227 oz. AGW   **Ruler:** Hung-hsien **Note:** K#1531.

Date	Mintage	VG	F	VF	XF	Unc
8 (1919)	—	—	—	2,000	2,850	4,000

Y# 331   20 DOLLARS

16.3000 g., 0.8500 Gold 0.4454 oz. AGW   **Ruler:** Hung-hsien **Note:** K#1530.

Date	Mintage	VG	F	VF	XF	Unc
8 (1919)	—	—	—	—	5,500	8,500

Y# 324a   FEN

Bronze

Date	Mintage	VG	F	VF	XF	Unc
22 (1933)	—	2.75	8.00	15.00	30.00	100

TOKEN COINAGE

KM# Tn1 FEN
Brass Mint: Shansi Arsenal

Date	Mintage	F	VF	XF	Unc	BU
17 (1928)	—	75.00	125	175	300	—

Note: This token is usually found with small punch marks near center on obverse and reverse

KM# Tn2 2 FEN
Brass Mint: Shansi Arsenal

Date	Mintage	F	VF	XF	Unc	BU
17 (1928)	—	150	250	400	650	—

Note: This token has always been found with small punch marks near center on obverse and reverse

KM# Tn3 5 FEN
Brass Mint: Shansi Arsenal Note: Similar to 2 Fen, KM#Tn2.

Date	Mintage	F	VF	XF	Unc	BU
17 (1928)	—	450	750	1,250	—	—

Note: This token has always been found with small punch marks near center on obverse and reverse

KM# Tn4 10 FEN
Brass Mint: Shansi Arsenal Note: Similar to 2 Fen, KM#Tn2.

Date	Mintage	F	VF	XF	Unc	BU
17 (1928)	—	450	750	1,250	—	—

Note: This token has always been found with small punch marks near center on obverse and reverse

PATTERNS
Including off metal strikes

KM#	Date	Mintage	Identification	Mkt Val
PnA7	ND(1912)	—	5 Cash. Copper. Crossed flags.	—
PnB7	ND(1912)	—	20 Cash. Copper. Crossed flags.	3,000
PnC7	ND(1912)	—	50 Cash. Copper. Crossed flags.	8,000
Pn2	ND(1912)	—	Cash. Copper Or Brass.	—
Pn3	ND(1912)	—	Cash. Zinc.	—
Pn4	ND(1912)	—	Cash. Iron.	—
Pn5	ND(1912)	—	10 Cash. Copper. Hsu13	1,000
PnA6	ND(1912)	—	10 Cash. Copper. Similar to Pn5 but larger bust; W972.	—
Pn6	ND(1912)	—	10 Cash. Gold.	—
Pn7	ND(1912)	—	20 Cents. Gold. Y#317	3,500
Pn8	ND(1912)	—	Dollar. Gold. Y#318	—
Pn9	ND(1912)	—	Dollar. Gold. Y#318 - K#1550	20,000
PnA10	ND(1912)	—	Dollar. Silver. Li Yuan-hung	—
Pn10	ND(1912)	—	Dollar. Silver. Chin Teh-chuen, K#672. Many counterfeits exist.	50,000
Pn11	ND(1912)	—	Dollar. Eyes in relief. Chin Teh-chuen, K#672a.	—

Note: All known examples are counterfeit.

| Pn12 | ND(1912) | — | Dollar. Bronze. K#672x | — |

Note: All known examples are counterfeit.

PnA13	ND(1914)	—	10 Cash. Copper. With L. GEORGI; Y#309.	800
Pn13	3(1914)	—	5 Cents. Nickel. K#815	—
Pn14	3(1914)	—	5 Cents. Nickel. Plain edge. Essay, K#815a	—
Pn15	3(1914)	—	5 Cents. Nickel. Milled edge. Essay K#815b; with G. L.	—
Pn16	3(1914)	—	5 Cents. Silver. Milled edge. Essay, K#815c; with G. L.	350
Pn17	3(1914)	—	5 Cents. Copper. Essay, K#815x	225
Pn18	3(1914)	—	5 Cents. Pewter. Plain edge. Essay, K#815y	—
Pn19	3(1914)	—	5 Cents. Copper. With G. L., essay, K#815z	—
Pn20	3(1914)	—	10 Cents. Silver. With G. L., K#659a	700
Pn21	3(1914)	—	10 Cents. Copper. Y#326	45.00
Pn22	3(1914)	—	10 Cents. Nickel. Y#326	350
Pn23	3(1914)	—	20 Cents. Silver. With G. L.; K#657a	900
Pn24	3(1914)	—	20 Cents. Copper. Y#327	65.00
Pn25	3(1914)	—	20 Cents. Nickel. Y#327	375
Pn26	3(1914)	—	20 Cents. Pewter. Y#327	300
Pn27	3(1914)	—	50 Cents. Silver. With L. GIORGI; Yuan Shih-kai, K#655a.	1,150
Pn28	ND(1914)	—	Dollar. Silver. With L. GIORGI; Yuan Shih-kai, K#642a.	9,500
Pn29	ND(1914)	—	Dollar. Gold. With L. GIORGI, Yuan Shih-kai; K#1558	25,000
Pn30	ND(1914)	—	Dollar. Silver. Yuan Shih-kai, plumes of hat touch rim; K#644.	10,500
Pn31	ND(1914)	—	Dollar. Silver. With L. GIORGI; Yuan Shih-kai, K#645	15,000
Pn32	3(1914)	—	Dollar. Silver. K#643	7,000
Pn33	3(1914)	—	Dollar. Silver. 26.1400 g. With L. GIORGI; K#643a	7,000
Pn34	ND(1914)	—	Dollar. Copper. K#322	500
Pn35	ND(1914)	—	Dollar. Brass. Y#322	600
Pn36	ND(1914)	—	Dollar. Gold. Y#329	25,000
Pn37	ND(1914)	—	Dollar. Copper. Y#329	450

KM#	Date	Mintage	Identification	Mkt Val
Pn38	ND(1914)	—	Dollar. Brass. Y#329	400
PnA39	ND(1914)	—	5 Dollars. Gold. K#1517	6,000
Pn39	5(1916)	—	1/2 Cent. Copper. Without center hole; Y#323	350
Pn40	5(1916)	—	10 Cash. Copper. Without center hole; Y#324	400
Pn41	5(1916)	—	10 Cash. Copper. With L. GIORGI; Y#324.3	—
Pn42	5(1916)	—	20 Cash. Copper. Hsu44	650
Pn43	5(1916)	—	20 Cents. Copper. Y#327	—
Pn44	ND(1916)	—	Dollar. Gold. Y#332. It has been verified that the San Francisco Mint actually struck 2 pieces in gold in 1928.	14,000
Pn45	ND(1916)	—	Dollar. White Metal. Y#332	—
Pn47	ND(1916)	—	Dollar. Silver. With L. GIORGI; plumes don't touch rim; K#663a.	25,000
Pn48	ND(1916)	—	Dollar. Silver. With L. GIORGI; K#663d	15,000
Pn50	1(1916)	—	10 Dollars. Gold. with L. G. Hung-hsien, near shoulder; K#1515a	—
Pn51	1(1916)	—	10 Dollars. Copper. with L. G. Hung-hsien, near shoulder; K#1515y	—
Pn52	ND(1916)	—	Dollar. Silver. Plumes of hat touch rim; K#664	10,500
Pn53	ND(1916)	—	Dollar. Gold. With L. GIORGI; K#1560	50,000
Pn54	1(1916)	—	10 Dollars. Silver. Y#333	—
Pn55	1(1916)	—	10 Dollars. Gold. Y#333	375
Pn56	8(1919)	—	10 Cash. Copper. Hsu29	1,000
Pn57	8(1919)	—	10 Cash. Copper. Hsu30	1,000
Pn59	8(1919)	—	10 Dollars. Gold. Y#330	325
Pn60	8(1919)	—	10 Dollars. Brass. Y#330	325
Pn61	8(1919)	—	20 Dollars. Copper. Y#331	485
Pn62	10(1921)	—	Dollar. Gold. K#1570	24,000
Pn63	10(1921)	—	Dollar. Silver. Reeded edge. K#676a.1	2,500
Pn64	10(1921)	—	Dollar. Silver. Plain edge. K#676a.2	2,500
Pn65	10(1921)	—	Dollar. Gold. Reeded edge. K#1570	25,000
Pn66	10(1921)	—	Dollar. Gold. Plain edge. K#1570a	25,000
Pn67	ND(1923)	—	Dollar. Gold. K#1572	17,500
Pn68	ND(1923)	—	Dollar. Copper. K#677x	450
Pn69	ND(1923)	—	Dollar. Brass. K#677y	450
Pn70	12(1923)	—	Dollar. Gold. Y#336	25,000
Pn71	12(1923)	—	Dollar. Copper. Y#336	—
Pn72	12(1923)	—	Dollar. Gold. Y#336.1	—
Pn73	12(1924)	—	Dollar. Gold. K#1577	20,000
Pn74	ND(1924)	—	Dollar. Copper. K#683x	700
Pn75	ND(1924)	—	Dollar. Pewter. K#683y	700
Pn76	15(1926)	—	10 Cents. Copper. Y#334	125
Pn77	15(1926)	—	10 Cents. Lead. Y#334	90.00
Pn78	15(1926)	—	20 Cents. Copper. Y#335	65.00
PnA79	15(1926)	—	20 Cents. Silver. K#604	150,000
Pn79	15(1926)	—	Dollar. Silver. K#685	27,500
Pn80	16(1927)	—	10 Cents. Copper. Y#339	—
Pn81	16(1927)	—	10 Cents. Gold. Y#339	—
Pn82	ND(1927)	—	Dollar. Gold. Y#318	—
Pn83	ND(1927)	—	Dollar. Copper. Y#318	225
Pn84	ND(1927)	—	Dollar. Silver. K#687	60,000
Pn85	16(1927)	—	Dollar. Silver. K#686	65,000
Pn86	ND(1928)	—	20 Cash. Copper. Y#337	—
Pn87	ND(1928)	—	20 Cash. Copper. Similar to 1 Chiao.	—
Pn90	17(1928)	—	Dollar. Silver. K#688	50,000
Pn91	17(1928)	—	Dollar. Copper. K#688x	3,500
PnA92	17(1928)	—	Dollar. Gold. K#688z	—
Pn92	17(1928)	—	Dollar. Pewter. K#688y	6,500
Pn93	18(1929)	—	20 Cents. Silver. K#611	—
Pn94	18(1929)	—	10 Cents. Copper-Nickel. Vienna; K#617yVI	850
Pn95	18(1929)	—	20 Cents. Copper-Nickel. Vienna; K#617yV	—
Pn96	18(1929)	—	50 Cents. Copper-Nickel. Vienna; K#617yIV	—
Pn97	18(1929)	—	Dollar. Silver. Italian; K#614	4,000
Pn98	18(1929)	—	Dollar. Silver. With designer's name. K#614a	6,000
Pn99	18(1929)	—	Dollar. Silver. English; K#615	2,750
Pn100	18(1929)	—	Dollar. Silver. American; K#616	2,750
Pn101	18(1929)	—	Dollar. Silver. Austrian; K#61	2,200
Pn102	18(1929)	—	Dollar. Silver. Japanese; K#618	900

Note: In 1929 China invited several mints to submit designs for a new Sun Yat-sen Dollar, with his bust on one side and a junk on the other. All designs were very much alike, differing mainly in details of the portrait, the waves, and the junk.

Pn103	18(1929)	—	10 Cents. Silver. K#617yIII	850
Pn104	18(1929)	—	20 Cents. Silver. K#617yII	850
Pn105	18(1929)	—	50 Cents. Silver. K#617yI	850
Pn106	18(1929)	—	Dollar. Silver. K#610	50,000
Pn107	18(1929)	—	20 Cents. Silver. K#611	5,000
Pn108	18(1929)	—	Dollar. Silver. Wreath. K#612	—
Pn109	ND(1929)	—	Dollar. Silver. Memento. K#620	—
Pn110	ND(1929)	—	Dollar. Copper. K#620x	—
Pn111	ND(1929)	—	Dollar. White Metal. K#620y	—
Pn112	ND(1929)	—	Dollar. Silver. Wreath. K#620k	—
Pn113	ND(1929)	—	Dollar. White Metal. K#620m	—
Pn114	21(1932)	—	Cent. Bronze.	—
Pn115	21(1932)	—	Cent. Bronze. Without center hole	—
Pn118	21(1932)	—	2 Cents. Nickel. Milled edge. K#830	1,200

KM#	Date	Mintage	Identification	Mkt Val
Pn119	21(1932)	—	2 Cents. Nickel. Plain edge. K#830a	1,200
Pn120	21(1932)	—	2 Cents. Nickel. Without center hole; K#830b	2,000
Pn121	21(1932)	—	5 Cents. Nickel. Milled edge. K#829	550
Pn122	21(1932)	—	5 Cents. Nickel. Plain edge. K#829a	550
Pn123	21(1932)	—	5 Cents. Nickel. Without center; K#829b	550
Pn136	21(1932)	—	Dollar. Copper. K#628x	—
Pn137	21(1932)	—	Dollar. Copper. Y#344, K#622x.	275
Pn138	22(1933)	—	Dollar. Copper. K#345	—
Pn139	23(1934)	—	Dollar. Copper. Y#345	—
Pn140	24(1935)	—	5 Cents. Nickel. K#833	400
Pn141	24(1935)	—	5 Cents. Copper. K#833x	—
Pn142	24(1935)	—	10 Cents. Nickel. K#832	400
Pn143	24(1935)	—	10 Cents. Copper. K#832x	—
Pn144	24(1935)	—	20 Cents. Nickel. K#831	400
Pn145	24(1935)	—	20 Cents. Copper. K#831x	—
PnA146	24(1935)	—	1/2 Dollar. Silver. K#625k	—
PnB146	24(1935)	—	1/2 Dollar. Copper. K#625x	—
Pn146	24(1935)	—	Dollar. Silver. K#625	—
Pn146a	24(1935)	—	Dollar. Copper Or Brass. Reduced size Pn146	1,550
Pn147	24(1935)	—	Dollar. Copper. Y#345	—
Pn148	25//1936	—	Mei. Copper. Character "Chin".	—
Pn149	25//1936	—	Mei. Copper.	—
Pn150	25//1936	—	2 Mei. Copper.	—
Pn151	25//1936	—	5 Mei. Copper.	—
Pn152	25//1936	—	10 Mei. Copper.	—
Pn153	25//1936	—	50 Mei. Copper.	—
Pn154	25//1936	—	20 Wen. Copper.	—
PnA155	25//1936	—	1/2 Fen. Copper. Character "P'ing" lower.	—

Note: This may also exist with character under spade on reverse

Pn155	25(1936)	—	Fen. Copper.	—
PnA156	25//1936	—	Fen. Copper. Character "P'ing" lower.	—
PnB156	25//1936	—	Fen. Copper. Character "P'ing" under spade.	—
PnC156	25//1936	—	Fen. Copper. Character "Ch'ing" lower.	—
PnD156	25//1936	—	Fen. Copper. Character "Ch'ing" under spade.	—
Pn156	25(1936)	—	5 Cents. Copper. Y#348	—
Pn157	25(1936)	—	10 Cents. Nickel. Character "Ch'ing" in field or on portrait.	450
Pn158	25(1936)	—	10 Cents. Nickel. Character "P'ing" in field or on portrait.	450
Pn159	25(1936)	—	10 Cents. Nickel. Character "Ch'ing" on side of portrait.	450
Pn160	25(1936)	—	10 Cents. Nickel. Character "P'ing" on side of portrait.	450
Pn161	25(1936)	—	10 Cents. Copper. Y#349	—
Pn162	25(1936)	—	10 Cents. Aluminum. Y#349	—
Pn163	25(1936)	—	10 Cents. Aluminum-Bronze. Y#349	—
Pn164	25(1936)	—	10 Cents. Lead. Y#349	—
Pn165	25(1936)	—	20 Cents. Copper. Y#350	—
Pn166	25(1936)	—	20 Cents. Aluminum. Y#350	—
Pn167	25(1936)	—	20 Cents. Aluminum-Bronze. Y#350	—
Pn168	25(1936)	—	20 Cents. Pewter. Y#350	75.00
Pn169	25(1936)	—	50 Cents. Silver. K#635	—
Pn170	25(1936)	—	50 Cents. Silver. K#633	—
Pn171	25(1936)	—	50 Cents. Silver. Similar to K#633 without Greek border.	—
Pn172	25(1936)	—	Dollar. Silver. K#634	—
Pn173	25(1936)	—	Dollar. Silver. Similar to K#632 without Greek border.	—
Pn174	25(1936)	—	Dollar. Silver. K#632	9,000
Pn175	25(1936)	—	Dollar. Copper. K#632x	2,500
Pn176	25(1936)	—	Dollar. Nickel. K#632y	2,500
Pn177	25(1936)	—	Dollar. Brass. K#632z	2,500
Pn178	25(1936)	—	Dollar. Silver. Chiang Kai-shek	40,000
Pn179	25(1936)	—	Dollar. Copper. Chiang Kai-shek	7,500
Pn180	26(1937)	—	5 Cents. Nickel. Y#348.2	—
Pn181	26(1937)	—	10 Cents. Nickel. "P'ing" on side of portrait; Y#349.7	—
Pn183	26(1937)	—	20 Cents. Nickel. Y#350.1	—
Pn184	26(1937)S	—	50 Cents. Silver. K#637	—
Pn185	26(1937)S	—	Dollar. Silver. K#636	—
Pn186	27(1938)	—	5 Cents. Copper. Y#348	—
Pn187	27(1938)	—	10 Cents. Copper. Y#349	—
Pn188	27(1938)	—	20 Cents. Copper. Y#350	—
Pn189	27(1938)	—	20 Cents. Pewter. Y#350	150
Pn190	28(1939)	—	5 Cents. Copper. Y#348	—
Pn191	28(1939)	—	5 Cents. Brass. Y#348	—
PnA192	28(1939)	—	20 Cents. Copper. K#857x	175
PnB192	29(1940)	—	1/2 Dollar. Copper.	250
Pn192	30(1941)	—	10 Cents. Copper. Y#360	250
Pn193	30(1941)	—	10 Cents. Brass. Y#360	—
PnA194	30(1941)	—	20 Cents. Nickel. K#863 IV	250
PnB194	30(1941)	—	1/2 Dollar. Silver. K#696x	—
PnC194	30(1941)	—	1/2 Dollar. Nickel. K#863 III	2,000
Pn194	31(1942)	—	10 Cents. Copper-Nickel. Character "Kuei" below the spade.	—
Pn195	31(1942)	—	10 Cents. Copper. Y#360	—
Pn196	31(1942)	—	10 Cents. Brass. Y#360	—
Pn197	31(1942)	—	20 Cents. Copper-Nickel. Character "Kuei" below spade.	—
Pn198	31(1942)	—	20 Cents. Copper. Y#361	—

KM#	Date	Mintage	Identification	Mkt Val
Pn199	31(1942)	—	50 Cents. Copper-Nickel. Character "Kuei" between legs of space. K#866m	—
Pn200	31(1942)	—	50 Cents. Copper. Y#362	200
Pn201	31(1942)	—	50 Cents. Bronze. Y#362	200
Pn202	31(1942)	—	50 Cents. Silver. Y#362	1,500
PnA203	32(1943)	—	50 Cents. Copper-Nickel. Character "Kuei" between legs of spade.	—
Pn203	32(1943)	—	50 Cents. Copper. Y#362	200
Pn204	32(1943)	—	50 Cents. Bronze. Y#362	200
PnA205	37(1948)	—	50 Cents. Silver. Ch'ing right; K#698	—
Pn205	37(1948)	—	Dollar. Silver. K#637yII	—
Pn206	37(1948)	—	2 Dollars. Silver. K#637yI; denomination	200

PATTERNS
Gold Standard

KM#Pn124-135 were intended to be a gold standard coinage, but was not adopted. Though inscribed One Yuan Dollar, the proposed unit was called a Sun.

KM#	Date	Mintage	Identification	Mkt Val
Pn124	21(1932)	—	10 Cents. Silver. K#631	—
Pn125	21(1932)	—	10 Cents. Silver. Plain edge. K#631a	—
Pn126	21(1932)	—	10 Cents. Copper. K#631	—
Pn127	21(1932)	—	20 Cents. Silver. Milled edge. K#630	—
Pn128	21(1932)	—	20 Cents. Silver. Plain edge. K#630a	—
Pn129	21(1932)	—	20 Cents. Copper. K#630x	—
Pn130	21(1932)	—	1/2 Dollar. Silver. Milled edge. K#629	4,500
Pn131	21(1932)	—	1/2 Dollar. Silver. Plain edge. K#629a	4,500
Pn132	21(1932)	—	1/2 Dollar. Copper. K#629x	—
Pn133	21(1932)	—	Dollar. Silver. Milled edge. K#628	—
Pn134	21(1932)	—	Dollar. Silver. Plain edge. K#628a	10,000
Pn135	21(1932)	—	Dollar. Silver. Cherry blossom edge	10,000

TRIAL STRIKES

KM#	Date	Mintage	Identification	Mkt Val
TS1	ND(1912)	—	Dollar. Silver. Uniface. Chin Te-chuan; K#672b	8,000
TS2	37(1948)	—	50 Cents. Silver. 4.9800 g. K#698w	750

TAIWAN

REPUBLIC

STANDARD COINAGE

Y# 531   CHIAO
Bronze **Obv:** Bust of Sun Yat-sen left **Rev:** Map, symbols on sides

Date	Mintage	F	VF	XF	Unc	BU
38(1949)	157,600,000	0.15	0.30	1.00	4.00	5.00

Y# 533   CHIAO
1.1400 g., Aluminum, 19 mm. **Obv:** Bust of Sun Yat-sen left **Rev:** Map, symbols on sides **Edge:** Reeded

Date	Mintage	F	VF	XF	Unc	BU
44(1955)	583,980,000	—	0.10	0.15	1.00	1.50

Y# 545   CHIAO
1.1000 g., Aluminum **Obv:** Single-heart orchid **Rev:** Two Chinese symbols

Date	Mintage	F	VF	XF	Unc	BU
56(1967)	89,999,000	—	0.10	0.15	0.75	1.00
59(1970)	30,000,000	—	0.10	0.25	1.00	1.25
60(1971)	19,925,000	—	0.20	0.40	1.50	2.00
61(1972)	11,141,000	0.10	0.40	0.60	2.00	2.50
62(1973)	111,400,000	—	—	0.10	0.75	1.00
63(1974)	71,930,000	—	0.10	0.25	1.00	1.25

Y# 534   2 CHIAO
1.8000 g., Aluminum, 22.9 mm. **Obv:** Bust of Sun Yat-sen left **Rev:** Map, symbols at sides **Edge:** Smooth

Date	Mintage	F	VF	XF	Unc	BU
39(1950)	327,495,000	—	0.10	0.50	3.00	3.50

Y# 532   5 CHIAO
5.0000 g., 0.7200 Silver 0.1157 oz. ASW **Obv:** Bust of Sun Yat-sen left **Rev:** Map, symbols at sides

Date	Mintage	F	VF	XF	Unc	BU
38(1949)	—	1.85	2.25	3.75	5.50	7.00

Y# 535   5 CHIAO
Brass, 27 mm. **Obv:** Bust of Sun Yat-sen left **Rev:** Map, symbols at sides **Edge:** Reeded

Date	Mintage	F	VF	XF	Unc	BU
43(1954)	279,624,000	—	0.10	0.25	1.00	1.50

Y# 546   5 CHIAO
3.4000 g., Brass, 22.5 mm. **Obv:** Mayling orchid **Edge:** Reeded

Date	Mintage	F	VF	XF	Unc	BU
56(1967)	109,999,000	—	0.10	0.15	0.50	0.75
59(1970)	6,010,000	0.15	0.30	0.60	1.25	1.50
60(1971)	4,434,000	0.20	0.40	0.80	1.50	1.75
61(1972)	21,171,000	—	0.10	0.20	1.00	1.25
62(1973)	88,840,000	—	0.10	0.20	1.00	1.25
69(1980)	3,972,000	—	0.10	0.20	1.00	1.25
70(1981)	100,000,000	—	0.10	0.20	1.00	1.25

Y# 550   1/2 YUAN
3.0000 g., Bronze, 18 mm. **Obv:** Orchid **Rev:** Value and Chinese symbols **Edge:** Plain

Date	Mintage	F	VF	XF	Unc	BU
70(1981)	103,800,000	—	0.10	0.20	1.00	1.25
70(1981) Proof	—	Value: 10.00				
75(1986)	22,000,000	—	0.10	0.20	1.00	1.25
77(1988)	10,000,000	—	0.15	0.30	1.25	1.50
84(1995)	—	—	0.15	0.30	1.00	1.25
84(1995) Proof	—	Value: 10.00				
85(1996)	—	—	0.15	0.30	1.00	1.25
85(1996) Proof	—	Value: 10.00				
86(1997)	—	—	0.15	0.30	1.00	1.25
86(1997) Proof	—	Value: 10.00				
87(1998)	—	—	0.15	0.30	1.00	1.25
87(1998) Proof	—	Value: 10.00				
88(1999)	—	—	0.15	0.30	1.00	1.25
88(1999) Proof	—	Value: 10.00				
89(2000)	—	—	0.15	0.30	1.00	1.25
89(2000) Proof	—	Value: 10.00				

Y# 536   YUAN
5.9300 g., Copper-Nickel-Zinc, 25 mm. **Obv:** Plum blossom **Rev:** Orchid **Edge:** Reeded

Date	Mintage	F	VF	XF	Unc	BU
49(1960)	321,717,000	—	0.10	0.20	0.50	0.65
59(1970)	48,800,000	0.10	0.20	0.50	1.00	1.25
60(1971)	41,532,000	0.10	0.20	0.50	1.00	1.25
61(1972)	105,309,000	—	0.10	0.20	0.50	0.65
62(1973)	353,924,000	—	0.10	0.20	0.50	0.65
63(1974)	535,605,000	—	0.10	0.20	0.50	0.65
64(1975)	456,874,000	—	0.10	0.20	0.50	0.65
65(1976)	634,497,000	—	0.10	0.20	0.50	0.65
66(1977)	116,900,000	—	0.10	0.20	0.50	0.65
67(1978)	104,245,000	—	0.10	0.20	0.50	0.65
68(1979)	—	0.10	0.20	0.50	0.80	1.00
69(1980)	113,900,000	—	0.10	0.20	0.50	0.65

Y# A537   YUAN
Silver **Subject:** 50th Anniversary of the Republic **Obv:** Chiang Kai-shek left **Rev:** Value at center within flower wreath

Date	Mintage	F	VF	XF	Unc	BU
50(1961)	—	—	—	—	285	325

Note: This coin was released accidentally or was released and quickly withdrawn and is very scarce today

Y# 543   YUAN
Copper-Nickel **Subject:** 80th Birthday of Chiang Kai-shek **Obv:** Bust of Chiang Kai-shek **Rev:** Chinese value in center

Date	Mintage	F	VF	XF	Unc	BU
55(1966)	—	0.25	0.35	0.50	1.00	1.50

Y# 547   YUAN
Copper-Nickel-Zinc, 25 mm. **Series:** F.A.O. **Obv:** Orchid **Rev:** Farmer in field, value below **Edge:** Reeded

Date	Mintage	F	VF	XF	Unc	BU
58(1969)	10,000,000	0.25	0.35	0.50	1.00	1.50

Y# 551   YUAN
3.8000 g., Bronze, 19.92 mm. **Obv:** Bust of Chiang Kai-shek left **Rev:** Chinese value in center, 1 below **Edge:** Reeded

Date	Mintage	F	VF	XF	Unc	BU
70(1981)	1,080,000,000	—	—	0.10	0.15	0.25
70(1981) Proof	—	Value: 12.50				
71(1982)	780,000,000	—	—	0.10	0.15	0.25
72(1983)	420,000,000	—	—	0.10	0.15	0.25
73(1984)	110,000,000	—	—	0.10	0.15	0.25
74(1985)	200,000,000	—	—	0.10	0.15	0.25
75(1986)	200,000,000	—	—	0.10	0.15	0.25
76(1987)	110,000,000	—	—	0.10	0.15	0.25
77(1988)	40,000,000	—	—	0.20	0.50	0.65

Date	Mintage	F	VF	XF	Unc	BU
81(1992)	—	—	—	0.15	0.25	0.35
82(1993)	—	—	—	0.15	0.25	0.35
83(1994)	—	—	—	0.15	0.25	0.35
84(1995)	—	—	—	0.15	0.25	0.35
84(1995) Proof	—	Value: 12.50				
85(1996)	—	—	—	0.15	0.25	0.35
85(1996) Proof	—	Value: 12.50				
86(1997)	—	—	—	0.15	0.25	0.35
86(1997) Proof	—	Value: 12.50				
87(1998)	—	—	—	0.15	0.30	0.35
87(1998) Proof	—	Value: 12.50				
88(1999)	—	—	—	0.15	0.30	0.35
88(1999) Proof	—	Value: 12.50				
89(2000)	—	—	—	0.15	0.30	0.35
89(2000) Proof	—	Value: 12.50				

Y# 537 5 YUAN
Copper-Nickel **Obv:** Bust of Sun Yat-sen left **Rev:** Mausoleum in Nanking **Edge:** Reeded

Date	Mintage	F	VF	XF	Unc	BU
54(1965)	—	0.35	0.75	1.50	5.00	6.50

Y# 548 5 YUAN
9.5000 g., Copper-Nickel, 28.9 mm. **Obv:** Bust of Chiang Kai-shek left **Rev:** Chinese symbols in center **Edge:** Reeded

Date	Mintage	F	VF	XF	Unc	BU
59(1970)	12,360,000	0.20	0.40	0.80	1.50	2.00
60(1971)	20,575,000	0.20	0.35	0.50	1.00	1.50
61(1972)	27,998,000	0.20	0.35	0.50	1.00	1.50
62(1973)	50,122,000	0.20	0.35	0.50	0.80	1.25
63(1974)	418,068,000	0.20	0.35	0.50	0.80	1.25
64(1975)	39,520,000	0.20	0.35	0.50	0.80	1.25
65(1976)	140,000,000	0.20	0.35	0.50	0.80	1.25
66(1977)	50,260,000	0.20	0.35	0.50	0.80	1.25
67(1978)	78,082,000	0.20	0.35	0.50	0.80	1.25
68(1979)	—	0.20	0.35	0.50	0.80	1.25
69(1980)	273,000,000	0.20	0.35	0.50	0.80	1.25
70(1981)	162,000,000	0.20	0.35	0.50	0.80	1.25

Y# 552 5 YUAN
Copper-Nickel **Obv:** Bust of Chiang Kai-shek left **Rev:** Chinese symbols in center, 5 below

Date	Mintage	F	VF	XF	Unc	BU
70(1981)	522,432,000	—	0.15	0.20	0.50	0.75
70(1981) Proof	—	Value: 12.50				
71(1982)	6,600,000	—	0.15	0.20	0.50	0.75
72(1983)	34,000,000	—	0.15	0.20	0.50	0.75
73(1984)	280,000,000	—	0.15	0.20	0.50	0.75
77(1988)	200,000,000	—	0.15	0.20	0.50	0.75
78(1989)	—	—	0.15	0.20	0.50	0.75
84(1995)	—	—	0.15		0.25	0.50	0.75
84(1995) Proof	—	Value: 12.50				
85(1996)	—	—	0.15		0.25	0.50	0.75
85(1996) Proof	—	Value: 12.50				
86(1997)	—	—	0.15		0.25	0.50	0.75
86(1997) Proof	—	Value: 12.50				
87(1998)	—	—	0.15		0.25	0.50	0.75
87(1998) Proof	—	Value: 12.50				
88(1999)	—	—	0.15		0.25	0.50	0.75
88(1999) Proof	—	Value: 12.50				
89(2000)	—	—	0.15		0.25	0.50	0.75
89(2000) Proof	—	Value: 12.50				

Y# 538 10 YUAN
Copper-Nickel, 26 mm. **Obv:** Bust of Sun Yat-sen left **Rev:** Mausoleum in Nanking

Date	Mintage	F	VF	XF	Unc	BU
54(1965)	—	0.50	1.00	2.00	6.00	7.50

Y# 553 10 YUAN
7.5000 g., Copper-Nickel, 26 mm. **Obv:** Bust of Chiang Kai-shek left **Rev:** Chinese symbols in center, 10 below

Date	Mintage	F	VF	XF	Unc	BU
70(1981)	123,000,000	—	0.30	0.45	0.75	1.00
70(1981) Proof	—	Value: 15.00				
71(1982)	361,000,000	—	0.30	0.45	0.75	1.00
72(1983)	196,000,000	—	0.30	0.45	0.75	1.00
73(1984)	220,000,000	—	0.30	0.45	0.75	1.00
74(1985)	200,000,000	—	0.30	0.45	0.75	1.00
75(1986)	100,000,000	—	0.30	0.45	0.75	1.00
76(1987)	90,000,000	—	0.30	0.45	0.75	1.00
77(1988)	100,000,000	—	0.30	0.45	0.75	1.00
78(1989)	—	—	0.30	0.45	0.75	1.00
79(1990)	—	—	0.30	0.45	0.75	1.00
80(1991)	—	—	0.30	0.45	0.75	1.00
81(1992)	—	—	0.30	0.45	0.75	1.00
82(1993)	—	—	0.30	0.45	0.75	1.00
83(1994)	—	—	0.30	0.45	0.75	1.00
84(1995)	—	—	0.25	0.45	0.75	1.00
84(1995) Proof	—	Value: 15.00				
85(1996)	—	—	0.25	0.45	0.75	1.00
85(1996) Proof	—	Value: 15.00				
86(1997)	—	—	0.25	0.45	0.75	1.00
86(1997) Proof	—	Value: 15.00				
87(1998)	—	—	0.25	0.45	0.75	1.00
87(1998) Proof	—	Value: 15.00				
88(1999)	—	—	0.25	0.45	0.75	1.00
88(1999) Proof	—	Value: 15.00				
89(2000)	—	—	0.25	0.45	0.75	1.00
89(2000) Proof	—	Value: 15.00				

Y# 555 10 YUAN
Copper-Nickel, 26 mm. **Subject:** 50th Anniversary - Taiwan's Liberation from Japan **Obv:** Map with dates flanking **Rev:** Chinese symbols in center, 10 below

Date	Mintage	F	VF	XF	Unc	BU
84(1995)	—	—	—	—	2.50	3.00

Y# 558 10 YUAN
Copper-Nickel, 26 mm. **Subject:** 50th Anniversary - Taiwan Yuan (Dollar) **Obv:** Coins **Rev:** Anniversary dates above denomination **Edge:** Reeded

Date	Mintage	F	VF	XF	Unc	BU
88(1999)	30,000,000	—	—	—	2.75	3.50

Y# 560 10 YUAN
7.5000 g., Copper-Nickel, 26 mm. **Subject:** Year of the Dragon **Obv:** Stylized dragon above denomination **Rev:** Dragon

Date	Mintage	F	VF	XF	Unc	BU
89(2000)	—	—	—	—	3.00	3.50

Y# 539 50 YUAN
17.1000 g., 0.7500 Silver 0.4123 oz. ASW **Obv:** Bust of Sun Yat-sen left **Rev:** Chinese symbols in center, bird above, deer below

Date	Mintage	F	VF	XF	Unc	BU
54(1965)	—	—	12.50	25.00	32.50

Y# 554 50 YUAN
Brass **Obv:** Orchid burst **Rev:** Chinese symbols center, 50 below, flower wreath circle

Date	Mintage	F	VF	XF	Unc	BU
81-1992 (1992)	—	—	0.50	1.00	3.50	4.00
82-1993 (1993)	—	—	0.50	1.00	3.50	4.00
84-1995 (1995)	—	—	0.50	1.00	3.50	4.00
84-1995 (1995) Proof	—	—	—	—	—	—
85-1996 (1996)	—	—	0.50	1.00	3.50	4.00
85-1996 (1996) Proof	—	—	—	—	—	—
86-1997 (1997)	—	—	0.50	1.00	3.50	4.00
86-1997 (1997) ,Proof	—	—	—	—	—	—
87-1998 (1998)	—	—	0.50	1.00	3.50	4.00
87-1998 (1998) Proof	—	—	—	—	—	—
88-1999 (1999)	—	—	0.50	1.00	3.50	4.00
88-1999 (1999) Proof	—	—	—	—	—	—
89-2000 (2000)	—	—	0.50	1.00	3.50	4.00
89-2000 (2000) Proof	—	—	—	—	—	—

Y# 556 50 YUAN
Bi-Metallic Brass center in Copper-Nickel ring **Obv:** Parliament building **Rev:** Value left, Chinese symbols at bottom

Date	Mintage	F	VF	XF	Unc	BU
84-1995 (1995)	—	—	—	—	5.75	6.50
84-1995 (1995) Proof	—	—	—	—	—	—
85-1996 (1996)	—	—	—	—	5.75	6.50
85-1996 (1996) Proof	—	—	—	—	—	—
86-1997 (1997)	—	—	—	—	5.75	6.50
86-1997 (1997) Proof	—	—	—	—	—	—
87-1998 (1998)	—	—	—	—	5.75	6.50
87-1998 (1998) Proof	—	—	—	—	—	—
88-1999 (1999)	—	—	—	—	5.75	6.50
88-1999 (1999) Proof	—	—	—	—	—	—
89-2000 (2000)	—	—	—	—	5.75	6.50
89-2000 (2000) Proof	—	—	—	—	—	—

Y# 562 50 YUAN
15.5680 g., 0.9990 Silver 0.5000 oz. ASW, 33 mm.
Subject: Late President - Chiang Ching-Kuo **Obv:** Bust of Ching-kuo facing **Rev:** Mausoleum above denomination **Edge:** Reeded **Mint:** Central Mint of China

Date	Mintage	F	VF	XF	Unc	BU
87 (1998)	70,000	—	—	—	25.00	28.00

Y# 559　50 YUAN
15.5500 g., 0.9250 Silver 0.4624 oz. ASW　**Subject:** 50 Years - Taiwan Yuan (Dollar) **Obv:** Coins **Rev:** Denomination including coin design and date

Date	Mintage	F	VF	XF	Unc	BU
88(1999)	390,000	—	—	—	20.00	22.50

Y# 564　50 YUAN
15.5680 g., 0.9990 Silver 0.5000 oz. ASW, 33 mm.
Subject: Year 2000 **Obv:** Celestial globe **Rev:** Dragon **Edge:** Reeded **Mint:** Central Mint of China

Date	Mintage	F	VF	XF	Unc	BU
89 (2000)	120,000	—	—	—	25.00	28.00

Y# 540　100 YUAN
22.2100 g., 0.7500 Silver 0.5355 oz. ASW　**Obv:** Bust of Sun Yat-sen left

Date	Mintage	F	VF	XF	Unc	BU
54(1965)	—	—	—	13.50	27.50	35.00

Y# 561　100 YUAN
15.5680 g., 0.9990 Silver 0.5000 oz. ASW, 33 mm.
Subject: 50th Anniversary - 2-28 Incident **Obv:** Monument **Rev:** Geometrical design **Edge:** Reeded **Mint:** Central Mint of China

Date	Mintage	F	VF	XF	Unc	BU
86(1997)	55,000	—	—	—	25.00	28.00

Y# 557　200 YUAN
31.1350 g., 0.9990 Silver 100000 oz. ASW　**Subject:** First Popular Election Vote **Obv:** Bust of President Lee Teng-hui and Vice President Lien Chan **Rev:** National emblem above text

Date	Mintage	F	VF	XF	Unc	BU
85(1996) Proof	—	Value: 65.00				

Y# 566　200 YUAN
31.3500 g., 0.9990 Silver 1.0069 oz. ASW, 38 mm.
Subject: Second Popular Vote Presidential Election **Obv:** Bust of the President and Vice-president **Rev:** National emblem above inscription **Edge:** Reeded

Date	Mintage	F	VF	XF	Unc	BU
89 (2000)	—	—	—	—	75.00	85.00

Y# 541　1000 YUAN
15.0000 g., 0.9000 Gold 0.4340 oz. AGW　**Obv:** Bust of Sun Yat-sen left

Date	Mintage	F	VF	XF	Unc	BU
54(1965)	—	—	—	—	425	475

Y# 563　1000 YUAN
15.5540 g., 0.9990 Gold 0.4996 oz. AGW, 25 mm.　**Subject:** Late President - Chiang Ching-kuo **Obv:** Bust of Ching-kuo facing **Rev:** Mausoleum **Edge:** Reeded **Mint:** Central Mint of China

Date	Mintage	F	VF	XF	Unc	BU
87(1998)	30,000	—	—	—	475	500

Y# 542　2000 YUAN
30.0000 g., 0.9000 Gold 0.8680 oz. AGW　**Obv:** Bust of Sun Yat-sen left **Rev:** Chinese symbols at center, budding branch wrapped around

Date	Mintage	F	VF	XF	Unc	BU
54(1965)	—	—	—	—	850	900

Y# 544　2000 YUAN
31.0600 g., 0.9000 Gold 0.8987 oz. AGW　**Subject:** 80th Birthday of Chiang Kai-shek **Rev:** Two cranes standing on rock

Date	Mintage	F	VF	XF	Unc	BU
55(1966)	—	—	—	—	875	925

PATTERNS
Yuan System; Including off metal strikes

KG numbers in reference to Coinage of the Chinese Emigre Government 1949-1957 by E. Kann and D. Graham.

KM#	Date	Mintage	Identification	Mkt Val
Pn1	ND38(1949)	—	Chiao. Bronze. KG#12a	150
Pn2	38(1949)	—	Chiao. Aluminum. KG#12b	150
Pn3	38(1949)	—	Chiao. Copper. KG#12c	150
Pn4	38(1949)	—	Chiao. Copper. KG#12d	150
Pn5	38(1949)	—	Chiao. Aluminum. K#12e; without reeded edge	150
Pn6	38(1949)	—	Chiao. Copper. k#13	150
Pn7	38(1949)	—	Chiao. Copper. K#14	150
Pn8	38(1949)	—	5 Chiao. Aluminum-Bronze. KG#15a	350
Pn9	38(1949)	—	5 Chiao. Aluminum. KG#15b	250
Pn10	38(1949)	—	5 Chiao. Silver. KG#16	400
Pn11	38(1949)	—	5 Chiao. Copper. KG#16a	300
Pn12	38(1949)	—	5 Chiao. Silver. KG#17	375
Pn13	38(1949)	—	5 Chiao. Silver. KG#18	600
Pn14	38(1949)	—	5 Chiao. Silver. KG#19	725
Pn15	38(1949)	—	5 Chiao. Silver. KG#20	400
Pn16	38(1949)	—	Yuan. Silver. KG#21i	400
PnA17	38(1949)	—	Yuan. Nickel. Plain edge.	—
PnB17	38(1949)	—	20 Yuan. Bronze.	1,200
Pn17	39(1950)	—	2 Chiao. Aluminum. Reeded edge. KG#21a	150
Pn18	39(1950)	—	2 Chiao. Aluminum-Bronze. KG#21b	150
Pn19	39(1950)	—	2 Chiao. Aluminum-Bronze. KG#21c; without reeded edge	150
Pn20	39(1950)	—	2 Chiao. Copper. KG#21d	150
Pn21	39(1950)	—	Yuan. Silver.	700
Pn22	39(1950)	—	Yuan. Copper-Nickel.	300
Pn23	39(1950)	—	Yuan. Copper-Nickel.	300
Pn24	39(1950)	—	Yuan. Aluminum-Bronze. KG#22a	200
Pn25	39(1950)	—	Yuan. Aluminum. KG#22b	350
Pn26	43(1954)	—	5 Chiao. Aluminum-Bronze. KG#23	300
Pn27	43(1954)	—	5 Chiao. Aluminum-Bronze. Reeded edge. KG#23a	300
Pn28	43(1954)	—	5 Chiao. Copper. KG#23b	300
Pn29	43(1954)	—	5 Chiao. Aluminum-Bronze. KG#23c	300
Pn30	43(1954)	—	5 Chiao. Aluminum-Bronze. KG#24	300
Pn31	43(1954)	—	5 Chiao. Aluminum-Bronze. KG#25	300
Pn32	43(1954)	—	5 Chiao. Aluminum-Bronze. KG#25a	300
Pn33	43(1954)	—	5 Chiao. Bronze. KG#26a	300
Pn34	44(1955)	—	Chiao. Aluminum. Simplified "TAI", KG#27a	175
Pn35	44(1955)	—	Chiao. Bronze. KG#27b	175
PnA36	45(1956)	—	2 Chiao. Aluminum-Bronze.	
Pn36	45(1956)	—	2 Chiao. Copper-Nickel. Y#534	175
PnA37	45(1956)	—	Yuan. Copper-Nickel. Ocean unlined.	
PnB37	45(1956)	—	Yuan. Aluminum-Bronze. Pn37 with simplified "TAI" character.	
Pn37	45(1956)	—	Yuan. Copper-Nickel.	300
Pn38	48(1959)	—	Yuan. Nickel.	350
Pn39	48(1959)	—	Yuan. Nickel-Silver.	250
Pn40	49(1960)	—	Yuan. Nickel-Silver. Y#536	250
Pn41	49(1960)	—	Yuan. Nickel-Silver. Large flan	275
Pn42	49(1960)	—	Yuan. Nickel-Silver. With Taiwan-sheng	275
Pn43	49(1960)	—	Yuan. Nickel-Silver. With 1 Yuan	275
Pn44	49(1960)	—	Yuan. Nickel-Silver. With 1 Kinmen	275
Pn45	49(1960)	—	5 Yuan. Nickel.	—
Pn46	49(1960)	—	5 Yuan. Nickel. Ancient Chinese symbols	—
PnA47	50(1961)	—	Yuan. Copper-Nickel. Reeded edge. Y#536	650
Pn47	50(1961)	—	Yuan. Nickel-Silver. Sun Yat-sen.	225
Pn48	50(1961)	—	Yuan. Nickel-Aluminum. Chiang Kai-shek.	225
Pn49	50(1961)	—	Yuan. Nickel-Silver. Similar to Pn48 but eleven characters above bust.	225
PnA49	50(1961)	—	Yuan. Nickel. Chiang Kai-shek.	225
PnB49	50(1961)	—	Yuan. Nickel-Aluminum. Chiang Kai-shek.	225
Pn50	51(1962)	—	5 Yuan. Nickel.	300
Pn51	53(1964)	—	5 Yuan. Copper-Nickel.	300
Pn52	54(1965)	—	10 Yuan. Copper-Nickel. Clouds replace mountains. Y#538	400
Pn53	54(1965)	—	10 Yuan. Copper-Nickel. Without clouds. Y#538	400
Pn54	55(1966)	—	2000 Yuan. Gilt Silver. Madam and President Chiang. Y#544	650
Pn65	62(1973)	—	5 Yuan. Gold. Y#548	1,350
Pn66	64(1975)	—	Yuan. Gold. Y#536	950
Pn67	64(1975)	—	Yuan. Aluminum. Y#536	200

PATTERNS
Tael System; Including off metal strikes

KG numbers in reference to Coinage of the Chinese Emigre Government 1949-1957 by E. Kann and D. Graham.

KM#	Date	Mintage	Identification	Mkt Val
Pn55	38(1949)	—	Chien. Aluminum-Bronze. KG#7b	350
Pn56	38(1949)	—	Chien. Silver. KG#6a	500
Pn57	38(1949)	—	Chien. Aluminum-Bronze. KG#6b	350
Pn58	38(1949)	—	2 Chien. Aluminum-Bronze. KG#4b	350
Pn59	38(1949)	—	2 Chien. Aluminum-Bronze. KG#3b	350
Pn60	38(1949)	—	5 Chien. Aluminum-Bronze. KG#2b	350
Pn62	45(1956)	—	2 Chien. Copper-Nickel.	250
Pn63	45(1956)	—	2 Chien. Aluminum-Bronze.	250
Pn64	45(1956)	—	2 Chien. Aluminum.	250

MINT SETS

KM#	Date	Mintage	Identification	Issue Price	Mkt Val
MS1	54(1965) (4)	—	Y#537-540	—	75.00
MS2	70(1981) (4)	—	Y#550-553	—	—
MS3	84(1995) (5)	—	Y#550-554	—	—
MS4	85(1996) (5)	—	Y#550-554	—	—
MS5	86(1997) (5)	—	Y#550-554	—	—
MS6	87(1998) (5)	—	Y#550-554	—	—
MS7	88(1999) (5)	—	Y#550-554	—	—
MSA7	88(1999) (2)	260,000	Y#558-559	—	25.00
MS8	89(2000) (5)	—	Y#550-554	—	—
MS9	92(2003) (6)	—	Y550-553, 565, 568 plus C-N Year of the Goat medal	—	20.00

PROOF SETS

KM#	Date	Mintage	Identification	Issue Price	Mkt Val
PS1	70(1981) (4)	—	Y#550-553	—	50.00
PS2	82(1993) (5)	50,000	Y#550-554	14.75	300
PS3	83(1994) (5)	70,000	Y#550-554	14.75	80.00
PS4	84(1995) (5)	70,000	Y#550-554	17.65	57.50
PS5	85(1996) (10)	70,000	Y#550-553 & 556	17.65	62.50
PS6	86(1997) (10)	70,000	Y#550-553 & 556	17.65	62.50
PS7	87(1998) (10)	100,000	Y#550-553 & 556	20.60	35.00
PS8	88(1999) (10)	100,000	Y#550-554	20.60	35.00
PS9	89(2000) (5)	100,000	Y#550-553 & 556	22.05	62.50

CHINA-JAPANESE PUPPET STATES

Shortly after World War I the greatest external threat to the territorial integrity of China was posed by Japan, which urgently needed room for an expanding population and raw materials for its industrial and military machines, and which recognized the necessity of controlling all of China if it was to realize its plan of dominating the rest of the Asiatic and South Sea countries. The Japanese had large investments in Manchuria (a name given by non-Chinese to the three northeastern provinces of China), which allowed them privileges that compromised Chinese sovereignty. The educated of China were not reconciled to Japan's growing power in Manchuria, and the resultant friction occasioned a series of vexing incidents, which Japan decided to circumvent by direct action. On the night of Sept. 18-19, 1931, with a contrived incident for an excuse, Japanese forces seized the city of Mukden (Shenyang), and within a few weeks completely demolished Chinese power north of the Great Wall.

In Feb. 1932, after the Japanese occupation of Manchuria, they set up Manchoukuo as an independent republic. Jehol (Rehe) was occupied by the Japanese in 1933 and added to Manchoukuo. Manchoukuo was established as an empire in 1934 with the deposed Manchu emperor Hsuan T'ung (the late Henry Pu Yi) as the puppet emperor K'ang Te. Lacking the means to face the Japanese armies in the field, the Chinese could only trade space for time.

Not content with confining its control of China to the areas north of the Great Wall, the Japanese launched a major campaign in 1937, and by the fall of 1938 had occupied in addition to Manchuria the provinces of Hopei (Hebei) and Chahar, most of the port cities, and the major cities as far west as Hankow (Hankou), now part of Wuhan. In addition, they dominated or threatened the provinces of Suiyuan, Shansi (Shanxi) and Shantung (Shandong).

Still the Chinese did not yield. The struggle was prolonged until the advent of World War II, which brought about the defeat of Japan and the return of the puppet states to Chinese control.

As the victorious Japanese armies swept deeper into China, Japan established central banks under control of the Bank of Japan in the conquered provinces for the purpose of establishing control over banking and finance in the puppet states, and eventually in all of China. These included the Chi Tung Bank, which had its main office in Tientsin (Tianjin) with branches in Peking (Beijing), Chinan (Jinan) and Tangshan, the Federal Reserve Bank of China with its main office in Peking (Beijing) and branches in 37 other cities; and the Hua Hsing Bank with its main office in Shanghai and two branches. The puppet states of Manchukuo, previously detailed in this introduction, and Mengchiang, which comprised a greater part of Inner Mongolia, were also major coin-issuing entities.

EAST HOPEI

AUTONOMOUS

The Chi Tung Bank was the banking institution of the "East Hopei Anti-Comintern Autonomous Government" established by the Japanese in 1936 to undermine the political position of China in the northwest provinces. It issued both coins and notes between 1937 and 1939 with a restraint uncharacteristic of the puppet banks of the China-Japanese puppet states.

ANTI-COMINTERN AUTONOMOUS GOVERNMENT

STANDARD COINAGE

Y# 516   5 LI
Copper **Issuer:** Chi Tung Bank **Obv:** Japanese character "first"
Rev: Value in grain stalks

Date	Mintage	VG	F	VF	XF	Unc
26(1937)	—	8.00	20.00	40.00	70.00	200

Y# 517   FEN
Copper **Issuer:** Chi Tung Bank **Obv:** Japanese character "first"
Rev: Value in grain stalks

Date	Mintage	VG	F	VF	XF	Unc
26(1937)	—	2.50	6.00	12.00	18.00	60.00

Y# 518   5 FEN
Copper-Nickel **Issuer:** Chi Tung Bank **Obv:** Japanese character "first" **Rev:** Value in grain stalks

Date	Mintage	VG	F	VF	XF	Unc
26(1937)	—	2.00	5.00	9.00	13.00	50.00

Y# 519   CHIAO
Copper-Nickel **Issuer:** Chi Tung Bank **Obv:** T'ien-ning Pagoda in Peking **Rev:** Value in grain stalks

Date	Mintage	VG	F	VF	XF	Unc
26(1937)	—	2.00	5.00	9.00	13.00	45.00

Y# 520   2 CHIAO
Copper-Nickel **Issuer:** Chi Tung Bank **Obv:** T'ien-ning Pagoda in Peking **Rev:** Value in grain stalks

Date	Mintage	VG	F	VF	XF	Unc
26(1937)	—	2.50	6.00	12.00	20.00	70.00

MANCHOUKUO

(Manchukuo)

The former Japanese puppet state of Manchoukuo (largely Manchuria), comprising the northeastern Chinese provinces of Fengtien (Liaoning), Kirin (Jilin), Heilungkiang (Heilongjiang) and Jehol (Rehe), had an area of 503,143 sq. mi. (1,303,134 sq. km.) and a population of 43.3 million. Capital: Changchun, renamed Hsinking. The area is rich in fertile soil, timber and mineral resources, including coal, iron and gold.

Until the closing years of the 19th century when Chinese influence became predominant, Manchuria was chiefly a domain of the tribal Manchus and their Mongol allies. Coincident with the rise of Chinese influence, foreign imperialistic powers began to appreciate the value of the area to their expansionist philosophy. Japan, overpopulated and poor in resources, desired it as a source of raw materials and for increased living area. Russia wanted it as the eastern terminus of the Trans-Siberian railway that was to unite its Asian empire. The inevitable conflict of Japanese, Chinese and Russian interests required that one or more of the powers be eliminated. After eliminating Russia in their war of 1904-05, Japan eliminated China on the night of Sept. 18, 1931, when, on the pretext of a contrived incident, it moved militarily to seize control of the Three Eastern Provinces. Early in 1932 Japan declared Manchuria independent by virtue of a voluntary separatist movement and established the state of Manchoukuo. To give the puppet state an aura of legitimacy, the deposed emperor of the former Manchu dynasty was recalled from retirement and designated "chief executive". The area was restored to China at the end of World War II.

RULERS
Ta T'ung, 1932-1934
K'ang Te, 1934-1945

The puppet emperor under the assumed name of K'ang Te was previously the last emperor of China (P'u-yi, or Hsuan T'ung, 1909-11).

MONETARY SYSTEM
10 Li = 1 Fen
10 Fen = 1 Chiao

IDENTIFICATION OF REIGN CHARACTERS

'Nien' Year	1932-1934	Ta T'ung

'Nien' Year	1934-1945	K'ang Te

DATE ABBREVIATIONS
TT - Ta T'ung
KT - K'ang Te

GREEK RIM BORDER VARIETIES

Narrow Design   Wide Design

MARKET VALUATIONS
Uncirculated aluminum coins without any planchet defects are worth up to twice the market valuations given.

JAPANESE OCCUPATION

STANDARD COINAGE

Y# 1   5 LI
Bronze **Ruler:** Ta-t'ung **Obv:** Flag **Rev:** Value in floral sprays

Date	Mintage	VG	F	VF	XF	Unc
TT 2(1933)	—	16.00	40.00	70.00	100	200
TT 3(1934)	—	3.00	8.00	18.00	30.00	60.00

Y# 5   5 LI
Bronze **Ruler:** K'ang-te **Obv:** Character Yuan for "first", flag **Rev:** Value in floral sprays

Date	Mintage	VG	F	VF	XF	Unc
KT 1(1934)	—	2.50	6.00	15.00	20.00	50.00
KT 2(1935)	—	2.50	6.00	15.00	20.00	50.00
KT 3(1936)	—	12.00	27.50	42.50	60.00	110
KT 4(1937)	—	3.00	8.00	20.00	25.00	55.00
KT 6(1939)	—	75.00	150	200	275	375

Y# 2   FEN
5.0100 g., Bronze, 23.97 mm. **Ruler:** Ta-t'ung **Obv:** Flag **Rev:** Value in floral sprays

Date	Mintage	VG	F	VF	XF	Unc
TT 2(1933)	—	1.50	4.00	8.00	16.00	50.00
TT 3(1934)	—	1.25	3.00	6.00	10.00	40.00

Y# 6 FEN
Bronze **Ruler:** K'ang-te **Obv:** Character Yuan for "first", flag
Rev: Value in floral sprays

Date	Mintage	VG	F	VF	XF	Unc
KT 1(1934)	—	0.80	2.00	6.00	12.00	30.00
KT 2(1935)	—	0.80	2.00	6.00	10.00	20.00
KT 3(1936)	—	0.80	2.00	6.00	10.00	20.00
KT 4(1937)	—	0.80	2.00	6.00	10.00	20.00
KT 5(1938)	—	0.80	2.00	6.00	10.00	20.00
KT 6(1939)	—	0.80	2.00	6.00	12.00	30.00

Y# 9 FEN
Aluminum, 19 mm. **Ruler:** K'ang-te **Obv:** National symbol
Rev: Value in floral wreath

Date	Mintage	VG	F	VF	XF	Unc
KT 6(1939)	—	0.30	0.80	1.50	4.00	10.00
KT 7(1940)	—	0.30	0.80	1.50	4.00	10.00
KT 8(1941)	—	0.30	0.80	1.50	4.00	10.00
KT 9(1942)	—	0.30	0.80	1.50	4.00	10.00
KT 10(1943)	—	0.30	0.80	1.50	4.00	10.00

Y# 13 FEN
Aluminum **Ruler:** K'ang-te **Obv:** Legend around large "1"
Rev: Floral wreath

Date	Mintage	VG	F	VF	XF	Unc
KT 10(1943)	—	0.70	1.50	4.00	10.00	20.00
KT 11(1944)	—	0.70	1.50	4.00	10.00	20.00

Y# 13a FEN
Red Fiber **Ruler:** K'ang-te **Obv:** Legend around large "1" **Rev:**
Floral wreath

Date	Mintage	Good	VG	F	VF	XF
KT 12(1945)	—	4.00	6.00	9.00	18.00	30.00

Y# 13a.1 FEN
Brown Fiber **Ruler:** K'ang-te **Obv:** Legend around large "1" **Rev:**
Floral wreath

Date	Mintage	Good	VG	F	VF	XF
KT 12(1945)	—	4.00	6.00	14.00	30.00	40.00

Y# 3 5 FEN
3.5000 g., Copper-Nickel **Ruler:** Ta-t'ung **Obv:** Lotus flower
Rev: Pearl above value between facing dragons

Date	Mintage	VG	F	VF	XF	Unc
TT 2(1933)	—	0.70	1.50	4.00	10.00	30.00
TT 3(1934)	—	0.30	0.80	2.00	4.00	20.00

Y# 7 5 FEN
Copper-Nickel **Ruler:** K'ang-te **Rev:** Pearl above value between
facing dragons

Date	Mintage	VG	F	VF	XF	Unc
KT 1(1934)	—	0.50	1.25	3.00	6.00	12.00
Note: Character Yuan for "first".						
KT 2(1935)	—	0.50	1.25	3.00	6.00	12.00

Date	Mintage	VG	F	VF	XF	Unc
KT 3(1936)	—	0.50	1.25	3.00	6.00	12.00
Note: Narrow border design						
KT 3(1936)	—	1.00	2.50	6.00	12.00	25.00
Note: Wide border design						
KT 4(1937)	—	0.80	2.00	4.00	8.00	15.00
KT 6(1939)	—	0.80	2.00	4.00	8.00	15.00

Y# 11 5 FEN
Aluminum **Ruler:** K'ang-te **Obv:** Legend around large "5"
Rev: National symbol above value in floral sprays

Date	Mintage	VG	F	VF	XF	Unc
KT 7 (1940)	—	0.50	1.25	3.00	6.00	12.00
KT 8 (1941)	—	0.30	0.80	1.50	4.00	8.00
KT 9 (1942)	—	0.30	0.80	1.50	4.00	8.00
KT 10 (1943)	—	0.30	0.80	1.50	4.00	8.00

Y# A13 5 FEN
Aluminum **Ruler:** K'ang-te **Obv:** Legend around small "5"
Rev: Wreath

Date	Mintage	VG	F	VF	XF	Unc
KT 10 (1943)	—	0.80	2.00	5.00	10.00	25.00
KT 11 (1944)	—	0.80	2.00	5.00	10.00	25.00

Y# A13a 5 FEN
Red Fiber **Ruler:** K'ang-te **Obv:** Legend around small "5"
Rev: Wreath

Date	Mintage	VG	F	VF	XF	Unc
KT 11 (1944)	—	5.00	9.00	18.00	30.00	—
KT 12 (1945)	—	85.00	115	150	—	—

Y# A13a.1 5 FEN
Brown Fiber **Ruler:** K'ang-te **Obv:** Legend around small "5"
Rev: Floral wreath

Date	Mintage	VG	F	VF	XF	Unc
KT 11 (1944)	—	10.00	20.00	30.00	50.00	—

Y# 4 CHIAO (10 Fen)
Copper-Nickel **Ruler:** Ta-t'ung **Obv:** Lotus flower **Rev:** Pearl
above value between facing dragons

Date	Mintage	VG	F	VF	XF	Unc
TT 2 (1933)	—	1.25	3.00	6.00	14.00	30.00
TT 3 (1934)	—	0.60	1.50	4.00	8.00	25.00

Y# 8 CHIAO (10 Fen)
Copper-Nickel **Ruler:** K'ang-te **Rev:** Pearl above value between
facing dragons

Date	Mintage	VG	F	VF	XF	Unc
KT 1 (1934)	—	0.60	1.50	4.00	6.00	16.00
Note: Character Yuan for "first".						
KT 2 (1935)	—	0.60	1.50	4.00	6.00	16.00
KT 5 (1938)	—	0.60	1.50	4.00	6.00	16.00
KT 6 (1939)	—	0.60	1.50	4.00	6.00	16.00
KT 6 (1939) Proof	—	—	—	—	—	—

Y# 10 CHIAO (10 Fen)
Copper-Nickel **Ruler:** K'ang-te **Obv:** Dragon head facing
Rev: National symbol above value in floral sprays

Date	Mintage	VG	F	VF	XF	Unc
KT 7 (1940)	—	4.00	6.00	10.00	20.00	50.00

Y# 12 CHIAO (10 Fen)
Aluminum **Ruler:** K'ang-te **Obv:** Legend around "10" on "Fundo"
weight outline **Rev:** National symbol above value in floral sprays

Date	Mintage	VG	F	VF	XF	Unc
KT 7 (1940)	—	0.70	1.50	4.00	6.00	16.00
KT 8 (1941)	—	0.70	1.50	4.00	6.00	16.00
KT 9 (1942)	—	0.70	1.50	4.00	6.00	16.00
KT 10 (1943)	—	115	275	400	500	600

Y# 14 CHIAO (10 Fen)
Aluminum **Ruler:** K'ang-te **Rev:** Legend around large "10"

Date	Mintage	VG	F	VF	XF	Unc
KT 10 (1943)	—	1.25	3.00	6.00	10.00	25.00

PATTERNS
Including off metal strikes

KM# Date	Mintage	Identification	Mkt Val
Pn1 KT5(1938)	—	5 Chiao. Copper-Nickel. Medieval emperor's bust. Portrait.	—
Pn2 KT5(1938)	—	5 Chiao. Copper-Nickel. Two facing phoenix. Chinese characters.	—
Pn3 KT9(1942)	—	Chiao. Silver. Specimen	600
Pn4 KT9(1942)	—	Chiao. Copper-Nickel. Specimen	375
Pn5 KT9(1942)	—	Chiao. Brass. Specimen	300
Pn6 KT9(1942)	—	Chiao. Nickel-Bronze. Specimen	300
Pn7 KT12(1945)	—	Fen. Copper Plated Steel. Y#13a	—

MENG CHIANG

As Japanese troops moved into North China in 1937, the political situation became fluid in several provinces bordering on Manchoukuo, which were sometimes referred to as Inner Mongolia. On September 27, 1937, the Chanan Bank was established. As the situation became more settled the Japanese effected the merger of two local banks with the Bank of Chanan under a new title, Meng Chiang (Mongolian Borderlands or Mongol Territory) Bank. The Meng Chiang Bank was organized on November 27 and opened on December 1, 1937, with headquarters in Kalgan (Zhangjiakou) and branch offices in about a dozen locations throughout the region. Its notes were declared the exclusive currency for the area. The bank closed at the end of the war.

JAPANESE OCCUPATION
STANDARD COINAGE

Y# 521 5 CHIAO
Copper-Nickel **Obv:** Legend in floral design **Rev:** Value in facing
dragons

Date	Mintage	VG	F	VF	XF	Unc
27(1938)	—	1.75	3.50	6.50	12.00	28.00

PATTERNS
Including off metal strikes

Note: KK indicates Kublai Khan dating system

KM#	Date	Mintage	Identification	Mkt Val
Pn1	738(1943)	—	Fen. Aluminum. Ram's head. Value above phoenix. This coin uses the Kublai Khan (KK) dating system.	—
Pn2	738(1943)	—	5 Fen. Aluminum. Ram's head. Value above phoenix. This coin uses the Kublai Khan (KK) dating system.	1,650
Pn3	738(1943)	—	Chiao. Aluminum. Ram's head. Value above phoenix. This coin uses the Kublai Khan (KK) dating system.	2,250

PROVISIONAL GOVT. OF CHINA

In late 1937 the Japanese North China Expeditionary Army established the "Provisional Government of China" at Peking (Beijing).

FEDERAL RESERVE BANK
The Federal Reserve Bank of China was opened in 1938 by Japanese military authorities in Peking (Beijing). It was the puppet financial agency of the Japanese in northeast China. The puppet bank issued both coins and currency, but in modest amounts.

JAPANESE OCCUPATION
STANDARD COINAGE

Y# 523   FEN
Aluminum Issuer: Federal Reserve Bank Obv: Legend around FR Bank symbol Rev: Temple of Heaven

Date	Mintage	VG	F	VF	XF	Unc
30 (1941)	—	1.00	2.00	4.00	5.00	15.00
31 (1942)	—	0.50	1.00	2.00	4.00	12.00
32 (1943)	—	2.00	5.00	10.00	20.00	40.00

Y# 524   5 FEN
Aluminum Issuer: Federal Reserve Bank Obv: Legend around FR Bank symbol Rev: Temple of Heaven Note: The 5 Fen pieces were struck on thick (1 gram) and thin (.8 gram) planchets.

Date	Mintage	VG	F	VF	XF	Unc
30 (1941)	—	1.00	2.00	4.00	5.00	15.00
31 (1942)	—	0.50	1.00	2.00	4.00	12.00
32 (1943)	—	2.00	5.00	10.00	20.00	40.00

Y# 525   CHIAO
Aluminum, 22 mm. Issuer: Federal Reserve Bank Obv: Legend around FR Bank symbol Rev: Temple of Heaven Note: The 1 Chiao pieces were struck on thick (1.5 gram), thin (1.2 gram), and very thin (1.0 gram) planchets.

Date	Mintage	VG	F	VF	XF	Unc
30 (1941)	—	1.00	2.00	4.00	5.00	15.00
31 (1942)	—	0.50	1.00	2.00	4.00	12.00
32 (1943)	—	1.50	3.00	5.00	9.00	35.00

PATTERNS
Including off metal strikes

KM#	Date	Mintage	Identification	Mkt Val
Pn1	30(1941)	—	Fen. Silver. KM#523, R.Y.30.	700
Pn2	30(1941)	—	5 Fen. Silver. KM#524, R.Y.30.	700

REFORMED GOVT. OF CHINA

On March 28, 1938 the Japanese Central China Expeditionary Army established the Reformed Government of the Republic of China at Nanking (Nanjing).

HUA HSING COMMERCIAL BANK
The Hua Hsing Commerce Bank was a financial agency created and established by the government of Japan and its puppet authorities in Shanghai in May 1939. Notes and coins were issued until sometime in 1941, with the quantities restricted by Chinese aversion to accepting them.

JAPANESE OCCUPATION
STANDARD COINAGE

Y# A522   FEN
Bronze Obv: Legend around character "Hua" above pair of wings Rev: Stylized character divides value

Date	Mintage	VG	F	VF	XF	Unc
29(1940)	—	50.00	100	200	300	400

Y# 522   10 FEN
Copper-Nickel Obv: Legend around character "Hua" above pair of wings Rev: Floral bouquet divides value

Date	Mintage	VG	F	VF	XF	Unc
29(1940)	—	0.40	1.00	2.00	3.50	7.00

Note: Metal alloys vary

PATTERNS
Including off metal strikes

KM#	Date	Mintage	Identification	Mkt Val
Pn1	29(1940)	—	Fen. Copper-Nickel.	650
Pn2	29(1940)	—	Fen. Silver.	750
Pn3	29(1940)	—	5 Fen. Copper-Nickel. Liu-ho Pagoda.	650
Pn4	29(1940)	—	20 Fen. Copper-Nickel. Junk.	2,250

CHINA, PEOPLE'S REPUBLIC

The Peoples Republic of China, located in eastern Asia, has an area of 3,696,100 sq. mi. (9,596,960 sq. km.) (including Manchuria and Tibet) and a population of *1.20 billion. Capital: Peking (Beijing). The economy is based on agriculture, mining, and manufacturing. Textiles, clothing, metal ores, tea and rice are exported.

China's ancient civilization began in east-central Henan's Huayang county, 2800-2300 B.C. The warring feudal states comprising early China were first united under Emperor Ch'in Shih (246-210 B.C.) who gave China its name and first central government. Subsequent dynasties alternated brilliant cultural achievements with internal disorder until the Empire was brought down by the revolution of 1911, and the Republic of China installed in its place. Chinese culture attained a pre-eminence in art, literature and philosophy, but a traditional backwardness in industry and administration ill prepared China for the demands of 19th century Western expansionism which exposed it to military and political humiliations, and mandated a drastic revision of political practice in order to secure an accommodation with the modern world.

The Republic of 1911 barely survived the stress of World War I, and was subsequently all but shattered by the rise of nationalism and the emergence of the Chinese Communist movement. Moscow, which practiced a policy of cooperation between Communists and other parties in movements for national liberation, sought to establish an entente between the Chinese Communist Party and the Kuomintang ('National Peoples Party') of Sun Yat-sen. The ensuing cooperation was based on little more than the hope each had of using the other.

An increasingly uneasy association between the Kuomintang and the Chinese Communist Party developed and continued until April 12, 1927, when Chiang Kai-shek, Sun Yat-sen's political heir, instituted a bloody purge to stamp out the Communists within the Kuomintang and the government and virtually paralyzed their ranks throughout China. Some time after the mid-1927 purges, the Chinese Communist Party turned to armed force to resist Chiang Kai-shek and during the period of 1930-34 acquired control over large parts of Kiangsi (Jiangxi), Fukien (Fujian), Hunan and Hupeh (Hubei). The Nationalist Nanking government responded with a series of campaigns against the soviet power bases and, by October of 1934, succeeded in driving the remnants of the Communist army to a refuge in Shensi (Shaanxi) Province. There the Communists reorganized under the leadership of Mao Tse-tung, defeated the Nationalist forces, and on Sept. 21, 1949, established the Peoples Republic of China. Thereafter relations between Russia and Communist China steadily deteriorated until 1958, when China emerged as an independent center of Communist power.

MONETARY SYSTEM
After 1949

10 Fen (Cents) = 1 Jiao
10 Jiao = 1 Renminbi Yuan

MINT MARKS
(b) - Beijing (Peking)
(s) - Shanghai
(y) - Shenyang (Mukden)

OBVERSE LEGENDS

中华人民共和国

ZHONGHUA RENMIN GONGHEGUO
(Peoples Republic of China)

中国人民银行

ZHONGHUA RENMIN YINHANG
(Peoples Bank of China)

NOTICE
Peoples Republic of China has been completely renumbered.

Cross References are included in note.

PEOPLES REPUBLIC
STANDARD COINAGE

KM# 1   FEN
0.6500 g., Aluminum, 17.97 mm. Obv: National emblem Rev: Value in sprays, date below Edge: Reeded Note: Prev. Y#1.

Date	Mintage	F	VF	XF	Unc	BU
1955	—	0.20	0.50	1.50	5.00	—
1956	—	0.40	1.00	2.50	7.50	—
1957	—	0.60	1.50	3.50	10.00	—
1958	—	0.10	0.25	0.75	2.50	—
1959	—	0.10	0.25	0.75	2.50	—
1961	—	0.10	0.25	0.75	2.50	—
1963	—	0.10	0.25	0.50	1.50	—
1964	—	0.10	0.25	0.50	1.00	—
1971	—	0.10	0.25	0.50	1.00	—
1972	—	0.10	0.25	0.50	1.00	—
1973	—	0.10	0.25	0.50	1.50	—
1974	—	0.10	0.25	0.50	1.00	—
1975	500,000	0.10	0.25	0.50	1.00	—
1976	—	—	0.10	0.25	0.50	—
1977	—	—	0.10	0.25	0.50	—
1978	—	—	0.10	0.25	0.50	—
1979	—	—	0.25	1.00	5.00	—
1980	—	—	0.10	0.25	0.50	—
1980 Proof	—	Value: 1.00				
1981	—	—	0.10	0.25	0.50	—
1981 Proof	—	Value: 1.00				
1982	—	—	—	0.25	0.50	—
1982 Proof	—	Value: 1.00				
1983	2,412,000	—	—	0.10	0.25	—
1983 Proof	—	Value: 1.00				
1984	3,283,000	—	—	0.10	0.25	—
1984 Proof	—	Value: 1.00				
1985	—	—	—	0.10	0.25	—
1985 Proof	—	Value: 1.00				
1986	—	—	—	0.10	0.25	—
1986 Proof	—	Value: 1.00				
1987	—	—	—	0.10	0.25	—
1991	—	—	—	0.10	0.25	—
1991 Proof	—	Value: 1.00				
1992	—	—	—	0.10	0.25	—
1992 Proof	—	Value: 1.00				
1993	—	—	—	—	0.75	—
Note: In sets only						
1993 Proof	—	Value: 1.00				
1994	—	—	—	—	0.75	—
Note: In sets only						
1994 Proof	—	Value: 1.00				
1995	—	—	—	—	0.75	—
Note: In sets only						
1995 Proof	—	Value: 1.00				
1996	—	—	—	—	0.75	—
Note: In sets only						
1996 Proof	—	Value: 1.00				
1997	—	—	—	0.10	0.15	0.25
1998	—	—	—	0.10	0.15	0.25
1999	—	—	—	0.10	0.15	0.25
2000	—	—	—	0.10	0.15	0.25

KM# 2   2 FEN

1.0500 g., Aluminum, 21 mm. **Obv:** National emblem
Rev: Denomination above wreath, date below **Note:** Prev. Y#2.

Date	Mintage	F	VF	XF	Unc	BU
1956	—	0.10	0.25	0.75	1.50	—
1959	—	0.20	0.50	1.00	4.00	—
1960	—	0.20	0.50	1.00	4.00	—
1961	—	0.10	0.25	0.75	1.50	—
1962	—	0.10	0.25	0.75	1.50	—
1963	—	0.10	0.25	0.75	1.50	—
1964	—	0.10	0.25	0.50	1.25	—
1974	—	0.10	0.25	0.50	1.50	—
1975	—	0.10	0.25	0.50	1.00	—
1976	—	0.10	0.25	0.50	1.00	—
1977	360,000	0.10	0.25	0.50	0.75	—
1978	—	0.10	0.20	0.40	0.60	—
1979	—	0.10	0.20	0.40	0.60	—
1980	—	0.10	0.20	0.40	0.60	—
1980 Proof	—	Value: 1.00				
1981	—	0.10	0.20	0.40	0.60	—
1981 Proof	—	Value: 1.00				
1982	—	0.10	0.20	0.40	0.60	—
1982 Proof	—	Value: 1.00				
1983	1,790,000	—	0.10	0.20	0.35	—
1983 Proof	—	Value: 1.00				
1984	1,963,000	—	0.10	0.20	0.35	—
1984 Proof	—	Value: 1.00				
1985	—	—	0.10	0.20	0.35	—
1985 Proof	—	Value: 1.00				
1986	—	—	0.15	0.35	0.75	—
1986 Proof	—	Value: 1.00				
1987	—	—	0.10	0.20	0.35	—
1988	—	—	0.10	0.20	0.35	—
1989	—	—	0.10	0.20	0.35	—
1990	—	—	0.10	0.20	0.35	—
1991	—	—	0.10	0.20	0.35	—
1991 Proof	—	Value: 1.00				
1992	—	—	0.10	0.20	0.35	—
1992 Proof	—	Value: 1.00				
1993	—	—	—	—	0.75	—
Note: In sets only						
1993 Proof	—	Value: 1.00				
1994	—	—	—	—	0.75	—
Note: In sets only						
1994 Proof	—	Value: 1.00				
1995	—	—	—	—	0.75	—
Note: In sets only						
1995 Proof	—	Value: 1.00				
1996	—	—	—	—	0.75	—
Note: In sets only						
1996 Proof	—	Value: 1.00				
1997	—	—	—	—	0.75	—
1998	—	—	—	—	0.75	—
1999	—	—	—	—	0.75	—
2000	—	—	—	—	0.75	—

KM# 3   5 FEN

1.6000 g., Aluminum, 24 mm. **Obv:** National emblem
Rev: Denomination above wreath, date below **Note:** Prev. Y#3.

Date	Mintage	F	VF	XF	Unc	BU
1955	—	0.30	0.75	2.00	10.00	—
1956	—	0.15	0.35	0.75	2.00	—
1957	—	0.15	0.35	0.75	2.50	—
1974	—	0.15	0.25	0.50	1.50	—
1975	—	0.15	0.25	0.50	1.50	—
1976	350,000	0.15	0.25	0.50	0.75	—
1979	—	0.15	0.50	1.25	10.00	—
1980	—	0.15	0.25	0.50	0.75	—
1980 Proof	—	Value: 1.00				
1981	—	0.15	0.25	0.50	0.75	—
1981 Proof	—	Value: 1.00				
1982	—	0.15	0.25	0.50	0.75	—
1982 Proof	—	Value: 1.00				
1983	484,000	—	0.15	0.25	0.45	—
1983 Proof	—	Value: 1.00				
1984	600,000	—	0.15	0.25	0.45	—
1984 Proof	—	Value: 1.00				
1985	—	—	0.15	0.25	0.45	—
1985 Proof	—	Value: 1.00				
1986	—	—	0.15	0.25	0.45	—
1986 Proof	—	Value: 1.00				
1987	—	—	0.15	0.25	0.45	—
1988	—	—	0.15	0.25	0.45	—

KM# 15   JIAO

2.6000 g., Copper-Zinc, 20 mm. **Obv:** National emblem
Rev: Denomination above wreath, date below **Note:** Prev. Y#24.

Date	Mintage	F	VF	XF	Unc	BU
1980	—	—	—	—	0.50	—
1980 Proof	—	Value: 1.00				
1981	—	—	—	—	0.50	—
1981 Proof	—	Value: 1.00				
1982 Proof	—	Value: 1.00				
1983	3,100,000	—	—	—	0.50	—
1983 Proof	—	Value: 1.00				
1984	3,500,000	—	—	—	0.50	—
1984 Proof	—	Value: 1.00				
1985	—	—	—	—	0.50	—
1985 Proof	—	Value: 1.00				
1986 Proof	—	Value: 1.00				

KM# 155   JIAO

Brass **Series:** 6th National Games **Subject:** Gymnast
Obv: Stylized torch divides date below **Rev:** Gymnast above
date, denomination at left **Note:** Prev. Y#148.

Date	Mintage	F	VF	XF	Unc	BU
1987	10,570,000	—	—	1.00	2.00	3.00

KM# 156   JIAO

Brass **Series:** 6th National Games **Subject:** Soccer
Obv: Stylized torch divides date below **Rev:** Soccer player
divides date and denomination **Note:** Prev. Y#149.

Date	Mintage	F	VF	XF	Unc	BU
1987	Inc. above	—	—	1.00	2.00	3.00

KM# 157   JIAO

Brass **Series:** 6th National Games **Subject:** Volleyball
Obv: Stylized torch divides date below **Rev:** Volleyball player,
date below, denomination at right **Note:** Prev. Y#150.

Date	Mintage	F	VF	XF	Unc	BU
1987	Inc. above	—	—	1.00	2.00	3.00

KM# 335   JIAO

Aluminum, 22.5 mm. **Obv:** National emblem, date below
Rev: Peony blossom, denomination at right **Note:** Prev. Y#328.

Date	Mintage	F	VF	XF	Unc	BU
1991	—	—	—	—	0.50	—
1991 Proof	—	Value: 1.00				
1992	—	—	—	—	0.50	—
1992 Proof	—	Value: 1.00				
1993	—	—	—	—	0.50	—
1993 Proof	—	Value: 1.00				
1994	—	—	—	—	0.50	—
1994 Proof	—	Value: 1.00				
1995	—	—	—	—	0.50	—
1995 Proof	—	Value: 1.00				
1996	—	—	—	—	0.50	—
1996 Proof	—	Value: 1.00				
1997	—	—	—	—	0.50	—
1998	—	—	—	—	0.50	—
1999	—	—	—	—	0.50	—
1999 Proof	—	Value: 1.00				

KM# 1210   JIAO

1.1200 g., Aluminum, 19 mm. **Obv:** Denomination, date below
Rev: Orchid **Rev. Leg.:** ZHONGGUA RENMIN YINHANG
Edge: Plain **Note:** Prev. Y#1068.

Date	Mintage	F	VF	XF	Unc	BU
1999	—	—	—	—	0.50	—
2000	—	—	—	—	0.50	—

KM# 16   2 JIAO

4.1500 g., Copper-Zinc, 23 mm. **Obv:** National emblem
Rev: Denomination above wreath, date below **Note:** Prev. Y#25.

Date	Mintage	F	VF	XF	Unc	BU
1980	—	—	—	—	0.60	—
1980 Proof	—	Value: 1.25				
1981	—	—	—	—	0.60	—
1981 Proof	—	Value: 1.25				
1982 Proof	—	Value: 1.25				
1983	4,200,000	—	—	—	0.60	—
1983 Proof	—	Value: 1.25				
1984	2,500,000	—	—	—	0.60	—
1984 Proof	—	Value: 1.25				
1985 Proof	—	Value: 1.25				
1986 Proof	—	Value: 1.25				

KM# 17   5 JIAO

6.0000 g., Copper-Zinc, 26 mm. **Obv:** National emblem
Rev: Denomination above wreath, date below **Note:** Prev. Y#26.

Date	Mintage	F	VF	XF	Unc	BU
1980	—	—	—	—	0.75	—
1980 Proof	—	Value: 1.50				
1981	—	—	—	—	0.75	—
1981 Proof	—	Value: 1.50				
1982 Proof	—	Value: 1.50				
1983	3,000,000	—	—	—	0.75	—
1983 Proof	—	Value: 1.50				
1984	3,500,000	—	—	—	0.75	—
1984 Proof	—	Value: 1.50				
1985	—	—	—	—	0.75	—
1985 Proof	—	Value: 1.50				
1986 Proof	—	Value: 1.50				

KM# 65 5 JIAO
2.2000 g., 0.9000 Silver 0.0637 oz. ASW, 14 mm. **Obv:** Building divides date and denomination **Rev:** Marco Polo looking left, two dates below **Note:** Prev. Y#53.

Date	Mintage	F	VF	XF	Unc	BU
1983 Proof	7,050	Value: 90.00				

KM# 265 5 JIAO
2.0000 g., 0.9990 Silver 0.0642 oz. ASW, 14 mm. **Obv:** Great wall, date below **Rev:** Denomination divides phoenix and dragon representing good luck **Note:** Prev. Y#205.

Date	Mintage	F	VF	XF	Unc	BU
1990 Proof	55,000	Value: 10.00				

KM# 336 5 JIAO
3.8300 g., Brass, 20.5 mm. **Obv:** National emblem, date below **Rev:** Denomination above flowers **Edge:** Segmented reeding **Note:** Prev. Y#329.

Date	Mintage	F	VF	XF	Unc	BU
1991	—	—	—	—	1.00	—
1991 Proof	—	Value: 1.50				
1992	—	—	—	—	1.00	—
1992 Proof	—	Value: 1.50				
1993	—	—	—	—	1.00	—
1993 Proof	—	Value: 1.50				
1994	—	—	—	—	1.00	—
1994 Proof	—	Value: 1.50				
1995	—	—	—	—	1.00	—
1995 Proof	—	Value: 1.50				
1996	—	—	—	—	1.00	—
1996 Proof	—	Value: 1.50				
1997	—	—	—	—	1.00	—
1998	—	—	—	—	1.00	—
1999	—	—	—	—	1.00	—
2000	—	—	—	—	1.00	—

KM# 29 YUAN
Brass, 30 mm. **Series:** 1980 Olympics **Subject:** Archery **Obv:** National emblem above denomination **Rev:** Archers, date below, Olympic logo upper left **Note:** Prev. Y#10.

Date	Mintage	F	VF	XF	Unc	BU
1980 Proof	40,000	Value: 12.50				

KM# 30 YUAN
Brass, 30 mm. **Series:** 1980 Olympics **Subject:** Wrestling **Obv:** National emblem, denomination below **Rev:** Wrestlers, date below, Olympic logo upper left **Note:** Prev. Y#11.

Date	Mintage	F	VF	XF	Unc	BU
1980 Proof	40,000	Value: 12.50				

KM# 31 YUAN
Brass, 30 mm. **Series:** 1980 Olympics **Subject:** Equestrian **Obv:** National emblem, denomination below **Rev:** Equestrians, date below, Olympic logo, upper left **Note:** Prev. Y#12.

Date	Mintage	F	VF	XF	Unc	BU
1980 Proof	40,000	Value: 12.50				

KM# 32 YUAN
Brass, 30 mm. **Series:** 1980 Olympics **Subject:** Soccer **Obv:** National emblem, denomination below **Rev:** Two soccer players in ancient garb **Note:** Prev. Y#13.

Date	Mintage	F	VF	XF	Unc	BU
1980 Proof	40,000	Value: 12.50				

KM# 21 YUAN
Brass, 30 mm. **Series:** Lake Placid - 13th Winter Olympic Games **Subject:** Alpine Skiing **Obv:** National emblem , Olympic logo at left, denomination below **Rev:** Skier within snowflake design **Note:** Prev. Y#14.

Date	Mintage	F	VF	XF	Unc	BU
1980 Proof	29,000	Value: 14.50				

KM# 19 YUAN
Brass **Series:** Lake Placid - 13th Winter Olympic Games **Subject:** Figure skating **Obv:** National emblem, Olympic logo at left, denomination below **Rev:** Woman figure skater within snowflake design **Note:** Prev. Y#16.

Date	Mintage	F	VF	XF	Unc	BU
1980 Proof	29,000	Value: 14.50				

KM# 20 YUAN
Brass **Series:** Lake Placid - 13th Winter Olympic Games **Subject:** Biathlon **Obv:** National emblem, Olympic logo at left, denomination below **Rev:** Biathlete within snowflake **Note:** Prev. Y#17.

Date	Mintage	F	VF	XF	Unc	BU
1980 Proof	29,000	Value: 14.50				

KM# 18 YUAN
9.3000 g., Copper-Nickel, 30 mm. **Obv:** National emblem, date below **Rev:** Great wall **Note:** Prev. Y#27.

Date	Mintage	F	VF	XF	Unc	BU
1980	—	—	—	—	2.00	—
1980 Proof	—	Value: 3.00				
1981	—	—	—	—	2.00	—
1981 Proof	—	Value: 3.00				

Date	Mintage	F	VF	XF	Unc	BU
1982 Proof	—	Value: 3.00				
1983	3,100,000	—	—	—	2.00	—
1983 Proof	—	Value: 3.00				
1984	4,100,000	—	—	—	2.00	—
1984 Proof	—	Value: 3.00				
1985	—	—	—	—	2.00	—
1985 Proof	—	Value: 3.00				
1986 Proof	—	Value: 3.00				

KM# 22 YUAN
Brass **Series:** Lake Placid - 13th Winter Olympic Games **Subject:** Women's speed Skating **Obv:** National emblem, Olympic logo at left, denomination below **Rev:** Speed skater within snowflake design **Note:** Prev. Y#15.

Date	Mintage	F	VF	XF	Unc	BU
1980 Proof	29,000	Value: 14.50				

KM# 58 YUAN
Brass **Subject:** World Cup Soccer **Obv:** National emblem, date below **Rev:** Soccer player, within ring, kicking the ball, denomination bottom right **Note:** Prev. Y#34.

Date	Mintage	F	VF	XF	Unc	BU
1982 Proof	20,000	Value: 10.00				

KM# 66 YUAN
12.7000 g., Brass, 32 mm. **Rev:** Panda seated with bamboo branch, within octagon line border

Date	Mintage	F	VF	XF	Unc	BU
1983 proof	30,000	Value: 15.00				

KM# 85 YUAN
Brass **Obv:** National emblem, date below **Rev:** Panda within octagon **Note:** Prev. Y#58.

Date	Mintage	F	VF	XF	Unc	BU
1983 Proof	30,000	Value: 40.00				
1984 Proof	30,000	Value: 40.00				

KM# 104 YUAN
Copper-Nickel **Subject:** 35th Anniversary - Peoples Republic **Obv:** National emblem above buildings, dates below **Rev:** Republic figures **Note:** Prev. Y#85.

Date	Mintage	F	VF	XF	Unc	BU
ND(1984)	20,410,000	—	—	—	6.00	—
ND(1984) Proof	—	Value: 7.50				

KM# 105 YUAN
Copper-Nickel **Subject:** 35th Anniversary - Peoples Republic **Obv:** National emblem **Rev:** Dancers **Note:** Prev. Y#86.

Date	Mintage	F	VF	XF	Unc	BU
ND(1984)	Inc. above	—	—	—	6.00	—
ND(1984) Proof	—	Value: 7.50				

KM# 106 YUAN
Copper-Nickel **Subject:** 35th Anniversary - Peoples Republic **Obv:** National emblem above buildings, dates below **Rev:** Monument amid cranes in flight **Note:** Prev. Y#87.

Date	Mintage	F	VF	XF	Unc	BU
ND(1984)	Inc. above	—	—	—	6.00	—
ND(1984) Proof	—	Value: 7.50				

KM# 112 YUAN
12.7000 g., 0.9990 Brass 0.4079 oz., 32 mm. **Rev:** Panda seated with bamboo in octagon linear border

Date	Mintage	F	VF	XF	Unc	BU
1984 Proof	30,000	Value: 15.00				

KM# 110 YUAN
Copper-Nickel **Subject:** 20th Anniversary - Tibet Autonomous Region **Obv:** National emblem, date below **Rev:** Potala Palace **Note:** Prev. Y#96.

Date	Mintage	F	VF	XF	Unc	BU
1985	2,612,000	—	—	—	3.00	8.50
1985 Proof	10,000	Value: 15.00				

KM# 111 YUAN
Copper-Nickel **Subject:** 30th Anniversary - Xinjiang Autonomous Region **Note:** Prev. Y#109.

Date	Mintage	F	VF	XF	Unc	BU
1985	4,500,000	—	—	2.00	6.00	—
1985 Proof	10,000	Value: 15.00				

KM# 130 YUAN
Copper-Nickel **Subject:** Year of Peace **Obv:** National emblem, date below **Rev:** Seated woman with doves **Note:** Prev. Y#151.

Date	Mintage	F	VF	XF	Unc	BU
1986	27,048,000	—	—	—	5.00	—

KM# 158 YUAN
Copper-Nickel **Subject:** 40th Anniversary - Mongolian Autonomous Region **Obv:** Building, date below **Rev:** Riders, sheep below, denomination at left **Note:** Prev. Y#140.

Date	Mintage	F	VF	XF	Unc	BU
1987	9,054,000	—	—	2.00	6.00	—

KM# 180 YUAN
Copper-Nickel **Subject:** 30th Anniversary - Kwangsi Autonomous Region **Obv:** Mountains and water, inscription and date below **Rev:** Native dancers, denomination at right, two dates upper left **Note:** Prev. Y#198.

Date	Mintage	F	VF	XF	Unc	BU
1988	4,072,000	—	—	—	7.00	—

KM# 181 YUAN
Copper-Nickel **Subject:** 30th Anniversary - Ningxia Autonomous Region **Rev:** Women with plants, denomination at right, within circle, dates below **Note:** Prev. Y#211.

Date	Mintage	F	VF	XF	Unc	BU
1988	1,560,000	—	—	—	15.00	—

KM# 182 YUAN
Copper-Nickel **Subject:** 40th Anniversary - Peoples Bank **Obv:** National emblem, date below **Rev:** Building divides dates **Note:** Prev. Y#212.

Date	Mintage	F	VF	XF	Unc	BU
1988	2,068,000	—	—	15.00	75.00	—

KM# 220 YUAN
Copper-Nickel **Subject:** 40th Anniversary - Peoples Republic **Obv:** National emblem above buildings, date below **Rev:** Music score divides artistic year and dates **Note:** Prev. Y#204.

Date	Mintage	F	VF	XF	Unc	BU
1989	2,000,000	—	—	—	4.00	—

KM# 264 YUAN
Nickel Clad Steel **Series:** 11th Asian Games - Beijing 1990 **Obv:** Building, Roman numeral above, inscription and date below **Rev:** Female archer, denomination above, panda archer below **Note:** Prev. Y#256.

Date	Mintage	F	VF	XF	Unc	BU
1990	Inc. above	—	—	—	4.00	—

KM# 266 YUAN
Nickel Clad Steel **Series:** XI Asian Games **Obv:** Building, Roman numerals above, inscription and date below **Rev:** Sword Dancer, panda dancer at left, denomination at right **Note:** Prev. Y#264.

Date	Mintage	F	VF	XF	Unc	BU
1990	25,608,000	—	—	—	4.00	—

KM# 338 YUAN
Nickel Clad Steel, 25 mm. **Subject:** Planting Trees Festival **Rev:** Head of young woman **Note:** Prev. Y#279.

Date	Mintage	F	VF	XF	Unc	BU
1991	10,000,000	—	—	—	2.25	—

KM# 339 YUAN
Nickel Clad Steel, 25 mm. **Subject:** Planting Trees Festival **Obv:** Trees, inscription, and numbers within circle **Rev:** Monument on globe divides birds in flight, date below **Note:** Prev. Y#280.

Date	Mintage	F	VF	XF	Unc	BU
1991	10,000,000	—	—	—	2.25	—

KM# 340 YUAN
Nickel Clad Steel, 25 mm. **Subject:** Planting Trees Festival **Obv:** Trees, inscription, and numbers within circle **Rev:** Seedling, date below **Note:** Prev. Y#281.

Date	Mintage	F	VF	XF	Unc	BU
1991	10,000,000	—	—	—	2.25	—

KM# 341 YUAN
5.9100 g., Nickel Plated Steel, 25 mm. **Subject:** 70th Anniversary of the Founding of the Chinese Communist Party **Obv:** National emblem, date below **Rev:** House of Shanghai **Note:** Prev. Y#284.

Date	Mintage	F	VF	XF	Unc	BU
1991	30,000,000	—	—	—	2.25	—

KM# 342 YUAN
5.8100 g., Nickel Plated Steel, 25 mm. **Subject:** 70th Anniversary of the Founding of the Chinese Communist Party **Rev:** House in Tsun-i (Zunyi), Kweichow Province **Note:** Prev. Y#285.

Date	Mintage	F	VF	XF	Unc	BU
1991	30,000,000	—	—	—	2.25	—

KM# 343 YUAN
5.8400 g., Nickel Plated Steel, 25 mm. **Subject:** 70th Anniversary of the Founding of the Chinese Communist Party - Meeting in Tiananmen Square, 1978 **Obv:** National emblem, date below **Rev:** Flags, monument, and building **Note:** Prev. Y#286.

Date	Mintage	F	VF	XF	Unc	BU
1991	30,000,000	—	—	—	2.25	—

KM# 344 YUAN
Nickel Plated Steel, 25 mm. **Subject:** 1st Women's World Football Cup **Obv:** Conjoined soccer balls, artistic woman design on top **Rev:** Goalie, date at right **Note:** Prev. Y#316.

Date	Mintage	F	VF	XF	Unc	BU
1991	10,000,000	—	—	—	2.50	—

KM# 345 YUAN
Nickel Plated Steel, 25 mm. **Subject:** 1st Women's World Football Cup **Obv:** Conjoined soccer balls, artistic woman design on top **Rev:** Player, soccer ball background, date at lower right **Note:** Prev. Y#317.

Date	Mintage	F	VF	XF	Unc	BU
1991	10,000,000	—	—	—	2.50	—

KM# 337 YUAN
Nickel Clad Steel, 25 mm. **Obv:** National emblem, date below **Rev:** Denomination above flowers **Note:** Prev. Y#330.

Date	Mintage	F	VF	XF	Unc	BU
1991	—	—	—	—	1.50	—
1991 Proof	—	Value: 2.50				
1992	—	—	—	—	1.50	—
1992 Proof	—	Value: 2.50				
1993	—	—	—	—	1.50	—
1993 Proof	—	Value: 2.50				
1994	—	—	—	—	1.50	—
1994 Proof	—	Value: 2.50				
1995	—	—	—	—	1.50	—
1995 Proof	—	Value: 2.50				
1996	—	—	—	—	1.50	—
1996 Proof	—	Value: 2.50				
1997	—	—	—	—	1.50	—
1997 Proof	—	Value: 2.50				
1998	—	—	—	—	1.50	—
1998 Proof	—	Value: 2.50				
1999	—	—	—	—	1.50	—
1999 Proof	—	Value: 2.50				

KM# 390 YUAN
Nickel Clad Steel, 25 mm. **Subject:** 10th Anniversary - Constitution **Obv:** National emblem, date below **Rev:** Constitution, denomination at right, dates and flower below **Note:** Prev. Y#364.

Date	Mintage	F	VF	XF	Unc	BU
1992	10,000,000	—	—	—	2.50	—

KM# 470 YUAN
Nickel Clad Steel, 25 mm. **Subject:** 100th Birthday of Soong Ching Ling - Second Wife of Sun Yat-sen **Obv:** Building, date below **Rev:** Bust of Ching-ling, 1892-1981, half left, revolutionary stateswoman **Note:** Prev. Y#365.

Date	Mintage	F	VF	XF	Unc	BU
1993	10,448,000	—	—	—	3.50	—
1993 Proof	—	Value: 5.00				

KM# 471 YUAN
Nickel Clad Steel, 25 mm. **Subject:** 100th Anniversary - Birth of Chairman Mao **Obv:** Buildings and mountains, date below **Rev:** Mao's head, left **Note:** Prev. Y#399.

Date	Mintage	F	VF	XF	Unc	BU
1993	20,000,000	—	—	—	3.50	—
1993 Prooflike	—	—	—	—	5.00	—

KM# 610 YUAN
Nickel Clad Steel, 25 mm. **Series:** Children's Year **Subject:** Project Hope **Obv:** National emblem, date below **Rev:** Two children, denomination lower left **Note:** Prev. Y#455.

Date	Mintage	F	VF	XF	Unc	BU
1994	—	—	—	—	2.50	—

KM# 710 YUAN
Nickel Plated Steel, 25 mm. **Subject:** Table Tennis **Obv:** Building divides design and date **Rev:** Table tennis player, denomination lower left **Note:** Prev. Y#487.

Date	Mintage	F	VF	XF	Unc	BU
1995	10,000,000	—	—	—	3.50	—
1995 Proof	20,000	Value: 10.00				

KM# 711 YUAN
5.9400 g., Nickel Plated Steel, 25 mm. **Subject:** 50th Anniversary - Defeat of Fascism and Japan **Obv:** Great Wall and mountains, date below **Rev:** Statue of rock and soldiers, dates and denomination below **Note:** Prev. Y#528.

Date	Mintage	F	VF	XF	Unc	BU
1995	10,000,000	—	—	—	3.50	—

KM# 712 YUAN
6.0300 g., Nickel Plated Steel, 25 mm. **Subject:** 50th Anniversary - United Nations **Obv:** National emblem above wall, denomination below **Rev:** United Nations logo and anniversary numbers, date lower right **Note:** Prev. Y#529.

Date	Mintage	F	VF	XF	Unc	BU
1995	10,000,000	—	—	—	3.00	—

KM# 713 YUAN
Nickel Plated Steel, 25 mm. **Subject:** 4th UN Women's Conference **Obv:** Small building within design **Rev:** Half moon and dove above inscription, denomination and dates below **Note:** Prev. Y#530.

Date	Mintage	F	VF	XF	Unc	BU
1995	10,000,000	—	—	—	3.00	—

KM# 880 YUAN
6.0500 g., Nickel Plated Steel, 25 mm. **Obv:** Zhu De's home in Sichuan, date below **Rev:** Marshal Zhu De, 3/4 left **Edge:** Lettered, "ZHONGGUO" twice **Mint:** Shanghai **Note:** Prev. Y#1124.

Date	Mintage	F	VF	XF	Unc	BU
1996	580,000	—	—	—	3.50	—

KM# 1121 YUAN
6.1000 g., Nickel Clad Steel, 24.9 mm. **Subject:** Liu Shao-chi **Obv:** Building, denomination and date **Rev:** Bust of Liu left, ZHONGGUO twice **Note:** Prev. Y#1057.

Date	Mintage	F	VF	XF	Unc	BU
1998	—				3.75	—

KM# 1120 YUAN
Nickel Clad Steel, 25 mm. **Subject:** 100th Birthday - Chou (Zhou) Enlai **Obv:** Chou (Zhou) birth place, date below **Rev:** Chou (Zhou) bust left **Note:** Prev. Y#721.

Date	Mintage	F	VF	XF	Unc	BU
1998	—				3.50	—

KM# 1211 YUAN
6.1000 g., Nickel Clad Steel, 24.9 mm. **Subject:** 50th Anniversary - People's Political Consultative Conference **Obv:** Emblem, date within, above inscription and dates **Rev:** Building, date below **Note:** Prev. Y#1058.

Date	Mintage	F	VF	XF	Unc	BU
1999	—				3.75	—

KM# 1212 YUAN
6.1000 g., Nickel Plated Steel, 24.9 mm. **Obv:** Denomination, date below **Rev:** Chrysanthemum **Rev. Leg.:** ZHONGGUA RENMIN YINHANG **Edge:** "RMB" three times **Note:** Prev. Y#1069.

Date	Mintage	F	VF	XF	Unc	BU
1999	—	—	—	—	—	1.50
2000	—	—	—	—	—	1.50

KM# 1301 YUAN
6.1000 g., Nickel Clad Steel, 25 mm. **Subject:** Dunhuang Cave **Obv:** Pagoda, date below **Rev:** Standing and floating figures **Edge:** "RMB" 3 times **Note:** Prev. Y#1037.

Date	Mintage	F	VF	XF	Unc	BU
2000	—	—	—	—	4.00	—

KM# 403 3 YUAN
15.0000 g., 0.9000 Silver 0.4340 oz. ASW **Subject:** Ancient Chinese Coins **Note:** Prev. Y#362.

Date	Mintage	F	VF	XF	Unc	BU
1992 Proof	23,000	Value: 16.50				

KM# 402 3 YUAN
15.0000 g., 0.9000 Silver 0.4340 oz. ASW **Subject:** Ancient Chinese Paper **Note:** Prev. Y#363.

Date	Mintage	F	VF	XF	Unc	BU
1992 Proof	Est. 20,000	Value: 16.50				

KM# 472 3 YUAN
15.0000 g., 0.9000 Silver 0.4340 oz. ASW **Rev:** Chinese Gods Fu, Lu and Shu **Note:** Prev. Y#403.

Date	Mintage	F	VF	XF	Unc	BU
1993 Proof	20,000	Value: 18.50				

KM# 734 3 YUAN
15.0000 g., 0.9000 Silver 0.4340 oz. ASW **Subject:** Yin and Yang Concept **Obv:** Great Wall tower, date below **Rev:** Chinese gods Fu, Lu and Shu with Yin Yang symbol, denomination below **Note:** Prev. Y#733.

Date	Mintage	F	VF	XF	Unc	BU
1995 Proof	—	Value: 16.50				

KM# 824 3 YUAN
15.0000 g., 0.9000 Silver 0.4340 oz. ASW **Subject:** Great Wall of China **Obv:** Great Wall view, date below **Rev:** Great Wall construction scene, denomination above **Note:** Prev. Y#734.

Date	Mintage	F	VF	XF	Unc	BU
1995 Proof	—	Value: 16.50				

KM# 1035 3 YUAN
15.0000 g., 0.9000 Silver 0.4340 oz. ASW, 30 mm. **Subject:** World Wildlife Federation **Obv:** State emblem, date below **Rev:** Panda seated right eating leaves, denomination at right **Edge:** Reeded **Note:** Prev. Y#1081.

Date	Mintage	F	VF	XF	Unc	BU
1997 Proof	50,000	Value: 17.50				

KM# 45 5 YUAN
15.0000 g., 0.9000 Silver 0.4340 oz. ASW, 33 mm. **Series:** Artifacts **Rev:** Lizard statue

Date	Mintage	F	VF	XF	Unc	BU
1981 Proof	5,000	Value: 30.00				

KM# 42 5 YUAN
15.0000 g., 0.9000 Silver 0.4340 oz. ASW, 33 mm. **Series:** Artifacts **Rev:** Elephant statue

Date	Mintage	F	VF	XF	Unc	BU
1981 Proof	5,000	Value: 30.00				

KM# 43 5 YUAN
15.0000 g., 0.9990 Silver 0.4818 oz. ASW, 33 mm. **Series:** Artifacts **Rev:** Rhino statue

Date	Mintage	F	VF	XF	Unc	BU
1981 Proof	5,000	Value: 30.00				

KM# 44 5 YUAN
15.0000 g., 0.9000 Silver 0.4340 oz. ASW, 33 mm. **Series:** Artifacts **Rev:** Dragon statue

Date	Mintage	F	VF	XF	Unc	BU
1981 Proof	5,000	Value: 30.00				

KM# 77 5 YUAN
22.2200 g., 0.9000 Silver 0.6429 oz. ASW **Obv:** Building **Rev:** Marco Polo bust, right, facing left, above ships, denomination below, dates at left of bust **Note:** Prev. Y#54.

Date	Mintage	F	VF	XF	Unc	BU
1983 Proof	15,000	Value: 55.00				

KM# 99 5 YUAN
22.2200 g., 0.9000 Silver 0.6429 oz. ASW **Rev:** Soldier statue, 3/4 left, from archaeological discovery, denomination lower left **Note:** Prev. Y#68.

Date	Mintage	F	VF	XF	Unc	BU
1984 Proof	14,000	Value: 20.00				

KM# 101 5 YUAN
22.2200 g., 0.9000 Silver 0.6429 oz. ASW **Rev:** Soldier statue, right, from archaeological discovery, denomination lower right **Note:** Prev. Y#69.

Date	Mintage	F	VF	XF	Unc	BU
1984 Proof	14,000	Value: 20.00				

KM# 98 5 YUAN
22.2200 g., 0.9000 Silver 0.6429 oz. ASW **Rev:** Soldier statue from archaeological discovery, kneeling, right, denomination lower right **Note:** Prev. Y#70.

Date	Mintage	F	VF	XF	Unc	BU
1984 Proof	14,000	Value: 20.00				

KM# 100 5 YUAN
22.2200 g., 0.9000 Silver 0.6429 oz. ASW **Rev:** Soldier statue with horse, right, from archaeological discovery, denomination below **Note:** Prev. Y#71.

Date	Mintage	F	VF	XF	Unc	BU
1984 Proof	14,000	Value: 20.00				

KM# 97   5 YUAN
8.4500 g., 0.8000 Silver 0.2173 oz. ASW **Series:** 1984 Summer
and Winter Olympics **Obv:** Mural of athletes divides emblem and
date **Rev:** High jumper, Olympic torch below, denomination at
left **Note:** Prev. Y#61.

Date	Mintage	F	VF	XF	Unc	BU
1984 Proof	10,000		Value: 25.00			

KM# 76   5 YUAN
22.0000 g., 0.9000 Silver 0.6366 oz. ASW, 22 mm.
Subject: Marco Polo

Date	Mintage	F	VF	XF	Unc	BU
1984 Proof	15,000		Value: 35.00			

KM# 121   5 YUAN
22.2200 g., 0.9000 Silver 0.6429 oz. ASW **Subject:** Founders
of Chinese Culture **Obv:** State seal **Rev:** Lao-Tse riding water
buffalo **Note:** Prev. Y#90.

Date	Mintage	F	VF	XF	Unc	BU
1985 Proof	8,175		Value: 30.00			

KM# 123   5 YUAN
22.2200 g., 0.9000 Silver 0.6429 oz. ASW **Subject:** Founders
of Chinese Culture **Rev:** Qu Yuan, left, facing , denomination at
right **Note:** Prev. Y#91.

Date	Mintage	F	VF	XF	Unc	BU
1985 Proof	8,175		Value: 30.00			

KM# 122   5 YUAN
22.2200 g., 0.9000 Silver 0.6429 oz. ASW **Subject:** Founders
of Chinese Culture **Rev:** Sun Wu, right, denomination at left
Note: Prev. Y#92.

Date	Mintage	F	VF	XF	Unc	BU
1985 Proof	8,175		Value: 30.00			

KM# 124   5 YUAN
22.2200 g., 0.9000 Silver 0.6429 oz. ASW **Subject:** Founders
of Chinese Culture **Rev:** Chen Sheng and Wu Guang,
denomination at left **Note:** Prev. Y#93.

Date	Mintage	F	VF	XF	Unc	BU
1985 Proof	8,175		Value: 30.00			

KM# 150   5 YUAN
22.2200 g., 0.9000 Silver 0.6429 oz. ASW **Subject:** 25th
Anniversary, World Wildlife Fund **Obv:** National emblem, date
below **Rev:** Giant panda divides mountains and denomination
Note: Prev. Y#106.

Date	Mintage	F	VF	XF	Unc	BU
1986	20,000	—	—	—	—	35.00
1986 Proof	20,000		Value: 50.00			

KM# 139   5 YUAN
18.6100 g., 0.9250 Silver 0.5534 oz. ASW **Subject:** Soccer
Obv: National emblem, inscription and date below **Rev:** Soccer
player, denomination lower right **Note:** Prev. Y#112.

Date	Mintage	F	VF	XF	Unc	BU
1986 Proof	8,500		Value: 35.00			

KM# 142   5 YUAN
22.2200 g., 0.9000 Silver 0.6429 oz. ASW **Subject:** Chinese
Culture **Rev:** Zhang Heng, Astronomer, left, denomination lower
right **Note:** Prev. Y#114.

Date	Mintage	F	VF	XF	Unc	BU
1986 Proof	9,675		Value: 25.00			

KM# 144   5 YUAN
22.2200 g., 0.9000 Silver 0.6429 oz. ASW **Subject:** Chinese
Culture **Rev:** Zu Chong Zhi, Mathematician, denomination at right
Note: Prev. Y#115.

Date	Mintage	F	VF	XF	Unc	BU
1986 Proof	9,675		Value: 25.00			

KM# 141   5 YUAN
22.2200 g., 0.9000 Silver 0.6429 oz. ASW **Subject:** Chinese
Culture **Rev:** Sima Qian, Historian, denomination below
Note: Prev. Y#116.

Date	Mintage	F	VF	XF	Unc	BU
1986 Proof	9,675		Value: 25.00			

KM# 139a   5 YUAN
17.0600 g., 0.8000 Silver 0.4388 oz. ASW **Note:** Prev. Y#112a.

Date	Mintage	F	VF	XF	Unc	BU
1986	1,000	—	—	—	—	125
Note: Satin finish						

KM# 143   5 YUAN
22.2200 g., 0.9000 Silver 0.6429 oz. ASW **Subject:** Chinese
Culture **Rev:** Cai Lun - papermaking, denomination upper right
Note: Prev. Y#113.

Date	Mintage	F	VF	XF	Unc	BU
1986 Proof	9,675		Value: 25.00			

KM# 148   5 YUAN
18.6100 g., 0.9250 Silver 0.5534 oz. ASW **Subject:** Year of
Peace **Obv:** National emblem, date below **Rev:** Seated woman,
doves in flight, denomination at left **Note:** Prev. Y#119.

Date	Mintage	F	VF	XF	Unc	BU
1986 Proof	1,350		Value: 250			

KM# 140   5 YUAN
18.6100 g., 0.9250 Silver 0.5534 oz. ASW   **Subject:** Soccer
Obv: National emblem above inscription and date **Rev:** Two
players, denomination above right **Note:** Prev. Y#197.

Date	Mintage	F	VF	XF	Unc	BU
1986 Proof	10,000	Value: 35.00				

KM# 140a   5 YUAN
16.8300 g., 0.8000 Silver 0.4329 oz. ASW   **Note:** Prev. Y#197a.

Date	Mintage	F	VF	XF	Unc	BU
1986 Satin finish	1,000	—	—	—	—	150

KM# 152   5 YUAN
22.2200 g., 0.9000 Silver 0.6429 oz. ASW   **Obv:** Great Wall,
date below **Rev:** The Empress of China, first American ship to
make a trade voyage to China. Denomination below **Note:** Prev.
Y#132.

Date	Mintage	F	VF	XF	Unc	BU
1986	75,000	—	—	—	—	35.00

KM# 174   5 YUAN
31.4700 g., 0.9000 Silver 0.9106 oz. ASW   **Rev:** Poet Li Bai, left,
denomination at right **Note:** Prev. Y#135.

Date	Mintage	F	VF	XF	Unc	BU
1987 Proof	4,000	Value: 27.50				

KM# 175   5 YUAN
31.4700 g., 0.9000 Silver 0.9106 oz. ASW   **Rev:** Poet Du Fu
walking right, denomination at left **Note:** Prev. Y#136.

Date	Mintage	F	VF	XF	Unc	BU
1987 Proof	4,000	Value: 27.50				

KM# 173   5 YUAN
31.4700 g., 0.9000 Silver 0.9106 oz. ASW   **Subject:** Bridge
Builder - Li Chun **Rev:** Li Chun, left, denomination lower left
Note: Prev. Y#137.

Date	Mintage	F	VF	XF	Unc	BU
1987 Proof	4,000	Value: 27.50				

KM# 172   5 YUAN
31.4700 g., 0.9000 Silver 0.9106 oz. ASW   **Rev:** Princess Chen
Wen and Song Zan Gan Bu strolling to left, denomination at left
Note: Prev. Y#138.

Date	Mintage	F	VF	XF	Unc	BU
1987 Proof	4,000	Value: 27.50				

KM# 210   5 YUAN
22.2200 g., 0.9000 Silver 0.6429 oz. ASW   **Subject:** Military
Hero of Song Dynasty - Yue Fei **Rev:** Yue Fei, left, denomination
at lower left **Note:** Prev. Y#160.

Date	Mintage	F	VF	XF	Unc	BU
1988 Proof	13,000	Value: 25.00				

KM# 209   5 YUAN
22.2200 g., 0.9000 Silver 0.6429 oz. ASW   **Subject:** Inventor of
Movable-type Printing **Rev:** Bi Sheng, 3/4 facing, denomination
at right **Note:** Prev. Y#161.

Date	Mintage	F	VF	XF	Unc	BU
1988 Proof	14,000	Value: 25.00				

KM# 207   5 YUAN
22.2200 g., 0.9000 Silver 0.6429 oz. ASW   **Subject:** Song
Dynasty Poet **Rev:** Su Shi, waving, 3/4 facing, denomination at
right **Note:** Prev. Y#162.

Date	Mintage	F	VF	XF	Unc	BU
1988 Proof	9,500	Value: 25.00				

KM# 208   5 YUAN
22.2200 g., 0.9000 Silver 0.6429 oz. ASW   **Subject:** Poetess of
Song Dynasty **Rev:** Li Qingzhao, facing, looking left,
denomination at left **Note:** Prev. Y#163.

Date	Mintage	F	VF	XF	Unc	BU
1988 Proof	13,000	Value: 25.00				

KM# 203   5 YUAN
27.0000 g., 0.9000 Silver 0.7812 oz. ASW   **Series:** Olympics
Obv: National emblem, date below **Rev:** Sailboat racing,
denomination at left **Note:** Prev. Y#171.

Date	Mintage	F	VF	XF	Unc	BU
1988 Proof	20,000	Value: 30.00				

KM# 204   5 YUAN
27.0000 g., 0.9000 Silver 0.7812 oz. ASW   **Series:** Seoul 1988
- 24th Summer Olympic Games **Obv:** National emblem, date
below **Rev:** Woman fencer, date at left, denomination below
Note: Prev. Y#172.

Date	Mintage	F	VF	XF	Unc	BU
1988 Proof	20,000	Value: 30.00				

KM# 201   5 YUAN
31.4700 g., 0.9000 Silver 0.9106 oz. ASW **Series:** Winter
Olympics **Obv:** National emblem, date below **Rev:** Downhill skier
with snowflakes, denomination at left **Note:** Prev. Y#129.

Date	Mintage	F	VF	XF	Unc	BU
1988 Proof	10,000	Value: 50.00				

KM# 202   5 YUAN
31.4700 g., 0.9000 Silver 0.9106 oz. ASW **Series:** Seoul 1988
- 24th Summer Olympic Games **Obv:** National emblem, date
below **Rev:** Woman hurdler, denomination below **Note:** Prev.
Y#130.

Date	Mintage	F	VF	XF	Unc	BU
1988 Proof	20,000	Value: 32.50				

KM# 248   5 YUAN
22.2200 g., 0.9000 Silver 0.6429 oz. ASW **Obv:** National
emblem, date below **Rev:** Kublai Khan, Emperor **Note:** Prev.
Y#213.

Date	Mintage	F	VF	XF	Unc	BU
1989 Proof	10,000	Value: 35.00				

KM# 249   5 YUAN
22.2200 g., 0.9000 Silver 0.6429 oz. ASW **Rev:** Guan Hanqing,
Playwright, denomination at left **Note:** Prev. Y#214.

Date	Mintage	F	VF	XF	Unc	BU
1989 Proof	8,000	Value: 30.00				

KM# 250   5 YUAN
22.2200 g., 0.9000 Silver 0.6429 oz. ASW **Rev:** Guo Shoujing,
Scientist, right, denomination at left **Note:** Prev. Y#215.

Date	Mintage	F	VF	XF	Unc	BU
1989 Proof	8,500	Value: 30.00				

KM# 251   5 YUAN
22.2200 g., 0.9000 Silver 0.6429 oz. ASW **Obv:** National
emblem, date below **Rev:** Huang Dao-po, facing, loooking left,
13th century inventor of hydraulic spinning, denomination at right
Note: Prev. Y#216.

Date	Mintage	F	VF	XF	Unc	BU
1989 Proof	8,000	Value: 30.00				

KM# 260   5 YUAN
22.2200 g., 0.9000 Silver 0.6429 oz. ASW **Series:** Save The
Children Fund **Obv:** National emblem, date below **Rev:** Children
and panda, denomination at right **Note:** Prev. Y#230.

Date	Mintage	F	VF	XF	Unc	BU
1989	20,000	—	—	—	—	30.00

KM# 245   5 YUAN
27.0000 g., 0.9250 Silver 0.8029 oz. ASW **Subject:** Soccer
Rev: 2 soccer players, date upper left, denomination below
Note: Prev. Y#243.

Date	Mintage	F	VF	XF	Unc	BU
1989 Proof	30,000	Value: 35.00				

KM# 246   5 YUAN
27.0000 g., 0.9250 Silver 0.8029 oz. ASW **Subject:** Soccer
Obv: National emblem, date below **Rev:** 2 soccer players,
denomination below **Note:** Prev. Y#297.

Date	Mintage	F	VF	XF	Unc	BU
1989 Proof	30,000	Value: 30.00				

KM# 247   5 YUAN
27.0000 g., 0.9250 Silver 0.8029 oz. ASW **Subject:** Soccer
Rev: Goalie, denomination at left **Note:** Prev. Y#298.

Date	Mintage	F	VF	XF	Unc	BU
1989 Proof	30,000	Value: 30.00				

KM# 313   5 YUAN
22.2200 g., 0.9000 Silver 0.6429 oz. ASW **Rev:** Luo
Guanzhong, Historian, seated left, denomination at right
Note: Prev. Y#302.

Date	Mintage	F	VF	XF	Unc	BU
1990 Proof	Est. 30,000	Value: 27.50				

KM# 310   5 YUAN
22.2200 g., 0.9000 Silver 0.6429 oz. ASW **Rev:** Li Zicheng,
Revolutionary, right, denomination upper right **Note:** Prev.
Y#303.

Date	Mintage	F	VF	XF	Unc	BU
1990 Proof	Est. 30,500	Value: 27.50				

KM# 311   5 YUAN
22.2200 g., 0.9000 Silver 0.6429 oz. ASW **Rev:** Li Shi Zhen,
Herbalist, seated left, denomination upper left **Note:** Prev. Y#304.

Date	Mintage	F	VF	XF	Unc	BU
1990 Proof	Est. 30,500	Value: 27.50				

KM# 312   5 YUAN
22.2200 g., 0.9000 Silver 0.6429 oz. ASW **Rev:** Zheng He, Seafarer, looking left, denomination at left **Note:** Prev. Y#305.

Date	Mintage	F	VF	XF	Unc	BU
1990 Proof	Est. 30,500	Value: 27.50				

KM# 262   5 YUAN
15.0000 g., 0.9000 Silver 0.4340 oz. ASW **Subject:** Bronze Archaeological Finds **Rev:** Elephant pitcher, left, denomination below

Date	Mintage	F	VF	XF	Unc	BU
1990 Proof	5,000	Value: 30.00				

KM# 263   5 YUAN
15.0000 g., 0.9000 Silver 0.4340 oz. ASW **Subject:** Bronze Archaeological Finds **Rev:** Mythical creature

Date	Mintage	F	VF	XF	Unc	BU
1990 Proof	5,000	Value: 30.00				

KM# A263   5 YUAN
15.0000 g., 0.9000 Silver 0.4340 oz. ASW **Subject:** Bronze Archaeological Finds **Rev:** Rhinoceros, left, denomination below

Date	Mintage	F	VF	XF	Unc	BU
1990 Proof	5,000	Value: 30.00				

KM# A264   5 YUAN
15.0000 g., 0.9000 Silver 0.4340 oz. ASW **Subject:** Bronze Archaeological Finds **Rev:** Leopard, left, denomination below

Date	Mintage	F	VF	XF	Unc	BU
1990 Proof	5,000	Value: 30.00				

KM# 324   5 YUAN
15.0000 g., 0.9000 Silver 0.4340 oz. ASW **Subject:** Taiwan Scenery Series **Obv:** Great Wall **Rev:** Tall, narrow building, denomination below **Note:** Prev. Y#676.

Date	Mintage	F	VF	XF	Unc	BU
1990 Proof	2,000	Value: 37.50				

KM# 323   5 YUAN
15.0000 g., 0.9000 Silver 0.4340 oz. ASW **Rev:** Pondside building, denomination below **Note:** Prev. Y#677.

Date	Mintage	F	VF	XF	Unc	BU
1990 Proof	2,000	Value: 37.50				

KM# 325   5 YUAN
15.0000 g., 0.9000 Silver 0.4340 oz. ASW **Rev:** Hillside building, denomination below **Note:** Prev. Y#678.

Date	Mintage	F	VF	XF	Unc	BU
1990 Proof	2,000	Value: 37.50				

KM# 322   5 YUAN
15.0000 g., 0.9000 Silver 0.4340 oz. ASW **Rev:** 3 buildings joined by bridges, denomination below **Note:** Prev. Y#679.

Date	Mintage	F	VF	XF	Unc	BU
1990 Proof	2,000	Value: 37.50				

KM# 315   5 YUAN
2.0000 g., 0.9990 Silver 0.0642 oz. ASW, 15 mm. **Rev:** Dragon and Phoenix

Date	Mintage	F	VF	XF	Unc	BU
1990 Proof	50,000	Value: 25.00				

KM# 377   5 YUAN
22.2200 g., 0.9000 Silver 0.6429 oz. ASW **Rev:** Song Yingxing, Scientist **Note:** Prev. Y#322.

Date	Mintage	F	VF	XF	Unc	BU
1991 Proof	Est. 25,000	Value: 27.50				

KM# 378   5 YUAN
22.2200 g., 0.9000 Silver 0.6429 oz. ASW **Rev:** Cao Xueqin, Writer **Note:** Prev. Y#323.

Date	Mintage	F	VF	XF	Unc	BU
1991 Proof	Est. 25,000	Value: 27.50				

KM# 379   5 YUAN
22.2200 g., 0.9000 Silver 0.6429 oz. ASW **Rev:** Lin Zexu, high ranking official **Note:** Prev. Y#324.

Date	Mintage	F	VF	XF	Unc	BU
1991 Proof	Est. 25,000	Value: 27.50				

KM# 380   5 YUAN
22.2200 g., 0.9000 Silver 0.6429 oz. ASW **Rev:** Hong Xuquan, Revolutionary **Note:** Prev. Y#325.

Date	Mintage	F	VF	XF	Unc	BU
1991 Proof	Est. 25,000	Value: 27.50				

KM# 404   5 YUAN
22.2200 g., 0.9000 Silver 0.6429 oz. ASW **Subject:** Archaeological Finds **Obv:** Great Wall, date below **Rev:** Ancient ships and shipbuilding, denomination at left **Note:** Prev. Y#331.

Date	Mintage	F	VF	XF	Unc	BU
1992 Proof	15,000	Value: 27.50				

KM# 407   5 YUAN
22.2200 g., 0.9000 Silver 0.6429 oz. ASW **Subject:** First Compass **Obv:** Great Wall, date below **Rev:** Ancient compass, men on horseback, empty biga, denomination below **Note:** Prev. Y#332.

Date	Mintage	F	VF	XF	Unc	BU
1992 Proof	15,000	Value: 25.00				

KM# 405   5 YUAN
22.2200 g., 0.9000 Silver 0.6429 oz. ASW **Subject:** First Seismograph **Obv:** Great wall, date below **Rev:** First seismograph **Note:** Prev. Y#333.

Date	Mintage	F	VF	XF	Unc	BU
1992 Proof	15,000	Value: 25.00				

KM# 406   5 YUAN
22.2200 g., 0.9000 Silver 0.6429 oz. ASW **Subject:** Ancient Kite Flying **Obv:** Great Wall, date below **Rev:** Butterfly, kites in background, denomination below **Note:** Prev. Y#334.

Date	Mintage	F	VF	XF	Unc	BU
1992 Proof	15,000	Value: 30.00				

KM# 408   5 YUAN
22.2200 g., 0.9000 Silver 0.6429 oz. ASW **Obv:** Great Wall, date below **Rev:** Bronze Age metal working scene, denomination below **Edge:** Fine or coarse reeding

Date	Mintage	F	VF	XF	Unc	BU
1992 Proof	15,000	Value: 25.00				

KM# 467   5 YUAN
15.0000 g., 0.9000 Silver 0.4340 oz. ASW **Obv:** National emblem, date below **Rev:** Marco Polo bust, looking right, buildings and dates at right, denomination below

Date	Mintage	F	VF	XF	Unc	BU
1992 Proof	12,000			Value: 25.00		

KM# 459   5 YUAN
15.0000 g., 0.9000 Silver 0.4340 oz. ASW **Subject:** Archaeological Finds **Obv:** National emblem **Rev:** Resting deer with long antlers **Note:** Prev. Y#750.

Date	Mintage	F	VF	XF	Unc	BU
1992 Proof	3,000			Value: 35.00		

KM# 465   5 YUAN
22.2200 g., 0.9000 Silver 0.6429 oz. ASW **Subject:** United Nations Environmental Protection **Obv:** National emblem, date below **Rev:** Woman drawing water from stream, denomination below **Note:** Prev. Y#548.

Date	Mintage	F	VF	XF	Unc	BU
1992 Proof	20,000			Value: 20.00		

KM# 450   5 YUAN
22.2200 g., 0.9000 Silver 0.6429 oz. ASW **Obv:** National emblem, date below **Rev:** Zheng Chenggong portrait, pointing right, denomination upper left **Note:** Prev. Y#549.

Date	Mintage	F	VF	XF	Unc	BU
1992 Proof	—			Value: 30.00		

KM# 448   5 YUAN
22.2200 g., 0.9000 Silver 0.6429 oz. ASW **Obv:** National emblem **Rev:** Cai Wenji, 177-254AD, Poet, kneeling left, denomination at right **Note:** Prev. Y#550.

Date	Mintage	F	VF	XF	Unc	BU
1992 Proof	Est. 7,000			Value: 30.00		

KM# 447   5 YUAN
22.2200 g., 0.9000 Silver 0.6429 oz. ASW **Obv:** National emblem **Rev:** Hua Mulan, soldier, 2nd Century Heroine on horseback, denomination upper right **Note:** Prev. Y#551.

Date	Mintage	F	VF	XF	Unc	BU
1992 Proof	Est. 7,000			Value: 30.00		

KM# 446   5 YUAN
22.2200 g., 0.9000 Silver 0.6429 oz. ASW **Obv:** National emblem **Rev:** Wang Zhaojun, Princess, Peacemaker, Sponsor of the Arts, denomination at right **Note:** Prev. Y#552.

Date	Mintage	F	VF	XF	Unc	BU
1992 Proof	Est. 7,000			Value: 30.00		

KM# 449   5 YUAN
22.2200 g., 0.9000 Silver 0.6429 oz. ASW **Obv:** National emblem **Rev:** Xiao Zhuo, 953-1009AD, Strategist, left, denomination below **Note:** Prev. Y#553.

Date	Mintage	F	VF	XF	Unc	BU
1992 Proof	Est. 7,000			Value: 28.00		

KM# 458   5 YUAN
15.0000 g., 0.9000 Silver 0.4340 oz. ASW **Subject:** Archeological Finds **Obv:** National emblem **Rev:** Panther sculpture **Note:** Prev. Y#751.

Date	Mintage	F	VF	XF	Unc	BU
1992 Proof	3,000			Value: 35.00		

KM# 457   5 YUAN
15.0000 g., 0.9000 Silver 0.4340 oz. ASW **Subject:** Archaeological Finds **Obv:** National emblem **Rev:** Bighorn sheep **Note:** Prev. Y#752.

Date	Mintage	F	VF	XF	Unc	BU
1992 Proof	3,000			Value: 35.00		

KM# 460   5 YUAN
15.0000 g., 0.9000 Silver 0.4340 oz. ASW **Subject:** Archaeological Finds **Obv:** National emblem **Rev:** Changzin court lantern **Note:** Prev. Y#753.

Date	Mintage	F	VF	XF	Unc	BU
1992 Proof	3,000			Value: 35.00		

KM# 75   5 YUAN
15.0000 g., 0.9000 Silver 0.4340 oz. ASW, 33 mm. **Subject:** Marco Polo **Rev:** Bust and two temples

Date	Mintage	F	VF	XF	Unc	BU
1992 Proof	30,000			Value: 25.00		

KM# 469   5 YUAN
Copper **Obv:** National emblem, date below **Obv. Leg.:** ZHONGCHUA RENMIN GONGHEFUO **Rev:** 2 Pandas eating bamboo, denomination below **Note:** Prev. Y#359.

Date	Mintage	F	VF	XF	Unc	BU
1993	2,000,000	—	—	—	15.00	25.00

KM# 489   5 YUAN
22.2200 g., 0.9000 Silver 0.6429 oz. ASW **Subject:** Chin-Yin Yang **Rev:** Two figures, one standing and one kneeling, denomination below **Note:** Prev. Y#377.

Date	Mintage	F	VF	XF	Unc	BU
1993 Proof	15,000			Value: 35.00		

KM# 491   5 YUAN
22.2200 g., 0.9000 Silver 0.6429 oz. ASW **Subject:** Invention of the Umbrella **Obv:** Great Wall, date below **Rev:** Figures with umbrellas above umbrella makers, denomination at right **Note:** Prev. Y#400.

Date	Mintage	F	VF	XF	Unc	BU
1993 Proof	15,000			Value: 20.00		

KM# 545   5 YUAN
1.5552 g., 0.9990 Gold 0.0499 oz. AGW **Subject:** Goddess of Mercy **Obv:** Great Wall, date below **Rev:** Goddess left, denomination at right **Note:** Prev. Y#498.

Date	Mintage	F	VF	XF	Unc	BU
1993 Prooflike	40,000	—	—	—	—	50.00

KM# 546   5 YUAN
1.5552 g., 0.9990 Gold 0.0499 oz. AGW **Rev:** Goddess Kuan Yin - Seated in Flowers **Note:** Prev. Y#500.

Date	Mintage	F	VF	XF	Unc	BU
1993 Proof	1,000			Value: 65.00		

KM# 567   5 YUAN
15.0000 g., 0.9000 Silver 0.4340 oz. ASW **Subject:** Archeological Finds **Obv:** National emblem **Rev:** Ox lantern **Note:** Prev. Y#768.

Date	Mintage	F	VF	XF	Unc	BU
1993 Proof	2,000			Value: 37.50		

KM# 568   5 YUAN
15.0000 g., 0.9000 Silver 0.4340 oz. ASW **Subject:** Archaeological Finds **Obv:** National emblem **Rev:** Human figure lantern **Note:** Prev. Y#769.

Date	Mintage	F	VF	XF	Unc	BU
1993 Proof	2,000			Value: 37.50		

KM# 570 5 YUAN
15.0000 g., 0.9000 Silver 0.4340 oz. ASW
Subject: Archeological Finds **Obv:** National emblem **Rev:** Horse statue **Note:** Prev. Y#770.

Date	Mintage	F	VF	XF	Unc	BU
1993 Proof	2,000	Value: 37.50				

KM# 569 5 YUAN
15.0000 g., 0.9000 Silver 0.4340 oz. ASW
Subject: Archeological Finds **Obv:** National emblem **Rev:** Pig statue **Note:** Prev. Y#771.

Date	Mintage	F	VF	XF	Unc	BU
1993 Proof	2,000	Value: 37.50				

KM# 583 5 YUAN
1.5552 g., 0.9990 Gold 0.0499 oz. AGW **Subject:** Homeland Scenery **Obv:** Great Wall **Rev:** Temple at Mount Song **Note:** Prev. Y#773.

Date	Mintage	F	VF	XF	Unc	BU
1993 Proof	8,888	Value: 50.00				

KM# 488 5 YUAN
22.2200 g., 0.9000 Silver 0.6429 oz. ASW
Subject: Mathematical Definition of Zero **Obv:** Great Wall, date below **Rev:** Mathematicians, abacus, denomination lower right **Note:** Prev. Y#558.

Date	Mintage	F	VF	XF	Unc	BU
1993 Proof	15,000	Value: 22.00				

KM# 490 5 YUAN
22.2200 g., 0.9000 Silver 0.6429 oz. ASW **Subject:** Invention of the Stirrup **Obv:** Great Wall **Rev:** Early polo game, denomination below **Note:** Prev. Y#559.

Date	Mintage	F	VF	XF	Unc	BU
1993 Proof	15,000	Value: 22.00				

KM# 492 5 YUAN
22.2200 g., 0.9000 Silver 0.6429 oz. ASW **Subject:** The Terracotta Army **Obv:** Great Wall, date below **Rev:** The unearthing of the terracotta figurines, denomination at right **Note:** Prev. Y#560.

Date	Mintage	F	VF	XF	Unc	BU
1993 Proof	15,000	Value: 22.00				

KM# 578 5 YUAN
15.0000 g., 0.9000 Silver 0.4340 oz. ASW **Obv:** Great Wall **Rev:** Taiwan Temple Buddha Statue **Note:** Prev. Y#441.

Date	Mintage	F	VF	XF	Unc	BU
1993 Proof	2,000	Value: 27.50				

KM# 576 5 YUAN
15.0000 g., 0.9000 Silver 0.4340 oz. ASW **Subject:** Taiwan Temple **Obv:** Great Wall **Rev:** Large temple **Note:** Prev. Y#442.

Date	Mintage	F	VF	XF	Unc	BU
1993 Proof	2,000	Value: 27.50				

KM# 577 5 YUAN
15.0000 g., 0.9000 Silver 0.4340 oz. ASW **Subject:** Taiwan Temple **Obv:** Great Wall **Rev:** Small temple **Note:** Prev. Y#443.

Date	Mintage	F	VF	XF	Unc	BU
1993 Proof	2,000	Value: 27.50				

KM# 575 5 YUAN
15.0000 g., 0.9000 Silver 0.4340 oz. ASW **Subject:** Taiwan Temple **Obv:** Great Wall **Rev:** Tower temple **Note:** Prev. Y#444.

Date	Mintage	F	VF	XF	Unc	BU
1993 Proof	2,000	Value: 27.50				

KM# 530 5 YUAN
22.2200 g., 0.9000 Silver 0.6429 oz. ASW **Obv:** National emblem **Rev:** Chou En-Lai, facing, denomination upper left **Note:** Prev. Y#534.

Date	Mintage	F	VF	XF	Unc	BU
1993 Proof	Est. 25,000	Value: 30.00				

KM# 532 5 YUAN
22.2200 g., 0.9000 Silver 0.6429 oz. ASW **Obv:** National emblem **Rev:** Liu Shaoqi, 3/4 left, denomination at left **Note:** Prev. Y#535.

Date	Mintage	F	VF	XF	Unc	BU
1993 Proof	Est. 25,000	Value: 30.00				

KM# 531 5 YUAN
22.2200 g., 0.9000 Silver 0.6429 oz. ASW **Obv:** National emblem **Rev:** Chu Teh, 3/4 facing, arm raised, denomination upper right **Note:** Prev. Y#536.

Date	Mintage	F	VF	XF	Unc	BU
1993 Proof	Est. 25,000	Value: 30.00				

KM# 533 5 YUAN
22.2200 g., 0.9000 Silver 0.6429 oz. ASW **Obv:** National emblem **Rev:** Li Da-Chao, facing, denomination at right **Note:** Prev. Y#537.

Date	Mintage	F	VF	XF	Unc	BU
1993 Proof	Est. 25,000	Value: 30.00				

KM# 628 5 YUAN
22.2200 g., 0.9000 Silver 0.6429 oz. ASW **Subject:** Oriental Inventions **Obv:** Great Wall, date below **Rev:** First tuned bells, denomination at left **Note:** Prev. Y#616.

Date	Mintage	F	VF	XF	Unc	BU
1994 Proof	15,000	Value: 18.00				

KM# 629 5 YUAN
22.2200 g., 0.9000 Silver 0.6429 oz. ASW **Subject:** Oriental Inventions **Obv:** Great Wall, date below **Rev:** First silken fabric, denomination lower right **Note:** Prev. Y#617.

Date	Mintage	F	VF	XF	Unc	BU
1994 Proof	15,000	Value: 20.00				

KM# 627 5 YUAN
22.2200 g., 0.9000 Silver 0.6429 oz. ASW **Subject:** Oriental Invention **Obv:** Great Wall, date below **Rev:** First records of comets, denomination at right **Note:** Prev. Y#618.

Date	Mintage	F	VF	XF	Unc	BU
1994 Proof	15,000	Value: 20.00				

KM# 631 5 YUAN
22.2200 g., 0.9000 Silver 0.6429 oz. ASW **Subject:** Oriental Inventions **Obv:** Great Wall, date below **Rev:** First masts for sailing, denomination lower right **Note:** Prev. Y#619.

Date	Mintage	F	VF	XF	Unc	BU
1994 Proof	15,000	Value: 20.00				

KM# 630   5 YUAN
22.2200 g., 0.9000 Silver 0.6429 oz. ASW   **Subject:** Oriental
Inventions **Obv:** Great Wall, date below **Rev:** First chain pumps
used to draw water, denomination below **Note:** Prev. Y#620.

Date	Mintage	F	VF	XF	Unc	BU
1994 Proof	15,000				Value: 18.00	

KM# 661   5 YUAN
15.5517 g., 0.9990 Silver 0.4995 oz. ASW   **Rev:** Goddess Kuan
Yin - with child, denomination at left **Note:** Prev. Y#506.

Date	Mintage	F	VF	XF	Unc	BU
1994 Proof	3,000				Value: 28.50	

KM# 659   5 YUAN
15.5517 g., 0.9990 Silver 0.4995 oz. ASW   **Rev:** Goddess Kuan
Yin - with bottle **Note:** Prev. Y#507.

Date	Mintage	F	VF	XF	Unc	BU
1994 Proof	3,000				Value: 28.50	

KM# 660   5 YUAN
15.5517 g., 0.9990 Silver 0.4995 oz. ASW   **Rev:** Goddess Kuan
Yin - standing, denomination at right **Note:** Prev. Y#508.

Date	Mintage	F	VF	XF	Unc	BU
1994 Proof	3,000				Value: 28.50	

KM# 674   5 YUAN
1.5552 g., 0.9990 Gold 0.0499 oz. AGW   **Obv:** Crowned figure
on horseback, date lower right **Rev:** Unicorn, denomination at
left **Note:** Prev. Y#419.

Date	Mintage	F	VF	XF	Unc	BU
1994 Proof	31,000				Value: 65.00	

KM# 778   5 YUAN
22.2200 g., 0.9000 Silver 0.6429 oz. ASW   **Obv:** Temple, date
below **Rev:** Goddess Kuan Yin, facing, - with Lotus flower,
denomination at left **Note:** Prev. Y#516.

Date	Mintage	F	VF	XF	Unc	BU
1995 Proof	3,000				Value: 28.50	

KM# 781A   5 YUAN
22.2200 g., 0.9000 Silver 0.6429 oz. ASW   **Obv:** Temple, date
below **Rev:** Goddess Kuan Yin - with wheel, 3/4 left, denomination
at right **Note:** Prev. Y#517.

Date	Mintage	F	VF	XF	Unc	BU
1995 Proof	3,000				Value: 28.50	

KM# 779   5 YUAN
22.2200 g., 0.9000 Silver 0.6429 oz. ASW   **Obv:** Temple, date
below **Rev:** Goddess Kuan Yin, 3/4 left, - with sceptre,
denomination at left **Note:** Prev. Y#518.

Date	Mintage	F	VF	XF	Unc	BU
1995 Proof	3,000				Value: 28.50	

KM# 781   5 YUAN
22.2200 g., 0.9000 Silver 0.6429 oz. ASW   **Obv:** Temple, date
below **Rev:** Goddess Kuan Yin - with bowl, 3/4 left, denomination
at right **Note:** Prev. Y#519.

Date	Mintage	F	VF	XF	Unc	BU
1995 Proof	3,000				Value: 28.50	

KM# 774   5 YUAN
22.2200 g., 0.9000 Silver 0.6429 oz. ASW   **Obv:** Temple, date
below **Rev:** Sea goddess bust, 3/4 left, denomination at right
Note: Prev. Y#481.

Date	Mintage	F	VF	XF	Unc	BU
1995 Proof	8,000,000				Value: 27.50	

KM# 868   5 YUAN
22.2200 g., 0.9000 Silver 0.6429 oz. ASW   **Rev:** 2 men leading
camel, denomination below **Note:** Prev. Y#600.

Date	Mintage	F	VF	XF	Unc	BU
1995 Proof	15,000				Value: 35.00	

KM# 869   5 YUAN
22.2200 g., 0.9000 Silver 0.6429 oz. ASW   **Rev:** Dancer,
denomination lower right **Note:** Prev. Y#601.

Date	Mintage	F	VF	XF	Unc	BU
1995 Proof	15,000				Value: 27.50	

KM# 867   5 YUAN
22.2200 g., 0.9000 Silver 0.6429 oz. ASW   **Rev:** Silk merchant
and customer, denomination at right **Note:** Prev. Y#602.

Date	Mintage	F	VF	XF	Unc	BU
1995 Proof	15,000				Value: 25.00	

KM# 866   5 YUAN
22.2200 g., 0.9000 Silver 0.6429 oz. ASW   **Rev:** Silk spinner,
denomination at right **Note:** Prev. Y#603.

Date	Mintage	F	VF	XF	Unc	BU
1995 Proof	Est. 15,000				Value: 25.00	

KM# 714   5 YUAN
Bronze   **Obv:** National emblem, date below **Obv. Leg.:**
ZHONGHUA RENMIN GONGHEGUO **Rev:** Golden monkey,
denomination at right **Note:** Prev. Y#547.

Date	Mintage	F	VF	XF	Unc	BU
1995	—	—	—	—	12.00	15.00

KM# 735   5 YUAN
22.2200 g., 0.9000 Silver 0.6429 oz. ASW   **Subject:** Oriental
Inventions **Obv:** Great Wall, date below **Rev:** Soldiers with cannon
and gunpowder, denomination lower left **Note:** Prev. Y#627.

Date	Mintage	F	VF	XF	Unc	BU
1995 Proof	15,000				Value: 25.00	

KM# 737 5 YUAN
22.2200 g., 0.9000 Silver 0.6429 oz. ASW **Subject:** Oriental Inventions **Obv:** Great Wall, date below **Rev:** Individual block printing, denomination at right **Note:** Prev. Y#628.

Date	Mintage	F	VF	XF	Unc	BU
1995 Proof	15,000	Value: 25.00				

KM# 739 5 YUAN
20.0000 g., 0.9000 Silver 0.5787 oz. ASW, 36 mm. **Subject:** Oriental Inventions - Chess **Obv:** The Great Wall, date below **Rev:** Chess players, denomination upper right **Note:** Prev. Y#629.

Date	Mintage	F	VF	XF	Unc	BU
1995 Proof	—	Value: 25.00				

KM# 736 5 YUAN
22.2200 g., 0.9000 Silver 0.6429 oz. ASW **Subject:** Oriental Inventions **Obv:** Great Wall, date below **Rev:** Potter, denomination lower left **Note:** Prev. Y#630.

Date	Mintage	F	VF	XF	Unc	BU
1995 Proof	15,000	Value: 25.00				

KM# 738 5 YUAN
22.2200 g., 0.9000 Silver 0.6429 oz. ASW **Subject:** Oriental Inventions **Obv:** Great Wall **Rev:** Teacher with chart of human body **Note:** Prev. Y#631.

Date	Mintage	F	VF	XF	Unc	BU
1995 Proof	15,000	Value: 25.00				

KM# 794 5 YUAN
1.5552 g., 0.9990 Gold 0.0499 oz. AGW **Obv:** Eastern unicorn rearing, left, date below **Rev:** Western unicorn with offspring, denomination at left **Note:** Prev. Y#736.

Date	Mintage	F	VF	XF	Unc	BU
1995 Proof	20,000	Value: 95.00				

KM# 828 5 YUAN
22.2223 g., 0.9000 Silver 0.6430 oz. ASW **Subject:** Chinese Culture Series **Obv:** Great Wall seen through arch, date below

---

Rev: Pagoda of Six Harmonies, denomination at left
Note: Prev. Y#794.

Date	Mintage	F	VF	XF	Unc	BU
1995 Proof	20,000	Value: 25.00				

KM# 827 5 YUAN
22.2223 g., 0.9000 Silver 0.6430 oz. ASW **Subject:** Chinese Culture Series **Obv:** Great Wall seen through arch, date below **Rev:** Mencius seated at table, denomination below **Note:** Prev. Y#795.

Date	Mintage	F	VF	XF	Unc	BU
1995 Proof	20,000	Value: 25.00				

KM# 825 5 YUAN
22.2223 g., 0.9000 Silver 0.6430 oz. ASW **Subject:** Chinese Culture Series **Obv:** Great Wall seen through arch, date below **Rev:** Tang Taizong seated, denomination at left **Note:** Prev. Y#796.

Date	Mintage	F	VF	XF	Unc	BU
1995 Proof	20,000	Value: 25.00				

KM# 826 5 YUAN
22.2223 g., 0.9000 Silver 0.6430 oz. ASW **Subject:** Chinese Culture Series **Obv:** Great Wall seen through arch **Rev:** Lion dance **Note:** Prev. Y#797.

Date	Mintage	F	VF	XF	Unc	BU
1995 Proof	20,000	Value: 25.00				

KM# 823 5 YUAN
22.2223 g., 0.9000 Silver 0.6430 oz. ASW **Subject:** Chinese Culture Series **Obv:** Great Wall seen through arch, date below **Rev:** Female opera role, denomination upper right **Note:** Prev. Y#798.

Date	Mintage	F	VF	XF	Unc	BU
1995 Proof	20,000	Value: 25.00				

KM# 910 5 YUAN
22.2223 g., 0.9000 Silver 0.6430 oz. ASW **Subject:** Chinese Inventions and Discoveries Series **Obv:** Great Wall, date below **Rev:** Three musicians, denomination at left **Note:** Prev. Y#871.

Date	Mintage	F	VF	XF	Unc	BU
1996 Proof	15,000	Value: 30.00				

KM# 912 5 YUAN
22.2223 g., 0.9000 Silver 0.6430 oz. ASW **Subject:** Chinese Inventions and Discoveries Series **Obv:** Great Wall, date below **Rev:** Suspension bridge, denomination at right **Note:** Prev. Y#872.

Date	Mintage	F	VF	XF	Unc	BU
1996 Proof	15,000	Value: 30.00				

KM# 913 5 YUAN
22.2223 g., 0.9000 Silver 0.6430 oz. ASW **Subject:** Chinese Inventions and Discoveries Series **Obv:** Great Wall **Rev:** Astronomical clock, denomination at right **Note:** Prev. Y#873.

Date	Mintage	F	VF	XF	Unc	BU
1996 Proof	15,000	Value: 30.00				

KM# 911 5 YUAN
22.2223 g., 0.9000 Silver 0.6430 oz. ASW **Subject:** Chinese Inventions and Discoveries Series **Obv:** Great Wall **Rev:** Sailing ship, denomination at right **Note:** Prev. Y#874.

Date	Mintage	F	VF	XF	Unc	BU
1996 Proof	15,000	Value: 30.00				

KM# 909 5 YUAN
22.2223 g., 0.9000 Silver 0.6430 oz. ASW **Subject:** Chinese Inventions and Discoveries Series **Obv:** Great Wall **Rev:** Horse cart, denomination below **Note:** Prev. Y#875.

Date	Mintage	F	VF	XF	Unc	BU
1996 Proof	15,000	Value: 30.00				

KM# 938   5 YUAN
15.5517 g., 0.9990 Silver 0.4995 oz. ASW **Obv:** Eastern unicorn, date below **Rev:** Western unicorn rearing, left, denomination lower left **Note:** Prev. Y#883.

Date	Mintage	F	VF	XF	Unc	BU
1996	—	—	—	—	—	25.00

KM# 933   5 YUAN
1.5552 g., 0.9990 Gold 0.0499 oz. AGW **Subject:** Goddess Guanyin **Obv:** Temple, date below **Rev:** Goddess holding flower, denomination at left **Note:** Prev. Y#885.

Date	Mintage	F	VF	XF	Unc	BU
1996 Proof	5,000	Value: 50.00				

KM# 939   5 YUAN
1.5552 g., 0.9990 Gold 0.0499 oz. AGW **Obv:** Eastern unicorn, date below **Rev:** Head of western unicorn, right, denomination at right **Note:** Prev. Y#740.

Date	Mintage	F	VF	XF	Unc	BU
1996	—	—	—	—	—	60.00
1996 Proof	5,000	Value: 130				

KM# 881   5 YUAN
Bronze **Obv:** National emblem, date below **Obv. Leg.:** ZONGHUA RENMIN GONGHEGUO **Rev:** Tiger, denomination at left **Note:** Prev. Y#729.

Date	Mintage	F	VF	XF	Unc	BU
1996	—	—	—	—	12.00	15.00

KM# 882   5 YUAN
Bronze **Obv:** National emblem, date below **Rev:** Pair of baiji dolphins, denomination above **Note:** Prev. Y#730.

Date	Mintage	F	VF	XF	Unc	BU
1996	—	—	—	—	12.00	15.00

KM# 974   5 YUAN
22.2200 g., 0.9000 Silver 0.6429 oz. ASW **Rev:** Caravan route market scene, denomination below **Note:** Prev. Y#604.

Date	Mintage	F	VF	XF	Unc	BU
1996 Proof	15,000	Value: 25.00				

KM# 972   5 YUAN
22.2200 g., 0.9000 Silver 0.6429 oz. ASW **Rev:** Fairy above Magao Sanctuary, denomination upper right **Note:** Prev. Y#605.

Date	Mintage	F	VF	XF	Unc	BU
1996 Proof	15,000	Value: 25.00				

KM# 973   5 YUAN
22.2200 g., 0.9000 Silver 0.6429 oz. ASW **Rev:** Various historic sculptures, denomination lower left **Note:** Prev. Y#606.

Date	Mintage	F	VF	XF	Unc	BU
1996 Proof	15,000	Value: 25.00				

KM# 971   5 YUAN
22.2200 g., 0.9000 Silver 0.6429 oz. ASW **Rev:** Musicians on camel, denomination at left **Note:** Prev. Y#607.

Date	Mintage	F	VF	XF	Unc	BU
1996 Proof	15,000	Value: 25.00				

KM# 934   5 YUAN
15.5500 g., 0.9990 Silver 0.4994 oz. ASW, 33 mm.
Obv: Temple, date below **Rev:** Goddess holding vase and twig, denomination at right **Edge:** Reeded **Note:** Prev. Y#1196.

Date	Mintage	F	VF	XF	Unc	BU
1996 Proof	5,000	Value: 35.00				

KM# 935   5 YUAN
1.5550 g., 0.9990 Gold 0.0499 oz. AGW, 14 mm.
Subject: Goddess Guanyin **Obv:** Temple **Rev:** Goddess holding vase and twig **Edge:** Reeded **Note:** Prev. Y#1197.

Date	Mintage	F	VF	XF	Unc	BU
1996 Proof	35,000	Value: 50.00				

KM# 1057   5 YUAN
1.5550 g., 0.9990 Gold 0.0499 oz. AGW, 14 mm.
Obv: Ornamental column **Rev:** Child holding a carp **Edge:** Reeded **Note:** Prev. Y#1198.

Date	Mintage	F	VF	XF	Unc	BU
1997	100,000	—	—	—	—	50.00

KM# 1067   5 YUAN
22.0000 g., 0.9000 Silver 0.6366 oz. ASW, 36 mm. **Obv:** Great Wall **Rev:** Building, denomination below **Edge:** Reeded **Mint:** Shenyang **Note:** Prev. Y#1190.

Date	Mintage	F	VF	XF	Unc	BU
1997(y)	35,000	—	—	—	22.50	—

KM# 1071   5 YUAN
22.0000 g., 0.9000 Silver 0.6366 oz. ASW, 36 mm. **Obv:** Great Wall view, date below **Rev:** Man with flag, denomination lower left **Edge:** Reeded **Mint:** Shenyang **Note:** Prev. Y#1186.

Date	Mintage	F	VF	XF	Unc	BU
1997(y)	35,000	—	—	—	22.50	—

KM# 1069   5 YUAN
22.0000 g., 0.9000 Silver 0.6366 oz. ASW, 36 mm. **Obv:** Great Wall **Rev:** Man with extended open hand, denomination at right **Edge:** Reeded **Mint:** Shenyang **Note:** Prev. Y#1187.

Date	Mintage	F	VF	XF	Unc	BU
1997(y)	35,000	—	—	—	22.50	—

KM# 1070   5 YUAN
22.0000 g., 0.9000 Silver 0.6366 oz. ASW, 36 mm. **Obv:** Great Wall **Rev:** Astronomer, denomination at left **Edge:** Reeded **Mint:** Shenyang **Note:** Prev. Y#1188.

Date	Mintage	F	VF	XF	Unc	BU
1997(y)	35,000	—	—	—	22.50	—

KM# 1068 5 YUAN
22.0000 g., 0.9000 Silver 0.6366 oz. ASW, 36 mm. **Obv:** Great Wall **Rev:** Gymnast, denomination at right **Edge:** Reeded **Mint:** Shenyang **Note:** Prev. Y#1189.

Date	Mintage	F	VF	XF	Unc	BU
1997(y)	35,000	—	—	—	22.50	—

KM# 1103 5 YUAN
22.0000 g., 0.9000 Silver 0.6366 oz. ASW, 36 mm. **Series:** Silk Road **Rev:** Camels entering gate

Date	Mintage	F	VF	XF	Unc	BU
1997 Proof	15,000	Value: 40.00				

KM# 1105 5 YUAN
22.0000 g., 0.9000 Silver 0.6366 oz. ASW, 36 mm. **Series:** Silk Road **Rev:** People inspecting cloth

Date	Mintage	F	VF	XF	Unc	BU
1997 Proof	15,000	Value: 40.00				

KM# 1106 5 YUAN
22.0000 g., 0.9000 Silver 0.6366 oz. ASW, 36 mm. **Series:** Silk Road **Rev:** Musicians and dancer

Date	Mintage	F	VF	XF	Unc	BU
1997 Proof	15,000	Value: 40.00				

KM# 980 5 YUAN
Bronze **Obv:** National emblem, date below **Obv. Leg.:** ZHONGHUA RENMIN GONGHEGUO **Rev:** Crested Ibis, left, denomination at left **Note:** Prev. Y#731.

Date	Mintage	F	VF	XF	Unc	BU
1997	—	—	—	—	14.50	17.50

KM# 981 5 YUAN
Bronze **Obv:** National emblem, date below **Obv. Leg.:** ZHONGHUA RENMIN GONGHEGUO **Rev:** Red-crowned Crane, right, denomination at right **Note:** Prev. Y#732.

Date	Mintage	F	VF	XF	Unc	BU
1997	—	—	—	—	14.50	17.50

KM# 1030 5 YUAN
15.5517 g., 0.9990 Silver 0.4995 oz. ASW **Obv:** 2 Eastern unicorns, date below **Rev:** 1 Western unicorn, denomination below **Note:** Prev. Y#911.

Date	Mintage	F	VF	XF	Unc	BU
1997 Proof	—	Value: 20.00				

KM# 1058 5 YUAN
15.5517 g., 0.9990 Silver 0.4995 oz. ASW **Subject:** Traditional Chinese Mascot **Obv:** Ornamental column **Rev:** Child holding carp **Note:** Prev. Y#916.1

Date	Mintage	F	VF	XF	Unc	BU
1997	80,000	—	—	—	22.00	—

KM# 1058a 5 YUAN
15.5500 g., 0.9990 Silver 0.4994 oz. ASW, 36 mm. **Obv:** Ornamental column **Rev:** Multicolor child holding carp **Edge:** Reeded **Note:** Prev. Y#916.2.

Date	Mintage	F	VF	XF	Unc	BU
1997 Proof	100,000	Value: 35.00				

KM# 1025 5 YUAN
15.5100 g., 0.9990 Silver 0.4981 oz. ASW, 33 mm. **Series:** Kuan Yin **Rev:** Female holding plant and jug

Date	Mintage	F	VF	XF	Unc	BU
1997 Proof	10,000	Value: 30.00				

KM# 1026 5 YUAN
15.5100 g., 0.9990 Silver 0.4981 oz. ASW, 33 mm. **Series:** Kuan Yin **Rev:** Female holding jug and plant

Date	Mintage	F	VF	XF	Unc	BU
1997 Proof	10,000	Value: 30.00				

KM# 1027 5 YUAN
1.5500 g., 0.9990 Gold 0.0498 oz. AGW, 14 mm. **Series:** Kuan Yin **Rev:** Female holding jug and plant

Date	Mintage	F	VF	XF	Unc	BU
1997 Proof	35,000	Value: 50.00				

KM# 1104 5 YUAN
22.0000 g., 0.9000 Silver 0.6366 oz. ASW, 36 mm. **Series:** Silk Road **Rev:** Statue within nitch

Date	Mintage	F	VF	XF	Unc	BU
1997 Proof	15,000	Value: 40.00				

KM# 1173 5 YUAN
15.6000 g., 0.9990 Silver 0.5010 oz. ASW, 33 mm. **Obv:** Radiant winged pillar monument above flowers **Rev:** Child holding vase, elephant at left **Edge:** Reeded **Note:** Prev. Y#1129.

Date	Mintage	F	VF	XF	Unc	BU
1998	80,000	—	—	—	25.00	—

KM# 1172 5 YUAN
15.6000 g., 0.9990 Silver 0.5010 oz. ASW, 36 mm. **Obv:** Radiant winged pillar monument above flowers **Rev:** Multicolor child holding vase, elephant at left **Edge:** Reeded **Note:** Prev. Y#1130.

Date	Mintage	F	VF	XF	Unc	BU
1998 Proof	100,000	Value: 35.00				

KM# 1123 5 YUAN
Bronze **Subject:** Brown-eared Pheasant **Obv:** National emblem, date below **Rev:** Pheasant, left, denomination above **Note:** Prev. Y#940.

Date	Mintage	F	VF	XF	Unc	BU
1998	—	—	—	—	12.50	17.50

KM# 1122 5 YUAN
Bronze **Subject:** Chinese Alligator **Obv:** National emblem, date below **Obv. Leg.:** ZHONGHUA RENMIN GONGHEGUO **Rev:** Alligator, right, denomination above **Note:** Prev. Y#941.

Date	Mintage	F	VF	XF	Unc	BU
1998	—	—	—	—	15.00	20.00

KM# A1134 5 YUAN
51.5000 g., 0.9990 Silver 1.6540 oz. ASW, 33 mm. **Subject:** Honk Kong International Coin Convention **Rev:** Panda seated eating bamboo leaves

Date	Mintage	F	VF	XF	Unc	BU
1998 Proof	30,000	Value: 25.00				

KM# 1158 5 YUAN
51.5000 g., 0.9990 Silver 1.6540 oz. ASW, 33 mm. **Series:** Kuan Yin **Rev:** Female standing holding branch

Date	Mintage	F	VF	XF	Unc	BU
1998 Proof	10,000	Value: 25.00				

KM# 1159 5 YUAN
51.5100 g., 0.9990 Silver 1.6544 oz. ASW, 33 mm. **Series:** Kuan Yin **Rev:** Female with hands in prayer

Date	Mintage	F	VF	XF	Unc	BU
1998 Proof	10,000	Value: 25.00				

KM# 1213 5 YUAN
13.3000 g., Bronze, 31.9 mm. **Obv:** State emblem **Rev:** Butterfly **Edge:** Reeded and plain sections **Note:** Prev. Y#1053.

Date	Mintage	F	VF	XF	Unc	BU
1999	—	—	—	—	12.00	17.50

KM# 1214 5 YUAN
13.3000 g., Bronze, 31.9 mm. **Obv:** State emblem **Rev:** Sturgeon **Edge:** Plain and reeded sections **Note:** Prev. Y#1054.

Date	Mintage	F	VF	XF	Unc	BU
1999	—	—	—	—	12.00	14.50

KM# 78 10 YUAN
1.2000 g., 0.9000 Gold 0.0347 oz. AGW, 14 mm. **Obv:** Building, denomination at right **Rev:** Marco Polo bust, left, dates below **Note:** Prev. Y#55.

Date	Mintage	F	VF	XF	Unc	BU
1983 Proof	50,000	Value: 55.00				

KM# 126 10 YUAN
16.8100 g., 0.9250 Silver 0.4999 oz. ASW **Subject:** Women's Decade **Obv:** National emblem, denomination below **Rev:** Heads of three women, dates upper right **Note:** Prev. Y#62.

Date	Mintage	F	VF	XF	Unc	BU
ND(1984) Proof	4,000	Value: 60.00				

KM# 96 10 YUAN
16.8100 g., 0.9250 Silver 0.4999 oz. ASW **Series:** Los Angeles 1984 - 23rd Summer Olympic Games **Obv:** National emblem, date below **Rev:** Volleyball player serving, denomination at left **Note:** Prev. Y#63.

Date	Mintage	F	VF	XF	Unc	BU
1984 Matte	1,000	—	—	—	80.00	—

KM# 96a 10 YUAN
17.0600 g., 0.8000 Silver 0.4388 oz. ASW **Note:** Prev. Y#63a.

Date	Mintage	F	VF	XF	Unc	BU
1984 Proof	4,500	Value: 50.00				

KM# 95 10 YUAN
17.0600 g., 0.8000 Silver 0.4388 oz. ASW **Series:** Olympics **Obv:** National emblem, date below **Rev:** Speed skater, denomination lower right **Note:** Prev. Y#64.

Date	Mintage	F	VF	XF	Unc	BU
1984 Proof	6,000	Value: 40.00				

KM# 103   10 YUAN
27.0000 g., 0.9000 Silver 0.7812 oz. ASW **Subject:** 110th Anniversary - Birth of Dr. Cheng Jiageng **Obv:** Jie Mei School **Rev:** Bust, facing, divides dates **Note:** Prev. Y#88.

Date	Mintage	F	VF	XF	Unc	BU
1984 Proof	6,000	Value: 75.00				

KM# 127   10 YUAN
34.5600 g., 0.9000 Silver 100000 oz. ASW **Subject:** 20th Anniversary - Tibet Autonomous Region **Obv:** National emblem, date below **Rev:** Potala Palace, denomination upper right **Note:** Prev. Y#97.

Date	Mintage	F	VF	XF	Unc	BU
1985 Proof	3,000	Value: 60.00				

KM# 128   10 YUAN
34.5600 g., 0.9000 Silver 100000 oz. ASW **Subject:** 30th Anniversary - Xinjiang Autonomous Region **Obv:** Building, date below **Rev:** Woman carrying tray, animals below, denomination at right, circle surrounds **Note:** Prev. Y#110.

Date	Mintage	F	VF	XF	Unc	BU
1985 Proof	1,400	Value: 100				

KM# 146   10 YUAN
29.1900 g., 0.9250 Silver 0.8681 oz. ASW **Subject:** 120th Anniversary - Birth of Sun Yat-sen **Obv:** Bust, facing, divides dates, date below **Rev:** Sun Yat-sen's residence, denomination below **Note:** Prev. Y#111.

Date	Mintage	F	VF	XF	Unc	BU
1986 Proof	8,450	Value: 50.00				

KM# 213   10 YUAN
27.0000 g., 0.9250 Silver 0.8029 oz. ASW **Subject:** Rare Animal Protection **Rev:** Crested Ibis, right, denomination at right **Note:** Prev. Y#165.

Date	Mintage	F	VF	XF	Unc	BU
1988 Proof	35,000	Value: 35.00				

KM# 212   10 YUAN
27.0000 g., 0.9250 Silver 0.8029 oz. ASW **Subject:** Rare Animal Protection **Rev:** Baiji dolphins, denomination above **Note:** Prev. Y#166.

Date	Mintage	F	VF	XF	Unc	BU
1988 Proof	35,000	Value: 35.00				

KM# 231   10 YUAN
15.0000 g., 0.8500 Silver 0.4099 oz. ASW **Subject:** Year of the Snake **Obv:** Shanhaiguan City Gate, date below **Rev:** Snake left, denomination below **Note:** Prev. Y#177.

Date	Mintage	F	VF	XF	Unc	BU
1989 Proof	15,000	Value: 40.00				

KM# 242   10 YUAN
27.0000 g., 0.9250 Silver 0.8029 oz. ASW **Subject:** 1990 Asian Games **Obv:** Monument, stadium, Great Wall segment and sun **Rev:** Weight lifter, left, denomination at left **Note:** Prev. Y#199.

Date	Mintage	F	VF	XF	Unc	BU
1989 Proof	20,000	Value: 30.00				

KM# 243   10 YUAN
27.0000 g., 0.9250 Silver 0.8029 oz. ASW **Subject:** 11th Asian Games - Beijing 1990 **Obv:** Monument, stadium, Great Wall segment and sun **Rev:** Platform diver, denomination at left **Note:** Prev. Y#200.

Date	Mintage	F	VF	XF	Unc	BU
1989 Proof	20,000	Value: 30.00				

KM# 240   10 YUAN
27.0000 g., 0.9250 Silver 0.8029 oz. ASW **Subject:** 1990 Asian Games **Obv:** Monument, stadium, Great Wall segment and sun **Rev:** Tennis player, denomination above **Note:** Prev. Y#201.

Date	Mintage	F	VF	XF	Unc	BU
1989 Proof	20,000	Value: 30.00				

KM# 241   10 YUAN
27.0000 g., 0.9250 Silver 0.8029 oz. ASW **Subject:** 1990 Asian Games **Obv:** Monument, stadium, Great Wall segment and sun **Rev:** Bicyclist, denomination lower right **Note:** Prev. Y#202.

Date	Mintage	F	VF	XF	Unc	BU
1989 Proof	20,000	Value: 30.00				

KM# 254   10 YUAN
27.0000 g., 0.9250 Silver 0.8029 oz. ASW **Subject:** Endangered Animals **Obv:** National emblem, date below **Rev:** Skia deer, denomination at left **Note:** Prev. Y#248.

Date	Mintage	F	VF	XF	Unc	BU
1989 Proof	10,000	Value: 35.00				

KM# 253   10 YUAN
27.0000 g., 0.9250 Silver 0.8029 oz. ASW **Subject:** Endangered Animals **Obv:** National emblem, date below **Rev:** Red-crowned crane, right, wings spread, denomination at left **Note:** Prev. Y#249.

Date	Mintage	F	VF	XF	Unc	BU
1989 Proof	10,000	Value: 37.50				

KM# 257   10 YUAN
27.0000 g., 0.9250 Silver 0.8029 oz. ASW **Subject:** 40th Anniversary of Peoples Republic **Rev:** Tiananmen Square, birds flying above, denomination at right **Note:** Prev. Y#235.

Date	Mintage	F	VF	XF	Unc	BU
ND(1989) Proof	5,000	Value: 40.00				

KM# 256   10 YUAN
27.0000 g., 0.9250 Silver 0.8029 oz. ASW **Subject:** 40th Anniversary of Peoples Republic **Obv:** National emblem divides dates **Rev:** Great Wall with eagles in flight above, denomination at left **Note:** Prev. Y#236.

Date	Mintage	F	VF	XF	Unc	BU
ND(1989) Proof	5,000	Value: 40.00				

KM# 308   10 YUAN
27.0000 g., 0.9250 Silver 0.8029 oz. ASW **Obv:** National emblem, date below **Rev:** Half figure of Homer, Poet, denomination at right **Note:** Prev. Y#244.

Date	Mintage	F	VF	XF	Unc	BU
1990 Proof	30,000	Value: 25.00				

KM# 306   10 YUAN
27.0000 g., 0.9250 Silver 0.8029 oz. ASW **Obv:** National emblem, date below **Rev:** William Shakespeare, seated, denomination upper left **Note:** Prev. Y#245.

Date	Mintage	F	VF	XF	Unc	BU
1990 Proof	30,000	Value: 25.00				

KM# 307   10 YUAN
27.0000 g., 0.9250 Silver 0.8029 oz. ASW **Obv:** National emblem, date below **Rev:** Ludwig van Beethoven, seated at piano, denomination above **Note:** Prev. Y#246.

Date	Mintage	F	VF	XF	Unc	BU
1990 Proof	30,000	Value: 25.00				

KM# 305   10 YUAN
27.0000 g., 0.9250 Silver 0.8029 oz. ASW **Obv:** National emblem, date below **Rev:** Thomas Alva Edison holding lightbulb, facing, denomination at right **Note:** Prev. Y#247.

Date	Mintage	F	VF	XF	Unc	BU
1990 Proof	30,000	Value: 25.00				

KM# 301   10 YUAN
30.0000 g., 0.9000 Silver 0.8680 oz. ASW **Series:** Barcelona 1992 - 25th Summer Olympic Games **Obv:** National emblem, date below **Rev:** Platform diver, denomination lower left **Note:** Prev. Y#366.

Date	Mintage	F	VF	XF	Unc	BU
1990 Proof	30,000	Value: 27.50				

KM# 292   10 YUAN
27.0000 g., 0.9250 Silver 0.8029 oz. ASW **Subject:** XI Asian Games **Rev:** Javelin thrower, denomination below **Note:** Prev. Y#251.

Date	Mintage	F	VF	XF	Unc	BU
1990 Proof	20,000	Value: 30.00				

KM# 294   10 YUAN
27.0000 g., 0.9250 Silver 0.8029 oz. ASW **Subject:** XI Asian Games **Rev:** Baseball player, denomination at left **Note:** Prev. Y#252.

Date	Mintage	F	VF	XF	Unc	BU
1990 Proof	20,000	Value: 30.00				

KM# 291   10 YUAN
27.0000 g., 0.9250 Silver 0.8029 oz. ASW **Subject:** XI Asian Games **Obv:** Roman numerals above building, date below **Rev:** Gymnast on rings, denomination lower right **Note:** Prev. Y#253.

Date	Mintage	F	VF	XF	Unc	BU
1990 Proof	20,000	Value: 30.00				

KM# 293 10 YUAN
27.0000 g., 0.9250 Silver 0.8029 oz. ASW **Subject:** XI Asian Games **Obv:** Roman numeral above building, date below **Rev:** Soccer player, denomination lower right **Note:** Prev. Y#254.

Date	Mintage	F	VF	XF	Unc	BU
1990 Proof	20,000		Value: 30.00			

KM# 302 10 YUAN
27.0000 g., 0.9000 Silver 0.7812 oz. ASW **Series:** Barcelona 1992 - 25th Summer Olympic Games **Obv:** National emblem, date below **Rev:** Woman high jumper, denomination at right **Note:** Prev. Y#300.

Date	Mintage	F	VF	XF	Unc	BU
1990 Proof	30,000		Value: 27.50			

KM# 317 10 YUAN
1.0000 g., 0.9990 Gold 0.0321 oz. AGW, 14 mm. **Obv:** Great Wall, date below **Rev:** Phoenix and dragon, denomination at left **Note:** Prev. Y#206.

Date	Mintage	F	VF	XF	Unc	BU
1990 Proof	34,000		Value: 50.00			

KM# 316 10 YUAN
31.1000 g., 0.9990 Silver 0.9988 oz. ASW **Obv:** Great Wall, date below **Rev:** Phoenix and dragon, denomination at right **Note:** Prev. Y#261.

Date	Mintage	F	VF	XF	Unc	BU
1990 Proof	12,000		Value: 35.00			

KM# 300 10 YUAN
27.0000 g., 0.9000 Silver 0.7812 oz. ASW **Series:** Summer Olympics **Obv:** National emblem, date below **Rev:** Bicycle racers, denomination below **Note:** Prev. Y#283.

Date	Mintage	F	VF	XF	Unc	BU
1990 Proof	30,000		Value: 22.50			

KM# 370 10 YUAN
27.0800 g., 0.9250 Silver 0.8053 oz. ASW **Subject:** 1st Women's World Football Championship **Obv:** 5 story building, date below **Rev:** Women's soccer, 2 players, denomination at right **Note:** Prev. Y#318.

Date	Mintage	F	VF	XF	Unc	BU
1991 Proof	2,800		Value: 45.00			

KM# 369 10 YUAN
27.0800 g., 0.9250 Silver 0.8053 oz. ASW **Subject:** Women's 1st World Football Championships **Obv:** 5 story building, date below **Rev:** Women's soccer, 3 players, denomination below **Note:** Prev. Y#319.

Date	Mintage	F	VF	XF	Unc	BU
1991 Proof	2,800		Value: 45.00			

KM# 374 10 YUAN
27.0800 g., 0.9250 Silver 0.8053 oz. ASW **Rev:** Mozart seated at piano, two dates upper right, denomination at left **Note:** Prev. Y#347.

Date	Mintage	F	VF	XF	Unc	BU
1991 Proof	—		Value: 25.00			

KM# 372 10 YUAN
27.0800 g., 0.9250 Silver 0.8053 oz. ASW **Rev:** Columbus **Note:** Prev. Y#348.

Date	Mintage	F	VF	XF	Unc	BU
1991 Proof	—		Value: 25.00			

KM# 375 10 YUAN
27.0800 g., 0.9250 Silver 0.8053 oz. ASW **Rev:** Einstein **Note:** Prev. Y#349.

Date	Mintage	F	VF	XF	Unc	BU
1991 Proof	—		Value: 25.00			

KM# 373 10 YUAN
27.0800 g., 0.9250 Silver 0.8053 oz. ASW **Obv:** National emblem, date below **Rev:** Mark Twain seated with book, denomination at left **Note:** Prev. Y#350.

Date	Mintage	F	VF	XF	Unc	BU
1991 Proof	—		Value: 25.00			

KM# 296 10 YUAN
30.0000 g., 0.9000 Silver 0.8680 oz. ASW **Series:** Olympics **Obv:** National emblem, date below **Rev:** Downhill skier, denomination lower left **Note:** Prev. Y#367.

Date	Mintage	F	VF	XF	Unc	BU
1991 Proof	30,000		Value: 25.00			

KM# 299 10 YUAN

30.0000 g., 0.9000 Silver 0.8680 oz. ASW **Series:** Barcelona 1992 - 25th Summer Olympic Games **Obv:** National emblem, date below **Rev:** Woman playing table tennis, denomination at right **Note:** Prev. Y#456.

Date	Mintage	F	VF	XF	Unc	BU
1991 Proof	30,000	Value: 35.00				

KM# 383 10 YUAN

31.1035 g., 0.9990 Silver 0.9990 oz. ASW **Subject:** 80th Anniversary - 1911 Revolution **Obv:** Building, two dates below **Rev:** Sun Yat Sen in civilian clothes, denomination at right **Note:** Prev. Y#476.

Date	Mintage	F	VF	XF	Unc	BU
ND(1991) Proof	2,500	Value: 50.00				

KM# 454 10 YUAN

27.0000 g., 0.9250 Silver 0.8029 oz. ASW **Subject:** Wildlife **Obv:** National emblem **Rev:** White storks, denomination at right **Note:** Prev. Y#486.

Date	Mintage	F	VF	XF	Unc	BU
1992 Proof	7,260	Value: 47.50				

KM# 439 10 YUAN

26.8300 g., 0.9000 Silver 0.7763 oz. ASW **Series:** 1994 Winter Olympics **Obv:** National emblem, date below **Rev:** Cross country skier, denomination at right **Note:** Prev. Y#368.

Date	Mintage	F	VF	XF	Unc	BU
1992 Proof	7,500	Value: 50.00				

KM# 466 10 YUAN

31.1035 g., 0.9990 Silver 0.9990 oz. ASW **Subject:** Environmental Protection **Obv:** National emblem, date below **Rev:** Kneeling woman fetching water at stream, denomination below **Note:** Prev. Y#942.

Date	Mintage	F	VF	XF	Unc	BU
1992	60,000	—	—	—	30.00	32.50

KM# 455 10 YUAN

26.9500 g., 0.9000 Silver 0.7798 oz. ASW **Obv:** National emblem, date below **Rev:** Snow leopard, denomination above **Note:** Prev. Y#584.

Date	Mintage	F	VF	XF	Unc	BU
1992 Proof	7,260	Value: 47.50				

KM# 438 10 YUAN

26.9500 g., 0.9000 Silver 0.7798 oz. ASW **Series:** Lillehammer 1994 - 17th Winter Olympic Games **Obv:** National emblem, date below **Rev:** Ski jumper, denomination at right **Note:** Prev. Y#490.

Date	Mintage	F	VF	XF	Unc	BU
1992 Proof	30,000	Value: 30.00				

KM# 443 10 YUAN

27.1100 g., 0.9000 Silver 0.7844 oz. ASW **Obv:** National emblem, date below **Rev:** Tschaikovsky leaning against piano, denomination lower left **Note:** Prev. Y#709.

Date	Mintage	F	VF	XF	Unc	BU
1992 Proof	30,000	Value: 30.00				

KM# 441 10 YUAN

27.0000 g., 0.9250 Silver 0.8029 oz. ASW **Subject:** International Celebrities **Obv:** National emblem, date below **Rev:** Leonardo Da Vinci with painting of Mona Lisa, denomination below **Note:** Prev. Y#755.

Date	Mintage	F	VF	XF	Unc	BU
1992 Proof	30,000	Value: 30.00				

KM# 442 10 YUAN

27.0000 g., 0.9250 Silver 0.8029 oz. ASW **Subject:** International Celebrities **Obv:** National emblem, date below **Rev:** Wolfgang Von Goethe, denomination at right **Note:** Prev. Y#756.

Date	Mintage	F	VF	XF	Unc	BU
1992 Proof	30,000	Value: 30.00				

KM# 444 10 YUAN

27.0000 g., 0.9250 Silver 0.8029 oz. ASW **Subject:** International Celebrities **Obv:** National emblem, date below **Rev:** Alfred Nobel, denomination at left **Note:** Prev. Y#757.

Date	Mintage	F	VF	XF	Unc	BU
1992 Proof	30,000	Value: 30.00				

KM# 538 10 YUAN

30.0000 g., 0.9000 Silver 0.8680 oz. ASW **Obv:** National emblem **Rev:** Song Qingling, seated, denomination st right **Note:** Prev. Y#758.

Date	Mintage	F	VF	XF	Unc	BU
1993 Proof	20,000	Value: 35.00				

KM# 537   10 YUAN
30.0000 g., 0.9000 Silver 0.8680 oz. ASW **Obv:** National emblem **Rev:** 3/4-length figure of Soong Ching-ling, 1892-1981, half left, birds in background, denomination at right **Note:** Prev. Y#759.

Date	Mintage	F	VF	XF	Unc	BU
1993 Proof	20,000	Value: 35.00				

KM# 588   10 YUAN
3.1030 g., 0.9990 Gold 0.0997 oz. AGW, 18 mm. **Subject:** Homeland Scenery **Obv:** Great Wall **Rev:** Cliffside building **Note:** Prev. Y#774.

Date	Mintage	F	VF	XF	Unc	BU
1993 Proof	8,888	Value: 90.00				

KM# 521   10 YUAN
27.0000 g., 0.9250 Silver 0.8029 oz. ASW **Subject:** World Cup Soccer **Obv:** National emblem, date below **Rev:** 3 soccer players, denomination below **Note:** Prev. Y#779.

Date	Mintage	F	VF	XF	Unc	BU
1993 Proof	30,000	Value: 32.50				

KM# 563   10 YUAN
27.0000 g., 0.9250 Silver 0.8029 oz. ASW **Rev:** 2 Bactrian camels, denomination below **Note:** Prev. Y#579.

Date	Mintage	F	VF	XF	Unc	BU
1993 Proof	4,825	Value: 40.00				

KM# 564   10 YUAN
27.0000 g., 0.9250 Silver 0.8029 oz. ASW **Rev:** Pere David deer, denomination above **Note:** Prev. Y#580.

Date	Mintage	F	VF	XF	Unc	BU
1993 Proof	4,825	Value: 40.00				

KM# 585   10 YUAN
31.1050 g., 0.9990 Silver 0.9990 oz. ASW **Subject:** Mt. Tai **Obv:** Great Wall, date below **Rev:** Small building with long staircase, denomination upper left **Note:** Prev. Y#933.

Date	Mintage	F	VF	XF	Unc	BU
1993 Proof	60,000	Value: 35.00				

KM# 525   10 YUAN
30.0000 g., 0.9000 Silver 0.8680 oz. ASW **Series:** Olympics **Obv:** National emblem, date below **Rev:** Runners, denomination below **Note:** Prev. Y#492.

Date	Mintage	F	VF	XF	Unc	BU
1993 Proof	30,000	Value: 30.00				

KM# 524   10 YUAN
30.0000 g., 0.9000 Silver 0.8680 oz. ASW **Subject:** Olympics Centennial **Obv:** National emblem, date below **Rev:** Fencing, denomination below **Note:** Prev. Y#493.

Date	Mintage	F	VF	XF	Unc	BU
1993 Proof	30,000	Value: 30.00				

KM# 586   10 YUAN
31.1050 g., 0.9990 Silver 0.9990 oz. ASW **Subject:** Mt. Hua **Obv:** Great Wall, date below **Rev:** Bird's eye view of mountain tops, shelter, denomination at left **Note:** Prev. Y#934.

Date	Mintage	F	VF	XF	Unc	BU
1993 Proof	60,000	Value: 35.00				

KM# 589   10 YUAN
31.1050 g., 0.9990 Silver 0.9990 oz. ASW **Subject:** Mt. Song **Obv:** Great Wall, date below **Rev:** Tall domed building, denomination at right **Note:** Prev. Y#935.

Date	Mintage	F	VF	XF	Unc	BU
1993 Proof	60,000	Value: 35.00				

KM# 587   10 YUAN
31.1050 g., 0.9990 Silver 0.9990 oz. ASW **Subject:** Homeland scenery **Obv:** Great Wall, date below **Rev:** Large building, islands in background, denomination upper right **Note:** Prev. Y#932.

Date	Mintage	F	VF	XF	Unc	BU
1993 Proof	60,000	Value: 35.00				

KM# 540.1   10 YUAN
27.0000 g., 0.9250 Silver 0.8029 oz. ASW **Subject:** Mao Tse Tung **Obv:** Building on cliff **Rev:** Bust facing, denomination at right **Note:** Prev. Y#412.1.

Date	Mintage	F	VF	XF	Unc	BU
1993	30,000	—	—	—	—	45.00

KM# 540.2   10 YUAN
27.0000 g., 0.9250 Silver 0.8029 oz. ASW **Obv:** Building on cliff, date at right **Rev:** Revised bust facing, denomination at right **Note:** Prev. Y#412.2.

Date	Mintage	F	VF	XF	Unc	BU
1993	—	—	—	—	—	45.00

KM# 520   10 YUAN
24.2550 g., 0.9000 Silver 0.7018 oz. ASW **Subject:** World Cup Soccer - 1994 **Obv:** National emblem, date below **Rev:** Soccer players, denomination lower left **Note:** Prev. Y#418.

Date	Mintage	F	VF	XF	Unc	BU
1993 Proof	30,000	Value: 35.00				

KM# 584   10 YUAN
31.1050 g., 0.9990 Silver 0.9990 oz. ASW, 39.9 mm. **Subject:** Mt. Heng **Obv:** Great Wall, date below **Rev:** Cliffside building, denomination below **Edge:** Reeded **Note:** Prev. Y#1229.

Date	Mintage	F	VF	XF	Unc	BU
1993 Proof	60,000	Value: 35.00				

KM# 594   10 YUAN
3.1103 g., 0.9990 Gold 0.0999 oz. AGW **Obv:** Temple of Harmony **Rev:** 2 peacocks, denomination above **Note:** Prev. Y#474.

Date	Mintage	F	VF	XF	Unc	BU
1993 Prooflike	—	—	—	—	—	100

KM# 548   10 YUAN
3.1103 g., 0.9990 Gold 0.0999 oz. AGW **Obv:** Building above date **Rev:** Goddess of Mercy holding flower, denomination at left **Note:** Prev. Y#499.

Date	Mintage	F	VF	XF	Unc	BU
1993 Prooflike	20,000	—	—	—	—	100

KM# 547   10 YUAN
3.1103 g., 0.9990 Gold 0.0999 oz. AGW **Rev:** Goddess Guanyin seated in flowers, denomination at left **Note:** Prev. Y#501.

Date	Mintage	F	VF	XF	Unc	BU
1993 Proof	1,000	Value: 100				

KM# 595   10 YUAN
31.1000 g., 0.9990 Silver 0.9988 oz. ASW **Obv:** Temple of Harmony, date below **Rev:** Peacocks, denomination above **Note:** Prev. Y#352.

Date	Mintage	F	VF	XF	Unc	BU
1993 Proof	7,000	Value: 55.00				
1997 Matte	50,000	—	—	—	—	40.00

KM# 493   10 YUAN
30.0000 g., 0.9000 Silver 0.8680 oz. ASW, 40 mm. **Subject:** Yin and Yang Concept **Obv:** Great Wall blockhouse, date below **Rev:** Four men studying the symbol, denomination below **Edge:** Reeded **Note:** Prev. Y#1077.

Date	Mintage	F	VF	XF	Unc	BU
1993	—	—	—	—	27.50	30.00

Note: Probably minted at a much later date.

KM# 494   10 YUAN
31.1035 g., 0.9990 Silver 0.9990 oz. ASW, 40 mm.
Series: Scientific and technical inventions **Rev:** Four men standing around scroll

Date	Mintage	F	VF	XF	Unc	BU
1993 Proof	11,800	Value: 50.00				

KM# 522   10 YUAN
27.2000 g., 0.9250 Silver 0.8089 oz. ASW **Obv:** National emblem, date below **Rev:** Soccer player, denomination at left

Date	Mintage	F	VF	XF	Unc	BU
1994 Proof	30,000	Value: 30.00				

KM# 662   10 YUAN
3.1103 g., 0.9990 Gold 0.0999 oz. AGW **Obv:** Great Wall above date **Rev:** Guanyin-Goddess of Mercy, holding child, facing, denomination at left **Note:** Prev. Y#510.

Date	Mintage	F	VF	XF	Unc	BU
1994 Prooflike	8,000	—	—	—	—	100

KM# 663   10 YUAN
31.1035 g., 0.9990 Silver 0.9990 oz. ASW **Obv:** Great Wall, date below **Rev:** Guanyin - Goddess of Mercy, holding child, facing, denomination at left **Note:** Prev. Y#482.

Date	Mintage	F	VF	XF	Unc	BU
1994 Proof	30,000	Value: 30.00				

KM# 675   10 YUAN
31.1000 g., 0.9990 Silver 0.9988 oz. ASW **Obv:** Figure on Eastern unicorn, date below **Rev:** Unicorn, sprays of roses below, denomination at left **Note:** Prev. Y#420.

Date	Mintage	F	VF	XF	Unc	BU
1994	50,000	—	—	—	—	27.50
1994 Proof	4,000	Value: 40.00				

KM# 676   10 YUAN
3.1103 g., 0.9990 Gold 0.0999 oz. AGW **Rev:** Unicorn looking back towards right **Note:** Prev. Y#421.

Date	Mintage	F	VF	XF	Unc	BU
1994 Proof	5,100	Value: 110				

KM# 652   10 YUAN
27.0000 g., 0.9250 Silver 0.8029 oz. ASW **Subject:** Hiroshima 1994 - 12th Asian Games **Obv:** National emblem, athletic figures above date **Rev:** Swimming, denomination at left **Note:** Prev. Y#438.

Date	Mintage	F	VF	XF	Unc	BU
1994 Proof	5,000	Value: 30.00				

KM# 651   10 YUAN
27.0000 g., 0.9250 Silver 0.8029 oz. ASW **Subject:** Hiroshima 1994 - 12th Asian Games **Rev:** Runners, denomination lower right **Note:** Prev. Y#439.

Date	Mintage	F	VF	XF	Unc	BU
1994 Proof	5,000	Value: 30.00				

KM# 692   10 YUAN
31.1035 g., 0.9990 Silver 0.9990 oz. ASW **Subject:** Children at Play **Rev:** 2 children and cat, denomination below **Note:** Prev. Y#457.

Date	Mintage	F	VF	XF	Unc	BU
1994 Proof	8,500	Value: 30.00				

KM# 693   10 YUAN
31.1035 g., 0.9990 Silver 0.9990 oz. ASW **Subject:** Children at Play **Obv:** Building, date below **Rev:** 3 children and toy boat, denomination below **Note:** Prev. Y#458.

Date	Mintage	F	VF	XF	Unc	BU
1994 Proof	8,500	Value: 30.00				

KM# 527   10 YUAN
31.1035 g., 0.9990 Silver 0.9990 oz. ASW **Series:** Olympics **Obv:** National emblem, date below **Rev:** Basketball player, denomination at left **Note:** Prev. Y#494.

Date	Mintage	F	VF	XF	Unc	BU
1994 Proof	30,000	Value: 35.00				

KM# 526   10 YUAN
31.1035 g., 0.9990 Silver 0.9990 oz. ASW **Series:** Olympics Centennial **Obv:** National emblem, date below **Rev:** Female archer shooting, denomination lower left **Note:** Prev. Y#495.

Date	Mintage	F	VF	XF	Unc	BU
1994 Proof	30,000	Value: 35.00				

KM# 528   10 YUAN
31.1035 g., 0.9990 Silver 0.9990 oz. ASW **Series:** Olympics **Obv:** National emblem, date below **Rev:** Boxing match, denomination at right **Note:** Prev. Y#496.

Date	Mintage	F	VF	XF	Unc	BU
1994 Proof	30,000	Value: 35.00				

KM# 654   10 YUAN
27.0000 g., 0.9250 Silver 0.8029 oz. ASW **Obv:** National emblem **Rev:** Confucius, denomination at right **Note:** Prev. Y#539.

Date	Mintage	F	VF	XF	Unc	BU
1994 Proof	—	Value: 30.00				

KM# 655   10 YUAN
27.0000 g., 0.9250 Silver 0.8029 oz. ASW **Rev:** Socrates, denomination lower left **Note:** Prev. Y#540.

Date	Mintage	F	VF	XF	Unc	BU
1994 Proof	—	Value: 30.00				

KM# 656   10 YUAN
27.0000 g., 0.9250 Silver 0.8029 oz. ASW **Rev:** Rembrandt, denomination at left **Note:** Prev. Y#541.

Date	Mintage	F	VF	XF	Unc	BU
1994 Proof	—	Value: 30.00				

KM# 657   10 YUAN
27.0000 g., 0.9250 Silver 0.8029 oz. ASW **Rev:** Verdi, denomination at right **Note:** Prev. Y#542.

Date	Mintage	F	VF	XF	Unc	BU
1994 Proof	—	Value: 30.00				

KM# 686   10 YUAN
31.1035 g., 0.9990 Silver 0.9990 oz. ASW **Subject:** Sino - Singapore Friendship **Obv:** Great Wall, date below **Rev:** City view of Singapore, denomination below **Note:** Prev. Y#710.

Date	Mintage	F	VF	XF	Unc	BU
1994 Proof	30,000	Value: 30.00				

KM# 671   10 YUAN
20.7360 g., 0.9000 Silver 0.6000 oz. ASW **Obv:** Building, date below **Rev:** Black-billed Magpies on branch, denomination below **Note:** Prev. Y#681.

Date	Mintage	F	VF	XF	Unc	BU
1994 Proof	3,900	Value: 45.00				

KM# 690 10 YUAN
31.1035 g., 0.9990 Silver 0.9990 oz. ASW **Subject:** Children at Play **Obv:** Imperial Palace, corner building **Rev:** Three children carrying tray, denomination below **Note:** Prev. Y#783.

Date	Mintage	F	VF	XF	Unc	BU
1994 Proof	2,500	Value: 50.00				

KM# 691 10 YUAN
31.1035 g., 0.9990 Silver 0.9990 oz. ASW **Subject:** Children at Play **Obv:** Imperial Palace, corner building **Rev:** Three children playing on ground, denomination above **Note:** Prev. Y#784.

Date	Mintage	F	VF	XF	Unc	BU
1994 Proof	2,500	Value: 50.00				

KM# 673 10 YUAN
4.0000 g., 0.9990 Bi-Metallic Gold center in silver ring 0.1285 oz., 23 mm. **Rev:** Dragon and Phoenix

Date	Mintage	F	VF	XF	Unc	BU
1994 Proof	2,500	Value: 200				

KM# 791 10 YUAN
27.0000 g., 0.9250 Silver 0.8029 oz. ASW **Subject:** Dinosaurs **Rev:** Pterodactylus, denomination at right **Note:** Prev. Y#469.

Date	Mintage	F	VF	XF	Unc	BU
1995 Proof	Est. 5,000	Value: 50.00				

KM# 792 10 YUAN
27.0000 g., 0.9250 Silver 0.8029 oz. ASW **Subject:** Dinosaurs **Rev:** Stegosaurus, denomination below **Note:** Prev. Y#470.

Date	Mintage	F	VF	XF	Unc	BU
1995 Proof	Est. 5,000	Value: 47.50				

KM# 786 10 YUAN
31.1035 g., 0.9990 Silver 0.9990 oz. ASW **Obv:** Building, date below **Rev:** Guanyin, Goddess of Mercy with sceptre, denomination at left **Note:** Prev. Y#489.

Date	Mintage	F	VF	XF	Unc	BU
1995 Prooflike	30,000	—	—	—	—	30.00

KM# 782 10 YUAN
3.1103 g., 0.9990 Gold 0.0999 oz. AGW **Obv:** Building, date below **Rev:** Guanyin - Goddess of Mercy with lotus flower, facing, denomination at left **Note:** Prev. Y#520.

Date	Mintage	F	VF	XF	Unc	BU
1995 Proof	3,000	Value: 115				

KM# 785 10 YUAN
3.1103 g., 0.9990 Gold 0.0999 oz. AGW **Obv:** Building, date below **Rev:** Guanyin, Goddess of Mercy with wheel, denomination at left **Note:** Prev. Y#521.

Date	Mintage	F	VF	XF	Unc	BU
1995 Proof	3,000	Value: 115				

KM# 783 10 YUAN
3.1103 g., 0.9990 Gold 0.0999 oz. AGW **Obv:** Building, date below **Rev:** Guanyin - Goddess of Mercy with sceptre, denomination at left **Note:** Prev. Y#522.

Date	Mintage	F	VF	XF	Unc	BU
1995 Proof	3,000	Value: 115				

KM# 784 10 YUAN
3.1103 g., 0.9990 Gold 0.0999 oz. AGW **Obv:** Building, date below **Rev:** Guanyin, Goddess of Mercy with bowl, denomination at left **Note:** Prev. Y#523.

Date	Mintage	F	VF	XF	Unc	BU
1995 Proof	3,000	Value: 115				

KM# 815 10 YUAN
31.1035 g., 0.9990 Silver 0.9990 oz. ASW **Subject:** Return of Hong Kong to China **Obv:** Tiananmen Square, date below **Rev:** Deng Xiao Ping bust, left, buildings below, denomination at bottom **Note:** Prev. Y#531.

Date	Mintage	F	VF	XF	Unc	BU
1995 Proof	88,000	Value: 42.50				

KM# 840 10 YUAN
27.0000 g., 0.9250 Silver 0.8029 oz. ASW **Obv:** Dragon in inner circle, date below **Rev:** Huang Di in chariot, denomination at lower right **Note:** Prev. Y#588.

Date	Mintage	F	VF	XF	Unc	BU
1995 Proof	5,000	Value: 40.00				

KM# 841 10 YUAN
27.0000 g., 0.9250 Silver 0.8029 oz. ASW **Obv:** Dragon in inner circle **Rev:** Half figure of Yan Di, wearing skins, facing, denomination lower right **Note:** Prev. Y#589.

Date	Mintage	F	VF	XF	Unc	BU
1995 Proof	5,000	Value: 40.00				

KM# 842 10 YUAN
27.0000 g., 0.9250 Silver 0.8029 oz. ASW **Obv:** Dragon in inner circle **Rev:** Half figure of Yao holding feathers, facing, denomination lower right **Note:** Prev. Y#590.

Date	Mintage	F	VF	XF	Unc	BU
1995 Proof	5,000	Value: 40.00				

KM# 843   10 YUAN
27.0000 g., 0.9250 Silver 0.8029 oz. ASW **Obv:** Dragon in inner circle **Rev:** Half figure of Shun with urn, facing, denomination lower left **Note:** Prev. Y#591.

Date	Mintage	F	VF	XF	Unc	BU
1995 Proof	5,000	Value: 40.00				

KM# 818   10 YUAN
27.0000 g., 0.9250 Silver 0.8029 oz. ASW **Rev:** Sailing ship, denomination above **Note:** Prev. Y#647.

Date	Mintage	F	VF	XF	Unc	BU
1995 Proof	10,000	Value: 75.00				

KM# 819   10 YUAN
27.0000 g., 0.9250 Silver 0.8029 oz. ASW **Rev:** Junk, denomination below **Note:** Prev. Y#650.

Date	Mintage	F	VF	XF	Unc	BU
1995 Proof	10,000	Value: 75.00				

KM# 813   10 YUAN
27.0000 g., 0.9250 Silver 0.8029 oz. ASW **Series:** 50th Anniversary - United Nations **Obv:** UN logo **Rev:** UN building **Note:** Prev. Y#682.

Date	Mintage	F	VF	XF	Unc	BU
1995 Proof	115,000	Value: 30.00				

KM# 795   10 YUAN
31.1050 g., 0.9990 Silver 0.9990 oz. ASW **Obv:** Eastern Unicorn, date below **Rev:** Unicorn with offspring, denomination at left **Note:** Prev. Y#683.

Date	Mintage	F	VF	XF	Unc	BU
1995 Proof	—	Value: 35.00				

KM# 806   10 YUAN
31.1050 g., 0.9990 Silver 0.9990 oz. ASW **Subject:** 50th Anniversary of Anti-Japanese War **Obv:** National emblem, date below **Rev:** Chou and Mao above soldiers, denomination below **Note:** Prev. Y#684.

Date	Mintage	F	VF	XF	Unc	BU
1995 Proof	3,750	Value: 50.00				

KM# 807   10 YUAN
31.1050 g., 0.9990 Silver 0.9990 oz. ASW **Obv:** National emblem, date below **Rev:** Attacking soldiers above bridge guarded by lion, denomination at right **Note:** Prev. Y#685.

Date	Mintage	F	VF	XF	Unc	BU
1995 Proof	3,750	Value: 50.00				

KM# 811   10 YUAN
31.1050 g., 0.9990 Silver 0.9990 oz. ASW **Subject:** 4th UN World Women's Congress **Obv:** Logo above building **Rev:** Three women with flowers and birds **Note:** Prev. Y#686.

Date	Mintage	F	VF	XF	Unc	BU
1995 Proof	30,500	Value: 35.00				

KM# 759   10 YUAN
27.0000 g., 0.9250 Silver 0.8029 oz. ASW **Series:** 1996 Olympics **Obv:** National emblem, date below **Rev:** Handball player, denomination lower right **Note:** Prev. Y#713.

Date	Mintage	F	VF	XF	Unc	BU
1995 Proof	—	Value: 30.00				

KM# 758   10 YUAN
27.0000 g., 0.9250 Silver 0.8029 oz. ASW **Series:** 1996 Olympics **Obv:** National emblem, date below **Rev:** Kick boxer, denomination at right **Note:** Prev. Y#714.

Date	Mintage	F	VF	XF	Unc	BU
1995 Proof	—	Value: 30.00				

KM# 796   10 YUAN
3.1100 g., 0.9990 Gold 0.0999 oz. AGW **Obv:** Eastern unicorn, date below **Rev:** Western unicorn with offspring, denomination at left **Note:** Prev. Y#737.

Date	Mintage	F	VF	XF	Unc	BU
1995 Proof	5,000	Value: 110				

KM# 833   10 YUAN
3.1103 g., 0.9990 Gold 0.0999 oz. AGW **Subject:** Chinese Culture Series **Obv:** Great Wall seen through arch, date below **Rev:** Pagoda of six harmonies, denomination at left **Note:** Prev. Y#799.

Date	Mintage	F	VF	XF	Unc	BU
1995 Proof	25,000	Value: 100				

KM# 830   10 YUAN
3.1103 g., 0.9990 Gold 0.0999 oz. AGW **Subject:** Chinese Culture Series **Obv:** Great Wall seen through arch **Rev:** Mencius seated at table, denomination below **Note:** Prev. Y#800.

Date	Mintage	F	VF	XF	Unc	BU
1995 Proof	25,000	Value: 100				

KM# 832   10 YUAN
3.1103 g., 0.9990 Gold 0.0999 oz. AGW **Subject:** Chinese Culture Series **Obv:** Great Wall seen through arch **Rev:** Tang Taizong seated, denomination at left **Note:** Prev. Y#801.

Date	Mintage	F	VF	XF	Unc	BU
1995 Proof	25,000	Value: 100				

KM# 834   10 YUAN
3.1103 g., 0.9990 Gold 0.0999 oz. AGW **Subject:** Chinese Culture Series **Obv:** Great Wall seen through arch **Rev:** Lion dance, denomination lower left **Note:** Prev. Y#802.

Date	Mintage	F	VF	XF	Unc	BU
1995 Proof	25,000	Value: 100				

KM# 831   10 YUAN
3.1103 g., 0.9990 Gold 0.0999 oz. AGW   **Subject:** Chinese Culture Series **Obv:** Great Wall seen through arch **Rev:** Female opera role **Note:** Prev. Y#803.

Date	Mintage	F	VF	XF	Unc	BU
1995 Proof	25,000	Value: 100				

KM# 871   10 YUAN
20.7333 g., 0.9000 Silver 0.5999 oz. ASW   **Obv:** Great Wall, date below **Rev:** Eagle in flight, denomination at left **Note:** Prev. Y#809.

Date	Mintage	F	VF	XF	Unc	BU
1995 Proof	3,900	Value: 65.00				

KM# 859   10 YUAN
31.1035 g., 0.9990 Silver 0.9990 oz. ASW   **Subject:** 50th Anniversary - Return of Taiwan to China **Obv:** Great Wall **Rev:** Taiwan and China maps **Note:** Prev. Y#811.

Date	Mintage	F	VF	XF	Unc	BU
1995 Proof	5,000	Value: 75.00				

KM# 858   10 YUAN
31.1035 g., 0.9990 Silver 0.9990 oz. ASW   **Subject:** 50th Anniversary - Return of Taiwan to China **Obv:** Great Wall **Rev:** Zhongshan Hall **Note:** Prev. Y#812.

Date	Mintage	F	VF	XF	Unc	BU
1995 Proof	5,000	Value: 75.00				

KM# 767   10 YUAN
27.0000 g., 0.9250 Silver 0.8029 oz. ASW   **Subject:** Painter Zu Beihong **Obv:** Portrait, facing, divides dates **Rev:** Cat stalking, denomination at left **Note:** Prev. Y#819.

Date	Mintage	F	VF	XF	Unc	BU
1995 Proof	8,000	Value: 40.00				

KM# 766   10 YUAN
27.0000 g., 0.9250 Silver 0.8029 oz. ASW   **Subject:** Painter Zu Beihong **Obv:** Portrait **Rev:** Horse running left, denomination at left **Note:** Prev. Y#820.

Date	Mintage	F	VF	XF	Unc	BU
1995 Proof	8,000	Value: 40.00				

KM# 847   10 YUAN
27.0000 g., 0.9250 Silver 0.8029 oz. ASW   **Subject:** Romance of the Three Kingdoms Series **Obv:** Luo Guanzhong bust, facing, date below **Rev:** Liu Bei standing holding rod, denomination at right **Note:** Prev. Y#825.

Date	Mintage	F	VF	XF	Unc	BU
1995 Proof	7,000	Value: 60.00				

KM# 849   10 YUAN
27.0000 g., 0.9250 Silver 0.8029 oz. ASW   **Subject:** Romance of the Three Kingdoms Series **Obv:** Luo Guanzhong bust **Rev:** Guan Yo reading, denomination above **Note:** Prev. Y#826.

Date	Mintage	F	VF	XF	Unc	BU
1995 Proof	7,000	Value: 60.00				

KM# 850   10 YUAN
27.0000 g., 0.9250 Silver 0.8029 oz. ASW   **Subject:** Romance of the Three Kingdoms Series **Obv:** Luo Guanzhong bust **Rev:** Zhang Fei on horse, denomination at left **Note:** Prev. Y#827.

Date	Mintage	F	VF	XF	Unc	BU
1995 Proof	7,000	Value: 60.00				

KM# 848   10 YUAN
27.0000 g., 0.9250 Silver 0.8029 oz. ASW   **Subject:** Romance of the Three Kingdoms Series **Obv:** Luo Guanzhong bust **Rev:** Zhuge Liang on throne, denomination at right **Note:** Prev. Y#828.

Date	Mintage	F	VF	XF	Unc	BU
1995 Proof	7,000	Value: 60.00				

KM# 756   10 YUAN
31.1035 g., 0.9990 Silver 0.9990 oz. ASW   **Subject:** Table Tennis **Obv:** Tianjing Stadium **Rev:** Table tennis player, denomination at left **Note:** Prev. Y#836.

Date	Mintage	F	VF	XF	Unc	BU
1995 Proof	3,000	Value: 75.00				

KM# 755   10 YUAN
31.1035 g., 0.9990 Silver 0.9990 oz. ASW   **Subject:** Table Tennis **Obv:** Tianjing Stadium **Rev:** Two table tennis players, denomination at left **Note:** Prev. Y#837.

Date	Mintage	F	VF	XF	Unc	BU
1995 Proof	3,000	Value: 75.00				

KM# 761   10 YUAN
31.1035 g., 0.9990 Silver 0.9990 oz. ASW   **Series:** Olympics **Obv:** National emblem, date below **Rev:** Gymnast, denomination at right **Note:** Prev. Y#841.

Date	Mintage	F	VF	XF	Unc	BU
1995 Proof	30,000	Value: 30.00				

KM# 760   10 YUAN
31.1035 g., 0.9990 Silver 0.9990 oz. ASW   **Series:** 1996 Olympics **Obv:** National emblem, date below **Rev:** Female shooter, denomination below **Note:** Prev. Y#842.

Date	Mintage	F	VF	XF	Unc	BU
1995 Proof	30,000	Value: 30.00				

KM# 775   10 YUAN
31.1035 g., 0.9990 Silver 0.9990 oz. ASW, 40 mm. **Subject:**
Goddess of Mazu **Rev:** Female bust right with flat topped hat

Date	Mintage	F	VF	XF	Unc	BU
1995 Proof	50,000			Value: 60.00		

KM# 776   10 YUAN
31.1035 g., 0.9990 Silver 0.9990 oz. ASW, 40 mm. **Subject:**
Goddess of Mazu **Rev:** Female bust facing

Date	Mintage	F	VF	XF	Unc	BU
1995 Proof	50,000			Value: 60.00		

KM# 903   10 YUAN
27.0000 g., 0.9250 Silver 0.8029 oz. ASW **Subject:** Ninth Asian
Stamp Exhibition **Obv:** Temple of Heaven, date below, within
circle, with additional legend **Rev:** Seated panda eating with cub
Note: Prev. Y#845.

Date	Mintage	F	VF	XF	Unc	BU
1996 Proof	2,000			Value: 50.00		

KM# 902   10 YUAN
27.0000 g., 0.9250 Silver 0.8029 oz. ASW **Subject:** Beijing Coin
Fair **Obv:** Temple of Heaven within inner circle with additional
legend **Rev:** Seated panda eating with cub, gold insert
Note: Prev. Y#846.

Date	Mintage	F	VF	XF	Unc	BU
1996 Proof	2,000			Value: 50.00		

KM# 931   10 YUAN
31.1035 g., 0.9990 Silver 0.9990 oz. ASW **Obv:** Building **Rev:**
Sun Yat-Sen bust, facing, denomination below, 3/4 wreath of fans
surrounds **Note:** Prev. Y#858.

Date	Mintage	F	VF	XF	Unc	BU
1996 Proof	20,000			Value: 30.00		

KM# 956   10 YUAN
31.1035 g., 0.9990 Silver 0.9990 oz. ASW **Subject:** Return of
Hong Kong to China **Obv:** Tiananmen Square, date below
Rev: Law book above Hong Kong harbor view, denomination
below **Note:** Prev. Y#860.

Date	Mintage	F	VF	XF	Unc	BU
1996 Proof	88,000			Value: 30.00		

KM# 906   10 YUAN
31.1035 g., 0.9990 Silver 0.9990 oz. ASW **Subject:** 45th
Anniversary - Chinese Aviation Industry **Obv:** National emblem,
date below **Rev:** Propeller airplane, denomination below
Note: Prev. Y#861.

Date	Mintage	F	VF	XF	Unc	BU
1996 Proof	20,000			Value: 30.00		

KM# 905   10 YUAN
31.1035 g., 0.9990 Silver 0.9990 oz. ASW **Subject:** 45th
Anniversary - Chinese Aviation Industry **Obv:** National emblem
Rev: Jet airplane, denomination at right **Note:** Prev. Y#862.

Date	Mintage	F	VF	XF	Unc	BU
1996 Proof	20,000			Value: 30.00		

KM# 908   10 YUAN
31.1035 g., 0.9990 Silver 0.9990 oz. ASW **Subject:** 40th
Anniversary - Chinese Aviation Industry **Obv:** National emblem
above Great Wall **Rev:** Satellites, denomination at left **Note:** Prev.
Y#863.

Date	Mintage	F	VF	XF	Unc	BU
1996 Proof	20,000			Value: 30.00		

KM# 907   10 YUAN
31.1035 g., 0.9990 Silver 0.9990 oz. ASW **Subject:** 40th
Anniversary - Chinese Aviation Industry **Obv:** National emblem
above Great Wall **Rev:** Rocket and satellites, denomination at
right **Note:** Prev. Y#864.

Date	Mintage	F	VF	XF	Unc	BU
1996 Proof	20,000			Value: 30.00		

KM# 954   10 YUAN
31.1035 g., 0.9990 Silver 0.9990 oz. ASW **Subject:** Centennial
of Chinese Post Office **Obv:** Modern stamp **Rev:** Radiant Imperial
stamp, no legend above **Note:** Prev. Y#865.

Date	Mintage	F	VF	XF	Unc	BU
1996 Proof	20,000			Value: 25.00		

KM# 904   10 YUAN
31.1035 g., 0.9990 Silver 0.9990 oz. ASW **Subject:** 9th Asian
Stamp Exhibition **Obv:** Stamp, date below **Rev:** Radiant Imperial
Stamp, with additional legend above and to right **Note:** Prev.
Y#866.

Date	Mintage	F	VF	XF	Unc	BU
1996 Proof	20,000			Value: 55.00		

KM# 951   10 YUAN
31.1035 g., 0.9990 Silver 0.9990 oz. ASW **Subject:** 60th
Anniversary - Long March **Obv:** Flag above building, date below
Rev: Chairman Mao on horse, denomination above horse head
Note: Prev. Y#868.

Date	Mintage	F	VF	XF	Unc	BU
1996 Proof	20,000			Value: 40.00		

KM# 952   10 YUAN
31.1035 g., 0.9990 Silver 0.9990 oz. ASW **Subject:** 60th
Anniversary - Long March **Obv:** Flag above Baota Mountain, date
below **Rev:** Two armies enjoined in battle, denomination below
Note: Prev. Y#869.

Date	Mintage	F	VF	XF	Unc	BU
1996 Proof	20,000	Value: 40.00				

KM# 959   10 YUAN
27.0000 g., 0.9250 Silver 0.8029 oz. ASW **Subject:** Romance
of the Three Kingdoms Series **Obv:** Luo Guanzhong portrait
Rev: Cao Cao standing with spear, denomination at right
Note: Prev. Y#876.

Date	Mintage	F	VF	XF	Unc	BU
1996 Proof	7,000	Value: 35.00				

KM# 960   10 YUAN
27.0000 g., 0.9250 Silver 0.8029 oz. ASW **Subject:** Romance
of the Three Kingdoms Series **Obv:** Luo Guanzhong portrait **Rev:**
Cao Pi seated at desk, denomination at right **Note:** Prev. Y#877.

Date	Mintage	F	VF	XF	Unc	BU
1996 Proof	7,000	Value: 35.00				

KM# 961   10 YUAN
27.0000 g., 0.9250 Silver 0.8029 oz. ASW **Subject:** Romance
of the Three Kingdoms Series **Obv:** Luo Guanzhong portrait
Rev: Cao Zhi standing with scroll and flags, denomination lower
left **Note:** Prev. Y#878.

Date	Mintage	F	VF	XF	Unc	BU
1996 Proof	7,000	Value: 35.00				

KM# 962   10 YUAN
27.0000 g., 0.9250 Silver 0.8029 oz. ASW **Subject:** Romance
of the Three Kingdoms Series **Obv:** Luo Guanzhong portrait
Rev: Sima Yi on horse with spear, denomination at left
Note: Prev. Y#879.

Date	Mintage	F	VF	XF	Unc	BU
1996 Proof	7,000	Value: 35.00				

KM# 941   10 YUAN
31.1050 g., 0.9990 Silver 0.9990 oz. ASW **Obv:** Eastern
unicorn, date below **Rev:** Western unicorn in wreath,
denomination lower left **Note:** Prev. Y#741.

Date	Mintage	F	VF	XF	Unc	BU
1996 Proof	8,000	Value: 50.00				

KM# 942   10 YUAN
3.1100 g., 0.9990 Gold 0.0999 oz. AGW **Obv:** Eastern unicorn,
date below **Rev:** Western unicorn in wreath, denomination lower
left **Note:** Prev. Y#742.

Date	Mintage	F	VF	XF	Unc	BU
1996 Proof	5,000	Value: 110				

KM# 936   10 YUAN
31.1035 g., 0.9990 Silver 0.9990 oz. ASW **Subject:** Goddess
of Mercy - Guanyin **Obv:** Temple, date below **Rev:** Goddess
holding flower, denomination at left **Note:** Prev. Y#886.

Date	Mintage	F	VF	XF	Unc	BU
1996 Proof	30,000	Value: 27.50				

KM# 937   10 YUAN
3.1101 g., 0.9990 Gold 0.0999 oz. AGW **Subject:** Goddess
Guanyin **Obv:** Temple **Rev:** Goddess holding flower **Note:** Prev.
Y#887.

Date	Mintage	F	VF	XF	Unc	BU
1996 Proof	10,000	Value: 90.00				

KM# 762   10 YUAN
27.0000 g., 0.9250 Silver 0.8029 oz. ASW **Series:** Olympics
Obv: National emblem, date below **Rev:** Sailboarder,
denomination at left **Note:** Prev. Y#890.

Date	Mintage	F	VF	XF	Unc	BU
1996 Proof	30,000	Value: 30.00				

KM# 1004   10 YUAN
31.1035 g., 0.9990 Silver 0.9990 oz. ASW **Subject:** Shanghai
International Stamp & Coin Expo **Obv:** Building within circle,
legend outside **Rev:** Panda, left, denomination below, gold insert
Note: Prev. Y#895.

Date	Mintage	F	VF	XF	Unc	BU
1997 Proof	30,000	Value: 50.00				

KM# 1045   10 YUAN
31.1035 g., 0.9990 Silver 0.9990 oz. ASW **Subject:** Return of
Hong Kong to China **Obv:** Tiananmen Square, date below
Rev: Flag and fireworks over city, denomination below
Note: Prev. Y#902.

Date	Mintage	F	VF	XF	Unc	BU
1997	800,000	—	—	—	—	35.00
1997 Proof	88,000	Value: 50.00				

KM# 1047 10 YUAN

31.1035 g., 0.9990 Silver 0.9990 oz. ASW **Subject:** Return of Macao to China **Obv:** Tiananmen Square **Rev:** Deng Xiaoping viewing Macao, denomination at right **Note:** Prev. Y#905.

Date	Mintage	F	VF	XF	Unc	BU
1997 Proof	88,000	Value: 40.00				

KM# 1041 10 YUAN

31.1035 g., 0.9990 Silver 0.9990 oz. ASW **Subject:** Peoples Liberation Army **Obv:** Radiant star above Great Wall, date below **Rev:** Founding of PLA scene, denomination below **Note:** Prev. Y#908.

Date	Mintage	F	VF	XF	Unc	BU
1997 Proof	30,000	Value: 25.00				

KM# 1042 10 YUAN

31.1035 g., 0.9990 Silver 0.9990 oz. ASW **Obv:** Radiant star above Great Wall, date below **Rev:** Three members of the PRC Army, Air Force and Navy Airplanes, boats and missile in background, denomination at left **Note:** Prev. Y#909.

Date	Mintage	F	VF	XF	Unc	BU
1997 Proof	30,000	Value: 25.00				

KM# 1032 10 YUAN

3.1100 g., 0.9990 Gold 0.0999 oz. AGW **Obv:** Eastern unicorn **Rev:** Western unicorn **Note:** Prev. Y#912a.

Date	Mintage	F	VF	XF	Unc	BU
1997 Proof	5,000	Value: 120				

KM# 1029 10 YUAN

3.1100 g., 0.9990 Gold 0.0999 oz. AGW **Subject:** Goddess Guanyin **Obv:** Putuo Hill Temple **Rev:** Goddess holding jug of dew **Note:** Prev. Y#913, 985.

Date	Mintage	F	VF	XF	Unc	BU
1997 Proof	10,000	Value: 100				

KM# 1062 10 YUAN

31.1035 g., 0.9990 Silver 0.9990 oz. ASW **Subject:** Celebrating Spring **Obv:** Radiant lantern, date below **Rev:** Children setting off firecrackers, denomination above **Note:** Prev. Y#914.1.

Date	Mintage	F	VF	XF	Unc	BU
1997	60,000	—	—	—	30.00	
1997 Proof	60,000	Value: 30.00				

KM# 1059 10 YUAN

31.1035 g., 0.9990 Silver 0.9990 oz. ASW **Subject:** Traditional Chinese Mascot **Obv:** Monument in Tiananmen Square, sprays below **Rev:** Child holding carp, denomination below **Note:** Prev. Y#917.1.

Date	Mintage	F	VF	XF	Unc	BU
1997 Proof	80,000	Value: 30.00				

KM# 1059a 10 YUAN

31.1035 g., 0.9990 Silver 0.9990 oz. ASW **Subject:** Traditional Chinese Mascot **Obv:** Monument in Tiananmen Square, sprays below, circle surrounds, date below **Rev:** Multicolor version of child holding carp, denomination below **Note:** Prev. Y#917.2.

Date	Mintage	F	VF	XF	Unc	BU
1997 Proof	100,000	Value: 35.00				

KM# 1038 10 YUAN

31.1035 g., 0.9990 Silver 0.9990 oz. ASW **Subject:** Wildlife of China **Obv:** National emblem, date below **Rev:** Chinese white dolphins, denomination lower right **Note:** Prev. Y#919.

Date	Mintage	F	VF	XF	Unc	BU
1997 Proof	68,000	Value: 40.00				

KM# 1037 10 YUAN

31.1035 g., 0.9990 Silver 0.9990 oz. ASW **Subject:** Wildlife of China **Obv:** National emblem, date below **Rev:** Swan with young, denomination lowe left **Note:** Prev. Y#920.

Date	Mintage	F	VF	XF	Unc	BU
1997 Proof	68,000	Value: 40.00				

KM# 1054 10 YUAN

31.2000 g., 0.9990 Silver 1.0021 oz. ASW **Subject:** Gesal, King of Tibet **Obv:** Towered building, date below **Rev:** King on horseback, denomination at right, figures in a row below **Note:** Prev. Y#936.

Date	Mintage	F	VF	XF	Unc	BU
1997 Proof	28,000	Value: 25.00				

KM# 1056 10 YUAN
31.2000 g., 0.9990 Silver 1.0021 oz. ASW **Subject:** Gadamellin of Mongolia **Obv:** Towered building, date below **Rev:** Cavalry attack with swords, denomination at right **Note:** Prev. Y#937.

Date	Mintage	F	VF	XF	Unc	BU
1997 Proof	28,000	Value: 25.00				

KM# 1053 10 YUAN
31.2000 g., 0.9990 Silver 1.0021 oz. ASW **Subject:** Yi Nationality **Obv:** Towered building, date below **Rev:** Madame She Ziang with sword, soldiers at right above denomination **Note:** Prev. Y#938.

Date	Mintage	F	VF	XF	Unc	BU
1997 Proof	28,000	Value: 25.00				

KM# 1055 10 YUAN
31.2000 g., 0.9990 Silver 1.0021 oz. ASW **Subject:** Li Nationality **Obv:** Towered building, date below **Rev:** Madame Zian reading scroll, denomination at right **Note:** Prev. Y#939.

Date	Mintage	F	VF	XF	Unc	BU
1997 Proof	28,000	Value: 25.00				

KM# 1063 10 YUAN
3.1103 g., 0.9990 Gold 0.0999 oz. AGW **Subject:** Celebrating Spring **Obv:** Lantern **Rev:** Children setting off firecrackers **Note:** Prev. Y#983.

Date	Mintage	F	VF	XF	Unc	BU
1997	100,000	—	—	—	—	100

KM# 1097 10 YUAN
3.1103 g., 0.9990 Gold 0.0999 oz. AGW **Obv:** Forbidden city, date below **Rev:** Bronze chinze, denomination upper right **Note:** Prev. Y#984; 1094.

Date	Mintage	F	VF	XF	Unc	BU
1997 Proof	11,000	Value: 100				

KM# 982 10 YUAN
Bi-Metallic Copper-Nickel center in Brass ring **Subject:** Return of Hong Kong **Obv:** Stylized flower within circle, date below **Rev:** City view, denom. above, circle surrounds **Note:** Prev. Y#722.

Date	Mintage	F	VF	XF	Unc	BU
1997		—	—	—	5.00	—

Note: 5,000 pieces were struck and issued in boxes with certificates and are valued at $350

KM# 983 10 YUAN
Bi-Metallic Brass center in Copper-Nickel ring **Subject:** Hong Kong - Constitution **Obv:** Stylized flower within circle, date below **Rev:** Document with state emblem within circle, denomination below **Note:** Prev. Y#723.

Date	Mintage	F	VF	XF	Unc	BU
1997		—	—	—	5.00	—

KM# 1051 10 YUAN
31.1035 g., 0.9990 Silver 0.9990 oz. ASW **Subject:** Sino - Thailand Friendship **Obv:** Forbidden City and Thai Royal Palace, date below **Rev:** Two Buddha statues, one in cameo, denomination lower left **Note:** Prev. Y#711.

Date	Mintage	F	VF	XF	Unc	BU
1997 Proof	45,000	Value: 22.50				

KM# 1091 10 YUAN
20.7333 g., 0.9000 Silver 0.5999 oz. ASW, 35 mm. **Subject:** Wildlife of China **Obv:** The Great Wall, date below **Rev:** Two penguins, denomination upper left **Edge:** Plain **Note:** Prev. Y#1079.

Date	Mintage	F	VF	XF	Unc	BU
1997 Proof	8,800	Value: 60.00				

KM# 1093 10 YUAN
31.4400 g., 0.9990 Silver 1.0098 oz. ASW, 39.8 mm. **Subject:** Forbidden City **Obv:** Exterior view of the Forbidden City **Rev:** Main interior approach and gatehouse to the palaces **Edge:** Reeded **Note:** Prev. Y#1092.

Date	Mintage	F	VF	XF	Unc	BU
1997 Proof	—	Value: 40.00				

KM# 1094 10 YUAN
31.1350 g., 0.9990 Silver 100000 oz. ASW, 39.8 mm. **Subject:** Forbidden City **Obv:** Exterior view of the Forbidden City **Rev:** Causeway to palace **Edge:** Reeded **Note:** Prev. Y#1093.

Date	Mintage	F	VF	XF	Unc	BU
1997 Proof	—	Value: 40.00				

KM# 1095 10 YUAN
31.1350 g., 0.9990 Silver 100000 oz. ASW, 39.8 mm. **Subject:** Forbidden City **Obv:** Exterior view of the Forbidden City **Rev:** Interior view **Edge:** Reeded **Note:** Prev. Y#1095.

Date	Mintage	F	VF	XF	Unc	BU
1997 Proof	—	Value: 40.00				

KM# 1077 10 YUAN
27.0000 g., 0.9250 Silver 0.8029 oz. ASW, 38 mm. **Subject:** Ancient Chinese Culture Series **Obv:** Dragon seal **Rev:** Bronze wares **Edge:** Reeded **Note:** Prev. Y#1099.

Date	Mintage	F	VF	XF	Unc	BU
1997 Proof	10,000	Value: 45.00				

KM# 1080 10 YUAN
27.0000 g., 0.9250 Silver 0.8029 oz. ASW, 38 mm. **Subject:** Ancient Chinese Culture Series **Obv:** Dragon seal **Rev:** Pottery **Edge:** Reeded **Note:** Prev. Y#1100.

Date	Mintage	F	VF	XF	Unc	BU
1997 Proof	10,000	Value: 45.00				

KM# 1079 10 YUAN
27.0000 g., 0.9250 Silver 0.8029 oz. ASW, 38 mm. **Subject:** Ancient Chinese Culture Series **Obv:** Dragon seal **Rev:** Calligraphy **Edge:** Reeded **Note:** Prev. Y#1101.

Date	Mintage	F	VF	XF	Unc	BU
1997 Proof	10,000	Value: 45.00				

KM# 1078 10 YUAN
27.0000 g., 0.9250 Silver 0.8029 oz. ASW, 38 mm. **Subject:** Ancient Chinese Culture Series **Obv:** Dragon seal **Rev:** Coinage **Edge:** Reeded **Note:** Prev. Y#1102.

Date	Mintage	F	VF	XF	Unc	BU
1997 Proof	10,000	Value: 45.00				

KM# 1076 10 YUAN
3.1100 g., 0.9990 Gold 0.0999 oz. AGW, 18 mm. **Obv:** Great Wall, date below **Rev:** Man with flag, denomination at left **Edge:** Reeded **Mint:** Shenyang **Note:** Prev. Y#1191.

Date	Mintage	F	VF	XF	Unc	BU
1997(y)	16,000	—	—	—	—	100

KM# 1074 10 YUAN
3.1100 g., 0.9990 Gold 0.0999 oz. AGW, 18 mm. **Obv:** Great Wall, date below **Rev:** Man with extended open hand, denomination at right **Edge:** Reeded **Mint:** Shenyang **Note:** Prev. Y#1192.

Date	Mintage	F	VF	XF	Unc	BU
1997(y)	16,000	—	—	—	—	100

KM# 1072 10 YUAN
3.1100 g., 0.9990 Gold 0.0999 oz. AGW, 18 mm. **Obv:** Great Wall, date below **Rev:** Astronomer, denomination upper left **Edge:** Reeded **Mint:** Shenyang **Note:** Prev. Y#1193.

Date	Mintage	F	VF	XF	Unc	BU
1997(y)	16,000	—	—	—	—	100

KM# 1073 10 YUAN
3.1100 g., 0.9990 Gold 0.0999 oz. AGW, 18 mm. **Obv:** Great Wall, date below **Rev:** Gymnast, denomination at right **Edge:** Reeded **Mint:** Shenyang **Note:** Prev. Y#1194.

Date	Mintage	F	VF	XF	Unc	BU
1997(y)	16,000	—	—	—	—	100

KM# 1075   10 YUAN
3.1100 g., 0.9990 Gold 0.0999 oz. AGW, 18 mm.   **Obv:** Great
Wall, date below **Rev:** Building, denomination below
Edge: Reeded **Mint:** Shenyang **Note:** Prev. Y#1195.

Date	Mintage	F	VF	XF	Unc	BU
1997(y)	16,000	—	—	—	—	100

KM# 1060   10 YUAN
3.1100 g., 0.9990 Gold 0.0999 oz. AGW, 18 mm.
Obv: Ornamental column **Rev:** Child holding a carp
Edge: Reeded **Note:** Prev. Y#1199.1

Date	Mintage	F	VF	XF	Unc	BU
1997	100,000	—	—	—	—	100

KM# 1060a   10 YUAN
3.1100 g., 0.9990 Gold 0.0999 oz. AGW, 18 mm.
Obv: Ornamental column **Rev:** Multicolor child holding a carp
Edge: Reeded **Note:** Prev. Y#1199.2

Date	Mintage	F	VF	XF	Unc	BU
1997 Proof	20,000	Value: 100				

KM# 1031   10 YUAN
31.1035 g., 0.9990 Silver 0.9990 oz. ASW   **Obv:** Eastern
unicorn, date below **Rev:** Western unicorn, denomination below
Note: Prev. Y#912.

Date	Mintage	F	VF	XF	Unc	BU
1997 Prooflike	—	—	—	—	—	30.00
1997 Proof	8,000	Value: 60.00				

KM# 1017   10 YUAN
31.1035 g., 0.9990 Silver 0.9990 oz. ASW, 27.2 x 42 mm.
Subject: Painting Master Qi Baishi **Rev:** Ants

Date.	Mintage	F	VF	XF	Unc	BU
1997 Proof	11,800	Value: 50.00				

KM# 1018   10 YUAN
31.1035 g., 0.9990 Silver 0.9990 oz. ASW, 27.5 x 42 mm.
Subject: Painting Master Qi Baishi **Rev:** Two squirrels

Date	Mintage	F	VF	XF	Unc	BU
1997 Proof	11,800	Value: 60.00				

KM# 1028   10 YUAN
31.1035 g., 0.9990 Silver 0.9990 oz. ASW, 40 mm.
Series: Kuan Yin **Rev:** Female holding jug

Date	Mintage	F	VF	XF	Unc	BU
1997 Proof	30,000	Value: 50.00				

KM# 1033   10 YUAN
3.1100 g., 0.9990 Gold 0.0999 oz. AGW, 18 mm.   **Rev:** Unicorn

Date	Mintage	F	VF	XF	Unc	BU
1997 Proof	5,000	Value: 100				

KM# 1039   10 YUAN
31.1035 g., 0.9990 Silver 0.9990 oz. ASW, 40 mm.
Series: Endangered wildlife **Rev:** Swan

Date	Mintage	F	VF	XF	Unc	BU
1997 Proof	68,000	Value: 60.00				

KM# 1084   10 YUAN
27.0000 g., 0.9250 Silver 0.8029 oz. ASW, 38.6 mm.
Series: Classic literature

Date	Mintage	F	VF	XF	Unc	BU
1997 Proof	10,000	Value: 50.00				

KM# 1085   10 YUAN
27.0000 g., 0.9250 Silver 0.8029 oz. ASW, 38.6 mm.
Series: Classic literature **Rev:** Man seated, incense burning at
right

Date	Mintage	F	VF	XF	Unc	BU
1997 Proof	—	Value: 50.00				

KM# 1087   10 YUAN
27.0000 g., 0.9250 Silver 0.8029 oz. ASW, 38.6 mm.
Series: Classical literature **Rev:** Bearded man standing, dragon
in background

Date	Mintage	F	VF	XF	Unc	BU
1997 Proof	10,000	Value: 50.00				

KM# 1096   10 YUAN
31.1035 g., 0.9990 Silver 0.9990 oz. ASW, 40 mm.
Series: Forbidden City **Rev:** Garden pagoda

Date	Mintage	F	VF	XF	Unc	BU
1997 Proof	80,000	Value: 50.00				

KM# 1101   10 YUAN
3.1100 g., 0.9990 Gold 0.0999 oz. AGW, 18 mm.
Series: Forbidden city **Rev:** Lion statue

Date	Mintage	F	VF	XF	Unc	BU
1997 Proof	11,000	Value: 100				

KM# 1161   10 YUAN
31.1035 g., 0.9990 Silver 0.9990 oz. ASW, 40 mm.
Series: Kuan Yin **Rev:** Seated figure on lotis

Date	Mintage	F	VF	XF	Unc	BU
1998 Proof	88,000	Value: 50.00				

KM# 1151   10 YUAN
31.0220 g., 0.9990 Silver 0.9963 oz. ASW   **Subject:** 100th
Birthday - Zhou Enlai **Obv:** Zhou Enlai Memorial Hall, date below
Rev: Zhou on horseback, denomination at right, two dates at left
Note: Prev. Y#724.

Date	Mintage	F	VF	XF	Unc	BU
1998 Proof	38,000	Value: 30.00				

KM# 1152   10 YUAN
31.0220 g., 0.9990 Silver 0.9963 oz. ASW   **Subject:** 100th
Birthday - Zhou Enlai **Obv:** Zhou Enlai Memorial Hall, date below
Rev: Zhou standing facing 3/4 right, denomination at right
Note: Prev. Y#725.

Date	Mintage	F	VF	XF	Unc	BU
1998 Proof	38,000	Value: 30.00				

KM# 1157   10 YUAN
31.3900 g., 0.9990 Silver 1.0082 oz. ASW   **Obv:** National
emblem, date below **Rev:** Portrait of Dr. Norman Bethune with
surgery scene, denomination at left **Note:** Prev. Y#727.

Date	Mintage	F	VF	XF	Unc	BU
1998 Proof	61,000	Value: 20.00				

KM# 1176   10 YUAN
31.4700 g., 0.9990 Silver 1.0107 oz. ASW **Subject:** Celebrating
Spring **Obv:** Radiant lantern, date below **Rev:** Three children
about to fly kites, denomination below **Note:** Prev. Y#744.

Date	Mintage	F	VF	XF	Unc	BU
1998	80,000	—	—	—	—	25.00
1998 Proof	60,000	Value: 27.50				

KM# 1163   10 YUAN
3.1103 g., 0.9990 Gold 0.0999 oz. AGW   **Subject:** Culture of
Dragons **Note:** Prev. Y#987.

Date	Mintage	F	VF	XF	Unc	BU
1998 Proof	6,000	Value: 100				

KM# 1036   10 YUAN
31.1035 g., 0.9990 Silver 0.9990 oz. ASW, 38 mm.
Subject: World Wildlife Fund **Obv:** National emblem, date below
Rev: Clouded leopard on branch, denomination below
Edge: Reeded **Note:** Prev. Y#1063.

Date	Mintage	F	VF	XF	Unc	BU
1998 Proof	40,000	Value: 35.00				

KM# 1196   10 YUAN
31.1035 g., 0.9990 Silver 0.9990 oz. ASW, 40 mm.
Subject: Vault Protector **Obv:** Denomination, inscription and
ornamental design, square cutout at center **Rev:** Old cash coin
characters, square cutout at center **Edge:** Reeded **Note:** Square
holed cash coin design. Prev. Y#1064.

Date	Mintage	F	VF	XF	Unc	BU
1998 Proof	100,000	Value: 22.50				

KM# 1197   10 YUAN
3.1100 g., 0.9990 Gold 0.0999 oz. AGW, 18 mm. **Subject:** Vault
Protector **Obv:** Denomination, inscription and ornamental design
Rev: Old cash coin characters **Edge:** Reeded **Note:** Square
holed cash coin design. Prev. Y#1065.

Date	Mintage	F	VF	XF	Unc	BU
1998 Proof	6,000	Value: 120				

KM# 1174.1   10 YUAN
31.1000 g., 0.9990 Silver 0.9988 oz. ASW, 40 mm.
Obv: Radiant winged pillar monument above flowers **Rev:** Child
holding vase, elephant at left **Edge:** Reeded **Note:** Prev. Y#1131.1.

Date	Mintage	F	VF	XF	Unc	BU
1998	80,000	—	—	—	—	27.50

KM# 1174.2 10 YUAN
31.1000 g., 0.9990 Silver 0.9988 oz. ASW, 40 mm.
Obv: Radiant winged pillar monument above flowers
Rev: Multicolor child holding vase, elephant at left **Edge:** Reeded
Note: Prev. Y#1131.2.

Date	Mintage	F	VF	XF	Unc	BU
1998 Proof	100,000			Value: 40.00		

KM# A1135 10 YUAN
31.1035 g., 0.9990 Silver 0.9990 oz. ASW, 40 mm. **Subject:**
Bejing International Coin Exposition **Rev:** Gilt panda seated

Date	Mintage	F	VF	XF	Unc	BU
1998 Proof	30,000			Value: 50.00		

KM# 1136 10 YUAN
31.1035 g., 0.9990 Silver 0.9990 oz. ASW, 40 mm.
Subject: China International Aviation & Aerospace Exposition
Rev: Panda seated on rock, gift insert at left

Date	Mintage	F	VF	XF	Unc	BU
1998 Proof	50,000			Value: 50.00		

KM# 1154 10 YUAN
31.1035 g., 0.9990 Silver 0.9990 oz. ASW, 40 mm.
Series: 100th Anniversary Birth of Liu Shaoqi **Rev:** Bust facing
wearing neckerchief

Date	Mintage	F	VF	XF	Unc	BU
1998 Proof	3,000			Value: 50.00		

KM# 1155 10 YUAN
31.1035 g., 0.9990 Silver 0.9990 oz. ASW, 40 mm.
Subject: 100th Anniversary Birth of Liu Shaoqi **Rev:** Liu
Shaoqui standing at microphone

Date	Mintage	F	VF	XF	Unc	BU
1998 Proof	30,000			Value: 50.00		

KM# 1162 10 YUAN
3.1100 g., 0.9990 Gold 0.0999 oz. AGW, 18 mm.
Subject: Dragon culture **Rev:** Dragon circle

Date	Mintage	F	VF	XF	Unc	BU
1998 Proof	6,000			Value: 100		

KM# 1168 10 YUAN
31.1035 g., 0.9990 Silver 0.9990 oz. ASW, 40 mm.
Subject: Macao's return to China **Rev:** Birds flying over lablet,
lighthouse at left, gate at right

Date	Mintage	F	VF	XF	Unc	BU
1998 Proof	88,000			Value: 50.00		

KM# 1175 10 YUAN
3.1100 g., 0.9990 Gold Colorized 0.0999 oz. AGW, 18 mm.
Series: Traditional Chinese auspicious matter **Rev:** White
elephant and man in red outfit

Date	Mintage	F	VF	XF	Unc	BU
1998 Proof	20,000			Value: 100		

KM# A1178 10 YUAN
3.1100 g., 0.9990 Gold 0.0999 oz. AGW, 18 mm. **Subject:**
Spring greeting **Obv:** Lantern and rays **Rev:** Three figures

Date	Mintage	F	VF	XF	Unc	BU
1998 Proof	60,000			Value: 100		

KM# A1179 10 YUAN
31.1035 g., 0.9990 Silver 0.9990 oz. ASW, 40 mm. **Subject:**
Spring greetings **Obv:** Lantern and rays **Rev:** Three figures

Date	Mintage	F	VF	XF	Unc	BU
1998 Proof	60,000			Value: 50.00		

KM# 1257 10 YUAN
31.1035 g., 0.9990 Silver 0.9990 oz. ASW, 40 mm.
Series: Traditional Chinese suspicious matters **Rev:** Boy holding
up large carp

Date	Mintage	F	VF	XF	Unc	BU
1999 Proof	100,000			Value: 50.00		

KM# 1259 10 YUAN
31.2600 g., 0.9990 Silver 1.0040 oz. ASW **Subject:** Celebrating
Spring **Obv:** Radiant lantern, date below **Rev:** Multicolor, children
lighting firecrackers, denomination above **Note:** Prev. Y#914.2.

Date	Mintage	F	VF	XF	Unc	BU
1999 Proof	—			Value: 42.50		

KM# 1252 10 YUAN
31.1035 g., 0.9990 Silver 0.9990 oz. ASW **Obv:** Wan Chun
Pavilion, date below **Rev:** Gold-plated Chinese roses,
denomination at lower left **Note:** Prev. Y#943.

Date	Mintage	F	VF	XF	Unc	BU
1999	100,000	—	—	—		50.00

KM# 1253 10 YUAN
31.1035 g., 0.9990 Silver 0.9990 oz. ASW **Obv:** Da Guan Tower
in Kunming, date below **Rev:** Multicolor camellias, denomination
upper right **Note:** Prev. Y#944.

Date	Mintage	F	VF	XF	Unc	BU
1999 Proof	100,000			Value: 50.00		

KM# 1279 10 YUAN
7.7800 g., Bi-Metallic Brass center in Copper-Nickel ring,
25.48 mm. **Subject:** Return of Macau **Obv:** Stylized water lily
Rev: Modern harbor, junk and city view, birds and banner above
Edge: Segmented reeding **Note:** Prev. Y#1056.

Date	Mintage	F	VF	XF	Unc	BU
1999	—	—	—	—	6.00	

KM# 1247 10 YUAN
7.8000 g., Bi-Metallic Brass center in Copper-Nickel ring,
25.5 mm. **Subject:** 50th Anniversary - People's Republic
Obv: Fireworks above building **Rev:** Birds above "50"
Edge: Reeded and plain sections **Note:** Prev. Y#1059.

Date	Mintage	F	VF	XF	Unc	BU
1999	—	—	—	—	8.00	

KM# 1242 10 YUAN
30.9200 g., 0.9990 Silver 0.9931 oz. ASW, 40 mm.
Subject: Yin and Yang Concept **Obv:** Gate, date below
Rev: Gold-plated standing goddess, denomination at right
Edge: Reeded **Note:** Prev. Y#1078.

Date	Mintage	F	VF	XF	Unc	BU
1999	—			Value: 50.00		

KM# 1243 10 YUAN
31.1035 g., 0.9990 Silver 0.9990 oz. ASW, 40 mm.
Obv: Building on top of E Mei Mountain, date below **Rev:** The
Kuan Yin Buddha, denomination at left **Edge:** Reeded
Mint: Shanghai **Note:** Prev. Y#1207.

Date	Mintage	F	VF	XF	Unc	BU
1999	60,000	—	—	—	—	40.00

KM# 1258 10 YUAN
31.1035 g., 0.9990 Silver 0.9990 oz. ASW, 40 mm. **Obv:**
Radiant winged pillar above flowers **Rev:** Multicolor child holding
a red carp above his head **Edge:** Reeded **Note:** Prev. Y#1228.

Date	Mintage	F	VF	XF	Unc	BU
1999 Proof	—			Value: 40.00		

KM# 1224 10 YUAN
31.1035 g., 0.9990 Silver 0.9990 oz. ASW, 40 mm. **Subject:**
Bejing Coin and Stamp Fair **Rev:** Gilt panda seated on rock

Date	Mintage	F	VF	XF	Unc	BU
1999 Proof	40,000			Value: 60.00		

KM# 1240 10 YUAN
31.1035 g., 0.9990 Silver 0.9990 oz. ASW, 27.5 x 42 mm.
Subject: Master Painter Zhang Daqian **Obv:** Bust facing
Rev: Large flower

Date	Mintage	F	VF	XF	Unc	BU
1999 Proof	10,000			Value: 60.00		

KM# 1241 10 YUAN
31.1035 g., 0.9990 Silver 0.9990 oz. ASW, 27.5 x 42 mm.
Subject: Master Painter Zhang Daiqian **Obv:** Portrait facing
Rev: Bud on flora bench

Date	Mintage	F	VF	XF	Unc	BU
1999 Proof	10,000			Value: 60.00		

KM# 1246 10 YUAN
31.1035 g., 0.9990 Silver 0.9990 oz. ASW **Subject:** 50
Anniversary PRC **Rev:** Three soldiers

Date	Mintage	F	VF	XF	Unc	BU
1999 Proof	84,900			Value: 50.00		

KM# 1248 10 YUAN
31.1035 g., 0.9990 Silver 0.9990 oz. ASW **Subject:** 50th
Anniversary PRC **Rev:** Arrow, progress scenes

Date	Mintage	F	VF	XF	Unc	BU
1999 Proof	84,900			Value: 50.00		

KM# 1254 10 YUAN
31.1035 g., 0.9990 Silver 0.9990 oz. ASW, 40 mm.
Subject: 22nd World Philatelic Congress **Rev:** UPO logo

Date	Mintage	F	VF	XF	Unc	BU
1999 Proof	50,000			Value: 45.00		

KM# 1255 10 YUAN
31.1035 g., 0.9990 Silver 0.9990 oz. ASW, 40 mm.
Subject: 22nd World Philatelic Congress **Obv:** Logo
Rev: Congress arch, stamps

Date	Mintage	F	VF	XF	Unc	BU
1999 Proof	50,000			Value: 40.00		

KM# 1260   10 YUAN
31.1035 g., 0.9990 Silver Colorized 0.9990 oz. ASW, 40 mm.
Series: Rare bird **Rev:** Bird amongst flora **Note:** Colorized

Date	Mintage	F	VF	XF	Unc	BU
1999 Proof	100,000	Value: 50.00				

KM# 1262   10 YUAN
31.1035 g., 0.9990 Silver 0.9990 oz. ASW, 42 x 27.5 mm.
Series: Ancient Chinese famous paintings **Obv:** Two horse carts one right other left **Rev:** Warrior chariot left

Date	Mintage	F	VF	XF	Unc	BU
1999 Proof	13,800	Value: 50.00				

KM# 1263   10 YUAN
31.1035 g., 0.9990 Silver 0.9990 oz. ASW, 42 x 27.5 mm.
Series: Ancient Chinese famous paintings **Obv:** Two horse carts one right other left **Rev:** Royal boat left

Date	Mintage	F	VF	XF	Unc	BU
1999 Proof	13,800	Value: 50.00				

KM# 1264   10 YUAN
31.1035 g., 0.9990 Silver 0.9990 oz. ASW, 42 x 27.5 mm.
Series: Ancient Chinese famous paintings **Rev:** Horseman left

Date	Mintage	F	VF	XF	Unc	BU
1999 Proof	13,800	Value: 50.00				

KM# 1265   10 YUAN
31.1035 g., 0.9990 Silver 0.9990 oz. ASW, 42 x 27.5 mm.
Series: Ancient Chinese famous paintings **Obv:** Two horse carts one right other left **Rev:** Trees

Date	Mintage	F	VF	XF	Unc	BU
1999 Proof	13,800	Value: 50.00				

KM# 1266   10 YUAN
31.1035 g., 0.9990 Silver 0.9990 oz. ASW, 42 x 27.5 mm.
Series: Ancient Chinese famous paintings **Obv:** Two horse carts one right other left **Rev:** Trees and groups of people

Date	Mintage	F	VF	XF	Unc	BU
1999 Proof	13,800	Value: 50.00				

KM# 1267   10 YUAN
31.1035 g., 0.9990 Silver 0.9990 oz. ASW, 42 x 27.5 mm.
Series: Ancient Chinese famous paintings **Obv:** Two horse carts one right other left **Rev:** Trees and river

Date	Mintage	F	VF	XF	Unc	BU
1999 Proof	13,800	Value: 50.00				

KM# 1268   10 YUAN
31.1035 g., 0.9990 Silver 0.9990 oz. ASW, 42 x 27.5 mm.
Series: Ancient Chinese famous paintings **Obv:** Two horse carts one right other left **Rev:** Rocks in river

Date	Mintage	F	VF	XF	Unc	BU
1999 Proof	13,800	Value: 50.00				

KM# 1269   10 YUAN
31.1035 g., 0.9990 Silver 0.9990 oz. ASW, 42 x 27.5 mm.
Series: Ancient Chinese famous paintings **Obv:** Two horse carts one right other left **Rev:** People and horses

Date	Mintage	F	VF	XF	Unc	BU
1999 Proof	13,800	Value: 50.00				

KM# 1270   10 YUAN
31.1035 g., 0.9990 Silver 0.9990 oz. ASW, 42 x 27.5 mm.
Series: Tall tower in arc **Subject:** Suzhou Gardens **Obv:** Bridge and river, temple

Date	Mintage	F	VF	XF	Unc	BU
1999 Proof	11,800	Value: 50.00				

KM# 1271   10 YUAN
31.1035 g., 0.9990 Silver 0.9990 oz. ASW, 42 x 27.5 mm.
Subject: Suzhou Gardens **Obv:** Two tall towered temple **Rev:** Water side temple

Date	Mintage	F	VF	XF	Unc	BU
1999 Proof	11,800	Value: 50.00				

KM# 1272   10 YUAN
31.1035 g., 0.9990 Silver 0.9990 oz. ASW, 42 x 27.5 mm.
Series: Temple at right in arc **Subject:** Suzhou Gardens **Obv:** Lakeside temple with reflection

Date	Mintage	F	VF	XF	Unc	BU
1999 Proof	11,800	Value: 50.00				

KM# 1273   10 YUAN
31.1035 g., 0.9990 Silver 0.9990 oz. ASW, 42 x 27.5 mm.
Subject: Suzhou Garden **Obv:** Temple in arc **Rev:** Temple by bridge and rock formation

Date	Mintage	F	VF	XF	Unc	BU
1999 Proof	11,800	Value: 50.00				

KM# 1274   10 YUAN
31.1035 g., 0.9990 Silver 0.9990 oz. ASW, 40 mm.
Subject: 10th Anniversary of Hope Project **Obv:** Logo and flora below **Rev:** Two children holding plaque

Date	Mintage	F	VF	XF	Unc	BU
1999 Proof	60,000	Value: 50.00				

KM# 1275   10 YUAN
31.1035 g., 0.9990 Silver 0.9990 oz. ASW, 14 x 120 mm.
Subject: Fan paintings **Obv:** Rice plant design in arc **Rev:** Flora plants

Date	Mintage	F	VF	XF	Unc	BU
1999 Proof	11,800	Value: 40.00				

KM# 1276   10 YUAN
31.1035 g., 0.9990 Silver 0.9990 oz. ASW, 14 x 120 mm.
Subject: Fan paintings **Obv:** Rice plant desing in arc **Rev:** Boat, trees and mountain scene

Date	Mintage	F	VF	XF	Unc	BU
1999 Proof	11,800	Value: 40.00				

KM# 1277   10 YUAN
31.1035 g., 0.9990 Silver 0.9990 oz. ASW, 14 x 120 mm.
Subject: Fan paintings **Obv:** Rice plant desing in arc **Rev:** One tree

Date	Mintage	F	VF	XF	Unc	BU
1999 Proof	11,800	Value: 40.00				

KM# 1278   10 YUAN
31.1035 g., 0.9990 Silver 0.9990 oz. ASW, 31.1035 mm.
Subject: Fan paintings **Obv:** Rice plant in arc **Rev:** Fisherman and fish

Date	Mintage	F	VF	XF	Unc	BU
1999 Proof	11,800	Value: 40.00				

KM# A1279   10 YUAN
31.1035 g., 0.9990 Silver 0.9990 oz. ASW, 40 mm.
Subject: Return of Macao **Rev:** Large 99 above buildings

Date	Mintage	F	VF	XF	Unc	BU
1999 Proof	88,000	Value: 50.00				

KM# 1283   10 YUAN
31.1035 g., 0.9990 Silver 0.9990 oz. ASW, 40 mm. **Subject:** Bejing opera **Rev:** Actress with long red ribbon **Note:** Colorized

Date	Mintage	F	VF	XF	Unc	BU
1999 Proof	38,000	Value: 50.00				

KM# 1284   10 YUAN
31.1035 g., 0.9990 Silver 0.9990 oz. ASW, 40 mm.
Subject: Bejing opera **Rev:** Female standing holding round fan **Note:** Colorized

Date	Mintage	F	VF	XF	Unc	BU
1999 Proof	38,000	Value: 50.00				

KM# 1285   10 YUAN
31.1035 g., 0.9990 Silver 0.9990 oz. ASW, 40 mm. **Subject:** Bejing opera **Rev:** Figure standing holding whip **Note:** Colorized

Date	Mintage	F	VF	XF	Unc	BU
1999 Proof	38,000	Value: 50.00				

KM# 1286   10 YUAN
31.1035 g., 0.9990 Silver 0.9990 oz. ASW, 40 mm.
Subject: Bejing opera **Rev:** Actor standing holding sword

Date	Mintage	F	VF	XF	Unc	BU
1999 Proof	38,000	Value: 50.00				

KM# 1331   10 YUAN
31.1035 g., 0.9990 Silver 0.9990 oz. ASW, 40 mm.
Subject: Y2K **Obv:** Monument **Rev:** World Golbe as an eye above value **Edge:** Reeded **Note:** Prev. Y#1235.

Date	Mintage	F	VF	XF	Unc	BU
2000 Proof	88,000	Value: 40.00				

KM# 1318   10 YUAN
23.0375 g., 0.9000 Silver 0.6666 oz. ASW, 40 mm.
Obv: Building within circle, date below **Rev:** Multicolor dragon, denomination at right **Note:** Prev. Y#993.

Date	Mintage	F	VF	XF	Unc	BU
2000	100,000	—	—	—	—	50.00

KM# 1332   10 YUAN
3.1103 g., 0.9990 Gold 0.0999 oz. AGW   **Subject:** Y2K
Note: Prev. Y#994.

Date	Mintage	F	VF	XF	Unc	BU
2000	50,000	—	—	—	—	100

KM# 1330   10 YUAN
3.1103 g., 0.9990 Gold 0.0999 oz. AGW, 18 mm.
Subject: Goddess Kuan Yin **Obv:** Putuo Mountain Gate **Rev:** Standing Kuan Yin with holographic background **Edge:** Reeded **Note:** Prev. Y#996.

Date	Mintage	F	VF	XF	Unc	BU
2000	33,000	—	—	—	—	135

KM# 1317   10 YUAN
31.1035 g., 0.9990 Silver 0.9990 oz. ASW, 40 mm.
Subject: Dragons **Note:** Prev. Y#1048.

Date	Mintage	F	VF	XF	Unc	BU
2000	50,000	—	—	—	—	40.00

KM# 1300   10 YUAN
7.8000 g., Bi-Metallic Copper-Nickel center in Brass ring, 25.5 mm. **Obv:** Rocket and city view above wheel **Rev:** Number two and eye above map of China **Edge:** Segmented reeding **Note:** Prev. Y#1123.

Date	Mintage	F	VF	XF	Unc	BU
2000	—	—	—	—	—	8.00

KM# 1311. 10 YUAN
31.1035 g., 0.9990 Silver 0.9990 oz. ASW, 40 mm. **Series:** Classic literature **Subject:** Dream of red mansion **Rev:** Female seated, child standing, three herons **Note:** Colorized

Date	Mintage	F	VF	XF	Unc	BU
2000 Proof	38,000	Value: 50.00				

KM# 1312   10 YUAN
31.1035 g., 0.9990 Silver 0.9990 oz. ASW, 40 mm.
Series: Classical literature **Subject:** Dream of red mansion **Rev:** Female standing by red fence **Note:** Colorized

Date	Mintage	F	VF	XF	Unc	BU
2000	38,000	Value: 50.00				

KM# 1313   10 YUAN
31.1035 g., 0.9990 Silver 0.9990 oz. ASW, 40 mm. **Series:** Classical literature **Subject:** Dream of red mansion **Rev:** Female in yellow kimono in room with red curtains **Note:** Colorized

Date	Mintage	F	VF	XF	Unc	BU
2000 Proof	38,000	Value: 50.00				

KM# 1314   10 YUAN
31.1035 g., 0.9990 Silver 0.9990 oz. ASW, 40 mm.
Series: Classical literature **Subject:** Dream of red mansion **Rev:** Female in blue kimono, cherry blossom **Note:** Colorized

Date	Mintage	F	VF	XF	Unc	BU
2000 Proof	38,000	Value: 50.00				

KM# 1328   10 YUAN
31.1035 g., 0.9990 Silver 0.9990 oz. ASW, 40 mm. **Series:** Rare bird **Rev:** Bird on pink blossom **Note:** Colorized

Date	Mintage	F	VF	XF	Unc	BU
2000 Proof	100,000	Value: 50.00				

KM# 1338   10 YUAN
31.1035 g., 0.9990 Silver 0.9990 oz. ASW, 40 mm. **Subject:** Beijing opera **Rev:** 2 figures with chairs **Note:** Colorized

Date	Mintage	F	VF	XF	Unc	BU
2000 Proof	38,000	Value: 50.00				

KM# 1339   10 YUAN
31.1035 g., 0.9990 Silver 0.9990 oz. ASW, 40 mm. **Subject:** Beijing opera **Rev:** 2 figures one with sword **Note:** Colorized

Date	Mintage	F	VF	XF	Unc	BU
2000 Proof	38,000	Value: 50.00				

KM# 1340   10 YUAN
31.1035 g., 0.9990 Silver 0.9990 oz. ASW, 40 mm.
Subject: Beijing opera **Rev:** Two figures both in yellow kimonos **Note:** Colorized

Date	Mintage	F	VF	XF	Unc	BU
2000 Proof	38,000	Value: 50.00				

KM# 1341   10 YUAN
31.1035 g., 0.9990 Silver 0.9990 oz. ASW, 40 mm.
Subject: Beijing opera **Rev:** Two figures one with blue and white diamond kimono **Note:** Colorized

Date	Mintage	F	VF	XF	Unc	BU
2000 Proof	38,000	Value: 50.00				

KM# 33 15 YUAN
10.0000 g., 0.8000 Silver 0.2572 oz. ASW **Series:** Olympics **Obv:** National emblem, denomination below **Rev:** Ancient archers, date below **Note:** Piedfort-type planchet. Prev. Y#745.

Date	Mintage	F	VF	XF	Unc	BU
1980	15,000				30.00	

KM# 34 20 YUAN
10.3500 g., 0.8500 Silver 0.2828 oz. ASW **Series:** 1980 Olympics **Subject:** Wrestling **Obv:** National emblem, denomination below **Rev:** Wrestlers, date below **Note:** Prev. Y#18.

Date	Mintage	F	VF	XF	Unc	BU
1980 Proof	29,000	Value: 20.00				

KM# 318 20 YUAN
62.2060 g., 0.9990 Silver 1.9979 oz. ASW **Rev:** Phoenix and dragon **Note:** Prev. Y#207.

Date	Mintage	F	VF	XF	Unc	BU
1990 Proof	5,000	Value: 90.00				

KM# 452 20 YUAN
62.2060 g., 0.9990 Silver 1.9979 oz. ASW **Obv:** Great Wall, date below **Rev:** Horse and dragon, denomination at right **Note:** Prev. Y#888.

Date	Mintage	F	VF	XF	Unc	BU
1992 Proof	6,000	Value: 100				
	Note: Issued in 1996					

KM# 966 20 YUAN
62.2060 g., 0.9990 Silver 1.9979 oz. ASW **Obv:** Bai Di city gate, date at bottom **Rev:** Yangtze River scene, denomination at bottom **Note:** Prev. Y#595.

Date	Mintage	F	VF	XF	Unc	BU
1996 Proof	8,000	Value: 65.00				

KM# 967 20 YUAN
62.2060 g., 0.9990 Silver 1.9979 oz. ASW **Obv:** Qu Yuan Temple, date at bottom **Rev:** River scene, denomination below **Note:** Prev. Y#596.

Date	Mintage	F	VF	XF	Unc	BU
1996 Proof	8,000	Value: 65.00				

KM# 968 20 YUAN
62.2060 g., 0.9990 Silver 1.9979 oz. ASW **Obv:** Zhang Fei Temple, date at bottom **Rev:** River scene, denomination below **Note:** Prev. Y#597.

Date	Mintage	F	VF	XF	Unc	BU
1996 Proof	8,000	Value: 65.00				

KM# 969 20 YUAN
62.2060 g., 0.9990 Silver 1.9979 oz. ASW **Obv:** Zhao Jun Temple, date at bottom **Rev:** River scene, denomination below **Note:** Prev. Y#598.

Date	Mintage	F	VF	XF	Unc	BU
1996 Proof	8,000	Value: 65.00				

KM# A1191 20 YUAN
62.2060 g., 0.9990 Silver 1.9979 oz. ASW, 19 x 29 mm. **Series:** Guilien scenery **Obv:** Tall out crop with pagoda at top **Rev:** Tall coastal islands

Date	Mintage	F	VF	XF	Unc	BU
1998 Proof	18,800	Value: 100				

KM# 1185 20 YUAN
62.2060 g., 0.9990 Silver 1.9979 oz. ASW, 55 x 36 mm. **Series:** Ancient paintings **Obv:** Tall temple and buildings **Rev:** Arch and buildings

Date	Mintage	F	VF	XF	Unc	BU
1998 Proof	18,800	Value: 100				

KM# 1190 20 YUAN
62.2060 g., 0.9990 Silver 1.9979 oz. ASW, 19 x 29 mm. **Series:** Guilien scenery **Obv:** 4 arched bridge **Rev:** Tall coastal islands

Date	Mintage	F	VF	XF	Unc	BU
1998 Proof	18,800	Value: 100				

KM# 1164 20 YUAN
62.2070 g., 0.9990 Silver 1.9979 oz. ASW, 55 x 36 mm. **Subject:** New look of Hong Kong **Obv:** Two flags, sprigs below **Rev:** Suspension bridge

Date	Mintage	F	VF	XF	Unc	BU
1998 Proof	11,800	Value: 100				

KM# 1165 20 YUAN
62.2510 g., 0.9990 Silver 1.9993 oz. ASW, 55 x 36 mm. **Subject:** New look of Hong Kong **Obv:** Two flags, sprigs below **Rev:** Modern tower and buildings

Date	Mintage	F	VF	XF	Unc	BU
1998 Proof	11,800	Value: 100				

KM# 1166 20 YUAN
62.2070 g., 0.9990 Silver 1.9979 oz. ASW, 55 x 36 mm. **Subject:** New look of Hong Kong **Obv:** Two flags, sprigs below **Rev:** Modern domed building, skyline

Date	Mintage	F	VF	XF	Unc	BU
1998 Proof	11,800	Value: 100				

KM# 1167 20 YUAN
62.2070 g., 0.9990 Silver 1.9979 oz. ASW, 55 x 36 mm. **Subject:** New look of Hong Kong **Obv:** Two flags, sprigs below **Rev:** Large buda statue

Date	Mintage	F	VF	XF	Unc	BU
1998 Proof	11,800	Value: 100				

KM# 1181 20 YUAN
62.2060 g., 0.9990 Silver 1.9979 oz. ASW, 55 x 36 mm. **Series:** Ancient paintings **Obv:** Tall temple and buildings **Rev:** Large black horse in rural scene

Date	Mintage	F	VF	XF	Unc	BU
1998 Proof	18,800	Value: 100				

KM# 1182 20 YUAN
62.2060 g., 0.9990 Silver 1.9979 oz. ASW, 55 x 36 mm. **Series:** Ancient paintings **Obv:** Tall temple and buildings **Rev:** Buildings in rural scene

Date	Mintage	F	VF	XF	Unc	BU
1998 Proof	18,800	Value: 100				

KM# 1183 20 YUAN
62.2060 g., 0.9990 Silver 1.9979 oz. ASW, 55 x 36 mm. **Series:** Ancient paintings **Obv:** Tall temple and buildings **Rev:** More buildings in rural scene

Date	Mintage	F	VF	XF	Unc	BU
1998 Proof	18,800	Value: 100				

KM# 1184 20 YUAN
62.2060 g., 0.9990 Silver 1.9979 oz. ASW, 55 x 36 mm. **Series:** Ancient paintings **Obv:** Tall temple and buildings **Rev:** Buildings and ships in scene

Date	Mintage	F	VF	XF	Unc	BU
1998 Proof	18,800	Value: 100				

KM# 1186 20 YUAN
62.2060 g., 0.9990 Silver 1.9979 oz. ASW, 55 x 36 mm. **Series:** Ancient paintings **Obv:** Tall temple and buildings **Rev:** Ships and rural scene

Date	Mintage	F	VF	XF	Unc	BU
1998 Proof	18,800	Value: 100				

KM# 1189 20 YUAN
62.2060 g., 0.9990 Silver 1.9979 oz. ASW, 19 x 29 mm. **Series:** Guilien scenery **Obv:** Natural bridge archway at sea shore **Rev:** Tall coastal islands

Date	Mintage	F	VF	XF	Unc	BU
1998 Proof	18,800	Value: 100				

KM# 1191 20 YUAN
62.2060 g., 0.9990 Silver 1.9979 oz. ASW, 19 x 29 mm. **Series:** Guilien scenery **Obv:** Long arched bridge **Rev:** Tall coastal islands

Date	Mintage	F	VF	XF	Unc	BU
1998 Proof	18,800	Value: 100				

KM# 1349 20 YUAN
62.2070 g., 0.9990 Silver 1.9979 oz. ASW, 55 x 36 mm. **Subject:** 100th Anniversary of finding Dun Huang Grottoes Scripture Cave **Rev:** Figure in flight right, with tray service

Date	Mintage	F	VF	XF	Unc	BU
2000 Proof	11,800	Value: 80.00				

KM# 1344 20 YUAN
62.2070 g., 0.9990 Silver 1.9979 oz. ASW, 55 x 36 mm. **Subject:** 100th Anniversary of finding Dun Huang Grottoes scripture cave **Obv:** Temple **Rev:** Figure in flight left

Date	Mintage	F	VF	XF	Unc	BU
2000 Proof	11,800	Value: 80.00				

KM# 1345 20 YUAN
62.2070 g., 0.9990 Silver 1.9979 oz. ASW, 55 x 36 mm. **Subject:** 100th Anniversary of finding Dun Huang Grottoes Scripture Cave **Rev:** Figure in flight right, circled around

Date	Mintage	F	VF	XF	Unc	BU
2000 Proof	11,800	Value: 80.00				

KM# 1346 20 YUAN
62.2070 g., 0.9990 Silver 1.9979 oz. ASW, 55 x 36 mm. **Subject:** 100th Anniversary of finding Duan Huang Grottoes Scripture Cave **Obv:** Temple **Rev:** Figure in flight right holding lyre

Date	Mintage	F	VF	XF	Unc	BU
2000 Proof	11,800	Value: 80.00				

KM# 1347   20 YUAN
62.2070 g., 0.9990 Silver 1.9979 oz. ASW, 55 x 36 mm.
Subject: 100th Anniversary of finding Dun Huang Grottoes
Scripture Cave **Obv:** Temple **Rev:** Figure in flight left, hand
outstretched right

Date	Mintage	F	VF	XF	Unc	BU
2000 Proof	11,800	Value: 80.00				

KM# 1348   20 YUAN
62.2070 g., 0.9990 Silver 1.9979 oz. ASW, 55 x 36 mm.
Subject: 100th Anniversary of finding Dun Huang Grottoes
Scripture Cave **Rev:** Figure in flight left, playing lyre

Date	Mintage	F	VF	XF	Unc	BU
2000 Proof	11,800	Value: 80.00				

KM# 60   25 YUAN
19.4400 g., 0.8000 Silver 0.5000 oz. ASW **Subject:** World
Soccer Cup **Obv:** National emblem, date below **Rev:** Soccer
players, denomination upper right **Note:** Prev. Y#35.

Date	Mintage	F	VF	XF	Unc	BU
1982 Proof	40,000	Value: 27.50				

KM# 59   25 YUAN
19.4400 g., 0.8000 Silver 0.5000 oz. ASW **Subject:** World
Soccer Cup **Obv:** National emblem, date below **Rev:** Soccer
players, denomination below **Note:** Prev. Y#36.

Date	Mintage	F	VF	XF	Unc	BU
1982 Proof	40,000	Value: 27.50				

KM# 461   25 YUAN
8.4800 g., 0.9170 Gold 0.2500 oz. AGW **Subject:** Bronze Age
Sculptures **Obv:** National emblem **Rev:** Ram **Note:** Prev. Y#555.

Date	Mintage	F	VF	XF	Unc	BU
1992 Proof	500	Value: 400				

KM# 462   25 YUAN
8.4800 g., 0.9170 Gold 0.2500 oz. AGW **Subject:** Bronze Age
Sculptures **Rev:** Panther **Note:** Prev. Y#556.

Date	Mintage	F	VF	XF	Unc	BU
1992 Proof	500	Value: 400				

KM# 453   25 YUAN
7.7759 g., 0.9990 Gold 0.2497 oz. AGW **Obv:** Great Wall
Rev: Horse and dragon **Note:** Prev. Y#889.

Date	Mintage	F	VF	XF	Unc	BU
1992 Proof	5,000	Value: 250				
Note: Issued in 1996						

KM# 590   25 YUAN
7.7758 g., 0.9990 Gold 0.2497 oz. AGW **Subject:** Homeland
Scenery **Obv:** Great Wall **Rev:** Large temple at Mount Heng
Note: Prev. Y#775.

Date	Mintage	F	VF	XF	Unc	BU
1993 Proof	8,888	Value: 250				

KM# 596   25 YUAN
7.7758 g., 0.9990 Gold 0.2497 oz. AGW **Obv:** Temple of Heaven
Rev: Two peacocks, denomination above **Note:** Prev. Y#475.

Date	Mintage	F	VF	XF	Unc	BU
1993 Prooflike	—	—	—	—	—	250

KM# 549   25 YUAN
7.7758 g., 0.9990 Gold 0.2497 oz. AGW **Rev:** Goddess Kuan
Yin seated in flower, denomination at left **Note:** Prev. Y#502.

Date	Mintage	F	VF	XF	Unc	BU
1993 Proof	1,000	Value: 250				

KM# 495   25 YUAN
7.7759 g., 0.9990 Gold 0.2497 oz. AGW **Rev:** Chinese Gods:
Fu, Lu, and Shu **Note:** Prev. Y#404.

Date	Mintage	F	VF	XF	Unc	BU
1993	Est. 3,000	—	—	—	—	250

KM# 572   25 YUAN
8.4900 g., 0.9170 Gold 0.2503 oz. AGW **Subject:** Bronze Age
Sculptures **Obv:** National emblem, date below **Rev:** Unicorn,
right, denomination lower right **Note:** Prev. Y#408.

Date	Mintage	F	VF	XF	Unc	BU
1993 Proof	350	Value: 600				

KM# 571   25 YUAN
8.4900 g., 0.9170 Gold 0.2503 oz. AGW **Subject:** Bronze Age
Sculptures **Obv:** National emblem, date below **Rev:** Pig, left,
denomination below **Note:** Prev. Y#409.

Date	Mintage	F	VF	XF	Unc	BU
1993 Proof	350	Value: 600				

KM# 498   25 YUAN
7.7758 g., 0.9995 Platinum 0.2499 oz. APW, 21.95 mm. **Series:**
Chinese Inventions and Discoveries **Obv:** Great Wall **Rev:** Stirrup
and equestrians **Edge:** Reeded **Note:** Prev. Y#1072.

Date	Mintage	F	VF	XF	Unc	BU
1993 Proof	100	Value: 950				

KM# 499   25 YUAN
7.7758 g., 0.9995 Platinum 0.2499 oz. APW **Series:** Chinese
Inventions and Discoveries **Obv:** Great Wall **Rev:** Umbrella use
and repair scene **Note:** Prev. Y#1073.

Date	Mintage	F	VF	XF	Unc	BU
1993 Proof	100	Value: 950				

KM# 496   25 YUAN
7.7758 g., 0.9995 Platinum 0.2499 oz. APW **Series:** Chinese
Inventions and Discoveries **Obv:** Great Wall **Rev:**
Mathematicians using an abacus **Note:** Prev. Y#1074.

Date	Mintage	F	VF	XF	Unc	BU
1993 Proof	100	Value: 950				

KM# 497   25 YUAN
7.7758 g., 0.9995 Platinum 0.2499 oz. APW **Series:** Chinese
Inventions and Discoveries **Obv:** Great Wall **Rev:** Two men and
Yin and Yang symbol **Note:** Prev. Y#1075.

Date	Mintage	F	VF	XF	Unc	BU
1993 Proof	100	Value: 950				

KM# 500   25 YUAN
7.7758 g., 0.9995 Platinum 0.2499 oz. APW **Series:** Chinese
Inventions and Discoveries **Obv:** Great Wall **Rev:** Excavating the
Terra-cotta army **Note:** Prev. Y#1076.

Date	Mintage	F	VF	XF	Unc	BU
1993 Proof	100	Value: 950				

KM# 633   25 YUAN
7.7758 g., 0.9995 Platinum 0.2499 oz. APW, 21.95 mm.
Subject: Oriental Inventions **Obv:** Great Wall **Rev:** First tuned
bells **Note:** Prev. Y#1118; 1181.

Date	Mintage	F	VF	XF	Unc	BU
1994 Proof	100	Value: 950				

KM# 634   25 YUAN
7.7758 g., 0.9995 Platinum 0.2499 oz. APW, 21.95 mm.
Subject: Oriental Inventions **Obv:** Great Wall **Rev:** First silken
fabric **Note:** Prev. Y#1119; 1182.

Date	Mintage	F	VF	XF	Unc	BU
1994 Proof	100	Value: 950				

KM# 632   25 YUAN
7.7758 g., 0.9995 Platinum 0.2499 oz. APW, 21.95 mm.
Subject: Oriental Inventions **Obv:** Great Wall **Rev:** First records
of comets **Note:** Prev. Y#1120; 1183.

Date	Mintage	F	VF	XF	Unc	BU
1994 Proof	100	Value: 950				

KM# 636   25 YUAN
7.7758 g., 0.9995 Platinum 0.2499 oz. APW, 21.95 mm.
Subject: Oriental Inventions **Obv:** Great Wall **Rev:** First masts
for sailing **Note:** Prev. Y#1121.

Date	Mintage	F	VF	XF	Unc	BU
1994 Proof	100	Value: 950				

KM# 635   25 YUAN
7.7758 g., 0.9995 Platinum 0.2499 oz. APW, 21.95 mm.
Subject: Oriental Inventions **Obv:** Great Wall **Rev:** First chain
pumps used to draw water **Note:** Prev. Y#1122; 1185.

Date	Mintage	F	VF	XF	Unc	BU
1994 Proof	100	Value: 950				

KM# 677   25 YUAN
7.7758 g., Bi-Metallic Gold center in Silver ring **Obv:** Building
within circle, date below **Rev:** Unicorn, denomination at left, within
circle **Note:** Prev. Y#422.

Date	Mintage	F	VF	XF	Unc	BU
1994 Proof	1,100	Value: 230				

KM# 678   25 YUAN
7.7758 g., 0.9990 Gold 0.2497 oz. AGW **Obv:** Figure on Eastern
unicorn, date below **Rev:** Unicorn, denomination at left, rose
sprays below **Note:** Prev. Y#423.

Date	Mintage	F	VF	XF	Unc	BU
1994 Proof	5,100	Value: 250				

KM# 664   25 YUAN
3.1103 g., 0.9990 Gold 0.0999 oz. AGW **Obv:** Great Wall, date
below **Rev:** Goddess Kuan Yin holding child, facing,
denomination at left **Note:** Prev. Y#511.

Date	Mintage	F	VF	XF	Unc	BU
1994 Proof	1,000	Value: 230				

KM# 666   25 YUAN
3.1103 g., 0.9990 Gold 0.0999 oz. AGW **Obv:** Great Wall, date
below **Rev:** Goddess Kuan Yin with bottle, 3/4 left, denomination
at right **Note:** Prev. Y#512.

Date	Mintage	F	VF	XF	Unc	BU
1994 Proof	1,000	Value: 230				

KM# 665   25 YUAN
3.1103 g., 0.9990 Gold 0.0999 oz. AGW **Obv:** Great Wall, date
below **Rev:** Goddess Kuan Yin standing, denomination at right
Note: Prev. Y#513.

Date	Mintage	F	VF	XF	Unc	BU
1994 Proof	1,000	Value: 230				

KM# 667   25 YUAN
3.1103 g., 0.9990 Gold 0.0999 oz. AGW **Obv:** Great Wall, date
below **Rev:** Goddess Kuan Yin seated, denomination at right
Note: Prev. Y#514.

Date	Mintage	F	VF	XF	Unc	BU
1994 Proof	1,000	Value: 230				

KM# 694   25 YUAN
7.7800 g., 0.9990 Gold 0.2499 oz. AGW, 22 mm. **Series:**
Famous paintings **Rev:** Three children playing with model ship

Date	Mintage	F	VF	XF	Unc	BU
1994 Proof	1,000	Value: 250				

KM# 695   25 YUAN
7.7800 g., 0.9990 Gold 0.2499 oz. AGW, 22 mm.
Series: Famous paintings **Rev:** Two children with dog

Date	Mintage	F	VF	XF	Unc	BU
1994 Proof	1,000	Value: 250				

KM# 787   25 YUAN
7.7758 g., 0.9990 Gold 0.2497 oz. AGW, 22 mm. **Obv:** Pu-Tow
temple **Rev:** Goddess of Mercy - with Lotus flower **Note:** Prev.
Y#524.

Date	Mintage	F	VF	XF	Unc	BU
1995 Proof	1,000	Value: 250				

KM# 790   25 YUAN
7.7758 g., 0.9990 Gold 0.2497 oz. AGW **Rev:** Goddess of Mercy
with wheel **Note:** Prev. Y#525.

Date	Mintage	F	VF	XF	Unc	BU
1995 Proof	1,000	Value: 250				

KM# 788   25 YUAN
7.7758 g., 0.9990 Gold 0.2497 oz. AGW **Rev:** Goddess of Mercy
with sceptre **Note:** Prev. Y#526.

Date	Mintage	F	VF	XF	Unc	BU
1995 Proof	1,000	Value: 250				

KM# 789   25 YUAN
7.7758 g., 0.9990 Gold 0.2497 oz. AGW **Rev:** Goddess of Mercy
with bowl **Note:** Prev. Y#527.

Date	Mintage	F	VF	XF	Unc	BU
1995 Proof	1,000	Value: 250				

KM# 777   25 YUAN
7.8300 g., 0.9990 Gold 0.2515 oz. AGW **Subject:** Sea Goddess
Mazhu **Obv:** Mazhu Temple **Rev:** Mazhu's portrayal **Note:** Prev.
Y#835.

Date	Mintage	F	VF	XF	Unc	BU
1995 Proof	3,000	Value: 250				

KM# 797   25 YUAN
7.7758 g., Bi-Metallic Gold center in Silver ring **Obv:** Building
within circle, date below **Rev:** Unicorn with offspring,
denomination at left, circle surrounds **Note:** Prev. Y#687; 1061.

Date	Mintage	F	VF	XF	Unc	BU
1995 Proof	2,000	Value: 230				

KM# 798   25 YUAN
7.8300 g., 0.9990 Gold 0.2515 oz. AGW **Obv:** Eastern unicorn
rearing, date below **Rev:** Western unicorn with offspring,
denomination at left **Note:** Prev. Y#738.

Date	Mintage	F	VF	XF	Unc	BU
1995 Proof	5,000	Value: 250				

KM# 943   25 YUAN
7.7759 g., 0.9990 Gold 0.2497 oz. AGW **Obv:** Eastern unicorn,
date below **Rev:** Western unicorn and maiden, denomination at
left **Note:** Prev. Y#743.

Date	Mintage	F	VF	XF	Unc	BU
1996 Proof	3,000	Value: 300				

KM# 955   25 YUAN
7.7759 g., 0.9990 Gold 0.2497 oz. AGW **Subject:** Centennial
of Chinese Post Office **Obv:** Modern postal stamp, date below
Rev: Imperial postal stamp, denomination at right **Note:** Prev.
Y#867.

Date	Mintage	F	VF	XF	Unc	BU
1996 Proof	3,000	Value: 250				

KM# 944   25 YUAN
7.7758 g., 0.9995 Platinum 0.2499 oz. APW, 21.9 mm.
Subject: Unicorn **Obv:** Eastern unicorn, full body, date below
Rev: Western unicorn head, right, denomination at right
Edge: Reeded **Note:** Prev. Y#955.

Date	Mintage	F	VF	XF	Unc	BU
1996 Proof	500	Value: 500				

KM# 1099   25 YUAN
7.7759 g., 0.9990 Gold 0.2497 oz. AGW **Subject:** China Palace
Museum **Obv:** Forbidden City **Rev:** Imperial Gardens **Note:** Prev.
Y#997.

Date	Mintage	F	VF	XF	Unc	BU
1997 Proof	4,000	Value: 250				

KM# 1100   25 YUAN
7.7759 g., 0.9990 Gold 0.2497 oz. AGW **Subject:** China Palace
Museum **Obv:** Forbidden City **Rev:** Jin Shui **Note:** Prev. Y#998.

Date	Mintage	F	VF	XF	Unc	BU
1997 Proof	4,000	Value: 250				

KM# 1102   25 YUAN
7.7759 g., 0.9990 Gold 0.2497 oz. AGW **Subject:** China Palace
Museum **Obv:** Forbidden City **Rev:** Quan Quin Palace
Note: Prev. Y#999.

Date	Mintage	F	VF	XF	Unc	BU
1997 Proof	4,000	Value: 250				

KM# 1064   25 YUAN
7.7759 g., 0.9990 Gold 0.2497 oz. AGW **Subject:** Celebrating
Spring **Obv:** Radiant lantern, date below **Rev:** Children setting
off firecrackers, denomination above **Note:** Prev. Y#915.

Date	Mintage	F	VF	XF	Unc	BU
1997 Proof	10,000	Value: 250				

KM# 1098   25 YUAN
7.7759 g., 0.9990 Gold 0.2497 oz. AGW **Subject:** China Palace
Museum **Obv:** Forbidden City **Rev:** Inner view of palace
Note: Prev. Y#1000.

Date	Mintage	F	VF	XF	Unc	BU
1997 Proof	4,000	Value: 250				

KM# 1178   25 YUAN
7.7758 g., 0.9999 Gold 0.2500 oz. AGW **Subject:** Greeting
Spring **Note:** Prev. Y#1135.

Date	Mintage	F	VF	XF	Unc	BU
1998	10,000	—	—	—	—	250

KM# A1180   25 YUAN
7.6500 g., 0.9990 Gold 0.2457 oz. AGW, 22 mm. **Subject:**
Spring greeting **Obv:** Lantern in rays **Rev:** Three figures dancing

Date	Mintage	F	VF	XF	Unc	BU
1998 Proof	10,000	Value: 200				

KM# 1329   25 YUAN
7.7758 g., 0.9999 Gold 0.2500 oz. AGW **Subject:** Bird
Rev: Multicolored. **Note:** Prev. Y#1136.

Date	Mintage	F	VF	XF	Unc	BU
2000	8,800	—	—	—	—	330

KM# 35   30 YUAN
15.0000 g., 0.8500 Silver 0.4099 oz. ASW **Series:** 1980
Olympics **Subject:** Equestrian **Obv:** National emblem,
denomination below **Rev:** Horse racing, date below **Note:** Prev.
Y#19.

Date	Mintage	F	VF	XF	Unc	BU
1980 Proof	29,000	Value: 20.00				

KM# 36   30 YUAN
15.0000 g., 0.8500 Silver 0.4099 oz. ASW **Series:** 1980
Olympics **Obv:** National emblem, denomination below
Rev: Soccer, date below **Note:** Prev. Y#20.

Date	Mintage	F	VF	XF	Unc	BU
1980 Proof	29,000	Value: 20.00				

KM# 26   30 YUAN
15.0000 g., 0.8500 Silver 0.4099 oz. ASW **Series:** Lake Placid
1980 - 13th Winter Olympic Games **Obv:** National emblem,
denomination below **Rev:** Woman speed skater, within snowflake
Note: Prev. Y#21.

Date	Mintage	F	VF	XF	Unc	BU
1980 Proof	20,000	Value: 20.00				

KM# 25   30 YUAN
16.0000 g., Silver **Series:** 1980 Olympics **Obv:** National
emblem, denomination below **Rev:** Downhill skier, within
snowflake **Note:** Prev. Y#746.

Date	Mintage	F	VF	XF	Unc	BU
1980 Proof	20,000	Value: 20.00				

KM# 23   30 YUAN
16.0000 g., Silver **Series:** Lake Placid 1980 - 13th Winter
Olympic Games **Obv:** National emblem, denomination below
Rev: Woman figure skater, within snowflake **Note:** Prev. Y#747.

Date	Mintage	F	VF	XF	Unc	BU
1980 Proof	20,000	Value: 20.00				

KM# 24   30 YUAN

16.0000 g., Silver **Series:** 1980 Olympics **Obv:** National emblem, denomination below **Rev:** Biathalon skier, within snowflake **Note:** Prev. Y#748.

Date	Mintage	F	VF	XF	Unc	BU
1980 Proof	20,000	Value: 20.00				

KM# 8   35 YUAN

19.4400 g., 0.8000 Silver 0.5000 oz. ASW **Subject:** UNICEF and IYC **Obv:** National emblem and date above sprays **Rev:** Children planting a flower, denomination below **Note:** Prev. Y#8.

Date	Mintage	F	VF	XF	Unc	BU
1979 Matte	1,000	—	—	—	150	—
1979 Proof	14,000	Value: 65.00				

KM# 50   35 YUAN

33.5800 g., 0.8000 Silver 0.8637 oz. ASW **Subject:** 70th Anniversary - 1911 Revolution **Obv:** Statue of Sun Yat-sen divides dates **Rev:** Mausoleum, denomination below **Note:** Prev. Y#46.

Date	Mintage	F	VF	XF	Unc	BU
1981 Proof	3,885	Value: 250				

KM# 147   50 YUAN

155.5000 g., 0.9990 Silver 4.9942 oz. ASW, 70 mm. **Subject:** 120th Anniversary - Birth of Sun Yat-sen **Rev:** Sun Yat-sen standing, facing, denomination at left, circle surrounds **Note:** Illustration reduced. Prev. Y#108.

Date	Mintage	F	VF	XF	Unc	BU
1986 Proof	3,000	Value: 200				

KM# 205   50 YUAN

155.5000 g., 0.9990 Silver 4.9942 oz. ASW, 70 mm. **Series:** Seoul 1988 - 24th Summer Olympic Games **Rev:** Volleyball game, denomination below **Note:** Illustration reduced. Prev. Y#170.

Date	Mintage	F	VF	XF	Unc	BU
1988 Proof	3,898	Value: 250				

KM# 297   50 YUAN

155.6800 g., 0.9990 Silver 500000 oz. ASW **Series:** Albertville 1992 - 16th Winter Olympic Games **Obv:** National emblem, date below **Rev:** 3 speed skaters, denomination above **Note:** Illustration reduced. Prev. Y#321.

Date	Mintage	F	VF	XF	Unc	BU
1990 Proof	10,000	Value: 165				

KM# 328   50 YUAN

15.5517 g., 0.9990 Gold 0.4995 oz. AGW **Subject:** Taiwan Scenery Series **Obv:** Great Wall **Rev:** Pagoda **Note:** Prev. Y#704.

Date	Mintage	F	VF	XF	Unc	BU
1990 Proof	4,000	Value: 500				
1997	—	—	—	—	—	—
1998	—	—	—	—	—	—
1999	—	—	—	—	—	—
2000	—	—	—	—	—	—

KM# 327   50 YUAN

15.5517 g., 0.9990 Gold 0.4995 oz. AGW **Subject:** Taiwan Scenery Series **Obv:** Great Wall **Rev:** Pondside building **Note:** Prev. Y#705.

Date	Mintage	F	VF	XF	Unc	BU
1990 Proof	4,000	Value: 500				

KM# 329   50 YUAN

15.5517 g., 0.9990 Gold 0.4995 oz. AGW **Subject:** Taiwan Scenery Series **Obv:** Great Wall **Rev:** Hillside building **Note:** Prev. Y#706.

Date	Mintage	F	VF	XF	Unc	BU
1990 Proof	4,000	Value: 500				
1997	—	—	—	—	—	—
1998	—	—	—	—	—	—
1999	—	—	—	—	—	—
2000	—	—	—	—	—	—

KM# 326   50 YUAN

15.5517 g., 0.9990 Gold 0.4995 oz. AGW **Subject:** Taiwan Scenery Series **Obv:** Great Wall **Rev:** Three buildings joined by docks and bridge **Note:** Prev. Y#707.

Date	Mintage	F	VF	XF	Unc	BU
1990 Proof	4,000	Value: 500				

KM# 303   50 YUAN

155.5000 g., 0.9990 Silver 4.9942 oz. ASW **Series:** Barcelona 1992 - 25th Summer Olympic Games **Obv:** National emblem, date below **Rev:** Female runners, denomination above **Note:** Prev. Y#472.

Date	Mintage	F	VF	XF	Unc	BU
1991 Proof	10,000	Value: 225				

KM# 382   50 YUAN

155.5000 g., 0.9990 Silver 4.9942 oz. ASW **Subject:** 80th Anniversary - 1911 Revolution **Obv:** Similar to 10 Yuan, Y#476,(building with two dates below) **Rev:** Sun Yat-Sen in uniform, facing, denomination at left **Note:** Prev. Y#477.

Date	Mintage	F	VF	XF	Unc	BU
1991 Proof	1,000	Value: 350				

KM# 463 50 YUAN
16.9600 g., 0.9170 Gold 0.5000 oz. AGW **Subject:** Bronze Age Sculptures **Obv:** National emblem, date below **Rev:** Kneeling figure, denomination below **Note:** Prev. Y#557.

Date	Mintage	F	VF	XF	Unc	BU
1992 Proof	500	Value: 775				

KM# 409 50 YUAN
155.5000 g., 0.9990 Silver 4.9942 oz. ASW, 70 mm. **Series:** Scientific and technical inventions **Rev:** Spoon on table

Date	Mintage	F	VF	XF	Unc	BU
1992 Proof	3,000	Value: 150				

KM# 543 50 YUAN
155.5175 g., 0.9990 Silver 4.9948 oz. ASW, 70 mm. **Rev:** Chairman Mao writing, denomination at right **Note:** Illustration reduced. Prev. Y#413.

Date	Mintage	F	VF	XF	Unc	BU
1993	1,500	—	—	—	300	—

KM# 565 50 YUAN
155.5518 g., 0.9990 Silver 4.9959 oz. ASW **Subject:** Chinese Wildlife **Obv:** National emblem, date below **Rev:** Brown bear and cub, denomination at right **Note:** Illustration reduced. Prev. Y#772.

Date	Mintage	F	VF	XF	Unc	BU
1993 Proof	4,500	Value: 350				

KM# 550 50 YUAN
15.5517 g., 0.9990 Gold 0.4995 oz. AGW **Obv:** Great Wall, date below **Rev:** Goddess Kuan Yin - seated in flower, denomination at left **Note:** Prev. Y#503.

Date	Mintage	F	VF	XF	Unc	BU
1993 Proof	1,000	Value: 525				

KM# 597 50 YUAN
155.5000 g., 0.9990 Silver 4.9942 oz. ASW **Obv:** Temple of Harmony **Rev:** Two peacocks **Note:** Prev. Y#353.

Date	Mintage	F	VF	XF	Unc	BU
1993 Proof	888	Value: 275				

KM# 501 50 YUAN
15.5517 g., 0.9990 Gold 0.4995 oz. AGW **Subject:** Chinese Inventions and Discoveries **Obv:** Great Wall, denomination below **Rev:** Chin with Yin Yang, denomination below **Note:** Prev. Y#378.

Date	Mintage	F	VF	XF	Unc	BU
1993 Proof	1,200	Value: 525				

KM# 504 50 YUAN
15.5517 g., 0.9990 Gold 0.4995 oz. AGW **Subject:** Chinese Inventions and Discoveries **Obv:** Great Wall, date below **Rev:** Invention of the Umbrella, denomination at right **Note:** Prev. Y#401.

Date	Mintage	F	VF	XF	Unc	BU
1993 Proof	1,200	Value: 525				

KM# 507 50 YUAN
155.5175 g., 0.9990 Silver 4.9948 oz. ASW **Subject:** Chinese Gods: Fu, Lu and Shu **Obv:** Building and Great Wall, date below **Rev:** Three gods with symbol on panel and child **Note:** Prev. Y#405.

Date	Mintage	F	VF	XF	Unc	BU
1993 Proof	1,000	Value: 325				

KM# 573 50 YUAN
16.9800 g., 0.9170 Gold 0.5006 oz. AGW **Subject:** Bronze Age Sculptures **Obv:** National emblem, date below **Rev:** Kneeling man lantern, denomination at right **Note:** Prev. Y#410.

Date	Mintage	F	VF	XF	Unc	BU
1993 Proof	350	Value: 850				

KM# 542 50 YUAN
15.5517 g., 0.9990 Gold 0.4995 oz. AGW **Subject:** Chairman Mao **Rev:** Bust, 3/4 left, denomination at left **Note:** Prev. Y#414.

Date	Mintage	F	VF	XF	Unc	BU
1993 Proof	5,000	Value: 550				
1993(s) Proof	2,500	Value: 600				

KM# 582 50 YUAN
15.5517 g., 0.9990 Gold 0.4995 oz. AGW **Subject:** Taiwan Temples **Obv:** Great Wall, date below **Rev:** Buddha statue, denomination below **Note:** Prev. Y#445.

Date	Mintage	F	VF	XF	Unc	BU
1993 Proof	1,000	Value: 525				

KM# 579 50 YUAN
15.5517 g., 0.9990 Gold 0.4995 oz. AGW **Subject:** Taiwan Temples **Obv:** Great Wall, date below **Rev:** Large temple, denomination below **Note:** Prev. Y#446.

Date	Mintage	F	VF	XF	Unc	BU
1993 Proof	1,000	Value: 525				

KM# 580 50 YUAN
15.5517 g., 0.9990 Gold 0.4995 oz. AGW **Subject:** Taiwan Temples **Obv:** Great Wall, date below **Rev:** Small temple, denomination below **Note:** Prev. Y#447.

Date	Mintage	F	VF	XF	Unc	BU
1993 Proof	1,000	Value: 525				

KM# 581 50 YUAN
15.5517 g., 0.9990 Gold 0.4995 oz. AGW **Subject:** Taiwan Temples **Obv:** Great Wall, date below **Rev:** Tower temple, denomination below **Note:** Prev. Y#448.

Date	Mintage	F	VF	XF	Unc	BU
1993 Proof	—	Value: 525				

KM# 503 50 YUAN
15.5517 g., 0.9990 Gold 0.4995 oz. AGW **Subject:** Chinese Inventions and Discoveries **Obv:** Great Wall **Rev:** Stirrup **Note:** Prev. Y#765.

Date	Mintage	F	VF	XF	Unc	BU
1993 Proof	1,200	Value: 525				

KM# 505 50 YUAN
15.5517 g., 0.9990 Gold 0.4995 oz. AGW **Subject:** Chinese Inventions and Discoveries **Obv:** Great Wall **Rev:** Excavation of the Terra-cotta Army **Note:** Prev. Y#766.

Date	Mintage	F	VF	XF	Unc	BU
1993 Proof	1,200	Value: 525				

KM# 506 50 YUAN
15.5517 g., 0.9990 Gold 0.4995 oz. AGW **Subject:** Chinese Inventions and Discoveries **Obv:** Great Wall **Rev:** Discovery of mathematical zero **Note:** Prev. Y#767.

Date	Mintage	F	VF	XF	Unc	BU
1993 Proof	1,200	Value: 525				

KM# 591 50 YUAN
155.5518 g., 0.9990 Silver 4.9959 oz. ASW **Obv:** Great Wall **Rev:** Mount Hau and river **Note:** Prev. Y#776.

Date	Mintage	F	VF	XF	Unc	BU
1993 Proof	8,888	Value: 275				

KM# 502 50 YUAN
15.5600 g., 0.9990 Gold 0.4997 oz. AGW, 40 mm. **Series:** Scientific and technical inventions **Rev:** Three men standing over printing form

Date	Mintage	F	VF	XF	Unc	BU
1993 Proof	1,200	Value: 450				

KM# 698 50 YUAN
15.5517 g., 0.9990 Gold 0.4995 oz. AGW **Subject:** Children At Play **Rev:** Two children with cat, denomination below **Note:** Prev. Y#459.

Date	Mintage	F	VF	XF	Unc	BU
1994 Proof	1,888	Value: 525				

KM# 697 50 YUAN
15.5517 g., 0.9990 Gold 0.4995 oz. AGW **Subject:** Children At Play **Obv:** Temple of Heaven **Rev:** Three children with toy boat, denomination below **Note:** Prev. Y#460.

Date	Mintage	F	VF	XF	Unc	BU
1994 Proof	1,888	Value: 525				

KM# 696 50 YUAN
155.5000 g., 0.9990 Silver 4.9942 oz. ASW **Subject:** Children At Play **Obv:** Temple of Heaven **Rev:** Two children with cat **Note:** Prev. Y#461.

Date	Mintage	F	VF	XF	Unc	BU
1994 Proof	500	Value: 375				

KM# 679 50 YUAN
155.5000 g., 0.9990 Silver 4.9942 oz. ASW **Obv:** Figure on Eastern unicorn, date below **Rev:** Unicorn looking right, denomination at left, rose sprays below **Note:** Prev. Y#424.

Date	Mintage	F	VF	XF	Unc	BU
1994 Proof	1,100	Value: 150				

KM# 680 50 YUAN
15.5517 g., 0.9990 Gold 0.4995 oz. AGW **Obv:** Figure on Eastern unicorn, date below **Rev:** Unicorn looking right, rose sprays below, denomination at left **Note:** Prev. Y#425.

Date	Mintage	F	VF	XF	Unc	BU
1994 Proof	1,100	Value: 450				

KM# 638 50 YUAN
15.5517 g., 0.9990 Gold 0.4995 oz. AGW **Subject:** Oriental Inventions **Obv:** Great Wall **Rev:** First tuned bells **Note:** Prev. Y#621.

Date	Mintage	F	VF	XF	Unc	BU
1994 Proof	1,200	Value: 525				

KM# 639 50 YUAN
15.5517 g., 0.9990 Gold 0.4995 oz. AGW **Subject:** Oriental Inventions **Obv:** Great Wall **Rev:** First silken fabric **Note:** Prev. Y#622.

Date	Mintage	F	VF	XF	Unc	BU
1994 Proof	1,200	Value: 525				

KM# 637 50 YUAN
15.5517 g., 0.9990 Gold 0.4995 oz. AGW **Subject:** Oriental Inventions - Astronomy **Obv:** Great Wall **Rev:** First records of comets **Note:** Prev. Y#623.

Date	Mintage	F	VF	XF	Unc	BU
1994 Proof	1,200	Value: 525				

KM# 641 50 YUAN
15.5517 g., 0.9990 Gold 0.4995 oz. AGW **Subject:** Oriental Inventions **Obv:** Great Wall **Rev:** First masts for sailing **Note:** Prev. Y#624.

Date	Mintage	F	VF	XF	Unc	BU
1994 Proof	1,200	Value: 525				

KM# 640 50 YUAN
15.5517 g., 0.9990 Gold 0.4995 oz. AGW **Subject:** Oriental Inventions **Obv:** Great Wall **Rev:** First chain pumps used to draw water **Note:** Prev. Y#625.

Date	Mintage	F	VF	XF	Unc	BU
1994 Proof	1,200	Value: 525				

KM# 687 50 YUAN
155.5175 g., 0.9990 Silver 4.9948 oz. ASW **Subject:** Sino-Singapore Friendship **Obv:** Great Wall **Rev:** Singapore harbor view **Note:** Prev. Y#785.

Date	Mintage	F	VF	XF	Unc	BU
1994 Proof	300	Value: 800				

KM# 669 50 YUAN
155.5175 g., 0.9990 Silver 4.9948 oz. ASW **Rev:** Taiwan temple **Note:** Prev. Y#708.

Date	Mintage	F	VF	XF	Unc	BU
1994 Proof	500	Value: 250				

KM# 79 50 YUAN
155.5000 g., 0.9990 Silver 4.9942 oz. ASW, 70 mm. **Subject:** Marco Polo **Rev:** Bust and two temples

Date	Mintage	F	VF	XF	Unc	BU
1994 Proof	1,500	Value: 250				

KM# 757 50 YUAN
155.5175 g., 0.9990 Silver 4.9948 oz. ASW **Series:** 1996 Summer Olympics **Obv:** National emblem, date below **Rev:** Table tennis player, date at right, denomination at left **Note:** Illustration reduced. Prev. Y#891.

Date	Mintage	F	VF	XF	Unc	BU
1995 Proof	—	Value: 125				
1996 Proof	3,000	Value: 140				

KM# 845 50 YUAN
1555.5175 g., 0.9990 Silver 49.958 oz. ASW, 70 mm. **Rev:** Da Yu walking through water, denomination at left **Note:** Illustration reduced. Prev. Y#592.

Date	Mintage	F	VF	XF	Unc	BU
1995 Proof	500	Value: 325				

KM# 800 50 YUAN
155.5000 g., 0.9990 Silver 4.9942 oz. ASW, 69 mm. **Rev:** Unicorn with offspring, denomination at left **Note:** Illustration reduced. Prev. Y#688.

Date	Mintage	F	VF	XF	Unc	BU
1995 Proof	—	Value: 150				

KM# 822 50 YUAN
155.5000 g., 0.9990 Silver 4.9942 oz. ASW, 70 mm. **Rev:** Junk, denomination below **Note:** Illustration reduced. Prev. Y#689.

Date	Mintage	F	VF	XF	Unc	BU
1995 Proof	1,000	Value: 300				

KM# 740 50 YUAN
15.5517 g., 0.9990 Gold 0.4995 oz. AGW **Subject:** Oriental Inventions **Obv:** Great Wall, date below **Rev:** Soldiers with cannon and gunpowder, denomination lower left **Note:** Prev. Y#632.

Date	Mintage	F	VF	XF	Unc	BU
1995 Proof	1,200	Value: 525				

KM# 742 50 YUAN
15.5517 g., 0.9990 Gold 0.4995 oz. AGW **Subject:** Oriental Inventions **Obv:** Great Wall, date below **Rev:** Individual block printing, denomination at right **Note:** Prev. Y#633.

Date	Mintage	F	VF	XF	Unc	BU
1995 Proof	1,200	Value: 525				

KM# 741 50 YUAN
15.5517 g., 0.9990 Gold 0.4995 oz. AGW **Subject:** Oriental Inventions **Obv:** Great Wall **Rev:** Potter **Note:** Prev. Y#634.

Date	Mintage	F	VF	XF	Unc	BU
1995 Proof	1,200	Value: 525				

KM# 744 50 YUAN
15.5517 g., 0.9990 Gold 0.4995 oz. AGW **Subject:** Oriental Inventions **Obv:** Great Wall **Rev:** Chess players **Note:** Prev. Y#635.

Date	Mintage	F	VF	XF	Unc	BU
1995 Proof	1,200	Value: 525				

KM# 743 50 YUAN
15.5517 g., 0.9990 Gold 0.4995 oz. AGW **Subject:** Oriental Inventions **Obv:** Great Wall, date below **Rev:** Teacher with anatomy chart of human body, denomination at left **Note:** Prev. Y#636.

Date	Mintage	F	VF	XF	Unc	BU
1995 Proof	1,200	Value: 525				

KM# 820 50 YUAN
15.5517 g., 0.9990 Gold 0.4995 oz. AGW **Rev:** Sailing ship **Note:** Prev. Y#648.

Date	Mintage	F	VF	XF	Unc	BU
1995 Proof	1,000	Value: 550				

KM# 821 50 YUAN
15.5517 g., 0.9990 Gold 0.4995 oz. AGW **Rev:** Junk **Note:** Prev. Y#651.

Date	Mintage	F	VF	XF	Unc	BU
1995 Proof	1,000	Value: 550				

KM# 816 50 YUAN
15.5517 g., 0.9990 Gold 0.4995 oz. AGW **Subject:** Return of Hong Kong to China - Series I **Obv:** Tiananmen building and monument **Rev:** Deng Xiaoping's portrait above Hong Kong skyline **Note:** Prev. Y#532.

Date	Mintage	F	VF	XF	Unc	BU
1995 Proof	11,800	Value: 500				

KM# 814 50 YUAN
15.5517 g., 0.9990 Gold 0.4995 oz. AGW **Series:** 50th Anniversary - United Nations **Obv:** United Nations logo, date below **Rev:** United Nations building, denomination upper left, dates at right **Note:** Prev. Y#488.

Date	Mintage	F	VF	XF	Unc	BU
1995 Proof	17,500	Value: 500				

KM# 793 50 YUAN
15.5517 g., 0.9990 Gold 0.4995 oz. AGW **Subject:** Dinosaur **Obv:** Tall building, date below **Rev:** Brontosaurus, denomination at left **Note:** Prev. Y#471.

Date	Mintage	F	VF	XF	Unc	BU
1995 Proof	2,000	Value: 500				

KM# 801 50 YUAN
15.5517 g., 0.9990 Gold 0.4995 oz. AGW **Obv:** Eastern unicorn, rearing, date below **Rev:** Western unicorn with offspring, denomination at left **Note:** Prev. Y#739.

Date	Mintage	F	VF	XF	Unc	BU
1995 Proof	2,000	Value: 525				

KM# 799 50 YUAN
15.5517 g., 0.9995 Platinum 0.4997 oz. APW, 26.8 mm. **Subject:** Unicorn **Obv:** Eastern unicorn, rearing, date below **Rev:** Western unicorn with offspring, denomination at left **Edge:** Reeded **Note:** Prev. Y#739a.

Date	Mintage	F	VF	XF	Unc	BU
1995 Proof	1,015	Value: 1,000				

KM# 844 50 YUAN
15.5517 g., 0.9990 Gold 0.4995 oz. AGW **Subject:** Yellow River culture **Rev:** Nu Wa Rising, denomination below **Note:** Prev. Y#593.

Date	Mintage	F	VF	XF	Unc	BU
1995 Proof	2,500	Value: 525				

KM# 870 50 YUAN
11.3180 g., 0.9160 Gold 0.3333 oz. AGW **Subject:** Silk Road **Obv:** National emblem, date below **Rev:** Man riding camel, denomination at right **Note:** Prev. Y#608.

Date	Mintage	F	VF	XF	Unc	BU
1995 Proof	10,000	Value: 325				

KM# 808 50 YUAN
15.5517 g., 0.9990 Gold 0.4995 oz. AGW **Subject:** 50th Anniversary - Anti-Japanese War **Obv:** National emblem, date below **Rev:** Zhou and Mao above soldiers, denomination below **Note:** Prev. Y#690.

Date	Mintage	F	VF	XF	Unc	BU
1995 Proof	2,500	Value: 500				

KM# 812 50 YUAN
10.3600 g., Bi-Metallic Gold center in Silver ring **Subject:** World Women's Conference **Obv:** Logo above building **Rev:** Three women, denomination above within circle **Note:** Prev. Y#691.

Date	Mintage	F	VF	XF	Unc	BU
1995 Proof	3,000	Value: 400				

KM# 862 50 YUAN
155.5175 g., 0.9990 Silver 4.9948 oz. ASW **Subject:** 50th Anniversary - For the return of Taiwan to China **Obv:** Great Wall **Rev:** Taiwan and China maps **Note:** Prev. Y#813.

Date	Mintage	F	VF	XF	Unc	BU
1995 Proof	999	Value: 575				

KM# 861 50 YUAN
15.5517 g., 0.9990 Gold 0.4995 oz. AGW **Subject:** 50th Anniversary - For the return of Taiwan to China **Obv:** Great Wall **Rev:** Taiwan and China maps **Note:** Prev. Y#814.

Date	Mintage	F	VF	XF	Unc	BU
1995 Proof	3,000	Value: 500				

KM# 860 50 YUAN
15.5517 g., 0.9990 Gold 0.4995 oz. AGW **Subject:** 50th Anniversary - For the return of Taiwan to China **Obv:** Great Wall **Rev:** Zhongshan Hall **Note:** Prev. Y#815.

Date	Mintage	F	VF	XF	Unc	BU
1995 Proof	3,000	Value: 500				

KM# 768 50 YUAN
7.9020 g., 0.9160 Gold 0.2327 oz. AGW **Obv:** Bust of painter Xu Beihong, facing, date below **Rev:** Lion, denomination lower right **Note:** Prev. Y#821.

Date	Mintage	F	VF	XF	Unc	BU
1995 Proof	3,000	Value: 250				

KM# 771 50 YUAN
155.5175 g., 0.9990 Silver 4.9948 oz. ASW **Obv:** Chiqian building **Rev:** Zheng Chenggong standing with flag and ships **Note:** Prev. Y#822.

Date	Mintage	F	VF	XF	Unc	BU
1995 Proof	250	Value: 475				

KM# 852 50 YUAN
155.5175 g., 0.9990 Silver 4.9948 oz. ASW **Subject:** Romance of Three Kingdoms **Obv:** Luo Guanzhong **Rev:** Three figures **Note:** Prev. Y#829.

Date	Mintage	F	VF	XF	Unc	BU
1995 Proof	7,000	Value: 475				

KM# 851 50 YUAN
15.5517 g., 0.9990 Gold 0.2497 oz. AGW **Subject:** Romance of Three Kingdoms **Obv:** Luo Guanzhong **Rev:** Three figures **Note:** Prev. Y#829a.

Date	Mintage	F	VF	XF	Unc	BU
1995 Proof	2,000	Value: 425				

KM# 763 50 YUAN
10.3678 g., 0.9990 Gold 0.3330 oz. AGW **Subject:** Table Tennis **Obv:** Tianjing Stadium **Rev:** Table tennis player **Note:** Prev. Y#838.

Date	Mintage	F	VF	XF	Unc	BU
1995 Proof	2,000	Value: 325				

KM# 769 50 YUAN
151.0000 g., 0.9990 Silver 4.8497 oz. ASW, 70 mm. **Subject:** 100th Anniversary Birth of Xu Beihong **Rev:** Figure riding oxen

Date	Mintage	F	VF	XF	Unc	BU
1995 Proof	300	Value: 250				

KM# 916 50 YUAN
15.5000 g., 0.9990 Gold 0.4978 oz. AGW, 27 mm. **Subject:** Scientific and technical inventions **Obv:** Tower on Great Wall **Rev:** Boat in river

Date	Mintage	F	VF	XF	Unc	BU
1996 Proof	1,200	Value: 450				

KM# 964 50 YUAN
155.5175 g., 0.9990 Silver 4.9948 oz. ASW, 80 mm. **Subject:** Romance of the Three Kingdoms Series **Obv:** Bust of Luo Guanzhong, 3/4 right, date below **Rev:** Battle scene, denomination below **Note:** Illustration reduced. Prev. Y#880.

Date	Mintage	F	VF	XF	Unc	BU
1996 Proof	500	Value: 325				

KM# 946   50 YUAN
15.5517 g., 0.9990 Gold 0.4995 oz. AGW, 27 mm. **Subject:**
Unicorn **Obv:** Eastern unicorn, full body **Rev:** Western unicorn
in wreath **Edge:** Reeded **Note:** Prev. Y#1039; 1091.

Date	Mintage	F	VF	XF	Unc	BU
1996 Proof	1,000	Value: 550				

KM# 957   50 YUAN
15.5517 g., 0.9990 Gold 0.4995 oz. AGW **Subject:** Return of
Hong Kong to China Series II **Obv:** Hong Kong Harbor
Note: Prev. Y#658.

Date	Mintage	F	VF	XF	Unc	BU
1996 Proof	11,800	Value: 500				

KM# 932   50 YUAN
15.5517 g., 0.9990 Gold 0.4995 oz. AGW **Obv:** Building, date
below **Rev:** Sun Yat-sen bust facing, denomination below, fan
sprays 3/4 around **Note:** Prev. Y#859.

Date	Mintage	F	VF	XF	Unc	BU
1996 Proof	3,000	Value: 500				

KM# 953   50 YUAN
15.5517 g., 0.9990 Gold 0.4995 oz. AGW **Subject:** 60th
Anniversary - Long March **Obv:** Flag above building, date below
Rev: Chairman Mao portrait, denomination at right **Note:** Prev.
Y#870.

Date	Mintage	F	VF	XF	Unc	BU
1996 Proof	6,000	Value: 500				

KM# 963   50 YUAN
15.5517 g., 0.9990 Gold 0.4995 oz. AGW **Subject:** Romance
of the Three Kingdoms Series **Obv:** Luo Guanzhong portrait **Rev:**
Guand Du on horseback, leading his troops **Note:** Prev. Y#881.

Date	Mintage	F	VF	XF	Unc	BU
1996 Proof	2,000	Value: 500				

KM# 945   50 YUAN
155.5175 g., 0.9990 Silver 4.9948 oz. ASW, 70.2 mm.
Subject: Unicorn **Obv:** Eastern unicorn, full body, date below
Rev: Western unicorn with maiden, denomination at left
Edge: Reeded **Note:** Illustration reduced. Prev. Y#1038.

Date	Mintage	F	VF	XF	Unc	BU
1996 Proof	—	Value: 325				

KM# 975   50 YUAN
11.3180 g., 0.9160 Gold 0.3333 oz. AGW **Subject:** Silk Road
Obv: National emblem, date below **Rev:** Water vendor,
denomination lower right **Note:** Prev. Y#609.

Date	Mintage	F	VF	XF	Unc	BU
1996 Proof	10,000	Value: 325				

KM# 970   50 YUAN
15.5517 g., 0.9990 Gold 0.4995 oz. AGW **Obv:** Yangtze River
scene, denomination lower left corner **Rev:** Large dam
Note: Prev. Y#599.

Date	Mintage	F	VF	XF	Unc	BU
1996 Proof	6,000	Value: 550				

KM# 914   50 YUAN
15.5000 g., 0.9990 Gold 0.4978 oz. AGW, 27 mm.
Series: Scientific and technical inventions **Obv:** Tower on Great
Wall **Rev:** Man in two horse cart

Date	Mintage	F	VF	XF	Unc	BU
1996 Proof	1,200	Value: 450				

KM# A915   50 YUAN
15.5000 g., 0.9990 Gold 0.4978 oz. AGW, 27 mm.
Series: Scientific and techiniacl inventions **Obv:** Tower on Great
Wall **Rev:** Three men seated playing musical instruments

Date	Mintage	F	VF	XF	Unc	BU
1996 Proof	1,200	Value: 450				

KM# 915   50 YUAN
15.5000 g., 0.9990 Gold 0.4978 oz. AGW, 27 mm.
Series: Scientific and technical inventions **Obv:** Tower on Great
Wall **Rev:** Three men seated playing musical instruments

Date	Mintage	F	VF	XF	Unc	BU
1996 Proof	1,200	Value: 450				

KM# 917   50 YUAN
51.5000 g., 0.9990 Gold 1.6540 oz. AGW, 27 mm.
Series: Scientific and techinical inventions **Obv:** Tower on Great
Wall **Rev:** Bridge

Date	Mintage	F	VF	XF	Unc	BU
1996 Proof	1,200	Value: 450				

KM# 918   50 YUAN
15.5000 g., 0.9990 Gold 0.4978 oz. AGW, 27 mm.
Series: Scientific and techinical inventions **Obv:** Tower on Great
Wall **Rev:** Tower

Date	Mintage	F	VF	XF	Unc	BU
1996 Proof	1,200	Value: 450				

KM# 1048   50 YUAN
155.5175 g., 0.9990 Silver 4.9948 oz. ASW, 80 mm.
Subject: Return of Macao to China **Obv:** Tiananmen Square -
Forbidden City, date above leaf sprays below **Rev:** Deng
Xiaoping viewing Macao, denomination at right **Note:** Illustration
reduced. Prev. Y#906.

Date	Mintage	F	VF	XF	Unc	BU
1997 Proof	—	Value: 200				

KM# 1081   50 YUAN
15.5517 g., 0.9990 Gold 0.4995 oz. AGW **Subject:** Huang
(Yellow) River Culture **Obv:** Archer **Rev:** Dragon **Note:** Prev.
Y#1004.

Date	Mintage	F	VF	XF	Unc	BU
1997 Proof	3,000	Value: 500				

KM# 1020   50 YUAN
15.5517 g., 0.9990 Gold 0.4995 oz. AGW **Obv:** Portrait of Qi
Bashi **Rev:** Squirrels eating grapes **Note:** Prev. Y#1005, 1029.

Date	Mintage	F	VF	XF	Unc	BU
1997 Proof	5,000	Value: 520				

KM# 1088   50 YUAN
15.5517 g., 0.9990 Gold 0.4999 oz. AGW **Subject:** Romance
of the Three Kingdoms **Rev:** Soldiers on a boat **Note:** Prev.
Y#1179.

Date	Mintage	F	VF	XF	Unc	BU
1997 Proof	3,000	Value: 500				

KM# 1044   50 YUAN
15.5517 g., 0.9990 Gold 0.4995 oz. AGW **Subject:** Return of
Hong Kong to China - Series III **Obv:** Tiananmen Square -
Forbidden City **Rev:** Flag and fireworks above Hong Kong,
denomination below **Note:** Prev. Y#903.

Date	Mintage	F	VF	XF	Unc	BU
1997 Proof	11,800	Value: 500				

KM# 1049   50 YUAN
155.5517 g., 0.9990 Gold 4.9959 oz. AGW **Subject:** Return of
Macao to China **Obv:** Tiananmen Square - Forbidden City
Rev: Deng Xiaoping viewing Macao **Note:** Prev. Y#906a.

Date	Mintage	F	VF	XF	Unc	BU
1997 Proof	11,800	Value: 500				

KM# 1043   50 YUAN
155.5175 g., 0.9990 Gold 4.9959 oz. AGW **Subject:** People's
Liberation Army **Obv:** Radiant star above Great Wall
Rev: Youthful Chairman Mao standing **Note:** Prev. Y#910.

Date	Mintage	F	VF	XF	Unc	BU
1997 Proof	12,000	Value: 500				

KM# 1061   50 YUAN
155.5175 g., 0.9990 Silver 4.9948 oz. ASW **Subject:** Traditional
Chinese Mascot **Obv:** Ornamental column **Rev:** Child holding
carp **Note:** Prev. Y#918.

Date	Mintage	F	VF	XF	Unc	BU
1997 Proof	3,800	Value: 125				

KM# 1040   50 YUAN
15.5517 g., 0.9990 Gold 0.4995 oz. AGW **Subject:** Chinese
Wildlife **Obv:** National emblem, date below **Rev:** Two white
dolphins, denomination at right **Note:** Prev. Y#921.

Date	Mintage	F	VF	XF	Unc	BU
1997 Proof	30,000	Value: 500				

KM# 1019   50 YUAN
151.2600 g., 0.9990 Silver 4.8581 oz. ASW, 70 mm.
Subject: Painting Master Qi Baishi **Rev:** Basket

Date	Mintage	F	VF	XF	Unc	BU
1997 Proof	999	Value: 150				

KM# 1082   50 YUAN
155.5000 g., 0.9990 Silver 4.9942 oz. ASW, 70 mm.
Series: Yellow river culture **Rev:** Female in flight

Date	Mintage	F	VF	XF	Unc	BU
1997 Proof	1,000	Value: 260				

KM# 1089   50 YUAN
151.5000 g., 0.9990 Silver 4.8658 oz. ASW, 70 mm.
Series: Classic literature **Rev:** Man and woman and 4 others
standing by banners

Date	Mintage	F	VF	XF	Unc	BU
1997 Proof	1,500	Value: 260				

KM# 1107   50 YUAN
10.1000 g., 0.9160 Gold 0.2974 oz. AGW, 23 mm. **Series:** Silk
Road **Rev:** Man with horse

Date	Mintage	F	VF	XF	Unc	BU
1997 Proof	10,000	Value: 300				

KM# 1195   50 YUAN
15.5000 g., 0.9990 Gold 0.4978 oz. AGW, 19 x 29 mm.
Series: Guilien scenery **Obv:** Tall out crop with pagoda at top
Rev: Tall coastal islands

Date	Mintage	F	VF	XF	Unc	BU
1998 Proof	1,600	Value: 450				

KM# 1153   50 YUAN
15.5517 g., 0.9990 Gold 0.4995 oz. AGW   **Subject:** Zhou Enlai
Note: Prev. Y#1007.

Date	Mintage	F	VF	XF	Unc	BU
1998 Proof	8,000	Value: 520				

KM# 1156   50 YUAN
15.5517 g., 0.9999 Gold 0.4999 oz. AGW   **Subject:** Liu Shao Qi
Obv: Portrait **Rev:** Temple **Note:** Prev. Y#1180.

Date	Mintage	F	VF	XF	Unc	BU
1998 Proof	8,000	Value: 500				

KM# 1160   50 YUAN
100.0000 g., 0.9990 Silver 3.2117 oz. ASW, 60 mm.
Series: Kuan Yin **Rev:** Multi armed seated statue

Date	Mintage	F	VF	XF	Unc	BU
1998 Proof	—	Value: 125				

KM# 1169   50 YUAN
15.5600 g., 0.9990 Gold 0.4997 oz. AGW, 27 mm.
Subject: Macao's return to China **Rev:** Birds flying over lablet, lighthouse at left, gate at right

Date	Mintage	F	VF	XF	Unc	BU
1998 Proof	11,800	Value: 450				

KM# 1170   50 YUAN
151.5000 g., 0.9990 Silver 4.8658 oz. ASW, 70 mm.
Subject: Macao's return to China **Rev:** Birds flying over lablet, lighthouse at left, gate at right

Date	Mintage	F	VF	XF	Unc	BU
1998 Proof	5,000	Value: 250				

KM# 1179   50 YUAN
155.5000 g., 0.9990 Silver 4.9942 oz. ASW, 70 mm.   **Subject:** Spring greeting **Obv:** Lantern and rays **Rev:** Three figures

Date	Mintage	F	VF	XF	Unc	BU
1998 Proof	1,500	Value: 250				

KM# 1187   50 YUAN
155.5000 g., 0.9990 Silver Colorized 4.9942 oz. ASW, 90 x 40 mm.   **Obv:** Long budding **Rev:** Six females

Date	Mintage	F	VF	XF	Unc	BU
1998 Proof	18,800	Value: 250				

KM# 1192   50 YUAN
15.5000 g., 0.9990 Gold 0.4978 oz. AGW, 19 x 29 mm.
Series: Guilien scenery **Obv:** Pastural bridge archway at sea shore **Rev:** Tall coastal islands

Date	Mintage	F	VF	XF	Unc	BU
1998 Proof	1,600	Value: 450				

KM# 1193   50 YUAN
15.5000 g., 0.9990 Gold 0.4978 oz. AGW, 19 x 29 mm.   **Series:** Guilien scenery **Obv:** 4 arched bridge **Rev:** Tall coastal islands

Date	Mintage	F	VF	XF	Unc	BU
1998 Proof	1,600	Value: 450				

KM# 1194   50 YUAN
15.5000 g., 0.9990 Gold 0.4978 oz. AGW, 19 x 29 mm.
Series: Guilien scenery **Obv:** Long arched bridge **Rev:** Tall coastal islands

Date	Mintage	F	VF	XF	Unc	BU
1998 Proof	1,600	Value: 450				

KM# 1250   50 YUAN
15.5517 g., 0.9990 Gold 0.4995 oz. AGW   **Subject:** 50th Anniversary of People's Republic **Note:** Prev. Y#1008.

Date	Mintage	F	VF	XF	Unc	BU
1999 Proof	15,700	Value: 500				

KM# 1245   50 YUAN
15.5600 g., 0.9990 Gold 0.4997 oz. AGW, 19 x 29 mm.
Subject: Master Painter Zhang Daqian **Obv:** Bust facing
Rev: Two riders on oxen

Date	Mintage	F	VF	XF	Unc	BU
1999 Proof	6,000	Value: 450				

KM# 1249   50 YUAN
15.5600 g., 0.9990 Gold 0.4997 oz. AGW, 27 mm.
Subject: 50th Anniversary of PRC **Rev:** Winged column

Date	Mintage	F	VF	XF	Unc	BU
1999 Proof	15,700	Value: 450				

KM# A1259   50 YUAN
151.5000 g., 0.9990 Silver 4.8658 oz. ASW, 70 mm.
Series: Traditional Chinese suspicious matters **Obv:** Winged column and rays

Date	Mintage	F	VF	XF	Unc	BU
1999 Proof	5,000	Value: 250				

KM# 1261   50 YUAN
151.5000 g., 0.9990 Silver 4.8658 oz. ASW, 90 x 40 mm.
Series: Ancient Chinese painting **Rev:** Men on horseback right
Note: Colorized

Date	Mintage	F	VF	XF	Unc	BU
1999 Proof	18,800	Value: 250				

KM# 1280   50 YUAN
15.5000 g., 0.9990 Gold 0.4978 oz. AGW, 27 mm.
Subject: Return of Macao **Rev:** 99 above buildings

Date	Mintage	F	VF	XF	Unc	BU
1999 Proof	11,800	Value: 450				

KM# 1281   50 YUAN
155.5000 g., 0.9990 Silver 4.9942 oz. ASW, 70 mm.
Subject: Rdturn of Macao **Rev:** Views of Macao

Date	Mintage	F	VF	XF	Unc	BU
1999 Proof	5,000	Value: 250				

KM# 1287   50 YUAN
15.5000 g., 0.9990 Gold 0.4978 oz. AGW, 27 mm.
Subject: Bejing opera **Rev:** Actor bowing

Date	Mintage	F	VF	XF	Unc	BU
1999 Proof	8,000	Value: 450				

KM# 1288   50 YUAN
155.0000 g., 0.9990 Silver 4.9782 oz. ASW, 90 x 40 mm.
Rev: 5 actors, one with banner **Note:** Colorized

Date	Mintage	F	VF	XF	Unc	BU
1999 Proof	11,800	Value: 250				

KM# 1342   50 YUAN
15.5000 g., 0.9990 Gold 0.4978 oz. AGW, 27 mm.   **Subject:** Beijing opera **Rev:** Performer and kettle drum **Note:** Colorized

Date	Mintage	F	VF	XF	Unc	BU
2000 Proof	8,000	Value: 450				

KM# 1333   50 YUAN
17.0000 g., 0.9990 Gold 0.5460 oz. AGW, 27 mm.   **Subject:** Y2K **Obv:** Monument **Rev:** World Globe as an eye above value within silver plated outer ring **Edge:** Reeded **Note:** Prev. Y#1236.

Date	Mintage	F	VF	XF	Unc	BU
2000 Proof	20,000	Value: 575				

KM# 1323   50 YUAN
155.5175 g., 0.9990 Silver 4.9948 oz. ASW   **Rev:** Dragons
Note: Prev. Y#1049.

Date	Mintage	F	VF	XF	Unc	BU
2000 Proof	1,888	Value: 360				

KM# 1334   50 YUAN
Bi-Metallic Gold center in Silver ring   **Subject:** Y-2-K **Note:** Prev. Y#1137.

Date	Mintage	F	VF	XF	Unc	BU
2000	20,000	Value: 400				

KM# 1315   50 YUAN
15.5000 g., 0.9990 Gold 0.4978 oz. AGW, 27 mm.
Series: Classic literature **Subject:** Dream of red mansion
Rev: Female standing looking at flora, parrots **Note:** Colorized

Date	Mintage	F	VF	XF	Unc	BU
2000 Proof	8,800	Value: 450				

KM# 1316   50 YUAN
155.5000 g., 0.9990 Silver 4.9942 oz. ASW, 28.5 x 120 mm.
Series: Classic literature **Subject:** Dream of red mansion
Rev: Two figures standing around basin **Note:** Colorized

Date	Mintage	F	VF	XF	Unc	BU
2000 Proof	11,800	Value: 250				

KM# 1343   50 YUAN
155.5000 g., 0.9990 Silver 4.9942 oz. ASW, 90 x 40 mm.
Subject: Bejing opera **Rev:** Five performers **Note:** Colorized

Date	Mintage	F	VF	XF	Unc	BU
2000 Proof	11,800	Value: 250				

KM# 80   100 YUAN
11.0000 g., 0.9000 Gold 0.3183 oz. AGW   **Obv:** Building, date at right **Rev:** Marco Polo bust, top right, ship below, denomination at bottom **Note:** Prev. Y#56.

Date	Mintage	F	VF	XF	Unc	BU
1983 Proof	1,030	Value: 600				

KM# 102   100 YUAN
11.3180 g., 0.9170 Gold 0.3337 oz. AGW   **Obv:** National emblem, date below **Rev:** Emperor Huang Di, denomination below **Note:** Prev. Y#72.

Date	Mintage	F	VF	XF	Unc	BU
1984 Proof	10,000	Value: 325				

KM# 125   100 YUAN
11.3180 g., 0.9170 Gold 0.3337 oz. AGW, 23 mm.
Subject: Founders of Chinese Culture **Rev:** Confucius, denomination at right **Note:** Prev. Y#94.

Date	Mintage	F	VF	XF	Unc	BU
1985 Proof	7,000	Value: 325				

KM# 151   100 YUAN
11.3180 g., 0.9170 Gold 0.3337 oz. AGW   **Subject:** Wildlife
Obv: National emblem, date below **Rev:** Wild Yak, left, denomination at left **Note:** Prev. Y#107.

Date	Mintage	F	VF	XF	Unc	BU
1986 Proof	3,000	Value: 325				

KM# 145   100 YUAN
11.3180 g., 0.9170 Gold 0.3337 oz. AGW, 23 mm.
Subject: Chinese Culture **Obv:** National emblem, date below
Rev: Revolutionary Soldier, Liu Bang on horseback, denomination at left **Note:** Prev. Y#117.

Date	Mintage	F	VF	XF	Unc	BU
1986 Proof	7,000	Value: 325				

KM# 149   100 YUAN
11.3180 g., 0.9170 Gold 0.3337 oz. AGW   **Subject:** Year of Peace **Rev:** Statue of seated female **Note:** Prev. Y#120.

Date	Mintage	F	VF	XF	Unc	BU
1986 Proof	1,000	Value: 660				

KM# 176   100 YUAN
11.3180 g., 0.9170 Gold 0.3337 oz. AGW   **Obv:** National emblem, date below **Rev:** Emperor Li Shih on horseback, denomination at right **Note:** Prev. Y#139.

Date	Mintage	F	VF	XF	Unc	BU
1987 Proof	7,000	Value: 350				

KM# 177   100 YUAN
373.2360 g., 0.9990 Silver 11.987 oz. ASW, 80 mm.
Subject: 125th Anniversary - Birth of Zhan Tianyou **Obv:** National emblem, date below **Rev:** Bust of Zhan Tianyou facing above steam locomotive on bridge, denomination below, dates above
Note: Illustration reduced. Prev. Y#131.

Date	Mintage	F	VF	XF	Unc	BU
1987 Proof	2,911	Value: 275				

KM# 211 100 YUAN
11.3180 g., 0.9170 Gold 0.3337 oz. AGW **Rev:** Empéror Zhao Kuangyin, denomination at right **Note:** Prev. Y#164.

Date	Mintage	F	VF	XF	Unc	BU
1988 Proof	Est. 7,000	Value: 350				

KM# 214 100 YUAN
8.0000 g., 0.9170 Gold 0.2358 oz. AGW **Subject:** Rare Animal Protection **Obv:** National emblem, date below **Rev:** Golden monkey, denomination at left **Note:** Prev. Y#167.

Date	Mintage	F	VF	XF	Unc	BU
1988 Proof	29,000	Value: 250				

KM# 206 100 YUAN
15.5500 g., 0.9990 Gold 0.4994 oz. AGW **Series:** Seoul 1988 - 24th Summer Olympic Games **Obv:** National emblem, date below **Rev:** Rhythmic gymnast, denomination at right **Note:** Prev. Y#173.

Date	Mintage	F	VF	XF	Unc	BU
1988 Proof	5,500	Value: 525				

KM# 244 100 YUAN
8.0000 g., 0.9170 Gold 0.2358 oz. AGW **Subject:** 11th Asian Games - Beijing 1990 **Obv:** Stadium **Rev:** Ribbon dancer, denomination below **Note:** Prev. Y#203.

Date	Mintage	F	VF	XF	Unc	BU
1989 Proof	Est. 7,000	Value: 250				

KM# 252 100 YUAN
11.3180 g., 0.9170 Gold 0.3337 oz. AGW **Obv:** National emblem, date below **Rev:** Genghis Khan on horseback, denomination at left **Note:** Prev. Y#217.

Date	Mintage	F	VF	XF	Unc	BU
1989 Proof	Est. 7,000	Value: 350				

KM# 261 100 YUAN
11.3180 g., 0.9170 Gold 0.3337 oz. AGW **Series:** Save the Children Fund **Obv:** National emblem, date below **Rev:** Child running flying kites, denomination lower right **Note:** Prev. Y#231.

Date	Mintage	F	VF	XF	Unc	BU
1989 Proof	5,000	Value: 325				

KM# 255 100 YUAN
8.0000 g., 0.9170 Gold 0.2358 oz. AGW **Series:** Endangered Animals **Obv:** National emblem, date below **Rev:** Chinese tiger, denomination at left **Note:** Prev. Y#250.

Date	Mintage	F	VF	XF	Unc	BU
1989 Proof	14,000	Value: 250				

KM# 258 100 YUAN
7.7750 g., 0.9990 Gold 0.2497 oz. AGW **Subject:** 40th Anniversary of People's Republic **Obv:** National emblem, date at right **Rev:** Pair of flying cranes, denomination at left **Note:** Prev. Y#299.

Date	Mintage	F	VF	XF	Unc	BU
1989 Proof	1,000	Value: 315				

KM# 314 100 YUAN
11.3180 g., 0.9170 Gold 0.3337 oz. AGW **Obv:** National emblem, date below **Rev:** Emperor Zhu Yuanzhang seated, denomination upper left **Note:** Prev. Y#306.

Date	Mintage	F	VF	XF	Unc	BU
1990	Est. 7,000	—	—	—	—	350

KM# 304 100 YUAN
11.3180 g., 0.9170 Gold 0.3337 oz. AGW **Series:** Barcelona 1992 - 25th Summer Olympic Games **Obv:** National emblem, date below **Rev:** 2 women playing basketball, denomination at right **Note:** Prev. Y#327.

Date	Mintage	F	VF	XF	Unc	BU
1990	10,000	—	—	—	—	325

KM# 267 100 YUAN
8.0000 g., 0.9170 Gold 0.2358 oz. AGW **Subject:** XI Asian Games - Beijing 1990 **Obv:** Roman numeral above stadium, date below **Rev:** Swimmer, denomination lower left **Note:** Prev. Y#256.

Date	Mintage	F	VF	XF	Unc	BU
1990 Proof	10,000	Value: 250				

KM# 309 100 YUAN
10.3700 g., 0.9170 Gold 0.3057 oz. AGW **Obv:** National emblem, date below **Rev:** First emperor, Huang Di standing, denomination at right **Note:** Prev. Y#287.

Date	Mintage	F	VF	XF	Unc	BU
1990 Proof	20,000	Value: 325				

KM# 371 100 YUAN
8.0000 g., 0.9160 Gold 0.2356 oz. AGW **Subject:** Women's 1st World Football Cup **Obv:** Stadium, date below **Rev:** Woman kicking ball, denomination at right **Note:** Prev. Y#320.

Date	Mintage	F	VF	XF	Unc	BU
1991 Proof	1,400	Value: 250				

KM# 381 100 YUAN
8.0000 g., 0.9160 Gold 0.2356 oz. AGW **Subject:** Emperor Kang Xi, denomination at left **Obv:** National emblem, date below **Note:** Prev. Y#326.

Date	Mintage	F	VF	XF	Unc	BU
1991 Proof	Est. 7,000	Value: 320				

KM# 384 100 YUAN
31.1035 g., 0.9990 Gold 0.9990 oz. AGW **Obv:** Building, two dates below **Rev:** Sun Yat-sen in uniform, facing, denomination at left **Note:** Illustration reduced. Prev. Y#479.

Date	Mintage	F	VF	XF	Unc	BU
ND(1991) Proof	1,000	Value: 1,100				

KM# 298 100 YUAN
11.3180 g., 0.9170 Gold 0.3337 oz. AGW **Series:** Albertville 1992 - 16th Winter Olympic Games **Obv:** National emblem, date below **Rev:** Pairs figure skating, denomination lower right **Note:** Prev. Y#473.

Date	Mintage	F	VF	XF	Unc	BU
1991 Proof	10,000	Value: 325				

KM# 385 100 YUAN
8.6000 g., 0.9170 Gold 0.2535 oz. AGW **Subject:** 80th Anniversary - 1911 Revolution **Obv:** Building **Rev:** Sun Yat-sen writing, denomination at right **Note:** Prev. Y#478.

Date	Mintage	F	VF	XF	Unc	BU
1991 Proof	2,500	Value: 325				

KM# 376 100 YUAN
11.3180 g., 0.9170 Gold 0.3337 oz. AGW **Rev:** Emperor Yan Di, denomination upper right **Note:** Prev. Y#545.

Date	Mintage	F	VF	XF	Unc	BU
1991 Proof	10,000	Value: 350				

KM# 445   100 YUAN
10.3700 g., 0.9170 Gold 0.3057 oz. AGW **Obv:** National
emblem, date below **Rev:** Emperor Da Yu, denomination at right
Note: Prev. Y#546.

Date	Mintage	F	VF	XF	Unc	BU
1992 Proof	10,000	Value: 350				

KM# 451   100 YUAN
11.3180 g., 0.9170 Gold 0.3337 oz. AGW **Obv:** National
emblem, date below **Rev:** Wu Zetian "The Iron Lady" 603-705AD,
Stateswoman, denomination at right **Note:** Prev. Y#554.

Date	Mintage	F	VF	XF	Unc	BU
1992 Proof	25,000	Value: 325				

KM# 440   100 YUAN
11.3180 g., 0.9170 Gold 0.3337 oz. AGW **Series:** 1994
Olympics **Obv:** Temple of Heaven **Rev:** Male figure skater,
denomination below **Note:** Prev. Y#692.

Date	Mintage	F	VF	XF	Unc	BU
1992 Proof	10,000	Value: 325				

KM# 456   100 YUAN
8.0000 g., 0.9170 Gold 0.2358 oz. AGW **Series:** Endangered
Wildlife **Rev:** Mountain sheep, denomination below **Note:** Prev.
Y#693.

Date	Mintage	F	VF	XF	Unc	BU
1992 Proof	5,000	Value: 325				

KM# 464   100 YUAN
33.9600 g., 0.9160 Gold 1.0000 oz. AGW **Subject:** Archeological
Finds **Obv:** National emblem **Rev:** Resting deer with long antlers
Note: Prev. Y#754.

Date	Mintage	F	VF	XF	Unc	BU
1992 Proof	500	Value: 1,375				

KM# 415   100 YUAN
31.1035 g., 0.9990 Gold 0.9990 oz. AGW **Subject:** Chinese
Inventions **Obv:** Great Wall, date below **Rev:** Ancient ships and
shipbuilding, denomination lower left **Note:** Prev. Y#336.

Date	Mintage	F	VF	XF	Unc	BU
1992 Proof	1,000	Value: 1,000				

KM# 418   100 YUAN
31.1035 g., 0.9990 Gold 0.9990 oz. AGW **Subject:** Chinese
Inventions **Rev:** First compass, denomination below **Note:** Prev.
Y#337.

Date	Mintage	F	VF	XF	Unc	BU
1992 Proof	1,000	Value: 1,000				

KM# 416   100 YUAN
31.1035 g., 0.9990 Gold 0.9990 oz. AGW **Subject:** Chinese
Inventions **Rev:** First seismograph, denomination below
Note: Prev. Y#338.

Date	Mintage	F	VF	XF	Unc	BU
1992 Proof	1,000	Value: 1,000				

KM# 417   100 YUAN
31.1035 g., 0.9990 Gold 0.9990 oz. AGW **Subject:** Chinese
Inventions **Obv:** Great Wall **Rev:** First kite, denomination below
Note: Prev. Y#339.

Date	Mintage	F	VF	XF	Unc	BU
1992 Proof	1,000	Value: 1,000				

KM# 419   100 YUAN
31.1035 g., 0.9990 Gold 0.9990 oz. AGW **Obv:** Great Wall, date
below **Rev:** Bronze Age Metal Working, large urn, denomination
below **Note:** Prev. Y#340.

Date	Mintage	F	VF	XF	Unc	BU
1992 Proof	1,000	Value: 1,000				

KM# 410   100 YUAN
31.1035 g., 0.9995 Platinum 0.9995 oz. APW, 32 mm.
Series: Scientific and technical inventions **Rev:** Ship

Date	Mintage	F	VF	XF	Unc	BU
1992 Proof	100	Value: 1,000				

KM# 411   100 YUAN
31.1035 g., 0.9995 Platinum 0.9995 oz. APW, 32 mm.
Series: Scientific and technical inventions **Rev:** Large urn

Date	Mintage	F	VF	XF	Unc	BU
1992 Proof	100	Value: 1,000				

KM# 412   100 YUAN
31.1035 g., 0.9995 Platinum 0.9995 oz. APW, 32 mm.
Series: Scientific and technical inventions **Rev:** Kite flying

Date	Mintage	F	VF	XF	Unc	BU
1992 Proof	100	Value: 1,000				

KM# 413   100 YUAN
31.1035 g., 0.9995 Platinum 0.9995 oz. APW, 32 mm.
Series: Scientific and technical inventions

Date	Mintage	F	VF	XF	Unc	BU
1992 Proof	100	Value: 1,000				

KM# 414   100 YUAN
31.1035 g., 0.9995 Platinum 0.9995 oz. APW, 32 mm.
Series: Scientific and technical inventions **Rev:** Large urn with
flange

Date	Mintage	F	VF	XF	Unc	BU
1992 Proof	100	Value: 1,000				

KM# 598   100 YUAN
31.1320 g., 0.9990 Gold 0.9999 oz. AGW **Obv:** Temple, date
below **Rev:** Two peacocks, denomination above **Note:** Prev.
Y#354.

Date	Mintage	F	VF	XF	Unc	BU
1993 Proof	1,200	Value: 1,000				

KM# 508   100 YUAN
31.1035 g., 0.9990 Gold 0.9990 oz. AGW **Obv:** Building and
Great Wall **Rev:** Chinese Gods: Fu, Lu, and Shu **Note:** Prev.
Y#406.

Date	Mintage	F	VF	XF	Unc	BU
1993 Proof	888	Value: 1,100				

KM# 574   100 YUAN
33.9500 g., 0.9170 Gold 1.0009 oz. AGW **Subject:** Bronze Age
Sculptures **Obv:** National emblem, date below **Rev:** Bull lantern,
denomination at left **Note:** Prev. Y#411.

Date	Mintage	F	VF	XF	Unc	BU
1993 Proof	350	Value: 1,675				

KM# 539   100 YUAN
8.0000 g., 0.9160 Gold 0.2356 oz. AGW **Obv:** National emblem,
date below **Rev:** Bust of Soong Ching-ling half left, 1892-1981,
Revolutionary Stateswoman, denomination at right **Note:** Prev.
Y#760.

Date	Mintage	F	VF	XF	Unc	BU
1993 Proof	2,000	Value: 260				

KM# 535   100 YUAN
31.1035 g., 0.9990 Gold 0.9990 oz. AGW **Obv:** Home of Sun
Yat-sen **Rev:** Bust of Sun Yat-sen, facing, denomination at right
Note: Prev. Y#763.

Date	Mintage	F	VF	XF	Unc	BU
1993 Proof	8,888	Value: 1,000				

KM# 592   100 YUAN
31.1035 g., 0.9990 Gold 0.9990 oz. AGW **Subject:** Mount Tai
Obv: Great Wall **Rev:** Temple **Note:** Prev. Y#777.

Date	Mintage	F	VF	XF	Unc	BU
1993 Proof	8,888	Value: 1,000				

KM# 523   100 YUAN
10.3600 g., 0.9170 Gold 0.3054 oz. AGW **Subject:** World Cup Soccer **Obv:** National emblem, date below **Rev:** Player kicking ball, denomination at left **Note:** Prev. Y#491.

Date	Mintage	F	VF	XF	Unc	BU
1993 Proof	5,000	Value: 300				

KM# 551   100 YUAN
31.1035 g., 0.9990 Gold 0.9990 oz. AGW **Obv:** Great Wall, date below **Rev:** Guanyin, Goddess of Mercy, seated in flower, denomination at left **Note:** Prev. Y#504.

Date	Mintage	F	VF	XF	Unc	BU
1993 Proof	1,000	Value: 1,000				

KM# 534   100 YUAN
11.3180 g., 0.9170 Gold 0.3337 oz. AGW **Obv:** National emblem, date below **Rev:** Bust of Chairman Mao Zedong, right, denomination at left **Note:** Prev. Y#538.

Date	Mintage	F	VF	XF	Unc	BU
1993 Proof	Est. 7,000	Value: 345				

KM# 566   100 YUAN
8.0000 g., 0.9160 Gold 0.2356 oz. AGW, 23 mm. **Series:** Endangered wildlife **Rev:** Panda climbing tree

Date	Mintage	F	VF	XF	Unc	BU
1993 Proof	5,000	Value: 250				

KM# 682   100 YUAN
31.1035 g., 0.9990 Gold 0.9990 oz. AGW **Obv:** Child riding Eastern Unicorn, date below **Rev:** Unicorn, denomination at left, rose sprays below **Note:** Prev. Y#427.

Date	Mintage	F	VF	XF	Unc	BU
1994 Proof	1,100	Value: 1,000				

KM# 653   100 YUAN
8.0000 g., 0.9170 Gold 0.2358 oz. AGW **Subject:** 12th Asian Games **Obv:** National emblem, row of athletic figures below, date at bottom **Rev:** Gymnast on bars, denomination at right **Note:** Prev. Y#440.

Date	Mintage	F	VF	XF	Unc	BU
1994 Proof	3,000	Value: 250				

KM# 681   100 YUAN
373.2360 g., 0.9990 Silver 11.987 oz. ASW, 85 mm. **Rev:** Unicorn with offspring, denomination at left **Note:** Illustration reduced. Prev. Y#426.

Date	Mintage	F	VF	XF	Unc	BU
1994 Proof	2,000	Value: 300				

KM# 658   100 YUAN
10.3600 g., 0.9170 Gold 0.3054 oz. AGW **Obv:** National emblem **Rev:** Emperor Zhou Wenwang, denomination at left **Note:** Prev. Y#543.

Date	Mintage	F	VF	XF	Unc	BU
1994 Proof	10,000	Value: 375				

KM# 529   100 YUAN
10.3000 g., 0.9990 Gold 0.3308 oz. AGW **Series:** Centennial Olympics, Atlanta 1994 - 26th Summer Olympic Games **Rev:** Female torch runner, denomination lower left **Note:** Prev. Y#497.

Date	Mintage	F	VF	XF	Unc	BU
1994 Proof	5,000	Value: 300				

KM# 672   100 YUAN
15.5500 g., 0.9160 Gold 0.4579 oz. AGW **Obv:** Building, date below **Rev:** Black-billed magpie on branch, denomination below **Note:** Prev. Y#695.

Date	Mintage	F	VF	XF	Unc	BU
1994 Proof	1,300	Value: 500				

KM# 699   100 YUAN
373.2400 g., 0.9990 Silver 11.987 oz. ASW, 80 mm. **Rev:** Two children with dog

Date	Mintage	F	VF	XF	Unc	BU
1994 Proof	400	Value: 500				

KM# 802   100 YUAN
373.2360 g., 0.9990 Silver 11.987 oz. ASW, 98 mm. **Rev:** Unicorn with offspring, denomination at left **Note:** Illustration reduced. Prev. Y#698.

Date	Mintage	F	VF	XF	Unc	BU
1995 Proof	—	Value: 325				

KM# 803   100 YUAN
31.1035 g., 0.9990 Gold 0.9990 oz. AGW, 32 mm. **Subject:** Unicorn **Obv:** Eastern unicorn **Rev:** Western unicorn with offspring **Edge:** Reeded **Note:** Prev. Y#1012; 1062.

Date	Mintage	F	VF	XF	Unc	BU
1995 Proof	—	Value: 1,000				

KM# 810   100 YUAN
31.1035 g., 0.9990 Gold 0.9990 oz. AGW **Subject:** 50th Anniversary - Anti-Japanese War **Rev:** People at wall, denomination below **Note:** Prev. Y#696.

Date	Mintage	F	VF	XF	Unc	BU
1995 Proof	1,400	Value: 1,000				

KM# 809   100 YUAN
31.1035 g., 0.9990 Gold 0.9990 oz. AGW **Rev:** Soldiers above bridge guarded by chinze, denomination at right **Note:** Prev. Y#697.

Date	Mintage	F	VF	XF	Unc	BU
1995 Proof	1,400	Value: 1,000				

KM# 838   100 YUAN
31.1035 g., 0.9990 Gold 0.9990 oz. AGW **Subject:** Chinese Culture Series **Obv:** Great Wall seen through arch **Rev:** Pagoda of Six Harmonies **Note:** Prev. Y#804.

Date	Mintage	F	VF	XF	Unc	BU
1995 Proof	1,000	Value: 975				

KM# 835   100 YUAN
31.0103 g., 0.9990 Gold 0.9960 oz. AGW **Subject:** Chinese Culture Series **Obv:** Great Wall seen through arch **Rev:** Mencius seated at table **Note:** Prev. Y#805.

Date	Mintage	F	VF	XF	Unc	BU
1995 Proof	1,000	Value: 975				

KM# 837   100 YUAN
31.0103 g., 0.9990 Gold 0.9960 oz. AGW **Subject:** Chinese Culture Series **Obv:** Great Wall seen through arch **Rev:** Tang Taizong seated **Note:** Prev. Y#806.

Date	Mintage	F	VF	XF	Unc	BU
1995 Proof	1,000	Value: 975				

KM# 836   100 YUAN
31.0103 g., 0.9990 Gold 0.9960 oz. AGW **Subject:** Chinese Culture Series **Obv:** Great Wall seen through arch **Rev:** Lion dance **Note:** Prev. Y#807.

Date	Mintage	F	VF	XF	Unc	BU
1995 Proof	1,000	Value: 975				

KM# 839   100 YUAN
31.1035 g., 0.9990 Gold 0.9990 oz. AGW **Subject:** Chinese Culture Series **Obv:** Great Wall seen through arch **Rev:** Female opera role **Note:** Prev. Y#808.

Date	Mintage	F	VF	XF	Unc	BU
1995 Proof	1,000	Value: 975				

KM# 872   100 YUAN
16.9779 g., 0.9160 Gold 0.5000 oz. AGW **Obv:** Great Wall, date below **Rev:** Perched eagle, denomination lower right **Note:** Prev. Y#810.

Date	Mintage	F	VF	XF	Unc	BU
1995 Proof	1,300	Value: 500				

KM# 772   100 YUAN
373.2420 g., 0.9990 Silver 11.987 oz. ASW **Subject:** Zheng Chenggong **Obv:** Chiqian building **Rev:** Standing figure with flag and ships **Note:** Prev. Y#823.

Date	Mintage	F	VF	XF	Unc	BU
1995 Proof	150	Value: 900				

KM# 853   100 YUAN
31.1035 g., 0.9990 Gold 0.9990 oz. AGW **Subject:** Romance of the Three Kingdoms **Obv:** Luo Guanzhong **Rev:** Standing Liu Bei with flags **Note:** Prev. Y#830.

Date	Mintage	F	VF	XF	Unc	BU
1995 Proof	1,500	Value: 1,000				

KM# 854   100 YUAN
31.1035 g., 0.9990 Gold 0.9990 oz. AGW **Subject:** Romance of the Three Kingdoms **Obv:** Luo Guanzhong **Rev:** Seated Guan Yu reading **Note:** Prev. Y#831.

Date	Mintage	F	VF	XF	Unc	BU
1995 Proof	1,500	Value: 975				

KM# 856   100 YUAN
31.1035 g., 0.9990 Gold 0.9990 oz. AGW **Subject:** Romance of the Three Kingdoms **Obv:** Luo Guanzhong **Rev:** Zhang Fei on horseback **Note:** Prev. Y#832.

Date	Mintage	F	VF	XF	Unc	BU
1995 Proof	1,500	Value: 1,000				

KM# 855   100 YUAN
31.1035 g., 0.9990 Gold 0.9990 oz. AGW **Subject:** Romance of the Three Kingdoms **Obv:** Luo Guanzhong **Rev:** Zhuge Liang seated on throne **Note:** Prev. Y#833.

Date	Mintage	F	VF	XF	Unc	BU
1995 Proof	1,500	Value: 1,000				

KM# 765   100 YUAN
10.3678 g., 0.9990 Gold 0.3330 oz. AGW **Series:** 1996 Olympics **Obv:** National emblem, date below **Rev:** High diver, denomination below **Note:** Prev. Y#843.

Date	Mintage	F	VF	XF	Unc	BU
1995 Proof	10,000	Value: 325				

KM# 764   100 YUAN
10.3678 g., 0.9990 Gold 0.3330 oz. AGW **Series:** Olympics **Obv:** National emblem, date below **Rev:** Ribbon dancer, denomination at right **Note:** Prev. Y#844.

Date	Mintage	F	VF	XF	Unc	BU
1995 Proof	10,000	Value: 325				

KM# 947   100 YUAN
31.1035 g., 0.9990 Gold 0.9990 oz. AGW, 32 mm. **Obv:** Eastern unicorn **Rev:** Western unicorn in wreath **Edge:** Reeded **Note:** Prev. Y#956, 1014.

Date	Mintage	F	VF	XF	Unc	BU
1996 Proof	1,250	Value: 1,000				

KM# 948   100 YUAN
31.1035 g., 0.9990 Platinum 0.9990 oz. APW, 32 mm. **Subject:** Unicorn **Obv:** Eastern unicorn, full body **Rev:** Western unicorn and maiden **Edge:** Reeded **Note:** Prev. Y#956a.

Date	Mintage	F	VF	XF	Unc	BU
1996 Proof	500	Value: 2,000				

KM# 1034   100 YUAN
31.1035 g., 0.9995 Platinum 0.9995 oz. APW **Obv:** Eastern unicorn **Rev:** Western unicorn **Note:** Prev. Y#966.

Date	Mintage	F	VF	XF	Unc	BU
1997 Proof	500	Value: 2,000				

KM# 1092   100 YUAN
16.9779 g., 0.9160 Gold 0.5000 oz. AGW, 26.5 mm. **Subject:** Wildlife of China **Obv:** The Great Wall **Rev:** Penguin **Edge:** Plain **Note:** Prev. Y#1080.

Date	Mintage	F	VF	XF	Unc	BU
1997 Proof	2,800	Value: 500				

KM# 1021   100 YUAN
373.2400 g., 0.9990 Silver 11.987 oz. ASW, 80 mm. **Subject:** Painting Master Qi Baishi **Rev:** Leaves & praying mantis

Date	Mintage	F	VF	XF	Unc	BU
1997 Proof	80	Value: 250				

KM# 319   150 YUAN
622.0400 g., 0.9990 Silver 19.978 oz. ASW **Rev:** Phoenix and dragon **Note:** Prev. Y#208.

Date	Mintage	F	VF	XF	Unc	BU
1990 Proof	1,500	Value: 650				

KM# 599   150 YUAN
622.0400 g., 0.9990 Silver 19.978 oz. ASW **Obv:** Temple of Harmony **Rev:** Two peacocks, denomination below **Note:** Prev. Y#355.

Date	Mintage	F	VF	XF	Unc	BU
1993 Proof	500	Value: 650				

KM# 683   150 YUAN
622.0400 g., 0.9990 Silver 19.978 oz. ASW **Obv:** Figure on Eastern unicorn, date below **Rev:** Unicorn, denomination at left, rose sprays below **Note:** Prev. Y#428.

Date	Mintage	F	VF	XF	Unc	BU
1994 Proof	500	Value: 500				

KM# 804   150 YUAN
622.0400 g., 0.9990 Silver 19.978 oz. ASW, 98 mm. **Obv:** Eastern unicorn, rearing, date below **Rev:** Unicorn with offspring **Note:** Illustration reduced. Prev. Y#699.

Date	Mintage	F	VF	XF	Unc	BU
1995	—	—	—	—	450	—

KM# 976   150 YUAN
622.0400 g., 0.9990 Silver 19.978 oz. ASW **Obv:** Eastern unicorn, date below **Rev:** Western unicorn, rearing, denomination below **Note:** Prev. Y#884.

Date	Mintage	F	VF	XF	Unc	BU
1996 Proof	500	Value: 600				

KM# 46   200 YUAN
8.4700 g., 0.9170 Gold 0.2497 oz. AGW **Subject:** Chinese Bronze Age Finds **Obv:** National emblem **Rev:** Leopard, denomination below **Note:** Prev. Y#28.

Date	Mintage	F	VF	XF	Unc	BU
1981 Proof	1,000	Value: 420				

KM# 47   200 YUAN
8.4700 g., 0.9170 Gold 0.2497 oz. AGW **Subject:** Chinese Bronze Age Finds **Obv:** National emblem **Rev:** Winged creature, denomination below **Note:** Prev. Y#29.

Date	Mintage	F	VF	XF	Unc	BU
1981 Proof	1,000	Value: 650				

KM# 61   200 YUAN
8.4700 g., 0.9170 Gold 0.2497 oz. AGW **Subject:** World Cup
Soccer **Obv:** National emblem, date below **Rev:** Player kicking,
denomination below **Note:** Prev. Y#37.

Date	Mintage	F	VF	XF	Unc	BU
1982 Proof	1,261	Value: 500				

KM# 320   200 YUAN
62.2060 g., 0.9990 Gold 1.9979 oz. AGW **Obv:** Great Wall, date
below **Rev:** Denomination between Phoenix and dragon
Note: Prev. Y#209.

Date	Mintage	F	VF	XF	Unc	BU
1990 Proof	2,538	Value: 2,000				

KM# 420   200 YUAN
1000.0000 g., 0.9990 Silver 32.117 oz. ASW, 100 mm.
Series: Scientific and technical inventions **Rev:** Ship

Date	Mintage	F	VF	XF	Unc	BU
1992 Proof	250	Value: 400				

KM# 421   200 YUAN
1000.0000 g., 0.9990 Silver 32.117 oz. ASW, 100 mm.
Series: Scientific and technical inventions **Rev:** Large urn

Date	Mintage	F	VF	XF	Unc	BU
1992 Proof	250	Value: 400				

KM# 422   200 YUAN
1000.0000 g., 0.9990 Silver 32.117 oz. ASW, 100 mm.
Series: Scientific and technical inventions **Rev:** Kite flying

Date	Mintage	F	VF	XF	Unc	BU
1992	250	Value: 400				

KM# 423   200 YUAN
1000.0000 g., 0.9990 Silver 32.117 oz. ASW, 100 mm.
Series: Scientific and technical inventions **Rev:** Spoon on table

Date	Mintage	F	VF	XF	Unc	BU
1992 Proof	250	Value: 400				

KM# 424   200 YUAN
1000.0000 g., 0.9990 Silver 32.117 oz. ASW, 100 mm. **Series:**
Scientific and technical inventions **Rev:** Large urn with flags

Date	Mintage	F	VF	XF	Unc	BU
1992 Proof	250	Value: 400				

KM# 863   200 YUAN
1000.0000 g., 0.9990 Silver 32.117 oz. ASW, 100 mm.
Subject: 50th Anniversary - Return of Taiwan to China **Obv:**
Great Wall **Rev:** Taiwan and China maps **Note:** Prev. Y#816.

Date	Mintage	F	VF	XF	Unc	BU
1995 Proof	100	Value: 2,150				

KM# 1052   200 YUAN
1000.0000 g., 0.9990 Silver 32.117 oz. ASW **Subject:** Sino -
Thailand Friendship **Obv:** Forbidden City and Thai Royal Palace
Rev: 2 Buddha statues, one in cameo **Note:** Prev. Y#712.

Date	Mintage	F	VF	XF	Unc	BU
1997 Proof	880	Value: 1,000				

KM# 1022   200 YUAN
1000.0000 g., 0.9990 Silver 32.117 oz. ASW, 100 mm.
Subject: Painting Master Qui Baishi **Rev:** Two baskets

Date	Mintage	F	VF	XF	Unc	BU
1997 Proof	188	Value: 500				

KM# 1198   200 YUAN
1000.0000 g., 0.9990 Silver 32.117 oz. ASW **Subject:** Vault
protector of the Tang Dynasty **Obv:** Cash coin **Rev:** Value and
flora

Date	Mintage	F	VF	XF	Unc	BU
1998 Proof	2,800	Value: 1,750				

KM# 28   250 YUAN
8.0000 g., 0.9170 Gold 0.2358 oz. AGW **Subject:** 1980 Winter
Olympics **Obv:** State seal **Rev:** Alpine skiing **Note:** Prev. Y#22.

Date	Mintage	F	VF	XF	Unc	BU
1980 Proof	10,000	Value: 225				

KM# 27   250 YUAN
8.0000 g., 0.9160 Gold 0.2356 oz. AGW, 23 mm.   **Rev:** Down
hill skier

Date	Mintage	F	VF	XF	Unc	BU
1980 Proof	20,000	Value: 250				

KM# 37   300 YUAN
10.0000 g., 0.9170 Gold 0.2948 oz. AGW **Series:** 1980
Olympics **Subject:** Archery **Obv:** National emblem,
denomination below **Rev:** Two archers, date below **Note:** Prev.
Y#23.

Date	Mintage	F	VF	XF	Unc	BU
1980 Proof	15,000	Value: 275				

KM# 668   300 YUAN
103.1250 g., 0.9990 Gold 3.3121 oz. AGW. **Obv:** Great Wall,
date below **Rev:** Guanyin, Goddess of Mercy, holding child,
facing, denomination at left **Note:** Prev. Y#515.

Date	Mintage	F	VF	XF	Unc	BU
1994 Proof	128	Value: 3,250				

KM# 1335   300 YUAN
1000.0000 g., 0.9990 Silver 32.117 oz. ASW, 100 mm. **Subject:**
The millennium **Rev:** Globe within eye design

Date	Mintage	F	VF	XF	Unc	BU
2000 Proof	3,000	Value: 1,000				

KM# 4   400 YUAN
16.9500 g., 0.9170 Gold 0.4997 oz. AGW **Obv:** National
emblem, two dates below **Rev:** 30th Anniversary of People's
Republic - Tiananmen, denomination below **Note:** Prev. Y#4.

Date	Mintage	F	VF	XF	Unc	BU
ND(1979) Proof	Est. 23,000	Value: 485				

KM# 5   400 YUAN
16.9500 g., 0.9170 Gold 0.4997 oz. AGW **Subject:** 30th
Anniversary of People's Republic **Obv:** National emblem, two
dates below **Rev:** People's Heroes Monument, denomination
below **Note:** Prev. Y#5.

Date	Mintage	F	VF	XF	Unc	BU
ND(1979) Proof	Est. 23,000	Value: 485				

KM# 6   400 YUAN
16.9500 g., 0.9170 Gold 0.4997 oz. AGW **Subject:** 30th
Anniversary of People's Republic **Obv:** National emblem, two
dates below **Rev:** Chairman Mao Memorial Hall, denomination
below **Note:** Prev. Y#6.

Date	Mintage	F	VF	XF	Unc	BU
ND(1979) Proof	Est. 23,000	Value: 485				

KM# 7   400 YUAN
16.9500 g., 0.9170 Gold 0.4997 oz. AGW **Subject:** 30th
Anniversary of People's Republic **Obv:** National emblem
Rev: Great Hall of the People **Note:** Prev. Y#7.

Date	Mintage	F	VF	XF	Unc	BU
ND(1979) Proof	Est. 23,000	Value: 485				

KM# 51   400 YUAN
13.3600 g., 0.9170 Gold 0.3939 oz. AGW **Subject:** 70th
Anniversary of 1911 Revolution **Obv:** Bust of Sun-Yat-sen,
facing, two dates below **Rev:** Nationalist troops attacking,
denomination and date below **Note:** Prev. Y#47.

Date	Mintage	F	VF	XF	Unc	BU
1981 Proof	1,338	Value: 1,100				

KM# 48   400 YUAN
16.9500 g., 0.9170 Gold 0.4997 oz. AGW **Subject:** Chinese
Bronze Age Finds **Obv:** State seal **Rev:** Rhinoceros, left,
denomination below **Note:** Prev. Y#30.

Date	Mintage	F	VF	XF	Unc	BU
1981 Proof	1,000	Value: 700				

KM# 9   450 YUAN
17.1700 g., 0.9000 Gold 0.4968 oz. AGW **Series:** International
Year of the Child **Obv:** State seal above floral sprays **Rev:** Two
children planting flower **Note:** Prev. Y#9.

Date	Mintage	F	VF	XF	Unc	BU
1979 Proof	Est. 12,000	Value: 485				

KM# 81   500 YUAN
155.5150 g., 0.9990 Gold 4.9947 oz. AGW, 60 mm.
Subject: Marco Polo bust on left, looking right, buildings at right, denomination below **Note:** Illustration reduced. Prev. Y#395.

Date	Mintage	F	VF	XF	Unc	BU
1983 Proof	100	Value: 5,000				

KM# 536   500 YUAN
155.5150 g., 0.9990 Gold 4.9947 oz. AGW **Subject:** Sun Yat-sen **Obv:** Home of Sun Yat-sen, date below **Rev:** Bust of Sun Yat-sen, facing, denomination at right **Note:** Prev. Y#764.

Date	Mintage	F	VF	XF	Unc	BU
1993 Proof	99	Value: 5,200				

KM# 544   500 YUAN
155.5150 g., 0.9990 Gold 4.9947 oz. AGW, 60 mm.
Subject: Chairman Mao **Obv:** Tall building, date at right **Rev:** 3/4 figure of Mao looking left, denomination at right **Note:** Illustration reduced. Prev. Y#415.

Date	Mintage	F	VF	XF	Unc	BU
1993 Proof	100	Value: 5,200				

KM# 593   500 YUAN
155.5150 g., 0.9990 Gold 4.9947 oz. AGW **Subject:** Tomb of Emperor Huang **Obv:** Great Wall, date below **Rev:** Tomb, denomination below **Note:** Prev. Y#778.

Date	Mintage	F	VF	XF	Unc	BU
1993 Proof	99	Value: 5,000				

KM# 509   500 YUAN
155.5150 g., 0.9990 Gold 4.9947 oz. AGW, 60 mm.
Subject: Chinese Gods: Fu, Lu and Shu, denomination below **Obv:** Building and Great Wall, date below **Rev:** Three gods with symbol on panel and child **Note:** Illustration reduced. Prev. Y#407.

Date	Mintage	F	VF	XF	Unc	BU
1993 Proof	99	Value: 5,000				

KM# 519   500 YUAN
155.5150 g., 0.9990 Gold 4.9947 oz. AGW, 60 mm.
Subject: Yandi, Semi-mythical First Emperor **Obv:** National emblem **Rev:** 3/4 figure looking left, denomination over right shoulder **Note:** Illustration reduced. Prev. Y#417.

Date	Mintage	F	VF	XF	Unc	BU
1993 Proof	99	Value: 5,000				

KM# 600   500 YUAN
155.5150 g., 0.9990 Gold 4.9947 oz. AGW **Obv:** Temple of Harmony **Rev:** Two peacocks **Note:** Prev. Y#356.

Date	Mintage	F	VF	XF	Unc	BU
1993 Proof	99	Value: 5,000				

KM# 684   500 YUAN
155.5150 g., 0.9990 Gold 4.9947 oz. AGW **Obv:** Eastern unicorn with rider, date below **Rev:** Unicorn above sprays of roses, denomination at left **Note:** Prev. Y#429.

Date	Mintage	F	VF	XF	Unc	BU
1994 Proof	99	Value: 5,000				

KM# 670   500 YUAN
155.5150 g., 0.9990 Gold 4.9947 oz. AGW, 60 mm.
Obv: Taiwan Temple, date below **Rev:** Buddha statue,
denomination below **Note:** Illustration reduced. Prev. Y#449.

Date	Mintage	F	VF	XF	Unc	BU
1994 Proof	76	Value: 5,000				

KM# 700   500 YUAN
155.5150 g., 0.9990 Gold 4.9947 oz. AGW, 60 mm. **Subject:**
Children At Play **Rev:** Two children with cat, denomination below
Note: Illustration reduced. Prev. Y#462.

Date	Mintage	F	VF	XF	Unc	BU
1994 Proof	99	Value: 5,000				

KM# 688   500 YUAN
155.5150 g., 0.9990 Gold 4.9947 oz. AGW **Subject:** Sino-
Singapore Friendship **Obv:** Great Wall, date below
Rev: Singapore Harbor, denomination below **Note:** Illustration
reduced. Prev. Y#701.

Date	Mintage	F	VF	XF	Unc	BU
1994 Proof	91	Value: 5,000				

KM# 864   500 YUAN
155.5175 g., 0.9999 Gold 4.9993 oz. AGW **Subject:** 50th
Anniversary - Taiwan's Return to China **Obv:** Great Wall, date
below **Rev:** Taiwan and China maps, date at right, denomination
lower left **Note:** Illustration reduced. Prev. Y#817.

Date	Mintage	F	VF	XF	Unc	BU
1995 Proof	99	Value: 5,000				

KM# 846   500 YUAN
155.5150 g., 0.9990 Gold 4.9947 oz. AGW, 60 mm.
Subject: Yellow River culture **Rev:** Nu Wa Rising, denomination
below **Note:** Illustration reduced. Prev. Y#594.

Date	Mintage	F	VF	XF	Unc	BU
1995 Proof	99	Value: 5,000				

KM# 823A   500 YUAN
155.5150 g., 0.9990 Gold 4.9947 oz. AGW, 60 mm.
Rev: Dragon boat, denomination below **Note:** Illustration
reduced. Prev. Y#649.

Date	Mintage	F	VF	XF	Unc	BU
1995 Proof	99	Value: 5,000				

KM# 817   500 YUAN
155.5150 g., 0.9990 Gold 4.9947 oz. AGW **Subject:** Return of
Hong Kong to China - Series I **Obv:** Tiananmen Square, date
below **Rev:** Bust of Deng Xiaoping over Hong Kong city view
Note: Prev. Y#533.

Date	Mintage	F	VF	XF	Unc	BU
1995 Proof	228	Value: 5,000				

KM# 805   500 YUAN
155.5150 g., 0.9990 Gold 4.9947 oz. AGW, 60 mm.
Subject: Unicorn **Obv:** Eastern unicorn **Rev:** Unicorn mother
and baby **Edge:** Reeded **Note:** Prev. Y#656.

Date	Mintage	F	VF	XF	Unc	BU
1995 Proof	99	Value: 5,000				

KM# 773   500 YUAN
155.5175 g., 0.9999 Gold 4.9993 oz. AGW **Subject:** Zheng
Chenggong **Obv:** Chiqian Building **Rev:** Standing figure with flag,
war ships in background, two dates upper right, denomination
lower right **Note:** Prev. Y#824.

Date	Mintage	F	VF	XF	Unc	BU
1995 Proof	99	Value: 5,000				

KM# 857   500 YUAN
155.5175 g., 0.9999 Gold 4.9993 oz. AGW **Subject:** Romance
of the Three Kingdoms Series **Obv:** Bust of Luo Guanzhong,
looking right **Rev:** Three heroes of Shu Han, denomination above
Note: Prev. Y#834.

Date	Mintage	F	VF	XF	Unc	BU
1995 Proof	99	Value: 5,000				

KM# 770   500 YUAN
151.0000 g., 0.9990 Gold 4.8497 oz. AGW, 60 mm. **Subject:**
100th Anniversary Birth of Xu Beihong **Rev:** Figure riding oxen

Date	Mintage	F	VF	XF	Unc	BU
1995 Proof	100	Value: 5,000				

KM# 965   500 YUAN
155.5175 g., 0.9990 Gold 4.9948 oz. AGW **Subject:** Romance
of the Three Kingdoms Series **Obv:** Bust of Luo Guanzhong
Rev: Guan Du on horseback leading troops, denomination at left
Note: Illustration reduced. Prev. Y#882.

Date	Mintage	F	VF	XF	Unc	BU
1996 Proof	99	Value: 5,000				

KM# 949   500 YUAN
155.5175 g., 0.9999 Gold 4.9993 oz. AGW **Obv:** Western unicorn on hind legs, surrounded by roses **Rev:** Eastern unicorn standing **Note:** Prev. Y#657.

Date	Mintage	F	VF	XF	Unc	BU
1996 Proof	108	Value: 5,000				

KM# 958   500 YUAN
155.5175 g., 0.9999 Gold 4.9993 oz. AGW **Subject:** Return of Hong Kong to China - Series II **Note:** Prev. Y#659.

Date	Mintage	F	VF	XF	Unc	BU
1996 Proof	228	Value: 5,000				

KM# 1046   500 YUAN
155.5175 g., 0.9990 Gold 4.9948 oz. AGW **Subject:** Return of Hong Kong to China - Series III **Obv:** Tiananmen Square **Rev:** Bust of Deng Xiaoping above city, denomination at left **Note:** Prev. Y#904.

Date	Mintage	F	VF	XF	Unc	BU
1997 Proof	228	Value: 5,000				

KM# 1050   500 YUAN
155.5175 g., 0.9990 Gold 4.9948 oz. AGW **Subject:** Return of Macao to China **Obv:** Tiananmen Square **Rev:** Deng Xiaoping standing viewing Macao, denomination at right **Note:** Prev. Y#907.

Date	Mintage	F	VF	XF	Unc	BU
1997 Proof	228	Value: 5,200				

KM# 1066   500 YUAN
155.5175 g., 0.9990 Gold 4.9948 oz. AGW **Subject:** Greeting Spring **Obv:** Lantern **Rev:** Children lighting firecrackers **Note:** Prev. Y#1022.

Date	Mintage	F	VF	XF	Unc	BU
1997 Proof	108	Value: 5,000				

KM# 1023   500 YUAN
155.5100 g., 0.9990 Gold 4.9946 oz. AGW, 60 mm.
Subject: Painting Master Qi Baishi

Date	Mintage	F	VF	XF	Unc	BU
1997 Proof	99	Value: 5,000				

KM# 1083   500 YUAN
151.5000 g., 0.9990 Gold 4.8658 oz. AGW, 60 mm. **Series:** Yellow river culture **Rev:** Kneeling archer shooting skyward right

Date	Mintage	F	VF	XF	Unc	BU
1997 Proof	128	Value: 5,000				

KM# 1090   500 YUAN
151.5000 g., 0.9990 Gold 4.8658 oz. AGW, 60 mm.
Series: Classic literature **Rev:** Warrior standing on prow

Date	Mintage	F	VF	XF	Unc	BU
1997 Proof	168	Value: 5,000				

KM# 1180   500 YUAN
155.5175 g., 0.9990 Gold 4.9948 oz. AGW **Subject:** Greeting Spring **Obv:** Lantern **Rev:** Children making kites **Note:** Prev. Y#1023.

Date	Mintage	F	VF	XF	Unc	BU
1998 Proof	128	Value: 5,000				

KM# 1171   500 YUAN
151.5000 g., 0.9990 Gold 4.8658 oz. AGW, 60 mm.
Subject: Macao's return to China **Rev:** Birds flying over lablet, lighthouse at left, gate at right

Date	Mintage	F	VF	XF	Unc	BU
1998 Proof	228	Value: 5,000				

KM# 1251   500 YUAN
155.5175 g., 0.9990 Gold 4.9948 oz. AGW **Subject:** 50th Anniversary of People's Republic Founding Ceremony **Note:** Prev. Y#1026.

Date	Mintage	F	VF	XF	Unc	BU
1999 Proof	990	Value: 5,000				

KM# 1282   500 YUAN
155.5000 g., 0.9990 Gold 4.9942 oz. AGW, 60 mm.
Subject: Return of Macao **Rev:** Views of Macao

Date	Mintage	F	VF	XF	Unc	BU
1999 Proof	228	Value: 5,000				

KM# 1336   500 YUAN
155.5175 g., 0.9990 Gold 4.9948 oz. AGW **Subject:** Y2K **Note:** Prev. Y#1028.

Date	Mintage	F	VF	XF	Unc	BU
2000 Proof	1,000	Value: 5,000				

KM# 49   800 YUAN
33.2000 g., 0.9170 Gold 0.9788 oz. AGW **Subject:** Chinese Bronze Age Finds **Obv:** National emblem, date below **Rev:** Elephant statue, left, denomination below **Note:** Prev. #Y31.

Date	Mintage	F	VF	XF	Unc	BU
1981 Proof	1,000	Value: 1,150				

KM# 259   1500 YUAN
622.6000 g., 0.9990 Gold 19.996 oz. AGW, 90 mm.
Subject: Anniversary of People's Republic **Obv:** National emblem above city view with fireworks in sky **Rev:** Man giving speech, people in background, denomination below **Note:** Illustration reduced. Prev. #Y232.

Date	Mintage	F	VF	XF	Unc	BU
1989 Proof	100	Value: 31,000				

KM# 321   1500 YUAN
622.6000 g., 0.9990 Gold 19.996 oz. AGW **Obv:** Great Wall **Rev:** Denomination divides Phoenix and dragon **Note:** Prev. #Y210.

Date	Mintage	F	VF	XF	Unc	BU
1989 Proof	250	Value: 20,000				

KM# 601   1500 YUAN
622.6000 g., 0.9990 Gold 19.996 oz. AGW **Obv:** Temple of Harmony **Rev:** Two peacocks **Note:** Prev. #Y357.

Date	Mintage	F	VF	XF	Unc	BU
1993 Proof	66	Value: 20,000				

KM# 552   1500 YUAN
562.5068 g., 0.9990 Gold 18.066 oz. AGW, 85 mm. **Rev:** Guanyin, Goddess of Mercy, seated in flower, denomination at left **Note:** Illustration reduced. Prev. #Y505.

Date	Mintage	F	VF	XF	Unc	BU
1993 Proof	88	Value: 17,500				

KM# 426   2000 YUAN
1000.0000 g., 0.9990 Gold 32.117 oz. AGW, 100 mm.
Subject: Chinese inventions **Rev:** First compass, denomination below **Note:** Illustration reduced. Prev. #Y402.

Date	Mintage	F	VF	XF	Unc	BU
1992 Proof	10	Value: 30,500				

KM# 425   2000 YUAN
1000.0000 g., 0.9990 Gold 32.117 oz. AGW **Subject:** Chinese Inventions and Discoveries **Obv:** Great Wall **Rev:** Seismograph **Note:** Prev. #Y749.

Date	Mintage	F	VF	XF	Unc	BU
1992 Proof	Est. 4	Value: 31,500				

KM# 689   2000 YUAN
1000.0000 g., 0.9990 Gold 32.117 oz. AGW, 112 mm.
Subject: Sino-Singapore Friendship **Obv:** Great Wall, date
below **Rev:** Singapore Harbor, denomination below
Note: Illustration reduced. Prev. #Y703.

Date	Mintage	F	VF	XF	Unc	BU
1994	15	—	—	—	—	30,500

KM# 685   2000 YUAN
1000.0000 g., 0.9990 Gold 32.117 oz. AGW **Obv:** Figure on
Eastern unicorn, date below **Rev:** Unicorn, denomination below,
rose sprays below **Note:** Prev. #Y430.

Date	Mintage	F	VF	XF	Unc	BU
1994 Proof	20	Value: 30,500				

KM# 865   2000 YUAN
1000.0000 g., 0.9990 Gold 32.117 oz. AGW **Subject:** 50th
Anniversary - Taiwan's Return to China **Obv:** Great Wall
Rev: Taiwan and China maps **Note:** Prev. #Y818.

Date	Mintage	F	VF	XF	Unc	BU
1995 Proof	25	Value: 30,500				

KM# 950   2000 YUAN
1000.0000 g., 0.9990 Gold 32.117 oz. AGW **Obv:** Eastern
unicorn **Rev:** Western unicorn with maiden **Note:** Prev. #Y957.

Date	Mintage	F	VF	XF	Unc	BU
1996 Proof	18	Value: 30,500				

KM# 1024   2000 YUAN
1000.0000 g., 0.9990 Gold 32.117 oz. AGW, 100 mm.
Subject: Painting Master Qi Baishi **Rev:** Two fruit baskets

Date	Mintage	F	VF	XF	Unc	BU
1997 Proof	25	Value: 70,000				

KM# 1199   2000 YUAN
1000.0000 g., 0.9990 Gold 32.117 oz. AGW, 100 mm.
Subject: Vault protector of the Tang Dynasty **Obv:** Cash coin
Rev: Value and flora

Date	Mintage	F	VF	XF	Unc	BU
1998 Proof	68	Value: 50,000				

KM# 1337   30000 YUAN
10000.0000 g., 0.9999 Gold 321.46 oz. AGW, 180 mm.
Subject: Third Millennium **Obv:** China Centenary Altar
Rev: Denominations **Edge:** Plain **Note:** Previous Y # 1070.

Date	Mintage	F	VF	XF	Unc	BU
2000	20	—	—	—	—	315,000

SILVER BULLION COINAGE
Lunar Series

KM# 73   10 YUAN
15.0000 g., 0.8500 Silver 0.4099 oz. ASW **Subject:** Year of the
Pig **Rev:** Pigs, denomination below **Note:** Prev. Y#44.

Date	Mintage	F	VF	XF	Unc	BU
1983 Proof	6,790	Value: 325				

KM# 93   10 YUAN
15.0000 g., 0.8500 Silver 0.4099 oz. ASW **Subject:** Year of the
Rat **Obv:** Building, date below **Rev:** Rat eating squash,
denomination below **Note:** Prev. Y#59.

Date	Mintage	F	VF	XF	Unc	BU
1984 Proof	11,000	Value: 90.00				

KM# 119   10 YUAN
15.0000 g., 0.9000 Silver 0.4340 oz. ASW **Subject:** Year of the
Ox **Rev:** Ox above denomination **Note:** Prev. Y#78.

Date	Mintage	F	VF	XF	Unc	BU
1985 Proof	22,000	Value: 45.00				

KM# 137   10 YUAN
15.0000 g., 0.9000 Silver 0.4340 oz. ASW **Subject:** Year of the
Tiger **Obv:** Qing Dynasty Palace, date below **Rev:** Tiger, after a
painting by He Ziang Ning, denomination upper left **Note:** Prev.
Y#98.

Date	Mintage	F	VF	XF	Unc	BU
1986 Proof	15,000	Value: 45.00				

KM# 169   10 YUAN
15.0000 g., 0.9000 Silver 0.4340 oz. ASW **Subject:** Year of the
Rabbit **Obv:** Yellow Crane Pavilion above legend **Rev:** 2 rabbits
above denomination **Note:** Prev. Y#121.

Date	Mintage	F	VF	XF	Unc	BU
1987 Proof	14,000	Value: 75.00				

KM# A193   10 YUAN
31.1000 g., 0.9990 Silver 0.9988 oz. ASW **Subject:** Year of the
Dragon **Obv:** Temple of Heaven, date below **Rev:** Dragons,
denomination below center

Date	Mintage	F	VF	XF	Unc	BU
1988 Proof	20,000	Value: 65.00				

KM# 193   10 YUAN
15.0000 g., 0.9000 Silver 0.4340 oz. ASW **Subject:** Year of the
Dragon **Obv:** Great Wall, date below **Rev:** Dragon above
denomination **Note:** Prev. Y#141.

Date	Mintage	F	VF	XF	Unc	BU
1988 Proof	15,000	Value: 65.00				

KM# 232   10 YUAN
31.1000 g., 0.9990 Silver 0.9988 oz. ASW **Subject:** Year of the
Snake **Obv:** National emblem **Rev:** Snake above denomination
Note: Prev. Y#183.

Date	Mintage	F	VF	XF	Unc	BU
1989 Proof	6,000	Value: 110				

KM# 282   10 YUAN
15.0000 g., 0.8500 Silver 0.4099 oz. ASW **Subject:** Year of the
Horse **Obv:** Temple of Confucius, date below **Rev:** Horse
galloping left, denomination below **Note:** Prev. Y#221.

Date	Mintage	F	VF	XF	Unc	BU
1990 Proof	15,000	Value: 45.00				

KM# 283   10 YUAN
31.1000 g., 0.9990 Silver 0.9988 oz. ASW **Subject:** Year of the
Horse **Rev:** Saddled horse, left, denomination lower right
Note: Prev. Y#222.

Date	Mintage	F	VF	XF	Unc	BU
1990 Proof	12,000	Value: 50.00				

KM# 360   10 YUAN
15.0000 g., 0.9000 Silver 0.4340 oz. ASW **Subject:** Year of the
Goat **Obv:** Chinese building and legend **Rev:** Goat, denomination
upper left **Note:** Prev. Y#270.

Date	Mintage	F	VF	XF	Unc	BU
1991 Proof	15,000	Value: 40.00				

KM# 361   10 YUAN
31.1000 g., 0.9990 Silver 0.9988 oz. ASW **Subject:** Year of the
Goat **Obv:** National emblem, date below **Rev:** Three goats,
denomination below **Note:** Prev. Y#271.

Date	Mintage	F	VF	XF	Unc	BU
1991 Proof	8,000	Value: 100				

KM# 427 10 YUAN
15.0000 g., 0.9000 Silver 0.4340 oz. ASW **Subject:** Year of the Monkey **Obv:** Building, date below **Rev:** Seated monkey, denomination at right **Note:** Prev. Y#288.

Date	Mintage	F	VF	XF	Unc	BU
1992 Proof	—			Value: 50.00		

KM# 428 10 YUAN
31.1000 g., 0.9988 Silver 0.9988 oz. ASW **Subject:** Year of the Monkey **Rev:** Monkey, denomination at left **Note:** Prev. Y#294.

Date	Mintage	F	VF	XF	Unc	BU
1992 Proof	8,000			Value: 60.00		

KM# 511 10 YUAN
20.7500 g., 0.9990 Silver 0.6664 oz. ASW **Subject:** Year of the Rooster **Obv:** Building, date below **Rev:** Rooster and sunflowers, denomination at left **Note:** Prev. Y#480.

Date	Mintage	F	VF	XF	Unc	BU
1993 Proof	6,800			Value: 125		

KM# 510 10 YUAN
31.1000 g., 0.9990 Silver 0.9988 oz. ASW **Subject:** Year of the Rooster **Obv:** National emblem, date below **Rev:** Rooster and hen, denomination at left **Note:** Prev. Y#567.

Date	Mintage	F	VF	XF	Unc	BU
1993 Proof	Est. 9,000			Value: 75.00		

KM# 643 10 YUAN
31.1000 g., 0.9990 Silver 0.9988 oz. ASW **Subject:** Year of the Dog **Note:** Prev. Y#396.

Date	Mintage	F	VF	XF	Unc	BU
1994 Proof	8,000			Value: 65.00		

KM# 642 10 YUAN
20.7500 g., 0.9990 Silver 0.6664 oz. ASW, 36 mm. **Subject:** Year of the Dog **Obv:** Traditional style building **Rev:** Value and dog **Edge:** Plain **Note:** Prev. Y#1246.

Date	Mintage	F	VF	XF	Unc	BU
1994 Proof	—			Value: 100		

KM# 745 10 YUAN
31.1050 g., 0.9990 Silver 0.9990 oz. ASW **Subject:** Year of the Pig **Obv:** National emblem, date below **Rev:** Pig, denomination at right **Note:** Prev. Y#450.

Date	Mintage	F	VF	XF	Unc	BU
1995 Proof	8,000			Value: 85.00		

KM# 752 10 YUAN
20.7500 g., 0.9990 Silver 0.6664 oz. ASW **Subject:** Year of the Pig **Obv:** Building, date below **Rev:** Two pigs, denomination lower left **Note:** Prev. Y#452.

Date	Mintage	F	VF	XF	Unc	BU
1995 Proof	6,800			Value: 110		

KM# 927 10 YUAN
31.1035 g., 0.9990 Silver 0.9990 oz. ASW **Subject:** Year of the Rat **Rev:** Rat by oil lamp, denomination below **Note:** Prev. Y#585.

Date	Mintage	F	VF	XF	Unc	BU
1996 Proof	8,000			Value: 60.00		

KM# 928 10 YUAN
23.0375 g., 0.9000 Silver 0.6666 oz. ASW **Subject:** Year of the Rat **Obv:** Dengdu Pavilion **Rev:** Rat eating corn cob **Note:** Prev. Y#854.

Date	Mintage	F	VF	XF	Unc	BU
1996 Proof	6,800			Value: 70.00		

KM# 1014 10 YUAN
23.0375 g., 0.9000 Silver 0.6666 oz. ASW **Subject:** Year of the Ox **Obv:** Mingyuan Pavilion **Rev:** Bull, denomination below **Note:** Prev. Y#896.

Date	Mintage	F	VF	XF	Unc	BU
1997 Proof	6,800			Value: 75.00		

KM# 1013.1 10 YUAN
31.1035 g., 0.9990 Silver 0.9990 oz. ASW **Subject:** Year of the Ox **Obv:** State seal **Rev:** Water buffalo **Note:** Prev. Y#899.1.

Date	Mintage	F	VF	XF	Unc	BU
1997 Proof	8,000			Value: 70.00		

KM# 1013.2 10 YUAN
31.1035 g., 0.9990 Silver 0.9990 oz. ASW, 40 mm. **Subject:** Year of the Ox **Obv:** National emblem, date below **Rev:** Bull, drinking, denomination below **Note:** Increased size. Prev. Y#899.2.

Date	Mintage	F	VF	XF	Unc	BU
1997	50,000	—	—	—	—	35.00

KM# 1138 10 YUAN
31.1035 g., 0.9990 Silver 0.9990 oz. ASW **Subject:** Year of the Tiger **Obv:** National emblem **Rev:** Tiger on rock, denomination at right **Note:** Prev. Y#922.

Date	Mintage	F	VF	XF	Unc	BU
1998	50,000	—	—	—	—	40.00

KM# 1138a 10 YUAN
31.1035 g., 0.9990 Silver 0.9990 oz. ASW **Subject:** Year of the
Tiger **Obv:** Badaling building **Rev:** Multicolor tiger cub,
denomination at right **Note:** Prev. Y#923.

Date	Mintage	F	VF	XF	Unc	BU
1998	100,000	—	—	—	—	40.00

KM# 1148 10 YUAN
23.0375 g., 0.9000 Silver 0.6666 oz. ASW **Subject:** Year of the
Tiger **Obv:** Badaling building, date below **Rev:** Tiger **Note:** Prev.
Y#926.

Date	Mintage	F	VF	XF	Unc	BU
1998 Proof	6,800	Value: 65.00				

KM# 1137 10 YUAN
31.1035 g., 0.9990 Silver 0.9990 oz. ASW, 32 mm. **Rev:** Tiger
on rock outcrop

Date	Mintage	F	VF	XF	Unc	BU
1998 Proof	8,000	Value: 50.00				

KM# 1225 10 YUAN
31.1035 g., 0.9990 Silver 0.9990 oz. ASW, 32 mm.
Subject: Year of the rabbit

Date	Mintage	F	VF	XF	Unc	BU
1999 Proof	8,000	Value: 75.00				

KM# 1226 10 YUAN
31.1035 g., 0.9990 Silver 0.9990 oz. ASW, 40 mm.
Subject: Year of the rabbit

Date	Mintage	F	VF	XF	Unc	BU
1999 Proof	100,000	Value: 50.00				

KM# A1227 10 YUAN
31.1035 g., 0.9990 Silver 0.9990 oz. ASW, 40 mm.
Subject: Year of the rabbit **Note:** Colorized

Date	Mintage	F	VF	XF	Unc	BU
1999 Proof	50,000	Value: 75.00				

KM# 1236 10 YUAN
20.5300 g., 0.9000 Silver 0.5940 oz. ASW, 36 mm.
Subject: Year of the rabbit

Date	Mintage	F	VF	XF	Unc	BU
1999 Proof	6,800	Value: 40.00				

KM# 1321 10 YUAN
31.1035 g., 0.9990 Silver 0.9990 oz. ASW, 43.2 x 26.5 mm.
Subject: Year of the Dragon **Obv:** Shanhaiguan gate tower of
the Great, date above **Rev:** Dragon, denomination lower right
Edge: Plain **Note:** Prev. Y#1110.

Date	Mintage	F	VF	XF	Unc	BU
2000 Proof	66,000	Value: 50.00				

KM# 1325 10 YUAN
23.0375 g., 0.9000 Silver 0.6666 oz. ASW **Subject:** Year of the
Dragon **Obv:** Building **Rev:** Dragon **Note:** Prev. Y#978.

Date	Mintage	F	VF	XF	Unc	BU
2000 Proof	6,800	Value: 95.00				

KM# 56 20 YUAN
15.0000 g., 0.8500 Silver 0.4099 oz. ASW **Subject:** Year of the
Dog **Obv:** Temple of Heaven, date lower right **Rev:** Dog above
denomination **Note:** Prev. Y#38.

Date	Mintage	F	VF	XF	Unc	BU
1982 Proof	8,825	Value: 125				

KM# 40 30 YUAN
15.0000 g., 0.8500 Silver 0.4099 oz. ASW **Subject:** Year of the
Rooster **Obv:** Shoreline temple, date lower left **Rev:** Rooster,
denomination at left **Note:** Prev. Y#32.

Date	Mintage	F	VF	XF	Unc	BU
1981 Proof	10,000	Value: 200				

KM# 170 50 YUAN
155.5000 g., 0.9990 Silver 4.9942 oz. ASW **Subject:** Year of
the Rabbit **Obv:** Pagoda, date below **Rev:** Two rabbits,
denomination below **Note:** Prev. Y#122.

Date	Mintage	F	VF	XF	Unc	BU
1987 Proof	4,000	Value: 275				

KM# 194 50 YUAN
155.5000 g., 0.9990 Silver 4.9942 oz. ASW, 70 mm.
Subject: Year of the Dragon **Obv:** Great Wall, date below
Rev: Inner circle holds three dragons, four dragons surround,
denomination below **Note:** Illustration reduced. Prev. Y#142.

Date	Mintage	F	VF	XF	Unc	BU
1988 Proof	5,000	Value: 265				

KM# 233 50 YUAN
155.5000 g., 0.9990 Silver 4.9942 oz. ASW, 70 mm. **Subject:**
Year of the Snake **Obv:** Shanhaiguan Pass Gate **Rev:** Snake
left, denomination below **Note:** Illustration reduced. Prev. Y#178.

Date	Mintage	F	VF	XF	Unc	BU
1989 Proof	1,000	Value: 365				

KM# 284 50 YUAN
155.5000 g., 0.9990 Silver 4.9942 oz. ASW, 70 mm.
Subject: Year of the Horse **Obv:** Temple of Confucius **Rev:** Two
horses drinking at stream, denomination below **Note:** Illustration
reduced. Prev. Y#223.

Date	Mintage	F	VF	XF	Unc	BU
1990 Proof	2,000	Value: 225				

KM# 362 50 YUAN
155.5000 g., 0.9990 Silver 4.9942 oz. ASW, 60 mm. **Subject:**
Year of the Goat **Obv:** Chinese building and legend **Rev:** Goats,
denomination above **Note:** Illustration reduced. Prev. Y#272.

Date	Mintage	F	VF	XF	Unc	BU
1991 Proof	2,000	Value: 275				

KM# 429 50 YUAN
155.5000 g., 0.9990 Silver 4.9942 oz. ASW **Subject:** Year of
the Monkey **Obv:** Building **Rev:** Monkey **Note:** Prev. Y#289.

Date	Mintage	F	VF	XF	Unc	BU
1992 Proof	1,000	Value: 325				

KM# 512   50 YUAN
155.5000 g., 0.9990 Silver 4.9942 oz. ASW **Subject:** Year of
the Rooster **Note:** Prev. Y#381.

Date	Mintage	F	VF	XF	Unc	BU
1993 Proof	1,000	Value: 285				

KM# 644   50 YUAN
155.5000 g., 0.9990 Silver 4.9942 oz. ASW **Subject:** Year of
the Dog **Note:** Prev. Y#386.

Date	Mintage	F	VF	XF	Unc	BU
1994 Proof	1,000	Value: 245				

KM# 746   50 YUAN
155.5175 g., 0.9990 Silver 4.9948 oz. ASW **Subject:** Year of
the Pig **Obv:** Traditional building **Rev:** Sow and 4 piglets
Note: Prev. Y#464.

Date	Mintage	F	VF	XF	Unc	BU
1995 Proof	1,000	Value: 245				

KM# 926   50 YUAN
155.5175 g., 0.9990 Silver 4.9948 oz. ASW **Subject:** Year of
the Rat **Obv:** Dengdu Pavilion **Rev:** Rat and grapes,
denomination above **Note:** Prev. Y#855.

Date	Mintage	F	VF	XF	Unc	BU
1996 Proof	1,000	Value: 255				

KM# 1011   50 YUAN
155.5175 g., 0.9990 Silver 4.9948 oz. ASW, 80 mm.
Subject: Year of the Ox **Obv:** Mingyuan Pavilion, date below
Rev: Bull ox, left, denomination above **Note:** Illustration reduced.
Prev. Y#897.

Date	Mintage	F	VF	XF	Unc	BU
1997 Proof	1,000	Value: 325				

KM# 1140   50 YUAN
155.5175 g., 0.9990 Silver 4.9948 oz. ASW **Subject:** Year of
the Tiger **Obv:** Badaling building **Rev:** Tiger on rock,
denomination at right **Note:** Prev. Y#927.

Date	Mintage	F	VF	XF	Unc	BU
1998 Proof	1,000	Value: 325				

KM# 1230   50 YUAN
151.5000 g., 0.9990 Silver 4.8658 oz. ASW, 70 mm.
Subject: Year of the rabbit

Date	Mintage	F	VF	XF	Unc	BU
1999 Proof	1,000	Value: 250				

KM# 195   100 YUAN
373.2360 g., 0.9990 Silver 11.987 oz. ASW, 80 mm.
Subject: Year of the Dragon **Obv:** Great Wall, date below
Rev: Two dragons facing, denomination below **Note:** Illustration
reduced. Prev. Y#143.

Date	Mintage	F	VF	XF	Unc	BU
1988 Proof	3,000	Value: 450				

KM# 234   100 YUAN
373.2360 g., 0.9990 Silver 11.987 oz. ASW **Subject:** Year of
the Snake **Obv:** Shanhaiguan Pass Gate **Rev:** Snake left within
beaded circle, denomination below **Note:** Illustration reduced.
Prev. Y#179.

Date	Mintage	F	VF	XF	Unc	BU
1989 Proof	400	Value: 800				

KM# 285   100 YUAN
373.2360 g., 0.9990 Silver 11.987 oz. ASW, 80 mm.
Subject: Year of the Horse **Obv:** Temple of Confucius **Rev:** Two
horses galloping left, denomination below **Note:** Illustration
reduced. Prev. Y#285.

Date	Mintage	F	VF	XF	Unc	BU
1990 Proof	1,000	Value: 385				

KM# 363   100 YUAN
373.2360 g., 0.9990 Silver 11.987 oz. ASW, 80 mm.
Subject: Year of the Goat **Rev:** Two goats, denomination at left
Note: Illustration reduced. Prev. Y#273.

Date	Mintage	F	VF	XF	Unc	BU
1991 Proof	1,000	Value: 385				

KM# 431   100 YUAN
373.2360 g., 0.9990 Silver 11.987 oz. ASW **Subject:** Year of
the Monkey **Obv:** Building **Rev:** Family of monkeys **Note:** Prev.
Y#290.

Date	Mintage	F	VF	XF	Unc	BU
1992 Proof	500	Value: 475				

KM# 514   100 YUAN
373.2360 g., 0.9990 Silver 11.987 oz. ASW **Subject:** Year of
the Rooster **Note:** Prev. Y#383.

Date	Mintage	F	VF	XF	Unc	BU
1993 Proof	500	Value: 425				

KM# 646   100 YUAN
373.2360 g., 0.9990 Silver 11.987 oz. ASW **Subject:** Year of
the Dog **Note:** Prev. Y#388.

Date	Mintage	F	VF	XF	Unc	BU
1994 Proof	500	Value: 425				

KM# 747   100 YUAN
373.2420 g., 0.9990 Silver 11.987 oz. ASW, 80 mm.
Subject: Year of the Pig **Rev:** Sow and five piglets **Note:** Prev.
Y#466.

Date	Mintage	F	VF	XF	Unc	BU
1995 Proof	500	Value: 400				

KM# 925   100 YUAN
373.2400 g., 0.9990 Silver 11.987 oz. ASW, 80 mm.
Subject: Year of the rat **Rev:** Rat on balance scale

Date	Mintage	F	VF	XF	Unc	BU
1996 Proof	500	Value: 250				

KM# 1010   100 YUAN
373.2360 g., 0.9990 Silver 11.987 oz. ASW **Subject:** Year of
the Ox **Note:** Prev. Y#669.

Date	Mintage	F	VF	XF	Unc	BU
1997	500	—	—	—	—	450

KM# 1141 100 YUAN
373.2420 g., 0.9990 Silver 11.987 oz. ASW **Subject:** Year of the Tiger **Obv:** Badaling building **Rev:** Tiger on rock, denomination at right **Note:** Prev. Y#928.

Date	Mintage	F	VF	XF	Unc	BU
1998 Proof	500	Value: 600				

KM# 1231 100 YUAN
373.0000 g., 0.9990 Silver 11.979 oz. ASW, 80 mm. **Subject:** Year of the rabbit

Date	Mintage	F	VF	XF	Unc	BU
1999 Proof	500	Value: 1,000				

KM# 436 200 YUAN
1000.0000 g., 0.9990 Silver 32.117 oz. ASW, 120 mm. **Subject:** Completion of 150 Yuan Lunar - Animal Coin Series **Obv:** Monument divides date and denomination within circle **Rev:** Ying/Yang symbols within octagon surrounded by twelve animal coins **Note:** Illustration reduced. Prev. Y#700.

Date	Mintage	F	VF	XF	Unc	BU
1992 Proof	185	Value: 1,250				

KM# 1239 200 YUAN
1000.0000 g., 0.9990 Silver 32.117 oz. ASW **Subject:** Completion of 12-Year Lunar Cycle **Note:** Prev. Y#976.

Date	Mintage	F	VF	XF	Unc	BU
1999 Proof	1,000	Value: 1,200				

SILVER BULLION COINAGE
Panda Series

KM# 483 5 YUAN
15.5517 g., 0.9990 Silver 0.4995 oz. ASW **Obv:** Temple of Heaven within circle, date below **Rev:** Panda facing forward, denomination below **Note:** Prev. Y#392.

Date	Mintage	F	VF	XF	Unc	BU
1993	—	—	—	—	—	22.50

KM# 621 5 YUAN
15.5517 g., 0.9990 Silver 0.4995 oz. ASW **Rev:** Panda approaching water, denomination above **Note:** Prev. Y#436.

Date	Mintage	F	VF	XF	Unc	BU
1994	—	—	—	—	—	25.00

KM# 731 5 YUAN
15.7717 g., 0.9990 Silver 0.5065 oz. ASW **Obv:** Temple of Heaven **Rev:** Panda climbing tree branch **Note:** Prev. Y#791.

Date	Mintage	F	VF	XF	Unc	BU
1995 Proof	—	Value: 27.50				

KM# 898 5 YUAN
15.5517 g., 0.9990 Silver 0.4995 oz. ASW **Obv:** Temple of Heaven **Rev:** Panda seated on shore **Note:** Large and small date varieties exist. Prev. Y#847.

Date	Mintage	F	VF	XF	Unc	BU
1996	—	—	—	—	13.50	20.00

KM# 1005 5 YUAN
15.5517 g., 0.9990 Silver 0.4995 oz. ASW **Obv:** Temple of Heaven with additional legend on Hong Kong's return **Rev:** Panda crossing stream, denomination lower left **Note:** Large and small date varieties exist. Prev. Y#893.

Date	Mintage	F	VF	XF	Unc	BU
1997 Proof	30,000	Value: 50.00				

KM# 995 5 YUAN
15.6000 g., 0.9990 Silver 0.5010 oz. ASW, 36 mm. **Obv:** Temple of Heaven **Rev:** Multicolor panda and flora **Edge:** Reeded **Note:** Large and small date varieties exist. Prev. Y#962.

Date	Mintage	F	VF	XF	Unc	BU
1997	100,000	—	—	—	—	24.00

KM# 993 5 YUAN
15.6300 g., 0.9990 Silver 0.5020 oz. ASW **Obv:** Temple of Heaven within circle, date below **Rev:** Panda crossing stream, denomination at lower left **Note:** Large and small date varieties exist. Prev. Y#728; 892.

Date	Mintage	F	VF	XF	Unc	BU
1997 Proof	—	Value: 22.00				

KM# 1131 5 YUAN
15.5517 g., 0.9990 Silver 0.4995 oz. ASW **Rev:** Multicolor panda **Note:** Large and small date varieties exist. Prev. Y#964.

Date	Mintage	F	VF	XF	Unc	BU
1998	100,000	—	—	—	—	24.00

KM# 1124 5 YUAN
15.5600 g., 0.9990 Silver 0.4997 oz. ASW, 33 mm. **Rev:** Panda seated eating bamboo leaf

Date	Mintage	F	VF	XF	Unc	BU
1998 Proof	200,000	Value: 25.00				

KM# 67 10 YUAN
27.0000 g., 0.9000 Silver 0.7812 oz. ASW **Obv:** Temple of Heaven, date below **Rev:** Two pandas, denomination below **Note:** Prev. Y#57.

Date	Mintage	F	VF	XF	Unc	BU
1983 Proof	10,000	Value: 225				
1983 Frosted Proof	Inc. above	Value: 235				

KM# 87 10 YUAN
27.0000 g., 0.9250 Silver 0.8029 oz. ASW **Obv:** Temple of Heaven, date below **Rev:** Panda and cub, denomination at right **Note:** Prev. Y#67.

Date	Mintage	F	VF	XF	Unc	BU
1984 Proof	10,000	Value: 150				

KM# 114 10 YUAN
27.0000 g., 0.9000 Silver 0.7812 oz. ASW **Obv:** Temple of Heaven, date below **Rev:** Panda with cub on back, denomination below **Note:** Prev. Y#95.

Date	Mintage	F	VF	XF	Unc	BU
1985 Proof	10,000	Value: 225				

KM# 167 10 YUAN
31.1000 g., 0.9990 Silver 0.9988 oz. ASW **Obv:** Temple of Heaven, date below **Rev:** Panda climbing tree, denomination at right **Note:** Prev. Y#133.

Date	Mintage	F	VF	XF	Unc	BU
1987 Proof	31,000	Value: 80.00				

KM# A221 10 YUAN
31.1000 g., 0.9990 Silver 0.9988 oz. ASW **Obv:** Temple of
Heaven, date below **Rev:** Baby panda on grid background, date
at bottom

Date	Mintage	F	VF	XF	Unc	BU
1989	250,000	—	—	—	—	30.00
1989 Proof	25,000	Value: 40.00				

KM# 276 10 YUAN
31.1000 g., 0.9990 Silver 0.9988 oz. ASW **Obv:** Temple of
Heaven, date below **Rev:** Panda, denomination below
Note: Prev. Y#237.

Date	Mintage	F	VF	XF	Unc	BU
1990	200,000	—	—	—	—	30.00
1990 Proof	20,000	Value: 40.00				

KM# 386.1 10 YUAN
31.1000 g., 0.9990 Silver 0.9988 oz. ASW **Obv:** Temple of
Heaven, date below with bottom serifs **Rev:** Panda sitting with
hind feet in water, denomination at left **Note:** Prev. Y#308.1.

Date	Mintage	F	VF	XF	Unc	BU
1991	100,000	—	—	—	—	85.00

KM# 386.2 10 YUAN
31.1000 g., 0.9990 Silver 0.9988 oz. ASW **Obv:** Temple of
Heaven, date below **Rev:** P behind panda **Note:** Prev. Y#308.2.

Date	Mintage	F	VF	XF	Unc	BU
1991 Proof	20,000	Value: 100				

KM# 386.3 10 YUAN
31.1000 g., 0.9990 Silver 0.9988 oz. ASW **Obv:** Building, date
below without bottom serifs **Note:** Prev. Y#308.3.

Date	Mintage	F	VF	XF	Unc	BU
1991	Inc. above	—	—	—	—	40.00

KM# 356 10 YUAN
62.2000 g., 0.9990 Silver 1.9977 oz. ASW **Obv:** Temple of
Heaven, date below **Rev:** Panda climbing bamboo branch,
denomination upper right **Note:** Prev. Y#314.

Date	Mintage	F	VF	XF	Unc	BU
1991 Proof	10,000	Value: 100				

KM# 397 10 YUAN
31.1000 g., 0.9990 Silver 0.9988 oz. ASW **Obv:** Temple of
Heaven within circle, date below **Rev:** Panda climbing right on
eucalyptus branch, denomination above **Note:** Prev. Y#346.

Date	Mintage	F	VF	XF	Unc	BU
1992	100,000	—	—	—	—	47.50
1992 Proof	5,202	Value: 65.00				

KM# A397 10 YUAN
31.1035 g., 0.9990 Silver 0.9990 oz. ASW, 40 mm. **Rev:** Panda
on tree branch

Date	Mintage	F	VF	XF	Unc	BU
1992 Proof	20,000	Value: 30.00				
1992 Proof	—	Value: 40.00				

KM# 478 10 YUAN
31.1000 g., 0.9990 Silver 0.9988 oz. ASW **Obv:** Temple of
Heaven, date below **Rev:** Mother panda nurturing cub
Note: Prev. Y#360.

Date	Mintage	F	VF	XF	Unc	BU
1993 Proof	20,000	Value: 55.00				

KM# 485 10 YUAN
31.1000 g., 0.9990 Silver 0.9988 oz. ASW **Obv:** Temple of
Heaven, date below **Rev:** Panda on flat rock **Note:** Prev. Y#361.

Date	Mintage	F	VF	XF	Unc	BU
1993	120,000	—	—	—	—	45.00

KM# 616 10 YUAN
31.1000 g., 0.9990 Silver 0.9988 oz. ASW **Obv:** Temple of
Heaven, date below **Rev:** Panda sitting on branch of tree **Note:**
Prev. Y#437.

Date	Mintage	F	VF	XF	Unc	BU
1994 Proof	20,000	Value: 55.00				

KM# A623 10 YUAN
31.1000 g., 0.9990 Silver 0.9988 oz. ASW **Obv:** Temple of
Heaven within circle, date below **Rev:** Seated panda eating,
denomination below

Date	Mintage	F	VF	XF	Unc	BU
1994	120,000	—	—	—	—	50.00

KM# 732.1 10 YUAN
31.1035 g., 0.9990 Silver 0.9990 oz. ASW **Obv:** Temple of
Heaven **Rev:** Panda sitting on branch eating large twig
Mint: Shanghai **Note:** Prev. Y#485.1.

Date	Mintage	F	VF	XF	Unc	BU
1995	—	—	—	—	—	40.00

KM# 732.2 10 YUAN
31.1035 g., 0.9990 Silver 0.9990 oz. ASW **Obv:** Temple of
Heaven, date below **Rev:** Panda eating small twig
Mint: Shenyang **Note:** Prev. Y#485.2.

Date	Mintage	F	VF	XF	Unc	BU
1995	—	—	—	—	—	37.00

KM# 723 10 YUAN
31.1035 g., 0.9990 Silver 0.9990 oz. ASW **Obv:** Temple of
Heaven **Rev:** Panda approaching water from right **Note:** Prev.
Y#787.

Date	Mintage	F	VF	XF	Unc	BU
1995 Proof	10,000	Value: 40.00				

KM# 733 10 YUAN
31.1035 g., 0.9990 Silver 0.9990 oz. ASW **Subject:** Beijing
Stamp Fair **Obv:** Temple of Heaven with additional legend below
Rev: Panda approaching water from right **Note:** Prev. Y#792.

Date	Mintage	F	VF	XF	Unc	BU
1995 Proof	18,000	Value: 40.00				

KM# 900 10 YUAN
31.2300 g., 0.9990 Silver 1.0030 oz. ASW, 39.8 mm.
Obv: Temple of Heaven **Rev:** Seated panda facing left
Edge: Reeded **Note:** Large and small date varieties exist. Prev.
Y#1096.

Date	Mintage	F	VF	XF	Unc	BU
1996 Proof	8,000	Value: 75.00				

KM# 892 10 YUAN
31.1035 g., 0.9990 Silver 0.9990 oz. ASW **Obv:** Temple of
Heaven within circle, date below **Rev:** Seated panda mother and
cub, denomination upper left **Note:** Large and small date varieties
exist. Prev. Y#583.

Date	Mintage	F	VF	XF	Unc	BU
1996 Prooflike	—	—	—	—	—	35.00

KM# 986 10 YUAN
31.1035 g., 0.9990 Silver 0.9990 oz. ASW **Obv:** Temple of
Heaven within circle, date below **Rev:** Panda on thick branch,
left, denomination below **Note:** Large and small date varieties
exist. Prev. Y#715.

Date	Mintage	F	VF	XF	Unc	BU
1997	50,000	—	—	—	—	30.00

KM# 1002   10 YUAN

31.2200 g., 0.9990 Silver 1.0027 oz. ASW **Obv:** Temple of
Heaven and date within circle, - "Visit China '97" around outside
Rev: Panda on large tree branch, denomination below
Note: Large and small date varieties exist. Prev. Y#726.

Date	Mintage	F	VF	XF	Unc	BU
1997	50,000					30.00

KM# 1003   10 YUAN

31.1035 g., 0.9990 Silver 0.9990 oz. ASW **Obv:** Temple of
Heaven - "Founding of Chongqing Municipality" **Rev:** Panda on
branch **Note:** Large and small date varieties exist. Prev. Y#894.

Date	Mintage	F	VF	XF	Unc	BU
1997 Proof	50,000	Value: 35.00				

KM# 996   10 YUAN

31.1035 g., 0.9990 Silver 0.9990 oz. ASW, 40 mm. **Obv:** Temple
of Heaven within circle, date below **Rev:** Multicolor panda and
flora, denomination at right **Edge:** Reeded **Note:** Large and small
date varieties exist. Prev. #Y1060.

Date	Mintage	F	VF	XF	Unc	BU
1997	—	—	—	—	45.00	55.00

KM# 1126   10 YUAN

31.1035 g., 0.9990 Silver 0.9990 oz. ASW **Obv:** Temple of
Heaven, date below **Rev:** Panda **Note:** Large and small date
varieties exist. Prev. Y#969.

Date	Mintage	F	VF	XF	Unc	BU
1998	250,000	—	—	—	—	45.00

KM# 1132   10 YUAN

31.1035 g., 0.9990 Silver 0.9990 oz. ASW **Obv:** Temple of
Heaven, date below **Rev:** Multicolor panda **Note:** Large and small
date varieties exist. Prev. Y#970.

Date	Mintage	F	VF	XF	Unc	BU
1998	100,000	—	—	—	—	45.00

KM# 1134   10 YUAN

31.0600 g., 0.9990 Silver 0.9976 oz. ASW, 39.9 mm.
Subject: 1998 Beijing Internatipnal Coin Exposition **Obv:** Temple
of Heaven **Rev:** Gilt Panda reclining on rock **Edge:** Reeded

Date	Mintage	F	VF	XF	Unc	BU
1998	30,000	—	—	—	—	60.00

KM# 1135   10 YUAN

31.0500 g., 0.9990 Silver 0.9972 oz. ASW, 39.91 mm. **Subject:**
1999 Beijing International Coin Exposition **Obv:** Temple of
Heaven **Rev:** Gilt Panda laying on rock **Edge:** Reeded

Date	Mintage	F	VF	XF	Unc	BU
1999	40,000					50.00

KM# 1216   10 YUAN

31.1035 g., 0.9990 Silver 0.9990 oz. ASW **Obv:** Temple of
Heaven within circle, date below **Rev:** Panda on rock,
denomination at left **Note:** Large and small date varieties exist.
Prev. Y#931.

Date	Mintage	F	VF	XF	Unc	BU
1999	—	Value: 60.00				

KM# 1217   10 YUAN

31.1035 g., 0.9990 Silver 0.9990 oz. ASW **Obv:** Temple of
Heaven, date below **Rev:** Multicolor panda **Note:** Large and small
date varieties exist. Prev. Y#974.

Date	Mintage	F	VF	XF	Unc	BU
1999	100,000	—	—	—	—	40.00

KM# 1310   10 YUAN

31.1035 g., 0.9990 Silver 0.9990 oz. ASW **Obv:** Temple of
Heaven within circle, date below **Rev:** Panda seated, holding
bamboo branch, denomination below **Note:** Large and small date
varieties exist. Prev. Y#979.

Date	Mintage	F	VF	XF	Unc	BU
2000	—	—	—	—	—	40.00

Note: Domestic Chinese examples struck with mirror fields,
overseas examples struck with frosted fields

KM# 168   50 YUAN

155.5000 g., 0.9990 Silver 4.9942 oz. ASW, 70 mm.
Obv: Temple of Heaven **Rev:** Panda clinging to tree trunk
Note: Prev. Y#134.

Date	Mintage	F	VF	XF	Unc	BU
1987 Proof	8,540	Value: 110				

KM# 188   50 YUAN

155.5000 g., 0.9990 Silver 4.9942 oz. ASW **Obv:** Temple of
Heaven **Rev:** Two pandas in tree **Note:** Prev. Y#168.

Date	Mintage	F	VF	XF	Unc	BU
1988 Proof	11,000	Value: 120				

KM# 222   50 YUAN

155.5000 g., 0.9990 Silver 4.9942 oz. ASW **Obv:** Temple of
Heaven **Rev:** Mother panda with cub **Note:** Prev. Y#218.

Date	Mintage	F	VF	XF	Unc	BU
1989 Proof	9,599	Value: 130				

KM# 273   50 YUAN

155.5000 g., 0.9990 Silver 4.9942 oz. ASW **Obv:** Temple of
Heaven **Rev:** Two pandas, one in tree **Note:** Prev. Y#262.

Date	Mintage	F	VF	XF	Unc	BU
1990 Proof	4,000	Value: 130				

KM# 353   50 YUAN

155.5000 g., 0.9990 Silver 4.9942 oz. ASW **Obv:** Temple of
Heaven, date below **Rev:** Pandas at waters edge, denomination
above **Note:** Prev. Y#373.

Date	Mintage	F	VF	XF	Unc	BU
1991 Proof	5,000	Value: 145				

KM# 398   50 YUAN

155.5000 g., 0.9990 Silver 4.9942 oz. ASW **Obv:** Temple of
Heaven, date below **Rev:** Pandas **Note:** Prev. Y#374.

Date	Mintage	F	VF	XF	Unc	BU
1992 Proof	4,000	Value: 145				

KM# 475   50 YUAN

155.5000 g., 0.9990 Silver 4.9942 oz. ASW **Obv:** Temple of
Heaven **Rev:** Pandas, denomination at left **Note:** Prev. Y#379.

Date	Mintage	F	VF	XF	Unc	BU
1993 Proof	Est. 3,000	Value: 165				

KM# 479   50 YUAN

155.5000 g., 0.9990 Silver 4.9942 oz. ASW, 70 mm. **Rev:** Two
panda playing on stump

Date	Mintage	F	VF	XF	Unc	BU
1993 Proof	3,000	Value: 250				

KM# 617   50 YUAN

155.5000 g., 0.9990 Silver 4.9942 oz. ASW **Obv:** Temple of
Heaven **Rev:** Two pandas, one in tree **Note:** Prev. Y#638.

Date	Mintage	F	VF	XF	Unc	BU
1994 Proof	3,000	Value: 200				

KM# 727 50 YUAN
155.5000 g., 0.9990 Silver 4.9942 oz. ASW **Obv:** Temple of Heaven **Rev:** Two pandas on river bank, denomination above **Note:** Prev. Y#645.

Date	Mintage	F	VF	XF	Unc	BU
1995 Proof	3,000	Value: 200				

KM# 189 100 YUAN
373.2360 g., 0.9990 Silver 11.987 oz. ASW, 70 mm. **Obv:** Temple of Heaven **Rev:** Two pandas in tree **Note:** Prev. Y#169.

Date	Mintage	F	VF	XF	Unc	BU
1988 Proof	5,000	Value: 300				

KM# 225 100 YUAN
373.2360 g., 0.9990 Silver 11.987 oz. ASW **Obv:** Temple of Heaven **Rev:** Panda with two cubs **Note:** Prev. Y#219.

Date	Mintage	F	VF	XF	Unc	BU
1989 Proof	3,670	Value: 310				

KM# 228 100 YUAN
373.2400 g., 0.9990 Silver 11.987 oz. ASW, 80 mm. **Rev:** Panda seated with two cubs

Date	Mintage	F	VF	XF	Unc	BU
1989 Proof	6,000	Value: 750				

KM# 274 100 YUAN
373.2360 g., 0.9990 Silver 11.987 oz. ASW **Obv:** Temple of Heaven **Rev:** Three curious pandas **Note:** Prev. Y#263.

Date	Mintage	F	VF	XF	Unc	BU
1990 Proof	2,500	Value: 325				

KM# 352 100 YUAN
373.2360 g., 0.9990 Silver 11.987 oz. ASW **Obv:** Temple of Heaven **Rev:** Pandas **Note:** Prev. Y#375.

Date	Mintage	F	VF	XF	Unc	BU
1991 Proof	Est. 2,500	Value: 350				

KM# 354 100 YUAN
373.2400 g., 0.9990 Silver 11.987 oz. ASW, 80 mm. **Rev:** Panda with two cubs, one in tree

Date	Mintage	F	VF	XF	Unc	BU
1991 Proof	2,500	Value: 900				

KM# 399 100 YUAN
373.2360 g., 0.9990 Silver 11.987 oz. ASW, 80 mm. **Obv:** Temple of Heaven, date below **Rev:** Pandas **Note:** Prev. Y#376.

Date	Mintage	F	VF	XF	Unc	BU
1992 Proof	Est. 2,500	Value: 350				

KM# 480 100 YUAN
373.2360 g., 0.9990 Silver 11.987 oz. ASW **Obv:** Temple of Heaven **Rev:** Pandas **Note:** Prev. Y#380.

Date	Mintage	F	VF	XF	Unc	BU
1993 Proof	Est. 2,500	Value: 375				

KM# 618 100 YUAN
373.2360 g., 0.9990 Silver 11.987 oz. ASW **Obv:** Temple of Heaven **Rev:** Panda with two cubs at waters edge, denomination lower right, circle surrounds **Note:** Prev. Y#652.

Date	Mintage	F	VF	XF	Unc	BU
1994 Proof	2,500	Value: 350				

KM# 720 100 YUAN
373.2360 g., 0.9990 Silver 11.987 oz. ASW **Obv:** Temple of Heaven **Rev:** Panda family **Note:** Prev. Y#646.

Date	Mintage	F	VF	XF	Unc	BU
1995 Proof	500	Value: 500				

KM# 899 100 YUAN
373.2400 g., 0.9990 Silver 11.987 oz. ASW, 80 mm. **Rev:** Three panda playing

Date	Mintage	F	VF	XF	Unc	BU
1996 Proof	800	Value: 900				

KM# 994 100 YUAN
373.2400 g., 0.9990 Silver 11.987 oz. ASW, 80 mm. **Rev:** Three panda playing

Date	Mintage	F	VF	XF	Unc	BU
1997 Proof	2,500	Value: 250				

KM# 1133 200 YUAN
1000.0000 g., 0.9990 Silver 32.117 oz. ASW **Obv:** Temple of Heaven **Rev:** Panda **Note:** Large and small date varieties exist. Prev. Y#968.

Date	Mintage	F	VF	XF	Unc	BU
1998 Proof	1,998	Value: 775				

KM# 1222 200 YUAN
1000.2108 g., 0.9990 Silver 32.124 oz. ASW, 100 mm. **Obv:** Temple of Heaven within circle **Rev:** Panda on rock left, denomination at left **Note:** Illustration reduced. Large and small date varieties exist. Prev. Y#971.

Date	Mintage	F	VF	XF	Unc	BU
1999 Proof	—	Value: 850				

KM# 1303 300 YUAN
1000.0000 g., 0.9990 Silver 32.117 oz. ASW, 100 mm. **Obv:** Temple of Heaven **Rev:** Panda seated on leaves **Edge:** Plain **Note:** Large and small date varieties exist. Prev. Y#1071.

Date	Mintage	F	VF	XF	Unc	BU
2000 Proof	2,000	Value: 850				

KM# 1308 300 YUAN
1000.0000 g., 0.9990 Silver 32.117 oz. ASW, 100 mm. **Rev:** Panda seated eating bamboo

Date	Mintage
	2,000 Value: 1,000

GOLD BULLION COINAGE
Panda Series

KM# 351 3 YUAN
1.0000 g., 0.9990 Gold 0.0321 oz. AGW **Obv:** Temple of Heaven **Rev:** Seated panda left, denomination at left **Note:** Prev. Y#307.

Date	Mintage	F	VF	XF	Unc	BU
1991 Proof	110,000	Value: 37.50				

KM# 68 5 YUAN
1.5552 g., 0.9990 Gold 0.0499 oz. AGW **Obv:** Temple of Heaven, date below **Rev:** Panda on all fours right, within circle **Note:** Prev. Y#48.

Date	Mintage	F	VF	XF	Unc	BU
1983 Proof	Est. 58,000	Value: 70.00				

KM# 86 5 YUAN
1.5552 g., 0.9990 Gold 0.0499 oz. AGW **Obv:** Temple of Heaven, date below **Rev:** Panda holding bamboo branch, reclined, denomination at right **Note:** Prev. Y#73.

Date	Mintage	F	VF	XF	Unc	BU
1984 Proof	Est. 86,000	Value: 50.00				

KM# 113 5 YUAN
1.5552 g., 0.9990 Gold 0.0499 oz. AGW **Obv:** Temple of Heaven, date below **Rev:** Panda hanging from branch, denomination upper left **Note:** Prev. Y#80.

Date	Mintage	F	VF	XF	Unc	BU
1985 Proof	Est. 217,000	Value: 50.00				

KM# 131 5 YUAN
1.5552 g., 0.9990 Gold 0.0499 oz. AGW **Obv:** Temple of Heaven, date below **Rev:** Panda, denomination below **Note:** Prev. Y#101.

Date	Mintage	F	VF	XF	Unc	BU
1986	Est. 87,500	—	—	—	—	47.50
1986 P Proof	10,000	Value: 50.00				

KM# 159 5 YUAN
1.5552 g., 0.9990 Gold 0.0499 oz. AGW **Obv:** Temple of Heaven, date below **Rev:** Panda left, denomination below **Note:** Prev. Y#124.

Date	Mintage	F	VF	XF	Unc	BU
1987(s)	Est. 103,000	—	—	—	—	47.50
1987(y)	Est. 39,000	—	—	—	—	47.50
1987 P Proof	10,000	Value: 50.00				

KM# 221 5 YUAN
1.5552 g., 0.9990 Gold 0.0499 oz. AGW **Obv:** Temple of Heaven, date below **Rev:** Panda pawing bamboo **Note:** Prev. Y#152.

Date	Mintage	F	VF	XF	Unc	BU
1988	Est. 482,000	—	—	—	—	47.50
1988 Proof	10,000	Value: 50.00				

KM# 183 5 YUAN
1.5500 g., 0.9990 Gold 0.0498 oz. AGW, 14 mm. **Rev:** Panda seated with bamboo

Date	Mintage	F	VF	XF	Unc	BU
1988 Proof	—	Value: 50.00				

KM# 268 5 YUAN
1.5552 g., 0.9990 Gold 0.0499 oz. AGW **Obv:** Temple of Heaven, date below **Rev:** Panda climbing rock, denomination below **Note:** Prev. Y#238.

Date	Mintage	F	VF	XF	Unc	BU
1990	Est. 337,000	—	—	—	—	47.50
1990 Proof	5,000	Value: 50.00				

KM# 346 5 YUAN
1.5552 g., 0.9990 Gold 0.0499 oz. AGW **Obv:** Temple of Heaven **Rev:** Panda with hind feet in water eating bamboo **Note:** Prev. Y#309.

Date	Mintage	F	VF	XF	Unc	BU
1991		—	—	—	—	50.00
1991 Proof	3,500	Value: 60.00				

KM# 391 5 YUAN
1.5552 g., 0.9990 Gold 0.0499 oz. AGW **Obv:** Temple of Heaven **Rev:** Panda on branch **Note:** Prev. Y#341.

Date	Mintage	F	VF	XF	Unc	BU
1992		—	—	—	—	50.00
1992 Proof	2,000	Value: 65.00				

KM# 473 5 YUAN
1.5552 g., 0.9990 Gold 0.0499 oz. AGW **Obv:** Temple of Heaven, date below **Rev:** Panda pawing bamboo **Note:** Prev. Y#610.

Date	Mintage	F	VF	XF	Unc	BU
1993		—	—	—	—	47.50
1993 Proof	2,500	Value: 55.00				

KM# 611   5 YUAN
1.5552 g., 0.9990 Gold 0.0499 oz. AGW Obv: Temple of Heaven, date below Rev: Panda sitting, denomination below Note: Prev. Y#431.

Date	Mintage	F	VF	XF	Unc	BU
1994	—	—	—	—	—	47.50
1994 Proof	—	Value: 55.00				

KM# 715   5 YUAN
1.5552 g., 0.9990 Gold 0.0499 oz. AGW Obv: Temple of Heaven, date below Rev: Panda holding bamboo stick, denomination at left Note: Prev. Y#640.

Date	Mintage	F	VF	XF	Unc	BU
1995	—	—	—	—	—	47.50

KM# 984   5 YUAN
1.5552 g., 0.9990 Gold 0.0499 oz. AGW Obv: Temple of Heaven Rev: Panda on branch Note: Large and small date varieties exist. Prev. Y#716.

Date	Mintage	F	VF	XF	Unc	BU
1997	—	—	—	—	—	47.50

Note: Exists in large and small date varieties

KM# 1125   5 YUAN
1.5600 g., 0.9990 Gold 0.0501 oz. AGW Obv: Temple of Heaven Rev: Panda seated on rock Note: Prev. Y#990.

Date	Mintage	F	VF	XF	Unc	BU
1998	—	—	—	—	—	47.50

KM# 1215   5 YUAN
1.5600 g., 0.9990 Gold 0.0501 oz. AGW Obv: Temple of Heaven Rev: Panda on ledge Note: Prev. Y#981.

Date	Mintage	F	VF	XF	Unc	BU
1999	—	—	—	—	—	47.50

Note: Exists in Large and Small date varieties.

KM# 1302   5 YUAN
1.5600 g., 0.9990 Gold 0.0501 oz. AGW Obv: Temple of Heaven Rev: Panda seated on leaves Note: Large and small date varieties exist. Prev. Y#945.

Date	Mintage	F	VF	XF	Unc	BU
2000	—	—	—	—	—	47.50

Note: Domestic Chinese examples struck with mirror fields, overseas examples struck with frosted fields

KM# 69   10 YUAN
3.1103 g., 0.9990 Gold 0.0999 oz. AGW Obv: Temple of Heaven, date below Rev: Panda right Note: Prev. Y#49.

Date	Mintage	F	VF	XF	Unc	BU
1983	Est. 74,000	—	—	—	—	100

KM# 88   10 YUAN
3.1103 g., 0.9990 Gold 0.0999 oz. AGW Obv: Temple of Heaven Rev: Panda holding bamboo branch, reclined, denomination at right Note: Prev. Y#74.

Date	Mintage	F	VF	XF	Unc	BU
1984	10,000	—	—	—	—	185

KM# 115   10 YUAN
3.1103 g., 0.9990 Gold 0.0999 oz. AGW Obv: Temple of Heaven, date below Rev: Panda hanging from branch, denomination upper left Note: Prev. Y#81.

Date	Mintage	F	VF	XF	Unc	BU
1985	Est. 150,000	—	—	—	—	100

KM# 132   10 YUAN
3.1103 g., 0.9990 Gold 0.0999 oz. AGW Obv: Temple of Heaven Rev: Panda, denomination below Note: Prev. Y#102.

Date	Mintage	F	VF	XF	Unc	BU
1986	Est. 45,000	—	—	—	—	100
1986 P Proof	10,000	Value: 90.00				

KM# 163   10 YUAN
3.1103 g., 0.9990 Gold 0.0999 oz. AGW Obv: Temple of Heaven, date below Rev: Panda, denomination below Note: Prev. Y#125.

Date	Mintage	F	VF	XF	Unc	BU
1987(s)	Est. 108,000	—	—	—	—	100
1987(y)	Est. 37,000	—	—	—	—	100
1987 P Proof	10,000	Value: 110				

KM# 184   10 YUAN
3.1103 g., 0.9990 Gold 0.0999 oz. AGW Obv: Temple of Heaven, date below Rev: Panda pawing bamboo, denomination below Note: Prev. Y#153.

Date	Mintage	F	VF	XF	Unc	BU
1988	Est. 290,000	—	—	—	—	100
1988 Proof	10,000	Value: 110				

KM# 223   10 YUAN
3.1103 g., 0.9990 Gold 0.0999 oz. AGW, 14 mm. Rev: Panda seated with bamboo, linear grid background

Date	Mintage	F	VF	XF	Unc	BU
1989	Est. 128,000	—	—	—	25.00	—
1989 Proof	8,000	Value: 45.00				

KM# 269   10 YUAN
3.1103 g., 0.9990 Gold 0.0999 oz. AGW Obv: Temple of Heaven, date below Rev: Panda, denomination below Note: Prev. Y#239.

Date	Mintage	F	VF	XF	Unc	BU
1990	Est. 214,000	—	—	—	—	100
1990 Proof	5,000	Value: 110				

KM# 347   10 YUAN
3.1100 g., 0.9990 Gold 0.0999 oz. AGW Obv: Temple of Heaven Rev: Panda with hind feet in water eating bamboo Note: Similar to 100 Yuan, KM# 350. Prev. Y#310.

Date	Mintage	F	VF	XF	Unc	BU
1991	—	—	—	—	—	100
1991 Proof	3,500	Value: 110				

KM# 392   10 YUAN
3.1103 g., 0.9990 Gold 0.0999 oz. AGW Obv: Temple of Heaven, date below Rev: Panda climbing right on eucalyptus branch Note: Prev. Y#342.

Date	Mintage	F	VF	XF	Unc	BU
1992	—	—	—	—	—	100
1992 Proof	2,000	Value: 110				

KM# 474   10 YUAN
3.1103 g., 0.9990 Gold 0.0999 oz. AGW Obv: Temple of Heaven Rev: Panda on flat rock Note: Prev. Y#484; 611; 1203.

Date	Mintage	F	VF	XF	Unc	BU
1993	—	—	—	—	—	100
1993 Proof	2,500	Value: 110				

KM# 612   10 YUAN
3.1103 g., 0.9990 Gold 0.0999 oz. AGW Obv: Temple of Heaven, date below Rev: Seated panda eating, denomination below Note: Prev. Y#432.

Date	Mintage	F	VF	XF	Unc	BU
1994	—	—	—	—	—	100
1994 Proof	2,500	Value: 110				

KM# 716   10 YUAN
3.1103 g., 0.9990 Gold 0.0999 oz. AGW Obv: Temple of Heaven Rev: Panda eating bamboo, denomination at left Note: Prev. Y#641.

Date	Mintage	F	VF	XF	Unc	BU
1995	—	—	—	—	—	100

KM# 889   10 YUAN
3.1103 g., 0.9990 Gold 0.0999 oz. AGW Subject: 15th Anniversary - Gold Panda Coins Obv: Temple of Heaven with additional legend Rev: Panda in tree Note: Large and small date varieties exist. Prev. Y#848.

Date	Mintage	F	VF	XF	Unc	BU
1996 Proof	20,000	Value: 110				

KM# 884   10 YUAN
3.1103 g., 0.9990 Gold 0.0999 oz. AGW Obv: Temple of Heaven, date below Rev: Panda in tree Note: Large and small date varieties exist. Prev. Y#575.

Date	Mintage	F	VF	XF	Unc	BU
1996	—	—	—	—	—	100

KM# 883   10 YUAN
1.5552 g., 0.9990 Gold 0.0499 oz. AGW Obv: Temple of Heaven, date below Rev: Panda in tree looking down, denomination lower left Note: Large and small date varieties exist. Prev. Y#581.

Date	Mintage	F	VF	XF	Unc	BU
1996	—	—	—	—	—	55.00

KM# 987   10 YUAN
3.1103 g., 0.9990 Gold 0.0999 oz. AGW Obv: Temple of Heaven Rev: Panda on branch Note: Large and small date varieties exist. Prev. Y#717.

Date	Mintage	F	VF	XF	Unc	BU
1997	—	—	—	—	—	100

KM# 1127   10 YUAN
3.1103 g., 0.9990 Gold 0.0999 oz. AGW Obv: Temple of Heaven Rev: Panda seated on rock Note: Large and small date varieties exist. Prev. Y#988.

Date	Mintage	F	VF	XF	Unc	BU
1998	—	—	—	—	—	100

KM# 1218   10 YUAN
3.1103 g., 0.9990 Gold 0.0999 oz. AGW Obv: Temple of Heaven Rev: Panda on ledge Note: Prev. Y#989.

Date	Mintage	F	VF	XF	Unc	BU
1999	—	—	—	—	—	100

Note: Exists in Large and Small date varieties.

KM# 1304   10 YUAN
3.1103 g., 0.9990 Gold 0.0999 oz. AGW Obv: Temple of Heaven Rev: Panda seated on leaves Note: Large and small date varieties exist. Prev. Y#946.

Date	Mintage	F	VF	XF	Unc	BU
2000 Proof	—	Value: 110				

KM# 70   25 YUAN
7.7758 g., 0.9990 Gold 0.2497 oz. AGW Obv: Temple of Heaven, date below Rev: Panda walking right, in inner circle, denomination below Note: Prev. Y#50.

Date	Mintage	F	VF	XF	Unc	BU
1983	Est. 39,000	—	—	—	—	250

KM# 89   25 YUAN
7.7758 g., 0.9990 Gold 0.2497 oz. AGW Obv: Temple of Heaven, date below Rev: Lounging Panda with bamboo Note: Prev. Y#75.

Date	Mintage	F	VF	XF	Unc	BU
1984	Est. 38,000	—	—	—	—	250

KM# 116   25 YUAN
7.7758 g., 0.9990 Gold 0.2497 oz. AGW **Obv:** Temple of Heaven, date below **Rev:** Panda hanging on bamboo branch, denomination upper left **Note:** Prev. Y#82.

Date	Mintage	F	VF	XF	Unc	BU
1985	Est. 95,000	—	—	—	—	250

KM# 133   25 YUAN
7.7758 g., 0.9990 Gold 0.2497 oz. AGW **Obv:** Temple of Heaven **Rev:** Facing panda standing, denomination below **Note:** Prev. Y#103.

Date	Mintage	F	VF	XF	Unc	BU
1986	Est. 33,000	—	—	—	—	250
1986 P Proof	10,000	Value: 260				

KM# 161   25 YUAN
7.7758 g., 0.9990 Gold 0.2497 oz. AGW **Obv:** Temple of Heaven, date below **Rev:** Panda drinking, denomination below **Note:** Prev. Y#126.

Date	Mintage	F	VF	XF	Unc	BU
1987(s)	Est. 81,000	—	—	—	—	250
1987(y)	Est. 31,000	—	—	—	—	250
1987 P Proof	10,000	Value: 260				

KM# 185   25 YUAN
7.7758 g., 0.9990 Gold 0.2497 oz. AGW **Obv:** Temple of Heaven **Rev:** Panda pawing bamboo **Note:** Prev. Y#154.

Date	Mintage	F	VF	XF	Unc	BU
1988	Est. 122,000	—	—	—	—	250
1988 Proof	10,000	Value: 260				

KM# 224   25 YUAN
7.7758 g., 0.9990 Gold 0.2497 oz. AGW **Obv:** Temple of Heaven, date below **Rev:** Panda reclining, grid behind, denomination below **Note:** Prev. Y#189.

Date	Mintage	F	VF	XF	Unc	BU
1989	Est. 71,000	—	—	—	—	250
1989 Proof	8,000	Value: 260				

KM# 270   25 YUAN
7.7758 g., 0.9990 Gold 0.2497 oz. AGW **Obv:** Temple of Heaven, date below **Rev:** Panda, denomination lower right **Note:** Prev. Y#240.

Date	Mintage	F	VF	XF	Unc	BU
1990	—	—	—	—	—	250
1990 Proof	5,000	Value: 260				

KM# 359   25 YUAN
7.7758 g., 0.9990 Gold 0.2497 oz. AGW, 22 mm. **Obv:** Temple of Heaven, date below **Edge:** Reeded **Note:** Prev. Y#311.

Date	Mintage	F	VF	XF	Unc	BU
1991	—	—	—	—	—	250
1991 Proof	—	Value: 260				

KM# 393   25 YUAN
7.7758 g., 0.9990 Gold 0.2497 oz. AGW **Obv:** Temple of Heaven, date below **Rev:** Panda on limb **Note:** Prev. Y#343.

Date	Mintage	F	VF	XF	Unc	BU
1992	—	—	—	—	—	250
1992 Proof	—	Value: 260				

KM# A613   25 YUAN
7.7758 g., 0.9990 Gold 0.2497 oz. AGW, 22 mm. **Obv:** Temple of Heaven **Rev:** Panda seated on flat rock **Edge:** Reeded **Mint:** Shenyang

Date	Mintage	F	VF	XF	Unc	BU
1993(y)	—	—	—	—	—	250
1993P(y) Proof	2,500	Value: 260				

KM# 613   25 YUAN
7.7758 g., 0.9990 Gold 0.2497 oz. AGW **Obv:** Temple of Heaven, date below **Rev:** Panda tugging on bamboo sprig **Note:** Prev. Y#433.

Date	Mintage	F	VF	XF	Unc	BU
1994	35,000	—	—	—	—	250
1994 Proof	—	Value: 260				

KM# 717   25 YUAN
7.7600 g., 0.9990 Gold 0.2492 oz. AGW **Obv:** Temple of Heaven, date below **Rev:** Panda **Note:** Prev. Y#642.

Date	Mintage	F	VF	XF	Unc	BU
1995	—	—	—	—	—	250

KM# 885   25 YUAN
7.8300 g., 0.9990 Gold 0.2515 oz. AGW **Obv:** Temple of Heaven, date below **Rev:** Panda **Note:** Large and small date varieties exist. Prev. Y#576.

Date	Mintage	F	VF	XF	Unc	BU
1996	—	—	—	—	—	250

KM# 891   25 YUAN
7.7759 g., 0.9990 Gold 0.2497 oz. AGW **Subject:** 15th Anniversary - Gold Panda Coinage **Obv:** Temple of Heaven with additional legend **Rev:** Panda in tree **Note:** Large and small date varieties exist. Prev. Y#849.

Date	Mintage	F	VF	XF	Unc	BU
1996 Proof	8,000	Value: 260				

KM# 989   25 YUAN
7.7759 g., 0.9990 Gold 0.2497 oz. AGW **Obv:** Temple of Heaven **Rev:** Panda on branch **Note:** Prev. Y#718.

Date	Mintage	F	VF	XF	Unc	BU
1997	—	—	—	—	—	250

Note: Exists in Large and Small date varieties.

KM# 1128   25 YUAN
7.7758 g., 0.9990 Gold 0.2497 oz. AGW **Obv:** Temple of Heaven **Rev:** Panda seated on rock **Note:** Large and small date varieties exist. Prev. Y#1002.

Date	Mintage	F	VF	XF	Unc	BU
1998	—	—	—	—	—	250

Note: Exists in both large and small date varieties

KM# 1219   25 YUAN
7.7758 g., 0.9990 Gold 0.2497 oz. AGW **Obv:** Temple of Heaven **Rev:** Panda on ledge **Note:** Large and small date varieties exist. Prev. Y#1003.

Date	Mintage	F	VF	XF	Unc	BU
1999	—	—	—	—	—	250

KM# 1305   25 YUAN
7.7758 g., 0.9990 Gold 0.2497 oz. AGW **Obv:** Temple of Heaven **Rev:** Panda seated on leaves **Note:** Large and small date varieties exist. Prev. Y#947.

Date	Mintage	F	VF	XF	Unc	BU
2000	—	—	—	—	—	250

Note: Domestic Chinese examples struck with mirror fields, overseas examples struck with frosted fields

KM# 71   50 YUAN
15.5517 g., 0.9990 Gold 0.4995 oz. AGW **Obv:** Temple of Heaven, date below **Rev:** Panda walking right, in inner circle, date below **Note:** Prev. Y#51.

Date	Mintage	F	VF	XF	Unc	BU
1983 Proof	Est. 23,000	Value: 500				

KM# 90   50 YUAN
15.5517 g., 0.9990 Gold 0.4995 oz. AGW **Obv:** Temple of Heaven, date below **Rev:** Lounging panda with bamboo sprig, denomination at right **Note:** Prev. Y#76.

Date	Mintage	F	VF	XF	Unc	BU
1984 Proof	Est. 17,000	Value: 500				

KM# 117   50 YUAN
15.5517 g., 0.9990 Gold 0.4995 oz. AGW **Obv:** Temple of Heaven, date below **Rev:** Panda hanging from bamboo branch, denomination upper left **Note:** Prev. Y#83.

Date	Mintage	F	VF	XF	Unc	BU
1985	Est. 76,000	—	—	—	—	500

KM# 134   50 YUAN
15.5517 g., 0.9990 Gold 0.4995 oz. AGW **Obv:** Temple of Heaven, date below **Rev:** Facing panda standing, denomination below **Note:** Prev. Y#104.

Date	Mintage	F	VF	XF	Unc	BU
1986	Est. 60,000	—	—	—	—	500
1986 P Proof	10,000	Value: 520				

KM# 162   50 YUAN
15.5517 g., 0.9990 Gold 0.4995 oz. AGW **Obv:** Temple of Heaven, date below **Rev:** Panda drinking water, denomination below **Note:** Prev. Y#127.

Date	Mintage	F	VF	XF	Unc	BU
1987(s)	Est. 91,000	—	—	—	—	500
1987(y)	Est. 17,000	—	—	—	—	500
1987 P Proof	10,000	Value: 520				

KM# 186   50 YUAN
15.5517 g., 0.9990 Gold 0.4995 oz. AGW **Obv:** Temple of Heaven, date below **Rev:** Panda pawing bamboo within circle, denomination below **Note:** Prev. Y#155.

Date	Mintage	F	VF	XF	Unc	BU
1988	Est. 104,000	—	—	—	—	500
1988 Proof	10,000	Value: 520				

KM# 226   50 YUAN
15.5517 g., 0.9990 Gold 0.4995 oz. AGW **Obv:** Temple of Heaven **Rev:** Grid behind panda **Note:** Prev. Y#190.

Date	Mintage	F	VF	XF	Unc	BU
1989	Est. 46,000	—	—	—	—	500
1989 Proof	8,000	Value: 520				

KM# 227   50 YUAN
31.1030 g., 0.9990 Palladium 0.9989 oz. **Obv:** Building, date below **Rev:** Panda on grid background, denomination lower right **Note:** Prev. Y#220.

Date	Mintage	F	VF	XF	Unc	BU
1989	3,000	—	—	—	—	500

KM# 271   50 YUAN
15.5517 g., 0.9990 Gold 0.4995 oz. AGW **Obv:** Temple of Heaven, date below **Rev:** Panda **Note:** Prev. Y#241.

Date	Mintage	F	VF	XF	Unc	BU
1990	Est. 35,000					500
1990 Proof	5,000	Value: 520				

KM# 349   50 YUAN
15.5517 g., 0.9990 Gold 0.4995 oz. AGW **Obv:** Temple of Heaven, date below **Rev:** Panda tugging on bamboo sprig, denomination below, within circle, date below **Note:** Prev. Y#312.

Date	Mintage	F	VF	XF	Unc	BU
1991	—					500
1991 Proof	3,500	Value: 520				

KM# 357   50 YUAN
31.1035 g., 0.9990 Gold 0.9990 oz. AGW **Subject:** 10th Anniversary of Panda Coinage **Obv:** Temple of Heaven, date below **Rev:** Panda climbing bamboo branch **Note:** Double thickness. Prev. Y#315.

Date	Mintage	F	VF	XF	Unc	BU
1991 Proof	2,500	Value: 975				

KM# 476   50 YUAN
15.5517 g., 0.9990 Gold 0.4995 oz. AGW **Obv:** Temple of Heaven **Rev:** Pandas **Note:** Prev. Y#613.

Date	Mintage	F	VF	XF	Unc	BU
1993	—					500
1993 Proof	2,500	Value: 520				

KM# A614   50 YUAN
15.5500 g., 0.9990 Gold 0.4994 oz. AGW, 27 mm. **Obv:** Temple of Heaven **Rev:** Panda seated on flat rock **Edge:** Reeded **Mint:** Shenyang

Date	Mintage	F	VF	XF	Unc	BU
1993(y)	—					500
1993P(y) Proof	2,500	Value: 520				

KM# 614   50 YUAN
15.5517 g., 0.9990 Gold 0.4995 oz. AGW **Obv:** Temple of Heaven **Rev:** Panda seated, eating bamboo shoots, denomination below **Note:** Prev. Y#434.

Date	Mintage	F	VF	XF	Unc	BU
1994	—					500
1994 Proof	2,500	Value: 520				

KM# 718   50 YUAN
15.5517 g., 0.9990 Gold 0.4995 oz. AGW **Obv:** Temple of Heaven **Rev:** Panda eating bamboo, denomination at left **Note:** Prev. Y#643.

Date	Mintage	F	VF	XF	Unc	BU
1995	—					500

KM# 886   50 YUAN
15.5517 g., 0.9990 Gold 0.4995 oz. AGW **Obv:** Temple of Heaven, date below **Rev:** Panda in tree **Note:** Large and small date varieties exist. Prev. Y#577.

Date	Mintage	F	VF	XF	Unc	BU
1996	—					500

KM# 990   50 YUAN
15.5517 g., 0.9990 Gold 0.4995 oz. AGW **Obv:** Temple of Heaven within circle, date below **Rev:** Panda on large tree branch, denomination below **Note:** Prev. Y#719.

Date	Mintage	F	VF	XF	Unc	BU
1997	—					500

Note: Exists in Large and Small date varieties

KM# 1129   50 YUAN
15.5517 g., 0.9990 Gold 0.4995 oz. AGW **Obv:** Temple of Heaven **Rev:** Panda seated on rock **Note:** Prev. Y#1010.

Date	Mintage	F	VF	XF	Unc	BU
1998	—					500

Note: Exists in Large and Small date varieties

KM# 1220   50 YUAN
15.5517 g., 0.9990 Gold 0.4995 oz. AGW **Obv:** Temple of Heaven **Rev:** Panda on ledge **Note:** Prev. Y#1011.

Date	Mintage	F	VF	XF	Unc	BU
1999	—					500

Note: Exists in Large and Small date varieties

KM# 1306   50 YUAN
15.5518 g., 0.9990 Gold 0.4995 oz. AGW **Obv:** Temple of Heaven, date below **Rev:** Panda seated on leaves **Note:** Large and small date varieties exist. Prev. Y#948.

Date	Mintage	F	VF	XF	Unc	BU
2000 Proof	—	Value: 520				

Note: Domestic Chinese examples struck with mirror fields, overseas examples struck with frosted fields.

KM# 72   100 YUAN
31.1320 g., 0.9990 Gold 0.9999 oz. AGW **Obv:** Temple of Heaven, date below **Rev:** Panda right within circle, date below **Note:** Prev. Y#52.

Date	Mintage	F	VF	XF	Unc	BU
1983	22,000				—	BV+10%

KM# 91   100 YUAN
31.1320 g., 0.9990 Gold 0.9999 oz. AGW **Obv:** Temple of Heaven, date below **Rev:** Lounging panda with bamboo sprigs, denomination at right **Note:** Prev. Y#77.

Date	Mintage	F	VF	XF	Unc	BU
1984	23,000				—	BV+10%

KM# 118   100 YUAN
31.1320 g., 0.9990 Gold 0.9999 oz. AGW **Obv:** Temple of Heaven, date below **Rev:** Panda hanging from branch, denomination upper left **Note:** Prev. Y#84.

Date	Mintage	F	VF	XF	Unc	BU
1985	164,000				—	BV+10%

KM# 135   100 YUAN
31.1320 g., 0.9990 Gold 0.9999 oz. AGW **Obv:** Temple of Heaven, date below **Rev:** Panda amongst bamboo plants **Note:** Prev. Y#105.

Date	Mintage	F	VF	XF	Unc	BU
1986	97,000				—	BV+10%
1986 P Proof	10,000	BV+15%				

KM# 166   100 YUAN
31.1320 g., 0.9990 Gold 0.9999 oz. AGW **Obv:** Temple of Heaven, date below **Rev:** Panda drinking at stream, denomination below **Note:** Prev. Y#128.

Date	Mintage	F	VF	XF	Unc	BU
1987(s)	84,000				—	BV+10%
1987(y)	47,000				—	BV+10%
1987 P Proof	10,000	BV+15%				

KM# 187   100 YUAN
31.1320 g., 0.9990 Gold 0.9999 oz. AGW **Obv:** Temple of Heaven, date below **Rev:** Panda pawing bamboo within circle, denomination below **Note:** Prev. Y#156.

Date	Mintage	F	VF	XF	Unc	BU
1988	167,000				—	BV+10%
1988 Proof	10,000	BV+15%				

KM# 229   100 YUAN
31.1320 g., 0.9990 Gold 0.9999 oz. AGW **Obv:** Temple of Heaven, date below **Rev:** Panda reclining, grid behind, denomination below **Note:** Prev. Y#191.

Date	Mintage	F	VF	XF	Unc	BU
1989	—				—	BV+10%
1989 Proof	8,000	BV+15%				

KM# 272   100 YUAN
31.1320 g., 0.9990 Gold 0.9999 oz. AGW **Obv:** Temple of Heaven, date below **Rev:** Panda climbing rock, denomination below **Note:** Prev. Y#242.

Date	Mintage	F	VF	XF	Unc	BU
1990	—				—	BV+10%
1990 Proof	5,000	BV+15%				

KM# 350   100 YUAN
31.1320 g., 0.9990 Gold 0.9999 oz. AGW **Obv:** Temple of Heaven, date below **Rev:** Seated panda with hind feet in water, eating bamboo, denomination at left **Note:** Prev. Y#313.

Date	Mintage	F	VF	XF	Unc	BU
1991	—				—	BV+10%
1991 Proof	3,500	BV+15%				

KM# 395   100 YUAN
31.1035 g., 0.9990 Gold 0.9990 oz. AGW **Obv:** Temple of Heaven within circle, date below **Rev:** Panda on branch, denomination above **Note:** Prev. Y#345.

Date	Mintage	F	VF	XF	Unc	BU
1992	—				—	BV+10%
1992 Proof	2,000	BV+15%				

KM# 477   100 YUAN
31.1035 g., 0.9990 Gold 0.9990 oz. AGW   **Obv:** Temple of
Heaven **Rev:** Panda seated on rock **Note:** Prev. Y#614.

Date	Mintage	F	VF	XF	Unc	BU
1993					—	BV+10%

KM# A615   100 YUAN
8.0000 g., 0.9160 Gold 0.2356 oz. AGW   **Obv:** National emblem,
date below **Rev:** Panda climbing tree, denomination at right

Date	Mintage	F	VF	XF	Unc	BU
1994 Proof	5,000	Value: 250				

KM# 615   100 YUAN
31.1035 g., 0.9990 Gold 0.9990 oz. AGW   **Obv:** Temple of
Heaven, date below **Rev:** Panda seated, eating bamboo shoots,
denomination below **Note:** Prev. Y#435.

Date	Mintage	F	VF	XF	Unc	BU
1994					—	BV+10%

KM# 719   100 YUAN
31.1030 g., 0.9990 Gold 0.9989 oz. AGW   **Obv:** Temple of
Heaven **Rev:** Panda eating bamboo **Note:** Prev. Y#644.

Date	Mintage	F	VF	XF	Unc	BU
1995					—	BV+10%

KM# 726   100 YUAN
31.0103 g., 0.9990 Gold 0.9960 oz. AGW   **Obv:** Temple of
Heaven within circle, date below **Rev:** Panda approaching water
from right, denomination below **Note:** Prev. Y#790.

Date	Mintage	F	VF	XF	Unc	BU
1995 Proof	2,000	BV+15%				

KM# 896   100 YUAN
31.1035 g., 0.9990 Gold 0.9990 oz. AGW   **Subject:** 15th
Anniversary - Gold Panda Coins **Obv:** Temple of Heaven with
additional legend **Rev:** Panda in tree **Note:** Large and small
varieties exist. Previous Y # 850.

Date	Mintage	F	VF	XF	Unc	BU
1996 Proof	1,500	BV+15%				

KM# 887   100 YUAN
31.1035 g., 0.9990 Gold 0.9990 oz. AGW   **Obv:** Temple of
Heaven within circle, date below **Rev:** Panda in tree,
denomination at left **Note:** Large and small date varieties exist.
Prev. Y#578.

Date	Mintage	F	VF	XF	Unc	BU
1996					—	BV+10%

KM# 901   100 YUAN
31.1035 g., 0.9990 Gold 0.9990 oz. AGW   **Obv:** Temple of
Heaven **Rev:** Panda sitting on rock **Note:** Large and small date
varieties exist. Prev. Y#1013.

Date	Mintage	F	VF	XF	Unc	BU
1996 Proof	1,500	BV+15%				

KM# 991   100 YUAN
31.1035 g., 0.9990 Gold 0.9990 oz. AGW   **Obv:** Temple of
Heaven **Rev:** Panda on large branch, denomination below
Note: Large and small date varieties exist. Prev. Y#720.

Date	Mintage	F	VF	XF	Unc	BU
1997					—	BV+10%

Note: Exists in large and small date varieties

KM# 1130   100 YUAN
31.1320 g., 0.9990 Gold 0.9999 oz. AGW   **Obv:** Temple of
Heaven **Rev:** Panda seated on rock **Note:** Large and small date
varieties exist. Prev. Y#1016.

Date	Mintage	F	VF	XF	Unc	BU
1998					—	BV+10%

KM# 1221   100 YUAN
31.1320 g., 0.9990 Gold 0.9999 oz. AGW   **Obv:** Temple of
Heaven **Rev:** Panda on ledge **Note:** Large and small date
varieties exist. Prev. Y#1017.

Date	Mintage	F	VF	XF	Unc	BU
1999					—	BV+10%

KM# 1307   100 YUAN
31.1036 g., 0.9990 Gold 0.9990 oz. AGW   **Obv:** Temple of
Heaven **Rev:** Panda seated on leaves **Note:** Large and small
date varieties exist. Prev. Y#949.

Date	Mintage	F	VF	XF	Unc	BU
2000					—	BV+10%

Note: Domestic Chinese examples struck with mirror fields,
overseas examples struck with frosted fields

KM# 164   500 YUAN
155.5150 g., 0.9990 Gold 4.9947 oz. AGW, 60 mm.
Obv: Temple of Heaven **Rev:** Panda with cub, denomination
below **Note:** Illustration reduced. Prev. Y#147.

Date	Mintage	F	VF	XF	Unc	BU
1987 Proof	3,000	BV+15%				

KM# 190   500 YUAN
155.5150 g., 0.9990 Gold 4.9947 oz. AGW   **Obv:** Temple of
Heaven **Rev:** Two pandas in tree, denomination upper left
Note: Prev. Y#233.

Date	Mintage	F	VF	XF	Unc	BU
1988 Proof	3,000	BV+15%				

KM# 400   500 YUAN
155.5150 g., 0.9990 Gold 4.9947 oz. AGW   **Obv:** Temple of
Heaven, date below **Rev:** Pandas **Note:** Prev. Y#369.

Date	Mintage	F	VF	XF	Unc	BU
1992 Proof	99	BV+25%				

KM# 481   500 YUAN
155.5150 g., 0.9990 Gold 4.9947 oz. AGW   **Obv:** Temple of
Heaven **Rev:** Two pandas climbing tree stumps **Note:** Prev.
Y#761.

Date	Mintage	F	VF	XF	Unc	BU
1993 Proof	99	BV+25%				

KM# 619   500 YUAN
155.5150 g., 0.9990 Gold 4.9947 oz. AGW   **Obv:** Temple of
Heaven **Rev:** Two pandas, one in tree, denomination above
Note: Prev. Y#639.

Date	Mintage	F	VF	XF	Unc	BU
1994 Proof.	99	BV+25%				

KM# 92   1000 YUAN
373.2360 g., 0.9990 Gold 11.987 oz. AGW, 70 mm.
Obv: Temple of Heaven **Rev:** Panda seated left, denomination
belo0w **Note:** Illustration reduced. Prev. #Y66.

Date	Mintage	F	VF	XF	Unc	BU
1984 Proof	250	BV+25%				

Note: A typical sealed proof exhibits some scuffing and is
valued as above, while perfect examples can bring up
to a 50% premium

KM# 136.1 1000 YUAN
373.2360 g., 0.9990 Gold 11.987 oz. AGW, 70 mm. **Obv:**
Temple of Heaven **Rev:** Panda eating bamboo shoot with cub,
denomination at right **Note:** Illustration reduced. Prev. #Y118.1.

Date	Mintage	F	VF	XF	Unc	BU
1986 Proof	2,550	BV+15%				

KM# 136.2 1000 YUAN
373.2360 g., 0.9990 Gold 11.987 oz. AGW **Obv:** Temple of
Heaven **Rev:** Panda eating bamboo shoot with cub **Edge:** Plain
Note: Prev. #Y118.2.

Date	Mintage	F	VF	XF	Unc	BU
1986 Proof	—	—	—	—	—	—

Note: 2 known; Last traded privately at $45,000

KM# 165 1000 YUAN
373.2360 g., 0.9990 Gold 11.987 oz. AGW **Obv:** Temple of
Heaven **Rev:** Panda with cub, denomination below
Note: Illustration reduced. Prev. #Y157.

Date	Mintage	F	VF	XF	Unc	BU
1987 Proof	2,445	BV+15%				

KM# 191 1000 YUAN
373.2360 g., 0.9990 Gold 11.987 oz. AGW **Obv:** Temple of
Heaven **Rev:** Pandas in tree **Note:** Similar to 500 Yuan, KM #
190. Prev. #Y234.

Date	Mintage	F	VF	XF	Unc	BU
1988 Proof	1,650	BV+15%				

KM# 275 1000 YUAN
373.2360 g., 0.9990 Gold 11.987 oz. AGW, 70 mm. **Obv:** Temple
of Heaven **Rev:** Three pandas, denomination upper right **Note:**
Prev. #Y282.

Date	Mintage	F	VF	XF	Unc	BU
1990 Proof	500	BV+20%				

KM# 355 1000 YUAN
373.2360 g., 0.9990 Gold 11.987 oz. AGW **Obv:** Temple of
Heaven, date below **Rev:** Pandas **Note:** Prev. #Y371.

Date	Mintage	F	VF	XF	Unc	BU
1991 Proof	400	BV+20%				

KM# 401 1000 YUAN
373.2360 g., 0.9990 Gold 11.987 oz. AGW **Obv:** Temple of
Heaven **Rev:** Pandas **Note:** Prev. #Y372.

Date	Mintage	F	VF	XF	Unc	BU
1992 Proof	99	BV+30%				

KM# 482 1000 YUAN
373.2360 g., 0.9990 Gold 11.987 oz. AGW **Obv:** Temple of
Heaven **Rev:** Panda family of three **Note:** Prev. #Y762.

Date	Mintage	F	VF	XF	Unc	BU
1993 Proof	99	BV+30%				

KM# 620 1000 YUAN
373.2420 g., 0.9990 Gold 11.987 oz. AGW, 70 mm.
Obv: Temple of Heaven **Rev:** Panda and two cubs at water's
edge **Edge:** Reeded **Note:** Prev. #Y1089.

Date	Mintage	F	VF	XF	Unc	BU
1994 Proof	99	BV+30%				

KM# 721 1000 YUAN
373.2420 g., 0.9990 Gold 11.987 oz. AGW, 70 mm.
Obv: Temple of Heaven **Rev:** Two adult pandas with cub
Edge: Reeded **Note:** Illustration reduced. Prev. #Y1090.

Date	Mintage	F	VF	XF	Unc	BU
1995 Proof	99	BV+30%				

KM# 992 2000 YUAN
1000.0000 g., 0.9990 Gold 32.117 oz. AGW **Obv:** Temple of
Heaven **Rev:** Panda **Note:** Large and small date varieties exist.
Prev. #Y961.

Date	Mintage	F	VF	XF	Unc	BU
1997 Proof	58	BV+30%				

KM# A1130 2000 YUAN
1000.0000 g., 0.9990 Gold 32.117 oz. AGW **Obv:** Temple of
Heaven **Rev:** Panda **Note:** Large and small date varieties exist.

Date	Mintage	F	VF	XF	Unc	BU
1998 Proof	58	BV+20%				

KM# 1223 2000 YUAN
1000.2108 g., 0.9990 Gold 32.124 oz. AGW **Obv:** Temple of
Heaven **Rev:** Panda on rock **Note:** Large and small date varieties
exist. Prev. #Y972.

Date	Mintage	F	VF	XF	Unc	BU
1999 Proof	68	BV+30%				

KM# 358 10000 YUAN
4851.6001 g., 0.9990 Gold 155.82 oz. AGW **Subject:** 10th
Anniversary of Gold Panda Issue **Obv:** Temple of Heaven
Rev: Panda on branch, denomination at right, in center of 10
panda coin designs **Note:** Prev. #Y358.

Date	Mintage	F	VF	XF	Unc	BU
1991 Proof, Rare	10	—	—	—	—	—

KM# 1309 30000 YUAN
1000.0000 g., 0.9990 Gold 32.117 oz. AGW, 90 mm.
Rev: Panda seated eating bamboo

Date	Mintage	F	VF	XF	Unc	BU
2000 Proof	68	Value: 70,000				

GOLD BULLION COINAGE
Lunar Series

KM# 1012 10 YUAN
3.1103 g., 0.9990 Gold 0.0999 oz. AGW **Subject:** Year of the
Ox **Obv:** Mingyuan Pavilion **Rev:** Calf **Note:** Prev. Y#901.

Date	Mintage	F	VF	XF	Unc	BU
1997 Proof	48,000	Value: 100				

KM# 1139 10 YUAN
3.1103 g., 0.9990 Gold 0.0999 oz. AGW **Subject:** Year of the
Tiger **Obv:** Badaling building, date below **Rev:** Tiger cub,
denomination at right **Note:** Prev. Y#924.

Date	Mintage	F	VF	XF	Unc	BU
1998 Proof	48,000	Value: 110				

KM# 1139a 10 YUAN
3.1103 g., 0.9990 Gold 0.0999 oz. AGW **Subject:** Year of the
Tiger **Obv:** Badaling building, date below **Rev:** Multicolor tiger
head, facing, denomination at right **Note:** Prev. Y#925.

Date	Mintage	F	VF	XF	Unc	BU
1998 Proof	30,000	Value: 265				

KM# 1228 10 YUAN
3.1103 g., 0.9990 Gold 0.0999 oz. AGW **Subject:** Year of the
Rabbit **Note:** Prev. Y#980.

Date	Mintage	F	VF	XF	Unc	BU
1999 Proof	48,000	Value: 100				

KM# 1229A 10 YUAN
3.1103 g., 0.9990 Gold 0.0999 oz. AGW **Rev:** Multicolor rabbit
Note: Prev. Y#991.

Date	Mintage	F	VF	XF	Unc	BU
1999 Proof	30,000	Value: 225				

KM# 1319 10 YUAN
3.1103 g., 0.9990 Gold 0.0999 oz. AGW **Subject:** Year of the
Dragon **Note:** Prev. Y#992.

Date	Mintage	F	VF	XF	Unc	BU
2000 Proof	48,000	Value: 165				

KM# 1320 10 YUAN
3.1100 g., 0.9990 Gold 0.0999 oz. AGW, 18 mm. **Subject:** Year
of the dragon **Note:** Colorized

Date	Mintage	F	VF	XF	Unc	BU
2000 Proof	30,000	Value: 100				

KM# 1322 50 YUAN
15.5518 g., 0.9990 Gold 0.4995 oz. AGW **Subject:** Year of the
Dragon **Note:** Prev. Y#1006; 1050.

Date	Mintage	F	VF	XF	Unc	BU
2000	6,600	—	—	—	—	575

KM# 196 100 YUAN
31.1320 g., 0.9990 Gold 0.9999 oz. AGW **Subject:** Year of the
Dragon **Obv:** Temple of Heaven **Rev:** 2 floating dragons **Note:**
Prev. Y#175.

Date	Mintage	F	VF	XF	Unc	BU
1988 Proof	10,000	BV+10%				

KM# 235 100 YUAN
31.1320 g., 0.9990 Gold 0.9999 oz. AGW **Subject:** Year of the
Snake **Obv:** National emblem **Rev:** Snake left, denomination
below **Note:** Prev. Y#184.

Date	Mintage	F	VF	XF	Unc	BU
1989 Proof	3,000	BV+10%				

KM# 286   100 YUAN
31.1320 g., 0.9990 Gold 0.9999 oz. AGW **Subject:** Year of the Horse **Obv:** National emblem, date below **Rev:** Prancing horse left, denomination lower right **Note:** Prev. Y#225.

Date	Mintage	F	VF	XF	Unc	BU
1990 Proof	6,000	BV+10%				

KM# 364   100 YUAN
31.1320 g., 0.9990 Gold 0.9999 oz. AGW **Subject:** Year of the Goat **Obv:** National emblem **Rev:** Two goats butting heads, denomination below **Note:** Prev. Y#274.

Date	Mintage	F	VF	XF	Unc	BU
1991 Proof	1,800	BV+15%				

KM# 432   100 YUAN
31.1035 g., 0.9990 Gold 0.9990 oz. AGW **Subject:** Year of the Monkey **Rev:** Monkey seated on branch, denomination at left **Note:** Prev. Y#295.

Date	Mintage	F	VF	XF	Unc	BU
1992 Proof	1,800	BV+15%				

KM# 515   100 YUAN
15.5517 g., 0.9170 Gold 0.4585 oz. AGW **Subject:** Year of the Rooster **Obv:** City gate, date below **Rev:** Rooster with sunflowers, denomination at left **Note:** Prev. Y#568.

Date	Mintage	F	VF	XF	Unc	BU
1993 Proof	2,300	BV+15%				

KM# 516   100 YUAN
31.1035 g., 0.9990 Gold 0.9990 oz. AGW **Subject:** Year of the Rooster **Obv:** National emblem **Rev:** Rooster and hen, denomination at left **Note:** Prev. Y#570.

Date	Mintage	F	VF	XF	Unc	BU
1993 Proof	1,900	BV+15%				

KM# 648   100 YUAN
31.1320 g., 0.9990 Gold 0.9999 oz. AGW **Subject:** Year of the Dog **Rev:** Two dogs, denomination lower left **Note:** Prev. Y#397.

Date	Mintage	F	VF	XF	Unc	BU
1994 Proof	1,800	BV+15%				

KM# 647   100 YUAN
16.3980 g., 0.9160 Gold 0.4829 oz. AGW **Subject:** Year of the Dog **Obv:** Phoenix Pavilion, date below **Rev:** Lap dog, denomination at left **Note:** Prev. Y#780.

Date	Mintage	F	VF	XF	Unc	BU
1994 Proof	2,300	BV+20%				

KM# 748   100 YUAN
31.1030 g., 0.9990 Gold 0.9989 oz. AGW **Subject:** Year of the Pig **Obv:** National emblem, date below **Rev:** Pig, denomination at right **Note:** Prev. Y#451.

Date	Mintage	F	VF	XF	Unc	BU
1995 Proof	1,800	BV+15%				

KM# 753   100 YUAN
15.5557 g., 0.9990 Gold 0.4996 oz. AGW **Subject:** Year of the Pig **Obv:** Building, date below **Rev:** Two pigs, denomination at lower left **Note:** Prev. Y#453.

Date	Mintage	F	VF	XF	Unc	BU
1995 Proof	2,300	BV+20%				

KM# 924   100 YUAN
31.1035 g., 0.9990 Gold 0.9990 oz. AGW **Subject:** Year of the Rat **Rev:** Rat by oil lamp, denomination below **Note:** Prev. Y#586.

Date	Mintage	F	VF	XF	Unc	BU
1996 Proof	1,800	BV+20%				

KM# 929   100 YUAN
16.9779 g., 0.9160 Gold 0.5000 oz. AGW **Subject:** Year of the Rat **Obv:** Dengdu Pavilion, date below **Rev:** Rat on corn cob, denomination upper left **Note:** Prev. Y#856.

Date	Mintage	F	VF	XF	Unc	BU
1996 Proof	2,300	BV+25%				

KM# 1009   100 YUAN
31.1035 g., 0.9990 Gold 0.9990 oz. AGW **Subject:** Year of the Ox **Obv:** National emblem, date below **Rev:** Ox, denomination below **Note:** Prev. Y#900.

Date	Mintage	F	VF	XF	Unc	BU
1997 Proof	1,600	BV+15%				

KM# 1015   100 YUAN
15.5557 g., 0.9990 Gold 0.4996 oz. AGW **Subject:** Year of the Ox **Note:** Prev. Y#670.

Date	Mintage	F	VF	XF	Unc	BU
1997 Proof	2,300	BV+20%				

KM# 1149   100 YUAN
15.5557 g., 0.9990 Gold 0.4996 oz. AGW **Subject:** Year of the Tiger **Note:** Prev. Y#1015.

Date	Mintage	F	VF	XF	Unc	BU
1998 Proof	2,300	BV+20%				

KM# 1142   100 YUAN
31.1035 g., 0.9990 Gold 0.9990 oz. AGW **Subject:** Year of the Tiger **Obv:** State seal **Rev:** Tiger **Note:** Prev. Y#929.

Date	Mintage	F	VF	XF	Unc	BU
1998 Proof	1,600	BV+15%				

KM# 1232   100 YUAN
31.1035 g., 0.9990 Gold 0.9990 oz. AGW **Subject:** Year of the Rabbit **Note:** Prev. Y#1018.

Date	Mintage	F	VF	XF	Unc	BU
1999 Proof	—	BV+25%				

KM# 1229   100 YUAN
15.5551 g., 0.9990 Gold 0.4996 oz. AGW **Subject:** Year of the Rabbit **Note:** Prev. Y#1019.

Date	Mintage	F	VF	XF	Unc	BU
1999 Prof	—	BV+20%				

KM# 1326   100 YUAN
15.5518 g., 0.9160 Gold 0.4580 oz. AGW **Rev:** Dragons **Note:** Prev. Y#1051.

Date	Mintage	F	VF	XF	Unc	BU
2000 Proof	2,300	Value: 750				

KM# 74   150 YUAN
8.0000 g., 0.9170 Gold 0.2358 oz. AGW **Subject:** Year of the Pig **Obv:** Hillside pagoda, waterfront, date lower right **Rev:** Two pigs, denomination below **Note:** Prev. Y#45.

Date	Mintage	F	VF	XF	Unc	BU
1983 Proof	2,035	Value: 900				

KM# 94   150 YUAN
8.0000 g., 0.9170 Gold 0.2358 oz. AGW **Subject:** Year of the Rat **Obv:** Fortress, date lower right **Rev:** Rat with squash, denomination below **Note:** Prev. Y#60.

Date	Mintage	F	VF	XF	Unc	BU
1984 Proof	2,248	Value: 2,400				

KM# 120 150 YUAN
8.0000 g., 0.9170 Gold 0.2358 oz. AGW **Subject:** Year of the Ox **Obv:** Houseboat in harbor **Rev:** Ox left, denomination below **Note:** Prev. Y#79.

Date	Mintage	F	VF	XF	Unc	BU
1985 Proof	Est. 16,000	Value: 250				

Note: 5,000 pieces were struck and issued in boxes with certificates and are valued at $350

KM# 138 150 YUAN
8.0000 g., 0.9170 Gold 0.2358 oz. AGW **Subject:** Year of the Tiger **Obv:** Qing Dynasty Palace, date below **Rev:** Tiger advancing left, after a painting by He Ziang Ning, denomination above **Note:** Prev. Y#99.

Date	Mintage	F	VF	XF	Unc	BU
1986 Proof	5,480	Value: 400				

KM# 171 150 YUAN
8.0000 g., 0.9170 Gold 0.2358 oz. AGW **Subject:** Year of the Rabbit **Obv:** Pagoda, date below **Rev:** Two rabbits, denomination below **Note:** Prev. Y#123.

Date	Mintage	F	VF	XF	Unc	BU
1987 Proof	4,780	Value: 285				

KM# 198 150 YUAN
8.0000 g., 0.9170 Gold 0.2358 oz. AGW **Subject:** Year of the Dragon **Obv:** Great Wall of China, date below **Rev:** Dragon attacking, denomination below **Note:** Prev. Y#144.

Date	Mintage	F	VF	XF	Unc	BU
1988 Proof	7,600	Value: 285				

KM# 237 150 YUAN
8.0000 g., 0.9170 Gold 0.2358 oz. AGW **Subject:** Year of the Snake **Obv:** Shanhaiguan Pass Gate, date below **Rev:** Snake left, denomination below **Note:** Prev. Y#180.

Date	Mintage	F	VF	XF	Unc	BU
1989 Proof	7,500	Value: 250				

KM# 288 150 YUAN
8.0000 g., 0.9170 Gold 0.2358 oz. AGW **Subject:** Year of the Horse **Obv:** Temple of Confucius, date below **Rev:** Horse galloping, denomination at left **Note:** Prev. Y#227.

Date	Mintage	F	VF	XF	Unc	BU
1990 Proof	7,500	Value: 260				

KM# 366 150 YUAN
8.0000 g., 0.9170 Gold 0.2358 oz. AGW **Subject:** Year of the Goat **Obv:** Chinese building and legend **Rev:** Goat reclining, denomination below **Note:** Prev. Y#276.

Date	Mintage	F	VF	XF	Unc	BU
1991 Proof	7,500	Value: 250				

KM# 433 150 YUAN
8.0000 g., 0.9170 Gold 0.2358 oz. AGW **Subject:** Year of the Monkey **Obv:** Pavilion of Emperor Teng **Rev:** Monkey sitting, denomination at right **Note:** Prev. Y#291.

Date	Mintage	F	VF	XF	Unc	BU
1992 Proof	5,000	Value: 285				

KM# 57 200 YUAN
8.4700 g., 0.9170 Gold 0.2497 oz. AGW **Subject:** Year of the Dog **Obv:** Temple of Heaven, date below **Rev:** Dog, denomination below **Note:** Prev. Y#39.

Date	Mintage	F	VF	XF	Unc	BU
1982 Proof	2,500	Value: 525				

KM# 41 250 YUAN
8.0000 g., 0.9170 Gold 0.2358 oz. AGW **Subject:** Year of the Rooster **Obv:** Monument, date lower left **Rev:** Rooster left, denomination at left **Note:** Prev. Y#33.

Date	Mintage	F	VF	XF	Unc	BU
1981 Proof	5,015	Value: 475				

KM# 199 500 YUAN
155.5150 g., 0.9990 Gold 4.9947 oz. AGW, 60 mm.
Subject: Year of the Dragon **Obv:** Great Wall **Rev:** Inner circle holds three dragons, four dragons surround, denomination below **Note:** Illustration reduced. Prev. Y#145.

Date	Mintage	F	VF	XF	Unc	BU
1988 Proof	3,000	Value: 4,850				

KM# 238 500 YUAN
155.5150 g., 0.9990 Gold 4.9947 oz. AGW, 60 mm.
Subject: Year of the Snake **Obv:** National emblem **Rev:** Snake left, denomination below, within beaded circle **Note:** Illustration reduced. Prev. Y#181.

Date	Mintage	F	VF	XF	Unc	BU
1989 Proof	500	Value: 5,000				

KM# 289 500 YUAN
155.5150 g., 0.9990 Gold 4.9947 oz. AGW, 60 mm.
Obv: Temple of Confucius **Rev:** Two horses drinking water, denomination below **Note:** Illustration reduced. Prev. Y#228.

Date	Mintage	F	VF	XF	Unc	BU
1990 Proof	500	Value: 5,000				

KM# 367 500 YUAN
155.5150 g., 0.9990 Gold 4.9947 oz. AGW, 60 mm.
Subject: Year of the Goat **Obv:** Two goats, one nursing offspring, denomination above **Note:** Prev. Y#277.

Date	Mintage	F	VF	XF	Unc	BU
1991 Proof	250	Value: 5,000				

KM# 434 500 YUAN
155.5150 g., 0.9990 Gold 4.9947 oz. AGW, 60 mm.
Subject: Year of the Monkey **Obv:** Chinese building **Rev:** Monkey seated, denomination at right **Note:** Illustration reduced. Prev. Y#292.

Date	Mintage	F	VF	XF	Unc	BU
1992 Proof	99	Value: 6,000				

KM# 517 500 YUAN
155.5150 g., 0.9990 Gold 4.9947 oz. AGW **Subject:** Year of the Rooster **Note:** Prev. Y#384.

Date	Mintage	F	VF	XF	Unc	BU
1993 Proof	99	Value: 5,500				

KM# 649 500 YUAN
155.5150 g., 0.9990 Gold 4.9947 oz. AGW **Subject:** Year of the Dog **Note:** Prev. Y#389.

Date	Mintage	F	VF	XF	Unc	BU
1994 Proof	99	Value: 5,500				

KM# 750 500 YUAN
155.5150 g., 0.9990 Gold 4.9947 oz. AGW **Subject:** Year of the Pig **Note:** Prev. Y#467.

Date	Mintage	F	VF	XF	Unc	BU
1995 Proof	99	Value: 5,500				

KM# 922 500 YUAN
155.5175 g., 0.9999 Gold 4.9993 oz. AGW **Subject:** Year of the Rat **Rev:** Rat eating grapes, denomination above **Note:** Prev. Y#663.

Date	Mintage	F	VF	XF	Unc	BU
1996 Proof	99	Value: 5,500				

KM# 1007 500 YUAN
155.5175 g., 0.9990 Gold 4.9948 oz. AGW **Subject:** Year of the Ox **Note:** Prev. Y#672.

Date	Mintage	F	VF	XF	Unc	BU
1997 Proof	99	Value: 5,000				

KM# 1144 500 YUAN
155.5175 g., 0.9990 Gold 4.9948 oz. AGW **Subject:** Year of the Tiger **Note:** Prev. Y#1024.

Date	Mintage	F	VF	XF	Unc	BU
1998 Proof	99	Value: 5,500				

KM# 1227 500 YUAN
155.5175 g., 0.9990 Gold 4.9948 oz. AGW **Subject:** Year of the Rabbit **Note:** Prev. Y#1025.

Date	Mintage	F	VF	XF	Unc	BU
1999 Proof	99	Value: 5,000				

KM# 1324 500 YUAN
155.5175 g., 0.9990 Gold 4.9948 oz. AGW **Subject:** Year of the Dragon **Note:** Prev. Y#1027.

Date	Mintage	F	VF	XF	Unc	BU
2000 Proof	108	Value: 5,500				

KM# 200 1000 YUAN
373.2360 g., 0.9990 Gold 11.987 oz. AGW, 70 mm.
Subject: Year of the Dragon **Obv:** Great Wall **Rev:** Two facing dragons, denomination below **Note:** Illustration reduced. Prev. #Y146.

Date	Mintage	F	VF	XF	Unc	BU
1988 Proof	518	Value: 12,000				

KM# 239 1000 YUAN
373.2360 g., 0.9990 Gold 11.987 oz. AGW, 70 mm.
Subject: Year of the Snake **Obv:** National emblem **Rev:** Snake left within beaded circle, denomination below **Note:** Illustration reduced. Prev. #Y182.

Date	Mintage	F	VF	XF	Unc	BU
1989 Proof	200	Value: 12,000				

KM# 290 1000 YUAN
373.2360 g., 0.9990 Gold 11.987 oz. AGW, 70 mm. **Subject:** Year of the Horse **Obv:** Temple of Confucius **Rev:** Two horses running, denomination below **Note:** Illustration reduced. Prev. #Y229.

Date	Mintage	F	VF	XF	Unc	BU
1990 Proof	500	Value: 12,000				

KM# 368 1000 YUAN
373.2360 g., 0.9990 Gold 11.987 oz. AGW **Subject:** Year of the Goat **Obv:** Chinese building and legend **Rev:** Three goats, denomination at left **Note:** Illustration reduced. Prev. #Y278.

Date	Mintage	F	VF	XF	Unc	BU
1991 Proof	200	Value: 12,000				

KM# 435 1000 YUAN
373.2360 g., 0.9990 Gold 11.987 oz. AGW **Subject:** Year of the Monkey **Obv:** Chinese building **Rev:** Five monkeys, denomination at left **Note:** Illustration reduced. Prev. #Y293.

Date	Mintage	F	VF	XF	Unc	BU
1992 Proof	99	Value: 12,000				

KM# 518 1000 YUAN
373.2360 g., 0.9990 Gold 11.987 oz. AGW **Subject:** Year of the Rooster **Note:** Prev. #Y385.

Date	Mintage	F	VF	XF	Unc	BU
1993 Proof	99	Value: 12,000				

KM# 650 1000 YUAN
373.2360 g., 0.9990 Gold 11.987 oz. AGW **Subject:** Year of the Dog **Note:** Prev. #Y390.

Date	Mintage	F	VF	XF	Unc	BU
1994 Proof	99	Value: 12,000				

KM# 751 1000 YUAN
373.2360 g., 0.9990 Gold 11.987 oz. AGW **Subject:** Year of the Pig **Note:** Prev. #Y468.

Date	Mintage	F	VF	XF	Unc	BU
1995 Proof	99	Value: 12,000				

KM# 921 1000 YUAN
373.2360 g., 0.9990 Gold 11.987 oz. AGW **Subject:** Year of the Rat **Note:** Prev. #Y664.

Date	Mintage	F	VF	XF	Unc	BU
1996 Proof	99	Value: 12,000				

KM# 1006 1000 YUAN
373.2360 g., 0.9990 Gold 11.987 oz. AGW **Subject:** Year of the Ox **Note:** Prev. #Y673.

Date	Mintage	F	VF	XF	Unc	BU
1997 Proof	99	Value: 12,000				

KM# 1145 1000 YUAN
373.2360 g., 0.9990 Gold 11.987 oz. AGW **Subject:** Year of the Tiger **Note:** Prev. #Y1030.

Date	Mintage	F	VF	XF	Unc	BU
1998 Proof	99	Value: 12,000				

KM# 1235 1000 YUAN
373.2360 g., 0.9990 Gold 11.987 oz. AGW **Subject:** Year of the Rabbit **Note:** Prev. #Y1031.

Date	Mintage	F	VF	XF	Unc	BU
1999 Proof	99	Value: 12,000				

KM# 437 2000 YUAN
1000.0000 g., 0.9990 Gold 32.117 oz. AGW, 100 mm.
Subject: Completion of 150 Yuan Lunar Animal Coin Series **Obv:** Monument divides date and denomination within circle **Rev:** Ying/Yang symbol within octagon, twelve animal coins surround **Note:** Illustration reduced. Prev. #Y702.

Date	Mintage	F	VF	XF	Unc	BU
1992 Proof	21	Value: 35,000				

KM# 754 2000 YUAN
1000.0000 g., 0.9990 Gold 32.117 oz. AGW **Subject:** Year of the Pig **Edge:** Scalloped **Note:** Prev. #Y660.

Date	Mintage	F	VF	XF	Unc	BU
1995 Proof	15	Value: 30,500				

KM# 930 2000 YUAN
1000.0000 g., 0.9990 Gold 32.117 oz. AGW **Subject:** Year of the Rat **Note:** Prev. #Y665.

Date	Mintage	F	VF	XF	Unc	BU
1996 Proof	15	Value: 30,500				

KM# 1016 2000 YUAN
1000.0000 g., 0.9990 Gold 32.117 oz. AGW **Subject:** Year of the Ox **Note:** Prev. #Y674.

Date	Mintage	F	VF	XF	Unc	BU
1997 Proof	15	Value: 30,500				

KM# 1150 2000 YUAN
1000.0000 g., 0.9990 Gold 32.117 oz. AGW **Subject:** Year of the Tiger **Note:** Prev. #Y967.

Date	Mintage	F	VF	XF	Unc	BU
1998 Proof	15	Value: 30,500				

KM# 1238 2000 YUAN
1000.0000 g., 0.9990 Gold 32.117 oz. AGW **Subject:** Year of the Rabbit **Note:** Prev. #Y975.

Date	Mintage	F	VF	XF	Unc	BU
1999 Proof	15	Value: 30,500				

KM# 1327 2000 YUAN
1000.2108 g., 0.9990 Gold 32.124 oz. AGW, Scalloped mm.
Subject: Year of the Dragon **Note:** Prev. #Y977.

Date	Mintage	F	VF	XF	Unc	BU
2000 Proof	15	Value: 32,000				

KM# A1327 10000 YUAN
1000.2108 g., 0.9990 Gold 32.124 oz. AGW **Subject:** Year of the Snake **Rev:** Dragons

Date	Mintage	F	VF	XF	Unc	BU
2000 Proof	15	Value: 32,000				

PLATINUM BULLION COINAGE
Panda Series

KM# 624 10 YUAN
3.1000 g., 0.9995 Platinum 0.0996 oz. APW, 18 mm.
Rev: Panda seated bending bamboo

Date	Mintage	F	VF	XF	Unc	BU
1994 Proof	2,500	Value: 100				

PLATINUM BULLION COINAGE
Lunar Series

KM# 197   100 YUAN
31.1030 g., 0.9995 Platinum 0.9994 oz. APW **Subject:** Year of the Dragon **Obv:** Temple of Heaven **Rev:** 2 floating dragons **Note:** Prev. Y#176.

Date	Mintage	F	VF	XF	Unc	BU
1988 Proof	2,000	BV+20%				

KM# 236   100 YUAN
31.1030 g., 0.9995 Platinum 0.9994 oz. APW **Subject:** Year of the Snake **Obv:** National emblem **Rev:** Snake, left, denomination below **Note:** Prev. Y#185.

Date	Mintage	F	VF	XF	Unc	BU
1989 Proof	1,000	BV+20%				

KM# 287   100 YUAN
31.1030 g., 0.9995 Platinum 0.9994 oz. APW **Subject:** Year of the Horse **Obv:** National emblem **Rev:** Prancing horse **Note:** Prev. Y#225a.

Date	Mintage	F	VF	XF	Unc	BU
1990 Proof	2,000	—	—	—	—	BV+ 20%

KM# 365   100 YUAN
31.1030 g., 0.9995 Platinum 0.9994 oz. APW **Subject:** Year of the Goat **Obv:** National emblem **Rev:** Two goats butting heads, denomination below **Note:** Prev. Y#274a.

Date	Mintage	F	VF	XF	Unc	BU
1991 Proof	500	BV+30%				

KM# 430   100 YUAN
31.1030 g., 0.9995 Platinum 0.9994 oz. APW **Subject:** Year of the Monkey **Rev:** Monkey seated on branch, denomination at left **Note:** Prev. Y#295a.

Date	Mintage	F	VF	XF	Unc	BU
1992 Proof	300	BV+35%				

KM# 513   100 YUAN
31.1030 g., 0.9995 Platinum 0.9994 oz. APW **Subject:** Year of the Rooster **Note:** Prev. Y#382.

Date	Mintage	F	VF	XF	Unc	BU
1993 Proof	300	BV+35%				

KM# 645   100 YUAN
31.1030 g., 0.9995 Platinum 0.9994 oz. APW **Subject:** Year of the Dog **Note:** Prev. Y#397a.

Date	Mintage	F	VF	XF	Unc	BU
1994 Proof	300	BV+35%				

KM# 749   100 YUAN
31.1030 g., 0.9995 Platinum 0.9994 oz. APW **Subject:** Year of the Pig **Note:** Prev. Y#465.

Date	Mintage	F	VF	XF	Unc	BU
1995 Proof	300	BV+35%				

KM# 923   100 YUAN
31.1035 g., 0.9995 Platinum 0.9995 oz. APW **Subject:** Year of the Rat **Rev:** Rat by oil lamp, denomination below **Note:** Prev. Y#586a.

Date	Mintage	F	VF	XF	Unc	BU
1996 Proof	300	BV+35%				

KM# 1008   100 YUAN
31.1035 g., 0.9995 Platinum 0.9995 oz. APW **Subject:** Year of the Ox **Obv:** National emblem **Rev:** Ox, denomination below **Note:** Prev. Y#900a.

Date	Mintage	F	VF	XF	Unc	BU
1997 Proof	300	BV+35%				

KM# 1143   100 YUAN
31.1035 g., 0.9990 Platinum 0.9990 oz. APW **Subject:** Year of the Tiger **Obv:** National emblem **Rev:** Tiger **Note:** Prev. Y#929a.

Date	Mintage	F	VF	XF	Unc	BU
1998 Proof	300	BV+35%				

KM# 1233   100 YUAN
31.1035 g., 0.9990 Platinum 0.9990 oz. APW **Subject:** Year of the Rabbit **Note:** Prev. Y#1018a.

Date	Mintage	F	VF	XF	Unc	BU
1999 Proof		BV+35%				

PLATINUM BULLION COINAGE
Panda Series

KM# 484   5 YUAN
1.5552 g., 0.9995 Platinum 0.0500 oz. APW **Obv:** Temple of Heaven within circle, date below **Rev:** Panda seated on rock, denomination upper left **Note:** Prev. Y#483.

Date	Mintage	F	VF	XF	Unc	BU
1993 Proof	2,500	Value: 125				

KM# 729   5 YUAN
1.5500 g., 0.9995 Platinum 0.0498 oz. APW, 14 mm. **Rev:** Panda with bamboo staff

Date	Mintage	F	VF	XF	Unc	BU
1995 Proof	10,000	Value: 150				

KM# 940   5 YUAN
1.5552 g., 0.9990 Platinum 0.0499 oz. APW **Obv:** Eastern unicorn, date below **Rev:** Head of western unicorn, right, denomination at right **Note:** Prev. Y#740a.

Date	Mintage	F	VF	XF	Unc	BU
1996	8,000	—	—	—	—	135

KM# 888   5 YUAN
1.5552 g., 0.9990 Platinum 0.0499 oz. APW **Obv:** Temple of Heaven, date below **Rev:** Panda in tree looking down, denomination lower left **Note:** Prev. Y#581a.

Date	Mintage	F	VF	XF	Unc	BU
1996	5,000	—	—	—	—	145

KM# 985   5 YUAN
1.5552 g., 0.9990 Platinum 0.0499 oz. APW **Obv:** Temple of Heaven **Rev:** Panda on branch **Note:** Prev. Y#716a.

Date	Mintage	F	VF	XF	Unc	BU
1997 Prooflike	5,000	—	—	—	—	135

KM# 277   10 YUAN
3.1100 g., 0.9995 Platinum 0.0999 oz. APW **Obv:** Temple of Heaven, date below **Rev:** Panda with branch, denomination below **Note:** Prev. Y#267.

Date	Mintage	F	VF	XF	Unc	BU
1990 Proof	4,500	Value: 225				

KM# 486   10 YUAN
3.1100 g., 0.9995 Platinum 0.0999 oz. APW **Obv:** Temple of Heaven within circle, date below **Rev:** Panda seated on rock, denomination upper left **Note:** Prev. Y#484a.

Date	Mintage	F	VF	XF	Unc	BU
1993 Proof	2,500	Value: 225				

KM# 623   10 YUAN
3.1103 g., 0.9990 Platinum 0.0999 oz. APW **Obv:** Temple of Heaven, date below **Rev:** Seated panda eating, denomination below **Note:** Prev. Y#432a.

Date	Mintage	F	VF	XF	Unc	BU
1994 Prooflike	2,500	—	—	—	—	250

KM# 730   10 YUAN
3.1103 g., 0.9990 Platinum 0.0999 oz. APW **Obv:** Temple of Heaven, date below **Rev:** Panda eating bamboo, denomination at left **Note:** Prev. Y#641a.

Date	Mintage	F	VF	XF	Unc	BU
1995 Prooflike	5,000	—	—	—	—	235

KM# 890   10 YUAN
3.1103 g., 0.9990 Platinum 0.0999 oz. APW **Obv:** Temple of Heaven, date below **Rev:** Panda in tree **Note:** Prev. Y#575a.

Date	Mintage	F	VF	XF	Unc	BU
1996 Prooflike	2,500	—	—	—	—	250

KM# 988   10 YUAN
3.1100 g., 0.9990 Platinum 0.0999 oz. APW **Obv:** Temple of Heaven **Rev:** Panda on branch **Note:** Prev. Y#717a.

Date	Mintage	F	VF	XF	Unc	BU
1997 Prooflike	2,500	—	—	—	—	225

KM# 278   25 YUAN
7.7758 g., 0.9995 Platinum 0.2499 oz. APW **Obv:** Temple of Heaven, date below **Rev:** Panda climbing tree, denomination at right **Note:** Prev. Y#268.

Date	Mintage	F	VF	XF	Unc	BU
1990 Proof	3,500	Value: 525				

KM# 279   50 YUAN
15.5517 g., 0.9995 Platinum 0.4997 oz. APW **Obv:** Temple of Heaven, date below **Rev:** Panda eating bamboo on rock, denomination below **Note:** Prev. Y#269.

Date	Mintage	F	VF	XF	Unc	BU
1990 Proof	2,500	Value: 725				

KM# A163   100 YUAN
31.1030 g., 0.9995 Platinum 0.9994 oz. APW **Obv:** Temple of Heaven, date below **Rev:** Panda drinking at stream, denomination below **Note:** Prev. Y#158.

Date	Mintage	F	VF	XF	Unc	BU
1987 Proof	2,000	BV+20%				

KM# 192   100 YUAN
31.1030 g., 0.9995 Platinum 0.9994 oz. APW **Obv:** Temple of Heaven, date below **Rev:** Panda grasping bamboo shoot, within circle, denomination below **Note:** Prev. Y#159.

Date	Mintage	F	VF	XF	Unc	BU
1988 Proof	2,000	BV+20%				

KM# 230 100 YUAN

31.1030 g., 0.9995 Platinum 0.9994 oz. APW **Obv:** Temple of Heaven, date below **Rev:** Panda reclining, grid behind, denomination lower right **Note:** Prev. Y#191a.

Date	Mintage	F	VF	XF	Unc	BU
1989 Proof	3,000	—	—	—	—	BV+ 20%

KM# 280 100 YUAN

31.1400 g., 0.9995 Platinum 1.0006 oz. APW **Obv:** Temple of Heaven, date below **Rev:** Panda on rock, denomination below **Note:** Prev. Y#735.

Date	Mintage	F	VF	XF	Unc	BU
1990 Proof	1,300	—	—	—	—	BV+ 30%

BI-METALLIC MEDALLIC BULLION COINAGE
Silver / Gold

KM# 396 10 YUAN

3.1103 g., Bi-Metallic Gold center in Silver ring **Obv:** Temple of Heaven within circle, date below **Rev:** Panda on branch, denomination above, within circle **Note:** Prev. Y#391.

Date	Mintage	F	VF	XF	Unc	BU
1992 Proof	2,000	Value: 150				

KM# 625 10 YUAN

3.1103 g., Bi-Metallic Gold center in Silver ring **Rev:** Phoenix and dragon **Note:** Prev. Y#463.

Date	Mintage	F	VF	XF	Unc	BU
1994	2,500	—	—	—	—	150

KM# A625 10 YUAN

3.1103 g., Bi-Metallic Gold center in Silver ring **Obv:** Temple of Heaven within circle, date below **Rev:** Panda tugging bamboo sprig, denomination below, within circle **Note:** Prev. Y#680.

Date	Mintage	F	VF	XF	Unc	BU
1994 Proof	3,000	Value: 150				

KM# 722 10 YUAN

3.1103 g., Bi-Metallic Gold center in Silver ring **Obv:** Temple of Heaven, date below **Rev:** Panda at stream, denomination below **Note:** Prev. Y#571.

Date	Mintage	F	VF	XF	Unc	BU
1995 Proof set	2,000	Value: 150				

KM# 893 10 YUAN

3.1103 g., Bi-Metallic Gold center in Silver ring **Obv:** Temple of Heaven **Rev:** Panda seated In rock **Note:** Prev. Y#851.

Date	Mintage	F	VF	XF	Unc	BU
1996 Proof	2,500	Value: 150				

KM# 998 10 YUAN

3.1103 g., Bi-Metallic Gold center in Silver ring **Obv:** Temple of Heaven, date below **Rev:** Panda climbing tree **Note:** Prev. Y#986.

Date	Mintage	F	VF	XF	Unc	BU
1997 Proof	2,800	Value: 135				

KM# 348 25 YUAN

7.7758 g., Bi-Metallic Gold center in Silver ring **Obv:** Temple of Heaven, date below **Rev:** Seated panda, denomination at left, date below **Note:** Prev. Y#301.

Date	Mintage	F	VF	XF	Unc	BU
1991 Proof	2,000	Value: 285				

KM# 487 25 YUAN

7.7758 g., Bi-Metallic Gold center in Silver ring **Obv:** Temple of Heaven, date below **Rev:** Panda on rock **Note:** Prev. Y#930.

Date	Mintage	F	VF	XF	Unc	BU
1993 Proof	2,500	Value: 285				

KM# 626 25 YUAN

7.7758 g., Bi-Metallic Gold center in Silver ring **Obv:** Temple of Heaven within circle, date below **Rev:** Panda tugging on bamboo sprig, denomination below, within circle, date below **Note:** Prev. Y#544.

Date	Mintage	F	VF	XF	Unc	BU
1994 Proof	2,500	Value: 255				

KM# 724 25 YUAN

7.7758 g., Bi-Metallic Gold center in Silver ring **Obv:** Temple of Heaven, date below **Rev:** Panda at stream, denomination below, within circle **Note:** Prev. Y#572.

Date	Mintage	F	VF	XF	Unc	BU
1995 Proof	2,000	Value: 260				

KM# 894 25 YUAN

7.7759 g., Bi-Metallic Gold center in Silver ring **Obv:** Temple of Heaven **Rev:** Panda seated on rock **Note:** Prev. Y#852.

Date	Mintage	F	VF	XF	Unc	BU
1996 Proof	2,500	Value: 255				

KM# 999 25 YUAN

7.7758 g., 0.9990 Bi-Metallic Gold center in Silver ring 0.2497 oz. **Obv:** Temple of Heaven; date below **Rev:** Panda climbing tree **Note:** Prev. Y#1001.

Date	Mintage	F	VF	XF	Unc	BU
1997 Proof	2,800	Value: 260				

KM# 281 50 YUAN

15.5517 g., 0.9990 Bi-Metallic Gold center in Silver ring 0.4995 oz. **Obv:** Temple of Heaven, date below, within circle **Rev:** Panda walking, denomination below, within circle, date below **Note:** Prev. Y#266.

Date	Mintage	F	VF	XF	Unc	BU
1990 Proof	2,000	Value: 385				

KM# 725 50 YUAN

21.7724 g., 0.9990 Bi-Metallic Gold center in Silver ring 0.6993 oz. **Obv:** Temple of Heaven within circle, date below **Rev:** Panda at stream, denomination below, within circle **Note:** Prev. Y#573.

Date	Mintage	F	VF	XF	Unc	BU
1995 Proof	2,000	Value: 425				

KM# 895 50 YUAN

15.5517 g., 0.9990 Bi-Metallic Gold center in Silver ring 0.4995 oz. **Obv:** Temple of Heaven **Rev:** Panda seated on rock **Note:** Prev. Y#853.

Date	Mintage	F	VF	XF	Unc	BU
1996 Proof	2,500	Value: 425				

KM# 1000 50 YUAN

15.5517 g., 0.9990 Bi-Metallic Gold center in Silver ring 0.4995 oz. **Obv:** Temple of Heaven, date below **Rev:** Panda climbing tree **Note:** Prev. Y#1009.

Date	Mintage	F	VF	XF	Unc	BU
1997 Proof	2,800	Value: 425				

KM# 728 500 YUAN

155.5175 g., 0.9999 Bi-Metallic Gold center in Silver ring 4.9993 oz. **Obv:** Temple of Heaven **Rev:** Two pandas sitting on rock, denomination above, within circle **Note:** Prev. Y#793.

Date	Mintage	F	VF	XF	Unc	BU
1995 Proof	199	Value: 4,250				

KM# 897 500 YUAN

155.5175 g., 0.9990 Bi-Metallic Gold center in Silver ring 4.9948 oz. **Obv:** Temple of Heaven, date below **Rev:** Panda **Note:** Prev. Y#1020.

Date	Mintage	F	VF	XF	Unc	BU
1996 Proof	199	Value: 4,250				

KM# 997 500 YUAN

155.5175 g., 0.9990 Bi-Metallic Gold center in Silver ring 4.9948 oz. **Obv:** Temple of Heaven **Rev:** Two pandas resting near stream **Note:** Prev. Y#1021.

Date	Mintage	F	VF	XF	Unc	BU
1997 Proof	199	Value: 4,250				

MEDALLIC BULLION COINAGE
Gold

KM# 52 1/10 OUNCE

3.1010 g., 0.9990 Gold 0.0996 oz. AGW, 18 mm. **Rev:** Panda seated with bamboo branch

Date	Mintage	F	VF	XF	Unc	BU
1982 Proof	—	Value: 100				

KM# 53 1/4 OUNCE

7.7758 g., 0.9990 Gold 0.2497 oz. AGW **Obv:** Temple of Heaven **Rev:** Panda with bamboo shoot **Note:** Prev. #Y41.

Date	Mintage	F	VF	XF	Unc	BU
1982	40,000	—	—	—	—	220

KM# 54 1/2 OUNCE

15.5160 g., 0.9990 Gold 0.4983 oz. AGW, 27 mm. **Rev:** Panda seated with bamboo branch

Date	Mintage	F	VF	XF	Unc	BU
1982 Proof	—	Value: 450				

KM# 55 OUNCE

31.1035 g., 0.9990 Gold 0.9990 oz. AGW, 32 mm. **Rev:** Panda seated with bamboo branch

Date	Mintage	F	VF	XF	Unc	BU
1982 Proof	—	Value: 900				

PATTERNS
Including off metal strikes

KM#	Date	Mintage	Identification	Issue Price	Mkt Val
Pn1	1983	—	5 Yuan. Denomination between sprays. Marco Polo bust at upper right, ships below, dates at left, denomination below. Silvered base metal, Marco Polo.		600
Pn2	1983	—	100 Yuan. Gilt Bronze.	—	600
Pn3	1985	—	200 Yuan. Gold. Decade for Women.	—	—
Pn4	1991	—	Yuan. Nickel Plated Steel. Raised character "pattern". KM#341.		100
Pn5	1991	—	Yuan. Nickel Plated Steel. Raised character "pattern". KM#342.		100
Pn6	1991	—	Yuan. Nickel Plated Steel. Raised character "pattern".		100
Pn7	1991	—	Yuan. Nickel Plated Steel. Raised character "pattern". KM#357.		150
Pn8	1991	—	Yuan. Nickel Plated Steel. Raised character "pattern". KM#345.		150
Pn9	1991	—	10000 Yuan. Gold.	—	—

PIEFORTS

KM#	Date	Mintage	Identification	Issue Price	Mkt Val
P1	1979	3,500	35 Yuan. 0.8000 Silver. KM#8.	—	200
P2	1979	500	450 Yuan. 0.9000 Gold. KM#9.	—	2,350
P3	1980	2,500	Yuan. Copper. KM#29.	—	30.00
P4	1980	2,500	Yuan. Copper. KM#30.	—	30.00
P5	1980	2,500	Yuan. Copper. KM#31.	—	30.00
P6	1980	2,500	Yuan. Copper. KM#32.	—	30.00
P7	1980	1,000	Yuan. Copper. KM#21.	—	30.00
P8	1980	1,000	Yuan. Copper. KM#22.	—	30.00
P9	1980	1,000	Yuan. Copper. KM#19.	—	30.00
P10	1980	1,000	Yuan. Copper. KM#20.	—	30.00
P11	1980	2,000	15 Yuan. 0.8000 Silver. KM#33. Archery.	—	100
P12	1980	2,000	20 Yuan. 0.8000 Silver. KM#34, Wrestling.	—	100
P13	1980	1,000	30 Yuan. 0.8000 Silver. KM#35. Equestrian.	249	100
P14	1980	1,000	30 Yuan. 0.8000 Silver. KM#36. Soccer.	249	100
P15	1980	2,000	30 Yuan. 0.8000 Silver. KM#26. Speed skating.	249	100
P16	1980	2,000	30 Yuan. 0.8000 Silver. KM#25. Alpine skiing.	—	100
P17	1980	2,000	30 Yuan. 0.8000 Silver. KM#24. Biathalon.	—	100
P18	1980	2,000	30 Yuan. 0.8000 Silver. KM#23. Figure skating.	—	100
P19	1980	360	250 Yuan. 0.9170 Gold. KM#28. Alpine skiing.	1,750	1,000
P19	1980	360	250 Yuan. 0.9170 Gold. KM#28. Alpine skiing.	1,750	1,000
P20	1980	500	300 Yuan. 0.9170 Gold. KM#37. Archery.	—	1,500
P20	1980	500	300 Yuan. 0.9170 Gold. KM#37. Archery.	—	1,500
PA21	1991	—	10 Yuan. 0.9990 Silver. 62.2000 g. Panda - Hind feet in water. KM#347.	—	200
P21	1992	—	5 Yuan. 0.9000 Silver. KM#404. Ancient ship building.	—	60.00
P22	1992	—	5 Yuan. 0.9000 Silver. KM#407. First compass.	—	60.00
P23	1992	—	5 Yuan. 0.9000 Silver. KM#405. First seismograph.	—	60.00
P24	1992	—	5 Yuan. 0.9000 Silver. KM#406. Ancient kite flying.	—	60.00
P25	1992	—	5 Yuan. 0.9000 Silver. KM#408. Bronze metal working.	—	60.00
P26	1996	5,000	5 Yuan. 0.9990 Silver. KM#933. Goddess holding flower.	—	—
P27	1996	5,000	5 Yuan. 0.9990 Silver. KM#934. Goddess holding vase and twig.	—	—
P28	1997	80,000	5 Yuan. 0.9990 Silver. KM#1058.	—	75.00
P29	1997	80,000	5 Yuan. 0.9990 Silver. KM#1058. Child w/carp.	—	—
P30	1997	80,000	10 Yuan. 0.9990 Silver. KM#1059. Child w/carp.	—	—
P31	1998	—	10 Yuan. 0.9990 Silver. KM#1138.	—	60.00
P32	1998	100,000	10 Yuan. 0.9990 Silver. KM#1059.	—	40.00

MINT SETS

KM#	Date	Mintage	Identification	Issue Price	Mkt Val
MS1	1979 (s) (3)	—	KM#1-3, Medal	—	15.00
MS2	1980(b) (7)	—	KM#1-3, 15-17	—	20.00
MS3	1982 (3)	—	KM-53, X MB10-11	750	3,400
MS4	1986 (2)	—	KM#130 (2)	—	12.50
MS5	1990 (2)	—	KM#266-267	—	8.00
MS7	1991 (2)	—	KM344-345	—	5.00
MS6	1991 (6)	—	KM#1-3, 335-337	—	5.50
MS8	1992 (6)	—	Y#1-3, 335-337	—	5.50
MS9	1993 (6)	—	KM#1-3, 335-337	—	5.50
MS10	1994 (6)	—	KM#1-3, 335-337	—	5.50
MS11	1995 (6)	—	KM#1-3, 335-337	—	5.50
MS12	1996 (6)	—	KM#1-3, 335-337	—	5.50
MS13	1997 (5)	—	KM#1-3, 328-330	—	—
MS14	1998 (5)	—	KM#1-3, 328-330	—	—
MS15	1999 (5)	—	KM#1-3, 328-330	—	—
MS16	2000 (5)	—	KM#1-3, 328-330	—	—

PROOF SETS

KM#	Date	Mintage	Identification	Issue Price	Mkt Val
PS1	1979 (4)	70,000	KM#4-7	1,695	1,650
PS2	1980 (14)	1,000	KM#19-22, 26-28, 29-32, 34-37	1,750	700
PS3	1980 (7)	—	KM#1-3, 15-18	—	10.00
PS4	1980 (4)	—	KM#29-32	—	50.00
PS5	1980 (4)	—	KM#19-22	—	50.00
PS6	1980 (3)	1,000	KM#34-36	—	50.00
PS8	1981 (4)	1,000	KM#46-49	2,950	2,550
PS7	1981(s) (7)	10,000	KM#1-3, 15-18, Medal	2.00	100
PS9	1982(s) (7)	—	KM#1-3, 15-18, Medal	2.00	50.00
PS10	1983(s) (7)	—	KM#1-3, 15-18, Book	2.00	40.00
PS11	1983(s) (7)	—	KM#1-3, 15-18, Medal (paper cover)	2.00	40.00
PS12	1984(y) (7)	—	KM#1-3, 15-18, Medal	—	100
PS13	1984 (4)	—	KM#98-101	—	90.00
PS14	1984 (3)	—	KM#104-106	—	22.50
PS15	1985 (2)	—	KM#110, 127	45.00	70.00
PS16	1985(y) (7)	—	KM#1-3, 15-18, Medal	—	100
PS17	1985 (2)	—	KM#111, 128	45.00	120
PS18	1985 (4)	—	KM#121-124	—	115
PS19	1986(y) (7)	—	KM#1-3, 15-18, Medal	10.00	500
PS20	1986 (5)	10,000	KM#131-135	—	800
PS21	1986 (4)	—	KM#141-144	—	110
PS22	1987 (5)	10,000	KM#159, 161-162, 166	—	800
PS23	1987 (2)	—	KM#167-168	278	175
PS24	1987 (4)	—	KM#172-175	—	120
PS25	1988 (4)	—	KM#207-210	200	110
PS26	1988 (5)	10,000	KM#184-187, 221	—	900
PS27	1989 (5)	8,000	KM224-229	—	850
PS28	1989 (4)	—	KM#248-251	—	130
PS29	1990 (5)	5,000	KM#268-272	—	1,000
PS30	1990 (3)	2,500	KM#277-279	1,095	750
PS31	1990 (1)	2,000	Y#281 and medal	995	500
PSA32	1990 (5)	10,000	KM#267, 291-294	—	265
PS32	1991 (6)	—	KM#1-3, 335-337	—	6.50
PS33	1991 (1)	2,000	KM#348 and medal	575	350
PS34	1991 (5)	350	KM#346-347, 349-350, 359	—	1,000
PS35	1992 (6)	—	KM#1-3, 335-337	—	6.50
PS36	1992	2,500	KMP#21-25 Piefort	—	350
PS37	1992 (5)	1,000	KM#415-419	—	4,500
PS38	1992 (5)	—	KM#391-395	—	1,000
PS39	1993 (4)	2,000	KM#575-578	200	140
PS40	1993 (4)	1,000	KM#579-582	1,600	1,350
PS41	1993 (3)	—	KM#595, 597-598	—	925
PS42	1993 (5)	—	KM#473, 476, 477	—	600
PS43	1993 (6)	—	KM#1-3, 335-337	—	8.00
PSA44	1993 (5)	2,500	KM#486-487.	—	850
PS44	1993 (5)	100	KM#496-500	1,875	2,000
PS45	1994 (11)	50	KM#674-684	—	6,000
PS46	1994 (10)	50	KM#674-683	—	4,500
PS47	1994 (5)	1,000	KM#674, 676-678, 680	—	1,385
PS48	1994 (4)	2,500	KM#674-676, 678	645	655
PS49	1994 (6)	1,000	kM#675-679, 681	—	845
PS50	1994 (2)	400	KM#675, 683	—	1,270
PS51	1994 (5)	—	KM#611-614, 626	—	600
PS52	1994 (6)	—	KM#1-3, 335-337	—	8.00
PS53	1995 (3)	2,000	KM#791-793	485	500
PS54	1995 (3)	2,000	KM#772, 724-725	—	710
PS55	1995 (2)	3,000	KM#791-792	89.00	90.00
PS56	1995 (4)	15,000	KM#866-869	—	150
PS57	1995 (4)	9,000	KM#840-843	—	160
PS58	1995 (6)	—	KM#1-3, 335-337	—	8.00
PS59	1995 (5)	1,000	KM#794, 796, 797-798, 801	—	1,385
PS60	1996 (4)	15,000	KM#971-974	—	180
PS61	1996 (4)	8,000	KM#966-969	—	240
PS62	1996 (6)	—	KM#1-3, 335-337	—	8.00
PS63	1996 (4)	750	KM#939, 941-943, plus bottle	—	625
PS64	1997 (4)	28,000	KM#1053-1056	—	200
PS65	1997 (4)	10,000	KM#1077-1080	—	180
PS66	1998 (1)	61,000	China KM#1157 and Canada KM#316	72.50	50.00

CHINESE SOVIET REPUBLIC

In November, 1931, the first congress of the Chinese Soviet proclaimed and established the "Chinese Soviet Republic" under the Chairmanship of Mao Tse-Tung.

Prior to 1949, the People's Republic of China did not exist as such, but the Communists did control areas known as Soviets. Most of the Soviets were established on the borders of two or more provinces and were named according to the provinces involved. Thus there were such soviets as the Kiangsi-Hunan Soviet, the Hunan-Hupeh-Kiangsi Soviet, the Hupeh-Honan-Anhwei Soviet and others. In 1931 some of the soviets in the southern Kiangsi area were consolidated into the Chinese Soviet Republic, which lasted until the Long March of 1934.

MONETARY SYSTEM
10 Cash (Wen) = 1 Cent (Fen)
100 Cents (Fen) = 1 Dollar (Yuan)

CONSOLIDATED SOVIET REPUBLIC
(Kiangsi)
STANDARD COINAGE

Y# 506 CENT
Copper **Ruler:** Mao Tse-tung **Obv:** Large "1" on hammer and sickle **Rev:** Star above value in wheat stalks

Date	Mintage	VG	F	VF	XF	Unc
ND(ca.1932)	—	10.00	20.00	35.00	65.00	—

Y# 506a CENT
Copper **Ruler:** Mao Tse-tung **Obv:** Large "1" on hammer and sickle **Rev:** Star above value in wheat stalks

Date	Mintage	F	VF	XF	Unc	BU
ND(ca.1960) Restrike	—	—	8.00	20.00	30.00	

Y# 507 5 CENTS
Copper **Ruler:** Mao Tse-tung **Obv:** Hammer and sickle on map outline **Rev:** Star over value in wheat stalks **Edge:** Plain
Note: Varieties exist.

Date	Mintage	VG	F	VF	XF	Unc
ND(ca.1932)	—	20.00	30.00	50.00	90.00	—

Y# 507.1 5 CENTS
Copper **Ruler:** Mao Tse-tung **Obv:** Hammer and sickle on map outline **Rev:** Star over value in wheat stalks **Edge:** Reeded
Note: Varieties exist.

Date	Mintage	VG	F	VF	XF	Unc
ND(ca.1932)	—	20.00	30.00	50.00	90.00	—

Y# 507a 5 CENTS
Copper **Ruler:** Mao Tse-tung **Obv:** Hammer and sickle on map outline **Rev:** Star over value in wheat stalks

Date	Mintage	F	VF	XF	Unc	BU
ND(ca.1960) Restrike	—	—	—	10.00	25.00	35.00

Y# 508 20 CENTS
5.5000 g., Silver **Ruler:** Mao Tse-tung **Obv:** Star over hammer and sickle on globe in wheat stalks **Rev:** Denomination
Note: Many minor varieties exist.

Date	Mintage	VG	F	VF	XF	Unc
1932	—	20.00	35.00	55.00	100	—
1933	—	20.00	35.00	45.00	85.00	—

KM# 5   DOLLAR
Silver **Ruler:** Mao Tse-tung **Obv:** Crude facing portrait of Lenin
Rev: Hammer, sickle, and value within ornamental wreath

Date	Mintage	VG	F	VF	XF	Unc
1931 Rare	—	—	—	—	—	—

PATTERNS
Including off metal strikes

KM#	Date	Mintage	Identification	Mkt Val
Pn1	1932	—	20 Cents. Copper. Y#508.	265

HSIANG-O-HSI SOVIET
(Kiangsi-West Hupeh)

SOVIET CONTROLLED PROVINCE
STANDARD COINAGE

KM# 1   FEN
Copper **Obv:** Legend around large star **Rev:** Denomination within wreath, legend around

Date	Mintage	VG	F	VF	XF	Unc
ND(1931) Rare	—	—	—	—	—	—

HUNAN SOVIET
SOVIET CONTROLLED PROVINCE
STANDARD COINAGE

KM# 1.1   DOLLAR
Silver **Obv:** Large star **Obv. Leg.:** "Hu-nan Sheng Su-wei-ai Cheng-fu" **Rev:** Denomination within sprays

Date	Mintage	VG	F	VF	XF	Unc
1931	—	200	350	—	—	—

KM# 1.2   DOLLAR
Silver **Obv:** Hammer and sickle within small star
Rev: Denomination within sprays

Date	Mintage	VG	F	VF	XF	Unc
1931	—	100	300	500	—	—

HUPEH-HONAN-ANWHEI SOVIET

The Hupeh-Honan-Anhwei Soviet District was a large revolutionary base. It was formerly made up of three separate special districts: East Hupeh, South Honan and West Anhwei which united until after 1930. Between 1931 and 1932 this Bank has issued a quantity of copper and silver coins as well as banknotes.

SOVIET CONTROLLED PROVINCE
STANDARD COINAGE

Y# 503   DOLLAR
26.8000 g., Silver **Obv:** Hammer and sickle on globe at center
Rev: Lower legend appears in crude Russian, denomination within circle at center **Rev. Leg.:** "SOVETS...."

Date	Mintage	VG	F	VF	XF	Unc
1932	—	250	575	750	1,000	—

Note: Attribution of Y#503 to the Hupeh-Honan-Anhwei Soviet is not definite.

Y# 504   DOLLAR
27.2000 g., Silver **Obv:** Hammer and sickle on globe at center
Rev: Denomination within center circle

Date	Mintage	VG	F	VF	XF	Unc
1932	—	175	275	400	700	—

P'ING CHIANG COUNTY SOVIET
SOVIET CONTROLLED PROVINCE
STANDARD COINAGE

KM# 1   DOLLAR
Silver **Obv:** Star in center circle holds sickle and hammer, legend in 8 Chinese characters **Obv. Leg.:** "P'ing Chiang..."
Rev: Denomination within wreath

Date	Mintage	VG	F	VF	XF	Unc
1931 Rare	—	—	—	—	—	—

SHENSI-NORTH SOVIET
SOVIET CONTROLLED PROVINCE
STANDARD COINAGE

Date is given in the 5th year of the Chinese Soviet Republic. They were issued after the Long March.

KM# 1.1   DOLLAR
Silver **Obv:** Large hammer and sickle **Rev:** Value in plain field, yr.5 at bottom

Date	Mintage	VG	F	VF	XF	Unc
5 (1936)	—	1,750	2,250	2,850	—	—

KM# 1.2   DOLLAR
Silver **Obv:** Star at left, slightly lower **Rev:** Denomination within center circle, legend rotated with yr.5 at top

Date	Mintage	VG	F	VF	XF	Unc
5 (1936)	—	1,750	2,250	2,850	—	—

KM# 2   DOLLAR

Silver **Obv:** Large hammer and sickle **Rev:** Value within wheat stalks

Date	Mintage	VG	F	VF	XF	Unc
5 (1936)	—	2,500	3,200	4,000	—	—

SZECHUAN-SHENSI SOVIET

SOVIET CONTROLLED PROVINCES

STANDARD COINAGE

Y# 510   200 CASH

Copper **Obv:** Three stars around hammer and sickle **Rev:** Denomination at center

Date	Mintage	Good	VG	F	VF	XF
1933	—	25.00	50.00	85.00	150	—

Y# 510.1   200 CASH

Copper **Obv:** Three stars around hammer and sickle **Rev:** Small "200" at center

Date	Mintage	Good	VG	F	VF	XF
1933	—	25.00	50.00	85.00	150	—

Y# 510.2   200 CASH

Copper **Obv:** Three stars around hammer and sickle **Rev:** Large "200" at center

Date	Mintage	Good	VG	F	VF	XF
1933	—	25.00	50.00	85.00	150	—

Y# 510.3   200 CASH

Copper **Obv:** Three stars around hammer and sickle **Rev:** Square 0's in "200" at center

Date	Mintage	Good	VG	F	VF	XF
1933	—	30.00	60.00	100	185	—

Y# 510.4   200 CASH

Copper **Obv:** Solid hammer and sickle reversed **Rev:** 200 retrograde at center'

Date	Mintage	Good	VG	F	VF	XF
1933	—	35.00	75.00	125	250	—

Y# 510.5   200 CASH

Copper **Obv:** Shaded hammer and sickle reversed, three stars above **Rev:** Denomination within wreath at center **Note:** Varieties exist.

Date	Mintage	Good	VG	F	VF	XF
1933	—	30.00	60.00	100	185	—

Y# 511.1   200 CASH

Copper **Obv:** Hammer and sickle within large star, date with open 3 and backwards 4 **Rev:** Denomination within circle

Date	Mintage	VG	F	VF	XF	Unc
1934	—	22.50	45.00	75.00	150	—

Y# 511.2   200 CASH

Copper **Obv:** Hammer and sickle within large star, date with 4 corrected **Rev:** Denomination within circle

Date	Mintage	VG	F	VF	XF	Unc
1934	—	22.50	45.00	75.00	150	—

Y# 511   200 CASH

Copper **Obv:** Hammer and sickle at center of large star, date with closed 3 and backwards 4 **Rev:** Denomination within circle **Note:** Modern forgeries of this variety exist.

Date	Mintage	VG	F	VF	XF	Unc
1934	—	22.50	45.00	75.00	150	—

Y# 511a   200 CASH

Copper **Obv:** Hammer and sickle within large star, date with 4 corrected **Rev:** Denomination within circle

Date	Mintage	F	VF	XF	Unc	BU
1934 Restrike	—	—	12.50	25.00	35.00	

Note: Many varieties of 200 Cash pieces exist; well struck, usually found in choice condition; unlisted varieties do not carry a premium

Y# 512   500 CASH

Copper **Obv:** Hammer and sickle within small star, small stars flanking date **Rev:** Denomination within circle

Date	Mintage	VG	F	VF	XF	Unc
1934	—	75.00	100	175	285	—

Y# 512.1   500 CASH

Copper **Obv:** Large stars flanking date; hammer handle across lower leg of star **Rev:** Denomination within circle

Date	Mintage	VG	F	VF	XF	Unc
1934	—	50.00	100	175	275	—

Y# 512.2   500 CASH

Copper, 33-34 mm. **Obv:** Hammer handle extends between right leg of star **Rev:** Denomination within circle

Date	Mintage	VG	F	VF	XF	Unc
1934	—	50.00	100	150	250	—

Note: Many varieties of 500 Cash pieces exist; unlisted varieties do not carry a premium

Y# 513 DOLLAR
26.3000 g., Silver **Obv:** Globe with hammer and sickle
Rev: Denomination within circle, large, decorative, solid stars

Date	Mintage	VG	F	VF	XF	Unc
1934	—	125	225	325	500	—

Y# 513.6 DOLLAR
26.3000 g., Silver **Obv:** Globe with outlined hammer and sickle, sickle blade over hammer handle **Rev:** Denomination within circle, small solid stars

Date	Mintage	VG	F	VF	XF	Unc
1934	—	100	200	275	450	—

Y# 513.1 DOLLAR
26.3000 g., Silver **Obv:** Globe with outlined hammer and sickle, hammer handle over sickle blade **Rev:** Denomination within circle, medium solid stars

Date	Mintage	VG	F	VF	XF	Unc
1934	—	100	175	250	450	—

Y# 513.2 DOLLAR
26.3000 g., Silver **Obv:** Globe with outlined hammer and sickle
Rev: Denomination within circle, small solid stars

Date	Mintage	VG	F	VF	XF	Unc
1933 Rare	—	—	—	—	—	—
1934	—	100	175	250	450	—

Y# 513.3 DOLLAR
26.3000 g., Silver **Obv:** Globe with hammer and sickle
Rev: Denomination within circle, outlined stars

Date	Mintage	VG	F	VF	XF	Unc
1934	—	100	225	300	500	—

Y# 513.5 DOLLAR
26.3000 g., Silver **Obv:** Globe with outlined hammer and sickle
Rev: Denomination within circle, large solid stars

Date	Mintage	VG	F	VF	XF	Unc
1934	—	100	225	300	500	—

Y# 513.4 DOLLAR
26.3000 g., Silver **Obv:** Globe with hammer and sickle
Rev: Denomination within circle, pentagram stars **Note:** Many minor varieties exist.

Date	Mintage	VG	F	VF	XF	Unc
1934	—	100	175	250	400	—

COUNTERMARKED COINAGE

K# 650k DOLLAR
26.4000 g., Silver **Countermark:** Three Chinese characters in rectangular box **Obv:** Bust, left, countermark of uncertain origin meaning "SOVIET" **Rev:** Denomination within wreath
Note: Countermark on Y#329.

CM Date	Host Date	Good	VG	F	VF	XF
ND(1934)	ND	62.50	125	200	325	600

(Northwest Anhwei)

SOVIET CONTROLLED PROVINCE
STANDARD COINAGE

KM# 1 50 CASH
Brass **Obv:** Legend around globe with hammer and sickle
Rev: Value in star within wreath, all within legend

Date	Mintage	Good	VG	F	VF	XF
1931	—	150	250	—	—	—

KM# 2 50 CASH
Copper **Obv:** Legend around globe with hammer and sickle
Rev: Value in circle, Chinese legend above, Western legend below

Date	Mintage	VG	F	VF	XF	Unc
ND(1931-32) Rare	—	—	—	—	—	—

COLOMBIA

The Republic of Colombia, in the northwestern corner of South America, has an area of 440,831 sq. mi. (1,138,910 sq. km.) and a population of*42.3 million. Capital: Bogota. The economy is primarily agricultural with a mild, rich coffee being the chief crop. Colombia has the world's largest platinum deposits and important reserves of coal, iron ore, petroleum and limestone; other precious metals and emeralds are also mined. Coffee, crude oil, bananas, sugar and emeralds are exported.

The northern coast of present Colombia was one of the first parts of the American continent to be visited by Spanish navigators. At Darien in Panama is the site of the first permanent European settlement on the American mainland in 1510. New Granada, as Colombia was known until 1861, stemmed from the settlement of Santa Marta in 1525. New Granada was established as a Spanish colony in 1549. Independence was declared in 1810, and secured in 1819 when Simon Bolivar united Colombia, Venezuela, Panama and Ecuador as the Republic of Gran Colombia. Venezuela withdrew from the Republic in 1829; Ecuador in 1830; and Panama in 1903.

MINT MARKS
A, M – Medellin (capital), Antioquia (state)
B - BOGOTA
(D) Denver, USA
H – Birmingham (Heaton & Sons)
(m) - Medellin, w/o mint mark
(Mo) - Mexico City
NI - Numismatica Italiana, Arezzo, Italy
  mint marks stylized in wreath
(P) - Philadelphia
(S) - San Francisco, USA.
(W) - Waterbury, CT (USA, Scoville mint)

REPUBLIC

DECIMAL COINAGE
100 Centavos = 1 Peso

KM# 275 CENTAVO
2.0000 g., Copper-Nickel, 17 mm. **Obv:** Liberty head right **Rev:** Denomination within wreath **Note:** Erratically punched final two digits of date are common on these issues, especially 1935-1948. A very faint "17" is often observable beneath the final two digits on many dates of this type.

Date	Mintage	F	VF	XF	Unc	BU
1918	430,000	6.00	15.00	35.00	125	—
1919	Inc. above	8.00	25.00	60.00	140	—
1920(D)	7,540,000	6.50	13.50	32.00	120	—
1921(D)	12,460,000	6.50	12.50	30.00	60.00	—
1933(P)	3,000,000	0.50	3.00	5.00	10.00	—
1935(P)	5,000,000	0.50	3.00	7.00	15.00	—
1936	1,540,000	2.00	5.00	15.00	45.00	—
1938(P)	7,920,000	0.25	0.50	2.00	6.00	—
1941B	1,000,000	0.50	1.00	3.00	10.00	—
1946B	2,096,000	0.35	0.75	2.50	6.50	—
1947/17B	1,835,000	1.00	3.50	6.00	12.00	—
1947/37B	Inc. above	1.00	3.50	6.00	12.00	—
1947/6B	Inc. above	1.00	3.50	6.00	12.00	—
1947B	Inc. above	0.50	1.00	2.00	5.00	—
1948/38B	1,139,000	1.00	3.50	6.00	12.00	—
1948B	Inc. above	0.50	1.00	2.00	5.00	—

KM# 205 CENTAVO
2.0000 g., Bronze, 17 mm. **Obv:** Liberty cap within wreath **Rev:** Coffee bean sprigs flank denomination, cornucopia above **Note:** Several date varieties exist.

Date	Mintage	F	VF	XF	Unc	BU
1942	1,000,000	1.00	2.00	4.50	12.50	—
1942B	Inc. above	1.00	3.50	9.00	28.00	—
1943	—	0.50	1.00	2.50	7.00	—
1943B	4,515,000	0.50	1.00	2.50	7.00	—
1944B	4,515,000	0.35	0.65	1.50	5.00	—
1945B	3,769,000	0.50	1.00	2.50	7.00	—
1945B over reversed B	—	0.35	0.65	1.50	5.00	—
1948B	585,000	0.50	1.00	3.00	10.00	—
1949B	4,255,000	0.35	0.65	1.50	5.00	—
1950B	5,827,000	0.45	0.75	2.50	8.00	—
1951B	Inc. above	0.35	0.65	1.75	5.50	—
1957	2,500,000	0.25	0.45	0.75	2.00	—
1958	590,000	0.25	0.45	1.00	2.25	—
1959	2,677,000	0.15	0.25	0.50	1.25	—
1960	2,500,000	0.15	0.25	0.50	1.25	—
1961 Widely spaced date	3,673,000	0.15	0.25	0.50	1.25	—
1961 Narrowly spaced date	Inc. above	0.15	0.25	0.45	1.00	—
1962	4,065,000	0.15	0.25	0.50	1.25	—
1963	1,845,000	0.15	0.25	0.75	2.00	—
1964/44	3,165,000	0.50	1.50	2.50	5.00	—
1964	Inc. above	0.15	0.25	0.50	1.25	—
1965 Large date	5,510,000	0.15	0.25	0.50	1.00	—
1965 Small date	Inc. above	0.15	0.25	0.45	1.00	—
1966	3,910,000	0.15	0.25	0.50	1.25	—

KM# 275a CENTAVO
2.0000 g., Nickel Clad Steel, 17 mm. **Obv:** Liberty head right **Rev:** Denomination within wreath **Note:** Erratically punched final two digits of date are common on these issues.

Date	Mintage	F	VF	XF	Unc	BU
1952/12B	—	0.20	0.50	1.50	4.00	—
1952B	Inc. above	0.10	0.15	0.75	3.00	—
1954B	5,080,000	0.10	0.15	0.50	2.00	—
1956	1,315,000	0.10	0.20	1.00	5.00	—
1957	900,000	0.35	0.75	2.50	7.50	—
1958/48	—	0.35	0.75	2.00	4.00	—
1958	1,596,000	0.20	0.45	1.00	3.00	—

KM# 218 CENTAVO
Bronze, 17 mm. **Subject:** Uprising Sesquicentennial **Obv:** Liberty cap within wreath **Rev:** Coffee bean sprigs flank denomination, cornucopia above **Note:** This and the other issues in the uprising commemorative series offer the usual design of the period with the dates 1810-1960 added at the bottom of the obverse.

Date	Mintage	F	VF	XF	Unc	BU
ND(1960)	500,000	0.60	1.50	3.00	8.00	—

KM# 205a CENTAVO
Copper Clad Steel, 17 mm. **Obv:** Liberty cap within wreath **Rev:** Coffee bean sprigs flank denomination, cornucopia above **Note:** Several date varieties exist.

Date	Mintage	F	VF	XF	Unc	BU
1967	5,730,000	—	0.10	0.15	0.45	—
1968	7,390,000	—	0.10	0.15	0.45	—
1969	6,870,000	—	0.10	0.15	0.45	—
1970	3,839,000	—	0.10	0.20	0.60	—
1971	3,020,000	—	0.10	0.20	0.60	—
1972	3,100,000	—	0.10	0.20	0.60	—
1973	—			0.10	0.35	—
1974	2,000,000			0.10	0.35	—
1975	1,000,000			0.10	0.35	—
1976	1,000,000			0.10	0.35	—
1977	900,000			0.10	0.45	—
1978	224,000			0.10	0.20	0.65

KM# 198 2 CENTAVOS
3.0000 g., Copper-Nickel **Obv:** Liberty head right, date below **Rev:** Denomination within wreath **Note:** Erratically punched final two digits exist for 1946-1947. A very faint "17" is often observable beneath the final two digits on many dates of this type.

Date	Mintage	F	VF	XF	Unc	BU
1918	930,000	7.00	15.00	30.00	80.00	—
1919	Inc. above.	16.50	30.00	60.00	135	—
1920	3,855,000	3.00	6.50	18.50	50.00	—
1921(D)	11,145,000	2.50	5.00	15.00	40.00	—
1922 10 pieces known	—	1,350	2,800	—	—	—
1933(P)	3,500,000	0.50	1.50	4.00	10.00	—
1935(P)	2,500,000	0.35	1.00	3.50	8.00	—
1938(P)	3,872,000	0.35	1.00	3.25	7.00	—
1941B	500,000	1.00	2.00	7.00	20.00	—
1942B	500,000	1.50	2.50	8.00	16.50	—
1946/36B	2,593,000	1.00	2.50	6.00	12.50	—
1946B	Inc. above	0.75	1.50	4.75	11.00	—
1947/3B	1,337,000	0.75	1.50	4.00	10.00	—
1947/36B	Inc. above	0.75	1.50	4.00	10.00	—
1947B	Inc. above	0.35	1.00	3.00	8.00	—

KM# 210 2 CENTAVOS
3.0300 g., Bronze, 19.04 mm. **Obv:** Liberty cap within wreath, date below **Rev:** Coffee bean sprigs flank denomination, cornucopia above **Mint:** Bogota

Date	Mintage	F	VF	XF	Unc	BU
1948B	2,648,000	0.35	1.00	4.00	10.00	—
1949B	1,278,000	0.75	2.00	7.00	15.00	—
1950B	2,285,000	0.75	1.50	7.00	18.00	—

KM# 211 2 CENTAVOS
3.1000 g., Aluminum-Bronze **Obv:** Head left, date below, divided legend **Rev:** Denomination within wreath

Date	Mintage	F	VF	XF	Unc	BU
1952B Small date	5,038,000	0.15	0.25	0.50	2.00	—

Date	Mintage	F	VF	XF	Unc	BU
1965/3	1,830,000	0.10	0.20	0.40	1.00	—
1965 Large date	Inc. above	0.15	0.25	0.50	2.00	—

KM# 214 2 CENTAVOS
2.9300 g., Aluminum-Bronze **Obv:** Head left, date below, continuous legend **Rev:** Denomination within wreath **Mint:** Bogota

Date	Mintage	F	VF	XF	Unc	BU
1955 Large date	2,513,000	0.15	0.30	1.00	3.00	—
1955B Large date	Inc. above	0.15	0.30	0.75	2.00	—
1959 Small date	4,609,000	0.10	0.20	0.50	1.50	—

KM# 219 2 CENTAVOS
Aluminum-Bronze **Subject:** Uprising Sesquicentennial **Obv:** Head left, date below **Rev:** Denomination within wreath **Mint:** Bogota

Date	Mintage	F	VF	XF	Unc	BU
ND(1960)	250,000	1.00	2.00	3.00	8.00	—

KM# 190 2-1/2 CENTAVOS
Copper-Nickel, 14.3 mm. **Obv:** Liberty cap within circle **Rev:** Denomination within circle **Mint:** Waterbury **Note:** It is probable the scarcity of this coin, & KM#184, result from their being placed incirculation within the then - Columbian state of Panama. After a brief US aided rebellion gained independence for Panama & the US gained canal rights, US-made silver coinage replaced the short-lived c-n Columbian coinage.

Date	Mintage	F	VF	XF	Unc	BU
1902(W)	Est. 400,000			500	900	—

KM# 191 5 CENTAVOS
1.2500 g., 0.6660 Silver 0.0268 oz. ASW, 14 mm. **Obv:** Head left, date below **Rev:** Small denomination within two cornucopias **Edge:** Plain **Mint:** Philadelphia

Date	Mintage	F	VF	XF	Unc	BU
1902(P)	400,000	0.75	1.50	3.50	8.00	—

KM# 184 5 CENTAVOS
Copper-Nickel, 20 mm. **Obv:** Head left **Rev:** Large denomination, sprays flank **Mint:** Waterbury **Note:** It is probable the scarcity of this coin & KM#190, result from their being placed in circulation within the then-Columbian state of Panama. After a biref US aided rebellion gained independence from Panama & the US gained canal rights, US-made silver coinage replaced the short-lived c-n Columbian coinage.

Date	Mintage	F	VF	XF	Unc	BU
1902(W)	Est. 400,000		400	650	1,000	—

KM# 199 5 CENTAVOS
4.0000 g., Copper-Nickel, 21 mm. **Obv:** Head right, date below **Rev:** Denomination within wreath **Note:** Varieties exist. Erratically punched final two digits of date are common on these issues, especially 1935-1950. A very faint "17" is often observable beneath the final two digits on many dates of this type. A cursive numeral form is found on some 1941 strikes or is obvious for the one's in the date. May only occur on some with "B" mm on reverse.

Date	Mintage	F	VF	XF	Unc	BU
1918	767,000	11.00	25.00	50.00	100	—
1919	1,926,000	16.50	30.00	65.00	125	—

Date	Mintage	F	VF	XF	Unc	BU
1920	2,062,000	11.00	25.00	50.00	100	—
1920H			10.00	27.50	45.00	100	—
1921	1,574,000	16.50	30.00	65.00	125	—
1921H			16.50	30.00	65.00	125	—
1922	2,623,000	16.50	30.00	65.00	125	—
1922H			16.50	30.00	65.00	125	—
1924	120,000	18.50	35.00	70.00	125	—
1933(P)	2,000,000	1.00	2.00	6.00	15.00	—
1935/24	1,616,000	5.00	12.00	30.00	60.00	—
1935(P)	10,000,000	0.75	1.75	3.50	10.00	—
1936			45.00	75.00	150	350	—
1938B	2,000,000	1.00	2.50	5.50	13.00	—
1938	3,867,000	2.00	3.75	8.00	15.00	—
1938 Large 38 in date	Inc. above	2.00	4.50	10.00	20.00	—
1939/5	2,000,000	1.75	3.00	6.00	13.00	—
1939	Inc. above	0.75	1.50	3.50	8.00	—
1941			2.50	5.50	9.00	23.00	—
1941B	500,000	3.00	6.00	10.00	25.00	—
1946(P) (S) Small date	40,000,000	0.20	0.50	1.00	3.00	—
1946(m) Large date	3,330,000	2.00	4.00	8.50	23.00	—
1949B	2,750,000	0.45	1.00	1.50	6.00	—
1950B Large 50 in date	3,611,000	6.00	12.00	25.00	45.00	—
1950B Small 50 in date	Inc. above	0.45	1.00	3.00	6.00	—

KM# 206 5 CENTAVOS
4.0200 g., Bronze, 21 mm. **Obv:** Liberty cap within wreath, date below **Rev:** Coffee bean sprigs flank denomination, cornucopia above **Note:** Some coins of 1942-1956 have weak "B" mint mark.

Date	Mintage	F	VF	XF	Unc	BU
1942	—	2.00	4.00	12.00	30.00	—
1942B	800,000	1.00	2.50	4.50	12.00	—
1943			5.00	9.00	18.00	35.00	—
1943B	6,053,000	0.75	1.50	3.00	10.00	—
1944			0.75	1.50	3.00	10.00	—
1944B	9,013,000	0.75	1.50	3.00	10.00	—
1945/4			0.75	1.50	3.00	10.00	—
1945			0.75	1.50	3.00	10.00	—
1945B	11,101,000	0.25	0.75	1.25	4.00	—
1946/5	—	1.25	3.50	4.50	12.50	—
1946	—	0.50	1.25	2.00	7.00	—
1952	—	1.25	2.50	3.50	10.00	—
1952B	3,985,000	0.15	0.40	1.00	2.50	—
1953B	5,180,000	0.10	0.25	0.75	2.00	—
1954B	1,159,000	0.10	0.25	0.75	2.00	—
1955B	6,819,000	0.10	0.25	0.75	2.00	—
1956	8,772,000	0.10	0.25	0.50	1.00	—
1956B			0.75	1.50	4.50	12.50	—
1957	8,912,000	0.10	0.25	0.50	2.00	—
1958	15,016,000	0.10	0.25	0.50	1.50	—
1959	14,271,000	0.10	0.25	0.50	1.50	—
1960/660	11,716,000	0.25	0.75	1.00	2.25	—
1960/70	Inc. above	0.25	0.75	1.00	2.25	—
1960	Inc. above	0.10	0.25	0.50	1.25	—
1961	11,200,000	0.10	0.25	0.50	1.25	—
CD1962	10,928,000	—	0.10	0.35	1.00	—
1963/53	15,113,000	—	—	—	—	—
1963	Inc. above	—	0.10	0.35	1.00	—
1964	9,336,000	—	0.10	0.35	1.00	—
1965	6,460,000	—	0.10	0.35	1.00	—
1966	7,170,000	—	0.10	0.35	1.00	—

KM# 206a 5 CENTAVOS
3.2300 g., Copper Clad Steel, 21.29 mm. **Obv:** Liberty cap within wreath, date below **Rev:** Coffee bean sprigs flank denomination, cornucopia above **Note:** Varieties exist for 1967, 1970, and 1973.

Date	Mintage	F	VF	XF	Unc	BU
1967	10,280,000	—	—	0.10	1.00	—
1968	8,900,000	—	—	0.10	1.00	—
1969	17,800,000	—	—	0.10	1.00	—
1970	14,842,000	—	—	0.10	0.50	—
1971	10,730,000	—	—	0.10	0.50	—
1972	10,170,000	—	—	0.10	0.50	—
1973	10,525,000	—	—	0.10	0.50	—
1974	5,310,000	—	—	0.10	0.50	—
1975	5,631,000	—	—	0.10	0.50	—
1976	3,009,000	—	—	0.10	0.50	—
1977	2,000,000	—	—	0.10	0.50	—
1978	468,000	—	—	0.10	0.50	—
1979	8,087,000					—

KM# 220 5 CENTAVOS
Bronze, 21 mm. **Subject:** Uprising Sesquicentennial **Obv:** Liberty cap within wreath **Rev:** Coffee bean sprigs flank denomination, cornucopia above

Date	Mintage	F	VF	XF	Unc	BU
ND(1960)	400,000	1.75	3.50	7.50	28.00	—

KM# 196.1 10 CENTAVOS
2.5000 g., 0.9000 Silver 0.0723 oz. ASW, 18 mm. **Obv:** Simon Bolivar head right, date below **Rev:** Arms and value **Note:** Varieties exist.

Date	Mintage	F	VF	XF	Unc	BU
1911	5,065,000	1.00	1.75	10.00	25.00	—
1913	8,305,000	1.00	1.75	9.00	20.00	—
1914	3,840,000	1.00	1.75	10.00	25.00	—
1920	2,149,000	1.00	1.75	10.00	25.00	—
1934B B on obverse	140,000	3.00	7.00	18.00	40.00	—
1934/24	Inc. above	6.25	13.50	28.00	60.00	—
1934	Inc. above	6.00	12.50	28.00	60.00	—
1937B			5.00	11.50	22.50	45.00	—
1938/7B	2,055,000	1.75	3.75	6.50	20.00	—
1938B Wide date	Inc. above	1.00	2.00	4.00	10.00	—
1938 Narrow date	Inc. above	1.00	2.00	4.00	10.00	—
1940	450,000	1.50	2.50	4.50	15.00	—
1941	4,415,000	1.00	1.50	3.00	8.00	—
1942	3,140,000	5.00	10.00	16.50	38.00	—
1942B B on reverse	Inc. above	1.00	1.50	3.00	7.50	—

KM# 196.2 10 CENTAVOS
2.5000 g., 0.9000 Silver 0.0723 oz. ASW, 18 mm. **Obv:** Simon Bolivar head right **Rev:** National arms recut

Date	Mintage	F	VF	XF	Unc	BU
1920	Inc. above	2.00	6.00	12.00	30.00	—

KM# 207.1 10 CENTAVOS
2.5000 g., 0.5000 Silver 0.0402 oz. ASW, 18 mm. **Obv:** Francisco de Paula Santander head right **Rev:** Denomination within wreath, mint mark at bottom

Date	Mintage	F	VF	XF	Unc	BU
1945B	4,830,000	0.75	1.50	3.50	10.00	—
1945 B-B	—					—
1945 Backwards B	—	1.00	2.00	4.00	10.00	—
1946/5B	—	0.65	1.50	4.50	13.00	—
1946B	—	0.65	1.50	4.50	13.00	—
1947/5B	7,366,000	1.50	3.00	5.00	15.00	—
1947/6B	Inc. above	1.50	3.00	5.00	15.00	—
1947B	Inc. above	1.50	3.00	5.00	15.00	—

KM# 207.2 10 CENTAVOS
2.5000 g., 0.5000 Silver 0.0402 oz. ASW, 18 mm. **Obv:** Head of Santander right, date below **Rev:** Denomination within wreath, mint mark at top **Note:** Varieties exist. Almost all dies for 1946-1951 show at least faint traces of overdating from 1945. Coins with absolutely no underdate, and those with very bold underdate, are generally worth more to advanced specialists.

Date	Mintage	F	VF	XF	Unc	BU
1947/5B	Inc. above	2.00	4.00	7.50	20.00	—
1947B	Inc. above	2.00	4.00	7.50	20.00	—
1948/5B	3,629,000	0.75	1.50	5.00	15.00	—
1948B	Inc. above	0.65	1.25	3.00	10.00	—
1949/5B	5,923,000	3.00	6.50	12.50	28.00	—
1949B	Inc. above	0.65	1.25	2.25	8.00	—
1950B	6,783,000	0.65	1.50	2.75	9.00	—
1951/5B	5,185,000	0.65	1.50	2.75	9.00	—
1951B	Inc. above	0.65	1.25	2.25	8.00	—
1952B	1,060,000	1.25	2.25	4.50	13.00	—

KM# 212.1 10 CENTAVOS
Copper-Nickel, 18 mm. **Obv:** Arms above date **Rev:** Head of Chief Calarca right divides denomination **Mint:** Bogota

Date	Mintage	F	VF	XF	Unc	BU
1952B	6,035,000	0.35	1.00	3.50	15.00	—
1953B	6,985,000	0.25	0.50	1.50	6.00	—

KM# 212.2 10 CENTAVOS
2.3300 g., Copper-Nickel, 18.5 mm. **Obv:** Arms above date **Rev:** Head of Chief Calarca right divides denomination **Mint:** Bogota **Note:** Varieties exist.

Date	Mintage	F	VF	XF	Unc	BU
1954B	13,006,000	0.20	0.50	1.25	3.00	—
1955B	9,968,000	0.20	0.50	1.25	3.00	—
1956	36,010,000	0.10	0.20	0.50	1.50	—
1956B			0.10	0.20	0.50	1.50	—

Date	Mintage	F	VF	XF	Unc	BU
1958	41,695,000					—
1959	36,653,000	0.10	0.20	0.50	1.50	—
1960	32,290,000	0.10	0.20	0.50	2.00	—
1961	17,780,000	0.10	0.20	0.50	2.00	—
1962	8,930,000	0.10	0.20	0.50	2.00	—
1963	37,540,000	0.10	0.20	0.50	1.50	—
1964	61,672,000	0.10	0.20	0.50	1.50	—
1965	12,804,000	0.10	0.25	0.75	3.00	—
1966 Large date	23,544,000	0.10	0.20	0.50	1.50	—

KM# 221 10 CENTAVOS
Copper-Nickel, 18.5 mm. **Subject:** Uprising Sesquicentennial **Obv:** Arms above two dates **Rev:** Head of Chief Calarca right divides denomination

Date	Mintage	F	VF	XF	Unc	BU
ND(1960)	1,000,000	1.00	2.00	3.50	8.00	—

KM# 226 10 CENTAVOS
2.5100 g., Nickel Clad Steel, 18.3 mm. **Obv:** Head of Santander right, date below **Rev:** Denomination within circular wreath

Date	Mintage	F	VF	XF	Unc	BU
1967	26,980,000		0.10	0.20	1.00	—
1968	23,670,000		0.10	0.20	1.00	—
1969	29,450,000		0.10	0.20	1.00	—

KM# 236 10 CENTAVOS
2.5200 g., Nickel Clad Steel, 18.3 mm. **Obv:** Head of Santander right, date below **Rev:** Denomination within wreath

Date	Mintage	F	VF	XF	Unc	BU
1969	Inc. above	—	0.10	0.20	1.00	—
1970	38,935,000	—	0.10	0.20	1.00	—
1971	53,314,000	—	0.10	0.20	1.00	—

KM# 243 10 CENTAVOS
Nickel Clad Steel, 18.3 mm. **Obv:** Legend divided after REPUBLICA

Date	Mintage	F	VF	XF	Unc	BU
1970						—
1971						—

KM# 253 10 CENTAVOS
2.5200 g., Nickel Clad Steel, 18.4 mm. **Obv:** Head right, date below, continuous legend **Rev:** Denomination within wreath **Note:** Varieties exist.

Date	Mintage	F	VF	XF	Unc	BU
1972	58,000,000	—	0.10	0.15	0.35	—
1973	46,549,000	—	0.10	0.15	0.35	—
1974	49,740,000	—	0.10	0.15	0.35	—
1975	46,037,000	—	0.10	0.15	0.35	—
1976	46,084,000	—	0.10	0.15	0.35	—
1977	8,127,000	—	0.10	0.15	0.35	—
1978	97,081,000	—	0.10	0.15	0.35	—
1980	18,929,000	—	0.10	0.15	0.35	—

KM# 197 20 CENTAVOS
5.0000 g., 0.9000 Silver 0.1447 oz. ASW **Obv:** Head of Simon Bolivar right, date below **Rev:** Arms, denomination above

Date	Mintage	F	VF	XF	Unc	BU
1911	1,206,000	2.00	3.50	7.50	17.50	—
1913	1,630,000	2.00	3.50	7.50	22.50	—
1914	2,560,000	2.00	3.50	9.00	25.00	—
1920 Wide date	1,242,000	2.50	6.00	12.50	32.50	—

Date	Mintage	F	VF	XF	Unc	BU
1920 Narrow date	Inc. above	2.50	6.00	12.50	32.50	—
1921	372,000	7.00	15.00	35.00	85.00	—
1922	45,000	30.00	55.00	85.00	225	—
1933B	330,000	3.50	7.50	15.00	35.00	—

Note: Mint mark on obverse

| 1933B | Inc. above | 12.50 | 25.00 | 45.00 | 125 | — |

Note: Mint mark on reverse

| 1933B | Inc. above | 5.00 | 10.00 | 20.00 | 50.00 | — |

Note: Mint mark on both sides

1938/1	1,410,000	4.00	8.00	17.00	35.00	—
1938	Inc. above	2.25	5.00	10.00	22.00	—
1941	—	2.50	6.00	12.00	28.00	—
1942	155,000	9.00	20.00	32.50	65.00	—
1942B	Inc. above	2.00	3.50	7.50	20.00	—

Note: Mint mark on reverse

KM# 208.1   20 CENTAVOS
5.0000 g., 0.5000 Silver 0.0804 oz. ASW **Obv:** Francisco de Paula Santander **Rev:** Mint mark in field below CENTAVOS

Date	Mintage	F	VF	XF	Unc	BU
1945B	1,675,000	1.25	3.00	7.00	15.00	—
1945BB	Inc. above	6.00	12.00	25.00	50.00	—

Note: 1945BB has extra B in wreath at bottom

1946/5B	6,599,000	1.25	2.50	6.50	15.00	—
1946B	Inc. above	1.50	3.00	9.00	20.00	—
1947/5B	9,708,000	1.50	6.00	12.00	28.00	—
1947B	—	3.00	6.00	12.00	28.00	—

KM# 208.3   20 CENTAVOS
5.0000 g., 0.5000 Silver 0.0804 oz. ASW **Obv:** Francisco de Paula Santander **Rev:** Without mint mark

Date	Mintage	F	VF	XF	Unc	BU
1946(m)	—	3.00	7.50	15.00	32.50	—
1946/5(m)	—	3.75	9.50	16.50	37.50	—
1947(m)	1,748,000	5.00	8.50	15.00	35.00	—

KM# 208.2   20 CENTAVOS
5.0000 g., 0.5000 Silver 0.0804 oz. ASW **Obv:** Francisco de Paula Santander **Rev:** Mint mark on wreath at top **Note:** Almost all dies for 1946-1951 show at least faint traces of overdating from 1945. Coins with absolutely no underdate, and those with very bold underdate, are generally worth more to advanced specialists. Varieties exist.

Date	Mintage	F	VF	XF	Unc	BU
1947/5B	Inc. above	5.00	10.00	20.00	50.00	—
1948/5B	Inc. above	1.25	3.00	5.00	12.00	—
1948B	Inc. above	1.50	3.00	5.00	14.00	—
1949/5B	403,000	3.75	8.50	17.50	45.00	—
1949B	Inc. above	2.50	5.00	10.00	32.50	—
1950/45B	1,899,000	2.75	6.75	15.00	50.00	—
1950B	Inc. above	2.75	6.00	13.50	37.50	—
1951/45B	7,498,000	1.25	3.00	6.50	13.50	—
1951B	Inc. above	1.25	3.00	6.00	12.50	—

KM# 213   20 CENTAVOS
5.0000 g., 0.3000 Silver 0.0482 oz. ASW **Obv:** Arms, date below **Rev:** Bust of Simon Bolivar left, divides denomination

Date	Mintage	F	VF	XF	Unc	BU
1952B Rare	3,887	—	—	—	—	—
1953B	17,819,000	1.00	1.50	3.50	7.50	—

KM# 215.1   20 CENTAVOS
Copper-Nickel, 23.4 mm. **Obv:** Head of Simon Bolivar right, small date below **Rev:** Denomination above arms, half circle of stars below

Date	Mintage	F	VF	XF	Unc	BU
1956	39,778,000	0.10	0.15	0.50	1.50	—
1959	55,519,000	0.10	0.15	0.50	1.50	—

KM# 215.2   20 CENTAVOS
4.9300 g., Copper-Nickel, 23.4 mm. **Obv:** Head of Simon Bolivar right, large date below **Rev:** Denomination above arms, half circle of stars below

Date	Mintage	F	VF	XF	Unc	BU
1963	12,035,000	—	0.10	0.50	1.50	—

Date	Mintage	F	VF	XF	Unc	BU
1964	29,075,000	—	0.10	0.50	1.50	—
1965	19,180,000	0.10	0.25	0.75	2.50	—

KM# 215.3   20 CENTAVOS
Copper-Nickel, 23.4 mm. **Obv:** Head of Simon Bolivar right, medium date **Rev:** Denomination above arms, half circle of stars below

Date	Mintage	F	VF	XF	Unc	BU
1966	23,060,000	0.10	0.15	0.50	1.50	—

KM# 222   20 CENTAVOS
Copper-Nickel **Subject:** Uprising Sesquicentennial **Obv:** Head right divides dates below **Rev:** Denomination above arms, half circle of stars below

Date	Mintage	F	VF	XF	Unc	BU
ND(1960)	500,000	0.75	1.50	3.00	9.00	—

KM# 224   20 CENTAVOS
Copper-Nickel **Obv:** Arms above denomination **Rev:** Bust of Jorge Eliecer Gaitan left, date below

Date	Mintage	F	VF	XF	Unc	BU
1965	1,000,000	—	0.10	0.50	1.50	—

KM# 227   20 CENTAVOS
Nickel Clad Steel **Obv:** Head of Santander right, large date and continuous legend **Rev:** Denomination within wreath

Date	Mintage	F	VF	XF	Unc	BU
1967	15,720,000	—	0.10	0.20	1.00	—
1968	26,680,000	—	0.10	0.20	1.00	—
1969	22,470,000	—	0.10	0.20	1.00	—

KM# 237   20 CENTAVOS
Nickel Clad Steel **Obv:** Refined detailed portrait of Santander right, with smaller date and legend **Rev:** Denomination within wreath

Date	Mintage	F	VF	XF	Unc	BU
1969	Inc. above	—	—	—	—	—
1970	44,358,000	—	0.10	0.20	1.00	—

KM# 245   20 CENTAVOS
Nickel Clad Steel **Obv:** Head right, legend divided after REPUBLICA DE **Rev:** Denomination within wreath

Date	Mintage	F	VF	XF	Unc	BU
1971	77,526,000	—	—	0.10	0.35	—

KM# 246.1   20 CENTAVOS
Nickel Clad Steel **Obv:** Head right, date below, legend continuous **Rev:** Denomination within wreath **Note:** Varieties exist with and without dots.

Date	Mintage	F	VF	XF	Unc	BU
1971	Inc. above	—	—	0.10	0.35	—
1972	41,891,000	—	—	0.10	0.35	—
1973/1	41,440,000	—	—	0.10	0.35	—
1973	Inc. above	—	—	0.15	0.50	—
1974/1	45,941,000	—	—	0.35	1.00	—

Date	Mintage	F	VF	XF	Unc	BU
1974	Inc. above	—	—	0.10	0.35	—
1975	28,635,000	—	—	0.10	0.35	—
1976	29,590,000	—	—	0.10	0.35	—
1977	2,054,000	—	—	0.15	0.50	—
1978	10,630,000	—	—	0.10	0.35	—

KM# 246.2   20 CENTAVOS
Nickel Clad Steel **Obv:** Head right, date below, smaller letters in legend **Rev:** Wreath with larger 20 and smaller CENTAVOS

Date	Mintage	F	VF	XF	Unc	BU
1979	16,655,000	—	—	0.10	0.20	—

KM# 267   25 CENTAVOS
Aluminum-Bronze **Obv:** Head of Simon Bolivar right, date below **Rev:** Denomination within lines

Date	Mintage	F	VF	XF	Unc	BU
1979	88,874,000	—	0.10	0.15	0.25	—
1980	46,168,000	—	0.10	0.15	0.25	—

KM# 186.2   50 CENTAVOS
12.5000 g., 0.8350 Silver 0.3356 oz. ASW, 30 mm. **Obv:** Liberty head left, incuse lettering on headband, date below **Rev:** Denomination above arms, DIOS LEI LIBERTAD **Mint:** Bogota **Note:** Similar to KM#186.1a.

Date	Mintage	VG	F	VF	XF	Unc
1906	446,000	7.50	14.00	25.00	40.00	80.00
1907	1,126,000	6.50	10.00	16.50	30.00	65.00
1908/7	871,000	20.00	30.00	45.00	65.00	145
1908	Inc. above	7.00	12.00	20.00	35.00	75.00

KM# 192   50 CENTAVOS
12.5000 g., 0.8350 Silver 0.3356 oz. ASW, 30 mm. **Obv:** Liberty head left, date below **Rev:** Denomination above arms **Mint:** Philadelphia

Date	Mintage	F	VF	XF	Unc	BU
1902(P)	960,000	15.00	30.00	60.00	125	—

KM# 193.1   50 CENTAVOS
12.5000 g., 0.9000 Silver 0.3617 oz. ASW, 30 mm. **Obv:** Simon Bolivar, sharper featured head right, date below **Rev:** Denomination above arms, left wing and flags far from legend **Note:** Struck at Birmingham and Bogota mints. Date varieties exist.

Date	Mintage	F	VF	XF	Unc	BU
1912	1,207,000	6.00	12.50	35.00	75.00	—
1912 Proof; rare	—	—	—	—	—	—

Date	Mintage	F	VF	XF	Unc	BU
1913	417,000	6.00	12.50	35.00	75.00	—
1914 Closed 4	769,000	7.00	15.00	40.00	85.00	—
1915 Small date	946,000	6.00	12.50	30.00	70.00	—
1915 Small date; Proof; rare	—	—	—	—	—	—
1915 Large date	Inc. above	—	—	—	—	—
1915 Proof; rare	—	—	—	—	—	—
1916 Small date	1,060,000	5.00	10.00	22.50	50.00	—
1917 Normal 7	99,000	10.00	20.00	45.00	90.00	—
1917 Foot on 7	Inc. above	10.00	20.00	45.00	90.00	—
1917 Curved top	Inc. above	10.00	20.00	50.00	100	—
1918	400,000	5.00	10.00	25.00	75.00	—
1919	Inc. above	15.00	25.00	40.00	85.00	—
1922	150,000	10.00	15.00	30.00	75.00	—
1923	150,000	10.00	15.00	30.00	75.00	—
1931/21B	—	5.00	10.00	22.50	50.00	—
1931B	700,000	5.00	10.00	22.50	50.00	—
1931	Inc. above	65.00	120	185	350	—
1932/12B	300,000	8.00	14.00	30.00	75.00	—
1932/22B	Inc. above	7.00	15.00	35.00	80.00	—
1932B	Inc. above	5.00	10.00	22.50	50.00	—
1932 Flat top 3, no B	Inc. above	20.00	30.00	45.00	90.00	—
1933/13B	1,000,000	5.00	10.00	20.00	45.00	—
1933/23B	Inc. above	5.00	10.00	25.00	50.00	—
1933B	Inc. above	BV	5.00	10.00	28.00	—

KM# 193.2 50 CENTAVOS
12.5000 g., 0.9000 Silver 0.3617 oz. ASW, 30 mm. **Obv:** Simon Bolivar, sharper featured head right, date below
Rev: Denomination above arms, larger letters, left wing and flags close to legend **Mint:** Medellin **Note:** Date varieties exist.

Date	Mintage	F	VF	XF	Unc	BU
1914 Open 4	—	5.00	10.00	30.00	80.00	—
1915/4 Large date	—	45.00	75.00	125	200	—
1915 Large date	—	55.00	100	150	250	—
1918/4	—	10.00	20.00	35.00	75.00	—
1918	—	5.00	10.00	25.00	65.00	—
1919/8	—	7.50	15.00	30.00	70.00	—
1919	—	7.50	15.00	30.00	70.00	—
1921	300,000	7.50	15.00	30.00	70.00	—
1922	—	5.00	10.00	25.00	65.00	—
1932/22M	1,200,000	20.00	40.00	70.00	145	—
1932M	Inc. above	BV	5.00	15.00	30.00	—
1932 Round top 3, no M	Inc. above	18.00	35.00	60.00	125	—
1933M	800,000	BV	7.50	15.00	50.00	—
1933/23 Round top 3s, no M	Inc. above	15.00	25.00	35.00	75.00	—

KM# 274 50 CENTAVOS
12.5000 g., 0.9000 Silver 0.3617 oz. ASW, 30 mm. **Obv:** Simon Bolivar, rounder featured head right, date below **Rev:** Denomination above arms **Note:** Struck at the Philadelphia and San Francisco mints. Sculptor of this Bolivar bust was Roulin.

Date	Mintage	F	VF	XF	Unc	BU
1916(P)	1,300,000	BV	7.50	25.00	50.00	—
1917(P)	142,000	6.00	18.00	37.50	75.00	—
1921(P)	1,000,000	BV	6.00	20.00	45.00	—
1922(P)	3,000,000	BV	5.00	15.00	40.00	—
1934(S)	10,000,000	BV	5.00	15.00	40.00	—

KM# 209 50 CENTAVOS
12.5000 g., 0.5000 Silver 0.2009 oz. ASW, 30 mm. **Obv:** Simon Bolivar (in military uniform) bust left, date below
Rev: Denomination within circular wreath **Mint:** Bogota

Date	Mintage	F	VF	XF	Unc	BU
1947/6	1,240,000	4.50	7.00	20.00	50.00	—
1947	Inc. above	10.00	15.00	30.00	75.00	—
1948/6	707,000	4.50	7.00	20.00	50.00	—
1948 inverted B	Inc. above	25.00	40.00	60.00	120	—
1948	Inc. above	7.50	12.50	25.00	65.00	—

KM# 217 50 CENTAVOS
12.5600 g., Copper-Nickel, 30.5 mm. **Obv:** Denomination below arms **Rev:** Head of Simon Bolivar by Tererani, right, date below **Note:** Various sizes of date exist.

Date	Mintage	F	VF	XF	Unc	BU
1958	3,596,000	0.15	0.50	1.25	3.50	—
1958 Medal Rotation	Inc. above	6.00	12.00	22.00	40.00	—
1959	13,466,000	0.15	0.30	1.00	3.00	—
1959 Medal Rotation	Inc. above	2.00	3.50	6.00	10.00	—
1960	4,360,000	0.15	0.30	1.50	4.00	—
1961	3,260,000	0.15	0.30	1.50	4.00	—
1962	2,336,000	0.15	0.30	1.50	4.00	—
1963	4,098,000	0.15	0.30	1.00	3.00	—
1964	9,274,000	0.15	0.30	1.00	3.00	—
1965	5,800,000	0.15	0.30	1.00	3.00	—
1966	2,820,000	0.15	0.30	1.00	3.00	—

KM# 223 50 CENTAVOS
Copper-Nickel, 30.5 mm. **Subject:** Uprising Sesquicentennial **Obv:** Denomination below arms **Rev:** Head right, two dates below

Date	Mintage	F	VF	XF	Unc	BU
ND(1960)	200,000	1.50	3.00	7.50	15.00	—

KM# 225 50 CENTAVOS
Copper-Nickel, 30.5 mm. **Obv:** Arms and denomination **Rev:** Jorge Eliecer Gaitan bust left, date below

Date	Mintage	F	VF	XF	Unc	BU
1965	600,000	0.10	0.20	0.50	1.50	—

KM# 228 50 CENTAVOS
Nickel Clad Steel, 30 mm. **Obv:** Head of Francisco de Paula Santander (from bust by Pierre-Jean David d'Angers), right, date below **Rev:** Denomination within circular wreath

Date	Mintage	F	VF	XF	Unc	BU
1967	3,460,000	0.10	0.15	0.25	1.00	—
1968	5,460,000	0.10	0.15	0.25	1.00	—
1969	1,590,000	0.10	0.15	0.25	1.00	—

KM# 244.1 50 CENTAVOS
Nickel Clad Steel **Obv:** Head right, flat truncation, date below **Rev:** Denomination within wreath, 5 far from wreath **Note:** Date varieties exist.

Date	Mintage	F	VF	XF	Unc	BU
1970	30,906,000	—	0.10	0.15	0.50	—
1971	32,650,000	—	0.10	0.15	0.50	—
1972	25,290,000	—	0.10	0.15	0.50	—
1973	8,060,000	—	0.10	0.15	0.50	—
1974	19,541,000	—	0.10	0.15	0.50	—
1975	4,325,000	—	0.10	0.15	0.60	—
1976	13,181,000	—	0.10	0.15	0.45	—
1977	10,413,000	—	0.10	0.15	0.45	—
1978	10,736,000	—	0.10	0.15	0.45	—

KM# 244.3 50 CENTAVOS
Nickel Clad Steel **Obv:** Head right, angled truncation, date below **Rev:** Denomination within wreath, 5 far from wreath **Note:** Mule.

Date	Mintage	F	VF	XF	Unc	BU
1979	—	10.00	20.00	30.00	50.00	—

KM# 244.2 50 CENTAVOS
Nickel Clad Steel **Obv:** Head right, angled truncation, date below **Rev:** Denomination within wreath, 5 close to wreath **Note:** Various sizes of dates exist.

Date	Mintage	F	VF	XF	Unc	BU
1979	22,584,000	—	0.10	0.15	0.45	—
1980	16,433,000	—	0.10	0.15	0.45	—
1982	10,107,000	—	0.10	0.15	0.45	—

KM# 216 PESO
25.0000 g., 0.9000 Silver 0.7234 oz. ASW, 37 mm. **Subject:** 200th Anniversary of Popayan Mint **Obv:** Arms above denomination **Rev:** Monument, sprays flank, date above **Mint:** Mexico City

Date	Mintage	F	VF	XF	Unc	BU
ND(1956)(Mo)	12,000	BV	15.00	18.00	25.00	—

KM# 229 PESO
Copper-Nickel, 30 mm. **Obv:** Head of Simon Bolivar right, date below **Rev:** Denomination within circular wreath

Date	Mintage	F	VF	XF	Unc	BU
1967	4,000,000	0.15	0.30	0.50	1.00	—

KM# 258.1 PESO
Copper-Nickel, 25.3 mm. **Obv:** Bust of Simon Bolivar 3/4 facing, small date below **Rev:** Denomination, ears of corn flank

Date	Mintage	F	VF	XF	Unc	BU
1974	56,020,000	—	0.10	0.15	0.50	—
1975 medium date	117,714,000	—	0.10	0.15	0.40	—
1976	98,728,000	—	0.10	0.15	0.40	—

KM# 258.2 PESO
Copper-Nickel **Obv:** Bust of Simon Bolivar 3/4 facing, large date below **Rev:** Denomination, ears of corn flank

Date	Mintage	F	VF	XF	Unc	BU
1976	Inc. above	—	0.10	0.15	0.40	—
1977	62,083,000	—	0.10	0.15	0.40	—
1978	48,624,000	—	0.10	0.15	0.40	—
1979	83,908,000	—	0.10	0.15	0.40	—
1980	93,406,000	—	0.10	0.15	0.40	—
1981	65,219,800	—	0.10	0.15	0.40	—

KM# 263 2 PESOS
7.5000 g., Bronze, 23.8 mm. **Obv:** Bust of Simon Bolivar 3/4 facing, date below **Rev:** Denomination within wreath **Note:** Varieties exist.

Date	Mintage	F	VF	XF	Unc	BU
1977	76,661,000	0.10	0.15	0.25	0.50	—
1978	69,575,000	0.10	0.15	0.25	0.50	—
1979	56,537,000	0.10	0.15	0.25	0.50	—
1980	108,521,000	0.10	0.15	0.25	0.50	—
1981	40,368,000	0.10	0.15	0.25	0.50	—
1983	8,358,000	0.10	0.15	0.25	0.50	—
1987	—	0.10	0.15	0.25	0.50	—
1988	16,200,000	0.10	0.15	0.25	0.50	—

KM# 194 2-1/2 PESOS
3.9940 g., 0.9170 Gold 0.1177 oz. AGW **Obv:** Native, date below **Rev:** Arms and denomination

Date	Mintage	F	VF	XF	Unc	BU
1913	18,000	—	BV	110	125	—

KM# 200 2-1/2 PESOS
3.9940 g., 0.9170 Gold 0.1177 oz. AGW **Obv:** Simon Bolivar large head right, date below **Rev:** Arms and denomination

Date	Mintage	F	VF	XF	Unc	BU
1919A	—	—	BV	110	120	—
Note: Two varieties, with large or small first 1 in date						
1919B	—	—	—	—	—	—
1919	34,000	—	BV	110	120	—
1920/19A	—	—	BV	110	120	—
1920A	—	—	BV	110	120	—
1920	34,000	—	BV	115	150	—

KM# 203 2-1/2 PESOS
3.9940 g., 0.9170 Gold 0.1177 oz. AGW **Obv:** Simon Bolivar small head, MEDELLIN below, date at bottom **Rev:** Arms and denomination

Date	Mintage	F	VF	XF	Unc	BU
1924	—	—	BV	110	120	—
1925 Rare	—	—	—	—	—	—
1927	—	—	BV	110	125	—
1928	14,000	—	BV	120	175	—
1929 Rare	—	—	—	—	—	—

KM# 195.2 5 PESOS
7.9881 g., 0.9170 Gold 0.2355 oz. AGW **Obv:** Native, date below **Rev:** Arms and denomination **Note:** Medallic die rotation.

Date	Mintage	F	VF	XF	Unc	BU
1913	Inc. above	—	—	BV	215	225
1917	43,000	—	—	BV	215	225
1918	Inc. above	—	—	BV	215	225
1919	Inc. above	—	—	BV	215	225

KM# 195.1 5 PESOS
7.9881 g., 0.9170 Gold 0.2355 oz. AGW **Obv:** Native, date below **Rev:** Arms and denomination **Note:** Various rotations of dies exist.

Date	Mintage	F	VF	XF	Unc	BU
1913	17,000	—	BV	215	225	240
1918/3	423,000	—	—	BV	215	225
1918	Inc. above	—	—	BV	215	225
1919	2,181,000	—	—	BV	215	225
1919 Long-tail 9	Inc. above	—	—	BV	215	225
1919 Dot over 9	Inc. above	—	—	BV	215	225

KM# 201.1 5 PESOS
7.9881 g., 0.9170 Gold 0.2355 oz. AGW **Obv:** Simon Bolivar, large head right **Rev:** Arms and den. **Note:** 1920A dated coins come with mint mark centered or on right side of coat of arms; 1923B dated coins come with B on the left or right of coat of arms. The 1923B mint mark to right carries a 25% premium in value. Various rotations of dies exist.

Date	Mintage	F	VF	XF	Unc	BU
1919	Inc. above	—	—	BV	215	225
Note: Narrow or wide dates, with multiple varieties of numeral alignment						
1919A	—	—	—	BV	215	225
Note: Narrow or wide date						
1919B	—	—	—	BV	215	225
1920	870,000	—	—	BV	215	225
1920A	Inc. above	—	—	BV	215	225
Note: Placement of A below coat of arms varies						
1920B	108,000	—	—	BV	215	225
Note: Placement of B varies						
1921A	—	—	—	BV	215	225
1922B	29,000	—	—	BV	215	225
Note: Two varieties known, with B touching or separated from coat of arms						
1923B	74,000	—	—	BV	215	225
1924B	705,000	—	—	BV	215	225
Note: Placement of B varies						

KM# 201.2 5 PESOS
7.9881 g., 0.9170 Gold 0.2355 oz. AGW **Obv:** Simon Bolivar, large head **Rev:** Arms and denomination **Note:** Medallic die rotation.

Date	Mintage	F	VF	XF	Unc	BU
1920	Inc. above	—	—	BV	215	225

KM# 204 5 PESOS
7.9881 g., 0.9170 Gold 0.2355 oz. AGW **Obv:** Simon Bolivar, small head, MEDELLIN below, date at bottom **Rev:** Arms and denomination **Note:** 1924 dated coins have several varieties in size of 2 and 4. 1925 dated coins exist with an Arabic and a Spanish style 5. 1930 dated coins have three varieties in size and placement of 3.

Date	Mintage	F	VF	XF	Unc	BU
1924 Large 2	120,000	—	—	BV	215	225
1924 Large 4	Inc. above	—	—	BV	215	225
1924 Small 4	Inc. above	—	—	BV	215	225
1924 MEDELLIN	Inc. above	—	—	BV	215	235
1925/4	668,000	—	—	BV	215	225
1925 MEDELLIN	Inc. above	—	—	BV	215	225
Note: Wide or narrow date						
1925 MEDFLLIN	Inc. above	—	—	BV	215	225
Note: Wide or narrow date						
1926	383,000	—	—	BV	215	225
1926 MEDFLLIN	Inc. above	—	—	BV	215	225
1926 MEDFLLIN	Inc. above	—	—	BV	215	225
Note: With large 6 in date						
1927 MEDFLLIN	365,000	—	—	BV	215	225
Note: Wide or narrow date						
1928 MEDFLLIN	314,000	—	—	BV	215	225
Note: Narrow or wide date with large or normal 2						
1929 MEDFLLIN	321,000	—	—	BV	215	225
Note: Narrow or wide date						
1930 MEDFLLIN	502,000	—	—	BV	215	225
Note: Varieties known with aligned date or dropped 3 in date						

KM# 230 5 PESOS
Copper-Nickel, 34 mm. **Subject:** International Eucharistic Congress **Obv:** Denomination within wheat stalks, date below **Rev:** Design within circle, within square, at center

Date	Mintage	F	VF	XF	Unc	BU
1968B	660,000	0.25	0.50	0.75	1.75	—

KM# 247 5 PESOS
Nickel Clad Steel, 30 mm. **Subject:** 6th Pan-American Games in Cali **Obv:** Torches flank denomination at center, date below **Rev:** Games logo

Date	Mintage	F	VF	XF	Unc	BU
1971	2,000,000	0.15	0.35	0.60	1.50	—

KM# 268 5 PESOS
Bronze, 26.3 mm. **Obv:** Seated figure right **Rev:** Denomination and buildings

Date	Mintage	F	VF	XF	Unc	BU
1980	146,268,000	0.25	0.50	0.75	1.50	—
1.981	9,148,000	0.25	0.50	0.75	1.50	—
1.982	—	0.25	0.50	0.75	1.50	—
1983	84,107,000	0.25	0.50	0.75	1.50	—
1985	—	0.25	0.50	0.75	1.50	—
1986	14,700,000	0.25	0.50	0.75	1.50	—
1987	—	0.25	0.50	0.75	1.50	—
1988 Large inverted date	Inc. above	0.25	0.50	0.75	1.50	—
1988 Small date	45,000,000	0.25	0.50	0.75	1.50	—
1989	—	0.25	0.50	0.75	1.50	—

KM# 280 5 PESOS
2.6000 g., Copper-Aluminum-Nickel, 17.3 mm. **Obv:** Arms above date **Rev:** Denomination within wreath **Note:** Varieties exist, such as 1989 where some have 72 beads on the obverse and reverse and some have 66 beads.

Date	Mintage	F	VF	XF	Unc	BU
1989	—	—	—	—	0.50	0.75
1990	—	—	—	—	0.50	0.75

Date	Mintage	F	VF	XF	Unc	BU
1991	—	—	—	—	0.50	0.75
1992	—	—	—	—	0.35	0.65
1993	—	—	—	—	0.35	0.65

KM# 202 10 PESOS
15.9761 g., 0.9170 Gold 0.4710 oz. AGW **Obv:** Head of Simon Bolivar right, date below **Rev:** Arms and denomination

Date	Mintage	F	VF	XF	Unc	BU
1919	101,000	—	BV	400	425	—
1924B	55,000	—	BV	400	425	—

Note: Varieties with aligned date and dropped 4 in date

KM# 270 10 PESOS
9.9600 g., Copper-Nickel-Zinc, 28 mm. **Obv:** Figure on horseback and standing, date at left **Rev:** Map showing San Andreas Island and Providencia, denomination below **Note:** Date varieties exist.

Date	Mintage	F	VF	XF	Unc	BU
1.981	104,554,000	—	0.15	0.25	1.25	—
1.982	83,605,000	—	0.15	0.25	1.25	—
1983	104,051,000	—	0.15	0.25	1.25	—
1985	80,000,000	—	0.15	0.25	1.25	—
1988	50,700,000	—	0.15	0.25	1.25	—
1989	—	—	0.15	0.25	1.25	—

KM# 281.1 10 PESOS
3.3000 g., Copper-Nickel-Zinc, 18.75 mm. **Obv:** Flagged arms, date below **Rev:** Denomination within wreath, wide 10 (5mm) - wreath nearly touches beads in rim **Edge:** Reeded **Note:** Varieties exist.

Date	Mintage	F	VF	XF	Unc	BU
1989	—	—	—	—	0.75	1.00
1990	—	—	—	—	0.75	1.00
1991	—	—	—	—	0.75	1.00
1992	—	—	—	—	0.50	0.75
1993	—	—	—	—	0.50	0.75
1994	—	—	—	—	0.50	0.75

KM# 281.2 10 PESOS
3.3000 g., Copper-Nickel-Zinc, 18.75 mm. **Obv:** Flagged arms, date below **Rev:** Narrow 10 (4.5mm) - wreath is 1 mm away from beads in rim

Date	Mintage	F	VF	XF	Unc	BU
1993	—	—	—	3.00	7.00	—
1994	—	—	—	3.00	7.00	—

KM# 271 20 PESOS
Aluminum-Bronze, 25 mm. **Obv:** Vase, date below **Rev:** Denomination within wreath **Note:** 1985 and 1988 coins exist with large and small dates.

Date	Mintage	F	VF	XF	Unc	BU
1982	—	—	0.15	0.20	0.30	0.50
1984	64,066,000	—	0.15	0.20	0.30	0.50
1985	100,690,000	—	0.15	0.20	0.30	0.50
1986	18,300,000	—	0.15	0.20	0.30	0.50
1987	—	—	0.15	0.20	0.30	0.50
1988	72,000,000	—	0.15	0.20	0.30	0.50
1989	—	—	0.15	0.20	0.30	0.50

KM# 282.1 20 PESOS
3.6000 g., Copper-Aluminum-Nickel, 20.25 mm. **Obv:** Flagged arms above date, 72 beads circle around the rim **Rev:** Denomination within wreath **Note:** Varieties exist.

Date	Mintage	F	VF	XF	Unc	BU
1989	—	—	—	—	0.75	1.00
1990	—	—	—	—	0.75	1.00
1991	—	—	—	—	0.75	1.00
1992	—	—	—	—	0.75	1.00
1993	—	—	—	—	0.75	1.00
1994	—	—	—	—	0.75	1.00

KM# 282.2 20 PESOS
3.6000 g., Copper-Aluminum-Nickel, 20.25 mm. **Obv:** Flagged arms, 68 beads circle around the rim **Rev:** Denomination within wreath

Date	Mintage	F	VF	XF	Unc	BU
1994	—	—	—	—	0.50	0.75

KM# 272 50 PESOS
8.4000 g., Copper-Nickel, 26.8 mm. **Subject:** National Constitution **Obv:** Arms above denomination, sprigs flank date below **Rev:** Building, stars below, within circle

Date	Mintage	F	VF	XF	Unc	BU
1986	14,900,000	—	—	—	1.25	1.50
1987 Large date	—	—	—	—	1.25	1.50
1988 Small date	100,000,000	—	—	—	1.25	1.50
1989	—	—	—	—	1.25	1.50

KM# 283.1 50 PESOS
4.5000 g., Copper-Nickel-Zinc, 21.8 mm. **Obv:** Flagged arms above date **Rev:** Denomination within wreath, 66 beads circle around rim **Note:** Varieties exist.

Date	Mintage	F	VF	XF	Unc	BU
1989	—	—	—	—	1.00	1.25
1990	—	—	—	—	1.00	1.25
1991	—	—	—	—	1.00	1.25
1992	—	—	—	—	1.00	1.25
1993	—	—	—	—	1.00	1.25
1994	—	—	—	—	1.00	1.25

KM# 283.2 50 PESOS
4.5600 g., Copper-Nickel-Zinc, 21.58 mm. **Obv:** National arms, date below **Rev:** Denomination within wreath, 72 beads circle around rim **Edge:** Reeded

Date	Mintage	F	VF	XF	Unc	BU
1990	—	—	—	0.30	0.80	1.20
1994	—	—	—	0.30	0.80	1.20

KM# 231 100 PESOS
4.3000 g., 0.9000 Gold 0.1244 oz. AGW **Subject:** International Eucharistic Congress **Obv:** Arms divide denomination **Rev:** Bust of Pope Paul VI left and Bogota's Cathedral at left, date below

Date	Mintage	F	VF	XF	Unc	BU
1968	108,000	—	—	—	100	110
1968 Proof	8,000	Value: 120				

KM# 238 100 PESOS
4.3000 g., 0.9000 Gold 0.1244 oz. AGW **Subject:** Battle of Boyaca - Joachim Paris **Obv:** Bust of Bolivar 3/4 facing **Rev:** Bust of Paris 3/4 facing, dates above, denomination below

Date	Mintage	F	VF	XF	Unc	BU
ND(1969)B Proof	6,000	Value: 135				
ND(1969)NI Proof	Inc. above	Value: 135				

KM# 248 100 PESOS
4.3000 g., 0.9000 Gold 0.1244 oz. AGW **Subject:** 6th Pan-American Games **Obv:** Games logo, date below **Rev:** Javelin thrower within circle, denomination below, 3/4 circle of athletes surround

Date	Mintage	F	VF	XF	Unc	BU
1971 Proof	6,000	Value: 145				

KM# 285.1 100 PESOS
Brass **Obv:** Flagged arms above date **Rev:** Denomination within wreath, numerals 4.5mm tall

Date	Mintage	F	VF	XF	Unc	BU
1992	—	—	—	—	1.75	2.00
1993	—	—	—	—	1.75	2.00
1994	—	—	—	—	1.75	2.00
1995	—	—	—	—	1.75	2.00

KM# 285.2 100 PESOS
5.3100 g., Brass, 23 mm. **Obv:** Flagged arms above date **Rev:** Denomination within wreath, numerals 6mm tall **Edge:** Lettered and segmented reeding, CIEN PESOS (twice) **Note:** Edge varieties exist.

Date	Mintage	F	VF	XF	Unc	BU
1994	—	—	—	0.60	1.50	2.00
1995	—	—	—	0.60	1.50	2.00

KM# 232 200 PESOS
8.6000 g., 0.9000 Gold 0.2488 oz. AGW **Subject:** International Eucharistic Congress **Obv:** Bust of Pope Paul VI left and Bogota's Cathedral at left, date below **Rev:** Arms divide denomination

Date	Mintage	F	VF	XF	Unc	BU
1968	108,000	—	—	—	—	250
1968 Proof	8,000	Value: 270				

KM# 239 200 PESOS
8.6000 g., 0.9000 Gold 0.2488 oz. AGW **Subject:** Battle of Boyaca - Carlos Soublette **Obv:** Bust of Bolivar 3/4 facing **Rev:** Bust of Soublette 3/4 facing, dates above, denomination below

Date	Mintage	F	VF	XF	Unc	BU
1969B Proof	6,000	Value: 260				
1969NI Proof	Inc. above	Value: 260				

KM# 249 200 PESOS
8.6000 g., 0.9000 Gold 0.2488 oz. AGW **Subject:** 6th Pan-American Games in Cali **Obv:** Games logo, date below **Rev:** Runner within circle, denomination below, 3/4 circle of athletes surround

Date	Mintage	F	VF	XF	Unc	BU
1971 Proof	6,000	Value: 275				

KM# 287   200 PESOS
7.0800 g., Copper-Zinc-Nickel, 24.39 mm. **Obv:** Denomination within lined circle, date below **Rev:** Quimbaya artwork **Edge:** Lettered, MOTIVO QUIMBAYA - 200 PESOS

Date	Mintage	F	VF	XF	Unc	BU
1994	—	—	—	0.60	1.50	2.00
1995	—	—	—	0.60	1.50	2.00
1996	—	—	—	0.60	1.50	2.00

KM# 233   300 PESOS
12.9000 g., 0.9000 Gold 0.3733 oz. AGW **Subject:** International Eucharistic Congress **Obv:** Bust of Pope Paul VI 3/4 left and Bogota's Cathedral at left, date below **Rev:** Arms above denomination

Date	Mintage	F	VF	XF	Unc	BU
1968	62,000					365
1968 Proof	8,000	Value: 385				

KM# 240   300 PESOS
12.9000 g., 0.9000 Gold 0.3733 oz. AGW **Subject:** Battle of Boyaca - Jose Anzoategui **Obv:** Bust of Bolivar 3/4 facing **Rev:** Bust of Anzoategui 3/4 facing, dates above, denomination below

Date	Mintage	F	VF	XF	Unc	BU
1969B Proof	6,000	Value: 375				
1969NI Proof	Inc. above	Value: 375				

KM# 250   300 PESOS
12.9000 g., 0.9000 Gold 0.3733 oz. AGW **Subject:** 6th Pan-American Games **Obv:** Games logo, date below **Rev:** Two figures within circle, denomination below, 3/4 circle of athletes surround

Date	Mintage	F	VF	XF	Unc	BU
1971 Proof	6,000	Value: 420				

KM# 234   500 PESOS
21.5000 g., 0.9000 Gold 0.6221 oz. AGW **Subject:** International Eucharistic Congress **Obv:** Bust of Pope Paul VI 3/4 left and Bogota's Cathedral left, date below **Rev:** Arms above denomination

Date	Mintage	F	VF	XF	Unc	BU
1968	14,000	—	—			625
1968 Proof	8,000	Value: 650				

KM# 241   500 PESOS
21.5000 g., 0.9000 Gold 0.6221 oz. AGW **Subject:** Battle of Boyaca **Obv:** Bust of Simon Bolivar 3/4 facing **Rev:** Bust of Juan Jose Rondon 3/4 facing, dates above, denomination below

Date	Mintage	F	VF	XF	Unc	BU
ND(1969)B Proof	6,000	Value: 650				
ND(1969)NI Proof	Inc. above	Value: 650				

KM# 251   500 PESOS
21.5000 g., 0.9000 Gold 0.6221 oz. AGW **Subject:** 6th Pan-American Games in Cali **Obv:** Games logo, date below **Rev:** Two figures within circle, denomination below, 3/4 circle of athletes surround

Date	Mintage	F	VF	XF	Unc	BU
1971 Proof	6,000	Value: 685				

KM# 264   500 PESOS
28.2800 g., 0.9250 Silver 0.8410 oz. ASW **Subject:** Conservation **Obv:** Tomas Cipriano de Mosquera bust left, dates below **Rev:** Orinoco Crocodile, denomination below

Date	Mintage	F	VF	XF	Unc	BU
1978	2,678	—	—		28.00	30.00
1978 Proof	3,233	Value: 35.00				
1979 Proof	—	Value: 35.00				

KM# 286   500 PESOS
7.4300 g., Bi-Metallic Aluminum-Bronze center in Copper-Nickel ring, 23.58 mm. **Obv:** Guacari tree within circle **Rev:** Denomination within circle, date below **Edge:** Segmented reeding

Date	Mintage	F	VF	XF	Unc	BU
1993	—	—	—	1.20	3.00	4.00
1994	—	—	—	1.20	3.00	4.00
1995	—	—	—	1.20	3.00	4.00
1996	—	—	—	1.20	3.00	4.00
1997	—	—	—	1.20	3.00	4.00

KM# 265   750 PESOS
35.0000 g., 0.9250 Silver 1.0408 oz. ASW **Subject:** Conservation **Obv:** Tomas Cipriano de Mosquera bust left **Rev:** Chestnut-bellied hummingbird, denomination below

Date	Mintage	F	VF	XF	Unc	BU
1978	2,656	—	—	—	30.00	32.00
1978 Proof	3,100	Value: 38.00				
1979 Proof	—	Value: 38.00				

KM# 254   1000 PESOS
4.3000 g., 0.9000 Gold 0.1244 oz. AGW **Subject:** 100th Anniversary - Birth of Guillermo Valencia **Obv:** Shield above denomination **Rev:** Head right

Date	Mintage	F	VF	XF	Unc	BU
1973 Proof	10,003	Value: 125				

KM# 259   1000 PESOS
4.3000 g., 0.9000 Gold 0.1244 oz. AGW **Subject:** 450th Anniversary - City of Santa Marta **Obv:** Bust 3/4 right, denomination below **Rev:** Symbol at center, dates below

Date	Mintage	F	VF	XF	Unc	BU
ND(1975) Proof	2,500	Value: 140				

KM# 260   1000 PESOS
4.3000 g., 0.9000 Gold 0.1244 oz. AGW **Subject:** Tricentennial - City of Medellin **Obv:** City gate on shield, sprays flank, dates below **Rev:** Symbol at center, denomination below

Date	Mintage	F	VF	XF	Unc	BU
ND(1975) Proof	4,000	Value: 125				

KM# 288   1000 PESOS
7.3000 g., Copper-Aluminum-Nickel, 21.67 mm. **Obv:** Value and date **Rev:** Filagreed design **Edge:** Reeded and lettered, CULTURA SINU MIL PESOS

Date	Mintage	F	VF	XF	Unc	BU
1996	—	—	—	—	3.75	4.00
1997	—	—	—	—	3.75	4.00
1998	—	—	—	—	3.75	4.00

KM# 235   1500 PESOS
64.5000 g., 0.9000 Gold 1.8663 oz. AGW **Subject:** International Eucharistic Congress **Obv:** Pope's bust 3/4 left, cathedral at left **Rev:** Arms above denomination

Date	Mintage	F	VF	XF	Unc	BU
1968	5,722	—	—	—	—	1,800
1968 Proof	8,000	Value: 1,850				

KM# 242   1500 PESOS
64.5000 g., 0.9000 Gold 1.8663 oz. AGW **Subject:** Battle of Boyaca **Obv:** Armored bust of Bolivar 3/4 facing **Rev:** Head of Santander right, arms divide dates above, denomination below

Date	Mintage	F	VF	XF	Unc	BU
ND(1969)B Proof	6,000	Value: 1,875				
ND(1969)NI Proof	Inc. above	Value: 1,875				

KM# 252   1500 PESOS
64.5000 g., 0.9000 Gold 1.8663 oz. AGW **Subject:** 6th Pan-American Games **Obv:** Games logo, date below **Rev:** Symbols on raft within circle, denomination below, 3/4 circle of athletes surrounds

Date	Mintage	F	VF	XF	Unc	BU
1971 Proof	6,000	Value: 1,900				

KM# 255   1500 PESOS
19.1000 g., 0.9000 Gold 0.5526 oz. AGW **Subject:** 50th Anniversary - Gold Museum of Central Bank of Bogota **Rev:** Pre-Columbian urn made by Chibcha Indians

Date	Mintage	F	VF	XF	Unc	BU
ND(1973) Proof	4,911	Value: 545				

KM# 257   2000 PESOS
12.9000 g., 0.9000 Gold 0.3733 oz. AGW **Subject:** 100th Anniversary - Birth of Guillermo Valencia **Obv:** Shield above denomination, date below **Rev:** Bust right, two dates below

Date	Mintage	F	VF	XF	Unc	BU
1973 Proof	5,003	Value: 375				

KM# 261   2000 PESOS
8.6000 g., 0.9000 Gold 0.2488 oz. AGW **Subject:** 450th Anniversary - City of Santa Marta **Obv:** Bust 3/4 right, denomination below **Rev:** Symbol, dates below

Date	Mintage	F	VF	XF	Unc	BU
ND(1975) Proof	2,500	Value: 250				

KM# 262   2000 PESOS
8.6000 g., 0.9000 Gold 0.2488 oz. AGW **Subject:** Tricentennial - City of Medellin **Obv:** City gate on shield, sprays flank, two dates below **Rev:** Symbol at center, denomination below

Date	Mintage	F	VF	XF	Unc	BU
ND(1975) Proof	4,000	Value: 245				

KM# 293   5000 PESOS
15.3000 g., Nickel **Subject:** 50th Anniversary - Organization of American States **Obv:** Denomination, date below **Rev:** Circle of flags

Date	Mintage	F	VF	XF	Unc	BU
1998	—	—	—	—	5.50	6.50

KM# 284   10000 PESOS
27.0000 g., 0.9250 Silver 0.8029 oz. ASW **Series:** Ibero - American **Subject:** Bogota Mint **Obv:** Arms at center, denomination below, shields surround **Rev:** Ancient coin, two dates below

Date	Mintage	F	VF	XF	Unc	BU
1991 Proof	70,000	Value: 55.00				

KM# 266   15000 PESOS
33.4370 g., 0.9000 Gold 0.9675 oz. AGW **Subject:** Conservation **Obv:** Armored bust left **Rev:** Ocelot left, denomination below

Date	Mintage	F	VF	XF	Unc	BU
1978	490	—	—	—	950	1,000
1978 Proof	148	Value: 2,000				

KM# 276   15000 PESOS
17.2900 g., 0.9000 Gold 0.5003 oz. AGW **Subject:** 150th Anniversary - Death of Antonio Jose De Sucre **Obv:** Armored bust 3/4 left divides dates **Rev:** Cornucopias enclose symbol at center, denomination below

Date	Mintage	F	VF	XF	Unc	BU
1980 Proof	250	Value: 500				

KM# 278   15000 PESOS
17.2900 g., 0.9000 Gold 0.5003 oz. AGW **Subject:** 150th Anniversary - Death of Jose Maria Cordova **Obv:** Bust 3/4 facing, divides dates **Rev:** Cornucopias enclose symbol at center, denomination below

Date	Mintage	F	VF	XF	Unc	BU
1980 Proof	250	Value: 500				

KM# 289   20000 PESOS
8.6400 g., 0.9000 Gold 0.2500 oz. AGW **Subject:** Birth Centennial **Obv:** Bust of Alfonso Lopez-Pumarejo facing divides dates **Rev:** Building, denomination below

Date	Mintage	F	VF	XF	Unc	BU
ND(1986) Proof	1,351	Value: 250				

KM# 269   30000 PESOS
34.5800 g., 0.9000 Gold 1.0006 oz. AGW **Subject:** Death of Bolivar **Obv:** Funeral scene, dates below **Rev:** Cornucopias flank symbol at center, denomination below

Date	Mintage	F	VF	XF	Unc	BU
1980 Proof	500	Value: 1,000				

KM# 273   35000 PESOS
8.6400 g., 0.9000 Gold 0.2500 oz. AGW **Subject:** 100th Anniversary - Birth of President Santos **Obv:** Bust facing divides dates **Rev:** Inscription within wreath

Date	Mintage	F	VF	XF	Unc	BU
ND(1988) Proof	900	Value: 250				

KM# 292   40000 PESOS
17.2800 g., 0.9000 Gold 0.5000 oz. AGW **Subject:** Centennial - Birthday of Alfonso Lopez-Pumarejo **Obv:** Bust facing divides dates **Rev:** Building, denomination below

Date	Mintage	F	VF	XF	Unc	BU
ND(1986) Proof	1,351	Value: 500				

KM# 290   50000 PESOS
8.6400 g., 0.9000 Gold 0.2500 oz. AGW **Subject:** Centennial - Birthday of Mariano Ospina P **Obv:** Portrait facing divides dates **Rev:** Inscription within wreath

Date	Mintage	F	VF	XF	Unc	BU
ND(1991) Proof	900	Value: 250				

KM# 277   70000 PESOS
17.2800 g., 0.9000 Gold 0.5000 oz. AGW **Subject:** 100th Anniversary - Birth of President Santos **Obv:** Bust 3/4 facing divides dates **Rev:** Inscription within wreath

Date	Mintage	F	VF	XF	Unc	BU
ND(1988) Proof	600	Value: 500				

KM# 291   100000 PESOS
17.2800 g., 0.9000 Gold 0.5000 oz. AGW **Subject:** Centennial - Birthday of Mariano Ospina P **Obv:** Head facing divides dates **Rev:** Inscription within wreath

Date	Mintage	F	VF	XF	Unc	BU
ND(1991) Proof	600	Value: 500				

INFLATIONARY COINAGE
P/M - Papel Moneda

Beginning about 1886, Colombia fell victim to rampant printing press inflation and a debased, vanishing coinage. Left without solid backing, the peso gradually fell until it was worth 1 centavo of the old silver-based currency. The copper-nickel 1, 2, and 5 peso p/m coins reflected this inflation, and later circulated at par with the newer 1, 2, and 5 centavo coins.

KM# A279   PESO (Papel Moneda)
2.0000 g., Copper-Nickel, 17 mm. **Obv:** Liberty head right **Rev:** Denomination, p/m below, within wreath

Date	Mintage	F	VF	XF	Unc	BU
1907 AM	2,860,000	1.25	3.50	13.50	22.50	40.00
1907 AM Proof	—	Value: 100				
1910 AM	1,205,000	3.50	9.00	17.50	25.00	47.50
1911 AM	2,816,000	2.75	6.50	13.50	20.00	45.00
1912 AM	6,094,000	2.00	5.00	11.00	18.50	37.50
1912 H Without crossbar	2,000,000	1.50	3.50	12.50	22.00	38.50
1912 H With crossbar	Inc. above	1.50	3.75	12.50	22.00	38.50
1913 AM	306,000	6.50	12.50	22.50	50.00	75.00
1914 AM	552,000	6.00	10.00	18.50	42.50	62.50
1916/4 AM	234,000	11.00	20.00	35.00	65.00	100
1916 AM	Inc. above	11.00	20.00	35.00	65.00	100

KM# B279   2 PESOS (Papel Moneda)
3.0000 g., Copper-Nickel, 19 mm. **Obv:** Liberty head right, date below **Rev:** Denomination, p/m below, within wreath **Note:** Date varieties exist.

Date	Mintage	F	VF	XF	Unc	BU
1907 AM	4,161,000	1.75	3.75	15.00	25.00	37.50
1907 AM Proof	—	Value: 100				
1910/07 AM	1,189,000	7.50	13.50	22.50	42.50	—
1910 AM	Inc. above	6.75	12.50	30.00	40.00	—
1914 AM	1,000,000	4.50	12.00	21.50	40.00	—

KM# 279   5 PESOS (Papel Moneda)
4.0000 g., Copper-Nickel, 21 mm. **Obv:** Liberty head right, date below **Rev:** Denomination, p/m below, within wreath

Date	Mintage	F	VF	XF	Unc	BU
1907 AM	6,143,000	2.50	7.50	15.00	22.50	40.00
1907 AM Proof	—	Value: 100				

Date	Mintage	F	VF	XF	Unc	BU
1909 AM	4,000,000	2.75	8.50	18.50	37.50	—
1912 H	2,000,000	3.50	10.00	20.00	42.00	—
1912 AM	1,897,000	3.75	10.00	25.00	45.00	—
1913 AM	Inc. above	3.75	10.00	26.50	50.00	—
1914 AM	Inc. above	10.00	20.00	38.50	70.00	—

LEPROSARIUM COINAGE
Bogota Mint

Special coinage for use in the three government leper colonies of Agua de Dios, Cano de Lord, and Contratacion. The hospitals were closed in the late 1950s and patients were allowed to exchange these special coins for regular currency at any bank.

KM# L9   CENTAVO
2.0000 g., Copper-Nickel **Obv:** LAZARETO on cross with circles at quarters, date below **Rev:** Denomination within wreath

Date	Mintage	Good	VG	F	VF	XF
1921 RH	300,000	0.75	1.50	3.50	7.00	—

KM# L10   2 CENTAVOS
3.0000 g., Copper-Nickel, 18.89 mm. **Obv:** LAZARETO on cross with circles at quarters, date below **Rev:** Denomination within wreath

Date	Mintage	Good	VG	F	VF	XF
1921 RH	350,000	0.50	0.65	1.75	6.75	—

KM# L1   2-1/2 CENTAVOS
1.3000 g., Brass **Obv:** Denomination within circle, date below **Rev:** LAZARETO on cross with circles at quarters

Date	Mintage	Good	VG	F	VF	XF
1901 Rare	20,000					3,500

Note: Only a few examples of this type are currently known to have survived.

KM# L2   5 CENTAVOS
Brass **Obv:** Denomination within circle **Rev:** LAZARETO on cross with circles at quarters, date below **Note:** Weight varies: 2.3-2.55 g.

Date	Mintage	Good	VG	F	VF	XF
1901 B	15,000	6.00	12.50	22.00	45.00	—

KM# L11   5 CENTAVOS
4.0000 g., Copper-Nickel, 22.88 mm. **Obv:** LAZARETO on cross with circles at quarters, date below **Rev:** Denomination within wreath, large 5

Date	Mintage	Good	VG	F	VF	XF
1921 H	200,000	1.00	2.00	4.50	9.00	—

KM# L3   10 CENTAVOS
Brass **Obv:** Denomination above date **Rev:** LAZARETO on cross with circles at quarters **Note:** Weight varies: 3.3-3.69 g.

Date	Mintage	Good	VG	F	VF	XF
1901 B	10,000	10.00	15.00	28.00	50.00	—

KM# L12 10 CENTAVOS
5.1000 g., Copper-Nickel, 22.89 mm. **Obv:** LAZARETO on cross with circles at quarters, date below **Rev:** Denomination within wreath

Date	Mintage	Good	VG	F	VF	XF
1921 RH	200,000	1.00	2.00	4.50	9.00	—

KM# L4 20 CENTAVOS
Brass **Obv:** LAZARETO on cross with circles at quarters, date below **Rev:** Denomination above arms **Note:** Weight varies: 4.85-5.1 g.

Date	Mintage	Good	VG	F	VF	XF
1901 B	30,000	10.00	15.00	28.00	50.00	—

KM# L5 50 CENTAVOS
Brass **Obv:** LAZARETO on cross with circles at quarters, date below **Rev:** Denomination above arms **Note:** Weight varies: 12-12.4 g.

Date	Mintage	Good	VG	F	VF	XF
1901 B	26,000	13.50	20.00	35.00	75.00	—

KM# L5a 50 CENTAVOS
Copper **Obv:** LAZARETO on cross with circles at quarters, date below **Rev:** Denomination above arms **Note:** Weight varies: 12-12.4 g.

Date	Mintage	Good	VG	F	VF	XF
1901 2 known	—	—	—	—	—	—

KM# L13 50 CENTAVOS
9.8000 g., Copper-Nickel

Date	Mintage	Good	VG	F	VF	XF
1921 RH	120,000	2.00	4.00	7.50	16.00	—

KM# L14 50 CENTAVOS
9.8000 g., Brass

Date	Mintage	Good	VG	F	VF	XF
1928 RH	50,000	2.00	4.50	9.00	18.00	—

KM# L14a 50 CENTAVOS
9.8000 g., Copper

Date	Mintage	Good	VG	F	VF	XF
1928 Proof; Rare	Inc. above	—	—	—	—	—

INFLATIONARY LEPROSARIUM COINAGE
P/M - Papel Moneda

1 Peso was equal in value to 1 Centavo of the old silver currency. It later circulated at par with the newer 1 Centavo coins.

KM# L6 PESO (Papel Moneda)
Copper-Nickel **Obv:** Denomination, P.M., below, within wreath **Rev:** LAZARETO within circle **Note:** Weight varies: 2.45-2.65 g.

Date	Mintage	Good	VG	F	VF	XF
1907/0	792,000					
1907	Inc. above	5.00	10.00	20.00	45.00	—

KM# L7 5 PESOS (Papel Moneda)
4.7500 g., Copper-Nickel

Date	Mintage	Good	VG	F	VF	XF
1907	159,000	30.00	60.00	100	200	—

KM# L8 10 PESOS (Papal Moneda)
9.5000 g., Copper-Nickel

Date	Mintage	Good	VG	F	VF	XF
1907	129,000	40.00	75.00	125	250	—

PROVINCE OF SANTANDER

CIVIL WAR COINAGE

KM# A1 10 CENTAVOS
0.5000 g., Brass **Obv:** Numeric denomination above 'C'
Note: Uniface.

Date	Mintage	VG	F	VF	XF	Unc
ND(1902)	—	10.00	18.50	28.50	60.00	—

KM# A2 20 CENTAVOS
0.7000 g., Brass **Obv:** Numeric denomination within "C"
Note: Uniface.

Date	Mintage	VG	F	VF	XF	Unc
1902	—	18.00	35.00	55.00	80.00	—

KM# A3 50 CENTAVOS
1.4500 g., Brass **Obv:** Numeric denomination within "C"
Note: Uniface. Varieties exist in shape of "0" in denomination: a fully rounded zero commands double the listed values. Later 20th Century counterfeits are known.

Date	Mintage	VG	F	VF	XF	Unc
1902	—	2.00	4.00	7.50	16.50	—

PATTERNS
Including off metal strikes

KM#	Date	Mintage	Identification	Mkt Val
Pn84	1909	—	5 Centavos. Copper-Nickel.	—
Pn85	1913	—	5 Decimos. Thin Bolivar head.	—
Pn86	1913	—	5 Decimos. Thin Bolivar head, canceled obverse die.	—
Pn87	1913	—	2-1/2 Pesos. Gold. ENSAYO; KM#194.	—
Pn88	1913	—	5 Pesos. Gold. ENSAYO; KM#195.	—
Pn89	1915	—	2-1/2 Pesos. Gold. ENSAYO; KM#194.	—
Pn90	1917	—	5 Centavos. Copper-Nickel. PAZ on cap band; otherwise as KM#199.	—
Pn91	1917	—	5 Centavos. Copper-Nickel. KM#199.	—
Pn92	1923	—	2-1/2 Pesos. Gold. ENSAYO; KM#203.	2,450
Pn93	1923	—	2-1/2 Pesos. Silver. ESSAI; KM#203.	—
Pn94	1923	—	5 Pesos. Gold. ENSAYO, KM#204.	—
Pn95	1923	—	5 Pesos. Silver. ESSAI; KM#204.	—
Pn96	1941	—	5 Centavos. Copper-Nickel.	—
Pn97	1946	—	50 Centavos. Copper-Nickel. 10-sided planchet.	—
Pn98	1946	—	50 Centavos. 0.5000 Silver. Reeded edge.	—
Pn99	1950	—	20 Centavos. 0.5000 Silver.	100
Pn100	1950	—	50 Centavos. 0.9000 Silver. Bolivar military bust, condor over large shield.	100
Pn101	1950	—	50 Centavos. 0.9000 Silver. Condor over small shield.	100
Pn102	1950	—	50 Centavos. 0.9000 Silver.	—
Pn103	1951	—	50 Centavos. Silver.	100
Pn104	1952	—	50 Centavos. Silver.	100
PnA105	1956	—	20 Centavos. Copper-Nickel. 4.9400 g. 23.73 mm. Reeded edge.	—
Pn105	1956	—	50 Centavos. Copper-Nickel.	125
Pn106	1956	—	Peso. Gold.	—
Pn107	1957	—	50 Centavos. Copper-Nickel.	125
Pn108	1963	—	Peso. Copper-Nickel. Prev. KM#Pn57.	125
Pn109	1968	—	Peso. Copper-Nickel. Prev. KM#Pn58.	125
Pn110	1969	—	50 Centavos. Copper-Nickel. Prev. KM#Pn59.	75.00
Pn111	1969	—	50 Centavos. Copper-Nickel. Prev. KM#Pn60.	75.00
Pn112	1969	—	Peso. Copper-Nickel. Prev. KM#Pn61.	125

KM#	Date	Mintage	Identification	Mkt Val
Pn114	1969	—	Peso. Copper-Nickel. Prev. KM#Pn63.	125
Pn113	1969	—	Peso. Copper-Nickel. Prev. KM#Pn62.	125
Pn115	1970	—	Centavo. Aluminum. Prev. KM#Pn64.	25.00
Pn116	1970	—	5 Centavos. Aluminum. Prev. KM#Pn65.	25.00
Pn117	1971	—	10 Centavos. Aluminum. Prev. KM#Pn66.	30.00
Pn118	1971	—	50 Centavos. Copper-Nickel. Prev. KM#Pn67.	65.00
Pn119	1974	—	Peso. Silver. 6.7000 g. Prev. KM#Pn68.	150
Pn120	1979	—	5 Pesos. Copper-Nickel. Inverted date. Prev. KM#Pn69.	—

PIEFORTS

KM#	Date	Mintage	Identification	Mkt Val
P3	1913	—	50 Centavos. 0.9000 Silver. Ensayo	2,500
P4	1915	—	10 Centavos. 0.9000 Silver. Ensayo	—
P5	1915	—	20 Centavos. 0.9000 Silver. Ensayo	—

TRIAL STRIKES

KM#	Date	Mintage	Identification	Mkt Val
TS14	ND	—	50 Centavos. Lead.	—
TS15	1911	—	10 Centavos. Lead. Uniface.	—
TS16	1911	—	20 Centavos. Lead. Uniface.	—
TS17	1946	—	20 Centavos. Nickel.	—
TS18	1946	—	20 Centavos. Nickel.	—

PROOF SETS

KM#	Date	Mintage	Identification	Issue Price	Mkt Val
PS1	1968 (5)	8,000	KM#231-235	340	2,150
PS2	1969 (5)	6,000	KM#238-242	—	2,150
PS3	1971 (5)	6,000	KM#248-252	—	2,500
PS4	1973 (3)	—	KM#254, 256, 257	—	475
PS5	1975 (2)	2,500	KM#260, 262	195	245
PS6	1975 (2)	4,000	KM#259, 261	195	265
PS7	1979 (2)	—	KM#264-265	—	75.00

COMOROS

The Federal Islamic Republic of the Comoros, a volcanic archipelago located in the Mozambique Channel of the Indian Ocean 300 miles (483 km.) northwest of Madagascar, has an area of 719 sq. mi. (2,171 sq. km.) and a population of *714,000. Capital: Moroni. The economy of the islands is based on agriculture. There are practically no mineral resources. Vanilla, essence for perfumes, copra, and sisal are exported.

Ancient Phoenician traders were probably the first visitors to the Comoro Islands, but the first detailed knowledge of the area was gathered by Arab sailors. Arab dominion and culture were firmly established when the Portuguese, Dutch, and French arrived in the 16th century. In 1843 a Malagasy ruler ceded the island of Mayotte to France; the other three principal islands of the archipelago-Anjouan, Moheli, and Grand Comore came under French protection in 1886. The islands were joined administratively with Madagascar in 1912. The Comoros became partially autonomous, with the status of a French overseas territory, in 1946, and achieved complete internal autonomy in 1961. On Dec. 31, 1975, after 133 years of French association, the Comoro Islands became the independent Republic of the Comoros.

Mayotte retained the option of determining its future ties and in 1976 voted to remain French. Its present status is that of a French Territorial Collectivity. French currency now circulates there.

TITLES

دولة انجزنجية

Daulat Anjazanchiyah

RULERS
French, 1886-1975

MINT MARKS
(a) - Paris, privy marks only
A - Paris

MONETARY SYSTEM
100 Centimes = 1 Franc

FRENCH COLONIAL
TOKEN COINAGE

KM# Tn1 25 CENTIMES
1.2000 g., Aluminum **Issuer:** Societe Anonyme **Obv:** Legend at center and surrounding **Rev:** Denomination

Date	Mintage	F	VF	XF	Unc	BU
ND(1915)	—	30.00	60.00	125	250	450

KM# Tn1a 25 CENTIMES
4.6000 g., Brass **Issuer:** Societe Anonyme **Obv:** Legend at center and surrounding **Rev:** Denomination

Date	Mintage	F	VF	XF	Unc	BU
ND(1922)	—	—	—	250	450	—

KM# Tn2 50 CENTIMES
Aluminum **Obv:** Legend at center and surrounding **Rev:** Denomination

Date	Mintage	F	VF	XF	Unc	BU
ND(1915)	—	35.00	70.00	125	250	450

KM# Tn2a 50 CENTIMES
Brass **Obv:** Legend at center and surrounding **Rev:** Denomination

Date	Mintage	F	VF	XF	Unc	BU
ND(1915)	—	—	—	450	600	—

KM# Tn3 FRANC
1.3000 g., Aluminum **Obv:** Legend at center and surrounding **Rev:** Denomination

Date	Mintage	F	VF	XF	Unc	BU
ND(1915)	—	40.00	80.00	135	260	500

KM# Tn3a FRANC
Brass **Obv:** Legend at center and surrounding **Rev:** Denomination

Date	Mintage	F	VF	XF	Unc	BU
ND(1922)	—	—	—	300	500	—

KM# Tn4 2 FRANCS
Aluminum **Obv:** Legend at center and surrounding **Rev:** Denomination

Date	Mintage	F	VF	XF	Unc	BU
ND(1915)	—	50.00	100	185	350	—

KM# Tn5 2 FRANCS
Aluminum **Note:** Uniface.

Date	Mintage	F	VF	XF	Unc	BU
1915	—	50.00	100	185	350	500

DECIMAL COINAGE

KM# 4 FRANC
0.9000 Aluminum **Obv:** Winged Liberty bust left, cargo ships in background, date below **Rev:** Trees surrounding denomination

Date	Mintage	F	VF	XF	Unc	BU
1964(a)	500,000	0.15	0.25	0.40	1.25	4.00

KM# 5 2 FRANCS
2.2100 g., Aluminum, 27.1 mm. **Obv:** Winged Liberty bust left, date below, cargo ships in background **Rev:** Trees surround denomination

Date	Mintage	F	VF	XF	Unc	BU
1964(a)	600,000	0.15	0.25	0.50	1.50	5.00

KM# 6 5 FRANCS
3.7300 g., Aluminum, 31.1 mm. **Obv:** Winged Liberty bust left, date below, cargo ships in background **Rev:** Trees surround denomination

Date	Mintage	F	VF	XF	Unc	BU
1964(a)	1,000,000	0.20	0.40	0.65	2.00	6.00

KM# 7 10 FRANCS
3.0100 g., Aluminum-Bronze **Obv:** Winged Liberty bust left, date below, cargo ships in background **Rev:** Plants on mantle with shells flanking, denomination at center, fish below

Date	Mintage	F	VF	XF	Unc	BU
1964(a)	600,000	0.20	0.50	1.00	2.50	4.00

KM# 8 20 FRANCS
3.8900 g., Aluminum-Bronze, 23.8 mm. **Obv:** Winged Liberty bust left, date below, cargo ships in background **Rev:** Plants on mantle, shells flank, denomination at center, fish below

Date	Mintage	F	VF	XF	Unc	BU
1964(a)	500,000	0.30	0.65	1.25	3.00	6.00

FEDERAL ISLAMIC REPUBLIC
STANDARD COINAGE

KM# 10 5000 FRANCS
44.8300 g., 0.9250 Silver 1.3332 oz. ASW **Issuer:** Etat Comorien **Obv:** Flowers, date at left, denomination below **Rev:** Bust of Said Mohamed Cheikh facing divides dates

Date	Mintage	F	VF	XF	Unc	BU
1976	700	—	—	—	100	135
1976 Proof	1,000	Value: 160				

KM# 11 10000 FRANCS
3.0700 g., 0.9000 Gold 0.0888 oz. AGW **Issuer:** Etat Comorien **Obv:** Anjouan sunbird, denomination below **Rev:** Bust of Said Mohamed Cheikh facing divides dates

Date	Mintage	F	VF	XF	Unc	BU
1976	500	—	—	—	100	130
1976 Proof	500	Value: 140				

KM# 12 20000 FRANCS
6.1400 g., 0.9000 Gold 0.1777 oz. AGW **Issuer:** Etat Comorien **Obv:** Coelacanth fish right, denomination below **Rev:** Bust of Said Mohamed Cheikh facing divides dates

Date	Mintage	F	VF	XF	Unc	BU
1976	500	—	—	—	250	285
1976 Proof	500	Value: 300				

INSTITUT D'EMISSION COINAGE

KM# 9 50 FRANCS
6.0900 g., Nickel, 24.1 mm. **Subject:** Independence of Republic **Obv:** Building with tall tower **Rev:** Half moon on cross above denomination, date below

Date	Mintage	F	VF	XF	Unc	BU
1975(a)	1,200,000	0.40	0.75	1.25	2.25	3.00

KM# 13 100 FRANCS
Nickel **Series:** F.A.O. **Obv:** Half moon and stars above denomination, date below **Rev:** Boat and fish

Date	Mintage	F	VF	XF	Unc	BU
1977(a)	1,500,000	0.60	1.00	2.00	3.75	5.00

BANQUE CENTRAL COINAGE

KM# 15 5 FRANCS
3.8500 g., Aluminum, 31 mm. **Subject:** World Fisheries Conference **Obv:** Trees surround denomination, date upper right **Rev:** Coelacanth fish left

Date	Mintage	F	VF	XF	Unc	BU
1984(a)	1,010,000	0.25	0.50	1.50	6.00	10.00
1992(a)	—	0.25	0.50	1.50	6.00	10.00

KM# 17 10 FRANCS
3.9100 g., Aluminum-Bronze, 22.4 mm. **Obv:** Half moon with four stars vertical from point to point **Rev:** Denomination above date

Date	Mintage	F	VF	XF	Unc	BU
1992(a)	—	—	—	—	1.65	2.00

KM# 14 25 FRANCS
3.9700 g., Nickel, 20 mm. **Series:** F.A.O. **Obv:** Chickens
Rev: Denomination above date

Date	Mintage	F	VF	XF	Unc	BU
1981(a)	1,000,000	1.50	3.00	6.00	16.00	—
1982(a)	2,007,000	0.20	0.40	0.80	2.00	4.00

KM# 16 50 FRANCS
6.0300 g., Stainless Steel, 23.93 mm. **Obv:** Crescent and stars above denomination, date below **Rev:** Building with tall tower
Edge: Reeded

Date	Mintage	F	VF	XF	Unc	BU
1990(a)	—	0.25	0.50	1.00	2.50	3.50
1994(a)	—	0.25	0.50	1.00	2.50	3.50

KM# 18 100 FRANCS
10.0000 g., Brass, 28 mm. **Subject:** Circulation Type
Obv: Denomination, crescent and stars above, date below
Rev: Boat and fish **Edge:** Plain

Date	Mintage	F	VF	XF	Unc	BU
1999(a)	—	—	—	—	3.50	5.00

ESSAIS
Standard metals unless otherwise noted

KM#	Date	Mintage	Identification	Mkt Val
E1	1964(a)	1,700	Franc. KM4.	15.00
E2	1964(a)	1,700	2 Francs. KM5.	15.00
E3	1964(a)	1,700	5 Francs. KM6.	15.00
E4	1964(a)	1,700	10 Francs. KM7.	15.00
E5	1964(a)	1,700	20 Francs. KM8.	17.50
E6	1975(a)	1,800	50 Francs. KM9.	25.00
E7	1977(a)	1,900	100 Francs. KM13.	30.00
E8	1982(a)	1,900	25 Francs.	20.00
E9	1984(a)	1,700	5 Francs. KM15.	17.50

"FDC" SETS

KM#	Date	Mintage	Identification	Issue Price	Mkt Val
SS1	1964 (5)	—	KM4-8. Issued with Reunion set.	—	15.00

MINT SETS

KM#	Date	Mintage	Identification	Issue Price	Mkt Val
MS1	1976 (3)	500	KM10-12	—	450

PROOF SETS

KM#	Date	Mintage	Identification	Issue Price	Mkt Val
PS1	1976 (3)	500	KM10-12	229	600

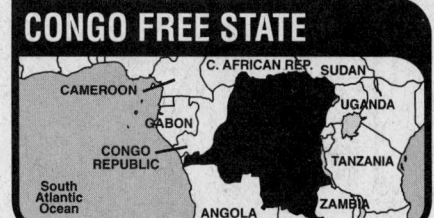

CONGO FREE STATE

In ancient times the territory comprising former Zaire was occupied by Negrito peoples (Pygmies) pushed into the mountains by Bantu and Nilotic invaders. The interior was first explored by the American correspondent Henry Stanley, who was subsequently commissioned by King Leopold II of Belgium to conclude development treaties with the local chiefs. The Berlin conference of 1885 awarded the area to Leopold, who administered and exploited it as his private property until it was annexed to Belgium in 1908.

For later issues, see Belgian Congo.

RULER
Leopold II

ROYAL DOMAIN
1865-1908
STANDARD COINAGE

KM# 9 5 CENTIMES
Copper-Nickel **Ruler:** Leopold II **Obv:** Crowned monograms surround center hole, within circle **Rev:** Hole at center of radiant star, denomination above, date below

Date	Mintage	F	VF	XF	Unc	BU
1906	100,000	5.00	10.00	25.00	60.00	—
1908	180,000	4.00	8.00	20.00	50.00	—
1908/6	—	—	—	—	—	—

KM# 10 10 CENTIMES
Copper-Nickel **Ruler:** Leopold II **Obv:** Hole at center of crowned monograms within circle **Rev:** Hole at center of radiant star, denomination above, date below

Date	Mintage	F	VF	XF	Unc	BU
1906	100,000	5.00	12.00	35.00	90.00	—
1908	800,000	3.00	8.00	30.00	80.00	—

KM# 11 20 CENTIMES
Copper-Nickel **Ruler:** Leopold II **Obv:** Hole at center of crowned monograms within circle **Rev:** Hole at center of radiant star, denomination above, date below

Date	Mintage	F	VF	XF	Unc	BU
1906	100,000	5.00	12.00	40.00	110	—
1908	400,000	4.00	8.00	35.00	95.00	—

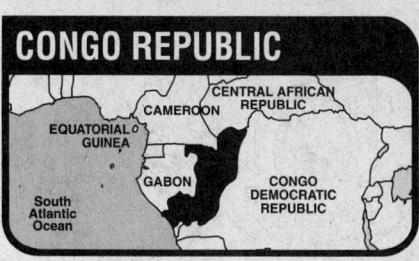

CONGO REPUBLIC

The Republic of the Congo (formerly the Peoples Republic of the Congo), located on the equator in west-central Africa, has an area of 132,047 sq. mi. (342,000 sq. km.) and a population of *2.98 million. Capital: Brazzaville. Agriculture forestry, mining, and food processing are the principal industries. Timber, industrial diamonds, potash, peanuts, and cocoa beans are exported.

The Portuguese were the first Europeans to explore the Congo (Brazzaville) area, 14th century. They conducted a slave trade with the tribal kingdoms of Teke, Loango, and Kongo without attempting developmental colonization. French influence was established in 1883 when the king of Teke signed a treaty with Savorgnan de Brazza, thereby placing his kingdom under the protection of France. While a French protectorate, the area was known as Middle Congo. In 1910 Middle Congo became a part of French Equatorial Africa, which also included Gabon, Ubangi-Shari (now the Central African Republic), and Chad. Following World War II, during which it was an important center of Free French activities, the Middle Congo was given a large measure of internal autonomy, and its inhabitants were made French citizens. Upon approval of the constitution of the Fifth French Republic, 1958, it became a member of the new French Community. On Aug. 15, 1960, Middle Congo became the independent Republic of the Congo-Brazzaville. In Jan. 1970 the country's name was changed to Peoples Republic of the Congo. A new constitution which asserts the government's advocacy of socialism was adopted in 1973.

In June and July of 1992, a new 125-member National Assembly was elected. Later that year a new president, Pascal Lissouba was elected. In November, President Lissouba dismissed the previous government and dissolved the National Assembly. A new 23-member government, including members of the opposition, was formed in December, 1992, and the name was changed to Republique du Congo.

NOTE: For earlier and related coinage see French Equatorial Africa and the Equatorial African States. For later coinage see Central African States.

RULER
French until 1960

MINT MARK
(a) - Paris, privy marks only

MONETARY SYSTEM
100 Centimes = 1 Franc

PEOPLE'S REPUBLIC
Republique Populaire du Congo
DECIMAL COINAGE

KM# 1 100 FRANCS
Nickel **Obv:** Three Giant Eland left **Rev:** Denomination within circle, date below

Date	Mintage	F	VF	XF	Unc	BU
1971(a)	2,700,000	8.00	15.00	25.00	40.00	—
1972(a)	2,500,000	8.00	15.00	25.00	40.00	—

KM# 2 100 FRANCS
Nickel **Obv:** Three Giant Eland left **Rev:** Denomination within circle, date below

Date	Mintage	F	VF	XF	Unc	BU
1975(a)	—	4.00	8.00	16.50	30.00	—
1982(a)	—	2.50	4.50	8.00	12.50	—
1983(a)	—	2.50	5.00	8.00	12.50	—
1985(a)	—	2.00	3.00	6.00	10.00	—
1990(a)	—	2.00	3.00	4.00	6.00	—

KM# 7   100 FRANCS
Nickel Plated Steel   **Subject:** Olympics **Obv:** National arms, denomination below **Rev:** Boxers, date below

Date	Mintage	F	VF	XF	Unc	BU
1991	5,000	—	—	—	15.00	17.00	—

KM# 8   100 FRANCS
Nickel Plated Steel   **Subject:** Olympics **Obv:** National arms, denomination below **Rev:** Hurdler, date lower right

Date	Mintage	F	VF	XF	Unc	BU
1991	5,000	—	—	—	15.00	17.00

KM# 10   100 FRANCS
Nickel Plated Steel   **Series:** Old Ships **Obv:** National arms, denomination below **Rev:** Spanish galleon, date below

Date	Mintage	F	VF	XF	Unc	BU
1991	—	—	—	—	14.00	16.00

KM# 30   100 FRANCS
Copper   **Series:** Old ships **Obv:** National arms, denomination below **Obv. Leg.:** Republique Populaire du Congo **Rev:** Spanish galleon, date below

Date	Mintage	F	VF	XF	Unc	BU
1991 Proof	100	Value: 55.00				

KM# 22   100 FRANCS
Copper   **Series:** Protection of Nature **Obv:** National arms, denomination below **Rev:** Congolese peacock

Date	Mintage	F	VF	XF	Unc	BU
1992	—	—	—	—	20.00	24.00

KM# 31   100 FRANCS
Copper-Nickel **Series:** Protection of Nature **Obv:** National arms, denomination below **Obv. Leg.:** Republique Populaire du Congo **Rev:** Congolese peacock

Date	Mintage	F	VF	XF	Unc	BU
1992	333	—	—	—	50.00	55.00

KM# 4   500 FRANCS
Copper-Nickel   **Obv:** Plants divide date and denomination, within octagon **Rev:** Inscription lower right of woman's head 3/4 left, within octagon

Date	Mintage	F	VF	XF	Unc	BU
1985(a)	—	3.50	6.50	10.00	18.50	—
1986(a)	—	3.50	6.50	10.00	18.50	—

KM# 5   500 FRANCS
16.0000 g., 0.9990 Silver 0.5139 oz. ASW   **Series:** Old Ships **Obv:** National arms, denomination below **Rev:** Spanish galleon, date below

Date	Mintage	F	VF	XF	Unc	BU
1991 Proof	—	Value: 30.00				

KM# 6   500 FRANCS
12.0000 g., 0.9990 Silver 0.3854 oz. ASW   **Subject:** World Cup Soccer **Obv:** National arms, denomination below **Rev:** Soccer players, date at left

Date	Mintage	F	VF	XF	Unc	BU
1991	—	—	—	—	27.50	32.50

KM# 9   500 FRANCS
16.0700 g., 0.9990 Silver 0.5161 oz. ASW   **Subject:** Olympics **Obv:** National arms, denomination below **Rev:** Hurdler

Date	Mintage	F	VF	XF	Unc	BU
1991 Proof	—	Value: 25.00				

KM# 9a   500 FRANCS
20.0000 g., 0.9990 Silver 0.6423 oz. ASW   **Subject:** Olympics **Obv:** National arms, denomination below **Rev:** Hurdler

Date	Mintage	F	VF	XF	Unc	BU
1991	5,000	—	—	—	27.50	32.50

KM# 11   500 FRANCS
20.0000 g., 0.9990 Silver 0.6423 oz. ASW   **Subject:** World Cup Soccer **Obv:** National arms, denomination below **Rev:** Player and date left of Statue of Liberty

Date	Mintage	F	VF	XF	Unc	BU
1992 Proof	—	Value: 25.00				

KM# 12   500 FRANCS
19.9500 g., 0.9990 Silver 0.6407 oz. ASW   **Subject:** Protection of Nature **Obv:** National arms, denomination below **Rev:** Congolese peacock

Date	Mintage	F	VF	XF	Unc	BU
1992 Proof	—	Value: 35.00				

REPUBLIC
Republique du Congo
DECIMAL COINAGE

KM# 18   100 FRANCS
Copper Nickel **Obv:** Woman seated with tablet, denomination below
Rev: Four-masted sailing ship - "Herzogin Cecilie", date below

Date	Mintage	F	VF	XF	Unc	BU
1993	—	—	—	—	10.00	12.00

KM# 20   100 FRANCS
Copper **Subject:** Preservation of Nature **Obv:** Woman seated
with tablet, denomination below **Rev:** Four elephants, tusks
below, date at lower left

Date	Mintage	F	VF	XF	Unc	BU
1993	—	—	—	—	25.00	28.00

KM# 32   100 FRANCS
Copper **Obv:** Woman seated with tablet, denomination below
Rev: Four-masted sailing ship - "Herzogin Cecilie", date below

Date	Mintage	F	VF	XF	Unc	BU
1993 Proof	100	Value: 50.00				

KM# 33   100 FRANCS
Copper **Subject:** Prehistoric Animals **Obv:** Woman seated with
tablet, denomination below **Rev:** Brachiosaurus in water, date below

Date	Mintage	F	VF	XF	Unc	BU
1993 Proof	100	Value: 50.00				

KM# 16   100 FRANCS
Copper-Nickel **Subject:** Prehistoric Animals **Obv:** Woman seated
with tablet, denomination below **Rev:** Polacanthus left, date below

Date	Mintage	F	VF	XF	Unc	BU
1994	—	—	—	—	30.00	35.00

KM# 19   100 FRANCS
Copper-Nickel **Subject:** Prehistoric Animals **Obv:** Woman
seated with tablet, denomination below **Rev:** Spinosaurus left,
date lower left

Date	Mintage	F	VF	XF	Unc	BU
1994	—	—	—	—	30.00	35.00

KM# 34   100 FRANCS
Copper-Nickel **Subject:** Prehistoric Animals **Obv:** Woman seated
with tablet, denomination below **Rev:** Mammuthus 3/4 facing

Date	Mintage	F	VF	XF	Unc	BU
1994 Proof	100	Value: 50.00				

KM# 21   100 FRANCS
Copper-Nickel **Obv:** Woman seated with tablet, denomination
below **Rev:** Junkers JU52 trimotor airplane left, date at right
Note: Multicolored.

Date	Mintage	F	VF	XF	Unc	BU
1995	25,000	—	—	—	25.00	30.00

KM# 35   100 FRANCS
Copper-Nickel **Subject:** XXVII Olympiade **Obv:** Woman seated
with tablet, denomination below **Rev:** Shot putter, date at left
Note: Prev. KM#45.

Date	Mintage	F	VF	XF	Unc	BU
1999	10,000	—	—	—	7.00	9.00

KM# 42   500 FRANCS
13.8100 g., 0.9990 Silver 0.4435 oz. ASW, 30 mm.
Obv: Woman seated with tablet, denomination below
Rev: Multicolor lion head, date at right **Edge:** Plain

Date	Mintage	F	VF	XF	Unc	BU
1996 Proof	—	Value: 40.00				

KM# 38   500 FRANCS
9.9600 g., Silver, 29.9 mm. **Series:** 2000 Olympics
Subject: Basketball **Obv:** Seated woman with tablet
Rev: Basketball player and map of Australia

Date	Mintage	F	VF	XF	Unc	BU
1998 Proof	—	Value: 22.00				

KM# 13   1000 FRANCS
20.0000 g., 0.9990 Silver 0.6423 oz. ASW **Subject:**
Preservation of Nature **Obv:** Woman seated with tablet,
denomination below **Rev:** Elephants, tusks below, date lower left

Date	Mintage	F	VF	XF	Unc	BU
1993 Proof	—	Value: 45.00				

KM# 14   1000 FRANCS
15.9000 g., 0.9990 Silver 0.5107 oz. ASW **Subject:** Prehistoric
Animals **Obv:** Woman seated with tablet, denomination below
Rev: Brachiosaurus, date below

Date	Mintage	F	VF	XF	Unc	BU
1993 Proof	—	Value: 40.00				

KM# 15   1000 FRANCS
20.1000 g., 0.9990 Silver 0.6456 oz. ASW **Obv:** Woman seated
with tablet, denomination below **Rev:** 4-masted sailing ship -
"Herzogin Cecilie", date below

Date	Mintage	F	VF	XF	Unc	BU
1993	100	—	—	—	100	120
1993 Proof	—	Value: 40.00				

KM# 17   1000 FRANCS
15.8800 g., 0.9990 Silver 0.5100 oz. ASW **Subject:** Prehistoric Animals **Obv:** Woman seated with tablet, denomination below **Rev:** Mammoth, date lower left

Date	Mintage	F	VF	XF	Unc	BU
1994 Proof	—	Value: 40.00				

KM# 23   1000 FRANCS
20.0000 g., 0.9990 Silver 0.6423 oz. ASW **Subject:** 1996 Olympics **Obv:** Woman seated with tablet **Rev:** Discus throwing, date at left

Date	Mintage	F	VF	XF	Unc	BU
1995 Proof	15,000	Value: 30.00				

KM# 24   1000 FRANCS
20.0000 g., 0.9990 Silver 0.6423 oz. ASW **Obv:** Woman seated with tablet **Rev:** Multicolor Swiss airliner - Junkers JU 52, left, date at right

Date	Mintage	F	VF	XF	Unc	BU
1995 Proof	15,000	Value: 60.00				

KM# 25   1000 FRANCS
20.0000 g., 0.9990 Silver 0.6423 oz. ASW **Obv:** Woman seated with tablet, denomination below **Rev:** Multicolor Panther head facing, date upper right

Date	Mintage	F	VF	XF	Unc	BU
1996 Proof	—	Value: 60.00				

KM# 40   1000 FRANCS
20.0000 g., 0.9990 Silver 0.6423 oz. ASW, 38.1 mm. **Obv:** Woman seated with tablet, denomination below **Rev:** Multicolor elephant **Edge:** Reeded

Date	Mintage	F	VF	XF	Unc	BU
1996 Proof	—	Value: 60.00				

KM# 26   1000 FRANCS
20.0000 g., 0.9990 Silver 0.6423 oz. ASW **Subject:** World Cup Soccer **Obv:** Woman seated with tablet, denomination below **Rev:** Two soccer players, date at right

Date	Mintage	F	VF	XF	Unc	BU
1996	100	—	—	—	75.00	90.00
1996 Proof	—	Value: 45.00				

KM# 27   1000 FRANCS
20.0000 g., 0.9990 Silver 0.6423 oz. ASW **Subject:** World Cup Soccer **Obv:** Woman seated with tablet, denomination below **Rev:** Multicolor Eiffel Tower, soccer ball and French flag,

Date	Mintage	F	VF	XF	Unc	BU
1996 Proof	—	Value: 45.00				

KM# 28.1   1000 FRANCS
20.0000 g., 0.9990 Silver 0.6423 oz. ASW **Subject:** XXVII Olympiade **Obv:** Woman seated with tablet, denomination below **Rev:** Multicolored boxers

Date	Mintage	F	VF	XF	Unc	BU
1997	100	—	—	—	100	120
1997 Proof	500	Value: 55.00				

KM# 41   1000 FRANCS
31.1000 g., 0.9990 Silver 0.9988 oz. ASW, 45 mm. **Obv:** Woman seated with tablet, denomination below **Rev:** Map of East Central African countries with two elephants and a crocodile **Edge:** Plain

Date	Mintage	F	VF	XF	Unc	BU
1997 Proof	—	Value: 150				

KM# 29   1000 FRANCS
15.0000 g., 0.9990 Silver 0.4818 oz. ASW **Obv:** Woman seated with tablet, denomination below **Rev:** Ancient Roman ship, date below

Date	Mintage	F	VF	XF	Unc	BU
1997 Proof	5,000	Value: 40.00				

KM# 39   1000 FRANCS
15.0000 g., 0.9990 Silver 0.4818 oz. ASW, 35 mm. **Obv:** Woman seated with tablet, denomination below **Rev:** Soccer player, date lower right **Edge:** Plain

Date	Mintage	F	VF	XF	Unc	BU
1997 Proof	—	Value: 40.00				

KM# 37   1000 FRANCS
15.0000 g., 0.9990 Silver 0.4818 oz. ASW, 34.9 mm. **Subject:** Graf Zeppelin **Obv:** Woman with tablet **Rev:** Multicolor New York City view with Zeppelin in flight and a cameo insert at lower right of Count Zeppelin **Edge:** Plain **Note:** Prev. KM#107.

Date	Mintage	F	VF	XF	Unc	BU
ND(1997) Proof	—	Value: 45.00				

KM# 28.2   1000 FRANCS
15.8800 g., 0.9990 Silver 0.5100 oz. ASW **Subject:** XXVII Olympiade **Obv:** Woman seated with tablet, denomination below **Rev:** Multicolored boxers

Date	Mintage	F	VF	XF	Unc	BU
1998	100	—	—	—	100	120
1998 Proof	5,000	Value: 45.00				

KM# 36   1000 FRANCS
20.1000 g., 0.9990 Silver 0.6456 oz. ASW **Subject:** XXVII Olympiade **Obv:** Woman seated with tablet, denomination below **Rev:** Shot putter, date at left

Date	Mintage	F	VF	XF	Unc	BU
1999 Proof	5,000	Value: 32.50				

KM# 43   1000 FRANCS
15.0000 g., 0.9990 Silver 0.4818 oz. ASW, 35 mm. **Obv:** Woman seated with tablet, denomination below **Rev:** Charles Darwin **Edge:** Plain

Date	Mintage	F	VF	XF	Unc	BU
1999 Proof	—	Value: 40.00				

KM# 44   1000 FRANCS
15.0000 g., 0.9990 Silver 0.4818 oz. ASW, 35 mm. **Obv:** Woman seated with tablet, denomination below **Rev:** Graf Ferdinand von Zeppelin **Edge:** Plain

Date	Mintage	F	VF	XF	Unc	BU
ND(2000) Proof	—	Value: 40.00				

KM# 45   1000 FRANCS
15.0000 g., 0.9990 Silver 0.4818 oz. ASW, 35 mm. **Obv:** Woman seated with tablet, denomination below **Rev:** Ciconia bird, date at right **Edge:** Plain

Date	Mintage	F	VF	XF	Unc	BU
2000	—			—	35.00	40.00

ESSAIS

Standard metals unless otherwise noted

KM#	Date	Mintage	Identification			Mkt Val
E1	1971(a)	1,450	100 Francs.			25.00
E2	1971(a)	4	100 Francs. Gold.			1,350
E3	1975(a)	1,700	100 Francs.			20.00
E5	1985(a)	1,700	500 Francs. Plants between denomination and date within octagon. Inscription at lower right of womans head.			35.00

PIEFORTS

KM#	Date	Mintage	Identification	Mkt Val
P1	1991	110	500 Francs. 0.9990 Silver. National arms, denomination below. Spanish galleon, date below. KM5.	125

TRIAL STRIKES

KM#	Date	Mintage	Identification	Mkt Val
TS1	1984	3	10 Francs. Silver. Fencing. Uniface.	600
TS2	1984	3	50 Francs. Silver. Shot put. Uniface.	600

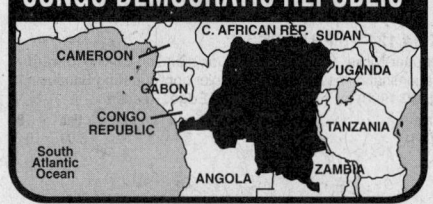

CONGO DEMOCRATIC REPUBLIC

The Democratic Republic of the Congo (formerly the Republic of Zaire, and earlier the Belgian Congo), located in the south-central part of Africa, has an area of 905,568 sq. mi. (2,345,410 sq. km.) and a population of *47.4 million. Capital: Kinshasa. The mineral-rich country produces copper, tin, diamonds, gold, zinc, cobalt and uranium.

In ancient times the territory comprising former Zaire was occupied by Negrito peoples (Pygmies) pushed into the mountains by Bantu and Nilotic invaders. The interior was first explored by the American correspondent Henry Stanley, who was subsequently commissioned by King Leopold II of Belgium to conclude development treaties with the local chiefs. The Berlin conference of 1885 awarded the area to Leopold, who administered and exploited it as his private property until it was annexed to Belgium in 1908. Belgium received the mandate for the German territory of Ruanda-Urundi as a result of the international treaties after WWI. During World War II, Belgian Congolese troops fought on the side of the Allies, notably in Ethiopia. Following the eruption of bloody independence riots in 1959, Belgium granted the Belgian Congo independence as the Republic of the Congo on June 30, 1960. The nation officially changed its name to Zaire on Oct. 27, 1971, and following a Civil War in 1997 changed its name to the "Democratic Republic of the Congo."

MINT MARKS
(b) – Brussels, privy marks only

REPUBLIC
1960 - 1971

DECIMAL COINAGE

KM# 1 10 FRANCS
3.2700 g., Aluminum, 29.8 mm. **Obv:** Denomination above date **Rev:** Lion face **Note:** Most recalled and melted.

Date	Mintage	F	VF	XF	Unc	BU
1965(b)	Est. 100,000,000	0.60	1.50	3.00	8.00	20.00

KM# 2 10 FRANCS
3.2260 g., 0.9000 Gold 0.0933 oz. AGW **Subject:** 5th Anniversary of Independence **Obv:** President Joseph Kasa-Vubu **Rev:** Crossed palm trees, denomination below **Note:** Approximately 70 percent melted.

Date	Mintage	F	VF	XF	Unc	BU
1965 Proof	Est. 3,000	Value: 120				

KM# 3 20 FRANCS
6.4520 g., 0.9000 Gold 0.1867 oz. AGW **Subject:** 5th Anniversary of Independence **Obv:** Uniformed bust of President Joseph Kasa-Vubu 3/4 right **Rev:** Crossed palm trees, denomination below **Note:** Approximately 70 percent melted.

Date	Mintage	F	VF	XF	Unc	BU
1965 Proof	Est. 3,000	Value: 230				

KM# 4 25 FRANCS
8.0640 g., 0.9000 Gold 0.2333 oz. AGW **Subject:** 5th Anniversary of Independence **Rev:** Elephant left **Note:** Approximately 70 percent melted.

Date	Mintage	F	VF	XF	Unc	BU
1965 Proof	Est. 3,000	Value: 300				

KM# 4a 25 FRANCS
Silver **Subject:** 5th Anniversary of Independence **Rev:** Elephant left

Date	Mintage	F	VF	XF	Unc	BU
1965 Proof	—	Value: 60.00				

KM# 5 50 FRANCS
16.1290 g., 0.9000 Gold 0.4667 oz. AGW **Subject:** 5th Anniversary of Independence **Obv:** Uniformed President's bust 3/4 right **Rev:** Elephant left, denomination and date below **Note:** Approximately 70 percent melted.

Date	Mintage	F	VF	XF	Unc	BU
1965 Proof	Est. 3,000	Value: 500				

KM# 6 100 FRANCS
32.2580 g., 0.9000 Gold 0.9334 oz. AGW **Subject:** 5th Anniversary of Independence **Obv:** Uniformed bust of President Joseph Kasa-Vubu 3/4 right **Rev:** Elephant left **Note:** Approximately 70 percent melted.

Date	Mintage	F	VF	XF	Unc	BU
1965 Proof	Est. 3,000	Value: 950				

KM# 6a 100 FRANCS
Silver **Subject:** 5th Anniversary of Independence **Obv:** President Joseph Kasa-Vubu **Rev:** Elephant left

Date	Mintage	F	VF	XF	Unc	BU
1965 Proof	—	Value: 100				

REFORM COINAGE

100 Sengis = 1 Likuta; 100 Makuta (plural of Likuta) = 1 Zaire

KM# 7 10 SENGIS
0.7000 g., Aluminum, 17 mm. **Obv:** Denomination within circle **Rev:** Leopard crouching on branch, date below **Edge:** Reeded

Date	Mintage	F	VF	XF	Unc	BU
1967	90,996,000	—	0.15	0.45	1.00	3.00
1967 Proof	—	Value: 250				

KM# 10 10 SENGIS
3.2000 g., 0.9000 Gold 0.0926 oz. AGW **Subject:** 5th Year of Mobutu Presidency **Obv:** Arms above denomination **Rev:** Military bust of President Joseph Desire Mobutu 3/4 facing, date below

Date	Mintage	F	VF	XF	Unc	BU
1970	1,000	—	—	—	100	110
1970 Proof	—	Value: 125				

KM# 10a 10 SENGIS
Gilt Brass **Subject:** 5th Year of Mobutu Presidency **Obv:** Arms **Rev:** Bust of President Joseph Desire Mobutu

Date	Mintage	F	VF	XF	Unc	BU
1970 Proof	—	Value: 70.00				

KM# 8 LIKUTA
1.2700 g., Aluminum, 20.9 mm. **Obv:** Denomination within circle **Rev:** Arms above date

Date	Mintage	F	VF	XF	Unc	BU
1967	49,180,000	—	0.15	0.50	1.25	—
1967 Proof	—	Value: 250				

KM# 9 5 MAKUTA
6.4100 g., Copper-Nickel, 25 mm. **Obv:** Denomination within circle **Rev:** Bust of President Mobutu 3/4 left, date below

Date	Mintage	F	VF	XF	Unc	BU
1967	2,470,000	0.25	0.50	1.00	3.00	—
1967 Proof	—	Value: 250				

KM# 11 25 MAKUTAS
Gilt Brass **Subject:** 5th Year of Mobutu Presidency **Obv:** Arms above denomination **Rev:** President's bust 3/4 facing, date below

Date	Mintage	F	VF	XF	Unc	BU
1970 Proof	—	Value: 100				

KM# 11a 25 MAKUTAS
8.0000 g., 0.9000 Gold 0.2315 oz. AGW **Subject:** 5th Year of Mobutu Presidency **Obv:** Arms above denomination **Rev:** President's bust facing

Date	Mintage	F	VF	XF	Unc	BU
1970	1,000	—	—	—	300	315
1970 Proof	—	Value: 325				

KM# 12 50 MAKUTAS
Gilt Brass **Subject:** 5th Year of Mobutu Presidency **Obv:** Arms above denomination **Rev:** President's bust 3/4 facing

Date	Mintage	F	VF	XF	Unc	BU
1970 Proof	—	Value: 125				

KM# 12a 50 MAKUTAS
16.0000 g., 0.9000 Gold 0.4630 oz. AGW **Subject:** 5th Year of Mobutu Presidency **Obv:** Arms above denomination **Rev:** President's bust 3/4 facing, date below

Date	Mintage	F	VF	XF	Unc	BU
1970	1,000	—	—	—	500	515
1970 Proof	1,000	Value: 525				

KM# 13 ZAIRE
Gilt Brass **Subject:** 5th Year of Mobutu Presidency **Obv:** Arms above denomination **Rev:** President's bust 3/4 facing

Date	Mintage	F	VF	XF	Unc	BU
1970 Proof	—	Value: 150				

KM# 13a ZAIRE
32.0000 g., 0.9000 Gold 0.9259 oz. AGW **Subject:** 5th Year of
Mobutu Presidency **Obv:** Arms above denomination
Rev: President's bust, 3/4 facing, date below

Date	Mintage	F	VF	XF	Unc	BU
1970	1,000	—	—	—	950	965
1970 Proof	1,000	Value: 975				

DEMOCRATIC REPUBLIC
1998 -

REFORM COINAGE
Congo Francs replace Zaire; July 1998

KM# 73 5 FRANCS
24.3000 g., Copper Nickel, 38.5 mm. **Subject:** Royals of Europe
Obv: Lion **Rev:** Multicolor portrait of Queen Juliana (1948-80)
and crowned arms **Edge:** Reeded

Date	Mintage	F	VF	XF	Unc	BU
1999 Proof	—	—	—	—	12.00	—

KM# 84 5 FRANCS
24.3000 g., Copper Nickel, 38.5 mm. **Subject:** Anna Paulowna
Obv: Lion within inner circle, denomination below in outer circle
Rev: Multicolor portrait applique within inner circle **Edge:** Reeded

Date	Mintage	F	VF	XF	Unc	BU
1999 Proof	—	Value: 10.00				

KM# 85 5 FRANCS
24.3000 g., Copper Nickel, 38.5 mm. **Subject:** Willem I
Obv: Lion within inner circle, denomination below in outer circle
Rev: Multicolor portrait applique within inner circle **Edge:** Reeded

Date	Mintage	F	VF	XF	Unc	BU
1999 Proof	—	Value: 10.00				

KM# 86 5 FRANCS
24.3000 g., Copper Nickel, 38.5 mm. **Subject:** Willem III
Obv: Lion within inner circle, denomination below in outer circle
Rev: Multicolor portrait applique within inner circle **Edge:** Reeded

Date	Mintage	F	VF	XF	Unc	BU
1999 Proof	—	Value: 10.00				

KM# 87 5 FRANCS
24.3000 g., Copper Nickel, 38.5 mm. **Subject:** Wilhelmina
Obv: Lion within inner circle, denomination below in outer circle
Rev: Multicolor portrait applique within inner circle **Edge:** Reeded

Date	Mintage	F	VF	XF	Unc	BU
1999 Proof	—	Value: 10.00				

KM# 88 5 FRANCS
24.3000 g., Copper Nickel, 38.5 mm. **Subject:** Bernhard
Obv: Lion within inner circle, denomination in outer circle
Rev: Multicolor portrait applique within inner circle **Edge:** Reeded

Date	Mintage	F	VF	XF	Unc	BU
1999 Proof	—	Value: 10.00				

KM# 89 5 FRANCS
24.3000 g., Copper-Nickel, 38.5 mm. **Subject:** Claus **Obv:** Lion
within inner circle, denomination below in outer circle
Rev: Multicolor portrait applique within inner circle **Edge:** Reeded

Date	Mintage	F	VF	XF	Unc	BU
1999 Proof	—	Value: 10.00				

KM# 90 5 FRANCS
24.3000 g., Copper-Nickel, 38.5 mm. **Subject:** Willem-Alexander
Obv: Lion within inner circle, denomination below in outer circle
Rev: Multicolor portrait applique within inner circle **Edge:** Reeded

Date	Mintage	F	VF	XF	Unc	BU
1999 Proof	—	Value: 10.00				

KM# 121 5 FRANCS
Copper-Nickel, 40 mm. **Obv:** Lion standing looking forward,
denomination below **Rev:** Multicolor applique King Baudouin I
(1930-1993) facing, dates at right **Edge:** Reeded

Date	Mintage	F	VF	XF	Unc	BU
2000	—	—	—	—	8.00	10.00

KM# 160 5 FRANCS
26.5300 g., Copper-Nickel, 37.3 mm. **Subject:** Marine-Life
Protection **Obv:** Standing lion facing, denomination below
Rev: Multicolor fish scene, date below **Edge:** Reeded

Date	Mintage	F	VF	XF	Unc	BU
2000 Proof	—	Value: 25.00				

KM# 24 5 FRANCS
Copper-Nickel **Subject:** Panama Canal **Obv:** Standing lion
facing, denomination below **Rev:** Sailing ship above inscription
and map **Note:** Prev. KM#47.

Date	Mintage	F	VF	XF	Unc	BU
2000	—	—	—	—	10.00	12.00

KM# 39 5 FRANCS
27.1600 g., Copper Nickel, 37.3 mm. **Series:** Wild Life
Protection **Obv:** Standing lion facing, denomination below
Rev: Multicolor holographic parrot with folded wings right
Edge: Reeded **Note:** Prev. KM#62.

Date	Mintage	F	VF	XF	Unc	BU
2000 Proof	—	Value: 30.00				

KM# 40 5 FRANCS
Copper Nickel 27.16, 37.3 mm. **Series:** Wild Life Protection
Obv: Standing lion facing, denomination below **Rev:** Multicolor
holographic parrot with open wings left **Edge:** Reeded
Note: Prev. KM#63.

Date	Mintage	F	VF	XF	Unc	BU
2000 Proof	—	Value: 30.00				

KM# 41 5 FRANCS
27.1600 g., Copper Nickel, 37.3 mm. **Series:** Wild Life
Protection **Obv:** Standing lion facing, denomination below
Rev: Multicolor holographic toucan left **Note:** Prev. KM#64.

Date	Mintage	F	VF	XF	Unc	BU
2000 Proof	—	Value: 30.00				

KM# 63 5 FRANCS
28.7500 g., Copper-Nickel, 38 mm. **Subject:** Lady Diana - Visit
to India **Obv:** Standing lion facing, denomination below **Rev:** Lady
Diana at left, Taj Mahal at right, cameo of Queen Mother top
center **Edge:** Reeded **Note:** Prev. KM#86.

Date	Mintage	F	VF	XF	Unc	BU
ND(2000) Proof	—	Value: 45.00				

KM# 64 5 FRANCS
28.7500 g., Copper-Nickel, 38 mm. **Subject:** Lady Diana -
Meeting with Pope John Paul II **Obv:** Standing lion facing,
denomination below **Rev:** Lady Diana front left, Pope John Paul
II facing left, cameo of Queen Mother top center **Edge:** Reeded
Note: Prev. KM#87.

Date	Mintage	F	VF	XF	Unc	BU
ND(2000) Proof	—	Value: 45.00				

KM# 17 10 FRANCS
20.0000 g., 0.9250 Silver 0.5948 oz. ASW **Series:** Endangered
Wildlife **Obv:** Lion within inner circle, date below in outer circle
Rev: Water chevrotain left, denomination below **Note:** Prev. KM#38.

Date	Mintage	F	VF	XF	Unc	BU
1999 Proof	10,000	Value: 40.00				

KM# 14 10 FRANCS
20.0000 g., 0.9250 Silver 0.5948 oz. ASW **Series:** Endangered
Wildlife **Obv:** Lion within inner circle, date below in outer circle
Rev: Bonobos female chimpanzee with young, denomination
below **Note:** Prev. KM#35.

Date	Mintage	F	VF	XF	Unc	BU
1999 Proof	10,000	Value: 40.00				

KM# 15 10 FRANCS
20.0000 g., 0.9250 Silver 0.5948 oz. ASW **Series:** Endangered
Wildlife **Obv:** Lion within inner circle, date below in outer circle
Rev: Pygmy hippopotamus right, denomination below
Note: Prev. KM#36.

Date	Mintage	F	VF	XF	Unc	BU
1999 Proof	10,000	Value: 40.00				

KM# 16 10 FRANCS
20.0000 g., 0.9250 Silver 0.5948 oz. ASW **Series:** Endangered
Wildlife **Obv:** Lion within inner circle, date below in outer circle
Rev: Crocodile left, denomination below **Note:** Prev. KM#37.

Date	Mintage	F	VF	XF	Unc	BU
1999 Proof	10,000	Value: 40.00				

KM# 18 10 FRANCS
20.0000 g., 0.9250 Silver 0.5948 oz. ASW **Series:** Endangered
Wildlife **Obv:** Lion within inner circle, date below in outer circle
Rev: Tree pangolin on branch right, denomination below
Note: Prev. KM#39.

Date	Mintage	F	VF	XF	Unc	BU
1999 Proof	10,000	Value: 40.00				

KM# 19 10 FRANCS
20.0000 g., 0.9250 Silver 0.5948 oz. ASW **Series:** Endangered
Wildlife **Obv:** Lion within inner circle, date below in outer circle **Rev:**
Poto hanging on branches, denomination below **Note:** Prev. KM#40.

Date	Mintage	F	VF	XF	Unc	BU
1999 Proof	10,000	Value: 40.00				

KM# 20 10 FRANCS
25.3100 g., 0.9250 Silver 0.7527 oz. ASW **Subject:** Explorers
of Africa-Dr. David Livingstone **Obv:** Lion within inner circle, date
below in outer circle **Rev:** Head facing, land and ship in
background, denomination at left **Note:** Prev. KM#41.

Date	Mintage	F	VF	XF	Unc	BU
1999 Proof	10,000	Value: 37.50				

KM# 21 10 FRANCS
25.3100 g., 0.9250 Silver 0.7527 oz. ASW **Subject:**
Explorers of Africa-Sir Henry Morton Stanley **Obv:** Lion within inner circle,
date below in outer circle **Rev:** Bust facing, denomination at right
Note: Prev. KM#42.

Date	Mintage	F	VF	XF	Unc	BU
1999 Proof	10,000	Value: 37.50				

KM# 22 10 FRANCS
25.3100 g., 0.9250 Silver 0.7527 oz. ASW **Subject:** 30th
Anniversary of the Lunar Landing **Obv:** Lion within inner circle,
date below in outer circle **Rev:** First lunar landing scene,
denomination at left, two dates above **Note:** Prev. KM#43.

Date	Mintage	F	VF	XF	Unc	BU
1999 Proof	10,000	Value: 37.50				

KM# 23 10 FRANCS
25.3100 g., 0.9250 Silver 0.7527 oz. ASW **Subject:** Sydney 2000 **Obv:** Roaring lion bust left within inner circle, date below in outer circle **Rev:** Diver and opera house, denomination at left **Note:** Prev. KM#44.

Date	Mintage	F	VF	XF	Unc	BU
1999 Proof	10,000	Value: 37.50				

KM# 25 10 FRANCS
25.1300 g., 0.9250 Silver 0.7473 oz. ASW **Subject:** Panama Canal **Obv:** Standing lion facing, denomination below **Rev:** Sailing ship above inscription and map **Note:** Prev. KM#48.

Date	Mintage	F	VF	XF	Unc	BU
2000 Proof	—	Value: 35.00				

KM# 26 10 FRANCS
25.1300 g., 0.9250 Silver 0.7473 oz. ASW **Subject:** Panama Canal **Obv:** Standing lion facing, denomination below **Rev:** Cargo ship over map of Panama, date at left **Note:** Prev. KM#49.

Date	Mintage	F	VF	XF	Unc	BU
2000 Proof	—	Value: 35.00				

KM# 27 10 FRANCS
25.1300 g., 0.9250 Silver 0.7473 oz. ASW **Subject:** 25th Anniversary - Visit of Pope John Paul II **Obv:** Standing lion facing, denomination below **Rev:** Bust 3/4 right of Pope John Paul II, date below **Note:** Prev. KM#50.

Date	Mintage	F	VF	XF	Unc	BU
2000 Proof	—	Value: 35.00				

KM# 28 10 FRANCS
25.1300 g., 0.9250 Silver 0.7473 oz. ASW **Subject:** 25th Anniversary - Visit of Pope John Paul II **Obv:** Standing lion facing, denomination below **Rev:** Half-length bust of Pope John Paul II facing, date below **Note:** Prev. KM#51.

Date	Mintage	F	VF	XF	Unc	BU
2000 Proof	—	Value: 35.00				

KM# 30 10 FRANCS
25.4500 g., 0.9250 Silver 0.7568 oz. ASW, 37.3 mm. **Subject:** Wild Life Protection **Obv:** Standing lion facing, denomination below **Rev:** Multicolor parrot with open wings left **Edge:** Reeded **Note:** Prev. KM#53.

Date	Mintage	F	VF	XF	Unc	BU
2000 Proof	—	Value: 50.00				

KM# 31 10 FRANCS
25.4500 g., 0.9250 Silver 0.7568 oz. ASW, 37.3 mm. **Subject:** Wild Life Protection **Obv:** Standing lion facing, denomination below **Rev:** Toucan with folded wings right **Edge:** Reeded **Note:** Prev. KM#54.

Date	Mintage	F	VF	XF	Unc	BU
2000 Proof	—	Value: 50.00				

KM# 32 10 FRANCS
31.2600 g., 0.9990 Silver 1.0040 oz. ASW, 47.7 x 27.1 mm. **Subject:** Millennium - space travel **Obv:** Standing lion facing, denomination below **Rev:** Footprint on the moon **Edge:** Plain **Note:** Prev. KM#55.

Date	Mintage	F	VF	XF	Unc	BU
2000 Proof	—	Value: 32.50				

KM# 33 10 FRANCS
31.2600 g., 0.9990 Silver 1.0040 oz. ASW, 45.1 x 23.4 mm. **Subject:** Animal Protection **Obv:** Standing lion facing within triangle, denomination below **Rev:** Chimpanzee hanging from branches **Edge:** Plain **Note:** Prev. KM#56.

Date	Mintage	F	VF	XF	Unc	BU
2000 Proof	—	Value: 35.00				

KM# 34 10 FRANCS
31.2600 g., 0.9990 Silver 1.0040 oz. ASW, 45.1 x 23.4 mm. **Subject:** Animal Protection **Obv:** Standing lion facing within triangle, denomination below **Rev:** 2 chimpanzees in trees **Edge:** Plain **Note:** Prev. KM#57.

Date	Mintage	F	VF	XF	Unc	BU
2000 Proof	—	Value: 35.00				

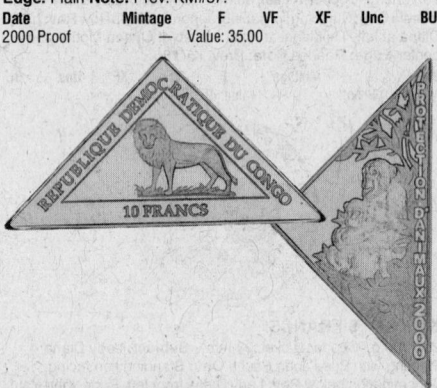

KM# 35 10 FRANCS
31.2600 g., 0.9990 Silver 1.0040 oz. ASW, 45.1 x 23.4 mm. **Subject:** Animal Protection **Obv:** Standing lion facing within triangle, denomination below **Rev:** Female chimpanzee with young one **Edge:** Plain **Note:** Prev. KM#58.

Date	Mintage	F	VF	XF	Unc	BU
2000 Proof	—	Value: 35.00				

KM# 36 10 FRANCS
31.2600 g., 0.9990 Silver 1.0040 oz. ASW, 45.1 x 23.4 mm. **Subject:** Animal Protection **Obv:** Standing lion facing within triangle, denomination below **Rev:** 2 chimpanzees on the ground **Edge:** Plain **Note:** Prev. KM#59.

Date	Mintage	F	VF	XF	Unc	BU
2000 Proof	—	Value: 35.00				

KM# 37   10 FRANCS
20.0000 g., 0.9250 Silver 0.5948 oz. ASW, 38 mm.
Subject: Millennium - Jesus **Obv:** Standing lion facing,
denomination below **Rev:** Portrait of Jesus facing within beaded
circles, date below **Edge:** Plain **Note:** Prev. KM#60.

Date	Mintage	F	VF	XF	Unc	BU
2000 Proof	—			Value: 40.00		

KM# 44   10 FRANCS
19.9200 g., 0.9250 Silver 0.5924 oz. ASW, 41.1 mm.
Series: Olympics **Obv:** Standing lion facing, date below
Rev: Long jumper, denomination at right **Edge:** Reeded
Note: Prev. KM#67.

Date	Mintage	F	VF	XF	Unc	BU
2000 Proof	—			Value: 40.00		

KM# 45   10 FRANCS
19.9200 g., 0.9250 Silver 0.5924 oz. ASW, 41.1 mm. **Series:**
Olympics **Obv:** Standing lion facing, date below **Rev:** Two divers,
denomination at left **Edge:** Reeded **Note:** Prev. KM#68.

Date	Mintage	F	VF	XF	Unc	BU
2000 Proof	—			Value: 40.00		

KM# 46   10 FRANCS
19.9200 g., 0.9250 Silver 0.5924 oz. ASW, 41.1 mm. **Series:**
Olympics **Obv:** Standing lion facing, date below **Rev:** Tennis
player, denomination at right **Edge:** Reeded **Note:** Prev. KM#69.

Date	Mintage	F	VF	XF	Unc	BU
2000 Proof	—			Value: 40.00		

KM# 47   10 FRANCS
19.9200 g., 0.9250 Silver 0.5924 oz. ASW, 41.1 mm. **Series:**
Olympics **Obv:** Standing lion facing, date below **Rev:** Weight
lifter, denomination at left **Edge:** Reeded **Note:** Prev. KM#70.

Date	Mintage	F	VF	XF	Unc	BU
2000 Proof	—			Value: 40.00		

KM# 48   10 FRANCS
19.9200 g., 0.9250 Silver 0.5924 oz. ASW, 41.1 mm.
Series: Olympics **Obv:** Standing lion facing, date below
Rev: Two fencers, denomination below **Edge:** Plain **Note:** Prev.
KM#71.

Date	Mintage	F	VF	XF	Unc	BU
2000 Proof	—			Value: 40.00		

KM# 49   10 FRANCS
19.9200 g., 0.9250 Silver 0.5924 oz. ASW, 41.1 mm.
Series: Olympics **Obv:** Standing lion facing, date below
Rev: Two boxers, denomination below **Edge:** Reeded
Note: Prev. KM#72.

Date	Mintage	F	VF	XF	Unc	BU
2000 Proof	—			Value: 40.00		

KM# 50   10 FRANCS
19.9200 g., 0.9250 Silver 0.5924 oz. ASW, 41.1 mm.
Series: Olympics **Obv:** Standing lion facing, date below
Rev: Rowing, denomination below **Edge:** Reeded **Note:** Prev.
KM#73.

Date	Mintage	F	VF	XF	Unc	BU
2000 Proof	—			Value: 40.00		

KM# 51   10 FRANCS
19.9200 g., 0.9250 Silver 0.5924 oz. ASW, 41.1 mm.
Series: Olympics **Obv:** Standing lion facing, date below
Rev: Archer, denomination at lower left **Edge:** Reeded
Note: Prev. KM#74.

Date	Mintage	F	VF	XF	Unc	BU
2000 Proof	—			Value: 40.00		

KM# 52   10 FRANCS
19.9200 g., 0.9250 Silver 0.5924 oz. ASW, 41.1 mm.
Series: Olympics **Obv:** Standing lion facing, date below
Rev: Judo match, denomination below **Edge:** Reeded
Note: Prev. KM#75.

Date	Mintage	F	VF	XF	Unc	BU
2000 Proof	—			Value: 40.00		

KM# 53   10 FRANCS
19.9200 g., 0.9250 Silver 0.5924 oz. ASW, 41.1 mm. **Series:**
Olympics **Obv:** Standing lion facing, date below **Rev:** Ribbon
dancer, denomination at right **Edge:** Reeded **Note:** Prev. KM#76.

Date	Mintage	F	VF	XF	Unc	BU
2000 Proof	—			Value: 40.00		

KM# 54   10 FRANCS
19.9200 g., 0.9250 Silver 0.5924 oz. ASW, 41.1 mm. **Series:**
Olympics **Obv:** Standing lion facing, date below **Rev:** Badminton
player, denomination below **Edge:** Reeded **Note:** Prev. KM#77.

Date	Mintage	F	VF	XF	Unc	BU
2000 Proof	—			Value: 40.00		

KM# 55   10 FRANCS
25.4500 g., 0.9250 Silver 0.7568 oz. ASW, 37.2 mm.
Series: Wild Life Protection **Obv:** Standing lion facing,
denomination below **Rev:** Multicolored toucan hologram left
Edge: Reeded **Note:** Prev. KM#78.

Date	Mintage	F	VF	XF	Unc	BU
2000 Proof	—			Value: 50.00		

KM# 92   10 FRANCS
30.8700 g., 0.9990 Silver 0.9915 oz. ASW, 38.7 mm.
Obv: Standing lion facing, date below **Rev:** African crocodile left,
denomination below **Edge:** Reeded

Date	Mintage	F	VF	XF	Unc	BU
2000 Proof	—			Value: 45.00		

KM# 98   10 FRANCS
31.5500 g., 0.9250 Silver 0.9382 oz. ASW, 38.7 mm.
Subject: Diogo Cao 1482 **Obv:** Standing lion facing,
denomination below **Rev:** Portuguese sailing ship, date at right
Edge: Reeded

Date	Mintage	F	VF	XF	Unc	BU
2000 Proof	—	Value: 40.00				

KM# 161   10 FRANCS
19.7600 g., 0.9250 Silver 0.5876 oz. ASW, 38.6 mm.
Obv: Standing lion facing, denomination below **Rev:** Gorilla on
all fours facing, date below **Edge:** Reeded

Date	Mintage	F	VF	XF	Unc	BU
2000 Proof	—	Value: 50.00				

KM# 183   20 FRANCS
1.2200 g., Gold, 13.85 mm.   **Subject:** Arican art **Obv:** Lion
standing right **Rev:** statue at right **Edge:** Reeded

Date	Mintage	F	VF	XF	Unc	BU
2000 Proof	—	Value: 55.00				

KM# 29   20 FRANCS
1.5300 g., 0.9990 Gold 0.0491 oz. AGW **Subject:** 25th Anniversary
- Visit of Pope John Paul II **Obv:** Standing lion facing, denomination
below **Rev:** Bust right of Pope John Paul II **Note:** Prev. KM#52.

Date	Mintage	F	VF	XF	Unc	BU
2000 Proof	—	Value: 50.00				

KM# 62   20 FRANCS
62.2000 g., 0.9999 Silver 1.9995 oz. ASW, 40 mm.
Subject: Japanese New 500 Yen Coin **Obv:** Standing lion facing,
denomination below **Rev:** Japanese 500 yen coin Y-125,
embedded over the obverse and reverse design of the Y-99 500
yen coin **Edge:** Reeded **Note:** Prev. KM#85.

Date	Mintage	F	VF	XF	Unc	BU
2000	1,500	—	—	—	65.00	75.00

KM# 177   100 FRANCS
39.2000 g., Gold   **Obv:** Roaring lion **Rev:** Dr. Livingstone and
river boat **Edge:** Reeded

Date	Mintage	F	VF	XF	Unc	BU
1999 Proof	—	Value: 1,250				

KM# 42   100 FRANCS
31.5400 g., 0.9999 Gold 1.0139 oz. AGW, 37.3 mm.
Subject: Wild Life Protection **Obv:** Standing lion facing,
denomination below **Rev:** Multicolor holographic parrot with
folded wings right **Edge:** Reeded **Note:** Prev. KM#65.

Date	Mintage	F	VF	XF	Unc	BU
2000 Proof	25	Value: 1,200				

KM# 43   100 FRANCS
31.5400 g., 0.9999 Gold 1.0139 oz. AGW, 37.3 mm.
Subject: Wild Life Protection **Obv:** Standing lion facing,
denomination below **Rev:** Multicolor holographic parrot with open
wings left **Edge:** Reeded **Note:** Prev. KM#66.

Date	Mintage	F	VF	XF	Unc	BU
2000 Proof	25	Value: 1,200				

ESSAIS

KM#	Date	Mintage	Identification	Mkt Val
E1	1965	—	10 Francs. Silver.	—
E2	1965(b)	—	10 Francs. Gold.	—

Note: Aluminum and copper-nickel essais of the 10 Francs
are valued at $350 and $450 respectively. These are
considered off-metal pieces created as die trials or setup strikes in the process of producing the official silver
and gold coins.

KM#	Date	Mintage	Identification	Mkt Val
E3	1970	—	50 Makutas. Pewter. KM12.	250
E4	1970	—	Zaire. Pewter. KM13.	325
E5	1970	—	Zaire. Silver. KM13.	165
E6	1970	—	10 Zaire. Gold. ESSAI.	1,000

PATTERNS
Including off metal strikes

KM#	Date	Mintage	Identification	Mkt Val
Pn1	1965	—	100 Francs. KM#6, Type II variety.	—
Pn5	1999	—	100 Francs. Gilt. Stanley	350
Pn6	1999	—	100 Francs. Gilt. Livingston	350

PIEFORTS WITH ESSAI

KM#	Date	Mintage	Identification	Mkt Val
PE1	1970	—	10 Zaire. Silver. 2.4 mm thick.	250
PE2	1970	—	10 Zaire. Silver. 4.7 mm thick.	600

MINT SETS

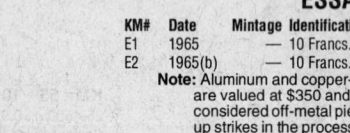

KM#	Date	Mintage	Identification	Issue Price	Mkt Val
MS1	1970 (4)	1,000	KM10-13	1,300	1,850

PROOF SETS

KM#	Date	Mintage	Identification	Issue Price	Mkt Val
PS1	1965 (5)	3,000	KM2-6. Approximately 70 percent melted.	490	2,100
PS2	1970 (4)	1,000	KM10-13	—	1,950
PS3	2000 (4)	—	KM#33-36	—	130

COOK ISLANDS

Cook Islands, a self-governing dependency of New Zealand
consisting of 15 islands, is located in the South Pacific Ocean
about 2,000 miles (3,218 km.) northeast of New Zealand. It has
an area of 93 sq. mi. (234 sq. km.) and a population of 17,185.
Capital: Avarua. The United States claims the islands of Danger,
Manahiki, Penrhyn, and Rakahanga atolls. Citrus and canned
fruits and juices, copra, clothing, jewelry, and mother-of-pearl
shell are exported.

Spanish navigator Alvaro de Mendada first sighted the
islands in 1595. Portuguese navigator Pedro Fernandes de
Quieros landed on Rakahanga in 1606. English navigator Capt.
James Cook sailed to the islands on three occasions: 1773, 1774
and 1777. He named them Hervey Islands, in honor of Augustus
John Hervey, a lord of the Admiralty. The islands were declared
a British protectorate in 1888, and were annexed to New Zealand
in 1901. They were granted internal self-government in 1965.
New Zealand provides an annual subsidy and retains responsibility for defense and foreign affairs.

RULER
British

MINT MARKS
(b) - British Royal Mint
FM - Franklin Mint, U.S.A. *
PM - Pobjoy Mint
   *NOTE: From 1975-1985 the Franklin Mint produced coin-
age in up to three different qualities. Qualities of issue are designated in () after each date and are defined as follows:
   (M) MATTE - Normal circulation strike or a dull finish produced by sandblasting special uncirculated (polish finish) or
proof quality dies.
   (U) SPECIAL UNCIRCULATED - Polished or proof-like in
appearance without any frosted features.
   (P) PROOF - The highest quality obtainable having mirror-
like fields and frosted features.

MONETARY SYSTEM
                        (Until 1967)
12 Pence = 1 Shilling
20 Shillings = 1 Pound
                        (Commencing 1967)
100 Cents = 1 Dollar

DEPENDENCY OF NEW ZEALAND
DECIMAL COINAGE

KM# 1   CENT
Bronze **Ruler:** Elizabeth II **Obv:** Young bust right, date below
Rev: Taro leaf, denomination at right

Date	Mintage	F	VF	XF	Unc	BU
1972	117,000	—	—	0.10	0.20	0.35
1972 Proof	17,000	Value: 0.50				
1973	8,500	—	—	0.10	0.20	0.35
1973 Proof	13,000	Value: 0.50				
1974	300,000	—	—	0.10	0.20	0.35
1974 Proof	7,300	Value: 0.50				
1975	429,000	—	—	0.10	0.20	0.35
1975FM (M)	1,000	—	—	—	0.50	0.65
1975FM (P)	21,000	Value: 0.50				
1975FM (U)	2,251	—	—	—	0.20	0.35
1976FM (M)	1,001	—	—	—	0.50	0.65
1976FM (P)	18,000	Value: 0.50				
1976FM (U)	1,066	—	—	—	0.20	0.35
1977FM (M)	1,171	—	—	—	0.50	0.65
1977FM (P)	5,986	Value: 0.50				
1977FM (U)	1,002	—	—	—	0.50	0.65
1979FM (M)	1,000	—	—	—	0.50	0.65
1979FM (P)	4,058	Value: 0.50				
1979FM (U)	500	—	—	—	1.00	1.25
1983	—	—	—	0.10	0.20	0.35
1983 Proof	10,000	Value: 0.50				

KM# 1a   CENT
Bronze **Ruler:** Elizabeth II **Obv:** Young bust right, date below
Rev: Taro leaf, denomination, 1728 • CAPT. JAMES COOK • 1978

Date	Mintage	F	VF	XF	Unc	BU
1978FM (M)	1,000	—	—	—	0.85	1.15
1978FM (P)	6,287	Value: 0.50				
1978FM (U)	767	—	—	—	0.75	1.00

KM# 1b CENT
Bronze **Ruler:** Elizabeth II **Subject:** Wedding of Prince Charles and Lady Diana **Obv:** Young bust right, THE ROYAL WEDDING 29 JULY 1981

Date	Mintage	F	VF	XF	Unc	BU
1981FM (M)	1,000	—	—	—	0.50	0.65
1981FM (P)	9,205	Value: 0.40				
1981FM (U)	1,100	—	—	—	0.50	0.65

KM# 2 2 CENTS
Bronze **Ruler:** Elizabeth II **Obv:** Young bust right, date below **Rev:** Pineapple, denomination at right

Date	Mintage	F	VF	XF	Unc	BU
1972	63,000	—	0.10	0.15	0.30	0.50
1972 Proof	17,000	Value: 0.75				
1973	8,500	—	0.15	0.20	0.40	0.60
1973 Proof	13,000	Value: 0.75				
1974	120,000	—	0.10	0.15	0.30	0.40
1974 Proof	7,300	Value: 0.75				
1975	129,000	—	0.10	0.15	0.25	0.45
1975FM (M)	1,000	—	—	—	0.50	0.75
1975FM (P)	21,000	Value: 0.75				
1975FM (U)	2,251	—	—	—	0.30	0.50
1976FM (M)	1,001	—	—	—	0.75	1.00
1976FM (P)	18,000	Value: 0.75				
1976FM (U)	1,066	—	—	—	0.30	0.50
1977FM (M)	1,171	—	—	—	0.75	1.00
1977FM (P)	5,986	Value: 0.75				
1977FM (U)	1,002	—	—	—	0.30	0.50
1979FM (M)	1,000	—	—	—	0.75	1.00
1979FM (P)	4,058	Value: 0.75				
1979FM (U)	500	—	—	—	0.30	0.50
1983	—	—	0.10	0.15	0.25	0.45
1983 Proof	10,000	Value: 0.75				

KM# 2a 2 CENTS
Bronze **Ruler:** Elizabeth II **Obv:** Young bust right **Rev:** Pineapple, denomination at right, 1728 • CAPT. JAMES COOK • 1978

Date	Mintage	F	VF	XF	Unc	BU
1978FM (M)	1,000	—	—	—	0.75	1.00
1978FM (P)	6,287	Value: 0.50				
1978FM (U)	767	—	—	—	0.85	1.15

KM# 2b 2 CENTS
Bronze **Ruler:** Elizabeth II **Subject:** Wedding of Prince Charles and Lady Diana **Obv:** Young bust right, date below, THE ROYAL WEDDING 29 JULY 1981

Date	Mintage	F	VF	XF	Unc	BU
1981FM (M)	1,000	—	—	—	0.75	1.00
1981FM (P)	9,205	Value: 0.50				
1981FM (U)	1,100	—	—	—	0.75	1.00

KM# 3 5 CENTS
Copper-Nickel, 19.41 mm. **Ruler:** Elizabeth II **Obv:** Young bust right, date below **Rev:** Hibiscus, denomination below

Date	Mintage	F	VF	XF	Unc	BU
1972	32,000	—	0.10	0.20	0.40	0.60
1972 Proof	17,000	Value: 1.00				
1973	8,500	—	0.15	0.25	0.50	0.75
1973 Proof	13,000	Value: 1.00				
1974	80,000	—	0.10	0.20	0.40	0.60
1974 Proof	7,300	Value: 1.00				
1975	89,000	—	0.10	0.20	0.40	0.60
1975FM (M)	1,000	—	—	—	1.00	1.25
1975FM (P)	21,000	Value: 0.85				
1975FM (U)	2,251	—	—	—	0.40	0.60
1976FM (M)	1,001	—	—	—	1.00	1.25
1976FM (P)	18,000	Value: 0.85				
1976FM (U)	1,066	—	—	—	0.40	0.60
1977FM (M)	1,171	—	—	—	1.00	1.25
1977FM (P)	5,986	Value: 1.00				
1977FM (U)	1,002	—	—	—	0.40	0.60
1979FM (M)	1,000	—	—	—	1.00	1.25
1979FM (P)	4,058	Value: 1.00				
1979FM (U)	500	—	—	—	0.40	0.60
1983	—	—	0.10	0.20	0.40	0.60
1983 Proof	10,000	Value: 1.00				

KM# 3a 5 CENTS
Copper-Nickel **Ruler:** Elizabeth II **Obv:** Young bust right, date below **Rev:** Hibiscus, denomination below, 1728 • CAPT. JAMES COOK • 1978

Date	Mintage	F	VF	XF	Unc	BU
1978FM (M)	1,000	—	—	—	1.00	1.25
1978FM (P)	6,287	Value: 0.50				
1978FM (U)	767	—	—	—	0.75	1.00

KM# 3b 5 CENTS
Copper-Nickel, 19.41 mm. **Ruler:** Elizabeth II **Subject:** Wedding of Prince Charles and Lady Diana **Obv:** Young bust right, date below, THE ROYAL WEDDING 29 JULY 1981

Date	Mintage	F	VF	XF	Unc	BU
1981FM (M)	1,000	—	—	—	1.00	1.25
1981FM (P)	9,205	Value: 0.50				
1981FM (U)	1,100	—	—	—	1.00	1.25

KM# 33 5 CENTS
Copper-Nickel, 19.41 mm. **Ruler:** Elizabeth II **Obv:** Crowned head right, date below **Rev:** Hibiscus

Date	Mintage	F	VF	XF	Unc	BU
1987	—	—	—	0.15	0.35	0.50
1987 Proof	—	Value: 1.00				
1988	—	—	—	0.15	0.35	0.50
1988 Proof	—	Value: 1.00				
1992	—	—	—	0.15	0.35	0.50
1992 Proof	—	Value: 1.00				
1994	20,000	—	—	0.15	0.35	0.50
1994 Proof	200	Value: 1.50				

KM# 369 5 CENTS
4.4300 g., Nickel Clad Steel, 24.05 mm. **Ruler:** Elizabeth II **Subject:** F.A.O. **Obv:** Head with tiara right, date below **Rev:** Statue of Tangaroa divides denomination **Edge:** Plain

Date	Mintage	F	VF	XF	Unc	BU
2000	—	—	—	—	1.00	1.50
2000 Proof	—	Value: 3.50				

KM# 4 10 CENTS
Copper-Nickel, 23.6 mm. **Ruler:** Elizabeth II **Obv:** Young bust right, date below **Rev:** Orange, denomination above

Date	Mintage	F	VF	XF	Unc	BU
1972	35,000	—	0.10	0.20	0.65	0.85
1972 Proof	17,000	Value: 1.25				
1973	59,000	—	0.10	0.20	0.65	0.85
1973 Proof	13,000	Value: 1.25				
1974	50,000	—	0.10	0.20	0.50	0.85
1974 Proof	7,300	Value: 1.25				
1975	59,000	—	0.10	0.20	0.50	0.85
1975FM (M)	1,000	—	—	—	1.25	1.50
1975FM (P)	21,000	Value: 1.25				
1975FM (U)	2,251	—	—	—	0.50	0.85
1976FM (M)	1,001	—	—	—	1.25	1.50
1976FM (P)	18,000	Value: 1.25				
1976FM (U)	1,066	—	—	—	0.50	0.65
1977FM (M)	1,171	—	—	—	1.25	1.50
1977FM (P)	5,986	Value: 1.25				
1977FM (U)	1,002	—	—	—	0.50	0.65
1983	—	—	0.10	0.20	0.50	0.65
1983 Proof	10,000	Value: 1.25				

KM# 4a 10 CENTS
Copper-Nickel, 23.6 mm. **Ruler:** Elizabeth II **Obv:** Young bust right, date below **Rev:** Orange, denomination above, 1728 • CAPT. JAMES COOK • 1978

Date	Mintage	F	VF	XF	Unc	BU
1978FM (M)	1,000	—	—	—	1.25	1.50
1978FM (P)	6,287	Value: 1.00				
1978FM (U)	767	—	—	—	1.25	1.50

KM# 4b 10 CENTS
Copper-Nickel, 23.6 mm. **Ruler:** Elizabeth II **Series:** F.A.O. **Obv:** Young bust right, date below **Rev:** Orange, denomination above

Date	Mintage	F	VF	XF	Unc	BU
1979FM (M)	9,000	—	—	—	1.00	1.25
1979FM (P)	4,058	Value: 1.25				
1979FM (U)	500	—	—	—	1.50	1.75

KM# 4c 10 CENTS
Copper-Nickel, 23.6 mm. **Ruler:** Elizabeth II **Subject:** Wedding of Prince Charles and Lady Diana **Obv:** Young bust right, date below, THE ROYAL WEDDING 29 JULY 1981

Date	Mintage	F	VF	XF	Unc	BU
1981FM (M)	1,000	—	—	—	1.25	1.50
1981FM (P)	9,205	Value: 0.75				
1981FM (U)	1,100	—	—	—	1.25	1.50

KM# 34 10 CENTS
5.6800 g., Copper-Nickel, 23.6 mm. **Ruler:** Elizabeth II **Obv:** Crowned head right, date below **Rev:** Orange, denomination above

Date	Mintage	F	VF	XF	Unc	BU
1987	—	—	—	0.20	0.50	0.75
1987 Proof	—	Value: 1.25				
1988	—	—	—	0.20	0.50	0.75
1988 Proof	—	Value: 1.25				
1992	—	—	—	0.20	0.50	0.75
1992 Proof	—	Value: 1.25				
1994	20,000	—	—	0.20	0.50	0.75
1994 Proof	200	Value: 1.75				

KM# 5 20 CENTS
Copper-Nickel, 28.52 mm. **Ruler:** Elizabeth II **Obv:** Young bust right, date below **Rev:** Fairy Tern right, denomination below

Date	Mintage	F	VF	XF	Unc	BU
1972	31,000	—	0.20	0.40	0.75	1.00
1972 Proof	17,000	Value: 1.50				
1973	49,000	—	0.20	0.40	0.75	1.00
1973 Proof	13,000	Value: 1.50				
1974	5,500	—	0.20	0.45	0.75	1.25
1974 Proof	7,300	Value: 1.50				
1975	60,000	—	0.20	0.40	0.75	1.00
1975FM (M)	1,000	—	—	—	1.50	1.75
1975FM (P)	21,000	Value: 1.50				
1975FM (U)	2,251	—	—	—	0.85	1.25
1983	—	—	0.20	0.40	0.85	1.25
1983 Proof	10,000	Value: 1.50				

KM# 14 20 CENTS
Copper-Nickel, 28.52 mm. **Ruler:** Elizabeth II **Obv:** Young bust right, date below **Rev:** Two Pacific Triton shells, denomination lower right

Date	Mintage	F	VF	XF	Unc	BU
1976FM (M)	1,001	—	—	—	1.50	1.75
1976FM (P)	18,000	Value: 1.50				
1976FM (U)	1,066	—	—	—	1.00	1.25
1977FM (M)	1,171	—	—	—	1.50	1.75
1977FM (P)	5,986	Value: 1.50				
1977FM (U)	1,002	—	—	—	1.00	1.25
1979FM (M)	1,000	—	—	—	1.50	1.75
1979FM (P)	4,058	Value: 1.50				
1979FM (U)	500	—	—	—	2.00	1.50

KM# 14a 20 CENTS
Copper-Nickel, 28.52 mm. **Ruler:** Elizabeth II **Obv:** Young bust right, date below **Rev:** Shells, denomination at right, 1728 • CAPT. JAMES COOK • 1978

Date	Mintage	F	VF	XF	Unc	BU
1978FM (M)	1,000	—	—	—	1.50	1.75
1978FM (P)	6,287	Value: 1.50				
1978FM (U)	767	—	—	—	2.00	2.50

KM# 14b 20 CENTS
Copper-Nickel, 28.52 mm. **Ruler:** Elizabeth II **Subject:** Wedding of Prince Charles and Lady Diana **Obv:** Young bust right, date below **Rev:** Shells, denomination at right, THE ROYAL WEDDING 29 JULY 1981

Date	Mintage	F	VF	XF	Unc	BU
1981FM (M)	1,000	—	—	—	1.50	1.75
1981FM (P)	9,205	Value: 1.00				
1981FM (U)	1,100	—	—	—	1.50	1.75

KM# 35 20 CENTS
11.3100 g., Copper-Nickel, 28.52 mm. **Ruler:** Elizabeth II
Obv: Crowned head right, date below **Rev:** Fairy Tern,
denomination below

Date	Mintage	F	VF	XF	Unc	BU
1987	—	—	—	0.25	0.75	1.00
1987 Proof	—	Value: 1.50				
1988	—	—	—	0.25	0.75	1.00
1988 Proof	—	Value: 1.50				
1992	—	—	—	0.25	0.75	1.00
1992 Proof	—	Value: 1.50				
1994	20,000	—	—	0.25	0.75	1.00
1994 Proof	200	Value: 2.00				

KM# 6.1 50 CENTS
Copper-Nickel, 31.75 mm. **Ruler:** Elizabeth II **Obv:** Young bust
right, date below **Rev:** Bonito fish, denomination upper left

Date	Mintage	F	VF	XF	Unc	BU
1972	31,000	—	—	0.65	1.25	2.00
1972 Proof	17,000	Value: 3.00				
1973	19,000	—	—	0.65	1.25	2.00
1973 Proof	13,000	Value: 3.00				
1974	10,000	—	—	0.65	1.25	2.00
1974 Proof	7,300	Value: 3.00				
1975	19,000	—	—	0.65	1.25	2.00
1975FM (M)	1,000	—	—	—	2.00	3.00
1975FM (P)	21,000	Value: 2.50				
1975FM (U)	2,251	—	—	—	1.50	2.00
1976FM (M)	1,001	—	—	—	2.00	3.00
1976FM (P)	18,000	Value: 2.50				
1976FM (U)	1,066	—	—	—	1.50	2.00
1977FM (M)	1,171	—	—	—	2.00	3.00
1977FM (P)	5,986	Value: 3.00				
1977FM (U)	1,002	—	—	—	1.50	2.00
1983	—	—	—	0.65	1.25	2.00
1983 Proof	10,000	Value: 3.50				

KM# 6.2 50 CENTS
Copper-Nickel, 31.75 mm. **Ruler:** Elizabeth II **Obv:** Young bust
right, date below, 1728 • CAPT. JAMES COOK • 1978

Date	Mintage	F	VF	XF	Unc	BU
1978FM (M)	1,000	—	—	—	2.00	3.00
1978FM (P)	6,287	Value: 2.00				
1978FM (U)	767	—	—	—	2.00	3.00

KM# 6.3 50 CENTS
Copper-Nickel, 31.75 mm. **Ruler:** Elizabeth II **Series:** F.A.O.
Obv: Young bust right, date below **Rev:** F.A.O. logo, Bonito fish,
denomination upper left

Date	Mintage	F	VF	XF	Unc	BU
1979FM (M)	9,000	—	—	0.75	1.25	2.00
1979FM (P)	4,058	Value: 2.25				
1979FM (U)	500	—	—	—	2.50	3.50

KM# 6.4 50 CENTS
Copper-Nickel, 31.75 mm. **Ruler:** Elizabeth II **Subject:**
Wedding of Prince Charles and Lady Diana **Obv:** Young bust
right, date below, THE ROYAL WEDDING 29 JULY 1981

Date	Mintage	F	VF	XF	Unc	BU
1981FM (M)	1,000	—	—	—	2.00	3.00
1981FM (P)	9,205	Value: 1.50				
1981FM (U)	1,100	—	—	—	2.00	3.00

KM# 36 50 CENTS
13.5400 g., Copper-Nickel, 31.75 mm. **Ruler:** Elizabeth II
Obv: Crowned head right, date below **Rev:** Bonito fish,
denomination upper left

Date	Mintage	F	VF	XF	Unc	BU
1987	—	—	—	0.65	1.50	2.00
1987 Proof	—	Value: 2.00				
1992	—	—	—	0.65	1.50	2.00

KM# 307 50 CENTS
Copper-Nickel **Ruler:** Elizabeth II **Obv:** Crowned head right,
date below **Rev:** Head 3/4 facing, dates and denomination below

Date	Mintage	F	VF	XF	Unc	BU
1997	—	—	—	—	6.00	
1997 Proof	—	—	Value: 8.50			

KM# 338 50 CENTS
26.9000 g., Copper-Nickel **Ruler:** Elizabeth II **Obv:** Crowned
head right, date below **Rev:** Multicolor cartoon cat "Garfield",
denomination below **Edge:** Reeded

Date	Mintage	F	VF	XF	Unc	BU
1999 Proof	—	Value: 7.50				

KM# 7 DOLLAR
27.2000 g., Copper-Nickel, 38.5 mm. **Ruler:** Elizabeth II
Obv: Young bust right, date below **Rev:** Tangaroa, Polynesian
God of Creation, divides denominations

Date	Mintage	F	VF	XF	Unc	BU
1972	31,000	—	1.00	1.50	2.50	4.00
1972 Proof	27,000	Value: 4.00				
1973	49,000	—	1.00	1.50	2.50	4.00
1973 Proof	13,000	Value: 6.00				
1974	20,000	—	1.00	1.50	2.50	4.00
1974 Proof	7,300	Value: 6.00				
1975	29,000	—	1.00	1.50	2.50	4.00
1975FM (M)	1,000	—	—	—	4.50	6.00
1975FM (P)	21,000	Value: 6.00				
1975FM (U)	2,251	—	—	—	3.50	5.00
1976FM (M)	1,001	—	—	—	4.50	6.00
1976FM (P)	18,000	Value: 5.00				
1976FM (U)	1,066	—	—	—	4.50	6.00
1977FM (M)	1,171	—	—	—	4.50	6.00
1977FM (P)	5,986	Value: 6.50				
1977FM (U)	1,002	—	—	—	4.50	6.00
1979FM (M)	1,000	—	—	—	4.50	6.00
1979FM (P)	4,058	Value: 6.50				
1979FM (U)	500	—	—	—	5.50	7.00
1983	—	—	1.00	1.50	3.50	5.00
1983 Proof	10,000	Value: 5.00				

KM# 7a DOLLAR
27.2000 g., Copper-Nickel, 38.5 mm. **Ruler:** Elizabeth II
Obv: Young bust right, date below **Rev:** Tangaroa, Polynesian
God of Creation, divides denominations, 1728 • CAPT. JAMES
COOK • 1978

Date	Mintage	F	VF	XF	Unc	BU
1978FM (M)	1,000	—	—	—	6.00	7.50
1978FM (P)	6,287	Value: 5.50				
1978FM (U)	767	—	—	—	6.00	7.50

KM# 7b DOLLAR
27.2000 g., Copper-Nickel, 38.5 mm. **Ruler:** Elizabeth II
Subject: Wedding of Prince Charles and Lady Diana **Obv:** Young
bust right, date below **Rev:** Tangaroa, Polynesian God of Creation,
divides denominations, THE ROYAL WEDDING 29 JULY 1981

Date	Mintage	F	VF	XF	Unc	BU
1981FM (M)	1,000	—	—	—	5.00	6.50
1981FM (P)	9,205	Value: 5.00				
1981FM (U)	1,100	—	—	—	5.00	6.50

KM# 30 DOLLAR
27.2000 g., Copper-Nickel, 38.5 mm. **Ruler:** Elizabeth II
Subject: 16th Forum, 2nd P.I.C. and Mini Games **Obv:** Young bust
right, date below **Rev:** Tangaroa, Polynesian God of Creation

Date	Mintage	F	VF	XF	Unc	BU
1985	—	—	—	—	3.50	5.00

KM# 30a DOLLAR
27.2200 g., 0.9250 Silver 0.8095 oz. ASW, 38.5 mm.
Ruler: Elizabeth II **Subject:** 16th Forum, 2nd P.I.C. and Mini
Games **Obv:** Young bust right, date below **Rev:** Tangaroa,
Polynesian God of Creation

Date	Mintage	F	VF	XF	Unc	BU
1985 Proof	Est. 2,500	Value: 16.50				

KM# 41 50 TENE
13.6000 g., Copper-Nickel, 31.75 mm. **Ruler:** Elizabeth II
Obv: Crowned head right, date below **Rev:** Hawksbill turtle right,
denomination above

Date	Mintage	F	VF	XF	Unc	BU
1988	60,000	—	—	0.50	2.00	3.50
1988 Proof	1,000	Value: 3.50				
1992	—	—	—	—	2.00	3.50
1992 Proof	—	Value: 3.50				
1994	20,000	—	—	—	2.00	3.50
1994 Proof	200	Value: 4.00				

KM# 30b DOLLAR
39.8000 g., 0.9170 Gold 1.1733 oz. AGW, 38.5 mm.
Ruler: Elizabeth II **Subject:** 16th Forum, 2nd P.I.C. and Mini Games **Obv:** Young bust right, date below **Rev:** Tangaroa, Polynesian God of Creation

Date	Mintage	F	VF	XF	Unc	BU
1985 Proof	Est. 25				Value: 1,750	

KM# 31 DOLLAR
27.2000 g., Copper-Nickel, 38.5 mm. **Ruler:** Elizabeth II **Subject:** 60th Birthday of Queen Elizabeth II **Obv:** Crowned bust right, date below **Rev:** Cameos of family members in circle

Date	Mintage	F	VF	XF	Unc	BU
1986	20,000				2.75	3.50

KM# 32 DOLLAR
27.2000 g., Copper-Nickel, 38.5 mm. **Ruler:** Elizabeth II **Subject:** Prince Andrew's Wedding **Obv:** Crowned head right, date below **Rev:** Busts of Andrew and Sarah facing each other within wreath

Date	Mintage	F	VF	XF	Unc	BU
1986	Est. 20,000				2.75	3.50

KM# 31a DOLLAR
27.2200 g., 0.9250 Silver 0.8095 oz. ASW, 38.5 mm.
Ruler: Elizabeth II **Subject:** 60th Birthday of Queen Elizabeth II **Obv:** Crowned bust right, date below **Rev:** Busts of Andrew and Sarah facing each other within wreath

Date	Mintage	F	VF	XF	Unc	BU
1986 Proof	Est. 2,500				Value: 16.50	

KM# 32a DOLLAR
27.2200 g., 0.9250 Silver 0.8095 oz. ASW, 38.5 mm.
Ruler: Elizabeth II **Subject:** Prince Andrews Wedding **Obv:** Crowned bust right, date below **Rev:** Busts of Andrew and Sarah facing each other within wreath

Date	Mintage	F	VF	XF	Unc	BU
1986 Proof	Est. 2,500				Value: 16.50	

KM# 31b DOLLAR
44.0000 g., 0.9170 Gold 1.2972 oz. AGW, 38.5 mm.
Ruler: Elizabeth II **Subject:** 60th Birthday of Queen Elizabeth II **Obv:** Crowned bust right, date below **Rev:** Busts of Andrew and Sarah facing each other within wreath

Date	Mintage	F	VF	XF	Unc	BU
1986 Proof	Est. 60				Value: 1,250	

KM# 32b DOLLAR
44.0000 g., 0.9170 Gold 1.2972 oz. AGW, 38.5 mm.
Ruler: Elizabeth II **Subject:** Prince Andrews Wedding **Obv:** Crowned bust right, date below **Rev:** Busts of Andrew and Sarah facing each other within wreath

Date	Mintage	F	VF	XF	Unc	BU
1986 Proof	Est. 75				Value: 1,250	

KM# 37 DOLLAR
Copper-Nickel, 28.52 mm. **Ruler:** Elizabeth II **Obv:** Crowned head right, date below **Rev:** Tangaroa statue divides denominations

Date	Mintage	F	VF	XF	Unc	BU
1987	—	—	—	1.00	2.50	3.50
1987 Proof	—	Value: 4.50				
1988	—	—	—	1.00	2.50	3.50
1988 Proof	—	Value: 4.50				
1992	—	—	—	1.00	2.50	3.50
1992 Proof	—	Value: 4.50				
1994	20,000	—	—	1.00	2.50	3.50
1994 Proof	200	Value: 5.50				

KM# 147 DOLLAR
27.2000 g., Copper-Nickel, 38.5 mm. **Ruler:** Elizabeth II **Obv:** Crowned head right, date below **Rev:** Tangaroa, Polynesian God of Fertility

Date	Mintage	F	VF	XF	Unc	BU
1992	—	—	—	—	2.75	

KM# 266 DOLLAR
27.2000 g., Copper-Nickel, 38.5 mm. **Ruler:** Elizabeth II **Obv:** Crowned head right, date below **Rev:** Queen Mother and daughters within circle, denomination below

Date	Mintage	F	VF	XF	Unc	BU
1995 Proof	Est. 30,000				Value: 3.00	

KM# 267 DOLLAR
10.0000 g., 0.5000 Silver 0.1607 oz. ASW **Ruler:** Elizabeth II **Subject:** 1996 Summer Olympics **Obv:** Crowned head right, date below **Rev:** Horse jumping left within circle, denomination below

Date	Mintage	F	VF	XF	Unc	BU
1996 Proof	Est. 10,000				Value: 4.50	

KM# 326 DOLLAR
31.1035 g., 0.9990 Silver 0.9990 oz. ASW **Ruler:** Elizabeth II **Subject:** Lunar Year of the Mouse **Obv:** Crowned head right, date below **Rev:** Mouse in basket

Date	Mintage	F	VF	XF	Unc	BU
1996 Proof	—				Value: 20.00	

KM# 327 DOLLAR
31.1035 g., 0.9990 Silver 0.9990 oz. ASW **Ruler:** Elizabeth II **Obv:** Crowned head right, date below **Rev:** Multicolor carnation

Date	Mintage	F	VF	XF	Unc	BU
1996 Proof	—				Value: 22.00	

KM# 268 DOLLAR
Copper-Nickel **Ruler:** Elizabeth II **Obv:** Crowned head right, date below **Rev:** Sir Francis Drake left and sailing ship right, denomination below

Date	Mintage	F	VF	XF	Unc	BU
1996 Proof	Est. 25,000				Value: 3.00	

KM# 277 DOLLAR
Copper-Nickel **Ruler:** Elizabeth II **Subject:** Yellowstone National Park **Obv:** Crowned head right, date below **Rev:** Multi-colored Grizzly Bear and cub

Date	Mintage	F	VF	XF	Unc	BU
1996	—	—	—	—	5.50	7.00

KM# 278 DOLLAR
Copper-Nickel **Ruler:** Elizabeth II **Subject:** Olympic National Park **Obv:** Crowned head right, date below **Rev:** Multicolor Bald Eagle in flight

Date	Mintage	F	VF	XF	Unc	BU
1996	—	—	—	—	5.50	7.00

KM# 341 DOLLAR
Copper-Nickel **Ruler:** Elizabeth II **Subject:** Endangered Wildlife **Obv:** Crowned head right, date below **Rev:** Senegalese lion, denomination below

Date	Mintage	F	VF	XF	Unc	BU
1996	—	—	—	—	12.00	14.00

KM# 311 DOLLAR
9.9700 g., 0.5000 Silver 0.1603 oz. ASW **Ruler:** Elizabeth II
Subject: Endangered Wildlife **Obv:** Crowned head right, date
below **Rev:** Mother elephant with calf, denomination below

Date	Mintage	F	VF	XF	Unc	BU
1996 Proof	—	Value: 12.00				

KM# 342 DOLLAR
28.4300 g., Copper-Nickel, 38.68 mm. **Ruler:** Elizabeth II
Subject: Endangered Wildlife **Obv:** Crowned head right
Rev: European otters **Edge:** Reeded

Date	Mintage	F	VF	XF	Unc	BU
1996	—	—	—	—	12.00	14.00

KM# 343 DOLLAR
28.4300 g., Copper-Nickel, 38.68 mm. **Ruler:** Elizabeth II
Subject: Endangered Wildlife **Obv:** Crowned head right
Rev: Jackass penguins **Edge:** Reeded

Date	Mintage	F	VF	XF	Unc	BU
1996	—	—	—	—	12.00	14.00

KM# 344 DOLLAR
28.4300 g., Copper-Nickel, 38.68 mm. **Ruler:** Elizabeth II
Subject: Endangered Wildlife **Obv:** Crowned head right
Rev: Fallow deer **Edge:** Reeded

Date	Mintage	F	VF	XF	Unc	BU
1996	—	—	—	—	12.00	14.00

KM# 345 DOLLAR
28.4300 g., Copper-Nickel, 38.68 mm. **Ruler:** Elizabeth II
Subject: Endangered Wildlife **Obv:** Crowned head right
Rev: Heaviside's dolphins **Edge:** Reeded

Date	Mintage	F	VF	XF	Unc	BU
1996	—	—	—	—	12.00	14.00

KM# 346 DOLLAR
28.4300 g., Copper-Nickel, 38.68 mm. **Ruler:** Elizabeth II
Subject: Endangered Wildlife **Obv:** Crowned head right
Rev: Cougar and cub **Edge:** Reeded

Date	Mintage	F	VF	XF	Unc	BU
1996	—	—	—	—	12.00	14.00

KM# 347 DOLLAR
28.4300 g., Copper-Nickel, 38.68 mm. **Ruler:** Elizabeth II
Subject: Endangered Wildlife **Obv:** Crowned head right
Rev: Lowland gorilla **Edge:** Reeded

Date	Mintage	F	VF	XF	Unc	BU
1996	—	—	—	—	12.00	14.00

KM# 348 DOLLAR
28.4300 g., Copper-Nickel, 38.68 mm. **Ruler:** Elizabeth II
Subject: Endangered Wildlife **Obv:** Crowned head right
Rev: Peregrine falcon **Edge:** Reeded

Date	Mintage	F	VF	XF	Unc	BU
1996	—	—	—	—	12.00	14.00

KM# 349 DOLLAR
28.4300 g., Copper-Nickel, 38.68 mm. **Ruler:** Elizabeth II
Subject: Endangered Wildlife **Obv:** Crowned head right
Rev: Kangaroo **Edge:** Reeded

Date	Mintage	F	VF	XF	Unc	BU
1996	—	—	—	—	12.00	14.00

KM# 350 DOLLAR
28.4300 g., Copper-Nickel, 38.68 mm. **Ruler:** Elizabeth II
Subject: Endangered Wildlife **Obv:** Crowned head right
Rev: Bee hummingbird **Edge:** Reeded

Date	Mintage	F	VF	XF	Unc	BU
1996	—	—	—	—	12.00	14.00

KM# 351 DOLLAR
28.4300 g., Copper-Nickel, 38.68 mm. **Ruler:** Elizabeth II
Subject: Endangered Wildlife **Obv:** Crowned head right
Rev: Butterfly and thistle **Edge:** Reeded

Date	Mintage	F	VF	XF	Unc	BU
1996	—	—	—	—	12.00	14.00

KM# 352 DOLLAR
28.4300 g., Copper-Nickel, 38.68 mm. **Ruler:** Elizabeth II
Subject: Endangered Wildlife **Obv:** Crowned head right
Rev: Ring-tailed lemurs **Edge:** Reeded

Date	Mintage	F	VF	XF	Unc	BU
1996	—	—	—	—	12.00	14.00

KM# 353 DOLLAR
28.4300 g., Copper-Nickel, 38.68 mm. **Ruler:** Elizabeth II
Subject: Endangered Wildlife **Obv:** Crowned head right
Rev: Szechuan takins **Edge:** Reeded

Date	Mintage	F	VF	XF	Unc	BU
1996	—	—	—	—	12.00	14.00

KM# 354 DOLLAR
28.4300 g., Copper-Nickel, 38.68 mm. **Ruler:** Elizabeth II
Subject: Endangered Wildlife **Obv:** Crowned head right
Rev: Eagle owl **Edge:** Reeded

Date	Mintage	F	VF	XF	Unc	BU
1996	—	—	—	—	12.00	14.00

KM# 355 DOLLAR
28.4300 g., Copper-Nickel, 38.68 mm. **Ruler:** Elizabeth II
Subject: Endangered Wildlife **Obv:** Crowned head right
Rev: White-tailed deer **Edge:** Reeded

Date	Mintage	F	VF	XF	Unc	BU
1996	—	—	—	—	12.00	14.00

KM# 356 DOLLAR
28.4300 g., Copper-Nickel, 38.68 mm. **Ruler:** Elizabeth II
Subject: Endangered Wildlife **Obv:** Crowned head right
Rev: Drill monkey **Edge:** Reeded

Date	Mintage	F	VF	XF	Unc	BU
1996	—	—	—	—	12.00	14.00

KM# 387 DOLLAR
28.4300 g., Copper-Nickel, 38.68 mm. **Ruler:** Elizabeth II
Subject: Endangered Wildlife **Obv:** Crowned head right
Rev: Alpine Ibex on mountain **Edge:** Reeded

Date	Mintage	F	VF	XF	Unc	BU
1996	—	—	—	—	12.00	14.00

KM# 308.1 DOLLAR
31.4600 g., 0.9990 Silver 1.0104 oz. ASW **Ruler:** Elizabeth II
Obv: Crowned head right, date below **Rev:** Princess Diana's
portrait, dates **Note:** Polished fields with matte portraits.

Date	Mintage	F	VF	XF	Unc	BU
1997 Proof	—	Value: 22.50				

KM# 308.2 DOLLAR
34.4600 g., 0.9990 Silver 1.1068 oz. ASW **Ruler:** Elizabeth II
Obv: Crowned head right, date below **Rev:** Princess Diana's bust
facing, dates **Note:** Matte fields with polished portraits.

Date	Mintage	F	VF	XF	Unc	BU
1997 Matte Proof	—	Value: 22.50				

KM# 314 DOLLAR
31.6350 g., 0.9990 Silver 1.0160 oz. ASW **Ruler:** Elizabeth II
Subject: Australian Fauna **Obv:** Crowned head right, date below
Rev: Multicolor ring-tailed gecko, in beaded circle, denomination
lower right

Date	Mintage	F	VF	XF	Unc	BU
1998 Proof	Est. 4,000	Value: 45.00				

KM# 315 DOLLAR
31.6350 g., 0.9990 Silver 1.0160 oz. ASW **Ruler:** Elizabeth II
Subject: Australian Fauna **Obv:** Crowned head right, date below
Rev: Multicolor bilby (mouse)

Date	Mintage	F	VF	XF	Unc	BU
1998 Proof	Est. 4,000	Value: 30.00				

KM# 316 DOLLAR
31.6350 g., 0.9990 Silver 1.0160 oz. ASW **Ruler:** Elizabeth II
Subject: Australian Fauna **Obv:** Crowned head right, date below
Rev: Multicolor platypus

Date	Mintage	F	VF	XF	Unc	BU
1998 Proof	Est. 4,000	Value: 35.00				

KM# 317 DOLLAR
31.6350 g., 0.9990 Silver 1.0160 oz. ASW **Ruler:** Elizabeth II
Subject: Australian Fauna **Obv:** Crowned head right, date below
Rev: Multicolor ghost bat

Date	Mintage	F	VF	XF	Unc	BU
1998 Proof	Est. 4,000	Value: 45.00				

KM# 318 DOLLAR
31.6350 g., 0.9990 Silver 1.0160 oz. ASW **Ruler:** Elizabeth II
Subject: Australian Fauna **Obv:** Crowned head right, date below
Rev: Multicolor hatback turtle

Date	Mintage	F	VF	XF	Unc	BU
1998 Proof	Est. 4,000	Value: 45.00				

KM# 361   DOLLAR
31.6800 g., 0.9990 Silver 1.0175 oz. ASW **Ruler:** Elizabeth II
Subject: Tropical Fish **Obv:** Crowned head right, date below
Rev: Multicolored lemonpeel angelfish **Edge:** Reeded

Date	Mintage	F	VF	XF	Unc	BU
1999 Proof	—	Value: 30.00				

KM# 365   DOLLAR
31.6800 g., 0.9990 Silver 1.0175 oz. ASW **Ruler:** Elizabeth II
Subject: Tropical Fish **Obv:** Crowned head right, date below
Rev: Multicolor clown fish on anemone **Edge:** Reeded

Date	Mintage	F	VF	XF	Unc	BU
1999 Proof	—	Value: 30.00				

KM# 362   DOLLAR
31.6800 g., 0.9990 Silver 1.0175 oz. ASW **Ruler:** Elizabeth II
Subject: Tropical Fish **Obv:** Crowned head right, date below
Rev: Multicolor clown triggerfish **Edge:** Reeded

Date	Mintage	F	VF	XF	Unc	BU
1999 Proof	—	Value: 30.00				

KM# 363   DOLLAR
31.6800 g., 0.9990 Silver 1.0175 oz. ASW **Ruler:** Elizabeth II
Subject: Tropical Fish **Obv:** Crowned head right, date below
Rev: Multicolor regal angelfish **Edge:** Reeded

Date	Mintage	F	VF	XF	Unc	BU
1999 Proof	—	Value: 30.00				

KM# 364   DOLLAR
Center Weight: 31.6800 g. **Center:** 0.9990 Silver 1.0175 oz. ASW
Ruler: Elizabeth II **Subject:** Tropical Fish **Obv:** Crowned head right,
date below **Rev:** Multicolor serpent starfish **Edge:** Reeded

Date	Mintage	F	VF	XF	Unc	BU
1999 Proof	—	Value: 35.00				

KM# 380   DOLLAR
28.2800 g., 0.9250 Silver 0.8410 oz. ASW, 38.6 mm.
Ruler: Elizabeth II **Subject:** Queen's Golden Jubilee
Obv: Crowned head right, date below **Rev:** Flags over roof tops,
denomination below **Edge:** Reeded

Date	Mintage	F	VF	XF	Unc	BU
2000 Proof	15,000	Value: 18.00				

KM# 437   DOLLAR
31.8000 g., 0.9990 Silver 1.0213 oz. ASW, 40.5 mm.
Ruler: Elizabeth II **Obv:** Crowned head right, date below
Rev: Queen Mother multicolor portrait **Edge:** Reeded

Date	Mintage	F	VF	XF	Unc	BU
2000 Proof	19,500	Value: 22.00				

KM# 8   2 DOLLARS
25.7000 g., 0.9250 Silver 0.7643 oz. ASW **Ruler:** Elizabeth II
Subject: 20th Anniversary of Coronation **Obv:** Young bust right,
date below

Date	Mintage	F	VF	XF	Unc	BU
1973	16,000	—	—	—	16.50	—
1973 Proof	46,000	Value: 17.50				

KM# 38   2 DOLLARS
Copper-Nickel, 28.52 mm. **Ruler:** Elizabeth II **Obv:** Crowned
head right, date below **Rev:** Kumete table, morter and pestle from
Atiu Island, denomination above

Date	Mintage	F	VF	XF	Unc	BU
1987	—	—	—	2.25	3.50	5.00
1987 Proof	—	Value: 6.00				
1988	—	—	—	2.25	3.50	5.00
1988 Proof	—	Value: 6.00				
1992	—	—	—	2.25	3.25	4.50
1992 Proof	—	Value: 6.00				
1994	20,000	—	—	2.25	3.25	4.50
1994 Proof	200	Value: 6.50				

KM# 279   2 DOLLARS
10.0000 g., 0.5000 Silver 0.1607 oz. ASW **Ruler:** Elizabeth II
Subject: Yellowstone National Park **Obv:** Crowned head right,
date below **Rev:** Grizzly bears, denomination below

Date	Mintage	F	VF	XF	Unc	BU
1996 Proof	—	Value: 12.00				

KM# 280   2 DOLLARS
10.0000 g., 0.5000 Silver 0.1607 oz. ASW **Ruler:** Elizabeth II
Subject: Olympic National Park **Obv:** Crowned head right, date
below **Rev:** Eagle flying in the mountain tops

Date	Mintage	F	VF	XF	Unc	BU
1996 Proof	—	Value: 12.00				

KM# 328   2 DOLLARS
10.0000 g., 0.5000 Silver 0.1607 oz. ASW **Ruler:** Elizabeth II
Subject: Petrified Forest National Park **Obv:** Crowned head right,
date below **Rev:** Pronghorn antelope

Date	Mintage	F	VF	XF	Unc	BU
1997 Proof	—					
1998 Proof	—	Value: 12.00				

KM# 329   2 DOLLARS
10.0000 g., 0.5000 Silver 0.1607 oz. ASW **Ruler:** Elizabeth II
Subject: Crater Lake National Park **Obv:** Crowned head right,
date below **Rev:** White-tailed deer

Date	Mintage	F	VF	XF	Unc	BU
1997 Proof	—					
1998 Proof	—	Value: 12.00				

KM# 376   2 DOLLARS
15.8400 g., 0.9990 Silver 0.5087 oz. ASW, 28.3 mm.
Ruler: Elizabeth II **Subject:** British Queen Mother **Obv:** Crowned
head right, date below **Rev:** Queen Mother and daughters, circa
1936 within circle, denomination below **Edge:** Reeded

Date	Mintage	F	VF	XF	Unc	BU
1997 Proof	—	Value: 10.00				

KM# 371   2 DOLLARS
10.0000 g., 0.5000 Silver 0.1607 oz. ASW, 30 mm.
Ruler: Elizabeth II **Subject:** Great Smoky Mountains National
Park **Obv:** Crowned head right, date below **Rev:** Red wolf and
two cubs **Edge:** Reeded

Date	Mintage	F	VF	XF	Unc	BU
1997 Proof	—				Value: 12.00	

KM# 372   2 DOLLARS
10.0000 g., 0.5000 Silver 0.1607 oz. ASW, 30 mm.
Ruler: Elizabeth II **Subject:** Theodore Roosevelt National Park
Obv: Crowned head right, date below **Rev:** Bison, denomination
below **Edge:** Reeded

Date	Mintage	F	VF	XF	Unc	BU
1997 Proof	—				Value: 12.00	

KM# 373   2 DOLLARS
10.0000 g., 0.5000 Silver 0.1607 oz. ASW, 30 mm.
Ruler: Elizabeth II **Subject:** Yosemite National Park
Obv: Crowned head right, date below **Rev:** Peregrine falcon
Edge: Reeded

Date	Mintage	F	VF	XF	Unc	BU
1997 Proof	—				Value: 10.00	

KM# 436   2 DOLLARS
20.4000 g., 0.5000 Silver 0.3279 oz. ASW, 33.9 mm.
Ruler: Elizabeth II **Obv:** Crowned head right, date below
Rev: Queen Mother and daughters circa 1980 **Edge:** Reeded

Date	Mintage	F	VF	XF	Unc	BU
1997 Proof	—				Value: 7.50	

KM# 374   2 DOLLARS
10.0000 g., 0.5000 Silver 0.1607 oz. ASW, 30 mm.
Ruler: Elizabeth II **Subject:** North Cascades National Park
Obv: Crowned head right, date below **Rev:** Spotted owl,
denomination below **Edge:** Reeded

Date	Mintage	F	VF	XF	Unc	BU
1998 Proof	—				Value: 12.00	

KM# 321   2 DOLLARS
42.4139 g., 0.9250 Silver 1.2613 oz. ASW **Ruler:** Elizabeth II
Obv: Crowned head right, date below **Rev:** Cook Islands
attractions and features, denomination at right

Date	Mintage	F	VF	XF	Unc	BU
1998 Proof	Est. 20,000				Value: 28.00	

Note: This coin is part of a tri-national, three coin matching
set with Fiji and Western Samoa

KM# 339   2 DOLLARS
31.1035 g., 0.9990 Silver 0.9990 oz. ASW **Ruler:** Elizabeth II
Obv: Crowned head right, date below **Rev:** Multicolor cartoon
cat, Garfield, flipping coin **Edge:** Reeded

Date	Mintage	F	VF	XF	Unc	BU
1999 Proof	—				Value: 18.50	

KM# 340   2 DOLLARS
31.1035 g., 0.9990 Silver 0.9990 oz. ASW **Ruler:** Elizabeth II
Obv: Crowned head right, date below **Rev:** Multicolor cartoon
cat, Garfield, tricking Odie **Edge:** Reeded

Date	Mintage	F	VF	XF	Unc	BU
1999 Proof	—				Value: 18.50	

KM# 9   2-1/2 DOLLARS
27.3500 g., 0.9250 Silver 0.8133 oz. ASW **Ruler:** Elizabeth II
Subject: Captain James Cook's 2nd Pacific Voyage **Obv:** Young
bust right, date below **Rev:** H.M.S. Resolution and H.M.S.
Adventure above world globe

Date	Mintage	F	VF	XF	Unc	BU
1973	6,000	—	—	—	17.00	—
1973 Proof	12,000		Value: 16.00			
1974	2,000	—	—	—	20.00	—
1974 Proof	12,000		Value: 16.00			

KM# 15   5 DOLLARS
27.3000 g., 0.5000 Silver 0.4388 oz. ASW **Ruler:** Elizabeth II
Subject: Wildlife Conservation **Obv:** Young bust right, date below
Rev: Mangara kingfisher, denomination below

Date	Mintage	F	VF	XF	Unc	BU
1976FM (M)	251	—	—	—	22.50	—
1976FM (P)	28,000		Value: 9.00			
1976FM (U)	2,192	—	—	—	15.00	—

KM# 17   5 DOLLARS
27.3000 g., 0.5000 Silver 0.4388 oz. ASW **Ruler:** Elizabeth II
Obv: Young bust right, date below **Rev:** Atiu swiftlet,
denomination below, Wildlife Conservation

Date	Mintage	F	VF	XF	Unc	BU
1977FM (M)	252	—	—	—	30.00	—
1977FM (P)	11,000		Value: 12.00			
1977FM (U)	4,032	—	—	—	15.00	—

KM# 20   5 DOLLARS
27.3000 g., 0.5000 Silver 0.4388 oz. ASW **Ruler:** Elizabeth II
Subject: Wildlife Conservation **Obv:** Young bust right, date below
Rev: Polynesian warblers by nest in branches, denomination
below, 1728 • CAPT. JAMES COOK • 1978

Date	Mintage	F	VF	XF	Unc	BU
1978FM (M)	250	—	—	—	20.00	—
1978FM (P)	11,000		Value: 12.00			
1978FM (U)	3,659	—	—	—	12.50	—

KM# 24   5 DOLLARS
27.3000 g., 0.5000 Silver 0.4388 oz. ASW **Ruler:** Elizabeth II
Subject: Wildlife Conservation **Obv:** Young bust right, date below
Rev: Rarotongan fruit doves on branch, denomination below

Date	Mintage	F	VF	XF	Unc	BU
1979FM (P)	8,612		Value: 10.00			
1979FM (U)	2,500	—	—	—	22.00	—

KM# 39   5 DOLLARS
Aluminum-Bronze, 31.51 mm.   **Ruler:** Elizabeth II
Obv: Crowned head right, date below **Rev:** Conch shell, denomination above

Date	Mintage	F	VF	XF	Unc	BU
1987	—	—	—	3.50	5.50	7.50
1987 Proof	—	Value: 9.00				
1988	—	—	—	3.50	5.50	7.50
1988 Proof	—	Value: 9.00				
1992	—	—	—	3.50	5.50	7.50
1992 Proof	—	Value: 9.00				
1994	20,000	—	—	3.50	5.50	7.50
1994 Proof	200	Value: 12.00				

KM# 39a   5 DOLLARS
Copper-Nickel, 31.51 mm.   **Ruler:** Elizabeth II **Obv:** Crowned head right, date below **Rev:** Conch shell **Note:** Mint error, struck on Australian 50 cents planchet.

Date	Mintage	F	VF	XF	Unc	BU
1988						

KM# 181   5 DOLLARS
Copper-Nickel   **Ruler:** Elizabeth II **Subject:** Endangered World Wildlife **Obv:** Crowned head right, date below **Rev:** Tiger

Date	Mintage	F	VF	XF	Unc	BU
1990	—	—	—	—	8.50	22.00

KM# 149   5 DOLLARS
9.9500 g., 0.5000 Silver 0.1599 oz. ASW   **Ruler:** Elizabeth II
Subject: World Cup Soccer **Obv:** Crowned head right, below **Rev:** Three soccer players

Date	Mintage	F	VF	XF	Unc	BU
1991 Proof	150,000	Value: 4.50				

KM# 217   5 DOLLARS
9.8500 g., 0.5000 Silver 0.1583 oz. ASW   **Ruler:** Elizabeth II
Obv: Crowned head right, date below **Rev:** Christopher Columbus 3/4 facing, ship at left, denomination below

Date	Mintage	F	VF	XF	Unc	BU
1991	Est. 50,000	—	—	—	6.00	8.00

KM# 218   5 DOLLARS
9.9500 g., 0.5000 Silver 0.1599 oz. ASW   **Ruler:** Elizabeth II
Subject: Endangered Wildlife **Obv:** Crowned head right, date below **Rev:** European otters

Date	Mintage	F	VF	XF	Unc	BU
1991	Est. 100,000	—	—	—	8.50	15.00

KM# 219   5 DOLLARS
9.9500 g., 0.5000 Silver 0.1599 oz. ASW   **Ruler:** Elizabeth II
Subject: Endangered Wildlife **Obv:** Crowned head right, date below **Rev:** Penguins

Date	Mintage	F	VF	XF	Unc	BU
1991	Est. 100,000	—	—	—	8.50	15.00

KM# 220   5 DOLLARS
9.9500 g., 0.5000 Silver 0.1599 oz. ASW   **Ruler:** Elizabeth II
Subject: Endangered Wildlife **Obv:** Crowned head right, date below **Rev:** Deer

Date	Mintage	F	VF	XF	Unc	BU
1991	Est. 100,000	—	—	—	8.50	15.00

KM# 221   5 DOLLARS
9.9500 g., 0.5000 Silver 0.1599 oz. ASW   **Ruler:** Elizabeth II
Subject: Endangered Wildlife **Obv:** Crowned head right, date below **Rev:** Cape dolphins

Date	Mintage	F	VF	XF	Unc	BU
1991	Est. 100,000	—	—	—	8.50	15.00

KM# 222   5 DOLLARS
9.9500 g., 0.5000 Silver 0.1599 oz. ASW   **Ruler:** Elizabeth II
Subject: Endangered Wildlife **Obv:** Crowned head right, date below **Rev:** Cougar

Date	Mintage	F	VF	XF	Unc	BU
1991	Est. 100,000	—	—	—	8.50	15.00

KM# 223   5 DOLLARS
9.9500 g., 0.5000 Silver 0.1599 oz. ASW   **Ruler:** Elizabeth II
Subject: Endangered Wildlife **Obv:** Crowned head right, date below **Rev:** Ibex

Date	Mintage	F	VF	XF	Unc	BU
1991	Est. 100,000	—	—	—	8.50	15.00

KM# 224   5 DOLLARS
9.9500 g., 0.5000 Silver 0.1599 oz. ASW   **Ruler:** Elizabeth II
Subject: Endangered Wildlife **Obv:** Crowned head right, date below **Rev:** Eagle owl

Date	Mintage	F	VF	XF	Unc	BU
1991	Est. 100,000	—	—	—	8.50	15.00

KM# 225   5 DOLLARS
9.9500 g., 0.5000 Silver 0.1599 oz. ASW   **Ruler:** Elizabeth II
Subject: Endangered Wildlife **Obv:** Crowned head right, date below **Rev:** Peregrine falcon

Date	Mintage	F	VF	XF	Unc	BU
1991	Est. 100,000	—	—	—	8.50	15.00

KM# 226   5 DOLLARS
9.9500 g., 0.5000 Silver 0.1599 oz. ASW   **Ruler:** Elizabeth II
Subject: Endangered Wildlife **Obv:** Crowned head right, date below **Rev:** African lion

Date	Mintage	F	VF	XF	Unc	BU
1991	Est. 100,000	—	—	—	8.50	15.00

KM# 227   5 DOLLARS
9.9500 g., 0.5000 Silver 0.1599 oz. ASW   **Ruler:** Elizabeth II
Subject: Endangered Wildlife **Obv:** Crowned head right, date below **Rev:** Bee hummingbird

Date	Mintage	F	VF	XF	Unc	BU
1991	Est. 100,000	—	—	—	8.50	15.00

KM# 228   5 DOLLARS
9.9500 g., 0.5000 Silver 0.1599 oz. ASW   **Ruler:** Elizabeth II
Subject: Endangered Wildlife **Obv:** Crowned head right, date below **Rev:** Kangaroo

Date	Mintage	F	VF	XF	Unc	BU
1991	Est. 100,000	—	—	—	8.50	15.00

KM# 229   5 DOLLARS
9.9500 g., 0.5000 Silver 0.1599 oz. ASW   **Ruler:** Elizabeth II
Subject: Endangered Wildlife **Obv:** Crowned head right, date below **Rev:** Persian fallow deer

Date	Mintage	F	VF	XF	Unc	BU
1991	Est. 100,000	—	—	—	8.50	15.00

KM# 230   5 DOLLARS
9.9500 g., 0.5000 Silver 0.1599 oz. ASW   **Ruler:** Elizabeth II
Subject: Endangered Wildlife **Obv:** Crowned head right, date below **Rev:** Lowland gorilla

Date	Mintage	F	VF	XF	Unc	BU
1991	Est. 100,000	—	—	—	8.50	15.00

KM# 253   5 DOLLARS
10.1300 g., 0.5000 Silver 0.1628 oz. ASW   **Ruler:** Elizabeth II
Obv: Crowned head right, date below **Rev:** First man on the moon, denomination below

Date	Mintage	F	VF	XF	Unc	BU
1991 Proof	—	Value: 6.00				

KM# 137   5 DOLLARS
10.0000 g., 0.5000 Silver 0.1607 oz. ASW   **Ruler:** Elizabeth II
Subject: Environmental Protection **Obv:** Crowned head right, date below **Rev:** Child watching butterfly

Date	Mintage	F	VF	XF	Unc	BU
1992 Proof	Est. 25,000	Value: 5.50				

KM# 150   5 DOLLARS
10.0000 g., 0.5000 Silver 0.1607 oz. ASW   **Ruler:** Elizabeth II
Obv: Crowned head right, date below **Rev:** Johann Sebastian Bach

Date	Mintage	F	VF	XF	Unc	BU
1992 Proof	—	Value: 5.50				

KM# 160   5 DOLLARS
10.0000 g., 0.5000 Silver 0.1607 oz. ASW   **Ruler:** Elizabeth II
Obv: Crowned head right, date below **Rev:** Sailing ship Astrolabe

Date	Mintage	F	VF	XF	Unc	BU
1992 Proof	—	Value: 5.50				

KM# 231 5 DOLLARS
10.0000 g., 0.5000 Silver 0.1607 oz. ASW **Ruler:** Elizabeth II **Subject:** Endangered Wildlife **Obv:** Crowned head right, date below **Rev:** Mandrill right, denomination below

Date	Mintage	F	VF	XF	Unc	BU
1992	Est. 100,000	—	—	—	8.50	15.00

KM# 232 5 DOLLARS
10.0000 g., 0.5000 Silver 0.1607 oz. ASW **Ruler:** Elizabeth II **Subject:** Endangered Wildlife **Obv:** Crowned head right, date below **Rev:** Butterfly

Date	Mintage	F	VF	XF	Unc	BU
1992	Est. 100,000	—	—	—	5.00	7.00

KM# 233 5 DOLLARS
10.0000 g., 0.5000 Silver 0.1607 oz. ASW **Ruler:** Elizabeth II **Subject:** Endangered Wildlife **Obv:** Crowned head right, date below **Rev:** Takin

Date	Mintage	F	VF	XF	Unc	BU
1992	Est. 100,000	—	—	—	5.00	7.00

KM# 252 5 DOLLARS
9.9500 g., 0.5000 Silver 0.1599 oz. ASW **Ruler:** Elizabeth II **Subject:** 1992 Olympics **Obv:** Crowned head right, date below **Rev:** High jump, denomination below

Date	Mintage	F	VF	XF	Unc	BU
1992 Proof	150,000	Value: 5.50				

KM# 255 5 DOLLARS
31.4700 g., 0.9250 Silver 0.9359 oz. ASW **Ruler:** Elizabeth II **Subject:** Queen Elizabeth II's 25th Wedding Anniversary **Obv:** Crowned head right, date below **Rev:** St. Paul's Cathedral

Date	Mintage	F	VF	XF	Unc	BU
1995 Proof	Est. 30,000	Value: 18.50				

KM# 234 5 DOLLARS
10.0000 g., 0.5000 Silver 0.1607 oz. ASW **Ruler:** Elizabeth II **Subject:** Endangered Wildlife **Obv:** Crowned head right, date below **Rev:** African elephant

Date	Mintage	F	VF	XF	Unc	BU
1995 Proof	Est. 25,000	Value: 12.00				

KM# 269 5 DOLLARS
31.4700 g., 0.9250 Silver 0.9359 oz. ASW **Ruler:** Elizabeth II **Subject:** Endangered Wildlife **Obv:** Crowned head right, date below **Rev:** Cheetah

Date	Mintage	F	VF	XF	Unc	BU
1996 Proof	Est. 15,000	Value: 22.00				

KM# 281 5 DOLLARS
28.0000 g., 0.9250 Silver 0.8327 oz. ASW **Ruler:** Elizabeth II **Subject:** Yellowstone National Park **Obv:** Crowned head right, date below **Rev:** Multicolor grizzly bear and cub

Date	Mintage	F	VF	XF	Unc	BU
1996 Proof	25,000	Value: 27.50				

KM# 282 5 DOLLARS
28.0000 g., 0.9250 Silver 0.8327 oz. ASW **Ruler:** Elizabeth II **Subject:** Olympic National Park **Obv:** Crowned head right, date below **Rev:** Multicolor bald eagle in flight

Date	Mintage	F	VF	XF	Unc	BU
1996 Proof	25,000	Value: 27.50				

KM# 301 5 DOLLARS
28.0000 g., 0.9250 Silver 0.8327 oz. ASW **Ruler:** Elizabeth II **Subject:** Endangered Wildlife **Obv:** Crowned head right, date below **Rev:** Crocodile on river bank

Date	Mintage	F	VF	XF	Unc	BU
1996 Proof	—	Value: 27.50				

KM# 302 5 DOLLARS
28.0000 g., 0.9250 Silver 0.8327 oz. ASW **Ruler:** Elizabeth II **Subject:** Endangered Wildlife **Obv:** Crowned head right, date below **Rev:** Lion, lioness and cubs

Date	Mintage	F	VF	XF	Unc	BU
1996 Proof	—	Value: 24.00				

KM# 303 5 DOLLARS
28.0000 g., 0.9250 Silver 0.8327 oz. ASW **Ruler:** Elizabeth II **Subject:** Endangered Wildlife **Obv:** Crowned head right, date below **Rev:** Female gorilla and offspring

Date	Mintage	F	VF	XF	Unc	BU
1996 Proof	—	Value: 22.00				

KM# 304 5 DOLLARS
28.0000 g., 0.9250 Silver 0.8327 oz. ASW **Ruler:** Elizabeth II **Subject:** Endangered Wildlife **Obv:** Crowned head right, date below **Rev:** Penguin family

Date	Mintage	F	VF	XF	Unc	BU
1996 Proof	—	Value: 24.00				

KM# 368 5 DOLLARS
28.0000 g., 0.9250 Silver 0.8327 oz. ASW **Ruler:** Elizabeth II **Subject:** Great Smoky Mountains National Park **Obv:** Crowned head right, date below **Rev:** Red wolf and two cubs **Edge:** Reeded

Date	Mintage	F	VF	XF	Unc	BU
1996 Proof	—	Value: 27.50				

KM# 366 5 DOLLARS
31.4700 g., 0.9250 Silver 0.9359 oz. ASW **Ruler:** Elizabeth II **Subject:** Protect Our World **Obv:** Crowned head right, date below **Rev:** Charles Darwin bust at right, map and tortoise, denomination below **Edge:** Reeded

Date	Mintage	F	VF	XF	Unc	BU
1996 Proof	—	Value: 25.00				

KM# 379   5 DOLLARS
31.4700 g., 0.9250 Silver 0.9359 oz. ASW, 38.6 mm.
Ruler: Elizabeth II **Subject:** Queen Mother **Obv:** Crowned head right, date below **Rev:** Queen Mother and daughters, circa 1936, within circle, denomination below **Edge:** Reeded

Date	Mintage	F	VF	XF	Unc	BU
1996 Proof	—	Value: 18.50				

KM# 370   5 DOLLARS
31.5000 g., 0.9250 Silver 0.9368 oz. ASW, 38.6 mm.
Ruler: Elizabeth II **Subject:** Olympics **Obv:** Crowned head right, date below **Rev:** Pole vaulter and runner **Edge:** Reeded

Date	Mintage	F	VF	XF	Unc	BU
1996 Proof	—	Value: 20.00				

KM# 377   5 DOLLARS
31.5000 g., 0.9250 Silver 0.9368 oz. ASW, 38.6 mm.
Ruler: Elizabeth II **Subject:** Endangered Wildlife **Obv:** Crowned head right, date below **Rev:** Two adult polar bears with cub **Edge:** Reeded

Date	Mintage	F	VF	XF	Unc	BU
1996 Proof	—	Value: 24.00				

KM# 457   5 DOLLARS
1.2000 g., 0.9995 Platinum 0.0386 oz. APW **Ruler:** Elizabeth II **Subject:** Love Angels

Date	Mintage	F	VF	XF	Unc	BU
1997 Proof	250	Value: 85.00				

KM# 335   5 DOLLARS
15.5200 g., 0.9990 Silver 0.4985 oz. ASW **Ruler:** Elizabeth II **Subject:** Japanese Samurai **Obv:** Crowned head right, date below **Rev:** 3/4 bust Yoshinobu Tokugawa facing, denomination at right, 3/4 braided circle surrounds **Edge:** Reeded

Date	Mintage	F	VF	XF	Unc	BU
1997FM Proof	—	Value: 12.00				

KM# 312   5 DOLLARS
1.2441 g., 0.9999 Gold 0.0400 oz. AGW **Ruler:** Elizabeth II **Obv:** Crowned head right, date below **Rev:** Portrait of Princess Diana, dates, denomination below

Date	Mintage	F	VF	XF	Unc	BU
1997 Proof	—	Value: 45.00				

KM# 367   5 DOLLARS
31.4500 g., 0.9250 Silver 0.9353 oz. ASW **Ruler:** Elizabeth II **Subject:** Millennium - 2000 A.D. **Obv:** Crowned head right, date below **Rev:** Christian symbol above Tangaroa, Pagan God of Creation, denomination below **Edge:** Plain

Date	Mintage	F	VF	XF	Unc	BU
1999 Proof	—	Value: 22.00				

KM# 444   5 DOLLARS
62.2070 g., 0.9990 Silver 1.9979 oz. ASW, 50 mm.
Ruler: Elizabeth II **Obv:** Crowned head right, date below **Rev:** SS Sofia Jane, steam and sail ship **Edge:** Reeded

Date	Mintage	F	VF	XF	Unc	BU
1999 Antiqued	5,000	—	—	—	65.00	—

KM# 445   5 DOLLARS
62.2070 g., 0.9990 Silver 1.9979 oz. ASW, 50 mm.
Ruler: Elizabeth II **Obv:** Crowned head right, date below **Rev:** Scottish Bard, barque type ship **Edge:** Reeded

Date	Mintage	F	VF	XF	Unc	BU
1999 Antiqued finish	5,000	—	—	—	65.00	—

KM# 446   5 DOLLARS
62.2070 g., 0.9990 Silver 1.9979 oz. ASW, 50 mm.
Ruler: Elizabeth II **Obv:** Crowned head right, date below **Rev:** Cutty Sark, clipper ship **Edge:** Reeded

Date	Mintage	F	VF	XF	Unc	BU
1999 Antiqued finish	5,000	—	—	—	65.00	—

KM# 447   5 DOLLARS
62.2070 g., 0.9990 Silver 1.9979 oz. ASW, 50 mm.
Ruler: Elizabeth II **Obv:** Crowned head right, date below **Rev:** HMS Sirius, 20 gun naval ship circa 1788 **Edge:** Reeded

Date	Mintage	F	VF	XF	Unc	BU
1999 Antiqued finish	5,000	—	—	—	65.00	—

KM# 448   5 DOLLARS
62.2070 g., 0.9990 Silver 1.9979 oz. ASW, 50 mm.
Ruler: Elizabeth II **Obv:** Crowned head right, date below **Rev:** 18 ft. Skiff **Edge:** Reeded

Date	Mintage	F	VF	XF	Unc	BU
1999 Antiqued finish	5,000	—	—	—	65.00	—

KM# 456   5 DOLLARS
31.5000 g., 0.9250 Silver 0.9368 oz. ASW, 38.6 mm.
Ruler: Elizabeth II **Obv:** Crowned head right, date below **Rev:** Sail Ship Archimedes **Edge:** Reeded

Date	Mintage	F	VF	XF	Unc	BU
1999 Proof	—	Value: 32.50				

KM# 378   5 DOLLARS
31.5000 g., 0.9250 Silver 0.9368 oz. ASW, 38.6 mm.
Ruler: Elizabeth II **Subject:** Takitumu Conservation Area **Obv:** Crowned head right, date below **Rev:** Rarotongan Monarch Flycatcher, denomination at left **Edge:** Reeded

Date	Mintage	F	VF	XF	Unc	BU
1999 Proof	—	Value: 30.00				

KM# 375   5 DOLLARS
28.1000 g., 0.9250 Silver with gold plated outer circle 0.8356 oz. ASW, 38.6 mm. **Ruler:** Elizabeth II **Subject:** Queen Mother's 100th Birthday **Obv:** Crowned head right, date below **Rev:** Queen Mother and daughters, circa 1980 **Edge:** Reeded

Date	Mintage	F	VF	XF	Unc	BU
2000 Proof	1,000	Value: 27.50				

KM# 10   7-1/2 DOLLARS
33.8000 g., 0.9250 Silver 1.0052 oz. ASW **Ruler:** Elizabeth II **Subject:** Capt. James Cook's 2nd Pacific Voyage **Obv:** Young bust right, date below **Rev:** H.M.S. Resolution and Cook's profile above map of Hervey Islands

Date	Mintage	F	VF	XF	Unc	BU
1973	6,000	—	—	—	22.00	—
1973 Proof	12,000	Value: 20.00				
1974	2,000	—	—	—	25.00	—
1974 Proof	13,000	Value: 20.00				

KM# 21   10 DOLLARS
27.9000 g., 0.9250 Silver 0.8297 oz. ASW **Ruler:** Elizabeth II
Subject: 25th Anniversary of Coronation **Obv:** Young bust right,
date below **Rev:** Crown with supporters, dates below,
denomination at bottom

Date	Mintage	F	VF	XF	Unc	BU
1978FM (U)	5,350	—	—	—	20.00	—
1978FM Proof	11,000	Value: 18.00				

KM# 72   10 DOLLARS
10.0000 g., 0.9250 Silver 0.2974 oz. ASW **Ruler:** Elizabeth II
Subject: Endangered World Wildlife **Obv:** Crowned head right,
date below **Rev:** Elephants head left

Date	Mintage	F	VF	XF	Unc	BU
1990 Proof	25,000	Value: 12.50				

KM# 73   10 DOLLARS
10.0000 g., 0.9250 Silver 0.2974 oz. ASW **Ruler:** Elizabeth II
Subject: Endangered World Wildlife **Obv:** Crowned head right,
date below **Rev:** Tiger

Date	Mintage	F	VF	XF	Unc	BU
1990 Proof	Est. 25,000	Value: 12.50				

KM# 79   10 DOLLARS
10.0000 g., 0.9250 Silver 0.2974 oz. ASW **Ruler:** Elizabeth II
Subject: Olympics **Obv:** Crowned head right, date below
Rev: Runner

Date	Mintage	F	VF	XF	Unc	BU
1990 Proof	150,000	Value: 7.50				

KM# 80   10 DOLLARS
10.0000 g., 0.9250 Silver 0.2974 oz. ASW **Ruler:** Elizabeth II
Subject: Endangered World Wildlife **Obv:** Crowned head right,
date below **Rev:** African elephants

Date	Mintage	F	VF	XF	Unc	BU
1990 Proof	Est. 25,000	Value: 12.50				

KM# 81   10 DOLLARS
28.0000 g., 0.9250 Silver 0.8327 oz. ASW **Ruler:** Elizabeth II
Subject: Save the Children **Obv:** Crowned head right, date below
Rev: Grass-skirted dancers

Date	Mintage	F	VF	XF	Unc	BU
1990 Proof	20,000	Value: 18.50				

KM# 90   10 DOLLARS
10.0000 g., 0.9250 Silver 0.2974 oz. ASW **Ruler:** Elizabeth II
Subject: 500 Years of America **Obv:** Crowned head right, date
below **Rev:** Bust at left looking right, ship at right, denomination below

Date	Mintage	F	VF	XF	Unc	BU
1990 Proof	Est. 150,000	Value: 7.50				

KM# 91   10 DOLLARS
10.0000 g., 0.9250 Silver 0.2974 oz. ASW **Ruler:** Elizabeth II
Subject: 1991 Winter Olympics **Obv:** Crowned head right, date
below **Rev:** Cross-country skier, denomination below

Date	Mintage	F	VF	XF	Unc	BU
1990 Proof	150,000	Value: 8.00				

KM# 121   10 DOLLARS
10.0000 g., 0.9250 Silver 0.2974 oz. ASW **Ruler:** Elizabeth II
Subject: 500 Years of America **Obv:** Crowned head right, date
below **Rev:** Columbus and ship

Date	Mintage	F	VF	XF	Unc	BU
1990 Proof	Est. 150,000	Value: 7.50				

KM# 136   10 DOLLARS
31.4700 g., 0.9250 Silver 0.9359 oz. ASW **Ruler:** Elizabeth II
Obv: Crowned head right, date below **Rev:** Bust with planet earth
revolving around radiant sun in background

Date	Mintage	F	VF	XF	Unc	BU
1992 Proof	—	Value: 18.50				

KM# 254   10 DOLLARS
31.4700 g., 0.9250 Silver 0.9359 oz. ASW **Ruler:** Elizabeth II
Subject: World Cup '94 **Obv:** Crowned head right, date below
Rev: Goalie catching ball

Date	Mintage	F	VF	XF	Unc	BU
1992 Proof	Est. 20,000	Value: 20.00				

KM# 358   10 DOLLARS
14.8000 g., 0.9250 Silver 0.4401 oz. ASW **Ruler:** Elizabeth II
Subject: Captain Cook **Obv:** Crowned head right, date below
Rev: Captain Cook wading ashore, denomination at right
Edge: Reeded

Date	Mintage	F	VF	XF	Unc	BU
1994FM Proof	—	Value: 10.00				

KM# 283   10 DOLLARS
28.0000 g., 0.9250 Silver 0.8327 oz. ASW **Ruler:** Elizabeth II
Subject: Olympic National Park **Obv:** Crowned head right, date
below **Rev:** Multicolor Bald eagle in flight over mountain tops,
denomination below

Date	Mintage	F	VF	XF	Unc	BU
1996 Proof	10,000	Value: 25.00				

KM# 284   10 DOLLARS
28.0000 g., 0.9250 Silver 0.8327 oz. ASW **Ruler:** Elizabeth II
Subject: Yellowstone National Park **Obv:** Crowned head right,
date below **Rev:** Multicolor Grizzly bear and cub

Date	Mintage	F	VF	XF	Unc	BU
1996 Proof	10,000	Value: 27.50				

KM# 359   10 DOLLARS
28.0000 g., 0.9250 Silver 0.8327 oz. ASW **Ruler:** Elizabeth II
Subject: Theodore Roosevelt National Park **Obv:** Crowned head
right, date below **Rev:** Multicolor bison **Edge:** Reeded

Date	Mintage	F	VF	XF	Unc	BU
1996 Proof	—	Value: 27.00				
1997 Proof	—	Value: 27.00				

KM# 285   10 DOLLARS
1.2441 g., 0.9990 Gold 0.0400 oz. AGW **Ruler:** Elizabeth II
Subject: Olympic National Park **Obv:** Crowned head right, date
below **Rev:** Eagle's head right, denomination below

Date	Mintage	F	VF	XF	Unc	BU
1996 Proof	—	Value: 45.00				

KM# 286   10 DOLLARS
1.2441 g., 0.9990 Gold 0.0400 oz. AGW **Ruler:** Elizabeth II
Subject: Yellowstone National Park **Obv:** Crowned head right,
date below

Date	Mintage	F	VF	XF	Unc	BU
1996 Proof	—	Value: 45.00				

KM# 330   10 DOLLARS
28.0000 g., 0.9250 Silver 0.8327 oz. ASW **Ruler:** Elizabeth II
Subject: Great Smoky Mountains National Park **Obv:** Crowned
head right, date below **Rev:** Multicolor red wolf with two cubs

Date	Mintage	F	VF	XF	Unc	BU
1997 Proof	—	Value: 35.00				

KM# 331   10 DOLLARS
28.0000 g., 0.9250 Silver 0.8327 oz. ASW **Ruler:** Elizabeth II
Subject: Yosemite National Park **Obv:** Crowned head right, date
below **Rev:** Multicolor Peregrine falcon

Date	Mintage	F	VF	XF	Unc	BU
1997 Proof	—	Value: 35.00				

KM# 360   10 DOLLARS
28.0000 g., 0.9250 Silver 0.8327 oz. ASW **Ruler:** Elizabeth II
Subject: Glacier Bay National Park **Obv:** Crowned head right,
date below **Rev:** Multicolor Humpback whale breaking the water

Date	Mintage	F	VF	XF	Unc	BU
1997 Proof	—	Value: 27.50				

KM# 458   10 DOLLARS
2.5000 g., 0.9995 Platinum 0.0803 oz. APW **Ruler:** Elizabeth II
Subject: Love Angels

Date	Mintage	F	VF	XF	Unc	BU
1997 Proof	250	Value: 175				

KM# 332   10 DOLLARS
28.0000 g., 0.9250 Silver 0.8327 oz. ASW **Ruler:** Elizabeth II
Subject: Grand Teton National park **Obv:** Crowned head right,
date below **Rev:** Multicolor Whooping crane

Date	Mintage	F	VF	XF	Unc	BU
1998 Proof	—	Value: 35.00				

KM# 333   10 DOLLARS
28.0000 g., 0.9250 Silver 0.8327 oz. ASW **Ruler:** Elizabeth II
Subject: Grand Canyon National Park **Obv:** Crowned head right,
date below **Rev:** Multicolor California condor in flight over canyon

Date	Mintage	F	VF	XF	Unc	BU
1998 Proof	—	Value: 35.00				

KM# 476   10 DOLLARS
1.2200 g., Gold, 13.88 mm. **Ruler:** Elizabeth II **Subject:** 1996
Solar Eclipse **Obv:** Crowned bust right **Rev:** Outlined earth
latitudes in rays **Edge:** Reeded

Date	Mintage	F	VF	XF	Unc	BU
1999 Proof	—	Value: 55.00				

KM# 477   10 DOLLARS
1.2200 g., Gold, 1.22 mm. **Ruler:** Elizabeth II **Obv:** Crowned
bust right **Rev:** Bottle-nosed Dolphin **Edge:** Reeded

Date	Mintage	F	VF	XF	Unc	BU
2000 Proof	—	Value: 55.00				

KM# 28   20 DOLLARS
28.2800 g., 0.9250 Silver 0.8410 oz. ASW **Ruler:** Elizabeth II
Subject: International Year of the Scout **Obv:** Young bust right,
date below **Rev:** Boy Scouts, dates at left, denomination at right

Date	Mintage	F	VF	XF	Unc	BU
1983	10,000	—	—	—	22.50	
1983 Proof	10,000	Value: 25.00				

KM# 151   20 DOLLARS
31.4700 g., 0.9250 Silver 0.9359 oz. ASW **Ruler:** Elizabeth II
Obv: Crowned head right, date below **Rev:** Friedrich von Schiller

Date	Mintage	F	VF	XF	Unc	BU
1993 Proof	—	Value: 18.50				

KM# 152   20 DOLLARS
31.4700 g., 0.9250 Silver 0.9359 oz. ASW **Ruler:** Elizabeth II
Obv: Crowned head right, date below **Rev:** Bust of Charles
Darwin facing left, tortoise and map, denomination below

Date	Mintage	F	VF	XF	Unc	BU
1993 Proof	10,000	Value: 18.50				

KM# 161 20 DOLLARS
31.4700 g., 0.9250 Silver 0.9359 oz. ASW **Ruler:** Elizabeth II
Subject: 1996 Olympics **Obv:** Crowned head right, date below
Rev: Pole vaulter and sprinter

Date	Mintage	F	VF	XF	Unc	BU
1993 Proof	50,000	Value: 17.50				

KM# 235 20 DOLLARS
31.4700 g., 0.9250 Silver 0.9359 oz. ASW **Ruler:** Elizabeth II
Obv: Crowned head right, date below **Rev:** Tainui Catamaran

Date	Mintage	F	VF	XF	Unc	BU
1995 Proof	Est. 15,000	Value: 17.50				

KM# 236 20 DOLLARS
1.2441 g., 0.9990 Gold 0.0400 oz. AGW **Ruler:** Elizabeth II
Subject: 500 Years of America **Obv:** Crowned head right, date
below **Rev:** Columbus claims the New World, denomination below

Date	Mintage	F	VF	XF	Unc	BU
1995	Est. 25,000	—	—	—	45.00	50.00

KM# 237 20 DOLLARS
1.2441 g., 0.9990 Gilt Silver 0.0400 oz. **Ruler:** Elizabeth II
Subject: 500 Years of America **Obv:** Crowned head right, date
below **Rev:** Washington crossing the Delaware, denomination below

Date	Mintage	F	VF	XF	Unc	BU
1995	Est. 25,000	—	—	—	45.00	50.00

KM# 256 20 DOLLARS
31.4700 g., 0.9250 Silver 0.9359 oz. ASW **Ruler:** Elizabeth II
Obv: Crowned head right, date below **Rev:** Queen Mother and
daughters within circle, denomination below

Date	Mintage	F	VF	XF	Unc	BU
1995 Proof	Est. 30,000	Value: 20.00				

KM# 257 20 DOLLARS
1.2441 g., 0.9999 Gold 0.0400 oz. AGW **Ruler:** Elizabeth II
Subject: 500 Years of America **Obv:** Crowned head right, date
below **Rev:** Statue of Liberty, denomination below

Date	Mintage	F	VF	XF	Unc	BU
1995	Est. 25,000	—	—	—	45.00	50.00

KM# 258 20 DOLLARS
1.2441 g., 0.9999 Gold 0.0400 oz. AGW **Ruler:** Elizabeth II
Subject: 500 Years of America **Obv:** Crowned head right, date
below **Rev:** Capt. James Cook bust right, denomination below

Date	Mintage	F	VF	XF	Unc	BU
1995 Proof	Est. 25,000	Value: 50.00				

KM# 270 20 DOLLARS
1.2441 g., 0.9999 Gold 0.0400 oz. AGW **Ruler:** Elizabeth II
Subject: 500 Years of America **Obv:** Crowned head right, date
below **Rev:** Astronaut on moon, denomination below

Date	Mintage	F	VF	XF	Unc	BU
1995 Proof	Est. 25,000	Value: 50.00				

KM# 288 20 DOLLARS
155.5175 g., 0.9990 Silver 4.9948 oz. ASW **Ruler:** Elizabeth II
Subject: Yellowstone National Park **Obv:** Crowned head right,
date below **Rev:** Grizzly bear

Date	Mintage	F	VF	XF	Unc	BU
1996 Proof	1,000	Value: 100				

KM# 298 20 DOLLARS
3.0000 g., 0.9999 Gold 0.0964 oz. AGW **Ruler:** Elizabeth II
Subject: Year of the Mouse **Obv:** Crowned head right, date below
Rev: Multicolor Mickey Mouse portrait facing, denomination below

Date	Mintage	F	VF	XF	Unc	BU
1996 Proof	—	Value: 85.00				

KM# 475 20 DOLLARS
1.2200 g., Gold, 13.89 mm. **Ruler:** Elizabeth II **Obv:** Crowned
bust right **Rev:** 1/2 length figure of Friedrich von Schiller at right
seated at table, bell at left **Edge:** Reeded

Date	Mintage	F	VF	XF	Unc	BU
1996 Proof	—	Value: 55.00				

KM# 287 20 DOLLARS
155.5175 g., 0.9990 Silver 4.9948 oz. ASW, 82 mm. **Ruler:**
Elizabeth II **Subject:** Olympic National Park **Obv:** Crowned head
right, date below **Rev:** Bald eagle **Note:** Illustration reduced.

Date	Mintage	F	VF	XF	Unc	BU
1996 Proof	1,000	Value: 100				

KM# 334 20 DOLLARS
32.0200 g., 0.9250 Silver 0.9522 oz. ASW **Ruler:** Elizabeth II
Subject: 12th Century **Obv:** Crowned head right, date below
Rev: Genghis Khan on horse left, soldier on camel at right,
denominaition at left

Date	Mintage	F	VF	XF	Unc	BU
1997 Proof	—	Value: 20.00				

KM# 336 20 DOLLARS
31.8800 g., 0.9250 Silver 0.9481 oz. ASW **Ruler:** Elizabeth II
Subject: 18th Century **Obv:** Crowned head right, date below
Rev: Signing of the Declaration of Independence, denomination
lower right **Edge:** Reeded

Date	Mintage	F	VF	XF	Unc	BU
1997FM Proof	—	Value: 20.00				

KM# 337 20 DOLLARS
31.8800 g., 0.9250 Silver 0.9481 oz. ASW **Ruler:** Elizabeth II
Subject: 19th Century **Obv:** Crowned head right, date below
Rev: Waving driver with two passengers in horseless carriage,
bicycle at right in back, denomination at left **Edge:** Reeded

Date	Mintage	F	VF	XF	Unc	BU
1997FM Proof	—	Value: 18.50				

KM# 459 20 DOLLARS
5.0000 g., 0.9995 Platinum 0.1607 oz. APW **Ruler:** Elizabeth II
Subject: Love Angels

Date	Mintage	F	VF	XF	Unc	BU
1997 Proof	250	Value: 325				

KM# 18 25 DOLLARS
48.8500 g., 0.9250 Silver 1.4527 oz. ASW **Ruler:** Elizabeth II
Subject: Queen's Silver Jubilee **Obv:** Crowned head right, date
below **Rev:** Crowned EIIR monogram between flowers

Date	Mintage	F	VF	XF	Unc	BU
1977FM (M)	100	—	—	—	47.50	—
1977FM (U)	4,068	—	—	—	32.50	—
1977FM Proof	17,000	Value: 30.00				

KM# 42 25 DOLLARS
37.0000 g., 0.9250 Silver 1.1003 oz. ASW **Ruler:** Elizabeth II
Subject: 100th Ann. of British Rule **Obv:** Crowned head right,
date below **Rev:** Sailing ship at bottom right, bust of Makea Takau
Ariki, island chief at left, mountains behind, denomination below

Date	Mintage	F	VF	XF	Unc	BU
1988 Proof	3,000	Value: 25.00				

KM# 83   25 DOLLARS
1.2144 g., 0.9990 Gold 0.0390 oz. AGW **Ruler:** Elizabeth II
Subject: Endangered Wildlife **Obv:** Crowned head right, date
below **Rev:** Bison head left, denomination below

Date	Mintage	F	VF	XF	Unc	BU
1990 Proof	100,000	Value: 47.50				

KM# 84   25 DOLLARS
1.2144 g., 0.9990 Gold 0.0390 oz. AGW **Ruler:** Elizabeth II
Subject: Endangered Wildlife **Obv:** Crowned head right, date
below **Rev:** Longhorn sheep head facing, denomination below

Date	Mintage	F	VF	XF	Unc	BU
1990 Proof	Est. 100,000	Value: 47.50				

KM# 85   25 DOLLARS
1.2144 g., 0.9990 Gold 0.0390 oz. AGW **Ruler:** Elizabeth II
Subject: Endangered Wildlife **Obv:** Crowned head right, date
below **Rev:** Tiger head, denomination below

Date	Mintage	F	VF	XF	Unc	BU
1990 Proof	—	Value: 47.50				

KM# 86   25 DOLLARS
1.2144 g., 0.9990 Gold 0.0390 oz. AGW **Ruler:** Elizabeth II
Subject: Endangered Wildlife **Obv:** Crowned head right, date
below **Rev:** Eagle

Date	Mintage	F	VF	XF	Unc	BU
1990 Proof	Est. 100,000	Value: 47.50				

KM# 87   25 DOLLARS
1.2144 g., 0.9990 Gold 0.0390 oz. AGW **Ruler:** Elizabeth II
Subject: Endangered Wildlife **Obv:** Crowned head right, date
below **Rev:** Elephant head left, denomination below

Date	Mintage	F	VF	XF	Unc	BU
1990 Proof	Est. 100,000	Value: 47.50				

KM# 88   25 DOLLARS
1.2144 g., 0.9990 Gold 0.0390 oz. AGW **Ruler:** Elizabeth II
Subject: Endangered Wildlife **Obv:** Crowned head right, date
below **Rev:** Lynx head left, denomination below

Date	Mintage	F	VF	XF	Unc	BU
1990 Proof	Est. 100,000	Value: 47.50				

KM# 239   25 DOLLARS
1.2144 g., 0.9990 Gold 0.0390 oz. AGW **Ruler:** Elizabeth II
Subject: Endangered Wildlife **Obv:** Crowned head right, date
below **Rev:** Bee hummingbird right, denomination below

Date	Mintage	F	VF	XF	Unc	BU
1990 Proof	Est. 100,000	Value: 47.50				

KM# 240   25 DOLLARS
1.2144 g., 0.9990 Gold 0.0390 oz. AGW **Ruler:** Elizabeth II
Subject: Endangered Wildlife **Obv:** Crowned head right, date
below **Rev:** Koala bear, denomination below

Date	Mintage	F	VF	XF	Unc	BU
1991 Proof	Est. 100,000	Value: 47.50				

KM# 241   25 DOLLARS
1.2144 g., 0.9990 Gold 0.0390 oz. AGW **Ruler:** Elizabeth II
Subject: Endangered Wildlife **Obv:** Crowned head right, date
below **Rev:** Panda bear, denomination below

Date	Mintage	F	VF	XF	Unc	BU
1991 Proof	Est. 100,000	Value: 47.50				
1997PM Proof	—	Value: 50.00				

KM# 138   25 DOLLARS
1.2144 g., 0.9990 Gold 0.0390 oz. AGW **Ruler:** Elizabeth II
Subject: Endangered Wildlife **Obv:** Crowned head right, date below
Rev: Przewalski's horse galloping right, denomination below

Date	Mintage	F	VF	XF	Unc	BU
1992 Proof	—	Value: 47.50				

KM# 242   25 DOLLARS
1.2144 g., 0.9990 Gold 0.0390 oz. AGW **Ruler:** Elizabeth II
Subject: Endangered Wildlife **Obv:** Crowned head right, date
below **Rev:** African lion, denomination below

Date	Mintage	F	VF	XF	Unc	BU
1992 Proof	Est. 100,000	Value: 47.50				

KM# 243   25 DOLLARS
1.2144 g., 0.9990 Gold 0.0390 oz. AGW **Ruler:** Elizabeth II
Subject: Endangered Wildlife **Obv:** Crowned head right, date
below **Rev:** Butterfly, denomination below

Date	Mintage	F	VF	XF	Unc	BU
1992 Proof	Est. 100,000	Value: 47.50				

KM# 238   25 DOLLARS
6.2200 g., 0.5830 Gold 0.1166 oz. AGW **Ruler:** Elizabeth II
Subject: 1996 Olympics **Obv:** Crowned head right, date below
Rev: Ancient archer within circle, denomination below

Date	Mintage	F	VF	XF	Unc	BU
1995 Proof	Est. 5,000	Value: 120				

KM# 271   25 DOLLARS
155.5175 g., 0.9990 Silver 4.9948 oz. ASW **Ruler:** Elizabeth II
Subject: Endangered Wildlife **Obv:** Crowned head right, date
below **Rev:** Koala bear and baby, denomination below

Date	Mintage	F	VF	XF	Unc	BU
1996 Proof	Est. 10,000	Value: 110				

KM# 272   25 DOLLARS
155.5175 g., 0.9990 Silver 4.9948 oz. ASW **Ruler:** Elizabeth II
Subject: Endangered Wildlife **Obv:** Crowned head right, date
below **Rev:** Family of chimpanzees

Date	Mintage	F	VF	XF	Unc	BU
1996 Proof	Est. 10,000	Value: 110				

KM# 273   25 DOLLARS
155.5175 g., 0.9990 Silver 4.9948 oz. ASW **Ruler:** Elizabeth II
Subject: Endangered Wildlife **Obv:** Crowned head right, date
below **Rev:** Family of elephants

Date	Mintage	F	VF	XF	Unc	BU
1996 Proof	Est. 10,000	Value: 110				

KM# 274   25 DOLLARS
155.5175 g., 0.9990 Silver 4.9948 oz. ASW **Ruler:** Elizabeth II
Subject: Endangered Wildlife **Obv:** Crowned head right, date
below **Rev:** Family of whooping cranes

Date	Mintage	F	VF	XF	Unc	BU
1996 Proof	Est. 10,000	Value: 110				

KM# 289   25 DOLLARS
155.5175 g., 0.9990 Silver 4.9948 oz. ASW **Ruler:** Elizabeth II
Subject: Olympic National Park **Obv:** Crowned head right, date
below **Rev:** Multicolor Bald eagle in flight

Date	Mintage	F	VF	XF	Unc	BU
1996 Proof	1,000	Value: 110				

KM# 290   25 DOLLARS
155.5175 g., 0.9990 Silver 4.9948 oz. ASW **Ruler:** Elizabeth II
Subject: Yellowstone Natonal Park **Obv:** Crowned head right,
date below **Rev:** Multicolor Grizzly bear and cub

Date	Mintage	F	VF	XF	Unc	BU
1996 Proof	1,000	Value: 110				

KM# 291 25 DOLLARS
3.1103 g., 0.9990 Gold 0.0999 oz. AGW **Ruler:** Elizabeth II
Subject: Olympic National Park **Obv:** Crowned head right, date
below **Rev:** Bald eagle head right, denomination below

Date	Mintage	F	VF	XF	Unc	BU
1996 Proof	—				Value: 100	

KM# 292 25 DOLLARS
3.1103 g., 0.9990 Gold 0.0999 oz. AGW **Ruler:** Elizabeth II
Subject: Yellowstone National Park **Obv:** Crowned head right,
date below **Rev:** Grizzly bear

Date	Mintage	F	VF	XF	Unc	BU
1996 Proof	—				Value: 100	

KM# 474 25 DOLLARS
7.8200 g., 0.9999 Gold 0.2514 oz. AGW, 19.97 mm.
Ruler: Elizabeth II **Subject:** Death of Princess Diana
Obv: Crowned bust right **Rev:** Head of Diana 3/4 right
Edge: Reeded

Date	Mintage	F	VF	XF	Unc	BU
1997 Proof	—				Value: 300	

KM# 309 30 DOLLARS
1000.1000 g., 0.9990 Silver 32.120 oz. ASW **Ruler:** Elizabeth II
Obv: Crowned head right, date below **Rev:** Princess Diana's
portrait, dates

Date	Mintage	F	VF	XF	Unc	BU
1997 Matte Proof	—				Value: 650	

KM# 11 50 DOLLARS
97.2000 g., 0.9250 Silver 2.8906 oz. ASW **Ruler:** Elizabeth II
Subject: Winston Churchill Centenary **Obv:** Young bust right,
date below **Rev:** Churchill head at right looking left, castle, Big
Ben clock, flag, denomination below

Date	Mintage	F	VF	XF	Unc	BU
1974	1,202	—	—	BV	60.00	65.00
1974 Proof	2,502				Value: 62.50	

KM# 11a 50 DOLLARS
97.2000 g., 0.9250 Silver Gilt 2.8906 oz. ASW **Ruler:**
Elizabeth II **Subject:** Winston Churchill Centenary **Obv:** Young
bust right, date below **Rev:** Churchill head at right looking left,
flag above castle and clock tower

Date	Mintage	F	VF	XF	Unc	BU
1974 Proof	2,002				Value: 60.00	

KM# 203 50 DOLLARS
3.9450 g., 0.5000 Gold 0.0634 oz. AGW **Ruler:** Elizabeth II
Obv: Young bust right, date below **Rev:** Denomination above plant

Date	Mintage	F	VF	XF	Unc	BU
1980 Proof	—				Value: 65.00	

KM# 27 50 DOLLARS
3.9450 g., 0.5000 Gold 0.0634 oz. AGW **Ruler:** Elizabeth II
Subject: Wedding of Prince Charles and Lady Diana **Obv:** Young
bust right, date below **Rev:** Denomination below symbol

Date	Mintage	F	VF	XF	Unc	BU
1981	220				65.00	—
1981 Proof	1,309		Value: 70.00			

KM# 40 50 DOLLARS
28.2800 g., 0.9250 Silver 0.8410 oz. ASW **Ruler:** Elizabeth II
Subject: 1988 Olympics **Obv:** Crowned bust right, date below
Rev: Torch bearer, globe in background

Date	Mintage	F	VF	XF	Unc	BU
1987PM Proof	20,000		Value: 18.00			

KM# 61 50 DOLLARS
20.9400 g., 0.9250 Silver 0.6227 oz. ASW **Ruler:** Elizabeth II
Subject: Great Explorers **Obv:** Crowned head right, date below
Rev: Stanley and Livingstone, denomination lower right

Date	Mintage	F	VF	XF	Unc	BU
1988 (P)	—				Value: 15.00	

KM# 62 50 DOLLARS
20.9400 g., 0.9250 Silver 0.6227 oz. ASW **Ruler:** Elizabeth II
Subject: Great Explorers **Obv:** Crowned head right, date below
Rev: Capt. James Cook

Date	Mintage	F	VF	XF	Unc	BU
1988FM (P)	—				Value: 15.00	

KM# 63 50 DOLLARS
20.9400 g., 0.9250 Silver 0.6227 oz. ASW **Ruler:** Elizabeth II
Subject: Great Explorers **Obv:** Crowned head right, date below
Rev: Vasco Nuñez de Balboa

Date	Mintage	F	VF	XF	Unc	BU
1988FM (P)	—				Value: 15.00	

KM# 64 50 DOLLARS
20.9400 g., 0.9250 Silver 0.6227 oz. ASW **Ruler:** Elizabeth II
Subject: Great Explorers **Obv:** Crowned head right, date below
Rev: Ferdinand Magellan's ships: Vittoria and Trinidad

Date	Mintage	F	VF	XF	Unc	BU
1988FM (P)	—				Value: 15.00	

KM# 65 50 DOLLARS
20.9400 g., 0.9250 Silver 0.6227 oz. ASW **Ruler:** Elizabeth II
Subject: Great Explorers **Obv:** Crowned head right, date below
Rev: Marco Polo on camel, denomination at right

Date	Mintage	F	VF	XF	Unc	BU
1988FM (P)	—				Value: 15.00	

KM# 66 50 DOLLARS
20.9400 g., 0.9250 Silver 0.6227 oz. ASW **Ruler:** Elizabeth II
Subject: Great Explorers **Obv:** Crowned head right, date below
Rev: Vasco da Gama

Date	Mintage	F	VF	XF	Unc	BU
1988FM (P)	—				Value: 15.00	

KM# 67   50 DOLLARS
20.9400 g., 0.9250 Silver 0.6227 oz. ASW   **Ruler:** Elizabeth II
Subject: Great Explorers **Obv:** Crowned head right, date below
Rev: Christopher Columbus

Date	Mintage	F	VF	XF	Unc	BU
1988FM (P)	—				Value: 15.00	

KM# 68   50 DOLLARS
20.9400 g., 0.9250 Silver 0.6227 oz. ASW   **Ruler:** Elizabeth II
Subject: Great Explorers **Obv:** Crowned head right, date below
Rev: Sir Francis Drake

Date	Mintage	F	VF	XF	Unc	BU
1988FM (P)	—				Value: 15.00	

KM# 69   50 DOLLARS
20.9400 g., 0.9250 Silver 0.6227 oz. ASW   **Ruler:** Elizabeth II
Subject: Great Explorers **Obv:** Crowned head right, date below
Rev: Sieur de la Salle

Date	Mintage	F	VF	XF	Unc	BU
1988FM (P)	—				Value: 15.00	

KM# 96   50 DOLLARS
20.9400 g., 0.9250 Silver 0.6227 oz. ASW   **Ruler:** Elizabeth II
Subject: Great Explorers **Obv:** Crowned head right, date below
Rev: Alexander the Great

Date	Mintage	F	VF	XF	Unc	BU
1988FM (P)	—				Value: 15.00	

KM# 97   50 DOLLARS
20.9400 g., 0.9250 Silver 0.6227 oz. ASW   **Ruler:** Elizabeth II
Subject: Great Explorers **Obv:** Crowned head right, date below
Rev: Leif Ericson, denomination at right

Date	Mintage	F	VF	XF	Unc	BU
1988FM (P)	—				Value: 15.00	

KM# 98   50 DOLLARS
20.9400 g., 0.9250 Silver 0.6227 oz. ASW   **Ruler:** Elizabeth II
Subject: Great Explorers **Obv:** Crowned head right, date below
Rev: Amerigo Vespucci

Date	Mintage	F	VF	XF	Unc	BU
1988FM (P)	—				Value: 15.00	

KM# 99   50 DOLLARS
20.9400 g., 0.9250 Silver 0.6227 oz. ASW   **Ruler:** Elizabeth II
Subject: Great Explorers **Obv:** Crowned head right, date below
Rev: Bartolomeu Diaz

Date	Mintage	F	VF	XF	Unc	BU
1988FM (P)	—				Value: 15.00	

KM# 100   50 DOLLARS
20.9400 g., 0.9250 Silver 0.6227 oz. ASW   **Ruler:** Elizabeth II
Subject: Great Explorers **Obv:** Crowned head right, date below
Rev: Juan Ponce de Léon

Date	Mintage	F	VF	XF	Unc	BU
1988FM (P)	—				Value: 15.00	

KM# 101   50 DOLLARS
20.9400 g., 0.9250 Silver 0.6227 oz. ASW   **Ruler:** Elizabeth II
Subject: Great Explorers **Obv:** Crowned head right, date below
Rev: Hernando Cortés

Date	Mintage	F	VF	XF	Unc	BU
1988FM (P)	—				Value: 15.00	

KM# 102   50 DOLLARS
20.9400 g., 0.9250 Silver 0.6227 oz. ASW   **Ruler:** Elizabeth II
Subject: Great Explorers **Obv:** Crowned head right, date below
Rev: Francisco Coronado

Date	Mintage	F	VF	XF	Unc	BU
1988FM (P)	—				Value: 15.00	

KM# 103   50 DOLLARS
20.9400 g., 0.9250 Silver 0.6227 oz. ASW   **Ruler:** Elizabeth II
Subject: Great Explorers **Obv:** Crowned head right, date below
Rev: Francisco Pizarro and map, denomination at left

Date	Mintage	F	VF	XF	Unc	BU
1988FM (P)	—				Value: 15.00	

KM# 104   50 DOLLARS
20.9400 g., 0.9250 Silver 0.6227 oz. ASW   **Ruler:** Elizabeth II
Subject: Great Explorers **Obv:** Crowned head right, date below
Rev: Samuel de Champlain

Date	Mintage	F	VF	XF	Unc	BU
1988FM (P)	—				Value: 15.00	

KM# 105   50 DOLLARS
20.9400 g., 0.9250 Silver 0.6227 oz. ASW   **Ruler:** Elizabeth II
Subject: Great Explorers **Obv:** Crowned head right, date below
Rev: John Cabot

Date	Mintage	F	VF	XF	Unc	BU
1988FM (P)	—				Value: 15.00	

KM# 106   50 DOLLARS
20.9400 g., 0.9250 Silver 0.6227 oz. ASW   **Ruler:** Elizabeth II
Subject: Great Explorers **Obv:** Crowned head right, date below
Rev: Abel Janszoon Tasman

Date	Mintage	F	VF	XF	Unc	BU
1988FM (P)	—				Value: 15.00	

KM# 107   50 DOLLARS
20.9400 g., 0.9250 Silver 0.6227 oz. ASW   **Ruler:** Elizabeth II
Subject: Great Explorers **Obv:** Crowned head right, date below
Rev: Lewis and Clark, denomination at left

Date	Mintage	F	VF	XF	Unc	BU
1988FM (P)	—				Value: 15.00	

KM# 108   50 DOLLARS
20.9400 g., 0.9250 Silver 0.6227 oz. ASW   **Ruler:** Elizabeth II
Subject: Great Explorers **Obv:** Crowned head right, date below
Rev: Fridtjof Nansen

Date	Mintage	F	VF	XF	Unc	BU
1988FM (P)	—				Value: 15.00	

KM# 109   50 DOLLARS
20.9400 g., 0.9250 Silver 0.6227 oz. ASW   **Ruler:** Elizabeth II
Subject: Great Explorers **Obv:** Crowned head right, date below
Rev: Robert Peary

Date	Mintage	F	VF	XF	Unc	BU
1988FM (P)	—				Value: 15.00	

KM# 110   50 DOLLARS
20.9400 g., 0.9250 Silver 0.6227 oz. ASW   **Ruler:** Elizabeth II
Subject: Great Explorers **Obv:** Crowned head right, date below
Rev: Roald Amundsen

Date	Mintage	F	VF	XF	Unc	BU
1988FM (P); Proof	—				Value: 15.00	

KM# 111   50 DOLLARS
20.9400 g., 0.9250 Silver 0.6227 oz. ASW   **Ruler:** Elizabeth II
Subject: Great Explorers **Obv:** Crowned head right, date below
Rev: Richard Byrd, map at left, denomination above

Date	Mintage	F	VF	XF	Unc	BU
1988FM (P)	—				Value: 15.00	

KM# 45   50 DOLLARS
19.4000 g., 0.9250 Silver 0.5769 oz. ASW   **Ruler:** Elizabeth II
Subject: 500 Years of America **Obv:** Crowned head right, date
below **Rev:** Sir Francis Drake

Date	Mintage	F	VF	XF	Unc	BU
1989 Proof	15,000		Value: 15.00			
1990 Proof	—		Value: 14.00			

KM# 49   50 DOLLARS
31.1000 g., 0.9250 Silver 0.9249 oz. ASW   **Ruler:** Elizabeth II
Subject: 500 Years of America **Obv:** Crowned head right, date
below **Rev:** Ferdinand Magellan at right, map at left,
denomination below

Date	Mintage	F	VF	XF	Unc	BU
1989 Proof	15,000		Value: 20.00			
1991 Proof	Est. 60,000		Value: 18.50			

KM# 46   50 DOLLARS
31.1000 g., 0.9990 Silver 0.9988 oz. ASW   **Ruler:** Elizabeth II
Subject: 500 Years of America **Obv:** Crowned head right, date
below **Rev:** Capt. James Cook

Date	Mintage	F	VF	XF	Unc	BU
1989 Proof	15,000		Value: 20.00			

KM# 47   50 DOLLARS
29.9000 g., 0.9250 Silver 0.8892 oz. ASW   **Ruler:** Elizabeth II
Subject: 500 Years of America **Obv:** Crowned head right, date
below **Rev:** Christopher Columbus, CHRISTOPHER
COLUMBUS WITH THE SANTA MARIA

Date	Mintage	F	VF	XF	Unc	BU
1989 Proof	Est. 15,000		Value: 18.50			

Note: Prior to the 27th edition, the illustration for KM#47
was incorrect. Please see KM#182 for correct listing.

KM# 60   50 DOLLARS
28.2800 g., 0.9250 Silver 0.8410 oz. ASW   **Ruler:** Elizabeth II
Subject: 1990 Olympics **Obv:** Crowned bust right, date below
Rev: Runners and biathalon

Date	Mintage	F	VF	XF	Unc	BU
1989 Proof	40,000		Value: 17.50			

KM# 70   50 DOLLARS
28.2800 g., 0.9250 Silver 0.8410 oz. ASW   **Ruler:** Elizabeth II
Subject: Soccer World Championship **Obv:** Crowned bust right,
date below **Rev:** Two soccer players and ball

Date	Mintage	F	VF	XF	Unc	BU
1989 Proof	—		Value: 17.50			

KM# 43   50 DOLLARS
31.1000 g., 0.9250 Silver 0.9249 oz. ASW   **Ruler:** Elizabeth II
Subject: 500 Years of America **Obv:** Crowned head right, date
below **Rev:** Jacques Cartier

Date	Mintage	F	VF	XF	Unc	BU
1990 Proof	60,000		Value: 20.00			
1991 Proof	—		Value: 18.50			

KM# 44   50 DOLLARS
31.1000 g., 0.9990 Silver 0.9988 oz. ASW   **Ruler:** Elizabeth II
Subject: 500 Years of America **Obv:** Crowned head right, date
below **Rev:** Vasco Nunez de Balboa, left, denomination below

Date	Mintage	F	VF	XF	Unc	BU
1990 Proof	15,000	Value: 22.00				
1991 Proof	—	Value: 20.00				

KM# 53   50 DOLLARS
19.4000 g., 0.9250 Silver 0.5769 oz. ASW   **Ruler:** Elizabeth II
Subject: Endangered World Wildlife **Obv:** Crowned head right,
date below **Rev:** African elephant

Date	Mintage	F	VF	XF	Unc	BU
1990 Matte Proof	1,000	Value: 35.00				
1990 Proof	25,000	Value: 25.00				

KM# 57   50 DOLLARS
19.4000 g., 0.9250 Silver 0.5769 oz. ASW   **Ruler:** Elizabeth II
Subject: Endangered World Wildlife **Obv:** Crowned head right,
date below **Rev:** Koala bear

Date	Mintage	F	VF	XF	Unc	BU
1990 Proof	Est. 25,000	Value: 25.00				

KM# 265   50 DOLLARS
28.3000 g., 0.9250 Silver 0.8416 oz. ASW   **Ruler:** Elizabeth II
Subject: World Cup Soccer **Obv:** Crowned head right, date
below **Rev:** Soccer players, denomination below

Date	Mintage	F	VF	XF	Unc	BU
1990 Proof	—	Value: 17.50				

KM# 54   50 DOLLARS
19.4000 g., 0.9250 Silver 0.5769 oz. ASW   **Ruler:** Elizabeth II
Subject: Endangered World Wildlife **Obv:** Crowned head right,
date below **Rev:** Lynx

Date	Mintage	F	VF	XF	Unc	BU
1990 Proof	25,000	Value: 25.00				

KM# 58   50 DOLLARS
19.4000 g., 0.9250 Silver 0.5769 oz. ASW   **Ruler:** Elizabeth II
Subject: Endangered World Wildlife **Obv:** Crowned head right,
date below **Rev:** Buffalo, denomination below

Date	Mintage	F	VF	XF	Unc	BU
1990	600		—	—	40.00	45.00
1990 Proof	25,000	Value: 25.00				

KM# 52   50 DOLLARS
19.4000 g., 0.9250 Silver 0.5769 oz. ASW   **Ruler:** Elizabeth II
Subject: Endangered World Wildlife **Obv:** Crowned head right,
date below **Rev:** Grizzly bear

Date	Mintage	F	VF	XF	Unc	BU
1990PM Matte Proof	550	Value: 45.00				
1990PM Proof	2,500	Value: 25.00				

KM# 55   50 DOLLARS
19.4000 g., 0.9250 Silver 0.5769 oz. ASW   **Ruler:** Elizabeth II
Subject: Endangered World Wildlife **Obv:** Crowned head right,
date below **Rev:** Black rhinoceros

Date	Mintage	F	VF	XF	Unc	BU
1990 Proof	Est. 25,000	Value: 25.00				

KM# 59   50 DOLLARS
19.4000 g., 0.9250 Silver 0.5769 oz. ASW   **Ruler:** Elizabeth II
Subject: Endangered World Wildlife **Obv:** Crowned head right,
date below **Rev:** Chimpanzee, denomination below

Date	Mintage	F	VF	XF	Unc	BU
1990 Proof	Est. 25,000	Value: 25.00				

KM# 48   50 DOLLARS
31.1000 g., 0.9990 Silver 0.9988 oz. ASW   **Ruler:** Elizabeth II
Subject: 500 Years of America **Obv:** Crowned head right, date
below **Rev:** President Abraham Lincoln in foreground of capitol

Date	Mintage	F	VF	XF	Unc	BU
1990 Proof	15,000	Value: 22.00				
1991 Proof	—	Value: 20.00				

KM# 56   50 DOLLARS
19.4000 g., 0.9250 Silver 0.5769 oz. ASW   **Ruler:** Elizabeth II
Subject: Endangered World Wildlife **Obv:** Crowned head right,
date below **Rev:** Bighorn sheep, denomination below

Date	Mintage	F	VF	XF	Unc	BU
1990 Proof	Est. 25,000	Value: 25.00				

KM# 89   50 DOLLARS
31.1000 g., 0.9250 Silver 0.9249 oz. ASW   **Ruler:** Elizabeth II
Subject: 500 Years of America **Obv:** Crowned head right, date
below **Rev:** 3/4 figure of Henry Hudson at right looking left, ship
at left, denomination below

Date	Mintage	F	VF	XF	Unc	BU
1990 Proof	60,000	Value: 20.00				

KM# 134 50 DOLLARS
31.1000 g., 0.9250 Silver 0.9249 oz. ASW **Ruler:** Elizabeth II
Subject: 500 Years of America **Obv:** Crowned head right, date
below **Rev:** Cabral bust at right, two figures with cross at left,
denomination below

Date	Mintage	F	VF	XF	Unc	BU
1990 Proof	Est. 60,000	Value: 20.00				

KM# 135 50 DOLLARS
31.1000 g., 0.9250 Silver 0.9249 oz. ASW **Ruler:** Elizabeth II
Subject: 500 Years of America **Obv:** Crowned head right, date
below **Rev:** Half figure of Bolivar at left facing right, denomination
below

Date	Mintage	F	VF	XF	Unc	BU
1990 Proof	Est. 60,000	Value: 20.00				

KM# 139 50 DOLLARS
31.2600 g., 0.9250 Silver 0.9296 oz. ASW **Ruler:** Elizabeth II
Subject: 500 Years of America **Obv:** Crowned head right, date
below **Rev:** Samuel Clemens at left looking right, steamboat in
background, denomination below

Date	Mintage	F	VF	XF	Unc	BU
1990 Proof	Est. 60,000	Value: 20.00				

KM# 182 50 DOLLARS
31.3500 g., 0.9250 Silver 0.9323 oz. ASW **Ruler:** Elizabeth II
Subject: 500 Years of America **Obv:** Crowned head right, date
below **Rev:** Columbus' portrait with Santa Maria in background

Date	Mintage	F	VF	XF	Unc	BU
1990 Proof	—	Value: 20.00				

KM# 184 50 DOLLARS
31.3500 g., 0.9250 Silver 0.9323 oz. ASW **Ruler:** Elizabeth II
Subject: 500 Years of America **Obv:** Crowned head right, date
below **Rev:** Inca Prince

Date	Mintage	F	VF	XF	Unc	BU
1990 Proof	Est. 60,000	Value: 20.00				

KM# 185 50 DOLLARS
31.3500 g., 0.9250 Silver 0.9323 oz. ASW **Ruler:** Elizabeth II
Subject: 500 Years of America **Obv:** Crowned head right, date
below **Rev:** Cortez and Montezuma, denomination below

Date	Mintage	F	VF	XF	Unc	BU
1990 Proof	Est. 60,000	Value: 20.00				

KM# 186 50 DOLLARS
31.3500 g., 0.9250 Silver 0.9323 oz. ASW **Ruler:** Elizabeth II
Subject: 500 Years of America **Obv:** Crowned head right, date
below **Rev:** Samuel de Champlain bust looking right,
denomination below

Date	Mintage	F	VF	XF	Unc	BU
1990 Proof	Est. 60,000	Value: 20.00				

KM# 188 50 DOLLARS
31.3500 g., 0.9250 Silver 0.9323 oz. ASW **Ruler:** Elizabeth II
Subject: 500 Years of America **Obv:** Crowned head right, date
below **Rev:** Sir Walter Raleigh at right facing left, ship at left,
denomination below

Date	Mintage	F	VF	XF	Unc	BU
1990 Proof	Est. 60,000	Value: 20.00				

KM# 112 50 DOLLARS
19.2000 g., 0.9250 Silver 0.5710 oz. ASW **Ruler:** Elizabeth II
Subject: 1992 Olympics **Obv:** Crowned head right, date below
Rev: Runner

Date	Mintage	F	VF	XF	Unc	BU
1990 Proof	40,000	Value: 14.00				

KM# 115 50 DOLLARS
19.8000 g., 0.9250 Silver 0.5888 oz. ASW **Ruler:** Elizabeth II
Subject: Endangered World Wildlife **Obv:** Crowned head right,
date below **Rev:** Blackbuck left, denomination below

Date	Mintage	F	VF	XF	Unc	BU
1990 Proof	—	Value: 25.00				

KM# 117 50 DOLLARS
19.8000 g., 0.9250 Silver 0.5888 oz. ASW **Ruler:** Elizabeth II
Subject: Endangered World Wildlife **Obv:** Crowned head right,
date below **Rev:** Whooping crane, denomination below

Date	Mintage	F	VF	XF	Unc	BU
1990 Proof	—	Value: 25.00				

KM# 144 50 DOLLARS
19.4000 g., 0.9250 Silver 0.5769 oz. ASW **Ruler:** Elizabeth II
Subject: Endangered World Wildlife **Obv:** Crowned head right,
date below **Rev:** European hedgehog left, denomination below

Date	Mintage	F	VF	XF	Unc	BU
1990 Proof	Est. 25,000	Value: 25.00				

KM# 205   50 DOLLARS
19.2000 g., 0.9250 Silver 0.5710 oz. ASW   **Ruler:** Elizabeth II
Subject: Endangered World Wildlife **Obv:** PM mint mark below
truncation **Rev:** European bison and calf

Date	Mintage	F	VF	XF	Unc	BU
1990PM Proof	Est. 25,000			Value: 25.00		

KM# 206   50 DOLLARS
19.2000 g., 0.9250 Silver 0.5710 oz. ASW   **Ruler:** Elizabeth II
Subject: Endangered World Wildlife **Obv:** Crowned head right,
date below **Rev:** Tiger

Date	Mintage	F	VF	XF	Unc	BU
1990 Proof	Est. 25,000			Value: 25.00		

KM# 207   50 DOLLARS
19.2000 g., 0.9250 Silver 0.5710 oz. ASW   **Ruler:** Elizabeth II
Subject: Endangered World Wildlife **Obv:** Crowned head right,
date below **Rev:** Dama gazelles, denomination below

Date	Mintage	F	VF	XF	Unc	BU
1990 Proof	Est. 25,000			Value: 25.00		

KM# 208   50 DOLLARS
19.2000 g., 0.9250 Silver 0.5710 oz. ASW   **Ruler:** Elizabeth II
Subject: Endangered World Wildlife **Obv:** Crowned head right,
date below **Rev:** Cougars

Date	Mintage	F	VF	XF	Unc	BU
1990PM Proof				Value: 27.00		

KM# 209   50 DOLLARS
19.2000 g., 0.9250 Silver 0.5710 oz. ASW   **Ruler:** Elizabeth II
Subject: Endangered World Wildlife **Obv:** Crowned head right,
date below **Rev:** Eagle Owl, denomination below

Date	Mintage	F	VF	XF	Unc	BU
1990(b) Proof				Value: 27.00		

KM# 210   50 DOLLARS
19.2000 g., 0.9250 Silver 0.5710 oz. ASW   **Ruler:** Elizabeth II
Subject: Endangered World Wildlife **Obv:** Crowned head right,
date below **Rev:** Heaviside's dolphins

Date	Mintage	F	VF	XF	Unc	BU
1990(b) Proof				Value: 27.00		

KM# 211   50 DOLLARS
19.2000 g., 0.9250 Silver 0.5710 oz. ASW   **Ruler:** Elizabeth II
Subject: Endangered World Wildlife **Obv:** Crowned head right,
date below **Rev:** European otters

Date	Mintage	F	VF	XF	Unc	BU
1990 Proof				Value: 25.00		

KM# 357   50 DOLLARS
19.2000 g., 0.9250 Silver 0.5710 oz. ASW   **Ruler:** Elizabeth II
Subject: Endangered World Wildlife **Obv:** Crowned head right,
date below **Rev:** Peregrine falcon

Date	Mintage	F	VF	XF	Unc	BU
1990(b) Proof				Value: 25.00		

KM# 212   50 DOLLARS
19.2000 g., 0.9250 Silver 0.5710 oz. ASW   **Ruler:** Elizabeth II
Subject: Endangered World Wildlife **Obv:** Crowned head right,
date below **Rev:** Alpine ibex

Date	Mintage	F	VF	XF	Unc	BU
1990 Proof				Value: 25.00		

KM# 213   50 DOLLARS
19.2000 g., 0.9250 Silver 0.5710 oz. ASW   **Ruler:** Elizabeth II
Subject: Endangered World Wildlife **Obv:** Crowned head right,
date below **Rev:** Senegalese lion, denomination below

Date	Mintage	F	VF	XF	Unc	BU
1990 Proof				Value: 25.00		

KM# 214   50 DOLLARS
19.2000 g., 0.9250 Silver 0.5710 oz. ASW   **Ruler:** Elizabeth II
Subject: Endangered World Wildlife **Obv:** Crowned head right,
date below **Rev:** Fallow deer, denomination below

Date	Mintage	F	VF	XF	Unc	BU
1990 Proof				Value: 25.00		

KM# 215   50 DOLLARS
19.2000 g., 0.9250 Silver 0.5710 oz. ASW   **Ruler:** Elizabeth II
Subject: Endangered World Wildlife **Obv:** Crowned head right,
date below **Rev:** Bee hummingbird

Date	Mintage	F	VF	XF	Unc	BU
1990 Proof				Value: 25.00		

KM# 216 50 DOLLARS
19.2000 g., 0.9250 Silver 0.5710 oz. ASW **Ruler:** Elizabeth II
Subject: Endangered World Wildlife **Obv:** Crowned head right,
date below **Rev:** Jackass penguins

Date	Mintage	F	VF	XF	Unc	BU
1990 Proof	—				Value: 25.00	

KM# 93 50 DOLLARS
19.8000 g., 0.9250 Silver 0.5888 oz.. ASW **Ruler:** Elizabeth II
Subject: Endangered Wildlife **Obv:** Crowned head right, date
below **Rev:** Eagle owl

Date	Mintage	F	VF	XF	Unc	BU
1991 Proof	Est. 25,000				Value: 25.00	

KM# 95 50 DOLLARS
19.2000 g., 0.9250 Silver 0.5710 oz. ASW **Ruler:** Elizabeth II
Subject: Endangered Wildlife **Obv:** Crowned head right, date
below **Rev:** Heaviside's dolphins

Date	Mintage	F	VF	XF	Unc	BU
1991 Proof	Est. 25,000				Value: 25.00	

KM# 118 50 DOLLARS
19.2000 g., 0.9250 Silver 0.5710 oz. ASW **Ruler:** Elizabeth II
Subject: Endangered Wildlife **Obv:** Crowned head right, date
below **Rev:** European otters

Date	Mintage	F	VF	XF	Unc	BU
1991 Proof	—				Value: 25.00	

KM# 119 50 DOLLARS
19.2000 g., 0.9250 Silver 0.5710 oz. ASW **Ruler:** Elizabeth II
Subject: Endangered Wildlife **Obv:** Crowned head right, date
below **Rev:** Peregrine falcon

Date	Mintage	F	VF	XF	Unc	BU
1991 Proof	Est. 25,000				Value: 25.00	

KM# 120 50 DOLLARS
19.2000 g., 0.9250 Silver 0.5710 oz. ASW **Ruler:** Elizabeth II
Subject: Endangered Wildlife **Obv:** Crowned head right, date
below **Rev:** Alpine ibex

Date	Mintage	F	VF	XF	Unc	BU
1991 Proof	Est. 25,000				Value: 25.00	

KM# 122 50 DOLLARS
19.2000 g., 0.9250 Silver 0.5710 oz. ASW **Ruler:** Elizabeth II
Subject: Endangered Wildlife **Obv:** Crowned head right,
below **Rev:** Senegalese lion

Date	Mintage	F	VF	XF	Unc	BU
1991 Proof	Est. 25,000				Value: 25.00	

KM# 123 50 DOLLARS
19.2000 g., 0.9250 Silver 0.5710 oz. ASW **Ruler:** Elizabeth II
Subject: Endangered Wildlife **Obv:** Crowned head right, date
below **Rev:** Deer

Date	Mintage	F	VF	XF	Unc	BU
1991 Proof	Est. 25,000				Value: 25.00	

KM# 124 50 DOLLARS
19.2000 g., 0.9250 Silver 0.5710 oz. ASW **Ruler:** Elizabeth II
Subject: Endangered Wildlife **Obv:** Crowned head right, date
below **Rev:** Kangaroo

Date	Mintage	F	VF	XF	Unc	BU
1991 Proof	Est. 25,000				Value: 25.00	

KM# 125 50 DOLLARS
19.2000 g., 0.9250 Silver 0.5710 oz. ASW **Ruler:** Elizabeth II
Subject: Endangered Wildlife **Obv:** Crowned head right, date
below **Rev:** Cougar and cub

Date	Mintage	F	VF	XF	Unc	BU
1991 Proof	Est. 25,000				Value: 25.00	

KM# 126 50 DOLLARS
19.2000 g., 0.9250 Silver 0.5710 oz. ASW **Ruler:** Elizabeth II
Subject: Endangered Wildlife **Obv:** Crowned head right, date
below **Rev:** Fallow deer

Date	Mintage	F	VF	XF	Unc	BU
1991 Proof	Est. 25,000				Value: 25.00	

KM# 127 50 DOLLARS
19.2000 g., 0.9250 Silver 0.5710 oz. ASW **Ruler:** Elizabeth II
Subject: Endangered Wildlife **Obv:** Crowned head right, date
below **Rev:** Bee hummingbird

Date	Mintage	F	VF	XF	Unc	BU
1991 Proof	Est. 25,000				Value: 25.00	

KM# 128   50 DOLLARS
19.2000 g., 0.9250 Silver 0.5710 oz. ASW   **Ruler:** Elizabeth II
Subject: Endangered Wildlife **Obv:** Crowned head right, date
below **Rev:** Jackass penguins

Date	Mintage	F	VF	XF	Unc	BU
1991 Proof	Est. 25,000				Value: 25.00	

KM# 94   50 DOLLARS
31.1000 g., 0.9250 Silver 0.9249 oz. ASW   **Ruler:** Elizabeth II
Subject: 500 Years of America **Obv:** Crowned head right, date
below **Rev:** Sitting Bull, denomination below

Date	Mintage	F	VF	XF	Unc	BU
1991 Proof	Est. 15,000				Value: 22.00	

KM# 140   50 DOLLARS
31.2600 g., 0.9250 Silver 0.9296 oz. ASW   **Ruler:** Elizabeth II
Subject: 500 Years of America **Obv:** Crowned head right, date
below **Rev:** Mayflower and pilgrims, denomination below

Date	Mintage	F	VF	XF	Unc	BU
1991 Proof	—				Value: 20.00	
1992 Proof	60,000				Value: 20.00	

KM# 141   50 DOLLARS
31.2600 g., 0.9250 Silver 0.9296 oz. ASW   **Ruler:** Elizabeth II
Subject: 500 Years of America **Obv:** Crowned head right, date
below **Rev:** Alexander Mackenzie bust looking right, figure in
canoe at right, denomination below

Date	Mintage	F	VF	XF	Unc	BU
1991 Proof	60,000				Value: 20.00	

KM# 145   50 DOLLARS
7.7750 g., 0.5833 Gold 0.1458 oz. AGW   **Ruler:** Elizabeth II
Subject: 500 Years of America **Obv:** Crowned head right, date
below **Rev:** Columbus kneeling with flag, denomination below

Date	Mintage	F	VF	XF	Unc	BU
1991 Proof	Est. 60,000				Value: 145	

KM# 148   50 DOLLARS
31.1000 g., 0.9250 Silver 0.9249 oz. ASW   **Ruler:** Elizabeth II
Subject: 500 Years of America **Obv:** Crowned head right, date
below **Rev:** Aztec Priest, denomination below

Date	Mintage	F	VF	XF	Unc	BU
1991 Proof	Est. 15,000				Value: 20.00	

KM# 189   50 DOLLARS
31.1000 g., 0.9250 Silver 0.9249 oz. ASW   **Ruler:** Elizabeth II
Subject: 500 Years of America **Obv:** Crowned head right, date
below **Rev:** Francisco Pizarro bust at left looking right, arms at
right, denomination below

Date	Mintage	F	VF	XF	Unc	BU
1991 Proof	Est. 60,000				Value: 20.00	

KM# 190   50 DOLLARS
31.1000 g., 0.9250 Silver 0.9249 oz. ASW   **Ruler:** Elizabeth II
Subject: 500 Years of America **Obv:** Crowned head right, date
below **Rev:** Jesuit Church in Cuzco, denomination below

Date	Mintage	F	VF	XF	Unc	BU
1991 Proof	Est. 60,000				Value: 20.00	

KM# 191   50 DOLLARS
31.1000 g., 0.9250 Silver 0.9249 oz. ASW   **Ruler:** Elizabeth II
Subject: 500 Years of America **Obv:** Crowned head right, date
below **Rev:** Peter Minuit's purchase of Manhattan Island,
denomination below

Date	Mintage	F	VF	XF	Unc	BU
1991 Proof	Est. 60,000				Value: 20.00	

KM# 192   50 DOLLARS
31.1000 g., 0.9250 Silver 0.9249 oz. ASW   **Ruler:** Elizabeth II
Subject: 500 Years of America **Obv:** Crowned head right, date
below **Rev:** Boston Tea Party, denomination below

Date	Mintage	F	VF	XF	Unc	BU
1991 Proof	Est. 60,000				Value: 20.00	

KM# 193   50 DOLLARS
31.1000 g., 0.9250 Silver 0.9249 oz. ASW   **Ruler:** Elizabeth II
Subject: 500 Years of America **Obv:** Crowned head right, date
below **Rev:** Marquis de Lafayette bust at right looking left, figures
at left, denomination below

Date	Mintage	F	VF	XF	Unc	BU
1991 Proof	Est. 60,000				Value: 20.00	

KM# 194   50 DOLLARS
31.1000 g., 0.9250 Silver 0.9249 oz. ASW   **Ruler:** Elizabeth II
Subject: 500 Years of America **Obv:** Crowned head right, date
below **Rev:** Robert Fulton, denomination below

Date	Mintage	F	VF	XF	Unc	BU
1991 Proof	Est. 60,000				Value: 20.00	

KM# 195 50 DOLLARS
31.1000 g., 0.9250 Silver 0.9249 oz. ASW **Ruler:** Elizabeth II
Subject: 500 Years of America **Obv:** Crowned head right, date
below **Rev:** First U.S. transcontinental railroad, two busts above
at left, denomination below

Date	Mintage	F	VF	XF	Unc	BU
1991 Proof	Est. 60,000	Value: 20.00				

KM# 196 50 DOLLARS
31.1000 g., 0.9250 Silver 0.9249 oz. ASW **Ruler:** Elizabeth II
Subject: 500 Years of America **Obv:** Crowned head right, date
below **Rev:** Emperor Maximilian of Mexico on horseback,
denomination below

Date	Mintage	F	VF	XF	Unc	BU
1991 Proof	Est. 60,000	Value: 20.00				

KM# 305 50 DOLLARS
31.1000 g., 0.9250 Silver 0.9249 oz. ASW **Ruler:** Elizabeth II
Subject: 500 Years of America **Obv:** Crowned head right, date
below **Rev:** Capt. James Cook

Date	Mintage	F	VF	XF	Unc	BU
1991 Proof	Est. 60,000	Value: 20.00				

KM# 44a 50 DOLLARS
31.1000 g., 0.9250 Silver 0.9249 oz. ASW **Ruler:** Elizabeth II
Subject: 500 Years of America **Obv:** Crowned head right, date
below **Rev:** Vasco Nuñez de Balboa

Date	Mintage	F	VF	XF	Unc	BU
1991 Proof	60,000	Value: 22.00				

KM# 46a 50 DOLLARS
31.1000 g., 0.9250 Silver 0.9249 oz. ASW **Ruler:** Elizabeth II
Subject: 500 Years of America **Obv:** Crowned head right, date
below **Rev:** Capt. James Cook

Date	Mintage	F	VF	XF	Unc	BU
1991 Proof	Est. 60,000	Value: 22.00				

KM# 114 50 DOLLARS
31.1000 g., 0.9250 Silver 0.9249 oz. ASW **Ruler:** Elizabeth II
Subject: 500 Years of America **Obv:** Crowned head right, date
below **Rev:** Coronado's discovery of the Grand Canyon,
denomination below

Date	Mintage	F	VF	XF	Unc	BU
1992 Proof	Est. 15,000	Value: 22.00				

KM# 129 50 DOLLARS
7.7760 g., 0.5830 Gold 0.1457 oz. AGW **Ruler:** Elizabeth II
Subject: Endangered Wildlife **Obv:** Crowned head right, date
below **Rev:** Eagles head

Date	Mintage	F	VF	XF	Unc	BU
1992 Proof	—	Value: 145				

KM# 131 50 DOLLARS
7.7760 g., 0.5830 Gold 0.1457 oz. AGW **Ruler:** Elizabeth II
Subject: Endangered Wildlife **Obv:** Crowned head right, date
below **Rev:** Elephant head

Date	Mintage	F	VF	XF	Unc	BU
1992 Proof	—	Value: 145				

KM# 132 50 DOLLARS
7.7760 g., 0.5830 Gold 0.1457 oz. AGW **Ruler:** Elizabeth II
Subject: Endangered Wildlife **Obv:** Crowned head right, date
below **Rev:** Tiger head

Date	Mintage	F	VF	XF	Unc	BU
1992 Proof	—	Value: 145				

KM# 142 50 DOLLARS
31.2600 g., 0.9250 Silver 0.9296 oz. ASW **Ruler:** Elizabeth II
Subject: 500 Years of America **Obv:** Crowned head right, date
below **Rev:** John Davis' strait marked on map, ship at right,
denomination below

Date	Mintage	F	VF	XF	Unc	BU
1992 Proof	Est. 60,000	Value: 20.00				

KM# 143 50 DOLLARS
31.2600 g., 0.9250 Silver 0.9296 oz. ASW **Ruler:** Elizabeth II
Subject: 500 Years of America **Obv:** Crowned head right, date
below **Rev:** Vitus Bering, denomination below

Date	Mintage	F	VF	XF	Unc	BU
1992 Proof	Est. 60,000	Value: 20.00				

KM# 156 50 DOLLARS
31.1035 g., 0.9250 Silver 0.9250 oz. ASW **Ruler:** Elizabeth II
Subject: 500 Years of America **Obv:** Crowned head right, date
below **Rev:** Pedro de Valdivia bust at left looking right,
denomination below

Date	Mintage	F	VF	XF	Unc	BU
1992 Proof	—	Value: 20.00				

KM# 157 50 DOLLARS
31.1035 g., 0.9250 Silver 0.9250 oz. ASW **Ruler:** Elizabeth II
Subject: 500 Years of America **Obv:** Crowned head right, date
below **Rev:** Diego de Almagro, denomination below

Date	Mintage	F	VF	XF	Unc	BU
1992 Proof	—	Value: 20.00				

KM# 162 50 DOLLARS
31.1035 g., 0.9250 Silver 0.9250 oz. ASW **Ruler:** Elizabeth II
Subject: 500 Years of America **Obv:** Crowned head right, date
below **Rev:** Francisco de Coronado

Date	Mintage	F	VF	XF	Unc	BU
1992 Proof	—	Value: 20.00				

KM# 176 50 DOLLARS
7.7760 g., 0.5833 Gold 0.1458 oz. AGW **Ruler:** Elizabeth II
Subject: 500 Years of America **Obv:** Crowned head right, date
below **Rev:** Robert de La Salle

Date	Mintage	F	VF	XF	Unc	BU
1992 Proof	—	Value: 145				

KM# 183 50 DOLLARS
31.1035 g., 0.9250 Silver 0.9250 oz. ASW **Ruler:** Elizabeth II
Subject: 500 Years of America **Obv:** Crowned head right, date
below **Rev:** Giovanni da Verrazano, denomination below

Date	Mintage	F	VF	XF	Unc	BU
1992 Proof	Est. 60,000	Value: 20.00				

KM# 197 50 DOLLARS
31.1035 g., 0.9250 Silver 0.9250 oz. ASW **Ruler:** Elizabeth II
Subject: 500 Years of America **Obv:** Crowned head right, date
below **Rev:** Juan Ponce de Leon, denomination below

Date	Mintage	F	VF	XF	Unc	BU
1992 Proof	Est. 60,000	Value: 20.00				

KM# 198   50 DOLLARS
31.1035 g., 0.9250 Silver 0.9250 oz. ASW **Ruler:** Elizabeth II
Subject: 500 Years of America **Obv:** Crowned head right, date
below **Rev:** 3/4 bust of Pedro de Mendoza at left, historic
monuments at right, denomination below

Date	Mintage	F	VF	XF	Unc	BU
1992 Proof	Est. 60,000	Value: 20.00				

KM# 199   50 DOLLARS
31.1035 g., 0.9250 Silver 0.9250 oz. ASW **Ruler:** Elizabeth II
Subject: 500 Years of America **Obv:** Crowned head right, date
below **Rev:** Pedro Menendez de Aviles on horseback at lower
right, monument at left, denomination below

Date	Mintage	F	VF	XF	Unc	BU
1992 Proof	—	Value: 20.00				

KM# 200   50 DOLLARS
31.1035 g., 0.9250 Silver 0.9250 oz. ASW **Ruler:** Elizabeth II
Subject: 500 Years of America **Obv:** Crowned head right, date
below **Rev:** Independence Hall, figures above denomination

Date	Mintage	F	VF	XF	Unc	BU
1992 Proof	—	Value: 22.00				

KM# 201   50 DOLLARS
31.1035 g., 0.9250 Silver 0.9250 oz. ASW **Ruler:** Elizabeth II
Subject: 500 Years of America **Obv:** Crowned head right, date
below **Rev:** Sacagawea guiding Lewis and Clark, denomination
below

Date	Mintage	F	VF	XF	Unc	BU
1992 Proof	Est. 60,000	Value: 20.00				

KM# 202   50 DOLLARS
31.1035 g., 0.9250 Silver 0.9250 oz. ASW **Ruler:** Elizabeth II
Subject: 500 Years of America **Obv:** Crowned head right, date
below **Rev:** Oregon Trail, conestoga wagon in front of U.S. map
outline, denomination below

Date	Mintage	F	VF	XF	Unc	BU
1992 Proof	Est. 60,000	Value: 20.00				

KM# 204   50 DOLLARS
7.7760 g., 0.5833 Gold 0.1458 oz. AGW **Ruler:** Elizabeth II
Subject: 500 Years of America **Obv:** Crowned head right, date
below **Rev:** Bust of John Cabot at left, ship at right, denomination
below

Date	Mintage	F	VF	XF	Unc	BU
1992 Proof	5,000	Value: 145				

KM# 249   50 DOLLARS
7.7760 g., 0.5830 Gold 0.1457 oz. AGW **Ruler:** Elizabeth II
Subject: 500 Years of America **Obv:** Crowned head right, date
below **Rev:** Busts of Ferdinand and Isabella half right,
denomination below

Date	Mintage	F	VF	XF	Unc	BU
1992 Proof	Est. 5,000	Value: 145				

KM# 259   50 DOLLARS
7.7760 g., 0.5830 Gold 0.1457 oz. AGW **Ruler:** Elizabeth II
Subject: 500 Years of America **Obv:** Crowned head right, date
below **Rev:** Paul de Maisonneuve, map and city view,
denomination below

Date	Mintage	F	VF	XF	Unc	BU
1992 Proof	Est. 5,000	Value: 145				

KM# 260   50 DOLLARS
7.7760 g., 0.5830 Gold 0.1457 oz. AGW **Ruler:** Elizabeth II
Subject: 500 Years of America **Obv:** Crowned head right, date
below **Rev:** Jakob le Maire, ship and map, denomination below

Date	Mintage	F	VF	XF	Unc	BU
1992 Proof	Est. 5,000	Value: 145				

KM# 244   50 DOLLARS
19.2000 g., 0.9250 Silver 0.5710 oz. ASW **Ruler:** Elizabeth II
Obv: Crowned head right, date below **Rev:** Poplar Admiral
Butterfly and thistle, denomination below

Date	Mintage	F	VF	XF	Unc	BU
1992 Proof	Est. 25,000	Value: 25.00				

KM# 261   50 DOLLARS
19.2000 g., 0.9250 Silver 0.5710 oz. ASW **Ruler:** Elizabeth II
Subject: Endangered Wildlife **Obv:** Crowned head right, date
below **Rev:** Szechuan Takins, denomination below

Date	Mintage	F	VF	XF	Unc	BU
1992 Proof	25,000	Value: 25.00				

KM# 262   50 DOLLARS
19.2000 g., 0.9250 Silver 0.5710 oz. ASW **Ruler:** Elizabeth II
Subject: Endangered Wildlife **Obv:** Crowned head right, date
below **Rev:** Ring-tailed lemurs

Date	Mintage	F	VF	XF	Unc	BU
1992 Proof	25,000	Value: 25.00				

KM# 263   50 DOLLARS
19.2000 g., 0.9250 Silver 0.5710 oz. ASW **Ruler:** Elizabeth II
Subject: Endangered Wildlife **Obv:** Crowned head right, date
below **Rev:** Mandrill, denomination below

Date	Mintage	F	VF	XF	Unc	BU
1992 Proof	25,000	Value: 25.00				

KM# 264 50 DOLLARS
19.2000 g., 0.9250 Silver 0.5710 oz. ASW **Ruler:** Elizabeth II
Subject: Endangered Wildlife **Obv:** Crowned head right, date
below **Rev:** Lowland gorilla

Date	Mintage	F	VF	XF	Unc	BU
1992 Proof	25,000	Value: 25.00				

KM# 310 50 DOLLARS
31.0000 g., 0.9250 Silver 0.9219 oz. ASW **Ruler:** Elizabeth II
Obv: Crowned head right, date below **Rev:** Aztec kneels before
Alvarado, denomination below, PEDRO DE ALVARADO
CONQUEROR of the AZTEC EMPIRE

Date	Mintage	F	VF	XF	Unc	BU
1992 Proof	—	Value: 20.00				

KM# 153 50 DOLLARS
7.7760 g., 0.5833 Gold 0.1458 oz. AGW **Ruler:** Elizabeth II
Subject: Endangered Wildlife **Obv:** Crowned head right, date
below **Rev:** Ibex

Date	Mintage	F	VF	XF	Unc	BU
1993 Proof	—	Value: 150				

KM# 154 50 DOLLARS
7.7760 g., 0.5833 Gold 0.1458 oz. AGW **Ruler:** Elizabeth II
Subject: Endangered Wildlife **Obv:** Crowned head right, date
below **Rev:** Owl and parrot

Date	Mintage	F	VF	XF	Unc	BU
1993 Proof	—	Value: 150				

KM# 164 50 DOLLARS
31.1035 g., 0.9250 Silver 0.9250 oz. ASW **Ruler:** Elizabeth II
Subject: 500 Years of America **Obv:** Crowned head right, date
below **Rev:** Pinzon brothers, denomination below

Date	Mintage	F	VF	XF	Unc	BU
1993 Proof	—	Value: 20.00				

KM# 165 50 DOLLARS
31.1035 g., 0.9250 Silver 0.9250 oz. ASW **Ruler:** Elizabeth II
Subject: 500 Years of America **Obv:** Crowned head right, date
below **Rev:** Juan de la Cosa

Date	Mintage	F	VF	XF	Unc	BU
1993 Proof	—	Value: 20.00				

KM# 166 50 DOLLARS
31.1035 g., 0.9250 Silver 0.9250 oz. ASW **Ruler:** Elizabeth II
Subject: 500 Years of America **Obv:** Crowned head right, date
below **Rev:** William Penn

Date	Mintage	F	VF	XF	Unc	BU
1993 Proof	—	Value: 20.00				

KM# 167 50 DOLLARS
31.1035 g., 0.9250 Silver 0.9250 oz. ASW **Ruler:** Elizabeth II
Subject: 500 Years of America **Obv:** Crowned head right, date
below **Rev:** Diego de Velasquez

Date	Mintage	F	VF	XF	Unc	BU
1993 Proof	—	Value: 20.00				

KM# 168 50 DOLLARS
31.1035 g., 0.9250 Silver 0.9250 oz. ASW **Ruler:** Elizabeth II
Subject: 500 Years of America **Obv:** Crowned head right, date
below **Rev:** Miner panning for gold

Date	Mintage	F	VF	XF	Unc	BU
1993 Proof	—	Value: 20.00				

KM# 169 50 DOLLARS
31.1035 g., 0.9250 Silver 0.9250 oz. ASW **Ruler:** Elizabeth II
Subject: 500 Years of America **Obv:** Crowned head right, date
below **Rev:** Sir Martin Frobisher bust at left facing right, rocks at
right, denomination below

Date	Mintage	F	VF	XF	Unc	BU
1993 Proof	—	Value: 20.00				

KM# 170 50 DOLLARS
31.1035 g., 0.9250 Silver 0.9250 oz. ASW **Ruler:** Elizabeth II
Subject: 500 Years of America **Obv:** Crowned head right, date
below **Rev:** George Vancouver

Date	Mintage	F	VF	XF	Unc	BU
1993 Proof	—	Value: 20.00				

KM# 171 50 DOLLARS
31.1035 g., 0.9250 Silver 0.9250 oz. ASW **Ruler:** Elizabeth II
Subject: 500 Years of America **Obv:** Crowned head right, date
below **Rev:** John Hawkins at right, ship at left, denomination below

Date	Mintage	F	VF	XF	Unc	BU
1993 Proof	—	Value: 20.00				

KM# 172 50 DOLLARS
31.1035 g., 0.9250 Silver 0.9250 oz. ASW **Ruler:** Elizabeth II
Subject: 500 Years of America **Obv:** Crowned head right, date
below **Rev:** Amerigo Vespucci head within map outline, ship at
right, denomination below

Date	Mintage	F	VF	XF	Unc	BU
1993 Proof	—	Value: 20.00				

KM# 173 50 DOLLARS
7.7760 g., 0.5833 Gold 0.1458 oz. AGW **Ruler:** Elizabeth II
Subject: 500 Years of America **Obv:** Crowned head right, date
below **Rev:** George Washington

Date	Mintage	F	VF	XF	Unc	BU
1993 Proof	—	Value: 145				

KM# 174 50 DOLLARS
7.7760 g., 0.5833 Gold 0.1458 oz. AGW **Ruler:** Elizabeth II
Subject: 500 Years of America **Obv:** Crowned head right, date
below **Rev:** Alonso de Hojeda

Date	Mintage	F	VF	XF	Unc	BU
1993 Proof	—	Value: 145				

KM# 175 50 DOLLARS
7.7760 g., 0.5833 Gold 0.1458 oz. AGW **Ruler:** Elizabeth II
Subject: 500 Years of America **Obv:** Crowned head right, date
below **Rev:** Thomas Jefferson

Date	Mintage	F	VF	XF	Unc	BU
1993 Proof	—	Value: 145				

KM# 177 50 DOLLARS
7.7760 g., 0.5833 Gold 0.1458 oz. AGW **Ruler:** Elizabeth II
Subject: 500 Years of America **Obv:** Crowned head right, date
below **Rev:** Captain James Cook

Date	Mintage	F	VF	XF	Unc	BU
1993 Proof	—	Value: 145				

KM# 178 50 DOLLARS
7.7760 g., 0.5833 Gold 0.1458 oz. AGW **Ruler:** Elizabeth II
Subject: 500 Years of America **Obv:** Crowned head right, date
below **Rev:** Christopher Columbus

Date	Mintage	F	VF	XF	Unc	BU
1993 Proof	—	Value: 145				

KM# 179 50 DOLLARS
7.7760 g., 0.5833 Gold 0.1458 oz. AGW **Ruler:** Elizabeth II
Subject: 500 Years of America **Obv:** Crowned head right, date
below **Rev:** Statue of Liberty

Date	Mintage	F	VF	XF	Unc	BU
1993 Proof	—	Value: 145				

KM# 180 50 DOLLARS
7.7760 g., 0.5833 Gold 0.1458 oz. AGW **Ruler:** Elizabeth II
Subject: 1996 Olympics **Obv:** Crowned head right, date below
Rev: Ribbon dancer, denomination below

Date	Mintage	F	VF	XF	Unc	BU
1993 Proof	Est. 5,000	Value: 145				

KM# 245   50 DOLLARS
7.7760 g., 0.5833 Gold 0.1458 oz. AGW **Ruler:** Elizabeth II
Subject: Endangered Wildlife **Obv:** Crowned head right, date
below **Rev:** African lion, denomination below

Date	Mintage	F	VF	XF	Unc	BU
1993 Proof	Est. 10,000				Value: 150	

KM# 248   50 DOLLARS
31.1035 g., 0.9250 Silver 0.9250 oz. ASW **Ruler:** Elizabeth II
Subject: 500 Years of America **Obv:** Crowned head right, date
below **Rev:** Jose de San Martin at right, figures on horseback at
left, denomination below

Date	Mintage	F	VF	XF	Unc	BU
1993 Proof	Est. 60,000				Value: 20.00	

KM# 155   50 DOLLARS
31.1035 g., 0.9250 Silver 0.9250 oz. ASW **Ruler:** Elizabeth II
Subject: 500 Years of America **Obv:** Crowned head right, date
below **Rev:** Father Jacques Marquette, denomination below

Date	Mintage	F	VF	XF	Unc	BU
1993 Proof	—				Value: 20.00	

KM# 163   50 DOLLARS
31.1035 g., 0.9250 Silver 0.9250 oz. ASW **Ruler:** Elizabeth II
Subject: 500 Years of America **Obv:** Crowned head right, date
below **Rev:** Francisco de Orellana bust at right looking left, ship
at left, denomination below

Date	Mintage	F	VF	XF	Unc	BU
1993 Proof	—				Value: 20.00	

KM# 472   50 DOLLARS
7.6500 g., 0.5830 Gold 0.1434 oz. AGW, 24.96 mm.
Ruler: Elizabeth II **Obv:** Crowned bust right **Rev:** Parrot's head
Edge: Reeded

Date	Mintage	F	VF	XF	Unc	BU
1993 Proof	—				Value: 200	

KM# 246   50 DOLLARS
7.7760 g., 0.5830 Gold 0.1457 oz. AGW **Ruler:** Elizabeth II
Subject: Endangered Wildlife **Obv:** Crowned head right, date
below **Rev:** Sea otter head, denomination below

Date	Mintage	F	VF	XF	Unc	BU
1994 Proof	Est. 10,000				Value: 150	

KM# 247   50 DOLLARS
7.7760 g., 0.5830 Gold 0.1457 oz. AGW **Ruler:** Elizabeth II
Subject: Endangered Wildlife **Obv:** Crowned head right, date
below **Rev:** Przewalski's horse

Date	Mintage	F	VF	XF	Unc	BU
1994 Proof	Est. 10,000				Value: 150	

KM# 275   50 DOLLARS
7.7760 g., 0.5830 Gold 0.1457 oz. AGW **Ruler:** Elizabeth II
Subject: Endangered Wildlife **Obv:** Crowned head right, date
below **Rev:** Poplar Admiral butterflies

Date	Mintage	F	VF	XF	Unc	BU
1994 Proof	Est. 10,000				Value: 150	

KM# 276   50 DOLLARS
7.7760 g., 0.5830 Gold 0.1457 oz. AGW **Ruler:** Elizabeth II **Obv:**
Crowned head right, date below **Rev:** Queen Mother and daughters

Date	Mintage	F	VF	XF	Unc	BU
1995 Proof	Est. 5,000				Value: 150	

KM# 299   50 DOLLARS
8.0000 g., 0.9999 Gold 0.2572 oz. AGW **Ruler:** Elizabeth II
Subject: Year of the Mouse **Obv:** Crowned head right, date below
Rev: Mickey and Minnie Mouse portrait, denomination below

Date	Mintage	F	VF	XF	Unc	BU
1996 Proof	—				Value: 250	

KM# 322   50 DOLLARS
32.2225 g., 0.9250 Silver 0.9582 oz. ASW **Ruler:** Elizabeth II
Subject: 2nd Century **Obv:** Crowned head right, date below
Rev: Chinese papermaker, denomination at left

Date	Mintage	F	VF	XF	Unc	BU
1997 Proof	—				Value: 25.00	

KM# 323   50 DOLLARS
32.2225 g., 0.9250 Silver 0.9582 oz. ASW **Ruler:** Elizabeth II
Subject: 8th Century **Obv:** Crowned head right, date below
Rev: Coronation of Charlemagne

Date	Mintage	F	VF	XF	Unc	BU
1997 Proof	—				Value: 22.50	

KM# 324   50 DOLLARS
32.2225 g., 0.9250 Silver 0.9582 oz. ASW **Ruler:** Elizabeth II
Subject: 12th Century **Obv:** Crowned head right, date below
Rev: Genghis Khan **Rev. Insc.:** GENGHIS KHAN BEGINS
ASIAN CONQUEST

Date	Mintage	F	VF	XF	Unc	BU
1997 Proof	—				Value: 22.50	

KM# 325.1   50 DOLLARS
32.2225 g., 0.9250 Silver 0.9582 oz. ASW **Ruler:** Elizabeth II
Subject: 13th Century **Obv:** Crowned head right, date below
Rev: Marco Polo and Kublai Khan **Note:** Prev. KM#325.

Date	Mintage	F	VF	XF	Unc	BU
1997 Proof	—				Value: 20.00	

KM# 325.2   50 DOLLARS
32.3400 g., 0.9250 Silver 0.9617 oz. ASW, 38.7 mm.
Ruler: Elizabeth II **Subject:** 13th Century **Obv:** Crowned head
right, date below **Rev:** Inscription in polished rectangle
Rev. Insc.: MARCO POLO AT KUBLAI KHAN'S COURT
Edge: Reeded

Date	Mintage	F	VF	XF	Unc	BU
1997FM Proof	—				Value: 20.00	

KM# 306 50 DOLLARS
Bi-Metallic Platinum center in Gold ring **Ruler:** Elizabeth II **Obv:** Crowned head right within circle, date below **Rev:** Mother seal with pup within circle, date below

Date	Mintage	F	VF	XF	Unc	BU
1997 Proof	—	Value: 300				

KM# 381 50 DOLLARS
4.1200 g., 0.5833 Gold 0.0773 oz. AGW, 20.9 mm. **Ruler:** Elizabeth II **Subject:** Explorers **Obv:** Crowned head right, date below **Rev:** Leif Ericson with battle axe facing, denomination at right **Edge:** Reeded

Date	Mintage	F	VF	XF	Unc	BU
1997 Proof	—	Value: 75.00				
1997FM Proof	—	Value: 85.00				

KM# 382 50 DOLLARS
4.6000 g., 0.5833 Gold 0.0863 oz. AGW, 20.9 mm. **Ruler:** Elizabeth II **Subject:** Explorers **Obv:** Crowned head right, date below **Rev:** Marco Polo on camel **Edge:** Reeded

Date	Mintage	F	VF	XF	Unc	BU
1997FM Proof	—	Value: 85.00				

KM# 383 50 DOLLARS
4.6000 g., 0.5833 Gold 0.0863 oz. AGW, 20.9 mm. **Ruler:** Elizabeth II **Subject:** Explorers **Obv:** Crowned head right, date below **Rev:** Vasco da Gama **Edge:** Reeded

Date	Mintage	F	VF	XF	Unc	BU
1997FM Proof	—	Value: 85.00				

KM# 384 50 DOLLARS
4.6000 g., 0.5833 Gold 0.0863 oz. AGW **Ruler:** Elizabeth II **Subject:** Explorers **Obv:** Crowned head right, date below **Rev:** Vasco de Nuñez Balboa **Edge:** Reeded

Date	Mintage	F	VF	XF	Unc	BU
1997FM Proof	—	Value: 85.00				

KM# 385 50 DOLLARS
4.6000 g., 0.5833 Gold 0.0863 oz. AGW, 20.9 mm. **Ruler:** Elizabeth II **Subject:** Explorers **Obv:** Crowned head right, date below **Rev:** Hernando Cortes **Edge:** Reeded

Date	Mintage	F	VF	XF	Unc	BU
1997FM Proof	—	Value: 85.00				

KM# 386 50 DOLLARS
4.6000 g., 0.5833 Gold 0.0863 oz. AGW, 20.9 mm. **Ruler:** Elizabeth II **Subject:** Explorers **Obv:** Crowned head right, date below **Rev:** Magellan's ships: Vittoria and Trinidad **Edge:** Reeded

Date	Mintage	F	VF	XF	Unc	BU
1997FM Proof	—	Value: 85.00				

KM# 390 50 DOLLARS
4.6000 g., 0.5833 Gold 0.0863 oz. AGW, 20.9 mm. **Ruler:** Elizabeth II **Subject:** Explorers **Obv:** Crowned head right, date below **Rev:** Alexander the Great with sword on horseback, denomination above **Edge:** Reeded

Date	Mintage	F	VF	XF	Unc	BU
1997FM Proof	—	Value: 85.00				

KM# 391 50 DOLLARS
4.6000 g., 0.5833 Gold 0.0863 oz. AGW, 20.9 mm. **Ruler:** Elizabeth II **Subject:** Explorers **Obv:** Crowned head right, date below **Rev:** Christopher Columbus **Edge:** Reeded

Date	Mintage	F	VF	XF	Unc	BU
1997FM Proof	—	Value: 85.00				

KM# 392 50 DOLLARS
4.6000 g., 0.5833 Gold 0.0863 oz. AGW, 20.9 mm. **Ruler:** Elizabeth II **Subject:** Explorers **Obv:** Crowned head right, date below **Rev:** Sir Francis Drake **Edge:** Reeded

Date	Mintage	F	VF	XF	Unc	BU
1997FM Proof	—	Value: 85.00				

KM# 393 50 DOLLARS
4.6000 g., 0.5833 Gold 0.0863 oz. AGW, 20.9 mm. **Ruler:** Elizabeth II **Subject:** Explorers **Obv:** Crowned head right, date below **Rev:** Abel Janszoon Tasman **Edge:** Reeded

Date	Mintage	F	VF	XF	Unc	BU
1997FM Proof	—	Value: 85.00				

KM# 394 50 DOLLARS
4.6000 g., 0.5833 Gold 0.0863 oz. AGW, 20.9 mm. **Ruler:** Elizabeth II **Subject:** Explorers **Obv:** Crowned head right, date below **Rev:** Capt. James Cook **Edge:** Reeded

Date	Mintage	F	VF	XF	Unc	BU
1997FM Proof	—	Value: 85.00				

KM# 395 50 DOLLARS
4.6000 g., 0.5833 Gold 0.0863 oz. AGW, 20.9 mm. **Ruler:** Elizabeth II **Subject:** Explorers **Obv:** Crowned head right, date below **Rev:** Richard E. Byrd **Edge:** Reeded

Date	Mintage	F	VF	XF	Unc	BU
1997FM Proof	—	Value: 85.00				

KM# 395.1 50 DOLLARS
6.3700 g., 0.5833 Gold 0.1195 oz. AGW, 21 mm. **Ruler:** Elizabeth II **Obv:** Crowned head right, date below **Rev:** Admiral Richard C. Byrd **Edge:** Reeded

Date	Mintage	F	VF	XF	Unc	BU
1997FM Proof	8	Value: 400				

Note: Struck on thicker than normal planchet resulting in a 38.5% heavier weight. 8 Pieces known.

KM# 399 50 DOLLARS
31.9000 g., 0.9250 Silver 0.9486 oz. ASW, 38.7 mm. **Ruler:** Elizabeth II **Subject:** 1st Century **Obv:** Crowned head right, date below **Rev:** Nativity scene **Edge:** Reeded

Date	Mintage	F	VF	XF	Unc	BU
1997FM Proof	—	Value: 22.50				

KM# 400 50 DOLLARS
32.1000 g., 0.9250 Silver 0.9546 oz. ASW, 38.7 mm. **Ruler:** Elizabeth II **Subject:** 3rd Century **Obv:** Crowned head right, date below **Rev:** Roman citizens **Edge:** Reeded

Date	Mintage	F	VF	XF	Unc	BU
1997FM Proof	—	Value: 22.50				

KM# 401 50 DOLLARS
30.9100 g., 0.9250 Silver 0.9192 oz. ASW, 38.7 mm. **Ruler:** Elizabeth II **Subject:** 4th Century **Obv:** Crowned head right, date below **Rev:** Constantine the Great **Edge:** Reeded

Date	Mintage	F	VF	XF	Unc	BU
1997FM Proof	—	Value: 22.50				

KM# 402 50 DOLLARS
32.3200 g., 0.9250 Silver 0.9611 oz. ASW, 38.7 mm. **Ruler:** Elizabeth II **Subject:** 5th Century **Obv:** Crowned head right, date below **Rev:** The sacking of Rome **Edge:** Reeded

Date	Mintage	F	VF	XF	Unc	BU
1997FM Proof	—	Value: 22.50				

KM# 403 50 DOLLARS
30.8200 g., 0.9250 Silver 0.9165 oz. ASW, 38.7 mm. **Ruler:** Elizabeth II **Subject:** 6th Century **Obv:** Crowned head right, date below **Rev:** Emperor Justinian **Edge:** Reeded

Date	Mintage	F	VF	XF	Unc	BU
1997FM Proof	—	Value: 22.50				

KM# 404 50 DOLLARS
31.1000 g., 0.9250 Silver 0.9249 oz. ASW, 38.7 mm. **Ruler:** Elizabeth II **Subject:** 7th Century **Obv:** Crowned head right, date below **Rev:** Establishment of Islam, domed building, denomination at left **Edge:** Reeded

Date	Mintage	F	VF	XF	Unc	BU
1997FM Proof	—	Value: 22.50				

KM# 405 50 DOLLARS
29.5300 g., 0.9250 Silver 0.8782 oz. ASW, 38.7 mm. **Ruler:** Elizabeth II **Subject:** 9th Century **Obv:** Crowned head right, date below **Rev:** Caliph of Baghdad **Edge:** Reeded

Date	Mintage	F	VF	XF	Unc	BU
1997FM Proof	—	Value: 22.50				

KM# 406   50 DOLLARS
32.1300 g., 0.9250 Silver 0.9555 oz. ASW, 38.7 mm.
Ruler: Elizabeth II **Subject:** 10th Century **Obv:** Crowned head right, date below **Rev:** Monk writing **Rev. Insc.:** THE DARK AGES OF EUROPE **Edge:** Reeded

Date	Mintage	F	VF	XF	Unc	BU
1997FM Proof	—	Value: 25.00				

KM# 407   50 DOLLARS
31.7600 g., 0.9250 Silver 0.9445 oz. ASW, 38.7 mm.
Ruler: Elizabeth II **Subject:** 11th Century **Obv:** Crowned head right, date below **Rev:** Norman landing scene **Rev. Insc.:** THE NORMAN CONQUEST **Edge:** Reeded

Date	Mintage	F	VF	XF	Unc	BU
1997FM Proof	—	Value: 22.50				

KM# 460   50 DOLLARS
10.0000 g., 0.9995 Platinum 0.3213 oz. APW **Ruler:** Elizabeth II **Subject:** Love Angels

Date	Mintage	F	VF	XF	Unc	BU
1997 Proof	250	Value: 650				

KM# 408   50 DOLLARS
31.7500 g., 0.9250 Silver 0.9442 oz. ASW, 38.7 mm. **Ruler:** Elizabeth II **Subject:** 14th Century **Obv:** Crowned head right, date below **Rev:** Renaissance buildings **Rev. Insc.:** BIRTH OF THE RENAISSANCE **Edge:** Reeded

Date	Mintage	F	VF	XF	Unc	BU
1997FM Proof	—	Value: 22.50				

KM# 409   50 DOLLARS
31.4400 g., 0.9250 Silver 0.9350 oz. ASW, 38.7 mm.
Ruler: Elizabeth II **Subject:** 15th Century **Obv:** Crowned head right, date below **Rev:** Columbus and ship **Rev. Insc.:** AGE OF EXPLORATION: CHRISTOPHER COLUMBUS **Edge:** Reeded

Date	Mintage	F	VF	XF	Unc	BU
1997FM Proof	—	Value: 22.50				

KM# 410   50 DOLLARS
32.6100 g., 0.9250 Silver 0.9698 oz. ASW, 38.7 mm.
Ruler: Elizabeth II **Subject:** 16th Century **Obv:** Crowned head right, date below **Rev:** William Shakespeare **Edge:** Reeded

Date	Mintage	F	VF	XF	Unc	BU
1997FM Proof	—	Value: 22.50				

KM# 411   50 DOLLARS
32.0500 g., 0.9250 Silver 0.9531 oz. ASW, 38.7 mm.
Ruler: Elizabeth II **Subject:** 17th Century **Obv:** Crowned head right, date below **Rev:** Isaac Newton **Edge:** Reeded

Date	Mintage	F	VF	XF	Unc	BU
1997FM Proof	—	Value: 22.50				

KM# 412   50 DOLLARS
32.3400 g., 0.9250 Silver 0.9617 oz. ASW, 38.7 mm.
Ruler: Elizabeth II **Subject:** 18th Century **Obv:** Crowned head right, date below **Rev:** Declaration of Independence signing scene **Edge:** Reeded

Date	Mintage	F	VF	XF	Unc	BU
1997FM Proof	—	Value: 22.50				

KM# 413   50 DOLLARS
31.6300 g., 0.9250 Silver 0.9406 oz. ASW, 38.7 mm.
Ruler: Elizabeth II **Subject:** 19th Century **Obv:** Crowned head right, date below **Rev:** Early automobile **Edge:** Reeded

Date	Mintage	F	VF	XF	Unc	BU
1997FM Proof	—	Value: 22.50				

KM# 414   50 DOLLARS
31.2400 g., 0.9250 Silver 0.9290 oz. ASW, 38.7 mm. **Ruler:** Elizabeth II **Subject:** 20th Century **Obv:** Crowned head right, date below **Rev:** Moon landing scene, denomination at left **Edge:** Reeded

Date	Mintage	F	VF	XF	Unc	BU
1997FM Proof	—	Value: 22.50				

KM# 461   75 DOLLARS
15.0000 g., 0.9995 Platinum 0.4820 oz. APW **Ruler:** Elizabeth II **Subject:** Love Angels

Date	Mintage	F	VF	XF	Unc	BU
1997 Proof	250	Value: 1,000				

KM# 12   100 DOLLARS
16.7185 g., 0.9170 Gold 0.4929 oz. AGW, 27 mm.
Ruler: Elizabeth II **Subject:** Winston Churchill Centenary **Obv:** Young bust right, date below **Rev:** Churchill head at right looking left, Big Ben and flag at left, denomination below

Date	Mintage	F	VF	XF	Unc	BU
1974	368	—	—	—	475	—
1974 Proof	1,453	Value: 475				

KM# 13   100 DOLLARS
9.6000 g., 0.9000 Gold 0.2778 oz. AGW, 26 mm. **Ruler:** Elizabeth II **Subject:** Bicentennial - Return of Captain James Cook from Second Pacific Voyage **Obv:** Young bust right, date below **Rev:** Ship divides portraits in cameos, denomination below

Date	Mintage	F	VF	XF	Unc	BU
1975FM (M)	100	—	—	—	285	—
1975FM (U)	7,447	—	—	—	275	—
1975FM Proof	17,000	Value: 270				

KM# 16   100 DOLLARS
9.6000 g., 0.9000 Gold 0.2778 oz. AGW, 26 mm.
Ruler: Elizabeth II **Subject:** U.S. Bicentennial **Obv:** Young bust right, date below **Rev:** Conjoined heads of Benjamin Franklin and James Cook left, denomination below

Date	Mintage	F	VF	XF	Unc	BU
1976FM (M)	50	—	—	—	300	—
1976FM (U)	852	—	—	—	275	—
1976FM Proof	9,373	Value: 270				

KM# 19   100 DOLLARS
9.6000 g., 0.9000 Gold 0.2778 oz. AGW, 26 mm.
Ruler: Elizabeth II **Subject:** Queen's Silver Jubilee **Obv:** Young bust right, date below **Rev:** Crowned EIIR monogram

Date	Mintage	F	VF	XF	Unc	BU
1977FM (M)	50	—	—	—	300	—
1977FM (P)	562	—	—	—	275	—
1977FM Proof	9,364	Value: 270				

KM# 25   100 DOLLARS
9.6000 g., 0.9000 Gold 0.2778 oz. AGW, 26 mm.
Ruler: Elizabeth II **Subject:** Membership in Commonwealth of Nations **Obv:** Young bust right, date below **Rev:** Tangaroa head left, divides denomination, circle surrounds

Date	Mintage	F	VF	XF	Unc	BU
1979FM (U)	400	—	—	—	275	—
1979FM Proof	3,367	Value: 270				

KM# 74   100 DOLLARS
1.2441 g., 0.9990 Gold 0.0400 oz. AGW **Ruler:** Elizabeth II **Subject:** Endangered World Wildlife **Obv:** Crowned head right, date below **Rev:** American bald eagle head left, beak open, denomination below

Date	Mintage	F	VF	XF	Unc	BU
1990 Prooflike	1,320	—	—	—	45.00	50.00

KM# 75   100 DOLLARS
1.2441 g., 0.9990 Gold 0.0400 oz. AGW, 14 mm.
Ruler: Elizabeth II **Subject:** Endangered World Wildlife **Obv:** Crowned head right, date below **Rev:** Bison

Date	Mintage	F	VF	XF	Unc	BU
1990 Prooflike	320	—	—	—	47.50	55.00

KM# 76   100 DOLLARS
1.2441 g., 0.9990 Gold 0.0400 oz. AGW, 14 mm.
Ruler: Elizabeth II **Subject:** Endangered World Wildlife **Obv:** Crowned head right, date below **Rev:** Elephant

Date	Mintage	F	VF	XF	Unc	BU
1990 Prooflike	720	—	—	—	47.50	55.00

KM# 77   100 DOLLARS
1.2441 g., 0.9990 Gold 0.0400 oz. AGW, 14 mm.
Ruler: Elizabeth II **Subject:** Endangered World Wildlife
Obv: Crowned head right, date below **Rev:** Tiger

Date	Mintage	F	VF	XF	Unc	BU
1990 Prooflike	420	—	—	—	65.00	75.00

KM# 78   100 DOLLARS
1.2441 g., 0.9990 Gold 0.0400 oz. AGW, 14 mm.
Ruler: Elizabeth II **Subject:** Endangered World Wildlife
Obv: Crowned head right, date below **Rev:** European Mouflon

Date	Mintage	F	VF	XF	Unc	BU
1990 Prooflike	320	—	—	—	47.50	55.00

KM# 92   100 DOLLARS
3.4550 g., 0.9000 Gold 0.1000 oz. AGW, 18 mm. **Ruler:**
Elizabeth II **Subject:** 1992 Summer Olympics **Obv:** Crowned
head right, date below **Rev:** Bicyclists, denomination below

Date	Mintage	F	VF	XF	Unc	BU
1990 Proof	Est. 5,000	Value: 125				

KM# 113   100 DOLLARS
172.1100 g., 0.9250 Silver 5.1182 oz. ASW, 65 mm.
Ruler: Elizabeth II **Subject:** 500 Years of America **Obv:** Crowned
head right, date below **Rev:** Ferdinand Magellan **Note:** Photo
reduced.

Date	Mintage	F	VF	XF	Unc	BU
1990 Proof	Est. 3,000	Value: 135				

KM# 319   100 DOLLARS
170.6000 g., 0.9250 Silver 5.0733 oz. ASW, 65 mm.
Ruler: Elizabeth II **Subject:** 500 Years of America **Obv:** Crowned
head right, date below **Rev:** Mt. Rushmore, eagle with wings
spread below, denomination at bottom **Note:** Illustration reduced.

Date	Mintage	F	VF	XF	Unc	BU
1991 Proof	—	Value: 125				

KM# 297   100 DOLLARS
155.6500 g., 0.9990 Silver 4.9991 oz. ASW **Ruler:** Elizabeth II
Subject: Endangered Wildlife **Obv:** Crowned head right, date
below **Rev:** Three elephants **Note:** Illustration reduced.

Date	Mintage	F	VF	XF	Unc	BU
1991 Proof	—	Value: 165				

KM# 320   100 DOLLARS
170.6000 g., 0.9250 Silver 5.0733 oz. ASW **Ruler:** Elizabeth II
Subject: 500 Years of America **Obv:** Crowned head right, date
below **Rev:** Bust of Columbus at left facing right, three ships at
right, denomination below **Note:** Illustration reduced.

Date	Mintage	F	VF	XF	Unc	BU
1992 Proof	—	Value: 125				

KM# 159   100 DOLLARS
155.5175 g., 0.9990 Silver 4.9948 oz. ASW **Ruler:** Elizabeth II
Subject: 500 Years of America **Obv:** Crowned head right, date
below **Rev:** Hudson's "Half Moon" and New York City skyline,
denomination below **Note:** Illustration reduced.

Date	Mintage	F	VF	XF	Unc	BU
1993 Proof	—	Value: 125				

KM# 158   100 DOLLARS
155.5176 g., 0.9990 Silver 4.9948 oz. ASW **Ruler:** Elizabeth II
Subject: Endangered Wildlife **Obv:** Crowned head right, date
below **Rev:** Manchurian cranes **Note:** Illustration reduced.

Date	Mintage	F	VF	XF	Unc	BU
1993 Proof	—	Value: 145				

KM# 250   100 DOLLARS
7.7761 g., 0.9990 Platinum 0.2497 oz. APW **Ruler:** Elizabeth II
Obv: Crowned head right, date below **Rev:** Javelin throwing

Date	Mintage	F	VF	XF	Unc	BU
1995 Proof	Est. 1,000	Value: 500				

KM# 293   100 DOLLARS
7.7800 g., 0.9990 Gold 0.2499 oz. AGW **Ruler:** Elizabeth II
Subject: Olympic National Park **Obv:** Crowned head right, date
below **Rev:** Eagles head right, denomination below

Date	Mintage	F	VF	XF	Unc	BU
1996 Proof	—	Value: 245				

KM# 294   100 DOLLARS
7.7800 g., 0.9990 Gold 0.2499 oz. AGW **Ruler:** Elizabeth II
Subject: Yellowstone National Park **Obv:** Crowned head right,
date below **Rev:** Grizzly Bear, denomination below

Date	Mintage	F	VF	XF	Unc	BU
1996 Proof	—	Value: 245				

KM# 300   100 DOLLARS
15.0000 g., 0.9999 Gold 0.4822 oz. AGW **Ruler:** Elizabeth II
Subject: Year of the Mouse **Obv:** Crowned head right, date below
Rev: Mickey Mouse sailboarding, denomination below

Date	Mintage	F	VF	XF	Unc	BU
1996 Proof	—	Value: 475				

KM# 388   100 DOLLARS
7.7800 g., 0.9990 Gold 0.2499 oz. AGW, 22 mm. **Ruler:**
Elizabeth II **Subject:** Yellowstone National Park **Obv:** Crowned
head right, date below **Rev:** Bear on tree branch **Edge:** Reeded

Date	Mintage	F	VF	XF	Unc	BU
1996 Proof	—	Value: 245				

KM# 22   200 DOLLARS
16.6000 g., 0.9000 Gold 0.4803 oz. AGW **Ruler:** Elizabeth II

Subject: Bicentennial - Discovery of Hawaii by Capt. James Cook **Obv:** Young bust right, date below **Rev:** Capt. James Cook with crew, denomination below

Date	Mintage	F	VF	XF	Unc	BU
1978FM (M)	26	—	—	—	530	—
1978FM (U)	621	—	—	—	475	—
1978FM Proof	3,216	Value: 470				

KM# 26 200 DOLLARS
16.6000 g., 0.9000 Gold 0.4803 oz. AGW **Ruler:** Elizabeth II **Subject:** Legacy of Capt. James Cook **Obv:** Young bust right, date below **Rev:** Bird flying right above banner, denomination below

Date	Mintage	F	VF	XF	Unc	BU
1979FM (U)	271	—	—	—	475	—
1979FM Proof	1,939	Value: 470				

KM# 29 200 DOLLARS
15.9800 g., 0.9170 Gold 0.4711 oz. AGW **Ruler:** Elizabeth II **Subject:** International Year of the Scout **Obv:** Young bust right, date below **Rev:** Circle of stars around symbol at center, dates at lower left, denomination at lower right

Date	Mintage	F	VF	XF	Unc	BU
1983 Proof	—	Value: 465				

KM# 251 200 DOLLARS
15.5520 g., 0.9990 Platinum 0.4995 oz. APW **Ruler:** Elizabeth II **Obv:** Crowned head right, date below **Rev:** Wrestling

Date	Mintage	F	VF	XF	Unc	BU
1995 Proof	1,000	Value: 1,000				

KM# 23 250 DOLLARS
17.9000 g., 0.9000 Gold 0.5179 oz. AGW **Ruler:** Elizabeth II **Subject:** 250th Anniversary - Birth of James Cook **Obv:** Young bust right, date below **Rev:** Head left, denomination below

Date	Mintage	F	VF	XF	Unc	BU
1978FM (M)	25	—	—	—	530	—
1978FM (U)	200	—	—	—	520	—
1978FM Proof	1,757	Value: 500				

KM# 50 250 DOLLARS
7.7750 g., 0.9990 Gold 0.2497 oz. AGW **Ruler:** Elizabeth II **Subject:** 500 Years of America **Obv:** Crowned head right, date below **Rev:** Cameos of Cook and Franklin flank sailing ship, denomination below

Date	Mintage	F	VF	XF	Unc	BU
1989 Proof	3,000	Value: 245				
1990 Proof	3,000	Value: 245				

KM# 51 250 DOLLARS
7.7750 g., 0.9990 Gold 0.2497 oz. AGW **Ruler:** Elizabeth II **Subject:** 500 Years of America **Obv:** Crowned head right, date below **Rev:** Amerigo Vespucci bust at right looking left, ship at left

Date	Mintage	F	VF	XF	Unc	BU
1990 Proof	Est. 3,000	Value: 245				

KM# 82 250 DOLLARS
9.6000 g., 0.9000 Gold 0.2778 oz. AGW **Ruler:** Elizabeth II **Subject:** Save the Children **Obv:** Crowned head right, date below **Rev:** Child behind large shell, denomination below

Date	Mintage	F	VF	XF	Unc	BU
1990 Proof	3,000	Value: 275				

KM# 71 250 DOLLARS
7.7750 g., 0.9990 Gold 0.2497 oz. AGW **Ruler:** Elizabeth II **Subject:** 1992 Olympics **Obv:** Crowned head right, date below **Rev:** Torch, denomination below

Date	Mintage	F	VF	XF	Unc	BU
1991 Proof	Est. 5,000	Value: 245				

KM# 295 250 DOLLARS
31.1035 g., 0.9990 Gold 0.9990 oz. AGW **Ruler:** Elizabeth II **Subject:** Olympic National Park **Obv:** Crowned head right, date below **Rev:** Multicolor bald eagle in flight

Date	Mintage	F	VF	XF	Unc	BU
1996 Proof	1,000	Value: 1,000				

KM# 296 250 DOLLARS
31.1035 g., 0.9990 Gold 0.9990 oz. AGW **Ruler:** Elizabeth II **Subject:** Yellowstone National Park **Obv:** Crowned head right, date below **Rev:** Multicolored grizzly bear and cub

Date	Mintage	F	VF	XF	Unc	BU
1996 Proof	1,000	Value: 1,000				

KM# 313 500 DOLLARS
14.7400 g., 0.9990 Platinum 0.4734 oz. APW **Ruler:** Elizabeth II **Obv:** Crowned head right, date below **Rev:** Marco Polo, oriental building in background, denomination below

Date	Mintage	F	VF	XF	Unc	BU
1995 Proof	Est. 1,000	Value: 850				

KM# 415 500 DOLLARS
14.7400 g., 0.9990 Platinum 0.4734 oz. APW, 25.8 mm. **Ruler:** Elizabeth II **Obv:** Crowned head right, date below **Rev:** Two of Ferdinand Magellan's ships **Edge:** Reeded

Date	Mintage	F	VF	XF	Unc	BU
1995FM Proof	1,000	Value: 850				

PIEFORTS

KM#	Date	Mintage	Identification	Mkt Val
P1	1985	250	Dollar. 0.9250 Silver.	200
P2	1986	500	Dollar. 0.9250 Silver.	45.00
P3	1986	500	Dollar. 0.9250 Silver.	45.00

MINT SETS

KM#	Date	Mintage	Identification	Issue Price	Mkt Val
MS1	1972 (7)	11,045	KM1-5, 6.1, 7	7.50	5.00
MS2	1973 (9)	3,652	KM1-5, 6.1, 7, 9, 10	52.50	40.00
MS3	1973 (7)	3,023	KM1-5, 6.1, 7	10.00	8.00
MS4	1973 (2)	2,348	KM9, 10	45.00	35.00
MS5	1974 (9)	913	KM1-5, 6.1, 7. 9. 10	5,250	50.00
MS6	1974 (7)	2,087	KM1-5, 6.1, 7	10.00	6.00
MS7	1974 (2)	587	KM9, 10	45.00	45.00
MS8	1975 (7)	2,251	KM1-5, 6.1, 7	10.00	6.00
MS9	1976 (8)	1,066	KM1-4, 6.1,7, 14, 15	20.00	25.00
MS10	1977 (8)	1,171	KM1-4, 6.1, 7, 14, 17	20.00	25.00
MS11	1978 (8)	767	KM1a-4a, 6.2, 7a, 14a, 20	20.00	30.00
MS12	1979 (8)	500	KM1-3, 4b, 6.3 7, 14, 24	—	30.00
MS13	1981 (7)	1,100	KM1b-3b, 4c, 6.4, 7b, 14b	—	16.00
MS14	1983	—	KM1-5, 6.1, 7	—	6.00
MS15	1987 (7)	—	KM33-39	—	15.00
MS16	1988 (7)	—	KM33-35, 37-39, 41	—	16.00
MS17	1992 (7)	—	KM33-35, 37-39, 41	—	16.00
MS18	1999 (5)	5,000	KM#444-448	418	418

PROOF SETS

KM#	Date	Mintage	Identification	Issue Price	Mkt Val
PS1	1972 (7)	17,101	KM1-5, 6.1, 7	20.00	9.00
PS2	1973 (9)	7,395	KM1-5, 6.1, 7, 9-10	89.50	45.00
PS3	1973 (7)	5,136	KM1-5, 6.1, 7	29.50	10.00
PS4	1973 (2)	4,754	KM9-10	60.00	35.00
PS5	1974 (9)	4,444	KM1-5, 6.1, 7, 9-10	95.00	50.00
PS6	1974 (7)	5,300	KM1-5, 6.1, 7	32.50	10.00
PS7	1974 (2)	2,856	KM9-10	65.00	35.00
PS8	1975 (7)	21,290	KM-15, 6.1, 7	31.50	10.00
PS9	1976 (8)	17,658	KM1-4, 6.1, 7, 14-15	40.00	22.50
PS10	1977 (8)	5,986	KM1-4, 6.1, 7, 14, 17	42.00	25.00
PS11	1978 (8)	6,287	KM1a-4a, 6.2, 7a, 14a, 20	42.00	25.00
PS12	1979 (8)	4,058	KM1-3,4b, 6.3, 7, 14; 24	44.00	25.00
PS13	1981 (7)	9,205	KM1b-3b, 4c, 6.4, 7b, 14b	39.50	12.50
PS14	1983 (7)	10,000	KM1-5, 6.1, 7	29.95	10.00
PS15	1987 (7)	—	KM33-39	—	32.50
PS16	1988 (7)	—	KM33-35, 37-39, 41	—	32.50
PSA16	1988 (25)	—	KM#61-69, 96-111	—	550
PS17	1991 (12)	1,000	KM93, 95, 118-120, 122-128	—	300
PS18	1992 (7)	—	KM33-35, 37-39, 41	—	32.50
PS19	1994 (7)	200	KM33-35, 37-39, 41	—	37.50
PS20	1996 (3)	—	KM298-300	—	500
PS21	1996 (6)	—	KM284, 286, 288, 292, 294, 296	—	935
PS22	1998 (5)	4,000	KM314-318	185	225
PS23	1999 (3)	—	KM338-340	98.00	110
PS24	1999 (5)	4,000	KM361-365	122	225

PROOF-LIKE SETS (PL)

KM#	Date	Mintage	Identification	Issue Price	Mkt Val
PLS1	1990 (5)	—	KM74-78	325	250
PLS2	1997 (5)	250	KM#457-461	—	1,575

COSTA RICA

The Republic of Costa Rica, located in southern Central America between Nicaragua and Panama, has an area of 19,730 sq. mi. (51,100 sq. km.) and a population of 3.4 million. Capital: San Jose. Agriculture predominates; tourism and coffee, bananas, beef and sugar contribute heavily to the country's export earnings.

Costa Rica was discovered by Christopher Columbus in 1502, during his last voyage to the New World, and was a colony of Spain from 1522 until independence in 1821. Established as a republic in 1848, Costa Rica adopted democratic reforms in the 1870's and 80's. Today, Costa Rica remains a model of orderly democracy in Latin America, although, like most of the hemisphere - its economy is in stress.

MINT MARKS
CR - San Jose 1825-1947
(P) – Philadelphia, 1905-1961
(L) – London, 1937, 1948

ISSUING BANK INITIALS - MINTS
BCCR - Philadelphia 1951-1958,1961
BICR - Philadelphia 1935
BNCR - London 1937,1948
BNCR - San Jose 1942-1947
GCR - Philadelphia 1905-1908,1929
GCR - San Jose 1917-1941

KEY TO MINT IDENTIFICATION

Key Letter	Mint
(a)	Armant Metalurgica, Santiago, Chile
(c)	Casa de Moneda, Mexico City Mint
(cc)	Casa de Moneda, Brazil
(co)	Colombia Republican Banko
(g)	Guatemala Mint
(i)	Italcambio Mint
(p) or (P)	Philadelphia Mint, USA
®	RCM – Royal Canadian Mint
(rm)	Royal Mint, London
(s)	San Francisco
(sj)	San Jose
(sm)	Sherrit Mint, Toronto
(v)	Vereingte Deutsche Metallwerke, Karlsruhe
(w)	Westain, Toronto

ASSAYERS' INITIALS
CY – Carlos Yglesias, 1902
JCV – Jesus Cubrero Vargas, 1903
GCR – Gobierno de Costa Rica

MONETARY SYSTEM
8 Reales = 1 Peso
16 Pesos = 8 Escudos = 1 Onza

REPUBLIC

REFORM COINAGE
1897, 100 Centimos = 1 Colon

KM# 144   2 CENTIMOS
1.0000 g., Copper-Nickel **Obv:** Large numeral above date
Rev: Denomination above sprays **Edge:** Plain

Date	Mintage	F	VF	XF	Unc	BU
1903(P)	630,000	0.50	1.00	3.00	10.00	15.00

Note: 274,342 of this type were used as planchets for KM178 in 1942.

KM# 145   5 CENTIMOS
1.0000 g., 0.9000 Silver 0.0289 oz. ASW **Obv:** National arms, date below **Rev:** Denomination within wreath **Edge:** Reeded

Date	Mintage	F	VF	XF	Unc	BU
1905(P)	500,000	BV	0.75	2.50	12.00	15.00
1910(P)	400,000	BV	0.75	2.50	15.00	20.00
1912(P)	540,000	BV	0.75	2.00	9.00	12.00
1914(P)	510,000	BV	0.75	2.00	8.00	10.00

KM# 146   10 CENTIMOS
2.0000 g., 0.9000 Silver 0.0579 oz. ASW, 18 mm. **Obv:** National arms, date below **Rev:** Denomination within wreath

Date	Mintage	F	VF	XF	Unc	BU
1905(P)	400,000	0.80	2.00	4.00	12.00	20.00
1910(P)	400,000	0.80	2.00	5.00	15.00	25.00
1912(P)	270,000	0.80	2.00	5.00	20.00	30.00
1914(P)	150,000	1.00	2.50	6.00	22.00	35.00

KM# 143   50 CENTIMOS
10.0000 g., 0.9000 Silver 0.2893 oz. ASW, 29 mm.
Obv: National arms, date below **Rev:** Denomination within wreath

Date	Mintage	F	VF	XF	Unc	BU
1902 CY	120,000	35.00	80.00	150	300	500
1903 JCV	380,000	25.00	60.00	125	250	350

Note: Of the total mintage for this date, San Jose Mint struck 132,140 in 1903 and Philadelphia Mint struck an additional 250,000 in 1904 with the 1903 date; the two strikings are indistinguishable, because all the dies were reportedly made in Philddelphia.

Date	Mintage	F	VF	XF	Unc	BU
1914(P) GCR	200,000	—	1,000	2,000	2,500	3,000

Note: Most coins dated 1914 were later counterstamped UN COLON/ 1923; See KM#164.

KM# 139   2 COLONES
1.5560 g., 0.9000 Gold 0.0450 oz. AGW **Obv:** National arms **Rev:** Bust of Colombus right

Date	Mintage	F	VF	XF	Unc	BU
1915(P)	5,000	BV	50.00	90.00	160	200
1916(P)	5,000	BV	55.00	90.00	160	200
1921(P)	3,000	BV	65.00	110	225	300
1922(P)	13,000	BV	45.00	70.00	125	175
1926(P)	15,000	BV	45.00	60.00	110	150
1928(P)	25,000	BV	45.00	55.00	100	125

REFORM COINAGE
1917, 100 Centavos = 1 Colon

KM# 147   5 CENTAVOS
1.0000 g., Brass **Obv:** National arms, date below
Rev: Denomination within wreath **Edge:** Plain

Date	Mintage	F	VF	XF	Unc	BU
1917(sj) Rare	400,000	25.00	50.00	100	200	350
1918(sj)	1,000,000	4.00	12.00	30.00	70.00	100
1919(sj)	500,000	3.00	10.00	25.00	60.00	100

KM# 148   10 CENTAVOS
2.0000 g., 0.5000 Silver 0.0321 oz. ASW, 18 mm. **Obv:** National arms, date below **Rev:** Denomination within wreath **Edge:** Reeded

Date	Mintage	F	VF	XF	Unc	BU
1917(sj)	100,000	1.50	2.50	5.00	10.00	15.00

KM# 149.1   10 CENTAVOS
2.0000 g., Brass, 18 mm. **Obv:** National arms, date below
Rev: Denomination within wreath, GCR at lower right

Date	Mintage	F	VF	XF	Unc	BU
1917 GCR	500,000	8.00	20.00	50.00	150	—

KM# 149.2   10 CENTAVOS
2.0000 g., Brass **Obv:** National arms, date below
Rev: Denomination within wreath, GCR at bottom center

Date	Mintage	F	VF	XF	Unc	BU
1917 GCR	Inc. above	6.00	15.00	40.00	100	200
1918 GCR	900,000	4.00	10.00	20.00	70.00	125
1919 GCR	250,000	2.00	6.00	10.00	60.00	100

KM# 150   50 CENTAVOS
10.0000 g., 0.5000 Silver 0.1607 oz. ASW, 29 mm.
Obv: National arms **Note:** All but 10 examples of the 1917 issue and the complete 1918 mintage were counterstamped UN COLON/1923. See KM#165.

Date	Mintage	F	VF	XF	Unc	BU
1917 GCR	9,400	—	—	2,000	3,000	4,000
1918 GCR	30,000	—	—	—	—	—

COUNTERSTAMPED COINAGE
Type VIII • 1923

In the financially stressful years between 1914 and 1925 many Latin American countries saw their currencies lose much of its former purchasing power. Governments reacted in several ways: In Peru, Chile, Brazil and most of Central America, this took the form of devaluing their monetary unit relative to such standards as the U.S. dollar and Swiss franc. Costa Rica began issuing coins of .500 fine silver and brass to replace the .900 fine silver issues of the past. A decree of 1923 also made provisions for the old .900 fine silver coins to be revalued, doubling their previous face values, by dated counterstamping conducted at the San Jose Mint through 1923 and into 1924.

Obverse counterstamp: 1923 in 11mm circle.

Reverse counterstamp: 50/CENTIMOS in 11mm circle.

NOTE: The total mintage for KM#154-159 was 1,866,000 pieces.

KM# 154   50 CENTIMOS
6.4000 g., 0.9030 Silver 0.1858 oz. ASW **Counterstamp:** Type VIII **Obv:** '1923' an old shield **Rev:** '50 centimos' within circle

CS Date	Host Date	Good	VG	F	VF	XF
1923	1850 JB	200	400	700	—	—

KM# 155   50 CENTIMOS
6.2500 g., 0.0750 Silver 0.0151 oz. ASW, 25 mm. **Counterstamp:** Type VIII **Obv:** '1923' an old shield **Rev:** '50 centimos' in circle

CS Date	Host Date	Good	VG	F	VF	XF
1923	1864 GW	150	300	500	—	—

KM# 156   50 CENTIMOS
6.2500 g., 0.7500 Silver 0.1507 oz. ASW, 25 mm. **Counterstamp:** Type VIII **Obv:** '1923' an old shield **Rev:** '50 centimos' in circle

CS Date	Host Date	Good	VG	F	VF	XF
1923	1864 GW	150	300	—	—	—
1923	1865 GW	50.00	100	150	—	—
1923	1875 GW	40.00	80.00	125	—	—

KM# 157   50 CENTIMOS
6.2500 g., 0.7500 Silver 0.1507 oz. ASW, 25 mm. **Counterstamp:** Type VIII **Obv:** '1923' an old shield **Rev:** '50 centimos' in circle

CS Date	Host Date	Good	VG	F	VF	XF
1923	1886 GW	—	6.00	8.00	12.00	20.00
1923	1887 GW	—	4.00	6.00	10.00	15.00

KM# 158   50 CENTIMOS
6.2500 g., 0.7500 Silver 0.1507 oz. ASW, 25 mm. **Counterstamp:** Type VIII **Obv:** '1923' an old shield **Rev:** '50 centimos' in circle

CS Date	Host Date	Good	VG	F	VF	XF
1923	1886 GW	—	8.00	10.00	15.00	30.00
1923	1887 GW	—	4.00	6.00	10.00	15.00

KM# 159   50 CENTIMOS
6.3000 g., 0.7500 Silver 0.1519 oz. ASW, 25 mm. **Counterstamp:** Type VIII **Obv:** '1923' an old shield **Rev:** '50 centimos' within circle
Note: Counterstamped on 25 Centavos, KM#130.

CS Date	Host Date	Good	VG	F	VF	XF
1923	1889HEATON	—	3.50	3.00	4.00	7.00
1923	1890/80HEATON	—	3.50	3.00	4.00	7.00
1923	1890HEATON	—	3.50	3.00	4.00	7.00
1923	1892HEATON	—	3.50	3.00	4.00	7.00
1923	1893HEATON	—	3.50	3.00	4.00	7.00

COUNTERSTAMPED COINAGE
Type IX • 1923

Obverse counterstamp: 1923 in 14mm circle.

Reverse counterstamp: UN/COLON in 14mm circle.

NOTE: The total mintage for KM#162-164 was 421,810 pieces. Host dates of 1867 GW, 1870 GW and 1872 GW are listed, but no examples are currently known to exist.

KM# 162   COLON
12.5000 g., 0.7500 Silver 0.3014 oz. ASW **Counterstamp:** Type IX **Note:** Counterstamped on 50 Centavos, KM#112.

CS Date	Host Date	Good	VG	F	VF	XF
1923	1866/5 GW	50.00	100	—	—	—
1923	1865 GW	50.00	—	—	—	—
1923	1867 GW	100	200	—	—	—
1923	1870 GW	400	—	—	—	—
1923	1872 GW	800	—	—	—	—
1923	1875 GW	50.00	100	250	—	—

KM# 165 COLON

10.0000 g., 0.5000 Silver 0.1607 oz. ASW, 29 mm.
Counterstamp: Type I **Obv:** Denomination on shield, date below
Rev: Date within circle, wreath surrounds **Note:** Counterstamped
on 50 Centavos, KM#112.

CS Date	Host Date	Good	VG	F	VF	XF
1923	1917 GCR	—	—	8.00	15.00	30.00
1923	1918 GCR	—	—	12.00	25.00	40.00

KM# 163 COLON (Un)

12.5000 g., 0.7500 Silver 0.3014 oz. ASW **Counterstamp:** Type
IX **Obv:** Date within circle, wreath surrounds **Rev:** Liberty cap
and flags above shield, turned 3/4 right, denomination within circle
on shield **Note:** Counterstamped on 50 Centavos, KM#112.

CS Date	Host Date	Good	VG	F	VF	XF
1923	1880 GW	—	7.50	7.50	10.00	25.00
1923	1885 GW	—	7.50	7.50	10.00	25.00
1923	1886 GW	—	9.00	9.00	17.50	30.00
1923	1887 GW	—	7.50	7.50	10.00	25.00
1923	1890 GW	—	7.50	7.00	10.00	20.00

KM# 164 COLON (Un)

10.0000 g., 0.9000 Silver 0.2893 oz. ASW, 29 mm.
Counterstamp: Type IX **Obv:** Date within circle, wreath
surrounds **Rev:** Denomination within circle on shield
Note: Counterstamped on 50 Centavos, KM#112.

CS Date	Host Date	Good	VG	F	VF	XF
1923	1902 CY	—	6.00	9.00	15.00	22.50
1923	1903 JCV	—	6.00	7.00	10.00	17.50
1923	1914 GCR	—	6.00	8.00	12.00	20.00

REFORM COINAGE
1920, 100 Centimos = 1 Colon

KM# 151 5 CENTIMOS

1.0000 g., Brass **Obv:** National arms, date below
Rev: Denomination within wreath, G.C.R. lower right **Edge:** Plain

Date	Mintage	F	VF	XF	Unc	BU
1920	500,000	3.00	9.00	25.00	60.00	100
1921	500,000	4.00	10.00	30.00	75.00	125
1922	500,000	3.00	8.00	20.00	40.00	75.00
1936	1,500,000	1.00	2.00	5.00	15.00	35.00
1938	1,000,000	1.00	2.00	10.00	25.00	40.00
1940	1,300,000	1.00	2.00	4.00	15.00	35.00
1941	1,000,000	1.00	3.00	6.00	25.00	40.00

KM# 169 5 CENTIMOS

1.0000 g., Bronze **Obv:** National arms, date below
Rev: Denomination within wreath, G.C.R. lower right

Date	Mintage	F	VF	XF	Unc	BU
1929(P)	1,500,000	1.00	3.00	8.00	20.00	40.00

KM# 179 5 CENTIMOS

1.0000 g., Brass **Obv:** National arms, date below
Rev: Denomination within wreath, star below divides B.N. at left
from C.R. at right

Date	Mintage	F	VF	XF	Unc	BU
1942	1,730,000	0.50	1.50	4.00	15.00	35.00
1943	1,000,000	0.50	1.50	4.50	15.00	45.00
1946	1,000,000	0.50	1.50	5.00	17.50	55.00
1947	3,000,000	0.50	1.00	3.00	10.00	20.00

KM# 178 5 CENTIMOS

1.0000 g., Copper-Nickel **Obv:** National arms, date below
Rev: Denomination within wreath, star below divides B.N. at left
from C.R. at right

Date	Mintage	F	VF	XF	Unc	BU
1942	274,000	0.65	1.00	4.00	10.00	22.50

Note: Struck over 2 Centimos, KM#144. Overstrikes with
clear evidence of the undertype command a 10-15%
premium.

KM# A184 5 CENTIMOS

1.0000 g., Copper-Nickel **Obv:** National arms, date below
Rev: Denomination within wreath, star below divides B.C. at left
from C.R. at right **Note:** Struck in Philadelphia 1951-52.

Date	Mintage	F	VF	XF	Unc	BU
1951(P)	3,000,000	0.35	0.75	1.50	3.00	6.50

KM# 184.1 5 CENTIMOS

1.0000 g., Copper-Nickel **Obv:** National arms, ribbon above,
date below **Rev:** Denomination within wreath, B.C.C.R. below
Note: Struck in Philadelphia, 1952.

Date	Mintage	F	VF	XF	Unc	BU
1951(P)	7,000,000	0.10	0.15	0.40	1.00	1.75

KM# 184.1a 5 CENTIMOS

0.8750 g., Stainless Steel, 14.92 mm. **Obv:** National arms,
ribbon above, date below **Rev:** Denomination within wreath,
B.C.C.R. below **Note:** 1967 date struck in San Francisco.

Date	Mintage	F	VF	XF	Unc	BU
1953(P)	9,040,000	—	—	0.10	0.25	—
1958(P)	19,940,000	—	—	0.10	0.15	—
	Note: Struck in 1959					
1967(s)	10,900,000	—	—	0.10	0.20	—

KM# 184.2 5 CENTIMOS

1.0100 g., Copper-Nickel, 14.99 mm. **Obv:** Small ships, 7 stars on
arms, no flag on near ship, date below **Rev:** Denomination within
wreath, B.C.C.R. below **Note:** Varieties exist for shields of each date.

Date	Mintage	F	VF	XF	Unc	BU
1969	20,000,000	—	—	0.10	0.15	—
1976		—	—	0.10	0.15	—
1976 Proof	5,000	Value: 2.50				
1978	7,520,000	—	—	0.10	0.15	—

KM# 184.3 5 CENTIMOS

1.0200 g., Copper-Nickel, 14.98 mm. **Obv:** Large ships, 7 stars
on arms, flag on near ship, date below arms **Rev:** Denomination
within wreath, B.C.C.R. below **Note:** Dies vary for each date.

Date	Mintage	F	VF	XF	Unc	BU
1972(g)	12,550,000	—	—	0.10	0.15	—
1973(g)	20,000,000	—	—	0.10	0.15	—
1976(g)	15,000,000	—	—	0.10	0.15	—

KM# 184.3a 5 CENTIMOS

0.9800 g., Brass, 15.0 mm. **Obv:** National arms, ribbon above, large
date below **Rev:** Denomination within wreath, B.C.C.R. below

Date	Mintage	F	VF	XF	Unc	BU
1979(g)	60,000,000	—	—	0.10	0.15	—

KM# 152 10 CENTIMOS

2.0000 g., Brass, 18 mm. **Obv:** National arms, date below
Rev: Denomination within wreath, G.C.R. at lower right

Date	Mintage	F	VF	XF	Unc	BU
1920 GCR	850,000	3.00	10.00	25.00	50.00	100
1921 GCR	750,000	3.00	10.00	30.00	75.00	150
1922 GCR	750,000	1.00	6.00	12.00	25.00	60.00

KM# 170 10 CENTIMOS

2.0000 g., Bronze, 18 mm. **Obv:** National arms, date below
Rev: Denomination within wreath, G.C.R. at bottom

Date	Mintage	F	VF	XF	Unc	BU
1929(P) GCR	500,000	1.50	3.50	10.00	30.00	50.00

KM# 174 10 CENTIMOS

Brass, 18 mm. **Obv:** National arms, date below
Rev: Denomination within wreath, G.C.R. below

Date	Mintage	F	VF	XF	Unc	BU
1936(sj)	750,000	1.00	2.00	5.00	15.00	35.00
1941(sj)	500,000	1.00	3.00	8.00	25.00	50.00

KM# 180 10 CENTIMOS

2.0000 g., Brass, 18 mm. **Obv:** National arms, date below
Rev: Denomination within wreath, B.N. - C.R. divided below

Date	Mintage	F	VF	XF	Unc	BU
1942(sj)	1,000,000	1.00	3.00	8.00	18.00	40.00
1943(sj)	500,000	1.00	3.50	9.00	20.00	45.00
1946(sj)	500,000	1.00	4.00	10.00	25.00	45.00
1947(sj)	1,500,000	0.50	1.00	3.00	10.00	20.00

Note: Edge varieties exist on 1947 strikes

KM# 185.1 10 CENTIMOS

2.0000 g., Copper-Nickel, 18 mm. **Obv:** Small ships, 5 stars in
shield, date below arms **Rev:** Denomination within wreath,
B.C.C.R. below

Date	Mintage	F	VF	XF	Unc	BU
1951(P)	2,500,000	0.10	0.20	0.70	2.00	5.00

Note: Struck in 1952

KM# 185.1a 10 CENTIMOS

1.7500 g., Stainless Steel, 18 mm. **Obv:** National arms, date
below **Rev:** Denomination within wreath, B.C.C.R. below

Date	Mintage	F	VF	XF	Unc	BU
1953(P)	5,290,000	—	—	0.10	0.75	—
1958(P)	10,470,000	—	—	0.10	0.25	—
Note: Struck in 1959						
1967(s)	5,500,000	—	—	0.10	0.25	—

KM# 185.2 10 CENTIMOS
2.0200 g., Copper-Nickel, 17.91 mm. **Obv:** Small ships, 7 stars in field, date below arms **Rev:** Denomination within wreath, B.C.C.R. below **Note:** Dies vary for each date

Date	Mintage	F	VF	XF	Unc	BU
1969(d)	10,000,000	—	—	—	0.10	0.15	—
1976(sm)	40,000,000	—	—	0.10	0.15	—
1976 Proof	5,000	Value: 2.50				

KM# 185.2a 10 CENTIMOS
Aluminum, 18 mm. **Obv:** National arms, small ships, 7 stars in field **Rev:** Denomination within wreath, B.C.C.R. below

Date	Mintage	F	VF	XF	Unc	BU
1982(v)	40,000,000	—	—	0.10	0.15	—

KM# 185.2b 10 CENTIMOS
2.0200 g., Nickel Clad Steel, 17.97 mm. **Obv:** National arms **Rev:** Denomination within wreath, B.C.C.R. below

Date	Mintage	F	VF	XF	Unc	BU
1979(sm)	10,000,000	—	—	0.10	0.15	—

KM# 185.3 10 CENTIMOS
1.9700 g., Copper-Nickel, 17.98 mm. **Obv:** Large ships, 7 stars in field, date below arms **Rev:** Denomination within wreath B.C.C.R. below

Date	Mintage	F	VF	XF	Unc	BU
1972(g)	20,000,000	—	—	0.10	0.15	—
1975(g)	5,000,000	—	—	0.10	0.15	—

KM# 168 25 CENTIMOS
3.4500 g., 0.6500 Silver 0.0721 oz. ASW **Obv:** National arms, date below **Rev:** Denomination within wreath, G.C.R. below at right **Edge:** Reeded

Date	Mintage	F	VF	XF	Unc	BU
1924	1,340,000	1.25	2.50	6.50	15.00	25.00

Note: Typical examples of KM#168 are weak at centers, fully struck up XF and Unc pieces command a 50% premium.

KM# 171 25 CENTIMOS
3.4500 g., Copper-Nickel **Obv:** National arms, date below **Rev:** Denomination within wreath, B.I.C.R. below **Edge:** Incuse lettered

Date	Mintage	F	VF	XF	Unc	BU
1935(P)	1,200,000	0.25	0.75	2.50	15.00	30.00

KM# 175 25 CENTIMOS
3.3300 g., Copper-Nickel **Obv:** National arms, date below **Rev:** Denomination within wreath, B.N.C.R. below

Date	Mintage	F	VF	XF	Unc	BU
1937(L)	1,600,000	0.25	0.75	2.00	8.00	15.00
1937(L) Proof	—	Value: 100				
Note: In proof sets only.						
1948(L)	9,200,000	0.10	0.20	0.40	2.00	4.00
1948(L) Specimen	—	—	—	—	—	250

KM# 181 25 CENTIMOS
3.5000 g., Yellow Brass **Obv:** National arms, date below **Rev:** Denomination within wreath, star divides B.N. from C.R. **Edge:** Reeded

Date	Mintage	F	VF	XF	Unc	BU
1944(sj)	800,000	0.50	1.00	4.00	12.00	20.00
1945(sj)	1,200,000	0.50	1.00	3.00	12.00	20.00
1946(sj)	1,200,000	0.50	1.00	3.00	10.00	15.00

KM# 181a 25 CENTIMOS
3.5000 g., Red Brass **Obv:** National arms, date below **Rev:** Denomination within wreath, star below divides B.N. and C.R. **Edge:** Reeded

Date	Mintage	F	VF	XF	Unc	BU
1945(sj)	Inc. above	2.00	4.00	10.00	20.00	35.00

KM# 188.1 25 CENTIMOS
3.4600 g., Copper-Nickel, 23.03 mm. **Obv:** Small ships, 7 stars on arms, date below **Rev:** Denomination within wreath, B.C.C.R. below **Note:** Dies vary for each date.

Date	Mintage	F	VF	XF	Unc	BU
1967(L)	4,000,000	—	—	0.10	0.50	—
1969(d)	4,000,000	—	—	0.10	0.50	—
1974(v)	—	—	—	0.10	0.30	—
1976(sm)	12,000,000	—	—	0.10	0.30	—
1976 Proof	5,000	Value: 2.50				
1978(a)	10,000,000	—	—	0.10	0.30	—

KM# 188.1a 25 CENTIMOS
Nickel Clad Steel **Obv:** National arms, date below **Rev:** Denomination within wreath, B.C.C.R. below **Note:** Beaded rims.

Date	Mintage	F	VF	XF	Unc	BU
1980(sm)	30,000,000	—	—	0.10	0.25	—

KM# 188.1b 25 CENTIMOS
Aluminum **Obv:** National arms, date below **Rev:** Denomination within wreath, B.C.C.R. below **Edge:** Plain

Date	Mintage	F	VF	XF	Unc	BU
1982(r)	30,000,000	—	—	0.10	0.25	—

KM# 188.3 25 CENTIMOS
1.0500 g., Aluminum, 17 mm. **Obv:** National arms, date below **Rev:** Denomination within wreath, B.C.C.R. below **Edge:** Reeded **Note:** Reduced size. Dies vary for each date.

Date	Mintage	F	VF	XF	Unc	BU
1983(r)	60,000,000	—	—	0.10	0.20	—
1986(c)	60,000,000	—	—	0.10	0.20	—
1989(c)	60,000,000	—	—	0.10	0.20	—

KM# 172 50 CENTIMOS
6.2500 g., Copper-Nickel, 25.02 mm. **Obv:** National arms, date below **Rev:** Denomination within wreath, B.I.C.R. below

Date	Mintage	F	VF	XF	Unc	BU
1935(P)	700,000	0.50	2.00	8.00	35.00	60.00

KM# 176 50 CENTIMOS
Copper-Nickel **Obv:** National arms, date below **Rev:** Denomination within wreath, B.N.C.R. below

Date	Mintage	F	VF	XF	Unc	BU
1937(L)	600,000	0.50	1.50	4.00	20.00	40.00
1937(L) Proof	—	Value: 150				
Note: In proof sets only.						
1948(L)	4,000,000	—	0.25	0.50	3.00	5.00
1948(L) Specimen	—	—	—	—	—	250

KM# 189.1 50 CENTIMOS
Copper-Nickel, 26 mm. **Obv:** Small ships, 7 stars on shield, date below arms **Rev:** Denomination within wreath, B.C.C.R. below **Note:** Medal rotation.

Date	Mintage	F	VF	XF	Unc	BU
1965(L)	1,000,000	—	0.10	0.25	1.00	—

KM# 189.3 50 CENTIMOS
7.2900 g., Copper-Nickel, 26 mm. **Obv:** National arms, date below **Rev:** Denomination within wreath, B.C.C.R. below, large 50, -BCCR- (repeated) **Note:** Dies vary for each date - the main varieties are an open or closed "5" in "50", or large and small dates.

Date	Mintage	F	VF	XF	Unc	BU
1968(P)	2,000,000	—	0.10	0.15	0.50	—
1970(P)	4,000,000	—	0.10	0.15	0.35	—
1976(sm)	6,000,000	—	0.10	0.15	0.35	—
1976 Proof	5,000	Value: 2.50				
1978(v)	10,000,000	—	0.10	0.15	0.35	—

KM# 189.2 50 CENTIMOS
7.0100 g., Copper-Nickel, 26 mm. **Obv:** Large ships, 7 stars in shield, date below arms **Rev:** Denomination within wreath, B.C.C.R. below, large 50

Date	Mintage	F	VF	XF	Unc	BU
1972(g) Large date	4,000,000	—	0.10	0.15	0.35	—
1975(g) Large date	524,000	—	0.10	0.15	0.35	—
1975 Small date	Inc. above	—	0.10	0.15	0.35	—

KM# 209.1   50 CENTIMOS
2.1800 g., Stainless Steel, 19.11 mm. **Obv:** Large ships, letters incuse on ribbon, date below arms **Rev:** Denomination within wreath, B.C.C.R. below, thick 50 **Edge:** Plain

Date	Mintage	F	VF	XF	Unc	BU
1982(c)	12,000,000	—	—	0.10	0.25	—
1983(c)	24,000,000	—	—	0.10	0.25	—
1990(c)	24,000,000	—	—	0.10	0.25	—

KM# 209.2   50 CENTIMOS
2.2000 g., Stainless Steel, 18.95 mm. **Obv:** Small ships, letters in relief on ribbon **Rev:** Denomination within wreath

Date	Mintage	F	VF	XF	Unc	BU
1984(L)	42,000,000	—	—	0.10	0.25	—

KM# 173   COLON
10.0000 g., Copper-Nickel, 29 mm. **Obv:** National arms, date below **Rev:** Denomination within wreath, B.I.C.R below **Edge:** Incuse BICR; plain **Note:** Beaded rims.

Date	Mintage	F	VF	XF	Unc	BU
1935(P)	350,000	1.00	3.00	10.00	50.00	100

Note: Struck in 1936.

KM# 177   COLON
Copper-Nickel, 29 mm. **Obv:** National arms, date below **Rev:** Denomination within wreath, B.N.C.R. below, -BNCR- (repeated)

Date	Mintage	F	VF	XF	Unc	BU
1937(L)	300,000	0.75	2.00	5.00	30.00	50.00
1937(L) Proof	—	Value: 200				
1948(L)	1,350,000	0.20	0.40	1.00	3.00	8.00
1948(L) Specimen	—					250

KM# 186.1   COLON
8.6670 g., Stainless Steel, 29 mm. **Obv:** Small ships, 5 stars in shield, date below **Rev:** Denomination within wreath, B.C.C.R. below, -BCCR- (repeated)

Date	Mintage	F	VF	XF	Unc	BU
1954(P)	987,000	0.20	0.35	1.00	10.00	12.00

KM# 186.1a   COLON
10.0000 g., Copper-Nickel, 29 mm. **Obv:** National arms, date below **Rev:** Denomination within wreath, B.C.C.R below

Date	Mintage	F	VF	XF	Unc	BU
1961(P)	1,000,000	0.10	0.20	0.50	2.00	—

KM# 186.2   COLON
10.3200 g., Copper-Nickel, 29 mm. **Obv:** Small ships, 7 stars in shield, date below **Rev:** Denomination within wreath, B.C.C.R. below, -BCCR- (repeated)

Date	Mintage	F	VF	XF	Unc	BU
1965(v)	1,000,000	0.10	0.20	0.40	1.00	—
1968(P)	2,000,000	0.10	0.20	0.30	0.65	—
1970(P)	2,000,000	0.10	0.20	0.30	0.65	—
1974(v)	2,000,000	0.10	0.20	0.30	0.65	—
1978(v)	10,000,000	0.10	0.20	0.30	0.65	—

KM# 186.3   COLON
9.7400 g., Copper-Nickel, 29 mm. **Obv:** Large ships, 7 stars in shield, date below **Rev:** Denomination within wreath, B.C.C.R. below

Date	Mintage	F	VF	XF	Unc	BU
1972(g)	2,000,000	0.10	0.20	0.30	0.65	—
1975(g)	1,028,000	0.10	0.20	0.30	0.65	—

KM# 186.4   COLON
9.7400 g., Copper-Nickel, 29 mm. **Obv:** Small ships, 7 stars in shield **Rev:** Denomination within wreath, large "1", -BCCR- (repeated) **Note:** Dies vary for each date.

Date	Mintage	F	VF	XF	Unc	BU
1976(sm)	12,000,000	0.10	0.20	0.30	0.65	—
1976(sm) Proof	5,000	Value: 2.50				
1977(sm)	22,000,000	0.10	0.20	0.30	0.65	—

KM# 210.1   COLON
3.2000 g., Stainless Steel, 21 mm. **Obv:** Large ships, letters incuse on ribbon, date below arms **Rev:** Denomination within wreath, B.C.C.R. below

Date	Mintage	F	VF	XF	Unc	BU
1982(cc)	12,000,000	—	—	0.15	0.35	—
1983(cc)	24,000,000	—	—	0.15	0.35	—
1984(L)	60,000,000	—	—	0.15	0.35	—
1991(cc)	30,000,000	—	—	0.15	0.35	—

KM# 210.2   COLON
3.2000 g., Stainless Steel, 21 mm. **Obv:** Small ships, letters in relief on ribbon, date below arms **Rev:** Denomination within wreath, B.C.C.R. below **Note:** Varieties exist with a "slim 1" in the value for 1984 & 1989, and a "fat 1" in the value for 1993 & 1994.

Date	Mintage	F	VF	XF	Unc	BU
1984(L)	Inc. above	—	—	0.15	0.35	—
1989(c)	50,000,000	—	—	0.15	0.35	—
1993(sm)	50,000,000	—	—	0.15	0.35	—
1994(v)	15,000,000	—	—	0.15	0.35	—

KM# 233   COLON
2.7800 g., Brass, 15.04 mm. **Obv:** National arms, date below **Rev:** Denomination above spray, B.C.C.R. below

Date	Mintage	F	VF	XF	Unc	BU
1998(a)				1.50	3.50	—

KM# 183   2 COLONES
Copper-Nickel, 32 mm. **Obv:** National arms, date below **Rev:** Denomination within wreath, B.N.C.R. below, -BNCR- (repeated)

Date	Mintage	F	VF	XF	Unc	BU
1948(L)	1,380,000	0.50	1.00	3.00	8.00	15.00
1948(L) Proof	—	Value: 350				

KM# 187.1   2 COLONES
12.0000 g., Stainless Steel, 32 mm. **Obv:** National arms with small ships, 5 stars in shield, date below arms **Rev:** Denomination within wreath, B.C.C.R. below, -BCCR- (repeated)

Date	Mintage	F	VF	XF	Unc	BU
1954(P)	1,028,000	0.50	1.00	3.00	15.00	20.00

KM# 187.1a   2 COLONES
Copper-Nickel, 32 mm. **Obv:** National arms, date below **Rev:** Denomination within wreath, B.C.C.R. below, -BCCR- (repeated)

Date	Mintage	F	VF	XF	Unc	BU
1961(P)	1,000,000	0.15	0.30	0.50	1.25	—

KM# 187.2   2 COLONES
Copper-Nickel, 32 mm. **Obv:** Small ships, 7 stars in shield, date below arms **Rev:** Denomination within wreath, B.C.C.R. below, -BCCR- (repeated) **Note:** Dies vary for each date.

Date	Mintage	F	VF	XF	Unc	BU
1968(L)	2,000,000	0.15	0.30	0.45	1.00	—
1970(P)	1,000,000	0.15	0.30	0.45	1.25	—
1972(v)	2,000,000	0.15	0.30	0.45	1.00	—
1978(v)	10,000,000	0.15	0.30	0.45	1.00	—

KM# 190   2 COLONES
4.3000 g., 0.9990 Silver 0.1381 oz. ASW **Subject:** 20th Anniversary of the Central Bank **Rev:** Bank above denomination

Date	Mintage	F	VF	XF	Unc	BU
1970 Proof	5,157	Value: 16.50				

Note: Also exists with a small oval with 1000 inside above the S in COLONES.

KM# 211.1 2 COLONES
4.2500 g., Stainless Steel, 23.1 mm. **Obv:** Large ships, letters incuse on ribbon, date below arms **Rev:** Denomination within wreath, B.C.C.R. below

Date	Mintage	F	VF	XF	Unc	BU
1982(cc)	12,000,000	—	—	0.20	0.60	—
1983(cc)	24,000,000	—	—	0.20	0.60	—

KM# 211.2 2 COLONES
4.2500 g., Stainless Steel, 23.1 mm. **Obv:** Small ship, letters in relief on ribbon, date below arms **Rev:** Denomination within wreath, B.C.C.R. below

Date	Mintage	F	VF	XF	Unc	BU
1984(L)	72,000,000	—	—	0.20	0.60	—

KM# 191 5 COLONES
10.7800 g., 0.9990 Silver 0.3462 oz. ASW **Subject:** 400th Year - The Founding of New Carthage Juan Vazquez de Coronado **Obv:** National arms, date below **Rev:** Bust with ruffled collar facing, raised 1000 hallmark in oval below "o" of "Cartago" **Edge:** Reeded

Date	Mintage	F	VF	XF	Unc	BU
1970 Proof	5,157	Value: 22.50				

KM# 203 5 COLONES
Nickel **Subject:** 25th Anniversary of the Central Bank **Obv:** National arms, denomination below **Rev:** Plants with two dates at right

Date	Mintage	F	VF	XF	Unc	BU
ND(1975)	2,000,000	—	0.15	0.35	1.25	—
ND(1975) Proof	5,000	Value: 2.00				

KM# 214.1 5 COLONES
7.2500 g., Stainless Steel, 25.9 mm. **Obv:** Small ship, letters in relief on ribbon, date below arms **Rev:** Denomination above spray, B.C.C.R. below, thick '5' on lined background

Date	Mintage	F	VF	XF	Unc	BU
1983(cc)	24,000,000	—	0.10	0.25	0.75	—
1989(v)	20,000,000	—	0.10	0.25	0.75	—

KM# 214.2 5 COLONES
7.2500 g., Stainless Steel, 25.9 mm. **Obv:** Large ship, letters incuse on ribbon **Rev:** Numeral on lined background, B.C.C.R. below sprays

Date	Mintage	F	VF	XF	Unc	BU
1985(cc)	25,000,000	—	0.10	0.25	0.75	—

KM# 214.3 5 COLONES
7.2500 g., Nickel Clad Steel, 25.9 mm. **Obv:** Small ship, letters in relief on ribbon **Rev:** Numeral on lined bakground, B.C.C.R. below sprays

Date	Mintage	F	VF	XF	Unc	BU
1993(L)	20,000,000	—	0.10	0.25	0.75	1.25

KM# 227 5 COLONES
4.0300 g., Brass Plated Steel, 21.5 mm. **Obv:** National arms, date below **Obv. Leg.:** REPUBLICA DE COSTA RICA **Rev:** Denomination above sprays, B.C.C.R. below **Edge:** Segmented reeding

Date	Mintage	F	VF	XF	Unc	BU
1995(w)	15,000,000	—	—	0.25	0.75	—

KM# 227a 5 COLONES
4.0000 g., Brass, 21.6 mm. **Obv:** National arms, large date below **Rev:** Denomination above spray, B.C.C.R. below, large letters in legends **Edge:** Segmented reeding

Date	Mintage	F	VF	XF	Unc	BU
1997(a)		—	—	—	0.50	—

KM# 227a.1 5 COLONES
4.0000 g., Brass, 21.6 mm. **Obv:** National arms, date below, smaller letters in legend and smaller date, shield is outlined **Obv. Leg.:** REPUBLICA DE COSTA RICA **Rev:** Denomination above sprays, B.C.C.R. below, smaller letters in legend **Edge:** Segmented reeding

Date	Mintage	F	VF	XF	Unc	BU
1999(co)		—	—	—	0.65	—

KM# 192 10 COLONES
21.7000 g., 0.9990 Silver 0.6969 oz. ASW **Subject:** Attempt of Unification of Middle America **Obv:** National arms, date below **Rev:** Kapok tree (ceiba petandra), five mountains in background, denomination below

Date	Mintage	F	VF	XF	Unc	BU
1970 Proof	5,157	Value: 35.00				

KM# 204 10 COLONES
Nickel, 32 mm. **Subject:** 25th Anniversary of the Central Bank **Obv:** National arms, denomination below **Rev:** Two dates above tree at center

Date	Mintage	F	VF	XF	Unc	BU
ND(1975)(v)	495,115	1.00	2.00	5.00	10.00	—
ND(1975)(v) Proof	5,000	Value: 15.00				

KM# 215.1 10 COLONES
8.4500 g., Stainless Steel, 28.3 mm. **Obv:** Small ship, letters in relief on ribbon, date below arms **Rev:** Denomination above spray, B.C.C.R. below, thick number on lined background

Date	Mintage	F	VF	XF	Unc	BU
1983(v)	12,000,000	—	0.20	0.35	1.25	—
1992(v)	25,000,000	—	0.20	0.35	1.25	—

KM# 215.2 10 COLONES
8.4500 g., Stainless Steel, 28.3 mm. **Obv:** Large ship, letters incuse on ribbon, date below arms **Rev:** Denomination above spray, B.C.C.R. below, thick number on lined background

Date	Mintage	F	VF	XF	Unc	BU
1985(cc)	20,000,000	—	0.20	0.35	1.25	—

KM# 228 10 COLONES
4.0200 g., Brass Plated Steel, 23.5 mm. **Obv:** National arms, date below **Rev:** Denomination above spray, B.C.C.R. below, thick 1 in numeral **Edge:** Segmented reeding

Date	Mintage	F	VF	XF	Unc	BU
1995(w)	15,000,000	—	—	0.35	1.25	—

KM# 228a 10 COLONES
5.0500 g., Brass, 23.5 mm. **Obv:** National arms, date below, large letters in legend and date, shield outlined **Obv. Leg.:** REPUBLICA DE COSTA RICA **Rev:** Denomination above sprays, B.C.C.R. below, thick 1 in numeral **Edge:** Segmented reeding

Date	Mintage	F	VF	XF	Unc	BU
1997(a)		—	—	—	1.00	—

KM# 228a.1 10 COLONES
5.0000 g., Brass, 23.5 mm. **Obv:** National arms and date below, small letters in legend **Rev:** Thin "1" in value above spray, B.C.C.R. below. Legends smaller than on KM#228a. **Edge:** Segmented reeding

Date	Mintage	F	VF	XF	Unc	BU
1999(co)		—	—	—	1.15	—

KM# 193 20 COLONES
43.7000 g., 0.9990 Silver 1.4035 oz. ASW, 50.8 mm. **Rev:** Venus de Milo statue, raised 1000 hallmark in oval below "O" in "MILO"

Date	Mintage	F	VF	XF	Unc	BU
1970 Proof	7,500	Value: 55.00				

KM# 205   20 COLONES
Nickel, 36 mm.   **Subject:** 25th Anniversary of the Central Bank
Obv: National arms above denomination **Rev:** Flowers divide
dates **Edge:** Reeded

Date	Mintage	F	VF	XF	Unc	BU
ND(1975)(v)	1,995,111	1.00	1.50	2.50	5.00	—
ND(1975)(v) Proof	5,000	Value: 9.00				

KM# 216.1   20 COLONES
9.7000 g., Stainless Steel, 31.25 mm.   **Obv:** Letters in relief on
ribbon, date below arms **Rev:** Denomination above spray,
B.C.C.R. below, thick numerals on patterned background

Date	Mintage	F	VF	XF	Unc	BU
1983(v)	16,000,000	—	0.35	0.65	1.75	—

KM# 216.2   20 COLONES
9.7000 g., Stainless Steel, 31.25 mm.   **Obv:** Letters incuse on
ribbon, date below arms **Rev:** Denomination above spray,
B.C.C.R. below, thick numerals on patterned background

Date	Mintage	F	VF	XF	Unc	BU
1985(cc)	25,000,000	—	0.35	0.65	1.75	—

KM# 216.3   20 COLONES
9.7500 g., Nickel Plated Steel, 31.25 mm.   **Obv:** National arms,
date below, letters in relief on ribbons **Rev:** Denomination above
spray, B.C.C.R. below, numerals on patterned background

Date	Mintage	F	VF	XF	Unc	BU
1994(sm)	10,000,000	—	0.35	0.65	1.75	—

KM# 194   25 COLONES
53.9000 g., 0.9990 Silver 1.7311 oz. ASW   **Subject:** 25 Years
of Social Legislation **Obv:** National arms, date below
Rev: "Materniad" sculpture by F. Zuniga, denomination below

Date	Mintage	F	VF	XF	Unc	BU
1970 Proof	6,800	Value: 75.00				

KM# 229   25 COLONES
Brass Plated Steel   **Obv:** National arms, date below
Rev: Denomination above spray, B.C.C.R. below
Edge: Segmented reeding

Date	Mintage	F	VF	XF	Unc	BU
1995	—	—	—	—	2.50	—

KM# 195.1   50 COLONES
7.4500 g., 0.9000 Gold 0.2156 oz. AGW   **Subject:** Inter-
American Human Rights Convention **Obv:** National arms, date
below **Rev:** Nude on globe background, denomination below

Date	Mintage	F	VF	XF	Unc	BU
1970 Proof	3,507	Value: 210				

KM# 195.2   50 COLONES
7.4500 g., 0.9000 Gold 0.2156 oz. AGW   **Obv:** National arms,
date below **Rev:** "1 AR" countermark above fineness statement

Date	Mintage	F	VF	XF	Unc	BU
1970 Proof	Inc. above	Value: 220				

KM# 200   50 COLONES
25.5500 g., 0.5000 Silver 0.4107 oz. ASW
Subject: Conservation **Obv:** National arms, date below
Rev: Green turtles, denomination below

Date	Mintage	F	VF	XF	Unc	BU
1974(L)	7,599	—	—	—	25.00	—

KM# 200a   50 COLONES
28.2800 g., 0.9250 Silver 0.8410 oz. ASW
Subject: Conservation **Obv:** National arms, date below
Rev: Green Turtle, denomination below

Date	Mintage	F	VF	XF	Unc	BU
1974(L) Proof	11,000	Value: 30.00				

KM# 231   50 COLONES
7.8000 g., Brass, 27.5 mm.   **Obv:** National arms, large date below,
shield outlined **Obv. Leg.:** REPUBLICA DE COSTA RICA **Rev:**
Value above spray **Rev. Leg.:** B. C. C. R. **Edge:** Segmented reeding

Date	Mintage	F	VF	XF	Unc	BU
1997(a)	—	—	—	—	3.00	—

KM# 231.1   50 COLONES
7.8000 g., Brass, 27.5 mm.   **Obv:** National arms, date below,
small letters and numerals in legend and date

Obv. Leg.: REPUBLICA DE COSTA RICA **Rev:** Value above
spray, smaller letters in legend **Rev. Leg.:** B. C. C. R.
Edge: Segmented reeding

Date	Mintage	F	VF	XF	Unc	BU
1999	—	—	—	—	3.00	—

KM# 196   100 COLONES
14.9000 g., 0.9000 Gold 0.4311 oz. AGW   **Obv:** National arms
Rev: Gold Vulture pendant in the style of the Chibcha Indians,
denomination below

Date	Mintage	F	VF	XF	Unc	BU
1970 Proof	3,507	Value: 425				

KM# 201   100 COLONES
32.1000 g., 0.5000 Silver 0.5160 oz. ASW
Subject: Conservation **Obv:** National arms, date below divides
BC from CR **Rev:** Manatee, denomination below

Date	Mintage	F	VF	XF	Unc	BU
1974(L)	7,599	—	—	—	27.00	—

KM# 201a   100 COLONES
35.0000 g., 0.9250 Silver 1.0408 oz. ASW
Subject: Conservation **Obv:** National arms **Rev:** Manatee

Date	Mintage	F	VF	XF	Unc	BU
1974(L) Proof	11,000	Value: 30.00				

KM# 206   100 COLONES
35.0000 g., 0.9250 Silver 1.0408 oz. ASW   **Subject:** International
Year of the Child **Rev:** Three birds in nest, date below

Date	Mintage	F	VF	XF	Unc	BU
1979	9,500	—	—	—	22.00	—
1979 Proof	5,000	Value: 28.00				

KM# 224   100 COLONES
Nickel   **Obv:** National arms, denomination below **Rev:** Bust of
President Dr. Oscar Arias S. divides dates

Date	Mintage	F	VF	XF	Unc	BU
1987(sm)	25,000	—	—	—	7.50	—

KM# 230   100 COLONES
Brass Plated Steel **Obv:** National arms above date
Rev: Denomination above spray, B.C.C.R. below
Edge: Segmented reeding

Date	Mintage	F	VF	XF	Unc	BU
1995(w)	—	—	—	—	4.50	—

KM# 230a   100 COLONES
Brass **Obv:** National arms, date below, large letters in legend
and date, shield outlined **Rev:** Value above spray, B.C.C.R. below
Edge: Segmented reeding

Date	Mintage	F	VF	XF	Unc	BU
1997(a)	—	—	—	—	4.50	—
1998(a)	—	—	—	—	4.50	—

KM# 230a.1   100 COLONES
9.0000 g., Brass, 29.5 mm. **Obv:** National arms, date below,
small letters in legend **Rev:** Denomination above spray, B.C.C.R.
below, small letters in legend **Edge:** Segmented reeding

Date	Mintage	F	VF	XF	Unc	BU
1999(co)	—	—	—	—	4.50	—

KM# 240   100 COLONES
9.1000 g., Brass, 29.5 mm. **Obv:** New design with much smaller
legend and date **Rev:** Value **Edge:** Segmented reeding

Date	Mintage	F	VF	XF	Unc	BU
2000(a)	—	—	—	—	4.50	—

KM# 197   200 COLONES
29.8000 g., 0.9000 Gold 0.8622 oz. AGW **Obv:** National arms
Rev: Juan Santamaria and cannon

Date	Mintage	F	VF	XF	Unc	BU
1970(i) Proof	3,507	Value: 750				

KM# 212   250 COLONES
30.3300 g., 0.9250 Silver 0.9020 oz. ASW
Subject: Conservation **Obv:** National arms **Rev:** Jaguar head
facing

Date	Mintage	F	VF	XF	Unc	BU
1982 FM Proof	1,109	Value: 140				

KM# 217   250 COLONES
30.3300 g., 0.9250 Silver 0.9020 oz. ASW **Obv:** National arms
Rev: National flower, denomination below

Date	Mintage	F	VF	XF	Unc	BU
1983(P) FM Proof	393	Value: 75.00				

KM# 207   300 COLONES
10.9700 g., 0.9250 Silver 0.3262 oz. ASW **Subject:** 125th
Anniversary - Death of Juan Santamaria **Obv:** National arms,
denomination below **Rev:** Juan Santamaria standing with torch
and rifle divides dates

Date	Mintage	F	VF	XF	Unc	BU
1981(sm) Proof	10,000	Value: 12.50				

KM# 223   300 COLONES
10.9700 g., 0.9250 Silver 0.3262 oz. ASW **Subject:** 200th
Anniversary - Founding of Alajuela **Obv:** National arms,
denomination below **Rev:** Head facing, divides dates

Date	Mintage	F	VF	XF	Unc	BU
1981(sm) Proof	—	Value: 12.50				

KM# 198   500 COLONES
74.5200 g., 0.9000 Gold 2.1562 oz. AGW **Subject:** 100th
Anniversary of Public Education **Obv:** National arms **Rev:** Jesus
Jimenez and students at desks

Date	Mintage	F	VF	XF	Unc	BU
1970(i) Proof	3,507	Value: 2,150				

KM# 236   500 COLONES
9.8000 g., Brass **Subject:** 50 Years - Central Bank **Obv:** National
arms, date below **Rev:** Bank building, value below

Date	Mintage	F	VF	XF	Unc	BU
2000(a)	5,000,000	—	—	—	2.50	3.50
2000(a) Proof	500	Value: 10.00				

KM# 199   1000 COLONES
149.0400 g., 0.9000 Gold 4.3124 oz. AGW **Subject:** 150th
Anniversary of Central American Independence **Obv:** National
arms **Rev:** Face on radiant sun above mountains, water and map,
denomination below **Note:** Illustration reduced.

Date	Mintage	F	VF	XF	Unc	BU
1970(i) Proof	3,507	Value: 4,200				

KM# 225   1000 COLONES
10.9700 g., 0.9250 Silver 0.3262 oz. ASW **Obv:** National arms,
denomination below **Rev:** Head of President Dr. Oscar Arias S.
divides dates

Date	Mintage	F	VF	XF	Unc	BU
1987(sm)	10,000	—	—	—	30.00	—

KM# 202   1500 COLONES
33.4370 g., 0.9000 Gold 0.9675 oz. AGW
Subject: Conservation **Obv:** National arms, date below divides
B.C. from C.R. **Rev:** Giant anteater, denomination below

Date	Mintage	F	VF	XF	Unc	BU
1974(L)	2,418	—	—	—	945	—
1974(L) Proof	726	Value: 975				

KM# 213   1500 COLONES
6.9800 g., 0.5000 Gold 0.1122 oz. AGW **Rev:** Busts of Francisco Coronado and Christopher Columbus, denomination above **Note:** Although considered legal tender, these coins were never officially authorized for circulation.

Date	Mintage	F	VF	XF	Unc	BU
1982FM (P)	724	Value: 125				

KM# 218   1500 COLONES
6.9800 g., 0.5000 Gold 0.1122 oz. AGW **Obv:** National arms, date below **Rev:** Native figurine, denomination above, spray below

Date	Mintage	F	VF	XF	Unc	BU
1983FM (P)	272	Value: 275				

KM# 234   3000 COLONES
25.3600 g., 0.9250 Silver 0.7542 oz. ASW **Subject:** 150th Anniversary San Juan de Dios Hospital **Obv:** National arms, denomination below **Rev:** Hospital building divides dates

Date	Mintage	F	VF	XF	Unc	BU
1994(rm) Proof	—	Value: 50.00				

KM# 208   5000 COLONES
15.0000 g., 0.9000 Gold 0.4340 oz. AGW **Subject:** 125th Anniversary - Death of Juan Santamaria **Obv:** National arms, denomination below **Rev:** Figure standing with torch and rifle divides dates

Date	Mintage	F	VF	XF	Unc	BU
1981(sm)	—	—	—	—	425	—
1981(sm) Proof	2,000	Value: 450				

KM# 232   5000 COLONES
15.0000 g., 0.9000 Gold 0.4340 oz. AGW **Subject:** Founding of Alajuela **Obv:** National arms **Rev:** Portrait of Ramirez

Date	Mintage	F	VF	XF	Unc	BU
1981(sm) Proof	2,000	Value: 450				

KM# 235   5000 COLONES
25.0600 g., 0.9250 Silver 0.7452 oz. ASW **Subject:** Centennial of the Colon **Obv:** National arms, denomination below **Rev:** Bust of Columbus right, two dates below denomination

Date	Mintage	F	VF	XF	Unc	BU
1997(a) Proof	—	Value: 50.00				

KM# 237   5000 COLONES
31.1000 g., 0.9250 Silver 0.9249 oz. ASW **Subject:** 50 Years - Central Bank **Obv:** National arms, date below **Rev:** Man working screw press, denomination at right

Date	Mintage	F	VF	XF	Unc	BU
2000(a) Proof	7,500	Value: 30.00				

KM# 226   25000 COLONES
15.0000 g., 0.9000 Gold 0.4340 oz. AGW **Obv:** National arms, denomination below **Rev:** Bust of President Dr. Oscar Arias S., divides dates

Date	Mintage	F	VF	XF	Unc	BU
1987(sm) Proof	5,000	Value: 425				

KM# 238   100000 COLONES
15.5500 g., 0.9000 Gold 0.4499 oz. AGW **Subject:** 50 Years - Central Bank **Obv:** National arms **Rev:** Three standing citizens, denomination at right

Date	Mintage	F	VF	XF	Unc	BU
2000(a) Proof	2,500	Value: 450				

LEPROSARIUM COINAGE

KM# L1   5 CENTIMOS
Copper Nickel **Note:** 4mm hole punched through 5 Centimos, KM#178.

Date	Mintage	VG	F	VF	XF	Unc
1942 (1944)	2,000	—	—	—	—	—

Note: Prospective buyers should proceed with caution, as many examples were produced in the early 1970's and no definitive proof of original examples currently exists.

KM# L2   25 CENTIMOS
Copper Nickel **Note:** 6mm hole punched through 25 Centimos, KM#171. Prospective buyers should proceed with caution, as modern fabrications are prevalent.

Date	Mintage	VG	F	VF	XF	Unc
1935 (1944) Rare	2,000	—	—	—	—	—

KM# L3   25 CENTIMOS
Copper-Nickel **Note:** 6mm hole punched through 25 Centimos, KM#175. Prospective buyers should proceed with caution, as modern fabrications are prevalent.

Date	Mintage	VG	F	VF	XF	Unc
1937 (1944) Rare Inc. above	—	—	—	—	—	—

KM# L4   50 CENTIMOS
Copper Nickel **Note:** 8mm hole punched through 50 Centimos, KM#172. Prospective buyers should proceed with caution, as modern fabrications are prevalent.

Date	Mintage	VG	F	VF	XF	Unc
1935 (1944) Rare	800	—	—	—	—	—

KM# L5   50 CENTIMOS
Copper Nickel **Note:** 8mm hole punched through 50 Centimos, KM#176. Prospective buyers should proceed with caution, as modern fabrications are prevalent.

Date	Mintage	VG	F	VF	XF	Unc
1937 (1944) Rare Inc. above	—	—	—	—	—	—

KM# L6   COLON
Copper Nickel **Note:** 9mm hole punched through 1 Colon, KM#173. Prospective buyers should proceed with caution, as modern fabrications are prevalent.

Date	Mintage	VG	F	VF	XF	Unc
1935 (1944) Rare	1,000	—	—	—	—	—

KM# L7   COLON
Copper Nickel **Note:** 9mm hole punched through 1 Colon, KM#177. Prospective buyers should proceed with caution, as modern fabrications are prevalent.

Date	Mintage	VG	F	VF	XF	Unc
1937 (1944) Rare Inc. above	—	—	—	—	—	—

PATTERNS
Including off metal strikes

KM#	Date	Mintage	Identification	Mkt Val
Pn11	1923	—	25 Centimos. Brass. Obverse of gold 5 pesos type KM#117 or 118, reverse as KM#168	—
Pn12	1924	—	25 Centimos. Brass. KM#168. Considered false.	—
Pn13	19xx	—	5 Centimos. Copper Nickel. Similar to 1929 issue	50.00
Pn14	19xx	—	5 Centimos. Brass. Similar to KM#151 type, 1936-1941 issues.	—
Pn15	19xx	—	10 Centimos. Copper-Nickel. Similar to 1929 issue. Prev.# KMPn10.	60.00
Pn16	1944	—	25 Centimos. Silver.	—
Pn17	1944	—	25 Centimos. Brass. Polished dies.	100

PIEFORTS

KM#	Date	Mintage	Identification	Mkt Val
P6	1946	—	25 Centimos. Brass.	200
P7	1946	—	25 Centimos. Copper Nickel. 7.4000 g. 50 pieces	300

MINT SETS

KM#	Date	Mintage	Identification	Issue Price	Mkt Val
MS1	1972 (6)	—	KM#184.4, 185.3-186.3, 187.2, 188.2-189.2	—	10.00
MS2	1975 (3)	—	KM#203-205	—	7.50

PROOF SETS

KM#	Date	Mintage	Identification	Issue Price	Mkt Val
PS1	1889 (4)	—	KM#128-131	—	—
PS2	1937 (3)	—	KM#175-177	—	450
PS3	1970 (10)	570	KM#190-199	—	5,500
PS4	1970 (5)	4,650	KM#190-194	52.00	220
PS5	1970 (5)	3,000	KM#195-199	832	5,225
PS6	1974 (2)	30,000	KM#200a-201a	50.00	50.00
PS7	1975 (3)	—	KM#203-205	—	15.00
PS8	1976 (5)	5,000	KM#184.3, 185.2, 186.4, 188.1, 189.1	10.00	7.50
PS9	2000 (3)	500	KM#236-238	—	—

CRETE

The island of Crete (Kriti), located 60 miles southeast of the Peloponnesus, was the center of a brilliant civilization that flourished before the advent of Greek culture. After being conquered by the Romans, Byzantines, Moslems and Venetians, Crete became part of the Turkish Empire in 1669. As a consequence of the Greek Revolution of the 1820s, it was ceded to Egypt. Egypt returned the island to the Turks in 1840, and they ceded it to Greece in 1913, after the Second Balkan War.

RULER
Prince George, 1898-1906

MINT MARKS
A - Paris
(a) - Paris (privy marks only)

GREEK ADMINISTRATION
STANDARD COINAGE

KM# 1 LEPTON
Bronze, 15 mm. **Ruler:** Prince George **Obv:** Crown
Rev: Denomination within wreath

Date	Mintage	F	VF	XF	Unc	BU
1901A	1,710,717	6.00	12.00	27.50	100	200

KM# 2 2 LEPTA
Bronze **Ruler:** Prince George **Obv:** Crown **Rev:** Denomination within wreath

Date	Mintage	F	VF	XF	Unc	BU
1901A	707,000	6.00	12.50	40.00	175	250

KM# 6 50 LEPTA
2.5000 g., 0.8350 Silver 0.0671 oz. ASW **Ruler:** Prince George
Obv: Head right **Rev:** Crowned arms, denomination below

Date	Mintage	F	VF	XF	Unc	BU
1901(a)	600,000	25.00	55.00	135	900	1,300

KM# 7 DRACHMA
5.0000 g., 0.8350 Silver 0.1342 oz. ASW **Ruler:** Prince George
Obv: Head right **Rev:** Crowned, mantled and supported arms, denomination below

Date	Mintage	F	VF	XF	Unc	BU
1901(a)	500,000	35.00	60.00	500	2,500	3,500

KM# 8 2 DRACHMAI
10.0000 g., 0.8350 Silver 0.2684 oz. ASW **Ruler:** Prince George
Obv: Head right **Rev:** Crowned, mantled and supported arms, denomination below

Date	Mintage	F	VF	XF	Unc	BU
1901(a)	175,000	75.00	150	1,000	7,500	10,000

KM# 9 5 DRACHMAI
25.0000 g., 0.9000 Silver 0.7234 oz. ASW **Ruler:** Prince George
Obv: Head right **Rev:** Crowned, mantled and supported arms, denomination below

Date	Mintage	F	VF	XF	Unc	BU
1901(a)	150,000	100	200	1,200	12,000	20,000

CROATIA

The Republic of Croatia, (Hrvatska) bordered on the west by the Adriatic Sea and the northeast by Hungary, has an area of 21,829 sq. mi. (56,538 sq. km.) and a population of 4.7 million. Capital: Zagreb.

The country was attached to the Kingdom of Hungary until Dec. 1, 1918, when it joined with the Serbs and Slovenes to form the Kingdom of the Serbs, Croats and Slovenes, which changed its name to the Kingdom of Yugoslavia on Oct. 3, 1929. On April 6, 1941, Hitler, angered by the coup d'etat that overthrew the pro-Nazi regime of regent Prince Paul, sent the Nazi armies crashing across the Yugoslav borders from Germany, Hungary, Romania and Bulgaria. Within a week the army of the Balkan Kingdom was prostrate and broken. Yugoslavia was dismembered to reward Hitler's Balkan allies. Croatia, reconstituted as a nominal kingdom, was given to the administration of an Italian princeling, who wisely decided to remain in Italy. By 1947 it was again totally part of the 6 Yugoslav Socialist Republics.

Croatia proclaimed their independence from Yugoslavia on Oct. 8, 1991.

Local Serbian forces, supported by the Yugoslav Federal Army, had developed a military stronghold and proclaimed an independent "SRPSKEKRAJINA" State in the area around Knin, located in southern Croatia having an estimated population of 350,000 Croat Serbs. In September 1995, Croat forces overwhelmed Croat Serb forces ending the short life of their proclaimed Serbian Republic.

NOTE: Coin dates starting with 1994 are followed with a period. Example: 1994.

MONETARY SYSTEM
100 Banica = 1 Kuna

The word kunas', related to the Russian Kunitsa, which means marten, reflects the use of furs for money in medieval Eastern Europe.

KINGDOM
DECIMAL COINAGE

KM# 1 KUNA
Zinc **Note:** Similar to 2 Kune, KM#2.

Date	Mintage	F	VF	XF	Unc	BU
1941 Rare	—	—	—	—	—	—

Note: Possibly unique

KM# 2 2 KUNE
2.2600 g., Zinc, 19.1 mm. **Edge:** Plain **Note:** Medal rotation

Date	Mintage	F	VF	XF	Unc	BU
1941	—	5.00	20.00	28.00	45.00	—
1941 Proof	—	Value: 80.00				

KM# A3 500 KUNA
9.9500 g., 0.9000 Gold 0.2879 oz. AGW **Obv:** Ante Pavelió, date below **Rev:** Denomination above arms within braided circle

Date	Mintage	F	VF	XF	Unc	BU
1941	170	—	1,750	2,250	3,000	—

KM# B3 500 KUNA
9.9500 g., 0.9000 Gold 0.2879 oz. AGW **Obv:** Kneeling figure with sheaf of grain, date below **Rev:** Denomination above arms within braided circle

Date	Mintage	F	VF	XF	Unc	BU
1941	—	—	—	—	3,400	—

REPUBLIC
REFORM COINAGE
May 30, 1994 - 1000 Dinara = 1 Kuna; 100 Lipa = 1 Kuna

For the circulating minor coins, the reverse legend (name of item) is in Croatian for odd dated years and Latin for even dated years.

KM# 3 LIPA
0.8000 g., Aluminum, 16 mm. **Obv:** Denomination above crowned arms **Obv. Leg.:** REPUBLIKA HRVATSKA **Rev:** Ears of corn, date below **Rev. Leg.:** KUKURUZ **Edge:** Plain

Date	Mintage	F	VF	XF	Unc	BU
1993	57,834,100	—	—	0.20	0.50	—
1993 Proof	17,000	Value: 1.00				
1995.	7,101,000	—	—	0.20	0.50	—
1995. With dot	—	—	—	0.20	0.50	—
1995. With dot, Proof	4,000	Value: 2.00				
1997.	5,019,000	—	—	0.20	0.50	—
1997. Proof	—	Value: 1.00				
1999.	8,000,000	—	—	0.20	0.50	—
1999. Proof	2,000	Value: 1.50				

KM# 3a LIPA
Silver, 17 mm. **Obv:** Denomination above arms **Rev:** Ears of corn

Date	Mintage	F	VF	XF	Unc	BU
1993 Proof, rare	5	—	—	—	—	—

KM# 3b LIPA
Gold, 17 mm. **Obv:** Denomination above arms **Rev:** Ears of corn

Date	Mintage	F	VF	XF	Unc	BU
1993 Proof, rare	5	—	—	—	—	—

KM# 12 LIPA
0.7000 g., Aluminum, 17 mm. **Obv:** Denomination above crowned arms **Obv. Leg.:** REPUBLIKA HRVATSKA **Rev:** Ears of corn, date below **Rev. Leg.:** ZEA MAYS **Edge:** Plain

Date	Mintage	F	VF	XF	Unc	BU
1994.	2,003,097	—	—	0.40	1.00	—
1994. Proof	4,000	Value: 2.00				
1996.	2,000,000	—	—	0.40	1.00	—
1996. Proof	5,000	Value: 1.00				
1998.	2,000,000	—	—	0.40	1.00	—
1998. Proof	2,000	Value: 2.50				
2000.	2,000,000	—	—	0.40	1.00	—
2000. Proof	1,000	Value: 2.50				

KM# 13 LIPA
Aluminum, 17 mm. **Obv:** Denomination above crowned arms **Rev:** Ears of corn, date below **Rev. Leg.:** FAO

Date	Mintage	F	VF	XF	Unc	BU
ND(1995)	1,000,000	—	—	0.35	1.00	—
ND(1995) Proof	5,000	Value: 1.50				

KM# 4 2 LIPE
0.9000 g., Aluminum, 18.97 mm. **Obv:** Denomination above crowned arms on half braid **Obv. Leg.:** REPUBLIKA HRVATSKA **Rev:** Grapevine, date below **Rev. Leg.:** VINOVA LOZA **Edge:** Plain

Date	Mintage	F	VF	XF	Unc	BU
1993	17,958,962	—	—	0.40	1.00	—
1993 Proof	17,000	Value: 2.00				
1995.	7,498,000	—	—	0.40	1.00	—
1995. Proof	4,000	Value: 2.00				
1997.	4,996,000	—	—	0.40	1.00	—
1997. Proof	2,000	Value: 2.50				
1999.	8,000,000	—	—	0.40	1.00	—
1999. Proof	2,000	Value: 2.50				

KM# 4a 2 LIPE
Silver, 19 mm. **Obv:** Denomination above crowned arms on half braid **Rev:** Grapevine above date

Date	Mintage	F	VF	XF	Unc	BU
1993 Proof, rare	5	—	—	—	—	—

KM# 4b 2 LIPE
Gold, 19 mm. **Obv:** Denomination above crowned arms on half braid **Rev:** Grapevine

Date	Mintage	F	VF	XF	Unc	BU
1993 Proof, rare	5	—	—	—	—	—

KM# 14 2 LIPE
0.9200 g., Aluminum, 19 mm. **Obv:** Denomination above crowned arms on half braid **Obv. Leg.:** REPUBLIKA HRVATSKA **Rev:** Grapevine, date below **Rev. Leg.:** VITIS VINIFERA **Edge:** Plain

Date	Mintage	F	VF	XF	Unc	BU
1994.	2,000,163	—	—	0.80	2.00	—
1994. Proof	4,000	Value: 2.25				
1996.	2,006,000	—	—	0.80	2.00	—
1996. Proof	5,000	Value: 2.25				
1998.	2,000,000	—	—	0.80	2.00	—
1998. Proof	2,000	Value: 2.50				
2000.	2,000,000	—	—	0.80	2.00	—
2000. Proof	1,000	Value: 3.00				

KM# 36 2 LIPE
0.9400 g., Aluminum, 18.97 mm. **Subject:** Olympics **Obv:** Denomination above crowned arms on half braid **Rev:** Olympic logo, torch above date below **Edge:** Plain

Date	Mintage	F	VF	XF	Unc	BU
1996.	1,000,000	—	—	0.30	0.75	—
1996. Proof	5,000	Value: 1.50				

KM# 5 5 LIPA
2.5400 g., Brass Plated Steel, 17.99 mm. **Obv:** Denomination above crowned arms **Obv. Leg.:** REPUBLIKA HRVATSKA **Rev:** Oak leaves, date below **Rev. Leg.:** HRAST LUZNJAK **Edge:** Plain

Date	Mintage	F	VF	XF	Unc	BU
1993	42,686,969	—	—	0.40	1.50	—
1993 Proof	17,000	Value: 2.00				
1995.	17,308,000	—	—	0.40	1.00	—
1995. Proof	4,000	Value: 3.00				
1997.	29,964,000	—	—	0.40	1.00	—
1997. Proof	2,000	Value: 3.50				
1999.	25,402,000	—	—	0.40	1.00	—
1999. Proof	2,000	Value: 3.50				

KM# 5a 5 LIPA
Silver, 18 mm. **Obv:** Denomination above crowned arms **Rev:** Oak leaves, date below

Date	Mintage	F	VF	XF	Unc	BU
1993 Proof, rare	5	—	—	—	—	—

KM# 5b 5 LIPA
Gold, 18 mm. **Obv:** Denomination above crowned arms **Rev:** Oak leaves, date below

Date	Mintage	F	VF	XF	Unc	BU
1993 Proof, rare	5	—	—	—	—	—

KM# 15 5 LIPA
2.4200 g., Brass Plated Steel, 17.99 mm. **Obv:** Denomination above crowned arms **Obv. Leg.:** REPUBLIKA HRVATSKA **Rev:** Oak leaves, date below **Rev. Leg.:** QUERCUS ROBUR **Edge:** Plain

Date	Mintage	F	VF	XF	Unc	BU
1994.	2,005,346	—	—	0.80	2.00	—
1994. Proof	4,000	Value: 2.25				
1996.	2,004,000	—	—	0.80	2.00	—
1996. Proof	5,000	Value: 2.50				
1998.	2,000,000	—	—	0.80	2.00	—
1998. Proof	2,000	Value: 3.00				
2000.	4,500,000	—	—	0.80	2.00	—
2000. Proof	1,000	Value: 4.00				

KM# 37 5 LIPA
Brass Plated Steel, 18 mm. **Subject:** Olympics **Obv:** Denomination above crowned arms **Rev:** Olympic logo, torch above, date below

Date	Mintage	F	VF	XF	Unc	BU
1996.	900,000	—	—	0.60	1.25	—
1996. Proof	5,000	Value: 2.00				

KM# 6 10 LIPA
3.3200 g., Brass Plated Steel, 20 mm. **Obv:** Denomination above crowned arms **Obv. Leg.:** REPUBLIKA HRVATSKA **Rev:** Tobacco plant, date below **Rev. Leg.:** DUHAN **Edge:** Plain

Date	Mintage	F	VF	XF	Unc	BU
1993	63,689,778	—	—	0.40	1.50	—
1993 Proof	17,000	Value: 3.00				
1995.	26,335,500	—	—	0.40	1.50	—
1995. Proof	4,000	Value: 4.00				
1997.	39,995,500	—	—	0.40	1.50	—
1997. Proof	1,000	Value: 4.50				
1999.	49,500,000	—	—	0.40	1.50	—
1999. Proof	2,000	Value: 4.50				

KM# 6a 10 LIPA
Silver, 20 mm. **Obv:** Denomination above crowned arms on half braid **Rev:** Tobacco plant, date below

Date	Mintage	F	VF	XF	Unc	BU
1993 Proof, rare	5	—	—	—	—	—

KM# 6b 10 LIPA
Gold, 20 mm. **Obv:** Denomination above crowned arms on half braid **Rev:** Oak leaves, date below

Date	Mintage	F	VF	XF	Unc	BU
1993 Proof, rare	5	—	—	—	—	—

KM# 16 10 LIPA
Brass Plated Steel, 20 mm. **Obv:** Denomination above crowned arms on half braid **Obv. Leg.:** REPUBLIKA HRVATSKA **Rev:** Tobacco plant, date below **Rev. Leg.:** NICOTIANA TABACUM **Edge:** Plain

Date	Mintage	F	VF	XF	Unc	BU
1994.	2,000,127	—	—	0.80	2.50	—
1994. Proof	4,000	Value: 4.00				
1996.	2,000,000	—	—	0.80	2.50	—
1996. Proof	5,000	Value: 3.50				
1998.	2,000,000	—	—	0.80	2.50	—
1998. Proof	2,000	Value: 4.50				
2000.	3,000,000	—	—	0.80	2.50	—
2000. Proof	1,000	Value: 5.00				

KM# 38 10 LIPA
Brass, 20 mm. **Subject:** 50th Anniversary - UN **Obv:** Denomination above crowned arms above half braid **Rev:** UN logo, dates below

Date	Mintage	F	VF	XF	Unc	BU
ND(1995)	900,000	—	—	0.50	1.20	—
ND(1995)	5,000	Value: 4.00				

KM# 7 20 LIPA
2.9000 g., Nickel Plated Steel, 18.5 mm. **Obv:** Denomination above crowned arms on half braid **Obv. Leg.:** REPUBLIKA HRVATSKA **Rev:** Olive branch, date below **Rev. Leg.:** MASLINA **Edge:** Plain

Date	Mintage	F	VF	XF	Unc	BU
1993	25,206,442	—	—	0.50	1.50	—
1993 Proof	17,000	Value: 3.00				

Date	Mintage	F	VF	XF	Unc	BU
1995.	39,718,500	—	—	0.50	1.50	—
1995. Proof	4,000	Value: 4.00				
1997.	9,999,000	—	—	0.45	1.50	—
1997. Proof	2,000	Value: 4.50				
1999.	33,500,000	—	—	0.45	1.50	—
1999. Proof	2,000	Value: 4.50				

KM# 7a 20 LIPA
Silver, 18.5 mm. **Obv:** Denomination above crowned arms on half braid **Rev:** Olive branch, date below

Date	Mintage	F	VF	XF	Unc	BU
1993 Proof, rare	5	—	—	—	—	—

KM# 7b 20 LIPA
Gold, 18.5 mm. **Obv:** Denomination above crowned arms on half braid **Rev:** Olive branch, date below

Date	Mintage	F	VF	XF	Unc	BU
1993 Proof, rare	5	—	—	—	—	—

KM# 17 20 LIPA
2.8800 g., Nickel Plated Steel, 18.5 mm. **Obv:** Denomination above crowned arms on half braid **Obv. Leg.:** REPUBLIKA HRVATSKA **Rev:** Olive branch, date below **Rev. Leg.:** OLEA EUROPAEA **Edge:** Plain

Date	Mintage	F	VF	XF	Unc	BU
1994.	2,072,862	—	—	0.80	2.50	—
1994. Proof	4,000	Value: 3.00				
1996.	2,000,000	—	—	0.80	2.50	—
1996. Proof	5,000	Value: 4.00				
1998.	2,000,000	—	—	0.80	2.50	—
1998. Proof	2,000	Value: 4.50				
2000.	2,000,000	—	—	0.80	2.50	—
2000. Proof	1,000	Value: 5.00				

KM# 18 20 LIPA
2.9000 g., Nickel Plated Steel, 18.5 mm. **Subject:** F.A.O. **Obv:** Denomination above crowned arms on half braid **Rev:** Olive branch, date below

Date	Mintage	F	VF	XF	Unc	BU
ND(1995)	1,000,000	—	—	0.65	1.50	—
ND(1995) Proof	5,000	Value: 4.50				

KM# 8 50 LIPA
3.6500 g., Nickel Plated Steel, 20.5 mm. **Obv:** Denomination above crowned arms on half braid **Obv. Leg.:** REPUBLIKA HRVATSKA **Rev:** Flowers, date below **Rev. Leg.:** VELEBITSKA DEGENIJA **Edge:** Plain

Date	Mintage	F	VF	XF	Unc	BU
1993	51,456,267	—	—	0.60	1.50	—
1993 Proof	17,000	Value: 4.00				
1995.	23,077,000	—	—	0.60	1.50	—
1995. Proof	4,000	Value: 4.50				
1997.	1,473,000	—	—	0.60	1.50	—
1997. Proof	2,000	Value: 5.00				
1999.	1,000,000	—	—	0.60	1.50	—
1999. Proof	2,000	Value: 5.00				

KM# 8a 50 LIPA
Silver, 20.5 mm. **Obv:** Denomination above crowned arms on half braid **Rev:** Flowers, date below

Date	Mintage	F	VF	XF	Unc	BU
1993 Proof, rare	5	—	—	—	—	—

KM# 8b 50 LIPA
Gold, 20.5 mm. **Obv:** Denomination above crowned arms on half braid **Rev:** Flowers, date below

Date	Mintage	F	VF	XF	Unc	BU
1993 Proof, rare	5	—	—	—	—	—

KM# 19 50 LIPA
3.6500 g., Nickel Plated Steel, 20.5 mm. **Obv:** Denomination above crowned arms on half braid **Obv. Leg.:** REPUBLIKA HRVATSKA **Rev:** Flowers, date below **Rev. Leg.:** DEGENIA VELEBITICA **Edge:** Plain

Date	Mintage	F	VF	XF	Unc	BU
1994.	2,001,131	—	—	0.80	2.50	—
1994. Proof	4,000	Value: 4.00				
1996.	2,000,000	—	—	0.80	2.50	—
1996. Proof	5,000	Value: 4.00				
1998.	2,000,000	—	—	0.80	2.50	—
1998. Proof	2,000	Value: 4.50				
2000.	3,500,000	—	—	0.80	2.50	—
2000. Proof	1,000	Value: 5.00				

KM# 39 50 LIPA
3.6500 g., Nickel Plated Steel, 20.5 mm. **Subject:** European soccer **Obv:** Denomination above crowned arms on half braid **Rev:** Checkered shield, soccer ball at bottom, date above

Date	Mintage	F	VF	XF	Unc	BU
1996.	900,000	—	—	0.65	1.50	—
1996. Proof	5,000	Value: 4.00				

KM# 9.1 KUNA
5.0000 g., Copper-Nickel, 22.5 mm. **Obv:** Marten back of numeral, arms divide branches below **Obv. Leg.:** REPUBLIKA HRVATSKA **Rev:** Nightingale left, two dates **Rev. Leg.:** SLAVUJ **Edge:** Reeded

Date	Mintage	F	VF	XF	Unc	BU
1993	49,913,770	—	—	0.75	1.65	1.75
1993 Proof	17,000	Value: 3.00				
1995.	32,707,000	—	—	0.75	1.65	1.75
1995. Proof	4,000	Value: 3.50				
1997.	6,205,000	—	—	0.75	1.65	1.75
1997. Proof	2,000	Value: 4.00				

KM# 9.1a KUNA
Silver, 22.5 mm. **Obv:** Marten back of numeral, arms divide branches below **Rev:** Nightingale left

Date	Mintage	F	VF	XF	Unc	BU
1993 Proof, rare	5	—	—	—	—	—

KM# 9.1b KUNA
Gold, 22.5 mm. **Obv:** Marten back of numeral, arms divide branches below **Rev:** Nightingale left

Date	Mintage	F	VF	XF	Unc	BU
1993 Proof, rare	5	—	—	—	—	—

KM# 9.2 KUNA
4.9300 g., Copper-Nickel, 22.5 mm. **Obv:** Crowned arms flanked by sprays, denomination above on marten **Rev:** Nightingale, left, '1994' above, date below **Edge:** Reeded

Date	Mintage	F	VF	XF	Unc	BU
1999.	18,000,000	—	—	0.75	1.75	—
1999. Proof	2,000	Value: 4.00				

KM# 9b KUNA
Gold **Obv:** Marten back of numeral, arms divide branches below **Rev:** Nightingale left

Date	Mintage	F	VF	XF	Unc	BU
1993 Proof, rare	5	—	—	—	—	—

KM# 20.1 KUNA
5.0000 g., Copper-Nickel, 22.5 mm. **Obv:** Marten back of numeral, arms divide branches below **Rev:** Nightingale left, date below **Rev. Leg.:** Error spelling "LUSCINNIA" MEGARHYNCHOS **Note:** Formerly KM-20

Date	Mintage	F	VF	XF	Unc	BU
1994.	2,000,133	—	—	0.50	2.00	—
1994. Proof	4,000	Value: 4.00				
1996.	—	—	—	—	—	—

KM# 20.2 KUNA
5.0000 g., Copper-Nickel, 22.5 mm. **Obv:** Marten back of numeral, arms divide branches below **Obv. Leg.:** REPUBLIKA HRVATSKA **Rev:** Nightingale left, date below **Rev. Leg.:** Correct spelling "LUSCINIA" MEGARHYNCHOS **Edge:** Reeded

Date	Mintage	F	VF	XF	Unc	BU
1996.	2,000,000	—	—	1.00	3.00	—
1996. Proof	5,000	Value: 5.00				
1998.	2,000,000	—	—	1.00	3.00	—
1998. Proof	1,000	Value: 5.00				
2000.	2,000,000	—	—	1.00	3.00	—
2000. Proof	1,000	Value: 5.00				

KM# 40 KUNA
Copper-Nickel, 22.5 mm. **Subject:** Olympics **Obv:** Marten back of numeral, arms divide branches below **Rev:** Olympic logo, torch above, date below

Date	Mintage	F	VF	XF	Unc	BU
1996.	1,000,000	—	—	0.65	1.50	—
1996. Proof	5,000	Value: 3.00				

KM# 10 2 KUNE
6.2000 g., Copper-Nickel, 24.5 mm. **Obv:** Marten back of numeral, arms divide branches below **Obv. Leg.:** REPUBLIKA HRVATSKA **Rev:** Bluefin tuna right, date below **Rev. Leg.:** TUNJ **Edge:** Reeded

Date	Mintage	F	VF	XF	Unc	BU
1993	19,774,119	—	—	1.00	2.00	—
1993 Proof	17,000	Value: 4.50				
1995.	9,304,000	—	—	1.00	2.00	—
1995. Proof	4,000	Value: 5.50				
1997.	1,305,000	—	—	1.00	2.00	—
1997. Proof	1,000	Value: 6.00				
1999.	2,500,000	—	—	1.00	2.00	—
1999. Proof	2,000	Value: 6.00				

KM# 10a 2 KUNE
Silver, 24.5 mm. **Obv:** Marten back of numeral, arms divide branches below **Rev:** Tuna right, date below

Date	Mintage	F	VF	XF	Unc	BU
1993 Proof, rare	5	—	—	—	—	—

KM# 10b 2 KUNE
Gold, 24.5 mm. **Obv:** Marten back of numeral, arms divide branches below **Rev:** Tuna right, date below

Date	Mintage	F	VF	XF	Unc	BU
1993 Proof, rare	5	—	—	—	—	—

KM# 21 2 KUNE
6.2000 g., Copper-Nickel, 24.5 mm. **Obv:** Marten back of numeral, arms divide branches below **Obv. Leg.:** REPUBLIKA HRVATSKA **Rev:** Bluefin tuna right, date below **Rev. Leg.:** THUNNUS - THYNNUS **Edge:** Reeded

Date	Mintage	F	VF	XF	Unc	BU
1994.	2,000,758	—	—	1.50	3.00	—
1994. Proof	4,000	Value: 5.00				
1996.	2,000,000	—	—	1.50	3.00	—
1996. Proof	5,000	Value: 4.50				
1998.	2,000,000	—	—	1.50	3.00	—
1998. Proof	1,000	Value: 5.50				
2000.	2,000,000	—	—	1.50	3.00	—
2000. Proof	1,000	Value: 6.00				

KM# 22 2 KUNE
6.2000 g., Copper-Nickel, 24.5 mm. **Obv:** Marten back of numeral, arms divide branches below **Rev:** Bluefin tuna right, date below **Rev. Leg.:** FAO

Date	Mintage	F	VF	XF	Unc	BU
ND(1995)	500,000	—	—	0.75	2.00	—
ND(1995) Proof	5,000	Value: 5.50				

KM# 11 5 KUNA
7.5000 g., Copper-Nickel, 26.7 mm. **Obv:** Marten back of numeral, arms divide branches below **Obv. Leg.:** REPUBLIKA HRVATSKA **Rev:** Brown bear left, date below **Rev. Leg.:** MRKI MEDVJRD **Edge:** Reeded

Date	Mintage	F	VF	XF	Unc	BU
1993	4,989,300	—	—	1.50	5.00	8.00
1993 Proof	17,000	Value: 7.50				
1995.	3,724,000	—	—	1.50	5.00	8.00
1995. Proof	4,000	Value: 7.50				
1997.	1,165,000	—	—	1.50	5.00	8.00
1997. Proof	2,000	Value: 7.50				
1999.	4,000,000	—	—	1.50	5.00	8.00
1999. Proof	2,000	Value: 7.50				

KM# 11a 5 KUNA
Silver, 26.7 mm. **Obv:** Marten back of numeral, arms divide branches below **Rev:** Brown bear left, date below

Date	Mintage	F	VF	XF	Unc	BU
1993 Proof, rare	5	—	—	—	—	—

KM# 11b 5 KUNA
Gold, 26.7 mm. **Obv:** Marten back of numeral, arms divide branches below **Rev:** Brown bear left, date below

Date	Mintage	F	VF	XF	Unc	BU
1993 Proof, rare	5	—	—	—	—	—

KM# 23 5 KUNA
7.5000 g., Copper-Nickel, 26.7 mm. **Obv:** Marten back of numeral, arms divide branches below **Obv. Leg.:** REPUBLIKA HRVATSKA **Rev:** Brown bear left, date below **Rev. Leg.:** URSUS ARCTOS **Edge:** Reeded

Date	Mintage	F	VF	XF	Unc	BU
1994.	2,001,442	—	—	2.00	—	8.00
1994. Proof	4,000	Value: 7.50				
1996.	2,000,000	—	—	2.00	—	8.00
1996. Proof	5,000	Value: 7.50				
1998. Proof	—	Value: 7.50				
2000.	7,700,000	—	—	2.00	—	8.00
2000. Proof	1,000	Value: 9.00				

KM# 24 5 KUNA
Copper-Nickel, 26.7 mm. **Subject:** 500th Anniversary - Senj **Obv:** Denomination on square divides arms above from shield below, circle surrounds **Rev:** Anniversary dates on symbol within circle

Date	Mintage	F	VF	XF	Unc	BU
1994.	1,000,000	—	—	—	3.50	—
1994. Proof	5,000	Value: 8.00				

KM# 24a 5 KUNA
Silver, 26.7 mm. **Subject:** 500th Anniversary - Senj **Obv:**
Denomination on square divides arms above from shield below,
circle surrounds **Rev:** Anniversary dates on symbols within circle

Date	Mintage	F	VF	XF	Unc	BU
1994. Proof	500	Value: 270				
Note: Reported not confirmed						

KM# 24b 5 KUNA
12.0000 g., 0.9000 Gold 0.3472 oz. AGW, 26.7 mm.
Subject: 500th Anniversary - Senj **Obv:** Denomination on square
divides arms above from shield below, circle surrounds
Rev: Anniversary dates on symbols within circle

Date	Mintage	F	VF	XF	Unc	BU
1994.	200	—	—	—	450	—

KM# 47 25 KUNA
Bi-Metallic Brass center in Copper-Nickel ring, 31 mm.
Subject: Danube Border Region **Obv:** 3D denomination on
marten within circle, crowned arms below divide branches
Rev: Regional map, date below

Date	Mintage	F	VF	XF	Unc	BU
1997.	300,000	—	—	—	11.50	—
1997. Proof	2,000	Value: 22.50				

KM# 48 25 KUNA
Bi-Metallic Brass center in Copper-Nickel ring, 31 mm.
Subject: 5th Anniversary - UN Membership **Obv:** 3D
denomination on marten within circle, crowned arms divide
branches below **Rev:** UN emblem within wreath, date below

Date	Mintage	F	VF	XF	Unc	BU
1997. Proof	2,000	Value: 22.50				
1997.	300,000	—	—	—	11.50	—

KM# 49 25 KUNA
Bi-Metallic Brass center in Copper-Nickel ring, 31 mm.
Subject: First Croatian Esperanto Congress **Obv:** 3D
denomination on marten within circle, crowned arms below divide
branches **Rev:** Logo, date below

Date	Mintage	F	VF	XF	Unc	BU
1997. Proof	2,000	Value: 22.50				
1997.	300,000	—	—	—	11.50	—

KM# 63 25 KUNA
Bi-Metallic Brass center in Copper-Nickel ring, 31 mm.
Subject: Lisbon Expo **Obv:** 3D denomination on marten within
circle, crowned arms below divide branches **Rev:** Sailboat, date
upper right

Date	Mintage	F	VF	XF	Unc	BU
1998.	300,000	—	—	—	11.50	—
1998. Proof	1,000	Value: 25.00				

KM# 64 25 KUNA
Bi-Metallic Brass center in Copper-Nickel ring, 31 mm.
Subject: European Union **Obv:** 3D denomination on marten
within circle, crowned arms below divide branches **Rev:** 12 stars
on a large "E", date below **Edge:** Plain

Date	Mintage	F	VF	XF	Unc	BU
1999.	300,000	—	—	—	11.50	—
1999. Proof	1,000	Value: 25.00				

KM# 65 25 KUNA
Bi-Metallic Brass center in Copper-Nickel ring, 31 mm. **Obv:** 3D
denomination on marten within circle, crowned arms below divide
branches **Rev:** Human fetus within radiant circle, date below
Edge: Plain

Date	Mintage	F	VF	XF	Unc	BU
2000.	300,000	—	—	—	11.50	—
2000. Proof	1,000	Value: 25.00				

KM# 25.1 100 KUNA
15.0000 g., Silver **Subject:** 900th Anniversary - St. Blaza Church
Obv: Buildings divide arms and denomination **Rev:** Altar at St.
Blaza divides dates

Date	Mintage	F	VF	XF	Unc	BU
ND(1994) Proof	3,000	Value: 50.00				

KM# 25.2 100 KUNA
15.0000 g., Silver **Subject:** 900th Anniversary - St. Blaza Church
Obv: Buildings divide denomination and arms, series II mark
added **Rev:** Altar at St. Blaza divides dates

Date	Mintage	F	VF	XF	Unc	BU
ND(1994) Proof	1,000	Value: 80.00				

KM# 26 100 KUNA
33.6300 g., Silver **Rev:** Half-length bust of Pope John Paul II

Date	Mintage	F	VF	XF	Unc	BU
1994. Proof	10,000	Value: 70.00				

KM# 27 100 KUNA
20.0000 g., 0.9250 Silver 0.5948 oz. ASW **Subject:** 5th
Anniversary of Independence

Date	Mintage	F	VF	XF	Unc	BU
ND(1995) Proof	6,000	Value: 35.00				

KM# 50 100 KUNA
20.0000 g., 0.9250 Silver 0.5948 oz. ASW **Subject:** City of Split
Obv: Towered building, denomination at left **Rev:** Ancient
depiction of king on throne, dates at left

Date	Mintage	F	VF	XF	Unc	BU
ND(1995) Proof	2,950	Value: 32.00				

KM# 41 100 KUNA
20.0000 g., 0.9250 Silver 0.5948 oz. ASW **Subject:** Olympics
Obv: Sailboat racing, denomination above **Rev:** Wheelchair-
bound javelin thrower, crowned arms above

Date	Mintage	F	VF	XF	Unc	BU
1996. Proof	2,000	Value: 40.00				

KM# 42 100 KUNA
20.0000 g., 0.9250 Silver 0.5948 oz. ASW **Subject:** Olympics
Obv: Rowing, denomination above **Rev:** Water polo player,
crowned arms above

Date	Mintage	F	VF	XF	Unc	BU
1996. Proof	2,000	Value: 40.00				

KM# 28 150 KUNA
24.0000 g., 0.9250 Silver 0.7137 oz. ASW **Subject:** 5th
Anniversary of Independence **Obv:** Denomination below
crowned arms **Rev:** Assorted symbols on portioned background

Date	Mintage	F	VF	XF	Unc	BU
1995. Proof	5,000	Value: 42.50				

KM# 43 150 KUNA
24.0000 g., 0.9250 Silver 0.7137 oz. ASW **Subject:** Olympics
Obv: Gymnast, denomination at right **Rev:** Basketball players,
crowned arms above

Date	Mintage	F	VF	XF	Unc	BU
1996. Proof	2,000	Value: 42.50				

KM# 44 150 KUNA
24.0000 g., 0.9250 Silver 0.7137 oz. ASW **Subject:** Olympics **Obv:**
Table tennis and paddle, denomination at top **Rev:** Marksmanship
eye design, crowned arms divide date above, circle surrounds

Date	Mintage	F	VF	XF	Unc	BU
1996.	2,000	Value: 42.50				

KM# 56 150 KUNA
24.0000 g., 0.9250 Silver 0.7137 oz. ASW **Subject:** 800th
Anniversary - City of Osijek **Obv:** Crowned arms above
denomination **Rev:** City view

Date	Mintage	F	VF	XF	Unc	BU
ND(1996) Proof	1,000	Value: 40.00				

KM# 59 150 KUNA
24.0000 g., 0.9250 Silver 0.7137 oz. ASW **Obv:** Denomination
above arms, date divided below **Rev:** Bust left

Date	Mintage	F	VF	XF	Unc	BU
1997. Proof	10,000	Value: 40.00				

KM# 67 150 KUNA
24.0000 g., 0.9250 Silver 0.7137 oz. ASW, 37 mm.
Subject: Vukovar **Obv:** Ceramic container, arms below
Rev: Courtyard, date at right **Edge:** Plain

Date	Mintage	F	VF	XF	Unc	BU
1997. Proof	1,000	Value: 35.00				

KM# 69 150 KUNA
24.0000 g., 0.9250 Silver 0.7137 oz. ASW, 37 mm. **Obv:** Wild
flowers, denomination at right, arms at top **Rev:** Eagle on branch
Edge: Plain

Date	Mintage	F	VF	XF	Unc	BU
1997. Proof	1,000	Value: 45.00				

KM# 75 150 KUNA
24.0000 g., 0.9250 Silver 0.7137 oz. ASW, 37 mm.
Subject: 150 Years of Croatian as an Official Language
Obv: Two hands writing **Rev:** Old document **Edge:** Plain

Date	Mintage	F	VF	XF	Unc	BU
1997. Proof	1,000	Value: 40.00				

KM# 73 150 KUNA
24.0000 g., 0.9250 Silver 0.7137 oz. ASW, 37 mm. **Obv:** Small
national arms above religious arms and value **Rev:** Cardinal
Stepinac (1898-1960) right **Edge:** Plain

Date	Mintage	F	VF	XF	Unc	BU
1998. Proof	2,000	Value: 37.50				

KM# 29.1 200 KUNA
33.6300 g., 0.9250 Silver 1.0000 oz. ASW **Obv:** St. Marka
Church **Rev:** Portal of St. Marka Church

Date	Mintage	F	VF	XF	Unc	BU
ND(1994) Proof	3,000	Value: 75.00				

KM# 29.2 200 KUNA
33.6300 g., 0.9250 Silver 1.0000 oz. ASW **Obv:** St. Marka
Church, Series II mark added **Rev:** Portal of St. Marka Church

Date	Mintage	F	VF	XF	Unc	BU
ND(1994) Proof	1,000	Value: 95.00				

KM# 30 200 KUNA
33.6300 g., 0.9250 Silver 1.0000 oz. ASW **Subject:** 5th
Anniversary of Independence

Date	Mintage	F	VF	XF	Unc	BU
ND(1995) Proof	4,000	Value: 75.00				

KM# 51 200 KUNA
33.6300 g., 0.9250 Silver 1.0000 oz. ASW **Subject:** Spalatum
Obv: Diocletian's palace, denomination and arms above
Rev: Sarcophagus, two dates above

Date	Mintage	F	VF	XF	Unc	BU
ND(1995) Proof	2,950	Value: 45.00				

KM# 45   200 KUNA
33.6300 g., 0.9250 Silver 1.0000 oz. ASW **Subject:** Olympics
Obv: High jumper **Rev:** Tennis player

Date	Mintage	F	VF	XF	Unc	BU
ND Proof	2,000	Value: 50.00				

KM# 46   200 KUNA
33.6300 g., 0.9250 Silver 1.0000 oz. ASW **Subject:** Olympics
Obv: Diving swimmers, denomination above **Rev:** Basketball
game, crowned arms above

Date	Mintage	F	VF	XF	Unc	BU
1996. Proof	2,000	Value: 50.00				

KM# 54   200 KUNA
33.6300 g., 0.9250 Silver 1.0000 oz. ASW **Subject:** University
in Zadar **Obv:** Circle of arches, denomination at top, arms below
Rev: Saint reading within circle, dates below

Date	Mintage	F	VF	XF	Unc	BU
ND(1996) Proof	1,000	Value: 55.00				

KM# 57   200 KUNA
33.6300 g., 0.9250 Silver 1.0000 oz. ASW **Subject:** 500th
Anniversary - City of Osijek **Obv:** National arms above
denomination **Rev:** City view

Date	Mintage	F	VF	XF	Unc	BU
ND(1996) Proof	1,000	Value: 52.00				

KM# 60   200 KUNA
33.6300 g., 0.9250 Silver 1.0000 oz. ASW **Obv:** Denomination
above national arms **Rev:** Bust left

Date	Mintage	F	VF	XF	Unc	BU
1997. Proof	5,000	Value: 45.00				

KM# 71   200 KUNA
33.6300 g., 0.9250 Silver 1.0000 oz. ASW, 40 mm. **Obv:** Wild
flowers **Obv. Leg.:** REPUBLIKA HRVATSKA **Rev:** Three black
storks **Rev. Leg.:** CRNA RODA **Edge:** Plain

Date	Mintage	F	VF	XF	Unc	BU
1997. Proof	1,000	Value: 60.00				

KM# 76   200 KUNA
33.6300 g., 0.9250 Silver 1.0000 oz. ASW, 40 mm. **Obv:** National
arms above a page of illuminated text, denomination below
Rev: Juraj Julija Klovic, 1498-1578, looking right **Edge:** Plain

Date	Mintage	F	VF	XF	Unc	BU
1998. Proof	2,000	Value: 47.50				

KM# 77   200 KUNA
33.6300 g., 0.9250 Silver 1.0000 oz. ASW, 40 mm.
Obv: National arms and value above book, quill and oil lamp
Rev: Ivana Brlic Mazuranic, seated looking right **Edge:** Plain

Date	Mintage	F	VF	XF	Unc	BU
1998. Proof	2,000	Value: 47.50				

KM# 80   200 KUNA
33.6300 g., 0.9250 Silver 1.0000 oz. ASW **Obv:** Cakovec old
town view **Rev:** Katarina Zrinska **Edge:** Plain

Date	Mintage	F	VF	XF	Unc	BU
1999. Proof	2,000	Value: 47.50				

KM# 81   200 KUNA
33.6300 g., 0.9250 Silver 1.0000 oz. ASW **Obv:** Aquarelle
painting **Rev:** Zlava Raskaj

Date	Mintage	F	VF	XF	Unc	BU
2000. Proof	2,000	Value: 47.50				

KM# 31.1   500 KUNA
3.5000 g., 0.9860 Gold 0.1109 oz. AGW **Obv:** Izborna Cathedral,
denomination below **Rev:** Arms at top and bottom, cherubs flank

Date	Mintage	F	VF	XF	Unc	BU
1994. Proof	1,000	Value: 200				

KM# 31.2 500 KUNA
3.5000 g., 0.9860 Gold 0.1109 oz. AGW **Obv:** Izborna Cathedral, Series II added **Rev:** Arms at top and bottom, cherubs flank

Date	Mintage	F	VF	XF	Unc	BU
1994. Proof	1,000	Value: 185				

KM# 32 500 KUNA
3.5000 g., 0.9860 Gold 0.1109 oz. AGW **Subject:** 5th Anniversary of Independence

Date	Mintage	F	VF	XF	Unc	BU
1995. Proof	4,000	Value: 175				

KM# 52 500 KUNA
3.5000 g., 0.9860 Gold 0.1109 oz. AGW **Subject:** City of Split **Obv:** Towered building, denomination at left **Rev:** Ancient depiction of king on throne, dates at left

Date	Mintage	F	VF	XF	Unc	BU
ND(1995) Proof	3,950	Value: 150				

KM# 55 500 KUNA
3.5000 g., 0.9860 Gold 0.1109 oz. AGW **Subject:** University of Zadar **Obv:** Circle of arches, denomination at top, arms below **Rev:** Saint reading within circle, dates below

Date	Mintage	F	VF	XF	Unc	BU
ND(1996) Proof	1,000	Value: 185				

KM# 58 500 KUNA
3.5000 g., 0.9860 Gold 0.1109 oz. AGW **Subject:** 800th Anniversary - City of Osijek **Obv:** Crowned arms, denomination below **Rev:** City view

Date	Mintage	F	VF	XF	Unc	BU
ND(1996) Proof	1,000	Value: 185				

KM# 68 500 KUNA
3.5000 g., 0.9860 Gold 0.1109 oz. AGW, 18 mm. **Subject:** Vukovar **Obv:** Ceramic container, denomination at upper right **Rev:** Courtyard, date at right **Edge:** Plain

Date	Mintage	F	VF	XF	Unc	BU
1997. Proof	2,000	Value: 115				

KM# 70 500 KUNA
3.5000 g., 0.9860 Gold 0.1109 oz. AGW, 18 mm. **Obv:** Wild flowers, denomination at right, arms above **Rev:** Eagle on branch **Edge:** Plain

Date	Mintage	F	VF	XF	Unc	BU
1997. Proof	1,000	Value: 125				

KM# 74 500 KUNA
3.5000 g., 0.9860 Gold 0.1109 oz. AGW, 18 mm. **Obv:** Small national arms above religious arms and value, date divided **Rev:** Bust of Cardinal Stepinac (1898-1960) right **Edge:** Plain

Date	Mintage	F	VF	XF	Unc	BU
1998. Proof	2,000	Value: 115				

KM# 82 500 KUNA
3.5000 g., 0.9860 Gold 0.1109 oz. AGW **Subject:** 10th Anniversary of Parliament **Obv:** View of session **Rev:** Parliament building

Date	Mintage	F	VF	XF	Unc	BU
ND (2000) Proof	500	Value: 135				

KM# 33 1000 KUNA
7.0000 g., 0.9860 Gold 0.2219 oz. AGW **Obv:** Crowned arms divides date above denomination **Rev:** Half-length portrait of Pope John Paul II, looking left

Date	Mintage	F	VF	XF	Unc	BU
1994. Proof	4,000	Value: 285				

KM# 34 1000 KUNA
7.0000 g., 0.9860 Gold 0.2219 oz. AGW **Subject:** 5th Anniversary of Independence **Obv:** Arms divide sprays below denomination, dotted background **Rev:** Map, inscription, and dates, dotted background

Date	Mintage	F	VF	XF	Unc	BU
ND(1995) Proof	4,000	Value: 285				

KM# 53 1000 KUNA
7.0000 g., 0.9860 Gold 0.2219 oz. AGW **Subject:** Spalatum **Obv:** Diocletian's palace, denomination and arms above **Rev:** Sarcophagus, dates above

Date	Mintage	F	VF	XF	Unc	BU
ND(1995) Proof	1,950	Value: 285				

KM# 72 1000 KUNA
7.0000 g., 0.9860 Gold 0.2219 oz. AGW, 22 mm. **Obv:** Wild flowers, arms above, denomination at right **Obv. Leg.:** REPUBLIKA HRVATSKA **Rev:** Three Black Storks **Rev. Leg.:** CRNA RODA **Edge:** Plain

Date	Mintage	F	VF	XF	Unc	BU
1997. Proof	1,000	Value: 275				

KM# 61 1000 KUNA
7.0000 g., 0.9860 Gold 0.2219 oz. AGW, 22 mm. **Obv:** National arms **Rev:** Dr. Tudman **Edge:** Plain **Subject:** Death of Dr. Tudman

Date	Mintage	F	VF	XF	Unc	BU
1997. Proof	3,000	Value: 245				

TRADE COINAGE

KM# 35 DUCAT
3.5000 g., 0.9860 Gold 0.1109 oz. AGW, 20 mm. **Obv:** Crowned arms with supporters, denomination below **Rev:** Ruder Boskovic bust at left facing, dates at left

Date	Mintage	F	VF	XF	Unc	BU
1994. Proof	5,000	Value: 160				

KM# 62 DUCAT
3.5000 g., 0.9860 Gold 0.1109 oz. AGW **Subject:** Liberation of Knin **Obv:** Crowned arms, denomination below **Rev:** Regional view within circle

Date	Mintage	F	VF	XF	Unc	BU
ND(1995)	3,000	—	—	—	160	—

PATTERNS
Including off metal strikes

KM#	Date	Mintage	Identification	Mkt Val
Pn5	1934	—	5 Kuna. Bronze.	350
Pn6	1934	—	5 Kuna. Copper Nickel.	400
Pn7	1934	—	5 Kuna. 0.9000 Silver.	450
Pn8	1934	—	5 Kuna. Zinc.	—
Pn9	1941	—	25 Banica. Zinc. With initials. 16 or 17 mm.	—
Pn10	1941	—	25 Banica. Zinc. Without initials. 16 or 17 mm.	—
Pn11	1941	—	25 Banica. Nickel. 16 or 17 mm.	—
Pn12	1941	—	25 Banica. Gold. 16 or 17 mm.	3,500
Pn13	1941	—	50 Banica. Nickel.	—
Pn14	1941	—	50 Banica. Zinc.	—
Pn15	1941	—	50 Banica. Silver.	—
Pn16	1941	—	50 Banica. Gold.	4,500
Pn17	1941	—	Kuna. Zinc.	—
Pn18	1941	—	Kuna. Copper.	—
Pn19	1941	—	Kuna. Aluminum.	175
Pn20	1941	—	Kuna. Nickel.	—
Pn21	1941	—	Kuna. Silver.	450
Pn22	1941	—	Kuna. Gold.	3,500
Pn23	1941	—	Kuna. Silver. 4.3800 g. 20 mm. Without undulating background.	—
Pn24	1941	—	2 Kune. Aluminum.	—
Pn25	1941	—	2 Kune. Nickel.	—
Pn26	1941	—	2 Kune. Silver. 4.8900 g. 22 mm.	—
Pn27	1941	—	2 Kune. Gold.	4,500
Pn28	1941	—	10 Kuna. Similar to Pn 19. 10 Kuna above shield within wheat border. Reported, not confirmed.	—
Pn29	1941	—	500 Kuna. Aluminum. Pn 26. Similar to B3.	—
Pn30	1941	—	500 Kuna. Copper Nickel. Pn 26. Similar to B3.	—
Pn31	1941	—	500 Kuna. Aluminum. Chain.	—
Pn32	1941	—	500 Kuna. Aluminum-Bronze.	—
Pn33	1941	—	500 Kuna. Copper.	—
Pn34	1941	—	500 Kuna. Copper Nickel.	—
Pn35	1941	—	500 Kuna. Silver.	—
Pn36	1941	—	500 Kuna. Aluminum. 1.6700 g. 22 mm. Head left, date below. Denomination above arms, wheat chain surrounds.	600
Pn37	1941	—	500 Kuna. Gold. 27 mm. Chain. KMA3.	—
Pn38	1941	—	500 Kuna. Nickel. 22 mm. KMA3.	—
Pn39	1941	—	500 Kuna. Aluminum. KMA3.	—
Pn40	1941	—	500 Kuna. Brass. 7.1100 g. 23 mm. KMA3.	400
Pn41	1943	—	5 Kuna.	—
Pn42	1943	—	10 Kuna.	—

MINT SETS

KM#	Date	Mintage	Identification	Issue Price	Mkt Val
MS1	1993 (9)	50,000	KM3-11	8.00	14.00

PROOF SETS

KM#	Date	Mintage	Identification	Issue Price	Mkt Val
PS1	1993 (9)	17,000	KM3-11	15.20	28.50
PS2	1993 (9)	10	KM3a-11a, rare		
PS3		5	KM3b-11b, rare		
PS4	1994 (9)	4,000	KM12, 14-17, 19-21, 23	15.20	32.50
PS5	1994 (3)	500	KM21, 23, 24a	—	280
PS6	1994 (3)	250	KM21, 23, 24b	—	475
PS7	1994 (2)	1,000	KM26, 33	240	360
PS8	ND (1994) (3)	250	KM25.1, 29.1, 31.1	154	325
PS9	ND (1994) (3)	500	KM25.2, 29.2, 31.2	154	350
PS10	1994-95 (2)	1,000	KM22, 25.2	—	85.00
PS11	1994-95 (4)	—	KM13, 18, 22, 24	—	40.00
PS12	1994-96 (9)	5,000	KM13, 18, 22, 24, 36-40	8.00	33.50
PS13	1995 (9)	4,000	KM3-11	15.20	34.50
PS14	1995 (5)	—	KM27, 28, 30, 32, 34	—	625
PS15	ND (1995) (2)	1,000	KM50-53	375	525
PS16	ND (1995) (2)	1,000	KM50, 51	62.50	75.00
PS17	ND (1995) (2)	1,000	KM50, 52	125	190
PS18	ND (1995) (2)	1,000	KM51, 53	250	345
PS19	ND (1995) (2)	1,000	KM52, 53	312	445
PS20	ND (1995) (5)	1,000	KM 27, 28, 30, 32, 34	406	620
PS21	ND (1995) (3)	2,000	KM 27, 30, 34	270	400
PS22	1995 (2)	2,000	KM28, 32	135	225
PS23	1996 (6)	1,000	KM41-46	-187	265
PS24	1996 (9)	5,000	KM12, 14-17, 19-21, 23	8.00	32.00
PS25	ND (1996) (2)	500	KM54-55	146	250
PS26	ND (1996) (3)	300	KM56-58	177	285
PS27	1997 (3)	300	KM59-61	281	370
PS28	1997 (2)	300	KM#69, 70	141	170

KM#	Date	Mintage	Identification	Issue Price	Mkt Val
PS29	1997 (2)	300	KM#71, 72	260	325
PS30	1997 (4)	300	KM#69, 70, 71, 72	401	500
PS31	1998 (2)	500	KM#73, 74	141	150
PS39	1997 (9)	—	KM#3-8, 9.1, 10-11	—	—
PS40	1998 (9)	—	KM#12, 14-17, 19, 20.2, 21, 23	—	—
PS41	1999 (9)	—	KM#3-8, 9.2, 10-11	—	—
PS42	2000 (9)	—	KM#12, 14-17, 19, 20.2, 21, 23	—	—

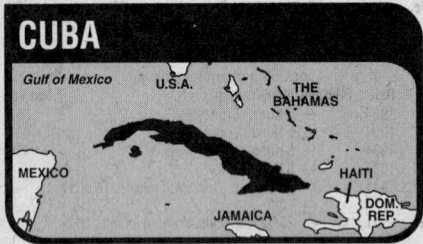

CUBA

The Republic of Cuba, situated at the northern edge of the Caribbean Sea about 90 miles (145 km.) south of Florida, has an area of 42,804 sq. mi. (110,860 sq. km.) and a population of *11.2 million. Capital: Havana. The Cuban economy is based on the cultivation and refining of sugar, which provides 80 percent of export earnings.

Discovered by Columbus in 1492 and settled by Diego Velasquez in the early 1500s, Cuba remained a Spanish possession until 1898, except for a brief British occupancy of Havana in 1762-63. Cuban attempts to gain freedom were crushed, even while Spain was granting independence to its other American possessions. Ten years of warfare, 1868-78, between Spanish troops and Cuban rebels exacted guarantees of rights which were never implemented. The final revolt, begun in 1895, evoked American sympathy, and with the aid of U.S. troops independence was proclaimed on May 20, 1902. Fulgencio Batista seized the government in 1952 and established a dictatorship. Opposition to Batista, led by Fidel Castro, drove him into exile on Jan. 1, 1959. A communist-type, 25-member collective leadership headed by Castro was inaugurated in March, 1962.

RULER
Spanish, until 1898

MINT MARK
Key - Havana, 1977-

MONETARY SYSTEM
100 Centavos = 1 Peso

FIRST REPUBLIC
1902 - 1962
DECIMAL COINAGE

KM# 9.1   CENTAVO
2.5200 g., Copper-Nickel   **Obv:** National arms within wreath, denomination below **Rev:** Roman denomination within circle of star, date below, 2.5 G. 250M

Date	Mintage	F	VF	XF	Unc	BU
1915	9,396,000	—	1.00	2.00	30.00	100
1915 Proof	200	Value: 1,000				
1916	9,318,000	—	1.00	2.00	30.00	100
1916 Proof	104	Value: 1,000				
1920	19,378,000	—	1.50	3.00	30.00	100
1938	2,000,000	—	2.50	6.00	45.00	125

KM# 9.2a   CENTAVO
Brass   **Obv:** National arms within wreath, denomination below **Rev:** Roman denomination within circle of star, 2.3 GR. 300M

Date	Mintage	F	VF	XF	Unc	BU
1943	20,000,000	—	0.40	1.25	7.00	50.00

KM# 9.2   CENTAVO
2.5500 g., Copper-Nickel   **Obv:** National arms within wreath, denomination below **Rev:** Roman denomination within circle of star, 2.5 GR. 250M

Date	Mintage	F	VF	XF	Unc	BU
1946	50,000,000	—	0.20	1.00	4.00	50.00
1961	100,000,000	—	0.25	0.60	1.50	10.00

KM# 26   CENTAVO
Brass, 17 mm.   **Subject:** Birth of Jose Marti Centennial **Obv:** Star on triangular shield divides denomination **Rev:** Bust, left

Date	Mintage	F	VF	XF	Unc	BU
1953	50,000,000	—	0.15	0.75	5.00	40.00
1953 Proof; Rare	100	—	—	—	—	—

KM# 30   CENTAVO
Copper-Nickel, 17 mm.   **Obv:** Star on triangular shield divides denomination **Rev:** Bust of Jose Marti left, date at left

Date	Mintage	F	VF	XF	Unc	BU
1958	50,000,000	—	0.15	0.75	30.00	120

KM# A10   2 CENTAVOS
Copper-Nickel   **Obv:** National arms within wreath, denomination below **Rev:** Roman denomination within circle of star, date below

Date	Mintage	F	VF	XF	Unc	BU
1915	6,090,000	—	1.25	3.00	40.00	175
1915 Proof	150	Value: 1,000				
1916	5,322,000	—	1.25	3.50	45.00	180
1916 Proof	100	Value: 1,000				

KM# 11.1   5 CENTAVOS
4.9000 g., Copper-Nickel, 21 mm.   **Obv:** National arms within wreath above denomination **Rev:** Roman denomination within circle of star, date below, 5.0 G. 250M

Date	Mintage	F	VF	XF	Unc	BU
1915	5,096,000	—	1.50	4.00	40.00	150
1915 Proof	150	Value: 1,000				
1916	1,714,000	—	1.50	5.00	50.00	210
1916 Proof	100	Value: 1,000				
1920	10,000,000	—	1.50	4.50	40.00	150

KM# 11.2   5 CENTAVOS
Copper-Nickel, 21 mm.   **Obv:** National arms within wreath, denomination below **Rev:** Roman denomination within circle of star, 5.0 G 250M **Note:** No period after G

Date	Mintage	F	VF	XF	Unc	BU
1920	—	—	1.75	5.00	100	400

KM# 11.3a   5 CENTAVOS
5.0000 g., Brass   **Rev:** 4.6 GR. 300M **Note:** Prev. KM#11.2a.

Date	Mintage	F	VF	XF	Unc	BU
1943	6,000,000	—	1.00	3.50	20.00	60.00

KM# 11.3   5 CENTAVOS
5.0000 g., Copper-Nickel, 21 mm.   **Obv:** National arms within wreath, denomination below **Rev:** Roman denomination within circle of star, date below, 5 GR. 250M **Note:** Prev. KM#11.2.

Date	Mintage	F	VF	XF	Unc	BU
1946	40,000,000	—	0.50	0.75	5.00	45.00
1960	20,000,000	—	0.75	1.25	15.00	70.00
1961	70,000,000	—	0.15	0.40	1.00	2.00

KM# A12   10 CENTAVOS
2.5000 g., 0.9000 Silver 0.0723 oz. ASW, 17.8 mm. **Obv:** National arms within wreath, denomination below **Rev:** Star

Date	Mintage	F	VF	XF	Unc	BU
1915	5,690,000	1.50	4.00	8.00	70.00	350
1915 Proof	125	Value: 1,500				
1916	560,000	7.00	20.00	50.00	350	1,200
1916 Proof	50	Value: 2,000				
1920	3,090,000	2.50	6.00	20.00	125	450
1948	5,120,000	—	1.25	2.00	9.00	25.00
1949	9,880,000	—	1.25	1.75	9.00	20.00

KM# 23   10 CENTAVOS
2.5000 g., 0.9000 Silver 0.0723 oz. ASW, 18 mm. **Subject:** 50th Year of Republic **Obv:** Two dates left of flag, tower at right, denomination below **Rev:** Star above tree, spoked wheel below

Date	Mintage	F	VF	XF	Unc	BU
1952	10,000,000	—	1.25	2.50	4.50	20.00

KM# 13.2   20 CENTAVOS
5.0000 g., 0.9000 Silver 0.1447 oz. ASW, 23 mm.   **Obv:** National arms within wreath, denomination below **Rev:** Low relief star, date below **Note:** Coins with high relief stars normally exhibit a weak key and palm tree on the reverse. Coins with low relief stars tend to exhibit much more distinct lines in the valleys running towards the center of the star.

Date	Mintage	F	VF	XF	Unc	BU
1915 Coarse reeding	7,915,150	3.25	5.00	15.00	50.00	250
Note: Mintage included in KM#13.1						
1915 Fine reeding	—	15.00	50.00	175	1,400	4,000
Note: Mintage included in KM#13.1						
1916	2,535,000	3.50	6.50	18.00	250	700
1916 Proof	50	Value: 3,200				
1920	6,130,000	—	4.00	8.00	50.00	250
1932	184,000	22.00	75.00	300	1,000	1,750
1948	6,830,000	—	3.00	5.00	10.00	20.00
1949	13,170,000	—	3.00	5.00	8.00	20.00

KM# 13.1   20 CENTAVOS
5.0000 g., 0.9000 Silver 0.1447 oz. ASW, 23 mm. **Obv:** National arms within wreath **Rev:** High relief star

Date	Mintage	F	VF	XF	Unc	BU
1915 Fine reeding	7,915,000	4.00	8.00	35.00	175	600
1915 Coarse reeding	Inc. above	75.00	225	450	1,000	2,000
1915 Proof	125	Value: 2,200				

KM# 24   20 CENTAVOS
5.0000 g., 0.9000 Silver 0.1447 oz. ASW, 23 mm. **Subject:** 50th Year of Republic **Obv:** Two dates left of flag, tower at right, denomination below **Rev:** Star above tree, spoked wheel below

Date	Mintage	F	VF	XF	Unc	BU
1952	8,700,000	—	2.00	4.00	6.00	25.00

KM# 27   25 CENTAVOS
6.2500 g., 0.9000 Silver 0.1808 oz. ASW, 24 mm.   **Subject:** Centennial - Birth of Jose Marti **Obv:** Liberty cap on post, denomination at right **Rev:** Bust, left

Date	Mintage	F	VF	XF	Unc	BU
1953	19,000,000	—	2.00	4.00	6.00	16.00
1953 Proof; Rare	—	—	—	—	—	—

KM# 14   40 CENTAVOS
10.0000 g., 0.9000 Silver 0.2893 oz. ASW   **Obv:** National arms within wreath, denomination below **Rev:** High relief star, date below

Date	Mintage	F	VF	XF	Unc	BU
1915	2,633,000	6.00	12.00	25.00	300	800
1915 Proof	100	Value: 1,300				
1920	540,000	15.00	50.00	120	400	1,000
1920 Proof; Rare	—	—	—	—	—	—

KM# 14.2   40 CENTAVOS
10.0000 g., 0.9000 Silver 0.2893 oz. ASW   **Obv:** National arms within wreath, denomination below **Rev:** Medium relief star, date below

Date	Mintage	F	VF	XF	Unc	BU
1915	Inc. above	30.00	100	275	1,250	1,750

KM# 14.3   40 CENTAVOS
10.0000 g., 0.9000 Silver 0.2893 oz. ASW   **Obv:** National arms within wreath, denomination below **Rev:** Low relief star, date

below **Note:** Coins with high relief stars normally exhibit a weak key and palm tree on the reverse. Coins with low relief stars tend to exhibit much more distinct lines in the valleys running towards the center of the star.

Date	Mintage	F	VF	XF	Unc	BU
1915	Inc. above	6.50	15.00	35.00	200	800
1916	188,000	18.00	75.00	300	1,000	2,500
1916 Proof	50	Value: 2,500				
1920	Inc. above	20.00	75.00	175	500	1,700

KM# 25 40 CENTAVOS
10.0000 g., 0.9000 Silver 0.2893 oz. ASW, 28 mm. **Subject:** 50th Year of Republic **Obv:** Two dates left of flag, tower at right, denomination below **Rev:** Star abovetree, spoked wheel below

Date	Mintage	F	VF	XF	Unc	BU
1952	1,250,000	—	4.00	6.00	20.00	50.00

KM# 28 50 CENTAVOS
12.5000 g., 0.9000 Silver 0.3617 oz. ASW, 31 mm. **Subject:** Centennial - Birth of Jose Marti **Obv:** Inscription on scroll, denomination at right **Rev:** Bust, left

Date	Mintage	F	VF	XF	Unc	BU
ND(1953)	2,000,000	—	4.00	6.00	15.00	35.00
ND(1953) Proof; Rare	—	—	—	—	—	—

KM# 15.1 PESO
26.7295 g., 0.9000 Silver 0.7734 oz. ASW **Obv:** National arms within wreath, denomination below **Rev:** High relief star, date below

Date	Mintage	F	VF	XF	Unc	BU
1915	1,976,000	15.00	20.00	85.00	300	1,500
1915 Proof	100	Value: 2,000				

KM# 15.2 PESO
26.7295 g., 0.9000 Silver 0.7734 oz. ASW **Obv:** National arms within wreath, denomination below **Rev:** Low relief star, date below **Note:** Coins with high relief stars normally exhibit a weak key and palm tree on the obverse. Coins with low relief stars tend to exhibit much more distinct lines in the valleys running towards the center of the star.

Date	Mintage	F	VF	XF	Unc	BU
1915	Inc. above	40.00	80.00	500	2,500	8,500
1916	843,000	15.00	20.00	70.00	700	2,500
1916 Proof	50	Value: 3,500				
1932	3,550,000	—	16.50	28.00	125	550
1933	6,000,000	—	15.00	20.00	90.00	175
1934	3,000,000	—	15.00	20.00	90.00	175

KM# 16 PESO
1.6718 g., 0.9000 Gold 0.0484 oz. AGW **Obv:** National arms within wreath, denomination below **Rev:** Head of Jose Marti right, date below

Date	Mintage	F	VF	XF	Unc	BU
1915	6,850	50.00	100	150	225	500
1915 Proof	140	Value: 2,500				
1916	11,000	50.00	100	150	300	900
1916 Proof	100	Value: 2,500				

KM# 22 PESO
26.7295 g., 0.9000 Silver 0.7734 oz. ASW **Obv:** National arms within wreath at right, denomination at left **Rev:** Laureate bust right, date lower right **Note:** Known as the "ABC" Peso.

Date	Mintage	F	VF	XF	Unc	BU
1934	7,000,000	16.50	25.00	50.00	175	450
1934 Matte proof	—	Value: 5,250				
1935	12,500,000	16.50	25.00	50.00	150	450
1936	16,000,000	16.50	25.00	50.00	150	500
1937	11,500,000	85.00	250	400	1,100	3,500
1938	10,800,000	15.00	22.50	45.00	125	450
1939	9,200,000	15.00	22.50	45.00	125	400

KM# 29 PESO
26.7295 g., 0.9000 Silver 0.7734 oz. ASW, 38 mm. **Subject:** Centennial of Jose Marti **Obv:** Radiant sun rising above water, denomination below **Rev:** Bust left, two dates

Date	Mintage	F	VF	XF	Unc	BU
ND(1953)	1,000,000	—	BV	15.00	30.00	150
ND(1953) Proof; Rare	—	—	—	—	—	—

KM# 17 2 PESOS
3.3436 g., 0.9000 Gold 0.0967 oz. AGW **Obv:** National arms within wreath, denomination below **Rev:** Head right, date below

Date	Mintage	F	VF	XF	Unc	BU
1915	10,000	85.00	95.00	175	500	1,000
1915 Proof	100	Value: 4,200				
1916	150,000	BV	85.00	95.00	175	350
1916 Proof; Rare	8	—	—	—	—	—

KM# 18 4 PESOS
6.6872 g., 0.9000 Gold 0.1935 oz. AGW **Obv:** National arms within wreath, denomination below **Rev:** Head right, date below

Date	Mintage	F	VF	XF	Unc	BU
1915	6,300	165	185	375	1,200	2,000
1915 Proof	100	Value: 3,000				
1916	129,000	BV	165	185	350	800
1916 Proof	90	Value: 4,500				

KM# 19 5 PESOS
8.3592 g., 0.9000 Gold 0.2419 oz. AGW **Obv:** National arms within wreath, denomination below **Rev:** Head right, date below

Date	Mintage	F	VF	XF	Unc	BU
1915	696,000	—	BV	225	250	475
1915 Proof	—	Value: 3,200				
1916	1,132,000	—	—	BV	225	450
1916 Proof	—	Value: 6,500				

Note: American Numismatic Rarities Eliasberg sale 4-05, Proof 65 realized $13,800.

KM# 20 10 PESOS
16.7185 g., 0.9000 Gold 0.4837 oz. AGW **Obv:** National arms within wreath, denomination below **Rev:** Head right, date below

Date	Mintage	F	VF	XF	Unc	BU
1915	95,000	—	BV	475	575	850
1915 Proof	—	Value: 7,500				
Proof	—	—	—	—	—	—
1916	1,169,000	—	—	BV	475	800
1916 Proof, Rare	—	—	—	—	—	—

Note: David Akers John Jay Pittman sale 8-99 very choice Proof realized $19,550, choice Proof realized $14,950. American Numismatic Rarities Eliasberg sale 4-05, Proof 62 realized $29,900.

KM# 21 20 PESOS
33.4370 g., 0.9000 Gold 0.9675 oz. AGW **Subject:** Jose Marti **Obv:** National arms within wreath, denomination below **Rev:** Head right, date below

Date	Mintage	F	VF	XF	Unc	BU
1915	57,000	—	BV	950	1,500	4,500
1915 Proof; Rare	—	—	—	—	—	—

Note: David Akers John Jay Pittman sale 8-99 very choice proof 1915 realized $11,500.

1916 Proof; Rare	10	—	—	—	—	—

Note: David Akers John Jay Pittman sale 8-99 nearly choice Proof 1916 realized $43,125.

SECOND REPUBLIC
1962 - Present
DECIMAL COINAGE

KM# 33.1 CENTAVO
0.7300 g., Aluminum **Obv:** National arms within wreath,

denomination below **Rev:** Roman denomination within circle of star, date below **Rev. Leg.:** PATRIA Y LIBERTAD **Note:** Shield varieties exist.

Date	Mintage	F	VF	XF	Unc	BU
1963	200,020,000	—	0.10	0.30	0.60	1.25
1966	50,000,000	—	0.10	0.40	0.80	1.75
1969	50,000,000	—	0.10	0.40	0.80	1.75
1970	50,000,000	—	0.10	0.40	0.80	1.75
1971	49,960,000	—	0.40	0.80	1.50	3.00
1972	100,000,000	—	0.10	0.40	0.80	1.75
1978	50,000,000	—	0.10	0.40	0.80	1.75
1979	100,000,000	—	0.10	0.40	0.80	1.75
1981	100,000,000	—	0.10	0.40	0.80	1.75
1982	50,000,000	—	0.10	0.40	0.80	1.75

KM# 33.2   CENTAVO
Aluminum   **Obv:** National arms within wreath, denomination below **Rev:** Roman denomination within circle of star, date below **Rev. Leg.:** PATRIA O MUERTE **Note:** Shield varieties exist.

Date	Mintage	F	VF	XF	Unc	BU
1983	—	—	0.10	0.40	0.80	1.75
1984	—	—	0.10	0.40	0.80	1.75
1985	—	—	0.10	0.40	0.80	1.75
1986	—	—	0.10	0.40	0.80	1.75
1987	—	—	0.10	0.40	0.80	1.75
1988	—	—	0.10	0.40	0.80	1.75

KM# 33.3   CENTAVO
0.7500 g., Aluminum, 16.76 mm.   **Obv:** Cuban arms within wreath, denomination below **Rev:** Roman denomination within circle of star, date below **Edge:** Plain **Note:** Shield varieties exist.

Date	Mintage	F	VF	XF	Unc	BU
1998	—	—	0.10	0.40	0.80	1.75

KM# 104.2   2 CENTAVOS
1.0000 g., Aluminum   **Obv:** National arms within wreath, denomination below **Rev:** Roman denomination within circle of star, date below **Note:** Large lettered legends, short edge denticles on both sides of coin

Date	Mintage	F	VF	XF	Unc	BU
1983	50,010,000	—	0.10	0.20	0.50	1.00
1984	62,500,000	—	0.10	0.25	1.00	2.00
1985	70,000,000	—	0.10	0.20	0.50	1.00
1986	15,000,000	—	0.10	0.20	0.50	1.00

KM# 104.1   2 CENTAVOS
Aluminum   **Obv:** National arms within wreath, denomination below **Rev:** Roman denomination within circle of star, date below **Note:** Small lettered legends, long edge denticles on both sides of coin

Date	Mintage	F	VF	XF	Unc	BU
1983	3,996,000	—	0.10	0.25	1.00	2.00

KM# 34   5 CENTAVOS
Aluminum, 21 mm.   **Obv:** National arms within wreath, denomination below **Rev:** Roman denomination within circle of star, date below **Note:** Shield varieties exist.

Date	Mintage	F	VF	XF	Unc	BU
1963	80,000,000	—	0.10	0.25	0.75	1.50
1966	50,000,000	—	0.15	0.35	1.50	3.00
1968 Kremnica	100,000,000	—	0.15	0.35	1.50	3.00
1968 Leningrad	103,000,000	—	0.25	0.50	2.50	5.00
1971	100,020,000	—	0.10	0.25	0.75	1.50
1972	100,000,000	—	0.10	0.25	0.75	1.50

KM# 31   20 CENTAVOS
Copper-Nickel, 24 mm.   **Subject:** Jose Marti **Obv:** National arms within wreath, denomination below **Rev:** Bust left, date lower left

Date	Mintage	F	VF	XF	Unc	BU
1962	83,860,000	—	1.00	1.50	3.00	6.00
1968	25,750,000	—	1.25	2.00	4.00	8.00

KM# 35.1   20 CENTAVOS
2.0000 g., Aluminum, 24 mm.   **Obv:** Cuban arms within wreath, denomination below **Rev:** Roman denomination within circle of star, date below **Note:** Shield varieties exist.

Date	Mintage	F	VF	XF	Unc	BU
1969	25,000,000	—	1.00	1.50	2.50	5.00
1971	29,560,000	—	1.00	1.50	2.50	5.00
1972	25,000,000	—	1.00	1.50	2.50	5.00

KM# 35.2   20 CENTAVOS
Aluminum, 24 mm.   **Obv:** National arms, revised shield **Rev:** Roman denomination within circle of star

Date	Mintage	F	VF	XF	Unc	BU
ND	—	4.00	7.00	10.00	15.00	—

KM# 360   25 CENTAVOS
Copper-Nickel   **Subject:** Carlos J. Finlay **Obv:** National arms within wreath, denomination below **Rev:** Bust at right looking left, dates below

Date	Mintage	F	VF	XF	Unc	BU
ND	—	—	5.00	10.00	15.00	

KM# 361   25 CENTAVOS
Copper-Nickel   **Subject:** Alexander von Humboldt **Obv:** National arms within wreath, denomination below **Rev:** Bust in cameo at left and bird at right divide dates

Date	Mintage	F	VF	XF	Unc	BU
1989	—	—	5.00	10.00	15.00	

KM# 32   40 CENTAVOS
9.6000 g., Copper-Nickel   **Subject:** Camilo Cienfuegos Gornaran **Obv:** National arms within wreath, denomination below **Rev:** Uniformed bust right, date at left

Date	Mintage	F	VF	XF	Unc	BU
1962	15,250,000	—	3.00	5.00	7.00	12.00

KM# 186   PESO
11.4000 g., Copper-Nickel, 29.98 mm.   **Subject:** Carlos Manuel de Cespedes **Obv:** National arms **Rev:** Bust facing **Edge:** Plain

Date	Mintage	F	VF	XF	Unc	BU
ND(1977)	3,000	—	—	—	10.00	15.00

KM# 187   PESO
Copper-Nickel, 30 mm.   **Subject:** Ignacio Agramonte **Obv:** National arms within wreath, denomination below **Rev:** Bust facing, date at left

Date	Mintage	F	VF	XF	Unc	BU
1977	3,000	—	—	—	10.00	15.00

KM# 188   PESO
Copper-Nickel, 30 mm.   **Subject:** Maximo Gomez

Date	Mintage	F	VF	XF	Unc	BU
1977	3,000	—	—	—	10.00	15.00

KM# 189   PESO
Copper-Nickel, 30 mm.   **Subject:** Antonio Maceo

Date	Mintage	F	VF	XF	Unc	BU
1977	3,000	—	—	—	10.00	15.00

KM# 190   PESO
Copper-Nickel, 30 mm.   **Subject:** 60th Anniversary of Socialist Revolution - Lenin **Obv:** National arms within wreath, denomination below **Rev:** Bust left divides dates

Date	Mintage	F	VF	XF	Unc	BU
ND(1977)	6,000	—	—	—	25.00	—

KM# 191   PESO

Copper-Nickel, 30 mm.   **Subject:** Nonaligned Nations Conference **Obv:** National arms within wreath, denomination below **Rev:** Design left of date

Date	Mintage	F	VF	XF	Unc	BU
1979	3,000	—	—	—	7.00	—

KM# 46   PESO

Copper-Nickel, 30 mm.   **Subject:** Cuban Flower - Mariposa

Date	Mintage	F	VF	XF	Unc	BU
1980	3,000	—	—	—	8.00	—

KM# 192   PESO

Copper-Nickel, 30 mm.   **Series:** Olympics **Obv:** National arms within wreath, denomination below **Rev:** Athletes in frames

Date	Mintage	F	VF	XF	Unc	BU
1980	3,000	—	—	—	6.50	—

KM# 193   PESO

Copper-Nickel, 30 mm.   **Series:** Olympics **Rev:** Three athletic figures

Date	Mintage	F	VF	XF	Unc	BU
1980	3,000	—	—	—	6.50	—

KM# 194   PESO

Copper-Nickel, 30 mm.   **Subject:** Soviet - Cuban Space Flight **Obv:** National arms within wreath, denomination below **Rev:** Shuttle orbiting planet, date below

Date	Mintage	F	VF	XF	Unc	BU
1980	3,000	—	—	—	7.50	—

KM# 53   PESO

Copper-Nickel, 30 mm.   **Subject:** Cuban Flowers **Rev:** Azahar flower

Date	Mintage	F	VF	XF	Unc	BU
1981	3,000	—	—	—	8.00	—

KM# 54   PESO

Copper-Nickel, 30 mm.   **Subject:** Cuban Flowers **Rev:** Orquidea flower

Date	Mintage	F	VF	XF	Unc	BU
1981	3,000	—	—	—	9.00	—

KM# 55   PESO

Copper-Nickel, 30 mm.   **Subject:** Cuban Fauna **Obv:** National arms within wreath, denomination below **Rev:** Cuban Crocodiles, date above

Date	Mintage	F	VF	XF	Unc	BU
1981	5,000	—	—	—	10.00	—

KM# 56   PESO

Copper-Nickel, 30 mm.   **Subject:** Cuban Fauna **Rev:** Emerald Hummingbird

Date	Mintage	F	VF	XF	Unc	BU
1981	5,000	—	—	—	10.00	—

KM# 57   PESO

Copper-Nickel, 30 mm.   **Subject:** Cuban Fauna **Rev:** Bee Hummingbird

Date	Mintage	F	VF	XF	Unc	BU
1981	5,000	—	—	—	10.00	—

KM# 58   PESO

Copper-Nickel, 30 mm.   **Subject:** Soccer World Championship - Spain 1982 **Obv:** National arms within wreath, denomination below **Rev:** Soccer player kicking ball, soccer ball background, date at right

Date	Mintage	F	VF	XF	Unc	BU
1981	10,000	—	—	—	8.00	—

KM# 59   PESO

Copper-Nickel, 30 mm.   **Subject:** World Food Day - Sugar Production **Obv:** National arms within wreath, denomination below **Rev:** Sugarcane plants, date lower right

Date	Mintage	F	VF	XF	Unc	BU
1981	10,000	—	—	—	8.00	—

KM# 60   PESO

Copper-Nickel, 30 mm.   **Subject:** XIV Central American and Caribbean Games **Obv:** National arms within wreath, denomination below **Rev:** Cartoon crocodile, date at left

Date	Mintage	F	VF	XF	Unc	BU
1981	5,000	—	—	—	10.00	—

KM# 61   PESO

Copper-Nickel, 30 mm.   **Subject:** XIV Central American and Caribbean Games **Obv:** National arms within wreath, denomination below **Rev:** Three athletes

Date	Mintage	F	VF	XF	Unc	BU
1981	5,000	—	—	—	8.00	—

KM# 62   PESO

Copper-Nickel, 30 mm.   **Subject:** XIV Central American and Caribbean Games **Obv:** National arms within wreath, denomination below **Rev:** Boxers

Date	Mintage	F	VF	XF	Unc	BU
1981	5,000	—	—	—	8.00	—

KM# 63 PESO
Copper-Nickel, 30 mm. **Subject:** Cuban Fauna **Obv:** National arms within wreath, denomination below **Rev:** Cuban Trogon

Date	Mintage	F	VF	XF	Unc	BU
1981	5,000	—	—	—	10.00	—

KM# 64 PESO
Copper-Nickel, 30 mm. **Subject:** Cuban Fauna **Obv:** National arms within wreath, denomination below **Rev:** Cuban Solendodon

Date	Mintage	F	VF	XF	Unc	BU
1981	5,000	—	—	—	10.00	—

KM# 65 PESO
Copper-Nickel, 30 mm. **Subject:** Cuban Fauna **Obv:** National arms within wreath, denomination below **Rev:** Giant Gar Fish

Date	Mintage	F	VF	XF	Unc	BU
1981	5,000	—	—	—	10.00	—

KM# 66 PESO
Copper-Nickel, 30 mm. **Obv:** National arms within wreath, denomination below **Rev:** Columbus' ship - Nina, date at right

Date	Mintage	F	VF	XF	Unc	BU
1981	10,000	—	—	—	12.00	—

KM# 67 PESO
Copper-Nickel, 30 mm. **Obv:** National arms within wreath, denomination below **Rev:** Columbus' ship - Pinta

Date	Mintage	F	VF	XF	Unc	BU
1981	10,000	—	—	—	12.00	—

KM# 68 PESO
Copper-Nickel, 30 mm. **Obv:** National arms within wreath, denomination below **Rev:** Columbus' ship - Santa Maria

Date	Mintage	F	VF	XF	Unc	BU
1981	10,000	—	—	—	12.00	—

KM# 88 PESO
Copper-Nickel, 30 mm. **Subject:** Ernest Hemingway **Obv:** National arms within wreath, denomination below **Rev:** Bust facing, three dates

Date	Mintage	F	VF	XF	Unc	BU
1982	7,000	—	—	—	15.00	—

KM# 89 PESO
Copper-Nickel, 30 mm. **Subject:** Ernest Hemingway **Obv:** National arms within wreath, denomination below **Rev:** Fishing yacht

Date	Mintage	F	VF	XF	Unc	BU
1982	7,000	—	—	—	15.00	—

KM# 90 PESO
Copper-Nickel, 30 mm. **Subject:** Ernest Hemingway **Obv:** National arms within wreath, denomination below **Rev:** Small boat

Date	Mintage	F	VF	XF	Unc	BU
ND(1982)	7,000	—	—	—	15.00	—

KM# 91 PESO
Copper-Nickel, 30 mm. **Subject:** Miquel De Cervantes **Obv:** National arms within wreath, denomination below **Rev:** Bust with ruffled collar 3/4 right, three dates

Date	Mintage	F	VF	XF	Unc	BU
1982	7,000	—	—	—	9.00	—

KM# 92 PESO
Copper-Nickel, 30 mm. **Subject:** Hidalgo Don Quijote **Obv:** National arms within wreath, denomination below **Rev:** Figure on horseback with lance divides dates

Date	Mintage	F	VF	XF	Unc	BU
1982	7,000	—	—	—	9.00	—

KM# 93 PESO
Copper-Nickel, 30 mm. **Subject:** Hidalgo Don Quijote and Sancho Panza **Obv:** National arms within wreath **Rev:** Small figure on mule, larger figure with lance on horse

Date	Mintage	F	VF	XF	Unc	BU
1982	7,000	—	—	—	9.00	—

KM# 94 PESO
Copper-Nickel, 30 mm. **Series:** F.A.O. **Rev:** Citrus fruit

Date	Mintage	F	VF	XF	Unc	BU
1982	6,609	—	—	—	8.00	—

KM# 95 PESO
Copper-Nickel, 30 mm. **Series:** F.A.O. **Obv:** National arms within wreath **Rev:** Cow on grass left

Date	Mintage	F	VF	XF	Unc	BU
1982	5,684	—	—	—	9.00	—

KM# 105 PESO
6.0000 g., Brass, 24.5 mm. **Obv:** National arms within wreath, denomination below **Rev:** Star, date below

Date	Mintage	F	VF	XF	Unc	BU
1983	10,000,000	0.25	0.50	1.00	2.50	—
1984	10,000,000	0.25	0.50	1.00	2.50	—
1985	10,300,000	0.25	0.50	1.00	2.50	—
1986	20,000,000	0.25	0.50	1.00	2.50	—
1987	10,000,000	0.25	0.50	1.00	2.50	—
1988	15,000,000	0.25	0.50	1.00	2.50	—
1989	15,000,000	0.25	0.50	1.00	2.50	—

KM# 106 PESO
Copper-Nickel, 30 mm. **Subject:** Railroad **Obv:** National arms within wreath, denomination below **Rev:** Train engine, date below

Date	Mintage	F	VF	XF	Unc	BU
1983	7,000	—	—	—	9.00	—

KM# 195 PESO
Copper-Nickel, 30 mm. **Series:** Olympics **Obv:** National arms within wreath, denomination **Rev:** Woman holding torch

Date	Mintage	F	VF	XF	Unc	BU
1983	3,000	—	—	—	8.00	—

KM# 130 PESO
Copper-Nickel, 30 mm. **Subject:** Transportation **Obv:** National arms within wreath, denomination **Rev:** Volanta coach

Date	Mintage	F	VF	XF	Unc	BU
1984	5,000	—	—	—	8.00	—

KM# 107 PESO
Copper-Nickel, 30 mm. **Subject:** World Fisheries Conference **Obv:** National arms within wreath, denomination below **Rev:** Spiny lobster

Date	Mintage	F	VF	XF	Unc	BU
1983	5,000	—	—	—	9.00	—

KM# 196 PESO
Copper-Nickel, 30 mm. **Series:** Olympics **Rev:** Two hockey players

Date	Mintage	F	VF	XF	Unc	BU
1983	3,000	—	—	—	8.00	—

KM# 140 PESO
Copper-Nickel, 30 mm. **Subject:** Castillos **Obv:** National arms within wreath, denomination below **Rev:** El Morro La Habana

Date	Mintage	F	VF	XF	Unc	BU
1984	5,000	—	—	—	8.00	—

KM# 173 PESO
Copper-Nickel, 30 mm. **Series:** 1984 Olympics **Obv:** National arms within wreath, denomination **Rev:** Runner

Date	Mintage	F	VF	XF	Unc	BU
1983	3,000	—	—	—	8.00	—

KM# 197 PESO
Copper-Nickel, 30 mm. **Series:** Olympics **Obv:** National arms within wreath, denomination **Rev:** Downhill skier

Date	Mintage	F	VF	XF	Unc	BU
1983	3,000	—	—	—	7.00	—

KM# 142 PESO
Copper-Nickel, 30 mm. **Subject:** Castillos **Obv:** National arms within wreath, denomination below **Rev:** La Fuerza La Habana

Date	Mintage	F	VF	XF	Unc	BU
1984	5,000	—	—	—	10.00	—

KM# 174 PESO
Copper-Nickel, 30 mm. **Series:** 1984 Olympics **Obv:** National arms within wreath, denomination **Rev:** Discus thrower

Date	Mintage	F	VF	XF	Unc	BU
1983	3,000	—	—	—	8.00	—

KM# 116 PESO
Copper-Nickel, 30 mm. **Subject:** Transportation **Obv:** National arms within wreath, denomination **Rev:** Freighter

Date	Mintage	F	VF	XF	Unc	BU
1984	5,000	—	—	—	8.00	—

KM# 144 PESO
Copper-Nickel, 30 mm. **Subject:** Castillos **Obv:** National arms within wreath, denomination below **Rev:** El Morro Santiago De Cuba

Date	Mintage	F	VF	XF	Unc	BU
1984	5,000	—	—	—	8.00	—

KM# 175 PESO
Copper-Nickel, 30 mm. **Series:** 1984 Olympics **Obv:** National arms within wreath, denomination below **Rev:** Judo, date upper right

Date	Mintage	F	VF	XF	Unc	BU
1983	3,000	—	—	—	8.00	—

KM# 118 PESO
Copper-Nickel, 30 mm. **Subject:** Santisima Trinidad **Obv:** National arms within wreath, denomination below **Rev:** Ship with full sails, date at left

Date	Mintage	F	VF	XF	Unc	BU
1984	3,000	—	—	—	12.00	—

KM# 172 PESO
Copper-Nickel, 30 mm. **Subject:** Transportation **Obv:** National arms within wreath, denomination below **Rev:** Hot air balloon, date at left

Date	Mintage	F	VF	XF	Unc	BU
1984	23	—	—	—	1,800	—

KM# 120   PESO
Copper-Nickel, 30 mm.   **Subject:** International Year of Music
Obv: National arms within wreath, denomination **Rev:** Bust of
Bach at left, musical score at right

Date	Mintage	F	VF	XF	Unc	BU
1985	2,000	—	—	—	10.00	—

KM# 124   PESO
Copper-Nickel, 30 mm.   **Subject:** Wildlife Preservation
Obv: National arms within wreath, denomination below
Rev: Cuban crocodile (head only)

Date	Mintage	F	VF	XF	Unc	BU
1985	5,000	—	—	—	20.00	—

KM# 126   PESO
Copper-Nickel, 30 mm.   **Subject:** Wildlife Preservation **Obv:**
National arms within wreath, denomination below **Rev:** Cuban
rock iguana (half body)

Date	Mintage	F	VF	XF	Unc	BU
1985	5,000	—	—	—	20.00	—

KM# 128   PESO
Copper-Nickel, 30 mm.   **Subject:** Wildlife Preservation
Obv: National arms within wreath, denomination below
Rev: Cuban amazon parrot (head)

Date	Mintage	F	VF	XF	Unc	BU
1985	5,000	—	—	—	20.00	—

KM# 132   PESO
Copper-Nickel, 30 mm.   **Subject:** 40th Anniversary of F.A.O.
Obv: National arms within wreath, denomination below
Rev: Sugar cane, lobster, palm tree, and F.A.O. logo

Date	Mintage	F	VF	XF	Unc	BU
ND(1985)	5,000	—	—	—	7.00	—

KM# 133   PESO
Copper-Nickel, 30 mm.   **Series:** F.A.O. **Obv:** National arms
within wreath, denomination below **Rev:** Two people amid forest

Date	Mintage	F	VF	XF	Unc	BU
1985	5,000	—	—	—	7.00	—

KM# 181   PESO
11.2600 g., Copper-Nickel, 30 mm.   **Series:** Wildlife
Preservation **Obv:** National arms **Rev:** Crocodile **Edge:** Plain

Date	Mintage	F	VF	XF	Unc	BU
1985	Est. 3,000	—	—	—	25.00	35.00

KM# 182   PESO
11.2600 g., Copper-Nickel, 30 mm.   **Series:** Wildlife Preservation
Obv: National arms **Rev:** Cuban rock iguana **Edge:** Plain

Date	Mintage	F	VF	XF	Unc	BU
1985	Est. 3,000	—	—	—	25.00	35.00

KM# 183   PESO
11.2600 g., Copper-Nickel, 30 mm.   **Series:** Wildlife
Preservation **Obv:** National arms **Rev:** Parrot perched on branch
right **Edge:** Plain

Date	Mintage	F	VF	XF	Unc	BU
1985	Est. 3,000	—	—	—	25.00	35.00

KM# 134   PESO
Copper-Nickel, 30 mm.   **Subject:** 100th Anniversary of
Automobile **Obv:** National arms within wreath, denomination
below **Rev:** Daimler-Benz, two dates below

Date	Mintage	F	VF	XF	Unc	BU
ND(1986)	3,000	—	—	—	12.00	—

KM# 136   PESO
Copper-Nickel, 30 mm.   **Subject:** 30th Anniversary - Voyage of
the Granma **Obv:** National arms within wreath, denomination
Rev: Large ship at sea, dates above

Date	Mintage	F	VF	XF	Unc	BU
ND(1986)	3,000	—	—	—	10.00	—

KM# 138   PESO
Copper-Nickel, 30 mm.   **Series:** Olympics **Obv:** National arms
within wreath, denomination **Rev:** Speed skater

Date	Mintage	F	VF	XF	Unc	BU
1986	1,000	—	—	—	22.00	—

KM# 198   PESO
Copper-Nickel, 30 mm.   **Obv:** National arms within wreath,
denomination below **Rev:** Speed skater, without rings above
skater, date lower left

Date	Mintage	F	VF	XF	Unc	BU
1986	3,000	—	—	—	8.00	—

KM# 122   PESO
Copper-Nickel, 30 mm.   **Subject:** Soccer World Championship
- Mexico '85 **Obv:** National arms within wreath, denomination
Rev: Two soccer players

Date	Mintage	F	VF	XF	Unc	BU
ND(1986)	5,000	—	—	—	8.00	—

KM# 156   PESO
Copper-Nickel, 30 mm.   **Subject:** International Year of Peace
Obv: National arms within wreath, denomination below
Rev: Dove with olive branch in flight, date at right

Date	Mintage	F	VF	XF	Unc	BU
1986	5,000	—	—	—	9.00	—
1986 Proof	5,000	Value: 15.00				

KM# 148 PESO
Copper-Nickel, 30 mm. **Obv:** National arms within wreath, denomination below **Rev:** Cathedral in Santiago

Date	Mintage	F	VF	XF	Unc	BU
1987	3,000	—	—	—	12.00	—

KM# 150 PESO
Copper-Nickel, 30 mm. **Obv:** National arms within wreath, denomination below **Rev:** Cathedral in Caridad del Cobre

Date	Mintage	F	VF	XF	Unc	BU
1987	3,000	—	—	—	12.00	—

KM# 152 PESO
Copper-Nickel, 30 mm. **Obv:** National arms within wreath, denomination below **Rev:** Cathedral in Trinidad, date below

Date	Mintage	F	VF	XF	Unc	BU
1987	3,000	—	—	—	12.00	—

KM# 154 PESO
Copper Nickel, 30 mm. **Subject:** 40th Anniversary - Expedition of Kon-Tiki **Obv:** National arms within wreath, denomination **Rev:** Full masted ships, dates

Date	Mintage	F	VF	XF	Unc	BU
ND(1987)	3,000	—	—	—	12.00	—

KM# 158 PESO
Copper-Nickel, 30 mm. **Subject:** 20th Anniversary - Demise of Ernesto Che Guevara **Obv:** National arms within wreath, denomination **Rev:** Facing bust divides dates

Date	Mintage	F	VF	XF	Unc	BU
ND(1987)	6,000	—	—	—	30.00	—
ND(1987) Proof	200	Value: 90.00				

KM# 160 PESO
Copper-Nickel, 30 mm. **Subject:** 70th Anniversary of Bolshevik Revolution **Obv:** National arms within wreath, denomination below **Rev:** Ship at sea, date at right

Date	Mintage	F	VF	XF	Unc	BU
1987	5,000	—	—	—	10.00	—

KM# 165 PESO
Copper-Nickel, 30 mm. **Subject:** 100th Anniversary of the Souvenir Peso **Obv:** National arms within wreath, denomination below **Rev:** Womans head right

Date	Mintage	F	VF	XF	Unc	BU
1987	3,000	—	—	—	12.00	—
1987 Proof	3,000	Value: 25.00				

KM# 167 PESO
Copper-Nickel, 30 mm. **Subject:** 100th Anniversary - Abolition of Slavery **Obv:** National arms within wreath, denomination below **Rev:** Half figure of slave breaking chains, three dates

Date	Mintage	F	VF	XF	Unc	BU
1987	2,000	—	—	—	15.00	—

KM# 179 PESO
Copper-Nickel, 30 mm. **Subject:** Chess Centennial **Obv:** National arms within wreath, denomination **Rev:** Jose Capablanca at match

Date	Mintage	F	VF	XF	Unc	BU
ND(1988)	1,000	—	—	—	20.00	—

KM# 184 PESO
Copper-Nickel, 30 mm. **Subject:** Soccer - 1986 Mexico **Obv:** National arms within wreath, denomination below **Rev:** Soccer players, date at left

Date	Mintage	F	VF	XF	Unc	BU
1988	1,000	—	—	—	20.00	—

KM# 200 PESO
Copper-Nickel, 30 mm. **Subject:** Chess Centennial **Rev:** Chess pieces

Date	Mintage	F	VF	XF	Unc	BU
ND(1988)	6,000	—	—	—	10.00	—

KM# 244 PESO
Copper-Nickel, 30 mm. **Subject:** Soccer World Championship - Italy 1990 **Obv:** Three towers above key on crowned shield within wreath **Rev:** Soccer players, date above

Date	Mintage	F	VF	XF	Unc	BU
1988	2,000	—	—	—	12.00	—

KM# 245 PESO
Copper-Nickel, 30 mm. **Subject:** European World Soccer Championship - Federal Republic of Germany **Obv:** National arms within wreath, denomination below **Rev:** Three players

Date	Mintage	F	VF	XF	Unc	BU
1988	2,000	—	—	—	12.00	—

KM# 246 PESO
Copper-Nickel, 30 mm. **Subject:** European World Soccer Championship - Federal Republic of Germany **Obv:** National arms within wreath, denomination below **Rev:** Four players

Date	Mintage	F	VF	XF	Unc	BU
1988	2,000	—	—	—	14.50	—

KM# 276 PESO
Copper-Nickel, 30 mm. **Subject:** 40th Anniversary of Cuban National Ballet **Obv:** National arms within wreath, denomination below **Rev:** Womans head right, looking up

Date	Mintage	F	VF	XF	Unc	BU
ND(1988)	2,000	—	—	—	12.00	—

KM# 277   PESO
Copper-Nickel, 30 mm.   **Subject:** 150th Anniversary of Havana
Grand Theater **Obv:** National arms within wreath, denomination
below **Rev:** Theater building, dates at left

Date	Mintage	F	VF	XF	Unc	BU
ND(1977)	2,000	—	—	—	12.00	—

KM# 282   PESO
Copper-Nickel, 30 mm.   **Obv:** National arms within wreath,
denomination **Rev:** Carlos J. Finlay

Date	Mintage	F	VF.	XF	Unc	BU
ND(1988)	2,000	—	—	—	12.00	—

KM# 512   PESO
Copper   **Obv:** National arms within wreath, denomination
Rev: Bust at lower right looking left, dates below

Date	Mintage	F	VF	XF	Unc	BU
ND(1988)	2,500	—	—	—	12.00	—

KM# 258   PESO
Copper-Nickel, 30 mm.   **Subject:** World Health Organization
Obv: National arms within wreath, denomination below
Rev: Nurse with baby, building in background

Date	Mintage	F	VF	XF	Unc	BU
1988	2,000	—	—	—	10.00	—

KM# 269   PESO
Copper-Nickel, 30 mm.   **Subject:** Transportation **Obv:** National
arms within wreath, denomination **Rev:** Zeppelin

Date	Mintage	F	VF	XF	Unc	BU
1988	1,000	—	—	—	50.00	—

KM# 324   PESO
Copper-Nickel, 30 mm.   **Subject:** Assault of the Moncada Garrison
Obv: National arms within wreath, denomination below **Rev:** Battle scene

Date	Mintage	F	VF	XF	Unc	BU
1988	2,000	—	—	—	12.00	—

KM# 363   PESO
Brass, 30 mm.   **Obv:** National arms within wreath, denomination
below **Rev:** Head of Jose Marti right, date below

Date	Mintage	F	VF	XF	Unc	BU
1988		—	—	—	15.00	—

KM# 513   PESO
Copper   **Subject:** Transportation **Obv:** National arms within
wreath, denomination **Rev:** Zeppelin, date lower left

Date	Mintage	F	VF	XF	Unc	BU
1988	2,500	—	—	—	30.00	—

KM# 247   PESO
Copper-Nickel, 30 mm.   **Subject:** World Soccer Championship
- Italy 1990 **Obv:** National arms within wreath, denomination
below **Rev:** Three players

Date	Mintage	F	VF	XF	Unc	BU
1989	4,000	—	—	—	10.00	—

KM# 248   PESO
Copper-Nickel, 30 mm.   **Subject:** World Soccer Championship
- Italy 1990 **Obv:** National arms within wreath, denomination
below **Rev:** Colosseum

Date	Mintage	F	VF	XF	Unc	BU
1989	2,000	—	—	—	20.00	—

KM# 253   PESO
Copper-Nickel, 30 mm.   **Subject:** 30th Anniversary of Revolution
Obv: National arms within wreath, denomination below
Rev: Castro with gun standing before radiant sun, dates at left

Date	Mintage	F	VF	XF	Unc	BU
ND(1989)	5,000	—	—	—	15.00	—

KM# 254   PESO
Copper-Nickel, 30 mm.   **Subject:** 30th Anniversary of Revolution
Obv: National arms within wreath, denomination below
Rev: Facing busts of Jose Marti and Castro

Date	Mintage	F	VF	XF	Unc	BU
1989	5,000	—	—	—	15.00	—

KM# 255   PESO
Copper-Nickel, 30 mm.   **Subject:** 30th Anniversary of Revolution
Obv: National arms within wreath, denomination below
Rev: Cienfuegos and Castro, dates at right

Date	Mintage	F	VF	XF	Unc	BU
ND(1989)	5,000	—	—	—	15.00	—

KM# 257   PESO
Copper-Nickel, 30 mm.   **Subject:** Triumph of the Revolution
Obv: National arms within wreath, denomination below
Rev: Castro with revolutionaries, dates below

Date	Mintage	F	VF	XF	Unc	BU
1989	2,000	—	—	—	15.00	—

KM# 259   PESO
Copper-Nickel, 30 mm.   **Subject:** Cuban Tobacco **Obv:** National
arms within wreath, denomination below **Rev:** Native smoking
above tobacco plant, parrot at right, date below

Date	Mintage	F	VF	XF	Unc	BU
1989	1,000	—	—	—	18.00	—

KM# 260 PESO
Copper-Nickel, 30 mm. **Subject:** 160th Anniversary of First Railroad in England **Obv:** National arms within wreath, denomination below **Rev:** Railroad carts, dates below and above

Date	Mintage	F	VF	XF	Unc	BU
1989	2,000	—	—	—	15.00	—

KM# 261 PESO
Copper-Nickel, 30 mm. **Subject:** 500th Anniversary - Discovery of America **Obv:** National arms within wreath, denomination below **Rev:** Three ships, date at left

Date	Mintage	F	VF	XF	Unc	BU
1989	3,145	—	—	—	15.00	—

KM# 270 PESO
Copper-Nickel, 30 mm. **Subject:** 30th Anniversary - The March to Victory **Obv:** National arms within wreath, denomination **Rev:** Uniformed figures marching, dates

Date	Mintage	F	VF	XF	Unc	BU
1989	2,000	—	—	—	12.00	—

KM# 271 PESO
Copper-Nickel, 30 mm. **Subject:** 200th Anniversary of French Revolution **Obv:** National arms within wreath, denomination below **Rev:** Female Allegory of Revolution

Date	Mintage	F	VF	XF	Unc	BU
ND(1989)	2,000	—	—	—	12.00	—

KM# 272 PESO
Copper-Nickel, 30 mm. **Subject:** 200th Anniversary of French Revolution - Bastille **Obv:** National arms within wreath, denomination below **Rev:** Castle scene, dates below

Date	Mintage	F	VF	XF	Unc	BU
ND(1989)	2,000	—	—	—	12.00	—

KM# 274 PESO
Copper-Nickel, 30 mm. **Subject:** First Spanish Railroad **Obv:** National arms within wreath, denomination below **Rev:** Train on track, three dates

Date	Mintage	F	VF	XF	Unc	BU
1989	2,000	—	—	—	12.00	—

KM# 275 PESO
Copper-Nickel, 30 mm. **Subject:** First Cuban Railroad **Obv:** National arms within wreath, denomination below **Rev:** Train engine divides dates

Date	Mintage	F	VF	XF	Unc	BU
1989	2,000	—	—	—	15.00	—

KM# 278 PESO
Copper-Nickel, 30 mm. **Subject:** 5th Centennial - Discovery of America **Obv:** National arms within wreath, denomination below **Rev:** Three ships at sea, date at left

Date	Mintage	F	VF	XF	Unc	BU
1989	2,000	—	—	—	12.00	—

KM# 283 PESO
Copper-Nickel, 30 mm. **Subject:** Alexander von Humboldt **Obv:** National arms within wreath, denomination below **Rev:** Cameo of Alexander von Humboldt, birds on branch

Date	Mintage	F	VF	XF	Unc	BU
1989	2,000	—	—	—	12.50	—

KM# 284 PESO
Copper-Nickel, 30 mm. **Series:** 1992 Olympics **Obv:** National arms within wreath, denomination below **Rev:** Two boxers

Date	Mintage	F	VF	XF	Unc	BU
1989	1,000	—	—	—	15.00	—

KM# 285 PESO
Copper-Nickel, 30 mm. **Obv:** National arms within wreath, denomination below **Rev:** Facing bust, date at left

Date	Mintage	F	VF	XF	Unc	BU
1989	2,000	—	—	—	15.00	—

KM# 286 PESO
Copper-Nickel, 30 mm. **Obv:** National arms within wreath, denomination below **Rev:** Profile of Ernesto Che Guevara

Date	Mintage	F	VF	XF	Unc	BU
1989	2,000	—	—	—	25.00	—

KM# 287 PESO
Copper-Nickel, 30 mm. **Obv:** National arms within wreath, denomination below **Rev:** Bust of Tania La Guerrillera, Argentinian revolutionary

Date	Mintage	F	VF	XF	Unc	BU
1989	2,000	—	—	—	15.00	—

KM# 436 PESO
Copper **Obv:** National arms within wreath, denomination below **Rev:** Cameo of Alexander von Humboldt, Condors

Date	Mintage	F	VF	XF	Unc	BU
1989	—	—	—	—	12.00	—

KM# 250 PESO
Copper, 30 mm. **Obv:** National arms within wreath, denomination below **Rev:** Esperanto at right, world globe at left

Date	Mintage	F	VF	XF	Unc	BU
1990	6,000	—	—	—	12.00	—

KM# 273 PESO
Copper, 30 mm. **Subject:** Discovery of America **Obv:** National arms within wreath, denomination below **Rev:** Scene depicting Columbus departing from Spain

Date	Mintage	F	VF	XF	Unc	BU
1990	12,000	—	—	—	12.00	—

KM# 279 PESO
Copper-Nickel, 30 mm. **Subject:** 5th Centennial of Columbus' Arrival in Cuba **Obv:** National arms within wreath, denomination below **Rev:** Ship at sea, map in background, date at right

Date	Mintage	F	VF	XF	Unc	BU
1990	2,000	—	—	—	12.00	—

KM# 288 PESO
Copper-Nickel, 30 mm. **Obv:** National arms within wreath, denomination below **Rev:** Columbus meeting natives

Date	Mintage	F	VF	XF	Unc	BU
1990	2,000	—	—	—	12.00	—

KM# 289 PESO
Copper-Nickel, 30 mm. **Obv:** National arms within wreath, denomination below **Rev:** Three soccer balls at left, map of Italy at right

Date	Mintage	F	VF	XF	Unc	BU
1990	—	—	—	—	9.00	—

KM# 306 PESO
Copper-Nickel, 30 mm. **Subject:** 500th Anniversary - Discovery of America **Obv:** National arms within wreath, denomination below **Rev:** King Ferdinand of Spain

Date	Mintage	F	VF	XF	Unc	BU
1990	3,000	—	—	—	10.00	—

KM# 307 PESO
Copper-Nickel, 30 mm. **Subject:** 500th Anniversary - Discovery of America **Obv:** National arms within wreath, denomination below **Rev:** Queen Isabella of Spain

Date	Mintage	F	VF	XF	Unc	BU
1990	3,000	—	—	—	10.00	—

KM# 308 PESO
Copper-Nickel, 30 mm. **Subject:** 500th Anniversary - Discovery of America **Obv:** National arms within wreath, denomination below **Rev:** Christopher Columbus 3/4 left

Date	Mintage	F	VF	XF	Unc	BU
1990	3,000	—	—	—	10.00	—

KM# 309 PESO
Copper Nickel, 30 mm. **Subject:** 500th Anniversary - Discovery of America **Obv:** National arms within wreath, denomination below **Rev:** Juan de la Cosa

Date	Mintage	F	VF	XF	Unc	BU
1990	3,000	—	—	—	8.00	—

KM# 310 PESO
Copper-Nickel, 30 mm. **Subject:** Pan American Games **Obv:** National arms within wreath, denomination below **Rev:** High jumper

Date	Mintage	F	VF	XF	Unc	BU
1990	5,000	—	—	—	8.00	—

KM# 311 PESO
Copper-Nickel, 30 mm. **Subject:** Pan American Games **Obv:** National arms within wreath, denomination below **Rev:** Volleyball

Date	Mintage	F	VF	XF	Unc	BU
1990	5,000	—	—	—	8.00	—

KM# 312 PESO
Copper-Nickel, 30 mm. **Subject:** Pan American Games **Obv:** National arms within wreath, denomination below **Rev:** Baseball game on baseball background

Date	Mintage	F	VF	XF	Unc	BU
1990	5,000	—	—	—	10.00	—

KM# 325 PESO
Copper-Nickel, 30 mm. **Obv:** National arms within wreath, denomination below **Rev:** Columbus' ships sailing west

Date	Mintage	F	VF	XF	Unc	BU
1990	12,000	—	—	—	9.00	—

KM# 340 PESO
Copper-Nickel, 30 mm. **Subject:** Celia Sanchez Manduley 1920-80, revolutionary **Obv:** National arms within wreath, denomination below **Rev:** Head looking left, dates below

Date	Mintage	F	VF	XF	Unc	BU
1990	—	—	—	—	8.00	—

KM# 387 PESO
Copper-Nickel, 30 mm. **Obv:** National arms within wreath, denomination below **Rev:** Route of first voyage by Columbus

Date	Mintage	F	VF	XF	Unc	BU
1990	2,000	—	—	—	12.00	—

KM# 471 PESO
Copper, 30 mm. **Obv:** National arms within wreath, denomination below **Rev:** Columbus meeting natives

Date	Mintage	F	VF	XF	Unc	BU
1990	—	—	—	—	12.00	—

KM# 514 PESO
Copper-Nickel, 30 mm. **Subject:** Simon Bolivar - Libertador **Obv:** National arms within wreath, denomination **Rev:** Uniformed bust facing, dates

Date	Mintage	F	VF	XF	Unc	BU
1990	2,000	—	—	—	10.00	—

KM# 364 PESO
Nickel Bonded Steel, 30 mm. **Obv:** National arms within wreath, denomination below **Rev:** Hatuey tribesman head left, date at right

Date	Mintage	F	VF	XF	Unc	BU
1991	3,000	—	—	—	10.00	—

KM# 365 PESO
Nickel Bonded Steel, 30 mm. **Obv:** National arms within wreath, denomination below **Rev:** Pinzon brothers

Date	Mintage	F	VF	XF	Unc	BU
1991	3,000	—	—	—	9.00	—

KM# 366 PESO
Nickel Bonded Steel, 30 mm. **Subject:** 500th Anniversary of New World **Obv:** National arms within wreath, denomination below **Rev:** Bust of Queen Joanna, 1479-1555, daughter of Isabella I

Date	Mintage	F	VF	XF	Unc	BU
1991	3,000	—	—	—	9.00	—

KM# 367 PESO
Nickel Bonded Steel, 30 mm. **Obv:** National arms within wreath, denomination below **Rev:** Diego Velazquez

Date	Mintage	F	VF	XF	Unc	BU
1991	3,000	—	—	—	9.00	—

KM# 388 PESO
Nickel Bonded Steel, 30 mm. **Subject:** Madrid **Obv:** National arms within wreath, denomination below **Rev:** Alcala Gate

Date	Mintage	F	VF	XF	Unc	BU
1991	10,000	—	—	—	9.00	—

KM# 389 PESO
Nickel Bonded Steel, 30 mm. **Subject:** Barcelona **Obv:** National arms within wreath, denomination below **Rev:** Olympic stadium

Date	Mintage	F	VF	XF	Unc	BU
1991		—	—	—	9.00	—

KM# 390 PESO
Nickel Bonded Steel, 30 mm. **Subject:** Seville **Obv:** National arms within wreath, denomination below **Rev:** La Giralda Tower

Date	Mintage	F	VF	XF	Unc	BU
1991		—	—	—	9.00	—

KM# 347 PESO
5.5000 g., Brass Plated Steel, 24.4 mm. **Subject:** Jose Marti **Obv:** National arms within wreath, denomination below **Rev:** Smaller Bust facing, denomination at left **Rev. Leg.:** PATRIA O MUERTE **Note:** Rim varieties exist.

Date	Mintage	F	VF	XF	Unc	BU
1991		—	—	1.00	2.50	5.00
1992		—	—	1.00	2.00	4.00
1992 Proof		—	—	—	—	—
1994		—	—	1.00	2.00	4.00

KM# 368 PESO
Copper-Nickel, 30 mm. **Subject:** Postal Ship **Obv:** National arms within wreath, denomination below **Rev:** Ship at sea, date at left

Date	Mintage	F	VF	XF	Unc	BU
1992		—	—	—	12.00	—

KM# 391 PESO
Nickel Bonded Steel, 30 mm. **Subject:** 25th Anniversary - Death of Ernesto Che Guevara **Obv:** National arms within wreath, denomination below **Rev:** Ernesto Che Guevara

Date	Mintage	F	VF	XF	Unc	BU
1992		—	—	—	12.00	—

KM# 392 PESO
Nickel Bonded Steel, 30 mm. **Obv:** National arms within wreath, denomination below **Rev:** Bartolome de Las Casas

Date	Mintage	F	VF	XF	Unc	BU
1992	3,000	—	—	—	9.00	—

KM# 393 PESO
Nickel Bonded Steel, 30 mm. **Obv:** National arms within wreath, denomination below **Rev:** Half figure of Chief Guama blowing shell, date at left

Date	Mintage	F	VF	XF	Unc	BU
1992	3,000	—	—	—	10.00	—

KM# 394 PESO
Nickel Bonded Steel, 30 mm. **Obv:** National arms within wreath, denomination below **Rev:** King Philipp of Spain

Date	Mintage	F	VF	XF	Unc	BU
1992	3,000	—	—	—	9.00	—

KM# 395 PESO
Nickel Bonded Steel, 30 mm. **Subject:** Spanish Royalty **Obv:** National arms within wreath, denomination below **Rev:** Banners below royal busts at top and bottom, dates flanking

Date	Mintage	F	VF	XF	Unc	BU
ND(1992)	3,000	—	—	—	9.00	—

KM# 401 PESO
Copper-Nickel, 30 mm. **Obv:** National arms within wreath, denomination below **Rev:** Seville Tower of Gold

Date	Mintage	F	VF	XF	Unc	BU
1992		—	—	—	9.00	—

KM# 402 PESO
Copper-Nickel, 30 mm. **Subject:** El Escorial **Obv:** National arms within wreath, denomination below **Rev:** City view, date below

Date	Mintage	F	VF	XF	Unc	BU
1992	—			—	9.00	

KM# 403 PESO
Copper-Nickel, 30 mm. **Obv:** National arms within wreath, denomination below **Rev:** St. Jorge Palace, date below

Date	Mintage	F	VF	XF	Unc	BU
1992	10,000			—	9.00	

KM# 437 PESO
Copper **Subject:** 25th Anniversary - Death of Ernesto Che Guevara **Obv:** National arms within wreath, denomination **Rev:** Uniformed bust facing, dates

Date	Mintage	F	VF	XF	Unc	BU
ND(1992)	—			—	15.00	

KM# 462 PESO
Nickel Bonded Steel, 30 mm. **Subject:** Introduction of Africans to America **Obv:** National arms within wreath, denomination below **Rev:** Figure with back facing at left, ship at sea at right, inscription below

Date	Mintage	F	VF	XF	Unc	BU
1992	—			—	11.50	

KM# 396 PESO
Copper **Subject:** Millennium of St. Jacobi **Obv:** National arms within wreath, denomination **Rev:** Armored figure on rearing horse right

Date	Mintage	F	VF	XF	Unc	BU
1993	—			—	10.00	

KM# 397.1 PESO
29.4300 g., Copper Plated Bronze, 37.9 mm. **Subject:** 40th Anniversary of the attack on Moncada Barracks by revolutionaries led by Fidel Castro on July 26, 1953. **Obv:** National arms, denomination below **Obv. Leg.:** REPUBLICA DE CUBA **Rev:** Uniformed bust of Castro left **Rev. Leg.:** 40 ANIVERSARIO DEL MONCADA **Edge:** Plain, beveled rim

Date	Mintage	F	VF	XF	Unc	BU
1993	—			—	20.00	30.00

KM# 404 PESO
Copper-Nickel, 30 mm. **Series:** Prehistoric Animals **Obv:** National arms within wreath, denomination below **Rev:** Chalicotherium standing with tree, date below

Date	Mintage	F	VF	XF	Unc	BU
1993	—			—	25.00	

KM# 429 PESO
Copper-Nickel, 30 mm. **Subject:** Federico Garcia Lorca **Obv:** National arms within wreath, denomination **Rev:** Bust facing, dates at left

Date	Mintage	F	VF	XF	Unc	BU
1993	—			—	10.00	

KM# 509 PESO
Copper **Obv:** National arms within wreath, denomination below **Rev:** President Abraham Lincoln, map of United States behind

Date	Mintage	F	VF	XF	Unc	BU
1993	—			—	10.00	

KM# 515 PESO
Copper **Obv:** National arms within wreath, denomination below **Rev:** Bolivar and Marti

Date	Mintage	F	VF	XF	Unc	BU
1993 Plain finish	—			—	10.00	—
1993 Antiqued finish	—			—	12.00	—

KM# 397.2 PESO
30.0200 g., Copper Plated Bronze, 37.9 mm. **Subject:** 40th Anniversary of the attack on Moncada Barracks by revolutionaries led by Fidel Castro on July 26, 1953 **Obv:** National arms, denomination below **Obv. Leg.:** REPUBLICA DE CUBA **Rev:** Uniformed bust of Castro left **Rev. Leg.:** 40 ANIVERSARIO DEL MONCADA **Edge:** Plain, flat rim

Date	Mintage	F	VF	XF	Unc	BU
1993	—			—	20.00	30.00

KM# 438 PESO
Copper-Nickel Plated Steel, 30 mm. **Series:** Prehistoric Animals **Obv:** National arms within wreath, denomination below **Rev:** Stegosaurus

Date	Mintage	F	VF	XF	Unc	BU
1994	—			—	25.00	

KM# 439 PESO
Copper-Nickel, 30 mm. **Series:** Caribbean Fauna **Obv:** National arms within wreath, denomination below **Rev:** Multicolored Bottle-nosed Dolphins

Date	Mintage	F	VF	XF	Unc	BU
1994	25,000			—	15.00	

KM# 460 PESO
Copper-Nickel, 30 mm. **Series:** Caribbean Fauna **Obv:** National arms within wreath, denomination below **Rev:** Multicolored Spotted Eagle Ray left, date below

Date	Mintage	F	VF	XF	Unc	BU
1994	25,000			—	15.00	

KM# 463 PESO
Nickel Bonded Steel, 30 mm. **Subject:** Isla del Evangelista
Obv: National arms within wreath, denomination below
Rev: Parrot, ship, and sea chest

Date	Mintage	F	VF	XF	Unc	BU
1994	—	—	—	—	12.00	—

KM# 464 PESO
Nickel Bonded Steel, 30 mm. **Subject:** Sailing Ships **Obv:** National arms within wreath, denomination below **Rev:** NAO VICTORIA

Date	Mintage	F	VF	XF	Unc	BU
1994	—	—	—	—	9.00	—

KM# 465 PESO
Nickel Bonded Steel, 30 mm. **Subject:** Sailing Ships **Obv:** National arms within wreath, denomination below **Rev:** LA INDIA

Date	Mintage	F	VF	XF	Unc	BU
1994	—	—	—	—	9.00	—

KM# 466.1 PESO
Copper-Nickel, 30 mm. **Series:** Caribbean Fauna **Obv:** National arms within wreath, denomination below **Rev:** Multicolored Yellow Sea Bass (Coney), 7 lines in the tail, slimmer fish

Date	Mintage	F	VF	XF	Unc	BU
1994	25,000	—	—	—	25.00	—

KM# 467.1 PESO
Copper-Nickel, 30 mm. **Series:** Caribbean Fauna **Obv:** National arms within wreath, denomination below **Rev:** Multicolored sailfish, small water splashes, thin nose

Date	Mintage	F	VF	XF	Unc	BU
1994	25,000	—	—	—	25.00	—

KM# 497 PESO
Copper-Nickel, 30 mm. **Series:** Caribbean Fauna **Obv:** National arms within wreath, denomination below **Rev:** Multicolor pelican

Date	Mintage	F	VF	XF	Unc	BU
1994	25,000	—	—	—	15.00	—

KM# 498.1 PESO
Copper-Nickel, 30 mm. **Series:** Caribbean Fauna **Obv:** National arms within wreath, denomination below **Rev:** Multicolored flamingos, thin water splashes

Date	Mintage	F	VF	XF	Unc	BU
1994	25,000	—	—	—	25.00	—

KM# 516 PESO
Copper **Subject:** Montecristi Manifesto **Obv:** National arms within wreath, denomination below **Rev:** Two seated figures facing each other, date lower left

Date	Mintage	F	VF	XF	Unc	BU
1994 Plain finish	—	—	—	—	12.00	—
1994 Antiqued finish	—	—	—	—	12.00	—

KM# 517 PESO
Copper **Obv:** National arms within wreath, denomination below **Rev:** Nao Victoria

Date	Mintage	F	VF	XF	Unc	BU
1994	2,500	—	—	—	12.00	—

KM# 518 PESO
12.7000 g., Nickel Bonded Steel, 32.68 mm. **Series:** World War I fighter airplanes **Obv:** National arms **Rev:** German Fokker Dr.I multicolor **Edge:** Plain

Date	Mintage	F	VF	XF	Unc	BU
1994	—	—	—	—	18.50	—

KM# 547 PESO
12.7000 g., Nickel Bonded Steel, 32.68 mm. **Series:** World War I fighter airplanes **Obv:** National arms **Rev:** English Albatross II multicolor **Edge:** Plain

Date	Mintage	F	VF	XF	Unc	BU
1994	25,000	—	—	—	18.50	—

KM# 606 PESO
Copper **Subject:** 500th Anniversary - Discovery of Evangelista Island **Obv:** National arms within wreath, denomination below **Rev:** Parrot, chest, and ship

Date	Mintage	F	VF	XF	Unc	BU
1994	—	—	—	—	12.50	—

KM# 466.2 PESO
Copper-Nickel, 30 mm. **Subject:** Caribbean Fauna **Obv:** National arms within wreath, denomination below **Rev:** Multicolored Yellow Sea Bass (Coney), 5 lines in the tail

Date	Mintage	F	VF	XF	Unc	BU
1994	Inc. above	—	—	—	15.00	—

KM# 467.2 PESO
Copper Nickel, 30 mm. **Subject:** Caribbean Fauna **Obv:** National arms within wreath, denomination below **Rev:** Multicolored Swordfish, large water splashes, wider nose

Date	Mintage	F	VF	XF	Unc	BU
1994	Inc. above	—	—	—	15.00	—

KM# 498.2 PESO
Copper-Nickel, 30 mm. **Subject:** Caribbean Fauna **Obv:** National arms within wreath, denomination below **Rev:** Multicolored flamingos, wide water splashes

Date	Mintage	F	VF	XF	Unc	BU
1994	Inc. above	—	—	—	15.00	—

KM# 472.1 PESO
Copper-Nickel, 30 mm. **Subject:** Pirates of the Caribbean **Obv:** Roman I in denomination, lower relief, more refined shield **Rev:** Blackbeard

Date	Mintage	F	VF	XF	Unc	BU
1995	Est. 25,000	—	—	—	12.00	—

KM# 472.2 PESO
Copper Nickel, 30 mm. **Subject:** Pirates of the Caribbean **Obv:** Arabic 1 in denomination, higher relief shield **Rev:** Blackbeard

Date	Mintage	F	VF	XF	Unc	BU
1995	Inc. above	—	—	—	12.00	—

KM# 472.3 PESO
Copper Nickel, 30 mm. **Subject:** Pirates of the Caribbean **Obv:** National arms within wreath, denomination below **Rev:** Blackbeard **Rev. Leg.:** Mariposas del Caribe **Note:** Struck on trial planchet

Date	Mintage	F	VF	XF	Unc	BU
1995 Rare	—	—	—	—	—	—

KM# 473.1 PESO
Copper-Nickel, 30 mm. **Subject:** Pirates of the Caribbean **Obv:** Roman I in denomination, lower relief, more refined shield **Rev:** Sir Henry Morgan

Date	Mintage	F	VF	XF	Unc	BU
1995	25,000	—	—	—	12.00	—

KM# 473.2 PESO
Copper Nickel, 30 mm. **Subject:** Pirates of the Caribbean **Obv:** Arabic 1 in denomination, higher relief shield **Rev:** Sir Henry Morgan

Date	Mintage	F	VF	XF	Unc	BU
1995	Inc. above	—	—	—	12.00	—

KM# 473.3 PESO
Copper Nickel, 30 mm. **Subject:** Pirates of the Caribbean **Obv:** National arms within wreath, denomination below **Rev:** Sir Henry Morgan **Rev. Leg.:** Mariposas del Caribe **Note:** Struck on trial planchet.

Date	Mintage	F	VF	XF	Unc	BU
1995 Rare	—	—	—	—	—	—

KM# 474.1 PESO
Copper-Nickel, 30 mm. **Subject:** Pirates of the Caribbean **Obv:** Roman I in denomination, lower relief, more refined shield **Rev:** Anne Bonny

Date	Mintage	F	VF	XF	Unc	BU
1995	Est. 25,000	—	—	—	12.00	—

KM# 474.2 PESO
Copper Nickel, 30 mm. **Subject:** Pirates of the Caribbean **Obv:** Arabic 1 in denomination, higher relief shield **Rev:** Anne Bonny

Date	Mintage	F	VF	XF	Unc	BU
1995	Inc. above	—	—	—	12.00	—

KM# 474.3 PESO
Copper Nickel, 30 mm. **Subject:** Pirates of the Caribbean **Obv:** National arms within wreath, denomination **Rev:** Anne Bonny **Rev. Leg.:** Mariposas del Caribe **Note:** Struck on trial planchet.

Date	Mintage	F	VF	XF	Unc	BU
1995 Rare	—	—	—	—	—	—

KM# 475.1 PESO
Copper-Nickel, 30 mm. **Subject:** Pirates of the Caribbean **Obv:** Roman I in denomination, lower relief, more refined shield **Rev:** Mary Read

Date	Mintage	F	VF	XF	Unc	BU
1995	Est. 25,000	—	—	—	12.00	—

KM# 475.2 PESO
Copper Nickel, 30 mm. **Subject:** Pirates of the Caribbean **Obv:** Arabic 1 in denomination, higher relief shield **Rev:** Mary Read

Date	Mintage	F	VF	XF	Unc	BU
1995	Inc. above	—	—	—	12.00	—

KM# 475.3 PESO
Copper Nickel, 30 mm. **Subject:** Pirates of the Caribbean **Obv:** National arms within wreath, denomination below **Rev:** Mary Read **Rev. Leg.:** Mariposas del caribe **Note:** Struck on trial planchet.

Date	Mintage	F	VF	XF	Unc	BU
1995 Rare	—	—	—	—	—	—

KM# 476.1 PESO
Copper-Nickel, 30 mm. **Subject:** Pirates of the Caribbean **Obv:** Roman I in denomination, lower relief, more refined shield **Rev:** Captain Kidd

Date	Mintage	F	VF	XF	Unc	BU
1995	Est. 25,000	—	—	—	12.00	—

KM# 476.2 PESO
Copper Nickel, 30 mm. **Subject:** Pirates of the Caribbean **Obv:** Arabic 1 in denomination, higher relief shield **Rev:** Captain Kidd

Date	Mintage	F	VF	XF	Unc	BU
1995	Inc. above	—	—	—	12.00	—

KM# 476.3 PESO
Copper Nickel, 30 mm. **Subject:** Pirates of the Caribbean **Obv:** National arms within wreath, denomination below **Rev:** Captain Kidd **Rev. Leg.:** Mariposas del Caribe **Note:** Struck on trial planchet.

Date	Mintage	F	VF	XF	Unc	BU
1995 Rare	—	—	—	—	—	—

KM# 477.1 PESO
Copper-Nickel, 30 mm. **Subject:** Pirates of the Caribbean **Obv:** Roman I in denomination, lower relief, more refined shield **Rev:** Piet Heyn

Date	Mintage	F	VF	XF	Unc	BU
1995	Est. 25,000	—	—	—	12.00	—

KM# 477.2 PESO
Copper Nickel, 30 mm. **Subject:** Pirates of the Caribbean **Obv:** Arabic 1 in denomination, higher relief shield **Rev:** Piet Heyn

Date	Mintage	F	VF	XF	Unc	BU
1995	Inc. above	—	—	—	12.00	—

KM# 477.3 PESO
Copper Nickel, 30 mm. **Subject:** Pirates of the Caribbean **Obv:** National arms within wreath, denomination below **Rev:** Piet Heyn **Rev. Leg.:** Mariposas del Caribe **Note:** Struck on trial planchet.

Date	Mintage	F	VF	XF	Unc	BU
1995 Rare	—	—	—	—	—	—

KM# 519 PESO
Copper **Subject:** Centennial - Death of Jose Marti in combat **Obv:** National arms within wreath, denomination below **Rev:** Bust of Marti facing, date at right

Date	Mintage	F	VF	XF	Unc	BU
1995 Plain finish	—	—	—	—	12.00	—
1995 Antiqued finish	3,000	—	—	—	12.00	—

KM# 520 PESO
Copper **Subject:** Centennial 1895-1995 **Obv:** National arms within wreath, denomination below **Rev:** Three conjoined busts, right of sword, facing right, dates below

Date	Mintage	F	VF	XF	Unc	BU
ND(1995) Plain finish	Inc. below	—	—	—	12.00	—
ND(1995) Antiqued finish	2,000	—	—	—	12.00	—

KM# 521 PESO
Nickel Bonded Steel, 30 mm. **Subject:** Centennial - Jose Marti in combat **Obv:** National arms within wreath, denomination below **Rev:** Bust of Marti looking left, date at right

Date	Mintage	F	VF	XF	Unc	BU
1995	—	—	—	—	7.50	—

KM# 522 PESO
12.7000 g., Nickel-Bonded Steel, 32.5 mm. **Obv:** National arms within wreath, denomination below **Rev:** Multicolored SIAI Marchetti Seaplane, date at left

Date	Mintage	F	VF	XF	Unc	BU
1995	—	—	—	—	18.50	—

KM# 523 PESO
Copper-Nickel **Subject:** 50th Anniversary - United Nations **Obv:** National arms within wreath, denomination below **Rev:** Five people, assorted ages and race, UN logo in front, dove outline behind, dates below

Date	Mintage	F	VF	XF	Unc	BU
ND(1995)	—	—	—	—	15.00	—

KM# 607 PESO
Nickel Bonded Steel, 30 mm. **Subject:** 50th Anniversary - F.A.O.
Obv: National arms within wreath, denomination below
Rev: Farmer plowing behind two oxen

Date	Mintage	F	VF	XF	Unc	BU
ND(1995)	—	—	—	—	17.00	—

KM# 562 PESO
13.0400 g., Nickel Bonded Steel, 32.78 mm. **Series:** Caribbean Fauna **Obv:** National arms **Rev:** Multicolored Vaca Anil Fish **Edge:** Plain

Date	Mintage	F	VF	XF	Unc	BU
1996	10,000	—	—	—	20.00	—

KM# 620 PESO
12.9200 g., Nickel-Bonded Steel, 32.61 mm. **Subject:** Turnera Ulmifola **Obv:** National arms **Rev:** Multicolor flower **Edge:** Plain

Date	Mintage	F	VF	XF	Unc	BU
1997	5,000	—	—	—	10.00	—

KM# 549 PESO
Nickel-Bonded Steel, 30 mm. **Series:** Caribbean Fauna
Obv: National arms within wreath, denomination below
Rev: Multicolored Purple-throated Carib Hummingbird

Date	Mintage	F	VF	XF	Unc	BU
1996	10,000	—	—	—	20.00	—

KM# 565 PESO
Nickel Bonded Steel, 30 mm. **Series:** Caribbean Fauna
Obv: National arms within wreath, denomination below
Rev: Multicolored Papilio butterfly

Date	Mintage	F	VF	XF	Unc	BU
1996	10,000	—	—	—	20.00	—

KM# 621 PESO
12.9200 g., Nickel-Bonded Steel, 32.61 mm. **Subject:** Cordia Sebestena **Obv:** National arms **Rev:** Multicolor flower **Edge:** Plain

Date	Mintage	F	VF	XF	Unc	BU
1997	5,000	—	—	—	10.00	—

KM# 550 PESO
Nickel Bonded Steel, 30 mm. **Series:** Caribbean Fauna
Obv: National arms within wreath, denomination below
Rev: Multicolored Yellow Perch

Date	Mintage	F	VF	XF	Unc	BU
1996	10,000	—	—	—	20.00	—

KM# 614 PESO
25.9100 Copper-Nickel, 37.9 mm. **Subject:** 40th Anniversary of the "Granma" Landing **Obv:** National arms within wreath, denomination below **Rev:** Portrait above ship **Edge:** Plain

Date	Mintage	F	VF	XF	Unc	BU
ND(1996)	—	Value: 15.00				

KM# 737 PESO
12.9200 g., Nickel-Bonded Steel, 32.61 mm. **Subject:** Lochnera Rosea **Obv:** National arms **Rev:** Multicolor flower **Edge:** Plain

Date	Mintage	F	VF	XF	Unc	BU
1997	5,000	—	—	—	10.00	—

KM# 551 PESO
Nickel Bonded Steel, 30 mm. **Series:** Caribbean Fauna
Obv: National arms within wreath, denomination below
Rev: Multicolored Cuban Tody Bird

Date	Mintage	F	VF	XF	Unc	BU
1996	10,000	—	—	—	20.00	—

KM# 731 PESO
25.8300 g., Copper-Nickel, 37.9 mm. **Series:** F.A.O.
Obv: National arms within wreath, denomination below
Rev: Woman picking fruit **Edge:** Plain

Date	Mintage	F	VF	XF	Unc	BU
1996	—	—	—	—	18.50	—

KM# 738 PESO
12.9200 g., Nickel-Bonded Steel, 32.61 mm. **Subject:** Bidens Pilosa **Obv:** National arms **Rev:** Multicolor flower **Edge:** Plain

Date	Mintage	F	VF	XF	Unc	BU
1997	5,000	—	—	—	10.00	—

KM# 552 PESO
Nickel Bonded Steel, 30 mm. **Series:** Caribbean Fauna
Obv: National arms within wreath, denomination below
Rev: Multicolored Wood Duck

Date	Mintage	F	VF	XF	Unc	BU
1996	10,000	—	—	—	20.00	—

KM# 619 PESO
12.9200 g., Copper-Nickel, 32.61 mm. **Subject:** Ruellia Tuberosa **Obv:** National arms **Rev:** Multicolor flower **Edge:** Plain

KM# 722 PESO
12.9200 g., Nickel-Bonded Steel, 32.61 mm. **Subject:** Hibiscus Elatus **Obv:** National arms **Rev:** Multicolored flower **Edge:** Plain

Date	Mintage	F	VF	XF	Unc	BU
1997	5,000	Value: 12.00				

KM# 617 PESO
Copper-Nickel, 37 mm. **Subject:** 30th Anniversary - Death of Ernesto Che Guevara **Obv:** National arms within wreath, denomination below **Rev:** Full figure of Guevara with rifle walking down road between anniversary dates, mountains behind

Date	Mintage	F	VF	XF	Unc	BU
1997	—	—	—	—	15.00	—

KM# 612 PESO
Copper-Nickel **Subject:** Fidel Castro's visit to the Vatican **Obv:** National arms within wreath, denomination below **Rev:** Pope and Castro meeting

Date	Mintage	F	VF	XF	Unc	BU
1997	—	—	—	—	15.00	—

KM# 618 PESO
25.8600 g., Copper-Nickel, 37.92 mm. **Subject:** Che Guevara's Death **Obv:** National arms, inscription **Rev:** Bearded portrait **Edge:** Plain

Date	Mintage	F	VF	XF	Unc	BU
ND(1997)	—	—	—	—	15.00	—

KM# 622 PESO
11.3000 g., Copper-Nickel, 30 mm. **Subject:** AIDS **Obv:** National arms within wreath, denomination below **Rev:** AIDS ribbon on silhouette before world map

Date	Mintage	F	VF	XF	Unc	BU
1998	50,000	—	—	—	15.00	—

KM# 732 PESO
25.8300 g., Copper-Nickel, 37.9 mm. **Subject:** Papal Visit **Obv:** National arms within wreath, denomination below **Rev:** Half figure of Pope John Paul II facing left, cathedral at left **Edge:** Plain

Date	Mintage	F	VF	XF	Unc	BU
1998	20,000	—	—	—	16.50	—

KM# 662 PESO
26.0000 g., Copper-Nickel, 38 mm. **Subject:** 40th Anniversary - The Triumph of the Revolution

Date	Mintage	F	VF	XF	Unc	BU
1999	10,000	—	—	—	15.00	—

KM# 663 PESO
Copper Nickel **Subject:** Hacia un Nuevo Milenio - Towards a New Millennium

Date	Mintage	F	VF	XF	Unc	BU
2000	—	—	—	—	15.00	—

KM# 664 PESO
26.0000 g., Copper Nickel, 38 mm. **Subject:** Welcome the Third Millennium

Date	Mintage	F	VF	XF	Unc	BU
2000	—	—	—	—	15.00	—

KM# 665 PESO
26.0000 g., Copper-Nickel, 38 mm. **Subject:** Welcome to the New Millennium

Date	Mintage	F	VF	XF	Unc	BU
2000	—	—	—	—	15.00	—

KM# 823 PESO
Copper-Nickel, 37.9 mm. **Series:** Shipbuilding Relics **Obv:** National arms **Rev:** Submarine "Peral" **Rev. Leg.:** RELIQUIAS DE LA NAVEGÀCIÓN

Date	Mintage	F	VF	XF	Unc	BU
2000	—	—	—	—	10.00	12.00

KM# 824 PESO
Copper-Nickel, 37.9 mm. **Series:** Shipbuilding Relics **Obv:** National arms **Rev:** Sailing ship "Juan Sebastion Elcano" **Rev. Leg.:** RELIQUIAS DE LA NAVEGÀCIÓN

Date	Mintage	F	VF	XF	Unc	BU
2000	—	—	—	—	10.00	12.00

KM# 825 PESO
Copper-Nickel, 37.9 mm. **Series:** Shipbuilding Relics **Obv:** National arms **Rev:** Ship "Galatea" **Rev. Leg.:** RELIQUIAS DE LA NAVEGÀCIÓN

Date	Mintage	F	VF	XF	Unc	BU
2000	—	—	—	—	10.00	12.00

KM# 826 PESO
Copper-Nickel, 37.9 mm. **Series:** Shipbuilding Relics **Obv:** National arms **Rev:** Steam paddleboat "BUENAVENTURA" **Rev. Leg.:** RELIQUIAS DE LA NAVEGÀCIÓN

Date	Mintage	F	VF	XF	Unc	BU
2000	—	—	—	—	10.00	12.00

KM# 827 PESO
Copper-Nickel, 37.9 mm. **Series:** Shipbuilding Relics **Obv:** National arms **Rev:** Nativity scene in center of ship's compass **Rev. Leg.:** RELIQUIAS DE LA NAVEGÀCIÓN

Date	Mintage	F	VF	XF	Unc	BU
2000	—	—	—	—	10.00	12.00

KM# 346 3 PESOS
9.0000 g., Copper-Nickel, 26.3 mm. **Subject:** Ernesto Che Guevara **Obv:** National arms within wreath, denomination below **Rev:** Head facing, date below **Note:** Shield varieties exist.

Date	Mintage	F	VF	XF	Unc	BU
1990	4,050,000	—	—	3.00	6.00	8.00
1992 Proof	500	Value: 12.50				

KM# 346a 3 PESOS
8.2000 g., Nickel Clad Steel, 26.3 mm. **Obv:** National arms within wreath, denomination below **Rev:** Head facing, date below **Note:** Shield varieties exist.

Date	Mintage	F	VF	XF	Unc	BU
1992	—	—	—	3.00	6.00	8.00
1995	—	—	—	3.00	6.00	8.00

KM# 36 5 PESOS
13.3300 g., 0.9000 Silver 0.3857 oz. ASW **Subject:** 25th Anniversary - National Bank of Cuba **Obv:** Star behind arms above 1/2 wreath, denomination below **Rev:** Multi-storied building

Date	Mintage	F	VF	XF	Unc	BU
ND(1975) Proof	50,000	Value: 16.50				

KM# 47 5 PESOS
12.0000 g., 0.9990 Silver 0.3854 oz. ASW **Subject:** First Soviet-Cuban Space Flight **Obv:** National arms within wreath, denomination below **Rev:** Shuttle orbiting planet, date below

Date	Mintage	F	VF	XF	Unc	BU
1980	10,000	—	—	—	12.50	—
1980 Proof	5,000	Value: 60.00				

KM# 48 5 PESOS
12.0000 g., 0.9990 Silver 0.3854 oz. ASW **Subject:** Moscow Olympics **Obv:** National arms within wreath, denomination **Rev:** Three small squares depict athletes

Date	Mintage	F	VF	XF	Unc	BU
1980	10,000	—	—	—	10.00	—

KM# 49 5 PESOS
12.0000 g., 0.9990 Silver 0.3854 oz. ASW **Obv:** National arms within wreath, denomination below **Rev:** Cuban flower - Mariposa

Date	Mintage	F	VF	XF	Unc	BU
1980	10,000	—	—	—	12.50	—
1980 Proof	2,000	Value: 25.00				

KM# 69 5 PESOS
12.0000 g., 0.9990 Silver 0.3854 oz. ASW **Obv:** National arms within wreath, denomination below **Rev:** Cuban flower - Azahar

Date	Mintage	F	VF	XF	Unc	BU
1981	10,000	—	—	—	12.50	—
1981 Proof	2,000	Value: 25.00				

KM# 70 5 PESOS
12.0000 g., 0.9990 Silver 0.3854 oz. ASW **Obv:** National arms within wreath, denomination below **Rev:** Cuban flower - Orquidea

Date	Mintage	F	VF	XF	Unc	BU
1981	10,000	—	—	—	12.50	—
1981 Proof	2,000	Value: 25.00				

KM# 71 5 PESOS
12.0000 g., 0.9990 Silver 0.3854 oz. ASW **Obv:** National arms within wreath, denomination below **Rev:** Columbus' ship - Nina

Date	Mintage	F	VF	XF	Unc	BU
1981	10,000	—	—	—	22.50	—
1981 Proof	1,000	Value: 60.00				

KM# 72 5 PESOS
12.0000 g., 0.9990 Silver 0.3854 oz. ASW **Obv:** National arms within wreath, denomination below **Rev:** Columbus' ship - Pinta

Date	Mintage	F	VF	XF	Unc	BU
1981	10,000	—	—	—	22.50	—
1981 Proof	1,000	Value: 60.00				

KM# 73 5 PESOS
12.0000 g., 0.9990 Silver 0.3854 oz. ASW **Obv:** National arms within wreath, denomination below **Rev:** Columbus' ship - Santa Maria

Date	Mintage	F	VF	XF	Unc	BU
1981	10,000	—	—	—	22.50	—
1981 Proof	1,000	Value: 60.00				

KM# 74 5 PESOS
12.0000 g., 0.9990 Silver 0.3854 oz. ASW **Series:** Cuban Fauna **Obv:** National arms within wreath, denomination below **Rev:** Crocodiles, date above

Date	Mintage	F	VF	XF	Unc	BU
1981	5,000	—	—	—	20.00	—
1981 Proof	1,000	Value: 35.00				

KM# 75 5 PESOS
12.0000 g., 0.9990 Silver 0.3854 oz. ASW **Series:** Cuban Fauna **Obv:** National arms within wreath, denomination below **Rev:** Emerald Hummingbird

Date	Mintage	F	VF	XF	Unc	BU
1981	5,000	—	—	—	20.00	—
1981 Proof	1,000	Value: 35.00				

KM# 76 5 PESOS
12.0000 g., 0.9990 Silver 0.3854 oz. ASW **Series:** Cuban Fauna **Obv:** National arms within wreath, denomination below **Rev:** Bee Hummingbird

Date	Mintage	F	VF	XF	Unc	BU
1981	5,000	—	—	—	20.00	—
1981 Proof	1,000	Value: 35.00				

KM# 77 5 PESOS
12.0000 g., 0.9990 Silver 0.3854 oz. ASW **Subject:** Soccer Games - Spain 1982 **Obv:** National arms within wreath, denomination below **Rev:** Soccer player

Date	Mintage	F	VF	XF	Unc	BU
1981 Proof	4,000	Value: 22.50				

KM# 78 5 PESOS
12.0000 g., 0.9990 Silver 0.3854 oz. ASW **Subject:** World Food Day - Sugar Production **Obv:** National arms within wreath, denomination below **Rev:** Sugarcane plant, date at right

Date	Mintage	F	VF	XF	Unc	BU
1981	7,000	—	—	—	18.00	—
1981 Proof	1,560	Value: 25.00				

KM# 79 5 PESOS
12.0000 g., 0.9990 Silver 0.3854 oz. ASW **Subject:** XIV Central American and Caribbean Games **Obv:** National arms within wreath, denomination below **Rev:** Animated Mascot

Date	Mintage	F	VF	XF	Unc	BU
1981	5,000	—	—	—	12.00	—
1981 Proof	2,000	Value: 32.50				

KM# 80 5 PESOS
12.0000 g., 0.9990 Silver 0.3854 oz. ASW **Subject:** XIV Central American and Caribbean Games **Obv:** National arms within wreath, denomination below **Rev:** Three athletes

Date	Mintage	F	VF	XF	Unc	BU
1981	5,000	—	—	—	12.00	—
1981 Proof	2,000	Value: 30.00				

KM# 81 5 PESOS
12.0000 g., 0.9990 Silver 0.3854 oz. ASW **Subject:** XIV Central American and Caribbean Games **Obv:** National arms within wreath, denomination below **Rev:** Boxers

Date	Mintage	F	VF	XF	Unc	BU
1981	5,000	—	—	—	12.00	—
1981 Proof	2,000	Value: 30.00				

KM# 82 5 PESOS
12.0000 g., 0.9990 Silver 0.3854 oz. ASW **Series:** Cuban Fauna **Obv:** National arms within wreath, denomination below **Rev:** Cuban Tocororo

Date	Mintage	F	VF	XF	Unc	BU
1981	5,000	—	—	—	15.00	—
1981 Proof	1,000	Value: 30.00				

KM# 83 5 PESOS
12.0000 g., 0.9990 Silver 0.3854 oz. ASW **Series:** Cuban Fauna **Obv:** National arms within wreath, denomination below **Rev:** Cuban Solenodon left, date below

Date	Mintage	F	VF	XF	Unc	BU
1981	5,000	—	—	—	15.00	—
1981 Proof	1,000	Value: 30.00				

KM# 84 5 PESOS
12.0000 g., 0.9990 Silver 0.3854 oz. ASW **Series:** Cuban Fauna **Obv:** National arms within wreath, denomination below **Rev:** Giant Garfish left, date above

Date	Mintage	F	VF	XF	Unc	BU
1981	5,000	—	—	—	15.00	—
1981 Proof	1,000	Value: 30.00				

KM# 96   5 PESOS
12.0000 g., 0.9990 Silver 0.3854 oz. ASW **Obv:** National arms within wreath, denomination below **Rev:** Bust facing, three dates

Date	Mintage	F	VF	XF	Unc	BU
1982	5,000	—	—	—	20.00	—
1982 Proof	1,000	Value: 50.00				

KM# 97   5 PESOS
12.0000 g., 0.9990 Silver 0.3854 oz. ASW **Obv:** National arms within wreath, denomination below **Rev:** Ernest Hemingway's fishing yacht

Date	Mintage	F	VF	XF	Unc	BU
1982	5,000	—	—	—	20.00	—
1982 Proof	1,000	Value: 50.00				

KM# 98   5 PESOS
12.0000 g., 0.9990 Silver 0.3854 oz. ASW **Obv:** National arms within wreath, denomination below **Rev:** Ernest Hemingway - small boat

Date	Mintage	F	VF	XF	Unc	BU
1982	5,000	—	—	—	20.00	—
1982 Proof	1,000	Value: 50.00				

KM# 99   5 PESOS
12.0000 g., 0.9990 Silver 0.3854 oz. ASW, 29.8 mm.
Obv: National arms **Rev:** Bust of Miguel De Cervantes Saavedra 3/4 right **Edge:** Reeded

Date	Mintage	F	VF	XF	Unc	BU
1982	7,000	—	—	—	15.00	—
1982 Proof	2,000	Value: 40.00				

KM# 100   5 PESOS
12.0000 g., 0.9990 Silver 0.3854 oz. ASW **Obv:** National arms within wreath, denomination below **Rev:** Hidalgo Don Quijote on horse

Date	Mintage	F	VF	XF	Unc	BU
1982	7,000	—	—	—	15.00	—
1982 Proof	2,000	Value: 40.00				

KM# 101   5 PESOS
12.0000 g., 0.9990 Silver 0.3854 oz. ASW **Subject:** Hidalgo Don Quijote and Sancho Panza **Obv:** National arms within wreath, denomination below **Rev:** Small figure on mule, larger figure with lance on horse

Date	Mintage	F	VF	XF	Unc	BU
1982	7,000	—	—	—	15.00	—
1982 Proof	2,000	Value: 40.00				

KM# 102   5 PESOS
12.0000 g., 0.9990 Silver 0.3854 oz. ASW **Series:** F.A.O. **Obv:** National arms within wreath, denomination below **Rev:** Citrus fruit

Date	Mintage	F	VF	XF	Unc	BU
1982	3,125	—	—	—	20.00	—
1982 Proof	1,040	Value: 32.50				

KM# 103   5 PESOS
12.0000 g., 0.9990 Silver 0.3854 oz. ASW **Series:** F.A.O. **Obv:** National arms within wreath, denomination below **Rev:** Cow on grass left

Date	Mintage	F	VF	XF	Unc	BU
1982	4,177	—	—	—	20.00	—
1982 Proof	1,000	Value: 32.50				

KM# 108   5 PESOS
12.0000 g., 0.9990 Silver 0.3854 oz. ASW **Series:** 1984 Winter Olympics - Hockey **Obv:** National arms within wreath, denomination below

Date	Mintage	F	VF	XF	Unc	BU
1983 Proof	5,000	Value: 15.00				

KM# 109   5 PESOS
12.0000 g., 0.9990 Silver 0.3854 oz. ASW **Series:** 1984 Summer Olympics **Obv:** National arms within wreath, denomination below **Rev:** Runner

Date	Mintage	F	VF	XF	Unc	BU
1983 Proof	5,000	Value: 15.00				

KM# 110   5 PESOS
12.0000 g., 0.9990 Silver 0.3854 oz. ASW **Obv:** National arms within wreath, denomination below **Rev:** Train on track, date below

Date	Mintage	F	VF	XF	Unc	BU
1983	5,000	—	—	—	15.00	—
1983 Proof	2,000	Value: 30.00				

KM# 111   5 PESOS
12.0000 g., 0.9990 Silver 0.3854 oz. ASW **Subject:** World Fisheries **Obv:** National arms within wreath, denomination below **Rev:** Spiny lobster

Date	Mintage	F	VF	XF	Unc	BU
1983	5,000	—	—	—	20.00	—
1983 Proof	1,000	Value: 40.00				

KM# 112   5 PESOS
12.0000 g., 0.9990 Silver 0.3854 oz. ASW **Subject:** Winter Olympics **Obv:** National arms within wreath, denomination below **Rev:** Woman holding torch

Date	Mintage	F	VF	XF	Unc	BU
1983 Proof	5,000	Value: 15.00				

KM# 113   5 PESOS
12.0000 g., 0.9990 Silver 0.3854 oz. ASW **Series:** Winter Olympics **Obv:** National arms within wreath, denomination below **Rev:** Downhill skier

Date	Mintage	F	VF	XF	Unc	BU
1983 Proof	5,000	Value: 15.00				

KM# 114   5 PESOS
12.0000 g., 0.9990 Silver 0.3854 oz. ASW **Series:** Summer Olympics **Obv:** National arms within wreath, denomination below **Rev:** Discus thrower

Date	Mintage	F	VF	XF	Unc	BU
1983 Proof	5,000	Value: 15.00				

KM# 115   5 PESOS
12.0000 g., 0.9990 Silver 0.3854 oz. ASW **Series:** Summer Olympics **Obv:** National arms within wreath, denomination below **Rev:** Judo match, date at right

Date	Mintage	F	VF	XF	Unc	BU
1983 Proof	5,000	Value: 15.00				

KM# 117   5 PESOS
12.0000 g., 0.9990 Silver 0.3854 oz. ASW **Subject:** Transportation **Obv:** National arms within wreath, denomination below **Rev:** Freighter, date below

Date	Mintage	F	VF	XF	Unc	BU
1984	5,000	—	—	—	18.00	—
1984 Proof	1,000	Value: 40.00				

KM# 119   5 PESOS
12.0000 g., 0.9990 Silver 0.3854 oz. ASW **Obv:** National arms within wreath, denomination below **Rev:** Santisimo Trinidad, date at left

Date	Mintage	F	VF	XF	Unc	BU
1984	5,000	—	—	—	18.00	—

KM# 131   5 PESOS
12.0000 g., 0.9990 Silver 0.3854 oz. ASW **Subject:** Transportation **Obv:** National arms within wreath, denomination below **Rev:** Volanta coach

Date	Mintage	F	VF	XF	Unc	BU
1984	5,000	—	—	—	14.00	—
1984 Proof	1,000	Value: 40.00				

KM# 666   5 PESOS
12.0000 g., 0.9990 Silver 0.3854 oz. ASW **Subject:** Transportation **Obv:** National arms within wreath, denomination below **Rev:** Hot air balloon

Date	Mintage	F	VF	XF	Unc	BU
1984	2	—	—	—	4,000	—

KM# 141   5 PESOS
12.0000 g., 0.9990 Silver 0.3854 oz. ASW **Subject:** Fortress - El Morro La Habana **Obv:** National arms within wreath, denomination below **Rev:** Fortress, date at left

Date	Mintage	F	VF	XF	Unc	BU
1984	5,000	—	—	—	15.00	—
1984 Proof	1,000	Value: 45.00				

KM# 143   5 PESOS
12.0000 g., 0.9990 Silver 0.3854 oz. ASW **Subject:** La Fuerza La Habana **Obv:** National arms within wreath, denomination below **Rev:** Fortress

Date	Mintage	F	VF	XF	Unc	BU
1984	5,000	—	—	—	15.00	—
1984 Proof	1,000	Value: 45.00				

KM# 145   5 PESOS
12.0000 g., 0.9990 Silver 0.3854 oz. ASW **Subject:** El Morro Santiago De Cuba **Obv:** National arms within wreath, denomination below **Rev:** Fortress

Date	Mintage	F	VF	XF	Unc	BU
1984	5,000	—	—	—	15.00	—
1984 Proof	1,000	Value: 45.00				

KM# 121   5 PESOS
12.0000 g., 0.9990 Silver 0.3854 oz. ASW **Subject:** International Year of Music - Bach

Date	Mintage	F	VF	XF	Unc	BU
1985	2,000	—	—	—	32.50	—
1985 Proof		Value: 45.00				

KM# 123   5 PESOS
12.0000 g., 0.9990 Silver 0.3854 oz. ASW, 29.83 mm. **Subject:** XIII World Football Championship - Mexico 1986 **Obv:** National arms **Rev:** Two soccer players **Edge:** Reeded

Date	Mintage	F	VF	XF	Unc	BU
1985	5,000	—	—	—	18.00	—
1985 Proof		Value: 35.00				

KM# 125   5 PESOS
12.0000 g., 0.9990 Silver 0.3854 oz. ASW **Subject:** Wildlife Preservation **Obv:** National arms within wreath, denomination below **Rev:** Cuban crocodile

Date	Mintage	F	VF	XF	Unc	BU
1985	5,000	—	—	—	40.00	—

KM# 127   5 PESOS
12.0000 g., 0.9990 Silver 0.3854 oz. ASW **Subject:** Wildlife Preservation **Obv:** National arms within wreath, denomination below **Rev:** Cuban Rock Iguana

Date	Mintage	F	VF	XF	Unc	BU
1985	5,000	—	—	—	40.00	—

KM# 129   5 PESOS
12.0000 g., 0.9990 Silver 0.3854 oz. ASW **Subject:** Wildlife Preservation **Obv:** National arms within wreath, denomination below **Rev:** Cuban Amazon Parrot

Date	Mintage	F	VF	XF	Unc	BU
1985	5,000	—	—	—	35.00	—

KM# 146   5 PESOS
12.0000 g., 0.9990 Silver 0.3854 oz. ASW **Subject:** 40th Anniversary of F.A.O. **Obv:** National arms within wreath, denomination below **Rev:** Lobster, palm tree, and sugar cane

Date	Mintage	F	VF	XF	Unc	BU
ND(1985)	4,500	—	—	—	15.00	—
ND(1985) Proof	500	Value: 45.00				

KM# 147   5 PESOS
12.0000 g., 0.9990 Silver 0.3854 oz. ASW **Series:** F.A.O. **Subject:** Forestry **Obv:** National arms within wreath, denomination below **Rev:** Stylized forest

Date	Mintage	F	VF	XF	Unc	BU
ND(1985)	4,500	—	—	—	15.00	—
ND(1985) Proof	500	Value: 40.00				

KM# 135   5 PESOS
12.0000 g., 0.9990 Silver 0.3854 oz. ASW **Subject:** 100th Anniversary of the Automobile **Obv:** National arms within wreath, denomination below **Rev:** Daimler-Benz

Date	Mintage	F	VF	XF	Unc	BU
ND(1986)	2,500	—	—	—	22.50	—

KM# 137   5 PESOS
12.0000 g., 0.9990 Silver 0.3854 oz. ASW **Subject:** 30th Anniversary - Voyage of the Granma **Obv:** National arms within wreath, denomination below **Rev:** Large ship at sea, dates

Date	Mintage	F	VF	XF	Unc	BU
ND(1986)	2,500	—	—	—	20.00	—

KM# 139   5 PESOS
12.0000 g., 0.9990 Silver 0.3854 oz. ASW **Series:** Olympics **Obv:** National arms within wreath, denomination below **Rev:** Skater

Date	Mintage	F	VF	XF	Unc	BU
1986	2,500	—	—	—	30.00	—

KM# 199   5 PESOS
12.0000 g., 0.9990 Silver 0.3854 oz. ASW **Series:** Olympics **Obv:** National arms within wreath, denomination below **Rev:** Without rings above skater

Date	Mintage	F	VF	XF	Unc	BU
1986	10,000	—	—	—	12.00	—

KM# 157 5 PESOS
12.0000 g., 0.9990 Silver 0.3854 oz. ASW **Series:** F.A.O.
Subject: International Year of Peace **Obv:** National arms within wreath, denomination below

Date	Mintage	F	VF	XF	Unc	BU
1986	10,000	—	—	—	22.50	—
1986 Proof	2,000	Value: 32.50				

KM# 149 5 PESOS
12.0000 g., 0.9990 Silver 0.3854 oz. ASW **Subject:** Cathedral in Santiago **Obv:** National arms within wreath, denomination below **Rev:** Cathedral, date above

Date	Mintage	F	VF	XF	Unc	BU
1987	2,500	—	—	—	25.00	—

KM# 151 5 PESOS
12.0000 g., 0.9990 Silver 0.3854 oz. ASW **Subject:** Cathedral in Caridad del Cobre **Obv:** National arms within wreath, denomination below **Rev:** Cathedral

Date	Mintage	F	VF	XF	Unc	BU
1987	2,500	—	—	—	25.00	—

KM# 153 5 PESOS
12.0000 g., 0.9990 Silver 0.3854 oz. ASW **Subject:** Cathedral in Trinidad **Obv:** National arms within wreath, denomination below **Rev:** Cathedral

Date	Mintage	F	VF	XF	Unc	BU
1987	2,500	—	—	—	25.00	—

KM# 155 5 PESOS
12.0000 g., 0.9990 Silver 0.3854 oz. ASW **Subject:** 40th Anniversary - Expedition of Kon-Tiki **Obv:** National arms within wreath, denomination below **Rev:** Full masted ships, dates

Date	Mintage	F	VF	XF	Unc	BU
ND(1987)	5,000	—	—	—	20.00	—

KM# 159 5 PESOS
12.0000 g., 0.9990 Silver 0.3854 oz. ASW **Subject:** 20th Anniversary - Demise of Ernesto Che Guevara **Obv:** National arms within wreath, denomination below **Rev:** Bust facing divides dates

Date	Mintage	F	VF	XF	Unc	BU
ND(1987)	5,000	—	—	—	35.00	—
ND(1987) Proof	200	Value: 150				

KM# 161 5 PESOS
12.0000 g., 0.9990 Silver 0.3854 oz. ASW **Subject:** 70th Anniversary - Bolshevik Revolution **Obv:** National arms within wreath, denomination below **Rev:** Ship at sea, date at right

Date	Mintage	F	VF	XF	Unc	BU
1987	3,000	—	—	—	22.50	—
1987 Proof	1,000	Value: 45.00				

KM# 166 5 PESOS
12.0000 g., 0.9990 Silver 0.3854 oz. ASW **Subject:** 100th Anniversary - Souvenir Peso **Obv:** National arms within wreath, denomination **Rev:** Head right

Date	Mintage	F	VF	XF	Unc	BU
1987	3,000	—	—	—	25.00	—

KM# 326 5 PESOS
12.0000 g., 0.9990 Silver 0.3854 oz. ASW **Subject:** Abolition of Slavery **Obv:** National arms within wreath, denomination **Rev:** Slave breaking chains, dates

Date	Mintage	F	VF	XF	Unc	BU
1987	2,000	—	—	—	32.50	—

KM# 180 5 PESOS
12.0000 g., 0.9990 Silver 0.3854 oz. ASW **Subject:** Jose Capablanca Chess Championship - Player **Obv:** National arms within wreath, denomination below **Rev:** Man with chessboard, dates at right

Date	Mintage	F	VF	XF	Unc	BU
ND	5,000	—	—	—	22.50	—

KM# 185 5 PESOS
12.0000 g., 0.9990 Silver 0.3854 oz. ASW **Subject:** Soccer - Mexico 1986 **Obv:** National arms within wreath, denomination below **Rev:** Soccer players, date at left

Date	Mintage	F	VF	XF	Unc	BU
1988	5,000	—	—	—	16.50	—
1988 Proof	—	Value: 30.00				

KM# 216 5 PESOS
6.0000 g., 0.9990 Silver 0.1927 oz. ASW **Subject:** Soccer - Italy 1990 **Obv:** Three towers above key on crowned shield within wreath **Rev:** Soccer players, date above

Date	Mintage	F	VF	XF	Unc	BU
1988	—	—	—	—	12.00	—

KM# 216a 5 PESOS
12.0000 g., 0.9990 Silver 0.3854 oz. ASW **Subject:** Soccer - Italy 1990 **Obv:** Three towers above key on crowned shield within wreath **Rev:** Soccer players, two dates

Date	Mintage	F	VF	XF	Unc	BU
1988	5,000	—	—	—	—	—

Note: Existence in doubt.

KM# 217 5 PESOS
12.0000 g., 0.9990 Silver 0.3854 oz. ASW **Subject:** Soccer - West Germany **Obv:** Three towers above key on crowned shield within wreath, denomination below **Rev:** Three players

Date	Mintage	F	VF	XF	Unc	BU
1988	5,000	—	—	—	18.50	—

KM# 218 5 PESOS
12.0000 g., 0.9990 Silver 0.3854 oz. ASW **Subject:** Soccer - West Germany **Obv:** Three towers above key on crowned shield within wreath, denomination below **Rev:** Four players

Date	Mintage	F	VF	XF	Unc	BU
1988	5,000	—	—	—	18.50	—

KM# 219   5 PESOS
16.0000 g., 0.9990 Silver 0.5139 oz. ASW   **Subject:** 40th Anniversary - Cuban National Ballet **Obv:** National arms within wreath, denomination **Rev:** Head of Alicia Alonso right, ballet dancer, dates below

Date	Mintage	F	VF	XF	Unc	BU
ND(1988) Proof	2,000	Value: 47.50				

KM# 220.1   5 PESOS
16.0000 g., 0.9990 Silver 0.5139 oz. ASW   **Obv:** National arms within wreath, denomination **Rev:** Graf Zeppelin

Date	Mintage	F	VF	XF	Unc	BU
1988 Proof	3,000	Value: 200				

KM# 220.2   5 PESOS
15.9400 g., 0.9990 Silver 0.5119 oz. ASW   **Obv:** National arms within wreath, thicker wreath **Rev:** Graf Zeppelin

Date	Mintage	F	VF	XF	Unc	BU
1988 Proof	—	Value: 120				

KM# 221   5 PESOS
16.0000 g., 0.9990 Silver 0.5139 oz. ASW   **Obv:** National arms within wreath, denomination below **Rev:** Carlos J. Finlay

Date	Mintage	F	VF	XF	Unc	BU
ND(1988) Proof	2,000	Value: 47.50				

KM# 222   5 PESOS
16.0000 g., 0.9990 Silver 0.5139 oz. ASW   **Subject:** World Health Organization **Obv:** National arms within wreath, denomination **Rev:** Nurse with baby, building in background

Date	Mintage	F	VF	XF	Unc	BU
ND(1988) Proof	2,000	Value: 47.50				

KM# 223   5 PESOS
16.0000 g., 0.9990 Silver 0.5139 oz. ASW   **Subject:** 150th Anniversary - Grand National Theater in Havana **Obv:** National arms within wreath, denomination below **Rev:** Theater building, dates and inscription at left

Date	Mintage	F	VF	XF	Unc	BU
ND(1988) Proof	2,000	Value: 55.00				

KM# 224.1   5 PESOS
16.0000 g., 0.9990 Silver 0.5139 oz. ASW   **Series:** Olympics - Barcelona **Obv:** National arms within wreath, plain bars **Rev:** Boxing

Date	Mintage	F	VF	XF	Unc	BU
1989 Proof	10,000	Value: 30.00				

KM# 224.2   5 PESOS
16.0000 g., 0.9990 Silver 0.5139 oz. ASW   **Subject:** Olympics - Barcelona **Obv:** National arms within wreath, striped bars **Rev:** Boxing

Date	Mintage	F	VF	XF	Unc	BU
1989 Proof	Inc. above	Value: 30.00				

KM# 225.1   5 PESOS
16.0000 g., 0.9990 Silver 0.5139 oz. ASW   **Series:** Olympics - Italy **Obv:** Small thin towers, lower relief, larger rectangular indentations in the tower and the crown **Rev:** Three soccer players

Date	Mintage	F	VF	XF	Unc	BU
1989 Proof	10,000	Value: 30.00				

KM# 225.2   5 PESOS
16.0000 g., 0.9990 Silver 0.5139 oz. ASW   **Subject:** Olympics - Italy **Obv:** Large, thick towers, higher relief, smaller oval indentations in the tower and the crown **Rev:** Three players

Date	Mintage	F	VF	XF	Unc	BU
1989 Proof	Inc. above	Value: 30.00				

KM# 226.1   5 PESOS
16.0000 g., 0.9990 Silver 0.5139 oz. ASW   **Series:** Olympics - Italy **Obv:** Small, thin towers, lower relief, larger rectangular indentations in the towers and crown **Rev:** Colosseum

Date	Mintage	F	VF	XF	Unc	BU
1989 Proof	10,000	Value: 32.00				

KM# 226.2   5 PESOS
16.0000 g., 0.9990 Silver 0.5139 oz. ASW   **Subject:** Olympics - Italy **Obv:** Large, thick towers, lower relief, smaller oval indentations in the towers and crown **Rev:** Colosseum

Date	Mintage	F	VF	XF	Unc	BU
1989 Proof	Inc. above	Value: 32.00				

KM# 226.3   5 PESOS
16.0000 g., 0.9990 Silver 0.5139 oz. ASW   **Subject:** Olympics - Italy **Obv:** High relief **Rev:** Colosseum

Date	Mintage	F	VF	XF	Unc	BU
1989 Proof	Inc. above	Value: 35.00				

KM# 227.1   5 PESOS
16.0000 g., 0.9990 Silver 0.5139 oz. ASW   **Subject:** Cuban tobacco **Obv:** Arms with plain field at lower right, thin wreath surrounds, denomination below **Rev:** Native smoking above tobacco plant, parrot at right, date below

Date	Mintage	F	VF	XF	Unc	BU
1989 Proof	2,000	Value: 55.00				

KM# 227.2   5 PESOS
16.0000 g., 0.9990 Silver 0.5139 oz. ASW   **Subject:** Cuban tobacco **Obv:** Arms with striped field at lower right, thick wreath **Rev:** Native smoking above tobacco plant, parrot at right, date below

Date	Mintage	F	VF	XF	Unc	BU
1989 Proof	Inc. above	Value: 55.00				

KM# 231   5 PESOS
16.0000 g., 0.9990 Silver 0.5139 oz. ASW   **Subject:** Alexander von Humboldt **Obv:** National arms within wreath, denomination **Rev:** Bust in cameo left of birds, dates

Date	Mintage	F	VF	XF	Unc	BU
1989 Proof	3,000	Value: 50.00				

KM# 251.1   5 PESOS
16.0000 g., 0.9990 Silver 0.5139 oz. ASW   **Subject:** Universal Congress of Esperanto **Obv:** Arms with plain field at lower right, thin wreath surrounds, denomination below **Rev:** Bust to right of globe looking left, date below

Date	Mintage	F	VF	XF	Unc	BU
1990 Proof	6,000	Value: 45.00				

KM# 251.2   5 PESOS
16.0000 g., 0.9990 Silver 0.5139 oz. ASW   **Subject:** Universal Congress of Esperanto **Obv:** Arms with striped field at lower right, thick wreath **Rev:** Bust to right of globe looking left

Date	Mintage	F	VF	XF	Unc	BU
1990 Proof	Inc. above	Value: 45.00				

KM# 290.1   5 PESOS
16.0000 g., 0.9990 Silver 0.5139 oz. ASW   **Subject:** Soccer **Obv:** Small, thin towers, lower relief, larger rectangular indentations in the towers and crown **Rev:** Map of Italy and soccer balls

Date	Mintage	F	VF	XF	Unc	BU
1990 Proof	10,000	Value: 30.00				

KM# 290.2   5 PESOS
16.0000 g., 0.9990 Silver 0.5139 oz. ASW   **Subject:** Soccer **Obv:** Large, thick towers, higher relief, smaller oval indentations in the towers and the crown **Rev:** Map of Italy and soccer balls

Date	Mintage	F	VF	XF	Unc	BU
1990 Proof	Inc. above	Value: 30.00				

KM# 290.3   5 PESOS
16.0000 g., 0.9990 Silver 0.5139 oz. ASW   **Subject:** Soccer **Obv:** National arms within wreath, denomination **Rev:** Map of Italy and soccer balls **Note:** Mule

Date	Mintage	F	VF	XF	Unc	BU
1990 Proof	—	Value: 100				

KM# 338   5 PESOS
12.0000 g., 0.9990 Silver 0.3854 oz. ASW   **Subject:** Soccer Championship **Obv:** National arms within wreath, denomination **Rev:** Two players

Date	Mintage	F	VF	XF	Unc	BU
1991 Proof	10,000	—	—	—	30.00	—

KM# 405   5 PESOS
6.0000 g., 0.9990 Silver 0.1927 oz. ASW   **Series:** Prehistoric Animals **Obv:** National arms within wreath, denomination below **Rev:** Apatosaurus

Date	Mintage	F	VF	XF	Unc	BU
1993 Proof	30,000	Value: 27.50				

KM# 524.1   5 PESOS
15.0000 g., 0.9990 Silver 0.4818 oz. ASW   **Subject:** Historia Postal de Cuba Steamship **Obv:** National arms within wreath, denomination below, thin letters **Rev:** Side-wheel steamship, date below, straight end 9's

Date	Mintage	F	VF	XF	Unc	BU
1993 Proof	25,000	Value: 25.00				

KM# 524.2   5 PESOS
15.0000 g., 0.9990 Silver 0.4818 oz. ASW   **Subject:** Historia Postal de Cuba Steamship **Obv:** National arms, thin letters and wreath **Rev:** Side-wheel steamship, curved end 9's in date

Date	Mintage	F	VF	XF	Unc	BU
1993 Proof	Inc. above	Value: 25.00				

KM# 524.4   5 PESOS
15.0000 g., 0.9990 Silver 0.4818 oz. ASW   **Subject:** Historia Postal de Cuba Steamship **Obv:** National arms, thin letters and wreath, large (5mm) gap between 15 and G **Rev:** Side-Wheel steamship, curved end 9's in date

Date	Mintage	F	VF	XF	Unc	BU
1993 Proof	—	Value: 50.00				

KM# 524.3   5 PESOS
15.0000 g., 0.9990 Silver 0.4818 oz. ASW, 33 mm.   **Subject:** Historia Postal de Cuba Steamship **Obv:** National arms, thick letters and wreath **Rev:** Side-wheel steamship, curved end 9's in date **Edge:** Reeded

Date	Mintage	F	VF	XF	Unc	BU
1993 Proof	—	Value: 50.00				

KM# 440   5 PESOS
16.0000 g., 0.9990 Silver 0.5139 oz. ASW   **Series:** Prehistoric Animals **Obv:** National arms within wreath, denomination below **Rev:** Triceratops

Date	Mintage	F	VF	XF	Unc	BU
1994 Proof	10,000	Value: 50.00				

KM# 573   5 PESOS
16.0000 g., 0.9990 Silver 0.5139 oz. ASW   **Series:** Prehistoric Animals **Obv:** National arms within wreath, denomination below **Rev:** Maiasaura

Date	Mintage	F	VF	XF	Unc	BU
1994 Proof	—	Value: 50.00				

KM# 581   5 PESOS
7.0000 g., 0.9990 Silver 0.2248 oz. ASW   **Obv:** National arms within wreath, denomination below **Rev:** Multicolored hibiscus

Date	Mintage	F	VF	XF	Unc	BU
1997 Proof	—	Value: 20.00				

KM# 623   5 PESOS
7.0000 g., 0.9990 Silver 0.2248 oz. ASW, 30 mm.   **Subject:** AIDS **Obv:** National arms within wreath, denomination below **Rev:** AIDS ribbon on silhouette before world map

Date	Mintage	F	VF	XF	Unc	BU
1998 Proof	50,000	Value: 18.50				

KM# 655   5 PESOS
7.0000 g., 0.9990 Silver 0.2248 oz. ASW   **Subject:** Expo 2000 - Philadelphia **Obv:** National arms within wreath, denomination below **Rev:** Cartoon above building

Date	Mintage	F	VF	XF	Unc	BU
1999 Proof	31,250	Value: 16.50				

KM# 656   5 PESOS
7.0000 g., 0.9990 Silver 0.2248 oz. ASW   **Subject:** Expo 2000 - Hannover **Obv:** National arms within wreath, denomination below **Rev:** Cartoon above city hall

Date	Mintage	F	VF	XF	Unc	BU
1999 Proof	31,250	Value: 16.50				

KM# 657   5 PESOS
7.0000 g., 0.9990 Silver 0.2248 oz. ASW   **Subject:** Expo 2000 - Osaka **Obv:** National arms within wreath, denomination below **Rev:** Cartoon above city view

Date	Mintage	F	VF	XF	Unc	BU
1999 Proof	31,250	Value: 16.50				

KM# 658   5 PESOS
7.0000 g., 0.9990 Silver 0.2248 oz. ASW   **Subject:** Expo 2000 - Montreal **Obv:** National arms within wreath, denomination below **Rev:** Cartoon above sports buildings

Date	Mintage	F	VF	XF	Unc	BU
1999 Proof	31,250	Value: 16.50				

KM# 659   5 PESOS
7.0000 g., 0.9990 Silver 0.2248 oz. ASW   **Subject:** Expo 2000 - Twipsy **Obv:** National arms within wreath, denomination below **Rev:** "Twipsy" in square

Date	Mintage	F	VF	XF	Unc	BU
1999 Proof	31,250	Value: 16.50				

KM# 660   5 PESOS
7.0000 g., 0.9990 Silver 0.2248 oz. ASW   **Subject:** Expo 2000 **Obv:** National arms within wreath, denomination below **Rev:** World map with logo center square

Date	Mintage	F	VF	XF	Unc	BU
1999 Proof	31,250	Value: 16.50				

KM# 673   5 PESOS
1.5500 g., 0.9990 Gold 0.0498 oz. AGW, 14 mm.   **Subject:** Zunzuncita **Obv:** National arms within wreath, denomination **Rev:** Hummingbird

Date	Mintage	F	VF	XF	Unc	BU
Proof						
1999 Proof	1,000	Value: 75.00				

KM# 37   10 PESOS
26.6600 g., 0.9000 Silver 0.7714 oz. ASW   **Subject:** 25th Anniversary - National Bank of Cuba **Obv:** Star behind national arms above half wreat, denomination below **Rev:** Multi-storied building

Date	Mintage	F	VF	XF	Unc	BU
1975 Proof	55,000	Value: 32.50				

KM# 50 10 PESOS
18.0000 g., 0.9990 Silver 0.5781 oz. ASW **Subject:** First Soviet-Cuban Space Flight **Obv:** National arms within wreath, denomination below **Rev:** Shuttle orbiting planet, date below

Date	Mintage	F	VF	XF	Unc	BU
1980	10,000	—	—	—	20.00	
1980 Proof	5,000	Value: 40.00				
1980 Matte proof	—				45.00	

KM# 51 10 PESOS
18.0000 g., 0.9990 Silver 0.5781 oz. ASW **Subject:** Moscow Olympics **Obv:** National arms within wreath, denomination **Rev:** Three athletic symbols in relief, date below

Date	Mintage	F	VF	XF	Unc	BU
1980	10,000	—	—	—	15.00	
1980 Matte proof	—	Value: 65.00				

KM# 162 10 PESOS
31.1000 g., 0.9990 Silver 0.9988 oz. ASW **Subject:** Triumph of the Revolution **Obv:** National arms on star background above half wreath, denomination below **Rev:** Castro with revolutionaries divide dates

Date	Mintage	F	VF	XF	Unc	BU
1987 Proof	2,000	Value: 47.50				
1988 Proof	4,000	Value: 37.50				
1989 Proof	2,000	Value: 47.50				

KM# 163 10 PESOS
31.1000 g., 0.9990 Silver 0.9988 oz. ASW **Subject:** 60th Anniversary - Birth of Ernesto Che Guevara **Obv:** National arms on star background above half wreath, denomination below **Rev:** Bust right, date at left

Date	Mintage	F	VF	XF	Unc	BU
1987 Proof	2,000	Value: 55.00				
1988 Proof	4,000	Value: 45.00				
1989 Proof	2,000	Value: 55.00				

KM# 164 10 PESOS
31.1000 g., 0.9990 Silver 0.9988 oz. ASW **Subject:** 30th Anniversary - The March to Victory **Obv:** National arms on star background above half wreath, denomination below **Rev:** Uniformed figures on march

Date	Mintage	F	VF	XF	Unc	BU
1987 Proof	2,000	Value: 47.50				
1988 Proof	4,000	Value: 37.50				
1989 Proof	2,000	Value: 47.50				

KM# 205 10 PESOS
31.1000 g., 0.9990 Silver 0.9988 oz. ASW **Subject:** 150th Anniversary - First Railroad in Spanish America **Obv:** National arms on star background above half wreath, denomination below **Rev:** Train engine on track divides dates

Date	Mintage	F	VF	XF	Unc	BU
1988 Proof	5,000	Value: 45.00				

KM# 206 10 PESOS
31.1000 g., 0.9990 Silver 0.9988 oz. ASW **Subject:** 140th Anniversary - First Railroad in Spain **Obv:** National arms on star background above half wreath, denomination below **Rev:** Train on track, dates below

Date	Mintage	F	VF	XF	Unc	BU
1988 Proof	5,000	Value: 45.00				

KM# 207 10 PESOS
31.1000 g., 0.9990 Silver 0.9988 oz. ASW **Subject:** 160th Anniversary - World's First Railroad **Obv:** National arms on star background above half wreath, denomination below **Rev:** Railroad carts divide dates

Date	Mintage	F	VF	XF	Unc	BU
1988 Proof	5,000	Value: 45.00				

KM# 211 10 PESOS
3.1100 g., 0.9990 Gold 0.0999 oz. AGW **Obv:** National arms within wreath, denomination below **Rev:** Jose Marti

Date	Mintage	F	VF	XF	Unc	BU
1988	50	—	—	—	140	250
1988 Proof	10	Value: 250				
1989	50	—	—	—	140	250
1989 Proof	15	Value: 250				
1990	15	—	—	—	140	250
1990 Proof	12	Value: 250				

KM# 228 10 PESOS
31.1000 g., 0.9990 Silver 0.9988 oz. ASW **Subject:** Tania La Guerrillera, Argentinian revolutionary **Obv:** National arms on star background above half wreath, denomination below **Rev:** Bust facing

Date	Mintage	F	VF	XF	Unc	BU
1988 Proof	5,000	Value: 45.00				

KM# 229 10 PESOS
31.1000 g., 0.9990 Silver 0.9988 oz. ASW **Subject:** Camilo Cienfuegos **Obv:** National arms on star background above half wreath, denomination below **Rev:** Bust facing

Date	Mintage	F	VF	XF	Unc	BU
1988 Proof	5,000	Value: 45.00				

KM# 230 10 PESOS
31.1000 g., 0.9990 Silver 0.9988 oz. ASW **Subject:** 35th Anniversary - Assault of the Moncada Garrison **Obv:** National arms on star background above half wreat, denomination below **Rev:** Armed figures, dates below

Date	Mintage	F	VF	XF	Unc	BU
ND(1988) Proof	5,000	Value: 42.50				

KM# 238 10 PESOS
20.0000 g., 0.9990 Silver 0.6423 oz. ASW **Subject:** 5th Centennial - Discovery of America **Obv:** National arms within wreath, denomination below **Rev:** Three ships at sea, date below and at left

Date	Mintage	F	VF	XF	Unc	BU
1989	3,145	—	—	—	47.50	—

KM# 239 10 PESOS
26.7200 g., 0.9990 Silver 0.8582 oz. ASW **Subject:** 200th Anniversary of French Revolution - Lady Justice **Obv:** National arms within wreath, denomination below **Rev:** 3/4 Figure of Lady Justice, dates above

Date	Mintage	F	VF	XF	Unc	BU
ND(1989)	500	—	—	—	75.00	—
ND(1989) Proof	2,000	Value: 50.00				

KM# 240 10 PESOS
26.7200 g., 0.9990 Silver 0.8582 oz. ASW **Subject:** 200th Anniversary of French Revolution **Obv:** Small national arms within wreath, denomination below **Rev:** Bastille

Date	Mintage	F	VF	XF	Unc	BU
ND(1989)	500	—	—	—	75.00	—
ND(1989) Proof	2,000	Value: 50.00				

KM# 241.1 10 PESOS
31.1000 g., 0.9990 Silver 0.9988 oz. ASW **Subject:** 30th Anniversary of Revolution **Obv:** Arms with plain field at lower right, thin wreath **Rev:** Castro

Date	Mintage	F	VF	XF	Unc	BU
ND(1989)	5,000	—	—	—	40.00	—
ND(1989) Proof	5,000	Value: 50.00				

KM# 242.1 10 PESOS
31.1000 g., 0.9990 Silver 0.9988 oz. ASW **Subject:** 30th Anniversary of Revolution **Obv:** Arms with plain field at lower right, thin wreath **Rev:** Jose Marti and Castro

Date	Mintage	F	VF	XF	Unc	BU
1989	5,000	—	—	—	40.00	—
1989 Proof	5,000	Value: 50.00				

KM# 243.1 10 PESOS
31.1000 g., 0.9990 Silver 0.9988 oz. ASW **Subject:** 30th Anniversary of Revolution **Obv:** Arms with plain field at lower right, thin wreath **Rev:** Camilo Cienfuegos and Fidel Castro, inscription above, dates at right

Date	Mintage	F	VF	XF	Unc	BU
ND(1989)	5,000	—	—	—	40.00	—
ND(1989) Proof	5,000	Value: 70.00				

KM# 249.1 10 PESOS
20.0000 g., 0.9990 Silver 0.6423 oz. ASW **Subject:** Discovery of America **Obv:** Arms with plain field at lower right, thin wreath, denomination below **Rev:** Three sailing ships, date below and at left

Date	Mintage	F	VF	XF	Unc	BU
1989 Proof	8,855	Value: 40.00				

KM# 249.2 10 PESOS
20.0000 g., 0.9990 Silver 0.6423 oz. ASW **Subject:** Discovery of America **Obv:** Arms with striped field at lower right, thick wreath **Rev:** Three sailing ships

Date	Mintage	F	VF	XF	Unc	BU
1989 Proof	Inc. above	Value: 40.00				

KM# 383 10 PESOS
3.1100 g., 0.9990 Gold 0.0999 oz. AGW **Obv:** National arms within wreath, denomination below **Rev:** Alexander von Humboldt

Date	Mintage	F	VF	XF	Unc	BU
1989	500	—	—	—	—	125
1989 Proof	—	Value: 100				

KM# 241.2 10 PESOS
31.1000 g., 0.9990 Silver 0.9988 oz. ASW **Subject:** 30th Anniversary of Revolution **Obv:** Arms with striped field at lower right, thick wreath **Rev:** Castro

Date	Mintage	F	VF	XF	Unc	BU
ND(1989)	Inc. above	—	—	—	40.00	—
ND(1989) Proof	Inc. above	Value: 50.00				

KM# 242.2 10 PESOS
31.1000 g., 0.9990 Silver 0.9988 oz. ASW **Subject:** 30th Anniversary of Revolution **Obv:** Arms with striped field at lower right, thick wreath **Rev:** Jose Marti and Castro

Date	Mintage	F	VF	XF	Unc	BU
1989	Inc. above	—	—	—	40.00	—
1989 Proof	—	Value: 70.00				

KM# 243.2 10 PESOS
31.1000 g., 0.9990 Silver 0.9988 oz. ASW **Subject:** 30th Anniversary of Revolution **Obv:** Arms with striped field at lower right, thick wreath **Rev:** Camilo Cienfuegos and Fidel Castro

Date	Mintage	F	VF	XF	Unc	BU
ND(1989)	Inc. above	—	—	—	40.00	—
ND(1989) Proof	Inc. above	Value: 50.00				

KM# 252.2 10 PESOS
20.0000 g., 0.9990 Silver 0.6423 oz. ASW **Subject:** Discovery of America **Obv:** Arms with striped field at lower right, thick wreath **Rev:** Ship and map of Cuba

Date	Mintage	F	VF	XF	Unc	BU
1990 Proof	—	Value: 40.00				

KM# 256.2 10 PESOS
20.0000 g., 0.9990 Silver 0.6423 oz. ASW **Subject:** 500th Anniversary of Columbus Meeting Native Americans **Obv:** Arms with striped field at lower right, thick wreath

Date	Mintage	F	VF	XF	Unc	BU
1990 Proof	—	Value: 40.00				

KM# 262.2 10 PESOS
31.1030 g., 0.9990 Silver 0.9989 oz. ASW **Obv:** Arms with striped bars at lower right, thick wreath **Rev:** Celia Sanchez Manduley

Date	Mintage	F	VF	XF	Unc	BU
1990 Proof	—	Value: 55.00				

KM# 267.2 10 PESOS
20.0000 g., 0.9990 Silver 0.6423 oz. ASW **Subject:** Discovery of America **Obv:** Arms with striped field at lower right, thick wreath **Rev:** Map of Columbus' route

Date	Mintage	F	VF	XF	Unc	BU
1990 Proof	—	Value: 35.00				

KM# 336.2 10 PESOS
28.0000 g., 0.9250 Silver 0.8327 oz. ASW **Subject:** Summer Olympics **Obv:** Tall (4mm) characters **Rev:** Hurdler

Date	Mintage	F	VF	XF	Unc	BU
1990 Proof	—	Value: 50.00				

KM# 344.2 10 PESOS
28.0000 g., 0.9250 Silver 0.8327 oz. ASW **Subject:** Summer Olympics **Obv:** Tall (4mm) characters **Rev:** Volleyball

Date	Mintage	F	VF	XF	Unc	BU
1990 Proof	—	Value: 100				

KM# 362.2 10 PESOS
28.0000 g., 0.9250 Silver 0.8327 oz. ASW **Subject:** Olympics **Obv:** Tall (4mm) characters **Rev:** Basketball

Date	Mintage	F	VF	XF	Unc	BU
1990 Proof	—	Value: 50.00				

KM# 252.1 10 PESOS
20.0000 g., 0.9990 Silver 0.6423 oz. ASW **Subject:** Discovery of America **Obv:** Arms with plain field at lower right, thin wreath **Rev:** Ship and map of Cuba, date at right

Date	Mintage	F	VF	XF	Unc	BU
1990 Proof	10,000	Value: 40.00				

KM# 256.1 10 PESOS
20.0000 g., 0.9990 Silver 0.6423 oz. ASW **Subject:** 500th Anniversary of Columbus Meeting Native Americans **Obv:** Arms with plain field at lower right, thin wreath **Rev:** Columbus meeting natives, date below

Date	Mintage	F	VF	XF	Unc	BU
1990 Proof	10,000	Value: 45.00				

KM# 262.1   10 PESOS
31.1030 g., 0.9990 Silver 0.9989 oz. ASW   **Obv:** Arms with plain field at lower right, thin wreath   **Rev:** Celia Sanchez Manduley

Date	Mintage	F	VF	XF	Unc	BU
1990 Proof	2,000	Value: 55.00				

KM# 263   10 PESOS
31.1030 g., 0.9990 Silver 0.9989 oz. ASW   **Subject:** Discovery of America   **Obv:** National arms within wreath, denomination   **Rev:** King Ferdinand bust 3/4 right within wreath, two dates

Date	Mintage	F	VF	XF	Unc	BU
1990 Proof	5,000	Value: 50.00				

KM# 264   10 PESOS
31.1030 g., 0.9990 Silver 0.9989 oz. ASW   **Subject:** Discovery of America   **Obv:** National arms within wreath, denomination   **Rev:** Queen Isabella

Date	Mintage	F	VF	XF	Unc	BU
1990 Proof	5,000	Value: 50.00				

KM# 265   10 PESOS
31.1030 g., 0.9990 Silver 0.9989 oz. ASW   **Subject:** Discovery of America   **Obv:** National arms within wreath, denomination below   **Rev:** Christopher Columbus

Date	Mintage	F	VF	XF	Unc	BU
1990 Proof	5,000	Value: 50.00				

KM# 266   10 PESOS
31.1030 g., 0.9990 Silver 0.9989 oz. ASW   **Subject:** Discovery of America   **Obv:** National arms within wreath, denomination below   **Rev:** Juan de la Casa

Date	Mintage	F	VF	XF	Unc	BU
1990 Proof	5,000	Value: 50.00				

KM# 267.1   10 PESOS
20.0000 g., 0.9990 Silver 0.6423 oz. ASW   **Subject:** Discovery of America   **Obv:** Arms with plain field at lower right, thin wreath   **Rev:** Map of Columbus' route

Date	Mintage	F	VF	XF	Unc	BU
1990 Proof	10,000	Value: 35.00				

KM# 280   10 PESOS
25.0000 g., 0.9990 Silver 0.8029 oz. ASW   **Subject:** Simon Bolivar   **Obv:** National arms within wreath, denomination   **Rev:** Uniformed bust right

Date	Mintage	F	VF	XF	Unc	BU
1990 Proof	3,300	Value: 47.50				

KM# 291   10 PESOS
31.1000 g., 0.9990 Silver 0.9988 oz. ASW   **Subject:** Pan American Games   **Obv:** National arms within wreath, denomination   **Rev:** High jumper

Date	Mintage	F	VF	XF	Unc	BU
1990 Proof	3,000	Value: 55.00				

KM# 292   10 PESOS
31.1000 g., 0.9990 Silver 0.9988 oz. ASW   **Subject:** Pan American Games   **Obv:** National arms within wreath, denomination   **Rev:** Volleyball

Date	Mintage	F	VF	XF	Unc	BU
1990 Proof	3,000	Value: 55.00				

KM# 293   10 PESOS
31.1000 g., 0.9990 Silver 0.9988 oz. ASW   **Subject:** Pan American Games   **Obv:** National arms within wreath, denomination   **Rev:** Baseball game scene

Date	Mintage	F	VF	XF	Unc	BU
1990 Proof	3,000	Value: 57.50				

KM# 336.1   10 PESOS
28.0000 g., 0.9250 Silver 0.8327 oz. ASW   **Series:** Summer Olympics   **Obv:** Small characters   **Rev:** Hurdler, tiny date at left

Date	Mintage	F	VF	XF	Unc	BU
1990 Proof	25,000	Value: 25.00				

KM# 342   10 PESOS
3.1100 g., 0.9990 Gold 0.0999 oz. AGW   **Series:** Olympics   **Obv:** National arms within wreath, denomination below   **Rev:** Basketball hoop, ball and hands, small date between arms below

Date	Mintage	F	VF	XF	Unc	BU
1990 Proof	Est. 5,000	Value: 110				

KM# 344.1   10 PESOS
28.0000 g., 0.9250 Silver 0.8327 oz. ASW   **Series:** Summer Olympics   **Obv:** Small characters   **Rev:** Volleyball

Date	Mintage	F	VF	XF	Unc	BU
1990 Proof	25,000	Value: 25.00				

KM# 345   10 PESOS
28.0000 g., 0.9250 Silver 0.8327 oz. ASW **Series:** Summer
Olympics **Obv:** Small characters **Rev:** High jumper

Date	Mintage	F	VF	XF	Unc	BU
1990 Proof	25,000	Value: 25.00				

KM# 362.1   10 PESOS
28.0000 g., 0.9250 Silver 0.8327 oz. ASW **Series:** Olympics
Obv: Small characters **Rev:** Basketball players

Date	Mintage	F	VF	XF	Unc	BU
1990 Proof	25,000	Value: 25.00				

KM# 369   10 PESOS
28.0000 g., 0.9990 Silver 0.8993 oz. ASW **Series:** Olympics
Rev: Figure on pommel horse, date below

Date	Mintage	F	VF	XF	Unc	BU
1990 Proof	Est. 25,000	Value: 25.00				

KM# 327   10 PESOS
31.1000 g., 0.9990 Silver 0.9988 oz. ASW **Obv:** National arms
within wreath, denomination **Rev:** Vicente and Martin Pinzon in
cameos

Date	Mintage	F	VF	XF	Unc	BU
1991 Proof	3,000	Value: 55.00				

KM# 328   10 PESOS
31.1000 g., 0.9990 Silver 0.9988 oz. ASW **Obv:** National arms
within wreath, denomination **Rev:** Hatuey tribesman

Date	Mintage	F	VF	XF	Unc	BU
1991 Proof	3,000	Value: 55.00				

KM# 329   10 PESOS
25.0000 g., 0.9990 Silver 0.8029 oz. ASW **Subject:** American
International Monetary Conference **Obv:** National arms within
wreath, denomination divided above **Rev:** Bust facing, dates below

Date	Mintage	F	VF	XF	Unc	BU
ND(1991) Proof	3,300	Value: 55.00				

KM# 337   10 PESOS
27.0000 g., 0.9990 Silver 0.8672 oz. ASW **Subject:** Ibero -
American **Obv:** National arms within wreath, denomination below
within inner circle, circle of arms surround **Rev:** Statue of
Columbus at Gardenas, dates at right

Date	Mintage	F	VF	XF	Unc	BU
1991 Proof	51,000	Value: 40.00				

KM# 348   10 PESOS
31.1000 g., 0.9990 Silver 0.9988 oz. ASW **Subject:** Madrid
Obv: National arms within wreath, denomination **Rev:** Alcala Gate

Date	Mintage	F	VF	XF	Unc	BU
1991 Proof	Est. 3,250	Value: 55.00				

KM# 349   10 PESOS
31.1000 g., 0.9990 Silver 0.9988 oz. ASW **Subject:** Seville
Obv: National arms within wreath, denomination **Rev:** La Giralda
Tower

Date	Mintage	F	VF	XF	Unc	BU
1991 Proof	Est. 3,250	Value: 55.00				

KM# 350   10 PESOS
31.1000 g., 0.9990 Silver 0.9988 oz. ASW **Subject:** Barcelona
Obv: National arms within wreath, denomination **Rev:** Olympic
Stadium

Date	Mintage	F	VF	XF	Unc	BU
1991 Proof	3,250	Value: 47.50				

KM# 525   10 PESOS
31.1000 g., 0.9990 Silver 0.9988 oz. ASW **Obv:** National arms
within wreath, denomination **Rev:** Diego Velazquez

Date	Mintage	F	VF	XF	Unc	BU
1991 Proof	3,000	Value: 55.00				

KM# 526   10 PESOS
31.1000 g., 0.9990 Silver 0.9988 oz. ASW **Subject:** 500th
Anniversary of New World **Obv:** National arms within wreath,
denomination **Rev:** Head of Queen Joanna, right, 1479-1555,
daughter of Isabella I

Date	Mintage	F	VF	XF	Unc	BU
1991 Proof	3,000	Value: 55.00				

KM# 341.1 10 PESOS
20.0000 g., 0.9990 Silver 0.6423 oz. ASW **Subject:** Postal
History of Cuba **Obv:** 1992 style national arms **Rev:** Spanish
galleon sailship, 1765 date

Date	Mintage	F	VF	XF	Unc	BU
1992 Proof	10,000	Value: 35.00				

KM# 341.2 10 PESOS
20.0000 g., 0.9990 Silver 0.6423 oz. ASW **Subject:** Postal
History **Obv:** Pre-1990 detailed, styled arms **Rev:** Sailing ship

Date	Mintage	F	VF	XF	Unc	BU
1992 Proof	—	Value: 37.50				

KM# 351 10 PESOS
31.1000 g., 0.9990 Silver 0.9988 oz. ASW **Subject:** Seville **Obv:**
National arms within wreath, denomination **Rev:** Tower of Gold

Date	Mintage	F	VF	XF	Unc	BU
1992 Proof	2,050	Value: 55.00				

KM# 352 10 PESOS
31.1000 g., 0.9990 Silver 0.9988 oz. ASW **Obv:** National arms
within wreath, denomination **Rev:** El Escorial

Date	Mintage	F	VF	XF	Unc	BU
1992 Proof	2,050	Value: 55.00				

KM# 353 10 PESOS
31.1000 g., 0.9990 Silver 0.9988 oz. ASW **Subject:** 500th
Anniversary of Philipp's rule **Obv:** National arms within wreath,
denomination **Rev:** Bust of Philip I 3/4 right, date at right, within wreath

Date	Mintage	F	VF	XF	Unc	BU
1992 Proof	3,000	Value: 55.00				

KM# 354.1 10 PESOS
20.0000 g., 0.9990 Silver 0.6423 oz. ASW **Subject:** Ptolomeo and
Toscanelli **Obv:** National arms within wreath, denomination **Rev:**
Medieval symbolic table, figure at top with globe, bust lower right

Date	Mintage	F	VF	XF	Unc	BU
1992 Proof	—	Value: 37.50				

KM# 354.2 10 PESOS
20.0000 g., 0.9990 Silver 0.6423 oz. ASW **Obv:** Arms with thick
wreath of the pre-1990 style **Rev:** Medieval symbolic table, figure
at top with globe, bust lower right

Date	Mintage	F	VF	XF	Unc	BU
1992 Proof	—	Value: 35.00				

KM# 355 10 PESOS
31.1000 g., 0.9990 Silver 0.9988 oz. ASW **Obv:** National arms
within wreath, denomination **Rev:** Guama tribesman

Date	Mintage	F	VF	XF	Unc	BU
1992 Proof	2,050	Value: 55.00				

KM# 370 10 PESOS
20.0000 g., 0.9990 Silver 0.6423 oz. ASW **Subject:** Postal
History **Obv:** National arms within wreath, denomination
Rev: Steam powered sailing ship, date below

Date	Mintage	F	VF	XF	Unc	BU
1992 Proof	10,000	Value: 37.50				

KM# 372 10 PESOS
31.0000 g., 0.9990 Silver 0.9956 oz. ASW **Obv:** National arms
within wreath, denomination below **Rev:** Seated figure left,
writing, date at left

Date	Mintage	F	VF	XF	Unc	BU
1992 Proof	2,050	Value: 50.00				

KM# 373 10 PESOS
31.0000 g., 0.9990 Silver 0.9956 oz. ASW **Subject:** Spanish
Kings and Queens **Obv:** National arms within wreath **Rev:** Two
heads left above and below banners

Date	Mintage	F	VF	XF	Unc	BU
ND(1992) Proof	2,050	Value: 55.00				

KM# 374 10 PESOS
31.0000 g., 0.9990 Silver 0.9956 oz. ASW **Subject:** San Jorge
Palace **Obv:** National arms within wreath, denomination
Rev: Palace view

Date	Mintage	F	VF	XF	Unc	BU
1992 Proof	2,050	Value: 55.00				

KM# 458.1 10 PESOS
20.0000 g., 0.9990 Silver 0.6423 oz. ASW **Subject:** World Cup
Soccer **Obv:** Arms with plain field at lower right, thin wreath, thick
characters **Rev:** Native in headdress on left, soccer player and
date at right

Date	Mintage	F	VF	XF	Unc	BU
1992 Proof	—	Value: 35.00				

KM# 458.2 10 PESOS
20.0000 g., 0.9990 Silver 0.6423 oz. ASW **Subject:** World Cup
Soccer **Obv:** Arms with plain field at lower right, thin wreath, thin
characters **Rev:** Native in headdress on left, soccer player and
date at right

Date	Mintage	F	VF	XF	Unc	BU
1992 Proof	—	Value: 35.00				

KM# 527.2 10 PESOS
20.0000 g., 0.9990 Silver 0.6423 oz. ASW **Subject:** 25th
Anniversary - Death of Ernesto Che Guevara **Obv:** Arms with
striped field at lower right, thick wreath **Rev:** Bust facing, dates

Date	Mintage	F	VF	XF	Unc	BU
ND(1992) Proof	Inc. above	Value: 45.00				

KM# 561 10 PESOS
20.0000 g., 0.9990 Silver 0.6423 oz. ASW **Subject:** Postal
History **Obv:** National arms within wreath, denomination
Rev: Old steam and sailship, date at right

Date	Mintage	F	VF	XF	Unc	BU
1992 Proof	—	Value: 37.50				

KM# 527.1 10 PESOS
20.0000 g., 0.9990 Silver 0.6423 oz. ASW **Subject:** 25th
Anniversary - Death of Ernesto Che Guevara **Obv:** Arms with
plain field at lower right, thin wreath **Rev:** Bust facing, dates

Date	Mintage	F	VF	XF	Unc	BU
ND(1992) Proof	10,000	Value: 65.00				

KM# 458.3 10 PESOS
20.0000 g., 0.9990 Silver 0.6423 oz. ASW **Subject:** World Cup
Soccer **Obv:** Arms with striped field at lower right, thick wreath
Rev: Native in headdress at left, soccer player and date at right

Date	Mintage	F	VF	XF	Unc	BU
1992 Proof	—	Value: 35.00				

KM# 371.1 10 PESOS
20.0000 g., 0.9990 Silver 0.6423 oz. ASW **Subject:** Introduction
of Africans into America **Obv:** National arms within thin wreath
Rev: Native at left, ship at sea on right

Date	Mintage	F	VF	XF	Unc	BU
1992 Proof	10,000	Value: 45.00				

KM# 371.2 10 PESOS
20.0000 g., 0.9990 Silver 0.6423 oz. ASW **Obv:** National arms
within thick wreath **Rev:** Native at left, ship at sea at right

Date	Mintage	F	VF	XF	Unc	BU
1992 Proof	—	Value: 45.00				

KM# 375.1 10 PESOS
20.0000 g., 0.9990 Silver 0.6423 oz. ASW **Obv:** Arms with plain
field at lower right, thin wreath **Rev:** President Abraham Lincoln

Date	Mintage	F	VF	XF	Unc	BU
1993 Proof	—	Value: 60.00				

KM# 398 10 PESOS
31.1000 g., 0.9990 Silver 0.9988 oz. ASW **Obv:** National arms
within wreath, denomination **Rev:** Frosted bust of Fidel Castro left

Date	Mintage	F	VF	XF	Unc	BU
1993 Proof	5,000	Value: 60.00				

KM# 399 10 PESOS
31.1000 g., 0.9990 Silver 0.9988 oz. ASW **Subject:** St. Jacobi
Obv: Two sets of shielded arms, denomination **Rev:** Armored
figure on rearing horse right

Date	Mintage	F	VF	XF	Unc	BU
1993 Proof	5,000	Value: 50.00				

KM# 407.1 10 PESOS
31.1000 g., 0.9990 Silver 0.9988 oz. ASW **Subject:** Federico
Garcia Lorca **Obv:** Arms with plain field at lower right, thin wreath
Rev: Bust facing, dates at left

Date	Mintage	F	VF	XF	Unc	BU
1993 Proof	3,300	Value: 60.00				

KM# 496 10 PESOS
19.9600 g., 0.9990 Silver 0.6411 oz. ASW **Subject:** Postal
History **Rev:** Steamship Almendares

Date	Mintage	F	VF	XF	Unc	BU
1993 Proof	—	Value: 45.00				

KM# 375.2 10 PESOS
20.0000 g., 0.9990 Silver 0.6423 oz. ASW **Obv:** Arms with striped
field at lower right, thick wreath **Rev:** President Abraham Lincoln

Date	Mintage	F	VF	XF	Unc	BU
1993 Proof	—	Value: 40.00				

KM# 407.2 10 PESOS
31.1000 g., 0.9990 Silver 0.9988 oz. ASW **Obv:** Arms with striped
field at lower right, thick wreath **Rev:** Frederico Garcia Lorca

Date	Mintage	F	VF	XF	Unc	BU
1993 Proof	Inc. above	Value: 45.00				

KM# 406.1 10 PESOS
31.1035 g., 0.9990 Silver 0.9990 oz. ASW **Obv:** Arms with plain field at lower right, thin wreath **Rev:** Bolivar and Marti

Date	Mintage	F	VF	XF	Unc	BU
1993 Proof	3,000	Value: 60.00				

KM# 406.2 10 PESOS
31.1035 g., 0.9990 Silver 0.9990 oz. ASW **Obv:** Arms with striped field at lower right, thick wreath **Rev:** Bolivar and Marti

Date	Mintage	F	VF	XF	Unc	BU
1993 Proof	Inc. above	Value: 45.00				

KM# 502.1 10 PESOS
20.0000 g., 0.9990 Silver 0.6423 oz. ASW **Series:** Caribbean Fauna **Obv:** Thin characters **Rev:** Multicolored Spotted Eagle Ray

Date	Mintage	F	VF	XF	Unc	BU
1994 Proof	10,000	Value: 45.00				

KM# 541 10 PESOS
27.0000 g., 0.9250 Silver 0.8029 oz. ASW **Subject:** Environmental Protection **Obv:** National arms within wreath, denomination **Rev:** Ivory-billed Woodpecker

Date	Mintage	F	VF	XF	Unc	BU
1994 Proof	20,000	Value: 45.00				

KM# 502.2 10 PESOS
20.0000 g., 0.9990 Silver 0.6423 oz. ASW **Subject:** Caribbean Fauna **Obv:** Thick characters **Rev:** Multicolored Spotter Eagle Ray

Date	Mintage	F	VF	XF	Unc	BU
1994 Proof	Inc. above	Value: 40.00				

KM# 408 10 PESOS
19.9600 g., 0.9990 Silver 0.6411 oz. ASW **Subject:** Montecristi Manifesto **Obv:** National arms within wreath, denomination below **Rev:** Two seated figures facing each other, date lower left

Date	Mintage	F	VF	XF	Unc	BU
1994 Proof	3,300	Value: 45.00				

KM# 427 10 PESOS
20.0000 g., 0.9990 Silver 0.6423 oz. ASW **Obv:** National arms within wreath, denomination below **Rev:** Sailing ship - LA INDIA

Date	Mintage	F	VF	XF	Unc	BU
1994 Proof	10,000	Value: 40.00				

KM# 428 10 PESOS
20.0000 g., 0.9990 Silver 0.6423 oz. ASW **Obv:** National arms within wreath, denomination below **Rev:** Sailing ship - NAO VICTORIA

Date	Mintage	F	VF	XF	Unc	BU
1994 Proof	10,000	Value: 40.00				

KM# 441 10 PESOS
20.0000 g., 0.9990 Silver 0.6423 oz. ASW **Subject:** Evangelista Island **Obv:** Map of island, small arms lower right **Rev:** Ship at sea, treasure chest, parrot

Date	Mintage	F	VF	XF	Unc	BU
1994 Proof	—	Value: 40.00				

KM# 442.1 10 PESOS
20.0000 g., 0.9990 Silver 0.6423 oz. ASW **Series:** Caribbean Fauna **Obv:** Thin characters **Rev:** Multicolored flamingos, thin water splashes

Date	Mintage	F	VF	XF	Unc	BU
1994 Proof	10,000	Value: 50.00				

KM# 442.2 10 PESOS
20.0000 g., 0.9990 Silver 0.6423 oz. ASW **Subject:** Caribbean Fauna **Obv:** Thick characters **Rev:** Multicolored flamingos, wide water splashes

Date	Mintage	F	VF	XF	Unc	BU
1994 Proof	Inc. above	Value: 40.00				

KM# 443.1 10 PESOS
20.0000 g., 0.9990 Silver 0.6423 oz. ASW **Series:** Caribbean Fauna **Obv:** Thin characters **Rev:** Multicolored Yellow Sea Bass (Coney), 7 lines in tail, slimmer fish

Date	Mintage	F	VF	XF	Unc	BU
1994 Proof	10,000	Value: 50.00				

KM# 443.2 10 PESOS
20.0000 g., 0.9990 Silver 0.6423 oz. ASW **Subject:** Caribbean Fauna **Obv:** Thin characters **Rev:** Multicolored Yellow Sea Bass (Coney), 5 lines in tail

Date	Mintage	F	VF	XF	Unc	BU
1994 Proof	Inc. above	Value: 40.00				

KM# 468 10 PESOS
20.0000 g., 0.9990 Silver 0.6423 oz. ASW **Subject:** Environmental Protection **Obv:** National arms within wreath, denomination **Rev:** Scale on left joined with tree on right, date lower right

Date	Mintage	F	VF	XF	Unc	BU
1994 Proof	Est. 5,000	Value: 45.00				

KM# 469 10 PESOS
20.0000 g., 0.9990 Silver 0.6423 oz. ASW **Series:** 1996 Olympics **Obv:** National arms within wreath, denomination **Rev:** Boxers

Date	Mintage	F	VF	XF	Unc	BU
1994 Proof	Est. 30,000	Value: 27.50				

KM# 470 10 PESOS
20.0000 g., 0.9990 Silver 0.6423 oz. ASW **Rev:** Red Baron Plane - multicolored Fokker Dr. I

Date	Mintage	F	VF	XF	Unc	BU
1994 Proof	—	Value: 55.00				

KM# 499.1 10 PESOS
20.0000 g., 0.9990 Silver 0.6423 oz. ASW **Series:** Caribbean Fauna **Obv:** Thin characters **Rev:** Multicolored bottle-nosed dolphins

Date	Mintage	F	VF	XF	Unc	BU
1994 Proof	Est. 10,000	Value: 45.00				

KM# 499.2 10 PESOS
20.0000 g., 0.9990 Silver 0.6423 oz. ASW **Subject:** Caribbean Fauna **Obv:** Thick characters **Rev:** Multicolored bottle-nosed dolphins

Date	Mintage	F	VF	XF	Unc	BU
1994 Proof	Inc. above	Value: 40.00				

KM# 500.1 10 PESOS
20.0000 g., 0.9990 Silver 0.6423 oz. ASW **Series:** Caribbean Fauna **Obv:** Thin characters **Rev:** Multicolored sailfish, smaller water splashes

Date	Mintage	F	VF	XF	Unc	BU
1994 Proof	10,000	Value: 50.00				

KM# 500.2 10 PESOS
20.0000 g., 0.9990 Silver 0.6423 oz. ASW **Subject:** Caribbean Fauna **Obv:** Thick characters **Rev:** Multicolored swordfish, larger water splashes

Date	Mintage	F	VF	XF	Unc	BU
1994 Proof	Inc. above	Value: 40.00				

KM# 501.1 10 PESOS
20.0000 g., 0.9990 Silver 0.6423 oz. ASW **Series:** Caribbean Fauna **Obv:** Thin characters **Rev:** Multicolored Brown Pelican

Date	Mintage	F	VF	XF	Unc	BU
1994 Proof	10,000	Value: 45.00				

KM# 501.2 10 PESOS
20.0000 g., 0.9990 Silver 0.6423 oz. ASW **Subject:** Caribbean Fauna **Obv:** Thick characters **Rev:** Multicolored Brown Pelican

Date	Mintage	F	VF	XF	Unc	BU
1994 Proof	Inc. above	Value: 40.00				

KM# 510.1 10 PESOS
20.0000 g., 0.9990 Silver 0.6423 oz. ASW **Subject:** World Cup Soccer **Obv:** Thin characters **Rev:** Two players with bridge in background, date above

Date	Mintage	F	VF	XF	Unc	BU
1994 Proof	Est. 10,000	Value: 40.00				

KM# 510.2 10 PESOS
20.0000 g., 0.9990 Silver 0.6423 oz. ASW **Subject:** World Cup Soccer **Obv:** Thick characters **Rev:** Two players with bridge in background, date above

Date	Mintage	F	VF	XF	Unc	BU
1994 Proof	Inc. above	Value: 40.00				

KM# 528 10 PESOS
20.0000 g., 0.9990 Silver 0.6423 oz. ASW **Obv:** National arms within wreath, denomination **Rev:** Multicolored Albatross DII fighter plane

Date	Mintage	F	VF	XF	Unc	BU
1994 Proof	—	Value: 50.00				

KM# 548 10 PESOS
Silver **Subject:** Seaplane **Obv:** National arms within wreath, denomination **Rev:** Multicolored SIAI Marchetti S55

Date	Mintage	F	VF	XF	Unc	BU
1995 Proof	15,000	Value: 50.00				

KM# 574 10 PESOS
20.0000 g., 0.9990 Silver 0.6423 oz. ASW **Subject:** Death of Jose Marti **Obv:** National arms within wreath, denomination below

Date	Mintage	F	VF	XF	Unc	BU
1995	—	—	—	—	45.00	—

KM# 600 10 PESOS
15.0000 g., 0.9990 Silver 0.4818 oz. ASW **Subject:** Caribbean Flora **Obv:** National arms within wreath, denomination below **Rev:** Multicolor flower, Ruelia tuberosa

Date	Mintage	F	VF	XF	Unc	BU
ND(1995) Proof	3,000	Value: 35.00				

KM# 478 10 PESOS
20.0000 g., 0.9990 Silver 0.6423 oz. ASW **Subject:** Pirates of the Caribbean **Obv:** National arms within wreath, denomination below **Rev:** Blackbeard within circle, date below

Date	Mintage	F	VF	XF	Unc	BU
1995 Proof	Est. 10,000	Value: 70.00				

KM# 479 10 PESOS
20.0000 g., 0.9990 Silver 0.6423 oz. ASW **Subject:** Pirates of the Caribbean **Obv:** National arms within wreath, denomination below **Rev:** Sir Henry Morgan

Date	Mintage	F	VF	XF	Unc	BU
1995 Proof	Est. 10,000	Value: 70.00				

KM# 480 10 PESOS
20.0000 g., 0.9990 Silver 0.6423 oz. ASW **Subject:** Pirates of the Caribbean **Obv:** National arms within wreath, denomination below **Rev:** Anne Bonny

Date	Mintage	F	VF	XF	Unc	BU
1995 Proof	Est. 10,000	Value: 70.00				

KM# 481   10 PESOS
20.0000 g., 0.9990 Silver 0.6423 oz. ASW **Subject:** Pirates of the Caribbean **Obv:** National arms within wreath, denomination below **Rev:** Mary Read

Date	Mintage	F	VF	XF	Unc	BU
1995 Proof	Est. 10,000			Value: 70.00		

KM# 482   10 PESOS
20.0000 g., 0.9990 Silver 0.6423 oz. ASW **Subject:** Pirates of the Caribbean **Obv:** National arms within wreath, denomination below **Rev:** Captain Kidd

Date	Mintage	F	VF	XF	Unc	BU
1995 Proof	Est. 10,000			Value: 70.00		

KM# 483   10 PESOS
20.0000 g., 0.9990 Silver 0.6423 oz. ASW **Subject:** Pirates of the Caribbean **Obv:** National arms within wreath, denomination below **Rev:** Piet Heyn

Date	Mintage	F	VF	XF	Unc	BU
1995 Proof	Est. 10,000			Value: 70.00		

KM# 511   10 PESOS
20.0000 g., 0.9990 Silver 0.6423 oz. ASW **Obv:** National arms within wreath, denomination **Rev:** Arnaldo Tamayo Mendez

Date	Mintage	F	VF	XF	Unc	BU
1995 Proof	Est. 5,000			Value: 45.00		

KM# 529   10 PESOS
20.0000 g., 0.9990 Silver 0.6423 oz. ASW **Subject:** F.A.O. 50th Anniversary **Obv:** National arms within wreath, denomination below **Rev:** Farmer plowing with two oxen, logo and dates above

Date	Mintage	F	VF	XF	Unc	BU
ND(1995) Proof	3,000			Value: 35.00		

KM# 530   10 PESOS
31.1000 g., 0.9990 Silver 0.9988 oz. ASW **Subject:** Centennial 1895-1995 **Obv:** National arms within wreath, denomination **Rev:** Sword to right of three conjoined busts right, dates below

Date	Mintage	F	VF	XF	Unc	BU
ND(1995) Proof	500			Value: 65.00		

KM# 540   10 PESOS
28.2800 g., 0.9250 Silver 0.8410 oz. ASW **Subject:** 50th Anniversary - United Nations **Obv:** National arms within wreath, denomination below **Rev:** Five persons of assorted ages and race, UN logo in front, outline of dove in back

Date	Mintage	F	VF	XF	Unc	BU
ND(1995) Proof	Est. 105,000			Value: 40.00		

KM# 584   10 PESOS
15.0000 g., 0.9990 Silver 0.4818 oz. ASW **Subject:** First Railroads - Switzerland **Obv:** National arms within wreath, denomination below **Rev:** First Swiss locomotive, date 1847-1997

Date	Mintage	F	VF	XF	Unc	BU
1996 Proof	—			Value: 32.50		

KM# 585   10 PESOS
15.0000 g., 0.9990 Silver 0.4818 oz. ASW **Subject:** El Mundo de la Aventura **Obv:** National arms within wreath, denomination below **Rev:** Multicolor submarine and cameo portrait of Capt. Nemo

Date	Mintage	F	VF	XF	Unc	BU
1996 Proof	—			Value: 40.00		

KM# 586   10 PESOS
20.0000 g., 0.9990 Silver 0.6423 oz. ASW **Subject:** Campeonato Mundial de Futbol - Francia **Obv:** National arms within wreath, denomination below **Rev:** Joan of Arc with France's flag before soccer ball

Date	Mintage	F	VF	XF	Unc	BU
1996 Proof	—			Value: 40.00		

KM# 587   10 PESOS
20.0000 g., 0.9990 Silver 0.6423 oz. ASW **Subject:** America - El Nuevo Mundo **Obv:** National arms within wreath, denomination below **Rev:** Ship and cameo portrait of Amerigo Vespucci

Date	Mintage	F	VF	XF	Unc	BU
1996 Proof	—			Value: 35.00		

KM# 588   10 PESOS
20.0000 g., 0.9990 Silver 0.6423 oz. ASW **Subject:** World Food Summit **Obv:** National arms within wreath, denomination below **Rev:** Woman picking fruit, F.A.O. logo, dates

Date	Mintage	F	VF	XF	Unc	BU
1996 Proof	—			Value: 40.00		

KM# 589   10 PESOS
31.1035 g., 0.9990 Silver 0.9990 oz. ASW **Subject:** 40th
Anniversary of the Granma's Landing **Obv:** National arms within
wreath, denomination below **Rev:** Castro's portrait above the
Granma

Date	Mintage	F	VF	XF	Unc	BU
1996 Proof	—	Value: 50.00				

KM# 553   10 PESOS
20.0000 g., 0.9990 Silver 0.6423 oz. ASW **Series:** Caribbean
Fauna **Obv:** National arms within wreath, denomination below
Rev: Multicolored Purple Throated Carib Hummingbird, right, date
at right

Date	Mintage	F	VF	XF	Unc	BU
1996 Proof	5,000	Value: 50.00				

KM# 554   10 PESOS
Silver **Series:** Caribbean Fauna **Obv:** National arms within
wreath, denomination below **Rev:** Multicolored Yellow Perch

Date	Mintage	F	VF	XF	Unc	BU
1996 Proof	5,000	Value: 45.00				

KM# 555   10 PESOS
20.0000 g., 0.9990 Silver 0.6423 oz. ASW **Series:** Caribbean
Fauna **Obv:** National arms within wreath, denomination below
Rev: Multicolored Cuban Tody Bird

Date	Mintage	F	VF	XF	Unc	BU
1996 Proof	5,000	Value: 45.00				

KM# 556   10 PESOS
20.0000 g., 0.9990 Silver 0.6423 oz. ASW **Series:** Caribbean
Fauna **Obv:** National arms within wreath, denomination below
Rev: Multicolored Wood Duck

Date	Mintage	F	VF	XF	Unc	BU
1996 Proof	5,000	—	—	—	45.00	

KM# 566   10 PESOS
20.0000 g., 0.9990 Silver 0.6423 oz. ASW **Series:** Caribbean
Fauna **Obv:** National arms within wreath, denomination below
Rev: Multicolored Papilio Butterfly

Date	Mintage	F	VF	XF	Unc	BU
1996	5,000	Value: 55.00				

KM# 563   10 PESOS
20.0000 g., 0.9990 Silver 0.6423 oz. ASW **Series:** Caribbean
Fauna **Obv:** National arms within wreath, denomination below
Rev: Multicolored Vaca Anil (Blue Cow) Fish

Date	Mintage	F	VF	XF	Unc	BU
1996 Proof	5,000	Value: 45.00				

KM# 582   10 PESOS
15.0000 g., 0.9990 Silver 0.4818 oz. ASW **Subject:** First Railroads
- Germany **Obv:** National arms within wreath, denomination below
Rev: First German locomotive, date 1835-1996

Date	Mintage	F	VF	XF	Unc	BU
1996 Proof	—	Value: 32.50				

KM# 583   10 PESOS
15.0000 g., 0.9990 Silver 0.4818 oz. ASW **Subject:** First Railroads
- Austria **Obv:** National arms within wreath, denomination below
Rev: First Austrian locomotive, date 1848-1996

Date	Mintage	F	VF	XF	Unc	BU
1996 Proof	—	Value: 32.50				

KM# 593   10 PESOS
15.0000 g., 0.9990 Silver 0.4818 oz. ASW **Subject:** Wonders
of the Ancient World **Obv:** National arms within wreath,
denomination below **Rev:** Hanging Gardens of Babylon

Date	Mintage	F	VF	XF	Unc	BU
1997 Proof	—	Value: 35.00				

KM# 594   10 PESOS
15.0000 g., 0.9990 Silver 0.4818 oz. ASW **Subject:** Wonders
of the Ancient World **Obv:** National arms within wreath,
denomination below **Rev:** Temple of Artemis

Date	Mintage	F	VF	XF	Unc	BU
1997 Proof	—	Value: 35.00				

KM# 595   10 PESOS
15.0000 g., 0.9990 Silver 0.4818 oz. ASW **Subject:** Wonders
of the Ancient World **Obv:** National arms within wreath,
denomination below **Rev:** Lighthouse of Alexandria

Date	Mintage	F	VF	XF	Unc	BU
1997 Proof	—	Value: 35.00				

KM# 596   10 PESOS
15.0000 g., 0.9990 Silver 0.4818 oz. ASW **Subject:** Wonders of
the Ancient World **Obv:** National arms within wreath, denomination
below **Rev:** Statue of Colossus of Rhodes over breakwater

Date	Mintage	F	VF	XF	Unc	BU
1997 Proof	—	Value: 35.00				

KM# 597   10 PESOS
15.0000 g., 0.9990 Silver 0.4818 oz. ASW **Subject:** Wonders of
the Ancient World **Obv:** National arms within wreath, denomination
below **Rev:** Painting above Egyptian pyramids and excavation

Date	Mintage	F	VF	XF	Unc	BU
1997 Proof	—	Value: 35.00				

KM# 598   10 PESOS
15.0000 g., 0.9990 Silver 0.4818 oz. ASW **Subject:** Wonders of the Ancient World - Temple of Jupiter **Obv:** National arms within wreath, denomination below **Rev:** Statue of Jupiter inside temple

Date	Mintage	F	VF	XF	Unc	BU
1997 Proof	—	Value: 35.00				

KM# 601   10 PESOS
15.0000 g., 0.9990 Silver 0.4818 oz. ASW **Subject:** Caribbean Flora **Obv:** National arms within wreath, denomination below **Rev:** Multicolored flower, "Cordia sebestena"

Date	Mintage	F	VF	XF	Unc	BU
1997 Proof	—	Value: 35.00				

KM# 602   10 PESOS
15.0000 g., 0.9990 Silver 0.4818 oz. ASW **Subject:** Caribbean Flora **Obv:** National arms within wreath, denomination below **Rev:** Multicolor flower, "Lochnera rosea"

Date	Mintage	F	VF	XF	Unc	BU
1997 Proof	—	Value: 35.00				

KM# 603   10 PESOS
15.0000 g., 0.9990 Silver 0.4818 oz. ASW **Subject:** Caribbena Flora **Obv:** National arms within wreath, denomination below **Rev:** Multicolored flower, "Turnera ulmifolia"

Date	Mintage	F	VF	XF	Unc	BU
1997 Proof	—	Value: 35.00				

KM# 604   10 PESOS
15.0000 g., 0.9990 Silver 0.4818 oz. ASW **Subject:** Caribbean Flora **Obv:** National arms within wreath, denomination below **Rev:** Multicolored flower, "Bidens pilosa"

Date	Mintage	F	VF	XF	Unc	BU
1997 Proof	—	Value: 35.00				

KM# 609   10 PESOS
15.0000 g., 0.9990 Silver 0.4818 oz. ASW **Subject:** Sesquicentennial of First Steam/Sail Powered Ship **Obv:** National arms within wreath, denomination below **Rev:** Ship, date

Date	Mintage	F	VF	XF	Unc	BU
1997 Proof	5,000	Value: 40.00				

KM# 613   10 PESOS
31.1035 g., 0.9990 Silver 0.9990 oz. ASW **Subject:** Castro Visit to Vatican **Obv:** National arms within wreath, denomination below **Rev:** Pope and Castro meeting

Date	Mintage	F	VF	XF	Unc	BU
1997	—	—	—	—	55.00	—

KM# 667   10 PESOS
15.0000 g., 0.9990 Silver 0.4818 oz. ASW **Subject:** 450th Anniversary - Birth of Cervantes

Date	Mintage	F	VF	XF	Unc	BU
1997 Proof	—	Value: 60.00				

KM# 625   10 PESOS
27.0000 g., 0.9250 Silver 0.8029 oz. ASW **Subject:** Ibero - American **Obv:** National arms and denomination within circle of arms **Rev:** Two rumba dancers, bongo drummer at left

Date	Mintage	F	VF	XF	Unc	BU
1997	—	—	—	—	55.00	—

KM# 723   10 PESOS
31.1035 g., 0.9990 Silver 0.9990 oz. ASW, 42 mm. **Subject:** 25th Anniversary - Ernesto Che Guevara's Death **Obv:** National arms and inscription **Rev:** Ernesto Che Guevara walking

Date	Mintage	F	VF	XF	Unc	BU
ND(1997) Proof	10,000	Value: 50.00				

KM# 724   10 PESOS
31.1035 g., 0.9990 Silver 0.9990 oz. ASW, 42 mm. **Subject:** 30th Anniversary - Ernesto Che Guevara's Death **Obv:** National arms within wreath, denomination **Rev:** Bust left **Edge:** Reeded

Date	Mintage	F	VF	XF	Unc	BU
ND(1997) Proof	10,000	Value: 50.00				

KM# 599   10 PESOS
15.0000 g., 0.9990 Silver 0.4818 oz. ASW **Subject:** Wonders of the Ancient World **Obv:** National arms within wreath, denomination below **Rev:** Mausoleum of Halicarnas

Date	Mintage	F	VF	XF	Unc	BU
1997 Proof	—	Value: 37.50				

KM# 590   10 PESOS
20.0000 g., 0.9990 Silver 0.6423 oz. ASW **Subject:** Circumnavigation of Cuba - Pinzon **Obv:** National arms within wreath, denomination below **Rev:** Sailship and cameo portrait of Vincente Pinzon

Date	Mintage	F	VF	XF	Unc	BU
1997 Proof	—	Value: 35.00				

KM# 591   10 PESOS
15.0000 g., 0.9990 Silver 0.4818 oz. ASW **Subject:** XXVII Olympics **Obv:** National arms within wreath, denomination below **Rev:** Two fencers

Date	Mintage	F	VF	XF	Unc	BU
1997 Proof	—	Value: 35.00				

KM# 592   10 PESOS
15.0000 g., 0.9990 Silver 0.4818 oz. ASW **Subject:** XXVII
Olympics **Obv:** National arms within wreath, denomination below
Rev: Multicolored baseball player at bat, baseball background,
small date below

Date	Mintage	F	VF	XF	Unc	BU
1997 Proof	—	Value: 40.00				

KM# 747   10 PESOS
3.1100 g., Gold, 16 mm. **Obv:** National arms and inscription
Rev: Che Guevara standing

Date	Mintage	F	VF	XF	Unc	BU
1997 Proof	500	Value: 195				

KM# 748   10 PESOS
3.1100 g., Gold, 16 mm. **Obv:** National arms within wreath,
denomination **Rev:** Bust of Che Guevara

Date	Mintage	F	VF	XF	Unc	BU
1997 Proof	500	Value: 195				

KM# 635   10 PESOS
31.1000 g., 0.9990 Silver 0.9988 oz. ASW, 38 mm. **Obv:**
National arms within wreath, denomination **Rev:** Pope John Paul
II, cathedral

Date	Mintage	F	VF	XF	Unc	BU
1997 Proof	10,000	Value: 50.00				

KM# 624   10 PESOS
31.1000 g., 0.9990 Silver 0.9988 oz. ASW, 38 mm. **Obv:**
National arms within wreath, denomination **Rev:** Deng Xiaoping
bust facing

Date	Mintage	F	VF	XF	Unc	BU
1997 Proof	10,000	Value: 45.00				

KM# 750   10 PESOS
31.1000 g., 0.9990 Silver 0.9988 oz. ASW, 38 mm.
Obv: National arms within wreath, denomination **Rev:** Deng
Xiaoping viewing Hong Kong

Date	Mintage	F	VF	XF	Unc	BU
1997 Proof	10,000	Value: 45.00				

KM# 751   10 PESOS
20.0000 g., 0.9990 Silver 0.6423 oz. ASW, 24x42 mm.
Obv: National arms within wreath, denomination **Rev:** Cruise ship
Hanseatic

Date	Mintage	F	VF	XF	Unc	BU
1998 Proof	2,500	Value: 50.00				

KM# 610   10 PESOS
15.0000 g., 0.9990 Silver 0.4818 oz. ASW **Subject:** Mississippi
Obv: National arms within wreath, denomination below
Rev: Riverboat

Date	Mintage	F	VF	XF	Unc	BU
1998 Proof	5,000	Value: 37.50				

KM# 644   10 PESOS
31.1035 g., 0.9990 Silver 0.9990 oz. ASW **Subject:** Centenary
- Explosion del Maine **Obv:** National arms within wreath,
denomination below **Rev:** Explosion scene

Date	Mintage	F	VF	XF	Unc	BU
1998 Proof	5,000	Value: 65.00				

KM# 611   10 PESOS
15.0000 g., 0.9990 Silver 0.4818 oz. ASW **Obv:** National arms
within wreath, denomination below **Rev:** The ship Rio Bravo

Date	Mintage	F	VF	XF	Unc	BU
1998 Proof	—	Value: 37.50				

KM# 645   10 PESOS
31.1035 g., 0.9990 Silver 0.9990 oz. ASW **Subject:** Centenary
- Naval battle of Santiago **Obv:** National arms within wreath,
denomination below **Rev:** Cameo of Admiral Cervera and burning
ship

Date	Mintage	F	VF	XF	Unc	BU
1998 Proof	5,000	Value: 65.00				

KM# 646   10 PESOS
31.1035 g., 0.9990 Silver 0.9990 oz. ASW **Subject:** Centenary
- Calixto Garcia - Combate en Oriente **Obv:** National arms within
wreath, denomination below **Rev:** Portrait above three Cuban
cavalry troopers

Date	Mintage	F	VF	XF	Unc	BU
1998 Proof	5,000	Value: 65.00				

KM# 647   10 PESOS
31.1035 g., 0.9990 Silver 0.9990 oz. ASW **Obv:** National arms
within wreath, denomination **Rev:** Souvenir peso design, bust of
Leonor Molina right

Date	Mintage	F	VF	XF	Unc	BU
1998 Proof	5,000	Value: 60.00				

KM# 648   10 PESOS
15.0000 g., 0.9990 Silver 0.4818 oz. ASW **Subject:** Expo 2000
- Twipsy **Obv:** National arms within wreath, denomination below
Rev: "Twipsy" cartoon logo

Date	Mintage	F	VF	XF	Unc	BU
1998 Proof	18,750	Value: 35.00				

KM# 649   10 PESOS
15.0000 g., 0.9990 Silver 0.4818 oz. ASW **Subject:** Expo 2000
- Germany **Obv:** National arms within wreath, denomination
below **Rev:** German map

Date	Mintage	F	VF	XF	Unc	BU
1998 Proof	18,750	Value: 35.00				

KM# 650 10 PESOS
15.0000 g., 0.9990 Silver 0.4818 oz. ASW **Subject:** Expo 2000 - London **Obv:** National arms within wreath, denomination below **Rev:** Cartoon over exhibit hall

Date	Mintage	F	VF	XF	Unc	BU
1998 Proof	18,750	Value: 35.00				

KM# 651 10 PESOS
15.0000 g., 0.9990 Silver 0.4818 oz. ASW **Subject:** Expo 2000 - Paris **Obv:** National arms within wreath, denomination below **Rev:** Cartoon and Eiffel Tower

Date	Mintage	F	VF	XF	Unc	BU
1998 Proof	18,750	Value: 35.00				

KM# 652 10 PESOS
15.0000 g., 0.9990 Silver 0.4818 oz. ASW **Subject:** Expo 2000 - Brussels **Obv:** National arms within wreath, denomination below **Rev:** Cartoon and Atomium structure

Date	Mintage	F	VF	XF	Unc	BU
1998 Proof	18,750	Value: 35.00				

KM# 653 10 PESOS
15.0000 g., 0.9990 Silver 0.4818 oz. ASW **Subject:** Expo 2000 - Postrimerias **Obv:** National arms within wreath, denomination below **Rev:** Cartoon on tree bearing world globe

Date	Mintage	F	VF	XF	Unc	BU
1998 Proof	18,750	Value: 35.00				

KM# 668 10 PESOS
31.1035 g., 0.9990 Silver 0.9990 oz. ASW, 45.2 x 35.1 mm. **Subject:** Havana Puzzle - Frigate Oquendo **Obv:** National arms within wreath, denomination below **Rev:** Two sailing ships **Edge:** Plain

Date	Mintage	F	VF	XF	Unc	BU
1998 Proof	—	Value: 60.00				

KM# 669 10 PESOS
31.1035 g., 0.9990 Silver 0.9990 oz. ASW, 45.2 x 35.1 mm. **Subject:** Havana Puzzle - City of Havana **Obv:** National arms within wreath, denomination below **Rev:** Havana city view **Edge:** Plain

Date	Mintage	F	VF	XF	Unc	BU
1998 Proof	3,000	Value: 60.00				

KM# 670 10 PESOS
31.1800 g., 0.9990 Silver 1.0014 oz. ASW, 45.2 x 35.1 mm. **Subject:** Havana Puzzle - Sailing Ship San Genaro **Obv:** National arms within wreath, denomination below **Rev:** Three sailing ships **Edge:** Plain

Date	Mintage	F	VF	XF	Unc	BU
1998 Proof	3,000	Value: 60.00				

KM# 671 10 PESOS
31.1800 g., 0.9990 Silver 1.0014 oz. ASW, 45.2 x 35.1 mm. **Subject:** Havana Puzzle - El Morro **Obv:** National arms within wreath, denomination below **Rev:** Light house and sailing ships **Edge:** Plain

Date	Mintage	F	VF	XF	Unc	BU
1998 Proof	3,000	Value: 60.00				

KM# 672 10 PESOS
31.1035 g., 0.9990 Silver 0.9990 oz. ASW **Subject:** 40th Anniversary - Triumph of the Revolution

Date	Mintage	F	VF	XF	Unc	BU
1999 Proof	—	Value: 45.00				

KM# 674 10 PESOS
31.1035 g., 0.9990 Silver 0.9990 oz. ASW **Subject:** Spanish Royal Visit - Fidel Castro receives King Juan Carlos I

Date	Mintage	F	VF	XF	Unc	BU
1999 Proof	5,000	Value: 75.00				

KM# 675 10 PESOS
31.1035 g., 0.9990 Silver 0.9990 oz. ASW **Subject:** Spanish Royal Visit - King Juan Carlos and Queen Sofia

Date	Mintage	F	VF	XF	Unc	BU
1999 Proof	5,000	Value: 75.00				

KM# 676 10 PESOS
31.1035 g., 0.9990 Silver 0.9990 oz. ASW **Subject:** Spanish Royal Visit - 2 Peoples United

Date	Mintage	F	VF	XF	Unc	BU
1999 Proof	—	Value: 75.00				

KM# 677 10 PESOS
31.1035 g., 0.9990 Silver 0.9990 oz. ASW **Subject:** Spanish Royal Visit - Homage to the Spanish Soldier

Date	Mintage	F	VF	XF	Unc	BU
1999 Proof	—	Value: 75.00				

KM# 661 10 PESOS
31.1035 g., 0.9990 Silver 0.9990 oz. ASW **Subject:** Zunzuncito **Obv:** National arms **Rev:** Hummingbird **Edge:** Plain

Date	Mintage	F	VF	XF	Unc	BU
1999 Proof	2,000	Value: 50.00				

KM# 725 10 PESOS
3.1100 g., 0.9990 Gold 0.0999 oz. AGW, 18 mm. **Subject:** Zunzuncito **Obv:** National arms **Rev:** Hummingbird **Edge:** Reeded

Date	Mintage	F	VF	XF	Unc	BU
1999 Proof	1,000	Value: 110				

KM# 752 10 PESOS
20.0000 g., 0.9990 Silver 0.6423 oz. ASW, 38 mm. **Subject:** First International Globalization Conference **Obv:** National arms within wreath, denomination **Rev:** World map

Date	Mintage	F	VF	XF	Unc	BU
1999 Proof	200	Value: 100				

KM# 753 10 PESOS
15.0000 g., 0.9990 Silver 0.4818 oz. ASW, 35 mm. **Subject:** Goethe's birthplace **Obv:** National arms within wreath, denomination **Rev:** Building at left, bust at right looking left

Date	Mintage	F	VF	XF	Unc	BU
1999 Proof	1,749	Value: 45.00				

KM# 754 10 PESOS
15.0000 g., 0.9990 Silver 0.4818 oz. ASW, 35 mm. **Subject:** Goeth's Weimar home **Obv:** National arms within wreath, denomination **Rev:** Building at right, bust at left looking right

Date	Mintage	F	VF	XF	Unc	BU
1999 Proof	1,749	Value: 45.00				

KM# 755 10 PESOS
15.0000 g., 0.9990 Silver 0.4818 oz. ASW, 35 mm. **Obv:** National arms within wreath, denomination **Rev:** Christopher Columbus, ship, and arms

Date	Mintage	F	VF	XF	Unc	BU
1999 Proof	1,950	Value: 45.00				

KM# 749   10 PESOS
3.1100 g., Gold, 18 mm. **Obv:** National arms within wreath,
denomination **Rev:** Hummingbird in flight

Date	Mintage	F	VF	XF	Unc	BU
1999 Proof	1,000	Value: 110				

KM# 736   10 PESOS
14.9300 g., 0.9990 Silver 0.4795 oz. ASW, 35.1 mm.
Subject: Johann Wolfgang von Goethe **Obv:** National arms
Rev: Seated figure outdoors **Edge:** Plain

Date	Mintage	F	VF	XF	Unc	BU
1999 Proof	1,749	Value: 45.00				

KM# 756   10 PESOS
31.1035 g., 0.9990 Silver 0.9990 oz. ASW, 38 mm.
Obv: National arms within wreath, denomination
Rev: Hummingbird feeding nestlings

Date	Mintage	F	VF	XF	Unc	BU
2000 Proof	20,000	Value: 37.50				

KM# 757   10 PESOS
20.0000 g., 0.9990 Silver 0.6423 oz. ASW, 38 mm.
Subject: Second International Globalization Conference
Obv: National arms within wreath, denomination **Rev:** World map

Date	Mintage	F	VF	XF	Unc	BU
2000 Proof	100	Value: 125				

KM# 758   10 PESOS
15.0000 g., 0.9990 Silver 0.4818 oz. ASW, 35 mm.
Obv: National arms within wreath, denomination **Rev:** Sailing
ship Santisima Trinidad

Date	Mintage	F	VF	XF	Unc	BU
2000 Proof	2,500	Value: 45.00				

KM# 759   10 PESOS
15.0000 g., 0.9990 Silver 0.4818 oz. ASW, 35 mm. **Obv:** National
arms within wreath, denomination **Rev:** Ship Vecero Rayo

Date	Mintage	F	VF	XF	Unc	BU
2000 Proof	2,500	Value: 45.00				

KM# 760   10 PESOS
15.0000 g., 0.9990 Silver 0.4818 oz. ASW, 35 mm.
Obv: National arms within wreath, denomination **Rev:** Sailing
ship, San Pedro De Alcantara

Date	Mintage	F	VF	XF	Unc	BU
2000 Proof	2,500	Value: 45.00				

KM# 761   10 PESOS
20.0000 g., 0.9990 Silver 0.6423 oz. ASW, 38 mm.
Obv: National arms within wreath, denomination **Rev:** "50" in design

Date	Mintage	F	VF	XF	Unc	BU
2000 Proof	1,250	Value: 50.00				

KM# 679   10 PESOS
31.1035 g., 0.9990 Silver 0.9990 oz. ASW **Subject:** Maritime
Relics - School Ship Galatea **Obv:** National arms within wreath,
denomination **Rev:** Ship with full sails at sea

Date	Mintage	F	VF	XF	Unc	BU
2000 Proof	1,500	Value: 35.00				

KM# 678   10 PESOS
31.1035 g., 0.9990 Silver 0.9990 oz. ASW **Subject:** Maritime
Relics - Peral Submarine **Obv:** National arms within wreath,
denomination **Rev:** Submarine under water, small ship above

Date	Mintage	F	VF	XF	Unc	BU
2000 Proof	1,500	Value: 35.00				

KM# 680   10 PESOS
31.1035 g., 0.9990 Silver 0.9990 oz. ASW **Subject:** Maritime
Relics - School Ship JS Elcano **Obv:** National arms within wreath,
denomination **Rev:** Ship with many full sails at sea

Date	Mintage	F	VF	XF	Unc	BU
2000 Proof	1,500	Value: 35.00				

KM# 681   10 PESOS
31.1035 g., 0.9990 Silver 0.9990 oz. ASW **Subject:** Maritime
Relics - Maritime Ambulance Buena Ventura **Obv:** National arms
within wreath, denomination **Rev:** Two ships at sea

Date	Mintage	F	VF	XF	Unc	BU
2000 Proof	1,500	Value: 35.00				

KM# 683   10 PESOS
20.0000 g., 0.9990 Silver 0.6423 oz. ASW **Subject:** Hacia un
Nuevo Milenio (Towards a New Millennium) **Obv:** National arms
within wreath, denomination below **Rev:** Dove of Peace covering
world map

Date	Mintage	F	VF	XF	Unc	BU
2000 Proof	3,000	Value: 50.00				

KM# 682   10 PESOS
20.0000 g., 0.9990 Silver 0.6423 oz. ASW **Subject:** Maritime
Relics - Nautical Rose of Juan de la Cosa **Obv:** National arms
within wreath, denomination **Rev:** Madonna and child with angels
at center of radiant sun design

Date	Mintage	F	VF	XF	Unc	BU
2000 Proof	1,500	Value: 35.00				

Date	Mintage	F	VF	XF	Unc	BU
2000 Proof	1,500	Value: 35.00				

KM# 684 10 PESOS
20.0000 g., 0.9990 Silver 0.6423 oz. ASW **Subject:** Welcome to the New Millennium **Obv:** National arms within wreath, denomination below **Rev:** Hot air balloons above earth

Date	Mintage	F	VF	XF	Unc	BU
2000 Proof	3,000	Value: 50.00				

KM# 685 10 PESOS
20.0000 g., 0.9990 Silver 0.6423 oz. ASW **Subject:** Welcome to the New Millennium **Obv:** National arms within wreath, denomination below **Rev:** Stars and Solar System

Date	Mintage	F	VF	XF	Unc	BU
2000 Proof	3,000	Value: 50.00				

KM# 687 10 PESOS
15.0000 g., 0.9990 Silver 0.4818 oz. ASW **Subject:** Palaces of the World **Obv:** National arms within wreath, denomination **Rev:** Windsor Palace

Date	Mintage	F	VF	XF	Unc	BU
2000 Proof	—	Value: 35.00				

KM# 688 10 PESOS
15.0000 g., 0.9990 Silver 0.4818 oz. ASW **Subject:** Palaces of the World **Obv:** National arms within wreath, denomination **Rev:** San Soucci Palace

Date	Mintage	F	VF	XF	Unc	BU
2000 Proof	—	Value: 35.00				

KM# 689 10 PESOS
15.0000 g., 0.9990 Silver 0.4818 oz. ASW **Subject:** Palaces of

the World **Obv:** National arms within wreath, denomination **Rev:** Schonbrunn Palace

Date	Mintage	F	VF	XF	Unc	BU
2000 Proof	—	Value: 35.00				

KM# 690 10 PESOS
15.0000 g., 0.9990 Silver 0.4818 oz. ASW **Subject:** Palaces of the World - Neuschwanstein Castles

Date	Mintage	F	VF	XF	Unc	BU
2000 Proof	—	Value: 35.00				

KM# 691 10 PESOS
15.0000 g., 0.9990 Silver 0.4818 oz. ASW **Subject:** Palaces of the World - Hradschinn Castle

Date	Mintage	F	VF	XF	Unc	BU
2000 Proof	—	Value: 35.00				

KM# 735 10 PESOS
27.0000 g., 0.9250 Silver 0.8029 oz. ASW, 40.1 mm.
Subject: Ibero-America - Man and Horse **Obv:** National arms and denomination within circle of arms **Rev:** Horse in center within pictures of horses being ridden **Edge:** Reeded

Date	Mintage	F	VF	XF	Unc	BU
2000 Proof	—	Value: 65.00				

KM# 686 10 PESOS
15.0000 g., 0.9990 Silver 0.4818 oz. ASW **Subject:** Palaces of the World **Obv:** National arms within wreath, denomination **Rev:** Versailles Palace

Date	Mintage	F	VF	XF	Unc	BU
2000 Proof	—	Value: 35.00				

KM# 212 15 PESOS
3.8800 g., 0.9990 Gold 0.1246 oz. AGW **Obv:** National arms within wreath, denomination below **Rev:** Jose Marti head right, date below

Date	Mintage	F	VF	XF	Unc	BU
1988	50	—	—	—	200	250
1988 Proof	15	Value: 270				

Date	Mintage	F	VF	XF	Unc	BU
1989	50	—	—	—	200	250
1989 Proof	15	Value: 270				
1990	15	—	—	—	250	260
1990 Proof	12	Value: 270				

KM# 38 20 PESOS
26.0000 g., 0.9250 Silver 0.7732 oz. ASW **Subject:** Ignacio Agramonte **Obv:** Flagged arms, liberty cap above **Rev:** Bust 3/4 facing, date at left

Date	Mintage	F	VF	XF	Unc	BU
1977 Proof	25,000	Value: 32.50				

KM# 39 20 PESOS
26.0000 g., 0.9250 Silver 0.7732 oz. ASW **Subject:** Maximo Gomez **Obv:** Liberty cap above flagged arms **Rev:** Bust facing

Date	Mintage	F	VF	XF	Unc	BU
1977 Proof	75,000	Value: 28.00				

KM# 40 20 PESOS
26.0000 g., 0.9250 Silver 0.7732 oz. ASW **Subject:** Antonio Maceo **Obv:** Liberty cap above flagged arms **Rev:** Bust facing looking right

Date	Mintage	F	VF	XF	Unc	BU
1977 Proof	75,000	Value: 28.00				

KM# 41 20 PESOS
26.0000 g., 0.9250 Silver 0.7732 oz. ASW **Subject:** 60th Anniversary Socialist Revolution - Lenin **Obv:** National arms within wreath, denomination **Rev:** Bust left

Date	Mintage	F	VF	XF	Unc	BU
1977 Proof	100	Value: 1,400				

KM# 44   20 PESOS
26.0000 g., 0.9250 Silver 0.7732 oz. ASW **Subject:** Nonaligned
Nations Conference **Obv:** National arms within wreath,
denomination below **Rev:** Design left of date

Date	Mintage	F	VF	XF	Unc	BU
1979	20,000	—	—	—	17.50	20.00
1979 Proof	—	Value: 60.00				
1979 Matte Proof	—	Value: 100				

KM# 169   20 PESOS
62.2000 g., 0.9990 Silver 1.9977 oz. ASW **Subject:** Triumph of
the Revolution **Obv:** Arms on star background above half wreath
Rev: Rejoicing scene

Date	Mintage	F	VF	XF	Unc	BU
1987 Proof	500	Value: 85.00				
1988 Proof	1,000	Value: 75.00				
1989 Proof	500	Value: 85.00				

KM# 170   20 PESOS
62.2000 g., 0.9990 Silver 1.9977 oz. ASW **Subject:** 60th
Anniversary - Birth of Ernesto Che Guevara **Obv:** Arms on star
background above half wreath **Rev:** Bust right

Date	Mintage	F	VF	XF	Unc	BU
1987 Proof	500	Value: 95.00				
1988 Proof	1,000	Value: 80.00				
1989 Proof	500	Value: 95.00				

KM# 171   20 PESOS
62.2000 g., 0.9990 Silver 1.9977 oz. ASW **Subject:** 30th
Anniversary - The March to Victory **Obv:** Arms on star background
above half wreath **Rev:** Soldiers on the march

Date	Mintage	F	VF	XF	Unc	BU
1987 Proof	333	Value: 85.00				
1988 Proof	1,000	Value: 75.00				
1989 Proof	500	Value: 85.00				

KM# 232   20 PESOS
62.2000 g., 0.9990 Silver 1.9977 oz. ASW **Subject:** 150th
Anniversary - First Railroad in Cuba **Obv:** Arms on star background
above wreath **Rev:** Train engine right

Date	Mintage	F	VF	XF	Unc	BU
1988 Proof	Est. 1,000	Value: 80.00				

KM# 233   20 PESOS
62.2000 g., 0.9990 Silver 1.9977 oz. ASW **Subject:** 140th
Anniversary - First Railroad in Spain **Obv:** Arms on star background
above half wreath **Rev:** Train left, dates

Date	Mintage	F	VF	XF	Unc	BU
ND(1988) Proof	Est. 1,000	Value: 80.00				

KM# 234   20 PESOS
62.2000 g., 0.9990 Silver 1.9977 oz. ASW **Subject:** 160th
Anniversary - First Railroad in England **Obv:** Arms on star
background above half wreath **Rev:** Ancient train with boxcar, dates

Date	Mintage	F	VF	XF	Unc	BU
1988 Proof	Est. 1,000	Value: 80.00				

KM# 235   20 PESOS
62.2000 g., 0.9990 Silver 1.9977 oz. ASW **Subject:** Tania La
Guerrillera, Argentinian revolutionary **Obv:** Arms on star
background above half wreath **Rev:** Bust facing

Date	Mintage	F	VF	XF	Unc	BU
1988 Proof	1,000	Value: 75.00				

KM# 236   20 PESOS
62.2000 g., 0.9990 Silver 1.9977 oz. ASW **Subject:** Camilo
Cienfuegos **Obv:** Arms on star background above half wreath
Rev: Bust facing, dates

Date	Mintage	F	VF	XF	Unc	BU
1988 Proof	1,000	Value: 75.00				

KM# 237   20 PESOS
62.2000 g., 0.9990 Silver 1.9977 oz. ASW **Subject:** 35th
Anniversary - Assault of the Moncada Garrison **Obv:** Arms on star
background above half wreath **Rev:** Armed figures, dates below

Date	Mintage	F	VF	XF	Unc	BU
ND(1988) Proof	1,000	Value: 75.00				

KM# 531   20 PESOS
62.2000 g., 0.9990 Silver 1.9977 oz. ASW **Obv:** National arms
within wreath, denomination **Rev:** Jose Raul playing chess

Date	Mintage	F	VF	XF	Unc	BU
ND(1988) Proof	1,000	Value: 90.00				

KM# 532   20 PESOS
62.2000 g., 0.9990 Silver 1.9977 oz. ASW **Subject:** 25th
Anniversary - Death of Ernesto Che Guevara **Obv:** National arms
Rev: Head facing, dates

Date	Mintage	F	VF	XF	Unc	BU
ND(1992) Proof	1,000	Value: 90.00				

KM# 471.1   20 PESOS
62.2000 g., 0.9990 Silver 1.9977 oz. ASW **Subject:** Fidel Castro
- 40th Anniversary of Moncada **Obv:** National arms within wreath,
denomination **Rev:** Uniformed bust left

Date	Mintage	F	VF	XF	Unc	BU
1993 Proof	—	Value: 90.00				

KM# 459   20 PESOS
62.2000 g., 0.9990 Silver 1.9977 oz. ASW **Subject:** Cuban
Railroad **Obv:** National arms **Rev:** Train engine, date below

Date	Mintage	F	VF	XF	Unc	BU
1994 Proof	—	Value: 90.00				

KM# 533   20 PESOS
62.2000 g., 0.9990 Silver 1.9977 oz. ASW **Subject:**
Transportation **Obv:** National arms **Rev:** Zeppelin, date below

Date	Mintage	F	VF	XF	Unc	BU
1995 Proof	1,000	Value: 110				

KM# 213   25 PESOS
7.7700 g., 0.9990 Gold 0.2496 oz. AGW **Subject:** Jose Marti
Obv: National arms within wreath, denomination below **Rev:** Head
right

Date	Mintage	F	VF	XF	Unc	BU
1988	50	—	—	—	—	350
1988 Proof	15	Value: 450				
1989	50	—	—	—	—	350
1989 Proof	15	Value: 450				
1990	12	—	—	—	—	400
1990 Proof	12	Value: 450				

KM# 692   25 PESOS
7.7759 g., 0.9990 Gold 0.2497 oz. AGW, 20 mm. **Subject:**
Zunzuncito **Obv:** National arms **Rev:** Hummingbird **Edge:** Reeded

Date	Mintage	F	VF	XF	Unc	BU
1999 Proof	1,000	Value: 250				

KM# 422   30 PESOS
93.2500 g., 0.9990 Silver 2.9949 oz. ASW **Rev:** Vincente and
Martin Pinzon

Date	Mintage	F	VF	XF	Unc	BU
1991 Proof	1,000	Value: 150				

KM# 423   30 PESOS
93.2500 g., 0.9990 Silver 2.9949 oz. ASW **Rev:** Hatuey People

Date	Mintage	F	VF	XF	Unc	BU
1991 Proof	1,000	Value: 125				

KM# 430   30 PESOS
93.3000 g., 0.9990 Silver 2.9965 oz. ASW **Series:** 500th
Anniversary of the New World **Subject:** Queen Joanna 1479-
1555, dughter of Isabella I **Obv:** National arms within wreath
Rev: Bust 3/4 right above half wreath

Date	Mintage	F	VF	XF	Unc	BU
1991 Proof	1,000	Value: 165				

KM# 431   30 PESOS
93.3000 g., 0.9990 Silver 2.9965 oz. ASW **Series:** 500th
Anniversary of the New World **Subject:** Diego Velazquez
Obv: National arms within wreath **Rev:** Bust 3/4 left above wreath

Date	Mintage	F	VF	XF	Unc	BU
1991 Proof	1,000	Value: 165				

KM# 376   30 PESOS
93.2500 g., 0.9990 Silver 2.9949 oz. ASW **Series:** 500th
Anniversary of the New World **Subject:** Guama native
Obv: National arms within wreath **Rev:** Native figure drinking
from large shell

Date	Mintage	F	VF	XF	Unc	BU
1992 Proof	550	Value: 125				

KM# 377   30 PESOS
93.2500 g., 0.9990 Silver 2.9949 oz. ASW **Series:** 500th
Anniversary of the New World **Subject:** Bartolome de Las Casas
Obv: National arms within wreath **Rev:** Figure at desk writing a
letter with a quill pen

Date	Mintage	F	VF	XF	Unc	BU
1992 Proof	550	Value: 125				

KM# 378   30 PESOS
93.2500 g., 0.9990 Silver 2.9949 oz. ASW **Series:** 500th
Anniversary of the New World **Subject:** King Philipp
Obv: National arms within wreath **Rev:** Bust 3/4 right above
half wreath

Date	Mintage	F	VF	XF	Unc	BU
1992 Proof	550	Value: 125				

KM# 379 30 PESOS
93.2500 g., 0.9990 Silver 2.9949 oz. ASW **Series:** 500th Anniversary of the New World **Subject:** Fernando and Elisabeth, Philipp and Johanna **Obv:** National arms within wreath **Rev:** Spanish kings and queens

Date	Mintage	F	VF	XF	Unc	BU
ND(1992) Proof	550	Value: 125				

KM# 208 50 PESOS
15.5500 g., 0.9990 Gold 0.4994 oz. AGW **Subject:** 30th Anniversary - The March to Victory **Obv:** Arms on star background above half wreath **Rev:** Soldiers on the march, date above

Date	Mintage	F	VF	XF	Unc	BU
1988 Proof	150	Value: 475				

KM# 209 50 PESOS
15.5500 g., 0.9990 Gold 0.4994 oz. AGW **Subject:** 60th Anniversary - Birth of Ernesto Che Guevara **Obv:** Arms on star background above half wreath **Rev:** Bust right, date at left

Date	Mintage	F	VF	XF	Unc	BU
1988 Proof	150	Value: 475				

KM# 210 50 PESOS
15.5500 g., 0.9990 Gold 0.4994 oz. AGW **Subject:** Triumph of the Revolutionary **Obv:** Arms on star background above half wreath **Rev:** Castro with revolutionaries, divide dates

Date	Mintage	F	VF	XF	Unc	BU
1988 Proof	150	Value: 475				

KM# 214 50 PESOS
15.5500 g., 0.9990 Gold 0.4994 oz. AGW **Subject:** Jose Marti **Obv:** National arms within wreath, denomination **Rev:** Head right

Date	Mintage	F	VF	XF	Unc	BU
1988	12	—	—	—	500	550
1988 Proof	15	Value: 650				
1989	150	—	—	—	475	525

Date	Mintage	F	VF	XF	Unc	BU
1989 Proof	15	Value: 650				
1990	15	—	—	—	500	550
1990 Proof	12	Value: 650				

KM# 313 50 PESOS
15.5500 g., 0.9990 Gold 0.4994 oz. AGW **Subject:** 160th Anniversary - First Train in England **Rev:** Train, Liverpool - Manchester

Date	Mintage	F	VF	XF	Unc	BU
1989 Proof	150	Value: 485				

KM# 314 50 PESOS
15.5500 g., 0.9990 Gold 0.4994 oz. AGW **Subject:** 150th Anniversary - First Train in Spanish America **Rev:** Train **Rev. Leg.:** HABANA-BEJUCAL

Date	Mintage	F	VF	XF	Unc	BU
1989 Proof	150	Value: 485				

KM# 315 50 PESOS
15.5500 g., 0.9990 Gold 0.4994 oz. AGW **Subject:** 140th Anniversary - First Train in Spain **Rev:** Train **Rev. Leg.:** BARCELONA-MATARD

Date	Mintage	F	VF	XF	Unc	BU
1989 Proof	150	Value: 485				

KM# 330 50 PESOS
15.5500 g., 0.9990 Gold 0.4994 oz. AGW **Subject:** Tania La Guerrillera **Rev:** Portrait of female guerilla fighter

Date	Mintage	F	VF	XF	Unc	BU
1989 Proof	150	Value: 485				

KM# 331 50 PESOS
15.5500 g., 0.9990 Gold 0.4994 oz. AGW **Subject:** Camilo Cienfuegos Gornaran **Rev:** Portrait of Camilo Cienfuegos

Date	Mintage	F	VF	XF	Unc	BU
1989 Proof	150	Value: 485				

KM# 332 50 PESOS
15.5500 g., 0.9990 Gold 0.4994 oz. AGW **Subject:** Assault of the Moncada Garrison **Rev:** Battle scene

Date	Mintage	F	VF	XF	Unc	BU
1989 Proof	150	Value: 485				

KM# 281 50 PESOS
15.5500 g., 0.9990 Gold 0.4994 oz. AGW **Subject:** Simon Bolivar **Rev:** Portrait of Simon Bolivar

Date	Mintage	F	VF	XF	Unc	BU
1990 Proof	50	Value: 485				

KM# 294 50 PESOS
155.5150 g., 0.9990 Silver 4.9947 oz. ASW **Subject:** 500th Anniversary - Discovery of America **Obv:** National arms within wreath **Rev:** Christopher Columbus

Date	Mintage	F	VF	XF	Unc	BU
1990 Proof	2,000	Value: 115				

KM# 295 50 PESOS
155.5150 g., 0.9990 Silver 4.9947 oz. ASW **Subject:** 500th Anniversary - Discovery of America **Obv:** National arms within wreath **Rev:** King Ferdinand of Spain

Date	Mintage	F	VF	XF	Unc	BU
1990 Proof	2,000	Value: 145				

KM# 296 50 PESOS
155.5150 g., 0.9990 Silver 4.9947 oz. ASW **Subject:** 500th Anniversary - Discovery of America **Obv:** National arms within wreath **Rev:** Queen Isabella of Spain

Date	Mintage	F	VF	XF	Unc	BU
1990 Proof	2,000	Value: 115				

KM# 297 50 PESOS
155.5150 g., 0.9990 Silver 4.9947 oz. ASW **Subject:** 500th Anniversary - Discovery of America **Obv:** National arms within wreath **Rev:** Juan de la Cosa

Date	Mintage	F	VF	XF	Unc	BU
1990 Proof	2,000	Value: 115				

KM# 298 50 PESOS
15.5500 g., 0.9990 Gold 0.4994 oz. AGW **Subject:** 500th Anniversary - Discovery of America **Obv:** National arms within wreath **Rev:** Portrait of Christopher Columbus

Date	Mintage	F	VF	XF	Unc	BU
1990 Proof	250	Value: 485				

KM# 299 50 PESOS
15.5500 g., 0.9990 Gold 0.4994 oz. AGW **Subject:** 500th Anniversary - Discovery of America **Obv:** National arms within wreath **Rev:** Portrait of King Ferdinand V

Date	Mintage	F	VF	XF	Unc	BU
1990 Proof	250	Value: 485				

KM# 300 50 PESOS
15.5500 g., 0.9990 Gold 0.4994 oz. AGW **Subject:** 500th Anniversary - Discovery of America **Obv:** National arms within wreath **Rev:** Portrait of Queen Isabella of Spain

Date	Mintage	F	VF	XF	Unc	BU
1990 Proof	250	Value: 485				

KM# 301 50 PESOS
15.5500 g., 0.9990 Gold 0.4994 oz. AGW **Subject:** 500th Anniversary - Discovery of America **Obv:** National arms within wreath **Rev:** Portrait of Juan de la Cosa

Date	Mintage	F	VF	XF	Unc	BU
1990 Proof	250	Value: 485				

KM# 321 50 PESOS
15.5500 g., 0.9990 Gold 0.4994 oz. AGW **Subject:** Pan American Games - Baseball **Obv:** National arms within wreath, denomination **Rev:** Baseball players

Date	Mintage	F	VF	XF	Unc	BU
1990 Proof	15	Value: 485				

KM# 322 50 PESOS
15.5500 g., 0.9990 Gold 0.4994 oz. AGW **Subject:** Pan American Games - High Jump **Obv:** National arms within wreath, denomination **Rev:** High jumper clearing pole

Date	Mintage	F	VF	XF	Unc	BU
1990 Proof	15	Value: 500				

KM# 323 50 PESOS
15.5500 g., 0.9990 Gold 0.4994 oz. AGW **Subject:** Pan American Games - Volleyball **Obv:** National arms within wreath, denomination **Rev:** Volleyball players

Date	Mintage	F	VF	XF	Unc	BU
1990 Proof	15	Value: 500				

KM# 339 50 PESOS
15.5500 g., 0.9990 Gold 0.4994 oz. AGW **Rev:** Hatuey tribesman

Date	Mintage	F	VF	XF	Unc	BU
1991 Proof	200	Value: 485				

KM# 343 50 PESOS
155.5000 g., 0.9990 Silver 4.9942 oz. ASW **Series:** Olympics **Obv:** National arms within wreath **Rev:** Stadium

Date	Mintage	F	VF	XF	Unc	BU
1991 Proof	1,050	Value: 240				

KM# 356 50 PESOS
155.5000 g., 0.9990 Silver 4.9942 oz. ASW **Subject:** Madrid - Alcala Gate **Obv:** National arms within wreath **Rev:** Building with arches

Date	Mintage	F	VF	XF	Unc	BU
1991 Proof	550	Value: 285				

KM# 357 50 PESOS
155.5000 g., 0.9990 Silver 4.9942 oz. ASW **Subject:** Seville - La Giralda Tower **Obv:** National arms within wreath **Rev:** Tower, date at right

Date	Mintage	F	VF	XF	Unc	BU
1991 Proof	550	Value: 285				

KM# 432 50 PESOS
155.5000 g., 0.9990 Silver 4.9942 oz. ASW **Series:** 500th Anniversary of the New World **Subject:** Queen Joanna 1479-1555, daughter of Isabella I **Obv:** National arms within wreath **Rev:** Head 3/4 right above half wreath

Date	Mintage	F	VF	XF	Unc	BU
1991 Proof	1,000	Value: 165				

KM# 433 50 PESOS
155.5000 g., 0.9990 Silver 4.9942 oz. ASW **Series:** 500th Anniversary of the New World **Subject:** Diego Valezquez **Obv:** National arms within wreath **Rev:** Bust 3/4 left above half wreath

Date	Mintage	F	VF	XF	Unc	BU
1991 Proof	1,000	Value: 165				

KM# 434 50 PESOS
155.5000 g., 0.9990 Silver 4.9942 oz. ASW **Series:** 500th Anneversary of the New World **Subject:** Pinzon Brothers **Obv:** National arms within wreath, denomination below **Rev:** Portraits in cameos, small ship above

Date	Mintage	F	VF	XF	Unc	BU
1991 Proof	1,000	Value: 165				

KM# 435 50 PESOS
155.5000 g., 0.9990 Silver 4.9942 oz. ASW **Series:** 500th Anniversary of the New World **Subject:** Hatuey Tribesman **Obv:** National arms within wreath, denomination **Rev:** Head stretching left

Date	Mintage	F	VF	XF	Unc	BU
1991 Proof	1,000	Value: 195				

KM# 444 50 PESOS
15.5500 g., 0.9990 Gold 0.4994 oz. AGW **Subject:** Queen Joanna

Date	Mintage	F	VF	XF	Unc	BU
1991 Proof	200	Value: 485				

KM# 445 50 PESOS
15.5500 g., 0.9990 Gold 0.4994 oz. AGW **Subject:** Diego Valezquez

Date	Mintage	F	VF	XF	Unc	BU
1991 Proof	200	Value: 485				

KM# 446 50 PESOS
15.5500 g., 0.9990 Gold 0.4994 oz. AGW **Subject:** Pinzon Brothers

Date	Mintage	F	VF	XF	Unc	BU
1991 Proof	200	Value: 485				

KM# 358 50 PESOS
155.5000 g., 0.9990 Silver 4.9942 oz. ASW **Series:** 500th Anniversary of the New World **Subject:** Philipp I **Obv:** National arms within wreath **Rev:** Bust right above half wreath

Date	Mintage	F	VF	XF	Unc	BU
1992 Proof	550	Value: 185				

KM# 359 50 PESOS
155.5000 g., 0.9990 Silver 4.9942 oz. ASW **Series:** 500th Anniversary of the New World **Subject:** Chief Guama **Obv:** National arms within wreath **Rev:** Native drinking from large shell

Date	Mintage	F	VF	XF	Unc	BU
1992 Proof	550	Value: 185				

KM# 380 50 PESOS
155.7300 g., 0.9990 Silver 5.0016 oz. ASW **Series:** 500th Anniversary of the New World **Subject:** Bartolome de Las Casas **Obv:** National arms within wreath, denomination below **Rev:** Seated figure writing with quill

Date	Mintage	F	VF	XF	Unc	BU
1992 Proof	550	Value: 185				

KM# 381 50 PESOS
155.7300 g., 0.9990 Silver 5.0016 oz. ASW **Series:** 500th
Anniversary of the New World **Subject:** Ferdinand and Elisabeth,
Philipp and Joanna **Obv:** National arms within wreath,
denomination below **Rev:** Busts of Spanish Kings and Queens left

Date	Mintage	F	VF	XF	Unc	BU
ND(1992) Proof	550	Value: 185				

KM# 382 50 PESOS
155.7300 g., 0.9990 Silver 5.0016 oz. ASW **Obv:** National arms
within wreath, denomination below **Rev:** San Jorge Palace

Date	Mintage	F	VF	XF	Unc	BU
1992 Proof	550	Value: 185				

KM# 568 50 PESOS
155.7300 g., 0.9990 Silver 5.0016 oz. ASW **Subject:** Cuban
Fauna **Obv:** National arms within wreath, denomination below
Rev: Multicolored Papilio butterfly

Date	Mintage	F	VF	XF	Unc	BU
1992 Proof	—	Value: 200				

KM# 641 50 PESOS
155.7300 g., 0.9990 Silver 5.0016 oz. ASW **Subject:** 1982 -
Ano de Espana **Obv:** National arms within wreath, denomination
below **Rev:** Seville's Tower of Gold

Date	Mintage	F	VF	XF	Unc	BU
1992 Proof	—	Value: 200				

KM# 400 50 PESOS
155.5150 g., 0.9990 Silver 4.9947 oz. ASW **Obv:** National arms,
denomination below on left, crowned arms on right **Rev:** St.
Jacobi on rearing horse

Date	Mintage	F	VF	XF	Unc	BU
1993 Proof	1,000	Value: 175				

KM# 693 50 PESOS
15.5518 g., 0.9990 Gold 0.4995 oz. AGW **Subject:** 40th
Anniversary - Assault on Moncada Garrison

Date	Mintage	F	VF	XF	Unc	BU
1993 Proof	—	Value: 485				

KM# 503 50 PESOS
155.5150 g., 0.9990 Silver 4.9947 oz. ASW **Subject:** Caribbean
Fauna **Obv:** National arms within wreath, denomination below
Rev: Multicolor bottle-nosed dolphins **Edge:** Reeded

Date	Mintage	F	VF	XF	Unc	BU
1994 Proof	2,500	Value: 200				

KM# 504 50 PESOS
155.5150 g., 0.9990 Silver 4.9947 oz. ASW **Subject:** Caribbean
Fauna **Obv:** National arms within wreath, denomination below
Rev: Multicolor sailfish

Date	Mintage	F	VF	XF	Unc	BU
1994 Proof	2,500	Value: 200				

KM# 505 50 PESOS
155.5150 g., 0.9990 Silver 4.9947 oz. ASW **Subject:** Caribbean
Fauna **Obv:** National arms within wreath, denomination below
Rev: Multicolored brown pelican

Date	Mintage	F	VF	XF	Unc	BU
1994 Proof	2,500	Value: 200				

KM# 506 50 PESOS
155.5150 g., 0.9990 Silver 4.9947 oz. ASW **Subject:** Caribbean
Fauna **Obv:** National arms within wreath, denomination below
Rev: Multicolored flamingos

Date	Mintage	F	VF	XF	Unc	BU
1994 Proof	2,500	Value: 200				

KM# 507   50 PESOS
155.5150 g., 0.9990 Silver 4.9947 oz. ASW **Subject:** Caribbean
Fauna **Obv:** National arms within wreath, denomination below
Rev: Multicolored Yellow Grouper

Date	Mintage	F	VF	XF	Unc	BU
1994 Proof	2,500	Value: 200				

KM# 508   50 PESOS
155.5150 g., 0.9990 Silver 4.9947 oz. ASW **Subject:** Caribbean
Fauna **Obv:** National arms within wreath, denomination below
Rev: Multicolored spotted eagle ray

Date	Mintage	F	VF	XF	Unc	BU
1994 Proof	2,500	Value: 200				

KM# 484   50 PESOS
155.5150 g., 0.9990 Silver 4.9947 oz. ASW **Subject:** Pirates of
the Caribbean **Obv:** National arms within wreath, denomination
below **Rev:** Blackbeard within circle, date below

Date	Mintage	F	VF	XF	Unc	BU
1995 Proof	Est. 3,000	Value: 265				

KM# 485   50 PESOS
155.5150 g., 0.9990 Silver 4.9947 oz. ASW **Series:** Pirates of
the Caribbean **Subject:** Sir Henry Morgan **Obv:** National arms
within wreath, denomination below **Rev:** Pirate with rifle over right
shoulder left

Date	Mintage	F	VF	XF	Unc	BU
1995 Proof	Est. 3,000	Value: 265				

KM# 486   50 PESOS
155.5150 g., 0.9990 Silver 4.9947 oz. ASW **Series:** Pirates of
the Caribbean **Subject:** Anne Bonny **Obv:** National arms within
wreath, denomination below **Rev:** Bare-breasted woman and
pirates drinking within circle, date below

Date	Mintage	F	VF	XF	Unc	BU
1995 Proof	Est. 3,000	Value: 265				

KM# 487   50 PESOS
155.5150 g., 0.9990 Silver 4.9947 oz. ASW **Series:** Pirates of
the Caribbean **Subject:** Mary Read **Obv:** National arms within
wreath, denomination below **Rev:** Pirates fighting on the beach

Date	Mintage	F	VF	XF	Unc	BU
1995 Proof	Est. 3,000	Value: 265				

KM# 488   50 PESOS
155.5150 g., 0.9990 Silver 4.9947 oz. ASW **Series:** Pirates of
the Caribbean **Subject:** Captain Kidd **Obv:** National arms within
wreath, denomination below **Rev:** Pirates aboard ship

Date	Mintage	F	VF	XF	Unc	BU
1995 Proof	Est. 3,000	Value: 265				

KM# 489   50 PESOS
155.5150 g., 0.9990 Silver 4.9947 oz. ASW **Subject:** Piet Heyn
Obv: National arms within wreath, denomination below
Rev: Pirates having sword fight

Date	Mintage	F	VF	XF	Unc	BU
1995 Proof	Est. 3,000	Value: 265				

KM# 490   50 PESOS
13.0000 g., 0.9170 Gold 0.3833 oz. AGW **Series:** Pirates of the
Caribbean **Subject:** Blackbeard **Obv:** National arms within wreath,
denomination below **Rev:** Bust 3/4 facing within circle, date below

Date	Mintage	F	VF	XF	Unc	BU
1995 Proof	Est. 1,000	Value: 375				

KM# 491   50 PESOS
13.0000 g., 0.9170 Gold 0.3833 oz. AGW **Series:** Pirates of the
Caribbean **Subject:** Sir Henry Morgan **Obv:** National arms within
wreath, denomination below **Rev:** Bust 3/4 right

Date	Mintage	F	VF	XF	Unc	BU
1995 Proof	Est. 1,000	Value: 375				

KM# 492   50 PESOS
13.0000 g., 0.9170 Gold 0.3833 oz. AGW Series: Pirates of the Caribbean Subject: Anne Bonny Obv: National arms within wreath, denomination below Rev: Half-length female figure facing, ship in distance

Date	Mintage	F	VF	XF	Unc	BU
1995 Proof	Est. 1,000	Value: 375				

KM# 493   50 PESOS
13.0000 g., 0.9170 Gold 0.3833 oz. AGW Series: Pirates of the Caribbean Subject: Mary Read Obv: National arms within wreath, denomination below Rev: Half-length female figure facing, ship in distance

Date	Mintage	F	VF	XF	Unc	BU
1995 Proof	Est. 1,000	Value: 375				

KM# 494   50 PESOS
13.0000 g., 0.9170 Gold 0.3833 oz. AGW Series: Pirates of the Caribbean Subject: Captain Kidd Obv: National arms within wreath, denomination below Rev: Half-length figure looking right, ships in distance

Date	Mintage	F	VF	XF	Unc	BU
1995 Proof	Est. 1,000	Value: 375				

KM# 495   50 PESOS
13.0000 g., 0.9170 Gold 0.3833 oz. AGW Series: Pirates of the Caribbean Subject: Piet Heyn Obv: National arms within wreath, denomination below Rev: Half-length bust facing, ships in distance

Date	Mintage	F	VF	XF	Unc	BU
1995 Proof	Est. 1,000	Value: 375				

KM# 557   50 PESOS
155.0000 g., 0.9990 Silver 4.9782 oz. ASW Series: Caribbean Fauna Obv: National arms within wreath, denomination below Rev: Purple-throated Carib Hummingbird

Date	Mintage	F	VF	XF	Unc	BU
1996 Proof	950	Value: 300				

KM# 558   50 PESOS
155.0000 g., 0.9990 Silver 4.9782 oz. ASW Series: Caribbean Fauna Obv: National arms within wreath, denomination below Rev: Yellow perch

Date	Mintage	F	VF	XF	Unc	BU
1996 Proof	950	Value: 300				

KM# 559   50 PESOS
155.0000 g., 0.9990 Silver 4.9782 oz. ASW Series: Caribbean Fauna Obv: National arms within wreath, denomination below Rev: Cuban Tody bird

Date	Mintage	F	VF	XF	Unc	BU
1996 Proof	950	Value: 300				

KM# 560   50 PESOS
155.0000 g., 0.9990 Silver 4.9782 oz. ASW Series: Caribbean Fauna Obv: National arms within wreath, denomination below Rev: Wood duck

Date	Mintage	F	VF	XF	Unc	BU
1996 Proof	950	Value: 300				

KM# 564   50 PESOS
155.0000 g., 0.9990 Silver 4.9782 oz. ASW Series: Caribbean Fauna Obv: National arms within wreath, denomination below Rev: Vaca anil fish

Date	Mintage	F	VF	XF	Unc	BU
1996 Proof	950	Value: 300				

KM# 567   50 PESOS
155.0000 g., 0.9990 Silver 4.9782 oz. ASW Series: Caribbean Fauna Obv: National arms within wreath, denomination below Rev: Papilio butterfly

Date	Mintage	F	VF	XF	Unc	BU
1996 Proof	950	Value: 300				

KM# 694   50 PESOS
155.0000 g., 0.9990 Silver 4.9782 oz. ASW Subject: Caribbean Flora Obv: National arms within wreath, denomination below Rev: Multicolor flower, "Bidens Romerillo"

Date	Mintage	F	VF	XF	Unc	BU
1997 Proof	—	Value: 300				

KM# 695   50 PESOS
155.0000 g., 0.9990 Silver 4.9782 oz. ASW Subject: Caribbean Flora Obv: National arms within wreath, denomination below Rev: Multicolor flower, "Cordia Vomitel"

Date	Mintage	F	VF	XF	Unc	BU
1997 Proof	—	Value: 300				

KM# 697   50 PESOS
155.0000 g., 0.9990 Silver 4.9782 oz. ASW Subject: Wonders of the Ancient World Rev: Temple of Artemis

Date	Mintage	F	VF	XF	Unc	BU
1997 Proof	—	Value: 250				

KM# 698   50 PESOS
155.0000 g., 0.9990 Silver 4.9782 oz. ASW Subject: Wonders of the Ancient World Rev: Pyramids

Date	Mintage	F	VF	XF	Unc	BU
1997 Proof	—	Value: 250				

KM# 699   50 PESOS
155.0000 g., 0.9990 Silver 4.9782 oz. ASW Subject: Wonders of the Ancient World Rev: Hanging Gardens of Babylon

Date	Mintage	F	VF	XF	Unc	BU
1997 Proof	—	Value: 250				

KM# 700   50 PESOS
155.0000 g., 0.9990 Silver 4.9782 oz. ASW Subject: Wonders of the Ancient World Rev: Statue of Jupiter at Olympus

Date	Mintage	F	VF	XF	Unc	BU
1997 Proof	—	Value: 250				

KM# 701   50 PESOS
155.0000 g., 0.9990 Silver 4.9782 oz. ASW Subject: Wonders of the Ancient World Rev: Colossus of Rhodes

Date	Mintage	F	VF	XF	Unc	BU
1997 Proof	—	Value: 250				

KM# 702   50 PESOS
155.0000 g., 0.9990 Silver 4.9782 oz. ASW Subject: Wonders of the Ancient World Rev: Mausoleum at Halicarnasos

Date	Mintage	F	VF	XF	Unc	BU
1997 Proof	—	Value: 250				

KM# 654   50 PESOS
15.5500 g., 0.9990 Gold 0.4994 oz. AGW Subject: Expo 2000 Obv: National arms within wreath Rev: Twipsy cartoon logo

Date	Mintage	F	VF	XF	Unc	BU
1998 Proof	3,125	Value: 475				

KM# 638   50 PESOS
15.5500 g., 0.9990 Gold 0.4994 oz. AGW, 30 mm. Subject: AIDS Obv: National arms within wreath Rev: AIDS ribbon on silhouette before world map

Date	Mintage	F	VF	XF	Unc	BU
1998 Proof	2,000	Value: 475				

KM# 704   50 PESOS
15.5518 g., 0.9990 Gold 0.4995 oz. AGW, 32.5 mm. Obv: National arms Rev: Hummingbird Edge: Reeded

Date	Mintage	F	VF	XF	Unc	BU
1999 Proof	1,000	Value: 485				

KM# 703   50 PESOS
15.5500 g., 0.9990 Gold 0.4994 oz. AGW Subject: 40th Anniversary - Triumph of the Revolution

Date	Mintage	F	VF	XF	Unc	BU
1999 Proof	—	Value: 475				

KM# 705   50 PESOS
15.5500 g., 0.9990 Gold 0.4994 oz. AGW Subject: Welcome the New Millennium

Date	Mintage	F	VF	XF	Unc	BU
2000 Proof	—	Value: 350				

KM# 706   50 PESOS
15.5500 g., 0.9990 Gold 0.4994 oz. AGW Subject: Welcome the Third Millennium

Date	Mintage	F	VF	XF	Unc	BU
2000 Proof	—	Value: 350				

KM# 707   50 PESOS
15.5500 g., 0.9990 Gold 0.4994 oz. AGW Subject: Hacia un Nuevo Milenio (Towards a new Millennium)

Date	Mintage	F	VF	XF	Unc	BU
2000 Proof	—	Value: 350				

KM# 42   100 PESOS
12.0000 g., 0.9170 Gold 0.3538 oz. AGW Subject: 60th Anniversary of Socialist Revolution - Lenin Obv: National arms within wreath, denomination below Rev: Bust left divides dates

Date	Mintage	F	VF	XF	Unc	BU
ND(1977) Proof	10	Value: 10,000				

KM# 43   100 PESOS
12.0000 g., 0.9170 Gold 0.3538 oz. AGW Obv: Liberty cap above flagged arms, denomination Rev: Carlos Manuel de Cespedes

Date	Mintage	F	VF	XF	Unc	BU
ND(1977) Proof	25,000	Value: 350				

KM# 45   100 PESOS
12.0000 g., 0.9170 Gold 0.3538 oz. AGW Subject: Nonaligned Nations Conference Obv: National arms within wreath Rev: Number six within design

Date	Mintage	F	VF	XF	Unc	BU
1979	2,000	—	—	—	375	425
1979 Proof	20,000	Value: 350				

KM# 52   100 PESOS
12.0000 g., 0.9170 Gold 0.3538 oz. AGW Subject: First Soviet-Cuban space flight Obv: Arms Rev: Shuttle orbiting planet, date below

Date	Mintage	F	VF	XF	Unc	BU
1980	1,000	—	—	—	375	425

KM# 85   100 PESOS
12.0000 g., 0.9170 Gold 0.3538 oz. AGW Obv: National arms within wreath, denomination below Rev: Columbus' ship - Niña

Date	Mintage	F	VF	XF	Unc	BU
1981	2,000	—	—	—	350	400

KM# 86   100 PESOS
12.0000 g., 0.9170 Gold 0.3538 oz. AGW **Obv:** National arms within wreath, denomination below **Rev:** Columbus' ship - Pinta

Date	Mintage	F	VF	XF	Unc	BU
1981	2,000	—	—	—	350	400

KM# 87   100 PESOS
12.0000 g., 0.9170 Gold 0.3538 oz. AGW **Obv:** National arms within wreath, denomination below **Rev:** Columbus' ship - Santa Maria

Date	Mintage	F	VF	XF	Unc	BU
1981	2,000	—	—	—	350	400

KM# 202   100 PESOS
31.1030 g., 0.9990 Gold 0.9989 oz. AGW **Subject:** 30th Anniversary of March to Victory **Obv:** Arms on star background above half wreath **Rev:** Soldiers on the march

Date	Mintage	F	VF	XF	Unc	BU
1988 Proof	100	Value: 975				

KM# 203   100 PESOS
31.1030 g., 0.9990 Gold 0.9989 oz. AGW **Subject:** 60th Anniversary - Birth of Ernesto Che Guevara **Obv:** Arms on star background above half wreath **Rev:** Bust right, dates at left

Date	Mintage	F	VF	XF	Unc	BU
1988 Proof	100	Value: 975				

KM# 204   100 PESOS
31.1030 g., 0.9990 Gold 0.9989 oz. AGW **Subject:** 30th Anniversary - Triumph of the Revolution **Obv:** Arms on star background above half wreath **Rev:** Scene of triumph, dates

Date	Mintage	F	VF	XF	Unc	BU
1988 Proof	100	Value: 975				

KM# 215   100 PESOS
31.1030 g., 0.9990 Gold 0.9989 oz. AGW **Subject:** Jose Marti **Obv:** National arms within wreath, denomination below **Rev:** Head right, date below

Date	Mintage	F	VF	XF	Unc	BU
1988	50	—	—	—	1,150	—
1988 Proof	15	Value: 1,300				
1989	150	—	—	—	1,100	—
1989 Proof	15	Value: 1,300				
1990	15	—	—	—	1,250	—
1990 Proof	12	Value: 1,350				

KM# 316   100 PESOS
31.1030 g., 0.9990 Gold 0.9989 oz. AGW **Subject:** 160th Anniversary - First train in England **Rev:** Train **Rev. Leg.:** LIVERPOOL-MANCHESTER

Date	Mintage	F	VF	XF	Unc	BU
1989 Proof	150	Value: 975				

KM# 317   100 PESOS
31.1030 g., 0.9990 Gold 0.9989 oz. AGW **Subject:** 150th Anniversary - First train in Spanish America **Rev:** Train **Rev. Leg.:** HABANA-BEJUCAL

Date	Mintage	F	VF	XF	Unc	BU
1989 Proof	150	Value: 975				

KM# 318   100 PESOS
31.1030 g., 0.9990 Gold 0.9989 oz. AGW **Subject:** 140th Anniversary - First train in Spain **Rev:** Train **Rev. Leg.:** BARCELONA-MATARO

Date	Mintage	F	VF	XF	Unc	BU
1989 Proof	150	Value: 975				

KM# 319   100 PESOS
31.1030 g., 0.9990 Gold 0.9989 oz. AGW **Subject:** 200th Anniversary of French Revolution - Lady Justice **Rev:** Female revolutionary raising flag

Date	Mintage	F	VF	XF	Unc	BU
1989 Proof	150	Value: 975				

KM# 320   100 PESOS
31.1030 g., 0.9990 Gold 0.9989 oz. AGW **Subject:** 200th Anniversary of French Revolution - Bastille **Rev:** Bastille, soldiers in foreground

Date	Mintage	F	VF	XF	Unc	BU
1989	150	—	—	—	985	—

KM# 333   100 PESOS
31.1030 g., 0.9990 Gold 0.9989 oz. AGW **Subject:** Tania La Guerrillera **Rev:** Portrait of female guerilla fighter

Date	Mintage	F	VF	XF	Unc	BU
1989 Proof	150	Value: 985				

KM# 334   100 PESOS
31.1030 g., 0.9990 Gold 0.9989 oz. AGW **Subject:** Camilo Cienfuegos Gornaran **Rev:** Portrait of Camilo Cienfuegos

Date	Mintage	F	VF	XF	Unc	BU
1989 Proof	150	Value: 985				

KM# 335   100 PESOS
31.1030 g., 0.9990 Gold 0.9989 oz. AGW **Subject:** 35th Anniversary - Assault of the Moncada Garrison **Rev:** Battle scene

Date	Mintage	F	VF	XF	Unc	BU
1989 Proof	150	Value: 985				

KM# 447   100 PESOS
31.1030 g., 0.9990 Gold 0.9989 oz. AGW **Subject:** 30th Anniversary of Revolution **Obv:** National arms within wreath, denomination **Rev:** Armed, uniformed figure standing right

Date	Mintage	F	VF	XF	Unc	BU
1989 Proof	250	Value: 975				

KM# 448   100 PESOS
31.1030 g., 0.9990 Gold 0.9989 oz. AGW **Subject:** 30th Anniversary of Revolution **Obv:** National arms within wreath, denomination **Rev:** Armed, uniformed figure standing right

Date	Mintage	F	VF	XF	Unc	BU
1989 Proof	250	Value: 975				

KM# 449   100 PESOS
31.1030 g., 0.9990 Gold 0.9989 oz. AGW **Subject:** 30th Anniversary of Revolution **Obv:** National arms within wreath, denomination **Rev:** Armed, uniformed figure standing right

Date	Mintage	F	VF	XF	Unc	BU
1989 Proof	250	Value: 975				

KM# 302   100 PESOS
31.1030 g., 0.9990 Gold 0.9989 oz. AGW **Subject:** 500th Anniversary - Discovery of America **Rev:** Portrait of Columbus

Date	Mintage	F	VF	XF	Unc	BU
1990 Proof	250	Value: 1,000				

KM# 303   100 PESOS
31.1030 g., 0.9990 Gold 0.9989 oz. AGW **Subject:** 500th Anniversary - Discovery of America **Rev:** Portrait of King Ferdinand V

Date	Mintage	F	VF	XF	Unc	BU
1990 Proof	250	Value: 1,000			•	

KM# 304   100 PESOS
31.1030 g., 0.9990 Gold 0.9989 oz. AGW **Subject:** 500th Anniversary - Discovery of America **Rev:** Portrait of Queen Isabella

Date	Mintage	F	VF	XF	Unc	BU
1990 Proof	250	Value: 1,000				

KM# 305   100 PESOS
31.1030 g., 0.9990 Gold 0.9989 oz. AGW **Subject:** 500th Anniversary - Discovery of America **Rev:** Portrait of Juan de la Cosa

Date	Mintage	F	VF	XF	Unc	BU
1990 Proof	250	Value: 1,000				

KM# 450   100 PESOS
31.1030 g., 0.9990 Gold 0.9989 oz. AGW **Subject:** Pinzon brothers **Obv:** National arms within wreath

Date	Mintage	F	VF	XF	Unc	BU
1991 Proof	200	Value: 975				

KM# 451   100 PESOS
31.1030 g., 0.9990 Gold 0.9989 oz. AGW **Subject:** 500th Anniversary of the New World **Rev:** Head of Queen Joanna half right, 1479-1555, daughter of Queen Isabella I

Date	Mintage	F	VF	XF	Unc	BU
1991 Proof	200	Value: 975				

KM# 452   100 PESOS
31.1030 g., 0.9990 Gold 0.9989 oz. AGW **Subject:** 500th Anniversary **Obv:** National arms within wreath **Rev:** Diego Velazquez

Date	Mintage	F	VF	XF	Unc	BU
1991 Proof	200	Value: 975				

KM# 534   100 PESOS
31.1030 g., 0.9990 Gold 0.9989 oz. AGW **Series:** Olympics **Rev:** Stadium

Date	Mintage	F	VF	XF	Unc	BU
1991 Proof	225	Value: 1,000				

KM# 535   100 PESOS
31.1030 g., 0.9990 Gold 0.9989 oz. AGW **Subject:** Madrid - Alcala Gate **Rev:** Building with arches

Date	Mintage	F	VF	XF	Unc	BU
1991 Proof	225	Value: 1,000				

KM# 569   100 PESOS
31.1030 g., 0.9990 Gold 0.9989 oz. AGW **Subject:** Hatuey People

Date	Mintage	F	VF	XF	Unc	BU
1991 Proof	—	Value: 1,000				

KM# 384   100 PESOS
31.1030 g., 0.9990 Gold 0.9989 oz. AGW **Subject:** Seville - Tower of Gold **Rev:** Tower of Gold in Seville

Date	Mintage	F	VF	XF	Unc	BU
1992 Proof	225	Value: 1,000				

KM# 385   100 PESOS
31.1030 g., 0.9990 Gold 0.9989 oz. AGW **Subject:** El Escorial **Rev:** El Escorial palace

Date	Mintage	F	VF	XF	Unc	BU
1992 Proof	225	Value: 1,000				

KM# 453   100 PESOS
31.1030 g., 0.9990 Gold 0.9989 oz. AGW **Subject:** 500th Anniversary **Obv:** National arms within wreath **Rev:** Bartolome de las Casas

Date	Mintage	F	VF	XF	Unc	BU
1992 Proof	100	Value: 975				

KM# 454   100 PESOS
31.1030 g., 0.9990 Gold 0.9989 oz. AGW **Subject:** 500th Anniversary **Obv:** National arms within wreath **Rev:** Guama Tribesman

Date	Mintage	F	VF	XF	Unc	BU
1992 Proof	100	Value: 975				

KM# 455   100 PESOS
31.1030 g., 0.9990 Gold 0.9989 oz. AGW **Subject:** 500th
Anniversary **Obv:** National arms within wreath **Rev:** King Philipp

Date	Mintage	F	VF	XF	Unc	BU
1992 Proof	100	Value: 975				

KM# 456   100 PESOS
31.1030 g., 0.9990 Gold 0.9989 oz. AGW **Subject:** 500th
Anniversary **Obv:** National arms within wreath **Rev:** Spanish
kings and queens

Date	Mintage	F	VF	XF	Unc	BU
1992 Proof	100	Value: 975				

KM# 536   100 PESOS
31.1030 g., 0.9990 Gold 0.9989 oz. AGW **Subject:** San Jorge
Palace

Date	Mintage	F	VF	XF	Unc	BU
1992 Proof	225	Value: 1,000				

KM# 570   100 PESOS
31.1030 g., 0.9990 Gold 0.9989 oz. AGW **Subject:** Ernesto Che
Guevara **Obv:** National arms within wreath

Date	Mintage	F	VF	XF	Unc	BU
1992 Proof	—	Value: 975				

KM# 537   100 PESOS
31.1030 g., 0.9990 Gold 0.9989 oz. AGW **Subject:** 40th
Anniversary of Moncada **Rev:** Fidel Castro

Date	Mintage	F	VF	XF	Unc	BU
1993 Proof	100	Value: 1,000				

KM# 538   100 PESOS
31.1030 g., 0.9990 Gold 0.9989 oz. AGW **Obv:** Two sets of
arms and denomination **Rev:** St. Jacobi

Date	Mintage	F	VF	XF	Unc	BU
1993 Proof	100	Value: 1,000				

KM# 539   100 PESOS
31.1030 g., 0.9990 Gold 0.9989 oz. AGW **Rev:** Federico Garcia
Lorca

Date	Mintage	F	VF	XF	Unc	BU
1993 Proof	100	Value: 975				

KM# 571   100 PESOS
31.1030 g., 0.9990 Gold 0.9989 oz. AGW **Obv:** National arms
within wreath **Rev:** Jose Marti

Date	Mintage	F	VF	XF	Unc	BU
1994 Proof	—	Value: 975				

KM# 572   100 PESOS
31.1030 g., 0.9990 Gold 0.9989 oz. AGW **Subject:** Centennial
of the Necessary War

Date	Mintage	F	VF	XF	Unc	BU
1995 Proof	—	Value: 975				

KM# 708   100 PESOS
31.1030 g., 0.9990 Gold 0.9989 oz. AGW **Subject:** Meeting of
Fidel Castro and Pope John Paul II in the Vatican

Date	Mintage	F	VF	XF	Unc	BU
1997 Proof	—	Value: 975				

KM# 709   100 PESOS
31.1030 g., 0.9990 Gold 0.9989 oz. AGW **Subject:** Papal visit
to Cuba

Date	Mintage	F	VF	XF	Unc	BU
1997 Proof	—	Value: 975				

KM# 710   100 PESOS
31.1030 g., 0.9990 Gold 0.9989 oz. AGW **Subject:** 90th
Anniversary - Triumph of the Revolution

Date	Mintage	F	VF	XF	Unc	BU
1999 Proof	—	Value: 975				

KM# 719   100 PESOS
31.1035 g., 0.9990 Gold 0.9990 oz. AGW, 38 mm. **Obv:** National
arms **Rev:** Hummingbird **Edge:** Reeded **Note:** Prev. KM#728.

Date	Mintage	F	VF	XF	Unc	BU
1999 Proof	1,000	Value: 975				

KM# 711   100 PESOS
31.1030 g., 0.9990 Gold 0.9989 oz. AGW **Subject:** Macia un
Nuevo Milenio (Towards a new millennium)

Date	Mintage	F	VF	XF	Unc	BU
2000 Proof	—	Value: 900				

KM# 712   100 PESOS
31.1030 g., 0.9990 Gold 0.9989 oz. AGW **Subject:** Welcome
to the third millennium

Date	Mintage	F	VF	XF	Unc	BU
2000 Proof	—	Value: 900				

KM# 713   100 PESOS
31.1030 g., 0.9990 Gold 0.9989 oz. AGW **Subject:** Welcome
to the new millennium

Date	Mintage	F	VF	XF	Unc	BU
2000 Proof	—	Value: 900				

KM# 714   100 PESOS
31.1030 g., 0.9990 Gold 0.9989 oz. AGW **Subject:** Maritime
relics - school ship Galatea

Date	Mintage	F	VF	XF	Unc	BU
2000 Proof	—	Value: 900				

KM# 715   100 PESOS
31.1030 g., 0.9990 Gold 0.9989 oz. AGW **Subject:** Maritime
relics - maritime ambulance Buena Ventura

Date	Mintage	F	VF	XF	Unc	BU
2000 Proof	—	Value: 900				

KM# 716   100 PESOS
31.1030 g., 0.9990 Gold 0.9989 oz. AGW **Subject:** Maritime
relics - nautical rise of Juan de la Cosa

Date	Mintage	F	VF	XF	Unc	BU
2000 Proof	—	Value: 900				

KM# 717   100 PESOS
31.1030 g., 0.9990 Gold 0.9989 oz. AGW **Subject:** Maritime
relics - school ship JS Elcana

Date	Mintage	F	VF	XF	Unc	BU
2000 Proof	—	Value: 900				

KM# 718   100 PESOS
31.1030 g., 0.9990 Gold 0.9989 oz. AGW **Subject:** Maritime
relics - Peral submarine

Date	Mintage	F	VF	XF	Unc	BU
2000 Proof	—	Value: 900				

KM# 642   150 PESOS
411.4225 g., 0.9990 Silver 13.213 oz. ASW **Series:** Cuban Fauna
Obv: National arms within wreath **Rev:** Multicolored Cuban Trogon
Note: The Cuban Trogon is the Cuban National Bird.

Date	Mintage	F	VF	XF	Unc	BU
1996 Proof	Est. 420	Value: 600				

KM# 542   200 PESOS
31.1000 g., Gold **Obv:** National arms within wreath **Rev:** Bolivar
and Marti

Date	Mintage	F	VF	XF	Unc	BU
1993	100	—	—	—	950	—
1993 Proof	100	Value: 1,000				

KM# 543   200 PESOS
31.1000 g., Gold **Series:** Prehistoric Animals **Obv:** National
arms within wreath **Rev:** Apatosaurus

Date	Mintage	F	VF	XF	Unc	BU
1993 Proof	100	Value: 975				

KM# 544   200 PESOS
31.1000 g., Gold **Series:** Prehistoric Animals **Rev:** Chalicotherium

Date	Mintage	F	VF	XF	Unc	BU
1993 Proof	100	Value: 1,000				

KM# 545   200 PESOS
31.1000 g., Gold   **Subject:** Montecristi Manifesto **Rev:** Two seated figures facing each other, date lower left

Date	Mintage	F	VF	XF	Unc	BU
1994 Proof	100	Value: 1,000				

KM# 643   300 PESOS
822.8449 g., 0.9990 Silver 26.427 oz. ASW   **Series:** Cuban Fauna **Obv:** National arms within wreath **Rev:** Multicolor Mariposa butterfly

Date	Mintage	F	VF	XF	Unc	BU
1996 Proof	Est. 420	Value: 975				

KM# 457   500 PESOS
155.5500 g., 0.9990 Gold 4.9958 oz. AGW   **Rev:** Christopher Columbus

Date	Mintage	F	VF	XF	Unc	BU
1990 Proof	15	Value: 5,500				

KM# 386   500 PESOS
155.5500 g., 0.9990 Gold 4.9958 oz. AGW   **Subject:** 500th Anniversary **Obv:** National arms within wreath **Rev:** Spanish Kings and Queens

Date	Mintage	F	VF	XF	Unc	BU
ND(1992) Proof	15	Value: 5,500				

KM# 605   500 PESOS
155.5500 g., 0.9990 Platinum 4.9958 oz. APW   **Subject:** Castro **Rev:** Fidel Castro

Date	Mintage	F	VF	XF	Unc	BU
1993 Proof		Value: 10,500				

KM# 720   500 PESOS
49.0000 g., 0.9990 Gold-Silver 1.5737 oz.   **Subject:** Che Guevara

Date	Mintage	F	VF	XF	Unc	BU
2000 Proof	101	Value: 1,950				

PESO CONVERTIBLE SERIES

KM# 729   CENTAVO
1.7000 g., Copper Plated Steel, 15 mm.   **Obv:** National arms within wreath, denomination below **Rev:** Tower and denomination **Edge:** Reeded

Date	Mintage	F	VF	XF	Unc	BU
2000	—	—	—	—	3.00	—

KM# 575.1   5 CENTAVOS
2.6300 g., Nickel-Plated Steel, 17.9 mm.   **Obv:** National arms within wreath, denomination and date below **Rev:** Casa Colonial, denomination above **Note:** Medal alignment

Date	Mintage	F	VF	XF	Unc	BU
1994	—	—	—	—	1.00	—

KM# 575.2   5 CENTAVOS
2.6500 g., Nickel-Plated Steel, 18 mm.   **Obv:** National arms **Rev:** Casa Colonial **Note:** Coin alignment, recut designs.

Date	Mintage	F	VF	XF	Unc	BU
1996	—	—	—	—	1.00	—
1998	—	—	—	—	1.00	—
1999	—	—	—	—	1.00	—
2000	—	—	—	—	1.00	—

KM# 576.1   10 CENTAVOS
Nickel-Bonded Steel, 20 mm.   **Obv:** National arms within wreath, denomination and date below **Rev:** Castillo de la Fuerza, denomination above **Note:** Medal alignment.

Date	Mintage	F	VF	XF	Unc	BU
1994	—	—	—	—	2.00	—

KM# 576.2   10 CENTAVOS
3.9400 g., Nickel Plated Steel   **Obv:** National arms **Rev:** Castillo de la Fuerza **Note:** Coin alignment, recut designs.

Date	Mintage	F	VF	XF	Unc	BU
1996	—	—	—	—	2.00	—
1999	—	—	—	—	2.00	—
2000	—	—	—	—	2.00	—

KM# 577.1   25 CENTAVOS
Nickel Bonded Steel, 23 mm.   **Obv:** National arms within wreath, denomination and date below **Rev:** Trinidad, denomination upper right **Note:** Medal alignment. Prev. KM#577.

Date	Mintage	F	VF	XF	Unc	BU
1994	—	—	—	—	3.00	—

KM# 577.2   25 CENTAVOS
5.7000 g., Nickel Plated Steel, 23 mm.   **Obv:** National arms **Rev:** Trinidad **Note:** Coin alignment.

Date	Mintage	F	VF	XF	Unc	BU
1998	—	—	—	—	3.00	—
2000	—	—	—	—	3.00	—

KM# 578.1   50 CENTAVOS
7.5000 g., Nickel Plated Steel, 25 mm.   **Obv:** National arms within wreath, denomination and date below **Rev:** Cathedral of Havana, denomination above **Note:** Medal alignment.

Date	Mintage	F	VF	XF	Unc	BU
1994	—	—	—	—	5.00	—

KM# 579.1   PESO
8.5000 g., Nickel Plated Steel, 27 mm.   **Obv:** National arms within wreath, denomination and date below **Rev:** Guama, denomination upper left **Note:** Medal alignment.

Date	Mintage	F	VF	XF	Unc	BU
1994	—	—	—	—	5.00	—

KM# 579.2   PESO
8.5000 g., Nickel Plated Steel, 27 mm.   **Obv:** National arms **Rev:** Guama **Note:** Coin alignment.

Date	Mintage	F	VF	XF	Unc	BU
1998	—	—	—	—	5.00	—
2000	—	—	—	—	5.00	—

KM# 730   5 PESOS
4.4600 g., Bi-Metallic Nickel Plated Steel center in Brass Plated Steel ring, 23 mm.   **Obv:** National arms within wreath, denomination below **Rev:** Bust right, denomination at right, within circle **Edge:** Reeded **Note:** Medal alignment.

Date	Mintage	F	VF	XF	Unc	BU
1999	—	—	—	—	25.00	—

VISITOR'S COINAGE

KM# 409   CENTAVO
Copper-Nickel   **Obv:** Stag, date below **Rev:** Palm tree within logo and denomination

Date	Mintage	F	VF	XF	Unc	BU
1988	—	—	0.50	1.50	3.00	—

KM# 410   CENTAVO
Aluminum   **Obv:** Palm tree within logo **Rev:** Denomination

Date	Mintage	F	VF	XF	Unc	BU
1988	—	—	0.50	1.50	5.00	—

KM# 411   5 CENTAVOS
Copper-Nickel   **Obv:** Mollusk and date **Rev:** Palm tree within logo, denomination

Date	Mintage	F	VF	XF	Unc	BU
1981	—	0.45	0.75	2.00	4.00	—

KM# 412.1   5 CENTAVOS
Copper-Nickel   **Obv:** Mollusk and date **Rev:** Palm tree within logo, denomination

Date	Mintage	F	VF	XF	Unc	BU
1981	—	0.45	0.75	2.00	4.00	—

KM# 412.2   5 CENTAVOS
Copper-Nickel   **Obv:** Mollusk and date **Rev:** Palm tree within logo, denomination

Date	Mintage	F	VF	XF	Unc	BU
1981	—	0.45	0.75	2.00	4.00	—

KM# 412.3   5 CENTAVOS
Copper-Nickel   **Obv:** Mollusk and date **Rev:** Palm tree within logo, small 5

Date	Mintage	F	VF	XF	Unc	BU
1989	—	0.35	0.50	1.50	3.00	—

KM# 412.3a   5 CENTAVOS
Copper-Nickel   **Obv:** Palm tree within logo, denomination **Rev:** Mollusk and date

Date	Mintage	F	VF	XF	Unc	BU
1989	—	—	1.00	3.00	6.00	—

KM# 413   5 CENTAVOS
Aluminum   **Obv:** Palm tree within logo, date below **Rev:** Denomination

Date	Mintage	F	VF	XF	Unc	BU
1988	—	0.50	1.00	3.00	5.00	—

KM# 414   10 CENTAVOS
Copper-Nickel   **Obv:** Hummingbird in flight right, date below **Rev:** Palm tree within logo, denomination

Date	Mintage	F	VF	XF	Unc	BU
1981	—	0.65	2.00	4.00	5.00	

KM# 415.1   10 CENTAVOS
Copper-Nickel   **Obv:** Hummingbird in flight right, date below **Rev:** Palm tree within logo, large "10"

Date	Mintage	F	VF	XF	Unc	BU
1981	—	0.50	1.00	3.00	5.00	7.00

KM# 415.2   10 CENTAVOS
Copper-Nickel   **Obv:** Hummingbird in flight right, date below **Rev:** Palm tree within logo, small "10"

Date	Mintage	F	VF	XF	Unc	BU
1981	—	0.65	2.00	4.00	15.00	

KM# 416   10 CENTAVOS
Aluminum   **Obv:** Palm tree within logo, date below **Rev:** Denomination

Date	Mintage	F	VF	XF	Unc	BU
1988	—	0.65	2.00	4.00		

KM# 415.2a   10 CENTAVOS
Stainless Steel   **Obv:** Hummingbird in flight right **Rev:** Palm tree within logo, small 10

Date	Mintage	F	VF	XF	Unc	BU
1989	—	1.25	4.00	9.00	30.00	

KM# 415.3   10 CENTAVOS
Copper-Nickel   **Obv:** Hummingbird in flight right **Rev:** Palm tree within logo, denomination **Note:** Reduced size.

Date	Mintage	F	VF	XF	Unc	BU
1989	—	1.25	4.50	10.00		

KM# 417   25 CENTAVOS
6.3200 g., Copper-Nickel   **Obv:** Flower, date below **Rev:** Palm tree within logo, denomination

Date	Mintage	F	VF	XF	Unc	BU
1981	—	0.50	1.00	2.50	6.00	

KM# 418.1   25 CENTAVOS
Copper-Nickel   **Obv:** Flower, date below **Rev:** Palm tree within logo, large 25

Date	Mintage	F	VF	XF	Unc	BU
1981	—	1.00	3.00	7.00		

KM# 418.2   25 CENTAVOS
Copper-Nickel   **Obv:** Flower, date below **Rev:** Palm tree within logo, small 25

Date	Mintage	F	VF	XF	Unc	BU
1989	—	1.00	3.00	7.00		

KM# 418.2a   25 CENTAVOS
Stainless Steel   **Obv:** Flower and date **Rev:** Palm tree within logo, denomination

Date	Mintage	F	VF	XF	Unc	BU
1989	—	2.00	5.50	12.00		

KM# 419   25 CENTAVOS
Aluminum   **Obv:** Palm tree within logo, date below **Rev:** Denomination

Date	Mintage	F	VF	XF	Unc	BU
1988	—	0.75	2.50	5.00		

KM# 420   50 CENTAVOS
Copper-Nickel   **Obv:** Palm tree within logo, date below **Rev:** Denomination and logo

Date	Mintage	F	VF	XF	Unc	BU
1981	—	2.50	7.50	15.00		

Note: Varieties exist in the number of lines below the palm tree.

KM# 461   50 CENTAVOS
Copper-Nickel   **Obv:** Palm tree within logo, denomination **Rev:** Denomination and logo

Date	Mintage	F	VF	XF	Unc	BU
1989	—	5.00	15.00	30.00		

KM# 421   PESO
Copper-Nickel   **Obv:** Lighthouse **Rev:** Palm tree within logo, denomination

Date	Mintage	F	VF	XF	Unc	BU
1981	—	4.00	12.00	24.00		

KM# 580   PESO
Copper-Nickel   **Obv:** Lighthouse **Rev:** Palm tree within logo, denomination

Date	Mintage	F	VF	XF	Unc	BU
1989	—	4.00	12.00	24.00		

TRIAL STRIKES

KM#	Date	Mintage	Identification	Mkt Val
TS1	1977	—	20 Pesos. Brass. Antonio Maceo, KM40. Prev. KM#TS5.	300
TS2	1977	—	20 Pesos. Brass. Maximo Gomez, KM39. Prev. KM#TS6.	300
TS3	1977	—	20 Pesos. Brass. Ignacio Aramonte, KM38. Prev. KM#TS7.	300
TS4	1977	—	20 Pesos. Copper-Nickel. Antonio Maceo, KM40. Prev. KM#TS8.	500
TS5	1977	—	100 Pesos. Brass. de Cespedes, KM43. Prev. KM#TS9.	300
TS6	1994	10	100 Pesos. Gold. Reverse of KM467, uniface. Prev. KM#TS2.	2,000
TS7	1994	1	50 Pesos. Silver. KM503; dolphins green and red. Prev. KM#TS3.	—
TS8	1994	1	50 Pesos. Silver. KM503, dolphins green and red.	—

PATTERNS
Including off metal strikes

KM#	Date	Mintage	Identification	Mkt Val
PnA10	1915	—	Centavo. Bronze.	
PnC10	1915	—	2 Centavos. Bronze.	2,000
PnA11	1970	—	Peso. 0.9990 Silver. KM158.	500
PnB11	1970	—	Peso. 0.9990 Silver. KM158.	500
PnC11	1986	—	5 Pesos. 0.9000 Copper. KM326.	—
PnD11	1986	—	5 Pesos. 0.0500 Silver. KM326.	—
PnE11	1986	—	5 Pesos. 0.0500 Gold. KM326.	—
PnF11	1987	—	5 Pesos. Copper. KM166.	—
PnG11	1987	—	5 Pesos. Copper. .900 Copper, 050 Silver, .050 Gold, KM#26.	—
Pn11	1987	3	5 Pesos. 0.9990 Gold. KM159.	6,500
PnA12	1988	6	5 Pesos. 0.9990 Silver.	1,150
Pn12	1988	6	5 Pesos. Silver.	1,150
PnA13	1988	6	100 Pesos. 0.9990 Gold.	5,500
PnB13	1988	—	100 Pesos. 0.9990 Gold.	5,500
Pn13	1988	6	100 Pesos. Gold.	—
Pn14	1993	34	10 Pesos. Silver. Mirror bust with frosted field. KM398.	600
Pn15	1994	25	10 Pesos. Silver. KM510, player's #9 on the back is matte.	385
Pn16	1995	22	10 Pesos. Silver. Key mint mark in proof.	385
Pn17	1995	100	Peso. Copper Nickel. Pirates del Carib, Sir Francis Drake, proof.	120
Pn106	1999	—	Peso. Copper-Nickel. KM662.	100
Pn107	1999	—	10 Pesos. Silver. KM672.	200
Pn108	1999	—	100 Pesos. Gold. KM710.	1,500

KM#	Date	Mintage	Identification	Mkt Val
Pn109	2000	—	Peso. Copper-Nickel. KM665.	
Pn110	2000	—	Peso. Copper-Nickel. KM664.	100
Pn111	2000	—	Peso. Copper-Nickel. KM663.	100
Pn112	2000	—	10 Pesos. Silver. KM685.	200
Pn113	2000	—	10 Pesos. Silver. KM681.	200
Pn114	2000	—	10 Pesos. Silver. KM678	200
Pn115	2000	—	10 Pesos. Silver. KM678.	200
Pn116	2000	—	10 Pesos. Silver. KM680.	200
Pn118	2000	—	10 Pesos. Silver. KM691.	200
Pn119	2000	—	10 Pesos. Silver. KM689.	200
Pn120	2000	—	10 Pesos. Silver. KM688.	200
Pn121	2000	—	10 Pesos. Silver. KM687.	200
Pn122	2000	—	10 Pesos. Silver. KM686.	200
Pn123	2000	—	10 Pesos. Silver. KM690.	200
Pn124	2000	—	10 Pesos. Silver. Ship Rays 1749-1805.	200
Pn125	2000	—	10 Pesos. Silver. Ship: Sand Pedro de Alcantara	200
Pn126	2000	—	10 Pesos. Silver. Ship: Santisma Trinidad.	200
Pn127	2000	—	10 Pesos. Silver. KM684.	200
Pn128	2000	—	10 Pesos. Silver. KM683.	200
Pn129	2000	—	100 Pesos. Gold. KM712.	1,500
Pn130	2000	—	100 Pesos. Gold. KM711.	1,500
Pn131	2000	—	100 Pesos. Gold. KM713.	1,500
Pn132	2000	—	100 Pesos. Gold. KM718.	1,500
Pn133	2000	—	100 Pesos. Gold. KM717.	1,250
Pn134	2000	—	100 Pesos. Gold. KM714.	1,500
Pn135	2000	—	100 Pesos. Gold. KM715.	1,500
Pn136	2000	—	100 Pesos. Gold. KM716.	1,500

PIEFORTS

KM#	Date	Mintage	Identification	Mkt Val
P3	1983	100	5 Pesos. Silver. KM10.	200
P4	1988	30	10 Pesos. Gold. KM211.	1,200
P5	1988	30	10 Pesos. Gold. KM211.	1,200
P6	1988	15	15 Pesos. Gold. KM212.	1,200
P7	1988	15	15 Pesos. Gold. KM212.	1,200
P8	1988	10	25 Pesos. Gold. KM213.	1,600
P9	1988	10	25 Pesos. Gold. KM213.	1,600
P10	1988	10	50 Pesos. Gold. KM214.	1,600
P11	1988	10	50 Pesos. Gold. KM214.	1,600
P12	1988	10	100 Pesos. Gold. KM215.	2,200
P13	1988	10	100 Pesos. Gold. KM215.	2,200
P14	1989	30	10 Pesos. Gold. KM211.	1,200
P15	1989	30	10 Pesos. Gold. KM211.	1,200
P16	1989	150	10 Pesos. Silver. KM239.	200
P17	1989	150	10 Pesos. Silver. KM240.	200
P18	1989	15	15 Pesos. Gold. KM212.	1,200
P19	1989	15	15 Pesos. Gold. KM212.	1,200
P20	1989	10	25 Pesos. Gold. KM213.	1,600
P21	1989	15	25 Pesos. Gold. KM213.	1,600
P22	1989	10	50 Pesos. Gold. KM214.	2,200
P23	1989	15	50 Pesos. Gold. KM214.	2,200
P24	1989	12	50 Pesos. Gold. KM313.	1,800
P25	1989	12	50 Pesos. Gold. KM314.	1,800
P26	1989	12	50 Pesos. Gold. KM315.	1,800
P27	1989	15	100 Pesos. Silver. KM215.	—
P28	1989	15	100 Pesos. Gold. KM215.	2,200
P29	1989	15	100 Pesos. Gold. KM215.	2,200
P30	1989	12	100 Pesos. Gold. KM316.	1,800
P31	1989	12	100 Pesos. Gold. KM317.	1,800
P32	1989	12	100 Pesos. Gold. KM318.	1,800
P33	1989	12	100 Pesos. Gold. KM319.	2,200
P34	1989	12	100 Pesos. Gold. KM320.	2,200
P35	1990	50	10 Pesos. Silver. Ship and Cub; KM252.	400
P36	1990	15	10 Pesos. Silver. KM280.	900
P37	1990	100	10 Pesos. Silver. KM291.	250
P38	1990	100	10 Pesos. Silver. KM292.	160
P39	1990	100	10 Pesos. Silver. KM293.	160
P40	1990	12	10 Pesos. Gold. KM211.	1,200
P41	1990	12	10 Pesos. Gold. KM211.	1,200
P42	1990	12	15 Pesos. Gold. KM212.	1,200
P43	1990	12	15 Pesos. Gold. KM212.	1,200
P44	1990	12	25 Pesos. Gold. 15.5400 g. KM213.	—
P45	1990	12	25 Pesos. Gold. 15.5400 g. KM213.	—
P46	1990	12	50 Pesos. Gold. KM214.	2,200
P47	1990	12	50 Pesos. Gold. KM214.	2,200
P48	1990	12	50 Pesos. Gold. KM321.	2,200
P49	1990	12	50 Pesos. Gold. KM322.	2,200
P50	1990	12	50 Pesos. Gold. KM323.	2,200
P51	1990	12	100 Pesos. Gold. KM215.	2,200
P52	1990	15	100 Pesos. Gold. KM215.	2,200
P53	1992	50	10 Pesos. Silver. KM341.	150
P54	1993	150	5 Pesos. Silver. KM405.	200
P55	1993	—	5 Pesos. Silver. KM406.	250
P56	1993	15	200 Pesos. Gold. KM542.	2,200
P58	1993	—	100 Pesos. Gold. Similar to 200 Pesos; KM542.	—
P57	1994	10	100 Pesos. Gold. KM545.	1,750
P65	1999	—	10 Pesos. Silver. KM672.	200
P66	2000	—	10 Pesos. Silver. KM684.	200
P67	2000	—	10 Pesos. Silver. KM685.	200
P68	2000	—	10 Pesos. Silver. KM683.	200

MINT SETS

KM#	Date	Mintage	Identification	Issue Price	Mkt Val
MS1	1953 (4)	—	KM#26-29	—	125
MS2	1994 (5)	—	KM#575.1-576.1, 577-579	—	35.00

PROOF SETS

KM#	Date	Mintage	Identification	Issue Price	Mkt Val
PS1	1915 (7)	20	KM#9-15	—	3,600
PS2	1915 (6)	24	KM#16-21; Rare	—	—
PS3	1916 (7)	20	KM#9-15	—	6,250
PS4	1916 (6)	—	KM#16-21; Rare	—	—
PS5	1953 (4)	—	KM#26-29; Rare	—	—
PS6	1975 (2)	—	KM#36, 37	—	30.00
PSA7	1977 (3)	—	KM#38-40	—	110
PS7	1977 (4)	—	KM#38-40, 43	290	335
PS8	1979 (2)	—	KM#44, 45	240	260
PS9	1988 (5)	15	KM#211-215	—	1,650
PS10	1998 (4)	—	KM#668-671	—	200
PS11	1999 (5)	—	KM#671, 673, 692, 704, 719	—	1,250

CURACAO

The island of Curacao, the largest of the six islands that comprise the Netherlands Antilles, which is an autonomous part of the Kingdom of the Netherlands located in the Caribbean Sea 40 miles off the coast of Venezuela, has an area of 173 sq. mi. (472 sq. km.) and a population of 127,900. Capital: Willemstad. The chief industries are banking and tourism. Salt, phosphates and cattle are exported.

Curacao was discovered by Spanish navigator Alonsode Ojeda in 1499 and was settled by Spain in 1527. The Dutch West India Company took the island from Spain in 1634 and administered it until 1787, when it was surrendered to the United Netherlands. The Dutch held it thereafter except for two periods during the Napoleonic Wars, 1800-1803 and 1807-16, when it was occupied by the British. During World War II, Curacao refined 60 percent of the oil used by the Allies; the refineries were protected by U.S. troops after Germany invaded the Netherlands in1940.

During the second occupation of the Napoleonic period, the British created an emergency coinage for Curacao by cutting the Spanish dollar into 5 equal segments and countermarking each piece with a rosette indent.

MINT MARKS
D - Denver
P - Philadelphia
(u) - Utrecht

KINGDOM OF NETHERLANDS

MODERN COINAGE
100 Cents = 1 Gulden

KM# 39   CENT
2.5000 g., Bronze, 19 mm. **Obv:** Rampant lion left within circle, date below **Rev:** Denomination within wreath **Edge:** Reeded

Date	Mintage	F	VF	XF	Unc	BU
1942P	2,500,000	1.25	2.50	5.00	10.00	25.00

Note: This coin was also circulated in Suriname. For similar coins dated 1943P & 1957-1960, see Suriname.

KM# 41   CENT
Bronze **Obv:** Rampant lion left within circle, date below **Rev:** Denomination within wreath

Date	Mintage	F	VF	XF	Unc	BU
1944D	3,000,000	1.00	2.00	5.00	12.00	20.00
1947 (u)	1,500,000	2.00	3.25	7.00	15.00	30.00
1947 (u) Proof	80	Value: 50.00				

KM# 42   2-1/2 CENTS
4.0000 g., Bronze, 23 mm. **Obv:** Rampant lion left within circle, date below **Rev:** Denomination within wreath **Edge:** Reeded

Date	Mintage	F	VF	XF	Unc	BU
1944D	1,000,000	1.00	2.00	5.00	12.00	20.00
1947 (u)	500,000	1.25	3.00	6.50	15.00	25.00
1947 (u) Proof	80	Value: 50.00				
1948 (u)	1,000,000	1.00	2.00	5.00	12.00	20.00
1948 (u) Proof	75	Value: 50.00				

KM# 40   5 CENTS
4.5000 g., Copper-Nickel, 18 mm. **Obv:** Flower within inner circle **Rev:** Denomination within circle divides date at sides, shells at corners of coin **Edge:** Plain

Date	Mintage	F	VF	XF	Unc	BU
1943	8,595,000	1.25	2.50	4.00	8.50	19.00

Note: The above piece does not bear either a palm tree privy mark or a mint mark, but it was struck expressly for use in Curacao and Surinam. This homeland type of KM#153 was last issued in the Netherlands in 1940

KM# 47   5 CENTS
4.4800 g., Copper-Nickel, 18 mm. **Obv:** Flower within inner circle **Rev:** Denomination within circle divides date at sides, shells at corners

Date	Mintage	F	VF	XF	Unc	BU
1948	1,000,000	1.25	2.50	6.00	12.00	20.00
1948 Proof	75	Value: 50.00				

KM# 37   10 CENTS
1.4000 g., 0.6400 Silver 0.0288 oz. ASW, 15 mm. **Obv:** Head left **Rev:** Denomination and date within wreath **Edge:** Reeded

Date	Mintage	F	VF	XF	Unc	BU
1941P	800,000	4.00	9.00	18.00	36.00	50.00
1942P	1,500,100	3.00	7.00	16.00	32.00	45.00
1943P	4,500,000	2.50	6.00	15.00	30.00	40.00

Note: Both these coins were also circulated in Surinam. For coins dated 1942P, see Surinam.

KM# 38   25 CENTS
3.5800 g., 0.6400 Silver 0.0737 oz. ASW, 19 mm. **Obv:** Head left **Rev:** Denomination above date within wreath **Edge:** Reeded

Date	Mintage	F	VF	XF	Unc	BU
1941P	1,100,000	3.00	6.00	12.50	25.00	35.00
1943/1P	2,500,000	45.00	90.00	175	220	350
1943P	Inc. above	1.75	4.00	7.50	15.00	25.00

Note: Both coins were also circulated in Surinam. For similar coins dated 1943, 1944 & 1945-P with acorn mint mark, see Netherlands.

KM# 36   1/10 GULDEN
1.4000 g., 0.6400 Silver 0.0288 oz. ASW **Obv:** Head left **Rev:** Crowned arms divide denomination, date below

Date	Mintage	F	VF	XF	Unc	BU
1901	300,000	10.00	20.00	40.00	85.00	140
1901 Proof	40	Value: 250				

KM# 43 1/10 GULDEN

1.4000 g., 0.6400 Silver 0.0288 oz. ASW, 15 mm. **Obv:** Head left **Rev:** Denomination, date below **Edge:** Reeded

Date	Mintage	F	VF	XF	Unc	BU
1944D	1,500,000	1.25	3.50	7.50	15.00	30.00
1947	1,000,000	1.25	3.50	7.50	12.50	25.00
1947 Proof	80	Value: 70.00				

KM# 48 1/10 GULDEN

1.4000 g., 0.6400 Silver 0.0288 oz. ASW, 15 mm. **Obv:** Head left **Rev:** Denomination, date below **Edge:** Reeded

Date	Mintage	F	VF	XF	Unc	BU
1948	1,000,000	1.25	3.50	7.50	12.50	25.00
1948 Proof	75	Value: 70.00				

KM# 44 1/4 GULDEN

3.5800 g., 0.6400 Silver 0.0737 oz. ASW, 18.8 mm. **Obv:** Head left **Rev:** Denomination, date below **Edge:** Reeded

Date	Mintage	F	VF	XF	Unc	BU
1944D	1,500,000	1.50	3.75	8.50	17.50	35.00
1947 (u)	1,000,000	1.50	3.50	7.50	12.50	25.00
1947 (u) Proof	80	Value: 80.00				

KM# 45 GULDEN

10.0000 g., 0.7200 Silver 0.2315 oz. ASW, 28 mm. **Obv:** Head left, GOD * ZU * MET * ONS *

Date	Mintage	F	VF	XF	Unc	BU
1944D	500,000	4.00	12.00	25.00	50.00	75.00

KM# 46 2-1/2 GULDEN

25.0000 g., 0.7200 Silver 0.5787 oz. ASW, 38 mm. **Obv:** Head left **Rev:** Crowned arms divide denomination, date belw, GOD * ZU * MET * ONS *

Date	Mintage	F	VF	XF	Unc	BU
1944D	200,000	—	BV	12.00	15.00	20.00

Note: 60,000 coins melted down after minting.

PROOF SETS

KM#	Date	Mintage	Identification	Issue Price	Mkt Val
PS1	1901 (2)	40	KM36(1901), KM35(1900)	—	500
PS2	1947 (4)	80	KM41-44	—	225
PS3	1948 (3)	75	KM42, 47-48	—	170

CYPRUS

The island of Cyprus lies in the eastern Mediterranean Sea 44 miles (71 km.) south of Turkey and 60 miles (97 km.) off the Syrian coast. It is the third largest island in the Mediterranean Sea, having an area of 3,572 sq. mi. (9,251 sq. km.) and a population of 736,636. Capital: Nicosia. Agriculture, light manufacturing and tourism are the chief industries. Citrus fruit, potatoes, footwear and clothing are exported

The importance of Cyprus dates from the Bronze Age when it was desired as a principal source of copper (from which the island derived its name) and as a strategic trading center. It was during this period that large numbers of Greeks settled on the island and gave it the predominantly Greek character. Its role as an international marketplace made it a prime disseminator of the then prevalent cultures, a role that still influences the civilization of Western man. Because of its fortuitous position and influential role, Cyprus was conquered by a succession of empires: the Assyrian, Egyptian, Persian, Macedonian, Ptolemaic, Roman and Byzantine. It was taken from Isaac Comnenus by Richard the Lion-Heart in 1191, sold to the Templar Knights and for the following 7 centuries was ruled by the Franks, the Venetians and the Ottomans. During the Ottoman period Cyprus acquired its Turkish community (18 percent of its population). In 1878 the island fell into British hands and was made a crown colony of Britain in 1925. Finally, on Aug. 16, 1960, it became an independent republic.

In 1964, the ethnic Turks withdrew from active participation in the government. Turkish forces invaded Cyprus in 1974, gained control of 40 percent of the island and forcibly separated the Greek and Turkish communities. In 1983, Turkish Cypriots proclaimed their own state in northern Cyprus, which remains without international recognition.

Cyprus is a member of the Commonwealth of Nations. The president is Chief of State and Head of Government. Cyprus is also a member of the European Union.

RULER
British, until 1960

MINT MARKS
no mint mark - Royal Mint, London, England
H - Birmingham, England

MONETARY SYSTEM
9 Piastres = 1 Shilling
20 Shillings = 1 Pound

BRITISH COLONY
PIASTRE COINAGE

KM# 1.2 1/4 PIASTRE

Bronze, 21 mm. **Obv:** Crowned head left **Rev:** Denomination within circle

Date	Mintage	F	VF	XF	Unc	BU
1901	72,000	20.00	50.00	100	200	—

KM# 8 1/4 PIASTRE

Bronze **Obv:** Crowned bust right **Rev:** Denomination within circle, date below

Date	Mintage	F	VF	XF	Unc	BU
1902	72,000	20.00	30.00	50.00	150	—
1905	422,000	10.00	30.00	40.00	100	—
1908	36,000	50.00	100	200	350	—

KM# 16 1/4 PIASTRE

Bronze **Obv:** Crowned bust left **Rev:** Denomination within circle, date below

Date	Mintage	F	VF	XF	Unc	BU
1922	72,000	10.00	25.00	40.00	100	—
1926	360,000	5.00	10.00	20.00	65.00	—
1926 Proof	—	Value: 365				

KM# 11 1/2 PIASTRE

Bronze **Obv:** Crowned bust right **Rev:** Denomination within circle, date at right

Date	Mintage	F	VF	XF	Unc	BU
1908	36,000	80.00	200	400	650	—

KM# 17 1/2 PIASTRE

Bronze **Obv:** Crowned bust left **Rev:** Denomination within circle, date at right

Date	Mintage	F	VF	XF	Unc	BU
1922	36,000	40.00	80.00	150	300	—
1927	108,000	10.00	20.00	50.00	120	—
1927 Proof	—	Value: 375				
1930	180,000	10.00	20.00	50.00	100	—
1930 Proof	—	Value: 365				
1931	90,000	15.00	30.00	80.00	140	—
1931 Proof	—	Value: 425				

KM# 20 1/2 PIASTRE

Copper-Nickel, 19.4 mm. **Obv:** Crowned bust left **Rev:** Denomination, date at right

Date	Mintage	F	VF	XF	Unc	BU
1934	1,440,000	0.75	2.50	6.50	20.00	—
1934 Proof	—	Value: 325				

KM# 22 1/2 PIASTRE

Copper-Nickel, 19.4 mm. **Obv:** Crowned head left **Rev:** Denomination, date at right

Date	Mintage	F	VF	XF	Unc	BU
1938	1,080,000	0.35	2.00	5.00	12.50	—
1938 Proof	—	Value: 325				

KM# 22a 1/2 PIASTRE

2.5000 g., Bronze, 19.4 mm. **Obv:** Crowned head left **Rev:** Denomination, date at right

Date	Mintage	F	VF	XF	Unc	BU
1942	1,080,000	2.00	4.00	10.00	25.00	—

Note: A large portion of the mintage was destroyed during WWII

Date	Mintage	F	VF	XF	Unc	BU
1942 Proof	—	Value: 400				
1943	1,620,000	0.25	1.00	2.50	15.00	—
1944	2,160,000	0.25	1.00	2.50	12.50	—
1945	1,080,000	0.25	1.00	2.50	15.00	—
1945 Proof	—	Value: 200				

KM# 29 1/2 PIASTRE

Bronze, 19.4 mm. **Obv:** Crowned head left **Rev:** Denom., date at right

Date	Mintage	F	VF	XF	Unc	BU
1949	1,080,000	0.15	0.35	1.00	3.50	—
1949 Proof	—	Value: 150				

KM# 12 PIASTRE
Bronze **Obv:** Crowned bust right **Rev:** Denomination within circle, date at right

Date	Mintage	F	VF	XF	Unc	BU
1908	27,000	100	200	350	750	—

KM# 18 PIASTRE
Bronze **Obv:** Crowned bust left **Rev:** Denomination within circle, date at right

Date	Mintage	F	VF	XF	Unc	BU
1922	54,000	15.00	50.00	150	300	—
1927	127,000	10.00	20.00	60.00	150	—
1927 Proof	—	Value: 400				
1930	96,000	10.00	25.00	100	200	—
1930 Proof	—	Value: 400				
1931	45,000	20.00	50.00	100	200	—
1931 Proof	—	Value: 725				

KM# 21 PIASTRE
Copper-Nickel **Obv:** Crowned bust left **Rev:** Denomination, date at right

Date	Mintage	F	VF	XF	Unc	BU
1934	1,440,000	1.00	2.50	6.50	16.50	—
1934 Proof	—	Value: 325				

KM# 23 PIASTRE
Copper-Nickel **Obv:** Crowned head left **Rev:** Denomination, date at right

Date	Mintage	F	VF	XF	Unc	BU
1938	2,700,000	0.60	1.50	3.00	12.50	—
1938 Proof	—	Value: 325				

KM# 23a PIASTRE
5.2200 g., Bronze **Obv:** Crowned head left **Rev:** Denomination, date at right

Date	Mintage	F	VF	XF	Unc	BU
1942	1,260,000	1.00	2.00	5.00	20.00	—
1942 Proof	—	Value: 225				
1943	2,520,000	0.50	1.00	2.50	15.00	—
1944	3,240,000	0.50	1.00	2.50	10.00	—
1945	1,080,000	0.60	1.50	3.00	20.00	—
1945 Proof	—	Value: 200				

Date	Mintage	F	VF	XF	Unc	BU
1946	1,080,000	0.60	1.50	3.00	20.00	—
1946 Proof	—	Value: 200				

KM# 30 PIASTRE
Bronze **Obv:** Crowned head left **Obv. Leg.:** Legend ends ...DEI GRATIA REX **Rev:** Denomination, date at right

Date	Mintage	F	VF	XF	Unc	BU
1949	1,080,000	0.25	0.75	2.00	4.00	—
1949 Proof	—	Value: 150				

KM# 4 3 PIASTRES
1.8851 g., 0.9250 Silver 0.0561 oz. ASW **Obv:** Crowned and veiled bust left **Rev:** Crown over denomination divides date, circle surrounds

Date	Mintage	F	VF	XF	Unc	BU
1901	300,000	8.00	25.00	50.00	100	—
1901 Proof	—	Value: 800				

KM# 5 4-1/2 PIASTRES
2.8276 g., 0.9250 Silver 0.0841 oz. ASW, 19 mm. **Obv:** Crowned and veiled bust left **Rev:** Crowned arms divide date, denomination below

Date	Mintage	F	VF	XF	Unc	BU
1901	400,000	10.00	20.00	40.00	100	—
1901 Proof	—	Value: 950				

KM# 15 4-1/2 PIASTRES
2.8276 g., 0.9250 Silver 0.0841 oz. ASW, 19 mm. **Obv:** Crowned bust left **Rev:** Crowned arms divide date, denomination below

Date	Mintage	F	VF	XF	Unc	BU
1921	600,000	5.00	10.00	30.00	80.00	—

KM# 24 4-1/2 PIASTRES
2.8276 g., 0.9250 Silver 0.0841 oz. ASW, 19 mm. **Obv:** Crowned head left **Rev:** Two stylized rampant lions left, denomination and date 3/4 surround

Date	Mintage	F	VF	XF	Unc	BU
1938	192,000	2.00	6.00	15.00	30.00	—
1938 Proof	—	Value: 400				

KM# 6 9 PIASTRES
5.6552 g., 0.9250 Silver 0.1682 oz. ASW **Obv:** Crowned and veiled bust left **Rev:** Crowned arms divide date, denomination below

Date	Mintage	F	VF	XF	Unc	BU
1901	600,000	15.00	40.00	100	200	—
1901 Proof	—	Value: 1,250				

KM# 9 9 PIASTRES
5.6552 g., 0.9250 Silver 0.1682 oz. ASW **Obv:** Crowned bust right **Rev:** Crowned arms divide date, denomination below

Date	Mintage	F	VF	XF	Unc	BU
1907	60,000	35.00	100	275	500	—

KM# 13 9 PIASTRES
5.6552 g., 0.9250 Silver 0.1682 oz. ASW **Obv:** Crowned bust left **Rev:** Crowned arms divide date, denomination below

Date	Mintage	F	VF	XF	Unc	BU
1913	50,000	40.00	125	300	650	—
1919	400,000	5.00	10.00	30.00	100	—
1921	490,000	5.00	10.00	30.00	100	—

KM# 25 9 PIASTRES
5.6552 g., 0.9250 Silver 0.1682 oz. ASW **Obv:** Crowned head left **Rev:** Two stylized rampant lions left, date at right, denomination below

Date	Mintage	F	VF	XF	Unc	BU
1938	504,000	5.00	8.00	12.00	30.00	—
1938 Proof	—	Value: 400				
1940	800,000	2.75	5.00	10.00	27.50	—
1940 Proof	—	Value: 400				

KM# 27 SHILLING
5.6300 g., Copper-Nickel **Obv:** Crowned head left **Rev:** Two stylized rampant lions left, date below, denomination above

Date	Mintage	F	VF	XF	Unc	BU
1947	1,440,000	2.00	4.00	10.00	30.00	—
1947 Proof	—	Value: 300				

KM# 31 SHILLING
Copper-Nickel **Obv:** Crowned head left **Obv. Leg.:** Legend ends; DEI GRATIA REX **Rev:** Two stylized rampant lions left, date below, denomination above

Date	Mintage	F	VF	XF	Unc	BU
1949	1,440,000	2.00	4.00	10.00	30.00	—
1949 Proof	—	Value: 300				

KM# 7 18 PIASTRES
11.3104 g., 0.9250 Silver 0.3364 oz. ASW **Obv:** Crowned and veiled bust left **Rev:** Crowned arms divide date and denomination below

Date	Mintage	F	VF	XF	Unc	BU
1901	200,000	40.00	150	300	550	
1901 Proof	—	Value: 2,500				

KM# 10   18 PIASTRES
11.3104 g., 0.9250 Silver 0.3364 oz. ASW **Obv:** Crowned bust right **Rev:** Crowned arms divide date and denomination below

Date	Mintage	F	VF	XF	Unc	BU
1907	20,000	85.00	225	500	1,350	

KM# 14   18 PIASTRES
11.3104 g., 0.9250 Silver 0.3364 oz. ASW **Obv:** Crowned bust left **Rev:** Crowned arms divide date and denomination below

Date	Mintage	F	VF	XF	Unc	BU
1913	25,000	70.00	140	350	700	
1921	155,000	25.00	60.00	150	350	

KM# 26   18 PIASTRES
11.3104 g., 0.9250 Silver 0.3364 oz. ASW **Obv:** Crowned head left **Rev:** Two stylized rampant lions left, date and denomination 3/4 surround

Date	Mintage	F	VF	XF	Unc	BU
1938	200,000	5.50	20.00	30.00	50.00	
1938 Proof	—	Value: 450				
1940	100,000	15.00	30.00	50.00	80.00	
1940 Proof	—	Value: 450				

KM# 28   2 SHILLING
4.0000 g., Copper-Nickel, 28.3 mm. **Obv:** Crowned head left **Rev:** Two stylized rampant lions left, date below, denomination above

Date	Mintage	F	VF	XF	Unc	BU
1947	720,000	2.00	4.00	10.00	35.00	
1947 Proof	—	Value: 400				

KM# 32   2 SHILLING
Copper-Nickel, 28.3 mm. **Obv:** Crowned head left **Rev:** Two stylized rampant lions left, date below, denomination above

Date	Mintage	F	VF	XF	Unc	BU
1949	720,000	4.00	8.00	15.00	40.00	
1949 Proof	—	Value: 400				

KM# 19   45 PIASTRES
28.2759 g., 0.9250 Silver 0.8409 oz. ASW, 38 mm.   **Subject:** 50th Anniversary of British Rule **Obv:** Crowned bust left **Rev:** Two stylized rampant lions left, date at right, denomination below

Date	Mintage	F	VF	XF	Unc	BU
ND(1928)	80,000	25.00	35.00	60.00	150	
ND(1928) Proof	517	Value: 550				

DECIMAL COINAGE
50 Mils = 1 Shilling; 20 Shillings = 1 Pound;
1000 Mils = 1 Pound

KM# 33   3 MILS
2.8000 g., Bronze, 20 mm. **Obv:** Crowned bust right **Rev:** Flying fish divides date and denomination

Date	Mintage	F	VF	XF	Unc	BU
1955	6,250,000	—	—	0.10	0.25	
1955 Proof	2,000	Value: 2.50				

KM# 34   5 MILS
Bronze **Obv:** Crowned bust right **Rev:** Standing figure with open arms, date and denomination below

Date	Mintage	F	VF	XF	Unc	BU
1955	10,000,000	—	0.15	0.25	0.40	
1955 Proof	2,000	Value: 3.00				
1956	2,950,000	—	0.15	0.30	0.50	
1956 Proof	—	Value: 300				

KM# 35   25 MILS
Copper-Nickel **Obv:** Crowned bust right **Rev:** Bulls head above denomination, date below

Date	Mintage	F	VF	XF	Unc	BU
1955	2,500,000	—	0.25	0.35	1.00	
1955 Proof	2,000	Value: 3.00				

KM# 36   50 MILS
Copper-Nickel **Obv:** Crowned bust right **Rev:** Fern leaves divide denomination, date below

Date	Mintage	F	VF	XF	Unc	BU
1955	4,000,000	—	0.35	0.50	1.00	
1955 Proof	2,000	Value: 3.00				

KM# 37   100 MILS
Copper-Nickel, 28 mm. **Obv:** Crowned bust right **Rev:** Stylized ancient merchant ship, denomination upper left, date below

Date	Mintage	F	VF	XF	Unc	BU
1955	2,500,000	—	0.50	0.75	1.50	
1955 Proof	2,000	Value: 4.50				
1957	Est. 500,000	—	10.00	15.00	50.00	
1957 Proof	—	Value: 440				

Note: All but 10,000 of 1957 issue were melted down.

REPUBLIC
DECIMAL COINAGE
50 Mils = 1 Shilling; 20 Shillings = 1 Pound;
1000 Mils = 1 Pound

KM# 38   MIL
Aluminum, 18.5 mm. **Obv:** Shielded arms within wreath, date above **Rev:** Denomination within wreath

Date	Mintage	F	VF	XF	Unc	BU
1963	5,000,000	—	—	—	0.15	
1963 Proof	25,000	Value: 1.00				
1971	500,000	—	—	0.10	0.25	
1972	500,000	—	—	0.10	0.25	
1972 Proof	—	Value: 2.00				

KM# 39   5 MILS
5.7400 g., Bronze **Obv:** Shielded arms within wreath, date above **Rev:** Stylized ancient merchant ship, denomination upper left

Date	Mintage	F	VF	XF	Unc	BU
1963	12,000,000	—	—	0.10	0.35	
1963 Proof	25,000	Value: 1.25				
1970	2,500,000	—	—	0.10	1.00	
1971	2,500,000	—	—	0.10	0.35	
1972	2,500,000	—	—	0.10	0.35	
1973	5,000,000	—	—	0.10	0.35	
1974	2,500,000	—	—	0.10	0.35	
1976	2,000,000	—	—	0.10	0.35	
1977	2,000,000	—	—	0.10	0.35	
1978	2,000,000	—	—	0.10	0.35	
1979	2,000,000	—	—	0.10	0.35	
1980	4,000,000	—	—	0.10	0.35	
1980 Proof	—	Value: 2.50				

KM# 50.1   5 MILS
1.2000 g., Aluminum, 20 mm. **Obv:** Shielded arms within wreath, date above **Rev:** Stylized ancient merchant ship, denomination upper left

Date	Mintage	F	VF	XF	Unc	BU
1981	12,500,000	—	—	—	0.25	

KM# 50.2   5 MILS
1.2000 g., Aluminum, 20 mm. **Obv:** Shielded arms within wreath, date above **Rev:** Stylized ancient merchant ship, denomination upper left

Date	Mintage	F	VF	XF	Unc	BU
1982	15,000,000				0.25	—
1982 Proof	—	Value: 2.00				

KM# 40 25 MILS
2.8000 g., Copper-Nickel, 19.4 mm. **Obv:** Shielded arms within wreath, date above **Rev:** Cedar of Lebanon, denomination at left

Date	Mintage	F	VF	XF	Unc	BU
1963	2,500,000	—	0.10	0.15	0.45	—
1963 Proof	25,000	Value: 1.50				
1968	1,500,000	—	0.10	0.15	2.00	—
1971	1,000,000	—	0.10	0.15	0.45	—
1972	500,000	—	0.10	0.15	0.50	—
1973	1,000,000	—	0.10	0.15	0.45	—
1974	1,000,000	—	0.10	0.15	0.45	—
1976	2,000,000	—	0.10	0.15	0.45	—
1977	500,000	—	0.10	0.15	0.45	—
1978	500,000	—	0.10	0.15	0.45	—
1979	1,000,000	—	0.10	0.15	0.45	—
1980	2,000,000	—	0.10	0.15	0.45	—
1981	3,000,000	—	0.10	0.15	0.45	—
1982	1,000,000	—	0.10	0.15	0.45	—
1982 Proof	—	Value: 3.00				

KM# 41 50 MILS
5.6000 g., Copper-Nickel, 23.5 mm. **Obv:** Shielded arms within wreath, date above **Rev:** Grape cluster above denomination

Date	Mintage	F	VF	XF	Unc	BU
1963	2,800,000	—	0.20	0.30	1.00	—
1963 Proof	25,000	Value: 1.75				
1970	500,000	—	0.20	0.35	2.00	—
1971	500,000	—	0.20	0.35	1.25	—
1972	750,000	—	0.20	0.30	1.00	—
1973	750,000	—	0.20	0.30	1.00	—
1974	1,500,000	—	0.20	0.30	1.00	—
1976	1,500,000	—	0.20	0.30	1.00	—
1977	500,000	—	0.20	0.30	1.00	—
1978	500,000	—	0.20	0.30	3.00	—
1979	1,000,000	—	0.20	0.30	1.00	—
1980	3,000,000	—	0.20	0.30	1.00	—
1981	4,000,000	—	0.20	0.30	1.00	—
1982	2,000,000	—	0.20	0.30	1.00	—
1982 Proof	—	Value: 3.50				

KM# 42 100 MILS
11.3000 g., Copper-Nickel, 28.45 mm. **Obv:** Shielded arms within wreath, date above **Rev:** Cyprus Mouflon left, denomination below

Date	Mintage	F	VF	XF	Unc	BU
1963	1,750,000	—	0.40	0.70	2.00	3.00
1963 Proof	25,000	Value: 2.50				
1971	500,000	—	0.50	0.75	2.00	3.00
1973	750,000	—	0.40	0.70	2.00	3.00
1974	1,000,000	—	0.50	0.75	2.00	3.00
1976	1,500,000	—	0.40	0.70	2.00	3.00
1977	500,000	—	0.50	0.75	2.00	3.00
1978	1,000,000	—	0.50	0.75	2.00	3.00
1979	1,000,000	—	0.40	0.70	2.00	3.00
1980	1,000,000	—	0.40	0.70	2.00	3.00
1981	2,000,000	—	0.40	0.70	2.00	3.00
1982	2,000,000	—	0.40	0.70	2.00	3.00
1982 Proof	—	Value: 5.00				

KM# 43 500 MILS
Copper-Nickel **Series:** F.A.O. **Obv:** Double cornucopia, as on the ancient coins of Ptolemy II **Rev:** Figure holding tray of fruit, denomination at right

Date	Mintage	F	VF	XF	Unc	BU
1970	80,000	—	2.00	5.00	10.00	—

KM# 43a 500 MILS
22.6200 g., 0.8000 Silver 0.5818 oz. ASW **Series:** F.A.O **Obv:** Double cornucopia, as on the ancient coins of Ptolemy **Rev:** Figure holding tray of fruit, denomination

Date	Mintage	F	VF	XF	Unc	BU
1970 Proof	5,000	Value: 55.00				

KM# 44 500 MILS
Copper-Nickel **Obv:** Shielded arms within wreath, date above **Rev:** Hercules, denomination at right

Date	Mintage	F	VF	XF	Unc	BU
1975	500,000	—	1.25	1.75	4.00	—
1977	300,000	—	1.25	1.75	5.00	—
1977 Proof	—	Value: 15.00				

KM# 44a 500 MILS
14.1400 g., 0.8000 Silver 0.3637 oz. ASW **Obv:** Shielded arms within wreath **Rev:** Hercules and denomination

Date	Mintage	F	VF	XF	Unc	BU
1975 Proof	10,000	Value: 25.00				

KM# 45 500 MILS
Copper-Nickel **Subject:** Refugees, denomination and date at right **Obv:** Shielded arms within wreath, date above

Date	Mintage	F	VF	XF	Unc	BU
1976	25,000	—	1.25	2.00	4.00	—

KM# 45a 500 MILS
14.1400 g., 0.9250 Silver 0.4205 oz. ASW **Obv:** Shielded arms within wreath **Rev:** Refugees, denomination at right

Date	Mintage	F	VF	XF	Unc	BU
1976 Proof	25,000	Value: 25.00				

KM# 48 500 MILS
Copper-Nickel **Subject:** Human Rights **Obv:** Flame within wreath divides dates **Rev:** Stylized crying dove above denomination

Date	Mintage	F	VF	XF	Unc	BU
ND(1978)	50,000	—	1.25	2.00	4.00	—

KM# 48a 500 MILS
14.1400 g., 0.9250 Silver 0.4205 oz. ASW **Subject:** Human Rights **Obv:** Flame within wreath divides denomination **Rev:** Crying dove above denomination

Date	Mintage	F	VF	XF	Unc	BU
ND(1978) Proof	5,000	Value: 65.00				

KM# 49 500 MILS
Copper-Nickel **Series:** Summer Olympic Games **Obv:** Shielded arms within wreath, date above **Rev:** Olympic logo divides date and denomination, sprays surround

Date	Mintage	F	VF	XF	Unc	BU
1980	50,000	—	1.25	2.50	6.50	—

KM# 49a 500 MILS
14.1400 g., 0.9250 Silver 0.4205 oz. ASW **Obv:** Shielded arms within wreath **Rev:** Olympic logo divides date and denomination, sprays surround

Date	Mintage	F	VF	XF	Unc	BU
1980 Proof	7,500	Value: 50.00				

KM# 51 500 MILS
Copper-Nickel **Subject:** World Food Day **Obv:** Shielded arms within wreath, date above **Rev:** Denomination divides swordfish and grain sprig, date above

Date	Mintage	F	VF	XF	Unc	BU
ND(1981)	50,000	—	1.25	2.00	6.00	10.00

KM# 51a 500 MILS
14.1400 g., 0.9250 Silver 0.4205 oz. ASW **Obv:** Shielded arms within wreath **Rev:** Denomination divides swordfish and grain sprig

Date	Mintage	F	VF	XF	Unc	BU
ND(1978) Proof	7,500	Value: 50.00				

KM# 46 POUND
Copper-Nickel, 38.5 mm. **Subject:** Refugee Commemorative **Obv:** Shielded arms within wreath, date above **Rev:** Refugees, date and denomination at right **Note:** Also known with a doubled die reverse, especially noticeable with the date.

Date	Mintage	F	VF	XF	Unc	BU
1976	25,000	—	2.00	2.50	5.50	—

KM# 46a POUND
28.2800 g., 0.9250 Silver 0.8410 oz. ASW **Obv:** Shielded arms within wreath **Rev:** Refugees, denomination at right **Note:** Refugee Commemorative.

Date	Mintage	F	VF	XF	Unc	BU
1976 Proof	25,000	Value: 40.00				

KM# 47 50 POUNDS
15.9800 g., 0.9170 Gold 0.4711 oz. AGW **Obv:** Archbishop Makarios right, two dates **Rev:** Ship above map, dolphins, date and denomination below

Date	Mintage	F	VF	XF	Unc	BU
1977	39,000	—	—	—	—	500
1977 Proof	51,000	Value: 550				

REFORM COINAGE
100 Cents = 1 Pound

KM# 52 HALF CENT
Aluminum **Obv:** Shielded arms within wreath, date below **Rev:** Cyclamen, denomination at right

Date	Mintage	F	VF	XF	Unc	BU
1983	10,000,000	—	—	0.10	0.15	0.25
1983 Proof	6,250	Value: 1.50				

KM# 53.1 CENT
Nickel-Brass **Obv:** Shielded arms within wreath, date below **Rev:** Stylized bird on a branch, value number surrounded by single line

Date	Mintage	F	VF	XF	Unc	BU
1983	15,000,000	—	—	0.10	0.20	0.30
1983 Proof	6,250	Value: 1.50				

KM# 53.2 CENT
Nickel-Brass **Obv:** Shielded arms within wreath, date below **Rev:** Stylized bird on a branch, value number surrounded by double line

Date	Mintage	F	VF	XF	Unc	BU
1985	5,000,000	—	—	0.10	0.20	0.30
1987	5,000,000	—	—	0.10	0.20	0.30
1988	5,000,000	—	—	0.10	0.20	0.30
1990	4,000,000	—	—	0.10	0.20	0.30

KM# 53.3 CENT
2.0300 g., Nickel-Brass, 16.48 mm. **Obv:** Shielded arms within altered wreath, date below **Rev:** Stylized bird on a branch, denomination at left **Edge:** Plain

Date	Mintage	F	VF	XF	Unc	BU
1991	4,000,000	—	—	0.10	0.20	0.30
1992	4,000,000	—	—	0.10	0.20	0.30
1993	7,000,000	—	—	0.10	0.20	0.30
1994	10,000,000	—	—	0.10	0.20	0.30
1996	12,000,000	—	—	0.10	0.20	0.30
1998	15,000,000	—	—	0.10	0.20	0.30

KM# 54.1 2 CENTS
Nickel-Brass, 19 mm. **Obv:** Shielded arms within wreath, date below **Rev:** Stylized goats, value number surrounded by single line

Date	Mintage	F	VF	XF	Unc	BU
1983	12,000,000	—	—	0.15	0.25	0.35
1983 Proof	6,250	Value: 1.50				

KM# 54.2 2 CENTS
Nickel-Brass, 19 mm. **Obv:** Shielded arms within wreath, date below **Rev:** Stylized goats; value number surrounded by double line

Date	Mintage	F	VF	XF	Unc	BU
1985	8,000,000	—	—	0.15	0.25	0.35
1988	5,150,000	—	—	0.15	0.25	0.35
1990	4,000,000	—	—	0.15	0.25	0.35

KM# 54.3 2 CENTS
2.5800 g., Nickel-Brass, 18.95 mm. **Obv:** Shielded arms within altered wreath, date below **Rev:** Stylized goats, denomination upper right **Edge:** Plain

Date	Mintage	F	VF	XF	Unc	BU
1991	4,000,000	—	—	0.15	0.25	0.35
1992	4,000,000	—	—	0.15	0.25	0.35
1993	4,000,000	—	—	0.15	0.25	0.35
1994	10,000,000	—	—	0.15	0.25	0.35
1996	12,000,000	—	—	0.15	0.25	0.35
1998	10,000,000	—	—	0.15	0.25	0.35

KM# 55.1 5 CENTS
Nickel-Brass, 22 mm. **Obv:** Shielded arms within wreath, date below **Rev:** Stylized bulls head, value number surrounded by single line **Note:** REV: Value number surrounded by single line

Date	Mintage	F	VF	XF	Unc	BU
1983	15,000,000	—	—	0.20	0.50	0.75
1983 Proof	6,250	Value: 2.00				

KM# 55.2 5 CENTS
Nickel-Brass, 22 mm. **Obv:** Shielded arms within wreath, date below **Rev:** Value number surrounded by double line

Date	Mintage	F	VF	XF	Unc	BU
1985	5,000,000	—	—	0.20	0.50	0.75
1987	5,000,000	—	—	0.20	0.50	0.75
1988	5,060,000	—	—	0.20	0.50	0.75
1990		—	—	0.20	0.50	0.75

KM# 55.3 5 CENTS
3.8000 g., Nickel-Brass, 20.37 mm. **Obv:** Altered wreath around arms **Rev:** Stylized bulls head above denomination **Edge:** Plain

Date	Mintage	F	VF	XF	Unc	BU
1991	4,000,000	—	—	0.20	0.50	0.75
1992	4,000,000	—	—	0.20	0.50	0.75
1993	5,000,000	—	—	0.20	0.50	0.75
1994	8,000,000	—	—	0.20	0.50	0.75
1998	1,000,000	—	—	0.20	0.50	0.75

KM# 56.1 10 CENTS
Nickel-Brass **Obv:** Shielded arms within wreath, date below **Rev:** Decorative vase, value number surrounded by single line

Date	Mintage	F	VF	XF	Unc	BU
1983	10,000,000	—	—	0.35	0.75	1.00
1983 Proof	6,250	Value: 3.00				

KM# 56.2 10 CENTS
Nickel-Brass **Obv:** Shielded arms within wreath, date below **Rev:** Value number framed by double line

Date	Mintage	F	VF	XF	Unc	BU
1985	5,000,000	—	—	0.35	0.75	1.00
1988	5,035,000	—	—	0.35	0.75	1.00
1990	4,000,000	—	—	0.35	0.75	1.00

KM# 56.3 10 CENTS
5.5700 g., Nickel-Brass, 24.4 mm. **Obv:** Altered wreath around arms **Rev:** Decorative vase, denomination above

Date	Mintage	F	VF	XF	Unc	BU
1991	4,000,000	—	—	0.35	0.75	1.00
1992	3,000,000	—	—	0.35	0.75	1.00
1993	3,000,000	—	—	0.35	0.75	1.00
1994	8,000,000	—	—	0.35	0.75	1.00
1998	5,000,000	—	—	0.35	0.75	1.00

KM# 57.1 20 CENTS
Nickel-Brass, 27 mm. **Obv:** Shielded arms within wreath, date below **Rev:** Value number framed by single line

Date	Mintage	F	VF	XF	Unc	BU
1983	10,000,000	—	—	0.50	2.00	3.50
1983 Proof	6,200	Value: 5.00				

KM# 57.2 20 CENTS
Nickel-Brass, 27 mm. **Obv:** Shielded arms within wreath, date below **Rev:** Value number framed by double line

Date	Mintage	F	VF	XF	Unc	BU
1985	5,040,000	—	—	0.50	2.50	3.00
1988	1,000,000	—	—	0.50	2.50	3.00

KM# 62.1 20 CENTS
Bronze, 27 mm. **Obv:** Shielded arms within wreath, date below **Rev:** Head left, denomination at right

Date	Mintage	F	VF	XF	Unc	BU
1989	2,000,000	—	—	—	1.00	1.50
1989 Proof	—	Value: 30.00				
1990	3,000,000	—	—	—	1.00	1.50

KM# 62.2 20 CENTS
7.7500 g., Nickel-Brass, 27 mm. **Obv:** Altered wreath around arms **Rev:** Head left, denomination at right

Date	Mintage	F	VF	XF	Unc	BU
1991	4,000,000	—	—	—	1.00	1.50
1992	3,000,000	—	—	—	1.00	1.50
1993	4,000,000	—	—	—	1.00	1.50
1994	8,000,000	—	—	—	1.00	1.50
1998	5,000,000	—	—	—	1.00	1.50

KM# 58 50 CENTS
Copper-Nickel, 32 mm. **Series:** F.A.O. **Subject:** Forestry **Obv:** Shielded arms within wreath, date above **Rev:** Goddess Diana in the shape of a stylized tree, denomination at right

Date	Mintage	F	VF	XF	Unc	BU
1985	33,000	—	2.50	5.00	16.50	22.50

KM# 58a 50 CENTS
14.1400 g., 0.9250 Silver 0.4205 oz. ASW, 32 mm. **Series:** F.A.O. **Obv:** Shielded arms within wreath, date below **Rev:** Goddess Diana in the shape of a stylized tree

Date	Mintage	F	VF	XF	Unc	BU
1985 Proof	4,000	Value: 50.00				

Table (top right column):

Date	Mintage	F	VF	XF	Unc	BU
1993	3,000,000	—	—	0.35	0.75	1.00
1994	8,000,000	—	—	0.35	0.75	1.00
1998	5,000,000	—	—	0.35	0.75	1.00

KM# 60 50 CENTS
Copper-Nickel **Subject:** Olympics **Obv:** Shielded arms within wreath, date below **Rev:** Symbols divide denomination, Olympic logo at right

Date	Mintage	F	VF	XF	Unc	BU
1988	14,000	—	—	—	3.50	5.00

KM# 60a 50 CENTS
14.1400 g., 0.9250 Silver 0.4205 oz. ASW **Obv:** Shielded arms within wreath, date below **Rev:** Symbols divide denomination, logo at right

Date	Mintage	F	VF	XF	Unc	BU
1988 Proof	4,000	Value: 45.00				

KM# 66 50 CENTS
7.0000 g., Copper-Nickel, 26.11 mm. **Subject:** Abduction of Europa **Obv:** National arms, date below **Rev:** Female figure riding bull right within square, denomination below **Edge:** Plain

Date	Mintage	F	VF	XF	Unc	BU
1991 narrow date	3,005,000	—	—	—	2.50	3.25
1993 wide date	300,000	—	—	—	2.50	3.25
1994 wide date	500,000	—	—	—	2.50	3.25
1996	5,000,000	—	—	—	2.50	3.25
1998	5,000,000	—	—	—	2.50	3.25

KM# 66a 50 CENTS
7.0000 g., 0.9250 Silver 0.2082 oz. ASW, 26 mm. **Obv:** Shielded arms within wreath, date below **Rev:** Figure riding bull within square, denomination below

Date	Mintage	F	VF	XF	Unc	BU
1991 Proof	5,000	Value: 35.00				

KM# 59 POUND
Copper-Nickel **Subject:** World Wildlife Fund **Obv:** Shielded arms within wreath, date below **Rev:** Cyprian wild sheep (Moufflon), denomination below

Date	Mintage	F	VF	XF	Unc	BU
1986	39,000	—	—	—	10.00	15.00

KM# 59a POUND
0.9250 Silver **Obv:** Shielded arms within wreath, date below **Rev:** Wild sheep, denomination below

Date	Mintage	F	VF	XF	Unc	BU
1986 Proof	13,000	Value: 40.00				

KM# 61 POUND
Copper-Nickel **Series:** Olympics **Obv:** Shielded arms within wreath, date below **Rev:** Symbols, denomination below

Date	Mintage	F	VF	XF	Unc	BU
1988	14,000	—	—	—	6.50	8.00

KM# 61a POUND
28.2800 g., 0.9250 Silver 0.8410 oz. ASW **Obv:** Shielded arms within wreath, date below **Rev:** Symbols and denomination

Date	Mintage	F	VF	XF	Unc	BU
1988 Proof	4,000	Value: 55.00				

KM# 64 POUND
Copper-Nickel **Series:** Save the Children Fund **Obv:** Shielded arms within wreath **Rev:** Two boys at play

Date	Mintage	F	VF	XF	Unc	BU
1989	19,000	—	—	—	5.50	7.50

Note: 4,000 issued in plastic case, 15,000 issued uncased

KM# 64a POUND
28.2800 g., 0.9250 Silver 0.8410 oz. ASW **Series:** Save the Children Fund **Obv:** Shielded arms within wreath **Rev:** Two boys at play

Date	Mintage	F	VF	XF	Unc	BU
1989 Proof	4,000	Value: 42.50				

KM# 63 POUND
Copper-Nickel **Subject:** Small European States Games **Rev:** Winged figure divides Olympic logos, denomination below

Date	Mintage	F	VF	XF	Unc	BU
1989	19,000	—	—	—	5.50	7.50

Note: 4,000 issued in plastic case, 15,000 issued uncased

KM# 63a POUND
28.2800 g., 0.9250 Silver 0.8410 oz. ASW **Subject:** Small European States Games **Rev:** Winged figure divides logos, denomination below

Date	Mintage	F	VF	XF	Unc	BU
1989 Proof	4,000	Value: 50.00				

KM# 67 POUND
Copper-Nickel **Series:** Olympics **Obv:** Small arms **Rev:** Relay Racing, denomination above Olympic logo

Date	Mintage	F	VF	XF	Unc	BU
1992	8,000	—	—	—	8.50	10.00

KM# 67a POUND
28.2800 g., 0.9250 Silver 0.8410 oz. ASW **Series:** Olympics **Obv:** Small arms **Rev:** Relay racing, denomination above logo

Date	Mintage	F	VF	XF	Unc	BU
1992 Proof	4,000	Value: 50.00				

KM# 69 POUND
Copper-Nickel **Subject:** 50th Anniversary - United Nations **Obv:** Shielded arms within wreath, date below **Rev:** Tree of flag shields divides denomination and logo

Date	Mintage	F	VF	XF	Unc	BU
1995	—	—	—	—	8.50	10.00

KM# 69a POUND
28.2800 g., 0.9250 Silver 0.8410 oz. ASW **Series:** 50th Anniversary - United Nations **Obv:** Shielded arms within wreath, date below **Rev:** Tree of flag shields, denomination and logo

Date	Mintage	F	VF	XF	Unc	BU
1995	—	Value: 42.00				

KM# 70 POUND
Copper-Nickel **Series:** F.A.O. **Subject:** 50th Anniversary - United Nations **Obv:** Shielded arms within wreath, date below **Rev:** Bovine portrait, wheat and denominaton

Date	Mintage	F	VF	XF	Unc	BU
1995	—	—	—	—	12.50	14.50

KM# 70a POUND
28.2800 g., 0.9250 Silver 0.8410 oz. ASW **Series:** 50th Anniversary - F.A.O. **Obv:** Shielded arms within wreath, date below **Rev:** Bovine Portrait, wheat and denomination

Date	Mintage	F	VF	XF	Unc	BU
1995	4,000	Value: 55.00				

KM# 71 POUND
Copper-Nickel **Series:** 1996 Olympics **Obv:** Shielded arms within wreath, date below **Rev:** Olympic rings, stylized flames, olive branch, denomination above

Date	Mintage	F	VF	XF	Unc	BU
1996	3,000	—	—	—	20.00	22.50

KM# 71a POUND
28.2800 g., 0.9250 Silver 0.8410 oz. ASW **Series:** 1996 Olympics **Obv:** Shielded arms within wreath, date below **Rev:** Olympic rings, stylized flames, olive branch

Date	Mintage	F	VF	XF	Unc	BU
1996	4,000	Value: 47.50				

KM# 72 POUND
Copper-Nickel **Subject:** World Wildlife Fund - Conserving Nature **Obv:** Shielded arms within wreath, date below **Rev:** Green turtle, denomination above

Date	Mintage	F	VF	XF	Unc	BU
1997	3,000	—	—	—	25.00	35.00

KM# 72a POUND
28.2800 g., 0.9250 Silver 0.8410 oz. ASW **Obv:** Shielded arms within wreath, date below **Rev:** Green turtle

Date	Mintage	F	VF	XF	Unc	BU
1997 Proof	Est. 15,000	Value: 50.00				

KM# 73 2 POUNDS
Bronze, 44.5 x 25 mm. **Subject:** Millennium **Obv:** National arms and denomination at right **Rev:** Three line inscription

Date	Mintage	F	VF	XF	Unc	BU
2000	1,000	—	—	—	50.00	52.50

KM# 73a 2 POUNDS
15.0000 g., 0.9250 Silver 0.4461 oz. ASW, 44.5 x 25 mm. **Subject:** Millennium **Obv:** National arms and denomination **Rev:** Three line inscription **Edge:** Plain

Date	Mintage	F	VF	XF	Unc	BU
2000	32,000	—	—	—	50.00	52.50

KM# 65 20 POUNDS
7.9881 g., 0.9170 Gold 0.2355 oz. AGW, 22 mm. **Subject:** 30th Anniversary of the Republic **Obv:** Shielded arms within wreath, date below **Rev:** Denomination within circle on stylized bird

Date	Mintage	F	VF	XF	Unc	BU
1990 Proof	5,000	Value: 275				

KM# 68 20 POUNDS
7.9881 g., 0.9170 Gold 0.2355 oz. AGW **Subject:** Museum Building Fund **Obv:** Shielded arms within wreath, date below **Rev:** Winged statue, left, denomination below

Date	Mintage	F	VF	XF	Unc	BU
1992 Proof	5,000	Value: 250				

KM# 74 100 POUNDS
Gold **Subject:** Millennium **Obv:** National arms and denomination at right **Rev:** Three line inscription

Date	Mintage	F	VF	XF	Unc	BU
2000	750	—	—	—	1,000	—

TRIAL STRIKES

KM#	Date	Mintage	Identification	Mkt Val
TS2	ND	—	45 Piastres. 0.9170 Gold. 40.0000 g. Uniface.	3,000

Note: 1 known

MINT SETS

KM#	Date	Mintage	Identification	Issue Price	Mkt Val
MS1	1955 (5)	2,550	KM33-37	2.20	6.50
MS2	1963 (5)	8,050	KM38-42	1.95	6.00
MS3	1971 (5)	3,000	KM38-42	1.65	5.00
MS4	1972 (4)	30,000	KM38-41	2.35	5.00
MS5	1973 (4)	5,000	KM39-42	2.75	5.00
MS6	1974 (4)	5,000	KM39-42	3.25	5.00
MS7	1976 (3)	5,000	KM40-42	1.25	4.50
MS8	1976 (4)	25,000	KM45-46	6.50	6.00
MS9	1977 (5)	10,000	KM39-42, 44	—	6.50
MS10	1978 (5)	—	KM39-42, 48	5.50	6.50
MS11	1979 (4)	—	KM39-42	—	6.50
MS12	1980 (4)	—	KM39-42	—	6.50
MS13	1981 (5)	—	KM40-42, 50.1, 51	5.00	6.50
MS14	1981 (4)	—	KM40-42, 50.1	5.00	6.50
MS15	1982 (4)	5,000	KM40-42, 50.2	5.00	6.50
MS16	1983 (6)	11,400	KM52,53.1-57.1	15.00	10.00
MS17	1988 (5)	—	KM53.2-57.2	—	10.00
MS18	1989 (5)	—	KM53.2-56.2, 62.1	—	10.00
MS19	1990 (5)	—	KM53.2-56.2, 62.1	10.00	10.00

PROOF SETS

KM#	Date	Mintage	Identification	Issue Price	Mkt Val
PS4	1901 (4)	—	KM4-7	—	5,500
PS5	1931 (2)	—	KM17-18	—	1,175
PS6	1934 (2)	—	KM20-21	—	650
PS7	1938 (5)	—	KM-22-26	—	2,000
PS8	1947 (2)	—	KM27-28	—	700
PS9	1949 (2)	—	KM31-32	—	700
PS10	1949 (4)	—	KM29-32	—	950
PS11	1955 (5)	2,000	KM33-37	5.50	16.00
PS12	1963 (5)	24,501	KM38-42	9.00	8.50
PS13	1963 (5)	500	KM38-42	8.70	8.00
PS14	1972, 1980, 1982 (6)	—	KM38(72), 39(80), 40-42(82), 50.2(82)	30.00	30.00
PS15	1976 (2)	25,000	KM45a-46a	50.00	35.00
PS16	1983 (6)	6,250	KM52, 53.1-57.1	20.00	40.00

CZECH REPUBLIC

The Czech Republic was formerly united with Slovakia as Czechoslovakia. It is bordered in the west by Germany, to the north by Poland, to the east by Slovakia and to the south by Austria. It consists of 3 major regions: Bohemia, Moravia and Silesia and has an area of 30,450 sq. mi. (78,864 sq. km.) and a population of 10.4 million. Capital: Prague (Praha). Agriculture and livestock are chief occupations while coal deposits are the main mineral resources.

The Czech lands were united with the Slovaks to form the Czechoslovak State, which came into existence on Oct. 28, 1918 upon the dissolution of the Austrian-Hungarian Empire. In 1938, this territory was broken up for the benefit of Germany, Poland, and Hungary by the Munich (Munchen) Agreement. In March 1939 the German influenced Slovak government proclaimed Slovakia independent. Germany incorporated the Czech lands into the Third Reich as the "Protectorate of Bohemia and Moravia." A Czech government-in-exile was set up in London in July 1940. The Soviets and USA forces liberated the area by May 1945. Communist influence increased steadily while pressure for liberalization culminated in the overthrow of the Stalinist leader Antonin Novotny and his associates in 1968. The Communist Party then introduced far reaching reforms which resulted in warnings from Moscow (Moskva), followed by occupation and stationing of Soviet forces. Mass demonstrations for reform began again in Nov. 1989 and the Federal Assembly abolished the Communist Party's sole right to govern. The new government formed was the Czech and Slovak Federal Republic. A movement for Democratic Slovakia was apparent in the June 1992 elections and on December 31, 1992, the CSFR was dissolved and the two new republics came into being on Jan. 1, 1993.

NOTE: For earlier issues see Czechoslovakia, Bohemia and Moravia or Slovakia listings.

MINT MARKS
(c) - castle = Hamburg
(cr) - cross = British Royal Mint
(l) - leaf = Royal Canadian
(m) - crowned *b* or *CM* = Jablonec nad Nisou
(mk) - *MK* in circle = Kremnica
(o) - broken circle = Vienna (Wien)

MONETARY SYSTEM
1 Czechoslovak Koruna (Kcs) = 1 Czech Koruna (Kc)
1 Koruna = 100 Haleru

REPUBLIC
STANDARD COINAGE

KM# 6 10 HALERU
0.6000 g., Aluminum, 15.5 mm. **Obv:** Crowned Czech lion left, date below **Rev:** Denomination and stylized river **Edge:** Plain **Note:** Two varieties of mint marks exist for 1994.

Date	Mintage	F	VF	XF	Unc	BU
1993(c)	100,000,000	—	—	—	0.20	—
Note: 200 pieces destroyed						
1993(m)	94,902,000	—	—	—	0.20	—
1994(c) In sets only	—	—	—	—	2.50	—
1994(m)	53,127,024	—	—	—	0.20	—
1994(m) Proof, dull	2,000	—	—	—	2.50	—
1994(m) Proof, bright	27,500	—	—	—	—	—
1995(m)	106,918,596	—	—	—	0.20	—
1996(m)	61,498,678	—	—	—	0.20	—
1997(m)	40,968,395	—	—	—	0.20	—
Note: 85,778 pieces destroyed						
1997(m) Proof	1,500	Value: 3.50				
1998(m)	41,027,073	—	—	—	0.20	—
1998(m) Proof	2,600	Value: 2.00				
1999(m)	54,428,800	—	—	—	0.20	—
1999(m) Proof	2,000	Value: 2.00				
2000(m)	52,497,440	—	—	—	0.20	—
2000(m) Proof	2,500	Value: 2.00				

KM# 2.1 20 HALERU
0.7400 g., Aluminum, 17 mm. **Obv:** Crowned Czech lion left, date above **Rev:** Linden leaf within denomination; closed 2, "h" above flat line **Edge:** Milled **Note:** Medallic coin alignment.

Date	Mintage	F	VF	XF	Unc	BU
1993(c)	80,000,000	—	—	—	0.30	—
1993(m)	30,558,000	—	—	—	0.30	—
1994(c)	9,310,000	—	—	—	0.30	—
1994(m)	81,291,201	—	—	—	0.30	—
1994(m) Proof, dull	2,500	—	—	—	3.00	—
1994(m) Proof, bright	17,500	—	—	—	1.00	—
1995(c)	450,000	—	—	—	1.75	—
1995(m)	80,960,374	—	—	—	0.30	—
1996(m)	61,086,142	—	—	—	0.30	—
1997(m)	51,013,450	—	—	—	0.30	—
Note: 78,835 pieces destroyed						
1997(m) Proof	1,500	Value: 5.00				

KM# 2.2 20 HALERU
Aluminum, 17 mm. **Obv:** Crowned Czech lion **Rev:** Linden leaf and value, "h" above flat line, closed 2 in denomination **Note:** Coin alignment.

Date	Mintage	F	VF	XF	Unc	BU
1993(m)	Inc. above	—	—	—	4.00	—

KM# 2.3 20 HALERU
0.7400 g., Aluminum **Obv:** Crowned Czech lion left, date above **Rev:** Open 2 in denomination, "h" above angle line **Note:** Medal alignment.

Date	Mintage	F	VF	XF	Unc	BU
1998(m)	51,135,904	—	—	—	0.30	—
1998(m) Proof	2,600	Value: 3.00				
1999(m)	20,820,612	—	—	—	0.30	—
1999(m) Proof	2,000	Value: 3.00				
2000(m)	31,466,085	—	—	—	0.30	—
2000(m) Proof	2,500	Value: 3.00				

KM# 3.1 50 HALERU
0.9000 g., Aluminum, 19 mm. **Obv:** Crowned Czech lion left, date below **Rev:** Large denomination **Edge:** Part plain, part milled repeated **Note:** Prev. KM#3.

Date	Mintage	F	VF	XF	Unc	BU
1993(c)	70,003,000	—	—	—	0.50	—

Note: 201 pieces destroyed

Date	Mintage	F	VF	XF	Unc	BU
1993(m)	30,474,000	—	—	—	0.50	—
1994(m)	21,109,425	—	—	—	0.50	—

Note: Open and closed 9 varieties exist in date

Date	Mintage	F	VF	XF	Unc	BU
1994(m) Proof, dull	2,500	—	—	—	3.00	—
1994(m) Proof, bright	27,500	—	—	—	1.00	—
1995(m)	30,940,000	—	—	—	0.50	—
1996(m)	35,904,000	—	—	—	0.50	—
1997(m)	25,713,443	—	—	—	0.50	—

Note: 35,610 pieces destroyed

Date	Mintage	F	VF	XF	Unc	BU
1997(m) Proof	1,500	Value: 5.00				
1998(m)	25,000	—	—	—	0.50	—
1998(m) Proof	2,600	Value: 3.00				
1999(m)	21,024,800	—	—	—	0.50	—

Note: 8,687 pieces destroyed

Date	Mintage	F	VF	XF	Unc	BU
1999(m) Proof	2,000	Value: 3.00				
2000(m)	15,753,440	—	—	—	0.50	—
2000(m) Proof	2,500	Value: 3.00				

KM# 7 KORUNA

Nickel Clad Steel, 20 mm. **Obv:** Crowned Czech lion left, date below **Rev:** Denomination above crown **Edge:** Milled **Note:** Two varieties of mint marks exist for 1996. 2000-03 have two varieties in the artisit monogram.

Date	Mintage	F	VF	XF	Unc	BU
1993(l)	102,431,000	—	—	—	0.60	—
1994(m)	52,162,620	—	—	—	0.60	—
1995(m)	40,668,280	—	—	—	0.60	—
1996(m)	35,344,913	—	—	—	0.60	—

Note: Figure 1 with and without serif, three varieties of designer's signature.

Date	Mintage	F	VF	XF	Unc	BU
1997(m)	15,055,501	—	—	—	0.60	—
1997(m) Proof	1,500	Value: 6.50				
1998(m)	25,000	—	—	—	0.60	—
1998(m) Proof	2,600	Value: 4.00				

Note: 90 pieces destroyed.

Date	Mintage	F	VF	XF	Unc	BU
1999(m)	24,904	—	—	—	0.60	—
1999(m) Proof	2,000	Value: 4.00				
2000(m)	15,568,697	—	—	—	0.60	—
2000(m) Proof	2,500	Value: 4.00				

KM# 9 2 KORUN

3.7000 g., Nickel Clad Steel, 21.5 mm. **Obv:** Crowned Czech lion left, date below **Rev:** Large denomination, pendant design at left **Edge:** Plain **Note:** Two varieties of designer monograms exist for 2001-04.

Date	Mintage	F	VF	XF	Unc	BU
1993(l)	80,001,000	—	—	—	0.65	—
1994(l)	18,360,000	—	—	—	0.65	—
1994(m)	30,310,000	—	—	—	0.65	—
1995(m)	30,520,405	—	—	—	0.65	—
1996(m)	15,201,750	—	—	—	0.65	—
1997(m)	15,040,245	—	—	—	0.65	—
1997(m) Proof	1,500	Value: 8.50				
1998(m)	10,455,480	—	—	—	0.65	—
1998(m) Proof	2,600	Value: 5.00				
1999(m)	28,768	—	—	—	0.65	—

Note: 1098 pieces destroyed.

Date	Mintage	F	VF	XF	Unc	BU
1999(m) Proof	2,000	Value: 5.00				
2000(m)	25,000	—	—	—	0.65	—
2000(m) Proof	2,500	Value: 5.00				

KM# 8 5 KORUN

4.8000 g., Nickel Plated Steel, 23 mm. **Obv:** Crowned Czech lion left, date below **Rev:** Large denomination, Charles bridge and linden leaf **Edge:** Plain

Date	Mintage	F	VF	XF	Unc	BU
1993(l)	70,001,000	—	—	—	1.00	—
1994(l)	14,400,000	—	—	—	1.00	—
1994(m)	30,475,491	—	—	—	1.00	—
1995(m)	20,155,218	—	—	—	1.00	—

Note: Two varieties of figure 5 and designer's signature.

Date	Mintage	F	VF	XF	Unc	BU
1996(m)	5,053,730	—	—	—	1.00	—
1997(m)	40,000	—	—	—	1.00	—

Date	Mintage	F	VF	XF	Unc	BU
1997(m) Proof	1,500	Value: 10.00				
1998(m)	25,000	—	—	—	1.00	—

Note: 10,207 pieces destroyed

Date	Mintage	F	VF	XF	Unc	BU
1998(m) Proof	2,600	Value: 6.00				

Note: 90 Pieces destroyed.

Date	Mintage	F	VF	XF	Unc	BU
1999(m)	29,490	—	—	—	1.00	—
1999(m) Proof	2,000	Value: 6.00				
2000(m)	26,431	—	—	—	1.00	—
2000(m) Proof	2,500	Value: 6.00				

KM# 4 10 KORUN

7.6200 g., Copper Plated Steel, 24.5 mm. **Obv:** Crowned Czech lion left, date below **Rev:** Brno Cathedral, denomination below **Edge:** Milled **Note:** Position of designer's initials on reverse change during the 1995 strike.

Date	Mintage	F	VF	XF	Unc	BU
1993(c)	70,001,000	—	—	—	2.00	—
1993(c) Small 10	1,000	25.00	75.00	150	250	—
1994(m)	20,677,220	—	—	—	1.50	—
1994(m) bright	30,000	—	—	—	2.00	—
1995(m)	152,388	—	—	—	1.50	—
1995(m) LK below	20,530,459	—	—	—	1.50	—
1996(m)	20,644,143	—	—	—	1.50	—
1997(m)	48,215	—	—	—	1.50	—
1997(m) Proof	1,500	Value: 12.00				
1998(m)	25,000	—	—	—	1.50	—

Note: 142,465 pieces melted.

Date	Mintage	F	VF	XF	Unc	BU
1998(m) Proof	2,600	Value: 7.00				

Note: 90 pieces melted.

Date	Mintage	F	VF	XF	Unc	BU
1999(m)	29,490	—	—	—	1.50	—

Note: 2,036 pieces melted.

Date	Mintage	F	VF	XF	Unc	BU
1999(m) Proof	2,000	Value: 7.00				
2000(m)	25,000	—	—	—	1.50	—
2000(m) Proof	2,500	Value: 7.00				

KM# 42 10 KORUN

7.5200 g., Copper Plated Steel, 24.5 mm. **Subject:** Year 2000 **Obv:** Crowned Czech lion left, date below **Rev:** Clock works above denomination, within circle **Edge:** Reeded

Date	Mintage	F	VF	XF	Unc	BU
2000	10,032,799	—	—	—	1.50	—
2000 Proof	2,500	Value: 7.50				

KM# 5 20 KORUN

8.4300 g., Brass Plated Steel, 26 mm. **Obv:** Crowned Czech lion left, date below **Rev:** St. Wenceslas (Duke Vaclav) on horse **Edge:** Plain **Note:** Two varieties of mint marks and style of 9's exist for 1997.

Date	Mintage	F	VF	XF	Unc	BU
1993(c)	55,001,000	—	—	1.00	3.00	—
1994(c)	100,000	—	—	—	3.50	—
1995(m)	101,837	—	—	—	2.50	—
1996(m)	101,150	—	—	—	2.50	—
1997(m)	8,091,219	—	—	—	2.50	—
1997(m) Proof	1,500	Value: 16.50				
1998(m)	15,725,000	—	—	—	2.50	—

Note: 41,786 pieces destroyed.

Date	Mintage	F	VF	XF	Unc	BU
1998(m) Proof	2,600	Value: 10.00				

Note: 90 pieces destroyed

Date	Mintage	F	VF	XF	Unc	BU
1999(m)	26,274,900	—	—	—	2.50	—

Note: 1,422 pieces destroyed.

Date	Mintage	F	VF	XF	Unc	BU
1999(m) Proof	2,000	Value: 10.00				
2000(m)	5,694,581	—	—	—	2.50	—
2000(m) Proof	2,500					

KM# 43 20 KORUN

8.4300 g., Brass Plated Steel, 26 mm. **Subject:** Year 2000 **Obv:** Crowned Czech lion left, date below **Rev:** Astrolab and denomination within circle **Edge:** Plain

Date	Mintage	F	VF	XF	Unc	BU
2000	10,015,000	—	—	—	2.50	—
2000 Proof	2,500	Value: 10.00				

KM# 1 50 KORUN

9.7000 g., Bi-Metallic Brass plated Steel center in Copper plated Steel ring, 27.5 mm. **Obv:** Crowned Czech lion left **Rev:** Prague city view **Edge:** Plain

Date	Mintage	F	VF	XF	Unc	BU
1993(c)	35,001,000	—	—	2.50	7.50	—
1994(c)	100,000	—	—	—	9.00	—
1995(m)	102,977	—	—	—	9.00	—
1996(m)	103,073	—	—	—	9.00	—
1997(m)	40,002	—	—	—	9.00	—
1997(m) Proof	1,500	Value: 35.00				
1998(m)	25,000	—	—	—	9.00	—

Note: 2,600 pieces destroyed.

Date	Mintage	F	VF	XF	Unc	BU
1998(m) Proof	2,600	Value: 20.00				

Note: 90 pieces destroyed

Date	Mintage	F	VF	XF	Unc	BU
1999(m)	29,490	—	—	—	9.00	—
1999(m) Proof	2,000	Value: 20.00				
2000(m)	26,436	—	—	—	9.00	—
2000(m) Proof	2,500	Value: 20.00				

KM# 10 200 KORUN

13.0000 g., 0.9000 Silver 0.3761 oz. ASW, 31 mm. **Subject:** 1st Anniversary of Constitution **Obv:** Quartered stylized arms above denomination and date **Rev:** Inscription above vertical dates **Note:** 7,420 pieces, uncirculated and 1,433 proof, were melted by the Czech National Bank in 1997.

Date	Mintage	F	VF	XF	Unc	BU
1993(o)	23,475	—	—	—	12.50	14.50

Note: Milled edge

Date	Mintage	F	VF	XF	Unc	BU
1993(o) Proof	3,968	Value: 30.00				

Note: Edge: CESKA NARODNI BANKA

KM# 11 200 KORUN

13.0000 g., 0.9000 Silver 0.3761 oz. ASW, 31 mm. **Subject:** 650th Anniversary **Obv:** Quartered arms above denomination **Rev:** St. Vitus Cathedral and Archbishop's arms **Note:** 6,940 pieces uncircualted melted.

Date	Mintage	F	VF	XF	Unc	BU
ND(1994)(o)	23,888	—	—	—	12.50	14.50

Note: Milled edge.

Date	Mintage	F	VF	XF	Unc	BU
ND(1994) Proof	2,500	Value: 400				

Note: Plain edge.

KM# 12 200 KORUN
13.0000 g., 0.9000 Silver 0.3761 oz. ASW, 31 mm.
Subject: 50th Anniversary - Normandy Invasion **Obv:** Quartered arms, denomination at left, date below **Rev:** Spitfires in formation **Note:** 6,940 pieces, Unc and Proof, were melted by the Czech National Bank in 1997.

Date	Mintage	F	VF	XF	Unc	BU
1994(cr)	29,980	—	—	—	16.50	18.50
Note: Milled edge						
1994(cr) Proof	5,000	Value: 150				
Note: Plain edge with CESKA NARODNI BANKA *0.900*						

KM# 13 200 KORUN
13.0000 g., 0.9000 Silver 0.3761 oz. ASW, 31 mm. **Subject:** 125th Anniversary of Brno Tramway **Obv:** Stylized, unbordered, quartered arms above date and denomination **Rev:** Tramway **Note:** 5,420 pieces uncirculated and 40 proof were remelted.

Date	Mintage	F	VF	XF	Unc	BU
1994(mk)	20,138	—	—	—	14.00	16.00
Note: Reeded edge						
1994 Proof	1,960	Value: 50.00				
Note: Plain edge						

KM# 14 200 KORUN
13.0000 g., 0.9000 Silver 0.3761 oz. ASW, 31 mm.
Subject: Environmental Protection **Obv:** Stylized quartered arms divide date, denomination below **Rev:** Nude on globe, animals and plants in background **Note:** 4400 pieces uncirculated, were melted by the Czech National Bank in 1997.

Date	Mintage	F	VF	XF	Unc	BU
1994(m)	21,236	—	—	—	14.00	16.00
Note: Milled edge						
1994(m) Proof	2,000	Value: 200				
Note: Edge: Plain with CESKA NARODNI BANKA *0.900*						

KM# 15 200 KORUN
13.0000 g., 0.9000 Silver 0.3761 oz. ASW, 31 mm.
Subject: 50th Anniversary - Victory Over Fascism **Note:** 5,830 pieces, uncirculated, were melted by the Czech National Bank in 1997.

Date	Mintage	F	VF	XF	Unc	BU
ND(1995)	19,852	—	—	—	14.00	16.00
Note: Plain edge						
ND(1995) Proof	2,000	Value: 250				
Note: Plain edge with CESKA NARODNI BANKA *0.900*						

KM# 16 200 KORUN
13.0000 g., 0.9000 Silver 0.3761 oz. ASW, 31 mm.
Subject: 200th Anniversary - Birth of Pavel Josef Safarik **Note:** 6,450 pieces, uncirculated and 7 proof, were melted by the Czech National Bank in 1997.

Date	Mintage	F	VF	XF	Unc	BU
1995	19,192	—	—	—	14.00	16.00
Note: Plain edge						
1995 Proof	1,998	Value: 42.00				
Note: Plain edge with CESKA NARODNI BANKA *0.900*						

KM# 17 200 KORUN
13.0000 g., 0.9000 Silver 0.3761 oz. ASW, 31 mm.
Subject: 50th Anniversary - United Nations **Obv:** Quartered arms above denomination **Rev:** UN logo, dates within wreath at left **Note:** 5,130 pieces, uncirculated and 53 proof, were melted by the Czech National Bank in 1997.

Date	Mintage	F	VF	XF	Unc	BU
ND(1995)	19,968	—	—	—	14.00	16.00
Note: Milled edge						
ND(1995) Proof	2,500	Value: 40.00				
Note: Plain edge with CESKA NARODNI BANKA *0.900*						

KM# 23 200 KORUN
13.0000 g., 0.9000 Silver 0.3761 oz. ASW, 31 mm. **Subject:** Karel Svolinsky **Obv:** Stylized quartered arms above denomination **Rev:** Bird on vase holding bouquet **Note:** 6,120 pieces, uncirculated and 1 proof, were melted by the Czech National Bank in 1997.

Date	Mintage	F	VF	XF	Unc	BU
ND(1996)	18,994	—	—	—	14.00	16.00
Note: Milled edge						
ND(1996) Proof	2,000	Value: 75.00				
Note: Plain edge with CESKA NARODNI BANKA *0.900*						

KM# 25 200 KORUN
13.0000 g., 0.9000 Silver 0.3761 oz. ASW, 31 mm. **Subject:** 200th Anniversary - Czech Christmas Mass by Jakub J. Ryba
Obv: Quartered arms within circle, denomination below **Rev:** Angel with horn, stars above, church lower left, circle surrounds, dates at right **Note:** 6,170 pieces uncirculated and 1 proof were remelted.

Date	Mintage	F	VF	XF	Unc	BU
ND(1996)	19,311	—	—	—	14.00	16.00
Note: Milled edge						
ND(1996) Proof	2,500	Value: 40.00				
Note: Plain edge with CESKA NARODNI BANKA *0.900*						

KM# 24 200 KORUN
13.0000 g., 0.9000 Silver 0.3761 oz. ASW, 31 mm.
Subject: Jean-Baptiste Gaspard Deburau **Obv:** Elongated, stylized, unbordered, quartered arms, denomination and date below **Rev:** Seated artistic portrait of Deburau **Note:** 7,380 pieces uncirculated and 1 proof were remelted.

Date	Mintage	F	VF	XF	Unc	BU
1996	16,659	—	—	—	15.00	17.00
Note: Milled edge						
1996 Proof	2,000	Value: 40.00				
Note: Plain edge with CESKA NARODNI BANKA *0.900*						

KM# 22 200 KORUN
13.0000 g., 0.9000 Silver 0.3761 oz. ASW, 31 mm. **Subject:** Czech Philharmonic **Obv:** Quartered arms above denomination
Rev: Building and musical instruments, dates above **Note:** Three varieties in the artisit's monogram exist. 5,820 pieces, uncirculated and 1 proof, were melted by the Czech National Bank in 1997.

Date	Mintage	F	VF	XF	Unc	BU
1996	19,231	—	—	—	14.00	16.00
Note: Milled edge						
1996 Proof	2,500	Value: 75.00				
Note: Plain edge with CESKA NARODNI BANKA *0.900*						

KM# 26 200 KORUN
13.0000 g., 0.9000 Silver 0.3761 oz. ASW, 31 mm.
Subject: Centennial - First Automobile in Bohemia **Obv:** National arms **Rev:** Side view of antique automobile - President **Note:** 4,380 uncirculated and 1 proof were remelted.

Date	Mintage	F	VF	XF	Unc	BU
ND(1997)	18,778	—	—	—	14.00	16.00
Note: Milled edge						
ND(1997) Proof	3,000	Value: 32.00				
Note: Plain edge with CESKA NARODNI BANKA *0.900*						

KM# 28 200 KORUN
13.0000 g., 0.9000 Silver 0.3761 oz. ASW, 31 mm. **Subject:** Czech Amateur Athletic Union **Obv:** Unbordered arms **Rev:** Runners **Note:** 5,930 pieces uncirculated and 617 proof were remelted.

Date	Mintage	F	VF	XF	Unc	BU
ND(1997)	17,215	—	—	—	14.00	16.00
ND(1997) Proof	3,000	Value: 35.00				

KM# 29 200 KORUN
13.0000 g., 0.9000 Silver 0.3761 oz. ASW, 31 mm.
Subject: 650th Anniversary - Na Slovanech-Emauzy Monastery **Obv:** Unbordered, quartered arms above denomination **Rev:** Seated saintly figure, date above **Note:** 5,060 pieces uncirculated and 49 proof were remelted.

Date	Mintage	F	VF	XF	Unc	BU
ND(1997)	18,100	—	—	—	14.00	16.00
Note: Milled edge						

ND(1997) Proof 2,966 Value: 32.00
Note: Plain edge with CESKA NARODNI BANKA *0.900*

KM# 27   200 KORUN
13.0000 g., 0.9000 Silver 0.3761 oz. ASW, 31 mm. **Subject:** Millennium - St. Adalbert's Death **Obv:** Unbordered quartered arms, denomination below **Rev:** Bishop's portrait right, dates at right **Note:** 2,370 pieces uncirculated were remelted.

Date	Mintage	F	VF	XF	Unc	BU
ND(1997)	20,567	—	—	—	14.00	16.00

Note: Milled edge
ND(1997) Proof 3,000 Value: 32.00
Note: Plain edge with CESKA NARODNI BANKA *0.900*

KM# 32   200 KORUN
13.0000 g., 0.9000 Silver 0.3761 oz. ASW, 31 mm. **Subject:** 800th Anniversary - Coronation of King Premysl I Otakar **Obv:** Quartered arms above denomination **Rev:** Half facing head at right, coin design at left **Note:** 3,110 pieces uncirculated and 6 proof were remelted.

Date	Mintage	F	VF	XF	Unc	BU
ND(1998)(m)	17,392	—	—	—	14.00	16.00

Note: Milled edge
ND(1998) Proof 3,000 Value: 30.00
Note: Plain edge with CESKA NARODNI BANKA *0.900*

KM# 31   200 KORUN
13.0000 g., 0.9000 Silver 0.3761 oz. ASW, 31 mm.
Subject: 200th Aniversary - Birth of Frantisek Palacky **Obv:** National arms **Rev:** Head of Palacky left **Note:** 3,700 pieces uncirculated and 359 proof were remelted.

Date	Mintage	F	VF	XF	Unc	BU
ND(1998)	16,881	—	—	—	14.00	16.00

Note: Milled edge
ND(1998) Proof 2,941 Value: 30.00
Note: Plain edge with CESKA NARODNI BANKA *0.900*

KM# 33   200 KORUN
13.0000 g., 0.9000 Silver 0.3761 oz. ASW, 31 mm. **Subject:** 150th Anniversary - Birth of Frantisek Kmoch **Obv:** National arms **Rev:** Head of Kmoch facing left, dates **Note:** 4,120 pieces uncirculated and 580 proof were remelted.

Date	Mintage	F	VF	XF	Unc	BU
ND(1998)(m)	16,522	—	—	—	11.50	13.50

Note: Milled edge
ND(1998)(m) 2,875 Value: 28.00
Note: Plain edge with CESKA NARODNI BANKA *0.900*

KM# 30   200 KORUN
13.0000 g., 0.9000 Silver 0.3761 oz. ASW, 31 mm. **Subject:** 650th Anniversary - Charles University in Prague **Obv:** Quartered arms within circle, patterned circle surrounds **Rev:** Charles IV portrait and document seal **Note:** 96 pieces uncirculated were remelted.

Date	Mintage	F	VF	XF	Unc	BU
ND(1998)	26,553	—	—	—	14.00	16.00

Note: Milled edge
ND(1998) Proof 3,000 Value: 95.00
Note: Plain edge with CESKA NARODNI BANKA *0.900*

KM# 35   200 KORUN
13.0000 g., 0.9000 Silver 0.3761 oz. ASW, 31 mm. **Subject:** 200 Years - Prague Fine Arts Academy **Obv:** Stylized and quartered national arms within 1/2 circle, denomination at left **Rev:** Stylized design, dates at left **Edge:** Reeded **Note:** 2,740 pieces uncirculated and 198 proof were remelted.

Date	Mintage	F	VF	XF	Unc	BU
ND(1999)	15,012	—	—	—	14.00	16.00

Note: Milled edge
ND(1999) Proof 2,881 Value: 28.00
Note: Plain edge with CESKA NARODNI BANKA *0.900*

KM# 34   200 KORUN
13.0000 g., 0.9000 Silver 0.3761 oz. ASW, 31 mm.
Subject: 50th Anniversary - NATO **Obv:** Unbordered, quartered arms, denomination below **Rev:** NATO style cross with dates on horizontals, CESKA REPUBLIKA CLENSKA ZEME NATO 1996 **Note:** 245 pieces uncirculated and 1 proof were remelted.

Date	Mintage	F	VF	XF	Unc	BU
ND(1999)	18,133	—	—	—	14.00	16.00

Note: Edge: CESKA REPUBLIKA...
ND(1999) Proof 3,000 Value: 30.00
Note: Plain edge with CESKA NARODNI BANKA *0.900*

KM# 37   200 KORUN
13.0000 g., 0.9000 Silver 0.3761 oz. ASW, 31 mm. **Subject:** 100th Birthday - Ondrej Sekora **Obv:** National arms **Rev:** Ant holding flowers **Note:** 1,150 pieces uncirculated and 15 proof were remelted.

Date	Mintage	F	VF	XF	Unc	BU
ND(1999)	15,548	—	—	—	14.00	16.00

Note: Milled edge
ND(1999) Proof 2,697 Value: 28.00
Note: Plain edge with CESKA NARODNI BANKA *0.900*

KM# 36   200 KORUN
13.0000 g., 0.9000 Silver 0.3761 oz. ASW, 31 mm. **Subject:** 100 Years - Brno University of Technology **Obv:** Unbordered, quartered arms, denomination below **Rev:** Stylized design, dates below **Note:** 1,790 pieces uncirculated were remelted.

Date	Mintage	F	VF	XF	Unc	BU
ND(1999)	17,304	—	—	—	14.00	16.00

Note: Milled edge
ND(1999) Proof 3,181 Value: 28.00
Note: Plain edge with CESKA NARODNI BANKA *0.900*

KM# 46   200 KORUN
13.0000 g., 0.9000 Silver 0.3761 oz. ASW **Subject:** 700th Anniversary - Currency Reform **Obv:** Quartered arms above coin design which divides denomination **Rev:** Seated figure divides coin designs **Note:** 1,750 pieces uncirculated were remelted.

Date	Mintage	F	VF	XF	Unc	BU
2000	14,855	—	—	—	15.00	

Note: Milled edge
2000 Proof 3,400 — — — 25.00
Note: Plain edge with CESKA NARODNI BANKA *0.900*

KM# 47   200 KORUN
13.0000 g., 0.9000 Silver 0.3761 oz. ASW **Subject:** 100th Anniversary - Birth of Poet Vitezslav Nezval **Obv:** Quartered arms above denomination **Rev:** Stylized head left, dates at right **Note:** 3,180 pieces uncirculated were remelted.

Date	Mintage	F	VF	XF	Unc	BU
2000	13,486	—	—	—	15.00	16.50

Note: Milled edge
2000 Proof 2,900 Value: 25.00
Note: Plain edge with CESKA NARODNI BANKA *0.900*

KM# 48   200 KORUN
13.0000 g., 0.9000 Silver 0.3761 oz. ASW, 31 mm.
Subject: 150th Anniversary - Birth of Zdenek Fibich, Musical Composer **Obv:** National arms **Rev:** Portrait **Note:** 1,900 pieces uncirculated and 1 proof were remelted.

Date	Mintage	F	VF	XF	Unc	BU
2000	13,694	—	—	—	14.00	16.00

Note: Milled edge
2000 Proof 2,900 Value: 28.00
Note: Plain edge with CESKA NARODNI BANKA *0.900*

KM# 49   200 KORUN
13.0000 g., 0.9000 Silver 0.3761 oz. ASW, 31 mm.
Subject: International Monetary Fund and Prague World Bank Group **Obv:** Crowned lion in swirling dots **Rev:** Circle of swirling dots **Note:** 519 pieces uncirculated and 3 proof were remelted.

Date	Mintage	F	VF	XF	Unc	BU
2000	15,249	—	—	—	14.00	16.00

Note: Milled edge
| 2000 Proof | 4,299 | | Value: 28.00 | | | |

Note: Plain edge with CESKA NARODNI BANKA *0.900*

KM# 50   200 KORUN
13.0000 g., 0.9000 Silver 0.3761 oz. ASW, 31 mm.
Subject: New Millennium **Obv:** Elongated, stylized, unbordered arms, denomination below **Rev:** Stylized phoenix design, date below **Note:** 99 pieces uncirculated and 1 proof remelted.

Date	Mintage	F	VF	XF	Unc	BU
2000	16,775	—	—	—	14.00	16.00

Note: Milled edge
| 2000 Proof | 3,500 | | Value: 28.00 | | | |

Note: Plain edge with CESKA NARODNI BANKA *0.900*

GOLD BULLION COINAGE

KM# 18   1000 KORUN
3.1103 g., 0.9999 Gold 0.1000 oz. AGW, 16 mm.
Subject: Historic Coins - Tolar of Silesian Estates 12-1/2 tolar 1620. **Obv:** Imperial eagle, denomination below **Rev:** Tablet with four line inscription within circle

Date	Mintage	F	VF	XF	Unc	BU
1995	1,997	—	—	—	—	115
1996	3,252	—	—	—	—	115
1996 Proof	741		Value: 145			
1997 Proof	2,247		Value: 125			

KM# 38   1000 KORUN
3.1103 g., 0.9999 Gold 0.1000 oz. AGW, 16 mm.
Subject: Karlstejn Castle **Obv:** Three shielded arms, dates below **Rev:** Old coin design at right, quartered design in center

Date	Mintage	F	VF	XF	Unc	BU
1998	2,200	—	—	—	—	110

Note: Milled edge
| 1998 Proof | 2,206 | | Value: 125 | | | |

Note: Plain edge
| 1999 Proof | 1,997 | | Value: 125 | | | |

KM# 44   2000 KORUN
34.2140 g., 0.9990 Bi-Metallic Gold plated insert on silver planchet. 1.0989 oz., 40 mm. **Subject:** Millennium **Obv:** National arms hologram on gold inlay **Rev:** Stylized 2000, *CNB* Ag 0.999* 31.103 g *CNB* AU 999.9 *3. 111 g* **Note:** With a 3.1110 gram, .999 gold, .0999 ounce actual gold weight gold inlay.

Date	Mintage	F	VF	XF	Unc	BU
ND(1999)(m)	11,358	—	—	—	95.00	110
ND(1999)(m) Proof	2,999		Value: 175			

KM# 19   2500 KORUN
7.7759 g., 0.9999 Gold 0.2500 oz. AGW, 22 mm. **Subject:** Historic Coins - 1620 Tolar of Moravian Estates **Obv:** Imperial eagle within circle, denomination below **Rev:** Vine climbing tower within circle

Date	Mintage	F	VF	XF	Unc	BU
1995	1,997	—	—	—	—	265
1996	1,253	—	—	—	—	265

Date	Mintage	F	VF	XF	Unc	BU
1996 Proof	741		Value: 300			
1997 Proof	1,697		Value: 275			

KM# 39   2500 KORUN
7.7759 g., 0.9999 Gold 0.2500 oz. AGW, 22 mm. **Rev:** Seal of Karel IV with legal document

Date	Mintage	F	VF	XF	Unc	BU
1998	1,122	—	—	—	—	245

Note: Milled edge
| 1998 Proof | 1,855 | | Value: 265 | | | |

Note: Plain edge
| 1999 Proof | 1,497 | | Value: 250 | | | |

KM# 20   5000 KORUN
15.5517 g., 0.9999 Gold 0.4999 oz. AGW, 28 mm.
Subject: Historic Coins **Obv:** Czech lion left within circle, denomination below **Rev:** Bohemian Maley Gros of 1587

Date	Mintage	F	VF	XF	Unc	BU
1995	997	—	—	—	—	560
1996	1,253	—	—	—	—	560
1996 Proof	741		Value: 625			
1997 Proof	1,496		Value: 575			

KM# 40   5000 KORUN
15.5530 g., 0.9999 Gold 0.5000 oz. AGW, 28 mm. **Obv:** Three shielded arms, date above, denomination below **Rev:** Karel IV, Charles University founder

Date	Mintage	F	VF	XF	Unc	BU
1998	1,045	—	—	—	—	475

Note: Milled edge
| 1998 Proof | 1,854 | | Value: 500 | | | |

Note: Edge: CESKA NARODNI BANKA 18.553 g.
| 1999 Proof | 1,497 | | Value: 475 | | | |

Note: Edge: CESKA NARODNI BANKA 18.553 g.

KM# 21   10000 KORUN
31.1035 g., 0.9999 Gold 0.9999 oz. AGW, 34 mm. **Subject:** Historic Coins **Obv:** Elongated, stylized, unbordered arms, date and denomination below **Rev:** Lion holding Prague Groschen

Date	Mintage	F	VF	XF	Unc	BU
1995	997	—	—	—	—	975
1996	1,251	—	—	—	—	975
1996 Proof	740		Value: 1,100			
1997 Proof	1,497		Value: 1,000			

KM# 41   10000 KORUN
31.1070 g., 0.9999 Gold 100000 oz. AGW, 34 mm. **Rev:** Karel IV and seals of Nove Mesto

Date	Mintage	F	VF	XF	Unc	BU
1998	2,200	—	—	—	—	975

Note: Milled edge
| 1998 Proof | 1,996 | | Value: 1,000 | | | |

Note: Edge: CESKA NARODNI BANKA 31.107 g.
| 1999 Proof | 1,297 | | Value: 1,000 | | | |

Note: Edge: CESKA NARODNI BANKA 31.107 g.

KM# 45   10000 KORUN
31.1070 g., 0.9990 Gold 0.9991 oz. AGW **Subject:** Karl IV **Obv:** 3 coats of arms **Rev:** Karl IV with 3 coin designs, *CESKA NARODNI BANKA8 31.107 g*

Date	Mintage	F	VF	XF	Unc	BU
1999(m) Proof	6,000		Value: 965			

MINT SETS

KM#	Date	Mintage	Identification	Issue Price	Mkt Val
MS1	1993 (9)	20,000	KM1, 2.1, 3-9	—	14.00
MS2	1994 (9)	13,400	KM1, 2.1, 3-9	—	14.00
MS3	1995 (9)	19,400	KM1, 2.1, 3-9	—	14.00
MS4	1996 (9)	14,188	KM1, 2.1, 3-9	—	14.00
MS5	1996 (9)	11,052	KM1, 2.1, 3-9 w/EURO 96 medal	—	15.50
MS6	1997 (9)	15,000	KM1, 2.1, 3-9	—	14.00
MS7	1998 (9)	5,000	KM1, 2.3, 3-9, Olympic Hockey Folder	—	14.00
MS8	1998 (9)	—	KM1, 2.3, 3-9, Summer Winter Scene Folder	—	—
MS9	1999 (9)	5,000	KM1, 2.3, 3-9, Parler Folder	—	14.00
MS10	1999 (9)	2,500	KM1, 2.3, 3-9, Nato Folder	—	14.00

KM#	Date	Mintage	Identification	Issue Price	Mkt Val
MS11	1999 (9)	2,500	KM1, 2.3, 3-9, Childrens Motif Folder	—	14.00
MS12	2000 (9)	6,000	KM#1, 2.3, 3.1, 6-9, 42-43 International Monetary Fund Folder	—	14.00

PROOF SETS

KM#	Date	Mintage	Identification	Issue Price	Mkt Val
PS1	1994 (3)	2,000	KM2.1, 3, 6	—	—
PS2	1997 (9)	1,500	KM1, 2.1, 3-9, plus silver medal	35.00	300
PS3	1998 (9)	2,500	KM1, 2.3, 3-9, plus silver medal	35.00	60.00
PS4	1999 (9)	2,000	KM1, 2.3, 3-9, plus silver medal	35.00	60.00
PS5	2000 (11)	2,500	KM#1, 2.3, 3.1, 4-9, 42-43	35.00	60.00

CZECHOSLOVAKIA

The Republic of Czechoslovakia, founded at the end of World War I, was part of the old Austrian-Hungarian Empire. It had an area of 49,371 sq. mi. (127,870 sq. km.) and a population of 15.6 million. Capital: Prague (Praha).

Czechoslovakia proclaimed itself a republic on Oct. 28, 1918, with Tomas G. Masaryk as President. Hitler's rise to power in Germany provoked Czechoslovakia's German minority in the Sudetenland to agitate for autonomy. At Munich (Munchen) in Sept. of 1938, France and Britain, seeking to avoid World War II, forced the cession of the Sudetenland to Germany. In March, 1939, Germany invaded Czechoslovakia and established the "protectorate of Bohemia and Moravia". Bohemia is a historic province in northwest Czechoslovakia that includes the city of Prague, one of the oldest continually occupied sites in Europe. Moravia is an area of considerable mineral wealth in central Czechoslovakia. Slovakia, a province in southeastern Czechoslovakia under Nazi influence was constituted as a republic. The end of World War II saw the re-established independence of Czechoslovakia, while bringing it within the Russian sphere of influence. On Feb. 23-25, 1948, the Communists seized control of the government in a coup d'etat, and adopted a constitution making the country a 'people's republic'. A new constitution adopted June 11, 1960, converted the country into a 'socialist republic', which lasted until 1989. On Nov. 11, 1989, demonstrations against the communist government began and in Dec. of that same year, communism was overthrown, and the Czech and Slovak Federal Republic was formed. In 1993 the CSFR split into the Czech Republic and The Republic of Slovakia.

NOTE: For additional listings see Bohemia and Moravia, Czech Republic and Slovakia.

MINT MARKS
(k) - Kremnica
(l) - Leningrad

MONETARY SYSTEM
100 Haleru = 1 Koruna

REPUBLIC
DECIMAL COINAGE

KM# 5   2 HALERE
2.0000 g., Zinc, 17 mm. **Obv:** Czech lion with Slovak shield **Rev:** Charles Bridge in Praha, denomination below **Edge:** Plain

Date	Mintage	F	VF	XF	Unc	BU
1923	2,700,000	3.00	5.00	10.00	16.00	—
1924	17,300,000	2.25	3.50	5.00	9.00	—
1925	2,000,000	3.00	5.00	7.50	17.00	—

KM# 6   5 HALERU
1.6600 g., Bronze, 16 mm. **Obv:** Czech lion with Slovak shield, date below **Rev:** Charles Bridge in Praha, denomination below **Edge:** Plain

Date	Mintage	F	VF	XF	Unc	BU
1923	37,800,000	0.20	0.30	0.50	2.00	—
1924	10	—	—	2,500	5,000	—

Note: There are two varieties of the number 4 in 1924 dated coins: with and without seraphs

1925	12,000,000	0.20	0.30	0.50	2.50	—
1926	1,084,000	1.50	4.00	20.00	60.00	—
1927	8,916,000	0.25	0.35	0.75	2.50	—
1928	5,320,000	0.30	0.45	0.75	2.50	—

Date	Mintage	F	VF	XF	Unc	BU
1929	12,680,000	0.25	0.35	0.75	2.50	—
1930	5,000,000	0.35	3.50	15.00	50.00	—
1931	7,448,000	0.25	0.35	0.75	2.50	—
1932	3,556,000	0.65	3.50	12.00	35.00	—
1938	14,244,000	0.25	0.35	0.75	2.00	—

KM# 3   10 HALERU
1.9600 g., Bronze, 18 mm. **Obv:** Czech lion with Slovak shield, date below **Rev:** Charles Bridge of Praha, denomination below **Edge:** Plain

Date	Mintage	F	VF	XF	Unc	BU
1922	6,000,000	0.30	0.45	1.00	2.75	—
1923	24,000,000	0.25	0.35	0.75	2.00	—
1924	5,320,000	0.30	0.45	1.00	3.00	—
1925	24,680,000	0.25	0.35	0.60	2.25	—
1926	10,000,000	0.25	0.35	0.75	2.25	—
1927	10,000,000	0.25	0.35	0.75	2.25	—
1928	14,290,000	0.25	0.35	0.75	2.25	—
1929	5,710,000	1.25	2.50	10.00	25.00	—
1930	6,980,000	0.30	0.45	1.00	2.50	—
1931	6,740,000	0.30	0.45	1.00	2.50	—
1932	11,280,000	0.25	0.35	0.75	2.00	—
1933	4,190,000	1.50	3.50	12.00	25.00	—
1934	13,200,000	0.25	0.35	0.75	2.00	—
1935	3,420,000	1.50	3.50	12.00	25.00	—
1936	8,560,000	0.25	0.35	0.75	2.00	—
1937	20,200,000	0.25	0.35	0.75	2.00	—
1938	21,400,000	0.25	0.35	0.75	2.00	—

KM# 1   20 HALERU
3.3300 g., Copper-Nickel, 20 mm. **Obv:** Czech lion with Slovak shield, date below **Rev:** Sheaf with sickle, linden branch, denomination at left **Edge:** Plain

Date	Mintage	F	VF	XF	Unc	BU
1921	40,000,000	0.25	0.35	0.60	2.50	—
1922	9,100,000	0.25	0.35	0.60	2.50	—
1924	20,931,000	0.25	0.35	0.60	2.50	—
1925	4,244,000	1.50	3.40	12.00	25.00	—
1926	14,825,000	0.25	0.35	0.60	2.50	—
1927	11,757,000	0.25	0.35	0.60	2.50	—
1928	14,018,000	0.25	0.35	0.60	2.50	—
1929	4,225,000	0.30	0.50	1.25	3.50	—
1930	—	1.00	2.00	5.00	14.00	—
1931	5,000,000	0.30	0.40	0.75	3.00	—
1933	Inc. above	9.00	25.00	80.00	160	—
1937	8,208,000	0.25	0.35	0.60	2.50	—
1938	18,787,000	0.25	0.35	0.60	2.50	—

KM# 16   25 HALERU
4.0000 g., Copper-Nickel, 21 mm. **Obv:** Czech lion with Slovak shield, date below **Rev:** Large denomination **Edge:** Milled

Date	Mintage	F	VF	XF	Unc	BU
1932	—	—	1,250	2,250	3,000	—
1933	22,711,000	0.50	1.00	2.00	4.00	—

KM# 2   50 HALERU
5.0000 g., Copper-Nickel, 22 mm. **Obv:** Czech lion with Slovak shield, date below **Rev:** Linden branches and wheat sprigs bound with ribbon **Edge:** Milled

Date	Mintage	F	VF	XF	Unc	BU
1921	3,000,000	0.25	0.50	1.00	3.00	—
1922	37,000,000	0.20	0.40	0.60	2.50	—
1924	10,000,000	0.20	0.40	0.60	3.00	—
1925	1,415,000	0.50	1.00	2.50	10.00	—
1926	1,585,000	3.50	9.00	20.00	45.00	—
1927	2,000,000	0.50	1.00	2.00	9.00	—
1931	6,000,000	0.25	0.50	1.00	2.50	—

KM# 4   KORUNA
6.6600 g., Copper-Nickel, 25 mm. **Obv:** Czech lion with Slovak shield, date below **Rev:** Woman with sheaf and sickle, denomination at left **Edge:** Milled

Date	Mintage	F	VF	XF	Unc	BU
1922	50,000,000	0.30	0.50	0.75	2.00	—
1923	15,385,000	0.30	0.50	0.75	2.00	—
1924	21,041,000	0.30	0.50	0.75	2.00	—
1925	8,574,000	0.40	0.60	1.25	4.00	—
1929	5,000,000	0.50	0.75	1.25	3.50	—
1930	5,000,000	0.40	0.60	1.25	5.00	—
1937	3,806,000	0.40	0.60	1.00	3.00	—
1938	8,582,000	0.40	0.60	1.00	3.00	—

KM# 10   5 KORUN
10.0000 g., Copper-Nickel, 30 mm. **Obv:** Czech lion with Slovak shield, date below **Rev:** Industrial factory and large value

Date	Mintage	F	VF	XF	Unc	BU
1925	16,474,500	1.50	2.50	3.50	10.00	—
1926	8,912,000	1.75	2.75	4.00	12.00	—
1927	4,613,500	8.00	20.00	80.00	165	—

KM# 11   5 KORUN
7.0000 g., 0.5000 Silver 0.1125 oz. ASW, 27 mm. **Obv:** Czech lion with Slovak shield, date below **Rev:** Industrial factory and large value **Edge:** Plain with crosses and waves

Date	Mintage	F	VF	XF	Unc	BU
1928	1,710,000	2.00	3.00	5.00	10.00	—
Note: Edge varieties exist for 1928						
1929	12,861,000	1.65	2.50	4.00	8.50	—
1930	10,429,000	1.65	2.50	4.00	8.50	—
1931	2,000,000	3.00	5.00	15.00	45.00	—
1932	1,000,000	5.00	7.50	20.00	60.00	—

KM# 11a   5 KORUN
7.0000 g., Nickel, 27 mm. **Obv:** Czech lion with Slovak shield, date below **Rev:** Industrial factory and large value

Date	Mintage	F	VF	XF	Unc	BU
1937	36,000	400	900	1,850	3,500	—
1938	17,200,000	1.25	2.50	4.00	6.50	—

KM# 12   10 KORUN
10.0000 g., 0.7000 Silver 0.2250 oz. ASW, 30 mm. **Subject:** 10th Anniversary of Independence **Obv:** Denomination

above state shield within circle, dates below **Rev:** Bust right **Edge:** Milled

Date	Mintage	F	VF	XF	Unc	BU
ND(1928)	1,000,000	4.00	5.00	7.00	12.00	—

KM# 15   10 KORUN
10.0000 g., 0.7000 Silver 0.2250 oz. ASW, 30 mm. **Obv:** State emblem, date below **Rev:** Republic holding linden tree, denomination above **Edge:** Milled

Date	Mintage	F	VF	XF	Unc	BU
1930	4,949,000	4.00	5.50	7.50	11.50	—
1931	6,689,000	3.75	5.00	7.00	10.00	—
1932	11,447,500	BV	3.50	5.00	9.00	—
1933	915,000	350	850	1,750	3,000	—

KM# 17   20 KORUN
12.0000 g., 0.7000 Silver 0.2701 oz. ASW, 34 mm. **Obv:** State emblem, date above **Rev:** Three figures: Industry, Agriculture, and Business, divide denomination **Edge:** Plain with crosses and waves

Date	Mintage	F	VF	XF	Unc	BU
1933	2,280,000	—	6.50	10.00	15.00	—
1934	3,280,000	—	6.50	10.00	15.00	—

KM# 18   20 KORUN
12.0000 g., 0.7000 Silver 0.2701 oz. ASW, 34 mm. **Subject:** Death of President Masaryk **Obv:** Denomination above state emblem **Rev:** Bust right, dates at left **Edge:** Plain with crosses and waves

Date	Mintage	F	VF	XF	Unc	BU
ND(1937)	1,000,000	—	5.00	8.00	11.50	—

TRADE COINAGE

KM# 7   DUKAT
3.4900 g., 0.9860 Gold 0.1106 oz. AGW **Subject:** 5th Anniversary of the Republic **Obv:** Shield with Czech lion and Slovak shield **Rev:** Duke Wenceslas (Vaclav) half-length figure facing **Edge:** Milled **Note:** Serially numbered below the duke. The number is in the die.

Date	Mintage	F	VF	XF	Unc	BU
1923	1,000	—	1,000	2,500	5,000	—

KM# 8   DUKAT
3.4900 g., 0.9860 Gold 0.1106 oz. AGW **Obv:** Czech lion with Slovak shield, date below **Rev:** Duke Wenceslas (Vaclav) half-length figure facing **Edge:** Milled **Note:** Similar to KM#7 but without serial numbers.

Date	Mintage	F	VF	XF	Unc	BU
1923	61,861	—	BV	140	200	—
1924	32,814	—	BV	140	200	—

Date	Mintage	F	VF	XF	Unc	BU
1925	66,279	—	BV	140	200	—
1926	58,669	—	BV	140	200	—
1927	25,774	—	BV	140	200	—
1928	18,983	—	BV	140	225	—
1929	10,253	—	BV	140	250	—
1930	11,338	—	BV	140	250	—
1931	43,482	—	BV	140	200	—
1932	26,617	—	BV	140	200	—
1933	57,597	—	BV	140	200	—
1934	9,729	—	110	160	250	—
1935	13,178	—	BV	140	225	—
1936	14,566	—	BV	140	225	—
1937	324	—	—	2,400	3,000	—
1938	56	—	—	1,750	16,500	—
1939	276	—	—	—	17,500	—

Note: Czech reports show mintage of 20 for Czechoslovakia and 256 for state of Slovakia

| 1951 | 500 | — | — | 2,400 | 3,000 | — |

KM# 9 2 DUKATY
6.9800 g., 0.9860 Gold 0.2213 oz. AGW, 25 mm. **Obv:** Czech lion with Slovak shield, denomination divides date below **Rev:** Duke Wenceslas (Vaclav) half-length figure facing **Edge:** Milled

Date	Mintage	F	VF	XF	Unc	BU
1923	4,000	—	275	600	1,000	—
1929	3,262	—	275	600	1,000	—
1930	Inc. above	—	275	700	1,200	—
1931	2,994	—	275	600	1,000	—
1932	5,496	—	275	600	1,000	—
1933	4,671	—	275	600	1,000	—
1934	2,403	—	275	700	1,200	—
1935	2,577	—	275	700	1,200	—
1936	819	—	400	1,000	1,800	—
1937	8	—	—	—	60,000	—
1938	186	—	—	—	8,000	—

Note: Czech reports show mintage of 14 for Czechoslovakia and 172 for state of Slovakia

| 1951 | 200 | — | — | — | 5,000 | — |

KM# 13 5 DUKATU
17.4500 g., 0.9860 Gold 0.5532 oz. AGW, 34 mm. **Obv:** Czech lion with Slovak shield, denomination and date below **Rev:** Duke Wenceslas (Vaclav) on horseback right **Edge:** Milled

Date	Mintage	F	VF	XF	Unc	BU
1929	1,827	—	750	1,500	2,250	—
1930	543	—	850	2,000	3,000	—
1931	1,528	—	750	1,500	2,250	—
1932	1,827	—	750	1,500	2,250	—
1933	1,752	—	750	1,500	2,250	—
1934	1,101	—	750	1,500	2,250	—
1935	1,037	—	750	1,500	2,250	—
1936	728	—	—	1,000	4,200	5,000
1937 Rare	4	—	—	—	—	—
1938	56	—	—	—	20,000	—

Note: Czech reports show mintage of 12 for Czechoslovakia and 44 for state of Slovakia

| 1951 | 100 | — | — | — | 10,000 | — |

KM# 14 10 DUKATU
34.9000 g., 0.9860 Gold 1.1063 oz. AGW, 42 mm. **Obv:** Czech lion with Slovak shield, denomination and date below **Rev:** Duke Wenceslas (Vaclav) on horseback right

Date	Mintage	F	VF	XF	Unc	BU
1929	1,564	—	2,000	3,500	5,000	—
1930	394	—	2,500	6,000	8,000	—
1931	1,239	—	2,000	3,500	5,000	—
1932	1,035	—	2,000	3,500	5,000	—
1933	1,780	—	2,000	3,500	5,000	—
1934	1,298	—	2,000	3,500	5,000	—
1935	600	—	2,500	4,000	6,000	—
1936	633	—	2,500	5,000	7,500	—
1937 Rare	34	—	—	—	—	—
1938	192	—	—	—	45,000	—
1951	100	—	—	—	17,500	—

Note: Czech reports show mintage of 20 for Czechoslovakia and 172 for state of Slovakia.

POST WAR COINAGE

KM# 20 20 HALERU
2.0000 g., Bronze, 18 mm. **Obv:** Czech lion with Slovak shield, date below **Rev:** Sheaf with sickle, linden branch, denomination at left **Edge:** Plain

Date	Mintage	F	VF	XF	Unc	BU
1947	—	65.00	125	200	300	—
1948	24,340,000	0.10	0.15	0.40	1.50	—
1949	25,660,000	0.10	0.15	0.40	1.50	—
1950	11,132,000	0.10	0.15	0.40	2.00	—

KM# 31 20 HALERU
0.5300 g., Aluminum, 16 mm. **Obv:** Czech lion with Slovak shield, date below **Rev:** Wheat sheaf, sickle, linden branch, denomination at left **Edge:** Plain

Date	Mintage	F	VF	XF	Unc	BU
1951	46,800,000	0.10	0.15	0.25	1.00	—
1952	80,340,000	0.10	0.15	0.25	1.00	—

KM# 21 50 HALERU
Bronze, 20 mm. **Obv:** Czech lion with Slovak shield, date below **Rev:** Linden branches and wheat sprigs bound with ribbon **Edge:** Plain

Date	Mintage	F	VF	XF	Unc	BU
1947	50,000,000	0.15	0.25	0.40	1.00	—
1948	20,000,000	0.15	0.25	0.40	1.50	—
1949	12,715,000	0.15	0.25	0.40	2.00	—
1950	17,415,000	0.15	0.25	0.40	1.80	—

KM# 32 50 HALERU
Aluminum, 18 mm. **Obv:** Czech lion with Slovak shield, date below **Rev:** Linden branches and wheat sprigs bound with ribbon **Edge:** Plain

Date	Mintage	F	VF	XF	Unc	BU
1951	60,000,000	0.15	0.35	0.50	0.75	—
1952	60,000,000	0.25	0.45	0.60	1.00	—
1953	34,920,000	1.00	2.50	6.00	10.00	—

KM# 19 KORUNA
Copper-Nickel, 21 mm. **Obv:** Czech lion with Slovak shield, date below **Rev:** Woman with sheaf and sickle, denomination at left **Edge:** Milled

Date	Mintage	F	VF	XF	Unc	BU
1946	88,000,000	0.15	0.25	0.50	1.00	—
1947	12,550,000	1.50	2.50	3.75	6.50	—

Note: Varieties exist for "4" in 1946 strikes

KM# 22 KORUNA
1.3400 g., Aluminum, 21 mm. **Obv:** Czech lion with Slovak shield, date below **Rev:** Woman with sheaf and sickle, denomination at left **Edge:** Milled

Date	Mintage	F	VF	XF	Unc	BU
1947	—	150	450	1,000	2,000	—

Note: Counterfeits, with prooflike fields, are known.

1950	62,190,000	0.20	0.35	0.45	1.00	—
1951	61,395,000	0.20	0.35	0.45	1.25	—
1952	101,105,000	0.20	0.30	0.40	0.80	—
1953	73,905,000	0.40	0.75	1.75	4.50	—

KM# 23 2 KORUNY
Copper-Nickel, 23.5 mm. **Obv:** Czech lion with Slovak shield, date below **Rev:** Juraj Janosik bust right, wearing hat, denomination at right **Edge:** Milled

Date	Mintage	F	VF	XF	Unc	BU
1947	20,000,000	0.20	0.40	0.60	1.25	—
1948	20,476,000	0.20	0.40	0.60	1.50	—

KM# 23a 2 KORUNY
Aluminum-Bronze, 23 mm. **Obv:** Czech lion with Slovak shield, date below **Rev:** Juraj Janosik bust right, wearing hat, denomination at right **Edge:** Milled

Date	Mintage	F	VF	XF	Unc	BU
1948	Est. 10,000,000	—	—	—	—	—

Note: Nearly entire mintage remelted, less than 20 known

KM# 34 5 KORUN
Aluminum, 23 mm. **Obv:** Czech lion with Slovak shield, date below **Rev:** Industrial factory and large value

Date	Mintage	F	VF	XF	Unc	BU
1951	—	—	300	700	1,500	—

Note: Not released for circulation. Almost the entire mintage was melted

| 1952 | 40,715,000 | 25.00 | 50.00 | 90.00 | 140 | — |

Note: Weakly struck counterfeits are known

KM# 24 50 KORUN
10.0000 g., 0.5000 Silver 0.1607 oz. ASW, 28 mm.
Subject: 1944 Slovak Uprising **Obv:** Czech lion with Slovak
shield **Rev:** Veiled female standing, holding linden branch,
denomination at left **Edge:** Plain with stars and waves

Date	Mintage	F	VF	XF	Unc	BU
ND(1947)	1,000,000	—	2.75	4.50	6.50	—

KM# 25 50 KORUN
10.0000 g., 0.5000 Silver 0.1607 oz. ASW, 28 mm.
Subject: 3rd Anniversary - Prague Uprising **Obv:** Czech lion with
Slovak shield **Rev:** Liberator divides denomination, date at right
Edge: Plain with stars and waves

Date	Mintage	F	VF	XF	Unc	BU
ND(1948)	1,000,000	—	2.75	4.50	6.50	—

KM# 28 50 KORUN
10.0000 g., 0.5000 Silver 0.1607 oz. ASW, 28 mm.
Subject: 70th Birthday - Josef Stalin **Obv:** Czech lion with Slovak
shield within lined frame, denomination above **Rev:** Uniformed
bust left **Edge:** Plain with stars and waves

Date	Mintage	F	VF	XF	Unc	BU
ND(1949)	1,000,000	—	2.75	4.50	7.00	—

KM# 26 100 KORUN
14.0000 g., 0.5000 Silver 0.2250 oz. ASW, 31 mm. **Subject:**
600th Anniversary - Charles University **Obv:** Czech lion with
Slovak shield, date below **Rev:** King Charles kneeling before
Duke Wenceslas, two shields at left, denomination below

Date	Mintage	F	VF	XF	Unc	BU
1948	1,000,000	—	3.25	4.75	7.50	—

KM# 29 100 KORUN
14.0000 g., 0.5000 Silver 0.2250 oz. ASW, 31 mm. **Subject:**
700th Anniversary - Jihlava Mining Privileges **Obv:** Czech lion
with Slovak shield above inscription and date **Rev:** Seated figure,
denomination below **Edge:** Plain with stars and waves

Date	Mintage	F	VF	XF	Unc	BU
1949	1,000,000	—	3.25	4.75	7.50	—

KM# 30 100 KORUN
14.0000 g., 0.5000 Silver 0.2250 oz. ASW, 31 mm.
Subject: 70th Birthday - Josef V. Stalin **Obv:** Czech lion with
Slovak shield, denomination above **Rev:** Uniformed bust left, date
at right **Edge:** Plain with stars and waves

Date	Mintage	F	VF	XF	Unc	BU
ND(1949)	1,000,000	—	3.25	4.75	7.50	—

KM# 33 100 KORUN
14.0000 g., 0.5000 Silver 0.2250 oz. ASW, 31 mm.
Subject: 30th Anniversary - Communist party **Obv:** Czech lion
with Slovak shield, denomination above **Rev:** Party Chairman
bust right divides dates **Edge:** Plain with stars and waves

Date	Mintage	F	VF	XF	Unc	BU
ND(1951)	1,000,000	—	3.25	4.75	7.50	—

PEOPLES REPUBLIC
DECIMAL COINAGE

KM# 35 HALER
0.4900 g., Aluminum, 16 mm. **Obv:** Czech lion with Slovak
shield, date below **Rev:** Large denomination within linden wreath,
star above **Edge:** Plain

Date	Mintage	F	VF	XF	Unc	BU
1953	188,885,000	—	—	0.10	0.25	—
1954	—	—	—	0.10	0.25	—
1955	—	—	—	0.15	0.50	—
1956	—	—	—	0.10	0.25	—
1957	—	—	—	0.10	0.25	—
1958	—	—	0.10	0.25	0.35	0.75	—
1959	—	—	—	0.15	0.50	—
1960	—	—	—	0.10	0.25	—

KM# 36 3 HALERE
0.6500 g., Aluminum, 18 mm. **Obv:** Czech lion with Slovak
shield, date below **Rev:** Large denomination within linden wreath,
star above **Edge:** Plain

Date	Mintage	F	VF	XF	Unc	BU
1953	90,001,000	—	—	0.10	0.15	0.30	—
1954	Inc. above	—	—	0.10	0.15	0.30	—

KM# 37 5 HALERU
Aluminum, 20 mm. **Obv:** Czech lion with Slovak shield, date
below **Rev:** Large denomination within linden wreath, star above
Edge: Plain

Date	Mintage	F	VF	XF	Unc	BU
1953	160,233,000	0.10	0.15	0.25	0.50	—
1954	Inc. above	0.10	0.15	0.25	0.50	—
1955	Inc. above	1.50	3.50	30.00	120	—

KM# 38 10 HALERU
Aluminum, 22 mm. **Obv:** Czech lion with Slovak shield, date
below **Rev:** Large denomination within linden wreath, star above

Date	Mintage	F	VF	XF	Unc	BU
1953	160,000	0.10	0.15	1.00	5.00	—

Note: Leningrad Mint-133 notches in milled edge

Date	Mintage	F	VF	XF	Unc	BU
1953	—	0.10	0.15	1.00	5.00	—

Note: Unknown Mint-125 notches in milled edge

Date	Mintage	F	VF	XF	Unc	BU
1954	—	0.25	0.50	2.00	7.00	—
1955	—	0.50	2.50	12.00	50.00	—
1956	—	0.10	0.15	1.00	5.00	—
1958	—	2.00	5.00	25.00	70.00	—

KM# 39 25 HALERU
1.4600 g., Aluminum, 24 mm. **Obv:** Czech lion with Slovak
shield, date below **Rev:** Large denomination within linden wreath,
star above

Date	Mintage	F	VF	XF	Unc	BU
1953	215,002,000	0.10	0.20	0.30	4.00	—

Note: Kremnica Mint - 134 notches in milled edge

Date	Mintage	F	VF	XF	Unc	BU
1953	—	0.30	0.50	0.60	6.00	—

Note: Leningrad Mint - 145 notches in milled edge

Date	Mintage	F	VF	XF	Unc	BU
1954	Inc. above	9.00	18.00	35.00	140	—

KM# 46 KORUNA
4.0000 g., Aluminum-Bronze, 23 mm. **Obv:** Czech lion with
Slovak shield, date below **Rev:** Woman kneeling planting linden
tree, denomination at left **Edge:** Milled

Date	Mintage	F	VF	XF	Unc	BU
1957	137,000,000	0.20	0.30	0.45	5.00	—
1958	Inc. above	0.20	0.30	0.45	7.00	—
1959	Inc. above	0.15	0.25	0.35	4.50	—
1960	Inc. above	0.15	0.25	0.35	4.50	—

KM# 27 100 KORUN
14.0000 g., 0.5000 Silver 0.2250 oz. ASW, 31 mm. **Subject:** 30th
Anniversary of Independence **Obv:** Czech lion with Slovak shield
within lined frame **Rev:** Man with flag and laurel branch divides dates,
denomination below **Edge:** Plain with stars and waves

Date	Mintage	F	VF	XF	Unc	BU
ND(1948)	1,000,000	—	3.25	4.75	7.50	—

KM# 40 10 KORUN
12.0000 g., 0.5000 Silver 0.1929 oz. ASW, 30 mm.
Subject: 10th Anniversary - Slovak Uprising **Obv:** Czech lion
with Slovak shield **Rev:** Soldier standing right, train and
construction site in background, denomination at left, dates below
Edge: Milled **Note:** 65,810 pieces, Unc and Proof, were melted
by the Czech National Bank in 1999.

Date	Mintage	F	VF	XF	Unc	BU
ND(1954)	250,000	—	2.75	3.75	6.50	—
ND(1954) Proof	5,000	Value: 12.00				

KM# 42 10 KORUN
12.0000 g., 0.5000 Silver 0.1929 oz. ASW, 30 mm. **Subject:** 10th Anniversary - Liberation from Germany **Obv:** Czech lion with Slovak shield **Rev:** Soldier kneeling left holding child, denomination below, dates at right **Edge:** Milled **Note:** 95,552 pieces Unc and Proof, were melted by the Czech National Bank in 1999.

Date	Mintage	F	VF	XF	Unc	BU
ND(1955)	300,000	—	2.75	3.75	6.50	—
ND(1955) Proof	5,000	Value: 14.50				

KM# 48 10 KORUN
12.0000 g., 0.5000 Silver 0.1929 oz. ASW, 30 mm. **Obv:** Czech lion with Slovak shield, date above **Rev:** Bust right of the Bishop of the Moravian Brotherhood, denomination below **Edge:** Milled **Note:** 7,854 pieces Unc and Proof, were melted by the Czech National Bank in 1999.

Date	Mintage	F	VF	XF	Unc	BU
1957	150,000	—	2.75	3.75	7.00	—
1957 Proof	5,000	Value: 14.50				

KM# 47.1 10 KORUN
12.0000 g., 0.5000 Silver 0.1929 oz. ASW, 30 mm. **Subject:** 250th Anniversary - Technical College **Obv:** Czech lion with Slovak shield, denomination below **Rev:** Bust left, hand on chin **Edge:** Plain with stars and waves **Note:** Raised designer initials.

Date	Mintage	F	VF	XF	Unc	BU
1957	75,000	—	2.75	3.75	7.50	—

Note: See note below KM#47.2

KM# 47.2 10 KORUN
12.0000 g., 0.5000 Silver 0.1929 oz. ASW, 30 mm. **Obv:** Czech lion with Slovak shield **Rev:** Bust left, hand on chin **Note:** Incuse designer initials.

Date	Mintage	F	VF	XF	Unc	BU
1957 Proof	Est. 5,000	Value: 14.50				

Note: 238 pieces, Unc and Proof, were melted by the Czech National Bank in 1999

KM# 41 25 KORUN
16.0000 g., 0.5000 Silver 0.2572 oz. ASW, 34 mm. **Subject:** 10th Anniversary - Slovak Unprising **Obv:** State emblem: Czech lion with Slovak shield **Rev:** Soldier standing right, train and construction site in background, denomination at left, dates below **Edge:** Milled **Note:** 110,933 Pieces, Unc and Proof, were melted by the Czech National Bank in 1999.

Date	Mintage	F	VF	XF	Unc	BU
ND(1954)	250,000	—	—	5.00	8.00	12.00
ND(1954) Proof	Est. 5,000	Value: 25.00				

KM# 43 25 KORUN
16.0000 g., 0.5000 Silver 0.2572 oz. ASW, 34 mm. **Subject:** 10th Anniversary - Liberation from Germany **Obv:** Czech lion with Slovak shield **Rev:** Mother and child greeting soldier divides dates and denomination **Edge:** Milled **Note:** 78,643 pieces, Unc and Proof, were melted by the Czech National Bank in 1999.

Date	Mintage	F	VF	XF	Unc	BU
ND(1955)	200,000	—	—	5.00	8.00	12.00
ND(1955) Proof	5,000	Value: 25.00				

KM# 44 50 KORUN
20.0000 g., 0.9000 Silver 0.5787 oz. ASW, 37 mm. **Subject:** 10th Anniversary - Liberation from Germany **Obv:** Czech lion with Slovak shield **Rev:** Soldier with rifle raised divides dates, denomination lower right **Edge:** Milled **Note:** 36,650 pieces were melted by the Czech National Bank in 1999.

Date	Mintage	F	VF	XF	Unc	BU
1955	120,000	—	8.50	12.00	18.00	25.00

KM# 45 100 KORUN
24.0000 g., 0.9000 Silver 0.6944 oz. ASW, 40 mm. **Subject:** 10th Anniversary - Liberation from Germany **Obv:** Czech lion with Slovak shield within circle **Rev:** Father and young boy greeting two returning soldiers, dates divided at top, denomination below **Note:** 22,244 pieces were melted by the Czech National Bank in 1999.

Date	Mintage	F	VF	XF	Unc	BU
ND(1955)	Est. 75,000	—	11.50	16.50	32.50	40.00

SOCIALIST REPUBLIC

DECIMAL COINAGE

KM# 51 HALER
0.5200 g., Aluminum, 16 mm. **Obv:** Czech lion with socialist shield within shield, date below **Rev:** Denomination within linden wreath, star above **Edge:** Plain

Date	Mintage	F	VF	XF	Unc	BU
1962	20,056,000	—	—	0.10	0.15	—

Date	Mintage	F	VF	XF	Unc	BU
1963	Inc. above	—	—	0.10	0.15	—
1986	3,360,000	—	—	—	1.00	—

KM# 52 3 HALERE
0.6400 g., Aluminum, 18 mm. **Obv:** Czech lion with socialist shield within shield, date below **Rev:** Denomination within linden wreath, star above **Edge:** Plain

Date	Mintage	F	VF	XF	Unc	BU
1962	Inc. below	100	150	200	280	—

Note: Counterfeits, with prooflike fields, are known.

Date	Mintage	F	VF	XF	Unc	BU
1963	5,130,000	—	—	0.10	0.15	—

KM# 53 5 HALERU
Aluminum, 20 mm. **Obv:** Czech lion with socialist shield within shield, date below **Rev:** Denomination within linden wreath, star above **Edge:** Plain

Date	Mintage	F	VF	XF	Unc	BU
1962	55,150,000	—	0.10	0.15	0.25	—
1963	Inc. above	—	0.10	0.15	0.25	—
1966	Inc. above	—	0.10	0.15	0.25	—
1967	20,770,000	—	0.10	0.15	0.25	—
1970	5,090,000	—	0.10	0.15	0.20	—
1972	10,090,000	—	0.10	0.15	0.20	—
1973	10,140,000	—	0.10	0.15	0.20	—
1974	15,510,000	—	0.10	0.15	0.20	—
1975	15,510,000	—	0.10	0.15	0.20	—
1976	15,550,000	—	0.10	0.15	0.20	—

KM# 53a 5 HALERU
2.0000 g., Brass **Obv:** Czech lion with socialist shield within shield **Rev:** Value within linden wreath, star above

Date	Mintage	F	VF	XF	Unc	BU
1967	Est. 20	—	—	300	500	—

KM# 86 5 HALERU
Aluminum, 16.2 mm. **Obv:** Czech lion with socialist shield within shield, date below **Rev:** Large denomination, star above **Edge:** Plain

Date	Mintage	F	VF	XF	Unc	BU
1977	26,710,000	—	—	0.10	0.25	—
1978	51,110,000	—	—	0.10	0.25	—
1979	72,380,000	—	—	0.10	0.25	—
1980	50,600	—	—	—	0.25	—
	Note: In sets only					
1981	66,160	—	—	—	0.50	—
	Note: In sets only					
1982	53,847	—	—	—	1.00	—
	Note: In sets only					
1983	60,000	—	—	—	0.50	—
	Note: In sets only					
1984	39,957	—	—	—	0.75	—
	Note: In sets only					
1985	39,791	—	—	—	0.75	—
	Note: In sets only					
1986	20,020,000	—	—	0.10	0.25	—
1987	520,000	—	—	0.10	0.35	—
1988	8,029,999	—	—	0.10	0.25	—
1989	110,000	—	—	0.10	0.50	—
1990	13,950,000	—	—	0.10	0.25	—

KM# 49.1 10 HALERU
Aluminum **Obv:** Star above Czech lion with socialist shield within shield **Rev:** Large denomination within linden wreath, star above

Date	Mintage	F	VF	XF	Unc	BU
1961	314,480,000	—	0.10	0.20	0.35	—
1962	Inc. above	—	0.10	0.20	0.35	—
1963	Inc. above	—	0.10	0.20	0.35	—
1964	Inc. above	—	0.10	0.20	0.35	—
1965	Inc. above	—	0.10	0.20	0.35	—
1966	Inc. above	—	0.10	0.20	0.35	—

Date	Mintage	F	VF	XF	Unc	BU
1967	46,990,000	—	0.10	0.20	0.35	—
1968	37,275,000	—	0.10	0.20	0.35	—
1969	80,000,000	—	0.10	0.15	0.35	—
1970	50,005,000	—	0.10	0.20	0.35	—
1971	30,450,000	—	0.10	0.20	0.35	—

KM# 49.2 10 HALERU
Aluminum, 22 mm. **Obv:** Star above Czech lion with socialist shield within shield, flat-top 3 in date below **Rev:** Denomination within linden wreath, star above **Note:** Obverse muled from 50 Haleru, KM 55.1.

Date	Mintage	F	VF	XF	Unc	BU
1963	Est. 3,600	12.50	25.00	60.00	150	—

Note: Weakly struck counterfeits are known.

KM# 49.1a 10 HALERU
2.4000 g., Brass **Obv:** Star above Czech lion with socialist shield within shield **Rev:** Large denomination within linden wreath, star above

Date	Mintage	F	VF	XF	Unc	BU
1968	Est. 20	—	—	300	500	—

KM# 80 10 HALERU
Aluminum, 18.2 mm. **Obv:** Czech lion with socialist shield within shield, fat date below **Rev:** Large thick denomination, star above **Note:** Varieties exist.

Date	Mintage	F	VF	XF	Unc	BU
1974	11,470,000	—	—	0.10	0.25	—
1975	41,002,000	—	—	0.10	0.25	—
1976	182,000,000	—	—	0.10	0.25	—
1977	151,760,000	—	—	0.10	0.25	—
1978	62,620,000	—	—	0.10	0.25	—
1979	30,240,000	—	—	0.10	0.25	—
1980	31,280,000	—	—	0.10	0.25	—
1981	43,616,160	—	—	0.10	0.25	—
1982	74,568,847	—	—	0.10	0.25	—
1983	50,560,000	—	—	0.10	0.25	—
1984	40,369,957	—	—	0.10	0.25	—
1985	92,929,791	—	—	0.10	0.25	—
1986	87,260,000	—	—	0.10	0.25	—
1987	30,030,000	—	—	0.10	0.25	—
1988	47,479,999	—	—	0.10	0.25	—
1989	50,300,000	—	—	0.10	0.25	—
1990	25,220,000	—	—	0.10	0.25	—

KM# 74 20 HALERU
Brass, 19.5 mm. **Obv:** Czech lion with socialist shield within shield, thick date below **Rev:** Large thick denomination, star above **Note:** Varieties exist.

Date	Mintage	F	VF	XF	Unc	BU
1972	25,820,000	—	0.10	0.20	0.40	—
1973	39,095,000	—	0.10	0.20	0.40	—
1974	24,795,000	—	0.10	0.20	0.40	—
1975	30,025,000	—	0.10	0.20	0.40	—
1976	30,540,000	—	0.10	0.20	0.40	—
1977	30,655,000	—	0.10	0.20	0.40	—
1978	30,095,000	—	0.10	0.20	0.40	—
1979	12,120,000	—	0.10	0.20	0.40	—
1980	52,301,000	—	0.10	0.15	0.30	—
1981	35,126,160	—	0.10	0.15	0.30	—
1982	41,238,847	—	0.10	0.15	0.30	—
1983	50,160,000	—	0.10	0.15	0.30	—
1984	33,684,957	—	0.10	0.15	0.30	—
1985	40,454,791	—	0.10	0.15	0.30	—
1986	37,055,000	—	0.10	0.15	0.30	—
1987	26,975,000	—	0.10	0.15	0.30	—
1988	18,259,999	—	0.10	0.15	0.30	—
1989	29,980,000	—	0.10	0.15	0.30	—
1990	15,030,000	—	0.10	0.15	0.30	—

KM# 54 25 HALERU
Aluminum, 24 mm. **Obv:** Czech lion with socialist shield within shield, date below **Rev:** Large denomination within linden wreath, star above **Edge:** Milled **Note:** This denomination ceased to be legal tender in 1972.

Date	Mintage	F	VF	XF	Unc	BU
1962	69,880,000	0.10	0.15	0.20	0.35	—
1963	Inc. above	0.10	0.15	0.20	0.35	—
1964	Inc. above	0.10	0.15	0.20	0.35	—

KM# 55.1 50 HALERU
Bronze, 21.5 mm. **Obv:** Czech lion with socialist shield within shield, date below **Rev:** Large denomination within linden wreath, star above

Date	Mintage	F	VF	XF	Unc	BU
1963	80,560,000	0.10	0.20	0.30	0.45	—
1964	Inc. above	0.10	0.20	0.30	0.45	—
1965	Inc. above	0.10	0.20	0.30	0.45	—
1969	9,876,000	0.10	0.20	0.30	0.45	—
1970	31,536,000	0.10	0.20	0.30	0.40	—
1971	20,800,000	0.10	0.20	0.30	0.40	—

KM# 55.2 50 HALERU
Bronze, 21.5 mm. **Obv:** Czech lion with socialist shield within shield, small date, without dots **Rev:** Value within linden wreath, star above **Note:** Obverse muled with 10 Haleru, KM 49.1.

Date	Mintage	F	VF	XF	Unc	BU
1969	—	12.50	22.50	40.00	75.00	—

KM# 89 50 HALERU
Copper-Nickel, 20.8 mm. **Obv:** Czech lion with socialist shield within shield, thick date below **Rev:** Thick denomination, star above **Edge:** Milled **Note:** Date varieties exist.

Date	Mintage	F	VF	XF	Unc	BU
1977	Est. 5	—	—	500	1,000	—
1978	40,480,000	—	—	0.10	0.50	—
1979	76,116,000	—	—	0.10	0.50	—
1980	51,000	—	—	—	1.50	—
	Note: In sets only					
1981	66,000	—	—	—	1.50	—
	Note: In sets only					
1982	14,261,847	—	—	0.10	0.50	—
1983	16,168,000	—	—	0.10	0.50	—
1984	16,207,957	—	—	0.10	0.50	—
1985	10,467,791	—	—	0.10	0.50	—
1986	10,020,000	—	—	0.10	0.50	—
1987	5,138,000	—	—	0.10	0.50	—
1988	5,089,999	—	—	0.10	0.50	—
1989	13,030,000	—	—	0.10	0.50	—
1990	7,742,000	—	—	0.10	0.50	—

KM# 50 KORUNA
Aluminum-Bronze, 23 mm. **Obv:** Czech lion with socialist shield within shield, date below **Rev:** Woman planting linden tree, denomination at left **Edge:** Milled **Note:** Date varieties exist.

Date	Mintage	F	VF	XF	Unc	BU
1961	146,964,000	—	0.15	0.30	0.60	—
1962	Inc. above	—	0.15	0.30	0.60	—
1963	Inc. above	—	0.15	0.30	0.60	—
1964	Inc. above	—	0.15	0.30	0.60	—
1965	Inc. above	—	0.15	0.30	0.60	—
1966	Inc. above	0.40	0.65	0.90	1.25	—
1967	7,924,000	—	0.15	0.30	0.60	—
1968	10,696,000	—	0.15	0.30	0.60	—
1969	21,820,000	—	0.15	0.30	0.60	—

Date	Mintage	F	VF	XF	Unc	BU
1970	31,036,000	—	0.15	0.30	0.60	—
1971	10,152,000	—	0.15	0.30	0.60	—
1975	6,657,000	—	0.15	0.30	0.60	—
1976	14,211,000	—	0.15	0.30	0.60	—
1977	10,434,000	—	0.15	0.30	0.75	—
1979	Inc. below	—	0.15	0.30	0.75	—
1980	24,513,000	—	0.15	0.30	0.75	—
1981	7,179,000	—	0.15	0.30	0.75	—
1982	17,162,847	—	0.15	0.30	0.75	—
1983	4,758,000	—	0.15	0.30	0.75	—
1984	9,732,957	—	0.15	0.30	0.75	—
1985	10,545,751	—	0.15	0.30	0.75	—
1986	2,789,000	—	0.15	0.30	0.75	—
1987	30,000	—	—	—	2.50	—
	Note: In sets only					
1988	29,999	—	—	—	2.50	—
	Note: In sets only					
1989	1,038,000	—	0.15	0.30	0.75	—
1990	19,368,000	—	0.15	0.30	0.75	—

KM# 75 2 KORUNY
Copper-Nickel, 24 mm. **Obv:** Czech lion with socialist shield within shield, date below **Rev:** Star above hammer and sickle, large value at right **Edge:** Plain with crosses and waves

Date	Mintage	F	VF	XF	Unc	BU
1972	20,344,000	—	0.25	0.45	1.00	—
1973	21,087,000	—	0.25	0.45	1.00	—
	Note: 1973 date exists with edge of 5 Korun KM#60, value: $15.00					
1974	27,957,000	—	0.25	0.45	1.00	—
1975	35,094,000	—	0.25	0.45	1.00	—
1976	1,100,000	—	0.25	0.45	1.00	—
1977	4,201,000	—	0.25	0.65	1.50	—
1980	14,943,000	—	0.25	0.35	0.75	—
1981	17,264,000	—	0.25	0.35	0.75	—
1982	8,108,000	—	0.25	0.35	0.75	—
1983	10,190,000	—	0.25	0.35	0.75	—
1984	8,634,000	—	0.25	0.35	0.75	—
1985	6,772,000	—	0.25	0.35	0.75	—
1986	10,262,000	—	0.25	0.35	0.75	—
1987	30,000	—	—	—	2.50	—
	Note: In sets only					
1988	30,000	—	—	—	2.50	—
	Note: In sets only					
1989	9,092,000	—	0.25	0.35	0.75	—
1990	10,672,000	—	0.25	0.35	0.75	—

KM# 57 3 KORUNY
5.5800 g., Copper-Nickel, 23.5 mm. **Obv:** Czech lion with socialist shield within shield, date below **Rev:** Branch of five linden leaves within banner, large value at right **Edge:** Plain with lime leaves and waves

Date	Mintage	F	VF	XF	Unc	BU
1965	15,000,000	—	0.50	1.00	2.50	—
1966	Inc. above	—	0.50	1.00	2.50	—
1968	7,000,000	—	0.45	0.85	2.00	—
1969	10,080,000	—	0.40	0.75	1.50	—

KM# 60 5 KORUN
7.2200 g., Copper-Nickel, 26 mm. **Obv:** Czech lion with socialist shield within shield, date below **Rev:** Geometric design and large denomination **Edge:** Plain with rhombs and waves

Date	Mintage	F	VF	XF	Unc	BU
1966	6,383,000	—	0.75	1.00	2.00	—

Note: 1966 varieties on obverse of coin: large date: no space between letter B in REPUBLIC and coat of arms; small date: space between letter B in REPUBLIC and coat of arms; plain edge: no ornamental inscription on edge (error coin). So far there has been no indication of any of the varieties as being scarce

Date	Mintage	F	VF	XF	Unc	BU
1967	4,544,000	—	—	0.75	1.50	—
1968	14,120,000	—	—	0.75	1.50	—
1969	Inc. above	0.75	1.50	5.00	9.00	—
Note: Date in semi-circle						
1969	5,486,000	—	—	0.75	1.50	—
Note: Straight date						
1970	10,073,000	—	—	0.75	1.50	—
1973	15,620,000	—	—	0.75	1.25	—
Note: Two variations in 3 of date						
1974	20,053,000	—	—	0.75	1.25	—
Note: Three variations in 4 of date						
1975	17,158,000	—	—	0.75	1.25	—
1978	5,317,000	—	—	0.75	1.25	—
1979	9,219,000	—	—	0.75	1.25	—
1980	12,559,000	—	—	0.75	1.25	—
1981	8,620,160	—	—	0.75	1.25	—
1982	6,903,847	—	—	0.75	1.25	—
1983	6,704,000	—	—	0.75	1.25	—
1984	6,856,957	—	—	0.75	1.25	—
1985	6,763,791	—	—	0.75	1.25	—
1986	20,000	—	—	—	35.00	—
Note: In sets only						
1987	30,000	—	—	—	7.00	—
Note: In sets only						
1988	29,999	—	—	—	5.00	—
1989	5,039,000	—	—	0.75	1.25	—
1990	2,783,000	—	—	0.75	1.25	—

KM# 56   10 KORUN
12.0000 g., 0.5000 Silver 0.1929 oz. ASW, 30 mm.
Subject: 20th Anniversary - 1944 Slovak Uprising **Obv:** Star above Czech lion with socialist shield within shield **Rev:** Three hands and linden sprig divide dates and denomination, SLOVENSKE NARODNE POVSTANIE **Note:** 11,476 pieces were melted by the Czech National Bank in 1999.

Date	Mintage	F	VF	XF	Unc	BU
ND(1964)	120,000	—	—	3.50	5.50	—

KM# 58   10 KORUN
12.0000 g., 0.5000 Silver 0.1929 oz. ASW, 30 mm. **Subject:** 550th Anniversary - Death of Jan Hus **Obv:** Star above Czech lion with socialist shield within shield **Rev:** Bust right, denomination below, 550 LET UPALENI M, JANA HUSA **Note:** 380 pieces, Unc and Proof, were melted by the Czech National Bank in 1999.

Date	Mintage	F	VF	XF	Unc	BU
ND(1965)	55,000	—	—	7.00	15.00	—
ND(1965) Proof	5,000	Value: 20.00				

KM# 61   10 KORUN
12.0000 g., 0.5000 Silver 0.1929 oz. ASW, 30 mm.
Subject: 1100th Anniversary of Great Moravia **Obv:** Star above Czech lion with socialist shield within shield **Rev:** Medal with horseman with falcon and plot of church, denomination upper right **Edge:** Plain with ellipse and rings **Note:** 9,446 pieces, Unc and Proof, were melted by the Czech National Bank in 1999.

Date	Mintage	F	VF	XF	Unc	BU
1966	115,000	—	—	4.00	6.50	—
1966 Proof	5,000	Value: 12.50				

KM# 62   10 KORUN
12.0000 g., 0.5000 Silver 0.1929 oz. ASW, 30 mm. **Subject:** 500th Anniversary - Bratislava University **Obv:** Czech lion with socialist shield above stylized three mountains and river, denomination below **Rev:** University seal and building, date lower right **Edge:** Plain with Rhombs and waves **Note:** 103 pieces, Unc and Proof, were melted by the Czech National Bank in 1999.

Date	Mintage	F	VF	XF	Unc	BU
ND(1967)	45,000	—	—	10.00	20.00	—
ND(1967) Proof	500	Value: 22.50				

KM# 63   10 KORUN
12.0000 g., 0.5000 Silver 0.1929 oz. ASW, 30 mm.
Subject: Centennial - Prague (Praha) National Theater **Obv:** Czech lion with socialist shield within shield, denomination below **Rev:** Female goddess in three-horse chariot, dates below **Edge:** Plain with crosses and waves **Note:** 50 pieces, Unc and Proof, were melted by the Czech National Bank in 1999.

Date	Mintage	F	VF	XF	Unc	BU
ND(1968)	55,000	—	—	15.00	20.00	—
ND(1968) Proof	5,000	Value: 40.00				

KM# 76   20 KORUN
9.0000 g., 0.5000 Silver 0.1447 oz. ASW, 29 mm. **Subject:** Centennial - Death of Andrej Sladkovic **Obv:** Czech lion with socialist shield within shield, denomination below **Rev:** Head left, dates below **Note:** 3,842 pieces, Unc and Proof, were melted by the Czech National Bank in 1999.

Date	Mintage	F	VF	XF	Unc	BU
ND(1972)	55,000	—	—	3.50	5.50	—
ND(1972) Proof	5,000	Value: 12.50				

KM# 59   25 KORUN
16.0000 g., 0.5000 Silver 0.2572 oz. ASW, 34 mm. **Subject:** 20th Anniversary - Czechoslovakian Liberation **Obv:** Czech lion with socialist shield within shield **Rev:** Female head left, dove with linden branch, denomination below, dates above and left, 20 LET OSVOBOZENI CSSR **Note:** 18,114 pieces, Unc and Proof, were melted by the Czech National Bank in 1999.

Date	Mintage	F	VF	XF	Unc	BU
ND(1965)	150,000	—	—	4.00	6.50	—
ND(1965) Proof	5,000	Value: 12.50				

KM# 64   25 KORUN
16.0000 g., 0.5000 Silver 0.2572 oz. ASW, 34 mm.
Subject: 150th Anniversary - Prague (Praha) National Museum **Obv:** Czech lion with socialist shield within shield, three line inscription below **Rev:** National Museum building, denomination below **Edge:** Plain with crosses and waves **Note:** 151 pieces, Unc and Proof, were melted by the Czech National Bank in 1999.

Date	Mintage	F	VF	XF	Unc	BU
ND(1968)	51,000	—	—	4.50	9.00	—
ND(1968) Proof	5,000	Value: 40.00				

KM# 66   25 KORUN
16.0000 g., 0.5000 Silver 0.2572 oz. ASW, 34 mm. **Subject:** 100th Anniversary - Death of J. E. Purkyne **Obv:** Czech lion with socialist shield within shield, denomination below **Rev:** Head right, dates at right, FYSIOLOG, FILOSOF, BUDITEL, BASNIK **Note:** Edge varieties exist; 140 pieces, Unc and Proof, were melted by the Czech National Bank in 1999.

Date	Mintage	F	VF	XF	Unc	BU
ND(1969)	45,000	—	—	4.00	8.00	—
ND(1969) Proof	5,000	Value: 28.00				

KM# 67   25 KORUN
16.0000 g., 0.5000 Silver 0.2572 oz. ASW, 34 mm.
Subject: 25th Anniversary - 1944 Slovak Uprising **Obv:** Czech lion with socialist shield within shield, three line inscription and denomination below **Rev:** Three mountains and plant, date at top, 25. VYROCIE SLOVENSKEHO NARODNEHO POVSTANIA **Note:** Edge varieties exist; 40 pieces, Unc and Proof, were melted by the Czech National Bank in 1999.

Date	Mintage	F	VF	XF	Unc	BU
ND(1969)	25,000	—	—	45.00	75.00	—
ND(1969) Proof	5,000	Value: 95.00				

KM# 68   25 KORUN
10.0000 g., 0.5000 Silver 0.1607 oz. ASW, 30 mm.
Subject: 50th Anniversary - Slovak National Theater **Obv:** Czech lion with socialist shield within square, denomination below **Rev:** Stylized head of muse within square divides dates **Note:** 4,923 pieces, Unc and Proof, were melted by the Czech National Bank in 1999.

Date	Mintage	F	VF	XF	Unc	BU
ND(1970)	45,000	—	—	5.00	10.00	—
ND(1970) Proof	5,000	Value: 60.00				

KM# 69 25 KORUN
10.0000 g., 0.5000 Silver 0.1607 oz. ASW, 30 mm. **Subject:** 25th Anniversary of Liberation **Obv:** Czech lion with socialist shield within shield, three line inscription below **Rev:** Sun of Liberation, landscape, denomination below **Edge:** - x - **Note:** 23,777 pieces, Unc and Proof, were melted by the Czech National Bank in 1999.

Date	Mintage	F	VF	XF	Unc	BU
ND(1970)	95,000	—	—	4.00	6.00	—
ND(1970) Proof	5,000	Value: 15.00				

KM# 65 50 KORUN
20.0000 g., 0.9000 Silver 0.5787 oz. ASW, 37 mm. **Subject:** 50th Anniversary of Czechoslovakia 20th Anniversary - People's Republic **Obv:** Czech lion with socialist shield divides dates, inscription and denomination below **Rev:** Woman's head left, wearing linden and floral wreath, date at left **Note:** 650 pieces, Unc and Proof, were melted by the Czech National Bank in 1999.

Date	Mintage	F	VF	XF	Unc	BU
ND(1968)	58,000	—	—	18.00	32.00	40.00
ND(1968) Proof	2,000	Value: 75.00				

KM# 70 50 KORUN
13.0000 g., 0.7000 Silver 0.2926 oz. ASW, 31 mm. **Subject:** Centennial - Birth of Lenin **Obv:** Czech lion with socialist shield within shield, denomination below **Rev:** Head right, date at left **Note:** 451 pieces, Unc and Proof, were melted by the Czech National Bank in 1999.

Date	Mintage	F	VF	XF	Unc	BU
ND(1970)	44,000	—	—	4.50	8.50	—
ND(1970) Proof	6,200	Value: 30.00				

KM# 71 50 KORUN
13.0000 g., 0.7000 Silver 0.2926 oz. ASW, 31 mm. **Subject:** 50th Anniversary - Czechoslovak Communist Party **Obv:** Czech lion with socialist shield within shield, denomination below **Rev:** Five figures standing within hammer and sickle, star above, dates below **Edge:** Wave, star, wave **Note:** 4,850 pieces, Unc and Proof, were melted by the Czech National Bank in 1999.

Date	Mintage	F	VF	XF	Unc	BU
ND(1971)	45,000	—	—	4.50	8.50	—
ND(1971) Proof	5,000	Value: 22.00				

KM# 72 50 KORUN
13.0000 g., 0.7000 Silver 0.2926 oz. ASW, 31 mm. **Subject:** 50th Anniversary - Death of Pavol Orsagh-Hviezdoslav **Obv:** Czech lion with socialist shield within shield, denomination below **Rev:** Head left, dates at right **Note:** 4,300 pieces, Unc and Proof, were melted by the Czech National Bank in 1999.

Date	Mintage	F	VF	XF	Unc	BU
ND(1971)	45,000	—	—	4.25	7.50	—
ND(1971) Proof	5,000	Value: 20.00				

KM# 77 50 KORUN
13.0000 g., 0.7000 Silver 0.2926 oz. ASW, 31 mm. **Subject:** 50th Anniversary - Death of J. V. Myslbek **Obv:** Czech lion with socialist shield within shield, denomination below **Rev:** Head left, dates at right, J. V. MYSLBEK *1922-1972* **Note:** 6,439 pieces, Unc and Proof, were melted by the Czech National Bank in 1999.

Date	Mintage	F	VF	XF	Unc	BU
ND(1972)	45,000	—	—	4.25	7.50	—
ND(1972) Proof	5,000	Value: 20.00				

KM# 78 50 KORUN
13.0000 g., 0.7000 Silver 0.2926 oz. ASW, 31 mm. **Subject:** 25th Anniversary - Victory of Communist Party **Obv:** Czech lion with socialist shield within shield **Rev:** Soldier standing before large star, hammer and sickle at right, 25. VYROCI VITEZNEHO UNORA* **Note:** 5,340 pieces, Unc and Proof, were melted by the Czech National Bank in 1999.

Date	Mintage	F	VF	XF	Unc	BU
ND(1973)	55,000	—	—	4.25	7.50	—
ND(1973) Proof	5,000	Value: 20.00				

KM# 79 50 KORUN
13.0000 g., 0.7000 Silver 0.2926 oz. ASW, 31 mm. **Subject:** 200th Anniversary - Birth of Josef Jungmann **Obv:** Czech lion with socialist shield within shield, denomination below **Rev:** Head right, dates below **Note:** 2,084 pieces, Unc and Proof, were melted by the Czech National Bank in 1999.

Date	Mintage	F	VF	XF	Unc	BU
ND(1973)	45,000	—	—	4.25	7.50	—
ND(1973) Proof	5,000	Value: 11.50				

KM# 81 50 KORUN
13.0000 g., 0.7000 Silver 0.2926 oz. ASW, 31 mm. **Subject:** Centennial - Birth of Janko Jesensky **Obv:** Czech lion with socialist shield within shield, denomination below **Rev:** Head 3/4 right, date at right **Edge:** Plain with wave star wave **Note:** 112,038 pieces, Unc and Proof, were melted by the Czech National Bank in 1999.

Date	Mintage	F	VF	XF	Unc	BU
ND(1974)	55,000	—	—	4.25	6.75	—
ND(1974) Proof	5,000	Value: 11.50				

KM# 83 50 KORUN
13.0000 g., 0.7000 Silver 0.2926 oz. ASW, 31 mm. **Subject:** Centennial - Birth of S. K. Neumann **Obv:** Czech lion with socialist shield within shield, denomination below **Rev:** Head right, dates at right **Note:** 11,537 pieces, Unc and Proof, were melted by the Czech National Bank in 1999.

Date	Mintage	F	VF	XF	Unc	BU
ND(1975)	55,000	—	—	4.25	6.75	—
ND(1975) Proof	5,000	Value: 11.50				

KM# 87 50 KORUN
13.0000 g., 0.7000 Silver 0.2926 oz. ASW, 31 mm. **Subject:** 125th Anniversary - Death of Jan Kollar **Obv:** Czech lion with socialist shield within shield, denomination below **Rev:** Head facing, dates below **Edge:** Milled **Note:** 19,743 pieces, Unc and Proof, were melted by the Czech National Bank in 1999.

Date	Mintage	F	VF	XF	Unc	BU
ND(1977)	75,000	—	—	4.25	6.75	—
ND(1977) Proof	5,000	Value: 11.50				

KM# 90 50 KORUN
13.0000 g., 0.7000 Silver 0.2926 oz. ASW, 31 mm. **Subject:** Centennial - Birth of Zdenek Nejedly **Obv:** Czech lion with socialist shield within shield, denomination below **Rev:** Bust right, dates at left **Edge:** Milled **Note:** 20,538 pieces, Unc and Proof, were melted by the Czech National Bank in 1999.

Date	Mintage	F	VF	XF	Unc	BU
ND(1978)	75,000	—	—	4.25	6.75	—
ND(1978) Proof	5,000	Value: 11.50				

KM# 91 50 KORUN
13.0000 g., 0.7000 Silver 0.2926 oz. ASW, 31 mm. **Subject:** 650th Anniversary of Kremnica Mint **Obv:** Czech lion with socialist shield within shield, denomination below **Rev:** Montage of five coin designs, dates below **Note:** 22,037 pieces, Unc and Proof, were melted by the Czech National Bank in 1999.

Date	Mintage	F	VF	XF	Unc	BU
ND(1978)	93,000	—	—	4.25	6.75	—
ND(1978) Proof	7,000	Value: 11.50				

KM# 98 50 KORUN
13.0000 g., 0.7000 Silver 0.2926 oz. ASW, 31 mm. **Subject:** 30th Anniversary of 9th Congress **Obv:** Czech lion with socialist shield within shield, linden leaves flanking, three line inscription above denomination below **Rev:** Hammer and sickle in gear at center, linden leaves at left, dates below **Edge:** Milled **Note:** 30,089 pieces, Unc and Proof, were melted by the Czech National Bank in 1999.

Date	Mintage	F	VF	XF	Unc	BU
ND(1979)	94,000	—	—	4.25	6.75	—
ND(1979) Proof	6,000	Value: 11.50				

KM# 121 50 KORUN
7.0000 g., 0.5000 Silver 0.1125 oz. ASW, 27 mm. **Obv:** Czech lion with socialist shield within shield, denomination and dates below **Rev:** Prague (Praha) city view **Note:** 6,838 pieces, Unc and Proof, were melted by the Czech National Bank in 1999.

Date	Mintage	F	VF	XF	Unc	BU
1986	90,000	—	—	—	6.00	—
1986 Proof	10,000	Value: 12.50				

KM# 122 50 KORUN
7.0000 g., 0.5000 Silver 0.1125 oz. ASW, 27 mm. **Obv:** Czech lion with socialist shield divides denomination, three line inscription and date below **Rev:** Levoca city view above three statues **Note:** 9,438 pieces Unc and Proof, were melted by the Czech National Bank in 1999.

Date	Mintage	F	VF	XF	Unc	BU
1986	69,000	—	—	—	6.00	—
1986 Proof	10,000	Value: 11.50				

KM# 124 50 KORUN
7.0000 g., 0.5000 Silver 0.1125 oz. ASW, 27 mm. **Obv:** Czech lion with socialist shield divides denomination, three line inscription and date below **Rev:** Three building facades in Telc **Note:** 13,438 pieces Unc and Proof, were melted by the Czech National Bank in 1999.

Date	Mintage	F	VF	XF	Unc	BU
1986	69,000	—	—	—	6.00	—
1986 Proof	10,000	Value: 11.50				

KM# 125 50 KORUN
7.0000 g., 0.5000 Silver 0.1125 oz. ASW, 27 mm. **Obv:** Czech lion with socialist shield divides denomination, three line inscription and date below **Rev:** Bratislava city view **Note:** 12,188 pieces, Unc and Proof, were melted by the Czech National Bank in 1999.

Date	Mintage	F	VF	XF	Unc	BU
1986	69,000	—	—	—	6.00	—
1986 Proof	10,000	Value: 11.50				

KM# 126 50 KORUN
7.0000 g., 0.5000 Silver 0.1125 oz. ASW, 27 mm. **Obv:** Czech lion with socialist shield within shield, date and denomination below **Rev:** Cesky Krumlov city view **Note:** 11,338 pieces Unc and Proof, were melted by the Czech National Bank in 1999.

Date	Mintage	F	VF	XF	Unc	BU
1986	69,000	—	—	—	6.00	—
1986 Proof	10,000	Value: 11.50				

KM# 127 50 KORUN
7.0000 g., 0.5000 Silver 0.1125 oz. ASW, 27 mm. **Subject:** Environmental Protection **Obv:** Czech lion with socialist shield within shield, date and denomination below **Rev:** Two Przewalski's horses **Note:** 338 pieces Unc and Proof, were melted by the Czech National Bank in 1999.

Date	Mintage	F	VF	XF	Unc	BU
1987	55,000	—	—	—	27.50	—
1987 Proof	5,000	Value: 35.00				

KM# 129 50 KORUN
7.0000 g., 0.5000 Silver 0.1125 oz. ASW, 27 mm. **Subject:** 300th Anniversary - Birth of Juraj Janosik **Obv:** Czech lion with socialist shield divides denomination, three line inscription below **Rev:** Standing, caped man divides dates, bird at left **Note:** 735 pieces Unc and Proof, were melted by the Czech National Bank in 1999.

Date	Mintage	F	VF	XF	Unc	BU
ND(1988)	53,000	—	—	—	7.00	—
ND(1988) Proof	5,000	Value: 15.00				

KM# 133 50 KORUN
7.0000 g., 0.5000 Silver 0.1125 oz. ASW, 27 mm. **Subject:** 150th Anniversary - Breclav to Brno Railroad **Obv:** Czech lion with socialist shield within shield, denomination below **Rev:** Early steam locomotive, dates below **Note:** 1,835 pieces Unc and Proof, were melted by the Czech National Bank in 1999.

Date	Mintage	F	VF	XF	Unc	BU
ND(1989)	67,000	—	—	—	7.00	—
ND(1989) Proof	3,000	Value: 16.00				

KM# 73 100 KORUN
15.0000 g., 0.7000 Silver 0.3376 oz. ASW, 33 mm. **Subject:** Centennial - Death of Josef Manes **Obv:** Czech lion

with socialist shield within shield, three line inscription and denomination below **Rev:** Bust right divides dates **Note:** 6,803 pieces, Unc and Proof, were melted by the Czech National Bank in 1999.

Date	Mintage	F	VF	XF	Unc	BU
ND(1971)	45,000	—	—	10.00	13.50	—
ND(1971) Proof	5,000	Value: 17.50				

KM# 82 100 KORUN
15.0000 g., 0.7000 Silver 0.3376 oz. ASW, 33 mm. **Subject:** Sesquicentennial - Birth of Bedrich Smetana **Obv:** Czech lion with socialist shield within shield, denomination below **Rev:** Head right, dates at left **Edge:** Plain with 150 LET OD NAROZENI **Note:** 6,201 pieces, Unc and Proof, were melted by the Czech National Bank in 1999.

Date	Mintage	F	VF	XF	Unc	BU
ND(1974)	75,000	—	—	10.00	12.00	—
ND(1974) Proof	5,000	Value: 17.50				

KM# 84 100 KORUN
15.0000 g., 0.7000 Silver 0.3376 oz. ASW, 33 mm. **Subject:** Centennial - Death of Janko Kral **Obv:** Czech lion with socialist shield within shield, denomination below **Rev:** Head right, dates lower right, BASNIK * REVOLUCIONAR **Note:** 19,839 pieces, Unc and Proof, were melted by the Czech National Bank in 1999.

Date	Mintage	F	VF	XF	Unc	BU
ND(1976)	75,000	—	—	10.00	12.00	—
ND(1976) Proof	5,000	Value: 17.50				

KM# 85 100 KORUN
15.0000 g., 0.7000 Silver 0.3376 oz. ASW, 33 mm. **Subject:** Centennial - Birth of Viktor Kaplan **Obv:** Czech lion with socialist shield within shield, denomination below **Rev:** Bust right, dates at left **Edge:** - * - **Note:** 22,339 pieces, Unc and Proof, were melted by the Czech National Bank in 1999.

Date	Mintage	F	VF	XF	Unc	BU
ND(1976)	75,000	—	—	10.00	12.00	—
ND(1976) Proof	5,000	Value: 17.50				

KM# 88 100 KORUN
15.0000 g., 0.7000 Silver 0.3376 oz. ASW, 33 mm. **Subject:** 300th Anniversary - Death of Vaclav Hollar **Obv:** Czech lion with socialist shield within shield, denomination below **Rev:** Head left, dates lower left **Edge:** Plain with waves and dots **Note:** 32,789 pieces, Unc and Proof, were melted by the Czech National Bank in 1999.

Date	Mintage	F	VF	XF	Unc	BU
ND(1977)	95,000	—	—	10.00	12.00	—
ND(1977) Proof	5,000	Value: 17.50				

KM# 93 100 KORUN
15.0000 g., 0.7000 Silver 0.3376 oz. ASW, 33 mm. **Subject:** 600th Anniversary - Death of Charles IV **Obv:** Czech lion with socialist shield within shield, three line inscription, denomination and date below **Rev:** Crowned bust right, dates below **Note:** 32,638 pieces, Unc and Proof, were melted by the Czech National Bank in 1999.

Date	Mintage	F	VF	XF	Unc	BU
1978	90,000	—	—	10.00	12.00	—
1978 Proof	10,000	Value: 17.50				

KM# 92 100 KORUN
15.0000 g., 0.7000 Silver 0.3376 oz. ASW, 33 mm. **Subject:** 75th Anniversary - Birth of Julius Fucik **Obv:** Czech lion with socialist shield within shield, denomination below **Rev:** Head left, dates at right, LIDE, MEL JSEM VAS RAD, BDETE! **Note:** 24,840 pieces, Unc and Proof, were melted by the Czech National Bank in 1999.

Date	Mintage	F	VF	XF	Unc	BU
ND(1978)	75,000	—	—	10.00	12.00	—
ND(1978) Proof	5,000	Value: 17.50				

KM# 99 100 KORUN
15.0000 g., 0.7000 Silver 0.3376 oz. ASW, 33 mm. **Subject:** 150th Anniversary - Birth of Jan Botto **Obv:** Czech lion with socialist shield within shield, three line inscription above denomination below **Rev:** Head 3/4 left, date below **Edge:** ooo star ooo **Note:** 26,740 pieces, Unc and Proof, were melted by the Czech National Bank in 1999.

Date	Mintage	F	VF	XF	Unc	BU
ND(1979)	75,000	—	—	10.00	12.00	—
ND(1979) Proof	5,000	Value: 17.50				

KM# 100 100 KORUN
15.0000 g., 0.7000 Silver 0.3376 oz. ASW, 33 mm. **Subject:** 150th Anniversary - Birth of Peter Parler **Obv:** Czech lion with socialist shield within shield, medieval arches in background, three line inscription above denomination below **Rev:** Bust facing, medieval arches in background, date at left and below **Edge:** Plain with waves and dots **Note:** 54,738 pieces, Unc and Proof, were melted by the Czech National Bank in 1999.

Date	Mintage	F	VF	XF	Unc	BU
ND(1980)	91,000	—	—	10.00	12.00	—
ND(1980) Proof	9,000	Value: 17.50				

KM# 101 100 KORUN
9.0000 g., 0.5000 Silver 0.1447 oz. ASW, 29 mm. **Subject:** Fifth Spartakiade Games **Obv:** Czech lion with socialist shield within shield divides denomination, inscription below **Rev:** Seven female gymnastic figures, shadowing, date at left **Note:** 50,391 pieces, Unc and Proof, were melted by the Czech National Bank in 1999.

Date	Mintage	F	VF	XF	Unc	BU
1980	110,000	—	—	—	12.00	—
1980 Proof	10,000	Value: 18.50				

KM# 102 100 KORUN
9.0000 g., 0.5000 Silver 0.1447 oz. ASW, 29 mm. **Subject:** Centennial - Birth of Bohumir Smeral **Obv:** Czech lion with socialist shield within shield, denomination below **Rev:** Bust 3/4 facing, dates lower right **Edge:** Milled **Note:** 29,943 pieces, Unc and Proof, were melted by the Czech National Bank in 1999.

Date	Mintage	F	VF	XF	Unc	BU
ND(1980)	74,000	—	—	—	12.00	—
ND(1980) Proof	6,000	Value: 17.50				

KM# 103 100 KORUN
9.0000 g., 0.5000 Silver 0.1447 oz. ASW, 29 mm. **Subject:** 20th Anniversary - Manned Space Flight **Obv:** Czech lion with socialist shield within shield, denomination below **Rev:** Cosmonaut Gagarin left, dates at right **Edge:** Milled **Note:** 31,639 pieces, Unc and Proof, were melted by the Czech National Bank in 1999.

Date	Mintage	F	VF	XF	Unc	BU
ND(1981)	95,000	—	—	—	9.00	—
ND(1981) Proof	5,000	Value: 17.50				

KM# 104 100 KORUN
9.0000 g., 0.5000 Silver 0.1447 oz. ASW, 29 mm. **Subject:** Centennial - Birth of Prof. Otakar Spaniel **Obv:** Czech lion with socialist shield within shield, denomination below **Rev:** Head left, dates below **Edge:** Milled **Note:** 56,189 pieces, Unc and Proof, were melted by the Czech National Bank in 1999.

Date	Mintage	F	VF	XF	Unc	BU
ND(1981)	115,000	—	—	—	9.00	—
ND(1981) Proof	5,000	Value: 17.50				

KM# 106 100 KORUN
9.0000 g., 0.5000 Silver 0.1447 oz. ASW, 29 mm.

Subject: Centennial - Birth of Ivan Olbracht **Obv:** Czech lion with socialist shield within shield divides denomination **Rev:** Head with hat left, dates at right **Edge:** Milled **Note:** 24,140 pieces, Unc and Proof, were melted by the Czech National Bank in 1999.

Date	Mintage	F	VF	XF	Unc	BU
ND(1982)	76,000	—	—	—	12.00	—
ND(1982) Proof	4,000	Value: 20.00				

KM# 107 100 KORUN
9.0000 g., 0.5000 Silver 0.1447 oz. ASW, 29 mm. **Subject:** 150th Anniversary - Ceske Budejovice Horse Drawn Railway **Obv:** Czech lion with socialist shield within shield, denomination and inscription below **Rev:** Horse-drawn train carriage, dates below **Note:** 14,939 pieces, Unc and Proof, were melted by the Czech National Bank in 1999.

Date	Mintage	F	VF	XF	Unc	BU
ND(1982)	76,000	—	—	—	12.00	—
ND(1982) Proof	7,000	Value: 17.50				

KM# 108 100 KORUN
9.0000 g., 0.5000 Silver 0.1447 oz. ASW, 29 mm. **Subject:** 100th Anniversary - Death of Karl Marx **Obv:** Czech lion with socialist shield within shield divides denomination, inscription below **Rev:** Head facing, dates at left **Edge:** Milled **Note:** 23,793 pieces, Unc and Proof, were melted by the Czech National Bank in 1999.

Date	Mintage	F	VF	XF	Unc	BU
ND(1983)	76,000	—	—	—	12.00	—
ND(1983) Proof	4,000	Value: 20.00				

KM# 109 100 KORUN
9.0000 g., 0.5000 Silver 0.1447 oz. ASW, 29 mm. **Subject:** Centennial - Birth of Jaroslav Hasek **Obv:** Czech lion with socialist shield within shield, denomination below **Rev:** Bust facing, date below **Edge:** Milled **Note:** 21,538 pieces, Unc and Proof, were melted by the Czech National Bank in 1999.

Date	Mintage	F	VF	XF	Unc	BU
ND(1983)	76,000	—	—	—	12.00	—
ND(1983) Proof	4,000	Value: 20.00				

KM# 110 100 KORUN
9.0000 g., 0.5000 Silver 0.1447 oz. ASW, 29 mm. **Subject:** Centennial - Death of Samo Chalupka **Obv:** Czech lion with socialist shield within shield, inscription and denomination below **Rev:** Bust 3/4 facing, dates at left **Edge:** Milled **Note:** 27,938 pieces, Unc and Proof, were melted by the Czech National Bank in 1999.

Date	Mintage	F	VF	XF	Unc	BU
ND(1983)	76,000	—	—	—	12.00	—
ND(1983) Proof	4,000	Value: 20.00				

KM# 111   100 KORUN
9.0000 g., 0.5000 Silver 0.1447 oz. ASW, 29 mm.   **Subject:** 100th Anniversary of National Theater of Prague **Obv:** Czech lion with socialist shield within shield, denomination below **Rev:** View of the National Theater in Prague, dates below **Edge:** Milled **Note:** 23,538 pieces, Unc and Proof, were melted by the Czech National Bank in 1999.

Date	Mintage	F	VF	XF	Unc	BU
ND(1983)	140,000	—	—	—	9.00	—
ND(1983) Proof	10,000	Value: 17.50				

KM# 113   100 KORUN
9.0000 g., 0.5000 Silver 0.1447 oz. ASW, 29 mm.   **Subject:** 300th Anniversary - Birth of Matej Bel **Obv:** Czech lion with socialist shield within shield, denomination below **Rev:** Seated figure, dates at right **Edge:** Milled **Note:** 5288 pieces, Unc and Proof, were melted by the Czech National Bank in 1999.

Date	Mintage	F	VF	XF	Unc	BU
ND(1984)	57,000	—	—	—	12.50	—
ND(1984) Proof	3,000	Value: 20.00				

KM# 114   100 KORUN
9.0000 g., 0.5000 Silver 0.1447 oz. ASW, 29 mm.   **Subject:** 150th Anniversary - Birth of Jan Neruda **Obv:** Czech lion with socialist shield within shield, denomination below **Rev:** Head 3/4 left, house and dates at left **Edge:** Milled **Note:** 12,539 pieces, Unc and Proof, were melted by the Czech National Bank in 1999.

Date	Mintage	F	VF	XF	Unc	BU
ND(1984)	76,000	—	—	—	12.00	—
ND(1984) Proof	4,000	Value: 20.00				

KM# 115   100 KORUN
9.0000 g., 0.5000 Silver 0.1447 oz. ASW, 29 mm.   **Subject:** Centennial - Birth of Antonin Zapotocky **Obv:** Czech lion with socialist shield within shield divides denomination, inscription below **Rev:** Head 3/4 right, dates at left **Edge:** Milled **Note:** 19,938 pieces, Unc and Proof, were melted by the Czech National Bank in 1999.

Date	Mintage	F	VF	XF	Unc	BU
ND(1984)	76,000	—	—	—	12.00	—
ND(1984) Proof	4,000	Value: 20.00				

KM# 120   100 KORUN
9.0000 g., 0.5000 Silver 0.1447 oz. ASW, 29 mm.   **Subject:** 250th Anniversary - Death of Petr Brandl **Obv:** Czech lion with socialist shield within shield, denomination below **Rev:** Bust facing, large rock in background, dates at right **Edge:** Milled **Note:** 16,038 pieces, Unc and Proof, were melted by the Czech National Bank in 1999.

Date	Mintage	F	VF	XF	Unc	BU
ND(1985)	71,000	—	—	—	10.00	—
ND(1985) Proof	4,000	Value: 20.00				

KM# 119   100 KORUN
9.0000 g., 0.5000 Silver 0.1447 oz. ASW, 29 mm.   **Subject:** 10th Anniversary of Helsinki Conference **Obv:** Czech lion with socialist shield within shield divides denomination, inscription below **Rev:** Stylized dove embracing European map, dates at lower left **Edge:** Milled **Note:** 18,838 pieces, Unc and Proof, were melted by the Czech National Bank in 1999.

Date	Mintage	F	VF	XF	Unc	BU
ND(1985)	75,000	—	—	—	12.00	—
ND(1985) Proof	5,000	Value: 20.00				

KM# 118   100 KORUN
9.0000 g., 0.5000 Silver 0.1447 oz. ASW, 29 mm.   **Subject:** 125th Anniversary - Birth of Martin Kukucin **Obv:** Czech lion with socialist shield within shield, denomination below **Rev:** Bust facing, dates at left **Edge:** Milled **Note:** 11,838 pieces, Unc and Proof, were melted by the Czech National Bank in 1999.

Date	Mintage	F	VF	XF	Unc	BU
ND(1985)	62,000	—	—	—	12.00	—
ND(1985) Proof	3,000	Value: 20.00				

KM# 116   100 KORUN
9.0000 g., 0.5000 Silver 0.1447 oz. ASW, 29 mm.   **Subject:** 200th Anniversary - Birth of Jan Holly **Obv:** Czech lion with socialist shield within shield divides denomination, inscription below **Rev:** Head 3/4 facing, dates at left **Edge:** Milled **Note:** 9,338 pieces, Unc and Proof, were melted by the Czech National Bank in 1999.

Date	Mintage	F	VF	XF	Unc	BU
ND(1985)	62,000	—	—	—	12.00	—
ND(1985) Proof	3,000	Value: 20.00				

KM# 117   100 KORUN
9.0000 g., 0.5000 Silver 0.1447 oz. ASW, 29 mm.   **Subject:** 1985 Ice Hockey Championships **Obv:** Czech lion with socialist shield within shield, denomination below **Rev:** Hockey player skating left, dates at left **Edge:** Milled **Note:** 2,788 pieces, Unc and Proof, were melted by the Czech National Bank in 1999.

Date	Mintage	F	VF	XF	Unc	BU
1985	66,000	—	—	—	12.50	—
1985 Proof	4,000	Value: 20.00				

KM# 123   100 KORUN
13.0000 g., 0.5000 Silver 0.2090 oz. ASW, 31 mm.   **Subject:** 150th Anniversary - Death of Karel Hynek Macha **Obv:** Czech lion with socialist shield within shield divides denomination, inscription below **Rev:** Head 3/4 left, dates at right **Edge:** Milled **Note:** 10,288 pieces, Unc and Proof, were melted by the Czech National Bank in 1999.

Date	Mintage	F	VF	XF	Unc	BU
ND(1986)	63,000	—	—	—	10.00	—
ND(1986) Proof	5,000	Value: 20.00				

KM# 128   100 KORUN
13.0000 g., 0.5000 Silver 0.2090 oz. ASW, 31 mm.   **Subject:** 225th Anniversary of Mining Academy **Obv:** Czech lion with socialist shield within shield, denomination below **Rev:** Mining equipment, dates above small shield at right **Edge:** Milled **Note:** 6,438 pieces, Unc and Proof, were melted by the Czech National Bank in 1999.

Date	Mintage	F	VF	XF	Unc	BU
ND(1987)	55,000	—	—	—	12.00	—
ND(1987) Proof	5,000	Value: 22.50				

KM# 130   100 KORUN
13.0000 g., 0.5000 Silver 0.2090 oz. ASW, 31 mm.   **Subject:** Prague Philatelic Exposition **Obv:** Czech lion with socialist shield within shield, denomination and date below **Rev:** City views of Prague presented as four stamps **Edge:** Milled **Note:** 4,235 pieces, Unc and Proof, were melted by the Czech National Bank in 1999.

Date	Mintage	F	VF	XF	Unc	BU
1988	66,000	—	—	—	14.00	—
1988 Proof	5,000	Value: 25.00				

KM# 132   100 KORUN
13.0000 g., 0.5000 Silver 0.2090 oz. ASW, 31 mm. **Subject:**
Centennial - Birth of Martin Benka **Obv:** Czech lion with socialist
shield within shield, denomination below **Rev:** Young Slovak
woman in national costume with dove, dates at right, based on
painting by Martin Benko **Edge:** Milled **Note:** 8,635 pieces, Unc
and Proof, were melted by the Czech National Bank in 1999.

Date	Mintage	F	VF	XF	Unc	BU
ND(1988)	55,000	—	—	—	12.50	—
ND(1988) Proof	5,000	Value: 28.00				

KM# 135   100 KORUN
13.0000 g., 0.5000 Silver 0.2090 oz. ASW, 31 mm. **Subject:**
50th Anniversary of Student Organization Against Occupation
and Fascism **Obv:** Czech lion with socialist shield within shield,
denomination below **Rev:** Barbed wire and medieval document
seal, dates above **Edge:** Milled **Note:** 4,335 pieces, Unc and
Proof, were melted by the Czech National Bank in 1999.

Date	Mintage	F	VF	XF	Unc	BU
ND(1989)	67,000	—	—	—	14.00	—
ND(1989) Proof	Est. 3,000	Value: 25.00				

KM# 137   100 KORUN
13.0000 g., 0.5000 Silver 0.2090 oz. ASW, 31 mm. **Subject:**
100th Anniversary - Birth of Karel Capek **Obv:** Czech lion with
socialist shield within shield, inscription and denomination below
Rev: Head left, dates at right **Edge:** Milled **Note:** 7,920 pieces,
Unc and Proof, were melted by the Czech National Bank in 1999.

Date	Mintage	F	VF	XF	Unc	BU
ND(1990)	67,000	—	—	—	14.00	—
ND(1990) Proof	3,500	Value: 25.00				

KM# 138   100 KORUN
13.0000 g., 0.5000 Silver 0.2090 oz. ASW, 31 mm. **Subject:**
250th Anniversary - Death of Jan Kupecky **Obv:** Czech lion with
socialist shield within shield, denomination below **Rev:** Half-
length figure holding paintbrush and palette right, dates at left
Edge: Milled **Note:** 7,570 pieces, Unc and Proof, were melted
by the Czech National Bank in 1999.

Date	Mintage	F	VF	XF	Unc	BU
ND(1990)	58,000	—	—	—	15.00	—
ND(1990) Proof	2,500	Value: 28.00				

KM# 105   500 KORUN
24.0000 g., 0.9000 Silver 0.6944 oz. ASW, 40 mm. **Subject:**
125th Anniversary - Death of Ludovit Stur **Obv:** Czech lion with
socialist shield within shield, inscription and denomination below
Rev: Head facing, dates below, 125 ROKOV OD SMRTI L'
STURA **Note:** 7,057 pieces, Unc and Proof, were melted by the
Czech National Bank in 1999.

Date	Mintage	F	VF	XF	Unc	BU
ND(1981)	51,000	—	—	—	40.00	—
ND(1981) Proof	4,000	Value: 70.00				

KM# 112   500 KORUN
24.0000 g., 0.9000 Silver 0.6944 oz. ASW, 40 mm. **Subject:**
100th Anniversary of National Theater in Prague **Obv:** Czech lion
with socialist shield within shield, denomination below **Rev:**
Woman with lyre, theater facade at right, dates below, NAROD
SOBE **Note:** 4,740 pieces, Unc and Proof, were melted by the
Czech National Bank in 1999.

Date	Mintage	F	VF	XF	Unc	BU
ND(1983)	55,000	—	—	—	45.00	—
ND(1983) Proof	5,000	Value: 80.00				

KM# 136   500 KORUN
24.0000 g., 0.9000 Silver 0.6944 oz. ASW, 40 mm. **Subject:**
100th Anniversary - Birth of Josef Lada **Obv:** Czech lion with
socialist shield within shield divides denomination, inscription
below **Rev:** Town view, children building snowmen divide dates,
CESKY MALIR   NARODNI UMELEC **Note:** 2,238 pieces, Unc
and Proof, were melted by the Czech National Bank in 1999.

Date	Mintage	F	VF	XF	Unc	BU
ND(1987)	48,000	—	—	—	50.00	—
ND(1987) Proof	5,000	Value: 75.00				

KM# 131   500 KORUN
24.0000 g., 0.9000 Silver 0.6944 oz. ASW, 40 mm. **Subject:**
20th Anniversary of National Federation **Obv:** Czech lion with
socialist shield within shield, inscription and denomination below
Rev: Stylized linden tree encircled by ribbon in shape of country,
dates below, 20. VYROCIE CESKOSLOVENSKEJ FEDERACIE
oM **Note:** 6,435 pieces, Unc and Proof, were melted by the Czech
National Bank in 1999.

Date	Mintage	F	VF	XF	Unc	BU
ND(1988)	46,000	—	—	—	45.00	—
ND(1988) Proof	3,000	Value: 80.00				

KM# 134   500 KORUN
24.0000 g., 0.9000 Silver 0.6944 oz. ASW, 40 mm. **Subject:** 125th
Anniversary of Matica Slovenska Institute **Obv:** Czech lion with
socialist shield within shield, denomination below **Rev:** Woman
standing in national costume holding book and linden sprigs, dates
at right, HOJ VLAST MOJA   TY ZEM DRAHA **Note:** 6,338 pieces,
Unc and Proof, were melted by the Czech National Bank in 1999.

Date	Mintage	F	VF	XF	Unc	BU
ND(1988)	44,000	—	—	—	45.00	—
ND(1988) Proof	5,000	Value: 75.00				

CZECH SLOVAK
FEDERAL REPUBLIC

DECIMAL COINAGE

KM# 149   HALER
0.7900 g., Aluminum, 16 mm. **Obv:** CSFR above quartered
shield, linden leaves flanking, date below **Rev:** Denomination
within linden wreath **Edge:** Plain

Date	Mintage	F	VF	XF	Unc	BU
1991	55,000	—	—	—	2.50	—
1992	50,000	—	—	—	2.50	—

KM# 150   5 HALERU
0.7500 g., Aluminum, 16.2 mm. **Obv:** CSFR above quartered
shield, linden leaves flanking, date below **Rev:** Large, thick,
denomination **Edge:** Plain

Date	Mintage	F	VF	XF	Unc	BU
1991	10,055,000	—	—	0.10	0.25	—
1992	50,000	—	—	—	2.00	—
Note: In sets only						

KM# 146 10 HALERU
Aluminum, 18.2 mm. **Obv:** CSFR above quartered shield, linden leaves flanking, date below **Rev:** Large, thick denomination

Date	Mintage	F	VF	XF	Unc	BU
1991	40,055,000	—	—	—	0.50	—
1992	45,050,000	—	—	—	0.50	—

KM# 143 20 HALERU
Aluminum-Bronze, 19.5 mm. **Obv:** CSFR above quartered shield, linden leaves flanking, date below **Rev:** Large, thick denomination **Edge:** Milled

Date	Mintage	F	VF	XF	Unc	BU
1991	41,105,000	—	—	0.20	0.50	—
1992	35,050,000	—	—	0.20	0.50	—

KM# 144 50 HALERU
Copper-Nickel, 20.8 mm. **Obv:** CSFR above quartered shield, linden leaves flanking, date below **Rev:** Large, thick denomination **Edge:** Milled

Date	Mintage	F	VF	XF	Unc	BU
1991	24,463,000	—	—	0.35	0.75	—
1992	15,062,000	—	—	0.35	0.75	—

KM# 151 KORUNA
4.0800 g., Copper-Aluminum, 23 mm. **Obv:** CSFR above quartered shield, linden leaves flanking, date below **Rev:** Female planting linden tree, denomination at left **Edge:** Reeded

Date	Mintage	F	VF	XF	Unc	BU
1991	20,056,000	—	—	0.50	1.00	—
1992	20,387,000	—	—	0.50	1.00	—

KM# 148 2 KORUNY
Copper-Nickel, 24 mm. **Obv:** CSFR above quartered shield, linden leaves flanking, date below **Rev:** Linden leaf, large value at right **Edge:** Plain with wave x wave

Date	Mintage	F	VF	XF	Unc	BU
1991(k)	25,201,000	—	—	0.60	1.25	—
1991(l)	20,000,000	—	—	0.60	1.25	—
1992	1,051,000	—	—	—	1.25	•

KM# 152 5 KORUN
Copper-Nickel, 26 mm. **Obv:** CSFR above quartered shield, linden leaves flanking, date below **Rev:** Geometric design, large value **Edge:** Eight plain and eight milled areas

Date	Mintage	F	VF	XF	Unc	BU
1991(k)	18,564,000	—	—	0.75	2.00	—
1991(l)	10,000,750	—	—	0.75	2.00	—

Date	Mintage	F	VF	XF	Unc	BU
1992	50,000	—	—	—	2.50	6.00

Note: In sets only

KM# 139.1 10 KORUN
Nickel-Bronze, 24.5 mm. **Obv:** CSFR above quartered shield, date below, denomination at left **Rev:** Bust right, dates at left **Edge:** Eight plain and eight milled areas **Note:** Designer initials (MR) below bust, four varieties exist.

Date	Mintage	F	VF	XF	Unc	BU
1990	9,990,000	—	—	2.00	7.00	—
1993	2,500,000	—	—	2.00	6.00	—

KM# 139.2 10 KORUN
Nickel-Bronze, 24.5 mm. **Obv:** CSFR above shield, date below, denomination at left **Rev:** Tomas G. Masaryk bust, right, dates at left **Note:** Designer name below bust: RONAI.

Date	Mintage	F	VF	XF	Unc	BU
1990	Inc. above	—	2.00	5.00	10.00	—

KM# 153 10 KORUN
Nickel-Bronze, 24.5 mm. **Obv:** CSFR above quartered shield, date below, denomination at left **Rev:** Uniformed bust left, dates at right

Date	Mintage	F	VF	XF	Unc	BU
1991	10,036,000	—	—	2.00	5.00	—
1993	2,500,000	—	—	2.50	6.00	—

KM# 159 10 KORUN
Nickel-Bronze, 24.5 mm. **Obv:** CSFR above quartered shield, date below, denomination at left **Rev:** Bust right, dates at left **Edge:** Eight plain and eight milled areas

Date	Mintage	F	VF	XF	Unc	BU
1992	5,050,000	—	—	2.00	5.00	—

KM# 140.1 50 KORUN
7.0000 g., 0.5000 Silver 0.1125 oz. ASW, 27 mm. **Obv:** CSFR quartered shield with designer's initials (LK) below denomination **Rev:** Veiled head left, date upper left **Edge:** Milled **Note:** See note with KM#140.2. Designer emblem exists with and without initials.

Date	Mintage	F	VF	XF	Unc	BU
1990	147,000	—	—	—	7.00	—
1990 Proof	3,000	Value: 18.00				

KM# 140.2 50 KORUN
7.0000 g., 0.5000 Silver 0.1125 oz. ASW, 27 mm. **Obv:** CSFR quartered shield, without designer's initials (LK) **Rev:** Veiled head left **Note:** 12,070 pieces, Unc and Proof of either KM#140.1 or 140.2, were melted by the Czech National Bank in 1999.

Date	Mintage	F	VF	XF	Unc	BU
1990	Inc. above	—	—	10.00	25.00	—

KM# 155 50 KORUN
7.0000 g., 0.7000 Silver 0.1575 oz. ASW, 27 mm. **Obv:** CSFR quartered shield, denomination below **Rev:** Piestany Spa building, shield below **Edge:** Milled **Note:** 17,920 pieces, Unc and Proof, were melted by the Czech National Bank in 1999.

Date	Mintage	F	VF	XF	Unc	BU
1991	75,000	—	—	—	7.50	—
1991 Proof	Est. 5,000	Value: 16.50				

KM# 145 50 KORUN
7.0000 g., 0.5000 Silver 0.1125 oz. ASW, 27 mm. **Obv:** CSFR quartered shield, denomination below **Rev:** Steamship Bohemia, dates below **Edge:** Milled **Note:** 4,470 pieces, Unc and Proof, were melted by the Czech National Bank in 1999.

Date	Mintage	F	VF	XF	Unc	BU
ND(1991)	77,000	—	—	—	8.00	—
ND(1991) Proof	3,000	Value: 18.00				

KM# 156 50 KORUN
7.0000 g., 0.7000 Silver 0.1575 oz. ASW, 27 mm. **Obv:** CSFR quartered shield, denomination below, date above **Rev:** Marianske Lazne Spa buildings **Edge:** Milled **Note:** 16,520 pieces, Unc and Proof, were melted by the Czech National Bank in 1999.

Date	Mintage	F	VF	XF	Unc	BU
1991	75,000	—	—	—	7.50	—
1991 Proof	5,000	Value: 16.50				

KM# 157 50 KORUN
7.0000 g., 0.7000 Silver 0.1575 oz. ASW, 27 mm. **Obv:** CSFR quartered shield, denomination above, date below **Rev:** Chamois on rock, Karlovy Vary Spa buildings **Edge:** Milled **Note:** 15,920, pieces, Unc and Proof, were melted by the Czech National Bank in 1999.

Date	Mintage	F	VF	XF	Unc	BU
1991	75,000	—	—	—	12.00	—
1991 Proof	5,000	Value: 20.00				

KM# 141 100 KORUN
13.0000 g., 0.5000 Silver 0.2090 oz. ASW, 31 mm. **Obv:** CSFR quartered shield, denomination at right **Rev:** Two horsemen right, date below **Edge:** Milled **Note:** 3,170 pieces, Unc and Proof, were melted by the Czech National Bank in 1999.

Date	Mintage	F	VF	XF	Unc	BU
1990	67,000	—	—	—	15.00	—
1990 Proof	3,000	Value: 25.00				

KM# 142   100 KORUN
13.0000 g., 0.5000 Silver 0.2090 oz. ASW, 31 mm. **Subject:**
100th Anniversary - Birth of Bohuslav Martinu **Obv:** CSFR
quartered shield, denomination below **Rev:** Head facing, dates
at right **Edge:** Milled **Note:** 8,170 pieces, Unc and Proof, were
melted by the Czech National Bank in 1999.

Date	Mintage	F	VF	XF	Unc	BU
ND(1990)	53,000	—	—	—	15.00	—
ND(1990) Proof	2,000	Value: 22.00				

KM# 147   100 KORUN
13.0000 g., 0.5000 Silver 0.2090 oz. ASW, 31 mm. **Subject:**
150th Anniversary - Birth of A. Dvorak **Obv:** CSFR quartered
shield, inscription and denomination below **Rev:** Stylized head
right, dates below **Edge:** Milled **Note:** 16,220 pieces, Unc and
Proof, were melted by the Czech National Bank in 1999.

Date	Mintage	F	VF	XF	Unc	BU
1991	75,000	—	—	—	12.00	—
1991 Proof	5,000	Value: 20.00				

KM# 154   100 KORUN
13.0000 g., 0.7000 Silver 0.2926 oz. ASW, 31 mm. **Subject:**
200th Anniversary - Death of Wolfgang A. Mozart **Obv:** CSFR
quartered shield, denomination below **Rev:** Bust right, dates
below **Edge:** Milled **Note:** 2,620 pieces, Unc and Proof, were
melted by the Czech National Bank in 1999.

Date	Mintage	F	VF	XF	Unc	BU
ND(1991)	75,000	—	—	—	12.00	—
ND(1991) Proof	5,000	Value: 45.00				

KM# 160   100 KORUN
13.0000 g., 0.5000 Silver 0.2090 oz. ASW, 31 mm. **Subject:**
175th Anniversary - Moravian Museum **Obv:** CSFR quartered
shield, denomination above, date below **Rev:** Moravian Museum,
Moravian eagle **Edge:** Milled **Note:** 226,977 pieces, Unc and
Proof, were melted by the Czech National Bank in 1999.

Date	Mintage	F	VF	XF	Unc	BU
1992	73,000	—	—	—	10.00	—
1992 Proof	5,000	Value: 22.00				

KM# 161   100 KORUN
13.0000 g., 0.5000 Silver 0.2090 oz. ASW, 31 mm. **Subject:**
Nazi Massacres at Lidice and Lezaky **Obv:** CSFR quartered
shield, denomination below, date above **Rev:** Cross with barbed
wire loop **Edge:** Milled **Note:** 24,620 pieces, Unc and Proof, were
melted by the Czech National Bank in 1999.

Date	Mintage	F	VF	XF	Unc	BU
1992	70,000	—	—	—	10.00	—
1992 Proof	3,000	Value: 22.00				

KM# 162   100 KORUN
13.0000 g., 0.5000 Silver 0.2090 oz. ASW, 31 mm. **Subject:**
1000 Years of Brevnov Monastery **Obv:** CSFR quartered
shield, denomination below **Rev:** Church and cloister columns, dates at
left **Edge:** Milled **Note:** 25,932 pieces, Unc and Proof, were
melted by the Czech National Bank in 1999.

Date	Mintage	F	VF	XF	Unc	BU
ND(1993)	70,000	—	—	—	8.00	—
ND(1993) Proof	3,000	Value: 22.00				

KM# 163   100 KORUN
13.0000 g., 0.5000 Silver 0.2090 oz. ASW, 31 mm. **Subject:**
Slovak Museum Centennial **Obv:** CSFR quartered shield,
inscription and denomination below **Rev:** Historic folk art designs,
dates lower left **Edge:** Milled **Note:** 31,932 pieces, Unc and Proof,
were melted by the Czech National Bank in 1999.

Date	Mintage	F	VF	XF	Unc	BU
ND(1993)	70,000	—	—	—	8.00	—
ND(1993) Proof	3,000	Value: 22.00				

KM# 158   500 KORUN
24.0000 g., 0.9000 Silver 0.6944 oz. ASW, 40 mm. **Subject:** 400th
Anniversary - Birth of J. A. Komensky **Obv:** CSFR quartered shield,
date above, denomination below **Rev:** J. A. Komensky standing,
dates at left **Edge:** Milled **Note:** 14,820 pieces, Unc and Proof, were
melted by the Czech National Bank in 1999.

Date	Mintage	F	VF	XF	Unc	BU
1992	60,000	—	—	—	35.00	—
1992 Proof	5,000	Value: 60.00				

KM# 164   500 KORUN
24.0000 g., 0.9000 Silver 0.6944 oz. ASW, 40 mm. **Subject:**
100th Year of Czech Tennis **Obv:** CSFR quartered shield,
inscription and denomination below **Rev:** Male tennis player,
stadium at left, dates above **Edge:** Milled **Note:** 27,074 pieces,
Unc and Proof, were melted by the Czech National Bank in 1999.

Date	Mintage	F	VF	XF	Unc	BU
ND(1993)	62,000	—	—	—	37.50	—
ND(1993) Proof	3,000	Value: 70.00				

PROBA

KM#	Date	Mintage	Identification	Mkt Val
Pr1	1922	—	Koruna. Aluminum.	—
Pr2	1922	—	Koruna. Copper-Nickel.	—
Pr3	1951	—	5 Koruna. Aluminum-Copper Magnesium.	—
Pr4	1932	2	25 Haleru. Copper-Nickel. W/dense notches.	—
Pr5	1932	2	25 Haleru. Copper-Nickel. Thin notches.	—
Pr6	1932	10	25 Haleru. Copper-Nickel.	—
Pr7	1976	—	3 Koruny.	—
Pr8	ND(1990)	2,500	100 Korun.	200

MINT SETS

KM#	Date	Mintage	Identification	Issue Price	Mkt Val
MS1	1980 (7)	50,000	KM50, 60, 74-75, 80, 86, 89	5.00	3.50
MS2	1981 (7)	66,000	KM50, 60, 74-75, 80, 86, 89	—	3.50
MS3	1982 (7)	53,000	KM50, 60, 74-75, 80, 86, 89	—	5.50
MS4	1983 (7)	50,000	KM50, 60, 74-75, 80, 86, 89	—	4.50
MS5	1984 (7)	39,000	KM50, 60, 74-75, 80, 86, 89	—	6.50
MS6	1985 (7)	39,000	KM50, 60, 74-75, 80, 86, 89	—	6.50
MS7	1986 (7)	20,000	KM50, 60, 74-75, 80, 86, 89	—	50.00
MS8	1987 (7)	30,000	km50, 60, 74-75, 80, 86, 89	—	15.00
MS9	1988 (7)	29,000	KM50, 60, 74-75, 80, 86, 89	—	10.00
MS10	1989 (7)	30,000	KM50, 60, 74-75, 80, 86, 89	—	10.00
MS11	1990 (7)	30,000	KM50, 60, 74-75, 80, 86, 89	—	10.00
MS12	1991 (9)	25,000	KM143-144, 146, 148-153	—	12.50
MS13	1991 (8)	30,000	KM143-144, 146, 148-152	—	12.50
MS14	1992 (9)	49,000	KM143-144, 146, 148-152, 159	—	15.00
MS15	1992 (8)	49,000	KM143-144,146, 148-152	—	10.00

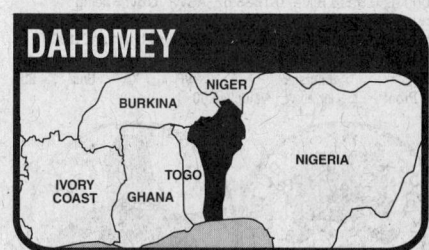

DAHOMEY

Porto-Novo, on the Bight of Benin, was founded as a trading
post by the Portuguese in the 17th century. At that time, Dahomey
(Benin) was composed of an aggregation of mutually suspicious
tribes, the majority of which were tributary to the powerful northern Kingdom of Abomey. In 1863, the King of Porto-Novo petitioned France for protection from Abomey. The French subjugated other militant tribes as well, and in 1892 organized the
area as a protectorate of France; in 1904 it was incorporated into
French West Africa as the Territory of Dahomey. After the establishment of the Fifth French Republic, the Territory at Dahomey
became an autonomous state within the French community. On
Aug. 1, 1960, it became the fully independent Republic of Dahomey. In 1974, the republic began a transition to a socialist society
with Marxism-Leninism as its revolutionary philosophy under Col.
Ahmed Kerekow. On Nov. 30, 1975, the name of the Republic of
Dahomey was changed to the Peoples Republic of Benin. As a
result of Benin's first free presidential election in 30 years, Nicephore Soglo defeated Colonel Kerekou.

Porto-Novo, on the Bight of Benin, was founded as a trading post by the Portuguese in the 17th century. At that time, Dahomey (Benin) was composed of an aggregation of mutually suspicious tribes, the majority of which were tributary to the powerful northern Kingdom of Abomey. In 1863, the King of Porto-Novo petitioned France for protection from Abomey. The French subjugated other militant tribes as well, and in 1892 organized the area as a protectorate of France; in 1904 it was incorporated into French West Africa as the Territory of Dahomey. After the establishment of the Fifth French Republic, the Territory at Dahomey became an autonomous state within the French community. On Aug. 1, 1960, it became the fully independent Republic of Dahomey. In 1974, the republic began a transition to a socialist society with Marxism-Leninism as its revolutionary philosophy under Col. Ahmed Kerekow. On Nov. 30, 1975, the name of the Republic of Dahomey was changed to the Peoples Republic of Benin. As a result of Benin's first free presidential election in 30 years, Nicephore Soglo defeated Colonel Kerekou.

MINT MARK
1 AR - Uno-A-Erre, Arezzo, Italy

REPUBLIC

STANDARD COINAGE

KM# 1.1 100 FRANCS
5.1000 g., 0.9990 Silver 0.1638 oz. ASW **Subject:** 10th Anniversary of Independence **Obv:** Facing cornucopias top supported arms, date above, denomination below **Rev:** Buildings on Lake Ganvié **Note:** Hallmark "999.9" above denomination.

Date	Mintage	F	VF	XF	Unc	BU
1971 Proof	4,650	Value: 45.00				

KM# 1.2 100 FRANCS
5.1000 g., 0.9990 Silver 0.1638 oz. ASW **Obv:** Facing cornucopias top supported arms, date above, denomination below **Rev:** Buildings on Lake Ganvié **Note:** Hallmark "999.9" right of denomination.

Date	Mintage	F	VF	XF	Unc	BU
1971 Proof	Inc. above	Value: 45.00				

KM# 1.3 100 FRANCS
5.1000 g., 0.9990 Silver 0.1638 oz. ASW **Obv:** Facing cornucopias top supported arms, date above, denomination below **Rev:** Buildings on Lake Ganvié **Note:** Hallmark "1000" lower right "S" in "FRANCS".

Date	Mintage	F	VF	XF	Unc	BU
1971 Proof	Inc. above	Value: 45.00				

KM# 2.1 200 FRANCS
10.2500 g., 0.9990 Silver 0.3292 oz. ASW **Subject:** 10th Anniversary of Independence **Obv:** Facing cornucopias top supported arms, date above, denomination below **Rev:** Abomey woman 3/4 left **Note:** Hallmark "999.9" between "200" and "FRANCS".

Date	Mintage	F	VF	XF	Unc	BU
1971 Proof	5,150	Value: 55.00				

KM# 2.2 200 FRANCS
10.2500 g., 0.9990 Silver 0.3292 oz. ASW **Obv:** Facing cornucopias top supported arms, date above, denomination below **Rev:** Abomey woman 3/4 left **Note:** Hallmark "1000" lower right of "S" in "FRANCS".

Date	Mintage	F	VF	XF	Unc	BU
1971 Proof	Inc. above	Value: 55.00				

KM# 2.3 200 FRANCS
10.2500 g., 0.9990 Silver 0.3292 oz. ASW **Obv:** Facing cornucopias top supported arms, date above, denomination below **Rev:** Abomey woman 3/4 left **Note:** Hallmark "999.9" lower right of "S" in "FRANCS".

Date	Mintage	F	VF	XF	Unc	BU
1971 Proof	Inc. above	Value: 55.00				

KM# 2.4 200 FRANCS
10.2500 g., 0.9990 Silver 0.3292 oz. ASW **Obv:** Facing cornucopias top supported arms, date above, denomination below **Rev:** Abomey woman 3/4 left **Note:** Hallmark "999.9" in oval below "F" in "CFA".

Date	Mintage	F	VF	XF	Unc	BU
1971 Proof	Inc. above	Value: 65.00				

KM# 3.1 500 FRANCS
25.2000 g., 0.9990 Silver 0.8094 oz. ASW **Subject:** 10th Anniversary of Independence **Obv:** Facing cornucopias top supported arms, date above, denomination below **Rev:** Ouémé woman right **Note:** "1000" in oval below "S" in "FRANCS".

Date	Mintage	F	VF	XF	Unc	BU
1971 Proof	5,550	Value: 100				

KM# 3.2 500 FRANCS
25.2000 g., 0.9990 Silver 0.8094 oz. ASW **Obv:** Facing cornucopias top supported arms, date above, denomination below **Rev:** Ouémé woman right **Note:** "1 AR" and "1000" to right of "CFA".

Date	Mintage	F	VF	XF	Unc	BU
1971 Proof	Inc. above	Value: 100				

KM# 4.1 1000 FRANCS
51.5000 g., 0.9990 Silver 1.6540 oz. ASW **Subject:** 10th Anniversary of Independence **Obv:** Facing cornucopias top supported arms, date above, denomination below **Rev:** Somba woman facing **Note:** "1000" in oval below "S" in "FRANCS".

Date	Mintage	F	VF	XF	Unc	BU
1971 Proof	6,500	Value: 165				

KM# 4.2 1000 FRANCS
51.5000 g., 0.9990 Silver 1.6540 oz. ASW **Obv:** Facing cornucopias top supported arms, date above, denomination below **Rev:** Somba woman facing **Note:** "1 AR" and "1000" to right of "CFA".

Date	Mintage	F	VF	XF	Unc	BU
1971 Proof	Inc. above	Value: 150				

KM# 6 2500 FRANCS
8.8800 g., 0.9000 Gold 0.2569 oz. AGW **Subject:** 10th Anniversary of Independence **Rev:** Dancers

Date	Mintage	F	VF	XF	Unc	BU
1971 Proof	960	Value: 300				

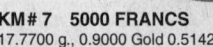

KM# 7 5000 FRANCS
17.7700 g., 0.9000 Gold 0.5142 oz. AGW **Subject:** 10th Anniversary of Independence **Obv:** Similar to 2500 Francs, KM#6 **Rev:** Water buffalos (suncerus caffer-bovidae)

Date	Mintage	F	VF	XF	Unc	BU
1971 Proof	610	Value: 575				

KM# 8   10000 FRANCS
35.5500 g., 0.9000 Gold 1.0286 oz. AGW   **Subject:** 10th
Anniversary of Independence **Obv:** Facing cornucopias top
supported arms, date above, denomination below **Rev:**
Acanthopholis

Date	Mintage	F	VF	XF	Unc	BU
1971 Proof	470	Value: 1,000				

KM# 9   25000 FRANCS
88.8800 g., 0.9000 Gold 2.5717 oz. AGW   **Subject:** 10th
Anniversary of Independence **Obv:** Facing cornucopias top
supported arms, date above, denomination below **Rev:** Aligned
Presidents busts, left **Rev. Leg.:** TROIS PRESIDENTS above,
S.M. APITY - J. AHOMADEGBE T. - H. MAGA below

Date	Mintage	F	VF	XF	Unc	BU
1971 Proof	380	Value: 2,500				

PROOF SETS

KM#	Date	Mintage	Identification	Issue Price	Mkt Val
PS1	1971 (8)	380	KM#1.1-4.1, 6-9	—	4,175
PS2	1971 (4)	4,270	KM#1.1-4.1	36.00	345

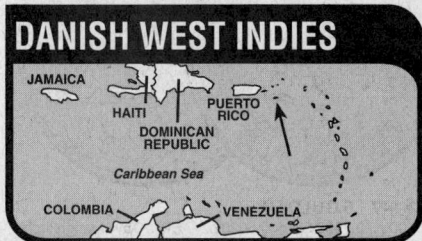

DANISH WEST INDIES

The Danish West Indies (now the U.S. organized unincorporated territory of the Virgin Islands of the United States) consisted of the islands of St. Thomas, St. John, St. Croix, and 62
islets in the Caribbean Sea roughly 40 miles (64 km.) east of
Puerto Rico. The islands have a combined area of 133 sq. mi.
(352 sq. km.) and a population of *106,000. Capital: Charlotte
Amalie. Tourism is the principal industry. Watch movements,
costume jewelry, pharmaceuticals, and rum are exported.

The Virgin Islands were discovered by Columbus, in 1493,
during his second voyage to America. During the 17th century,
individual islands, actually the peaks of a submerged mountain
range, were held by Spain, Holland, England, France and Denmark. These islands were also the favorite resorts of the buccaneers operating in the Caribbean and the coastal waters of
eastern North America. Control of most of the 100-island group

finally passed to Denmark, with England securing the easterly
remainder. The Danish islands had their own coinage from the
early 18th century, based on but unequal to, Denmark's homeland system. In the late 18th and early 19th centuries, Danish
minor copper and silver coinage augmented the islands currency. The Danish islands were purchased by the United States
in 1917 for $25 million, mainly to forestall their acquisition by Ger-
many and because they command the Anegada Passage into the
Caribbean Sea, a strategic point on the defense perimeter of the
Panama Canal.

RULER
Danish, until 1917

MINTMASTERS' NITIALS

Letter	Date	Name
P, VBP	1893-1918	Vilhelm Burchard Poulsen

MONEYERS' INITIALS

Letter	Date	Name
GJ	1901-1933	(Knud) Gunnar Jensen
AH	1908-1924	Andreas Frederik Vilhelm Hansen

MONETARY SYSTEM
(1904-1934)
5 Bit = 1 Cent
100 Bit = 1 Franc
5 Francs = 1 Daler

DANISH COLONY
DECIMAL COINAGE
20 Cents = 1 Franc

KM# 74   1/2 CENT (2-1/2 Bit)
Bronze   **Ruler:** Christian IX **Obv:** Crowned monogram above
date **Rev:** Denominations divided by trident, caduceus and sickle
Note: Mintmaster's initial: P. Moneyer's initials: GJ.

Date	Mintage	F	VF	XF	Unc	BU
1905(h)	190,000	2.75	5.50	13.00	35.00	—
1905(h) Prooflike	—	—	—	—	—	—
Note: Specimen strike						

KM# 75   CENT (5 Bit)
Bronze, 23 mm.   **Ruler:** Christian IX **Rev:** Denominations divided
by trident, caduceus and sickle **Note:** Mintmaster's initial: P.
Moneyer's initials: GJ.

Date	Mintage	F	VF	XF	Unc	BU
1905(h)	500,000	3.50	7.50	23.00	62.50	—

KM# 83   CENT (5 Bit)
Bronze   **Obv:** Crowned monogram above date **Rev:** Denominations
divided by trident, caduceus and sickle **Note:** Mintmaster's initials:
VBP. Moneyer's initials: AH-GJ.

Date	Mintage	F	VF	XF	Unc	BU
1913(h)	200,000	9.00	17.50	42.50	93.50	—

KM# 76   2 CENTS (10 Bit)
Bronze   **Ruler:** Christian IX **Obv:** Crowned monogram above
date **Rev:** Denominations divided by trident, caduceus and sickle
Note: Mintmaster's initial: P. Moneyer's initials: GJ.

Date	Mintage	F	VF	XF	Unc	BU
1905(h)	150,000	5.00	13.50	32.00	80.00	—
1905(h) Prooflike	20	—	—	—	—	—
Note: Specimen strike						

KM# 77   5 CENTS (25 Bit)
Nickel   **Ruler:** Christian IX **Obv:** Crowned monogram above date
Rev: Denominations divided by trident, caduceus and sickle
Note: Mintmaster's initial: P. Moneyer's initials: GJ.

Date	Mintage	F	VF	XF	Unc	BU
1905(h)	199,000	3.00	7.50	20.00	67.50	—
1905(h) Prooflike	20	—	—	—	—	—
Note: Specimen strike						

KM# 78   10 CENTS (50 Bit)
2.5000 g., 0.8000 Silver 0.0643 oz. ASW   **Ruler:** Christian IX
Obv: Head left **Rev:** Plant divides denominations
Note: Mintmaster's initial: P. Moneyer's initials: GJ.

Date	Mintage	F	VF	XF	Unc	BU
1905(h)	175,000	4.00	8.50	20.00	70.00	—
1905(h) Prooflike	20	—	—	—	—	—
Note: Specimen strike						

KM# 79   20 CENTS (1 Franc)
5.0000 g., 0.8000 Silver 0.1286 oz. ASW   **Ruler:** Christian IX
Obv: Uniformed bust left **Rev:** Three liberty figures divide
denominations, date below **Note:** Mintmaster's initial: P.
Moneyer's initials: GJ.

Date	Mintage	F	VF	XF	Unc	BU
1905(h)	150,000	12.50	27.50	72.50	145	—
1905(h) Prooflike	20	—	—	—	—	—
Note: Specimen strike						

KM# 81   20 CENTS (1 Franc)
5.0000 g., 0.8000 Silver 0.1286 oz. ASW   **Obv:** Head left
Rev: Three liberty figures divide denominations, date below
Note: Mintmaster's initial: P. Moneyer's initials: GJ.

Date	Mintage	F	VF	XF	Unc	BU
1907(h)	101,000	15.00	35.00	90.00	185	—
1907(h) Prooflike	10	—	—	—	—	—
Note: Specimen strike						

KM# 80   40 CENTS (2 Francs)
10.0000 g., 0.8000 Silver 0.2572 oz. ASW   **Ruler:** Christian IX
Note: Mintmaster's initial: P. Moneyer's initials: GJ.

Date	Mintage	F	VF	XF	Unc	BU
1905(h)	38,000	30.00	62.50	165	345	—
1905(h) Prooflike	20	—	—	—	—	—
Note: Specimen strike						

KM# 82   40 CENTS (2 Francs)
10.0000 g., 0.8000 Silver 0.2572 oz. ASW   **Obv:** Head left
Rev: Three liberty figures divide denominations, date below
Note: Mintmaster's initial: P. Moneyer's initials: GJ.

Date	Mintage	F	VF	XF	Unc	BU
1907(h)	25,000	55.00	120	235	460	—
1907(h) Prooflike	10	—	—	—	—	1,100
Note: Specimen strike						

KM# 72   4 DALER (20 Francs)
6.4516 g., 0.9000 Gold 0.1867 oz. AGW   **Ruler:** Christian IX
Obv: Head left **Rev:** Seated liberty figure divides denominations
Note: Mintmaster's initial: P. Moneyer's initials: GJ.

Date	Mintage	F	VF	XF	Unc	BU
1904(h)	121,000	165	250	420	675	—
1905(h)	Inc. above	175	275	435	800	—

KM# 73   10 DALER (50 Francs)
16.1290 g., 0.9000 Gold 0.4667 oz. AGW   **Ruler:** Christian IX
Obv: Head left **Rev:** Seated liberty figure divides denominations,
date below **Note:** Mintmaster's initial: P. Moneyer's initials: GJ.

Date	Mintage	F	VF	XF	Unc	BU
1904(h)	2,005	1,250	2,000	4,350	7,200	—

TRIAL STRIKES

KM#	Date	Mintage	Identification		Mkt Val
TS1	1904	—	20 Francs. Copper. 10.8000 g. KM#72.		—
TS2	1904	—	20 Francs. Copper. 10.8000 g. KM#72.		—

PROOF-LIKE SETS (PL)

KM#	Date	Mintage	Identification	Issue Price	Mkt Val
PL4	1905 (5)	20	KM#76-80	—	—
PL5	1907 (2)	10	KM#81-82	—	—

DANZIG

Danzig is an important seaport on the northern coast of
Poland with access to the Baltic Sea. It has at different times
belonged to the Teutonic Knights, Pomerania, Russia, and Prussia. It was part of the Polish Kingdom from 1587-1772.
Danzig (Gdansk) was a free city from 1919 to 1939 during
which most of its modern coinage was made.

MONETARY SYSTEM

Until 1923
100 Pfennig = 1 Mark

Commencing 1923
100 Pfennig = 1 Gulden

FREE CITY

STANDARD COINAGE

KM# 140   PFENNIG
1.6300 g., Bronze, 17.03 mm.   **Obv:** Denomination **Rev:** Arms
divide date

Date	Mintage	F	VF	XF	Unc	BU
1923	4,000,000	1.50	4.00	8.00	20.00	38.00
1923 Proof	—	Value: 300				
1926	1,500,000	2.25	6.00	12.00	32.00	70.00
1929	1,000,000	4.00	12.00	20.00	40.00	80.00
1930	2,000,000	2.00	5.00	10.00	25.00	45.00
1937	3,000,000	2.00	5.00	10.00	25.00	45.00

KM# 141   2 PFENNIG
Bronze   **Obv:** Denomination **Rev:** Arms divide date

Date	Mintage	F	VF	XF	Unc	BU
1923	1,000,000	2.75	7.00	15.00	30.00	70.00
1923 Proof	—	Value: 350				
1926	1,750,000	2.75	7.00	15.00	30.00	70.00
1937	500,000	4.00	10.00	20.00	40.00	80.00

KM# 142   5 PFENNIG
Copper-Nickel   **Obv:** Denomination **Rev:** Arms divide date within
snowflake design

Date	Mintage	F	VF	XF	Unc	BU
1923	3,000,000	2.00	4.00	9.00	25.00	45.00
1923 Proof	—	Value: 1,500				
1928	1,000,000	5.00	15.00	30.00	60.00	120
1928 Proof	—	Value: 1,800				

KM# 151   5 PFENNIG
Aluminum-Bronze   **Obv:** Denomination **Rev:** Turbot left, date below

Date	Mintage	F	VF	XF	Unc	BU
1932	4,000,000	2.50	5.00	20.00	60.00	125

KM# 143   10 PFENNIG
Copper-Nickel   **Obv:** Denomination **Rev:** Arms divide date within
snowflake design

Date	Mintage	F	VF	XF	Unc	BU
1923	5,000,000	3.50	7.00	18.00	36.00	75.00
1923 Proof	—	Value: 500				

KM# 152   10 PFENNIG
Aluminum-Bronze   **Obv:** Denomination **Rev:** Codfish (godus
morrhua) left, date below

Date	Mintage	F	VF	XF	Unc	BU
1932	5,000,000	3.00	7.00	30.00	80.00	135

KM# 144   1/2 GULDEN
2.5000 g., 0.7500 Silver 0.0603 oz. ASW   **Obv:** Date divided by
shielded arms, denomination above **Rev:** Ship at sea

Date	Mintage	F	VF	XF	Unc	BU
1923	1,000,000	12.00	30.00	75.00	200	—
1923 Proof	—	Value: 2,000				
1927	400,000	27.50	55.00	150	350	—
1927 Proof	—	Value: 2,500				

KM# 153   1/2 GULDEN
Nickel   **Obv:** Crowned vertical crosses **Rev:** Denomination above
date

Date	Mintage	F	VF	XF	Unc	BU
1932	1,400,000	12.00	35.00	75.00	225	—

KM# 145   GULDEN
5.0000 g., 0.7500 Silver 0.1206 oz. ASW   **Obv:** Ship and star
divide denomination **Rev:** Shielded arms with supporters, star,
date below

Date	Mintage	F	VF	XF	Unc	BU
1923	2,500,000	15.00	40.00	90.00	245	—
1923 Proof	—	Value: 1,850				

KM# 154   GULDEN
Nickel   **Obv:** Large numeric denomination within circle **Rev:** Arms
divide date

Date	Mintage	F	VF	XF	Unc	BU
1932	2,500,000	12.00	35.00	55.00	125	350

KM# 146   2 GULDEN
10.0000 g., 0.7500 Silver 0.2411 oz. ASW   **Obv:** Ship and star
divide denomination **Rev:** Shielded arms with supporters, star
above, date below

Date	Mintage	F	VF	XF	Unc	BU
1923	1,250,000	60.00	120	300	700	—
1923 Proof	—	Value: 2,250				

KM# 155   2 GULDEN
10.0000 g., 0.5000 Silver 0.1607 oz. ASW   **Obv:** Ship afloat
within circle, denomination below **Rev:** Shielded arms with
supporters, date above

Date	Mintage	F	VF	XF	Unc	BU
1932	1,250,000	145	285	450	1,200	2,000

KM# 147   5 GULDEN
25.0000 g., 0.7500 Silver 0.6028 oz. ASW   **Obv:** Marienkirche
within circle **Rev:** Shielded arms with supporters, denomination
below, star above

Date	Mintage	F	VF	XF	Unc	BU
1923	700,000	125	270	675	1,450	—
1923 Proof	—	Value: 2,250				
1927	160,000	300	500	1,150	2,150	—
1927 Proof	—	Value: 4,500				

KM# 156   5 GULDEN
14.8200 g., 0.5000 Silver 0.2382 oz. ASW   **Obv:** Marienkirche
within circle, denomination below **Rev:** Shielded arms with
supporters, date above

Date	Mintage	F	VF	XF	Unc	BU
1932	430,000	475	900	1,650	2,750	—

KM# 157 5 GULDEN
14.8200 g., 0.5000 Silver 0.2382 oz. ASW **Obv:** Grain elevator by harbor within circle, denomination below **Rev:** Shielded arms with supporters, date above

Date	Mintage	F	VF	XF	Unc	BU
1932	430,000	225	525	1,700	3,000	—

KM# 158 5 GULDEN
Nickel **Obv:** Ship with three crowns asea, numeric denomination at left, circle surrounds, denomination below circle, date at right **Rev:** Arms with supporters on oval shield

Date	Mintage	F	VF	XF	Unc	BU
1935	800,000	150	300	650	1,200	2,000

KM# 159 10 GULDEN
Nickel **Obv:** Town hall tower, numeric denomination at right, circle surrounds, denomination below, date at right **Rev:** Arms with supporters on oval shield

Date	Mintage	F	VF	XF	Unc	BU
1935	380,000	650	1,250	2,250	3,750	7,500

KM# 148 25 GULDEN
7.9881 g., 0.9170 Gold 0.2355 oz. AGW **Obv:** Arms between columns with supporters, date below **Rev:** Statue from the Nepture fountain, denomination at left and divided below **Note:** Presented to senate members.

Date	Mintage	F	VF	XF	Unc	BU
1923	800	—	1,650	2,500	4,000	—
1923 Proof	200	Value: 8,500				

KM# 150 25 GULDEN
7.9881 g., 0.9170 Gold 0.2355 oz. AGW **Obv:** Arms with supporters, date below **Rev:** Statue from the Neptune fountain, denomination at left and divided below **Note:** Never offcially released for circulation. A few were distributed on Sept. 1, 1939, in VIP presentation cases. A small hoard was discovered in the early 21st century making hundreds of the coins available to the numismatic market and driving prices down to current levels.

Date	Mintage	F	VF	XF	Unc	BU
1930	Est. 4,000	—	—	1,500	2,000	2,500

TOKEN COINAGE

KM# Tn1 10 PFENNIG
Zinc **Obv:** Angel head above oval arms within circle, date below **Rev:** Denomination within cartouche **Note:** Small "10" in cartouche.

Date	Mintage	F	VF	XF	Unc	BU
1920	876,000	18.00	30.00	60.00	125	—

KM# Tn2 10 PFENNIG
Zinc **Note:** Large "10".

Date	Mintage	F	VF	XF	Unc	BU
1920	124,000	100	150	250	375	—

PATTERNS
Including off metal strikes

KM#	Date	Mintage	Identification	Mkt Val
Pn43	1920	30	10 Pfennig. Silver.	3,250
Pn44	1920	30	10 Pfennig. Silver. Large 10.	3,250
Pn45	1923	—	5 Pfennig. Brass.	165
Pn46	1923	—	10 Pfennig. Brass.	170
Pn47	1923	10	Gulden. Gold. KM145.	7,500
Pn48	1927	—	2 Pfennig. Brass.	—
Pn49	1935	—	5 Gulden. Nickel. PROBE.	—
Pn50	1935	—	10 Gulden. Nickel. PROBE.	—
Pn51	1935	—	10 Gulden. Tin.	110

PROOF SETS

KM#	Date	Mintage	Identification	Issue Price	Mkt Val
PS1	1923 (8)	—	KM140-147	—	1,600

DENMARK

The Kingdom of Denmark (Danmark), a constitutional monarchy located at the mouth of the Baltic Sea, has an area of 16,639 sq. mi. (43,070 sq. km.) and a population of 5.2 million. Capital: Copenhagen. Most of the country is arable. Agriculture is conducted by large farms served by cooperatives. The largest industries are food processing, iron and metal, and shipping. Machinery, meats (chiefly bacon), dairy products and chemicals are exported.

The present decimal system of currency was introduced in 1874. As a result of a referendum held September 28, 2000, the currency of the European Monetary Union, the Euro, will not be introduced in Denmark in the foreseeable future.

RULERS
Christian IX, 1863-1906
Frederik VIII, 1906-1912
Christian X, 1912-1947
Frederik IX, 1947-1972
Margrethe II, 1972—

MINT MARKS
(h) - Copenhagen, heart

MINT OFFICIALS' INITIALS
Copenhagen

Letter	Date	Name
*P, VBP	1893-1918	Vilhelm Buchard Poulsen
HCN	1919-1927	Hans Christian Nielsen
N	1927-1955	Niels Peter Nielsen
C	1956-1971	Alfred Frederik Christiansen
S	1971-1978	Vagn Sorensen
B	1978-1981	Peter M Bjarno
R, NR	1982-1989	N. Norregaard Rasmussen
LG - JP	1990-2001	Laust Grove / J Petersen

NOTE: The letter P was only used on Danish West Indies coins and on Denmark, KM#802.

MONEYERS' INITIALS
Copenhagen

Letter	Date	Name
GI, GJ	1901-1933	Knud Gunnar Jensen
AH	1908-1924	Andreas Frederik Vilhelm Hansen
HS, S	1933-1968	Harald Salomon
B	1968-1983	Frode Bahnsen
A	1986-	Johan Alkjaer (designer)
HV	1986-	Hanne Varming (sculptor)
JP	1989-	Jan Petersen

MONETARY SYSTEM
100 Øre = 1 Krone

KINGDOM
DECIMAL COINAGE
100 Øre = 1 Krone; 1874-present

KM# 792.2 ORE
2.0000 g., Bronze **Ruler:** Christian IX **Obv:** Crowned CIX monogram, date at lower lerft, mintmark and initials VBP at lower right **Rev:** Denomination above porpoise and barley stalk

Date	Mintage	F	VF	XF	Unc	BU
1902/802(h) VBP	2,977,000	2.75	4.50	10.00	32.50	—
1902(h) VBP	Inc. above	1.75	2.75	6.50	28.00	—
1904/804(h) VBP	4,962,000	1.75	3.50	6.25	20.00	—
1904(h) VBP	Inc. above	1.25	2.25	4.75	18.00	—

KM# 804 ORE
2.0000 g., Bronze **Ruler:** Frederik VIII **Obv:** Crowned F8F monogram, initials GJ at lower right **Rev:** Denomination within circle, date and initials VBP below **Rev. Leg.:** "THE KINGDOM OF DENMARK"

Date	Mintage	F	VF	XF	Unc	BU
1907(h) VBP, GJ	5,975,000	1.25	2.75	5.50	16.00	—
1909(h) VBP, GJ	2,985,000	1.25	2.75	5.50	18.50	—
1910(h) VBP; GJ	2,994,000	1.75	4.50	12.00	30.00	—
1912(h) VBP; GJ	3,006,000	1.25	3.75	8.00	25.00	—

KM# 812.1 ORE
2.0000 g., Bronze **Ruler:** Christian X **Obv:** Crowned CX monogram, initials VBP and mint mark at lower left, date and initials GJ at lower right **Rev:** Thick denomination, ornaments flanking

Date	Mintage	F	VF	XF	Unc	BU
1913(h) VBP; GJ	5,011,000	1.00	1.50	2.00	6.00	—
1915(h) VBP; GJ	4,940,000	1.35	2.25	3.75	10.00	—
1916(h) VBP; GJ	2,439,000	1.35	2.75	5.00	14.00	—
1917(h) VBP; GJ	4,564,000	16.00	25.00	45.00	90.00	—

KM# 812.1a ORE
1.7400 g., Iron **Ruler:** Christian X **Obv:** Crowned CX monogram, initials VBP and mint mark at lower left, date and initials GJ at lower right **Rev:** Thick denomination, ornaments flanking

Date	Mintage	F	VF	XF	Unc	BU
1918(h) VBP; GJ	6,776,000	2.00	5.50	20.00	65.00	—

KM# 812.2 ORE
2.0000 g., Bronze **Ruler:** Christian X **Obv:** Crowned CX monogram, initials HCN and mint mark at lower left, date and initials GJ at lower right **Rev:** Value, ornaments flanking

Date	Mintage	F	VF	XF	Unc	BU
1919(h) HCN; GJ	4,586,000	1.00	1.50	4.00	8.50	—
1920(h) HCN; GJ	2,367,000	6.00	12.50	30.00	60.00	—
1921(h) HCN; GJ	3,121,000	1.35	2.25	3.25	8.50	—
1922(h) HCN; GJ	3,267,000	1.75	2.50	4.00	9.50	—
1923(h) HCN; GJ	2,938,000	1.75	2.50	3.75	8.50	—

KM# 812.2a ORE
1.7400 g., Iron **Ruler:** Christian X **Obv:** Crowned CX monogram, initials HCN and mint mark at lower left, date and initials GJ at lower right **Rev:** Value, ornaments flanking

Date	Mintage	F	VF	XF	Unc	BU
1919(h) HCN; GJ	931,000	5.00	15.00	42.50	110	—

KM# 826.1 ORE
1.9000 g., Bronze **Ruler:** Christian X **Obv:** Crowned CXC monogram within title "KING OF DENMARK", initials GJ below **Rev:** Country name and date above center hole, denomination, mint mark, and initials HCN below

Date	Mintage	F	VF	XF	Unc	BU
1926(h) HCN; GJ	1,572,000	3.00	6.50	20.00	65.00	—
1927(h) HCN; GJ	Inc. above	0.10	0.30	4.50	25.00	—

KM# 826.2 ORE
1.9000 g., Bronze **Ruler:** Christian X **Obv:** Crowned CXC monogram within title "KING OF DENMARK", initials GJ below **Rev:** Country name and date above center hole, denomination, mint mark, and initial N below **Note:** For coins dated 1941 refer to Faeroe Islands listings.

Date	Mintage	F	VF	XF	Unc	BU
1927(h) N; GJ	Inc. above	4.00	11.00	30.00	90.00	—
1928(h) N; GJ	29,691,000	0.10	0.25	2.75	12.50	—
1929(h) N; GJ	5,172,000	0.10	0.25	2.75	17.50	—
1930(h) N; GJ	5,306,000	0.10	0.20	2.75	20.00	—
1932(h) N; GJ	5,089,000	0.10	0.20	2.75	18.00	—
1933(h) N; GJ	2,095,000	0.25	1.50	5.50	35.00	—
1934(h) N; GJ	3,665,000	—	0.15	1.00	10.00	25.00
1935(h) N; GJ	5,668,000	—	0.15	1.00	7.00	—
1936(h) N; GJ	5,584,000	—	0.15	0.40	4.00	—
1937(h) N; GJ	6,877,000	—	0.15	0.40	3.25	—
1938(h) N; GJ	3,850,000	—	0.15	0.40	2.50	—
1939(h) N; GJ	5,662,000	—	0.15	0.30	2.50	—
1940(h) N; GJ	1,965,000	—	0.15	0.30	2.00	—

KM# 832 ORE
1.6000 g., Zinc **Ruler:** Christian X **Obv:** Crowned CX monogram divides date, mint mark and initials N-S below **Rev:** Oak and beech leaves divide value

Date	Mintage	F	VF	XF	Unc	BU
1941(h) N; S	21,570,000	0.10	0.30	9.00	40.00	—
1942(h) N; S	6,997,000	0.10	0.30	9.00	40.00	—
1943(h) N; S	15,082,000	0.10	0.30	9.00	40.00	—
1944(h) N; S	11,981,000	0.10	0.30	9.00	40.00	—
1945(h) N; S	916,000	1.00	2.00	20.00	60.00	—
1946(h) N; S	712,000	3.00	7.50	25.00	75.00	—

KM# 839.1 ORE
1.6000 g., Zinc, 16 mm. **Ruler:** Frederik IX **Obv:** Crowned F IX R monogram divides date **Rev:** Mint mark, initials N-S below value

Date	Mintage	F	VF	XF	Unc	BU
1948(h) N; S	460,000	1.00	2.25	9.50	55.00	—
1949(h) N; S	2,513,000	0.35	0.80	3.50	45.00	—

Date	Mintage	F	VF	XF	Unc	BU
1950(h) N; S	9,453,000	0.25	0.40	3.25	40.00	—
1951(h) N; S	2,931,000	0.35	1.00	3.50	55.00	—
1952(h) N; S	7,626,000	0.15	0.30	2.25	30.00	—
1953(h) N; S	11,994,000	0.10	0.20	2.25	30.00	—
1954(h) N; S	12,642,000	0.10	0.20	2.25	25.00	—
1955(h) N; S	14,177,000	0.10	0.20	1.75	25.00	—

KM# 839.2 ORE
1.6000 g., Zinc, 16 mm. **Ruler:** Frederik IX **Obv:** Crowned FIXR monogram divides date **Rev:** Mint mark, initials C-S below value

Date	Mintage	F	VF	XF	Unc	BU
1956(h) C; S	20,211,000	0.10	0.20	0.80	7.00	—
1957(h) C; S	20,900,000	0.10	0.20	0.80	7.00	—
1958(h) C; S	16,021,000	—	0.10	0.60	6.00	—
1959(h) C; S	15,929,000	—	0.10	0.60	6.00	—
1960(h) C; S	23,982,000	—	0.10	0.60	4.00	—
1961(h) C; S	18,986,000	—	0.10	0.50	3.00	—
1962(h) C; S	16,992,000	—	0.10	0.50	1.75	—
1963(h) C; S	28,986,000	—	0.10	0.40	1.75	—
1964(h) C; S	21,971,000	—	0.10	0.40	1.75	—
1965(h) C; S	29,943,000	—	0.10	0.30	1.75	—
1966(h) C; S	35,907,000	—	0.10	0.20	1.75	—
1967(h) C; S	32,959,000	—	0.10	0.20	1.75	—
1968(h) C; S	21,889,000	—	—	0.20	0.80	—
1969(h) C; S	29,243,000	—	—	0.10	0.80	—
1970(h) C; S	22,970,000	—	—	0.10	0.50	—
1971(h) C; S	21,983,000	—	—	0.10	0.50	—

KM# 839.3 ORE
1.6000 g., Zinc, 16 mm. **Ruler:** Frederik IX **Obv:** Crowned F IX R monogram divides date **Rev:** Mint mark, initials S-S below value

Date	Mintage	F	VF	XF	Unc	BU
1972(h) S; S	13,000,000	—	—	0.10	0.60	—

KM# 846 ORE
1.8000 g., Bronze **Ruler:** Frederik IX **Obv:** Crowned F IX R monogram divides date **Rev:** Two barley stalks around value, initials below **Note:** Never released for circulation, see note at 2 Ore, KM#847.

Date	Mintage	F	VF	XF	Unc	BU
1960(h) C; S	8,990,000	—	—	1.00	1.50	—
1962(h) C; S	Inc. above	—	—	1.00	1.50	—
1963(h) C; S	9,980,000	—	—	1.00	1.50	—
1964(h) C; S	2,990,000	—	—	1.00	1.50	—

KM# 793.2 2 ORE
4.0000 g., Bronze **Ruler:** Christian IX **Obv:** Crowned CIX monogram, date at lower lerft, mintmark and initials VBP at lower right **Rev:** Denomination above porpoise and barley stalk

Date	Mintage	F	VF	XF	Unc	BU
1902/802(h) VBP	3,502,000	3.00	6.00	12.00	45.00	—
1902(h) VBP	Inc. above	1.50	3.00	6.00	37.50	—
1906(h) VBP	2,498,000	3.50	10.00	22.50	45.00	—

KM# 805 2 ORE
4.0000 g., Bronze **Ruler:** Frederik VIII **Obv:** Crowned F8F monogram, initials GJ at lower right **Rev:** Denomination within circle, date and initials VBP below

Date	Mintage	F	VF	XF	Unc	BU
1907(h) VBP; GJ	2,502,000	1.50	3.00	12.00	32.50	—
1909(h) VBP; GJ	2,485,000	2.25	5.00	20.00	70.00	—
1912(h) VBP; GJ	2,480,000	2.25	5.00	14.00	45.00	—

KM# 813.1 2 ORE
4.0000 g., Bronze **Ruler:** Christian X **Obv:** Crowned CX monogram, initials VBP and mint mark at lower left, date and initials GJ at lower right **Rev:** Value, ornament flanking

Date	Mintage	F	VF	XF	Unc	BU
1913(h) VBP; GJ	373,000	27.50	50.00	85.00	220	—
1914(h) VBP; GJ	2,126,000	2.25	4.00	6.50	25.00	—
1915(h) VBP; GJ	2,485,000	1.75	4.00	6.50	27.50	—
1916(h) VBP; GJ	1,383,000	2.75	4.00	7.50	30.00	—
1917(h) VBP; GJ	1,837,000	14.00	27.50	45.00	100	135

KM# 813.1a 2 ORE
3.4700 g., Iron **Ruler:** Christian X **Obv:** Crowned CX monogram, initials VBP and mint mark at lower left, date and initials GJ at lower right **Rev:** Value, ornament flanking

Date	Mintage	F	VF	XF	Unc	BU
1918(h) VBP; GJ	4,160,999	2.25	7.50	30.00	90.00	—

KM# 813.2 2 ORE
4.0000 g., Bronze **Ruler:** Christian X **Obv:** Crowned CX monogram, initials HCN and mint mark at lower left, date and initials GJ at lower right **Rev:** Thick denomination, ornaments flanking

Date	Mintage	F	VF	XF	Unc	BU
1919(h) HCN; GJ	5,503,000	6.00	12.00	27.50	60.00	—
1920(h) HCN; GJ	2,528,000	1.00	1.50	3.50	22.50	—
1921(h) HCN; GJ	2,158,000	3.25	5.00	8.50	20.00	—
1923(h) HCN; GJ	2,625,000	2.25	4.00	7.00	20.00	—

KM# 813.2a 2 ORE
3.4700 g., Iron **Ruler:** Christian X **Obv:** Crowned CX monogram, initials HCN and mint mark at lower left, date and initials GJ at lower right **Rev:** Value, ornament flanking

Date	Mintage	F	VF	XF	Unc	BU
1919(h) HCN; GJ	1,944,000	20.00	45.00	100	250	—

KM# 827.1 2 ORE
3.8000 g., Bronze **Ruler:** Christian X **Obv:** Crowned CXC monogram within title "KING OF DENMARK", initials GJ below **Rev:** Country name and date above center hole, denomination, mint mark, and initials HCN below

Date	Mintage	F	VF	XF	Unc	BU
1926(h) HCN; GJ	301,000	42.50	80.00	250	1,050	—
1927(h) HCN; GJ	15,359,000	0.10	0.20	3.25	25.00	—

KM# 827.2 2 ORE
3.8000 g., Bronze **Ruler:** Christian X **Obv:** Crowned CXC monogram within title "KING OF DENMARK", initials GJ below **Rev:** Country name and date above center hole, denomination, mint mark, and initial N below **Note:** For coins dated 1941 refer to Faeroe Islands listings.

Date	Mintage	F	VF	XF	Unc	BU
1927(h) N; GJ	Inc. above	1.00	2.25	55.00	190	290
1928(h) N; GJ	5,758,000	0.10	0.20	2.50	22.50	50.00
1929(h) N; GJ	6,817,000	0.10	0.20	2.50	42.50	—
1930(h) N; GJ	2,327,000	0.75	1.50	8.50	80.00	—
1931(h) N; GJ	5,135,000	0.10	0.20	2.25	30.00	55.00
1932(h) N; GJ	Inc. above	1.25	2.25	35.00	150	—
1934(h) N; GJ	756,000	0.50	1.00	8.00	42.50	—
1935(h) N; GJ	1,391,000	0.10	0.20	2.00	27.50	—
1936(h) N; GJ	2,973,000	0.10	0.20	1.00	25.00	—
1937(h) N; GJ	3,437,000	0.10	0.20	1.00	12.50	—
1938(h) N; GJ	2,177,000	—	0.10	0.50	5.50	—
1939(h) N; GJ	3,165,000	—	0.10	0.50	3.25	—
1940(h) N; GJ	1,582,000	—	0.10	0.50	2.25	—

KM# 833 2 ORE
1.2000 g., Aluminum **Ruler:** Christian X **Obv:** Crowned CX monogram divides date within title: "KING OF DENMARK"; mint mark and initials N-S below **Rev:** Oak and beach leaves divide value

Date	Mintage	F	VF	XF	Unc	BU
1941(h) N; S	26,205,000	0.10	0.60	2.25	14.00	—
1941(h) N; S Proof	—	Value: 150				

KM# 833a 2 ORE
3.2000 g., Zinc **Ruler:** Christian X **Obv:** Crowned CX monogram divides date, mint mark and initials N-S below **Rev:** Oak and beach leaves divide value

---

Date	Mintage	F	VF	XF	Unc	BU
1942(h) N; S	12,934,000	0.10	0.40	10.00	55.00	—
1943(h) N; S	9,603,000	0.10	0.40	10.00	55.00	—
1944(h) N; S	6,069,000	0.10	0.40	10.00	55.00	—
1945(h) N; S	329,000	4.25	8.50	45.00	120	—
1947(h) N; S	589,000	1.50	3.00	22.50	90.00	—

KM# 840.1 2 ORE
3.2000 g., Zinc, 20.8 mm. **Ruler:** Frederik IX **Obv:** Crowned F IX R monogram and date **Rev:** Mint mark, initials N-S below value

Date	Mintage	F	VF	XF	Unc	BU
1948(h) N; S	1,927,000	0.40	1.00	6.50	55.00	—
1949(h) N; S	1,603,000	3.75	14.50	60.00	250	—
1950(h) N; S	4,544,000	0.75	1.35	6.50	60.00	—
1951(h) N; S	3,766,000	1.50	2.50	12.50	95.00	—
1952(h) N; S	4,874,000	0.10	0.20	2.50	45.00	—
1953(h) N; S	8,112,000	0.10	0.20	2.50	35.00	—
1954(h) N; S	6,497,000	0.10	0.20	2.50	25.00	—
1955(h) N; S	6,968,000	—	0.10	1.50	15.00	—

KM# 840.2 2 ORE
3.2000 g., Zinc, 20.8 mm. **Ruler:** Frederik IX **Obv:** Crowned FIXR monogram divides date **Rev:** Mint mark, initials C-S below value

Date	Mintage	F	VF	XF	Unc	BU
1956(h) C; S	10,004,000	—	0.10	1.00	7.50	—
1957(h) C; S	15,329,000	—	0.10	1.00	6.00	—
1958(h) C; S	8,119,999	—	0.10	1.00	5.00	—
1959(h) C; S	10,462,000	—	0.10	1.00	4.00	—
1960(h) C; S	16,504,000	—	0.10	0.80	3.00	—
1961(h) C; S	15,504,000	—	0.10	0.80	2.50	—
1962(h) C; S	10,980,000	—	0.10	0.80	2.50	—
1963(h) C; S	19,470,000	—	0.10	0.30	1.50	—
1964(h) C; S	15,411,000	—	0.10	0.30	1.00	—
1965(h) C; S	20,173,000	—	0.10	0.20	1.00	—
1966(h) C; S	21,949,000	—	0.10	0.20	1.00	—
1967(h) C; S	22,439,000	—	0.10	0.20	1.00	—
1968(h) C; S	17,632,000	—	—	0.10	0.80	—
1969(h) C; S	29,276,000	—	—	0.10	0.80	—
1970(h) C; S	23,864,000	—	—	0.10	0.50	—
1971(h) C; S	35,811,000	—	—	0.10	0.50	—

KM# 847 2 ORE
3.6000 g., Bronze **Ruler:** Frederik IX **Obv:** Crowned F IX R monogram, date **Rev:** Two barley stalks around value, mint mark and initials C-S below **Note:** KM#847 was never released for circulation. Together with the 4 dates of 1 Øre, KM#846, they were sold as a 10 coin set to collectors by the mint. Approximately 100,000 sets were sold, remaining coins were melted. The date 1963 was produced exclusively for the set in 1973

Date	Mintage	F	VF	XF	Unc	BU
1960(h) C; S	Inc. above	—	—	1.00	1.50	—
1962(h) C; S	Inc. above	—	—	1.00	1.50	—
1963(h) C; S	100,000	—	—	1.00	1.50	—
1964(h) C; S	3,990,000	—	—	1.00	1.50	—
1965(h) C; S	11,980,000	—	—	1.00	1.50	—
1966(h) C; S	12,000,000	—	—	1.00	1.50	—

KM# 840.3 2 ORE
3.2000 g., Zinc **Ruler:** Frederik IX **Obv:** Crowned F IX R monogram and date **Rev:** Mint mark, initials S-S below value

Date	Mintage	F	VF	XF	Unc	BU
1972(h) S; S	6,496,000	—	0.15	0.30	0.85	—

KM# 794.2 5 ORE
8.0000 g., Bronze **Ruler:** Christian IX **Obv:** Crowned CIX monogram, date at lower left, mintmark and initials VBP at lower right **Rev:** Value above porpoise and barley stalk

Date	Mintage	F	VF	XF	Unc	BU
1902(h) VBP	601,000	12.50	25.00	47.50	140	—
1904(h) VBP	397,000	25.00	50.00	125	275	—
1906(h) VBP	1,000,000	17.50	40.00	85.00	200	—

KM# 806 5 ORE
8.0000 g., Bronze **Ruler:** Frederik VIII **Obv:** Crowned F VIII F monogram, initials VBP at lower right **Rev:** Value within circle, date and initials VP below

Date	Mintage	F	VF	XF	Unc	BU
1907(h) VBP; GJ	1,000,000	8.00	15.00	40.00	95.00	—
1908(h) VBP; GJ	1,198,000	9.00	17.00	45.00	105	—
1912(h) VBP; GJ	999,000	10.00	19.00	50.00	120	160

KM# 814.1 5 ORE
8.0000 g., Bronze **Ruler:** Christian X **Obv:** Crowned CX monogram, initials VBP and mint mark lower at left, date and initials GJ at lower right **Rev:** Thick value, ornaments flanking

Date	Mintage	F	VF	XF	Unc	BU
1913(h) VBP; GJ	216,000	60.00	110	150	275	425
1914(h) VBP; GJ	785,000	8.00	16.00	20.00	45.00	—
1916(h) VBP; GJ	887,000	10.00	20.00	30.00	60.00	—
1917(h) VBP; GJ	494,000	12.50	30.00	50.00	100	250

KM# 814.1a 5 ORE
6.9400 g., Iron **Ruler:** Christian X **Obv:** Crowned CX monogram, initials VBP and mint mark at lower left, date and initials GJ at lower right **Rev:** Value, ornament flanking

Date	Mintage	F	VF	XF	Unc	BU
1918(h) VBP; GJ	1,918,000	8.00	16.00	45.00	140	—

KM# 814.2 5 ORE
8.0000 g., Bronze **Ruler:** Christian X **Obv:** Crowned CX monogram, initials HCN and mint mark at lower left, date and initials GJ at lower right **Rev:** Thick value, ornaments flanking

Date	Mintage	F	VF	XF	Unc	BU
1919(h) HCN; GJ	994,000	3.25	5.50	8.50	22.50	—
1920(h) HCN; GJ	2,618,000	7.00	13.50	22.50	45.00	—
1921(h) HCN; GJ	3,248,000	4.50	8.00	11.50	25.00	—
1923(h) HCN; GJ	369,000	85.00	175	240	425	—

KM# 814.2a 5 ORE
6.9400 g., Iron **Ruler:** Christian X **Obv:** Crowned CX monogram, initials HCN and mint mark at lower left, date and initials GJ at lower right **Rev:** Value, ornament flanking

Date	Mintage	F	VF	XF	Unc	BU
1919(h) HCN; GJ	1,034,999	25.00	75.00	140	300	—

KM# 828.1 5 ORE
7.6000 g., Bronze, 27.4 mm. **Ruler:** Christian X **Obv:** Crowned CXC monogram within title "KING OF DENMARK", initials GJ below **Rev:** Country name and date above center hole, denomination, mint mark, and initials HCN below

Date	Mintage	F	VF	XF	Unc	BU
1927(h) HCN; GJ	7,129,000	0.10	0.25	3.50	30.00	—

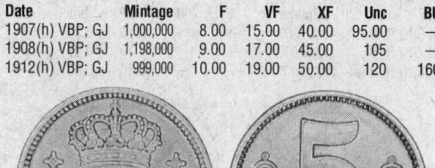

KM# 828.2 5 ORE
7.6000 g., Bronze **Ruler:** Christian X **Obv:** Crowned CXC monogram within title "KING OF DENMARK", initials GJ below **Rev:** Country name and date above center hole, denomination, mint mark, and initial N below **Note:** For coins dated 1941 refer to Faeroe Islands.

Date	Mintage	F	VF	XF	Unc	BU
1927(h) N; GJ	Inc. above	4.00	8.00	90.00	700	1,000
1928(h) N; GJ	4,685,000	0.10	0.40	3.50	32.50	—
1929(h) N; GJ	1,387,000	0.30	0.60	5.00	75.00	—
1930(h) N; GJ	1,339,000	0.40	0.80	15.00	80.00	—
1932(h) N; GJ	1,010,999	0.30	0.60	9.50	75.00	100

Date	Mintage	F	VF	XF	Unc	BU
1932(h) N; GJ Proof	—	Value: 150				
1934(h) N; GJ	524,000	0.30	0.60	8.00	55.00	—
1935(h) N; GJ	1,124,000	2.25	4.50	27.50	125	—
1936(h) N; GJ	1,091,000	0.20	0.40	3.25	37.50	—
1937(h) N; GJ	1,209,000	0.20	0.40	1.50	50.00	—
1938(h) N; GJ	1,093,000	0.40	1.00	2.25	15.00	—
1939(h) N; GJ	1,402,000	0.15	0.20	0.50	4.25	—
1940(h) N; GJ	2,735,000	0.15	0.20	0.50	4.25	—

KM# 834 5 ORE
2.4000 g., Aluminum **Ruler:** Christian X **Obv:** Crowned CX monogram divides date, mint mark and initials N-S below **Rev:** Oak and beech leaves divide value

Date	Mintage	F	VF	XF	Unc	BU
1941(h) N; S	16,984,000	0.10	1.00	3.75	20.00	—
1941(h) N; S Proof	—	Value: 150				

KM# 834a 5 ORE
6.4000 g., Zinc **Ruler:** Christian X **Obv:** Crowned CX monogram and date within title: "KING OF DENMARK"; mint mark and initials N-S below **Rev:** Value between oak and beech leaves

Date	Mintage	F	VF	XF	Unc	BU
1942(h) N; S	2,963,000	1.50	3.00	30.00	90.00	—
1943(h) N; S	4,522,000	0.50	1.75	22.50	75.00	—
1944(h) N; S	3,744,000	0.60	2.00	22.50	75.00	—
1945(h) N; GJ	864,000	4.00	10.00	45.00	125	—

KM# 843.1 5 ORE
6.4000 g., Zinc **Ruler:** Frederik IX **Obv:** Crowned FIXR monogram, IX, and date **Rev:** Mint mark, initials N-S below value

Date	Mintage	F	VF	XF	Unc	BU
1950(h) N; S	657,000	6.00	12.50	50.00	120	—
1951(h) N; S Straight 5	1,858,000	1.25	3.00	14.00	60.00	—
1951(h) N; S Slant 5	Inc. above	1.00	2.50	12.00	55.00	—
1952(h) N; S	3,562,000	0.60	1.00	6.50	35.00	—
1953(h) N; S	5,944,000	0.60	1.00	4.50	30.00	—
1954(h) N; S	3,060,000	0.40	1.25	4.00	25.00	—
1955(h) N; S	2,314,000	1.00	2.00	6.00	25.00	—

KM# 843.2 5 ORE
6.4000 g., Zinc **Ruler:** Frederik IX **Obv:** Crowned FIXR monogram, divides date **Rev:** Mint mark, initials C-S below value

Date	Mintage	F	VF	XF	Unc	BU
1956(h) C; S	5,888,000	0.40	1.25	2.75	11.00	—
1957(h) C; S	8,606,000	0.20	0.50	1.50	6.50	—
1958(h) C; S	9,598,000	0.20	0.50	1.50	5.50	—
1959(h) C; S	6,110,000	0.10	0.20	1.00	5.50	—
1960(h) C; S	11,800,000	0.10	0.20	1.00	3.50	—
1961(h) C; S	8,995,000	0.20	0.40	1.00	2.75	—
1962(h) C; S	9,729,000	0.10	0.20	0.80	2.75	—
1963(h) C; S	8,980,000	0.10	0.20	0.80	2.50	—
1964(h) C; S	6,738,000	0.75	1.25	3.50	7.00	—

KM# 848.1 5 ORE
6.0000 g., Bronze, 24 mm. **Ruler:** Frederik IX **Obv:** Crowned FIXR monogram, divides date **Rev:** Two barley stalks around denomination, initials C-S below

Date	Mintage	F	VF	XF	Unc	BU
1960(h) C; S	3,760,000	0.10	0.25	1.25	6.00	—
1962(h) C; S	5,873,000	0.25	0.75	2.25	20.00	—
1963(h) C; S	23,287,000	—	0.10	0.50	2.75	—
1964(h) C; S	41,521,000	—	0.10	0.50	2.75	—
1965(h) C; S	14,229,000	—	0.10	0.50	2.75	—
1966(h) C; S	23,410,000	—	0.10	0.50	2.75	—
1967(h) C; S	15,094,000	—	0.10	0.50	2.75	—
1968(h) C; S	16,105,000	—	0.10	0.40	1.75	—
1969(h) C; S	23,594,000	—	0.10	0.30	1.00	—
1970(h) C; S	26,176,000	—	—	0.10	1.00	—
1971(h) C; S	10,076,000	—	—	0.10	1.00	—

KM# 848.2 5 ORE
6.0000 g., Bronze, 24 mm. **Ruler:** Frederik IX **Obv:** Crowned F IX R monogram, date **Rev:** Two barley stalks around value, initials S-S below

Date	Mintage	F	VF	XF	Unc	BU
1972(h) S; S	27,938,000	—	—	0.10	1.00	—

KM# 859.1 5 ORE
1.6000 g., Copper Clad Iron, 15.5 mm. **Ruler:** Margrethe II **Obv:** Crowned MIIR monogram divides date; mint mark, initials S-B **Rev:** "DANMARK" above denomination

Date	Mintage	F	VF	XF	Unc	BU
1973(h) S; B	75,138,000	—	—	0.10	0.70	—
1974(h) S; B	71,796,000	—	—	0.10	0.70	—
1975(h) S; B	45,004,000	—	—	0.10	0.70	—
1976(h) S; B	73,296,000	—	—	0.10	0.70	—
1977(h) S; B	74,066,000	—	—	0.10	0.70	—
1978(h) S; B	52,425,000	—	—	0.10	0.70	—

KM# 859.2 5 ORE
1.6000 g., Copper Clad Iron, 15.5 mm. **Ruler:** Margrethe II **Obv:** Crowned MIIR monogram divides date; mint mark, initials B-B **Rev:** "DANMARK" above denomination

Date	Mintage	F	VF	XF	Unc	BU
1979(h) B; B	58,953,000	—	—	0.10	0.70	—
1980(h) B; B	54,362,000	—	—	0.10	0.70	—
1981(h) B; B	52,201,000	—	—	0.10	0.35	—

KM# 859.3 5 ORE
1.6000 g., Copper Clad Iron, 15.5 mm. **Ruler:** Margrethe II **Obv:** Crowned MIIR monogram divides date; mint mark, initials R-B **Rev:** "DANMARK" above value

Date	Mintage	F	VF	XF	Unc	BU
1982(h) R; B	74,296,000	—	—	0.10	0.30	—
1983(h) R; B	70,655,000	—	—	0.10	0.30	—
1984(h) R; B	27,599,000	—	—	0.10	0.30	—
1985(h) R; B	56,676,000	—	—	0.10	0.30	—
1986(h) R; B	62,496,000	—	—	0.10	0.30	—
1987(h) R; B	71,798,000	—	—	0.10	0.30	—
1988(h) R; B	48,925,000	—	—	0.10	0.30	—

KM# 795.2 10 ORE
1.4500 g., 0.4000 Silver 0.0186 oz. ASW **Ruler:** Christian IX **Obv:** Head right, date mintmark and initials below **Rev:** Denomination above porpoise and barley stalk, star at top

Date	Mintage	F	VF	XF	Unc	BU
1903/803(h) VBP	3,007,000	4.50	8.00	15.00	35.00	—
1903(h) VBP	Inc. above	3.00	6.00	12.00	27.50	—
1904(h) VBP	2,449,000	20.00	30.00	47.50	95.00	—
1905(h) VBP	1,571,000	2.50	5.00	10.00	27.50	—

KM# 807 10 ORE
1.4500 g., 0.4000 Silver 0.0186 oz. ASW **Ruler:** Frederik VIII **Obv:** Head left, initials GJ below **Rev:** Value, date, mint mark, initials VBP within circle, lily ornamentation surrounds

Date	Mintage	F	VF	XF	Unc	BU
1907(h) VBP; GJ	3,068,000	3.25	5.50	11.50	30.00	50.00
1910(h) VBP; GJ	2,530,000	3.50	5.00	10.00	27.50	—
1911(h) VBP; GJ	579,000	27.50	45.00	70.00	140	—
1912(h) VBP; GJ	1,951,000	3.75	7.00	12.00	30.00	—

KM# 818.1 10 ORE
1.4500 g., 0.4000 Silver 0.0186 oz. ASW **Ruler:** Christian X **Obv:** Crowned CX monogram, initials VBP and mint mark at lower left, date and initials GJ at lower right **Rev:** Value, ornaments flanking

Date	Mintage	F	VF	XF	Unc	BU
1914(h) VBP; GJ	2,128,000	4.00	7.00	11.00	22.50	35.00
1915(h) VBP; GJ	915,000	5.50	10.00	14.00	25.00	—

Date	Mintage	F	VF	XF	Unc	BU
1916(h) VBP; GJ	2,699,000	4.00	7.00	11.50	20.00	—
1917(h) VBP; GJ	6,003,000	2.25	4.00	6.00	12.50	—
1918(h) VBP; GJ	5,042,000	1.35	2.50	4.25	4.00	—

KM# 818.2   10 ORE
1.4500 g., 0.4000 Silver 0.0186 oz. ASW **Ruler:** Christian X
Obv: Crowned CX monogram, initials HCN and mint mark at lower left, date and initials GJ at lower right **Rev:** Value, ornament flanking

Date	Mintage	F	VF	XF	Unc	BU
1919(h) HCN; GJ	10,184,000	1.00	1.50	2.75	4.75	—

KM# 818.2a   10 ORE
1.5000 g., Copper-Nickel, 15 mm. **Ruler:** Christian X **Obv:** Crowned CX monogram, initials HCN and mint mark at lower left, date and initials GJ at lower right **Rev:** Value, ornaments flanking

Date	Mintage	F	VF	XF	Unc	BU
1920(h) HCN; GJ	10,234,000	2.75	4.00	9.50	40.00	—
1921(h) HCN; GJ	8,064,000	2.75	3.75	8.00	32.50	—
1922(h) HCN; GJ	3,065,000	20.00	30.00	50.00	95.00	—
1923(h) HCN; GJ	1,790,000	325	475	650	900	—

KM# 822.1   10 ORE
3.0000 g., Copper-Nickel **Ruler:** Christian X **Obv:** Crowned CXR monogram around center hole, date, mint mark and initials HCN-GJ below hole **Rev:** Center hole flanked by spiral ornamentation dividing value

Date	Mintage	F	VF	XF	Unc	BU
1924(h) HCN; GJ	14,661,000	0.25	1.50	3.00	20.00	—
1925(h) HCN; GJ	Inc. above	0.30	1.50	8.00	40.00	—
1925(h) HCN; G	8,678,000	0.35	1.75	9.00	47.50	—
1926(h) HCN; GJ	4,107,000	0.30	1.50	8.00	45.00	—

KM# 822.2   10 ORE
3.0000 g., Copper-Nickel **Ruler:** Christian X **Obv:** Crowned CXR monogram around center hole, date, mint mark and initial N-GJ below hole **Rev:** Center hole flanked by spiral ornamentation dividing value **Note:** For coins dated 1941 without mint mark or initials refer to Faeroe Islands listings.

Date	Mintage	F	VF	XF	Unc	BU
1929(h) N; GJ	5,037,000	0.75	1.25	8.00	45.00	—
1931(h) N; GJ Large N	Inc. above	1.35	2.50	11.00	55.00	—
1931(h) N; GJ Small N	3,054,000	1.35	2.50	11.00	55.00	—
1933(h) N; GJ	1,274,000	7.50	15.00	35.00	90.00	—
1934(h) N; GJ	2,013,000	1.00	2.50	8.00	30.00	—
1935(h) N; GJ	2,848,000	1.35	2.50	7.00	27.50	—
1936(h) N; GJ	3,320,000	1.35	2.50	6.00	45.00	—
1937(h) N; GJ	2,234,000	1.00	1.75	6.00	20.00	—
1938(h) N; GJ	2,991,000	1.75	3.00	5.50	17.50	—
1939(h) N; GJ	2,973,000	1.00	2.00	5.50	17.50	—
1940(h) N; GJ	2,998,000	0.50	1.00	2.00	12.50	—
1941(h) N; GJ	748,000	2.75	4.50	8.00	20.00	—
1946(h) N; GJ	460,000	2.50	4.25	6.00	10.00	—
1947(h) N; GJ	1,292,000	85.00	115	170	230	—

KM# 822.2a   10 ORE
2.4000 g., Zinc **Ruler:** Christian X **Obv:** Crowned CXR monogram around center hole, date, mint mark and initials N-GJ below hole **Rev:** Center hole flanked by spiral ornamentation dividing value

Date	Mintage	F	VF	XF	Unc	BU
1941(h) N; GJ	7,706,000	1.00	2.00	14.00	40.00	—
1942(h) N; GJ	8,676,000	1.00	2.00	14.00	40.00	—
1943(h) N; GJ	2,181,000	1.75	3.25	15.00	42.50	—
1944(h) N; GJ	7,994,000	1.35	2.50	10.00	32.50	—
1945(h) N; GJ	1,280,000	45.00	70.00	110	225	325

KM# 841.1   10 ORE
3.0000 g., Copper-Nickel, 18 mm. **Ruler:** Frederik IX **Obv:** Crowned FIXR monogram divides date, oak and beech branches below **Rev:** Denomination, country name, mint mark, initials N-S

Date	Mintage	F	VF	XF	Unc	BU
1948(h) N; S	5,317,000	0.20	0.60	1.40	25.00	—
1949(h) N; S	7,595,000	0.10	0.20	3.00	22.50	—
1950(h) N; S	6,886,000	0.10	0.20	3.00	20.00	—

Date	Mintage	F	VF	XF	Unc	BU
1951(h) N; S	8,763,000	0.10	0.20	4.00	30.00	—
1952(h) N; S	6,810,000	0.10	0.20	3.00	22.50	—
1953(h) N; S	11,946,000	0.10	0.20	3.00	20.00	—
1954(h) N; S	19,739,000	—	0.10	1.50	10.00	—
1955(h) N; S	17,623,000	—	0.10	1.50	10.00	—

KM# 841.2   10 ORE
3.0000 g., Copper-Nickel, 18 mm. **Ruler:** Frederik IX **Obv:** Crowned FIXR monogram divides date, oak and beech branches below **Rev:** Denomination, country name, mint mark, initials C-S

Date	Mintage	F	VF	XF	Unc	BU
1956(h) C; S	12,323,000	—	0.10	2.25	12.50	—
1957(h) C; S	13,227,000	—	0.10	1.00	6.50	—
1958(h) C; S	10,870,000	—	0.10	1.00	6.50	—
1959(h) C; S	1,255,000	30.00	45.00	65.00	140	—
1960(h) C; S	5,107,000	0.10	0.30	1.00	4.25	—

KM# 849.1   10 ORE
3.0000 g., Copper-Nickel, 18 mm. **Ruler:** Frederik IX **Obv:** Crowned FIXR monogram divides date, mint mark and initials C-S below **Rev:** Denomination, country name above oak branches

Date	Mintage	F	VF	XF	Unc	BU
1960(h) C; S	Inc. above	0.10	0.30	0.75	4.00	—
1961(h) C; S	20,258,000	—	0.15	0.40	5.00	—
1962(h) C; S	12,785,000	—	0.15	0.40	5.00	—
1963(h) C; S	17,171,000	—	0.15	0.40	4.00	—
1964(h) C; S	14,282,000	—	0.15	0.40	3.25	—
1965(h) C; S	21,857,000	—	0.15	0.40	3.25	—
1966(h) C; S	24,160,000	—	0.15	0.20	2.75	—
1967(h) C; S	21,544,000	—	0.15	0.20	1.75	—
1968(h) C; S	7,586,000	—	0.15	0.20	1.50	—
1969(h) C; S	31,534,000	—	—	0.10	1.00	—
1970(h) C; S	37,813,000	—	—	0.10	0.30	—
1971(h) C; S	17,719,000	—	—	0.10	0.30	—

KM# 849.2   10 ORE
3.0000 g., Copper-Nickel, 18 mm. **Ruler:** Frederik IX **Obv:** Crowned FIXR above mint mark and initials S-S **Rev:** Value, country name above oak branches

Date	Mintage	F	VF	XF	Unc	BU
1972(h) S; S	46,959,000	—	—	0.10	0.30	—

KM# 860.1   10 ORE
3.0000 g., Copper-Nickel, 18 mm. **Ruler:** Margrethe II **Obv:** Crowned MIIR monogram divides date, mint mark and initials S-B below **Rev:** Value flanked by oak leaves

Date	Mintage	F	VF	XF	Unc	BU
1973(h) S; B	37,538,000	—	—	0.10	0.30	—
1974(h) S; B	38,570,000	—	—	0.10	0.30	—
1975(h) S; B	62,633,000	—	—	0.10	0.50	—
1976(h) S; B	64,358,999	—	—	0.10	0.50	—
1977(h) S; B	61,994,000	—	—	0.10	0.50	—
1978(h) S; B	30,302,000	—	—	0.10	0.50	—

KM# 860.2   10 ORE
3.0000 g., Copper-Nickel, 18 mm. **Ruler:** Margrethe II **Obv:** Crowned MIIR monogram divides date, mint mark and initials B-B below **Rev:** Value flanked by oak leaves

Date	Mintage	F	VF	XF	Unc	BU
1979(h) B; B	10,224,000	—	—	0.10	0.30	—
1980(h) B; B	37,233,000	—	—	0.10	0.30	—
1981(h) B; B	51,565,000	—	—	0.10	0.20	—

KM# 860.3   10 ORE
3.0000 g., Copper-Nickel, 18 mm. **Ruler:** Margrethe II **Obv:** Crowned MIIR monogram divides date, mint mark and initials R-B below **Rev:** Value flanked by oak leaves

Date	Mintage	F	VF	XF	Unc	BU
1982(h) R; B	40,195,000	—	—	0.10	0.20	—
1983(h) R; B	35,634,000	—	—	0.10	0.20	—
1984(h) R; B	17,828,000	—	—	0.10	0.20	—
1985(h) R; B	29,317,000	—	—	0.10	0.20	—

Date	Mintage	F	VF	XF	Unc	BU
1986(h) R; B	46,254,000	—	—	0.10	0.20	—
1987(h) R; B	27,898,000	—	—	0.10	0.20	—
1988(h) R; B	29,400,000	—	—	0.10	0.20	—

KM# 796.2   25 ORE
2.4200 g., 0.6000 Silver 0.0467 oz. ASW **Ruler:** Christian IX **Obv:** Head right, date mint mark and initials below **Rev:** Value above porpoise and barley stalk, star at top

Date	Mintage	F	VF	XF	Unc	BU
1904(h) VBP	1,922,000	22.00	40.00	55.00	115	—
1905/805(h) VBP	1,722,000	15.00	27.50	47.50	90.00	—
1905(h) VBP	Inc. above	12.50	22.50	42.50	70.00	—

KM# 808   25 ORE
2.4200 g., 0.6000 Silver 0.0467 oz. ASW **Ruler:** Frederik VIII **Obv:** Head left, initials GJ below **Rev:** Value, date, mint mark, initials VBP within circle, lily ornamentation surrounds

Date	Mintage	F	VF	XF	Unc	BU
1907(h) VBP; GJ	2,009,000	8.00	15.00	30.00	60.00	—
1911(h) VBP; GJ	2,015,000	8.00	15.00	30.00	60.00	—

KM# 815.1   25 ORE
2.4200 g., 0.6000 Silver 0.0467 oz. ASW **Ruler:** Christian X **Obv:** Crowned CX monogram, initials VBP and mint mark lower left, date and initials GJ lower right **Rev:** Value, ornaments flanking

Date	Mintage	F	VF	XF	Unc	BU
1913(h) VBP; GJ	2,016,000	4.00	7.50	12.50	25.00	—
1914(h) VBP; GJ	347,000	95.00	150	210	325	—
1915(h) VBP; GJ	2,862,000	3.25	6.00	10.00	20.00	—
1916(h) VBP; GJ	938,000	10.00	16.00	27.50	40.00	—
1917(h) VBP; GJ	1,354,000	42.50	70.00	105	170	—
1918(h) VBP; GJ	2,089,999	6.00	9.50	15.00	23.00	—

KM# 815.2   25 ORE
2.4200 g., 0.6000 Silver 0.0467 oz. ASW **Ruler:** Christian X **Obv:** Crowned CX monogram, initials HCN and mint mark lower left, date and initials GJ lower right **Rev:** Value, ornament flanking

Date	Mintage	F	VF	XF	Unc	BU
1919(h) HCN; GJ	9,295,000	1.25	2.00	3.00	6.00	—

KM# 815.2a   25 ORE
2.4000 g., Copper-Nickel **Ruler:** Christian X **Obv:** Crowned CX monogram, initials HCN and mint mark lower left, date and initials GJ lower right **Rev:** Value, ornament flanking

Date	Mintage	F	VF	XF	Unc	BU
1920(h) HCN; GJ	12,288,000	3.00	5.00	16.00	50.00	—
1921(h) HCN; GJ	9,444,000	2.50	4.00	16.00	50.00	—
1922(h) HCN; GJ	5,701,000	32.50	45.00	65.00	110	—

KM# 823.1   25 ORE
4.5000 g., Copper-Nickel **Ruler:** Christian X **Obv:** Crowned CXR monogram around center hole, date, mint mark and initials HCN-GJ below hole **Rev:** Center hole flanked by designs divide value

Date	Mintage	F	VF	XF	Unc	BU
1924(h) HCN; GJ	8,035,000	0.30	1.75	4.50	17.50	—
1925(h) HCN; GJ	1,906,000	5.00	9.00	20.00	70.00	240
1926(h) HCN; GJ	2,659,000	1.50	2.75	8.00	50.00	—

KM# 823.2 25 ORE

4.5000 g., Copper-Nickel **Ruler:** Christian X **Obv:** Crowned CXR monogram around center hole, date, mint mark and initials N-GJ below hole **Rev:** Center hole flanked by spiral ornamentations dividing value **Note:** For coins dated 1941 refer to Faeroe Islands listings.

Date	Mintage	F	VF	XF	Unc	BU
1929(h) N; GJ	886,000	1.75	3.75	10.00	50.00	—
1930(h) N; GJ	3,423,000	2.25	4.50	15.00	60.00	—
1932(h) N; GJ	846,000	8.50	12.50	22.50	75.00	—
1933(h) N; GJ	479,000	30.00	42.50	60.00	140	—
1934(h) N; GJ	1,660,000	2.75	5.50	15.00	55.00	—
1935(h) N; GJ	1,032,000	12.50	25.00	42.50	95.00	—
1936(h) N; GJ	1,453,000	1.75	2.75	7.50	37.50	—
1937(h) N; GJ	1,612,000	3.25	5.50	9.50	25.00	—
1938(h) N; GJ	1,794,000	2.75	4.00	8.00	25.00	—
1939(h) N; GJ	1,972,000	12.50	22.50	37.50	75.00	—
1940(h) N; GJ	1,356,000	1.35	2.25	4.00	15.00	—
1946(h) N; GJ	2,323,000	1.25	2.75	4.00	10.00	—
1947(h) N; GJ	1,751,000	5.00	10.00	16.00	25.00	—

KM# 823.2a 25 ORE

3.6000 g., Zinc **Ruler:** Christian X **Obv:** Crowned CXR monogram around center hole, date, mint mark and initials N-GJ below hole **Rev:** Center hole flanked by spiral ornamentations dividing value

Date	Mintage	F	VF	XF	Unc	BU
1941(h) N; GJ	15,332,000	4.00	7.50	20.00	50.00	—
1942(h) N; GJ	997,000	1.50	3.50	12.50	40.00	—
1943(h) N; GJ	5,784,000	4.00	9.00	20.00	45.00	—
1944(h) N; GJ	10,665,000	1.50	4.00	12.50	40.00	60.00
1945(h) N; GJ	4,543,000	2.50	5.00	12.50	40.00	60.00

KM# 842.1 25 ORE

4.5000 g., Copper-Nickel, 23 mm. **Ruler:** Frederik IX **Obv:** Crowned FIXR monogram divides value, oak and beech branches below **Rev:** Value, country name, mint mark, initials N-S

Date	Mintage	F	VF	XF	Unc	BU
1948(h) N; S	1,853,000	2.25	5.00	10.00	55.00	—
1949(h) N; S	15,000,000	0.20	0.50	2.25	17.50	—
1950(h) N; S	13,771,000	0.20	0.50	3.75	30.00	—
1951(h) N; S	5,045,000	0.20	0.50	4.50	35.00	—
1952(h) N; S	2,017,999	0.75	3.00	14.00	45.00	—
1953(h) N; S	9,553,000	0.20	0.50	2.25	11.00	—
1954(h) N; S	11,337,000	0.20	0.50	1.50	6.50	—
1955(h) N; S	6,385,000	0.20	0.50	1.50	6.50	—

KM# 842.2 25 ORE

4.5000 g., Copper-Nickel, 23 mm. **Ruler:** Frederik IX **Obv:** Crowned FIXR monogram divides value, oak and beech branches below **Rev:** Value, country name, mint mark, initials C-S

Date	Mintage	F	VF	XF	Unc	BU
1956(h) C; S	10,228,000	0.20	0.50	1.00	5.50	—
1957(h) C; S	7,421,000	0.20	0.50	0.75	4.50	—
1958(h) C; S	3,600,000	0.30	0.60	1.00	5.00	—
1959(h) C; S	2,211,000	2.25	4.25	7.00	11.00	20.00
1960(h) C; S	3,453,000	0.30	0.60	1.25	6.00	—

KM# 850 25 ORE

4.5000 g., Copper-Nickel, 23 mm. **Ruler:** Frederik IX **Obv:** Crowned FIXR monogram divides date, oak and beech branches below **Rev:** Value, country name, mint mark, initials C-S

Date	Mintage	F	VF	XF	Unc	BU
1960(h) C; S	Inc. above	6.50	11.00	15.00	27.50	—
1961(h) C; S	20,860,000	0.20	0.35	1.00	6.00	—

Date	Mintage	F	VF	XF	Unc	BU
1962(h) C; S	12,563,000	0.20	0.35	1.00	5.00	—
1964(h) C; S	6,175,000	0.20	0.35	1.00	5.00	—
1965(h) C; S	13,492,000	0.20	0.35	1.00	5.00	—
1966(h) C; S	50,220,000	0.20	0.35	1.00	5.00	—
1967(h) C; S	87,468,000	6.00	12.50	16.00	27.50	—

KM# 855.1 25 ORE

4.3000 g., Copper-Nickel, 23 mm. **Ruler:** Frederik IX **Obv:** Crowned F IX R monogram, date below, to left of center hole, beech branch to right, initials C-S and mint mark at bottom **Rev:** Value, country name and 2 stalks of barley around center hole

Date	Mintage	F	VF	XF	Unc	BU
1966(h) C; S	Inc. above	—	0.20	0.40	3.00	—
1967(h) C; S	Inc. above	—	0.20	0.40	2.50	—
1968(h) C; S	39,142,000	—	0.20	0.40	1.50	—
1969(h) C; S	16,974,000	—	0.20	0.40	1.25	—
1970(h) C; S	5,393,000	—	—	0.20	0.80	—
1971(h) C; S	12,725,000	—	—	0.20	0.70	—

KM# 855.2 25 ORE

4.3000 g., Copper-Nickel, 23 mm. **Ruler:** Frederik IX **Obv:** Crowned F IX R monogram and date to left of center hole, beech branch to right, initial S-S and mint mark at bottom **Rev:** Value, country name and 2 stalks of barley around center hole

Date	Mintage	F	VF	XF	Unc	BU
1972(h) S; S	31,422,000	—	—	0.20	0.50	—

KM# 861.1 25 ORE

4.3000 g., Copper-Nickel, 23 mm. **Ruler:** Margrethe II **Obv:** Crowned MIIR monogram to left, oak branch to right of center hole, date above, mint mark and initials S-B below **Rev:** Denomination divided by center hole, stylized stalks flank

Date	Mintage	F	VF	XF	Unc	BU
1973(h) S; B	30,834,000	—	—	0.20	0.50	—
1974(h) S; B	22,178,000	—	—	0.20	0.50	—
1975(h) S; B	28,798,000	—	—	0.20	0.50	—
1976(h) S; B	48,388,000	—	—	0.20	0.50	—
1977(h) S; B	32,238,999	—	—	0.20	0.50	—
1978(h) S; B	17,444,000	—	—	0.20	0.50	—

KM# 861.2 25 ORE

4.3000 g., Copper-Nickel, 23 mm. **Ruler:** Margrethe II **Obv:** Crowned MIIR monogram to left, oak branch to right of center hole, date above, mint mark and initials B-B below **Rev:** Value divided by center hole, stylized stalks flank

Date	Mintage	F	VF	XF	Unc	BU
1979(h) B; B	24,261,000	—	—	0.20	0.50	—
1980(h) B; B	30,448,000	—	—	0.20	0.50	—
1981(h) B; B	1,427,000	—	—	0.20	0.50	—

KM# 861.3 25 ORE

4.3000 g., Copper-Nickel, 23 mm. **Ruler:** Margrethe II **Obv:** Crowned MIIR monogram to left, oak branch to right of center hole, date above, mint mark and initials B-B below **Rev:** Value divided by center hole, stylized stalks flank

Date	Mintage	F	VF	XF	Unc	BU
1982(h) R; B	24,671,000	—	—	0.20	0.50	—
1983(h) R; B	32,706,000	—	—	0.20	0.50	—
1984(h) R; B	22,882,000	—	—	0.20	0.50	—
1985(h) R; B	29,048,000	—	—	0.20	0.50	—
1986(h) R; B	53,496,000	—	—	0.20	0.50	—
1987(h) R; B	30,575,000	—	—	0.20	0.50	—
1988(h) R; B	23,370,000	—	—	0.20	0.50	—

KM# 868.1 25 ORE

2.8000 g., Bronze, 17.5 mm. **Ruler:** Margrethe II **Obv:** Large crown divides date above, initial to right of country **Rev:** Denomination, small heart above, mint mark and initials LG-

JP below **Note:** Beginning in 1996 and ending with 1998, the words "DANMARK" and "ØRE" have raised edges. Heart mint mark under "ØRE"; Prev. KM#868.

Date	Mintage	F	VF	XF	Unc	BU
1990 LG; JP; A	109,084,000	—	—	—	0.40	—
1991 LG; JP; A	102,162,000	—	—	—	0.40	—
1992 LG; JP; A	6,293,000	—	—	—	1.25	—
1993 LG; JP; A	14,756,000	—	—	—	0.40	—
1994 LG; JP; A	35,750,000	—	—	—	0.40	—
1995 LG; JP; A	40,000,000	—	—	—	0.40	—
1996 LG; JP; A	46,760,000	—	—	—	0.15	—
1997 LG; JP; A	30,306,000	—	—	—	0.15	—
1998 LG; JP; A	17,200,000	—	—	—	0.15	—
1999 LG; JP; A	18,748,000	—	—	—	0.15	—
2000 LG; JP; A	14,500,000	—	—	—	0.15	—

KM# 866.1 50 ORE

4.3000 g., Bronze, 21.5 mm. **Ruler:** Margrethe II **Obv:** Date above large crown, country name below, initial A to right **Rev:** Large heart above value, mint mark and initials NR-JP below **Note:** Heart mint mark under the word "Øre".

Date	Mintage	F	VF	XF	Unc	BU
1989 NR; JP; A	92,236,000	—	—	—	0.50	—

KM# 866.2 50 ORE

4.3000 g., Bronze, 21.5 mm. **Ruler:** Margrethe II **Obv:** Large crown divides date above, initial to right of country name **Rev:** Large heart above value, mint mark and initials LG-JP below **Note:** Beginning in 1996 and ending with 1998, the words "DANMARK" and "ØRE" have raised edges. Heart mint mark under the word "ØRE".

Date	Mintage	F	VF	XF	Unc	BU
1990 LG; JP; A	63,518,000	—	—	—	0.50	—
1991 LG; JP; A	11,115,000	—	—	—	0.50	—
1992 LG; JP; A	14,397,000	—	—	—	0.50	—
1993 LG; JP; A	14,328,000	—	—	—	0.50	—
1994 LG; JP; A	25,055,000	—	—	—	0.35	—
1995 LG; JP; A	15,988,000	—	—	—	0.35	—
1996 LG; JP; A	11,536,000	—	—	—	0.35	—
1997 LG; JP; A	15,574,000	—	—	—	0.25	—
1998 LG; JP; A	13,120,000	—	—	—	0.25	—
1999 LG; JP; A	14,186,000	—	—	—	0.25	—
2000 LG; JP; A	15,500,000	—	—	—	0.25	—

KM# 831.1 1/2 KRONE

3.0000 g., Aluminum-Bronze **Ruler:** Christian X **Obv:** Crowned CXC monogram, date, mint mark, and initials HCN-GJ **Rev:** Value above, country name below large crown

Date	Mintage	F	VF	XF	Unc	BU
1924(h) HCN; GJ	2,150,000	4.00	9.00	17.50	72.50	—
1925(h) HCN; GJ	3,432,000	4.00	9.00	20.00	80.00	—
1926(h) HCN; GJ	716,000	11.50	25.00	40.00	95.00	—

KM# 831.2 1/2 KRONE

3.0000 g., Aluminum-Bronze **Ruler:** Christian X **Obv:** Crowned CXC monogram, date, mint mark, and initial N-GJ **Rev:** Value above, country name below large crown

Date	Mintage	F	VF	XF	Unc	BU
1939(h) N; GJ	226,000	70.00	100	130	200	—
1940(h) N; GJ	1,871,000	4.50	8.50	12.50	22.50	—

KM# 819 KRONE

7.5000 g., 0.8000 Silver 0.1929 oz. ASW **Ruler:** Christian X **Obv:** Head of Christian X, right, with titles, date, mint mark and initials AH at neck, and VBP at date **Rev:** Crowned royal arms with porpoise to left, barley stalk to right, value below

Date	Mintage	F	VF	XF	Unc	BU
1915(h) VBP; AH	1,410,000	10.00	20.00	30.00	50.00	—
1916(h) VBP; AH	992,000	12.50	22.50	35.00	60.00	—

KM# 824.1 KRONE
6.5000 g., Aluminum-Bronze, 25.5 mm. **Ruler:** Christian X **Obv:** Crowned CXC monogram, date, mint mark, and initials HCN-GJ **Rev:** Denomination above large crown, country name below

Date	Mintage	F	VF	XF	Unc	BU
1924(h) HCN; GJ	999,000	200	700	1,500	3,000	—
1925(h) HCN; GJ	6,314,000	2.50	10.00	45.00	120	—
1926(h) HCN; GJ	2,706,000	2.50	10.00	50.00	135	—

KM# 824.2 KRONE
6.5000 g., Aluminum-Bronze, 25.5 mm. **Ruler:** Christian X **Obv:** Crowned CXC monogram, date, mint mark, and initials N-GJ **Rev:** Denomination above large crown, country name below

Date	Mintage	F	VF	XF	Unc	BU
1929(h) N; GJ	501,000	8.00	15.00	85.00	210	—
1930(h) N; GJ	540,000	22.50	42.50	115	340	—
1931(h) N; GJ	540,000	9.00	20.00	60.00	190	—
1934(h) N; GJ	529,000	6.50	11.50	40.00	150	265
1935(h) N; GJ	505,000	35.00	50.00	110	250	—
1936(h) N; GJ	558,000	10.00	20.00	60.00	185	—
1938(h) N; GJ	407,000	17.50	27.50	55.00	170	270
1939(h) N; GJ	1,517,000	2.75	4.50	10.00	50.00	—
1940(h) N; GJ	1,496,000	2.75	5.00	90.00	55.00	—
1941(h) N; GJ	661,000	10.00	20.00	70.00	275	—

KM# 835 KRONE
6.5000 g., Aluminum-Bronze, 25.5 mm. **Ruler:** Christian X **Obv:** Head right, with titles, mint mark, initials N-S **Rev:** Value divided by stalk of wheat and oats crossed, date

Date	Mintage	F	VF	XF	Unc	BU
1942(h) N; S	3,952,000	2.00	3.25	10.00	55.00	—
1943(h) N; S	798,000	12.50	32.50	100	350	—
1944(h) N; S	1,760,000	2.00	4.00	17.50	72.50	—
1945(h) N; S	2,581,000	2.00	3.00	8.00	55.00	—
1946(h) N; S	4,321,000	2.00	3.00	5.00	32.50	—
1947(h) N; S	5,060,000	2.00	2.50	3.00	12.50	—

KM# 837.1 KRONE
6.5000 g., Aluminum-Bronze, 25.5 mm. **Ruler:** Frederik IX **Obv:** Head right, titles, mint mark, initials N-S **Rev:** Crowned royal arms divide date, value above

Date	Mintage	F	VF	XF	Unc	BU
1947(h) N; S	Inc. above	3.00	6.00	11.50	30.00	—
1948(h) N; S	4,248,000	2.00	3.00	6.50	14.00	—
1949(h) N; S	1,300,000	4.25	8.50	18.00	45.00	—
1952(h) N; S	2,124,000	3.00	5.00	10.00	24.00	—
1953(h) N; S	573,000	4.25	7.00	13.00	26.00	—
1954(h) N; S	584,000	14.00	22.50	45.00	75.00	140
1955(h) N; S	1,359,000	5.50	8.75	13.00	25.00	—

KM# 837.2 KRONE
6.5000 g., Aluminum-Bronze, 25.5 mm. **Ruler:** Frederik IX **Obv:** Head right, titles, mint mark, initials C-S **Rev:** Crowned royal arms divide date, value above

Date	Mintage	F	VF	XF	Unc	BU
1956(h) C; S	2,858,000	1.75	2.75	4.00	8.00	—
1957(h) C; S	10,896,000	0.60	1.00	1.50	4.00	—
1958(h) C; S	1,507,000	1.00	1.75	2.25	4.25	—
1959(h) C; S	243,000	15.00	25.00	30.00	42.50	—
1960(h) C; S	100	—	—	3,000	3,750	—

Note: 1960 dated coins were not released into circulation, however, approximately 50 pieces did eventually make their way into the collector's market in 1969.

KM# 851.1 KRONE
6.8000 g., Copper-Nickel, 25.5 mm. **Ruler:** Frederik IX **Obv:** Older head right, titles, mint mark, initials C-S **Rev:** Crowned and quartered royal arms divide date, value above

Date	Mintage	F	VF	XF	Unc	BU
1960(h) C; S	1,000,000	1.00	1.50	2.75	9.00	—
1961(h) C; S	10,348,000	—	0.50	1.75	14.00	—
1962(h) C; S	27,068,000	—	0.50	1.75	12.00	—
1963(h) C; S	32,083,000	—	0.50	1.50	6.50	—
1964(h) C; S	5,984,000	—	0.50	1.50	6.50	—
1965(h) C; S	13,799,000	—	0.50	1.25	7.00	—
1966(h) C; S	10,890,000	—	0.50	1.25	5.00	—
1967(h) C; S	18,304,000	—	0.50	1.25	5.00	—
1968(h) C; S	8,212,999	—	0.50	1.00	3.75	—
1969(h) C; S	9,597,000	—	0.50	1.00	2.00	—
1970(h) C; S	9,460,000	—	—	0.50	2.00	—
1971(h) C; S	13,985,000	—	—	0.50	2.00	—

KM# 851.2 KRONE
6.8000 g., Copper-Nickel, 25.5 mm. **Ruler:** Frederik IX **Obv:** Older head right, titles, mint mark, initials S-S **Rev:** Crowned royal arms divide date, value above

Date	Mintage	F	VF	XF	Unc	BU
1972(h) S; S	21,019,000	—	—	0.40	1.25	—

KM# 862.1 KRONE
6.8000 g., Copper-Nickel, 25.5 mm. **Ruler:** Margrethe II **Obv:** Head right, with titles, mint mark, initials S-B **Rev:** Crowned and quartered royal arms divide date, value below

Date	Mintage	F	VF	XF	Unc	BU
1973(h) S; B	18,268,000	—	—	0.40	1.00	—
Note: Narrow rim (0.7mm)						
1973(h) S; B	Inc. above	—	—	0.40	1.00	—
Note: Wide rim (1.1mm)						
1974(h) S; B	17,742,000	—	—	0.40	0.80	—
1975(h) S; B	20,136,000	—	—	0.40	0.80	—
1976(h) S; B	28,049,000	—	—	0.40	0.80	—
1977(h) S; B	25,685,000	—	—	0.40	0.80	—
1978(h) S; B	11,286,000	—	—	0.40	0.80	—

KM# 862.2 KRONE
6.8000 g., Copper-Nickel, 25.5 mm. **Ruler:** Margrethe II **Obv:** Head right, with titles, mint mark, initials S-B **Rev:** Crowned and quartered royal arms divide date, value below

Date	Mintage	F	VF	XF	Unc	BU
1979(h) B; B	25,216,000	—	—	0.35	0.80	—
1980(h) B; B	25,825,000	—	—	0.35	0.80	—
1981(h) B; B	8,889,000	—	—	0.35	0.80	—

KM# 862.3 KRONE
6.8000 g., Copper-Nickel, 25.5 mm. **Ruler:** Margrethe II **Obv:** Head right with titles, mint mark, initials R; B **Rev:** Crowned and quartered royal arms divide date, value below

Date	Mintage	F	VF	XF	Unc	BU
1982(h) R; B	5,011,000	—	—	0.35	0.80	—
1983(h) R; B	13,946,000	—	—	0.35	0.80	—
1984(h) R; B	36,439,000	—	—	0.35	0.70	—
1985(h) R; B	10,843,000	—	—	0.35	0.70	—
1986(h) R; B	12,556,000	—	—	0.35	0.70	—
1987(h) R; B	20,120,000	—	—	0.35	0.70	—
1988(h) R; B	32,073,999	—	—	0.35	0.70	—
1989(h) R; B	15,704,000	—	—	0.35	0.70	—

KM# 873.1 KRONE
3.6000 g., Copper-Nickel, 20.25 mm. **Ruler:** Margrethe II **Obv:** Wave design surrounds center hole, value above, hearts flank **Rev:** 3 crowned MII monograms around center hole, date, mint mark, and initials LG-JP-A below **Note:** Prev. KM#873.

Date	Mintage	F	VF	XF	Unc	BU
1992 LG; JP; A	81,621,000	—	—	—	0.60	—
1993 LG; JP; A	15,844,000	—	—	—	0.60	—
1994 LG; JP; A	23,658,000	—	—	—	0.60	—
1995 LG; JP; A	34,966,000	—	—	—	0.60	—
1996 LG; JP; A	10,081,000	—	—	—	0.60	—
1997 LG; JP; A	10,121,807	—	—	—	0.60	—
1998 LG; JP; A	13,100,000	—	—	—	0.60	—
1999 LG; JP; A	6,479,000	—	—	—	0.60	—
2000 LG; JP; A	21,500,000	—	—	—	0.60	—

KM# 802 2 KRONER
15.0000 g., 0.8000 Silver 0.3858 oz. ASW, 31 mm. **Ruler:** Christian IX **Subject:** 40th Anniversary of Reign **Obv:** Armored bust right, with titles and anniversary dates, date and "P" below bust **Rev:** Seated woman holding royal shield; flying dove to the left; Motto: "With God for honor and justice"; value in exergue

Date	Mintage	F	VF	XF	Unc	BU
1903(h) P; GJ	103,392	15.00	27.50	65.00	110	180

KM# 803 2 KRONER
15.0000 g., 0.8000 Silver 0.3858 oz. ASW, 31 mm. **Ruler:** Frederik VIII **Subject:** Death of Christian IX and Accession of Frederik VIII **Obv:** Armored bust left with titles, motto, date, initials VBP **Rev:** Bust left with titles, date of death, value, initials GJ

Date	Mintage	F	VF	XF	Unc	BU
1906(h) VBP GJ	151,000	6.00	9.00	30.00	55.00	110

KM# 811 2 KRONER
15.0000 g., 0.8000 Silver 0.3858 oz. ASW, 31 mm. **Ruler:** Christian X **Subject:** Death of Frederik VIII and Accession of Christian X **Obv:** Head right with initials AH at neck, date, mint mark and initials VBP below **Rev:** Head right with initials AH, value below, date of death **Note:** Coin rotation.

Date	Mintage	F	VF	XF	Unc	BU
1912(h) VBP; AH	101,917	15.00	30.00	60.00	100	165

KM# 820 2 KRONER
15.0000 g., 0.8000 Silver 0.3858 oz. ASW, 31 mm.
Ruler: Christian X **Obv:** Head right with initials AH at neck, date, mint mark and initial VBP below **Rev:** Crowned royal arms, porpoise and barley stalk flanking, value below

Date	Mintage	F	VF	XF	Unc	BU
1915(h) VBP; AH	657,000	22.50	40.00	70.00	175	—
1916(h) VBP; AH	402,000	18.00	30.00	45.00	160	—

KM# 821 2 KRONER
15.0000 g., 0.8000 Silver 0.3858 oz. ASW, 31 mm.
Ruler: Christian X **Subject:** Silver Wedding Anniversary
Obv: Heads of Christian X and Queen Alexandrine right, initials GJ **Rev:** Crowned arms within anniversary dates, initials HCN, denomination below

Date	Mintage	F	VF	XF	Unc	BU
1923(h) HCN; GJ	203,357	—	15.00	25.00	40.00	90.00

KM# 825.1 2 KRONER
13.0000 g., Aluminum-Bronze, 31 mm. **Ruler:** Christian X
Obv: Crowned CXC monogram, date, mint mark and initials HCN-GJ **Rev:** Denomination above large crown, country name below

Date	Mintage	F	VF	XF	Unc	BU
1924(h) HCN; GJ	1,138,000	40.00	300	900	2,600	—
1925(h) HCN; GJ	3,248,000	2.50	15.00	50.00	135	—
1926(h) HCN; GJ	1,126,000	2.50	15.00	50.00	185	—

KM# 825.2 2 KRONER
13.0000 g., Aluminum-Bronze, 31 mm. **Ruler:** Christian X
Obv: Crowned CXC monogram, date, mint mark, and initials N-GJ **Rev:** Denomination above large crown, country name below

Date	Mintage	F	VF	XF	Unc	BU
1936(h) N; GJ	400,000	7.00	17.00	75.00	400	—
1938(h) N; GJ	191,000	17.50	27.50	105	325	—
1939(h) N; GJ	723,000	2.00	3.75	10.00	50.00	—
1940(h) N; GJ	743,000	7.00	12.00	25.00	75.00	—
1941(h) N; GJ	129,000	40.00	75.00	275	600	—

KM# 829 2 KRONER
15.0000 g., 0.8000 Silver 0.3858 oz. ASW, 31 mm.
Ruler: Christian X **Subject:** King's 60th Birthday **Obv:** Head right, date, mint mark, initials AH at neck, N below **Rev:** Draped and supported national arms, value below, initials HS, two dates at top

Date	Mintage	F	VF	XF	Unc	BU
1930(h) N; AH/HS	302,640	—	—	10.00	17.50	35.00

KM# 830 2 KRONER
15.0000 g., 0.8000 Silver 0.3858 oz. ASW, 31 mm.
Ruler: Christian X **Subject:** 25th Anniversary of Reign
Obv: Head right, mint mark and initials N-S below **Rev:** Crowned royal arms, value below

Date	Mintage	F	VF	XF	Unc	BU
ND(1937)(h) N; S	208,699	—	8.50	12.00	18.00	40.00

KM# 836 2 KRONER
15.0000 g., 0.8000 Silver 0.3858 oz. ASW, 31 mm. **Ruler:** Christian X **Subject:** King's 75th Birthday **Obv:** Head right, mint mark and initials N-S below **Rev:** Dates of birth and 75th birthday year within wreath, legend around, denomination below **Rev. Leg.:** "IN ONE WITH HIS PEOPLE IN SORROW AND VICTORY"

Date	Mintage	F	VF	XF	Unc	BU
ND(1945)(h) N; S	156,642	—	12.00	18.00	35.00	70.00

KM# 838.1 2 KRONER
13.0000 g., Aluminum-Bronze, 31.4 mm. **Ruler:** Frederik IX
Obv: Head right, mint mark and initials N-S below **Rev:** Crowned royal arms divide date, value above

Date	Mintage	F	VF	XF	Unc	BU
1947(h) N; S	1,151,000	2.25	4.50	12.50	40.00	—
1948(h) N; S	857,000	1.75	3.00	8.00	32.50	—
1949(h) N; S	272,000	4.50	9.50	30.00	85.00	—
1951(h) N; S	1,576,000	1.35	2.25	4.50	22.50	—
1952(h) N; S	1,958,000	1.00	2.00	5.00	20.00	—
1953(h) N; S	432,000	2.25	4.50	12.50	45.00	—
1954(h) N; S	716,000	2.25	4.00	9.50	37.50	—
1955(h) N; S	457,000	3.75	6.50	11.00	37.50	—

KM# 838.2 2 KRONER
13.0000 g., Aluminum-Bronze, 31.4 mm. **Ruler:** Frederik IX
Obv: Head right, mint mark and initials C-S below **Rev:** Crowned royal arms divide date, value above

Date	Mintage	F	VF	XF	Unc	BU
1956(h) C; S	1,444,000	2.00	3.25	5.50	11.50	—
1957(h) C; S	2,610,000	1.50	2.25	3.50	7.00	—
1958(h) C; S	2,605,000	1.50	2.25	3.25	8.00	—
1959(h) C; S	192,000	17.50	25.00	35.00	55.00	—

KM# 844 2 KRONER
15.0000 g., 0.8000 Silver 0.3858 oz. ASW, 31 mm.
Ruler: Frederik IX **Subject:** Foundation for the Campaign against Tuberculosis in Greenland **Obv:** Conjoined heads right, date, mint mark and initials N-S below **Rev:** Map of Greenland, country name in Greenlandic language, denomination below **Note:** Greenland Commemorative.

Date	Mintage	F	VF	XF	Unc	BU
1953(h) N; S	151,710	—	10.00	30.00	70.00	150

KM# 845 2 KRONER
15.0000 g., 0.8000 Silver 0.3858 oz. ASW, 31 mm.
Ruler: Frederik IX **Subject:** Princess Margrethe's 18th Birthday **Obv:** Head right with titles, mint mark and initials C-S below **Rev:** Head left, date of 18th birthday, value below

Date	Mintage	F	VF	XF	Unc	BU
ND(1958)(h) C; S	301,426	—	8.50	15.00	30.00	45.00

KM# 874.1 2 KRONER
5.9000 g., Copper-Nickel, 24.5 mm. **Ruler:** Margrethe II
Obv: 3 crowned MII monograms around center hole, date and initials LG-JP-A below **Rev:** Design surrounds center hole, denomination above, hearts flank **Note:** Prev. KM#874.

Date	Mintage	F	VF	XF	Unc	BU
1992 LG; JP; A	41,648,000				0.75	—
1993 LG; JP; A	43,864,000				0.75	—
1994 LG; JP; A	27,629,000				0.75	—
1995 LG; JP; A	19,850,000				0.75	—
1996 LG; JP; A	2,884,000				0.75	—
1997 LG; JP; A	25,874,000				0.75	—
1998 LG; JP; A	4,360,000				0.75	—
1999 LG; JP; A	20,608,000				0.60	—
2000 LG; JP; A	10,400,000				0.60	—

KM# 852 5 KRONER
17.0000 g., 0.8000 Silver 0.4372 oz. ASW, 33 mm.
Ruler: Frederik IX **Subject:** Silver Wedding Anniversary
Obv: Conjoined heads right, within titles **Rev:** Crowned double FI monogram, silver anniversary dates above, 2 barley stalks, value, mint mark and initials C-S below

Date	Mintage	F	VF	XF	Unc	BU
ND(1960)(h) C; S	409,858	—	8.50	12.50	25.00	42.50

KM# 853.1 5 KRONER
15.0000 g., Copper-Nickel, 33 mm. **Ruler:** Frederik IX
Obv: Head right, titles, mint mark and initials C-S **Rev:** Crowned and quartered arms divide date within two oak branches, value above

Date	Mintage	F	VF	XF	Unc	BU
1960(h) C; S	6,418,000	—	2.25	4.00	17.50	—
1961(h) C; S	9,744,000	—	2.25	4.00	22.50	—
1962(h) C; S	2,073,999	—	2.75	4.50	27.50	50.00
1963(h) C; S	709,000	—	2.75	4.50	30.00	45.00
1964(h) C; S	1,443,000	—	2.25	4.00	25.00	40.00
1965(h) C; S	2,574,000	—	2.25	2.50	20.00	35.00
1966(h) C; S	4,370,000	—	2.00	2.25	12.50	—
1967(h) C; S	1,864,000	—	2.00	2.25	9.00	—
1968(h) C; S	4,131,999	—	2.00	2.25	9.00	—
1969(h) C; S	72,000	2.25	4.50	7.50	15.00	—
1970(h) C; S	2,246,000	—	—	2.00	4.00	—
1971(h) C; S	4,767,000	—	—	2.00	3.50	—

KM# 853.2   5 KRONER
15.0000 g., Copper-Nickel, 33 mm. **Ruler:** Frederik IX
Obv: Head right, mint mark and initials S-S **Rev:** Crowned and quartered arms divide date within two oak branches, value above

Date	Mintage	F	VF	XF	Unc	BU
1972(h) S; S	2,599,000	—	—	2.00	3.25	—

KM# 854   5 KRONER
17.0000 g., 0.8000 Silver 0.4372 oz. ASW, 33 mm.
Ruler: Frederik IX **Subject:** Wedding of Princess Anne Marie
Obv: Head right, mint mark and initials C-S **Rev:** Head left within title and wedding date

Date	Mintage	F	VF	XF	Unc	BU
1964(h) C; S	359,473	—	8.50	15.00	22.50	37.50

KM# 863.1   5 KRONER
15.0000 g., Copper-Nickel, 33 mm. **Ruler:** Margrethe II
Obv: Head right, mint mark and initial S-B below **Rev:** Crowned and quartered royal arms divide date and oak leaves, value below

Date	Mintage	F	VF	XF	Unc	BU
1973(h) S; B	3,774,000	—	—	2.00	4.00	—
Note: Narrow rim (1.0mm)						
1973(h) S; B	Inc. above	—	—	2.00	4.00	—
Note: Wide rim (1.5mm)						
1974(h) S; B	5,239,000	—	—	2.00	4.00	—
1975(h) S; B	5,810,000	—	—	3.50	8.00	—
1976(h) S; B	7,651,000	—	—	2.00	5.00	—
1977(h) S; B	6,885,000	—	—	2.00	5.00	—
1978(h) S; B	2,984,000	—	—	2.00	5.00	—

KM# 863.2   5 KRONER
15.0000 g., Copper-Nickel, 33 mm. **Ruler:** Margrethe II
Obv: Head right, mint mark and initials B-B below **Rev:** Crowned and quartered royal arms divide date and oak leaves, value below

Date	Mintage	F	VF	XF	Unc	BU
1979(h) B; B	2,861,000	—	—	2.00	4.00	—
1980(h) B; B	3,622,000	—	—	2.50	6.50	—
1981(h) B; B	1,057,000	—	—	2.00	4.00	—

KM# 863.3   5 KRONER
15.0000 g., Copper-Nickel, 33 mm. **Ruler:** Margrethe II
Obv: Head right, mint mark and initials R-B below **Rev:** Crowned and quartered royal arms divide date and oak leaves, value below

Date	Mintage	F	VF	XF	Unc	BU
1982(h) R; B	1,002,000	—	—	2.50	6.50	—
1983(h) R; B	1,044,000	—	—	2.00	3.50	—
1984(h) R; B	713,000	—	—	2.00	4.00	—
1985(h) R; B	621,000	—	—	2.00	4.00	—
1986(h) R; B	1,042,000	—	—	2.00	3.50	—
1987(h) R; B	611,000	—	—	2.00	3.50	—
1988(h) R; B	648,000	—	—	2.00	3.50	—

KM# 869.1   5 KRONER
9.2000 g., Copper-Nickel, 28.5 mm. **Ruler:** Margrethe II **Obv:** 3 crowned MII monograms around center hole, date and initials LG-JP-A below **Rev:** Wave design surrounds center hole, denomination above, hearts flank **Note:** Large and small date varieties exist.

Date	Mintage	F	VF	XF	Unc	BU
1990 LG; JP; A	46,745,000	—	—	—	2.25	—
1991 LG; JP; A	3,752,000	—	—	—	2.25	—
1992 LG; JP; A	2,426,000	—	—	—	2.25	—
1993 LG; JP; A	1,538,000	—	—	—	2.25	—
1994 LG; JP; A	7,920,000	—	—	—	2.25	—
1995 LG; JP; A	5,850,000	—	—	—	2.25	—
1997 LG; JP; A	5,258,000	—	—	—	2.00	—
1998 LG; JP; A	6,450,000	—	—	—	2.00	—
1999 LG; JP; A	4,786,000	—	—	—	2.00	—
2000 LG; JP; A	2,800,000	—	—	—	2.00	—

KM# 809   10 KRONER
4.4803 g., 0.9000 Gold 0.1296 oz. AGW **Ruler:** Frederik VIII **Obv:** Head left with titles **Rev:** Draped crowned national arms above date, value, mint mark and initials VBP

Date	Mintage	F	VF	XF	Unc	BU
1908(h) VBP; GJ	308,000	—	160	225	300	—
1909(h) VBP; GJ	153,000	—	165	235	320	—

KM# 816   10 KRONER
4.4803 g., 0.9000 Gold 0.1296 oz. AGW **Ruler:** Christian X **Obv:** Head right with title, date, mint mark, initials VBP. Initials AH at neck **Rev:** Draped crowned national arms above date, value, mint mark and initials VBP

Date	Mintage	F	VF	XF	Unc	BU
1913(h) AH/ GJ	312,000	—	160	225	300	—
1917(h) AH/ GJ	132,000	—	160	225	300	—

KM# 856   10 KRONER
20.4000 g., 0.8000 Silver 0.5247 oz. ASW **Ruler:** Frederik IX **Subject:** Wedding of Princess Margrethe **Obv:** Head right with titles, mint mark, initials C-S **Rev:** Heads of Prince and Princess right, value below

Date	Mintage	F	VF	XF	Unc	BU
ND(1967)(h) C; S	419,542	—	12.50	20.00	30.00	55.00
Note: 78,383 pieces were melted.						

KM# 857   10 KRONER
20.4000 g., 0.8000 Silver 0.5247 oz. ASW **Ruler:** Frederik IX **Subject:** Wedding of Princess Benedikte **Obv:** Head right, mint mark and initials C-S below **Rev:** Head left, value below

Date	Mintage	F	VF	XF	Unc	BU
ND(1968)(h) C; S	253,837	—	14.00	22.50	32.50	60.00
Note: 42,923 were melted.						

KM# 858   10 KRONER
20.4000 g., 0.8000 Silver 0.5247 oz. ASW **Ruler:** Margrethe II **Subject:** Death of Frederik IX and Accession of Margrethe II **Obv:** Head right, motto, titles, mint mark and initials S-B **Rev:** Head right with titles, date of death, value below

Date	Mintage	F	VF	XF	Unc	BU
1972(h) S; S	402,000	—	9.00	12.00	17.50	25.00

KM# 864.1   10 KRONER
12.5000 g., Copper-Nickel, 28 mm. **Ruler:** Margrethe II **Obv:** Head right with tiara, mint mark and initials B-B below **Rev:** Large 10 on horizontal grid, two rye stalks flanking, date above

Date	Mintage	F	VF	XF	Unc	BU
1979(h) B; B	76,801,000	—	—	2.00	5.00	—
1981(h) B; B	10,520,000	—	2.50	5.00	13.00	—

KM# 864.2   10 KRONER
12.5000 g., Copper-Nickel, 28 mm. **Ruler:** Margrethe II **Obv:** Head right with tiara, mint mark and initials R-B below **Rev:** Large 10 on horizontal grid, two rye stalks flanking, date above

Date	Mintage	F	VF	XF	Unc	BU
1982(h) R; B	1,065,000	—	2.50	5.00	13.50	—
1983(h) R; B	1,123,000	—	2.50	5.00	13.50	—
1984(h) R; B	748,000	—	3.00	6.00	16.00	22.50
1985(h) R; B	720,000	—	3.00	6.00	16.00	22.50
1987(h) R; B	719,000	—	2.50	4.75	13.50	20.00
1988(h) R; B	718,000	—	2.25	4.50	12.50	—

KM# 865   10 KRONER
12.5000 g., Copper-Nickel, 28 mm. **Ruler:** Margrethe II **Subject:** Crown Prince's 18th Birthday **Obv:** Head of Margrethe II with tiara right, mint mark and initials R-A below **Rev:** Head of crown prince Frederik left, date of 18th birthday, value below **Edge:** Plain

Date	Mintage	F	VF	XF	Unc	BU
ND(1986)(h) R; A	1,090,351	—	—	5.00	10.00	—
ND(1986)(h) R; A Proof	2,000	Value: 180				
Note: In folder						

KM# 865a   10 KRONER
14.3000 g., 0.8000 Silver 0.3678 oz. ASW, 28 mm.
Ruler: Margrethe II **Obv:** Head with tiara right, mint mark and initials R-A below **Rev:** Head of Crown Prince Frederik left, date of 18th birthday, value below

Date	Mintage	F	VF	XF	Unc	BU
1986(h) R; A Proof	24,000	Value: 140				

KM# 867.1   10 KRONER
7.0000 g., Aluminum-Bronze, 23.35 mm. **Ruler:** Margrethe II **Obv:** Head with tiara right, titles, date, initials NR-JP-A **Rev:** Crowned arms within ornaments, value below **Edge:** Plain

Date	Mintage	F	VF	XF	Unc	BU
1989 NR; JP; A	38,346,000	—	—	—	4.00	—

KM# 867.2 10 KRONER
7.0000 g., Aluminum-Bronze, 23.35 mm. **Ruler:** Margrethe II
Obv: Head with tiara right, titles, date, initials LG-JP-A **R**
ev: Crowned arms within ornaments, value below **Edge:** Plain

Date	Mintage	F	VF	XF	Unc	BU
1990 LG; JP; A	12,193,000	—	—	—	4.00	—
1991 LG; JP; A	1,065,000	—	—	—	6.00	—
1992 LG; JP; A	484,000	—	—	4.00	9.00	—
1993 LG; JP; A	1,069,000	—	—	—	3.00	7.00

KM# 877 10 KRONER
7.0000 g., Aluminum-Bronze, 23.35 mm. **Ruler:** Margrethe II
Obv: New portrait right, date below **Rev:** Crowned arms within
ornaments, value below **Edge:** Plain **Note:** Beginning with strikes
in 1995 and ending in 1998, letters and numbers on reverse have
raised edges.

Date	Mintage	F	VF	XF	Unc	BU
1994 LG; JP; A	4,058,000	—	—	—	5.00	—
1995 LG; JP; A	9,461,000	—	—	—	5.00	—
1997 LG; JP; A	3,725,000	—	—	—	5.00	—
1998 LG; JP; A	6,000,000	—	—	—	4.25	—
1999 LG; JP; A	4,034,749	—	—	—	4.25	—

KM# 810 20 KRONER
8.9606 g., 0.9000 Gold 0.2593 oz. AGW **Ruler:** Frederik VIII
Obv: Head left, with titles **Rev:** Crowned and mantled arms above
date, value, mint mark and initials VBP

Date	Mintage	F	VF	XF	Unc	BU
1908(h) VBP; GJ	243,000	—	290	365	500	—
1909(h) VBP; GJ	365,000	—	300	375	520	—
1910(h) VBP; GJ	200,000	—	310	380	540	—
1911(h) VBP; GJ	183,000	—	300	375	510	—
1912(h) VBP; GJ	184,000	—	300	375	510	—

KM# 817.1 20 KRONER
8.9606 g., 0.9000 Gold 0.2593 oz. AGW **Ruler:** Christian X
Obv: Head right with title, date, mint mark, initials VBP, initials
AH at neck **Rev:** Crowned and mantled arms above date, value,
mint mark and initials VBP

Date	Mintage	F	VF	XF	Unc	BU
1913(h) AH/GJ	815,000	—	300	365	500	—
1914(h) AH/GJ	920,000	—	300	365	500	—
1915(h) AH/GJ	532,000	—	300	370	510	—
1916(h) AH/GJ	1,401,000	—	300	370	510	—
1917(h) AH/GJ	Inc. above	—	300	370	510	—

KM# 817.2 20 KRONER
8.9606 g., 0.9000 Gold 0.2593 oz. AGW **Ruler:** Christian X
Obv: Head right with title, date, mint mark, and initials HCN,
initials AH at neck **Rev:** Crowned and mantled arms above date,
value, mint mark, and initials HCN **Note:** 1926-1927 dated 20
Kroners were not released for circulation.

Date	Mintage	F	VF	XF	Unc	BU
1926(h) HCN	358,000	—	—	4,500	9,000	—
1927(h) HCN	Inc. above	—	—	4,500	9,000	—

KM# 817.3 20 KRONER
8.9606 g., 0.9000 Gold 0.2593 oz. AGW **Ruler:** Christian X
Obv: Head right with title, date, mint mark, and initials HCN.
Initials AH at neck **Rev:** Crowned and mantled arms above date,
value, mint mark and initials HCN **Note:** The 1930-1931 dated
20 Kroners were not released for circulation.

Date	Mintage	F	VF	XF	Unc	BU
1930(h) N	1,285,000	—	—	4,500	9,000	—
1931(h) N	Inc. above	—	—	4,500	9,000	—

KM# 870 20 KRONER
9.3000 g., Aluminum-Bronze, 27 mm. **Ruler:** Margrethe II
Subject: 50th Birthday of Queen Margrethe **Obv:** Head with hat
right, mint mark after 2 in legend, initials LG left of shoulder
Rev: Large crown above daisy flower divides dates, value below
Edge: Alternate reeded and plain sections

Date	Mintage	F	VF	XF	Unc	BU
ND(1990)(h) LG	1,101,000	—	—	—	6.00	—

KM# 871 20 KRONER
9.3000 g., Aluminum-Bronze **Ruler:** Margrethe II **Obv:** Head
with tiara right, titles, date, initials LG-JP-A, mint mark after II in
legend **Rev:** Crowned arms within ornaments and value
Edge: Alternate reeded and plain sections **Note:** Large and small
date varieties exist.

Date	Mintage	F	VF	XF	Unc	BU
1990(h) LG; JP ; A	34,368,000	—	—	—	8.00	—
1991(h) LG; JP; A	11,563,000	—	—	—	9.00	—
1993(h) LG; JP; A	674,000	—	—	—	10.00	—

KM# 875 20 KRONER
9.3000 g., Aluminum-Bronze **Ruler:** Margrethe II **Subject:**
Silver Wedding Anniversary **Obv:** Heads of Prince Henrik and
Margrethe II facing each other, anniversary dates below
Rev: Fairy tale house, mint mark and initials LG at lower left,
denomination at left **Edge:** Alternate reeded and plain sections

Date	Mintage	F	VF	XF	Unc	BU
ND(1992)(h) LG	994,000	—	—	—	6.00	—

KM# 878 20 KRONER
9.3000 g., Aluminum-Bronze **Ruler:** Margrethe II **Obv:** New
portrait right, date, mint mark and initials LG-JP-A below
Rev: Crowned arms within ornament and value **Edge:** Alternating
reeded and plain sections **Note:** Strikes dated 1996 and 1998
have letters and numbers on reverse with raised edges.

Date	Mintage	F	VF	XF	Unc	BU
1994(h) LG, JP; A	2,565,000	—	—	—	7.00	—
1996(h) LG, JP; A	8,651,000	—	—	—	6.50	—
1998(h) LG, JP; A	4,000,000	—	—	—	6.50	—
1999(h) LG, JP; A	4,133,363	—	—	—	6.50	—

KM# 879 20 KRONER
9.3000 g., Aluminum-Bronze **Ruler:** Margrethe II **Subject:** 1000
Years of Danish Coinage **Obv:** Head with cloche left, inner legend
in runic letters **Rev:** Large crown on cross, mint mark and initials
LG **Edge:** Alternate reeded and plain sections

Date	Mintage	F	VF	XF	Unc	BU
ND(1995)(h) LG; JP; A	1,000,000	—	—	—	6.00	—

KM# 881 20 KRONER
9.3000 g., Aluminum-Bronze **Ruler:** Margrethe II **Subject:**
Wedding of Prince Joachim **Obv:** New portrait right, mint mark after
II in legend, initials LG below at date **Rev:** Schackenborg castle at
center, value below **Edge:** Alternate reeded and plain sections

Date	Mintage	F	VF	XF	Unc	BU
1995(h) LG, JP	1,000,000	—	—	—	6.00	—

Note: Although dated 1995, this coin was minted at the end
of the year and included in a 1996 mint set.

KM# 883 20 KRONER
9.3000 g., Aluminum-Bronze **Ruler:** Margrethe II **Subject:** 25th
Anniversary - Queen's Reign **Obv:** Full-length portrait, mint mark
and initials LG **Rev:** Crowned arms within anniversary date and
value **Edge:** Alternate reeded and plain sections

Date	Mintage	F	VF	XF	Unc	BU
ND(1997)(h) LG; JP	1,000,000	—	—	—	6.00	—

KM# 885 20 KRONER
9.3000 g., Aluminum-Bronze **Ruler:** Margrethe II **Subject:** 60th
Birthday of Queen Margrethe II **Obv:** Bust right **Rev:** Crown
divides dates above daisy flowers, denomination below
Edge: Alternating reeded and plain sections

Date	Mintage	F	VF	XF	Unc	BU
ND(2000)(h) LG	1,000,000	—	—	—	5.75	—

KM# 872 200 KRONER
31.1000 g., 0.8000 Silver 0.7999 oz. ASW, 38 mm.
Ruler: Margrethe II **Subject:** 50th Birthday of Queen Margrethe
Obv: Bust with hat right, mint mark after 2 in legend, initials LG
and Fox mark above shoulder **Rev:** Large crown above daisy
flower divides dates, value below **Edge:** Plain

Date	Mintage	F	VF	XF	Unc	BU
ND(1990)(h) LG	128,855	—	—	—	55.00	—

KM# 876 200 KRONER
31.1000 g., 0.9990 Silver 0.9988 oz. ASW, 38 mm. **Ruler:** Margrethe II **Subject:** Silver Wedding Anniversary **Obv:** Heads of Prince Henrik and Queen Margrethe II facing each other, anniversary dates below **Rev:** Fairy tale house, mint mark and initials LG at lower left, denomination **Edge:** Plain

Date	Mintage	F	VF	XF	Unc	BU
ND(1992)(h) LG	58,750	—	—	—	55.00	—

KM# 880 200 KRONER
31.1000 g., 0.9990 Silver 0.9988 oz. ASW, 38 mm. **Ruler:** Margrethe II **Subject:** 1000 Year of Danish Coinage **Obv:** Head with cloche left, runic lettering within legend **Rev:** Large crown on cross, mint mark at left, initials LG at bottom, denomination at left **Edge:** Plain

Date	Mintage	F	VF	XF	Unc	BU
ND(1995)(h) LG	27,727	—	—	—	80.00	—

KM# 882 200 KRONER
31.1000 g., 0.9990 Silver 0.9988 oz. ASW, 38 mm. **Ruler:** Margrethe II **Subject:** Wedding of Prince Joachim **Obv:** New portrait right, date below **Rev:** Schackenburg Castle, denomination below **Edge:** Plain

Date	Mintage	F	VF	XF	Unc	BU
1995(h) LG	55,100	—	—	—	55.00	—

KM# 884 200 KRONER
31.1000 g., 0.9990 Silver 0.9988 oz. ASW, 38 mm. **Ruler:** Margrethe II **Subject:** 25th Anniversary - Queen's Reign **Obv:** Full-length portrait **Rev:** Quartered arms, denomination below, anniversary date at right **Edge:** Plain

Date	Mintage	F	VF	XF	Unc	BU
ND(1997)(h) LG	62,022	—	—	—	60.00	—

KM# 886 200 KRONER
31.1000 g., 0.9990 Silver 0.9988 oz. ASW, 38 mm. **Ruler:** Margrethe II **Subject:** 60th Birthday of Queen Margrethe II **Obv:** Bust with tiara right **Rev:** Crown above flowers divides dates, denomination below **Edge:** Plain

Date	Mintage	F	VF	XF	Unc	BU
ND(2000)(h) LG	60,000	—	—	—	55.00	—

PATTERNS
Including off metal strikes

KM#	Date	Mintage	Identification	Mkt Val
PnB63	1940	—	25 Ore. Zinc. KM#823.	—
Pn63	1941	—	Ore. Aluminum. KM#832.	3,300
PnA64	1941	—	2 Ore. Zinc. KM#833.	—
PnB64	1941	—	5 Ore. Zinc. KM#834.	—
Pn64	19xxC	—	Krone. Copper-Nickel. KM#837.2.	700

KM#	Date	Mintage	Identification	Mkt Val
Pn65	1947	—	5 Kroner. Nickel. Without denomination.	3,650
Pn66	1948N	—	5 Ore. Zinc. KM#843. Unique.	—
Pn67	1926(h) HCN; GJ	—	5 Ore. Bronze. KM#828.1. Thomas Holland Sale 11-00 $8600. Beware of counterfeits. Another example of the 1926 5 Øre was auctioned at Thomas Høiland Auction 20, lot 1574. The coin was defaced on the obv. which the catalogers see as a proof that the coin is a pattern.	—

PROVAS

KM#	Date	Mintage	Identification	Mkt Val

| Pr3 | 1983 | 6 | 25 Ore. Bronze. Crowned MIIR monogram. Value on circlular grid. I. | 2,900 |

| Pr4 | 1983 | 5 | 25 Ore. Bronze. II. | 3,000 |

| Pr5 | 1983 | 7 | 50 Ore. Bronze. II. | 2,900 |

| Pr6 | 1983 | 6 | 50 Ore. Bronze. II. | 2,900 |
| Pr7 | 1983 | — | 50 Ore. Bronze. Without Roman numeral. | — |

KM#	Date	Mintage	Identification	Mkt Val
Pr8	1983	4	50 Ore. Bronze. 22.5 mm. Wide rim.	—
Pr9	1983	4	Krone. Copper-Nickel. Head of Margrethe II. Crowned arms, date, value. Similar to Pr11.	—
Pr10	1983	4	2 Kroner. Copper-Nickel. Similar to Pr11.	—
PrA111	1983	4	5 Kroner. Copper-Nickel. 27.2 mm.	1,600
PrB111	1983	6	5 Kroner. Copper-Nickel.	1,300

| Pr11 | 1983 | 3 | 5 Kroner. Copper-Nickel. Head right. Crowned and quartered arms divide denomination, date below. | — |
| Pr12 | 1983 | 6 | 10 Kroner. Aluminum-Bronze. Supported national arms, date, value. I. | 2,000 |

| Pr13 | 1983 | 7 | 10 Kroner. Aluminum-Bronze. II. | 1,575 |

| Pr14 | 1983 | 7 | 10 Kroner. Aluminum-Bronze. Head right. Crowned arms with supporters, date and denomination below. III. | 2,400 |

| Pr15 | 1983 | 6 | 10 Kroner. Aluminum-Bronze. III. | 2,400 |
| Pr16 | 1983 | — | 10 Kroner. Aluminum-Bronze. Without Roman numeral. | — |

| Pr17 | 1983 | 7 | 20 Kroner. Aluminum-Bronze. I. | 2,300 |

| Pr18 | 1983 | 7 | 20 Kroner. Aluminum-Bronze. II. | 2,300 |

| Pr19 | 1983 | 7 | 20 Kroner. Aluminum-Bronze. III. | 2,300 |

KM#	Date	Mintage	Identification	Mkt Val
Pr20	1983	6	20 Kroner. Aluminum-Bronze. IIII.	2,650
Pr21	1983	—	20 Kroner. Aluminum-Bronze. Without Roman numeral.	—
Pr23	1983	7	50 Kroner. Aluminum-Bronze. II.	2,100
Pr24	1983	7	50 Kroner. Aluminum-Bronze. III.	2,100
Pr25	1983	6	50 Kroner. Aluminum-Bronze. IIII.	2,400
Pr26	1983	22	50 Kroner. Aluminum-Bronze. Without Roman numeral.	1,475
Pr27	1984	81	25 Ore. Bronze. 17.25 mm. Large crown, date above. Denomination, hearts above and below.	90.00
Pr1	1900	9	10 Kroner. Aluminum-Bronze. Head right, date below. Crowned arms within circle, denomination below. Issued: 1984-1986.	1,200
Pr2	1900	16	20 Kroner. Aluminum-Bronze. Head right, date below. Crowned arms within circle, denomination below. Issued: 1984-1986.	1,000

KM#	Date	Mintage	Identification	Mkt Val
Pr28	1984	81	50 Ore. Bronze. 19.75 mm. Value below heart.	85.00
Pr29	1984	99	Krone. Copper-Nickel. Three crowned MIIR monograms. Ornaments around center hole.	75.00
Pr45	19(84)	23	50 Ore. Bronze. 19.75 mm.	300
Pr30	1984	118	Krone. Copper-Nickel. Large crown above date divided by center hole, MIIR below.	65.00
Pr31	1984	203	Krone. Copper-Nickel. Ornaments surround center hole, hearts flank, denomination above country name below. Center hole divides date, crown above, MIIR below. Reverse of 1988.	40.00
Pr32	1984	—	Krone. Copper-Nickel. Similar to Pr30 but without hole.	550
Pr33	1984	191	2 Kroner. Copper-Nickel. Triple monogram. Ornaments around center hole, value above.	50.00
Pr34	1984	103	2 Kroner. Copper-Nickel. Milled edge.	90.00
Pr35	1984	201	2 Kroner. Copper-Nickel. Interrupted milling 6 or 7 notches.	50.00

KM#	Date	Mintage	Identification	Mkt Val
Pr36	1984	85	5 Kroner. Copper-Nickel. Triple monogram. Ornament around center hole, value.	75.00
Pr37	1984	108	5 Kroner. Copper-Nickel. Milled edge.	90.00
Pr38	1984	202	5 Kroner. Copper-Nickel. Milled edge.	45.00
Pr39	1984	6	5 Kroner. Copper-Nickel. As Pr36 except for added date at top and country name at bottom. Large 5 above ornament and denomination.	2,000
Pr40	1984	85	10 Kroner. Aluminum-Bronze. Crowned arms, ornament, value.	100
PrA41	1984	4	10 Kroner. Aluminum-Bronze. Without "Prove".	—
PrB41	1984	3	10 Kroner. Aluminum-Bronze. Different ornaments and value style. Without "Prove".	—
Pr41	1984	112	20 Kroner. Aluminum-Bronze. Head right, date below. Crowned arms within circle, denomination below.	85.00
Pr42	1984	4	20 Kroner. Aluminum-Bronze. Without "PROVE".	—
PrA43	1984	51	20 Kroner. Aluminum-Bronze. Without "Prove".	165

KM#	Date	Mintage	Identification	Mkt Val
Pr43	1986	183	25 Ore. Bronze. 17.5 mm.	65.00
Pr44	1986	210	25 Ore. Bronze. 18 mm.	55.00
Pr46	1986	181	50 Ore. Bronze. 21 mm.	75.00
Pr47	19(86)	1	Krone. Copper-Nickel. Crowned MIIR monogram, date. Ornaments around center hole, value, country name. Crown lacks lower rim.	500
Pr48	19(86)	1	Krone. Copper-Nickel. Center hole within crowned monogram. Full crown (miscolored).	600
Pr49	198(6)	6	Krone. Copper-Nickel. Three digits in date.	1,400
Pr50	198(6)	9	Krone. Copper-Nickel. Without hole.	850
Pr51	1986	183	Krone. Copper-Nickel. Full date.	45.00
PrA521	1986	2	Krone. Copper-Nickel. Without hole.	—
Pr52a	1986	91	2 Kroner. Copper-Nickel. Two crowned MIIR monograms, date. Ornaments around center hole, value, country name. With hole interrupted milling 7x5 grooves.	100
Pr52b	1986	196	2 Kroner. Copper-Nickel. Without hole, interrupted milling, 6x6 grooves.	25.00
Pr52c	1986	196	2 Kroner. Copper-Nickel. Without hole, interrupted milling, 8x7 grooves, widely spaced notches.	30.00
Pr52d	1986	196	2 Kroner. Copper-Nickel. Without hole, interrupted milling, 8x9 grooves.	30.00
Pr52e	1986	196	2 Kroner. Copper-Nickel. Without hole, interrupted milling, 8x8 grooves, no notches.	30.00
Pr52f	1986	196	2 Kroner. Copper-Nickel. Without hole, interrupted milling, 8x8 grooves, with notches.	30.00
Pr52g	1986	196	2 Kroner. Copper-Nickel. Without hole, interrupted milling, 6x7 grooves.	30.00
Pr52h	1986	196	2 Kroner. Copper-Nickel. Interrupted milling, 8x7 grooves, narrowly spaced notches.	30.00
Pr53	1986	2	2 Kroner. Copper-Nickel. Three crowned MIIR monograms, date. Ornaments around center hole, denomination. Without hole.	—
Pr54	1986	190	2 Kroner. Copper-Nickel. With hole.	30.00
Pr55	1986	102	5 Kroner. Copper-Nickel. Three crowned MIIr monograms, mint mark, date. Ornaments with value and country name.	140
Pr56	1986	212	5 Kroner. Copper-Nickel. Turned 120 degrees.	30.00
Pr57	1986	5	5 Kroner. Copper-Nickel. Without hole.	2,100
Pr58	1986	302	10 Kroner. Aluminum-Bronze. 23 mm. Head of Margrethe II. Crowned arms, ornaments, value.	80.00
Pr59a	1986	198	20 Kroner. Aluminum-Bronze. Interrupted milling, 12x4 grooves.	30.00
Pr59b	1986	198	20 Kroner. Aluminum-Bronze. Interrupted milling, 8x8 grooves, notches widely spaced.	30.00
Pr59c	1986	198	20 Kroner. Aluminum-Bronze. Interrupted milling, 8x6 grooves.	30.00
Pr59d	1986	198	20 Kroner. Aluminum-Bronze. Interrupted milling, 16x3 grooves, no notches.	30.00
Pr59e	1986	198	20 Kroner. Aluminum-Bronze. Interrupted milling, 8x8 grooves, notches narrowly spaced.	30.00
Pr59f	1986	198	20 Kroner. Aluminum-Bronze. Interrupted milling, 8x8 grooves.	30.00
Pr60	1987	190	50 Ore. Bronze.	30.00
Pr61	1988	171	25 Ore. Bronze.	70.00
Pr62	1988	178	50 Ore. Bronze.	75.00
Pr63	1988	56	50 Ore. Bronze. A above cross on crown.	80.00
Pr64	1988	187	Krone. Copper-Nickel. Three crowned MIIR monograms, date, mint mark. Ornaments around center hole, value, country name.	75.00
Pr65	1988	175	2 Kroner. Copper-Nickel.	75.00
Pr66	1988	174	5 Kroner. Copper-Nickel. Ornaments surround center hole, hearts flank, denomination above country name below. Three crowns and monograms surround center hole, date below, hearts at top sides.	75.00
Pr67	1988	171	10 Kroner. Aluminum-Bronze.	55.00
Pr68	1988	171	20 Kroner. Aluminum-Bronze.	32.00

KM#	Date	Mintage	Identification	Mkt Val
Pr69	1990 LG-JP	—	Krone. Copper-Nickel.	8.00
Pr70	1990 LG-JP	—	2 Kroner. Copper-Nickel.	8.00

TRIAL STRIKES

KM#	Date	Mintage	Identification	Mkt Val
TS3	1907	—	10 Kroner. Bronze. KM#809.	800
TS4	1907	—	10 Kroner. Bronze. KM#809.	800
TS5	1907	—	20 Kroner. Bronze. KM#810.	—
TS6	1907	—	20 Kroner. Bronze. KM#810.	—

MINT SETS

KM#	Date	Mintage	Identification	Issue Price	Mkt Val
MS1	1956 (7)	—	KM#837.2-843.2	—	120
MS2	1957 (7)	—	KM#837.2-843.2	—	90.00
MS3	1958 (7)	—	KM#837.2-843.2	—	90.00
MS4	1959 (7)	—	KM#837.2-843.2	—	245
MS5	1960 (8)	—	KM#837.2, 839.2-843.2, 849.1, 850	—	135
MSA12	1960-66 (10)	10,000	KM#846 (1960, 1962, 1963, 1964), KM#847 (1960, 1962, 1963, 1964, 1965, 1966)	—	9.00
MS6	1961 (7)	—	KM#839.2-840.2, 843.2, 849.1, 850, 851.1, 853.1	—	80.00
MS7	1962 (8)	—	KM#839.2-840.2, 843.2, 848.1-849.1, 850, 851.1, 853.1	—	65.00
MS8	1963 (7)	—	KM#839.2-840.2, 843.2, 848.1-849.1, 851.1, 853.1	—	40.00
MS9	1964 (8)	—	KM#839.2-840.2, 843.2, 848.1-849.1, 850, 851.1, 853.1	—	40.00
MS10	1965 (7)	—	KM#839.2-840.2, 848.1-849.1, 850, 851.1, 853.1	—	40.00
MS11	1966 (8)	—	KM#839.2-840.2, 848.1-849.1, 850, 851.1, 853.1, 855.1	—	35.00
MS12	1967 (8)	—	KM#839.2-840.2, 848.1-849.1, 850, 851.1, 853.1, 855.1	—	45.00
MS13	1968 (7)	—	KM#839.2-840.2, 848.1-849.1, 851.1, 853.1, 855.1	—	28.00
MS14	1969 (7)	—	KM#839.2-840.2, 848.1-849.1, 851.1, 853.1, 855.1	—	28.00
MS15	1970 (7)	—	KM#839.2-840.2, 848.1-849.1, 851.1, 853.1, 855.1	—	13.50
MS16	1971 (7)	—	KM#839.2-840.2, 848.1-849.1, 851.1, 853.1, 855.1	—	13.50
MS17	1972 (7)	—	KM#839.3-840.3, 848.2-849.2, 851.2, 853.2, 855.2	—	9.00
MS18	1973 (5)	—	KM#859.1-863.1	—	10.00
MS19	1974 (5)	—	KM#859.1-863.1	6.00	9.00
MS20	1975 (5)	4,300	KM#859.1-863.1	6.00	100
MS21	1976 (5)	6,000	KM#859.1-863.1	3.55	45.00
MS22	1977 (5)	6,000	KM#859.1-863.1	—	45.00
MS23	1978 (5)	6,000	KM#859.1-863.1	—	20.00
MS24	1979 (6)	6,000	KM#859.2-863.2, 864.1	—	18.00
MS25	1980 (5)	4,000	KM#859.2-863.2	—	150
MS26	1981 (6)	15,767	KM#859.3-863.2, 864.1	—	16.50
MS27	1982 (6)	17,031	KM#859.3-863.3, 864.2	—	14.00
MS28	1983 (6)	14,595	KM#859.3-863.3, 864.2	—	14.00
MS29	1984 (6)	14,041	KM#859.3-863.3, 864.2	—	14.00
MS30	1985 (6)	14,003	KM#859.3-863.3, 864.2	—	14.00
MS31	1986 (6)	20,000	KM#859.3-863.3, 865	—	25.00
MS32	1987 (6)	15,000	KM#859.3-863.3, 864.2	—	25.00
MS33	1988 (6)	19,692	KM#859.3-863.3, 864.2	—	14.00
MS34	1989 (3)	27,123	KM#862.3, 866.1, 867.1	12.00	12.00
MS35	1990 (6)	39,258	KM#866.2, 867.2, 868-871	15.00	16.50
MS36	1991 (5)	33,258	KM#866.2, 867.2, 868-869, 871	15.00	22.50
MS37	1992 (7)	40,000	KM#866.2, 867.2, 868-869, 873-875	15.00	25.00
MS38	1993 (7)	35,000	KM#866.2, 867.2, 868-869, 871, 873-874	15.00	20.00
MS39	1994 (7)	30,000	K#866.2, 868-869, 873-874, 877-878	15.00	16.50
MS40	1995 (7)	25,000	KM#866.2, 868-869, 873-874, 877, 879	15.00	16.50
MS41	1996 (6)	25,000	KM#866.2, 868, 873-874, 878, 881 (1995 date)	15.00	16.50
MS42	1997 (7)	25,000	KM#866.2, 868-869, 873-874, 877, 883	15.00	25.00
MS43	1998 (7)	28,000	KM#866.2, 868, 869, 873-874, 877, 878	15.00	22.50
MS44	1999 (7)	30,100	KM#866.2, 868-869, 873-874, 877, 878	15.00	22.50
MS45	2000 (6)	28,000	KM#866.2, 868, 869, 873, 874, 885	15.00	50.00

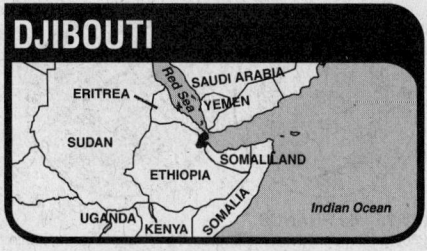

The Republic of Djibouti (formerly French Somaliland and the French Overseas Territory of Afars and Issas), located in northeast Africa at the Bab el Mandeb Strait connecting the Suez Canal and the Red Sea with the Gulf of Aden and the Indian Ocean, has an area of 8,950 sq. mi. (22,000 sq. km.) and a population of 421,320. Capital: Djibouti. The tiny nation has less than one sq. mi. of arable land, and no natural resources except salt, sand, and camels. The commercial activities of the transshipment port of Djibouti and the Addis Abada-Djibouti railroad are the basis of the economy. Salt, fish and hides are exported.

French interest in former French Somaliland began in 1839 with concessions obtained by a French naval lieutenant from the provincial sultans. French Somaliland was made a protectorate in 1884 and its boundaries were delimited by the Franco-British and Ethiopian accords of 1887 and 1897. It became a colony in 1896 and a territory within the French Union in 1946. In 1958 it voted to join the new French Community as an overseas territory, and reaffirmed that choice by a referendum in March, 1967. Its name was changed from French Somaliland to the French Territory of Afars and Issas on July 5, 1967.

The French Tricolor, which had flown over the strategically important territory for 115 years, was lowered for the last time on June 27, 1977, when French Afars and Issas became Africa's 49th independent state, under the name of the Republic of Djibouti.

Djibouti, a seaport and capital city of the Republic of Djibouti (and formerly of French Somaliland and French Afars and Issas) is located on the east coast of Africa at the southernmost entrance to the Red Sea. The capital was moved from Obok to Djibouti in 1892 and established as the transshipment point for Ethiopia's foreign trade via the Franco-Ethiopian railway linking Djibouti and Addis Ababa.

RULER
French, until 1977

COLONY

TOKEN COINAGE

KM# Tn1 5 CENTIMES
Zinc **Issuer:** Chamber of Commerce

Date	Mintage	VG	F	VF	XF	Unc
1920	—	12.00	25.00	70.00	150	300

KM# Tn5 5 CENTIMES
Aluminum **Issuer:** Chamber of Commerce **Obv:** Horned deer left of tree, date below **Rev:** Denomination within wreath

Date	Mintage	VG	F	VF	XF	Unc
1921	—	10.00	20.00	50.00	100	225

KM# Tn2 10 CENTIMES
Zinc **Issuer:** Chamber of Commerce

Date	Mintage	VG	F	VF	XF	Unc
1920	—	15.00	30.00	80.00	165	325

KM# Tn6 10 CENTIMES
Aluminum **Issuer:** Chamber of Commerce

Date	Mintage	VG	F	VF	XF	Unc
1921	—	12.00	25.00	65.00	125	250

KM# Tn7 25 CENTIMES
Aluminum **Issuer:** Chamber of Commerce **Obv:** Horned deer left of tree, date below **Rev:** Denomination within wreath

Date	Mintage	VG	F	VF	XF	Unc
1921	—	15.00	30.00	80.00	165	325

KM# Tn3 50 CENTIMES
Zinc **Issuer:** Chamber of Commerce

Date	Mintage	VG	F	VF	XF	Unc
1920	—	20.00	40.00	100	200	450

KM# Tn8 50 CENTIMES
Bronze-Aluminum **Issuer:** Chamber of Commerce **Obv:** Country name between hearts at center, date below, beaded outline surrounds **Rev:** Large denomination

Date	Mintage	VG	F	VF	XF	Unc
1921	—	15.00	30.00	80.00	160	320

KM# Tn9 50 CENTIMES
Bronze **Issuer:** Chamber of Commerce

Date	Mintage	VG	F	VF	XF	Unc
1921	—	20.00	40.00	100	200	400

KM# Tn10 50 CENTIMES
Aluminum **Issuer:** Chamber of Commerce

Date	Mintage	VG	F	VF	XF	Unc
1922	—	22.50	45.00	120	250	500

KM# Tn4 FRANC
Aluminum **Issuer:** Chamber of Commerce

Date	Mintage	VG	F	VF	XF	Unc
1920	—	25.00	50.00	135	275	550

REPUBLIC

STANDARD COINAGE

KM# 20 FRANC
1.3000 g., Aluminum, 23 mm. **Obv:** National arms within wreath, date below **Rev:** Giant eland head with headdress facing, divides denomination, shell on fish flank below

Date	Mintage	F	VF	XF	Unc	BU
1977(a)	300,000	0.50	0.75	1.50	3.00	5.00
1996(a)	—	0.50	0.75	1.50	3.00	5.00
1997(a)	350	—	—	—	16.00	18.00
	Note: In sets only					
1999(a)	1,800	—	—	—	7.00	9.00
	Note: In sets only					

KM# 37 FRANC
33.0000 g., Aluminum-Bronze, 40.9 mm. **Subject:** 50th Anniversary French Djibouti **Obv:** National arms **Obv. Leg.:** REPUBLIQUE DE DJIBOUTI **Rev:** Large value above 50e ANNIVERSAIRE **Rev. Leg.:** UNITÉ - ÉGALITÉ - PAIX **Edge:** Plain

Date	Mintage	F	VF	XF	Unc	BU
1999(a) Proof	500	Value: 35.00				

KM# 21   2 FRANCS
2.2000 g., Aluminum, 27.1 mm. **Obv:** National arms within wreath, date below **Rev:** Giant eland head with headdress facing, divides denomination, shell on fish flank below

Date	Mintage	F	VF	XF	Unc	BU
1977(a)	200,000	0.75	1.00	1.75	3.50	5.50
1991(a)	—	0.75	1.00	1.75	3.50	5.50
1996(a)	—	0.75	1.00	1.75	3.50	5.50
1997(a)	350	—	—	—	16.00	18.00
Note: In sets only
1999(a)	1,800	—	—	—	7.00	9.00
Note: In sets only

KM# 22   5 FRANCS
3.7500 g., Aluminum, 31.1 mm. **Obv:** National arms within wreath, date below **Rev:** Giant eland head with headdress facing, divides denomination, shell on fish flank below

Date	Mintage	F	VF	XF	Unc	BU
1977(a)	400,000	0.75	1.25	2.00	4.00	6.00
1986(a)	—	0.75	1.00	1.75	3.50	5.50
1989(a)	—	0.75	1.00	1.75	3.50	5.50
1991(a)	—	0.75	1.00	1.75	3.50	5.50
1996(a)	—	0.75	1.00	1.75	3.50	5.50
1997(a)	350	—	—	—	16.00	18.00
Note: In sets only
1999(a)	1,800	—	—	—	7.00	9.00
Note: In sets only

KM# 23   10 FRANCS
3.0000 g., Aluminum-Bronze, 20 mm. **Obv:** National arms within wreath, date below **Rev:** Boats on water, denomination above **Note:** Varieties exist.

Date	Mintage	F	VF	XF	Unc	BU
1977(a)	600,000	0.45	0.85	1.50	3.00	5.00
1983(a)	—	0.50	1.00	1.75	3.50	5.50
1989(a)	—	0.45	0.75	1.25	2.50	4.50
1991(a)	—	0.45	0.75	1.25	2.50	4.50
1996(a)	—	0.45	0.75	1.25	2.50	4.50
1997(a)	350	—	—	—	16.00	18.00
Note: In sets only
1999(a)	1,800	—	—	—	7.00	9.00
Note: In sets only

KM# 24   20 FRANCS
4.0000 g., Aluminum-Bronze, 23.5 mm. **Obv:** National arms within wreath, date below **Rev:** Boats on water, denomination above **Note:** Varieties exist.

Date	Mintage	F	VF	XF	Unc	BU
1977(a)	700,000	0.50	1.00	1.50	3.00	5.00
1982(a)	—	0.50	1.00	1.75	3.50	5.50
1983(a)	—	0.50	1.00	1.50	3.00	5.00
1986(a)	—	0.45	0.75	1.25	2.50	4.50
1991(a)	—	0.45	0.75	1.25	2.50	4.50
1996(a)	—	0.45	0.75	1.25	2.50	4.50
1997(a)	350	—	—	—	16.00	18.00
Note: In sets only
1999(a)	1,800	—	—	—	7.00	9.00
Note: In sets only

KM# 25   50 FRANCS
7.0500 g., Copper-Nickel, 25.7 mm. **Obv:** National arms within wreath, date below **Rev:** Pair of dromedary camels right, denomination above

Date	Mintage	F	VF	XF	Unc	BU
1977(a)	1,500,000	0.75	1.50	3.00	6.00	9.00
1982(a)	—	0.75	1.50	3.00	6.00	9.00
1983(a)	—	0.50	1.00	2.25	6.00	9.00
1986(a)	—	0.50	1.00	2.25	6.00	9.00
1989(a)	—	0.50	1.00	2.25	6.00	9.00
1991(a)	—	0.50	1.00	2.25	6.00	9.00
1997(a)	350	—	—	—	16.00	18.00
Note: In sets only
1999(a)	1,800	—	—	—	7.00	9.00
Note: In sets only

KM# 26   100 FRANCS
12.0000 g., Copper-Nickel, 30 mm. **Obv:** National arms within wreath, date below **Rev:** Pair of dromedary camels right, denomination above

Date	Mintage	F	VF	XF	Unc	BU
1977(a)	1,500,000	1.00	2.00	3.00	7.50	10.00
1983(a)	—	1.00	2.50	3.50	8.00	10.00
1991(a)	—	1.00	1.75	2.75	7.50	8.00
1996(a)	—	1.00	1.75	2.25	7.00	8.00
1997(a)	350	—	—	—	18.00	20.00
Note: In sets only
1999(a)	1,800	—	—	—	8.00	10.00
Note: In sets only

KM# 29   100 FRANCS
31.4700 g., 0.9250 Silver 0.9359 oz. ASW **Subject:** World Cup Soccer **Obv:** National arms within wreath, date below **Rev:** Soccer player divides maps, denomination below

Date	Mintage	F	VF	XF	Unc	BU
1994 Proof	Est. 15,000	Value: 40.00				

KM# 30   100 FRANCS
31.4700 g., 0.9250 Silver 0.9359 oz. ASW **Series:** 1996 Olympic Games **Obv:** National arms within wreath, date below **Rev:** Runner, denomination at right

Date	Mintage	F	VF	XF	Unc	BU
1994 Proof	Est. 30,000	Value: 37.50				

KM# 31   100 FRANCS
31.4700 g., 0.9250 Silver 0.9359 oz. ASW **Obv:** National arms within wreath, date below **Rev:** Frigate "Bateau" flag and denomination below

Date	Mintage	F	VF	XF	Unc	BU
1994 Proof	Est. 15,000	Value: 45.00				

KM# 32   100 FRANCS
31.4700 g., 0.9250 Silver 0.9359 oz. ASW **Subject:** Endangered Wildlife **Obv:** National arms within wreath, date below **Rev:** Grevy zebras running right, denomination below

Date	Mintage	F	VF	XF	Unc	BU
1994 Proof	Est. 15,000	Value: 45.00				

KM# 33   100 FRANCS
31.4700 g., 0.9250 Silver 0.9359 oz. ASW **Obv:** National arms within wreath, date below **Rev:** Portuguese "Nao" ship within circle, denomination below

Date	Mintage	F	VF	XF	Unc	BU
1996 Proof	Est. 15,000	Value: 45.00				

KM# 36   250 FRANCS
1.2440 g., 0.9990 Gold 0.0400 oz. AGW, 13.95 mm. **Obv:** National arms within wreath, date below **Rev:** Old Portuguese Ship

Date	Mintage	F	VF	XF	Unc	BU
1996 Proof	—	Value: 75.00				

KM# 27   500 FRANCS
Aluminum-Bronze **Obv:** National arms within wreath, date below **Rev:** Denomination within sprays

Date	Mintage	F	VF	XF	Unc	BU
1989(a)	—	3.00	4.00	6.00	10.00	12.00
1991(a)	—	3.00	4.00	6.00	10.00	12.00
1997(a)	350	—	—	—	18.00	20.00
Note: In sets only

Date	Mintage	F	VF	XF	Unc	BU
1999(a)	1,800	—	—	—	12.00	15.00

Note: In sets only

KM# 35   500 FRANCS
0.9250 Silver **Subject:** Wildlife of Africa **Rev:** One lion in a tree, two lions under a tree

Date	Mintage	F	VF	XF	Unc	BU
1997 Proof	—	Value: 70.00				

KM# 28   15000 FRANCS
24.3000 g., 0.9990 Silver 0.7804 oz. ASW **Obv:** National arms within wreath, date below **Rev:** Map at center, denomination below

Date	Mintage	F	VF	XF	Unc	BU
1991	Est. 10,000	—	—	—	100	—

ESSAIS
Standard metals unless otherwise noted

KM#	Date	Mintage	Identification	Mkt Val
E1	1977	1,700	Franc. KM20.	12.50
E2	1977	1,700	2 Francs. KM21.	12.50
E3	1977	1,700	5 Francs. KM22.	12.50
E4	1977	1,700	10 Francs. KM23.	14.50
E5	1977	1,700	20 Francs. KM24.	14.50
E6	1977	1,700	50 Francs. KM25.	17.50
E7	1977	1,700	100 Francs. KM26.	20.00

MINT SETS

KM#	Date	Mintage	Identification	Issue Price	Mkt Val
MS1	1997 (8)	350	KM#20-27	—	150
MS2	1999 (8)	1,800	KM#20-27	—	75.00

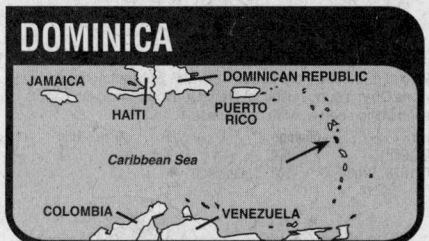

DOMINICA

The Commonwealth of Dominica, situated in the Lesser Antilles midway between Guadeloupe to the north and Martinique to the south, has an area of 290 sq. mi. (750 sq. km.) and a population of 82,608. Capital: Roseau. Agriculture is the chief economic activity of the mountainous island. Bananas are the chief export.

Columbus discovered and named the island on Nov. 3, 1493. Spain neglected it and it was finally colonized by the French in 1632. The British drove the French from the island in 1756. Thereafter it changed hands between the French and British a dozen or more times before becoming permanently British in 1805. Around 1761, pierced or mutilated silver from Martinique was used on the island. A council in 1798 acknowledged and established value for these mutilated coins and ordered other cut and countermarked to be made in Dominica. These remained in use until 1862, when they were demonetized and sterling became the standard. Throughout the greater part of its British history, Dominica was a presidency of the Leeward Islands. In 1940 its administration was transferred to the Windward Islands and it was established as a separate colony with considerable local autonomy. From 1955, Dominica was a member of the currency board of the British Caribbean Territories (Eastern Group), which issued its own coins until 1965. Dominica became a West Indies associated state with a built in option for independence in 1967. Full independence was attained on Nov. 3, 1978. Dominica, which has a republican form of government, is a member of the Commonwealth of Nations.

RULER
British, until 1978

MINT MARKS
CHI in circle - Valcambi, Chiasso, Italy
(ml) - maple leaf - Canadian Royal Mint

MONETARY SYSTEM
(Commencing 1813)
16 Bits = 12 Shillings = 1 Dollar (Spanish)
100 Cents = 1 Dollar (Dominican)

BRITISH COLONY
MODERN COINAGE

KM# 11   4 DOLLARS
Copper-Nickel, 38.5 mm. **Series:** F.A.O. **Rev:** Sugar cane and banana tree branch, denomination below **Note:** This 4-dollar F.A.O. commemorative coin is part of a group. The others are listed individually under their respective country names: Antigua, Barbados, Dominica, Grenada, Montserrat, St. Kitts, St. Lucia, and St. Vincent.

Date	Mintage	F	VF	XF	Unc	BU
1970	13,000	4.00	6.00	10.00	20.00	30.00
1970 Proof	2,000	Value: 35.00				

COMMONWEALTH
MODERN COINAGE

KM# 12.1   10 DOLLARS
20.5000 g., 0.9250 Silver 0.6096 oz. ASW **Subject:** Independence - History of Carnival **Obv:** Young bust right **Rev:** Six dancing women, denomination below, with mint mark

Date	Mintage	F	VF	XF	Unc	BU
ND(1978)CHI	1,500	—	—	12.00	18.50	22.00
ND(1978)CHI Proof	2,000	Value: 25.00				

KM# 12.2   10 DOLLARS
20.5000 g., 0.9250 Silver 0.6096 oz. ASW **Subject:** Independence - History of Carnival **Obv:** Young bust right **Rev:** Six dancing women, denomination below, without mint mark

Date	Mintage	F	VF	XF	Unc	BU
ND(1978)	—	—	—	12.00	18.50	22.00

KM# 12.3   10 DOLLARS
20.5000 g., 0.9250 Silver 0.6096 oz. ASW **Subject:** Independence - History of Carnival **Obv:** Young bust right **Rev:** Six dancing women, denomination below, Canadian mint mark and fineness

Date	Mintage	F	VF	XF	Unc	BU
ND(1978)(ml)	18	—	—	—	—	—
ND(1978)(ml) Proof	233	Value: 80.00				

KM# 16   10 DOLLARS
20.5000 g., 0.9250 Silver 0.6096 oz. ASW **Subject:** Visit of Pope John Paul II **Obv:** Young bust right **Rev:** Head with beanie left, denomination below

Date	Mintage	F	VF	XF	Unc	BU
ND(1979)CHI	1,150	—	—	12.50	20.00	25.00
ND(1979)CHI Proof	3,450	Value: 28.00				

KM# 20   10 DOLLARS
Copper Nickel **Subject:** Royal Visit **Obv:** Crowned bust right **Rev:** Lion tops arms with parrots, circle surrounds

Date	Mintage	F	VF	XF	Unc	BU
1985	Est. 100,000	—	—	6.00	10.00	17.50

KM# 20a   10 DOLLARS
28.2800 g., 0.9250 Silver 0.8410 oz. ASW **Subject:** Royal Visit **Obv:** Crowned bust right **Rev:** Lion tops arms with parrots, circle surrounds

Date	Mintage	F	VF	XF	Unc	BU
1985 Proof	Est. 5,000	Value: 30.00				

KM# 13.1   20 DOLLARS
40.9100 g., 0.9250 Silver 1.2166 oz. ASW   **Subject:**
Independence and 50th Anniversary of Graf Zeppelin **Obv:**
Young bust right divides dates **Rev:** Blimp above denomination

Date	Mintage	F	VF	XF	Unc	BU
ND(1978)CHI	500	—	—	35.00	65.00	75.00
ND(1978)CHI Proof	1,000	Value: 90.00				

KM# 13.2   20 DOLLARS
40.9100 g., 0.9250 Silver 1.2166 oz. ASW   **Subject:**
Independence and 50th Anniversary of Graf Zeppelin **Obv:**
Young bust right divides dates **Rev:** Blimp above denomination,
Canadian mint mark and .925 fineness stamp added

Date	Mintage	F	VF	XF	Unc	BU
ND(1978)(ml)	—	—	—	—	—	—
ND(1978)(ml) Proof	233	Value: 125				

KM# 13.3   20 DOLLARS
Silver, 45.2 mm.   **Obv:** Young bust right **Rev:** Blimp above
denomination **Edge:** Reeded **Note:** No mint marks or fineness.

Date	Mintage	F	VF	XF	Unc	BU
ND(1978) Proof	—	Value: 150				

KM# 17   20 DOLLARS
40.9100 g., 0.9250 Silver 1.2166 oz. ASW   **Subject:** Israel and
Egypt Peace Treaty **Obv:** Young bust right **Rev:** Portrait of Sadat,
Begin, and Carter, with small flags, denomination below

Date	Mintage	F	VF	XF	Unc	BU
ND(1979)CHI	200	—	—	40.00	75.00	85.00
ND(1979)CHI Proof	200	Value: 100				

KM# 21   100 DOLLARS
129.5900 g., 0.9250 Silver 3.8538 oz. ASW, 63 mm.
Subject: Tropical Birds - Imperial Parrots **Obv:** Lion tops arms
with parrots, circle surrounds, date below **Rev:** Parrots in trees,
denomination above **Note:** Illustration reduced.

Date	Mintage	F	VF	XF	Unc	BU
1988 Proof	Est. 10,000	Value: 125				

KM# 14.1   150 DOLLARS
9.6000 g., 0.9000 Gold 0.2778 oz. AGW   **Subject:** Independence
- Imperial Parrot **Obv:** Young bust right **Rev:** Map of Dominica and
parrot, without fineness, denomination at left

Date	Mintage	F	VF	XF	Unc	BU
ND(1978)	300	—	—	—	300	—
ND(1978) Proof	400	Value: 350				

KM# 14.2   150 DOLLARS
9.6000 g., 0.9000 Gold 0.2778 oz. AGW   **Subject:** Independence
- Imperial Parrot **Obv:** Young bust right **Rev:** Parrot and map,
denomination at left, Canadian mint mark and .900 fineness added

Date	Mintage	F	VF	XF	Unc	BU
ND(1978)(ml)	18	—	—	—	—	—
ND(1978)(ml) Proof	116	Value: 345				

KM# 18   150 DOLLARS
9.6000 g., 0.9000 Gold 0.2778 oz. AGW   **Subject:** Israel and
Egypt Peace Treaty **Obv:** Young bust right **Rev:** Heads of Carter,
Sadat, and Begin with flags, denomination below

Date	Mintage	F	VF	XF	Unc	BU
ND(1979)CHI	100	—	—	—	500	—
ND(1979)CHI Proof	100	Value: 550				

KM# 15.1   300 DOLLARS
19.2000 g., 0.9000 Gold 0.5555 oz. AGW   **Subject:** Independence
- Arms **Obv:** Young bust right **Rev:** Lion tops arms with parrots,
denomination below, without fineness

Date	Mintage	F	VF	XF	Unc	BU
ND(1978)	500	—	—	—	550	—
ND(1978) Proof	800	Value: 600				

KM# 15.2   300 DOLLARS
19.2000 g., 0.9000 Gold 0.5555 oz. AGW   **Subject:** Independence
- Arms **Obv:** Young bust right **Rev:** National arms, Canadian mint
mark and .900 fineness added

Date	Mintage	F	VF	XF	Unc	BU
ND(1978)(ml)	18	—	—	—	—	—
ND(1978)(ml) Proof	82	Value: 650				

KM# 19   300 DOLLARS
19.2000 g., 0.9000 Gold 0.5555 oz. AGW   **Subject:** Visit of Pope
John Paul II **Obv:** Young bust right **Rev:** Head with beanie left,
denomination below

Date	Mintage	F	VF	XF	Unc	BU
ND(1979)CHI	5,000	—	—	—	525	—
ND(1979)CHI	300	—	—	—	575	—

KM# 22 500 DOLLARS
47.5400 g., 0.9170 Gold 1.4015 oz. AGW **Subject:** Royal Visit **Obv:** Crowned bust right **Rev:** Lion tops arms with parrots, circle surrounds

Date	Mintage	F	VF	XF	Unc	BU
1985 Proof	Est. 250	Value: 1,350				

PROOF SETS

KM#	Date	Mintage	Identification	Issue Price	Mkt Val
PS1	1978 (2)	—	KM#12.3, 13.2	—	200
PS2	1978 (4)	—	KM#12.3, 13.2, 14.2, 15.2	—	1,125

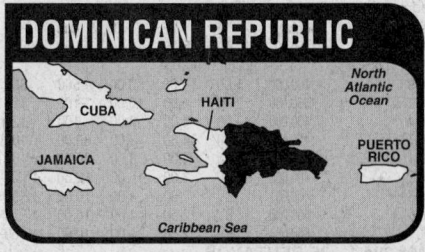

DOMINICAN REPUBLIC

The Dominican Republic, which occupies the eastern two-thirds of the island of Hispaniola, has an area of 18,704 sq. mi. (48,734 sq. km.) and a population of 7.9 million. Capital: Santo Domingo. The largely agricultural economy produces sugar, coffee, tobacco and cocoa. Tourism and casino gaming are also a rising source of revenue.

Columbus discovered Hispaniola in 1492, and named it La Isla Espanola - 'the Spanish Island'. Santo Domingo, the oldest white settlement in the Western Hemisphere, was the base from which Spain conducted its exploration of the New World. Later, French buccaneers settled the western third of Hispaniola, naming the colony St. Dominique, which in 1697, was ceded to France by Spain. In 1804, following a bloody revolt by former slaves, the French colony became the Republic of Haiti - mountainous country'. The Spanish called their part of Hispaniola Santo Domingo. In 1822, the Haitians conquered the entire island and held it until 1844, when Juan Pablo Duarte, the national hero of the Dominican Republic, drove them out of Santo Domingo and established an independent Dominican Republic. The republic returned voluntarily to Spanish dominion from 1861 to 1865, after being rejected by France, Britain and the United States. Independence was reclaimed in 1866.

MINT MARKS
(c) - Stylized maple leaf, Royal Canadian Mint
Mo – Mexico City
(o) - CHI in oval - Valcambi, Chiasso, Italy
(t) - Tower, Tower Mint, London

MONETARY SYSTEM
100 Centavos = 1 Peso Oro

REPUBLIC

REFORM COINAGE
1937

100 Centavos = 1 Peso Oro

KM# 17 CENTAVO
3.1100 g., Bronze **Obv:** National arms **Rev:** Palm tree divides denomination and weight, date below

Date	Mintage	F	VF	XF	Unc	BU
1937	1,000,000	0.50	1.50	7.50	75.00	100
1937 Proof	—	Value: 350				
1939	2,000,000	0.50	1.25	5.00	40.00	60.00
1941	2,000,000	0.25	0.50	3.00	12.00	25.00
1942	2,000,000	0.25	0.50	3.00	15.00	30.00
1944	5,000,000	0.20	0.50	1.50	10.00	20.00
1947	3,000,000	0.20	0.50	1.00	8.00	15.00
1949	3,000,000	0.20	0.40	1.00	8.00	15.00
1951	3,000,000	0.20	0.35	0.75	8.00	15.00
1952	3,000,000	0.20	0.35	0.75	8.00	15.00
1955	3,000,000	0.15	0.35	0.75	6.00	12.00
1956	3,000,000	0.15	0.35	0.75	6.00	12.00
1957	5,000,000	0.10	0.25	0.75	5.00	10.00
1959	5,000,000	0.10	0.25	0.75	5.00	10.00
1961	5,000,000	0.10	0.20	0.50	2.00	5.00
1961 10 known; Proof	—	Value: 500				

KM# 25 CENTAVO
Bronze **Subject:** 100th Anniversary - Restoration of the Republic **Obv:** National arms, date below **Rev:** Taino Indian divides denomination and weight

Date	Mintage	F	VF	XF	Unc	BU
1963	13,000,000	—	—	0.10	0.40	0.80

KM# 31 CENTAVO
3.0200 g., Bronze **Obv:** National arms **Rev:** Profile of native princess left divides denomination and weight, date below

Date	Mintage	F	VF	XF	Unc	BU
1968	5,000,000	—	—	0.10	0.20	0.50
1971	6,000,000	—	—	0.10	0.20	0.50
1972	3,000,000	—	—	0.10	0.20	0.50
1972 Proof	500	Value: 15.00				
1975	500,000	—	0.10	0.20	0.30	0.60

KM# 32 CENTAVO
3.0200 g., Bronze **Series:** F.A.O. **Obv:** National arms, date below **Rev:** Profile of native princess left divides denomination and weight, date below

Date	Mintage	F	VF	XF	Unc	BU
1969	5,000,000	—	—	0.10	0.30	0.60

KM# 40 CENTAVO
Bronze **Subject:** Centennial - Death of Juan Pablo Duarte **Obv:** National arms, two dates below **Rev:** Bust facing divides denomination and weight, date below

Date	Mintage	F	VF	XF	Unc	BU
1976	3,995,000	—	—	0.10	0.20	0.50
1976 Proof	5,000	Value: 1.00				

KM# 48 CENTAVO
Bronze **Subject:** Death of Juan Pablo Duarte **Obv:** National arms without memorial legend **Rev:** Bust facing divides denomination and weight, date below

Date	Mintage	F	VF	XF	Unc	BU
1978	2,995,000	—	—	0.10	0.15	0.30
1978 Proof	5,000	Value: 2.00				
1979	2,985,000	—	—	0.10	0.15	0.30
1979 Proof	500	Value: 15.00				
1980	200,000	—	—	0.10	0.15	0.30
1980 Proof	3,000	Value: 1.00				
1981 Proof	3,000	Value: 1.00				

Note: KM#48a previously listed here has been moved to the Pattern section

KM# 64 CENTAVO
2.0000 g., Copper Plated Zinc, 19.03 mm. **Subject:** Human Rights **Obv:** National arms **Rev:** Bust of Caonabo right **Edge:** Plain

Date	Mintage	F	VF	XF	Unc	BU
1984Mo	10,000,000	—	—	0.10	0.25	0.50
1984Mo Proof	1,600	Value: 1.50				
1986	18,067,000	—	—	0.10	0.25	0.50

Date	Mintage	F	VF	XF	Unc	BU
1986 Proof	1,600	Value: 1.50				
1987	15,000,000	—	—	0.10	0.25	0.50
1987(t) Proof	1,600	Value: 1.50				

KM# 64a CENTAVO
2.0000 g., 0.9000 Silver 0.0579 oz. ASW, 19.03 mm. **Subject:** Human Rights **Obv:** National arms **Rev:** Bust of Caonabo right **Edge:** Plain

Date	Mintage	F	VF	XF	Unc	BU
1984Mo Proof	100	Value: 20.00				
1986 Proof	100	Value: 20.00				

KM# 72 CENTAVO
Copper Plated Zinc, 19.1 mm. **Obv:** National arms, date below **Rev:** Triangular artifact, denomination below

Date	Mintage	F	VF	XF	Unc	BU
1989	1,115	—	—	—	1.25	1.75

KM# 72a CENTAVO
3.7000 g., 0.9250 Silver 0.1100 oz. ASW, 19.1 mm. **Obv:** National arms, date below **Rev:** Triangular artifact

Date	Mintage	F	VF	XF	Unc	BU
1989 Proof	2,600	—	—	—	—	—

KM# 18 5 CENTAVOS
Copper-Nickel, 21 mm. **Obv:** National arms **Rev:** Profile of native princess left divides denomination and weight, date below

Date	Mintage	F	VF	XF	Unc	BU
1937	2,000,000	1.00	1.75	5.00	50.00	65.00
1937 Proof	—	Value: 600				
1939	200,000	5.00	15.00	60.00	350	400
1951	2,000,000	0.75	1.25	2.00	20.00	35.00
1956	1,000,000	0.20	0.50	0.80	3.50	5.00
1959	1,000,000	0.20	0.50	0.80	3.50	5.00
1961	4,000,000	0.10	0.20	0.35	0.75	1.25
1961 10 known; Proof	—	Value: 700				
1971	440,000	0.20	0.40	0.60	1.50	2.05
1972	2,000,000	0.10	0.15	0.20	0.40	0.90
1972 Proof	500	Value: 15.00				
1974	5,000,000	—	—	0.10	0.40	0.90
1974 Proof	500	Value: 15.00				

KM# 18a 5 CENTAVOS
5.0000 g., 0.3500 Silver 0.0563 oz. ASW, 21 mm. **Obv:** National arms **Rev:** Profile of native princess left divides denomination and weight, date below

Date	Mintage	F	VF	XF	Unc	BU
1944	2,000,000	1.50	3.50	7.50	50.00	75.00

KM# 26 5 CENTAVOS
Copper-Nickel, 21 mm. **Subject:** 100th Anniversary - Restoration of the Republic **Obv:** National arms, two dates below **Rev:** Profile of native princess left divides denomination and weight, date below

Date	Mintage	F	VF	XF	Unc	BU
1963	4,000,000	—	0.10	0.15	0.60	1.25

KM# 41 5 CENTAVOS
Copper-Nickel, 41 mm. **Subject:** Centennial - Death of Juan Pablo Duarte **Obv:** National arms, two dates below **Rev:** Bust facing divides denomination and weight, date below

Date	Mintage	F	VF	XF	Unc	BU
1976	5,595,000	—	—	0.10	0.50	1.00
1976 Proof	5,000	Value: 2.00				

KM# 49 5 CENTAVOS

Copper-Nickel, 21 mm. **Obv:** National arms without memorial legend **Rev:** Bust facing divides denomination and weight, date below

Date	Mintage	F	VF	XF	Unc	BU
1978	1,996,000	—	—	0.10	0.35	0.90
1978 Proof	5,000	Value: 1.50				
1979	2,988,000	—	—	0.10	0.35	0.90
1979 Proof	500	Value: 15.00				
1980	5,300,000	—	—	0.10	0.35	0.90
1980 Proof	3,000	Value: 2.00				
1981	4,500,000	—	—	0.10	0.35	0.90
1981 Proof	3,000	Value: 2.00				

Note: KM#49a previously listed here has been moved to the Pattern section

KM# 59 5 CENTAVOS

5.0000 g., Copper Nickel, 21.19 mm. **Subject:** Human Rights **Obv:** National arms **Rev:** Conjoined busts right, denomination above **Edge:** Plain

Date	Mintage	F	VF	XF	Unc	BU
1983	3,998,000	—	—	0.10	0.30	0.90
1983(t) Proof	1,600	Value: 2.00				
1984Mo	10,000,000	—	—	0.10	0.30	0.90
1984Mo Proof	1,600	Value: 2.00				
1986	12,898,000	—	—	0.10	0.30	0.90
1986 Proof	1,600	Value: 2.00				
1987	10,000,000	—	—	0.10	0.30	0.90
1987(t) Proof	1,700	Value: 2.00				

KM# 59a 5 CENTAVOS

5.0000 g., 0.9000 Silver 0.1447 oz. ASW, 21.19 mm. **Subject:** Human Rights **Obv:** National arms **Rev:** Conjoined busts right, denomination above **Edge:** Plain

Date	Mintage	F	VF	XF	Unc	BU
1983(t) Proof	100	Value: 30.00				
1984Mo Proof	100	Value: 30.00				
1986 Proof	100	Value: 30.00				

KM# 69 5 CENTAVOS

Nickel Clad Steel, 21 mm. **Subject:** Native Culture **Obv:** National arms, date below **Rev:** Native drummer, denomination at left

Date	Mintage	F	VF	XF	Unc	BU
1989	50,000,000	—	—	—	0.35	0.90

KM# 69a 5 CENTAVOS

5.8300 g., 0.9250 Silver 0.1734 oz. ASW, 21 mm. **Subject:** Native Culture **Obv:** National arms, date below **Rev:** Native drummer, denomination at left

Date	Mintage	F	VF	XF	Unc	BU
1989 Proof	2,600	—	—	—	—	—

KM# 19 10 CENTAVOS

2.5000 g., 0.9000 Silver 0.0723 oz. ASW, 17.9 mm. **Obv:** National arms **Rev:** Profile of native princess left divides denomination and weight

Date	Mintage	F	VF	XF	Unc	BU
1937	1,000,000	BV	2.00	5.00	40.00	60.00
1937 Proof	—	Value: 700				
1939	150,000	5.00	15.00	40.00	300	350
1942	2,000,000	1.25	2.00	3.00	30.00	40.00
1944	1,000,000	1.25	2.00	4.00	75.00	95.00
1951	500,000	1.25	2.00	3.00	10.00	17.50
1952	500,000	1.25	2.00	3.00	10.00	17.50
1953	750,000	1.25	2.00	3.00	8.00	15.00
1956	1,000,000	1.00	1.75	2.50	8.00	15.00
1959	2,000,000	BV	1.25	2.25	7.00	12.50
1961	2,000,000	BV	1.25	2.00	6.00	12.00

KM# 19a 10 CENTAVOS

2.4900 g., Copper-Nickel, 17.9 mm. **Obv:** National arms **Rev:** Profile of native princess left divides denomination and weight, date below **Edge:** Plain

Date	Mintage	F	VF	XF	Unc	BU
1967	10,000,000	—	—	0.15	0.50	1.00
1973	8,000,000	—	—	0.15	0.50	1.00
1973 Proof	500	Value: 20.00				
1975	8,000,000	—	—	0.15	0.50	1.00

KM# 27 10 CENTAVOS

2.5000 g., 0.6500 Silver 0.0522 oz. ASW, 17.9 mm. **Subject:** 100th Anniversary - Restoration of the Republic **Obv:** National arms **Rev:** Profile of native princess left divides denomination and weight

Date	Mintage	F	VF	XF	Unc	BU
1963	4,000,000	—	BV	1.00	2.00	3.00

KM# 42 10 CENTAVOS

Copper-Nickel, 17.9 mm. **Subject:** Centennial - Death of Juan Pablo Duarte **Obv:** National arms **Rev:** Bust facing, date below

Date	Mintage	F	VF	XF	Unc	BU
1976	5,595,000	—	—	0.10	0.75	1.50
1976 Proof	5,000	Value: 2.00				

KM# 50 10 CENTAVOS

2.5600 g., Copper-Nickel, 17.9 mm. **Obv:** National arms **Rev:** Bust facing divides denomination and weight, date below

Date	Mintage	F	VF	XF	Unc	BU
1978	3,000,000	—	—	0.10	0.50	1.00
1978 Proof	5,000	Value: 2.00				
1979	4,020,000	—	—	0.10	0.50	1.00
1979 Proof	500	Value: 20.00				
1980	4,400,000	—	—	0.10	0.35	1.00
1980 Proof	3,000	Value: 3.00				
1981	6,000,000	—	—	0.10	0.35	1.00
1981 Proof	3,000	Value: 3.00				

Note: KM#50a previously listed here has been moved to the Pattern section

KM# 60 10 CENTAVOS

2.5000 g., Copper-Nickel, 17.88 mm. **Subject:** Human Rights **Obv:** National arms, date below **Rev:** Head left, denomination above **Edge:** Reeded

Date	Mintage	F	VF	XF	Unc	BU
1983	4,998,000	—	—	0.10	0.35	0.90
1983(t)	4,000,000	—	—	0.10	0.35	0.90
1983(t) Proof	1,600	Value: 2.50				
1984Mo	15,000,000	—	—	0.10	0.25	0.75

Note: Coarse reeding

1984Mo Proof	1,600	Value: 2.50				

Note: Coarse reeding

1986	15,515,000	—	—	0.10	0.25	0.75
1986 Proof	1,600	Value: 2.50				
1987	20,000,000	—	—	0.10	0.25	0.75
1987(t) Proof	1,700	Value: 2.50				

KM# 60a 10 CENTAVOS

2.5000 g., 0.9000 Silver 0.0723 oz. ASW, 17.88 mm. **Subject:** Human Rights **Obv:** National arms **Rev:** Head left, denomination above **Edge:** Reeded

Date	Mintage	F	VF	XF	Unc	BU
1983(t) Proof	100	Value: 30.00				
1984Mo Proof	100	Value: 30.00				
1986 Proof	100	Value: 30.00				

KM# 70 10 CENTAVOS

Nickel Clad Steel, 17.9 mm. **Obv:** National arms, date below **Rev:** Indigenous fruits and vegetables divide denomination

Date	Mintage	F	VF	XF	Unc	BU
1989	40,000,000	—	—	—	0.40	0.90
1991	3,500,000	—	—	—	0.40	0.90

KM# 70a 10 CENTAVOS

2.9000 g., 925.0000 Silver 86.240 oz. ASW, 17.9 mm. **Obv:** National arms **Rev:** Indigenous fruits and vegetables divide denomination

Date	Mintage	F	VF	XF	Unc	BU
1989 Proof	2,600	—	—	—	—	—

KM# 20 25 CENTAVOS

6.2500 g., 0.9000 Silver 0.1808 oz. ASW, 24 mm. **Obv:** National arms **Rev:** Profile of native princess left divides denomination and weight, date below

Date	Mintage	F	VF	XF	Unc	BU
1937	560,000	BV	5.00	15.00	65.00	75.00
1937 Proof	—	Value: 1,000				
1939	160,000	5.00	15.00	50.00	500	650
1942	560,000	2.50	4.00	10.00	100	125
1944	400,000	2.50	4.00	8.00	100	125
1947	400,000	2.50	4.00	8.00	80.00	100
1951	400,000	2.50	4.00	8.00	80.00	100
1952	400,000	BV	3.00	5.00	12.50	15.00
1956	400,000	BV	2.50	4.00	10.00	12.50
1960	600,000	BV	2.50	4.00	10.00	12.50
1961	800,000	BV	2.50	4.00	10.00	12.50

KM# 20a.1 25 CENTAVOS

6.2500 g., Copper Nickel, 24 mm. **Obv:** National arms **Rev:** Profile of native princess left divides denomination and weight, date below **Edge:** Plain

Date	Mintage	F	VF	XF	Unc	BU
1967	5,000,000	—	0.10	0.20	0.75	1.00
1972	800,000	—	0.10	0.40	1.00	1.50
1972 Proof	500	Value: 20.00				

KM# 20a.2 25 CENTAVOS

5.9500 g., Copper-Nickel, 24 mm. **Obv:** National arms **Rev:** Profile of native princess left divides denomination and weight, date below **Edge:** Reeded

Date	Mintage	F	VF	XF	Unc	BU
1974	2,000,000	—	0.10	0.40	1.00	1.50
1974 Proof	500	Value: 20.00				

KM# 28 25 CENTAVOS

6.2500 g., 0.9000 Silver 0.1306 oz. ASW, 24 mm. **Subject:** 100th Anniversary - Restoration of the Republic **Obv:** National arms, two dates below **Rev:** Profile of native princess left divides denomination and weight, date below

Date	Mintage	F	VF	XF	Unc	BU
1963	2,400,000	—	BV	2.00	3.00	5.00

KM# 43 25 CENTAVOS

Copper-Nickel, 24 mm. **Subject:** Centennial - Death of Juan Pablo Duarte **Obv:** National arms, two dates below **Rev:** Bust facing divides denomination and weight, date below

Date	Mintage	F	VF	XF	Unc	BU
1976	3,195,000	—	0.10	0.40	1.00	1.50
1976 Proof	5,000	Value: 2.50				

KM# 51 25 CENTAVOS

6.2700 g., Copper-Nickel, 24 mm. **Obv:** National arms without memorial legend **Rev:** Bust facing divides denomination and weight, date below

Date	Mintage	F	VF	XF	Unc	BU
1978	996,000	—	—	0.35	0.75	1.00
1978 Proof	5,000	Value: 3.00				
1979	2,089,000	—	—	0.15	0.50	0.75
1979 Proof	500	Value: 25.00				
1980	2,600,000	—	—	0.15	0.50	0.75
1980 Proof	3,000	Value: 3.00				
1981	3,200,000	—	—	0.15	0.50	0.75
1981 Proof	3,000	Value: 3.00				

Note: KM#51a previously listed here has been moved to the Pattern section

KM# 61.1 25 CENTAVOS
6.2500 g., Copper-Nickel, 24.45 mm. **Subject:** Human Rights
Obv: National arms, date below, denomination at left
Rev: Profiles of the Mirabel sisters left, Patria, Minerva & Maria
Teresa, human rights martyrs murdered 25.11.1960 by Trujillo
Edge: Fine reeding **Note:** Medal rotation.

Date	Mintage	F	VF	XF	Unc	BU
1983	793,000	—	0.10	0.20	0.50	1.00
1983(t)	5,000	—	—	2.50	4.00	
1983(t) Proof	1,600	Value: 8.00				
1984Mo Coarse reeding	6,400,000	—	—	0.15	0.40	1.00
1984Mo Proof; coarse reeding	1,600	Value: 8.00				

KM# 61.1a 25 CENTAVOS
6.2500 g., 0.9000 Silver 0.1808 oz. ASW, 24 mm.
Subject: Human Rights **Obv:** National arms **Rev:** Profile of the
Mirabel sisters left

Date	Mintage	F	VF	XF	Unc	BU
1983(t) Proof	100	Value: 40.00				
1984Mo Proof	100	Value: 40.00				

KM# 61.2a 25 CENTAVOS
Silver **Subject:** Human Rights **Obv:** National arms **Rev:** Profile
of the Mirabel sisters left

Date	Mintage	F	VF	XF	Unc	BU
1986 Proof	—	Value: 40.00				

KM# 61.2 25 CENTAVOS
6.2500 g., Copper-Nickel, 24 mm. **Subject:** Human Rights
Obv: National arms, date below, denomination at left
Rev: Profiles of the Mirabel sisters left, Patria, Minerva and Maria
Teresa, human rights martyrs murdered 25.11.1960 by Trujillo
Edge: Fine reeding **Note:** Coin rotation.

Date	Mintage	F	VF	XF	Unc	BU
1986 Coarse reeding	10,132,000	—	—	0.15	0.40	1.00
1986 Proof	1,600	Value: 8.00				
1987	6,000,000	—	—	0.15	0.40	1.00
1987(t) Proof	1,700	Value: 8.00				

KM# 71.1 25 CENTAVOS
Nickel Clad Steel, 24 mm. **Subject:** Native Culture **Obv:** National
arms, date below **Rev:** Two oxen pulling cart, denomination above

Date	Mintage	F	VF	XF	Unc	BU
1989 Coarse reeding	16,000,000	—	—	—	0.60	1.25
1991 Fine reeding	38,000,000	—	—	—	0.60	1.25

KM# 71.1a 25 CENTAVOS
6.7400 g., 0.9250 Silver 0.2004 oz. ASW, 24 mm.
Subject: Native Culture **Obv:** National arms **Rev:** Two oxen
pulling cart

Date	Mintage	F	VF	XF	Unc	BU
1989 Proof	2,600	—	—	—	—	—

KM# 71.2 25 CENTAVOS
Nickel Clad Steel, 24 mm. **Subject:** Native Culture **Obv:** National
arms, date below **Rev:** Two oxen pulling cart, denomination
above **Edge:** Coarse reeding **Note:** Obverse and reverse legends
and designs in beaded circle. Varieties exist.

Date	Mintage	F	VF	XF	Unc	BU
1990	20,000,000	—	—	—	0.60	1.25

KM# 21 1/2 PESO
12.5000 g., 0.9000 Silver 0.3617 oz. ASW, 30.5 mm.
Obv: National arms **Rev:** Profile of native princess left divides
denomination and weight

Date	Mintage	F	VF	XF	Unc	BU
1937	500,000	BV	7.50	12.50	70.00	100
1937 Proof	—	Value: 1,500				
1944	100,000	BV	15.00	40.00	400	450
1947	200,000	BV	10.00	30.00	350	500
1951	200,000	BV	7.50	15.00	150	200
1952	140,000	BV	7.50	12.50	70.00	100
1959	100,000	BV	6.00	10.00	40.00	75.00
1960	100,000	BV	6.00	9.00	30.00	55.00
1961	400,000	BV	5.00	7.00	25.00	50.00

KM# 21a.1 1/2 PESO
Copper-Nickel, 30.5 mm. **Obv:** National arms **Rev:** Profile of
native princess left divides denomination and weight **Edge:** Plain

Date	Mintage	F	VF	XF	Unc	BU
1967	1,500,000	—	0.20	0.40	1.50	3.00
1968	600,000	—	0.30	0.50	2.50	5.00

KM# 29 1/2 PESO
12.5000 g., 0.6500 Silver 0.2612 oz. ASW, 30.5 mm. **Subject:**
100th Anniversary - Restoration of the Republic **Obv:** National arms
Rev: Profile of native princess left divides denomination and weight

Date	Mintage	F	VF	XF	Unc	BU
1963	300,000	—	BV	4.50	7.50	9.00

KM# 21a.2 1/2 PESO
Copper-Nickel, 30.5 mm. **Obv:** National arms **Rev:** Profile of native
princess left divides denomination and weight **Edge:** Reeded

Date	Mintage	F	VF	XF	Unc	BU
1973	600,000	—	0.20	0.40	1.50	2.00
1973 Proof	500	Value: 30.00				
1975	600,000	—	0.20	0.40	1.50	2.00

KM# 44 1/2 PESO
Copper-Nickel, 30.5 mm. **Subject:** Centennial - Death of Juan
Pablo Duarte **Obv:** National arms, two dates below **Rev:** Bust
facing divides denomination and weight, date below

Date	Mintage	F	VF	XF	Unc	BU
1976	195,000	—	0.20	0.40	1.50	2.00
1976 Proof	5,000	Value: 3.00				

KM# 52 1/2 PESO
12.3800 g., Copper-Nickel, 30.5 mm. **Obv:** National arms
without memorial legend **Rev:** Bust facing divides denomination
and weight, date below

Date	Mintage	F	VF	XF	Unc	BU
1978	296,000	—	0.20	0.40	1.50	2.00
1978 Proof	5,000	Value: 4.00				
1979	967,000	—	0.20	0.40	1.50	2.00
1979 Proof	500	Value: 30.00				

Date	Mintage	F	VF	XF	Unc	BU
1980	1,000,000	—	0.20	0.40	1.50	2.00
1980 Proof	3,000	Value: 5.00				
1981	1,300,000	—	0.20	0.40	1.50	2.00
1981 Proof	3,000	Value: 5.00				

Note: KM#52a listed here has been moved to the Pattern section

KM# 62.1a 1/2 PESO
12.5000 g., 0.9000 Silver 0.3617 oz. ASW, 30.5 mm.
Subject: Human Rights **Obv:** National arms, date below
Rev: Three profiles right

Date	Mintage	F	VF	XF	Unc	BU
1983(t) Proof	100	Value: 50.00				
1984Mo Proof	100	Value: 50.00				

KM# 62.1 1/2 PESO
12.5000 g., Copper-Nickel, 30.87 mm. **Subject:** Human Rights
Obv: National arms, date below, denomination at left **Rev:** Three
profiles right **Edge:** Fine reeding **Note:** Medal rotation.

Date	Mintage	F	VF	XF	Unc	BU
1983	393,000	—	0.20	0.40	1.50	2.00
1983(t)	5,000	—	—	4.00	5.00	
1983(t) Proof	1,600	Value: 15.00				
1984Mo Coarse reeding	3,200,000	—	0.20	0.40	1.50	2.00
1984Mo Proof; coarse reeding	1,600	Value: 15.00				

KM# 62.2a 1/2 PESO
12.5000 g., 0.9000 Silver 0.3617 oz. ASW **Subject:** Human
rights **Obv:** National arms, date below **Rev:** 3 profiles right

Date	Mintage	F	VF	XF	Unc	BU
1986 Proof	100	Value: 50.00				

KM# 62.2 1/2 PESO
12.5000 g., Copper-Nickel, 30.5 mm. **Subject:** Human Rights
Obv: National arms, date below, denomination at left **Rev:** Three
profiles right **Edge:** Fine reeding **Note:** Coin rotation.

Date	Mintage	F	VF	XF	Unc	BU
1986	5,225,000	—	0.20	0.40	2.00	1.50
1986 Proof	1,600	Value: 15.00				
1987	3,000,000	—	0.20	0.40	2.00	1.50
1987(t) Proof	1,700	Value: 15.00				

KM# 73.1 1/2 PESO
Nickel Clad Steel, 30.5 mm. **Subject:** National Culture
Obv: National arms **Rev:** Beacon at Colon

Date	Mintage	F	VF	XF	Unc	BU
1989	8,000,000	—	—	—	2.00	3.00

KM# 73.1a 1/2 PESO
14.6500 g., 0.9250 Silver 0.4357 oz. ASW, 30.5 mm. **Subject:**
National Culture **Obv:** National arms **Rev:** Beacon at Colon

Date	Mintage	F	VF	XF	Unc	BU
1989 Proof	2,600	—	—	—	—	—

KM# 73.2 1/2 PESO
Nickel-Clad Steel, 30.5 mm. **Subject:** National Culture
Obv: National arms, date below **Rev:** Beacon at Colon,
denomination at left

Date	Mintage	F	VF	XF	Unc	BU
1990	1,500,000	—	—	—	2.00	3.00

KM# 22 PESO
26.7000 g., 0.9000 Silver 0.7726 oz. ASW **Obv:** National arms
Rev: HP below head of native princess left

Date	Mintage	F	VF	XF	Unc	BU
1939	15,000	18.00	45.00	200	1,500	
1939 Proof	—	Value: 2,250				
1952	20,000	—	BV	15.00	18.00	30.00

KM# 23   PESO
26.7000 g., 0.9000 Silver 0.7726 oz. ASW, 38 mm.
Subject: 25th Anniversary of Trujillo Regime **Obv:** National arms
Rev: Bust right divides date and denomination **Note:** 30,550
officially melted following Trujillo's assassination in 1961.

Date	Mintage	F	VF	XF	Unc	BU
1955	50,000	10.00	12.00	15.00	25.00	35.00

KM# 30   PESO
26.7000 g., 0.6500 Silver 0.5580 oz. ASW **Subject:** 100th
Anniversary - Restoration of the Republic **Obv:** Memorial legend
around national arms, two dates below **Rev:** Profile of native
princess left divides denomination and weight, date below

Date	Mintage	F	VF	XF	Unc	BU
1963	20,000	—	—	10.00	12.00	16.00
1963 Proof						

KM# 33   PESO
Copper-Nickel, 38 mm. **Subject:** 125th Anniversary of the
Republic **Obv:** Memorial legend around national arms, two dates
below **Rev:** Pueblo entrance within circle holding legend divides
denomination and weight, date below

Date	Mintage	F	VF	XF	Unc	BU
1969	30,000	—	—	2.00	4.50	6.00

KM# 34   PESO
26.7000 g., 0.9000 Silver 0.7726 oz. ASW **Subject:** 25th
Anniversary - Central Bank **Obv:** Memorial legend around
national arms **Rev:** Bank door in inner circle divides denomination
and weight, date below

Date	Mintage	F	VF	XF	Unc	BU
1972	27,000	—	—	—	14.00	16.00
1972 Proof	3,000	Value: 18.00				

KM# 35   PESO
26.7000 g., 0.9000 Silver 0.7726 oz. ASW **Subject:** 12th Central
American and Caribbean Games **Obv:** National arms without
memorial legend **Rev:** Coat of arms within circle, on map,
denomination and date below

Date	Mintage	F	VF	XF	Unc	BU
1974	50,000	—	—	14.00	16.00	
1974 Proof	5,000	Value: 18.00				

KM# 45   PESO
Copper-Nickel **Subject:** Centennial - Death of Juan Pablo Duarte
Obv: National arms, two dates below **Rev:** Bust facing divides
denomination and weight, date below

Date	Mintage	F	VF	XF	Unc	BU
1976	25,000	—	1.00	2.00	4.00	
1976 Proof	5,000	Value: 7.50				

KM# 53   PESO
Copper-Nickel   **Obv:** National arms without memorial legend
Rev: Bust facing divides denomination and weight, date below

Date	Mintage	F	VF	XF	Unc	BU
1978	35,000	—	1.00	2.00	4.00	
1978 Proof	5,000	Value: 7.50				
1979	45,000	—	1.00	2.00	4.00	
1979 Proof	500	Value: 35.00				
1980	20,000	—	1.00	2.00	4.00	
1980 Proof	3,000	Value: 6.50				
1981 Proof	3,000	Value: 6.50				

Note: KM#53a previously listed here has been moved to
the Pattern section

KM# 63.1a   PESO
17.0000 g., 0.9000 Silver 0.4919 oz. ASW **Subject:** Human Rights
Obv: National arms, denomination **Rev:** Three profiles right

Date	Mintage	F	VF	XF	Unc	BU
1983(t) Proof	100	Value: 100				
1984 Proof	100	Value: 100				

KM# 63.1   PESO
16.9000 g., Copper Nickel, 33.54 mm. **Subject:** Human Rights
Obv: National arms, date below, denomination at left **Rev:** Three
profiles right **Edge:** Fine reeding **Note:** Medal rotation.

Date	Mintage	F	VF	XF	Unc	BU
1983	5,000	—	—	—	6.00	12.00
1983(t)	93,000	—	—	1.00	2.50	4.00

Date	Mintage	F	VF	XF	Unc	BU
1983(t) Proof	1,600	Value: 15.00				
1984Mo Coarse reeding	120,000	—	—	1.00	2.50	4.00
1984Mo Proof; coarse reeding	1,600	Value: 15.00				

KM# 63.2   PESO
16.9000 g., Copper-Nickel, 33.2 mm. **Subject:** Human Rights
Obv: National arms, date below, denomination at left **Rev:** Three
profiles right **Edge:** Fine reeding **Note:** Coin rotation.

Date	Mintage	F	VF	XF	Unc	BU
1986	—	—	—	1.00	2.50	4.00

KM# 65   PESO
Nickel Bonded Steel   **Subject:** 15th Central American and
Caribbean Games **Obv:** National arms, date below,
denomination at left **Rev:** St. George and coat of arms

Date	Mintage	F	VF	XF	Unc	BU
1986	100,000	—	—	1.00	3.00	5.00
1986 Proof	2,000	Value: 15.00				

KM# 65a   PESO
6.5000 g., Copper-Nickel **Subject:** 15th Central American and
Caribbean Games **Obv:** National arms, denomination **Rev:** St.
George and coat of arms

Date	Mintage	F	VF	XF	Unc	BU
1986	548	—	—	—	40.00	60.00
1986 Proof	48	—	—	—	—	

KM# 65b   PESO
10.0000 g., Copper-Nickel **Subject:** 15th Central American and
Caribbean Games **Obv:** National arms and denomination
Rev: St. George and coat of arms

Date	Mintage	F	VF	XF	Unc	BU
1986	550	—	—	—	40.00	60.00
1986 Proof	50	—	—	—	—	

KM# 66   PESO
19.8400 g., Copper-Nickel **Subject:** 500th Anniversary -
Discovery and Evangelization **Obv:** National arms, date below,
denomination at left **Rev:** 3 ships at sea, date below

Date	Mintage	F	VF	XF	Unc	BU
1988(c)	150,000	—	—	—	2.50	3.50
1988(c) Proof	1,500	Value: 12.50				

KM# 66a   PESO
21.1035 g., 0.9990 Silver 0.6778 oz. ASW **Subject:** 500th
Anniversary - Discovery and Evangelization **Obv:** Denomination,
national arms **Rev:** 3 ships at sea

Date	Mintage	F	VF	XF	Unc	BU
1988 Proof	10,000	Value: 18.50				

KM# 66b   PESO
31.1035 g., 0.9990 Gold 0.9990 oz. AGW **Subject:** 500th
Anniversary - Discovery and Evangelization **Obv:** Denomination,
national arms **Rev:** 3 ships at sea

Date	Mintage	F	VF	XF	Unc	BU
1988 Proof	—	Value: 1,250				

KM# 74   PESO
Copper-Nickel **Subject:** 500th Anniversary - Discovery and
Evangelization **Obv:** Denomination, national arms **Rev:** Sailship
landing

Date	Mintage	F	VF	XF	Unc	BU
1989(c)		—	—	—	2.50	3.50

KM# 74a   PESO
31.1035 g., 0.9990 Silver 0.9990 oz. ASW **Subject:** 500th
Anniversary - Discovery and Evangelization **Obv:** Denomination,
national arms **Rev:** Sailship landing

Date	Mintage	F	VF	XF	Unc	BU
1989 Proof	10,000	Value: 20.00				

KM# 74b   PESO
31.1035 g., 0.9990 Gold 0.9990 oz. AGW **Subject:** 500th
Anniversary - Discovery and Evangelization **Obv:** Denomination,
national arms **Rev:** Sailship landing

Date	Mintage	F	VF	XF	Unc	BU
1989(c) Proof	30	Value: 1,250				

KM# 77 PESO
Copper-Nickel **Subject:** 500th Anniversary - Discovery and Evangelization **Obv:** National arms, date below, denomination at left **Rev:** Two standing figures, date below

Date	Mintage	F	VF	XF	Unc	BU
1990(c)	30,000	—	—	—	2.50	3.50

KM# 77a PESO
31.1035 g., 0.9990 Silver 0.9990 oz. ASW **Subject:** 500th Anniversary - Discovery and Evangelization **Obv:** National arms and denomination **Rev:** Two standing figures

Date	Mintage	F	VF	XF	Unc	BU
1990 Proof	10,000	Value: 20.00				

KM# 77b PESO
31.1035 g., 0.9990 Gold 0.9990 oz. AGW **Subject:** 500th Anniversary - Discovery and Evangelization **Obv:** National arms **Rev:** Two standing figures

Date	Mintage	F	VF	XF	Unc	BU
1990 Proof	50	—	—	—	1,000	—

KM# 80.1 PESO
Copper-Zinc, 25 mm. **Subject:** Juan Pablo Duarte **Obv:** National arms and denomination **Rev:** DUARTE on bust 3/4 left, date below **Note:** Coin die alignment.

Date	Mintage	F	VF	XF	Unc	BU
1991	40,000,000	—	—	—	2.00	2.50
1992	35,000,000	—	—	—	2.00	2.50

KM# 81 PESO
Copper-Nickel **Subject:** Pinzon brothers on ship at sea **Obv:** National arms, date below, denomination at left **Rev:** Conjoined busts 3/4 left, on ship at sea, date below

Date	Mintage	F	VF	XF	Unc	BU
1991(c)	50,000	—	—	—	2.50	3.50

KM# 81a PESO
31.1035 g., 0.9990 Silver 0.9990 oz. ASW **Subject:** Pinzon brothers on ship at sea **Obv:** Denomination, national arms **Rev:** Conjoined busts left on ship at sea

Date	Mintage	F	VF	XF	Unc	BU
1991 Proof	10,000	Value: 20.00				

KM# 81b PESO
31.1035 g., 0.9990 Gold 0.9990 oz. AGW **Subject:** Pinzon brothers on ship at sea **Obv:** Denomination, national arms **Rev:** Conjoined busts left on ship at sea

Date	Mintage	F	VF	XF	Unc	BU
1991 Proof	35	Value: 1,150				

KM# 80.2 PESO
6.4900 g., Copper-Zinc, 25 mm. **Subject:** Juan Pablo Duarte **Obv:** National arms and denomination **Rev:** DUARTE below bust, date below **Note:** Coin die alignment.

Date	Mintage	F	VF	XF	Unc	BU
1992	35,000,000	—	—	—	2.00	2.50

Date	Mintage	F	VF	XF	Unc	BU
1993	40,000,000	—	—	—	2.00	2.50
2000		—	—	—	2.00	2.50

KM# 82 PESO
Copper-Nickel **Subject:** Christopher Columbus **Obv:** National arms, date below, denomination at left **Rev:** Bust 3/4 left, date below

Date	Mintage	F	VF	XF	Unc	BU
1992(c)	50,000	—	—	—	2.50	3.50

KM# 82a PESO
31.1035 g., 0.9990 Silver 0.9990 oz. ASW **Subject:** Christopher Columbus **Obv:** Denomination, national arms **Rev:** Bust 3/4 left

Date	Mintage	F	VF	XF	Unc	BU
1992 Proof	10,000	Value: 20.00				

KM# 82b PESO
31.1035 g., 0.9990 Gold 0.9990 oz. AGW **Subject:** Christopher Columbus **Obv:** Denomination, national arms **Rev:** Bust 3/4 left

Date	Mintage	F	VF	XF	Unc	BU
1992(c) Proof	35	Value: 1,150				

KM# 87 PESO
Copper-Nickel **Subject:** UN - Peace **Obv:** National arms, stars flank date below, denomination at left, **Rev:** UN logo, two doves, two dates above

Date	Mintage	F	VF	XF	Unc	BU
1995		—	—	—	9.00	10.00

KM# 87a PESO
28.4400 g., 0.9250 Silver 0.8458 oz. ASW **Subject:** UN - Peace **Obv:** Denomination, arms, stars **Rev:** UN logo, two doves

Date	Mintage	F	VF	XF	Unc	BU
1995 Proof	—	Value: 35.00				

KM# 80.3 PESO
Copper-Zinc, 25 mm. **Subject:** Juan Pablo Duarte **Obv:** National arms and denomination **Rev:** DUARTE below bust **Note:** Medal die alignment

Date	Mintage	F	VF	XF	Unc	BU
1997		—	—	—	2.00	2.50

KM# 88 5 PESOS
Bi-Metallic Stainless Steel center in Brass ring, 23 mm. **Subject:** 50th Anniversary - Central Bank **Obv:** Denomination and national arms within circle, date below **Rev:** Head facing within circle, two dates below

Date	Mintage	F	VF	XF	Unc	BU
1997		—	—	—	2.50	3.00

KM# 37 10 PESOS
28.0000 g., 0.9000 Silver 0.8102 oz. ASW **Subject:** International Bankers' Conference - First Hispaniola Coinage of Carlos and Johanna **Obv:** National arms, denomination and date below **Rev:** Arms of Castille in inner ring

Date	Mintage	F	VF	XF	Unc	BU
1975	26,000	—	—	—	17.50	20.00
1975 Proof	4,000	Value: 27.50				

KM# 38 10 PESOS
30.0000 g., 0.9000 Silver 0.8680 oz. ASW **Subject:** Taino Art **Obv:** National arms **Rev:** Ancient figurine "Pueblo Viejo Mine" divides dates, date below

Date	Mintage	F	VF	XF	Unc	BU
1975	Est. 45,000					
	Note: Reported, not confirmed					
1975 Proof	5,000	Value: 25.00				

KM# 57 10 PESOS
23.3300 g., 0.9250 Silver 0.6938 oz. ASW, 38.61 mm. **Subject:** International Year of the Child **Obv:** National arms **Rev:** 1/2 length figure of child drawing a house, small logos at left and right **Rev. Leg.:** AÑO INTERNACIONAL DEL NIÑO **Edge:** Reeded

Date	Mintage	F	VF	XF	Unc	BU
1982(o) Proof	8,712	Value: 14.50				

KM# 91 10 PESOS
2.4500 g., 0.9990 Silver 0.0787 oz. ASW, 18 mm. **Obv:** National arms **Rev:** St. Andrews Chapel

Date	Mintage	F	VF	XF	Unc	BU
2000 Proof	3,000	Value: 22.50				

KM# 92 10 PESOS
2.4500 g., 0.9990 Silver 0.0787 oz. ASW, 18 mm. **Obv:** National arms **Rev:** Our Lady of Carmen Church

Date	Mintage	F	VF	XF	Unc	BU
2000 Proof	3,000	Value: 22.50				

KM# 93 10 PESOS
2.4500 g., 0.9990 Silver 0.0787 oz. ASW, 18 mm. **Obv:** National arms **Rev:** Regina Angelorum Church

Date	Mintage	F	VF	XF	Unc	BU
2000 Proof	3,000	Value: 22.50				

KM# 94 10 PESOS
2.4500 g., 0.9990 Silver 0.0787 oz. ASW, 18 mm. **Obv:** National arms **Rev:** Chapel of the Remedies

Date	Mintage	F	VF	XF	Unc	BU
2000 Proof	3,000	Value: 22.50				

KM# 95 10 PESOS
2.4500 g., 0.9990 Silver 0.0787 oz. ASW, 18 mm. **Obv:** National arms **Rev:** St. Lazarus Church

Date	Mintage	F	VF	XF	Unc	BU
2000 Proof	3,000	Value: 22.50				

KM# 96 10 PESOS
2.4500 g., 0.9990 Silver 0.0787 oz. ASW, 18 mm. **Obv:** National arms **Rev:** St. Michael's Church

Date	Mintage	F	VF	XF	Unc	BU
2000 Proof	3,000	Value: 22.50				

KM# 97 10 PESOS
2.4500 g., 0.9990 Silver 0.0787 oz. ASW, 18 mm. **Obv:** National arms **Rev:** Church of Santa Barbara

Date	Mintage	F	VF	XF	Unc	BU
2000 Proof	3,000	Value: 22.50				

KM# 98 10 PESOS
2.4500 g., 0.9990 Silver 0.0787 oz. ASW, 18 mm. **Obv:** National arms **Rev:** Our Lady of the Rosary Church

Date	Mintage	F	VF	XF	Unc	BU
2000 Proof	3,000	Value: 22.50				

KM# 99 10 PESOS
2.4500 g., 0.9990 Silver 0.0787 oz. ASW, 18 mm. **Obv:** National arms **Rev:** Church of Banica

Date	Mintage	F	VF	XF	Unc	BU
2000 Proof	3,000	Value: 22.50				

KM# 100 10 PESOS
2.4500 g., 0.9990 Silver 0.0787 oz. ASW, 18 mm. **Obv:** National arms **Rev:** Church of Boya

Date	Mintage	F	VF	XF	Unc	BU
2000 Proof	3,000	Value: 22.50				

KM# 101 10 PESOS
2.4500 g., 0.9990 Silver 0.0787 oz. ASW, 18 mm. **Obv:** National arms **Rev:** Santo Domingo Cathedral

Date	Mintage	F	VF	XF	Unc	BU
2000 Proof	3,000	Value: 22.50				

KM# 102 10 PESOS
2.4500 g., 0.9990 Silver 0.0787 oz. ASW, 18 mm. **Obv:** National arms **Rev:** Holy Cross Cathedral of El Seibo

Date	Mintage	F	VF	XF	Unc	BU
2000 Proof	3,000	Value: 22.50				

KM# 103 10 PESOS
2.4500 g., 0.9990 Silver 0.0787 oz. ASW, 18 mm. **Obv:** National arms **Rev:** Higney Sanctuary

Date	Mintage	F	VF	XF	Unc	BU
2000 Proof	3,000	Value: 22.50				

KM# 110 10 PESOS
3.1360 g., 0.9999 Gold 0.1008 oz. AGW, 16 mm. **Obv:** National arms **Rev:** Santa María de la Encarnación cathedral

Date	Mintage	F	VF	XF	Unc	BU
2000	2,000	—	—	—	120	—

KM# 111 10 PESOS
3.1360 g., 0.9999 Gold 0.1008 oz. AGW, 16 mm. **Obv:** National arms **Rev:** Banica church

Date	Mintage	F	VF	XF	Unc	BU
2000	2,000	—	—	—	120	—

KM# 112 10 PESOS
3.1360 g., 0.9999 Gold 0.1008 oz. AGW, 16 mm. **Obv:** National arms **Rev:** Boya church

Date	Mintage	F	VF	XF	Unc	BU
2000	2,000	—	—	—	120	—

KM# 113 10 PESOS
3.1360 g., 0.9999 Gold 0.1008 oz. AGW, 16 mm. **Obv:** National arms **Rev:** Nuestra Señora del Carmen church

Date	Mintage	F	VF	XF	Unc	BU
2000	2,000	—	—	—	120	—

KM# 114 10 PESOS
3.1360 g., 0.9999 Gold 0.1008 oz. AGW, 16 mm. **Obv:** National arms **Rev:** Nuestra Señora del Rosario church

Date	Mintage	F	VF	XF	Unc	BU
2000	2,000	—	—	—	120	—

KM# 115 10 PESOS
3.1360 g., 0.9999 Gold 0.1008 oz. AGW, 16 mm. **Obv:** National arms **Rev:** Santa Barbara church

Date	Mintage	F	VF	XF	Unc	BU
2000	2,000	—	—	—	120	—

KM# 116 10 PESOS
3.1360 g., 0.9999 Gold 0.1008 oz. AGW, 16 mm. **Obv:** National arms **Rev:** Santa Cruz de El Seibo church

Date	Mintage	F	VF	XF	Unc	BU
2000	2,000	—	—	—	120	—

KM# 117 10 PESOS
3.1360 g., 0.9999 Gold 0.1008 oz. AGW, 16 mm. **Obv:** National arms **Rev:** San Lázaro church

Date	Mintage	F	VF	XF	Unc	BU
2000	2,000	—	—	—	—	120

KM# 118 10 PESOS
3.1360 g., 0.9999 Gold 0.1008 oz. AGW, 16 mm. **Obv:** National arms **Rev:** San Miguel church

Date	Mintage	F	VF	XF	Unc	BU
2000	2,000	—	—	—	120	—

KM# 119 10 PESOS
3.1360 g., 0.9999 Gold 0.1008 oz. AGW, 16 mm. **Obv:** National arms **Rev:** Regina Angelorum chuch

Date	Mintage	F	VF	XF	Unc	BU
2000	2,000	—	—	—	120	—

KM# 120 10 PESOS
3.1360 g., 0.9999 Gold 0.1008 oz. AGW, 16 mm. **Obv:** National arms **Rev:** Sanctuary at Higuey

Date	Mintage	F	VF	XF	Unc	BU
2000	2,000	—	—	—	120	—

KM# 121 10 PESOS
3.1360 g., 0.9999 Gold 0.1008 oz. AGW, 16 mm. **Obv:** National arms **Rev:** Chapel of the Remedios

Date	Mintage	F	VF	XF	Unc	BU
2000	2,000	—	—	—	120	—

KM# 122 10 PESOS
3.1360 g., 0.9999 Gold 0.1008 oz. AGW, 16 mm. **Obv:** National arms **Rev:** Chapel of San Andrés

Date	Mintage	F	VF	XF	Unc	BU
2000	2,000	—	—	—	120	—

KM# 54 25 PESOS
65.0000 g., 0.9250 Silver 1.9330 oz. ASW **Subject:** Pope John Paul II's Visit **Obv:** National arms, denomination below **Rev:** Bust left, Vatican City and date at left

Date	Mintage	F	VF	XF	Unc	BU
ND(1979)	3,000	—	—	—	40.00	45.00
ND(1979) Proof	6,000	Value: 50.00				

KM# 24 30 PESOS
29.6220 g., 0.9000 Gold 0.8571 oz. AGW, 32 mm. **Subject:** 25th Anniversary of Trujillo regime **Obv:** National arms, denomination below **Rev:** Head left, date below

Date	Mintage	F	VF	XF	Unc	BU
1955	33,000	—	—	BV	825	850

KM# 36 30 PESOS
11.7000 g., 0.9000 Gold 0.3385 oz. AGW **Subject:** 12th Central American and Caribbean Games **Obv:** National arms **Rev:** Games symbol, denomination and date below

Date	Mintage	F	VF	XF	Unc	BU
1974	25,000	—	—	—	325	345
1974 Proof	5,000	Value: 375				

KM# 46 30 PESOS
78.0000 g., 0.9250 Silver 2.3196 oz. ASW **Subject:** 30th Anniversary of Central Bank **Obv:** National arms, denomination at left, date below **Rev:** Bank building, two dates below

Date	Mintage	F	VF	XF	Unc	BU
1977	5,000	—	—	—	42.50	47.50
1977 Proof	2,000	Value: 55.00				

KM# 104 50 PESOS
28.3500 g., 0.9250 Silver 0.8431 oz. ASW, 38 mm. **Subject:** 50th Anniversary - Central Bank **Obv:** National arms **Rev:** Seated woman holding up coin **Edge:** Reeded

Date	Mintage	F	VF	XF	Unc	BU
ND (1997)	3,000	—	—	—	—	35.00
ND (1997) Proof	2,000	Value: 50.00				

KM# 39 100 PESOS
10.0000 g., 0.9000 Gold 0.2893 oz. AGW **Subject:** Taino Art **Obv:** National arms, date below **Rev:** Native art divides denomination, date below

Date	Mintage	F	VF	XF	Unc	BU
1975	18,000	—	—	—	275	285
1975 Proof	2,000	Value: 300				

KM# 55 100 PESOS
12.0000 g., 0.9000 Gold 0.3472 oz. AGW **Subject:** Pope John Paul II's Visit **Obv:** National arms, denomination below **Rev:** Bust left, Vatican City and date at left

Date	Mintage	F	VF	XF	Unc	BU
ND(1979)	1,000	—	—	—	320	330
ND(1979) Proof	3,000	Value: 350				

KM# 67 100 PESOS
155.5000 g., 0.9990 Silver 4.9942 oz. ASW, 65 mm.
Subject: Discovery of America - Native Americans

Date	Mintage	F	VF	XF	Unc	BU
1988 Proof	5,300	Value: 110				

KM# 75 100 PESOS
155.5000 g., 0.9990 Silver 4.9942 oz. ASW **Subject:** 500th Anniversary of Discovery and Evangelization of America **Obv:** Arms **Rev:** Columbus and crew, date below

Date	Mintage	F	VF	XF	Unc	BU
1989(c) Proof	1,500	Value: 125				

KM# 75a 100 PESOS
155.5000 g., 0.9990 Gold 4.9942 oz. AGW **Subject:** 500th Anniversary of Discovery and Evangelization of America **Obv:** Arms **Rev:** Columbus and crew

Date	Mintage	F	VF	XF	Unc	BU
1989 Proof	30	Value: 5,000				

KM# 78 100 PESOS
155.5000 g., 0.9990 Silver 4.9942 oz. ASW, 65 mm. **Subject:** 500th Anniversary of Discovery and Evangelization of America **Obv:** National arms **Rev:** Building a stockade, date below **Note:** Illustration reduced.

Date	Mintage	F	VF	XF	Unc	BU
1990 Proof	1,000	Value: 145				

KM# 78a 100 PESOS
155.5300 g., 0.9990 Gold 4.9952 oz. AGW, 65 mm. **Subject:** 500th Anniversary of Discovery and Evangelization of America **Obv:** National arms **Rev:** Building a stockade **Note:** Illustration reduced.

Date	Mintage	F	VF	XF	Unc	BU
1990 Proof	50	Value: 5,000				

KM# 83 100 PESOS
155.5300 g., 0.9990 Silver 4.9952 oz. ASW, 65 mm. **Subject:** 500th Anniversary of Discovery and Evangelization of America **Obv:** National arms **Rev:** Columbus Presenting Native American to Court **Note:** Illustration reduced.

Date	Mintage	F	VF	XF	Unc	BU
1991 Proof	1,500	Value: 125				

KM# 83a 100 PESOS
155.5300 g., 0.9990 Gold 4.9952 oz. AGW, 65 mm. **Subject:** 500th Anniversary of Discovery and Evangelization of America **Obv:** National arms **Rev:** Columbus Presenting Native American to Court **Note:** Illustration reduced.

Date	Mintage	F	VF	XF	Unc	BU
1991 Proof	35	Value: 5,000				

KM# 84 100 PESOS
155.5300 g., 0.9990 Silver 4.9952 oz. ASW, 65 mm. **Subject:** 500th Anniversary - Discovery and Evangelization of America **Obv:** National arms **Rev:** Columbus bust left, and anchored ship, date below **Note:** Illustration reduced.

Date	Mintage	F	VF	XF	Unc	BU
1992 Proof	1,500	Value: 135				

KM# 84a 100 PESOS
155.5300 g., 0.9990 Gold 4.9952 oz. AGW, 65 mm. **Subject:** 500th Anniversary - Discovery and Evangelization of America **Obv:** National arms **Rev:** Bust left and anchored ship

Date	Mintage	F	VF	XF	Unc	BU
1992 Proof	35	Value: 5,000				

KM# 47 200 PESOS
31.0000 g., 0.8000 Gold 0.7973 oz. AGW **Subject:** Centennial - Death of Juan Pablo Duarte **Obv:** National arms, date below **Rev:** Head facing divides denomination, two dates below **Note:** Large quantities of both varieties were melted for bullion.

Date	Mintage	F	VF	XF	Unc	BU
1977	1,000	—	—	—	775	800
1977 Proof	2,000	Value: 850				

KM# 58 200 PESOS
17.1700 g., 0.9000 Gold 0.4968 oz. AGW **Subject:** International Year of the Child **Obv:** National arms, date below **Rev:** Children dancing, denomination below

Date	Mintage	F	VF	XF	Unc	BU
1982 Proof	4,303	Value: 475				

KM# 105 200 PESOS
12.0000 g., 0.9000 Gold 0.3472 oz. AGW, 25 mm. **Subject:** 50th Anniversary - Central Bank **Obv:** National arms **Rev:** Seated woman holding up coin **Edge:** Reeded

Date	Mintage	F	VF	XF	Unc	BU
ND (1997)	500	—	—	—	—	385
ND (1997) Proof	2,000	Value: 450				

KM# 56 250 PESOS
31.1000 g., 0.9000 Gold 0.8999 oz. AGW **Subject:** Visit of Pope John Paul II

Date	Mintage	F	VF	XF	Unc	BU
1979	1,000	—	—	—	850	875
1979 Proof	3,000	Value: 900				

KM# 68 500 PESOS
31.1000 g., 0.9990 Gold 0.9988 oz. AGW **Subject:** Discovery of America - Columbus

Date	Mintage	F	VF	XF	Unc	BU
1988 Proof	2,600	Value: 950				

KM# 76 500 PESOS
31.1000 g., 0.9990 Gold 0.9988 oz. AGW **Subject:** 500th Anniversary - Discovery and Evangelization of America **Obv:** National arms, denomination below **Rev:** Portraits of Ferdinand and Isabella, date below

Date	Mintage	F	VF	XF	Unc	BU
1989 Proof	600	Value: 1,000				

KM# 76a 500 PESOS
31.1000 g., 0.9990 Platinum 0.9988 oz. APW **Subject:** 500th Anniversary - Discovery and Evangelization of America **Obv:** National arms **Rev:** Portraits of Ferdinand and Isabella

Date	Mintage	F	VF	XF	Unc	BU
1989 Proof	—	Value: 2,000				

KM# 79 500 PESOS
16.9600 g., 0.9170 Gold 0.5000 oz. AGW **Subject:** 500th Anniversary - Discovery and Evangelization of America **Obv:** National arms, denomination below **Rev:** Santa Maria and landing crew, date below

Date	Mintage	F	VF	XF	Unc	BU
1990 Proof	1,500	Value: 500				

KM# 79a 500 PESOS
15.5500 g., 0.9990 Platinum 0.4994 oz. APW **Subject:** 500th Anniversary - Discovery and Evangelization of America **Obv:** National arms **Rev:** Santa Maria and landing crew

Date	Mintage	F	VF	XF	Unc	BU
1990 Proof	50	Value: 1,000				

KM# 85 500 PESOS
16.9600 g., 0.9170 Gold 0.5000 oz. AGW **Subject:** 500th Anniversary - Discovery and Evangelization of America **Obv:** National arms, denomination below **Rev:** American fruits, date below

Date	Mintage	F	VF	XF	Unc	BU
1991 Proof	1,500	Value: 500				

KM# 85a 500 PESOS

15.5500 g., 0.9990 Platinum 0.4994 oz. APW **Subject:** 500th Anniversary - Discovery and Evangelization of America
Obv: National arms **Rev:** American fruits

Date	Mintage	F	VF	XF	Unc	BU
1991 Proof	35	Value: 1,000				

KM# 86 500 PESOS

16.9600 g., 0.9170 Gold 0.5000 oz. AGW **Subject:** 500th Anniversary - Discovery and Evangelization of America
Obv: National arms, denomination below **Rev:** Enshrined tomb of Christopher Columbus, date below

Date	Mintage	F	VF	XF	Unc	BU
1992 Proof	2,000	Value: 500				

KM# 86a 500 PESOS

15.5500 g., 0.9990 Platinum 0.4978 oz. APW **Subject:** 500th Anniversary - Discovery and Evangelization of America **Obv:** National arms **Rev:** Enshrined tomb of Christopher Columbus

Date	Mintage	F	VF	XF	Unc	BU
1992 Proof	35	Value: 1,000				

KM# 108 2000 PESOS

62.7670 g., 0.9167 Gold 1.8498 oz. AGW, 38 mm. **Subject:** Third Millennium of Christianity **Obv:** National arms **Rev:** Doves, globe **Rev. Leg.:** TERCER MILENO - DEL CRISTIANISMO

Date	Mintage	F	VF	XF	Unc	BU
2000 Proof	2,000	Value: 1,800				

KM# 109 2000 PESOS

31.1600 g., 0.9995 Platinum 1.0013 oz. APW, 30 mm. **Subject:** Third Millenium of Christianity **Obv:** National arms **Rev:** Doves, globe **Rev. Leg.:** TERCER MILENO - DEL CRISTIANISMO

Date	Mintage	F	VF	XF	Unc	BU
2000 Proof	200	Value: 2,200				

PATTERNS

Including off metal strikes

KM#	Date	Mintage	Identification	Mkt Val
Pn6	1937	—	50 Centavos. Silver. Obverse only.	—
Pn7	1937	—	50 Centavos. Copper. Obverse only.	—
Pn8	1937	—	50 Centavos. Silver. Reverse only.	—
Pn9	1961	—	5 Centavos. Copper-Bonded Steel.	—
Pn10	1961	—	5 Centavos. Copper-Bonded Steel.	—
Pn11	1961	—	5 Centavos. Copper-Bonded Steel. Same design both sides.	—
Pn12	1961	—	10 Centavos. Copper-Bonded Steel.	—
Pn13	1961	—	25 Centavos. Chrome Plated Steel.	—
Pn14	1968	3	50 Centavos. Reeded edge.	—
Pn15	1972	1	25 Centavos. Reeded edge.	—
Pn16	1975	1	10 Pesos. Silver.	—
Pn17	1975	11	10 Pesos. 0.5000 Gold.	—
Pn18	1975	1	10 Pesos. 0.2940 Gold.	—
Pn19	1975	1	10 Pesos. 0.4000 Gold.	—
Pn20	1975	1	10 Pesos. 0.8000 Gold.	—
Pn21	1975	1	100 Pesos. 0.9000 Gold. without matte details.	—
Pn22	1975	1	100 Pesos. 0.8000 Gold. alloyed with .050 Silver and .150 Copper.	—
Pn23	1975	5	100 Pesos. 0.8000 Gold. alloyed with .150 Silver.	—
Pn24	1975	5	100 Pesos. 0.8000 Gold. alloyed with .150 Silver and .050 Copper, Proof.	—
Pn25	1976	3	10 Centavos. Plain rim.	—
Pn26	1977	5	30 Pesos. Gold. Proof.	—
Pn27	1978	3	Centavo. Aluminum.	—
Pn28	1978	3	Centavo. Copper And Zinc.	100
Pn29	1978	—	Centavo. 0.9000 Silver. 3.5800 g.	125
Pn30	1978	—	5 Centavos. 0.9000 Silver. 5.8600 g. Without memorial legend.	125
Pn31	1978	—	10 Centavos. 0.9000 Silver. 2.9500 g. Without memorial legend.	125
Pn32	1978	3	25 Centavos. 6-1/2 Gramos.	—
Pn33	1978	—	25 Centavos. 0.9000 Silver. 7.3200 g. Without memorial legend.	150
Pn34	1978	—	1/2 Peso. 0.9000 Silver. 14.5500 g. Without memorial legend.	150
Pn35	1978	—	Peso. 0.9000 Silver. 30.9200 g. Without memorial legend. Portrait of Duarte.	300
Pn36	1979	—	Centavo. 0.9000 Silver. 3.5800 g.	125
Pn37	1979	—	5 Centavos. 0.9000 Silver. 5.8600 g. Without memorial legend.	125
Pn38	1979	—	10 Centavos. 0.9000 Silver. 2.9500 g. Without memorial legend.	125
Pn39	1979	3	25 Centavos. 6-1/2 Gramos.	—
Pn40	1979	—	25 Centavos. 0.9000 Silver. 7.3200 g. Without memorial legend.	150
Pn41	1979	—	1/2 Peso. 0.9000 Silver. 14.5500 g. Without memorial legend.	150
Pn42	1979	—	Peso. 0.9000 Silver. 30.9200 g. Without memorial legend. Portrait of Duarte.	300
Pn43	1980	—	Centavo. 0.9000 Silver. 3.5800 g.	125
Pn44	1980	—	5 Centavos. 0.9000 Silver. 5.8600 g. Without memorial legend.	125

KM#	Date	Mintage	Identification	Mkt Val
Pn45	1980	—	10 Centavos. 0.9000 Silver. 2.9500 g. Without memorial legend.	125
Pn46	1980	—	25 Centavos. 0.9000 Silver. 7.3200 g. Without memorial legend.	150
Pn47	1980	—	1/2 Peso. 0.9000 Silver. 14.5500 g. Without memorial legend.	150
Pn48	1980	—	Peso. 0.9000 Silver. 30.9200 g. Without memorial legend. Portrait of Duarte.	300
Pn49	1981	—	Centavo. 0.9000 Silver. 3.5800 g.	125
Pn50	1981	—	5 Centavos. 0.9000 Silver. 5.8600 g.	125
Pn51	1981	—	10 Centavos. 0.9000 Silver. 2.9500 g. Without memorial legend.	125
Pn52	1981	—	25 Centavos. 0.9000 Silver. 7.3200 g. Without memorial legend.	150
Pn53	1981	—	1/2 Peso. 0.9000 Silver. 14.5500 g. Without memorial legend.	150
Pn54	1981	—	Peso. 0.9000 Silver. 30.9200 g. Without memorial legend. Portrait of Duarte.	300
Pn55	1982	80	10 Pesos. Silver. KM#57.	—
Pn56	1983	15	25 Centavos. Nickel Bonded Steel.	200
Pn57	1984	3	25 Centavos. Nickel Bonded Steel.	200
Pn58	1984	5	Peso. Nickel Bonded Steel.	—
Pn59	1986	500	Peso. Copper-Nickel.	—

Note: Several issues previously listed under Patterns have now been correctly identified as commercially inspired, privately contracted Medallic Issues and have been moved to that section. The remaining patterns have been renumbered

PIEFORTS

KM#	Date	Mintage	Identification	Mkt Val
P1	1977	5	30 Pesos. Gold. Piefort.	—
P2	1982	262	10 Pesos.	150
P3	1982	42	200 Pesos.	2,250
P4	1983 H	300	5 Centavos.	20.00
P5	1983 H	300	10 Centavos. Nickel Bonded Steel.	30.00
P6	1983	300	25 Centavos. Copper-Nickel. KM#61.	35.00
P7	1983 H	300	25 Centavos. Copper-Nickel.	35.00
P8	1983	300	1/2 Peso. Copper-Nickel center. KM#62.	40.00
P9	1983	300	Peso. Copper-Nickel. KM#63.	50.00
P10	1984Mo	300	Centavo. KM64.	5.00
P11	1984Mo	300	5 Centavos. KM59.	5.00
P12	1984Mo	300	10 Centavos. KM60.	5.00
P13	1984Mo	300	25 Centavos. KM61.1.	8.00
P14	1984Mo	300	1/2 Peso. KM62.1.	10.00
P15	1984Mo	300	Peso. KM63.1.	12.00
P16	1986	300	Peso. Nickel Bonded Steel.	15.00
P17	1986	50	Peso. Copper Nickel. 20.0000 g.	—
P18	1986	300	Centavo. Copper Plated Zinc.	5.00
P19	1986	300	5 Centavos. Copper-Nickel.	5.00
P20	1986	300	10 Centavos. Copper-Nickel.	8.00
P21	1986	300	25 Centavos. Copper-Nickel.	10.00
P22	1986	300	1/2 Peso. Copper-Nickel.	12.00
P23	1987	300	Centavo. 0.9250 Silver.	—
P24	1987	300	5 Centavos. 0.9250 Silver.	—
P25	1987	300	10 Centavos. 0.9250 Silver.	—
P26	1987	300	25 Centavos. 0.9250 Silver.	—
P27	1987	300	1/2 Peso. 0.9250 Silver.	—
P28	1988	100	Peso. 0.9990 Silver. KM#67.	50.00
P29	1988	100	100 Pesos. 0.9990 Silver. KM#67.	325
P30	1989	300	Centavo. 0.9250 Silver. KM#72a.	—
P31	1989	300	5 Centavos. 0.9250 Silver. KM#69a.	—
P32	1989	300	10 Centavos. 0.9250 Silver. KM#70a.	—
P33	1989	300	25 Centavos. 0.9250 Silver. KM#71a.	—
P34	1989	300	1/2 Peso. 0.9250 Silver. KM#73a.	—
P35	1989	10,000	Peso. 0.9990 Silver. KM#74.	40.00
P36	1989	200	100 Pesos. 0.9990 Silver. KM#75.	375
P37	1990	10,000	Peso. 0.9990 Silver. KM#77.	40.00
P38	1990	200	100 Pesos. 0.9990 Silver. KM#78.	300
P39	1991	10,000	Peso. 0.9990 Silver. KM#81.	40.00
P40	1992	10,000	Peso. 0.9990 Silver. KM#82.	40.00

MINT SETS

KM#	Date	Mintage	Identification	Issue Price	Mkt Val
MS1	1983 (5)	2,000	KM#59-63	10.00	15.00
MS2	1984 (6)	2,000	KM#59-64	—	15.00
MS3	1986 (5)	2,000	KM#59-62, 64	10.00	14.00
MS4	1987 (5)	1,000	KM#59-62, 64	10.00	14.00
MS5	1989 (5)	1,000	KM#69,70,71.1,72,73.1	—	14.00

PROOF SETS

KM#	Date	Mintage	Identification	Issue Price	Mkt Val
PS1	1937 (5)	—	KM#17-21	—	5,000
PS2	1972 (4)	500	KM#18, 20a.1, 31, 34	20.00	65.00
PS3	1973 (2)	500	KM#19a, 21a.2	5.00	50.00
PS4	1974 (2)	500	KM#18, 20a.2	5.00	35.00
PS5	1974 (2)	500	KM#35-36	120	190
PS6	1975 (2)	500	KM#38-39	200	165
PS7	1976 (6)	5,000	KM#40-45	10.00	20.00
PS8	1978 (6)	5,000	KM#48-53	10.00	20.00
PS9	1978 (6)	15	KM#Pn29-31, Pn33-35	175	900
PS10	1979 (6)	500	KM#48-53	15.00	135
PS11	1979 (6)	15	KM#Pn36-38, Pn40-42	255	900
PS12	1980 (6)	3,000	KM#48-53	15.00	20.00
PS13	1980 (6)	15	KM#Pn43-48	255	900
PS14	1981 (6)	3,000	KM#48-53	15.00	20.00
PS15	1981 (6)	15	KM#Pn49-54	300	900
PS18	1983 (2)	100	KM#59a, 60a	45.00	45.00

KM#	Date	Mintage	Identification	Issue Price	Mkt Val
PS16	1983 (2)	1,600	KM#59-60	10.00	10.00
PS17	1983 (2)	300	KM-P4, P5	25.00	50.00
PS19	1983 (3)	1,570	KM#61-63	20.00	20.00
PS21	1983 (3)	70	KM#61.1a-63.1a	125	125
PS20	1983 (3)	270	KM-P7, 8, 9	45.00	115
PS22	1984 (6)	1,570	KM#59-64	20.00	45.00
PS23	1984 (6)	270	KM-P10, 11, 12, 13, 14, 15	30.00	30.00
PS24	1984 (6)	70	KM#59a-60a, 61.1a, 62.1a, 63.1a, 64a	250	250
PS25	1986 (5)	1,570	KM#59-62, 64	30.00	20.00
PS26	1986 (5)	270	KM-P17, 19, 20, 21, 22	40.00	40.00
PS27	1986 (5)	70	KM#59a-60a, 61.1a, 62.1a, 64a	150	150
PS28	1987 (5)	1,600	KM#59-62, 64	—	30.00
PS29	1987 (5)	300	KM-P23, 24, 25, 26, 27	—	75.00
PS30	1989 (5)	2,500	KM#69a-70a, 71.1a, 72a, 73.1a	—	—
PS31	1989 (5)	300	KM-P30, 31, 32, 33, 34	—	—
PS32	2000 (13)	—	KM#91-103	—	195

SPECIAL SETS

KM#	Date	Mintage	Identification	Issue Price	Mkt Val
SS1	1983 (15)	30	KM#61-63, 61a-63a, all mint marks, including Pieforts	200	200
SS2	1984 (24)	30	KM#59-64, including Pieforts	400	400
SS3	1986 (20)	30	KM#59-64	300	300
SS4	1986 (2)	1,700	KM#65, Proof & Unc.	35.00	25.00
SS5	1986 (3)	300	KM#65, Proof & Unc., KM-P16	75.00	75.00
SS6	1986 (2)	23	KM#65a, Proof & Unc.	—	—
SS7	1986 (3)	25	KM#65a, Proof & Unc., KM-P17	—	—
SS8	1986 (3)	25	KM#65b, Proof & Unc., P#17	—	—
SS9	1986 (3)	25	KM#65b, Proof & Unc., P#17	—	—
SS10	1987 (15)	100	KM#59-62, 64, KM-P23, 24, 25, 26, 27	—	125
SS11	1989 (15)	100	KM#69-73, KM-P31, 32, 33, 34, 35	—	—

EAST AFRICA

East Africa was an administrative grouping of five separate British territories: Kenya, Uganda, the Sultanate of Zanzibar and British Somaliland.

The common interest of Kenya, Tanganyika and Uganda invited cooperation in economic matters and consideration of political union. The territorial governors, organized as the East Africa High Commission, met periodically to administer such common activities as taxation, industrial development and education. The authority of the Commission did not infringe upon the constitution and internal autonomy of the individual colonies. A common coinage and banknotes, which were also legal tender in Aden, were provided for use of the member colonies by the East Africa Currency Board. The coinage through 1919 had the legend "East Africa and Uganda Protectorate".

NOTE: For later coinage see Kenya, Tanzania and Uganda.

RULER
British

MINT MARKS
A - Ackroyd & Best, Morley
I - Bombay Mint
H - Heaton Mint, Birmingham, England
K, KN - King's Norton Mint, Birmingham, England
SA - Pretoria Mint, South Africa
No mint mark — British Royal Mint, London

EAST AFRICA AND UGANDA PROTECTORATES

DECIMAL COINAGE

50 Cents = 1 Shilling; 100 Cents = 1 Florin

KM# 6 1/2 CENT
Aluminum **Ruler:** Edward VII **Edge:** Plain

Date	Mintage	F	VF	XF	Unc	BU
1908	900,000	15.00	25.00	60.00	90.00	—

KM# 6a 1/2 CENT
Copper-Nickel **Ruler:** Edward VII **Obv:** Center hole divides crown and denomination, fleurs flank center hole, denomination above, circle surrounds **Edge:** Plain

Date	Mintage	F	VF	XF	Unc	BU
1909	900,000	6.00	12.00	35.00	60.00	95.00

KM# 5 CENT
Aluminum **Ruler:** Edward VII **Obv:** Center hole divides crown and denomination, fleurs flank center hole, denomination above, circle surrounds **Edge:** Plain

Date	Mintage	F	VF	XF	Unc	BU
1907	6,948,000	5.00	10.00	30.00	50.00	—
1908	2,871,000	8.00	16.00	35.00	60.00	—

KM# 5a CENT
2.8800 g., Copper-Nickel **Ruler:** Edward VII **Obv:** Center hole divides crown and denomination, fleurs flank center hole, denomination above, circle surrounds **Edge:** Plain

Date	Mintage	F	VF	XF	Unc	BU
1909	25,000,000	0.50	1.25	3.00	7.00	—
1910	6,000,000	0.50	1.25	4.00	12.00	—

KM# 7 CENT
Copper-Nickel **Ruler:** George V **Obv:** Center hole divides crown and denomination, fleurs flank center hole, denomination above, circle surrounds **Edge:** Plain

Date	Mintage	F	VF	XF	Unc	BU
1911H	25,000,000	0.25	1.00	5.00	15.00	—
1912H	20,000,000	0.25	1.00	3.00	8.00	—
1913	4,529,000	0.75	1.50	8.00	20.00	—
1914 S	6,000,000	0.75	1.75	5.00	15.00	—
1914H	2,500,000	1.00	3.00	8.00	20.00	—
1916H	1,824,000	1.25	4.00	10.00	25.00	—
1917H	3,176,000	0.75	2.00	5.00	15.00	—
1918H	10,000,000	0.50	1.00	3.25	12.00	—

KM# A11 5 CENTS
Copper-Nickel **Ruler:** Edward VII

Date	Mintage	F	VF	XF	Unc	BU
1907 Rare	—	—	—	—	—	—

KM# 11 5 CENTS
Copper-Nickel **Ruler:** George V **Obv:** Center hole divides crown and denomination, fleurs flank center hole, denomination above, circle surrounds **Edge:** Plain

Date	Mintage	F	VF	XF	Unc	BU
1913H	300,000	1.50	4.00	20.00	35.00	—
1914K	1,240,000	0.75	3.25	12.00	22.50	—
1914K Proof	— Value: 200					

Note: The 1914K was issued with British West Africa KM#8 in a double (4 pieces) Specimen Set

Date	Mintage	F	VF	XF	Unc	BU
1919H	200,000	10.00	15.00	40.00	120	—

KM# 2 10 CENTS
Copper-Nickel **Ruler:** Edward VII **Obv:** Center hole divides crown and denomination, fleurs flank center hole, denomination above, circle surrounds **Edge:** Plain

Date	Mintage	F	VF	XF	Unc	BU
1906	—	1,000	1,500	2,000	3,000	—
1907	1,000,000	1.50	4.00	16.00	30.00	50.00
1910	500,000	4.00	8.00	35.00	60.00	—

KM# 8 10 CENTS
Copper-Nickel **Ruler:** George V **Obv:** Center hole divides crown and denomination, fleurs flank center hole, denomination above, circle surrounds **Edge:** Plain

Date	Mintage	F	VF	XF	Unc	BU
1911H	1,250,000	2.00	5.00	25.00	40.00	—
1912H	1,050,000	2.00	5.00	30.00	55.00	—
1913	50,000	75.00	150	300	500	—
1918H	400,000	10.00	20.00	80.00	150	—

KM# 3 25 CENTS
2.9160 g., 0.8000 Silver 0.0750 oz. ASW **Ruler:** Edward VII **Obv:** Bust of King Edward VII right **Rev:** Lion and mountains within 3/4 circle with fleur ends, denomination and date below **Edge:** Reeded

Date	Mintage	F	VF	XF	Unc	BU
1906	400,000	3.00	7.00	35.00	60.00	—
1910H	200,000	4.00	8.00	50.00	90.00	—

KM# 10 25 CENTS
2.9160 g., 0.8000 Silver 0.0750 oz. ASW **Ruler:** George V **Obv:** Bust of King George V left **Rev:** Lion and mountains within 3/4 circle with fleur ends, date and denomination below **Edge:** Reeded

Date	Mintage	F	VF	XF	Unc	BU
1912	180,000	4.00	15.00	45.00	80.00	—
1913	300,000	3.50	10.00	35.00	60.00	—
1914H	80,000	20.00	35.00	60.00	100	—
1914H Proof	— Value: 400					
1918H	40,000	150	300	500	900	—

KM# 4 50 CENTS
5.8319 g., 0.8000 Silver 0.1500 oz. ASW **Ruler:** Edward VII **Obv:** Bust of King Edward VII right **Rev:** Lion and mountains within circle with fleur ends, denomination and date below **Edge:** Reeded

Date	Mintage	F	VF	XF	Unc	BU
1906	200,000	4.50	30.00	80.00	140	—
1906 Proof	— Value: 400					

Date	Mintage	F	VF	XF	Unc	BU
1909	100,000	15.00	50.00	155	300	—
1910	100,000	10.00	45.00	110	225	—

KM# 9 50 CENTS
5.8319 g., 0.8000 Silver 0.1500 oz. ASW **Ruler:** George V **Obv:** Bust of King George V left **Rev:** Lion and mountains within circle with fleur ends, denomination and date below **Edge:** Reeded

Date	Mintage	F	VF	XF	Unc	BU
1911	150,000	7.50	35.00	85.00	140	—
1911 Proof	— Value: 250					
1912	100,000	8.00	45.00	125	200	—
1913	200,000	5.00	30.00	65.00	135	—
1914H	180,000	5.00	30.00	65.00	135	—
1918H	60,000	60.00	200	350	500	—
1919	100,000	250	350	900	1,500	—

BRITISH COLONIES

DECIMAL COINAGE

50 Cents = 1 Shilling; 100 Cents = 1 Florin

KM# 12 CENT
Copper-Nickel **Ruler:** George V **Obv:** Center hole divides crown and denomination, fleurs flank center hole, denomination above, circle surrounds **Edge:** Plain

Date	Mintage	F	VF	XF	Unc	BU
1920H	Est. 2,908,000	30.00	60.00	110	225	—

Note: Only about 30% of the total mintage was released into circulation

Date	Mintage	F	VF	XF	Unc	BU
1920H Proof	— Value: 300					

Note: 20-30 pcs

Date	Mintage	F	VF	XF	Unc	BU
1920	—	—	—	—	750	—
1921	920,000	—	—	—	3,000	—

Note: Not released for circulation

KM# 13 5 CENTS
Copper-Nickel **Ruler:** George V **Obv:** Center hole divides crown and denomination, fleurs flank center hole, denomination above, circle surrounds **Edge:** Plain

Date	Mintage	F	VF	XF	Unc	BU
1920H	Est. 550,000	75.00	250	300	425	—

Note: Only about 30% of the total mintage was released into circulation

Date	Mintage	F	VF	XF	Unc	BU
1920H Proof	— Value: 475					

Note: 20-30 pcs

KM# 14 10 CENTS
Copper-Nickel **Ruler:** George V **Obv:** Center hole divides crown and denomination, fleurs flank center hole, denomination above, circle surrounds **Edge:** Plain

Date	Mintage	F	VF	XF	Unc	BU
1920H	Est. 700,000	120	150	225	375	—
1920H Proof	— Value: 600					

Note: 20-30 pcs

KM# 15   25 CENTS

2.9160 g., 0.5000 Silver 0.0469 oz. ASW **Ruler:** George V **Obv:** Bust of King George V left **Rev:** Lion and mountains within circle with fleur ends, date and denomination below **Edge:** Reeded

Date	Mintage	F	VF	XF	Unc	BU
1920H	748,000	25.00	35.00	75.00	150	—
1920H Proof	—	Value: 250				

Note: 20-30 pieces

KM# 16   50 CENTS

5.8319 g., 0.5000 Silver 0.0937 oz. ASW **Ruler:** George V **Obv:** Bust of King George V left **Rev:** Lion and mountains within circle with fleur ends; date and denomination below **Edge:** Reeded **Note:** Not released for circulation.

Date	Mintage	F	VF	XF	Unc	BU
1920A	12,000	1,500	2,000	3,000	4,000	—
1920H	62,000	500	1,000	1,500	2,500	—
1920H Proof	—	Value: 600				

Note: 20-30 pieces

KM# 17   FLORIN

11.6638 g., 0.5000 Silver 0.1875 oz. ASW **Ruler:** George V **Obv:** Bust of King George V left **Rev:** Lion and mountains within circle with fleur ends, denomination and date below **Edge:** Reeded

Date	Mintage	F	VF	XF	Unc	BU
1920	1,479,000	15.00	75.00	200	325	—
1920A	542,000	200	500	1,100	2,000	—
1920H	9,689,000	12.50	60.00	125	275	—
1920H Proof	—	Value: 800				

Note: 20-30 pieces

1921	2	—	—	—	4,500	—

REFORM COINAGE
Commencing May 1921

100 Cents = 1 Shilling

KM# 22   CENT

1.9100 g., Bronze **Ruler:** George V **Obv:** Center hole divides crown and denomination, fleurs flank **Rev:** Tusks flank center hole, denomination above, circle surrounds **Edge:** Plain

Date	Mintage	F	VF	XF	Unc	BU
1922	8,250,000	0.25	0.50	3.50	15.00	22.00
1922H	43,750,000	0.25	0.50	3.50	6.50	9.00
1923	50,000,000	0.25	0.50	3.50	6.50	9.00
1924	Inc. above	0.25	0.75	5.00	10.00	15.00
1924H	17,500,000	0.25	0.75	4.00	8.00	11.00
1924KN	10,720,000	0.25	0.75	4.00	8.00	11.00
1924KN Proof	—	Value: 125				
1925	6,000,000	50.00	100	225	350	—
1925KN	6,780,000	2.00	4.00	18.00	35.00	52.00
1927	10,000,000	0.25	0.75	5.00	10.00	15.00
1927 Proof	—	Value: 125				
1928H	12,000,000	0.25	0.75	4.00	8.00	11.00
1928KN	11,764,000	0.50	2.00	8.00	18.00	27.00
1928KN Proof	—	Value: 125				
1930	15,000,000	0.25	0.50	2.50	5.00	8.00
1930 Proof	—	Value: 125				
1935	10,000,000	0.25	0.50	1.75	3.50	6.00

KM# 29   CENT

1.9500 g., Bronze **Ruler:** George VI **Obv:** Center hole divides crown and denomination, fleurs flank **Rev:** Tusks flank center hole, denomination above, circle surrounds **Edge:** Plain

Date	Mintage	F	VF	XF	Unc	BU
1942	25,000,000	0.10	0.25	1.25	2.50	4.00
1942I	15,000,000	0.15	0.30	1.50	3.00	5.00

KM# 32   CENT

1.7000 g., Bronze **Ruler:** George VI **Obv:** Center hole divides crown and denomination, fleurs flank **Obv. Leg.:** ET IND. IMP. dropped from legend **Rev:** Tusks flank center hole, denomination above, circle surrounds **Edge:** Plain

Date	Mintage	F	VF	XF	Unc	BU
1949	4,000,000	0.35	0.75	2.00	4.00	7.00
1949 Proof	—	Value: 125				
1950	16,000,000	0.10	0.25	1.25	2.50	5.00
1950 Proof	—	Value: 150				
1951H	9,000,000	0.10	0.25	1.25	2.50	5.00
1951H Proof	—	Value: 125				
1951KN	11,140,000	0.10	0.25	1.25	2.50	5.00
1951KN Proof	—	Value: 125				
1952	7,000,000	0.10	0.25	1.25	2.50	5.00
1952 Proof	—	Value: 150				
1952H	13,000,000	0.10	0.25	1.25	2.50	5.00
1952H Proof	—	Value: 125				
1952KN	5,230,000	0.10	0.25	1.50	5.00	8.00

KM# 35   CENT

2.0000 g., Bronze, 20 mm. **Ruler:** Elizabeth II **Obv:** Center hole divides crown and denomination, fleurs flank **Rev:** Tusks flank center hole, denomination above, circle surrounds **Edge:** Plain

Date	Mintage	F	VF	XF	Unc	BU
1954	8,000,000	0.10	0.25	0.85	2.50	5.00
1954 Proof	—	Value: 150				
1955	5,000,000	0.10	0.25	0.50	1.75	3.00
1955H	6,384,000	0.10	0.20	0.65	1.75	3.00
1955KN	4,000,000	0.10	0.20	0.65	1.75	3.00
1956H	15,616,000	0.10	0.15	0.30	1.25	3.00
1956KN	9,680,000	0.10	0.20	0.40	1.25	3.00
1957	15,000,000	0.10	0.20	0.65	1.75	3.00
1957H	5,000,000	1.50	3.00	6.00	15.00	21.00
1957KN	Inc. above	0.10	0.20	0.65	1.75	3.00
1959	10,000,000	0.10	0.20	0.40	1.25	2.00
1959KN	10,000,000	0.10	0.20	0.40	1.25	2.00
1961	1,800,000	0.15	0.40	2.00	3.50	5.00
1961 Proof	—	Value: 100				
1961H	1,800,000	0.15	0.40	2.00	3.50	5.00
1962H	10,320,000	0.10	0.20	0.40	1.25	2.00

KM# 18   5 CENTS

6.2400 g., Bronze, 25.3 mm. **Ruler:** George V **Edge:** Plain

Date	Mintage	F	VF	XF	Unc	BU
1921	1,000,000	2.00	4.00	15.00	32.00	50.00
1922	2,500,000	0.50	1.25	4.50	12.50	15.00
1923	2,400,000	0.50	1.25	6.00	15.00	18.00
1923 Proof	—	Value: 150				
1924	4,800,000	0.50	1.00	5.00	15.00	21.00
1925	6,600,000	0.50	1.00	4.00	10.00	15.00
1925 Proof	—	Value: 125				
1928	1,200,000	1.50	3.00	10.00	25.00	35.00
1928 Proof	—	Value: 150				
1933	5,000,000	—	0.50	5.00	10.00	15.00
1934	3,910,000	0.50	1.00	7.50	15.00	21.00
1934 Proof	—	Value: 150				
1935	5,800,000	0.50	1.00	5.00	10.00	15.00

Date	Mintage	F	VF	XF	Unc	BU
1935 Proof	—	Value: 150				
1936	1,000,000	2.00	15.00	30.00	50.00	—

KM# 23   5 CENTS

Bronze, 26 mm. **Ruler:** Edward VIII **Obv:** Center hole divides crown and denomination, fleurs flank **Rev:** Tusks flank center hole, denomination above, circle surrounds **Edge:** Plain

Date	Mintage	F	VF	XF	Unc	BU
1936H	3,500,000	0.25	0.50	2.00	5.50	9.00
1936H Proof	—	Value: 150				
1936KN	2,150,000	0.25	0.50	2.00	5.50	9.00
1936KN Proof	—	Value: 150				

KM# 25.1   5 CENTS

6.3200 g., Bronze **Ruler:** George VI **Obv:** Center hole divides crown and denomination, fleurs flank **Rev:** Tusks flank center hole, denomination above, circle surrounds **Edge:** Plain **Note:** Thick flan.

Date	Mintage	F	VF	XF	Unc	BU
1937H	3,000,000	0.50	1.00	2.00	4.00	7.00
1937KN	3,000,000	0.50	1.00	2.00	6.00	10.00
1939	2,000,000	0.50	1.00	5.00	13.50	20.00
1939KN	2,000,000	0.50	1.00	5.00	13.50	20.00
1941	—	3.00	10.00	25.00	40.00	65.00
1941I	20,000,000	0.50	1.00	2.00	5.00	8.00

KM# 25.2   5 CENTS

5.6700 g., Bronze **Ruler:** George VI **Obv:** Center hole divides crown and denomination, fleurs flank **Rev:** Tusks flank center hole, denomination above, circle surrounds **Edge:** Plain **Note:** Thin flan, reduced weight.

Date	Mintage	F	VF	XF	Unc	BU
1941I	Inc. above	0.50	1.00	2.00	5.00	8.00
1942	16,000,000	0.50	1.00	2.00	4.00	7.00
1942SA	4,120,000	1.00	6.00	15.00	30.00	42.00
1943SA	17,880,000	Value: 3.00				

KM# 25.3   5 CENTS

Bronze **Ruler:** George VI **Edge:** Plain **Note:** Similar to KM#25.2, but hole not punched.

Date	Mintage	F	VF	XF	Unc	BU
1942	—	—	—	—	100	—

KM# 33   5 CENTS

5.7700 g., Bronze **Ruler:** George VI **Obv:** Center hole divides crown and denomination, fleurs flank **Obv. Leg.:** ET IND. IMP. dropped from legend **Rev:** Tusks flank center hole, denomination above, circle surrounds **Edge:** Plain

Date	Mintage	F	VF	XF	Unc	BU
1949	4,000,000	0.25	0.50	3.00	6.00	10.00
1949 Proof	—	Value: 175				
1951H	6,000,000	0.25	0.50	2.00	5.00	8.00
1951H Proof	—	Value: 175				
1952	11,200,000	0.20	0.40	1.00	3.00	6.00
1952 Proof	—	Value: 200				

KM# 37   5 CENTS

5.7700 g., Bronze **Ruler:** Elizabeth II **Obv:** Center hole divides crown and denomination, fleurs flank **Rev:** Tusks flank center hole, denomination above, circle surrounds **Edge:** Plain

Date	Mintage	F	VF	XF	Unc	BU
1955	2,000,000	0.10	0.25	0.75	2.00	3.50
1955 Proof	—	Value: 150				

Date	Mintage	F	VF	XF	Unc	BU
1955H	4,000,000	0.20	0.50	1.25	3.50	5.00
1955H Proof	—	Value: 150				
1955KN	2,000,000	0.35	0.80	2.50	5.00	8.00
1956H	3,000,000	0.15	0.35	1.00	3.00	5.00
1956KN	3,000,000	3.00	5.00	8.00	10.00	15.00
1956KN Proof	—	Value: 125				
1957H	5,000,000	0.10	0.25	0.75	2.00	3.50
1957KN	5,000,000	0.10	0.25	0.75	2.00	3.50
1961H	4,000,000	0.15	0.35	1.00	3.00	5.50
1963	12,600,000	—	0.10	0.30	0.75	1.50
1963 Proof	—	Value: 150				

KM# 39   5 CENTS
5.6900 g., Bronze **Ruler:** Elizabeth II **Obv:** Fleurs flank center hole, country name below, denomination above and right **Rev:** Tusks flank center hole, denomination above, circle surrounds **Edge:** Plain **Note:** Post-independence issue.

Date	Mintage	F	VF	XF	Unc	BU
1964	7,600,000	—	0.10	0.20	0.50	0.85

KM# 19   10 CENTS
11.1400 g., Bronze **Ruler:** George V **Obv:** Center hole divides crown and denomination, fleurs flank **Rev:** Tusks flank center hole, denomination above, circle surrounds **Edge:** Plain

Date	Mintage	F	VF	XF	Unc	BU
1921	130,000	5.00	20.00	45.00	80.00	—
1922	7,120,000	1.00	3.00	8.00	20.00	—
1923	1,200,000	1.25	4.00	20.00	40.00	—
1924	4,900,000	0.65	2.25	14.00	25.00	—
1925	4,800,000	0.65	2.25	14.00	25.00	—
1927	2,000,000	0.75	2.50	12.50	20.00	—
1928	3,800,000	0.75	2.50	15.00	30.00	—
1928 Proof	—	Value: 175				
1933	6,260,000	0.75	2.50	6.50	17.50	—
1934	3,649,000	0.75	2.50	15.00	30.00	—
1935	7,300,000	0.65	2.00	8.00	18.00	—
1936	500,000	1.50	15.00	30.00	50.00	—

KM# 24   10 CENTS
10.7400 g., Bronze, 30.5 mm. **Ruler:** Edward VIII **Obv:** Center hole divides crown and denomination, fleurs flank **Rev:** Tusks flank center hole, denomination above, circle surrounds **Edge:** Plain **Note:** For listing of mule dated 1936H with obverse of KM#24 and reverse of British West Africa KM#16 refer to British West Africa listings.

Date	Mintage	F	VF	XF	Unc	BU
1936	2,000,000	1.00	3.50	8.00	25.00	40.00
1936 Proof	—	Value: 200				
1936H	4,330,000	0.25	0.50	1.50	6.50	10.00
1936H Proof	—	Value: 325				
1936KN	4,142,000	0.25	0.50	1.50	6.50	10.00
1936KN Proof	—	Value: 145				

KM# 24a   10 CENTS
Copper-Nickel **Ruler:** Edward VIII **Obv:** Center hole divides crown and denomination, fleurs flank **Rev:** Tusks flank center hole, denomination above, circle surrounds **Edge:** Plain

Date	Mintage	F	VF	XF	Unc	BU
1936KN	—	—	—	—	—	—

KM# 26.1   10 CENTS
11.3400 g., Bronze **Ruler:** George VI **Obv:** Center hole divides crown and denomination, fleurs flank **Rev:** Tusks flank center hole, denomination above, circle surrounds **Edge:** Plain **Note:** Thick flan.

Date	Mintage	F	VF	XF	Unc	BU
1937	2,000,000	0.25	0.75	2.50	6.00	9.00
1937 Proof	—	Value: 175				
1937H	2,500,000	0.25	0.75	2.50	8.00	13.00
1937H Proof	—	Value: 175				
1937KN	2,500,000	0.25	0.75	2.50	8.00	13.00
1937KN Proof	—	Value: 175				
1939H	2,000,000	0.25	0.70	5.50	15.00	21.00
1939KN	2,029,999	0.25	0.70	12.50	16.00	
1939KN Proof	—	Value: 175				
1941I	15,682,000	0.35	1.00	6.00	15.00	23.00
1941I Proof	—	Value: 175				
1941		0.50	1.50	7.50	16.00	21.00
1941 Proof	—	Value: 175				

KM# 26.2   10 CENTS
Bronze **Ruler:** George VI **Obv:** Center hole divides crown and denomination, fleurs flank **Rev:** Tusks flank center hole, denomination above, circle surrounds **Edge:** Plain **Note:** Thin flan, reduced weight.

Date	Mintage	F	VF	XF	Unc	BU
1942	12,000,000	0.20	0.50	1.75	4.00	7.00
1942I	4,317,000	3.00	5.00	12.00	20.00	28.00
1942 Proof	—	Value: 175				
1943SA	14,093,000	0.25	0.50	4.50	10.00	15.00
1945SA	5,000,000	0.25	0.50	5.00	12.50	16.00

KM# 34   10 CENTS
9.5000 g., Bronze **Ruler:** George VI **Obv:** Center hole divides crown and denomination, fleurs flank **Obv. Leg.:** ET IND. IMP. dropped from legend **Rev:** Tusks flank center hole, denomination above, circle surrounds **Edge:** Plain

Date	Mintage	F	VF	XF	Unc	BU
1949	4,000,000	0.25	2.50	5.00	15.00	21.00
1949 Proof	—	Value: 175				
1950	8,000,000	0.20	0.40	1.75	4.00	7.00
1950 Proof	—	Value: 200				
1951	14,500,000	0.20	0.40	1.25	3.00	6.00
1951 Proof	—	Value: 175				
1952	15,800,000	0.20	0.40	1.25	3.00	6.00
1952 Proof	—	Value: 250				
1952H	2,000,000	3.00	5.00	10.00	20.00	30.00

KM# 38   10 CENTS
9.3600 g., Bronze **Ruler:** Elizabeth II **Obv:** Center hole divides crown and denomination, fleurs flank **Rev:** Tusks flank center hole, denomination above, circle surrounds **Edge:** Plain

Date	Mintage	F	VF	XF	Unc	BU
1956	6,001,000	0.35	1.00	2.50	10.00	15.00
1956 Proof	—	Value: 175				
1964H Rare						

KM# 40   10 CENTS
9.4000 g., Bronze **Ruler:** Elizabeth II **Obv:** Fleurs flank center hole, country name below, denomination above and right **Rev:** Tusks flank center hole, denomination above, circle surrounds **Edge:** Plain **Note:** Post-independence issue.

Date	Mintage	F	VF	XF	Unc	BU
1964H	10,002,000	0.10	0.15	0.30	1.00	1.50

KM# 20   50 CENTS
3.8879 g., 0.2500 Silver 0.0312 oz. ASW **Ruler:** George V **Obv:** Crowned bust of King George V left **Rev:** Lion and mountains within 3/4 circle with fleur ends, date below divides denominations **Edge:** Reeded

Date	Mintage	F	VF	XF	Unc	BU
1921	6,200,000	1.00	5.00	17.50	30.00	—
1922	Inc. above	1.00	4.00	16.00	27.50	—
1923	396,000	5.00	18.00	55.00	80.00	—
1924	1,000,000	2.00	14.00	25.00	40.00	—

KM# 27   50 CENTS
3.8879 g., 0.2500 Silver 0.0312 oz. ASW **Ruler:** George VI **Obv:** Crowned head of King George VI left **Rev:** Lion and mountains within 3/4 circle with fleur ends, date and denomination below and right **Edge:** Reeded

Date	Mintage	F	VF	XF	Unc	BU
1937H	4,000,000	0.75	1.25	5.50	12.50	—
1937H Proof	—	Value: 275				
1942H	5,000,000	0.75	1.25	9.00	20.00	—
1943I	2,000,000	1.50	5.00	17.50	30.00	—
1944SA	1,000,000	2.00	6.00	18.00	32.50	—

KM# 30   50 CENTS
3.8900 g., Copper-Nickel **Ruler:** George VI **Obv:** Crowned head of King George VI left **Obv. Leg.:** ET INDIA IMPERATOR dropped from legend **Rev:** Lion and mountains within 3/4 circle with fleur ends, date divides denominations below **Edge:** Reeded

Date	Mintage	F	VF	XF	Unc	BU
1948	7,290,000	0.20	0.40	2.00	6.00	10.00
1948 Proof	—	Value: 250				
1949	12,960,000	0.15	0.30	1.50	5.00	10.00
1949 Proof	—	Value: 325				
1952KN	2,000,000	0.20	0.40	2.00	.7.50	10.00

KM# 36   50 CENTS
Copper-Nickel **Ruler:** Elizabeth II **Obv:** Crowned bust right **Rev:** Lion and mountains within 3/4 circle with fleur ends, date divides denominations below **Edge:** Reeded **Note:** The KHN mint marks above exist because the master dies were produced with both the KN and H mint marks for use at either mint. Each mint was required to remove the other's mint mark before striking, but this was not always meticulously done. When one or the other mint mark was not fully removed a weak trace would remain creating the

appearance of a wide space K N with a weak H in the middle or an H flanked by a weak K and N, in the field below the lion.

Date	Mintage	F	VF	XF	Unc	BU
1954	3,720,000	0.15	0.35	1.00	4.00	8.00
1954 Proof	—	Value: 225				
1955H	1,600,000	1.00	3.00	6.00	15.00	8.00
1955H Proof	—	Value: 225				
1955KHN	—	10.00	20.00	55.00	85.00	8.00
1955KN	—	0.15	0.35	1.75	5.00	8.00
1956H	2,000,000	0.15	0.25	1.25	4.00	8.00
1956H Proof	—	Value: 225				
1956KHN	—	10.00	20.00	35.00	65.00	8.00
1956KN	2,000,000	0.15	0.35	1.75	5.00	8.00
1958H	2,600,000	0.15	0.40	2.00	5.00	8.00
1960	4,000,000	0.10	0.25	1.25	4.00	8.00
1962KN	4,000,000	0.15	0.35	1.75	5.00	8.00
1963	6,000,000	0.10	0.25	1.25	4.00	8.00

KM# 21   SHILLING
7.7759 g., 0.2500 Silver 0.0625 oz. ASW, 27.8 mm.
Ruler: George V **Obv:** Bust of King George V left **Edge:** Reeded

Date	Mintage	F	VF	XF	Unc	BU
1921	6,141,000	1.50	5.75	18.00	30.00	—
1921H	4,240,000	1.75	3.00	25.00	40.00	—
1922	18,858,000	1.25	2.25	13.00	28.00	—
1922H	20,052,000	1.25	2.25	13.00	28.00	—
1923	4,000,000	5.00	10.00	30.00	45.00	—
1924	44,604,000	1.00	2.00	7.00	18.00	—
1925	28,405,000	1.00	2.00	7.00	20.00	—
1925 Proof	—	Value: 250				

KM# 28.1   SHILLING
7.7759 g., 0.2500 Silver 0.0625 oz. ASW **Ruler:** George VI **Obv:** Crowned head of King George VI left **Rev:** Lion and mountains within 3/4 circle with fleur ends, date divides denominations below **Edge:** Reeded **Note:** REV; Type I, thin rim and short milling, EAST AFRICA further from edge than Type II, larger loop on right side of coin below diamond in legend. Edge reeding spaced out

Date	Mintage	F	VF	XF	Unc	BU
1937H	7,672,000	1.00	2.00	12.50	22.00	25.00
1937H Proof	—	Value: 300				
1941I	7,000,000	1.25	2.25	14.00	28.00	—
1942H	4,430,000	1.25	2.25	14.00	28.00	—
1942H Proof	—	Value: 300				
1944H	10,000,000	1.25	2.25	17.00	32.00	—

KM# 28.2   SHILLING
7.7759 g., 0.2500 Silver 0.0625 oz. ASW **Ruler:** George VI
Obv: Crowned head left **Rev:** Type II, thicker rim and larger milling, EAST AFRICA and leaves very near the edge, small leaf (loop) under diamond on right side **Edge:** Reeded

Date	Mintage	F	VF	XF	Unc	BU
1941I Rare	—	—	—	—	—	—

KM# 28.3   SHILLING
7.7759 g., 0.2500 Silver 0.0625 oz. ASW **Ruler:** George VI
Obv: Crowned head left **Rev:** Type III, retouched central image, especially tuft of grass in front of lion **Edge:** Reeded

Date	Mintage	F	VF	XF	Unc	BU
1942I	3,900,000	1.00	2.00	13.00	25.00	—
1943I	—	500	750	1,200	1,500	—

Note: 25-50 pieces

KM# 28.4   SHILLING
7.7759 g., 0.2500 Silver 0.0625 oz. ASW **Ruler:** George VI **Obv:** Crowned head left **Rev:** Lion and mountains within 3/4 circle with fleur ends, date divides denominations below **Edge:** Reeded **Note:** Obverse and reverse as KM#28.1, edge reeding close. For more in-depth comparison of these reverse variety types, see The Guidebook and Catalogue of British Commonwealth Coins, 1649-1971, 3rd Edition, Remick, J. Winnipeg, Regency Coin and Stamp, 1971.

Date	Mintage	F	VF	XF	Unc	BU
1944SA	5,820,000	1.25	2.25	17.00	30.00	—
1945SA	10,080,000	1.25	2.25	13.00	27.50	—
1946SA	18,260,000	1.00	2.00	12.00	20.00	—

KM# 31   SHILLING
7.8100 g., Copper-Nickel, 27.8 mm. **Ruler:** George VI
Obv: Crowned head of King George VI left **Obv. Leg.:** ET INDIA IMPERATOR dropped from legend **Rev:** Lion and mountains within 3/4 circle with fleur ends, date and denomination below **Edge:** Reeded

Date	Mintage	F	VF	XF	Unc	BU
1948	19,704,000	0.50	0.90	2.00	6.50	12.00
1949	38,318,000	0.50	0.90	2.00	6.50	12.00
1949 Proof	—	Value: 250				
1949H	12,584,000	0.50	0.90	2.25	7.50	12.50
1949KN	15,060,000	0.50	0.90	3.25	7.50	12.50
1950	56,362,000	0.35	0.60	1.50	5.00	12.00
1950 Proof	—	Value: 250				
1950H	12,416,000	0.50	0.90	3.25	6.00	12.00
1950KN	10,040,000	0.40	0.70	2.00	5.00	12.00
1952	55,605,000	0.35	0.60	1.50	5.00	12.00
1952 Proof	—	Value: 175				
1952H	8,023,999	0.35	0.60	1.75	5.00	12.00
1952KN	9,360,000	0.35	0.60	1.75	5.00	12.00

PATTERNS
Including off metal strikes

KM#	Date	Mintage	Identification	Mkt Val
Pn6	1906	—	Cent. Aluminum. KM#5.	1,500
Pn7	1907	5	1/2 Cent. Aluminum. KM#6.	2,000
Pn8	1907	—	5 Cents. Copper-Nickel. KM#11.	2,500
Pn9	1908	—	Cent. Copper-Nickel. KM#5a.	
Pn10	1920 (a)	—	50 Cents. Aluminum. KM#16.	3,000
Pn11	1920 (a)	—	Florin. Aluminum. KM#17.	2,000
Pn12	1925KN	—	Cent. Bronze. Uniface.	250
Pn13	1929KN	—	Cent. Bronze. Uniface.	250

MINT SETS

KM#	Date	Mintage	Identification	Issue Price	Mkt Val
MS1	1921-1922 (5)	—	KM#18-22. The 5 cent coin is dated 1921, all others are 1922.	—	2,000

PROOF SETS

KM#	Date	Mintage	Identification	Issue Price	Mkt Val
PS1	1906-1907 (4)	—	KM#2-5, Pn7-8; Rare	—	—
PSA1	1920H (6)	—	KM#12-17; 20-30 pieces	—	3,000
PS2	1949 (5)	—	KM#30-34	—	1,000
PS3	1950 (3)	—	KM#31, 32, 34	—	600
PS4	1952 (3)	—	KM#32, 33, 34	—	600

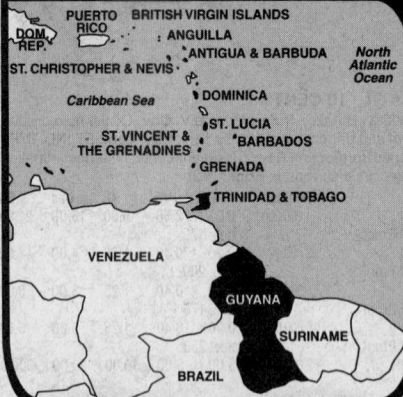

EAST CARIBBEAN STATES

PUERTO RICO
DOM. REP.
BRITISH VIRGIN ISLANDS
ANGUILLA
ANTIGUA & BARBUDA
ST. CHRISTOPHER & NEVIS
North Atlantic Ocean
Caribbean Sea
DOMINICA
ST. LUCIA
ST. VINCENT & THE GRENADINES
BARBADOS
GRENADA
TRINIDAD & TOBAGO
VENEZUELA
GUYANA
SURINAME
BRAZIL

The East Caribbean States, formerly the British Caribbean Territories (Eastern Group), formed a currency board in 1950 to provide the constituent territories of Trinidad & Tobago, Barbados, British Guiana (now Guyana), British Virgin Islands, Anguilla, St. Kitts, Nevis, Antigua, Dominica, St. Lucia, St. Vincent and Grenada with a common currency, thereby permitting withdrawal of the regular British Pound currency. This was dissolved in 1965 and after the breakup, the East Caribbean Territories, a grouping including Barbados, the Leeward and Windward Islands, came into being. Coinage of the dissolved 'Eastern Group' continues to circulate. Paper currency of the East Caribbean Authority was first issued in 1965 and although Barbados withdrew from the group they continued using them prior to 1973 when Barbados issued a decimal coinage.

A series of 4-dollar coins tied to the FAO coinage program were released in 1970 under the name of the Caribbean Development Bank by eight loosely federated island groupings in the eastern Caribbean. These issues are listed individually in this volume under Antigua, Barbados, Dominica, Grenada, Montserrat, St. Kitts, St. Lucia and St. Vincent.

BRITISH CARIBBEAN TERRITORIES
STANDARD COINAGE
100 Cents = 1 British West Indies Dollar

KM# 1   1/2 CENT
5.6300 g., Bronze, 20.4 mm. **Ruler:** Elizabeth II **Obv:** Crowned bust right **Rev:** Denomination above date

Date	Mintage	F	VF	XF	Unc	BU
1955	500,000	0.30	0.50	1.00	2.50	—
1955 Proof	2,000	Value: 3.00				
1958	200,000	0.50	0.75	1.50	3.00	—
1958 Proof	20	Value: 145				

KM# 2   CENT
5.6400 g., Bronze **Ruler:** Elizabeth II **Obv:** Crowned bust right **Rev:** Denomination within wreath, date below

Date	Mintage	F	VF	XF	Unc	BU
1955	8,000,000	0.15	0.25	0.60	1.00	—
1955 Proof	2,000	Value: 3.00				
1957	3,000,000	0.15	0.25	1.75	3.00	—
1957 Proof	—	Value: 100				
1958	1,500,000	0.35	0.50	4.50	7.50	—
1958 Proof	20	Value: 165				
1959	500,000	0.40	0.60	6.00	20.00	—
1959 Proof	—	Value: 100				
1960	2,500,000	0.15	0.25	0.60	1.25	—
1960 Proof	—	Value: 100				
1961	2,280,000	0.25	0.35	0.75	1.25	—
1961 Proof	—	Value: 100				
1962	2,000,000	0.15	0.25	0.50	1.25	—
1962 Proof	—	Value: 100				
1963	750,000	0.45	0.70	1.20	2.50	—
1963 Proof	—	Value: 100				
1964	2,500,000					—
1964 Proof	—	Value: 100				
1965	4,800,000			0.20	0.35	—
1965 Prooflike	—				0.75	—
1965 Proof	—	Value: 5.00				

KM# 3   2 CENTS
9.5500 g., Bronze, 30.5 mm. **Ruler:** Elizabeth II **Obv:** Crowned bust right **Rev:** Denomination within wreath, date below

Date	Mintage	F	VF	XF	Unc	BU
1955	5,500,000	0.15	0.25	0.50	1.00	—
1955 Proof	2,000	Value: 3.00				
1957	1,250,000	0.15	0.25	1.25	2.50	—
1957 Proof	—	Value: 110				
1958	1,250,000	0.15	0.25	2.50	5.00	—
1958 Proof	20	Value: 185				
1960	750,000	0.15	0.25	1.75	3.50	—
1960 Proof	—	Value: 110				
1961	788,000	0.15	0.25	1.75	3.50	—
1961 Proof	—	Value: 110				
1962	1,060,000	0.10	0.20	0.30	0.85	—
1962 Proof	—	Value: 110				
1963	250,000	0.50	0.75	1.50	5.00	—
1963 Proof	—	Value: 110				
1964	1,188,000	0.10	0.20	0.30	0.75	—
1964 Proof	—	Value: 110				
1965	2,001,000	—	0.10	0.20	0.45	—
1965 Prooflike	—				0.75	—
1965 Proof	—	Value: 5.00				

KM# 4   5 CENTS
Nickel-Brass, 21 mm. **Ruler:** Elizabeth II **Obv:** Crowned head right **Rev:** Sir Francis Drake's Golden Hind divides denomination, date below

Date	Mintage	F	VF	XF	Unc	BU
1955	8,600,000	0.15	0.25	0.60	1.25	—
1955 Proof	2,000	Value: 4.50				
1956	2,000,000	0.15	0.25	0.60	1.00	—
1956 Proof	—	Value: 300				
1960	1,000,000	0.20	0.30	0.90	1.50	—
1960 Proof	—	Value: 150				
1962	1,300,000	0.15	0.25	0.50	1.00	—
1962 Proof	—	Value: 150				
1963	200,000	0.25	0.35	1.20	2.00	—
1963 Proof	—	Value: 150				
1964	1,350,000	—	0.10	0.30	0.75	—
1964 Proof	—	Value: 150				
1965	2,400,000	—	0.10	0.20	0.50	—
1965 Prooflike	—	—	—	—	0.75	—
1965 Proof	—	Value: 5.00				

KM# 5   10 CENTS
2.5900 g., Copper-Nickel, 18 mm. **Ruler:** Elizabeth II **Obv:** Crowned head right **Rev:** Sir Francis Drake's Golden Hind divides denomination, date below

Date	Mintage	F	VF	XF	Unc	BU
1955	5,000,000	0.15	0.25	0.45	0.75	—
1955 Proof	2,000	Value: 4.50				
1956	4,000,000	0.15	0.25	0.45	0.75	—
1956 Proof	—	Value: 175				
1959	2,000,000	0.15	0.25	0.60	1.00	—
1959 Proof	—	Value: 175				
1961	1,260,000	0.20	0.30	0.50	1.00	—
1961 Proof	—	Value: 175				
1962	1,200,000	0.15	0.25	0.50	1.00	—
1962 Proof	—	Value: 175				
1964	1,400,000	0.10	0.20	0.35	0.65	—
1965	3,200,000	0.10	0.20	0.30	0.50	—
1965 Prooflike	—	—	—	—	0.75	—
1965 Proof	—	Value: 5.00				

KM# 6   25 CENTS
6.5100 g., Copper-Nickel **Ruler:** Elizabeth II **Obv:** Crowned bust right **Rev:** Sir Francis Drake's Golden Hind divides denomination, date below

Date	Mintage	F	VF	XF	Unc	BU
1955	7,000,000	0.35	0.50	0.70	1.00	—
1955 Proof	2,000	Value: 6.50				
1957	800,000	0.75	1.00	2.25	4.50	—
1957 Proof	—	Value: 225				
1959	1,000,000	0.35	0.50	1.25	2.25	—
1959 Proof	—	Value: 225				
1961	744,000	0.50	0.75	2.50	5.00	—
1961 Proof	—	Value: 225				
1962	480,000	0.25	0.50	1.25	2.50	—
1962 Proof	—	Value: 225				
1963	480,000	0.25	0.50	1.25	2.50	—
1963 Proof	—	Value: 225				
1964	480,000	0.25	0.50	1.00	1.75	—
1964 Proof	—	Value: 225				
1965	1,280,000	0.25	0.50	0.75	1.00	—
1965 Prooflike	—	—	—	—	1.50	—
1965 Proof	—	Value: 7.50				

KM# 7   50 CENTS
13.0000 g., Copper-Nickel, 30 mm. **Ruler:** Elizabeth II **Obv:** Crowned bust right **Rev:** Figure and horseheads above shielded arms and circular pictures, denomination and date divided below

Date	Mintage	F	VF	XF	Unc	BU
1955	1,500,000	1.00	1.50	2.00	3.50	5.00
1955 Proof	2,000	Value: 12.50				
1965	100,000	2.00	5.00	7.50	15.00	—
1965 Prooflike	—	—	—	—	7.50	—
1965 Proof	—	Value: 10.00				

EAST CARIBBEAN TERRITORIES

STANDARD COINAGE
100 Cents = 1 Dollar

KM# 8   10 DOLLARS
Copper-Nickel, 38.8 mm. **Ruler:** Elizabeth II **Subject:** 10th Anniversary of Caribbean Development Bank **Obv:** Sir Francis Drake's Golden Hind divides denomination, date below **Rev:** Map on grid within circle, dates below **Note:** Prev. KM#1.

Date	Mintage	F	VF	XF	Unc	BU
1980	—	—	—	—	7.00	9.00

KM# 8a   10 DOLLARS
28.2800 g., 0.9250 Silver 0.8410 oz. ASW, 38.8 mm. **Ruler:** Elizabeth II **Obv:** Sir Francis Drake's Golden Hind divides denomination, date below **Rev:** Map on grid within circle, two dates below **Note:** Prev. KM#1a.

Date	Mintage	F	VF	XF	Unc	BU
1980 Proof	10,000	Value: 45.00				

KM# 9   10 DOLLARS
Copper-Nickel, 38.8 mm. **Ruler:** Elizabeth II **Subject:** Wedding of Prince Charles and Lady Diana **Obv:** Young bust right **Rev:** Sir Francis Drake's Golden Hind and map of island chain, denomination below **Note:** Prev. KM#2.

Date	Mintage	F	VF	XF	Unc	BU
1981	50,000	—	—	—	7.00	9.00

KM# 9a   10 DOLLARS
28.2800 g., 0.9250 Silver 0.8410 oz. ASW, 38.8 mm. **Ruler:** Elizabeth II **Obv:** Young bust right **Rev:** Sir Francis Drake's Golden Hind and map of island chain, denomination below **Note:** Prev. KM#2a.

Date	Mintage	F	VF	XF	Unc	BU
1981 Proof	30,000	Value: 30.00				

EAST CARIBBEAN STATES

STANDARD COINAGE
100 Cents = 1 Dollar

KM# 10   CENT
0.9000 g., Aluminum, 18.4 mm. **Ruler:** Elizabeth II **Obv:** Young bust right **Rev:** Wreath divides denomination, date upper right **Note:** Prev. KM#1.

Date	Mintage	F	VF	XF	Unc	BU
1981	—	—	—	—	0.20	0.30
1981 Proof	5,000	Value: 1.25				
1983	—	—	—	—	0.20	0.30
1984	—	—	—	—	0.20	0.30
1986	—	—	—	—	0.20	0.30
1986 Proof	2,500	Value: 1.25				
1987	—	—	—	—	0.20	0.30
1989	—	—	—	—	0.20	0.30
1991	—	—	—	—	0.20	0.30
1992	—	—	—	—	0.20	0.30
1993	—	—	—	—	0.20	0.30
1994	—	—	—	—	0.20	0.30
1995	—	—	—	—	0.20	0.30
1996	—	—	—	—	0.20	0.30
1997	—	—	—	—	0.20	0.30
1998	—	—	—	—	0.20	0.30
1999	—	—	—	—	0.20	0.30
2000	—	—	—	—	0.20	0.30

KM# 11   2 CENTS
1.1000 g., Aluminum, 18.25 mm. **Ruler:** Elizabeth II **Obv:** Young bust right **Rev:** Wreath divides denomination, date upper right **Note:** Prev. KM#2.

Date	Mintage	F	VF	XF	Unc	BU
1981	—	—	—	0.10	0.25	0.35
1981 Proof	5,000	Value: 1.50				
1984	—	—	—	0.10	0.25	0.35
1986	—	—	—	0.10	0.25	0.35
1986 Proof	2,500	Value: 1.50				
1987	—	—	—	0.10	0.25	0.35
1989	—	—	—	0.10	0.25	0.35
1991	—	—	—	0.10	0.25	0.35
1992	—	—	—	0.10	0.25	0.35
1993	—	—	—	0.10	0.25	0.35
1994	—	—	—	0.10	0.25	0.35
1995	—	—	—	0.10	0.25	0.35
1996	—	—	—	0.10	0.25	0.35
1997	—	—	—	0.10	0.25	0.35
1998	—	—	—	0.10	0.25	0.35
1999	—	—	—	0.10	0.25	0.35
2000	—	—	—	0.10	0.25	0.35

KM# 12   5 CENTS
1.3100 g., Aluminum, 23.1 mm. **Ruler:** Elizabeth II **Obv:** Young bust right **Rev:** Wreath divides denomination, date upper right **Note:** Prev. KM#3.

Date	Mintage	F	VF	XF	Unc	BU
1981	—	—	—	0.10	0.30	0.45
1981 Proof	5,000	Value: 2.25				
1984	—	—	—	0.10	0.30	0.45
1986	—	—	—	0.10	0.30	0.45
1986 Proof	2,500	Value: 2.25				
1987	—	—	—	0.10	0.30	0.45
1989	—	—	—	0.10	0.30	0.45
1991	—	—	—	0.10	0.30	0.45
1992	—	—	—	0.10	0.30	0.45
1993	—	—	—	0.10	0.30	0.45
1994	—	—	—	0.10	0.30	0.45
1995	—	—	—	0.10	0.30	0.45
1996	—	—	—	0.10	0.30	0.45

Date	Mintage	F	VF	XF	Unc	BU
1997	—	—	—	0.10	0.30	0.45
1998	—	—	—	0.10	0.30	0.45
1999	—	—	—	0.10	0.30	0.45
2000	—	—	—	0.10	0.30	0.45

KM# 13   10 CENTS
2.6000 g., Copper-Nickel, 18.1 mm. **Ruler:** Elizabeth II
Obv: Young bust right **Rev:** Sir Francis Drake's Golden Hind, denomination below and left, date at right **Note:** Prev. KM#4.

Date	Mintage	F	VF	XF	Unc	BU
1981	—	—	0.10	0.15	0.40	0.60
1981 Proof	5,000	Value: 3.00				
1986	—	—	0.10	0.15	0.40	0.60
1986 Proof	2,500	Value: 3.00				
1987	—	—	0.10	0.15	0.40	0.60
1989	—	—	0.10	0.15	0.40	0.60
1991	—	—	0.10	0.15	0.40	0.60
1992	—	—	0.10	0.15	0.40	0.60
1993	—	—	0.10	0.15	0.40	0.60
1994	—	—	0.10	0.15	0.40	0.60
1995	—	—	0.10	0.15	0.40	0.60
1996	—	—	0.10	0.15	0.40	0.60
1997	—	—	0.10	0.15	0.40	0.60
1998	—	—	0.10	0.15	0.40	0.60
1999	—	—	0.10	0.15	0.40	0.60
2000	—	—	0.10	0.15	0.40	0.60

KM# 14   25 CENTS
6.5000 g., Copper-Nickel, 24 mm. **Ruler:** Elizabeth II
Obv: Young bust right **Rev:** Sir Francis Drake's Golden Hind, divides denomination, date at right **Note:** Prev. KM#5.

Date	Mintage	F	VF	XF	Unc	BU
1981	—	—	0.15	0.20	0.50	0.75
1981 Proof	5,000	Value: 4.00				
1986	—	—	0.15	0.20	0.50	0.75
1986 Proof	2,500	Value: 4.00				
1987	—	—	0.15	0.20	0.50	0.75
1989	—	—	0.15	0.20	0.50	0.75
1991	—	—	0.15	0.20	0.50	0.75
1992	—	—	0.15	0.20	0.50	0.75
1993	—	—	0.15	0.20	0.50	0.75
1994	—	—	0.15	0.20	0.50	0.75
1995	—	—	0.15	0.20	0.50	0.75
1996	—	—	0.15	0.20	0.50	0.75
1997	—	—	0.15	0.20	0.50	0.75
1998	—	—	0.15	0.20	0.50	0.75
1999	—	—	0.15	0.20	0.50	0.75
2000	—	—	0.15	0.20	0.50	0.75

KM# 15   DOLLAR
8.2000 g., Aluminum-Bronze, 26.9 mm. **Ruler:** Elizabeth II
Obv: Young bust right **Rev:** Sir Francis Drake's Golden Hind divides denomination, date at right **Note:** Prev. KM#6.

Date	Mintage	F	VF	XF	Unc	BU
1981	—	—	0.50	0.75	1.50	2.50
1981 Proof	5,000	Value: 8.00				
1986	—	—	0.50	0.75	1.50	2.50
1986 Proof	2,500	Value: 8.00				

KM# 20   DOLLAR
7.9300 g., Copper-Nickel, 27.5 mm. **Ruler:** Elizabeth II
Obv: Young bust right **Rev:** Sir Francis Drake's Golden Hind divides denomination, date at right **Note:** Prev. KM#11.

Date	Mintage	F	VF	XF	Unc	BU
1989	—	—	—	—	2.25	3.25
1991	—	—	—	—	2.25	3.25
1992	—	—	—	—	2.25	3.25
1993	—	—	—	—	2.25	3.25
1994	—	—	—	—	2.25	3.25
1995	—	—	—	—	2.25	3.25
1996	—	—	—	—	2.25	3.25
1997	—	—	—	—	2.00	3.00
1998	—	—	—	—	2.00	3.00
1999	—	—	—	—	2.00	3.00
2000	—	—	—	—	2.00	3.00

KM# 24   2 DOLLARS
Copper-Nickel **Ruler:** Elizabeth II **Subject:** 10th Anniversary of Central Bank **Obv:** Bank building, dates below **Rev:** Bust facing, denomination below **Note:** Prev. KM#15.

Date	Mintage	F	VF	XF	Unc	BU
ND(1993)	—	—	—	—	8.50	10.00

KM# 16   10 DOLLARS
Copper-Nickel **Ruler:** Elizabeth II **Series:** F.A.O. **Subject:** World Food Day **Obv:** Denomination within wreath, date below **Rev:** Grain sprig within circle divides date and FAO logo **Note:** Prev. KM#7.

Date	Mintage	F	VF	XF	Unc	BU
1981	—	—	—	—	14.50	16.50

KM# 16a   10 DOLLARS
28.2800 g., 0.5000 Silver 0.4546 oz. ASW **Ruler:** Elizabeth II
Obv: Denomination within wreath, date below **Rev:** Grain sprig within circle divides date and FAO logo **Note:** Prev. KM#7a.

Date	Mintage	F	VF	XF	Unc	BU
1981	10,000	—	—	—	17.50	20.00
1981 Proof	5,000	Value: 47.50				

KM# 22   10 DOLLARS
28.2800 g., 0.9250 Silver 0.8410 oz. ASW **Ruler:** Elizabeth II
Subject: Queen Mother's 90th Birthday **Obv:** Crowned bust right, denomination below **Rev:** Crowned monogram with flowers flanking, dates below **Note:** Prev. KM#13.

Date	Mintage	F	VF	XF	Unc	BU
ND(1990) Proof	—	Value: 50.00				

KM# 23   10 DOLLARS
28.2800 g., 0.9250 Silver 0.8410 oz. ASW **Ruler:** Elizabeth II
Subject: 40th Anniversary - Coronation of Queen Elizabeth **Obv:** Crowned bust right, denomination below **Rev:** Crowned and seated 1/2 figure holding scepter and royal orb, dates below **Note:** Prev. KM#14.

Date	Mintage	F	VF	XF	Unc	BU
ND(1993) Proof	10,000	Value: 47.50				

KM# 25 10 DOLLARS
28.2800 g., 0.9250 Silver 0.8410 oz. ASW **Ruler:** Elizabeth II
Subject: 10th Anniversary of Central Bank **Obv:** Bank building,
dates below **Rev:** Bust facing, denomination below **Note:** Prev.
KM#16.

Date	Mintage	F	VF	XF	Unc	BU
ND(1993) Proof	2,500	Value: 55.00				

KM# 27 10 DOLLARS
31.4700 g., 0.9250 Silver 0.9359 oz. ASW **Ruler:** Elizabeth II
Subject: World Cup Soccer **Rev:** Buildings, soccer ball at right,
denomination below **Note:** Prev. KM#18.

Date	Mintage	F	VF	XF	Unc	BU
1994 Proof	10,000	Value: 45.00				

KM# 33 10 DOLLARS
28.5000 g., 0.9250 Silver 0.8475 oz. ASW, 38.5 mm. **Ruler:**
Elizabeth II **Subject:** Reeded **Obv:** Queens portrait **Rev:** The
Royal Launch, denomination divides dates below **Edge:** Reeded

Date	Mintage	F	VF	XF	Unc	BU
1996 Proof	—	Value: 50.00				

KM# 32 10 DOLLARS
28.5000 g., 0.9250 Silver 0.8475 oz. ASW, 38.5 mm.
Ruler: Elizabeth II **Subject:** Queen Elizabeth and Philip's Golden
Wedding Anniversary **Obv:** Crowned bust right, date below
Rev: The royal couple waving behind gold inset shield, within
circle, denomination below **Edge:** Reeded

Date	Mintage	F	VF	XF	Unc	BU
1997 Proof	—	Value: 45.00				

KM# 30 10 DOLLARS
28.2800 g., 0.9250 Silver 0.8410 oz. ASW **Ruler:** Elizabeth II
Subject: Montserrat Volcano Appeal Fund **Obv:** Queens portrait
Rev: Multicolor rainbow and volcano, date below **Note:** Prev.
KM#30.

Date	Mintage	F	VF	XF	Unc	BU
1998 Proof	10,000	Value: 60.00				

KM# 28 10 DOLLARS
28.2800 g., 0.9250 Silver 0.8410 oz. ASW **Ruler:** Elizabeth II
Subject: 50th Anniversary - University of the West Indies
Obv: Bust facing, denomination below **Rev:** University arms,
dates below, Pelican above **Note:** Prev. KM#19.

Date	Mintage	F	VF	XF	Unc	BU
ND(1999) Proof	1,000	Value: 60.00				

KM# 31 2000 CENTS (20 Dollars)
7.9800 g., 0.9170 Gold 0.2353 oz. AGW **Ruler:** Elizabeth II
Series: Millennium **Subject:** British Royal Mint **Obv:** Young bust
right **Rev:** Ship, palm trees and radiant sun within circle divided
by words "millennium", denomination below **Edge:** Reeded
Note: Prev. KM#22.

Date	Mintage	F	VF	XF	Unc	BU
2000	—	—	—	—	225	250

KM# 19 50 DOLLARS
28.2800 g., 0.9250 Silver 0.8410 oz. ASW **Ruler:** Elizabeth II
Series: International Year of Disabled Persons **Obv:** Young bust
right **Rev:** Two winged figures divide date and denomination
Note: Prev. KM#10.

Date	Mintage	F	VF	XF	Unc	BU
1981	10,000	—	—	—	30.00	—
1981 Proof	10,000	Value: 45.00				

KM# 17 50 DOLLARS
28.2800 g., 0.9250 Silver 0.8410 oz. ASW **Ruler:** Elizabeth II
Series: International Year of the Scout **Rev:** Boy scouts,
denomination below, date at left **Note:** Prev. KM#8.

Date	Mintage	F	VF	XF	Unc	BU
ND(1983)	10,000	—	—	—	30.00	35.00
ND(1983) Proof	10,000	Value: 47.50				

KM# 26 100 DOLLARS
15.9760 g., 0.9170 Gold 0.4710 oz. AGW **Ruler:** Elizabeth II
Subject: 10th Anniversary of Central Bank **Obv:** Bank building,
dates below **Rev:** Bust facing, denomination below **Note:** Prev.
KM#17.

Date	Mintage	F	VF	XF	Unc	BU
1993 Proof	150	Value: 550				

KM# 29 100 DOLLARS
15.9760 g., 0.9170 Gold 0.4710 oz. AGW **Ruler:** Elizabeth II
Subject: 50th Anniversary - University of West Indies **Obv:** Bust
facing, denomination below **Rev:** University arms, pelican above,
dates below **Note:** Prev. KM#20.

Date	Mintage	F	VF	XF	Unc	BU
ND(1999) Proof	300	Value: 550				

KM# 21 500 DOLLARS
15.9800 g., 0.9170 Gold 0.4711 oz. AGW **Ruler:** Elizabeth II
Series: International Year of Disabled Persons **Obv:** Young bust
right **Rev:** Two figures raising center figure, denomination above,
date at right **Note:** Prev. KM#12.

Date	Mintage	F	VF	XF	Unc	BU
1981	—	—	—	—	525	550
1981 Proof	—	Value: 750				

KM# 18 500 DOLLARS
15.9800 g., 0.9170 Gold 0.4711 oz. AGW **Ruler:** Elizabeth II
Series: International Year of the Scout **Obv:** Queens portrait
Rev: One scout standing, pointing; one scout kneeling with map,
denomination below, date at right **Note:** Prev. KM#9.

Date	Mintage	F	VF	XF	Unc	BU
ND(1983)	2,000	—	—	—	450	475
ND(1983) Proof	2,000	Value: 575				

PIEFORTS

KM#	Date	Mintage	Identification	Mkt Val
P1	1981	1,000	50 Dollars. Silver. KM#19.	65.00
P2	1981	—	500 Dollars. Gold. KM#21.	1,600

MINT SETS

KM#	Date	Mintage	Identification	Issue Price	Mkt Val
MS1	1986 (6)	—	KM#10-15	—	7.50
MS2	1991 (6)	—	KM#10-14, 20	19.95	20.00
MS3	1992 (6)	—	KM#10-14, 20	—	15.00
MS4	1993 (6)	—	KM#10-14, 20	30.00	15.00
MS5	1994 (6)	—	KM#10-14,20	30.00	15.00
MS6	1995 (6)	—	KM#10-14, 20	30.00	15.00
MS7	1995-97 (6)	—	KM#10-11 (1995), 12-14, 20 (1997)	25.00	25.00
MS8	1996 (6)	—	KM#10-14, 20	30.00	15.00
MS9	1997 (6)	—	KM#10-14, 20	30.00	15.00
MS10	1998 (6)	—	KM#10-14, 20	30.00	15.00
MS11	1999 (6)	—	KM#10-14, 20	25.00	25.00
MS12	2000 (7)	—	KM#10-14, 20, 31	139	145

PROOF SETS

KM#	Date	Mintage	Identification	Issue Price	Mkt Val
PS1	1955 (7)	2,000	KM#1-7	—	30.00
PS2	1958 (3)	20	KM#1-3	—	500
PS3	1965 (6)	—	KM#2-7	—	35.00
PS5	1981 (6)	5,000	KM#10-15	29.00	20.00
PS6	1986 (6)	2,500	KM#10-15	30.75	20.00

ECUADOR

The Republic of Ecuador, located astride the equator on the Pacific Coast of South America, has an area of 105,037 sq. mi. (283,560 sq. km.) and a population of 10.9 million. Capital: Quito. Agriculture is the mainstay of the economy but there are appreciable deposits of minerals and petroleum. It is one of the world's largest exporters of bananas and balsa wood. Coffee, cacao, sugar and petroleum are also valuable exports.

Ecuador was first sighted in 1526 by Francisco Pizarro. Conquest was undertaken by Sebastian de Benalcazar, who founded Quito in 1534. Ecuador was part of the Viceroyalty of New Granada through the 16th and 17th centuries. After previous attempts to attain independence were crushed, Antonio Sucre, the able lieutenant of Bolivar, secured Ecuador's freedom in the Battle of Pinchincha, May 24, 1822. It then joined Venezuela and Colombia in a confederation known as Gran Colombia, and became an independent republic when it left the confederacy in 1830.

MINT MARKS
BIRMm - Birmingham, Heaton
Birmingham - Birmingham
D - Denver
H - Heaton, Birmingham
HF - LeLocle (Swiss)
LIMA - Lima
Mo - Mexico
PHILA.U.S.A. - Philadelphia
PHILADELPHIA - Philadelphia
PHILA - Philadelphia

MONETARY SYSTEM
10 Centavos = 1 Decimo
10 Decimos = 1 Sucre
25 Sucres = 1 Condor

REPUBLIC

DECIMAL COINAGE
10 Centavos = 1 Decimo; 10 Decimos = 1 Sucre;
25 Sucres = 1 Condor

KM# 57   1/2 CENTAVO (Medio)
Copper-Nickel **Obv:** Flag draped arms, date below
Rev: Denomination within laurels

Date	Mintage	F	VF	XF	Unc	BU
1909H	4,000,000	4.00	9.00	20.00	40.00	—

KM# 58   CENTAVO (Un)
Copper-Nickel **Obv:** Flag draped arms, date below
Rev: Denomination within laurels

Date	Mintage	F	VF	XF	Unc	BU
1909H	3,000,000	4.50	10.00	22.00	45.00	—

KM# 67   CENTAVO (Un)
6.2500 g., Bronze **Obv:** Flag draped arms, date below
Rev: Denomination within laurels

Date	Mintage	F	VF	XF	Unc	BU
1928	2,016,000	1.00	2.00	7.50	25.00	—

KM# 59   2 CENTAVOS (Dos)
Copper-Nickel **Obv:** Flag draped arms, date below
Rev: Denomination within laurels

Date	Mintage	F	VF	XF	Unc	BU
1909H	2,500,000	5.00	12.00	25.00	60.00	—
1909H Proof	—	Value: 200				

KM# 61   2-1/2 CENTAVOS
Copper-Nickel **Obv:** Flag draped arms, date below
Rev: Denomination within laurels

Date	Mintage	F	VF	XF	Unc	BU
1917	1,600,000	6.00	15.00	55.00	175	—

KM# 68   2-1/2 CENTAVOS
Nickel **Obv:** Flag draped arms, date below **Rev:** Denomination within laurels

Date	Mintage	F	VF	XF	Unc	BU
1928	4,000,000	2.00	4.00	20.00	50.00	—

KM# 55.1   1/2 DECIMO (Medio)
1.2500 g., 0.9000 Silver 0.0362 oz. ASW **Obv:** Head of Sucre left **Rev:** Flag-draped arms, denomination upper left

Date	Mintage	F	VF	XF	Unc	BU
1902/892LIMA JF	1,000,000	1.00	2.00	8.50	20.00	—
1902/802LIMA JF	Inc. above	1.00	2.00	8.50	20.00	—
1902LIMA JF	Inc. above	0.75	1.50	6.00	20.00	—
1905/805LIMA JF	500,000	3.00	5.00	15.00	40.00	—
1905/2LIMA JF	Inc. above	3.50	6.00	18.00	50.00	—
1905LIMA JF	Inc. above	0.75	1.50	7.00	15.00	—
1912/05LIMA FG	20,000	3.00	6.00	18.00	50.00	—
1912LIMA FG	Inc. above	0.75	1.50	6.00	15.00	—
1912LIMA FG	Inc. above	2.00	3.00	8.50	20.00	—

Note: FCUADOR (obverse error)

KM# 55.2   1/2 DECIMO (Medio)
1.2500 g., 0.9000 Silver 0.0362 oz. ASW **Obv:** Head of Sucre left, date below **Rev:** Modified flag draped arms, denomination upper left

Date	Mintage	F	VF	XF	Unc	BU
1915BIRMm	2,000,000	0.75	1.25	5.00	10.00	—
1915BIRMm Proof	—	Value: 200				

KM# 60.1   5 CENTAVOS (Cinco)
Copper-Nickel **Obv:** Flag draped arms with tails on flagpoles pointing outward, date below **Rev:** Denomination within laurels

Date	Mintage	F	VF	XF	Unc	BU
1909H	2,000,000	4.50	10.00	30.00	80.00	—

KM# 60.2   5 CENTAVOS (Cinco)
Copper-Nickel **Obv:** Flag draped arms with tails on flagpoles pointing downward, date below **Rev:** Denomination within laurels
Note: Thin planchet.

Date	Mintage	F	VF	XF	Unc	BU
1917	1,200,000	8.50	25.00	80.00	200	—
1918	7,980,000	4.00	8.50	17.50	75.00	—

KM# 63   5 CENTAVOS (Cinco)
Copper-Nickel **Obv:** Flag draped arms, date below
Rev: Denomination within laurels

Date	Mintage	F	VF	XF	Unc	BU
1919	12,000,000	1.00	2.00	8.00	15.00	—

Note: 3 berries to left of "C" on reverse

1919	Inc. above	1.25	2.50	20.00	40.00	—

Note: 4 berries loose to left of "C" on reverse

1919	Inc. above	1.25	2.50	20.00	40.00	—

Note: 4 berries tight to left of "C" on reverse

KM# 65   5 CENTAVOS (Cinco)
Copper-Nickel **Obv:** Flag draped arms, date below **Rev:** Head right within wreath, denomination below

Date	Mintage	F	VF	XF	Unc	BU
1924H	10,000,000	2.00	5.00	15.00	35.00	—

KM# 69   5 CENTAVOS (Cinco)
Nickel **Obv:** Flag draped arms, date below **Rev:** Head right within wreath, denomination below

Date	Mintage	F	VF	XF	Unc	BU
1928	16,000,000	1.00	2.00	3.00	6.50	—

KM# 75   5 CENTAVOS (Cinco)
Nickel **Obv:** Flag draped arms, date below **Rev:** Denomination within wreath

Date	Mintage	F	VF	XF	Unc	BU
1937HF	15,000,000	0.10	0.20	0.75	2.00	—

KM# 75a   5 CENTAVOS (Cinco)
Brass **Obv:** Flag draped arms, date below **Rev:** Denomination within wreath

Date	Mintage	F	VF	XF	Unc	BU
1942	2,000,000	1.00	2.00	6.00	15.00	—
1944D	3,000,000	1.00	2.00	5.00	10.00	—

KM# 75b   5 CENTAVOS (Cinco)
1.9400 g., Copper-Nickel, 17.1 mm. **Obv:** Flag draped arms
Rev: Denomination within wreath

Date	Mintage	F	VF	XF	Unc	BU
1946	40,000,000	—	—	0.40	1.00	—

KM# 75c 5 CENTAVOS (Cinco)
Nickel Clad Steel **Obv:** Flag draped arms, date below
Rev: Denomination within wreath

Date	Mintage	F	VF	XF	Unc	BU
1970	—	—	—	0.15	0.50	—
1970	—	—	—	—	—	—

Note: ECADOR (obverse legend error)

KM# 50.3 DECIMO (Un)
2.5000 g., 0.9000 Silver 0.0723 oz. ASW **Obv:** Head left, legend without "LEY" **Rev. Leg.:** Flag draped arms

Date	Mintage	VG	F	VF	XF	Unc
1902LIMA JF	519,000	—	1.75	4.50	10.00	22.00

Note: With JR below fasces on reverse

| 1902LIMA JF | Inc. above | — | 1.75 | 4.50 | 10.00 | 22.00 |

Note: Without JR below fasces on reverse

1902LIMA JF/TF	—	—	1.50	3.00	10.00	20.00
1905LIMA JF	250,000	—	1.50	3.00	10.00	20.00
1912LIMA FG	30,000	—	3.00	6.00	15.00	35.00

KM# 50.4 DECIMO (Un)
2.5000 g., 0.9000 Silver 0.0723 oz. ASW **Obv:** Head of Sucre left, date below **Rev:** Flag draped arms, denomination upper left

Date	Mintage	VG	F	VF	XF	Unc
1915BIRMm	1,000,000	—	BV	1.25	2.00	7.00
1915BIRMm Proof	—	Value: 300				

KM# 50.5 DECIMO (Un)
2.5000 g., 0.9000 Silver 0.0723 oz. ASW **Obv:** Head of Sucre left **Rev:** Flag draped arms

Date	Mintage	VG	F	VF	XF	Unc
1916PHILA	2,000,000	—	BV	1.25	2.00	7.00

KM# 62 10 CENTAVOS (Diez)
Copper-Nickel **Obv:** Flag draped arms, date below
Rev: Denomination within wreath

Date	Mintage	F	VF	XF	Unc	BU
1918	1,000,000	10.00	20.00	40.00	90.00	—

KM# 64 10 CENTAVOS (Diez)
Copper-Nickel **Obv:** Flag draped arms, date below
Rev: Denomination within wreath

Date	Mintage	F	VF	XF	Unc	BU
1919	2,000,000	2.00	4.00	10.00	25.00	—
1919 Proof	—	Value: 300				

KM# 66 10 CENTAVOS (Diez)
Copper-Nickel **Obv:** Flag draped arms, date below **Rev:** Head of Bolivar left within wreath, denomination below **Note:** The H mint mark is very small and is located above the date.

Date	Mintage	F	VF	XF	Unc	BU
1924H	5,000,000	1.25	2.50	7.50	20.00	—
1924H Proof	—	Value: 100				

KM# 70 10 CENTAVOS (Diez)
Nickel **Obv:** Flag draped arms, date below **Rev:** Head of Bolivar right within wreath, denomination below

Date	Mintage	F	VF	XF	Unc	BU
1928	16,000,000	1.00	2.00	6.50	20.00	—

KM# 76 10 CENTAVOS (Diez)
Nickel **Obv:** Flag draped arms **Rev:** Denomination in wreath

Date	Mintage	F	VF	XF	Unc	BU
1937HF	7,500,000	0.25	0.50	1.00	3.50	—

KM# 76a 10 CENTAVOS (Diez)
Brass **Obv:** Flag draped arms, date below **Rev:** Denomination within wreath

Date	Mintage	F	VF	XF	Unc	BU
1942	5,000,000	0.60	1.00	5.00	15.00	—

KM# 76b 10 CENTAVOS (Diez)
Copper-Nickel **Obv:** Flag draped arms, date below
Rev: Denomination within wreath

Date	Mintage	F	VF	XF	Unc	BU
1946	40,000,000	0.10	0.15	0.25	1.00	—

KM# 76c 10 CENTAVOS (Diez)
2.8000 g., Nickel Clad Steel, 19.3 mm. **Obv:** Flag draped arms, date below **Rev:** Denomination within wreath **Note:** Varieties exist.

Date	Mintage	F	VF	XF	Unc	BU
1964	20,000,000	—	—	0.20	0.75	—
1968	15,000,000	—	—	0.20	0.75	—
1972	20,000,000	—	—	0.15	0.65	—

KM# 76d 10 CENTAVOS (Diez)
Copper-Nickel Clad Steel **Obv:** Flag draped arms, date below
Rev: Denomination within wreath

Date	Mintage	F	VF	XF	Unc	BU
1976	10,000,000	—	—	0.15	0.65	—

KM# 51.3 2 DECIMOS (Dos)
5.0000 g., 0.9000 Silver 0.1447 oz. ASW **Obv:** Head of Sucre left **Rev:** Flag-draped arms, legend without "LEI"

Date	Mintage	F	VF	XF	Unc	BU
1912/18 FG	50,000	5.00	12.50	30.00	75.00	—
1912 FG	Inc. above	2.75	6.00	20.00	50.00	—
1914 FG LIMA	110,000	3.00	7.00	14.50	40.00	—
1914 FG LIMA	Inc. above	2.50	5.50	11.50	30.00	—
1915 FG	157,000	5.00	15.00	50.00	100	—

Note: Small "R" below fasces on reverse

KM# 51.4 2 DECIMOS (Dos)
5.0000 g., 0.9000 Silver 0.1447 oz. ASW **Obv:** Head of Sucre left **Rev:** Flag-draped arms, mint name in legend below
Rev. Leg.: ...PHILADELPHIA...

Date	Mintage	F	VF	XF	Unc	BU
1914 TF	2,500,000	2.25	3.50	7.50	15.00	—
1916 TF	1,000,000	2.25	3.50	7.50	15.00	—

KM# 77.1 20 CENTAVOS
3.9000 g., Nickel, 21 mm. **Obv:** Flag draped arms, date below
Rev: Denomination within wreath

Date	Mintage	F	VF	XF	Unc	BU
1937HF	7,500,000	0.25	0.50	1.00	5.00	—

KM# 77.1a 20 CENTAVOS
3.7200 g., Brass, 21 mm. **Obv:** Flag draped arms, date below
Rev: Denomination within wreath

Date	Mintage	F	VF	XF	Unc	BU
1942	5,000,000	0.60	1.00	6.00	15.00	—
1944 D	15,000,000	0.40	0.75	4.00	10.00	—

KM# 77.1b 20 CENTAVOS
Copper Nickel, 21 mm. **Obv:** Flag draped arms
Rev: Denomination within wreath

Date	Mintage	F	VF	XF	Unc	BU
1946	30,000,000	0.25	0.75	2.00	5.00	—

KM# 77.1c 20 CENTAVOS
Nickel Clad Steel, 21 mm. **Obv:** Flag draped arms
Rev: Denomination within wreath

Date	Mintage	F	VF	XF	Unc	BU
1959	14,400,000	—	—	0.20	1.00	—
1962	14,400,000	—	—	0.20	1.00	—
1966	24,000,000	—	—	0.20	1.00	—
1969	24,000,000	—	—	0.20	1.00	—
1971	12,000,000	—	—	0.20	1.00	—
1972	48,432,000	—	—	0.20	1.00	—

KM# 77.2 20 CENTAVOS
Copper-Nickel, 21 mm. **Obv:** Modified flag draped arms, date below **Rev:** Denomination within wreath

Date	Mintage	F	VF	XF	Unc	BU
1974	19,562,000	—	—	0.15	0.50	—

KM# 77.2a 20 CENTAVOS
Nickel Coated Steel, 21 mm. **Obv:** Flag draped arms, date below
Rev: Denomination within wreath

Date	Mintage	F	VF	XF	Unc	BU
1975	52,437,000	—	—	0.15	0.35	—
1978	37,500,000	—	—	0.15	0.35	—
1980	18,000,000	—	—	0.15	0.35	—
1981	21,000,000	—	—	0.15	0.35	—

KM# 71 50 CENTAVOS (Cincuenta)
2.5000 g., 0.7200 Silver 0.0579 oz. ASW **Obv:** Head of Sucre left, date below **Rev:** Flag draped arms, denomination above, mint name below **Rev. Leg.:** ...PHILA•U•S•A...

Date	Mintage	F	VF	XF	Unc	BU
1928	1,000,000	1.50	3.00	15.00	40.00	—
1930	155,000	2.00	5.00	25.00	60.00	—

KM# 81   50 CENTAVOS (Cincuenta)
4.9200 g., Nickel Clad Steel **Obv:** Flag draped arms, date below
Rev: Denomination within wreath

Date	Mintage	F	VF	XF	Unc	BU
1963	20,000,000	—	0.15	0.25	0.85	—
1971	5,000,000	—	0.15	0.25	0.85	—
1974	—	—	0.15	0.25	0.85	—
1975	—	—	0.15	0.25	0.85	—
1977	40,000,000	—	0.10	0.20	0.75	—
1979	25,000,000	—	0.10	0.20	0.75	—
1982	20,000,000	—	0.10	0.20	0.75	—

KM# 87   50 CENTAVOS (Cincuenta)
Nickel Clad Steel **Obv:** Modified flag draped arms, date below
Rev: Denomination within wreath

Date	Mintage	F	VF	XF	Unc	BU
1985	30,000,000	—	0.10	0.20	0.40	—

KM# 90   50 CENTAVOS (Cincuenta)
Nickel Clad Steel **Obv:** Flag draped arms, date below
Rev: Denomination within square **Note:** The circulation strikes
were withdrawn from circulation and remelted. Approximately
100,000 pieces were released.

Date	Mintage	F	VF	XF	Unc	BU
1988	—	—	—	—	0.30	—
1988 Proof	25					

KM# 72   SUCRE (Un)
5.0000 g., 0.7200 Silver 0.1157 oz. ASW **Obv:** Head of Sucre
left, date below **Rev:** Flag draped arms, denomination above,
mint name in legend below **Rev. Leg.:** ...PHILA•U•S•A...

Date	Mintage	F	VF	XF	Unc	BU
1928	3,000,000	2.00	4.00	12.50	35.00	—
1930	400,000	3.00	10.00	30.00	70.00	—
1934	2,000,000	BV	2.00	10.00	30.00	—

KM# 78.1   SUCRE (Un)
Nickel, 26.5 mm. **Obv:** Flag draped arms, date below **Rev:** Head
of Sucre left within wreath, denomination below

Date	Mintage	F	VF	XF	Unc	BU
1937 HF	9,000,000	0.50	1.00	2.00	7.00	—

KM# 78.2   SUCRE (Un)
Nickel, 25.9 mm. **Obv:** Flag draped arms **Rev:** Head of Sucre left

Date	Mintage	F	VF	XF	Unc	BU
1946	18,000,000	0.40	0.60	0.80	2.00	—

KM# 78a   SUCRE (Un)
Copper-Nickel, 26 mm. **Obv:** Different ship in flag draped arms,
date below **Rev:** Head of Sucre left within wreath, denomination
below

Date	Mintage	F	VF	XF	Unc	BU
1959	8,400,000	0.25	0.50	0.65	1.00	—
1959 Proof	—	Value: 250				

KM# 78b   SUCRE (Un)
5.7500 g., Nickel Clad Steel, 26 mm. **Obv:** Flag draped arms,
date below **Rev:** Head left within wreath, denomination below
Note: Ship in arms similar to KM#78

Date	Mintage	F	VF	XF	Unc	BU
1964	20,000,000	—	0.10	0.25	0.75	—
1970	24,000,000	—	0.10	0.25	0.75	—
1971	8,092,000	—	0.10	0.25	0.75	—
1974	40,308,000	—	0.10	0.25	0.50	—
1978	32,000,000	—	0.10	0.25	0.50	—
1979	32,000,000	—	0.10	0.25	0.50	—
1980	110,000,000	—	0.10	0.25	0.50	—
1981	70,000,000	—	0.10	0.25	0.50	—

KM# 83   SUCRE (Un)
Nickel Clad Steel, 26 mm. **Obv:** Modified flag draped arms, date
below **Rev:** Head left within wreath, denomination below
Note: Ship in arms similar to KM #78

Date	Mintage	F	VF	XF	Unc	BU
1974	32,000,000	—	0.10	0.20	0.40	—
1975	32,000,000	—	0.10	0.20	0.40	—
1975 Proof	—	Value: 150				
1977	32,000,000	—	0.10	0.20	0.35	—

KM# 85.1   SUCRE (Un)
Nickel Clad Steel, 26 mm. **Obv:** Modified coat of arms
Rev: Large head right within wreath

Date	Mintage	F	VF	XF	Unc	BU
1985	—	—	—	—	0.50	—

KM# 85.2   SUCRE (Un)
Nickel Clad Steel, 26 mm. **Obv:** Flag draped arms, date below
Rev: Small head left within wreath, denomination below

Date	Mintage	F	VF	XF	Unc	BU
1986	—	—	—	—	0.50	—

KM# 89   SUCRE (Un)
Nickel Clad Steel **Obv:** Flag draped arms, date below **Rev:** Head
left within wreath, denomination below **Note:** The 1988 circulation
strikes were reportedly withdrawn from circulation and remelted.
Approximately 100,000 pieces were released.

Date	Mintage	F	VF	XF	Unc	BU
1988	—	—	—	—	0.40	—
1988 Proof	25					

Date	Mintage	F	VF	XF	Unc	BU
1990	—	—	—	—	0.40	—
1992	—	—	—	—	0.40	—

KM# 111   SUCRE (Un)
31.1000 g., 0.9000 Gold 0.8999 oz. AGW, 40 mm. **Subject:**
Central Bank's 70th Anniversary **Obv:** Partial view of bank
building **Rev:** Coin designs of 1 escudo KM-15 **Edge:** Reeded

Date	Mintage	F	VF	XF	Unc	BU
ND (1997) Proof	2,000	Value: 825				

KM# 73   2 SUCRES (Dos)
10.0000 g., 0.7200 Silver 0.2315 oz. ASW **Obv:** Head of Sucre
left, date below **Rev:** Flag draped arms, denomination above,
mint name below **Rev. Leg.:** ...PHILA•U•S•A...

Date	Mintage	F	VF	XF	Unc	BU
1928	500,000	3.50	10.00	30.00	70.00	—
1930	100,000	7.00	25.00	50.00	90.00	—

KM# 80   2 SUCRES (Dos)
10.0000 g., 0.7200 Silver 0.2315 oz. ASW **Obv:** Head of Sucre
left, date below **Rev:** Flag draped arms, denomination above

Date	Mintage	F	VF	XF	Unc	BU
1944Mo	1,000,000	3.50	5.00	8.00	16.00	—

KM# 82   2 SUCRES (Dos)
Copper-Nickel **Obv:** Flag draped arms, date below **Rev:** Head
3/4 facing, divides denomination **Note:** Not released to
circulation. All but approximatley 35 pieces remelted.

Date	Mintage	F	VF	XF	Unc	BU
1973	2,000,000	—	—	200	300	—

KM# 79   5 SUCRES (Cinco)
25.0000 g., 0.7200 Silver 0.5787 oz. ASW **Obv:** Head of Sucre
left, date below **Rev:** Flag draped arms, denomination above

Date	Mintage	F	VF	XF	Unc	BU
1943Mo	1,000,000	—	BV	12.00	16.50	27.50
1944Mo	2,600,000	—	BV	11.50	14.00	22.50

KM# 84   5 SUCRES (Cinco)
Copper-Nickel **Obv:** Flag draped arms, date below **Rev:** Head
of Sucre left within wreath, denomination below

Date	Mintage	F	VF	XF	Unc	BU
1973	500	—	—	—	1,200	—

Note: Only 7 pieces were distributed to Ecuadorian government officials, while 8 pieces (5 of these cancelled) reside in the Central Bank Collection; the remaining 485 pieces have been remelted

KM# 91   5 SUCRES (Cinco)
5.2900 g., Nickel Clad Steel, 22 mm.   **Obv:** Flag draped arms, date below **Rev:** Denomination within lines, design in background **Note:** The 1988 circulation strikes were reportedly withdrawn from circulation and remelted. Approximately 100,000 pieces released.

Date	Mintage	F	VF	XF	Unc	BU
1988	—	—	—	—	0.50	—
1988 Proof	25	—	—	—	—	—
1991	—	—	—	—	0.50	—

KM# 92.1   10 SUCRES (Diez)
Nickel Clad Steel, 24 mm.   **Obv:** Flag draped arms, date below **Rev:** Denomination to right of statuette **Note:** Similar to KM#92.2 but small arms and letters. The circulation strikes were withdrawn from circulation and remelted. Approximately 100,000 pieces were released.

Date	Mintage	F	VF	XF	Unc	BU
1988	—	—	—	—	1.00	—
1988 Proof	25	—	—	—	—	—

KM# 92.2   10 SUCRES (Diez)
6.1700 g., Nickel Clad Steel, 24 mm.   **Obv:** Flag draped arms, date below, large arms and letters **Rev:** Denomination to right of statuette

Date	Mintage	F	VF	XF	Unc	BU
1991	—	—	—	—	1.00	—

KM# 94.1   20 SUCRES
Nickel Clad Steel, 26 mm.   **Obv:** Flag draped arms, date below **Rev:** Denomination to right of small monument **Note:** The circulation strikes were withdrawn from circulation and remelted. Approximately 100,000 pieces released.

Date	Mintage	F	VF	XF	Unc	BU
1988	—	—	—	—	1.75	—
1988 Proof	25	—	—	—	—	—

KM# 94.2   20 SUCRES
Nickel Clad Steel, 26 mm.   **Obv:** Modified coat of arms **Rev:** Denomination to right of small monument

Date	Mintage	F	VF	XF	Unc	BU
1991	—	—	—	—	1.75	—

KM# 93   50 SUCRES
Nickel Clad Steel, 29 mm.   **Obv:** Flag draped arms, date below **Rev:** Denomination to left of native mask **Note:** The 1988 circulation strikes were withdrawn from circulation and remelted. Approximately 100,000 pieces released.

Date	Mintage	F	VF	XF	Unc	BU
1988 Narrow date	—	—	—	—	3.00	—
Note: 141 denticles in obverse border						
1988 Proof	25	—	—	—	—	—
1991 Wide date	—	—	—	—	3.00	—
Note: 141 denticles in obverse border						
1991 Narrow date	—	—	—	—	3.00	—
Note: 161 denticles in obverse border						

KM# 96   100 SUCRES
Bi-Metallic Bronze plated Steel center in Nickel plated Steel ring, 19 mm.   **Subject:** National Bicentennial **Obv:** Flag draped arms within circle, date below **Rev:** Bust left within circle, denomination below

Date	Mintage	F	VF	XF	Unc	BU
1995	—	—	0.35	0.55	2.00	3.00

KM# 101   100 SUCRES
3.6000 g., Bi-Metallic Brass clad steel center in Stainless Steel ring, 19.9 mm.   **Subject:** 70th Anniversary - Central Bank **Obv:** Bust of Antonio Jose de Sucre left within circle, dates below **Rev:** Denomination within circle, grain sprigs flank

Date	Mintage	F	VF	XF	Unc	BU
ND(1997)	—	—	0.25	0.50	2.00	3.00

KM# 97   500 SUCRES
Bi-Metallic Bronze plated Steel center in Nickel plated Steel ring, 21.5 mm.   **Subject:** State Reform **Obv:** Flag draped arms within circle, date below **Rev:** Isidro Ayora facing within circle, denomination below

Date	Mintage	F	VF	XF	Unc	BU
1995	—	—	—	—	3.00	4.00

KM# 102   500 SUCRES
5.7500 g., Bi-Metallic Aluminumn-Bronze center in Copper-Nickel ring, 21.5 mm.   **Subject:** 70th Anniversary - Central Bank **Obv:** Isidro Ayora head facing within circle, dates below **Rev:** Denomination within circle, grain sprigs flank

Date	Mintage	F	VF	XF	Unc	BU
ND(1997)	—	—	—	—	3.00	4.00

KM# 86   1000 SUCRES
23.3300 g., 0.9250 Silver 0.6938 oz. ASW **Subject:** Championship Soccer **Obv:** Flag draped arms, date below **Rev:** Soccer player, globe in background, denomination below

Date	Mintage	F	VF	XF	Unc	BU
1986 Proof	8,125	Value: 50.00				

KM# 88   1000 SUCRES
23.3300 g., 0.9250 Silver 0.6938 oz. ASW **Subject:** Championship Soccer **Obv:** Flag draped arms, date below **Rev:** Soccer players, globe in background, denomination below

Date	Mintage	F	VF	XF	Unc	BU
1986 Proof	Est. 10,000	Value: 50.00				

KM# 99   1000 SUCRES
Bi-Metallic Brass center in Stainless Steel ring, 23.5 mm.   **Obv:** Flag draped arms within circle, date below **Rev:** Eugenio Espejo head right within circle, denomination below

Date	Mintage	F	VF	XF	Unc	BU
1996	—	—	—	—	5.00	6.00

KM# 103   1000 SUCRES
7.1900 g., Bi-Metallic Aluminumn-Bronze center in Copper-Nickel ring, 23.9 mm.   **Subject:** 70th Anniversary - Central Bank **Obv:** Eugenio Espejo head right within circle, dates below **Rev:** Denomination within circle, grain sprigs flank

Date	Mintage	F	VF	XF	Unc	BU
ND(1997)	—	—	—	—	5.00	6.00

KM# 95   5000 SUCRES
27.0000 g., 0.9250 Silver 0.8029 oz. ASW   **Subject:** Ibero - American Series **Obv:** Flag draped arms and date within inner circle, circle of shields surround **Rev:** Native mask and dates above three ships, denomination below

Date	Mintage	F	VF	XF	Unc	BU
1991 Proof	50,000	Value: 75.00				

KM# 98   5000 SUCRES
27.0000 g., 0.9250 Silver 0.8029 oz. ASW **Subject:** Environmental Protection - Galapagos Penguins **Rev:** Two penguins, date at right, denomination below

Date	Mintage	F	VF	XF	Unc	BU
1994 Proof	20,000		Value: 75.00			

KM# 100   5000 SUCRES
27.0000 g., 0.9250 Silver 0.8029 oz. ASW **Subject:** Ibero-American Series - Native Costumes

Date	Mintage	F	VF	XF	Unc	BU
1997 Proof	20,000		Value: 60.00			

KM# 109   5000 SUCRES
27.1000 g., 0.9250 Silver 0.8059 oz. ASW, 40 mm.
Subject: Ibero-America Series **Obv:** Flag draped arms within a circle of arms **Rev:** Man on horse with condor in background, date at left, denomination below **Edge:** Reeded

Date	Mintage	F	VF	XF	Unc	BU
1999 Proof	—		Value: 60.00			

KM# 74   CONDOR (Un)
8.3592 g., 0.9000 Gold 0.2419 oz. AGW **Obv:** Head of Bolivar left, date below **Rev:** Flag draped arms, denomination above, mint name below **Rev. Leg.:** ...BIRMINGHAM... **Note:** 5,000 were released into circulation; the remainder are held as the Central Bank gold reserve.

Date	Mintage	F	VF	XF	Unc	BU
1928	20,000		BV	220	350	425

REFORM COINAGE
100 Centavos = 1 Dollar

KM# 104   CENTAVO (Un)
2.5200 g., Brass, 19 mm. **Obv:** Map of the Americas within circle **Rev:** Denomination **Edge:** Plain

Date	Mintage	F	VF	XF	Unc	BU
2000	—		—	—	0.20	0.40

KM# 105   5 CENTAVOS (Cinco)
5.0000 g., Steel, 21.2 mm. **Subject:** Juan Montalvo **Obv:** Bust 3/4 facing and arms **Rev:** Denomination **Edge:** Plain

Date	Mintage	F	VF	XF	Unc	BU
2000	—		—	—	0.50	0.75

KM# 106   10 CENTAVOS (Diez)
2.2400 g., Steel, 17.9 mm. **Subject:** Eugenio Espejo **Obv:** Bust 3/4 left and arms **Rev:** Denomination **Edge:** Plain

Date	Mintage	F	VF	XF	Unc	BU
2000	—		—	—	0.75	1.00

KM# 107   25 CENTAVOS
5.6500 g., Steel, 24.2 mm. **Subject:** Jose Joaquin De Olmedo **Obv:** Bust facing and arms **Rev:** Denomination **Edge:** Reeded

Date	Mintage	F	VF	XF	Unc	BU
2000	—		—	—	1.00	1.50

KM# 108   50 CENTAVOS (Cincuenta)
11.3200 g., Steel, 30.6 mm. **Subject:** Eloy Alfaro **Obv:** Head at left 3/4 facing and arms **Rev:** Denomination **Edge:** Reeded

Date	Mintage	F	VF	XF	Unc	BU
2000	—		—	2.00	5.00	6.50

KM# 110   SUCRE (Un)
11.2500 g., Nickel Clad Steel, 30.5 mm. **Obv:** Denomination **Rev:** Antonio Jose De Sucre and small national arms **Edge:** Reeded

Date	Mintage	F	VF	XF	Unc	BU
2000	—		—	2.50	5.50	7.00

PATTERNS
Including off metal strikes

KM#	Date	Mintage	Identification	Mkt Val
Pn11	1928	—	Condor. Copper-Nickel. KM#74.	
Pn12	1928	—	Condor. Copper. KM#74.	
Pn13	1974	—	20 Centavos. Brass. 3.6000 g. KM#77.2	150
Pn14	1975	—	50 Centavos. Brass. 5.2100 g. KM#81.	150
Pn15	1975	—	Sucre. Brass. 6.7900 g. KM#83.	150
Pn16	1976	—	10 Centavos. Brass. 2.9100 g. KM#76d.	150

PIEFORTS

KM#	Date	Mintage	Identification	Mkt Val
P1	1915H	—	1/2 Decimo. Copper Nickel.	
P2	1915H	—	Decimo. Copper Nickel.	

MINT SETS

KM#	Date	Mintage	Identification	Issue Price	Mkt Val
MS35	1975	10,000	8 circulating coins and 1 commemorative dollar Polo	30.00	42.00
MS36	2000 (5)	—	KM#104-108	30.00	28.00

PROOF SETS

KM#	Date	Mintage	Identification	Issue Price	Mkt Val
PS2	1988 (6)	25	KM#89-94		

EGYPT

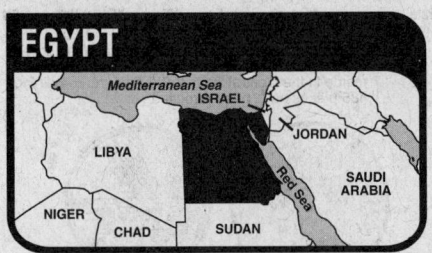

The Arab Republic of Egypt, located on the northeastern corner of Africa, has an area of 385,229 sq. mi. (1,1001,450 sq. km.) and a population of 62.4 million. Capital: Cairo. Although Egypt is an almost rainless expanse of desert, its economy is predominantly agricultural. Cotton, rice and petroleum are exported. Other main sources of income are revenues from the Suez Canal, remittances of Egyptian workers abroad and tourism.

Egyptian history dates back to about 3000 B.C. when the empire was established by uniting the upper and lower kingdoms. Following its 'Golden Age' (16th to 13th centuries B.C.), Egypt was conquered by Persia (525 B.C.) and Alexander the Great (332 B.C.). The Ptolemies, descended from one of Alexander's generals, ruled until the suicide of Cleopatra (30 B.C.) when Egypt became the private domain of the Roman emperor, and subsequently part of the Byzantine world. Various Muslim dynasties ruled Egypt from 641 on, including Ayyubid Sultans to 1250 and Mamluks to 1517, when it was conquered by the Ottoman Turks, interrupted by the occupation of Napoleon (1798-1801). A semi-independent dynasty was founded by Muhammad Ali in 1805 which lasted until 1952. Turkish rule became increasingly casual, permitting Great Britain to inject its influence by purchasing shares in the Suez Canal. British troops occupied Egypt in 1882, becoming the de facto rulers. On Dec. 14, 1914, Egypt was made a protectorate of Britain. British occupation ended on Feb. 28, 1922, when Egypt became a sovereign, independent kingdom. The monarchy was abolished and a republic proclaimed on June 18, 1953.

On Feb. 1, 1958, Egypt and Syria formed the United Arab Republic. Yemen joined on March 8 in an association known as the United Arab States. Syria withdrew from the United Arab Republic on Sept. 29, 1961, and on Dec. 26 Egypt dissolved its ties with Yemen in the United Arab States. On Sept. 2, 1971, Egypt finally shed the name United Arab Republic in favor of the Arab Republic of Egypt.

RULERS
British, 1882-1922
Kingdom, 1922-1953
Ahmed Fuad I, 1922-1936
Farouk, 1936-1952
Fuad II, 1952-1953
Republic, 1953-
MONETARY SYSTEM

(1885-1916)
10 Ushr-al-Qirsh = 1 Piastre
(Commencing 1916)
10 Milliemes = 1 Piastre (Qirsh)
100 Piastres = 1 Pound (Gunayh)

MINT MARKS
Egyptian coins issued prior to the advent of the British Protectorate series of Sultan Hussein Kamil introduced in 1916 were very similar to Turkish coins of the same period. They can best be distinguished by the presence of the Arabic word *Misr* Egypt) on the reverse, which generally appears immediately above the Muslim accession date of the ruler, which is presented in Arabic numerals. Each coin is individually dated according to the regnal years.
BP - Budapest, Hungary
H - Birmingham, England
KN - King's Norton, England

ENGRAVER
W - Emil Weigand, Berlin

INITIAL LETTERS
Letters, symbols and numerals were placed on coins during the reigns of Mustafa II (1695) until Selim III (1789). They have been observed in various positions but the most common position being over *bin* in the third row of the obverse. In Egypt these letters and others used on the Paras (Medins) above the word *duribe* on the reverse during this period.

REGNAL YEAR IDENTIFICATION

4
Duriba fi

| Misr | Accession Date |

DENOMINATIONS

| Para | Qirsh |

NOTE: The unit of value on coins of this period is generally presented on the obverse immediately below the toughra, as shown in the illustrations above.

Piastres 1916-1933

| Milliemes | Piastres 1934 – |

TITLES

المملكة   المصرية
al-Mamlaka   al-Misriya
(The Kingdom of Egypt)

U.A.R. EGYPT

The legend illustrated is *Jumhuriyat Misr al-Arabiyya* which translates to 'The Arab Republic of Egypt'. Similar legends are found on the modern issues of Syria.

OTTOMAN EMPIRE
Rsumed
Abdul Hamid II
AH1293-1327/1876-1909AD
REFORM COINAGE

KM# 287   1/40 QIRSH
Bronze **Obv:** Tughra **Rev:** Legend

Date	Mintage	F	VF	XF	Unc	BU
AH1293/27 (1901)	1,200,000	1.50	4.00	11.00	18.00	—
AH1293/29 (1903)	2,000,000	1.00	3.00	6.00	15.00	—
AH1293/31 (1905) H	2,400,000	1.00	3.00	6.00	15.00	—
AH1293/32 (1906) H	Inc. below	1.00	4.00	11.00	18.00	—
AH1293/33 (1907) H	1,200,000	1.00	4.00	11.00	18.00	—
AH1293/35 (1909) H	1,200,000	2.00	5.00	7.00	15.00	—

KM# 288   1/20 QIRSH
3.1200 g., Bronze **Obv:** Tughra **Rev:** Legend

Date	Mintage	F	VF	XF	Unc	BU
AH1293/27 (1901)	1,402,000	1.00	3.00	5.00	12.00	—
AH1293/29 (1903)	3,200,000	1.00	3.00	5.00	12.00	—
AH1293/31 (1905) H	3,000,000	1.00	3.00	5.00	12.00	—
AH1293/32 (1906) H	Inc. below	1.00	3.00	5.00	12.00	—
AH1293/33 (1907) H	1,400,000	2.00	3.00	7.00	15.00	—
AH1293/35 (1909) H	1,400,000	3.00	6.00	12.00	20.00	—

KM# 289   1/10 QIRSH
1.7200 g., Copper-Nickel **Obv:** Tughra **Rev:** Denomination

Date	Mintage	F	VF	XF	Unc	BU
AH1293/27-35 (1901) Proof	—	Value: 100				

Note: Above value for common date proof

AH1293/27 (1901)	3,010,000	1.00	2.00	5.00	10.00	—
AH1293/28 (1902)	6,000,000	1.00	2.00	5.00	10.00	—
AH1293/29 (1903)	1,500,000	1.00	3.00	6.00	15.00	—
AH1293/30 (1904)	1,000,000	1.00	3.00	6.00	15.00	—
AH1293/31 (1905) H	3,000,000	1.00	3.00	6.00	15.00	—
AH1293/32 (1906) H	Inc. below	1.00	3.00	6.00	15.00	—
AH1293/33 (1907) H	2,000,000	1.00	5.00	5.00	10.00	—
AH1293/35 (1909) H	2,000,000	1.25	5.00	12.00	20.00	—

KM# 290   2/10 QIRSH
2.3900 g., Copper-Nickel **Obv:** Tughra **Rev:** Denomination

Date	Mintage	F	VF	XF	Unc	BU
AH1293/27 (1901)	1,002,000	1.00	5.00	12.00	20.00	—
AH1293/28 (1902)	2,000,000	1.00	5.00	12.00	20.00	—
AH1293/29 (1903)	1,500,000	1.00	5.00	12.00	20.00	—
AH1293/30 (1904)	—	3.00	12.00	22.00	40.00	—
AH1293/31 (1905) H	1,000,000	1.00	5.00	12.00	20.00	—
AH1293/33 (1907) H	1,500,000	1.00	5.00	12.00	20.00	—
AH1293/35 (1909) H	750,000	2.00	10.00	20.00	35.00	—

KM# 291   5/10 QIRSH
3.9100 g., Copper-Nickel

Date	Mintage	F	VF	XF	Unc	BU
AH1293/27 (1901)	4,999,000	0.30	5.00	11.00	20.00	—
AH1293/29 (1903)	12,000,000	0.30	2.00	6.00	12.00	—
AH1293/30 (1904)	2,000,000	0.50	4.00	12.00	25.00	—
AH1293/33 (1907) H	1,000,000	2.00	9.00	22.50	40.00	—
AH1293/27-33 (1908) Proof	—	Value: 145				

Note: Above value for common date proof

KM# 292   QIRSH
1.4000 g., 0.8330 Silver 0.0375 oz. ASW **Obv:** Tughra

Date	Mintage	F	VF	XF	Unc	BU
AH1293/27-33 (1901) Proof	—	Value: 135				

Note: Above value for common date proof

AH1293/27 (1901) W	200,000	1.25	7.00	15.00	27.50	—
AH1293/29 (1903) W	100,000	1.50	7.00	16.00	30.00	—
AH1293/29 (1903) H	100,000	1.25	5.00	12.00	25.00	—
AH1293/33 (1907) H	100,000	1.25	5.00	12.00	25.00	—

KM# 299   QIRSH
Copper-Nickel **Obv:** Tughra **Rev:** Stars surround legend

Date	Mintage	F	VF	XF	Unc	BU
AH1293/27 (1901)	999,000	2.00	12.00	32.00	50.00	—
AH1293/29 (1903)	3,500,000	2.00	5.00	15.00	30.00	—
AH1293/30 (1904)	500,000	2.50	14.00	35.00	55.00	—
AH1293/33 (1907) H	1,000,000	2.00	8.00	21.00	40.00	—

KM# 293   2 QIRSH
2.8000 g., 0.8330 Silver 0.0750 oz. ASW, 19 mm. **Obv:** Flower to right of tughra **Rev:** Denomination

Date	Mintage	F	VF	XF	Unc	BU
AH1293/17-33 (1901) Proof	—	Value: 145				

Note: Above value for common date of proof

AH1293/27 (1901) W	1,000,000	2.00	8.00	21.00	35.00	—
AH1293/29 (1903) W	450,000	2.00	10.00	25.00	45.00	—
AH1293/29 (1903) H	1,250,000	2.00	6.00	15.00	30.00	—
AH1293/30 (1904) H	500,000	3.00	10.00	22.00	40.00	—
AH1293/31 (1905) H	Inc. above	3.00	10.00	22.00	40.00	—
AH1293/33 (1907) H	450,000	2.00	10.00	22.00	35.00	—

KM# 294   5 QIRSH
7.0000 g., 0.8330 Silver 0.1875 oz. ASW **Obv:** Flower at right of toughra

Date	Mintage	F	VF	XF	Unc	BU
AH1293/27 (1901) W	448,000	5.00	12.50	30.00	50.00	—
AH1293/29 (1903) W	600,000	5.00	10.00	30.00	50.00	—
AH1293/29 (1903) H	3,465,000	5.00	10.00	30.00	50.00	—
AH1293/30 (1904) H	1,213,000	5.00	10.00	32.50	60.00	—
AH1293/31 (1905) H	1,959,000	5.00	10.00	32.50	60.00	—
AH1293/32 (1906) H	Inc. above	5.00	10.00	30.00	50.00	—
AH1293/33 (1907) H	2,800,000	3.00	7.50	30.00	50.00	—

KM# 298   5 QIRSH
0.4200 g., 0.8750 Gold 0.0118 oz. AGW **Obv:** "Al-Ghazi" at right of tughra **Rev:** Denomination

Date	Mintage	F	VF	XF	Unc	BU
AH1293//34 (1908)	8,000	45.00	120	150	180	—

KM# 295   10 QIRSH
14.0000 g., 0.8330 Silver 0.3749 oz. ASW **Obv:** Flower at right of tughra **Rev:** Denomination

Date	Mintage	F	VF	XF	Unc	BU
AH1293/27-33 (1901) Proof	—	Value: 435				

Note: Above value for common date of proof

AH1293/27 (1901) W	250,000	15.00	50.00	95.00	150	—
AH1293/29 (1903) W Est.	2,450,000	8.00	25.00	60.00	100	—
AH1293/29 (1903) H	2,950,000	8.00	25.00	65.00	100	—
AH1293/30 (1904) H	1,000,000	8.00	25.00	65.00	100	—
AH1293/31 (1905) H	1,250,000	10.00	28.00	65.00	150	—
AH1293/32 (1906) H	Inc. below	8.00	16.00	65.00	100	—
AH1293/33 (1907) H	2,400,000	8.00	16.50	65.00	100	—

KM# 282   10 QIRSH
0.8544 g., 0.8750 Gold 0.0240 oz. AGW **Obv:** Al-Ghazi at right of tughra **Rev:** Denomination

Date	Mintage	F	VF	XF	Unc	BU
AH1293/34 (1908)	5,000	60.00	180	250	450	—

KM# 296 20 QIRSH
28.0000 g., 0.8330 Silver 0.7499 oz. ASW **Obv:** Tughra
Rev: Legend within wreath

Date	Mintage	F	VF	XF	Unc	BU
AH1293/27-33 (1901) Proof	—	Value: 825				

Note: Above value for common date of proof

Date	Mintage	F	VF	XF	Unc	BU
AH1293/27 (1901) W	25,000	17.50	70.00	250	500	—
AH1293/29 (1903) W	50,000	15.00	60.00	200	425	—
AH1293/29 (1903) H	425,000	12.00	50.00	180	400	—
AH1293/30 (1904) H	200,000	12.00	55.00	200	400	—
AH1293/31 (1905) H	250,000	12.00	55.00	200	400	—
AH1293/32 (1906) H	Inc. below	12.00	55.00	200	400	—
AH1293/33 (1907) H	300,000	12.00	45.00	175	350	—

Muhammad V
AH1327-1332/1909-1914AD

MILLED COINAGE

KM# 300 1/40 QIRSH
Bronze **Obv:** Tughra **Rev:** Denomination

Date	Mintage	F	VF	XF	Unc	BU
AH1327/2 (1910) H	2,000,000	1.50	3.00	10.00	25.00	—
AH1327/3 (1911) H	2,000,000	1.50	3.00	10.00	25.00	—
AH1327/4 (1911) H	1,200,000	1.50	3.00	10.00	25.00	—
AH1327/6 (1913) H	1,200,000	1.00	2.00	8.00	20.00	—

KM# 301 1/20 QIRSH
Bronze **Obv:** Tughra **Rev:** Denomination

Date	Mintage	F	VF	XF	Unc	BU
AH1327/2 (1910) H	2,000,000	1.00	5.00	11.00	18.00	—
AH1327/3 (1911) H	2,000,000	1.50	5.00	15.00	25.00	—
AH1327/4 (1911) H	2,400,000	1.00	5.00	11.00	18.00	—
AH1327/6 (1913) H	1,400,000	0.75	4.00	11.00	18.00	—

KM# 302 1/10 QIRSH
Copper-Nickel **Obv:** Tughra **Rev:** Denomination

Date	Mintage	F	VF	XF	Unc	BU
AH1327/2-6 (1910) H Proof	—	Value: 110				

Note: Above value for common date of proof

Date	Mintage	F	VF	XF	Unc	BU
AH1327/2 (1910) H	3,000,000	3.00	6.00	15.00	25.00	—
AH1327/3 (1911)	1,000,000	5.00	12.00	30.00	50.00	—
AH1327/4 (1911) H	3,000,000	1.00	2.00	5.00	12.50	—
AH1327/6 (1913) H	3,000,000	0.75	1.50	3.00	12.50	—

KM# 303 2/10 QIRSH
2.4200 g., Copper-Nickel **Obv:** Tughra within wreath
Rev: Denomination

Date	Mintage	F	VF	XF	Unc	BU
AH1327/2 (1910) H	1,000,000	2.00	6.00	15.00	25.00	—
AH1327/3 (1911)	500,000	3.00	10.00	15.00	35.00	—
AH1327/4 (1911) H	1,000,000	2.00	6.00	15.00	25.00	—
AH1327/6 (1913) H	1,000,000	1.25	6.00	15.00	25.00	—
AH1327/2-6 (1914) H Proof	—	Value: 120				

Note: Above value for common date of proof

KM# 304 5/10 QIRSH
Copper-Nickel **Obv:** Tughra within wreath **Rev:** Denomination

Date	Mintage	F	VF	XF	Unc	BU
AH1327/2 (1910) H	2,131,000	2.50	12.00	20.00	50.00	—
AH1327/3 (1911)	1,000,000	5.00	22.00	45.00	75.00	—
AH1327/4 (1911) H	3,327,000	1.00	5.00	11.00	25.00	—
AH1327/6 (1913)	3,000,000	1.00	5.00	11.00	25.00	—

KM# 305 QIRSH
1.4000 g., 0.8330 Silver 0.0375 oz. ASW **Obv:** Tughra
Rev: Denomination

Date	Mintage	F	VF	XF	Unc	BU
AH1327/2 (1910) H	251,000	2.00	6.00	18.00	28.00	—
AH1327/3 (1911) H	171,000	2.25	6.00	18.00	35.00	—

KM# 306 QIRSH
Copper-Nickel **Obv:** Tughra within wreath **Rev:** Denomination
within circle of stars

Date	Mintage	F	VF	XF	Unc	BU
AH1327/2 (1910) H	1,000,000	2.00	7.00	18.00	35.00	—
AH1327/3 (1911)	300,000	20.00	40.00	95.00	150	—
AH1327/4 (1911) H	500,000	4.00	15.00	40.00	65.00	—
AH1327/6 (1913) H	2,500,000	2.00	4.00	8.00	20.00	—

KM# 307 2 QIRSH
2.8000 g., 0.8330 Silver 0.0750 oz. ASW **Obv:** Tughra, spray
below **Rev:** Denomination within wreath

Date	Mintage	F	VF	XF	Unc	BU
AH1327/2 (1910) H	250,000	5.00	15.00	45.00	90.00	—
AH1327/3 (1911) H	300,000	5.00	15.00	45.00	90.00	—

KM# 308 5 QIRSH
7.0000 g., 0.8330 Silver 0.1875 oz. ASW **Obv:** Tughra above
spray **Rev:** Denomination within wreath

Date	Mintage	F	VF	XF	Unc	BU
AH1327/2-6 (1910) H Proof	—	Value: 350				

Note: Above value for common date of proof

Date	Mintage	F	VF	XF	Unc	BU
AH1327/2 (1910) H	5/4,000	10.00	40.00	90.00	150	—
AH1327/3 (1911) H	2,400,000	5.00	20.00	40.00	70.00	—
AH1327/4 (1911) H	1,351,000	6.00	22.00	40.00	85.00	—
AH1327/6 (1913) H	7,400,000	4.00	15.00	27.00	55.00	—

KM# 309 10 QIRSH
14.0000 g., 0.8330 Silver 0.3749 oz. ASW **Obv:** Tughra, spray
below **Rev:** Denomination within wreath

Date	Mintage	F	VF	XF	Unc	BU
AH1327/2-6 (1910) H Proof	—	Value: 475				

Note: Above value for common date of proof

Date	Mintage	F	VF	XF	Unc	BU
AH1327/2 (1910) H	300,000	20.00	50.00	110	200	—
AH1327/3 (1911) H	1,300,000	8.00	25.00	75.00	115	—
AH1327/4 (1911) H	300,000	10.00	50.00	110	200	—
AH1327/6 (1913) H	4,212,000	6.00	15.00	35.00	80.00	—

KM# 310 20 QIRSH
28.0000 g., 0.8330 Silver 0.7499 oz. ASW **Obv:** Tughra, spray
below **Rev:** Denomination within wreath

Date	Mintage	F	VF	XF	Unc	BU
AH1327/2-6 (1910) H Proof	—	Value: 950				

Note: Above value for common date of proof

Date	Mintage	F	VF	XF	Unc	BU
AH1327/2 (1910) H	75,000	35.00	65.00	210	500	—
AH1327/3 (1911) H	600,000	22.50	65.00	100	325	—
AH1327/4 (1911) H	100,000	30.00	55.00	135	425	—
AH1327/6 (1913) H	875,000	21.50	32.50	70.00	300	—

BRITISH PROTECTORATE
AH1333-1341 / 1914-1922AD

Hussein Kamil
As Sultan, AH1333-1336/1914-1917AD

OCCUPATION COINAGE
French

KM# 312 1/2 MILLIEME
Bronze **Obv:** Tughra, date below **Rev:** Dates below
denominations **Note:** Accession date: AH1333.

Date	Mintage	F	VF	XF	Unc	BU
AH1335-1917	4,000,000	1.35	5.00	12.50	25.00	—

KM# 313 MILLIEME
Copper-Nickel **Obv:** Center hole divides date and legend **Rev:** Center hole divides denomination, date below **Note:** Accession date: AH1333.

Date	Mintage	F	VF	XF	Unc	BU
AH1335-1917H	12,000,000	0.40	2.00	7.00	12.00	—
AH1335-1917	4,002,000	1.25	4.00	11.00	20.00	—

KM# 314 2 MILLIEMES
Copper-Nickel **Obv:** Center hole divides date **Rev:** Center hole divides denomination, date below **Note:** Accession date: AH1333.

Date	Mintage	F	VF	XF	Unc	BU
AH1335-1916H	300,000	1.25	8.00	15.00	30.00	—
AH1335-1917H	9,000,000	0.40	2.00	5.00	14.00	—
AH1335-1917	3,006,000	1.00	4.00	12.00	22.00	—

KM# 315 5 MILLIEMES
4.7500 g., Copper-Nickel **Obv:** Center hole divides dates **Rev:** Center hole divides denomination **Note:** Accession date: AH1333.

Date	Mintage	F	VF	XF	Unc	BU
AH1335-1916H	3,000,000	1.35	5.50	25.00	50.00	—
AH1335-1916	3,000,000	2.00	5.00	25.00	50.00	—
AH1335-1917H	37,000,000	0.60	1.50	2.50	8.00	—
AH1335-1917	6,776,000	1.00	2.50	6.00	15.00	—

KM# 316 10 MILLIEMES
Copper-Nickel **Obv:** Center hole divides dates **Rev:** Center hole divides denomination **Note:** Accession date: AH1333.

Date	Mintage	F	VF	XF	Unc	BU
AH1335-1916	1,006,999	2.00	6.00	40.00	100	—
AH1335-1916H	1,000,000	1.50	6.00	40.00	100	—
AH1335-1917	1,010,999	2.00	6.00	18.00	35.00	—
AH1335-1917H	6,000,000	0.75	2.00	7.00	15.00	—
AH1335-1917KN	4,000,000	1.25	3.00	8.00	20.00	—

KM# 317.1 2 PIASTRES
2.8000 g., 0.8330 Silver 0.0750 oz. ASW **Obv:** Text above date and sprays **Rev:** Denomination, legend within wreath **Note:** Accession date: AH1333.

Date	Mintage	F	VF	XF	Unc	BU
AH1335-1916	2,505,000	2.00	6.00	15.00	30.00	—
AH1335-1917	4,461,000	1.50	4.50	10.00	20.00	—

KM# 317.2 2 PIASTRES
2.8000 g., 0.8330 Silver 0.0750 oz. ASW **Obv:** Without inner circle **Rev:** Without inner circle **Note:** Accession date: AH1333.

Date	Mintage	F	VF	XF	Unc	BU
AH1335-1917H	2,180,000	1.50	4.00	8.00	15.00	—

KM# 318.1 5 PIASTRES
7.0000 g., 0.8330 Silver 0.1875 oz. ASW **Obv:** Text within wreath **Rev:** Denomination within wreath **Note:** Accession date: AH1333.

Date	Mintage	F	VF	XF	Unc	BU
AH1335-1916	6,000,000	3.50	9.00	20.00	35.00	—
AH1335-1917	9,218,000	2.75	5.00	17.50	32.00	—

KM# 318.2 5 PIASTRES
7.0000 g., 0.8330 Silver 0.1875 oz. ASW **Obv:** Without inner circle **Rev:** Without inner circle **Note:** Accession date: AH1333.

Date	Mintage	F	VF	XF	Unc	BU
AH1335-1917H	5,036,000	3.50	9.00	22.00	45.00	—
AH1335-1917H Proof	—	Value: 325				

KM# 319 10 PIASTRES
14.0000 g., 0.8330 Silver 0.3749 oz. ASW **Obv:** Text above date within wreath **Rev:** Denomination within wreath, dates below **Note:** Accession date: AH1333.

Date	Mintage	F	VF	XF	Unc	BU
AH1335-1916	2,900,000	6.00	15.00	40.00	95.00	—
AH1335-1917	4,859,000	6.00	12.00	22.00	85.00	—

KM# 320 10 PIASTRES
14.0000 g., 0.8330 Silver 0.3749 oz. ASW **Obv:** Text above date within wreath, without inner circle **Rev:** Denomination within wreath, without inner circle **Note:** Accession date: AH1333.

Date	Mintage	F	VF	XF	Unc	BU
AH1335-1917H	2,000,000	6.00	15.00	45.00	100	—

KM# 321 20 PIASTRES
28.0000 g., 0.8330 Silver 0.7499 oz. ASW **Obv:** Text above date within wreath **Rev:** Denomination within wreath, dates below **Note:** Accession date: AH1333.

Date	Mintage	F	VF	XF	Unc	BU
AH1335-1916	1,500,000	12.00	25.00	85.00	160	—
AH1335-1917	840,000	12.00	20.00	95.00	180	—
AH1335-1917 Proof	—	Value: 750				

KM# 322 20 PIASTRES
28.0000 g., 0.8330 Silver 0.7499 oz. ASW **Obv:** Without inner circle **Rev:** Without inner circle **Note:** Accession date: AH1333.

Date	Mintage	F	VF	XF	Unc	BU
AH1335-1917H	250,000	22.00	65.00	155	300	—

KM# 324 100 PIASTRES
8.5000 g., 0.8750 Gold 0.2391 oz. AGW **Obv:** Text above date within wreath **Rev:** Denomination within wreath, dates below **Note:** Accession date: AH1333.

Date	Mintage	F	VF	XF	Unc	BU
AH1335-1916	10,000	—	150	275	425	—
AH1335-1916 Proof	—	Value: 1,500				

Note: Restrikes may exist

Fuad I
As Sultan, AH1336-1341/1917-1922AD
OCCUPATION COINAGE
French

KM# 325 2 PIASTRES
2.8000 g., 0.8330 Silver 0.0750 oz. ASW **Obv:** Text above date **Rev:** Denomination and dates **Note:** Accession date: AH1335.

Date	Mintage	F	VF	XF	Unc	BU
AH1338-1920H	2,820,000	37.50	110	200	365	—

KM# 326 5 PIASTRES
7.0000 g., 0.8330 Silver 0.1875 oz. ASW **Obv:** Text above date **Rev:** Denomination and dates **Note:** Accession date: AH1335.

Date	Mintage	F	VF	XF	Unc	BU
AH1338-1920H	1,000,000	17.50	55.00	165	340	—

KM# 327 10 PIASTRES
14.0000 g., 0.8330 Silver 0.3749 oz. ASW **Obv:** Text above date **Rev:** Denomination and dates **Note:** Accession date: AH1335.

Date	Mintage	F	VF	XF	Unc	BU
AH1338-1920H	500,000	17.50	65.00	200	350	—

KM# 328   20 PIASTRES
28.0000 g., 0.8330 Silver 0.7499 oz. ASW **Obv:** Text above date
Rev: Denomination and dates **Note:** Accession date: AH1335.

Date	Mintage	F	VF	XF	Unc	BU
AH1338-1920H Rare	2					

KINGDOM
AH1341-1372 / 1922-1952AD

Fuad I
As King, AH1341-1355/1922-1936AD
DECIMAL COINAGE

KM# 330   1/2 MILLIEME
Bronze **Obv:** Bust right **Rev:** Denomination, dates above

Date	Mintage	F	VF	XF	Unc	BU
AH1342-1924H	3,000,000	2.00	5.00	14.00	25.00	—
AH1342-1924H Proof	—	Value: 120				

KM# 343   1/2 MILLIEME
Bronze **Obv:** Uniformed bust left **Rev:** Dates above denomination

Date	Mintage	F	VF	XF	Unc	BU
AH1348-1929BP	1,000,000	6.00	20.00	30.00	50.00	—
AH1351-1932H	1,000,000	3.00	20.00	30.00	50.00	—
AH1351-1932H Proof	—	Value: 160				

KM# 331   MILLIEME
Bronze **Obv:** Bust right **Rev:** Denomination divides dates

Date	Mintage	F	VF	XF	Unc	BU
AH1342-1924H	6,500,000	1.25	3.00	6.00	15.00	—

KM# 344   MILLIEME
4.2400 g., Bronze **Obv:** Uniformed bust left **Rev:** Denomination divides dates

Date	Mintage	F	VF	XF	Unc	BU
AH1348-1929BP	4,500,000	1.50	4.00	10.00	20.00	—
AH1351-1932H	2,500,000	0.50	1.25	6.00	15.00	—

Date	Mintage	F	VF	XF	Unc	BU
AH1351-1932H Proof	—	Value: 120				
AH1352-1933H	5,110,000	1.25	3.00	15.00	40.00	—
AH1354-1935H	18,000,000	0.20	0.50	2.00	8.00	—

KM# 332   2 MILLIEMES
Copper-Nickel **Obv:** Bust right **Rev:** Denomination divides dates

Date	Mintage	F	VF	XF	Unc	BU
AH1342-1924H	4,500,000	1.25	3.00	10.00	20.00	—
AH1342-1924H Proof	—	Value: 120				

KM# 345   2 MILLIEMES
Copper-Nickel **Obv:** Uniformed bust left **Rev:** Denomination divides dates

Date	Mintage	F	VF	XF	Unc	BU
AH1348-1929BP Est.	3,500,000	0.40	1.00	3.00	10.00	—

KM# 356   2-1/2 MILLIEMES
Copper-Nickel **Obv:** Uniformed bust left **Rev:** Denomination divides dates

Date	Mintage	F	VF	XF	Unc	BU
AH1352-1933	4,000,000	1.25	7.00	10.00	30.00	—

KM# 333   5 MILLIEMES
Copper-Nickel **Obv:** Bust right **Rev:** Denomination divides dates

Date	Mintage	F	VF	XF	Unc	BU
AH1342-1924	6,000,000	1.25	6.00	17.50	28.00	—

KM# 346   5 MILLIEMES
Copper-Nickel **Obv:** Uniformed bust left **Rev:** Denomination divides dates

Date	Mintage	F	VF	XF	Unc	BU
AH1348-1929BP	4,000,000	0.75	5.00	14.00	25.00	—
AH1352-1933H	3,000,000	1.50	4.00	18.00	35.00	—
AH1354-1935H	8,000,000	0.80	1.00	6.00	12.50	—
AH1354-1935H Proof	—	Value: 120				

KM# 334   10 MILLIEMES
5.1900 g., Copper-Nickel **Obv:** Bust right **Rev:** Denomination divides dates

Date	Mintage	F	VF	XF	Unc	BU
AH1342-1924	2,000,000	2.00	15.00	30.00	100	—

KM# 347   10 MILLIEMES
5.2200 g., Copper-Nickel **Obv:** Uniformed bust left
Rev: Denomination divides dates

Date	Mintage	F	VF	XF	Unc	BU
AH1348-1929BP	1,500,000	1.35	8.50	20.00	38.00	—
AH1352-1933H	1,500,000	1.35	8.50	25.00	45.00	—
AH1354-1935H	4,000,000	0.75	3.00	11.50	20.00	—

KM# 335   2 PIASTRES
2.8000 g., 0.8330 Silver 0.0750 oz. ASW **Obv:** Bust right
Rev: Denomination above center circle, dates flank below

Date	Mintage	F	VF	XF	Unc	BU
AH1342-1923H	2,500,000	2.00	6.00	11.00	35.00	—

KM# 348   2 PIASTRES
2.8000 g., 0.8330 Silver 0.0750 oz. ASW **Obv:** Uniformed bust left **Rev:** Denomination above center circle, dates flank below

Date	Mintage	F	VF	XF	Unc	BU
AH1348-1929BP	500,000	2.00	5.00	11.00	20.00	—
Note: Edge varieties exist						

KM# 336   5 PIASTRES
7.0000 g., 0.8330 Silver 0.1875 oz. ASW **Obv:** Bust right
Rev: Denomination above center circle, dates flank below

Date	Mintage	F	VF	XF	Unc	BU
AH1341-1923H	1,800,000	3.50	10.00	30.00	60.00	—
AH1341-1923	800,000	4.50	15.00	35.00	60.00	—
AH1341-1923H Proof	—	Value: 250				

KM# 349   5 PIASTRES
7.0000 g., 0.8330 Silver 0.1875 oz. ASW **Obv:** Uniformed bust left **Rev:** Denomination above center circle, dates flank below

Date	Mintage	F	VF	XF	Unc	BU
AH1348-1929BP	800,000	4.50	15.00	35.00	65.00	—
AH1352-1933	1,300,000	3.50	7.50	25.00	55.00	—
AH1352-1933 Proof	—	Value: 250				

KM# 337   10 PIASTRES
14.0000 g., 0.8330 Silver 0.3749 oz. ASW, 32.5 mm. **Obv:** Bust right **Rev:** Denomination above center circle, dates flank below

Date	Mintage	F	VF	XF	Unc	BU
AH1341-1923	400,000	7.00	22.50	70.00	120	—
AH1341-1923H	1,000,000	7.00	22.50	60.00	100	—
AH1341-1923H Proof	—	Value: 450				

KM# 350 10 PIASTRES
14.0000 g., 0.8330 Silver 0.3749 oz. ASW **Obv:** Uniformed bust left **Rev:** Denomination above center circle, dates flank below

Date	Mintage	F	VF	XF	Unc	BU
AH1348-1929BP	400,000	6.50	20.00	55.00	100	—
AH1352-1933	Est. 350,000	6.50	20.00	55.00	100	—
AH1352-1933 Proof	—	Value: 475				

KM# 338 20 PIASTRES
28.0000 g., 0.8330 Silver 0.7499 oz. ASW **Obv:** Bust right **Rev:** Denomination above center circle, dates flank below

Date	Mintage	F	VF	XF	Unc	BU
AH1341-1923	100,000	20.00	60.00	210	425	—
AH1341-1923H	50,000	20.00	70.00	240	445	—
AH1341-1923H Proof	—	Value: 875				

KM# 339 20 PIASTRES
1.7000 g., 0.8750 Gold 0.0478 oz. AGW **Obv:** Bust right **Rev:** Denomination above center inscription, dates flank below

Date	Mintage	F	VF	XF	Unc	BU
AH1341-1923	65,000	50.00	85.00	145	325	—

KM# 351 20 PIASTRES
1.7000 g., 0.8750 Gold 0.0478 oz. AGW **Obv:** Bust left **Rev:** Denomination above center inscription, dates flank below

Date	Mintage	F	VF	XF	Unc	BU
AH1348 Proof	—	—	—	—	—	—
AH1348-1929	—	45.00	65.00	85.00	125	—
AH1349-1930	—	45.00	65.00	85.00	125	—
AH1349-1930 Proof	—	—	—	—	—	—

KM# 352 20 PIASTRES
28.0000 g., 0.8330 Silver 0.7499 oz. ASW **Obv:** Uniformed bust left **Rev:** Denomination above center circle, dates flank below

Date	Mintage	F	VF	XF	Unc	BU
AH1348-1929BP	50,000	15.00	70.00	165	350	—
AH1352-1933	25,000	12.50	70.00	150	300	—
AH1352-1933 Proof	—	—	—	—	—	—

KM# 340 50 PIASTRES
4.2500 g., 0.8750 Gold 0.1196 oz. AGW **Obv:** Bust right **Rev:** Denomination above inscription, dates flank

Date	Mintage	F	VF	XF	Unc	BU
AH1341-1923	18,000	BV	115	135	175	—

KM# 353 50 PIASTRES
4.2500 g., 0.8750 Gold 0.1196 oz. AGW **Obv:** Bust left **Rev:** Denomination above inscription, dates flank below

Date	Mintage	F	VF	XF	Unc	BU
AH1348-1929	—	BV	120	145	185	—
AH1348-1929 Proof	—	—	—	—	—	—
AH1349-1930	—	BV	115	135	165	—
AH1349-1930 Proof	—	—	—	—	—	—

KM# 341 100 PIASTRES
8.5000 g., 0.8750 Gold 0.2391 oz. AGW **Obv:** Bust right **Rev:** Denomination above center circle, dates flank below

Date	Mintage	F	VF	XF	Unc	BU
AH1340-1922	25,000	BV	215	235	275	—

KM# 354 100 PIASTRES
8.5000 g., 0.8750 Gold 0.2391 oz. AGW **Obv:** Bust left

Date	Mintage	F	VF	XF	Unc	BU
AH1348-1929	—	BV	220	245	295	—
AH1349-1930	—	BV	215	235	275	—
AH1349-1930 Proof	—	—	—	—	—	—

KM# 342 500 PIASTRES
42.5000 g., 0.8750 Gold 1.1956 oz. AGW **Obv:** Bust right **Rev:** Denomination above center circle, dates flank below

Date	Mintage	F	VF	XF	Unc	BU
AH1340-1922	1,800	—	—	1,250	1,500	—
AH1340-1922 Proof	—	Value: 1,750				

Note: Circulation coins were struck in both red and yellow gold

KM# 355 500 PIASTRES
42.5000 g., 0.8750 Gold 1.1956 oz. AGW **Obv:** Uniformed bust left **Rev:** Denomination above center circle, dates flank below

Date	Mintage	F	VF	XF	Unc	BU
AH1348-1929	—	—	—	1,200	1,400	—
AH1349-1930	—	—	—	1,200	1,400	—
AH1351-1932	—	—	—	1,200	1,400	—
AH1351-1932 Proof	—	Value: 1,650				

Farouk
AH1355-1372/1936-1952AD
DECIMAL COINAGE

KM# 357 1/2 MILLIEME
Bronze **Obv:** Uniformed bust looking left **Rev:** Denomination, dates below

Date	Mintage	F	VF	XF	Unc	BU
AH1357-1938	4,000,000	1.50	5.00	9.00	18.00	—
AH1357-1938 Proof	—	Value: 100				

KM# 358 MILLIEME
Bronze **Obv:** Uniformed bust looking left **Rev:** Denomination, dates below

Date	Mintage	F	VF	XF	Unc	BU
AH1357-1938	26,240,000	0.20	0.50	2.00	7.00	—
AH1357-1938 Proof	—	Value: 120				
AH1364-1945	10,000,000	1.25	7.00	26.00	50.00	—
AH1366-1947	—	1.25	7.00	26.00	50.00	—
AH1369-1950	5,000,000	0.40	1.00	3.00	10.00	—
AH1369-1950 Proof	—	Value: 85.00				

KM# 362 MILLIEME
3.9600 g., Copper-Nickel, 18.1 mm.

Date	Mintage	F	VF	XF	Unc	BU
AH1357-1938	3,500,000	1.00	3.50	8.00	15.00	—

KM# 359 2 MILLIEMES
2.5100 g., Copper-Nickel **Obv:** Uniformed bust looking left **Rev:** Denomination divides dates

Date	Mintage	F	VF	XF	Unc	BU
AH1357-1938	2,500,000	1.50	4.00	14.00	25.00	—
AH1357-1938 Proof	—	Value: 140				

KM# 360 5 MILLIEMES
Bronze **Obv:** Uniformed bust looking left **Rev:** Denomination divides dates

Date	Mintage	F	VF	XF	Unc	BU
AH1357-1938	—	0.40	1.00	3.00	10.00	—
AH1357-1938 Proof	—	Value: 65.00				
AH1362-1943	—	0.40	1.00	3.00	10.00	—

KM# 363   5 MILLIEMES
4.0000 g., Copper-Nickel **Obv:** Uniformed bust looking left
Rev: Denomination divides dates

Date	Mintage	F	VF	XF	Unc	BU
AH1357-1938	7,000,000	0.40	1.00	4.00	10.00	—
AH1357-1938 Proof	—	Value: 75.00				
AH1360-1941	11,500,000	0.20	1.00	4.00	8.00	—

KM# 361   10 MILLIEMES
5.7000 g., Bronze **Obv:** Uniformed bust looking left
Rev: Denomination divides dates

Date	Mintage	F	VF	XF	Unc	BU
AH1357-1938	—	0.40	1.00	4.00	10.00	—
AH1357-1938 Proof	—	Value: 140				
AH1362-1943	—	—	0.75	4.00	10.00	—

KM# 364   10 MILLIEMES
5.5500 g., Copper-Nickel, 23 mm. **Obv:** Uniformed bust looking
left **Rev:** Denomination divides dates

Date	Mintage	F	VF	XF	Unc	BU
AH1357-1938	3,500,000	0.40	1.00	5.00	12.50	—
AH1357-1938 Proof	—	Value: 85.00				
AH1360-1941	5,322,000	0.40	1.00	5.00	12.50	—

KM# 365   2 PIASTRES
2.8000 g., 0.8330 Silver 0.0750 oz. ASW

Date	Mintage	F	VF	XF	Unc	BU
AH1356-1937	500,000	1.25	1.75	3.00	8.00	—
Note: Fine and coarse edge reeding exist						
AH1356-1937 Proof	—	Value: 300				
AH1358-1939	500,000	1.50	4.00	10.00	75.00	—
AH1358-1939 Proof	—	Value: 200				
AH1361-1942	10,000,000	1.25	1.75	4.00	10.00	—
Note: Normal and flat rim varieties exist for AH1361 coins						

KM# 369   2 PIASTRES
2.8000 g., 0.5000 Silver 0.0450 oz. ASW **Obv:** Uniformed bust
left **Rev:** Denomination and dates within tasseled wreath

Date	Mintage	F	VF	XF	Unc	BU
AH1363-1944	32,000	0.85	1.45	2.75	5.50	—

KM# 366   5 PIASTRES
7.0000 g., 0.8330 Silver 0.1875 oz. ASW, 25.92 mm.
Obv: Uniformed bust left **Edge:** Security

Date	Mintage	F	VF	XF	Unc	BU
AH1356-1937	—	2.75	3.75	6.50	15.00	—
AH1356-1937 Proof	—	Value: 275				
AH1358-1939	8,000,000	2.75	3.75	6.50	15.00	—
AH1358-1939 Proof	—	Value: 275				

KM# 367   10 PIASTRES
14.0000 g., 0.8330 Silver 0.3749 oz. ASW

Date	Mintage	F	VF	XF	Unc	BU
AH1356-1937	2,800,000	5.50	9.00	17.50	35.00	—
AH1356-1937 Proof	—	Value: 375				
AH1358-1939	2,850,000	5.50	9.00	17.50	35.00	—
AH1358-1939 Proof	—	Value: 300				

KM# 368   20 PIASTRES
28.0000 g., 0.8330 Silver 0.7499 oz. ASW **Obv:** Uniformed bust
looking left **Rev:** Denomination and dates within tasseled wreath

Date	Mintage	F	VF	XF	Unc	BU
AH1356-1937	—	12.00	26.00	50.00	90.00	—
AH1356-1937 Proof	—	Value: 1,000				
AH1358-1939	—	12.00	26.00	50.00	90.00	—
AH1358-1939 Proof	—	Value: 1,200				

KM# 370   20 PIASTRES
1.7000 g., 0.8750 Gold 0.0478 oz. AGW **Subject:** Royal
Wedding **Obv:** Uniformed bust looking left **Rev:** Dates within
circle, denomination above, decorative vine surrounds

Date	Mintage	F	VF	XF	Unc	BU
AH1357-1938	20,000	BV	65.00	90.00	125	145

KM# 371   50 PIASTRES
4.2500 g., 0.8750 Gold 0.1196 oz. AGW **Subject:** Royal
Wedding **Obv:** Uniformed bust looking left **Rev:** Dates within
circle, denomination above, decorative vine surrounds

Date	Mintage	F	VF	XF	Unc	BU
AH1357-1938	10,000	BV	120	150	250	—

KM# 372   100 PIASTRES
8.5000 g., 0.8750 Gold 0.2391 oz. AGW **Subject:** Royal
Wedding **Obv:** Uniformed bust looking left **Rev:** Dates within
circle, denomination above, decorative vine surrounds

Date	Mintage	F	VF	XF	Unc	BU
AH1357-1938	5,000	—	BV	235	300	—
Note: Circulation coins were struck in both red and yellow gold						

KM# 373   500 PIASTRES
42.5000 g., 0.8750 Gold 1.1956 oz. AGW **Subject:** Royal
Wedding **Obv:** Uniformed bust looking left **Rev:** Dates within
circle, denomination above, decorative vine surrounds

Date	Mintage	F	VF	XF	Unc	BU
AH1357-1938	—	—	—	1,250	2,500	—
AH1357-1938 Proof	—	Value: 3,000				

FIRST REPUBLIC
AH1373-1378 / 1953-1958AD
DECIMAL COINAGE

KM# 375   MILLIEME
1.8000 g., Aluminum-Bronze **Obv:** Denomination divides dates
Rev: Small sphinx with outlined base

Date	Mintage	F	VF	XF	Unc	BU
AH1373-1954	—	10.00	20.00	100	250	—
AH1374-1954	—	1.25	3.25	8.00	20.00	—
AH1374-1955	—	0.80	2.00	5.00	12.50	—
AH1375-1956	—	0.80	2.00	5.00	12.50	—

KM# 376   MILLIEME
1.8000 g., Aluminum-Bronze **Obv:** Denomination divides dates
Rev: Small sphinx without base outlined

Date	Mintage	F	VF	XF	Unc	BU
AH1373-1954	—	5.00	12.50	30.00	50.00	—
AH1374-1954	—	1.25	3.25	8.00	20.00	—
AH1374-1955	—	0.60	1.50	4.00	10.00	—
AH1375-1956	—	0.60	1.50	4.00	10.00	—
AH1376-1957	—	20.00	50.00	100	150	—

KM# 377   MILLIEME
1.8000 g., Aluminum-Bronze **Rev:** Large sphinx with outlined base

Date	Mintage	F	VF	XF	Unc	BU
AH1375-1956	—	0.15	0.40	1.00	2.50	—
AH1376-1957	—	0.15	0.40	1.00	2.50	—
AH1377-1958	—	0.15	0.40	1.00	2.50	—

KM# 378   5 MILLIEMES
Aluminum-Bronze **Obv:** Denomination divides dates **Rev:** Small
sphinx with outlined base

Date	Mintage	F	VF	XF	Unc	BU
AH1373-1954	—	—	5.00	10.00	35.00	—
AH1374-1954	—	—	4.00	8.00	25.00	—
AH1374-1955	—	—	10.00	20.00	50.00	—
AH1375-1956	—	—	3.00	6.00	15.00	—

KM# 379 5 MILLIEMES
Aluminum-Bronze **Obv:** Denomination divides dates **Rev:** Large sphinx

Date	Mintage	F	VF	XF	Unc	BU
AH1376-1957	—	—	2.00	4.00	10.00	—
AH1377-1957	—	—	2.00	4.00	10.00	—
AH1377-1958	—	—	2.00	4.00	10.00	—

KM# 380.1 10 MILLIEMES
Aluminum-Bronze **Obv:** Denomination divides dates **Rev:** Small sphinx with base outlined **Note:** Thin milliemes.

Date	Mintage	F	VF	XF	Unc	BU
AH1373-1954	—	—	5.00	12.00	25.00	—

KM# 380.2 10 MILLIEMES
Aluminum-Bronze **Obv:** Denomination divides date **Rev:** Small sphinx with base outlined **Note:** Thick Milliemes.

Date	Mintage	F	VF	XF	Unc	BU
AH1374-1954	—	—	4.00	10.00	20.00	—
AH1374-1955	—	—	3.00	7.00	15.00	—

KM# 381 10 MILLIEMES
4.7400 g., Aluminum-Bronze, 23.0 mm. **Rev:** Large sphinx **Note:** Exists also with eagle, 2 stars.

Date	Mintage	F	VF	XF	Unc	BU
AH1374-1955	—	—	50.00	85.00	150	—
AH1375-1956	—	—	3.00	7.00	15.00	—
AH1376-1957	—	—	2.00	6.00	12.00	—
AH1377-1958	—	—	2.00	6.00	12.00	—

KM# 382 5 PIASTRES
3.5000 g., 0.7200 Silver 0.0810 oz. ASW **Obv:** Denomination within wings **Rev:** Small Sphinx with outlined base **Note:** Die varieties exist which appear to be lacking outlined base of Sphinx.

Date	Mintage	F	VF	XF	Unc	BU
AH1375-1956	—	BV	1.50	3.00	8.00	—
AH1376-1956	—	1.50	3.00	5.00	10.00	—
AH1376-1957	—	BV	1.50	3.00	8.00	—

KM# 383 10 PIASTRES
7.0000 g., 0.6250 Silver 0.1407 oz. ASW **Obv:** Denomination within wings **Rev:** Large sphinx

Date	Mintage	F	VF	XF	Unc	BU
AH1374-1955	1,408,000	2.00	4.00	9.00	18.00	—

Note: Varieties in date sizes exist

KM# 383a 10 PIASTRES
7.0000 g., 0.7200 Silver 0.1620 oz. ASW **Obv:** Denomination within wings **Rev:** Sphinx, dates

Date	Mintage	F	VF	XF	Unc	BU
AH1375-1956	—	BV	3.50	7.00	15.00	—
AH1376-1957	—	BV	3.50	6.00	12.00	—

KM# 384 20 PIASTRES
14.0000 g., 0.7200 Silver 0.3241 oz. ASW **Obv:** Denomination within wings

Date	Mintage	F	VF	XF	Unc	BU
AH1375-1956	—	BV	5.50	9.00	18.00	—

KM# 385 25 PIASTRES
17.5000 g., 0.7200 Silver 0.4051 oz. ASW, 35 mm. **Subject:** Suez Canal Nationalization **Obv:** Denomination and dates above wings **Rev:** Headquarter building in Port Said

Date	Mintage	F	VF	XF	Unc	BU
AH1375-1956	258,000	BV	8.00	10.00	20.00	—

KM# 389 25 PIASTRES
17.5000 g., 0.7200 Silver 0.4051 oz. ASW, 35 mm. **Subject:** National Assembly Inauguration **Obv:** Denomination and dates above wings **Rev:** Radiant sun behind building

Date	Mintage	F	VF	XF	Unc	BU
AH1376-1957	246,000	BV	7.50	9.00	17.00	—

KM# 386 50 PIASTRES
28.0000 g., 0.9000 Silver 0.8102 oz. ASW, 40 mm. **Subject:** Evacuation of the British **Obv:** Denomination and dates above wings **Rev:** Figure with torch and broken chains

Date	Mintage	F	VF	XF	Unc	BU
AH1375-1956	250,000	BV	15.00	18.00	22.50	—

KM# 387 POUND
8.5000 g., 0.8750 Gold 0.2391 oz. AGW **Subject:** 3rd and 5th Anniversaries of Revolution **Obv:** Denomination and dates above wings **Rev:** Pharoah Ramses II in a war chariot

Date	Mintage	F	VF	XF	Unc	BU
AH1374-1955	16,000	—	—	225	250	—
AH1377-1957	10,000	—	—	235	265	—

Note: Struck in red and yellow gold

KM# 388 5 POUNDS
42.5000 g., 0.8750 Gold 1.1956 oz. AGW **Subject:** 3rd and 5th Anniversaries of Revolution **Obv:** Denomination and dates above wings **Rev:** Horse, chariot, and archer

Date	Mintage	F	VF	XF	Unc	BU
AH1374-1955	—	—	—	1,200	1,400	—
AH1377-1957	—	—	—	1,250	1,500	—

Note: Struck in red and yellow gold

UNITED ARAB REPUBLIC
AH1378-1391 / 1958-1971AD

DECIMAL COINAGE

KM# 393 MILLIEME
Aluminum-Bronze **Obv:** Denomination divides dates, legend above **Rev:** Eagle with shield on breast

Date	Mintage	F	VF	XF	Unc	BU
AH1380-1960	—	—	0.10	0.15	0.30	—
AH1386-1966 Proof	—	Value: 3.00				

KM# 403 2 MILLIEMES
Aluminum-Bronze **Obv:** Denomination divides dates, legend above **Rev:** Eagle with shield on breast

Date	Mintage	F	VF	XF	Unc	BU
AH1381-1962	—	—	0.15	0.35	0.65	—
AH1386-1966 Proof	—	Value: 3.00				

KM# 394 5 MILLIEMES
Aluminum-Bronze **Obv:** Denomination divides dates, legend above **Rev:** Eagle with shield on breast

Date	Mintage	F	VF	XF	Unc	BU
AH1380-1960	—	—	0.15	0.45	0.85	—
AH1386-1966 Proof	—	Value: 3.00				

KM# 410 5 MILLIEMES
Aluminum

Date	Mintage	F	VF	XF	Unc	BU
AH1386-1967	—	—	0.15	0.40	0.75	—

KM# 395   10 MILLIEMES
Aluminum-Bronze **Obv:** Denomination divides dates, legend above **Obv. Leg.:** Misr **Rev:** Eagle with shield on breast

Date	Mintage	F	VF	XF	Unc	BU
AH1378-1958	—	—	15.00	20.00	40.00	—
AH1380-1960	16,079,999	—	0.80	1.20	2.25	—
AH1386-1966 Proof	—	Value: 4.00				

KM# 396   10 MILLIEMES
Aluminum-Bronze **Obv:** Denomination divides dates, legend above, without Misr above denomination **Rev:** Eagle with shield on breast

Date	Mintage	F	VF	XF	Unc	BU
AH1378-1958	—	—	15.00	25.00	40.00	—
AH1378-1958 Proof	—	Value: 300				

KM# 411   10 MILLIEMES
Aluminum **Obv:** Denomination divides dates **Rev:** Eagle with shield on breast

Date	Mintage	F	VF	XF	Unc	BU
AH1386-1967	—	—	0.15	0.35	0.75	—

KM# 390   20 MILLIEMES
Aluminum-Bronze, 24 mm. **Subject:** Agriculture and Industrial Fair in Cairo **Obv:** Denomination divides dates, legend above **Rev:** Symbols of agriculture and industry

Date	Mintage	F	VF	XF	Unc	BU
AH1378-1958	—	—	0.75	1.50	5.00	—

KM# 397   5 PIASTRES
3.5000 g., 0.7200 Silver 0.0810 oz. ASW **Obv:** Denomination divides dates, legend above **Rev:** Eagle with shield on breast

Date	Mintage	F	VF	XF	Unc	BU
AH1380-1960	—	—	1.75	3.00	5.00	—
AH1386-1966	—	Value: 8.00				

KM# 404   5 PIASTRES
2.5000 g., 0.7200 Silver 0.0579 oz. ASW **Subject:** Diversion of the Nile **Obv:** Denomination divides dates, legend above **Rev:** Sadd el-Ali Dam, Nile River basin scene

Date	Mintage	F	VF	XF	Unc	BU
AH1384-1964	500,000	—	1.25	2.50	4.00	—
AH1384-1964 Proof	2,000	Value: 8.00				

KM# 412   5 PIASTRES
Copper-Nickel, 25 mm. **Obv:** Denomination divides dates, legend above **Rev:** Eagle with shield on breast

Date	Mintage	F	VF	XF	Unc	BU
AH1387-1967	10,800,000	—	0.50	0.75	1.50	—

Note: Edge varieties, narrow and gapped milling, exist

KM# 414   5 PIASTRES
Copper-Nickel **Subject:** International Industrial Fair **Obv:** Denomination, legend above **Rev:** Globe with cogwheel section around, dates below

Date	Mintage	F	VF	XF	Unc	BU
AH1388-1968	500,000	—	0.75	1.00	2.50	—

KM# 417   5 PIASTRES
Copper-Nickel, 25 mm. **Subject:** 50th Anniversary - International Labor Organization **Obv:** Denomination, legend **Rev:** Hands holding open-ended wrenches within wreath, dates divided below

Date	Mintage	F	VF	XF	Unc	BU
AH1389-1969	500,000	—	0.75	1.00	2.50	—

KM# 392   10 PIASTRES
7.0000 g., 0.7200 Silver 0.1620 oz. ASW, 24 mm. **Subject:** First Anniversary of U.A.R. Founding **Obv:** Denomination divides dates, legend above **Rev:** Eagle with shield on breast

Date	Mintage	F	VF	XF	Unc	BU
AH1378-1959	—	—	3.25	6.00	17.50	—

KM# 398   10 PIASTRES
7.0000 g., 0.7200 Silver 0.1620 oz. ASW **Obv:** Denomination divides dates, legend above **Rev:** Eagle with shield on breast

Date	Mintage	F	VF	XF	Unc	BU
AH1380-1960	500,000	—	3.00	4.50	7.50	—
AH1386-1966 Proof	—	Value: 12.50				

KM# 405   10 PIASTRES
5.0000 g., 0.7200 Silver 0.1157 oz. ASW **Subject:** Diversion of the Nile **Obv:** Denomination divides dates, legend above **Rev:** Sadd el-Ali Dam, Nile River basin scene

Date	Mintage	F	VF	XF	Unc	BU
AH1384-1964	500,000	—	2.50	3.50	6.00	—
AH1384-1964 Proof	2,000	Value: 12.50				

KM# 413   10 PIASTRES
Copper-Nickel, 27 mm. **Obv:** Denomination divides dates, legend above **Rev:** Eagle with shield on breast

Date	Mintage	F	VF	XF	Unc	BU
AH1387-1967	13,200,000	—	0.60	0.90	2.00	—

KM# 419   10 PIASTRES
Copper-Nickel **Subject:** Cairo International Agricultural Fair **Obv:** Denomination divides dates, legend above **Rev:** Grain sprig above globe and name

Date	Mintage	F	VF	XF	Unc	BU
AH1389-1969	1,000,000	—	0.75	1.25	3.00	—

KM# 418   10 PIASTRES
Copper-Nickel **Series:** F.A.O. **Obv:** Denomination divides dates, legend above **Rev:** People with oxen, eagle above, logo below

Date	Mintage	F	VF	XF	Unc	BU
ND(1970)	500,000	—	0.75	1.25	3.50	—

KM# 420   10 PIASTRES
Copper-Nickel **Subject:** 50 Years - Banque Misr **Obv:** Crowned head within wreath left of denomination and date **Rev:** Sun above building

Date	Mintage	F	VF	XF	Unc	BU
AH1390-1970	500,000	—	0.60	1.00	2.00	—

KM# 421.1   10 PIASTRES
Copper-Nickel **Subject:** Cairo International Industrial Fair **Obv:** Denomination **Rev:** Ship within cogwheel, dates in box below

Date	Mintage	F	VF	XF	Unc	BU
AH1390-1970	500,000	—	0.60	1.00	3.25	—

KM# 421.2   10 PIASTRES
6.0200 g., Copper-Nickel, 27 mm. **Subject:** Cairo International Industrial Fair **Obv:** New shorter Arabic inscriptions, denomination at center **Rev:** Ship within cogwheel, dates in box below

Date	Mintage	F	VF	XF	Unc	BU
AH1391-1971	500,000	—	0.60	1.00	2.75	—

KM# 399   20 PIASTRES
14.0000 g., 0.7200 Silver 0.3241 oz. ASW **Obv:** Denomination divides dates, legend above **Rev:** Eagle with shield on breast

Date	Mintage	F	VF	XF	Unc	BU
AH1380-1960	400,000	—	7.00	15.00	25.00	—
AH1386-1966 Proof	—	Value: 32.50				

KM# 400   25 PIASTRES
17.5000 g., 0.7200 Silver 0.4051 oz. ASW **Subject:** 3rd Year of National Assembly **Obv:** Denomination and dates above wings **Rev:** Radiant sun back of building, hand on book in front

Date	Mintage	F	VF	XF	Unc	BU
AH1380-1960	250,000	—	6.50	9.00	18.00	—

KM# 406   25 PIASTRES
10.0000 g., 0.7200 Silver 0.2315 oz. ASW **Subject:** Diversion of the Nile **Obv:** Denomination divides dates, legend above **Rev:** Sadd el-Ali Dam, Nile River basin scene

Date	Mintage	F	VF	XF	Unc	BU
AH1384-1964	250,000	—	3.75	5.50	9.50	—
AH1384-1964 Proof	2,000	Value: 35.00				

KM# 422   25 PIASTRES
6.0000 g., 0.7200 Silver 0.1389 oz. ASW **Subject:** President Nasser **Obv:** Head of President Nasser right

Date	Mintage	F	VF	XF	Unc	BU
AH1390-1970	700,000	—	2.50	4.00	6.50	—

KM# 407   50 PIASTRES
20.0000 g., 0.7200 Silver 0.4630 oz. ASW **Subject:** Diversion of the Nile **Rev:** Nile River basin scene

Date	Mintage	F	VF	XF	Unc	BU
AH1384-1964	250,000	—	9.00	10.00	12.00	—
AH1384-1964 Proof	2,000	Value: 40.00				

KM# 423   50 PIASTRES
12.5000 g., 0.7200 Silver 0.2893 oz. ASW **Subject:** President Nasser **Obv:** Head of President Nasser right **Rev:** Denomination and dates

Date	Mintage	F	VF	XF	Unc	BU
AH1390-1970	400,000	—	6.00	7.00	9.00	—

KM# 391   1/2 POUND
4.2500 g., 0.8750 Gold 0.1196 oz. AGW, 20 mm. **Subject:** U.A.R. Founding **Obv:** Denomination and dates above wings **Rev:** Pharoah Ramses II in a war chariot

Date	Mintage	F	VF	XF	Unc	BU
AH1378-1958	30,000	—	—	—	200	—

KM# 401   POUND
8.5000 g., 0.8750 Gold 0.2391 oz. AGW **Rev:** Aswan Dam

Date	Mintage	F	VF	XF	Unc	BU
AH1379-1960	252,000	—	—	—	225	245

KM# 415   POUND
25.0000 g., 0.7200 Silver 0.5787 oz. ASW **Obv:** Denomination and dates **Rev:** Power station for Aswan Dam, grain sprigs flank

Date	Mintage	F	VF	XF	Unc	BU
AH1387-1968	100,000	—	9.00	10.00	12.00	—

KM# 424   POUND
25.0000 g., 0.7200 Silver 0.5787 oz. ASW **Subject:** 1000th Anniversary - Al Azhar Mosque **Obv:** Center circle divides dates **Rev:** Al Azhar Mosque

Date	Mintage	F	VF	XF	Unc	BU
AH1359-1361 - 1970-1972	100,000	—	9.00	10.00	13.00	—

KM# 425   POUND
25.0000 g., 0.7200 Silver 0.5787 oz. ASW **Subject:** President Nasser **Obv:** Head of President Nasser right **Rev:** Denomination divides dates, legend above

Date	Mintage	F	VF	XF	Unc	BU
AH1390-1970	400,000	—	9.00	10.00	12.00	—

KM# 426   POUND
8.0000 g., 0.8750 Gold 0.2250 oz. AGW **Subject:** President Nasser **Obv:** Head of President Nasser right **Rev:** Denomination divides dates, legend above

Date	Mintage	F	VF	XF	Unc	BU
AH1390-1970	10,000	—	—	—	220	—

KM# 402   5 POUNDS
42.5000 g., 0.8750 Gold 1.1956 oz. AGW **Obv:** Denomination and dates above wings **Rev:** Aswan Dam

Date	Mintage	F	VF	XF	Unc	BU
AH1379-1960	5,000	—	—	—	1,200	—

KM# 408   5 POUNDS
26.0000 g., 0.8750 Gold 0.7314 oz. AGW **Subject:** Diversion of the Nile **Obv:** Denomination divides dates, legend above **Rev:** Nile River basin scene

Date	Mintage	F	VF	XF	Unc	BU
AH1384-1964	—	—	—	—	750	—

KM# 416 5 POUNDS
26.0000 g., 0.8750 Gold 0.7314 oz. AGW **Subject:** 1400th Anniversary of the Koran **Obv:** Denomination and dates within center circle **Rev:** Open Koran book above globe with radiant sun in back

Date	Mintage	F	VF	XF	Unc	BU
AH1388-1968	10,000	—	—	—	745	—

KM# 427 5 POUNDS
26.0000 g., 0.8750 Gold 0.7314 oz. AGW **Subject:** 1000th Anniversary - Al Azhar Mosque **Rev:** Al Azhar Mosque

Date	Mintage	F	VF	XF	Unc	BU
AH1390-1970	—	—	—	—	765	—

KM# 428 5 POUNDS
26.0000 g., 0.8750 Gold 0.7314 oz. AGW **Subject:** President Nasser **Obv:** Head of President Nasser right

Date	Mintage	F	VF	XF	Unc	BU
AH1390-1970	3,000	—	—	—	765	—

KM# 409 10 POUNDS
52.0000 g., 0.8750 Gold 1.4628 oz. AGW **Subject:** Diversion of the Nile **Obv:** Denomination divides dates **Rev:** Nile River basin scene

Date	Mintage	F	VF	XF	Unc	BU
AH1384-1964	2,000	—	—	—	1,450	—

ARAB REPUBLIC
AH1391- / 1971- AD
DECIMAL COINAGE

KM# A423 MILLIEME
Aluminum **Obv:** Denomination divides dates, legend above **Rev:** Eagle with shield on breast

Date	Mintage	F	VF	XF	Unc	BU
AH1392-1972	—	—	0.10	0.30	0.50	—

KM# A425 5 MILLIEMES
Aluminum **Obv:** Denomination divides dates, legend above **Rev:** Eagle with shield on breast

Date	Mintage	F	VF	XF	Unc	BU
AH1392-1972	16,000,000	—	0.20	0.50	2.50	—

KM# A424 5 MILLIEMES
Aluminum **Obv:** Denomination divides dates, legend above **Rev:** Corn ears and grain sprigs encircle figure below sun **Note:** Mule - Obverse of KM#A425 and reverse of KM#433.

Date	Mintage	F	VF	XF	Unc	BU
AH1392-1972	—	—	10.00	20.00	45.00	—

KM# 432 5 MILLIEMES
2.0000 g., Brass, 18 mm. **Obv:** Denomination divides dates, legend above **Rev:** Eagle with shield on breast

Date	Mintage	F	VF	XF	Unc	BU
AH1393-1973	—	—	0.10	0.15	0.30	—

KM# A433 5 MILLIEMES
Aluminum, 18 mm. **Obv:** Denomination divides dates, legend above **Rev:** Eagle with shield on breast **Note:** Mule - Obverse of KM#433 and reverse of KM#A425.

Date	Mintage	F	VF	XF	Unc	BU
AH1393-1973	—	—	10.00	20.00	45.00	—

KM# 433 5 MILLIEMES
Aluminum **Series:** F.A.O. **Obv:** Denomination divides dates, legend above **Rev:** Corn ears and grain sprigs encircle figure below sun

Date	Mintage	F	VF	XF	Unc	BU
AH1393-1973	10,000,000	—	0.10	0.20	0.35	—

KM# 434 5 MILLIEMES
2.0000 g., Brass, 18 mm. **Obv:** Denomination divides dates, legend above **Rev:** Nefertiti head right and grain sprig **Note:** Mule.

Date	Mintage	F	VF	XF	Unc	BU
AH1393-1973	—	—	5.00	10.00	20.00	—

KM# 445 5 MILLIEMES
4.0000 g., Brass, 18 mm. **Series:** International Women's Year **Obv:** Denomination divides dates, legend above **Rev:** Nefertiti head right and grain sprig

Date	Mintage	F	VF	XF	Unc	BU
AH1395-1975	10,000,000	—	0.10	0.15	0.30	—

KM# 462 5 MILLIEMES
Brass, 18 mm. **Series:** F.A.O. **Obv:** Denomination divides dates, legend above **Rev:** People, animals, and building

Date	Mintage	F	VF	XF	Unc	BU
AH1397-1977	5,000,000	—	0.10	0.20	0.50	—

KM# 463 5 MILLIEMES
Brass **Subject:** 1971 Corrective Revolution **Obv:** Denomination divides dates, legend above **Rev:** City scene

Date	Mintage	F	VF	XF	Unc	BU
AH1397-1977	2,500,000	—	0.10	0.20	0.50	—
AH1399-1979	2,500,000	—	0.10	0.20	0.50	—

KM# A426 10 MILLIEMES
Aluminum, 21 mm.

Date	Mintage	F	VF	XF	Unc	BU
AH1392-1972	20,000,000	—	0.50	2.00	6.00	—

Note: Two varieties of edge letterings exist

KM# 435 10 MILLIEMES
3.2000 g., Brass, 21 mm.

Date	Mintage	F	VF	XF	Unc	BU
AH1393-1973	—	—	0.10	0.25	0.50	—
AH1396-1976	—	—	0.75	1.50	3.00	—

KM# 446 10 MILLIEMES
3.2000 g., Brass, 21 mm. **Series:** F.A.O. **Obv:** Denomination divides dates, legend above **Rev:** Family scene

Date	Mintage	F	VF	XF	Unc	BU
AH1395-1975	10,000,000	—	0.10	0.20	0.35	—

KM# 449 10 MILLIEMES
3.1100 g., Brass, 21 mm. **Series:** F.A.O. **Obv:** Denomination divides dates, legend above **Rev:** Osiris seated, wheat ear at right

Date	Mintage	F	VF	XF	Unc	BU
AH1396-1976	10,000,000	—	0.10	0.20	0.30	—

KM# 464 10 MILLIEMES
3.2800 g., Brass, 21 mm. **Series:** F.A.O. **Obv:** Denomination divides dates, legend above **Rev:** Various laborers surround center design

Date	Mintage	F	VF	XF	Unc	BU
AH1397-1977	10,000,000	—	0.10	0.20	0.85	—

KM# 465 10 MILLIEMES
Brass, 21 mm. **Subject:** 1971 Corrective Revolution **Obv:** Denomination divides dates, legend above **Rev:** Date and denomination left of head

Date	Mintage	F	VF	XF	Unc	BU
AH1397-1977	2,500,000	—	0.10	0.20	0.65	—
AH1399-1979	2,500,000	—	0.20	0.40	1.00	—

KM# 476 10 MILLIEMES
Brass, 21 mm. **Series:** F.A.O. **Obv:** Denomination divides dates, legend above **Rev:** Woman looking into microscope

Date	Mintage	F	VF	XF	Unc	BU
AH1398-1978	2,000,000	—	0.10	0.20	0.80	—

KM# 483 10 MILLIEMES
Brass, 21 mm. **Series:** International Year of the Child
Obv: Denomination divides dates, legend above **Rev:** Seated woman and child

Date	Mintage	F	VF	XF	Unc	BU
AH1399-1979	2,000,000	—	0.10	0.20	0.65	—

KM# 498 10 MILLIEMES
Aluminum-Bronze, 21 mm. **Subject:** Sadat's Corrective Revolution **Obv:** Fist raised holding grain stalk
Rev: Denomination divides dates, legend above

Date	Mintage	F	VF	XF	Unc	BU
AH1400-1980	2,500,000	—	0.10	0.25	1.00	—

KM# 499 10 MILLIEMES
Aluminum-Bronze, 21 mm. **Series:** F.A.O.

Date	Mintage	F	VF	XF	Unc	BU
AH1400-1980	2,000,000	—	0.10	0.20	0.60	—

KM# 553.1 PIASTRE
Aluminum-Bronze, 18 mm. **Obv:** Christian date left of denomination, tughra above **Rev:** Pyramids

Date	Mintage	F	VF	XF	Unc	BU
AH1404-1984	—	—	—	0.15	0.35	—

KM# 553.2 PIASTRE
Aluminum-Bronze, 18 mm. **Obv:** Islamic date left of denomination, tughra above **Rev:** Pyramids

Date	Mintage	F	VF	XF	Unc	BU
AH1404-1984	—	—	—	0.15	0.35	—

KM# 500 2 PIASTRES
4.9000 g., Aluminum-Bronze, 21 mm.

Date	Mintage	F	VF	XF	Unc	BU
AH1400-1980	—	—	0.20	0.30	0.60	—

KM# 554.1 2 PIASTRES
4.9000 g., Aluminum-Bronze, 21 mm. **Obv:** Christian date left of denomination

Date	Mintage	F	VF	XF	Unc	BU
AH1404-1984	—	—	—	0.20	0.50	—

KM# 554.2 2 PIASTRES
4.9000 g., Aluminum-Bronze, 21 mm. **Obv:** Islamic date left of denomination

Date	Mintage	F	VF	XF	Unc	BU
AH1404-1984	—	—	—	0.20	0.50	—

KM# A427 5 PIASTRES
4.5100 g., Copper-Nickel, 24.5 mm. **Subject:** 25th Anniversary of UNICEF

Date	Mintage	F	VF	XF	Unc	BU
AH1392-1972	500,000	—	0.75	1.00	3.00	—

Note: Error in spelling "UNICFE".

KM# A428 5 PIASTRES
4.5000 g., Copper-Nickel, 25 mm. **Obv:** Denomination divides dates, legend above **Rev:** Islamic falcon

Date	Mintage	F	VF	XF	Unc	BU
AH1392-1972	—	—	0.50	0.75	2.00	—

KM# 436 5 PIASTRES
Copper-Nickel, 25 mm. **Subject:** Cairo State Fair **Obv:** Denomination divides dates, legend above **Rev:** Stylized design

Date	Mintage	F	VF	XF	Unc	BU
AH1393-1973	500,000	—	0.60	0.75	2.25	—

KM# 437 5 PIASTRES
Copper-Nickel, 25 mm. **Subject:** 75th Anniversary - National Bank of Egypt **Obv:** Denomination divides dates, legend above **Rev:** Bank building in front of globe at left

Date	Mintage	F	VF	XF	Unc	BU
AH1393-1973	1,000,000	—	0.60	0.75	2.00	—

KM# A441 5 PIASTRES
4.5500 g., Copper-Nickel, 25 mm. **Subject:** First Anniversary - October War **Obv:** Denomination divides dates, legend above **Rev:** Soldier with gun facing right

Date	Mintage	F	VF	XF	Unc	BU
AH1394-1974	2,000,000	—	0.60	0.75	2.00	—

KM# 447 5 PIASTRES
4.4600 g., Copper-Nickel, 25 mm. **Series:** International Women's Year **Obv:** Denomination divides dates, legend above **Rev:** Bust of Nefertiti right, grain sprig at left

Date	Mintage	F	VF	XF	Unc	BU
AH1395-1975	2,000,000	—	0.50	0.65	1.25	—

KM# 451 5 PIASTRES
Copper-Nickel, 25 mm. **Subject:** 1976 Cairo Trade Fair **Obv:** Denomination divides dates, legend above **Rev:** Legend forms square around design, florals flank

Date	Mintage	F	VF	XF	Unc	BU
AH1396-1976	500,000	—	0.60	0.75	2.00	—

KM# 450 5 PIASTRES
Copper-Nickel, 25 mm. **Obv:** Denomination divides dates, legend above **Rev:** Islamic falcon **Note:** Mule.

Date	Mintage	F	VF	XF	Unc	BU
AH1396-1976	—	—	5.00	10.00	20.00	—

KM# 466 5 PIASTRES
Copper-Nickel, 25 mm. **Subject:** 1971 Corrective Revolution

Date	Mintage	F	VF	XF	Unc	BU
AH1397-1977	1,000,000	—	0.50	0.60	1.50	—
AH1399-1979	—	—	0.50	0.60	1.25	—

KM# 467 5 PIASTRES
Copper-Nickel, 25 mm. **Subject:** 50th Anniversary - Textile Industry **Obv:** Crowned head within wreath at right of denomination and dates **Rev:** Figure between dates

Date	Mintage	F	VF	XF	Unc	BU
AH1397-1977	1,000,000	—	0.50	0.75	1.65	—

KM# 468 5 PIASTRES
Copper-Nickel, 25 mm. **Series:** F.A.O. **Obv:** Denomination divides dates, legend above **Rev:** People, animals, and building

Date	Mintage	F	VF	XF	Unc	BU
AH1397-1977	—	—	0.50	0.75	1.65	—

Note: Edge varieties exist with narrow and wide milling

KM# 477 5 PIASTRES
Copper-Nickel, 25 mm. **Subject:** Portland Cement **Obv:** Denomination divides dates, legend above **Rev:** Cement factory, dates at top

Date	Mintage	F	VF	XF	Unc	BU
AH1398-1978	500,000	—	0.50	0.75	1.65	—

KM# 478 5 PIASTRES
4.4600 g., Copper-Nickel, 25 mm. **Series:** F.A.O. **Obv:** Denomination divides dates, legend above **Rev:** Woman looking into microscope

Date	Mintage	F	VF	XF	Unc	BU
AH1398-1978	1,000,000	—	0.50	0.75	1.65	—

KM# 484 5 PIASTRES
Copper-Nickel, 25 mm. **Series:** International Year of the Child **Obv:** Denomination divides dates, legend above **Rev:** Woman seated with child

Date	Mintage	F	VF	XF	Unc	BU
AH1399-1979	1,000,000	—	0.50	0.75	1.65	—

KM# 501 5 PIASTRES
Copper-Nickel, 25 mm. **Subject:** Applied Professions **Obv:** Denomination divides dates, legend above **Rev:** Various professions depicted, date and shield below

Date	Mintage	F	VF	XF	Unc	BU
AH1400-1980	500,000	—	0.50	0.75	1.35	—

KM# 502   5 PIASTRES
Copper-Nickel, 25 mm.   **Subject:** Sadat's Corrective Revolution of May 15, 1971 **Obv:** Denomination divides dates, legend above **Rev:** Raised fist holding stalk of grain

Date	Mintage	F	VF	XF	Unc	BU
AH1400-1980	1,000,000	—	0.25	0.60	1.50	2.00

KM# 555.1   5 PIASTRES
Aluminum-Bronze   **Obv:** Christian date left of denomination, tughra above **Rev:** Pyramids

Date	Mintage	F	VF	XF	Unc	BU
AH1404-1984	—	—	0.25	0.75	—	

Note: Varieties exist with wide and narrow rims

KM# 555.2   5 PIASTRES
Aluminum-Bronze   **Obv:** Islamic date left of denomination, tughra above **Rev:** Pyramids

Date	Mintage	F	VF	XF	Unc	BU
AH1404-1984	—	—	0.25	0.75	—	

KM# 622.1   5 PIASTRES
4.9100 g., Aluminum-Bronze, 23.39 mm.   **Obv:** Tughra below dates and denomination, denomination not shaded **Rev:** Pyramids **Edge:** Reeded

Date	Mintage	F	VF	XF	Unc	BU
AH1404-1984	—	—	0.25	0.85	—	

KM# 622.2   5 PIASTRES
Aluminum-Bronze, 23 mm.   **Obv:** Denomination shaded, tughra below **Rev:** Pyramids

Date	Mintage	F	VF	XF	Unc	BU
AH1404-1984	—	—	0.25	0.85	—	

KM# 731   5 PIASTRES
Brass, 21 mm.   **Obv:** Denomination divides dates, legend above **Rev:** Decorated vase

Date	Mintage	F	VF	XF	Unc	BU
AH1413-1992	—	—	—	—	0.50	0.75

KM# 429   10 PIASTRES
Copper-Nickel, 27 mm.   **Subject:** Cairo International Fair **Obv:** Denomination, legend **Rev:** Dates in box below ship with mast

Date	Mintage	F	VF	XF	Unc	BU
AH1392-1972	500,000	—	0.60	1.00	2.50	—

KM# 430   10 PIASTRES
Copper-Nickel, 27 mm.   **Rev:** Islamic falcon

Date	Mintage	F	VF	XF	Unc	BU
AH1392-1972	—	—	0.60	1.00	4.00	—

KM# 431   10 PIASTRES
Copper-Nickel, 27 mm.   **Obv:** Denomination divides dates, legend above **Rev:** Islamic falcon **Note:** Mule.

Date	Mintage	F	VF	XF	Unc	BU
AH1392-1972	—	—	5.50	17.50	27.50	—

Note: Wide and narrow inscriptions exist for obverse

KM# 442   10 PIASTRES
Copper-Nickel, 27 mm.   **Subject:** First Anniversary - October War **Obv:** Denomination divides dates, legend above **Rev:** Wreath above 3/4 figure of soldier, dates below

Date	Mintage	F	VF	XF	Unc	BU
AH1394-1974	2,000,000	—	0.60	1.00	4.00	—

KM# 448   10 PIASTRES
6.0000 g., Copper-Nickel, 27 mm.   **Series:** F.A.O. **Obv:** Denomination divides dates, legend above **Rev:** Family scene

Date	Mintage	F	VF	XF	Unc	BU
AH1395-1975	2,000,000	—	0.60	1.00	4.00	—

KM# 452   10 PIASTRES
Copper-Nickel, 27 mm.   **Subject:** Reopening of the Suez Canal **Obv:** Denomination divides dates, legend above **Rev:** Canal scene

Date	Mintage	F	VF	XF	Unc	BU
AH1396-1976	5,000,000	—	0.60	1.00	4.00	—

Note: Wide and narrow inscriptions exist for the obverse

KM# 469   10 PIASTRES
Copper-Nickel, 27 mm.   **Series:** F.A.O. **Obv:** Denomination divides dates, legend above **Rev:** Various laborers surround center design

Date	Mintage	F	VF	XF	Unc	BU
AH1397-1977	1,000,000	—	0.60	1.00	3.00	—

KM# 470   10 PIASTRES
5.9500 g., Copper-Nickel, 27 mm.   **Subject:** 1971 Corrective Revolution **Obv:** Denomination divides dates, legend above **Rev:** Date and denomination left of head

Date	Mintage	F	VF	XF	Unc	BU
AH1397-1977	1,000,000	—	0.50	0.85	3.00	—
AH1399-1979	1,000,000	—	0.50	0.85	3.00	—

KM# 471   10 PIASTRES
Copper-Nickel, 27 mm.   **Subject:** 20th Anniversary - Economic Union

Date	Mintage	F	VF	XF	Unc	BU
AH1397-1977	1,000,000	—	0.50	0.85	3.00	—

KM# 479   10 PIASTRES
Copper-Nickel, 27 mm.   **Subject:** Cairo International Fair **Obv:** Denomination divides dates, legend above **Rev:** Legend forms square around design at top

Date	Mintage	F	VF	XF	Unc	BU
AH1398-1978	—	—	0.50	0.85	3.50	—

KM# 485   10 PIASTRES
Copper-Nickel, 27 mm.   **Subject:** 25th Anniversary of Abbasia Mint **Obv:** Denomination divides dates, legend above **Rev:** Dates at top corners of building, cogwheel design above

Date	Mintage	F	VF	XF	Unc	BU
AH1399-1979	1,000,000	—	0.50	0.85	3.00	—

KM# 486   10 PIASTRES
Copper-Nickel, 27 mm.   **Subject:** National Education Day **Obv:** Denomination divides dates, legend above **Rev:** Teachers, back to back and students, wreath in background

Date	Mintage	F	VF	XF	Unc	BU
AH1399-1979	1,000,000	—	0.50	0.85	3.00	—

KM# 503   10 PIASTRES
Copper-Nickel, 27 mm.   **Subject:** Doctor's Day **Obv:** Denomination divides dates, legend above **Rev:** Seated Egyptian healer with staff left

Date	Mintage	F	VF	XF	Unc	BU
AH1400-1980	1,000,000	—	0.50	1.00	3.00	—

KM# 504   10 PIASTRES
Copper-Nickel, 27 mm.   **Subject:** Egyptian-Israeli Peace Treaty
Obv: Denomination divides dates, legend above **Rev:** Anwar Sadat
at right facing left, dove of peace, hand with quill signing treaty

Date	Mintage	F	VF	XF	Unc	BU
AH1400-1980	1,000,000	—	1.00	2.00	4.50	—

KM# 505   10 PIASTRES
Copper-Nickel, 27 mm.   **Series:** F.A.O.

Date	Mintage	F	VF	XF	Unc	BU
AH1400-1980	1,000,000	—	0.50	1.00	3.00	—

KM# 506   10 PIASTRES
Copper-Nickel, 27 mm.   **Series:** F.A.O.   **Subject:** Sadat's
Corrective Revolution of May 15, 1971 **Obv:** Denomination
divides dates, legend above **Rev:** Raised fist with grain stalk

Date	Mintage	F	VF	XF	Unc	BU
AH1400-1980	—	—	0.50	1.00	3.00	—
AH1401-1981	—	—	0.60	1.20	3.50	—

KM# 520   10 PIASTRES
Copper-Nickel, 27 mm.   **Subject:** Scientist's Day
Obv: Denomination, seated figure at left **Rev:** Cogwheel center
of spray below sun and satellite dish

Date	Mintage	F	VF	XF	Unc	BU
AH1401-1981	—	—	0.50	1.00	3.00	—

KM# 521   10 PIASTRES
6.1200 g., Copper-Nickel, 27 mm.   **Subject:** 25th Anniversary -
Trade Unions **Obv:** Denomination divides dates, legend above
Rev: Half cogwheel above shield

Date	Mintage	F	VF	XF	Unc	BU
AH1402-1981	—	—	1.00	2.00	4.50	—

KM# 599   10 PIASTRES
Copper-Nickel, 27 mm.   **Subject:** 50th Anniversary of Egyptian
Products Co. **Obv:** Denomination divides dates, legend above
Rev: Head within crowned wreath at top, triangle in background

Date	Mintage	F	VF	XF	Unc	BU
AH1402-1982	—	—	0.50	1.00	3.00	—

KM# 556   10 PIASTRES
4.4900 g., Copper-Nickel, 24.81 mm.   **Obv:** Denomination divides
dates, legend above **Rev:** Mohammad Ali Mosque **Edge:** Reeded

Date	Mintage	F	VF	XF	Unc	BU
AH1404-1984	—	—	—	0.50	1.00	—

KM# 570   10 PIASTRES
Copper-Nickel, 25 mm.   **Subject:** 25th Anniversary - National
Planning Institute **Obv:** Arabic legends, dates below **Rev:** Shield
divides dates

Date	Mintage	F	VF	XF	Unc	BU
AH1405-1985	100,000	—	—	—	2.00	—

KM# 573   10 PIASTRES
Copper-Nickel, 25 mm.   **Subject:** 60th Anniversary - Egyptian
Parliament **Obv:** Arabic legends, dates below **Rev:** Dates above
building

Date	Mintage	F	VF	XF	Unc	BU
AH1405-1985	250,000	—	—	—	2.00	—

KM# 675   10 PIASTRES
Copper-Nickel, 25 mm.   **Subject:** 1973 October War
Obv: Tughra below dates, denomination at right **Rev:** Figure with
flag left, building at right, dates below

Date	Mintage	F	VF	XF	Unc	BU
AH1410-1989	250,000	—	—	—	2.00	—

KM# 732   10 PIASTRES
Brass, 23 mm.   **Obv:** Denomination divides dates, legend above
Rev: Mohammad Ali Mosque

Date	Mintage	F	VF	XF	Unc	BU
AH1413-1992	—	—	—	—	2.00	—

KM# 507   20 PIASTRES
10.0500 g., Copper-Nickel, 30.04 mm.   **Obv:** Denomination
divides dates, legend above **Rev:** Eagle with shield on breast
Edge: Reeded

Date	Mintage	F	VF	XF	Unc	BU
AH1400-1980	—	—	0.75	1.00	3.00	—

KM# 557   20 PIASTRES
6.0000 g., Copper-Nickel, 27 mm.   **Obv:** Denomination divides
dates, legend above **Obv. Leg.:** Mohammad Ali Mosque
Rev: Mohammad Ali Mosque

Date	Mintage	F	VF	XF	Unc	BU
AH1404-1984	—	—	—	0.70	2.00	—

KM# 596   20 PIASTRES
6.0000 g., Copper-Nickel, 27 mm.   **Subject:** 25th Anniversary -
Cairo International Airport **Obv:** Arabic legends, dates below
Rev: Birds in flight, wings and tails form diamond at center

Date	Mintage	F	VF	XF	Unc	BU
AH1405-1985	50,000	—	—	—	5.00	—

KM# 597   20 PIASTRES
Copper-Nickel, 27 mm.   **Subject:** Professions **Obv:** Arabic
legends, dates below **Rev:** People doing various jobs

Date	Mintage	F	VF	XF	Unc	BU
AH1406-1985	100,000	—	—	—	3.00	—

KM# 606   20 PIASTRES
Copper-Nickel, 27 mm.   **Subject:** Warrior's Day **Obv:** Arabic
legends, dates below **Rev:** Torch on crossed swords within wreath

Date	Mintage	F	VF	XF	Unc	BU
AH1406-1986	50,000	—	—	—	5.00	—

KM# 607   20 PIASTRES
Copper-Nickel, 27 mm.   **Subject:** Census **Obv:** Arabic legends,
dates below **Rev:** City scene

Date	Mintage	F	VF	XF	Unc	BU
AH1407-1986	500,000	—	—	—	3.00	—

KM# 652   20 PIASTRES
Copper-Nickel, 27 mm. **Subject:** Investment Bank **Obv:** Tughra divides dates **Rev:** Design in center of toothed circle, within circle

Date	Mintage	F	VF	XF	Unc	BU
AH1407-1987	250,000	—	—	—	5.00	—

KM# 646   20 PIASTRES
Copper-Nickel, 27 mm. **Subject:** Police Day **Obv:** Arabic legends, dates below **Rev:** Eagle with wings spread on pedestal within wreath

Date	Mintage	F	VF	XF	Unc	BU
AH1408-1988	250,000	—	—	—	5.00	—

KM# 650   20 PIASTRES
Copper-Nickel, 27 mm. **Subject:** Dedication of Cairo Opera House **Obv:** Arabic legends, dates below **Rev:** Building

Date	Mintage	F	VF	XF	Unc	BU
AH1409-1988	250,000	—	—	—	5.00	—

KM# 676   20 PIASTRES
6.0000 g., Copper-Nickel, 27 mm. **Subject:** 1973 October War **Obv:** Tughra below denomination and dates **Rev:** Figure with flag at left, building at right, dates below **Edge:** Reeded

Date	Mintage	F	VF	XF	Unc	BU
AH1410-1989	250,000	—	—	—	5.00	—

KM# 685   20 PIASTRES
Copper-Nickel, 27 mm. **Subject:** National Health Insurance **Obv:** Denomination and dates within circle at top **Rev:** People within half moon design at left, rock in background, dates below

Date	Mintage	F	VF	XF	Unc	BU
AH1409-1989	250,000	—	—	—	5.00	—

KM# 690   20 PIASTRES
Copper-Nickel, 25 mm. **Subject:** Cairo Subway **Obv:** Four patterned tiles divide dates **Rev:** Designs within circles flank 3/4 wreath surrounding train

Date	Mintage	F	VF	XF	Unc	BU
AH1409-1989	250,000	—	—	—	5.00	—

KM# 733   20 PIASTRES
Copper-Nickel, 25 mm. **Subject:** Mosque **Obv:** Denomination divides dates

Date	Mintage	F	VF	XF	Unc	BU
AH1413-1992	—	—	—	—	2.50	—

KM# 438   25 PIASTRES
6.0000 g., 0.7200 Silver 0.1389 oz. ASW **Subject:** 75th Anniversary - National Bank of Egypt **Obv:** Denomination dates **Rev:** National Bank building, globe at back, divides dates

Date	Mintage	F	VF	XF	Unc	BU
AH1393-1973	100,000	—	4.00	6.00	9.00	—

KM# 734   25 PIASTRES
Copper-Nickel **Obv:** Chain surrounds center hole, dates below **Rev:** Chain surrounds center hole, denomination below

Date	Mintage	F	VF	XF	Unc	BU
AH1413-1993	—	—	—	—	2.75	—

KM# 834   1/2 POUND
4.0000 g., 0.8750 Gold 0.1125 oz. AGW **Subject:** El Akkad **Obv:** Legend and vase **Rev:** Portrait

Date	Mintage	F	VF	XF	Unc	BU
AH1413-1992	600	—	—	—	275	—

KM# 809   1/2 POUND
4.0000 g., 0.8750 Gold 0.1125 oz. AGW **Subject:** 20th Anniversary - October War **Obv:** Smoking chimney text **Rev:** Soldier with flag

Date	Mintage	F	VF	XF	Unc	BU
AH1414-1993	Est. 5,000	—	—	—	265	—

KM# 760   1/2 POUND
4.0000 g., 0.8750 Gold 0.1125 oz. AGW **Subject:** Salah El Din El-Ayubi **Obv:** Denomination **Rev:** Portrait

Date	Mintage	F	VF	XF	Unc	BU
AH1414-1994	500	—	—	—	275	—

KM# 439   POUND
25.0000 g., 0.7200 Silver 0.5787 oz. ASW **Series:** F.A.O. **Obv:** Denomination divides dates, legend above **Rev:** Corn ears and grain sprigs flank Aswan Dam

Date	Mintage	F	VF	XF	Unc	BU
AH1393-1973	50,000	—	9.00	10.00	15.00	—

KM# 440   POUND
8.0000 g., 0.8750 Gold 0.2250 oz. AGW **Subject:** 75th Anniversary - National Bank of Egypt **Obv:** Denomination divides dates **Rev:** National Bank of Egypt building, globe at back, divides dates

Date	Mintage	F	VF	XF	Unc	BU
AH1393-1973	7,000	—	—	—	220	—

KM# 443   POUND
15.0000 g., 0.7200 Silver 0.3472 oz. ASW **Subject:** First Anniversary - October War **Obv:** Denomination divides dates **Rev:** Half-figure of soldier within 3/4 wreath above

Date	Mintage	F	VF	XF	Unc	BU
AH1394-1974	50,000	—	—	—	22.00	—

KM# 453   POUND
15.0000 g., 0.7200 Silver 0.3472 oz. ASW **Series:** F.A.O. **Obv:** Denomination divides dates **Rev:** Osiris seated, wheat sprig at right

Date	Mintage	F	VF	XF	Unc	BU
AH1396-1976	50,000	—	—	—	20.00	—

KM# 454   POUND
15.0000 g., 0.7200 Silver 0.3472 oz. ASW **Subject:** Reopening of Suez Canal **Obv:** Denomination divides dates **Rev:** Sun above canal scene

Date	Mintage	F	VF	XF	Unc	BU
AH1396-1976	250,000	—	—	—	10.00	—

KM# 455   POUND
15.0000 g., 0.7200 Silver 0.3472 oz. ASW **Rev:** Om Kalsoum right, singer, music symbol in hair

Date	Mintage	F	VF	XF	Unc	BU
AH1396-1976	250,000	—	—	—	10.00	—

KM# 456 POUND
8.0000 g., 0.8750 Gold 0.2250 oz. AGW **Rev:** Om Kalsoum right

Date	Mintage	F	VF	XF	Unc	BU
AH1396-1976	5,000	—	—	—	220	—

KM# 457 POUND
15.0000 g., 0.7200 Silver 0.3472 oz. ASW **Obv:** Denomination divides dates **Rev:** Bust of King Faisal half right

Date	Mintage	F	VF	XF	Unc	BU
AH1396-1976	100,000	—	—	—	12.00	—

KM# 458 POUND
8.0000 g., 0.8750 Gold 0.2250 oz. AGW **Obv:** Denomination divides dates **Rev:** Bust of King Faisal half right

Date	Mintage	F	VF	XF	Unc	BU
AH1396-1976	8,000	—	—	—	225	—

KM# 472 POUND
15.0000 g., 0.7200 Silver 0.3472 oz. ASW **Series:** F.A.O. **Obv:** Denomination divides dates **Rev:** Various laborers surround center design

Date	Mintage	F	VF	XF	Unc	BU
AH1397-1977	50,000	—	—	—	10.00	—

KM# 473 POUND
15.0000 g., 0.7200 Silver 0.3472 oz. ASW **Subject:** 1971 Corrective Revolution **Obv:** Denomination divides dates **Rev:** Sun above head at right, date and denomination at left

Date	Mintage	F	VF	XF	Unc	BU
AH1397-1977	50,000	—	—	—	10.00	—
AH1399-1979	49,000	—	—	—	11.00	—
AH1399-1979 Proof	1,500	Value: 30.00				

KM# 474 POUND
15.0000 g., 0.7200 Silver 0.3472 oz. ASW **Subject:** 20th Anniversary - Economic Union **Obv:** Denomination divides dates **Rev:** Design above grasped hands divides dates, grain stalks divided by cogwheel below flank

---

Date	Mintage	F	VF	XF	Unc	BU
AH1397-1977	50,000	—	—	—	10.00	—

KM# 475 POUND
8.0000 g., 0.8750 Gold 0.2250 oz. AGW **Subject:** 20th Anniversary - Economic Union

Date	Mintage	F	VF	XF	Unc	BU
AH1397-1977	5,000	—	—	—	220	—

KM# 480 POUND
15.0000 g., 0.7200 Silver 0.3472 oz. ASW **Subject:** Portland Cement **Obv:** Denomination divides dates **Rev:** Cement factory

Date	Mintage	F	VF	XF	Unc	BU
AH1398-1978	50,000	—	—	—	10.00	—

KM# 481 POUND
15.0000 g., 0.7200 Silver 0.3472 oz. ASW **Subject:** 25th Anniversary - Ain Shams University **Obv:** Denomination divides dates **Rev:** Birds flank center design, dates below

Date	Mintage	F	VF	XF	Unc	BU
AH1398-1978	50,000	—	—	—	10.00	—

KM# 482 POUND
15.0000 g., 0.7200 Silver 0.3472 oz. ASW **Series:** F.A.O. **Rev:** Female looking into microscope

Date	Mintage	F	VF	XF	Unc	BU
AH1398-1978	50,000	—	—	—	10.00	—

KM# 488 POUND
15.0000 g., 0.7200 Silver 0.3472 oz. ASW **Subject:** 25th Anniversary - Abbasia Mint **Obv:** Denomination divides dates **Rev:** Dates above building at corners, cogwheel at top

Date	Mintage	F	VF	XF	Unc	BU
AH1399-1979	23,000	—	—	—	20.00	—
AH1399-1979 Proof	2,000	Value: 25.00				

KM# 489 POUND
15.0000 g., 0.7200 Silver 0.3472 oz. ASW **Series:** F.A.O. and I.Y.C. **Obv:** Denomination divides dates **Rev:** Seated woman with child, logo and designs at right, FAO below chair

Date	Mintage	F	VF	XF	Unc	BU
AH1399-1979	48,000	—	—	—	10.00	—
AH1399-1979 Proof	2,500	Value: 20.00				

KM# 490 POUND
15.0000 g., 0.7200 Silver 0.3472 oz. ASW **Subject:** National Education Day **Obv:** Denomination divides dates **Rev:** Back to back teachers and students, wreath in background

Date	Mintage	F	VF	XF	Unc	BU
AH1399-1979	98,000	—	—	—	11.00	—
AH1399-1979 Proof	2,000	Value: 20.00				

KM# 491 POUND
15.0000 g., 0.7200 Silver 0.3472 oz. ASW **Subject:** 100th Anniversary - Bank of Land Reform **Rev:** Seated figure, workers harvesting grain at back, farmers and oxen above

Date	Mintage	F	VF	XF	Unc	BU
AH1399-1979	98,000	—	—	—	11.00	—
AH1399-1979 Proof	2,000	Value: 20.00				

KM# 492 POUND
8.0000 g., 0.8750 Gold 0.2250 oz. AGW **Subject:** 100th Anniversary - Bank of Land Reform

Date	Mintage	F	VF	XF	Unc	BU
AH1399-1979	4,200	—	—	—	220	—
AH1399-1979 Proof	800	Value: 250				

KM# 493 POUND
15.0000 g., 0.7200 Silver 0.3472 oz. ASW **Subject:** 1400th Anniversary - Mohammed's Flight **Obv:** Denomination divides dates **Rev:** Birds and eggs in front of web design

Date	Mintage	F	VF	XF	Unc	BU
AH1400-1979	97,000	—	—	—	11.00	—
AH1400-1979 Proof	3,000	Value: 15.00				

KM# 494 POUND
8.0000 g., 0.8750 Gold 0.2250 oz. AGW **Subject:** 1400th Anniversary - Mohammed's Flight

Date	Mintage	F	VF	XF	Unc	BU
AH1400-1979	2,000	—	—	—	225	—
AH1400-1979 Proof	2,000	Value: 250				

KM# 508 POUND
15.0000 g., 0.7200 Silver 0.3472 oz. ASW **Subject:** Egyptian-Israeli Peace Treaty **Obv:** Denomination divides dates **Rev:** Head of Anwar Sadat at right facing left, with dove of peace at left

Date	Mintage	F	VF	XF	Unc	BU
AH1400-1980	95,000	—	—	—	10.00	—
AH1400-1980 Proof	5,000	Value: 15.50				

KM# 509 POUND
8.0000 g., 0.8750.Gold 0.2250 oz. AGW **Subject:** Egyptian-Israeli Peace Treaty **Obv:** Denomination divides dates **Rev:** Head of Anwar Sadat left, with dove of peace at left

Date	Mintage	F	VF	XF	Unc	BU
AH1400-1980	9,500	—	—	—	220	—
AH1400-1980 Proof	500	Value: 250				

KM# 510 POUND
15.0000 g., 0.7200 Silver 0.3472 oz. ASW **Subject:** Applied Professions in Egypt **Obv:** Denomination divides dates **Rev:** Various professions depicted, date and shield below

Date	Mintage	F	VF	XF	Unc	BU
AH1400-1980	22,000	—	—	—	20.00	—
AH1400-1980 Proof	3,000	Value: 15.00				

KM# 511 POUND
15.0000 g., 0.7200 Silver 0.3472 oz. ASW **Subject:** Doctor's Day **Obv:** Denomination divides dates **Rev:** Seated healer with staff facing left

Date	Mintage	F	VF	XF	Unc	BU
AH1400-1980	97,000	—	—	—	10.00	—
AH1400-1980 Proof	3,000	Value: 15.00				

KM# 512 POUND
8.0000 g., 0.8750 Gold 0.2250 oz. AGW **Subject:** Doctor's Day **Rev:** Seated healer with staff facing left

Date	Mintage	F	VF	XF	Unc	BU
AH1400-1980 Proof	5,000	Value: 235				

KM# 513 POUND
15.0000 g., 0.7200 Silver 0.3472 oz. ASW **Series:** F.A.O. **Obv:** Denomination divides dates **Rev:** Kneeling figure with book and birds, city scene at right, pyramids and tractor at left

Date	Mintage	F	VF	XF	Unc	BU
AH1400-1980	97,000	—	—	—	10.00	—
AH1400-1980 Proof	3,000	Value: 15.00				

KM# 514 POUND
15.0000 g., 0.7200 Silver 0.3472 oz. ASW **Subject:** Sadat's Corrective Revolution of May 15, 1971 **Obv:** Denomination divides dates **Rev:** Raised clenched fist holding grain sprig

Date	Mintage	F	VF	XF	Unc	BU
AH1400-1980	47,000	—	—	—	15.00	—
AH1400-1980 Proof	3,000	Value: 15.00				

KM# 515 POUND
15.0000 g., 0.7200 Silver 0.3472 oz. ASW **Obv:** Denomination divides dates **Rev:** Cairo University Law facility

Date	Mintage	F	VF	XF	Unc	BU
AH1400-1980	47,000	—	—	—	15.00	—
AH1400-1980 Proof	3,000	Value: 15.00				

KM# 516 POUND
8.0000 g., 0.8750 Gold 0.2250 oz. AGW **Obv:** Denomination divides dates **Rev:** Cairo University Law facility

Date	Mintage	F	VF	XF	Unc	BU
AH1400-1980	2,000	—	—	—	220	—
AH1400-1980 Proof	—	Value: 250				

KM# 522 POUND
15.0000 g., 0.7200 Silver 0.3472 oz. ASW **Subject:** Scientists' Day **Obv:** Denomination within circle, seated figure at left **Rev:** Sun above satellite dish, cogwheel divides spray below

Date	Mintage	F	VF	XF	Unc	BU
AH1401-1981	25,000	—	—	—	20.00	—

KM# 523 POUND
15.0000 g., 0.7200 Silver 0.3472 oz. ASW **Series:** World Food Day **Obv:** Denomination divides dates **Rev:** Standing figure with food tray, animals at right, figure harvesting grain at left

Date	Mintage	F	VF	XF	Unc	BU
AH1401-1981	50,000	—	—	—	10.50	—
AH1401-1981 Proof	1,500	Value: 30.00				

KM# 524 POUND
15.0000 g., 0.7200 Silver 0.3472 oz. ASW **Subject:** 3rd Anniversary - Suez Canal Reopening **Obv:** Denomination divides dates **Rev:** Grain stalk right of canal scene

Date	Mintage	F	VF	XF	Unc	BU
AH1401-1981	50,000	—	—	—	10.00	—
AH1401-1981 Proof	2,000	Value: 25.00				

KM# 525 POUND
8.0000 g., 0.8750 Gold 0.2250 oz. AGW **Subject:** 3rd Anniversary - Suez Canal Reopening

Date	Mintage	F	VF	XF	Unc	BU
AH1401-1981 Proof	150	Value: 275				

KM# 528 POUND
15.0000 g., 0.7200 Silver 0.3472 oz. ASW **Subject:** 25th Anniversary - Nationalization of Suez Canal **Obv:** Denomination divides dates **Rev:** Central design divides dates, grain spray below

Date	Mintage	F	VF	XF	Unc	BU
AH1401-1981	25,000	—	—	—	20.00	—
AH1401-1981 Proof	1,500	Value: 30.00				

KM# 529 POUND
8.0000 g., 0.8750 Gold 0.2250 oz. AGW **Subject:** 25th Anniversary - Nationalization of Suez Canal **Obv:** Denomination divides dates **Rev:** Central design divides dates, grain spray below

Date	Mintage	F	VF	XF	Unc	BU
AH1401-1981	3,000	—	—	—	225	—

KM# 532 POUND
15.0000 g., 0.7200 Silver 0.3472 oz. ASW **Series:** F.A.O. **Obv:** Denomination divides dates **Rev:** Figures flank design at center

Date	Mintage	F	VF	XF	Unc	BU
AH1401-1981	50,000	—	—	—	10.00	—

KM# 526 POUND
15.0000 g., 0.7200 Silver 0.3472 oz. ASW **Subject:** 25th Anniversary - Egyptian Industry

Date	Mintage	F	VF	XF	Unc	BU
AH1402-1981	25,000	—	—	—	15.00	—

KM# 527 POUND
15.0000 g., 0.7200 Silver 0.3472 oz. ASW **Subject:** 25th Anniversary - Trade Unions **Obv:** Denomination divides dates **Rev:** Hands holding up factories, flower below, all within oval on shield with 1/2 cogwheel above, dates at left

Date	Mintage	F	VF	XF	Unc	BU
AH1402-1981	25,000	—	—	—	15.00	—

KM# 530 POUND
15.0000 g., 0.7200 Silver 0.3472 oz. ASW **Subject:** 100th Anniversary - Revolt by Arabi Pasha **Rev:** Pasha mounted on horse in front of his followers

Date	Mintage	F	VF	XF	Unc	BU
AH1402-1981	50,000	—	—	—	10.00	—
AH1402-1981 Proof	1,500	Value: 30.00				

KM# 531 POUND
8.0000 g., 0.8750 Gold 0.2250 oz. AGW **Subject:** 100th Anniversary - Revolt by Arabi Pasha **Rev:** Pasha mounted on horse in front of his followers

Date	Mintage	F	VF	XF	Unc	BU
AH1402-1981	3,000	—	—	—	225	—

KM# 539 POUND
15.0000 g., 0.7200 Silver 0.3472 oz. ASW **Subject:** Golden Jubilee - Egypt Air **Obv:** Denomination divides dates **Rev:** Stylized bird on globe, dates above

Date	Mintage	F	VF	XF	Unc	BU
AH1402-1982	20,000	—	—	—	15.00	—

KM# 540 POUND
15.0000 g., 0.7200 Silver 0.3472 oz. ASW **Subject:** 1000th Anniversary - Al Azhar Mosque **Obv:** Denomination within circle, divides dates **Rev:** Mosque

Date	Mintage	F	VF	XF	Unc	BU
AH1402-1982	23,000	—	—	—	12.00	—
AH1402-1982 Proof	4,000	Value: 15.00				

KM# 541 POUND
8.0000 g., 0.8750 Gold 0.2250 oz. AGW **Subject:** 1000th Anniversary - Al Azhar Mosque **Rev:** Mosque

Date	Mintage	F	VF	XF	Unc	BU
AH1402-1982 Proof	2,000	Value: 235				

KM# 544 POUND
15.0000 g., 0.7200 Silver 0.3472 oz. ASW **Subject:** 50th Anniversary - Egyptian Products Co. **Obv:** Denomination divides dates **Rev:** Head within crowned wreath at top, triangle in background

Date	Mintage	F	VF	XF	Unc	BU
AH1402-1982	5,000	—	—	—	20.00	—
AH1402-1982 Proof	2,000	Value: 25.00				

KM# 545 POUND
15.0000 g., 0.7200 Silver 0.3472 oz. ASW **Subject:** Return of Sinai to Egypt **Obv:** Denomination divides dates **Rev:** Grain sprigs form 'V', bird above

Date	Mintage	F	VF	XF	Unc	BU
AH1402-1982(1983)	50,000	—	—	—	10.00	—
AH1402-1982(1983) Proof	2,000	Value: 25.00				

KM# 542 POUND
15.0000 g., 0.7200 Silver 0.3472 oz. ASW **Subject:** 50th Anniversary of Air Force **Rev:** Air Force insignia within wreath

Date	Mintage	F	VF	XF	Unc	BU
AH1403-1982	10,000	—	—	—	20.00	—
AH1403-1982 Proof	2,260	Value: 25.00				

KM# 543 POUND
8.0000 g., 0.8750 Gold 0.2250 oz. AGW **Subject:** 50th Anniversary of Air Force **Rev:** Air Force insignia within wreath

Date	Mintage	F	VF	XF	Unc	BU
AH1403-1982 Proof	2,000	Value: 235				

KM# 549 POUND
15.0000 g., 0.7200 Silver 0.3472 oz. ASW **Subject:** 50th Anniversary - Deaths of Shawky and Hafez **Obv:** Denomination divides dates **Rev:** Two busts, flowers flank

Date	Mintage	F	VF	XF	Unc	BU
AH1403-1983	25,000	—	—	—	15.00	—

KM# 551 POUND
15.0000 g., 0.7200 Silver 0.3472 oz. ASW **Subject:** Misr Insurance Company **Obv:** Denomination divides dates **Rev:** Design within center oval divides dates

Date	Mintage	F	VF	XF	Unc	BU
AH1404-1984	20,000	—	—	—	15.00	—

KM# 559 POUND
15.0000 g., 0.7200 Silver 0.3472 oz. ASW **Subject:** Helwan University Faculty of Fine Arts **Obv:** Flower head at top, denomination and dates **Rev:** Artist's tools within design

Date	Mintage	F	VF	XF	Unc	BU
AH1404-1984	25,000	—	—	—	15.00	—
AH1404-1984 Proof	25	Value: 200				

KM# 583 POUND
8.0000 g., 0.8750 Gold 0.2250 oz. AGW **Subject:** 50th Anniversary - Egyptian Radio Broadcasting

Date	Mintage	F	VF	XF	Unc	BU
AH1404-1984	2,000	—	—	—	235	—

KM# 571 POUND
8.0000 g., 0.8750 Gold 0.2250 oz. AGW **Subject:** 25th Anniversary - National Planning Institute

Date	Mintage	F	VF	XF	Unc	BU
AH1405-1985	200	—	—	—	300	—

KM# 574 POUND
8.0000 g., 0.8750 Gold 0.2250 oz. AGW **Subject:** 60th Anniversary - Egyptian Parliament **Rev:** Parliament building

Date	Mintage	F	VF	XF	Unc	BU
AH1405-1985	1,000	—	—	—	250	—

KM# 577 POUND
8.0000 g., 0.8750 Gold 0.2250 oz. AGW **Subject:** 25th Anniversary - Cairo Stadium **Rev:** Stadium

Date	Mintage	F	VF	XF	Unc	BU
AH1405-1985	300	—	—	—	300	—

KM# 580 POUND
8.0000 g., 0.8750 Gold 0.2250 oz. AGW **Subject:** 25th Anniversary - Egyptian Television

Date	Mintage	F	VF	XF	Unc	BU
AH1405-1985	150	—	—	—	325	—

KM# 604 POUND
8.0000 g., 0.8750 Gold 0.2250 oz. AGW **Subject:** Commerce Day **Rev:** Stylized depictions of commercial activity

Date	Mintage	F	VF	XF	Unc	BU
AH1405-1985 Proof	2,000	Value: 235				

KM# 605 POUND
8.0000 g., 0.8750 Gold 0.2250 oz. AGW **Subject:** Faculty of Economics and Political Science **Obv:** Arabic legends, seals, and date **Rev:** Graph within wreath, partial gear wheel

Date	Mintage	F	VF	XF	Unc	BU
AH1405-1985 Proof	250	Value: 275				

KM# 635 POUND
8.0000 g., 0.8750 Gold 0.2250 oz. AGW **Subject:** 25th Anniversary - Cairo International Airport **Obv:** Stylized legend above dates, dividing two seals **Rev:** Two circling vultures within Arabic and English legends

Date	Mintage	F	VF	XF	Unc	BU
AH1405-1985	200	—	—	—	275	—

KM# 632 POUND
8.0000 g., 0.8750 Gold 0.2250 oz. AGW **Subject:** Prophet's Mosque **Obv:** Minaret, globe, denomination, legends **Rev:** Crescent, mosque, minaret below legend arch

Date	Mintage	F	VF	XF	Unc	BU
AH1406-1985	800	—	—	—	250	—

KM# 636 POUND
8.0000 g., 0.8750 Gold 0.2250 oz. AGW **Subject:** Cairo University Faculty of Commerce **Obv:** Stylized legend above dates, dividing two seals **Rev:** Ancient Egyptian commerce related scenes

Date	Mintage	F	VF	XF	Unc	BU
AH1406-1986	200	—	—	—	275	—

KM# 637 POUND
8.0000 g., 0.8750 Gold 0.2250 oz. AGW **Subject:** 25th Anniversary - Egyptian Central Bank **Obv:** Stylized flowers, gear wheel and cotton within legend **Rev:** Ancient Egyptian sculptures, legends above and below within ornamental border

Date	Mintage	F	VF	XF	Unc	BU
AH1406-1986	200	—	—	—	285	—

KM# 638 POUND
8.0000 g., 0.8750 Gold 0.2250 oz. AGW **Subject:** 100th Anniversary - Petroleum Industry **Obv:** Stylized legend above dates, dividing two seals **Rev:** Oil well and landscape within ornamental circle

Date	Mintage	F	VF	XF	Unc	BU
AH1406-1986	800	—	—	—	250	—

KM# 640 POUND
8.0000 g., 0.8750 Gold 0.2250 oz. AGW **Subject:** 50th Anniversary - National Theater **Obv:** Stylized stage curtain, legend within **Rev:** Large building, two masks in foreground, legend above

Date	Mintage	F	VF	XF	Unc	BU
AH1406-1986	250	—	—	—	265	—

KM# 644 POUND
8.0000 g., 0.8750 Gold 0.2250 oz. AGW **Subject:** Restoration of Parliament Building **Obv:** Arabic legends **Rev:** Dome and tower with scaffolding

Date	Mintage	F	VF	XF	Unc	BU
AH1406-1986	400	—	—	—	250	—

KM# 639 POUND
8.0000 g., 0.8750 Gold 0.2250 oz. AGW **Subject:** Census **Obv:** Arabic legends, seals, date **Rev:** City view with paper doll cutout human figures

Date	Mintage	F	VF	XF	Unc	BU
AH1407-1986	200	—	—	—	260	—

KM# 643 POUND
8.0000 g., 0.8750 Gold 0.2250 oz. AGW **Subject:** 40th Anniversary - Engineer's Syndicate **Obv:** Arabic legends, seals, dates **Rev:** Three triangles, legend, ornamentation

Date	Mintage	F	VF	XF	Unc	BU
AH1407-1986	400	—	—	—	250	—

KM# 645 POUND
8.0000 g., 0.8750 Gold 0.2250 oz. AGW **Subject:** Parliament Museum **Obv:** Arabic legends, seals, dates **Rev:** Documents, quill, carriage, building with national emblem

Date	Mintage	F	VF	XF	Unc	BU
AH1407-1987	400	—	—	—	250	—

KM# 653 POUND
8.0000 g., 0.8750 Gold 0.2250 oz. AGW **Subject:** Investment Bank **Obv:** Toughra, legends above and below, dates **Rev:** Symbol within stylized circle, legend around

Date	Mintage	F	VF	XF	Unc	BU
AH1407-1987	600	—	—	—	250	—

KM# 673 POUND
8.0000 g., 0.8750 Gold 0.2250 oz. AGW **Subject:** First African Subway **Obv:** Stylized legends and denomination **Rev:** Subway emerging from tunnel with legend around rim

Date	Mintage	F	VF	XF	Unc	BU
AH1408-1987 Proof	500	Value: 260				

KM# 647 POUND
8.0000 g., 0.8750 Gold 0.2250 oz. AGW **Subject:** Police Day **Obv:** Arabic and English legends, seals, dates **Rev:** Police emblem - eagle in wreath, legends

Date	Mintage	F	VF	XF	Unc	BU
AH1408-1988	500	—	—	—	250	—

KM# 654 POUND
8.0000 g., 0.8750 Gold 0.2250 oz. AGW **Subject:** Dedication of Cairo Opera House **Obv:** Arabic legends, seals, dates **Rev:** Opera house, legends above and below

Date	Mintage	F	VF	XF	Unc	BU
AH1409-1988	1,500	—	—	—	250	—

KM# 661 POUND
8.0000 g., 0.8750 Gold 0.2250 oz. AGW **Subject:** Naquib Mahfouz, Nobel Laureate **Obv:** Stylized quill ink and paper design with legend above **Rev:** Head of Mahfouz left

Date	Mintage	F	VF	XF	Unc	BU
AH1409-1988 Proof	1,000	Value: 235				

KM# 664 POUND
8.0000 g., 0.8750 Gold 0.2250 oz. AGW **Subject:** United Parliamentary Union **Obv:** Kufic legend above denomination and dates **Rev:** Anniversary dates, map in wreath above domed building, and legend

Date	Mintage	F	VF	XF	Unc	BU
AH1409-1989 Proof	200	Value: 285				

KM# 666 POUND
8.0000 g., 0.8750 Gold 0.2250 oz. AGW **Subject:** First Arab Olympics **Obv:** Kufic legend above denomination and dates **Rev:** 5 Olympic rings and map as part of torch held by hand within wreath and legend

Date	Mintage	F	VF	XF	Unc	BU
AH1409-1989 Proof	300	Value: 265				

KM# 668 POUND
8.0000 g., 0.8750 Gold 0.2250 oz. AGW **Subject:** National Research Center **Obv:** Kufic legend above denomination and dates **Rev:** Stylized ancient and modern research elements

Date	Mintage	F	VF	XF	Unc	BU
AH1409-1989 Proof	250	Value: 265				

KM# 677 POUND
8.0000 g., 0.8750 Gold 0.2250 oz. AGW **Subject:** University of Cairo, School of Agriculture **Obv:** Denomination between wheat ears above legend **Rev:** Ancient farming scene and coat of arms, building in background

Date	Mintage	F	VF	XF	Unc	BU
AH1410-1989 Proof	200	Value: 285				

KM# 695 POUND
8.0000 g., 0.8750 Gold 0.2250 oz. AGW **Subject:** Export Trade Show **Obv:** Toughra, inscription above **Rev:** Display of symbols

Date	Mintage	F	VF	XF	Unc	BU
AH1410-1989 Proof	200	Value: 285				

KM# 696 POUND
8.0000 g., 0.8750 Gold 0.2250 oz. AGW **Subject:** Union of African Parliament **Obv:** Toughra, denomination, date within circle and legend **Rev:** Map of Africa, laurel branch and Parliament building

Date	Mintage	F	VF	XF	Unc	BU
AH1410-1990 Proof	200	Value: 285				

KM# 699 POUND
8.0000 g., 0.8750 Gold 0.2250 oz. AGW **Subject:** 5th African Games - Cairo **Obv:** Torch with legend and inscription **Rev:** Logo above rings within legend

Date	Mintage	F	VF	XF	Unc	BU
AH1411-1991 Proof	200	Value: 285				

KM# 832 POUND
8.0000 g., 0.8750 Gold 0.2250 oz. AGW **Subject:** Library of Alexandria **Obv:** Legend and inscription **Rev:** Waterfront building with tower

Date	Mintage	F	VF	XF	Unc	BU
AH1411-1991	300	—	—	—	400	—

KM# 726 POUND
8.0000 g., 0.8750 Gold 0.2250 oz. AGW **Subject:** Mohamed Abdel Wahab **Rev:** Bust of Mohamed Abdel Wahab left with music sheet in background

Date	Mintage	F	VF	XF	Unc	BU
AH1412-1991	1,000	—	—	—	235	—

KM# 835 POUND
15.0000 g., 0.7200 Silver 0.3472 oz. ASW **Subject:** Gorgui Zidane **Obv:** Legend and vase **Rev:** Portrait **Edge:** Reeded

Date	Mintage	F	VF	XF	Unc	BU
AH1413-1992	3,000	—	—	—	20.00	—

KM# 836 POUND
8.0000 g., 0.8750 Gold 0.2250 oz. AGW **Subject:** Rifa'a El Tahtaoui **Obv:** Legend and vase **Rev:** Portrait

Date	Mintage	F	VF	XF	Unc	BU
AH1413-1992	800	—	—	—	400	—

KM# 810 POUND
15.0000 g., 0.7200 Silver 0.3472 oz. ASW **Subject:** 20th Anniversary - October War **Obv:** Smoking chimneys divide dates, text **Rev:** Soldier with flag

Date	Mintage	F	VF	XF	Unc	BU
AH1414-1993	Est. 25,000	—	—	—	30.00	—

KM# 811 POUND
8.0000 g., 0.8750 Gold 0.2250 oz. AGW **Subject:** 20th Anniversary - October War **Obv:** Smoking chimney, text **Rev:** Soldier with flag

Date	Mintage	F	VF	XF	Unc	BU
AH1414-1993	Est. 3,000	—	—	—	400	—

KM# 761 POUND
15.0000 g., 0.7200 Silver 0.3472 oz. ASW **Subject:** Salah El Din El-Ayubi **Obv:** Denomination **Rev:** Portrait

Date	Mintage	F	VF	XF	Unc	BU
AH1414-1994	5,000	—	—	—	25.00	—

KM# 762 POUND
8.0000 g., 0.8750 Gold 0.2250 oz. AGW **Subject:** Salah El Din El-Ayubi **Obv:** Denomination **Rev:** Portrait

Date	Mintage	F	VF	XF	Unc	BU
AH1414-1994	300	—	—	—	400	—

KM# 764 POUND
15.0000 g., 0.7200 Silver 0.3472 oz. ASW **Subject:** 125 Years - Suez Canal **Obv:** Toughra **Rev:** Building and canal scenes

Date	Mintage	F	VF	XF	Unc	BU
AH1415-1994	3,000	—	—	—	20.00	—

KM# 766 POUND
15.0000 g., 0.7200 Silver 0.3472 oz. ASW **Subject:** 75 Years - Bank of Misr **Obv:** Inscription **Rev:** Bank building and emblem, dates upper left

Date	Mintage	F	VF	XF	Unc	BU
AH1415-1994	2,500	—	—	—	30.00	—

KM# 839 POUND
15.0000 g., 0.7200 Silver 0.3472 oz. ASW **Subject:** Abd Al Halem Hafez **Obv:** Tughra, date and denomination **Rev:** Head left

Date	Mintage	F	VF	XF	Unc	BU
AH1416-1995	3,000	—	—	—	20.00	—

KM# 767 POUND
8.0000 g., 0.8750 Gold 0.2250 oz. AGW **Subject:** 75 Years - Bank of Misr

Date	Mintage	F	VF	XF	Unc	BU
AH1415-1995	1,000	—	—	—	275	300

KM# 769 POUND
15.0000 g., 0.7200 Silver 0.3472 oz. ASW **Series:** F.A.O. **Rev:** Workers

Date	Mintage	F	VF	XF	Unc	BU
AH1415-1995	3,000	—	—	—	40.00	—

KM# 771 POUND
8.0000 g., 0.8750 Gold 0.2250 oz. AGW **Subject:** Pediatrics International Conference **Obv:** Tughra divides dates and denomination **Rev:** Children and pyramids on globe, dates divided below

Date	Mintage	F	VF	XF	Unc	BU
AH1416-1995	300	—	—	—	400	—

KM# 840 POUND
8.0000 g., 0.8750 Gold 0.2250 oz. AGW **Obv:** Denomination **Rev:** Abd Al Halem Hafez

Date	Mintage	F	VF	XF	Unc	BU
AH1416-1995	500	—	—	—	400	—

KM# 844 POUND
15.0000 g., 0.7200 Silver 0.3472 oz. ASW **Subject:** Centennial - Electrification **Obv:** Legend and inscription **Rev:** Electric bolt on Pyramid

Date	Mintage	F	VF	XF	Unc	BU
AH1417-1996	3,000	—	—	—	15.00	—

KM# 937 POUND
8.0000 g., 0.8750 Gold 0.2250 oz. AGW, 24 mm. **Subject:** Centennial of the Geological Survey Authority **Obv:** Toughra, value **Rev:** Ancient dig **Edge:** Reeded

Date	Mintage	F	VF	XF	Unc	BU
AH1416-1996	250	—	—	—	—	350

KM# 946 POUND
8.0000 g., 0.8750 Gold 0.2250 oz. AGW, 24 mm. **Subject:** Diamond Jubilee Electricity in Egypt **Obv:** Value **Rev:** Prism, gear teeth below **Edge:** Reeded

Date	Mintage	F	VF	XF	Unc	BU
AH1417-1996	1,000	—	—	—	280	—

KM# 947 POUND
8.0000 g., 0.8750 Gold 0.2250 oz. AGW, 24 mm. **Series:** 4th World Youth Cup **Obv:** Ornamental doorway, value **Rev:** Stylized player on soccer ball **Rev. Leg.:** WORLD CHAMPIONSHIP / FOR THE FIFA/IYC CUP EGYPT **Edge:** Reeded

Date	Mintage	F	VF	XF	Unc	BU
AH1418-1997	130	—	—	—	350	—

KM# 948 POUND
8.0000 g., 0.8750 Gold 0.2250 oz. AGW, 24 mm. **Subject:** Air Force Day **Obv:** Value **Rev:** Air Force emblem **Edge:** Reeded

Date	Mintage	F	VF	XF	Unc	BU
AH1418-1997	1,250	—	—	—	280	—

KM# 926 POUND
15.0000 g., 0.7200 Silver 0.3472 oz. ASW, 35 mm. **Subject:** Soccer FIFA-JVC Cup **Obv:** Value, ornamental design and inscription **Rev:** Games logo **Edge:** Reeded

Date	Mintage	F	VF	XF	Unc	BU
AH1418-1997	—	—	—	—	90.00	—

KM# 845 POUND
15.0000 g., 0.7200 Silver 0.3472 oz. ASW **Subject:** 65 Years - Egyptian Air Force **Obv:** Denomination **Rev:** Flying eagle in wreath

Date	Mintage	F	VF	XF	Unc	BU
AH1418-1997	226	—	—	—	85.00	—

KM# 847 POUND
15.0000 g., 0.7200 Silver 0.3472 oz. ASW **Subject:** 50 Years Arab Land Bank **Obv:** Denomination **Rev:** Arab Real Estate domed Bank building

Date	Mintage	F	VF	XF	Unc	BU
AH1418-1997	3,000	—	—	—	35.00	—

KM# 849 POUND
15.0000 g., 0.7200 Silver 0.3472 oz. ASW **Subject:** 95th Interparliamentary Union Conference **Obv:** Circular design above inscription **Rev:** Pyramids in wreath

Date	Mintage	F	VF	XF	Unc	BU
AH1418-1997	375	—	—	—	85.00	—

KM# 851 POUND
15.0000 g., 0.7200 Silver 0.3472 oz. ASW **Subject:** Centennial - Chemical Department **Obv:** Denomination **Rev:** Symbolic design

Date	Mintage	F	VF	XF	Unc	BU
AH1419-1998	1,000	—	—	—	35.00	—

KM# 855 POUND
15.0000 g., 0.7200 Silver 0.3472 oz. ASW **Series:** Centennial - National Bank **Obv:** Denomination **Rev:** Large "100"

Date	Mintage	F	VF	XF	Unc	BU
AH1419-1998	2,000	—	—	—	85.00	—

KM# 857 POUND
15.0000 g., 0.7200 Silver 0.3472 oz. ASW **Subject:** 25th Anniversary - October War **Obv:** Denomination **Rev:** Symbolic design

Date	Mintage	F	VF	XF	Unc	BU
AH1419-1998	2,000	—	—	—	40.00	—

KM# 859 POUND
15.0000 g., 0.7200 Silver 0.3472 oz. ASW **Subject:** Death of Imam Metwaly El Sharawi **Obv:** Open book **Rev:** Bust of El Sharawi facing

Date	Mintage	F	VF	XF	Unc	BU
AH1419-1998	2,000	—	—	—	40.00	—

KM# 861 POUND
15.0000 g., 0.7200 Silver 0.3472 oz. ASW **Subject:** Centennial - Land Surveying **Obv:** Denomination **Rev:** "100" above ancient surveyors

Date	Mintage	F	VF	XF	Unc	BU
AH1419-1998	1,000	—	—	—	35.00	—

KM# 863 POUND
15.0000 g., 0.7200 Silver 0.3472 oz. ASW **Series:** Centennial - Solidarity **Obv:** Denomination **Rev:** Symbolic design

Date	Mintage	F	VF	XF	Unc	BU
AH1419-1998	2,000	—	—	—	35.00	—

KM# 949 POUND
8.0000 g., 0.8750 Gold 0.2250 oz. AGW, 224 mm. **Subject:** Centennial National Bank of Egypt **Obv:** Value **Rev:** Sprig though large "100" **Edge:** Reeded

Date	Mintage	F	VF	XF	Unc	BU
AH1419-1998	1,000	—	—	—	280	—

KM# 950 POUND
8.0000 g., 0.8750 Gold 0.2250 oz. AGW, 24 mm. **Subject:** Silver Jubilee October War **Obv:** Value **Rev:** Monument **Edge:** Reeded

Date	Mintage	F	VF	XF	Unc	BU
AH1419-1998	1,000	—	—	—	280	—

KM# 951 POUND
8.0000 g., 0.8750 Gold 0.2250 oz. AGW, 24 mm. **Subject:** Sheikh Mohamed Metwally El-Shaarawi **Obv:** Open book with rays, value below **Rev:** Bust of shiekh facing holding open book **Edge:** Reeded

Date	Mintage	F	VF	XF	Unc	BU
AH1419-1998	1,200	—	—	—	350	—

KM# 952 POUND
8.0000 g., 0.8750 Gold 0.2250 oz. AGW, 24 mm. **Subject:** Nilesat **Obv:** Value **Rev:** Sphinx at lower right **Edge:** Reeded

Date	Mintage	F	VF	XF	Unc	BU
AH1419-1998	1,500	—	—	—	260	—

KM# 953 POUND
8.0000 g., 0.8750 Gold 0.2250 oz. AGW, 24 mm. **Subject:** Restoration of Al Azhar Mosque **Obv:** Value **Rev:** Mosque **Edge:** Reeded

Date	Mintage	F	VF	XF	Unc	BU
AH1419-1998	1,000	—	—	—	280	—

KM# 954 POUND
8.0000 g., 0.8750 Gold 0.2250 oz. AGW, 24 mm. **Subject:** Cairo Metro Tunnel under Nile River **Obv:** Value **Rev:** Water, Metro train below **Edge:** Reeded

Date	Mintage	F	VF	XF	Unc	BU
AH1420-1999	550	—	—	—	320	—

KM# 865 POUND
15.0000 g., 0.7200 Silver 0.3472 oz. ASW **Subject:** Golden Jubilee of Ash Shanns University **Obv:** Denomination **Rev:** Monument

Date	Mintage	F	VF	XF	Unc	BU
AH1420-1999	1,000	—	—	—	35.00	—

KM# 928 POUND
15.0000 g., 0.7200 Silver 0.3472 oz. ASW, 35 mm. **Subject:** National Insurance Company Centennial **Obv:** Value **Rev:** Ancient seated figure with "100" **Edge:** Reeded

Date	Mintage	F	VF	XF	Unc	BU
AH1421-2000	2,500	—	—	—	35.00	—

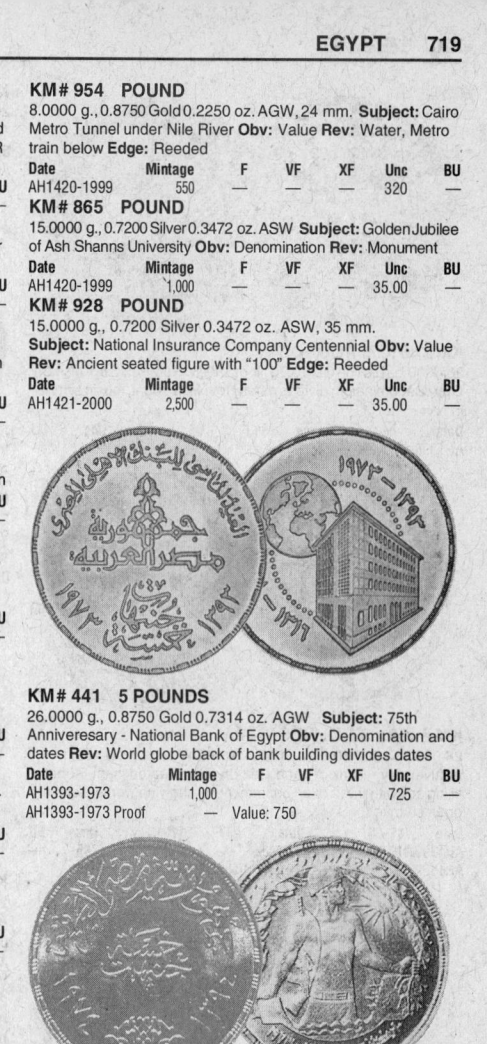

KM# 441 5 POUNDS
26.0000 g., 0.8750 Gold 0.7314 oz. AGW **Subject:** 75th Anniveresary - National Bank of Egypt **Obv:** Denomination and dates **Rev:** World globe back of bank building divides dates

Date	Mintage	F	VF	XF	Unc	BU
AH1393-1973	1,000	—	—	—	725	—
AH1393-1973 Proof	—	Value: 750				

KM# 444 5 POUNDS
26.0000 g., 0.8750 Gold 0.7314 oz. AGW **Subject:** 1973 October War **Obv:** Denomination, dates, and legend **Rev:** Half-figure of soldier, 3/4 wreath surrounds above

Date	Mintage	F	VF	XF	Unc	BU
AH1394-1974	1,000	—	—	—	775	—

KM# 459 5 POUNDS
26.0000 g., 0.8750 Gold 0.7314 oz. AGW **Subject:** King Faisal of Saudi Arabia **Obv:** Denomination divides dates **Rev:** Head 3/4 right

Date	Mintage	F	VF	XF	Unc	BU
AH1396-1976	2,500	—	—	—	825	—

KM# 460 5 POUNDS
26.0000 g., 0.8750 Gold 0.7314 oz. AGW **Subject:** Reopening of Suez Canal

Date	Mintage	F	VF	XF	Unc	BU
AH1396-1976	2,000	—	—	—	750	—

KM# 461 5 POUNDS
26.0000 g., 0.8750 Gold 0.7314 oz. AGW **Subject:** Om Kalsoum
Obv: Denomination divides dates **Rev:** Head right, music symbol in hair

Date	Mintage	F	VF	XF	Unc	BU
AH1396-1976	1,000	—	—	—	900	—

KM# 495 5 POUNDS
26.0000 g., 0.8750 Gold 0.7314 oz. AGW **Subject:** 100th Anniversary - Bank of Land Reform **Rev:** Seated man, farmer tilling soil with three oxen behind, mural showing workers cutting grain sheaves

Date	Mintage	F	VF	XF	Unc	BU
AH1399-1979	1,750	—	—	—	745	—
AH1399-1979 Proof	250	Value: 850				

KM# 496 5 POUNDS
26.0000 g., 0.8750 Gold 0.7314 oz. AGW **Subject:** 1400th Anniversary - Mohammed's Flight **Obv:** Denomination divides dates, legend above **Rev:** Two doves with eggs in front of spider web

Date	Mintage	F	VF	XF	Unc	BU
AH1400-1979	2,000	—	—	—	745	—

KM# 517 5 POUNDS
26.0000 g., 0.8750 Gold 0.7314 oz. AGW **Subject:** Egyptian-Israeli Peace Treaty **Obv:** Denomination divides dates, legend above **Rev:** Head of Anwar Sadat at right facing left, dove of peace at left behind

Date	Mintage	F	VF	XF	Unc	BU
AH1400-1980	2,375	—	—	—	745	—
AH1400-1980 Proof	125	Value: 875				

KM# 518 5 POUNDS
26.0000 g., 0.8750 Gold 0.7314 oz. AGW **Subject:** Doctors' Day

Date	Mintage	F	VF	XF	Unc	BU
AH1400-1980	1,000	—	—	—	760	—

KM# 534 5 POUNDS
26.0000 g., 0.8750 Gold 0.7314 oz. AGW **Subject:** 3rd Anniversary - Suez Canal Reopening

Date	Mintage	F	VF	XF	Unc	BU
AH1401-1981 Proof	75	Value: 900				
AH1401-1981	925	—	—	—	760	—

KM# 533 5 POUNDS
24.0000 g., 0.9250 Silver 0.7137 oz. ASW **Series:** International Year of the Child **Rev:** Children holding hands and dancing around stylistic globe

Date	Mintage	F	VF	XF	Unc	BU
AH1401-1981 Proof	10,000	Value: 30.00				

KM# 535 5 POUNDS
26.0000 g., 0.8750 Gold 0.7314 oz. AGW **Subject:** 25th Anniversary - Ministry of Industry

Date	Mintage	F	VF	XF	Unc	BU
AH1402-1981 Proof	1,500	Value: 745				

KM# 536 5 POUNDS
26.0000 g., 0.8750 Gold 0.7314 oz. AGW **Subject:** 100th Anniversary - Revolt by Arabi Pasha **Rev:** Pasha mounted on horse in front of his followers

Date	Mintage	F	VF	XF	Unc	BU
AH1402-1981	1,000	—	—	—	760	—

KM# 537 5 POUNDS
26.0000 g., 0.8750 Gold 0.7314 oz. AGW **Subject:** 25th Anniversary - Nationalization of Suez Canal **Obv:** Denomination divides dates, legend above **Rev:** Design at center, grain spray below

Date	Mintage	F	VF	XF	Unc	BU
AH1401-1981	1,000	—	—	—	760	—

KM# 546 5 POUNDS
26.0000 g., 0.8750 Gold 0.7314 oz. AGW **Subject:** 1000th Anniversary - Al Azhar Mosque **Rev:** Mosque

Date	Mintage	F	VF	XF	Unc	BU
AH1402-1982	1,500	—	—	—	745	—

KM# 547 5 POUNDS
26.0000 g., 0.8750 Gold 0.7314 oz. AGW **Subject:** 50th Anniversary - Air Force **Rev:** Air Force insignia within wreath

Date	Mintage	F	VF	XF	Unc	BU
AH1403-1982	1,000	—	—	—	760	—

KM# 552 5 POUNDS
17.5000 g., 0.7200 Silver 0.4051 oz. ASW **Subject:** 75th Anniversary - Cairo University **Obv:** Denomination within circle divides dates **Rev:** Buildings, shield within wreath at right

Date	Mintage	F	VF	XF	Unc	BU
AH1404-1983	25,000	—	—	—	18.00	—

KM# 558 5 POUNDS
17.5000 g., 0.7200 Silver 0.4051 oz. ASW **Subject:** Los Angeles Olympics **Obv:** Torch above Olympic rings, dates below **Rev:** Athletes above symbols

Date	Mintage	F	VF	XF	Unc	BU
AH1404-1984	20,000	—	—	—	13.50	—

KM# 560 5 POUNDS
17.5000 g., 0.7200 Silver 0.4051 oz. ASW **Subject:** Academy of Arabic Languages **Obv:** Denomination within circle divides dates **Rev:** World globe above book

Date	Mintage	F	VF	XF	Unc	BU
AH1404-1984	25,000	—	—	—	13.50	—

KM# 561 5 POUNDS
17.5000 g., 0.7200 Silver 0.4051 oz. ASW **Subject:** 50th Anniversary - Egyptian Radio Broadcasting **Obv:** Designs within small circles flank design at top, dates below **Rev:** Radio tower divides dates

Date	Mintage	F	VF	XF	Unc	BU
AH1404-1984	25,000	—	—	—	18.50	—

KM# 565   5 POUNDS
17.5000 g., 0.7200 Silver 0.4051 oz. ASW **Subject:** Sculptor
Mahmoud Mokhtar **Obv:** Denomination within circle divides dates
Rev: Bust left

Date	Mintage	F	VF	XF	Unc	BU
AH1404-1984	10,000	—	—	—	20.00	—

KM# 566   5 POUNDS
17.5000 g., 0.7200 Silver 0.4051 oz. ASW **Subject:** Golden
Jubilee of Petroleum Industry **Obv:** Denomination within circle
divides dates **Rev:** Radiant flame above three rings

Date	Mintage	F	VF	XF	Unc	BU
AH1404-1984	10,000	—	—	—	18.50	—

KM# 567   5 POUNDS
17.5000 g., 0.7200 Silver 0.4051 oz. ASW **Subject:** Diamond
Jubilee of Cooperation **Obv:** Arabic legends, dates below
Rev: Seven joined hexagons with different scenes

Date	Mintage	F	VF	XF	Unc	BU
AH1404-1984	10,000	—	—	—	20.00	—

KM# 671   5 POUNDS
26.0000 g., 0.8750 Gold 0.7314 oz. AGW **Subject:** 50th
Anniversary - Egyptian Radio **Obv:** Arabic legends **Rev:** Tall
buildings with transmitter

Date	Mintage	F	VF	XF	Unc	BU
AH1404-1984 Proof	500	Value: 750				

KM# 563   5 POUNDS
17.5000 g., 0.7200 Silver 0.4051 oz. ASW **Subject:** 100th
Anniversary - Moharram Printing Press Co. **Obv:** Arabic legends,
date below **Rev:** Printing design on shaded field that resembles
the letter 'B'

Date	Mintage	F	VF	XF	Unc	BU
AH1405-1985	20,000	—	—	—	18.50	—

KM# 564   5 POUNDS
40.0000 g., 0.8750 Gold 1.1252 oz. AGW **Subject:** 100th
Anniversary - Moharram Printing Press Co.

Date	Mintage	F	VF	XF	Unc	BU
AH1405-1985	200	—	—	—	1,850	—

KM# 572   5 POUNDS
17.5000 g., 0.7200 Silver 0.4051 oz. ASW **Subject:** 25th
Anniversary - National Planning Institute **Obv:** Arabic legends,
dates below **Rev:** Design on shield divides dates

Date	Mintage	F	VF	XF	Unc	BU
AH1405-1985	15,000	—	—	—	20.00	—

KM# 575   5 POUNDS
17.5000 g., 0.7200 Silver 0.4051 oz. ASW **Subject:** 60th
Anniversary - Egyptian Parliament **Obv:** Arabic legends, dates
below **Rev:** Parliament building, dates above

Date	Mintage	F	VF	XF	Unc	BU
AH1405-1985	25,000	—	—	—	18.00	—

KM# 576   5 POUNDS
26.0000 g., 0.8750 Gold 0.7314 oz. AGW **Subject:** 60th
Anniversary - Egyptian Parliament **Rev:** Parliament building

Date	Mintage	F	VF	XF	Unc	BU
AH1405-1985	500	—	—	—	1,750	—

KM# 578   5 POUNDS
17.5000 g., 0.7200 Silver 0.4051 oz. ASW **Subject:** 25th
Anniversary - Cairo Stadium **Obv:** Arabic legends, dates below
Rev: Stadium

Date	Mintage	F	VF	XF	Unc	BU
AH1405-1985	25,000	—	—	—	18.00	—

KM# 581   5 POUNDS
17.5000 g., 0.7200 Silver 0.4051 oz. ASW **Subject:** 25th
Anniversary - Egyptian Television **Obv:** Arabic legends, dates
below **Rev:** Television tower emitting signal divides dates

Date	Mintage	F	VF	XF	Unc	BU
AH1405-1985	5,000	—	—	—	30.00	—

KM# 585   5 POUNDS
17.5000 g., 0.7200 Silver 0.4051 oz. ASW **Subject:** 25th
Anniversary - Cairo International Airport **Rev:** Buzzards in flight
adapted from ancient Egyptian art

Date	Mintage	F	VF	XF	Unc	BU
AH1405-1985	20,000	—	—	—	14.00	—

KM# 592   5 POUNDS
17.5000 g., 0.7200 Silver 0.4051 oz. ASW **Subject:**
Tutankhamen **Obv:** Arabic legends, dates below **Rev:** Bust left

Date	Mintage	F	VF	XF	Unc	BU
AH1405-1985	6,000	—	—	—	25.00	—
AH1405-1985 Proof	2,000	Value: 30.00				

KM# 593   5 POUNDS
17.5000 g., 0.7200 Silver 0.4051 oz. ASW **Subject:** XV UIA
Congress **Obv:** Arabic legends, dates below **Rev:** Pyramid

Date	Mintage	F	VF	XF	Unc	BU
AH1405-1985	10,000	—	—	—	20.00	—
AH1405-1985 Proof	Est. 500	Value: 25.00				

KM# 598   5 POUNDS
17.5000 g., 0.7200 Silver 0.4051 oz. ASW **Subject:** Faculty of
Economics and Political Science **Obv:** Arabic legends, dates
below **Rev:** Grid on globe, dentiled arch above, spray below,
divides dates above

Date	Mintage	F	VF	XF	Unc	BU
AH1405-1985	8,000	—	—	—	22.00	—

KM# 600   5 POUNDS
17.5000 g., 0.7200 Silver 0.4051 oz. ASW   **Subject:** Commerce Day **Obv:** Arabic legends, dates below **Rev:** Ship above head on grid, vendors and shoppers flank

Date	Mintage	F	VF	XF	Unc	BU
AH1405-1985	20,000	—	—	—	18.00	—
AH1405-1985 Proof	1,000	Value: 40.00				

KM# 584   5 POUNDS
17.5000 g., 0.7200 Silver 0.4051 oz. ASW   **Subject:** The Prophet's Mosque **Obv:** Towers at left of stylized globe **Rev:** Mosque

Date	Mintage	F	VF	XF	Unc	BU
AH1406-1985	25,000	—	—	—	18.00	—
AH1406-1985 Proof	1,000	Value: 40.00				

KM# 587   5 POUNDS
17.5000 g., 0.7200 Silver 0.4051 oz. ASW   **Subject:** Professions **Obv:** Arabic legends, dates below **Rev:** Various professions illustrated on coin

Date	Mintage	F	VF	XF	Unc	BU
AH1406-1985	8,000	—	—	—	22.00	—

KM# 633   5 POUNDS
26.0000 g., 0.8750 Gold 0.7314 oz. AGW   **Subject:** Prophet's Mosque **Obv:** Minaret, globe, denomination, legends **Rev:** Crescent, mosque, minaret below legend arch

Date	Mintage	F	VF	XF	Unc	BU
AH1406-1985	400	—	—	—	750	—

KM# 579   5 POUNDS
26.0000 g., 0.8750 Gold 0.7314 oz. AGW   **Subject:** 25th Anniversary - Cairo Stadium **Rev:** Stadium

Date	Mintage	F	VF	XF	Unc	BU
AH1405-1985	200	—	—	—	1,850	—

KM# 582   5 POUNDS
26.0000 g., 0.8750 Gold 0.7314 oz. AGW   **Subject:** 25th Anniversary - Egyptian Television **Obv:** Arabic legends, dates below **Rev:** Television tower emitting signal divides dates

Date	Mintage	F	VF	XF	Unc	BU
AH1405-1985	100	—	—	—	1,150	—

KM# 615   5 POUNDS
17.5000 g., 0.7200 Silver 0.4051 oz. ASW   **Subject:** 30th Anniversary - Atomic Energy Organization **Obv:** Arabic legends, dates below **Rev:** Atoms within circle above center design, figures flank

Date	Mintage	F	VF	XF	Unc	BU
AH1406-1986	5,000	—	—	—	30.00	—

KM# 603   5 POUNDS
17.5000 g., 0.7200 Silver 0.4051 oz. ASW   **Subject:** Census **Obv:** Arabic legends, dates below **Rev:** Joined figures below city scene

Date	Mintage	F	VF	XF	Unc	BU
AH1407-1986	6,000	—	—	—	25.00	—

KM# 610   5 POUNDS
17.5000 g., 0.7200 Silver 0.4051 oz. ASW   **Subject:** 40th Anniversary - Engineer's Syndicate **Obv:** Arabic legends, dates below **Rev:** Stylized train and pyramids within square formed by outer designs

Date	Mintage	F	VF	XF	Unc	BU
AH1407-1986	6,000	—	—	—	25.00	—

KM# 616   5 POUNDS
17.5000 g., 0.7200 Silver 0.4051 oz. ASW   **Subject:** 30th Anniversary - Egyptian Industry **Obv:** Arabic legends, dates below **Rev:** Split dentiled design at center

Date	Mintage	F	VF	XF	Unc	BU
AH1407-1986	5,000	—	—	—	30.00	—

KM# 586   5 POUNDS
17.5000 g., 0.7200 Silver 0.4051 oz. ASW   **Subject:** Cairo University Faculty of Commerce **Obv:** Arabic legends, dates below **Rev:** Scribes and merchant vessel

Date	Mintage	F	VF	XF	Unc	BU
AH1406-1986	20,000	—	—	—	18.00	—

KM# 588   5 POUNDS
17.5000 g., 0.7200 Silver 0.4051 oz. ASW   **Subject:** 25th Anniversary - Egyptian National Bank **Obv:** Denomination divides dates, buds above, cogwheel at left **Rev:** Monument divides dates

Date	Mintage	F	VF	XF	Unc	BU
AH1406-1986	6,000	—	—	—	25.00	—

KM# 589   5 POUNDS
17.6800 g., 0.7200 Silver 0.4092 oz. ASW   **Subject:** World Soccer Championships **Obv:** Grain heads above denomination and dates **Rev:** Soccer ball, three pyramids

Date	Mintage	F	VF	XF	Unc	BU
AH1406-1986 Prooflike	5,000	—	—	—	—	30.00
AH1406-1986 Proof	2,150	Value: 30.00				

KM# 590 5 POUNDS
17.5000 g., 0.7200 Silver 0.4051 oz. ASW **Subject:** African Soccer Championship Games **Rev:** Two soccer players at right

Date	Mintage	F	VF	XF	Unc	BU
AH1406-1986	15,000	—	—	—	24.00	—
AH1406-1986 Proof	2,000	Value: 30.00				

KM# 594 5 POUNDS
17.5000 g., 0.7200 Silver 0.4051 oz. ASW **Subject:** 50th Anniversary - Ministry of Health **Obv:** Denomination and dates within circle **Rev:** Figures on heart, within half moon design, below surgeon holding snake and glass

Date	Mintage	F	VF	XF	Unc	BU
AH1406-1986	10,000	—	—	—	20.00	—
AH1406-1986 Proof	Est. 500	Value: 55.00				

KM# 601 5 POUNDS
17.5000 g., 0.7200 Silver 0.4051 oz. ASW **Subject:** Warrior's Day **Rev:** Crossed swords within wreath

Date	Mintage	F	VF	XF	Unc	BU
AH1406-1986	16,000	—	—	—	22.00	—

KM# 602 5 POUNDS
17.5000 g., 0.7200 Silver 0.4051 oz. ASW **Subject:** 100th Anniversary - Petroleum Industry **Obv:** Arabic legends, dates below **Rev:** Oil derrick with building behind

Date	Mintage	F	VF	XF	Unc	BU
AH1406-1986	6,000	—	—	—	25.00	—

KM# 608 5 POUNDS
17.5000 g., 0.7200 Silver 0.4051 oz. ASW **Subject:** 50th Anniversary - National Theater **Obv:** Drapes enclose text **Rev:** Theater building, masks below

Date	Mintage	F	VF	XF	Unc	BU
AH1406-1986	6,000	—	—	—	25.00	—

KM# 609 5 POUNDS
17.5000 g., 0.7200 Silver 0.4051 oz. ASW **Subject:** Mecca **Obv:** Denomination and dates **Rev:** Building within circle

Date	Mintage	F	VF	XF	Unc	BU
AH1406-1986	30,000	—	—	—	15.00	—
AH1406-1986 Proof	—	Value: 22.50				

KM# 614 5 POUNDS
17.5000 g., 0.7200 Silver 0.4051 oz. ASW **Subject:** Restoration of Parliament Building **Obv:** Arabic legends, dates below **Rev:** Dome and tower with scaffolding

Date	Mintage	F	VF	XF	Unc	BU
AH1406-1986	5,000	—	—	—	30.00	—

KM# 614a 5 POUNDS
26.0000 g., 0.8750 Gold 0.7314 oz. AGW **Subject:** Restoration of Parliament Building **Obv:** Arabic legends **Rev:** Dome and tower with scaffolding

Date	Mintage	F	VF	XF	Unc	BU
AH1406-1986	300	—	—	—	760	—

KM# 609a 5 POUNDS
26.0000 g., 0.8750 Gold 0.7314 oz. AGW **Subject:** Mecca **Obv:** Denomination and dates **Rev:** Building within circle

Date	Mintage	F	VF	XF	Unc	BU
AH1406-1986 Proof	1,400	Value: 745				

KM# 617a 5 POUNDS
26.0000 g., 0.8750 Gold 0.7314 oz. AGW **Subject:** Parliament Museum **Obv:** Arabic legends, seals and dates **Rev:** Documents, quill, carriage, building with national emblem

Date	Mintage	F	VF	XF	Unc	BU
AH1407-1987	300	—	—	—	760	—

KM# 674 5 POUNDS
26.0000 g., 0.8750 Gold 0.7314 oz. AGW **Subject:** First African Subway **Obv:** Stylized legends and denomination **Rev:** Subway emerging from tunnel with legend around rim

Date	Mintage	F	VF	XF	Unc	BU
AH1408-1987 Proof	200	Value: 800				

KM# 611 5 POUNDS
17.5000 g., 0.7200 Silver 0.4051 oz. ASW **Subject:** Aida Opera **Obv:** Towers, sun, date, names and inscriptions **Rev:** Scene from the opera, 'AIDA'

Date	Mintage	F	VF	XF	Unc	BU
ND(1407-1987)	25,000	—	—	—	35.00	—

KM# 617 5 POUNDS
17.5000 g., 0.7200 Silver 0.4051 oz. ASW **Subject:** Parliament Museum **Obv:** Arabic legends, seals and dates **Rev:** Documents, quill, carriage, building with national emblem

Date	Mintage	F	VF	XF	Unc	BU
AH1407-1987	5,000	—	—	—	30.00	—

KM# 618 5 POUNDS
17.5000 g., 0.7200 Silver 0.4051 oz. ASW **Subject:** Veterinarian Day **Obv:** Arabic legends, dates below **Rev:** Squatting figure with ox, caduceus within large 'V' above ox at left

Date	Mintage	F	VF	XF	Unc	BU
AH1407-1987	5,000	—	—	—	30.00	—

KM# 619 5 POUNDS
17.5000 g., 0.7200 Silver 0.4051 oz. ASW **Subject:** 75th Anniversary - Misr Petroleum Company **Obv:** Arabic legends, dates below **Rev:** Pyramids within circle divides dates

Date	Mintage	F	VF	XF	Unc	BU
AH1407-1987	10,000	—	—	—	20.00	—

KM# 630 5 POUNDS
17.5000 g., 0.7200 Silver 0.4051 oz. ASW **Subject:** Faculty of Fine Arts **Obv:** Denomination, dates and legend **Rev:** Design above dates

Date	Mintage	F	VF	XF	Unc	BU
AH1407-1987	5,000	—	—	—	30.00	—

KM# 651 5 POUNDS
17.7800 g., 0.7200 Silver 0.4116 oz. ASW **Subject:** Investment Bank **Obv:** Tughra divides dates **Rev:** Design within inner dentiled circle

Date	Mintage	F	VF	XF	Unc	BU
AH1407-1987	8,000	—	—	—	24.00	—

KM# 620 5 POUNDS
17.5000 g., 0.7200 Silver 0.4051 oz. ASW **Subject:** First African Subway **Obv:** Four square designs divide dates **Rev:** Train leaving tunnel

Date	Mintage	F	VF	XF	Unc	BU
AH1408-1987	15,000	—	—	—	18.00	—

KM# 623 5 POUNDS
17.5000 g., 0.7200 Silver 0.4051 oz. ASW **Subject:** 25th Anniversary - Hellwan Company **Obv:** Circles flank smoking towers at top, dates below **Rev:** Design within inner circle, legends and dentiled circle surrounds

Date	Mintage	F	VF	XF	Unc	BU
AH1408-1987	8,000	—	—	—	24.00	—

KM# 670 5 POUNDS
26.0000 g., 0.8750 Gold 0.7314 oz. AGW **Subject:** National Research Center **Obv:** Kufic legend above denomination and date **Rev:** Stylized ancient and modern research elements

Date	Mintage	F	VF	XF	Unc	BU
AH1408-1988 Proof	—	Value: 800				
AH1409-1989 Proof	200	Value: 800				

KM# 626 5 POUNDS
17.5000 g., 0.7200 Silver 0.4051 oz. ASW **Series:** Summer Olympics **Obv:** Denomination and date above design and legend **Rev:** Athletes and mythological figures, dates below

Date	Mintage	F	VF	XF	Unc	BU
AH1408-1988	24,000	—	—	—	15.00	—
AH1408-1988 Matte	—	—	—	—	55.00	—
AH1408-1988 Proof	5,000	Value: 30.00				

KM# 628 5 POUNDS
17.5000 g., 0.7200 Silver 0.4051 oz. ASW **Series:** Winter Olympics **Rev:** Ski jumper and figure skater

Date	Mintage	F	VF	XF	Unc	BU
AH1408-1988	8,000	—	—	—	24.00	—
AH1408-1988 Matte	—	—	—	—	55.00	—
AH1408-1988 Proof	2,000	Value: 30.00				

KM# 669 5 POUNDS
17.5000 g., 0.7200 Silver 0.4051 oz. ASW **Subject:** National Research Center **Rev:** Stylized ancient and modern research elements

Date	Mintage	F	VF	XF	Unc	BU
AH1408-1988	5,000	—	—	—	30.00	—

KM# 621 5 POUNDS
17.5000 g., 0.7200 Silver 0.4051 oz. ASW **Subject:** Police Day **Obv:** Arabic legends **Rev:** Eagle with wings spread within oval wreath

Date	Mintage	F	VF	XF	Unc	BU
AH1408-1988	35,000	—	—	—	14.00	—

KM# 624 5 POUNDS
17.5000 g., 0.7200 Silver 0.4051 oz. ASW **Series:** Summer Olympics **Obv:** Denomination and date above design and legend **Rev:** Pharoah and athletes

Date	Mintage	F	VF	XF	Unc	BU
AH1408-1988 Matte	—	—	—	—	55.00	—
AH1408-1988 Proof	2,000	Value: 27.50				
AH1408-1988	30,000	—	—	—	13.50	—

KM# 631 5 POUNDS
17.5000 g., 0.7200 Silver 0.4051 oz. ASW **Subject:** 50th Anniversary of Air Travel **Obv:** Torch above shield within eagles wings **Rev:** Stylized airplane above text divides dates

Date	Mintage	F	VF	XF	Unc	BU
AH1408-1988	5,000	—	—	—	30.00	—

KM# 649 5 POUNDS
17.5000 g., 0.7200 Silver 0.4051 oz. ASW **Subject:** Dedication of Cairo Opera House **Obv:** Arabic legends, seals and dates **Rev:** Opera house

Date	Mintage	F	VF	XF	Unc	BU
AH1409-1988	30,000	—	—	—	13.50	—

KM# 655 5 POUNDS
26.0000 g., 0.8750 Gold 0.7314 oz. AGW **Subject:** Dedication of Cairo Opera House **Obv:** Arabic legends, seals, dates **Rev:** Opera house, legends above and below

Date	Mintage	F	VF	XF	Unc	BU
AH1409-1988	200	—	—	—	775	—

KM# 660 5 POUNDS
17.5000 g., 0.7200 Silver 0.4051 oz. ASW **Subject:** Ministry of Agriculture **Obv:** Tughra divides dates and denomination **Rev:** Tractor above corn ears, within grain sprigs and flowers

Date	Mintage	F	VF	XF	Unc	BU
AH1409-1988	5,000	—	—	—	30.00	—

KM# 662   5 POUNDS
17.5000 g., 0.7200 Silver 0.4051 oz. ASW **Subject:** Naguib Mahfouz, Nobel Laureate **Obv:** Quill in inkwell designed as globe, divides date and denomination **Rev:** Head left

Date	Mintage	F	VF	XF	Unc	BU
AH1409-1988	15,000	—	—	—	20.00	—

KM# 663   5 POUNDS
17.5000 g., 0.7200 Silver 0.4051 oz. ASW **Subject:** Advista Arabia II **Obv:** Arabic legends, seals and dates **Rev:** Head with art tools left, date at right

Date	Mintage	F	VF	XF	Unc	BU
AH1409-1989	5,000	—	—	—	30.00	—

KM# 665   5 POUNDS
17.5000 g., 0.7200 Silver 0.4051 oz. ASW **Subject:** United Parliamentary Union **Obv:** Denomination divides dates below text **Rev:** Globe within wreath divides buildings, date on top building

Date	Mintage	F	VF	XF	Unc	BU
AH1409-1989	5,000	—	—	—	30.00	—

KM# 667   5 POUNDS
17.5000 g., 0.7200 Silver 0.4051 oz. ASW **Subject:** First Arab Olympics **Obv:** Kufic legend below denomination and date within circle **Rev:** Wreath surrounds hand holding pillar with map and rings on top

Date	Mintage	F	VF	XF	Unc	BU
AH1409-1989	8,000	—	—	—	24.00	—

KM# 686   5 POUNDS
17.5000 g., 0.7200 Silver 0.4051 oz. ASW **Subject:** National Health Insurance **Obv:** Dates and denomination within circle, text below **Rev:** Figures within half moon design on rock, dates below

Date	Mintage	F	VF	XF	Unc	BU
AH1409-1989	3,000	—	—	—	35.00	—

KM# 678   5 POUNDS
17.5000 g., 0.7200 Silver 0.4051 oz. ASW **Subject:** University of Cairo - School of Agriculture **Obv:** Denomination and dates within wreath of grain sprigs, text below **Rev:** Shield to right of farmers and oxen, building in background

Date	Mintage	F	VF	XF	Unc	BU
AH1410-1989	4,000	—	—	—	32.00	—

KM# 687   5 POUNDS
17.5000 g., 0.7200 Silver 0.4051 oz. ASW **Subject:** Export Drive **Obv:** Tughra, date and text **Rev:** Stylized symbols

Date	Mintage	F	VF	XF	Unc	BU
AH1410-1989	4,000	—	—	—	35.00	—

KM# 688   5 POUNDS
17.5000 g., 0.7200 Silver 0.4051 oz. ASW **Subject:** National Population Center **Obv:** Tughra below dates **Rev:** Repeated design of people forms square at center, which holds text

Date	Mintage	F	VF	XF	Unc	BU
AH1410-1990	5,000	—	—	—	30.00	—

KM# 689   5 POUNDS
17.5000 g., 0.7200 Silver 0.4051 oz. ASW **Subject:** Union of African Parliaments **Obv:** Tughra below dates and denomination, within circle **Rev:** Map in background divides grain sprig and building

Date	Mintage	F	VF	XF	Unc	BU
AH1410-1990	5,000	—	—	—	30.00	—

KM# 691   5 POUNDS
17.8200 g., 0.9000 Silver 0.5156 oz. ASW **Subject:** Dar-el-Eloun Faculty **Obv:** Denomination and dates within circle above text **Rev:** Bust and shield left of dates, text below

Date	Mintage	F	VF	XF	Unc	BU
AH1410-1990	5,000	—	—	—	30.00	—

KM# 697   5 POUNDS
17.5000 g., 0.7200 Silver 0.4051 oz. ASW **Subject:** Newly Populated Areas Organization

Date	Mintage	F	VF	XF	Unc	BU
AH1410-1990	2,000	—	—	—	45.00	—

KM# 698   5 POUNDS
17.5000 g., 0.7200 Silver 0.4051 oz. ASW **Subject:** Alexandria Sports Club **Obv:** Denomination and dates within circle above text **Rev:** Athletes surround center circles with text and designs

Date	Mintage	F	VF	XF	Unc	BU
AH1411-1990	5,000	—	—	—	30.00	—

KM# 679   5 POUNDS
17.5000 g., 0.7200 Silver 0.4051 oz. ASW **Series:** Soccer World Championship - Italy **Obv:** Circle of text at center of wings, denomination and dates above **Rev:** Ancient gods in front of pyramid with soccer ball above

Date	Mintage	F	VF	XF	Unc	BU
AH1410-1990	600	—	—	—	120	—
AH1410-1990 Proof	8,000	Value: 25.00				

KM# 682 5 POUNDS
17.5000 g., 0.7200 Silver 0.4051 oz. ASW **Series:** Soccer World Championship - Italy **Obv:** Text within circle at center of wings, denomination and dates above **Rev:** Player chasing ball

Date	Mintage	F	VF	XF	Unc	BU
AH1410-1990 Matte	400	—	—	—	150	—
AH1410-1990 Proof	4,000	Value: 35.00				

KM# 692 5 POUNDS
17.8200 g., 0.9000 Silver 0.5156 oz. ASW **Subject:** Islamic Development Bank **Obv:** Globe back of towered buildings above grasped hands, dentiled design below, grain stalks flank **Rev:** Tughra divided dates above inscription and denomination

Date	Mintage	F	VF	XF	Unc	BU
AH1411-1991	5,000	—	—	—	30.00	—

KM# 700 5 POUNDS
17.8200 g., 0.9000 Silver 0.5156 oz. ASW **Subject:** 5th African Games - Cairo

Date	Mintage	F	VF	XF	Unc	BU
AH1411-1991	3,000	—	—	—	35.00	—

KM# 727 5 POUNDS
17.5000 g., 0.7200 Silver 0.4051 oz. ASW **Subject:** Muhamed Abdel Wahab **Obv:** Arabic legends and inscriptions **Rev:** Bust left with music sheet in background

Date	Mintage	F	VF	XF	Unc	BU
AH1412-1991	30,000	—	—	—	13.50	—

KM# 728 5 POUNDS
26.0000 g., 0.8750 Gold 0.7314 oz. AGW **Subject:** Muhamed Abdel Wahab **Obv:** Arabic legends and inscriptions **Rev:** Bust left with music sheet in background

Date	Mintage	F	VF	XF	Unc	BU
AH1412-1991 Proof	400	—	—	—	765	—

KM# 791 5 POUNDS
17.4200 g., 0.7200 Silver 0.4032 oz. ASW **Subject:** National Zoo **Obv:** Zoo entrance, dates and denomination **Rev:** Five zoo animals

Date	Mintage	F	VF	XF	Unc	BU
AH1411-1991	—	—	—	—	40.00	—

KM# 804 5 POUNDS
17.5000 g., 0.7200 Silver 0.4051 oz. ASW **Subject:** Atomic Energy **Obv:** Denomination **Rev:** Ancient statue and pyramid within rings

Date	Mintage	F	VF	XF	Unc	BU
AH1411-1991	Est. 5,000	—	—	—	30.00	—

KM# 805 5 POUNDS
17.5000 g., 0.7200 Silver 0.4051 oz. ASW **Subject:** Library of Alexandria **Obv:** Arabic inscription, dates **Rev:** Library building complex

Date	Mintage	F	VF	XF	Unc	BU
AH1411-1991	Est. 8,000	—	—	—	24.00	—

KM# 805a 5 POUNDS
26.0000 g., 0.8750 Gold 0.7314 oz. AGW **Subject:** Library of Alexandria **Obv:** Arabic inscription **Rev:** Library building complex **Edge:** Reeded **Note:** Struck at Cairo.

Date	Mintage	F	VF	XF	Unc	BU
AH1411-1991 Proof	200	—	—	—	775	—

KM# 833 5 POUNDS
26.0000 g., 0.8750 Gold 0.7314 oz. AGW **Subject:** Library of Alexandria **Obv:** Legend and inscription **Rev:** Waterfront building with tower

Date	Mintage	F	VF	XF	Unc	BU
AH1411-1991	200	—	—	—	775	—

KM# 701 5 POUNDS
17.5000 g., 0.7200 Silver 0.4051 oz. ASW **Series:** Summer Olympics **Obv:** Text within circle at center of wings, denomination and dates above **Rev:** Two men fencing

Date	Mintage	F	VF	XF	Unc	BU
AH1412-1992	999	—	—	—	42.50	—
AH1412-1992 Proof	2,999	Value: 40.00				

KM# 702 5 POUNDS
17.5000 g., 0.7200 Silver 0.4051 oz. ASW **Series:** Summer Olympics **Obv:** Text within circle at center of wings, denomination and dates above **Rev:** Pairs wrestling, half globe below

Date	Mintage	F	VF	XF	Unc	BU
AH1412-1992	999	—	—	—	110	—
AH1412-1992 Proof	2,999	Value: 40.00				

KM# 703 5 POUNDS
17.5000 g., 0.7200 Silver 0.4051 oz. ASW **Series:** Summer Olympics **Obv:** Text within circle at center of wings, denomination and dates above **Rev:** Archery demonstrated

Date	Mintage	F	VF	XF	Unc	BU
AH1412-1992	999	—	—	—	110	—
AH1412-1992 Proof	2,999	Value: 40.00				

KM# 704 5 POUNDS
17.5000 g., 0.7200 Silver 0.4051 oz. ASW **Series:** Summer Olympics **Obv:** Text within circle at center of wings, denomination and dates above **Rev:** Many men wrestling an ox

Date	Mintage	F	VF	XF	Unc	BU
AH1412-1992	999	—	—	—	110	—
AH1412-1992 Proof	2,999	Value: 40.00				

KM# 705 5 POUNDS
17.5000 g., 0.7200 Silver 0.4051 oz. ASW **Series:** Summer Olympics **Obv:** Text within circle at center of wings, denomination and dates above **Rev:** Swimmer stalking a duck

Date	Mintage	F	VF	XF	Unc	BU
AH1412-1992	999	—	—	—	110	—
AH1412-1992 Proof	2,999	Value: 40.00				

KM# 706 5 POUNDS

17.5000 g., 0.7200 Silver 0.4051 oz. ASW **Series:** Summer Olympics **Rev:** Handball player

Date	Mintage	F	VF	XF	Unc	BU
AH1412-1992	999	—	—	—	110	—
AH1412-1992 Proof	25,000	Value: 20.00				

KM# 707 5 POUNDS

17.5000 g., 0.7200 Silver 0.4051 oz. ASW **Series:** Summer Olympics **Rev:** Field hockey player

Date	Mintage	F	VF	XF	Unc	BU
AH1412-1992	999	—	—	—	110	—
AH1412-1992 Proof	25,000	Value: 20.00				

KM# 708 5 POUNDS

17.5000 g., 0.7200 Silver 0.4051 oz. ASW **Series:** Summer Olympics **Obv:** Text within circle at center of wings, denomination and dates above **Rev:** Soccer player kicking ball

Date	Mintage	F	VF	XF	Unc	BU
AH1412-1992	999	—	—	—	110	—
AH1412-1992 Proof	25,000	Value: 20.00				

KM# 806 5 POUNDS

17.5000 g., 0.7200 Silver 0.4051 oz. ASW **Subject:** Lighthouse of Alexandria **Obv:** Denomination and dates within circle above text **Rev:** Ancient tower and Egyptian

Date	Mintage	F	VF	XF	Unc	BU
AH1412-1992	Est. 3,000	—	—	—	22.00	—

KM# 807 5 POUNDS

17.5000 g., 0.7200 Silver 0.4051 oz. ASW **Subject:** 50 Years - University of Alexandria **Obv:** Arabic inscription, dates **Rev:** University emblem divides dates

Date	Mintage	F	VF	XF	Unc	BU
AH1413-1992	Est. 3,000	—	—	—	22.00	—

KM# 808 5 POUNDS

17.5000 g., 0.7200 Silver 0.4051 oz. ASW **Subject:** Naguib Mahfouz, Nobel Laureate **Obv:** Vase and inscriptions, dates below **Rev:** Bust right

Date	Mintage	F	VF	XF	Unc	BU
AH1413-1992	Est. 6,000	—	—	—	24.00	—

KM# 746 5 POUNDS

22.5000 g., 0.9990 Silver 0.7226 oz. ASW **Subject:** Menkaure Triad **Obv:** Vulture, denomination above and dates below **Rev:** Three figures

Date	Mintage	F	VF	XF	Unc	BU
AH1414-1993 Proof	50,000	Value: 30.00				

KM# 735 5 POUNDS

22.5000 g., 0.9990 Silver 0.7226 oz. ASW **Subject:** Cleopatra - queen and statesperson, 69-30BC **Obv:** Vulture, denomination above and dates below **Rev:** Bust in formal headdress left

Date	Mintage	F	VF	XF	Unc	BU
AH1413-1993 Proof	50,000	Value: 36.50				

KM# 740 5 POUNDS

22.5000 g., 0.9990 Silver 0.7226 oz. ASW **Subject:** Pyramids **Obv:** Vulture, denomination above and dates below **Rev:** Three pyramids

Date	Mintage	F	VF	XF	Unc	BU
AH1414-1993 Proof	50,000	Value: 36.50				

KM# 741 5 POUNDS

22.5000 g., 0.9990 Silver 0.7226 oz. ASW **Obv:** Vulture, denomination above and dates below **Rev:** Sphinx

Date	Mintage	F	VF	XF	Unc	BU
AH1414-1993 Proof	50,000	Value: 36.50				

KM# 742 5 POUNDS

22.5000 g., 0.9990 Silver 0.7226 oz. ASW **Subject:** King Narmur Smiting a Foe **Obv:** Vulture, denomination above and dates below **Rev:** Decorative vase depicting punishment scene

Date	Mintage	F	VF	XF	Unc	BU
AH1414-1993 Proof	50,000	Value: 36.50				

KM# 743 5 POUNDS

22.5000 g., 0.9990 Silver 0.7226 oz. ASW **Obv:** Vulture, denomination above and dates below **Rev:** Guardian Goddess Serket

Date	Mintage	F	VF	XF	Unc	BU
AH1414-1993 Proof	50,000	Value: 36.50				

KM# 744   5 POUNDS
22.5000 g., 0.9990 Silver 0.7226 oz. ASW **Subject:** Amulet of Hathor **Obv:** Vulture, denomination above and dates below **Rev:** Sculpture of head

Date	Mintage	F	VF	XF	Unc	BU
AH1414-1993 Proof	50,000	Value: 36.50				

KM# 745   5 POUNDS
22.5000 g., 0.9990 Silver 0.7226 oz. ASW **Obv:** Vulture, denomination above and dates below **Rev:** Standing Ramses II

Date	Mintage	F	VF	XF	Unc	BU
AH1414-1993 Proof	50,000	Value: 36.50				

KM# 747   5 POUNDS
22.5000 g., 0.9990 Silver 0.7226 oz. ASW **Subject:** Symbol of Unification **Obv:** Vulture, denomination above and dates below **Rev:** Two females representing the upper and lower Nile

Date	Mintage	F	VF	XF	Unc	BU
AH1414-1993 Proof	50,000	Value: 36.50				

KM# 748   5 POUNDS
22.5000 g., 0.9990 Silver 0.7226 oz. ASW **Series:** World Cup Soccer **Obv:** Vulture, denomination above and dates below **Rev:** Kneeling King Pepi I facing

Date	Mintage	F	VF	XF	Unc	BU
AH1414-1993 Proof	—	Value: 40.00				
AH1415-1994 Proof	50,000	Value: 36.50				

KM# 759   5 POUNDS
17.5000 g., 0.7200 Silver 0.4051 oz. ASW **Subject:** Beram El Tunsi, Poet **Obv:** Inscription and seals, dates below **Rev:** Bust 3/4 left

Date	Mintage	F	VF	XF	Unc	BU
AH1413-1993	3,000	—	—	—	35.00	—

KM# 793   5 POUNDS
22.5000 g., 0.9990 Silver 0.7226 oz. ASW **Obv:** Vulture, denomination above and dates below **Rev:** Tutankhamen's burial mask

Date	Mintage	F	VF	XF	Unc	BU
AH1414-1993 Proof	—	Value: 37.50				

KM# 812   5 POUNDS
17.5000 g., 0.7200 Silver 0.4051 oz. ASW **Subject:** 20th Anniversary - October War **Obv:** Smoking towers divide dates **Rev:** Soldier with flag

Date	Mintage	F	VF	XF	Unc	BU
AH1414-1993	Est. 5,000	—	—	—	32.50	—

KM# 837   5 POUNDS
17.5000 g., 0.7200 Silver 0.4051 oz. ASW **Subject:** 125th Anniversary of Taalat Harb Birth **Obv:** Denomination and date in circle above inscription **Rev:** Taalat Harb wearing fez **Edge:** Reeded

Date	Mintage	F	VF	XF	Unc	BU
AH1413-1993	5,000	—	—	—	25.00	—

KM# 869   5 POUNDS
22.5500 g., 0.9990 Silver 0.7242 oz. ASW **Subject:** King Kha-Sekhem **Obv:** Vulture, denomination above and dates below **Rev:** Seated figure **Edge:** Reeded

Date	Mintage	F	VF	XF	Unc	BU
AH1414-1993 Proof	15,000	—	—	—	45.00	—

KM# 879   5 POUNDS
26.0000 g., 0.8750 Gold 0.7314 oz. AGW **Subject:** Symbol of Unification **Obv:** Vulture, denomination above and dates below **Rev:** Two females representing the upper and lower Nile

Date	Mintage	F	VF	XF	Unc	BU
AH1414-1993 Proof	3,000	—	—	—	745	—

KM# 969   5 POUNDS
17.5000 g., 0.9250 Silver 0.5204 oz. ASW, 37 mm. **Series:** Protect Our world **Obv:** Sculpture above winged inscription in circle **Rev:** Relief stone carving of 4 seated royalty **Edge:** Reeded

Date	Mintage	F	VF	XF	Unc	BU
AH1415-1994 Matte	5,000	—	—	—	70.00	—

KM# 970   5 POUNDS
17.5000 g., 0.9250 Silver 0.5204 oz. ASW, 37 mm. **Series:** Protect Our world **Obv:** Sculpture above winged inscription in circle **Rev:** Sphinx, pyramids **Edge:** Reeded

Date	Mintage	F	VF	XF	Unc	BU
AH1415-1994 Matte	—	—	—	—	70.00	—

KM# 971   5 POUNDS
17.5000 g., 0.9250 Silver 0.5204 oz. ASW, 37 mm. **Obv:** Relief stone sculpture above winged circle with inscription **Rev:** Ancient boat of Queen Chnemtamun **Edge:** Reeded

Date	Mintage	F	VF	XF	Unc	BU
AH1415-1994 Matte	—	—	—	—	70.00	—

KM# 972   5 POUNDS
17.5000 g., 0.9250 Silver 0.5204 oz. ASW, 37 mm. **Obv:** Relief stone sculpture above winged circle with inscription **Rev:** Suez canal scene, pyramids in background **Edge:** Reeded

Date	Mintage	F	VF	XF	Unc	BU
AH1415-1994 Matte	—	—	—	—	70.00	—

KM# 736   5 POUNDS
17.5000 g., 0.9250 Silver 0.5204 oz. ASW **Series:** World Cup Soccer **Obv:** Text within circle at center of wings, dates above divided by oval shield **Rev:** Two players, pyramid with Statue of Liberty at left

Date	Mintage	F	VF	XF	Unc	BU
AH1415-1994	499	—	—	—	150	—
AH1415-1994 Proof	15,000	Value: 40.00				

KM# 738   5 POUNDS
17.5000 g., 0.9250 Silver 0.5204 oz. ASW **Series:** World Cup Soccer **Rev:** Stylized player

Date	Mintage	F	VF	XF	Unc	BU
AH1415-1994	499	—	—	—	150	—
AH1415-1994 Proof	15,000	Value: 40.00				

KM# 749   5 POUNDS
22.5000 g., 0.9990 Silver 0.7226 oz. ASW **Obv:** Vulture, denomination above and dates below **Rev:** Sphinx and pyramids

Date	Mintage	F	VF	XF	Unc	BU
AH1414-1994 Proof	50,000	Value: 32.50				

KM# 750   5 POUNDS
22.5000 g., 0.9990 Silver 0.7226 oz. ASW **Obv:** Vulture, denomination above and dates below **Rev:** King Djoser wearing the Red Crown right

Date	Mintage	F	VF	XF	Unc	BU
AH1415-1994 Proof	50,000	Value: 30.00				

KM# 751   5 POUNDS
22.5000 g., 0.9990 Silver 0.7226 oz. ASW   **Obv:** Vulture, denomination above and dates below **Rev:** King Khonsu facing

Date	Mintage	F	VF	XF	Unc	BU
AH1415-1994 Proof	50,000	Value: 30.00				

KM# 752   5 POUNDS
22.5000 g., 0.9990 Silver 0.7226 oz. ASW   **Obv:** Vulture, denomination above and dates below **Rev:** RE (Sun God) presenting the Ankh (Symbol of Life) to Sesostris I wearing Double Crown

Date	Mintage	F	VF	XF	Unc	BU
AH1415-1994 Proof	50,000	Value: 30.00				

KM# 753   5 POUNDS
22.5000 g., 0.9990 Silver 0.7226 oz. ASW   **Obv:** Vulture, denomination above and dates below **Rev:** God Horus wearing Double Crown

Date	Mintage	F	VF	XF	Unc	BU
AH1415-1994 Proof	50,000	Value: 30.00				

KM# 754   5 POUNDS
22.5000 g., 0.9990 Silver 0.7226 oz. ASW   **Obv:** Vulture, denomination above and dates below **Rev:** Standing god Seth left

Date	Mintage	F	VF	XF	Unc	BU
AH1415-1994 Proof	50,000	Value: 30.00				

KM# 757   5 POUNDS
22.5000 g., 0.9990 Silver 0.7226 oz. ASW   **Obv:** Vulture, denomination above and dates below **Rev:** Queen Nefretari, wife of Ramses II kneeling right

Date	Mintage	F	VF	XF	Unc	BU
AH1415-1994 Proof	Est. 25,000	Value: 37.50				

KM# 763   5 POUNDS
17.5000 g., 0.7200 Silver 0.4051 oz. ASW   **Subject:** Salah El Din El-Ayubi **Obv:** Dates and denomination within circle above text **Rev:** Bust at center, mosque behind at left, mounted rider with sword at right

Date	Mintage	F	VF	XF	Unc	BU
AH1414-1994	5,000	—	—	—	30.00	—

KM# 783   5 POUNDS
22.5000 g., 0.9990 Silver 0.7226 oz. ASW   **Obv:** Ancient style vulture **Rev:** Bust of Nefertiti right

Date	Mintage	F	VF	XF	Unc	BU
AH1415-1994 Proof	50,000	Value: 36.50				

KM# 784   5 POUNDS
22.5000 g., 0.9990 Silver 0.7226 oz. ASW   **Obv:** Vulture, denomination above and dates below **Rev:** Archer in chariot

Date	Mintage	F	VF	XF	Unc	BU
AH1415-1994 Proof	50,000	Value: 37.50				

KM# 785   5 POUNDS
22.5000 g., 0.9990 Silver 0.7226 oz. ASW   **Obv:** Vulture, denomination above and dates below **Rev:** Five birds

Date	Mintage	F	VF	XF	Unc	BU
AH1415-1994 Proof	50,000	Value: 40.00				

KM# 786   5 POUNDS
22.5000 g., 0.9990 Silver 0.7226 oz. ASW   **Obv:** Vulture, denomination above and dates below **Rev:** Hippopotamus right

Date	Mintage	F	VF	XF	Unc	BU
AH1415-1994 Proof	50,000	Value: 45.00				

KM# 787   5 POUNDS
22.5000 g., 0.9990 Silver 0.7226 oz. ASW   **Obv:** Vulture, denomination above and dates below **Rev:** Ruins of Karnak

Date	Mintage	F	VF	XF	Unc	BU
AH1415-1994 Proof	50,000	Value: 30.00				

KM# 788   5 POUNDS
22.5000 g., 0.9990 Silver 0.7226 oz. ASW   **Obv:** Vulture, denomination above and dates below **Rev:** Standing Goddess Neith wearing the Red Crown

Date	Mintage	F	VF	XF	Unc	BU
AH1415-1994 Proof	50,000	Value: 30.00				

KM# 789   5 POUNDS
22.5000 g., 0.9990 Silver 0.7226 oz. ASW   **Obv:** Vulture, denomination above and dates below **Rev:** Statue of King Amenemhat III

Date	Mintage	F	VF	XF	Unc	BU
AH1415-1994 Proof	50,000	Value: 30.00				

KM# 790   5 POUNDS
22.5000 g., 0.9990 Silver 0.7226 oz. ASW **Obv:** Vulture, denomination above and dates below **Rev:** Ritual mask of Queen Hatshepsut, female Pharoah, peacemaker, died 1468BC

Date	Mintage	F	VF	XF	Unc	BU
AH1415-1994 Proof	50,000	Value: 30.00				

KM# 792   5 POUNDS
15.0000 g., 0.7200 Silver 0.3472 oz. ASW **Subject:** ICPD Cairo **Obv:** Inscription and seals **Rev:** Stylized design

Date	Mintage	F	VF	XF	Unc	BU
AH1415-1994	—			—	17.50	—

KM# 794   5 POUNDS
22.5950 g., 0.9990 Silver 0.7257 oz. ASW **Obv:** Vulture, denomination above and dates below **Rev:** Seated, jeweled cat

Date	Mintage	F	VF	XF	Unc	BU
AH1415-1994 Proof	—	Value: 45.00				

KM# 795   5 POUNDS
22.5950 g., 0.9990 Silver 0.7257 oz. ASW **Obv:** Vulture, denomination above and dates below **Rev:** Sacred falcon at Edfu

Date	Mintage	F	VF	XF	Unc	BU
AH1415-1994 Proof	—	Value: 45.00				

KM# 797   5 POUNDS
22.5950 g., 0.9990 Silver 0.7257 oz. ASW **Obv:** Vulture, denomination above and dates below **Rev:** Tutankhamen's throne

Date	Mintage	F	VF	XF	Unc	BU
AH1415-1994 Proof	—	Value: 31.50				

KM# 798   5 POUNDS
22.5950 g., 0.9990 Silver 0.7257 oz. ASW **Obv:** Vulture, denomination above and dates below **Rev:** King Au as high priest

Date	Mintage	F	VF	XF	Unc	BU
AH1415-1994 Proof	—	Value: 31.50				

KM# 799   5 POUNDS
22.5950 g., 0.9990 Silver 0.7257 oz. ASW **Obv:** Vulture, denomination above and dates below **Rev:** Akhnaton

Date	Mintage	F	VF	XF	Unc	BU
AH1415-1994 Proof	—	Value: 40.00				

KM# 800   5 POUNDS
22.5950 g., 0.9990 Silver 0.7257 oz. ASW **Obv:** Vulture, denomination above and dates below **Rev:** Osiris, seated right

Date	Mintage	F	VF	XF	Unc	BU
AH1415-1994 Proof	—	Value: 30.00				

KM# 801   5 POUNDS
22.5950 g., 0.9990 Silver 0.7257 oz. ASW **Obv:** Vulture, denomination above and dates below **Rev:** RE, the sun god, walking left

Date	Mintage	F	VF	XF	Unc	BU
AH1415-1994 Proof	—	Value: 30.00				

KM# 802   5 POUNDS
22.5950 g., 0.9990 Silver 0.7257 oz. ASW **Obv:** Vulture, denomination above and dates below **Rev:** The God Khnoum, walking right

Date	Mintage	F	VF	XF	Unc	BU
AH1415-1994 Proof	—	Value: 37.50				

KM# 803   5 POUNDS
22.5950 g., 0.9990 Silver 0.7257 oz. ASW **Obv:** Vulture, denomination above and dates below **Rev:** Sobek, Crocodile God, walking left

Date	Mintage	F	VF	XF	Unc	BU
AH1415-1994 Proof	—	Value: 37.50				

KM# 813   5 POUNDS
22.5500 g., 0.9990 Silver 0.7242 oz. ASW **Obv:** Vulture, denomination above and dates below **Rev:** Ancient seated scribe **Edge:** Reeded

Date	Mintage	F	VF	XF	Unc	BU
AH1415-1994 Proof	—	Value: 37.50				

KM# 823 5 POUNDS
22.5000 g., 0.9990 Silver 0.7226 oz. ASW **Obv:** Vulture,
denomination above and dates below **Rev:** Temple of Ramses II

Date	Mintage	F	VF	XF	Unc	BU
AH1415-1994 Proof	—		Value: 36.50			

KM# 824 5 POUNDS
22.5000 g., 0.9990 Silver 0.7226 oz. ASW **Obv:** Vulture,
denomination above and dates below **Rev:** Ancient ruins

Date	Mintage	F	VF	XF	Unc	BU
AH1415-1994 Proof	—		Value: 30.00			

KM# 825 5 POUNDS
22.5000 g., 0.9990 Silver 0.7226 oz. ASW **Obv:** Vulture,
denomination above and dates below **Rev:** Egyptian gazelle right

Date	Mintage	F	VF	XF	Unc	BU
AH1415-1994 Proof	—		Value: 40.00			

KM# 826 5 POUNDS
22.5000 g., 0.9990 Silver 0.7226 oz. ASW **Obv:** Vulture,
denomination above and dates below **Rev:** King Thoutmosis III,
kneeling, left

Date	Mintage	F	VF	XF	Unc	BU
AH1415-1994 Proof	—		Value: 30.00			

KM# 827 5 POUNDS
22.5000 g., 0.9990 Silver 0.7226 oz. ASW **Obv:** Vulture,
denomination above and dates below **Rev:** Seated King Khufu

Date	Mintage	F	VF	XF	Unc	BU
AH1415-1994 Proof	—		Value: 30.00			

KM# 828 5 POUNDS
22.5000 g., 0.9990 Silver 0.7226 oz. ASW **Obv:** Vulture,
denomination above and dates below **Rev:** Standing Goddess
Hathor left

Date	Mintage	F	VF	XF	Unc	BU
AH1415-1994 Proof	—		Value: 30.00			

KM# 829 5 POUNDS
22.5000 g., 0.9990 Silver 0.7226 oz. ASW **Obv:** Vulture,
denomination above and dates below **Rev:** Standing God Ptah
of Memphis right

Date	Mintage	F	VF	XF	Unc	BU
AH1415-1994 Proof	—		Value: 30.00			

KM# 830 5 POUNDS
22.5000 g., 0.9990 Silver 0.7226 oz. ASW **Obv:** Vulture,
denomination above and dates below **Rev:** Seated Goddess Isis
nursing child

Date	Mintage	F	VF	XF	Unc	BU
AH1415-1994 Proof	—		Value: 30.00			

KM# 831 5 POUNDS
22.5000 g., 0.9990 Silver 0.7226 oz. ASW **Obv:** Vulture,
denomination above and dates below **Rev:** Dwarf Seneb and family

Date	Mintage	F	VF	XF	Unc	BU
AH1415-1994 Proof	—		Value: 30.00			

KM# 874 5 POUNDS
26.0000 g., 0.8750 Gold 0.7314 oz. AGW **Rev:** Sphinx and
pyramids

Date	Mintage	F	VF	XF	Unc	BU
AH1415-1994 Proof	5,000		Value: 765			

KM# 875 5 POUNDS
22.5000 g., 0.9990 Silver 0.7226 oz. ASW **Rev:** 3/4-length
standing Sheikh El Balad

Date	Mintage	F	VF	XF	Unc	BU
AH1415-1994 Proof	15,000		Value: 40.00			

KM# 876 5 POUNDS
26.0000 g., 0.8750 Gold 0.7314 oz. AGW **Rev:** 3/4-length
standing Sheikh El Balad

Date	Mintage	F	VF	XF	Unc	BU
AH1415-1994 Proof	3,000		Value: 760			

KM# 878 5 POUNDS
26.0000 g., 0.8750 Gold 0.7314 oz. AGW **Obv:** Vulture,
denomination above and dates below **Rev:** Dwarf Seneb and family

Date	Mintage	F	VF	XF	Unc	BU
AH1415-1994 Proof	3,000		Value: 760			

KM# 880 5 POUNDS
26.0000 g., 0.8750 Gold 0.7314 oz. AGW **Rev:** Kneeling King
Pepi I facing

Date	Mintage	F	VF	XF	Unc	BU
AH1415-1994 Proof	3,000		Value: 760			

KM# 881 5 POUNDS
26.0000 g., 0.8750 Gold 0.7314 oz. AGW **Rev:** Statue of King
Amenemhat III

Date	Mintage	F	VF	XF	Unc	BU
AH1415-1994 Proof	3,000		Value: 760			

KM# 883 5 POUNDS
22.5000 g., 0.9990 Silver 0.7226 oz. ASW **Rev:** Seated King
Horemheb

Date	Mintage	F	VF	XF	Unc	BU
AH1415-1994 Proof	15,000		Value: 40.00			

KM# 889 5 POUNDS
22.5000 g., 0.9990 Silver 0.7226 oz. ASW **Obv:** Vulture,
denomination above and dates below **Rev:** Akhnaton and family

Date	Mintage	F	VF	XF	Unc	BU
AH1415-1994 Proof	15,000		Value: 40.00			

KM# 894 5 POUNDS
22.5000 g., 0.9990 Silver 0.7226 oz. ASW **Obv:** Vulture,
denomination above and dates below **Rev:** Bust amulet of Hathor

Date	Mintage	F	VF	XF	Unc	BU
AH1415-1994 Proof	15,000		Value: 40.00			

KM# 896 5 POUNDS
22.5000 g., 0.9990 Silver 0.7226 oz. ASW **Rev:** Pair of geese

Date	Mintage	F	VF	XF	Unc	BU
AH1415-1994 Proof	15,000		Value: 40.00			

KM# 765   5 POUNDS
17.5000 g., 0.7200 Silver 0.4051 oz. ASW **Subject:** 50 Years - Arab League **Obv:** Dates and denomination within circle above text **Rev:** Buildings and emblem

Date	Mintage	F	VF	XF	Unc	BU
AH1415-1995	5,000	—	—	—	22.50	—

KM# 768   5 POUNDS
17.5000 g., 0.7200 Silver 0.4051 oz. ASW **Subject:** 75 Years - Bank of Misr

Date	Mintage	F	VF	XF	Unc	BU
AH1415-1995	2,500	—	—	—	28.00	—

KM# 770   5 POUNDS
17.5000 g., 0.7200 Silver 0.4051 oz. ASW **Series:** F.A.O. **Obv:** Tughra above logo **Rev:** People working

Date	Mintage	F	VF	XF	Unc	BU
AH1415-1995	5,000	—	—	—	50.00	—

KM# 838   5 POUNDS
17.5000 g., 0.7200 Silver 0.4051 oz. ASW **Subject:** 75 Years - American University in Cairo **Rev:** Design in center surrounded by inscriptions and border

Date	Mintage	F	VF	XF	Unc	BU
AH1415-1995	3,000	—	—	—	25.00	—

KM# 772   5 POUNDS
17.5000 g., 0.7200 Silver 0.4051 oz. ASW **Subject:** Pediatrics International Conference

Date	Mintage	F	VF	XF	Unc	BU
AH1416-1995	4,000	—	—	—	25.00	—

KM# 774   5 POUNDS
26.0000 g., 0.8750 Gold 0.7314 oz. AGW **Subject:** 75 Years - Architects Association **Obv:** Tughra **Rev:** Head left

Date	Mintage	F	VF	XF	Unc	BU
AH1416-1995	300	—	—	—	775	—

KM# 841   5 POUNDS
17.5000 g., 0.7200 Silver 0.4051 oz. ASW **Obv:** Tughra **Rev:** Abd Al Halem Hafez left

Date	Mintage	F	VF	XF	Unc	BU
AH1416-1995	5,000	—	—	—	45.00	—

KM# 842   5 POUNDS
26.0000 g., 0.8750 Gold 0.7314 oz. AGW **Rev:** Abd Al Halem Hafez

Date	Mintage	F	VF	XF	Unc	BU
AH1416-1995	500	—	—	—	775	—

KM# 843   5 POUNDS
17.5000 g., 0.9000 Silver 0.5064 oz. ASW **Subject:** Centennial - Mining and Geology **Obv:** Denomination with toughra **Rev:** Building in circle

Date	Mintage	F	VF	XF	Unc	BU
AH1416-1996	700	—	—	—	75.00	—

KM# 973   5 POUNDS
17.5000 g., 0.7200 Silver 0.4051 oz. ASW, 37 mm. **Subject:** 4th World Youth Cup **Obv:** Ornate doorway **Rev:** Stylized player on soccer ball **Rev. Insc.:** 4th U.17 WORLD CHAMPIONSHIP / FOR THE FIFA/IYC CUP EGYPT 1997 **Edge:** Reeded

Date	Mintage	F	VF	XF	Unc	BU
AH1418-1997	850	—	—	—	—	125

KM# 846   5 POUNDS
17.5000 g., 0.9000 Silver 0.5064 oz. ASW **Subject:** 65 Years - Egyptian Air Force **Rev:** Flying eagle in wreath

Date	Mintage	F	VF	XF	Unc	BU
AH1418-1997	300	—	—	—	85.00	—

KM# 848   5 POUNDS
17.5000 g., 0.9000 Silver 0.5064 oz. ASW **Subject:** 50 Years Arab Land Bank **Rev:** Arab Real Estate domed Bank building

Date	Mintage	F	VF	XF	Unc	BU
AH1418-1997	3,000	—	—	—	37.50	—

KM# 850   5 POUNDS
17.5000 g., 0.9000 Silver 0.5064 oz. ASW **Subject:** 95th Interparliamentary Union Conference **Obv:** Circular design above inscription **Rev:** Pyramids in wreath

Date	Mintage	F	VF	XF	Unc	BU
AH1418-1997	375	—	—	—	85.00	—

KM# 852   5 POUNDS
17.5000 g., 0.9000 Silver 0.5064 oz. ASW **Subject:** Centennial - Chemical Department **Rev:** Symbolic design

Date	Mintage	F	VF	XF	Unc	BU
AH1419-1998	1,000	—	—	—	40.00	—

KM# 853   5 POUNDS
17.5000 g., 0.9000 Silver 0.5064 oz. ASW **Subject:** Restoration of Al Azhar Mosque

Date	Mintage	F	VF	XF	Unc	BU
AH1419-1998	4,000	—	—	—	37.50	—

KM# 856   5 POUNDS
17.5000 g., 0.9000 Silver 0.5064 oz. ASW **Subject:** Centennial of National Bank **Rev:** Large "100"

Date	Mintage	F	VF	XF	Unc	BU
AH1419-1998	2,000	—	—	—	85.00	—

KM# 858   5 POUNDS
17.5000 g., 0.9000 Silver 0.5064 oz. ASW **Subject:** 25th Anniversary - October War **Rev:** Symbolic design

Date	Mintage	F	VF	XF	Unc	BU
AH1419-1998	1,500	—	—	—	40.00	—

KM# 860   5 POUNDS
17.5000 g., 0.9000 Silver 0.5064 oz. ASW **Subject:** Death of El Sheikh M. Metwaly El Sharawy **Rev:** Bust of Imam Metwaly El Sharawi facing

Date	Mintage	F	VF	XF	Unc	BU
AH1419-1998	3,000	—	—	—	40.00	—

KM# 862   5 POUNDS
17.5000 g., 0.9000 Silver 0.5064 oz. ASW **Subject:** Centennial - Land Surveying **Rev:** "100" above ancient surveyors

Date	Mintage	F	VF	XF	Unc	BU
AH1419-1998	6,000	—	—	—	40.00	—

KM# 864   5 POUNDS
17.5000 g., 0.9000 Silver 0.5064 oz. ASW **Subject:** Centennial - Solidarity **Rev:** Symbolic design

Date	Mintage	F	VF	XF	Unc	BU
AH1419-1998	9,500	—	—	—	37.50	—

KM# 854   5 POUNDS
17.5000 g., 0.9000 Silver 0.5064 oz. ASW **Subject:** 16th Men's World Handball Championship **Obv:** Denomination and dates **Rev:** Handball game

Date	Mintage	F	VF	XF	Unc	BU
AH1420-1999	6,500	—	—	—	45.00	—

KM# 867   5 POUNDS
17.5000 g., 0.9000 Silver 0.5064 oz. ASW **Subject:** 50 Years Cairo Metropolitan Mass Transit System **Rev:** Water above subway train

Date	Mintage	F	VF	XF	Unc	BU
AH1420-1999	2,000	—	—	—	40.00	—

KM# 897   5 POUNDS
17.5000 g., 0.9000 Silver 0.5064 oz. ASW **Subject:** 75 Years - Dar El-Eloum University

Date	Mintage	F	VF	XF	Unc	BU
AH1420-1999	2,000	—	—	—	40.00	—

KM# 898   5 POUNDS
17.3300 g., 0.9750 Silver 0.5432 oz. ASW, 37 mm. **Subject:** Sacred falcon **Obv:** Denomination and inscription **Rev:** Ancient sacred falcon **Edge:** Reeded

Date	Mintage	F	VF	XF	Unc	BU
AH1420-1999 Proof	—	Value: 50.00				

KM# 899   5 POUNDS
17.3300 g., 0.9750 Silver 0.5432 oz. ASW, 37 mm. **Obv:** Denomination and inscription **Rev:** Two statues of Ramses II **Edge:** Reeded

Date	Mintage	F	VF	XF	Unc	BU
AH1420-1999 Proof	—	Value: 50.00				

KM# 773   5 POUNDS
17.5000 g., 0.7200 Silver 0.4051 oz. ASW **Subject:** 75 Years - Architects Association **Obv:** Outline of building divides dates **Rev:** Seated statue

Date	Mintage	F	VF	XF	Unc	BU
AH1416-1995	3,000	—	—	—	50.00	—

KM# 900 5 POUNDS
17.3300 g., 0.9750 Silver 0.5432 oz. ASW, 37 mm.
Obv: Denomination and inscription **Rev:** Tutankhamen's Death
Mask **Edge:** Reeded

Date	Mintage	F	VF	XF	Unc	BU
AH1420-1999 Proof	—	Value: 50.00				

KM# 901 5 POUNDS
17.3300 g., 0.9750 Silver 0.5432 oz. ASW, 37 mm. **Obv:** Denomination and inscription **Rev:** Bust of Nefertiti right **Edge:** Reeded

Date	Mintage	F	VF	XF	Unc	BU
AH1420-1999 Proof	—	Value: 50.00				

KM# 902 5 POUNDS
17.3300 g., 0.9750 Silver 0.5432 oz. ASW, 37 mm.
Obv: Denomination and inscription **Rev:** Imaginary bust of
Cleopatra left **Edge:** Reeded

Date	Mintage	F	VF	XF	Unc	BU
AH1420-1999 Proof	—	Value: 50.00				

KM# 927 5 POUNDS
17.5000 g., 0.7200 Silver 0.4051 oz. ASW, 37 mm.
Subject: Ain Shams University **Obv:** Value **Rev:** Shams
University logo above anniversary dates 2000-1950
Edge: Reeded

Date	Mintage	F	VF	XF	Unc	BU
AH1420-1999	1,000	—	—	—	45.00	—

KM# 929 5 POUNDS
17.5000 g., 0.7200 Silver 0.4051 oz. ASW, 37 mm.
Subject: National Insurance Company Centennial **Obv:** Value
Rev: Ancient seated figure with "100" **Edge:** Reeded

Date	Mintage	F	VF	XF	Unc	BU
AH1421-2000	2,500	—	—	—	45.00	—

KM# 519 10 POUNDS
40.0000 g., 0.8750 Gold 1.1252 oz. AGW **Subject:** Egyptian-
Israeli Peace Treaty **Obv:** Denomination divides dates **Rev:** Head
at right facing left, dove with olive branch at left

Date	Mintage	F	VF	XF	Unc	BU
AH1400-1980	950	—	—	—	1,100	1,150
AH1400-1980 Proof	50	Value: 1,350				

KM# 538 10 POUNDS
40.0000 g., 0.8750 Gold 1.1252 oz. AGW **Subject:** 25th
Anniversary - Ministry of Industry **Obv:** Text, denomination and
dates **Rev:** Factory building, cogwheel at right

Date	Mintage	F	VF	XF	Unc	BU
AH1402-1981	18	—	—	—	1,600	
AH1402-1981 Proof	1,000	Value: 1,100				

KM# 548 10 POUNDS
40.0000 g., 0.8750 Gold 1.1252 oz. AGW **Subject:** 1000th
Anniversary - Al Azhar Mosque **Obv:** Text within circle divides
dates **Rev:** Mosque

Date	Mintage	F	VF	XF	Unc	BU
AH1402-1982 Proof	1,322	Value: 1,050				

KM# 634 10 POUNDS
40.0000 g., 0.8750 Gold 1.1252 oz. AGW **Subject:** Prophet's
Mosque **Obv:** Minaret, globe, denomination, legends
Rev: Crescent, mosque, minaret below legend arch

Date	Mintage	F	VF	XF	Unc	BU
AH1406-1985 Proof	300	Value: 1,150				

KM# 672 50 POUNDS
8.5000 g., 0.9000 Gold 0.2459 oz. AGW **Series:** World Soccer
Championships **Obv:** Stylized flowers, denomination, date and
legends **Rev:** Soccer ball on road between Mexican and Egyptian
pyramids

Date	Mintage	F	VF	XF	Unc	BU
AH1406-1986	250	—	—	—	300	—
AH1406-1986 Proof	250	Value: 350				

KM# 641 50 POUNDS
8.5000 g., 0.9000 Gold 0.2459 oz. AGW **Subject:** Mecca **Obv:**
Arabic legend, ornamentation **Rev:** Interior view of the Kaaba

Date	Mintage	F	VF	XF	Unc	BU
AH1406-1986	14,000	—	—	—	250	—

KM# 612 50 POUNDS
8.5000 g., 0.9000 Gold 0.2459 oz. AGW **Subject:** Aida Opera
Obv: Radiant sun, pillars and inscriptions **Rev:** Ancient figures
among ruins

Date	Mintage	F	VF	XF	Unc	BU
AH1407-1987	40,000	—	—	—	275	—

KM# 625 50 POUNDS
8.5000 g., 0.9000 Gold 0.2459 oz. AGW **Series:** Summer
Olympics **Obv:** Arabic legend and ornamentation within English
legend **Rev:** Pharoah and athletes

Date	Mintage	F	VF	XF	Unc	BU
AH1408-1988	150	—	—	—	350	—
AH1408-1988 Proof	50	Value: 400				

KM# 627 50 POUNDS
8.5000 g., 0.9000 Gold 0.2459 oz. AGW **Series:** Summer
Olympics **Rev:** Athletes and mythological figures

Date	Mintage	F	VF	XF	Unc	BU
AH1408-1988	750	—	—	—	300	—
AH1408-1988 Proof	250	Value: 350				

KM# 629 50 POUNDS
8.5000 g., 0.9000 Gold 0.2459 oz. AGW **Series:** Winter
Olympics **Obv:** Winged design, English legend, Arabic inscription
Rev: Ski jumper and figure skater within Arabic legend

Date	Mintage	F	VF	XF	Unc	BU
AH1408-1988	150	—	—	—	350	—
AH1408-1988 Proof	50	Value: 400				

KM# 680 50 POUNDS
8.5000 g., 0.9000 Gold 0.2459 oz. AGW **Subject:** Soccer World
Championship - Italy **Obv:** Text within circle at center of wings,
denomination and dates above **Rev:** Ancient gods

Date	Mintage	F	VF	XF	Unc	BU
AH1410-1990 Proof	225	Value: 450				

KM# 683 50 POUNDS
8.5000 g., 0.9000 Gold 0.2459 oz. AGW **Subject:** Soccer World
Championship **Rev:** Player chasing ball

Date	Mintage	F	VF	XF	Unc	BU
AH1410-1990 Proof	75	Value: 525				

KM# 709 50 POUNDS
8.5000 g., 0.9000 Gold 0.2459 oz. AGW **Series:** Summer
Olympics **Obv:** Text within circle at center of wings, denomination
and dates above **Rev:** Fencing

Date	Mintage	F	VF	XF	Unc	BU
AH1412-1992	49	—	—	—	475	—
AH1412-1992 Proof	99	Value: 475				

KM# 710 50 POUNDS
8.5000 g., 0.9000 Gold 0.2459 oz. AGW **Series:** Summer
Olympics **Obv:** Text within circle at center of wings, denomination
and dates above **Rev:** Wrestling, half globe below

Date	Mintage	F	VF	XF	Unc	BU
AH1412-1992	49	—	—	—	475	—
AH1412-1992 Proof	99	Value: 475				

KM# 711 50 POUNDS
8.5000 g., 0.9000 Gold 0.2459 oz. AGW **Series:** Summer
Olympics **Obv:** Text within circle at center of wings, denomination
and dates above **Rev:** Archery

Date	Mintage	F	VF	XF	Unc	BU
AH1412-1992	49	—	—	—	475	—
AH1412-1992 Proof	99	Value: 475				

KM# 712 50 POUNDS
8.5000 g., 0.9000 Gold 0.2459 oz. AGW **Series:** Summer
Olympics **Obv:** Text within circle at center of wings, denomination
and dates above **Rev:** Many men wrestling an ox

Date	Mintage	F	VF	XF	Unc	BU
AH1412-1992	49	—	—	—	475	—
AH1412-1992 Proof	99	Value: 475				

KM# 713 50 POUNDS
8.5000 g., 0.9000 Gold 0.2459 oz. AGW **Series:** Summer Olympics **Obv:** Text within circle at center of wings, denomination and dates above **Rev:** Swimmer stalking a duck

Date	Mintage	F	VF	XF	Unc	BU
AH1412-1992	49	—	—	—	475	—
AH1412-1992 Proof	99	Value: 475				

KM# 714 50 POUNDS
8.5000 g., 0.9000 Gold 0.2459 oz. AGW **Series:** Summer Olympics **Obv:** Text within circle at center of wings, denomination and dates above **Rev:** Handball player

Date	Mintage	F	VF	XF	Unc	BU
AH1412-1992	49	—	—	—	475	—
AH1412-1992 Proof	99	Value: 475				

KM# 715 50 POUNDS
8.5000 g., 0.9000 Gold 0.2459 oz. AGW **Series:** Summer Olympics **Obv:** Text within circle at center of wings, denomination and dates above **Rev:** Field hockey player

Date	Mintage	F	VF	XF	Unc	BU
AH1412-1992	49	—	—	—	475	—
AH1412-1992 Proof	99	Value: 475				

KM# 716 50 POUNDS
8.5000 g., 0.9000 Gold 0.2459 oz. AGW **Series:** Summer Olympics **Obv:** Text within circle at center of wings, denomination and dates above **Rev:** Soccer player kicking ball

Date	Mintage	F	VF	XF	Unc	BU
AH1412-1992	49	—	—	—	475	—
AH1412-1992 Proof	115	Value: 475				

KM# 755 50 POUNDS
8.5000 g., 0.9000 Gold 0.2459 oz. AGW **Obv:** Vulture, denomination above and dates below **Rev:** King Tutankhamen's burial mask

Date	Mintage	F	VF	XF	Unc	BU
AH1414-1993 Proof	—	Value: 300				

KM# 756 50 POUNDS
8.5000 g., 0.9000 Gold 0.2459 oz. AGW **Subject:** Cleopatra **Obv:** Vulture, denomination above and dates below **Rev:** Bust left

Date	Mintage	F	VF	XF	Unc	BU
AH1414-1993 Proof	—	Value: 275				

KM# 776 50 POUNDS
8.5000 g., 0.9000 Gold 0.2459 oz. AGW **Obv:** Vulture, denomination above and dates below **Rev:** Sphinx head

Date	Mintage	F	VF	XF	Unc	BU
AH1414-1993 Proof	—	Value: 250				

KM# 777 50 POUNDS
8.5000 g., 0.9000 Gold 0.2459 oz. AGW **Obv:** Vulture, denomination above and dates below **Rev:** Standing Ramses II

Date	Mintage	F	VF	XF	Unc	BU
AH1414-1993 Proof	—	Value: 250				

KM# 868 50 POUNDS
8.5000 g., 0.9000 Gold 0.2459 oz. AGW **Subject:** King Narmer Palette **Obv:** Vulture, denomination above and dates below **Rev:** King killing a wounded foe

Date	Mintage	F	VF	XF	Unc	BU
AH1414-1993 Proof	3,000	Value: 285				

KM# 870 50 POUNDS
8.5000 g., 0.9000 Gold 0.2459 oz. AGW **Subject:** King Kna-Sekhem **Obv:** Vulture, denomination above and dates below **Rev:** Seated king

Date	Mintage	F	VF	XF	Unc	BU
AH1414-1993 Proof	3,000	Value: 285				

KM# 873 50 POUNDS
8.5000 g., 0.9000 Gold 0.2459 oz. AGW **Subject:** Menkaure Triad **Obv:** Vulture, denomination above and dates below **Rev:** Three carved figurines

Date	Mintage	F	VF	XF	Unc	BU
AH1414-1993 Proof	3,000	Value: 285				

KM# 885 50 POUNDS
8.5000 g., 0.9000 Gold 0.2459 oz. AGW **Subject:** Thoutmosis III **Obv:** Vulture, denomination above and dates below **Rev:** Kneeling figure holding jar

Date	Mintage	F	VF	XF	Unc	BU
AH1414-1993 Proof	3,000	Value: 285				

KM# 775 50 POUNDS
8.5000 g., 0.9000 Gold 0.2459 oz. AGW **Obv:** Vulture, denomination above and dates below **Rev:** Three pyramids

Date	Mintage	F	VF	XF	Unc	BU
AH1414-1993 Proof	—	Value: 250				

KM# 778 50 POUNDS
8.5000 g., 0.9000 Gold 0.2459 oz. AGW **Obv:** Vulture, denomination above and dates below **Rev:** Crowned falcon left

Date	Mintage	F	VF	XF	Unc	BU
AH1415-1994 Proof	—	Value: 275				

KM# 737 50 POUNDS
8.5000 g., 0.9000 Gold 0.2459 oz. AGW **Series:** World Cup Soccer **Obv:** Text within circle at center of wings, oval shield above divides dates **Rev:** Two players, pyramid and Statue of Liberty

Date	Mintage	F	VF	XF	Unc	BU
AH1415-1994	99	—	—	—	350	—
AH1415-1994 Proof	99	Value: 350				

KM# 739 50 POUNDS
8.5000 g., 0.9000 Gold 0.2459 oz. AGW **Series:** World Cup Soccer **Obv:** Text within circle at center of wings, oval shield above divides dates **Rev:** Stylized player

Date	Mintage	F	VF	XF	Unc	BU
AH1415-1994	99	—	—	—	350	—
AH1415-1994 Proof	99	Value: 350				

KM# 779 50 POUNDS
8.5000 g., 0.9000 Gold 0.2459 oz. AGW **Subject:** Queen Nefertiti **Obv:** Vulture, denomination above and dates below **Rev:** Bust right

Date	Mintage	F	VF	XF	Unc	BU
AH1415-1994 Proof	—	Value: 250				

KM# 780 50 POUNDS
8.5000 g., 0.9000 Gold 0.2459 oz. AGW **Obv:** Vulture, denomination above and dates below **Rev:** Seated cat right

Date	Mintage	F	VF	XF	Unc	BU
AH1415-1994 Proof	—	Value: 250				

KM# 781 50 POUNDS
8.5000 g., 0.9000 Gold 0.2459 oz. AGW **Obv:** Vulture, denomination above and dates below **Rev:** Archer in chariot

Date	Mintage	F	VF	XF	Unc	BU
AH1415-1994 Proof	—	Value: 265				

KM# 782 50 POUNDS
8.5000 g., 0.9000 Gold 0.2459 oz. AGW **Obv:** Vulture, denomination above and dates below **Rev:** Standing God Seth left

Date	Mintage	F	VF	XF	Unc	BU
AH1415-1994 Proof	—	Value: 245				

KM# 814 50 POUNDS
8.5000 g., 0.9000 Gold 0.2459 oz. AGW **Obv:** Vulture, denomination above and dates below **Rev:** Hippopotamus

Date	Mintage	F	VF	XF	Unc	BU
AH1415-1994 Proof	—	Value: 245				

KM# 815 50 POUNDS
8.5000 g., 0.9000 Gold 0.2459 oz. AGW **Obv:** Vulture, denomination above and dates below **Rev:** Egyptian gazelle

Date	Mintage	F	VF	XF	Unc	BU
AH1415-1994 Proof	—	Value: 245				

KM# 816 50 POUNDS
8.5000 g., 0.9000 Gold 0.2459 oz. AGW **Obv:** Vulture, denomination above and dates below **Rev:** Phoenix birds

Date	Mintage	F	VF	XF	Unc	BU
AH1415-1994 Proof	—	Value: 245				

KM# 817 50 POUNDS
8.5000 g., 0.9000 Gold 0.2459 oz. AGW **Obv:** Vulture, denomination above and dates below **Rev:** Egyptian geese

Date	Mintage	F	VF	XF	Unc	BU
AH1415-1994 Proof	—	Value: 245				

KM# 818 50 POUNDS
8.5000 g., 0.9000 Gold 0.2459 oz. AGW **Obv:** Vulture, denomination above and dates below **Rev:** King Taharqa

Date	Mintage	F	VF	XF	Unc	BU
AH1415-1994 Proof	—	Value: 245				

KM# 819 50 POUNDS
8.5000 g., 0.9000 Gold 0.2459 oz. AGW **Obv:** Vulture, denomination above and dates below **Rev:** Amenhotep Temple

Date	Mintage	F	VF	XF	Unc	BU
AH1415-1994 Proof	—	Value: 245				

KM# 820 50 POUNDS
8.5000 g., 0.9000 Gold 0.2459 oz. AGW **Obv:** Vulture, denomination above and dates below **Rev:** Karnak Temple

Date	Mintage	F	VF	XF	Unc	BU
AH1415-1994 Proof	—	Value: 245				

KM# 821 50 POUNDS
8.5000 g., 0.9000 Gold 0.2459 oz. AGW **Obv:** Vulture, denomination above and dates below **Rev:** Philae Temple

Date	Mintage	F	VF	XF	Unc	BU
AH1415-1994 Proof	—	Value: 245				

KM# 822 50 POUNDS
8.5000 g., 0.9000 Gold 0.2459 oz. AGW **Obv:** Vulture, denomination above and dates below **Rev:** Khonsu Temple

Date	Mintage	F	VF	XF	Unc	BU
AH1415-1994 Proof	—	Value: 245				

KM# 871 50 POUNDS
8.5000 g., 0.9000 Gold 0.2459 oz. AGW **Obv:** Vulture, denomination above and dates below **Rev:** King Djoser wearing the Red Crown

Date	Mintage	F	VF	XF	Unc	BU
AH1415-1994 Proof	3,000	Value: 275				

KM# 872 50 POUNDS
8.5000 g., 0.9000 Gold 0.2459 oz. AGW **Obv:** Vulture, denomination above and dates below **Rev:** Seated King Khufu with flat-top hat

Date	Mintage	F	VF	XF	Unc	BU
AH1415-1994 Proof	3,000	Value: 275				

KM# 882 50 POUNDS
8.5000 g., 0.9000 Gold 0.2459 oz. AGW **Subject:** King Sesostris I **Obv:** Vulture, denomination above and dates below **Rev:** RE (sun god) presenting the ANKH (symbol of life) to the king wearing the Double Crown

Date	Mintage	F	VF	XF	Unc	BU
AH1415-1994 Proof	3,000	Value: 275				

KM# 884 50 POUNDS
8.5000 g., 0.9000 Gold 0.2459 oz. AGW **Subject:** King Horemheb **Obv:** Vulture, denomination above and dates below **Rev:** Seated King Horemheb

Date	Mintage	F	VF	XF	Unc	BU
AH1415-1994 Proof	3,000	Value: 275				

KM# 886 50 POUNDS
8.5000 g., 0.9000 Gold 0.2459 oz. AGW **Subject:** King Khonsu **Obv:** Vulture, denomination above and dates below **Rev:** 1/2-length King Khonsu

Date	Mintage	F	VF	XF	Unc	BU
AH1415-1994 Proof	3,000	Value: 275				

KM# 887 50 POUNDS
8.5000 g., 0.9000 Gold 0.2459 oz. AGW **Subject:** Tutankhamen's Throne **Obv:** Vulture, denomination above and dates below **Rev:** King Tut seated on throne with servant

Date	Mintage	F	VF	XF	Unc	BU
AH1415-1994 Proof	3,000	Value: 300				

KM# 888 50 POUNDS
8.5000 g., 0.9000 Gold 0.2459 oz. AGW **Subject:** Queen Hatshepsut **Obv:** Vulture, denomination above and dates below **Rev:** Queen's facial sculpture

Date	Mintage	F	VF	XF	Unc	BU
AH1415-1994 Proof	3,000	Value: 275				

KM# 890 50 POUNDS
8.5000 g., 0.9000 Gold 0.2459 oz. AGW **Subject:** Akhnaton and Family **Obv:** Vulture, denomination above and dates below **Rev:** Family scene

Date	Mintage	F	VF	XF	Unc	BU
AH1415-1994 Proof	3,000	Value: 275				

KM# 891 50 POUNDS
8.5000 g., 0.9000 Gold 0.2459 oz. AGW **Obv:** Vulture, denomination above and dates below **Rev:** Akhnaton

Date	Mintage	F	VF	XF	Unc	BU
AH1415-1994 Proof	3,000	Value: 275				

KM# 892 50 POUNDS
8.5000 g., 0.9000 Gold 0.2459 oz. AGW **Subject:** Queen Nefertarl **Obv:** Vulture, denomination above and dates below **Rev:** Kneeling Queen Nefertarl

Date	Mintage	F	VF	XF	Unc	BU
AH1415-1994 Proof	5,000	Value: 275				

KM# 893 50 POUNDS
8.5000 g., 0.9000 Gold 0.2459 oz. AGW **Subject:** Ramses III **Obv:** Vulture, denomination above and dates below **Rev:** 3/4-length Ramses III

Date	Mintage	F	VF	XF	Unc	BU
AH1415-1994 Proof	3,000	Value: 300				

KM# 895 50 POUNDS
8.5000 g., 0.9000 Gold 0.2459 oz. AGW **Obv:** Vulture, denomination above and dates below **Rev:** Amulet of Hathor

Date	Mintage	F	VF	XF	Unc	BU
AH1415-1994 Proof	3,000	Value: 275				

KM# 877 50 POUNDS
26.0000 g., 0.8750 Gold 0.7314 oz. AGW **Obv:** Vulture, denomination above and dates below **Rev:** Ancient seated scribe

Date	Mintage	F	VF	XF	Unc	BU
AH1415-1994 Proof	3,000	Value: 750				

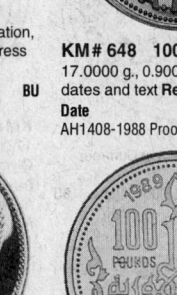

KM# 921 50 POUNDS
11.8000 g., 0.9000 Gold 0.3414 oz. AGW, 26 mm. **Obv:** Value and inscription **Rev:** Statue of Ramses II seated **Edge:** Reeded

Date	Mintage	F	VF	XF	Unc	BU
AH1420-1999 Proof	—	Value: 350				

KM# 550 100 POUNDS
17.1500 g., 0.9000 Gold 0.4962 oz. AGW **Obv:** Denomination, dates and text **Rev:** Bust of Queen Nefertiti right

Date	Mintage	F	VF	XF	Unc	BU
AH1404-1983 Proof	16,000	Value: 725				

KM# 562 100 POUNDS
17.1500 g., 0.9000 Gold 0.4962 oz. AGW **Obv:** Denomination, dates and text **Rev:** Bust of Cleopatra VII in formal headdress left 69-30BC, Queen and statesperson

Date	Mintage	F	VF	XF	Unc	BU
AH1404-1984 Proof	2,121	Value: 800				

KM# 569 100 POUNDS
17.1500 g., 0.9000 Gold 0.4962 oz. AGW **Obv:** Denomination, dates and text **Rev:** The golden falcon, from an ancient breastplate found in King Tutankhamen's tomb

Date	Mintage	F	VF	XF	Unc	BU
AH1405-1985 Proof	1,800	Value: 600				

KM# 591 100 POUNDS
17.1500 g., 0.9000 Gold 0.4962 oz. AGW **Rev:** Tutankhamen

Date	Mintage	F	VF	XF	Unc	BU
AH1406-1986 Proof	7,500	Value: 775				

KM# 642 100 POUNDS
17.0000 g., 0.9000 Gold 0.4919 oz. AGW **Subject:** Mecca **Obv:** Arabic legend, ornamentation **Rev:** Interior view of the Kaaba

Date	Mintage	F	VF	XF	Unc	BU
AH1406-1986	700	—	—	—	675	

KM# 613 100 POUNDS
17.0000 g., 0.9000 Gold 0.4919 oz. AGW **Obv:** Denomination, dates and text **Rev:** The golden ram

Date	Mintage	F	VF	XF	Unc	BU
AH1407-1987 Proof	7,500	Value: 600				

KM# 648 100 POUNDS
17.0000 g., 0.9000 Gold 0.4919 oz. AGW **Obv:** Denomination, dates and text **Rev:** The golden warrior

Date	Mintage	F	VF	XF	Unc	BU
AH1408-1988 Proof	5,500	Value: 600				

KM# 656 100 POUNDS
17.1500 g., 0.9000 Gold 0.4962 oz. AGW **Obv:** Denomination, dates and text **Rev:** The golden cat

Date	Mintage	F	VF	XF	Unc	BU
AH1409-1989 FM Proof	Est. 7,500	Value: 600				

KM# 681   100 POUNDS
17.0000 g., 0.9000 Gold 0.4919 oz. AGW **Series:** World Soccer Championship - Italy **Rev:** Ancient gods

Date	Mintage	F	VF	XF	.Unc	BU
AH1410-1990 Proof	125				Value: 800	

KM# 684   100 POUNDS
17.0000 g., 0.9000 Gold 0.4919 oz. AGW **Series:** World Soccer Championship - Italy **Rev:** Player chasing ball

Date	Mintage	F	VF	XF	BU
AH1410-1990 Proof	75			Value: 825	

KM# 693   100 POUNDS
17.0000 g., 0.9000 Gold 0.4919 oz. AGW **Series:** Ancient Egyptian Culture **Obv:** Denomination, dates and text **Rev:** Sphinx

Date	Mintage	F	VF	XF	Unc	BU
AH1410-1990 FM Proof	Est. 5,000			Value: 650		

KM# 729   100 POUNDS
17.0000 g., 0.9000 Gold 0.4919 oz. AGW **Series:** Ancient Egyptian Culture **Obv:** Denomination, dates and text **Rev:** Pyramids of Giza

Date	Mintage	F	VF	XF	Unc	BU
AH1411-1991 Proof	Est. 5,000			Value: 650		

KM# 717   100 POUNDS
17.0000 g., 0.9000 Gold 0.4919 oz. AGW **Series:** Summer Olympics **Rev:** Fencing

Date	Mintage	F	VF	XF	Unc	BU
AH1412-1992	49	—	—	—	845	—
AH1412-1992 Proof	99		Value: 850			

KM# 718   100 POUNDS
17.0000 g., 0.9000 Gold 0.4919 oz. AGW **Series:** Summer Olympics **Obv:** Text within circle at center of wings, denomination and dates above **Rev:** Wrestling matches

Date	Mintage	F	VF	XF	Unc	BU
AH1412-1992	49	—	—	—	850	—
AH1412-1992 Proof	99			Value: 845		

KM# 719   100 POUNDS
17.0000 g., 0.9000 Gold 0.4919 oz. AGW **Series:** Summer Olympics **Obv:** Text within circle at center of wings, denomination and dates above **Rev:** Archery demonstration

Date	Mintage	F	VF	XF	Unc	BU
AH1412-1992	49	—	—	—	845	—
AH1412-1992 Proof	99		Value: 850			

KM# 720   100 POUNDS
17.0000 g., 0.9000 Gold 0.4919 oz. AGW **Series:** Summer Olympics **Obv:** Text within circle at center of wings, denomination and dates above **Rev:** Many men wrestling an ox

Date	Mintage	F	VF	XF	Unc	BU
AH1412-1992	49	—	—	—	845	—
AH1412-1992 Proof	99		Value: 850			

KM# 721   100 POUNDS
17.0000 g., 0.9000 Gold 0.4919 oz. AGW **Series:** Summer Olympics **Rev:** Swimmer stalking a duck

Date	Mintage	F	VF	XF	Unc	BU
AH1412-1992	49	—	—	—	845	—
AH1412-1992 Proof	99		Value: 850			

KM# 722   100 POUNDS
17.0000 g., 0.9000 Gold 0.4919 oz. AGW **Series:** Summer Olympics **Rev:** Handball player

Date	Mintage	F	VF	XF	Unc	BU
AH1412-1992	49	—	—	—	845	—
AH1412-1992 Proof	99		Value: 850			

KM# 723   100 POUNDS
17.0000 g., 0.9000 Gold 0.4919 oz. AGW **Series:** Summer Olympics **Rev:** Field hockey player

Date	Mintage	F	VF	XF	Unc	BU
AH1412-1992	49	—	—	—	845	—
AH1412-1992 Proof	99		Value: 850			

KM# 724   100 POUNDS
17.0000 g., 0.9000 Gold 0.4919 oz. AGW **Series:** Summer Olympics **Rev:** Soccer player

Date	Mintage	F	VF	XF	Unc	BU
AH1412-1992	49	—	—	—	850	—
AH1412-1992 Proof	115		Value: 845			

KM# 730   100 POUNDS
17.1500 g., 0.9000 Gold 0.4962 oz. AGW **Subject:** The Golden Guardians **Obv:** Denomination, dates and text **Rev:** Two statues of Ramses II

Date	Mintage	F	VF	XF	Unc	BU
1992 Proof	Est. 5,000			Value: 650		

PATTERNS
Including off metal strikes

KM#	Date	Mintage	Identification	Mkt Val
Pn33	ND (1917)KN	—	10 Milliemes. Copper-Nickel. 5.7000 g. 25.9 mm. Blank. Design of KM-316 reverse. Plain edge. Reverse die trial of KM-316	
Pn32	1917	—	10 Milliemes. Copper-Nickel. 5.7200 g. 25.9 mm. Design of KM-316 obverse. Blank. Plain edge. Obverse die trial of KM-316	
Pn26	1917	—	1/2 Millieme. Copper-Nickel.	500
Pn27	1942	—	2 Piastres. Platinum. KM#365	—
Pn28	1960	—	25 Piastres. Silver. KM#400 but with hand pointing to right	—
Pn29	1962	—	5 Piastres. Bronze. ESSAi	—
Pn30	1962	—	5 Piastres. Brass Or Aluminum-Bronze. 7.3400 g.	1,600
Pn31	1964	—	10 Piastres. Copper-Nickel.	—

PIEFORTS

KM#	Date	Mintage	Identification	Mkt Val
P1	1981	152	5 Pounds. 0.9000 Silver. KM533	350

PROOF SETS

KM#	Date	Mintage	Identification	Issue Price	Mkt Val
PS1	1938 (4)	—	KM#370, 371, 372, 373	4,200	4,500
PS2	1964 (4)	2,000	KM#404, 405, 406, 407	18.00	90.00
PS3	1966 (7)	2,500	KM#393, 394, 395, 397, 398, 399, 403	9.00	75.00
PS4	1980 (4)	—	KM#508, 509, 517, 519	—	2,000
PS5	1980 (3)	—	KM#509, 517, 519	—	1,975

SPECIMEN SETS (SS)

KM#	Date	Mintage	Identification	Issue Price	Mkt Val
SS1	1916/7 (10)	—	KM#312-316, 317.1, 318.1, 319, 321, 324	—	1,700

EL SALVADOR

GUATEMALA
HONDURAS
NICARAGUA
North Pacific Ocean

The Republic of El Salvador, a Central American country bordered by Guatemala, Honduras and the Pacific Ocean, has an area of 8,124 sq. mi. (21,040 sq. km.) and a population of 6.0 million. Capital: San Salvador. This most intensely cultivated of Latin America countries produces coffee (the major crop), sugar and balsam for export. Gold, silver and other metals are largely unexploited.

The first Spanish attempt to subjugate the area was undertaken in 1523 by Pedro de Alvarado, Cortes' lieutenant. He was forced to retreat by Indian forces, but returned in 1525 and succeeded in bringing the region under control of the Captaincy General of Guatemala. In 1821, El Salvador and the other Central American provinces jointly declared independence from Spain. In 1823, the Republic of Central America was formed by the five Central American states; this federation dissolved in 1839. El Salvador then became an independent republic in 1841.

Since 1960, El Salvador has been a part of the Central American Common Market. During the 1980's El Salvador went through a 12 year Civil War that ended in 1992 with the signing of a United Nations-sponsored Peace Accord. Free elections, with full participation of all political parties, were held in 1994, 1997 and 1999. Armando Calderon-Sol was elected president in 1994 for a 5-year term and Francisco Flores was elected in 1999 for a 5-year term as well.

MINT MARKS
C.A.M. - Central American Mint, San Salvador
H - Heaton Mint, Birmingham
S - San Francisco
Mo - Mexico
(a) - British Royal Mint, England
(b) - Denver Mint, USA
(c) - Deutsche Nickel A.G., Germany
(d) - Guatemala City Mint, Guatemala
(e) - Mexico City Mint, Mexico
(f) - San Francisco Mint, USA
(g) - Sherrit Mint, Canada
(h) - Vereingte Deutsche Metall, Germany
(i) - Royal Canadian Mint, Canada
(P) – Philadelphia Mint, USA
NOTE: The Monetary Integration Law of November 2000 resulted in the elimination of the Colon coinage and notes by early October 2002. No new coins are expected to be minted.

REPUBLIC OF EL SALVADOR
DECIMAL COINAGE
100 Centavos = 1 Peso

KM# 120   1/4 REAL
3.2000 g., Bronze **Obv:** Flag draped arms within wreath, liberty cap on top, swords above cap **Rev:** Denomination and date within wreath **Note:** The decimal value of this coin was about 3 Centavos. It was apparently struck in response to the continuing use of the Reales monetary system in rural areas.

Date	Mintage	F	VF	XF	Unc	BU
1909	—	20.00	40.00	75.00	150	—

KM# 106   CENTAVO
2.5000 g., Copper-Nickel **Obv:** Head of Francisco Morazan left, date below **Obv. Leg.:** REPUBLICA DEL SALVADOR **Rev:** Denomination within wreath **Note:** Medal rotation.

Date	Mintage	F	VF	XF	Unc	BU
1913H	2,500,000	1.50	3.50	6.00	40.00	—

KM# 127   CENTAVO
2.5000 g., Copper-Nickel **Obv:** Head of Francisco Morazan left, date below **Rev:** Denomination within wreath **Note:** Medal rotation.

Date	Mintage	F	VF	XF	Unc	BU
1915(P)	5,000,000	1.25	4.50	12.50	35.00	—
1919(P)	1,000,000	2.25	-7.00	20.00	60.00	—
1920(P)	1,490,000	1.50	6.00	15.00	40.00	—
1925(f)	200,000	4.00	12.00	25.00	70.00	—
1926(f)	400,000	3.00	10.00	20.00	55.00	—
1928S	5,000,000	1.25	7.00	16.00	40.00	—

Note: Varieties exist with large or small "S"

1936(P)	2,500,000	1.25	4.50	12.50	35.00	—

KM# 107   3 CENTAVOS
3.3000 g., Copper-Nickel **Obv:** Head of Francisco Morazan left **Obv. Leg.:** REPUBLICA DEL SALVADOR **Rev:** Denomination within wreath **Note:** Medal rotation.

Date	Mintage	F	VF	XF	Unc	BU
1913H	1,000,000	2.00	8.00	20.00	65.00	125

KM# 128   3 CENTAVOS
3.5000 g., Copper Nickel **Obv:** Head of Francisco Morazan left, date below **Rev:** Denomination within wreath **Note:** Medal rotation.

Date	Mintage	F	VF	XF	Unc	BU
1915(P)	2,700,000	2.00	8.00	20.00	65.00	200

KM# 121   5 CENTAVOS
1.2500 g., 0.8350 Silver 0.0336 oz. ASW **Obv:** Arms **Rev:** Denomination within wreath

Date	Mintage	F	VF	XF	Unc	BU
1911	1,000,000	4.00	10.00	20.00	45.00	—

KM# 124   5 CENTAVOS
1.2500 g., 0.8350 Silver 0.0336 oz. ASW **Obv:** Flag draped triangular arms within wreath **Rev:** Denomination within wreath

Date	Mintage	F	VF	XF	Unc	BU
1914(P)	2,000,000	3.00	7.00	15.00	35.00	—
1914(P) Proof	20	Value: 750				

KM# 129   5 CENTAVOS
5.0000 g., Copper-Nickel **Obv:** Head of Francisco Morazan left, date below **Rev:** Denomination within wreath **Note:** Medal rotation.

Date	Mintage	F	VF	XF	Unc	BU
1915(P)	2,500,000	2.25	6.00	15.00	60.00	
1916(P)	1,500,000	2.50	7.00	20.00	65.00	
1917(P)	1,000,000	3.00	8.00	20.00	70.00	
1918/7(P)	1,000,000	2.50	7.00	20.00	60.00	
1918(P)	Inc. above	2.50	7.00	17.50	70.00	
1919/8(P)	—	2.50	7.00	17.50	70.00	
1919(P)	2,000,000	2.50	7.00	17.50	70.00	
1920(P)	2,000,000	1.75	4.50	10.00	50.00	
1921(f)	1,780,000	2.00	5.00	12.00	55.00	
1925(f)	4,000,000	1.25	3.50	10.00	55.00	

KM# 122   10 CENTAVOS
2.5000 g., 0.8350 Silver 0.0671 oz. ASW **Obv:** Flag draped arms, liberty cap on top, dates below **Rev:** Denomination within wreath

Date	Mintage	F	VF	XF	Unc	BU
1911	1,000,000	3.00	7.00	15.00	65.00	

KM# 125   10 CENTAVOS
2.5000 g., 0.8350 Silver 0.0671 oz. ASW **Obv:** Flag draped triangular arms within wreath, dates below **Rev:** Denomination within wreath

Date	Mintage	F	VF	XF	Unc	BU
1914(P)	1,500,000	2.50	6.50	12.50	45.00	—
1914(P) Proof	20	Value: 750				

KM# 123   25 CENTAVOS
6.2500 g., 0.8350 Silver 0.1678 oz. ASW **Obv:** Flag draped arms, liberty cap above, dates below **Rev:** Denomination within wreath

Date	Mintage	F	VF	XF	Unc	BU
1911	600,000	5.00	9.00	18.00	50.00	—

KM# 126   25 CENTAVOS
6.2500 g., 0.8350 Silver 0.1678 oz. ASW **Obv:** Flag draped triangular arms within wreath, dates below **Rev:** Denomination within wreath

Date	Mintage	F	VF	XF	Unc	BU
1914(P) 15 DE SEPT DE 1821	1,400,000	5.50	7.00	12.00	35.00	—
1914(P) 15 SET DE 1821	Inc. above	5.50	7.00	12.00	35.00	—
1914(P) Proof	20	Value: 1,500				

KM# 115.1   PESO (Colon)
25.0000 g., 0.9000 Silver 0.7234 oz. ASW **Obv:** Arms **Obv. Leg.:** REPUBLICA DEL SALVADOR **Rev:** Columbus bust left

Date	Mintage	F	VF	XF	Unc	BU
1904C.A.M.	600,000	12.50	15.00	30.00	160	—
1908C.A.M.	1,600,000	12.50	14.00	28.00	140	—
1911C.A.M.	500,000	12.50	15.00	30.00	150	—
1914C.A.M.	700,000				625	—

Note: 1914 struck at the Brussels mint, but then remelted

KM# 115.2   PESO (Colon)
25.0000 g., 0.9000 Silver 0.7234 oz. ASW **Obv:** Flag draped arms, liberty cap and swords above, dates below **Rev:** Columbus bust left, denomination below, heavier portrait (wider right shoulder) **Note:** Struck at United States mints.

Date	Mintage	F	VF	XF	Unc	BU
1904C.A.M. (f)	400,000	15.00	20.00	40.00	250	—
1909C.A.M. (f)	690,000	13.50	17.50	32.50	200	—
1911C.A.M. (P) (S)	1,020,000	12.50	15.00	30.00	175	—

Note: Of the total mintage, 510, 993 struck at Philadelphia Mint (P), and 511,108 were struck at San Francisco Mint (f)

Date	Mintage	F	VF	XF	Unc	BU
1914C.A.M. (P)	2,100,000	12.50	15.00	30.00	175	425
1914C.A.M. Proof	Est. 20	Value: 3,000				

REFORM COINAGE
100 Centavos = 1 Colon

KM# 133 CENTAVO
2.5000 g., Copper-Nickel **Obv:** Head of Francisco Morazan left **Rev:** Denomination within wreath **Note:** Medal rotation.

Date	Mintage	F	VF	XF	BU
1940(P)	1,000,000	2.00	6.00	15.00	45.00

KM# 135.1 CENTAVO
2.5000 g., Bronze, 15 mm. **Obv:** Head of Francisco Morazan left, date below **Rev:** Denomination within wreath

Date	Mintage	F	VF	XF	Unc	BU
1942(f)	5,000,000	0.20	0.50	1.00	4.50	—
Note: Struck in 1943						
1943(f)	5,000,000	0.20	0.50	1.00	4.50	—
Note: Struck in 1944						
1945(P)	5,000,000	0.20	0.40	0.75	3.50	—
1947(f)	5,000,000	0.20	0.50	1.00	4.00	—
1951(f)	10,000,000	0.10	0.30	0.75	2.50	—
1952(f)	10,000,000	0.10	0.20	0.40	2.00	—
Note: Struck in 1953						
1956(P)	10,000,000	0.10	0.20	0.40	2.00	—
Note: Struck in 1957						
1966	5,000,000	—		0.10	0.75	—
1968 (f)	5,000,000	—		0.10	0.75	—
1969 (b)	5,000,000	—		0.10	0.75	—
1972 (f)	20,000,000	—		0.10	0.50	—

KM# 135.1a CENTAVO
2.5000 g., Bronze Clad Steel **Obv:** Head of Francisco Morazan left **Rev:** Denomination within wreath **Note:** Prev. KM#135d. Medal rotation.

Date	Mintage	F	VF	XF	Unc	BU
1989(h)	36,000,000	—		0.10	0.20	0.35
1992(h)	—	—		0.10	0.20	0.35

KM# 135.2 CENTAVO
2.5000 g., Brass **Obv:** Head of Francisco Morazan left **Rev:** Denomination within wreath **Note:** Prev. KM#135a. Medal rotation.

Date	Mintage	F	VF	XF	Unc	BU
1976(g)	20,000,000	—		0.10	0.20	0.35
1977(g)	40,000,000	—		0.10	0.20	0.35

KM# 135.2a CENTAVO
2.5000 g., Copper-Zinc **Obv:** DH monogram at truncation, smaller Morazan portrait **Rev:** Denomination in wreath, SM at right base of 1 **Note:** Previously KM#135c.

Date	Mintage	F	VF	XF	Unc	BU
1981(d)	50,000,000	—		0.10	0.20	0.35

KM# 135.2b CENTAVO
2.5000 g., Copper Clad Steel **Obv:** DH monogram at truncation, smaller Morazan portrait **Rev:** Denomination in wreath, SM at right base of 1 **Note:** Prev. KM#135b.

Date	Mintage	F	VF	XF	Unc	BU
1986 (a)	30,000,000	—	—	0.10	0.20	0.35

KM# A154 CENTAVO
1.5000 g., Brass Plated Steel, 15 mm. **Obv:** Head of Francisco Morazan left **Rev:** Denomination in wreath

Date	Mintage	F	VF	XF	Unc	BU
1988(h) Proof	—	Value: 50.00				

KM# 135.2c CENTAVO
2.5000 g., Brass Clad Steel **Obv:** DH monogram at truncation, smaller portrait **Rev:** Denomination in wreath, SM at right base of 1

Date	Mintage	F	VF	XF	Unc	BU
1995(a)	—	—		0.10	0.20	0.35

KM# 147 2 CENTAVOS
2.6000 g., Nickel-Brass **Obv:** Head of Francisco Morazan left **Rev:** Denomination within wreath **Note:** Medal rotation.

Date	Mintage	F	VF	XF	Unc	BU
1974(a)	10,002,000	—	0.10	0.20	1.00	—
1974(a)	2,000	Value: 30.00				
Note: In proof sets only						

KM# 148 3 CENTAVOS
4.0000 g., Nickel-Brass, 19 mm. **Obv:** Head of Francisco Morazan left **Rev:** Denomination within wreath **Note:** Medal rotation.

Date	Mintage	F	VF	XF	Unc	BU
1974(a)	10,002,000	0.10	0.15	0.20	1.00	—
1974(a)	2,000	Value: 35.00				
Note: In proof sets only						

KM# 134 5 CENTAVOS
5.0000 g., Copper-Nickel, 23 mm. **Obv:** Head of Francisco Morazan left **Rev:** Denomination within wreath **Note:** Medal rotation.

Date	Mintage	F	VF	XF	Unc	BU
1939	—	—				—
1940(P)	800,000	1.00	3.00	10.00	30.00	—
1951	2,000,000	0.75	2.00	6.00	15.00	—
1956	8,000,000	0.10	0.15	0.25	1.00	—
1959	6,000,000	0.10	0.15	0.25	1.00	—
1963	10,000,000	—	0.10	0.15	0.50	—
1966	6,000,000	0.10	0.15	0.25	0.75	—
1967 (f)	10,000,000	—	0.10	0.15	0.50	—
1972 (f)	10,000,000	—	0.10	0.15	0.50	—
1974 (g)	10,002,000	—	0.10	0.15	0.50	—
1974 (g)	2,000	Value: 35.00				
Note: In proof sets only						

KM# 134a 5 CENTAVOS
5.0000 g., Nickel-Silver, 23 mm. **Obv:** Head of Francisco Morazan left, date below **Rev:** Denomination within wreath

Date	Mintage	F	VF	XF	Unc	BU
1944(f)	5,000,000	0.25	0.50	1.50	5.00	—
1948(f)	3,000,000	0.25	0.50	1.00	2.50	—
1950(f)	2,000,000	0.25	0.50	1.50	5.00	—
1952(f)	4,000,000	0.20	0.35	0.75	4.00	—
Note: Half the total mintage was struck in 1952, the remainder in 1953						

KM# 149 5 CENTAVOS
5.0000 g., Copper-Nickel Clad Steel, 23 mm. **Obv:** Head of Francisco Morazan left, date below **Rev:** Denomination within wreath **Note:** Medal rotation.

Date	Mintage	F	VF	XF	Unc	BU
1975 (a)	15,000,000	—	0.10	0.15	0.30	0.50
1975	2,000	Value: 40.00				
Note: In proof sets only						
1986 (h)	30,000,000	—		0.10	0.15	0.50

KM# 149a 5 CENTAVOS
5.0000 g., Nickel Clad Steel, 23 mm. **Obv:** Head of Francisco Morazan left **Rev:** Denomination within wreath

Date	Mintage	F	VF	XF	Unc	BU
1976 (g)	15,000,000	—	0.10	0.15	0.30	0.50
1984 (a)	15,000,000	—		0.10	0.15	0.50

KM# 149b 5 CENTAVOS
5.0000 g., Copper-Nickel-Zinc, 23 mm. **Obv:** Head of Francisco Morazan left **Rev:** Denomination within wreath **Note:** Prev. KM#149a.

Date	Mintage	F	VF	XF	Unc	BU
1977(h)	26,000,000	—	0.10	0.15	0.30	0.50

KM# 154 5 CENTAVOS
2.0000 g., Stainless Steel, 17 mm. **Obv:** Head of Francisco Morazan left, date below **Rev:** Denomination within wreath

Date	Mintage	F	VF	XF	Unc	BU
1987(h)	30,000,000	—	0.10	0.15	0.30	0.50
1987(h) Proof	—	Value: 50.00				
1999(h)	—	—	0.10	0.15	0.30	0.50

KM# 154a 5 CENTAVOS
2.0000 g., Copper-Nickel Clad Steel **Obv:** Head of Francisco Morazan left **Rev:** Denomination within wreath **Note:** Medal rotation.

Date	Mintage	F	VF	XF	Unc	BU
1991 (h)	—	—	0.10	0.15	0.30	0.50
1998 (c)	—	—	0.10	0.15	0.30	0.50

KM# 154b 5 CENTAVOS
2.0000 g., Nickel Clad Steel, 17 mm. **Obv:** Head of Francisco Morazan left, date below **Rev:** Denomination within wreath **Note:** Medal rotation.

Date	Mintage	F	VF	XF	Unc	BU
1992 (g)	—	—	0.10	0.15	0.30	0.50
1993 (g)	—	—	0.10	0.15	0.30	0.50
1994 (h)	—	—	0.10	0.15	0.30	0.50
1994(h) Proof	—	Value: 40.00				
1995 (g)	—	—	0.10	0.15	0.30	0.50
1998	—	—	0.10	0.15	0.30	0.50
1999	—	—	0.10	0.15	0.30	0.50

KM# 130 10 CENTAVOS
7.0000 g., Copper-Nickel, 26 mm. **Obv:** Head of Francisco Morazan left, date below **Rev:** Denomination within wreath **Note:** Medal rotation.

Date	Mintage	F	VF	XF	Unc	BU
1921(f)	2,000,000	4.50	10.00	30.00	200	300
1925(f)	2,000,000	5.00	12.50	55.00	—	—
1940(f)	500,000	6.50	15.00	40.00	90.00	—
1951(f)	1,000,000	1.00	3.50	12.50	30.00	—
1967(f)	2,000,000	—	0.10	0.50	2.00	—
1968(b)	3,000,000	—	0.10	0.40	1.25	—
1969(b)	3,000,000	—	0.10	0.40	1.25	—
1972(f)	7,000,000	—	0.10	0.25	1.00	—

KM# 130a 10 CENTAVOS
7.0000 g., Copper-Nickel-Zinc, 26 mm. **Obv:** Head of Francisco Morazan left **Rev:** Denomination within wreath

Date	Mintage	F	VF	XF	Unc	BU
1952(f)	2,000,000	0.15	0.25	0.75	4.00	—
Note: Of the 2,000,000 struck, 336,000 were struck in 1952 and the remaining 1,664,000 struck in 1953						
1985 Mo	15,000,000	—	0.10	0.15	0.30	—

KM# 150 10 CENTAVOS
7.0000 g., Copper-Nickel Clad Steel, 26 mm. **Obv:** Head of Francisco Morazan left date below **Rev:** Denomination within wreath **Note:** Medal rotation.

Date	Mintage	F	VF	XF	Unc	BU
1975(a)	15,000,000	—	0.15	0.25	0.50	—
1975(a)	2,000	Value: 35.00				
Note: In proof sets only						

KM# 150a 10 CENTAVOS
7.0000 g., Copper-Nickel-Zinc, 26 mm. **Obv:** Head of Francisco Morazan left **Rev:** Denomination within wreath **Note:** Medal rotation.

Date	Mintage	F	VF	XF	Unc	BU
1977(h)	24,000,000	—	0.10	0.20	0.45	—
1977(h) Proof	—	Value: 40.00				

KM# 155 10 CENTAVOS
3.0000 g., Stainless Steel, 20 mm. **Obv:** Head of Francisco Morazan left date below **Rev:** Denomination within wreath **Note:** Medal rotation.

Date	Mintage	F	VF	XF	Unc	BU
1987 (h)	30,000,000	—	0.10	0.20	0.40	0.60
1987(h) Proof	—	Value: 50.00				
1999 (i)	—	—	0.10	0.20	0.40	0.60

KM# 155a 10 CENTAVOS
Nickel Clad Steel **Obv:** Head of Francisco Morazan left **Rev:** Denomination within wreath **Note:** Medal rotation.

Date	Mintage	F	VF	XF	Unc	BU
1992 (a)	—	—	0.10	0.20	0.40	0.60
1993 (g)	—	—	0.10	0.20	0.40	0.60
1994 (h)	—	—	0.10	0.20	0.40	0.60
1994 Proof	—	Value: 40.00				

KM# 155b 10 CENTAVOS
Copper-Nickel Clad Steel **Obv:** Head of Francisco Morazan left **Rev:** Denomination within wreath

Date	Mintage	F	VF	XF	Unc	BU
1995 (c)	—	—	0.10	0.20	0.40	0.60
1998 (c)	—	—	0.10	0.20	0.40	0.60
1999	—	—	0.10	0.20	0.40	0.60

KM# 136 25 CENTAVOS
7.5000 g., 0.9000 Silver 0.2170 oz. ASW **Obv:** Head of Francisco Morazan left, date below **Rev:** Denomination within wreath

Date	Mintage	F	VF	XF	Unc	BU
1943	1,000,000	4.00	5.00	8.00	16.00	—
1944	1,000,000	4.00	5.00	8.00	16.00	—

KM# 137 25 CENTAVOS
2.5000 g., 0.9000 Silver 0.0723 oz. ASW **Obv:** Head of Jose Matias Delgado left, date below **Rev:** Denomination within wreath

Date	Mintage	F	VF	XF	Unc	BU
1953	14,000,000	1.00	1.50	2.50	4.50	—

KM# 139 25 CENTAVOS
2.5000 g., Nickel, 17.8 mm. **Obv:** Head of Jose Matias Delgado left, date below **Rev:** Denomination within wreath

Date	Mintage	F	VF	XF	Unc	BU
1970 (a)	14,000,000	—	0.10	0.20	0.60	0.80
1973 (g)	28,000,000	—	0.10	0.20	0.50	0.75
1975 (g)	20,000,000	—	0.10	0.20	0.50	0.75
1977 (a)	22,400,000	—	0.10	0.20	0.50	0.75

KM# 139a 25 CENTAVOS
2.5000 g., Copper-Nickel **Obv:** Head of Jose Matias Delgado left **Rev:** Denomination within wreath

Date	Mintage	F	VF	XF	Unc	BU
1986Mo	21,000,000	—	0.10	0.20	0.50	0.75
1986Mo Proof	—	Value: 50.00				

KM# 157 25 CENTAVOS
4.0000 g., Stainless Steel, 22.5 mm. **Obv:** Head of Jose Matias Delgado left, date below **Rev:** Denomination within wreath **Note:** Medal rotation.

Date	Mintage	F	VF	XF	Unc	BU
1988 (h)	20,000,000	—	0.10	0.20	0.50	0.75
1988(h) Proof	—	Value: 50.00				
1999 (i)	—	—	0.10	0.20	0.50	0.75

KM# 157a 25 CENTAVOS
4.0000 g., Copper-Nickel Clad Steel **Obv:** Bust of Jose Matias Delgado left **Rev:** Denomination

Date	Mintage	F	VF	XF	Unc	BU
1992(c)	—	—	0.10	0.20	0.50	0.75
1995(c)	—	—	0.10	0.20	0.50	0.75

KM# 157b 25 CENTAVOS
4.0000 g., Nickel Clad Steel **Obv:** Head of Jose Matias Delgado left, date below **Rev:** Denomination within wreath **Note:** Medal rotation.

Date	Mintage	F	VF	XF	Unc	BU
1993 (a)	—	—	0.10	0.20	0.50	0.75
1994 (g)	—	—	0.10	0.20	0.50	0.75
1998	—	—	0.10	0.20	0.50	0.75
1999	—	—	0.10	0.20	0.50	0.75

KM# 138 50 CENTAVOS
5.0000 g., 0.9000 Silver 0.1447 oz. ASW **Obv:** Head of Jose Matias Delgado left, date below **Rev:** Denomination within wreath

Date	Mintage	F	VF	XF	Unc	BU
1953	3,000,000	3.00	4.00	5.00	8.00	—

KM# 140.1 50 CENTAVOS
5.0000 g., Nickel, 20 mm. **Obv:** Head of Jose Matias Delgado left, date below **Rev:** Denomination within wreath **Note:** 1.65 millimeters thick.

Date	Mintage	F	VF	XF	Unc	BU
1970(a)	3,000,000	—	0.20	0.30	0.60	0.80

KM# 140.2 50 CENTAVOS
5.1000 g., Nickel, 20 mm. **Obv:** Head of Jose Matias Delgado left **Rev:** Denomination **Note:** Two millimeters thick.

Date	Mintage	F	VF	XF	Unc	BU
1977(a)	1,500,000	—	0.20	0.30	0.60	0.80

KM# 131 COLON
25.0000 g., 0.9000 Silver 0.7234 oz. ASW, 37 mm. **Subject:** 400th Anniversary - San Salvador **Obv:** Flags flank triangular arms within wreath, denomination below **Rev:** Alvarado and Quinonez busts left, dates above

Date	Mintage	F	VF	XF	Unc	BU
ND(1925)Mo	2,000	50.00	90.00	135	225	—

KM# 141 COLON
2.3000 g., 0.9990 Silver 0.0739 oz. ASW **Subject:** 150th Anniversary of Independence **Obv:** Flags flank triangular arms within wreath, bust at right **Rev:** Salvador Dali image, "La Fecandida" within circle, denomination below

Date	Mintage	F	VF	XF	Unc	BU
1971 Proof	21,000	Value: 7.50				

KM# 153 COLON
9.2500 g., Copper-Nickel, 29 mm. **Obv:** Head of Christopher Columbus left, date below **Rev:** Denomination within wreath

Date	Mintage	F	VF	XF	Unc	BU
1984Mo	10,000,000	—	0.50	1.00	2.50	3.50
1984Mo Proof	—	Value: 125				
1985Mo	20,000,000	—	0.50	1.00	2.50	3.50
1985Mo Proof	—	Value: 200				

KM# 156 COLON
6.0000 g., Stainless Steel, 25 mm. **Obv:** Head of Christopher Columbus left, date below **Rev:** Denomination within wreath

Date	Mintage	F	VF	XF	Unc	BU
1988 (h)	30,000,000	—	0.40	0.80	2.25	3.00
1988 (h) Proof	—	Value: 50.00				
1999 (i)	—	—	0.80	2.25	3.00	

KM# 156a COLON
6.0000 g., Copper-Nickel Clad Steel, 25 mm. **Obv:** Head of Christopher Columbus left **Rev:** Denomination within wreath **Note:** Medal rotation.

Date	Mintage	F	VF	XF	Unc	BU
1991(h)	—	—	0.40	0.80	2.25	3.00

KM# 156b COLON
6.0000 g., Nickel Clad Steel, 25 mm. **Obv:** Head of Christopher Columbus left **Rev:** Denomination within wreath **Note:** Medal rotation.

Date	Mintage	F	VF	XF	Unc	BU
1993 (a)	—	—	0.40	0.80	2.25	3.00
1994 (g)	—	—	0.40	0.80	2.25	3.00
1995 (h)	—	—	0.40	0.80	2.25	3.00
1998	—	—	0.40	0.80	2.25	3.00
1999	—	—	0.40	0.80	2.25	3.00

KM# 142 5 COLONES
11.5000 g., 0.9990 Silver 0.3693 oz. ASW **Subject:** 150th Anniversary of Independence **Obv:** Flags flank triangular arms within wreath, date below **Rev:** Liberty statue, Cañas bust at right, dates at left, denomination below

Date	Mintage	F	VF	XF	Unc	BU
1971 Proof	18,000	Value: 12.50				

KM# 162 5 COLONES
7.5000 g., Bi-Metallic Bronze Plated Steel center in Nickel-plated Steel ring, 26 mm. **Obv:** Columbus' ships sailing west on world map within circle, date below **Rev:** Denomination within circle, wreath surrounds **Edge:** Segmented reeding **Note:** Viridian mint. Not released for circulation.

Date	Mintage	F	VF	XF	Unc	BU
1997	—	—	—	—	—	—

KM# 163 5 COLONES
7.5000 g., Bi-Metallic, 25.9 mm. **Obv:** Y2K motif **Rev:** Denomination **Note:** Not released for circulation.

Date	Mintage	F	VF	XF	Unc	BU
2000	—	—	—	—	—	—

KM# 132 20 COLONES
15.5600 g., 0.9000 Gold 0.4502 oz. AGW, 27 mm. **Subject:** 400th Anniversary - San Salvador **Obv:** Flags flank triangular arms within wreath, denomination below **Rev:** Alvarado and Quinonez busts left, dates above

Date	Mintage	F	VF	XF	Unc	BU
ND(1925)Mo	200	—	800	1,600	2,500	—

KM# 143 25 COLONES
2.9400 g., 0.9000 Gold 0.0851 oz. AGW **Subject:** 150th Anniversary of Independence **Obv:** Flags flank triangular arms within wreath **Rev:** Salvador Dali image, "La Fecundida" within circle, denomination below

Date	Mintage	F	VF	XF	Unc	BU
1971 Proof	7,650	Value: 100				

KM# 151 25 COLONES
25.0000 g., 0.9000 Silver 0.7234 oz. ASW **Subject:** 18th Annual Governors' Assembly **Obv:** Flags flank triangular arms within wreath, denomination below **Rev:** First coin of C.A. Federation 1874, date below **Note:** Medal rotation.

Date	Mintage	F	VF	XF	Unc	BU
1977	2,000	—	—	—	27.50	32.50
1977 Proof	20,000	Value: 37.50				

KM# 144 50 COLONES
5.9000 g., 0.9000 Gold 0.1707 oz. AGW **Subject:** 150th Anniversary of Independence **Obv:** Flags flank triangular arms within wreath **Rev:** Liberty statue, Cañas bust at right, dates at left, denomination below

Date	Mintage	F	VF	XF	Unc	BU
1971 Proof	3,530	Value: 175				

KM# 145 100 COLONES
11.8000 g., 0.9000 Gold 0.3414 oz. AGW **Subject:** 150th Anniversary of Independence **Obv:** Flags flank triangular arms within wreath **Rev:** Map of El Salvador, denomination below

Date	Mintage	F	VF	XF	Unc	BU
1971 Proof	2,750	Value: 350				

KM# 158 150 COLONES
25.0000 g., 0.9000 Silver 0.7234 oz. ASW, 37 mm. **Subject:** Union for Peace **Obv:** Four clasped hands, date below **Rev:** Denomination within wreath **Edge:** Lettered

Date	Mintage	F	VF	XF	Unc	BU
1992	—	—	—	—	42.50	—

KM# 160 150 COLONES
25.0000 g., 0.9000 Silver 0.7234 oz. ASW, 37 mm. **Subject:** Discovery of America **Obv:** Columbus' ships and world map, date below **Rev:** Denomination within wreath **Edge:** Lettered

Date	Mintage	F	VF	XF	Unc	BU
1992	—	—	—	—	47.50	—

KM# 146 200 COLONES
23.6000 g., 0.9000 Gold 0.6829 oz. AGW **Subject:** 150th Anniversary of Independence **Obv:** Flags flank triangular arms within wreath, bust at right, date below **Rev:** Panchimalco Church, denomination below

Date	Mintage	F	VF	XF	Unc	BU
1971 Proof	2,245	Value: 675				

KM# 152 250 COLONES
16.0000 g., 0.9170 Gold 0.4717 oz. AGW **Subject:** 18th Annual Governors' Assembly **Obv:** Flags flank triangular arms within wreath, denomination below **Rev:** First coin of C.A. Federation 1824, dates below

Date	Mintage	F	VF	XF	Unc	BU
1977	4,000	—	—	—	450	475
1977 Proof	400	Value: 550				

KM# 159 2500 COLONES
16.0000 g., 0.9170 Gold 0.4717 oz. AGW **Subject:** Union for Peace **Obv:** Four clasped hands, date below **Rev:** Denomination within wreath

Date	Mintage	F	VF	XF	Unc	BU
1992	—	—	—	—	—	475
1992 Proof	—	Value: 750				

KM# 161 2500 COLONES
16.0000 g., 0.9170 Gold 0.4717 oz. AGW **Subject:** Discovery of America **Obv:** Columbus' ships and world map, date below **Rev:** Denomination within wreath

Date	Mintage	F	VF	XF	Unc	BU
1992	—	—	—	—	—	475
1992 Proof	—	Value: 750				

PATTERNS
Including off metal strikes

KM#	Date	Mintage	Identification	Mkt Val
Pn51	1996	—	5 Colones. Nickel-Plated Steel ring. 7.4000 g. 25.9 mm. Columbus' ships and world map, date below. Denomination within wreath. Prev.KM#Pn15.	400

PROOF SETS

KM#	Date	Mintage	Identification	Issue Price	Mkt Val
PS3	1914 (4)	—	KM#115.2, 124-126	—	6,000
PS4	1971 (6)	—	KM#141-146	—	1,325
PS5	1971 (4)	—	KM#143-146	250	1,300
PS6	1971 (2)	—	KM#141-142	6.00	20.00
PS7	1974 (3)	2,000	KM#134, 147-148	—	100
PS8	1975 (2)	2,000	KM#149.1, 150	—	70.00
PS9	1987-88 (5)	—	KM#A154, 154-157	—	250

EQUATORIAL AFRICAN STATES

For historical background, see the introduction to Central African States.

CURRENCY UNION

DECIMAL COINAGE

100 Centimes = 1 Franc

KM# 6 FRANC
Aluminum **Obv:** Three giant eland left, date below
Rev: Denomination within wreath

Date	Mintage	F	VF	XF	Unc	BU
1969(a)	2,500,000	0.25	0.65	1.00	2.25	—
1971(a)	3,000,000	0.25	0.65	1.00	2.25	—

KM# 1 5 FRANCS
Aluminum-Bronze **Obv:** Three giant eland left
Rev: Denomination within wreath

Date	Mintage	F	VF	XF	Unc	BU
1961(a)	10,000,000	0.35	1.00	1.50	2.50	—
1962(a)	5,000,000	0.35	1.00	1.50	2.50	—

KM# 1a 5 FRANCS
Aluminum-Nickel-Bronze **Obv:** Three giant eland left, date below **Rev:** Denomination within wreath

Date	Mintage	F	VF	XF	Unc	BU
1965(a)	7,000,000	0.35	1.00	1.50	3.00	—
1967(a)	4,000,000	0.35	1.00	1.25	2.50	—
1968(a)	5,000,000	0.35	1.00	1.25	2.50	—
1970(a)	9,000,000	0.35	1.00	1.25	2.50	—
1972(a)	5,000,000	0.35	1.00	1.25	2.50	—
1973(a)	5,010,000	0.35	1.00	1.25	2.50	—

KM# 2 10 FRANCS
Aluminum-Bronze **Obv:** Three giant eland left
Rev: Denomination within wreath

Date	Mintage	F	VF	XF	Unc	BU
1961(a)	10,000,000	0.40	1.00	1.75	3.00	—
1962(a)	5,000,000	0.40	1.00	1.75	3.00	—

KM# 2a 10 FRANCS
Aluminum-Nickel-Bronze **Obv:** Three giant eland left, date below
Rev: Denomination within wreath

Date	Mintage	F	VF	XF	Unc	BU
1965(a)	7,000,000	1.00	1.75	2.75	5.00	—
1967(a)	10,000,000	0.40	1.00	1.75	3.00	—
1968(a)	2,000,000	1.50	2.25	3.50	6.00	—
1969(a)	10,000,000	0.40	1.00	1.75	3.00	—
1972(a)	5,000,000	0.40	1.00	1.75	3.00	—
1973(a)	5,000,000	0.75	1.50	2.50	4.50	—

KM# 4 25 FRANCS
Aluminum-Bronze **Obv:** Three giant eland left, date below
Rev: Denomination within wreath

Date	Mintage	F	VF	XF	Unc	BU
1962(a)	6,000,000	0.50	1.25	2.25	4.00	—

KM# 4a 25 FRANCS
Aluminum-Nickel-Bronze **Obv:** Three giant eland left, date below
Rev: Denomination, within wreath

Date	Mintage	F	VF	XF	Unc	BU
1970(a)	3,019,000	0.50	1.25	2.25	4.00	—
1972(a)	5,000,000	0.50	1.25	2.00	3.00	—

KM# 3 50 FRANCS
Copper-Nickel, 30.7 mm. **Obv:** Three giant eland left, date below
Rev: Denomination within wreath

Date	Mintage	F	VF	XF	Unc	BU
1961(a)	5,000,000	2.00	4.00	6.00	10.00	—
1963(a)	5,000,000	2.00	4.00	6.00	10.00	—

KM# 5 100 FRANCS
11.7100 g., Nickel, 25.2 mm. **Obv:** Three giant eland left
Rev: Denomination, date above **Note:** KM#5 was issued double thick and should not be considered a piefort.

Date	Mintage	F	VF	XF	Unc	BU
1966(a)	6,000,000	2.00	4.00	7.00	12.00	—
1967(a)	5,800,000	2.00	4.00	7.00	12.00	—
1968(a)	6,200,000	2.00	4.00	7.00	12.00	—

ESSAIS
Standard metals unless otherwise noted

KM#	Date	Mintage	Identification	Issue Price	Mkt Val
E1	1961(a)	—	5 Francs. KM#1.	—	10.00
E2	1961(a)	—	10 Francs. KM#2.	—	15.00
E3	1961(a)	—	50 Francs. Three Giant Eland, left, date below. Denomination within wreath. KM#3.	—	50.00
E4	1961(a)	—	50 Francs. Gold. KM#4.	—	1,250
E4	1961(a)	—	50 Francs. Gold. KM#4.	—	1,250
E5	1962(a)	—	25 Francs. KM#4. This is a mule, having an old reverse die with a wing privy mark.	—	100
E6	1966(a)	—	100 Francs. KM#5.	—	20.00
E7	1969(a)	—	Franc. KM#6.	—	15.00

PIEFORTS

KM#	Date	Mintage	Identification	Issue Price	Mkt Val
P1	1965(a)	—	100 Francs. Gold. 23.4800 g. Three Giant Eland, left. Denomination, date above. KM#5. With ESSAI.	—	1,200

EQUATORIAL GUINEA

The Republic of Equatorial Guinea (formerly Spanish Guinea) consists of Rio Muni, located on the coast of West-Central Africa between Cameroon and Gabon, and the off-shore islands of Fernando Po, Annobon, Corisco, Elobey Grande and Elobey Chico. The equatorial country has an area of 10,831 sq. mi. (28,050 sq. km.) and a population of 420,293. Capital: Malabo. The economy is based on agriculture and forestry. Cacao, wood and coffee are exported.

Fernando Po was discovered between 1474 and 1496 by Portuguese navigators charting a route to the spice islands of the Far East. Portugal retained control of it and the adjacent islands until 1778 when they, together with trading rights to the African coast between the Ogooue and Niger Rivers, were ceded to Spain. Fernando Po was administered, with Spanish consent, by the British from 1827 to 1844 when it was reclaimed by Spain. Mainland Rio Muni was granted to Spain by the Berlin Conference of 1885. The name of the colony was changed from Spanish Guinea to Equatorial Guinea in Dec. of 1963. Independence was attained on Oct. 12, 1968.

Equatorial Guinea converted to the CFA currency system as issued for the Central African States issuing its first 100 Franc denomination in 1985.

NOTE: The 1969 coinage carries the actual minting date in the stars at the sides of the large date.

MINT MARK
(a) - Paris, privy marks only

REPUBLIC

PESETA COINAGE

KM# 1 PESETA
3.4200 g., Aluminum-Bronze, 19.5 mm. **Edge:** Reeded

Date	Mintage	F	VF	XF	Unc	BU
1969(69)	—	0.35	0.75	1.25	2.50	—

KM# 2 5 PESETAS
4.9000 g., Copper-Nickel, 22 mm. **Edge:** Reeded

Date	Mintage	F	VF	XF	Unc	BU
1969(69)	—	0.75	1.50	2.50	8.00	—

KM# 3 25 PESETAS
Copper-Nickel, 24 mm. **Obv:** Crossed tusks, date below **Rev:** Denomination at left, shielded arms at right, stars above arms

Date	Mintage	F	VF	XF	Unc	BU
1969(69)	—	1.50	2.50	6.50	12.00	—

KM# 5 25 PESETAS
5.0000 g., 0.9990 Silver 0.1606 oz. ASW **Subject:** World Bank **Obv:** Crossed tusks divide arms above and denomination below **Rev:** Banner crosses globe

Date	Mintage	F	VF	XF	Unc	BU
1970 Proof	2,475	Value: 10.00				

KM# 6   25 PESETAS
5.0000 g., 0.9990 Silver 0.1606 oz. ASW **Subject:** United Nations **Obv:** Crossed tusks divide arms above and denomination below **Rev:** UN logo

Date	Mintage	F	VF	XF	Unc	BU
1970 Proof	2,475	Value: 10.00				

KM# 4   50 PESETAS
Copper-Nickel **Obv:** Head right, date below **Rev:** Denomination at left, arms at right

Date	Mintage	F	VF	XF	Unc	BU
1969(69)	—	2.00	3.00	7.50	15.00	—

KM# 7   50 PESETAS
10.0000 g., 0.9990 Silver 0.3212 oz. ASW **Obv:** Crossed tusks divide arms above and denomination below **Rev:** Durer's Praying Hands

Date	Mintage	F	VF	XF	Unc	BU
1970 Proof	3,840	Value: 12.00				

KM# 8   75 PESETAS
15.0000 g., 0.9990 Silver 0.4818 oz. ASW **Obv:** Crossed tusks divide arms above and denomination below **Rev:** Pope John XXIII bust left

Date	Mintage	F	VF	XF	Unc	BU
1970 Proof	4,000	Value: 21.50				

KM# 9.1   75 PESETAS
15.0000 g., 0.9990 Silver 0.4818 oz. ASW **Subject:** Centennial - Birth of Vladimir Ilyich Lenin **Obv:** Crossed tusks divide arms above and denomination below, fineness stamp in field behind denomination **Rev:** Head left divides dates **Note:** Prev. KM#9.

Date	Mintage	F	VF	XF	Unc	BU
1970 Proof	4,000	Value: 21.50				

KM# 9.2   75 PESETAS
15.1400 g., 1.0000 Silver 0.4867 oz. ASW, 35.8 mm. **Subject:** Centennial of Lenin's birth **Obv:** Crossed tusks divide arms above and denomination below, fineness stamp at truncation of left tusk **Rev:** Head left divides dates

Date	Mintage	F	VF	XF	Unc	BU
1970 Proof	—	Value: 21.50				

KM# 10.1   75 PESETAS
15.0000 g., 0.9990 Silver 0.4818 oz. ASW **Subject:** Abraham Lincoln **Obv:** Crossed tusks divide arms above and denomination below, hallmark "1000" in oval at left tusk base **Rev:** Bust facing divides dates

Date	Mintage	F	VF	XF	Unc	BU
1970 Proof	4,390	Value: 30.00				

KM# 10.2   75 PESETAS
15.0000 g., 0.9990 Silver 0.4818 oz. ASW **Obv:** "1 AR" Hallmark above "E" in "Pesetas"

Date	Mintage	F	VF	XF	Unc	BU
1970 Proof	Inc. above	Value: 35.00				

KM# 11   75 PESETAS
15.0000 g., 0.9990 Silver 0.4818 oz. ASW **Subject:** Centennial - Birth of Mahatma Gandhi **Obv:** Crossed tusks divide arms above and denomination below **Rev:** Bust looking right divides dates

Date	Mintage	F	VF	XF	Unc	BU
1970 Proof	4,000	Value: 28.00				

KM# 12.1   100 PESETAS
20.0000 g., 0.9990 Silver 0.6423 oz. ASW **Obv:** Crossed tusk divide arms above and denomination below **Rev:** Durer's Praying Hands

Date	Mintage	F	VF	XF	Unc	BU
1970 Proof	4,000	Value: 30.00				

KM# 12.2   100 PESETAS
20.0000 g., 0.9990 Silver 0.6423 oz. ASW **Obv:** Crossed tusks divide arms above and denomination below, "1 AR" hallmark **Rev:** Durer's Praying Hands

Date	Mintage	F	VF	XF	Unc	BU
1970 Proof	Inc. above	Value: 27.50				

KM# 13.1   100 PESETAS
20.0000 g., 0.9990 Silver 0.6423 oz. ASW, 40 mm. **Obv:** Crossed tusks divide arms above and denomination below **Rev:** Goya's Naked Maja

Date	Mintage	F	VF	XF	Unc	BU
1970 Proof	30,000	Value: 35.00				

KM# 13.2   100 PESETAS
20.0000 g., 0.9990 Silver 0.6423 oz. ASW, 40 mm. **Obv:** Crossed tusks divide arms above and denomination below, fineness stamp at base of right tusk **Rev:** Goya's Naked Maja

Date	Mintage	F	VF	XF	Unc	BU
1970 Proof	Inc. above	Value: 35.00				

KM# 13.3   100 PESETAS
20.0000 g., 0.9990 Silver 0.6423 oz. ASW, 40 mm. **Obv:** Crossed tusks divide arms above and denomination below, fineness stamp below base of right tusk **Rev:** Goya's Naked Maja

Date	Mintage	F	VF	XF	Unc	BU
1970 Proof	Inc. above	Value: 35.00				

KM# 13.4   100 PESETAS
20.0000 g., 0.9990 Silver 0.6423 oz. ASW, 40 mm. **Obv:** Crossed tusks divide arms above and denomination below, fineness stamp above letters AN **Rev:** Goya's Naked Maja

Date	Mintage	F	VF	XF	Unc	BU
1970 Proof	Inc. above	Value: 35.00				

KM# 13.5   100 PESETAS
20.0000 g., 0.9990 Silver 0.6423 oz. ASW, 40 mm. **Obv:** Crossed tusks divide arms above and denomination below, 1000 in oval at base of right tusk **Rev:** Goya's Naked Maja

Date	Mintage	F	VF	XF	Unc	BU
1970 Proof	Inc. above	Value: 35.00				

KM# 20.1   250 PESETAS
3.5200 g., 0.9000 Gold 0.1018 oz. AGW **Obv:** Crossed tusks divide arms above and denomination below, fineness countermark at 8 o'clock by tusk base **Rev:** Goya's Naked Maja **Note:** Prev. KM#20.

Date	Mintage	F	VF	XF	Unc	BU
1970 Proof	3,500	Value: 110				

KM# 14   150 PESETAS
30.0000 g., 0.9990 Silver 0.9635 oz. ASW, 30 mm. **Subject:** Centennial of the Capital Rome **Obv:** Crossed tusks divide arms above and denomination below **Rev:** Symbols of Rome, dates at left

Date	Mintage	F	VF	XF	Unc	BU
1970 Proof	3,520	Value: 45.00				

KM# 17   150 PESETAS
30.0000 g., 0.9990 Silver 0.9635 oz. ASW **Subject:** Centennial of the Capital Rome **Obv:** Crossed tusks divide arms above and denomination below **Rev:** Mercury left, dates lower left

Date	Mintage	F	VF	XF	Unc	BU
1970 Proof	3,520	Value: 50.00				

KM# 20.2   250 PESETAS
3.5200 g., 0.9000 Gold 0.1018 oz. AGW **Obv:** Crossed tusks divide arms above and denomination below, fineness countermark at 4 o'clock by tusk base **Rev:** Goya's Naked Maja

Date	Mintage	F	VF	XF	Unc	BU
1970 Proof	—	Value: 110				

KM# 21   250 PESETAS
3.5200 g., 0.9000 Gold 0.1018 oz. AGW **Obv:** Crossed tusks divide arms and denomination below **Rev:** Durer's Praying Hands

Date	Mintage	F	VF	XF	Unc	BU
1970 Proof	2,000	Value: 100				

KM# 15   150 PESETAS
30.0000 g., 0.9990 Silver 0.9635 oz. ASW **Subject:** Centennial of the Capital Rome **Obv:** Crossed tusks divide arms above and denomination below **Rev:** Coliseum

Date	Mintage	F	VF	XF	Unc	BU
1970 Proof	3,520	Value: 45.00				

KM# 18.1   200 PESETAS
40.0000 g., 0.9990 Silver 1.2847 oz. ASW **Subject:** World Soccer Championship in Mexico **Obv:** Crossed tusks divide arms above and denomination below **Rev:** Statue flanked by countries with dates, four on each side

Date	Mintage	F	VF	XF	Unc	BU
1970 Proof	4,200	Value: 60.00				

KM# 18.2   200 PESETAS
40.0000 g., 0.9990 Silver 1.2847 oz. ASW **Subject:** World Soccer Championship in Mexico **Obv:** Fineness stamp in oval at base of right tusk; mint mark stamp "1 AR" at base of left tusk; incuse serial number below denomination **Rev:** Statue flanked by countries with dates, four on each side

Date	Mintage	F	VF	XF	Unc	BU
1970 Proof	Inc. above	Value: 75.00				

KM# 22   500 PESETAS
7.0500 g., 0.9000 Gold 0.2040 oz. AGW **Obv:** Crossed tusks divide arms above and denomination below **Rev:** Bust of Pope John XXIII

Date	Mintage	F	VF	XF	Unc	BU
1970 Proof	1,680	Value: 200				

KM# 23   500 PESETAS
7.0500 g., 0.9000 Gold 0.2040 oz. AGW **Subject:** Vladimer Illyich Lenin **Obv:** Crossed tusks divide arms above and denomination below **Rev:** Head left divides dates

Date	Mintage	F	VF	XF	Unc	BU
1970 Proof	1,680	Value: 200				

KM# 24   500 PESETAS
7.0500 g., 0.9000 Gold 0.2040 oz. AGW **Obv:** Crossed tusks divide arms and denomination below **Rev:** President Abraham Lincoln

Date	Mintage	F	VF	XF	Unc	BU
1970 Proof	1,700	Value: 200				

KM# 25   500 PESETAS
7.0500 g., 0.9000 Gold 0.2040 oz. AGW **Subject:** Centennial - Birth of Mahatma Gandhi **Obv:** Crossed tusks divide arms above and denomination below **Rev:** Portrait of Gandhi

Date	Mintage	F	VF	XF	Unc	BU
1970 Proof	1,680	Value: 200				

KM# 26   750 PESETAS
10.5700 g., 0.9000 Gold 0.3058 oz. AGW **Subject:** Centennial of the Capital Rome **Obv:** Crossed tusks divide arms above and denomination below **Rev:** Symbols of Rome

Date	Mintage	F	VF	XF	Unc	BU
1970 Proof	1,650	Value: 300				

KM# 27   750 PESETAS
10.5700 g., 0.9000 Gold 0.3058 oz. AGW **Subject:** Centennial of the Capital Rome **Obv:** Crossed tusks divide arms above and denomination below **Rev:** Coliseum

Date	Mintage	F	VF	XF	Unc	BU
1970 Proof	1,550	Value: 300				

KM# 28   750 PESETAS
10.5700 g., 0.9000 Gold 0.3058 oz. AGW **Subject:** Centennial of the Capital Rome **Obv:** Crossed tusks divide arms above and denomination below **Rev:** Athena divides dates and buildings

Date	Mintage	F	VF	XF	Unc	BU
1970 Proof	1,550	Value: 300				

KM# 16   150 PESETAS
30.0000 g., 0.9990 Silver 0.9635 oz. ASW **Subject:** Centennial of the Capital Rome **Obv:** Crossed tusks divide arms above and denomination below **Rev:** Athena divides dates and buildings

Date	Mintage	F	VF	XF	Unc	BU
1970 Proof	3,520	Value: 45.00				

KM# 29   750 PESETAS
10.5700 g., 0.9000 Gold 0.3058 oz. AGW **Subject:** Centennial of the Capital Rome **Obv:** Crossed tusks divide arms above and denomination below **Rev:** Head of Mercury left

Date	Mintage	F	VF	XF	Unc	BU
1970 Proof	1,550	Value: 300				

KM# 30   1000 PESETAS
14.1000 g., 0.9000 Gold 0.4080 oz. AGW **Subject:** World Soccer Championship in Mexico **Obv:** Crossed tusks divide arms above and denomination below **Rev:** Statue flanked by countries with dates, four on each side

Date	Mintage	F	VF	XF	Unc	BU
1970 Proof	1,190	Value: 400				

KM# 31   5000 PESETAS
70.5200 g., 0.9000 Gold 2.0405 oz. AGW **Subject:** First President - Francisco Macias **Obv:** Crossed tusks divide arms above and denomination below **Rev:** Head 3/4 right

Date	Mintage	F	VF	XF	Unc	BU
1970 Proof	330	Value: 2,000				

KM# 19   200 PESETAS
40.0000 g., 0.9990 Silver 1.2847 oz. ASW **Subject:** First President Francisco Macias **Obv:** Crossed tusks divide arms above and denomination below **Rev:** Head 3/4 right

Date	Mintage	F	VF	XF	Unc	BU
1970 Proof	4,000	Value: 55.00				

REFORM COINAGE
1975-1980

KM# 32 EKUELE
Brass **Obv:** Head left, date below **Rev:** Assorted tools divide denomination **Note:** Withdrawn from circulation.

Date	Mintage	F	VF	XF	Unc	BU
1975	3,000,000	1.00	2.00	3.00	5.00	7.00

KM# 33 5 EKUELE
Copper-Nickel **Obv:** Head left, date below **Rev:** Figures on split shields divide denomination **Note:** Withdrawn from circulation.

Date	Mintage	F	VF	XF	Unc	BU
1975	2,800,000	1.00	2.00	3.50	6.00	8.00

KM# 34 10 EKUELE
Copper-Nickel **Obv:** Head left, date below **Rev:** Rooster within shield divides denomination **Note:** Withdrawn from circulation.

Date	Mintage	F	VF	XF	Unc	BU
1975	1,300,000	1.50	2.50	4.50	9.00	12.00

KM# 35 1000 EKUELE
21.4300 g., 0.9250 Silver 0.6373 oz. ASW **Obv:** Bank building, denomination below **Rev:** Head right, date below

Date	Mintage	F	VF	XF	Unc	BU
1978 Proof	31,000	Value: 18.50				

KM# 36 2000 EKUELE
42.8700 g., 0.9250 Silver 1.2749 oz. ASW **Obv:** Assorted tools, denomination below, rooster above **Rev:** President Masie Nguema Biyogo head, right, date below

Date	Mintage	F	VF	XF	Unc	BU
1978 Proof	31,000	Value: 32.50				

KM# 37 2000 EKUELE
31.1000 g., 0.9270 Silver 0.9269 oz. ASW **Subject:** XXII Olympics **Rev:** Discus thrower, building at left, Olympic logo at right

Date	Mintage	F	VF	XF	Unc	BU
ND(1979) Proof	11,000	Value: 22.00				

KM# 56 2000 EKUELE
31.0000 g., 0.9270 Silver 0.9239 oz. ASW **Rev:** Impalas

Date	Mintage	F	VF	XF	Unc	BU
1980 (1983) Proof	1,000	Value: 32.50				

KM# 55 2000 EKUELE
31.0000 g., 0.9270 Silver 0.9239 oz. ASW **Rev:** Burchell's zebra

Date	Mintage	F	VF	XF	Unc	BU
1980 (1983) Proof	1,000	Value: 32.50				

KM# 57 2000 EKUELE
31.0000 g., 0.9270 Silver 0.9239 oz. ASW **Obv:** Bank building, denomination below **Rev:** Tiger's head 3/4 left, date below

Date	Mintage	F	VF	XF	Unc	BU
1980 (1983) Proof	1,000	Value: 35.00				

KM# 58 2000 EKUELE
31.0000 g., 0.9270 Silver 0.9239 oz. ASW **Rev:** Cheetah running left, date below

Date	Mintage	F	VF	XF	Unc	BU
1980 (1983) Proof	1,000	Value: 35.00				

KM# 39 5000 EKUELE
6.9600 g., 0.9170 Gold 0.2052 oz. AGW **Obv:** Bank building, denomination below **Rev:** Head right, date below

Date	Mintage	F	VF	XF	Unc	BU
1978 Proof	31,000	Value: 200				

KM# 40 10000 EKUELE
13.9200 g., 0.9170 Gold 0.4104 oz. AGW **Obv:** Assorted tools, denomination below, rooster above **Rev:** Head right, date below

Date	Mintage	F	VF	XF	Unc	BU
1978 Proof	31,000	Value: 385				

KM# 41 10000 EKUELE
13.9200 g., 0.9170 Gold 0.4104 oz. AGW **Subject:** Soccer Games - Argentina 1978 **Obv:** Assorted tools, denomination below, rooster above **Rev:** Country name and map at center, soccer players flank, shields above and below

Date	Mintage	F	VF	XF	Unc	BU
ND(1979) Proof	121	Value: 550				

REFORM COINAGE
1980-1982

KM# 50 EKUELE
Aluminum-Bronze **Obv:** T. E. Nkogo head right, date below **Rev:** Denomination at left, shielded arms at right, stars above arms **Note:** Two digit incuse date within star to left of date on obverse

Date	Mintage	F	VF	XF	Unc	BU
1980(80)	Est. 200,000	—	—	—	60.00	70.00

KM# 54 EKUELE
62.2900 g., 0.9990 Gold 2.0006 oz. AGW **Obv:** Coat of arms **Rev:** Pope John Paul II

Date	Mintage	F	VF	XF	Unc	BU
1982	—	—	—	—	1,850	

KM# 51 5 BIPKWELE
Copper-Nickel **Obv:** T. E. Nkogo right **Rev:** Value and arms **Note:** Two digit incuse date within star to left of date on obverse

Date	Mintage	F	VF	XF	Unc	BU
1980(80)	Est. 200,000	—	65.00	125	175	

KM# 52   25 BIPKWELE
6.3800 g., Copper-Nickel **Obv:** T. E. Nkogo head right, date below **Rev:** Denomination at left, arms at right **Note:** Two digit incuse date within star to left of date on obverse

Date	Mintage	F	VF	XF	Unc	BU
1980(80)	Est. 200,000	—	15.00	25.00	45.00	55.00
1981	Est. 800,000	—	—	—	—	—

KM# 53   50 BIPKWELE
Copper-Nickel **Obv:** T. E. Nkogo right **Rev:** Value and arms **Note:** Two digit incuse date within star to left of date on obverse

Date	Mintage	F	VF	XF	Unc	BU
1980(80)	Est. 200,000	—	—	—	50.00	60.00
1981	Est. 500,000	—	—	—	—	—

REFORM COINAGE
1985-

KM# 62   5 FRANCOS
Aluminum-Bronze **Obv:** Three Giant Eland left **Rev:** Denomination above date

Date	Mintage	F	VF	XF	Unc	BU
1985(a)	—	—	2.50	4.50	8.00	15.00

KM# 60   25 FRANCOS
Aluminum-Bronze **Obv:** Three Giant Eland left **Rev:** Denomination above date

Date	Mintage	F	VF	XF	Unc	BU
1985(a)	—	—	3.50	7.00	15.00	25.00

KM# 64   50 FRANCOS
Nickel **Obv:** Three Giant Eland left **Rev:** Denomination above date

Date	Mintage	F	VF	XF	Unc	BU
1985(a)	—	—	8.00	16.00	28.00	40.00
1986(a)	—	—	6.00	12.00	20.00	30.00

KM# 59   100 FRANCOS
Nickel **Obv:** Three Giant Eland left **Rev:** Denomination above date

Date	Mintage	F	VF	XF	Unc	BU
1985(a)	—	—	10.00	20.00	35.00	50.00
1986(a)	—	—	7.00	14.00	25.00	40.00

KM# 68   1000 FRANCOS
Copper-Nickel **Obv:** Arms above denomination **Rev:** Brandenburg Gate, dates below

Date	Mintage	F	VF	XF	Unc	BU
1991 Proof, Rare	5,150	Value: 30.00				

KM# 130   1000 FRANCOS
Copper-Nickel-Zinc **Obv:** National arms divide date, denomination below **Rev:** Lucerne city view **Rev. Leg.:** LUGARES FAMOSOS DEL MUNDO

Date	Mintage	F	VF	XF	Unc	BU
1993 Proof	—	Value: 22.50				

KM# 131   1000 FRANCOS
Copper-Nickel **Subject:** XV World Soccer Cup - USA 1994 **Obv:** National arms **Rev:** Playing field **Rev. Insc.:** 999 CuNi

Date	Mintage	F	VF	XF	Unc	BU
1993 Proof	—	Value: 30.00				

KM# 132   1000 FRANCOS
Copper-Nickel **Subject:** XV World Soccer Cup - USA 1994 **Obv:** National arms **Rev:** Soccer net and players **Rev. Insc.:** 999

Date	Mintage	F	VF	XF	Unc	BU
1993 Proof	—	Value: 30.00				
1994 Proof	—	Value: 30.00				

KM# 81   1000 FRANCOS
Copper-Nickel **Subject:** Jurassic Dinosaurs **Obv:** Arms divide date, denomination below **Rev:** Diplodocus **Note:** Multicolored.

Date	Mintage	F	VF	XF	Unc	BU
1993	—	—	—	—	30.00	—

KM# 115   1000 FRANCOS
25.5600 g., Copper-Nickel, 38 mm. **Subject:** Jurassic Dinosaurs **Obv:** Arms divide date, denomination below **Rev:** Multicolor stegosaurus **Edge:** Reeded

Date	Mintage	F	VF	XF	Unc	BU
1993	—	—	—	—	30.00	—

KM# 82   1000 FRANCOS
Copper-Nickel **Subject:** Jurassic Dinosaurs **Obv:** Arms divide date, denomination below **Rev:** Styracosaurus

Date	Mintage	F	VF	XF	Unc	BU
1993	—	—	—	—	30.00	—

KM# 83   1000 FRANCOS
Copper-Nickel **Subject:** Jurassic Dinosaurs **Obv:** Arms divide date, denomination below **Rev:** Tyrannosaurus

Date	Mintage	F	VF	XF	Unc	BU
1993	—	—	—	—	35.00	—

KM# 87   1000 FRANCOS
Copper-Nickel **Subject:** Jurassic Dinosaurs **Obv:** Arms divide date, denomination below **Rev:** Allosaurus

Date	Mintage	F	VF	XF	Unc	BU
1993	—	—	—	—	30.00	—

KM# 88   1000 FRANCOS
Copper-Nickel **Subject:** Jurassic Dinosaurs **Obv:** Arms divide date, denomination below **Rev:** Plateosaurus

Date	Mintage	F	VF	XF	Unc	BU
1993	—	—	—	—	30.00	—

KM# 89   1000 FRANCOS
Copper-Nickel **Subject:** African Bird Wildlife - Kingfisher **Obv:** Arms divide date, denomination below **Rev:** Pair of multicolored kingfishers

Date	Mintage	F	VF	XF	Unc	BU
1994	10,000	—	—	—	35.00	—

KM# 90   1000 FRANCOS
Copper-Nickel **Subject:** FIFA - XV World Soccer Championship - USA 1994 **Obv:** National arms divide date, denomination below **Rev:** Brazilian champion soccer players with trophy

Date	Mintage	F	VF	XF	Unc	BU
1994 Proof	—	Value: 27.50				

KM# 136   1000 FRANCOS
Copper-Nickel-Zinc **Series:** Famous World Places **Obv:** National arms **Rev:** Ruins of the Kaiser Wilhelm Gedächtnis Church, Berlin, multicolor

Date	Mintage	F	VF	XF	Unc	BU
1994 Proof	15,000	Value: 30.00				

KM# 138   1000 FRANCOS
Copper-Nickel **Subject:** FIFA - XV World Soccer Championship - USA 1994 **Obv:** National arms divide date, denomination below **Rev:** Brazilian champion soccer player's arms holding trophy, soccer ball outline in background

Date	Mintage	F	VF	XF	Unc	BU
1994 Proof	—	Value: 27.50				

KM# 139   1000 FRANCOS
Copper-Nickel-Zinc **Subject:** World's Famous Dogs **Obv:** National arms **Rev:** Dalmation, multicolor

Date	Mintage	F	VF	XF	Unc	BU
1994	—	—	—	—	25.00	—

KM# 93   1000 FRANCOS
Copper-Nickel-Zinc **Subject:** World's Famous Stamps **Obv:** National arms divide date, denomination below **Rev:** Swiss stamp of Jean Tinguely, multicolor

Date	Mintage	F	VF	XF	Unc	BU
1994	15,000	—	—	—	20.00	—
1995	Inc. above	—	—	—	20.00	—

KM# 112   1000 FRANCOS
26.0000 g., Copper-Nickel, 38 mm. **Obv:** Arms divide date,
denomination below **Rev:** Multicolor Spanish Salvador Dali
stamp design **Edge:** Reeded

Date	Mintage	F	VF	XF	Unc	BU
1994 Proof	15,000	Value: 20.00				

KM# 91   1000 FRANCOS
Copper-Nickel-Zinc **Series:** World's Famous Dogs **Obv:** Arms
divide date, denomination below **Rev:** St. Bernards, multicolor
Note: Multicolored.

Date	Mintage	F	VF	XF	Unc	BU
1994	10,000	—	—	—	30.00	—

KM# 92   1000 FRANCOS
Copper-Nickel **Subject:** 25th Anniversary - Moon Landing
Obv: Arms divide date, denomination below **Rev:** Placing the flag

Date	Mintage	F	VF	XF	Unc	BU
1994	15,000	—	—	—	22.50	—

KM# 84.1   1000 FRANCOS
Copper-Nickel **Subject:** 150th Anniversary - Basel "Taube"
Stamp **Obv:** Arms divide date, denomination below **Rev:** Stamp
within circle **Note:** Multicolored.

Date	Mintage	F	VF	XF	Unc	BU
1995	15,000	—	—	—	20.00	—

KM# 84.2   1000 FRANCOS
Copper-Nickel **Subject:** 150th Anniversary - Basel "Taube"
Stamp **Obv:** Arms divide date, denomination below **Rev. Leg.:**
Stamp within circle, error, "TAUBER" **Note:** Multicolored.

Date	Mintage	F	VF	XF	Unc	BU
1995	Inc. above	—	—	—	30.00	—

KM# 95   1000 FRANCOS
Copper-Nickel **Subject:** Famous Places in the World - Altdorf
Obv: Arms divide date, denomination below **Rev:** Multicolor
applique of Wilhelm Tell

Date	Mintage	F	VF	XF	Unc	BU
1996 Proof	—	Value: 27.50				

KM# 96   1000 FRANCOS
Copper-Nickel **Subject:** Famous Stamps of the World - Pintores
Famosos dei Mundo - Rolf Knie **Obv:** Arms divide date,
denomination below **Rev:** Multicolor applique of Swiss circus
stamp design

Date	Mintage	F	VF	XF	Unc	BU
1996 Proof	—	Value: 35.00				

KM# 97   1000 FRANCOS
Copper-Nickel **Subject:** Famous Stamps of the World - XXVI
Juegos Olimpicos de Verano **Obv:** Arms divide date,
denomination below **Rev:** Stamp with downhill skier

Date	Mintage	F	VF	XF	Unc	BU
1996 Proof	—	Value: 35.00				

KM# 118   1000 FRANCOS
29.5000 g., Copper-Nickel, 38 mm. **Subject:** Famous Places -
les Diablerets **Obv:** Arms divide date, denomination below
Rev: Multicolor stamp design **Edge:** Reeded

Date	Mintage	F	VF	XF	Unc	BU
1996	—	—	—	—	—	—

KM# 134   3000 FRANCOS
1.5500 g., 0.9990 Gold 0.0498 oz. AGW **Series:** Zodiac
Subject: Year of the Dog **Obv:** Flower blossom in sprays
Rev: Dog standing left

Date	Mintage	F	VF	XF	Unc	BU
1994 Proof	—	Value: 80.00				

KM# 66   7000 FRANCOS
26.3000 g., 0.9990 Silver 0.8447 oz. ASW **Obv:** Arms above
denomination **Rev:** President Mbasogo bust above three shields

Date	Mintage	F	VF	XF	Unc	BU
1991 Proof	—	Value: 42.50				

KM# 67   7000 FRANCOS
25.7000 g., 0.9990 Silver 0.8254 oz. ASW **Subject:** Soccer -
Italy 1990 **Obv:** Arms above denomination **Rev:** Soccer players,
small statue at left

Date	Mintage	F	VF	XF	Unc	BU
1991 Proof	6,000	Value: 45.00				

KM# 69   7000 FRANCOS
20.0000 g., 0.9990 Silver 0.6423 oz. ASW **Subject:** Discovery
of America **Obv:** Arms above denomination **Rev:** Santa Maria,
date below

Date	Mintage	F	VF	XF	Unc	BU
1991 Proof	15,000	Value: 40.00				

KM# 70 7000 FRANCOS
20.0000 g., 0.9990 Silver 0.6423 oz. ASW **Subject:** Seville Expo **Obv:** Arms above denomination **Rev:** Symbols from expo

Date	Mintage	F	VF	XF	Unc	BU
1991 Proof	15,000				40.00	

KM# 71 7000 FRANCOS
20.0000 g., 0.9990 Silver 0.6423 oz. ASW **Subject:** Barcelona Olympics **Obv:** Arms above denomination **Rev:** Athletes covering Olympic rings

Date	Mintage	F	VF	XF	Unc	BU
1991 Proof	15,000		Value: 42.50			

KM# 76 7000 FRANCOS
510.3000 g., 0.9990 Silver 16.389 oz. ASW, 75.1 mm. **Subject:** Endangered Wildlife **Obv:** Arms at lower left, figures and wildlife scene **Rev:** Lions, denomination below **Note:** Illustration reduced.

Date	Mintage	F	VF	XF	Unc	BU
1992 Proof	1,700		Value: 250			

KM# 80 7000 FRANCOS
10.4800 g., 0.9990 Silver 0.3366 oz. ASW **Subject:** Barcelona Olympics - 1992 **Obv:** Arms above denomination **Rev:** Katrin Krabbe, German sprinter

Date	Mintage	F	VF	XF	Unc	BU
1992 Proof	15,000		Value: 22.50			

KM# 105 7000 FRANCOS
7.7700 g., 0.9000 Gold 0.2248 oz. AGW **Subject:** Endangered Wildlife **Obv:** Arms above denomination **Rev:** Lions

Date	Mintage	F	VF	XF	Unc	BU
1992 Proof	450		Value: 450			

KM# 121 7000 FRANCOS
10.5100 g., 0.9990 Silver 0.3376 oz. ASW, 34.9 mm. **Obv:** National arms above denomination **Rev:** Elephant in profile, no trees or fineness statement in background **Edge:** Reeded

Date	Mintage	F	VF	XF	Unc	BU
1993 Proof	—		Value: 55.00			

KM# 122 7000 FRANCOS
10.2700 g., 0.9990 Silver 0.3298 oz. ASW, 34.8 mm. **Subject:** Protection of Endangered Wildlife **Obv:** Arms divide date, denomination below **Rev:** Two gorillas **Edge:** Reeded

Date	Mintage	F	VF	XF	Unc	BU
1993 Proof	—		Value: 55.00			

KM# 123 7000 FRANCOS
19.7300 g., 0.9990 Silver 0.6337 oz. ASW, 38.1 mm. **Obv:** National arms divide date, denomination below **Rev:** Lucerne city view **Rev. Leg.:** LUGARES FAMOSOS DEL MUNDO **Edge:** Reeded

Date	Mintage	F	VF	XF	Unc	BU
1993 Proof	—		Value: 45.00			

KM# 126 7000 FRANCOS
0.9990 Silver, 34.8 mm. **Subject:** Endangered Wildlife **Obv:** Arms divide date, denomination below **Rev:** Rhino **Edge:** Reeded

Date	Mintage	F	VF	XF	Unc	BU
1993	—		Value: 60.00			

KM# 127 7000 FRANCOS
0.9990 Silver, 34.8 mm. **Subject:** Endangered Wildlife **Obv:** Arms divide date, denomination below **Rev:** Buffalo **Edge:** Reeded

Date	Mintage	F	VF	XF	Unc	BU
1993 Proof	—		Value: 50.00			

KM# 128 7000 FRANCOS
0.9990 Silver, 34.8 mm. **Subject:** Endangered Wildlife **Obv:** Arms divide date, denomination below **Rev:** Lion **Edge:** Reeded

Date	Mintage	F	VF	XF	Unc	BU
1993 Proof	—		Value: 60.00			

KM# 129 7000 FRANCOS
0.9990 Silver, 34.8 mm. **Subject:** Endangered Wildlife **Obv:** Arms divide date, denomination below **Rev:** Springbok **Edge:** Reeded

Date	Mintage	F	VF	XF	Unc	BU
1993 Proof	—		Value: 50.00			

KM# 77 7000 FRANCOS
10.5100 g., 0.9990 Silver 0.3376 oz. ASW **Subject:** African Elephant Protection **Obv:** National arms divide date, denomination below **Rev:** Elephant

Date	Mintage	F	VF	XF	Unc	BU
1993 Proof	Est. 25,000		Value: 30.00			

KM# 78 7000 FRANCOS
20.0000 g., 0.9990 Silver 0.6423 oz. ASW **Subject:** Barcelona Olympics **Obv:** Arms divide date, denomination below **Rev:** Athletes covering Olympic rings

Date	Mintage	F	VF	XF	Unc	BU
1993 Proof	—		Value: 65.00			

KM# 94 7000 FRANCOS
20.1700 g., 0.9990 Silver 0.6478 oz. ASW **Subject:** Jurassic Dinosaurs **Obv:** Arms divide date, denomination below **Rev:** Multicolor stegosaurus scene applique

Date	Mintage	F	VF	XF	Unc	BU
1993 Proof	—		Value: 65.00			

KM# 114 7000 FRANCOS
9.9300 g., 0.7400 Silver 0.2362 oz. ASW, 34.8 mm. **Subject:** Endangered Wildlife **Obv:** Arms divide date, denomination below **Rev:** Giraffe family **Edge:** Reeded

Date	Mintage	F	VF	XF	Unc	BU
1993 Proof	—		Value: 50.00			

KM# 119 7000 FRANCOS
20.0000 g., 0.9990 Silver 0.6423 oz. ASW **Obv:** Arms divide date, denomination below **Rev:** Zebras

Date	Mintage	F	VF	XF	Unc	BU
1993 Proof	—		Value: 50.00			

KM# 133 7000 FRANCOS
20.0000 g., 0.9990 Silver 0.6423 oz. ASW **Subject:** XV World Soccer Cup - USA 1994 **Obv:** National arms **Rev:** Playing field

Date	Mintage	F	VF	XF	Unc	BU
1994 Proof	—		Value: 40.00			

KM# 137 7000 FRANCOS
20.0000 g., 0.9990 Silver 0.6423 oz. ASW **Series:** Famous World Places **Obv:** National arms **Rev:** Ruins of the Kaiser Wilhelm Gedächtnis Church - Berlin, multicolor

Date	Mintage	F	VF	XF	Unc	BU
1994 Proof	10,000		Value: 40.00			

KM# 140 7000 FRANCOS
20.0000 g., 0.9990 Silver 0.6423 oz. ASW **Subject:** World's Famous Dogs **Obv:** National arms **Rev:** Dalmation, multicolor

Date	Mintage	F	VF	XF	Unc	BU
1994 Proof	—		Value: 50.00			

KM# 86 7000 FRANCOS
20.1700 g., 0.9990 Silver 0.6478 oz. ASW **Subject:** XV World Cup Soccer - USA 1994 **Obv:** Arms divide date, denomination below **Rev:** Soccer net and players

Date	Mintage	F	VF	XF	Unc	BU
1994 Proof	—		Value: 40.00			

KM# 113 7000 FRANCOS
20.3500 g., 0.9990 Silver 0.6536 oz. ASW, 38 mm. **Obv:** Arms divide date, denomination below **Rev:** Multicolor Spanish Salvador Dali stamp design **Edge:** Reeded

Date	Mintage	F	VF	XF	Unc	BU
1994 Proof	—		Value: 50.00			

KM# 125 7000 FRANCOS
20.3500 g., 0.9990 Silver 0.6536 oz. ASW, 38.1 mm. **Obv:** Arms divide date, denomination below **Rev:** Multicolor Bulldog on cross **Edge:** Reeded

Date	Mintage	F	VF	XF	Unc	BU
1994 Proof	—		Value: 45.00			

KM# 98   7000 FRANCOS
20.3500 g., 0.9990 Silver 0.6536 oz. ASW **Subject:** African Bird
Wildlife - Kingfisher **Obv:** Arms divide date, denomination below
Rev: Pair of multicolor kingfishers

Date	Mintage	F	VF	XF	Unc	BU
1994 Proof	—	Value: 45.00				

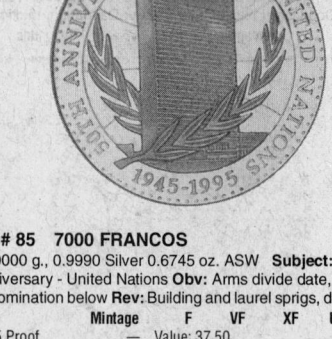

KM# 99   7000 FRANCOS
20.3500 g., 0.9990 Silver 0.6536 oz. ASW **Series:** World's
Famous Dogs **Obv:** Arms divide date, denomination below
Rev: Pair of St. Bernards, multicolor

Date	Mintage	F	VF	XF	Unc	BU
1994 Proof	7,500	Value: 50.00				

KM# 108   7000 FRANCOS
20.3500 g., 0.9990 Silver 0.6536 oz. ASW **Subject:** 25th
Anniversary - Moon Landing **Obv:** Arms divide date,
denomination below **Rev:** Multicolor moon landing scene

Date	Mintage	F	VF	XF	Unc	BU
1994 Proof	10,000	Value: 42.50				

KM# 141   7000 FRANCOS
20.0000 g., 0.9990 Silver 0.6423 oz. ASW **Subject:** World's
Famous Stamps **Obv:** National arms divide date, denomination
below **Rev:** Swiss stamp of Jean Tinguely, multicolor

Date	Mintage	F	VF	XF	Unc	BU
1995 Proof	7,500	Value: 50.00				

KM# 85   7000 FRANCOS
21.0000 g., 0.9990 Silver 0.6745 oz. ASW **Subject:** 50th
Anniversary - United Nations **Obv:** Arms divide date,
denomination below **Rev:** Building and laurel sprigs, dates below

Date	Mintage	F	VF	XF	Unc	BU
1995 Proof	—	Value: 37.50				

KM# 100   7000 FRANCOS
157.5500 g., 0.9990 Silver 5.0601 oz. ASW, 64.9 mm. **Subject:**
Endangered wildlife **Obv:** Topical map of Africa **Rev:** Elephant
head facing, denomination below **Note:** Illustration reduced.

Date	Mintage	F	VF	XF	Unc	BU
1995 Proof	555	Value: 165				

KM# 109   7000 FRANCOS
20.3500 g., 0.9990 Silver 0.6536 oz. ASW **Subject:** 150th
Anniversary - Basel "Taube" Stamp **Obv:** Arms divide date,
denomination below **Rev:** Multicolored stamp

Date	Mintage	F	VF	XF	Unc	BU
1995 Proof	7,500	Value: 30.00				

KM# 101   7000 FRANCOS
157.5500 g., 0.9990 Silver 5.0601 oz. ASW **Subject:** Endangered
wildlife **Obv:** Topical map of Africa **Rev:** Mother elephant with calf,
denomination below **Note:** Illustration reduced.

Date	Mintage	F	VF	XF	Unc	BU
1995 Proof	555	Value: 165				

KM# 102   7000 FRANCOS
157.5500 g., 0.9990 Silver 5.0601 oz. ASW **Subject:** Endangered
wildlife **Obv:** Topical map of Africa **Rev:** Elephants at watering hole,
denomination below **Note:** Illustration reduced.

Date	Mintage	F	VF	XF	Unc	BU
1995 Proof	555	Value: 165				

KM# 103   7000 FRANCOS
157.5500 g., 0.9990 Silver 5.0601 oz. ASW **Subject:** Endangered
wildlife **Obv:** Topical map of Africa **Rev:** Elephant family,
denomination below **Note:** Illustration reduced.

Date	Mintage	F	VF	XF	Unc	BU
1995 Proof	555	Value: 165				

KM# 104   7000 FRANCOS
157.5500 g., 0.9990 Silver 5.0601 oz. ASW **Subject:** Endangered
wildlife **Obv:** Topical map of Africa **Rev:** Adolescent elephant with
adult **Note:** Illustration reduced.

Date	Mintage	F	VF	XF	Unc	BU
1995 Proof	555	Value: 135				

KM# 120   7000 FRANCOS
19.6000 g., 0.9999 Silver 0.6301 oz. ASW, 37.9 mm.
Subject: Charlemagne **Obv:** Arms divide date, denomination
below **Rev:** King on horse **Edge:** Reeded

Date	Mintage	F	VF	XF	Unc	BU
1997 Proof	—	Value: 35.00				

KM# 116   8000 FRANCOS
7.7700 g., 0.9990 Gold 0.2496 oz. AGW, 26.9 mm.
Subject: World's Famous Dogs **Obv:** Arms divide date,
denomination below **Rev:** Pekingese dog and Chinese building
Edge: Reeded

Date	Mintage	F	VF	XF	Unc	BU
1994 Proof	—	Value: 250				

KM# 72 15000 FRANCOS
7.0000 g., 0.9170 Gold 0.2064 oz. AGW **Subject:** Discovery of America - Columbus **Obv:** Arms above denomination

Date	Mintage	F	VF	XF	Unc	BU
1991 Proof	1,500	Value: 215				

KM# 73 15000 FRANCOS
7.0000 g., 0.9170 Gold 0.2064 oz. AGW **Subject:** Expo Seville **Obv:** Arms above denomination **Rev:** Ship and Space Shuttle, dates below

Date	Mintage	F	VF	XF	Unc	BU
1991 Proof	1,500	Value: 215				

KM# 74 15000 FRANCOS
7.0000 g., 0.9170 Gold 0.2064 oz. AGW **Series:** Barcelona Olympics **Obv:** Arms above denomination **Rev:** Equestrian jumping

Date	Mintage	F	VF	XF	Unc	BU
1991 Proof	1,500	Value: 215				

KM# 74a 15000 FRANCOS
20.3300 g., 0.9990 Silver 0.6529 oz. ASW **Series:** Barcelona Olympics **Obv:** Arms above denomination **Rev:** Equestrian jumping

Date	Mintage	F	VF	XF	Unc	BU
1992 Proof	—	Value: 50.00				

KM# 79 15000 FRANCOS
855.3422 g., 0.9990 Silver 27.471 oz. ASW, 106 mm. **Subject:** Endangered Wildlife **Obv:** Topical map of Africa **Rev:** Elephant mother and calf, denomination below **Note:** Illustration reduced.

Date	Mintage	F	VF	XF	Unc	BU
1992 Proof	2,200	Value: 525				

KM# 106 15000 FRANCOS
15.5500 g., 0.9000 Gold 0.4499 oz. AGW **Subject:** Endangered Wildlife **Obv:** Topical map of Africa **Rev:** Elephant

Date	Mintage	F	VF	XF	Unc	BU
1992 Proof	450	Value: 450				

KM# 135 15000 FRANCOS
31.1000 g., 0.9990 Gold 0.9988 oz. AGW **Series:** Zodiac **Subject:** Year of the Dog **Obv:** Flower blossom in sprays **Rev:** Dog standing left

Date	Mintage	F	VF	XF	Unc	BU
1994 Proof	—	Value: 1,100				

KM# 107 30000 FRANCOS
33.9300 g., 0.9170 Gold 1.0003 oz. AGW, 32.8 mm. **Subject:** Elephant Protection **Obv:** Arms above denomination **Rev:** Elephant **Edge:** Reeded

Date	Mintage	F	VF	XF	Unc	BU
1993 Proof	700	Value: 1,000				

Note: 400 pieces remelted at mint

ESSAIS

KM#	Date	Mintage	Identification	Issue Price	Mkt Val
E1	1978	25	1000 Ekuele. Aluminum. KM#35.	—	45.00
E2	1978	20	1000 Ekuele. Copper. KM#35.	—	50.00
E3	1978	25	2000 Ekuele. Aluminum. KM#36.	—	55.00
E4	1978	—	2000 Ekuele. Copper. KM#36.	—	60.00
E5	1978	—	5000 Ekuele. Aluminum. KM#39.	—	35.00
E6	1978	—	5000 Ekuele. Copper. KM#39.	—	40.00
E7	1978	—	10000 Ekuele. Aluminum. KM#40.	—	45.00
E8	1978	—	10000 Ekuele. Copper. KM#40.	—	50.00
E9	ND(1979)	—	2000 Ekuele. Aluminum. KM#38.	—	25.00
E10	ND(1979)	—	2000 Ekuele. Copper. KM#38.	—	90.00
E11	ND(1979)	—	10000 Ekuele. Aluminum. KM#41.	—	25.00
E12	ND(1979)	—	10000 Ekuele. Copper. KM#41.	—	60.00
E13	1980	—	Bipkwele. Copper. KM#5.	—	20.00
E28	1985	—	5 Francos. Aluminum-Bronze. KM#62.	—	35.00
E29	1985	—	25 Francos. Aluminum-Bronze. Three Giant Eland, left. Denomination above date. KM#60.	—	40.00
E30	1985	—	50 Francos. Nickel. KM#64.	—	55.00
E31	1985	—	100 Francos. Nickel. Three Giant Eland, left. Denomination above date. KM#59.	—	27.50

PATTERNS
Including off metal strikes

KM#	Date	Mintage	Identification	Mkt Val
Pn17	1995	—	1000 Francos. Copper-Nickel. 26.4000 g. 38.2 mm. National arms. Large "UN" letters with German inscription on UN logo. Reeded edge. First reported in World Coin News Round-up in August 2003	100
Pn31	1992	—	15000 Francos. 0.9990 Gold Plated Silver. 12.6700 g.	—
Pn32	1993	—	1000 Francos. Copper Nickel. Soccer scene.	45.00
Pn33	1993	—	1000 Francos. Copper Nickel. Soccer players through net.	45.00
Pn34	1994	—	1000 Francos. Copper Nickel. Hands holding FIFA cup.	35.00
Pn35	1994	—	1000 Francos. Copper Nickel. Three players holding cup.	35.00
Pn36	1994	—	7000 Francos. 0.9990 Silver. 19.9100 g. Dalmations.	60.00
Pn37	1995	—	1000 Francos. Copper-Nickel. 26.4000 g. 38.2 mm. National arms. "UN" letters with German inscription and the UN logo in background. Reeded edge.	—
Pn38	1996	—	1000 Francos. Brass. 28.5000 g. 38 mm. National arms. French postage stamp design. Reeded edge.	300

PIEFORTS

KM#	Date	Mintage	Identification	Issue Price	Mkt Val
P1	1978	—	1000 Ekuele. Copper. KM#35.	—	200
P2	1978	—	1000 Ekuele. 0.9250 Silver. KM#35.	—	250
P3	1978	—	2000 Ekuele. Copper. 6.8 mm. Plain edge. KM#36.	—	300
P4	1978	—	5000 Ekuele. Copper. 2.6 mm. Milled edge. KM#39.	—	175
P5	1978	—	5000 Ekuele. Copper. 4.1 mm. Plain edge.	—	150
P6	1978	—	10000 Ekuele. Copper. 3.4 mm. Milled edge. KM#41.	—	110
P7	ND(1979)	—	2000 Ekuele. Copper. KM#38.	—	215
P8	ND(1979)	—	2000 Ekuele. 0.9250 Silver. KM#38.	—	300
P9	ND(1979)	—	2000 Ekuele. Gilt Copper.	—	215
P10	ND(1979)	—	10000 Ekuele. Copper. KM#41.	—	225
P11	ND(1979)	—	10000 Ekuele. Gold. KM#41.	—	1,250
P12	ND(1979)	—	10000 Ekuele. Gilt Copper. KM#41.	—	200

TRIAL STRIKES

KM#	Date	Mintage	Identification	Issue Price	Mkt Val
TS1	1978	—	2000 Ekuele. Copper. 3.9 mm. KM#36. PRUEBA.	—	150
TS2	1978	—	2000 Ekuele. Copper. 3.9 mm. PRUEBA. KM#36.	—	150
TS3	1978	—	5000 Ekuele. Copper. 2.8 mm. KM#39. PRUEBA.	—	75.00
TS3	1978	—	5000 Ekuele. Copper. 2.8 mm. KM#39. PRUEBA.	—	75.00
TS4	1978	—	5000 Ekuele. Copper. 2.8 mm. KM#39. PRUEBA.	—	75.00
TS5	1978	—	10000 Ekuele. Copper. 3.6 mm. KM#40. PRUEBA.	—	75.00
TS6	1978	—	10000 Ekuele. Copper. PRUEBA. KM#40.	—	75.00
TS6	1978	—	10000 Ekuele. Copper. PRUEBA. KM#40.	—	75.00
TS7	1978(80)	—	2000 Bipkwele. 0.9250 Silver. 25.2100 g. M2. PRUEBA.	—	150
TS8	1978(80)	—	2000 Bipkwele. 0.9250 Silver. 25.2100 g. PRUEBA. M3.	—	150

MINT SETS

KM#	Date	Mintage	Identification	Issue Price	Mkt Val
MS1	1975 (3)	—	KM#32-34	—	22.00

PROOF SETS

KM#	Date	Mintage	Identification	Issue Price	Mkt Val
PS1	1970 (27)	330	KM#5-31	—	4,750
PS2	1970 (15)	2,475	KM#5-19	127	450
PS3	1970 (12)	330	KM#20-31	—	4,300

ERITREA

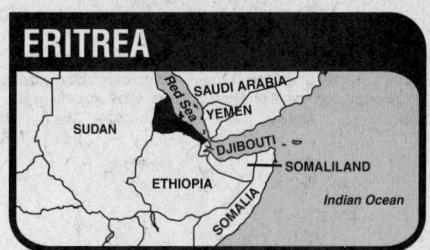

The State of Eritrea, a former Ethiopian province fronting on the Red Sea, has an area of 45,300 sq. mi. (117,600 sq. km.) and a population of 3.6 million. It was an Italian colony from 1889 until its incorporation into Italian East Africa in 1936. It was under the British Military Administration from 1941 to Sept. 15, 1952, when the United Nations designated it an autonomous unit within the federation of Ethiopia and Eritrea. On Nov. 14, 1962, it was annexed with Ethiopia. In 1991 the Eritrean Peoples Liberation Front extended its control over the entire territory of Eritrea. Following 2 years of provisional government, Eritrea held a referendum on independence in May 1993. Overwhelming popular approval led to the proclamation of an independent Republic of Eritrea on May 24.

RULERS
Vittorio Emanuele III, 1900-1945

MINT MARKS
M - Milan
PM - Pobjoy
R – Rome

MONETARY SYSTEM
100 Centesimi = 1 Lira
5 Lire = 1 Tallero
100 Cents = 1 Nakfa (from 1997)

ITALIAN COLONY
COLONIAL COINAGE

KM# 5   TALLERO
28.0668 g., 0.8350 Silver 0.7534 oz. ASW, 40 mm. **Ruler:**
Vittorio Emanuele III **Obv:** Bust with loose hair right, date at right
Rev: Crowned imperial eagle with shield on breast

Date	Mintage	F	VF	XF	Unc	BU
1918R	510,000	40.00	100	300	650	1,000

REPUBLIC
DECIMAL COINAGE

100 Cents = 1 Dollar

KM# 43   CENT
2.2000 g., Nickel Clad Steel, 17 mm. **Obv:** Red-fronted gazelle
right, divides denomination **Rev:** Soldiers with flag, date at left

Date	Mintage	F	VF	XF	Unc	BU
1997	—	—	—	—	0.50	1.00

KM# 44   5 CENTS
2.7000 g., Nickel Clad Steel, 18.9 mm. **Obv:** Leopard on log
divides denomination **Rev:** Soldiers with flag, date at left

Date	Mintage	F	VF	XF	Unc	BU
1997	—	—	—	—	0.75	1.50

KM# 45   10 CENTS
3.3000 g., Nickel Clad Steel, 20.95 mm. **Obv:** Ostrich left divides
denomination **Rev:** Soldiers with flag, date at left **Edge:** Reeded

Date	Mintage	F	VF	XF	Unc	BU
1997	—	—	—	—	1.00	1.75

KM# 46   25 CENTS
5.8000 g., Nickel Clad Steel, 23 mm. **Obv:** Grevy's zebra left
divides denomination **Rev:** Soldiers with flag, date at left

Date	Mintage	F	VF	XF	Unc	BU
1997	—	—	—	—	1.25	2.00

KM# 47   50 CENTS
7.8000 g., Nickel Clad Steel, 24.95 mm. **Obv:** Greater Kudu left
divides denomination **Rev:** Soldiers with flag, date at left

Date	Mintage	F	VF	XF	Unc	BU
1997	—	—	—	1.50	2.25	

KM# 48   100 CENTS
10.3000 g., Nickel Clad Steel, 26.2 mm. **Obv:** African elephant and
calf left, divide denomination **Rev:** Soldiers with flag, date at left

Date	Mintage	F	VF	XF	Unc	BU
1997	—	—	—	—	2.00	3.00

KM# 6   DOLLAR
Copper-Nickel **Subject:** Independence Day **Obv:** Dhow, camel
and palm tree, date below, all within circle **Rev:** Tree within laurel
wreath, dates below, circle surrounds, denomination below

Date	Mintage	F	VF	XF	Unc	BU
1993	—	—	—	—	8.50	

KM# 10   DOLLAR
Copper-Nickel **Subject:** Preserve Planet Earth **Obv:** Dhow,
camel and palm tree, date below, all within circle
Rev: Triceratops, denomination below

Date	Mintage	F	VF	XF	Unc	BU
1993	—	—	—	—	14.00	

KM# 13   DOLLAR
Copper-Nickel **Subject:** Preserve Planet Earth **Obv:** Dhow,
camel and palm tree, date below, all within circle
Rev: Ankylosaurus, denomination below

Date	Mintage	F	VF	XF	Unc	BU
1993	—	—	—	—	14.00	

KM# 14   DOLLAR
Copper-Nickel **Subject:** Preserve Planet Earth **Obv:** Dhow,
camel and palm tree, date below, all within circle
Rev: Pteranodon, denomination below

Date	Mintage	F	VF	XF	Unc	BU
1993	—	—	—	—	14.00	

KM# 15   DOLLAR
Copper-Nickel **Subject:** Preserve Planet Earth **Obv:** Dhow,
camel and palm tree, date below, all within circle **Rev:** Cheetah,
denomination below

Date	Mintage	F	VF	XF	Unc	BU
1994	—	—	—	—	14.00	

KM# 16   DOLLAR
Copper-Nickel **Subject:** Preserve Planet Earth **Obv:** Dhow,
camel and palm tree, date below, all within circle **Rev:** Black
Rhinoceros, denomination below

Date	Mintage	F	VF	XF	Unc	BU
1994	—	—	—	—	14.00	

KM# 17   DOLLAR
Copper-Nickel **Subject:** Preserve Planet Earth **Obv:** Dhow,
camel and palm tree, date below, all within circle **Rev:** Black and
White Colobus Monkey, denomination below

Date	Mintage	F	VF	XF	Unc	BU
1994	—	—	—	—	14.00	

KM# 28   DOLLAR
Copper-Nickel **Subject:** Preserve Planet Earth **Obv:** Dhow,
camel and palm tree, date below, all within circle **Rev:** Lions

Date	Mintage	F	VF	XF	Unc	BU
1995PM	—	—	—	—	14.00	

KM# 31   DOLLAR
Copper-Nickel **Subject:** Preserve Planet Earth **Obv:** Dhow, camel
and palm tree, date below, all within circle **Rev:** Cape Eagle owl

Date	Mintage	F	VF	XF	Unc	BU
1995PM	—	—	—	—	14.00	

KM# 34   DOLLAR
Copper-Nickel **Subject:** Preserve Planet Earth **Obv:** Dhow, camel and palm tree, date below, all within circle **Rev:** Wattled Cranes

Date	Mintage	F	VF	XF	Unc	BU
1996	—	—	—	—	14.00	—

KM# 37   DOLLAR
Copper-Nickel **Subject:** Preserve Planet Earth **Obv:** Dhow, camel and palm tree, date below, all within circle **Rev:** Laner falcon

Date	Mintage	F	VF	XF	Unc	BU
1996	—	—	—	—	14.00	—

KM# 40   DOLLAR
Copper-Nickel **Subject:** Jurassic Park **Obv:** Dhow, camel and palm tree, date below, all within circle **Rev:** Triceratops, Jurassic Park logo

Date	Mintage	F	VF	XF	Unc	BU
1997	—	—	—	—	14.00	—

KM# 7   10 DOLLARS
31.1030 g., 0.9999 Silver 0.9998 oz. ASW **Subject:** Independence Day **Obv:** Dhow, camel and palm tree, date below, within circle **Rev:** Tree within laurel wreath, dates below, circle surrounds, denomination below

Date	Mintage	F	VF	XF	Unc	BU
1993 Proof	Est. 30,000	Value: 45.00				

KM# 11   10 DOLLARS
28.2800 g., 0.9250 Silver 0.8410 oz. ASW **Subject:** Preserve Planet Earth **Obv:** Dhow, camel and palm tree, date below, all within circle **Rev:** Triceratops, denomination below

Date	Mintage	F	VF	XF	Unc	BU
1993 Proof	Est. 30,000	Value: 45.00				

KM# 24   10 DOLLARS
28.2800 g., 0.9250 Silver 0.8410 oz. ASW **Subject:** Preserve Planet Earth **Obv:** Dhow, camel and palm tree, date below, all within circle **Rev:** Ankylosaurus

Date	Mintage	F	VF	XF	Unc	BU
1993 Proof	Est. 30,000	Value: 45.00				

KM# 25   10 DOLLARS
28.2800 g., 0.9250 Silver 0.8410 oz. ASW **Subject:** Preserve Planet Earth **Obv:** Dhow, camel and palm tree, date below, all within circle **Rev:** Pteranodon

Date	Mintage	F	VF	XF	Unc	BU
1993 Proof	Est. 30,000	Value: 45.00				

KM# 18   10 DOLLARS
28.2800 g., 0.9250 Silver 0.8410 oz. ASW **Subject:** Preserve Planet Earth **Obv:** Dhow, camel and palm tree, date below, all within circle **Rev:** Cheetah, denomination below

Date	Mintage	F	VF	XF	Unc	BU
1994 Proof	Est. 30,000	Value: 45.00				

KM# 19   10 DOLLARS
28.2800 g., 0.9250 Silver 0.8410 oz. ASW **Subject:** Preserve Planet Earth **Obv:** Dhow, camel and palm tree, date below, all within circle **Rev:** Black rhinoceros, denomination below

Date	Mintage	F	VF	XF	Unc	BU
1994 Proof	Est. 30,000	Value: 45.00				

KM# 20   10 DOLLARS
28.2800 g., 0.9250 Silver 0.8410 oz. ASW **Subject:** Preserve Planet Earth **Obv:** Dhow, camel and palm tree, date below, all within circle **Rev:** Colobus monkey, denomination below

Date	Mintage	F	VF	XF	Unc	BU
1994 Proof	Est. 30,000	Value: 45.00				

KM# 29   10 DOLLARS
28.2800 g., 0.9250 Silver 0.8410 oz. ASW **Subject:** Preserve Planet Earth **Obv:** Dhow, camel and palm tree, date below, all within circle **Rev:** Lions, denomination below

Date	Mintage	F	VF	XF	Unc	BU
1995PM Proof	5,000	Value: 45.00				

KM# 32   10 DOLLARS
28.2800 g., 0.9250 Silver 0.8410 oz. ASW **Subject:** Preserve Planet Earth **Obv:** Dhow, camel and palm tree, date below, all within circle **Rev:** Cape Eagle owl, denomination below

Date	Mintage	F	VF	XF	Unc	BU
1995PM Proof	Est. 30,000	Value: 45.00				

KM# 35   10 DOLLARS
28.2800 g., 0.9250 Silver 0.8410 oz. ASW **Subject:** Preserve Planet Earth **Obv:** Dhow, camel and palm tree, date below, all within circle **Rev:** Wattled cranes, denomination below

Date	Mintage	F	VF	XF	Unc	BU
1996 Proof	Est. 30,000	Value: 45.00				

KM# 38   10 DOLLARS
28.2800 g., 0.9250 Silver 0.8410 oz. ASW **Subject:** Preserve Planet Earth **Obv:** Dhow, camel and palm tree, date below, all within circle **Rev:** Laner falcon, denomination below

Date	Mintage	F	VF	XF	Unc	BU
1996 Proof	Est. 30,000	Value: 45.00				

KM# 41   10 DOLLARS
28.2800 g., 0.9250 Silver 0.8410 oz. ASW **Subject:** Jurassic Park **Obv:** Dhow, camel and palm tree, date below, all within circle **Rev:** Triceratops, Jurassic Park logo, denomination below

Date	Mintage	F	VF	XF	Unc	BU
1997 Proof	Est. 10,000	Value: 45.00				

KM# 8   50 DOLLARS
3.1100 g., 0.9990 Gold 0.0999 oz. AGW **Subject:** Independence Day **Obv:** Dhow, camel and tree within circle, denomination below **Rev:** Tree within laurel wreath, dates below, circle surrounds, denomination below

Date	Mintage	F	VF	XF	Unc	BU
1993 Proof	Est. 20,000	Value: 115				

KM# 9 100 DOLLARS
6.2200 g., 0.9990 Gold 0.1998 oz. AGW **Subject:**
Independence Day **Obv:** Dhow, camel and palm tree, date below,
all within circle **Rev:** Tree within laurel wreath, dates below, circle
surrounds, denomination below

Date	Mintage	F	VF	XF	Unc	BU
1993 Proof	Est. 5,000			Value: 215		

KM# 12 100 DOLLARS
6.2200 g., 0.9990 Gold 0.1998 oz. AGW **Subject:** Preserve
Planet Earth **Obv:** Dhow, camel and tree within circle,
denomination below **Rev:** Triceratops, denomination below

Date	Mintage	F	VF	XF	Unc	BU
1993 Proof	Est. 5,000			Value: 195		

KM# 26 100 DOLLARS
6.2200 g., 0.9990 Gold 0.1998 oz. AGW **Subject:** Preserve
Planet Earth **Obv:** Dhow, camel and palm tree, date below, all
within circle **Rev:** Ankylosaurus

Date	Mintage	F	VF	XF	Unc	BU
1993 Proof	Est. 5,000			Value: 195		

KM# 27 100 DOLLARS
6.2200 g., 0.9990 Gold 0.1998 oz. AGW **Subject:** Preserve
Planet Earth **Obv:** Dhow, camel and palm tree, date below, all
within circle **Rev:** Pteranodon

Date	Mintage	F	VF	XF	Unc	BU
1993 Proof	Est. 5,000			Value: 195		

KM# 21 100 DOLLARS
6.2200 g., 0.9990 Gold 0.1998 oz. AGW **Subject:** Preserve
Planet Earth **Obv:** Dhow, camel and palm tree, date below, all
within circle **Rev:** Mother and baby cheetah

Date	Mintage	F	VF	XF	Unc	BU
1994 Proof	5,000			Value: 195		

KM# 22 100 DOLLARS
6.2200 g., 0.9990 Gold 0.1998 oz. AGW **Subject:** Preserve
Planet Earth **Obv:** Dhow, camel and palm tree, date below, all
within circle **Rev:** Rhinoceros head right

Date	Mintage	F	VF	XF	Unc	BU
1994 Proof	5,000			Value: 195		

KM# 23 100 DOLLARS
6.2200 g., 0.9990 Gold 0.1998 oz. AGW **Subject:** Preserve
Planet Earth **Obv:** Dhow, camel and palm tree, date below, all
within circle **Rev:** Colobus monkey

Date	Mintage	F	VF	XF	Unc	BU
1994 Proof	5,000			Value: 195		

KM# 30 100 DOLLARS
6.2200 g., 0.9990 Gold 0.1998 oz. AGW **Subject:** Preserve
Planet Earth **Obv:** Dhow, camel and palm tree, date below, all
within circle **Rev:** Female lion and cub

Date	Mintage	F	VF	XF	Unc	BU
1995 Proof	Est. 5,000			Value: 200		

KM# 33 100 DOLLARS
6.2200 g., 0.9990 Gold 0.1998 oz. AGW **Subject:** Preserve
Planet Earth **Obv:** Dhow, camel and palm tree, date below, all
within circle **Rev:** Cape eagle owl

Date	Mintage	F	VF	XF	Unc	BU
1995 Proof	Est. 5,000			Value: 195		

KM# 36 100 DOLLARS
6.2200 g., 0.9990 Gold 0.1998 oz. AGW **Subject:** Preserve
Planet Earth **Obv:** Dhow, camel and palm tree, date below, all
within circle **Rev:** Wattled cranes

Date	Mintage	F	VF	XF	Unc	BU
1996 Proof	Est. 5,000			Value: 195		

KM# 39 100 DOLLARS
6.2200 g., 0.9990 Gold 0.1998 oz. AGW **Subject:** Preserve
Planet Earth **Obv:** Dhow, camel and palm tree, date below, all
within circle **Rev:** Laner falcon

Date	Mintage	F	VF	XF	Unc	BU
1996 Proof	Est. 5,000			Value: 195		

KM# 42 100 DOLLARS
6.2200 g., 0.9990 Gold 0.1998 oz. AGW **Subject:** Jurassic Park
Obv: Dhow, camel and tree within circle, denomination below
Rev: Triceratops, Jurassic Park logo

Date	Mintage	F	VF	XF	Unc	BU
1997 Proof	Est. 2,500			Value: 200		

PROVAS

KM#	Date	Mintage	Identification		Mkt Val
PR1	1918R	—	Tallero. Bust with loose hair right. Crowned imperial eagle, shield on breast. KM5.		1,250

ESTONIA

The Republic of Estonia (formerly the Estonian Soviet
Socialist Republic of the U.S.S.R.) is the northernmost of the
three Baltic States in Eastern Europe. It has an area of 17,462
sq. mi. (45,100 sq. km.) and a population of 1.6 million. Capital:
Tallinn. Agriculture and dairy farming are the principal industries.
Butter, eggs, bacon, timber and petroleum are exported.

This small and ancient Baltic state had enjoyed but two
decades of independence since the 13th century until the present
time. After having been conquered by the Danes, the Livonian
Knights, the Teutonic Knights of Germany (who reduced the people to serfdom), the Swedes, the Poles and Russia, Estonia
declared itself an independent republic on Feb. 24, 1918 but was
not freed until Feb. 1919. The peace treaty was signed Feb. 2,
1920. Shortly after the start of World War II, it was again occupied
by Russia and incorporated as the 16th state of the U.S.S.R Germany occupied the tiny state from 1941 to 1944, after which it was
retaken by Russia. Most of the nations of the world, including the
United States and Great Britain, did not recognize Estonia's
incorporation into the Soviet Union.

The coinage, issued during the country's brief independence, is obsolete.

On August 20, 1991, the Parliament of the Estonian Soviet
Socialist Republic voted to reassert the republic's independence.

REPUBLIC
1918 - 1941
REPUBLIC COINAGE

KM# 1 MARK
Copper-Nickel, 18 mm. **Obv:** Three Czech lions left divide date
Rev: Denomination **Edge:** Milled

Date	Mintage	F	VF	XF	Unc	BU
1922	5,025,000	4.00	5.00	9.00	17.00	—

KM# 1a MARK
2.6000 g., Nickel-Bronze, 18 mm. **Obv:** Three Czech lions left
divide date **Rev:** Denomination **Edge:** Milled

Date	Mintage	F	VF	XF	Unc	BU
1924	1,985,000	4.00	8.00	12.00	25.00	—

KM# 5 MARK
Nickel-Bronze **Obv:** Three Czech lions left divide date
Rev: Denomination

Date	Mintage	F	VF	XF	Unc	BU
1926	3,979,000	7.00	10.00	17.00	34.00	—

KM# 2 3 MARKA
Copper-Nickel **Obv:** Three Czech lions left divide date
Rev: Denomination

Date	Mintage	F	VF	XF	Unc	BU
1922	2,089,000	4.00	7.00	9.00	15.00	

KM# 2a 3 MARKA
Nickel-Bronze **Obv:** Three Czech lions left divide date
Rev: Denomination

Date	Mintage	F	VF	XF	Unc	BU
1925	1,134,000	7.00	10.00	17.00	34.00	—

KM# 6 3 MARKA
Nickel-Bronze **Obv:** Three Czech lions on shield within wreath
Rev: Denomination, date below

Date	Mintage	F	VF	XF	Unc	BU
1926	903,000	30.00	60.00	90.00	170	—

KM# 3 5 MARKA
5.0000 g., Copper-Nickel, 23 mm. **Obv:** Three Czech lions left
divide date **Rev:** Denomination **Edge:** Milled

Date	Mintage	F	VF	XF	Unc	BU
1922	3,983,000	7.00	10.00	12.00	24.00	—

KM# 3a 5 MARKA
5.0000 g., Nickel-Bronze, 23 mm. **Obv:** Three Czech lions left
divide date **Rev:** Denomination **Edge:** Milled

Date	Mintage	F	VF	XF	Unc	BU
1924	1,335,000	7.00	10.00	17.00	27.00	—

KM# 7 5 MARKA
Nickel-Bronze **Obv:** Three Czech lions on shield within wreath
Rev: Denomination above date

Date	Mintage	F	VF	XF	Unc	BU
1926	1,038,000	90.00	170	220	370	—

KM# 4 10 MARKA
6.0000 g., Nickel-Bronze, 26 mm. **Obv:** Three Czech lions left
divide date **Rev:** Denomination **Edge:** Milled

Date	Mintage	F	VF	XF	Unc	BU
1925	2,200,000	10.00	15.00	25.00	45.00	—

KM# 8 10 MARKA
Nickel-Bronze **Obv:** Three Czech lions on shield within wreath
Rev: Denomination above date

Date	Mintage	F	VF	XF	Unc	BU
1926	2,789,000	700	1,100	1,600	2,200	—

Note: Most of this issue was melted down; Not released to
circulation

REFORM COINAGE
100 Senti = 1 Kroon

KM# 10 SENT
2.0000 g., Bronze, 17 mm. **Obv:** Three Czech lions left above
date **Rev:** Denomination, oak leaves in background **Edge:** Plain

Date	Mintage	F	VF	XF	Unc	BU
1929	23,553,000	2.00	3.00	4.00	5.00	—

KM# 19.1 SENT
2.0000 g., Bronze, 16 mm. **Obv:** Three Czech lions left above date **Rev:** Denomination **Edge:** Plain **Note:** 1mm thick planchet.

Date	Mintage	F	VF	XF	Unc	BU
1939	5,000,000	5.00	10.00	17.00	38.00	—

KM# 19.2 SENT
Bronze **Obv:** Three Czech lions left divide date **Rev:** Denomination **Note:** 0.9mm thick planchet.

Date	Mintage	F	VF	XF	Unc	BU
1939	Inc. above	8.00	12.00	18.00	39.00	—

KM# 15 2 SENTI
3.5000 g., Bronze, 19 mm. **Obv:** Three Czech lions left above date **Rev:** Denomination **Edge:** Plain

Date	Mintage	F	VF	XF	Unc	BU
1934	5,838,000	3.00	5.00	8.00	12.00	—

KM# 11 5 SENTI
3.5000 g., Bronze, 23.3 mm. **Obv:** Three Czech lions left above date **Rev:** Denomination **Edge:** Plain

Date	Mintage	F	VF	XF	Unc	BU
1931	11,000,000	3.00	4.00	9.00	17.00	—

KM# 12 10 SENTI
Nickel-Bronze, 18 mm. **Obv:** Three Czech lions within shield divide date **Rev:** Denomination **Edge:** Plain

Date	Mintage	F	VF	XF	Unc	BU
1931	4,089,000	3.00	4.00	12.00	20.00	—

KM# 17 20 SENTI
3.9200 g., Nickel-Bronze, 21 mm. **Obv:** Three Czech lions within shield divide date **Rev:** Denomination **Edge:** Plain

Date	Mintage	F	VF	XF	Unc	BU
1935	4,250,000	6.00	8.00	14.00	24.00	—

KM# 9 25 SENTI
Nickel-Bronze **Obv:** Three Czech lions within shield, wreath surrounds **Rev:** Denomination above date

Date	Mintage	F	VF	XF	Unc	BU
1928	2,025,000	7.00	11.00	28.00	45.00	—

KM# 18 50 SENTI
7.5000 g., Nickel-Bronze, 27.5 mm. **Obv:** Three Czech lions within shield divide date **Rev:** Denomination **Edge:** Plain

Date	Mintage	F	VF	XF	Unc	BU
1936	1,256,000	7.00	12.00	20.00	38.00	—

KM# 14 KROON
6.0000 g., 0.5000 Silver 0.0964 oz. ASW, 26 mm. **Subject:** 10th Singing Festival **Obv:** Three Czech lions within shield, wreath surrounds, date below **Rev:** Harp divides dates, denomination below

Date	Mintage	F	VF	XF	Unc	BU
1933	350,000	15.00	30.00	50.00	70.00	100

KM# 16 KROON
5.9600 g., Aluminum-Bronze, 25 mm. **Obv:** Three Czech lions within shield, wreath surrounds, date below **Rev:** Ship of Vikings, denomination below **Edge:** Plain **Note:** 1990 restrikes which exist are private issues.

Date	Mintage	F	VF	XF	Unc	BU
1934	3,304,000	7.00	10.00	18.00	50.00	70.00

KM# 20 2 KROONI
12.0000 g., 0.5000 Silver 0.1929 oz. ASW, 30 mm. **Subject:** Toompea Fortress at Tallinn **Obv:** Three Czech lions within shield, wreath surrounds, date below **Rev:** Castle denomination below **Edge:** Milled

Date	Mintage	F	VF	XF	Unc	BU
1930	1,276,000	7.00	12.00	20.00	50.00	80.00

KM# 13 2 KROONI
12.0000 g., 0.5000 Silver 0.1929 oz. ASW, 30 mm. **Subject:** Tercentenary - University of Tartu **Obv:** Three Czech lions within shield, wreath surrounds, date below **Rev:** University building, denomination below **Edge:** Plain

Date	Mintage	F	VF	XF	Unc	BU
1932	100,000	20.00	30.00	40.00	75.00	95.00

MODERN REPUBLIC
1991 - present
STANDARD COINAGE

KM# 21 5 SENTI
1.2900 g., Brass, 15.9 mm. **Obv:** Three Czech lions left divide date **Rev:** Denomination **Edge:** Plain

Date	Mintage	F	VF	XF	Unc	BU
1991	—	—	—	—	0.30	—
1992	—	—	—	—	0.30	—
1995	—	—	—	—	0.30	—

KM# 22 10 SENTI
1.8500 g., Copper-Aluminum-Nickel, 17.1 mm. **Obv:** National arms **Rev:** Denomination **Rev. Leg.:** EESTI VABARIIK **Edge:** Plain

Date	Mintage	F	VF	XF	Unc	BU
1991	—	—	—	0.20	0.50	0.75
1992	—	—	—	0.20	0.50	0.75
1994	—	—	—	0.20	0.50	0.75
1996	—	—	—	0.20	0.50	0.75
1997	—	—	—	0.20	0.50	0.75
1998	—	—	—	0.20	0.50	0.75

KM# 23 20 SENTI
2.2700 g., Brass, 18.9 mm. **Obv:** Three Czech lions left divide date **Rev:** Denomination **Edge:** Plain

Date	Mintage	F	VF	XF	Unc	BU
1992	—	—	—	—	1.00	—
1996	—	—	—	—	1.00	—

KM# 23a 20 SENTI
2.0000 g., Nickel Plated Steel, 18.9 mm. **Obv:** National arms **Rev:** Denomination **Rev. Leg.:** EESTI VABARIIK **Edge:** Plain

Date	Mintage	F	VF	XF	Unc	BU
1997	—	—	—	0.40	1.00	1.35
1999	—	—	—	0.40	1.00	1.35

KM# 24 50 SENTI
2.9000 g., Brass, 19.5 mm. **Obv:** National arms **Rev:** Denomination **Rev. Leg.:** EESTI VABARIIK **Edge:** Plain

Date	Mintage	F	VF	XF	Unc	BU
1992	—	—	—	0.60	1.50	2.00

KM# 28 KROON
5.4400 g., Copper-Nickel, 23.5 mm. **Obv:** Three Czech lions within shield divide date **Rev:** Large, thick denomination **Edge:** Plain

Date	Mintage	F	VF	XF	Unc	BU
1992	20,000	—	—	—	—	—
Note: In sets only						
1993	—	—	—	—	2.00	—
1995	—	—	—	—	2.00	—

KM# 35 KROON
5.0000 g., Brass, 23.5 mm. **Obv:** National arms **Rev:** Large, thick denomination **Rev. Leg.:** EESTI VABARIIK **Edge:** Segmented reeding

Date	Mintage	F	VF	XF	Unc	BU
1998	—	—	—	0.60	1.50	2.00
2000	—	—	—	0.60	1.50	2.00

KM# 36 KROON
Brass, 23.5 mm. **Obv:** Bird above date **Rev:** Festival building and denomination

Date	Mintage	F	VF	XF	Unc	BU
1999	100,000	—	—	—	6.00	—

KM# 29 5 KROONI
7.1000 g., Brass, 26.2 mm. **Subject:** 75th Anniversary - Declaration of Independence **Obv:** Three Czech lions within shield divide date **Rev:** Small deer right, denomination at right **Edge:** Plain

Date	Mintage	F	VF	XF	Unc	BU
1993	—	—	—	—	4.00	7.00
1993 Prooflike	—	Value: 6.00				

KM# 30 5 KROONI
7.1000 g., Brass, 26.1 mm. **Subject:** 75th Anniversary - Estonian National Bank **Obv:** Three Czech lions within shield divide date **Rev:** Denomination on design **Edge:** Plain

Date	Mintage	F	VF	XF	Unc	BU
1994	—	—	—	—	4.00	—

KM# 25 10 KROONI
28.2800 g., 0.9250 Silver 0.8410 oz. ASW **Series:** Olympics **Obv:** Three Czech lions within shield, wreath surrounds, date below **Rev:** Two sail boats, denomination below

Date	Mintage	F	VF	XF	Unc	BU
1992 Proof	Est. 20,000	Value: 50.00				

KM# 26 10 KROONI
28.2800 g., 0.9250 Silver 0.8410 oz. ASW **Obv:** Three Czech lions within shield, wreath surrounds, date below **Rev:** Barn Swallow, denomination below

Date	Mintage	F	VF	XF	Unc	BU
1992 Proof	Est. 10,000	Value: 55.00				

KM# 32 10 KROONI
16.0000 g., 0.9250 Silver 0.4758 oz. ASW **Subject:** 80th Anniversary of Nation **Obv:** Framed dates **Rev:** Farmer plowing field, denomination above

Date	Mintage	F	VF	XF	Unc	BU
ND(1998) Prooflike	Est. 15,000	—	—	—	22.50	—

KM# 37 15.65 KROONI
1.7300 g., 0.9000 Gold 0.0501 oz. AGW **Subject:** Estonia's Euro Equivalent **Obv:** Three Czech lions within shield, wreath surrounds, date below **Rev:** Cross and stars design, denomination below

Date	Mintage	F	VF	XF	Unc	BU
1999 Proof	Est. 5,000	Value: 50.00				

KM# 27 100 KROONI
24.0000 g., 0.9250 Silver 0.7137 oz. ASW **Obv:** Three Czech lions left **Rev:** Barn Swallows, date below, denomination above

Date	Mintage	F	VF	XF	Unc	BU
1992 Proof	Est. 50,000	Value: 45.00				

KM# 31 100 KROONI
28.2800 g., 0.9250 Silver 0.8410 oz. ASW **Obv:** Three Czech lions within shield, wreath surrounds, date below **Rev:** Olympics - Nike crowning Wrestler, denomination below

Date	Mintage	F	VF	XF	Unc	BU
1996	—	—	—	—	30.00	—
1996 Proof	10,000	Value: 40.00				

KM# 33 100 KROONI
27.0000 g., 0.9250 Silver 0.8029 oz. ASW **Subject:** 80th Anniversary of Nation **Obv:** Framed dates **Rev:** Male figure and stylized eagle head, denomination below

Date	Mintage	F	VF	XF	Unc	BU
ND(1998) Proof	Est. 12,000	Value: 50.00				
ND(1998)	—	—	—	—	35.00	—

KM# 34 500 KROONI
8.6400 g., 0.9000 Gold 0.2500 oz. AGW **Subject:** 80th Anniversary of Nation **Obv:** Framed dates **Rev:** Male figure on horse, denomination above

Date	Mintage	F	VF	XF	Unc	BU
ND(1998) Proof	Est. 3,000	Value: 245				

MINT SETS

KM#	Date	Mintage	Identification	Issue Price	Mkt Val
MS1	1992 (5)	20,000	KM#21-24, 28	—	40.00

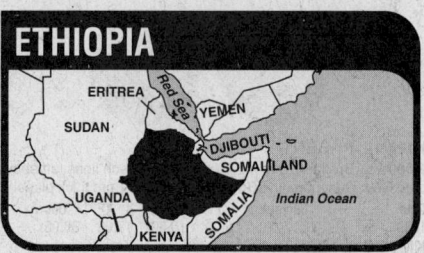

ETHIOPIA

The People's Federal Republic of Ethiopia (formerly the Peoples Democratic Republic and the Empire of Ethiopia), Africa's oldest independent nation, faces the Red Sea in East-Central Africa. The country has an area of 424,214 sq. mi. (1,004,390 sq. km.) and a population of 56 million people who are divided among 40 tribes that speak some 270 languages and dialects. Capital: Addis Ababa. The economy is predominantly agricultural and pastoral. Gold and platinum are mined and petroleum fields are being developed. Coffee, oilseeds, hides and cereals are exported.

Legend claims that Menelik I, the son born to Solomon, King of Israel, by the Queen of Sheba, settled in Axum in North Ethiopia to establish the dynasty, which reigned with only brief interruptions until 1974. Modern Ethiopian history began with the reign of Emperor Menelik II (1889-1913) under whose guidance the country emerged from medieval isolation. Progress continued throughout the reigns of Menelik's daughter, Empress Zauditu, and her successor Emperor Haile Selassie I who was coronated in 1930. Ethiopia was invaded by Italy in 1935, and together with Italian Somaliland and Eritrea became part of Italian East Africa. Victor Emmanuel III, as declared by Mussolini, would be Ethiopia's emperor as well as a king of Italy. Liberated by British and Ethiopian troops in 1941, Ethiopia reinstated Haile Selassie I to the throne. The 225th consecutive Solomonic ruler was deposed by a military committee on Sept 12, 1974. In July 1976 Ethiopia's military provisional government referred to the country as Socialist Ethiopia. After establishing a new regime in 1991, Ethiopia became a federated state and is now the Federal Republic of Ethiopia. Following 2 years of provisional government, the province of Eritrea held a referendum on independence in May 1993 leading to the proclamation of its independence on May 24.

No coins, patterns or presentation pieces are known bearing Emperor Lij Yasu's likeness or titles. Coins of Menelik II were struck during this period with dates frozen.

RULERS
Menelik II, 1889-1913
Lij Yasu, 1913-1916
Zauditu, Empress, 1916-1930
Haile Selassie I
 1930-36, 1941-1974
Victor Emmanuel III, of Italy
 1936-1941

MINT MARKS
A - Paris
 (a) - Paris, privy marks only
 (b)
 Coinage of Menelik II, 1889-1913
NOTE: The first national issue coinage, dated 1887 and 1888 E.E., carried a cornucopia, A, and fasces on the reverse. Subsequent dates have a torch substituted for the fasces, the A being dropped. All issues bearing these marks were struck at the Paris Mint. Coins without mint marks were struck in Addis Ababa.

MONETARY SYSTEM
(Until about 1903)
40 Besa = 20 Gersh = 1 Birr
(After 1903)
32 Besa = 16 Gersh = 1 Birr

DATING
Ethiopian coinage is dated by the Ethiopian Era calendar (E.E.), which commenced 7 years and 8 months after the advent of A.D. dating.

EXAMPLE
1900 (10 and 9 = 19 x 100)
 36 (Add 30 and 6)
1936 E.E.
 8 (Add)
1943/4 AD

EMPIRE OF ETHIOPIA
REFORM COINAGE

KM# 12 GERSH
1.4038 g., 0.8350 Silver 0.0377 oz. ASW, 16.5 mm. **Ruler:** Manelik II EE1882-1906 / 1889-1913AD **Obv:** Crowned bust right **Rev:** Crowned lion left, left foreleg raised holding ribboned cross

Date	Mintage	F	VF	XF	Unc	BU
EE1895A	44,789,000	2.00	3.50	15.00	35.00	—

Note: Struck between 1903-1928

KM# 3 1/4 BIRR
7.1088 g., 0.8350 Silver 0.1908 oz. ASW, 25 mm. **Ruler:** Manelik II EE1882-1906 / 1889-1913AD **Obv:** Crowned bust right **Rev:** Crowned lion left, left foreleg raised holding ribboned cross

Date	Mintage	F	VF	XF	Unc	BU
EE1895A	821,000	5.00	15.00	75.00	200	—

Note: Struck between 1903 and 1925

KM# 19 BIRR
28.0750 g., 0.8350 Silver 0.7537 oz. ASW, 40 mm. **Ruler:** Manelik II EE1882-1906 / 1889-1913AD **Obv:** Crowned bust right **Rev:** Crowned lion left, right foreleg raised holding ribboned cross

Date	Mintage	F	VF	XF	Unc	BU
EE1895	459,000	25.00	90.00	250	500	—
EE1895 Proof	—	Value: 1,200				

Note: Struck in 1901, 1903 and 1904

KM# 20 1/2 WERK
3.5000 g., 0.9000 Gold 0.1013 oz. AGW, 18 mm. **Ruler:** Empress Zauditu EE1909-1923 / 1916-1930AD **Obv:** Crowned bust left, laurels below **Rev:** St. George on horseback slaying the dragon

Date	Mintage	F	VF	XF	Unc	BU
EE1923	—	250	500	900	1,500	—

KM# 21 WERK
7.0000 g., 0.9000 Gold 0.2025 oz. AGW, 21 mm. **Ruler:** Empress Zauditu EE1909-1923 / 1916-1930AD **Obv:** Crowned bust left, laurels below **Rev:** St. George on horseback slaying the dragon

Date	Mintage	F	VF	XF	Unc	BU
EE1923	—	500	750	1,500	2,500	—

DECIMAL COINAGE

100 Santeems (Cents) = 1 Birr (Dollar)

100 Matonas = 100 Santeems

KM# 27 MATONA
Copper **Ruler:** Haile Selassie I EE1923-1929 / 1930-1936AD **Obv:** Crowned head right **Rev:** Crowned lion right, right foreleg raised holding ribboned cross

Date	Mintage	F	VF	XF	Unc	BU
EE1923	1,250,000	1.50	2.50	8.00	16.00	22.00

Note: Struck by ICI in Birmingham, England. Other denominations in the Matona series were struck in Addis Ababa

KM# 32 CENT (Ande Santeem)
Copper, 17 mm. **Ruler:** Haile Selassie I EE1923-1929 / 1930-36AD; Second Reign, EE1936-1966 / 1943-74AD **Obv:** Bust left, date below **Rev:** Crowned lion right, right foreleg raised holding ribboned cross

Date	Mintage	F	VF	XF	Unc	BU
EE1936	20,000,000	—	0.10	0.20	1.00	2.00

Note: Struck at Philadelphia, Birmingham and the Royal Mint, London between 1944 and 1975 with the date EE1936 frozen

KM# 28.1 5 MATONAS
Copper **Ruler:** Haile Selassie I EE1923-1929 / 1930-1936AD **Obv:** Crowned head right **Rev:** Crowned lion right, right foreleg raised holding ribboned cross **Edge:** Plain

Date	Mintage	F	VF	XF	Unc	BU
EE1923	1,363,000	2.00	3.50	6.00	20.00	25.00

KM# 28.2 5 MATONAS
Copper **Ruler:** Haile Selassie I EE1923-1929 / 1930-1936AD **Obv:** Crowned head right **Rev:** Crowned lion right, right foreleg raised holding ribboned cross **Edge:** Reeded

Date	Mintage	F	VF	XF	Unc	BU
EE1923	Inc. above	3.00	4.50	8.00	25.00	40.00

KM# 33 5 CENTS (Amist Santeem)
Copper, 20 mm. **Ruler:** Haile Selassie I EE1923-1929 / 1930-36AD; Second Reign, EE1936-1966 / 1943-74AD **Obv:** Bust left, date below **Rev:** Crowned lion right, right foreleg raised holding ribboned cross

Date	Mintage	F	VF	XF	Unc	BU
EE1936	219,000,000	—	0.10	0.20	0.50	1.50

Note: Struck between 1944-1962 in Philadelphia and 1964-1966 in Birmingham

KM# 29 10 MATONAS
Nickel **Ruler:** Haile Selassie I EE1923-1929 / 1930-1936AD **Obv:** Crowned bust right **Rev:** Crowned lion right, right foreleg raised holding ribboned cross

Date	Mintage	F	VF	XF	Unc	BU
EE1923	936,000	1.50	2.50	4.50	12.50	—

KM# 34 10 CENTS (Assir Santeem)
Copper, 23 mm. **Ruler:** Haile Selassie I EE1923-1929 /

1930-36AD; Second Reign, EE1936-1966 / 1943-74AD **Obv:** Bust left, date below **Rev:** Crowned lion right, right foreleg raised holding ribboned cross

Date	Mintage	F	VF	XF	Unc	BU
EE1936	348,998,000	—	0.10	0.25	1.00	2.00

Note: Struck between 1945-1963 in Philadelphia, 1964-1966 in Birmingham and 1974-1975 in London

KM# 30 25 MATONAS
Nickel **Ruler:** Haile Selassie I EE1923-1929 / 1930-1936AD **Obv:** Crowned head right **Rev:** Crowned lion right, right foreleg raised holding ribboned cross

Date	Mintage	F	VF	XF	Unc	BU
EE1923	2,742,000	1.25	2.00	5.00	10.00	—

KM# 35 25 CENTS (Haya Amist Santeem)
Copper, 26 mm. **Ruler:** Haile Selassie I EE1923-1929 / 1930-36AD; Second Reign, EE1936-1966 / 1943-74AD **Obv:** Bust left, date below **Rev:** Crowned lion right, right foreleg raised holding ribboned cross

Date	Mintage	F	VF	XF	Unc	BU
EE1936	10,000,000	5.00	10.00	20.00	45.00	60.00

Note: 421,500 issued and 1952 withdrawn and replaced by KM#36

KM# 36 25 CENTS (Haya Amist Santeem)
Copper, 25.5 mm. **Ruler:** Haile Selassie I EE1923-1929 / 1930-36AD; Second Reign, EE1936-1966 / 1943-74AD **Obv:** Bust left, date below **Rev:** Crowned lion right, right foreleg raised holding ribboned cross

Date	Mintage	F	VF	XF	Unc	BU
EE1936	30,000,000	0.25	0.50	1.00	4.00	10.00

Note: Issued in 1952 and 1953. Crude and refined edges

KM# 31 50 MATONAS
7.1100 g., Nickel **Ruler:** Haile Selassie I EE1923-1929 / 1930-1936AD **Obv:** Crowned head right **Rev:** Crowned lion right, right foreleg raised holding ribboned cross

Date	Mintage	F	VF	XF	Unc	BU
EE1923	1,621,000	1.50	3.00	8.00	15.00	—

KM# 37 50 CENTS (Hamsa Santeem)
7.0307 g., 0.8000 Silver 0.1808 oz. ASW **Ruler:** Haile Selassie I EE1923-1929 / 1930-36AD; Second Reign, EE1936-1966 / 1943-74AD **Obv:** Bust left, date below **Rev:** Crowned lion right, right foreleg raised holding ribboned cross

Date	Mintage	F	VF	XF	Unc	BU
EE1936	30,000,000	3.00	5.00	12.00	25.00	—

Note: Struck in 1944-1945

KM# 37a 50 CENTS (Hamsa Santeem)
7.0307 g., 0.7000 Silver 0.1582 oz. ASW Ruler: Haile Selassie I
EE1923-1929 / 1930-36AD; Second Reign, EE1936-1966 / 1943-
74AD Obv: Bust left, date below Rev: Crowned lion right, right
foreleg raised holding ribboned cross

Date	Mintage		VF	XF	Unc	BU
EE1936	20,434,000	2.50	4.50	12.00	25.00	—

Note: Struck in 1947

KM# 48 5 DOLLARS
20.0000 g., 0.9250 Silver 0.5948 oz. ASW Ruler: Haile Selassie
Second Reign Rev: Bust facing, dates below

Date	Mintage	F	VF	XF	Unc	BU
EE1964 F-NI	—	—	—	—	75.00	—
EE1964 NI Proof	55,000	Value: 40.00				

KM# 49 5 DOLLARS
20.0000 g., 0.9250 Silver 0.5948 oz. ASW Ruler: Haile Selassie
Second Reign Rev: Crowned bust facing, dates below

Date	Mintage	F	VF	XF	Unc	BU
EE1964 F-NI	—	—	—	—	75.00	—
EE1964 NI Proof	55,000	Value: 40.00				

KM# 50 5 DOLLARS
20.0000 g., 0.9250 Silver 0.5948 oz. ASW Ruler: Haile Selassie
Second Reign Rev: Crowned lion right, right foreleg raised
holding ribboned cross

Date	Mintage	F	VF	XF	Unc	BU
EE1964 F-NI	—	—	—	—	85.00	—
EE1964 NI Proof	60,000	Value: 40.00				

KM# 51 5 DOLLARS
20.0000 g., 0.9250 Silver 0.5948 oz. ASW Ruler: Haile Selassie
Second Reign Rev: Veiled bust left, dates at right

Date	Mintage	F	VF	XF	Unc	BU
EE1964 F-NI	—	—	—	—	90.00	—
EE1964 NI Proof	60,000	Value: 42.50				

KM# 52 5 DOLLARS
25.0000 g., 0.9999 Silver 0.8037 oz. ASW Ruler: Haile Selassie
Second Reign Obv: Uniformed bust right, crown at left, shield
at right Rev: Crowned lion right, right foreleg raised holding
ribboned cross

Date	Mintage	F	VF	XF	Unc	BU
1972 (1972) HF Proof	100,000	Value: 27.00				

KM# 38 10 DOLLARS
4.0000 g., 0.9000 Gold 0.1157 oz. AGW Ruler: Haile Selassie
Second Reign Subject: 75th Anniverary of Birth and 50th Jubilee
of Reign of Emperor Haile Selassie I Obv: Bust 3/4 left divides
crown and shield Rev: Crowned lion right, right foreleg raised
holding ribboned cross

Date	Mintage	F	VF	XF	Unc	BU
EE1958 (1966) NI Proof	28,000	Value: 125				

KM# 53 10 DOLLARS
40.0000 g., 0.9250 Silver 1.1895 oz. ASW Ruler: Haile Selassie
Second Reign Obv: Uniformed bust 3/4 facing Rev: Crowned
lion right, right foreleg raised holding ribboned cross

Date	Mintage	F	VF	XF	Unc	BU
EE1964 (1972) F-NI	—	—	—	—	175	—
EE1964 (1972) NI Proof	50,000	Value: 85.00				

KM# 39 20 DOLLARS
8.0000 g., 0.9000 Gold 0.2315 oz. AGW Ruler: Haile Selassie
Second Reign Subject: 75th Anniversary of Birth and 50th
Jubilee of Reign of Emperor Haile Selassie I Obv: Bust 3/4 left
divides crown and shield Rev: Crowned lion right, right foreleg
raised holding ribboned cross

Date	Mintage	F	VF	XF	Unc	BU
EE1958 (1966) NI Proof	25,000	Value: 245				

KM# 40 50 DOLLARS
20.0000 g., 0.9000 Gold 0.5787 oz. AGW Ruler: Haile Selassie
Second Reign Subject: 75th Anniversary of Birth and 50th
Jubilee of Reign of Emperor Haile Selassie I Obv: Bust 3/4 left
divides crown and shield Rev: Crowned lion right, right foreleg
raised holding ribboned cross

Date	Mintage	F	VF	XF	Unc	BU
EE1958 (1966) NI Proof	15,000	Value: 575				

KM# 55 50 DOLLARS
20.0000 g., 0.9000 Gold 0.5787 oz. AGW Ruler: Haile Selassie
Second Reign Obv: Bust of Theodros II, Emperor 1855-1866AD
Rev: Lion

Date	Mintage	F	VF	XF	Unc	BU
EE1964 (1972) NI Proof	12,000	Value: 600				

KM# 56 50 DOLLARS
20.0000 g., 0.9000 Gold 0.5787 oz. AGW Ruler: Haile Selassie
Second Reign Obv: Bust of Yohannes IV, Emperor, 1872-1889AD

Date	Mintage	F	VF	XF	Unc	BU
EE1964 (1972) NI Proof	12,000	Value: 600				

KM# 57 50 DOLLARS
20.0000 g., 0.9000 Gold 0.5787 oz. AGW Ruler: Haile Selassie
Second Reign Obv: Bust of Menelik II, Emperor, 1889-1913AD

Date	Mintage	F	VF	XF	Unc	BU
EE1964 (1972) NI Proof	20,000	Value: 600				

KM# 58 50 DOLLARS
20.0000 g., 0.9000 Gold 0.5787 oz. AGW Ruler: Haile Selassie
Second Reign Obv: Bust of Empress Zauditu, 1916-1930AD

Date	Mintage	F	VF	XF	Unc	BU
EE1964 (1972) NI Proof	16,000	Value: 600				

KM# 41 100 DOLLARS
40.0000 g., 0.9000 Gold 1.1574 oz. AGW Ruler: Haile Selassie
Second Reign Subject: 75th Anniversary of Birth and 50th
Jubilee of Reign of Emperor Haile Selassie I Rev: Crowned lion
right, right foreleg raised holding ribboned cross

Date	Mintage	F	VF	XF	Unc	BU
EE1958 (1966) NI Proof	11,000	Value: 1,150				

KM# 59 100 DOLLARS
40.0000 g., 0.9000 Gold 1.1574 oz. AGW Ruler: Haile Selassie
Second Reign Obv: Uniformed bust 3/4 facing Rev: Crowned
lion right, right foreleg raised holding ribboned cross

Date	Mintage	F	VF	XF	Unc	BU
EE1964 (1972) NI Proof	10,000	Value: 1,150				

KM# 42 200 DOLLARS
80.0000 g., 0.9000 Gold 2.3148 oz. AGW Ruler: Haile Selassie
Second Reign Subject: 75th Anniversary of Birth and 50th
Jubilee of Reign of Emperor Haile Selassie I Rev: Crowned lion
right, right foreleg raised holding ribboned cross

Date	Mintage	F	VF	XF	Unc	BU
EE1958 (1966) NI	8,823			Value: 2,250		
Proof						

TOKEN COINAGE

KM# Tn1 PIASTRE (1/16 Thaler)
Aluminum **Ruler:** Empress Zauditu EE1909-1923 / 1916-1930AD **Obv:** Seven line inscription **Rev:** Denomination and date

Date	Mintage	VG	F	VF	XF	Unc
1922	—	12.00	25.00	40.00	65.00	—

Note: Issued by a commercial syndicate in Dire Dawa

KM# Tn2 PIASTRE (1/16 Thaler)
Aluminum **Obv:** Legend within circle and surrounding **Rev:** Denomination

Date	Mintage	VG	F	VF	XF	Unc
ND	—	10.00	20.00	35.00	55.00	—

Note: Issued by P. P. Trohalis in Addis Ababa

KM# Tn3 PIASTRE (1/16 Thaler)
Copper-Nickel-Zinc **Obv:** Legend surrounds center **Rev:** Denomination

Date	Mintage	VG	F	VF	XF	Unc
ND	—	25.00	40.00	65.00	90.00	—

Note: Issued by Magdalinos Freres in Addis Ababa

KM# Tn4 PIASTRE (1/16 Thaler)
Aluminum **Rev:** Denomination

Date	Mintage	VG	F	VF	XF	Unc
ND	—	20.00	35.00	60.00	85.00	—

Note: Issued by Prasso Concessions En Abyssinie

KM# Tn5 PIASTRE (1/16 Thaler)
Aluminum **Note:** Uniface

Date	Mintage	VG	F	VF	XF	Unc
ND	—	25.00	45.00	75.00	100	—

Note: Issued by F. L. in Addis Abada

PEOPLES DEMOCRATIC REPUBLIC

We have two varieties for KM#43.1 to KM#46.1. One was minted at the British Royal Mint, the other at the Berlin Mint. The main difference is where the lion's chin whiskers end above the date (easiest to see on the 2nd, 3rd and 4th characters).

British Royal Mint

Berlin Mint

DECIMAL COINAGE

100 Santeems (Cents) = 1 Birr (Dollar)

100 Matonas = 100 Santeems

KM# 43.1 CENT
0.6000 g., Aluminum, 17 mm. **Series:** F.A.O. **Obv:** Small lion head right, uniform chin whiskers **Rev:** Farmer with two oxen, denomination above

Date	Mintage	F	VF	XF	Unc	BU
EE1969	35,034,000	0.20	0.30	0.50	1.00	—

KM# 43.2 CENT
0.6000 g., Aluminum, 17 mm. **Obv:** Small lion head right, two long chin whiskers at left nearly touch date **Rev:** Farmer with two oxen, denomination above

Date	Mintage	F	VF	XF	Unc	BU
EE1969	Inc. above	0.25	0.35	0.65	1.25	—

KM# 43.3 CENT
0.6000 g., Aluminum, 17 mm. **Obv:** Large lion head right **Rev:** Farmer with two oxen, denomination above

Date	Mintage	F	VF	XF	Unc	BU
EE1969 FM Proof	12,000			Value: 2.50		

KM# 44.1 5 CENTS
3.0000 g., Copper-Zinc, 20 mm. **Obv:** Small lion head right, uniform chin whiskers **Rev:** Denomination left of figure

Date	Mintage	F	VF	XF	Unc	BU
EE1969	201,275,000	0.20	0.30	0.50	1.00	—

KM# 44.2 5 CENTS
3.0000 g., Copper-Zinc, 20 mm. **Obv:** Lion head right, date below **Rev:** Denomination left of figure

Date	Mintage	F	VF	XF	Unc	BU
EE1969	Inc. above	0.25	0.35	0.65	1.25	—

KM# 44.3 5 CENTS
3.0000 g., Copper-Zinc, 20 mm. **Obv:** Large lion head, right **Rev:** Denomination left of figure

Date	Mintage	F	VF	XF	Unc	BU
EE1969 FM Proof	12,000			Value: 2.50		

KM# 45.1 10 CENTS
4.5000 g., Copper-Zinc, 23 mm. **Obv:** Small lion head right, uniform chin whiskers **Rev:** Mountain Nyala, denomination at right

Date	Mintage	F	VF	XF	Unc	BU
EE1969	202,722,000	0.20	0.30	0.60	1.50	3.00

KM# 45.2 10 CENTS
4.5000 g., Copper-Zinc, 23 mm. **Obv:** Small lion head, two long chin whiskers at left nearly touch date **Rev:** Mountain Nyala and denomination

Date	Mintage	F	VF	XF	Unc	BU
EE1969	Inc. above	0.25	0.40	0.75	1.75	3.00

KM# 45.3 10 CENTS
4.5000 g., Copper-Zinc, 23 mm. **Obv:** Large lion head right **Rev:** Mountain Nyala, denomination at right

Date	Mintage	F	VF	XF	Unc	BU
EE1969 FM					2.00	3.25
EE1969 FM Proof	12,000			Value: 4.00		

KM# 46.1 25 CENTS
3.7000 g., Copper-Nickel, 21.45 mm. **Obv:** Small lion head right, uniform chin whiskers **Rev:** Man and woman with arms raised divide denomination **Edge:** Reeded

Date	Mintage	F	VF	XF	Unc	BU
EE1969	44,983,000	0.20	0.30	0.60	1.25	2.00

KM# 46.2 25 CENTS
3.7000 g., Copper-Nickel, 21.45 mm. **Obv:** Small lion head, two long chin whiskers at left nearly touch date **Rev:** Man and woman with arms raised divide denomination

Date	Mintage	F	VF	XF	Unc	BU
EE1969	Inc. above	0.25	0.40	0.75	1.50	—

KM# 46.3 25 CENTS
3.7000 g., Copper-Nickel, 21.45 mm. **Obv:** Large lion head right **Rev:** Man and woman with arms raised divide denomination

Date	Mintage	F	VF	XF	Unc	BU
EE1969 FM Proof	12,000			Value: 4.50		

KM# 47.1 50 CENTS
6.0000 g., Copper-Nickel, 25 mm. **Obv:** Small lion head right, uniform chin whiskers **Rev:** People of the Republic, denomination above

Date	Mintage	F	VF	XF	Unc	BU
EE1969	27,772,000	0.40	0.75	1.25	3.00	—

KM# 47.2 50 CENTS
6.0000 g., Copper-Nickel, 25 mm. **Obv:** Small lion head, two long chin whiskers at left nearly touch date **Rev:** People of the republic, denomination above

Date	Mintage	F	VF	XF	Unc	BU
EE1969	Inc. above	0.50	0.85	1.50	3.00	—

KM# 47.3 50 CENTS
6.0000 g., Copper-Nickel, 25 mm. **Obv:** Large lion head **Rev:** People of the republic, denomination above **Note:** Prev. KM#47.2.

Date	Mintage	F	VF	XF	Unc	BU
EE1969 FM Proof	12,000				Value: 7.50	

KM# 64 2 BIRR
Copper-Nickel **Subject:** World Soccer Games 1982 **Obv:** Lion head right **Rev:** Soccer players in front of two joined globes, denomination above

Date	Mintage	F	VF	XF	Unc	BU
EE1964 (error)	7	—	—	—	145	—
EE1974		—	—	—	12.00	—

KM# 61 10 BIRR
25.3100 g., 0.9250 Silver 0.7527 oz. ASW **Subject:** Conservation **Obv:** Lion within circle divides wreath surrounding symbols in center **Rev:** Bearded Vulture

Date	Mintage	F	VF	XF	Unc	BU
EE1970	4,002	—	—	—	25.00	—

KM# 61a 10 BIRR
28.2800 g., 0.9250 Silver 0.8410 oz. ASW **Obv:** Lion within circle divides wreath surrounding symbols in center **Rev:** Bearded Vulture

Date	Mintage	F	VF	XF	Unc	BU
EE1970 Proof	3,460				Value: 35.00	

KM# 54 20 BIRR
23.3300 g., 0.9250 Silver 0.6938 oz. ASW **Subject:** International Year of the Child **Obv:** Silhouette of child flanked by laurels, logo above **Rev:** Children, logo above, denomination below

Date	Mintage	F	VF	XF	Unc	BU
EE1972 Proof	16,000				Value: 30.00	

KM# 65 20 BIRR
23.3300 g., 0.9250 Silver 0.6938 oz. ASW **Subject:** World Soccer Games 1982 **Obv:** Lion head right **Rev:** Soccer players in front of two joined globes, denomination above

Date	Mintage	F	VF	XF	Unc	BU
EE1974 Proof	10,000				Value: 40.00	

KM# 73 20 BIRR
23.3300 g., 0.9250 Silver 0.6938 oz. ASW **Subject:** Decade for Women **Rev:** Woman in field

Date	Mintage	F	VF	XF	Unc	BU
1984 Proof	372				Value: 175	

KM# 74 20 BIRR
23.3300 g., 0.9250 Silver 0.6938 oz. ASW **Subject:** 50th Anniversary UNICEF - Folk Dance **Obv:** Two dancing girls and huts, denomination below **Rev:** UNICEF logo divides date **Edge:** Reeded

Date	Mintage	F	VF	XF	Unc	BU
1998 Proof					Value: 50.00	

KM# 62 25 BIRR
31.6500 g., 0.9250 Silver 0.9412 oz. ASW **Subject:** Conservation **Obv:** Lion within circle divides wreath surrounding symbols in center **Rev:** Mountain Nyala left, right foreleg raised

Date	Mintage	F	VF	XF	Unc	BU
EE1970	4,002	—	—	—	30.00	—

KM# 62a 25 BIRR
35.0000 g., 0.9250 Silver 1.0408 oz. ASW **Obv:** Lion within circle divides wreath surrounding symbols in center **Rev:** Mountain Nyala left, right foreleg raised

Date	Mintage	F	VF	XF	Unc	BU
EE1970 Proof	3,295				Value: 40.00	

KM# 66 50 BIRR
56.0000 g., 0.9250 Silver 1.6653 oz. ASW, 38. mm. **Subject:** International Year of Disabled Persons **Obv:** Symbol within wreath **Rev:** Hand grasping wrist, denomination below, initials above

Date	Mintage	F	VF	XF	Unc	BU
EE1974	11,000	—	—	—	35.00	—
EE1974 Proof	10,000				Value: 45.00	

KM# 67 200 BIRR
7.1300 g., 0.9000 Gold 0.2063 oz. AGW **Subject:** World Soccer Games 1982 **Obv:** Lion head right **Rev:** Soccer players in front of two joined globes, denomination above

Date	Mintage	F	VF	XF	Unc	BU
1982 Proof	1,310				Value: 220	

KM# 72 200 BIRR
7.1300 g., 0.9000 Gold 0.2063 oz. AGW **Subject:** Decade for Women **Obv:** Small lion head right, denomination below **Rev:** Woman with child, writing

Date	Mintage	F	VF	XF	Unc	BU
1984 Proof	298				Value: 350	

KM# 60 400 BIRR
17.1700 g., 0.9000 Gold 0.4968 oz. AGW **Subject:** International Year of the Child **Obv:** Silhouette of child, laurels flanking, logo above **Rev:** Children playing, denomination below, logo above

Date	Mintage	F	VF	XF	Unc	BU
EE1972 Proof	3,387				Value: 465	

KM# 68 500 BIRR
15.9800 g., 0.9170 Gold 0.4711 oz. AGW **Subject:** International Year of the Disabled Persons **Obv:** Symbol within wreath **Rev:** Flanking figures on steps holding arms of central figure, denomination below

Date	Mintage	F	VF	XF	Unc	BU
EE1974	2,007	*	—	—	470	—
EE1974 Proof	2,042				Value: 485	

KM# 63 600 BIRR
33.4370 g., 0.9000 Gold 0.9675 oz. AGW **Subject:** Conservation **Obv:** Lion within circle divides wreath surrounding symbols at center **Rev:** Walia Ibex right

Date	Mintage	F	VF	XF	Unc	BU
EE1970	547	—	—	—	950	—
EE1970 Proof	160				Value: 1,100	

PATTERNS
Including off metal strikes

KM#	Date	Mintage	Identification	Mkt Val
Pn7	EE1921	—	Werk. Gold. Similar to KM20 (proof)	—
Pn8	EE1921	—	Werk. Gold. Similar to KM21 (proof)	—

TRIAL STRIKES

KM#	Date	Mintage	Identification	Mkt Val
TS9	EE1917	—	1/2 Birr. Pewter. KM M3. (thin)	300
TS10	EE1917	—	Birr. Pewter. KM M4. (thin)	500
TS11	1966	—	10 Dollars. Gilt Bronze. KM38	50.00
TS12	1966	—	20 Dollars. Gilt Bronze. KM39	80.00
TS13	1966	—	50 Dollars. Gilt Bronze. KM40	130
TS14	1966	—	100 Dollars. Gilt Bronze. KM41	240
TS15	1966	—	200 Dollars. Gilt Bronze. KM42	450

Note: Issued in cased set of five pieces.

PIEFORTS

KM#	Date	Mintage	Identification	Issue Price	Mkt Val
P1	1980	39	20 Birr. Silver. KM54	—	150
P2	1980	8	400 Birr. Gold. KM60	—	775
P3	1981	1,100	50 Birr. Silver. 56.0000 g. 38 mm. KM66	—	55.00
P4	1982	520	500 Birr. Gold. KM68	—	650

MINT SETS

KM#	Date	Mintage	Identification	Issue Price	Mkt Val
MS1	1972 (5)	—	KM48-51, 53	—	500

PROOF SETS

KM#	Date	Mintage	Identification	Issue Price	Mkt Val
PS2	1966 (5)	8,823	KM38-42	—	4,250
PS3	1972 (10)	—	KM48-51, 53, 55-59	—	3,800
PS5	1972 (5)	10,000	KM55-59	—	3,550
PS6	1972 (5)	50,000	KM48-51, 53	46.00	250
PS7	1977 (5)	11,724	KM43.2-47.2	25.00	25.00
PS8	1979 (2)	—	KM61a-62a	—	75.00

FAEROE ISLANDS

The Faeroe Islands, a self-governing community within the kingdom of Denmark, are situated in the North Atlantic between Iceland and the Shetland Islands. The 17 inhabited islands and numerous islets and reefs have an area of 540 sq. mi. (1,400 sq. km.) and a population of 46,000. Capital: Thorshavn. The principal industries are fishing and livestock. Fish and fish products are exported.

While it is thought that Irish hermits lived on the islands in the 7th and 8th centuries, the present inhabitants are descended from 6th century Norse settlers. The Faeroe Islands became a Norwegian fief in 1035 and became Danish in 1380 when Norway and Denmark were united. They have ever since remained in Danish possession and were granted self-government (except for an appointed governor-general) with their own legislature, executive and flag in 1948.

The islands were occupied by British troops during World War II, after the German occupation of Denmark. The Faeroe island coinage was struck in London during World War II.

RULER
Danish

MONETARY SYSTEM
100 Øre = 1 Krone

DANISH STATE
DECIMAL COINAGE

KM# 1   ORE
Bronze   Obv: Center hole divides date and denomination
Rev: Center hole within crowned monogram

Date	Mintage	F	VF	XF	Unc	BU
1941	Est. 200,000	25.00	50.00	75.00	110	—

Note: Also struck in 1942 with 1941 dies

| 1941 Proof | | | — | Value: 565 | | |

KM# 2   2 ORE
Bronze   Obv: Center hole divides date and denomination
Rev: Center hole within crowned monogram

Date	Mintage	F	VF	XF	Unc	BU
1941	Est. 200,000	10.00	20.00	32.50	75.00	—

Note: Also struck in 1942 with 1941 dies

| 1941 Proof | | | — | Value: 565 | | |

KM# 3   5 ORE
Bronze   Obv: Center hole divides date and denomination
Rev: Center hole within crowned monogram

Date	Mintage	F	VF	XF	Unc	BU
1941	Est. 200,000	6.00	12.00	22.50	70.00	—

Note: Also struck in 1942 with 1941 dies

| 1941 Proof | | | — | Value: 565 | | |

KM# 4   10 ORE
Copper-Nickel   Obv: Center hole divides crowned monogram, date below   Rev: Center hole with ornaments divides denomination

Date	Mintage	F	VF	XF	Unc	BU
1941	Est. 300,000	8.50	15.00	30.00	100	—

Note: Also struck in 1942 with 1941 dies

| 1941 Proof | | | — | Value: 585 | | |

KM# 5   25 ORE
Copper-Nickel   Obv: Center hole divides crowned monogram, date below   Rev: Center hole with ornaments divides denominatio

Date	Mintage	F	VF	XF	Unc	BU
1941	Est. 250,000	9.00	15.00	32.50	110	—

Note: Also struck in 1942 with 1941 dies

| 1941 Proof | | | — | Value: 585 | | |

PROOF SETS

KM#	Date	Mintage	Identification	Issue Price	Mkt Val
PS1	1941 (5)	—	KM1-5	—	2,850

FALKLAND ISLANDS

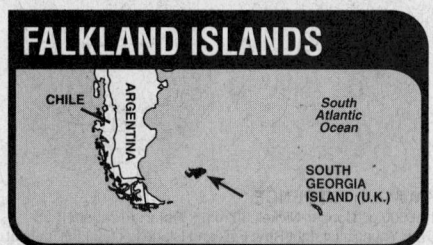

The Colony of the Falkland Islands and Dependencies, a British colony located in the South Atlantic about 500 miles northeast of Cape Horn, has an area of 4,700 sq. mi. (12,170 sq. km.) and a population of 2,121. East Falkland, West Falkland, South Georgia, and South Sandwich are the largest of the 200 islands. Capital: Stanley. Sheep grazing is the main industry. Wool, whale oil, and seal oil are exported.

The Falklands were discovered by British navigator John Davis (Davys) in 1592, and named by Capt. John Strong - for Viscount Falkland, treasurer of the British navy - in 1690. French navigator Louis De Bougainville established the first settlement, at Port Louis, in 1764. The following year Capt. John Byron claimed the islands for Britain and left a small party at Saunders Island. Spain later forced the French and British to abandon their settlements but did not implement its claim to the islands. In 1829 the Republic of Buenos Aires, which claimed to have inherited the Spanish rights, sent Louis Vernet to develop a colony on the islands. In 1831 he seized three American sealing vessels, whereupon the men of the corvette, the U.S.S. Lexington, destroyed his settlement and proclaimed the Falklands to be 'free of all governance'. Britain, which had never renounced its claim, then re-established its settlement in 1833.

RULER
British

MONETARY SYSTEM
100 Pence = 1 Pound

BRITISH COLONY
DECIMAL COINAGE

KM# 1   1/2 PENNY
1.7820 g., Bronze, 17.14 mm.   Ruler: Elizabeth II   Obv: Young bust right   Rev: Salmon behind denomination, date at right

Date	Mintage	F	VF	XF	Unc	BU
1974	140,000	—	—	0.10	0.35	0.50
1974 Proof	23,000	Value: 1.50				
1980	—	—		0.10	0.25	0.50
1980 Proof	10,000	Value: 1.50				
1982	—	—		0.10	0.25	0.50
1982 Proof	—	Value: 1.50				
1983	—	—		0.10	0.25	0.50

KM# 2   PENNY
3.6000 g., Bronze, 20.3 mm.   Ruler: Elizabeth II   Obv: Young bust right   Rev: Gentoo penguins flank denomination, date below

Date	Mintage	F	VF	XF	Unc	BU
1974	96,000	—	0.10	0.20	0.60	1.00
1974 Proof	23,000	Value: 2.00				
1980	—	—	0.10		0.60	1.00
1980 Proof	10,000	Value: 2.00				
1982	—	—	0.10		0.60	1.00
1982 Proof	—	Value: 2.00				
1983	—	—	0.10	0.20	0.60	1.00
1985	—	—	0.10	0.20	0.60	1.00
1987	111,000	—	—	0.20	0.60	1.00
1987 Proof	—	Value: 2.50				
1992	—	—	0.10		0.60	1.00
1992 Proof	—	Value: 2.50				

KM# 2a   PENNY
Copper Plated Steel, 20.3 mm.   Ruler: Elizabeth II   Obv: Young bust right   Rev: Denomination divides penguins, date below

Date	Mintage	F	VF	XF	Unc	BU
1998	2,500	—	—	—	0.50	0.75
1999	—	—	—	—	0.50	0.75
1999 Proof	2,500	Value: 2.00				

KM# 3   2 PENCE
7.1000 g., Bronze, 25.9 mm.   Ruler: Elizabeth II   Obv: Young bust right   Rev: Upland goose, wings open, denomination above, date at right

Date	Mintage	F	VF	XF	Unc	BU
1974	72,000	—	0.10	0.15	0.50	2.00
1974 Proof	23,000	Value: 3.00				
1980	—	—	0.10	0.15	0.50	2.00
1980 Proof	10,000	Value: 3.00				
1982	—	—	0.10	0.15	0.50	2.00
1982 Proof	—	Value: 3.00				
1983	—	—	0.10	0.15	0.50	2.00
1985	—	—	0.10	0.15	0.50	2.00
1987	106,000	—	—	0.15	0.50	2.00
1987 Proof	—	Value: 3.50				
1992	—	—	0.10	0.15	0.50	2.00
1992 Proof	—	Value: 3.50				

KM# 3a   2 PENCE
Copper Plated Steel, 25.9 mm.   Ruler: Elizabeth II   Obv: Young bust right   Rev: Upland goose, wings open, denomination above, date at right

Date	Mintage	F	VF	XF	Unc	BU
1998	—	—	—	—	0.35	1.00
1999	—	—	—	—	0.35	1.00
1999 Proof	2,500	Value: 3.00				

KM# 4.1 5 PENCE

5.6500 g., Copper-Nickel, 23.6 mm. **Ruler:** Elizabeth II
Obv: Young bust right **Rev:** Blackbrowed albatross in flight,
denomination and date below

Date	Mintage	F	VF	XF	Unc	BU
1974	67,000	—	0.10	0.25	0.75	1.00
1974 Proof	23,000	Value: 3.50				
1980	—	—	0.10	0.25	0.75	1.00
1980 Proof	10,000	Value: 4.00				
1982	—	—	0.10	0.25	0.75	1.00
1982 Proof	—	Value: 4.00				
1983	—	—	0.10	0.25	0.75	1.00
1985	—	—	0.10	0.20	0.75	1.00
1987	5,000	—	—	0.25	0.75	1.00
1987 Proof	—	Value: 4.50				
1992	—	—	0.10	0.25	0.75	1.00
1992 Proof	—	Value: 4.50				

KM# 4.2 5 PENCE

Copper-Nickel, 18 mm. **Ruler:** Elizabeth II **Obv:** Young bust right
Rev: Blackbrowed albatross in flight, denomination and date below

Date	Mintage	F	VF	XF	Unc	BU
1998	—	—	—	—	0.75	1.00
1999	—	—	—	—	0.75	1.00
1999 Proof	2,500	Value: 4.00				

KM# 5.1 10 PENCE

11.3100 g., Copper-Nickel, 28.5 mm. **Ruler:** Elizabeth II
Obv: Young bust right **Rev:** Ursine seal with cub, denomination
below, date at left

Date	Mintage	F	VF	XF	Unc	BU
1974	87,000	—	0.20	0.40	1.50	3.50
1974 Proof	23,000	Value: 5.00				
1980	—	—	0.20	0.40	1.50	3.50
1980 Proof	10,000	Value: 5.00				
1982	—	—	0.20	0.40	1.50	3.50
1982 Proof	—	Value: 5.00				
1983	—	—	0.20	0.40	1.50	3.50
1985	—	—	0.20	0.40	1.50	3.50
1987	4,000	—	—	0.40	1.50	3.50
1987 Proof	—	Value: 5.50				
1992	—	—	0.20	0.40	1.50	3.50
1992 Proof	—	Value: 5.50				

KM# 5.2 10 PENCE

Copper-Nickel, 24.5 mm. **Ruler:** Elizabeth II **Obv:** Young bust
right **Rev:** Ursine seal with cub, denomination below, date at left

Date	Mintage	F	VF	XF	Unc	BU
1998	—	—	—	—	1.50	3.00
1999	—	—	—	—	1.50	3.00
1999 Proof	2,500	Value: 5.00				

KM# 17 20 PENCE

5.0000 g., Copper-Nickel, 21.95 mm. **Ruler:** Elizabeth II
Obv: Young bust right **Rev:** Romney marsh sheep left,
denomination above

Date	Mintage	F	VF	XF	Unc	BU
1982	—	—	0.40	0.65	2.00	4.00
1982 Proof	—	Value: 5.00				
1983	—	—	0.40	0.65	2.00	4.00
1985	—	—	0.40	0.65	2.00	4.00
1987	4,250	—	0.40	0.65	2.00	4.00
1987 Proof	—	Value: 5.50				
1992	—	—	0.40	0.65	2.00	4.00
1992 Proof	—	Value: 5.50				
1998	—	—	0.40	0.65	2.00	4.00
1999	—	—	—	—	2.00	4.00
1999 Proof	2,500	Value: 5.00				

KM# 10 50 PENCE

Copper-Nickel, 38.5 mm. **Ruler:** Elizabeth II **Subject:** Queen's
Silver Jubilee **Obv:** Young bust right, dates at left **Rev:** Sheep
above ship on shield within wreath, denomination below

Date	Mintage	F	VF	XF	Unc	BU
ND(1977)	100,000	—	1.00	1.50	3.00	4.50

KM# 10a 50 PENCE

28.2800 g., 0.9250 Silver 0.8410 oz. ASW, 38.5 mm.
Ruler: Elizabeth II **Obv:** Young bust right **Rev:** Sheep above ship
on shield within wreath, denomination below

Date	Mintage	F	VF	XF	Unc	BU
ND(1977) Proof	22,000	Value: 17.50				

KM# 14.1 50 PENCE

13.6500 g., Copper-Nickel, 30 mm. **Ruler:** Elizabeth II
Obv: Young bust right **Rev:** Falkland Island fox (extinct), date at
right, denomination above

Date	Mintage	F	VF	XF	Unc	BU
1980	—	—	1.00	2.00	5.00	7.50
1980 Proof	—	Value: 8.00				
1982	—	—	1.00	2.00	5.00	7.50
1982 Proof	—	Value: 8.00				
1983	—	—	1.00	2.00	5.00	7.50
1985	—	—	1.00	2.00	5.00	7.50
1987	4,000	—	1.00	2.00	5.00	7.50
1987 Proof	—	Value: 9.00				
1992	—	—	1.00	2.00	5.00	7.50
1992 Proof	—	Value: 9.00				
1995	—	—	—	2.00	5.00	7.50

KM# 14.2 50 PENCE

Copper-Nickel, 27.3 mm. **Ruler:** Elizabeth II **Obv:** Young bust
right **Rev:** Falkland Island fox (extinct) **Note:** Reduced size.

Date	Mintage	F	VF	XF	Unc	BU
1998	—	—	—	2.00	5.00	7.50
1999	—	—	—	2.00	5.00	7.50
1999 Proof	2,500	Value: 8.00				

KM# 15 50 PENCE

Copper-Nickel, 38.5 mm. **Ruler:** Elizabeth II **Subject:** 80th
Anniversary - Birth of Queen Mother **Obv:** Young bust right
Rev: Queen Mother's bust left

Date	Mintage	F	VF	XF	Unc	BU
ND(1980)	—	—	1.00	1.50	3.50	6.00

KM# 15a 50 PENCE

28.2800 g., 0.9250 Silver 0.8410 oz. ASW, 38.5 mm.
Ruler: Elizabeth II **Subject:** 80th Anniversary of Queen
Mother **Obv:** Young bust right **Rev:** Queen Mother's bust left

Date	Mintage	F	VF	XF	Unc	BU
ND(1980) Proof	—	Value: 17.50				

KM# 16 50 PENCE

Copper-Nickel, 38.5 mm. **Ruler:** Elizabeth II **Subject:** Wedding
of Prince Charles and Lady Diana **Obv:** Young bust right **Rev:**
Conjoined busts of royal couple right

Date	Mintage	F	VF	XF	Unc	BU
1981	—	—	1.00	1.50	3.00	4.50

KM# 16a 50 PENCE

28.2800 g., 0.9250 Silver 0.8410 oz. ASW, 38.5 mm. **Ruler:**
Elizabeth II **Subject:** Wedding of Prince Charles and Lady Diana
Obv: Young bust right **Rev:** Conjoined busts of royal couple right

Date	Mintage	F	VF	XF	Unc	BU
1981 Proof	40,000	Value: 22.00				

KM# 18 50 PENCE

Copper-Nickel, 38.5 mm. **Subject:** Liberation from Argentina
Forces **Obv:** Young bust right, denomination below **Rev:** Flag
design in background, state shield at left, date below

Date	Mintage	F	VF	XF	Unc	BU
ND(1982)	—	—	1.00	1.50	3.00	4.50

KM# 18a 50 PENCE

28.2800 g., 0.9250 Silver 0.8410 oz. ASW, 38.5 mm.
Ruler: Elizabeth II **Obv:** Young bust right, denomination below
Rev: Flag design in background, state shield at left, date below

Date	Mintage	F	VF	XF	Unc	BU
ND(1982) Proof	Est. 25,000	Value: 20.00				

KM# 18b 50 PENCE

47.5000 g., 0.9170 Gold 1.4003 oz. AGW, 38.5 mm.
Ruler: Elizabeth II **Subject:** Liberation From Argentina Forces
Obv: Young bust right, denomination below **Rev:** Flag design in
background, state shield at left, date below

Date	Mintage	F	VF	XF	Unc	BU
ND(1982) Proof	25	Value: 5,500				

KM# 19 50 PENCE

Copper-Nickel, 38.5 mm. **Ruler:** Elizabeth II **Subject:** 150th
Anniversary of British Rule **Obv:** Young bust right **Rev:** Ship
divides dates

Date	Mintage	F	VF	XF	Unc	BU
ND(1983)	Est. 50,000	—	1.00	2.00	5.00	7.00

KM# 19a 50 PENCE

28.2800 g., 0.9250 Silver 0.8410 oz. ASW, 38.5 mm.
Ruler: Elizabeth II **Obv:** Young bust right **Rev:** Ship divides dates

Date	Mintage	F	VF	XF	Unc	BU
ND(1983) Proof	Est. 10,000	Value: 25.00				

KM# 19b   50 PENCE
47.5400 g., 0.9170 Gold 1.4015 oz. AGW, 38.5 mm. **Ruler:** Elizabeth II **Subject:** 150th Anniversary of British Rule **Obv:** Young bust right **Rev:** Ship divides dates

Date	Mintage	F	VF	XF	Unc	BU
ND(1983) Proof	150	Value: 1,450				

KM# 21   50 PENCE
Copper-Nickel, 38.5 mm. **Ruler:** Elizabeth II **Subject:** Opening of Mount Pleasant Airport **Obv:** Crowned bust right, denomination below **Rev:** Bust left, date at right

Date	Mintage	F	VF	XF	Unc	BU
ND(1985)	—	—	—	—	3.00	4.50

KM# 21a   50 PENCE
28.2750 g., 0.9250 Silver 0.8408 oz. ASW, 38.5 mm. **Obv:** Crowned bust right, denomination below **Rev:** Bust left

Date	Mintage	F	VF	XF	Unc	BU
ND (1985) Proof	Est. 5,000	Value: 20.00				

KM# 25   50 PENCE
Copper-Nickel, 38.5 mm. **Ruler:** Elizabeth II **Subject:** World Wildlife Fund **Obv:** Crowned bust right **Rev:** King penguins, denomination and date

Date	Mintage	F	VF	XF	Unc	BU
1987	—	—	—	—	7.00	14.00

KM# 25a   50 PENCE
28.2800 g., 0.9250 Silver 0.8410 oz. ASW, 38.5 mm. **Ruler:** Elizabeth II **Subject:** World Wildlife Fund **Obv:** Crowned bust right **Rev:** King Penguins, denomination and date

Date	Mintage	F	VF	XF	Unc	BU
1987 Proof	Est. 25,000	Value: 35.00				

KM# 26   50 PENCE
Copper-Nickel, 38.5 mm. **Ruler:** Elizabeth II **Subject:** Children's Fund **Obv:** Crowned bust right **Rev:** Woman on horseback, dog herding animals, denomination below

Date	Mintage	F	VF	XF	Unc	BU
1990	Est. 20,000	—	—	—	5.00	10.00

KM# 26a   50 PENCE
28.2800 g., 0.9250 Silver 0.8410 oz. ASW, 38.5 mm. **Ruler:** Elizabeth II **Subject:** Children's Fund **Obv:** Crowned bust right **Rev:** Woman on horseback, dog herding animals, denomination below

Date	Mintage	F	VF	XF	Unc	BU
1990 Proof	—	Value: 37.50				

KM# 34   50 PENCE
Copper-Nickel, 38.5 mm. **Ruler:** Elizabeth II **Subject:** 40th Anniversary - Reign of Queen Elizabeth II **Obv:** Crowned bust right **Rev:** Three figures, one at left is silhouette, dates below

Date	Mintage	F	VF	XF	Unc	BU
ND(1992)	—	—	—	—	4.50	6.50

KM# 34a   50 PENCE
28.2800 g., 0.9250 Silver 0.8410 oz. ASW, 38.5 mm. **Ruler:** Elizabeth II **Subject:** 40th Anniversary - Reign of Queen Elizabeth II **Obv:** Crowned bust right **Rev:** Three figures, one at left is silhouette, dates below

Date	Mintage	F	VF	XF	Unc	BU
ND(1992) Proof	5,000	Value: 50.00				

KM# 34b   50 PENCE
47.5400 g., 0.9170 Gold 1.4015 oz. AGW, 38.5 mm. **Ruler:** Elizabeth II **Subject:** 40th Anniversary - Reign of Queen Elizabeth II **Obv:** Crowned bust right **Rev:** Three figures, one at left is silhouette, dates below

Date	Mintage	F	VF	XF	Unc	BU
ND(1992) Proof	150	Value: 1,375				

KM# 43   50 PENCE
Copper-Nickel, 38.5 mm. **Ruler:** Elizabeth II **Subject:** 40th Anniversary - Coronation of Queen Elizabeth II **Obv:** Crowned bust right **Rev:** Queen on horseback, dates and denomination below

Date	Mintage	F	VF	XF	Unc	BU
ND(1993)	—	—	—	—	6.50	8.50

KM# 43a   50 PENCE
28.2800 g., 0.9250 Silver 0.8410 oz. ASW, 38.5 mm. **Ruler:** Elizabeth II **Subject:** 40th Anniversary - Coronation of Queen Elizabeth II **Obv:** Crowned bust right **Rev:** Queen on horseback, dates and denomination below

Date	Mintage	F	VF	XF	Unc	BU
ND(1993) Proof	Est. 10,000	Value: 55.00				

KM# 45   50 PENCE
Copper-Nickel, 38.5 mm. **Ruler:** Elizabeth II **Subject:** V. E. Day - 50th Anniversary **Obv:** Crowned bust right **Rev:** Denomination and dove divide flags, date below

Date	Mintage	F	VF	XF	Unc	BU
1995	—	—	—	—	5.50	7.50

KM# 45a   50 PENCE
28.2800 g., 0.9250 Silver 0.8410 oz. ASW, 38.5 mm. **Ruler:** Elizabeth II **Subject:** V. E. Day - 50th Anniversary **Obv:** Crowned bust right **Rev:** Denomination and dove divide flags, date below

Date	Mintage	F	VF	XF	Unc	BU
1995 Proof	Est. 10,000	Value: 50.00				

KM# 45b   50 PENCE
47.5400 g., 0.9170 Gold 1.4015 oz. AGW, 38.5 mm. **Ruler:** Elizabeth II **Subject:** V.E. Day - 50th Anniversary **Obv:** Crowned bust right **Rev:** Denomination and dove divide flags, date below

Date	Mintage	F	VF	XF	Unc	BU
1995 Proof	Est. 100	Value: 1,400				

KM# 46   50 PENCE
Copper-Nickel, 38.5 mm. **Ruler:** Elizabeth II **Subject:** Queen Elizabeth II's 70th Birthday **Obv:** Crowned bust right **Rev:** Queen and Prince Philip as young adults, denomination and date below

Date	Mintage	F	VF	XF	Unc	BU
1996	—	—	—	—	7.00	9.00

KM# 46a   50 PENCE
28.2800 g., 0.9250 Silver 0.8410 oz. ASW, 38.5 mm. **Ruler:** Elizabeth II **Subject:** Queen Elizabeth II's 70th Birthday **Obv:** Crowned bust right **Rev:** Queen and Prince Philip as young adults, denomination and date below

Date	Mintage	F	VF	XF	Unc	BU
1996 Proof	—	Value: 50.00				

KM# 72   50 PENCE
28.2800 g., Copper-Nickel, 38.6 mm. **Ruler:** Elizabeth II **Obv:** Crowned bust right, date below **Rev:** Queen Mother holding infant on lap, date below, circle surrounds, denmination below **Edge:** Reeded

Date	Mintage	F	VF	XF	Unc	BU
1995	—	—	—	—	7.00	9.00

KM# 72a   50 PENCE
28.2800 g., 0.9250 Silver 0.8410 oz. ASW, 38.6 mm. **Ruler:** Elizabeth II **Obv:** Crowned bust right, date below **Rev:** Queen Mother holding infant on lap, date below, circle surrounds, denmination below

Date	Mintage	F	VF	XF	Unc	BU
1995 Proof	—	Value: 35.00				

KM# 72a.1   50 PENCE
15.9200 g., 0.9250 Silver 0.4734 oz. ASW, 28.3 mm. **Ruler:** Elizabeth II **Obv:** Crowned bust right, date below **Rev:** Queen Mother holding the baby, date below, circle surrounds, denomination below **Edge:** Reeded

Date	Mintage	F	VF	XF	Unc	BU
1997 Proof	—	Value: 25.00				

KM# 59   50 PENCE
Copper-Nickel, 38.5 mm. **Ruler:** Elizabeth II **Subject:** WWF - Conserving Nature **Obv:** Crowned bust right **Rev:** Pair of Black-browed Albatross, date above

Date	Mintage	F	VF	XF	Unc	BU
1997	—	—	—	—	14.00	

KM# 59a 50 PENCE
28.2800 g., 0.9250 Silver 0.8410 oz. ASW, 38.5 mm. **Ruler:** Elizabeth II **Subject:** WWF - Conserving Nature **Obv:** Crowned bust right **Rev:** Pair of Black-browed Albatross, date above

Date	Mintage	F	VF	XF	Unc	BU
1997 Proof	Est. 15,000	Value: 40.00				

KM# 60a 50 PENCE
28.2800 g., 0.9250 Silver 0.8410 oz. ASW, 38.5 mm. **Ruler:** Elizabeth II **Subject:** WWF - Conserving Nature **Obv:** Crowned bust right **Rev:** Peale's dolphin

Date	Mintage	F	VF	XF	Unc	BU
1998 Proof	—	Value: 40.00				

KM# 60 50 PENCE
Copper-Nickel, 38.5 mm. **Ruler:** Elizabeth II **Subject:** WWF - Conserving Nature **Obv:** Crowned bust right **Rev:** Peale's dolphin, date above

Date	Mintage	F	VF	XF	Unc	BU
1998	—	—	—	—	14.00	—

KM# 71a 50 PENCE
28.2800 g., 0.9250 Silver 0.8410 oz. ASW, 38.5 mm. **Ruler:** Elizabeth II **Obv:** Crowned bust right **Rev:** Uncrowned portrait left **Edge:** Reeded

Date	Mintage	F	VF	XF	Unc	BU
1999 Proof	10,000	Value: 50.00				

KM# 66 50 PENCE
28.2800 g., Copper-Nickel, 38.5 mm. **Ruler:** Elizabeth II **Subject:** Winston Churchill **Obv:** Crowned bust right **Rev:** Churchill in Admiral's uniform, date below ship at left

Date	Mintage	F	VF	XF	Unc	BU
1999	—	—	—	—	7.00	9.00

KM# 66a 50 PENCE
28.2800 g., 0.9250 Silver 0.8410 oz. ASW, 38.5 mm. **Ruler:** Elizabeth II **Subject:** Winston Churchill **Obv:** Crowned bust right **Rev:** Churchill in Admiral's uniform

Date	Mintage	F	VF	XF	Unc	BU
1999 Proof	2,500	Value: 40.00				

KM# 66b 50 PENCE
47.5400 g., 0.9160 Gold 1.4000 oz. AGW, 38.5 mm. **Ruler:** Elizabeth II **Obv:** Crowned bust right **Rev:** Churchill in Admiral's uniform

Date	Mintage	F	VF	XF	Unc	BU
1999 Proof	125	Value: 1,500				

KM# 6 1/2 POUND
3.9900 g., 0.9170 Gold 0.1176 oz. AGW. **Ruler:** Elizabeth II **Obv:** Young bust right **Rev:** Romney marsh sheep left, date above

Date	Mintage	F	VF	XF	Unc	BU
1974 Proof	2,673	Value: 175				

KM# 7 POUND
7.9900 g., 0.9170 Gold 0.2356 oz. AGW. **Ruler:** Elizabeth II **Obv:** Young bust right **Rev:** Romney marsh sheep left, date above

Date	Mintage	F	VF	XF	Unc	BU
1974 Proof	2,675	Value: 275				

KM# 24 POUND
9.5000 g., Nickel-Brass, 22.5 mm. **Ruler:** Elizabeth II **Obv:** Crowned bust right **Rev:** State shield, date and denomination, DESIRE THE RIGHT

Date	Mintage	F	VF	XF	Unc	BU
1987	—	—	—	—	3.50	—
1987 Proof	2,500	Value: 12.50				
1992	—	—	—	—	3.50	—
1992 Proof	—	Value: 12.50				
1999	—	—	—	—	3.50	—
1999 Proof	2,500	Value: 12.50				

KM# 24a POUND
9.5000 g., 0.9250 Silver 0.2825 oz. ASW, 22.5 mm. **Ruler:** Elizabeth II **Obv:** Crowned bust right **Rev:** State shield, date and denomination

Date	Mintage	F	VF	XF	Unc	BU
1987 Proof	Est. 5,000	Value: 22.50				

KM# 24b POUND
19.6500 g., 0.9170 Gold 0.5793 oz. AGW, 22.5 mm. **Ruler:** Elizabeth II **Obv:** Crowned bust right **Rev:** State shield, date and denomination

Date	Mintage	F	VF	XF	Unc	BU
1987 Proof	Est. 200	Value: 625				

KM# 8 2 POUNDS
15.9800 g., 0.9170 Gold 0.4711 oz. AGW. **Ruler:** Elizabeth II **Obv:** Young bust right **Rev:** Romney marsh sheep left, date above

Date	Mintage	F	VF	XF	Unc	BU
1974 Proof	2,158	Value: 525				

KM# 22 2 POUNDS
28.2800 g., 0.5000 Silver 0.4546 oz. ASW, 38.61 mm. **Ruler:** Elizabeth II **Subject:** Commonweatlth Games **Obv:** Crowned bust right, denomination below **Rev:** Marksman

Date	Mintage	F	VF	XF	Unc	BU
1986	Est. 50,000	—	—	—	30.00	—

KM# 22a 2 POUNDS
28.2800 g., 0.9250 Silver 0.8410 oz. ASW, 38.61 mm. **Ruler:** Elizabeth II **Obv:** Crowned bust right, denomination below **Rev:** Marksman

Date	Mintage	F	VF	XF	Unc	BU
1986	Est. 20,000	Value: 40.00				

KM# 32 2 POUNDS
28.2800 g., 0.9250 Silver 0.8410 oz. ASW, 38.61 mm. **Ruler:** Elizabeth II **Subject:** 10th Wedding Anniversary - Prince Charles and Lady Diana **Obv:** Crowned bust right **Rev:** Facing cameos divide cathedral and crown design, wreath surrounds

Date	Mintage	F	VF	XF	Unc	BU
1991 Proof	Est. 10,000	Value: 40.00				

KM# 35 2 POUNDS
Copper-Nickel, 38.61 mm. **Ruler:** Elizabeth II **Subject:** Heritage Year **Obv:** Crowned bust right **Rev:** State shield below flowers, ferns flank

Date	Mintage	F	VF	XF	Unc	BU
1992	—	—	—	—	11.50	—

KM# 35a 2 POUNDS
28.2800 g., 0.9250 Silver 0.8410 oz. ASW, 38.61 mm. **Ruler:** Elizabeth II **Subject:** Heritage Year **Obv:** Crowned bust right **Rev:** State shield below flowers, ferns flank

Date	Mintage	F	VF	XF	Unc	BU
1992 Proof	Est. 7,500	Value: 37.50				

KM# 47b 2 POUNDS
28.2800 g., Copper-Nickel, 38.6 mm. **Ruler:** Elizabeth II **Subject:** Royal Heritage - Egbert of Wessex **Obv:** Crowned bust right **Rev:** Egbert in archway, dates divided **Edge:** Reeded

Date	Mintage	F	VF	XF	Unc	BU
1996	—	—	—	—	8.50	—

KM# 48b 2 POUNDS
28.2800 g., Copper-Nickel, 38.6 mm. **Ruler:** Elizabeth II **Subject:** Royal Heritage - Alfred the Great **Obv:** Crowned bust right **Rev:** Alfred with axe, scroll, ancient coin, dates divided **Edge:** Reeded

Date	Mintage	F	VF	XF	Unc	BU
1996	—	—	—	—	8.50	—

KM# 49b 2 POUNDS
28.2800 g., Copper-Nickel, 38.6 mm. **Ruler:** Elizabeth II **Subject:** Royal Heritage - Edward the Confessor 1042-66 **Obv:** Crowned bust right **Rev:** Edward with halo offering miniature church within wreath, dates divided **Edge:** Reeded

Date	Mintage	F	VF	XF	Unc	BU
1996	—	—	—	—	8.50	—

KM# 50b 2 POUNDS
28.2800 g., Copper-Nickel, 38.6 mm. **Ruler:** Elizabeth II **Subject:** Royal Heritage - William I the Conqueror 1066-87 **Obv:** Crowned bust right **Rev:** Seated William holding miniature church, Doomsday Book at left, shield at right, dates below **Edge:** Reeded

Date	Mintage	F	VF	XF	Unc	BU
1996	—	—	—	—	8.50	—

KM# 51b 2 POUNDS
28.2800 g., Copper-Nickel, 38.6 mm. **Ruler:** Elizabeth II **Subject:** Royal Heritage - Henry II 1154-89 **Obv:** Crowned bust right **Rev:** Crowned bust of Henry II 3/4 facing, dates at right **Edge:** Reeded

Date	Mintage	F	VF	XF	Unc	BU
1996	—	—	—	—	8.50	—

KM# 52b 2 POUNDS
28.2800 g., Copper-Nickel, 38.6 mm. **Ruler:** Elizabeth II **Subject:** Royal Heritage - Richard the Lionheart 1189-99 **Obv:** Crowned bust right **Rev:** Seated Richard flanked by sun and crescent moon, dates divided **Edge:** Reeded

Date	Mintage	F	VF	XF	Unc	BU
1996	—	—	—	—	8.50	—

KM# 53b 2 POUNDS
28.2800 g., Copper-Nickel, 38.6 mm. **Ruler:** Elizabeth II
Subject: Royal Heritage - Henry IV 1399-1413 **Obv:** Crowned
bust right **Rev:** Portrait of Henry in crown and cape right, dates
below **Edge:** Reeded

Date	Mintage	F	VF	XF	Unc	BU
1996	—	—	—	—	8.50	—

KM# 54b 2 POUNDS
28.2800 g., Copper-Nickel, 38.6 mm. **Ruler:** Elizabeth II
Subject: Royal Heritage - Edward IV 1461-83 **Obv:** Crowned
bust right **Rev:** Youthful Edward bust looking left, castle and ship
at left, dates divided **Edge:** Reeded

Date	Mintage	F	VF	XF	Unc	BU
1996	—	—	—	—	8.50	—

KM# 55b 2 POUNDS
28.2800 g., Copper-Nickel, 38.6 mm. **Ruler:** Elizabeth II **Subject:**
Royal Heritage - Henry VIII 1509-47 **Obv:** Crowned bust right
Rev: Standing Henry with shield; dates below at left **Edge:** Reeded

Date	Mintage	F	VF	XF	Unc	BU
1996	—	—	—	—	8.50	—

KM# 56b 2 POUNDS
28.2800 g., Copper-Nickel, 38.6 mm. **Ruler:** Elizabeth II
Subject: Royal Heritage - Elizabeth I 1558-1603 **Obv:** Crowned
bust right **Rev:** Bust with high ruffled collar 3/4 facing, dates below
Edge: Reeded

Date	Mintage	F	VF	XF	Unc	BU
1996	—	—	—	—	8.50	—

KM# 57b 2 POUNDS
28.2800 g., Copper-Nickel, 38.6 mm. **Ruler:** Elizabeth II
Subject: Royal Heritage - Charles I 1625-49 **Obv:** Crowned bust
right **Rev:** Smiling portrait of Charles 3/4 right, small shield and
dates at right **Edge:** Reeded

Date	Mintage	F	VF	XF	Unc	BU
1996	—	—	—	—	8.50	—

KM# 58b 2 POUNDS
28.2800 g., Copper-Nickel, 38.6 mm. **Ruler:** Elizabeth II
Subject: Royal Heritage - Victoria 1837-1901 **Obv:** Crowned bust
right **Rev:** Seated Queen Victoria with scepter and shield, dates
at right **Edge:** Reeded

Date	Mintage	F	VF	XF	Unc	BU
1996	—	—	—	—	8.50	—

KM# 47 2 POUNDS
28.2800 g., 0.9250 Silver 0.8410 oz. ASW, 38.61 mm.
Ruler: Elizabeth II **Subject:** Royal Heritage - Egbert of Wessex
Obv: Crowned bust right **Rev:** Egbert in archway, dates divided

Date	Mintage	F	VF	XF	Unc	BU
1996 Proof	10,000		Value: 50.00			

KM# 47a 2 POUNDS
28.1500 g., 0.9250 Bi-Metallic Silver center in Gold-plated Silver
ring 0.8371 oz., 38.61 mm. **Ruler:** Elizabeth II **Subject:** Royal
Heritage - Egbert of Wessex **Obv:** Crowned bust right **Rev:**
Egbert in archway, dates divided

Date	Mintage	F	VF	XF	Unc	BU
1996 Proof	Est. 10,000		Value: 45.00			

KM# 48 2 POUNDS
28.2800 g., 0.9250 Silver 0.8410 oz. ASW, 38.61 mm.
Ruler: Elizabeth II **Subject:** Royal Heritage - Alfred the Great
Obv: Crowned bust right **Rev:** Alfred with axe, scroll, ancient
coin, dates divided

Date	Mintage	F	VF	XF	Unc	BU
1996 Proof	10,000		Value: 50.00			

KM# 48a 2 POUNDS
28.1500 g., 0.9250 Bi-Metallic Silver center in Gold-plated Silver
ring 0.8371 oz., 38.61 mm. **Ruler:** Elizabeth II **Subject:** Royal
Heritage - Alfred the Great **Obv:** Crowned bust right **Rev:** Alfred
with axe, scroll, ancient coin, dates divided

Date	Mintage	F	VF	XF	Unc	BU
1996 Proof	Est. 10,000		Value: 35.00			

KM# 49 2 POUNDS
28.2800 g., 0.9250 Silver 0.8410 oz. ASW, 38.61 mm.
Ruler: Elizabeth II **Subject:** Royal Heritage - Edward the
Confessor **Obv:** Crowned bust right **Rev:** Edward with halo
offering miniature church within wreath, dates divided

Date	Mintage	F	VF	XF	Unc	BU
1996 Proof	10,000		Value: 50.00			

KM# 49a 2 POUNDS
28.1500 g., 0.9250 Bi-Metallic Silver center in Gold-plated Silver
ring 0.8371 oz., 38.61 mm. **Ruler:** Elizabeth II **Subject:** Royal
Heritage - Edward the Confessor **Obv:** Crowned bust right
Rev: Edward with halo offering miniature church; dates divided

Date	Mintage	F	VF	XF	Unc	BU
1996 Proof	Est. 10,000		Value: 35.00			

KM# 50 2 POUNDS
28.2800 g., 0.9250 Silver 0.8410 oz. ASW, 38.61 mm.
Ruler: Elizabeth II **Subject:** Royal Heritage - William I
Obv: Crowned bust right **Rev:** Seated William holding miniature
church, Doomsday Book at left, shield at right, dates below

Date	Mintage	F	VF	XF	Unc	BU
1996 Proof	10,000		Value: 50.00			

KM# 50a 2 POUNDS
28.1500 g., 0.9250 Bi-Metallic Silver center in Gold-plated ring
0.8371 oz., 38.61 mm. **Ruler:** Elizabeth II **Subject:** Royal Heritage
- William I **Obv:** Crowned bust right **Rev:** Seated William holding
miniature church, Doomsday Book at left, shield at right, dates below

Date	Mintage	F	VF	XF	Unc	BU
1996 Proof	Est. 10,000		Value: 35.00			

KM# 51 2 POUNDS
28.2800 g., 0.9250 Silver 0.8410 oz. ASW, 38.61 mm.
Ruler: Elizabeth II **Subject:** Royal Heritage - Henry II 1154-89
Obv: Crowned bust right **Rev:** Crowned bust of Henry II 3/4
facing, dates at right

Date	Mintage	F	VF	XF	Unc	BU
1996 Proof	10,000		Value: 50.00			

KM# 51a 2 POUNDS
28.1500 g., 0.9250 Bi-Metallic Silver center in Gold-plated Silver
ring 0.8371 oz., 38.61 mm. **Ruler:** Elizabeth II **Subject:** Royal
Heritage - Henry II 1154-89 **Obv:** Crowned bust right **Rev:**
Crowned bust of Henry II 3/4 facing, dates at right

Date	Mintage	F	VF	XF	Unc	BU
1996 Proof	Est. 10,000		Value: 35.00			

KM# 52 2 POUNDS
28.2800 g., 0.9250 Silver 0.8410 oz. ASW, 38.61 mm.
Ruler: Elizabeth II **Subject:** Royal Heritage - Richard I The
Lionheart 1189-99 **Obv:** Crowned bust right **Rev:** Seated Richard
flanked by sun and crescent moon, dates divided

Date	Mintage	F	VF	XF	Unc	BU
1996 Proof	10,000		Value: 50.00			

KM# 52a 2 POUNDS
28.1500 g., 0.9250 Bi-Metallic Silver center in Gold-plated Silver ring
0.8371 oz., 38.61 mm. **Ruler:** Elizabeth II **Subject:** Royal Heritage
- Richard I The Lionheart 1189-99 **Obv:** Crowned bust right
Rev: Seated Richard flanked by sun and crescent moon; dates
divided

Date	Mintage	F	VF	XF	Unc	BU
1996 Proof	Est. 10,000		Value: 35.00			

KM# 53 2 POUNDS
28.2800 g., 0.9250 Silver 0.8410 oz. ASW, 38.61 mm.
Ruler: Elizabeth II **Subject:** Royal Heritage - Henry IV 1399-1413
Obv: Crowned bust right **Rev:** Portrait of Henry in crown and
cape right, dates below

Date	Mintage	F	VF	XF	Unc	BU
1996 Proof	10,000		Value: 50.00			

KM# 53a 2 POUNDS
28.1500 g., 0.9250 Bi-Metallic Silver center in Gold-plated Silver
ring 0.8371 oz., 38.61 mm. **Ruler:** Elizabeth II **Subject:** Royal
Heritage - Henry IV 1399-1413 **Obv:** Crowned bust right **Rev:**
Portrait of Henry in crown and cape right, dates below

Date	Mintage	F	VF	XF	Unc	BU
1996 Proof	Est. 10,000		Value: 35.00			

KM# 54 2 POUNDS
28.2800 g., 0.9250 Silver 0.8410 oz. ASW, 38.61 mm.
Ruler: Elizabeth II **Subject:** Royal Heritage - Edward IV 1461-
83 **Obv:** Crowned bust right **Rev:** Youthful Edward bust looking
left, castle and ship at left, dates divided

Date	Mintage	F	VF	XF	Unc	BU
1996 Proof	10,000		Value: 50.00			

KM# 54a 2 POUNDS
28.1500 g., 0.9250 Bi-Metallic Silver center in Gold-plated Silver ring
0.8371 oz., 38.61 mm. **Ruler:** Elizabeth II **Subject:** Royal Heritage
- Edward IV 1461-83 **Obv:** Crowned bust right **Rev:** Youthful Edward
bust looking left, castle and ship at left, dates divided

Date	Mintage	F	VF	XF	Unc	BU
1996 Proof	Est. 10,000		Value: 35.00			

KM# 55   2 POUNDS
28.2800 g., 0.9250 Silver 0.8410 oz. ASW, 38.61 mm.
Ruler: Elizabeth II **Subject:** Royal Heritage - Henry VIII 1509-47
Obv: Crowned bust right **Rev:** Standing Henry with shield; dates
below at left

Date	Mintage	F	VF	XF	Unc	BU
1996 Proof	10,000	Value: 50.00				

KM# 55a   2 POUNDS
28.1500 g., 0.9250 Bi-Metallic Silver center in Gold-plated Silver
ring 0.8371 oz., 38.61 mm. **Ruler:** Elizabeth II **Subject:**
Royal Heritage - Henry VIII 1509-47 **Obv:** Crowned bust right
Rev: Standing Henry with shield; dates

Date	Mintage	F	VF	XF	Unc	BU
1996 Proof	Est. 10,000	Value: 35.00				

KM# 56   2 POUNDS
28.2800 g., 0.9250 Silver 0.8410 oz. ASW, 38.61 mm.
Ruler: Elizabeth II **Subject:** Royal Heritage - Elizabeth I 1558-
1603 **Obv:** Crowned bust right **Rev:** Bust with high ruffled collar
3/4 facing, dates below

Date	Mintage	F	VF	XF	Unc	BU
1996 Proof	10,000	Value: 50.00				

KM# 56a   2 POUNDS
28.1500 g., 0.9250 Bi-Metallic Silver center in Gold-plated Silver
ring 0.8371 oz., 38.61 mm. **Ruler:** Elizabeth II **Subject:**
Royal Heritage - Elizabeth I 1558-1603 **Obv:** Crowned bust right
Rev: Bust with high ruffled collar 3/4 facing, dates below

Date	Mintage	F	VF	XF	Unc	BU
1996 Proof	Est. 10,000	Value: 35.00				

KM# 57   2 POUNDS
28.2800 g., 0.9250 Silver 0.8410 oz. ASW, 38.61 mm.
Ruler: Elizabeth II **Subject:** Royal Heritage - Charles I 1625-49
Obv: Crowned bust right **Rev:** Smiling portrait of Charles 3/4
right, small shield and dates at right

Date	Mintage	F	VF	XF	Unc	BU
1996 Proof	10,000	Value: 50.00				

KM# 57a   2 POUNDS
28.1500 g., 0.9250 Bi-Metallic Silver center in Gold-plated Silver
ring 0.8371 oz., 38.61 mm. **Ruler:** Elizabeth II **Subject:** Royal
Heritage - Charles I 1625-49 **Obv:** Crowned bust right
Rev: Smiling portrait of Charles 3/4 right, small shield and dates
at right

Date	Mintage	F	VF	XF	Unc	BU
1996 Proof	Est. 10,000	Value: 35.00				

KM# 58   2 POUNDS
28.2800 g., 0.9250 Silver 0.8410 oz. ASW, 38.61 mm.
Ruler: Elizabeth II **Subject:** Royal Heritage 1837-1901
Obv: Crowned bust right **Rev:** Seated Queen Victoria with
scepter and shield, dates at right

Date	Mintage	F	VF	XF	Unc	BU
1996 Proof	10,000	Value: 50.00				

KM# 58a   2 POUNDS
28.1500 g., 0.9250 Bi-Metallic Silver center in Gold-plated Silver
ring 0.8371 oz., 38.61 mm.   **Ruler:** Elizabeth II **Subject:** Royal
Heritage - Victoria 1837-1901 **Obv:** Crowned bust right **Rev:**
Seated Queen Victoria with sceptre and shield, dates at right

Date	Mintage	F	VF	XF	Unc	BU
1996 Proof	Est. 10,000	Value: 35.00				

KM# 104   2 POUNDS
1.2428 g., 0.9990 Gold 0.0399 oz. AGW, 14 mm.
Ruler: Elizabeth II **Obv:** Crowned bust right **Rev:** Egbert of
Wessex 802-839 **Edge:** Reeded

Date	Mintage	F	VF	XF	Unc	BU
1997 Proof	—	Value: 45.00				

KM# 105   2 POUNDS
1.2428 g., 0.9990 Gold 0.0399 oz. AGW, 14 mm.
Ruler: Elizabeth II **Obv:** Crowned bust right **Rev:** Alfred the Great
871-899 **Edge:** Reeded

Date	Mintage	F	VF	XF	Unc	BU
1997 Proof	—	Value: 45.00				

KM# 106   2 POUNDS
1.2428 g., 0.9990 Gold 0.0399 oz. AGW, 14 mm.
Ruler: Elizabeth II **Obv:** Crowned bust right **Rev:** Edward the
Confessor **Edge:** Reeded

Date	Mintage	F	VF	XF	Unc	BU
1997 Proof	—	Value: 45.00				

KM# 107   2 POUNDS
1.2428 g., 0.9990 Gold 0.0399 oz. AGW, 14 mm.
Ruler: Elizabeth II **Obv:** Crowned bust right **Rev:** William I the
Conqueror 1066-87 **Edge:** Reeded

Date	Mintage	F	VF	XF	Unc	BU
1997 Proof	—	Value: 45.00				

KM# 108   2 POUNDS
1.2428 g., 0.9990 Gold 0.0399 oz. AGW, 14 mm. **Ruler:** Elizabeth II
Obv: Crowned bust right **Rev:** Henry II 1154-89 **Edge:** Reeded

Date	Mintage	F	VF	XF	Unc	BU
1997 Proof	—	Value: 45.00				

KM# 109   2 POUNDS
1.2428 g., 0.9990 Gold 0.0399 oz. AGW, 14 mm.
Ruler: Elizabeth II **Obv:** Crowned bust right **Rev:** Richard I the
Lion Hearted, 1189-99 **Edge:** Reeded

Date	Mintage	F	VF	XF	Unc	BU
1997 Proof	—	Value: 45.00				

KM# 110   2 POUNDS
1.2428 g., 0.9990 Gold 0.0399 oz. AGW, 14 mm. **Ruler:** Elizabeth II
Obv: Crowned bust right **Rev:** Henry IV 1399-1413 **Edge:** Reeded

Date	Mintage	F	VF	XF	Unc	BU
1997 Proof	—	Value: 45.00				

KM# 111   2 POUNDS
1.2428 g., 0.9990 Gold 0.0399 oz. AGW, 14 mm.
Ruler: Elizabeth II **Obv:** Crowned bust right **Rev:** Edward IV
1461-83 **Edge:** Reeded

Date	Mintage	F	VF	XF	Unc	BU
1997 Proof	—	Value: 45.00				

KM# 112   2 POUNDS
1.2428 g., 0.9990 Gold 0.0399 oz. AGW, 14 mm.
Ruler: Elizabeth II **Obv:** Crowned bust right **Rev:** Henry VIII
1509-47 **Edge:** Reeded

Date	Mintage	F	VF	XF	Unc	BU
1997 Proof	—	Value: 45.00				

KM# 113   2 POUNDS
1.2428 g., 0.9990 Gold 0.0399 oz. AGW, 14 mm.
Ruler: Elizabeth II **Obv:** Crowned bust right **Rev:** Elizabeth I
1558-1603 **Edge:** Reeded

Date	Mintage	F	VF	XF	Unc	BU
1997 Proof	—	Value: 45.00				

KM# 114   2 POUNDS
1.2428 g., 0.9990 Gold 0.0399 oz. AGW, 14 mm.
Ruler: Elizabeth II **Obv:** Crowned bust right **Rev:** Charles I 1625-
49 **Edge:** Reeded

Date	Mintage	F	VF	XF	Unc	BU
1997 Proof	—	Value: 45.00				

KM# 115   2 POUNDS
1.2428 g., 0.9990 Gold 0.0399 oz. AGW, 14 mm.
Ruler: Elizabeth II **Obv:** Crowned bust right **Rev:** Victoria 1837-
1901 **Edge:** Reeded

Date	Mintage	F	VF	XF	Unc	BU
1998 Proof	—	Value: 45.00				

KM# 116   2 POUNDS
7.8000 g., 0.5830 Gold 0.1462 oz. AGW, 24.9 mm.
Ruler: Elizabeth II **Subject:** Royal Heritage - Egbert of Wessex
802-839 **Obv:** Crowned bust right **Rev:** Egbert in archway, dates
divided **Edge:** Reeded

Date	Mintage	F	VF	XF	Unc	BU
1997 Proof	—	Value: 175				

KM# 117   2 POUNDS
7.8000 g., 0.5830 Gold 0.1462 oz. AGW, 24.9 mm.
Ruler: Elizabeth II **Obv:** Crowned bust right **Rev:** Alfred the Great
871-899 **Edge:** Reeded

Date	Mintage	F	VF	XF	Unc	BU
1997 Proof	—	Value: 175				

KM# 118   2 POUNDS
7.8000 g., 0.5830 Gold 0.1462 oz. AGW, 24.9 mm.
Ruler: Elizabeth II **Obv:** Crowned bust right **Rev:** Edward the
Confessor 1042-66 **Edge:** Reeded

Date	Mintage	F	VF	XF	Unc	BU
1997 Proof	—	Value: 175				

KM# 119   2 POUNDS
7.8000 g., 0.5830 Gold 0.1462 oz. AGW, 24.9 mm.
Ruler: Elizabeth II **Obv:** Crowned bust right **Rev:** William I the
Conqueror 1066-87 **Edge:** Reeded

Date	Mintage	F	VF	XF	Unc	BU
1997 Proof	—	Value: 175				

KM# 120   2 POUNDS
7.8000 g., 0.5830 Gold 0.1462 oz. AGW, 24.9 mm.
Ruler: Elizabeth II **Obv:** Crowned bust right **Rev:** Henry II 1154-
89 **Edge:** Reeded

Date	Mintage	F	VF	XF	Unc	BU
1997 Proof	—	Value: 175				

KM# 121   2 POUNDS
7.8000 g., 0.5830 Gold 0.1462 oz. AGW, 24.9 mm.
Ruler: Elizabeth II **Obv:** Crowned bust right **Rev:** Richard I the
Lion Hearted 1189-99 **Edge:** Reeded

Date	Mintage	F	VF	XF	Unc	BU
1997 Proof	—	Value: 175				

KM# 122   2 POUNDS
7.8000 g., 0.5830 Gold 0.1462 oz. AGW, 24.9 mm.
Ruler: Elizabeth II **Obv:** Crowned bust right **Rev:** Henry IV 1399-
1413 **Edge:** Reeded

Date	Mintage	F	VF	XF	Unc	BU
1997 Proof	—	Value: 175				

KM# 123   2 POUNDS
7.8000 g., 0.5830 Gold 0.1462 oz. AGW, 24.9 mm.
Ruler: Elizabeth II **Obv:** Crowned bust right **Rev:** Edward IV
1461-83 **Edge:** Reeded

Date	Mintage	F	VF	XF	Unc	BU
1997 Proof	—	Value: 175				

KM# 124   2 POUNDS
7.8700 g., 0.5830 Gold 0.1475 oz. AGW, 24.9 mm.
Ruler: Elizabeth II **Obv:** Crowned bust right **Rev:** Henry VIII
1509-47, shield at right, dates at left **Edge:** Reeded

Date	Mintage	F	VF	XF	Unc	BU
1997 Proof	—	Value: 175				

KM# 125   2 POUNDS
7.8000 g., 0.5830 Gold 0.1462 oz. AGW, 24.9 mm.
Ruler: Elizabeth II **Subject:** Royal Heritage - Elizabeth I 1558-
1603 **Obv:** Crowned bust right **Rev:** Bust with high ruffled collar
3/4 facing, dates below **Edge:** Reeded

Date	Mintage	F	VF	XF	Unc	BU
1998 Proof	—	Value: 175				

KM# 126   2 POUNDS
7.8000 g., 0.5830 Gold 0.1462 oz. AGW, 24.9 mm.
Ruler: Elizabeth II **Obv:** Crowned bust right **Rev:** Charles I 1625-
49 **Edge:** Reeded

Date	Mintage	F	VF	XF	Unc	BU
1998 Proof	—	Value: 175				

KM# 127   2 POUNDS
7.8000 g., 0.5830 Gold 0.1462 oz. AGW, 24.9 mm.
Ruler: Elizabeth II **Obv:** Crowned bust right **Rev:** Victoria 1837-
1901 **Edge:** Reeded

Date	Mintage	F	VF	XF	Unc	BU
1998 Proof	—	Value: 175				

KM# 61   2 POUNDS
Copper-Nickel   **Ruler:** Elizabeth II   **Subject:** Flying Doctor
Service   **Obv:** Crowned bust right   **Rev:** Two airplanes in flight,
denomination below

Date	Mintage	F	VF	XF	Unc	BU
1998	—	—	—	—	8.50	—

KM# 61a   2 POUNDS
28.2800 g., 0.9250 Silver 0.8410 oz. ASW   **Ruler:** Elizabeth II
Subject: Flying Doctor Service   **Obv:** Crowned bust right   **Rev:**
Two airplanes in flight

Date	Mintage	F	VF	XF	Unc	BU
1998 Proof	Est. 10,000	Value: 50.00				

KM# 128   2 POUNDS
7.6700 g., 0.5830 Gold 0.1438 oz. AGW, 24.9 mm.
Ruler: Elizabeth II   **Obv:** Crowned bust right, date below
Rev: Queen Mother holding the baby within circle, denomination
below   **Edge:** Reeded

Date	Mintage	F	VF	XF	Unc	BU
1998 Proof	—	Value: 160				

KM# 64   2 POUNDS
Copper-Nickel   **Ruler:** Elizabeth II   **Subject:** Sir Ernest Henry
Shackleton   **Obv:** Crowned bust right   **Rev:** Cameo portrait and
icebound ship "Endurance", denomination below divides dates

Date	Mintage	F	VF	XF	Unc	BU
1999	—	—	—	—	8.50	—

KM# 64a   2 POUNDS
28.2800 g., 0.9250 Silver 0.8410 oz. ASW   **Ruler:** Elizabeth II
Subject: Sir Ernest Henry Shackleton   **Obv:** Crowned bust right
Rev: Cameo portrait and icebound ship "Endurance"

Date	Mintage	F	VF	XF	Unc	BU
1999 Proof	Est. 10,000	Value: 50.00				

KM# 69   2 POUNDS
28.2800 g., Bi-Metallic Copper-Nickel center in Nickel-Brass ring,
38.61 mm.   **Ruler:** Elizabeth II   **Obv:** Crowned bust right
Rev: Island map, radiant sun and denomination within circle of
wildlife   **Edge:** Plain

Date	Mintage	F	VF	XF	Unc	BU
1999	—	—	—	—	10.00	—
1999 Proof	2,500	Value: 20.00				

KM# 69a   2 POUNDS
28.1500 g., 0.9250 Bi-Metallic Silver center in Gold-plated Silver
ring 0.8371 oz., 38.61 mm.   **Ruler:** Elizabeth II   **Obv:** Crowned
bust right within circle, dates below   **Rev:** Islands map, radiant
sun, and denomination within circle of local wildlife   **Edge:** Reeded

Date	Mintage	F	VF	XF	Unc	BU
1999-2000 Proof	—	Value: 55.00				

KM# 85   2 POUNDS
28.4000 g., 0.9250 Silver with gold gilt outer ring 0.8446 oz. ASW,
38.4 mm.   **Ruler:** Elizabeth II   **Subject:** Queen Mother
Obv: Crowned bust right within beaded circle, date below
Rev: Queen Mother holding baby and date within beaded circle,
denomination below   **Edge:** Reeded

Date	Mintage	F	VF	XF	Unc	BU
2000 Proof	10,000	Value: 50.00				

KM# 67   2 POUNDS
28.2800 g., Copper-Nickel   **Ruler:** Elizabeth II   **Subject:** The
Gold Rush - "Vicar of Bray" Ship   **Obv:** Crowned bust right, date
below   **Rev:** Ship in harbor, denomination below   **Edge:** Reeded

Date	Mintage	F	VF	XF	Unc	BU
2000	—	—	—	—	8.50	—

KM# 67a   2 POUNDS
28.2800 g., 0.9250 Silver 0.8410 oz. ASW   **Ruler:** Elizabeth II
Subject: The Gold Rush - "Vicar of Bray" Ship   **Obv:** Crowned
bust right   **Rev:** Ship in harbor, denomination below   **Edge:** Reeded

Date	Mintage	F	VF	XF	Unc	BU
2000 Proof	10,000	Value: 47.50				

KM# 9   5 POUNDS
39.9400 g., 0.9170 Gold 1.1775 oz. AGW   **Ruler:** Elizabeth II
Obv: Young bust right   **Rev:** Romney marsh sheep left, date above

Date	Mintage	F	VF	XF	Unc	BU
1974 Proof	2,158	Value: 1,250				

KM# 11   5 POUNDS
28.2800 g., 0.9250 Silver 0.8410 oz. ASW   **Ruler:** Elizabeth II
Subject: Conservation   **Obv:** Young bust right   **Rev:** Humpback
whale

Date	Mintage	F	VF	XF	Unc	BU
1979	3,998	—	—	—	30.00	—
1979 Proof	3,432	Value: 45.00				

KM# 27   5 POUNDS
Copper-Nickel   **Ruler:** Elizabeth II   **Subject:** 90th Birthday of
Queen Mother   **Obv:** Crowned bust right, denomination below
Rev: Crowned monogram, flowers flank, dates below

Date	Mintage	F	VF	XF	Unc	BU
1990	—	—	—	—	17.50	—

KM# 27a   5 POUNDS
28.2800 g., 0.9250 Silver 0.8410 oz. ASW   **Ruler:** Elizabeth II
Subject: 90th Birthday of Queen Mother   **Obv:** Crowned bust
right, denomination below   **Rev:** Flowers flank crowned
monogram, dates below

Date	Mintage	F	VF	XF	Unc	BU
1990 Proof	Est. 10,000	Value: 37.50				

KM# 33   5 POUNDS
39.9400 g., 0.9170 Gold 1.1775 oz. AGW   **Ruler:** Elizabeth II
Subject: 10th Wedding Anniversary - Prince Charles and Lady
Diana   **Obv:** Crowned bust right   **Rev:** Facing cameo portraits of
Prince Charles and Princess Diana

Date	Mintage	F	VF	XF	Unc	BU
1991 Proof	Est. 200	Value: 1,150				

KM# 36   5 POUNDS
Copper-Nickel   **Ruler:** Elizabeth II   **Subject:** 10th Anniversary of
Liberation   **Obv:** Crowned bust right   **Rev:** Statue at center,
inscription at right within 1/2 wreath

Date	Mintage	F	VF	XF	Unc	BU
1992	—	—	—	—	15.00	—

KM# 36a   5 POUNDS
28.2800 g., 0.9250 Silver 0.8410 oz. ASW, 38.61 mm.
Ruler: Elizabeth II   **Subject:** 10th Anniversary of Liberation
Obv: Crowned bust right   **Rev:** Statue at center, inscription at right

Date	Mintage	F	VF	XF	Unc	BU
1992 Proof	Est. 5,000	Value: 42.50				

KM# 36b   5 POUNDS
39.9400 g., 0.9170 Gold 1.1775 oz. AGW **Ruler:** Elizabeth II
Subject: 10th Anniversary of Liberation **Obv:** Crowned bust right
Rev: Statue at center, inscription at right

Date	Mintage	F	VF	XF	Unc	BU
1992 Proof	100	Value: 1,200				

KM# 37   5 POUNDS
28.2800 g., 0.9250 Silver 0.8410 oz. ASW **Ruler:** Elizabeth II
Subject: 400th Anniversary of Discovery - Ship "Desire"
Obv: Crowned bust right **Rev:** Map above ship, "Desire" at sea,
dates at right

Date	Mintage	F	VF	XF	Unc	BU
ND(1992) Proof	Est. 20,000	Value: 40.00				

KM# 63   5 POUNDS
Copper-Nickel **Ruler:** Elizabeth II **Subject:** Queen's Golden
Wedding Anniversary **Obv:** Crowned bust right **Rev:** Royal
couple with gold inlay shield, dates at right

Date	Mintage	F	VF	XF	Unc	BU
1997	—	—	—	—	20.00	—

KM# 63a   5 POUNDS
28.2800 g., 0.9250 Silver 0.8410 oz. ASW, 38.6 mm.
Ruler: Elizabeth II **Subject:** Queen's Golden Wedding
Anniversary **Obv:** Crowned bust right **Rev:** Royal couple with
gold inlay shield **Edge:** Reeded

Date	Mintage	F	VF	XF	Unc	BU
1997 Proof	—	Value: 45.00				

KM# 12   10 POUNDS
35.0000 g., 0.9250 Silver 1.0408 oz. ASW **Ruler:** Elizabeth II
Subject: Conservation **Obv:** Young bust right **Rev:** Flightless
steamer ducks, denomination below, date at right

Date	Mintage	F	VF	XF	Unc	BU
1979	3,996	—	—	—	35.00	—
1979 Proof	3,247	Value: 50.00				

KM# 28   10 POUNDS
3.1300 g., 0.9990 Gold 0.1005 oz. AGW **Ruler:** Elizabeth II
Subject: 90th Birthday of Queen Mother **Obv:** Crowned bust right
Rev: Crowned arms with supporters, dates below

Date	Mintage	F	VF	XF	Unc	BU
ND(1990) Proof	Est. 750	Value: 110				

KM# 38   10 POUNDS
3.1300 g., 0.9990 Gold 0.1005 oz. AGW **Ruler:** Elizabeth II
Subject: 400th Anniversary of Discovery - Ship "Desire"
Obv: Crowned bust right **Rev:** Map above ship "Desire" at sea,
dates at right

Date	Mintage	F	VF	XF	Unc	BU
ND(1992) Proof	Est. 400	Value: 110				

KM# 62   20 POUNDS
6.2200 g., 0.9990 Gold 0.1998 oz. AGW **Ruler:** Elizabeth II
Subject: Flying Doctor Service **Obv:** Crowned bust right
Rev: Two airplanes in flight

Date	Mintage	F	VF	XF	Unc	BU
1998 Proof	Est. 1,000	Value: 200				

KM# 65   20 POUNDS
6.2200 g., 0.9990 Gold 0.1998 oz. AGW **Ruler:** Elizabeth II
Subject: Sir Ernest H. Shackleton **Obv:** Crowned bust right
Rev: Cameo portrait and icebound ship

Date	Mintage	F	VF	XF	Unc	BU
1999 Proof	Est. 1,000	Value: 200				

KM# 68   20 POUNDS
6.2200 g., 0.9990 Gold 0.1998 oz. AGW **Ruler:** Elizabeth II
Subject: The Gold Rush **Obv:** Crowned bust right **Rev:** "Vicar
of Bray" in harbor **Edge:** Reeded

Date	Mintage	F	VF	XF	Unc	BU
2000PM Proof	1,000	Value: 200				

KM# 20   25 POUNDS
150.0000 g., 0.9250 Silver 4.4607 oz. ASW **Ruler:** Elizabeth II
Subject: 100 Years of Self Sufficiency **Obv:** Crowned bust right
Rev: S.S. Great Britain a steam and sailing ship which was
scuttled in the Falkland Islands, dates below

Date	Mintage	F	VF	XF	Unc	BU
ND(1985) Proof	Est. 20,000	Value: 165				

KM# 23   25 POUNDS
150.0000 g., 0.9250 Silver 4.4607 oz. ASW **Ruler:** Elizabeth II
Subject: Prince Andrew's Wedding **Obv:** Crowned bust right **Rev:**
Profiles of Prince Andrew and Sarah Ferguson facing, date above

Date	Mintage	F	VF	XF	Unc	BU
1986 Proof	Est. 20,000	Value: 115				

KM# 29   25 POUNDS
7.8100 g., 0.9990 Gold 0.2508 oz. AGW **Ruler:** Elizabeth II
Subject: 90th Birthday of Queen Mother **Obv:** Crowned bust right
Rev: Queen Mother head left, within wreath and flowers, dates below

Date	Mintage	F	VF	XF	Unc	BU
ND(1990) Proof	Est. 750	Value: 245				

KM# 40   25 POUNDS
7.8100 g., 0.9990 Gold 0.2508 oz. AGW, 22 mm.
Ruler: Elizabeth II **Subject:** 100th Anniversary of Christchurch
Cathedral **Obv:** Crowned bust right, denomination below
Rev: Cathedral, cross, scepter, and mitre, dates at left

Date	Mintage	F	VF	XF	Unc	BU
1992 Proof	Est. 400	Value: 235				

KM# 39   25 POUNDS
155.5800 g., 0.9250 Silver 4.6267 oz. ASW; 65 mm.
Ruler: Elizabeth II **Subject:** 400th Anniversary - First Sighting of
Falkland Islands **Obv:** Crowned bust right **Rev:** Map above ship
"Desire" at sea, dates at right

Date	Mintage	F	VF	XF	Unc	BU
ND(1992) Proof	Est. 3,000	Value: 200				

KM# 30   50 POUNDS
15.6100 g., 0.9990 Gold 0.5014 oz. AGW **Ruler:** Elizabeth II
Subject: 90th Birthday of Queen Mother **Obv:** Crowned bust right

Date	Mintage	F	VF	XF	Unc	BU
ND(1990) Proof	Est. 750	Value: 475				

KM# 41   50 POUNDS
15.6100 g., 0.9990 Gold 0.5014 oz. AGW, 27 mm.
Ruler: Elizabeth II **Subject:** 100th Anniversary of Defense Force
Obv: Crowned bust right **Rev:** Soldier with shield, dates at right

Date	Mintage	F	VF	XF	Unc	BU
ND(1992) Proof	Est. 400	Value: 465				

KM# 44   50 POUNDS
47.5400 g., 0.9170 Gold 1.4015 oz. AGW **Ruler:** Elizabeth II
Subject: 40th Anniversary - Coronation of Queen Elizabeth II

Date	Mintage	F	VF	XF	Unc	BU
ND(1993) Proof	Est. 100	Value: 1,350				

KM# 31   100 POUNDS
31.2100 g., 0.9990 Gold 1.0024 oz. AGW **Ruler:** Elizabeth II
Subject: 90th Birthday of Queen Mother **Obv:** Crowned bust right
Rev: Queen Mother's head left, within wreath and flowers, dates
below

Date	Mintage	F	VF	XF	Unc	BU
ND(1990) Proof	Est. 750	Value: 975				

KM# 42 100 POUNDS

31.2100 g., 0.9990 Gold 1.0024 oz. AGW, 32.69 mm.
Ruler: Elizabeth II **Subject:** 400th Anniversary of Discovery - Ship 'Desire' **Obv:** Crowned bust right **Rev:** Map above ship "Desire" at sea, dates at right

Date	Mintage	F	VF	XF	Unc	BU
ND(1992) Proof	Est. 400		Value: 975			

KM# 13 150 POUNDS

33.4370 g., 0.9000 Gold 0.9675 oz. AGW **Ruler:** Elizabeth II **Subject:** Conservation **Obv:** Young bust right **Rev:** Falkland Fur Seal, denomination below, date at right

Date	Mintage	F	VF	XF	Unc	BU
1979	488				1,100	
1979 Proof	164		Value: 1,750			

PIEFORTS

KM#	Date	Mintage	Identification		Mkt Val
P1	1987	2,500	Pound. 0.9250 Silver. KM24a.		42.50
P2	1992	750	50 Pence. 0.9250 Silver. KM34a		60.00
P3	1995	—	50 Pence. 0.9250 Silver. KM45a		85.00

MINT SETS

KM#	Date	Mintage	Identification	Issue Price	Mkt Val
MS1	1987 (7)	—	KM2-3, 4.1-5.1, 14.1, 17, 24	10.00	12.00
MS2	1992 (8)	—	KM2-3, 4.1-5.1, 14.1, 17, 24, 35	24.50	25.00
MS3	1999 (8)	—	KM2a-3a, 4.2-5.2, 14.2, 17, 24, 69	20.00	22.50

PROOF SETS

KM#	Date	Mintage	Identification	Issue Price	Mkt Val
PS1	1974 (5)	20,000	KM1-3, 4.1-5.1	12.00	15.50
PS2	1974 (4)	2,000	KM6-9		1,100	2,225
PS3	1979 (2)	10,000	KM11-12	—	110
PS4	1980 (6)	10,000	KM1-3, 4.1-5.1, 14.1	35.00	20.00
PS5	1982 (8)	5,000	KM1-3, 4.1-5.1, 14.1, 17, 18a	—	45.00
PS6	1982 (7)	5,000	KM1-3, 4.1-5.1, 14.1, 17	—	27.50
PS7	1987 (7)	2,500	KM2-3, 4.1-5.1, 14.1, 17, 24	35.00	40.00
PS8	1990 (4)	750	KM28-31	1,595	1,750
PS9	1992 (8)	2,500	KM2-3, 4.1-5.1, 14.1, 17, 24, 35a	89.50	90.00
PS10	1992 (4)	400	KM38, 40-42	1,595	1,725
PS11	1992 (6)	—	KM#35a, 36a, 39, 40-42		
PS12	1999 (8)	2,500	KM2a-3a, 4.2-5.2, 14.2, 17, 24, 69	50.00	60.00

FIJI ISLANDS

The Republic of Fiji, consists of about 320 islands located in the southwestern Pacific 1,100 miles (1,770 km.) north of New Zealand. The islands have a combined area of 7,056 sq. mi. (18,274 sq. km.) and a population of 772,891. Capital: Suva. Fiji's economy is based on agriculture and mining. Sugar, coconut products, manganese, and gold are exported.

The first European to sight Fiji was the Dutch navigator Abel Tasman in 1643 and the islands were visited by British naval captain James Cook in 1774. The first complete survey of the island was conducted by the United States in 1840. Settlement by mercenaries from Tonga, and traders attracted by the sandalwood trade, began in 1801. Following a lengthy period of intertribal warfare, the islands were unconditionally ceded to Great Britain in 1874 by King Cakobau. Fiji became a sovereign and independent nation on Oct. 10, 1970, the 96th anniversary of the cession of the islands to Queen Victoria.

Fiji was declared a Republic in 1987 following two military coups. It left the British Commonwealth and Queen Elizabeth ceased to be the Head of State. A new constitution was introduced in 1991. The country returned to the Commonwealth in 1997 with a revised constitution. Fiji is a member of the Commonwealth of Nations, but has been subject to periodic short suspensions.

RULER
British until 1970

MINT MARKS
(c) - Australian Mint, Canberra

(H) – The Mint, Birmingham
(I) – Royal Mint, Llatrisant
(o) – Royal Canadian Mint, Ottawa
S - San Francisco, U.S.A.

MONETARY SYSTEM
12 Pence = 1 Shilling
2 Shillings = 1 Florin
20 Shillings = 1 Pound

REPUBLIC
British Administration until 1970
POUND STERLING COINAGE

KM# 1 1/2 PENNY

Copper-Nickel **Ruler:** George V **Obv:** Crown above center hole **Rev:** Center hole divides date, denomination above

Date	Mintage	F	VF	XF	Unc	BU
1934	96,000	0.75	1.75	4.00	15.00	20.00
1934 Proof	—					

KM# 14 1/2 PENNY

Copper-Nickel **Ruler:** George VI **Obv:** Crown above center hole **Rev:** Center hole divides date, denomination above

Date	Mintage	F	VF	XF	Unc	BU
1940	24,000	2.50	7.50	12.50	30.00	50.00
1940 Proof	—	Value: 350				
1941	96,000	0.75	1.50	4.00	10.00	20.00
1941 Proof	—	Value: 200				

KM# 14a 1/2 PENNY

Brass **Ruler:** George VI **Obv:** Crown above center hole **Rev:** Center hole divides date, denomination above

Date	Mintage	F	VF	XF	Unc	BU
1942S	250,000	—	0.35	2.50	10.00	20.00
1943S	250,000	—	0.35	2.50	12.50	20.00

KM# 16 1/2 PENNY

Copper-Nickel **Ruler:** George VI **Obv:** Crown above center hole, EMPEROR dropped from legend **Rev:** Center hole divides date, denomination above

Date	Mintage	F	VF	XF	Unc	BU
1949	96,000	—	0.50	2.00	7.50	12.50
1949	—	Value: 210				
1950	115,000	—	0.35	1.50	6.00	10.00
1950 Proof	—	Value: 230				
1951	115,000	—	0.35	1.50	5.00	7.50
1951 Proof	—	Value: 190				
1952	228,000	—	0.25	0.75	1.50	2.00
1952 Proof	—					

KM# 20 1/2 PENNY

Copper-Nickel **Obv:** Crown above center hole **Rev:** Center hole divides date, denomination above

Date	Mintage	F	VF	XF	Unc	BU
1954	228,000	—	0.25	0.50	1.00	1.50
1954 Proof	—	Value: 180				

KM# 2 PENNY

Copper-Nickel, 26 mm. **Ruler:** George V **Obv:** Crown above center hole **Rev:** Center hole divides date, denomination below

Date	Mintage	F	VF	XF	Unc	BU
1934	480,000	0.50	1.00	5.00	12.50	22.50
1934 Proof	—					
1935	240,000	0.65	1.25	5.00	15.00	25.00
1935 Proof	—					
1936	240,000	0.65	1.25	5.00	17.50	27.50
1936 Proof	—					

KM# 6 PENNY

Copper-Nickel, 26 mm. **Ruler:** Edward VIII **Obv:** Crown above center hole **Rev:** Center hole divides date, denomination below

Date	Mintage	F	VF	XF	Unc	BU
1936	120,000	0.50	1.00	2.00	4.00	7.50
1936 Proof	—	Value: 225				

KM# 7 PENNY

Copper-Nickel, 26 mm. **Ruler:** George VI **Obv:** Crown above center hole **Rev:** Center hole divides date, denomination below

Date	Mintage	F	VF	XF	Unc	BU
1937	360,000	0.50	1.00	3.00	7.50	12.50
1937 Proof	—	Value: 225				
1940	144,000	1.50	3.00	15.00	45.00	75.00
1940 Proof	—	Value: 225				
1941	228,000	0.50	1.00	2.00	10.00	15.00
1941 Proof	—	Value: 225				
1945	240,000	1.00	2.00	6.00	15.00	25.00
1945 Proof	—	Value: 225				

KM# 7a PENNY

Brass, 26 mm. **Ruler:** George VI **Obv:** Crown above center hole **Rev:** Center hole divides date, denomination below

Date	Mintage	F	VF	XF	Unc	BU
1942S	1,000,000	0.25	1.00	3.50	10.00	20.00
1943S	1,000,000	0.25	1.00	3.50	7.50	20.00

KM# 17 PENNY

6.5000 g., Copper-Nickel, 26 mm. **Ruler:** George VI **Obv:** Crown above center hole, "EMPEROR" dropped from legend **Rev:** Center hole divides date, denomination below

Date	Mintage	F	VF	XF	Unc	BU
1949	120,000	0.25	0.50	1.00	4.50	7.50
1949 Proof	—	Value: 325				
1950	58,000	1.50	3.50	12.50	65.00	100
1950 Proof	—	Value: 200				
1952	230,000	0.25	0.50	1.00	3.75	7.00
1952 Proof	—	Value: 175				

KM# 21   PENNY

6.6400 g., Copper-Nickel, 26 mm. **Ruler:** Elizabeth II
Obv: Crown above center hole **Rev:** Center hole divides date, denomination below

Date	Mintage	F	VF	XF	Unc	BU
1954	511,000	0.20	0.50	1.00	3.00	4.50
1954 Proof	—	Value: 175				
1955	230,000	0.20	0.50	1.25	5.00	9.00
1955 Proof	—	Value: 175				
1956	230,000	0.20	0.50	1.25	3.50	7.50
1956 Proof	—	Value: 175				
1957	360,000	0.10	0.25	0.75	3.00	7.00
1957 Proof	—	Value: 175				
1959	864,000	—	0.20	0.35	2.00	3.50
1959 Proof	—	Value: 175				
1961	432,000	0.15	0.35	0.50	1.25	3.00
1961 Proof	—	Value: 175				
1963	432,000	0.15	0.35	0.50	1.25	3.00
1963 Proof	—	Value: 175				
1964	864,000	—	0.15	0.25	0.85	2.00
1964 Proof	—	Value: 150				
1965	1,440,000	—	—	0.20	0.75	2.00
1966	720,000	—	—	0.20	0.85	2.50
1967	720,000	—	—	0.20	0.75	1.50
1968	720,000	—	—	0.20	0.75	1.50

KM# 15   THREEPENCE

6.1700 g., Nickel-Brass, 21.19 mm. **Ruler:** George VI
Obv: Crowned head left **Rev:** Native dwelling, date above, denomination below

Date	Mintage	F	VF	XF	Unc	BU
1947	450,000	1.50	2.50	6.00	20.00	45.00
1947 Proof	—	Value: 190				

KM# 18   THREEPENCE

Nickel-Brass **Ruler:** George VI **Obv:** Crowned head left, EMPEROR dropped from legend **Rev:** Native dwelling, date above, denomination below

Date	Mintage	F	VF	XF	Unc	BU
1950	450,000	0.50	1.00	4.00	15.00	25.00
1950 Proof	—	Value: 190				
1952	400,000	0.50	1.00	5.00	22.50	35.00
1952 Proof	—	Value: 190				

KM# 22   THREEPENCE

Nickel-Brass **Ruler:** Elizabeth II **Obv:** Crowned head right
Rev: Native dwelling, date above, denomination below

Date	Mintage	F	VF	XF	Unc	BU
1955	400,000	0.50	1.00	4.00	17.50	35.00
1955 Proof	—	Value: 130				
1956	200,000	0.50	1.00	4.00	20.00	40.00
1956 Proof	—	Value: 155				
1958	200,000	0.50	1.00	4.00	20.00	40.00
1958 Proof	—	Value: 140				
1960	240,000	0.25	0.50		3.00	8.50	15.00
1960 Proof	—	Value: 125				
1961	240,000	0.25	0.50	1.25	6.00	12.50
1961 Proof	—	Value: 125				
1963	240,000	0.15	0.30	0.75	5.00	10.00
1963 Proof	—	Value: 115				
1964	240,000	0.15	0.30	0.50	2.00	5.00
1965	800,000	—	0.15	0.25	1.50	3.50
1967	800,000	—	0.15	0.25	1.50	3.50

KM# 3   SIXPENCE

2.8276 g., 0.5000 Silver 0.0455 oz. ASW, 19.5 mm.
Ruler: George V **Obv:** Crowned bust left **Rev:** Sea turtle divides date, denomination below

Date	Mintage	F	VF	XF	Unc	BU
1934	160,000	1.25	2.50	10.00	35.00	45.00
1934 Proof	—	Value: 450				
1935	120,000	1.50	3.50	12.50	45.00	55.00
1935 Proof	—	Value: 350				
1936	40,000	2.00	4.00	15.00	55.00	70.00
1936 Proof	—	Value: 350				

KM# 8   SIXPENCE

2.8276 g., 0.5000 Silver 0.0455 oz. ASW, 19.5 mm.
Ruler: George VI **Obv:** Crowned head left **Rev:** Sea turtle divides date, denomination below

Date	Mintage	F	VF	XF	Unc	BU
1937	40,000	2.00	4.00	16.00	50.00	75.00
1937 Proof	—	Value: 400				

KM# 11   SIXPENCE

2.8276 g., 0.5000 Silver 0.0455 oz. ASW, 19.5 mm.
Ruler: George VI **Obv:** Smaller head **Rev:** Sea turtle divides date, denomination below

Date	Mintage	F	VF	XF	Unc	BU
1938	40,000	2.00	4.00	13.50	45.00	60.00
1938 Proof	—	Value: 500				
1940	40,000	2.00	4.00	13.50	45.00	60.00
1940 Proof	—	Value: 350				
1941	40,000	3.00	8.00	20.00	60.00	85.00
1941 Proof	—	Value: 350				

KM# 11a   SIXPENCE

2.8276 g., 0.9000 Silver 0.0818 oz. ASW, 19.5 mm.
Ruler: George VI **Obv:** Crowned head left **Rev:** Sea turtle divides date, denomination below

Date	Mintage	F	VF	XF	Unc	BU
1942S	400,000	—	1.25	2.50	7.50	10.00
1943S	400,000	—	1.25	2.50	7.50	10.00

KM# 19   SIXPENCE

Copper-Nickel, 19.5 mm. **Ruler:** Elizabeth II **Obv:** Crowned head right **Rev:** Sea turtle divides date, denomination below

Date	Mintage	F	VF	XF	Unc	BU
1953	800,000	0.25	0.50	1.00	3.00	7.50
1953 Proof	—	Value: 210				
1958	400,000	0.25	0.50	1.50	4.50	8.00
1958 Proof	—	Value: 200				
1961	400,000	0.25	0.50	1.00	3.50	7.00
1961 Proof	—	Value: 200				
1962	400,000	0.25	0.50	1.00	3.00	7.00
1962 Proof	—	Value: 200				
1965	800,000	0.15	0.30	1.00	2.50	6.00
1967	800,000	0.15	0.30	1.00	2.50	6.00

KM# 4   SHILLING

5.6552 g., 0.5000 Silver 0.0909 oz. ASW, 23.5 mm.
Ruler: George V **Obv:** Crowned bust left **Rev:** Outrigger divides dates, denomination above

Date	Mintage	F	VF	XF	Unc	BU
1934	360,000	1.50	4.00	14.50	60.00	75.00
1934 Proof	—	Value: 650				

Date	Mintage	F	VF	XF	Unc	BU
1935	180,000	1.50	4.00	14.50	75.00	90.00
1935 Proof	—	Value: 550				
1936	140,000	1.50	6.00	15.50	75.00	90.00
1936 Proof	—	Value: 550				

KM# 9   SHILLING

5.6552 g., 0.5000 Silver 0.0909 oz. ASW, 23.5 mm.
Ruler: George VI **Obv:** Crowned head left **Rev:** Outrigger divides dates, denomination above

Date	Mintage	F	VF	XF	Unc	BU
1937	40,000	1.50	7.00	17.50	80.00	100
1937 Proof	—	Value: 500				

KM# 12   SHILLING

5.6552 g., 0.5000 Silver 0.0909 oz. ASW, 23.5 mm.
Ruler: George VI **Obv:** Smaller head **Rev:** Outrigger divides date, denomination above

Date	Mintage	F	VF	XF	Unc	BU
1938	40,000	1.50	7.00	17.50	80.00	100
1938 Proof	—	Value: 450				
1941	40,000	1.50	7.00	17.50	80.00	100
1941 Proof	—	Value: 450				

KM# 12a   SHILLING

5.6552 g., 0.9000 Silver 0.1636 oz. ASW, 23.5 mm.
Ruler: George VI **Obv:** Crowned head left **Rev:** Outrigger divides date, denomination above

Date	Mintage	F	VF	XF	Unc	BU
1942S	500,000	—	2.50	3.50	7.50	10.00
1943S	500,000	—	2.50	3.50	7.50	10.00

KM# 23   SHILLING

Copper-Nickel, 23.5 mm. **Ruler:** Elizabeth II **Obv:** Crowned head right **Rev:** Outrigger divides date, denomination above

Date	Mintage	F	VF	XF	Unc	BU
1957	400,000	0.50	0.75	2.00	10.00	12.50
1957 Proof	—	Value: 350				
1958	400,000	0.50	0.75	2.25	10.00	12.50
1958 Proof	—	Value: 300				
1961	200,000	0.75	1.00	2.25	7.50	10.00
1961 Proof	—	Value: 275				
1962	400,000	0.35	0.75	1.25	4.00	6.50
1962 Proof	—	Value: 250				
1965	800,000	0.25	0.50	0.75	2.00	3.50

KM# 5   FLORIN

11.3104 g., 0.5000 Silver 0.1818 oz. ASW **Ruler:** George V
Obv: Crowned bust left **Rev:** Shield of arms divides date, denomination below

Date	Mintage	F	VF	XF	Unc	BU
1934	200,000	2.50	4.50	17.50	125	145
1934 Proof	—	Value: 750				
1935	50,000	2.75	9.00	20.00	185	210
1935 Proof	—	Value: 700				
1936	65,000	2.75	9.00	20.00	170	190
1936 Proof	—	Value: 725				

KM# 10 FLORIN
11.3104 g., 0.5000 Silver 0.1818 oz. ASW **Ruler:** George VI **Obv:** Crowned head left **Rev:** Shield of arms divides date, denomination below

Date	Mintage	F	VF	XF	Unc	BU
1937	30,000	2.65	7.00	17.50	150	170
1937 Proof	—	Value: 850				

KM# 13 FLORIN
11.3104 g., 0.5000 Silver 0.1818 oz. ASW **Ruler:** George VI **Obv:** Smaller head **Rev:** Shield of arms divides dates, denomination below

Date	Mintage	F	VF	XF	Unc	BU
1938	20,000	4.00	12.00	25.00	190	215
1938 Proof	—	Value: 750				
1941	20,000	4.00	12.00	25.00	190	215
1941 Proof	—	Value: 775				
1945	100,000	9.00	20.00	35.00	230	275
1945 Proof	—	Value: 750				

KM# 13a FLORIN
11.3104 g., 0.9000 Silver 0.3273 oz. ASW **Ruler:** George VI **Obv:** Crowned head left **Rev:** Shield of arms divides date, denomination below

Date	Mintage	F	VF	XF	Unc	BU
1942S	250,000	—	6.00	7.00	12.50	17.50
1943S	250,000	—	6.00	7.50	15.00	20.00

Note: BU coins must display full face of leopard at top of arms

KM# 24 FLORIN
Copper-Nickel **Ruler:** Elizabeth II **Obv:** Crowned head right **Rev:** Shield of arms divides date, denomination below

Date	Mintage	F	VF	XF	Unc	BU
1957	300,000	0.50	1.00	4.00	15.00	20.00
1957 Proof	—	Value: 375				
1958	220,000	0.50	1.00	4.00	15.00	20.00
1958 Proof	—	Value: 375				
1962	200,000	0.25	0.50	2.00	10.00	15.00
1962 Proof	—	Value: 375				
1964	200,000	0.25	0.50	1.50	5.00	10.00
1964 Proof	—	Value: 400				
1965	400,000	0.25	0.50	1.00	3.00	5.00

DECIMAL COINAGE
100 Cents = 1 Dollar

KM# 27 CENT
1.9000 g., Bronze, 17.5 mm. **Ruler:** Elizabeth II **Rev:** Tanoa kava bowl divides denomination

Date	Mintage	F	VF	XF	Unc	BU
1969(h)	11,000,000	—	—	0.10	0.20	1.00
1969 Proof	10,000	Value: 0.50				
1973(c)	3,000,000	—	—	0.10	0.50	2.00
1975(c)	2,064,000	—	—	0.10	0.50	1.50
1976(c)	—	—	—	0.10	0.50	1.00
(c)	2,005,000	—	—	0.10	0.50	1.00
1983(c)	3,000,000	—	—	0.10	0.50	1.00
1983 Proof	3,000	Value: 1.00				
1984(c)	2,295,000	—	—	0.10	0.35	1.00
1985(c)	—	—	—	0.10	0.35	1.00

KM# 27a CENT
2.2600 g., 0.9250 Silver 0.0672 oz. ASW, 17.5 mm. **Ruler:** Elizabeth II **Rev:** Tanoa kava bowl divides denomination

Date	Mintage	F	VF	XF	Unc	BU
1976 Proof	3,012	Value: 3.50				

KM# 39 CENT
1.9000 g., Bronze, 17.5 mm. **Ruler:** Elizabeth II **Series:** F.A.O. **Obv:** Young bust right **Rev:** Rice plant at left, denomination at right

Date	Mintage	F	VF	XF	Unc	BU
1977(c)	3,000,000	—	—	0.10	0.50	1.50
1978(c)	3,032,000	—	—	0.10	0.50	1.50
1978 Proof	2,000	Value: 2.50				
1979(c)	2,500,000	—	—	0.10	2.00	4.00
1980(c)	314,000	—	—	0.10	0.50	1.50
1980 Proof	2,500	Value: 1.50				
1981(c)	4,040,000	—	—	0.10	0.50	1.00
1982(c)	5,000,000	—	—	0.10	0.50	1.00
1982 Proof	3,000	Value: 1.00				

KM# 49 CENT
1.9000 g., Bronze, 17.5 mm. **Ruler:** Elizabeth II **Obv:** Crowned head right, date at right **Rev:** Tanoa kava bowl divides denomination

Date	Mintage	F	VF	XF	Unc	BU
1986(c)	3,400,000	—	—	0.10	0.50	1.00
1987(c)	3,400,000	—	—	0.15	0.50	1.00

KM# 49a CENT
1.5400 g., Copper Plated Zinc, 17.5 mm. **Ruler:** Elizabeth II **Obv:** Crowned head right, date at right **Rev:** Tanoa kava bowl divides denomination

Date	Mintage	F	VF	XF	Unc	BU
1990(o)	8,500,000	—	—	0.10	0.25	0.75
1992(o)	16,200,000	—	—	0.10	0.25	0.75
1994(o)	7,800,000	—	—	—	0.25	0.75
1995(o)	6,000,000	—	—	—	0.25	2.00
1997(o)	12,000,000	—	—	—	0.25	1.00
1999(o)	14,000,000	—	—	—	0.25	0.75

KM# 28 2 CENTS
3.8500 g., Bronze, 21.1 mm. **Ruler:** Elizabeth II **Obv:** Young bust right, date at right **Rev:** Palm fan and denomination

Date	Mintage	F	VF	XF	Unc	BU
1969(h)	8,000,000	—	—	0.10	0.50	0.75
1969 Proof	10,000	Value: 0.75				
1973(c)	2,110,000	—	0.10	0.15	0.75	2.50
1975(c)	1,500,000	—	0.10	0.15	0.75	1.50
1976(c)	1,004,999	—	0.10	0.15	0.75	1.50
1977	1,250,000	—	—	0.10	0.75	1.50
1978(c)	1,502,000	—	—	0.10	0.75	1.50
1978 Proof	2,000	Value: 3.50				
1979(c)	500,000	—	—	0.10	2.50	5.00
1980(c)	4,019,999	—	—	0.10	1.00	1.75
1980 Proof	2,500	Value: 2.50				
1981(c)	3,250,000	—	—	0.10	1.00	2.00
1982(c)	4,000,000	—	—	0.10	1.00	1.75
1982 Proof	3,000	Value: 2.00				
1983(c)	3,000,000	—	—	0.10	0.75	1.75
1983 Proof	3,000	Value: 1.50				
1984(c)	1,845,000	—	—	0.10	0.75	1.75
1985(c)	1,700,000	—	—	0.10	0.75	2.00

KM# 28a 2 CENTS
4.5300 g., 0.9250 Silver 0.1347 oz. ASW, 21.1 mm. **Ruler:** Elizabeth II **Obv:** Young bust right **Rev:** Palm fan and denomination

Date	Mintage	F	VF	XF	Unc	BU
1976 Proof	3,012	Value: 4.50				

KM# 50 2 CENTS
3.8500 g., Bronze, 21.1 mm. **Ruler:** Elizabeth II **Obv:** Crowned head right, date at right **Rev:** Palm fan and denomination

Date	Mintage	F	VF	XF	Unc	BU
1986(c)	1,700,000	—	—	0.15	0.75	1.50
1987(c)	1,700,000	—	—	0.15	0.75	1.50

KM# 50a 2 CENTS
3.8500 g., Copper Plated Zinc, 21.1 mm. **Ruler:** Elizabeth II **Obv:** Crowned head right, date at right **Rev:** Palm fan and denomination

Date	Mintage	F	VF	XF	Unc	BU
1990(o)	5,500,000	—	—	—	0.75	1.00
1992(o)	10,000,000	—	—	—	0.50	1.00
1994(o)	6,000,000	—	—	—	0.35	2.00
1995(o)	5,000,000	—	—	—	0.35	1.00

KM# 29 5 CENTS
2.8000 g., Copper-Nickel, 19.35 mm. **Ruler:** Elizabeth II **Obv:** Young bust right, date at right **Rev:** Fijian drum - lali divides denomination

Date	Mintage	F	VF	XF	Unc	BU
1969(I)	9,200,000	—	0.10	0.20	0.75	1.00
1969 Proof	10,000	Value: 0.75				
1973(c)	600,000	—	0.10	0.30	1.50	2.00
1974(c)	608,000	—	0.10	0.30	1.25	2.00
1975(c)	1,008,000	—	0.10	0.20	1.00	2.00
1976(c)	1,205,000	—	0.10	0.20	1.00	2.00
1977	960,000	—	0.10	0.20	1.00	2.00
1978(c)	880,000	—	0.10	0.20	1.00	2.00
1978 Proof	2,000	Value: 5.00				
1979(c)	1,500,000	—	0.10	0.25	2.00	4.50
1980(c)	2,506,000	—	0.10	0.15	1.00	1.50
1980 Proof	2,500	Value: 3.50				
1981(c)	1,980,000	—	0.10	0.15	1.00	1.50
1982(c)	2,700,000	—	0.10	0.15	1.00	1.50
1982 Proof	3,000	Value: 3.00				
1983(c)	3,000,000	—	0.10	0.15	1.00	1.50
1983 Proof	3,000	Value: 2.00				
1984(c)	5,005,000	—	0.10	0.20	1.00	1.50

KM# 29a 5 CENTS
3.2800 g., 0.9250 Silver 0.0975 oz. ASW, 19.35 mm. **Ruler:** Elizabeth II **Series:** F.A.O. **Obv:** Young bust right **Rev:** Fijian drum - lali divides denomination

Date	Mintage	F	VF	XF	Unc	BU
1976 Proof	3,012	Value: 6.00				

KM# 51 5 CENTS
2.8000 g., Copper-Nickel, 19.35 mm. **Ruler:** Elizabeth II **Obv:** Crowned head right, date at right **Rev:** Fijian drum - lali divides denomination

Date	Mintage	F	VF	XF	Unc	BU
1986(c)	1,200,000	—	0.10	0.20	1.00	1.50
1987(c)	1,200,000	—	0.10	0.20	1.00	2.00

KM# 51a 5 CENTS
2.3700 g., Nickel Bonded Steel, 19.35 mm. **Ruler:** Elizabeth II **Obv:** Crowned head right **Rev:** Fijian drum - lali divides denomination

Date	Mintage	F	VF	XF	Unc	BU
1990(o)	4,000,000	—	—	—	1.00	1.50
1992(o)	7,700,000	—	—	—	0.75	1.00
1994(o)	500,000	—	—	—	0.75	1.00
1995	—	—	—	—	0.75	2.50
1997(I)	4,000,000	—	—	—	0.75	1.00
1998(I)	3,000,000	—	—	—	0.75	1.00
1999(I)	3,000,000	—	—	—	0.75	1.00
2000(I)	3,000,000	—	—	—	0.75	1.00

KM# 77 5 CENTS
Nickel Bonded Steel, 19.35 mm. **Ruler:** Elizabeth II **Series:** F.A.O. **Subject:** Harvest From the Sea **Obv:** Crowned head right, date at right **Rev:** Fish, F.A.O. logo below denomination

Date	Mintage	F	VF	XF	Unc	BU
1995(o)	300,000	—	—	—	1.00	1.50

KM# 30 10 CENTS
5.6000 g., Copper-Nickel, 23.6 mm. **Ruler:** Elizabeth II
Rev: Throwing club - ula tava tava

Date	Mintage	F	VF	XF	Unc	BU
1969	3,500,000	—	0.20	0.40	1.00	1.50
1969 Proof	10,000	Value: 1.00				
1973	750,000	—	0.20	0.50	2.50	4.00
1975	752,000	—	0.20	0.50	1.75	3.00
1976	805,000	—	0.20	0.50	1.50	2.50
1977	240,000	—	0.25	0.65	1.50	2.50
1978	664,000	—	0.20	0.50	1.50	2.50
1978 Proof	2,000	Value: 6.00				
1979	702,000	—	0.20	0.50	1.50	2.50
1980	1,000,000	—	0.15	0.30	1.50	2.50
1980 Proof	2,500	Value: 4.50				
1981	1,200,000	—	0.20	0.50	1.25	2.00
1982	1,500,000	—	0.20	0.50	1.25	2.00
1982 Proof	3,000	Value: 4.00				
1983	3,003,000	—	0.25	0.65	1.25	2.00
1983 Proof	3,000	Value: 3.00				
1984	5,000,000	—	0.25	0.65	1.25	2.00
1985	660,000	—	0.20	0.50	1.25	2.00

KM# 30a 10 CENTS
6.5500 g., 0.9250 Silver 0.1948 oz. ASW, 23.6 mm.
Ruler: Elizabeth II **Rev:** Throwing club - ula tava tava

Date	Mintage	F	VF	XF	Unc	BU
1976 Proof	3,012	Value: 6.50				

KM# 52 10 CENTS
5.6000 g., Copper-Nickel, 23.6 mm. **Ruler:** Elizabeth II **Obv:** Crowned head right, date at right **Rev:** Throwing club - ula tava tava divides denomination

Date	Mintage	F	VF	XF	Unc	BU
1986(c)	740,000	—	0.20	0.40	1.50	2.25
1987(c)	740,000	—	0.20	0.40	1.50	2.25

KM# 52a 10 CENTS
4.7600 g., Nickel Bonded Steel, 23.6 mm. **Ruler:** Elizabeth II **Obv:** Crowned head right **Rev:** Throwing club - ula tava tava

Date	Mintage	F	VF	XF	Unc	BU
1990	2,000,000	—	—	—	1.25	1.75
1992	31,640,000	—	—	—	1.25	1.75
1994	1,000,000	—	—	—	1.25	1.75
1995	736,000	—	—	—	1.25	2.00
1996	1,000,000	—	—	—	1.25	2.50
1997	2,000,000	—	—	—	1.00	1.50
1998(I)	2,000,000	—	—	—	1.00	1.25
1999(I)	2,000,000	—	—	—	1.00	1.25
2000(I)	1,340,000	—	—	—	1.00	1.25

KM# 31 20 CENTS
11.2500 g., Copper-Nickel, 28.5 mm. **Ruler:** Elizabeth II **Obv:** Young bust right, date at right **Rev:** Tabua on braided sennit cord divides denomination

Date	Mintage	F	VF	XF	Unc	BU
1969	2,000,000	—	0.30	0.80	1.50	2.00
1969 Proof	10,000	Value: 1.75				
1973	250,000	—	0.35	1.00	2.25	3.00
1974	252,000	—	0.35	0.75	2.00	2.75
1975	352,000	—	0.35	0.75	3.00	4.50
1976	405,000	—	0.25	0.65	1.75	2.25
1977	200,000	—	0.35	0.75	3.50	4.00
1978	406,000	—	0.25	0.50	1.75	2.25
1978 Proof	2,000	Value: 8.00				
1979	500,000	—	0.25	0.60	1.75	2.25
1980	1,014,000	—	0.25	0.60	1.75	2.25

Date	Mintage	F	VF	XF	Unc	BU
1980 Proof	2,500	Value: 6.50				
1981	1,200,000	—	0.25	0.60	1.75	2.25
1982	1,500,000	—	0.25	0.60	1.50	2.00
1982 Proof	3,000	Value: 6.00				
1983	3,003,000	—	0.35	0.75	1.50	2.00
1983 Proof	3,000	Value: 5.00				
1984	5,005,000	—	0.35	0.75	1.50	2.00
1985	240,000	—	0.20	0.35	1.75	2.25

KM# 31a 20 CENTS
13.0900 g., 0.9250 Silver 0.3893 oz. ASW, 28.5 mm.
Ruler: Elizabeth II **Obv:** Young bust right **Rev:** Tabua on braided sennit cord divides denomination

Date	Mintage	F	VF	XF	Unc	BU
1976 Proof	3,012	Value: 8.50				

KM# 53 20 CENTS
11.2500 g., Copper-Nickel, 28.5 mm. **Ruler:** Elizabeth II **Obv:** Crowned head right, date at right **Rev:** Tabua on braided sennit cord divides denomination

Date	Mintage	F	VF	XF	Unc	BU
1986(c)	360,000	—	0.25	0.60	2.00	2.50
1987(c)	360,000	—	0.25	0.60	2.00	2.50

KM# 53a 20 CENTS
11.2500 g., Nickel Bonded Steel, 28.5 mm. **Ruler:** Elizabeth II **Obv:** Crowned head right **Rev:** Tabua on braided sennit cord divides denomination

Date	Mintage	F	VF	XF	Unc	BU
1990	1,500,000	—	0.20	0.35	1.50	2.00
1992	1,000,000	—	0.20	0.35	1.75	3.50
1994	500,000	—	0.20	0.35	1.50	3.00
1995	200,000	—	0.20	0.35	1.50	2.00
1996(I)	1,000,000	—	0.20	0.35	1.25	1.50
1997(I)	153,000	—	0.20	0.35	1.50	3.00
1998	1,000,000	—	0.20	0.35	1.25	1.50
1999(I)	1,000,000	—	0.20	0.35	1.25	1.50
2000(I)	1,000,000	—	0.20	0.35	1.25	1.50

KM# 36 50 CENTS
15.5500 g., Copper-Nickel, 31.5 mm. **Ruler:** Elizabeth II **Obv:** Young bust right, date at right **Rev:** Sailing canoe - Takia, denomination below

Date	Mintage	F	VF	XF	Unc	BU
1975	1,000,000	—	0.75	1.50	4.00	6.50
1976	805,000	—	0.50	1.00	2.00	3.50
1978	4,006	—	1.25	2.00	5.00	6.50
1978 Proof	2,000	Value: 13.00				
1979(c)	258,000	—	0.75	1.00	5.00	6.50
1980	316,000	—	0.75	1.00	2.00	3.50
1980 Proof	2,500	Value: 11.50				
1981	511,000	—	0.75	1.00	4.00	7.00
1982	1,000,000	—	0.75	1.00	3.00	5.00
1982 Proof	3,000	Value: 10.00				
1983	3,000,000	—	0.65	1.00	2.50	4.00
1983 Proof	3,000	Value: 9.00				
1984	5,000,000	—	0.65	1.00	2.25	3.50

KM# 36a 50 CENTS
18.0000 g., 0.9250 Silver 0.5353 oz. ASW, 31.5 mm.
Ruler: Elizabeth II **Obv:** Young bust right **Rev:** Sailing canoe - Takia, denomination below

Date	Mintage	F	VF	XF	Unc	BU
1976 Proof	3,012	Value: 13.50				

KM# 44 50 CENTS
15.5500 g., Copper-Nickel, 31.5 mm. **Ruler:** Elizabeth II

Series: F.A.O. **Subject:** First Indians in Fiji Centennial
Obv: Young bust right, date at right **Rev:** Rice plants, denomination and date at right

Date	Mintage	F	VF	XF	Unc	BU
1979	258,000	—	—	—	2.50	—
1979 Proof	6,004	Value: 7.50				

KM# 45 50 CENTS
15.5500 g., Copper-Nickel, 31.5 mm. **Ruler:** Elizabeth II **Subject:** 10th Anniversary of Independence **Obv:** Arms with supporters, date below **Rev:** Prince Charles 3/4 facing, denomination below

Date	Mintage	F	VF	XF	Unc	BU
1980	10,000	—	—	—	2.50	—

KM# 54 50 CENTS
15.5500 g., Copper-Nickel, 31.5 mm. **Ruler:** Elizabeth II **Obv:** Crowned head right, date at right **Rev:** Sailing canoe - Takia, denomination below

Date	Mintage	F	VF	XF	Unc	BU
1986(c)	160,000	—	0.75	1.00	2.00	4.00
1987(c)	160,000	—	0.50	0.75	2.00	4.00

KM# 54a 50 CENTS
13.4300 g., Nickel Bonded Steel, 31.5 mm. **Ruler:** Elizabeth II **Obv:** Crowned head right **Rev:** Sailing canoe - Takia, denomination below

Date	Mintage	F	VF	XF	Unc	BU
1990(o)	800,000	—	—	0.60	1.75	2.50
1992(o)	280,000	—	—	0.60	1.75	2.50
1994(o)	480,000	—	—	0.60	1.50	2.50
1995(I)	480,000	—	—	0.60	1.50	2.50
1996(I)	560,000	—	—	0.60	1.50	2.50
1997(I)	536,000	—	—	0.60	1.50	2.50
1998(I)	536,000	—	—	0.60	1.50	2.50
1999(I)	536,000	—	—	0.60	1.50	2.50
2000(I)	536,000	—	—	0.60	1.50	2.50

KM# 32 DOLLAR
Copper-Nickel, 38.5 mm. **Ruler:** Elizabeth II **Obv:** Young bust right **Rev:** Arms with supporters, date below

Date	Mintage	F	VF	XF	Unc	BU
1969	70,000	—	—	1.00	3.50	—
1969 Proof	10,000	Value: 3.50				
1976	5,007	—	1.50	2.50	5.00	—

KM# 32a DOLLAR
28.2800 g., 0.9250 Silver 0.8410 oz. ASW **Ruler:** Elizabeth II **Obv:** Young bust right **Rev:** Arms with supporters divide denomination

Date	Mintage	F	VF	XF	Unc	BU
1976 Proof	3,012	Value: 20.00				

KM# 33a DOLLAR
28.2800 g., 0.9250 Silver 0.8410 oz. ASW **Ruler:** Elizabeth II **Subject:** Independence Commemorative **Obv:** Young bust right **Rev:** Crown above dove on shield, palm trees flank

Date	Mintage	F	VF	XF	Unc	BU
1970 Proof	1,000	Value: 75.00				

KM# 33 DOLLAR

Copper-Nickel **Ruler:** Elizabeth II **Subject:** Independence Commemorative **Obv:** Young bust right, date at right **Rev:** Dove with olive branch on shield, crown above, palm trees flank

Date	Mintage	F	VF	XF	Unc	BU
1970	15,000	—	—	—	3.00	—
1970 Proof	15,000	Value: 4.00				

Note: Variety with medallic alignment exists; Value: $100

KM# 71 DOLLAR

Copper-Nickel **Ruler:** Elizabeth II **Subject:** Move to Buckingham Palace **Obv:** Crowned head right **Rev:** Buckingham Palace and soldier within circle, denomination below

Date	Mintage	F	VF	XF	Unc	BU
1995	Est. 300,000	—	—	—	3.00	—

KM# 73 DOLLAR

8.0400 g., Brass **Ruler:** Elizabeth II **Obv:** Crowned head right, date at right **Rev:** "Saqamoli" drinking vessel, denomination above

Date	Mintage	F	VF	XF	Unc	BU
1995	5,000,000	—	—	1.00	2.00	3.50
1996(I)	1,000,000	—	—	1.00	2.00	3.50
1997(I)	1,000,000	—	—	1.00	2.00	3.50
1998(I)	1,000,000	—	—	1.00	2.00	3.50
1999(I)	1,000,000	—	—	1.00	2.00	3.50
2000(I)	1,000,000	—	—	1.00	2.00	3.50

KM# 78 2 DOLLARS

42.4139 g., 0.9250 Silver 1.2613 oz. ASW **Ruler:** Elizabeth II **Subject:** Soft Coral Capital of the World **Obv:** Crowned head at left facing right **Rev:** Denomination at right, coral industry scenes

Date	Mintage	F	VF	XF	Unc	BU
1998 Proof	20,000	Value: 30.00				

Note: Part of a tri-nation, three coin matching set with Cook Islands and Western Samoa

KM# 81 5 DOLLARS

20.0000 g., 0.5000 Silver 0.3215 oz. ASW **Ruler:** Elizabeth II **Subject:** Protect Our World **Obv:** Crowned head right **Rev:** Reef-heron, fish and tree, denomination below **Edge:** Reeded

Date	Mintage	F	VF	XF	Unc	BU
1993 Proof	25,000	Value: 9.00				

KM# 69 5 DOLLARS

20.0000 g., 0.5000 Silver 0.3215 oz. ASW **Ruler:** Elizabeth II **Subject:** Queen Mother's London House **Obv:** Crowned head right **Rev:** Clarence House within circle, denomination below

Date	Mintage	F	VF	XF	Unc	BU
1994 Proof	50,000	Value: 8.00				

KM# 80 5 DOLLARS

31.4400 g., 0.9250 Silver 0.9350 oz. ASW **Ruler:** Elizabeth II **Subject:** Millennium 2000 **Obv:** Crowned head right, date at right **Rev:** Woman, map of Tavenui with 180 meridian and branch, denomination above

Date	Mintage	F	VF	XF	Unc	BU
1999 Proof	10,000	Value: 25.00				

KM# 40 10 DOLLARS

30.3000 g., 0.9250 Silver 0.9011 oz. ASW **Ruler:** Elizabeth II **Subject:** Queen's Silver Jubilee **Obv:** Young bust right, date at right **Rev:** Arms with supporters, crown divides dates above, denomination below

Date	Mintage	F	VF	XF	Unc	BU
1977 Proof	3,010	Value: 20.00				

KM# 41 10 DOLLARS

28.2800 g., 0.5000 Silver 0.4546 oz. ASW **Ruler:** Elizabeth II **Subject:** Conservation **Obv:** Young bust right **Rev:** Pink-billed parrot finch on branch right

Date	Mintage	F	VF	XF	Unc	BU
1978	3,582	—	—	—	20.00	—

KM# 41a 10 DOLLARS

28.2800 g., 0.9250 Silver 0.8410 oz. ASW **Ruler:** Elizabeth II **Subject:** Conservation **Obv:** Young bust right **Rev:** Pink-billed parrot finch

Date	Mintage	F	VF	XF	Unc	BU
1978 Proof	4,026	Value: 24.00				

KM# 46 10 DOLLARS

28.4400 g., 0.5000 Silver 0.4572 oz. ASW **Ruler:** Elizabeth II **Subject:** 10th Anniversary of Independence **Obv:** Arms with supporters, date below **Rev:** Bust 3/4 left, denomination below

Date	Mintage	F	VF	XF	Unc	BU
1980	5,001	—	—	—	—	12.00

KM# 46a 10 DOLLARS

30.4800 g., 0.9250 Silver 0.9064 oz. ASW **Ruler:** Elizabeth II **Subject:** 10th Anniversary of Independence **Obv:** Arms with supporters **Rev:** Bust of Prince Charles 3/4 left

Date	Mintage	F	VF	XF	Unc	BU
1980 Proof	3,001	Value: 20.00				

KM# 48 10 DOLLARS

30.0000 g., 0.9250 Silver 0.8921 oz. ASW **Ruler:** Elizabeth II **Subject:** Wedding of Prince Charles and Lady Diana **Obv:** Young bust right **Rev:** Head 3/4 left

Date	Mintage	F	VF	XF	Unc	BU
1981 Proof	5,000	Value: 17.50				

KM# 55   10 DOLLARS
28.2800 g., 0.9250 Silver 0.8410 oz. ASW   **Ruler:** Elizabeth II
Subject: 25th Anniversary - World Wildlife Fund **Obv:** Crowned
head right **Rev:** Fijian ground frog, denomination at right

Date	Mintage	F	VF	XF	Unc	BU
1986 Proof	25,000	Value: 25.00				

KM# 60   10 DOLLARS
28.2800 g., 0.9250 Silver 0.8410 oz. ASW   **Ruler:** Elizabeth II
Subject: Save the Children Fund **Obv:** Crowned head right
Rev: Children reading by lantern light, denomination upper right

Date	Mintage	F	VF	XF	Unc	BU
1991 Proof	20,000	Value: 16.50				

KM# 62   10 DOLLARS
28.2800 g., 0.9250 Silver 0.8410 oz. ASW   **Ruler:** Elizabeth II
Subject: 40th Anniversary - Coronation of Queen Elizabeth II
Obv: Crowned head right **Rev:** Queen seated on throne flanked
by church figures

Date	Mintage	F	VF	XF	Unc	BU
1993 Proof	10,000	Value: 16.50				

KM# 63   10 DOLLARS
31.1035 g., 0.9250 Silver 0.9250 oz. ASW   **Ruler:** Elizabeth II
Subject: Discovery of Fiji **Obv:** Crowned head right **Rev:** Cameo
of Abel J. Tasman upper right, ships below

Date	Mintage	F	VF	XF	Unc	BU
1993 Proof	10,000	Value: 18.00				

KM# 64   10 DOLLARS
31.1035 g., 0.9250 Silver 0.9250 oz. ASW   **Ruler:** Elizabeth II
Subject: Discovery of Fiji **Obv:** Crowned head right **Rev:** Cameo
of William Bligh upper right, long boat with sailors, denomination
below

Date	Mintage	F	VF	XF	Unc	BU
1993 Proof	10,000	Value: 18.00				

KM# 66   10 DOLLARS
31.4600 g., 0.9250 Silver 0.9356 oz. ASW   **Ruler:** Elizabeth II
Subject: Protect Our World **Obv:** Crowned head right **Rev:** Island
scene within palm of hand, denomination below

Date	Mintage	F	VF	XF	Unc	BU
1993 Proof	—	Value: 18.00				

KM# 67   10 DOLLARS
31.4600 g., 0.9250 Silver 0.9356 oz. ASW   **Ruler:** Elizabeth II
Series: 1996 Olympics **Obv:** Crowned head right **Rev:** Judo
match, denomination below

Date	Mintage	F	VF	XF	Unc	BU
1993 Proof	20,000	Value: 18.00				

KM# 68   10 DOLLARS
31.6400 g., 0.9250 Silver 0.9409 oz. ASW   **Ruler:** Elizabeth II
Subject: World Cup Soccer **Obv:** Crowned head right
Rev: Soccer player

Date	Mintage	F	VF	XF	Unc	BU
Proof	30,000	Value: 18.00				

KM# 70   10 DOLLARS
31.4700 g., 0.9250 Silver 0.9359 oz. ASW   **Ruler:** Elizabeth II
Subject: Lunar Module "Eagle" **Obv:** Crowned head right
Rev: Lunar module on moon, eagle outline in background,
denomination below

Date	Mintage	F	VF	XF	Unc	BU
1994 Proof	Est. 10,000	Value: 18.00				

KM# 74   10 DOLLARS
31.3700 g., 0.9250 Silver 0.9329 oz. ASW   **Ruler:** Elizabeth II
Subject: Endangered Wildlife **Obv:** Crowned head right
Rev: Streaked Fantail on branch, denomination below

Date	Mintage	F	VF	XF	Unc	BU
1995 Proof	—	Value: 25.00				

KM# 75   10 DOLLARS
34.4600 g., 0.9250 Silver 1.0248 oz. ASW   **Ruler:** Elizabeth II
Subject: Silver Jubilee of Independence **Obv:** Crowned head
right **Rev:** Arms with supporters, crown above divides dates,
denomination below

Date	Mintage	F	VF	XF	Unc	BU
1995 Proof	—	Value: 20.00				

KM# 79   10 DOLLARS
31.5200 g., 0.9250 Silver 0.9373 oz. ASW   **Ruler:** Elizabeth II
Series: Olympic Games 1996 **Obv:** Crowned head right
Rev: Two sailboarders, denomination at right

Date	Mintage	F	VF	XF	Unc	BU
1995 Proof	—	Value: 18.00				

KM# 86   10 DOLLARS
31.3500 g., 0.9250 Silver 0.9323 oz. ASW, 38.7 mm.
Ruler: Elizabeth II **Subject:** Queen Elizabeth II and The Queen
Mother - Move to Buckingham Palace **Obv:** Crowned head right
Rev: 1/2 bust of soldier at right in front of Buckingham Palace
within circle, denomination below **Edge:** Reeded

Date	Mintage	F	VF	XF	Unc	BU
1995 Proof	—	Value: 18.00				

KM# 100   10 DOLLARS
31.4700 g., 0.9250 Silver 0.9359 oz. ASW, 38.61 mm.
Ruler: Elizabeth II **Subject:** Victorian Age - Queen Victoria's
Coronation, 28 June 1838 **Obv:** Crowned head right
Rev: Crowned Queen Victoria **Edge:** Reeded

Date	Mintage	F	VF	XF	Unc	BU
1996 Proof	10,000	Value: 18.00				

KM# 90   10 DOLLARS
28.5000 g., 0.9250 Silver 0.8475 oz. ASW, 38.5 mm.
Ruler: Elizabeth II **Subject:** Queen's 70th Birthday
Obv: Crowned head right **Rev:** Native dancer, denomination
divides dates below **Edge:** Reeded

Date	Mintage	F	VF	XF	Unc	BU
1996 Proof	—	Value: 17.50				

KM# 87   10 DOLLARS
19.7000 g., 0.9250 Silver 0.5858 oz. ASW, 33.9 mm.
Ruler: Elizabeth II **Subject:** Queen Elizabeth II's Golden Jubilee
Obv: Crowned head right **Rev:** The royal couple, shield and
treehouse **Edge:** Reeded

Date	Mintage	F	VF	XF	Unc	BU
1997 Proof	—	Value: 16.00				

KM# 92 10 DOLLARS
31.6000 g., 0.9250 Silver 0.9397 oz. ASW, 38.6 mm.
Ruler: Elizabeth II **Subject:** Princess Diana **Obv:** Crowned head right **Rev:** Diana with sick child **Edge:** Reeded

Date	Mintage	F	VF	XF	Unc	BU
1997 Proof	—	Value: 20.00				

KM# 76 10 DOLLARS
31.3300 g., 0.9250 Silver 0.9317 oz. ASW **Ruler:** Elizabeth II
Subject: Endangered Wildlife **Obv:** Crowned head right
Rev: Banded iguana left

Date	Mintage	F	VF	XF	Unc	BU
1997 Proof	—	Value: 27.50				

KM# 85 10 DOLLARS
28.2800 g., 0.9250 Silver 0.8410 oz. ASW, 38.6 mm. **Ruler:** Elizabeth II **Subject:** UNICEF **Obv:** Crowned head right **Rev:** Two young folk dancers, denomination below **Edge:** Reeded

Date	Mintage	F	VF	XF	Unc	BU
1997 Proof	25,000	Value: 16.50				

KM# 96 10 DOLLARS
34.4700 g., 0.9250 Silver 1.0251 oz. ASW, 38.6 mm.
Ruler: Elizabeth II **Subject:** HM Barge [sic] "Endeavour"
Obv: Crowned head right **Rev:** Endeavour **Edge:** Reeded

Date	Mintage	F	VF	XF	Unc	BU
1998(o) Proof	20,000	Value: 20.00				

KM# 97 10 DOLLARS
1.2500 g., 0.9990 Gold 0.0401 oz. AGW **Ruler:** Elizabeth II
Subject: Discovery of Gold in Fiji - 1932 **Obv:** Crowned head right **Rev:** Gold panning

Date	Mintage	F	VF	XF	Unc	BU
1998 Proof	—	Value: 45.00				

KM# 91 10 DOLLARS
28.1000 g., 0.9250 Silver Gold plated outer ring 0.8356 oz. ASW, 38.6 mm. **Ruler:** Elizabeth II **Subject:** Queen Mother's Centennial **Obv:** Crowned head right within beaded circle, date at right **Rev:** Elizabeth and David as children within beaded circle, denomination below **Edge:** Reeded

Date	Mintage	F	VF	XF	Unc	BU
2000 Proof	10,000	Value: 20.00				

KM# 103 10 DOLLARS
1.2400 g., 0.9990 Gold 0.0398 oz. AGW **Ruler:** Elizabeth II
Obv: Crowned head right **Obv. Leg.:** ELIZABETH II - FIJI
Rev: Dakuwaqa - Shark god

Date	Mintage	F	VF	XF	Unc	BU
2000 Proof	—	Value: 60.00				

KM# 42 20 DOLLARS
35.0000 g., 0.5000 Silver 0.5626 oz. ASW **Ruler:** Elizabeth II
Subject: Conservation **Obv:** Young bust right **Rev:** Golden cowrie, denomination below

Date	Mintage	F	VF	XF	Unc	BU
1978	3,584	—	—	—	20.00	—

KM# 42a 20 DOLLARS
35.0000 g., 0.9250 Silver 1.0408 oz. ASW **Ruler:** Elizabeth II
Subject: Conservation **Obv:** Young bust right **Rev:** Golden cowrie

Date	Mintage	F	VF	XF	Unc	BU
1978 Proof	3,869	Value: 27.50				

KM# 102 20 DOLLARS
3.1100 g., 0.5850 Gold 0.0585 oz. AGW **Ruler:** Elizabeth II
Subject: XXVII Summer Olympics - Sydney 2000 **Obv:** Crowned head right **Obv. Leg.:** ELIZABETH II - FIJI **Rev:** Sprinter

Date	Mintage	F	VF	XF	Unc	BU
1998 Proof	—	Value: 90.00				

KM# 34 25 DOLLARS
48.6000 g., 0.9250 Silver 1.4453 oz. ASW **Ruler:** Elizabeth II
Subject: 100th Anniversary - Cession to Great Britian
Obv: Young bust right **Rev:** Bust of King Cakobau, facing, denomination below, dates above

Date	Mintage	F	VF	XF	Unc	BU
1974	2,400	—	—	—	32.50	—
1974 Proof	8,299	Value: 30.00				

KM# 37 25 DOLLARS
48.6000 g., 0.9250 Silver 1.4453 oz. ASW **Ruler:** Elizabeth II
Obv: Young bust right **Rev:** King Cakobau bust facing, denomination below, dates above

Date	Mintage	F	VF	XF	Unc	BU
1975	836	—	—	—	40.00	—
1975 Proof	5,157	Value: 30.00				

KM# 57 25 DOLLARS
7.7750 g., 0.7500 Gold 0.1875 oz. AGW **Ruler:** Elizabeth II
Obv: Denomination at center of designs **Rev:** Balikula mint mark of Pacific Sovereign Mint, Fijian thatched temple

Date	Mintage	F	VF	XF	Unc	BU
ND(1990)	443	—	—	—	190	—
Note: Boar tusks						
ND(1991)	512	—	—	—	190	—
Note: War fan						
ND(1992)	50	—	—	—	210	—

KM# 58 50 DOLLARS
15.5500 g., 0.7500 Gold 0.3749 oz. AGW **Ruler:** Elizabeth II
Obv: Denomination at center of patterns **Rev:** Balikula mint mark of Pacific Sovereign Mint, Fijian warrior

Date	Mintage	F	VF	XF	Unc	BU
ND(1990)	168	—	—	—	365	—
Note: Boar tusks						
ND(1991)	141	—	—	—	365	—
Note: War fan						
ND(1992)	43	—	—	—	385	—

KM# 72 50 DOLLARS
7.7760 g., 0.5833 Gold 0.1458 oz. AGW **Ruler:** Elizabeth II
Subject: Olympics **Obv:** Crowned head right, date at right
Rev: Two field hockey players, denomination below

Date	Mintage	F	VF	XF	Unc	BU
1996	Est. 3,000	—	—	—	145	—

KM# 88 50 DOLLARS
1000.0000 g., 0.9990 Silver 32.117 oz. ASW, 100 mm.
Ruler: Elizabeth II **Subject:** 70th Birthday of Queen Elizabeth II
Obv: Crowned head right **Rev:** Queen and Queen mother side by side facing **Edge:** Reeded **Note:** Illustration reduced.

Date	Mintage	F	VF	XF	Unc	BU
1996 Proof	99	Value: 650				

KM# 35   100 DOLLARS
31.3600 g., 0.5000 Gold 0.5041 oz. AGW **Ruler:** Elizabeth II
Subject: 100th Anniversary - Cession to Great Britain **Obv:** Young
bust right **Rev:** Bust of King Cakobau facing, denomination below

Date	Mintage	F	VF	XF	Unc	BU
1974	1,109	—	—	—	475	—
1974 Proof	2,321	Value: 500				

KM# 38   100 DOLLARS
31.3000 g., 0.5000 Gold 0.5031 oz. AGW **Ruler:** Elizabeth II **Obv:**
Young bust right **Rev:** King Cakobau, facing denomination below

Date	Mintage	F	VF	XF	Unc	BU
1975	593	—	—	—	500	—
1975 Proof	3,197	Value: 475				

KM# 59   100 DOLLARS
31.1000 g., 0.7500 Gold 0.7499 oz. AGW **Ruler:** Elizabeth II
Obv: Denomination within center, diamonds on pattern at top,
bottom, right and left **Rev:** Balikula mint mark of Pacific Sovereign
Mint **Note:** Dates are privy marks; 1990 - Boar Tusks; 1991 - War
Fan; 1992 - ?.

Date	Mintage	F	VF	XF	Unc	BU
ND(1990)	161	—	—	—	735	—
ND(1991)	131	—	—	—	735	—
ND(1992)	41	—	—	—	765	—

KM# 65   100 DOLLARS
7.5000 g., 0.9170 Gold 0.2211 oz. AGW **Ruler:** Elizabeth II
Subject: Discovery of Fiji **Obv:** Crowned head right, date at right
Rev: James Cook in cameo right of sailing ship, denomination below

Date	Mintage	F	VF	XF	Unc	BU
1993 Proof	3,000	Value: 220				

KM# 98   100 DOLLARS
0.9990 Gold **Ruler:** Elizabeth II **Subject:** Silver Jubilee of
Independence **Obv:** Crowned head right **Rev:** Arms

Date	Mintage	F	VF	XF	Unc	BU
1995 Proof	—	Value: 225				

KM# 47   200 DOLLARS
15.9800 g., 0.9170 Gold 0.4711 oz. AGW **Ruler:** Elizabeth II
Subject: 10th Anniversary of Independence **Obv:** Arms with
supporters, date below **Rev:** Bust 3/4 facing, denomination below

Date	Mintage	F	VF	XF	Unc	BU
1980	500	—	—	—	500	—
1980 Proof	1,166	Value: 475				

KM# 56   200 DOLLARS
15.9800 g., 0.9170 Gold 0.4711 oz. AGW **Ruler:** Elizabeth II
Subject: 25th Anniversary - World Wildlife Fund **Obv:** Young
bust right **Rev:** Ogmodon

Date	Mintage	F	VF	XF	Unc	BU
1986 Proof	5,000	Value: 450				

KM# 61   200 DOLLARS
10.0000 g., 0.9170 Gold 0.2948 oz. AGW **Ruler:** Elizabeth II
Subject: Save the Children Fund **Obv:** King Cakobau facing
divides date **Rev:** Child with toy boat, figure in background with
spear, denomination below

Date	Mintage	F	VF	XF	Unc	BU
1991 Proof	32,000	Value: 315				

KM# 43   250 DOLLARS
33.4370 g., 0.9000 Gold 0.9675 oz. AGW **Ruler:** Elizabeth II
Subject: Conservation **Obv:** Young bust right **Rev:** Banded
iguana, denomination at right

Date	Mintage	F	VF	XF	Unc	BU
1978	810	—	—	—	975	—
1978 Proof	252	Value: 1,100				

TRIAL STRIKES

KM#	Date	Mintage	Identification	Mkt Val
TS1	1974	—	100 Dollars. Bronze. KM35.	950
TS2	1974	—	Cent. Bronze. Fijian planting taro.	275
TS3	1974	—	Cent. Copper-Nickel. Fijian planting taro.	310

MINT SETS

KM#	Date	Mintage	Identification	Issue Price	Mkt Val
MSA1	1934 (3)	—	KM3-5	—	750
MSB1	1969 (6)	—	KM27-32	—	5.00
MS1	1976 (7)	5,001	KM27-32, 36	9.00	11.50
MS2	1976 (6)	—	KM27-31, 36	—	6.50
MS3	1978 (6)	4,006	KM28-31, 36, 39	4.50	7.00
MS4	1978 (3)	—	KM41-43	444	750
MS5	1978 (2)	—	KM41-42	44.00	45.00
MS6	1983 (6)	3,000	KM27-31, 36	5.00	4.50
MS7	1984 (6)	5,000	KM27-31, 36	3.60	4.00
MS8	1990 (8)	—	KM49a-54a	—	5.00
MS9	1990 (3)	—	KM57-59	905	1,225

PROOF SETS

KM#	Date	Mintage	Identification	Issue Price	Mkt Val
PS1	1969 (6)	10,000	KM27-32	7.20	6.50
PS2	1976 (7)	3,023	KM27a-32a, 36a	87.50	35.00
PS3	1978 (6)	2,000	KM28-31, 36, 39	31.00	20.00
PS4	1978 (2)	—	KM#41a, 42a	76.00	55.00
PS5	1978 (3)	—	KM#41a, 42a, 43	726	1,000
PS6	1980 (6)	2,500	KM#28-31, 36, 39	45.00	20.00
PS7	1982 (6)	3,000	KM#28-31, 36	32.00	20.00
PS8	1983 (6)	3,000	KM#27-31, 36	27.00	20.00
PS9	1993 (3)	—	KM#63-65	370	230

FINLAND

The Republic of Finland, the third northernmost state of the
European continent, has an area of 130,559 sq. mi. (338,127 sq. km.)
and a population of 5.1 million. Capital: Helsinki. Lumbering, shipbuilding, metal and woodworking are the leading industries. Paper,
timber, wood pulp, plywood and metal products are exported.

The Finns, who probably originated in the Volga region of
Russia, took Finland from the Lapps late in the 7th century. They
were conquered in the 12th century by Eric IX of Sweden, and
brought into contact with Western Christendom. In 1809, Sweden
was conquered by Alexander I of Russia, and the peace terms
gave Finland to Russia which became a grand duchy, with autonomy, within the Russian Empire until Dec. 6, 1917, when, shortly
after the Bolshevik revolution it declared its independence. After
a brief but bitter civil war between the Russian communists and
Finnish nationalists in which the Whites (nationalists) were victorious, a new constitution was adopted, and on Dec. 6, 1917 Finland was established as a republic. In 1939 Soviet troops
attacked Finland over disputed territorial concessions which
were later granted in the peace treaty of 1940. When the Germans invaded Russia, Finland became involved and in the Armistice of 1944 lost the Petsamo area to the Soviets.

RULER
Nicholas II, 1894-1917

MONETARY SYSTEM
100 Pennia = 1 Markka

Commencing 1963
100 Old Markka = 1 New Markka

MINT MARKS
H - Birmingham 1921
Heart (h) - Copenhagen 1922
No mm – Helsinki

MINT OFFICIALS' INITIALS

Letter	Date	Name
H	1948-1958	Peippo Uolevi Helle
H-M	1990	Raimo Heino & Raimo Makkonen
K	1976-1983	Timo Koivuranta
K-H	1977, 1979	Timo Koivuranta & Heikki Haivaoja (Designer)
K-M	1983	Timo Koivuranta & Pertti Makinen
K-N	1978	Timo Koivuranta & Antti Neuvonen
K-T	1982	Timo Koivuranta & Erja Tielinen
L	1885-1912	Johan Conrad Lihr
L	1948	Vesa Uolevi Liuhto
L-M	1991	Arto Lappalainen & Raimo Makkonen
L-M	2000	Maija Lavonen & Raimo Makkonen
M	1987	Raimo Makkonen
M-G	1998	Raimo Makkonen & Henrik Gummerus
M-L	1997	Raimo Makkonen & Tero Lounas
M-L-L	1995	Raimo Makkonen & Arto Lappalainen & Marita Lappalainen
M-L-M	1989	Marjo Lahtinen & Raimo Makkonen
M-O	1998	Raimo Makkonen & Harri Ojala
M-S	1992, 1997	Raimo Makkonen & Erkki Salmela
N	1983-1987	Tapio Nevalainen
P-M	1989-1991, 1994-1995, 1997, 2000	Reijo Paavilainen & Raimo Makkonen
P-N	1985	Reijo Paavilainen & Tapio Nevalainen
P-V-M	1999	Juhani Pallasmaa, Jukka Veistola & Raimo Makkonen
R-M	1999	Jarkko Roth & Raimo Makkonen
S	1912-1947	Isak Gustaf Sundell
S	1958-1975	Allan Alarik Soiniemi
S-H	1967-1971	Allan Alarik Soiniemi & Heikki Haivaoja (Designer)
S-J	1960	Allan Alarik Soiniemi & Toivo Jaatinen
S-M	1995	Terho Sakki & Raimo Makkonen
T-M	1996, 2000	Erja Tielinen & Raimo Makkonen

GRAND DUCHY

DECIMAL COINAGE

KM# 13   PENNI
1.2800 g., Copper, 15 mm. **Ruler:** Nicholas II **Obv:** Crowned
monogram **Rev:** Denomination and date

Date	Mintage	F	VF	XF	Unc	BU
1901	1,520,000	0.75	1.25	2.50	10.00	—
1902	1,000,000	0.75	3.00	7.50	15.00	—
1903	1,145,000	0.75	3.00	7.50	15.00	—
Note: Small 3						
1903	Inc. above	1.50	5.00	10.00	20.00	—
Note: Large 3						
1904	500,000	2.50	7.00	12.00	25.00	—

Date	Mintage	F	VF	XF	Unc	BU
1905	1,390,000	0.50	1.00	2.00	6.00	—
1906	1,020,000	0.50	1.00	2.00	5.00	—
1907	2,490,000	0.75	1.25	2.50	4.00	—

Note: Normal 7

Date	Mintage	F	VF	XF	Unc	BU
1907	Inc. above	0.30	0.75	1.75	4.00	—

Note: Without serif on 7 arm

Date	Mintage	F	VF	XF	Unc	BU
1908	950,000	0.50	2.50	5.00	12.00	—
1909	3,060,000	0.25	0.65	1.25	2.50	—
1911	2,550,000	0.25	0.65	1.25	2.50	—
1912	2,450,000	0.25	0.65	1.25	2.50	—
1913	1,650,000	0.25	0.65	1.25	3.00	—
1914	1,900,000	0.25	0.65	1.25	3.50	—
1915	2,250,000	0.25	0.65	1.25	2.50	—
1916	3,040,000	0.25	0.50	1.00	2.00	—

KM# 15 5 PENNIA
6.4000 g., Copper, 25 mm. **Ruler:** Nicholas II **Obv:** Crowned monogram **Rev:** Denomination and date

Date	Mintage	F	VF	XF	Unc	BU
1901	990,000	2.00	7.50	30.00	100	—
1905	620,000	3.00	15.00	60.00	150	—
1906	960,000	2.00	7.50	30.00	120	—
1907	770,000	3.00	15.00	100	200	—
1908	1,660,000	1.50	5.00	25.00	70.00	—
1910	60,000	35.00	70.00	150	300	—
1911	1,050,000	1.00	3.00	10.00	50.00	—
1912	460,000	3.00	7.50	35.00	100	—
1913	1,060,000	0.75	2.00	6.00	25.00	—
1914	820,000	0.75	2.00	6.00	25.00	—
1915	2,080,000	0.30	1.00	5.00	15.00	—
1916	4,470,000	0.30	0.75	3.00	10.00	—
1917	4,070,000	0.30	0.75	3.00	10.00	—

KM# 14 10 PENNIA
12.8000 g., Copper, 30 mm. **Ruler:** Nicholas II **Obv:** Crowned monogram **Rev:** Denomination and date within wreath

Date	Mintage	F	VF	XF	Unc	BU
1905	500,000	3.00	15.00	100	250	—
1907	503,000	3.00	15.00	100	250	—
1908	320,000	2.00	12.00	50.00	150	—
1909	180,000	4.00	25.00	135	350	—
1910	241,000	2.50	12.00	50.00	120	—
1911	370,000	2.00	7.50	30.00	75.00	—
1912	191,000	2.50	10.00	35.00	120	—
1913	150,000	7.50	15.00	75.00	250	—
1914	605,000	1.00	3.00	12.00	40.00	—
1915	420,000	1.00	2.00	10.00	20.00	—
1916	1,952,000	0.50	1.00	5.00	12.00	—
1917	1,600,000	1.00	2.50	7.50	15.00	—

KM# 6.2 25 PENNIA
1.2747 g., 0.7500 Silver 0.0307 oz. ASW, 16 mm. **Ruler:** Nicholas II **Obv:** Crowned Imperial double eagle with sceptre and orb **Rev:** Denomination and date within wreath **Note:** Dentilated border.

Date	Mintage	F	VF	XF	Unc	BU
1901 L	993,000	1.00	3.00	10.00	50.00	—
1902 L	210,000	6.00	15.00	45.00	120	—
1906 L	281,000	2.00	7.50	20.00	90.00	—
1907 L	590,000	1.50	3.00	10.00	35.00	—
1908 L	340,000	2.00	7.50	30.00	90.00	—
1909 L	1,099,000	1.00	2.50	7.50	20.00	—
1910 L	392,000	5.00	15.00	25.00	100	—
1913 S	832,000	0.50	1.50	2.50	4.00	—
1915 S	2,400,000	0.50	0.75	1.00	1.50	—
1916 S	6,392,000	0.50	0.75	1.00	1.50	—
1917 S	5,820,000	0.50	0.75	1.00	1.50	—

KM# 2.2 50 PENNIA
2.5494 g., 0.7500 Silver 0.0615 oz. ASW, 18.6 mm. **Ruler:** Nicholas II **Obv:** Crowned imperial double eagle with sceptre and orb **Rev:** Denomination and date within wreath **Note:** Dentilated border.

Date	Mintage	F	VF	XF	Unc	BU
1907 L	260,000	2.00	7.50	35.00	110	—
1908 L	353,000	1.50	3.00	13.00	40.00	—
1911 L	616,000	1.00	1.50	3.50	7.50	—
1914 S	600,000	0.85	1.25	2.00	5.00	—
1915 S	1,000,000	0.85	1.00	1.50	2.50	—
1916 S	4,752,000	0.85	1.00	1.50	2.50	—
1917 S	3,972,000	0.85	1.00	1.50	2.50	—

KM# 3.2 MARKKA
5.1828 g., 0.8680 Silver 0.1446 oz. ASW, 24 mm. **Ruler:** Nicholas II **Obv:** Crowned imperial double eagle holding orb and scepter, fineness around (text in Finnish) **Rev:** Denomination and date within wreath **Note:** Obverse text translates to: "94.48 pieces from one pound of fine silver." Dentilated border.

Date	Mintage	F	VF	XF	Unc	BU
1907 L	350,000	7.50	10.00	15.00	35.00	—
1908 L	153,000	15.00	20.00	35.00	100	—
1915 S	1,212,000	7.50	10.00	15.00	35.00	—

KM# 7.2 2 MARKKAA
10.3657 g., 0.8680 Silver 0.2893 oz. ASW, 27.5 mm. **Ruler:** Nicholas II **Obv:** Crowned imperial double eagle holding orb and scepter, fineness around (Finnish text) **Rev:** Denomination and date within wreath **Note:** Obverse text translates to: "47.24 pieces from one pound of fine silver." Dentilated border.

Date	Mintage	F	VF	XF	Unc	BU
1905 L	24,000	200	250	700	2,000	—
1906 L	225,000	20.00	25.00	65.00	120	—
1907 L	125,000	20.00	30.00	90.00	275	—
1908 L	124,000	20.00	30.00	60.00	90.00	—

KM# 8.2 10 MARKKAA
3.2258 g., 0.9000 Gold 0.0933 oz. AGW, 18.9 mm. **Ruler:** Nicholas II **Obv:** Crowned imperial double eagle holding orb and scepter **Rev:** Denomination and date within circle, fineness around **Note:** Regal issues

Date	Mintage	F	VF	XF	Unc	BU
1904 L	102,000	500	750	1,000	1,200	—
1905 L	43,000	2,500	3,500	4,500	6,000	—
1913 S	396,000	175	200	250	300	—

KM# 9.2 20 MARKKAA
6.4516 g., 0.9000 Gold 0.1867 oz. AGW, 21.3 mm. **Ruler:** Nicholas II **Obv:** Crowned imperial double eagle holding orb and scepter **Rev:** Denomination and date within circle, fineness around **Note:** Regal issues.

Date	Mintage	F	VF	XF	Unc	BU
1903 L	112,000	275	350	450	500	—
1904 L	188,000	250	330	400	450	—
1910 L	201,000	250	330	400	450	—
1911 L	161,000	250	330	400	450	—
1912 L	881,000	6,500	8,000	12,000	15,000	—
1912 S	Inc. above	250	330	400	450	—
1913 S	214,000	250	330	400	450	—

CIVIL WAR COINAGE
Kerenski Government Issue

KM# 16 PENNI
1.2800 g., Copper, 15 mm. **Ruler:** Nicholas II

Date	Mintage	F	VF	XF	Unc	BU
1917	1,650,000	0.25	0.75	1.00	1.50	—

KM# 17 5 PENNIA
6.4000 g., Copper, 25 mm. **Ruler:** Nicholas II **Obv:** Imperial double eagle holding royal orb and scepter, shield on breast within circle **Rev:** Denomination above date

Date	Mintage	F	VF	XF	Unc	BU
1917	Inc. above	0.30	0.75	3.00	7.00	—

KM# 18 10 PENNIA
12.8000 g., Copper, 30 mm. **Ruler:** Nicholas II

Date	Mintage	F	VF	XF	Unc	BU
1917	Inc. above	0.50	1.00	4.00	10.00	—

KM# 19 25 PENNIA
1.2747 g., 0.7500 Silver 0.0307 oz. ASW, 16 mm. **Ruler:** Nicholas II **Obv:** Crown above eagle removed

Date	Mintage	F	VF	XF	Unc	BU
1917 S	2,310,000	—	BV	1.00	1.50	—

KM# 20 50 PENNIA
2.5494 g., 0.7500 Silver 0.0615 oz. ASW, 18.6 mm. **Ruler:** Nicholas II **Obv:** Imperial double eagle holding royal orb and scepter, shield on breast **Rev:** Denomination and date within wreath **Note:** No crown above eagle

Date	Mintage	F	VF	XF	Unc	BU
1917 S	570,000	—	BV	1.25	2.00	—

CIVIL WAR COINAGE
Liberated Finnish Government Issue

KM# 21 5 PENNIA
2.5000 g., Copper, 17.9 mm. **Obv:** Flag and 3 trumpets within wreath, wreath knot centered between 9 and 1 of date below **Obv. Leg.:** •KANSAN TYÖ, KANSAN VALTA•-SUOMI-FINLAND **Rev:** Large value flanked by flower heads **Note:** Prev. KM#21.1. For previously listed KM#21.2, refer to Unusual World Coins, X#B1.

Date	Mintage	F	VF	XF	Unc	BU
1918	35,000	30.00	45.00	55.00	65.00	—

REPUBLIC

DECIMAL COINAGE

KM# 23 PENNI
1.0000 g., Copper, 14 mm. **Rev:** Denomination flanked by rosettes

Date	Mintage	F	VF	XF	Unc	BU
1919	1,200,000	0.25	0.65	1.75	3.00	—
1920	720,000	0.25	0.65	1.75	3.00	—
1921	510,000	0.35	1.00	2.00	4.00	—
1922	1,060,000	0.25	0.65	1.75	3.00	—
1923	990,000	0.25	0.65	1.75	3.00	—
1924	2,180,000	0.25	0.65	1.75	3.00	—

KM# 22 5 PENNIA
2.5000 g., Copper, 18 mm. **Obv:** Rampant lion left with sword divides date **Rev:** Rosettes flank denomination

Date	Mintage	F	VF	XF	Unc	BU
1918	4,270,000	0.10	0.25	1.00	4.00	—
1919	4,640,000	0.10	0.25	1.00	4.00	—
1920	7,710,000	0.10	0.25	1.00	3.00	—
1921	5,910,000	0.10	0.25	1.00	3.00	—
1922	8,540,000	0.10	0.25	1.00	3.00	—
1927	1,520,000	0.75	1.50	3.50	15.00	—
1928	2,110,000	0.25	0.50	1.50	8.00	—
1929	1,500,000	0.25	0.50	1.50	8.00	—

Date	Mintage	F	VF	XF	Unc	BU
1930	2,140,000	0.75	1.25	3.00	12.00	—
1932	2,130,000	0.15	0.50	1.00	4.00	—
1934	2,180,000	0.15	0.50	1.00	4.00	—
1935	1,610,000	0.15	0.35	1.00	3.00	—
1936	2,610,000	0.15	0.35	1.00	3.00	—
1937	3,830,000	0.10	0.25	1.00	3.00	—
1938	4,300,000	0.10	0.25	1.00	3.00	—
1939	2,270,000	0.10	0.25	1.00	3.00	—
1940	1,610,000	0.25	0.50	1.50	5.00	—

KM# 64.1   5 PENNIA
1.2700 g., Copper, 16 mm. **Obv:** Rosette above center hole flanked by leaves dividing date below **Rev:** Center hole divides denomination, rosettes flank **Note:** Punched center hole.

Date	Mintage	F	VF	XF	Unc	BU
1941	5,950,000	0.10	0.20	0.50	1.25	—
1942	4,280,000	0.10	0.20	0.50	1.25	—
1943	1,530,000	0.10	0.50	1.25	2.50	—

KM# 64.2   5 PENNIA
Copper, 16 mm.   **Note:** Without punched center hole. These issues were not authorized by the government and any that exist were illegally removed from the mint.

Date	Mintage	F	VF	XF	Unc	BU
1941	Inc. above	25.00	30.00	70.00	100	—
1942	Inc. above	25.00	30.00	70.00	100	—
1943	Inc. above	50.00	70.00	100	125	—

KM# 24   10 PENNIA
5.0000 g., Copper, 22 mm. **Obv:** Rampant lion left, holding sword, divides date

Date	Mintage	F	VF	XF	Unc	BU
1919	3,670,000	0.10	0.25	1.00	5.00	—
1920	2,380,000	0.10	0.25	1.00	5.00	—
1921	3,970,000	0.10	0.25	1.00	5.00	—
1922	2,180,000	0.10	0.25	2.00	7.00	—
1923	910,000	1.00	2.00	15.00	45.00	—
1924	1,350,000	0.25	0.50	5.00	20.00	—
1926	1,690,000	0.25	0.50	3.50	15.00	—
1927	1,330,000	0.50	1.00	10.00	40.00	—
1928	1,006,000	0.50	1.00	5.00	20.00	—
1929	1,560,000	0.35	0.85	3.00	15.00	—
1930	650,000	0.75	1.50	12.50	25.00	—
1931	1,040,000	1.00	2.00	20.00	60.00	—
1934	1,680,000	0.35	0.85	5.00	12.00	—
1935	1,690,000	0.15	0.25	2.00	10.00	—
1936	2,009,999	0.15	0.25	1.00	7.50	—
1937	2,420,000	0.10	0.25	0.50	3.50	—
1938	2,940,000	0.10	0.25	0.50	3.50	—
1939	2,100,000	0.10	0.25	0.50	3.50	—
1940	2,009,999	0.25	0.50	1.00	5.00	—

KM# 33.1   10 PENNIA
2.5500 g., Copper, 18.5 mm. **Obv:** Rosette above center hole flanked by leaves dividing date below **Rev:** Center hole divides denomination, rosettes flank

Date	Mintage	F	VF	XF	Unc	BU
1941	3,610,000	0.10	0.25	0.50	1.25	—
1942	4,970,000	0.10	0.25	0.50	1.25	—
1943	1,860,000	0.25	0.75	1.50	2.50	—

KM# 33.2   10 PENNIA
2.6000 g., Copper, 18.5 mm. **Obv:** Rosette above center hole flanked by leaves dividing date below **Rev:** Center hole divides denomination, rosettes flank **Note:** Without punched center hole. These issues were not authorized by the government and any that exist were illegally removed from the mint.

Date	Mintage	F	VF	XF	Unc	BU
1941	Inc. above	30.00	50.00	75.00	100	—
1942	Inc. above	30.00	50.00	75.00	100	—
1943	Inc. above	35.00	75.00	90.00	120	—

KM# 34.2   10 PENNIA
Iron **Obv:** Sprigs divide date, rosette above **Rev:** Rosettes and denomination **Note:** Without punched center hole. These issues were not authorized by the government and any that exist were illegally removed from the mint.

Date	Mintage	F	VF	XF	Unc	BU
1943	Inc. above	50.00	75.00	100	125	—

Date	Mintage	F	VF	XF	Unc	BU
1944	Inc. above	50.00	75.00	100	125	—
1945	Inc. above	70.00	100	150	175	—

KM# 34.1   10 PENNIA
1.1200 g., Iron, 16 mm. **Obv:** Rosette above center hole flanked by leaves dividing date below **Rev:** Center hole flanked by rosettes divides denomination **Note:** Reduced planchet size.

Date	Mintage	F	VF	XF	Unc	BU
1943	1,430,000	0.10	0.25	1.00	5.00	—
1944	3,040,000	0.10	0.25	1.00	5.00	—
1945	1,810,000	0.25	0.50	2.00	10.00	—

KM# 25   25 PENNIA
1.2700 g., Copper-Nickel, 16 mm. **Obv:** Rampant lion left holding sword divides date **Rev:** Denomination flanked by grain sprigs

Date	Mintage	F	VF	XF	Unc	BU
1921 H	20,096,000	0.10	0.25	1.00	3.00	—
1925 S	1,250,000	0.50	1.50	15.00	25.00	—
1926 S	2,820,000	0.40	1.25	5.00	12.00	—
1927 S	1,120,000	0.50	1.50	10.00	20.00	—
1928 S	2,920,000	0.40	1.00	5.00	12.00	—
1929 S	200,000	3.00	6.50	35.00	65.00	—
1930 S	1,090,000	1.00	3.00	10.00	20.00	—
1934 S	1,260,000	0.40	0.75	3.00	12.00	—
1935 S	2,190,000	0.30	0.50	2.00	8.00	—
1936 S	2,300,000	0.20	0.40	2.00	7.50	—
1937 S	4,019,999	0.20	0.40	1.00	5.00	—
1938 S	4,500,000	0.20	0.40	1.00	3.00	—
1939 S	2,712,000	0.20	0.40	1.00	3.00	—
1940 S	4,840,000	0.15	0.30	0.75	2.00	—

KM# 25a   25 PENNIA
1.2700 g., Copper, 16 mm. **Obv:** Rampant lion left divides date **Rev:** Grain sprigs flank denomination

Date	Mintage	F	VF	XF	Unc	BU
1940 S	72,000	1.00	2.00	7.50	20.00	—
1941 S	5,980,000	0.10	0.35	2.00	5.00	—
1942 S	6,464,000	0.10	0.35	2.00	5.00	—
1943 S	4,912,000	0.25	0.50	3.00	7.00	—

KM# 25b   25 PENNIA
Iron, 16 mm. **Obv:** Rampant lion left divides dates **Rev:** Grain sprigs flank denomination

Date	Mintage	F	VF	XF	Unc	BU
1943 S	2,700,000	0.15	0.50	3.00	12.00	—
1944 S	5,480,000	0.15	0.50	2.00	8.00	—
	Note: Small closed 4's					
1944 S	Inc. above	0.15	0.50	2.00	8.00	—
	Note: Large open 4's					
1945 S	6,810,000	0.25	0.75	3.00	12.00	—

KM# 26   50 PENNIA
2.5500 g., Copper-Nickel, 18.5 mm. **Obv:** Rampant lion left divides date

Date	Mintage	F	VF	XF	Unc	BU
1921 H	10,072,000	0.15	0.30	1.00	3.00	—
1923 S	6,000,000	0.25	1.00	3.00	12.00	—
1929 S	984,000	1.00	2.00	15.00	50.00	—
1934 S	612,000	1.00	2.50	15.00	50.00	—
1935 S	610,000	1.00	2.50	10.00	40.00	—
1936 S	1,520,000	0.30	0.50	3.00	15.00	—
1937 S	2,350,000	0.15	0.25	1.00	7.50	—
1938 S	2,330,000	0.15	0.25	1.00	5.00	—
1939 S	1,280,000	0.15	0.25	1.00	5.00	—
1940 S	3,152,000	0.15	0.25	1.00	3.00	—

KM# 26a   50 PENNIA
2.5500 g., Copper, 18.5 mm. **Obv:** Rampant lion left divides date **Rev:** Grain sprigs flank denomination

Date	Mintage	F	VF	XF	Unc	BU
1940 S	480,000	1.25	2.50	8.00	20.00	—
1941 S	3,860,000	0.15	0.40	3.00	8.00	—
1942 S	5,900,000	0.15	0.40	3.00	8.00	—
1943 S	3,140,000	0.20	0.50	3.00	8.00	—

KM# 26b   50 PENNIA
2.2500 g., Iron, 18.5 mm. **Obv:** Rampant lion left divides date **Rev:** Grain sprigs flank denomination

Date	Mintage	F	VF	XF	Unc	BU
1943 S	1,580,000	0.25	0.50	5.00	20.00	—
1944 S	7,600,000	0.15	0.40	3.00	12.00	—
1945 S	4,700,000	0.15	0.40	3.00	15.00	—
1946 S	2,632,000	0.30	0.50	3.00	15.00	—

Date	Mintage	F	VF	XF	Unc	BU
1947 S	1,748,000	0.50	2.00	10.00	25.00	—
1948 L	1,112,000	3.00	10.00	20.00	35.00	—

KM# 27   MARKKA
5.1000 g., Copper-Nickel, 24 mm.

Date	Mintage	F	VF	XF	Unc	BU
1921 H	10,048,000	1.00	2.00	3.00	10.00	—
1922 Heart	10,000,000	1.00	2.00	5.00	15.00	—
1923 S	1,780,000	10.00	20.00	35.00	70.00	—
1924 S	3,270,000	5.00	10.00	20.00	40.00	—

KM# 30   MARKKA
4.0000 g., Copper-Nickel, 21 mm. **Obv:** Rampant lion left divides date **Rev:** Denomination flanked by branches **Note:** Reduced size.

Date	Mintage	F	VF	XF	Unc	BU
1928 S	3,000,000	0.15	1.00	5.00	20.00	—
1929 S	3,862,000	0.15	1.00	5.00	20.00	—
1930 S	10,284,000	0.15	1.00	5.00	15.00	—
1931 S	2,830,000	0.15	1.00	5.00	15.00	—
1932 S	4,140,000	0.15	1.00	5.00	15.00	—
1933 S	4,032,000	0.15	1.00	5.00	15.00	—
1936 S	562,000	1.00	3.00	20.00	65.00	—
1937 S	4,930,000	0.15	1.00	3.00	6.00	—
1938 S	4,410,000	0.15	1.00	3.00	6.00	—
1939 S	3,070,000	0.15	1.00	3.00	6.00	—
1940 S	3,372,000	0.15	1.00	3.00	6.00	—

Note: Coins dated 1928S, 1929S and 1930S are known to be restruck on 1921-24, KM#27 coins; 1928S: 2 or 3 known

KM# 30a   MARKKA
4.0000 g., Copper, 21 mm. **Obv:** Rampant lion left divides date **Rev:** Denomination flanked by branches

Date	Mintage	F	VF	XF	Unc	BU
1940 S	84,000	1.50	3.50	8.00	20.00	—
1941 S	8,970,000	0.15	0.50	2.00	8.00	—
1942 S	11,200,000	0.15	0.50	2.00	8.00	—
1943 S	7,460,000	0.15	0.50	2.00	8.00	—
1949 H	250	6,000	7,500	10,000	12,000	—
	Note: Counterfeits exist					
1950 H	320,000	0.50	1.00	3.00	10.00	—
1951 H	4,630,000	0.25	0.50	2.00	8.00	—

KM# 30b   MARKKA
3.5000 g., Iron, 21 mm. **Obv:** Rampant lion left divides date **Rev:** Branches flank denomination

Date	Mintage	F	VF	XF	Unc	BU
1943 S	7,460,000	0.15	0.25	5.00	20.00	—
1944 S	12,830,000	0.15	0.25	5.00	20.00	—
1945 S	21,950,000	0.15	0.25	5.00	20.00	—
1946 S	2,630,000	0.15	0.30	5.00	20.00	—
1947 S	1,750,000	0.25	0.50	5.00	25.00	—
1948 L	20,500,000	0.15	0.25	3.00	10.00	—
1949 H	17,358,000	0.15	0.25	2.00	8.00	—
1950 H	14,654,000	0.15	0.25	2.00	7.00	—
1951 H	21,414,000	0.15	0.25	2.00	7.00	—
1952 H	5,410,000	0.25	0.50	5.00	20.00	—

KM# 36   MARKKA
1.1500 g., Iron, 16 mm. **Obv:** Four joined loops form design, date below **Rev:** Grasped hands flank denomination

Date	Mintage	F	VF	XF	Unc	BU
1952	22,050,000	0.15	0.35	1.00	7.00	—
1953	28,618,000	0.15	0.35	1.00	7.00	—

KM# 36a   MARKKA
1.1500 g., Nickel Plated Iron, 16 mm. **Obv:** Four joined loops form design, date below **Rev:** Grasped hands flank denomination

Date	Mintage	F	VF	XF	Unc	BU
1953	6,000,000	5.00	8.00	15.00	25.00	—
1954	36,400,000	—	0.10	0.25	0.50	—
1955	38,100,000	—	0.10	0.25	0.50	—
1956	35,600,000	—	0.10	0.25	1.00	—
1957	29,100,000	—	0.10	0.25	0.50	—
1958	19,940,000	0.10	0.20	0.35	0.70	—
1959	23,920,000	—	0.10	0.25	0.50	—
	Note: Thick letters					
1959	Inc. above	—	0.10	0.25	1.00	—
	Note: Thin letters					
1960	22,020,000	—	0.10	0.25	0.50	—
1961	32,220,000	—	0.10	0.25	0.50	—
1962	29,040,000	—	0.10	0.25	0.50	—

KM# 31   5 MARKKAA
4.5000 g., Aluminum-Bronze, 23 mm. **Obv:** Wreath divides denomination **Rev:** Shielded arms within wreath divide date

Date	Mintage	F	VF	XF	Unc	BU
1928 S	580,000	65.00	90.00	175	350	—
1929 S	Inc. above	60.00	85.00	175	400	—
1930 S	592,000	1.00	3.00	40.00	100	—
1931 S	3,090,000	1.00	2.00	20.00	40.00	—
1932 S	964,000	12.00	30.00	200	400	—
1933 S	1,050,000	1.00	3.00	30.00	100	—
1935 S	440,000	2.00	5.00	30.00	100	—
1936 S	470,000	2.00	5.00	30.00	100	—
1937 S	1,032,000	1.00	3.00	20.00	40.00	—
1938 S	912,000	1.00	3.00	20.00	40.00	—
1939 S	752,000	1.00	3.00	20.00	40.00	—
1940 S	820,000	2.00	5.00	25.00	50.00	—
1941 S	1,452,000	1.00	3.00	12.00	25.00	—
1942 S	1,390,000	1.00	2.00	10.00	20.00	—
1946 S	618,000	5.00	10.00	30.00	100	—

KM# 31a   5 MARKKAA
4.5500 g., Brass, 23 mm. **Obv:** Denomination divided by wreath **Rev:** Shielded arms within wreath divides date below

Date	Mintage	F	VF	XF	Unc	BU
1946 S	5,538,000	0.50	1.00	2.00	7.00	—
1947 S	6,550,000	1.00	2.00	3.00	12.00	—
1948 L	8,210,000	0.50	1.00	2.00	10.00	—
1949 H	11,014,000	2.00	5.00	10.00	20.00	—
Note: Thin H						
1949 H	Inc. above	1.00	2.00	3.00	7.00	—
Note: Wide H						
1950 H	4,760,000	0.50	1.00	3.00	7.00	—
1951 H	7,800,000	0.50	1.00	2.00	5.00	—
1952 H	1,210,000	3.00	8.00	15.00	30.00	—

KM# 37   5 MARKKAA
2.5500 g., Iron, 18 mm. **Obv:** Four joined loops form design, date below **Rev:** Grasped hands flank denomination

Date	Mintage	F	VF	XF	Unc	BU
1952	10,820,000	0.20	0.35	2.00	8.00	—
1953	9,772,000	0.20	0.35	3.00	10.00	—

KM# 37a   5 MARKKAA
2.5500 g., Nickel Plated Iron, 18 mm. **Obv:** Four joined loops form design, date below **Rev:** Grasped hands flank denomination

Date	Mintage	F	VF	XF	Unc	BU
1953	Inc. above	75.00	125	200	300	—
1954	6,696,000	—	0.20	1.00	5.00	—
1955	9,894,000	—	0.20	1.00	5.00	—
1956	8,220,000	—	0.20	1.00	5.00	—
1957	4,276,000	—	0.20	1.00	5.00	—
1958	3,300,000	—	0.20	1.00	7.00	—
1959	5,874,000	—	0.20	1.00	5.00	—
1960	3,066,000	0.10	0.25	1.00	5.00	—
1961	7,254,000	0.10	0.25	0.50	3.00	—
1962	4,542,000	0.50	2.00	5.00	8.00	—

KM# 32A   10 MARKKAA
8.0000 g., Aluminum-Bronze, 27 mm. **Obv:** Wreath divides denomination **Rev:** Shielded arms within wreath divide date below **Note:** Prev. KM#63.

Date	Mintage	F	VF	XF	Unc	BU
1928 S	730,000	3.00	15.00	70.00	200	—
1929 S	Inc. above	2.00	8.00	50.00	150	—
1930 S	260,000	1.00	5.00	35.00	100	—
1931 S	1,530,000	1.00	3.00	20.00	120	—
1932 S	1,010,000	1.00	2.50	10.00	85.00	—
1934 S	154,000	2.00	8.00	50.00	120	—
1935 S	81,000	3.00	12.00	70.00	180	—
1936 S	304,000	2.00	8.00	50.00	100	—
1937 S	181,000	1.50	5.00	20.00	90.00	—
1938 S	631,000	1.00	3.00	15.00	60.00	—
1939 S	133,000	5.00	10.00	30.00	75.00	—

KM# 38   10 MARKKAA
3.0000 g., Aluminum-Bronze, 20 mm. **Obv:** Rampant lion left within circle, date below **Rev:** Tree right of denomination

Date	Mintage	F	VF	XF	Unc	BU
1952 H	6,390,000	0.20	1.00	5.00	12.00	—
1953 H	22,650,000	0.15	0.35	1.00	5.00	—
1954 H	2,452,000	0.50	1.00	5.00	15.00	—
1955 H	2,342,000	0.20	0.50	5.00	12.00	—
1956 H	4,240,000	0.20	0.40	3.00	10.00	—
1958 H	3,292,000	3.00	10.00	20.00	35.00	—
Note: Thin 1						
1958 H	Inc. above	0.20	0.40	3.00	8.00	—
Note: Wide 1						
1960 S	740,000	2.00	5.00	10.00	20.00	—
1961 S	3,580,000	2.00	5.00	10.00	20.00	—
Note: Wide 1						
1961 S	Inc. above	0.20	0.50	2.00	5.00	—
1962 S	1,852,000	0.30	1.00	3.00	7.00	—

Note: The "1" in the denomination on all 1952 to 1956 issues is the thin variety; 1960 issues are the wide variety, and 1961's and 1962's are thin; Varieties exist in root length of tree

KM# 32   20 MARKKAA
13.0000 g., Aluminum-Bronze, 31 mm. **Obv:** Wreath divides denomination **Rev:** Shielded arms within wreath divide date below

Date	Mintage	F	VF	XF	Unc	BU
1931 S	16,000	20.00	30.00	50.00	75.00	—
1932 S	14,000	30.00	40.00	60.00	90.00	—
1934 S	390,000	2.00	5.00	30.00	100	—
1935 S	250,000	2.00	10.00	50.00	100	—
1936 S	110,000	3.00	15.00	50.00	150	—
1937 S	510,000	1.50	5.00	15.00	50.00	—
1938 S	360,000	1.50	5.00	15.00	50.00	—
1939 S	960,000	1.00	2.00	6.00	20.00	—

KM# 39   20 MARKKAA
4.5000 g., Aluminum-Bronze, 25.5 mm. **Obv:** Rampant lion left within circle, date below **Rev:** Tree right of denomination

Date	Mintage	F	VF	XF	Unc	BU
1952 H	83,000	7.00	10.00	20.00	40.00	—
1953 H	2,880,000	0.25	0.50	3.00	15.00	—
1954 H	17,034,000	0.15	0.50	2.00	10.00	—
1955 H	2,800,000	0.25	0.50	5.00	15.00	—
1956 H	2,540,000	0.25	0.50	5.00	15.00	—
1957 H	1,050,000	0.50	1.00	8.00	20.00	—
1958 H	515,000	2.50	5.00	20.00	40.00	—
1959 S	1,580,000	0.25	0.50	5.00	15.00	—
1960 S	3,850,000	0.15	0.50	3.00	10.00	—
1961 S	4,430,000	0.15	0.50	3.00	10.00	—
1962 S	2,280,000	0.15	0.50	3.00	8.00	—

KM# 40   50 MARKKAA
5.5000 g., Aluminum-Bronze, 25 mm. **Obv:** Rampant lion left within circle, date below **Rev:** Tree right of denomination

Date	Mintage	F	VF	XF	Unc	BU
1952 H	991,000	2.00	5.00	20.00	40.00	—
1953 H	10,300,000	0.25	0.50	3.00	10.00	—
1954 H	1,170,000	2.00	5.00	20.00	40.00	—
1955 H	583,000	2.50	5.00	25.00	50.00	—
1956 H	792,000	2.00	5.00	20.00	40.00	—
1958 H	242,000	25.00	40.00	60.00	75.00	—

Date	Mintage	F	VF	XF	Unc	BU
1960 S	110,000	25.00	50.00	75.00	100	—
1961 S	1,811,000	1.00	2.00	5.00	15.00	—
1962 S	405,000	2.00	4.00	15.00	25.00	—

KM# 28   100 MARKKAA
4.2105 g., 0.9000 Gold 0.1218 oz. AGW, 18.5 mm. **Obv:** Rampant lion left divides date **Rev:** Denomination flanked by sprigs

Date	Mintage	F	VF	XF	Unc	BU
1926 S	50,000	—	1,000	1,250	1,450	—

KM# 41   100 MARKKAA
5.2000 g., 0.5000 Silver 0.0836 oz. ASW, 24 mm. **Obv:** Shielded arms above date **Rev:** Denomination surrounded by trees and tree tops

Date	Mintage	F	VF	XF	Unc	BU
1956 H	3,012,000	—	BV	1.50	3.00	—
1957 H	3,012,000	—	BV	1.50	3.00	—
1958 H	1,704,000	BV	2.00	5.00	8.00	—
1959 S	1,270,000	5.00	7.50	18.00	25.00	—
1960 S	290,000	3.50	7.00	15.00	20.00	—

KM# 29   200 MARKKAA
8.4210 g., 0.9000 Gold 0.2437 oz. AGW, 22.5 mm. **Obv:** Rampant lion left divides date **Rev:** Denomination flanked by sprigs

Date	Mintage	F	VF	XF	Unc	BU
1926 S	50,000	—	1,500	2,000	2,200	—

KM# 42   200 MARKKAA
8.3000 g., 0.5000 Silver 0.1334 oz. ASW, 27.5 mm. **Obv:** Shielded arms above date **Rev:** Denomination surrounded by trees and tree tops

Date	Mintage	F	VF	XF	Unc	BU
1956 H	1,552,000	—	BV	3.00	7.00	—
1957 H	2,157,000	—	BV	3.00	7.00	—
1958 H	1,477,000	BV	2.50	5.00	10.00	—
1958 S	34,000	400	600	750	850	—
1959 S	70,000	25.00	40.00	55.00	70.00	—

KM# 35   500 MARKKAA
12.0000 g., 0.5000 Silver 0.1929 oz. ASW, 32 mm. **Obv:** Wreath divides denomination **Rev:** Olympic logo above date

Date	Mintage	F	VF	XF	Unc	BU
1951 H	19,000	300	400	450	500	—
1952 H	586,000	20.00	28.00	40.00	50.00	—

KM# 43 1000 MARKKAA
14.0000 g., 0.8750 Silver 0.3938 oz. ASW, 32 mm.
Subject: Markka Currency System Centennial - Snellman
Obv: Head left, date below **Rev:** Denomination within wreath

Date	Mintage	F	VF	XF	Unc	BU
1960 S-J	201,000	7.00	10.00	20.00	30.00	—

REFORM COINAGE
100 Old Markka = 1 New Markka 1963

KM# 44 PENNI
1.6000 g., Copper, 15.8 mm. **Obv:** Four joined loops form design, date below **Rev:** Grasped hands flank denomination

Date	Mintage	F	VF	XF	Unc	BU
1963	171,333,000	—	0.15	0.25	1.50	—
	Note: Struck at Leningrad Mint					
1964	49,300,000	—	0.15	0.50	2.00	—
1965	43,112,000	—	0.15	0.50	2.00	—
1966	36,880,000	—	0.15	0.50	2.00	—
1967	62,792,000	—	0.15	0.50	2.00	—
1968	73,416,000	—	—	0.50	2.00	—
1969	51,748,000	—	—	0.50	2.00	—

KM# 44a PENNI
0.4500 g., Aluminum, 15.8 mm. **Obv:** Four joined loops form design, date below **Rev:** Grasped hands flank denomination

Date	Mintage	F	VF	XF	Unc	BU
1969	28,524,000	—	—	0.50	2.00	—
1970	85,140,000	—	—	0.20	1.00	—
1971	70,240,000	—	—	0.20	1.00	—
1972	95,096,000	—	—	0.20	1.00	—
1973	115,532,000	—	—	0.20	0.50	—
1974	100,132,000	—	—	0.20	0.50	—
1975	111,906,000	—	—	0.20	0.50	—
1976	34,965,000	—	—	0.20	0.50	—
1977	61,393,000	—	—	0.20	0.50	—
1978	90,132,000	—	—	0.20	0.50	—
1979	33,388,000	—	—	0.20	0.50	—

KM# 45 5 PENNIA
2.6000 g., Copper, 18.5 mm. **Obv:** Four joined loops form design, date below **Rev:** Grasped hands flank denomination

Date	Mintage	F	VF	XF	Unc	BU
1963	60,320,000	—	0.15	0.50	1.50	—
1964	4,634,000	0.50	1.00	5.00	15.00	—
1965	10,264,000	—	0.15	0.50	2.00	—
1966	8,064,000	—	0.15	0.50	3.00	—
1967	9,968,000	—	0.15	0.50	2.00	—
1968	6,144,000	—	0.15	0.50	2.00	—
1969	3,598,000	—	0.15	0.50	2.00	—
1970	13,772,000	—	0.15	0.25	1.00	—
1971	20,010,000	—	—	0.25	1.00	—
1972	24,122,000	—	—	0.25	1.00	—
1973	25,644,000	—	—	0.25	1.00	—
1974	21,530,000	—	—	0.25	1.00	—
1975	25,010,000	—	—	0.25	1.00	—
1976	25,551,000	—	—	0.25	1.00	—
1977	1,489,000	—	0.10	0.50	1.50	—

KM# 45a 5 PENNIA
0.8000 g., Aluminum, 18 mm. **Obv:** Four joined loops form design, date below **Rev:** Grasped hands flank denomination

---

Date	Mintage	F	VF	XF	Unc	BU
1977	30,552,000	—	—	0.15	0.50	—
1978	26,112,000	—	—	0.15	0.50	—
1979	40,042,000	—	—	0.15	0.50	—
1980	60,026,000	—	—	0.15	0.50	—
1981	2,044,000	—	0.20	0.40	1.00	—
1982	10,012,000	—	—	0.25	0.75	—
1983	33,885,000	—	—	—	0.25	—
1984	25,001,000	—	—	—	0.25	—
1985	25,000,000	—	—	—	0.25	—
1986	20,000,000	—	—	—	0.25	—
1987	2,020,000	—	—	—	0.25	—
1988	33,005,000	—	—	—	0.15	—
1989	2,200,000	—	—	—	0.50	—
1990	2,506,000	—	—	—	0.50	—

KM# 46 10 PENNIA
3.0000 g., Aluminum-Bronze, 20 mm. **Obv:** Rampant lion left, date below **Rev:** Tree right of denomination

Date	Mintage	F	VF	XF	Unc	BU
1963 S	38,420,000	—	0.15	0.50	1.50	—
1964 S	6,926,000	—	0.15	1.00	3.00	—
1965 S	4,524,000	—	0.15	0.50	3.00	—
1966 S	3,094,000	—	0.15	0.50	2.00	—
1967 S	1,050,000	0.15	0.30	3.00	10.00	—
1968 S	3,004,000	—	0.15	0.25	1.50	—
1969 S	5,046,000	—	—	0.20	1.50	—
1970 S	3,996,000	—	—	0.20	1.50	—
1971 S	15,026,000	—	—	0.10	1.00	—
1972 S	19,900,000	—	—	0.10	1.00	—
1973 S	9,196,000	—	—	0.10	1.00	—
1974 S	8,930,000	—	—	0.10	0.50	—
1975 S	15,064,000	—	—	0.10	0.50	—
1976 K	10,063,000	—	—	0.10	0.50	—
1977 K	10,043,000	—	—	0.10	0.50	—
1978 K	10,062,000	—	—	0.10	0.50	—
1979 K	13,072,000	—	—	0.10	0.50	—
1980 K	23,654,000	—	—	0.10	0.50	—
1981 K	30,036,000	—	—	0.10	0.50	—
1982 K	35,548,000	—	—	0.10	0.50	—

KM# 46a 10 PENNIA
1.0000 g., Aluminum, 20 mm. **Obv:** Rampant lion left, date below **Rev:** Tree right of denomination

Date	Mintage	F	VF	XF	Unc	BU
1983 K	6,320,000	—	—	0.25	1.00	—
1983 N	4,191,000	—	—	0.25	1.00	—
1984 N	20,061,000	—	—	0.10	0.50	—
1985 N	20,000,000	—	—	0.10	0.50	—
1986 N	15,000,000	—	—	0.10	0.50	—
1987 M	8,654,000	—	—	0.25	1.00	—
1987 N	1,400,000	—	—	0.25	1.00	—
1988 M	23,197,000	—	—	0.10	0.50	—
1989 M	2,400,000	—	—	0.25	0.50	—
1990 M	2,254,000	—	—	0.25	0.50	—

KM# 65 10 PENNIA
1.8000 g., Copper-Nickel, 16.3 mm. **Obv:** Flower pods and stems, date at right **Rev:** Denomination to right of honeycombs

Date	Mintage	F	VF	XF	Unc	BU
1990 M	338,100,000	—	—	0.10	0.15	—
1991 M	263,899,000	—	—	0.10	0.15	—
1992 M	136,131,000	—	—	0.10	0.15	—
1993 M	56,206,000	—	—	0.10	0.15	—
1994 M	59,946,000	—	—	0.10	0.15	—
1994 M Proof	5,000	Value: 7.00				
1995 M	85,000,000	—	—	0.10	0.15	—
1995 M Proof	3,000	Value: 7.00				
1996 M	123,000,000	—	—	0.10	0.15	—
1996 M Proof	1,200	Value: 7.00				
1997 M	43,406,000	—	—	0.10	0.15	—
1997 M Proof	2,000	Value: 7.00				
1998 M	95,322,000	—	—	0.10	0.15	—
1998 M Proof	2,000	Value: 7.00				
1999 M	46,375,000	—	—	0.10	0.15	—
1999 M Proof	—	Value: 7.00				
2000 M	114,903,000	—	—	—	0.15	—
2000 M Proof	—	Value: 7.00				

KM# 47 20 PENNIA
4.5000 g., Aluminum-Bronze, 22.5 mm. **Obv:** Rampant lion left, date below **Rev:** Tree right of denomination

---

Date	Mintage	F	VF	XF	Unc	BU
1963 S	39,970,000	—	0.15	0.20	1.50	—
1964 S	4,248,000	0.50	1.00	2.50	5.00	—
1965 S	5,704,000	0.10	0.50	1.00	3.00	—
1966 S	4,085,000	0.10	0.50	1.00	3.00	—
1967 S	1,716,000	0.10	0.50	1.00	3.00	—
1968 S	1,330,000	0.10	0.50	1.00	3.00	—
1969 S	201,000	0.50	1.00	2.00	4.00	—
1970 S	230,000	0.50	1.00	2.00	3.50	—
1971 S	5,150,000	—	0.25	0.50	1.00	—

Note: Some coins dated 1971 are magnetic and command a higher premium

Date	Mintage	F	VF	XF	Unc	BU
1972 S	10,001,000	—	0.25	0.50	1.00	—
1973 S	9,462,000	—	0.25	0.50	1.00	—
1974 S	12,705,000	—	0.25	0.50	1.00	—
1975 S	12,068,000	—	0.25	0.50	1.00	—
1976 K	20,058,000	—	0.25	0.50	1.00	—
1977 K	10,063,000	—	0.25	0.50	1.00	—
1978 K	10,014,000	—	0.25	0.50	1.00	—
1979 K	7,513,000	—	0.25	0.50	1.00	—
1980 K	20,047,000	—	—	0.25	0.50	—
1981 K	30,002,000	—	—	0.25	0.50	—
1982 K	35,050,000	—	—	0.25	0.50	—
1983 K	7,113,000	—	—	0.25	0.50	—
1983 N	12,889,000	—	—	0.25	0.50	—
1984 N	20,029,000	—	—	0.25	0.50	—
1985 N	15,004,000	—	—	0.25	0.50	—
1986 N	20,001,000	—	—	0.25	0.50	—
1987 M	25,670,000	—	—	0.25	0.50	—
1987 N	1,200,000	—	0.25	0.50	1.00	—
1988 M	13,853,000	—	—	0.25	0.50	—
1989 M	40,695,000	—	—	0.25	0.50	—
1990 M	9,168,000	—	—	0.25	0.50	—

KM# 48 50 PENNIA
5.5000 g., Aluminum-Bronze, 25.0 mm. **Obv:** Rampant lion left, date below **Rev:** Tree right of denomination

Date	Mintage	F	VF	XF	Unc	BU
1963 S	17,316,000	—	0.20	0.50	3.00	—
1964 S	3,101,000	—	0.25	3.00	10.00	—
1965 S	1,667,000	—	0.20	2.00	5.00	—
1966 S	1,051,000	—	0.20	2.00	7.50	—
1967 S	400,000	0.25	0.50	2.00	5.00	—
1968 S	816,000	—	0.25	1.00	4.00	—
1969 S	1,341,000	—	0.20	0.50	3.00	—
1970 S	2,250,000	—	0.20	0.50	2.00	—
1971 S	10,003,000	—	0.20	0.50	1.50	—

Note: Some coins dated 1971 are magnetic and command a higher premium

Date	Mintage	F	VF	XF	Unc	BU
1972 S	7,892,000	—	0.20	0.50	1.50	—
1973 S	5,428,000	—	0.20	0.50	1.50	—
1974 S	5,049,000	—	0.20	0.50	1.50	—
1975 S	4,305,000	—	0.20	0.50	1.50	—
1976 K	7,022,000	—	0.20	0.50	1.50	—
1977 K	8,077,000	—	0.20	0.50	1.50	—
1978 K	8,048,000	—	0.20	0.50	1.50	—
1979 K	8,004,000	—	0.20	0.50	1.50	—
1980 K	5,349,000	—	0.20	0.50	1.50	—
1981 K	20,031,000	—	0.20	0.50	1.00	—
1982 K	5,042,000	—	0.20	0.50	1.50	—
1983 K	4,043,999	—	—	0.25	1.50	—
1983 N	1,016,000	—	—	0.25	1.50	—
1984 N	3,006,000	—	—	0.25	1.00	—
1985 N	10,000,000	—	—	0.25	1.00	—
1986 N	9,002,000	—	—	0.25	1.00	—
1987 N	700,000	—	0.30	0.75	1.50	—
1987 M	4,305,000	—	—	0.25	1.00	—
1988 M	14,735,000	—	—	0.25	1.00	—
1989 M	10,651,000	—	—	0.25	1.00	—
1990 M	5,391,000	—	—	0.50	2.00	—

KM# 66 50 PENNIA
3.3000 g., Copper-Nickel, 19.7 mm. **Obv:** Polar bear, date below **Rev:** Denomination above flower heads

Date	Mintage	F	VF	XF	Unc	BU
1990 M	70,459,000	—	—	0.20	0.75	—
1991 M	90,480,000	—	—	0.20	0.75	—
1992 M	58,996,000	—	—	0.20	0.75	—
1993 M	10,066,000	—	—	0.20	0.75	—
1994 M	3,005,000	—	—	0.20	0.75	—
1994 M Proof	5,000	Value: 8.00				
1995 M	1,048,000	—	—	0.20	0.75	—
1995 M Proof	3,000	Value: 8.00				
1996 M	17,000,000	—	—	0.20	0.75	—
1996 M Proof	1,200	Value: 8.00				
1997 M	524,000	—	—	0.20	1.00	—
1997 M Proof	2,000	Value: 8.00				
1998 M	3,345,500	—	—	0.20	0.75	—
1998 M Proof	2,000	Value: 8.00				
1999 M	100,000	—	—	0.20	1.00	—
1999 M Proof	—	Value: 8.00				
2000 M	100,000	—	—	0.20	1.00	—
2000 M Proof	—	Value: 8.00				

KM# 49   MARKKA
6.4000 g., 0.3500 Silver 0.0720 oz. ASW, 24 mm.
Obv: Rampant lion left, date below **Rev:** Stylized fir trees with denomination in center, SUOMI FINLAND

Date	Mintage	F	VF	XF	Unc	BU
1964 S	9,999,000	BV	1.20	2.00	5.00	—
1965 S	15,107,000	—	BV	1.50	4.00	—
1966 S	15,183,000	—	BV	1.50	3.00	—
1967 S	6,249,000	—	BV	1.50	3.00	—
1968 S	3,063,000	—	BV	1.50	3.00	—

KM# 49a   MARKKA
6.1000 g., Copper-Nickel, 24 mm. **Obv:** Rampant lion left, date below **Rev:** Denomination flanked by stylized fir trees, SUOMI FINLAND

Date	Mintage	F	VF	XF	Unc	BU
1969 S	1,308,000	0.25	0.50	1.00	2.00	—
1970 S	12,255,000	—	0.35	0.50	1.00	—
1971 S	19,676,000	—	0.35	0.50	1.00	—
1972 S	19,885,000	—	0.35	0.50	1.00	—
1973 S	17,060,000	—	0.35	0.50	1.00	—
1974 S	18,065,000	—	0.35	0.50	1.00	—
1975 S	11,523,000	—	0.35	0.50	1.00	—
1976 K	12,048,000	—	0.35	0.50	1.00	—
1977 K	10,077,000	—	0.35	0.50	1.00	—
1978 K	10,022,000	—	0.35	0.50	1.00	—
1979 K	11,311,000	—	0.35	0.50	1.00	—
1980 K	19,306,000	—	—	0.35	0.75	—
1981 K	32,003,000	—	—	0.35	0.75	—
1982 K	30,001,000	—	—	0.35	0.75	—
1983 K	8,074,999	—	—	0.35	0.75	—
1983 N	11,927,000	—	—	0.35	0.75	—
1984 N	15,000,000	—	—	0.35	0.75	—
1985 N	19,001,000	—	—	0.35	0.75	—
1986 N	10,000,000	—	—	0.35	0.75	—
1987 M	9,303,000	—	—	0.35	0.75	—
1987 N	700,000	—	0.50	1.00	2.00	—
1988 M	27,535,000	—	—	0.35	0.75	—
1989 M	37,520,000	—	—	0.35	0.75	—
1990 M	50,305,000	—	—	0.35	0.75	—
1991 M	15,026,000	—	—	0.35	0.75	—
1992 M	3,628,000	—	—	0.35	0.75	—
1993 M	1,036,000	—	—	0.50	1.00	—

KM# 76   MARKKA
4.9000 g., Aluminum-Bronze, 22 mm. **Obv:** Rampant lion left within circle, date below **Rev:** Ornaments flank denomination within circle

Date	Mintage	F	VF	XF	Unc	BU
1993 M	91,588,000	—	—	0.35	0.75	—
1994 M	152,011,000	—	—	0.35	0.75	—
1994 M Proof	5,000	Value: 10.00				
1995 M	40,008,000	—	—	0.35	0.75	—
1995 M Proof	3,000	Value: 10.00				
1996 M	21,000,000	—	—	0.35	0.75	—
1996 M Proof	1,200	Value: 10.00				
1997 M	23,775,200	—	—	0.35	0.75	—
1997 M Proof	2,000	Value: 10.00				
1998 M	33,955,200	—	—	0.35	0.75	—
1998 M Proof	2,000	Value: 10.00				
1999 M	100,000	—	—	0.35	0.75	—
1999 M Proof	—	Value: 10.00				
2000 M	100,000	—	—	0.35	0.75	—
2000 M Proof	—	Value: 10.00				

KM# 76a   MARKKA
Copper-Nickel **Obv:** Rampant lion left within circle, date below **Rev:** Ornaments flank denomination

Date	Mintage	F	VF	XF	Unc	BU
1993 M	100,000	—	—	—	—	—

Note: In sets only

KM# 53   5 MARKKAA
8.0000 g., Aluminum-Bronze, 26.3 mm. **Obv:** Icebreaker "Varma", date below **Rev:** Stylized flock of birds, REPUBLIKEN FINLAND SUOMEN TASAVALTA

Date	Mintage	F	VF	XF	Unc	BU
1972 S	400,000	1.50	2.00	2.50	4.00	—
1973 S	2,188,000	—	1.25	2.00	3.00	—
1974 S	300,000	—	1.25	2.00	3.00	—
1975 S	300,000	—	1.25	2.00	3.00	—
1976 K	400,000	—	1.25	2.00	3.00	—
1977 K	300,000	—	1.25	2.00	3.00	—
1978 K	300,000	—	1.25	2.00	3.00	—

KM# 57   5 MARKKAA
8.0000 g., Aluminum-Bronze, 26.3 mm. **Obv:** Icebreaker "Urho", date below **Rev:** Stylized flock of birds with denomination at top

Date	Mintage	F	VF	XF	Unc	BU
1979 K	2,005,000	—	—	1.50	2.25	—
1980 K	501,000	—	1.50	2.00	3.00	—
1981 K	1,009,000	—	—	1.50	2.25	—
1982 K	3,004,000	—	—	1.50	2.25	—
1983 K	8,776,000	—	—	1.50	2.25	—
1983 N	11,230,000	—	—	1.50	2.25	—
1984 N	15,001,000	—	—	1.50	2.25	—
1985 N	8,005,000	—	—	1.50	2.25	—
1986 N	5,006,000	—	—	1.50	2.25	—
1987 N	660,000	—	1.50	2.00	3.00	—
1987 M	2,348,000	—	—	1.50	2.25	—
1988 M	3,042,000	—	—	1.50	2.25	—
1989 M	10,175,000	—	—	1.50	2.25	—
1990 M	9,925,000	—	—	1.50	2.25	—
1991 M	9,910,000	—	—	2.00	3.00	—
1992 M	547,000	—	—	2.00	3.00	—
1993 M	911,000	—	—	2.00	3.00	—

KM# 73   5 MARKKAA
5.5000 g., Copper-Aluminum-Nickel, 24.5 mm. **Obv:** Lake Saimaa ringed seal, date below **Rev:** Denomination, dragonfly and lily pad leaves

Date	Mintage	F	VF	XF	Unc	BU
1992 M	800,000	—	—	—	3.50	6.00
1993 M	46,034,000	—	—	—	2.00	5.00
1994 M	19,003,000	—	—	—	2.00	5.00
1994 M Proof	5,000	Value: 12.00				
1995 M	9,016,000	—	—	—	2.50	5.00
1995 M Proof	3,000	Value: 12.00				
1996 M	7,000,000	—	—	—	2.50	5.00
1996 M Proof	1,200	Value: 12.00				
1997 M	537,700	—	—	2.00	3.00	5.00
1997 M Proof	2,000	Value: 12.00				
1998 M	813,650	—	—	—	2.50	5.00
1998 M Proof	2,000	Value: 12.00				
1999 M	100,000	—	—	—	2.50	5.00
1999 M Proof	—	Value: 12.00				
2000 M	100,000	—	—	—	2.50	5.00
2000 M Proof	—	Value: 12.00				

KM# 50   10 MARKKAA
23.7500 g., 0.9000 Silver 0.6872 oz. ASW, 35 mm.
Subject: 50th Anniversary of Independence **Obv:** Five Whooper swans in flight, date above **Rev:** Design above denomination, ITSENAINEN SUOMI 50 FINLAND SJALVSTANDIGT 50

Date	Mintage	F	VF	XF	Unc	BU
1967 S-H	1,000,000	—	—	BV	8.00	10.00

KM# 51   10 MARKKAA
22.7500 g., 0.5000 Silver 0.3657 oz. ASW, 35 mm.
Subject: Centennial - Birth of President Paasikivi
Obv: Denomination below date, brick wall background **Rev:** Head facing

Date	Mintage	F	VF	XF	Unc	BU
1970 S-H	600,000	—	—	BV	4.50	5.00

KM# 52   10 MARKKAA
24.2000 g., 0.5000 Silver 0.3890 oz. ASW, 35 mm. **Subject:** 10th European Athletic Championships **Obv:** Denomination above city scene **Rev:** Runners on track, date lower right

Date	Mintage	F	VF	XF	Unc	BU
1971 S-H	1,000,000	—	—	BV	4.50	5.00

KM# 54   10 MARKKAA
23.5000 g., 0.5000 Silver 0.3778 oz. ASW, 35 mm. **Subject:** 75th Birthday of President Kekkonen **Obv:** Denomination below trees, hills in background **Rev:** Head facing

Date	Mintage	F	VF	XF	Unc	BU
1975 S-H	1,000,000	—	—	BV	4.50	5.00

KM# 55   10 MARKKAA
21.7800 g., 0.5000 Silver 0.3501 oz. ASW, 35 mm.
Subject: 60th Anniversary of Independence **Obv:** Four line inscription superimposed over five line inscription, date at left **Rev:** Crowds of people, denomination upper right

Date	Mintage	F	VF	XF	Unc	BU
1977 K-H	400,000	—	—	BV	4.50	5.00

KM# 77   10 MARKKAA
8.8000 g., Bi-Metallic Brass center in Copper-Nickel ring, 27.25 mm. **Obv:** Capercaillie bird within circle, date above **Rev:** Denomination and branches

Date	Mintage	F	VF	XF	Unc	BU
1993 M	30,002,000	—	—	2.00	3.50	5.00
1994 M	19,979,000	—	—	2.00	3.50	5.00
1994 M Proof	5,000	Value: 18.00				
1995 M	4,008,000	—	—	2.00	3.50	5.00
1995 M Proof	3,000	Value: 18.00				
1996 M	3,300,000	—	—	2.00	3.50	5.00
1996 M Proof	1,200	Value: 18.00				
1997 M	917,607	—	—	2.00	3.50	5.00
1997 M Proof	2,000	Value: 18.00				
1998 M	797,713	—	—	2.00	3.50	5.00
1998 M Proof	2,000	Value: 18.00				
1999 M	100,000	—	—	—	3.00	6.00
1999 M Proof	—	Value: 18.00				
2000 M	100,000	—	—	—	3.00	6.00
2000 M Proof	—	Value: 18.00				

KM# 82   10 MARKKAA
8.0000 g., Bi-Metallic Brass center in Copper-Nickel ring, 27.25 mm. **Subject:** European Unity **Obv:** Swan in flight within circle, date upper right **Rev:** Denomination and branches

Date	Mintage	F	VF	XF	Unc	BU
1995 M	500,000	—	—	2.50	4.50	6.00

KM# 82a   10 MARKKAA
Bi-Metallic Gold center in Silver ring, 27.25 mm. **Subject:** European Unity **Obv:** Swan in flight left within circle **Rev:** Denomination and branches **Note:** Total weight 12.200 grams.

Date	Mintage	F	VF	XF	Unc	BU
1995 M Proof	2,000	Value: 2,500				

KM# 91   10 MARKKAA
8.8200 g., Bi-Metallic Copper-Nickel center in Brass ring, 27.25 mm. **Obv:** Fire breathing profile left, date at right **Rev:** Denomination and branches **Note:** Finnish Presidency of the EU.

Date	Mintage	F	VF	XF	Unc	BU
1999M	100,000	—	—	—	10.00	12.50

KM# 91a   10 MARKKAA
13.2000 g., Bi-Metallic .925 Silver center in .75 Gold ring, 27.25 mm. **Obv:** Fire breathing profile left **Rev:** Denomination and branches **Edge:** Lettered **Note:** Total weight 13.200 grams.

Date	Mintage	F	VF	XF	Unc	BU
1999	3,000	—	—	—	1,000	1,150

KM# 56   25 MARKKAA
26.3000 g., 0.5000 Silver 0.4228 oz. ASW, 37 mm. **Subject:** Winter Games in Lahti **Obv:** Ski trail, denomination at left

Date	Mintage	F	VF	XF	Unc	BU
1978 K-N	500,000	—	—	5.00	7.00	9.00

KM# 58   25 MARKKAA
26.3000 g., 0.5000 Silver 0.4228 oz. ASW, 37 mm. **Subject:** 750th Anniversary of Turku **Obv:** School of fish, denomination above **Rev:** City scene with dates

Date	Mintage	F	VF	XF	Unc	BU
1979 K-H	300,000	—	—	5.00	7.00	9.00

KM# 85   25 MARKKAA
20.2000 g., Bi-Metallic Brass center in Copper-Nickel ring, 35 mm. **Subject:** 80th Anniversary of Independence **Obv:** Stylized landscape, dates below **Rev:** Stylized city view, denomination below

Date	Mintage	F	VF	XF	Unc	BU
ND(1997) M-L	100,000	—	—	12.50	15.00	
ND(1997) M-L Proof	2,000	Value: 16.50				

Note: In sets only

KM# 59   50 MARKKAA
20.0000 g., 0.5000 Silver 0.3215 oz. ASW, 30 mm. **Subject:** 80th Birthday of President Kekkonen **Obv:** Head 3/4 facing **Rev:** Horses, denomination above

Date	Mintage	F	VF	XF	Unc	BU
1981 K	500,000	—	—	5.00	7.00	9.00

KM# 60   50 MARKKAA
23.1000 g., 0.5000 Silver 0.3713 oz. ASW, 35 mm.
Subject: World Ice Hockey Championship Games
Obv: Denomination **Rev:** Hockey player, date at right

Date	Mintage	F	VF	XF	Unc	BU
1982 K-T	400,000	—	—	7.50	9.00	12.00

KM# 61   50 MARKKAA
21.8000 g., 0.5000 Silver 0.3504 oz. ASW, 35 mm.
Subject: 1st World Athletics Championships **Obv:** Trees divide denomination **Rev:** Hurdler, date at right

Date	Mintage	F	VF	XF	Unc	BU
1983 K-M	450,000	—	—	7.50	9.00	12.00

KM# 62   50 MARKKAA
19.9000 g., 0.5000 Silver 0.3199 oz. ASW, 35 mm.
Subject: National Epic - The Kalevala **Obv:** Trees with reflections, denomination at right **Rev:** Stylized waves with figure, dates below

Date	Mintage	F	VF	XF	Unc	BU
1985 P-N	300,000	—	—	8.00	10.00	14.50

KM# 74   100 MARKKAA
24.0000 g., 0.8300 Silver 0.6404 oz. ASW **Subject:** World Nordic Skiing Championships, Lahti, Finland 1989 **Obv:** Marjo Matikainen (5 km ski champion in 1988 Calgary Olympics)

Date	Mintage	F	VF	XF	Unc	BU
1989 M-L-M	100,000	—	—	25.00	35.00	

KM# 75   100 MARKKAA
24.0000 g., 0.8300 Silver 0.6404 oz. ASW **Subject:** Pictorial

Arts of Finland **Obv:** Artistic design, denomination above
Rev: Two figures holding artists palette, date at right

Date	Mintage	F	VF	XF	Unc	BU
1989 P-M	100,000	—	—	25.00	35.00	50.00

KM# 67   100 MARKKAA
24.0000 g., 0.8300 Silver 0.6404 oz. ASW **Subject:** 50th
Anniversary of Disabled War Veterans Association **Obv:** Home
and landscape scene, denomination above **Rev:** Cross
superimposed on people, date below

Date	Mintage	F	VF	XF	Unc	BU
1990 P-M	100,000	—	—	25.00	35.00	40.00

KM# 68   100 MARKKAA
24.0000 g., 0.8300 Silver 0.6404 oz. ASW **Subject:** 350th
Anniversary - University of Helsinki **Obv:** Owl, denomination
below **Rev:** Harp within square, dates below

Date	Mintage	F	VF	XF	Unc	BU
1990 H-M	150,000	—	—	30.00	40.00	60.00

KM# 69   100 MARKKAA
24.0000 g., 0.8300 Silver 0.6404 oz. ASW **Subject:** Ice Hockey
World Championship Games **Obv:** Stylized design, date lower
right **Rev:** Stylized hockey player, denomination below

Date	Mintage	F	VF	XF	Unc	BU
1991 L-M	150,000	—	—	25.00	35.00	40.00
1991 L-M Proof	200	Value: 500				

Note: Struck with polished dies to prooflike quality and encapsulated in hard plastic 60 mm x 83 mm square;
these pieces were given out as business gifts to selected mint visitors

KM# 70   100 MARKKAA
24.0000 g., 0.9250 Silver 0.7137 oz. ASW **Subject:** 70th
Anniversary - Autonomy of Aland **Obv:** Masted ship at sea,
denomination above **Rev:** Stag on crowned shield, dates below

Date	Mintage	F	VF	XF	Unc	BU
1991 P-M	100,000	—	—	25.00	35.00	40.00
1991 P-M	Est. 700	Value: 400				

Note: Encapsulated as KM#69 above, but struck to higher
prooflike quality

KM# 71   100 MARKKAA
24.0000 g., 0.9250 Silver 0.7137 oz. ASW **Subject:** 75th
Anniversary of Independence **Obv:** Pine trees **Rev:** Artistic
design, denomination below

Date	Mintage	F	VF	XF	Unc	BU
1992 M-S	300,000	—	—	20.00	22.50	25.00

KM# 78   100 MARKKAA
24.0000 g., 0.9250 Silver 0.7137 oz. ASW **Subject:** Stadium of
Friendship **Obv:** Laurel sprig, stylized stadium, denomination
above **Rev:** Sprinters, date above

Date	Mintage	F	VF	XF	Unc	BU
1994 P-M	80,000	—	—	—	22.50	25.00

Note: Encapsulated as KM#69 above, but struck to higher
proof quality
| 1994 P-M Proof | 15,000 | Value: 30.00 |

KM# 80   100 MARKKAA
24.0000 g., 0.9250 Silver 0.7137 oz. ASW **Subject:** 100th
Birthday - Artturi Ilmari Virtanen **Obv:** Budding branch,
denomination below **Rev:** Head right

Date	Mintage	F	VF	XF	Unc	BU
1995 S-M	40,000	—	—	30.00	35.00	40.00
1995 S-M Proof	3,000	Value: 65.00				

KM# 81   100 MARKKAA
24.0000 g., 0.9250 Silver 0.7137 oz. ASW **Subject:** 50th
Anniversary - United Nations **Obv:** Design, denomination at left,
date below **Rev:** Face foreward, dates at right

Date	Mintage	F	VF	XF	Unc	BU
1995 P-M	40,000	—	—	—	35.00	40.00
1995 P-M Proof	3,000	Value: 65.00				

KM# 83   100 MARKKAA
24.0000 g., 0.9250 Silver 0.7137 oz. ASW **Subject:** Helene
Schjerfbeck - Painter - 50th Anniversary of Her Death

Date	Mintage	F	VF	XF	Unc	BU
1996 T-M	300,000	—	—	—	60.00	75.00
1996 T-M Proof	3,000	Value: 150				

KM# 84   100 MARKKAA
22.0000 g., 0.9250 Silver 0.6542 oz. ASW **Subject:** 100th
Birthday - Paavo Nurmi **Obv:** Two gymnasts **Rev:** Facial portrait
and running Paavo Nurmi, denomination below

Date	Mintage	F	VF	XF	Unc	BU
1997 M-S	45,000	—	—	30.00	35.00	40.00
1997 M-S Proof	6,500	Value: 65.00				

KM# 87   100 MARKKAA
22.0000 g., 0.9250 Silver 0.6542 oz. ASW **Subject:** 100th
Birthday - Alvar Aalto **Obv:** Walls above cliffs and denominations
Rev: Mature rye plants, dates in vertical at right

Date	Mintage	F	VF	XF	Unc	BU
1998 M-G	Est. 44,000	—	—	—	25.00	30.00
1998 M-G Proof	4,000	Value: 65.00				

KM# 88   100 MARKKAA
22.0000 g., 0.9250 Silver 0.6542 oz. ASW **Subject:**
Suomenlinna Fortress **Obv:** Stylized island view, denomination
below **Rev:** Sailship and fortress gate, dates at right

Date	Mintage	F	VF	XF	Unc	BU
1998 M-O	30,000	—	—	25.00	30.00	35.00
1998 M-O Proof	3,300	Value: 65.00				

KM# 89   100 MARKKAA
22.0000 g., 0.9250 Silver 0.6542 oz. ASW **Subject:** Jean Sibelius - Composer **Obv:** Head left **Rev:** Finlandia musical score divides date and denomination

Date	Mintage	F	VF	XF	Unc	BU
1999 P-V-M	30,000	—	—	25.00	28.00	30.00
1999 P-V-M Proof	6,000	Value: 50.00				

KM# 92   100 MARKKAA
22.0000 g., 0.9250 Silver 0.6542 oz. ASW **Subject:** Jubilee Year 2000 **Obv:** Turku Cathedral vault ceiling design, denomination below **Rev:** Leaf within circle, date below **Edge:** Plain

Date	Mintage	F	VF	XF	Unc	BU
2000M L-M	15,000	—	—	50.00	60.00	70.00
2000M L-M Proof	3,000	Value: 80.00				

KM# 93   100 MARKKAA
22.0000 g., 0.9250 Silver 0.6542 oz. ASW **Subject:** 450th Anniversary - Helsinki Cultural Capital **Obv:** Symbolic column design **Rev:** Carved city view, denomination upper left **Edge:** Plain

Date	Mintage	F	VF	XF	Unc	BU
2000 P-M	10,000	—	—	35.00	50.00	60.00

KM# 94   100 MARKKAA
22.0000 g., 0.9250 Silver 0.6542 oz. ASW, 35 mm. **Subject:** Aleksis Kivi **Obv:** Books on shelves, denomination below **Rev:** Portrait on partial disc, facing left, date at left **Edge:** Plain

Date	Mintage	F	VF	XF	Unc	BU
2000M T-M	10,000	—	—	—	30.00	40.00
2000M T-M Proof	6,000	Value: 70.00				

KM# 72   1000 MARKKAA
9.0000 g., 0.9000 Gold 0.2604 oz. AGW, 22.1 mm. **Subject:** 75th Anniversary of Independence **Obv:** Dates above design **Rev:** Denomination below design

Date	Mintage	F	VF	XF	Unc	BU
1992 M-S	35,000	—	—	—	230	240

KM# 86   1000 MARKKAA
8.6400 g., 0.9000 Gold 0.2500 oz. AGW **Subject:** 80th Anniversary of Independence **Obv:** New shoot growing from tree stump, denomination above **Rev:** Symbolic design separating dates

Date	Mintage	F	VF	XF	Unc	BU
ND (1997) M-P Proof	20,000	Value: 300				

KM# 90   1000 MARKKAA
8.6400 g., 0.9000 Gold 0.2500 oz. AGW **Subject:** Jean Sibelius - Composer **Obv:** Head left **Rev:** Finlandia musical score, denomination above, date below

Date	Mintage	F	VF	XF	Unc	BU
1999 P-V-M Proof	25,000	Value: 350				

KM# 79   2000 MARKKAA
16.9700 g., 0.9000 Gold 0.4910 oz. AGW, 28 mm. **Subject:** 50 Years of Peace **Obv:** Design at center, date below **Rev:** Design above denomination

Date	Mintage	F	VF	XF	Unc	BU
1995 M-L-L	6,900	Value: 700				

EURO COINAGE
European Union Issues

KM# 98   EURO CENT
2.2700 g., Copper Plated Steel, 16.3 mm. **Obv:** Rampant lion left surrounded by stars, date at left **Rev:** Denomination and globe **Edge:** Plain

Date	Mintage	F	VF	XF	Unc	BU
1999M	8,100,000	—	—	—	1.25	—
1999M Proof	—	—	—	—	—	—
2000M	7,600,000	—	—	—	3.50	—
2000M Proof	—	—	—	—	—	—

KM# 99   2 EURO CENT
3.0000 g., Copper Plated Steel, 18.7 mm. **Obv:** Rampant lion surrounded by stars, date at left **Rev:** Denomination and globe **Edge:** Grooved

Date	Mintage	F	VF	XF	Unc	BU
1999M	1,785,000	—	—	—	1.25	—
1999M Proof	—	—	—	—	—	—
2000M	13,937,000	—	—	—	3.50	—
2000M Proof	—	—	—	—	—	—

KM# 100   5 EURO CENT
3.9400 g., Copper Plated Steel, 19.66 mm. **Obv:** Rampant lion left surrounded by stars, date at left **Rev:** Denomination and globe **Edge:** Plain

Date	Mintage	F	VF	XF	Unc	BU
1999M	63,380,000	—	—	—	1.00	—
1999M Proof	—	—	—	—	—	—
2000M	56,660,000	—	—	—	1.00	—
2000M Proof	—	—	—	—	—	—

KM# 101   10 EURO CENT
4.0000 g., Brass, 19.7 mm. **Obv:** Rampant lion left surrounded by stars, date at left **Rev:** Denomination and map **Edge:** Reeded

Date	Mintage	F	VF	XF	Unc	BU
1999M	133,520,000	—	—	—	1.25	—
1999M Proof	—	—	—	—	—	—
2000M	167,449,000	—	—	—	1.75	—
2000M Proof	—	—	—	—	—	—

KM# 102   20 EURO CENT
5.7300 g., Brass, 22.2 mm. **Obv:** Rampant lion left surrounded by stars, date at left **Rev:** Denomination and map **Edge:** Notched

Date	Mintage	F	VF	XF	Unc	BU
1999M	42,350,000	—	—	—	1.25	—
1999M Proof	—	—	—	—	—	—
2000M	500,000	—	—	—	12.00	—
2000M Proof	—	—	—	—	—	—

KM# 103   50 EURO CENT
7.8100 g., Brass, 24.2 mm. **Obv:** Rampant lion left surrounded by stars, date at left **Rev:** Denomination and map **Edge:** Reeded

Date	Mintage	F	VF	XF	Unc	BU
1999M	20,696,000	—	—	—	1.75	—
1999M Proof	—	—	—	—	—	—
2000M	67,097,000	—	—	—	1.50	—
2000M Proof	—	—	—	—	—	—

KM# 104   EURO
7.5000 g., Bi-Metallic Copper-nickel center in Brass ring, 23.2 mm. **Obv:** 2 flying swans, date below, surrounded by stars on outer ring **Rev:** Denomination and map **Edge:** Reeded and plain sections

Date	Mintage	F	VF	XF	Unc	BU
1999M	16,210,000	—	—	—	5.00	—
1999M Proof	—	—	—	—	—	—
2000M	36,639,000	—	—	—	5.00	—
2000M Proof	—	—	—	—	—	—

KM# 105   2 EURO
8.5200 g., Bi-Metallic Brass center in Copper-nickel ring, 25.6 mm. **Obv:** 2 cloudberry flowers surrounded by stars on outer ring **Rev:** Denomination and map **Edge:** Reeded and lettered, SUOMI FINLAND

Date	Mintage	F	VF	XF	Unc	BU
1999M	16,090,000	—	—	—	4.00	—
1999M Proof	—				—	—
2000M	8,680,000	—	—	—	4.00	—
2000M Proof	—				—	—

PATTERNS
Including off metal strikes

KM#	Date	Mintage Identification	Mkt Val
Pn11	1918	— 5 Pennia. Silver.	3,500
Pn12	1919	— Penni. Nickel.	—
Pn13	1921	— 10 Pennia. Iron.	—
Pn14	1922	— 5 Pennia. Silver.	—
Pn15	1923	— 50 Pennia. Copper.	—
Pn16	1923	— Markkaa. Copper.	—
Pn17	1924	— 10 Pennia. Nickel.	—
Pn18	1926	— 200 Markkaa. Copper.	—
Pn19	1927	— 10 Pennia. Copper.	—
Pn20	1936	— 25 Pennia. Copper.	—
Pn21	1936	— Markkaa. Iron.	—
Pn22	1941	— 10 Pennia. Iron.	250
Pn23	1942	— 25 Pennia. Aluminum.	—
Pn24	1942	— 50 Pennia. Aluminum.	—
Pn25	1942	— Markkaa. Aluminum.	—
Pn26	1942	— Markka. Iron-Blued.	—
Pn27	1942	— 5 Markkaa. Brass.	—
Pn28	1945	— Markkaa. Brass.	3,000
Pn29	1946	— 5 Markkaa. Nickel.	—
Pn30	1947	— 5 Markkaa. Iron.	—
Pn31	1948	— Markkaa. Aluminum.	—
Pn32	1948	— Markkaa. Bronze.	—
Pn33	1948	— 5 Markkaa. Nickel.	—
Pn34	1949	— Markkaa. Copper.	5,000
Pn35	1949	— 5 Markkaa. Iron.	—
Pn36	1950 H	— Markkaa. Brass.	2,500
Pn37	1951	— 500 Markkaa. Aluminum-Blued.	—
Pn38	1952	— Markkaa. Iron-Blued.	—
Pn39	1952	— 5 Markkaa. Iron-Blued.	—
Pn40	1952	— 10 Markkaa. Iron.	500
Pn41	1952	— 10 Markkaa. Copper.	—
Pn42	1953	— Markka. Aluminum. With pearls.	—
Pn43	1953	— Markka. Iron. Lion head.	—
Pn44	1953	— Markka. Iron. With pearls.	—
Pn45	1953	— 5 Markkaa. Iron-Blued.	—
Pn46	1953	— 50 Markkaa. Nickel.	—
Pn47	1954	— Markka. Nickel Plated Iron.	1,000
Pn48	1954	— Markkaa. Iron. With pearls.	—
Pn49	1954	— 5 Markkaa. Iron. With pearls.	—
Pn50	1954	— 20 Markkaa. Nickel.	—
Pn51	1956	— 20 Markkaa. Nickel.	—
Pn52	1956	— 20 Markkaa. Silver.	—
Pn53	1956	— 500 Markkaa. Silver. With waves.	—
Pn54	1956	— 500 Markkaa. Silver. With plain field.	—
Pn55	1969	— 5 Markkaa. Copper-Nickel.	—

TRIAL STRIKES

KM#	Date	Mintage Identification	Mkt Val
TS6	1918	— 5 Markkaa. Iron.	2,000
TS7	1960	— (1000 Markkaa). Brass.	—
TS8	1960	— (1000 Markkaa). Brass.	—

MINT SETS

KM#	Date	Mintage	Identification	Issue Price	Mkt Val
MS1	1973 (7)	9,978	KM#44a, 45-48, 49a, 53 Soft plastic holder	10.00	60.00
MS2	1973 (7)	10,029	KM#44a, 45-48, 49a, 53 Hard plastic holder	5.00	25.00
MS3	1974	79,258	KM#44a, 45-48, 49a, 53	3.75	8.00
MS4	1975 (7)	58,820	KM#44a, 45-48, 49a, 53	3.75	8.00
MS5	1976 (7)	45,263	KM#44a, 45-48, 49a, 53	3.75	8.00
MS6	1977 (7)	40,392	KM#44a, 45-48, 49a, 53	4.00	10.00
MS7	1978 (7)	39,745	KM#44a-45a, 46-48, 49a, 53	4.45	8.00
MS8	1979 (7)	36,000	KM#44a-45a, 46-48, 49a, 57	4.85	10.00
MS9	1980 (7)	33,805	KM#45a, 46-48, 49a, 57	5.00	8.00
MS10	1981 (6)	63,100	KM#45a, 46-48, 49a, 57	5.25	8.00
MS11	1982 (6)	35,500	KM#45a, 46-48, 49a, 57	5.50	8.00
MS12	1983 (6)	30,100	KM#45a-46a, 47-48, 49a, 57	3.25	8.00
MS13	1983 (6)	9,250	KM#45a-46a, 47-48, 49a, 57	3.25	20.00
MS14	1984 (6)	30,500	KM#45a-46a, 47-48, 49a, 57	3.25	6.00
MS15	1984 (6)	600	KM#45a-46a, 47-48, 49a, 57 Russian text	3.75	50.00
MS16	1985 (6)	38,385	KM#45a-46a, 47-48, 49a, 57 Finnish text	3.25	6.00
MS17	1985 (6)	1,500	KM#45a-46a, 47-48, 49a, 57 Russian text	4.65	20.00
MS18	1985 (6)	1,560	KM#45a-46a, 47-48, 49a, 57 English text	3.75	20.00
MS19	1986 (6)	37,100	KM#45a-46a, 47-48, 49a, 57 Finnish text	3.25	6.00
MS20	1986 (6)	1,300	KM#45a-46a, 47-48, 49a, 57 Russian text	5.00	20.00
MS21	1986 (6)	1,780	KM#45a-46a, 47-48, 49a, 57 English text	4.25	20.00
MS22	1987 (6)	34,300	KM#45a-46a, 47-48, 49a, 57 Finnish text	—	6.00
MS23	1987 (6)	1,120	KM#45a-46a, 47-48, 49a, 57 Russian text	—	20.00
MS24	1987 (6)	1,400	KM#45a-46a, 47-48, 49a, 57 English text	—	20.00
MS25	1987 (6)	15,900	KM#45a-46a, 47-48, 49a, 57 Finnish text	—	10.00
MS26	1987 (6)	300	KM#45a-46a, 47-48, 57 Russian text	—	50.00
MS27	1987 (6)	180	KM#45a-46a, 47-48, 49a, 57 English text	—	50.00

KM#	Date	Mintage	Identification	Issue Price	Mkt Val
MS28	1988 (6)	35,750	KM#45a-46a, 47-48, 49a, 57 Finnish text	—	6.00
MS29	1988 (6)	1,450	KM#45a-46a, 47-48, 49a, 57 English text	—	15.00
MS30	1988 (6)	1,220	KM#45a-46a, 47-48, 49a, 57 Russian text	—	15.00
MS31	1989 (6)	33,000	KM#45a-46a, 47-48, 49a, 57 Finnish text, bronze medal	—	6.00
MS32	1989 (6)	1,450	KM#45a-46a, 47-48, 49a, 57 English text, bronze medal	—	10.00
MS33	1989 (6)	1,700	KM#45a-46a, 47-48, 49a, 57 Russian text, bronze medal	—	10.00
MS34	1989 (6)	15,982	KM#45a-46a, 47-48, 49a, 57 Finnish text, silver medal	—	22.00
MS35	1989 (6)	1,000	KM#45a-46a, 47-48, 49a, 57 English text, silver medal	—	35.00
MS36	1989 (6)	1,150	KM#45a-46a, 47-48, 49a, 57 Russian text, silver medal	—	35.00
MS37	1990 (6)	29,400	KM#45a-46a, 47-48, 49a, 57 Finnish text	—	6.00
MS38	1990 (6)	1,000	KM#45a-46a, 47-48, 49a, 57 English text	—	10.00
MS39	1990 (6)	1,500	KM#45a-46a, 47-48, 49a, 57 Russian text	—	10.00
MS40	1990 (4)	41,750	KM#49a, 57, 65-66 Finnish text	—	9.00
MS41	1990 (4)	3,500	KM#49a, 57, 65-66 English text	—	10.00
MS42	1991 (4)	30,000	KM#49a, 57, 65-66 Finnish-Swedish text	—	10.00
MS43	1991 (4)	5,000	KM#49a, 57, 65-66 English text	—	10.00
MS44	1992 (5)	28,000	KM#49a, 57, 65-55, 73	—	12.50
MS45	1993 (6)	100,000	KM#49a, 65-66, 73, 76a, 77	—	21.50
MS46	1993 (5)	—	KM#65-66, 73, 76-77	13.30	13.50
MS47	1993 (4)	20,000	KM#49a, 65-66, 73 Silver medal	—	15.00
MS48	1994 (5)	25,000	KM#65-66, 73, 76-77 Medal (August Frederick Soldan)	—	18.00
MS49	1995 (5)	23,190	KM#65-66, 73, 76-77 Ecu medal	—	20.00
MS50	1995 (5)	15,000	KM#65-66, 73, 76-77 Medal (John Conrad Lihr)	—	20.00
MS51	1996 (5)	16,300	KM#65-66, 73, 76-77 Medal (Isak Gustaf Sundell)	—	20.00
MS52	1997 (5)	18,000	KM#65-66, 73, 76-77 Medal (Peippo Uolevi Helle)	—	20.00
MS53	1998 (5)	18,000	KM#65-66, 73, 76-77 Medal, (Allan Alarik Soiniemi)	—	20.00
MS54	1999 (5)	—	KM#65-66, 73, 76-77 Medal (Euro Summit)	—	20.00
MS55	1999 (5)	—	KM#65-66, 73, 76-77 Medal , Finnish presidency of the EU	12.50	20.00
MS56	2000 (5)	—	KM#65-66, 73, 76-77 Medal (Byzantine imitation coin found in Finland)	12.50	20.00
MS57	2000 (5)	—	KM#65-66, 73, 76-77 Medal (Time)	12.50	20.00

PROOF SETS

KM#	Date	Mintage	Identification	Issue Price	Mkt Val
PS1	1994 (5)	1,000	KM#65-66, 73, 76-77 Medal (August Frederik Soldan)	—	150
PS2	1995 (2)	500	KM#80, 82a	802	1,350
PS3	1995 (5)	1,810	KM#65-66, 73, 76-77 Medal (Ecu)	—	55.00
PS4	1996 (5)	1,200	KM#65-66, 73, 76-77 Medal (Johan Conrad Lihr)	—	55.00
PS5	1997 (6)	2,000	KM#65-66, 73, 76-77, 85	67.50	70.00
PS6	1998 (5)	1,600	KM#65-66, 73, 76-77 Medal (10 Euro Suomenlinna Fortress)	—	55.00
PS7	1999 (5)	—	KM#65-66, 73, 76-77 Medal (Euro Summit)	—	55.00
PS8	2000 (5)	—	KM#65-66, 73, 76-77, medal (Nykyaika)	—	55.00

FRANCE

The French Republic, largest of the West European nations, has an area of 210,026 sq. mi. (547,030 sq. km.) and a population of 58.1 million. Capital: Paris. Agriculture, manufacturing, tourist industry and financial services are the most important elements of France's diversified economy. Textiles and clothing, steel products, machinery and transportation equipment, chemicals, pharmaceuticals, nuclear electricity, agricultural products and wine are exported.

The monarchy was ousted by the Revolution of 1848 and the Second Republic proclaimed. Louis Napoleon Bonaparte (nephew of Napoleon I) was elected president of the Second Republic. He was proclaimed emperor in 1852. As Napoleon III, he gave France two decades of prosperity under a stable, autocratic regime, but led it to defeat in the Franco-Prussian War of 1870, after which the Third Republic was established.

The Third Republic endured until 1940 and the capitulation of France to the swiftly maneuvering German forces. Marshal Philippe Petain formed a puppet government that sued for peace and ruled unoccupied France until 1942 from Vichy. Meanwhile, General Charles de Gaulle escaped to London where he formed a wartime government in exile and the Free French army. De Gaulle's provisional exile government was officially recognized by the Allies after the liberation of Paris in 1944, and De Gaulle, who had been serving as head of the provisional government, tacitly maintained that position. In October 1945, the people overwhelmingly rejected a return to the prewar government, thus paving the way for the formation of the Fourth Republic in 1947 just after the dismissal of De Gaulle, at grips with a coalition of rival parties, the Communists especially.

In actual operation, the Fourth Republic was remarkably like the Third, with the National Assembly the focus of power causing a constant governmental instability. The later years of the Fourth Republic were marked by a burst of industrial expansion unmatched in modern French history. The growth rate, however, was marred by a two colonial wars, nagging inflationary trend that weakened the franc and undermined the betterment of the people's buying power. This and the Algerian conflict led to the recall of De Gaulle to power, the adoption of a new constitution vesting strong powers in the executive, and the establishment in 1959 of the current Fifth Republic.

RULERS
Third Republic, 1871-1940
Vichy State, 1940-1944
De Gaulle's Provisional Govt., 1944-1946
Fourth Republic, 1947-1958
Fifth Republic, 1959—

MINT MARKS AND PRIVY MARKS
In addition to the date and mint mark which are customary on western civilization coinage, most coins manufactured by the French Mints contain two or three small 'Marks or Differents' as the French call them. These privy marks represent the men responsible for the dies which struck the coins. One privy mark is sometimes for the Engraver General (since 1880 the title is Chief Engraver). The other privy mark is the signature of the Mint Director; another one is the different of the local engraver. Three other marks appeared at the end of Louis XIV's reign: one for the Director General of Mints, one for the General Engineer of Mechanical edge-marking, one identifying over struck coins in 1690-1705 and in 1715-1723. Equally amazing and unique is that sometimes the local assayer's or Judge-custody's 'different' or 'secret pellet' appears. Since 1880 this privy mark has represented the office rather than the personage of both the Administration of Coins & Medals and the Mint Director, and a standard privy mark has been used (cornucopia).

For most dates these privy marks are important though minor features for advanced collectors or local researchers. During some issue dates, however, the marks changed. To be even more accurate sometimes the marks changed when the date didn't, even though it should have. These coins can be attributed to the proper mintage report only by considering the privy marks. Previous references (before G. Sobin and F. Droulers) have by and large ignored these privy marks. It is entirely possible that unattributed varieties may exist for any privy mark transition. All transition years which may have two or three varieties or combinations of privy marks have the known attribution indicated after the date (if it has been confirmed).

ENGRAVER GENERAL'S PRIVY MARKS

Mark	Desc.	Date	Name
Torch	Torch	1896-1930	Henry Patey
Wing	Wing	1931-Oct. 1958	Lucien Bazor
Owl	Owl	1958-74	Raymond Joly
Dolphin	Dolphin	1974-94	Rousseau
Bee	Bee	1994-	Pierre Rodier

MINT DIRECTOR'S PRIVY MARKS

Some modern coins struck from dies produced at the Paris Mint have the 'A' mint mark. In the absence of a mint mark, the cornucopia privy mark serves to attribute a coin to Paris design.

A – Paris, Central Mint

B – Beaumont – Le Roger

Cornucopia		1943-58

(b) – Brussels

Legend ending BD, see PAU

C - Castelsarrasin

C	Cornucopia	1914, 1943-46

Thunderbolt (tb) - Poissy

	Cornucopia	1922-24

Star (s) - Madrid

★		1916

MONETARY SYSTEM
(Commencing 1960)
1 Old Franc = 1 New Centime
100 New Centimes = 1 New Franc

MODERN REPUBLICS
1870-
DECIMAL COINAGE

KM# 840   CENTIME
1.0000 g., Bronze, 15 mm. **Obv:** Liberty head right
Rev: Denomination above date within wreath **Note:** Without mint mark or privy mark.

Date	Mintage	F	VF	XF	Unc	BU
1901	1,000,000	1.00	2.00	15.00	35.00	50.00
1902	1,000,000	0.75	1.50	4.00	15.00	25.00
1903	2,000,000	0.50	1.50	3.00	15.00	25.00
1904	1,000,000	0.75	1.50	4.00	15.00	25.00
1908	4,500,000	2.00	4.00	10.00	20.00	35.00
1909	1,500,000	3.00	5.00	12.00	30.00	50.00
1910	1,500,000	10.00	20.00	40.00	100	185
1911	5,000,000	0.25	0.75	1.50	5.00	10.00
1912	2,000,000	0.50	1.00	2.00	7.00	12.00
1913	1,500,000	0.50	1.00	2.00	7.00	12.00
1914	1,000,000	0.75	1.50	3.00	9.50	15.00
1916	1,996,000	0.50	1.00	2.00	6.50	12.00
1919	2,407,000	0.25	0.75	1.50	4.00	9.00
1920	2,594,000	0.25	0.75	1.50	4.00	9.00

KM# 841   2 CENTIMES
2.0000 g., Bronze, 20.2 mm. **Obv:** Liberty head right
Rev: Denomination and date within wreath **Note:** Without mint mark or privy mark.

Date	Mintage	F	VF	XF	Unc	BU
1901	1,000,000	1.00	2.50	4.00	11.50	50.00
1902	750,000	1.50	3.50	5.50	15.00	55.00
1903	750,000	1.50	3.50	5.50	16.50	55.00
1904	500,000	2.00	4.50	7.50	18.50	60.00

Date	Mintage	F	VF	XF	Unc	BU
1907	250,000	10.00	25.00	55.00	130	200
1908	3,500,000	0.35	0.75	2.00	6.00	20.00
1909	1,750,000	6.00	12.00	30.00	50.00	90.00
1910	1,750,000	0.50	1.00	5.00	12.50	40.00
1911	5,000,000	0.15	0.50	1.25	5.00	15.00
1912	1,500,000	0.25	1.00	2.00	7.00	20.00
1913	1,750,000	0.25	1.00	2.00	7.00	20.00
1914	2,000,000	0.15	0.50	1.25	5.00	15.00
1916	500,000	0.75	1.50	3.00	9.00	30.00
1919	902,000	0.50	1.00	2.00	6.00	20.00
1920	598,000	0.75	1.50	3.00	8.00	25.00

KM# A933   2 CENTIMES
3.0000 g., Chrome Plated Steel, 17 mm. **Edge:** Plain

Date	Mintage	F	VF	XF	Unc	BU
1965	—	—	—	—	—	—

KM# 842   5 CENTIMES
5.0000 g., Bronze, 25.1 mm. **Obv:** Liberty head right
Rev: Republic protecting her child, denomination at right, date below **Note:** Without mint mark.

Date	Mintage	F	VF	XF	Unc	BU
1901 (c)	6,000,000	1.75	3.50	15.00	55.00	75.00
1902	7,900,000	1.75	3.50	10.00	50.00	70.00
1903	2,879,000	5.00	10.00	25.00	75.00	.100
1904	8,000,000	1.00	3.00	6.50	25.00	50.00
1905	2,100,000	6.00	16.00	45.00	115	225
1906	8,394,000	0.75	2.50	6.00	24.00	50.00
1907	7,900,000	0.75	2.50	6.00	24.00	50.00
1908	6,090,000	2.00	4.00	12.00	32.00	75.00
1909	8,000,000	0.75	2.50	6.00	25.00	50.00
1910	4,000,000	1.50	2.50	9.00	50.00	85.00
1911	15,386,000	0.25	0.75	1.75	9.00	15.00
1912	20,000,000	0.25	0.75	1.75	9.00	15.00
1913	12,603,000	0.25	0.75	1.75	9.00	15.00
1914	7,000,000	0.25	0.75	1.75	9.00	15.00
1915	6,032,000	0.25	0.75	1.75	9.00	15.00
1916	41,531,000	0.25	0.75	1.75	7.50	12.50
1916 (s)	Inc. above	0.25	0.75	1.75	7.50	12.50
1917	16,963,000	0.25	0.75	1.75	7.50	12.50
1920	8,151,999	2.00	4.00	9.00	28.00	55.00
1921	142,000	250	450	850	1,350	—

KM# 865   5 CENTIMES
3.0000 g., Copper-Nickel, 17 mm. **Obv:** Monogram within wreath divided by center hole, liberty cap above **Rev:** Denomination divided by plant and center hole

Date	Mintage	F	VF	XF	Unc	BU
1914 Rare	—	—	—	—	—	—
1917	10,458,000	1.00	1.75	4.00	18.00	40.00
1918	35,592,000	0.25	0.75	1.75	4.50	10.00
1919	43,848,000	0.25	0.75	1.75	4.00	9.00
1920	51,321,000	0.25	0.75	1.75	3.50	8.00

KM# 875   5 CENTIMES
2.0000 g., Copper-Nickel, 17 mm. **Obv:** Monogram divided by center hole, liberty cap above, wreath surrounds **Rev:** Denomination divided by plant and center hole, date below

Date	Mintage	F	VF	XF	Unc	BU
1920	Inc. above	5.00	15.00	28.00	75.00	150
1921	32,908,000	0.25	0.50	1.75	4.00	9.00
1922	31,700,000	0.25	0.50	1.75	4.00	9.00
1922 (tb)	17,717,000	1.50	2.50	5.00	13.50	28.00
1923	23,322,000	0.50	1.50	2.00	6.50	12.00
1923 (tb)	45,097,000	0.50	1.50	2.00	3.50	8.00
1924	47,018,000	0.25	0.50	1.00	3.50	8.00
1924 (tb)	21,210,000	0.50	1.50	2.00	5.50	10.00
1925	66,837,999	0.25	0.50	1.00	2.50	6.00
1926	19,820,000	0.25	0.50	1.00	5.50	10.00
1927	6,066,000	2.50	8.50	25.00	70.00	180
1930	31,902,000	0.20	0.50	1.00	2.25	5.00
1931	34,711,000	0.20	0.50	1.00	2.25	5.00
1932	31,112,000	0.20	0.50	1.00	2.25	5.00
1933	12,970,000	1.00	1.75	4.00	10.00	20.00
1934	27,144,000	0.30	0.65	2.00	5.00	10.00
1935	57,221,000	0.25	0.50	1.00	2.25	5.00

Date	Mintage	F	VF	XF	Unc	BU
1936	64,340,999	0.15	0.25	0.75	2.25	5.00
1937	26,329,000	0.15	0.25	0.75	2.25	5.00
1938	21,614,000	0.15	0.25	0.75	2.25	5.00

KM# 875a   5 CENTIMES
1.5000 g., Nickel-Bronze, 17 mm. **Obv:** Center hole divides monogram, liberty cap above, wreath surrounds **Rev:** Center hole and plant divide denomination, date below

Date	Mintage	F	VF	XF	Unc	BU
.1938.	26,330,000	0.15	0.50	1.00	3.00	—
.1938. star	Inc. above	100	200	300	425	—
.1939.	52,673,000	0.10	0.25	0.75	2.00	—

KM# 843   10 CENTIMES
10.0000 g., Bronze, 30 mm. **Obv:** Liberty head right
Rev: Republic protecting her child **Note:** Without mint mark.

Date	Mintage	F	VF	XF	Unc	BU
1901 (c)	2,700,000	1.50	3.00	20.00	50.00	75.00
1902	3,800,000	0.75	1.75	6.50	25.00	45.00
1903	3,650,000	0.75	1.75	6.50	25.00	45.00
1904	3,800,000	0.75	1.75	6.50	25.00	45.00
1905	950,000	25.00	50.00	125	275	450
1906	3,000,000	2.00	5.00	12.00	40.00	65.00
1907	4,000,000	0.75	1.75	4.50	20.00	35.00
1908	3,500,000	0.75	1.75	4.50	20.00	35.00
1909	2,933,000	0.75	1.75	4.50	25.00	40.00
1910	3,567,000	0.75	1.75	4.50	20.00	35.00
1911	7,903,000	0.50	1.25	2.75	12.00	20.00
1912	9,500,000	0.50	1.25	2.75	12.00	20.00
1913	9,000,000	0.50	1.25	2.75	12.00	20.00
1914	6,000,000	0.75	1.75	3.50	14.00	25.00
1915	4,362,000	0.50	1.25	2.75	12.00	20.00
1916	22,477,000	0.25	0.75	1.50	7.00	12.00
1916 (s)	Inc. above	0.25	0.75	1.50	7.00	12.00
1917	11,914,000	0.25	0.75	1.50	7.00	12.00
1920	4,119,000	1.50	3.00	10.00	40.00	65.00
1921	1,896,000	8.00	16.00	40.00	85.00	140

KM# 866   10 CENTIMES
4.0000 g., Nickel, 21.3 mm. **Obv:** Monogram divided by center hole, liberty cap above, wreath surrounds **Rev:** Denomination divided by plant and center hole, date below

Date	Mintage	F	VF	XF	Unc	BU
1914 dash	3,972	400	700	1,000	1,600	—

KM# 866a   10 CENTIMES
4.0000 g., Copper-Nickel, 21.3 mm. **Obv:** Center hole divides monogram, liberty cap above, wreath surrounds **Rev:** Center hole and plant divides denomination, date below **Note:** Varieties with small and large hole exist.

Date	Mintage	F	VF	XF	Unc	BU
1917	8,170,999	0.75	1.50	3.50	20.00	35.00
1918	30,605,000	0.25	0.50	1.00	3.50	6.50
1919	33,488,999	0.25	0.50	1.00	3.50	6.50
1920	38,845,000	0.25	0.50	1.00	3.50	6.50
1921	42,768,000	0.10	0.35	0.75	2.50	6.50
1922	23,033,000	0.35	0.75	1.25	4.00	7.00
1922 (tb)	12,412,000	0.75	1.50	2.50	6.50	12.00
1923	18,701,000	0.50	1.00	2.00	4.50	8.00
1923 (tb)	30,016,000	0.25	0.50	1.00	3.00	5.00
1924	43,949,000	0.10	0.35	0.75	2.00	3.00
1924 (tb)	13,591,000	1.50	4.50	12.50	40.00	65.00
1925	46,266,000	0.10	0.35	0.75	2.00	3.00
1926	25,660,000	0.25	0.50	1.00	3.00	5.00
1927	16,203,000	0.40	0.75	1.25	4.00	7.00
1928	6,967,000	1.00	2.50	8.00	28.00	55.00
1929	24,531,000	0.10	0.35	1.00	2.00	3.00
1930	22,146,000	0.10	0.35	1.00	2.00	3.00
1931	49,107,000	0.10	0.35	1.00	2.00	3.00
1932	30,317,000	0.10	0.35	1.00	2.00	3.00
1933	13,042,000	0.35	0.75	1.50	4.00	7.00
1934	24,067,000	0.10	0.50	1.00	2.00	3.00

Date	Mintage	F	VF	XF	Unc	BU
1935	47,487,000	0.10	0.50	1.00	2.00	3.00
1936	57,738,000	0.10	0.50	1.00	2.00	3.00
1937	25,308,000	0.10	0.50	1.00	2.00	3.00
1938	17,063,000	0.25	0.75	1.75	4.50	8.00

KM# 889.1   10 CENTIMES
3.0000 g., Nickel-Bronze, 21.3 mm. **Obv:** Monogram divided by center hole, liberty cap above, wreath surrounds **Rev:** Denomination divided by plant and center hole, date below

Date	Mintage	F	VF	XF	Unc	BU
.1938.	24,151,000	0.25	0.50	1.00	2.00	—
1938.	Inc. above					
.1939.	62,269,000	0.15	0.30	0.65	1.75	—

KM# 889.2   10 CENTIMES
Nickel-Bronze, 21.3 mm. **Obv:** Center hole divides monogram, liberty cap above **Rev:** Center hole and plant divide denomination **Note:** Thin flan: 1.35-1.45mm thickness

Date	Mintage	F	VF	XF	Unc	BU
.1939.	Inc. above	0.10	0.20	0.50	1.25	

KM# 898.2   10 CENTIMES
2.5000 g., Zinc, 21.3 mm. **Obv:** Grain sprigs flank center hole **Rev:** Center hole divides denomination, oak leaves flank, date below **Note:** Thin flan, 1.3mm.

Date	Mintage	F	VF	XF	Unc	BU
1941	Inc. above	0.25	0.50	1.25	3.00	—
1942	Inc. above	0.20	0.40	1.00	2.25	—
1943	Inc. above	0.75	1.50	2.75	6.00	—

KM# 898.1   10 CENTIMES
Zinc, 21 mm. **Obv:** Grain sprigs flank center hole **Rev:** Center hole divides denomination, oak leaves flank, date below **Note:** Issued for Vichy French State, thickness 1.5 mm. Varieties exist w/o hole.

Date	Mintage	F	VF	XF	Unc	BU
1941	70,860,000	0.35	0.65	1.50	6.00	—
1942	139,598,000	0.30	0.60	1.25	4.00	—
1943	48,957,600	1.00	2.00	4.00	15.00	—

KM# 895   10 CENTIMES
Zinc **Rev:** Without dash below MES in C MES

Date	Mintage	F	VF	XF	Unc	BU
1941	235,875,000	1.00	2.00	6.00	15.00	

KM# 896   10 CENTIMES
Zinc **Obv:** Monogram within wreath divided by center hole, liberty cap above **Rev:** Center hole within wreath divides denomination, date below, dash below MES in C MES

Date	Mintage	F	VF	XF	Unc	BU
1941	Inc. above	0.75	1.25	4.00	10.00	—

KM# 897   10 CENTIMES
Zinc, 21 mm. **Obv:** Monogram within wreath divided by center hole, liberty cap above **Rev:** Center hole within wreath divides denomination, dot before and after date below

Date	Mintage	F	VF	XF	Unc	BU
.1941.	Inc. above	0.25	0.50	1.00	4.00	—
1941.	Inc. above	0.25	0.50	1.00	4.00	—

KM# 903   10 CENTIMES
1.5000 g., Zinc, 17 mm. **Obv:** Grain sprigs flank center hole **Rev:** Center hole divides denomination, oak leaves flank, date below **Note:** Reduced size.

Date	Mintage	F	VF	XF	Unc	BU
1943	24,638,000	0.25	0.75	2.50	7.00	—
1944	58,463,000	0.25	0.50	2.00	5.00	—

KM# 906.1   10 CENTIMES
Zinc, 17 mm. **Obv:** Monogram divided by center hole, liberty cap above, wreath surrounds **Rev:** Center hole and plant divide denomination, date below **Note:** Reduced size.

Date	Mintage	F	VF	XF	Unc	BU
1945	38,174,000	1.00	1.75	3.25	12.00	—
1946 Rare						

KM# 906.2   10 CENTIMES
Zinc **Obv:** Monogram divided by center hole, liberty cap above, wreath surrounds **Rev:** Center hole and plant divide denomination

Date	Mintage	F	VF	XF	Unc	BU
1945B	7,246,000	1.50	3.00	6.00	16.00	—
1946B	10,566,000	2.50	5.00	10.00	25.00	60.00

KM# 906.3   10 CENTIMES
Zinc **Obv:** Monogram divided by center hole, liberty cap above, wreath surrounds **Rev:** Center hole and plant divide denomination

Date	Mintage	F	VF	XF	Unc	BU
1945C	8,379,000	2.00	4.00	8.00	20.00	45.00

KM# 899   20 CENTIMES
3.5000 g., Zinc, 24 mm. **Obv:** Grain sprigs flank center hole **Rev:** Center hole divides denomination, oak leaves flank, date below **Note:** Issued for Vichy French State.

Date	Mintage	F	VF	XF	Unc	BU
1941	54,044,000	1.00	2.00	4.00	17.00	—

KM# 900.1   20 CENTIMES
3.5000 g., Zinc **Obv:** Grain sprigs flank center hole **Rev:** Center hole divides denomination, oak leaves flank, date below **Note:** Thick flan.

Date	Mintage	F	VF	XF	Unc	BU
1941	31,397,000	1.00	2.00	4.00	15.00	—
1942	112,868,000	0.50	1.00	2.00	7.00	—
1943	64,138,000	0.75	1.50	2.50	8.50	—

KM# 900.2   20 CENTIMES
3.0000 g., Zinc **Obv:** Grain sprigs flank center hole **Rev:** Center hole divides denomination, leaves flank **Note:** Thin flan. Struck at Paris Mint.

Date	Mintage	F	VF	XF	Unc	BU
1941	Inc. above	0.50	0.75	2.00	8.50	—
1942	Inc. above	0.50	0.75	2.00	7.50	—
1943	Inc. above	0.50	0.75	2.00	6.50	—
1944	5,250,000	15.00	30.00	80.00	200	—

KM# 900.2a   20 CENTIMES
3.0000 g., Iron **Obv:** Grain sprigs flank center hole **Rev:** Center hole divides denomination, leaves flank

Date	Mintage	F	VF	XF	Unc	BU
1944	695,000	25.00	50.00	150	185	250

KM# 907.2   20 CENTIMES
3.0000 g., Zinc, 24 mm. **Obv:** Monogram divided by center hole, liberty cap above, wreath surrounds **Rev:** Center hole and plant divide denomination, date below

Date	Mintage	F	VF	XF	Unc	BU
1945B	100,000	85.00	165	285	470	—
1946B Rare	5,525,000	75.00	150	260	450	—

KM# 907.1   20 CENTIMES
Zinc **Obv:** Monogram divided by center hole, liberty cap above, wreath surrounds **Rev:** Center hole and plant divide denomination, date below **Note:** Fourth Republic.

Date	Mintage	F	VF	XF	Unc	BU
1945	6,003,000	2.00	4.00	9.00	22.00	45.00
1946	2,662,000	8.00	18.00	35.00	70.00	140

KM# 907.3   20 CENTIMES
Zinc **Obv:** Monogram divided by center hole, liberty cap above, wreath surrounds **Rev:** Center hole and plant divide denomination, date below

Date	Mintage	F	VF	XF	Unc	BU
1945C	299,000	20.00	40.00	85.00	150	220

KM# 855   25 CENTIMES
7.0000 g., Nickel, 24 mm. **Obv:** Laureate liberty head left **Rev:** Denomination and date flanked by cornucopias **Note:** Without mint mark.

Date	Mintage	F	VF	XF	Unc	BU
1903	16,000,000	0.25	1.00	2.00	11.50	—

KM# 856   25 CENTIMES
7.0000 g., Nickel, 24 mm. **Obv:** Laureate bust left **Rev:** Oak leaves divide date and denomination, column with axe head on top at left

Date	Mintage	F	VF	XF	Unc	BU
1904	16,000,000	0.25	0.75	2.00	13.50	—
1905	8,000,000	0.50	1.50	3.50	20.00	—

KM# 867   25 CENTIMES
5.0400 g., Nickel, 24 mm. **Obv:** Monogram divided by center hole, liberty cap above, wreath surrounds **Rev:** Center hole and plant divide denomination, dash under "MES" in denomination

Date	Mintage	F	VF	XF	Unc	BU
1914	941,000	1.50	3.00	7.00	22.50	40.00
1915	535,000	2.50	4.00	8.00	32.00	60.00
1916	100,000	15.00	30.00	60.00	120	245
1917	65,000	30.00	50.00	85.00	185	375

KM# 867a   25 CENTIMES
5.0000 g., Copper-Nickel, 24 mm. **Obv:** Monogram divided by center hole, liberty cap above, wreath surrounds **Rev:** Without dash under "MES" in denomination **Edge:** Plain **Note:** Varieties: Edges reeded on 1920, 1929, 1931, different size.

Date	Mintage	F	VF	XF	Unc	BU
1917	3,085,000	2.00	4.00	12.00	22.00	40.00
1918	18,330,000	0.25	0.50	1.50	3.50	6.00
1919	5,106,000	1.00	2.00	3.00	7.00	12.00
1920	18,108,000	0.15	0.50	1.00	3.00	5.00
1921	18,531,000	0.15	0.50	1.00	3.00	5.00
1922	17,766,000	0.15	0.50	1.00	3.00	5.00
1923	19,718,000	0.15	0.50	1.00	3.00	5.00
1924	24,535,000	0.15	0.50	1.00	3.00	5.00
1925	17,807,000	0.15	0.50	1.00	3.00	5.00
1926	13,226,000	0.15	0.50	1.00	3.00	5.00
1927	13,465,000	0.15	0.50	1.00	3.00	5.00
1928	9,960,000	0.25	0.50	1.50	3.50	6.50
1929	12,887,000	0.15	0.50	1.00	2.50	4.00
1930	28,363,000	0.15	0.50	1.00	2.50	4.00
1931	22,121,000	0.15	0.50	1.00	2.50	4.00
1932	30,364,000	0.15	0.50	1.00	2.50	4.00
1933	28,562,000	0.15	0.50	1.00	2.50	4.00
1936	4,657,000	1.50	3.00	8.00	18.00	35.00
1937	7,780,000	0.25	0.50	1.50	3.50	6.00

KM# 867b   25 CENTIMES
4.1600 g., Nickel-Bronze, 24 mm. **Rev:** Center hole and plant divide denomination, date below **Edge:** Plain **Note:** Listings below appear with a period before and after the date.

Date	Mintage	F	VF	XF	Unc	BU
1938	5,170,000	0.25	0.50	1.00	2.50	3.50
1939	42,964,000	0.15	0.35	0.75	1.50	2.50

Note: Thick flan (1.55mm)

Date	Mintage	F	VF	XF	Unc	BU
1939	Inc. above	0.15	0.35	0.75	1.50	2.50

Note: Thin flan (1.35mm)

Date	Mintage	F	VF	XF	Unc	BU
1940	3,446,000	6.00	12.00	18.00	35.00	55.00

KM# 854   50 CENTIMES
2.5000 g., 0.8350 Silver 0.0671 oz. ASW, 18 mm. **Obv:** Figure sowing seed **Rev:** Leafy branch divides date and denomination **Note:** Without mint mark.

Date	Mintage	F	VF	XF	Unc	BU
1901	4,960,000	2.00	4.00	12.00	45.00	90.00
1902	3,778,000	2.50	5.00	15.00	55.00	80.00
1903	2,222,000	12.00	25.00	50.00	150	215
1904	4,000,000	1.50	3.50	10.00	45.00	90.00
1905	2,381,000	5.00	9.00	20.00	100	200
1906	2,679,000	2.50	5.00	15.00	55.00	85.00
1907	7,332,000	1.50	3.50	10.00	30.00	50.00
1908	14,304,000	1.00	1.50	4.00	15.00	30.00
1909	9,900,000	1.00	1.50	4.00	15.00	30.00
1910	15,923,000	BV	1.25	3.00	10.00	20.00
1911	1,330,000	20.00	50.00	110	200	350
1912	16,000,000	BV	1.00	1.50	5.00	9.00
1913	14,000,000	BV	1.00	1.50	5.00	9.00
1914	9,657,000	BV	1.00	1.50	6.00	10.00
1915	20,893,000	BV	1.00	1.25	3.00	5.00
1916	52,963,000	BV	1.00	1.25	2.50	4.00
1917	48,629,000	BV	1.00	1.25	2.50	4.00
1918	36,492,000	BV	1.00	1.25	2.50	4.00
1919	24,299,000	BV	1.00	1.25	2.50	4.00
1920	8,509,000	1.00	1.50	3.00	6.00	10.00

KM# 884   50 CENTIMES
2.0000 g., Aluminum-Bronze, 18 mm. **Obv:** Denomination within circle **Rev:** Mercury seated left, caduceus at left, shield on right, date below **Note:** Varieties for 1924: Closed and open 4's.

Date	Mintage	F	VF	XF	Unc	BU
1921	8,692,000	0.75	2.00	6.00	18.00	35.00
1922	86,226,000	0.15	0.25	1.00	4.00	8.00
1923	119,584,000	0.15	0.25	0.75	2.50	5.00
1924	97,036,000	0.15	0.25	1.00	3.00	6.00
1925	48,017,000	0.25	0.50	1.25	5.00	10.00
1926	46,447,000	0.25	0.50	1.25	5.00	10.00
1927	23,703,000	0.75	1.50	3.00	8.50	16.50
1928	10,329,000	0.75	2.00	5.00	16.00	30.00
1929	6,669,000	2.50	6.00	12.50	25.00	60.00

KM# 894.1   50 CENTIMES
2.0000 g., Aluminum-Bronze, 18 mm. **Obv:** Laureate head left **Rev:** Denomination above date, cornucopias flank

Date	Mintage	F	VF	XF	Unc	BU
1931	62,775,000	0.15	0.25	1.00	3.00	5.00
1932 Closed 9	Inc. above	0.15	0.25	0.50	2.00	3.50
1932 Open 9	108,839,000	0.15	0.25	0.50	2.00	3.50
1933 Closed 9	Inc. above	0.15	0.25	0.75	3.00	5.00
1933 Open 9	41,937,000	0.15	0.25	0.75	3.00	5.00
1936	16,602,000	0.50	1.00	2.00	5.00	9.00
1937	43,950,000	0.15	0.25	0.75	3.00	5.00
1938	55,707,000	0.15	0.25	0.75	3.00	5.00
1939	96,594,000	0.15	0.25	0.50	2.00	3.50
1940	10,854,000	0.50	1.00	2.00	5.00	9.00
1941	82,958,000	0.15	0.25	1.00	3.00	5.00
1947	Est. 2,170,000	60.00	125	225	350	—

Note: 1947 date was struck for colonial use in Africa

KM# 894.1a   50 CENTIMES
Aluminum, 18 mm. **Obv:** Laureate liberty head left **Rev:** Cornucopias flank denomination and date **Note:** Without mint mark. Thick and thin planchets exist.

Date	Mintage	F	VF	XF	Unc	BU
1941	129,758,000	0.15	0.25	0.50	2.00	3.00
1944	9,898,000	0.50	1.00	2.50	6.00	9.00

Date	Mintage	F	VF	XF	Unc	BU
1945	26,224,000	0.15	0.25	1.00	3.00	5.00
1946	24,605,000	0.15	0.25	1.00	3.00	5.00
1947	51,744,000	0.15	0.25	0.60	2.00	3.00

KM# 894.2a   50 CENTIMES
0.7000 g., Aluminum, 18 mm. **Obv:** Laureate liberty head left **Rev:** Cornucopias flank denomination and date

Date	Mintage	F	VF	XF	Unc	BU
1944B	20,000	—	—	—	—	—

Note: Reported, not confirmed

Date	Mintage	F	VF	XF	Unc	BU
1945B	6,357,000	0.50	1.00	3.00	8.00	15.00
1946B	29,344,000	0.15	0.25	1.00	4.00	7.00
1947B	18,504,000	2.00	5.00	10.00	20.00	35.00

KM# 894.3a   50 CENTIMES
Aluminum, 18 mm. **Obv:** Laureate liberty head left **Rev:** Cornucopias flank denomination and date

Date	Mintage	F	VF	XF	Unc	BU
1944C	17,220,000	—	—	—	—	—

Note: Reported, not confirmed

Date	Mintage	F	VF	XF	Unc	BU
1945C	2,968,000	1.00	3.00	6.00	12.00	25.00

KM# 894.2   50 CENTIMES
Aluminum-Bronze, 18 mm. **Obv:** Laureate liberty head left **Rev:** Cornucopias flank denomination and date

Date	Mintage	F	VF	XF	Unc	BU
1939B	6,200,000	0.50	1.00	2.50	10.00	18.00

KM# 914.1   50 CENTIMES
Aluminum, 18 mm. **Obv:** Double bit axe, grain sprigs flank **Rev:** Denomination above date, oak leaves flank **Note:** Without mint mark. Vichy French State. Thick and thin planchets exist.

Date	Mintage	F	VF	XF	Unc	BU
1942	50,134,000	0.15	0.25	0.75	2.00	3.50
1943	84,462,000	0.15	0.25	0.75	1.50	2.50
1944	57,410,000	1.50	3.00	6.00	18.00	32.50

KM# 914.2   50 CENTIMES
0.8000 g., Aluminum, 18 mm. **Obv:** Grain sprigs flank double bit axe **Rev:** Denomination above date, oak leaves flank

Date	Mintage	F	VF	XF	Unc	BU
1943B	21,916,000	5.00	10.00	28.00	50.00	70.00
1944B	27,334,000	1.50	3.00	7.00	15.00	25.00

KM# 914.3   50 CENTIMES
Aluminum, 18 mm. **Obv:** Grain sprigs flank double bit axe **Rev:** Denomination above date, oak leaves flank

Date	Mintage	F	VF	XF	Unc	BU
1944C Small C	27,213,000	2.00	4.00	8.00	26.00	40.00
1944C Large C	Inc. above	—	—	—	—	—

KM# 914.4   50 CENTIMES
Aluminum, 18 mm. **Obv:** Grain sprigs flank double bit axe **Rev:** Denomination above date, oak leaves flank **Note:** Without mint mark. Thin flan. Struck at Paris Mint.

Date	Mintage	F	VF	XF	Unc	BU
1942	—	0.15	0.25	1.00	2.50	4.50
1943	—	0.15	0.25	0.50	1.25	2.00

KM# 844.1   FRANC
5.0000 g., 0.8350 Silver 0.1342 oz. ASW, 23 mm. **Obv:** Figure sowing seed **Rev:** Leafy branch divides date and denomination **Note:** Without mint mark.

Date	Mintage	F	VF	XF	Unc	BU
1901	6,200,000	Value: 140				
1902	6,000,000	2.00	4.00	20.00	75.00	140
1903	472,000	40.00	80.00	325	650	1,000
1904	7,000,000	2.00	4.00	17.50	75.00	130
1905	6,004,000	2.00	4.00	15.00	65.00	110
1906	1,908,000	6.00	20.00	40.00	100	175
1907	2,563,000	4.00	9.00	30.00	90.00	150
1908	3,961,000	2.50	5.00	20.00	65.00	110
1909	10,924,000	2.00	2.50	5.00	22.00	75.00
1910	7,725,000	2.00	2.50	5.00	22.00	75.00
1911	5,542,000	2.25	3.00	12.00	45.00	90.00
1912	10,001,000	2.00	2.50	5.00	22.00	75.00
1913	13,654,000	2.00	2.50	4.00	18.00	50.00
1914	14,361,000	2.00	2.50	3.50	15.00	45.00
1915	47,955,000	BV	1.85	2.25	5.50	10.00
1916	92,029,000	—	BV	2.00	3.50	9.00
1917	57,153,000	—	BV	2.00	3.50	9.00
1918	50,112,000	—	BV	2.00	3.50	9.00
1919	46,112,000	—	BV	2.00	3.50	9.00
1920	19,322,000	BV	1.85	2.50	5.50	10.00

KM# 844.2   FRANC
5.0000 g., 0.8350 Silver 0.1342 oz. ASW, 23 mm. **Obv:** Figure sowing seed **Rev:** Leafy branch divides date and denomination

Date	Mintage	F	VF	XF	Unc	BU
1914C	43,000	135	250	350	500	700

KM# 876   FRANC
4.0900 g., Aluminum-Bronze, 23 mm. **Obv:** Value **Obv. Leg.:** CHAMBRES • DE • COMMERCE • DE • FRANCE **Rev:** Mercury seated left **Rev. Leg.:** COMMERCE - INDUSTRIE **Edge:** Reeded **Note:** Without mint mark. Chamber of Commerce.

Date	Mintage	F	VF	XF	Unc	BU
1920	590,000	3.00	5.00	12.50	32.00	—
1921	54,572,000	0.25	0.50	1.50	5.50	9.00
1922	111,343,000	0.15	0.25	1.00	4.50	8.00
1923	140,138,000	0.15	0.25	1.00	3.50	7.00
1924 Closed 4	Inc. above	0.35	0.60	2.00	6.50	8.00
1924 Open 4	87,715,000	0.15	0.25	1.00	4.50	12.00
1925	36,523,000	0.25	0.50	1.50	5.50	9.00
1926	1,580,000	3.00	8.00	20.00	45.00	75.00
1927	11,330,000	0.50	1.50	3.50	8.50	16.00

KM# 885   FRANC
4.0000 g., Aluminum-Bronze, 23 mm. **Obv:** Laureate head left **Rev:** Cornucopias flank denomination and date **Edge:** Plain

Date	Mintage	F	VF	XF	Unc	BU
1931	15,504,000	0.25	0.50	2.00	6.50	10.00
1932	29,768,000	0.15	0.25	1.00	4.00	7.00
1933	15,356,000	0.25	0.50	2.00	6.50	10.00
1934	17,286,000	0.25	0.50	2.00	5.00	9.00
1935	1,166,000	6.00	15.00	25.00	60.00	100
1936	23,817,000	0.15	0.25	1.00	4.00	7.00
1937	30,940,000	0.15	0.25	1.00	3.00	5.00
1938	66,165,000	0.15	0.25	1.00	2.50	1.00
1939	48,434,000	0.15	0.25	1.00	3.00	5.00
1940	25,525,000	0.15	0.25	1.00	3.50	6.00
1941	34,705,000	0.15	0.25	1.00	3.00	5.00

KM# 885a.1   FRANC
1.3000 g., Aluminum, 23 mm. **Obv:** Laureate head left **Rev:** Cornucopias flank denomination and date **Edge:** Plain **Note:** Thick and thin planchets exist.

Date	Mintage	F	VF	XF	Unc	BU
1941	60,877,000	0.10	0.20	1.00	4.00	6.00
1943	4,400	1,200	1,500	2,250	4,000	6,000
1944	22,608,000	0.10	0.20	1.50	5.00	8.00
1945	61,780,000	0.10	0.15	0.50	2.00	3.00
1946	52,516,000	0.10	0.15	0.25	2.00	3.00
1947	110,448,000	0.10	0.15	0.25	2.00	3.00
1948	96,092,000	0.10	0.15	0.25	2.00	3.00
1949	41,090,000	0.10	0.15	0.25	2.00	3.00
1950	27,882,000	0.10	0.15	0.50	2.50	4.00
1957	16,497,000	0.10	0.15	0.75	3.00	5.00
1958	21,197,000	0.10	0.15	0.75	3.00	5.00
1959	41,985,000	0.10	0.15	0.25	1.25	2.00

KM# 902.1   FRANC
Aluminum, 23 mm. **Obv:** Double bit axe, grain sprigs flank **Rev:** Denomination above date, oak leaves flank **Note:** Without mint mark. Vichy French State Issues. Thick and thin planchets exist.

Date	Mintage	F	VF	XF	Unc	BU
1942	152,144,000	0.25	0.50	1.50	4.00	6.00
1942 Without LB	Inc. above	—	—	—	—	—

Date	Mintage	F	VF	XF	Unc	BU
1943	205,564,000	0.10	0.25	1.00	2.50	3.50
1943 Thin flan	Inc. above	0.10	0.25	1.00	2.50	3.50
1944	50,605,000	0.50	1.25	2.00	10.00	15.00

KM# 885b FRANC
Zinc, 23 mm. **Obv:** Laureate head left **Rev:** Cornucopias flank denomination and date **Note:** Struck for colonial use in Africa.

Date	Mintage	F	VF	XF	Unc	BU
1943A	Est. 17,000	750	1,100	1,700	3,200	—

KM# 902.2 FRANC
1.2800 g., Aluminum, 23 mm. **Obv:** Grain sprigs flank double bit axe **Rev:** Leaves flank denomination, date below

Date	Mintage	F	VF	XF	Unc	BU
1943B	68,082,000	5.00	9.00	28.00	80.00	120
1944B	13,622,000	1.50	3.00	12.00	25.00	40.00
1944 large C	74,859,000	0.50	1.50	3.50	12.50	20.00
1944 small C	—	50.00	100	200	400	600

KM# 885a.3 FRANC
Aluminum, 23 mm. **Obv:** Laureate head left **Rev:** Cornucopias flank denomination and date

Date	Mintage	F	VF	XF	Unc	BU
1944C	33,600,000	0.50	1.50	3.50	12.00	20.00
1945C	5,220,000	1.50	3.50	9.00	25.00	60.00

KM# 885a.2 FRANC
Aluminum, 23 mm. **Obv:** Laureate head left **Rev:** Cornucopias flank denomination and date

Date	Mintage	F	VF	XF	Unc	BU
1945B	4,251,000	1.00	3.50	9.00	28.00	75.00
1946B	26,493,000	0.10	0.20	1.50	5.00	8.00
1947B	31,562,000	0.10	0.20	1.00	4.00	7.00
1948B	45,481,000	0.10	0.20	1.00	3.50	5.00
1949B	35,840,000	0.10	0.20	1.00	4.00	7.00
1950B	18,800,000	1.00	2.00	3.50	15.00	22.00
1957B	63,976,000	0.10	0.20	1.00	4.00	7.00
1958B	13,412,000	0.25	0.75	2.00	5.50	9.00

KM# 902.3 FRANC
Aluminum, 23 mm. **Obv:** Grain sprigs flank double bit axe **Rev:** Leaves flank denomination, date below

Date	Mintage	F	VF	XF	Unc	BU
1944 Large C	74,859,000	0.25	0.75	1.50	5.50	9.00
1944 Small C	Inc. above	15.00	30.00	70.00	325	—

KM# 845.1 2 FRANCS
10.0000 g., 0.8350 Silver 0.2684 oz. ASW, 27 mm. **Obv:** Figure sowing seed **Rev:** Leafy branch divides denomination and date **Note:** Without mint mark.

Date	Mintage	F	VF	XF	Unc	BU
1901	1,860,000	6.50	18.00	50.00	150	275
1902	2,000,000	6.50	18.00	50.00	125	210
1904	1,500,000	7.50	18.00	40.00	175	250
1905	2,000,000	6.50	18.00	50.00	150	225
1908	2,502,000	3.75	6.00	20.00	75.00	100
1909	1,000,000	8.00	18.00	35.00	175	250
1910	2,190,000	3.75	6.00	20.00	75.00	100
1912	1,000,000	7.00	18.00	40.00	125	200
1913	500,000	15.00	25.00	45.00	150	225
1914	5,719,000	BV	3.75	7.00	25.00	50.00
1915	13,963,000	—	BV	4.00	18.00	25.00
1916	17,887,000	—	BV	4.00	18.00	25.00
1917	16,555,000	—	BV	4.00	18.00	25.00
1918	12,026,000	—	BV	4.00	18.00	25.00
1919	9,261,000	—	BV	4.00	15.00	22.00
1920	3,014,000	BV	4.00	7.00	25.00	35.00

KM# 845.2 2 FRANCS
10.0000 g., 0.8352 Silver 0.2685 oz. ASW, 27 mm. **Obv:** Figure sowing seed **Rev:** Leafy branch divides date and denomination

Date	Mintage	F	VF	XF	Unc	BU
1914C	462,000	9.00	16.00	35.00	65.00	160
1914C Matte Proof	—	Value: 650				

KM# 877 2 FRANCS
8.0000 g., Aluminum-Bronze, 27 mm. **Subject:** French Chamber of Commerce **Obv:** Denomination within circle **Rev:** Mercury seated left, caduceus at left, shield on right, date below **Note:** Without mint mark.

Date	Mintage	F	VF	XF	Unc	BU
1920	14,363,000	6.00	15.00	40.00	90.00	125
1921	Inc. above	0.75	1.50	4.00	12.50	20.00

Date	Mintage	F	VF	XF	Unc	BU
1922	29,463,000	0.50	1.00	2.00	7.50	12.00
1923	43,960,000	0.50	1.00	2.00	7.50	12.00
1924 Open 4	29,631,000	0.50	1.00	2.00	7.50	12.00
1924 Closed 4	Inc. above	0.65	1.50	3.00	10.00	18.00
1925/3	31,607,000	0.75	1.75	4.00	12.50	20.00
1925	Inc. above	0.50	1.00	2.00	8.00	14.00
1926	2,962,000	7.00	18.00	50.00	100	150
1927	1,678,000	100	150	300	700	—

KM# 886 2 FRANCS
8.0000 g., Aluminum-Bronze, 27 mm. **Obv:** Laureate head left **Rev:** Denomination and date flanked by cornucopias

Date	Mintage	F	VF	XF	Unc	BU
1931	1,717,000	3.00	6.00	12.00	35.00	50.00
1932	8,943,000	0.75	1.50	3.00	10.00	18.00
1933	8,413,000	0.75	1.50	3.00	10.00	18.00
1934	6,896,000	1.25	2.50	6.00	12.00	20.00
1935	298,000	12.00	20.00	40.00	90.00	125
1936	12,394,000	0.25	1.00	2.00	6.00	10.00
1937	11,055,000	0.25	1.00	2.00	6.00	10.00
1938	28,072,000	0.20	0.50	1.00	5.00	9.00
1939	25,403,000	0.20	0.50	1.00	5.00	9.00
1940	9,716,000	1.00	2.00	3.50	10.00	18.00
1941	16,684,000	0.25	1.00	2.00	6.00	10.00

KM# 886a.1 2 FRANCS
Aluminum, 27 mm. **Obv:** Laureate head left **Rev:** Denomination and date flanked by cornucopias

Date	Mintage	F	VF	XF	Unc	BU
1941	Inc. above	0.25	0.50	1.00	3.00	5.00
1944	7,224,000	0.75	1.00	4.00	12.00	20.00
1945	16,636,000	0.50	1.00	2.50	7.00	10.00
1946	34,930,000	0.20	0.50	1.00	3.50	5.00
1947	78,984,000	0.20	0.30	1.00	2.50	4.00
1948	32,354,000	0.20	0.50	1.00	3.50	5.00
1949	13,683,000	0.25	0.50	1.00	2.50	4.00
1950	12,191,000	0.25	0.50	1.00	2.50	4.00
1958	9,906,000	0.20	0.50	1.00	3.50	5.00
1959	17,774,000	0.20	0.50	1.00	3.50	5.00

KM# 904.2 2 FRANCS
2.2000 g., Aluminum, 27 mm. **Obv:** Grain sprigs flank double bit axe **Rev:** Oak leaves flank denomination, date below

Date	Mintage	F	VF	XF	Unc	BU
1943B	34,131,000	3.50	7.00	15.00	25.00	—
1944B	10,298,000	1.50	3.00	6.00	18.00	—

KM# 904.1 2 FRANCS
Aluminum, 27 mm. **Obv:** Double bit axe, grain sprigs flank **Rev:** Oak leaves flank denomination, date below **Note:** Without mint mark. Issued for Vichy French State.

Date	Mintage	F	VF	XF	Unc	BU
1943	106,997,000	0.20	0.50	1.00	10.00	—
1944	25,546,000	0.75	1.50	3.50	12.00	—

KM# 905 2 FRANCS
8.1500 g., Brass, 27 mm. **Obv:** FRANCE within wreath **Rev:** Large denomination above date **Note:** Without mint mark. Issued during Allied Occupation for circulation in Algeria and France.

Date	Mintage	F	VF	XF	Unc	BU
1944	50,000,000	1.00	2.00	5.00	25.00	60.00

KM# 886a.2 2 FRANCS
2.2000 g., Aluminum, 27 mm. **Obv:** Laureate head left **Rev:** Denomination and date flanked by cornucopias

Date	Mintage	F	VF	XF	Unc	BU
1944B	170,000	—				
1945B	1,726,000	3.00	7.00	15.00	35.00	50.00
1946B	6,018,000	2.00	4.00	8.00	20.00	30.00
1947B	26,220,000	0.20	0.50	1.00	3.50	5.00

Date	Mintage	F	VF	XF	Unc	BU
1948B	39,090,000	0.20	0.50	1.00	3.00	5.00
1949B	23,955,000	0.20	0.50	1.00	3.50	5.00
1950B	18,185,000	0.50	1.00	3.00	5.00	8.00

KM# 904.3 2 FRANCS
Aluminum, 27 mm. **Obv:** Grain sprigs flank double bit axe **Rev:** Oak leaves flank denomination, date below

Date	Mintage	F	VF	XF	Unc	BU
1944C	19,470,000	1.25	2.50	5.00	18.00	30.00

KM# 886a.3 2 FRANCS
Aluminum, 27 mm. **Obv:** Laureate head left **Rev:** Denomination and date flanked by cornucopias

Date	Mintage	F	VF	XF	Unc	BU
1945C	1,165,000	5.00	10.00	25.00	65.00	110

KM# 887 5 FRANCS
6.0000 g., Nickel, 23.7 mm. **Obv:** Head right, date below **Rev:** Denomination flanked by grain sprigs **Note:** Without mint mark.

Date	Mintage	F	VF	XF	Unc	BU
1933 (a)	105,029,373	0.75	1.50	3.50	9.00	15.00

KM# 888 5 FRANCS
12.0000 g., Nickel, 31 mm. **Obv:** Laureate head left **Rev:** Denomination above date within sectioned wreath **Note:** Without mint mark.

Date	Mintage	F	VF	XF	Unc	BU
1933 (a)	56,686,000	0.25	0.75	2.50	8.00	14.00
1935 (a)	54,164,000	0.25	0.75	2.50	8.00	14.00
1936 (a)	117,000	400	700	1,200	1,850	—
1937 (a)	157,000	35.00	60.00	120	225	—
1938 (a)	4,977,000	12.00	25.00	50.00	100	—
1939 (a)	—	700	1,200	2,000	4,000	—

KM# 888a.1 5 FRANCS
12.0000 g., Aluminum-Bronze, 31 mm. **Obv:** Laureate head left **Rev:** Denomination above date within sectioned wreath **Note:** Struck for Colonial use in Algeria.

Date	Mintage	F	VF	XF	Unc	BU
1938 (a)	10,144,000	6.00	10.00	18.00	85.00	120
1939 (a)	Inc. above	2.50	5.00	12.00	30.00	60.00
1940 (a)	38,758,000	1.00	2.00	3.50	10.00	40.00

KM# 901 5 FRANCS
4.0000 g., Copper-Nickel, 22 mm. **Obv:** Double bit axe divides denomination, date below **Rev:** Head with collar left **Note:** Without mint mark.

Date	Mintage	F	VF	XF	Unc	BU
1941	13,782,000	65.00	100	150	275	440

Note: Never released into circulation.

KM# 888b.1 5 FRANCS
3.5000 g., Aluminum, 31.5 mm. **Obv:** Laureate head left **Rev:** Denomination above date within sectioned wreath **Edge:** Plain **Note:** Without mint mark.

Date	Mintage	F	VF	XF	Unc	BU
1945 (a) Open 9	95,399,000	0.20	0.35	1.50	6.00	9.00
1946 (a) Open 9	61,332,000	0.20	0.35	1.50	6.00	9.00
1947 (a) Open 9	46,576,000	0.20	0.35	1.50	6.00	9.00
1947 (a) Closed 9	Inc. above	0.20	0.35	1.50	6.00	9.00
1948 (a) Open 9	104,473,000	1.00	3.00	6.00	12.50	—
1948 (a) Closed 9	Inc. above	5.00	10.00	30.00	50.00	—
1949 (a) Closed 9	203,252,000	0.20	0.35	0.75	3.00	5.00
1950 (a) Closed 9	128,372,000	0.20	0.35	0.75	3.00	5.00
1952 (a) Closed 9	4,000,000	20.00	40.00	100	225	—

KM# 888a.3 5 FRANCS
Aluminum-Bronze, 31 mm. **Obv:** Laureate head left **Rev:** Denomination above date within sectioned wreath

Date	Mintage	F	VF	XF	Unc	BU
1945C Open 9	Inc. above	3.00	7.00	15.00	30.00	—
1946C Open 9	Inc. above	5.00	15.00	30.00	60.00	—

KM# 888b.2 5 FRANCS
Aluminum, 31 mm. **Obv:** Laureate head left **Rev:** Denomination above date within sectioned wreath

Date	Mintage	F	VF	XF	Unc	BU
1945B Open 9	6,043,000	1.50	3.00	5.00	15.00	28.00
1946B Open 9	13,360,000	0.75	1.50	3.00	12.00	20.00
1947B Open 9	30,839,000	0.50	1.00	2.50	8.00	14.00
1947B Closed 9	Inc. above	0.50	1.00	2.50	8.00	14.00
1948B Open 9	28,047,000	20.00	40.00	100	175	—
B Closed 9	Inc. above	20.00	40.00	100	175	—
1949B Closed 9	48,414,000	0.50	1.00	2.50	8.00	14.00
1950B Closed 9	28,952,000	0.75	1.50	3.50	9.00	16.00

KM# 888b.3 5 FRANCS
Aluminum, 31 mm. **Obv:** Laureate head left **Rev:** Denomination above date within sectioned wreath

Date	Mintage	F	VF	XF	Unc	BU
1945C Open 9	2,208,000	7.00	15.00	28.00	60.00	85.00
1946C Open 9	1,269,000	8.00	18.00	38.00	75.00	95.00

KM# 888a.2 5 FRANCS
Aluminum-Bronze, 31 mm. **Obv:** Laureate head left **Rev:** Denomination above date within sectioned wreath **Note:** Struck for Colonial use in Africa.

Date	Mintage	F	VF	XF	Unc	BU
1945 (a) Open 9	13,044,000	1.00	2.00	4.00	11.00	18.00
1946 (a) Open 9	21,790,000	1.00	2.00	4.00	11.00	18.00
1947 (a)	2,662,000	165	400	600	1,200	—

Note: Date exists with both open and closed 9's.

KM# 846 10 FRANCS
3.2258 g., 0.9000 Gold 0.0933 oz. AGW

Date	Mintage	F	VF	XF	Unc	BU
1901	2,100,000	—	BV	90.00	125	180
1901	2,100,000	—	BV	90.00	125	180
1905	1,426,000	—	BV	90.00	125	180
1905	1,426,000	—	BV	90.00	125	180
1906	3,665,000	—	BV	90.00	125	180
1907	3,364,000	—	BV	90.00	125	180
1908	1,650,000	—	BV	90.00	125	180
1909	599,000	—	BV	90.00	250	410
1910	2,110,000	—	BV	90.00	125	180
1911	1,881,000	—	BV	90.00	125	180
1912	1,756,000	—	BV	90.00	150	200
1914	3,041,000	—	BV	85.00	120	180

KM# 878 10 FRANCS
10.0000 g., 0.6800 Silver 0.2186 oz. ASW, 28 mm. **Note:** Without mint mark.

Date	Mintage	F	VF	XF	Unc	BU
1929	16,292,000	BV	3.50	5.50	12.00	22.00
1930	36,986,000	BV	3.00	4.50	9.00	16.00
1931	35,468,000	BV	3.00	4.50	9.00	16.00
1932	40,288,000	BV	3.00	3.50	7.00	12.00
1933	31,146,000	BV	3.00	3.50	7.00	12.00
1934	52,001,000	BV	3.00	3.50	7.00	12.00
1936	—	—	—	—	—	—
1937	52,000	65.00	125	250	360	500
1938	14,090,000	BV	3.00	6.00	12.50	25.00
1939	8,298,999	3.00	4.00	8.00	17.50	32.00

KM# 908.1 10 FRANCS
7.0000 g., Copper-Nickel, 26 mm. **Obv:** Laureate head right, long leaves and short leaves **Rev:** Denomination above date, inscription below, grain columns flank **Edge:** Reeded **Note:** Large head.

Date	Mintage	F	VF	XF	Unc	BU
1945 (II)	6,557,000	0.25	0.75	2.00	6.00	9.00
1945 (sl)	Inc. above	15.00	30.00	50.00	90.00	140
1946 (II)	24,409,000	185	300	400	—	—
1946 (sl)	Inc. above	0.25	0.50	2.00	5.00	8.00
1947	41,627,000	0.25	0.50	1.00	3.00	5.00

KM# 908.2 10 FRANCS
Copper-Nickel, 26 mm. **Obv:** Laureate head right **Rev:** Denomination above date, inscription below, grain columns flank **Edge:** Reeded **Note:** Large head

Date	Mintage	F	VF	XF	Unc	BU
1946B (II)	8,452,000	20.00	35.00	50.00	85.00	—
1946B (sl)	Inc. above	0.25	0.75	2.00	9.00	—
1947B	17,188,000	0.25	0.50	2.00	8.00	—

KM# 909.2 10 FRANCS
7.0000 g., Copper-Nickel, 26 mm. **Obv:** Large head **Rev:** Denomination above date, inscription below, grain columns flank

Date	Mintage	F	VF	XF	Unc	BU
1947B	Inc. above	1.00	2.50	6.00	30.00	—
1948B	40,500,000	0.35	0.75	2.00	7.00	—
1949B	29,518,000	0.35	0.75	2.00	7.00	—

KM# 909.1 10 FRANCS
Copper-Nickel, 26 mm. **Obv:** Laureate head right, small head **Rev:** Denomination above date, inscription below, grain columns flank **Note:** Without mint mark.

Date	Mintage	F	VF	XF	Unc	BU
1947	Inc. above	0.30	0.75	1.50	3.50	5.00
1948	155,945,000	0.20	0.35	0.75	2.00	3.50
1949	118,149,000	0.20	0.35	0.75	2.00	3.50

KM# 915.1 10 FRANCS
3.0000 g., Aluminum-Bronze, 20 mm. **Obv:** Head left **Rev:** Denomination above date at right, rooster above laurel leaves at left **Edge:** Plain **Note:** Without mint mark.

Date	Mintage	F	VF	XF	Unc	BU
1950	13,534,000	0.35	0.65	1.50	5.00	8.00
1951	153,689,000	0.20	0.35	0.75	2.00	3.50
1952	76,810,000	0.20	0.35	0.75	2.00	3.50
1953	46,272,000	0.25	0.50	0.75	2.50	4.00
1954	2,207,000	4.00	12.00	30.00	50.00	80.00
1955	47,466,000	0.20	0.35	0.75	2.50	4.00
1956	2,570,000	—	—	—	—	—

Note: Reported, not confirmed.

1957	26,351,000	0.50	1.00	2.00	4.50	7.50
1958 (w)	27,213,000	0.50	1.00	2.00	4.50	7.50
1959	125,000	—	—	—	—	—

Note: Reported, not confirmed.

KM# 915.2 10 FRANCS
Aluminum-Bronze, 20 mm. **Obv:** Head left **Rev:** Rooster above laurel sprig, denominaton at right

Date	Mintage	F	VF	XF	Unc	BU
1950B	4,808,000	1.00	3.00	6.00	17.50	30.00
1951B	106,866,000	0.20	0.35	0.75	2.00	3.00
1952B	72,346,000	0.20	0.35	0.75	2.00	3.00
1953B	36,466,000	0.25	0.50	1.00	3.00	4.50
1954B	21,634,000	0.75	1.50	3.50	7.00	10.00
1958B	1,500,000	—	—	—	—	—

Note: Reported, not confirmed.

KM# 847 20 FRANCS
6.4516 g., 0.9000 Gold 0.1867 oz. AGW **Edge:** DIEU PROTEGE LA FRANCE

Date	Mintage	F	VF	XF	Unc	BU
1901A	2,643,000	—	—	BV	200	325
1901A	2,643,000	—	—	BV	200	325
1902A	2,394,000	—	—	BV	200	325
1902A	2,394,000	—	—	BV	200	325
1903A	4,405,000	—	—	BV	200	325
1904A	7,706,000	—	—	BV	200	325
1905A	9,158,000	—	—	BV	200	325
1906A	14,613,000	—	—	BV	200	325

KM# 857 20 FRANCS
6.4516 g., 0.9000 Gold 0.1867 oz. AGW **Obv:** Oak leaf wreath encircles liberty head right **Rev:** Rooster divides denomination, date below **Edge:** LIBERTE EGALITE FRATERNITE **Note:** All dates from 1907-1914 have been officially restruck.

Date	Mintage	F	VF	XF	Unc	BU
1906	—	—	—	BV	200	315
1907	17,716,000	—	—	BV	200	315
1908	6,721,000	—	—	BV	200	315
1909	9,637,000	—	—	BV	200	315
1910	5,779,000	—	—	BV	200	315
1911	5,346,000	—	—	BV	200	315
1912	10,332,000	—	—	BV	200	315
1913	12,163,000	—	—	BV	200	315
1914	6,518,000	—	—	BV	200	315

KM# 879 20 FRANCS
20.0000 g., 0.6800 Silver 0.4372 oz. ASW, 35 mm. **Obv:** Laureate head right, long and short leaves **Rev:** Denomination above date, inscription below, grain columns flank **Note:** Without mint mark.

Date	Mintage	F	VF	XF	Unc	BU
1929 (II)	3,234,000	BV	6.50	9.00	35.00	85.00
1932 Only 1 known	—	—	—	—	—	—
1933 (sl)		BV	6.00	7.00	18.00	40.00

Note: Counterfeits exist in bronze-aluminum with thin silver sheath.

1933 (II)	Inc. above	BV	6.00	7.00	18.00	40.00
1934 (sl)	11,785,000	BV	6.00	10.00	30.00	45.00
1936 (sl)	48,000	200	300	450	700	—
1937 (sl)	1,189,000	10.00	15.00	25.00	50.00	85.00
1938 (sl)	10,910,000	BV	6.00	7.50	20.00	35.00
1939	3,918	1,000	2,000	2,750	4,500	—

KM# 916.1 20 FRANCS
4.0000 g., Aluminum-Bronze, 23.5 mm. **Obv:** Head left, "GEORGES GUIRAUD" behind head **Rev:** Denomination above date at right, rooster above laurel branch at left **Edge:** Plain **Note:** The 4-plume variety has been identified as a counterfeit.

Date	Mintage	F	VF	XF	Unc	BU
1950	5,779,000	0.50	1.00	2.50	7.00	12.00

KM# 916.2 20 FRANCS
Aluminum-Bronze, 23 mm. **Obv:** Head left **Rev:** Rooster above laurel sprig, denomination at right **Note:** The 4-plume variety has been identified as a counterfeit.

Date	Mintage	F	VF	XF	Unc	BU
1950B		1.50	3.00	7.00	20.00	35.00

Note: 3 plumes

| 1950B | | 40.00 | 85.00 | 150 | 225 | — |

Note: 4 plumes

KM# 917.2 20 FRANCS
Aluminum-Bronze, 23 mm. **Obv:** "G. GUIRAUD" behind head **Rev:** Rooster above laurel sprig, denomination at right

Date	Mintage	F	VF	XF	Unc	BU
1950B	43,355,000	25.00	35.00	50.00	135	—

Note: 3 plumes

| 1950B | Inc. above | 0.50 | 1.00 | 3.00 | 6.50 | 10.00 |

Note: 4 plumes

| 1951B | 46,815,000 | 0.30 | 0.50 | 1.75 | 3.50 | 5.00 |

Note: 4 plumes

| 1952B | 54,381,000 | 0.30 | 0.50 | 1.75 | 3.50 | 5.00 |

Note: 4 plumes

| 1953B | 42,410,000 | 0.30 | 0.50 | 1.75 | 3.50 | 5.00 |

Note: 4 plumes

| 1954B | 1,573,000 | 125 | 200 | 350 | 800 | — |

Note: 4 plumes

KM# 917.1 20 FRANCS
Aluminum-Bronze, 23 mm. **Obv:** Head left, "G. GUIRAUD" behind head **Rev:** Denomination above date at right, rooster above laurel branch at left **Note:** Without mint mark.

Date	Mintage	F	VF	XF	Unc	BU
1950	120,656,000	2.00	6.00	12.00	40.00	—

Note: 3 plumes

Date	Mintage	F	VF	XF	Unc	BU
1950	Inc. above	0.25	0.40	1.00	2.50	3.50
Note: 4 plumes						
1951	97,922,000	0.25	0.40	1.00	2.50	3.50
Note: 4 plumes						
1952	130,281,000	0.25	0.40	1.00	2.50	3.50
Note: 4 plumes						
1953	60,158,000	0.30	0.50	1.00	2.50	3.50
Note: 4 plumes						

KM# 831 50 FRANCS
16.1290 g., 0.9000 Gold 0.4667 oz. AGW **Obv:** Standing Genius writing the Constitution, rooster at right, fasces at left **Rev:** Denomination above date within circular wreath

Date	Mintage	F	VF	XF	Unc	BU
1904A	20,000	425	575	950	1,650	2,400

KM# 918.2 50 FRANCS
Aluminum-Bronze, 27 mm. **Obv:** Head left **Rev:** Rooster above laurel, denomination at right

Date	Mintage	F	VF	XF	Unc	BU
1950B Rare	—					
1951B	11,829,000	0.75	1.50	3.00	9.00	16.00
1952B	13,432,000	1.00	2.00	5.00	15.00	28.00
1953B	23,376,000	0.65	1.25	2.50	8.00	14.00
1954B	6,531,000	3.00	5.50	11.50	30.00	50.00

KM# 918.1 50 FRANCS
8.0000 g., Aluminum-Bronze, 27 mm. **Obv:** Head left **Rev:** Denomination above date at right, rooster above laurel branch at left **Edge:** Plain **Note:** Without mint mark.

Date	Mintage	F	VF	XF	Unc	BU
1950	600,000	75.00	150	350	625	—
1951	68,630,000	0.50	1.00	2.25	5.50	9.00
1952	74,212,000	0.50	1.00	2.25	5.50	9.00
1953	63,172,000	0.50	1.00	2.25	5.50	9.00
1954	997,000	15.00	35.00	65.00	110	—
1958 (w)	501,000	25.00	50.00	85.00	240	—

KM# 832 100 FRANCS
32.2581 g., 0.9000 Gold 0.9334 oz. AGW **Obv:** Standing Genius writing the Constitution, rooster on right, fasces on left **Rev:** Denomination above date within circular wreath **Edge:** DIEU PROTEGE LA FRANCE

Date	Mintage	F	VF	XF	Unc	BU
1901A	10,000	—	—	BV	950	1,500
1901A	10,000	—	—	BV	950	1,500
1902A	10,000	—	—	BV	950	1,500
1902A	10,000	—	—	BV	950	1,500
1903A	10,000	—	—	BV	950	1,500
1904A	20,000	—	—	BV	950	1,500
1905A	10,000	—	—	BV	950	1,500
1906A	30,000	—	—	BV	950	1,500

KM# 858 100 FRANCS
32.2581 g., 0.9000 Gold 0.9334 oz. AGW **Obv:** Standing Genius writing the constitution, rooster on right, column on the left **Rev:** Denomination and date within wreath **Edge:** LIBERTE EGALITE FRATERNITE

Date	Mintage	F	VF	XF	Unc	BU
1907A	20,000	—	—	BV+5%	950	1,150
1908A	23,000	—	—	BV+5%	950	1,150
1909A	20,000	—	—	BV+5%	950	1,150
1910A	20,000	—	—	BV+5%	950	1,150
1911A	30,000	—	—	BV+5%	950	1,150
1912A	20,000	—	—	BV+5%	950	1,150
1913A	30,000	—	—	BV+5%	950	1,150
1914A Rare	1,281					

KM# 880 100 FRANCS
6.5500 g., 0.9000 Gold 0.1895 oz. AGW **Obv:** Winged head left **Rev:** Denomination above grain sprig, date below, laurel and oak branches flank **Note:** Without mint mark.

Date	Mintage	F	VF	XF	Unc	BU
1929	50	—	—	2,500	4,000	—
1932	Est. 50	—	—	3,250	4,750	—
1933	Est. 300	—	—	1,650	2,500	—
1934 Rare	—					
1935	6,102,000	—	—	BV+5%	350	750
1936	7,689,000	—	—	BV+5%	350	750

KM# 919.1 100 FRANCS
6.0000 g., Copper-Nickel, 24 mm. **Obv:** Liberty bust with torch right **Rev:** Denomination above date at left, grain sprigs at right **Edge:** Reeded

Date	Mintage	F	VF	XF	Unc	BU
1954	97,285,000	0.50	1.00	2.50	7.00	10.00
1955	152,517,000	0.25	0.75	1.50	4.50	6.00
1956	7,578,000	2.00	5.00	8.00	30.00	—
1957	11,312,000	1.50	3.00	6.00	18.00	30.00
1958 (w)	3,256,000	2.50	5.50	12.50	35.00	—
1958 (o)	Inc. above	20.00	40.00	90.00	175	—

KM# 919.2 100 FRANCS
Copper-Nickel, 24 mm. **Obv:** Liberty bust with torch right **Rev:** Denomination and date left of grain sprigs

Date	Mintage	F	VF	XF	Unc	BU
1954B	86,261,000	0.50	1.25	2.50	5.00	8.00
1955B	136,585,000	0.25	0.75	1.50	3.50	5.00
1956B	19,154,000	1.00	2.00	4.50	10.00	15.00
1957B	25,702,000	1.00	2.00	4.50	12.50	22.00
1958B	54,072,000	1.00	2.00	4.50	11.50	20.00

REFORM COINAGE
Commencing 1960
1 Old Franc = 1 New Centime; 100 New Centimes = 1 New Franc

KM# 928 CENTIME
1.6500 g., Chrome-Steel, 15 mm. **Obv:** Cursive legend surrounds grain sprig **Rev:** Cursive denomination, date at top **Edge:** Plain **Note:** 1991-1993 dated coins, non-Proof, exist in both coin and medal alignment. Values given here are for medal alignment examples. Pieces struck in coin alignment have been traded for as much as $50.00.

Date	Mintage	F	VF	XF	Unc	BU
1962	34,200,000	—	—	0.10	0.25	0.35
1963	16,811,000	—	0.10	0.15	0.35	0.50
1964	22,654,000	—	—	0.10	0.25	0.35
1965	47,799,000	—	—	0.10	0.25	0.35
1966	19,688,000	—	—	0.10	0.25	0.35
1967	52,308,000	—	—	0.10	0.25	0.35
1968	40,890,000	—	—	0.10	0.25	0.35
1969	35,430,000	—	—	0.10	0.25	0.35
1970	29,600,000	—	—	0.10	0.25	0.35
1971	3,082,000	—	—	0.10	0.25	0.35
1972	1,014,999	—	0.10	0.15	0.35	0.50
1973	1,806,000	—	0.10	0.15	0.35	0.50
1974	7,949,000	—	—	0.10	0.25	0.35
1975	771,000	—	0.10	0.25	1.00	1.50
1976	4,482,000	—	—	0.10	0.25	0.35
1977	6,425,000	—	—	0.10	0.25	0.35
1978	1,236,000	—	0.10	0.15	0.35	0.50
1979	2,213,000	—	—	0.10	0.25	0.35
1980	60,000	—	—	—	1.00	1.50
1981	50,000	—	—	—	1.00	1.50
1982	69,000	—	—	—	1.00	1.50
1983	101,000	—	—	—	1.00	1.50
1984	50,000	—	—	—	1.00	1.50
1985	20,000	—	—	—	1.00	1.50
1986	48,000	—	—	—	1.00	1.50
Note: In sets only						
1987	100,000	—	—	—	1.00	1.50
1988	100,000	—	—	—	1.00	1.50
1989	83,000	—	—	—	1.00	1.50
1990	15,000	—	—	—	1.00	1.50
1991	5,000	—	—	—	1.00	1.50
1991 Proof	10,000	Value: 2.00				
1992	85,000	—	—	—	1.00	1.50
1992 Proof	15,000	Value: 2.00				
1993	40,000	—	—	—	1.00	1.50
1993 Proof	10,000	Value: 2.00				
1994 bee	20,000	—	—	—	1.00	1.50
1994 fish	50,000	—	—	—	1.00	1.50
1995	25,000	—	—	—	1.00	1.50
1995 Proof	10,000	Value: 2.00				
1996	17,000	—	—	—	1.00	1.50
1996 Proof	8,000	Value: 2.00				
1997	15,000	—	—	—	1.00	1.50
Note: In sets only						
1997 Proof	10,000	Value: 2.00				
1998	—	—	—	—	1.00	1.50
Note: In sets only						
1998 Proof	—	Value: 2.00				
1999	—	—	—	—	1.00	1.50
Note: In sets only						
1999 Proof	—	Value: 2.00				
2000	—	—	—	—	1.00	1.50
Note: In sets only						
2000 Proof	—	Value: 2.00				

KM# 928a CENTIME
2.5000 g., 0.7500 Gold 0.0603 oz. AGW **Obv:** Cursive legend surrounds grain sprig, medallic alignment **Rev:** Cursive denomination, date above, medallic alignment **Edge:** Plain **Note:** Last Centime.

Date	Mintage	F	VF	XF	Unc	BU
2000	25,000	—	—	—	—	65.00

KM# 927 5 CENTIMES
Chrome-Steel **Obv:** Cursive legend surrounds grain sprig **Rev:** Cursive denomination, date above

Date	Mintage	F	VF	XF	Unc	BU
1961	39,000,000	0.10	0.20	0.50	2.00	3.00
1962	166,360,000	0.10	0.15	0.20	0.75	1.00

Date	Mintage	F	VF	XF	Unc	BU
1963	71,900,000	0.10	0.20	0.40	1.00	1.50
1964	126,480,000	0.10	0.15	0.30	0.75	1.00

KM# 933 5 CENTIMES
2.0000 g., Copper-Aluminum-Nickel, 17 mm. **Obv:** Liberty bust left **Rev:** Denomination above date, grain sprig below, laurel branch at left **Edge:** Plain **Note:** 1991-1993 dated coins, non-Proof exist in both coin and medal alignment.

Date	Mintage	F	VF	XF	Unc	BU
1966	502,512,000	—	—	—	0.10	0.15
1967	11,747,000	—	—	0.10	0.25	0.35
1968	110,395,000	—	—	—	0.10	0.15
1969	94,955,000	—	—	—	0.10	0.15
1970	58,900,000	—	—	—	0.10	0.15
1971	93,190,000	—	—	—	0.10	0.15
1972	100,515,000	—	—	—	0.10	0.15
1973	100,344,000	—	—	—	0.10	0.15
1974	103,890,000	—	—	—	0.10	0.15
1975	95,835,000	—	—	—	0.10	0.15
1976	148,395,000	—	—	—	0.10	0.15
1977	115,285,000	—	—	—	0.10	0.15
1978	189,804,000	—	—	—	0.10	0.15
1979	180,000,000	—	—	—	0.10	0.15
1980	180,010,000	—	—	—	0.10	0.15
1981	134,974,000	—	—	—	0.10	0.15
1982	138,000,000	—	—	—	0.10	0.15
1983	132,000,000	—	—	—	0.10	0.15
1984	150,000,000	—	—	—	0.10	0.15
1985	170,000,000	—	—	—	0.10	0.15
1986	280,000,000	—	—	—	0.10	0.15
1987	310,000,000	—	—	—	0.10	0.15
1988	200,000,000	—	—	—	0.10	0.15
1989	84,000	—	—	—	1.00	1.50
1990	79,992,000	—	—	—	0.20	0.30
1991	49,994,000	—	—	—	0.20	0.30
1991 Proof	10,000	Value: 1.00				
1992	179,996,000	—	—	—	0.20	0.30
1992 Proof	15,000	Value: 1.00				
1993	154,988,000	—	—	—	0.20	0.30
1993 Proof	10,000	Value: 1.00				
1994	—	—	—	—	0.20	0.30
1994 fish	60,000,000	—	—	—	0.20	0.30
1994 fish Proof	10,000	—	—	—	—	—
1994 bee	59,996,000	—	—	—	0.20	0.30
1995	129,991,999	—	—	—	0.20	0.30
1995 Proof	10,000	Value: 1.00				
1996	139,990,000	—	—	—	0.20	0.30
1996 Proof	8,000	Value: 1.00				
1997	199,995,000	—	—	—	0.20	0.30
1997 Proof	10,000	Value: 1.00				
1998	300,084,000	—	—	—	0.20	0.30
1998 Proof	—	Value: 1.00				
1999	—	—	—	—	1.50	2.50

Note: In sets only

Date	Mintage	F	VF	XF	Unc	BU
1999 Proof	—	Value: 1.00				
2000	—	—	—	—	1.50	2.50

Note: In sets only

Date	Mintage	F	VF	XF	Unc	BU
2000 Proof	—	Value: 1.00				

KM# 929 10 CENTIMES
3.0000 g., Copper-Aluminum-Nickel, 20 mm. **Obv:** Liberty bust left **Rev:** Denomination above date, grain sprig below, laurel branch at left **Edge:** Plain **Note:** Without mint mark. 1991-1993 dated coins, non-Proof, exist in both coin and medal alignment.

Date	Mintage	F	VF	XF	Unc	BU
1962	29,100,000	—	—	0.10	0.40	0.60
1963	217,601,000	—	—	—	0.10	0.15
1964	93,409,000	—	—	0.10	0.20	0.30
1965	41,220,000	—	—	0.10	0.30	0.50
1966	16,428,999	—	0.10	0.15	0.40	0.60
1967	196,728,000	—	—	—	0.10	0.15
1968	111,700,000	—	—	—	0.10	0.15
1969	129,530,000	—	—	—	0.10	0.15
1970	77,020,000	—	—	—	0.10	0.15
1971	26,280,000	—	—	—	0.10	0.15
1972	45,700,000	—	—	—	0.10	0.15
1973	58,000,000	—	—	—	0.10	0.15
1974	91,990,000	—	—	—	0.10	0.15
1975	74,450,000	—	—	—	0.10	0.15
1976	137,320,000	—	—	—	0.10	0.15
1977	140,110,000	—	—	—	0.10	0.15
1978	154,360,000	—	—	—	0.10	0.15
1979	140,000,000	—	—	—	0.10	0.15
1980	140,010,000	—	—	—	0.10	0.15
1981	135,000,000	—	—	—	0.10	0.15
1982	110,000,000	—	—	—	0.10	0.15
1983	150,000,000	—	—	—	0.10	0.15
1984	200,000,000	—	—	—	0.10	0.15
1985	170,000,000	—	—	—	0.10	0.15
1986	150,000,000	—	—	—	0.10	0.15
1987	150,000,000	—	—	—	0.10	0.15
1988	145,000,000	—	—	—	0.10	0.15
1989	179,984,000	—	—	—	0.10	0.15
1990	179,992,000	—	—	—	0.10	0.15
1991	179,986,000	—	—	—	0.10	0.15
1991 Proof	10,000	Value: 1.00				
1992	179,996,000	—	—	—	0.10	0.15
1992 Proof	15,000	Value: 1.00				
1993	154,988,000	—	—	—	0.10	0.15
1993 Proof	10,000	Value: 1.00				
1994	—	—	—	—	0.10	0.15
1994 Fish	103,000,000	—	—	—	0.10	0.15
1994 Fish Proof	10,000	Value: 1.00				
1994 Bee	76,988,000	—	—	—	0.10	0.15
1995	169,996,000	—	—	—	0.10	0.15
1995 Proof	10,000	Value: 1.00				
1996	179,981,000	—	—	—	0.10	0.15
1996 Proof	8,000	Value: 1.00				
1997	551,991,000	—	—	—	0.10	0.15
1997 Proof	10,000	Value: 1.00				
1998	350,000,000	—	—	—	0.10	0.15
1998 Proof	—	Value: 1.00				
1999	—	—	—	—	2.00	3.00

Note: In sets only

Date	Mintage	F	VF	XF	Unc	BU
1999 Proof	—	Value: 1.00				
2000	60,000,000	—	—	—	0.10	0.15
2000 Proof	—	Value: 1.00				

KM# 930 20 CENTIMES
4.0000 g., Copper-Aluminum-Nickel, 23.5 mm. **Obv:** Liberty bust left **Rev:** Denomination above date, grain sprig below, laurel branch at left **Edge:** Plain **Note:** Without mint mark. 1991-1993 dated coins, non-Proof, exist in both coin and medal alignment.

Date	Mintage	F	VF	XF	Unc	BU
1962	48,200,000	—	—	0.10	0.40	0.60
1963	190,330,000	—	—	0.10	0.30	0.50
1964	127,521,000	—	—	0.10	0.30	0.50
1965	27,024,000	—	0.10	0.20	0.40	0.60
1966	21,762,000	—	0.10	0.20	0.40	0.60
1967	138,780,000	—	—	0.10	0.15	0.25
1968	77,408,000	—	—	0.10	0.20	0.30
1969	50,570,000	—	—	0.10	0.20	0.30
1970	70,040,000	—	—	0.10	0.15	0.25
1971	31,080,000	—	—	0.10	0.15	0.25
1972	39,740,000	—	—	0.10	0.15	0.25
1973	45,240,000	—	—	0.10	0.15	0.25
1974	54,250,000	—	—	0.10	0.15	0.25
1975	40,570,000	—	—	0.10	0.15	0.25
1976	117,610,000	—	—	—	0.10	0.15
1977	100,340,000	—	—	—	0.10	0.15
1978	125,015,000	—	—	—	0.10	0.15
1979	70,000,000	—	—	—	0.10	0.15
1980	20,010,000	—	—	0.10	0.15	0.25
1981	125,000,000	—	—	—	0.10	0.15
1982	150,000,000	—	—	—	0.10	0.15
1983	110,000,000	—	—	—	0.10	0.15
1984	200,000,000	—	—	—	0.10	0.15
1985	150,000,000	—	—	—	0.10	0.15
1986	40,000,000	—	—	—	0.10	0.15
1987	60,000,000	—	—	—	0.10	0.15
1988	220,000,000	—	—	—	0.10	0.15
1989	139,985,000	—	—	—	0.10	0.15
1990	49,990,000	—	—	—	0.10	0.15
1991	39,992,000	—	—	—	0.10	0.15
1991 1 Proof	10,000	Value: 1.00				
1992	89,985,000	—	—	—	0.10	0.15
1992 1 Proof	15,000	Value: 1.00				
1993	10,990,000	—	—	—	0.10	0.15
1993 1 Proof	10,000	Value: 1.00				
1994	—	—	—	—	0.10	0.15
1994 Fish	60,000,000	—	—	—	0.10	0.15
1994 Fish Proof	10,000	Value: 1.00				
1994 Bee	79,900,000	—	—	—	0.10	0.15
1995	109,995,000	—	—	—	0.10	0.15
1995 Proof	10,000	Value: 1.00				
1996	139,987,000	—	—	—	0.10	0.15
1996 Proof	8,000	Value: 1.00				
1997	436,216,500	—	—	—	0.10	0.15
1997 Proof	10,000	Value: 1.00				
1998	—	—	—	—	2.00	3.00

Note: In sets only

Date	Mintage	F	VF	XF	Unc	BU
1998 Proof	—	Value: 1.00				
1999	—	—	—	—	2.00	3.00

Note: In sets only

Date	Mintage	F	VF	XF	Unc	BU
1999 Proof	—	Value: 1.00				

Date	Mintage	F	VF	XF	Unc	BU
2000	85,385,000	—	—	—	0.10	0.15
2000 Proof	—	Value: 1.00				

KM# 939.1 50 CENTIMES
4.5000 g., Aluminum-Bronze, 19.5 mm. **Obv:** Liberty bust left, 3 folds in collar **Rev:** Denomination above date, grain sprig below, laurel branch at left **Edge:** Reeded

Date	Mintage	F	VF	XF	Unc	BU
1962	37,560,000	0.30	0.60	1.50	3.00	5.00
1963	62,482,000	0.20	0.40	1.00	2.00	3.00

KM# 939.2 50 CENTIMES
Aluminum-Bronze, 25 mm. **Obv:** 4 folds in collar **Rev:** Denomination above grain sprig, laurel at left

Date	Mintage	F	VF	XF	Unc	BU
1962	Inc. above	30.00	70.00	120	170	275
1963	Inc. above	0.20	0.40	1.00	2.00	3.00
1964	41,471,000	0.45	0.90	2.00	6.00	9.00

KM# 931.1 1/2 FRANC
4.5000 g., Nickel, 19.5 mm. **Obv:** The seed sower **Rev:** Laurel divides denomination and date **Edge:** Reeded **Note:** Without mint mark.

Date	Mintage	F	VF	XF	Unc	BU
1965	184,834,000	—	—	0.15	0.30	0.50

Note: Small legends

Date	Mintage	F	VF	XF	Unc	BU
1965	Inc. above	—	—	0.15	0.30	0.50

Note: Large legends

Date	Mintage	F	VF	XF	Unc	BU
1966	88,890,000	—	—	0.15	0.30	0.50
1967	28,394,000	—	—	0.15	0.40	0.60
1968	57,548,000	—	—	0.15	0.30	0.50
1969	47,144,000	—	—	0.15	0.30	0.50
1970	42,298,000	—	—	0.15	0.30	0.50
1971	36,068,000	—	—	0.15	0.30	0.50
1972	42,302,000	—	—	0.15	0.30	0.50
1972	Inc. above	25.00	50.00	100	150	

Note: Without "O. ROTY"

Date	Mintage	F	VF	XF	Unc	BU
1973	48,372,000	—	—	0.15	0.30	0.60
1974	37,072,000	—	—	0.15	0.30	0.60
1975	22,803,000	—	—	0.15	0.40	0.60
1976	115,314,000	—	—	0.15	0.30	0.50
1977	131,644,000	—	—	0.15	0.30	0.60
1978	63,360,000	—	—	0.15	0.30	0.50
1979	51,000	—	—	—	0.50	0.75
1980	60,000	—	—	—	0.50	0.75

Note: In sets only

Date	Mintage	F	VF	XF	Unc	BU
1981	50,000	—	—	—	0.50	0.75
1982	78,000	—	—	—	0.50	0.75
1983	50,000,000	—	—	0.15	0.30	0.50
1984	80,000,000	—	—	0.15	0.30	0.50
1985	50,000,000	—	—	—	1.50	2.50
1986	110,000,000	—	—	—	1.50	2.50
1987	50,000,000	—	—	—	0.30	0.50
1988	100,000	—	—	—	0.40	0.60
1989	83,000	—	—	—	0.40	0.60
1990	15,000	—	—	—	0.40	0.60
1991	49,988,000	—	—	—	0.40	0.60

Note: Exists in both coin and medal alignment

Date	Mintage	F	VF	XF	Unc	BU
1992	29,968,000	—	—	—	0.40	0.60

Note: Exists in both coin and medal alignment

Date	Mintage	F	VF	XF	Unc	BU
1993	24,972,000	—	—	—	0.40	0.60
1994 Fish	10,000,000	—	—	—	0.40	0.60
1994 Bee	29,972,000	—	—	—	0.40	0.60
1995	29,976,000	—	—	—	0.40	0.60
1996	55,978,000	—	—	—	0.40	0.60
1997	99,976,000	—	—	—	0.40	0.60
1998	—	—	—	—	2.00	3.00

Note: In sets only

Date	Mintage	F	VF	XF	Unc	BU
1999	—	—	—	—	2.00	3.00

Note: In sets only

Date	Mintage	F	VF	XF	Unc	BU
2000	75,000,000	—	—	—	0.40	0.60

KM# 931.2 1/2 FRANC
4.5000 g., Nickel, 19.5 mm. **Obv:** Modified sower, engraver's signature: "O. ROTY" preceded by "D'AP" **Rev:** Laurel divides date and denomination **Edge:** Plain

Date	Mintage	F	VF	XF	Unc	BU
1991	—	—	—	—	0.40	0.60
1991 Proof	10,000	Value: 1.50				
1992	—	—	—	—	0.40	0.60
1992 Proof	15,000	Value: 1.50				
1993	—	—	—	—	0.40	0.60
1993 Proof	10,000	Value: 1.50				

Date	Mintage	F	VF	XF	Unc	BU
1994 Fish	—	—	—	—	0.40	0.60
1994 Fish Proof	10,000	Value: 1.50				
1994 Bee	—	—	—	—	0.40	0.60
1995	—	—	—	—	0.40	0.60
1995 Proof	10,000	Value: 1.50				
1996	—	—	—	—	0.40	0.60
1996 Proof	8,000	Value: 1.50				
1997	—	—	—	—	0.40	0.60
1997 Proof	10,000	Value: 1.50				
1998 Proof	—	Value: 1.50				
1999 Proof	—	Value: 1.50				
2000	—	—	—	—	0.40	0.60
2000 Proof	—	Value: 1.50				

KM# 925.1 FRANC
6.0000 g., Nickel, 24 mm. **Obv:** The seed sower **Rev:** Laurel branch divides denomination and date **Edge:** Reeded
Note: Without mint mark.

Date	Mintage	F	VF	XF	Unc	BU
1960	406,375,000	—	—	0.20	0.40	0.60
1961	119,611,000	—	—	0.20	0.40	0.60
1962	14,014,000	—	—	0.25	0.50	0.75
1964	77,425,000	—	—	0.20	0.40	0.60
1965	44,252,000	—	—	0.20	0.40	0.60
1966	38,038,000	—	—	0.20	0.40	0.60
1967	11,322,000	—	—	0.25	0.50	0.75
1968	51,550,000	—	—	0.20	0.40	0.60
1969	70,595,000	—	—	0.20	0.40	0.60
1970	42,560,000	—	—	0.20	0.40	0.60
1971	42,475,000	—	—	0.20	0.40	0.60
1972	48,250,000	—	—	0.20	0.40	0.60
1973	70,000,000	—	—	0.20	0.40	0.60
1974	82,235,000	—	—	0.20	0.40	0.60
1975	101,685,000	—	—	0.20	0.40	0.60
1976	192,520,000	—	—	0.20	0.40	0.60
1977	230,085,000	—	—	0.20	0.40	0.60
1978	136,580,000	—	—	0.20	0.40	0.60
1979	51,000	—	—	—	3.00	5.00
1980	60,000	—	—	—	3.00	5.00
	Note: In sets only					
1981	50,000	—	—	—	3.00	5.00
1982	92,000	—	—	—	3.00	5.00
1983	101,000	—	—	—	3.00	5.00
1984	50,000	—	—	—	3.00	5.00
1985	7,002,000	—	—	—	2.00	3.00
1986	48,000	—	—	—	3.00	5.00
1987	100,000	—	—	—	2.50	4.00
1988	100,000	—	—	—	2.50	4.00
1989	83,000	—	—	—	3.00	5.00
1990	15,000	—	—	—	4.00	6.00
1991	54,988,000	—	—	—	0.40	0.60
	Note: Exists in both coin and medal alignment					
1992	30,000,000	—	—	—	0.40	0.60
	Note: Exists in both coin and medal alignment					
1993	20,000	—	—	—	4.00	6.00
1994 Bee	4,792,000	—	—	—	0.40	0.60
1995	15,000	—	—	—	0.40	0.60
1996	—	—	—	—	3.00	5.00
	Note: In sets only					
1997	—	—	—	—	3.00	5.00
	Note: In sets only					
1998	—	—	—	—	3.00	5.00
	Note: In sets only					
1999	80,432,000	—	—	—	0.40	0.60
2000	—	—	—	—	3.00	5.00
	Note: In sets only					

KM# 963 FRANC
6.0000 g., Nickel, 24 mm. **Subject:** 30th Anniversary of Fifth Republic **Obv:** Head right **Rev:** Denomination within six sided wreath, dates below

Date	Mintage	F	VF	XF	Unc	BU
1988	49,921,000	—	—	—	1.00	2.00

KM# 978 FRANC
22.2000 g., 0.9000 Silver 0.6423 oz. ASW, 24 mm. **Subject:** 30th Anniversary of Fifth Republic

Date	Mintage	F	VF	XF	Unc	BU
1988 Proof	60,000	Value: 30.00				

KM# 979 FRANC
9.0000 g., 0.9200 Gold 0.2662 oz. AGW, 24 mm. **Subject:** 30th Anniversary of Fifth Republic

Date	Mintage	F	VF	XF	Unc	BU
1988 Proof	20,000	Value: 260				

KM# 967 FRANC
6.0000 g., Nickel, 24 mm. **Subject:** 200th Anniversary of Estates General **Obv:** Denomination within wreath, date below **Rev:** Three figure monument

Date	Mintage	F	VF	XF	Unc	BU
1989	5,010,000	—	—	—	2.50	4.50

KM# 925.2 FRANC
6.0000 g., Nickel, 24 mm. **Obv:** Modified sower, engraver's signature: O. ROTY, preceded by D'AP **Rev:** Laurel divides date and denomination **Edge:** Plain

Date	Mintage	F	VF	XF	Unc	BU
1991	—	—	—	—	0.40	0.60
1991 Proof	10,000	Value: 2.50				
1992	—	—	—	—	0.40	0.60
1992 Proof	15,000	Value: 2.50				
1993	—	—	—	—	0.40	0.60
1993 Proof	10,000	Value: 2.50				
1994 Bee	—	—	—	—	0.40	0.60
1994 Fish Proof	10,000	Value: 2.50				
1995	35,000	—	—	—	0.40	0.60
1995 Proof	10,000	Value: 2.50				
1996	5,000	—	—	—	0.40	0.60
1996 Proof	8,000	Value: 2.50				
1997	15,000	—	—	—	0.40	0.60
1997 Proof	—	Value: 2.50				
1998 Proof	—	Value: 2.50				
1999 Proof	—	Value: 2.50				
2000	—	—	—	—	0.40	0.60
2000 Proof	—	Value: 2.50				

KM# 1004.1 FRANC
6.0000 g., Nickel, 24 mm. **Subject:** 200th Anniversary of French Republic **Obv:** Liberty bust left **Rev:** Denomination within wreath, date below

Date	Mintage	F	VF	XF	Unc	BU
1992	30,000,000	—	—	—	1.25	2.00

KM# 1004.1a FRANC
9.0000 g., 0.9200 Gold 0.2662 oz. AGW, 24 mm. **Subject:** 200th Anniversary of the French Republic **Obv:** Liberty bust left **Rev:** Denomination within wreath

Date	Mintage	F	VF	XF	Unc	BU
1992 Proof	5,000	Value: 265				

KM# 1004.1b FRANC
11.0000 g., 0.9990 Platinum 0.3533 oz. APW, 24 mm. **Obv:** Liberty bust left **Rev:** Denomination within wreath

Date	Mintage	F	VF	XF	Unc	BU
1992 Proof	2,000	Value: 650				

KM# 1005 FRANC
15.5500 g., 0.9000 Silver 0.4499 oz. ASW **Obv:** Liberty bust left **Rev:** Denomination within wreath, date below

Date	Mintage	F	VF	XF	Unc	BU
1992	—	—	—	—	17.50	25.00
1992 Proof	30,000	Value: 35.00				

KM# 1014 FRANC
22.2000 g., 0.9000 Silver 0.6423 oz. ASW **Obv:** American soldiers storming Omaha Beach **Rev:** Head of Liberty Statue, flags, denomination and date

Date	Mintage	F	VF	XF	Unc	BU
1993	1,000,000	—	—	—	14.00	20.00
1993 Proof	150,000	Value: 30.00				

KM# 1015 FRANC
17.0000 g., 0.9250 Gold 0.5055 oz. AGW **Subject:** Normandy Invasion **Obv:** American soldiers storming Omaha beach **Rev:** Head of Liberty Statue, flags, denomination and date

Date	Mintage	F	VF	XF	Unc	BU
1993 Proof	Est. 20,000	Value: 485				

KM# 1133 FRANC
6.0000 g., Nickel, 24 mm. **Subject:** 200th Anniversary of Institute of France **Obv:** Institut de France building divides denomination, date below **Rev:** Framed arms, date below, branches flank three sides

Date	Mintage	F	VF	XF	Unc	BU
1995	4,976,000	—	—	—	1.50	2.00

KM# 1160 FRANC
6.0000 g., Nickel, 24 mm. **Subject:** 100th Anniversary - Birth of Jacques Rueff **Obv:** Head at right facing **Rev:** Figure at center, flanked by branches, divides denomination

Date	Mintage	F	VF	XF	Unc	BU
1996	2,976,000	—	—	—	1.50	2.50

KM# 1211 FRANC
12.0000 g., 0.9000 Silver 0.3472 oz. ASW **Subject:** 1998 World Cup Soccer Games **Obv:** Games logo above denomination **Rev:** Soccer ball on world globe

Date	Mintage	F	VF	XF	Unc	BU
1997	250,000	—	—	—	25.00	30.00

KM# 1214 FRANC
11.9400 g., 0.9000 Silver 0.3455 oz. ASW **Subject:** 125th Anniversary - Universal Postal Union **Obv:** Partial stamp design, monograms, dates above denomination **Rev:** Head left on stamp design, patterned coin background **Edge:** Reeded

Date	Mintage	F	VF	XF	Unc	BU
ND(1999)	—	—	—	—	20.00	25.00

KM# 1291   FRANC
13.0000 g., 0.9000 Silver 0.3761 oz. ASW, 30 mm.
Subject: Rugby **Obv:** Players in a scrum, date above **Rev:** Players jumping for a ball, denomination below **Edge:** Plain

Date	Mintage	F	VF	XF	Unc	BU
1999	50,000	—	—	—	25.00	30.00

KM# 925.1a   FRANC
8.0000 g., 0.7500 Gold 0.1929 oz. AGW, 24 mm. **Obv:** The seed sower **Rev:** Laurel divides date and denomination **Edge:** Reeded
Note: Medallic alignment.

Date	Mintage	F	VF	XF	Unc	BU
2000	5,000	—	—	—	220	250

KM# 1262   FRANC
13.0000 g., 0.9000 Silver 0.3761 oz. ASW **Subject:** World Soccer Championship **Obv:** Soccer ball design, denomination on ball divides "R" and "F", date below **Rev:** Soccer player **Edge:** Reeded

Date	Mintage	F	VF	XF	Unc	BU
2000	10,000	—	—	—	25.00	30.00

KM# 942.1   2 FRANCS
7.5000 g., Nickel, 26.5 mm. **Obv:** The seed sower **Rev:** Denomination on branches, date below **Edge:** Plain

Date	Mintage	F	VF	XF	Unc	BU
1979	130,000,000	—	—	0.40	0.65	1.00
1980	100,010,000	—	—	0.40	0.65	1.00
1981	120,000,000	—	—	0.40	0.65	1.00
1982	90,000,000	—	—	0.40	0.65	1.00
1983	90,000,000	—	—	0.40	0.65	1.00
1984	50,000	—	—	—	0.75	1.25
1985	20,000	—	—	—	2.00	3.00
1986	48,000	—	—	—	2.00	3.00
1987	100,000	—	—	—	0.75	1.25
1988	100,000	—	—	—	0.75	1.25
1989	83,000	—	—	—	0.75	1.25
1990	15,000	—	—	—	0.75	1.25
1994 Fish	—	—	—	—	0.75	1.25
1994 Bee	—	—	—	—	14.00	20.00
1995	—	—	—	—	0.75	1.25
1996	—	—	—	—	0.75	1.25
1997	—	—	—	—	0.75	1.25
1998	—	—	—	—	0.75	1.25
1999	—	—	—	—	0.75	1.25
2000	—	—	—	—	0.75	1.25

KM# 942.2   2 FRANCS
7.5000 g., Nickel, 26.5 mm. **Obv:** The seed sower **Rev:** Denomination on branches, date below **Edge:** Plain

Date	Mintage	F	VF	XF	Unc	BU
1991	5,000	—	—	—	—	—
1991 Proof	10,000	Value: 3.50				
1992	15,000	—	—	—	0.75	1.25
1992 Proof	85,000	Value: 3.50				
1993	40,000	—	—	—	0.75	1.25
1993 Proof	10,000	Value: 3.50				
1994 Fish	9,870,000	—	—	—	0.75	1.25
1994 Fish Proof	10,000	Value: 3.50				
1994 Bee	20,000	—	—	—	0.75	1.25
1995	20,000	—	—	—	0.75	1.25
1995 Proof	10,000	Value: 3.50				
1996	11,980,000	—	—	—	0.75	1.25
1996 Proof	8,000	Value: 3.50				
1997	9,990,000	—	—	—	0.75	1.25
1997 Proof	10,000	Value: 3.50				
1998	45,000,000	—	—	—	0.75	1.25
1998 Proof	—	Value: 3.50				
1999 Proof	—	Value: 3.50				

Date	Mintage	F	VF	XF	Unc	BU
2000	25,000,000	—	—	—	0.75	1.25
2000 Proof	—	Value: 3.50				

KM# 1062   2 FRANCS
7.5000 g., Nickel, 26.5 mm. **Obv:** Bust with hat facing, double cross in background **Rev:** Denomination on branches, date below **Edge:** Reeded

Date	Mintage	F	VF	XF	Unc	BU
1993	30,000,000	—	—	—	1.00	1.50

KM# 1119   2 FRANCS
7.5000 g., Nickel, 26.5 mm. **Obv:** Head of Louis Pasteur facing, building at left **Rev:** Denomination to right of bottles, date below

Date	Mintage	F	VF	XF	Unc	BU
1995	9,975,000	—	—	—	2.00	2.75

KM# 1187   2 FRANCS
7.5000 g., Nickel, 26.5 mm. **Obv:** Georges Guynemer, WWI ace fighter pilot, looking left, date below **Rev:** Guynemer's stork emblem below denomination

Date	Mintage	F	VF	XF	Unc	BU
1997	—	—	—	—	2.25	3.00

KM# 1213   2 FRANCS
7.5000 g., Nickel, 26.5 mm. **Subject:** 50th Anniversary- Declaration of Human Rights **Obv:** Rene Cassin head right, initials above inscription, dates and building below **Rev:** Denomination on world globe, laurel spray and date below

Date	Mintage	F	VF	XF	Unc	BU
1998	—	—	—	—	2.25	3.00

KM# 926   5 FRANCS
12.0000 g., 0.8350 Silver 0.3221 oz. ASW, 19 mm. **Obv:** Figure sowing seed **Rev:** Branches divide denomination and date **Edge:** LIBERTE EGALITE FRATERNITE

Date	Mintage	F	VF	XF	Unc	BU
1960	55,182,000	—	—	BV	5.00	6.50
1961	15,630,000	—	—	BV	5.00	6.50
1962	42,500,000	—	—	BV	5.00	6.50
1963	37,936,000	—	—	BV	5.00	6.50
1964	32,378,000	—	—	BV	5.00	6.50
1965	5,156,000	—	—	BV	6.00	7.50
1966	5,017,000	—	—	BV	6.00	7.50

Date	Mintage	F	VF	XF	Unc	BU
1967	502,000	—	BV	6.00	12.00	15.00
1968	557,000	—	—	BV	10.00	12.50
1969	504,000	—	—	BV	10.00	12.50

KM# 926a.1   5 FRANCS
10.0000 g., Nickel Clad Copper-Nickel, 29 mm. **Obv:** The seed sower **Rev:** Branches divide denomination and date **Edge:** Reeded

Date	Mintage	F	VF	XF	Unc	BU
1970	57,890,000	—	—	1.00	1.25	1.75
1971	142,204,000	—	—	1.00	1.25	1.75
1972	45,492,000	—	—	1.00	1.50	2.25
1973	45,079,000	—	—	1.00	1.25	1.75
1974	26,888,000	—	—	1.00	1.25	1.75
1975	16,712,000	—	—	1.00	1.25	1.75
1976	1,662,000	—	1.00	1.25	2.00	3.00
1977	485,000	—	1.00	1.50	2.25	3.50
1978	30,022,000	—	—	1.00	1.25	1.75
1979	51,000	—	—	2.00	3.50	5.50
1980	60,000	—	—	—	5.00	7.50
	Note: In sets only					
1981	50,000	—	—	2.00	3.00	5.50
1982	60,000	—	—	2.00	3.50	5.50
1983	101,000	—	—	2.00	3.50	5.50
1984	49,000	—	—	2.00	3.50	5.50
1985	20,000	—	—	2.00	6.00	9.00
1986	48,000	—	—	—	5.00	7.50
	Note: In sets only					
1987	20,000,000	—	—	—	1.65	2.50
1988	100,000	—	—	—	1.65	2.85
1989	83,000	—	—	—	1.65	3.00
1990	14,990,000	—	—	—	1.65	2.50
1991	7,488,000	—	—	—	1.65	2.50
1992	9,966,000	—	—	—	1.65	2.50
1993	14,970,000	—	—	—	1.65	2.50
1994 Bee	6,000,000	—	—	—	1.65	2.50
1994 Fish	3,990,000	—	—	—	1.65	2.50
1995	19,986,000	—	—	—	1.65	2.50
1996	12,000	—	—	3.00	5.00	7.50
1997	—	—	—	—	—	7.50
	Note: In sets only					
1998	—	—	—	—	5.00	7.50
	Note: In sets only					
1999	—	—	—	—	5.00	7.50
	Note: In sets only					
2000	—	—	—	—	5.00	7.50
	Note: In sets only					

KM# 968   5 FRANCS
10.0000 g., Copper-Nickel, 29 mm. **Subject:** Centennial - Erection of Eiffel Tower **Obv:** Base of tower, denomination above **Rev:** Eiffel Tower, dates at right

Date	Mintage	F	VF	XF	Unc	BU
1989	9,774,000	—	—	—	6.50	9.00

KM# 968a   5 FRANCS
12.0000 g., 0.9000 Silver 0.3472 oz. ASW, 29 mm.
Subject: Centennial - Erection of Eiffel Tower **Obv:** Denomination above tower base **Rev:** Tower view from bottom

Date	Mintage	F	VF	XF	Unc	BU
1989 Proof	80,000	Value: 28.00				

KM# 968b   5 FRANCS
14.0000 g., 0.9250 Gold 0.4163 oz. AGW, 29 mm.
Subject: Centennial - Erection of Eiffel Tower **Obv:** Denomination above tower base **Rev:** Tower view from bottom

Date	Mintage	F	VF	XF	Unc	BU
1989 Proof	30,000	Value: 450				

KM# 968c   5 FRANCS
16.0000 g., 0.9990 Platinum 0.5139 oz. APW, 29 mm.
Subject: Centennial - Erection of Eiffel Tower **Obv:** Denomination above base **Rev:** Tower view from base

Date	Mintage	F	VF	XF	Unc	BU
1989 Proof	Est. 3,000	Value: 750				

Note: 1,800 pieces were melted by MTB Banking

KM# 926a.2   5 FRANCS
6.5000 g., Nickel Clad Copper-Nickel, 29 mm. **Obv:** Modified sower, engraver's signature: "O. ROTY" preceded by "D'AP" **Rev:** Branches divide date and denomination **Edge:** Plain

Date	Mintage	F	VF	XF	Unc	BU
1991	7,490,000				1.65	2.50
1991 Proof	10,000	Value: 6.50				
1992	9,986,000				1.65	2.50
1992 Proof	15,000	Value: 6.50				
1993	14,990,000				1.65	2.50
1993 Proof	10,000	Value: 6.50				
1994 Fish	6,000,000				1.65	2.50
1994 Fish Proof	10,000	Value: 6.50				
1994 Bee	3,990,000				1.65	2.50
1995	20,006,000				1.65	2.50
1995 Proof	—	Value: 6.50				
1996	17,000				1.65	2.50
1996 Proof	8,000	Value: 6.50				
1997	15,000				1.65	2.50
1997 Proof	—	Value: 6.50				
1998 Proof	—	Value: 6.50				
1999 Proof	—	Value: 6.50				
2000	—				1.65	2.50
2000 Proof	—	Value: 6.50				

KM# 1006   5 FRANCS
10.0000 g., Copper-Nickel, 29 mm. **Obv:** Denomination within design **Rev:** Bust of Pierre Mendes France facing

Date	Mintage	F	VF	XF	Unc	BU
1992	10,000,000				4.50	6.00

KM# 1006a   5 FRANCS
12.0000 g., 0.9000 Silver 0.3472 oz. ASW, 29 mm. **Obv:** Denomination within design **Rev:** Bust of Pierre Mendes France facing

Date	Mintage	F	VF	XF	Unc	BU
1992 Proof	10,000	Value: 30.00				

KM# 1006b   5 FRANCS
14.0000 g., 0.9200 Gold 0.4141 oz. AGW, 29 mm. **Obv:** Denomination within design **Rev:** Bust of Pierre Mendes France facing

Date	Mintage	F	VF	XF	Unc	BU
1992 Proof	1,000	Value: 400				

KM# 1007   5 FRANCS
12.0000 g., 0.9000 Silver 0.3472 oz. ASW, 29 mm. **Subject:** French Antarctic Territories **Rev:** 3 albatross in flight

Date	Mintage	F	VF	XF	Unc	BU
1992 Proof	15,000	Value: 50.00				

KM# 1063   5 FRANCS
10.0000 g., Nickel Clad Copper-Nickel, 29 mm. **Obv:** Head of Voltaire the poet 3/4 facing **Rev:** Quill divides building and date from denomination **Edge:** Reeded

Date	Mintage	F	VF	XF	Unc	BU
1994	15,000,000				4.00	5.00

KM# 1118   5 FRANCS
12.0000 g., 0.9000 Silver 0.3472 oz. ASW, 29 mm. **Subject:** 50th Anniversary - United Nations **Obv:** Dove and branch at left, denomination at right **Rev:** UN logo, dates below

Date	Mintage	F	VF	XF	Unc	BU
1995 Proof	250,000	Value: 27.50				

KM# 1118a   5 FRANCS
14.0000 g., 0.9200 Gold 0.4141 oz. AGW, 29 mm. **Obv:** Dove and branch left of denomination **Rev:** UN logo and dates

Date	Mintage	F	VF	XF	Unc	BU
1995 Proof	125,000	Value: 400				

KM# 1155   5 FRANCS
10.0500 g., Nickel Clad Steel, 29 mm. **Obv:** Denomination and date within wreath **Rev:** Hercules group design **Edge:** Reeded

Date	Mintage	F	VF	XF	Unc	BU
1996	4,976,000				4.50	6.00

KM# 1212   5 FRANCS
12.0000 g., 0.9000 Silver 0.3472 oz. ASW, 29 mm. **Subject:** 1998 World Cup Soccer Games: French Victory **Obv:** Game logo above denomination **Rev:** Handheld trophy with stadium in background

Date	Mintage	F	VF	XF	Unc	BU
1998 Proof	Est. 100,000	Value: 45.00				

KM# 1215   5 FRANCS
12.0000 g., 0.9000 Silver 0.3472 oz. ASW, 29 mm. **Subject:** Yves St. Laurent **Obv:** RF monogram within entwined snake design, denomination below **Rev:** Fashion show scene

Date	Mintage	F	VF	XF	Unc	BU
2000	—				30.00	

KM# 1222   5 FRANCS
10.0000 g., Copper-Nickel Plated Nickel, 29 mm. **Subject:** 2000 Years of French Coinage **Obv:** Denomination and date within wreath **Rev:** 1st century B.C. Celtic Parisii Stater coin design **Edge:** Reeded

Date	Mintage	F	VF	XF	Unc	BU
2000	50,000	—			10.00	12.00

KM# 1223   5 FRANCS
10.0000 g., Copper-Nickel Plated Nickel, 29 mm. **Subject:** 2000 Years of French Coinage **Obv:** Denomination and date within wreath **Rev:** Charlemagne Denar coin design **Edge:** Reeded

Date	Mintage	F	VF	XF	Unc	BU
2000	50,000	—			10.00	12.00

KM# 1224   5 FRANCS
10.0000 g., Copper-Nickel Plated Nickel, 29 mm. **Subject:** 2000 Years of French Coinage **Obv:** Denomination and date within wreath **Rev:** Louis IX Gold Ecu design **Edge:** Reeded

Date	Mintage	F	VF	XF	Unc	BU
2000	50,000				9.50	11.50

KM# 1255   6.55957 FRANCS
22.2000 g., 0.9000 Silver 0.6423 oz. ASW **Obv:** Europa allegorical portrait **Rev:** Country names and euro-currency equivalents around RF and denomination in center plus French coin designs **Edge:** Plain

Date	Mintage	F	VF	XF	Unc	BU
1999 Proof	25,000	Value: 40.00				

KM# 1254   6.55957 FRANCS
13.0000 g., 0.9000 Silver 0.3761 oz. ASW **Subject:** Euro Conversion Series **Obv:** Europa allegorical portrait, denomination and date at left **Rev:** Country names and euro-currency equivalents around "RF" and denomination in center **Edge:** Plain **Note:** Struck at Paris Mint.

Date	Mintage	F	VF	XF	Unc	BU
1999	200,000	—			30.00	35.00

KM# 1225   6.55957 FRANCS
22.2000 g., 0.9000 Silver 0.6423 oz. ASW **Subject:** European Art Styles Renaissance **Obv:** Europa allegorical portrait, denomination and date at left **Rev:** Renaissance style buildings **Edge:** "Europa" repeated four times

Date	Mintage	F	VF	XF	Unc	BU
2000 Proof	15,000	Value: 35.00				

KM# 1226   6.55957 FRANCS
22.2000 g., 0.9000 Silver 0.6423 oz. ASW **Series:** European Art Styles - Renaissance Classic and Baroque **Obv:** Europa allegorical portrait, denomination and date at left **Rev:** Buildings, top and left of artistic design

Date	Mintage	F	VF	XF	Unc	BU
2000 Proof	15,000	Value: 35.00				

KM# 1227   6.55957 FRANCS
22.2000 g., 0.9000 Silver 0.6423 oz. ASW **Series:** European Art Styles Renaissance - Art Nouveau **Rev:** Artistic designs

Date	Mintage	F	VF	XF	Unc	BU
2000 Proof	15,000	Value: 35.00				

KM# 1228   6.55957 FRANCS
22.2000 g., 0.9000 Silver 0.6423 oz. ASW **Series:** European Art Styles Renaissance - Modern **Obv:** Europa allegorical portrait and denomination at left **Rev:** Modern artistic designs

Date	Mintage	F	VF	XF	Unc	BU
2000 Proof	15,000	Value: 35.00				

KM# 1244   6.55957 FRANCS
22.2000 g., 0.9000 Silver 0.6423 oz. ASW **Series:** European Art Styles Renaissance - Greek and Roman **Rev:** Greek and Roman columns

Date	Mintage	F	VF	XF	Unc	BU
2000 Proof	15,000	Value: 35.00				

KM# 1245   6.55957 FRANCS
22.2000 g., 0.9000 Silver 0.6423 oz. ASW **Series:** European Art Styles Renaissance - Roman Art and Structures **Rev:** Figure on shield, columns in background

Date	Mintage	F	VF	XF	Unc	BU
2000 Proof	15,000	Value: 35.00				

KM# 1246   6.55957 FRANCS
22.2000 g., 0.9000 Silver 0.6423 oz. ASW **Series:** European Art Styles Renaissance - Gothic **Rev:** Religious figure in foreground, designs in background

Date	Mintage	F	VF	XF	Unc	BU
2000 Proof	15,000	Value: 35.00				

KM# 1258   6.55957 FRANCS
13.0000 g., 0.9000 Silver 0.3761 oz. ASW **Obv:** Country names and euro-currency equivalents around "RF" and denomination **Rev:** Europa allegorical portrait, date below **Edge:** Plain

Date	Mintage	F	VF	XF	Unc	BU
2000	200,000	—			30.00	35.00

KM# 1259   6.55957 FRANCS
22.2000 g., 0.9000 Silver 0.6423 oz. ASW **Obv:** Country names and euro-currency equivalents around "RF", denomination and French euro coin designs **Edge:** Plain

Date	Mintage	F	VF	XF	Unc	BU
2000 Proof	10,000	Value: 40.00				

KM# 932 10 FRANCS
25.0000 g., 0.9000 Silver 0.7234 oz. ASW, 37 mm. **Obv:** Denomination and date within wreath **Rev:** Hercules group **Note:** Without mint mark.

Date	Mintage	F	VF	XF	Unc	BU
1965	8,051,000	—	BV	13.50	15.00	18.00
1966	9,800,000	—	BV	10.00	12.50	15.00
1967	10,100,000	—	BV	10.00	12.50	15.00
1968	3,887,000	—	BV	14.00	16.00	20.00
1969	761,000	—	BV	15.00	18.00	22.50
1970	5,013,000	—	BV	13.50	15.00	18.00
1971	513,000	—	BV	15.00	18.00	22.50
1972	915,000	—	BV	14.00	16.00	20.00
1973	207,000	—	BV	16.00	20.00	25.00

KM# 940 10 FRANCS
10.0000 g., Nickel-Brass, 26 mm. **Rev:** High tension towers and electric transmission wires, denomination at center **Edge:** Incuse, LIBERTÉ, EGALITÉ, FRATERNITÉ

Date	Mintage	F	VF	XF	Unc	BU
1974	22,447,000	—	—	1.50	2.00	2.50
1975	59,013,000	—	—	1.50	2.00	2.50
1976	104,093,000	—	—	1.50	2.00	2.50
1977	100,028,000	—	—	1.50	2.00	2.50
1978	97,590,000	—	—	1.50	2.00	2.50
1979	110,000,000	—	—	1.50	2.00	2.50
1980	80,010,000	—	—	1.50	2.00	2.50
1981	50,000	—	—	—	2.75	3.75
1982	74,000	—	—	—	2.75	3.75
1983	101,000	—	—	—	2.75	3.75
1984	39,988,000	—	—	1.50	2.00	2.50
1985	30,000,000	—	—	1.50	2.00	2.50
1987	Est. 50,000,000	—	—	—	2.50	2.50

KM# 950 10 FRANCS
10.0000 g., Nickel-Bronze, 26 mm. **Subject:** 100th Anniversary - Death of Leon Gambetta **Obv:** Denomination and date, flags in background **Rev:** Head left

Date	Mintage	F	VF	XF	Unc	BU
1982	3,045,000	—	—	2.50	4.00	5.00

KM# 952 10 FRANCS
Nickel-Bronze, 26 mm. **Subject:** 200th Anniversary - Montgolfier Balloon **Obv:** Denomination and date below balloon basket **Rev:** Balloon, figures and date below

Date	Mintage	F	VF	XF	Unc	BU
1983	3,001,000	—	—	2.50	4.00	5.00

KM# 953 10 FRANCS
Nickel-Bronze, 26 mm. **Subject:** 200th Anniversary - Birth of Stendhal **Obv:** Head 3/4 facing **Rev:** Quill, branch, book, and buildings divide date and denomination

Date	Mintage	F	VF	XF	Unc	BU
1983	2,951,000	—	—	2.50	4.00	5.00

KM# 954 10 FRANCS
Nickel-Bronze, 26 mm. **Subject:** 200th Anniversary - Birth of Francois Rude **Obv:** Head 3/4 right, RF below **Rev:** Armed figure divides denomination and date

Date	Mintage	F	VF	XF	Unc	BU
1984	10,000,000	—	—	2.50	3.50	4.50

KM# 956 10 FRANCS
Nickel-Bronze, 26 mm. **Subject:** Centennial - Death of Victor Hugo **Obv:** Denomination above armed figures, quill and book at right, date below **Rev:** Head facing

Date	Mintage	F	VF	XF	Unc	BU
1985	10,000,000	—	—	2.50	3.50	4.50

KM# 956a 10 FRANCS
12.0000 g., 0.9000 Silver 0.3472 oz. ASW, 26 mm. **Subject:** Centennial - Death of Victor Hugo **Obv:** Figures left of quill and book, denomination above **Rev:** Head facing

Date	Mintage	F	VF	XF	Unc	BU
1985	20,000	—	—	—	20.00	25.00

KM# 956b 10 FRANCS
12.0000 g., 0.9990 Silver 0.3854 oz. ASW, 26 mm. **Subject:** Centennial - Death of Victor Hugo **Obv:** Figures left of quill and book, denomination above **Rev:** Head facing

Date	Mintage	F	VF	XF	Unc	BU
1985 Proof	8,000	Value: 35.00				

KM# 959 10 FRANCS
6.5000 g., Nickel, 21 mm. **Obv:** Designs divide denomination and date **Rev:** Madam Republic head, map in background

Date	Mintage	F	VF	XF	Unc	BU
1986	110,015,000	—	—	3.00	10.00	15.00

Note: Recalled and melted, no longer legal tender

KM# 958 10 FRANCS
6.5000 g., Nickel, 21 mm. **Subject:** 100th Anniversary - Birth of Robert Schuman **Obv:** Rooster at left, denomination right **Rev:** Half head right

Date	Mintage	F	VF	XF	Unc	BU
1986	9,961,000	—	—	3.00	6.50	7.50

KM# 958a 10 FRANCS
7.0000 g., 0.9000 Silver 0.2025 oz. ASW **Obv:** Rooster at left, denomination right **Rev:** Half head right

Date	Mintage	F	VF	XF	Unc	BU
1986	20,000	—	—	—	18.50	22.50

KM# 958b 10 FRANCS
7.0000 g., 0.9500 Silver 0.2138 oz. ASW **Obv:** Rooster at left, denomination right **Rev:** Half head right

Date	Mintage	F	VF	XF	Unc	BU
1986 Proof	6,000	Value: 45.00				

KM# 958c 10 FRANCS
7.0000 g., 0.9200 Gold 0.2070 oz. AGW **Subject:** 100th Anniversary - Birth of Robert Schuman **Obv:** Rooster at left, denomination right **Rev:** Half head right

Date	Mintage	F	VF	XF	Unc	BU
1986 Proof	5,000	Value: 265				

KM# 961 10 FRANCS
12.0000 g., 0.9000 Silver 0.3472 oz. ASW **Subject:** Millennium of King Hugo Capet first King of France **Obv:** Denomination and date within circle **Rev:** Crowned figure standing at center divides dates below, rosettes in background

Date	Mintage	F	VF	XF	Unc	BU
1987	20,000	—	—	—	18.50	22.50

KM# 961a 10 FRANCS
12.0000 g., 0.9500 Silver 0.3665 oz. ASW **Subject:** Millennium of King Capet and France **Obv:** Denomination and date within circle **Rev:** Crowned figure standing at center, rosettes in background

Date	Mintage	F	VF	XF	Unc	BU
1987 Proof	10,000	Value: 40.00				

KM# 961b 10 FRANCS
12.0000 g., 0.9200 Gold 0.3549 oz. AGW **Subject:** Millennium of King Capet and France **Obv:** Denomination and date within circle **Rev:** Crowned figure standing at center, rosettes in background

Date	Mintage	F	VF	XF	Unc	BU
1987 Proof	6,000	Value: 350				

KM# 961c 10 FRANCS
14.0000 g., 0.9990 Platinum 0.4496 oz. APW **Subject:** Millennium of King Capet and France **Obv:** Denomination and date within circle **Rev:** Crowned figure standing at center, rosettes in background

Date	Mintage	F	VF	XF	Unc	BU
1987 Proof	1,000	Value: 850				

KM# 961d 10 FRANCS
Nickel-Bronze, 21 mm. **Subject:** Millennium of King Capet and France **Obv:** Denomination and date within circle **Rev:** Crowned figure standing at center, rosettes in background

Date	Mintage	F	VF	XF	Unc	BU
1987	70,000,000	—	—	3.00	6.50	9.00

KM# 964.1 10 FRANCS
6.5000 g., Bi-Metallic Nickel center in Aluminum-Bronze ring, 23 mm. **Subject:** Spirit of Bastille **Obv:** Winged figure divides RF within circle **Rev:** Patterned denomination above date within circle **Edge:** Plain or Reeded

Date	Mintage	F	VF	XF	Unc	BU
1988	100,000,000	—	—	2.50	6.00	7.50
1989	249,980,000	—	—	2.50	6.00	7.50
1990	250,000,000	—	—	2.50	6.00	7.50
1991	249,987,000	—	—	2.50	6.00	7.50
	Note: Exist in both medal and coin alignment					
1992	99,966,000	—	—	2.50	6.00	7.50
	Note: Exist in both medal and coin alignment					
1995	15,000	—	—	6.00	10.00	12.50
1996	12,000	—	—	6.00	10.00	12.50
2000	28,065,000	—	—	2.50	6.00	7.50

KM# 964.1a 10 FRANCS
Bi-Metallic .920 Gold center in Gold with Palladium and Silver alloy ring, 23 mm. **Subject:** Spirit of Bastille **Obv:** Winged figure divides RF **Rev:** Patterned denomination above date

Date	Mintage	F	VF	XF	Unc	BU
1988 Proof	5,000	Value: 350				

KM# 965   10 FRANCS
Aluminum-Bronze, 26 mm.   **Subject:** 100th Anniversary - Birth
of Roland Garros **Obv:** Denomination below wings **Rev:** Dates
and plane above head right

Date	Mintage	F	VF	XF	Unc	BU
1988	30,000,000	—	—	2.50	4.00	5.00

KM# 965a   10 FRANCS
12.0000 g., 0.9000 Silver 0.3472 oz. ASW, 26 mm.   **Obv:** Wings
above denomination **Rev:** Airplane above head right

Date	Mintage	F	VF	XF	Unc	BU
1988	10,000	—	—	—	18.50	22.50

KM# 965b   10 FRANCS
12.0000 g., 0.9500 Silver 0.3665 oz. ASW, 26 mm.   **Obv:** Wings
above denomination **Rev:** Airplane above head right

Date	Mintage	F	VF	XF	Unc	BU
1988 Proof	10,000	Value: 35.00				

KM# 965c   10 FRANCS
12.0000 g., 0.9200 Gold 0.3549 oz. AGW, 26 mm.
Subject: 100th Anniversary - Birth of Roland Garros **Obv:** Wings
above denomination **Rev:** Airplane above head right

Date	Mintage	F	VF	XF	Unc	BU
1988 Proof	3,000	Value: 350				

KM# 969   10 FRANCS
Bi-Metallic Steel center in Aluminum-Bronze ring, 23 mm.
Subject: 300th Anniversary - Birth of Montesquieu **Obv:** Bust
right **Rev:** Patterned denomination above date

Date	Mintage	F	VF	XF	Unc	BU
1989	15,000	—	—	6.50	17.50	20.00

KM# 969a   10 FRANCS
Bi-Metallic Gold, Palladium and Silver alloy center in .920 Gold
ring, 23 mm.   **Subject:** 300th Anniversary - Birth of Montesquieu
Obv: Bust right **Rev:** Patterned denomination above date

Date	Mintage	F	VF	XF	Unc	BU
1989 Proof	5,000	Value: 375				

KM# 964.2   10 FRANCS
Aluminum-Bronze, 23 mm.   **Obv:** Winged figure divides RF
Rev: Patterned denomination above date **Edge:** Plain

Date	Mintage	F	VF	XF	Unc	BU
1991	—	—	—	—	—	—
	Note: Exists in both medal and coin alignment.					
1991 Proof	10,000	Value: 15.00				
1992	—	—	—	—	6.00	7.50
	Note: Exists in both medal and coin alignment.					
1992 Proof	15,000	Value: 15.00				
1993	20,000	—	—	—	6.00	7.50
1993 Proof	10,000	Value: 15.00				
1994 Bee	20,000	—	—	—	6.00	7.50
1994 Fish Proof	10,000	Value: 15.00				
1995	25,000	—	—	—	6.00	7.50
1995 Proof	10,000	Value: 15.00				
1996	17,000	—	—	—	6.00	7.50
1996 Proof	8,000	Value: 15.00				
1997	15,000	—	—	—	6.00	7.50
1997 Proof	10,000	Value: 15.00				
1998	—	—	—	—	6.00	7.50
1998 Proof	—	Value: 15.00				
1999	—	—	—	—	6.00	7.50
1999 Proof	—	Value: 15.00				
2000	—	—	—	—	6.00	7.50
2000 Proof	—	Value: 15.00				

KM# 1144   10 FRANCS
21.1600 g., 0.9000 Silver 0.6123 oz. ASW   **Subject:** World Cup

- Coupe du Monde 1998 **Obv:** World Cup 1998 logo above
denomination **Rev:** Soccer ball breaking net, stylized dove, date
upper right

Date	Mintage	F	VF	XF	Unc	BU
1996 Proof	Est. 40,000	Value: 40.00				

KM# 1166   10 FRANCS
21.1600 g., 0.9000 Silver 0.6123 oz. ASW   **Subject:** World Cup -
Uruguay 1930 1958 **Obv:** World Cup 1998 logo above denomination
Rev: Stylized gaucho and soccer player, date below

Date	Mintage	F	VF	XF	Unc	BU
1996 Proof	100,000	Value: 35.00				

KM# 1161   10 FRANCS
21.1600 g., 0.9000 Silver 0.6123 oz. ASW   **Subject:** World Cup
- Argentina 1978 1986 **Obv:** World Cup 1998 logo above
denomination **Rev:** Stylized bull and soccer player, date below

Date	Mintage	F	VF	XF	Unc	BU
1997 Proof	100,000	Value: 35.00				

KM# 1163   10 FRANCS
21.1600 g., 0.9000 Silver 0.6123 oz. ASW   **Subject:** World Cup
- England 1966 **Obv:** World Cup 1998 logo above denomination
Rev: Big Ben and soccer player, date below

Date	Mintage	F	VF	XF	Unc	BU
1997 Proof	100,000	Value: 35.00				

KM# 1165   10 FRANCS
21.1600 g., 0.9000 Silver 0.6123 oz. ASW   **Subject:** World Cup
- Italy 1934 1938 1982 **Obv:** World Cup 1998 logo above
denomination and date **Rev:** Colosseum and soccer player, date
below

Date	Mintage	F	VF	XF	Unc	BU
1997 Proof	100,000	Value: 35.00				

KM# 1162   10 FRANCS
21.1600 g., 0.9000 Silver 0.6123 oz. ASW   **Subject:** World Cup
- Brazil 1958 1962 1970 1994 **Obv:** World Cup 1998 logo above
denomination **Rev:** Pavilion and soccer player, date below

Date	Mintage	F	VF	XF	Unc	BU
1998 Proof	100,000	Value: 35.00				

KM# 1167   10 FRANCS
21.1600 g., 0.9000 Silver 0.6123 oz. ASW   **Subject:** World Cup -
Coupe du Monte **Obv:** World Cup 1998 logo above denomination
and date **Rev:** World Cup trophy and 10 French city arms

Date	Mintage	F	VF	XF	Unc	BU
1998 Proof	100,000	Value: 35.00				

KM# 1205   10 FRANCS
22.2000 g., 0.9000 Silver 0.6423 oz. ASW   **Series:** Treasures
of the Nile - J.F. Champollion **Obv:** Portrait and obelisk
Rev: Sphinx and pyramids, date at left, denomination below

Date	Mintage	F	VF	XF	Unc	BU
1998 Proof	15,000	Value: 38.50				

KM# 1164   10 FRANCS
21.1600 g., 0.9000 Silver 0.6123 oz. ASW   **Subject:** World Cup
- Germany 1954 1974 1990 **Obv:** World Cup 1998 logo above
denomination **Rev:** Brandenburg gate, soccer player, date below

Date	Mintage	F	VF	XF	Unc	BU
1997 Proof	100,000	Value: 35.00				

KM# 1206   10 FRANCS
22.2000 g., 0.9000 Silver 0.6423 oz. ASW **Series:** Treasures
of the Nile **Subject:** Nefertiti 1372-1350BC, Queen and
monotheist **Obv:** Crowned bust 3/4 right **Rev:** Sphinx and
pyramids, date at left, denomination below

Date	Mintage	F	VF	XF	Unc	BU
1998 Proof	15,000	Value: 38.50				

KM# 1207   10 FRANCS
22.2000 g., 0.9000 Silver 0.6423 oz. ASW **Series:** Treasures
of the Nile **Subject:** Ramses II **Rev:** Kneeling figure right

Date	Mintage	F	VF	XF	Unc	BU
1998 Proof	15,000	Value: 38.50				

KM# 1294   10 FRANCS
22.2300 g., 0.9000 Silver 0.6432 oz. ASW, 36.9 mm.
Subject: Rugby **Obv:** Players in a "scrum" **Rev:** Players jumping
for a ball **Edge:** Plain

Date	Mintage	F	VF	XF	Unc	BU
1999A Proof	10,000	Value: 35.00				

KM# 1398   10 FRANCS
22.2000 g., 0.9000 Silver 0.6423 oz. ASW, 37 mm. **Obv:** Partial
postage stamp with denomination below, Initials, "RF" on wavy
field **Rev:** First French postage stamp **Edge:** Plain

Date	Mintage	F	VF	XF	Unc	BU
ND (1999)A Proof	—	Value: 45.00				

KM# 1400   10 FRANCS
22.2000 g., 0.9000 Silver 0.6423 oz. ASW, 36.9 mm.
Obv: Liberty bust by Dupre **Rev:** Value **Edge:** Plain

Date	Mintage	F	VF	XF	Unc	BU
2000 Proof	—	Value: 40.00				

KM# 1401   10 FRANCS
22.2000 g., 0.9000 Silver 0.6423 oz. ASW, 36.9 mm.
Obv: Liberty bust by Lagriffoul **Rev:** Value **Edge:** Plain

Date	Mintage	F	VF	XF	Unc	BU
2000 Proof	—	Value: 40.00				

KM# 1216   10 FRANCS
22.2300 g., 0.9000 Silver 0.6432 oz. ASW **Series:** XXth Century
- Biology and Medicine **Obv:** Double X design divides date and
denomination **Rev:** Parents, fetus, hands **Edge:** Plain

Date	Mintage	F	VF	XF	Unc	BU
2000 Proof	10,000	Value: 40.00				

KM# 1217   10 FRANCS
22.2300 g., 0.9000 Silver 0.6432 oz. ASW **Series:** XXth Century
- Physical Sciences **Rev:** Einstein's portrait, atom and planets

Date	Mintage	F	VF	XF	Unc	BU
2000 Proof	10,000	Value: 40.00				

KM# 1218   10 FRANCS
22.2300 g., 0.9000 Silver 0.6432 oz. ASW **Series:** XXth Century
- Communications **Rev:** World, satellites and keyboard

Date	Mintage	F	VF	XF	Unc	BU
2000 Proof	10,000	Value: 40.00				

KM# 1219   10 FRANCS
22.2300 g., 0.9000 Silver 0.6432 oz. ASW **Series:** XXth Century
- The Automobile **Rev:** Race cars above horse

Date	Mintage	F	VF	XF	Unc	BU
2000 Proof	10,000	Value: 40.00				

KM# 1220   10 FRANCS
22.2300 g., 0.9000 Silver 0.6432 oz. ASW **Series:** XXth Century
- Flight **Rev:** Icarus in flight above Bleriot monoplane

Date	Mintage	F	VF	XF	Unc	BU
2000 Proof	10,000	Value: 40.00				

KM# 1221   10 FRANCS
22.2300 g., 0.9000 Silver 0.6432 oz. ASW **Series:** XXth Century
- Space Travel **Rev:** Astronaut weightless in space amidst planets

Date	Mintage	F	VF	XF	Unc	BU
2000 Proof	10,000	Value: 40.00				

KM# 1229   10 FRANCS
22.2000 g., 0.9000 Silver 0.6423 oz. ASW **Subject:** 2000 Years
- French Coinage **Obv:** Denomination and date within wreath
Rev: 1st century B.C. Celtic Parisii Stater coin design **Edge:** Plain

Date	Mintage	F	VF	XF	Unc	BU
2000 Proof	10,000	Value: 40.00				

KM# 1230 10 FRANCS
22.2000 g., 0.9000 Silver 0.6423 oz. ASW **Rev:** Charlemagne Denar coin design, laureate head right

Date	Mintage	F	VF	XF	Unc	BU
2000 Proof	10,000	Value: 40.00				

KM# 1231 10 FRANCS
22.2000 g., 0.9000 Silver 0.6423 oz. ASW **Subject:** 2000 Years of French Coinage **Obv:** Denomination **Rev:** Louis IX gold ecu coin design, arms on shield within scalloped wreath **Edge:** Plain

Date	Mintage	F	VF	XF	Unc	BU
2000 Proof	10,000	Value: 40.00				

KM# 1235 10 FRANCS
22.2000 g., 0.9000 Silver 0.6423 oz. ASW **Subject:** Yves St. Laurent **Obv:** RF monogram within entwined snake design, date above, denomination lower right **Rev:** Fashion show scene

Date	Mintage	F	VF	XF	Unc	BU
2000 Proof	30,000	Value: 37.50				

KM# 1263 10 FRANCS
22.2000 g., 0.9000 Silver 0.6423 oz. ASW **Subject:** Antoine de St. Exupery **Obv:** RF Monogram, portrait and bi-plane **Rev:** Multicolor "Little Prince" character, denomination at left, date below

Date	Mintage	F	VF	XF	Unc	BU
2000 Proof	10,000	Value: 47.50				

KM# 1008.2 20 FRANCS
9.0000 g., Tri-Metallic Copper-Aluminum-Nickel center plug, Nickel inner ring, Copper-Aluminum-Nickel outer ring, 27 mm. **Obv:** Mont St. Michel **Rev:** Patterned denomination above date **Edge:** 5 milled bands, reeded or plain

Date	Mintage	F	VF	XF	Unc	BU
1992	Inc. above	—	—	—	6.50	8.50

Note: Open V in outer ring, exist in both coin and medal alignment

Date	Mintage	F	VF	XF	Unc	BU
1992 Proof	15,000	Value: 25.00				
1992	59,986,000	—	—	—	6.50	8.50

Note: Closed V in outer ring, exist in both coin and medal alignment

| 1993 | 54,990,000 | — | — | — | 7.00 | 9.00 |

Note: Exist in both coin and medal alignment

Date	Mintage	F	VF	XF	Unc	BU
1993 Proof	10,000	Value: 25.00				
1994	—	—	—	—	8.00	10.00
1994 Proof		Value: 25.00				
1994 Fish	5,000,000	—	—	—	10.00	12.50
1994 Fish Proof	10,000	Value: 25.00				
1994 Bee	9,990,000	—	—	—	9.00	11.00
1995	9,996,000	—	—	—	9.00	11.00
1995 Proof	10,000	Value: 25.00				
1996	17,000	—	—	—	6.50	8.50
1996 Proof	8,000	Value: 25.00				
1997	15,000	—	—	—	8.00	10.00
1997 Proof	10,000	Value: 25.00				
1998	—	—	—	—	8.00	10.00
1998 Proof		Value: 25.00				
1999	—	—	—	—	8.00	10.00
1999 Proof		Value: 25.00				
2000	—	—	—	—	8.00	10.00
2000 Proof		Value: 25.00				

KM# 1008.2a 20 FRANCS
12.6600 g., Tri-Metallic .720 Gold center plug, .950 Silver inner ring, .750 Gold outer ring., 27 mm. **Obv:** Mont St. Michel; 5 bands of stripes in outer ring **Rev:** Patterned denomination above date

Date	Mintage	F	VF	XF	Unc	BU
1992 Proof	15,000	Value: 225				

KM# 1008.2b 20 FRANCS
16.4600 g., Tri-Metallic .920 Gold center plug, .750 Gold inner ring, .920 Gold outer ring, 27 mm. **Obv:** Mont St. Michel **Rev:** Patterned denomination above date

Date	Mintage	F	VF	XF	Unc	BU
1992 Proof	5,000	Value: 400				

KM# 1008.1 20 FRANCS
Tri-Metallic Copper-Aluminum-Nickel center plug%2C Nickel inner ring%2C Copper-Aluminum-Nickel outer ring, 27 mm. **Obv:** Mont St. Michel **Rev:** Patterned denomination above date within circle **Edge:** 4 milled bands

Date	Mintage	F	VF	XF	Unc	BU
1992	Inc. above	—	—	—	15.00	18.00

Note: Open V in outer ring

| 1992 | 60,000,000 | — | — | — | 15.00 | 18.00 |

Note: Closed V in outer ring

KM# 1016 20 FRANCS
Tri-Metallic Aluminum-Bronze center plug, Nickel inner ring, Copper-Aluminum-Nickel outer ring, 27 mm. **Subject:** Mediterranean Games **Obv:** Tower of Adge **Rev:** Denomination flanked by laurels, wavy design below, rings divide date at bottom

Date	Mintage	F	VF	XF	Unc	BU
1993	5,001,000	—	—	—	10.00	12.00

KM# 1036 20 FRANCS
Tri-Metallic Aluminum-Bronze center plug, Nickel inner ring, Copper-Aluminum-Nickel outer ring, 26.8 mm. **Subject:** Founder of Modern Day Olympics - Pierre de Coubertin **Obv:** Head left, 'RF' below, torch at right **Rev:** Building at left, denomination and date divided by Olympic logo at right

Date	Mintage	F	VF	XF	Unc	BU
1994	15,000,000	—	—	—	10.00	12.00

KM# 941.1 50 FRANCS
30.0000 g., 0.9000 Silver 0.8680 oz. ASW **Obv:** Denomination within wreath **Rev:** Hercules group **Note:** Without mint mark.

Date	Mintage	F	VF	XF	Unc	BU
1974	4,299,000	—	—	BV	12.00	14.00
1975	4,551,000	—	—	BV	14.50	17.50
1976	7,739,000	—	—	BV	13.50	18.00
1977	7,884,000	—	—	BV	12.00	14.00
1978	12,028,000	—	—	BV	12.00	14.00
1979	12,041,000	—	—	BV	12.00	14.00
1980	60,000	—	—	25.00	50.00	65.00

Note: In sets only

KM# 941.2 50 FRANCS
30.0000 g., 0.9000 Silver 0.8680 oz. ASW **Obv:** Denomination within wreath **Rev:** Legend begins at the level of the beltline of the goddess of Hercules' at left

Date	Mintage	F	VF	XF	Unc	BU
1974	—	15.00	25.00	40.00	65.00	85.00

KM# 1145 50 FRANCS
8.4521 g., 0.9200 Gold 0.2500 oz. AGW **Subject:** World Class Soccer **Obv:** Soccer ball, denomination and date below **Rev:** Stylized dove, soccer ball

Date	Mintage	F	VF	XF	Unc	BU
1996 Proof	Est. 10,000	Value: 250				

KM# 1208 50 FRANCS
8.4521 g., 0.9200 Gold 0.2500 oz. AGW **Subject:** Treasures of the Nile **Obv:** Portrait above 'RF', obelisk at right **Rev:** Sphinx and pyramids, date at left, denomination below

Date	Mintage	F	VF	XF	Unc	BU
1998 Proof	3,000	Value: 275				

KM# 1236 50 FRANCS
8.4521 g., 0.9200 Gold 0.2500 oz. AGW **Subject:** Yves St. Laurent **Obv:** RF monogram, denomination **Rev:** Fashion show scene **Edge:** Plain

Date	Mintage	F	VF	XF	Unc	BU
2000 Proof	2,000	Value: 275				

KM# 1256 65.5997 FRANCS
8.4500 g., 0.9250 Gold 0.2513 oz. AGW **Series:** Euro Conversion Series **Obv:** Country names with euro currency equivalents around "RF", denomination and French coin designs **Rev:** Europa allegorical portrait **Edge:** Plain

Date	Mintage	F	VF	XF	Unc	BU
1999 Proof	10,000	Value: 275				

KM# 1260 65.5997 FRANCS
8.4500 g., 0.9250 Gold 0.2513 oz. AGW **Obv:** Country names with euro-currency equivalents around "RF", denomination and French euro coin designs

Date	Mintage	F	VF	XF	Unc	BU
2000 Proof	3,000	Value: 275				

KM# 951.1 100 FRANCS
15.0000 g., 0.9000 Silver 0.4340 oz. ASW **Obv:** Pantheon, date below **Rev:** Leafy design above denomination **Note:** Without mint mark.

Date	Mintage	F	VF	XF	Unc	BU
1982	3,030,000	—	—	—	27.50	37.50
1982 Proof	25,000	Value: 45.00				
1983	5,001,000	—	—	—	27.50	37.50
1983 Proof	17,000	Value: 45.00				
1984	5,000,000	—	—	—	27.50	37.50
1985	999,000	—	—	—	30.00	40.00
1985 Proof	13,000	Value: 45.00				
1986	519,000	—	—	—	30.00	40.00
1987	100,000	—	—	—	30.00	40.00
1988	100,000	—	—	—	30.00	40.00
1989	83,000	—	—	—	30.00	40.00
1990	15,000	—	—	—	35.00	45.00
1991	5,000	—	—	—	35.00	45.00
1991 Proof	10,000	Value: 55.00				
1992 Proof	15,000	Value: 45.00				
1993 Proof	15,000	Value: 45.00				
1994 Proof	15,000	Value: 45.00				
1995	4,011	—	—	—	32.00	42.00
1995 Proof	10,000	Value: 48.00				
1996	2,013	—	—	—	40.00	50.00
1996 Proof	8,000	Value: 60.00				
1997	—	—	—	—	40.00	50.00
1997 Proof	—	Value: 60.00				
1998	—	—	—	—	40.00	50.00
1998 Proof	—	Value: 60.00				
1999	—	—	—	—	40.00	50.00
1999 Proof	—	Value: 60.00				
2000	—	—	—	—	40.00	50.00
2000 Proof	—	Value: 60.00				

KM# 960 100 FRANCS
15.0000 g., 0.9000 Silver 0.4340 oz. ASW, 31 mm.
Subject: Centennial - Statue of Liberty **Obv:** Top of statue facing, dates at right **Rev:** Liberty cap over inscription above denomination, date below

Date	Mintage	F	VF	XF	Unc	BU
1986	4,427,000	—	—	—	11.50	16.50

KM# 960a 100 FRANCS
15.0000 g., 0.9500 Silver 0.4581 oz. ASW **Subject:** Centennial of Statue of Liberty **Obv:** Top of statue facing **Rev:** Liberty cap over inscription above denomination, date below

Date	Mintage	F	VF	XF	Unc	BU
1986 Proof	18,000	Value: 45.00				

KM# 960b 100 FRANCS
17.0000 g., 0.9200 Gold 0.5028 oz. AGW **Subject:** Centennial - Statue of Liberty **Obv:** Top of statue facing **Rev:** Liberty cap over inscription above denomination, date below

Date	Mintage	F	VF	XF	Unc	BU
1986	13,000	—	—	—	450	475
1986 Proof	17,000	Value: 500				

KM# 960c 100 FRANCS
20.0000 g., 0.9990 Platinum 0.6423 oz. APW **Subject:** Centennial - Statue of Liberty **Obv:** Top of statue facing **Rev:** Liberty cap over inscription above denomination, date below

Date	Mintage	F	VF	XF	Unc	BU
1986 Proof	9,500	Value: 1,300				

KM# 960d 100 FRANCS
17.0000 g., 0.9000 Palladium 0.4919 oz. **Subject:** Centennial - Statue of Liberty **Obv:** Top of statue facing **Rev:** Liberty cap over inscription above denomination, date below

Date	Mintage	F	VF	XF	Unc	BU
1986 Proof	1,250	Value: 425				

KM# 966 100 FRANCS
15.0000 g., 0.9000 Silver 0.4340 oz. ASW **Subject:** Fraternity **Obv:** Radiant head left with crown of cherubs **Rev:** Liberty cap over inscription above denomination, date below

Date	Mintage	F	VF	XF	Unc	BU
1988	4,853,000	—	—	—	26.50	32.50

KM# 966a 100 FRANCS
15.0000 g., 0.9500 Silver 0.4581 oz. ASW **Subject:** Fraternity **Obv:** Radiant head left with crown of cherubs

Date	Mintage	F	VF	XF	Unc	BU
1988 Proof	20,000	Value: 40.00				

KM# 966b 100 FRANCS
17.0000 g., 0.9200 Gold 0.5028 oz. AGW **Subject:** Fraternity **Obv:** Radiant head left with crown of cherubs **Rev:** Liberty cap over inscription above denomination, date below

Date	Mintage	F	VF	XF	Unc	BU
1988	3,000	—	—	—	465	485
1988 Proof	12,000	Value: 500				

KM# 966c 100 FRANCS
20.0000 g., 0.9990 Platinum 0.6423 oz. APW **Subject:** Fraternity **Obv:** Radiant head left with crown of cherubs **Rev:** Liberty cap over inscription above denomination, date below

Date	Mintage	F	VF	XF	Unc	BU
1988 Proof	5,000	Value: 1,300				

KM# 966d 100 FRANCS
17.0000 g., 0.9000 Palladium 0.4919 oz. **Subject:** Fraternity **Obv:** Radiant head left with crown of cherubs **Rev:** Liberty cap over inscription above denomination, date below

Date	Mintage	F	VF	XF	Unc	BU
1988 Proof	7,000	Value: 350				

KM# 955 100 FRANCS
15.0000 g., 0.9000 Silver 0.4340 oz. ASW **Subject:** 50th Anniversary - Death of Marie Curie **Obv:** Leafy branches divide date and denomination **Rev:** Head right, dates below

Date	Mintage	F	VF	XF	Unc	BU
1984	3,964,000	—	—	—	25.00	30.00

KM# 955a 100 FRANCS
15.0000 g., 0.9500 Silver 0.4581 oz. ASW **Obv:** Leafy branches divide date and denomination **Rev:** Head right, two dates

Date	Mintage	F	VF	XF	Unc	BU
1984 Proof	1,000	Value: 200				

KM# 955b 100 FRANCS
17.0000 g., 0.9200 Gold 0.5028 oz. AGW **Subject:** 50th Anniversary - Death of Marie Curie **Obv:** Leafy branches divide date and denomination **Rev:** Head right, two dates

Date	Mintage	F	VF	XF	Unc	BU
1984 Proof	5,000	Value: 500				

KM# 957 100 FRANCS
15.0000 g., 0.9000 Silver 0.4340 oz. ASW **Subject:** Centennial of Emile Zola's Novel **Rev:** Head right

Date	Mintage	F	VF	XF	Unc	BU
1985	3,980,000	—	—	—	28.00	35.00
1985 Proof	13,000	Value: 55.00				

KM# 957a 100 FRANCS
15.0000 g., 0.9500 Silver 0.4581 oz. ASW **Subject:** Centennial of Emile Zola's Novel **Rev:** Head right

Date	Mintage	F	VF	XF	Unc	BU
1985 Proof	5,000	Value: 115				

KM# 957b 100 FRANCS
17.0000 g., 0.9200 Gold 0.5028 oz. AGW **Subject:** Centennial of Emile Zola's Novel **Rev:** Head right

Date	Mintage	F	VF	XF	Unc	BU
1985 Proof	5,000	Value: 500				

KM# 962 100 FRANCS
15.0000 g., 0.9000 Silver 0.4340 oz. ASW, 31 mm.
Subject: 230th Anniversary - Birth of General Lafayette **Obv:** Bust left **Rev:** Liberty cap over inscription above denomination, date below

Date	Mintage	F	VF	XF	Unc	BU
1987	4,801,000	—	—	—	20.00	25.00

KM# 962a 100 FRANCS
15.0000 g., 0.9500 Silver 0.4581 oz. ASW **Subject:** 230th Anniversary - Birth of General Lafayette **Obv:** Bust left **Rev:** Liberty cap over inscription above denomination, date below

Date	Mintage	F	VF	XF	Unc	BU
1987 Proof	30,000	Value: 35.00				

KM# 962b 100 FRANCS
17.0000 g., 0.9200 Gold 0.5028 oz. AGW **Subject:** 230th Anniversary - Birth of General Lafayette **Obv:** Bust left **Rev:** Liberty cap over inscription above denomination, date below

Date	Mintage	F	VF	XF	Unc	BU
1987	10,000	—	—	—	450	475
1987 Proof	20,000	Value: 500				

KM# 962c 100 FRANCS
20.0000 g., 0.9990 Platinum 0.6423 oz. APW **Subject:** 230th Anniversary - Birth of General Lafayette **Obv:** Bust left **Rev:** Liberty cap over inscription above denomination, date below

Date	Mintage	F	VF	XF	Unc	BU
1987 Proof	8,500	Value: 1,300				

KM# 962d 100 FRANCS
17.0000 g., 0.9000 Palladium 0.4919 oz. **Subject:** 230th Anniversary - Birth of General Lafayette **Obv:** Bust left **Rev:** Liberty cap over inscription above denomination, date below

Date	Mintage	F	VF	XF	Unc	BU
1987 Proof	7,000	Value: 350				

KM# 970 100 FRANCS
15.0000 g., 0.9000 Silver 0.4340 oz. ASW **Subject:** Human Rights **Obv:** Standing Genius writing the constitution **Rev:** Liberty cap over inscription above denomination, date below

Date	Mintage	F	VF	XF	Unc	BU
1989	4,823,000	—	—	—	32.50	37.50

KM# 970a 100 FRANCS
15.0000 g., 0.9500 Silver 0.4581 oz. ASW **Subject:** Human Rights **Obv:** Standing Genius writing the constitution **Rev:** Liberty cap over inscription above denomination, date below

Date	Mintage	F	VF	XF	Unc	BU
1989 Proof	40,000	Value: 40.00				

KM# 971 100 FRANCS
22.2000 g., 0.9000 Silver 0.6423 oz. ASW **Subject:** 1992 Olympics **Obv:** Alpine skiing **Rev:** Cross on flame, date and denomination, logo below

Date	Mintage	F	VF	XF	Unc	BU
1989 Proof	136,000	Value: 30.00				

KM# 972 100 FRANCS
22.2000 g., 0.9000 Silver 0.6423 oz. ASW **Subject:** 1992 Olympics **Obv:** Ice Skating Couple **Rev:** Cross on flame, date and denomination, logo below

Date	Mintage	F	VF	XF	Unc	BU
1989 Proof	179,000	Value: 27.50				

KM# 970b 100 FRANCS
17.0000 g., 0.9200 Gold 0.5028 oz. AGW **Subject:** Human Rights **Obv:** Standing Genius writing the constitution **Rev:** Liberty cap over inscription above denomination, date below

Date	Mintage	F	VF	XF	Unc	BU
1989	1,000	—	—	—	600	650
1989 Proof	20,000	Value: 500				

KM# 970c 100 FRANCS
20.0000 g., 0.9990 Platinum 0.6423 oz. APW **Subject:** Human Rights **Obv:** Standing Genius writing the constitution **Rev:** Liberty cap over inscription above denomination, date below

Date	Mintage	F	VF	XF	Unc	BU
1989 Proof	1,000	Value: 1,350				

KM# 970d 100 FRANCS
17.0000 g., 0.9000 Palladium 0.4919 oz. **Subject:** Human Rights **Obv:** Standing Genius writing the constitution **Rev:** Liberty cap over inscription above denomination, date below

Date	Mintage	F	VF	XF	Unc	BU
1989 Proof	1,250	Value: 425				

Date	Mintage	F	VF	XF	Unc	BU
1990 Proof	110,000				Value: 30.00	

KM# 980   100 FRANCS
22.2000 g., 0.9000 Silver 0.6423 oz. ASW **Series:** 1992 Olympics **Obv:** Speed skaters and alpine marmot **Rev:** Crossed flame divides date and denomination, Olympic logo below

Date	Mintage	F	VF	XF	Unc	BU
1990 Proof	137,000				Value: 30.00	

KM# 981   100 FRANCS
22.2000 g., 0.9000 Silver 0.6423 oz. ASW **Series:** 1992 Olympics **Obv:** Bobsledding **Rev:** Games logo, value and legend

Date	Mintage	F	VF	XF	Unc	BU
1990 Proof	127,000				Value: 30.00	

KM# 982   100 FRANCS
15.0100 g., 0.9000 Silver 0.4343 oz. ASW **Subject:** Charlemagne **Obv:** Date and denomination divided by monogram, laurel spray below, circle surrounds **Rev:** Stylized head facing

Date	Mintage	F	VF	XF	Unc	BU
1990	4,950,000	—	—	—	37.50	40.00

KM# 983   100 FRANCS
22.2000 g., 0.9000 Silver 0.6423 oz. ASW **Series:** 1992 Olympics **Obv:** Free-style skier and chamois **Rev:** Crossed flame, date and denomination, logo below

Date	Mintage	F	VF	XF	Unc	BU
1990 Proof	110,000				Value: 32.50	

KM# 984   100 FRANCS
22.2000 g., 0.9000 Silver 0.6423 oz. ASW **Subject:** 1992 Olympics **Obv:** Slalom skiers **Rev:** Crossed flame, date and denomination, logo below

KM# 991   100 FRANCS
22.2000 g., 0.9000 Silver 0.6423 oz. ASW **Subject:** 100th Anniversary of Basketball **Obv:** 2 players **Rev:** Star, ring, and globe above denomination and date

Date	Mintage	F	VF	XF	Unc	BU
1991 Proof	13,000				Value: 50.00	

KM# 992   100 FRANCS
22.2000 g., 0.9000 Silver 0.6423 oz. ASW **Subject:** 100th Anniversary of Basketball **Obv:** 1 player, hoops in background

Date	Mintage	F	VF	XF	Unc	BU
1991 Proof	13,000				Value: 50.00	

KM# 993   100 FRANCS
22.2000 g., 0.9000 Silver 0.6423 oz. ASW **Series:** 1992 Olympics **Obv:** Hockey players and Ibex **Rev:** Crossed flame divides date and denomination, Olympic logo below

Date	Mintage	F	VF	XF	Unc	BU
1991 Proof	93,000				Value: 37.50	

KM# 994   100 FRANCS
22.2000 g., 0.9000 Silver 0.6423 oz. ASW **Series:** 1992 Olympics **Obv:** Cross-country skier, building at left **Rev:** Crossed flame, date and denomination, logo below

Date	Mintage	F	VF	XF	Unc	BU
1991 Proof	93,000				Value: 35.00	

KM# 995   100 FRANCS
22.2000 g., 0.9000 Silver 0.6423 oz. ASW **Series:** 1992 Olympics **Obv:** Ski jumpers **Rev:** Crossed flame, date and denomination, logo below

Date	Mintage	F	VF	XF	Unc	BU
1991 Proof	90,000				Value: 37.50	

KM# 996   100 FRANCS
15.0100 g., 0.9000 Silver 0.4343 oz. ASW **Obv:** Finger pointing on starred paper, denomination below **Rev:** Head 3/4 facing, date below

Date	Mintage	F	VF	XF	Unc	BU
1991	3,985,000	—	—	—	32.50	35.00

KM# 1009   100 FRANCS
22.2000 g., 0.9000 Silver 0.6423 oz. ASW **Subject:** Paralympics **Obv:** Segmented flying birds, denomination and date below **Rev:** Designs

Date	Mintage	F	VF	XF	Unc	BU
1992 Proof	5,000				Value: 60.00	

KM# 1010   100 FRANCS
22.2000 g., 0.9000 Silver 0.6423 oz. ASW **Subject:** French Antarctic Territories **Obv:** Head at left facing, ship, mountains and "RF" in background, denomination below **Rev:** Fur seals above date

Date	Mintage	F	VF	XF	Unc	BU
1992 Proof	15,000				Value: 75.00	

KM# 1011   100 FRANCS
22.2000 g., 0.9000 Silver 0.6423 oz. ASW **Subject:** French Antarctic Territories **Rev:** Emperor Penguins, date below

Date	Mintage	F	VF	XF	Unc	BU
1992 Proof	15,000	Value: 75.00				

KM# 1120 100 FRANCS
15.0100 g., 0.9000 Silver 0.4343 oz. ASW **Subject:** Jean Monet
Rev: Denomination above date within legend, rings surround, RF
at bottom

Date	Mintage	F	VF	XF	Unc	BU
1992	3,925,000	—	—	—	35.00	37.50

KM# 1017 100 FRANCS
22.2000 g., 0.9000 Silver 0.6423 oz. ASW **Series:** Bicentennial
of the Louvre **Obv:** Mona Lisa **Rev:** Patterned pyramids front
museum, date and denomination below

Date	Mintage	F	VF	XF	Unc	BU
1993	—	—	—	—	—	—
1993 Proof	200,000	Value: 45.00				

KM# 1018.1 100 FRANCS
15.0000 g., 0.9000 Silver 0.4340 oz. ASW, 31 mm.
Series: Bicentennial of the Louvre **Obv:** Liberty **Rev:** Patterned
pyramids front museum, date and denomination below

Date	Mintage	F	VF	XF	Unc	BU
1993	—	—	—	—	35.00	40.00

KM# 1018.2 100 FRANCS
22.2000 g., 0.9000 Silver 0.6423 oz. ASW **Series:** Bicentennial
of the Louvre **Obv:** Liberty **Rev:** Patterned pyramids front
museum, date and denomination below

Date	Mintage	F	VF	XF	Unc	BU
1993	—	—	—	—	—	—
1993 Proof	20,000	Value: 37.50				

KM# 1018.2a 100 FRANCS
17.0000 g., 0.9200 Gold 0.5028 oz. AGW **Series:** Bicentennial
of the Louvre **Obv:** Liberty **Rev:** Patterned pyramids front
museum, date and denomination below

Date	Mintage	F	VF	XF	Unc	BU
1993	—	—	—	—	475	500
1993 Proof	5,000	Value: 550				

KM# 1019 100 FRANCS
22.2000 g., 0.9000 Silver 0.6423 oz. ASW **Series:** Bicentennial
of the Louvre **Obv:** Victory **Rev:** Patterned pyramids front
museum, date and denomination below

Date	Mintage	F	VF	XF	Unc	BU
1993	—	—	—	—	—	—
1993 Proof	20,000	Value: 37.50				

KM# 1019a 100 FRANCS
17.0000 g., 0.9200 Gold 0.5028 oz. AGW **Series:** Bicentennial
of the Louvre **Obv:** Victory **Rev:** Patterned pyramids front
museum, date and denomination below

Date	Mintage	F	VF	XF	Unc	BU
1993	—	—	—	—	475	500
1993 Proof	5,000	Value: 550				

KM# 1020 100 FRANCS
22.2600 g., 0.9000 Silver 0.6441 oz. ASW **Series:** Bicentennial
of the Louvre **Obv:** Venus de Milo **Rev:** Patterned pyramids front
museum, date and denomination below

Date	Mintage	F	VF	XF	Unc	BU
1993	—	—	—	—	—	—
1993 Proof	20,000	Value: 40.00				

KM# 1021 100 FRANCS
22.2600 g., 0.9000 Silver 0.6441 oz. ASW **Series:** Bicentennial
of the Louvre **Obv:** Marie-Marguerite **Rev:** Patterned pyramids
front museum, date and denomination below

Date	Mintage	F	VF	XF	Unc	BU
1993	—	—	—	—	—	—
1993 Proof	20,000	Value: 35.00				

KM# 1021a 100 FRANCS
17.0000 g., 0.9200 Gold 0.5028 oz. AGW **Series:** Bicentennial
of the Louvre **Obv:** Marie-Marguerite **Rev:** Patterned pyramids
front museum, date and denomination below

Date	Mintage	F	VF	XF	Unc	BU
1993	—	—	—	—	475	500
1993 Proof	5,000	Value: 550				

KM# 1022 100 FRANCS
22.2600 g., 0.9000 Silver 0.6441 oz. ASW **Series:** Bicentennial
of the Louvre **Obv:** Napoleon crowning Josephine as Empress,
1763-1814 **Rev:** Patterned pyramids front museum, date and
denomination below

Date	Mintage	F	VF	XF	Unc	BU
1993	—	—	—	—	—	—
1993 Proof	20,000	Value: 42.50				

KM# 1022a 100 FRANCS
17.0000 g., 0.9200 Gold 0.5028 oz. AGW **Series:** Bicentennial
of the Louvre **Obv:** Napoleon crowning Josephine **Rev:** Patterned
pyramids front museum, date and denomination below

Date	Mintage	F	VF	XF	Unc	BU
1993	—	—	—	—	475	500
1993 Proof	5,000	Value: 550				

KM# 1023 100 FRANCS
22.2000 g., 0.9000 Silver 0.6423 oz. ASW **Obv:** Head with hat
facing **Rev:** Flaming torch, denomination below

Date	Mintage	F	VF	XF	Unc	BU
1993	100,000	—	—	—	25.00	28.00
1993 Proof	50,000	Value: 40.00				

KM# 1037 100 FRANCS
22.2000 g., 0.9000 Silver 0.6423 oz. ASW **Subject:** Winston
Churchill **Obv:** Uniformed bust right

Date	Mintage	F	VF	XF	Unc	BU
1994 Proof	Est. 30,000	Value: 42.50				

KM# 1038 100 FRANCS
22.2000 g., 0.9000 Silver 0.6423 oz. ASW **Subject:** General de
Gaulle **Obv:** Bust right at microphone **Rev:** Map of France,
inscription overlay

Date	Mintage	F	VF	XF	Unc	BU
1994 Proof	Est. 30,000	Value: 45.00				

KM# 1039 100 FRANCS
22.2000 g., 0.9000 Silver 0.6423 oz. ASW **Subject:** General
Leclerc **Obv:** Bust facing **Rev:** Flag, inscription, fort, denomination

Date	Mintage	F	VF	XF	Unc	BU
1994 Proof	Est. 30,000		Value: 42.50			

KM# 1040 100 FRANCS
22.2000 g., 0.9000 Silver 0.6423 oz. ASW **Subject:** General Marie
Pierre Koenig **Obv:** Bust facing looking left **Rev:** Battle scene

Date	Mintage	F	VF	XF	Unc	BU
1994 Proof	Est. 30,000		Value: 42.50			

KM# 1041 100 FRANCS
22.2000 g., 0.9000 Silver 0.6423 oz. ASW **Subject:** General Juin
Obv: Uniformed bust right, map of Italy at right, mountaintop building

Date	Mintage	F	VF	XF	Unc	BU
1994 Proof	Est. 30,000		Value: 42.50			

KM# 1042 100 FRANCS
22.2000 g., 0.9000 Silver 0.6423 oz. ASW **Subject:** General
Dwight David Eisenhower **Obv:** Bust 3/4 left **Rev:** Flags representing
allied countries under Supreme Commander Eisenhower

Date	Mintage	F	VF	XF	Unc	BU
1994 Proof	Est. 30,000		Value: 42.50			

KM# 1043 100 FRANCS
22.2000 g., 0.9000 Silver 0.6423 oz. ASW **Subject:** Sainte -
Mere - Eglise **Rev:** Church, parachute behind

Date	Mintage	F	VF	XF	Unc	BU
1994 Proof	Est. 30,000		Value: 42.50			

KM# 1044 100 FRANCS
22.2000 g., 0.9000 Silver 0.6423 oz. ASW **Subject:** General de
Lattre de Tassigny **Obv:** Face in profile right **Rev:** Waving flags
below denomination

Date	Mintage	F	VF	XF	Unc	BU
1994 Proof	Est. 30,000		Value: 42.50			

KM# 1046 100 FRANCS
22.2000 g., 0.9000 Silver 0.6423 oz. ASW **Subject:** De Gaulle
and Adenauer **Obv:** Facing busts, date below **Rev:** Two hands
joined in handshake

Date	Mintage	F	VF	XF	Unc	BU
1994 Proof	Est. 30,000		Value: 42.50			

KM# 1047 100 FRANCS
33.6300 g., 0.9250 Silver 1.0000 oz. ASW **Series:** 1996
Olympics **Obv:** Head facing, denomination and date below
Rev: Discus thrower **Edge:** CITIUS ALTIUS FORTIUS

Date	Mintage	F	VF	XF	Unc	BU
1994 Proof	250,000		Value: 32.50			

KM# 1048 100 FRANCS
33.6300 g., 0.9250 Silver 1.0000 oz. ASW **Subject:** 1996
Olympics **Obv:** Head facing, denomination and date below
Rev: Javelin Thrower **Edge:** CITIUS ALTIUS FORTIUS

Date	Mintage	F	VF	XF	Unc	BU
1994 Proof	250,000		Value: 32.50			

KM# 1072 100 FRANCS
22.2000 g., 0.9000 Silver 0.6423 oz. ASW **Series:** Centennial
of Cinema **Subject:** Lumiere Brothers **Obv:** Antique movie
camera, denomination at right **Rev:** Conjoined busts right

Date	Mintage	F	VF	XF	Unc	BU
1994 Proof	15,000		Value: 32.50			

KM# 1073 100 FRANCS
17.0000 g., 0.9200 Gold 0.5028 oz. AGW **Series:** Centennial
of Cinema **Subject:** Lumiere Brothers **Obv:** Antique movie
camera **Rev:** Conjoined busts right

Date	Mintage	F	VF	XF	Unc	BU
1994 Proof	5,000		Value: 550			

KM# 1076 100 FRANCS
22.2000 g., 0.9000 Silver 0.6423 oz. ASW **Series:** Centennial
of Cinema **Subject:** Charlie Chaplin **Obv:** Antique movie camera
Rev: Head facing

Date	Mintage	F	VF	XF	Unc	BU
1994 Proof	15,000		Value: 42.00			

KM# 1077 100 FRANCS
17.0000 g., 0.9200 Gold 0.5028 oz. AGW **Series:** Centennial
of Cinema **Subject:** Charlie Chaplin **Obv:** Antique movie camera
Rev: Head facing

Date	Mintage	F	VF	XF	Unc	BU
1994 Proof	5,000		Value: 550			

KM# 1182 100 FRANCS
22.2000 g., 0.9000 Silver 0.6423 oz. ASW **Rev:** Voltaire

Date	Mintage	F	VF	XF	Unc	BU
1994 Proof	3,000		Value: 60.00			

KM# 1045.1   100 FRANCS
15.0000 g., 0.9000 Silver 0.4340 oz. ASW, 31 mm.
Subject: Liberation of Paris **Obv:** Battle scene, denomination below **Rev:** Triumphant troops marching down Champs Elysees **Note:** Smaller size.

Date	Mintage	F	VF	XF	Unc	BU
1994	1,598,000	—	—	—	35.00	40.00

KM# 1045.2   100 FRANCS
22.2000 g., 0.9000 Silver 0.6423 oz. ASW **Subject:** Liberation of Paris **Obv:** Battle scene, denomination **Rev:** Triumphant troops marching down Champs Elysees

Date	Mintage	F	VF	XF	Unc	BU
1994 Proof	Est. 30,000	Value: 42.50				

KM# 1080   100 FRANCS
22.2000 g., 0.9000 Silver 0.6423 oz. ASW **Series:** Centennial of Cinema **Subject:** Leon Gaumont **Obv:** Antique movie camera **Rev:** Head facing

Date	Mintage	F	VF	XF	Unc	BU
1995 Proof	15,000	Value: 40.00				

KM# 1081   100 FRANCS
17.0000 g., 0.9200 Gold 0.5028 oz. AGW **Series:** Centennial of Cinema **Subject:** Leon Gaumont **Obv:** Antique movie camera **Rev:** Head facing

Date	Mintage	F	VF	XF	Unc	BU
1995 Proof	5,000	Value: 550				

KM# 1084   100 FRANCS
22.2000 g., 0.9000 Silver 0.6423 oz. ASW **Series:** Centennial of Cinema **Subject:** Jean Renoir **Obv:** Antique movie camera **Rev:** Head right

Date	Mintage	F	VF	XF	Unc	BU
1995 Proof	15,000	Value: 30.00				

KM# 1085   100 FRANCS
17.0000 g., 0.9200 Gold 0.5028 oz. AGW **Series:** Centennial of Cinema **Subject:** Jean Renoir **Obv:** Antique movie camera **Rev:** Head right

Date	Mintage	F	VF	XF	Unc	BU
1995 Proof	5,000	Value: 550				

KM# 1088   100 FRANCS
22.2000 g., 0.9000 Silver 0.6423 oz. ASW **Series:** Centennial of Cinema **Subject:** Alfred Hitchcock **Obv:** Antique movie camera **Rev:** Head 1/4 left

Date	Mintage	F	VF	XF	Unc	BU
1995 Proof	15,000	Value: 40.00				

KM# 1089   100 FRANCS
17.0000 g., 0.9200 Gold 0.5028 oz. AGW **Series:** Centennial of Cinema **Subject:** Alfred Hitchcock **Obv:** Antique movie camera **Rev:** Head 1/4 left

Date	Mintage	F	VF	XF	Unc	BU
1995 Proof	5,000	Value: 550				

KM# 1092   100 FRANCS
22.2000 g., 0.9000 Silver 0.6423 oz. ASW **Series:** Centennial of Cinema **Subject:** Greta Garbo **Obv:** Antique movie camera **Rev:** Head right

Date	Mintage	F	VF	XF	Unc	BU
1995 Proof	15,000	Value: 37.50				

KM# 1093   100 FRANCS
17.0000 g., 0.9200 Gold 0.5028 oz. AGW **Series:** Centennial of Cinema **Subject:** Greta Garbo 1905-1990, actress in "Camille & Ninotchka" **Obv:** Antique movie camera **Rev:** Head right

Date	Mintage	F	VF	XF	Unc	BU
1995 Proof	5,000	Value: 550				

KM# 1096   100 FRANCS
22.2000 g., 0.9000 Silver 0.6423 oz. ASW **Series:** Centennial of Cinema **Subject:** Audrey Hepburn **Obv:** Antique movie camera **Rev:** Head 3/4 left

Date	Mintage	F	VF	XF	Unc	BU
1994 Proof	15,000	Value: 37.50				

KM# 1097   100 FRANCS
17.0000 g., 0.9200 Gold 0.5028 oz. AGW **Series:** Centennial of Cinema **Subject:** Audrey Hepburn **Obv:** Antique movie camera **Rev:** Head 3/4 left

Date	Mintage	F	VF	XF	Unc	BU
1994 Proof	5,000	Value: 550				

KM# 1100   100 FRANCS
22.2000 g., 0.9000 Silver 0.6423 oz. ASW **Series:** Centennial of Cinema **Subject:** Federico Fellini **Obv:** Antique movie camera **Rev:** Bust 3/4 right

Date	Mintage	F	VF	XF	Unc	BU
1995 Proof	15,000	Value: 30.00				

KM# 1101   100 FRANCS
17.0000 g., 0.9200 Gold 0.5028 oz. AGW **Series:** Centennial of Cinema **Subject:** Federico Fellini **Obv:** Antique movie camera **Rev:** Bust 3/4 right

Date	Mintage	F	VF	XF	Unc	BU
1995 Proof	5,000	Value: 550				

KM# 1104   100 FRANCS
22.2000 g., 0.9000 Silver 0.6423 oz. ASW **Series:** Centennial of Cinema **Subject:** Yves Montand **Obv:** Antique movie camera **Rev:** Bust 3/4 facing

Date	Mintage	F	VF	XF	Unc	BU
1994 Proof	15,000	Value: 30.00				

KM# 1105   100 FRANCS
17.0000 g., 0.9200 Gold 0.5028 oz. AGW **Series:** Centennial of Cinema **Subject:** Yves Montand **Obv:** Antique movie camera **Rev:** Bust 3/4 facing

Date	Mintage	F	VF	XF	Unc	BU
1994 Proof	5,000	Value: 550				

KM# 1108   100 FRANCS
22.2000 g., 0.9000 Silver 0.6423 oz. ASW **Series:** Centennial of Cinema **Subject:** Romy Schneider **Obv:** Antique movie camera **Rev:** Bust 3/4 left

Date	Mintage	F	VF	XF	Unc	BU
1995 Proof	15,000	Value: 30.00				

KM# 1109   100 FRANCS
17.0000 g., 0.9200 Gold 0.5028 oz. AGW **Series:** Centennial of Cinema **Subject:** Romy Schneider **Obv:** Antique movie camera **Rev:** Bust 3/4 left

Date	Mintage	F	VF	XF	Unc	BU
1995 Proof	5,000	Value: 550				

KM# 1116.2   100 FRANCS
22.2000 g., 0.9000 Silver 0.6423 oz. ASW **Obv:** Victory in Europe date, May 8, 1945 **Rev:** Birds in flight above banners, PAX below

Date	Mintage	F	VF	XF	Unc	BU
1995 Proof	30,000	Value: 45.00				

KM# 1134   100 FRANCS
22.2000 g., 0.9000 Silver 0.6423 oz. ASW **Obv:** Bust facing **Rev:** Lab bottles, denomination and date

Date	Mintage	F	VF	XF	Unc	BU
1995 Proof	10,000	Value: 45.00				

KM# 1136   100 FRANCS
22.2000 g., 0.9000 Silver 0.6423 oz. ASW **Obv:** Bust 1/4 left **Rev:** Bird in tree, denomination at right, fox and date below

Date	Mintage	F	VF	XF	Unc	BU
1995 Proof	10,000	Value: 45.00				

KM# 1116.1   100 FRANCS
15.0000 g., 0.9000 Silver 0.4340 oz. ASW, 31 mm.
Subject: V.E. Day **Obv:** Victory in Europe date, May 8, 1945 **Rev:** Birds in flight above banners, PAX below **Note:** Smaller size.

Date	Mintage	F	VF	XF	Unc	BU
1995	1,990,000	—	—	—	40.00	45.00

KM# 1138   100 FRANCS
22.2000 g., 0.9000 Silver 0.6423 oz. ASW **Subject:** 300th Anniversary of the Death of Marie de Sevigne; letter writer, 1626-1696 **Obv:** Bust 1/4 left **Rev:** Crowned double arms with supporters divide date and denomination

Date	Mintage	F	VF	XF	Unc	BU
1996 Proof	5,000	Value: 65.00				

KM# 1180   100 FRANCS
15.0500 g., 0.9000 Silver 0.4355 oz. ASW **Subject:** King Clovis I **Obv:** Bust facing **Rev:** Baptism scene, date and denomination below

Date	Mintage	F	VF	XF	Unc	BU
1996	2,000,000	—	—	—	32.50	37.50
1996 Proof	—	Value: 60.00				

KM# 1172   100 FRANCS
17.0000 g., 0.9200 Gold 0.5028 oz. AGW **Subject:** Coupe du Monde 1998 - France **Obv:** World Cup 1998 logo above denomination and date **Rev:** Segment of Eiffel tower, soccer player

Date	Mintage	F	VF	XF	Unc	BU
1996 Proof	25,000	Value: 500				

KM# 1168   100 FRANCS
17.0000 g., 0.9200 Gold 0.5028 oz. AGW **Subject:** Coupe du Monde 1998 - Africa **Obv:** World Cup 1998 logo above denomination and date **Rev:** Soccer player and map of Africa, date below

Date	Mintage	F	VF	XF	Unc	BU
1997 Proof	25,000	Value: 500				

KM# 1169   100 FRANCS
17.0000 g., 0.9200 Gold 0.5028 oz. AGW **Subject:** Coupe du Monde 1998 - America **Obv:** World Cup 1998 logo above denomination and date below **Rev:** Soccer player and map of North & South America

Date	Mintage	F	VF	XF	Unc	BU
1997 Proof	25,000	Value: 500				

KM# 1170   100 FRANCS
17.0000 g., 0.9200 Gold 0.5028 oz. AGW **Subject:** Coupe du Monde 1998 - Asia **Rev:** Soccer player and map of Asia, date below

Date	Mintage	F	VF	XF	Unc	BU
1997 Proof	25,000	Value: 500				

KM# 1173   100 FRANCS
17.0000 g., 0.9200 Gold 0.5028 oz. AGW **Subject:** Coupe du Monde 1998 - Oceania **Rev:** Soccer player and map of the Pacific, with Australia highlighted in a box, date below

Date	Mintage	F	VF	XF	Unc	BU
1997 Proof	25,000	Value: 500				

KM# 1188   100 FRANCS
15.1500 g., 0.9000 Silver 0.4384 oz. ASW **Obv:** Head facing **Rev:** Two cats flanking denomination

Date	Mintage	F	VF	XF	Unc	BU
1997	3,000	—	—	—	32.50	37.50
1997 Proof	3,000	Value: 50.00				

KM# 1195   100 FRANCS
8.4500 g., 0.9200 Gold 0.2499 oz. AGW **Obv:** Pantheon, date below **Rev:** Denomination and tree design

Date	Mintage	F	VF	XF	Unc	BU
1997 Proof	500	Value: 350				

KM# 1196   100 FRANCS
22.2000 g., 0.9000 Silver 0.6423 oz. ASW **Subject:** Georges Guynemer **Obv:** Bust 3/4 facing **Rev:** Guynemer's stork and denomination

Date	Mintage	F	VF	XF	Unc	BU
1997 Proof	3,000	Value: 50.00				

KM# 1198   100 FRANCS
22.2000 g., 0.9000 Silver 0.6423 oz. ASW **Subject:** Pierre and Marie Curie, 1867-1934, physicist - chemist **Obv:** Conjoined busts left **Rev:** Denomination

Date	Mintage	F	VF	XF	Unc	BU
1997 Proof	3,000	Value: 50.00				

KM# 1171   100 FRANCS
17.0000 g., 0.9200 Gold 0.5028 oz. AGW **Subject:** Coupe du Monte 1998 - Europe **Obv:** World Cup 1998 logo, denomination and date below **Rev:** Soccer player and map of Europe, date below

Date	Mintage	F	VF	XF	Unc	BU
1998 Proof	25,000	Value: 500				

KM# 1201   100 FRANCS
22.2000 g., 0.9000 Silver 0.6423 oz. ASW **Subject:** Marie Caritat Marquis de Condorcet **Obv:** Bust 3/4 right **Rev:** Denomination

Date	Mintage	F	VF	XF	Unc	BU
1998 Proof	3,000	Value: 50.00				

KM# 1203   100 FRANCS
22.2000 g., 0.9000 Silver 0.6423 oz. ASW **Subject:** Gaspard Monge **Obv:** Bust 3/4 right, building at right **Rev:** Denomination

Date	Mintage	F	VF	XF	Unc	BU
1998 Proof	3,000	Value: 50.00				

KM# 1209   100 FRANCS
17.0000 g., 0.9200 Gold 0.5028 oz. AGW **Subject:** Treasures of the Nile - King Tutankhamon **Obv:** Burial mask and dog **Rev:** Sphinx and pyramids

Date	Mintage	F	VF	XF	Unc	BU
1998 Proof	2,000	Value: 575				

KM# 1210   100 FRANCS
17.0000 g., 0.9200 Gold 0.5028 oz. AGW **Subject:** Treasures of the Nile - The Scribe Accroupi **Obv:** Seated scribe **Rev:** Pyramids, Sphinx, date at left, denomination below

Date	Mintage	F	VF	XF	Unc	BU
1998 Proof	2,000	Value: 575				

KM# 1397   100 FRANCS
22.1400 g., 0.9000 Silver 0.6406 oz. ASW, 37 mm.   **Subject:** Human Rights Declaration **Obv:** Bust right, building and dates below **Rev:** Denomination on globe, laurel spray below **Edge:** Plain

Date	Mintage	F	VF	XF	Unc	BU
1998A Proof	—	Value: 50.00				

KM# 1295   100 FRANCS
22.3000 g., 0.9000 Silver 0.6452 oz. ASW, 36.7 mm. **Subject:** Louis Braille **Obv:** Portrait, dots and fingers **Rev:** Braille text, tools and fingers **Edge:** Plain

Date	Mintage	F	VF	XF	Unc	BU
1999 Proof	3,000	Value: 50.00				

KM# 1296   100 FRANCS
22.3000 g., 0.9000 Silver 0.6452 oz. ASW, 36.7 mm. **Subject:** Jean Jaures **Obv:** Bearded portrait **Rev:** Floor plan and dome **Edge:** Plain

Date	Mintage	F	VF	XF	Unc	BU
1999 Proof	3,000	Value: 50.00				

KM# 1232   100 FRANCS
17.0000 g., 0.9200 Gold 0.5028 oz. AGW **Subject:** 2000 Years - French Coinage **Obv:** Denomination **Rev:** 1st century B.C. Celtic Parisii Stater coin design **Edge:** Plain

Date	Mintage	F	VF	XF	Unc	BU
2000 Proof	1,000	Value: 575				

KM# 1233   100 FRANCS
17.0000 g., 0.9200 Gold 0.5028 oz. AGW **Subject:** 2000 Years - French Coinage **Rev:** Charlemagne Denar coin design

Date	Mintage	F	VF	XF	Unc	BU
2000 Proof	1,000	Value: 575				

KM# 1234   100 FRANCS
17.0000 g., 0.9200 Gold 0.5028 oz. AGW **Subject:** 2000 Years - French Coinage **Rev:** Louis IX gold Ecu coin design

Date	Mintage	F	VF	XF	Unc	BU
2000 Proof	1,000	Value: 575				

KM# 1238   100 FRANCS
17.0000 g., 0.9200 Gold 0.5028 oz. AGW **Series:** XXth Century **Subject:** Biology and Medicine **Obv:** Double X design **Rev:** Parents, fetus, hands

Date	Mintage	F	VF	XF	Unc	BU
2000 Proof	1,000	Value: 575				

KM# 1239   100 FRANCS
17.0000 g., 0.9200 Gold 0.5028 oz. AGW **Series:** XXth Century **Subject:** Physics **Rev:** Einstein's portrait, atom and formula

Date	Mintage	F	VF	XF	Unc	BU
2000 Proof	1,000	Value: 575				

KM# 1240   100 FRANCS
17.0000 g., 0.9200 Gold 0.5028 oz. AGW **Series:** XXth Century **Subject:** Communications **Rev:** World, satellites, keyboard

Date	Mintage	F	VF	XF	Unc	BU
2000 Proof	1,000	Value: 575				

KM# 1241   100 FRANCS
17.0000 g., 0.9200 Gold 0.5028 oz. AGW **Series:** XXth Century **Subject:** Automobile **Rev:** Race cars above horse

Date	Mintage	F	VF	XF	Unc	BU
2000 Proof	1,000	Value: 450				

KM# 1242   100 FRANCS
17.0000 g., 0.9200 Gold 0.5028 oz. AGW **Series:** XXth Century **Subject:** Flight **Rev:** Icarus in flight above Bleriot monoplane

Date	Mintage	F	VF	XF	Unc	BU
2000 Proof	1,000	Value: 575				

KM# 1243   100 FRANCS
17.0000 g., 0.9200 Gold 0.5028 oz. AGW **Series:** XXth Century **Subject:** Space Travel **Rev:** Astronaut, footprint on moon, planets

Date	Mintage	F	VF	XF	Unc	BU
2000 Proof	1,000	Value: 575				

KM# 1264   100 FRANCS
17.0000 g., 0.9200 Gold 0.5028 oz. AGW **Subject:** Antoine de St. Exupery **Obv:** Portrait, bi-plane **Rev:** The "Little Prince" standing on a small planet

Date	Mintage	F	VF	XF	Unc	BU
2000 Proof	1,000	Value: 575				

KM# 974   500 FRANCS
17.0000 g., 0.9200 Gold 0.5028 oz. AGW **Series:** 1992 Olympics **Obv:** Ice skating couple **Rev:** Cross on flame divides date and denomination, Olympic logo below

Date	Mintage	F	VF	XF	Unc	BU
1989 Proof	Est. 17,000	Value: 500				

KM# 973   500 FRANCS
17.0000 g., 0.9200 Gold 0.5028 oz. AGW **Series:** 1992 Olympics **Obv:** Alpine skiing **Rev:** Cross on flame, date and denomination, Olympic logo below **Note:** Without mint mark.

Date	Mintage	F	VF	XF	Unc	BU
1989 Proof	19,000	Value: 500				

KM# 985   500 FRANCS
17.0000 g., 0.9200 Gold 0.5028 oz. AGW **Series:** 1992 Olympics **Obv:** Speed skating **Rev:** Crossed flame, date and denomination, logo below

Date	Mintage	F	VF	XF	Unc	BU
1990 Proof	13,000	Value: 500				

KM# 986   500 FRANCS
17.0000 g., 0.9200 Gold 0.5028 oz. AGW **Series:** 1992 Olympics **Obv:** Bobsledding **Rev:** Games logo, value and legend

Date	Mintage	F	VF	XF	Unc	BU
1990 Proof	13,000	Value: 500				

KM# 987   500 FRANCS
17.0000 g., 0.9200 Gold 0.5028 oz. AGW **Series:** 1992 Olympics **Subject:** Pierre de Coubertin **Obv:** Free-style skier watched by chamois **Rev:** Head facing

Date	Mintage	F	VF	XF	Unc	BU
1990 Proof	8,000	Value: 500				

KM# 988   500 FRANCS
17.0000 g., 0.9200 Gold 0.5028 oz. AGW **Series:** 1992 Olympics **Obv:** Modern and old style slalom skiers

Date	Mintage	F	VF	XF	Unc	BU
1990 Proof	8,000	Value: 500				

KM# 977   500 FRANCS
17.0000 g., 0.9200 Gold 0.5028 oz. AGW **Subject:** 100th Anniversary of Basketball **Obv:** Player jumping for lay-up shot, hoop behind **Rev:** Star, ring, and globe, denomination and date below

Date	Mintage	F	VF	XF	Unc	BU
1991 Proof	5,000	Value: 500				

KM# 997   500 FRANCS
17.0000 g., 0.9200 Gold 0.5028 oz. AGW **Series:** 1992 Olympics **Obv:** 2 hockey players and large ibex ram

Date	Mintage	F	VF	XF	Unc	BU
1991 Proof	8,000	Value: 500				

KM# 998   500 FRANCS
17.0000 g., 0.9200 Gold 0.5028 oz. AGW

Date	Mintage	F	VF	XF	Unc	BU
1991 Proof	8,000	Value: 500				

KM# 999   500 FRANCS
17.0000 g., 0.9200 Gold 0.5028 oz. AGW **Series:** 1992 Olympics **Obv:** Old style and modern ski jumpers

Date	Mintage	F	VF	XF	Unc	BU
1991 Proof	8,000	Value: 500				

KM# 1000   500 FRANCS
17.0000 g., 0.9200 Gold 0.5028 oz. AGW   **Series:** 1992 Olympics
Subject: Pierre de Coubertin **Obv:** Head facing **Rev:** Cross on
flame divides date and denomination, Olympic logo below

Date	Mintage	F	VF	XF	Unc	BU
1991 Proof	28,000	Value: 500				

KM# 1001   500 FRANCS
17.0000 g., 0.9200 Gold 0.5028 oz. AGW   **Obv:** Building,.
denomination and date below **Rev:** Mozart in Paris at piano

Date	Mintage	F	VF	XF	Unc	BU
1991 Proof	Est. 5,000	Value: 500				

KM# 1024   500 FRANCS
31.1040 g., 0.9990 Gold 0.9990 oz. AGW   **Series:** Bicentennial
of the Louvre **Obv:** Mona Lisa **Rev:** Pyramids front building, date
and denomination below

Date	Mintage	F	VF	XF	Unc	BU
1993	—					—
1993 Proof	5,000	Value: 950				
1994 Proof	5,000	Value: 1,000				

KM# 1025.1   500 FRANCS
31.1040 g., 0.9990 Gold 0.9990 oz. AGW   **Series:** Bicentennial
of the Louvre **Obv:** Venus de Milo

Date	Mintage	F	VF	XF	Unc	BU
1993	—					—
1993 Proof	5,000	Value: 950				

KM# 1026   500 FRANCS
155.5175 g., 0.9990 Gold 4.9948 oz. AGW   **Series:** Bicentennial
of the Louvre **Obv:** Liberty **Rev:** Pyramids front building, date
and denomination below

Date	Mintage	F	VF	XF	Unc	BU
1993 Proof	99	Value: 4,650				
1994 Proof	99	Value: 4,750				

KM# 1027   500 FRANCS
155.5175 g., 0.9990 Gold 4.9948 oz. AGW   **Series:** Bicentennial
of the Louvre **Obv:** Mona Lisa **Rev:** Patterned pyramids front building

Date	Mintage	F	VF	XF	Unc	BU
1993 Proof	99	Value: 4,750				
1994 Proof	99	Value: 4,850				

KM# 1028   500 FRANCS
17.0000 g., 0.9200 Gold 0.5028 oz. AGW   **Subject:** Jean Moulin
Obv: Head facing

Date	Mintage	F	VF	XF	Unc	BU
1993 Proof	5,000	Value: 500				

KM# 1183   500 FRANCS
155.5175 g., 0.9990 Gold 4.9948 oz. AGW   **Series:** Bicentennial
of the Louvre **Obv:** Victory

Date	Mintage	F	VF	XF	Unc	BU
1993 Proof	99	Value: 4,500				
1994 Proof	99	Value: 4,600				

KM# 1184   500 FRANCS
155.5175 g., 0.9990 Gold 4.9948 oz. AGW   **Series:** Bicentennial
of the Louvre **Obv:** Napoleon and Josephine

Date	Mintage	F	VF	XF	Unc	BU
1993 Proof	99	Value: 4,600				
1994 Proof	99	Value: 4,700				

KM# 1185   500 FRANCS
155.5175 g., 0.9990 Gold 4.9948 oz. AGW   **Series:** Bicentennial
of the Louvre **Obv:** Marie Marguerite

Date	Mintage	F	VF	XF	Unc	BU
1993 Proof	99	Value: 4,600				
1994 Proof	99	Value: 4,700				

KM# 1025.2   500 FRANCS
155.5000 g., 0.9990 Gold 4.9942 oz. AGW, 50 mm.   **Obv:** Venus
de Milo **Rev:** The Louvre Building entrance above value

Date	Mintage	F	VF	XF	Unc	BU
1993 Proof	99	Value: 4,600				

KM# 1399   500 FRANCS
155.5175 g., 0.9990 Gold 4.9948 oz. AGW, 50 mm.
Subject: Venus De Milo **Edge:** Plain

Date	Mintage	F	VF	XF	Unc	BU
1993A Proof	99	Value: 4,600				

KM# 1049   500 FRANCS
17.0000 g., 0.9200 Gold 0.5028 oz. AGW   **Subject:** Winston
Churchill **Obv:** Bust right, denomination and date **Rev:** Eleven
line inscription on flag design, rampant lion at right

Date	Mintage	F	VF	XF	Unc	BU
1994 Proof	Est. 2,000	Value: 500				

KM# 1051   500 FRANCS
17.0000 g., 0.9200 Gold 0.5028 oz. AGW   **Subject:** General
Leclerc **Obv:** Bust facing

Date	Mintage	F	VF	XF	Unc	BU
1994 Proof	Est. 2,000	Value: 500				

KM# 1050   500 FRANCS
17.0000 g., 0.9200 Gold 0.5028 oz. AGW   **Subject:** General de
Gaulle **Obv:** 3/4 bust of General de Gaulle in front of microphone

Date	Mintage	F	VF	XF	Unc	BU
1994 Proof	Est. 5,000	Value: 500				

KM# 1052   500 FRANCS
17.0000 g., 0.9200 Gold 0.5028 oz. AGW   **Subject:** General
Marie Pierre Koenig **Obv:** Bust looking left

Date	Mintage	F	VF	XF	Unc	BU
1994 Proof	Est. 2,000	Value: 500				

KM# 1053   500 FRANCS
17.0000 g., 0.9200 Gold 0.5028 oz. AGW   **Subject:** General Juin
Obv: Bust right, map of Italy at right

Date	Mintage	F	VF	XF	Unc	BU
1994 Proof	Est. 2,000	Value: 500				

KM# 1054   500 FRANCS
17.0000 g., 0.9200 Gold 0.5028 oz. AGW   **Subject:** Dwight
David Eisenhower **Obv:** Uniformed bust left

Date	Mintage	F	VF	XF	Unc	BU
1994 Proof	Est. 2,000	Value: 500				

KM# 1055   500 FRANCS
17.0000 g., 0.9200 Gold 0.5028 oz. AGW **Rev:** Church of Sainte
- Mere - Eglise, parachute behind

Date	Mintage	F	VF	XF	Unc	BU
1994 Proof	Est. 2,000	Value: 500				

KM# 1056   500 FRANCS
17.0000 g., 0.9200 Gold 0.5028 oz. AGW **Subject:** General de
Lattre de Tassigny **Obv:** Head right

Date	Mintage	F	VF	XF	Unc	BU
1994 Proof	Est. 2,000	Value: 500				

KM# 1057   500 FRANCS
17.0000 g., 0.9200 Gold 0.5028 oz. AGW **Subject:** Liberation of
Paris **Obv:** Triumphant troops marching down Champs Elysees

Date	Mintage	F	VF	XF	Unc	BU
1994 Proof	Est. 5,000	Value: 500				

KM# 1058   500 FRANCS
17.0000 g., 0.9200 Gold 0.5028 oz. AGW **Obv:** Heads of de
Gaulle and Adenauer facing the center, date below

Date	Mintage	F	VF	XF	Unc	BU
1994 Proof	Est. 2,000	Value: 500				

KM# 1059   500 FRANCS
16.9700 g., 0.9170 Gold 0.5003 oz. AGW **Subject:** 1996
Olympics **Obv:** Head facing, date and denomination **Rev:** Archer
in front of Eiffel Tower **Edge:** CITIUS ALTIUS FORTTUS

Date	Mintage	F	VF	XF	Unc	BU
1994 Proof	60,000	Value: 500				

KM# 1074   500 FRANCS
31.0350 g., 0.9990 Gold 0.9968 oz. AGW **Series:** Centennial
of Cinema **Subject:** Lumiere Brothers **Obv:** Antique camera
Rev: Conjoined busts right

Date	Mintage	F	VF	XF	Unc	BU
1994 Proof	3,000	Value: 950				

KM# 1078   500 FRANCS
31.0350 g., 0.9990 Gold 0.9968 oz. AGW **Series:** Centennial
of Cinema **Subject:** Charlie Chaplin **Obv:** Antique movie camera
Rev: Head facing

Date	Mintage	F	VF	XF	Unc	BU
1994 Proof	3,000	Value: 950				

KM# 1079   500 FRANCS
155.5175 g., 0.9990 Gold 4.9948 oz. AGW **Series:** Centennial
of Cinema **Subject:** Charlie Chaplin **Obv:** Antique movie camera
Rev: Head facing

Date	Mintage	F	VF	XF	Unc	BU
1994 Proof	99	Value: 4,600				

KM# 1186   500 FRANCS
17.0000 g., 0.9200 Gold 0.5028 oz. AGW **Series:** Centennial
of Cinema **Rev:** Voltaire

Date	Mintage	F	VF	XF	Unc	BU
1994 Proof	350	Value: 500				

KM# 1082   500 FRANCS
31.0350 g., 0.9990 Gold 0.9968 oz. AGW **Series:** Centennial
of Cinema **Subject:** Leon Gaumont **Obv:** Antique movie camera
Rev: Head facing

Date	Mintage	F	VF	XF	Unc	BU
1995 Proof	3,000	Value: 950				

KM# 1083   500 FRANCS
155.5175 g., 0.9990 Gold 4.9948 oz. AGW **Series:** Centennial
of Cinema **Subject:** Leon Gaumont **Obv:** Antique movie camera
Rev: Head facing

Date	Mintage	F	VF	XF	Unc	BU
1995 Proof	99	Value: 4,600				

KM# 1086   500 FRANCS
31.0350 g., 0.9990 Gold 0.9968 oz. AGW **Series:** Centennial
of Cinema **Subject:** Jean Renoir **Obv:** Antique movie camera
Rev: Head 3/4 right

Date	Mintage	F	VF	XF	Unc	BU
1995 Proof	3,000	Value: 950				

KM# 1087   500 FRANCS
155.5175 g., 0.9990 Gold 4.9948 oz. AGW **Series:** Centennial
of Cinema **Subject:** Jean Renoir **Obv:** Antique movie camera
Rev: Head 3/4 right

Date	Mintage	F	VF	XF	Unc	BU
1995 Proof	99	Value: 4,600				

KM# 1090   500 FRANCS
31.0350 g., 0.9990 Gold 0.9968 oz. AGW **Series:** Centennial
of Cinema **Subject:** Alfred Hitchcock **Obv:** Antique movie camera
Rev: Bust 3/4 facing

Date	Mintage	F	VF	XF	Unc	BU
1995 Proof	3,000	Value: 950				

KM# 1091   500 FRANCS
155.5175 g., 0.9990 Gold 4.9948 oz. AGW **Series:** Centennial
of Cinema **Subject:** Alfred Hitchcock **Obv:** Antique movie camera
Rev: Bust 3/4 facing

Date	Mintage	F	VF	XF	Unc	BU
1995 Proof	99	Value: 4,600				

KM# 1094   500 FRANCS
31.0350 g., 0.9990 Gold 0.9968 oz. AGW **Series:** Centennial
of Cinema **Subject:** Greta Garbo 1905-1990; actress in "Camille
& Ninotchka" **Obv:** Antique movie camera **Rev:** Head with high
collar right

Date	Mintage	F	VF	XF	Unc	BU
1995 Proof	3,000	Value: 950				

KM# 1095   500 FRANCS
155.5175 g., 0.9990 Gold 4.9948 oz. AGW **Series:** Centennial
of Cinema **Subject:** Greta Garbo 1905-1990; actress in "Camille
& Ninotchka" **Obv:** Antique movie camera **Rev:** Head with high
collar right

Date	Mintage	F	VF	XF	Unc	BU
1995 Proof	99	Value: 4,600				

KM# 1098   500 FRANCS
31.0350 g., 0.9990 Gold 0.9968 oz. AGW **Series:** Centennial
of Cinema **Subject:** Audrey Hepburn **Obv:** Antique movie camera
Rev: Head 3/4 left

Date	Mintage	F	VF	XF	Unc	BU
1994 Proof	3,000	Value: 950				

KM# 1099   500 FRANCS
155.5175 g., 0.9990 Gold 4.9948 oz. AGW **Series:** Centennial
of Cinema **Subject:** Audrey Hepburn **Obv:** Antique movie camera
Rev: Head 3/4 left

Date	Mintage	F	VF	XF	Unc	BU
1994 Proof	99	Value: 4,600				

KM# 1102   500 FRANCS
31.0350 g., 0.9990 Gold 0.9968 oz. AGW **Series:** Centennial
of Cinema **Subject:** Federico Fellini **Obv:** Antique movie camera
Rev: Bust 3/4 right

Date	Mintage	F	VF	XF	Unc	BU
1995 Proof	3,000	Value: 950				

KM# 1103   500 FRANCS
155.5175 g., 0.9990 Gold 4.9948 oz. AGW **Series:** Centennial
of Cinema **Subject:** Federico Fellini **Obv:** Antique movie camera
Rev: Bust 3/4 right

Date	Mintage	F	VF	XF	Unc	BU
1995 Proof	99	Value: 4,600				

KM# 1106   500 FRANCS
31.0350 g., 0.9990 Gold 0.9968 oz. AGW **Series:** Centennial
of Cinema **Subject:** Yves Montand **Obv:** Antique movie camera
Rev: Bust 3/4 facing

Date	Mintage	F	VF	XF	Unc	BU
1994 Proof	3,000	Value: 950				

KM# 1107   500 FRANCS
155.5175 g., 0.9990 Gold 4.9948 oz. AGW **Series:** Centennial
of Cinema **Subject:** Yves Montand **Obv:** Antique movie camera
Rev: Bust 3/4 facing

Date	Mintage	F	VF	XF	Unc	BU
1994 Proof	99	Value: 4,600				

KM# 1110   500 FRANCS
31.0350 g., 0.9990 Gold 0.9968 oz. AGW **Series:** Centennial
of Cinema **Subject:** Romy Schneider **Obv:** Antique movie
camera **Rev:** Bust 3/4 left

Date	Mintage	F	VF	XF	Unc	BU
1995 Proof	3,000	Value: 950				

KM# 1111   500 FRANCS
155.5175 g., 0.9990 Gold 4.9948 oz. AGW **Series:** Centennial
of Cinema **Subject:** Romy Schneider **Obv:** Antique movie
camera **Rev:** Bust 3/4 left

Date	Mintage	F	VF	XF	Unc	BU
1995 Proof	99	Value: 4,600				

KM# 1117   500 FRANCS
17.0000 g., 0.9200 Gold 0.5028 oz. AGW **Subject:** V.E. Day
Obv: Victory in Europe date May 8, 1945, denomination
Rev: Birds in flight above banners, PAX below

Date	Mintage	F	VF	XF	Unc	BU
1995 Proof	5,000	Value: 500				

KM# 1135   500 FRANCS
17.0000 g., 0.9200 Gold 0.5028 oz. AGW **Obv:** Louis Pasteur

Date	Mintage	F	VF	XF	Unc	BU
1995 Proof	1,000	Value: 500				

KM# 1137   500 FRANCS
17.0000 g., 0.9200 Gold 0.5028 oz. AGW **Obv:** Jean de la Fountain

Date	Mintage	F	VF	XF	Unc	BU
1995 Proof	1,000	Value: 500				

KM# 1311   500 FRANCS
155.5000 g., 0.9990 Gold 4.9942 oz. AGW, 50 mm. **Series:**
Centennial of Cinema **Subject:** Gerard Philipe **Obv:** Antique
movie camera **Rev:** Bust 3/4 facing

Date	Mintage	F	VF	XF	Unc	BU
1995 Proof	99	Value: 4,600				

KM# 1312   500 FRANCS
155.5000 g., 0.9990 Gold 4.9942 oz. AGW, 50 mm.
Series: Centennial of Cinema **Subject:** George Melies
Obv: Antique movie camera **Rev:** Head facing

Date	Mintage	F	VF	XF	Unc	BU
1995 Proof	99	Value: 4,600				

KM# 1313   500 FRANCS
155.5000 g., 0.9990 Gold 4.9942 oz. AGW, 50 mm. **Series:**
Centennial of Cinema **Subject:** Arletty **Obv:** Antique movie
camera **Rev:** Head left

Date	Mintage	F	VF	XF	Unc	BU
1995 Proof	99	Value: 4,600				

KM# 1314   500 FRANCS
155.5000 g., 0.9990 Gold 4.9942 oz. AGW, 50 mm.
Series: Centennial of Cinema **Subject:** Marcel Pagnol **Obv:**
Antique movie camera **Rev:** Head 3/4 left

Date	Mintage	F	VF	XF	Unc	BU
1995 Proof	—	Value: 4,600				

KM# 1139   500 FRANCS
17.0000 g., 0.9200 Gold 0.5028 oz. AGW **Subject:** 300th
Anniversary - Death of Marie de Sevigne; letter writer, 1626-1696
Obv: Bust 1/2 left

Date	Mintage	F	VF	XF	Unc	BU
1996 Proof	500	Value: 600				

KM# 1181   500 FRANCS
17.0000 g., 0.9200 Gold 0.5028 oz. AGW **Subject:** King Clovis
I **Obv:** Bust facing

Date	Mintage	F	VF	XF	Unc	BU
1996 Proof	250	Value: 700				

KM# 1197   500 FRANCS
17.0000 g., 0.9200 Gold 0.5028 oz. AGW **Subject:** Georges
Guynemer **Obv:** Bust 3/4 facing **Rev:** Stork emblem and
denomination

Date	Mintage	F	VF	XF	Unc	BU
1997 Proof	300	Value: 575				

KM# 1199   500 FRANCS
17.0000 g., 0.9200 Gold 0.5028 oz. AGW **Subject:** Pierre and
Marie Curie 1867-1934, physicist - chemist **Obv:** Conjoined busts
left **Rev:** Denomination

Date	Mintage	F	VF	XF	Unc	BU
1997 Proof	300	Value: 575				

KM# 1200   500 FRANCS
17.0000 g., 0.9200 Gold 0.5028 oz. AGW **Subject:** Andre
Malraux **Obv:** Head facing **Rev:** Cats flanking denomination

Date	Mintage	F	VF	XF	Unc	BU
1997 Proof	300	Value: 575				

KM# 1202   500 FRANCS
17.0000 g., 0.9200 Gold 0.5028 oz. AGW **Subject:** Marquis de
Condorcet **Obv:** Head right **Rev:** Denomination

Date	Mintage	F	VF	XF	Unc	BU
1998 Proof	300	Value: 575				

KM# 1204   500 FRANCS
17.0000 g., 0.9200 Gold 0.5028 oz. AGW **Subject:** Gaspard
Monge **Obv:** Head 1/2 right **Rev:** Denomination

Date	Mintage	F	VF	XF	Unc	BU
1998 Proof	300	Value: 575				

KM# 1237   500 FRANCS
31.1040 g., 0.9990 Gold 0.9990 oz. AGW **Subject:** Yves St.
Laurent **Obv:** RF monogram within entwined snake design divides
denomination and date **Rev:** Fashion show scene **Edge:** Plain

Date	Mintage	F	VF	XF	Unc	BU
2000 Proof	1,000	Value: 900				

KM# 1315   500 FRANCS-75 EURO
155.5000 g., 0.9990 Gold 4.9942 oz. AGW, 50 mm.
Subject: "The Thinker" by Auguste Rodin **Obv:** Seated statue
left **Rev:** Denominations-(francs and euros)

Date	Mintage	F	VF	XF	Unc	BU
1996 Proof	99	Value: 4,600				

KM# 1316   500 FRANCS-75 EURO
155.5000 g., 0.9990 Gold 4.9942 oz. AGW, 50 mm.
Subject: Chinese Horseman **Obv:** Equestrian statue
Rev: Denominations-(francs and euros)

Date	Mintage	F	VF	XF	Unc	BU
1996 Proof	99	Value: 4,600				

KM# 1317   500 FRANCS-75 EURO
155.5000 g., 0.9990 Gold 4.9942 oz. AGW, 50 mm.
Subject: Klimt's "The Kiss" **Obv:** Two figures embraced
Rev: Denominations-(francs and euros)

Date	Mintage	F	VF	XF	Unc	BU
1997 Proof	—	Value: 4,600				

KM# 1318   500 FRANCS-75 EURO
155.5000 g., 0.9990 Gold 4.9942 oz. AGW, 50 mm.
Subject: Dürer's Self Portrait **Obv:** Bust facing
Rev: Denominations-(francs and euros)

Date	Mintage	F	VF	XF	Unc	BU
1997 Proof	99	Value: 4,600				

KM# 1319   500 FRANCS-75 EURO
155.5000 g., 0.9990 Gold 4.9942 oz. AGW, 50 mm. **Obv:** Japanese
woman carrying a case **Rev:** Denominations-(francs and euros)

Date	Mintage	F	VF	XF	Unc	BU
1997 Proof	99	Value: 4,600				

KM# 1320   500 FRANCS-75 EURO
155.5000 g., 0.9990 Gold 4.9942 oz. AGW, 50 mm.

Subject: "The Little Dancer" by Degas **Obv:** Figure in tutu left
Rev: Denominations-(francs and euros)

Date	Mintage	F	VF	XF	Unc	BU
1997 Proof	99	Value: 4,600				

KM# 1257   655.957 FRANCS
31.1040 g., 0.9990 Gold 0.9990 oz. AGW **Series:** Euro
conversion **Obv:** Country names with euro-currency equivalents
around "RF", denomination and French coin designs **Rev:** Europa
allegorical portrait **Edge:** Plain

Date	Mintage	F	VF	XF	Unc	BU
1999 Proof	2,000	Value: 950				

KM# 1261   655.957 FRANCS
31.1040 g., 0.9990 Gold 0.9990 oz. AGW **Obv:** Country names
with euro-currency equivalents around "RF", denomination and
French euro coin design

Date	Mintage	F	VF	XF	Unc	BU
2000 Proof	2,000	Value: 950				

KM# 1247   655.957 FRANCS
15.5520 g., 0.9990 Gold 0.4995 oz. AGW **Series:** European Art
Styles - Renaissance **Obv:** Europe allegorical portrait **Rev:** Greek
and Roman style buildings

Date	Mintage	F	VF	XF	Unc	BU
2000 Proof	2,000	Value: 525				

KM# 1248   655.957 FRANCS
15.5520 g., 0.9990 Gold 0.4995 oz. AGW **Series:** European Art
Styles - Roman **Rev:** Roman sculpture and ancient buildings

Date	Mintage	F	VF	XF	Unc	BU
2000 Proof	2,000	Value: 525				

KM# 1249   655.957 FRANCS
15.5520 g., 0.9990 Gold 0.4995 oz. AGW **Series:** European Art
Styles - Gothic **Rev:** Gothic sculpture and buildings

Date	Mintage	F	VF	XF	Unc	BU
2000 Proof	2,000	Value: 525				

KM# 1250   655.957 FRANCS
15.5520 g., 0.9990 Gold 0.4995 oz. AGW **Series:** European Art
Styles - Renaissance **Rev:** Renaissance buildings

Date	Mintage	F	VF	XF	Unc	BU
2000 Proof	2,000	Value: 525				

KM# 1251   655.957 FRANCS
15.5520 g., 0.9990 Gold 0.4995 oz. AGW **Series:** European Art
Styles - Classic and Baroque **Rev:** Classic and Baroque art

Date	Mintage	F	VF	XF	Unc	BU
2000 Proof	2,000	Value: 525				

KM# 1252   655.957 FRANCS
15.5520 g., 0.9990 Gold 0.4995 oz. AGW **Series:** European Art
Styles - Art Nouveau **Rev:** Arches and scrollwork

Date	Mintage	F	VF	XF	Unc	BU
2000 Proof	2,000	Value: 525				

KM# 1253   655.957 FRANCS
15.5520 g., 0.9990 Gold 0.4995 oz. AGW **Series:** European Art
Styles - Modern **Rev:** Modern artistic designs

Date	Mintage	F	VF	XF	Unc	BU
2000 Proof	2,000	Value: 525				

ECU / FRANCS COINAGE
European Currency Units

KM# 989   100 FRANCS-15 ECUS
22.2000 g., 0.9000 Silver 0.6423 oz. ASW **Obv:** Center
monogram divides date and denomination, laurel spray below
Rev: Stylized head facing, denomination below

Date	Mintage	F	VF	XF	Unc	BU
1990 Proof	30,000	Value: 85.00				

KM# 1002   100 FRANCS-15 ECUS
22.2000 g., 0.9000 Silver 0.6423 oz. ASW **Subject:** Descartes
Obv: Finger pointing to starred paper, denomination below
Rev: Head 3/4 facing, denomination and date below

Date	Mintage	F	VF	XF	Unc	BU
1991 Proof	20,000	Value: 65.00				

KM# 1012   100 FRANCS-15 ECUS
22.2000 g., 0.9000 Silver 0.6423 oz. ASW **Subject:** Jean Monet
Obv: Denomination in center within legend and chain above RF
Rev: Head left, denomination at right

Date	Mintage	F	VF	XF	Unc	BU
1992 Proof	30,000	Value: 55.00				

KM# 1029   100 FRANCS-15 ECUS
22.2000 g., 0.9000 Silver 0.6423 oz. ASW **Subject:**
Mediterranean Games **Obv:** Head left, denomination below **Rev:**
Swimming, denomination below, rings divide date below

Date	Mintage	F	VF	XF	Unc	BU
1993 Proof	15,000	Value: 47.50				

KM# 1030   100 FRANCS-15 ECUS
22.2000 g., 0.9000 Silver 0.6423 oz. ASW **Subject:**
Mediterranean Games **Obv:** Head left, denomination below **Rev:**
Soccer, denomination below, rings divide date below

Date	Mintage	F	VF	XF	Unc	BU
1993 Proof	15,000	Value: 47.50				

KM# 1031   100 FRANCS-15 ECUS
22.2000 g., 0.9000 Silver 0.6423 oz. ASW **Rev:** Arc de Triumph

Date	Mintage	F	VF	XF	Unc	BU
1993 Proof	20,000	Value: 42.50				

KM# 1032   100 FRANCS-15 ECUS
22.2000 g., 0.9000 Silver 0.6423 oz. ASW **Rev:** Brandenburg Gate

Date	Mintage	F	VF	XF	Unc	BU
1993 Proof	20,000	Value: 42.50				

KM# 1060 100 FRANCS-15 ECUS
22.2000 g., 0.9000 Silver 0.6423 oz. ASW **Rev:** Stylized Tunnel View - Map

Date	Mintage	F	VF	XF	Unc	BU
1994 Proof	20,000	Value: 32.50				

KM# 1068 100 FRANCS-15 ECUS
22.2000 g., 0.9000 Silver 0.6423 oz. ASW **Obv:** Denominations-(francs/ecus) **Rev:** St. Mark's Cathedral, Venice

Date	Mintage	F	VF	XF	Unc	BU
1994 Proof	20,000	Value: 32.50				

KM# 1070 100 FRANCS-15 ECUS
22.2000 g., 0.9000 Silver 0.6423 oz. ASW **Obv:** Stars surround denominations, (francs/euros) **Rev:** Big Ben, London, date below

Date	Mintage	F	VF	XF	Unc	BU
1994 Proof	20,000	Value: 32.50				

KM# 1112 100 FRANCS-15 ECUS
22.2000 g., 0.9000 Silver 0.6423 oz. ASW **Rev:** The Alhambra, Granada, date below

Date	Mintage	F	VF	XF	Unc	BU
1995 Proof	20,000	Value: 35.00				

KM# 1114 100 FRANCS-15 ECUS
22.2000 g., 0.9000 Silver 0.6423 oz. ASW **Rev:** The Parthenon, Greece, date below

Date	Mintage	F	VF	XF	Unc	BU
1995 Proof	20,000	Value: 35.00				

KM# 990 500 FRANCS-70 ECUS
17.0000 g., 0.9200 Gold 0.5028 oz. AGW **Obv:** Center monogram divides date and denomination, laurel spray below **Rev:** Stylized head facing above denomination

Date	Mintage	F	VF	XF	Unc	BU
1990 Proof	5,000	Value: 500				

KM# 990a 500 FRANCS-70 ECUS
20.0000 g., 0.9990 Platinum 0.6423 oz. APW **Obv:** Monogram divides denomination and date, spray below **Rev:** Stylized head facing, denominition below

Date	Mintage	F	VF	XF	Unc	BU
1990 Proof	2,000	Value: 1,300				

KM# 1003 500 FRANCS-70 ECUS
17.0000 g., 0.9200 Gold 0.5028 oz. AGW **Subject:** Descartes **Obv:** Finger pointing to page with stars **Rev:** Head 3/4 facing

Date	Mintage	F	VF	XF	Unc	BU
1991 Proof	3,000	Value: 500				

KM# 1003a 500 FRANCS-70 ECUS
20.0000 g., 0.9990 Platinum 0.6423 oz. APW **Subject:** Descartes **Obv:** Finger pointing to page with stars, denomination **Rev:** Head 3/4 facing

Date	Mintage	F	VF	XF	Unc	BU
1991 Proof	1,000	Value: 1,300				

KM# 1013 500 FRANCS-70 ECUS
17.0000 g., 0.9200 Gold 0.5028 oz. AGW **Subject:** Jean Monet **Obv:** Denomination and date within legend at center, chain surrounds, RF below **Rev:** Head left, denomination at right

Date	Mintage	F	VF	XF	Unc	BU
1992 Proof	5,000	Value: 500				

KM# 1013a 500 FRANCS-70 ECUS
20.0000 g., 0.9990 Platinum 0.6423 oz. APW **Subject:** Jean Monet **Obv:** Denomination and date within legend at center, chain surrounds, RF below **Rev:** Head 3/4 left

Date	Mintage	F	VF	XF	Unc	BU
1992 Proof	2,000	Value: 1,300				

KM# 1033 500 FRANCS-70 ECUS
17.0000 g., 0.9200 Gold 0.5028 oz. AGW **Subject:** Mediterranean Games **Obv:** Head left, denomination below **Rev:** Statue divides denomination above, rings divide date below

Date	Mintage	F	VF	XF	Unc	BU
1993 Proof	3,000	Value: 500				

KM# 1034 500 FRANCS-70 ECUS
17.0000 g., 0.9200 Gold 0.5028 oz. AGW **Obv:** Denominations-(francs/ecus) **Rev:** Arc de Triumph, date below

Date	Mintage	F	VF	XF	Unc	BU
1993 Proof	5,000	Value: 500				

KM# 1034a 500 FRANCS-70 ECUS
19.8000 g., 0.9900 Platinum 0.6302 oz. APW **Obv:** Denominations-(francs/ecus) **Rev:** Arc de Triumph

Date	Mintage	F	VF	XF	Unc	BU
1993 Proof	2,000	Value: 1,300				

KM# 1035 500 FRANCS-70 ECUS
17.0000 g., 0.9200 Gold 0.5028 oz. AGW **Obv:** Denominations-(francs/ecus) **Rev:** Brandenburg Gate, date above

Date	Mintage	F	VF	XF	Unc	BU
1993 Proof	5,000	Value: 500				

KM# 1035a 500 FRANCS-70 ECUS
19.8000 g., 0.9900 Platinum 0.6302 oz. APW **Obv:** Denominations-(francs/ecus) **Rev:** Brandenburg Gate

Date	Mintage	F	VF	XF	Unc	BU
1993 Proof	2,000	Value: 1,300				

KM# 1061 500 FRANCS-70 ECUS
17.0000 g., 0.9200 Gold 0.5028 oz. AGW **Obv:** Stars surround denominations, (francs/euros) **Rev:** Channel Tunnel

Date	Mintage	F	VF	XF	Unc	BU
1994 Proof	5,000	Value: 500				

KM# 1069 500 FRANCS-70 ECUS
17.0000 g., 0.9200 Gold 0.5028 oz. AGW **Obv:** Stars surround denominations, (francs/euros) **Rev:** St. Mark's Cathedral, Venice, date below

Date	Mintage	F	VF	XF	Unc	BU
1994 Proof	5,000	Value: 500				

KM# 1069a 500 FRANCS-70 ECUS
20.0000 g., 0.9990 Platinum 0.6423 oz. APW **Obv:** Stars surround denominations, (francs/euros) **Rev:** St. Mark's Cathedral, Venice

Date	Mintage	F	VF	XF	Unc	BU
1994 Proof	2,000	Value: 1,300				

KM# 1071   500 FRANCS-70 ECUS
17.0000 g., 0.9200 Gold 0.5028 oz. AGW **Obv:** Stars surround denominations, (francs/euros) **Rev:** Big Ben, London, date below

Date	Mintage	F	VF	XF	Unc	BU
1994 Proof	5,000	Value: 500				

KM# 1071a   500 FRANCS-70 ECUS
20.0000 g., 0.9990 Platinum 0.6423 oz. APW **Obv:** Stars surround denominations, (francs/euros) **Rev:** Big Ben, London

Date	Mintage	F	VF	XF	Unc	BU
1994 Proof	2,000	Value: 1,300				

KM# 1113   500 FRANCS-70 ECUS
17.0000 g., 0.9200 Gold 0.5028 oz. AGW **Obv:** Stars surround denominations, (francs/euros) **Rev:** The Alhambra, Granada

Date	Mintage	F	VF	XF	Unc	BU
1995 Proof	5,000	Value: 500				

KM# 1113a   500 FRANCS-70 ECUS
20.0000 g., 0.9990 Platinum 0.6423 oz. APW **Obv:** Stars surround denominations, (francs/euros) **Rev:** The Alhambra, Granada

Date	Mintage	F	VF	XF	Unc	BU
1995 Proof	2,000	Value: 1,300				

KM# 1115   500 FRANCS-70 ECUS
17.0000 g., 0.9200 Gold 0.5028 oz. AGW **Obv:** Stars surround denominations, (francs/euros) **Rev:** The Parthenon, Athens

Date	Mintage	F	VF	XF	Unc	BU
1995 Proof	5,000	Value: 500				

KM# 1115a   500 FRANCS-70 ECUS
20.0000 g., 0.9990 Platinum 0.6423 oz. APW **Obv:** Stars surround denominations, (francs/euros) **Rev:** The Parthenon, Athens

Date	Mintage	F	VF	XF	Unc	BU
1995 Proof	2,000	Value: 1,300				

EURO / FRANCS COINAGE

KM# 1121   10 FRANCS-1.5 EURO
22.2000 g., 0.9000 Silver 0.6423 oz. ASW **Series:** Museum Treasures **Subject:** La Source by Raphael Jean A.D. Ingres **Obv:** Standing nude facing, RF and date at left **Rev:** Denominations, (francs/euros), on lined field, stars surround

Date	Mintage	F	VF	XF	Unc	BU
1996 Proof	15,000	Value: 37.50				

KM# 1122   10 FRANCS-1.5 EURO
22.2000 g., 0.9000 Silver 0.6423 oz. ASW **Series:** Museum Treasures **Subject:** Fife player by Edouard Manet **Obv:** Standing figure facing, RF and date at left **Rev:** Denominations, (francs/euros), on lined field, stars surround

Date	Mintage	F	VF	XF	Unc	BU
1996 Proof	15,000	Value: 35.00				

KM# 1123   10 FRANCS-1.5 EURO
22.2000 g., 0.9000 Silver 0.6423 oz. ASW **Series:** Museum Treasures **Subject:** Shang Dynasty Elephant **Obv:** Elephant left, RF and date at left **Rev:** Denominations, (francs/euros), on lined field, stars surround

Date	Mintage	F	VF	XF	Unc	BU
1996 Proof	15,000	Value: 35.00				

KM# 1146   10 FRANCS-1.5 EURO
22.2000 g., 0.9000 Silver 0.6423 oz. ASW **Series:** Museum Treasures **Subject:** David by Michaelangelo **Obv:** Standing nude facing, RF and date at right **Rev:** Denominations, (francs/euros), on lined field, stars surround

Date	Mintage	F	VF	XF	Unc	BU
1996 Proof	15,000	Value: 32.50				

KM# 1147   10 FRANCS-1.5 EURO
22.2000 g., 0.9000 Silver 0.6423 oz. ASW **Series:** Museum Treasures **Subject:** Vincent Van Gogh, self portrait **Obv:** Bust 3/4 left, RF and date at left **Rev:** Denominations, (francs/euros), on lined field, stars surround

Date	Mintage	F	VF	XF	Unc	BU
1996 Proof	15,000	Value: 35.00				

KM# 1148   10 FRANCS-1.5 EURO
22.2000 g., 0.9000 Silver 0.6423 oz. ASW **Series:** Museum Treasures **Subject:** Clothed Maya by Goya **Obv:** Reclining figure, RF and date at left **Rev:** Denominations, (francs/euros), on lined field, stars surround

Date	Mintage	F	VF	XF	Unc	BU
1996 Proof	15,000	Value: 32.50				

KM# 1158   10 FRANCS-1.5 EURO
22.2000 g., 0.9000 Silver 0.6423 oz. ASW **Series:** Museum Treasures **Subject:** Chinese Horseman **Obv:** Equestrian statue right, RF and date at right **Rev:** Denominations, (francs/euros), on lined field, stars surround

Date	Mintage	F	VF	XF	Unc	BU
1996 Proof	15,000	Value: 32.50				

KM# 1124   10 FRANCS-1.5 EURO
22.2000 g., 0.9000 Silver 0.6423 oz. ASW **Series:** Museum Treasures **Subject:** "The Thinker" by Auguste Rodin **Obv:** Seated statue left, RF and date at left **Rev:** Denominations, (francs/euros), on lined field, stars surround **Note:** Silver coins sold as a set only.

Date	Mintage	F	VF	XF	Unc	BU
1996 Proof	15,000	Value: 35.00				

KM# 1292   10 FRANCS-1.5 EURO
22.2200 g., 0.9000 Silver 0.6429 oz. ASW, 36.9 mm. **Subject:** Museum Treasures **Obv:** Figure wearing tutu left, RF and date at right **Rev:** Denominations, (francs/euros), on lined field, stars surround **Edge:** Plain

Date	Mintage	F	VF	XF	Unc	BU
1997 Proof	15,000	Value: 35.00				

KM# 1297   10 FRANCS-1.5 EURO
22.2200 g., 0.9000 Silver 0.6429 oz. ASW **Series:** Museum Treasures **Obv:** Japanese woman carrying a glass box **Rev:** Denominations, (francs/euros), on lined field, stars surround

Date	Mintage	F	VF	XF	Unc	BU
1997 Proof	15,000	Value: 30.00				

KM# 1298   10 FRANCS-1.5 EURO
22.2200 g., 0.9000 Silver 0.6429 oz. ASW **Series:** Museum Treasures **Subject:** Durer's "Self Portrait" **Obv:** Bust facing **Rev:** Denominations, (francs/euros), on lined field, stars surround

Date	Mintage	F	VF	XF	Unc	BU
1997 Proof	15,000	Value: 30.00				

KM# 1299   10 FRANCS-1.5 EURO
22.2200 g., 0.9000 Silver 0.6429 oz. ASW **Series:** Museum Treasures **Subject:** Klimt's "The Kiss" **Obv:** Two figures embraced **Rev:** Denominations, (francs/euros), on lined field, stars surround

Date	Mintage	F	VF	XF	Unc	BU
1997 Proof	15,000	Value: 32.50				

KM# 1125   100 FRANCS-15 EURO
17.0000 g., 0.9200 Gold 0.5028 oz. AGW **Series:** Museum Treasures **Subject:** La Source by Raphael Jean A.D. Ingres **Obv:** Standing nude facing **Rev:** Denominations, (francs/euros), on lined field, stars surround

Date	Mintage	F	VF	XF	Unc	BU
1996 Proof	5,000	Value: 500				

KM# 1126   100 FRANCS-15 EURO
17.0000 g., 0.9200 Gold 0.5028 oz. AGW **Series:** Museum Treasures **Subject:** Fife Player by Edouard Manet **Obv:** Standing figure facing **Rev:** Denominations, (francs/euros), on lined field, stars surround

Date	Mintage	F	VF	XF	Unc	BU
1996 Proof	5,000	Value: 500				

KM# 1127   100 FRANCS-15 EURO
17.0000 g., 0.9200 Gold 0.5028 oz. AGW **Series:** Museum Treasures **Subject:** Shang Dynasty Elephant **Obv:** Elephant left **Rev:** Denominations, (francs/euros), on lined field, stars surround

Date	Mintage	F	VF	XF	Unc	BU
1996 Proof	5,000	Value: 500				

KM# 1140   100 FRANCS-15 EURO
22.2000 g., 0.9000 Silver 0.6423 oz. ASW **Obv:** Stars surround denominations, (francs/euros) **Rev:** St. Stephen's Cathedral, Vienna, date at right

Date	Mintage	F	VF	XF	Unc	BU
1996 Proof	20,000	Value: 50.00				

KM# 1142   100 FRANCS-15 EURO
22.2000 g., 0.9000 Silver 0.6423 oz. ASW **Obv:** Stars surround denominations, (francs/euros) **Rev:** Grand Place, Bruxelles, date below

Date	Mintage	F	VF	XF	Unc	BU
1996 Proof	20,000	Value: 37.50				

KM# 1149   100 FRANCS-15 EURO
17.0000 g., 0.9200 Gold 0.5028 oz. AGW **Series:** Museum Treasures **Subject:** Van Gogh, Self Portrait **Obv:** Bust 3/4 left **Rev:** Denominations, (francs/euros), on lined field, stars surround

Date	Mintage	F	VF	XF	Unc	BU
1996 Proof	5,000	Value: 500				

KM# 1150   100 FRANCS-15 EURO
17.0000 g., 0.9200 Gold 0.5028 oz. AGW **Series:** Museum Treasures **Subject:** Clothed Maya by Goya **Obv:** Reclined figure **Rev:** Stars surround denominations, (francs/euros), on lined field

Date	Mintage	F	VF	XF	Unc	BU
1996 Proof	5,000	Value: 500				

KM# 1156   100 FRANCS-15 EURO
22.2000 g., 0.9000 Silver 0.6423 oz. ASW **Subject:** Amsterdam - Magere Brug **Obv:** Denominations, (francs/euros), on field of stars **Rev:** Bridge, date below

Date	Mintage	F	VF	XF	Unc	BU
1996 Proof	20,000	Value: 37.50				

KM# 1159   100 FRANCS-15 EURO
17.0000 g., 0.9200 Gold 0.5028 oz. AGW **Series:** Museum Treasures **Subject:** Chinese Horseman **Obv:** Equestrian statue **Rev:** Stars surround denominations, (francs/euros), on lined field

Date	Mintage	F	VF	XF	Unc	BU
1996 Proof	5,000	Value: 500				

KM# 1174   100 FRANCS-15 EURO
22.2000 g., 0.9000 Silver 0.6423 oz. ASW **Subject:** Lisbon **Obv:** Denominations-(francs/ecus), on field of stars **Rev:** Castle-like building Tour de Belem, date below

Date	Mintage	F	VF	XF	Unc	BU
1997 Proof	20,000	Value: 50.00				

KM# 1176   100 FRANCS-15 EURO
22.2000 g., 0.9000 Silver 0.6423 oz. ASW **Subject:** Helsinki **Obv:** Denominations-(francs/ecus) **Rev:** Cathedral, Cathedrale Saint - Nicolas, date below

Date	Mintage	F	VF	XF	Unc	BU
1997 Proof	20,000	Value: 50.00				

KM# 1178   100 FRANCS-15 EURO
22.2000 g., 0.9000 Silver 0.6423 oz. ASW **Subject:** Copenhagen **Obv:** Denominations-(francs/ecus) **Rev:** Statue of the Copenhagen mermaid, Petite Sirene, date at right

Date	Mintage	F	VF	XF	Unc	BU
1997 Proof	20,000	Value: 55.00				

KM# 1189 100 FRANCS-15 EURO
22.2000 g., 0.9000 Silver 0.6423 oz. ASW **Subject:** Irlande - Rock of Cashel **Obv:** Denomination **Rev:** Celtic cross and castle, date below

Date	Mintage	F	VF	XF	Unc	BU
1997 Proof	20,000	Value: 50.00				

KM# 1191 100 FRANCS-15 EURO
22.2000 g., 0.9000 Silver 0.6423 oz. ASW **Subject:** Luxembourg - Wenceslaus Wall **Obv:** Denomination **Rev:** Walled palace, date above

Date	Mintage	F	VF	XF	Unc	BU
1997 Proof	20,000	Value: 50.00				

KM# 1193 100 FRANCS-15 EURO
22.2000 g., 0.9000 Silver 0.6423 oz. ASW **Subject:** Stockholm - Hotel de Ville **Obv:** Denomination **Rev:** Tower and building, date at right

Date	Mintage	F	VF	XF	Unc	BU
1997 Proof	20,000	Value: 50.00				

KM# 1128 500 FRANCS-75 EURO
31.1035 g., 0.9990 Gold 0.9990 oz. AGW **Series:** Museum Treasures **Subject:** "The Thinker", by Auguste Rodin **Obv:** Seated statue left **Rev:** Stars surround denominations, (francs/euros), on lined field

Date	Mintage	F	VF	XF	Unc	BU
1996 Proof	5,000	Value: 950				

KM# 1129 500 FRANCS-75 EURO
155.5175 g., 0.9990 Gold 4.9948 oz. AGW **Series:** Museum Treasures **Subject:** La Source by Raphael Jean A.D. Ingres **Obv:** Standing nude facing **Rev:** Stars surround denominations, (francs/euros), on lined field

Date	Mintage	F	VF	XF	Unc	BU
1996 Prof	99	Value: 4,650				

KM# 1130 500 FRANCS-75 EURO
155.5175 g., 0.9990 Gold 4.9948 oz. AGW **Series:** Museum Treasures **Subject:** Fife Player by Edouard Manet **Obv:** Standing figure facing **Rev:** Stars surround denominations, (francs/euros), on lined field

Date	Mintage	F	VF	XF	Unc	BU
1996 Proof	99	Value: 4,650				

KM# 1131 500 FRANCS-75 EURO
155.5175 g., 0.9990 Gold 4.9948 oz. AGW **Series:** Museum Treasures **Subject:** Shang Dynasty Elephant **Obv:** Elephant left **Rev:** Stars surround denominations, (francs/euros), on lined field

Date	Mintage	F	VF	XF	Unc	BU
1996 Proof	99	Value: 4,650				

KM# 1141 500 FRANCS-75 EURO
17.0000 g., 0.9200 Gold 0.5028 oz. AGW **Subject:** St. Stephen's Cathedral, Vienna **Obv:** Denominations, (francs/euro), on field of stars **Rev:** Cathedral, date at right

Date	Mintage	F	VF	XF	Unc	BU
1996 Proof	5,000	Value: 500				

KM# 1141a 500 FRANCS-75 EURO
20.0000 g., 0.9990 Platinum 0.6423 oz. APW **Subject:** St. Stephen's Cathedral, Vienna **Obv:** Denominations-(francs/ecus) **Rev:** Cathedral

Date	Mintage	F	VF	XF	Unc	BU
1996 Prof	2,000	Value: 1,300				

KM# 1143 500 FRANCS-75 EURO
17.0000 g., 0.9200 Gold 0.5028 oz. AGW **Subject:** Grand Place, Bruxelles **Obv:** Denominations-(francs/ecus) **Rev:** Buildings with tower, date below

Date	Mintage	F	VF	XF	Unc	BU
1996 Proof	5,000	Value: 500				

KM# 1143a 500 FRANCS-75 EURO
20.0000 g., 0.9990 Platinum 0.6423 oz. APW **Subject:** Grand Place, Bruxelles **Obv:** Denominations-(francs/ecus) **Rev:** Buildings with tower

Date	Mintage	F	VF	XF	Unc	BU
1996 Proof	2,000	Value: 1,300				

KM# 1151 500 FRANCS-75 EURO
31.1035 g., 0.9990 Gold 0.9990 oz. AGW **Series:** Museum Treasures **Subject:** David by Michaelangelo **Obv:** Standing nude **Rev:** Denominations, (francs/euros), on lined field, stars surround

Date	Mintage	F	VF	XF	Unc	BU
1996 Proof	5,000	Value: 950				

KM# 1152 500 FRANCS-75 EURO
155.5175 g., 0.9990 Gold 4.9948 oz. AGW **Series:** Museum Treasures **Subject:** David by Michaelangelo **Obv:** Standing nude **Rev:** Denominations-(francs/ecus), on lined field, stars surround

Date	Mintage	F	VF	XF	Unc	BU
1996 Proof	99	Value: 4,650				

KM# 1153 500 FRANCS-75 EURO
155.5175 g., 0.9990 Gold 4.9948 oz. AGW **Series:** Museum Treasures **Subject:** Vincent Van Gogh, Self Portrait **Obv:** Bust 3/4 left, RF and date at left **Rev:** Denominations-(francs/ecus), on lined field, stars surround

Date	Mintage	F	VF	XF	Unc	BU
1996 Proof	99	Value: 4,650				

KM# 1154 500 FRANCS-75 EURO
155.5175 g., 0.9990 Gold 4.9948 oz. AGW **Series:** Museum Treasures **Subject:** Clothed Maya by Goya **Obv:** Reclined figure, RF and date at left **Rev:** Denominations-(francs/ecus), on lined field, stars surround

Date	Mintage	F	VF	XF	Unc	BU
1996 Proof	99	Value: 4,650				

KM# 1157 500 FRANCS-75 EURO
17.0000 g., 0.9200 Gold 0.5028 oz. AGW **Subject:** Amsterdam Magere Brug

Date	Mintage	F	VF	XF	Unc	BU
1996 Proof	5,000	Value: 500				

KM# 1157a 500 FRANCS-75 EURO
20.0000 g., 0.9990 Platinum 0.6423 oz. APW **Subject:** Amsterdam Magere Brug

Date	Mintage	F	VF	XF	Unc	BU
1996 Proof	2,000	Value: 1,300				

KM# 1175 500 FRANCS-75 EURO
17.0000 g., 0.9200 Gold 0.5028 oz. AGW **Subject:** Lisbon **Obv:** Denominations **Rev:** Castle-like building Tour de Belem, date below

Date	Mintage	F	VF	XF	Unc	BU
1997 Proof	5,000	Value: 500				

KM# 1175a 500 FRANCS-75 EURO
20.0000 g., 0.9990 Platinum 0.6423 oz. APW **Subject:** Lisbon **Obv:** Denominations **Rev:** Castle-like building Tour de Belem

Date	Mintage	F	VF	XF	Unc	BU
1997 Proof	2,000	Value: 1,300				

KM# 1179 500 FRANCS-75 EURO
17.0000 g., 0.9200 Gold 0.5028 oz. AGW **Subject:** Copenhagen **Obv:** Denominations, (francs/euros), on field of stars **Rev:** Statue of Copenhagen's Little Mermaid, Petite Siren, date at right

Date	Mintage	F	VF	XF	Unc	BU
1997 Proof	5,000	Value: 525				

KM# 1179a 500 FRANCS-75 EURO
20.0000 g., 0.9990 Platinum 0.6423 oz. APW **Subject:** Copenhagen **Obv:** Denominations **Rev:** Statue of Copenhagen's Little Mermaid, Petite Siren

Date	Mintage	F	VF	XF	Unc	BU
1997 Proof	2,000	Value: 1,300				

KM# 1190 500 FRANCS-75 EURO
17.0000 g., 0.9200 Gold 0.5028 oz. AGW **Subject:** Ireland - Rock of Cashel **Obv:** Denomination **Rev:** Celtic cross and castle

Date	Mintage	F	VF	XF	Unc	BU
1997 Proof	5,000	Value: 500				

KM# 1190a 500 FRANCS-75 EURO
20.0000 g., 0.9990 Platinum 0.6423 oz. APW **Subject:** Ireland - Rock of Cashel **Obv:** Denomination **Rev:** Celtic cross and castle

Date	Mintage	F	VF	XF	Unc	BU
1997 Proof	2,000	Value: 1,300				

KM# 1192 500 FRANCS-75 EURO
17.0000 g., 0.9200 Gold 0.5028 oz. AGW **Subject:** Luxembourg - Wenceslas Wall **Obv:** Denomination **Rev:** Walled palace

Date	Mintage	F	VF	XF	Unc	BU
1997 Proof	5,000	Value: 500				

KM# 1192a 500 FRANCS-75 EURO
20.0000 g., 0.9990 Platinum 0.6423 oz. APW **Subject:** Luxembourg-Wenceslas Wall **Obv:** Denomination **Rev:** Walled palace

Date	Mintage	F	VF	XF	Unc	BU
1997 Proof	2,000	Value: 1,300				

KM# 1194 500 FRANCS-75 EURO
17.0000 g., 0.9990 Gold 0.5460 oz. AGW **Subject:** Stockholm - Hotel de Ville **Obv:** Denomination **Rev:** Tower and building

Date	Mintage	F	VF	XF	Unc	BU
1997 Proof	5,000	Value: 500				

KM# 1177 500 FRANCS-75 EURO
17.0000 g., 0.9200 Gold 0.5028 oz. AGW **Subject:** Helsinki **Obv:** Denominations **Rev:** Cathedrale Saint Nicholas, date below

Date	Mintage	F	VF	XF	Unc	BU
1997 Proof	5,000	Value: 500				

KM# 1177a 500 FRANCS-75 EURO
20.0000 g., 0.9990 Platinum 0.6423 oz. APW **Subject:** Helsinki **Obv:** Denominations **Rev:** Cathedral, Cathedrale Saint Nicholas

Date	Mintage	F	VF	XF	Unc	BU
1997 Proof	2,000	Value: 1,300				

KM# 1194a 500 FRANCS-75 EURO
20.0000 g., 0.9990 Platinum 0.6423 oz. APW **Subject:** Stockholm - Hotel de Ville **Obv:** Denomination **Rev:** Tower and building

Date	Mintage	F	VF	XF	Unc	BU
1997 Proof	2,000	Value: 1,300				

EURO COINAGE
European Union Issues

KM# 1282 EURO CENT
2.2700 g., Copper Plated Steel, 16.3 mm. **Obv:** Human face **Rev:** Denomination and globe **Edge:** Plain

Date	Mintage	F	VF	XF	Unc	BU
1999	794,054,000	—	—	—	0.35	0.50
1999 Proof	15,000	Value: 10.00				
2000	605,267,000	—	—	—	0.35	0.50
2000 Proof	15,000	Value: 10.00				

KM# 1283 2 EURO CENT
3.0300 g., Copper-Plated-Steel, 18.7 mm. **Obv:** Human face **Rev:** Denomination and globe **Edge:** Grooved

Date	Mintage	F	VF	XF	Unc	BU
1999	702,104,000	—	—	—	0.50	0.75
1999 Proof	Est. 15,000	Value: 10.00				
2000	510,155,000	—	—	—	0.50	0.75
2000 Proof	15,000	Value: 10.00				

KM# 1284 5 EURO CENT
3.8600 g., Copper-Plated-Steel, 21.2 mm. **Obv:** Human face **Rev:** Denomination and globe **Edge:** Plain

Date	Mintage	F	VF	XF	Unc	BU
1999	616,227,000	—	—	—	0.75	1.25
1999 Proof	Est. 15,000	Value: 12.00				
2000	280,099,000	—	—	—	0.75	1.25
2000 Proof	15,000	Value: 12.00				

KM# 1285 10 EURO CENT
4.0700 g., Brass, 19.7 mm. **Obv:** The seed sower divides date and RF **Rev:** Denomination and map **Edge:** Reeded

Date	Mintage	F	VF	XF	Unc	BU
1999	447,284,600	—	—	—	0.75	1.25
1999 Proof	15,000	Value: 12.00				
2000	297,467,000	—	—	—	0.75	1.25
2000 Proof	15,000	Value: 12.00				

KM# 1286 20 EURO CENT
5.7300 g., Brass, 22.2 mm. **Obv:** The seed sower divides date and RF **Rev:** Denomination and map **Edge:** Notched

Date	Mintage	F	VF	XF	Unc	BU
1999	454,326,200	—	—	—	1.00	1.50
1999 Proof	15,000	Value: 14.00				
2000	148,988,600	—	—	—	1.25	2.00
2000 Proof	15,000	Value: 14.00				

KM# 1287 50 EURO CENT
7.8100 g., Brass, 24.2 mm. **Obv:** The seed sower divides date and RF **Rev:** Denomination and map **Edge:** Reeded

Date	Mintage	F	VF	XF	Unc	BU
1999	150,788,600	—	—	—	1.50	2.25
1999 Proof	15,000	Value: 15.00				
2000	179,531,000	—	—	—	1.25	2.00
2000 Proof	15,000	Value: 15.00				

KM# 1288 EURO
7.5000 g., Bi-Metallic Copper-Nickel center in Brass ring, 23.3 mm. **Obv:** Stylized tree divides RF within circle, date below **Rev:** Denomination and map **Edge:** Reeded and plain sections

Date	Mintage	F	VF	XF	Unc	BU
1999	301,085,000	—	—	—	2.50	3.75
1999 Proof	15,000	Value: 18.00				
2000	297,305,000	—	—	—	2.50	3.75
2000 Proof	15,000	Value: 18.00				

KM# 1289 2 EURO
8.5200 g., Bi-Metallic Brass center in Copper-Nickel ring, 25.6 mm. **Obv:** Stylized tree divides RF within circle, date below **Rev:** Denomination and map **Edge:** Reeding with 2's and stars

Date	Mintage	F	VF	XF	Unc	BU
1999	56,730,000	—	—	—	4.50	7.00
1999 Proof	15,000	Value: 20.00				
2000	171,155,000	—	—	—	3.75	6.00
2000 Proof	15,000	Value: 20.00				

ESSAIS
Standard metals unless otherwise noted

KM#	Date	Mintage	Identification	Mkt Val
E38	1903 (a)	—	25 Centimes. Nickel. Denomination within square, date below. KM#855.	160
E-A39	1904 (a)	—	25 Centimes. Nickel. Laureate bust left. Denomination above date. Without square around denomination, 22 sided flan.	165
E39	1904 (a)	—	25 Centimes. Nickel. Laureate bust left. Leafy branch divides denomination and date, axe on column at left. KM#856.	150
E-A40	1904 (a)	—	25 Centimes. Nickel. 22 sided flan, KM#856.	150
E-B40	1904 (a)	—	25 Centimes. Nickel. 18 sided flan, KM#856.	150
E-C40	1908 (a)	—	5 Centimes. Bronze. Head right. Woman and child, denomination at right, date below. KM#842.	175
E40	1908 (a)	—	10 Centimes. Aluminum. KM#843.	150
E41	1910 (a)	—	5 Centimes. Bronze. KM#842.	160
E42	1913 (a)	—	25 Centimes. Nickel. KM#867.	110
E43	1914 (a)	104	5 Centimes. Copper-Nickel. KM#865.	550
E44	1914 (a)	—	25 Centimes. Nickel. KM#867.	110
E45	1929 (a)	—	10 Francs. Silver. Delannoy.	675
E46	1929 (a)	—	10 Francs. Aluminum-Bronze. Republic above denomination and date. Laureate head right.	60.00
E47	1929 (a)	—	10 Francs. Aluminum-Bronze. Oak leaves on head right, date at right. Hand holding supported torch divides denomination.	75.00
E48	1929 (a)	—	10 Francs. Silver. KM#878.	75.00
E49	1929 (a)	—	20 Francs. Silver. KM#879.	950
E50	1929 (a)	—	20 Francs. Aluminum-Bronze. KM#879.	120
E51	1929 (a)	15	100 Francs. Gold. Winged head left. Leafy branches flank grain sprig, denomination above, date below.	3,850
E52	1929	15	100 Francs. Gold. Globe with sprays flanking, denomination below.	3,850
E53	1929 (a)	15	100 Francs. Gold. Laureate head left. Grain sprig left and branch right divide denomination and date.	3,850
E54	1929 (a)	15	100 Francs. Gold. Laureate bust left. Ribboned branches and torch divide RF above denomination and date.	3,850
E55	1929 (a)	15	100 Francs. Gold. Braided head left. Caduceus divides denomination, cornucopias, and date below.	3,850
E56	1929 (a)	15	100 Francs. Gold. Laureate head left. Denomination and date within wreath.	3,850
E57	1929 (a)	15	100 Francs. Gold. Laureate head left. Denomination and date within wreath.	3,850
E58	1929 (a)	15	100 Francs. Gold. Laureate head left. Five grain sprigs divide denomination and date below.	3,850
E59	1929 (a)	15	100 Francs. Gold. Head left. Oak tree divides denomination.	3,850
E60	1929 (a)	15	100 Francs. Gold. Head left, hair in bun. Three grain sprigs divide date and denomination.	3,850
E62	1929 (a)	15	100 Francs. Gold. With Essai, KM#880.	3,900
E-A64	1931	—	50 Centimes. Aluminum-Bronze. KM#894.1, Morlon.	50.00
E-B64	1931	—	Franc. Aluminum-Bronze. KM#885, Morlon.	75.00
E64	1931	—	2 Francs. Aluminum-Bronze. KM#886.	90.00
E-A65	1933	—	5 Francs. Nickel. KM#887, Bazor.	200
E65	1933	—	5 Francs. Nickel. KM#888.	100
E66	1933	—	5 Francs. Seated Liberty, date below. 5 FRANCS at center, legend and wheat spears around.	450
E-A67	1933	—	5 Francs. Silver. Laureate head right. Denomination and date above inscription, grain columns flank. Turin.	775
E67	1934 (a)	—	5 Francs. Nickel. KM#888.	—
E68	1938 (a)	—	25 Centimes. Nickel-Bronze center. KM#867b.	150
E69	1938 (a)	—	10 Francs. Nickel. KM#908.1.	320
E70	1938 (a)	—	20 Francs. Nickel. KM#879.	320
E71	1938 (a)	—	20 Francs. Aluminum. KM#879.	275
E72	1939 (a)	—	20 Francs. Copper-Nickel. KM#879.	250
E73	1940 (a)	—	25 Centimes. Zinc. KM#867b.	125
E74	1941 (a)	—	10 Centimes. Zinc. KM#898.1.	115
E75	1941 (a)	—	20 Centimes. Zinc. KM#899.	135
E76	1941 (a)	—	20 Centimes. Zinc. KM#900.1.	135
E-A77	1941	—	2 Francs. Iron. KM#886, Morlon.	285
E77	1941	—	5 Francs. Copper-Nickel. Head left. Cross divides denomination. Bazor.	220
E78	1941	—	10 Francs. Aluminum. Head left. Shield divides denomination and date. Delannoy.	350
E79	1941	—	10 Francs. Nickel.	550
E-A80	1941	—	10 Francs. Aluminum. Head left. Grain sprig divides denomination, date below, wreath surrounds. Simon.	325
E80	1941 (a)	—	10 Francs. Nickel.	525

KM#	Date	Mintage	Identification	Mkt Val
E81	1941	—	10 Francs. Copper-Nickel. Face and inscription left. Denomination and date on center shield, family scenes flank. Galle.	375
E82	1941	—	20 Francs. Aluminum. Head left, date below. Leaves at center of grain sheaf divide denomination. Cochet.	285
E-A92	1941	—	20 Francs. Aluminum. Denomination and date below center inscription. Bouchard.	365
E83	1942	—	Franc. Aluminum. KM#902.1.	175
E84	1943 (a)	300	10 Centimes. Zinc. KM#903.	165
E85	1943 (a)	300	2 Francs. Aluminum. KM#904.	225
E86	1943	—	10 Francs. Copper-Nickel. Bazor.	265
E86a	1943	—	10 Francs. Aluminum. Head left. Statues below denomination, date at bottom. Bazor.	320
E87	1944 (a)	300	10 Centimes. Zinc. KM#906.	165
E88	1945 (a)	40	20 Centimes. Zinc. KM#907.	350
E89	1945 (a)	1,100	5 Francs. KM#888b.	110
E90	1945 (a)	1,100	10 Francs. Copper-Nickel. KM#909.	85.00
E91	1950 (g)	1,700	20 Francs. Aluminum-Bronze. KM#915.	40.00
E92	1950 (a)	25	20 Francs. Aluminum-Bronze. Georges Guiraud, KM#916.	550
E93	1950 (a)	1,700	20 Francs. Silver. G. Guiraud, KM#971.	40.00
E94	1950 (a)	1,700	50 Francs. Aluminum-Bronze. KM#918.	95.00
E95	1950 (a)	50	100 Francs. Silver.	250
E-A96	1950	—	100 Francs. Copper-Nickel. KM#919.1.	4,000
E96	1951 (a)	28	20 Francs. Aluminum-Bronze. KM#917.	625
E97	1954 (a)	1,200	10 Francs. Copper-Nickel. KM#919.	85.00
E98	1959 (a)	4,000	Franc. Nickel. KM#925.	65.00
E99	1959 (a)	4,000	Franc. Nickel. KM#925.	50.00
E100	1959	—	2 Francs. Silver. KM#845.1.	950
E101	1959 (a)	4,000	5 Francs. Silver. KM#926.	60.00
E102	1959 (a)	I.A.	5 Francs. Silver. Small 5 in date, KM#926.	65.00
E103	1961 (a)	3,500	Centime. Chrome-Steel. KM#928.	30.00
E104	1961 (a)	3,500	5 Centimes. Chrome-Steel. KM#927.	30.00
E105	1961	—	20 Centimes. Aluminum-Bronze. KM#930.	40.00
E106	1961	—	20 Centimes. Laureate head with short hair left. Denomination and date within wreath.	40.00
E107	1961	—	20 Centimes. Head with long hair left. Denomination above date within wreath.	75.00
E108	1962 (a)	3,500	10 Centimes. Aluminum-Bronze. KM#929.	25.00
E109	1962 (a)	3,500	20 Centimes. Aluminum-Bronze. KM#930.	25.00
E110	1962 (a)	3,500	50 Centimes. Aluminum-Bronze. KM#939.	25.00
E111	1964 (a)	3,500	10 Francs. Silver. KM#932.	150
E112	1965 (a)	4,700	1/2 Franc. Nickel. KM#931.	35.00
E113	1966 (a)	4,128	5 Centimes. Aluminum-Bronze. KM#933.	30.00
E114	1970 (a)	5,000	5 Francs. Silver. KM#926a.	40.00
E115	1974	7,300	10 Francs. Nickel-Brass. KM#940.	45.00
E116	1974	9	10 Francs. Gold. KM#940.	2,750
	1974	9	10 Francs. Gold. KM#940.	2,750
E117	1974	13,800	50 Francs. Silver. KM#941.	80.00
E118	1974	5	50 Francs. Gold. KM#941.	3,250
	1974	5	50 Francs. Gold. KM#941.	3,250
E119	1978	6,000	2 Francs. Nickel. KM#942.	45.00
E120	1978	22	2 Francs. Silver. KM#942.	450
E121	1978	12	2 Francs. Gold. KM#942.	1,350
	1978	12	2 Francs. Gold. KM#942.	1,350
E122	1982	—	10 Francs. Copper-Nickel. Gambetta, KM#950.	60.00
E123	1982	—	100 Francs. Silver. KM#951.	90.00
E124	1983	4,000	10 Francs. Nickel-Bronze. Baloon, KM#952.	45.00
E125	1983	9	10 Francs. Gold. Baloon, KM#952.	1,850
	1983	9	10 Francs. Gold. Baloon, KM#952.	1,850
E126	1983	4,000	10 Francs. Nickel-Bronze. Stendhal, KM#953.	45.00
E127	1983	9	10 Francs. Gold. Stendhal, KM#953.	1,850
	1983	9	10 Francs. Gold. Stendhal, KM#953.	1,850
E128	1984	—	10 Francs. Nickel-Bronze. Rude, KM#954.	45.00
E129	1984	—	100 Francs. Silver. Curie, KM#955.	75.00
E130	1985	1,700	10 Francs. Nickel-Bronze. Hugo, KM#956.	45.00
E131	1985	1,700	100 Francs. Silver. Zola, KM#957.	60.00
E132	1986	1,750	10 Francs. Nickel. KM#959.	45.00
E133	1986	9	10 Francs. Gold. KM#959.	1,850
	1986	9	10 Francs. Gold. KM#959.	1,850
E134	1986	1,750	10 Francs. Nickel. Schuman, KM#958d.	45.00
E135	1986	1,750	100 Francs. Silver. Liberty, KM#960.	100
E136	1987	1,850	10 Francs. Nickel-Bronze. Capet, KM#916.1.	50.00
E137	1987	1,850	100 Francs. Silver. Lafayette, KM#962.	150
E138	1988	1,850	Franc. Nickel. KM#963.	75.00
E139	1988	1,850	10 Francs. Aluminum-Bronze. Garros, KM#965.	35.00
E140	1988	1,850	10 Francs. Steel center. Aluminum-Bronze ring. Bastille, KM#964.	50.00
E141	1988	1,850	100 Francs. Silver. Fraternity, KM#966.	60.00
E142	1989	—	Franc. Nickel. KM#967.	45.00
E143	1989	—	5 Francs. Nickel. Eiffel TOwer, KM#968.	60.00
E144	1989	—	10 Francs. Steel center. Aluminum-Bronze ring. Montesquien, KM#969.	50.00
E145	1989	—	100 Francs. Silver. Human Rights, KM#970.	65.00
E146	1994	—	20 Francs. Aluminum-Bronze center. Nickel inner ring, Copper-Aluminum-Nickel outer ring, KM#1036.	75.00

PATTERNS
Including off metal strikes

KM#	Date	Mintage	Identification	Mkt Val
Pn102	1929	—	100 Francs. Aluminum-Bronze. Bust left. Date. CENT FRANCS.	140
Pn103	1933	—	5 Francs. Liberty bust left. Legend above, date below. CENT FRANCS.	180
Pn104	1939	—	20 Francs. Copper-Nickel.	600
Pn105	1941	—	10 Francs. Copper-Nickel. Petain bust left, legend in front. People working at sides. TRAVAIL / FAMILLE / PATRIE / 10 / FRANCS / 1941	325
Pn106	1941	—	20 Francs. Copper-Nickel. Petain bust left. Sheaves of wheat bent outward divide denomination, legend above.	325
Pn107	1941	—	20 Francs. Copper-Nickel. Petain bust left. Family group above FAMILLE divide 20-FR.	325
Pn108	1941	—	20 Francs. Nickel. Petain bust left. 3 figures, 2 standing, 1 sitting.	325
Pn109	1942	—	5 Francs. Copper-Nickel. Petain bust left. TRAVAIL / FAMILLE / PATRIE / 5 / FRANCS / 1942	325
Pn110	1943	—	10 Francs. Copper-Nickel. Petain bust left. 3 figures, 2 standing, 1 sitting.	325
Pn111	1950	—	20 Francs. Liberty left. 20-FR divided by symbol.	55.00
Pn112	1950	—	20 Francs. Liberty left. Inscription above 20 dividing flowers, FRANCS and date below.	55.00
Pn113	1950	—	20 Francs. Liberty bust left. 20 over branch at left, FRANCS in center at right, date below.	55.00
Pn114	1950	—	20 Francs. Liberty bust left. 20 in small circle of branches, 4 branches to edge of coin.	55.00
Pn115	1950	—	100 Francs. Copper-Nickel.	250
Pn116	1964	131	10 Francs. Silver. KM#756. KM#932.	300
Pn117	1964	3,500	10 Francs. Silver. KM#932.	100
Pn118	1977	253	2 Francs. Nickel. KM#942.	70.00

PIEFORTS
Standard metals unless otherwise noted

KM#	Date	Mintage	Identification	Mkt Val
P251	1903	—	25 Centimes. Copper-Nickel-Zinc.	150
P270	1914	—	10 Centimes. Nickel. KM#866.	120
P272	1914	—	25 Centimes. Nickel. KM#867.	165
P280	1920	—	5 Centimes. Copper-Nickel. KM#875.	135
P-A297	1920	—	2 Francs. Aluminum-Bronze. KM#877.	125
P297	1928	—	2 Francs. Silver. KM#845.	320
P300	1929	—	100 Francs. Gold. KM#880.	3,500
P305	1941	—	10 Centimes. Zinc. KM#895.	220
P341	1962	500	Centime. Chrome-Steel. KM#928.	25.00
P342	1962	50	Centime. Silver. KM#928.	65.00
P343	1962	20	Centime. Gold. KM#928.	325
P344	1962	500	10 Centimes. Aluminum-Bronze. KM#929.	25.00
P345	1962	50	10 Centimes. Silver. KM#929.	85.00
P346	1962	20	10 Centimes. Gold. KM#929.	375
P347	1962	500	20 Centimes. Aluminum-Bronze. KM#930.	25.00
P348	1962	50	20 Centimes. Silver. KM#930.	120
P349	1962	20	20 Centimes. Gold. KM#930.	400
P350	1962	500	50 Centimes. Aluminum-Bronze. KM#939.	25.00
P351	1962	50	50 Centimes. Silver. KM#939.	130
P352	1962	20	50 Centimes. Gold. KM#939.	500
P353	1965	500	1/2 Franc. Nickel. KM#931.	30.00
P354	1965	50	1/2 Franc. Silver. KM#931.	75.00
P355	1965	20	1/2 Franc. Gold. KM#931.	400
P356	1965	500	10 Francs. Silver center. KM#932.	75.00
P357	1965	50	10 Francs. Gold. KM#932.	2,500
P358	1966	500	5 Centimes. Aluminum-Bronze. KM#933.	20.00
P359	1966	50	5 Centimes. Silver. KM#933.	80.00
P360	1966	20	5 Centimes. Gold. KM#933.	350
P361	1967	500	Centime. Chrome-Steel center. KM#928.	20.00
P362	1967	50	Centime. Silver. KM#928.	35.00
P363	1967	20	Centime. Gold. KM#928.	375
P364	1967	500	5 Centimes. Aluminum-Bronze. KM#933.	20.00
P365	1967	50	5 Centimes. Silver. KM#933.	50.00
P366	1967	20	5 Centimes. Gold. KM#933.	350
P367	1967	500	10 Centimes. Aluminum-Bronze. KM#929.	20.00
P368	1967	50	10 Centimes. Silver. KM#929.	65.00
P369	1967	20	10 Centimes. Gold. KM#929.	350
P370	1967	500	20 Centimes. Aluminum-Bronze. KM#930.	20.00
P371	1967	50	20 Centimes. Silver. KM#930.	125

KM#	Date	Mintage	Identification	Mkt Val
P372	1967	20	20 Centimes. Gold. KM#930.	400
P373	1967	500	25 Centimes. Aluminum-Bronze. KM#939.	20.00
P374	1967	50	50 Centimes. Silver. KM#939.	125
P375	1967	20	50 Centimes. Gold. KM#939.	675
P376	1967	500	1/2 Franc. Nickel. KM#931.	25.00
P377	1967	50	1/2 Franc. Silver. KM#931.	85.00
P378	1967	20	1/2 Franc. Gold. KM#931.	450
P379	1967	500	Franc. Nickel. KM#925.	25.00
P380	1967	50	Franc. Silver. KM#925.	85.00
P382	1967	500	5 Francs. Silver. KM#926.	35.00
P383	1967	50	5 Francs. Gold. KM#926.	850
P384	1967	500	10 Francs. Silver. KM#932.	50.00
P385	1967	50	10 Francs. Gold. KM#932.	1,950
P386	1968	500	Centime. Chrome-Steel. KM#928.	35.00
P387	1968	50	Centime. Silver. KM#928.	60.00
P388	1968	20	Centime. Gold. KM#928.	375
P389	1968	500	5 Centimes. Aluminum-Bronze. KM#933.	35.00
P390	1968	50	5 Centimes. Silver. KM#933.	60.00
P391	1968	20	5 Centimes. Gold. KM#933.	225
P392	1968	500	10 Centimes. Aluminum-Bronze. KM#929.	35.00
P393	1968	50	10 Centimes. Silver. KM#929.	60.00
P394	1968	20	10 Centimes. Gold. KM#929.	325
P395	1968	500	20 Centimes. Aluminum-Bronze. KM#930.	35.00
P396	1968	50	20 Centimes. Silver. KM#930.	60.00
P397	1968	20	20 Centimes. Gold. KM#930.	425
P398	1968	500	1/2 Franc. Nickel. KM#931.	35.00
P399	1968	50	1/2 Franc. Silver. KM#931.	65.00
P400	1968	20	1/2 Franc. Gold. KM#931.	425
P401	1968	500	Franc. Nickel. KM#925.	35.00
P402	1968	50	Franc. Silver. KM#925.	65.00
P404	1968	500	5 Francs. Silver. KM#926.	35.00
P405	1968	50	5 Francs. Gold. KM#926.	875
P406	1968	500	10 Francs. Silver. KM#932.	45.00
P407	1968	50	10 Francs. Gold. KM#932.	2,500
P408	1970	500	5 Francs. Nickel Clad Copper-Nickel. KM#926a.	40.00
P409	1970	200	5 Francs. Silver. KM#926a.	60.00
P410	1970	100	5 Francs. Gold. KM#926a.	875
P411	1970	100	5 Francs. Platinum. KM#926a.	1,950
P412	1971	500	Centime. Chrome-Steel. KM#928.	20.00
P413	1971	250	Centime. Silver. KM#928.	30.00
P414	1971	100	Centime. Gold. KM#928.	140
P415	1971	500	5 Francs. Aluminum-Bronze. KM#933.	20.00
P416	1971	250	5 Francs. Silver. KM#933.	30.00
P417	1971	100	5 Centimes. Gold. KM#933.	165
P418	1971	500	10 Centimes. Aluminum-Bronze. KM#929.	20.00
P419	1971	250	10 Centimes. Silver. KM#929.	35.00
P420	1971	100	10 Centimes. Gold. KM#929.	250
P421	1971	500	20 Centimes. Aluminum-Bronze. KM#930.	20.00
P422	1971	250	20 Centimes. Silver. KM#930.	35.00
P423	1971	100	20 Centimes. Gold. KM#930.	375
P424	1971	500	1/2 Franc. Nickel. KM#931.	20.00
P425	1971	250	1/2 Franc. Silver. KM#931.	35.00
P426	1971	100	1/2 Franc. Gold. KM#931.	365
P427	1971	500	Franc. Nickel. KM#925.	25.00
P428	1971	250	Franc. Silver. KM#925.	35.00
P429	1971	100	Franc. Gold. KM#925.	450
P430	1971	1,000	5 Francs. Nickel Clad Copper-Nickel. KM#926a.	20.00
P431	1971	500	5 Francs. Silver. KM#926a.	30.00
P432	1971	250	5 Francs. Gold. KM#926a.	875
P433	1971	100	5 Francs. Platinum. KM#926a.	1,950
P435	1971	500	10 Francs. Silver. KM#932.	50.00
P436	1971	250	10 Francs. Gold. KM#932.	2,400
P437	1972	250	Centime. Chrome-Steel. KM#928.	20.00
P438	1972	150	Centime. Silver. KM#928.	25.00
P439	1972	75	Centime. Gold. KM#928.	140
P440	1972	250	5 Centimes. Aluminum-Bronze. KM#933.	20.00
P441	1972	150	5 Centimes. Silver. KM#933.	25.00
P442	1972	75	5 Centimes. Gold. KM#933.	200
P443	1972	250	10 Centimes. Aluminum-Bronze. KM#929.	20.00
P444	1972	150	10 Centimes. Silver. KM#929.	25.00
P445	1972	75	10 Centimes. Gold. KM#929.	285
P446	1972	250	20 Centimes. Aluminum-Bronze. KM#930.	25.00
P447	1972	150	20 Centimes. Silver. KM#930.	35.00
P448	1972	75	20 Centimes. Gold. KM#930.	345
P449	1972	250	1/2 Franc. Nickel. KM#931.	25.00
P450	1972	150	1/2 Franc. Silver. KM#931.	35.00
P451	1972	75	1/2 Franc. Gold. KM#931.	380
P452	1972	250	Franc. Nickel. KM#925.	25.00
P453	1972	150	Franc. Silver. KM#925.	40.00
P454	1972	75	Franc. Gold. KM#925.	500
P455	1972	500	5 Francs. Nickel Clad Copper-Nickel. KM#926a.	25.00
P456	1972	250	5 Francs. Silver. KM#926a.	35.00
P457	1972	200	5 Francs. Gold. KM#926a.	875
P458	1972	500	10 Francs. Silver. KM#932.	70.00
P459	1972	200	10 Francs. Gold. KM#932.	2,400
P460	1972	20	10 Francs. Platinum. KM#932.	3,950
P461	1973	250	Centime. Chrome-Steel. KM#928.	20.00
P462	1973	150	Centime. Silver. KM#928.	25.00
P463	1973	75	Centime. Gold. KM#928.	175
P464	1973	250	5 Centimes. Aluminum-Bronze center. KM#933.	20.00

KM#	Date	Mintage	Identification	Mkt Val
P465	1973	150	5 Centimes. Silver. KM#933.	25.00
P466	1973	75	5 Centimes. Gold. KM#933.	200
P467	1973	250	10 Centimes. Aluminum-Bronze. KM#929.	20.00
P468	1973	150	10 Centimes. Silver. KM#929.	25.00
P469	1973	75	10 Centimes. Gold. KM#929.	285
P470	1973	250	20 Centimes. Aluminum-Bronze. KM#930.	20.00
P471	1973	150	20 Centimes. Silver. KM#930.	25.00
P472	1973	75	20 Centimes. Gold. KM#930.	375
P473	1973	250	1/2 Franc. Nickel. KM#931.	20.00
P474	1973	150	1/2 Franc. Silver. KM#931.	25.00
P475	1973	75	1/2 Franc. Gold. KM#931.	385
P476	1973	250	Franc. Nickel. KM#925.	20.00
P477	1973	150	Franc. Silver. KM#925.	25.00
P478	1973	75	Franc. Gold. KM#925.	385
P479	1973	500	5 Francs. Nickel Clad Copper-Nickel. KM#926a.	20.00
P480	1973	250	5 Francs. Silver. KM#926a.	35.00
P481	1973	200	5 Francs. Gold. KM#926a.	875
P482	1973	500	10 Francs. Silver. KM#932.	25.00
P483	1973	200	10 Francs. Gold. KM#932.	2,400
P484	1973	20	10 Francs. Platinum. KM#932.	3,950
P485	1974	127	Centime. Chrome-Steel. KM#928.	30.00
P486	1974	242	Centime. Gold. KM#928.	35.00
P487	1974	96	Centime. Gold. KM#928.	160
P488	1974	98	5 Centimes. Aluminum-Bronze. KM#933.	30.00
P489	1974	247	5 Centimes. Silver. KM#933.	35.00
P490	1974	96	5 Centimes. Gold. KM#933.	200
P491	1974	97	10 Centimes. Aluminum-Bronze. KM#929.	30.00
P492	1974	246	10 Centimes. Silver. KM#929.	35.00
P493	1974	94	10 Centimes. Gold. KM#929.	275
P494	1974	101	20 Centimes. Aluminum-Bronze. KM#930.	30.00
P495	1974	247	20 Centimes. Silver. KM#930.	35.00
P496	1974	98	20 Centimes. Gold. KM#930.	365
P497	1974	102	1/2 Franc. Nickel. KM#931.	30.00
P498	1974	241	1/2 Franc. Silver. KM#931.	35.00
P499	1974	91	1/2 Franc. Gold. KM#931.	380
P500	1974	118	Franc. Nickel. KM#925.	35.00
P501	1974	246	Franc. Silver. KM#925.	40.00
P502	1974	95	Franc. Gold. KM#925.	485
P503	1974	162	5 Francs. Nickel Clad Copper-Nickel. KM#926a.	35.00
P504	1974	245	5 Francs. Silver. KM#926a.	40.00
P505	1974	107	5 Francs. Gold. KM#926a.	875
P506	1974	493	10 Francs. Nickel-Brass. KM#940.	35.00
P507	1974	491	10 Francs. Silver. KM#940.	40.00
P508	1974	172	10 Francs. Gold. KM#940.	875
P509	1974	982	50 Francs. Silver. KM#941.	100
P510	1974	241	50 Francs. Gold. KM#941.	3,250
P511	1974	18	50 Francs. Platinum. KM#941.	5,000
P512	1975	147	Centime. Chrome-Steel. KM#928.	20.00
P513	1975	228	Centime. Silver. KM#928.	25.00
P514	1975	67	Centime. Gold. KM#928.	160
P515	1975	129	5 Centimes. Aluminum-Bronze. KM#933.	20.00
P516	1975	203	5 Centimes. Silver. KM#933.	25.00
P517	1975	44	5 Centimes. Gold. KM#933.	200
P518	1975	127	10 Centimes. Aluminum-Bronze. KM#929.	20.00
P519	1975	198	10 Centimes. Silver. KM#929.	25.00
P520	1975	39	10 Centimes. Gold. KM#929.	270
P521	1975	133	20 Centimes. Aluminum-Bronze. KM#930.	20.00
P522	1975	212	20 Centimes. Silver. KM#930.	25.00
P523	1975	42	20 Centimes. Gold. KM#930.	365
P524	1975	131	1/2 Franc. Nickel. KM#931.	20.00
P525	1975	213	1/2 Franc. Silver. KM#931.	25.00
P526	1975	40	1/2 Franc. Gold. KM#931.	395
P527	1975	145	Franc. Nickel. KM#925.	20.00
P528	1975	250	Franc. Silver. KM#925.	25.00
P529	1975	51	Franc. Gold. KM#925.	500
P530	1975	202	5 Francs. Nickel Clad Copper-Nickel. KM#926a.	20.00
P531	1975	250	5 Francs. Silver. KM#926a.	30.00
P532	1975	60	5 Francs. Gold. KM#926a.	875
P533	1975	356	10 Francs. Nickel-Brass. KM#940.	25.00
P534	1975	500	10 Francs. Silver. KM#940.	35.00
P535	1975	62	10 Francs. Gold. KM#940.	875
P536	1975	955	50 Francs. Silver. KM#941.	100
P537	1975	74	50 Francs. Gold. KM#941.	3,400
P538	1975	10	50 Francs. Platinum. KM#941.	5,000
P539	1976	200	Centime. Chrome-Steel. KM#928.	20.00
P540	1976	300	Centime. Silver. KM#928.	25.00
P541	1976	100	Centime. Gold. KM#928.	160
P542	1976	200	5 Centimes. Aluminum-Bronze. KM#933.	20.00
P543	1976	300	5 Centimes. Silver. KM#933.	25.00
P544	1976	100	5 Centimes. Gold. KM#933.	160
P545	1976	200	10 Centimes. Aluminum-Bronze. KM#929.	20.00
P546	1976	300	10 Centimes. Silver. KM#929.	25.00
P547	1976	100	10 Centimes. Gold. KM#929.	270
P548	1976	200	20 Centimes. Aluminum-Bronze. KM#930.	20.00
P549	1976	300	20 Centimes. Silver. KM#930.	25.00
P550	1976	100	20 Centimes. Gold. KM#930.	365
P551	1976	200	1/2 Franc. Nickel. KM#931.	20.00
P552	1976	250	1/2 Franc. Silver. KM#931.	25.00
P553	1976	100	1/2 Franc. Gold. KM#931.	500
P554	1976	126	Franc. Nickel. KM#925.	30.00
P555	1976	88	Franc. Silver. KM#925.	35.00
P556	1976	38	Franc. Gold. KM#925.	500
P557	1976	178	5 Francs. Nickel Clad Copper-Nickel center. KM#926a.	30.00
P558	1976	104	5 Francs. Silver. KM#926a.	37.50
P559	1976	26	5 Francs. Gold. KM#926a.	875
P560	1976	175	10 Francs. Nickel-Brass. KM#940.	30.00
P561	1976	121	10 Francs. Silver. KM#940.	40.00
P562	1976	36	10 Francs. Gold. KM#940.	875
P563	1976	213	50 Francs. Silver. KM#941.	150
P564	1976	54	50 Francs. Gold. KM#941.	3,400
P565	1976	6	50 Francs. Platinum. KM#941.	7,000
P566	1977	118	Centime. Chrome-Steel. KM#928.	25.00
P567	1977	247	Centime. Silver. KM#928.	30.00
P568	1977	53	Centime. Gold. KM#928.	160
P569	1977	89	5 Centimes. Aluminum-Bronze. KM#933.	25.00
P570	1977	232	5 Centimes. Silver. KM#933.	30.00
P571	1977	41	5 Centimes. Gold. KM#933.	195
P572	1977	85	10 Centimes. Aluminum-Bronze. KM#929.	25.00
P573	1977	231	10 Centimes. Silver. KM#929.	30.00
P575	1977	88	20 Centimes. Aluminum-Bronze. KM#930.	30.00
P576	1977	243	20 Centimes. Silver. KM#930.	35.00
P577	1977	32	20 Centimes. Gold. KM#930.	365
P578	1977	89	1/2 Franc. Nickel. KM#931.	30.00
P579	1977	234	1/2 Franc. Silver. KM#931.	35.00
P580	1977	32	1/2 Franc. Gold. KM#931.	395
P581	1977	100	Franc. Nickel. KM#925.	30.00
P582	1977	259	Franc. Silver. KM#925.	35.00
P583	1977	42	Franc. Gold. KM#925.	500
P584	1977	139	5 Francs. Nickel Clad Copper-Nickel. KM#926a.	30.00
P585	1977	282	5 Francs. Silver. KM#926a.	35.00
P586	1977	35	5 Francs. Gold. KM#926a.	875
P587	1977	146	10 Francs. Nickel-Brass center. KM#940.	30.00
P588	1977	296	10 Francs. Silver. KM#940.	40.00
P589	1977	43	10 Francs. Gold. KM#940.	875
P590	1977	465	50 Francs. Silver. KM#941.	125
P591	1977	50	50 Francs. Gold. KM#941.	3,400
P592	1977	19	50 Francs. Platinum. KM#941.	5,000
P593	1978	150	Centime. Chrome-Steel. KM#928.	20.00
P594	1978	294	Centime. Silver. KM#928.	25.00
P595	1978	144	Centime. Gold. KM#928.	160
P596	1978	148	5 Centimes. Aluminum-Bronze center. KM#933.	20.00
P597	1978	295	5 Centimes. Silver. KM#933.	25.00
P598	1978	144	5 Centimes. Gold. KM#933.	195
P599	1978	147	10 Centimes. Aluminum-Bronze. KM#929.	20.00
P600	1978	290	10 Centimes. Silver. KM#929.	25.00
P601	1978	139	10 Centimes. Gold. KM#929.	270
P602	1978	148	20 Centimes. Aluminum-Bronze. KM#930.	20.00
P603	1978	296	20 Centimes. Silver. KM#930.	25.00
P604	1978	141	20 Centimes. Gold. KM#930.	365
P605	1978	149	1/2 Franc. Nickel. KM#931.	20.00
P606	1978	296	1/2 Franc. Silver. KM#931.	25.00
P607	1978	141	1/2 Franc. Gold. KM#931.	395
P608	1978	149	Franc. Nickel. KM#925.	20.00
P609	1978	297	Franc. Silver. KM#925.	25.00
P610	1978	142	Franc. Gold. KM#925.	500
P611	1978	350	2 Francs. Silver. KM#942.	30.00
P612	1978	—	2 Francs. Nickel. KM#942.	100
P613	1978	150	5 Francs. Nickel Clad Copper-Nickel. KM#926a.	20.00
P614	1978	306	5 Francs. Silver. KM#926a.	25.00
P615	1978	143	5 Francs. Gold. KM#926a.	875
P616	1978	174	10 Francs. Nickel-Brass. KM#940.	25.00
P617	1978	345	10 Francs. Silver. KM#940.	35.00
P618	1978	144	10 Francs. Gold. KM#940.	875
P619	1978	599	50 Francs. Silver. KM#941.	120
P620	1978	149	50 Francs. Gold. KM#941.	3,400
P621	1978	25	50 Francs. Platinum. KM#941.	5,000
P622	1979	300	Centime. Chrome-Steel. KM#928.	15.00
P623	1979	600	Centime. Silver. KM#928.	20.00
P624	1979	300	Centime. Gold. KM#928.	160
P625	1979	299	5 Centimes. Silver. KM#935.	15.00
P626	1979	600	5 Centimes. Silver. KM#933.	20.00
P627	1979	300	5 Centimes. Gold. KM#933.	160
P628	1979	300	10 Centimes. Aluminum-Bronze. KM#929.	15.00
P629	1979	600	10 Centimes. Silver. KM#929.	20.00
P630	1979	300	10 Centimes. Gold. KM#929.	270
P631	1979	300	20 Centimes. Aluminum-Bronze. KM#930.	15.00
P632	1979	600	20 Centimes. Silver. KM#930.	20.00
P633	1979	300	20 Centimes. Gold. KM#930.	365
P634	1979	300	1/2 Franc. Nickel. KM#931.	15.00
P635	1979	600	1/2 Franc. Silver. KM#931.	20.00
P636	1979	300	1/2 Franc. Gold. KM#931.	395
P637	1979	500	Franc. Nickel. KM#925.	20.00
P638	1979	1,250	Franc. Silver. KM#925.	85.00
P639	1979	600	Franc. Gold. KM#925.	500
P640	1979	500	2 Francs. Nickel. KM#942.	20.00
P641	1979	1,250	2 Francs. Silver. KM#942.	30.00
P642	1979	600	2 Francs. Gold. KM#942.	710
P643	1979	40	2 Francs. Platinum. KM#942.	1,325
P644	1979	300	5 Francs. Nickel Clad Copper-Nickel. KM#926a.	20.00
P645	1979	600	5 Francs. Silver. KM#926a.	30.00
P646	1979	300	5 Francs. Gold. KM#926a.	875
P647	1979	349	10 Francs. Nickel-Brass. KM#940.	25.00
P648	1979	700	10 Francs. Silver. KM#940.	35.00
P649	1979	300	10 Francs. Gold. KM#940.	895
P650	1979	2,250	50 Francs. Silver. KM#941.	100
P651	1979	400	50 Francs. Gold. KM#941.	3,150
P652	1979	30	50 Francs. Platinum. KM#941.	5,000
P653	1980	155	Centime. Chrome-Steel center. KM#928.	15.00
P654	1980	570	Centime. Silver. KM#928.	20.00
P655	1980	176	Centime. Gold. KM#928.	160
P656	1980	142	5 Centimes. Aluminum-Bronze center. KM#933.	15.00
P657	1980	547	5 Centimes. Silver. KM#933.	20.00
P658	1980	137	5 Centimes. Gold. KM#933.	195
P659	1980	148	10 Centimes. Aluminum-Bronze. KM#929.	15.00
P660	1980	528	10 Centimes. Silver. KM#929.	20.00
P661	1980	127	10 Centimes. Gold. KM#929.	270
P662	1980	140	20 Centimes. Aluminum-Bronze. KM#930.	15.00
P663	1980	569	20 Centimes. Silver. KM#930.	20.00
P664	1980	136	20 Centimes. Gold. KM#930.	365
P665	1980	156	1/2 Franc. Nickel. KM#931.	15.00
P666	1980	537	1/2 Franc. Silver. KM#931.	20.00
P667	1980	118	1/2 Franc. Gold. KM#931.	395
P668	1980	132	Franc. Nickel. KM#925.	15.00
P669	1980	563	Franc. Silver. KM#925.	20.00
P670	1980	193	Franc. Gold. KM#925.	500
P671	1980	194	2 Francs. Nickel. KM#942.	15.00
P672	1980	772	2 Francs. Silver. KM#942.	20.00
P673	1980	130	2 Francs. Gold. KM#942.	710
P674	1980	271	5 Francs. Nickel Clad Copper-Nickel. KM#926a.	15.00
P675	1980	580	5 Francs. Silver. KM#926a.	20.00
P676	1980	213	5 Francs. Gold. KM#926a.	895
P677	1980	148	10 Francs. Nickel-Brass. KM#940.	15.00
P678	1980	730	10 Francs. Silver. KM#940.	20.00
P679	1980	157	10 Francs. Gold. KM#940.	890
P680	1980	2,500	50 Francs. Silver. KM#941.	100
P681	1980	500	50 Francs. Gold. KM#941.	3,150
P682	1980	34	50 Francs. Platinum. KM#941.	5,000
P683	1981	150	Centime. Chrome-Steel. KM#928.	15.00
P684	1981	362	Centime. Silver. KM#928.	20.00
P685	1981	69	Centime. Gold. KM#928.	160
P686	1981	105	5 Centimes. Aluminum-Bronze. KM#933.	15.00
P687	1981	358	5 Centimes. Silver. KM#933.	20.00
P688	1981	42	5 Centimes. Gold. KM#933.	195
P689	1981	104	10 Centimes. Aluminum-Bronze. KM#929.	15.00
P690	1981	357	10 Centimes. Silver. KM#929.	20.00
P691	1981	32	10 Centimes. Gold. KM#929.	250
P692	1981	106	20 Centimes. Aluminum-Bronze. KM#930.	15.00
P693	1981	359	20 Centimes. Silver. KM#930.	20.00
P694	1981	30	20 Centimes. Gold. KM#930.	365
P695	1981	110	1/2 Franc. Nickel. KM#931.	15.00
P696	1981	358	1/2 Franc. Silver. KM#931.	20.00
P697	1981	33	1/2 Franc. Gold. KM#931.	395
P698	1981	16	1/2 Franc. Platinum. KM#931.	1,000
P699	1981	122	Franc. Nickel. KM#925.	15.00
P700	1981	358	Franc. Silver. KM#925.	20.00
P701	1981	42	Franc. Gold. KM#925.	450
P702	1981	16	Franc. Platinum. KM#925.	1,350
P703	1981	131	2 Francs. Nickel. KM#942.	15.00
P704	1981	359	2 Francs. Silver. KM#942.	25.00
P705	1981	37	2 Francs. Gold. KM#942.	710
P706	1981	16	2 Francs. Platinum. KM#942.	1,500
P707	1981	150	5 Francs. Nickel Clad Copper-Nickel. KM#926a.	15.00
P708	1981	261	5 Francs. Silver. KM#926a.	20.00
P709	1981	52	5 Francs. Gold. KM#926a.	890
P710	1981	16	5 Francs. Platinum. KM#926a.	1,750
P711	1981	150	10 Francs. Nickel-Brass. KM#940.	15.00
P712	1981	365	10 Francs. Silver. KM#940.	30.00
P713	1981	52	10 Francs. Gold. KM#940.	890
P714	1981	17	10 Francs. Platinum. KM#940.	1,850
P715	1982	70	Centime. Steel. KM#928.	20.00
P716	1982	195	Centime. Silver. KM#928.	25.00
P717	1982	36	Centime. Gold. KM#928.	225
P718	1982	53	5 Centimes. Aluminum-Bronze. KM#933.	25.00
P719	1982	164	5 Centimes. Silver. KM#933.	25.00
P720	1982	26	5 Centimes. Gold. KM#933.	250
P721	1982	53	10 Centimes. Aluminum-Bronze. KM#929.	25.00
P722	1982	163	10 Centimes. Silver. KM#929.	25.00
P723	1982	29	10 Centimes. Gold. KM#929.	275
P724	1982	53	20 Centimes. Aluminum-Bronze. KM#930.	25.00
P725	1982	171	20 Centimes. Silver. KM#930.	25.00
P726	1982	26	20 Centimes. Gold. KM#930.	385
P727	1982	54	1/2 Franc. Nickel. KM#931.	25.00
P728	1982	165	1/2 Franc. Silver. KM#931.	25.00
P729	1982	26	1/2 Franc. Gold. KM#931.	385
P730	1982	4	1/2 Franc. Platinum. KM#931.	3,000
P731	1982	57	Franc. Nickel. KM#925.	25.00
P732	1982	252	Franc. Silver. KM#925.	25.00
P733	1982	29	Franc. Gold. KM#925.	450
P734	1982	6	Franc. Platinum. KM#925.	1,800
P735	1982	62	2 Francs. Nickel. KM#942.	25.00
P736	1982	203	2 Francs. Silver. KM#942.	25.00
P737	1982	27	2 Francs. Gold. KM#942.	925

KM#	Date	Mintage	Identification	Mkt Val
P738	1982	4	2 Francs. Platinum. KM#942.	3,500
P739	1982	69	5 Francs. Nickel Clad Copper-Nickel. KM#926a.	25.00
P740	1982	188	5 Francs. Silver. KM#926a.	25.00
P741	1982	27	5 Francs. Gold. KM#926a.	950
P742	1982	4	5 Francs. Platinum. KM#926a.	3,750
P743	1982	80	10 Francs. Nickel-Brass. KM#940.	25.00
P744	1982	239	10 Francs. Silver. KM#940.	30.00
P745	1982	33	10 Francs. Gold. KM#940.	890
P746	1982	4	10 Francs. Platinum. KM#940.	4,000
P747	1982	326	10 Francs. Nickel-Bronze. KM#950.	20.00
P748	1982	812	10 Francs. Silver. KM#950.	30.00
P749	1982	87	10 Francs. Gold. KM#950.	890
P750	1982	14	10 Francs. Platinum. KM#950.	1,700
P751	1982	999	100 Francs. Silver. KM#951.	55.00
P752	1982	93	100 Francs. Gold. KM#951.	1,100
P753	1982	16	100 Francs. Platinum. KM#951.	2,250
P754	1983	50	Centime. Steel. KM#928.	20.00
P755	1983	98	Centime. Silver. KM#928.	25.00
P756	1983	17	Centime. Gold. KM#928.	225
P757	1983	42	Centime. Aluminum-Bronze. KM#933.	20.00
P758	1983	90	5 Centimes. Silver. KM#933.	25.00
P759	1983	7	5 Centimes. Gold. KM#933.	650
P760	1983	42	10 Centimes. Aluminum-Bronze. KM#929.	25.00
P761	1983	90	10 Centimes. Silver. KM#929.	30.00
P762	1983	6	10 Centimes. Gold. KM#929.	700
P763	1983	44	20 Centimes. Aluminum-Bronze. KM#930.	25.00
P764	1983	95	20 Centimes. Silver. KM#930.	30.00
P765	1983	5	20 Centimes. Gold. KM#930.	775
P766	1983	43	1/2 Franc. Nickel. KM#931.	25.00
P767	1983	89	1/2 Franc. Silver. KM#931.	35.00
P768	1983	5	1/2 Franc. Gold. KM#931.	825
P769	1983	3	1/2 Franc. Platinum. KM#931.	7,150
P770	1983	46	Franc. Nickel center. KM#925.	25.00
P771	1983	98	Franc. Silver. KM#925.	35.00
P772	1983	11	Franc. Gold. KM#925.	550
P773	1983	3	Franc. Platinum. KM#925.	7,150
P774	1983	51	2 Francs. Nickel. KM#942.	25.00
P775	1983	121	2 Francs. Silver. KM#942.	35.00
P776	1983	9	2 Francs. Gold. KM#942.	750
P777	1983	3	2 Francs. Platinum. KM#942.	6,950
P778	1983	58	5 Francs. Nickel Clad Copper-Nickel. KM#926a.	25.00
P779	1983	97	5 Francs. Silver. KM#926a.	35.00
P780	1983	8	5 Francs. Gold. KM#926a.	950
P781	1983	3	5 Francs. Platinum. KM#926a.	7,350
P782	1983	286	10 Francs. Nickel-Bronze. KM#952.	20.00
P783	1983	454	10 Francs. Silver. KM#952.	35.00
P784	1983	34	10 Francs. Gold. KM#952.	890
P785	1983	13	10 Francs. Platinum. KM#952.	2,350
P786	1983	74	10 Francs. Nickel-Brass. KM#940.	25.00
P787	1983	118	10 Francs. Silver. KM#940.	45.00
P788	1983	12	10 Francs. Gold. KM#940.	900
P789	1983	5	10 Francs. Platinum. KM#940.	2,800
P790	1983	206	10 Francs. Nickel-Bronze. KM#953.	20.00
P791	1983	314	10 Francs. Silver. KM#953.	45.00
P792	1983	29	10 Francs. Gold. KM#953.	890
P793	1983	5	10 Francs. Platinum. KM#953.	2,800
P794	1983	242	100 Francs. Silver. KM#951.	55.00
P795	1983	14	100 Francs. Gold. KM#951.	1,250
P796	1983	7	100 Francs. Platinum. KM#951.	2,350
P797	1984	56	Centime. Steel. KM#928.	25.00
P798	1984	64	Centime. Silver. KM#928.	25.00
P799	1984	10	Centime. Gold. KM#928.	225
P800	1984	36	5 Centimes. Copper-Nickel. KM#933.	30.00
P801	1984	49	5 Centimes. Silver. KM#933.	25.00
P802	1984	6	5 Centimes. Gold. KM#933.	650
P803	1984	34	10 Centimes. Copper-Nickel. KM#929.	30.00
P804	1984	54	10 Centimes. Silver. KM#929.	25.00
P805	1984	4	10 Centimes. Gold. KM#929.	1,200
P806	1984	34	20 Centimes. Copper-Nickel. KM#930.	30.00
P807	1984	60	20 Centimes. Silver. KM#930.	25.00
P808	1984	4	20 Centimes. Gold. KM#930.	1,400
P809	1984	34	1/2 Franc. Nickel. KM#931.	30.00
P900	1984	59	1/2 Franc. Silver. KM#931.	25.00
P901	1984	8	1/2 Franc. Gold. KM#931.	550
P902	1984	5	1/2 Franc. Platinum. KM#931.	1,450
P903	1984	40	Franc. Nickel. KM#925.	30.00
P904	1984	69	Franc. Silver. KM#925.	25.00
P905	1984	6	Franc. Gold. KM#925.	850
P906	1984	5	Franc. Platinum. KM#925.	2,500
P907	1984	42	2 Francs. Nickel. KM#942.	30.00
P908	1984	79	2 Francs. Silver. KM#942.	25.00
P909	1984	9	2 Francs. Gold. KM#942.	800
P910	1984	5	2 Francs. Platinum. KM#942.	1,750
P911	1984	55	5 Francs. Nickel Clad Copper-Nickel. KM#926a.	30.00
P912	1984	59	5 Francs. Silver. KM#926a.	30.00
P913	1984	4	5 Francs. Gold. KM#926a.	1,650
P914	1984	5	5 Francs. Platinum. KM#926a.	2,700
P915	1984	50	10 Francs. Copper-Nickel-Aluminum. KM#940.	30.00
P916	1984	79	10 Francs. Silver. KM#940.	30.00
P917	1984	6	10 Francs. Gold. KM#940.	1,000
P918	1984	5	10 Francs. Platinum. KM#940.	2,500
P919	1984	184	10 Francs. Copper-Nickel-Aluminum. KM#954.	25.00

KM#	Date	Mintage	Identification	Mkt Val
P920	1984	244	10 Francs. Silver. KM#954.	30.00
P921	1984	18	10 Francs. Gold. KM#954.	950
P922	1984	5	10 Francs. Platinum. KM#954.	2,200
P923	1984	500	100 Francs. Silver. KM#955.	50.00
P924	1984	34	100 Francs. Gold. KM#955.	1,300
P925	1984	9	100 Francs. Platinum. KM#955.	1,950
P926	1984	100	100 Francs. Silver. KM#951.	65.00
P927	1984	10	100 Francs. Gold. KM#951.	1,450
P928	1984	5	100 Francs. Platinum. KM#951.	3,200
P929	1985	100	Centime. 0.9250 Silver. KM#928.	20.00
P930	1985	18	Centime. 0.9200 Gold. KM#928.	225
P931	1985	60	5 Centimes. 0.9250 Silver. KM#933.	30.00
P932	1985	6	5 Centimes. 0.9200 Gold. KM#933.	500
P933	1985	65	10 Centimes. 0.9250 Silver. KM#929.	32.00
P934	1985	4	10 Centimes. 0.9200 Gold. KM#929.	1,200
P935	1985	85	20 Centimes. 0.9250 Silver. KM#930.	35.00
P936	1985	4	20 Centimes. 0.9200 Gold. KM#930.	1,400
P937	1985	80	1/2 Franc. 0.9250 Silver. KM#931.	35.00
P938	1985	16	1/2 Franc. 0.9200 Gold. KM#931.	475
P939	1985	5	1/2 Franc. Platinum. KM#931.	2,000
P940	1985	90	Franc. 0.9250 Silver. KM#925.	35.00
P941	1985	5	Franc. 0.9200 Gold. KM#925.	750
P942	1985	5	Franc. Platinum. KM#925.	1,600
P943	1985	90	2 Francs. 0.9250 Silver. KM#942.	35.00
P944	1985	17	2 Francs. 0.9200 Gold. KM#942.	750
P945	1985	5	2 Francs. Platinum. KM#942.	1,600
P946	1985	70	5 Francs. 0.9250 Silver. KM#926a.	50.00
P947	1985	4	5 Francs. 0.9200 Gold. KM#926a.	2,100
P948	1985	5	5 Francs. Platinum. KM#926a.	2,350
P949	1985	120	10 Francs. 0.9250 Silver. KM#940.	45.00
P950	1985	12	10 Francs. 0.9200 Gold. KM#940.	1,150
P951	1985	5	10 Francs. Platinum. KM#940.	2,150
P952	1985	8	10 Francs. 0.9200 Gold. KM#952.	1,150
P953	1985	8	10 Francs. 0.9200 Gold. KM#953.	1,150
P954	1985	45	10 Francs. 0.9250 Silver. KM#954.	60.00
P955	1985	8	10 Francs. 0.9200 Gold. KM#954.	1,100
P956	1985	215	10 Francs. 0.9250 Silver. KM#956.	45.00
P957	1985	17	10 Francs. 0.9200 Gold. KM#956.	1,000
P958	1985	15	10 Francs. Platinum. KM#956.	2,400
P959	1985	100	100 Francs. 0.9250 Silver. KM#951.	65.00
P960	1985	18	100 Francs. 0.9200 Gold. KM#951.	1,325
P961	1985	10	100 Francs. Platinum. KM#951.	2,850
P962	1985	200	100 Francs. 0.9250 Silver. KM#955a.	55.00
P963	1985	8	100 Francs. 0.9200 Gold. KM#955b.	1,650
P964	1985	440	100 Francs. 0.9250 Silver. KM#957.	45.00
P965	1985	30	100 Francs. 0.9200 Gold. KM#957.	1,225
P966	1985	15	100 Francs. Platinum. KM#957.	2,400
P967	1986	10	100 Francs. Platinum. KM#958.	1,850
P968	1986	200	10 Francs. 0.9500 Silver. KM#959.	50.00
P969	1986	5	10 Francs. Platinum. KM#959.	2,150
P970	1986	5	100 Francs. Platinum. KM#951.	3,000
P971	1986	250	100 Francs. Silver. KM#951.	50.00
P972	1986	5,000	100 Francs. 0.9000 Silver. KM#960.	12.50
P973	1986	15	100 Francs. Platinum. KM#960.	2,150
P973b	1986	50	100 Francs. Gold. KM#960b.	1,375
P974	1987	50	Centime. 0.9500 Silver. KM#928.	40.00
P975	1987	50	5 Centimes. 0.9500 Silver. KM#933.	50.00
P976	1987	50	10 Centimes. 0.9500 Silver. KM#929.	50.00
P977	1987	50	20 Centimes. 0.9500 Silver. KM#930.	50.00
P978	1987	50	1/2 Franc. 0.9500 Silver. KM#931.	50.00
P979	1987	50	Franc. 0.9500 Silver. KM#925.	40.00
P980	1987	50	2 Francs. 0.9500 Silver. KM#942.	50.00
P981	1987	50	5 Francs. 0.9500 Silver. KM#926a.	65.00
P982	1987	50	10 Francs. 0.9500 Silver. KM#940.	65.00
P983	1987	15	10 Francs. 0.9200 Gold. KM#940.	950
P984	1987	5	10 Francs. 0.9990 Platinum. KM#940.	2,200
P985	1987	1,000	10 Francs. 0.9500 Silver. KM#961.	45.00
P986	1987	25	10 Francs. 0.9200 Gold. KM#961.	890
P987	1987	10	10 Francs. 0.9990 Platinum. KM#961.	1,650
P988	1987	30	100 Francs. 0.9000 Silver. KM#951.	65.00
P989	1987	15	100 Francs. 0.9200 Gold. KM#951.	1,200
P990	1987	5	100 Francs. 0.9990 Platinum. KM#951.	2,850
P991	1987	51,000	100 Francs. 0.9500 Silver. KM#962, Proof.	20.00
P991a	1987	100,000	100 Francs. 0.9000 Silver. KM#962, Unc.	12.50
P992	1987	50	100 Francs. 0.9200 Gold. KM#962.	1,300
P993	1987	15	100 Francs. 0.9990 Platinum. KM#962.	2,400
P994	1988	5	Centime. Platinum. KM#928.	500
P995	1988	—	10 Francs. 0.9000 Silver. KM#965a, Proof.	100
P996	1988	—	10 Francs. Gold. KM#965c, Proof.	1,300
P997	1988	10	10 Francs. Platinum. KM#965.	1,150
P998	1988	5	100 Francs. Platinum. KM#951.	2,100
PSA999	1988	—	100 Francs. 0.9000 Silver. KM#966, Proof.	2,200
P999	1988	20,000	100 Francs. 0.9000 Silver. KM#966, Unc.	14.00
P1000	1988	100	100 Francs. Platinum. KM#966.	2,350
P1001	1989	5	Centime. Platinum. KM#928.	450
P1002	1989	10	Franc. Platinum. KM#925.	1,250
P1003	1989	300	Franc. Silver. KM#967.	35.00
P1004	1989	25	Franc. Gold. KM#967.	800
P1005	1989	10	Franc. Platinum. KM#967.	1,250
P1006	1989	10	5 Francs. Platinum. KM#968.	1,850
P1007	1989	5	100 Francs. Platinum. KM#951.	2,150
PA1008	1989	—	100 Francs. 0.9000 Silver. KM#970, Proof.	25.00
P1008	1989	10,000	100 Francs. 0.9000 Silver. KM#970, Unc.	16.00
P1009	1989	10	100 Francs. Platinum. KM#970.	2,150

KM#	Date	Mintage	Identification	Mkt Val
P1011	1990	10	Centime. Gold. KM#928.	440
P1012	1990	5	Centime. Platinum. KM#928.	550
P1013	1990	50	5 Centimes. Silver. KM#933.	40.00
P1014	1990	50	10 Centimes. Silver. KM#929.	40.00
P1015	1990	50	20 Centimes. Silver. KM#930.	40.00
P1016	1990	5	20 Centimes. Gold. KM#930.	700
P1017	1990	50	1/2 Franc. Silver. KM#931.	40.00
P1018	1990	50	Franc. Silver. KM#925.	40.00
P1019	1990	50	2 Francs. Silver. KM#942.	40.00
P1020	1990	5	2 Francs. Gold. KM#942.	1,000
P1021	1990	50	5 Francs. Silver. KM#926a.	40.00
P1022	1990	10	10 Francs. Gold. Gold Alloy Spirit of Bastille.	650
P1023	1990	50	100 Francs. Silver. KM#951.	65.00
P1024	1990	10	100 Francs. Gold. KM#951.	1,250
P1025	1990	5	100 Francs. Platinum. KM#951.	2,100
P1026	1990	100	100 Francs. Silver. KM#982.	60.00
P1027	1990	10	100 Francs. Gold. KM#982.	1,250
P1028	1990	5	100 Francs. Platinum. KM#982.	1,900
P1010	1990	50	Centime. Silver. KM#928.	—
P1029	1991	—	100 Francs. Silver. KM#951.	65.00
P1030	1991	—	100 Francs. Silver. KM#996.	65.00

PIEFORTS WITH ESSAI

Double thickness; standard metals unless otherwise noted

KM#	Date	Mintage	Identification	Mkt Val
PE271	1914	—	10 Centimes. Nickel. Center hole divides RF within wreath, liberty cap above. Denomination divided by plant and center hole, date below. KM#866.	600
PE272	1914	—	25 Centimes. Nickel. KM#867.	550
PE-A281	1920	—	5 Centimes. Copper-Nickel. KM#875.	120
PE281	1920	—	50 Centimes. Aluminum-Bronze. Denomination within circle, legend surrounds. Mercury seated left, caduceus on left, shield on right, date below. KM#875.	120
PE282	1920	—	Franc. Bronze-Aluminum. Denomination within circle, legend surrounds. Mercury seated left, caduceus on left, shield on right, date below.	120
PE298	1929	—	10 Francs. Silver. KM#878.	350
PE299	1929	—	20 Francs. Silver. KM#879.	400
PE301	1931	—	50 Centimes. Aluminum-Bronze. KM#894.1.	—
PE302	1931	—	Franc. Aluminum-Bronze. KM#885.	—
PE303	1931	—	2 Francs. Aluminum-Bronze. KM#886.	—
PE306	1941	—	10 Francs. Zinc. KM#898.	120
PE304	1941	—	20 Centimes. Zinc. KM#899.	140
PE307	1941	—	20 Centimes. Zinc. KM#900.	120
PE308	1941	—	5 Francs. Copper-Nickel. KM#901.	500
PE309	1943	—	2 Francs. Aluminum. KM#904.	150
PE310	1945	104	20 Centimes. Zinc. KM#907.	165
PE311	1945	104	5 Francs. Nickel. KM#888.	120
PE312	1945	104	20 Francs. Copper-Nickel. KM#879.	185
PE313	1946	104	50 Centimes. Aluminum. KM#894.1a.	90.00
PE314	1946	—	Franc. Aluminum. KM#885a.	100
PE315	1946	104	2 Francs. Aluminum. KM#886a.	120
PE316	1946	104	10 Francs. Copper-Nickel. Laureate head right. Denomination above date, inscription below, grain columns flank. KM#909.	175
PE317	1950	—	10 Francs. Aluminum-Bronze. KM#915.	70.00
PE318	1950	—	20 Francs. Aluminum-Bronze. KM#916.	85.00
PE319	1950	—	50 Francs. Aluminum-Bronze. KM#918.	135
PE320	1952	104	10 Francs. Aluminum-Bronze. KM#915.	70.00
PE321	1952	104	20 Francs. Aluminum-Bronze. KM#917.	85.00
PE322	1952	104	50 Francs. Aluminum-Bronze. KM#918.1.	115
PE323	1954	104	100 Francs. Copper-Nickel. KM#919.	115
PE324	1958	65	100 Francs. Silver. KM#919.	550
PE325		104	Franc. Nickel. KM#925.	85.00
PE326	1959	104	5 Francs. Silver. KM#926, Small 5.	135
PE327	1959	104	5 Francs. Silver. KM#926, Large 5.	375
PE328	1960	50	Franc. Nickel. KM#925.	165
PE329	1960	20	Franc. Gold. KM#925.	675
PE330	1960	500	Franc. Nickel. KM#925.	45.00
PE331	1960	500	5 Francs. Silver. KM#926.	115
PE332	1960	50	5 Francs. Gold. KM#926.	690
PE333	1961	104	Centime. Chrome-Steel. KM#928.	65.00
PE334	1961	104	5 Centimes. Chrome-Steel. KM#927.	65.00
PE335	1961	500	5 Centimes. Chrome-Steel. KM#927.	30.00
PE336	1961	50	5 Centimes. Silver. KM#927.	120
PE337	1961	20	5 Centimes. Gold. KM#927.	600
PE338	1962	104	10 Centimes. Aluminum-Bronze. KM#929.	50.00
PE339	1962	104	20 Centimes. Aluminum-Bronze. KM#930.	50.00
PE340	1962	104	50 Centimes. Aluminum-Bronze. KM#939.	85.00
PE434	1971	100	5 Francs. Platinum. KM#926a.	1,500

MINT SETS

KM#	Date	Mintage	Identification	Issue Price	Mkt Val
MS1	1986 (10)	20,000	KM#925.1, 926a, 928-931, 933, 942, 951.1, 959 (sets with perfect case and no PVC damage on coins command a 25% premium)	—	90.00
MS2	1987 (10)	4,000	KM#925.1, 926a, 928-931, 933, 940, 942, 961d	—	60.00
MS3	1988 (10)	2,000	KM#925.1, 926a, 928-931, 933, 942, 964-965	—	65.00
MS4	1989 (10)	2,000	KM#925.1, 926a, 928-931, 933, 942, 964, 969	—	65.00
MS6	1991 (9)	2,500	KM#925.1, 926a.1, 928-930, 931.1, 933, 942.1, 964.1, medal rotation	50.00	40.00
MS7	1992 (10)	20,000	KM#925.1, 926a.1, 928-930, 931.1, 933, 942.1, 964.1, 1008.2, medal rotation	—	45.00
MS8	1993 (10)	20,000	KM#925.1, 926a.1, 928-930, 931.1, 933, 942.1, 964.1, 1008.2, medal rotation	—	40.00
MS9	1994 (10)	20,000	KM#925.1, 926a.1, 928-930, 931.1, 933, 942.1, 964.2, 1008.2 bee privy mark	—	50.00
MS10	1995 (10)	20,000	KM#925.1, 926a.1, 928, 930, 931.1, 933, 942.1, 964.2, 1008.2	—	50.00
MS11	1996 (10)	5,000	KM#925.1, 926a.1, 928-930, 931.1, 933, 942.1, 964.2, 1008.2	—	60.00
MS12	1996 (3)	2,500	KM#1155, 1160, 1180	—	35.00
MS13	1997 (10)	15,000	KM#925.1, 926a.1, 928-930, 931.1, 933, 942.1, 964.2, 1008.2	—	50.00
MS14	1998 (10)	—	KM#925.1, 926a.1, 928-930, 931.1, 933, 942.1, 964.2, 1008.2	—	50.00
MS15	1999 (10)	—	KM#925.1, 926a.1, 928-930, 931.1, 933, 942.1, 964.2, 1008.2	—	50.00
MS16	2000 (3)	—	KM#1222-1224	—	30.00
MS17	2000 (10)	50,000	KM#925, 926a, 928-931, 933, 942, 964.2, 1008.2	—	50.00
MS18	1999 (8)	35,000	KM#1282-1289	20.25	50.00
MS19	2000 (8)	35,000	KM#1282-1289	20.25	50.00

PROOF SETS

KM#	Date	Mintage	Identification	Issue Price	Mkt Val
PS6	1990-91 (9)	—	KM#971-972, 980-981, 983-984, 993-995	—	500
PS7	1991 (10)	10,000	KM#925.2, 926a.2, 928-930, 931.2, 933, 942.2, 951.2, 964.2	160	145
PS8	1991 (3)	15,000	KM#977, 991-992	—	500
PS9	1992 (11)	15,000	KM#925.2, 926a.2, 928-930, 931.2, 933, 942.2, 951.2, 964.2, 1008.2	—	125
PS10	1992 (3)	2,000	KM#1007, 1010-1011	—	200
PS11	1993 (11)	10,000	KM#925.1, 926a.1, 928-930, 931.2, 933, 942.1, 964.1, 961.1, 1008.2	—	135
PS12	1994 (11)	10,000	KM#925.2, 926a.2, 928-930, 931.2, 933, 942.2, 951.1, 964.2, 1008.2, fish privy mark	—	135
PS13	1995 (11)	10,000	KM#925.2, 926a.2, 928-930, 931.2, 933, 942.2, 951.1, 964.2, 1008.2	—	135
PS14	1996 (11)	8,000	KM#925.2, 926a.2, 928-930, 931.2, 933, 942.2, 951.1, 964.2, 1008.2	—	140
PS15	1997 (11)	10,000	KM#925.2, 926a.2, 928-930, 931.2, 933, 942.2, 951.1, 964.2, 1008.2	—	135
PS16	1998 (11)	—	KM#925.2, 926a.2, 928-930, 931.2, 933, 942.2, 951.1, 964.2, 1008.2	—	135
PS17	1999 (11)	—	KM#925.2, 926a.2, 928-930, 941.2, 933, 942.2, 951.1, 964.2, 1008.2	—	135
PS18	2000 (11)	—	KM#925.2, 926a.2, 928-930, 931.2, 933, 942.2, 951.1, 964.2, 1008.2	—	135
PS19	1999 (8)	15,000	KM#1282-1289	59.00	110
PS20	2000 (8)	15,000	KM#1282-1289	59.00	110

SPECIMEN FDC SETS (FLEUR DE COIN)

KM#	Date	Mintage	Identification	Issue Price	Mkt Val
SS1	1964 (7)	25,600	KM#925-930, 939	4.00	25.00
SS2	1965 (7)	35,000	KM#925-926, 928-932	7.60	35.00
SS3	1966 (8)	7,171	KM#925-926, 928-933	9.00	70.00
SS4	1967 (8)	2,305	KM#925-926, 928-933	10.00	220
SS5	1968 (8)	3,000	With perfect box KM#925-926, 928-933	10.00	500
SS5A	1968 (8)	I.A.	KM#925-926, 928-933 without box	—	120
SS6	1969 (8)	6,050	KM#925-926, 928-933	10.00	120
SS7	1970 (8)	10,000	KM#925, 926a, 928-933	9.00	60.00
SS8	1971 (8)	12,000	KM#925, 926a, 928-933	9.00	60.00
SS9	1972 (8)	15,000	KM#925, 926a, 928-933	9.00	60.00
SS10	1973 (8)	79,000	KM#925, 926a, 928-933	12.00	35.00
SS11	1974 (9)	98,800	KM#925, 926a, 928-931, 933, 940-941	31.00	35.00
SS12	1975 (9)	52,000	KM#925, 926a, 928-931, 933, 940-941	35.00	37.50
SS13	1976 (9)	35,700	KM#925, 926a, 928-931, 933, 940-941	35.00	40.00
SS14	1977 (9)	25,000	KM#925, 926a, 928-931, 933, 940-941	36.00	45.00
SS15	1978 (9)	24,000	KM#925, 926a, 928-931, 933, 940-941	39.00	60.00
SS16	1979 (10)	40,500	KM#925, 926a, 928-931, 933, 940--942	55.00	70.00
SS17	1980 (10)	60,000	KM#925, 926a, 928-931, 933, 940-942	90.00	60.00
SS18	1981 (9)	26,000	KM#925, 926a, 928-931, 933, 940, 942	—	55.00
SS19	1982 (11)	27,500	KM#925, 926a, 928-931, 933, 940, 942, 950-951	—	85.00
SS20	1983 (12)	16,561	KM#925, 926a, 928-931, 933, 940, 942, 951-953	—	120
SS21	1984 (12)	13,388	KM#825, 926a, 928-931, 933, 940, 942, 951, 954, 955	—	175
SS22	1985 (12)	12,224	KM#925, 926a, 928-931, 933, 940, 942, 951, 956-957	—	150
SS23	1986 (12)	13,000	KM#925.1, 926a.1, 928-931.1, 933, 942.1, 951, 958, 959, 960	—	165
SS24	1987 (12)	15,000	KM#925.1, 926a.1, 928-931.1, 933, 940, 942.1, 951, 961, 962	68.00	165
SS25	1987 (2)	—	KMP991-991a, Proof and BU	120	60.00
SS26	1988 (13)	13,000	KM#925, 926a.1, 928-931.1, 933, 941.1, 951, 963-966	—	175
SS27	1989 (14)	10,000	KM#925.1, 926a.1, 928-931.1, 933, 942.1, 951, 964, 967-970	—	185
SS28	1990 (13)	10,000	KM#925.1, 926a.1, 928-931.1, 933, 942.1, 951, 964, 980-982	—	175
SS29	1990 (11)	10,000	KM#925.1, 926a.1, 928-931.1, 933, 942.1, 951, 964, 982	—	165

FRENCH AFARS & ISSAS

MINT MARK
(a) - Paris (privy marks only)

MONETARY SYSTEM
100 Centimes = 1 Franc

NOTE
For later coinage, see Djibouti
For earlier coinage, see French Somaliland

FRENCH COLONY
DECIMAL COINAGE

KM# 16   FRANC
1.3000 g., Aluminum, 24 mm. **Obv:** Winged bust left, date below **Rev:** Lyre antelope divides denomination

Date	Mintage	F	VF	XF	Unc	BU
1969(a)	100,000	1.00	2.00	3.50	6.00	—
1971(a)	100,000	1.00	2.00	3.50	6.00	—
1975(a)	300,000	0.75	1.25	2.00	3.00	—

KM# 13   2 FRANCS
2.2000 g., Aluminum, 27 mm. **Obv:** Winged bust left, date below **Rev:** Lyre antelope divides denomination

Date	Mintage	F	VF	XF	Unc	BU
1968(a)	100,000	1.00	2.00	3.50	6.00	—
1975(a)	180,000	0.75	1.50	2.50	5.00	—

KM# 14   5 FRANCS
3.8000 g., Aluminum, 31.1 mm. **Obv:** Winged bust left, date below **Rev:** Lyre antelope divides denomination

Date	Mintage	F	VF	XF	Unc	BU
1968(a)	100,000	1.00	2.00	3.50	6.00	—
1975(a)	300,000	0.75	1.25	2.00	4.00	—

KM# 17   10 FRANCS
3.0000 g., Aluminum-Bronze, 20 mm. **Obv:** Winged bust left, date below **Rev:** Dhow, ocean liner, denomination above

Date	Mintage	F	VF	XF	Unc	BU
1969(a)	100,000	1.50	3.00	6.00	9.00	—
1970(a)	300,000	1.00	2.00	4.00	7.00	—
1975(a)	360,000	0.75	1.50	3.00	5.00	—

KM# 15   20 FRANCS
4.1000 g., Aluminum-Bronze, 23.6 mm. **Obv:** Winged bust left, date below **Rev:** Dhow, ocean liner, denomination above

Date	Mintage	F	VF	XF	Unc	BU
1968(a)	300,000	1.50	2.50	4.50	8.00	—
1975(a)	300,000	1.25	2.00	4.00	7.00	—

KM# 18   50 FRANCS
7.0000 g., Copper Nickel, 25.5 mm. **Obv:** Hooded head left, date below **Rev:** Pair of dromedary camels, denomination above

Date	Mintage	F	VF	XF	Unc	BU
1970(a)	600,000	1.50	3.00	6.00	10.00	12.00
1975(a)	180,000	1.50	3.00	6.00	10.00	12.00

KM# 19   100 FRANCS
11.9000 g., Copper-Nickel, 30 mm. **Obv:** Hooded head left, date below **Rev:** Pair of dromedary camels, denomination below

Date	Mintage	F	VF	XF	Unc	BU
1970(a)	600,000	2.50	4.00	7.00	11.50	15.00
1975(a)	400,000	2.50	4.50	7.50	12.50	16.00

ESSAIS
Standard metals unless otherwise noted

KM#	Date	Mintage	Identification	Issue Price	Mkt Val
E1	1968(a)	1,700	2 Francs. KM13.	—	12.00
E2	1968(a)	1,700	5 Francs. KM14.	—	15.00
E3	1968(a)	1,700	20 Francs. KM15.	—	20.00
E4	1969(a)	1,700	Franc. KM16.	—	15.00
E5	1969(a)	1,700	10 Francs. KM17.	—	20.00
E6	1970(a)	1,700	50 Francs. KM18.	—	30.00
E7	1970(a)	1,700	100 Francs. KM19.	—	35.00

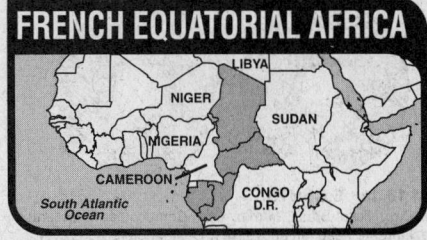

FRENCH EQUATORIAL AFRICA

French Equatorial Africa, an area consisting of four self governing dependencies (Middle Congo, Ubangi-Shari, Chad and Gabon) in West-Central Africa, had an area of 969,111 sq. mi. (2,509,987 sq. km.). Capital: Brazzaville. The area, rich in natural resources, exported cotton, timber, coffee, cacao, diamonds and gold.

Little is known of the history of these parts of Africa prior to French occupation - which began with no thought of territorial acquisition. France's initial intent was simply to establish a few supply stations along the west coast of Africa to service the warships assigned to combat the slave trade in the early part of the 19th century. French settlement began in 1839. Gabon (then Gabun) and the Middle Congo were secured between 1885 and 1891; Chad and Ubangi-Shari between 1894 and 1897. The four colonies were joined to form French Equatorial Africa in 1910. The dependencies were changed from colonies to territories within the French Union in 1946, and all the inhabitants were made French citizens. In 1958 they voted to become autonomous republics within the new French Community, and attained full independence in 1960.

For later coinage see Central African States, Congo Peoples Republic, Gabon and Chad.

RULER
French, until 1960

MINT MARKS
(a) - Paris, privy marks only
(t) - Poissy, privy marks only, thunderbolt
SA - Pretoria (1942-1943)

ENGRAVERS' INITIALS
GLS – Steynberg

MONETARY SYSTEM
100 Centimes = 1 Franc

FRENCH COLONY
DECIMAL COINAGE

KM# 3   5 CENTIMES
Aluminum-Bronze **Note:** Similar to 10 Centimes, KM#4.

Date	Mintage	F	VF	XF	Unc	BU
1943	Est. 44,000,000	90.00	150	325	600	900

Note: Not released for circulation

KM# 4   10 CENTIMES
Aluminum-Bronze

Date	Mintage	F	VF	XF	Unc	BU
1943	Est. 13,000,000	75.00	100	160	375	500

Note: Not released for circulation

KM# 5   25 CENTIMES
Aluminum-Bronze **Note:** Similar to 10 Centimes, KM#4.

Date	Mintage	F	VF	XF	Unc	BU
1943	Est. 4,160,000	200	350	550	800	1,200

Note: Not released for circulation

KM# 1   50 CENTIMES
Brass **Rev:** Double cross divides denomination, date below

Date	Mintage	F	VF	XF	Unc	BU
1942SA	8,000,000	1.50	3.00	8.00	20.00	30.00

KM# 1a   50 CENTIMES
Bronze **Rev:** Double cross divides denomination

Date	Mintage	F	VF	XF	Unc	BU
1943SA	16,000,000	1.25	2.50	7.00	18.00	25.00

KM# 2   FRANC
Brass **Obv:** Rooster, small shield above **Rev:** Double cross divides denomination, date below

Date	Mintage	F	VF	XF	Unc	BU
1942SA	3,000,000	2.00	3.50	10.00	22.50	30.00

KM# 2a   FRANC
Bronze **Obv:** Rooster left, small shield above **Rev:** Double cross divides denomination

Date	Mintage	F	VF	XF	Unc	BU
1943SA	6,000,000	1.75	2.75	9.00	20.00	30.00

KM# 6   FRANC
Aluminum, 23 mm. **Obv:** Winged bust left, date below **Rev:** Loder's gazelle divides denomination

Date	Mintage	F	VF	XF	Unc	BU
1948(a)	15,000,000	0.15	0.25	0.50	2.00	—

KM# 7   2 FRANCS
Aluminum **Obv:** Winged bust left, date below **Rev:** Loder's gazelle divides denomination

Date	Mintage	F	VF	XF	Unc	BU
1948(a)	5,040,000	0.25	0.50	1.50	4.00	—

TOKEN COINAGE
Middle Congo

KM# TnA1   NON-DENOMINATED
Aluminum **Obv:** Center hole, date below, MC above **Rev:** Center hole within Elephant walking left **Note:** Prev. KM#Tn1.

Date	Mintage	F	VF	XF	Unc	BU
1925(t)	—	35.00	65.00	115	300	425

KM# TnA2   NON-DENOMINATED
Aluminum **Rev:** Center hole within Leopard walking left **Note:** Previous KM#Tn2.

Date	Mintage	F	VF	XF	Unc	BU
1926	—	40.00	75.00	150	325	475

ESSAIS
Standard metals unless otherwise noted

KM#	Date	Mintage Identification			Mkt Val
E1	1948(a)	2,000	Franc. Copper-Nickel. KM#7		30.00
E2	1948(a)	2,000	2 Francs. Copper-Nickel. KM#7		35.00

PIEFORTS WITH ESSAI
Standard metals unless otherwise noted

KM#	Date	Mintage Identification			Mkt Val
PE1	1948(a)	104	Franc. Aluminum. KM#6		60.00
PE2	1948(a)	104	2 Francs. Aluminum. KM#7		70.00

FRENCH INDO-CHINA

French Indo-China, made up of the protectorates of Annam, Tonkin, Cambodia and Laos and the colony of Cochin-China was located on the Indo-Chinese peninsula of Southeast Asia. The colony had an area of 286,194 sq. mi. (741,242 sq. km.). and a population of 30 million. Principal cities: Saigon, Haiphong, Vientiane, Pnom-Penh and Hanoi.

The forebears of the modern Indo-Chinese people originated in the Yellow River Valley of Northern China. From there, they were driven into the Indo-Chinese peninsula by the Han Chinese. The Chinese followed southward in the second century B.C., conquering the peninsula and ruling it until 938, leaving a lingering heritage of Chinese learning and culture. Indo-Chinese independence was basically maintained until the arrival of the French in the mid-19th century who established control over all of Vietnam, Laos and Cambodia. Activities directed toward obtaining self-determination accelerated during the Japanese occupation of World War II. The dependencies were changed from colonies to territories within the French Union in 1946, and all the inhabitants were made French citizens.

In Aug. of 1945, an uprising erupted involving the French and Vietnamese Nationalists, culminated in the French military disaster at Dien Bien Phu (May, 1954) and the subsequent Geneva Conference that brought an end to French colonial rule in Indo-China.

For later coinage see Kampuchea, Laos and Vietnam.

RULER
French, until 1954

MINT MARKS
A - Paris
(a) - Paris, privy marks only
B - Beaumont-le-Roger
C - Castlesarrasin
H - Heaton, Birmingham
(p) - Thunderbolt - Poissy
S - San Francisco, U.S.A.
None - Osaka, Japan
None - Hanoi, Tonkin

MONETARY SYSTEM
5 Sapeques = 1 Cent
100 Cents = 1 Piastre

FRENCH COLONY
STANDARD COINAGE

KM# 6   2 SAPEQUE
Bronze

Date	Mintage	F	VF	XF	Unc	BU
1901A	4,843,000	2.50	7.50	15.00	45.00	100
1902A	2,500,000	7.50	20.00	40.00	125	200

KM# 25   1/4 CENT
Zinc **Obv:** Square surrounds center hole, grain sprigs flank, date below **Rev:** Square around center hole, corners section coin, denomination divided by hole **Note:** Lead counterfeits dated 1941 and 1942 are known.

Date	Mintage	F	VF	XF	Unc	BU
1941	—	12.00	25.00	35.00	—	—
1942	221,800,000	8.00	15.00	35.00	75.00	100
1943	279,450,000	15.00	35.00	55.00	125	150
1944	46,122,000	100	180	250	750	1,250

KM# 20   1/2 CENT
Bronze, 21 mm. **Obv:** Center hole divides RF, liberty cap above, wreath surrounds **Rev:** Denomination divided by grain sprigs around center hole, date below

Date	Mintage	F	VF	XF	Unc	BU
1935(a)	26,365,000	0.25	0.50	2.00	10.00	—
1936(a)	23,635,000	0.25	0.50	2.00	10.00	—
1937(a)	10,244,000	0.50	1.50	5.00	15.00	40.00
1938(a)	16,665,000	0.25	0.75	2.50	12.00	—

Date	Mintage	F	VF	XF	Unc	BU
1939(a)	17,305,000	0.25	0.75	2.50	12.00	—
1940(a)	11,218,000	4.00	8.00	20.00	40.00	75.00

KM# 20a 1/2 CENT
Zinc, 21 mm. **Obv:** Center hole divides RF, liberty cap above, wreath surrounds **Rev:** Denomination divided by center hole and grain sprigs

Date	Mintage	F	VF	XF	Unc	BU
1939(a)	185,000	200	400	600	900	—
1940(a)	Inc. above	350	500	800	1,200	—

KM# 8 CENT
7.5100 g., Bronze, 27.5 mm. **Obv:** Center hole within statue, denomination below **Rev:** Symbols at four sides of center hole within circle, date below

Date	Mintage	F	VF	XF	Unc	BU
1901	9,750,000	2.00	3.00	7.50	25.00	—
1902	6,050,000	4.00	7.00	15.00	50.00	—
1903	8,000,000	2.50	4.00	8.00	30.00	—
1906	2,000,000	15.00	20.00	35.00	100	—

KM# 12.1 CENT
Bronze, 26 mm. **Obv:** Center hole within statue, denomination below, mint mark "A" for Paris mint **Rev:** Symbols at four sides of center hole within circle, date below

Date	Mintage	F	VF	XF	Unc	BU
1908	3,000,000	10.00	20.00	55.00	235	350
1909	5,000,000	20.00	40.00	80.00	275	—
1910	7,703,000	2.00	5.00	15.00	35.00	—
1911	15,234,000	0.75	3.00	10.00	20.00	—
1912	17,027,000	0.75	2.00	7.50	20.00	—
1913	3,945,000	2.00	7.00	18.00	45.00	—
1914	11,027,000	0.75	3.00	15.00	30.00	—
1916	1,312,000	8.00	15.00	30.00	65.00	—
1917	9,762,000	1.00	4.00	10.00	20.00	—
1918	2,372,000	6.00	12.50	25.00	50.00	—
1919	9,148,000	1.00	4.00	7.50	20.00	—
1920	18,305,000	0.75	3.00	5.00	12.50	—
1921	14,272,000	0.75	2.00	3.00	10.00	—
1922	8,850,000	1.00	3.00	5.00	20.00	—
1923	1,079,000	40.00	90.00	180	350	—
1926	11,672,000	0.75	2.00	4.00	15.00	—
1927	3,328,000	5.00	15.00	35.00	70.00	—
1930	4,682,000	1.25	2.75	5.00	15.00	—
1931	5,318,000	30.00	85.00	200	550	—

Note: Torch privy mark

| 1931 | Inc. above | 60.00 | 120 | 300 | 800 | — |

Note: Wing privy mark

1937	8,902,000	1.50	3.00	6.00	25.00	—
1938	15,499,000	1.00	2.00	4.00	16.00	—
1939	17,589,000	1.00	2.00	4.00	16.00	—

KM# 12.2 CENT
Bronze, 26 mm. **Obv:** No mint mark at bottom, (San Francisco mint) **Rev:** Four symbols surround center hole **Note:** Without mint mark.

Date	Mintage	F	VF	XF	Unc	BU
1920	13,290,000	2.00	4.00	10.00	25.00	—
1921	1,710,000	15.00	70.00	180	350	—

KM# 12.3 CENT
Bronze, 26 mm. **Obv:** Center hole within statue, denomination below **Rev:** Four symbols surround center hole

Date	Mintage	F	VF	XF	Unc	BU
1922(p)	9,476,000	1.00	1.75	5.00	12.00	—
1923(p)	35,524,000	0.50	0.75	1.50	7.50	—

KM# 24.3 CENT
Zinc **Obv:** Wreath surrounds, cap above, denomination below **Rev:** Wreath surrounds center hole, denomination divided **Note:** Vichy Government issue. Type 2: Rosette on Phrygian cap. Variety 2: 11 petals.

Date	Mintage	F	VF	XF	Unc	BU
1940	2,360,000	8.00	18.00	35.00	70.00	—
1941	2,500,000	7.00	16.00	25.00	70.00	—

Circles

KM# 24.1 CENT
Zinc **Obv:** Wreath surrounds center hole, liberty cap above, denomination below **Rev:** Center hole divides denomination, wreath surrounds, date below **Note:** Vichy Government issue. Type 1: Circles on Phrygian cap.

Date	Mintage	F	VF	XF	Unc	BU
1940	1,990,000	10.00	16.00	40.00	75.00	—

Rosettes

KM# 24.2 CENT
Zinc **Obv:** Wreath surrounds center hole, liberty cap above, denomination below **Rev:** Center hole divides denomination, wreath surrounds, date below **Note:** Vichy Government issue. Type 2: Rosette on Phrygian cap, variety 2 with 12 petals.

Date	Mintage	F	VF	XF	Unc	BU
1940	150,000	18.00	35.00	70.00	140	—

KM# 26 CENT
Aluminum **Obv:** Center hole flanked by leafy sprays, date below **Rev:** Denomination left and top of center hole **Note:** Edge varieties exist - plain, grooved, and partially grooved.

Date	Mintage	F	VF	XF	Unc	BU
1943	15,000,000	0.75	2.00	4.00	8.00	—

KM# 18 5 CENTS
5.0000 g., Copper-Nickel, 24 mm. **Obv:** Cornucopias flank center hole, laureate head left above **Rev:** Center hole within wreath divides denomination, date below **Note:** 1.6 mm thick; prev. KM#18.1.

Date	Mintage	F	VF	XF	Unc	BU
1923(a)	1,611,000	5.00	10.00	20.00	40.00	—
1924(a)	3,389,000	6.00	12.00	24.00	45.00	—
1925(a)	6,000,000	5.00	10.00	20.00	35.00	—
1930(a) Torch	4,000,000	5.00	10.00	20.00	35.00	—
1937(a) Wing	10,000,000	2.00	5.00	10.00	20.00	—
1938(a)	1,480,000	15.00	30.00	75.00	160	—
1938(a) Proof	—		Value: 275			

KM# 18.1a 5 CENTS
4.0000 g., Nickel-Brass, 24 mm. **Obv:** Cornucopias flank center hole, laureate head left above **Rev:** Center hole divides denomination, wreath surrounds, date below **Note:** 1.3 mm thick.

Date	Mintage	F	VF	XF	Unc	BU
1938(a)	50,569,000	0.75	2.00	5.00	12.00	—
1939(a)	38,501,000	0.75	2.00	5.00	12.00	—

KM# 27 5 CENTS
Aluminum **Note:** Vichy Government issue. Edge varieties exist: reeded - rare, plain, grooved, and partially grooved.

Date	Mintage	F	VF	XF	Unc	BU
1943A	10,000,000	1.00	2.00	5.00	10.00	—

KM# 30.1 5 CENTS
Aluminum **Obv:** Bust right holding laurel, date below **Rev:** Plant divides denomination

Date	Mintage	F	VF	XF	Unc	BU
1946(a)	28,000,000	0.25	0.60	1.00	5.00	—

KM# 30.2 5 CENTS
Aluminum **Obv:** Bust right holding laurel, date below **Rev:** Plant divide denomination

Date	Mintage	F	VF	XF	Unc	BU
1946B	22,000,000	0.25	0.60	1.00	5.00	—

KM# 9 10 CENTS
2.7000 g., 0.8350 Silver 0.0725 oz. ASW **Obv:** Liberty seated left with fasces **Rev:** Denomination within wreath **Rev. Leg.:** TITRE 0.835. POIDS 2 GR. 7

Date	Mintage	F	VF	XF	Unc	BU
1901	2,950,000	7.00	25.00	60.00	200	350
1902	7,050,000	4.00	12.00	30.00	125	—
1903	1,300,000	12.00	30.00	80.00	325	—
1908	1,000,000	50.00	100	200	575	725
1909	1,000,000	30.00	75.00	130	425	—
1910	2,689,000	25.00	60.00	100	350	—
1911	2,311,000	25.00	40.00	80.00	325	—
1912	2,500,000	25.00	35.00	70.00	275	—
1913	4,847,000	7.50	12.50	30.00	125	—
1914	2,667,000	10.00	30.00	60.00	175	—
1916	2,000,000	10.00	30.00	60.00	185	—
1917	1,500,000	25.00	50.00	100	300	—
1919	1,500,000	30.00	60.00	125	350	—

KM# 14 10 CENTS
3.0000 g., 0.4000 Silver 0.0386 oz. ASW **Obv:** Liberty seated, date below **Rev:** Denomination within wreath, without fineness indicated **Note:** Without mint mark.

Date	Mintage	F	VF	XF	Unc	BU
1920	10,000,000	10.00	20.00	50.00	120	150

KM# 16.1 10 CENTS
2.7000 g., 0.6800 Silver 0.0590 oz. ASW **Obv:** Liberty seated, date below **Rev:** Denomination within wreath **Rev. Leg.:** TITRE 0.680 POIDS 2 GR. 7

Date	Mintage	F	VF	XF	Unc	BU
1921A	12,516,000	1.50	3.00	9.00	25.00	30.00
1922A	22,381,000	1.50	3.00	9.00	20.00	25.00
1923A	21,755,000	1.50	3.00	9.00	20.00	25.00
1924A	2,816,000	4.00	9.00	25.00	60.00	80.00
1925A	4,909,000	2.00	5.00	15.00	35.00	50.00
1927A	6,471,000	2.50	7.00	17.50	40.00	60.00
1928A	1,593,000	40.00	100	200	480	750
1929A	5,831,000	1.50	3.00	10.00	30.00	50.00
1930A	6,608,000	1.50	3.00	7.50	30.00	50.00
1931A Proof	100	Value: 400				

KM# 16.2 10 CENTS
2.7000 g., 0.6800 Silver 0.0590 oz. ASW **Obv:** Liberty seated left, date below **Rev:** Denomination within wreath **Rev. Leg.:** TITRE 0.680 POIDS 2 GR. 7

Date	Mintage	F	VF	XF	Unc	BU
1937(a)	25,000,000	1.00	1.50	3.00	8.00	10.00

KM# 21.1 10 CENTS
Nickel, 18 mm. **Obv:** Bust right holding laurel, date without dots **Rev:** Plant divides denomination **Note:** These coins are magnetic.

Date	Mintage	F	VF	XF	Unc	BU
1939(a)	16,841,000	0.50	1.00	2.00	8.00	10.00
1940(a)	25,505,000	0.50	1.00	2.00	8.00	10.00

KM# 21.1a 10 CENTS
3.0000 g., Copper-Nickel, 17.96 mm. **Obv:** Date without dots **Rev:** Plant divides denomination **Edge:** Reeded **Note:** These coins are not magnetic.

Date	Mintage	F	VF	XF	Unc	BU
1939(a)	—	45.00	100	100	375	—
Note: Mintage included in KM#21.2						
1941S	50,000,000	0.50	1.00	3.00	8.00	—

KM# 21.2 10 CENTS
Copper-Nickel, 18 mm. **Obv:** Date between two dots **Rev:** Plant divides denomination **Note:** These coins are not magnetic.

Date	Mintage	F	VF	XF	Unc	BU
.1939.(a)	2,237,000	65.00	140	250	475	—

KM# 28.1 10 CENTS
Aluminum, 23 mm. **Obv:** Bust right holding laurel, date below **Rev:** Plant divides denomination

Date	Mintage	F	VF	XF	Unc	BU
1945(a)	40,170,000	0.25	0.50	1.00	4.50	—

KM# 28.2 10 CENTS
Aluminum, 23 mm. **Obv:** Bust right holding laurel, date below **Rev:** Plant divides denomination

Date	Mintage	F	VF	XF	Unc	BU
1945B	9,830,000	1.00	2.00	5.00	12.50	—

KM# 10 20 CENTS
5.4000 g., 0.8350 Silver 0.1450 oz. ASW

Date	Mintage	F	VF	XF	Unc	BU
1901	1,375,000	20.00	50.00	100	300	—
1902	3,525,000	7.50	15.00	40.00	175	—
1903	675,000	50.00	100	150	600	—
1908	500,000	100	250	400	850	—
1909	500,000	100	200	350	850	—
1911	2,340,000	7.50	15.00	35.00	120	—
1912	160,000	100	200	400	900	1,100
1913	1,252,000	50.00	100	150	400	—
1914	2,500,000	7.50	15.00	25.00	120	—
1916	1,000,000	20.00	45.00	120	280	—

KM# 13 20 CENTS
0.8350 Silver **Obv:** KM#10 **Rev:** KM#3a **Note:** Mule.

Date	Mintage	F	VF	XF	Unc	BU
1909	—	100	250	650	1,000	1,400

KM# 15 20 CENTS
6.0000 g., 0.4000 Silver 0.0772 oz. ASW **Rev:** Without fineness indicated **Note:** Without mint mark.

Date	Mintage	F	VF	XF	Unc	BU
1920	4,000,000	12.50	25.00	50.00	125	—

KM# 17.1 20 CENTS
5.4000 g., 0.6800 Silver 0.1181 oz. ASW **Obv:** Seated liberty left, date below **Rev:** Denomination within wreath **Rev. Leg.:** TITRE O.680 POIDS 5 GR. 4

Date	Mintage	F	VF	XF	Unc	BU
1921A	3,663,000	4.00	10.00	20.00	40.00	—
1922A	5,812,000	3.00	6.00	12.00	25.00	—
1923A	7,109,000	3.00	6.00	12.00	25.00	—
1924A	1,400,000	8.00	20.00	40.00	90.00	—
1925A	2,556,000	6.00	15.00	30.00	75.00	—
1927A	3,245,000	4.00	10.00	20.00	40.00	—
1928A	794,000	15.00	40.00	80.00	225	—
1929A	644,000	20.00	50.00	100	275	—
1930A	5,576,000	3.00	6.00	12.00	25.00	—

KM# 17.2 20 CENTS
5.4000 g., 0.6800 Silver 0.1181 oz. ASW **Obv:** Liberty seated, date below **Rev:** Denomination within wreath **Rev. Leg.:** TITRE O.680 POIDS 5 GR. 4

Date	Mintage	F	VF	XF	Unc	BU
1937(a)	17,500,000	1.75	2.50	6.00	12.00	—

KM# 23 20 CENTS
Nickel, 24 mm. **Obv:** Bust right holding laurel, date below **Rev:** Plant divides denomination **Note:** Magnetic coin with security edge.

Date	Mintage	F	VF	XF	Unc	BU
1939(a)	344,500	15.00	30.00	40.00	125	—

KM# 23a.1 20 CENTS
Copper-Nickel, 24 mm. **Obv:** Bust right holding laurel, date below **Rev:** Plant divides denomination **Edge:** Reeded **Note:** Non-magnetic coin.

Date	Mintage	F	VF	XF	Unc	BU
1939(a)	14,676,000	0.50	1.00	2.00	10.00	—
Note: Date between dots						

KM# 23a.2 20 CENTS
Copper-Nickel, 24 mm. **Obv:** Bust right holding laurel, date below **Rev:** Plant divides denomination **Edge:** Reeded **Note:** Non-magnetic coin.

Date	Mintage	F	VF	XF	Unc	BU
1941S	25,000,000	0.50	1.00	2.00	5.00	—
Note: Date between dots						

KM# 29.1 20 CENTS
Aluminum **Obv:** Bust right holding laurel, date below **Rev:** Plant divides denomination

Date	Mintage	F	VF	XF	Unc	BU
1945(a)	15,412,000	0.50	1.00	2.50	10.00	—

KM# 29.2 20 CENTS
Aluminum **Obv:** Bust right holding laurel, date below **Rev:** Plant divides denomination

Date	Mintage	F	VF	XF	Unc	BU
1945B	6,665,000	2.00	4.00	8.00	25.00	—

KM# 29.3 20 CENTS
Aluminum **Obv:** Bust right holding laurel, date below **Rev:** Plant divides denomination

Date	Mintage	F	VF	XF	Unc	BU
1945C	22,423,000	0.50	1.00	3.00	15.00	—

KM# 4a.2 50 CENTS
13.5000 g., 0.9000 Silver 0.3906 oz. ASW **Obv:** Liberty seated, date below **Rev:** Denomination within wreath **Rev. Leg.:** TITRE 0.900. POIDS 13 GR. 5

Date	Mintage	F	VF	XF	Unc	BU
1936(a)	4,000,000	7.50	9.00	12.00	25.00	—

KM# 31 50 CENTS
12.4700 g., Copper-Nickel **Obv:** Liberty seated, date below **Rev:** Denomination within wreath **Rev. Leg.:** BRONZE DE NICKEL

Date	Mintage	F	VF	XF	Unc	BU
1946(a)	32,292,000	2.00	4.00	9.00	25.00	—

KM# 5a.1 PIASTRE
27.0000 g., 0.9000 Silver 0.7812 oz. ASW **Obv:** Liberty seated left with fasces **Rev:** Denomination within wreath **Rev. Leg.:** TITRE 0.900 POIDS 27 GR.

Date	Mintage	F	VF	XF	Unc	BU
1901A	3,150,000	15.00	18.00	25.00	200	275
1902A	3,327,000	15.00	18.00	25.00	200	275
1903A	10,077,000	15.00	18.00	22.50	180	—
1904A	5,751,000	15.00	18.00	22.50	180	—
1905A	3,561,000	15.00	18.00	22.50	180	—
1906A	10,194,000	15.00	18.00	22.50	180	—
1907A	14,062,000	15.00	18.00	22.50	180	—
1908A	13,986,000	15.00	18.00	22.50	180	—
1909A	9,201,000	15.00	18.00	22.50	180	—
1910A	761,000	25.00	40.00	120	400	475
1913A	3,244,000	15.00	18.00	22.50	180	—
1924A	2,831,000	15.00	18.00	25.00	200	—
1925A	2,882,000	15.00	18.00	25.00	200	—
1926A	6,383,000	15.00	18.00	22.50	180	—
1927A	8,183,999	15.00	18.00	22.50	180	100
1928A	5,290,000	15.00	18.00	22.50	250	—

KM# 5a.2 PIASTRE
27.0000 g., 0.9000 Silver 0.7812 oz. ASW **Rev:** Denomination within wreath **Note:** Without mint mark.

Date	Mintage	F	VF	XF	Unc	BU
1921	4,850,000	15.00	20.00	40.00	200	175
1922	1,150,000	15.00	30.00	75.00	350	325

KM# 5a.3 PIASTRE
27.0000 g., 0.9000 Silver 0.7812 oz. ASW **Rev:** Denomination within wreath

Date	Mintage	F	VF	XF	Unc	BU
1921H	3,580,000	15.00	20.00	40.00	250	—
1922H	7,420,000	15.00	18.00	22.50	180	—

KM# 19 PIASTRE
20.0000 g., 0.9000 Silver 0.5787 oz. ASW **Obv:** Laureate head left **Rev:** Denomination and date within keyhole shape wreath

Date	Mintage	F	VF	XF	Unc	BU
1931(a)	16,000,000	15.00	20.00	40.00	90.00	—

FEDERATED STATES
French Union
STANDARD COINAGE

KM# 32.1 PIASTRE
Copper-Nickel, 34.5 mm. **Obv:** Bust right holding laurel, date below **Rev:** Grain sprigs below denomination **Note:** Security edge.

Date	Mintage	F	VF	XF	Unc	BU
1946(a)	2,520,000	7.50	12.50	35.00	85.00	135
1947(a)	261,000	15.00	35.00	75.00	160	300

KM# 32.2 PIASTRE
18.1300 g., Copper-Nickel, 34.5 mm. **Obv:** Bust right holding laurel, date below **Rev:** Denomination above plants **Edge:** Reeded **Note:** Similar coins dated 1946 with reverse legend: INDOCHINE - FRANCAISE are Essais.

Date	Mintage	F	VF	XF	Unc	BU
1947(a)	54,480,000	2.00	4.00	7.50	10.00	30.00

PIEFORTS

KM#	Date	Mintage	Identification	Mkt Val
P2	1908	—	Cent. Bronze. KM#12.1	480
P3	1920	—	20 Cents. Brass. Reeded edge. Medallic alignment. KM#15.	—
P4	1923	—	Cent. Bronze. Filled center hole. KM#12.1.	—
P5	19(30)	—	Cent. Bronze. France Y#81. Filled center hole; KM#12.1.	—
P6	19(30)	—	Cent. Aluminum-Bronze. France Y#81. Filled center hole; KM#12.1.	750
P7	19(31)	—	20 Cents. Medallic alignment.	500
P8	1939	—	1/2 Cent. Zinc. KM#20a.	325

PIEFORTS WITH ESSAI
Double thickness - Standard metals unless otherwise noted

KM#	Date	Mintage	Identification	Mkt Val
PE1	1908	—	Cent. Bronze. KM#12.1.	235
PE2	1923	—	5 Cents. Nickel-Brass. KM#18.1.	350
PE3	1931(a)	—	Piastre. Silver. Laureate head left. Denomination and date within keyhole shape wreath. KM#19.	2,000
PE4	1945(a)	104	10 Cents. Aluminum. KM#28.1.	180
PE5	1945(a)	104	20 Cents. Aluminum. KM#29.1.	200
PE6	1946(a)	104	5 Cents. Aluminum. KM#30.1.	120
PE7	1946(a)	104	50 Cents. Copper-Nickel center. KM#31.	275
PE8	1947(a)	104	Piastre. Copper-Nickel. KM#32.	425

TRIAL STRIKES

KM#	Date	Mintage	Identification	Mkt Val
TS1	1921	—	Piastre. 0.9000 Silver. Without collar.	—
TS4	1931	—	Piastre. KM#19 but struck in aluminum.	—
TS2	ND(1931)	—	Piastre. Uniface.	1,200
TS3	1931	—	Piastre. Uniface, denomination and date within keyhole shape wreath.	650

FRENCH OCEANIA

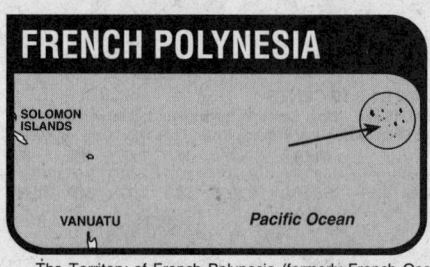

SOLOMON ISLANDS

NEW HEBRIDES   Pacific Ocean

The Colony of French Oceania (now the Territory of French Polynesia), comprising 130 basalt and coral islands scattered among five archipelagoes in the South Pacific, had an area of 1,544 sq. mi. (3,999 sq. km.). Capital: Papeete. The colony produced phosphates, copra and vanilla.

Tahiti of the Society Islands, the hub of French Oceania, was visited by Capt. Cook in 1769 and by Capt. Bligh on the Bounty 1788-89. The Society Islands were claimed by France in 1768, and in 1903 grouped with the Marquesas Islands, the Tuamotu Archipelago, the Gambier Islands and the Austral Islands under a single administrative head located at Papeete, Tahiti, to form the colony of French Oceania.

RULER
French

MINT MARKS
(a)   - Paris, privy marks only
(b)

MONETARY SYSTEM
100 Centimes = 1 Franc

FRENCH OVERSEAS TERRITORY
DECIMAL COINAGE

KM# 1 50 CENTIMES
Aluminum **Obv:** Seated Liberty with torch and cornucopia right, date below **Rev:** Inscription and island scene divide denomination

Date	Mintage	F	VF	XF	Unc	BU
1949(a)	795,000	0.50	0.75	1.50	3.00	6.50

KM# 2 FRANC
1.3100 g., Aluminum, 23.4 mm.

Date	Mintage	F	VF	XF	Unc	BU
1949(a)	2,000,000	0.20	0.35	1.00	2.00	3.00

KM# 3 2 FRANCS
Aluminum, 31 mm. **Obv:** Seated Liberty with torch and cornucopia right, date below

Date	Mintage	F	VF	XF	Unc	BU
1949(a)	1,000,000	0.40	0.60	1.25	2.50	4.00

KM# 4 5 FRANCS
Aluminum **Obv:** Seated Liberty with torch and cornucopia right, date below **Rev:** Inscription and island scene divide denomination

Date	Mintage	F	VF	XF	Unc	BU
1952	2,000,000	0.50	0.75	1.50	3.50	5.50

ESSAIS
Standard metals unless otherwise noted

KM#	Date	Mintage	Identification	Mkt Val
E1	1948	1,100	50 Centimes. Incuse design.	25.00
E2	1948	1,100	50 Centimes. Raised design.	25.00
E3	1948	1,100	Franc. Incuse design.	30.00
E4	1948	1,100	Franc. Raised design.	30.00
E5	1948	1,100	2 Francs. Copper-Nickel. 9.9800 g. 26.9 mm. Republic seated with grain spray and shield. Dhow divides denomination and date. Plain edge. Incuse design.	35.00
E6	1948	1,100	2 Francs. Copper-Nickel. 9.9800 g. 26.9 mm. Raised design.	35.00
E7	1949(a)	2,000	50 Centimes. Copper-Nickel. KM1	20.00
E8	1949(a)	2,000	Franc. Copper-Nickel. KM2	25.00
E9	1949(a)	2,000	2 Francs. Copper-Nickel. KM3	30.00
E10	1952(a)	1,200	5 Francs. Aluminum. KM4.	35.00

PIEFORTS WITH ESSAI
Double thickness - Standard metals unless otherwise noted

KM#	Date	Mintage	Identification	Mkt Val
PE1	1949(a)	104	50 Centimes.	60.00
PE2	1949(a)	104	Franc.	70.00
PE3	1949(a)	104	2 Francs.	80.00
PE4	1952(a)	104	5 Francs.	95.00

FRENCH POLYNESIA

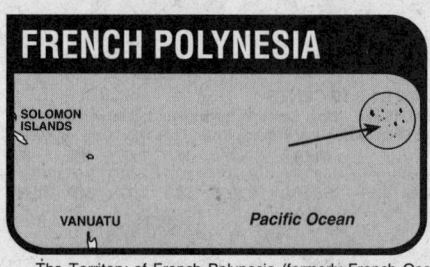

SOLOMON ISLANDS

VANUATU   Pacific Ocean

The Territory of French Polynesia (formerly French Oceania) has an area of 1,544 sq. mi. (3,941 sq. km.) and a population of 220,000. It is comprised of the same five archipelagoes that were grouped administratively to form French Oceania.

The colony of French Oceania became the Territory of French Polynesia by act of the French National Assembly in March, 1957. In Sept. of 1958 it voted in favor of the new constitution of the Fifth Republic, thereby electing to remain within the new French Community.

Picturesque, mountainous Tahiti, the setting of many tales of adventure and romance, is one of the most inspiringly beautiful islands in the world. Robert Louis Stevenson called it 'God's sweetest works'. It was there that Paul Gaugin, one of the pioneers of the Impressionist movement, painted the brilliant, exotic pictures that later made him famous. The arid coral atolls of Tuamotu comprise the most economically valuable area of French Polynesia. Pearl oysters thrive in the warm, limpid lagoons, and extensive portions of the atolls are valuable phosphate rock.

RULER
French

MINT MARKS
(a)   - Paris, privy marks only
(b)

MONETARY SYSTEM
100 Centimes = 1 Franc

FRENCH OVERSEAS TERRITORY
DECIMAL COINAGE

KM# 1 50 CENTIMES
Aluminum **Obv:** Seated Liberty with torch and cornucopia right, date below **Rev:** Legend and island scene divides denomination

Date	Mintage	F	VF	XF	Unc	BU
1965(a)	400,000	0.10	0.25	0.50	1.50	4.50

KM# 2 FRANC
Aluminum **Obv:** Seated Liberty with torch and cornucopia right, date below **Rev:** Legend and island scene divide denomination

Date	Mintage	F	VF	XF	Unc	BU
1965(a)	3,300,000	—	0.10	0.20	0.75	2.50

KM# 11   FRANC
1.3000 g., Aluminum, 23 mm. **Obv:** Seated Liberty with torch and cornucopia right, date below, legend added flanking figure's feet **Obv. Leg.:** I. E. O. M. **Rev:** Legend and island scene divide denomination

Date	Mintage	F	VF	XF	Unc	BU
1975(a)	2,000,000	—	0.10	0.15	0.45	2.50
1977(a)	2,000,000	—	0.10	0.15	0.45	1.75
1979(a)	1,500,000	—	0.10	0.15	0.45	1.25
1981(a)	2,000,000	—	0.10	0.15	0.45	1.25
1982(a)	1,000,000	—	0.10	0.15	0.45	1.25
1983(a)	2,200,000	—	0.10	0.15	0.45	1.25
1984(a)	1,500,000	—	0.10	0.15	0.45	1.25
1985(a)	2,000,000	—	0.10	0.15	0.45	1.25
1986(a)	2,000,000	—	0.10	0.15	0.45	1.25
1987(a)	2,000,000	—	0.10	0.15	0.45	1.25
1989(a)	1,000,000	—	0.10	0.15	0.45	1.25
1990(a)	1,500,000	—	0.10	0.15	0.45	1.00
1991(a)	1,400,000	—	0.10	0.15	0.35	1.00
1992(a)	800,000	—	0.10	0.15	0.35	1.00
1993(a)	2,300,000	—	0.10	0.15	0.35	1.00
1994(a)	1,000,000	—	0.10	0.15	0.30	1.00
1995(a)	1,000,000	—	0.10	0.15	0.30	1.00
1996(a)	2,700,000	—	0.10	0.15	0.30	1.00
1997(a)	1,100,000	—	0.10	0.15	0.25	0.75
1998(a)	1,600,000	—	0.10	0.15	0.25	0.75
1999(a)	2,600,000	—	0.10	0.15	0.25	0.75
2000(a)	3,000,000	—	0.10	0.15	0.25	0.75

KM# 3   2 FRANCS
Aluminum **Obv:** Seated Liberty with torch and cornucopia right, date below **Rev:** Legend and island scene divide denomination

Date	Mintage	F	VF	XF	Unc	BU
1965(a)	1,750,000	—	0.10	0.25	1.00	2.50

KM# 10   2 FRANCS
2.7000 g., Aluminum, 27 mm. **Obv:** Seated Liberty with torch and cornucopia right, date below, legend added flanking figure's feet **Obv. Leg.:** I. E. O. M. **Rev:** Legend and island scene divide denomination

Date	Mintage	F	VF	XF	Unc	BU
1973(a)	400,000	—	0.10	0.25	0.75	3.00
1975(a)	1,000,000	—	0.10	0.25	0.75	2.00
1977(a)	1,000,000	—	0.10	0.25	0.75	2.00
1979(a)	2,000,000	—	0.10	0.25	0.75	1.75
1982(a)	1,000,000	—	0.10	0.25	0.75	1.75
1983(a)	1,500,000	—	0.10	0.25	0.75	1.75
1984(a)	1,200,000	—	0.10	0.25	0.75	1.75
1985(a)	1,400,000	—	0.10	0.25	0.75	1.50
1986(a)	1,500,000	—	0.10	0.25	0.75	1.50
1987(a)	1,000,000	—	0.10	0.25	0.75	1.50
1988(a)	500,000	—	0.10	0.25	0.75	1.50
1989(a)	1,000,000	—	0.10	0.25	0.75	1.50
1990(a)	1,500,000	—	0.10	0.25	0.75	1.50
1991(a)	1,500,000	—	0.10	0.25	0.60	1.50
1992(a)	—	—	0.10	0.25	0.60	1.25
1993(a)	1,400,000	—	0.10	0.25	0.50	1.25
1995(a)	1,200,000	—	0.10	0.20	0.40	1.25
1996(a)	2,200,000	—	0.10	0.20	0.40	1.25
1997(a)	1,300,000	—	0.10	0.20	0.40	1.25
1998(a)	600,000	—	0.10	0.20	0.40	1.25
1999(a)	2,800,000	—	0.10	0.20	0.40	1.00
2000(a)	1,600,000	—	0.10	0.20	0.40	1.00

KM# 4   5 FRANCS
3.7500 g., Aluminum, 31 mm. **Obv:** Seated Liberty with torch and cornucopia right, date below **Rev:** Legend and island scene divide denomination

Date	Mintage	F	VF	XF	Unc	BU
1965(a)	1,520,000	0.10	0.25	0.50	1.75	3.50

KM# 12   5 FRANCS
3.7500 g., Aluminum, 31 mm. **Obv:** Seated Liberty with torch and cornucopia right, date below, legend added flanking figure's feet **Obv. Leg.:** I. E. O. M. **Rev:** Legend and island divide denomination

Date	Mintage	F	VF	XF	Unc	BU
1975(a)	500,000	0.10	0.20	0.40	1.25	3.25
1977(a)	500,000	0.10	0.20	0.40	1.25	2.25
1982(a)	500,000	0.10	0.20	0.40	1.25	2.25
1983(a)	800,000	0.10	0.20	0.40	1.25	2.00
1984(a)	600,000	0.10	0.20	0.40	1.25	2.00
1985(a)	—	0.10	0.20	0.40	1.25	2.00
1986(a)	600,000	0.10	0.20	0.40	1.25	2.00
1987(a)	400,000	0.10	0.20	0.40	1.25	1.75
1988(a)	400,000	0.10	0.20	0.40	1.25	1.75
1989(a)	—	0.10	0.20	0.40	1.25	1.75
1990(a)	500,000	0.10	0.20	0.40	1.25	1.75
1991(a)	700,000	0.10	0.20	0.40	1.00	1.50
1992(a)	500,000	0.10	0.20	0.40	1.00	1.50
1993(a)	400,000	0.10	0.20	0.35	0.85	1.25
1994(a)	500,000	0.10	0.20	0.35	0.70	1.25
1996(a)	100,000	0.10	0.20	0.35	0.75	1.25
1997(a)	500,000	0.10	0.20	0.35	0.85	1.25
1998(a)	800,000	0.10	0.20	0.35	0.70	1.25
1999(a)	600,000	0.10	0.20	0.35	0.65	1.25
2000(a)	900,000				0.50	1.00

KM# 5   10 FRANCS
Nickel **Obv:** Capped head left, date below **Rev:** Native art above denomination

Date	Mintage	F	VF	XF	Unc	BU
1967(a)	1,000,000	0.25	0.50	0.75	1.85	4.75

KM# 8   10 FRANCS
6.0000 g., Nickel, 24 mm. **Obv:** Capped head left, date and legend below **Obv. Leg.:** I. E. O. M. **Rev:** Native art, denomination below

Date	Mintage	F	VF	XF	Unc	BU
1972(a)	300,000	0.25	0.50	0.75	2.75	4.50
1973(a)	400,000	0.25	0.50	0.75	2.75	3.00
1975(a)	1,000,000	0.25	0.50	0.75	1.75	2.75
1979(a)	500,000	0.25	0.50	0.75	1.75	2.75
1982(a)	500,000	0.25	0.50	0.75	1.75	2.75
1983(a)	1,000,000	0.25	0.50	0.75	1.75	2.75
1984(a)	800,000	0.25	0.50	0.75	1.75	2.75
1985(a)	800,000	0.25	0.50	0.75	1.75	2.75
1986(a)	800,000	0.25	0.50	0.75	1.75	2.50
1991(a)	600,000	0.25	0.50	0.75	1.50	2.50
1992(a)	400,000	0.25	0.50	0.75	1.25	2.50
1993(a)	600,000	0.25	0.50	0.75	1.25	2.25

Date	Mintage	F	VF	XF	Unc	BU
1995(a)	500,000	0.25	0.50	0.70	1.00	2.00
1996(a)	300,000	0.25	0.50	0.70	1.00	2.00
1997(a)	300,000	0.25	0.50	0.70	1.00	2.00
1998(a)	1,000,000	0.25	0.45	0.65	0.85	1.75
1999(a)	2,000,000	0.25	0.45	0.65	0.85	1.75
2000(a)	1,200,000	0.25	0.45	0.65	0.85	1.75

KM# 6   20 FRANCS
10.0000 g., Nickel, 28.3 mm. **Obv:** Capped head left, date below **Rev:** Flowers, vanilla shoots, bread fruit

Date	Mintage	F	VF	XF	Unc	BU
1967(a)	750,000	0.35	0.75	1.25	3.00	4.50
1969(a)	250,000	0.35	1.00	2.00	7.00	9.00
1970(a)	500,000	0.35	0.75	1.25	3.25	3.75

KM# 9   20 FRANCS
10.0000 g., Nickel, 28.3 mm. **Obv:** Capped head left, date and legend below **Obv. Leg.:** I. E. O. M. **Rev:** Flowers, vanilla shoots, bread fruit

Date	Mintage	F	VF	XF	Unc	BU
1972(a)	300,000	0.30	0.50	1.00	3.00	5.50
1973(a)	300,000	0.30	0.50	1.00	3.00	4.50
1975(a)	700,000	0.30	0.50	1.00	2.25	3.50
1977(a)	350,000	0.35	0.75	1.50	4.50	7.50
1979(a)	500,000	0.30	0.50	1.00	2.25	3.50
1983(a)	800,000	0.30	0.50	1.00	2.25	3.50
1984(a)	600,000	0.30	0.50	1.00	2.25	3.50
1986(a)	400,000	0.30	0.50	1.00	2.25	3.00
1988(a)	250,000	0.30	0.50	1.00	2.25	3.00
1991(a)	—	0.30	0.50	1.00	2.00	3.00
1992(a)	—	0.30	0.50	1.00	2.00	3.00
1993(a)	—	0.30	0.50	1.00	1.75	2.50
1995(a)	—	0.30	0.50	1.00	1.75	2.50
1996(a)	—	0.30	0.50	0.85	1.50	2.25
1997(a)	—	0.30	0.50	0.85	1.50	2.25
1998(a)	—	0.30	0.50	0.85	1.35	2.00
1999(a)	—	0.30	0.50	0.85	1.35	2.00
2000(a)	—	—			1.25	1.75

KM# 7   50 FRANCS
15.0000 g., Nickel, 33 mm. **Obv:** Capped head left, date below **Rev:** Denomination above Moorea Harbor

Date	Mintage	F	VF	XF	Unc	BU
1967(a)	600,000	0.60	1.00	2.00	5.00	8.00

KM# 13   50 FRANCS
15.0000 g., Nickel, 33 mm. **Obv:** Capped head left, date and legend below **Obv. Leg.:** I. E. O. M. **Rev:** Denomination above Moorea Harbor

Date	Mintage	F	VF	XF	Unc	BU
1975(a)	500,000	0.60	0.80	1.25	4.00	7.50
1982(a)	500,000	0.60	0.80	1.25	4.00	6.00

Date	Mintage	F	VF	XF	Unc	BU
1985(a)	Inc. above	0.60	0.80	1.25	4.00	6.00
1988(a)	125,000	0.60	0.80	1.25	4.00	7.00
1991(a)	—	0.60	0.80	1.25	3.50	5.00
1995(a)	—	0.60	0.75	1.20	2.00	3.00
1996(a)	—	0.60	0.75	1.00	1.50	2.50
1998(a)	—	0.60	0.75	1.00	1.50	2.50
1999(a)	—	0.60	0.75	1.00	1.50	2.50
2000(a)	—	—	—	—	1.50	2.50

KM# 14   100 FRANCS
10.0000 g., Nickel-Bronze, 30 mm. **Obv:** Capped head left, date below **Rev:** Denomination above Moorea Harbor

Date	Mintage	F	VF	XF	Unc	BU
1976(a)	2,000,000	1.20	1.50	2.00	4.00	9.00
1979(a)	150	—	—	—	—	—
1982(a)	1,000,000	1.20	1.50	2.25	5.00	8.50
1984(a)	500,000	1.20	1.50	2.25	5.00	8.00
1986(a)	400,000	1.20	1.50	2.25	5.00	8.00
1987(a)	500,000	1.20	1.50	2.25	5.00	8.00
1988(a)	500,000	1.20	1.50	2.25	5.00	7.50
1991(a)	—	1.20	1.50	2.25	4.25	7.00
1992(a)	—	1.20	1.50	2.25	4.00	7.00
1995(a)	—	1.20	1.50	2.25	3.50	6.50
1996(a)	—	1.20	1.50	2.00	3.00	6.50
1997(a)	—	1.20	1.50	2.00	3.00	6.00
1998(a)	—	1.00	1.25	1.75	2.50	5.00
1999(a)	—	—	—	—	2.50	5.00
2000(a)	—	—	—	—	2.00	3.50

ESSAIS
Standard metals unless otherwise noted

KM#	Date	Mintage	Identification	Mkt Val
E1	1967(a)	1,700	100 Francs. Nickel. KM5.	20.00
E2	1967(a)	1,700	20 Francs. Nickel. KM6.	25.00
E3	1967(a)	1,700	50 Francs. Nickel. KM7.	30.00
E4	1976(a)	1,900	100 Francs. Nickel-Bronze. KM14.	35.00

PIEFORTS

KM#	Date	Mintage	Identification	Mkt Val
P1	1967(a)	500	10 Francs. Nickel. KM5.	25.00
P2	1967(a)	50	10 Francs. 0.9500 Silver. KM5.	120
P3	1967(a)	20	10 Francs. 0.9200 Gold. KM5.	950
P4	1967(a)	500	20 Francs. Nickel. KM6.	25.00
P5	1967(a)	50	20 Francs. 0.9500 Silver. KM6.	140
P6	1967(a)	20	20 Francs. 0.9200 Gold. KM6.	1,250
P7	1967(a)	500	50 Francs. Nickel. KM7.	30.00
P8	1967(a)	50	50 Francs. 0.9500 Silver. KM7.	180
P9	1967(a)	20	50 Francs. 0.9200 Gold. KM7.	1,450
P10	1979(a)	150	50 Centimes. Aluminum. KM11.	20.00
P11	1979(a)	250	50 Centimes. 0.9250 Silver. KM11.	75.00
P12	1979(a)	93	50 Centimes. 0.9200 Gold. KM11.	450
P13	1979(a)	150	2 Francs. Aluminum. KM10.	30.00
P14	1979(a)	250	2 Francs. 0.9250 Silver. KM10.	85.00
P15	1979(a)	94	2 Francs. 0.9200 Gold. KM10.	650
P16	1979(a)	150	5 Francs. Aluminum. KM12.	40.00
P17	1979(a)	250	5 Francs. 0.9250 Silver. KM12.	90.00
P18	1979(a)	95	5 Francs. 0.9200 Gold. KM12.	900
P19	1979(a)	150	10 Francs. Nickel. KM8.	50.00
P20	1979(a)	250	10 Francs. 0.9250 Silver. KM8.	90.00
P21	1979(a)	94	10 Francs. 0.9200 Gold. KM8.	700
P22	1979(a)	150	20 Francs. Nickel. KM9.	55.00
P23	1979(a)	250	20 Francs. 0.9250 Silver. KM9.	110
P24	1979(a)	93	20 Francs. 0.9200 Gold. KM9.	850
P25	1979(a)	150	50 Francs. Nickel. KM13.	60.00
P26	1979(a)	250	50 Francs. 0.9250 Silver. KM13.	130
P27	1979(a)	94	50 Francs. 0.9200 Gold. KM13.	1,900
P28	1979(a)	150	100 Francs. Nickel-Bronze. KM14.	75.00
P29	1979(a)	350	100 Francs. 0.9250 Silver. KM14.	150
P30	1979(a)	98	100 Francs. 0.9200 Gold. KM14.	2,000

"FDC" SETS

KM#	Date	Mintage	Identification	Issue Price	Mkt Val
SS1	1965 (4)	2,200	KM1-4	—	10.00
SS2	1967 (3)	2,200	K5-7	10.00	17.00

FRENCH SOMALILAND

French Somaliland is located in northeast Africa at the Bab el Mandeb Strait connecting the Suez Canal and the Red Sea with the Gulf of Aden and the Indian Ocean. French interest in French Somaliland began in 1839 with concessions obtained by a French naval lieutenant from the provincial sultans. French Somaliland was made a protectorate in 1884 and its boundaries were delimited by the Franco-British and Ethiopian accords of 1887 and 1897. It became a colony in 1896 and a territory within the French Union in 1946.

NOTE: For later coinage see French Afars & Issas.

MINT MARK
(a) - Paris (privy marks only)

MONETARY SYSTEM
100 Centimes = 1 Franc

FRENCH OVERSEAS TERRITORY

DECIMAL COINAGE

KM# 4   FRANC
Aluminum **Obv:** Winged head left, date below **Rev:** Lyre antelope divides denomination

Date	Mintage	F	VF	XF	Unc	BU
1948(a)	200,000	6.50	12.50	25.00	45.00	75.00
1949(a)	Inc. above	8.00	15.00	30.00	60.00	95.00

KM# 8   FRANC
1.3000 g., Aluminum, 22.8 mm. **Obv:** Winged head left, date below **Rev:** Lyre antelope divides denomination

Date	Mintage	F	VF	XF	Unc	BU
1959(a)	500,000	0.25	0.50	1.50	3.00	5.00
1965(a)	200,000	0.35	0.60	2.00	4.00	6.00

KM# 5   2 FRANCS
Aluminum **Obv:** Winged head left, date below **Rev:** Lyre antelope divides denomination

Date	Mintage	F	VF	XF	Unc	BU
1948(a)	200,000	6.50	12.50	25.00	60.00	80.00
1949(a)	Inc. above	8.00	15.00	30.00	70.00	95.00

KM# 9   2 FRANCS
2.2000 g., Aluminum **Obv:** Winged head left, date below **Rev:** Lyre antelope divides denomination

Date	Mintage	F	VF	XF	Unc	BU
1959(a)	200,000	0.25	0.75	2.50	5.00	7.00
1965(a)	240,000	0.25	0.75	2.50	5.00	7.00

KM# 6   5 FRANCS
Aluminum **Obv:** Winged head left, date below **Rev:** Lyre antelope divides denomination

Date	Mintage	F	VF	XF	Unc	BU
1948(a)	500,000	5.00	10.00	25.00	45.00	75.00

KM# 10   5 FRANCS
3.6600 g., Aluminum **Obv:** Winged head left, date below **Rev:** Lyre antelope divides denomination

Date	Mintage	F	VF	XF	Unc	BU
1959(a)	500,000	0.25	0.75	2.50	5.50	7.50
1965(a)	200,000	0.25	0.75	3.00	6.50	8.50

KM# 11   10 FRANCS
Aluminum-Bronze **Obv:** Winged head left, date below **Rev:** Dhow, ocean liner, denomination above

Date	Mintage	F	VF	XF	Unc	BU
1965(a)	250,000	0.50	1.00	3.00	6.00	8.00

KM# 7   20 FRANCS
3.9600 g., Aluminum-Bronze **Obv:** Winged head left, date below **Rev:** Dhow, ocean liner, denomination above

Date	Mintage	F	VF	XF	Unc	BU
1952(a)	500,000	1.25	2.50	4.50	10.00	12.00

KM# 12   20 FRANCS
Aluminum-Bronze **Obv:** Winged head left, date below **Rev:** Dhow, ocean liner, denomination above

Date	Mintage	F	VF	XF	Unc	BU
1965(a)	200,000	1.00	2.00	4.00	8.00	10.00

ESSAIS
Standard metals unless otherwise noted

KM#	Date	Mintage	Identification	Mkt Val
E1	1948(a)	2,000	Franc. Copper-Nickel. KM4.	12.00
E2	1948(a)	2,000	2 Francs. Copper-Nickel. KM5.	15.00
E3	1948(a)	2,000	5 Francs. Copper-Nickel. KM6	18.00
E4	1952(a)	1,200	20 Francs. Aluminum-Bronze. KM7	22.00
E5	1965(a)	2,000	10 Francs. Aluminum-Bronze center. KM11	20.00

PIEFORTS WITH ESSAI
Standard metals unless otherwise noted

KM#	Date	Mintage	Identification	Mkt Val
PE1	1948(a)	104	Franc.	70.00
PE2	1948(a)	104	2 Francs.	80.00
PE3	1948(a)	104	5 Francs.	90.00
PE4	1952(a)	104	20 Francs.	100

"FDC" SETS

KM#	Date	Mintage Identification	Issue Price	Mkt Val
SS1	1965 (5)	1,898 KM#8-12; Issued with French Polynesia	—	40.00

FRENCH WEST AFRICA

French West Africa (Afrique Occidentale Francaise), a former federation of French colonial territories on the northwest coast of Africa, had an area of 1,831,079 sq. mi. (4,742,495 sq. km.) and a population of about 17.4 million. Capital: Dakar. The constituent territories were Mauritania, Senegal, Dahomey, French Sudan, Ivory Coast, Upper Volta, Niger, French Guinea, and later on the mandated area of Togo. Peanuts, palm kernels, cacao, coffee and bananas were exported.

Prior to the mid-19th century, France, as the other European states, maintained establishments on the west coast of Africa for the purpose of trading in slaves and gum, but made no serious attempt at colonization. From 1854 onward, the coastal settlements were gradually extended into the interior until, by the opening of the 20th century, acquisition ended and organization and development began. French West Africa was formed in 1895 by grouping the several colonies under one administration (at Dakar) while retaining a large measure of autonomy to each of the constituent territories. The inhabitants of French West Africa were made French citizens in 1946. With the exception of French Guinea, all of the colonies voted in 1958 to become autonomous members of the new French Community. French Guinea voted to become the fully independent Republic of Guinea. The present-day independent states are members of the "Union Monetaire Ouest-Africaine". For later coinage see West African States.

RULERS
French

MINT MARKS
(a) - Paris, privy marks only
(L) – London

MONETARY SYSTEM
100 Centimes = 1 Franc
5 Francs = 1 Unit

FRENCH COLONIES

COLONIAL COINAGE

KM# 1   50 CENTIMES
Aluminum-Bronze **Obv:** Laureate head left **Rev:** Cornucopias flank denomination and date

Date	Mintage	F	VF	XF	Unc	BU
1944(L)	10,000,000	2.00	4.00	15.00	28.00	32.00
1944(L) Proof	—	Value: 200				

KM# 2   FRANC
Aluminum-Bronze **Obv:** Laureate head left **Rev:** Cornucopias flank denomination and date

Date	Mintage	F	VF	XF	Unc	BU
1944(L)	15,000,000	1.00	2.00	10.00	20.00	25.00
1944(L) Proof	—	Value: 250				

KM# 3   FRANC
Aluminum **Obv:** Winged head left, date below **Rev:** Rhim gazelle facing divides denomination

Date	Mintage	F	VF	XF	Unc	BU
1948(a)	30,110,000	0.15	0.20	2.00	4.00	5.00
1955(a)	5,200,000	0.20	0.35	1.00	3.00	4.00

KM# 4   2 FRANCS
2.2400 g., Aluminum, 27 mm. **Obv:** Winged head left, date below **Rev:** Rhim gazelle facing divides denomination

Date	Mintage	F	VF	XF	Unc	BU
1948(a)	12,665,000	0.20	0.30	0.50	1.75	2.75
1955(a)	1,400,000	0.25	0.40	5.00	12.00	14.00

KM# 5   5 FRANCS
Aluminum-Bronze **Obv:** Head left divides date above **Rev:** Rhim gazelle facing, divides denomination

Date	Mintage	F	VF	XF	Unc	BU
1956(a)	85,000,000	0.35	0.50	1.00	2.50	5.00

KM# 6   10 FRANCS
Aluminum-Bronze, 23.5 mm. **Obv:** Head left, divides date above **Rev:** Rhim gazelle facing divides denomination

Date	Mintage	F	VF	XF	Unc	BU
1956(a)	20,000,000	0.50	1.00	1.50	3.50	6.00

KM# 8   10 FRANCS
3.9200 g., Aluminum-Bronze, 23.9 mm. **Obv:** Fish divides denomination **Rev:** Rhim gazelle facing, date below **Note:** Issued for circulation in French West Africa, including Togo.

Date	Mintage	F	VF	XF	Unc	BU
1957(a)	30,000,000	0.50	1.00	1.50	3.00	5.00

KM# 7   25 FRANCS
Aluminum-Bronze **Obv:** Head left divides date above **Rev:** Rhim gazelle facing, divides denomination

Date	Mintage	F	VF	XF	Unc	BU
1956(a)	37,877,000	0.50	1.00	2.00	5.50	8.00

KM# 9   25 FRANCS
Aluminum-Bronze **Obv:** Fish divides denomination **Rev:** Rhim gazelle facing, date below **Note:** Also issued for circulation in Togo.

Date	Mintage	F	VF	XF	Unc	BU
1957(a)	30,000,000	0.50	1.00	3.00	5.00	7.00

ESSAIS
Standard metals unless otherwise noted

KM#	Date	Mintage Identification	Mkt Val
E1	1948(a)	2,000 Franc. Copper-Nickel. KM3.	25.00
E2	1948	2,000 2 Francs. Copper-Nickel. KM4.	30.00
E3	1956(a)	2,300 5 Francs. Aluminum-Bronze. KM5	16.00
E4	1956(a)	2,300 10 Francs. Aluminum-Bronze. KM6.	20.00
E5	1956(a)	2,300 25 Francs. Aluminum-Bronze. KM7	22.00
E6	1957(a)	— 10 Francs. Aluminum-Bronze. KM8	20.00
E7	1957(a)	— 25 Francs. Aluminum-Bronze. KM9	22.00

PIEFORTS WITH ESSAI
Double thickness - Standard metals unless otherwise noted

KM#	Date	Mintage Identification	Mkt Val
PE1	1948(a)	104 Franc. Aluminum. KM3.	50.00
PE2	1948(a)	104 2 Francs. Aluminum. KM4.	60.00

FUJAIRAH

An original member of the United Arab Emirates, al-Fujairah is the only emirate that does not have territory on the Persian Gulf. It is on the eastern side of the "horn" of Oman. It has an estimated area of 450 sq. mi. (1200 sq. km.) and a population of 27,000. Al-Fujairah has been, historically a frequent rival of Sharjah. As recently as 1952 Great Britain recognized al-Fujairah as an autonomous state.

TITLES

الفجيرة

al Fujaira(t)

RULERS
Muhammad bin Hamad al-Sharqi, 1952-74
Hamad bin Muhammad al-Sharqi, 1974--

EMIRATE
NON-CIRCULATING
LEGAL TENDER COINAGE

KM# 1   RIYAL
3.0000 g., 1.0000 Silver 0.0964 oz. ASW **Ruler:** Muhammad bin Hamad al-Sharqi **Subject:** Desert Fort **Obv:** Arms-flags above rifles on pointed shield **Rev:** Arms below fort

Date	Mintage	F	VF	XF	Unc	BU
AH1388-1969 Proof	4,050	Value: 25.00				
AH1389-1970 Proof	Inc. above	Value: 25.00				

KM# 2   2 RIYALS
6.0000 g., 1.0000 Silver 0.1929 oz. ASW **Ruler:** Muhammad bin Hamad al-Sharqi **Subject:** President Richard Nixon **Obv:** Arms-flags above rifles on pointed shield **Rev:** Head 3/4 right

Date	Mintage	F	VF	XF	Unc	BU
AH1388-1969 Proof	6,250	Value: 30.00				
AH1389-1970 Proof	Inc. above	Value: 30.00				

KM# 3   5 RIYALS
15.0000 g., 1.0000 Silver 0.4822 oz. ASW **Ruler:** Muhammad bin Hamad al-Sharqi **Series:** 1972 Munich Olympics **Obv:** Arms-flags above rifles on pointed shield **Rev:** Olympic rings, logo and torch

Date	Mintage	F	VF	XF	Unc	BU
AH1388-1969 Proof	3,550	Value: 55.00				
AH1389-1970 Proof	1,300	Value: 60.00				

KM# 7   25 RIYALS
5.1800 g., 0.9000 Gold 0.1499 oz. AGW **Ruler:** Muhammad bin Hamad al-Sharqi **Subject:** U.S. President Richard Nixon **Obv:** Arms-flags above rifles on pointed shield **Rev:** Head 3/4 right

Date	Mintage	F	VF	XF	Unc	BU
AH1388-1969 Proof	3,280	Value: 165				
Note: Fineness incuse						
AH1389-1970 Proof	Inc. above	Value: 165				
Note: Fineness both raised and incuse						

KM# 19   10 RIYALS
30.0000 g., 1.0000 Silver 0.9645 oz. ASW **Ruler:** Muhammad bin Hamad al-Sharqi **Obv:** Arms **Rev:** Five shields at left, Arab riders and sun at right

Date	Mintage	F	VF	XF	Unc	BU
AH1389-1969 Proof	15,000	Value: 55.00				

KM# 4.1   10 RIYALS
30.0000 g., 1.0000 Silver 0.9645 oz. ASW **Ruler:** Muhammad bin Hamad al-Sharqi **Subject:** Apollo XI **Obv:** Arms, fineness in oval at lower left, mintage figure at lower right **Rev:** Astronauts, moon and stars, dates at upper left

Date	Mintage	F	VF	XF	Unc	BU
AH1388-1969 Proof	14,000	Value: 60.00				

KM# 8   50 RIYALS
10.3600 g., 0.9000 Gold 0.2998 oz. AGW **Ruler:** Muhammad bin Hamad al-Sharqi **Series:** 1972 Munich Olympics **Obv:** Arms-flags above rifles on pointed shield **Rev:** Olympic logo and symbols with date

Date	Mintage	F	VF	XF	Unc	BU
AH1388-1969 Proof	1,230	Value: 280				
AH1389-1970 Proof	400	Value: 300				

KM# 20   10 RIYALS
30.0000 g., 1.0000 Silver 0.9645 oz. ASW **Ruler:** Muhammad bin Hamad al-Sharqi **Subject:** Visit of Pope Paul VI to Philippines **Obv:** Arms-flags above rifles on pointed shield **Rev:** Buildings, Pope's profile at right

Date	Mintage	F	VF	XF	Unc	BU
AH1389-1969 Proof	300	Value: 85.00				

KM# 4.2   10 RIYALS
30.0000 g., 1.0000 Silver 0.9645 oz. ASW **Ruler:** Muhammad bin Hamad al-Sharqi **Obv:** Arms, mintage figure stamped at lower left, fineness in oval at lower right **Rev:** Astronauts, moon and stars, dates upper left

Date	Mintage	F	VF	XF	Unc	BU
AH1389-1969 Proof	—	Value: 60.00				

KM# 9   100 RIYALS
20.7300 g., 0.9000 Gold 0.5998 oz. AGW **Ruler:** Muhammad bin Hamad al-Sharqi **Subject:** Apollo X **Obv:** Arms-flags above rifles on pointed shield **Rev:** Three astronauts and moon

Date	Mintage	F	VF	XF	Unc	BU
AH1388-1969 Proof	2,140	Value: 575				

KM# 21   10 RIYALS
30.0000 g., 1.0000 Silver 0.9645 oz. ASW **Ruler:** Muhammad bin Hamad al-Sharqi **Subject:** Visit of Pope Paul VI to Australia **Obv:** Arms-flags above rifles on pointed shield **Rev:** Pope's profile at left, crown with keys and kangaroo on map at right

Date	Mintage	F	VF	XF	Unc	BU
AH1389-1969 Proof	12,000	Value: 85.00				

KM# 5   10 RIYALS
30.0000 g., 1.0000 Silver 0.9645 oz. ASW **Ruler:** Muhammad bin Hamad al-Sharqi **Subject:** Apollo XII **Obv:** Arms **Rev:** Four shields on moon background at left, astronauts aligned on large shield at right

Date	Mintage	F	VF	XF	Unc	BU
AH1388-1969 Proof	15,000	Value: 50.00				
AH1389-1969 Proof	15,000	Value: 50.00				

KM# 10   100 RIYALS
20.7300 g., 0.9000 Gold 0.5998 oz. AGW **Ruler:** Muhammad bin Hamad al-Sharqi **Subject:** Apollo XII **Obv:** Arms-flags above rifles on pointed shield **Rev:** Four shields on moon surface at left, three astronauts on shield at right

Date	Mintage	F	VF	XF	Unc	BU
AH1388-1969 Proof	3,040	Value: 550				
AH1389-1970 Proof	—	Value: 550				

KM# 23   100 RIYALS
20.7300 g., 0.9000 Gold 0.5998 oz. AGW **Ruler:** Muhammad bin Hamad al-Sharqi **Subject:** Apollo XIII **Obv:** Arms-flags above rifles on pointed shield **Rev:** Five shields at left, Arab riders and sun at right

Date	Mintage	F	VF	XF	Unc	BU
AH1389-1970 Proof	600	Value: 600				

KM# 24   100 RIYALS
20.7300 g., 0.9000 Gold 0.5998 oz. AGW **Ruler:** Muhammad bin Hamad al-Sharqi **Subject:** Visit of Pope Paul VI to Philippines **Obv:** Arms-flags above rifles on pointed shield **Rev:** Buildings, Pope's profile at right

Date	Mintage	F	VF	XF	Unc	BU
AH1389-1970 Proof	290	Value: 650				

KM# 22   10 RIYALS
30.0000 g., 1.0000 Silver 0.9645 oz. ASW **Ruler:** Muhammad bin Hamad al-Sharqi **Subject:** Apollo XIV **Obv:** Arms-flags above rifles on pointed shield **Rev:** Moon above shooting star within ring, planet lower left

Date	Mintage	F	VF	XF	Unc	BU
AH1389-1969 Proof	14,000	Value: 75.00				

KM# 26   100 RIYALS
20.7300 g., 0.9000 Gold 0.5998 oz. AGW **Ruler:** Muhammad bin Hamad al-Sharqi **Subject:** Visit of Pope Paul VI to Australia **Obv:** Arms-flags above rifles on pointed shield **Rev:** Pope's profile at left, crown with keys and kangaroo on map at right

Date	Mintage	F	VF	XF	Unc	BU
AH1389-1970 Proof	250	Value: 650				

KM# 25   100 RIYALS
20.7300 g., 0.9000 Gold 0.5998 oz. AGW **Ruler:** Muhammad bin Hamad al-Sharqi **Subject:** Apollo XIV **Obv:** Arms-flags above rifles on pointed shield **Rev:** Moon above shooting star within ring, planet lower left

Date	Mintage	F	VF	XF	Unc	BU
AH1389-1971 Proof	550	Value: 550				

KM# 11   200 RIYALS
41.4600 g., 0.9000 Gold 1.1996 oz. AGW **Ruler:** Muhammad bin Hamad al-Sharqi **Subject:** Mohamad bin Hamad al-Sharqi **Obv:** Arms-flags above rifles on pointed shield **Rev:** Bust left

Date	Mintage	F	VF	XF	Unc	BU
AH1388-1969 Proof	680	Value: 1,250				

Note: Serially numbered on the obverse

PROOF SETS

KM#	Date	Mintage	Identification	Issue Price	Mkt Val
PS1	1969-71 (18)	—		—	
PS2	1969-71 (9)	—	KM#1-4.2, 5, 19-22	—	525
PS3	1969-71 (8)	—	KM#4.2, 5, 19, 22, 9, 10, 23, 25	—	2,525
PS4	1969 (8)	—	KM#1-4.2, 7-9, 11	—	2,400
PS5	1969 (5)	2,550	KM#1-4.2, 5	40.00	220
PS6	1969 (5)	5,000	KM#7-11	280	2,775
PS7	1969 (4)	—	KM#1-4.2	—	170
PS8	1970 (5)	200	KM#1-4.2, 5	40.00	225

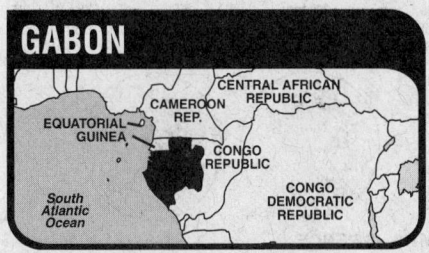

GABON

The Gabonese Republic, a member of the French Community, straddles the equator on the west coast of Africa. The hot and humid rain forest country has an area of 103,347 sq. mi. (267,670 sq. km.) and a population of 1.2 million, almost all of Bantu origin. Capital: Libreville. Extravagantly rich in resources, Gabon exports crude oil, manganese ore, gold and timbers.

Gabon was first visited by Portuguese navigator Diego Cam in the 15th century. Dutch, French and British traders, lured by the rich stands of hard woods and oil palms, quickly followed. The French founded their first settlement on the left bank of the Gabon River in 1839 and established their presence by signing treaties with the tribal chiefs. After gradually extending their influence into the interior during the last half of the 19th century, France occupied Gabon in 1885 and, in 1910, organized it as one of the four territories of French Equatorial Africa. It became an autonomous republic within the French Union in 1946, and on Aug. 17, 1960, became a completely independent republic within the new French Community.

For earlier coinage see French Equatorial Africa, Central African States and the Equatorial African States.

MINT MARKS
(a) - Paris, privy marks only
(t) - Poissy, privy marks only, thunderbolt

FRENCH EQUATORIAL AFRICAN TERRITORY
TOKEN COINAGE

Believed to be initially used for payment of taxes. These tokens do not show a denomination, but circulated until 1930 with varying values corresponding to the animals shown. All have center hole.

KM# Tn1   NON-DENOMINATED
Aluminum **Obv:** Date below center hole, "GABON" above **Rev:** Hole within elephant walking left

Date	Mintage	F	VF	XF	Unc	BU
1925(t)	—	55.00	100	200	400	750

KM# Tn2   NON-DENOMINATED
Aluminum **Obv:** Date below center hole, "GABON" above **Rev:** Center hole within leopard walking left

Date	Mintage	F	VF	XF	Unc	BU
1926	—	100	175	325	550	700

KM# Tn3   NON-DENOMINATED
Aluminum **Obv:** Date below center hole, "GABON" above **Rev:** Center hole within ox head facing

Date	Mintage	F	VF	XF	Unc	BU
1927(t)	—	75.00	150	250	450	650

KM# Tn4   NON-DENOMINATED
Aluminum **Obv:** Date below center hole, "GABON" above **Rev:** Center hole within pelican right

Date	Mintage	F	VF	XF	Unc	BU
1928	—	125	200	350	550	700

KM# Tn5   NON-DENOMINATED
Aluminum **Obv:** "Gabon" above center hole, date below **Rev:** Rhinoceros walking left

Date	Mintage	F	VF	XF	Unc	BU
1929	—	85.00	175	300	550	700

REPUBLIC
DECIMAL COINAGE

KM# 1   10 FRANCS
4.2000 g., 0.9000 Gold 0.1215 oz. AGW **Subject:** Independence **Obv:** Head of Mba right, date below **Rev:** Arms with supporters, denomination below

Date	Mintage	F	VF	XF	Unc	BU
1960 Proof	500	Value: 125				

KM# 2   25 FRANCS
8.0000 g., 0.9000 Gold 0.2315 oz. AGW **Subject:** Independence **Obv:** Head of Mba right, date below **Rev:** Arms with supporters, denomination below

Date	Mintage	F	VF	XF	Unc	BU
1960	10,000				220	
1960 Proof	500	Value: 235				

KM# 3   50 FRANCS
16.0000 g., 0.9000 Gold 0.4630 oz. AGW **Subject:** Independence **Obv:** Head of Mba right, date below **Rev:** Arms with supporters, denomination below

Date	Mintage	F	VF	XF	Unc	BU
1960 Proof	500	Value: 465				

KM# 4   100 FRANCS
32.0000 g., 0.9000 Gold 0.9259 oz. AGW **Subject:** Independence **Obv:** Head of Mba right, date below **Rev:** Arms with supporters, denomination

Date	Mintage	F	VF	XF	Unc	BU
1960 Proof	500	Value: 925				

KM# 12   100 FRANCS
Nickel, 25 mm. **Obv:** Three great eland left **Rev:** Denomination within circle, date below

Date	Mintage	F	VF	XF	Unc	BU
1971(a)	1,300,000	4.50	9.00	17.50	25.00	—
1972(a)	2,000,000	4.50	9.00	17.50	25.00	—

KM# 13   100 FRANCS
Nickel, 25 mm. **Obv:** Three great eland left **Rev:** Denomination within circle, date below

Date	Mintage	F	VF	XF	Unc	BU
1975(a)	—	2.00	4.00	7.50	15.00	22.00
1977(a)	—	3.00	6.50	12.50	24.00	30.00
1978(a)	—	2.50	4.50	9.00	18.50	26.00
1982(a)	—	1.75	3.50	6.50	10.00	15.00
1983(a)	—	1.75	3.50	6.50	10.00	15.00
1984(a)	—	1.75	3.50	6.50	10.00	15.00
1985(a)	—	1.75	3.50	6.50	10.00	15.00

KM# 14 500 FRANCS
Copper-Nickel **Obv:** Leafy plants divide denomination and date
Rev: Head left, inscription at right

Date	Mintage	F	VF	XF	Unc	BU
1985(a)	—	4.00	7.00	12.00	20.00	—

KM# 6 1000 FRANCS
3.5000 g., 0.9000 Gold 0.1013 oz. AGW **Obv:** Head of Bongo
left **Rev:** Stump of okume tree, denomination below, arms above

Date	Mintage	F	VF	XF	Unc	BU
1969 Proof	4,000	Value: 110				

KM# 7 3000 FRANCS
10.5000 g., 0.9000 Gold 0.3038 oz. AGW **Obv:** Head of Bongo
left **Rev:** Arms with supporters, denomination below

Date	Mintage	F	VF	XF	Unc	BU
1969 Proof	4,000	Value: 300				

KM# 8 5000 FRANCS
17.5000 g., 0.9000 Gold 0.5064 oz. AGW **Obv:** Head of Bongo left
Rev: Reliquary figure of Bakota, denomination below, arms above

Date	Mintage	F	VF	XF	Unc	BU
1969 Proof	4,000	Value: 500				

KM# 11 5000 FRANCS
17.5000 g., 0.9000 Gold 0.5064 oz. AGW **Subject:** Visit of
French President Georges Pompidou **Rev:** Head left

Date	Mintage	F	VF	XF	Unc	BU
1971 Proof	—	Value: 525				

KM# 9 10000 FRANCS
35.0000 g., 0.9000 Gold 1.0127 oz. AGW **Subject:** 1st Moon
landing **Obv:** Head of Bongo left **Rev:** Lunar module,
denomination below

Date	Mintage	F	VF	XF	Unc	BU
1969 Proof	4,000	Value: 950				

KM# 10 20000 FRANCS
70.0000 g., 0.9000 Gold 2.0254 oz. AGW **Subject:** 1st Moon
landing - Cape Kennedy **Obv:** Head of Bongo left **Rev:** Apollo XI
at launching pad, denomination below

Date	Mintage	F	VF	XF	Unc	BU
1969 Proof	4,000	Value: 1,950				

ESSAIS
Standard metals unless otherwise noted

KM#	Date	Mintage	Identification	Mkt Val
E1	1960	10	25 Francs. Gold. KM2.	750
E2	1960	—	25 Francs. Silver. KM2.	250
E3	1971(a)	1,450	100 Francs. KM12.	30.00
E4	1971(a)	4	100 Francs. Gold. KM12.	1,900
E5	1971(a)	—	5000 Francs. Copper-Aluminum-Nickel. KM11.	200
E6	1975(a)	1,700	100 Francs. Three great eland left. Denomination within circle, date below. KM13.	20.00
E7	1985(a)	1,700	500 Francs. Plants divide denomination and date. Head left, inscription at right. KM14.	30.00

PROOF SETS

KM#	Date	Mintage	Identification	Issue Price	Mkt Val
PS1	1960 (4)	500	KM1-4	—	1,750
PS2	1969 (5)	4,000	KM6-10	—	3,800

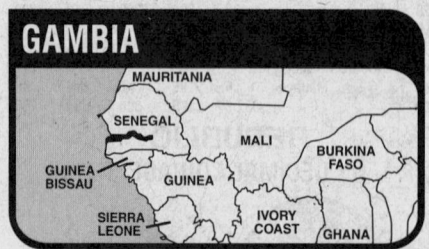

GAMBIA

The Republic of The Gambia, occupies a strip of land 7 miles
(11km.) to 20 miles (32 km.) wide and 200 miles (322 km.) long
encompassing both sides of West Africa's Gambia River, and
completely surrounded by Senegal. The republic, one of Africa's
smallest countries, has an area of 4,127 sq. mi. (11,300 sq. km.)
and a population of 989,273. Capital: Banjul. Agriculture and tourism are the principal industries. Peanuts constitute 95 per cent
of export earnings.

The Gambia was once part of the great empires of Ghana
and Songhay. When Portuguese gold seekers and slave traders
visited The Gambia in the 15th century, it was part of the Kingdom
of Mali. In 1588 the territory became, through purchase, the first
British colony in Africa. English slavers established Fort James,
the first settlement, on a small island a dozen miles up the Gambia River in 1664. After alternate periods of union with Sierra
Leone and existence as a separate colony The Gambia became
a British colony in 1888. On Feb. 18, 1965, The Gambia achieved
independence as a constitutional monarchy within the Commonwealth of Nations, with Elizabeth II as Head of State as
Queen of The Gambia. It became a republic on April 24, 1970,
remaining a member of the Commonwealth, but with the president as Chief of State and Head of Government.

Together with Senegal, The Gambia formed a confederation
on February 1, 1982. This confederation was officially dissolved
on September 21, 1989. In July, 1994 a military junta took control
of The Gambia and disbanded its elected government.

For earlier coinage see British West Africa.

RULER
British until 1970

MONETARY SYSTEM
12 Pence = 1 Shilling
20 Shillings = 1 Pound

COLONIAL
STERLING COINAGE

KM# 1 PENNY
Bronze, 25.5 mm. **Obv:** Young bust right **Rev:** Sailing vessel,
denomination at right **Edge:** Smooth

Date	Mintage	F	VF	XF	Unc	BU
1966	3,600,000	—	0.20	0.40	1.00	1.25
1966 Proof	6,600	Value: 1.00				

KM# 2 3 PENCE
Nickel-Brass, 21.5 mm. **Obv:** Young bust right **Rev:** Double-
spurred francolin, denomination above **Edge:** Smooth

Date	Mintage	F	VF	XF	Unc	BU
1966	2,000,000	—	0.30	0.50	1.50	2.00
1966 Proof	6,600	Value: 1.50				

KM# 3 6 PENCE
2.7700 g., Copper-Nickel, 19.5 mm. **Obv:** Young bust right
Rev: Peanuts divide denomination **Edge:** Reeded

Date	Mintage	F	VF	XF	Unc	BU
1966	1,500,000	—	0.30	0.50	1.75	2.00
1966 Proof	6,600	Value: 1.75				

KM# 4 SHILLING
5.8000 g., Copper-Nickel, 23.5 mm. **Obv:** Young bust right
Rev: Oil palm, denomination above **Edge:** Reeded

Date	Mintage	F	VF	XF	Unc	BU
1966	2,500,000	—	0.50	0.80	2.00	2.50
1966 Proof	6,600	Value: 2.00				

KM# 5   2 SHILLINGS

Copper-Nickel, 28.3 mm.   **Obv:** Young bust right **Rev:** African domestic ox divides denomination **Edge:** Reeded

Date	Mintage	F	VF	XF	Unc	BU
1966	1,600,000	—	0.75	1.50	2.50	3.00
1966 Proof	6,600	Value: 2.50				

KM# 6   4 SHILLINGS

Copper-Nickel, 34 mm.   **Obv:** Young bust right **Rev:** Slender-snouted crocodile, denomination at right **Edge:** Reeded

Date	Mintage	F	VF	XF	Unc	BU
1966	800,000	—	1.50	2.50	5.50	10.00
1966 Proof	6,600	Value: 8.00				

KM# 7   8 SHILLINGS

Copper-Nickel   **Obv:** Young bust right **Rev:** Hippopotamus, denomination above

Date	Mintage	F	VF	XF	Unc	BU
1970	25,000	—	2.00	4.00	12.00	17.50

KM# 7a   8 SHILLINGS

32.4000 g., 0.9250 Silver 0.9635 oz. ASW   **Obv:** Young bust right **Rev:** Hippopotamus, denomination above

Date	Mintage	F	VF	XF	Unc	BU
1970 Proof	4,500	Value: 35.00				

Note: VIP issued proofs have a frosted relief, value: $175.00.

REPUBLIC

DECIMAL COINAGE

100 Bututs = 1 Dalasi

KM# 8   BUTUT

1.8000 g., Bronze, 17.15 mm.   **Obv:** President's bust left **Rev:** Peanuts, denomination at right

Date	Mintage	F	VF	XF	Unc	BU
1971	12,449,000	—	—	0.10	0.20	0.30
1971 Proof	32,000	Value: 0.50				
1973	3,000,000	—	—	0.10	0.25	0.35
1974	19,060,000	—	0.25	0.50	1.50	2.00

KM# 14   BUTUT

Bronze   **Series:** F.A.O.   **Obv:** President's bust left **Rev:** Peanuts, denomination at right

---

Date	Mintage	F	VF	XF	Unc	BU
1974	26,062,000	—	—	0.10	0.20	0.30
1985	4,500,000	—	—	0.15	0.25	0.35

KM# 54   BUTUT

Copper Plated Steel, 17.6 mm.   **Obv:** National arms, date below **Rev:** Peanuts, denomination at right

Date	Mintage	F	VF	XF	Unc	BU
1998	—	—	—	—	0.20	0.30

KM# 9   5 BUTUTS

3.5500 g., Bronze, 20.3 mm.   **Obv:** President's bust left **Rev:** Sailing vessel, denomination at right

Date	Mintage	F	VF	XF	Unc	BU
1971	5,400,000	—	—	0.10	0.35	0.50
1971 Proof	32,000	Value: 0.60				

KM# 55   5 BUTUTS

Copper Plated Steel   **Obv:** National arms, date below **Rev:** Sailboat, denomination at right

Date	Mintage	F	VF	XF	Unc	BU
1998	—	—	—	—	0.35	0.50

KM# 10   10 BUTUTS

6.2000 g., Nickel-Brass, 25.9 mm.   **Obv:** President's bust left **Rev:** Double-spurred francolin, denomination at right

Date	Mintage	F	VF	XF	Unc	BU
1971	3,000,000	—	0.15	0.35	1.50	2.00
1971 Proof	32,000	Value: 2.00				

KM# 64   10 BUTUTS

24.7000 g., Copper-Nickel, 38.5 mm.   **Subject:** Marine Life Protection **Obv:** National arms **Rev:** Multicolor fish scene **Edge:** Reeded

Date	Mintage	F	VF	XF	Unc	BU
1997	—	—	—	—	27.50	—

KM# 56   10 BUTUTS

Brass Plated Steel, 26 mm.   **Obv:** National arms, date below **Rev:** Double-spurred francolin, denomination at right

Date	Mintage	F	VF	XF	Unc	BU
1998	—	—	—	—	1.00	1.50

KM# 11   25 BUTUTS

5.6500 g., Copper-Nickel, 23.6 mm.   **Obv:** President's bust left **Rev:** Oil palm, denomination above

Date	Mintage	F	VF	XF	Unc	BU
1971	3,040,000	—	0.15	0.30	0.75	1.00
1971 Proof	32,000	Value: 1.25				

KM# 57   25 BUTUTS

4.9700 g., Copper-Nickel, 23.9 mm.   **Obv:** National arms, date below **Rev:** Oil palm, denomination above

Date	Mintage	F	VF	XF	Unc	BU
1998	—	—	—	—	1.00	1.25

KM# 12   50 BUTUTS

11.3000 g., Copper-Nickel, 28.5 mm.   **Obv:** President's bust left **Rev:** African domestic ox divides denomination

Date	Mintage	F	VF	XF	Unc	BU
1971	1,700,000	—	0.35	0.65	1.75	2.50
1971 Proof	32,000	Value: 1.75				

KM# 60   50 BUTUTS

24.9700 g., 0.9800 Silver 0.7867 oz. ASW   **Subject:** Marine Life Protection **Obv:** National arms, date and denomination below **Rev:** Pair of multicolor fish

Date	Mintage	F	VF	XF	Unc	BU
1997 Proof	—	Value: 35.00				

KM# 58   50 BUTUTS

Copper-Nickel, 28.8 mm.   **Obv:** National arms, date below **Rev:** African domestic ox divides denomination

Date	Mintage	F	VF	XF	Unc	BU
1998	—	—	—	—	1.50	2.00

KM# 62   2000 BUTUTS

0.9250 g., Silver, 37.5 mm.   **Subject:** Millennium **Obv:** National arms, dates below **Rev:** Gambian map on radiant sun, denomination below **Edge:** Reeded **Note:** Struck at British Royal Mint.

Date	Mintage	F	VF	XF	Unc	BU
ND(1999) Proof	30,000	Value: 55.00				

KM# 13   DALASI
Copper-Nickel   **Obv:** President's bust left **Rev:** Slender-snouted crocodile, denomination at right

Date	Mintage	F	VF	XF	Unc	BU
1971	1,300,000	—	2.00	3.50	8.00	10.00
1971 Proof	32,000	Value: 5.00				

KM# 29   DALASI
12.2000 g., Copper-Nickel, 30.8 mm.   **Obv:** President's bust left **Rev:** Slender-snouted crocodile, denomination at right **Edge:** Reeded, smooth alternating edge

Date	Mintage	F	VF	XF	Unc	BU
1987	—	—	1.75	2.75	6.00	7.50

KM# 65   DALASI
28.1100 g., Copper Nickel, 38.6 mm.   **Subject:** Queen Mother **Obv:** National arms, date below **Rev:** Oval portraits of George V, Edward VIII and George VI within circle, denomination below **Edge:** Reeded

Date	Mintage	F	VF	XF	Unc	BU
1996	30,000	—	—	—	16.50	18.50

KM# 59   DALASI
8.8100 g., Copper Nickel, 28 mm.   **Obv:** National arms, date below **Rev:** Slender-snouted crocodile, denomination at right

Date	Mintage	F	VF	XF	Unc	BU
1998	—	—	1.75	2.75	6.00	7.50

KM# 46   2 DALASIS
9.9200 g., 0.5000 Silver 0.1595 oz. ASW   **Subject:** Olympic Games 1996 **Obv:** National arms, date below **Rev:** Two runners crossing a finish line, denomination at right

Date	Mintage	F	VF	XF	Unc	BU
1996 Proof	Est. 10,000	Value: 15.00				

KM# 49   2 DALASIS
Copper-Nickel   **Subject:** 70th Birthday of Queen Elizabeth II **Obv:** National arms

Date	Mintage	F	VF	XF	Unc	BU
1996	5,000	—	—	—	10.00	12.00

KM# 16   10 DALASIS
28.2800 g., 0.5000 Silver 0.4546 oz. ASW   **Subject:** 10th Anniversary of Independence **Obv:** President's bust left **Rev:** National arms, denomination below

Date	Mintage	F	VF	XF	Unc	BU
1975	50,000	—	—	—	10.00	12.50

KM# 16a   10 DALASIS
28.2800 g., 0.9250 Silver 0.8410 oz. ASW   **Subject:** 10th Anniversary of Independence **Obv:** President's bust left **Rev:** National arms, denomination

Date	Mintage	F	VF	XF	Unc	BU
1975 Proof	20,000	Value: 17.50				

KM# 23   10 DALASIS
28.2800 g., 0.5000 Silver 0.4546 oz. ASW, 38.61 mm.   **Subject:** Commonwealth Games **Obv:** President's bust left **Rev:** Hurdlers, denomination below

Date	Mintage	F	VF	XF	Unc	BU
1986	Est. 50,000	—	—	—	12.50	14.00

KM# 23a   10 DALASIS
28.2800 g., 0.9250 Silver 0.8410 oz. ASW, 38.61 mm.   **Subject:** Commonwealth Games **Obv:** President's bust left **Rev:** Hurdlers, denomination

Date	Mintage	F	VF	XF	Unc	BU
1986 Proof	Est. 20,000	Value: 22.50				

KM# 28   10 DALASIS
28.2800 g., 0.9250 Silver 0.8410 oz. ASW   **Subject:** Silver Jubilee of Independence **Obv:** President's bust left **Rev:** National arms, denomination below

Date	Mintage	F	VF	XF	Unc	BU
1990 Proof	2,000	Value: 42.50				

KM# 30   10 DALASIS
Copper-Nickel   **Subject:** Papal Visit **Obv:** National arms, denomination below **Rev:** Half-figure of Pope 3/4 facing, right arm raised

Date	Mintage	F	VF	XF	Unc	BU
1992	—	—	—	—	6.50	8.00

KM# 30a   10 DALASIS
28.2800 g., 0.9250 Silver 0.8410 oz. ASW   **Subject:** Papal Visit **Obv:** National arms, denomination **Rev:** Half figure of Pope 3/4 facing with right arm raised

Date	Mintage	F	VF	XF	Unc	BU
1992 Proof	5,000	Value: 55.00				

KM# 50   10 DALASIS
Copper Nickel   **Subject:** 70th Birthday of H.M. Queen Elizabeth II **Obv:** National arms, date **Rev:** Queen inspecting guard, denomination

Date	Mintage	F	VF	XF	Unc	BU
1996	—	—	—	—	8.00	10.00

KM# 50a   10 DALASIS
28.2800 g., 0.9250 Silver 0.8410 oz. ASW   **Subject:** 70th Birthday of H.M. Queen Elizabeth II **Obv:** National arms, date below **Rev:** Queen inspecting guard, denomination divides dates

Date	Mintage	F	VF	XF	Unc	BU
1996 Proof	70,000	Value: 42.50				

KM# 17   20 DALASIS
28.6300 g., 0.9250 Silver 0.8514 oz. ASW   **Subject:** Conservation **Obv:** President's bust left **Rev:** Spur-winged goose divides denomination

Date	Mintage	F	VF	XF	Unc	BU
1977	4,302	—	—	—	22.00	—

KM# 20   20 DALASIS
28.2800 g., 0.9250 Silver 0.8410 oz. ASW   **Subject:** World Food Day **Obv:** President's bust left **Rev:** Logo above field worker, denomination below

Date	Mintage	F	VF	XF	Unc	BU
1981	10,000	—	—	—	25.00	30.00
1981 Proof	5,000	Value: 45.00				

KM# 21   20 DALASIS
28.2800 g., 0.9250 Silver 0.8410 oz. ASW **Subject:** Year of the Scout **Obv:** President's bust in beret left **Rev:** Scout emblem above motto, denomination

Date	Mintage	F	VF	XF	Unc	BU
1983	Est. 10,000	—	—	—	25.00	30.00
1983 Proof	Inc. above	Value: 40.00				

KM# 24   20 DALASIS
28.3400 g., 0.9250 Silver 0.8428 oz. ASW, 38.66 mm.
Subject: World Wildlife Fund **Obv:** Bust of President Kairaba Jawara 3/4 left **Rev:** Temminck's colobus monkey divides denomination **Edge:** Reeded

Date	Mintage	F	VF	XF	Unc	BU
1987 Proof	Est. 25,000	Value: 27.50				
1989 Proof	—	Value: 60.00				

KM# 26   20 DALASIS
28.2800 g., 0.9250 Silver 0.8410 oz. ASW **Subject:** Save the Children Fund **Obv:** Bust of President Alhaji Sir Dawda Dairaba Jawara **Rev:** Girls playing "akara" (rythmic clapping and dancing game), denomination below

Date	Mintage	F	VF	XF	Unc	BU
1989	Est. 20,000	Value: 25.00				

KM# 32   20 DALASIS
31.4700 g., 0.9250 Silver 0.9359 oz. ASW **Subject:** 40th Anniversary - Coronation of Queen Elizabeth II **Obv:** President's bust left **Rev:** Royal crown above denomination

Date	Mintage	F	VF	XF	Unc	BU
1993 Proof	Est. 10,000	Value: 47.50				

KM# 38   20 DALASIS
31.4700 g., 0.9250 Silver 0.9359 oz. ASW **Subject:** Endangered Wildlife **Obv:** President's bust left **Rev:** Chimpanzee, denomination below

Date	Mintage	F	VF	XF	Unc	BU
1993 Proof	Est. 15,000	Value: 35.00				
1994 Proof	—	Value: 35.00				

KM# 33   20 DALASIS
31.2600 g., 0.9250 Silver 0.9296 oz. ASW **Series:** Olympics **Obv:** President's bust left **Rev:** Wrestlers, denomination below

Date	Mintage	F	VF	XF	Unc	BU
1993 Proof	Est. 40,000	Value: 22.50				

KM# 34   20 DALASIS
31.4700 g., 0.9250 Silver 0.9359 oz. ASW **Subject:** Prince Henry the Navigator **Obv:** President's bust left **Rev:** Ship at sea at left, 3/4 figure at right above denomination

Date	Mintage	F	VF	XF	Unc	BU
1993 Proof	Est. 15,000	Value: 22.50				

KM# 36   20 DALASIS
31.4700 g., 0.9250 Silver 0.9359 oz. ASW
Subject: Rendezvous in Space **Obv:** President's bust left **Rev:** Space Shuttle at left, astronauts at right, denomination below

Date	Mintage	F	VF	XF	Unc	BU
1993 Proof	Est. 10,000	Value: 35.00				

KM# 35   20 DALASIS
31.4700 g., 0.9250 Silver 0.9359 oz. ASW **Subject:** Soccer - World Cup 1994 **Obv:** President's bust left **Rev:** Maps on globe, soccer ball and players, denomination below

Date	Mintage	F	VF	XF	Unc	BU
1994 Proof	Est. 15,000	Value: 30.00				

KM# 40   20 DALASIS
31.4700 g., 0.9250 Silver 0.9359 oz. ASW **Subject:** Elizabeth, the Queen Mother **Obv:** National arms, date below **Rev:** Busts of Edward VIII, George V and George VI facing within circles, inscription above **Rev. Insc.:** Year of the Three Kings

Date	Mintage	F	VF	XF	Unc	BU
1994 Proof	Est. 30,000	Value: 37.50				

KM# 39   20 DALASIS
31.4700 g., 0.9250 Silver 0.9359 oz. ASW **Subject:** Mungo Park **Obv:** President's bust left **Rev:** Bust left at right, figures piloting raft at left, denomination above

Date	Mintage	F	VF	XF	Unc	BU
1994 Proof	Est. 10,000	Value: 32.50				

KM# 47   20 DALASIS
31.4700 g., 0.9250 Silver 0.9359 oz. ASW **Subject:** Olympic Games 1996 **Obv:** National arms, date below **Rev:** Two runners crossing a finish line, denomination at right

Date	Mintage	F	VF	XF	Unc	BU
1994 Proof	—	Value: 22.50				

KM# 37   20 DALASIS
Copper-Nickel   **Subject:** 50th Anniversary - United Nations
Obv: National arms, date below **Rev:** Dove with olive branch
above UN logo, map in background, denomination below

Date	Mintage	F	VF	XF	Unc	BU
1995	—	—	—	—	8.00	10.00

KM# 37a   20 DALASIS
28.2800 g., 0.9250 Silver 0.8410 oz. ASW   **Subject:** 50th
Anniversary - United Nations **Obv:** National arms, date
Rev: Dove with olive branch above logo, map in background

Date	Mintage	F	VF	XF	Unc	BU
1995 Proof	—	Value: 32.50				

KM# 41   20 DALASIS
31.4700 g., 0.9250 Silver 0.9359 oz. ASW   **Subject:** Protect Our
World **Obv:** National arms, date below **Rev:** Nudes in forest, birds
and snake in trees, denomination below

Date	Mintage	F	VF	XF	Unc	BU
1995 Proof	Est. 10,000	Value: 40.00				

KM# 42   20 DALASIS
7.7760 g., 0.5833 Gold 0.1458 oz. AGW   **Subject:** Endangered
Wildlife **Obv:** National arms, date below **Rev:** Black rhinoceros,
denomination below

Date	Mintage	F	VF	XF	Unc	BU
1995	Est. 2,000	—	—	—	145	165

KM# 43   20 DALASIS
7.7760 g., 0.5833 Gold 0.1458 oz. AGW   **Subject:** Endangered
Wildlife **Obv:** National arms, date below **Rev:** African elephant,
denomination below

Date	Mintage	F	VF	XF	Unc	BU
1995	Est. 2,000	—	—	—	145	165

KM# 44   20 DALASIS
31.4700 g., 0.9250 Silver 0.9359 oz. ASW   **Subject:** Victorian Age
Obv: National arms, date below **Rev:** Queen Victoria with first steam
locomotive in background within circle, denomination below

Date	Mintage	F	VF	XF	Unc	BU
1996	Est. 10,000	—	—	—	—	42.50

KM# 51   20 DALASIS
31.4700 g., 0.9990 Silver 1.0107 oz. ASW   **Subject:** World Cup
1998 **Obv:** National arms, date below **Rev:** Two soccer players,
denomination below

Date	Mintage	F	VF	XF	Unc	BU
1996 Proof	10,000	Value: 40.00				

KM# 63   20 DALASIS
31.3600 g., 0.9250 Silver 0.9326 oz. ASW, 38.5 mm.   **Subject:**
British Queen Mother **Obv:** National arms, date below **Rev:** 1909
Portrait of the Queen Mother, denomination below **Edge:** Reeded

Date	Mintage	F	VF	XF	Unc	BU
1996 Proof	—	Value: 40.00				

KM# 18   40 DALASIS
35.2900 g., 0.9250 Silver 1.0495 oz. ASW   **Subject:** Conservation
Obv: President's bust left **Rev:** Aardvark divides denomination

Date	Mintage	F	VF	XF	Unc	BU
1977	4,304	—	—	—	25.00	

KM# 18a   40 DALASIS
35.2900 g., 0.9250 Silver 1.0495 oz. ASW   **Subject:** Conservation
Obv: President's bust left **Rev:** Aardvark divides denomination

Date	Mintage	F	VF	XF	Unc	BU
1977 Proof	—	Value: 42.00				

KM# 52   50 DALASIS
1.2441 g., 0.9990 Gold 0.0400 oz. AGW   **Subject:** Kankan
Manga Musa **Obv:** National arms, date below **Rev:** Seated king
and supplicant, denomination below

Date	Mintage	F	VF	XF	Unc	BU
1997 Proof	—	Value: 45.00				

KM# 45   100 DALASIS
1000.0000 g., 0.9990 Silver 32.117 oz. ASW, 100 mm.   **Subject:**
Endangered Wildlife **Obv:** National arms, date below **Rev:** Lion
family within circle, denomination below **Note:** Illustration reduced.

Date	Mintage	F	VF	XF	Unc	BU
1996 Proof	1,000	Value: 650				

KM# 53   100 DALASIS
3.1100 g., 0.5833 Gold 0.0583 oz. AGW   **Series:** Olympic
Games 2000 **Obv:** National arms, date below **Rev:** Silhouette of
three runners, denomination below

Date	Mintage	F	VF	XF	Unc	BU
1997 Proof	5,000	Value: 65.00				

KM# 61   150 DALASIS
7.7760 g., 0.5830 Gold 0.1457 oz. AGW   **Subject:** British Year
of 3 Kings and Queen Mother **Obv:** National arms, date below
Rev: Busts of Edward VIII, George V and George VI facing within
circles

Date	Mintage	F	VF	XF	Unc	BU
1996 Proof	—	Value: 175				

KM# 48   200 DALASIS
31.1035 g., 0.9990 Gold 0.9990 oz. AGW   **Subject:** Endangered
Wildlife **Rev:** Lion right, denomination below

Date	Mintage	F	VF	XF	Unc	BU
1996 Proof	1,000	Value: 975				

KM# 22   250 DALASIS
15.9800 g., 0.9170 Gold 0.4711 oz. AGW   **Subject:** Year of the
Scout **Obv:** President's bust in beret left **Rev:** Scout emblem
above motto, denomination below

Date	Mintage	F	VF	XF	Unc	BU
1983	2,000	—	—	—	475	
1983 Proof	2,000	Value: 500				

KM# 31 250 DALASIS
47.5400 g., 0.9170 Gold 1.4015 oz. AGW **Subject:** Papal Visit **Obv:** National arms **Rev:** Pope John Paul II giving a blessing

Date	Mintage	F	VF	XF	Unc	BU
1992 Proof	100	Value: 1,350				

KM# 19 500 DALASIS
33.4370 g., 0.9000 Gold 0.9675 oz. AGW **Subject:** Conservation **Obv:** President's bust left **Rev:** Sitatunga divides denomination

Date	Mintage	F	VF	XF	Unc	BU
1977	699				935	950
1977 Proof	285	Value: 975				

KM# 25 1000 DALASIS
10.0000 g., 0.9170 Gold 0.2948 oz. AGW **Subject:** World Wildlife Fund **Obv:** President's bust left **Rev:** Gambian puffback bird divides denomination

Date	Mintage	F	VF	XF	Unc	BU
1987 Proof	Est. 5,000	Value: 285				

KM# 27 1000 DALASIS
10.0000 g., 0.9170 Gold 0.2948 oz. AGW **Subject:** Save the Children Fund **Obv:** President's bust left

Date	Mintage	F	VF	XF	Unc	BU
1989 Proof	Est. 3,000	Value: 300				

PROOF SETS

KM#	Date	Mintage	Identification	Issue Price	Mkt Val
PS4	1977 (2)	—	KM17a, 18a	60.00	60.00
PS1	1966 (6)	5,100	KM1-6	13.00	16.50
PS2	1966 and 1970 (7)	1,500	KM1-6, 7a	25.00	52.50
PS3	1971 (6)	26,249	KM8-13	—	11.50

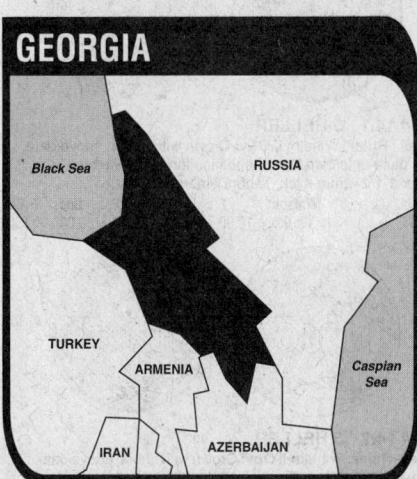

GEORGIA

Georgia (formerly the Georgian Social Democratic Republic under the U.S.S.R.), is bounded by the Black Sea to the west and by Turkey, Armenia and Azerbaijan. It occupies the western part of Transcaucasia covering an area of 26,900 sq. mi. (69,700 sq. km.) and a population of 5.7 million. Capitol: Tbilisi. Hydro-electricity, minerals, forestry and agriculture are the chief industries.

After the Russian Revolution the Georgians, Armenians, and Azerbaijanis formed the short-lived Transcaucasian Federal

Republic on Sept. 20, 1917, which broke up into three independent republics on May 26, 1918. A Germano-- Georgian treaty was signed on May 28, 1918, followed by a Turko-Georgian peace treaty on June 4. The end of WW I and the collapse of the central powers allowed free elections.

On May 20, 1920, Soviet Russia concluded a peace treaty, recognizing its independence, but later invaded on Feb. 11, 1921 and a soviet republic was proclaimed. On March 12, 1922 Stalin included Georgia in a newly formed Transcaucasian Soviet Federated Socialist Republic. On Dec. 5, 1936 the T.S.F.S.R. was dissolved and Georgia became a direct member of the U.S.S.R. The collapse of the U.S.S.R. allowed full transition to independence and on April 9, 1991 a unanimous vote declared the republic an independent state based on its original treaty of independence of May 1918.

INDEPENDENT STATE (C.I.S.)

STANDARD COINAGE
100 Thetri = 1 Lari

KM# 76 THETRI
1.3500 g., Stainless Steel, 14.9 mm. **Obv:** Stylized candelabra design divides date within circle **Rev:** Denomination above grapes **Edge:** Smooth

Date	Mintage	F	VF	XF	Unc	BU
1993	—	—	—	—	0.25	0.35

KM# 77 2 THETRI
1.8500 g., Stainless Steel, 17.4 mm. **Obv:** Stylized candelabra divides date within circle **Rev:** Stylized eagle above denomination **Edge:** Smooth

Date	Mintage	F	VF	XF	Unc	BU
1993	—	—	—	—	0.35	0.50

KM# 78 5 THETRI
2.4500 g., Stainless Steel, 19.9 mm. **Obv:** Stylized candelabra divides date within circle **Rev:** Stylized lion above denomination **Edge:** Smooth

Date	Mintage	F	VF	XF	Unc	BU
1993	—	—	—	—	0.75	1.00

KM# 79 10 THETRI
2.9500 g., Stainless Steel, 21.9 mm. **Obv:** Stylized candelabra divides date within circle **Rev:** St. Mamas riding lion right, denomination **Edge:** Smooth

Date	Mintage	F	VF	XF	Unc	BU
1993	—	—	—	—	1.25	1.50

KM# 80 20 THETRI
4.9500 g., Stainless Steel, 25 mm. **Obv:** Stylized candelabra divides date within circle **Rev:** Red Deer left, denomination **Edge:** Smooth

Date	Mintage	F	VF	XF	Unc	BU
1993	—	—	—	—	1.50	2.00

KM# 81 50 THETRI
2.4500 g., Brass, 19 mm. **Obv:** Stylized candelabra divides date within circle **Rev:** Stylized griffin left, above denomination **Edge:** Smooth

Date	Mintage	F	VF	XF	Unc	BU
1993					2.00	2.50

KM# 83 10 LARI
28.2800 g., 0.9250 Silver 0.8410 oz. ASW, 28.4 mm. **Subject:** State System 3,000 Years **Obv:** Denomination within circle **Rev:** Eagle and lion within circle **Edge:** Reeded

Date	Mintage	F	VF	XF	Unc	BU
2000 Proof	1,000	Value: 55.00				

KM# 84 10 LARI
28.2800 g., 0.9250 Silver 0.8410 oz. ASW **Subject:** Birth of Jesus 2,000th Anniversary **Obv:** Denomination within circle **Rev:** Christian arms within circle

Date	Mintage	F	VF	XF	Unc	BU
2000 Proof	1,000	Value: 55.00				

KM# 85 10 LARI
10.6000 g., Bi-Metallic Copper-Nickel center in Brass ring, 26 mm. **Subject:** State System: 3000 Years **Obv:** Denomination within circle **Rev:** Eagle above lion within circle **Edge:** Reeding over "GEORGIA . TEN LARI"

Date	Mintage	F	VF	XF	Unc	BU
2000	1,000	—	—	—	18.00	20.00

KM# 86 10 LARI
10.6000 g., Bi-Metallic Copper-Nickel center in Brass ring, 25.9 mm. **Subject:** Christianity: 2000 Years **Obv:** Denomination within circle **Rev:** Christian arms within circle **Edge:** Reeding over "GEORGIA . TEN LARI"

Date	Mintage	F	VF	XF	Unc	BU
2000	25,000	—	—	—	15.00	16.50

KM# 86a 10 LARI
16.0000 g., 0.9000 Silver 0.4630 oz. ASW, 28.3 mm.
Obv: Denomination **Rev:** Christian arms **Edge:** Reeded and lettered **Edge:** "GEORGIA TEN LARI"

Date	Mintage	F	VF	XF	Unc	BU
2000 Proof	— Value: 75.00					

KM# 87 10 LARI
28.2800 g., Copper-Nickel, 38.61 mm. **Subject:** 300th Anniversary of Statehood **Obv:** Eagle above lion **Rev:** Denomination

Date	Mintage	F	VF	XF	Unc	BU
2000	2,000	—	—	—	25.00	28.00

KM# 88 10 LARI
28.2800 g., Copper-Nickel, 38.61 mm. **Subject:** 2000th Anniversary of the Birth of Christ

Date	Mintage	F	VF	XF	Unc	BU
2000	2,000	—	—	—	25.00	28.00

KM# 82 500 LARI
17.0000 g., 0.9170 Gold 0.5012 oz. AGW **Subject:** 50th Anniversary - Defeat of Fascism **Obv:** Stylized candelabra divides date above denomination **Rev:** Profiles of Stalin, Roosevelt, Churchill and de Gaulle left, date below

Date	Mintage	F	VF	XF	Unc	BU
1995 Proof	2,000 Value: 520					

MINT SETS

KM#	Date	Mintage Identification	Issue Price	Mkt Val
MS1	1993 (6)	— KM76-81	—	7.50

GERMAN EAST AFRICA

German East Africa (Tanganyika), located on the coast of east-central Africa between British East Africa (now Kenya) and Portuguese East Africa (now Mozambique), had an area of 362,284 sq. mi. (938,216 sq. km.) and a population of about 6 million. Capital: Dar es Salaam. Chief products prior to German control were ivory and slaves; after German control, sisal, coffee, and rubber. Germany acquired control of the area by treaties with coastal chiefs in 1884, established it as a protectorate in 1891, and proclaimed it the Colony of German East Africa in 1897. After World War I, Tanganyika was entrusted to Great Britain as a League of Nations mandate, and after World War II as a United Nations trust territory. Tanganyika became an independent nation within the British Commonwealth on Dec. 9, 1961. Coins dated up until 1902 were issued by the German East Africa Company. From 1904 onwards, the government issued coins.
NOTE: For later coinage see East Africa.

TITLE

شراكة المانيا

Sharaka(t) Almania

RULER
Wilhelm II, 1888-1918

MINT MARKS
A - Berlin
J - Hamburg
T - Tabora

MONETARY SYSTEM
Until 1904
64 Pesa = 1 Rupie
Commencing 1904
100 Heller = 1 Rupie

COLONY
STANDARD COINAGE
German East Africa Company
1891-

KM# 3 1/4 RUPIE
2.9160 g., 0.9170 Silver 0.0860 oz. ASW **Ruler:** Wihelm II **Obv:** Armored bust left **Rev:** Shielded arms, denomination below

Date	Mintage	F	VF	XF	Unc	BU
1901	350,000	6.00	18.00	45.00	140	160

KM# 4 1/2 RUPIE
5.8319 g., 0.9170 Silver 0.1719 oz. ASW **Ruler:** Wihelm II **Obv:** Armored bust left **Rev:** Shielded arms, denomination below

Date	Mintage	F	VF	XF	Unc	BU
1901	215,000	15.00	40.00	100	250	325

KM# 2 RUPIE
11.6638 g., 0.9170 Silver 0.3439 oz. ASW **Ruler:** Wihelm II **Obv:** Armored bust left **Rev:** Shielded arms, denomination below

Date	Mintage	F	VF	XF	Unc	BU
1901	319,000	12.50	25.00	75.00	175	225
1902	151,000	20.00	40.00	125	450	575

STANDARD COINAGE
1904-

KM# 6 1/2 HELLER
Bronze **Ruler:** Wihelm II **Obv:** Crown with ribbon above date **Rev:** Denomination within wreath

Date	Mintage	F	VF	XF	Unc	BU
1904A	1,201,000	2.00	6.00	10.00	35.00	50.00
1905A	7,192,000	2.25	5.25	9.00	32.50	45.00
1905J	4,000,000	2.25	5.25	9.00	32.50	45.00
1906J	6,000,000	1.25	3.50	6.50	28.00	40.00
1906J Proof	— Value: 250					

KM# 7 HELLER
Bronze **Ruler:** Wihelm II **Obv:** Crown with ribbon above date **Rev:** Denomination within wreath

Date	Mintage	F	VF	XF	Unc	BU
1904A	10,256,000	0.75	2.25	4.00	20.00	30.00
1904A Proof	— Value: 125					
1904J	2,500,000	0.75	2.25	7.00	25.00	35.00
1905A	3,760,000	0.75	2.25	7.00	25.00	35.00
1905A Proof	— Value: 125					
1905J	7,556,000	0.75	2.25	4.00	25.00	35.00

Date	Mintage	F	VF	XF	Unc	BU
1906A	3,004,000	0.75	2.25	7.00	25.00	40.00
1906A Proof	— Value: 200					
1906J	1,962,000	0.75	2.25	7.00	30.00	50.00
1907J	17,790,000	0.75	1.50	4.00	20.00	25.00
1908J	12,205,000	0.75	1.50	4.00	20.00	25.00
1908J Proof	— Value: 135					
1909J	1,698,000	2.50	7.50	15.00	35.00	50.00
1909J Proof	— Value: 135					
1910J	5,096,000	0.75	1.50	4.00	20.00	25.00
1910J Proof	— Value: 135					
1911J	6,420,000	0.75	1.50	4.00	20.00	25.00
1911J Proof	— Value: 135					
1912J	7,012,000	0.75	1.50	4.00	25.00	40.00
1912J Proof	— Value: 135					
1913A		0.75	1.50	4.00	20.00	30.00
1913A Proof	— Value: 135					
1913J	5,186,000	0.75	1.50	4.00	20.00	30.00
1913J Proof	— Value: 150					

KM# 11 5 HELLER
Bronze **Ruler:** Wihelm II **Obv:** Crown with ribbon above date **Rev:** Denomination within wreath

Date	Mintage	F	VF	XF	Unc	BU
1908J	600,000	20.00	45.00	85.00	550	675
1908J Proof	— Value: 2,200					
1909J	756,000	22.00	50.00	90.00	550	675
1909J Proof	60 Value: 2,200					

KM# 13 5 HELLER
Copper-Nickel **Ruler:** Wihelm II **Obv:** Center hole divides date, crown with ribbon above, legend below **Rev:** Center hole divides denomination, sprigs flank

Date	Mintage	F	VF	XF	Unc	BU
1913A	1,000,000	6.00	15.00	25.00	55.00	100
1913A Proof	— Value: 250					
1913J	1,000,000	6.00	15.00	25.00	60.00	100
1913J Proof	— Value: 250					
1914J	1,000,000	5.00	12.00	22.00	50.00	100
1914J Proof	— Value: 250					

KM# 14.1 5 HELLER
Brass **Ruler:** Wihelm II **Obv:** Crown with ribbon above date, oval base on crown **Rev:** Denomination within wreath
Note: 1-1/2 -2mm thick. Tabora emergency issue.

Date	Mintage	F	VF	XF	Unc	BU
1916T	30,000	10.00	20.00	40.00	80.00	150

KM# 14.2 5 HELLER
Brass **Ruler:** Wihelm II **Obv:** Crown with ribbon above date, flat base on crown **Rev:** Denomination within wreath **Note:** 1mm or less thick.

Date	Mintage	F	VF	XF	Unc	BU
1916T	Inc. above	4.00	12.00	30.00	60.00	100

KM# 12 10 HELLER
Copper-Nickel **Ruler:** Wihelm II **Obv:** Center hole divides date, crown with ribbon above, legend below **Rev:** Center hole divides denomination, sprigs flank

Date	Mintage	F	VF	XF	Unc	BU
1908J	—	5.00	15.00	30.00	90.00	125
1908J Proof	—	Value: 350				
1909J	1,990,000	3.00	10.00	20.00	80.00	125
1909J Proof	—	Value: 275				
1910J	500,000	3.00	10.00	20.00	80.00	150
1910J Proof	—	Value: 275				
1911A	500,000	5.00	15.00	35.00	100	150
1911A Proof	—	Value: 300				
1914J	200,000	10.00	30.00	60.00	125	200
1914 Proof	—	Value: 285				

KM# 15 20 HELLER
Copper **Ruler:** Wihelm II **Obv:** Crown with ribbon above date **Rev:** Denomination within wreath **Note:** Tabora Emergency Coinage.

Date	Mintage	F	VF	XF	Unc	BU
1916T	300,000	6.00	10.00	20.00	85.00	100
Note: Obverse A and reverse A						
1916T	Inc. above	125	200	350	—	—
Note: Obverse A and reverse B						
1916T	Inc. above	60.00	85.00	140	—	—
Note: Obverse B and reverse A						
1916T	Inc. above	6.00	10.00	20.00	60.00	80.00
Note: Obverse B and reverse B						
1916T Rare	Inc. above	—	—	—	—	—
Note: Obverse A and reverse C						
1916T Rare	Inc. above	—	—	—	—	—
Note: Obverse B and reverse C						

KM# 15a 20 HELLER
Brass **Ruler:** Wihelm II **Obv:** Crown with ribbon above date **Rev:** Denomination within wreath **Note:** Tabora Emergency Issue.

Date	Mintage	F	VF	XF	Unc	BU
1916T	1,600,000	6.00	10.00	20.00	75.00	90.00
Note: Obverse A and reverse A; Curled tip on second L						
1916T	Inc. above	7.00	12.50	25.00	85.00	100
Note: Obverse A and reverse B; Pointed tips on L's						
1916T	Inc. above	7.00	12.50	25.00	85.00	100
Note: Obverse B and reverse A; Curled tip on second L						
1916T	Inc. above	6.00	10.00	20.00	65.00	80.00
Note: Obverse B and reverse B; Pointed tips on L's						
1916T	Inc. above	10.00	30.00	45.00	125	150
Note: Obverse A and reverse C; Curled tips on L's						
1916T	Inc. above	12.00	35.00	50.00	135	150
Note: Obverse B and reverse C; Curled tips on L's						

KM# 8 1/4 RUPIE
2.9160 g., 0.9170 Silver 0.0860 oz. ASW **Ruler:** Wihelm II **Obv:** Armored bust left **Rev:** Shielded arms, denomination below

Date	Mintage	F	VF	XF	Unc	BU
1904A	300,000	5.00	12.00	37.50	110	150
1904A Proof	—	Value: 300				
1906A	300,000	5.00	12.00	37.50	110	150
1906A Proof	—	Value: 300				
1906J	100,000	20.00	60.00	125	300	400
1907J	200,000	10.00	25.00	75.00	200	275
1907J Proof	—	Value: 375				
1909A	300,000	6.00	13.50	40.00	185	225
1910J	600,000	5.00	12.00	37.50	110	140
1910J Proof	—	Value: 350				
1912J	400,000	6.00	13.50	40.00	120	175
1912J Proof	—	Value: 350				
1913A	200,000	6.50	14.50	42.50	135	225
1913A Proof	—	Value: 350				
1913J	400,000	5.00	12.00	37.50	110	140
1913J Proof	—	Value: 300				
1914J	200,000	6.50	14.50	42.50	125	200
1914J Proof	—	Value: 300				

KM# 9 1/2 RUPIE
5.8319 g., 0.9170 Silver 0.1719 oz. ASW **Ruler:** Wihelm II **Obv:** Armored bust left **Rev:** Shielded arms, denomination below

Date	Mintage	F	VF	XF	Unc	BU
1904A	400,000	15.00	40.00	95.00	275	325
1904A Proof	—	Value: 450				
1906A	50,000	125	225	350	750	1,000
1906A Proof	—	Value: 1,000				
1906J	50,000	125	225	350	750	1,000
1907J	140,000	20.00	50.00	125	300	350
1907J Proof	—	Value: 550				
1909A	100,000	30.00	65.00	150	350	500
1910J	300,000	20.00	40.00	100	250	275
1910J Proof	—	Value: 450				
1912A	200,000	15.00	40.00	95.00	250	300
1913A	100,000	20.00	45.00	110	300	400
1913J	200,000	15.00	40.00	95.00	200	250
1914J	100,000	20.00	45.00	100	285	350

KM# 10 RUPIE
11.6638 g., 0.9170 Silver 0.3439 oz. ASW **Ruler:** Wihelm II **Obv:** Armored bust left **Rev:** Shielded arms, denomination below

Date	Mintage	F	VF	XF	Unc	BU
1904A	1,000,000	11.50	22.50	45.00	130	150
1904A Proof	—	Value: 425				
1905A	300,000	15.00	27.50	60.00	185	250
1905A Proof	—	Value: 450				
1905J	1,000,000	11.50	22.50	45.00	130	160
1905J Proof	—	Value: 400				
1906A	950,000	11.50	22.50	45.00	130	160
1906J	700,000	15.00	27.50	65.00	175	200
1907J	880,000	9.00	15.00	45.00	180	200
1908J	500,000	12.50	25.00	55.00	190	225
1908J Proof	—	Value: 450				
1909A	200,000	15.00	27.50	65.00	275	350
1910J	270,000	9.00	15.00	45.00	200	275
1911A	300,000	12.50	25.00	55.00	175	250
1911A Proof	—	Value: 450				
1911J	1,400,000	9.00	15.00	45.00	150	175
1911J Proof	—	Value: 400				
1912J	300,000	12.50	25.00	55.00	165	250
1912J Proof	—	Value: 450				
1913A	400,000	12.50	25.00	55.00	160	225
1913J	1,400,000	9.00	15.00	45.00	150	175
1913J Proof	—	Value: 400				
1914J	500,000	11.50	22.50	50.00	175	250

KM# 16.1 15 RUPIEN
7.1680 g., 0.7500 Gold 0.1728 oz. AGW **Ruler:** Wihelm II **Obv:** Crowned imperial eagle, right arabesque ends below "T" of "OSTAFRIKA" **Rev:** Elephant roaring right above date **Note:** Tabora Emergency Issue.

Date	Mintage	F	VF	XF	Unc	BU
1916T	9,803	650	950	1,400	2,350	2,850

KM# 16.2 15 RUPIEN
7.1680 g., 0.7500 Gold 0.1728 oz. AGW **Ruler:** Wihelm II **Obv:** Crowned imperial eagle above denomination, right arabesque ends below first "A" of "OSTAFRIKA" **Rev:** Elephant roaring right above date **Note:** Tabora Emergency Issue.

Date	Mintage	F	VF	XF	Unc	BU
1916T	6,395	675	1,000	1,500	2,350	2,850

PATTERNS
Including off metal strikes

KM#	Date	Mintage	Identification	Mkt Val
Pn1	1908	—	5 Heller. Bronze.	1,000
Pn2	1908	—	10 Heller. Copper-Nickel. Crown with ribbon above center hole dividing date. Center hole divides denomination.	350
Pn2a	1908/1908	—	10 Heller. Copper-Nickel. Two obverses.	375
Pn5	ND	—	5 Rupien. White Metal. Uniface.	450
Pn6	1913A	—	Rupie. Aluminum.	—

GERMAN STATES

Although the origin of the German Empire can be traced to the Treaty of Verdun that ceded Charlemagne's lands east of the Rhine to German Prince Louis, it was for centuries little more than a geographic expression, con- sisting of hundreds of effectively autonomous big and little states. Nominally the states owed their allegiance to the Holy Roman Emperor, who was also a German king, but as the Emperors exhibited less and less concern for Germany the actual power devolved on the lords of the individual states. The fragmentation of the empire climaxed with the tragic denouement of the Thirty Years War, 1618-48, which devastated much of Germany, destroyed its agriculture and medieval commercial eminence and ended the attempt of the Hapsburgs to unify Germany. Deprived of administrative capacity by a lack of resources, the imperial authority became utterly powerless. At this time Germany contained an estimated 1,800 individual states, some with a population of as little as 300. The German Empire of recent history (the creation of Bis- marck) was formed on April 14, 1871, when the king of Prussia became German Emperor William I. The new empire comprised 4 kingdoms, 6 grand duchies, 12 duchies and principalities, 3 free cities and the nonautonomous province of Alsace-Lorraine. The states had the right to issue gold and silver coins of higher value than 1 Mark; coins of 1 Mark and under were general issues of the empire.

MINT MARKS
A - Berlin, 1750-date
D - Munich (Germany), 1872-date
E - Muldenhutten (Germany), 1887-1953
F - Stuttgart (Germany) 1872-date
G - Karlsruhe (Germany) 1872-date
J - Hamburg (Germany) 1873-date

MONETARY SYSTEM
After the German unification in 1871 when the old Thaler system was abandoned in favor of the Mark system (100 Pfennig = 1 Mark) the Vereinsthaler continued to circulate as a legal tender 3 Mark coin, and the double Thaler as a 6 Mark coin until 1908. In 1908 the Vereinsthalers were officially demonetized and the Thaler coinage was replaced by the new 3 Mark coin which had the same specifications as the old Vereinsthaler. The double Thaler coinage was not replaced as there was no great demand for a 6 Mark coin. Until the 1930's the German public continued to refer to the 3 Mark piece as a "Thaler".

Commencing 1871
100 Pfennig = 1 Mark

VERRECHNUNGS & GUTSCHRIFTS TOKENS
These were metallic indebtedness receipts used for commercial and banking purposes due to the lack of available subsidiary coinage. These tokens could be redeemed in sufficient quantities.

ANHALT-DESSAU

Anhalt-Dessau was part of the 1252 division that included Zerbst and Köthen. In 1396, Anhalt-Zerbst was divided into Anhalt-Zerbst and Anhalt-Dessau. In 1508, Anhalt-Zerbst was absorbed into Anhalt-Dessau. The latter was given to the eldest son of Joachim Ernst in the division of 1603. As other lines became extinct, they fell to Anhalt-Dessau, which united all territories of the dynasty in 1863. The last ruler was forced to give up power at the end of World War I. Anhalt area: 2314 km. Capital: Dessau.

RULERS
Friedrich I, 1871-1904
Friedrich II, 1904-1918
Ernst, 1918

MINT MARK
A – Berlin Mint, 1839-1914

DUCHY
REFORM COINAGE

KM# 27   2 MARK
11.1110 g., 0.9000 Silver 0.3215 oz. ASW, 28 mm.
Ruler: Friedrich II **Obv:** Head left **Rev:** Crowned imperial German eagle, shield on breast **Edge:** Reeded

Date	Mintage	F	VF	XF	Unc	BU
1901A	—	150	325	500	1,200	1,600
1904A	50,000	150	375	500	1,000	1,400
1904A Proof	150	Value: 1,750				

KM# 29   3 MARK
16.6670 g., 0.9000 Silver 0.4823 oz. ASW, 33 mm.
Ruler: Friedrich II **Obv:** Head left **Rev:** Crowned imperial German eagle, shield on breast **Edge:** GOTT MIT UNS

Date	Mintage	F	VF	XF	Unc	BU
1909A	100,000	35.00	75.00	150	250	400
1911A	100,000	40.00	85.00	165	250	420
Common date Proof	—	Value: 550				
Common date Proof	—	Value: 400				

KM# 30   3 MARK
16.6670 g., 0.9000 Silver 0.4823 oz. ASW, 33 mm.
Ruler: Friedrich II **Subject:** Silver Wedding Anniversary
Obv: Jugate heads left **Rev:** Crowned imperial German eagle, shield on breast **Edge:** GOTT MIT UNS

Date	Mintage	F	VF	XF	Unc	BU
1914A	200,000	25.00	60.00	85.00	100	160
1914A Proof	1,000	Value: 325				

KM# 31   5 MARK
27.7770 g., 0.9000 Silver 0.8037 oz. ASW, 38 mm.
Ruler: Friedrich II **Subject:** Silver Wedding Anniversary
Obv: Jugate heads left **Rev:** Crowned imperial German eagle, shield on breast **Edge:** GOTT MIT UNS

Date	Mintage	F	VF	XF	Unc	BU
1901A	—	450	800	1,250	2,700	4,000
1914A	30,000	65.00	180	285	450	650
1914A Proof	1,000	Value: 1,000				

KM# 25   10 MARK
3.9820 g., 0.9000 Gold 0.1152 oz. AGW **Ruler:** Friedrich I
Obv: Head right **Obv. Leg.:** FRIEDRICH HERZOG VON
ANHALT **Rev:** Crowned imperial German eagle **Rev. Leg.:**
DEUTSCHES REICH date 10 MARK **Edge:** GOTT MIT UNS

Date	Mintage	F	VF	XF	Unc	BU
1901A	20,000	750	1,250	1,800	2,700	3,500
1901A Proof	200	Value: 4,250				

KM# 26   20 MARK
7.9650 g., 0.9000 Gold 0.2305 oz. AGW **Ruler:** Friedrich I
Obv: Small head right **Obv. Leg.:** FRIEDRICH HERZOG VON
ANHALT **Rev:** Crowned imperial German eagle
Rev. Leg.: DEUTSCHES REICH date ZWEI MARK

Date	Mintage	F	VF	XF	Unc	BU
1901A	15,000	750	1,250	1,800	2,700	3,500
1901A Proof	200	Value: 4,250				

KM# 28   20 MARK
7.9650 g., 0.9000 Gold 0.2305 oz. AGW **Ruler:** Friedrich II
Obv: Head left **Rev:** Crowned imperial German eagle, shield on breast **Edge:** GOTT MIT UNS

Date	Mintage	F	VF	XF	Unc	BU
1904A	25,000	600	1,000	1,400	2,500	3,500
1904A Proof	200	Value: 3,750				

PATTERNS
Including off metal strikes

KM#	Date	Mintage	Identification	Mkt Val
Pn1	1901A	—	2 Mark. Silver. KM23.	3,500
Pn2	1901A	—	5 Mark. Silver. KM24.	5,000
Pn3	1914	—	3 Mark. Silver. Wreath around rim. KM30.	—
Pn4	1914	—	3 Mark. Brass.	—
Pn5	1914	—	5 Mark. Silver. Pn6. KM31.	2,000
Pn6	1914	—	5 Mark. Silver. Lettered edge.	2,000
Pn7	1914	—	5 Mark. Silver. Plain edge.	2,000

BADEN

The earliest rulers of Baden, in the southwestern part of Germany along the Rhine, descended from the dukes of Zähringen in the late 11th century. The first division of the territory occurred in 1190, when separate lines of margraves were established in Baden and in Hachberg. Immediately prior to its extinction in 1418, Hachberg was sold back to Baden, which underwent several minor divisions itself during the next century. Baden acquired most of the countship of Sponheim from Electoral Pfalz near the end of the 15th century. In 1515, the most significant division of the patrimony took place, in which the Baden-Baden and Baden-(Pforzheim) Durlach lines were established.

Although Baden-Durlach was founded upon the division of Baden in 1515, the youngest son of Christoph I did not begin ruling in his own right until the demise of his father. This part of Baden was called Pforzheim until 1565, when the margrave moved his seat from the former to Durlach, located to the west and nearer the Rhine. After the male line of Baden-Baden failed in 1771 and the two parts of Baden were reunited, the fortunes of the margraviate continued to grow. Karlsruhe, near Durlach, was developed into a well-planned capital city. The ruler was given the rank of elector in 1803, only to be raised to grand duke three years later. The grand duchy came to an end in 1918, but had by this time become one of the largest states in Germany.

RULERS
Friedrich I, Prince Regent 1852-1856,
    Grand Duke 1856-1907
Friedrich II, 1907-1918

GRAND DUCHY
REFORM COINAGE

KM# 269   2 MARK
11.1110 g., 0.9000 Silver 0.3215 oz. ASW, 28 mm. **Ruler:**
Friedrich I as Grand Duke **Obv:** Head left **Obv. Leg.:** FRIEDRICH
GROSHERZOG VON BADEN **Rev:** Crowned imperial German
eagle **Rev. Leg.:** DEUTSCHES REICH date   ZWEI MARK

Date	Mintage	F	VF	XF	Unc	BU
1901G	401,322	40.00	90.00	275	1,200	2,250
1901G Proof	—	Value: 3,000				
1902G	5,368	275	700	1,500	4,000	6,000
1902G Proof, rare	—	Value: 7,500				

KM# 271   2 MARK
11.1110 g., 0.9000 Silver 0.3215 oz. ASW, 28 mm. **Ruler:**
Friedrich I as Grand Duke **Subject:** 50th Year of Reign **Obv:** Head
right **Rev:** Crowned imperial German eagle, shield on breast

Date	Mintage	F	VF	XF	Unc	BU
1902	375,018	12.00	25.00	35.00	50.00	70.00

KM# 272   2 MARK
11.1110 g., 0.9000 Silver 0.3215 oz. ASW, 28 mm.
Ruler: Friedrich I as Grand Duke **Obv:** Head right **Rev:** Crowned
imperial German eagle, shield on breast

Date	Mintage	F	VF	XF	Unc	BU
1902G	198,250	25.00	55.00	90.00	250	500
1903G	493,989	20.00	45.00	90.00	250	350
1904G	1,121,754	20.00	40.00	80.00	250	350
1905G	609,835	20.00	45.00	70.00	175	300
1906G Rare	107,549	45.00	90.00	225	700	1,400
1907G	913,024	20.00	40.00	65.00	150	225

KM# 276   2 MARK
11.1110 g., 0.9000 Silver 0.3215 oz. ASW, 28 mm.
Ruler: Friedrich I as Grand Duke **Subject:** Golden Wedding
Anniversary **Obv:** Heads of royal couple right **Rev:** Crowned
imperial German eagle, shield on breast

Date	Mintage	F	VF	XF	Unc	BU
1906	350,000	15.00	25.00	35.00	60.00	70.00
1906 Matte proof	200	—	—	—	—	—

KM# 278   2 MARK
11.1110 g., 0.9000 Silver 0.3215 oz. ASW, 28 mm.
Ruler: Friedrich I as Grand Duke **Subject:** Death of Friedrich
Obv: Head right **Rev:** Crowned imperial German eagle, shield
on breast

Date	Mintage	F	VF	XF	Unc	BU
1907	350,000	20.00	50.00	70.00	90.00	100
1907 Proof	— Value: 175					

KM# 283   2 MARK
11.1110 g., 0.9000 Silver 0.3215 oz. ASW, 28 mm.
Ruler: Friedrich II **Obv:** Head left **Rev:** Crowned imperial German eagle, shield on breast

Date	Mintage	F	VF	XF	Unc	BU
1911G	72,000	125	250	400	750	1,200
1913G	937,050	100	250	400	700	1,200
(1911-1913) Proof	— Value: 1,500					

KM# 280   3 MARK
16.6670 g., 0.9000 Silver 0.4823 oz. ASW, 33 mm.
Ruler: Friedrich II **Obv:** Head left **Rev:** Crowned imperial German eagle, shield on breast

Date	Mintage	F	VF	XF	Unc	BU
1908G	304,927	12.00	25.00	35.00	100	160
1909G	760,716	12.00	25.00	35.00	75.00	160
1910G	674,640	12.00	25.00	35.00	75.00	160
1911G	382,033	12.00	25.00	35.00	75.00	160
1912G	835,199	12.00	25.00	35.00	75.00	160
1914G	412,804	12.00	25.00	35.00	70.00	160
1915G	169,533	20.00	50.00	75.00	225	300
(1908-1915)G Proof	— Value: 250					

KM# 268   5 MARK
27.7770 g., 0.9000 Silver 0.8037 oz. ASW, 38 mm. **Ruler:** Friedrich I as Grand Duke **Obv:** Head left **Obv. Leg.:** FRIEDRICH GROSHERZOG VON BADEN **Rev:** Crowned imperial German eagle **Rev. Leg.:** DEUTSCHES REICH date FUNF MARK

Date	Mintage	F	VF	XF	Unc	BU
1901G	128,131	30.00	90.00	350	2,000	4,000
1902G	42,708	35.00	90.00	350	2,000	4,250
(1891-1902)G Proof	— Value: 5,000					

KM# 273   5 MARK
27.7770 g., 0.9000 Silver 0.8037 oz. ASW, 38 mm. **Ruler:** Friedrich I as Grand Duke **Subject:** 50th Year of Reign **Obv:** Head right **Rev:** Crowned imperial German eagle, shield on breast

Date	Mintage	F	VF	XF	Unc	BU
1902	50,024	45.00	90.00	150	225	300
1902 Proof	— Value: 625					

KM# 274   5 MARK
27.7770 g., 0.9000 Silver 0.8037 oz. ASW, 38 mm.
Ruler: Friedrich I as Grand Duke **Obv:** Head right **Rev:** Crowned imperial German eagle, shield on breast **Edge:** GOTT MIT UNS **Note:** Varieties exist.

Date	Mintage	F	VF	XF	Unc	BU
1902G	128,100	35.00	60.00	150	600	1,200
1903G	439,105	20.00	50.00	140	600	1,000
1904G	237,914	20.00	50.00	140	600	1,000
1907G	243,821	20.00	50.00	140	600	850
(1902-1907)G Proof	— Value: 1,250					

KM# 277   5 MARK
27.7770 g., 0.9000 Silver 0.8037 oz. ASW, 38 mm.
Ruler: Friedrich I as Grand Duke **Subject:** Golden Wedding Anniversary **Obv:** Jugate busts right **Rev:** Crowned imperial German eagle, shield on breast

Date	Mintage	F	VF	XF	Unc	BU
1906	60,000	40.00	80.00	145	220	325
1906 Proof	— Value: 400					

KM# 279   5 MARK
27.7770 g., 0.9000 Silver 0.8037 oz. ASW, 38 mm. **Ruler:** Friedrich I as Grand Duke **Subject:** Death of Friedrich **Obv:** Head right **Rev:** Crowned imperial German eagle, shield on breast

Date	Mintage	F	VF	XF	Unc	BU
1907	60,000	60.00	125	175	250	350
1907 Proof	— Value: 425					

KM# 281   5 MARK
27.7770 g., 0.9000 Silver 0.8037 oz. ASW, 38 mm. **Ruler:** Friedrich II **Obv:** Head left **Rev:** Crowned imperial German eagle, shield on breast

Date	Mintage	F	VF	XF	Unc	BU
1908G	184,000	40.00	60.00	200	600	1,100
1913G	244,000	30.00	50.00	175	400	900
(1908-1913)G Proof	— Value: 1,500					

KM# 267   10 MARK
3.9820 g., 0.9000 Gold 0.1152 oz. AGW **Ruler:** Friedrich I as Grand Duke **Obv:** Head left **Obv. Leg.:** FRIEDRICH GROSHERZOG VON BADEN **Rev:** Crowned imperial German eagle **Rev. Leg.:** DEUTSCHES REICH date 10 MARK

Date	Mintage	F	VF	XF	Unc	BU
1901G	91,248	145	225	300	500	700
1901G Proof	— Value: 2,000					

KM# 275   10 MARK
3.9820 g., 0.9000 Gold 0.1152 oz. AGW **Ruler:** Friedrich I as Grand Duke **Obv:** Head right **Rev:** Crowned imperial German eagle, shield on breast

Date	Mintage	F	VF	XF	Unc	BU
1902G	30,409	175	300	450	750	1,250
1903G	109,450	125	200	275	450	700
1904G	149,240	115	200	275	400	700
1905G	95,932	125	200	275	500	750
1906G	120,902	125	200	275	400	700
1907G	121,902	115	200	275	400	700
(1902-1907)G Proof	— Value: 2,000					

KM# 282   10 MARK
3.9820 g., 0.9000 Gold 0.1152 oz. AGW **Ruler:** Friedrich II **Obv:** Head right **Rev:** Crowned imperial German eagle, shield on breast

Date	Mintage	F	VF	XF	Unc	BU
1909G	86,000	225	500	700	950	1,300
1910G	60,649	225	500	700	950	1,300
1911G	29,488	2,000	4,000	5,000	6,750	8,000
1912G	25,975	700	850	1,400	2,000	3,000
1913G	41,567	500	700	850	1,250	2,000
(1909-1913)G Proof	— Value: 2,000					

KM# 284   20 MARK
7.9650 g., 0.9000 Gold 0.2305 oz. AGW **Ruler:** Friedrich II **Obv:** Head left **Rev:** Crowned imperial German eagle, shield on breast

Date	Mintage	F	VF	XF	Unc	BU
1911G	190,836	BV	215	240	320	425
1912G	311,063	BV	215	240	320	425
1913G	85,374	BV	215	250	350	450
1914G	280,520	BV	215	240	320	425
(1911-1914)G Proof	— Value: 1,750					

BAVARIA
(Bayern)

Located in south Germany. In 1180 the Duchy of Bavaria was given to the Count of Wittelsbach by the emperor. He is the ancestor of all who ruled in Bavaria until 1918. Primogeniture was proclaimed in 1506 and in 1623 the dukes of Bavaria were given the electoral right. Bavaria, which had been divided for the various heirs, was reunited in 1799. The title of king was granted to Bavaria in 1805. Captial: München, population-- 1905: 6,524,372.

RULERS
Otto, 1886-1913, Prince Regent Luitpold, 1886-1912
Ludwig III, 1913-1918

MINT MARKS
D - Munich

KINGDOM
REFORM COINAGE

KM# 913   2 MARK
11.1110 g., 0.9000 Silver 0.3215 oz. ASW, 28 mm. **Ruler:** Otto
Prince Regent Luitpold **Obv:** Head left **Obv. Leg.:** OTTO KOENIG
VON BAYERN **Rev:** Crowned imperial German eagle **Rev. Leg.:**
DEUTSCHES REICH, ZWEI MARK **Edge:** Reeded **Note:** Open
and closed curl varieties exist. Prev. KM#511. Varieites exist

Date	Mintage	F	VF	XF	Unc	BU
1901D	829,064	12.00	28.00	55.00	135	300
1902D	1,340,789	10.00	22.00	45.00	120	300
1903D	1,406,067	10.00	22.00	45.00	110	275
1904D	2,320,238	9.00	20.00	40.00	100	275
1905D	1,406,100	10.00	22.00	45.00	100	275
1906D	1,054,500	10.00	22.00	55.00	120	325
1907D	2,106,712	9.00	20.00	35.00	100	275
1908D	632,700	10.00	22.00	45.00	95.00	300
1912D	213,652	12.00	28.00	60.00	125	400
1913D	97,698	40.00	80.00	160	250	475

KM# 997   2 MARK
11.1110 g., 0.9000 Silver 0.3215 oz. ASW **Ruler:** Otto Prince
Regent Luitpold **Subject:** 90th Birthday of Prince Regent Luitpold
Obv: Head right **Rev:** Crowned imperial eagle, shield on breast
Edge: Reeded **Note:** Prev. KM#516.

Date	Mintage	F	VF	XF	Unc	BU
1911D	640,000	12.00	22.00	35.00	55.00	75.00
1911D Proof	—	Value: 125				

KM# 1002   2 MARK
11.1110 g., 0.9000 Silver 0.3215 oz. ASW, 28 mm.
Ruler: Ludwig III **Obv:** Head left **Rev:** Crowned imperial eagle,
shield on breast **Note:** Prev. KM#519.

Date	Mintage	F	VF	XF	Unc	BU
1914D	573,533	30.00	50.00	110	160	250
1914D Proof	—	Value: 450				

KM# 996   3 MARK
16.6670 g., 0.9000 Silver 0.4823 oz. ASW, 33 mm. **Ruler:** Otto
Prince Regent Luitpold **Obv:** Head left **Rev:** Crowned imperial
eagle, shield on breast **Edge:** GOTT MIT UNS **Note:** Prev. KM#515

Date	Mintage	F	VF	XF	Unc	BU
1908D	680,529	12.00	20.00	35.00	60.00	125
1909D	827,460	10.00	18.00	30.00	50.00	125
1910D	1,496,091	10.00	18.00	30.00	50.00	125
1911D	843,437	12.00	20.00	35.00	60.00	125
1912D	1,013,650	12.00	20.00	35.00	60.00	125
1913D	713,275	12.00	20.00	35.00	60.00	125
1913D Proof	—	Value: 250				

KM# 998   3 MARK
16.6670 g., 0.9000 Silver 0.4823 oz. ASW, 33 mm. **Ruler:** Otto
Prince Regent Luitpold **Subject:** 90th Birthday of Prince Regent
Luitpold **Obv:** Head right **Rev:** Crowned imperial eagle, shield
on breast **Edge:** GOTT MIT UNS **Note:** Prev. KM#517.

Date	Mintage	F	VF	XF	Unc	BU
1911D	639,721	12.00	22.00	35.00	50.00	65.00
1911D Proof	—	Value: 125				

KM# 1005   3 MARK
16.6670 g., 0.9000 Silver 0.4823 oz. ASW, 33 mm.
Ruler: Ludwig III **Obv:** Head left **Rev:** Crowned imperial eagle,
shield on breast **Edge:** GOTT MIT UNS **Note:** Prev. KM#520.

Date	Mintage	F	VF	XF	Unc	BU
1914D	717,460	17.50	32.50	50.00	75.00	130
1914D Proof	—	Value: 250				

KM# 1010   3 MARK
16.6670 g., 0.9000 Silver 0.4823 oz. ASW, 33 mm.
Ruler: Ludwig III **Subject:** Golden Wedding Anniversary
Obv: Jugate heads right **Rev:** Crowned imperial eagle, shield on
breast **Note:** Prev. KM#523.

Date	Mintage	F	VF	XF	Unc	BU
1918D	130	—	12,500	26,000	32,000	45,000

KM# 915   5 MARK
27.7770 g., 0.9000 Silver 0.8037 oz. ASW, 38 mm. **Ruler:** Otto
Obv: Head left **Obv. Leg.:** OTTO KOENIG VON BAYERN
Rev: Crowned imperial German eagle **Rev. Leg.:** DEUTSCHES
REICH, FUNF MARK **Edge:** GOTT MIT UNS **Note:** Varieties in
the hair locks and curls exist. Prev. KM#512.1-512.4.

Date	Mintage	F	VF	XF	Unc	BU
1901D	295,371	14.00	25.00	85.00	300	550
1902D	506,049	14.00	25.00	65.00	250	500
1903D	1,012,097	14.00	25.00	65.00	250	450
1904D	548,340	16.00	30.00	70.00	250	450
1906D	70,249	35.00	75.00	200	1,100	2,000
1907D	752,653	14.00	20.00	50.00	200	425
1908D	576,579	14.00	20.00	50.00	200	425
1913D	520,040	14.00	20.00	40.00	120	275
(1901-1913)D Proof	—	Value: 800				

KM# 999   5 MARK
27.7770 g., 0.9000 Silver 0.8037 oz. ASW, 38 mm. **Ruler:** Otto
Prince Regent Luitpold **Subject:** 90th Birthday of Prince Regent
Luitpold **Obv:** Head right **Rev:** Crowned imperial eagle, shield
on breast **Note:** Prev. KM#518.

Date	Mintage	F	VF	XF	Unc	BU
1911D	160,000	25.00	65.00	95.00	170	225
1911D Proof	—	Value: 275				

KM# 1007   5 MARK
27.7770 g., 0.9000 Silver 0.8037 oz. ASW, 38 mm.
Ruler: Ludwig III **Obv:** Head left **Note:** Prev. KM#521.

Date	Mintage	F	VF	XF	Unc	BU
1914D	142,600	40.00	90.00	175	250	375

KM# 994   10 MARK
3.9820 g., 0.9000 Gold 0.1152 oz. AGW **Ruler:** Otto **Obv:** Head
left **Obv. Leg.:** OTTO KOENIG V. BAYERN **Rev:** Crowned
imperial German eagle **Rev. Leg.:** DEUTSCHES REICH
Note: Prev. KM#514.

Date	Mintage	F	VF	XF	Unc	BU
1901D	140,639	110	135	175	275	425
1902D	70,308	110	135	175	275	425
1903D	534,426	110	130	175	275	425
1904D	210,112	110	130	175	275	425
1905D	281,231	110	130	175	275	425
1906D	140,512	110	135	180	300	425
1907D	211,211	110	130	175	275	425
1909D	208,970	110	130	175	275	425
1910D	140,753	110	130	175	275	425
1911D	71,616	110	135	185	325	425
1912D	140,874	110	135	185	300	425
(1901-1912)D Proof	71,616,140,874	Value: 1,000				

KM# 920   20 MARK
7.9650 g., 0.9000 Gold 0.2305 oz. AGW **Ruler:** Otto **Obv:** Head
left **Obv. Leg.:** OTTO KOENIG VON BAYERN **Rev:** Type III
Rev. Leg.: DEUTSCHES REICH **Edge:** GOTT MIT UNS
Note: Prev. KM#513.

Date	Mintage	F	VF	XF	Unc	BU
1905D	501,000	BV	210	225	275	375
1905D Proof	—	Value: 1,600				

Date	Mintage	F	VF	XF	Unc	BU
1913D	310,778	Value: 25,000				
1913D Proof		Value: 35,000				

KM# 1009 20 MARK

7.9650 g., 0.9000 Gold 0.2305 oz. AGW **Ruler:** Ludwig III
Obv: Head left **Rev:** Crowned imperial eagle, shield on breast
Note: Prev. KM#522. Never officially released.

Date	Mintage	F	VF	XF	Unc	BU
1914D	532,851	—	2,000	3,000	3,500	4,500
1914D Proof, rare		Value: 5,000				

PATTERNS
Including off metal strikes

KM#	Date	Mintage	Identification	Mkt Val
Pn14	1904	—	5 Mark. Silver. Eagle in ring. Reeded edge.	—
Pn15	1904D	—	5 Mark. Silver. Eagle in ring. Lettered edge.	—
Pn16	1904D	—	5 Mark. Silver. Without inner circle.	3,000
Pn17	1905D	—	5 Mark. Copper. Pn6. KM512.	—
Pn18	1911	—	3 Mark. Silver.	—
Pn19	1911D	—	3 Mark. Copper.	—
Pn25	1913D	—	3 Mark. Silver. Plain edge.	—
Pn35	1914D	—	3 Mark. Silver. Bust faces right.	2,000
Pn36	1914D	—	5 Mark. Silver. Larger lettering, KM521.	2,500
Pn37	1914D	—	5 Mark. Silver. Plain edge. KM521.	—
Pn38	1914D	—	20 Mark. Gold. Lettered edge.	10,000
Pn39	1914D	—	20 Mark. Silver Gilt. Hallmarked, plain edge.	150
Pn40	1914D	—	20 Mark. Silver Gilt. Hallmarked, plain edge. KM522.	—
Pn41	1914D	—	20 Mark. Gold. Denticled rim. KM522. Plain edge.	9,000
Pn42	1914D	—	20 Mark. Silver Gilt. Denticled rim. KM522. Hallmarked, plain edge.	—
Pn43	1914D	—	20 Mark. Gold. 18-millimeter bust. KM522. Lettered edge.	8,000
Pn44	1914D	—	20 Mark. Silver Gilt. 18-millimeter bust. KM522. Hallmarked, plain edge.	—
Pn45	1914D	—	20 Mark. Gold. Plain rim. KM522. Plain edge.	9,000
Pn46	1914D	—	20 Mark. Gold. Plain rim. KM522. Lettered edge.	9,000
Pn47	1914D	—	20 Mark. Gold. Round "O" in KOENIG. Lettered edge.	9,000
Pn48	1914D	—	20 Mark. Silver Gilt. Round "O" in KOENIG. KM522. Hallmarked, plain edge.	—
Pn49	ND J	—	Gulden. Gold. Bust of Ludwig III in uniform. Main bridge of Wurzburger.	—

BREMEN

Established at about the same time as the bishopric in 787, Bremen was under the control of the bishops and archbishops until joining the Hanseatic League in 1276. Archbishop Albrecht II granted the mint right to the city in 1369, but this was not formalized by imperial decree until 1541. In 1646, Bremen was raised to free imperial status and continued to strike its own coins into the early 20th century. The city lost its free imperial status in 1803 and was controlled by France from 1806 until 1813. Regaining it independence in 1815, Bremen joined the North German Confederation in 1867 and the German Empire in 1871. Since 1369, there was practically continuous coinage until 1907.

FREE CITY
REGULAR COINAGE

KM# 250 2 MARK

11.1110 g., 0.9000 Silver 0.3215 oz. ASW, 28 mm. **Obv:** Key on crowned shield with supporters **Rev:** Crowned imperial eagle, shield on breast, date at right, denomination below **Edge:** Reeded

Date	Mintage	F	VF	XF	Unc	BU
1904 J	100,000	30.00	70.00	100	150	225
1904 J Proof	200	Value: 400				

KM# 251 5 MARK

27.7770 g., 0.9000 Silver 0.8037 oz. ASW, 38 mm. **Obv:** Key on crowned shield with supporters **Rev:** Crowned imperial eagle, shield on breast, date at right, denomination below **Edge:** GOTT MIT UNS

Date	Mintage	F	VF	XF	Unc	BU
1906 J	40,846	85.00	200	300	450	550
1906 J Proof	600	Value: 1,000				

KM# 253 10 MARK

3.9820 g., 0.9000 Gold 0.1152 oz. AGW **Obv:** Key on crowned shield with supporters **Rev:** Crowned imperial eagle, shield on breast, date at right, denomination below

Date	Mintage	F	VF	XF	Unc	BU
1907 J	20,006	425	1,000	1,400	1,800	2,500
1907 J Proof		Value: 2,800				

KM# 252 20 MARK

7.9650 g., 0.9000 Gold 0.2305 oz. AGW **Edge:** GOTT MIT UNS

Date	Mintage	F	VF	XF	Unc	BU
1906 J	20,122	425	1,000	1,400	1,850	2,500
1906 J Proof		Value: 2,800				

TOKEN COINAGE
Reckoning Tokens

These vouchers, issued March 18, 1924, were based on the American dollar. Issued in conjunction with Bremens issue of treasury. Due to monies being held to purchase Bremens 5% Dollar Bond, they rarely circulated. The tokens were withdrawn September 30 of that same year.

KM# Tn1 2 VERRECHNUNGS-PFENNIG

Brass **Obv:** State arms-key within circle **Rev:** Denomination within circle

Date	Mintage	F	VF	XF	Unc	BU
ND(1924)	501,000	10.00	25.00	45.00	85.00	130

KM# Tn2 5 VERRECHNUNGS-PFENNIG

Aluminum **Obv:** State arms-key within circle **Rev:** Denomination within circle

Date	Mintage	F	VF	XF	Unc	BU
ND(1924)	669,000	9.00	18.00	30.00	70.00	125

KM# Tn3 10 VERRECHNUNGS-PFENNIG

Aluminum **Obv:** State arms-key within circle **Rev:** Denomination within circle

Date	Mintage	F	VF	XF	Unc	BU
ND(1924)	695,000	10.00	20.00	35.00	75.00	125

KM# Tn4 20 VERRECHNUNGS-PFENNIG

Aluminum **Obv:** State arms-key within circle **Rev:** Denomination within circle

Date	Mintage	F	VF	XF	Unc	BU
ND(1924)	382,000	17.00	35.00	60.00	120	200

KM# Tn5 50 VERRECHNUNGS-PFENNIG

Aluminum **Obv:** Key on crowned shield with supporters
Rev: Denomination within circle

Date	Mintage	F	VF	XF	Unc	BU
ND(1924)	483,000	30.00	75.00	125	200	300

KM# Tn6 VERRECHNUNGSMARK

Aluminum **Obv:** Crowned shield with supporters on pedestal, key on shield **Rev:** Large, thick denomination **Note:** This coin is listed in Jaeger & Funck as struck in aluminum. Kunker has listed it as having an iron core but doesn't indicate what metal clads or plates the piece.

Date	Mintage	F	VF	XF	Unc	BU
ND(1924)	382,000	75.00	150	275	500	—

PATTERNS
Including off metal strikes

KM#	Date	Mintage	Identification	Mkt Val
Pn40	1904 J	—	5 Mark. KM251.	25,000
Pn41	1905 J	—	2 Mark. KM250.	5,000
Pn42	1905 J	—	5 Mark. Silver. Larger lettering without beaded rim. KM251.	20,000
Pn43	1905 J	—	5 Mark. Tin.	2,000
Pn44	1906	—	5 Mark. Bronze.	5,000
Pn45	1906	—	5 Mark. Silver.	5,000
Pn46	1906	—	5 Mark. Tin.	—
Pn47	ND	—	S.M.. Copper.	—

BRUNSWICK-WOLFENBUTTEL

(Braunschweig-Wolfenbüttel)

Located in north-central Germany. Wolfenbüttel was annexed to Brunswick in 1257. One of the five surviving sons of Albrecht II founded the first line in Wolfenbüttel in 1318. A further division in Wolfenbüttel and Lüneburg was undertaken in 1373. Another division occurred in 1495, but the Wolfenbüttel duchy survived in the younger line. Heinrich IX was forced out of his territory during the religious wars of the mid-sixteenth century by Duke Johann Friedrich I of Saxony and Landgrave Philipp of Hessen in 1542, but was restored to his possessions in 1547. Duke Friedrich Ulrich was forced to cede the Grubenhagen lands, which had been acquired by Wolfenbüttel in 1596, to Lüneburg in 1617. When the succession died out in 1634, the lands and titles fell to the cadet line in Dannenberg. The line became extinct once again and passed to Brunswick-Bevern in 1735 from which a new succession of Wolfenbüttel dukes descended. The ducal family was beset by continual personal and political tragedy during the nineteenth century. Two of the dukes were killed in battles with Napoleon, the territories were occupied by the French and became part of the Kingdom of Westphalia, another duke was forced out by a revolt in 1823. From 1884 until 1913, Brunswick-Wolfenbüttel was governed by Prussia and then turned over to the only surviving (of 3) prince of Brunswick who married the only daughter of Kaiser Wilhelm II. His reign was short, however, as he was forced to abdicate at the end of World War I.

RULERS
Prussian rule, 1884-1913
Ernst August, 1913-1918

DUCHY
REFORM COINAGE

KM# 1161 3 MARK
16.6670 g., 0.9000 Silver 0.4823 oz. ASW, 33 mm.
Ruler: Ernst August **Subject:** Ernst August Wedding and
Accession **Obv:** Jugate heads right **Rev:** Crowned imperial eagle,
shield on breast **Edge:** GOTT MIT UNS

Date	Mintage	F	VF	XF	Unc	BU
1915A	1,700	600	1,200	2,000	2,750	3,500
1915A Proof	—	Value: 3,750				

KM# 1162 3 MARK
16.6670 g., 0.9000 Silver 0.4823 oz. ASW, 33 mm.
Ruler: Ernst August **Subject:** Ernst August Wedding and
Accession **Obv:** Jugate heads right **Obv. Leg.:** U LUNEB added
Rev: Crowned imperial eagle, shield on breast

Date	Mintage	F	VF	XF	Unc	BU
1915A	31,634	50.00	120	200	275	375
1915A Proof	—	Value: 450				

KM# 1163 5 MARK
27.7770 g., 0.9000 Silver 0.8037 oz. ASW, 38 mm.
Ruler: Ernst August **Subject:** Ernst August Wedding and
Accession **Obv:** Jugate heads right **Rev:** Crowned imperial eagle,
shield on breast **Edge:** GOTT MIT UNS

Date	Mintage	F	VF	XF	Unc	BU
1915A	1,400	800	1,750	3,000	3,750	4,500
1915A Proof	—	Value: 4,750				

KM# 1164 5 MARK
27.7770 g., 0.9000 Silver 0.8037 oz. ASW, 38 mm.
Ruler: Ernst August **Subject:** Ernst August Wedding and
Accession **Obv:** Jugate heads right **Obv. Leg.:** U. LUNEB added
Rev: Crowned imperial eagle, shield on breast

Date	Mintage	F	VF	XF	Unc	BU
1915A	8,600	185	400	700	1,200	1,500
1915A Proof	—	Value: 1,600				

PATTERNS
Including off metal strikes

KM#	Date	Mintage	Identification	Mkt Val
Pn54	1913	—	3 Mark. Silver.	3,500
Pn55	1913	—	5 Mark. Silver.	5,000
Pn56	1915A	—	3 Mark. Silver. Plain edge. KM1161.	—
Pn57	1915A	—	3 Mark. Silver. Beaded rim. Weak 5 in date. Plain edge. KM1162.	—
Pn58	191x	—	5 Mark. Silver. Beaded rim, wedding portraits facing left. Partial date. Plain edge.	—

HAMBURG

The city of Hamburg is located on the Elbe River about 75 miles (125 kilometers) from the North Sea. Tradition states that it was founded by Charlemagne in the early 9th century. At first, the town was controlled by the archbishopric of Bremen and Hamburg (see Bremen). In 1110, Hamburg and the territory of Holstein came under the rule of Count Adolf I of Schauenburg (Schaumburg, ruled 1106-1128), which inaugurated a period stretching for four centuries in which the Holstein dynasty exercised authority over the city. Hamburg joined with Lübeck in 1241 to form the first partnership in what was to become the Hanseatic League. Count Adolf VI of Schauenburg (1290-1315) gave civic autonomy to Hamburg in 1292 and leased the mint right to the citizens the next year. Local *hohlpfennige* had already been struck fifty years previous. From this early time, the city struck an almost continuous series of coins throughout the centuries up to World War I. In 1510, Hamburg was granted the status of a Free City of the Empire, although it had actually been free for about 250 years. It was occupied by the French during the period of the Napoleonic Wars. In 1866, Hamburg joined the North German Confederation and became a part of the German Empire in 1871.

FREE CITY
REFORM COINAGE

KM# 294 2 MARK
11.1110 g., 0.9000 Silver 0.3215 oz. ASW, 28 mm. **Obv:** Helmeted arms with lion supporters **Obv. Leg.:** FREIE UND HANSESTADT HAMBURG **Rev:** Crowned imperial eagle **Rev. Leg.:** DEUTSCHES REICH 1899, ZWEI MARK below **Edge:** Reeded

Date	Mintage	F	VF	XF	Unc	BU
1901J	482,408	15.00	25.00	60.00	200	300
1902J	778,880	12.50	25.00	60.00	200	300
1903J	817,215	12.50	25.00	50.00	200	300
1904J	1,248,330	12.50	25.00	50.00	180	300
1905J	204,040	35.00	65.00	125	550	1,000
1906J	1,224,910	12.50	25.00	50.00	180	300
1907J	1,225,503	12.50	25.00	50.00	180	300
1908J	367,750	12.50	30.00	55.00	180	325
1911J	204,250	12.50	30.00	55.00	180	325
1912J	78,500	20.00	50.00	110	300	600
1913J	105,325	12.50	30.00	65.00	180	550
1914J	327,758	10.00	25.00	50.00	140	300
(1901-1914)J Proof	—	Value: 400				

KM# 296 3 MARK
16.6670 g., 0.9000 Silver 0.4823 oz. ASW, 33 mm. **Obv:** Three tower castle on helmeted shield with supporters **Rev:** Crowned imperial eagle, shield on breast **Edge:** GOTT MIT UNS

Date	Mintage	F	VF	XF	Unc	BU
1908J	408,475	12.50	25.00	40.00	80.00	130
1909J	1,388,892	12.50	25.00	40.00	80.00	130
1910J	525,500	12.50	25.00	40.00	80.00	130
1911J	922,000	12.50	25.00	40.00	80.00	130
1912J	491,088	12.50	25.00	40.00	80.00	130
1913J	343,200	12.50	25.00	40.00	80.00	130
1914J	575,111	12.50	25.00	40.00	80.00	130
(1908-1914) Proof	—	Value: 250				

KM# 293 5 MARK
27.7770 g., 0.9000 Silver 0.8037 oz. ASW, 38 mm. **Obv:** Helmeted arms with lion supporters **Obv. Leg.:** FREIE UND HANSESTADT HAMBURG **Rev:** Crowned imperial eagle **Rev. Leg.:** DEUTSCHES REICH 1907, FUNF MARK below **Edge:** GOTT MIT UNS

Date	Mintage	F	VF	XF	Unc	BU
1901J	171,603	20.00	40.00	100	500	900
1902J	294,034	17.50	35.00	80.00	400	800
1903J	588,535	17.50	35.00	75.00	275	450
1904J	318,640	16.00	32.00	75.00	275	500
1907J	325,534	16.00	32.00	75.00	275	550
1908J	457,794	16.00	32.00	75.00	200	325
1913J	326,800	16.00	32.00	60.00	165	225
(1901-1913)J Proof	—	Value: 1,500				

KM# 292 10 MARK
3.9820 g., 0.9000 Gold 0.1152 oz. AGW **Obv:** Helmeted arms with lion supporters **Obv. Leg.:** FREIE UND HANSESTADT HAMBURG **Rev:** Crowned imperial eagle, type II
Rev. Leg.: DEUTSCHES REICH

Date	Mintage	F	VF	XF	Unc	BU
1901J	81,891	110	150	175	385	500
1902J	40,763	120	225	350	650	1,000
1903J	229,786	110	150	175	350	500
1905J	164,000	110	150	175	350	500
1906J	163,347	110	150	175	350	500
1907J	111,373	110	150	175	350	500
1908J	31,685	150	300	450	800	1,300
1909J	122,245	110	150	175	350	500
1909J Proof	—	Value: 1,600				
1910J	40,598	120	225	300	600	1,000
1910J Proof	—	Value: 2,000				
1911J	75,000	115	175	250	300	800
1911J Proof	—	Value: 3,500				
1912J	47,775	145	245	350	500	1,000
1912J Proof	—	Value: 2,000				
1913J	40,937	145	245	300	400	1,000
1913J Proof	—	Value: 2,000				

KM# 295 20 MARK
7.9650 g., 0.9000 Gold 0.2305 oz. AGW **Obv:** Helmeted arms with lion supporters **Obv. Leg.:** FREIE UND HANSESTADT HAMBURG **Rev:** Crowned imperial eagle, type III
Rev. Leg.: DEUTSCHES REICH **Edge:** GOTT MIT UNS

Date	Mintage	F	VF	XF	Unc	BU
1908J Rare	14	—	—	—	75,000	—
1913J Proof	—	Value: 1,000				
1913J	491,133	—	BV	210	220	275

TOKEN COINAGE
Reckoning Tokens

KM# Tn1 1/100 VERRECHNUNGSMARKE
Aluminum, 20.5 mm. **Issuer:** Hamburg Bank **Obv:** City arms-
three tower castle on helmeted shield with supporters **Rev:**
Denomination within circle

Date	Mintage	F	VF	XF	Unc	BU
1923	9,128,000	3.00	6.00	12.50	25.00	—

KM# Tn2 5/100 VERRECHNUNGSMARKE
Aluminum, 23 mm. **Issuer:** Hamburg Bank **Obv:** City arms-three
tower castle on helmeted shield with supporters **Rev:**
Denomination within circle

Date	Mintage	F	VF	XF	Unc	BU
1923	8,100,000	2.75	4.50	9.00	18.00	—

KM# Tn3 1/10 VERRECHNUNGSMARKE
Aluminum, 26.5 mm. **Issuer:** Hamburg Bank **Obv:** City arms-
three tower castle on helmeted shield with supporters
Rev: Denomination within circle

Date	Mintage	F	VF	XF	Unc	BU
1923	8,600,000	2.75	4.50	10.00	20.00	—

PATTERNS
Including off metal strikes

KM#	Date	Mintage	Identification	Mkt Val
Pn20	1906J	—	5 Mark. Copper. Plain edge. KM293.	—
Pn21	1913	—	5 Mark. Silver. Plain edge. KM293.	1,100
Pn22	1913J	—	5 Mark. Silver. Plain edge. KM293.	—
Pn23	1914J	—	3 Mark. Silver. Plain edge. KM296.	1,250
Pn24	1922J	—	1/2 Mark. Aluminum. Plain edge.	—
Pn25	1922J	—	1/2 Mark. Iron. Plain edge.	—
Pn26	1922J	—	1/2 Mark. Nickel. Plain edge.	—
Pn27	1922J	—	1/2 Mark. Copper. Plain edge. 19 mm.	225
Pn28	1922J	—	Mark. Aluminum. Plain edge.	—
Pn29	1922J	—	Mark. Copper. Plain edge.	—
Pn30	1922J	—	Mark. Nickel. Plain edge.	—
Pn31	1922J	—	Mark. Iron. Plain edge.	—
Pn32	1922J	—	2 Mark. Nickel. Plain edge.	—
Pn33	1922J	—	2 Mark. Aluminum. Plain edge.	—
Pn34	1922J	—	2 Mark. Zinc. Plain edge.	—
Pn35	1922J	—	3 Mark. Iron. Plain edge. Copper-nickel plated.	—
Pn36	1922J	—	3 Mark. Aluminum. Plain edge.	—
Pn37	1922J	—	3 Mark. Nickel. Plain edge.	—
Pn38	1922J	—	5 Mark. Nickel Plated Iron. Plain edge.	—
Pn39	1922J	—	5 Mark. Aluminum. Plain edge.	—
Pn40	1922J	—	5 Mark. Nickel. Plain edge.	—
Pn41	1922J	—	5 Mark. Zinc. Plain edge.	—

HESSE-DARMSTADT
(Hessen-Darmstadt)

Founded by the youngest of Philipp I's four sons
upon the death of their father in 1567, Hesse-Darmstadt was one
of the two main branches of the family which survived past the
beginning of the 17th century. The Countship of Hanau-Lich-
tenberg was through marriage when the male line failed in 1736.
Ludwig X was forced to cede that territory to France in 1801. In
1803, Darmstadt acquired part of the Palatinate, the city of Friedberg, part of the city of Mainz, and the Duchy of Westphalia in a
general settlement with France. The Landgrave was elevated to
the status of Grand Duke in 1806 and reacquired Hesse-Hom-
burg, which got its souverainty back in 1816. In 1815 the Congress of Vienna awarded Hesse-Darmstadt the city of Worms
and all of Mainz. These were relinquished, along with Hesse-
Homburg, to Prussia in 1866 and Hesse-Darmstadt was called
just Hesse from 1867 onwards. Hesse became part of the German Empire in 1871, but ceased to exist as a semi-sovereign
state at the end of World War I.

RULER
Ernst Ludwig, 1892-1918

GRAND DUCHY
REFORM COINAGE
Grossherzogtum within the German Empire

KM# 372 2 MARK
11.1110 g., 0.9000 Silver 0.3215 oz. ASW, 28 mm.
Ruler: Ernst Ludwig **Subject:** 400th Birthday of Philipp the
Magnanimous **Obv:** Jugate heads left, dates below **Rev:**
Crowned imperial eagle with shield on breast **Edge:** Reeded

Date	Mintage	F	VF	XF	Unc	BU
1904	100,000	30.00	65.00	100	150	200
1904 Proof	2,250	Value: 400				

Note: Obverse matte, reverse polished

KM# 375 3 MARK
16.6670 g., 0.9000 Silver 0.4823 oz. ASW, 33 mm.
Ruler: Ernst Ludwig **Obv:** Head left **Rev:** Crowned imperial
eagle, shield on breast **Edge:** GOTT MIT UNS

Date	Mintage	F	VF	XF	Unc	BU
1910A	200,000	50.00	100	175	400	550
1910A Proof	Est. 500	Value: 750				

KM# 376 3 MARK
16.6670 g., 0.9000 Silver 0.4823 oz. ASW, 33 mm.
Ruler: Ernst Ludwig **Subject:** 25-Year Jubilee **Obv:** Head left
Rev: Crowned imperial eagle, shield on breast **Note:** All minted
pieces are proof. Values in circulated grades are for impaired
proofs.

Date	Mintage	F	VF	XF	Unc	BU
1917A	1,333	—	3,400	5,200	7,000	9,500
1917A Proof	Inc. above	Value: 9,500				

KM# 373 5 MARK
27.7770 g., 0.9000 Silver 0.8037 oz. ASW, 38 mm.
Ruler: Ernst Ludwig **Subject:** 400th birthday of Philipp the
Magnanimous **Obv:** Jugate heads left, dates below **Rev:**
Crowned imperial eagle, shield on breast **Edge:** GOTT MIT UNS

Date	Mintage	F	VF	XF	Unc	BU
1904	40,000	70.00	140	260	370	500
1904 Proof	700	Value: 750				

Note: Obverse matte, reverse polished

KM# 371 20 MARK
7.9650 g., 0.9000 Gold 0.2305 oz. AGW **Ruler:** Ernst Ludwig
Obv: Head left **Obv. Leg.:** ERNST LUDWIG GROSHERZOG VON
HESSEN **Rev:** Crowned imperial eagle, shield on breast **Rev. Leg.:**
DEUTSCHES REICH date, 20 MARK below **Edge:** GOTT MIT UNS

Date	Mintage	F	VF	XF	Unc	BU
1901A	80,000	250	460	800	1,250	2,000
1901A Proof	600	Value: 3,200				
1903A	40,000	250	460	800	1,250	2,000
1903A Proof	100	Value: 3,200				

KM# 374 20 MARK
7.9650 g., 0.9000 Gold 0.2305 oz. AGW **Ruler:** Ernst Ludwig **Obv:**
Head left **Obv. Leg.:** ERNST LUDWIG GROSHERZOG VON
HESSEN **Rev:** Crowned imperial eagle, shield on breast **Rev. Leg.:**
DEUTSCHES REICH date, 20 MARK below **Edge:** GOTT MIT UNS

Date	Mintage	F	VF	XF	Unc	BU
1905A	45,000	300	420	600	1,200	1,400
1905A Proof	200	Value: 2,400				
1906A	85,000	210	360	460	1,000	1,400
1906A Proof	199	Value: 2,250				
1908A	40,000	250	400	750	1,200	1,400
1908A Proof	—	Value: 2,250				
1911A	150,000	210	360	550	1,000	1,400
1911A Proof	—	Value: 2,250				

PATTERNS
Including off metal strikes

KM#	Date	Mintage	Identification	Mkt Val
Pn31	1910A	—	3 Mark. Silver.	1,800
Pn33	1917A	—	3 Mark. Silver. Plain edge. Y82.	10,000
Pn32	1917	—	3 Mark. Silver.	—

LIPPE-DETMOLD

After the division of 1613, the Counts of Lippe-Detmold, as
the senior branch of the family, ruled over the largest portion of
Lippe (see), a small patrimony in northwestern Germany. In 1620,
Lippe-Sternberg became extinct and its lands and titles reverted
to Lippe-Detmold. The younger brother of Hermann Adolf
founded the line of Lippe-Sternberg-Schwalenberg (Biesterfeld)
in 1652, which lasted into the 20th century. In 1720, the count was
raised to the rank of prince, but did not use the title until 1789.
Lippe joined the North German Confederation in 1866 and
became part of the German Empire in 1871. Prince Alexander
was declared insane and placed under a regency during his entire
reign. There ensued a ten-year testamentary dispute between the
Lippe-Biesterfeld and the Schaumburg-Lippe lines over the succession to the childless Alexander - a Wilhelmine cause célèbre.
Leopold (V) of the Biesterfeld line gained the principality in 1905,
but was forced to abdicate in 1918, at the end of World War I. In
1947, Lippe was absorbed by the German state of North Rhine-
Westphalia.

RULERS
Alexander, 1895-1905
Leopold IV, 1905-1918
MINT MARK
A - Berlin mint, 1843-1918

PRINCIPALITY
REFORM COINAGE

KM# 270 2 MARK
11.1110 g., 0.9000 Silver 0.3215 oz. ASW, 28 mm.
Ruler: Leopold IV **Obv:** Head left **Rev:** Crowned imperial eagle,
shield on breast **Edge:** Reeded

Date	Mintage	F	VF	XF	Unc	BU
1906A	20,000	125	225	350	500	650
1906A Proof	1,100	Value: 750				

KM# 275   3 MARK
16.6670 g., 0.9000 Silver 0.4823 oz. ASW, 33 mm.   **Ruler:**
Leopold IV **Obv:** Head left **Rev:** Crowned imperial eagle, shield
on breast **Edge:** GOTT MIT UNS

Date	Mintage	F	VF	XF	Unc	BU
1913A	15,000	150	325	450	600	750
1913A Proof, rare	100	Value: 1,100				

LUBECK

The original settlement was called Liubice, the capital of a
Slavic principality. It was located at the confluence of the Schwar-
tau with the Trave Rivers and contained a castle with a merchant
town on a harbor. The town was burned down in 1138 and Count
Adolf II of Holstein (1128-64) refounded the city four miles (6.5
kilometers) up the Trave in 1143. Duke Heinirich III the Lion of
Saxony (1153-80) forced Adolf II to relinquish Lübeck to him as
his feudal overlord. Heinrich III no sooner had the city in his possession when a fire destroyed it. Heinrich III began rebuilding it
in 1159 and this is now considered the traditional date of it founding. As the city and its trade on the Baltic grew in importance, special rights and privileges were granted to it in 1188 by Emperor
Friedrich I Barbarossa. In 1226, Friedrich II raised Lübeck to the
status of a free imperial city and a long period of self-government
began. From about 1190 and into the 13th century, an imperial
mint operated in the town. Although Lübeck was granted the mint
right in 1188, reiterated in 1226 and 1340, its earliest civic coinage only began about 1350. The commercial importance of the
city became even greater when it joined with Hamburg in 1241
to form the nucleus of what was to become the Hanseatic
League. In 1358, the member cities of the League, which had
grown very powerful during the preceding century, elected
Lübeck as the administrative capital. By the beginning of the 15th
century, the city was second only to Cologne as the largest in
northern Germany.

The Protestant Reformation swept through Lübeck in 1529-
30 (see Bishopric) and changes came rapidly as the governing
city council was removed from office, only to be replaced by a revolutionary *burgomeister*, Jürgen Wullenwever. An unsuccessful
war ensued against Denmark, Sweden and the Netherlands and
caused the city to lose its powerful position in northern Europe.
This began the dismemberment of the Hanseatic League and
even a victorious war against Sweden during 1563-1570 was not
enough to prevent the decline of Lübeck's fortunes. The demise
of the League in 1630, during the Thirty Years' War, may have
actually been beneficial to the city as it was able to remain neutral
during the long years of struggle throughout Germany. The city
was able to regain much of its lost economic power during the 18th
century, partly due to increased trade with Russia through its new
Baltic port of St. Petersburg. Lübeck's economy was completely
ruined, however, during the Napoleonic Wars (1792-1815).
Occupied by the French from 1811 to 1813, it was restored as a
free city in the latter year. After 1815, the city was a member of
the German Confederation and joined the North German Confederation in 1866. It remained a free city as part of the German
Empire from 1871 until the end of World War I in 1918. However,
its status as a self-governing entity, which had begun in 1226, did
not end until 1937, when it was made a part of the province of
Schleswig-Holstein.

FREE CITY
REFORM COINAGE

KM# 210   2 MARK
11.1110 g., 0.9000 Silver 0.3215 oz. ASW, 28 mm.   **Obv:** Double
imperial eagle with divided shield on breast **Rev:** Crowned
imperial eagle, shield on breast **Edge:** Reeded

Date	Mintage	F	VF	XF	Unc	BU
1901A	25,000	100	225	300	475	700
1901A Proof	—	Value: 900				

KM# 212   2 MARK
11.1110 g., 0.9000 Silver 0.3215 oz. ASW, 28 mm.   **Obv:** Double
imperial eagle with divided shield on breast **Edge:** Reeded

Date	Mintage	F	VF	XF	Unc	BU
1904A	25,000	45.00	100	150	225	375
1904A Proof	200	Value: 500				
1905A	25,000	45.00	100	150	225	325
1905A Proof	178	Value: 500				
1906A	25,000	45.00	100	150	225	325
1906A Proof	200	Value: 500				
1907A	25,000	45.00	100	150	225	325
1907A Proof	—	Value: 500				
1911A	25,000	45.00	100	150	225	325
1911A Proof	—	Value: 500				
1912A	25,000	45.00	100	150	225	325
1912A Proof	—	Value: 500				

KM# 215   3 MARK
16.6670 g., 0.9000 Silver 0.4823 oz. ASW, 33 mm.   **Obv:** Double
imperial eagle with divided shield on breast **Rev:** Crowned
imperial eagle, shield on breast **Edge:** GOTT MIT UNS

Date	Mintage	F	VF	XF	Unc	BU
1908	33,334	25.00	70.00	125	200	350
1909A	33,334	25.00	70.00	125	200	350
1910A	33,334	25.00	70.00	125	200	350
1911A	33,334	25.00	70.00	125	200	350
1912A	34,000	25.00	70.00	125	200	350
1913A	30,000	25.00	70.00	125	200	350
1914A	10,000	35.00	85.00	150	250	350
(1908-1914)A Proof	—	Value: 400				

KM# 213   5 MARK
27.7770 g., 0.9000 Silver 0.8037 oz. ASW, 38 mm.   **Obv:** Double
imperial eagle with divided shield on breast **Rev:** Crowned
imperial eagle, shield on breast

Date	Mintage	F	VF	XF	Unc	BU
1904A	10,000	120	325	425	550	1,100
1904A Proof	200	Value: 1,500				
1907A	10,000	120	325	450	575	1,100
1907 Proof	—	Value: 1,700				
1908A	10,000	120	325	450	600	1,100
1908 Proof	—	Value: 1,600				
1913A	6,000	120	325	450	650	1,100
1913 Proof	—	Value: 1,750				

KM# 211   10 MARK
3.9820 g., 0.9000 Gold 0.1152 oz. AGW   **Obv:** Double imperial
eagle with divided shield on breast **Rev:** Crowned imperial eagle,
shield on breast **Edge:** ~ * ~

Date	Mintage	F	VF	XF	Unc	BU
1901A	10,000	375	1,100	1,350	1,650	2,700
1901A Proof	200	Value: 3,000				
1904A	10,000	375	1,100	1,350	1,650	2,700
1904A Proof	130	Value: 3,000				

KM# 214   10 MARK
3.9820 g., 0.9000 Gold 0.1152 oz. AGW   **Obv:** Double imperial
eagle with divided shield on breast **Rev:** Crowned imperial eagle,
shield on breast **Edge:** ~ * ~

Date	Mintage	F	VF	XF	Unc	BU
1905A	10,000	400	1,050	1,300	1,650	2,500
1905A Proof	247	Value: 3,250				
1906A	10,000	400	1,050	1,300	1,650	2,500
1906A Proof	216	Value: 3,250				
1909A	10,000	400	1,050	1,300	1,650	2,000
1909A Proof	—	Value: 2,750				
1910A	10,000	300	800	1,200	1,650	2,250
1910A Proof	—	Value: 3,000				

PATTERNS
Including off metal strikes

KM#	Date	Mintage	Identification	Mkt Val
Pn38	1915A	—	3 Mark. Copper. Aluminum plated.	—
Pn39	1915A	—	3 Mark. Zinc. Aluminum-plated.	—
Pn40	1915A	—	3 Mark. Silver.	3,000

MECKLENBURG-SCHWERIN

The Duchy of Mecklenburg was divided in 1592 to form the
branches of Mecklenburg-Schwerin and Mecklenburg-Güstrow.
During the Thirty Years' War, the several dukes of the Mecklenburg states sided with the Protestant forces against the
emperor. Albrecht von Wallenstein, Duke of Friedland and imperial general, ousted the Mecklenburg dukes from their territories
in 1628. The rightful rulers were each restored to their lands in
1632. In 1658, Mecklenburg-Schwerin was divided by the four
sons of Adolf Friedrich into the lines of Mecklenburg-Schwerin,
Mecklenburg-Grabow, Mecklenburg-Mirow (extinct in 1675) and
Mecklenburg-Strelitz (see). Mecklenburg-Schwerin and Mecklenburg-Güstrow fell extinct in the male line in 1692 and 1695
respectively, becoming a source of dispute between Mecklenburg-Grabow and Mecklenburg-Strelitz. Both parties finally
agreed to a settlement in 1701 which awarded about eighty percent of all Mecklenburg territory to Grabow, which became the
main Schwerin line, and the rest to Strelitz. No coinage was produced for Mecklenburg-Schwerin from 1708 until 1750. In 1815,
the Congress of Vienna elevated the ruler to the rank of Grand
Duke. Mecklenburg-Schwerin became a part of the German
Empire in 1871. The last grand duke abdicated at the end of
World War I in 1918.

RULER
Friedrich Franz IV, 1897-1918

MINT MARKS
A - Berlin mint, 1852-1915

GRAND DUCHY
REFORM COINAGE

KM# 330   2 MARK
11.1110 g., 0.9000 Silver 0.3215 oz. ASW, 28 mm.   **Ruler:**
Friedrich Franz IV **Subject:** Grand Duke Coming of Age **Obv:** Head
right **Rev:** Crowned imperial eagle, shield on breast **Edge:** Reeded

Date	Mintage	F	VF	XF	Unc	BU
1901A	50,000	125	350	500	1,100	1,600
1901A Proof	1,000	Value: 2,000				

KM# 333   2 MARK
11.1110 g., 0.9000 Silver 0.3215 oz. ASW, 28 mm.
Ruler: Friedrich Franz IV **Subject:** Friedrich Franz IV Wedding
Obv: Jugate heads left **Rev:** Crowned imperial eagle, shield on
breast **Edge:** Reeded

Date	Mintage	F	VF	XF	Unc	BU
1904A	100,000	18.00	40.00	65.00	100	150
1904A Proof	6,000	Value: 225				

KM# 340 3 MARK
16.6670 g., 0.9000 Silver 0.4823 oz. ASW, 33 mm.
Ruler: Friedrich Franz IV **Subject:** 100 Years as Grand Duchy
Obv: Uniformed jugate busts left **Rev:** Crowned imperial eagle,
shield on breast within circle **Edge:** GOTT MIT UNS

Date	Mintage	F	VF	XF	Unc	BU
1915A	33,334	50.00	100	175	250	350
1915A Proof	—	Value: 500				

KM# 334 5 MARK
27.7770 g., 0.9000 Silver 0.8037 oz. ASW, 38 mm.
Ruler: Friedrich Franz IV **Subject:** Friedrich Franz IV Wedding
Obv: Jugate heads left **Rev:** Crowned imperial eagle, shield on
breast **Edge:** GOTT MIT UNS

Date	Mintage	F	VF	XF	Unc	BU
1904A	40,000	45.00	100	175	250	375
1904A Proof	2,500	Value: 600				

KM# 341 5 MARK
27.7770 g., 0.9000 Silver 0.8037 oz. ASW, 38 mm.
Ruler: Friedrich Franz IV **Subject:** 100 Years as Grand Duchy
Obv: Uniformed jugate busts left **Rev:** Crowned imperial eagle,
shield on breast within circle **Edge:** GOTT MIT UNS

Date	Mintage	F	VF	XF	Unc	BU
1915A	10,000	135	375	500	900	1,500
1915A Proof	—	Value: 1,600				

KM# 331 10 MARK
3.9820 g., 0.9000 Gold 0.1152 oz. AGW **Ruler:** Friedrich Franz IV
Subject: Grand Duke Coming of Age **Obv:** Head right
Rev: Crowned imperial eagle, shield on breast, type III **Edge:** ~ * ~

Date	Mintage	F	VF	XF	Unc	BU
1901A	10,000	1,250	2,250	3,250	4,500	7,000
1901A Proof	200	Value: 8,000				

KM# 332 20 MARK
7.9650 g., 0.9000 Gold 0.2305 oz. AGW **Ruler:** Friedrich Franz IV
Subject: Grand Duke Coming of Age **Obv:** Head right
Rev: Crowned imperial eagle, shield on breast, type III
Edge: GOTT MIT UNS

Date	Mintage	F	VF	XF	Unc	BU
1901A	5,000	1,700	3,250	4,500	6,250	9,000
1901A Proof, rare	200	Value: 10,000				

PATTERNS
Including off metal strikes

KM#	Date	Mintage	Identification	Mkt Val
Pn26	1915A	—	3 Mark. Silver. Plain edge. KM340.	2,000
Pn27	1915A	—	3 Mark. Silver.	—
Pn28	1915A	—	5 Mark. Silver. KM341.	3,000

MECKLENBURG-STRELITZ

The Duchy of Mecklenburg-Strelitz was the youngest branch of the dynasty established when Mecklenburg-Schwerin was divided in 1658. Like its parent senior line, Mecklenburg-Strelitz became a grand duchy in 1815 as enacted by the Congress of Vienna. It became a constituent part of the German Empire in 1871, but all sovereignty ended with the conclusion of World War I in 1918.

RULERS
Friedrich Wilhelm, 1860-1904
Adolf Friedrich V, 1904-1914
Adolf Friedrich VI, 1914-1918

GRAND DUCHY
REFORM COINAGE

KM# 115 2 MARK
11.1110 g., 0.9000 Silver 0.3215 oz. ASW, 28 mm.
Ruler: Adolph Friedrich V **Obv:** Head left **Rev:** Crowned imperial
eagle, shield on breast **Edge:** Reeded

Date	Mintage	F	VF	XF	Unc	BU
1905A	10,000	150	400	575	1,000	1,400
1905A Proof	2,500	Value: 1,500				

KM# 120 3 MARK
16.6670 g., 0.9000 Silver 0.4823 oz. ASW, 33 mm.
Ruler: Adolph Friedrich V **Obv:** Head left **Rev:** Crowned imperial
eagle, shield on breast **Edge:** GOTT MIT UNS

Date	Mintage	F	VF	XF	Unc	BU
1913A	7,000	250	600	950	1,600	2,400
1913A Proof	—	Value: 2,800				

KM# 116 10 MARK
3.9820 g., 0.9000 Gold 0.1152 oz. AGW **Ruler:** Adolph
Friedrich V **Obv:** Head left **Rev:** Crowned imperial eagle, shield
on breast **Edge:** ~ * ~

Date	Mintage	F	VF	XF	Unc	BU
1905A	1,000	1,750	3,750	6,000	7,500	9,000
1905A Proof	150	Value: 10,000				

KM# 117 20 MARK
7.9650 g., 0.9000 Gold 0.2305 oz. AGW **Ruler:** Adolph
Friedrich V **Obv:** Head left **Rev:** Crowned imperial eagle, shield
on breast, type III **Edge:** GOTT MIT UNS

Date	Mintage	F	VF	XF	Unc	BU
1905A	1,000	3,000	5,500	8,000	11,500	15,000
1905A Proof	160	Value: 17,500				

PATTERNS
Including off metal strikes

KM#	Date	Mintage	Identification	Mkt Val
Pn41	1913	—	3 Mark. Silver. KM120.	3,000

OLDENBURG

The county of Oldenburg was situated on the North Seacoast, to the east of the principality of East Friesland. It was originally part of the old duchy of Saxony and the first recorded lord ruled from the beginning of the 11th century. The first count was named in 1091 and had already acquired the county of Delmenhorst prior to that time. The first identifiable Oldenburg coinage was struck in the first half of the 13th century. Oldenburg was divided into Oldenburg and Delmenhorst in 1270, but the two lines were reunited by marriage five generations later. Through another marriage to the heiress of the duchy of Schleswig and county of Holstein, the house of Denmark descended through the Oldenburg line beginning in 1448, while a junior branch continued as counts of Oldenburg. The lordship of Jever was added to the county's domains in 1575. In 1667, the last count died without a direct heir and Oldenburg reverted to Denmark until 1773. In the following year, Oldenburg was given to the bishop of Lübeck, of the Holstein-Gottorp line, and raised to the status of a duchy. Oldenburg was occupied several times during the Napoleonic Wars and became a grand duchy in 1829. In 1817, Oldenburg acquired the principality of Birkenfeld from Prussia and struck coins in denominations used there. World War I spelled the end of temporal power for the Grand Duke in 1918, but the title has continued up to the present time. Grand Duke Anton Günther was born in 1923.

RULER
Friedrich August, 1900-1918

MINT MARK
A - Berlin mint, 1891-1901

GRAND DUCHY
REFORM COINAGE

KM# 202 2 MARK
11.1110 g., 0.9000 Silver 0.3215 oz. ASW, 28 mm.
Ruler: Friedrich August **Obv:** Head left **Obv. Leg.:** FRIEDRICH
AUGUST GROSSHERZOG V. OLDENBURG **Rev:** Crowned
imperial eagle with wreathed arms on breast **Rev. Leg.:**
DEUTSCHES REICH date, ZWEI MARK below **Edge:** Reeded

Date	Mintage	F	VF	XF	Unc	BU
1901A	75,000	100	225	400	900	1,500
1901A Proof, rare	260	Value: 2,500				

KM# 203 5 MARK
27.7770 g., 0.9000 Silver 0.8037 oz. ASW, 38 mm.
Ruler: Friedrich August **Obv:** Head left **Obv. Leg.:** FRIEDRICH
AUGUST GROSSHERZOG V. OLDENBURG **Rev:** Crowned
imperial eagle with wreathed arms on breast **Rev. Leg.:**
DEUTSCHES REICH date, FUNF MARK below **Edge:** GOTT ~ MIT
~ UNS

Date	Mintage	F	VF	XF	Unc	BU
1901A	10,000	350	900	1,500	3,750	7,000
1901A Proof	170	Value: 8,000				

PRUSSIA

(Preussen)

Elector Friedrich III of Brandenburg-Prussia (1688-1713) was accorded the title of "King in Prussia" in 1701 as a reward for his support of Austria during the War of the Spanish Succession. Under successive strong leaders, Prussia gained increasing importance and added to its territories to become one of the leading countries of Europe in the course of the 18th century. As part of the reforms instituted by Friedrich II, the system of single letter mintmarks representing specific mints replaced the traditional incorporation of mint officials' symbols and/or initials as part of coin designs. Some of these very same mintmarks are still in use on modern German coins up to the present day. During the Napoleonic Wars (1792-1815), Prussia was allied with Saxony and they were soundly defeated at Jena in 1806. Prussia was forced to cede large portions of its territory at the time, but played a large part in the final defeat of Napoleon. The Congress of Vienna awarded Prussia part of Pomerania, the northern half of Saxony, much of Westphalia and the Rhineland, thus making it the largest state in Germany and a major power in European affairs. After defeating Denmark in 1864 and Austria in 1866, Prussia acquired Schleswig-Holstein, Hannover, Hesse-Cassel, Nassau and Frankfurt am Main. By this time, Prussia encompassed a large part of German territory and its population included two-thirds of all the German people. By winning the Franco-Prussian War (1870-71), Prussia became the pivotal state in the unification of Germany in 1871, King Wilhelm I was proclaimed Kaiser (Emperor) of all Germany, but World War I brought an end to both the Empire and the Kingdom of Prussia in 1918.

NOTE: For coins of Neuchatel previously listed here, see Switzerland.

RULER
Wilhelm II, 1888-1918

MINT MARK
A - Berlin = Prussia, East Friesland, East Prussia, Posen

KINGDOM

REFORM COINAGE

KM# 522 2 MARK

11.1110 g., 0.9000 Silver 0.3215 oz. ASW, 28 mm.
Ruler: Wilhelm II **Obv:** Head right **Obv. Leg.:** WILHELM II DEUTSCHER KAISER KONIG V. PREUSSEN **Rev:** Crowned imperial eagle **Rev. Leg.:** DEUTSCHES REICH date, ZWEI MARK below **Edge:** Reeded

Date	Mintage	F	VF	XF	Unc	BU
1901	398,486	70.00	160	300	1,000	2,250
1901 Proof	—	Value: 3,000				
1902	3,948,323	7.50	16.00	55.00	100	275
1903	4,078,709	7.50	16.00	55.00	100	275
1904A	9,981,031	7.50	16.00	55.00	100	250
1905A	6,423,135	7.00	15.00	50.00	100	275
1905A Proof	620	Value: 600				
1906A	4,000,000	7.00	15.00	50.00	100	300
1906A Proof	85	Value: 600				
1907A	8,085,264	7.00	15.00	50.00	100	250
1908A	2,389,550	7.00	15.00	45.00	100	300
1911A	1,181,475	10.00	22.00	55.00	110	300
1912A	732,813	12.00	28.00	58.00	125	325

KM# 525 2 MARK

11.1110 g., 0.9000 Silver 0.3215 oz. ASW, 28 mm.
Ruler: Wilhelm II **Subject:** 200th Anniversary - Kingdom of Prussia **Obv:** Friedrich I, Wilhelm II left **Rev:** Crowned imperial eagle with shield on breast **Edge:** Reeded

Date	Mintage	F	VF	XF	Unc	BU
1901A	2,600,000	7.50	15.00	22.00	35.00	50.00
1901A Proof	—	Value: 125				

KM# 532 2 MARK

11.1110 g., 0.9000 Silver 0.3215 oz. ASW, 28 mm. **Ruler:** Wilhelm II **Subject:** 100th Anniversary - victory over Napoleon at Leipzig **Obv:** Eagle with snake in talons, denomination below **Rev:** Figure on horseback surrounded by people **Edge:** Reeded

Date	Mintage	F	VF	XF	Unc	BU
1913A	1,500,000	7.50	15.00	22.00	40.00	50.00
1913A Proof	—	Value: 125				

KM# 533 2 MARK

11.1110 g., 0.9000 Silver 0.3215 oz. ASW, 28 mm. **Ruler:** Wilhelm II **Subject:** 25th Year of Reign **Obv:** Uniformed bust right **Rev:** Crowned imperial eagle with shield on breast **Edge:** Reeded

Date	Mintage	F	VF	XF	Unc	BU
1913A	1,500,000	7.50	15.00	22.00	40.00	50.00
1913A Proof	5,000	Value: 125				

KM# 527 3 MARK

16.6670 g., 0.9000 Silver 0.4823 oz. ASW, 33 mm.
Ruler: Wilhelm II **Obv:** Head right **Rev:** Crowned imperial eagle with shield on breast **Edge:** GOTT MIT UNS

Date	Mintage	F	VF	XF	Unc	BU
1908A	2,858,666	7.00	14.00	24.00	90.00	150
1909A	6,343,745	7.00	14.00	24.00	90.00	150
1910A	5,590,624	7.00	14.00	24.00	90.00	150
1911A	3,241,770	7.00	14.00	24.00	90.00	150
1912A	4,626,330	7.00	14.00	24.00	85.00	150
(1908-1912)A Proof	—	Value: 250				

KM# 530 3 MARK

16.6670 g., 0.9000 Silver 0.4823 oz. ASW, 33 mm.
Ruler: Wilhelm II **Subject:** Berlin University **Obv:** Friedrich Wilhelm III and Wilhelm II left divide dates **Rev:** Crowned imperial eagle with shield on breast **Edge:** GOTT MIT UNS

Date	Mintage	F	VF	XF	Unc	BU
1910A	200,000	22.00	55.00	85.00	125	225
1910A Proof	2,000	Value: 375				

KM# 531 3 MARK

16.6670 g., 0.9000 Silver 0.4823 oz. ASW, 33 mm.
Ruler: Wilhelm II **Subject:** Breslau University **Obv:** Friedrich Wilhelm III, Wilhelm II left within circle **Rev:** Crowned imperial eagle with shield on breast **Edge:** GOTT MIT UNS

Date	Mintage	F	VF	XF	Unc	BU
1911A	400,000	18.00	45.00	70.00	85.00	200
1911A Proof	—	Value: 300				

KM# 534 3 MARK

16.6670 g., 0.9000 Silver 0.4823 oz. ASW, 33 mm.
Ruler: Wilhelm II **Subject:** 100 Years - Defeat of Napoleon **Obv:** Eagle with snake in talons, denomination below **Rev:** Figure on horseback surrounded by people **Edge:** GOTT MIT UNS

Date	Mintage	F	VF	XF	Unc	BU
1913A	3,000,000	8.00	20.00	25.00	40.00	60.00
1913A Proof	—	Value: 150				

KM# 535 3 MARK

16.6670 g., 0.9000 Silver 0.4823 oz. ASW, 33 mm.
Ruler: Wilhelm II **Subject:** 25th Year of Reign **Obv:** Uniformed bust right **Rev:** Crowned imperial eagle with shield on breast **Edge:** GOTT MIT UNS

Date	Mintage	F	VF	XF	Unc	BU
1913A	1,000,000	8.00	20.00	25.00	40.00	60.00
1913A Proof	6,000	Value: 130				

KM# 538 3 MARK

16.6670 g., 0.9000 Silver 0.4823 oz. ASW, 33 mm.
Ruler: Wilhelm II **Obv:** Uniformed bust right **Rev:** Crowned imperial eagle with shield on breast **Edge:** GOTT MIT UNS

Date	Mintage	F	VF	XF	Unc	BU
1914A	2,022,000	10.00	20.00	25.00	70.00	300
1914A Proof	—	Value: 600				

KM# 539 3 MARK
16.6670 g., 0.9000 Silver 0.4823 oz. ASW, 33 mm.
Ruler: Wilhelm II **Subject:** Centenary - Absorption of Mansfeld **Obv:** St. George slaying the dragon **Rev:** Crowned imperial eagle with shield on breast **Edge:** GOTT MIT UNS

Date	Mintage	F	VF	XF	Unc	BU
1915A	30,000	220	400	600	1,100	1,300
1915A Proof	—	Value: 1,500				

KM# 523 5 MARK
27.7770 g., 0.9000 Silver 0.8037 oz. ASW, 38 mm.
Ruler: Wilhelm II **Obv:** Head right **Obv. Leg.:** WILHELM II DEUTSCHER KAISER KONIG V. PREUSSEN **Rev:** Crowned imperial eagle, type III **Rev. Leg.:** DEUTSCHES REICH date, FUNF MARK below **Edge:** GOTT MIT UNS

Date	Mintage	F	VF	XF	Unc	BU
1901A	667,990	9.00	17.50	80.00	450	1,250
1902A	1,950,840	8.00	17.50	80.00	300	1,250
1903A	3,855,795	8.00	17.50	80.00	300	110
1904A	2,060,410	8.00	17.50	95.00	300	1,100
1906A Rare	230,963	20.00	40.00	130	1,000	2,200
1907A	2,103,338	8.00	16.00	65.00	200	600
1908A	2,230,579	8.00	16.00	60.00	250	600
(1891-1908)A	—	Value: 1,500				
Common date proof						

KM# 526 5 MARK
27.7770 g., 0.9000 Silver 0.8037 oz. ASW, 38 mm.
Ruler: Wilhelm II **Subject:** 200 Years - Kingdom of Prussia **Obv:** Friedrich I, Wilhelm II left **Rev:** Crowned imperial eagle with shield on breast **Edge:** GOTT MIT UNS

Date	Mintage	F	VF	XF	Unc	BU
1901A	460,000	30.00	50.00	80.00	110	150
1901A Proof	—	Value: 275				

KM# 536 5 MARK
27.7770 g., 0.9000 Silver 0.8037 oz. ASW, 38 mm.
Ruler: Wilhelm II **Obv:** Uniformed bust right **Rev:** Crowned imperial eagle, shield on breast

Date	Mintage	F	VF	XF	Unc	BU
1913A	1,961,712	14.00	28.00	40.00	150	350
1914A	1,587,179	13.00	24.00	35.00	150	400
(1913-1914)A Proof	—	Value: 1,500				

KM# 520 10 MARK
3.9820 g., 0.9000 Gold 0.1152 oz. AGW **Ruler:** Wilhelm II **Obv:** Head right **Obv. Leg.:** WILHELM II DEUTSCHER KAISER KONIG V. PREUSSEN **Rev:** Crowned imperial eagle, type III **Rev. Leg.:** DEUTSCHES REICH date, 10 MARK below **Edge:** ~ * ~

Date	Mintage	F	VF	XF	Unc	BU
1901A	701,930	BV	110	125	250	500
1901A Proof	—	Value: 1,600				
1902A	270,911	BV	135	185	275	500
1902A Proof	—	Value: 1,600				
1903A	1,684,979	BV	110	125	250	450
1903A Proof	—	Value: 1,600				
1904A	1,178,129	BV	110	125	250	400
1905A	1,072,513	BV	110	125	250	400
1905A Proof	117	Value: 1,200				
1906A	541,970	BV	115	135	265	425
1906A Proof	150	Value: 1,200				
1907A	812,698	BV	110	125	250	400
1907A Proof	—	Value: 1,600				
1909A	531,934	BV	115	135	265	425
1909A Proof	—	Value: 1,600				
1910A	803,111	BV	110	125	250	400
1910 Proof	—	Value: 1,600				
1911A	270,798	BV	130	180	275	400
1911A Proof	—	Value: 1,600				
1912A	542,372	BV	110	125	250	400
1912A Proof	—	Value: 1,600				

KM# 521 20 MARK
7.9650 g., 0.9000 Gold 0.2305 oz. AGW **Ruler:** Wilhelm II **Obv:** Head right **Obv. Leg.:** WILHELM II DEUTSCHER KAISER KONIG V. PREUSSEN **Rev:** Crowned imperial eagle, type III **Rev. Leg.:** DEUTSCHES REICH date, 20 MARK below

Date	Mintage	F	VF	XF	Unc	BU
1901	5,188,340	—	—	BV+10%	245	400
1901 Proof	—	Value: 1,500				
1902	4,138,128	—	—	BV+10%	245	400
1902A Proof	—	Value: 1,500				
1903	2,870,073	—	—	BV+10%	245	400
1903A Proof	—	Value: 1,500				
1904	3,452,625	—	—	BV+10%	245	400
1904A Proof	—	Value: 1,500				
1905	4,220,793	—	—	BV+10%	245	400
1905 Proof	287	Value: 1,500				
1905	920,784	BV+5%	—	190	300	400
1906	7,788,922	—	—	BV+10%	250	400
1906 Proof	124	Value: 1,500				
1906	101,808	BV+5%	—	380	600	400
1907	2,576,286	—	—	BV+10%	245	400
1907A Proof	—	Value: 1,500				
1908	3,274,168	—	—	BV+10%	245	400
1908A Proof	—	Value: 1,500				
1909	5,212,836	—	—	BV+10%	245	400
1909A Proof	—	Value: 1,500				
1909	350,128	—	—	225	300	400
1909 Proof	—	Value: 1,750				
1910	8,645,549	—	—	BV+10%	245	400
1910	753,217	—	—	BV+10%	245	400
1910 Proof	—	Value: 1,500				
1911	4,745,790	—	—	BV+10%	245	400
1911 Proof	—	Value: 1,500				
1912 Proof	—	Value: 1,500				
1912	5,569,398	—	—	BV+10%	245	400
1912	502,530	BV+3%	BV+5%	225	300	400
1913	6,102,730	—	BV	160	245	400
1913 Proof	—	Value: 1,500				

KM# 537 20 MARK
7.9650 g., 0.9000 Gold 0.2305 oz. AGW **Ruler:** Wilhelm II **Obv:** Uniformed bust right **Rev:** Crowned imperial eagle with shield on breast

Date	Mintage	F	VF	XF	Unc	BU
1913A	—	BV	BV+5%	220	250	300
1913A Proof	—	Value: 1,500				
1914A	2,136,861	BV	BV+5%	220	250	300

Date	Mintage	F	VF	XF	Unc	BU
1914A Proof	—	Value: 1,500				
1915A	1,268,055	—	1,100	1,400	2,000	2,500

PATTERNS
Including off metal strikes

KM#	Date	Mintage	Identification	Mkt Val
Pn28	1901	—	5 Mark. Silver. Larger design. KM526.	3,000
Pn29	1901A	—	5 Mark. Silver. Larger design. KM526.	3,000
PnA30	1901A	—	20 Mark. Silver. Plain edge.	350
Pn30	1904A	—	2 Mark. Silver. Plain edge. Broader rim. KM522.	1,000
Pn31	1904A	—	5 Mark. Silver.	—
Pn32	1904A	—	5 Mark. Copper. "N.A." countermarked.	—
Pn33	1904A	—	5 Mark. Silver. Reeded edge. Without beaded rims. KM523.	—
Pn34	1904A	—	5 Mark. Silver. Smaller lettering. KM523.	—
Pn35	1904A	—	5 Mark. Silver. Eagle in ornamental in inner border.	3,000
Pn36	1905A	—	3 Mark. Silver.	3,500
Pn37	1905A	—	3 Mark. Silver. Legend in different position.	3,500
Pn38	1905A	—	3 Mark. Copper.	—
Pn39	1905A	—	3 Mark. Silver. KM527.	—
PnA40	1907A	—	20 Mark. Copper. 4.1100 g.	—
Pn40	1908A	—	5 Mark. Silver.	—
Pn41	1908A	—	5 Mark. Brass.	—
Pn42	1908J	—	20 Mark. Gold. KM521.2. Extra rare.	—
Pn43	1909A	—	2 Mark. Nickel. KM522.	—
Pn44	1910	—	3 Mark. Silver.	2,000
Pn45	1910	—	3 Mark. Copper.	—
Pn46	1911	—	3 Mark. Silver. KM531.	2,000
Pn47	1911	—	3 Mark. Copper.	—
Pn48	1911A	—	3 Mark. Silver. KM531.	1,000
Pn49	1912A	—	2 Mark. Silver. KM533.	1,000
Pn51	1912	—	3 Mark. Bronze.	—
Pn52	1912A	—	3 Mark. Bronze.	1,500
Pn53	1912A	—	3 Mark. Bronze.	—
Pn54	1913A	—	2 Mark. Silver. Dots above "O" in KONIG. KM533.	2,500
Pn55	1913	—	3 Mark. Silver.	2,000
Pn56	1913	—	3 Mark. Silver.	—
Pn57	1913A	—	3 Mark. Silver.	2,500
Pn58	1913A	—	3 Mark. Bronze.	—
Pn59	1913A	—	3 Mark. Silver. Dots above O in KONIG. KM535.	2,500
Pn60	1913A	—	3 Mark. Copper.	—
Pn61	1913A	—	5 Mark. Silver. Extra sharp design. KM536.	—
Pn62	1914A	—	3 Mark. Silver. Extra sharp design. KM538.	—
Pn63	1915	—	3 Mark. Silver. Gothic script. KM539.	3,500
Pn64	1915	—	3 Mark. White Metal.	—
Pn65	1915	—	3 Mark. Iron, Tinned. Tin-iron.	—

REUSS

The Reuss family, whose lands were located in Thuringia, was founded c. 1035. By the end of the 12th century, the custom of naming all males in the ruling house Heinrich had been established. The Elder Line modified this strange practice in the late 17th century to numbering all males from 1 to 100, then beginning over again. The Younger Line, meanwhile, decided to start the numbering of Heinrichs with the first male born in each century. Greiz was founded in 1303. Upper and Lower Greiz lines were founded in 1535 and the territories were divided until 1768. In 1778 the ruler was made a prince of the Holy Roman Empire. The principality endured until 1918.

MINT MARKS
A - Berlin
B - Hannover

REUSS-OBERGREIZ

The other branch of the division of 1635, Obergreiz went through a number of consolidations and further divisions. Upon the extinction of the Ruess-Untergreiz line in 1768, the latter passed to Reuss-Obergreiz and this line continued on into the 20th century, obtaining the rank of count back in 1673 and that of prince in 1778.

RULERS
Heinrich XXII, 1859-1902
Heinrich XXIV, 1902-1918

PRINCIPALITY
REFORM COINAGE

KM# 128 2 MARK
11.1110 g., 0.9000 Silver 0.3215 oz. ASW, 28 mm.
Ruler: Heinrich XXII **Obv:** Head right **Obv. Leg.:** HEINRICH XXII

v. G. G. ALT. L. SOUV. FÜRST REUSS **Rev:** Crowned imperial eagle with shield on breast **Rev. Leg.:** DEUTSCHES REICH date, ZWEI MARK below **Edge:** Reeded

Date	Mintage	F	VF	XF	Unc	BU
1901A	10,000	125	250	375	700	1,100
1901A Proof	—	Value: 1,200				

KM# 130 3 MARK
16.6670 g., 0.9000 Silver 0.4823 oz. ASW, 33 mm.
Ruler: Heinrich XXIV **Obv:** Head right **Rev:** Crowned imperial eagle with shield on breast

Date	Mintage	F	VF	XF	Unc	BU
1909A	10,000	140	325	450	800	1,300
1909A Proof	400	Value: 1,500				

PATTERNS
Including off metal strikes

KM#	Date	Mintage	Identification	Mkt Val
Pn4	1909A	—	3 Mark. Silver. Head faces left. KM130, Rare	—

SAXE-ALTENBURG
(Sachsen-Neu-Altenburg)

A new line was established at Altenburg when the Duke of Saxe-Hildburghausen exchanged Hildburghausen for Altenburg in 1826. This line lasted until the end of World War I, when the last duke was forced to abdicate.

RULERS
Ernst I, 1853-1908
Ernst II, 1908-1918

MINT MARK
A – Berlin Mint, 1886-1918

DUCHY
REFORM COINAGE

KM# 144 2 MARK
11.1110 g., 0.9000 Silver 0.3215 oz. ASW, 28 mm.
Ruler: Ernst I **Subject:** Ernst 75th Birthday **Obv:** Head right **Rev:** Crowned imperial eagle with shield on breast **Edge:** Reeded

Date	Mintage	F	VF	XF	Unc	BU
1901A	50,000	120	250	450	750	1,200
1901A Proof	500	Value: 1,400				

KM# 145 5 MARK
27.7770 g., 0.9000 Silver 0.8037 oz. ASW, 38 mm. **Ruler:** Ernst I **Subject:** Ernst 75th Birthday **Obv:** Head right **Rev:** Crowned imperial eagle with shield on breast **Edge:** GOTT MIT UNS

Date	Mintage	F	VF	XF	Unc	BU
1901A	20,000	200	500	750	1,450	2,300
1901A Proof	500	Value: 2,500				

KM# 147 5 MARK
27.7770 g., 0.9000 Silver 0.8037 oz. ASW, 38 mm.
Ruler: Ernst I **Subject:** Ernst's 50th Year of Reign **Obv:** Head right, date and sprays below **Rev:** Crowned imperial eagle with shield on breast **Edge:** GOTT MIT UNS

Date	Mintage	F	VF	XF	Unc	BU
1903A	20,000	100	200	325	500	700
1903A Proof	300	Value: 1,000				

SAXE-COBURG-GOTHA
(Sachsen-Coburg-Gotha)

Upon the extinction of the ducal line in Saxe-Gotha-Altenburg in 1826, Gotha was assigned to Saxe-Coburg-Saalfeld and Saxe-Meiningen received Saalfeld. The resulting duchy became called Saxe-Coburg-Gotha. Albert, the son of Ernst I and younger brother of Ernst II, married Queen Victoria of Great Britain and the British royal dynastic name was that of Saxe-Coburg-Gotha. Their son, Alfred was made the Duke of Edinburgh and succeeded his uncle, Ernst II, as Duke of Saxe-Coburg-Gotha. Alfred's older brother, Eduard Albert, followed their mother as King Edward VII (1901-1910). The last duke of Saxe-Coburg-Gotha was Alfred's nephew, Karl Eduard, forced to abdicate in 1918 as a result of World War I, which was fought in part against his cousin, King George V.

RULER
Karl Eduard, 1900-1918

MINT MARK
A – Berlin Mint, 1886-1911

DUCHY
REFORM COINAGE

KM# 152 2 MARK
11.1110 g., 0.9000 Silver 0.3215 oz. ASW, 28 mm.
Ruler: Karl Eduard **Obv:** Head right **Edge:** Reeded

Date	Mintage	F	VF	XF	Unc	BU
1905A	10,000	135	350	600	1,100	1,300
1905A Proof	2,000	Value: 1,400				
1911A Proof	100	Value: 14,000				

KM# 153 5 MARK
27.7770 g., 0.9000 Silver 0.8037 oz. ASW, 38 mm. **Ruler:** Karl Eduard **Obv:** Head right **Rev:** Crowned imperial eagle with shield on breast **Edge:** GOTT MIT UNS

Date	Mintage	F	VF	XF	Unc	BU
1907A	10,000	325	850	1,150	1,750	2,400
1907A Proof	—	Value: 3,250				

KM# 154 10 MARK
3.9820 g., 0.9000 Gold 0.1152 oz. AGW **Ruler:** Karl Eduard **Obv:** Head right **Rev:** Crowned imperial eagle with shield on breast **Edge:** ~ * ~

Date	Mintage	F	VF	XF	Unc	BU
1905A	10,000	1,000	1,600	2,000	2,600	3,750
1905A Proof	489	Value: 4,250				

KM# 155 20 MARK
7.9650 g., 0.9000 Gold 0.2305 oz. AGW **Ruler:** Karl Eduard **Obv:** Head, right **Rev:** Crowned imperial eagle with shield on breast, type I **Edge:** GOTT MIT UNS

Date	Mintage	F	VF	XF	Unc	BU
1905A	10,000	1,000	1,600	2,000	2,850	3,700
1905A Proof	484	Value: 5,000				

SAXE-MEININGEN
(Sachsen-Meiningen)

The duchy of Saxe-Meiningen was located in Thuringia (Thüringen), sandwiched between Saxe-Weimar-Eisenach on the west and north and the enclave of Schmalkalden belonging to Hesse-Cassel on the east. It was founded upon the division of the Ernestine line in Saxe-Gotha in 1680. In 1735, due to an exchange of some territory, the duchy became known as Saxe-Coburg-Meiningen. In 1826, Saxe-Coburg-Gotha assigned Saalfeld to Saxe-Meiningen. The duchy came under the strong influence of Prussia from 1866, when Bernhard II was forced to abdicate because of his support of Austria. The last duke was forced to give up his sovereign power at the end of World War I in 1918.

RULERS
Georg II, 1866-1914
Bernhard III, 1914-1918

DUCHY
REFORM COINAGE

KM# 196 2 MARK
11.1110 g., 0.9000 Silver 0.3215 oz. ASW, 28 mm.
Ruler: Georg II **Subject:** Duke's 75th Birthday **Obv:** Head right **Rev:** Crowned imperial eagle with shield on breast **Edge:** Reeded

Date	Mintage	F	VF	XF	Unc	BU
1901D	20,000	100	250	400	750	1,000
1901D Proof	—	Value: 1,250				

KM# 198 2 MARK
11.1110 g., 0.9000 Silver 0.3215 oz. ASW, 28 mm.
Ruler: Georg II **Obv:** Head left, long beard **Rev:** Crowned imperial eagle with shield on breast **Edge:** Reeded

Date	Mintage	F	VF	XF	Unc	BU
1902D	20,000	250	800	1,150	2,200	3,250

KM# 199 2 MARK
11.1110 g., 0.9000 Silver 0.3215 oz. ASW, 28 mm.
Ruler: Georg II **Obv:** Head left, short beard **Rev:** Crowned imperial eagle with shield on breast

Date	Mintage	F	VF	XF	Unc	BU
1902D	Inc. above	100	200	350	750	1,250
1913D Proof	—	Value: 1,800				
1913D	5,000	150	275	600	1,250	1,750

KM# 206 2 MARK
11.1110 g., 0.9000 Silver 0.3215 oz. ASW, 28 mm. **Ruler:** Bernhard III **Subject:** Death of Georg II **Obv:** Head left, long beard **Rev:** Crowned imperial eagle with shield on breast **Edge:** Reeded

Date	Mintage	F	VF	XF	Unc	BU
1915	30,000	35.00	75.00	150	220	325
1915 Proof	—	Value: 400				

KM# 203 3 MARK
16.6670 g., 0.9000 Silver 0.4823 oz. ASW, 33 mm.
Ruler: Georg II **Obv:** Head left, long beard **Rev:** Crowned imperial eagle with shield on breast **Edge:** GOTT MIT UNS

Date	Mintage	F	VF	XF	Unc	BU
1908D	35,000	35.00	110	165	250	350
1908D Proof	—	Value: 600				
1913D	20,000	35.00	110	165	300	400
1913D Proof	—	Value: 600				

KM# 207 3 MARK
16.6670 g., 0.9000 Silver 0.4823 oz. ASW, 33 mm.
Ruler: Bernhard III **Subject:** Death of Georg II **Obv:** Head left, long beard **Rev:** Crowned imperial eagle with shield on breast **Edge:** GOTT MIT UNS

Date	Mintage	F	VF	XF	Unc	BU
1915	30,000	30.00	70.00	150	220	325
1915 Proof	—	Value: 500				

KM# 197 5 MARK
27.7770 g., 0.9000 Silver 0.8037 oz. ASW, 38 mm.
Ruler: Georg II **Subject:** Duke's 75th Birthday **Obv:** Head right, long beard **Rev:** Crowned imperial eagle with shield on breast **Edge:** GOTT MIT UNS

Date	Mintage	F	VF	XF	Unc	BU
1901D	20,000	85.00	325	550	1,000	1,600
1901D Proof	—	Value: 2,000				

KM# 200 5 MARK
27.7770 g., 0.9000 Silver 0.8037 oz. ASW, 38 mm.
Ruler: Georg II **Obv:** Long beard **Rev:** Crowned imperial eagle with shield on breast **Edge:** GOTT MIT UNS

Date	Mintage	F	VF	XF	Unc	BU
1902D	20,000	60.00	200	350	1,000	1,500

KM# 201 5 MARK
27.7770 g., 0.9000 Silver 0.8037 oz. ASW, 38 mm.
Ruler: Georg II **Obv:** Head left, long beard **Rev:** Crowned imperial eagle with shield on breast

Date	Mintage	F	VF	XF	Unc	BU
1902D	Inc. above	60.00	175	475	1,200	1,800
1908D	60,000	50.00	160	275	850	1,350

KM# 202 10 MARK
3.9820 g., 0.9000 Gold 0.1152 oz. AGW **Ruler:** Georg II **Obv:** Head left, long beard **Rev:** Crowned imperial eagle with shield on breast **Edge:** ~ * ~

Date	Mintage	F	VF	XF	Unc	BU
1902D	2,000	1,250	2,500	3,750	4,500	6,250
1902D Proof	—	Value: 8,000				
1909D	2,000	1,250	2,500	3,750	4,500	6,250
1909D Proof	—	Value: 8,000				
1914D	1,002	1,500	3,000	4,000	5,500	7,000
1914D Proof	—	Value: 9,000				

KM# 195 20 MARK
7.9650 g., 0.9000 Gold 0.2305 oz. AGW **Ruler:** Georg II **Obv:** Head left, short beard **Obv. Leg.:** GEORG HERZOG VON SACHSEN MEININGEN **Rev:** Crowned imperial eagle, type III **Rev. Leg.:** DEUTSCHES REICH date, 20 MARK below **Edge:** GOTT MIT UNS

Date	Mintage	F	VF	XF	Unc	BU
1905D	1,000	3,000	6,000	8,500	12,500	17,000
1905D Proof	—	Value: 17,500				
1910D	1,004	—	—	—	—	—
1914D	1,001	—	—	—	—	—

KM# 205 20 MARK
7.9650 g., 0.9000 Gold 0.2305 oz. AGW **Ruler:** Georg II **Obv:** Head left, long beard **Rev:** Crowned imperial eagle with shield on breast **Edge:** GOTT MIT UNS

Date	Mintage	F	VF	XF	Unc	BU
1910D	1,004	2,000	3,750	5,500	7,000	9,000
1910D Proof	—	Value: 10,000				
1914D	1,000	2,000	3,750	5,500	7,000	9,000
1914D Proof	—	Value: 10,000				

PATTERNS
Including off metal strikes

KM#	Date	Mintage	Identification	Mkt Val
Pn16	1901D	—	10 Mark. Gold. With neck and beard variety. KM202. Extra rare.	—
Pn17	1901D	—	10 Mark. Gold. KM202.	—
Pn18	1915D	—	2 Mark. KM206.	1,250
Pn19	1915D	—	3 Mark. KM207.	1,250

SAXE-WEIMAR-EISENACH
(Sachsen-Weimar-Eisenach)

When the death of the duke of Saxe-Eisenach in 1741 heralded the extinction of that line, its possessions reverted to Saxe-Weimar, which henceforth was known as Saxe-Weimar-Eisenach. Because of the strong role played by the duke during the Napoleonic Wars, Saxe-Weimar-Eisenach was raised to the rank of a grand duchy in 1814 and granted the territory of Neustadt, taken from Saxony. The last grand duke abdicated at the end of World War I.

RULERS
Karl Alexander, 1853-1901
Wilhelm Ernst, 1901-1918

MINT MARK
A – Berlin Mint, 1840-1915

GRAND DUCHY
REFORM COINAGE

Y# 170 2 MARK
11.1110 g., 0.9000 Silver 0.3215 oz. ASW, 28 mm.
Ruler: Wilhelm Ernst **Obv:** Head left **Rev:** Crowned imperial eagle with shield on breast **Edge:** Reeded

Date	Mintage	F	VF	XF	Unc	BU
1901A	100,000	125	325	450	850	1,500
1901A Proof	—	Value: 2,000				

Y# 172 2 MARK
11.1110 g., 0.9000 Silver 0.3215 oz. ASW, 28 mm.
Ruler: Wilhelm Ernst **Subject:** Grand Duke's First Marriage - Caroline **Obv:** Jugate heads left **Rev:** Crowned imperial eagle with shield on breast **Edge:** Reeded

Date	Mintage	F	VF	XF	Unc	BU
1903A	40,000	35.00	60.00	100	160	225
1903A Proof	Est. 1,000	Value: 250				

Y# 174 2 MARK
11.1110 g., 0.9000 Silver 0.3215 oz. ASW, 28 mm.
Ruler: Wilhelm Ernst **Subject:** Jena University 350th Anniversary **Obv:** Johan Friedrich I the Magnanimous 3/4 right **Rev:** Crowned imperial eagle with shield on breast **Edge:** Reeded

Date	Mintage	F	VF	XF	Unc	BU
1908	50,000	25.00	55.00	110	135	200

Y# 176   3 MARK
16.6670 g., 0.9000 Silver 0.4823 oz. ASW, 33 mm.
Ruler: Wilhelm Ernst **Subject:** Grand Duke's Second Marriage
- Feodora **Obv:** Jugate heads left **Rev:** Crowned imperial eagle
with shield on breast **Edge:** GOTT MIT UNS

Date	Mintage	F	VF	XF	Unc	BU
1910	133,000	20.00	40.00	85.00	120	160
1910A Proof	—	Value: 250				

Y# 177   3 MARK
16.6670 g., 0.9000 Silver 0.4823 oz. ASW, 33 mm.
Ruler: Wilhelm Ernst **Subject:** Centenary of Grand Duchy
Obv: Wilhelm Ernst and Carl August right **Rev:** Crowned imperial
eagle with shield on breast **Edge:** GOTT MIT UNS

Date	Mintage	F	VF	XF	Unc	BU
1915A	50,000	25.00	50.00	140	150	250
1915A Proof	200	Value: 400				

Y# 173   5 MARK
27.7770 g., 0.9000 Silver 0.8037 oz. ASW, 38 mm. **Ruler:**
Wilhelm Ernst **Subject:** Grand Duke's First Marriage - Caroline
Obv: Jugate heads left **Rev:** Crowned imperial eagle with shield
on breast **Edge:** GOTT MIT UNS

Date	Mintage	F	VF	XF	Unc	BU
1903A	24,000	60.00	125	225	375	500
1903A Proof	Est. 1,000	Value: 750				

Y# 175   5 MARK
27.7770 g., 0.9000 Silver 0.8037 oz. ASW, 38 mm. **Ruler:**
Wilhelm Ernst **Subject:** Jena University 350th Anniversary **Obv:**
Johan Friedrich I the Magnanimous 3/4 right **Rev:** Crowned
imperial eagle with shield on breast **Edge:** GOTT MIT UNS

Date	Mintage	F	VF	XF	Unc	BU
1908	40,000	60.00	110	200	300	425
1908 Proof	—	Value: 750				

Y# 171   20 MARK
7.9650 g., 0.9000 Gold 0.2305 oz. AGW **Ruler:** Wilhelm Ernst
Subject: Golden Wedding of Carl Alexander **Obv:** Head left
Rev: Crowned imperial eagle with shield on breast **Edge:** GOTT
MIT UNS

Date	Mintage	F	VF	XF	Unc	BU
1901A	5,000	1,500	2,200	3,800	5,500	7,000
1901A Proof, rare	—	Value: 10,000				

PATTERNS
Including off metal strikes

KM#	Date	Mintage	Identification	Mkt Val
Pn1	1908	—	5 Mark. Silver. Figure smaller. Y#175, Rare.	—
Pn2	1910	—	3 Mark. Silver.	2,000
Pn3	1910	—	3 Mark. Brass.	—

SAXONY

Saxony, located in southeast Germany was founded in 850.
The first coinage was struck c. 990. It was divided into two lines
in 1464. The electoral right was obtained by the elder line in 1547.
During the time of the Reformation, Saxony was one of the more
powerful states in central Europe. It became a kingdom in 1806.
At the Congress of Vienna in 1815, they were forced to cede half
its territories to Prussia.

RULERS
Albert, 1873-1902
Georg, 1902-1904
Friedrich August III, 1904-1918

MINT MARK
L - Leipzig

KINGDOM
REFORM COINAGE

KM# 1245   2 MARK
11.1110 g., 0.9000 Silver 0.3215 oz. ASW **Ruler:** Albert
Edge: Reeded **Note:** Similar to KM#185.

Date	Mintage	F	VF	XF	Unc	BU
1901E	439,724	12.50	55.00	110	300	1,000
1902E	542,762	10.00	55.00	110	275	800
1902E Proof	—	Value: 1,750				

KM# 1255   2 MARK
11.1110 g., 0.9000 Silver 0.3215 oz. ASW, 28 mm. **Ruler:**
Georg **Subject:** Death of Albert **Obv:** Head right **Rev:** Crowned
imperial eagle with shield on breast **Edge:** Reeded

Date	Mintage	F	VF	XF	Unc	BU
1902E	167,625	15.00	40.00	65.00	125	175
1902E Proof	250	Value: 225				

KM# 1257   2 MARK
11.1110 g., 0.9000 Silver 0.3215 oz. ASW, 28 mm. **Ruler:** Georg
Obv: Head right **Rev:** Crowned imperial eagle with shield on breast

Date	Mintage	F	VF	XF	Unc	BU
1903E	745,551	30.00	60.00	140	250	600
1903E Proof	50	Value: 1,100				
1904E	1,265,533	17.50	40.00	100	200	600
1904E Proof	—	Value: 900				

KM# 1261   2 MARK
11.1110 g., 0.9000 Silver 0.3215 oz. ASW, 28 mm. **Ruler:**
Friedrich August III **Subject:** Death of Georg **Obv:** Head right
Rev: Crowned imperial eagle with shield on breast **Edge:** Reeded

Date	Mintage	F	VF	XF	Unc	BU
1904E	150,000	15.00	40.00	90.00	120	160
1904E Proof	55	Value: 250				

KM# 1263   2 MARK
11.1110 g., 0.9000 Silver 0.3215 oz. ASW, 28 mm. **Ruler:**
Friedrich August III **Obv:** Head right **Rev:** Crowned imperial
eagle with shield on breast **Edge:** Reeded

Date	Mintage	F	VF	XF	Unc	BU
1905E	558,951	20.00	45.00	75.00	160	350
1905E Proof	100	Value: 650				
1906E	558,750	20.00	45.00	75.00	160	350
1907E	1,112,519	20.00	45.00	70.00	155	350
1908E	335,689	20.00	45.00	70.00	155	350
1911E	186,250	20.00	45.00	75.00	200	350
1912E	167,625	20.00	45.00	75.00	200	350
1914E	298,000	20.00	45.00	70.00	125	350
(1905-1914)E Proof	—	Value: 500				

KM# 1268   2 MARK
11.1110 g., 0.9000 Silver 0.3215 oz. ASW, 28 mm. **Ruler:**
Friedrich August III **Subject:** 500th Anniversary - Leipzig
University **Obv:** Crown Prince Friedrich the Pugnacious and
Friedrich August III left **Rev:** Crowned imperial eagle with shield
on breast **Edge:** Reeded

Date	Mintage	F	VF	XF	Unc	BU
1909	125,000	15.00	35.00	65.00	100	130
1909 Proof	300	Value: 225				

KM# 1267   3 MARK
16.6670 g., 0.9000 Silver 0.4823 oz. ASW, 33 mm.
Ruler: Friedrich August III **Obv:** Head right **Rev:** Crowned
imperial eagle with shield on breast **Edge:** GOTT MIT UNS

Date	Mintage	F	VF	XF	Unc	BU
1908E	276,073	10.00	22.00	40.00	100	150
1909E	1,196,719	10.00	20.00	35.00	80.00	150
1910E	745,000	10.00	20.00	35.00	90.00	150
1911E	581,250	10.00	20.00	35.00	90.00	150
1912E	378,750	10.00	20.00	35.00	90.00	150
1913E	306,500	10.00	20.00	35.00	90.00	150
(1908-1913)E Proof	—	Value: 450				

KM# 1275   3 MARK
16.6670 g., 0.9000 Silver 0.4823 oz. ASW, 33 mm.
Ruler: Friedrich August III **Subject:** Battle of Leipzig Centennial
Obv: Monument divides date above **Rev:** Crowned imperial eagle
with shield on breast **Edge:** GOTT MIT UNS

Date	Mintage	F	VF	XF	Unc	BU
1913E	999,999	12.00	18.00	28.00	40.00	55.00
1913E Proof	17,000	Value: 200				

KM# 1276   3 MARK
16.6670 g., 0.9000 Silver 0.4823 oz. ASW, 33 mm.
Ruler: Friedrich August III **Subject:** Jubilee of Reformation
Obv: Friederich the Wise right, Protector of Martin Luther **Rev:**
Crowned imperial eagle with shield on breast **Edge:** GOTT MIT UNS

Date	Mintage	F	VF	XF	Unc	BU
1917E Proof	100	Value: 75,000				

KM# 1246   5 MARK
27.7770 g., 0.9000 Silver 0.8037 oz. ASW, 38 mm. **Ruler:** Albert
Obv: Head right **Obv. Leg.:** ALBERT KOENIG VON SACHSEN
Rev: Crowned imperial eagle **Rev. Leg.:** DEUTSCHES REICH
date, FUNF MARK below **Edge:** GOTT MIT UNS

Date	Mintage	F	VF	XF	Unc	BU
1901E	156,450	25.00	55.00	300	750	1,500
1901E Proof	—	Value: 2,750				
1902E Proof, rare	—	Value: 2,750				
1902E	168,200	20.00	45.00	275	650	1,200

KM# 1256   5 MARK
27.7770 g., 0.9000 Silver 0.8037 oz. ASW, 38 mm.
Ruler: Georg **Subject:** Death of Albert **Obv:** Head right
Rev: Crowned imperial eagle with shield on breast **Edge:** GOTT
MIT UNS

Date	Mintage	F	VF	XF	Unc	BU
1902E	100,000	30.00	65.00	125	300	345
1902E Proof	250	Value: 750				

KM# 1258   5 MARK
27.7770 g., 0.9000 Silver 0.8037 oz. ASW, 38 mm.
Ruler: Georg **Obv:** Head right **Rev:** Crowned imperial eagle with
shield on breast **Edge:** GOTT MIT UNS

Date	Mintage	F	VF	XF	Unc	BU
1903E	536,298	25.00	50.00	175	550	1,000
1903E Proof	50	Value: 2,000				
1904E	290,643	30.00	60.00	175	650	1,000
1904E Proof	—	Value: 1,500				

KM# 1262   5 MARK
27.7770 g., 0.9000 Silver 0.8037 oz. ASW, 38 mm. **Ruler:**
Friedrich August III **Subject:** Death of Georg **Obv:** Head right **Rev:**
Crowned imperial eagle with shield on breast **Edge:** GOTT MIT UNS

Date	Mintage	F	VF	XF	Unc	BU
1904E	37,200	45.00	150	225	350	450
1904E Proof	70	Value: 800				

KM# 1266   5 MARK
27.7770 g., 0.9000 Silver 0.8037 oz. ASW, 38 mm.
Ruler: Friedrich August III **Obv:** Head right **Rev:** Crowned
imperial eagle with shield on breast

Date	Mintage	F	VF	XF	Unc	BU
1907E	398,043	20.00	40.00	90.00	300	525
1908E	317,301	20.00	40.00	85.00	250	500
1914E	298,000	17.50	35.00	80.00	200	325
1914E Proof	—	Value: 1,500				

KM# 1269   5 MARK
27.7770 g., 0.9000 Silver 0.8037 oz. ASW, 38 mm.
Ruler: Friedrich August III **Subject:** 500th Anniversary - Leipzig
University **Obv:** Crown Prince Friedrich the Pugracious and
Friederich August III left **Rev:** Crowned imperial eagle with shield
on breast **Edge:** GOTT MIT UNS

Date	Mintage	F	VF	XF	Unc	BU
1909	50,000	50.00	100	190	275	350
1909 Proof	300	Value: 600				

KM# 1247   10 MARK
3.9820 g., 0.9000 Gold 0.1152 oz. AGW **Ruler:** Albert
Rev: Crowned imperial eagle, type III **Edge:** ~ * ~

Date	Mintage	F	VF	XF	Unc	BU
1901E	74,767	115	175	250	500	800
1902E	37,413	115	175	250	500	800
1902E Proof	—	Value: 2,000				

KM# 1259   10 MARK
3.9820 g., 0.9000 Gold 0.1152 oz. AGW **Ruler:** Georg
Obv: Head right **Rev:** Crowned imperial eagle with shield on
breast **Edge:** ~ * ~

Date	Mintage	F	VF	XF	Unc	BU
1903E	283,822	120	260	350	600	1,200
1903E Proof	100	Value: 2,750				
1904E	149,260	120	260	350	600	1,200
1904E Proof	—	Value: 2,250				

KM# 1264   10 MARK
3.9820 g., 0.9000 Gold 0.1152 oz. AGW **Ruler:** Friedrich
August III **Obv:** Head right **Rev:** Crowned imperial eagle with
shield on breast **Edge:** ~ * ~

Date	Mintage	F	VF	XF	Unc	BU
1905E	111,994	175	300	360	500	750
1905E Proof	100	Value: 2,500				
1906E Proof	—	Value: 2,500				
1906E	75,093	175	300	360	500	850
1907E	112,000	175	300	360	500	750
1907E Proof	111,878	Value: 2,500				
1909E	112,070	175	300	360	500	750
1910E	75,185	175	300	360	500	900
1910E Proof	—	Value: 2,500				
1911E	37,622	175	300	360	500	900
1912E	75,252	175	300	360	500	800
1912E Proof	—	Value: 2,500				

KM# 1260   20 MARK
7.9650 g., 0.9000 Gold 0.2305 oz. AGW **Ruler:** Georg
Obv: Head right **Rev:** Crowned imperial eagle with shield on
breast, type III **Edge:** GOTT MIT UNS

Date	Mintage	F	VF	XF	Unc	BU
1903E	250,000	BV	260	350	450	700
1903E Proof	—	Value: 2,500				

KM# 1265   20 MARK
7.9650 g., 0.9000 Gold 0.2305 oz. AGW **Ruler:** Friedrich
August III **Obv:** Head right **Rev:** Crowned imperial eagle with
shield on breast

Date	Mintage	F	VF	XF	Unc	BU
1905E	500,173	BV	220	400	500	600
1905E Proof	86	Value: 2,750				
1913E	121,002	BV	240	500	600	750
1914E	325,246	BV	240	375	450	600
1914E Proof	—	Value: 2,500				

PATTERNS
Including off metal strikes

KM#	Date	Mintage	Identification	Mkt Val
Pn78	1902 E	—	5 Mark. Silver. KM1258.	—
PnA78	1905E	—	20 Mark. Copper. 4.0600 g.	—
PnB78	1905E	—	20 Mark. Copper. 4.8900 g. Bust in uniform.	—
Pn79	1913	—	3 Mark. Silver.	—
Pn80	1917 E	—	3 Mark. Aluminum. KM1267.	—

SCHAUMBURG-LIPPE

The tiny countship of Schaumburg-Lippe, with an area of only 131 square miles (218 square kilometers) in northwest Germany, was surrounded by the larger states of Brunswick-Lüneburg-Calenberg, an enclave of Hesse-Cassel, and the bishopric of Minden (part of Brandenburg-Prussia from 1648). It was founded in 1640 when Schaumburg-Gehmen was divided between Hesse-Cassel and Lippe-Alverdissen. The two became known as Schaumburg-Hessen and Schaumburg-Lippe. Philipp II, the youngest son of Count Simon VI of Lippe came into the possession of Alverdissen and Lipperode upon his father's death in 1613. In 1640, he also inherited half of Schaumburg-Bückeburg, becoming the first Count of Schaumburg-Lippe. A separate line of Schaumburg-Alverdissen was established in 1681 and, upon the extinction of the elder line in 1777, the lands and titles devolved onto Alverdissen, becoming the ruling line in the countship. In 1807, the count was raised to the rank of prince and Schaumburg-Lippe was incorporated into the Rhine Confederation. It became a part of the German Confederation in 1815 and joined the North German Confederation in 1866. The principality became a member state in the German Empire in 1871. The last sovereign prince resigned as a result of World War I.

RULERS
Albrecht Georg, 1893-1911
Adolf II Bernhard, 1911-1918

MINT MARK
A - Berlin mint, 1858-1911

PRINCIPALITY
REFORM COINAGE

Y# 203   2 MARK
11.1110 g., 0.9000 Silver 0.3215 oz. ASW, 28 mm.   **Ruler:** Albrecht Georg **Subject:** Death of Prince Georg **Obv:** Head left **Obv. Leg.:** GEORG FURST ZU SCHAUMBURG-LIPPE **Rev:** Crowned imperial eagle with shield on breast **Rev. Leg.:** DEUTSCHES REICH date, ZWEI MARK below **Edge:** Reeded

Date	Mintage	F	VF	XF	Unc	BU
1904A	5,000	200	475	550	850	1,100
1904A Proof	200	Value: 1,750				

Y# 206   3 MARK
16.6670 g., 0.9000 Silver 0.4823 oz. ASW, 33 mm.
Ruler: Albrecht Georg **Subject:** Death of Prince Georg **Obv:** Head left **Rev:** Crowned imperial eagle with shield on breast **Edge:** GOTT MIT UNS

Date	Mintage	F	VF	XF	Unc	BU
1911A	50,000	30.00	65.00	100	250	300
1911A Proof	—	Value: 375				

Y# 204   5 MARK
27.7770 g., 0.9000 Silver 0.8037 oz. ASW, 38 mm.
Ruler: Albrecht Georg **Subject:** Death of Prince Georg **Obv:** Head left **Obv. Leg.:** GEORG FURST ZU SCHAUMBURG-LIPPE **Rev:** Crowned imperial eagle with shield on breast **Rev. Leg.:** DEUTSCHES REICH date, FUNF MARK below **Edge:** GOTT MIT UNS

Date	Mintage	F	VF	XF	Unc	BU
1904A	3,000	350	900	1,250	2,400	3,250
1904A Proof	200	Value: 3,750				

Y# 205   20 MARK
7.9650 g., 0.9000 Gold 0.2305 oz. AGW **Ruler:** Albrecht Georg **Subject:** Death of Prince Georg **Obv:** Head left **Obv. Leg.:** GEORG FURST ZU SCHAUMBURG-LIPPE **Rev:** Crowned imperial eagle with shield on breast **Rev. Leg.:** DEUTSCHES REICH date, 20 MARK below **Edge:** GOTT MIT UNS

Date	Mintage	F	VF	XF	Unc	BU
1904A	5,500	1,250	2,200	3,000	4,000	5,250
1904A Proof	132	Value: 6,000				

SCHLESWIG-HOLSTEIN

Schleswig-Holstein is located along the border area between Denmark and Germany. The Duchy of Schleswig was predominantly Danish while the Duchy of Holstein was mostly German. Holstein-Gottorp was the ruling line in most of the territory from 1533 and lost Schleswig to Denmark permanently in 1721. Holstein-Gottorp was transferred by the 1773 Treaty of Zarskoje Selo to Denmark in exchange for Oldenburg. There was a great deal of trouble in the area during the 19th century and as a result of a war with Denmark, Prussia annexed the territory in 1864. After World War I, a plebiscite was held and the area was divided in 1920. North Slesvig went to Denmark while South Schleswig and Holstein became a permanent part of Germany.

STATE
GUTSCHRIFTSMARKE COINAGE

KM# Tn1   5/100 GUTSCHRIFTSMARKE
Aluminum, 23 mm.   **Obv:** Provincial arms **Rev:** Denomination

Date	Mintage	F	VF	XF	Unc	BU
1923	3,330,000	3.00	7.00	14.00	20.00	25.00

KM# Tn2   10/100 GUTSCHRIFTSMARKE
Aluminum, 27 mm.   **Obv:** Provincial arms **Rev:** Denomination

Date	Mintage	F	VF	XF	Unc	BU
1923	4,500,000	4.00	8.00	16.00	20.00	25.00

SCHWARZBURG-RUDOLSTADT

Established upon the division of Schwarzburg-Sondershausen in 1552, the younger main branch of Schwarzburg, centered on the castle and town of Rudolstadt, 17 miles (29 kilometers) south of Weimar, flourished until the end of World War I. The count was raised to the rank of prince in 1711. The three sons of Albrecht VII, the first Count of Schwarzburg-Rudolstadt, ruled and issued coinage jointly, followed by a long succession of sole rulers descended from the middle son, Ludwig Günther I.

RULER
Günther Viktor, 1890-1918 (died 1925)
Arms: (See under Schwarzburg)

REFERENCES:
F = **Ernst Fischer**, *Die Münzen des Hauses Schwarzburg*, Heidelberg, 1904.
R = **Ernst Helmuth von Bethe**, *Schwarzburger Münzen und Medaillen: Sammlung des Schlossmuseums in Rudolstadt*, Halle (Saale), 1903.

MINT MARK
A - Berlin mint, 1841-1901

PATTERNS
Including off metal strikes

KM#	Date	Mintage	Identification	Mkt Val
Pn9	1901 A	—	2 Mark. Silver. Y207. Extra rare. Prev. KM#Pn3.	—

SCHWARZBURG-SONDERSHAUSEN

As the elder main line of Schwarzburg established in 1552, the counts of Schwarzburg-Sondershausen controlled their scattered territories from the castle of Sondershausen in northern Thuringia (Thüringen), 10 miles (16 kilometers) southeast of Nordhausen. Count Christian Wilhelm I was raised to the rank of prince in 1697 and the line descended from him until it finally became extinct in 1909. All titles and territories then passed to Schwarzburg-Rudolstadt.

RULER
Karl Günther, 1880-1909

Arms: (See under Schwarzburg)

REFERENCES:
F = **Ernst Fischer**, *Die Münzen des Hauses Schwarzburg*, Heidelberg, 1904.
R = **Ernst Helmuth von Bethe**, *Schwarzburger Münzen und Medaillen: Sammlung des Schlossmuseums in Rudolstadt*, Halle (Saale), 1903.

MINT MARK
A - Berlin mint, 1846-1909

PRINCIPALITY
REFORM COINAGE

KM# 152   2 MARK
11.1110 g., 0.9000 Silver 0.3215 oz. ASW, 28 mm.   **Ruler:** Karl Günther **Subject:** 25th Anniversary of Reign **Obv:** Head right, leafy spray below **Rev:** Crowned German imperial eagle with shield on breast **Edge:** Reeded **Note:** Thick rim. Prev. Y#211.

Date	Mintage	F	VF	XF	Unc	BU
1905	13,000	45.00	90.00	160	250	325
1905 Proof	5,000	Value: 400				

KM# 153   2 MARK
11.1110 g., 0.9000 Silver 0.3215 oz. ASW, 28 mm.
Ruler: Karl Günther **Subject:** 25th Anniversary of Reign **Obv:** Head right, leafy spray below **Rev:** Crowned German imperial eagle with shield on breast **Note:** Thin rim. Previous Y#211a.

Date	Mintage	F	VF	XF	Unc	BU
1905	62,000	25.00	70.00	95.00	150	275
1905 Proof	5,000	Value: 400				

KM# 154   3 MARK
16.6670 g., 0.9000 Silver 0.4823 oz. ASW, 33 mm.   **Ruler:** Karl Günther **Subject:** Death of Karl Gunther **Obv:** Head right **Rev:** Crowned German imperial eagle with shield on breast **Edge:** GOTT MIT UNS **Note:** Previous Y#212.

Date	Mintage	F	VF	XF	Unc	BU
1909A	70,000	30.00	60.00	100	175	325
1909A Proof	200	Value: 500				

PATTERNS
Including off metal strikes

KM#	Date	Mintage	Identification	Mkt Val
Pn1	1901A	—	2 Mark. Silver. Y209.	3,000
Pn2	1901A	—	2 Mark. Silver. Y211.	3,000
Pn3	1909A	—	3 Mark. Silver.	3,500

WALDECK-PYRMONT

The Count of Waldeck-Eisenberg inherited the Countship of Pyrmont, located between Lippe and Hannover, in 1625, thus creating an entity which encompassed about 672 square miles (1120 square kilometers). Waldeck and Pyrmont were permanently united in 1668, thus continuing the Eisenberg line as Waldeck-Pyrmont from that date. The count was raised to the rank of prince in 1712 and the unification of the two territories was confirmed in 1812. Waldeck-Pyrmont joined the German Confederation in 1815 and the North German Confederation in 1867. The prince renounced his sovereignty on 1 October of that year and Waldeck-Pyrmont was incorporated into Prussia. However, coinage was struck into the early 20th century for Waldeck-Pyrmont as a member of the German Empire. The hereditary territorial titles were lost along with the war in 1918. Some coins were struck for issue in Pyrmont only in the 18th through 20th centuries but those are listed separately under that name.

RULER
Friedrich, 1893-1918 (d.1946)

MINT OFFICIALS
AW - Albert Welle, mintmaster in Arolsen 1827-1840
FW, F*w, W, .W. – Friedrich Welle

MINT MARKS
A - Berlin mint, 1842-1903
B - Hannover mint, 1867

PRINCIPALITY
REFORM COINAGE

Y# 213 5 MARK
27.7770 g., 0.9000 Silver 0.8037 oz. ASW, 38 mm.
Ruler: Friedrich **Obv:** Head left **Rev:** Crowned imperial eagle with shield on breast **Edge:** GOTT MIT UNS

Date	Mintage	F	VF	XF	Unc	BU
1903A	2,000	—	3,000	4,000	5,000	7,500
1903A Proof	300	Value: 8,000				

Y# 214 20 MARK
7.9650 g., 0.9000 Gold 0.2305 oz. AGW **Ruler:** Friedrich **Obv:** Head left **Rev:** Crowned imperial eagle with shield on breast **Edge:** GOTT MIT UNS

Date	Mintage	F	VF	XF	Unc	BU
1903A	2,000	2,750	4,500	7,500	11,000	14,000
1903A Proof	150	Value: 16,000				

WURTTEMBERG

Located in South Germany, between Baden and Bavaria, Württemberg takes its name from the ancestral castle of the ruling dynasty. The early countship was located in the old duchy of Swabia, most of which was given to Count Ulrich II (1265-79) in 1268 by Conradin von Hohenstaufen. Ulrich's son, Eberhard II (1279-1325) moved the seat of his rule to Stuttgart. Württemberg obtained the mint right in 1374 and joined the Swabian monetary union two years later. The countship was divided into the lines of Württemberg-Urach and Württemberg-Stuttgart in 1441 and the elder Urach branch was raised to the rank of duke in 1495. It became extinct in the following year and the younger line in Württemberg-Stuttgart inherited the lands and ducal title. A cadet line of the family had been established in Mömpelgard in 1473 and, when the Württemberg-Stuttgart line fell extinct in 1593, the primacy of the dynasty fell to Württemberg-Mömpelgard. The latter took the Stuttgart title and spun off several cadet branches in Neustadt, Neuenburg and Weiltingen-Brenz. Meanwhile, the duke in Stuttgart succumbed to the French advances under Napoleon. Land west of the Rhine was exchanged with France for territories in and around Reutlingen, Heilbronn and seven other towns in 1802. More territories were added in Swabia at the expense of Austria in 1805. Napoleon elevated the duke to the status of elector in 1803 and then to king in 1806. Even more land was given to Württemberg that year, doubling the kingdom's size, and it joined the Confederation of the Rhine. At the close of the Napoleonic Wars (1792-1815), Württemberg joined the German Confederation, but sided with Austria in its war with Prussia in 1866. It sided with Prussia against France in 1870 and became a member of the German Empire in 1871. King Wilhelm II was forced to abdicate at the end of World War I in 1918.

RULER
Wilhelm II, 1891-1918

MINT MARKS
C, CT - Christophstal Mint
F - Freudenstadt Mint
S - Stuttgart Mint
T - Tübingen Mint

KINGDOM
REFORM COINAGE

KM# 631 2 MARK
11.1110 g., 0.9000 Silver 0.3215 oz. ASW, 28 mm.
Ruler: Wilhelm II **Obv:** Head right **Obv. Leg.:** WILHELM II

KOENIG VON WUERTTEMBERG **Rev:** Crowned imperial eagle with shield on breast **Rev. Leg.:** DEUTSCHES REICH date, ZWEI MARK below **Edge:** Reeded

Date	Mintage	F	VF	XF	Unc	BU
1901F	591,927	9.00	19.00	45.00	125	300
1902F	815,620	9.00	17.00	45.00	125	350
1903F	811,383	9.00	19.00	45.00	125	350
1904F	1,988,177	8.00	15.00	35.00	100	300
1905F	609,835	9.00	20.00	40.00	100	300
1906F	1,504,620	9.00	20.00	40.00	100	375
1907F	1,504,497	8.00	15.00	35.00	100	300
1908F	451,370	8.00	22.00	45.00	125	275
1912F	251,224	8.00	15.00	35.00	100	200
1913F	5,675	8.00	17.00	45.00	125	350
1914F	5,962	8.00	17.00	40.00	100	225
(1901-1914) Proof	—	Value: 275				

KM# 635 3 MARK
16.6670 g., 0.9000 Silver 0.4823 oz. ASW, 33 mm. **Ruler:** Wilhelm II **Obv:** Head right **Rev:** Crowned imperial eagle with shield on breast **Edge:** GOTT MIT UNS

Date	Mintage	F	VF	-XF	Unc	BU
1908F	300,000	10.00	20.00	30.00	70.00	150
1909F	1,906,698	10.00	20.00	30.00	65.00	150
1910F	837,230	10.00	20.00	30.00	65.00	150
1911F	424,820	10.00	20.00	30.00	65.00	150
1912F	849,100	10.00	17.50	25.00	60.00	150
1913F	267,700	10.00	20.00	30.00	75.00	150
1914F	733,121	10.00	17.50	25.00	60.00	125
(1908-1914)F Proof	—	Value: 300				

KM# 636 3 MARK
16.6670 g., 0.9000 Silver 0.4823 oz. ASW, 33 mm. **Ruler:** Wilhelm II **Subject:** Silver Wedding Anniversary **Obv:** Conjoined heads right, normal bar in "H" of "CHARLOTTE" **Rev:** Crowned imperial eagle with shield on breast **Edge:** GOTT MIT UNS

Date	Mintage	F	VF	XF	Unc	BU
1911F	493,000	12.00	18.00	35.00	45.00	65.00
1911F Proof	—	Value: 175				

KM# 637 3 MARK
16.6670 g., 0.9000 Silver 0.4823 oz. ASW, 33 mm. **Ruler:** Wilhelm II **Subject:** Silver Wedding Anniversary **Obv:** High bar in "H" of "CHARLOTTE" **Rev:** Crowned imperial eagle with shield on breast **Edge:** GOTT MIT UNS

Date	Mintage	F	VF	XF	Unc	BU
1911F	7,000	140	300	475	700	1,100
1911F Proof	—	Value: 1,250				

KM# 638 3 MARK
16.6670 g., 0.9000 Silver 0.4823 oz. ASW, 33 mm.
Ruler: Wilhelm II **Subject:** 25th Year of Reign **Obv:** Head right **Rev:** Crowned imperial eagle with shield on breast **Edge:** GOTT MIT UNS **Note:** 5,650 were melted.

Date	Mintage	F	VF	XF	Unc	BU
1916F Proof	1,000	Value: 8,500				

KM# 632 5 MARK
27.7770 g., 0.9000 Silver 0.8037 oz. ASW, 38 mm.
Ruler: Wilhelm II **Obv:** Head right **Obv. Leg.:** WILHELM II KOENIG VON WUERTTEMBERG **Rev:** Crowned imperial eagle with shield on breast **Rev. Leg.:** DEUTSCHES REICH date, FUNF MARK below **Edge:** GOTT MIT UNS

Date	Mintage	F	VF	XF	Unc	BU
1901F	210,700	15.00	35.00	90.00	600	1,250
1902F	360,889	15.00	35.00	90.00	400	1,400
1903F	722,182	15.00	30.00	75.00	375	1,100
1904F	391,317	15.00	30.00	75.00	375	1,100
1906F	45,000	25.00	65.00	200	1,200	2,500
1906F Proof	50	Value: 3,500				
1907F	436,321	15.00	30.00	65.00	300	800
1908F	521,716	15.00	30.00	55.00	250	500
1913F	341,200	15.00	30.00	50.00	200	375
(1901-1913)F Proof	—	Value: 1,300				

KM# 633 10 MARK
3.9820 g., 0.9000 Gold 0.1152 oz. AGW **Ruler:** Wilhelm II **Obv:** Head right **Obv. Leg.:** WILHELM II KOENIG VON WUERTTEMBERG **Rev:** Crowned imperial eagle with shield on breast **Rev. Leg.:** DEUTSCHES REICH **Edge:** ~ * ~

Date	Mintage	F	VF	XF	Unc	BU
1901F	110,262	110	135	175	300	550
1902F	50,112	125	150	200	400	700
1903F	180,402	110	125	175	300	550
1903F Proof	—	Value: 2,000				
1904F	349,631	110	140	175	300	550
1904F Proof	—	Value: 2,000				
1905F	199,312	110	140	175	300	500
1905F Proof	—	Value: 2,000				
1906F	100,164	110	140	175	300	550
1906F Proof	50	Value: 2,000				
1907F	149,921	110	140	175	300	500
1907F Proof	—	Value: 2,000				
1909F	100,189	110	140	175	300	500
1909F Proof	—	Value: 2,250				
1910F	150,229	110	140	175	300	500
1910F Proof	—	Value: 2,250				
1911F	50,337	140	275	350	600	800
1911F Proof	—	Value: 2,250				
1912F	49,353	140	275	335	600	1,000
1912F Proof	—	Value: 2,250				
1913F	50,038	140	275	375	600	1,000
1913F Proof	—	Value: 2,250				

KM# 634 20 MARK
7.9650 g., 0.9000 Gold 0.2305 oz. AGW **Ruler:** Wilhelm II **Obv:** Head right **Obv. Leg.:** WILHELM II KOENIG VON WUERTTEMBERG **Rev:** Crowned imperial eagle with shield on breast **Rev. Leg.:** DEUTSCHES REICH date, 20 MARK below **Edge:** GOTT MIT UNS

Date	Mintage	F	VF	XF	Unc	BU
1905F	500,594		BV	225	250	425
1905F Proof	—	Value: 2,000				
1913F	42,687	5,000	16,000	25,000	40,000	65,000
1913F Proof, rare	—	Value: 85,000				

Date	Mintage	F	VF	XF	Unc	BU
1914F	552,684	1,750	2,750	3,750	5,000	6,000
1914F Proof	—	Value: 8,000				

PATTERNS
Including off metal strikes

KM#	Date	Mintage Identification	Mkt Val
Pn42	19xxF	— 5 Mark. Copper. Lettered edge.	—
Pn43	1904	— 5 Mark. Silver.	2,500
Pn44	1904F	— 5 Mark. Copper. Y222. Eagle within irregular inner circle, countermarked "N.A.".	—
Pn45	1905	— 5 Mark. Silver.	3,500
Pn46	1905	— 5 Mark. Silver. Beaded rim.	5,500
Pn47	1905F	— 5 Mark. Silver. Lettered edge.	3,500
Pn48	1905F	— 5 Mark. Silver. Reeded edge.	3,500
Pn49	1910F	— 3 Mark. Silver. Irregular "LH" under neck. Y225a.	—
Pn50	1911	— 3 Mark. Silver.	—
Pn51	1911	— 3 Mark. Silver. Busts divide date.	—
Pn52	1911F	— 3 Mark. Aluminum.	—
PnA53	1911F	— 3 Mark. Iron. Aluminum-plated.	—
Pn53	1911F	— 3 Mark. Silver.	—
Pn54	1911F	— 3 Mark. Silver.	—
Pn55	1911F	— 3 Mark. Copper.	—
Pn56	1911F	— 3 Mark. Silver.	—
Pn57	1911F	— 3 Mark. Copper.	—
Pn58	1911F	— 3 Mark. Silver.	3,500
Pn59	1911F	— 3 Mark. Copper.	—
Pn60	1913F	— 2 Mark. Aluminum.	—
Pn61	1913	— 5 Mark. Nickel.	—
Pn62	1916F	— 3 Mark. Aluminum.	6,000
Pn63	1916F	— 3 Mark. Silver.	12,500

TRIAL STRIKES

KM#	Date	Mintage Identification	Mkt Val
TS3	1905	— 3 Mark. Silver. Uniface.	—
TS4	19xx	— 5 Mark. Silver. Uniface.	200

GERMANY

1871-1918
Germany, a nation of north-central Europe which from 1871 to 1945 was, successively, an empire, a republic and a totalitarian state, attained its territorial peak as an empire when it comprised a 208,780 sq. mi. (540,740 sq. km.) homeland and an overseas colonial empire.

As the power of the Roman Empire waned, several war-like tribes residing in northern Germany moved south and west, invading France, Belgium, England, Italy and Spain. In 800 A.D. the Frankish king Charlemagne, who ruled most of France and Germany, was crowned Emperor of the Holy Roman Empire, a loose federation of an estimated 1,800 German States that lasted until 1806. Modern Germany was formed from the eastern part of Charlemagne's empire.

After 1812, the German States were reduced to a federation of 32, of which Prussia was the strongest. In 1871, Prussian chancellor Otto von Bismarck united the German States into an empire ruled by William I, the Prussian king. The empire initiated a colonial endeavor and became one of the world's greatest powers. Germany disintegrated as a result of World War I.

It was reestablished as the Weimar Republic. The humiliation of defeat, economic depression, poverty and discontent gave rise to Adolf Hitler, 1933, who reconstituted Germany as the Third Reich and after initial diplomatic and military triumphs, expanded his goals beyond Europe into Africa and USSR which led it into final disaster in World War II, ending on VE Day, May 7, 1945.

RULERS
Wilhelm II, 1888-1918

MINT MARKS
A - Berlin
D - Munich
E - Muldenhutten (1887-1953)
F - Stuttgart
G - Karlsruhe
J - Hamburg

MONETARY SYSTEM
(Until 1923)
100 Pfennig = 1 Mark

(Commencing 1945)
100 Pfennig = 1 Mark

EMPIRE
STANDARD COINAGE

KM# 10   PFENNIG
2.0200 g., Copper   **Ruler:** Wilhelm II **Obv:** Denomination, date at right **Rev:** Crowned imperial eagle with shield on breast
Note: Struck from 1890-1916.

Date	Mintage	F	VF	XF	Unc	BU
1901A	21,045,000	0.20	1.25	4.00	22.00	25.00
1901D	5,337,000	0.50	2.00	9.00	40.00	45.00
1901E	1,397,000	1.00	6.00	27.50	80.00	100
1901F	2,925,000	0.60	4.00	17.50	60.00	80.00
1901G	1,977,000	2.50	9.00	32.50	110	130
1901J	2,011,000	4.00	12.50	40.00	180	225
1902A	7,474,000	0.50	2.00	4.00	25.00	30.00
1902D	2,811,000	0.60	3.50	6.00	40.00	45.00
1902E	1,183,000	1.00	6.00	25.00	110	130
1902F	1,250,000	1.00	6.00	25.00	100	120
1902G	881,000	4.00	22.50	60.00	200	230
1902J	150	475	1,600	2,200	5,000	6,000
1903A	12,690,000	0.20	1.00	4.00	30.00	35.00
1903D	3,140,000	0.80	2.00	8.00	40.00	50.00
1903E	1,956,000	1.50	3.00	10.00	50.00	60.00
1903F	2,945,000	0.80	2.00	10.00	45.00	55.00
1903G	1,377,000	3.00	6.00	25.00	100	125
1903J	2,832,000	1.00	4.00	20.00	60.00	80.00
1904A	28,625,000	0.20	1.00	3.00	25.00	30.00
1904D	4,118,000	0.80	2.00	8.00	40.00	45.00
1904E	2,778,000	1.00	3.00	9.00	40.00	50.00
1904F	4,520,000	1.00	3.00	8.00	40.00	50.00
1904G	3,232,000	2.00	6.00	18.00	80.00	90.00
1904J	4,467,000	1.00	2.50	10.00	40.00	50.00
1905A	19,631,000	0.20	1.00	3.50	18.00	22.00
1905D	6,084,000	0.50	2.00	5.50	30.00	35.00
1905E	3,564,000	0.50	2.00	5.50	30.00	35.00
1905E	Inc. above	—	—	2,500	—	—

Note: Cross under denomination

Date	Mintage	F	VF	XF	Unc	BU
1905F	4,153,000	0.80	3.00	6.50	40.00	45.00
1905G	3,051,000	0.80	3.00	18.00	70.00	80.00
1905J	4,085,000	1.00	5.00	12.00	55.00	65.00
1906A	46,921,000	0.20	0.80	2.50	18.00	20.00
1906D	5,633,000	0.20	0.80	5.00	30.00	35.00
1906E	7,278,000	0.20	0.80	5.00	20.00	25.00
1906F	7,173,000	0.20	0.80	5.00	25.00	30.00
1906G	5,194,000	0.20	0.80	5.00	40.00	45.00
1906J	3,622,000	0.20	1.00	6.00	45.00	55.00
1907A	33,711,000	0.20	0.80	1.50	14.00	16.00
1907D	14,691,000	0.20	1.00	2.00	20.00	23.00
1907E	3,719,000	0.20	1.50	5.00	20.00	25.00
1907F	7,026,000	0.20	1.00	3.00	20.00	23.00
1907G	3,052,000	0.20	1.50	6.00	30.00	35.00
1907J	6,722,000	0.20	1.50	6.00	20.00	25.00
1908A	21,922,000	0.20	0.60	1.25	12.00	15.00
1908D	10,629,000	0.20	0.80	2.25	20.00	23.00
1908E	3,400,000	0.20	1.50	5.00	22.00	26.00
1908F	6,112,000	0.20	1.50	5.00	20.00	26.00
1908G	3,663,000	0.20	2.00	6.00	40.00	45.00
1908J	5,581,000	0.20	1.50	5.00	22.00	26.00
1909A	21,430,000	0.20	0.75	3.00	20.00	23.00
1909D	2,814,000	0.20	1.25	7.00	55.00	65.00
1909E	2,562,000	1.00	3.00	8.00	45.00	50.00
1909F	2,425,000	1.50	4.00	10.00	50.00	60.00
1909G	1,220,000	1.50	5.00	12.00	80.00	90.00
1909J	1,634,000	1.50	5.00	11.00	80.00	90.00
1910A	10,761,000	0.20	0.75	2.50	15.00	18.00
1910D	4,221,000	0.20	1.00	3.00	20.00	24.00
1910E	1,600,000	0.50	3.00	5.00	38.00	42.00
1910F	3,009,000	0.30	2.00	6.00	30.00	35.00
1910G	1,834,000	0.50	3.00	16.00	85.00	95.00
1910J	2,450,000	0.50	3.00	9.00	60.00	70.00
1911A	38,172,000	0.20	0.75	2.00	14.00	16.00
1911D	8,657,000	0.20	1.00	3.00	20.00	23.00
1911E	5,236,000	0.20	1.00	3.00	20.00	23.00
1911F	5,780,000	0.20	1.00	3.00	20.00	23.00
1911G	2,075,000	0.20	1.50	5.00	35.00	40.00
1911J	5,594,000	0.20	1.00	3.00	15.00	18.00
1912A	42,693,000	0.10	0.75	1.50	10.00	13.00
1912D	10,173,000	0.10	0.80	2.00	12.00	15.00
1912E	5,689,000	0.10	0.80	2.50	13.00	16.00
1912F	7,441,000	0.10	0.80	3.00	13.00	16.00
1912G	5,526,000	0.10	0.80	3.00	15.00	20.00
1912J	5,615,000	0.10	0.80	3.00	25.00	30.00
1913A	32,671,000	0.10	0.50	2.00	10.00	13.00
1913D	8,161,000	0.20	1.00	3.00	12.00	15.00
1913E	2,258,000	1.00	3.00	4.00	20.00	23.00
1913F	6,620,000	0.20	1.00	3.00	14.00	16.00
1913G	3,209,000	0.20	1.00	2.00	25.00	30.00

Date	Mintage	F	VF	XF	Unc	BU
1913J	1,456,000	0.10	5.00	11.00	45.00	50.00
1914A	9,976,000	0.20	0.80	2.00	8.00	10.00
1914D	1,842,000	0.20	1.25	2.50	14.00	17.00
1914E	2,926,000	0.30	2.00	3.00	15.00	18.00
1914F	3,316,000	0.20	1.00	2.00	15.00	18.00
1914G	2,100,000	0.20	1.75	2.50	15.00	18.00
1914J	4,368,000	0.20	1.75	2.50	15.00	18.00
1915A	14,738,000	0.10	0.75	1.50	8.00	10.00
1915D	1,771,000	0.20	1.00	2.50	20.00	22.00
1915E	2,779,000	0.20	1.00	3.50	20.00	22.00
1915F	1,411,000	0.20	1.00	4.00	25.00	30.00
1915G	2,041,000	0.20	1.00	4.00	25.00	30.00
1915J	2,981,000	0.20	1.00	4.00	20.00	25.00
1916A	5,960,000	0.20	0.75	2.50	10.00	12.00
1916D	5,401,000	0.20	1.00	4.00	25.00	30.00
1916E	818,000	1.00	6.00	8.00	35.00	40.00
1916F	1,104,000	0.80	3.00	8.00	35.00	40.00
1916G	671,000	1.50	6.00	20.00	60.00	70.00
1916J	898,000	1.00	5.00	10.00	50.00	55.00
1901-16 Common date proof	—	Value: 100				

KM# 24   PFENNIG
Aluminum   **Ruler:** Wilhelm II **Obv:** Denomination, date at right **Rev:** Crowned imperial eagle with shield on breast

Date	Mintage	F	VF	XF	Unc	BU
1916G	—	—	260	380	8,000	1,000
1917A	27,159,000	0.15	0.75	2.00	6.00	8.00
1917A Proof	—	Value: 90.00				
1917D	6,940,000	0.15	0.75	2.50	10.00	12.00
1917E	3,862,000	0.50	2.00	5.00	15.00	18.00
1917E Proof	—	Value: 90.00				
1917F	5,125,000	0.25	2.00	3.00	10.00	12.00
1917G	3,139,000	0.25	2.00	4.00	10.00	13.00
1917G Proof	—	Value: 90.00				
1917J	4,182,000	0.50	2.50	3.00	24.00	28.00
1917J Proof	—	Value: 90.00				
1918A	—	—	2,000	3,000	4,000	5,000
1918D	318,000	10.00	20.00	45.00	100	125
1918F	—	—	2,500	4,000		

Note: The 1918F 1 Pfennigs are from the burned-out ruins of the Stuttgart Mint destroyed in World War II

1916-18 Common date proof	—	Value: 90.00				

KM# 16   2 PFENNIG
3.3000 g., Copper   **Ruler:** Wilhelm II **Obv:** Denomination, date at right **Rev:** Crowned imperial eagle with shield on breast

Date	Mintage	F	VF	XF	Unc	BU
1904A	5,414,000	0.20	1.00	5.00	25.00	30.00
1904D	1,404,000	0.50	2.00	10.00	30.00	35.00
1904E	744,000	2.00	6.00	16.00	70.00	80.00
1904F	1,002,000	0.20	3.50	12.00	45.00	55.00
1904G	495,000	3.00	7.00	28.00	140	160
1904J	444,000	2.00	11.00	25.00	180	200
1905A	5,172,000	0.10	0.50	2.50	20.00	22.00
1905D	1,570,000	0.20	2.00	10.00	30.00	35.00
1905E	924,000	0.40	3.50	12.00	55.00	65.00
1905F	1,115,000	0.40	1.00	10.00	60.00	70.00
1905G	1,030,000	0.40	3.50	16.00	80.00	100
1905J	1,609,000	0.40	3.00	12.00	90.00	100
1906A	8,459,000	0.20	1.00	5.00	30.00	35.00
1906D	3,539,000	0.20	1.75	6.00	35.00	40.00
1906E	2,055,000	0.20	1.50	7.50	40.00	45.00
1906F	2,840,000	0.20	1.50	6.50	35.00	40.00
1906G	1,527,000	0.40	2.00	12.00	80.00	90.00
1906J	1,908,000	0.40	2.00	12.00	60.00	70.00
1907A	13,468,000	0.10	0.50	3.00	16.00	20.00
1907D	1,921,000	0.20	0.75	4.50	28.00	30.00
1907E	744,000	0.50	2.50	8.00	55.00	65.00
1907F	1,059,000	0.20	2.50	12.00	70.00	80.00
1907G	610,000	0.50	3.00	12.00	70.00	80.00
1907J	952,000	0.20	2.50	10.00	60.00	65.00
1908A	5,421,000	0.10	1.00	4.00	20.00	25.00
1908D	1,407,000	0.10	2.00	7.00	25.00	30.00
1908E	745,000	1.00	3.00	10.00	50.00	55.00
1908F	1,003,000	0.10	3.00	10.00	50.00	55.00
1908G	610,000	0.25	4.00	14.00	70.00	80.00
1908J	817,000	0.10	3.00	12.00	60.00	70.00
1910A	5,421,000	0.20	5.00	18.00	22.00	
1910D	1,407,000	0.50	2.00	8.00	30.00	35.00
1910E	745,000	1.00	4.50	10.00	55.00	60.00
1910F	1,003,000	0.40	2.00	8.00	50.00	55.00
1910G	517,000	0.40	3.00	15.00	90.00	110
1910J	568,000	0.40	3.00	15.00	80.00	90.00
1911A	8,187,000	0.10	3.00	17.00	20.00	
1911D	2,100,000	0.20	1.00	4.00	22.00	26.00

Date	Mintage	F	VF	XF	Unc	BU
1911E	1,133,000	0.50	3.00	5.00	26.00	30.00
1911F	1,490,000	0.40	2.00	4.00	22.00	26.00
1911G	1,313,000	0.40	2.00	6.00	30.00	35.00
1911J	1,883,000	0.40	2.00	4.00	22.00	26.00
1912A	13,580,000	0.20	0.75	3.00	18.00	20.00
1912D	3,109,000	0.30	1.00	4.00	22.00	26.00
1912E	1,808,000	0.30	2.00	5.00	22.00	26.00
1912F	2,366,000	0.30	1.00	6.00	22.00	26.00
1912G	1,395,000	0.50	2.50	7.50	50.00	60.00
1912J	1,605,000	0.50	2.00	6.00	30.00	35.00
1913A	4,212,000	0.20	0.75	3.00	16.00	18.00
1913D	2,525,000	0.20	1.00	6.00	24.00	28.00
1913E	413,000	0.50	3.00	12.00	65.00	75.00
1913F	1,602,000	0.40	2.00	12.00	60.00	70.00
1913G	741,000	1.50	9.00	13.00	70.00	80.00
1913J	1,254,000	0.40	2.00	9.00	60.00	70.00
1914A	5,350,000	0.10	1.00	3.00	14.00	16.00
1914E	1,201,000	1.00	5.00	8.00	40.00	45.00
1914F	158,000	12.00	45.00	90.00	300	325
1914G	610,000	2.00	9.00	25.00	120	140
1914J	817,000	0.10	6.00	17.00	70.00	80.00
1915A	3,897,000	0.40	1.00	3.00	12.00	15.00
1915D	1,407,000	0.40	2.00	6.00	20.00	25.00
1915E	288,000	3.00	15.00	28.00	50.00	60.00
1915F	904,000	0.20	2.00	7.00	25.00	30.00
1916A	3,524,000	0.20	1.00	3.00	12.00	14.00
1916D	915,000	0.40	1.50	8.00	18.00	22.00
1916E	484,000	1.00	3.50	10.00	32.00	36.00
1916F	651,000	0.25	1.50	5.00	20.00	25.00
1916G	397,000	1.00	3.50	14.00	50.00	60.00
1916J	531,000	0.50	2.50	12.00	40.00	50.00
1904-16 Common date proof	—	Value: 150				

KM# 11 5 PFENNIG
2.4700 g., Copper-Nickel, 18 mm. **Ruler:** Wilhelm II
Obv: Denomination, date at right **Rev:** Crowned imperial eagle with shield on breast **Note:** Struck from 1890-1915.

Date	Mintage	F	VF	XF	Unc	BU
1901A	8,155,000	0.20	0.60	3.00	40.00	50.00
1901D	2,779,000	0.20	1.50	12.00	75.00	85.00
1901E	1,492,000	0.40	2.50	12.00	100	120
1901F	1,810,000	0.40	2.50	10.00	90.00	110
1901G	915,000	0.50	3.50	35.00	300	350
1901J	1,226,000	0.50	3.50	25.00	150	170
1902A	8,949,000	0.20	0.75	5.00	40.00	50.00
1902D	2,812,000	0.40	2.50	12.00	90.00	110
1902E	1,120,000	1.00	3.50	12.00	70.00	80.00
1902F	1,800,000	1.00	3.00	11.00	60.00	70.00
1902G	1,220,000	1.50	6.00	25.00	150	170
1902J	1,636,000	1.50	6.00	20.00	130	150
1903A	5,932,000	0.20	4.00	6.00	70.00	80.00
1903D	1,406,000	0.60	2.00	15.00	100	120
1903E	1,114,000	0.80	3.50	18.00	80.00	100
1903F	1,209,000	1.00	4.00	20.00	175	225
1903G	610,000	2.00	9.00	55.00	275	300
1903J	817,000	1.00	6.00	45.00	225	250
1904A	6,791,000	0.20	6.00	10.00	65.00	75.00
1904D	1,408,000	1.00	2.50	15.00	80.00	100
1904E	746,000	1.50	6.00	20.00	130	150
1904F	1,006,000	1.00	3.50	20.00	100	120
1904G	610,000	2.00	8.00	25.00	300	350
1904J	818,000	1.00	5.00	28.00	200	225
1905A	8,129,000	0.20	0.75	2.50	35.00	45.00
1905D	2,109,000	0.20	1.00	6.00	80.00	90.00
1905E	1,117,000	0.40	1.75	7.00	60.00	70.00
1905F	1,505,000	0.20	1.00	6.00	70.00	80.00
1905G	915,000	1.00	3.00	16.00	130	145
1905J	1,226,000	0.60	2.50	12.00	120	135
1906A	18,970,000	0.20	0.75	2.00	25.00	35.00
1906D	4,922,000	0.20	1.00	5.00	40.00	50.00
1906E	2,605,000	0.20	1.25	5.00	45.00	55.00
1906F	3,512,000	0.20	1.00	5.00	50.00	60.00
1906G	2,136,000	0.50	2.00	15.00	130	150
1906J	2,859,000	0.20	1.75	13.00	130	150
1907A	11,930,000	0.20	0.75	2.25	20.00	25.00
1907D	2,113,000	0.20	1.00	5.00	40.00	50.00
1907E	1,517,000	0.30	1.75	5.00	40.00	50.00
1907F	1,845,000	0.30	1.75	5.00	40.00	45.00
1907G	915,000	1.00	2.50	6.00	60.00	80.00
1907J	1,636,000	0.50	2.00	5.00	45.00	50.00
1908A	22,114,000	0.20	0.50	2.50	18.00	20.00
1908D	4,991,000	0.20	1.00	3.00	20.00	25.00
1908E	2,919,000	0.30	1.50	5.00	35.00	40.00
1908/7F	5,124,000	30.00	60.00	80.00	125	150
1908F	Inc. above	0.50	1.50	5.00	40.00	50.00
1908G	3,357,000	0.50	2.00	8.00	70.00	80.00
1908J	3,264,000	0.50	2.00	10.00	110	130
1909A	5,797,000	0.40	1.50	9.00	60.00	70.00
1909D	2,753,000	0.60	2.50	14.00	110	130
1909E	984,000	1.50	4.50	18.00	120	140
1909F	252,000	2.00	18.00	50.00	250	300
1909/8J	1,632,000	1.00	5.00	5.00	45.00	50.00
1909J	Inc. above	1.00	9.00	28.00	170	190

Date	Mintage	F	VF	XF	Unc	BU
1910A	7,344,000	0.20	0.50	3.00	25.00	30.00
1910D	2,814,000	0.20	0.80	6.00	40.00	50.00
1910E	1,290,000	0.20	1.00	9.00	60.00	70.00
1910F	1,721,000	0.20	1.50	11.00	65.00	75.00
1910G	1,222,000	0.30	1.75	20.00	120	130
1910J	152,000	30.00	42.50	70.00	150	175
1911A	15,660,000	0.20	0.50	1.50	10.00	12.00
1911D	2,221,000	0.20	1.00	2.50	15.00	18.00
1911E	1,770,000	0.40	2.00	3.00	15.00	18.00
1911F	2,714,000	0.40	2.00	3.00	15.00	18.00
1911G	1,833,000	0.40	1.00	2.50	15.00	18.00
1911J	3,116,000	0.20	1.00	2.00	18.00	22.00
1912A	19,320,000	0.20	0.80	2.00	12.00	15.00
1912D	4,015,000	0.20	0.80	2.50	16.00	18.00
1912E	2,568,000	0.20	1.00	2.50	20.00	25.00
1912F	3,679,000	0.20	1.00	2.50	22.00	25.00
1912G	2,440,000	0.20	1.00	3.00	30.00	35.00
1912J	3,020,000	0.20	1.00	2.50	20.00	25.00
1913A	15,506,000	0.20	0.50	1.50	12.00	15.00
1913D	5,519,000	0.20	0.50	3.00	15.00	18.00
1913E	2,373,000	0.50	2.00	3.00	17.00	20.00
1913F	2,054,000	0.50	2.00	3.00	17.00	20.00
1913G	1,221,000	1.00	5.00	9.00	70.00	80.00
1913J	253,000	10.00	16.00	35.00	160	180
1914A	23,605,000	0.20	0.50	1.00	9.00	10.00
1914D	3,014,000	0.20	0.80	1.50	12.00	15.00
1914E	1,710,000	0.20	1.00	3.50	12.00	15.00
1914F	2,206,000	0.20	1.00	2.50	18.00	22.00
1914G	1,218,000	0.20	1.00	3.00	20.00	25.00
1914J	3,235,000	0.20	1.00	2.50	20.00	25.00
1915D	3,516,000	0.10	1.00	2.00	18.00	22.00
1915E	834,000	1.00	8.00	13.00	60.00	70.00
1915F	1,894,000	0.10	2.00	5.00	35.00	40.00
1915G	894,000	0.50	7.00	18.00	70.00	80.00
1915J	1,669,000	0.10	6.00	14.00	60.00	70.00
1901-15 Common date proof	—	Value: 120				

KM# 19 5 PFENNIG
2.5100 g., Iron **Obv:** Denomination, date below **Rev:** Crowned imperial eagle with shield on breast

Date	Mintage	F	VF	XF	Unc	BU
1915A	34,631,000	0.20	0.50	3.00	15.00	20.00
1915D	2,021,000	2.00	7.00	13.00	60.00	70.00
1915E	4,670,000	1.00	4.00	9.00	40.00	45.00
1915F	3,500,000	0.80	3.00	6.00	35.00	40.00
1915G	3,676,000	0.80	3.00	6.00	35.00	40.00
1915J	2,100,000	1.50	6.00	12.00	50.00	60.00
1916A	51,003,000	0.20	0.50	2.50	12.00	15.00
1916D	19,590,000	0.20	0.50	3.00	18.00	22.00
1916E	2,271,000	2.00	6.00	15.00	50.00	60.00
1916F	10,479,000	0.20	0.80	5.00	25.00	30.00
1916G	5,599,000	0.50	1.50	5.50	35.00	40.00
1916J	10,253,000	0.30	1.00	4.00	30.00	35.00
1917A	87,315,000	0.10	0.30	1.50	12.00	15.00
1917D	19,581,000	0.20	1.00	2.50	14.00	17.00
1917E	11,092,000	0.10	1.00	3.00	18.00	20.00
1917F	10,930,000	0.20	0.50	3.50	20.00	22.00
1917F	—	600	1,000	1,600	2,250	2,500

Note: Mule with Polish reverse of Y#5, see Poland

Date	Mintage	F	VF	XF	Unc	BU
1917G	6,720,000	0.20	1.00	4.00	18.00	22.00
1917J	11,686,000	0.20	1.00	4.50	20.00	25.00
1918A	223,516,000	0.10	0.50	1.00	6.00	8.00
1918D	29,130,000	0.10	0.50	1.00	8.00	10.00
1918E	23,600,000	0.20	1.00	2.00	10.00	14.00
1918F	24,598,000	0.10	0.30	1.25	10.00	12.00
1918G	12,697,000	0.20	1.00	2.00	10.00	14.00
1918J	20,240,000	0.10	0.50	1.00	8.00	10.00
1919A	112,102,000	0.10	0.50	0.75	6.00	8.00
1919D	41,163,000	0.10	0.50	1.00	8.00	10.00
1919E	20,608,000	0.10	1.00	1.00	8.00	10.00
1919F	32,700,000	0.10	0.50	1.00	8.00	10.00
1919G	13,925,000	0.10	1.00	2.00	15.00	20.00
1919J	16,249,000	0.50	1.50	6.00	15.00	20.00
1920A	80,300,000	0.10	0.40	1.00	5.00	8.00
1920D	25,502,000	0.10	0.50	1.00	6.00	9.00
1920E	11,646,000	0.50	1.00	3.00	25.00	30.00
1920F	24,300,000	0.10	0.40	1.00	10.00	12.00
1920G	10,244,000	0.10	0.50	1.25	16.00	18.00
1920J	16,857,000	0.20	0.30	1.00	14.00	16.00
1921A	143,418,000	0.10	0.20	0.75	7.00	9.00
1921D	38,133,000	0.10	0.20	1.00	7.00	9.00
1921E	21,104,000	0.50	1.00	3.50	25.00	30.00
1921F	24,800,000	0.10	0.20	1.00	8.00	10.00
1921G	21,289,000	0.10	0.20	1.00	8.00	10.00
1921J	28,928,000	0.15	1.00	2.50	8.00	10.00
1922A Rare	89,062,000	—	—	—	—	—
1922D	31,240,000	0.10	0.20	0.50	12.00	14.00
1922E	19,156,000	0.50	1.00	8.00	20.00	25.00
1922F	16,436,000	0.10	0.20	1.00	12.00	14.00
1922G	19,708,000	0.10	0.25	1.00	8.00	10.00
1922J	16,820,000	0.10	0.20	1.25	15.00	18.00
1915-22 Common date proof	—	Value: 110				

KM# 12 10 PFENNIG
3.7200 g., Copper-Nickel, 21.11 mm. **Ruler:** Wilhelm II
Obv: Denomination, date at right **Rev:** Crowned imperial eagle with shield on breast **Note:** Struck from 1890-1916.

Date	Mintage	F	VF	XF	Unc	BU
1901A	10,200,000	0.20	1.00	8.00	70.00	—
1901D	3,259,000	1.00	4.00	22.00	150	—
1901E	1,863,000	1.00	5.00	20.00	170	—
1901F	2,594,000	1.00	5.00	16.00	130	—
1901G	1,527,000	2.00	17.00	60.00	280	—
1901J	1,225,000	2.00	14.00	60.00	280	—
1902A	5,878,000	0.20	1.00	4.00	60.00	—
1902D	1,406,000	0.20	1.00	15.00	120	—
1902E	502,000	1.00	5.00	45.00	280	—
1902F	1,003,000	0.20	1.00	15.00	110	—
1902G	610,000	0.20	10.00	50.00	280	—
1902J	815,000	1.50	8.00	30.00	220	—
1903A	5,131,000	0.20	0.50	5.00	90.00	—
1903D	1,406,000	0.40	1.00	15.00	150	—
1903E	988,000	0.40	1.00	15.00	120	—
1903F	1,003,000	0.50	2.00	22.00	175	—
1903G	610,000	0.20	8.00	50.00	250	—
1903J	816,000	1.50	6.00	45.00	250	—
1904A	5,189,000	0.20	0.50	4.00	70.00	—
1904D	1,056,000	0.20	1.50	14.00	140	—
1904E	559,000	0.20	1.50	14.00	130	—
1904F	753,000	0.20	1.50	16.00	180	—
1904G	457,000	2.00	10.00	50.00	280	—
1904J	612,000	2.00	8.00	40.00	250	—
1905A	8,650,000	0.20	0.50	3.00	48.00	—
1905A Proof	250	Value: 100				
1905D	1,846,000	0.20	1.00	6.00	100	—
1905E	980,000	0.40	1.50	16.00	150	—
1905F	1,310,000	0.40	1.50	16.00	150	—
1905J	642,000	1.50	8.00	50.00	250	—
1905J	1,430,000	1.50	8.00	40.00	220	—
1906A	14,470,000	0.20	0.50	4.00	50.00	—
1906D	4,132,000	0.20	1.00	5.00	80.00	—
1906E	2,189,000	0.20	1.00	6.00	80.00	—
1906F	2,953,000	0.20	1.00	6.00	75.00	—
1906G	1,952,000	1.00	5.00	40.00	260	—
1906J	2,042,000	1.00	5.00	30.00	220	—
1907A	17,971,000	0.20	0.50	2.00	25.00	—
1907D	2,813,000	0.20	1.00	3.00	40.00	—
1907E	2,291,000	0.20	1.00	3.00	45.00	—
1907F	3,206,000	0.20	1.00	6.00	60.00	—
1907G	1,889,000	0.50	2.00	15.00	140	—
1907J	2,750,000	0.40	1.00	12.00	90.00	—
1908A	20,410,000	0.20	0.50	2.00	35.00	—
1908D	6,773,000	0.20	1.00	2.00	28.00	—
1908E	2,490,000	0.20	1.00	5.00	80.00	—
1908F	3,535,000	0.20	1.00	6.00	80.00	—
1908G	1,708,000	0.40	2.00	15.00	130	—
1908J	2,649,000	0.20	1.00	12.00	90.00	—
1909A	2,270,000	0.40	1.00	8.00	35.00	—
1909D	966,000	0.60	2.00	15.00	120	—
1909E	806,000	1.00	3.00	13.00	130	—
1909F	780,000	3.00	12.00	36.00	180	—
1909G	980,000	2.00	9.00	40.00	240	—
1909J	725,000	3.00	15.00	60.00	350	—
1910A	3,734,000	0.20	6.00	2.00	30.00	—
1910D	1,406,000	0.30	1.00	4.00	35.00	—
1910E	300,000	2.50	10.00	28.00	160	—
1910F	1,003,000	0.50	2.00	12.00	60.00	—
1910G	610,000	2.50	10.00	33.00	220	—
1911A	13,554,000	0.10	0.50	1.50	25.00	—
1911D	2,508,000	0.20	0.80	2.50	25.00	—
1911E	2,246,000	0.30	0.80	3.00	30.00	—
1911F	2,235,000	0.30	0.80	3.00	30.00	—
1911G	1,678,000	0.20	1.50	6.00	45.00	—
1911J	3,062,000	0.20	0.80	3.00	38.00	—
1912A	21,312,000	0.10	0.40	2.00	18.00	—
1912D	6,988,000	0.20	0.80	2.00	24.00	—
1912E	2,649,000	0.20	0.80	3.00	28.00	—
1912F	3,787,000	0.10	0.40	3.00	22.00	—
1912G	2,441,000	0.40	0.40	3.00	30.00	—
1912J	2,730,000	0.10	0.40	4.00	30.00	—
1913A	13,466,000	0.10	0.50	1.00	18.00	—
1913D	3,164,000	0.20	0.80	2.00	22.00	—
1913E	1,478,000	0.20	1.00	2.50	25.00	—
1913F	1,991,000	0.20	1.00	2.50	30.00	—
1913G	1,373,000	0.20	1.50	4.00	35.00	—
1913J	1,550,000	0.20	1.50	4.00	35.00	—
1914A	18,570,000	0.10	0.50	2.00	18.00	—
1914D	2,301,000	0.10	0.50	2.00	22.00	—
1914E	3,478,000	0.10	0.60	3.00	22.00	—
1914F	4,515,000	0.20	1.00	3.00	22.00	—
1914G	2,689,000	0.20	1.00	3.00	30.00	—
1914J	1,589,000	0.20	1.00	3.00	28.00	—
1915A	10,639,000	0.10	0.50	3.00	18.00	—
1915D	2,277,000	0.10	0.50	3.00	22.00	—
1915E	1,027,000	0.20	1.00	3.00	30.00	—
1915F	1,508,000	0.20	1.00	3.00	30.00	—

Date	Mintage	F	VF	XF	Unc	BU
1915G	363,000	30.00	100	180	380	—
1915J	2,677,000	0.50	1.00	5.00	30.00	—
1916D	1,128,000	0.50	1.00	5.00	30.00	—
1901-16 Common date proof	—	Value: 80.00				

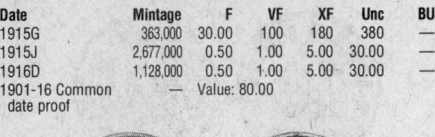

KM# 20 10 PFENNIG
3.6000 g., Iron **Obv:** Denomination, date below **Rev:** Crowned imperial eagle with shield on breast, beaded border

Date	Mintage	F	VF	XF	Unc	BU
1916A	69,143,000	0.20	0.60	1.50	8.00	—
1916D	11,609,000	0.20	0.60	1.50	12.00	—
1916E	8,280,000	0.30	1.00	2.50	12.00	—
1916F	7,473,000	0.30	2.00	4.50	15.00	—
1916G	5,878,000	0.30	2.00	4.50	18.00	—
1916J	11,683,000	0.30	1.00	2.50	15.00	—
1916 Rare	—	180	220	—	—	—
1917A	53,198,000	0.20	0.60	1.50	4.00	—
1917D	16,370,000	0.20	0.60	1.50	5.00	—
1917E	9,182,000	0.30	1.00	3.00	7.00	—
1917F	11,341,000	0.20	1.50	3.00	7.00	—
1917F						—

Note: Mule with Polish reverse of Y#6, see Poland

Date	Mintage	F	VF	XF	Unc	BU
1917G	7,088,000	0.30	1.50	8.00	25.00	—
1917J	9,205,000	0.30	1.00	8.00	25.00	—
1918D	42,000	0.50	1,250	2,400	—	—
1921A	16,265,000	0.80	3.00	8.00	33.00	—
1922D		2.00	6.00	12.00	45.00	—
1922E	2,235,000	10.00	30.00	60.00	200	—
1922F	1,928,000	2.00	6.00	12.00	45.00	—
1922G	1,358,000	10.00	30.00	60.00	200	—
1922J	2,420,000	2.00	6.00	15.00	60.00	—
1922		40.00	130	200	—	—

Note: There are several 1915A patterns for this type

| 1916-22 Common date proof | — | Value: 95.00 | | | | |

KM# 25 10 PFENNIG
Zinc **Ruler:** Wilhelm II **Rev:** Crowned imperial eagle with shield on breast, beaded border

Date	Mintage	F	VF	XF	Unc	BU
1917A	—	90.00	180	380	—	—
1917	—	90.00	180	380	—	—

KM# 26 10 PFENNIG
Zinc **Obv:** Denomination, date below **Rev:** Crowned imperial eagle with shield on breast **Note:** Weight varies: 3.10-3.60 grams. Without mint mark. Variations in planchet thickness exist.

Date	Mintage	F	VF	XF	Unc	BU
1917	75,073,000	0.10	0.20	1.00	8.00	—
1918	202,008,000	0.10	0.20	1.00	8.00	—
1918 Proof	28	Value: 300				
1919	147,800,000	0.10	0.20	1.00	8.00	—
1919 Proof	50	Value: 100				
1920	223,019,000	0.10	0.20	1.00	6.00	—
1920 Proof	40	Value: 100				
1921	319,334,000	0.10	0.20	1.00	4.00	—
1921 Proof	24	Value: 300				
1922	274,499,000	0.10	0.20	1.00	8.00	—
1922 Proof	12	Value: 400				

KM# 18 25 PFENNIG
4.0200 g., Nickel **Ruler:** Wilhelm II **Obv:** Crowned imperial eagle with shield on breast **Rev:** Denomination within wreath

Date	Mintage	F	VF	XF	Unc	BU
1909A	962,000	3.00	9.00	15.00	33.00	—
1909D	1,406,000	3.00	9.00	12.00	22.00	—
1909E	250,000	15.00	33.00	48.00	110	—
1909F	400,000	3.00	11.00	20.00	55.00	—
1909G	610,000	5.00	13.00	20.00	55.00	—
1909J	10,000	220	500	1,000	2,500	—
1910A	9,522,000	2.00	6.00	10.00	22.00	—
1910D	1,408,000	4.00	11.00	22.00	70.00	—
1910E	1,242,000	5.00	14.00	23.00	70.00	—
1910F	1,605,000	3.00	9.00	20.00	60.00	—
1910G	330,000	3.00	9.00	20.00	70.00	—

Date	Mintage	F	VF	XF	Unc	BU
1910J	1,561,000	3.00	9.00	17.00	50.00	—
1911A	3,179,000	2.50	8.00	14.00	25.00	—
1911D	506,000	5.00	14.00	28.00	60.00	—
1911E	747,000	4.00	11.00	22.00	70.00	—
1911G	892,000	4.00	11.00	22.00	70.00	—
1911J	516,000	6.00	11.00	26.00	80.00	—
1912A	2,590,000	3.00	9.00	12.00	35.00	—
1912D	900,000	4.50	12.00	15.00	45.00	—
1912F	1,003,000	4.50	12.00	15.00	45.00	—
1912J	362,000	12.50	25.00	35.00	90.00	—
1909-12 Common date proof	—	Value: 175				

KM# 15 50 PFENNIG
2.7770 g., 0.9000 Silver 0.0804 oz. ASW **Ruler:** Wilhelm II **Obv:** Denomination within wreath **Rev:** Crowned imperial eagle with shield on breast within wreath

Date	Mintage	F	VF	XF	Unc	BU
1901A	194,000	160	300	400	650	750
1902F	95,000	250	300	500	850	1,000
1902F Proof	—	Value: 800				
1903A	384,000	130	220	280	500	600
1901-03 Common date proof	—	Value: 500				

KM# 17 1/2 MARK
2.7770 g., 0.9000 Silver 0.0804 oz. ASW, 20 mm.
Obv: Denomination within wreath **Rev:** Crowned imperial eagle with shield on breast within wreath **Note:** Some coins dated from 1918-19 were issued with a black finish to prevent hoarding.

Date	Mintage	F	VF	XF	Unc	BU
1905A	37,766,000	0.85	1.25	2.50	22.00	—
1905D	7,636,000	0.85	1.25	3.00	33.00	—
1905E	4,908,000	0.85	1.25	3.00	30.00	—
1905F	6,310,000	0.85	1.25	4.00	28.00	—
1905G	3,886,000	1.00	4.00	6.00	45.00	—
1905J	6,316,000	1.00	3.00	9.00	75.00	—
1906A	29,754,000	0.80	1.50	3.00	25.00	—
1906D	11,977,000	0.90	2.00	4.00	30.00	—
1906E	5,821,000	0.90	2.00	4.00	30.00	—
1906F	8,036,000	1.00	3.00	6.00	30.00	—
1906G	4,273,000	1.00	3.00	6.00	30.00	—
1906J	2,179,000	2.00	8.00	25.00	250	—
1907A	14,168,000	0.80	1.25	3.00	85.00	—
1907D	2,884,000	0.90	1.50	4.50	33.00	—
1907E	600,000	2.00	10.00	28.00	90.00	—
1907F	1,202,000	1.50	5.00	20.00	165	—
1907G	927,000	1.50	4.00	30.00	165	—
1907J	3,268,000	1.00	3.00	18.00	110	—
1908A	5,018,000	0.90	3.00	15.00	100	—
1908D	400,000	5.00	15.00	50.00	200	—
1908E	591,000	3.00	10.00	18.00	140	—
1908F	1,000	2,000	5,000	8,000	10,000	—
1908G	675,000	3.00	30.00	60.00	500	—
1808/7J	1,309,000	3.00	30.00	60.00	500	—
1908J	Inc. above	3.00	26.00	100	1,200	—
1909A	5,404,000	0.85	2.00	9.00	100	—
1909/5D	1,001,000	1.00	4.00	20.00	120	—
1909D	Inc. above	1.00	4.00	20.00	120	—
1909E	745,000	3.00	9.00	20.00	120	—
1909F	999,000	1.00	4.00	20.00	130	—
1909G	607,000	4.00	15.00	24.00	400	—
1909J	816,000	3.00	10.00	20.00	180	—
1911A	2,710,000	1.00	2.00	9.00	90.00	—
1911/05D	703,000	1.00	3.00	12.00	85.00	—
1911D	Inc. above	3.00	12.00	20.00	85.00	—
1911E	376,000	1.00	4.00	14.00	70.00	—
1911F	502,000	3.00	9.00	22.00	140	—
1911G	610,000	3.00	9.00	22.00	110	—
1911J	418,000	5.00	15.00	40.00	380	—
1912A	2,709,000	1.00	3.00	9.00	45.00	—
1912/5D	703,000	3.00	10.00	20.00	60.00	—
1912D	Inc. above	3.00	10.00	20.00	60.00	—
1912E	369,000	3.00	10.00	30.00	170	—
1912F	501,000	4.00	12.00	22.00	170	—
1912J	399,000	11.00	30.00	60.00	350	—
1913A	5,419,000	0.90	2.00	7.00	25.00	—
1913/05D	1,406,000	1.00	3.00	9.00	30.00	—
1913D	Inc. above	1.00	3.00	9.00	30.00	—
1913E	745,000	2.00	5.00	10.00	55.00	—
1913F	1,003,000	1.50	4.00	8.00	55.00	—
1913G	610,000	3.00	9.00	18.00	80.00	—
1913J	817,000	3.00	10.00	20.00	140	—
1914A	13,525,000	0.85	1.50	4.00	24.00	—
1914/05D	328,000	3.00	10.00	25.00	50.00	—

Date	Mintage	F	VF	XF	Unc	BU
1914D	Inc. above	3.00	10.00	25.00	50.00	—
1914J	2,292,000	1.00	3.00	10.00	70.00	—
1915A	13,015,000	0.85	1.25	4.00	11.00	—
1915/05D	5,117,000	0.90	1.50	3.00	10.00	—
1915D	Inc. above	0.85	1.25	5.00	12.00	—
1915E	3,308,000	0.85	1.25	3.00	12.00	—
1915F	5,309,000	0.85	1.25	3.00	12.00	—
1915G	2,730,000	0.85	2.00	6.00	18.00	—
1915J	2,285,000	0.85	2.00	4.00	18.00	—
1916A	9,750,000	0.85	1.25	3.00	14.00	—
1916/616D	4,397,000	0.90	1.50	3.00	10.00	—
1916/05D	Inc. above	0.90	1.50	3.00	10.00	—
1916/5D	Inc. above	0.90	1.50	3.00	10.00	—
1916D	Inc. above	0.90	2.00	7.00	15.00	—
1916E	1,640,000	0.90	1.50	3.00	10.00	—
1916F	2,410,000	0.90	2.00	7.00	15.00	—
1916G	1,779,000	1.00	3.00	8.00	30.00	—
1916J	1,464,000	1.00	3.00	8.00	35.00	—
1917A	14,692,000	0.85	1.25	3.00	10.00	—
1917/05D	979,000	0.90	2.00	5.00	16.00	—
1917D	Inc. above	0.90	2.00	5.00	16.00	—
1917E	1,561,000	0.90	1.50	3.00	10.00	—
1917F	450,000	3.00	10.00	30.00	220	—
1917G	619,000	3.00	10.00	30.00	180	—
1917J	1,039,000	1.50	5.00	10.00	30.00	—
1918A	14,622,000	0.85	1.25	3.00	10.00	—
1918/05D	3,670,000	0.90	2.00	5.00	10.00	—
1918D	Inc. above	0.90	1.50	3.00	10.00	—
1918E	2,807,000	1.50	5.00	12.00	25.00	—
1918E Proof	19	—	—	—	—	—
1918F	4,010,000	3.00	9.00	20.00	80.00	—
1918G	1,032,000	2.00	6.00	14.00	60.00	—
1918J	3,452,000	1.50	5.00	12.00	30.00	—
1919A	9,124,000	0.85	1.25	4.00	12.00	—
1919/1619D	2,195,000	0.90	1.50	5.00	15.00	—
1919/05D	Inc. above	0.90	1.50	5.00	15.00	—
1919D	Inc. above	2.00	6.00	12.00	15.00	—
1919E	1,767,000	2.00	6.00	12.00	25.00	—
1919F	1,559,000	3.00	9.00	18.00	80.00	—
1919J	1,875,000	2.00	6.00	22.00	35.00	—
1905-19 Common date proof	—	Value: 150				

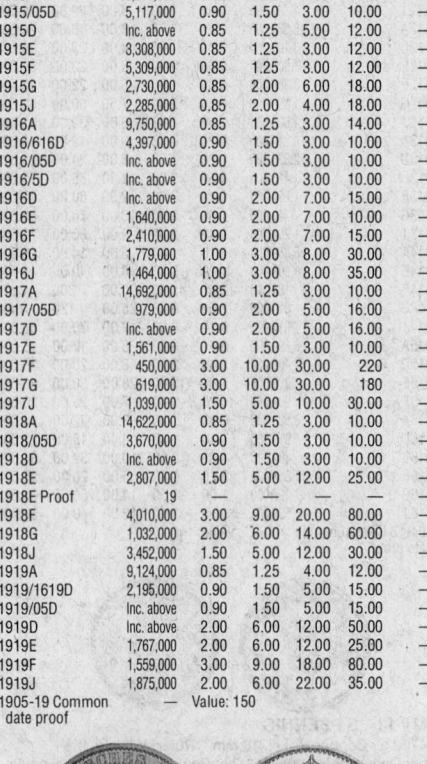

KM# 14 MARK
5.5500 g., 0.9000 Silver 0.1606 oz. ASW **Ruler:** Wilhelm II **Obv:** Denomination within wreath **Rev:** Crowned imperial eagle with shield on breast **Note:** Struck from 1890-1916.

Date	Mintage	F	VF	XF	Unc	BU
1901A	3,821,000	2.00	6.00	20.00	50.00	—
1901/800D	914,000	2.50	5.00	12.00	35.00	—
1901/801D	915,000	2.50	5.00	12.00	35.00	—
1901D	Inc. above	2.00	6.00	20.00	50.00	—
1901E	484,000	3.00	10.00	20.00	250	—
1901F	802,000	2.00	6.00	18.00	220	—
1901G	579,000	3.00	10.00	40.00	320	—
1901J	531,000	3.50	12.00	45.00	320	—
1902A	5,222,000	1.75	5.00	14.00	150	—
1902D	1,546,000	1.75	4.00	14.00	120	—
1902E	819,000	2.50	9.00	30.00	300	—
1902F	953,000	2.00	7.00	30.00	200	—
1902G	270,000	5.00	20.00	60.00	800	—
1902J	898,000	3.00	10.00	40.00	800	—
1903A	3,965,000	1.65	4.00	12.00	100	—
1903/803D	914,000	1.75	5.00	12.00	60.00	—
1903D	Inc. above	1.75	5.00	12.00	60.00	—
1903E	485,000	3.00	9.00	33.00	280	—
1903F	652,000	3.00	8.00	25.00	250	—
1903G	614,000	3.00	8.00	45.00	400	—
1903J	531,000	3.50	10.00	30.00	1,000	—
1904A	3,243,000	1.65	3.00	12.00	100	—
1904D	1,761,000	1.65	3.50	16.00	60.00	—
1904E	931,000	1.65	4.00	20.00	200	—
1904F	1,255,000	1.65	4.00	18.00	120	—
1904G	664,000	2.50	8.00	26.00	200	—
1904J	1,021,000	2.50	8.00	35.00	1,000	—
1905A	10,303,000	1.65	3.50	14.00	50.00	—
1905D	1,759,000	1.65	4.00	15.00	100	—
1905E	931,000	2.00	5.00	22.00	170	—
1905F	Inc. above	—	—	—	—	—
1905G	860,000	2.00	6.00	20.00	280	—
1905J	1,021,000	2.50	7.00	35.00	750	—
1906A	5,414,000	1.65	3.50	11.00	150	—
1906D	1,412,000	1.65	4.00	11.00	110	—
1906E	745,000	2.50	9.00	22.00	220	—
1906F	2,257,000	1.75	5.00	16.00	120	—
1906G	609,000	3.00	11.00	40.00	400	—
1906G Proof						—
1906J	372,000	5.00	15.00	50.00	2,000	—
1907A	9,201,000	1.65	2.50	5.00	55.00	—
1907D	2,387,000	1.65	2.75	9.00	50.00	—
1907E	1,265,000	1.65	3.00	11.00	80.00	—
1907F	1,704,000	1.65	3.00	8.00	65.00	—

Date	Mintage	F	VF	XF	Unc	BU
1907G	1,035,000	1.25	4.00	12.00	130	—
1907J	1,833,000	1.75	5.00	25.00	350	—
1908A	4,338,000	1.65	3.00	9.00	85.00	—
1908D	1,126,000	1.65	3.00	9.00	60.00	—
1908E	596,000	2.50	7.00	18.00	100	—
1908F	802,000	1.65	5.00	15.00	85.00	—
1908G	488,000	2.50	9.00	24.00	210	—
1908J	653,000	2.50	8.00	30.00	420	—
1909A	4,151,000	1.65	5.00	13.00	200	—
1909D	1,968,000	1.65	5.00	12.00	75.00	—
1909E	Inc. below	40.00	120	180	420	—
1909G	854,000	3.00	10.00	24.00	170	—
1909J	53,000	85.00	175	285	650	—
1910A	5,870,000	1.65	3.50	12.00	55.00	—
1910D	1,406,000	1.75	4.00	6.00	50.00	—
1910E	1,050,000	1.75	5.00	12.00	80.00	—
1910F	1,631,000	1.75	5.00	10.00	70.00	—
1910G	610,000	2.00	7.00	22.00	170	—
1910J	1,094,000	2.50	8.00	30.00	330	—
1911A	5,693,000	1.65	3.00	9.00	60.00	—
1911D	126,000	8.00	30.00	48.00	170	—
1911E	738,000	1.75	5.00	8.00	60.00	—
1911F	773,000	2.50	9.00	50.00	900	—
1911G	305,000	3.50	11.00	40.00	100	—
1911J	812,000	2.50	9.00	35.00	100	—
1912A	2,439,000	1.65	2.50	6.00	70.00	—
1912D	632,000	1.75	4.00	10.00	100	—
1912E	708,000	2.00	5.00	10.00	70.00	—
1912F	502,000	2.00	6.00	16.00	145	—
1912J	409,000	5.00	25.00	50.00	750	—
1913F	450,000	5.00	15.00	30.00	130	—
1913G	275,000	15.00	40.00	60.00	180	—
1913J	368,000	7.00	20.00	40.00	270	—
1914A	11,304,000	1.65	2.25	4.00	15.00	—
1914/9D	3,515,000	1.65	2.50	6.00	18.00	—
1914D	Inc. above	1.65	2.50	6.00	18.00	—
1914E	2,235,000	1.65	3.00	7.00	18.00	—
1914F	2,300,000	1.65	2.25	3.75	15.00	—
1914G	1,911,000	1.65	4.00	8.00	20.00	—
1914J	2,978,000	1.65	4.00	8.00	18.00	—
1915A	13,817,000	1.65	2.25	4.00	15.00	—
1915D	4,218,000	1.65	3.00	5.00	15.00	—
1915E	2,235,000	1.65	3.00	5.00	15.00	—
1915F	2,911,000	1.65	3.00	9.00	20.00	—
1915G	1,749,000	1.65	3.00	6.00	15.00	—
1915J	1,634,000	1.75	4.00	8.00	15.00	—
1916F	306,000	10.00	30.00	45.00	90.00	—
1901-16 Common date proof	—	Value: 150				

MILITARY COINAGE - WWI

Issued under the authority of the German Military Commander of the East for use in Estonia, Latvia, Lithuania, Poland, and Northwest Russia.

KM# 21 KOPEK

Iron **Ruler:** Wilhelm II **Obv:** Inscription **Rev:** Denomination and date within iron cross

Date	Mintage	F	VF	XF	Unc	BU
1916A	11,942,000	2.00	6.00	15.00	40.00	—
1916A Proof	—	Value: 150				
1916J	8,000,000	2.50	7.00	20.00	50.00	—
1916J Proof	—	Value: 150				

KM# 22 2 KOPEKS

Iron **Ruler:** Wilhelm II **Obv:** Inscription **Rev:** Denomination and date within iron cross

Date	Mintage	F	VF	XF	Unc	BU
1916A	6,973,000	2.00	6.00	15.00	40.00	—
1916A Proof	—	Value: 150				
1916J	8,000,000	2.50	6.00	15.00	40.00	—
1916J Proof	—	Value: 150				

KM# 23 3 KOPEKS

Iron **Ruler:** Wilhelm II **Obv:** Inscription **Rev:** Denomination and date within iron cross

Date	Mintage	F	VF	XF	Unc	BU
1916A	8,670,000	2.50	6.00	18.00	45.00	—
1916A Proof	—	Value: 150				
1916J	8,000,000	2.50	6.00	18.00	45.00	—
1916J Proof	—	Value: 150				

PATTERNS

Including off metal strikes

KM#	Date	Mintage	Identification	Mkt Val
Pn66	1901A	—	50 Pfennig. Silver. Plain 2mm edge. KM#15.	200
Pn67	1901A	—	50 Pfennig. Silver. Plain 3.5mm edge. KM#15.	200
Pn68	1901A	—	50 Pfennig. Silver. Coarse reeding. KM#15.	200
Pn69	1901A	—	50 Pfennig. Silver. Coarse wavy reeding. KM#15.	200
Pn70	1901A	—	1/2 Mark. Silver.	400
Pn71	1901D	—	1/2 Mark. Silver. Date.	400
Pn72	1901D	—	1/2 Mark. Silver. Incuse diamond.	400
Pn73	1901D	—	1/2 Mark. Brass. Incuse diamond.	200
Pn74	1901D	—	1/2 Mark. Brass. Incuse diamond, beaded circle.	200
Pn75	1901D	—	1/2 Mark. Silver. Diamond within beads.	375
Pn76	1901D	—	1/2 Mark. Brass. Beaded diamond.	200
Pn77	1901D	—	1/2 Mark. Silver. Beaded diamond.	375
Pn78	1901D	—	1/2 Mark. Silver. Beaded circle.	375
Pn79	1901D	—	1/2 Mark. Brass. Beaded circle.	200
Pn80	1901D	—	1/2 Mark. Silver. Diamond within beads.	375
Pn81	1901D	—	1/2 Mark. Silver. Incuse diamond.	375
Pn82	1901D	—	1/2 Mark. Silver. Incuse diamond.	200
Pn83	1901D	—	1/2 Mark. Silver. Date.	375
Pn84	1901D	—	1/2 Mark. Silver. Beaded circle.	375
Pn85	1901D	—	1/2 Mark. Brass. Beaded circle.	200
Pn86	1902A	—	50 Pfennig. Silver. Without beaded rims, coarse reeding; KM#15.	375
Pn87	1902A	—	50 Pfennig. Silver. Without beaded rims, reeded edge; KM#15.	375
Pn88	1902A	—	50 Pfennig. 0.7100 Silver. Incuse circle.	500
Pn89	1902A	—	1/2 Mark. Silver. Incuse circle.	400
Pn90	1903A	—	50 Pfennig. Silver. Without beaded rim, coarse reeding; KM#15.	375
Pn91	1903A	—	50 Pfennig. Silver. Coarse reeding; KM#15.	375
Pn92	1903D	—	50 Pfennig. Silver. Crown.	400
Pn93	1903D	—	50 Pfennig. Eagle.	400
Pn94	1903D	—	50 Pfennig. Brass. Otto of Bavaria.	375
Pn95	1903D	—	50 Pfennig. Copper. Otto of Bavaria.	375
Pn96	1903	—	50 Pfennig. Brass. Crown. Otto of Bavaria.	375
Pn97	1903D	—	50 Pfennig. Brass. Germania.	350
Pn98	1904A	—	1/2 Mark. Silver. KM#17.	400
Pn99	NDA	—	25 Pfennig. Nickel-Silver. Value within beaded circle.	200
Pn100	NDA	—	25 Pfennig. Copper-Nickel. Beaded circle.	200
Pn101	NDA	—	25 Pfennig. Tin Alloy. Beaded circle.	200
Pn102	1907	—	25 Pfennig. Nickel. Germania.	150
Pn103	1907A	—	25 Pfennig. Copper. Crown.	150
Pn104	1907A	—	25 Pfennig. Nickel. Crown.	150
Pn105	1907D	—	1/2 Mark. Silver. Coarse reeding; KM#17.	200
Pn106	1908A	—	25 Pfennig. Nickel.	300
Pn107	1908A	—	25 Pfennig. Nickel-Silver. Eagle plain.	200
Pn108	1908A	—	25 Pfennig. Silver. Eagle plain.	300
Pn109	1908A	—	25 Pfennig. Nickel-Silver. Eagle within beads.	200
Pn110	1908A	—	25 Pfennig. Nickel-Silver. Eagle within beads.	200
Pn111	1908A	—	25 Pfennig. Eagle plain.	200
Pn112	1908A	—	25 Pfennig. Copper-Nickel.	200
Pn113	1908A	—	25 Pfennig. Nickel-Silver.	200
Pn114	1908A	—	25 Pfennig. Nickel.	200
Pn115	1908A	—	25 Pfennig. Nickel-Silver.	200
Pn116	1908A	—	25 Pfennig. Aluminum.	200
Pn117	1908A	—	25 Pfennig. Copper-Nickel.	150
Pn118	1908A	—	25 Pfennig. Silver.	250
Pn119	1908A	—	25 Pfennig. Bronze.	150
Pn120	1908A	—	25 Pfennig. Copper.	150
Pn121	1908A	—	25 Pfennig. Silver. Eagle in crown.	400
Pn122	1908A	—	25 Pfennig. Silver. Cross in crown.	400
Pn123	1908A	—	25 Pfennig. Copper-Nickel.	400
Pn124	1908A	—	25 Pfennig. Copper-Nickel.	200
Pn125	1908A	—	25 Pfennig. Silver.	400
Pn126	1908A	—	25 Pfennig. Nickel.	200
Pn127	1908A	—	25 Pfennig. Copper-Nickel.	250
Pn128	1908A	—	25 Pfennig. Nickel.	250
Pn129	1908A	—	25 Pfennig. Nickel. Germania.	250
Pn130	1908A	—	25 Pfennig. Nickel. Kaiser Wilhelm.	225
Pn131	1908A	—	25 Pfennig. Iron. Kaiser Wilhelm.	200
Pn132	1908A	—	25 Pfennig. Copper. Kaiser Wilhelm.	250

KM#	Date	Mintage	Identification	Mkt Val
PnA133	1908D	—	25 Pfennig. Copper. Eagle head in order collar.	100
Pn133	1908D	—	25 Pfennig. Silvered Copper Alloy.	150
Pn134	1908D	—	25 Pfennig. Silvered Copper Alloy.	150
Pn135	1908A	—	25 Pfennig. Lead. Without circle around eagle, or crown above value.	150
PnA136	1908D	—	25 Pfennig. Nickel.	150
PnB136	1908J	—	25 Pfennig. Nickel. Previous German East Africa Pn3; with sprigs.	250
PnC136	1908J	—	25 Pfennig. Nickel. Previous German East Africa Pn4; with sprigs.	
Pn136	1908J	—	25 Pfennig. Copper-Nickel. Gothic style.	250
Pn137	1908J	—	25 Pfennig. Copper-Nickel. Block style.	250
Pn138	1908A	—	25 Pfennig. Copper-Nickel. Crown.	250
Pn139	1908A	—	25 Pfennig. Tin. Crown.	200
Pn140	1908A	—	25 Pfennig. Aluminum. Crown.	200
Pn141	1908	—	25 Pfennig. Silver. Eagle within beads.	350
Pn142	1908/09	—	25 Pfennig. Nickel-Silver. Eagle within beads.	250
Pn143	1909A	—	25 Pfennig. Silver. Large eagle.	300
Pn144	1909A	—	10 Pfennig. Nickel. 2mm rims, KM#12.	250
Pn145	1909	—	25 Pfennig. Nickel.	200
Pn146	1909	—	25 Pfennig. Bronze.	200
Pn147	1909A	—	25 Pfennig. Antique Silvered Copper Alloy.	175
Pn148	1909A	—	25 Pfennig. Cast	200
Pn149	1909A	—	25 Pfennig. Copper-Nickel.	200
Pn150	1909A	—	25 Pfennig. Nickel.	200
Pn151	1909A	—	25 Pfennig. Nickel.	200
Pn152	1909A	—	25 Pfennig. Nickel-Silver.	200
Pn153	1909A	—	25 Pfennig. Nickel.	200
Pn154	1909A	—	25 Pfennig. Iron.	175
Pn155	1909A	—	25 Pfennig. Nickel.	200
Pn156	1909A	—	25 Pfennig. Nickel.	200
Pn157	1909A	—	25 Pfennig. Silver.	350
Pn158	1909A	—	25 Pfennig. Silver. Standing eagle right.	350
Pn159	1909A	—	25 Pfennig. Silver.	350
Pn160	1909A	—	25 Pfennig. Silver. Standing eagle right.	350
Pn161	1909A	—	25 Pfennig. Silver.	300
Pn162	1909A	—	25 Pfennig. Nickel.	200
Pn163	1909A	—	25 Pfennig. Copper-Nickel.	200
Pn168	1909A	—	25 Pfennig. Silver. Eagle within legend.	300
Pn169	1909A	—	25 Pfennig. Silver. Large eagle, legend above crowned value.	300
Pn170	1909A	—	25 Pfennig. Silver.	350
PnA171	1909A	—	25 Pfennig.	250
Pn171	1909A	—	25 Pfennig. Silver.	300
Pn172	1909A	—	25 Pfennig. Silver.	300
Pn173	1909A	—	25 Pfennig. Nickel. GOTT MITUNS above crowned eagle with spread wings. DEUTSCHES REICH above large numerals.	250
Pn174	1909A	—	25 Pfennig. Nickel. Stockier eagle, countermarked mm. Large numerals and countermarked date.	250
Pn175	1909A	—	25 Pfennig.	250
Pn176	1909E	—	25 Pfennig. Silver Or Copper-Nickel.	300
Pn177	1909A	—	25 Pfennig. Antique Silvered Copper Alloy.	250
Pn178	NDA	—	25 Pfennig. Silver. Large eagle.	350
Pn179	1910E	—	25 Pfennig. Silver. Eagle within legend.	250
Pn180	1910A	—	1/2 Mark. Silver. KM#17.	350
Pn181	1910	—	Mark. Silver. Without mint mark, KM#7.	—
PnD182	1910A	—	3 Mark. Ernst Ludwig	—
PnA182	1911D	—	Mark. Aluminum Clad Zinc.	—
PnB182	1911D	—	2 Mark. Aluminum Clad Zinc. Bavaria	—
PnC182	1912D	—	3 Mark. Aluminum Clad Zinc. Bavaria	—
PnE182	1913	—	3 Mark. Silver. Without mint mark, Kaiser on horseback.	—
PnF182	1913	—	3 Mark. Copper.	—
Pn182	1914A	—	5 Pfennig. Unknown Metal. Reeded edge. KM#11	—
PnA183	1915	—	Non-Denominated. Gilt Bronze.	—
Pn183	1915A	—	Pfennig. Zinc. Reeded edge. KM#10	—
Pn184	1915A	—	Pfennig. Iron. Date below value, KM#24.	—
Pn185	1915A	—	Pfennig. Aluminum.	—
Pn186	1915	—	5 Pfennig. Copper-Nickel center. Without mint mark, KM#11.	—
Pn187	1915A	—	10 Pfennig. Brass. KM#17. KM#12.	—
Pn188	1915A	—	10 Pfennig. Brass. Broad rims, KM#12.	—
Pn189	1915A	—	10 Pfennig. Nickel. Broad rims.	—
Pn190	1915A	—	10 Pfennig. Copper-Nickel. Broad rims.	—
Pn191	1915A	—	10 Pfennig. Rusted Iron. Broad rims.	100
Pn192	1915A	—	10 Pfennig. Brass. Date above value.	—
Pn193	1915A	—	10 Pfennig. Nickel. Date above value.	—
Pn194	1915A	—	10 Pfennig. Iron. Date above value.	—
Pn195	1915A	—	10 Pfennig. Small "10".	—
Pn196	1915A	—	10 Pfennig. Large "10".	—
Pn197	1915A	—	10 Pfennig. Brass. Small "10", KM#20.	—
Pn198	1915A	—	10 Pfennig. Nickel. Small "10", KM#20.	—
Pn199	1915A	—	10 Pfennig. Iron. 67 beads on rim.	—
Pn200	1915A	—	10 Pfennig. Nickel. 67 beads on rim.	—
Pn201	1915A	—	10 Pfennig. Copper-Nickel. KM#20.	—
Pn202	1915A	—	10 Pfennig. Iron. KM#20.	500
Pn203	1915A	—	1/2 Mark. Silver. Large eagle.	—
Pn204	1915A	—	Mark. Aluminum. GOTT MIT UNS on rim, KM#14.	—
PnA205	ND	—	Pfennig. Copper. KM#24.	—
Pn205	1916A	—	Pfennig. Aluminum. KM#24.	—
Pn206	1916F	—	Pfennig. Aluminum. KM#24.	—
Pn207	1917	—	Pfennig. Aluminum. Without mint mark, KM#24.	—
Pn208	1917	—	10 Pfennig. Iron. W/out mint mark, KM#20.	—
Pn209	1917A	—	10 Pfennig. Zinc. Mint mark, KM#26.	—

WEIMAR REPUBLIC

1919-1933

The Imperial German government disintegrated in a flurry of royal abdications as World War I ended. Desperate German parliamentarians, fearful of impending anarchy and civil war, hastily declared a German Republic. The new National Assembly, which was convened Feb. 6, 1919 in Weimar had to establish a legal government, draft a constitution, and then conclude a peace treaty with the Allies. Friedrich Ebert was elected as Reichs President. The harsh terms of the peace treaty imposed on Germany were economically and psychologically unacceptable to the German population regardless of political persuasion and the problem of German treaty compliance was to plague the Republic until the worldwide Great Depression of 1929. The new constitution paid less attention to fundamental individual rights and concentrated more power in the President and Central Government to insure a more stable social and economic order. The German bureaucracy survived the transition intact and had a stifling effect on the democratic process. The army started training large numbers of reservists in conjunction with the U.S.S.R. thereby circumventing treaty limitations on the size of the German military.

New anti-democratic ideologies were forming. Communism and Fascism were spreading. The National Socialist German Workers Party, under Hitler's leadership, incorporated the ever-present anti-Semitism into a new virulent Nazi Catechism.

In spite of the historic German inflation, the French occupation of the Rhineland, and the loss of vast territories and resources, the republic survived. By 1929 the German economy had been restored to its pre-war level. Much of the economic gains however were dependent on the extensive assistance provided by the U.S.A. and collapsed along with the world economy in 1929. Even during the good times, the Republic was never able to muster any loyal public support or patriotism. By 1930, Nationalists, Nazis, and Communists held nearly half of the Reichstag seats and the government was forced to rely more and more on presidential decrees as the only means to effectuate policy. In 1932, the Nazis won 230 Reichstag seats. As head of the largest party, Hitler claimed the right to form the next government. President Hindenburg's opposition forced a second election in which the Nazis lost 34 seats. Von Papen, however, convinced Hindenburg to name Hitler Chancellor by arguing that Hitler could be controlled! Hitler formed his cabinet and immediately began consolidating his power and laying the groundwork for the Third Reich.

MONETARY SYSTEM

(During 1923-1924)
100 Rentenpfennig = 1 Rentenmark

(Commencing 1924)
100 Reichspfennig = 1 Reichsmark

WEIMAR REPUBLIC

MARK COINAGE
1922-1923

KM# 27 50 PFENNIG
Aluminum, 23 mm. **Obv:** Denomination above date **Rev:** Sheaf behind inscription

Date	Mintage	F	VF	XF	Unc	BU
1919A	7,173,000	0.25	1.00	3.50	20.00	25.00
1919D	791,000	5.00	11.00	22.00	70.00	90.00
1919E	930,000	2.00	6.00	15.00	60.00	80.00
1919E Proof	35	Value: 350				
1919F	160,000	10.00	20.00	40.00	120	150
1919G	660,000	2.00	4.00	10.00	40.00	48.00
1919J	800,000	5.00	10.00	24.00	70.00	85.00
1920A	119,793,000	0.10	0.50	1.00	7.00	10.00
1920D	28,306,000	0.10	0.50	1.50	9.00	12.00
1920E	14,400,000	0.25	1.00	2.50	12.00	15.00
1920E Proof	226	Value: 150				
1920F	10,932,000	0.25	1.00	2.50	12.00	15.00
1920G	5,040,000	0.25	1.00	3.00	20.00	25.00
1920J	15,423,000	0.25	1.00	3.00	12.00	15.00
1921A	184,468,000	0.10	0.15	0.50	3.00	5.00
1921D	48,729,000	0.10	0.15	0.75	6.00	8.00
1921E	31,210,000	0.15	1.00	2.00	10.00	12.00
1921E Proof	332	Value: 115				
1921F	46,950,000	0.10	0.15	0.75	10.00	12.00
1921G	19,107,000	0.10	0.25	1.00	6.00	8.00
1921J	28,013,000	0.10	0.25	1.00	6.00	8.00
1922A	145,215,000	0.10	0.25	1.00	6.00	8.00
1922D	58,019,000	0.10	0.25	1.00	6.00	8.00
1922E	33,930,000	0.15	1.00	2.00	10.00	14.00
1922E Proof	333	Value: 115				
1922F	33,000,000	0.10	0.25	1.00	6.00	8.00
1922G	36,745,000	0.10	0.25	1.00	6.00	8.00
1922J	36,202,000	0.10	0.25	1.00	6.00	8.00

KM# 28 3 MARK
Aluminum **Obv:** Denomination above date **Rev:** Eagle
Edge: Reeded

Date	Mintage	F	VF	XF	Unc	BU
1922A	15,497,000	0.25	2.50	7.00	14.00	20.00
1922A Proof	—	Value: 85.00				
1922E	2,000	60.00	100	200	600	700
1922E Proof	1,000	Value: 300				
1922F Rare	—	—	—	—	—	—

KM# 29 3 MARK
2.0300 g., Aluminum **Subject:** 3rd Anniversary Weimar Constitution

Date	Mintage	F	VF	XF	Unc	BU
1922A	32,514,000	0.25	1.00	3.00	10.00	12.00
1922D	8,441,000	140	200	300	800	1,000
1922D Proof	—	Value: 1,100				
1922E	2,440,000	0.50	2.00	4.00	12.00	15.00
1922E Proof	22,000	Value: 50.00				
1922F	6,023,000	2.00	6.00	12.00	35.00	45.00
1922G	3,655,000	0.50	2.00	4.00	12.00	15.00
1922J	4,896,000	0.50	2.00	4.00	12.00	15.00
1923E	2,060,000	6.00	12.00	25.00	70.00	80.00
1923E Proof	2,291	Value: 75.00				
1923F	—	300	650	1,000	2,250	2,750

Note: The 1923F 3 Mark pieces are from the burned-out ruin of the Stuttgart Mint, destroyed in World War II

KM# 35 200 MARK
1.0000 g., Aluminum, 23 mm. **Obv:** Denomination above date **Rev:** Eagle

Date	Mintage	F	VF	XF	Unc	BU
1923A	174,900,000	0.15	0.50	0.75	2.00	3.00
1923A Proof	—	Value: 125				
1923D	35,189,000	0.20	0.50	1.00	2.20	3.00
1923D Proof, unique	—	—	—	—	—	—
1923E	11,250,000	0.20	1.00	3.00	7.00	9.00
1923E Proof	4,095	Value: 100				
1923F	20,090,000	0.25	0.75	2.00	3.00	4.00
1923F Proof	—	Value: 125				
1923G	24,923,000	0.25	0.75	2.00	3.00	4.00
1923G Proof	—	Value: 125				
1923J	16,258,000	0.20	1.00	3.00	7.00	9.00
1923J Proof	—	Value: 125				

KM# 36 500 MARK
1.6700 g., Aluminum **Obv:** Denomination above date **Rev:** Eagle

Date	Mintage	F	VF	XF	Unc	BU
1923A	59,278,000	0.20	1.00	1.50	5.00	6.00
1923A Proof	—	Value: 125				
1923D	13,683,000	0.25	1.00	3.00	5.00	7.00
1923D Proof	—	Value: 125				
1923E	2,128,000	2.00	5.00	12.00	30.00	35.00
1923E Proof	2,053	Value: 100				
1923F	7,963,000	0.25	1.00	3.00	8.00	9.00
1923F Proof	—	Value: 125				
1923G	4,404,000	0.25	1.75	6.00	14.00	16.00
1923G Proof	—	Value: 125				
1923J	1,008,000	10.00	20.00	40.00	90.00	100
1923J Proof	—	Value: 250				

RENTENMARK COINAGE
1923-1929

KM# 30 RENTENPFENNIG
2.0000 g., Bronze **Obv:** Denomination within circle **Rev:** Wheat sheaf divides date

Date	Mintage	F	VF	XF	Unc	BU
1923A	12,629,000	0.25	1.00	3.00	15.00	16.00
1923D	Est. 2,314,000	0.25	2.00	7.00	30.00	33.00
1923E	2,200,000	1.00	3.00	8.00	30.00	33.00
1923F	160,000	2.00	8.00	24.00	80.00	90.00
1923G	1,004,000	1.00	4.00	8.00	30.00	33.00
1923J	1,470,000	2.00	8.00	20.00	85.00	100
1924A	55,273,000	0.25	0.50	3.00	12.00	14.00
1924D	17,540,000	0.25	1.50	4.00	15.00	17.00
1924E	6,838,000	1.00	1.50	6.00	24.00	27.00
1924F	10,347,000	1.00	2.50	6.00	24.00	27.00
1924G	7,366,000	1.00	3.00	9.00	30.00	33.00
1924J	11,024,000	1.00	2.50	6.00	24.00	26.00
1925A	—	750	1,250	2,500	—	—
1929F	—	150	250	500	1,000	1,200
1923-29 Common date proof	—	Value: 120				

KM# 31 2 RENTENPFENNIG
3.3000 g., Bronze, 20 mm. **Obv:** Denomination within circle **Rev:** Wheat sheaf divides date

Date	Mintage	F	VF	XF	Unc	BU
1923A	8,587,000	0.20	1.00	3.00	20.00	22.00
1923D	1,490,000	0.20	1.00	6.00	35.00	40.00
1923F	Inc. above	1.00	3.50	9.00	35.00	40.00
1923G	Inc. above	1.00	2.00	10.00	40.00	50.00
1923J	Inc. above	2.00	6.00	15.00	70.00	80.00
1924A	80,864,000	0.20	0.50	1.00	8.00	10.00
1924D	19,899,000	0.25	1.00	3.00	15.00	17.00
1924E	6,595,000	0.25	1.00	3.00	15.00	17.00
1923-24 Common date proof	—	Value: 140				
1924F	14,969,000	0.25	1.00	3.00	15.00	17.00
1924G	10,349,000	0.25	1.00	4.00	18.00	20.00
1924J	21,196,000	0.25	1.00	3.00	15.00	17.00

KM# 32 5 RENTENPFENNIG
2.5200 g., Aluminum-Bronze, 18 mm. **Obv:** Denomination within square, oak leaf on each side **Rev:** 6 grain sprigs form center triangle above date

Date	Mintage	F	VF	XF	Unc	BU
1923A	3,083,000	1.00	3.00	10.00	50.00	55.00
1923D	Inc. below	1.00	3.00	12.00	60.00	65.00
1923F	Inc. below	35.00	70.00	120	300	320
1923G	Inc. below	10.00	25.00	50.00	200	220
1924A	171,966,000	0.25	1.00	3.00	20.00	24.00
1924D	31,163,000	0.25	1.00	5.00	28.00	30.00
1924E	12,206,000	0.25	1.00	6.00	30.00	33.00
1924F	29,032,000	0.25	1.00	5.00	30.00	33.00
1924G	19,217,000	0.25	1.00	6.00	30.00	33.00
1924J	32,332,000	0.25	1.00	5.00	25.00	27.00
1925F 1 known	—	—	5,000	—	—	—
1923-25 Common date proof	—	Value: 160				

KM# 33 10 RENTENPFENNIG
3.9200 g., Aluminum-Bronze, 21 mm. **Obv:** Denomination within square, oak leaf on each side **Rev:** Six grain sprigs form center triangle above date

Date	Mintage	F	VF	XF	Unc	BU
1923A	Inc. below	0.25	3.00	10.00	30.00	33.00
1923D	Inc. below	0.50	6.00	12.00	48.00	53.00
1923F	Inc. below	70.00	100	180	400	420
1923G	Inc. below	2.50	15.00	25.00	120	140
1924A	169,956,000	0.25	1.00	3.00	15.00	17.00
1924D	33,894,000	0.25	1.00	4.00	18.00	20.00
1924E	18,679,000	0.25	1.50	4.50	22.00	24.00
1924F	42,237,000	0.25	1.50	5.00	22.00	24.00
1924F Proof	—	Value: 160				
1924G	18,758,000	0.25	1.50	5.00	22.00	25.00
1924J	33,928,000	0.25	1.50	6.00	25.00	28.00

Date	Mintage	F	VF	XF	Unc	BU
1925F	13,000	900	1,500	2,000	—	—
1923-1925 Common date proof	—	Value: 160				

KM# 34 50 RENTENPFENNIG
5.1700 g., Aluminum-Bronze **Obv:** Denomination within square, oak leaf on each side **Rev:** Six grain sprigs form center triangle above date

Date	Mintage	F	VF	XF	Unc	BU
1923A	451,000	10.00	20.00	32.00	80.00	90.00
1923D	192,000	15.00	30.00	48.00	180	200
1923F	120,000	40.00	90.00	125	420	450
1923G	120,000	20.00	40.00	55.00	220	240
1923J	4,000	500	800	1,600	2,500	2,800
1924A	117,365,000	5.00	12.00	20.00	60.00	70.00
1924D	30,971,000	6.00	15.00	25.00	80.00	90.00
1924E	14,668,000	6.00	15.00	25.00	80.00	90.00
1924F	21,968,000	10.00	15.00	25.00	85.00	100
1924G	13,349,000	12.00	22.00	36.00	130	150
1924J	17,252,000	10.00	20.00	35.00	100	120
1923-24 Common date proof	—	Value: 225				

REICHSMARK COINAGE
1924-1938

KM# 37 REICHSPFENNIG
2.0000 g., Bronze **Obv:** Denomination within circle **Rev:** Wheat sheaf divides date

Date	Mintage	F	VF	XF	Unc	BU
1924A	13,496,000	0.20	0.50	1.00	10.00	11.00
1924D	6,206,000	0.20	0.50	1.00	12.00	13.00
1924E	1,100,000	100	250	400	850	900
1924F	2,650,000	0.20	0.50	1.00	12.00	13.00
1924G	5,100,000	0.25	0.75	3.00	15.00	16.00
1924J	24,400,000	0.20	0.50	1.00	12.00	13.00
1925A	40,925,000	0.20	0.50	1.00	5.00	10.00
1925D	1,558,000	5.00	15.00	35.00	100	120
1925E	10,460,000	0.20	0.50	1.00	10.00	11.00
1925F	5,673,000	0.20	0.50	1.00	10.00	11.00
1925G	13,502,000	0.20	0.50	1.00	10.00	11.00
1925J	30,300,000	0.20	0.50	1.00	10.00	11.00
1927A	4,671,000	0.30	1.00	3.00	18.00	19.00
1927D	4,203,000	0.30	1.00	3.00	18.00	19.00
1927E	8,000,000	0.30	1.00	3.00	18.00	19.00
1927F	2,350,000	0.50	2.00	10.00	35.00	37.00
1927G	3,236,000	0.50	2.00	8.00	30.00	32.00
1928A	19,300,000	0.20	0.50	1.00	10.00	11.00
1928D	10,200,000	0.20	0.50	1.00	11.00	12.00
1928F	8,672,000	0.20	0.50	1.00	12.00	13.00
1928G	3,764,000	0.50	2.00	5.00	24.00	26.00
1929A	37,170,000	0.20	0.50	1.00	6.00	10.00
1929D	9,337,000	0.20	0.50	1.00	6.00	10.00
1929E	6,600,000	0.20	0.50	1.00	6.00	11.00
1929F	3,150,000	0.20	0.50	1.50	6.00	11.00
1929G	1,986,000	0.20	0.75	3.00	13.00	15.00
1930A	40,997,000	0.20	0.50	1.00	8.00	10.00
1930D	6,441,000	0.20	0.50	1.00	10.00	12.00
1930E	1,412,000	6.00	15.00	40.00	140	160
1930F	6,415,000	0.20	0.50	1.50	10.00	11.00
1930G	5,017,000	0.20	0.50	1.00	10.00	11.00
1931A	38,481,000	0.20	0.50	3.00	8.00	10.00
1931D	5,998,000	0.20	0.50	1.00	11.00	12.00
1931E	12,800,000	0.20	0.50	2.50	14.00	16.00
1931F	12,591,000	0.20	0.50	1.00	11.00	12.00
1931G	2,622,000	0.20	0.50	8.00	30.00	33.00
1932A	17,096,000	0.20	0.75	2.50	20.00	24.00
1933A	37,846,000	0.20	0.50	1.00	8.00	10.00
1933E	2,945,000	0.30	2.00	8.00	30.00	33.00
1933F	5,023,000	0.20	0.50	1.00	11.00	12.00
1934A	51,214,000	0.20	0.50	1.00	7.00	9.00
1934D	7,408,000	0.20	0.50	1.00	10.00	12.00
1934E	4,628,000	0.50	3.50	10.00	35.00	40.00
1934F	5,667,000	0.20	0.50	1.00	11.00	13.00
1934G	2,450,000	0.50	2.00	5.00	15.00	17.00
1934J	4,271,000	0.30	1.00	3.00	15.00	17.00
1935A	35,894,000	0.20	0.50	1.00	7.00	9.00
1935D	15,489,000	0.20	0.50	1.00	10.00	12.00
1935E	8,351,000	0.20	0.50	2.00	11.00	14.00
1935F	12,094,000	0.20	0.50	1.50	8.00	10.00
1935G	7,454,000	0.20	0.50	1.00	11.00	14.00
1935J	8,505,000	0.20	0.50	1.00	10.00	12.00
1936A	Est. 50,949,000	0.20	0.50	1.00	7.00	8.00
1936D	12,262,000	0.20	0.50	1.00	9.00	10.00
1936E	2,576,000	0.50	3.00	7.00	30.00	33.00

Date	Mintage	F	VF	XF	Unc	BU
1936F	6,915,000	0.20	0.50	1.00	10.00	12.00
1936G	Est. 2,940,000	0.20	0.50	1.00	11.00	13.00
1936J	Est. 5,421,000	0.20	0.50	1.00	11.00	13.00
1924-36 Common date proof	—	Value: 85.00				

KM# 38 2 REICHSPFENNIG
3.3400 g., Bronze **Obv:** Denomination within circle **Rev:** Wheat sheaf divides date

Date	Mintage	F	VF	XF	Unc	BU
1923F Proof	,	Value: 4,500				
1924A	19,620,000	0.20	0.50	1.00	10.00	12.00
1924D	3,482,000	0.30	1.00	2.00	20.00	22.00
1924E	4,253,000	0.30	2.00	5.00	25.00	28.00
1924F	4,567,000	0.30	0.60	1.50	15.00	17.00
1924G	7,560,000	0.30	0.60	1.50	15.00	17.00
1924J	7,489,000	0.30	0.50	1.00	15.00	17.00
1925A	22,433,000	0.20	0.50	1.00	7.00	8.00
1925D	2,412,000	0.20	1.00	4.00	30.00	32.00
1925E	5,414,000	0.30	0.60	2.00	18.00	20.00
1925F	4,851,000	0.30	0.60	2.00	18.00	20.00
1925G	2,456,000	2.00	7.00	15.00	75.00	80.00
1936A	3,220,000	0.50	2.00	5.00	24.00	26.00
1936D	6,525,000	0.20	0.50	1.50	8.00	10.00
1936E	573,000	5.00	12.00	22.00	80.00	90.00
1936F	3,100,000	0.20	0.60	4.00	23.00	25.00
1923-36 Common date proof	—	Value: 90.00				

KM# 75 4 REICHSPFENNIG
Bronze **Obv:** Large denomination within circle, date at right **Rev:** Eagle

Date	Mintage	F	VF	XF	Unc	BU
1932A	27,101,000	—	9.00	15.00	35.00	40.00
1932A Proof	—	Value: 150				
1932D	7,055,000	—	12.00	18.00	40.00	50.00
1932D Proof	—	Value: 150				
1932E	3,729,000	—	15.00	23.00	45.00	55.00
1932E Proof	—	Value: 150				
1932F	5,022,000	—	12.00	18.00	48.00	60.00
1932F Proof	—	Value: 150				
1932G	3,050,000	—	15.00	25.00	80.00	100
1932G Proof	—	Value: 150				
1932J	4,094,000	—	12.00	18.00	65.00	75.00
1932J Proof	—	Value: 150				

KM# 39 5 REICHSPFENNIG
2.5400 g., Aluminum-Bronze **Obv:** Denomination within square, oak leaf on each side **Rev:** Six grain sprigs form center triangle above date

Date	Mintage	F	VF	XF	Unc	BU
1924A	14,469,000	0.30	0.60	3.00	20.00	22.00
1924D	8,139,000	0.50	1.00	4.00	20.00	23.00
1924E	5,976,000	0.50	1.00	5.00	25.00	28.00
1924E Proof, Rare	166	—	—	—	—	—
1924F	3,134,000	0.50	1.00	4.00	25.00	28.00
1924G	4,790,000	0.50	1.00	7.00	30.00	33.00
1924J	2,200,000	0.50	2.00	10.00	40.00	44.00
1925A	85,239,000	0.20	0.50	2.50	13.00	15.00
1925D	39,750,000	0.20	0.50	2.50	15.00	17.00
1925E	17,554,000	0.20	1.00	4.00	18.00	20.00
1925E Proof, Rare	61	—	—	—	—	—
1925F Large 5	20,990,000	6.00	14.00	28.00	130	150
1925F Small 5	Inc. above	0.20	0.50	4.00	25.00	28.00
1925G	10,232,000	0.20	1.00	5.00	26.00	30.00
1925J	10,950,000	0.50	4.00	9.00	40.00	45.00
1926A	22,377,000	0.50	1.00	5.00	30.00	35.00
1926E	5,990,000	10.00	25.00	50.00	260	290
1926E Proof, Rare	33	—	—	—	—	—
1926F	2,871,000	5.00	16.00	38.00	190	220
1930A	7,418,000	0.30	3.00	6.00	25.00	30.00
1935A	19,178,000	0.20	0.50	1.00	10.00	12.00
1935D	5,480,000	0.20	1.00	2.00	12.00	14.00
1935E	2,384,000	0.30	0.60	3.00	20.00	22.00
1935F	4,585,000	0.20	1.00	2.00	16.00	18.00
1935G	2,652,000	0.30	3.00	6.00	20.00	22.00

Date	Mintage	F	VF	XF	Unc	BU
1935J	2,614,000	0.30	3.00	6.00	24.00	26.00
1936A	36,992,000	0.20	0.30	1.00	10.00	12.00
1936D	8,108,000	0.20	0.50	2.00	12.00	14.00
1936E	2,981,000	0.20	0.60	3.00	18.00	20.00
1936F	6,643,000	0.20	0.60	3.00	15.00	17.00
1936G	2,274,000	0.20	0.60	3.00	18.00	20.00
1936J	4,470,000	0.20	0.60	3.00	18.00	20.00
1924-36 Common date proof	—	Value: 100				

KM# 40 10 REICHSPFENNIG
4.0500 g., Aluminum-Bronze, 21 mm. Obv: Denomination within square, oak leaf on each side Rev: Six grain sprigs form center triangle above date

Date	Mintage	F	VF	XF	Unc	BU
1924A	20,883,000	0.20	1.00	6.00	32.00	35.00
1924D	9,639,000	0.20	1.00	9.00	52.00	60.00
1924E	5,185,000	0.20	1.00	6.00	35.00	40.00
1924E Proof, Rare	166	—	—	—	—	—
1924F	2,758,000	1.00	9.00	28.00	160	180
1924G	4,363,000	0.30	2.00	11.00	70.00	85.00
1924J	3,993,000	0.30	2.00	11.00	70.00	85.00
1925A	102,319,000	0.20	0.50	2.00	15.00	20.00
1925D	36,853,000	0.20	1.00	4.00	28.00	32.00
1925E	18,700,000	0.30	1.00	9.00	45.00	52.00
1925E Proof, Rare	61	—	—	—	—	—
1925F	12,516,000	0.20	3.00	15.00	55.00	62.00
1925G	10,360,000	0.30	4.00	15.00	60.00	70.00
1925J	8,755,000	1.00	5.00	17.00	80.00	90.00
1926A	14,390,000	0.30	2.00	10.00	50.00	55.00
1926G	1,481,000	2.00	10.00	28.00	130	150
1928A	2,308,000	2.00	6.00	12.00	45.00	60.00
1928G	Inc. below	50.00	120	200	600	700
1929A	25,712,000	0.20	1.00	2.00	22.00	25.00
1929D	7,049,000	0.20	1.00	2.00	35.00	40.00
1929E	3,138,000	0.30	2.00	12.00	75.00	90.00
1929F	3,740,000	0.30	2.00	12.00	65.00	75.00
1929G	2,729,000	0.30	4.00	18.00	90.00	100
1929J	4,086,000	0.30	2.00	12.00	75.00	85.00
1930A	7,540,000	0.20	1.00	3.00	20.00	24.00
1930D	2,148,000	0.30	2.00	5.00	35.00	40.00
1930E	2,090,000	1.00	4.00	13.00	90.00	110
1930F	2,006,000	1.00	4.00	13.00	60.00	75.00
1930G	1,542,000	2.00	5.00	20.00	100	130
1930J	1,637,000	2.00	4.00	12.00	100	120
1931A	9,661,000	0.30	2.00	4.00	25.00	35.00
1931D	664,000	15.00	35.00	70.00	180	200
1931F	1,482,000	7.50	20.00	45.00	150	180
1931G	38,000	170	260	430	1,600	2,000
1932A	4,528,000	0.30	2.00	4.00	24.00	28.00
1932D	2,812,000	0.50	4.00	10.00	50.00	60.00
1932E	1,491,000	2.50	5.00	12.00	75.00	90.00
1932F	1,806,000	3.00	8.00	15.00	90.00	115
1932G	137,000	350	850	1,250	2,000	2,500
1933A	1,349,000	15.00	25.00	45.00	170	200
1933G	1,046,000	5.00	15.00	30.00	80.00	100
1933J	1,634,000	3.00	9.00	20.00	60.00	75.00
1934A	3,200,000	0.30	1.00	6.00	30.00	35.00
1934D	1,252,000	2.00	7.00	18.00	110	125
1934E	Inc. below	18.00	35.00	65.00	180	215
1934F	100,000	12.00	30.00	55.00	170	205
1934G	150,000	15.00	40.00	75.00	290	335
1935A	35,890,000	0.20	0.50	2.00	15.00	17.00
1935D	8,960,000	0.20	0.50	2.00	18.00	20.00
1935E	5,966,000	0.20	0.50	2.00	20.00	22.00
1935F	7,944,000	0.20	0.30	1.50	18.00	20.00
1935G	4,847,000	0.20	0.50	3.00	20.00	22.00
1935J	8,995,000	0.20	0.50	3.00	16.00	18.00
1936A	24,527,000	0.20	0.80	2.00	18.00	20.00
1936D	8,092,000	0.20	1.00	3.00	23.00	25.00
1936E	2,441,000	0.20	1.00	6.00	28.00	31.00
1936F	4,889,000	0.20	1.00	3.00	24.00	27.00
1936G	1,715,000	0.20	3.00	12.00	50.00	56.00
1936J	1,632,000	0.50	4.00	18.00	70.00	80.00
1924-36 Common date proof	—	Value: 100				

KM# 41 50 REICHSPFENNIG
Aluminum-Bronze Obv: Denomination within square, oak leaf on each side Rev: Six grain sprigs form center triangle above date

Date	Mintage	F	VF	XF	Unc	BU
1924A	801,000	700	1,200	2,000	3,000	3,500
1924A	—	Value: 4,000				

Date	Mintage	F	VF	XF	Unc	BU
1924E	Inc. below	1,650	3,000	4,500	5,500	6,500
1924F	55,000	3,200	7,000	10,000	17,000	20,000
1924F Proof	—	Value: 22,500				

Note: Peus Auction #324 4-89 proof realized $10,360

Date	Mintage	F	VF	XF	Unc	BU
1924G	11,000	6,000	12,000	18,000	25,000	30,000
1924G Proof	—	Value: 15,000				
1925E	1,805,000	900	1,400	2,250	3,750	4,250
1925E Proof	196	Value: 5,500				
1925F	—	6,000	12,000	18,000	25,000	30,000
1925F Proof	—	Value: 35,000				

Note: Peus Auction #324 4-89 proof realized $23,830. Kurdfälzische Munzhandlung Mannheim 6-91 proof realized $37,600

KM# 49 50 REICHSPFENNIG
3.5100 g., Nickel Obv: Eagle within circle, leaf spray below Rev: Denomination within lined circle, oak leaves and acorns above

Date	Mintage	F	VF	XF	Unc	BU
1927A	16,309,000	2.00	3.00	7.00	23.00	25.00
1927D	2,228,000	3.00	7.00	15.00	65.00	75.00
1927E	1,070,000	4.00	9.00	18.00	70.00	80.00
1927F	1,940,000	2.50	6.00	12.00	60.00	70.00
1927G	1,756,000	5.00	15.00	25.00	100	120
1927J	4,056,000	2.50	6.00	12.00	60.00	70.00
1928A	43,864,000	0.80	2.00	4.00	18.00	20.00
1928D	14,088,000	1.00	3.00	6.00	30.00	35.00
1928E	8,618,000	1.00	3.00	6.00	30.00	35.00
1928F	9,954,000	1.00	3.00	6.00	30.00	35.00
1928G	6,177,000	1.00	3.50	7.00	40.00	50.00
1928J	6,565,000	1.00	3.00	6.00	40.00	50.00
1929A	10,298,000	1.00	3.00	7.00	40.00	50.00
1929D	1,965,000	2.00	6.00	15.00	70.00	85.00
1929F	1,162,000	9.00	20.00	45.00	150	170
1930A	4,128,000	1.00	4.00	8.00	40.00	48.00
1930D	1,406,000	4.00	8.00	15.00	75.00	88.00
1930E	745,000	20.00	35.00	70.00	220	250
1930F	320,000	50.00	100	140	360	420
1930G	610,000	18.00	40.00	80.00	250	280
1930J	526,000	20.00	50.00	100	280	320
1931A	5,624,000	1.00	4.00	8.00	21.00	24.00
1931D	1,125,000	2.00	7.00	16.00	32.00	35.00
1931F	1,484,000	2.00	6.00	15.00	30.00	33.00
1931G	60,000	190	290	420	900	1,000
1931J	291,000	45.00	120	200	400	500
1932E	598,000	40.00	90.00	150	400	500
1932G	96,000	800	1,300	1,900	2,900	3,500
1933G	333,000	55.00	120	180	430	475
1933J	654,000	45.00	100	155	360	390
1935A	6,390,000	1.00	4.00	9.00	32.00	36.00
1935D	2,812,000	3.00	7.00	15.00	42.00	48.00
1935E	745,000	10.00	25.00	40.00	130	150
1935F	2,006,000	3.00	6.00	12.00	40.00	50.00
1935G	650,000	15.00	35.00	48.00	140	180
1935J	1,635,000	3.00	14.00	34.00	100	120
1936A	7,696,000	2.00	4.00	10.00	25.00	35.00
1936D	844,000	7.00	20.00	42.00	155	175
1936E	1,190,000	7.00	20.00	40.00	165	190
1936F	602,000	9.00	25.00	52.00	180	220
1936G	936,000	6.00	18.00	35.00	110	130
1936J	490,000	30.00	70.00	120	260	290
1937A	10,842,000	1.00	2.50	5.00	12.00	14.00
1937D	2,814,000	1.00	4.00	12.00	36.00	40.00
1937F	1,700,000	1.00	4.00	12.00	36.00	40.00
1937J	300,000	60.00	120	200	380	420
1938E	1,200,000	8.00	15.00	30.00	110	125
1938G	1,299,000	7.00	13.00	26.00	90.00	105
1938J	1,333,000	7.00	13.00	26.00	90.00	105
1927-38 Common date proof	—	Value: 200				

KM# 42 MARK
5.0000 g., 0.5000 Silver 0.0804 oz. ASW Obv: Denomination above date Rev: Eagle

Date	Mintage	F	VF	XF	Unc	BU
1924A	75,536,000	5.00	12.00	24.00	65.00	75.00
1924D	17,099,000	6.00	13.00	26.00	75.00	90.00
1924E	12,293,000	7.00	16.00	32.00	170	190
1924E Proof	115	Value: 275				
1924F	16,550,000	6.00	13.00	26.00	120	140
1924G	10,065,000	7.00	15.00	30.00	160	190
1924J	13,481,000	6.00	12.00	25.00	110	130
1925A	13,878,000	14.00	28.00	56.00	270	290
1925D	6,100,000	9.00	20.00	40.00	130	150
1924-25 Common date proof	—	Value: 250				

KM# 43 3 MARK
15.0000 g., 0.5000 Silver 0.2411 oz. ASW, 30 mm. Obv: Denomination above date Rev: Eagle

Date	Mintage	F	VF	XF	Unc	BU
1924A	24,386,000	16.00	40.00	80.00	110	130
1924D	3,769,000	20.00	45.00	90.00	280	320
1924E	3,353,000	20.00	42.00	80.00	280	320
1924E Proof	115	Value: 450				
1924F	4,518,000	20.00	40.00	80.00	200	230
1924G	2,745,000	20.00	50.00	100	300	340
1924J	3,677,000	20.00	40.00	80.00	220	250
1925D	2,558,000	40.00	100	200	700	790
1924-25 Common date proof	—	Value: 280				

KM# 44 REICHSMARK
5.0000 g., 0.5000 Silver 0.0804 oz. ASW Obv: Eagle above date Rev: Denomination within wreath

Date	Mintage	F	VF	XF	Unc	BU
1925	34,527,000	5.00	12.00	24.00	50.00	55.00
1925A Proof	600	Value: 380				
1925D	13,854,000	6.00	16.00	28.00	60.00	70.00
1925E	6,460,000	8.00	20.00	32.00	110	125
1925F	8,035,000	8.00	17.00	27.00	135	155
1925G	4,520,000	9.00	23.00	38.00	120	140
1925J	6,800,000	9.00	22.00	36.00	115	135
1926A	35,555,000	8.00	17.00	26.00	95.00	110
1926D	4,424,000	10.00	21.00	38.00	120	140
1926E	3,225,000	14.00	32.00	70.00	230	260
1926E Proof	31	Value: 450				
1926F	3,045,000	12.00	30.00	50.00	190	210
1926G	3,410,000	14.00	32.00	55.00	240	260
1926J	1,290,000	50.00	110	180	480	540
1927A	364,000	250	390	600	1,300	1,400
1927F	1,959,000	40.00	70.00	110	280	310
1927J	2,451,000	30.00	55.00	100	240	265

KM# 45 2 REICHSMARK
10.0000 g., 0.5000 Silver 0.1607 oz. ASW, 28 mm. Obv: Eagle above date Rev: Denomination within wreath

Date	Mintage	F	VF	XF	Unc	BU
1925A	16,145,000	8.00	16.00	24.00	80.00	90.00
1925D	2,272,000	10.00	20.00	32.00	120	135
1925E	1,971,000	12.00	25.00	43.00	160	175
1925E Proof	101	Value: 350				
1925F	2,414,000	11.00	23.00	37.00	100	115
1925G	929,000	15.00	32.00	65.00	210	230
1925J	2,326,000	10.00	20.00	32.00	96.00	110
1926A	31,645,000	8.00	16.00	25.00	70.00	80.00
1926D	11,322,000	8.00	16.00	25.00	80.00	90.00
1926E	5,107,000	11.00	23.00	45.00	170	190
1926E Proof	30	—	750	—	—	—
1926F	7,115,000	8.00	16.00	32.00	105	120
1926G	5,171,000	10.00	20.00	42.00	150	170
1926J	5,305,000	10.00	18.00	38.00	115	130
1927A	6,399,000	12.00	25.00	40.00	135	150
1927D	466,000	800	1,200	2,000	5,000	6,000
1927E	373,000	200	325	700	1,400	1,600
1927E Proof	53	Value: 3,000				
1927F	502,000	60.00	200	300	950	1,100
1927J	540,000	45.00	100	185	500	580
1931D	2,109,000	20.00	36.00	53.00	160	180
1931E	1,118,000	26.00	50.00	85.00	240	270
1931F	1,505,000	22.00	40.00	65.00	190	230
1931G	915,000	30.00	55.00	100	250	300
1931J	1,226,000	30.00	55.00	100	520	600
1925-31 Common date proof	—	Value: 300				

KM# 46 3 REICHSMARK
15.0000 g., 0.5000 Silver 0.2411 oz. ASW, 30 mm. **Subject:**
1000th Year of the Rhineland **Obv:** Armored figure behind shield
divides date, right arm raised **Rev:** Denomination within wreath

Date	Mintage	F	VF	XF	Unc	BU
1925A	3,052,000	25.00	45.00	55.00	100	110
1925A Proof	—	Value: 200				
1925D	1,123,000	25.00	50.00	60.00	110	125
1925D Proof	—	Value: 240				
1925E	441,000	25.00	55.00	65.00	120	145
1925E Proof	229	Value: 250				
1925F	173,000	30.00	60.00	75.00	135	155
1925F Proof	—	Value: 280				
1925G	300,000	30.00	55.00	70.00	115	130
1925G Proof	—	Value: 240				
1925J	492,000	30.00	55.00	70.00	115	130
1925J Proof	—	Value: 240				

KM# 48 3 REICHSMARK
15.0000 g., 0.5000 Silver 0.2411 oz. ASW, 30 mm.
Subject: 700 Years of Freedom for Lubeck **Obv:** Denomination
within circle, leaf spray below **Rev:** Double-headed eagle on
shield within circle, dates above

Date	Mintage	F	VF	XF	Unc	BU
1926A	200,000	60.00	110	180	240	260
1926A Proof	—	Value: 300				

KM# 50 3 REICHSMARK
15.0000 g., 0.5000 Silver 0.2411 oz. ASW, 30 mm. **Subject:**
100th Anniversary of Bremerhaven **Obv:** Eagle on shield within
scalloped design **Rev:** Shield divides date below ship

Date	Mintage	F	VF	XF	Unc	BU
1927A	150,000	70.00	130	190	270	290
1927A Proof	—	Value: 360				

KM# 52 3 REICHSMARK
15.0000 g., 0.5000 Silver 0.2411 oz. ASW, 30 mm. **Subject:**
1000th Anniversary - Founding of Nordhausen **Obv:** Large
denomination within scalloped design **Rev:** Heinrich I and Mathilde

Date	Mintage	F	VF	XF	Unc	BU
1927A	100,000	60.00	120	190	260	290
1927A Proof	—	Value: 500				

KM# 53 3 REICHSMARK
15.0000 g., 0.5000 Silver 0.2411 oz. ASW, 30 mm. **Subject:**
400th Anniversary - Philipps University in Marburg **Obv:** Eagle,
denomination below **Rev:** Arms of Philip I the Magnanimous

Date	Mintage	F	VF	XF	Unc	BU
1927A	130,000	60.00	115	160	240	265
1927A Proof	—	Value: 290				

KM# 54 3 REICHSMARK
15.0000 g., 0.5000 Silver 0.2411 oz. ASW, 30 mm. **Subject:**
450th Anniversary - Tubingen University **Obv:** Eagle,
denomination below **Rev:** Count Eberhard the Bearded left

Date	Mintage	F	VF	XF	Unc	BU
1927F	50,000	190	380	520	720	765
1927F Proof	—	Value: 980				

KM# 57 3 REICHSMARK
15.0000 g., 0.5000 Silver 0.2411 oz. ASW, 30 mm.
Subject: 900th Anniversary - Founding of Naumburg **Obv:** Eagle
above denomination **Rev:** Margrave Hermann, City Founder

Date	Mintage	F	VF	XF	Unc	BU
1928A	100,000	70.00	115	170	230	250
1928A Matte proof	—	Value: 480				

KM# 58 3 REICHSMARK
15.0000 g., 0.5000 Silver 0.2411 oz. ASW, 30 mm. **Subject:**
400th Anniversary - Death of Albrecht Durer **Obv:** Eagle above
denomination **Rev:** Head left within circle, date below

Date	Mintage	F	VF	XF	Unc	BU
1928D	50,000	150	330	530	710	750
1928D Matte proof	—	Value: 900				

KM# 59 3 REICHSMARK
15.0000 g., 0.5000 Silver 0.2411 oz. ASW, 30 mm. **Subject:**
1000th Anniversary - Founding of Dinkelsbuhl **Obv:** Eagle above
denomination **Rev:** Shield below figure holding sickle and sheaf,
towers flank, date is divided in fourths by the above

Date	Mintage	F	VF	XF	Unc	BU
1928D	40,000	250	500	750	900	1,000

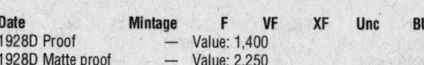

Date	Mintage	F	VF	XF	Unc	BU
1928D Proof	—	Value: 1,400				
1928D Matte proof	—	Value: 2,250				

KM# 65 3 REICHSMARK
15.0000 g., 0.5000 Silver 0.2411 oz. ASW, 30 mm.
Subject: 1000th Anniversary - Meissen **Obv:** Eagle within circle,
denomination below **Rev:** Central figure holding shields on poles
divides date, five crosses above

Date	Mintage	F	VF	XF	Unc	BU
1929E	200,000	30.00	50.00	75.00	115	125
1929E Proof	—	Value: 330				

KM# 62 3 REICHSMARK
15.0000 g., 0.5000 Silver 0.2411 oz. ASW, 30 mm. **Subject:**
Waldeck-Prussia Union **Obv:** Imperial eagle above denomination
Rev: Eagle with wings lowered holds shield at left, date below

Date	Mintage	F	VF	XF	Unc	BU
1929A	170,000	55.00	125	175	250	270
1929A Proof	—	Value: 450				

KM# 63 3 REICHSMARK
15.0000 g., 0.5000 Silver 0.2411 oz. ASW, 30 mm. **Subject:** 10th
Anniversary - Weimar Constitution **Obv:** Paul von Hindenburg
Rev: Hand with two fingers raised within circle, dates below

Date	Mintage	F	VF	XF	Unc	BU
1929A	1,421,000	20.00	35.00	65.00	80.00	70.00
1929A Proof	—	Value: 250				
1929A Matte proof	—					
1929D	499,000	20.00	40.00	75.00	90.00	98.00
1929D Proof	—	Value: 250				
1929E	122,000	24.00	50.00	85.00	100	110
1929E Proof	—	Value: 280				
1929F	370,000	20.00	40.00	80.00	95.00	105
1929F Proof	—	Value: 280				
1929G	256,000	20.00	40.00	80.00	95.00	105
1929G Proof	—	Value: 280				
1929J	342,000	20.00	40.00	75.00	90.00	105
1929J Proof	—	Value: 280				

KM# 60 3 REICHSMARK
15.0000 g., 0.5000 Silver 0.2411 oz. ASW, 30 mm.
Subject: 200th Anniversary - Birth of Gotthold Lessing **Obv:**
Small eagle, denomination below **Rev:** Head left divides dates

Date	Mintage	F	VF	XF	Unc	BU
1929A	217,000	25.00	50.00	80.00	130	140
1929A Proof	—	Value: 290				
1929D	56,000	30.00	55.00	85.00	145	155
1929D Proof	—	Value: 330				
1929E	30,000	30.00	65.00	95.00	160	170
1929E Proof	—	Value: 330				
1929F	40,000	25.00	45.00	90.00	140	150
1929F Proof	—	Value: 330				

Date	Mintage	F	VF	XF	Unc	BU
1929G	24,000	25.00	40.00	85.00	160	170
1929G Proof	—	Value: 330				
1929J	33,000	25.00	40.00	85.00	150	160
1929J Proof	—	Value: 330				

KM# 67 3 REICHSMARK
15.0000 g., 0.5000 Silver 0.2411 oz. ASW, 30 mm.
Subject: Graf Zeppelin Flight **Obv:** Eagle, denomination below
Rev: Zeppelin across globe, date below

Date	Mintage	F	VF	XF	Unc	BU
1930A	542,000	35.00	65.00	90.00	140	150
1930A Proof	—	Value: 325				
1930D	141,000	35.00	70.00	95.00	150	160
1930D Proof	—	Value: 360				
1930E	75,000	45.00	90.00	125	170	185
1930E Proof	—	Value: 360				
1930F	100,000	35.00	70.00	95.00	145	155
1930F Proof	—	Value: 325				
1930G	61,000	45.00	90.00	125	170	185
1930G Proof	—	Value: 360				
1930J	82,000	50.00	100	115	155	170
1930J Proof	—	Value: 360				

KM# 69 3 REICHSMARK
15.0000 g., 0.5000 Silver 0.2411 oz. ASW, 30 mm. **Subject:** 700th Anniversary - Death of Von Der Vogelweide **Obv:** Eagle on shield, design in background **Rev:** Figure of Walther von der Vogelweide sitting, left, with doves, harp on lower left. date at bottom

Date	Mintage	F	VF	XF	Unc	BU
1930A	163,000	35.00	55.00	95.00	120	130
1930A Proof	—	Value: 290				
1930A Matte proof	—	Value: 500				
1930D	42,000	35.00	65.00	100	140	150
1930D Proof	—	Value: 290				
1930E	22,000	37.50	75.00	120	160	175
1930E Proof	—	Value: 290				
1930F	30,000	37.50	85.00	110	200	220
1930F Proof	—	Value: 290				
1930G	18,000	45.00	80.00	130	175	190
1930G Proof	—	Value: 290				
1930J	25,000	45.00	80.00	120	165	180
1930J Proof	—	Value: 290				

KM# 70 3 REICHSMARK
15.0000 g., 0.5000 Silver 0.2411 oz. ASW, 30 mm.
Subject: Liberation of Rhineland **Obv:** Eagle on shield, design in background **Rev:** Eagle left on bridge divides date

Date	Mintage	F	VF	XF	Unc	BU
1930A	1,734,000	25.00	48.00	65.00	100	110
1930A Proof	—	Value: 240				
1930A Matte proof	—	—	—	—	—	—
1930D	450,000	25.00	55.00	75.00	120	135
1930D Proof	—	Value: 240				
1930E	38,000	75.00	120	200	330	360
1930E Proof	—	Value: 450				
1930F	321,000	35.00	60.00	90.00	110	125
1930F Proof	—	Value: 240				
1930G	195,000	35.00	65.00	100	130	145
1930J	261,000	35.00	60.00	90.00	120	135
1930J Proof	—	Value: 240				

KM# 72 3 REICHSMARK
15.0000 g., 0.5000 Silver 0.2411 oz. ASW, 30 mm.
Subject: 300th Anniversary - Magdeburg Rebuilding **Obv:** Eagle on shield, scalloped design in background **Rev:** Shield divides dates above city scene

Date	Mintage	F	VF	XF	Unc	BU
1931A	100,000	90.00	170	255	340	370
1931A Proof	—	Value: 450				

KM# 73 3 REICHSMARK
15.0000 g., 0.5000 Silver 0.2411 oz. ASW, 30 mm. **Subject:** Centenary - Death of von Stein **Obv:** Eagle divides dates, denomination below **Rev:** Head left, name below

Date	Mintage	F	VF	XF	Unc	BU
1931A	150,000	55.00	120	180	240	260
1931A Proof	—	Value: 380				

KM# 74 3 REICHSMARK
15.0000 g., 0.5000 Silver 0.2411 oz. ASW, 30 mm. **Obv:** Eagle above date **Rev:** Denomination within wreath

Date	Mintage	F	VF	XF	Unc	BU
1931A	13,324,000	130	260	360	660	750
1931D	2,232,000	160	300	400	790	900
1931E	2,235,000	190	330	430	1,050	1,200
1931F	2,357,000	160	300	400	730	860
1931G	1,468,000	190	360	490	1,160	1,320
1931J	1,115,000	230	330	460	1,140	1,300
1932A	2,933,000	140	260	400	730	860
1932D	1,986,000	150	280	460	900	1,050
1932F	653,000	230	430	880	2,100	2,600
1932G	210,000	500	900	1,700	4,500	5,800
1932J	1,336,000	190	320	470	970	1,060
1933G	152,000	900	1,750	3,100	7,200	9,000

Note: Less than 10 percent of issue was released

| 1931-33 Common date proof | — | Value: 1,400 | | | | |

KM# 76 3 REICHSMARK
15.0000 g., 0.5000 Silver 0.2411 oz. ASW, 30 mm.
Subject: Centenary - Death of Goethe **Obv:** Eagle divides dates, denomination below **Rev:** Head left, name below

Date	Mintage	F	VF	XF	Unc	BU
1932A	217,000	35.00	80.00	110	160	175
1932A Proof	—	Value: 240				
1932D	56,000	40.00	80.00	115	180	195
1932D Proof	—	Value: 240				
1932E	30,000	45.00	85.00	125	200	220
1932E Proof	—	Value: 280				
1932F	40,000	35.00	80.00	115	180	195
1932F Proof	—	Value: 240				
1932F Matte proof	—	Value: 600				
1932G	24,000	45.00	85.00	125	200	220
1932G Proof	—	Value: 320				

Date	Mintage	F	VF	XF	Unc	BU
1932J	33,000	45.00	80.00	115	180	195
1932J Proof	—	Value: 280				

KM# 47 5 REICHSMARK
25.0000 g., 0.5000 Silver 0.4019 oz. ASW, 37 mm. **Subject:** 1000th Year of the Rhineland **Obv:** Armored figure behind shield divides date, right arm raised **Rev:** Denomination within wreath

Date	Mintage	F	VF	XF	Unc	BU
1925A	684,000	50.00	95.00	125	210	225
1925A Proof	—	Value: 600				
1925D	452,000	50.00	95.00	140	240	265
1925D Proof	—	Value: 700				
1925E	204,000	55.00	110	160	255	285
1925E Proof	226	Value: 700				
1925F	212,000	55.00	105	150	245	275
1925F Proof	—	Value: 700				
1925G	89,000	60.00	120	170	300	350
1925G Proof	—	Value: 700				
1925J	43,000	95.00	190	290	520	580
1925J Proof	—	Value: 800				

KM# 51 5 REICHSMARK
25.0000 g., 0.5000 Silver 0.4019 oz. ASW, 37 mm. **Subject:** 100th Anniversary - Bremerhaven **Obv:** Eagle on shield, scalloped design in background **Rev:** Crowned shield divides date below ship

Date	Mintage	F	VF	XF	Unc	BU
1927A	50,000	220	420	580	760	850
1927A Proof	—	Value: 980				

KM# 55 5 REICHSMARK
25.0000 g., 0.5000 Silver 0.4019 oz. ASW, 37 mm. **Subject:** 450th Anniversary - University of Tubingen **Rev:** Bust left within circle

Date	Mintage	F	VF	XF	Unc	BU
1927F	40,000	130	290	550	725	860
1927F Proof	—	Value: 1,100				

KM# 56 5 REICHSMARK
25.0000 g., 0.5000 Silver 0.4019 oz. ASW, 37 mm. **Obv:** Eagle within circle, denomination below **Rev:** Oaktree divides date

Date	Mintage	F	VF	XF	Unc	BU
1927A	7,926,000	50.00	90.00	140	260	280
1927D	1,471,000	40.00	100	160	340	370
1927E	1,100,000	50.00	120	175	430	470
1927F	700,000	50.00	130	220	550	630
1927G	759,000	60.00	160	260	880	1,000
1927J	1,006,000	50.00	125	190	480	520
1928A	15,466,000	40.00	100	135	290	320
1928D	4,613,000	45.00	110	145	400	440
1928E	2,310,000	60.00	130	190	520	580
1928F	3,771,000	50.00	120	160	420	480

Date	Mintage	F	VF	XF	Unc	BU
1928G	1,923,000	65.00	145	180	450	500
1928J	2,450,000	60.00	125	170	430	490
1929A	6,730,000	45.00	100	130	300	330
1929D	2,020,000	50.00	130	190	490	535
1929E	860,000	140	320	540	1,650	1,900
1929F	814,000	70.00	175	260	760	850
1929G	950,000	90.00	190	290	880	990
1929J	779,000	90.00	190	300	800	890
1930A	3,790,000	60.00	120	170	410	440
1930D	606,000	175	450	600	1,700	1,900
1930E	354,000	500	1,550	2,200	5,100	5,700
1930F	630,000	300	650	930	1,650	1,800
1930G	367,000	600	1,350	1,850	4,600	5,100
1930J	740,000	300	660	880	1,800	2,000
1931A	14,651,000	40.00	100	140	270	300
1931D	3,254,000	50.00	120	165	385	420
1931E	2,245,000	60.00	135	180	450	490
1931F	4,152,000	50.00	120	165	385	420
1931G	1,620,000	75.00	190	330	950	1,080
1931J	3,092,000	60.00	140	210	460	500
1932A	32,303,000	40.00	100	140	270	300
1932D	8,556,000	45.00	115	160	300	340
1932E	4,013,000	55.00	125	180	320	360
1932F	5,019,000	50.00	120	170	310	350
1932G	3,504,000	60.00	150	220	500	570
1932J	3,752,000	60.00	150	220	520	590
1933J	423,000	700	1,400	2,600	5,400	6,000
1933J Proof	—	Value: 6,500				
1927-33 Common date proof	—	Value: 900				

KM# 66 5 REICHSMARK
25.0000 g., 0.5000 Silver 0.4019 oz. ASW, 37 mm.
Subject: 1000th Anniversary - Meissen **Obv:** Eagle **Rev:** Central figure holding shields on poles divides date, five crosses above

Date	Mintage	F	VF	XF	Unc	BU
1929E	120,000	160	250	400	550	600
1929E Proof	—	Value: 1,000				

KM# 61 5 REICHSMARK
25.0000 g., 0.5000 Silver 0.4019 oz. ASW, 37 mm.
Subject: 200th Anniversary - Birth of Gotthold Lessing **Obv:** Small eagle, denomination below **Rev:** Head left divides date

Date	Mintage	F	VF	XF	Unc	BU
1929A	87,000	60.00	100	145	255	275
1929A Proof	—	Value: 600				
1929D	22,000	60.00	110	160	280	310
1929D Proof	—	Value: 670				
1929E	12,000	60.00	125	200	300	330
1929E Proof	—	Value: 670				
1929F	16,000	60.00	120	180	290	320
1929F Proof	—	Value: 670				
1929G	9,760	80.00	150	225	350	400
1929G Proof	—	Value: 800				
1929J	13,000	70.00	130	210	330	360
1929J Proof	—	Value: 670				

KM# 64 5 REICHSMARK
25.0000 g., 0.5000 Silver 0.4019 oz. ASW, 37 mm. **Subject:** 10th Anniversary - Weimar Constitution **Obv:** Hand with two fingers raised, dates below **Rev:** Head left, denomination above

Date	Mintage	F	VF	XF	Unc	BU
1929A	325,000	55.00	100	160	260	290
1929A Proof	—	Value: 500				
1929D	84,000	60.00	120	180	290	330
1929D Proof	—	Value: 500				

Date	Mintage	F	VF	XF	Unc	BU
1929E	45,000	70.00	140	200	320	360
1929E Proof	—	Value: 500				
1929F	60,000	70.00	130	190	350	380
1929F Proof	—	Value: 500				
1929G	37,000	70.00	140	200	370	420
1929G Proof	—	Value: 500				
1929J	49,000	70.00	130	190	350	380
1929J Proof	—	Value: 500				

KM# 68 5 REICHSMARK
25.0000 g., 0.5000 Silver 0.4019 oz. ASW, 37 mm.
Subject: Graf Zeppelin Flight **Obv:** Eagle, denomination below **Rev:** Zeppelin across globe, date below

Date	Mintage	F	VF	XF	Unc	BU
1930A	217,000	70.00	120	190	300	330
1930A Proof	—	Value: 500				
1930A Matte proof	—	—	—	—	—	—
1930D	56,000	75.00	130	200	325	360
1930D Proof	—	Value: 700				
1930E	30,000	80.00	150	210	350	390
1930E Proof	—	Value: 550				
1930F	40,000	75.00	140	200	340	380
1930F Proof	—	Value: 500				
1930G	24,000	85.00	160	235	350	390
1930G Proof	—	Value: 660				
1930J	33,000	80.00	150	220	340	380
1930J Proof	—	Value: 660				

KM# 71 5 REICHSMARK
25.0000 g., 0.5000 Silver 0.4019 oz. ASW, 37 mm.
Subject: Liberation of Rhineland **Obv:** Eagle on shield, design in background **Rev:** Eagle left on bridge divides date

Date	Mintage	F	VF	XF	Unc	BU
1930A	325,000	70.00	125	190	310	340
1930A Proof	—	Value: 500				
1930D	84,000	70.00	135	220	375	400
1930D Proof	—	Value: 550				
1930E	45,000	80.00	150	275	420	450
1930E Proof	—	Value: 500				
1930F	60,000	70.00	135	235	400	440
1930F Proof	—	Value: 500				
1930G	37,000	90.00	170	280	440	500
1930G Proof	—	Value: 670				
1930J	49,000	80.00	150	250	420	470
1930J Proof	—	Value: 620				

KM# 77 5 REICHSMARK
25.0000 g., 0.5000 Silver 0.4019 oz. ASW, 37 mm.
Subject: Centenary - Death of Goethe **Obv:** Eagle divides dates, denomination below **Rev:** Head left, name below

Date	Mintage	F	VF	XF	Unc	BU
1932A	11,000	950	2,300	2,850	3,450	3,800
1932A Proof	—	Value: 4,500				
1932D	2,812	1,000	2,400	3,000	3,800	4,200
1932D Proof	—	Value: 5,000				
1932E	1,490	1,000	2,500	3,150	4,200	4,500

Date	Mintage	F	VF	XF	Unc	BU
1932E Proof	—	Value: 5,000				
1932F	2,006	1,000	2,400	3,000	4,000	4,500
1932F Proof	—	Value: 5,000				
1932G	1,220	1,050	2,550	3,200	4,250	4,750
1932G Proof	—	Value: 5,000				
1932J	1,634	1,000	2,450	3,100	4,100	4,500
1932J Proof	—	Value: 5,000				

PATTERNS
Including off metal strikes

KM#	Date	Mintage	Identification	Mkt Val
PnA331	1927	—	3 Mark. Silver. Justus Von Liebig; never issued.	—

Note: An XF-AU example brought $15,957 at the Emporium Hamburg 1987 sale.

KM#	Date	Mintage	Identification	Mkt Val
Pn212	1919A	—	50 Pfennig. Brass.	250
Pn213	1919A	—	50 Pfennig. Silver.	350
Pn214	1919A	—	50 Pfennig. Nickel.	175
Pn215	1919A	—	50 Pfennig. Aluminum.	175
Pn216	1919A	—	50 Pfennig. Zinc.	175
Pn217	1919A	—	50 Pfennig. Zinc. Reeded edge.	—
Pn218	1919A	—	50 Pfennig. Aluminum. Reeded edge.	125
Pn219	1919A	—	50 Pfennig. Aluminum. Plain edge.	—
Pn220	1919A	—	50 Pfennig. Alum. Ornamental edge.	—
Pn221	1919A	—	50 Pfennig. Zinc. Ornamental edge.	—
Pn222	1919G	—	1/2 Mark. KM#17.	—
Pn223	1919G	—	Mark. Copper. KM#14.	—
Pn224	19xxA	—	Mark. Aluminum.	—
Pn225	1921A	—	Mark. Brass Plated Aluminum.	—
Pn226	1921A	—	Mark. Zinc.	—
Pn227	1921A	—	Mark.	—
Pn228	1921A	—	Mark. Aluminum Plated Steel.	—
Pn229	1921A	—	Mark. Nickel.	150
Pn230	1921A	—	Mark. Silver.	—
Pn231	1921A	—	Mark. Iron.	—
Pn232	1921A	—	Mark. Copper Strips Inlaid On Silver Or Copper-Nickel.	—
Pn233	1921A	—	Mark. Copper Strips Inlaid On Alum.	—
PnA234	1922A	—	10 Pfennig. Iron.	225
Pn234	1922A	—	50 Pfennig. Iron. Plain with 6 ridges edge. KM#27.	—
Pn235	1922F	—	3 Mark. Alum. KM#28; GOTT MIT UNS.	850

Note: Most 1922F lettered-edge 3 Marks were recovered from the burned out ruins of the Stuttgart Mint destroyed in World War II; the above value is for the one known perfect example, blackened VF examples are valued between $200 and $400

KM#	Date	Mintage	Identification	Mkt Val
Pn236	1922F	—	3 Mark. Alum. Reeded edge. KM#28.	—
Pn237	1922F	—	3 Mark. Alum. Plain edge. KM#28.	—
Pn238	1922G	—	3 Mark. Alum. Reeded edge. KM#28.	—
Pn239	1922A	—	5 Mark. Aluminum.	125
Pn239a	1922A	—	5 Mark. Aluminum Plated Copper.	750
Pn240	1922A	—	5 Mark. Roman lettering.	—
Pn248	1923F	—	1000 Mark. Silver. Reeded edge.	—
Pn249	1923F	—	1000 Mark. Aluminum. Plain edge.	—
Pn241	1923	—	2 Pfennig. Bronze. Without mintmark; KM#31.	—
Pn242	1923	—	50 Pfennig. Aluminum-Bronze. Without mintmark; KM#34.	—
Pn243	1923F	—	3 Mark. KM#29.4.	250

Note: All pattern 1923F 3 Marks were recovered from the burned out ruins of the Stuttgart Mint destroyed in World War II; blackened VF examples range in value from $250 to $450

KM#	Date	Mintage	Identification	Mkt Val
Pn244	1923A	—	20 Mark. Aluminum.	—
Pn245	1923A	—	100 Mark. Aluminum.	—
Pn246	1923F	—	200 Mark. Aluminum. Doubled reeding; KM#35.	—
Pn247	1923F	—	1000 Mark. Alum. Reeded edge.	325
PnA250	1924	—	2 Pfennig. Brass. KM#31.	150
Pn250	1924E	—	2 Pfennig. Copper. Eagle head left.	—
Pn251	1924E	—	10 Pfennig. Copper.	—
Pn252	1924E	—	10 Pfennig. Aluminum.	—
Pn253	1924E	—	10 Pfennig. Copper. Full eagle	—
Pn254	1924E	—	10 Pfennig. Aluminum. Full eagle	—
Pn255	1924E	—	10 Pfennig. Nickel. Full eagle.	—
Pn256	1924D	—	50 Pfennig. Lead. KM#41.	—
Pn257	1924A	—	Mark. Silver. Reeded, lettered edge.	—
Pn258	1924A	—	3 Mark. 0.5000 Silver. Ornam. edge.	—
Pn259	1924E	—	5 Mark. Silver.	—
Pn260	1925E	—	Pfennig. Copper.	—
Pn261	1925E	—	2 Pfennig. Copper.	—
Pn262	1925E	—	5 Pfennig. Copper-Nickel.	—
Pn263	1925E	—	5 Pfennig. Copper-Nickel. Larger eagle head.	—
Pn264	1925E	—	10 Pfennig. Copper-Nickel.	—
Pn272	1925F	—	50 Pfennig. Brass. Mercury	—
Pn273	1925E	—	Mark. Silver. Thick wreath.	—
Pn274	1925E	—	Mark. Nickel. Thick wreath.	—
Pn275	1925E	—	Mark. 0.4500 Silver. Thin wreath.	—
PnA276	1925F	—	3 Mark. Brass.	—
PnA277	1925	—	3 Mark. Brass. Woman's head.	—
Pn277	1925J	—	3 Mark. Iron. KM#46.	—
Pn284	1925	—	20 Mark. Brass.	—
Pn265	1925	6	50 Pfennig. Alum.-Bronze. KM#41.	17,500

Note: An XF-AU example brought $15,957, Emporium Hamburg 1987 sale

KM#	Date	Mintage	Identification	Mkt Val
Pn266	1925F	—	50 Pfennig. Brass. Bundle.	125
Pn267	1925F	—	50 Pfennig. Bronze. Bundle.	125
Pn268	1925F	—	50 Pfennig. Copper-Nickel. Bundle.	125
Pn269	1925F	—	50 Pfennig. Nickel. Bundle.	125
Pn270	1925F	—	50 Pfennig. Nickel-Silver. Mercury	150
Pn271	1925F	—	50 Pfennig. Nickel. Mercury	150
Pn276	1925E	—	2 Mark. 0.5000 Silver. Thick wreath.	175

KM#	Date	Mintage	Identification	Mkt Val
Pn278	1925E	—	3 Mark. Silver.	450
Pn279	1925E	—	5 Reichsmark. Silver.	850
Pn280	1925E	—	5 Mark. Silver.	850
Pn281	1925F	—	5 Mark. Silver.	1,850
Pn281a	1925F	—	5 Mark. Silvered-Bronze.	175
Pn282	1925E	—	5 Mark. Silver.	1,500
Pn283	1925E	—	20 Mark. Gold.	7,500
	1925E	—	20 Mark. Gold.	7,500
Pn287	1926E	—	50 Pfennig. Copper-Nickel. Leaves through value	150
Pn291	1926E	—	50 Pfennig. Copper-Nickel. Cornucopia.	150
Pn305	1926J	—	50 Pfennig. Nickel.	125
Pn307	1926A	—	Mark. Brass.	125
Pn310	1926A	—	5 Mark. Silver.	850
Pn311	1926A	—	5 Mark. Silver.	850
Pn312	1926A	—	5 Mark. Silver.	1,000
Pn312a	1926D	—	5 Mark. Silver. Ship sailing right.	600
Pn313	1926E	—	5 Mark. Silver. Large eagle, small mint mark.	600
Pn314	1926	—	5 Mark. Silver. Small eagle, large mint mark.	600
Pn315	1926E	—	5 Mark. Silver.	850
Pn316	1926E	—	5 Mark. Silver.	850
Pn318	1926F	—	5 Mark. Silver. With motto.	700
Pn320	1926F	—	5 Mark. Silver. Without motto..	850
Pn285	1926E	—	50 Pfennig. Copper-Nickel.	—
Pn286	1926	—	50 Pfennig.	—
Pn288	1926A	—	50 Pfennig. Leaves below value	—
Pn289	1926E	—	50 Pfennig. Copper-Nickel. Leaves below value	—
Pn290	1926	—	50 Pfennig. Leaves below value.	—
Pn292	1926E	—	50 Pfennig. Copper-Nickel. Two leaves.	—
Pn293	1926E	—	50 Pfennig. Copper-Nickel. Wreath.	—
Pn294	1926E	—	50 Pfennig. Copper-Nickel. Wheat.	—
Pn295	1926E	—	50 Pfennig. Copper-Nickel. Eagle.	—
Pn296	1926E	—	50 Pfennig. Copper-Nickel. Two leaves.	—
Pn297	1926E	—	50 Pfennig. Copper-Nickel. Eagle.	—
Pn298	1926E	—	50 Pfennig. Copper-Nickel. Wheat.	—
Pn299	1926E	—	50 Pfennig. Copper-Nickel. Two leaves.	—
Pn300	1926E	—	50 Pfennig. Copper-Nickel. Eagle.	—
Pn301	1926E	—	50 Pfennig. Copper-Nickel. "Reichspfennig"	—
Pn302	1926E	—	50 Pfennig. Copper-Nickel.	—
Pn303	1926A	—	50 Pfennig. Nickel.	—
Pn304	1926E	—	50 Pfennig. Copper-Nickel.	—
Pn306	1926J	—	50 Pfennig. Nickel. Smaller eagle.	—
Pn307a	1926A	—	Mark. Silver.	—
PnA308	1926	—	3 Mark.	—
Pn308	1926A	—	5 Mark. Silver.	—
Pn309	1926	—	5 Mark. Silver. Wreath aaround eagle.	—
Pn317	1926F	—	5 Mark. Silver. "PROBE"; with motto.	—
Pn319	1926F	—	5 Mark. Silver. "PROBE" without motto.	—
Pn321	1927A	—	50 Pfennig. Nickel center. Deeper relief, KM#49.	—
Pn322	1927E	—	50 Pfennig. Nickel.	—
Pn324	1927	—	Mark. Brass. Pn307.	—
Pn327	1927A	—	3 Mark. 0.9930 Silver.	—
Pn328	1927F	—	3 Mark. Silver. Lettered edge. "PROBE"	—
Pn329	1927F	—	3 Mark. Silver, Lettered edge.	—
PnA331	1927F	—	3 Mark. Silver. Justus Von Liebig; never issued.	—
Pn331	1927A	—	5 Mark. Silver. Large eagle.	—
Pn332	NDA	—	5 Mark. Silvered Tin. Small eagle.	—
Pn334	1927A	—	5 Mark. Silver. 50 stars; KM#56.	—
Pn335	1927A	—	5 Mark. Silver. 47 stars; KM#56.	—
Pn336	1927A	—	5 Mark. Silver. 73 stars; KM#56.	—
Pn323	1927F	—	50 Pfennig. Copper-Nickel.	175
Pn325	1927F	—	Mark. 0.5000 Silver. Ornamental edge.	200
Pn326	1927F	—	Mark. 0.9930 Silver. Plain edge.	250
Pn327a	1927A	—	3 Mark. Copper-Nickel.	1,000
Pn330	1927F	—	3 Mark. Plain edge.	875
Pn337	1929A	—	3 Mark. Silver. Script on edge; KM#60.	875
Pn341	1929A	—	5 Mark. Silver. "PROBE".	1,850
Pn338	1929A	—	3 Mark. Silver. "PROBE"; KM#62.	—
Pn339	1929A	—	3 Mark. Silver. Plain rims; "PROBE".	—
Pn340	1929A	—	5 Mark. Silver. Star rims; "PROBE".	—
Pn342	1929A	—	5 Mark. Silver. Pn346.	—
PnA343	1929E	—	3 Mark. PROBE	—
Pn343	1930	—	3 Mark. Silver. "PROBE"; KM#70.	—
Pn346	1930A	—	5 Mark. Silver. "PROBE"; KM#68.	—
Pn347	1930	—	5 Mark. Silver.	—
Pn344	1930	—	3 Mark. Silver. "PROBE"	900
Pn345	1930A	—	3 Mark. Silver. "PROBE"; KM#69.	900
PnA347	1931G	—	Pfennig. Brass.	100
Pn348	1931A	—	3 Mark.	—
Pn349	1931	—	5 Mark.	—
Pn350	1932A	—	4 Pfennig. Silvered Copper. "PROBE"	—
PnA351	1932	—	3 Mark. Silver.	—
Pn352	1932F	—	3 Mark. Silver. Reeded edge. "PROBE"; KM#74.	—
Pn353	1932F	—	3 Mark. Silver. Reeded edge. Without "PROBE"; KM#74.	—
Pn351	1932D	—	3 Mark. 0.7500 Silver. KM#74.	750
Pn353a	1932A	—	5 Mark. Nickel. "PROBE". KM#76.	400

THIRD REICH

MINT MARKS
A - Berlin
B - Vienna, 1938-1944
D - Munich
E - Muldenhutten
F - Stuttgart
G - Karlsruhe
J - Hamburg

MONETARY SYSTEMS
(During 1923-1924)
100 Rentenpfennig = 1 Rentenmark

(Commencing 1924)
100 Reichspfennig = 1 Reichsmark

1933-1945

A wide range of factors, such as humiliation of defeat, economic depression, poverty, and a pervasive feeling of discontent aided Hitler in his climb to power. After the unsuccessful Putsch (uprising against the Bavarian Government) in 1923, Hitler was imprisoned in Landsberg Fortress. While imprisoned Hitler dictated his book *"Mein Kampf"* which became the cornerstone of Nazism espousing Hitler's irrational ideology and the manipulation of power without moral constraint as the basis of strategy.

Master propagandist Josef Goebbels tried to attract the sympathetic attention of the German public. The usual tactic was to have Hitler promise all things to all people provided that they in turn would pledge to him their complete faith and obedience.

Once in power, coercion was used to elicit the appearance of unanimous endorsement. Public works and military rearmament helped overcome the depression. It took the Nazis only about two years to consolidate their system politically. The combined terrorism of the storm troops and the police forces, including the Gestapo, stifled potential opposition. By 1935, Nazi affiliated organizations controlled all German cultural, professional, and economic fields, assuring strict compliance with the party line.

With the passage of the Nurnberg Laws in 1935, the more ominous aspects of Nazi anti-Semitism came to light. Jews were deprived of their citizenship and forbidden to marry non-Jews. This was followed by confiscation of property and the required wearing of the Star of David for identification purposes, eventually culminating in the mass deportation to concentration and death camps.

By 1936, unemployment was virtually eliminated and economic production was up to 1929 levels. All sources of information were under the control of Josef Goebbels, while all police power was in the hands of Heinrich Himmler. Himmler's Gestapo would silence Germans who were not convinced by Goebbel's propaganda machine. Usually the implied threat was enough. The majority of Germans did not suffer any ill effects at first and national pride stirred once again.

Hitler's audacity in foreign affairs met with success due to the trend of appeasement by the western powers. First, Germany withdrew from the League of Nations and the World Disarmament Council. In 1935, the Saar voted to return to Germany and Hitler renounced the reviled 1921 peace treaty and related pacts. In 1936, German forces reoccupied the Rhineland. In 1938, Austria was annexed and at the Munich Conference, which excluded Czechoslovakia, Great Britain and France agreed that the Sudetenland was to become German territory. In 1939, Slovakia became an independent Nazi Puppet State and the "Protectorate" of Bohemia and Moravia was established. Next came the German-Soviet non-aggression pact, which secretly divided up Poland between the two totalitarian powers. Great Britain and France finally declared war when Poland was invaded. The years of 1939-1942 were a period of impressive victories for Germany's well-trained and equipped forces. However, when Hitler expanded his war beyond Western Europe by invading Africa and Russia and declaring war on the U.S.A. it started the chain of events, which would culminate in the total and final German defeat on May 8, 1945, VE Day, ending the European theater of the Second World War and The Third Reich.

THIRD REICH

STANDARD COINAGE

KM# 89 REICHSPFENNIG
2.0100 g., Bronze, 17.43 mm. **Obv:** Eagle above swastika within wreath **Rev:** Denomination, oak leaves below

Date	Mintage	F	VF	XF	Unc	BU
1936A	—	2.00	5.50	15.00	50.00	75.00

Note: Mintage included with KM#37.

Date	Mintage	F	VF	XF	Unc	BU
1936E	150,000	27.50	55.00	110	165	275
1936F	4,600,000	25.00	50.00	90.00	200	300
1936G	—	15.00	25.00	60.00	110	200

Note: Mintage included with KM#37.

Date	Mintage	F	VF	XF	Unc	BU
1936J	—	10.00	22.50	50.00	100	125

Note: Mintage included with KM#37.

Date	Mintage	F	VF	XF	Unc	BU
1937A	67,180,000	0.20	0.35	1.00	3.50	6.00
1937D	14,060,000	0.20	0.35	1.25	6.00	12.00
1937E	10,700,000	0.20	0.40	1.25	6.00	12.00
1937F	11,058,000	0.20	0.35	1.25	6.00	12.00
1937G	4,250,000	0.20	0.40	2.50	6.00	14.00
1937J	6,714,000	0.20	0.40	1.25	6.00	12.00
1938A	75,707,000	0.15	0.35	0.50	5.00	9.00
1938B	2,378,000	0.50	4.00	6.50	15.00	30.00
1938D	13,930,000	0.15	0.35	0.60	6.00	9.00
1938E	14,503,000	0.15	0.35	0.60	6.00	9.00
1938F	11,714,000	0.15	0.35	0.60	6.00	9.00
1938G	8,390,000	0.15	0.35	1.25	6.00	11.00
1938J	15,458,000	0.15	0.35	0.60	6.00	9.00
1939A	97,541,000	0.15	0.35	0.60	4.00	9.00
1939B	22,732,000	0.20	0.40	0.90	6.00	11.00
1939D	20,760,000	0.15	0.30	0.60	5.00	9.00
1939E	12,478,000	0.15	0.35	0.60	6.00	11.00
1939F	12,482,000	0.15	0.35	0.60	5.00	9.00
1939G	12,250,000	0.15	0.35	0.60	6.00	9.00
1939J	8,368,000	0.15	0.35	0.60	6.00	11.00
1940A	27,094,000	0.15	0.35	0.60	5.00	10.00
1940F	7,850,000	0.20	0.45	1.25	7.00	12.00
1940G	3,875,000	1.00	4.00	11.00	20.00	35.00

Date	Mintage	F	VF	XF	Unc	BU
1940J	7,450,000	0.60	2.75	4.50	10.00	20.00
1936-1940 Common date proof	— Value: 140					

KM# 97 REICHSPFENNIG
1.8100 g., Zinc, 17 mm. **Obv:** Eagle above swastika within wreath **Rev:** Denomination, oak leaves below

Date	Mintage	F	VF	XF	Unc	BU
1940A	223,948,000	0.15	0.25	1.00	5.00	8.00
1940B	62,198,000	0.15	0.25	1.00	5.00	8.00
1940D	43,951,000	0.15	0.25	1.00	5.00	8.00
1940E	20,749,000	0.25	1.00	4.50	11.00	17.50
1940F	33,854,000	0.15	0.25	1.00	6.00	10.00
1940G	20,165,000	0.15	0.25	1.00	6.00	12.00
1940J	24,459,000	0.15	0.25	1.00	6.00	10.00
1941A	281,618,000	0.15	0.20	0.50	4.00	7.00
1941B	62,285,000	0.20	1.00	1.50	5.00	7.00
1941D	73,745,000	0.15	0.20	0.60	5.00	7.00
1941E	49,041,000	0.15	0.50	1.50	8.50	15.00
1941F	51,017,000	0.15	0.20	0.60	5.00	8.00
1941J	57,625,000	0.15	0.20	0.60	6.00	10.00
1942A	558,877,000	0.15	0.20	0.50	5.00	6.00
1942B	124,740,000	0.15	0.25	1.00	6.00	7.00
1942D	134,145,000	0.15	0.20	0.60	6.00	7.00
1942E	84,674,000	0.20	1.25	2.00	8.00	10.00
1942F	90,788,000	0.15	0.20	0.60	6.00	7.00
1942G	59,858,000	0.15	0.20	0.60	6.00	9.00
1942J	122,934,000	0.15	0.50	1.00	6.00	7.00
1943A	372,401,000	0.15	0.20	0.50	6.00	7.00
1943B	79,315,000	0.15	0.50	0.90	6.00	7.00
1943D	91,629,000	0.15	0.20	0.50	6.00	7.00
1943E	34,191,000	0.50	2.25	6.50	12.00	18.00
1943F	70,269,000	0.15	0.50	0.90	6.00	7.00
1943G	24,688,000	0.20	1.25	2.00	8.00	11.00
1943J	37,695,000	0.20	1.25	2.00	6.00	7.00
1944A	124,421,000	0.15	0.50	1.50	5.00	7.00
1944B	87,850,000	0.25	1.00	1.75	6.00	9.00
1944D	56,755,000	0.25	1.00	2.00	7.00	10.00
1944E	41,729,000	0.25	1.75	4.00	12.00	18.00
1944F	15,580,000	0.50	3.50	6.50	17.50	25.00
1944G	34,967,000	0.15	0.60	1.50	6.00	11.00
1945A	17,145,000	0.50	2.50	7.00	20.00	30.00
1945E	6,800,000	45.00	60.00	100	175	275
1940-1945 Common date proof	— Value: 140					

KM# 90 2 REICHSPFENNIG
3.3400 g., Bronze, 20.11 mm. **Obv:** Eagle above swastika within wreath **Rev:** Denomination, oak leaves below

Date	Mintage	F	VF	XF	Unc	BU
1936A	Inc. below	0.60	3.50	10.00	40.00	50.00
1936D	Inc. below	0.60	3.50	8.00	30.00	35.00
1936F	3,100,000	5.00	15.00	40.00	100	160
1937A	34,404,000	0.20	0.60	1.25	7.00	11.00
1937D	9,016,000	0.20	0.60	1.25	7.00	11.00
1937E	Inc. below	12.50	17.50	35.00	70.00	110
1937F	7,487,000	0.20	0.60	1.75	8.00	11.00
1937G	490,000	2.00	7.50	14.00	40.00	50.00
1937J	450,000	2.00	7.50	14.00	30.00	35.00
1938A	27,264,000	0.20	0.50	1.00	6.00	9.00
1938B	2,714,000	1.50	3.50	8.00	30.00	40.00
1938D	8,770,000	0.20	0.35	1.00	6.00	9.00
1938E	5,450,000	0.35	1.00	2.00	7.00	10.00
1938F	10,090,000	0.20	0.35	1.00	6.00	9.00
1938G	3,685,000	0.20	0.35	5.50	15.00	22.00
1938J	7,243,000	0.20	0.35	1.25	7.00	13.00
1939A	37,348,000	0.20	0.35	1.00	6.00	9.00
1939B	9,361,000	0.20	0.35	1.00	6.00	9.00
1939D	7,555,000	0.20	0.35	1.00	6.00	9.00
1939E	6,650,000	0.35	1.00	2.00	7.00	11.00
1939F	7,019,000	0.20	0.35	1.00	6.00	10.00
1939G	4,885,000	0.20	0.35	1.25	9.00	15.00
1939J	6,996,000	0.20	0.35	1.25	7.00	10.00
1940A	22,681,000	0.20	0.35	1.00	8.00	12.00
1940D	3,855,000	0.60	2.50	5.50	20.00	25.00
1940E	3,412,000	2.00	8.00	12.50	20.00	30.00
1940G	1,161,000	40.00	80.00	120	225	375
1940J	2,357,000	1.50	7.00	13.50	35.00	50.00
1936-1940 Common date proof	— Value: 175					

KM# 91 5 REICHSPFENNIG
2.5300 g., Aluminum-Bronze **Obv:** Eagle above swastika within wreath **Rev:** Denomination, oak leaves below

Date	Mintage	F	VF	XF	Unc	BU
1936A	Inc. below	30.00	65.00	90.00	130	180
1936D	Inc. below	30.00	65.00	90.00	160	225
1936G	Inc. below	50.00	90.00	150	300	375
1937A	29,700,000	0.50	1.00	2.00	7.00	10.00
1937D	4,992,000	0.50	1.00	2.00	12.50	20.00
1937E	4,474,000	0.50	1.50	3.50	20.00	30.00
1937F	2,092,000	0.50	1.00	6.00	20.00	40.00
1937G	2,749,000	2.50	6.50	12.50	35.00	50.00
1937J	6,991,000	0.50	2.50	5.00	20.00	30.00
1938A	54,012,000	0.50	2.50	4.00	9.00	12.50
1938B	3,447,000	0.50	2.00	4.00	15.00	20.00
1938D	17,708,000	0.50	1.00	2.00	8.00	10.00
1938E	8,602,000	0.50	1.00	4.00	12.00	20.00
1938F	8,147,000	0.50	1.00	2.00	10.00	20.00
1938G	7,323,000	0.50	1.00	2.00	10.00	20.00
1938J	7,646,000	0.50	1.00	2.00	10.00	20.00
1939A	35,337,000	0.50	1.00	2.00	7.00	10.00
1939B	8,313,000	0.50	1.00	1.50	7.00	10.00
1939D	8,304,000	0.50	1.00	2.00	7.50	12.00
1939E	5,138,000	0.50	1.00	1.50	7.50	12.00
1939F	10,339,000	0.50	1.00	1.50	7.00	10.00
1939G	4,266,000	0.50	2.50	6.50	15.00	22.00
1939J	4,177,000	0.50	2.00	6.50	12.50	22.00
1936-1939 Common date proof	— Value: 150					

KM# 100 5 REICHSPFENNIG
2.5000 g., Zinc, 19 mm. **Obv:** Eagle above swastika within wreath **Rev:** Denomination, oak leaves below

Date	Mintage	F	VF	XF	Unc	BU
1940A	174,684,000	0.20	0.25	0.75	6.00	8.00
1940B	63,469,000	0.25	1.00	1.50	6.00	8.00
1940D	44,364,000	0.25	1.00	1.50	6.00	8.00
1940E	25,800,000	0.30	1.00	3.50	7.00	10.00
1940F	31,381,000	0.25	1.00	2.00	7.00	10.00
1940G	24,148,000	0.25	1.00	2.75	8.00	15.00
1940J	30,518,000	0.25	1.00	2.00	7.00	10.00
1941A	246,216,000	0.20	0.25	0.75	5.00	7.00
1941B	60,297,000	0.20	0.40	1.75	7.50	10.00
1941D	51,100,000	0.20	0.40	1.75	7.50	10.00
1941E	26,354,000	0.20	0.40	1.75	7.50	10.00
1941F	36,725,000	0.20	0.40	1.75	7.50	10.00
1941G	21,276,000	0.20	0.40	2.00	8.50	12.00
1941J	52,872,000	0.20	0.40	2.00	7.50	10.00
1942A	161,042,000	0.20	0.25	0.75	6.00	9.00
1942B	12,405,000	0.25	1.50	4.50	10.00	15.00
1942D	15,486,000	0.20	0.45	2.25	8.00	12.00
1942E	8,800,000	6.00	15.00	20.00	40.00	50.00
1942F	24,662,000	0.20	0.35	1.50	8.00	12.00
1942G	12,749,000	0.20	0.40	2.25	10.00	15.00
1943A	46,830,000	0.20	0.50	1.75	7.00	10.00
1943B	833,000	30.00	50.00	75.00	160	200
1943D	13,650,000	0.20	0.50	3.50	9.00	13.00
1943E	16,581,000	2.00	6.00	10.00	20.00	25.00
1943F	9,891,000	0.25	1.00	2.50	8.00	12.00
1943G	7,237,000	0.20	0.75	2.25	9.00	15.00
1944A	23,699,000	3.50	12.50	25.00	40.00	50.00
1944D	26,340,000	0.25	1.25	2.50	7.00	10.00
1944E	19,720,000	0.50	2.50	5.00	10.00	14.00
1944F	6,853,000	0.25	1.50	2.75	8.00	12.00
1944G	3,540,000	100	200	275	400	500
1940-1944 Common date proof	— Value: 225					

KM# 92 10 REICHSPFENNIG
4.0300 g., Aluminum-Bronze **Obv:** Eagle above swastika within wreath **Rev:** Denomination, oak leaves below

Date	Mintage	F	VF	XF	Unc	BU
1936A	Inc. below	20.00	40.00	60.00	100	120
1936E	245,000	90.00	150	200	300	375
1936G	129,000	175	225	300	450	700
1937A	36,830,000	0.50	1.00	2.25	12.00	20.00
1937D	6,882,000	0.50	2.00	3.50	12.00	22.00
1937E	3,786,000	2.00	9.00	18.00	45.00	60.00
1937F	5,934,000	1.00	2.50	6.00	25.00	40.00
1937G	2,131,000	1.00	5.50	9.00	30.00	60.00
1937J	4,439,000	1.00	2.00	5.00	20.00	30.00
1938A	70,068,000	0.50	1.00	2.00	7.00	12.00
1938B	7,852,000	1.00	2.00	4.50	15.00	20.00
1938D	16,990,000	0.50	1.00	2.00	9.00	16.00
1938E	10,739,000	0.50	1.00	2.50	10.00	16.00
1938F	12,307,000	0.50	2.00	2.75	11.00	18.00
1938G	8,584,000	0.50	2.00	3.00	12.00	22.00
1938J	10,389,000	0.50	2.00	2.75	12.00	20.00
1939A	40,171,000	0.50	2.00	2.25	9.00	15.00
1939B	7,814,000	0.50	2.00	2.25	10.00	16.00
1939D	11,307,000	0.50	2.00	2.25	12.00	20.00
1939E	5,079,000	1.00	2.00	6.50	15.00	20.00
1939F	6,993,000	0.50	2.00	3.00	12.00	20.00
1939G	5,532,000	1.00	4.50	9.00	16.00	22.00
1939J	5,557,000	0.50	2.00	2.50	12.00	20.00
1936-1939 Common date proof	— Value: 175					

KM# 101 10 REICHSPFENNIG
3.5200 g., Zinc, 21 mm. **Obv:** Eagle above swastika within wreath **Rev:** Denomination, oak leaves below

Date	Mintage	F	VF	XF	Unc	BU
1940A	212,948,000	0.20	0.40	1.75	8.00	15.00
1940B	76,274,000	0.20	0.75	3.00	12.00	20.00
1940D	45,434,000	0.20	0.75	2.50	12.00	20.00
1940E	34,350,000	0.20	0.75	2.50	12.00	25.00
1940F	27,603,000	0.20	1.50	6.00	17.50	40.00
1940G	27,308,000	0.20	1.50	8.00	25.00	50.00
1940J	41,678,000	0.20	1.25	2.50	12.00	25.00
1941A	240,284,000	0.20	0.40	1.50	7.00	14.00
1941B	70,747,000	0.20	0.75	3.00	9.00	15.00
1941D	77,560,000	0.20	0.75	3.50	12.00	20.00
1941E	36,548,000	0.20	0.75	3.50	12.00	20.00
1941F	42,834,000	0.20	0.75	3.50	12.00	20.00
1941G	28,765,000	0.20	2.25	9.00	25.00	40.00
1941J	30,525,000	0.20	0.75	2.50	12.00	25.00
1942A	184,545,000	0.20	0.30	0.75	9.00	15.00
1942B	16,329,000	1.00	3.00	12.00	30.00	50.00
1942D	40,852,000	0.20	1.25	3.50	12.00	25.00
1942E	18,334,000	1.00	2.00	12.00	30.00	50.00
1942F	32,690,000	0.20	0.50	3.50	12.00	25.00
1942G	20,295,000	1.00	2.00	12.00	35.00	60.00
1942J	29,957,000	0.50	1.75	3.50	12.00	25.00
1943A	157,357,000	0.20	1.50	2.50	9.00	15.00
1943B	11,940,000	2.50	7.50	14.00	30.00	60.00
1943D	17,304,000	0.25	1.75	4.50	16.00	25.00
1943E	10,445,000	2.50	7.50	14.00	35.00	60.00
1943F	24,804,000	0.25	2.50	5.00	20.00	25.00
1943G	3,618,000	4.00	14.00	35.00	80.00	150
1943J	1,821,000	25.00	45.00	85.00	200	300
1944A	84,164,000	0.20	1.00	2.50	10.00	15.00
1944B	40,781,000	0.50	1.50	2.50	12.00	20.00
1944D	30,369,000	0.50	1.50	2.50	12.00	20.00
1944E	29,963,000	0.50	2.00	4.50	12.00	20.00
1944F	19,639,000	0.50	2.50	5.00	14.00	25.00
1944G	13,023,000	0.75	3.50	10.00	30.00	50.00
1945A	7,112,000	5.00	12.50	30.00	90.00	150
1945E	4,897,000	15.00	35.00	80.00	140	200
1940-1945 Common date proof	— Value: 250					

KM# 87 50 REICHSPFENNIG
Aluminum **Obv:** Eagle above date **Rev:** Denomination, oak leaves below

Date	Mintage	F	VF	XF	Unc	BU
1935A	75,912,000	1.00	2.25	9.00	35.00	80.00
1935A Proof	— Value: 250					
1935D	19,688,000	1.00	2.25	12.00	60.00	100
1935D Proof	— Value: 250					
1935E	10,418,000	1.00	3.50	12.00	60.00	100
1935E Proof	— Value: 250					
1935F	14,061,000	1.00	2.25	12.00	60.00	100
1935F Proof	— Value: 250					
1935G	8,540,000	2.00	4.50	14.00	65.00	110
1935G Proof	— Value: 250					
1935J	11,438,000	2.00	4.50	14.00	65.00	110
1935J Proof	— Value: 250					

KM# 95 50 REICHSPFENNIG

Nickel **Obv:** Eagle above swastika within wreath
Rev: Denomination within circle, oak leaves and acorns below

Date	Mintage	F	VF	XF	Unc	BU
1938A	5,051,000	17.50	32.50	42.50	55.00	75.00
1938B	1,124,000	25.00	40.00	50.00	80.00	100
1938D	1,260,000	25.00	40.00	55.00	80.00	100
1938E	949,000	25.00	40.00	60.00	100	125
1938F	1,210,000	15.00	30.00	50.00	90.00	125
1938G	460,000	30.00	70.00	90.00	160	225
1938J	730,000	30.00	90.00	120	225	300
1939A	15,037,000	20.00	30.00	40.00	50.00	60.00
1939B	2,826,000	20.00	35.00	45.00	60.00	90.00
1939D	3,648,000	17.50	35.00	45.00	60.00	90.00
1939E	1,924,000	17.50	35.00	50.00	85.00	100
1939F	2,602,000	17.50	35.00	50.00	70.00	90.00
1939G	1,565,000	17.50	35.00	75.00	130	170
1939J	2,114,000	17.50	35.00	60.00	100	120
1938-1939 Common date proof	—	Value: 275				

KM# 96 50 REICHSPFENNIG

1.3400 g., Aluminum **Obv:** Eagle above swastika within wreath
Rev: Denomination, oak leaves below

Date	Mintage	F	VF	XF	Unc	BU
1939A	5,000,000	2.50	6.00	20.00	65.00	100
1939B	5,482,000	2.50	6.00	20.00	65.00	100
1939D	600,000	6.00	16.00	35.00	120	170
1939E	2,000,000	2.50	6.00	25.00	70.00	110
1939F	3,600,000	2.50	11.00	30.00	70.00	120
1939G	560,000	12.50	22.50	60.00	150	200
1939J	1,000,000	12.50	22.50	50.00	150	200
1940A	56,128,000	2.50	4.50	11.00	35.00	50.00
1940B	10,016,000	5.00	9.00	25.00	70.00	100
1940D	13,800,000	8.00	15.00	30.00	100	150
1940E	5,618,000	8.00	15.00	30.00	100	150
1940F	6,663,000	5.00	10.00	25.00	65.00	100
1940G	5,616,000	15.00	27.00	55.00	130	200
1940J	7,335,000	8.00	15.00	30.00	100	150
1941A	31,263,000	5.00	9.00	20.00	65.00	100
1941B	4,291,000	3.00	10.00	25.00	80.00	110
1941D	7,200,000	2.00	10.00	25.00	80.00	110
1941E	3,806,000	5.00	15.00	27.50	85.00	125
1941F	5,128,000	2.50	10.00	25.00	65.00	100
1941G	3,091,000	10.00	20.00	40.00	110	150
1941J	4,165,000	10.00	20.00	35.00	110	150
1942A	11,580,000	2.00	5.00	10.00	30.00	50.00
1942B	2,876,000	5.00	12.00	25.00	70.00	100
1942D	2,247,000	2.00	20.00	35.00	80.00	120
1942E	3,810,000	5.00	20.00	40.00	110	150
1942F	5,133,000	2.00	15.00	30.00	80.00	120
1942G	1,400,000	10.00	25.00	70.00	125	200
1943A	29,325,000	2.00	5.00	10.00	30.00	40.00
1943B	8,229,000	2.00	5.00	10.00	25.00	40.00
1943D	5,315,000	2.00	7.00	16.00	50.00	75.00
1943G	2,892,000	10.00	20.00	50.00	110	180
1943J	4,166,000	5.00	9.00	14.00	30.00	45.00
1944B	5,622,000	2.50	8.00	12.00	50.00	70.00
1944D	4,886,000	7.50	16.00	40.00	100	130
1944F	3,739,000	5.00	10.00	20.00	75.00	100
1944G	1,190,000	60.00	100	180	400	600
1940-1944 Common date proof	—	Value: 275				

KM# 78 REICHSMARK

4.8500 g., Nickel **Obv:** Denomination within wreath, date below
Rev: Eagle

Date	Mintage	F	VF	XF	Unc	BU
1933A	6,030,000	1.00	2.75	8.00	35.00	45.00
1933D	4,562,000	1.00	3.50	10.00	35.00	45.00
1933E	3,500,000	2.50	7.50	10.00	25.00	45.00
1933F	1,400,000	4.00	8.50	16.00	45.00	65.00
1933G	2,000,000	2.50	10.00	20.00	90.00	130
1934A	52,345,000	1.00	1.75	3.00	10.00	15.00
1934D	30,597,000	1.00	1.75	5.00	16.00	22.00

Date	Mintage	F	VF	XF	Unc	BU
1934E	15,135,000	1.00	3.00	7.00	16.00	22.00
1934F	23,672,000	1.00	2.75	5.00	15.00	20.00
1934G	13,252,000	1.50	5.00	10.00	20.00	25.00
1934J	16,820,000	1.00	3.50	7.50	16.00	20.00
1935A	57,896,000	1.00	2.50	5.00	12.50	15.00
1935J	3,621,000	10.00	15.00	30.00	110	150
1936A	20,287,000	1.25	4.50	8.00	20.00	25.00
1936D	4,940,000	2.50	7.50	15.00	40.00	50.00
1936E	3,200,000	10.00	15.00	35.00	110	150
1936F	2,075,000	20.00	30.00	50.00	110	150
1936G	620,000	30.00	75.00	150	225	275
1936J	2,975,000	7.50	15.00	30.00	110	150
1937A	49,976,000	1.00	1.75	3.00	9.00	13.00
1937D	10,529,000	2.00	5.00	10.00	20.00	30.00
1937E	2,926,000	4.00	12.50	22.50	50.00	70.00
1937F	6,221,000	4.00	12.50	22.50	65.00	90.00
1937G	2,143,000	3.00	9.00	16.00	45.00	70.00
1937J	4,721,000	3.00	9.00	16.00	60.00	90.00
1938A	9,829,000	2.00	5.00	12.00	30.00	45.00
1938E	2,073,000	5.00	18.00	35.00	90.00	130
1938F	2,739,000	6.00	20.00	25.00	75.00	100
1938G	4,381,000	15.00	35.00	70.00	140	225
1938J	1,269,000	30.00	65.00	100	160	250
1939A	52,150,000	6.00	12.50	16.00	40.00	50.00
1939B	9,836,000	60.00	110	160	275	375
1939D	12,522,000	10.00	22.50	37.50	80.00	100
1939E	6,570,000	25.00	40.00	70.00	130	160
1939F	10,033,000	15.00	25.00	45.00	110	150
1939G	5,475,000	70.00	140	200	350	450
1939J	8,478,000	20.00	40.00	60.00	120	175
1933-1939 Common date proof	—	Value: 250				

KM# 79 2 REICHSMARK

8.0000 g., 0.6250 Silver 0.1607 oz. ASW, 27 mm.
Subject: 450th Anniversary - Birth of Martin Luther **Obv:** Eagle above denomination **Rev:** Head left, dates below

Date	Mintage	F	VF	XF	Unc	BU
1933A	542,000	10.00	22.50	30.00	50.00	70.00
1933A Proof	—	Value: 250				
1933D	141,000	12.00	25.00	35.00	60.00	75.00
1933D Proof	—	Value: 250				
1933E	75,000	15.00	30.00	40.00	60.00	90.00
1933E Proof	—	Value: 275				
1933F	100,000	12.00	25.00	35.00	60.00	80.00
1933F Proof	—	Value: 275				
1933G	61,000	16.00	30.00	42.00	75.00	120
1933G Proof	—	Value: 275				
1933J	82,000	12.00	25.00	40.00	60.00	85.00
1933J Proof	—	Value: 265				

KM# 81 2 REICHSMARK

8.0000 g., 0.6250 Silver 0.1607 oz. ASW, 27 mm. **Subject:** 1st Anniversary - Nazi Rule March 21, 1933 **Obv:** Eagle divides dates, denomination below **Rev:** Potsdam Garrison Church

Date	Mintage	F	VF	XF	Unc	BU
1934A	2,710,000	4.50	10.00	22.00	50.00	90.00
1934A Proof	—	Value: 250				
1934D	703,000	5.50	12.00	28.00	70.00	110
1934D Proof	—	Value: 250				
1934E	373,000	7.50	16.50	40.00	100	130
1934E Proof	—	Value: 250				
1934F	502,000	6.00	12.00	32.50	75.00	110
1934F Proof	—	Value: 250				
1934G	305,000	7.00	15.00	45.00	110	140
1934G Proof	—	Value: 250				
1934J	409,000	7.00	15.00	40.00	100	120
1934J Proof	—	Value: 250				

KM# 84 2 REICHSMARK

8.0000 g., 0.6250 Silver 0.1607 oz. ASW, 27 mm.

Subject: 175th Anniversary - Birth of Schiller **Obv:** Eagle, oak leaves flank, denomination below **Rev:** Head left, date below

Date	Mintage	F	VF	XF	Unc	BU
1934F	300,000	40.00	70.00	90.00	120	145
1934F Proof	—	Value: 250				

KM# 93 2 REICHSMARK

8.0000 g., 0.6250 Silver 0.1607 oz. ASW, 25 mm.
Subject: Swastika-Hindenburg Issue **Obv:** Eagle above swastika within wreath **Rev:** Large head, right

Date	Mintage	F	VF	XF	Unc	BU
1936D	840,000	4.00	7.00	20.00	60.00	90.00
1936E	Inc. below	9.00	28.00	45.00	110	175
1936G	Inc. below	8.00	18.00	30.00	80.00	145
1936J	Inc. below	30.00	70.00	160	400	550
1937A	23,425,000	2.50	3.00	4.50	11.00	16.00
1937D	6,190,000	2.50	3.00	4.50	16.00	20.00
1937E	3,725,000	2.50	3.50	6.00	22.00	30.00
1937F	5,015,000	2.50	3.00	6.00	16.00	22.00
1937G	1,913,000	2.50	4.50	10.00	30.00	45.00
1937J	2,756,000	2.50	3.50	5.50	20.00	35.00
1938A	13,201,000	2.50	3.00	5.00	11.00	20.00
1938B	13,163,000	2.50	3.00	5.00	15.00	22.00
1938D	3,711,000	2.50	3.00	5.00	16.00	30.00
1938E	4,731,000	2.50	3.00	6.00	16.00	30.00
1938F	1,882,000	3.00	4.00	6.50	20.00	40.00
1938G	2,313,000	2.50	3.50	5.50	17.00	30.00
1938J	2,306,000	2.50	3.50	5.50	17.00	30.00
1939A	26,855,000	2.25	3.00	4.50	11.00	15.00
1939B	3,522,000	2.50	3.25	5.50	14.00	30.00
1939D	5,357,000	2.50	3.25	5.00	14.00	25.00
1939E	251,000	15.00	30.00	45.00	100	160
1939F	3,180,000	2.50	3.25	5.50	14.00	30.00
1939G	2,305,000	2.50	3.50	7.50	20.00	40.00
1939J	3,414,000	2.50	3.25	7.00	17.50	30.00
1936-1939 Common date proof	—	Value: 225				

KM# 80 5 REICHSMARK

13.8800 g., 0.9000 Silver 0.4016 oz. ASW, 29 mm.
Subject: 450th Anniversary - Birth of Martin Luther **Obv:** Eagle, denomination below **Rev:** Head left, dates below

Date	Mintage	F	VF	XF	Unc	BU
1933A	108,000	60.00	100	150	200	275
1933A Proof	—	Value: 400				
1933D	28,000	60.00	125	175	200	300
1933D Proof	—	Value: 450				
1933E	12,000	80.00	145	190	225	300
1933E Proof	—	Value: 450				
1933F	20,000	60.00	125	160	200	300
1933F Proof	—	Value: 525				
1933G	12,000	100	175	250	300	400
1933G Proof	—	Value: 550				
1933J	16,000	85.00	145	180	250	350
1933J Proof	—	Value: 550				

KM# 82 5 REICHSMARK

13.8800 g., 0.9000 Silver 0.4016 oz. ASW, 29 mm.
Subject: 1st Anniversary - Nazi Rule **Obv:** Eagle divides date, denomination below **Rev:** Potsdam Garrison Church divides date

Date	Mintage	F	VF	XF	Unc	BU
1934A	2,168,000	10.00	12.00	40.00	100	120
1934D	562,000	10.00	15.00	45.00	120	140
1934E	298,000	10.00	18.00	50.00	150	180
1934F	401,000	10.00	14.00	40.00	120	160
1934G	244,000	10.00	20.00	50.00	160	190
1934J	327,000	10.00	18.00	45.00	160	190

Date	Mintage	F	VF	XF	Unc	BU
1934 Proof	—	Value: 300				

Note: Impaired proofs are common and valued around $200

KM# 83 5 REICHSMARK
13.8800 g., 0.9000 Silver 0.4016 oz. ASW, 29 mm.
Subject: 1st Anniversary - Nazi Rule **Obv:** Eagle divides date, denomination below **Rev:** Potsdam Garrison Church, date 21 MARZ 1933 dropped

Date	Mintage	F	VF	XF	Unc	BU
1934A	14,526,000	5.00	6.00	10.00	35.00	40.00
1934D	6,303,000	5.00	6.00	13.00	40.00	50.00
1934E	2,739,000	5.00	7.00	15.00	55.00	65.00
1934F	4,844,000	5.00	6.00	13.00	40.00	50.00
1934G	2,304,000	5.00	7.50	15.00	55.00	65.00
1934J	4,294,000	5.00	6.50	14.00	50.00	60.00
1935A	23,407,000	4.00	5.00	9.00	30.00	40.00
1935D	3,539,000	5.00	6.50	14.00	40.00	50.00
1935E	2,476,000	5.00	7.50	15.00	55.00	65.00
1935F	2,177,000	5.00	7.50	17.50	60.00	70.00
1935G	1,966,000	5.00	7.50	16.00	65.00	85.00
1935J	1,425,000	6.00	10.00	22.50	90.00	115
1934-1935 Common date proof	—	Value: 275				

KM# 85 5 REICHSMARK
13.8800 g., 0.9000 Silver 0.4016 oz. ASW, 29 mm.
Subject: 175th Anniversary - Birth of Schiller **Obv:** Eagle, oak leaves flank, denomination below **Rev:** Head left, dates below

Date	Mintage	F	VF	XF	Unc	BU
1934F	100,000	150	200	285	425	475
1934F Proof	—	Value: 750				

KM# 86 5 REICHSMARK
13.8800 g., 0.9000 Silver 0.4016 oz. ASW, 29 mm.
Subject: Hindenburg issue **Obv:** Eagle divides date, denomination below **Rev:** Large head, right

Date	Mintage	F	VF	XF	Unc	BU
1935A	19,325,000	4.00	5.00	9.00	16.00	20.00
1935D	6,596,000	4.00	6.00	9.00	20.00	25.00
1935E	3,260,000	4.00	6.00	11.00	25.00	30.00
1935F	4,372,000	4.00	6.00	9.00	25.00	30.00
1935G	2,371,000	4.00	6.50	12.50	35.00	45.00
1935J	2,830,000	4.00	6.50	12.50	40.00	60.00
1936A	30,611,000	4.00	5.50	9.00	16.00	20.00
1936D	7,032,000	4.00	6.00	9.00	20.00	25.00
1936E	3,320,000	4.00	6.00	11.00	25.00	30.00
1936F	4,926,000	4.00	6.00	11.00	25.00	30.00
1936G	2,734,000	4.00	6.50	15.00	50.00	70.00
1936J	3,706,000	4.00	6.50	14.00	40.00	50.00
1935-1936 Common date proof	—	Value: 250				

KM# 94 5 REICHSMARK
13.8800 g., 0.9000 Silver 0.4016 oz. ASW, 29 mm.
Subject: Swastika-Hindenburg Issue **Obv:** Eagle above swastika within wreath **Rev:** Large head, right

Date	Mintage	F	VF	XF	Unc	BU
1936A	8,430,000	4.00	6.00	10.00	20.00	30.00
1936D	1,872,000	4.00	7.00	14.00	30.00	40.00
1936E	870,000	5.00	8.00	16.00	35.00	50.00
1936F	1,732,000	4.00	7.00	14.00	40.00	50.00
1936G	743,000	5.00	9.00	20.00	65.00	80.00
1936J	640,000	8.00	18.00	30.00	90.00	110
1937A	6,662,000	4.00	6.00	9.00	20.00	30.00
1937D	2,173,000	4.00	6.00	10.00	25.00	35.00
1937E	1,490,000	5.00	8.00	14.00	30.00	50.00
1937F	1,578,000	4.00	7.50	14.00	35.00	45.00
1937G	1,472,000	5.00	8.00	14.00	35.00	45.00
1937J	2,191,000	4.00	6.00	12.50	30.00	40.00
1938A	6,789,000	4.00	6.00	9.00	20.00	25.00
1938D	1,304,000	4.00	6.00	12.50	25.00	35.00
1938E	425,000	5.00	8.00	14.00	40.00	60.00
1938F	740,000	4.00	6.50	12.50	40.00	60.00
1938G	861,000	4.00	7.50	14.00	40.00	60.00
1938J	1,302,000	4.00	6.50	12.50	30.00	40.00
1939A	3,428,000	4.00	7.50	13.00	25.00	40.00
1939B	1,942,000	5.00	8.00	14.00	25.00	50.00
1939D	1,216,000	7.00	11.00	18.00	40.00	50.00
1939E	1,320,000	15.00	20.00	40.00	80.00	110
1939F	1,060,000	7.50	12.50	25.00	70.00	100
1939G	567,000	12.50	20.00	35.00	100	140
1939J	1,710,000	5.00	10.00	20.00	60.00	75.00
1936-1939 Common date proof	—	Value: 250				

MILITARY COINAGE
WWII
KM# 98 5 REICHSPFENNIG
Zinc **Note:** Circulated only in occupied territories.

Date	Mintage	F	VF	XF	Unc	BU
1940A	—	15.00	20.00	30.00	60.00	90.00
1940B	3,020,000	100	160	325	550	750
1940D	—	30.00	45.00	75.00	120	190
1940E	2,445,000	100	200	325	550	750
1940F	—	200	300	425	675	900
1940G	—	6,000	10,000	—	—	—
1940J	—	100	225	325	500	750
1941A	—	300	500	800	1,500	2,500
1941F	—	5,000	10,000	—	—	—
1940-1941 Common date proof	—	Value: 850				

KM# 99 10 REICHSPFENNIG
Zinc **Rev:** Eagle head above center hole, denomination below
Note: Circulated only in occupied territories.

Date	Mintage	F	VF	XF	Unc	BU
1940A	—	15.00	20.00	30.00	50.00	80.00
1940B	840,000	200	325	650	950	1,250
1940D	—	5,000	6,000	10,000	15,000	20,000
1940E	5,100,000	3,000	4,500	6,000	10,000	12,000
1940F	—	300	450	1,250	1,750	2,250
1940G	150,000	100	125	225	400	550
1940J	—	400	900	1,400	2,500	2,750
1941A	—	600	1,100	1,800	2,500	2,750
1941F 2 known	—	—	12,000	—	15,000	—
1940-1941 Proof	—	Value: 1,150				

ALLIED OCCUPATION
POST WW II COINAGE
KM# A102 REICHSPFENNIG
Zinc **Obv:** Modified design, swastika and wreath removed
Rev: Eagle missing tail feathers

Date	Mintage	F	VF	XF	Unc	BU
1944D	—	—	—	10,000	—	—
Note: Possibly a pattern, only one known						

KM# A103 REICHSPFENNIG
Zinc **Obv:** Eagle above date **Rev:** Denomination

Date	Mintage	F	VF	XF	Unc	BU
1945F	2,984,000	6.00	12.00	20.00	40.00	60.00
1946F	1,633,000	20.00	40.00	70.00	140	165
1946G	1,500,000	40.00	70.00	110	170	225
1945-1946 Common date proof	—	Value: 250				

KM# A105 5 REICHSPFENNIG
Zinc **Obv:** Eagle, date below **Rev:** Denomination

Date	Mintage	F	VF	XF	Unc	BU
1947A	—	3.00	7.50	15.00	40.00	55.00
1947D	16,528,000	3.00	5.00	7.00	20.00	40.00
1948A	—	5.00	12.50	20.00	45.00	70.00
1948E	7,666,000	150	300	400	700	850
1947-1948 Proof	—	Value: 250				

KM# A104 10 REICHSPFENNIG
Zinc **Obv:** Eagle **Rev:** Denomination

Date	Mintage	F	VF	XF	Unc	BU
1945F	5,942,000	4.50	7.50	15.00	35.00	60.00
1946F	3,738,000	15.00	25.00	35.00	90.00	120
1946G	1,600,000	40.00	70.00	120	200	300
1947A	—	4.50	10.00	20.00	35.00	65.00
1947E	2,612,000	250	350	575	775	950
1947F	1,269,000	2.00	4.00	9.00	20.00	28.00
1948A	—	5.00	18.00	22.50	35.00	55.00
1948F	19,579,000	2.00	4.00	9.00	30.00	40.00
1946-1948 Common date proof	—	Value: 225				

PATTERNS
Including off metal strikes

KM#	Date	Mintage	Identification	Mkt Val
Pn354	1933	—	Mark. Nickel. Legend above eagle. PROBE.	300
Pn355	1933A	—	Mark. Nickel. "PROBE."	300
Pn356	1933A	—	Mark. Nickel. Rays above eagle.	300
Pn357	1933A	—	Mark. Nickel. Plain above eagle.	300
Pn358	1933A	—	Mark. Nickel. Large 1 with rays. "PROBE."	300
Pn359	1933A	—	Mark. Nickel. "PROBE."	300
Pn360	1933J	—	Mark. Nickel. KM78.	300
PnA361	1933/6	—	5 Mark. Copper-Nickel. Martin Luther. Eagle. KM94.	—
Pn361	1934	—	2 Mark. KM79. KM81.	—
Pn362	1934A	—	2 Mark. Silver. KM84.	—
Pn363	NDD	—	5 Mark. Silver. Similar to Pn351 edge. KM80.	—
Pn364	1934A	—	5 Mark. Silver. KM85. "PROBE".	—
Pn365	1934A	—	5 Pfennig. Brass. KM91.	—
Pn366	1934A	—	5 Pfennig. Aluminum-Bronze. KM91.1. "PROBE."	—
Pn367	1935A	—	50 Pfennig. Aluminum.	—
Pn370	1935A	—	5 Mark. Silver. "PROBE."	—
Pn371	1935A	—	5 Mark. Silver. "PROBE."	—
Pn368	1935A	—	50 Pfennig. Oak leaves next to date. "PROBE." Wavy edge.	—
Pn369	1935E	—	Mark. Nickel. KM78.	—
Pn372	1935A	—	5 Mark. Silver. Masses entering. "PROBE."	—
Pn373	1935A	—	5 Mark. 0.9000 Silver. Family entering. "PROBE."	—
Pn374	1935A	—	5 Mark. Electrotype.	—
Pn375	1936D	—	Pfennig. Copper Plated Iron. KM89.	—
PnA375	1936D	—	Reichspfennig. Copper Plated Iron. KM30.	—
Pn376	1937	—	5 Pfennig. Iron. KM91. Hindenburg.	—
Pn377	1937A	—	50 Pfennig. Nickel. KM95. "PROBE."	—
Pn378	1939A	—	5 Pfennig. Zinc. KM100.	—
Pn379	1939A	—	Mark. Nickel. "PROBE" on rim.	—
Pn380	1939A	—	Mark. Pn379. Pn381.	—
Pn381	1939A	—	Mark.	225
Pn382	1939A	—	Mark. Aluminum. KM78. Pn381.	—
Pn383	1939/40	—	Mark. Iron. "PROBE." Copper-nickel plated.	300
Pn384	1940	—	Mark. Silver.	400
Pn385	1942	—	5 Reichsmark. Silvered Copper.	—
Pn386	1942	—	5 Reichsmark. Copper. Klippe.	—
Pn388	1942A	—	5 Mark. Silvered Copper, Steel helmet in laurel wreath.	—
Pn387	1942	—	5 Reichsmark. Silver. Klippe.	6,500
PnB390	1946G	—	10 Pfennig. Brass.	900
PnA389	1946G	—	Pfennig. Aluminum.	—
Pn390	1947J	—	50 Pfennig. Aluminum.	—
Pn391	1947D	—	5 Pfennig. Aluminum.	—
Pn394	1947D	—	10 Pfennig. Aluminum.	—
PnC389	1947A	—	5 Pfennig. Aluminum. Reeded edge.	—
PnC390	1947A	—	10 Pfennig. Dur-Aluminum.	—
PnB389	1947J	—	5 Pfennig. Zinc. without swastika. KM100.	3,350
PnD389	1947A	—	10 Pfennig. Zinc. with slavic 7. KM104	6,000
Pn389	1947J	—	5 Pfennig. Zinc. Without swastika. KM101.	3,350
Pn395	1947D	—	10 Pfennig. Iron. Copper-nickel plated.	—
Pn392	1947	—	5 Pfennig. Brass Plated Aluminum.	—
Pn393	1947D	—	5 Pfennig. Copper-Nickel Plated Iron. Copper-nickel plated.	—
PnA390	1947D	—	10 Pfennig. Aluminum. Plain edge.	—
Pn396	1948F	—	10 Pfennig. Zinc.	—

GERMANY-FEDERAL REPUBLIC

1949-

The Federal Republic of Germany, located in north-central Europe, has an area of 137,744 sq. mi. (356,910 sq. km.) and a population of 81.1 million. Capital: Berlin. The economy centers about one of the world's foremost industrial establishments. Machinery, motor vehicles, iron, steel, yarns and fabrics are exported.

During the post-Normandy phase of World War II, Allied troops occupied the western German provinces of Schleswig-Holstein, Hamburg, Lower Saxony, Bremen, North Rhine-Westphalia, Hesse, Rhineland-Palatinate, Baden-Wurttemberg, Bavaria and Saarland. The conquered provinces were divided into American, British and French occupation zones. Five eastern German provinces were occupied and administered by the forces of the Soviet Union.

The post-World War II division of Germany was ended Oct. 3, 1990, when the German Democratic Republic (East Germany) ceased to exist and its five constituent provinces were formally admitted to the Federal Republic of Germany. An election Dec. 2, 1990, chose representatives to the united federal parliament (Bundestag), which then conducted its opening session in Berlin in the old Reichstag building. Berlin is again the capital of a United Germany.

MINT MARKS
A - Berlin
D - Munich
F - Stuttgart
G - Karlsruhe
J - Hamburg

MONETARY SYSTEM
100 Pfennig = 1 Deutsche Mark (DM)

FEDERAL REPUBLIC

STANDARD COINAGE

KM# A101 PFENNIG
Bronze Clad Steel, 16.5 mm. **Obv. Leg.:** BANK DEUTSCHER LÄNDER

Date	Mintage	F	VF	XF	Unc	BU
1948D	46,325,000	—	0.50	15.00	40.00	—
1948F	68,203,000	—	0.50	8.00	32.50	—
1948F Proof	250	Value: 150				
1948G	45,604,000	—	0.50	15.00	60.00	—
1948J	79,304,000	—	0.50	15.00	50.00	—
1949D	99,863,000	—	0.50	6.00	27.50	—
1949D Proof	—	Value: 100				
1949F	70,900,000	—	0.50	6.00	22.50	—
1949F Proof	250	Value: 60.00				
1949G	70,950,000	—	0.50	10.00	40.00	—
1949J	101,932,000	—	0.50	6.00	27.50	—
1949J Proof	—	Value: 85.00				

KM# 105 PFENNIG
2.0000 g., Copper Plated Steel, 16.5 mm. **Obv:** Five oak leaves, date below **Obv. Leg.:** BUNDES REPUBLIK DEUTSCHLAND **Rev:** Denomination

Date	Mintage	F	VF	XF	Unc	BU
1950D	772,592,000	—	—	0.10	2.00	—
1950F	898,277,000	—	—	0.10	2.00	—
1950F Proof	620	Value: 27.50				
1950G	515,673,000	—	—	0.10	3.00	—
1950G Proof	1,800	Value: 5.00				
1950J	784,424,000	—	—	0.10	2.00	—
1950J Proof	—	Value: 12.00				
1966D	65,063,000	—	—	0.10	3.00	—
1966F	75,031,000	—	—	0.10	3.00	—
1966F Proof	100	Value: 35.00				
1966G	48,261,000	—	—	0.10	5.00	—
1966G Proof	3,070	Value: 4.00				
1966J	66,842,000	—	—	0.10	3.00	—
1966J Proof	1,000	Value: 8.00				
1967D	39,082,000	—	0.10	2.00	8.00	—
1967F	45,003,000	—	0.10	1.50	8.00	—
1967F Proof	1,500	Value: 6.00				
1967G	20,787,000	—	0.20	4.50	17.00	—
1967G Proof	4,500	Value: 3.50				
1967J	42,583,000	—	0.10	1.50	8.00	—
1967J Proof	1,500	Value: 8.00				
1968D	32,796,999	—	0.10	1.50	7.00	—
1968F	26,338,000	—	0.10	1.50	7.00	—
1968F Proof	3,000	Value: 5.00				
1968G	20,382,000	—	0.10	1.50	8.00	—
1968G Proof	6,023	Value: 4.00				
1968J	23,414,000	—	0.10	1.50	8.00	—
1968J Proof	2,000	Value: 6.50				
1969D	78,177,000	—	—	0.10	1.00	—
1969F	90,172,000	—	—	0.10	1.00	—
1969F Proof	5,100	Value: 1.50				
1969G	61,836,000	—	—	0.10	2.00	—
1969G Proof	8,700	Value: 1.25				
1969J	80,221,000	—	—	0.10	1.00	—
1969J Proof	5,000	Value: 1.50				
1970D	91,151,000	—	—	0.10	1.00	—
1970F	105,236,000	—	—	0.10	1.00	—
1970F Proof	5,240	Value: 1.50				
1970G	82,421,000	—	—	0.10	1.00	—
1970G Proof	10,200	Value: 1.00				
1970 Small J	93,455,000	—	—	0.10	1.00	—
1970 Large J	Inc. above	—	—	0.10	1.00	—
1970J Proof	5,000	Value: 1.50				

Date	Mintage	F	VF	XF	Unc	BU
1971D	116,612,000	—	—	0.10	0.50	—
1971D Proof	8,000	Value: 1.00				
1971F	157,393,000	—	—	0.10	0.50	—
1971F Proof	8,000	Value: 1.00				
1971G	77,674,000	—	—	0.10	1.00	—
1971G Proof	10,200	Value: 1.00				
1971J	120,218,000	—	—	0.10	0.50	—
1971J Proof	8,000	Value: 1.00				
1972D	90,696,000	—	—	0.10	0.25	—
1972D Proof	8,000	Value: 1.00				
1972F	105,006,000	—	—	0.10	0.25	—
1972F Proof	8,000	Value: 1.00				
1972G	60,660,000	—	—	0.10	0.25	—
1972G Proof	10,000	Value: 1.00				
1972J	93,492,000	—	—	0.10	0.25	—
1972J Proof	8,000	Value: 1.00				
1973D	38,976,000	—	—	0.10	0.25	—
1973D Proof	9,000	Value: 1.00				
1973F	45,006,000	—	—	0.10	0.25	—
1973F Proof	9,000	Value: 1.00				
1973G	25,811,000	—	—	0.10	0.25	—
1973G Proof	9,000	Value: 1.00				
1973J	40,057,000	—	—	0.10	0.25	—
1973J Proof	9,000	Value: 1.00				
1974D	90,951,000	—	—	0.10	0.25	—
1974D Proof	35,000	Value: 0.40				
1974F	105,091,000	—	—	0.10	0.25	—
1974F Proof	35,000	Value: 0.40				
1974G	60,548,000	—	—	0.10	0.25	—
1974G Proof	35,000	Value: 0.40				
1974J	93,527,000	—	—	0.10	0.25	—
1974J Proof	35,000	Value: 0.40				
1975D	91,053,000	—	—	0.10	0.25	—
1975D Proof	43,000	Value: 0.40				
1975F	105,007,000	—	—	0.10	0.25	—
1975F Proof	43,000	Value: 0.40				
1975G	60,704,000	—	—	0.10	0.25	—
1975G Proof	43,000	Value: 0.40				
1975J	93,495,000	—	—	0.10	0.25	—
1975J Proof	43,000	Value: 0.40				
1976D	130,227,000	—	—	0.10	0.25	—
1976D Proof	43,000	Value: 0.40				
1976F	150,037,000	—	—	0.10	0.25	—
1976F Proof	43,000	Value: 0.40				
1976G	86,586,000	—	—	0.10	0.25	—
1976G Proof	43,000	Value: 0.40				
1976J	133,500,000	—	—	0.10	0.25	—
1976J Proof	43,000	Value: 0.40				
1977D	143,000,000	—	—	0.10	0.25	—
1977D Proof	52,000	Value: 0.40				
1977F	165,000,000	—	—	0.10	0.25	—
1977F Proof	51,000	Value: 0.40				
1977G	95,201,000	—	—	0.10	0.25	—
1977G Proof	51,000	Value: 0.40				
1977J	146,788,000	—	—	0.10	0.25	—
1977J Proof	51,000	Value: 0.40				
1978D	156,000,000	—	—	0.10	0.25	—
1978D Proof	54,000	Value: 0.40				
1978F	180,000,000	—	—	0.10	0.25	—
1978F Proof	54,000	Value: 0.40				
1978G	103,800,000	—	—	0.10	0.25	—
1978G Proof	54,000	Value: 0.40				
1978J	160,200,000	—	—	0.10	0.25	—
1978J Proof	54,000	Value: 0.40				
1979D	156,000,000	—	—	0.10	0.25	—
1979D Proof	89,000	Value: 0.40				
1979F	180,000,000	—	—	0.10	0.25	—
1979F Proof	89,000	Value: 0.40				
1979G	103,800,000	—	—	0.10	0.25	—
1979G Proof	89,000	Value: 0.40				
1979J	160,200,000	—	—	0.10	0.25	—
1979J Proof	89,000	Value: 0.40				
1980D	200,080,000	—	—	0.10	0.25	—
1980D Proof	110,000	Value: 0.40				
1980F	200,620,000	—	—	0.10	0.25	—
1980F Proof	110,000	Value: 0.40				
1980G	71,940,000	—	—	0.10	0.25	—
1980G Proof	110,000	Value: 0.40				
1980J	143,110,000	—	—	0.10	0.25	—
1980J Proof	110,000	Value: 0.40				
1981D	169,550,000	—	—	0.10	0.25	—
1981D Proof	91,000	Value: 0.40				
1981F	274,010,000	—	—	0.10	0.25	—
1981F Proof	91,000	Value: 0.40				
1981G	178,010,000	—	—	0.10	0.25	—
1981G Proof	91,000	Value: 0.40				
1981J	189,090,000	—	—	0.10	0.25	—
1981J Proof	91,000	Value: 0.40				
1982D	130,090,000	—	—	0.10	0.20	—
1982D Proof	78,000	Value: 0.40				
1982F	108,390,000	—	—	0.10	0.20	—
1982F Proof	78,000	Value: 0.40				
1982G	77,740,000	—	—	0.10	0.20	—
1982G Proof	78,000	Value: 0.40				
1982J	124,720,000	—	—	0.10	0.20	—
1982J Proof	78,000	Value: 0.40				
1983D	46,800,000	—	—	0.10	0.20	—
1983D Proof	75,000	Value: 0.40				
1983F	54,000,000	—	—	0.10	0.20	—
1983F Proof	75,000	Value: 0.40				
1983G	31,140,000	—	—	0.10	0.20	—
1983G Proof	75,000	Value: 0.40				

Date	Mintage	F	VF	XF	Unc	BU
1983J	48,060,000	—		0.10	0.20	—
1983J Proof	75,000	Value: 0.40				
1984D	58,500,000	—		0.10	0.20	—
1984D Proof	64,000	Value: 0.40				
1984F	67,500,000	—		0.10	0.20	—
1984F Proof	64,000	Value: 0.40				
1984G	38,900,000	—		0.10	0.20	—
1984G Proof	64,000	Value: 0.40				
1984J	60,100,000	—		0.10	0.20	—
1984J Proof	64,000	Value: 0.40				
1985D	19,500,000	—		0.10	0.20	—
1985D Proof	56,000	Value: 0.40				
1985F	22,500,000	—		0.10	0.20	—
1985F Proof	54,000	Value: 0.40				
1985G	13,000,000	—			0.10	—
1985G Proof	55,000	Value: 0.40				
1985J	20,000,000	—			0.10	—
1985J Proof	54,000	Value: 0.40				
1986D	39,000,000	—			0.10	—
1986D Proof	44,000	Value: 0.40				
1986F	45,000,000	—			0.10	—
1986F Proof	44,000	Value: 0.40				
1986G	25,900,000	—			0.10	—
1986G Proof	44,000	Value: 0.40				
1986J	40,100,000	—			0.10	—
1986J Proof	44,000	Value: 0.40				
1987D	6,500,000	—			0.10	—
1987D Proof	45,000	Value: 0.40				
1987F	7,500,000	—			0.10	—
1987F Proof	45,000	Value: 0.40				
1987G	4,330,000	—			0.10	—
1987G Proof	45,000	Value: 0.40				
1987J	6,680,000	—			0.10	—
1987J Proof	45,000	Value: 0.40				
1988D	52,000,000	—			0.10	—
1988D Proof	45,000	Value: 0.40				
1988F	60,000,000	—			0.10	—
1988F Proof	45,000	Value: 0.40				
1988G	34,600,000	—			0.10	—
1988G Proof	44,000	Value: 0.40				
1988J	53,400,000	—			0.10	—
1988J Proof	45,000	Value: 0.40				
1989D	104,000,000	—			0.10	—
1989D Proof	45,000	Value: 0.40				
1989F	120,000,000	—			0.10	—
1989F Proof	45,000	Value: 0.40				
1989G	69,200,000	—			0.10	—
1989G Proof	45,000	Value: 0.40				
1989J	106,800,000	—			0.10	—
1989J Proof	45,000	Value: 0.40				
1990D	169,000,000	—			0.10	—
1990D Proof	45,000	Value: 0.40				
1990F	195,000,000	—			0.10	—
1990F Proof	45,000	Value: 0.40				
1990G	112,450,000	—			0.10	—
1990G Proof	45,000	Value: 0.40				
1990J	173,550,000	—			0.10	—
1990J Proof	45,000	Value: 0.40				
1991A	260,000,000	—			0.10	—
1991A Proof	45,000	Value: 0.40				
1991D	273,000,000	—			0.10	—
1991D Proof	45,000	Value: 0.40				
1991F	312,000,000	—			0.10	—
1991F Proof	45,000	Value: 0.40				
1991G	182,000,000	—			0.10	—
1991G Proof	45,000	Value: 0.40				
1991J	273,000,000	—			0.10	—
1991J Proof	45,000	Value: 0.40				
1992A	40,000,000	—			0.10	—
1992A Proof	45,000	Value: 0.40				
1992D	42,000,000	—			0.10	—
1992D Proof	45,000	Value: 0.40				
1992F	48,000,000	—			0.10	—
1992F Proof	45,000	Value: 0.40				
1992G	28,000,000	—			0.10	—
1992G Proof	45,000	Value: 0.40				
1992J	42,000,000	—			0.10	—
1992J Proof	45,000	Value: 0.40				
1993A	40,000,000	—			0.10	—
1993A Proof	45,000	Value: 0.40				
1993D	42,000,000	—			0.10	—
1993D Proof	45,000	Value: 0.40				
1993F	48,000,000	—			0.10	—
1993F Proof	45,000	Value: 0.40				
1993G	28,000,000	—			0.10	—
1993G Proof	45,000	Value: 0.40				
1993J	42,000,000	—			0.10	—
1993J Proof	45,000	Value: 0.40				
1994A	100,000,000	—			0.10	—
1994A Proof	45,000	Value: 0.40				
1994D	105,000,000	—			0.10	—
1994D Proof	45,000	Value: 0.40				
1994F	120,000,000	—			0.10	—
1994F Proof	45,000	Value: 0.40				
1994G	70,000,000	—			0.10	—
1994G Proof	45,000	Value: 0.40				
1994J	105,000,000	—			0.10	—
1994J Proof	45,000	Value: 0.40				
1995A	100,000,000	—			0.15	—
1995A Proof	45,000	Value: 0.45				
1995D	105,000,000	—			0.15	—
1995D Proof	45,000	Value: 0.45				
1995F	120,000,000	—			0.15	—
1995F Proof	45,000	Value: 0.45				
1995G	70,000,000	—			0.15	—
1995G Proof	45,000	Value: 0.45				
1995J	105,000,000	—			0.15	—
1995J Proof	45,000	Value: 0.45				
1996A	80,000,000	—			0.20	—
1996A Proof	45,000	Value: 0.50				
1996D	84,000,000	—			0.20	—
1996D Proof	45,000	Value: 0.50				
1996F	96,000,000	—			0.20	—
1996F Proof	45,000	Value: 0.50				
1996G	56,000,000	—			0.20	—
1996G Proof	45,000	Value: 0.50				
1996J	84,000,000	—			0.20	—
1996J Proof	45,000	Value: 0.50				
1997A In sets only	70,000	—			1.75	—
1997A Proof	45,000	Value: 2.00				
1997D In sets only	70,000	—			1.75	—
1997D Proof	45,000	Value: 2.00				
1997F In sets only	70,000	—			1.75	—
1997F Proof	45,000	Value: 2.00				
1997G In sets only	70,000	—			1.75	—
1997G Proof	45,000	Value: 2.00				
1997J In sets only	70,000	—			1.75	—
1997J Proof	45,000	Value: 2.00				
1998A In sets only	70,000	—			1.75	—
1998A Proof	45,000	Value: 2.00				
1998D In sets only	70,000	—			1.75	—
1998D Proof	45,000	Value: 2.00				
1998F In sets only	70,000	—			1.75	—
1998F Proof	45,000	Value: 2.00				
1998G In sets only	70,000	—			1.75	—
1998G Proof	45,000	Value: 2.00				
1998J In sets only	70,000	—			1.75	—
1998J Proof	45,000	Value: 2.00				
1999A In sets only	70,000	—			1.75	—
1999A Proof	45,000	Value: 2.00				
1999D In sets only	70,000	—			1.75	—
1999D Proof	45,000	Value: 2.00				
1999F In sets only	70,000	—			1.75	—
1999F Proof	45,000	Value: 2.00				
1999G In sets only	70,000	—			1.75	—
1999G Proof	45,000	Value: 2.00				
1999J In sets only	70,000	—			1.75	—
1999J Proof	45,000	Value: 2.00				
2000A In sets only	20,000	—			1.75	—
2000A Proof	45,000	Value: 2.00				
2000D In sets only	20,000	—			1.75	—
2000D Proof	45,000	Value: 2.00				
2000F In sets only	20,000	—			1.75	—
2000F Proof	45,000	Value: 2.00				
2000G In sets only	20,000	—			1.75	—
2000G Proof	45,000	Value: 2.00				
2000J In sets only	20,000	—			1.75	—
2000J Proof	45,000	Value: 2.00				

KM# 106   2 PFENNIG

Bronze, 19.25 mm. **Obv:** Five oak leaves, date below **Rev:** Denomination

Date	Mintage	F	VF	XF	Unc	BU
1950D	26,263,000	—	0.10	2.50	12.00	—
1950D Proof	—	Value: 50.00				
1950F	30,278,000	—	0.10	2.00	10.00	—
1950F Proof	200					
1950G	17,151,000	—	0.10	25.00	75.00	—
1950G Proof	—	Value: 90.00				
1950J	27,216,000	—	0.10	2.50	12.00	—
1950J Proof	—	Value: 40.00				
1958D	19,440,000	—	0.10	3.00	14.00	—
1958F	24,122,000	—	0.10	2.00	10.00	—
1958F Proof	100	—	—	—	—	—
1958G	15,255,000	—	0.10	4.00	18.00	—
1958J	21,250,000	—	0.10	2.00	10.00	—
1959D	19,690,000	—	0.10	2.00	10.00	—
1959F	25,017,000	—	0.10	1.50	10.00	—
1959F Proof	75	—	—	—	—	—
1959G	12,899,000	—	0.10	3.00	14.00	—
1959J	25,482,000	—	0.10	2.00	10.00	—
1960D	21,979,000	—	0.10	1.50	9.00	—
1960F	13,060,000	—		0.10	10.00	—
1960F Proof	75	—	—	—	—	—
1960G	5,657,000	—	0.10	2.00	18.00	—
1960J	17,799,000	—	0.10	2.00	10.00	—
1961D	26,662,000	—	0.10	1.50	9.00	—
1961F	24,990,000	—	0.10	1.50	8.00	—
1961G	18,060,000	—	0.10	1.50	9.00	—
1961J	22,147,000	—	0.10	1.50	8.00	—
1962D	21,297,000	—	0.10	1.50	9.00	—
1962F	42,189,000	—	0.10	1.00	6.00	—
1962G	17,297,000	—	0.10	2.00	12.00	—
1962J	30,706,000	—	0.10	1.00	8.00	—
1963D	7,648,000	—	0.10	2.00	10.00	—
1963F	18,299,000	—	0.10	1.50	9.00	—
1963G	35,838,000	—	0.10	1.50	8.00	—
1963G Proof						
1963J	42,884,000	—	0.10	1.50	6.00	—
1964D	20,336,000	—	0.10	1.50	10.00	—
1964F	31,400,000	—	0.10	1.50	7.00	—
1964G	18,431,000	—	0.10	1.50	8.00	—
1964G Proof	Est. 600	Value: 12.00				
1964J	13,370,000	—	0.10	1.50	8.00	—
1965D	48,541,000	—	0.10	1.00	4.00	—
1965F	27,000,000	—	0.10	1.00	6.00	—
1965F Proof	Est. 80	Value: 70.00				
1965G	13,584,000	—	0.10	1.50	7.00	—
1965G Proof	1,200	Value: 5.00				
1965J	33,397,000	—	0.10	1.00	4.00	—
1966D	65,077,000	—		0.50	3.00	—
1966F	52,543,000	—		0.50	3.00	—
1966F Proof	100	Value: 80.00				
1966G	40,804,000	—		0.50	3.00	—
1966G Proof	3,070	Value: 5.50				
1966J	46,754,000	—		0.50	3.00	—
1966J Proof	1,000	Value: 40.00				
1967D	25,997,000	—	0.10	1.00	6.00	—
1967F	30,004,000	—	0.10	1.00	5.00	—
1967F Proof	1,500	Value: 7.00				
1967G	6,280,000	—	0.10	1.50	10.00	—
1967G Proof	4,500	Value: 4.50				
1967J	26,725,000	—	0.10	1.00	6.00	—
1967J Proof	1,500	Value: 10.00				
1968D	19,523,000	—	0.10	1.00	5.00	—
1968G	15,357,000	—	0.10	1.00	6.00	—
1968G Proof	3,651	Value: 4.00				
1968J	—	—	200	400	600	—

Note: A 1968J error of 1963J exists with coin alignment

Date	Mintage	F	VF	XF	Unc	BU
1969J	—	—	200	400	600	—

KM# 106a   2 PFENNIG

2.9000 g., Bronze Clad Steel, 19.25 mm. **Obv:** Five oak leaves, date below **Rev:** Denomination

Date	Mintage	F	VF	XF	Unc	BU
1967G Proof	520	Value: 950				
1968D	19,523,000	—	—	0.50	2.50	—
1968F	30,000,000	—	—	0.50	2.50	—
1968F Proof	3,000	Value: 6.00				
1968G	13,004,000	—	—	0.50	2.50	—
1968G Proof	2,372	Value: 4.00				
1968J	20,026,000	—	—	0.25	2.00	—
1968J Proof	2,000	Value: 7.50				
1969D	39,012,000	—	—	0.25	1.00	—
1969D Proof	—	Value: 1.25				
1969F	45,029,000	—	—	0.25	1.00	—
1969F Proof	5,100	Value: 1.25				
1969G	32,156,999	—	—	0.25	1.00	—
1969G Proof	8,700	Value: 1.25				
1969J	40,102,000	—	—	0.25	1.00	—
1969J Proof	5,000	Value: 2.50				
1970D	45,525,000	—	—	0.10	0.25	—
1970F	73,851,000	—	—	0.10	0.25	—
1970F Proof	5,140	Value: 1.25				
1970G	30,330,000	—	—	0.10	0.25	—
1970G Proof	10,200	Value: 1.25				
1970 Small J	46,730,000	—	—	0.10	0.25	—
1970 Large J	Inc. above	—	—	0.10	0.25	—
1970J Proof	5,000	Value: 1.75				
1971D	71,755,000	—	—	0.10	0.25	—
1971D Proof	8,000	Value: 1.25				
1971F	82,765,000	—	—	0.10	0.25	—
1971F Proof	8,000	Value: 1.25				
1971G	47,850,000	—	—	0.10	0.25	—
1971G Proof	10,000	Value: 1.25				
1971J	73,641,000	—	—	0.10	0.25	—
1971J Proof	8,000	Value: 1.25				
1972D	52,403,000	—	—	0.10	0.25	—
1972D Proof	8,000	Value: 1.00				
1972F	60,272,000	—	—	0.10	0.25	—
1972F Proof	8,000	Value: 1.00				
1972G	34,864,000	—	—	0.10	0.25	—
1972G Proof	10,000	Value: 1.00				
1972J	53,673,000	—	—	0.10	0.25	—
1972J Proof	8,000	Value: 1.00				
1973D	26,190,000	—	—	0.10	0.25	—
1973D Proof	9,000	Value: 1.00				
1973F	30,160,000	—	—	0.10	0.25	—
1973F Proof	9,000	Value: 1.00				
1973G	17,379,000	—	—	0.10	0.25	—
1973G Proof	9,000	Value: 1.00				
1973J	26,830,000	—	—	0.10	0.25	—
1973J Proof	9,000	Value: 1.00				
1974D	58,667,000	—	—	0.10	0.25	—
1974D Proof	35,000	Value: 0.50				
1974F	67,596,000	—	—	0.10	0.25	—
1974F Proof	35,000	Value: 0.50				
1974G	39,007,000	—	—	0.10	0.25	—
1974G Proof	35,000	Value: 0.50				

Date	Mintage	F	VF	XF	Unc	BU
1974J	60,195,000	—	—	0.10	0.25	—
1974J Proof	35,000	Value: 0.50				
1975D	58,634,000	—	—	0.10	0.25	—
1975D Proof	43,000	Value: 0.50				
1975F	67,685,000	—	—	0.10	0.25	—
1975F Proof	43,000	Value: 0.50				
1975G	39,391,000	—	—	0.10	0.25	—
1975G Proof	43,000	Value: 0.50				
1975J	60,207,000	—	—	0.10	0.25	—
1975J Proof	43,000	Value: 0.50				
1976D	78,074,000	—	—	0.10	0.25	—
1976D Proof	43,000	Value: 0.50				
1976F	90,130,000	—	—	0.10	0.25	—
1976F Proof	43,000	Value: 0.50				
1976G	51,988,000	—	—	0.10	0.25	—
1976G Proof	43,000	Value: 0.50				
1976J	80,145,000	—	—	0.10	0.25	—
1976J Proof	43,000	Value: 0.50				
1977D	84,516,000	—	—	0.10	0.20	—
1977D Proof	51,000	Value: 0.40				
1977F	97,504,000	—	—	0.10	0.20	—
1977F Proof	51,000	Value: 0.40				
1977G	56,276,000	—	—	0.10	0.20	—
1977G Proof	51,000	Value: 0.40				
1977J	86,888,000	—	—	0.10	0.20	—
1977J Proof	51,000	Value: 0.40				
1978D	84,500,000	—	—	0.10	0.20	—
1978D Proof	54,000	Value: 0.40				
1978F	97,500,000	—	—	0.10	0.20	—
1978F Proof	54,000	Value: 0.40				
1978G	56,225,000	—	—	0.10	0.20	—
1978G Proof	54,000	Value: 0.40				
1978J	86,775,000	—	—	0.10	0.20	—
1978J Proof	54,000	Value: 0.40				
1979D	91,000,000	—	—	0.10	0.20	—
1979D Proof	89,000	Value: 0.40				
1979F	105,000,000	—	—	0.10	0.20	—
1979F Proof	89,000	Value: 0.40				
1979G	60,550,000	—	—	0.10	0.20	—
1979G Proof	89,000	Value: 0.40				
1979J	93,480,000	—	—	0.10	0.20	—
1979J Proof	89,000	Value: 0.40				
1980D	93,360,000	—	—	0.10	0.20	—
1980D Proof	110,000	Value: 0.40				
1980F	120,360,000	—	—	0.10	0.20	—
1980F Proof	110,000	Value: 0.40				
1980G	50,830,000	—	—	0.10	0.20	—
1980G Proof	110,000	Value: 0.40				
1980J	102,260,000	—	—	0.10	0.20	—
1980J Proof	110,000	Value: 0.40				
1981D	93,910,000	—	—	0.10	0.20	—
1981D Proof	91,000	Value: 0.40				
1981F	83,710,000	—	—	0.10	0.20	—
1981F Proof	91,000	Value: 0.40				
1981G	89,850,000	—	—	0.10	0.20	—
1981G Proof	91,000	Value: 0.40				
1981J	87,250,000	—	—	0.10	0.20	—
1981J Proof	91,000	Value: 0.40				
1982D	64,390,000	—	—	—	—	—
1982D Proof	78,000	Value: 0.40				
1982F	36,870,000	—	—	0.10	0.20	—
1982F Proof	78,000	Value: 0.40				
1982G	58,590,000	—	—	0.10	0.20	—
1982G Proof	78,000	Value: 0.40				
1982J	57,690,000	—	—	0.10	0.20	—
1982J Proof	78,000	Value: 0.40				
1983D	71,500,000	—	—	0.10	0.20	—
1983D Proof	75,000	Value: 0.40				
1983F	82,500,000	—	—	0.10	0.20	—
1983F Proof	75,000	Value: 0.40				
1983G	47,575,000	—	—	0.10	0.20	—
1983G Proof	75,000	Value: 0.40				
1983J	73,425,000	—	—	0.10	0.20	—
1983J Proof	75,000	Value: 0.40				
1984D	58,500,000	—	—	—	—	—
1984D Proof	64,000	Value: 0.40				
1984F	67,500,000	—	—	0.10	0.20	—
1984F Proof	64,000	Value: 0.40				
1984G	38,900,000	—	—	0.10	0.20	—
1984G Proof	64,000	Value: 0.40				
1984J	60,100,000	—	—	0.10	0.20	—
1984J Proof	64,000	Value: 0.40				
1985D	19,500,000	—	0.10	1.00	3.00	—
1985D Proof	56,000	Value: 0.40				
1985F	22,500,000	—	0.25	1.00	3.00	—
1985F Proof	54,000	Value: 0.40				
1985G	13,000,000	0.25	0.75	2.50	8.00	—
1985G Proof	55,000	Value: 0.40				
1985J	20,000,000	0.25	0.50	2.00	7.00	—
1985J Proof	54,000	Value: 0.40				
1986D	39,000,000	—	—	—	0.25	—
1986D Proof	44,000	Value: 0.40				
1986F	45,000,000	—	—	—	0.25	—
1986F Proof	44,000	Value: 0.40				
1986G	25,900,000	—	—	—	0.50	—
1986G Proof	44,000	Value: 0.40				
1986J	40,100,000	—	—	—	0.25	—
1986J Proof	44,000	Value: 0.40				
1987D	6,500,000	0.50	1.00	2.50	5.00	—
1987D Proof	45,000	Value: 0.40				
1987F	7,500,000	0.50	1.00	2.50	5.00	—
1987F Proof	45,000	Value: 0.40				

Date	Mintage	F	VF	XF	Unc	BU
1987G	4,330,000	0.75	1.25	2.75	6.00	—
1987G Proof	45,000	Value: 0.40				
1987J	6,680,000	0.50	1.00	2.50	5.00	—
1987J Proof	45,000	Value: 0.40				
1988D	52,000,000	—	—	—	0.25	—
1988D Proof	45,000	Value: 0.40				
1988F	60,000,000	—	—	—	0.25	—
1988F Proof	45,000	Value: 0.40				
1988G	34,600,000	—	—	—	0.25	—
1988G Proof	45,000	Value: 0.40				
1988J	53,400,000	—	—	—	0.25	—
1988J Proof	45,000	Value: 0.40				
1989D	52,000,000	—	—	—	0.25	—
1989D Proof	45,000	Value: 0.40				
1989F	60,000,000	—	—	—	0.25	—
1989F Proof	45,000	Value: 0.40				
1989G	34,600,000	—	—	—	0.25	—
1989G Proof	45,000	Value: 0.40				
1989J	53,400,000	—	—	—	0.25	—
1989J Proof	45,000	Value: 0.40				
1990D	71,500,000	—	—	—	0.25	—
1990D Proof	45,000	Value: 0.40				
1990F	82,500,000	—	—	—	0.25	—
1990F Proof	45,000	Value: 0.40				
1990G	47,570,000	—	—	—	0.25	—
1990G Proof	45,000	Value: 0.40				
1990J	73,420,000	—	—	—	0.25	—
1990J Proof	45,000	Value: 0.40				
1991A	115,000,000	—	—	—	0.25	—
1991A Proof	45,000	Value: 0.40				
1991D	120,750,000	—	—	—	0.25	—
1991D Proof	45,000	Value: 0.40				
1991F	138,000,000	—	—	—	0.25	—
1991F Proof	45,000	Value: 0.40				
1991G	80,500,000	—	—	—	0.25	—
1991G Proof	45,000	Value: 0.40				
1991J	120,750,000	—	—	—	0.25	—
1991J Proof	45,000	Value: 0.40				
1992A	60,000,000	—	—	—	0.25	—
1992A Proof	45,000	Value: 0.40				
1992D	63,000,000	—	—	—	0.25	—
1992D Proof	45,000	Value: 0.40				
1992F	72,000,000	—	—	—	0.25	—
1992F Proof	45,000	Value: 0.40				
1992G	42,000,000	—	—	—	0.25	—
1992G Proof	45,000	Value: 0.40				
1992J	63,000,000	—	—	—	0.25	—
1992J Proof	45,000	Value: 0.40				
1993A	10,000,000	—	0.25	1.00	4.00	—
1993A Proof	45,000	Value: 0.40				
1993D	10,500,000	—	0.25	1.00	4.00	—
1993D Proof	45,000	Value: 0.40				
1993F	12,000,000	—	0.25	1.00	4.00	—
1993F Proof	45,000	Value: 0.40				
1993G	7,000,000	—	0.25	1.00	4.00	—
1993G Proof	45,000	Value: 0.40				
1993J	10,000,000	—	0.25	1.00	4.00	—
1993J Proof	45,000	Value: 0.40				
1994A	55,000,000	—	—	—	0.15	—
1994A Proof	45,000	Value: 0.40				
1994D	57,750,000	—	—	—	0.15	—
1994D Proof	45,000	Value: 0.40				
1994F	66,000,000	—	—	—	0.15	—
1994F Proof	45,000	Value: 0.40				
1994G	38,500,000	—	—	—	0.25	—
1994G Proof	45,000	Value: 0.40				
1994J	57,750,000	—	—	—	0.15	—
1994J Proof	45,000	Value: 0.40				
1995A	1,000,000,000	—	—	—	0.15	—
1995A Proof	45,000	Value: 0.45				
1995D	105,000,000	—	—	—	0.15	—
1995D Proof	45,000	Value: 0.45				
1995F	120,000,000	—	—	—	0.15	—
1995F Proof	45,000	Value: 0.45				
1995G	70,000,000	—	—	—	0.25	—
1995G Proof	45,000	Value: 0.45				
1995J	105,000,000	—	—	—	0.15	—
1995J Proof	45,000	Value: 0.45				
1996A	40,000,000	—	—	—	0.20	—
1996A Proof	45,000	Value: 0.50				
1996D	42,000,000	—	—	—	0.20	—
1996D Proof	45,000	Value: 0.50				
1996F	48,000,000	—	—	—	0.20	—
1996F Proof	45,000	Value: 0.50				
1996G	28,000,000	—	—	—	0.25	—
1996G Proof	45,000	Value: 0.50				
1996J	42,000,000	—	—	—	0.20	—
1996J Proof	45,000	Value: 0.50				
1997A In sets only	70,000	—	—	—	1.75	—
1997A Proof	45,000	Value: 2.00				
1997D In sets only	70,000	—	—	—	1.75	—
1997D Proof	45,000	Value: 2.00				
1997F In sets only	70,000	—	—	—	1.75	—
1997F Proof	45,000	Value: 2.00				
1997G In sets only	70,000	—	—	—	1.75	—
1997G Proof	45,000	Value: 2.00				
1997J In sets only	70,000	—	—	—	1.75	—
1997J Proof	45,000	Value: 2.00				
1998A In sets only	70,000	—	—	—	1.75	—
1998A Proof	45,000	Value: 2.00				
1998D In sets only	70,000	—	—	—	1.75	—
1998D Proof	45,000	Value: 2.00				

Date	Mintage	F	VF	XF	Unc	BU
1998F In sets only	70,000	—	—	—	1.75	—
1998F Proof	45,000	Value: 2.00				
1998G In sets only	70,000	—	—	—	1.75	—
1998G Proof	45,000	Value: 2.00				
1998J In sets only	70,000	—	—	—	1.75	—
1998J Proof	45,000	Value: 2.00				
1999A In sets only	70,000	—	—	—	1.75	—
1999A Proof	45,000	Value: 2.00				
1999D In sets only	70,000	—	—	—	1.75	—
1999D Proof	45,000	Value: 2.00				
1999F In sets only	70,000	—	—	—	1.75	—
1999F Proof	45,000	Value: 2.00				
1999G In sets only	70,000	—	—	—	1.75	—
1999G Proof	45,000	Value: 2.00				
1999J In sets only	70,000	—	—	—	1.75	—
1999J Proof	45,000	Value: 2.00				
2000A In sets only	70,000	—	—	—	1.75	—
2000A Proof	45,000	Value: 2.00				
2000D In sets only	70,000	—	—	—	1.75	—
2000D Proof	45,000	Value: 2.00				
2000F In sets only	70,000	—	—	—	1.75	—
2000F Proof	45,000	Value: 2.00				
2000G In sets only	70,000	—	—	—	1.75	—
2000G Proof	45,000	Value: 2.00				
2000J In sets only	70,000	—	—	—	1.75	—
2000J Proof	45,000	Value: 2.00				

KM# 102   5 PFENNIG
Bronze Clad Steel, 18.5 mm. **Obv:** Five oak leaves, date below **Obv. Leg.:** BANK DEUTSCHER LÄNDER **Rev:** Denomination

Date	Mintage	F	VF	XF	Unc	BU
1949D	60,026,000	0.25	1.00	10.00	45.00	—
1949D Proof	—	Value: 150				
1949F	66,081,999	0.25	1.00	7.50	35.00	—
1949F Proof	250	Value: 85.00				
1949G	57,356,000	0.25	1.50	12.50	50.00	—
1949J	68,977,000	0.25	1.00	10.00	40.00	—
1949J Proof	—	Value: 85.00				

KM# 107   5 PFENNIG
3.0000 g., Brass Plated Steel, 18.5 mm. **Obv:** Five oak leaves, date below **Obv. Leg.:** BUNDES REPUBLIK DEUTSCHLAND **Rev:** Denomination

Date	Mintage	F	VF	XF	Unc	BU
1950D	271,962,000	—	—	1.50	5.00	—
1950F	362,880,000	—	—	1.50	5.00	—
1950F Proof	500	Value: 65.00				
1950G	180,492,000	—	—	1.50	5.00	—
1950G Proof	1,800	Value: 25.00				
1950J Large J	285,283,000	—	—	1.50	5.00	—
1950J Small J	Inc. above	—	—	1.50	5.00	—
1950J Proof	—					
1966D	26,036,000	—	—	1.50	8.50	—
1966F	30,047,000	—	—	1.50	8.50	—
1966F Proof	100	Value: 60.00				
1966G	17,333,000	—	—	1.50	8.50	—
1966G Proof	3,070	Value: 7.50				
1966J	26,741,000	—	—	1.50	8.50	—
1966J Proof	1,000	Value: 17.50				
1967D	10,418,000	—	—	1.50	8.50	—
1967F	12,012,000	—	—	1.50	8.50	—
1967F Proof	1,500	Value: 15.00				
1967G	1,736,000	0.50	2.50	7.00	25.00	—
1967G Proof	4,500	Value: 7.50				
1967J	10,706,000	—	—	1.50	8.50	—
1967J Proof	1,500	Value: 15.00				
1968D	13,047,000	—	—	1.00	6.00	—
1968F	15,026,000	—	—	1.00	5.00	—
1968F Proof	3,000	Value: 9.00				
1968G	13,855,000	—	—	1.00	7.00	—
1968G Proof	6,023	Value: 6.00				
1968J	13,362,000	—	—	1.00	7.00	—
1968J Proof	2,000	Value: 15.00				
1969D	23,488,000	—	—	0.50	2.50	—
1969F	27,046,000	—	—	0.50	2.50	—
1969F Proof	5,000	Value: 3.00				
1969G	15,631,000	—	—	0.50	3.00	—
1969G Proof	8,700	Value: 2.50				
1969J	24,120,000	—	—	0.50	2.50	—
1969J Proof	5,000	Value: 2.00				
1970D	39,940,000	—	—	0.10	1.00	—
1970F	45,517,000	—	—	0.10	1.00	—
1970F Proof	5,140	Value: 2.50				
1970G	27,638,000	—	—	0.10	1.00	—
1970G Proof	10,200	Value: 1.50				

Date	Mintage	F	VF	XF	Unc	BU
1970J	40,873,000	—	—	0.10	1.00	—
1970J Proof	5,000	Value: 2.50				
1971D	57,345,000	—	—	0.10	1.00	—
1971D Proof	8,000	Value: 1.50				
1971F	66,426,000	—	—	0.10	1.00	—
1971F Proof	8,000	Value: 1.50				
1971G	38,284,000	—	—	0.10	1.00	—
1971G Proof	10,000	Value: 1.50				
1971J	58,566,000	—	—	0.10	1.00	—
1971J Proof	8,000	Value: 1.50				
1972D	52,325,000	—	—	0.10	1.00	—
1972D Proof	8,000	Value: 1.50				
1972F	60,292,000	—	—	0.10	1.00	—
1972F Proof	8,000	Value: 1.50				
1972G	34,719,000	—	—	0.10	1.00	—
1972G Proof	10,000	Value: 1.50				
1972J	54,218,000	—	—	0.10	1.00	—
1972J Proof	8,000	Value: 1.50				
1973D	15,596,000	—	—	0.10	1.00	—
1973D Proof	9,000	Value: 1.50				
1973F	18,039,000	—	—	0.10	1.00	—
1973F Proof	9,000	Value: 1.50				
1973G	10,391,000	—	—	0.10	1.00	—
1973G Proof	9,000	Value: 1.50				
1973J	16,035,000	—	—	0.10	1.00	—
1973J Proof	9,000	Value: 1.50				
1974D	15,769,000	—	—	0.10	1.00	—
1974D Proof	35,000	Value: 0.50				
1974F	18,143,000	—	—	0.10	1.00	—
1974F Proof	35,000	Value: 0.50				
1974G	10,508,000	—	—	0.10	1.00	—
1974G Proof	35,000	Value: 0.50				
1974J	16,055,000	—	—	0.10	1.00	—
1974J Proof	35,000	Value: 0.50				
1975D	15,715,000	—	—	0.10	1.00	—
1975D Proof	43,000	Value: 0.50				
1975F	18,013,000	—	—	0.10	0.35	—
1975F Proof	43,000	Value: 0.50				
1975G	10,466,000	—	—	0.10	0.35	—
1975G Proof	43,000	Value: 0.50				
1975J	16,201,000	—	—	0.10	0.35	—
1975J Proof	43,000	Value: 0.50				
1976D	47,091,000	—	—	0.10	0.35	—
1976D Proof	43,000	Value: 0.50				
1976F	54,370,000	—	—	0.10	0.35	—
1976F Proof	43,000	Value: 0.50				
1976G	31,367,000	—	—	0.10	0.35	—
1976G Proof	43,000	Value: 0.50				
1976J	48,321,000	—	—	0.10	0.35	—
1976J Proof	43,000	Value: 0.50				
1977D	52,159,000	—	—	0.10	0.35	—
1977D Proof	51,000	Value: 0.45				
1977F	60,124,000	—	—	0.10	0.35	—
1977F Proof	51,000	Value: 0.45				
1977G	34,600,000	—	—	0.10	0.35	—
1977G Proof	51,000	Value: 0.45				
1977J	53,481,000	—	—	0.10	0.35	—
1977J Proof	51,000	Value: 0.45				
1978D	41,600,000	—	—	0.10	0.35	—
1978D Proof	54,000	Value: 0.45				
1978F	48,000,000	—	—	0.10	0.35	—
1978F Proof	54,000	Value: 0.45				
1978G	27,680,000	—	—	0.10	0.35	—
1978G Proof	54,000	Value: 0.45				
1978J	42,720,000	—	—	0.10	0.35	—
1978J Proof	54,000	Value: 0.45				
1979D	41,600,000	—	—	0.10	0.20	—
1979D Proof	89,000	Value: 0.40				
1979F	48,000,000	—	—	0.10	0.20	—
1979F Proof	89,000	Value: 0.40				
1979G	27,680,000	—	—	0.10	0.20	—
1979G Proof	89,000	Value: 0.40				
1979J	42,711,000	—	—	0.10	0.20	—
1979J Proof	89,000	Value: 0.40				
1980D	39,880,000	—	—	0.10	0.20	—
1980D Proof	110,000	Value: 0.40				
1980F	53,270,000	—	—	0.10	0.20	—
1980F Proof	110,000	Value: 0.40				
1980G	43,070,000	—	—	0.10	0.20	—
1980G Proof	110,000	Value: 0.40				
1980J	59,130,000	—	—	0.10	0.20	—
1980J Proof	110,000	Value: 0.40				
1981D	82,250,000	—	—	0.10	0.20	—
1981D Proof	91,000	Value: 0.40				
1981F	84,910,000	—	—	0.10	0.20	—
1981F Proof	91,000	Value: 0.40				
1981G	41,910,000	—	—	0.10	0.20	—
1981G Proof	91,000	Value: 0.40				
1981J	49,290,000	—	—	0.10	0.20	—
1981J Proof	91,000	Value: 0.40				
1982D	57,500,000	—	—	0.10	0.20	—
1982D Proof	78,000	Value: 0.40				
1982F	53,290,000	—	—	0.10	0.20	—
1982F Proof	78,000	Value: 0.40				
1982G	23,750,000	—	—	0.10	0.20	—
1982G Proof	78,000	Value: 0.40				
1982J	62,000,000	—	—	0.10	0.20	—
1982J Proof	78,000	Value: 0.40				
1983D	46,800,000	—	—	0.10	0.20	—
1983D Proof	75,000	Value: 0.40				
1983F	54,000,000	—	—	0.10	0.20	—
1983F Proof	75,000	Value: 0.40				
1983G	31,140,000	—	—	0.10	0.20	—
1983G Proof	75,000	Value: 0.40				
1983J	48,060,000	—	—	0.10	0.20	—
1983J Proof	75,000	Value: 0.40				
1984D	36,400,000	—	—	0.10	0.20	—
1984D Proof	64,000	Value: 0.40				
1984F	42,000,000	—	—	0.10	0.20	—
1984F Proof	64,000	Value: 0.40				
1984G	24,200,000	—	—	0.10	0.20	—
1984G Proof	64,000	Value: 0.40				
1984J	37,400,000	—	—	0.10	0.20	—
1984J Proof	64,000	Value: 0.40				
1985D	15,600,000	—	—	0.10	0.50	—
1985D Proof	56,000	Value: 0.50				
1985F	18,000,000	—	—	0.10	0.50	—
1985F Proof	54,000	Value: 0.50				
1985G	10,400,000	—	—	0.10	0.50	—
1985G Proof	55,000	Value: 0.50				
1985J	16,000,000	—	—	0.10	0.50	—
1985J Proof	54,000	Value: 0.50				
1986D	36,400,000	—	—	—	0.25	—
1986D Proof	44,000	Value: 0.40				
1986F	42,000,000	—	—	—	0.25	—
1986F Proof	44,000	Value: 0.40				
1986G	24,200,000	—	—	—	0.25	—
1986G Proof	44,000	Value: 0.40				
1986J	37,400,000	—	—	—	0.25	—
1986J Proof	44,000	Value: 0.40				
1987D	52,000,000	—	—	—	0.25	—
1987D Proof	45,000	Value: 0.40				
1987F	60,000,000	—	—	—	0.25	—
1987F Proof	45,000	Value: 0.40				
1987G	34,600,000	—	—	—	0.25	—
1987G Proof	45,000	Value: 0.40				
1987J	53,400,000	—	—	—	0.25	—
1987J Proof	45,000	Value: 0.40				
1988D	52,400,000	—	—	—	0.25	—
1988D Proof	45,000	Value: 0.40				
1988F	72,000,000	—	—	—	0.25	—
1988F Proof	45,000	Value: 0.40				
1988G	41,500,000	—	—	—	0.25	—
1988G Proof	45,000	Value: 0.40				
1988J	64,099,999	—	—	—	0.25	—
1988J Proof	45,000	Value: 0.40				
1989D	93,600,000	—	—	—	0.25	—
1989D Proof	45,000	Value: 0.40				
1989F	108,000,000	—	—	—	0.25	—
1989F Proof	45,000	Value: 0.40				
1989G	62,280,000	—	—	—	0.25	—
1989G Proof	45,000	Value: 0.40				
1989J	96,120,000	—	—	—	0.25	—
1989J Proof	45,000	Value: 0.40				
1990A	70,000,000	—	—	—	0.10	—
1990D	93,600,000	—	—	—	0.10	—
1990D Proof	45,000	Value: 0.40				
1990F	108,000,000	—	—	—	0.10	—
1990F Proof	45,000	Value: 0.40				
1990G	62,280,000	—	—	—	0.10	—
1990G Proof	45,000	Value: 0.40				
1990J	96,120,000	—	—	—	0.10	—
1990J Proof	45,000	Value: 0.40				
1991A	128,000,000	—	—	—	0.10	—
1991A Proof	45,000	Value: 0.40				
1991D	134,400,000	—	—	—	0.10	—
1991D Proof	45,000	Value: 0.40				
1991F	153,600,000	—	—	—	0.10	—
1991F Proof	45,000	Value: 0.40				
1991G	89,600,000	—	—	—	0.10	—
1991G Proof	45,000	Value: 0.40				
1991J	134,400,000	—	—	—	0.10	—
1991J Proof	45,000	Value: 0.40				
1992A	28,000,000	—	—	—	0.10	—
1992A Proof	45,000	Value: 0.40				
1992D	29,400,000	—	—	—	0.10	—
1992D Proof	45,000	Value: 0.40				
1992F	33,600,000	—	—	—	0.10	—
1992F Proof	45,000	Value: 0.40				
1992G	19,600,000	—	—	—	0.10	—
1992G Proof	45,000	Value: 0.40				
1992J	29,400,000	—	—	—	0.10	—
1992J Proof	45,000	Value: 0.40				
1993A	36,000,000	—	—	—	0.10	—
1993A Proof	45,000	Value: 0.40				
1993D	37,800,000	—	—	—	0.10	—
1993D Proof	45,000	Value: 0.40				
1993F	43,200,000	—	—	—	0.10	—
1993F Proof	45,000	Value: 0.40				
1993G	25,200,000	—	—	—	0.10	—
1993G Proof	45,000	Value: 0.40				
1993J	37,800,000	—	—	—	0.10	—
1993J Proof	45,000	Value: 0.40				
1994A	38,000,000	—	—	—	0.10	—
1994A Proof	45,000	Value: 0.40				
1994D	39,900,000	—	—	—	0.10	—
1994D Proof	45,000	Value: 0.40				
1994F	45,600,000	—	—	—	0.10	—
1994F Proof	45,000	Value: 0.40				
1994G	26,600,000	—	—	—	0.10	—
1994G Proof	45,000	Value: 0.40				
1994J	39,900,000	—	—	—	0.10	—
1994J Proof	45,000	Value: 0.40				
1995A	48,000,000	—	—	—	0.15	—
1995A Proof	45,000	Value: 0.45				
1995D	50,400,000	—	—	—	0.15	—
1995D Proof	45,000	Value: 0.45				
1995F	57,600,000	—	—	—	0.15	—
1995F Proof	45,000	Value: 0.45				
1995G	33,600,000	—	—	—	0.15	—
1995G Proof	45,000	Value: 0.45				
1995J	50,400,000	—	—	—	0.15	—
1995J Proof	45,000	Value: 0.45				
1996A	48,000,000	—	—	—	0.20	—
1996A Proof	45,000	Value: 0.50				
1996D	50,400,000	—	—	—	0.20	—
1996D Proof	45,000	Value: 0.50				
1996F	57,600,000	—	—	—	0.20	—
1996F Proof	45,000	Value: 0.50				
1996G	33,600,000	—	—	—	0.20	—
1996G Proof	45,000	Value: 0.50				
1996J	50,400,000	—	—	—	0.20	—
1996J Proof	45,000	Value: 0.50				
1997A In sets only	70,000	—	—	—	1.75	—
1997A Proof	45,000	Value: 2.00				
1997D In sets only	70,000	—	—	—	1.75	—
1997D Proof	45,000	Value: 2.00				
1997F In sets only	70,000	—	—	—	1.75	—
1997F Proof	45,000	Value: 2.00				
1997G In sets only	70,000	—	—	—	1.75	—
1997G Proof	45,000	Value: 2.00				
1997J In sets only	70,000	—	—	—	1.75	—
1997J Proof	45,000	Value: 2.00				
1998A In sets only	70,000	—	—	—	1.75	—
1998A Proof	45,000	Value: 2.00				
1998D In sets only	70,000	—	—	—	1.75	—
1998D Proof	45,000	Value: 2.00				
1998F In sets only	70,000	—	—	—	1.75	—
1998F Proof	45,000	Value: 2.00				
1998G In sets only	70,000	—	—	—	1.75	—
1998G Proof	45,000	Value: 2.00				
1998J In sets only	70,000	—	—	—	1.75	—
1998J Proof	45,000	Value: 2.00				
1999A In sets only	70,000	—	—	—	1.75	—
1999A Proof	45,000	Value: 2.00				
1999D In sets only	70,000	—	—	—	1.75	—
1999D Proof	45,000	Value: 2.00				
1999F In sets only	70,000	—	—	—	1.75	—
1999F Proof	45,000	Value: 2.00				
1999G In sets only	70,000	—	—	—	1.75	—
1999G Proof	45,000	Value: 2.00				
1999J In sets only	70,000	—	—	—	1.75	—
1999J Proof	45,000	Value: 2.00				
2000A In sets only	70,000	—	—	—	1.75	—
2000A Proof	45,000	Value: 2.00				
2000D In sets only	70,000	—	—	—	1.75	—
2000D Proof	45,000	Value: 2.00				
2000F In sets only	70,000	—	—	—	1.75	—
2000F Proof	45,000	Value: 2.00				
2000G In sets only	45,000	—	—	—	1.75	—
2000G Proof	45,000	Value: 2.00				
2000J In sets only	45,000	—	—	—	1.75	—
2000J Proof	70,000	Value: 2.00				

KM# 103   10 PFENNIG
Brass Clad Steel, 21.5 mm. **Obv:** Five oak leaves, date below **Obv. Leg.:** BANK DEUTSCHER LÄNDER **Rev:** Denomination

Date	Mintage	F	VF	XF	Unc	BU
1949D	140,558,000	—	0.50	7.50	30.00	—
1949D Proof	—	Value: 150				
1949F	120,932,000	—	0.50	10.00	35.00	—
1949F Proof	250	Value: 140				
1949G	82,933,000	—	1.00	10.00	40.00	—
1949J Large J	154,095,000	—	0.50	7.50	30.00	—
1949J Proof	—	Value: 60.00				
1949J Small J	Inc. above	—	0.50	7.50	32.00	—
1949J Proof	—	Value: 60.00				

KM# 108   10 PFENNIG
4.0000 g., Brass Plated Steel, 21.5 mm. **Obv:** Five oak leaves, date below **Obv. Leg.:** BUNDES REPUBLIK DEUTSCHLAND **Rev:** Denomination **Edge:** Plain

Date	Mintage	F	VF	XF	Unc	BU
1950D	393,209,000	—	—	0.50	4.00	—
1950F	584,340,000	—	—	0.50	4.00	—
1950F Proof	500	Value: 45.00				
1950G	309,045,000	—	0.20	1.00	8.00	—

Date	Mintage	F	VF	XF	Unc	BU
1950G Proof	1,800	Value: 5.00				
1950J	402,452,000	—	—	0.50	4.00	—
1950J Proof	—	Value: 20.00				
1966D	31,220,000	—	0.20	1.50	8.00	—
1966F	36,097,000	—	0.20	1.50	8.00	—
1966F Proof	100	Value: 75.00				
1966G	25,338,000	—	0.20	1.50	9.00	—
1966G Proof	3,070	Value: 7.50				
1966J	32,116,000	—	0.20	1.50	8.00	—
1966J Proof	1,000	Value: 12.50				
1967D	15,632,000	—	0.20	3.00	10.00	—
1967F	18,049,000	—	0.20	2.00	9.00	—
1967F Proof	1,500	Value: 15.00				
1967G	1,518,000	0.20	2.00	7.00	30.00	—
1967G Proof	4,500	Value: 7.50				
1967J	16,050,999	—	0.20	3.00	10.00	—
1967J Proof	1,500	Value: 12.50				
1968D	5,207,000	—	0.20	2.00	10.00	—
1968F	6,010,000	—	0.20	2.00	8.00	—
1968F Proof	3,000	Value: 10.00				
1968G	12,384,000	—	0.15	1.50	7.00	—
1968G Proof	6,023	Value: 5.00				
1968J	5,422,000	—	0.20	2.00	10.00	—
1968J Proof	2,000	Value: 10.00				
1969D	41,693,000	—	—	0.15	2.00	—
1969F	48,084,000	—	—	0.15	2.00	—
1969F Proof	5,000	Value: 3.00				
1969G	48,760,000	—	—	0.15	2.00	—
1969G Proof	8,700	Value: 2.50				
1969J	42,756,000	—	—	0.15	2.00	—
1969J Proof	5,000	Value: 2.50				
1970D	54,085,000	—	—	0.15	2.00	—
1970F	60,086,000	—	—	0.15	2.00	—
1970F Proof	5,140	Value: 3.00				
1970G	35,900,000	—	—	0.15	1.00	—
1970G Proof	10,200	Value: 2.00				
1970J	40,115,000	—	—	0.15	1.00	—
1970J Proof	5,000	Value: 2.50				
1971D	54,022,000	—	—	0.15	0.25	—
1971D Proof	8,000	Value: 2.50				
1971F	92,534,000	—	—	0.15	0.25	—
1971F Proof	8,000	Value: 2.50				
1971G	88,614,000	—	—	0.15	0.25	—
1971G Proof	10,000	Value: 2.00				
1971 Small J	65,622,000	—	—	0.15	0.25	—
1971 Large J	Inc. above	—	—	0.15	0.25	—
1971J Proof	8,000	Value: 1.50				
1972D	104,345,000	—	—	0.15	0.25	—
1972D Proof	8,000	Value: 1.50				
1972F	110,177,000	—	—	0.15	0.25	—
1972F Proof	8,000	Value: 1.50				
1972G	71,766,000	—	—	0.15	0.25	—
1972G Proof	10,000	Value: 1.50				
1972J	96,991,000	—	—	0.15	0.25	—
1972J Proof	8,000	Value: 1.50				
1973D	26,052,000	—	—	0.15	0.25	—
1973D Proof	9,000	Value: 1.50				
1973F	30,070,000	—	—	0.15	0.25	—
1973F Proof	9,000	Value: 1.50				
1973G	17,294,000	—	—	0.15	0.25	—
1973G Proof	9,000	Value: 1.50				
1973J	26,774,000	—	—	0.15	0.25	—
1973J Proof	9,000	Value: 1.50				
1974D	15,707,000	—	—	0.15	0.25	—
1974D Proof	35,000	Value: 0.75				
1974F	18,135,000	—	—	0.15	0.25	—
1974F Proof	35,000	Value: 0.75				
1974G	10,450,000	—	—	0.15	0.25	—
1974G Proof	35,000	Value: 0.75				
1974J	16,056,000	—	—	0.15	0.25	—
1974J Proof	35,000	Value: 0.75				
1975D	15,654,000	—	—	0.15	0.25	—
1975D Proof	43,000	Value: 0.75				
1975F	18,043,000	—	—	0.15	0.25	—
1975F Proof	43,000	Value: 0.75				
1975G	10,403,000	—	—	0.15	0.25	—
1975G Proof	43,000	Value: 0.75				
1975J	16,111,000	—	—	0.15	0.25	—
1975J Proof	43,000	Value: 0.75				
1976D	65,200,000	—	—	0.15	0.25	—
1976D Proof	43,000	Value: 0.75				
1976F	75,282,000	—	—	0.15	0.25	—
1976F Proof	43,000	Value: 0.75				
1976G	43,372,000	—	—	0.15	0.25	—
1976G Proof	43,000	Value: 0.75				
1976J	66,930,000	—	—	0.15	0.25	—
1976J Proof	43,000	Value: 0.75				
1977D	64,989,000	—	—	0.10	0.20	—
1977D Proof	51,000	Value: 0.50				
1977F	75,052,000	—	—	0.10	0.20	—
1977F Proof	51,000	Value: 0.50				
1977G	43,300,000	—	—	0.10	0.20	—
1977G Proof	51,000	Value: 0.50				
1977J	66,800,000	—	—	0.10	0.20	—
1977J Proof	51,000	Value: 0.50				
1978D	91,000,000	—	—	0.10	0.20	—
1978D Proof	54,000	Value: 0.50				
1978F	105,000,000	—	—	0.10	0.20	—
1978F Proof	54,000	Value: 0.50				
1978G	60,590,000	—	—	0.10	0.20	—
1978J	93,490,000	—	—	0.10	0.20	—
1978J Proof	54,000	Value: 0.50				
1979D	104,000,000	—	—	0.10	0.20	—
1979D Proof	89,000	Value: 0.50				
1979F	120,000,000	—	—	0.10	0.20	—
1979F Proof	89,000	Value: 0.50				
1979G	69,200,000	—	—	0.10	0.20	—
1979G Proof	89,000	Value: 0.50				
1979J	106,800,000	—	—	0.10	0.20	—
1979J Proof	89,000	Value: 0.50				
1980D	65,450,000	—	—	0.10	0.20	—
1980D Proof	110,000	Value: 0.50				
1980F	122,780,000	—	—	0.10	0.20	—
1980F Proof	110,000	Value: 0.50				
1980G	75,410,000	—	—	0.10	0.20	—
1980G Proof	110,000	Value: 0.50				
1980J	70,960,000	—	—	0.10	0.20	—
1980J Proof	110,000	Value: 0.50				
1981D	135,200,000	—	—	0.10	0.20	—
1981D Proof	91,000	Value: 0.50				
1981F	117,410,000	—	—	0.10	0.20	—
1981F Proof	91,000	Value: 0.50				
1981G	69,440,000	—	—	0.10	0.20	—
1981G Proof	91,000	Value: 0.50				
1981J	138,360,000	—	—	0.10	0.20	—
1981J Proof	91,000	Value: 0.50				
1982D	74,690,000	—	—	0.10	0.20	—
1982D Proof	78,000	Value: 0.50				
1982F	85,140,000	—	—	0.10	0.20	—
1982F Proof	78,000	Value: 0.50				
1982G	50,840,000	—	—	0.10	0.20	—
1982G Proof	78,000	Value: 0.50				
1982J	80,620,000	—	—	0.10	0.20	—
1982J Proof	78,000	Value: 0.50				
1983D	33,800,000	—	—	0.10	0.20	—
1983D Proof	75,000	Value: 0.50				
1983F	39,000,000	—	—	0.10	0.20	—
1983F Proof	75,000	Value: 0.50				
1983G	22,490,000	—	—	0.10	0.20	—
1983G Proof	75,000	Value: 0.50				
1983J	34,710,000	—	—	0.10	0.20	—
1983J Proof	75,000	Value: 0.50				
1984D	52,000,000	—	—	0.10	0.20	—
1984D Proof	64,000	Value: 0.50				
1984F	60,000,000	—	—	0.10	0.20	—
1984F Proof	64,000	Value: 0.50				
1984G	34,600,000	—	—	0.10	0.20	—
1984G Proof	64,000	Value: 0.50				
1984J	53,400,000	—	—	0.10	0.20	—
1984J Proof	64,000	Value: 0.50				
1985D	78,000,000	—	—	—	0.15	—
1985D Proof	56,000	Value: 0.50				
1985F	90,000,000	—	—	—	0.15	—
1985F Proof	54,000	Value: 0.50				
1985G	51,900,000	—	—	—	0.15	—
1985G Proof	55,000	Value: 0.50				
1985J	80,100,000	—	—	—	0.15	—
1985J Proof	54,000	Value: 0.50				
1986D	41,600,000	—	—	—	0.15	—
1986D Proof	44,000	Value: 0.50				
1986F	48,000,000	—	—	—	0.15	—
1986F Proof	44,000	Value: 0.50				
1986G	27,700,000	—	—	—	0.15	—
1986G Proof	44,000	Value: 0.50				
1986J	42,700,000	—	—	—	0.15	—
1986J Proof	44,000	Value: 0.15				
1987D	58,500,000	—	—	—	0.10	—
1987D Proof	45,000	Value: 0.15				
1987F	67,500,000	—	—	—	0.10	—
1987F Proof	45,000	Value: 0.15				
1987G	38,900,000	—	—	—	0.10	—
1987G Proof	45,000	Value: 0.50				
1987J	60,100,000	—	—	—	0.15	—
1987J Proof	45,000	Value: 0.50				
1988D	109,200,000	—	—	—	0.15	—
1988D Proof	45,000	Value: 0.50				
1988F	126,000,000	—	—	—	0.15	—
1988F Proof	45,000	Value: 0.50				
1988G	72,700,000	—	—	—	0.15	—
1988G Proof	45,000	Value: 0.50				
1988J	112,100,000	—	—	—	0.15	—
1988J Proof	45,000	Value: 0.50				
1989D	119,600,000	—	—	—	0.15	—
1989D Proof	45,000	Value: 0.50				
1989F	138,000,000	—	—	—	0.15	—
1989F Proof	45,000	Value: 0.50				
1989G	79,580,000	—	—	—	0.15	—
1989G Proof	45,000	Value: 0.50				
1989J	122,820,000	—	—	—	0.15	—
1989J Proof	45,000	Value: 0.50				
1990A	100,000,000	—	—	—	0.15	—
1990D	156,000,000	—	—	—	0.15	—
1990D Proof	45,000	Value: 0.50				
1990F	180,000,000	—	—	—	0.15	—
1990F Proof	45,000	Value: 0.50				
1990G	103,800,000	—	—	—	0.15	—
1990G Proof	45,000	Value: 0.50				
1990J	160,200,000	—	—	—	0.15	—
1990J Proof	45,000	Value: 0.50				
1991A	170,000,000	—	—	—	0.15	—
1991A Proof	45,000	Value: 0.40				
1991D	178,550,000	—	—	—	0.15	—
1991D Proof	45,000	Value: 0.40				
1991F	204,000,000	—	—	—	0.15	—
1991F Proof	45,000	Value: 0.40				
1991G	119,000,000	—	—	—	0.15	—
1991G Proof	45,000	Value: 0.40				
1991J	178,500,000	—	—	—	0.15	—
1991J Proof	45,000	Value: 0.40				
1992A	80,000,000	—	—	—	0.10	—
1992A Proof	45,000	Value: 0.40				
1992D	84,000,000	—	—	—	0.10	—
1992D Proof	45,000	Value: 0.40				
1992F	96,000,000	—	—	—	0.10	—
1992F Proof	45,000	Value: 0.40				
1992G	56,000,000	—	—	—	0.10	—
1992G Proof	45,000	Value: 0.40				
1992J	84,000,000	—	—	—	0.10	—
1992J Proof	45,000	Value: 0.40				
1993A	80,000,000	—	—	—	0.10	—
1993A Proof	45,000	Value: 0.40				
1993D	84,000,000	—	—	—	0.10	—
1993D Proof	45,000	Value: 0.40				
1993F	96,000,000	—	—	—	0.10	—
1993F Proof	45,000	Value: 0.40				
1993G	56,000,000	—	—	—	0.10	—
1993G Proof	45,000	Value: 0.40				
1993J	84,000,000	—	—	—	0.10	—
1993J Proof	45,000	Value: 0.40				
1994A	100,000,000	—	—	—	0.10	—
1994A Proof	45,000	Value: 0.40				
1994D	105,000,000	—	—	—	0.10	—
1994D Proof	45,000	Value: 0.40				
1994F	120,000,000	—	—	—	0.10	—
1994F Proof	45,000	Value: 0.40				
1994G	70,000,000	—	—	—	0.10	—
1994G Proof	45,000	Value: 0.40				
1994J	105,000,000	—	—	—	0.10	—
1994J Proof	45,000	Value: 0.40				
1995A	110,000,000	—	—	—	0.15	—
1995A Proof	45,000	Value: 0.45				
1995D	115,000,000	—	—	—	0.15	—
1995D Proof	45,000	Value: 0.45				
1995F	132,000,000	—	—	—	0.15	—
1995F Proof	45,000	Value: 0.45				
1995G	77,000,000	—	—	—	0.15	—
1995G Proof	45,000	Value: 0.45				
1995J	115,500,000	—	—	—	0.15	—
1995J Proof	45,000	Value: 0.45				
1996A	90,000,000	—	—	—	0.20	—
1996A Proof	45,000	Value: 0.50				
1996D	94,500,000	—	—	—	0.20	—
1996D Proof	45,000	Value: 0.50				
1996F	108,000,000	—	—	—	0.20	—
1996F Proof	45,000	Value: 0.50				
1996G	63,000,000	—	—	—	0.20	—
1996G Proof	45,000	Value: 0.50				
1996J	94,500,000	—	—	—	0.20	—
1996J Proof	45,000	Value: 0.50				
1997A In sets only	70,000	—	—	—	1.75	—
1997A Proof	45,000	Value: 2.00				
1997D In sets only	70,000	—	—	—	1.75	—
1997D Proof	45,000	Value: 2.00				
1997F In sets only	70,000	—	—	—	1.75	—
1997F Proof	45,000	Value: 2.00				
1997G In sets only	70,000	—	—	—	1.75	—
1997G Proof	45,000	Value: 2.00				
1997J In sets only	70,000	—	—	—	1.75	—
1997J Proof	45,000	Value: 2.00				
1998A	—	—	—	—	1.75	—
1998A Proof	—	Value: 2.00				
1998D	—	—	—	—	1.75	—
1998D Proof	—	Value: 2.00				
1998F In sets only	70,000	—	—	—	1.75	—
1998F Proof	45,000	Value: 2.00				
1998G	—	—	—	—	1.75	—
1998G Proof	—	Value: 2.00				
1998J	—	—	—	—	1.75	—
1998J Proof	—	Value: 2.00				
1999A	—	—	—	—	1.75	—
1999A Proof	—	Value: 2.00				
1999D	—	—	—	—	1.75	—
1999D Proof	—	Value: 2.00				
1999F In sets only	70,000	—	—	—	1.75	—
1999F Proof	45,000	Value: 2.00				
1999G	—	—	—	—	1.75	—
1999G Proof	—	Value: 2.00				
1999J	—	—	—	—	1.75	—
1999J Proof	—	Value: 2.00				
2000A In sets only	70,000	—	—	—	1.75	—
2000A Proof	45,000	Value: 2.00				
2000D In sets only	70,000	—	—	—	1.75	—
2000D Proof	45,000	Value: 2.00				
2000F In sets only	70,000	—	—	—	1.75	—
2000F Proof	45,000	Value: 2.00				
2000G In sets only	70,000	—	—	—	1.75	—
2000G Proof	45,000	Value: 2.00				
2000J In sets only	70,000	—	—	—	1.75	—
2000J Proof	45,000	Value: 2.00				

KM# 104   50 PFENNIG
3.5000 g., Copper-Nickel, 20 mm. **Obv:** Denomination
Obv. Leg.: BANK DEUTSCHER LÄNDER **Rev:** Woman planting an oak seedling, date below

Date	Mintage	F	VF	XF	Unc	BU
1949D	39,108,000	—	0.75	4.50	45.00	—
1949F	45,118,000	—	0.50	3.00	35.00	—
1949F Proof	200	Value: 125				
1949G	25,924,000	—	0.75	5.00	55.00	—
1949J	42,303,000	—	0.75	3.50	35.00	—
1949J Proof	—	Value: 135				
1950G	30,000	—	—	350	475	750

Note: The 1950G dated coin was restruck without authorization by a mint official using genuine dies - quantity unknown

KM# 109.1   50 PFENNIG
3.5000 g., Copper-Nickel, 20 mm. **Obv:** Denomination
Obv. Leg.: BUNDESREPUBLIK DEUTSCHLAND **Rev:** Woman planting an oak seedling **Edge:** Reeded

Date	Mintage	F	VF	XF	Unc	BU
1950D	100,735,000	—	0.50	0.75	7.00	—
1950F	143,510,000	—	0.50	0.75	7.00	—
1950F Proof	450	Value: 85.00				
1950G	66,421,000	—	0.50	1.50	12.00	—
1950J	102,736,000	—	0.50	0.75	9.00	—
1950J Proof	—	Value: 25.00				
1966D	8,327,999	—	0.50	1.00	15.00	—
1966F	9,605,000	—	0.50	1.00	15.00	—
1966F Proof	100	Value: 125				
1966G	5,543,000	—	0.50	1.50	15.00	—
1966G Proof	3,070	Value: 10.00				
1966J	8,569,000	—	1.00	7.00	35.00	—
1966J Proof	1,000	Value: 20.00				
1967D	5,207,000	—	0.50	1.00	15.00	—
1967F	6,005,000	—	0.50	1.00	15.00	—
1967F Proof	1,500	Value: 18.00				
1967G	1,843,000	—	1.00	5.00	22.00	—
1967G Proof	4,500	Value: 15.00				
1967J	10,684,000	—	0.50	1.50	20.00	—
1967J Proof	1,500	Value: 18.00				
1968D	7,809,000	—	0.50	1.50	12.00	—
1968F	3,000,000	—	0.50	1.50	12.00	—
1968F Proof	3,000	Value: 15.00				
1968G	6,818,000	—	0.50	1.50	12.00	—
1968G Proof	6,023	Value: 8.00				
1968J	2,672,000	—	1.00	5.00	30.00	—
1968J Proof	2,000	Value: 15.00				
1969D	14,561,000	—	0.45	0.55	2.50	—
1969F	16,804,000	—	0.45	0.55	2.50	—
1969F Proof	5,000	Value: 4.00				
1969G	9,704,000	—	0.45	0.55	2.50	—
1969G Proof	8,700	Value: 3.50				
1969J	14,969,000	—	0.45	0.55	2.50	—
1969J Proof	5,000	Value: 10.00				
1970D	25,294,000	—	0.45	0.55	1.50	—
1970F	26,455,000	—	0.45	0.55	1.50	—
1970F Proof	5,140	Value: 3.50				
1970G	11,955,000	—	0.45	0.55	1.50	—
1970G Proof	10,200	Value: 3.00				
1970J	10,683,000	—	0.45	0.55	1.50	—
1970J Proof	5,000	Value: 3.50				
1971D	23,393,000	—	0.45	0.55	1.25	—
1971D Proof	8,000	Value: 3.00				
1971F	29,746,000	—	0.45	0.55	1.25	—
1971F Proof	8,000	Value: 3.00				
1971G	15,556,000	—	0.45	0.55	1.25	—
1971G Proof	10,000	Value: 3.00				
1971 Large J	24,044,000	—	0.45	0.55	1.25	—
1971 Small J	Inc. above	—	0.45	0.55	1.25	—
1971J Proof	8,000	Value: 3.00				

KM# 109.2   50 PFENNIG
3.5000 g., Copper-Nickel, 20 mm. **Obv:** Denomination
Rev: Woman planting an oak seedling **Edge:** Plain
Note: Counterfeits of 1972 dated coins with reeded edges exist.

Date	Mintage	F	VF	XF	Unc	BU
1972D	26,008,000	—	—	0.45	0.60	—
1972D Proof	8,000	Value: 2.00				
1972F	30,043,000	—	—	0.45	0.60	—
1972F Proof	8,000	Value: 2.00				
1972G	17,337,000	—	—	0.45	0.60	—
1972G Proof	10,000	Value: 2.00				
1972J	26,707,000	—	—	0.45	0.60	—
1972J Proof	8,000	Value: 2.00				
1973D	7,810,000	—	—	0.45	1.00	—
1973D Proof	9,000	Value: 2.00				
1973F	8,994,000	—	—	0.45	0.60	—
1973F Proof	9,000	Value: 2.00				
1973G	5,201,000	—	—	0.45	0.60	—
1973G Proof	9,000	Value: 2.00				
1973J	8,010,999	—	—	0.45	0.60	—
1973J Proof	9,000	Value: 2.00				
1974D	18,264,000	—	—	0.45	1.00	—
1974D Proof	35,000	Value: 1.00				
1974 Large F	21,036,000	—	—	0.45	1.00	—
1974 Small F	Inc. above	—	—	0.45	1.00	—
1974F Proof	35,000	Value: 1.00				
1974G	12,159,000	—	—	0.45	1.00	—
1974G Proof	35,000	Value: 1.00				
1974J	18,752,000	—	—	0.45	1.00	—
1974J Proof	35,000	Value: 1.00				
1975D	13,055,000	—	—	0.45	1.00	—
1975D Proof	43,000	Value: 1.00				
1975F	15,003,000	—	—	0.45	1.00	—
1975F Proof	43,000	Value: 1.00				
1975G	8,675,000	—	—	0.45	1.50	—
1975G Proof	43,000	Value: 1.00				
1975J	13,379,000	—	—	0.45	1.00	—
1975J Proof	43,000	Value: 1.00				
1976D	10,411,000	—	—	0.45	0.60	—
1976D Proof	43,000	Value: 1.00				
1976F	12,048,000	—	—	0.45	0.60	—
1976F Proof	43,000	Value: 1.00				
1976G	6,653,000	—	—	0.45	1.25	—
1976G Proof	43,000	Value: 1.00				
1976J	10,716,000	—	—	0.45	0.60	—
1976J Proof	43,000	Value: 1.00				
1977D	10,400,000	—	—	0.45	0.60	—
1977D Proof	51,000	Value: 0.75				
1977F	12,000,000	—	—	0.45	0.60	—
1977F Proof	51,000	Value: 0.75				
1977G	6,921,000	—	—	0.45	1.00	—
1977G Proof	51,000	Value: 0.75				
1977J	10,708,000	—	—	0.45	0.60	—
1977J Proof	51,000	Value: 0.75				
1978D	10,400,000	—	—	0.45	1.00	—
1978D Proof	54,000	Value: 0.75				
1978F	12,000,000	—	—	0.45	0.60	—
1978F Proof	54,000	Value: 0.75				
1978G	6,640,000	—	—	0.45	1.00	—
1978G Proof	54,000	Value: 0.75				
1978J	10,680,000	—	—	0.45	0.60	—
1978J Proof	54,000	Value: 0.75				
1979D	10,400,000	—	—	0.45	1.00	—
1979D Proof	89,000	Value: 0.75				
1979F	12,000,000	—	—	0.45	0.60	—
1979F Proof	89,000	Value: 0.75				
1979G	6,920,000	—	—	0.45	1.00	—
1979G Proof	89,000	Value: 0.75				
1979J	10,680,000	—	—	0.45	0.60	—
1979J Proof	89,000	Value: 0.75				
1980D	23,250,000	—	—	0.45	0.60	—
1980D Proof	110,000	Value: 0.75				
1980F	17,440,000	—	—	0.45	0.60	—
1980F Proof	110,000	Value: 0.75				
1980G	22,460,000	—	—	0.45	1.00	—
1980G Proof	110,000	Value: 0.75				
1980J	24,030,000	—	—	0.45	0.60	—
1980J Proof	110,000	Value: 0.75				
1981D	17,900,000	—	—	0.45	1.25	—
1981D Proof	91,000	Value: 0.75				
1981F	29,810,000	—	—	0.45	1.25	—
1981F Proof	91,000	Value: 0.75				
1981G	10,880,000	—	—	0.45	1.50	—
1981G Proof	91,000	Value: 0.75				
1981J	24,140,000	—	—	0.45	1.25	—
1981J Proof	91,000	Value: 0.75				
1982D	21,540,000	—	—	0.45	1.25	—
1982D Proof	78,000	Value: 0.75				
1982F	28,900,000	—	—	0.45	1.25	—
1982F Proof	78,000	Value: 0.75				
1982G	19,710,000	—	—	0.45	1.50	—
1982G Proof	78,000	Value: 0.75				
1982J	17,210,000	—	—	0.45	1.25	—
1982J Proof	78,000	Value: 0.75				
1983D	20,800,000	—	—	0.45	1.25	—
1983D Proof	75,000	Value: 0.75				
1983F	24,000,000	—	—	0.45	1.25	—
1983F Proof	75,000	Value: 0.75				
1983G	13,840,000	—	—	0.45	1.50	—
1983G Proof	75,000	Value: 0.75				
1983J	21,360,000	—	—	0.45	1.25	—
1983J Proof	75,000	Value: 0.75				
1984D	11,700,000	—	—	0.45	1.50	—
1984D Proof	64,000	Value: 0.75				
1984F	13,500,000	—	—	0.45	1.50	—
1984F Proof	64,000	Value: 0.75				
1984G	7,800,000	—	—	0.45	1.50	—
1984G Proof	64,000	Value: 0.75				
1984J	12,000,000	—	—	0.45	1.50	—
1984J Proof	64,000	Value: 0.75				
1985D	15,700,000	—	—	0.45	1.50	—
1985D Proof	56,000	Value: 0.75				
1985F	18,000,000	—	—	0.45	1.50	—
1985F Proof	54,000	Value: 0.75				
1985G	10,400,000	—	—	0.45	1.50	—
1985G Proof	55,000	Value: 0.75				
1985J	16,100,000	—	—	0.45	1.50	—
1985J Proof	54,000	Value: 0.75				
1986D	2,100,000	—	1.00	2.00	8.00	—
1986D Proof	44,000	Value: 0.75				
1986F	2,400,000	—	1.00	2.00	7.00	—
1986F Proof	44,000	Value: 0.75				
1986G	1,400,000	1.00	2.00	4.00	10.00	—
1986G Proof	44,000	Value: 0.75				
1986J	2,100,000	—	1.50	3.50	12.50	—
1986J Proof	44,000	Value: 0.75				
1987D	520,000	2.00	5.00	10.00	30.00	—
1987D Proof	45,000	Value: 0.75				
1987F	600,000	1.00	3.00	6.00	15.00	—
1987F Proof	45,000	Value: 0.75				
1987G	350,000	2.50	5.00	8.00	28.00	—
1987G Proof	45,000	Value: 0.75				
1987J	530,000	1.00	3.00	6.00	15.00	—
1987J Proof	45,000	Value: 0.75				
1988D	4,160,000	—	—	0.50	2.00	—
1988D Proof	45,000	Value: 0.75				
1988F	4,800,000	—	—	0.50	2.00	—
1988F Proof	45,000	Value: 0.75				
1988G	2,770,000	—	—	1.00	3.00	—
1988G Proof	45,000	Value: 0.75				
1988J	4,300,000	—	—	0.50	2.00	—
1988J Proof	45,000	Value: 0.75				
1989D	36,400,000	—	—	—	0.50	—
1989D Proof	45,000	Value: 0.75				
1989F	42,000,000	—	—	—	0.50	—
1989F Proof	45,000	Value: 0.75				
1989G	24,220,000	—	—	—	0.50	—
1989G Proof	45,000	Value: 0.75				
1989J	37,380,000	—	—	—	0.50	—
1989J Proof	45,000	Value: 0.75				
1990A	150,000,000	—	—	—	0.50	—
1990D	58,500,000	—	—	—	0.50	—
1990D Proof	45,000	Value: 0.75				
1990F	67,500,000	—	—	—	0.50	—
1990F Proof	45,000	Value: 0.75				
1990G	38,920,000	—	—	—	0.50	—
1990J	60,070,000	—	—	—	0.50	—
1990J Proof	45,000	Value: 0.75				
1991A	22,000,000	—	—	—	0.50	—
1991A Proof	45,000	Value: 0.75				
1991D	23,100,000	—	—	—	0.50	—
1991D Proof	45,000	Value: 0.75				
1991F	26,400,000	—	—	—	0.50	—
1991F Proof	45,000	Value: 0.75				
1991G	15,400,000	—	—	—	0.50	—
1991G Proof	45,000	Value: 0.75				
1991J	23,100,000	—	—	—	0.50	—
1991J Proof	45,000	Value: 0.75				
1992A	18,000,000	—	—	—	0.50	—
1992A Proof	45,000	Value: 0.75				
1992D	18,900,000	—	—	—	0.50	—
1992D Proof	45,000	Value: 0.75				
1992F	21,600,000	—	—	—	0.50	—
1992F Proof	45,000	Value: 0.75				
1992G	12,600,000	—	—	—	1.00	—
1992G Proof	45,000	Value: 0.75				
1992J	18,900,000	—	—	—	0.50	—
1992J Proof	45,000	Value: 0.75				
1993A	16,000,000	—	—	—	0.50	—
1993A Proof	45,000	Value: 0.75				
1993D	16,800,000	—	—	—	0.50	—
1993D Proof	45,000	Value: 0.75				
1993F	19,200,000	—	—	—	0.50	—
1993F Proof	45,000	Value: 0.75				
1993G	11,200,000	—	—	—	1.50	—
1993G Proof	45,000	Value: 0.75				
1993J	16,800,000	—	—	—	0.50	—
1993J Proof	45,000	Value: 0.75				
1994A	7,500,000	—	—	—	1.50	—
1994A Proof	45,000	Value: 0.75				
1994D	7,875,000	—	—	—	3.00	—
1994D Proof	45,000	Value: 0.75				
1994F	9,000,000	—	—	—	1.50	—
1994F Proof	45,000	Value: 0.75				
1994G	5,250,000	—	—	—	1.50	—
1994G Proof	45,000	Value: 0.75				
1994J	7,875,000	—	—	—	1.00	—
1994J Proof	45,000	Value: 0.75				
1995A	1,300,000	—	—	—	2.25	—
1995A Proof	45,000	Value: 6.00				
1995D	1,365,000	—	—	—	2.25	—
1995D Proof	45,000	Value: 6.00				
1995F	20,000	—	—	—	90.00	—
1995F Proof	45,000	Value: 12.00				
1995G	20,000	—	—	—	100	—
1995G Proof	45,000	Value: 12.00				
1995J	150,000	—	—	—	14.00	—
1995J Proof	45,000	Value: 12.00				

Date	Mintage	F	VF	XF	Unc	BU
1996A In sets only	50,000	—	—	—	12.00	—
1996A Proof	45,000	Value: 13.50				
1996D In sets only	50,000	—	—	—	12.00	—
1996D Proof	45,000	Value: 13.50				
1996F In sets only	50,000	—	—	—	12.00	—
1996F Proof	45,000	Value: 13.50				
1996G In sets only	50,000	—	—	—	12.00	—
1996G Proof	45,000	Value: 13.50				
1996J In sets only	50,000	—	—	—	12.00	—
1996J Proof	45,000	Value: 13.50				
1997A In sets only	70,000	—	—	—	4.75	—
1997A Proof	45,000	Value: 5.00				
1997D In sets only	70,000	—	—	—	4.75	—
1997D Proof	45,000	Value: 5.00				
1997F In sets only	70,000	—	—	—	4.75	—
1997F Proof	45,000	Value: 5.00				
1997G In sets only	70,000	—	—	—	4.75	—
1997G Proof	45,000	Value: 5.00				
1997J In sets only	70,000	—	—	—	4.75	—
1997J Proof	45,000	Value: 5.00				
1998A In sets only	70,000	—	—	—	4.75	—
1998A Proof	45,000	Value: 5.00				
1998D In sets only	70,000	—	—	—	4.75	—
1998D Proof	45,000	Value: 5.00				
1998F In sets only	70,000	—	—	—	4.75	—
1998F Proof	45,000	Value: 5.00				
1998G In sets only	70,000	—	—	—	4.75	—
1998G Proof	45,000	Value: 5.00				
1998J In sets only	70,000	—	—	—	4.75	—
1998J Proof	45,000	Value: 5.00				
1999A In sets only	70,000	—	—	—	4.75	—
1999A Proof	45,000	Value: 5.00				
1999D In sets only	70,000	—	—	—	4.75	—
1999D Proof	45,000	Value: 5.00				
1999F In sets only	70,000	—	—	—	4.75	—
1999F Proof	45,000	Value: 5.00				
1999G In sets only	70,000	—	—	—	4.75	—
1999G Proof	45,000	Value: 5.00				
1999J In sets only	70,000	—	—	—	4.75	—
1999J Proof	45,000	Value: 5.00				
2000A In sets only	70,000	—	—	—	5.00	—
2000A Proof	45,000	Value: 5.00				
2000D In sets only	70,000	—	—	—	5.00	—
2000D Proof	45,000	Value: 5.00				
2000F In sets only	70,000	—	—	—	5.00	—
2000F Proof	45,000	Value: 5.00				
2000G In sets only	70,000	—	—	—	5.00	—
2000G Proof	45,000	Value: 5.00				
2000J In sets only	70,000	—	—	—	5.00	—
2000J Proof	45,000	Value: 5.00				

KM# 110 MARK

5.5000 g., Copper-Nickel, 23.5 mm. **Obv:** Eagle
Rev: Denomination flanked by oak leaves, date below

Date	Mintage	F	VF	XF	Unc	BU
1950D	60,467,000	—	1.50	12.00	75.00	—
1950D Proof	—	Value: 200				
1950F	69,183,000	—	1.50	12.00	70.00	—
1950F Proof	150	Value: 450				
1950G	39,826,000	—	2.00	15.00	110	—
1950G Proof	Est. 200	Value: 375				
1950J	61,483,000	—	1.00	10.00	65.00	—
1950J Proof	—	Value: 200				
1954D	5,202,000	2.00	8.00	100	425	—
1954D Proof	—	Value: 925				
1954F	6,000,000	2.50	10.00	200	650	—
1954F Proof	175	Value: 1,000				
1954G	3,459,000	4.00	25.00	450	1,900	—
1954G Proof	15	Value: 2,250				
1954J	5,341,000	1.50	7.00	55.00	400	—
1954J Proof	—	Value: 1,000				
1955D	3,093,000	2.00	9.00	125	550	—
1955D Proof	—	Value: 900				
1955F	4,909,000	1.00	6.00	50.00	500	—
1955F Proof	Est. 20	Value: 750				
1955G	2,500,000	4.00	40.00	400	1,650	—
1955G Proof	—	Value: 2,750				
1955J	5,294,000	1.00	6.00	50.00	220	—
1955J Proof	—	Value: 650				
1956D	13,231,000	1.00	4.00	35.00	325	—
1956D Proof	—	Value: 525				
1956F	14,700,000	1.00	4.00	35.00	375	—
1956F Proof	100	Value: 500				
1956G	8,362,000	1.00	4.00	35.00	275	—
1956G Proof	—	Value: 650				
1956J	11,478,000	1.00	5.00	40.00	220	—
1956J Proof	—	Value: 850				
1957D	6,820,000	1.00	5.00	75.00	325	—
1957D Proof	100	Value: 475				
1957F	6,390,000	1.00	5.00	75.00	325	—
1957F Proof	100	Value: 485				
1957G	3,841,000	2.50	10.00	145	800	—
1957G Proof	27	Value: 1,350				
1957J	6,632,000	1.00	6.00	100	500	—
1957J Proof	200	Value: 385				
1958D	4,150,000	1.00	4.00	40.00	275	—
1958D Proof	200	Value: 400				
1958F	4,109,000	1.00	5.00	45.00	375	—
1958F Proof	100	Value: 525				
1958G	3,460,000	2.50	8.00	135	1,100	—
1958G Proof	20	Value: 2,100				
1958J	4,656,000	1.00	5.00	50.00	500	—
1958J Proof	37	Value: 850				
1959D	10,409,000	—	2.00	20.00	225	—
1959D Proof	40	Value: 850				
1959F	11,972,000	—	2.00	20.00	225	—
1959F Proof	100	Value: 475				
1959G	6,921,000	1.00	5.00	40.00	375	—
1959G Proof	20	Value: 2,100				
1959J	10,691,000	1.00	4.00	35.00	650	—
1959J Proof	25	Value: 1,250				
1960D	5,453,000	—	2.00	25.00	750	—
1960D Proof	100	Value: 550				
1960F	5,709,000	—	2.00	25.00	250	—
1960F Proof	100	Value: 800				
1960G	3,632,000	1.00	6.00	50.00	600	—
1960G Proof	100	Value: 650				
1960J	5,612,000	2.50	8.00	200	750	—
1960J Proof	36	Value: 1,650				
1961D	7,536,000	—	2.00	20.00	275	—
1961D Proof	60	Value: 800				
1961F	6,029,000	—	2.00	20.00	175	—
1961F Proof	50	Value: 800				
1961G	4,843,000	1.00	6.00	50.00	475	—
1961G Proof	70	Value: 700				
1961J	7,483,000	1.50	7.00	75.00	850	—
1961J Proof	28	Value: 1,000				
1962D	10,327,000	—	1.50	15.00	400	—
1962D Proof	40	Value: 800				
1962F	11,122,000	—	1.50	10.00	125	—
1962F Proof	45	Value: 750				
1962G	6,054,000	—	2.00	25.00	800	—
1962G Proof	100	Value: 550				
1962J	10,822,000	—	2.00	17.50	220	—
1962J Proof	28	Value: 1,100				
1963D	12,624,000	—	1.00	10.00	110	—
1963D Proof	40	Value: 550				
1963F	18,292,000	—	1.50	15.00	135	—
1963F Proof	45	Value: 650				
1963G	11,253,000	—	1.50	12.50	165	—
1963G Proof	200	Value: 300				
1963J	15,906,000	—	1.50	15.00	200	—
1963J Proof	28	Value: 1,200				
1964D	8,048,000	—	0.85	4.00	100	—
1964D Proof	30	Value: 1,000				
1964F	12,796,000	—	0.85	4.00	90.00	—
1964F Proof	25	Value: 1,900				
1964G	3,465,000	—	2.00	20.00	250	—
1964G Proof	368	Value: 275				
1964J	6,958,000	—	0.85	4.00	85.00	—
1964J Proof	33	Value: 900				
1965D	9,388,000	—	0.75	3.00	37.50	—
1965F	9,013,000	—	0.75	3.00	40.00	—
1965F Proof	Est. 80	Value: 175				
1965G	6,232,000	—	0.75	3.00	47.50	—
1965G Proof	1,200	Value: 65.00				
1965J	8,023,999	—	0.75	3.00	55.00	—
1966D	11,717,000	—	0.75	3.00	42.50	—
1966F	11,368,000	—	0.75	3.00	42.50	—
1966F Proof	100	Value: 200				
1966G	7,799,000	—	0.75	3.00	55.00	—
1966G Proof	3,070	Value: 45.00				
1966J	12,030,000	—	0.75	3.00	42.50	—
1966J Proof	1,000	Value: 85.00				
1967D	13,017,000	—	0.75	3.00	32.50	—
1967F	7,500,000	—	0.75	5.00	100	—
1967F Proof	1,500	Value: 95.00				
1967G	4,324,000	—	0.75	3.00	55.00	—
1967G Proof	4,500	Value: 50.00				
1967J	13,357,000	—	0.75	3.00	40.00	—
1967J Proof	1,500	Value: 85.00				
1968D	1,303,000	—	1.00	10.00	65.00	—
1968F	1,500,000	—	0.75	4.00	40.00	—
1968F Proof	2,000	Value: 65.00				
1968G	5,198,000	—	1.50	7.00	60.00	—
1968G Proof	6,023	Value: 35.00				
1968J	1,338,000	1.00	12.50	145	375	—
1968J Proof	2,000	Value: 85.00				
1969D	13,025,000	—	0.75	1.50	22.00	—
1969F	15,021,000	—	0.75	1.50	20.00	—
1969F Proof	5,000	Value: 15.00				
1969G	8,665,000	—	0.75	1.50	32.50	—
1969G Proof	8,700	Value: 14.50				
1969J	13,370,000	—	0.75	1.50	25.00	—
1969J Proof	5,000	Value: 18.00				
1970D	17,928,000	—	0.75	1.00	20.00	—
1970F	19,408,000	—	0.75	1.00	25.00	—
1970F Proof	5,140	Value: 15.00				
1970G	20,386,000	—	0.75	1.00	32.50	—
1970G Proof	10,200	Value: 9.00				
1970J	10,707,000	—	0.75	1.00	20.00	—
1970J Proof	5,000	Value: 15.00				
1971D	24,513,000	—	0.75	1.00	10.00	—
1971D Proof	8,000	Value: 8.00				
1971F	28,275,000	—	0.75	1.00	10.00	—
1971F Proof	8,000	Value: 8.00				
1971G	16,375,000	—	0.75	1.00	12.50	—
1971G Proof	10,000	Value: 8.00				
1971J	25,214,000	—	0.75	1.00	10.00	—
1971J Proof	8,000	Value: 8.00				
1972D	20,904,000	—	0.75	1.00	10.00	—
1972D Proof	8,000	Value: 7.00				
1972F	24,086,000	—	0.75	1.00	10.00	—
1972F Proof	8,000	Value: 7.00				
1972G	13,868,000	—	0.75	1.00	10.00	—
1972G Proof	10,000	Value: 7.00				
1972J	21,360,000	—	0.75	1.00	10.00	—
1972J Proof	8,000	Value: 7.00				
1973D	14,327,000	—	0.75	1.00	6.00	—
1973D Proof	9,000	Value: 5.00				
1973F	16,591,999	—	0.75	1.00	6.00	—
1973F Proof	9,000	Value: 5.00				
1973G	10,409,000	—	0.75	1.00	6.00	—
1973G Proof	9,000	Value: 5.00				
1973J	14,704,000	—	0.75	1.00	6.00	—
1973J Proof	9,000	Value: 5.00				
1974D	20,876,000	—	0.75	1.00	6.00	—
1974D Proof	35,000	Value: 4.00				
1974F	24,057,000	—	0.75	1.00	6.00	—
1974F Proof	35,000	Value: 4.00				
1974G	13,931,000	—	0.75	1.00	6.00	—
1974G Proof	35,000	Value: 4.00				
1974J	21,440,000	—	0.75	1.00	6.00	—
1974J Proof	35,000	Value: 4.00				
1975D	18,241,000	—	0.75	1.00	6.00	—
1975D Proof	43,000	Value: 4.00				
1975F	21,059,000	—	0.75	1.00	6.00	—
1975F Proof	43,000	Value: 4.00				
1975G	12,142,000	—	0.75	1.00	6.50	—
1975G Proof	43,000	Value: 4.00				
1975J	18,770,000	—	0.75	1.00	6.00	—
1975J Proof	43,000	Value: 4.00				
1976D	15,670,000	—	0.75	1.00	6.00	—
1976D Proof	43,000	Value: 4.00				
1976F	18,105,000	—	0.75	1.00	6.00	—
1976F Proof	43,000	Value: 4.00				
1976G	10,382,000	—	0.75	1.00	6.00	—
1976G Proof	43,000	Value: 4.00				
1976J	16,046,000	—	0.75	1.00	6.00	—
1976J Proof	43,000	Value: 4.00				
1977D	20,801,000	—	0.75	0.85	3.00	—
1977D Proof	51,000	Value: 2.00				
1977F	24,026,000	—	0.75	0.85	3.00	—
1977F Proof	51,000	Value: 2.00				
1977G	13,849,000	—	0.75	0.85	3.00	—
1977G Proof	51,000	Value: 2.00				
1977J	21,416,000	—	0.75	0.85	3.00	—
1977J Proof	51,000	Value: 2.00				
1978D	15,600,000	—	0.75	0.85	2.00	—
1978D Proof	54,000	Value: 1.25				
1978F	18,000,000	—	0.75	0.85	2.00	—
1978F Proof	54,000	Value: 1.25				
1978G	10,380,000	—	0.75	0.85	2.00	—
1978G Proof	54,000	Value: 1.25				
1978J	16,020,000	—	0.75	0.85	2.00	—
Note: Error with coin alignment exists						
1978J Proof	54,000	Value: 1.25				
1979D	18,200,000	—	0.75	0.85	2.00	—
1979D Proof	89,000	Value: 1.25				
1979F	21,000,000	—	0.75	0.85	2.00	—
1979F Proof	89,000	Value: 1.25				
1979G	12,110,000	—	0.75	0.85	2.00	—
1979G Proof	89,000	Value: 1.25				
1979J	18,690,000	—	0.75	0.85	2.00	—
1979J Proof	89,000	Value: 1.25				
1980D	24,330,000	—	—	0.75	0.90	—
1980D Proof	110,000	Value: 1.00				
1980F	9,670,000	—	—	0.75	0.90	—
1980F Proof	110,000	Value: 1.00				
1980G	8,540,000	—	—	0.75	0.90	—
1980G Proof	110,000	Value: 1.00				
1980J	16,010,000	—	—	0.75	0.90	—
1980J Proof	110,000	Value: 1.00				
1981D	21,150,000	—	—	1.50	4.00	—
1981D Proof	91,000	Value: 1.00				
1981F	25,910,000	—	—	1.50	4.00	—
1981F Proof	91,000	Value: 1.00				
1981G	14,090,000	—	—	1.50	4.00	—
1981G Proof	91,000	Value: 1.00				
1981J	18,800,000	—	—	1.50	4.00	—
1981J Proof	91,000	Value: 1.00				
1982D	20,590,000	—	—	1.50	4.00	—
1982D Proof	78,000	Value: 1.00				
1982F	22,990,000	—	—	1.50	4.00	—
1982F Proof	78,000	Value: 1.00				
1982G	14,900,000	—	—	1.50	4.00	—
1982G Proof	78,000	Value: 1.00				
1982J	11,520,000	—	—	1.50	4.00	—
1982J Proof	78,000	Value: 1.00				
1983D	18,200,000	—	—	1.50	4.00	—
1983D Proof	75,000	Value: 1.00				
1983F	21,000,000	—	—	1.50	4.00	—
1983F Proof	75,000	Value: 1.00				
1983G	12,100,000	—	—	1.50	4.00	—
1983G Proof	75,000	Value: 1.00				
1983J	18,690,000	—	—	1.50	4.00	—

Date	Mintage	F	VF	XF	Unc	BU
1983J Proof	75,000	Value: 1.00				
1984D	8,400,000	—	—	1.50	4.00	—
1984D Proof	64,000	Value: 1.50				
1984F	9,700,000	—	—	1.50	4.00	—
1984F Proof	64,000	Value: 1.50				
1984G	5,600,000	—	—	1.50	4.00	—
1984G Proof	64,000	Value: 1.50				
1984J	8,700,000	—	—	1.50	4.00	—
1984J Proof	64,000	Value: 1.50				
1985D	11,700,000	—	—	1.50	4.00	—
1985D Proof	56,000	Value: 1.50				
1985F	13,500,000	—	—	1.50	4.00	—
1985F Proof	54,000	Value: 1.50				
1985G	7,800,000	—	—	1.50	4.00	—
1985G Proof	55,000	Value: 1.50				
1985J	12,000,000	—	—	1.50	4.00	—
1985J Proof	54,000	Value: 1.50				
1986D	10,400,000	—	—	1.50	5.00	—
1986D Proof	44,000	Value: 1.50				
1986F	12,000,000	—	—	1.50	5.00	—
1986F Proof	44,000	Value: 1.50				
1986G	6,900,000	—	—	1.50	5.00	—
1986G Proof	44,000	Value: 1.50				
1986J	10,700,000	—	—	1.50	5.00	—
1986J Proof	44,000	Value: 1.50				
1987D	3,120,000	—	3.50	7.50	15.00	—
1987D Proof	45,000	Value: 1.50				
1987F	3,600,000	—	3.50	7.50	15.00	—
1987F Proof	45,000	Value: 1.50				
1987G	2,080,000	—	3.50	7.50	15.00	—
1987G Proof	45,000	Value: 1.50				
1987J	3,200,000	—	3.50	7.50	15.00	—
1987J Proof	45,000	Value: 1.50				
1988D	20,800,000	—	—	0.75	2.00	—
1988D Proof	45,000	Value: 1.50				
1988F	24,000,000	—	—	0.75	2.00	—
1988F Proof	45,000	Value: 1.50				
1988G	13,800,000	—	—	0.75	2.00	—
1988G Proof	45,000	Value: 1.50				
1988J	21,400,000	—	—	0.75	2.00	—
1988J Proof	45,000	Value: 1.50				
1989D	39,000,000	—	—	—	1.00	—
1989D Proof	45,000	Value: 1.50				
1989F	45,000,000	—	—	—	1.00	—
1989F Proof	45,000	Value: 1.50				
1989G	25,950,000	—	—	—	1.00	—
1989G Proof	45,000	Value: 1.50				
1989J	40,050,000	—	—	—	1.00	—
1989J Proof	45,000	Value: 1.50				
1990A	55,000,000	—	—	—	1.00	—
1990D	77,740,000	—	—	—	1.00	—
1990D Proof	45,000	Value: 1.50				
1990F	89,700,000	—	—	—	1.00	—
1990F Proof	45,000	Value: 1.50				
1990G	51,720,000	—	—	—	1.00	—
1990G Proof	45,000	Value: 1.50				
1990J	79,830,000	—	—	—	1.00	—
1990J Proof	45,000	Value: 1.50				
1991A	30,000,000	—	—	—	1.00	—
1991A Proof	45,000	Value: 1.50				
1991D	31,500,000	—	—	—	1.00	—
1991D Proof	45,000	Value: 1.50				
1991F	36,000,000	—	—	—	1.00	—
1991F Proof	45,000	Value: 1.50				
1991G	21,000,000	—	—	—	1.00	—
1991G Proof	45,000	Value: 1.50				
1991J	31,500,000	—	—	—	1.00	—
1991J Proof	45,000	Value: 1.50				
1992A	30,000,000	—	—	—	1.00	—
1992A Proof	45,000	Value: 1.50				
1992D	31,500,000	—	—	—	1.00	—
1992D Proof	45,000	Value: 1.50				
1992F	36,000,000	—	—	—	1.00	—
1992F Proof	45,000	Value: 1.50				
1992G	21,000,000	—	—	—	1.00	—
1992G Proof	45,000	Value: 1.50				
1992J	31,500,000	—	—	—	1.00	—
1992J Proof	45,000	Value: 1.50				
1993A	8,000,000	—	—	—	1.00	—
1993A Proof	45,000	Value: 1.50				
1993D	8,400,000	—	—	—	1.00	—
1993D Proof	45,000	Value: 1.50				
1993F	9,600,000	—	—	—	1.00	—
1993F Proof	45,000	Value: 1.50				
1993G	5,600,000	—	—	—	1.00	—
1993G Proof	45,000	Value: 1.50				
1993J	8,400,000	—	—	—	1.00	—
1993J Proof	45,000	Value: 1.50				
1994A	18,000,000	—	—	—	1.00	—
1994A Proof	45,000	Value: 1.50				
1994D	18,900,000	—	—	—	1.00	—
1994D Proof	45,000	Value: 1.50				
1994F	21,800,000	—	—	—	1.00	—
1994F Proof	45,000	Value: 1.50				
1994G	12,800,000	—	—	—	1.00	—
1994G Proof	45,000	Value: 1.50				
1994J	18,900,000	—	—	—	1.00	—
1994J Proof	45,000	Value: 1.50				
1995A	20,000	—	—	—	70.00	—

Note: In sets only

Date	Mintage	F	VF	XF	Unc	BU
1995A Proof	45,000	Value: 20.00				
1995D	20,000	—	—	—	70.00	—
Note: In sets only						
1995D Proof	45,000	Value: 20.00				
1995F	20,000	—	—	—	70.00	—
Note: In sets only						
1995F Proof	45,000	Value: 20.00				
1995G	20,000	—	—	—	70.00	—
Note: In sets only						
1995G Proof	45,000	Value: 20.00				
1995J	100,000	—	—	—	18.00	—
1995J Proof	45,000	Value: 20.00				
1996A In sets only	50,000	—	—	—	12.50	—
1996A Proof	45,000	Value: 14.00				
1996D In sets only	50,000	—	—	—	12.50	—
1996D Proof	45,000	Value: 14.00				
1996F In sets only	50,000	—	—	—	12.50	—
1996F Proof	45,000	Value: 14.00				
1996G In sets only	50,000	—	—	—	12.50	—
1996G Proof	45,000	Value: 14.00				
1996J In sets only	50,000	—	—	—	12.50	—
1996J Proof	45,000	Value: 14.00				
1997A In sets only	70,000	—	—	—	4.75	—
1997A Proof	45,000	Value: 5.00				
1997D In sets only	70,000	—	—	—	4.75	—
1997D Proof	45,000	Value: 5.00				
1997F In sets only	70,000	—	—	—	4.75	—
1997F Proof	45,000	Value: 5.00				
1997G In sets only	70,000	—	—	—	4.75	—
1997G Proof	45,000	Value: 5.00				
1997J In sets only	70,000	—	—	—	4.75	—
1997J Proof	45,000	Value: 5.00				
1998A In sets only	70,000	—	—	—	4.75	—
1998A Proof	45,000	Value: 5.00				
1998D	70,000	—	—	—	4.75	—
Note: In sets only						
1998D Proof	45,000	Value: 5.00				
1998F	70,000	—	—	—	4.75	—
Note: In sets only						
1998F Proof	45,000	Value: 5.00				
1998G	70,000	—	—	—	4.75	—
Note: In sets only						
1998G Proof	45,000	Value: 5.00				
1998J	70,000	—	—	—	4.75	—
Note: In sets only						
1998J Proof	45,000	Value: 5.00				
1999A	70,000	—	—	—	4.75	—
Note: In sets only						
1999A Proof	45,000	Value: 5.00				
1999D	70,000	—	—	—	4.75	—
Note: In sets only						
1999D Proof	45,000	Value: 5.00				
1999F	70,000	—	—	—	4.75	—
Note: In sets only						
1999F Proof	45,000	Value: 5.00				
1999G In sets only	70,000	—	—	—	4.75	—
1999G Proof	45,000	Value: 5.00				
1999J In sets only	70,000	—	—	—	4.75	—
1999J Proof	45,000	Value: 5.00				
2000A In sets only	70,000	—	—	—	5.00	—
2000A Proof	45,000	Value: 5.00				
2000D In sets only	70,000	—	—	—	5.00	—
2000D Proof	45,000	Value: 5.00				
2000F In sets only	70,000	—	—	—	5.00	—
2000F Proof	45,000	Value: 5.00				
2000G In sets only	70,000	—	—	—	5.00	—
2000G Proof	45,000	Value: 5.00				
2000J In sets only	70,000	—	—	—	5.00	—
2000J Proof	45,000	Value: 5.00				

KM# 111 2 MARK
7.0000 g., Copper-Nickel, 26.75 mm. **Obv:** Eagle
Rev: Denomination flanked by leaves, grapes, and grain sprigs, date above

Date	Mintage	F	VF	XF	Unc	BU
1951D	19,564,000	—	25.00	30.00	100	—
1951D Proof	200	Value: 450				
1951F	22,609,000	—	25.00	30.00	100	—
1951F Proof	150	Value: 500				
1951G	Est. 13,012,000	—	50.00	75.00	200	—

Note: The 1951G dated coin was restruck without authorization by a mint official using genuine dies - quantity unknown

Date	Mintage	F	VF	XF	Unc	BU
1951G Proof	33	Value: 1,200				
1951J	20,104,000	—	25.00	30.00	100	—
1951J Proof	180	Value: 450				

KM# 116 2 MARK
7.0000 g., Copper-Nickel, 26.75 mm. **Subject:** Max Planck
Obv: Eagle above denomination **Rev:** Head left, dates below

Date	Mintage	F	VF	XF	Unc	BU
1957D	7,452,000	—	2.00	6.00	65.00	—
1957D Proof	350	Value: 235				
1957F	6,337,000	—	2.00	6.00	65.00	—
1957F Proof	100	Value: 325				
1957G	2,598,000	—	3.00	7.50	135	—
1957G Proof	56	Value: 600				
1957J	11,210,000	—	2.00	6.00	60.00	—
1957J Proof	370	Value: 175				
1958D	12,623,000	—	1.50	5.00	50.00	—
1958D Proof	1,240	Value: 85.00				
1958F	16,825,000	—	1.50	4.00	45.00	—
1958F Proof	300	Value: 200				
1958G	10,744,000	—	1.50	4.00	45.00	—
1958G Proof	45	Value: 700				
1958J	9,408,000	—	1.50	4.00	45.00	—
1958J Proof	100	Value: 400				
1959D	1,020,000	—	4.00	15.00	240	—
1959D Proof	38	Value: 1,150				
1959F	203,000	—	15.00	60.00	425	—
1959F Proof	24	Value: 1,850				
1960D	3,535,000	—	1.50	4.00	35.00	—
1960D Proof	100	Value: 325				
1960F	3,692,000	—	1.50	4.00	35.00	—
1960F Proof	50	Value: 600				
1960G	2,695,000	—	2.00	4.00	35.00	—
1960G Proof	130	Value: 300				
1960J	4,676,000	—	1.50	4.00	35.00	—
1960J Proof	36	Value: 800				
1961D	3,918,000	—	1.50	4.00	35.00	—
1961D Proof	50	Value: 600				
1961F	3,872,000	—	1.50	4.00	35.00	—
1961F Proof	46	Value: 650				
1961G	2,776,000	—	2.00	4.00	35.00	—
1961G Proof	100	Value: 325				
1961J	2,940,000	—	1.50	4.00	35.00	—
1961J Proof	28	Value: 800				
1962D	4,105,000	—	2.00	6.00	35.00	—
1962D Proof	50	Value: 600				
1962F	3,344,000	—	2.00	6.00	35.00	—
1962F Proof	42	Value: 625				
1962G	1,800,000	—	2.00	6.00	45.00	—
1962G Proof	130	Value: 300				
1962J	3,609,000	—	2.00	6.00	25.00	—
1962J Proof	28	Value: 750				
1963D	4,411,000	—	1.50	4.00	25.00	—
1963D Proof	40	Value: 650				
1963F	3,752,000	—	1.50	4.00	25.00	—
1963F Proof	47	Value: 600				
1963G	3,448,000	—	1.50	4.00	25.00	—
1963G Proof	200	Value: 350				
1963J	7,348,000	—	1.50	4.00	25.00	—
1963J Proof	32	Value: 700				
1964D	5,205,000	—	1.50	4.00	20.00	—
1964D Proof	40	Value: 650				
1964F	4,834,000	—	1.50	4.00	20.00	—
1964F Proof	36	Value: 800				
1964G	3,044,000	5.00	10.00	25.00	125	—
1964G Proof	368	Value: 150				
1964J	2,681,000	—	1.50	4.00	20.00	—
1964J Proof	43	Value: 600				
1965D	3,903,000	—	1.50	2.50	15.00	—
1965D Proof	35	Value: 800				
1965F	4,045,000	—	1.50	2.50	15.00	—
1965F Proof	300	Value: 250				
1965G	2,599,000	—	1.50	2.50	15.00	—
1965G Proof	8,233	Value: 5.00				
1965J	4,006,999	—	1.50	2.50	15.00	—

Note: Error exists without edge inscription

Date	Mintage	F	VF	XF	Unc	BU
1965J Proof	36	Value: 750				
1966D	5,855,000	—	1.50	2.50	12.00	—
1966D Proof	20	Value: 900				
1966F	3,750,000	—	1.50	2.50	12.00	—
1966F Proof	450	Value: 250				
1966G	3,895,000	—	1.50	2.50	12.00	—
1966G Proof	3,070	Value: 20.00				
1966J	6,014,000	—	1.50	2.50	12.00	—
1966J Proof	1,000	Value: 35.00				
1967D	3,254,000	—	1.50	2.50	12.00	—
1967D Proof	20	Value: 900				
1967F	3,758,000	—	1.50	2.50	12.00	—
1967F Proof	1,600	Value: 32.00				
1967G	1,878,000	—	1.50	4.00	16.50	—
1967G Proof	5,363	Value: 28.00				
1967J	6,684,000	—	1.25	2.50	12.00	—
1967J Proof	1,500	Value: 32.00				
1968D	4,166,000	—	1.50	2.50	15.00	—
1968D Proof	30	Value: 850				

Date	Mintage	F	VF	XF	Unc	BU
1968F	1,050,000	—	2.00	5.00	20.00	—
1968F Proof	3,100	Value: 22.00				
1968G	3,060,000	—	2.00	2.50	12.00	—
1968G Proof	6,023	Value: 15.00				
1968J	939,000	—	2.00	4.00	20.00	—
1968J Proof	2,000	Value: 28.00				
1969D	2,602,000	—	2.00	2.50	15.00	—
1969F	3,005,000	—	2.00	2.50	15.00	—
1969F Proof	5,100	Value: 6.00				
1969G	1,754,000	—	2.00	2.50	16.50	—
1969G Proof	8,700	Value: 6.00				
1969J	2,680,000	—	2.00	2.50	10.00	—
1969J Proof	5,000	Value: 6.00				
1970D	5,203,000	—	1.50	2.00	4.00	—
1970F	6,018,000	—	1.50	2.00	4.00	—
1970F Proof	5,140	Value: 7.50				
1970G	3,461,000	—	1.50	2.00	4.00	—
1970G Proof	10,000	Value: 5.00				
1970J	5,691,000	—	1.50	2.00	4.00	—
1970J Proof	5,000	Value: 6.00				
1971D	8,451,000	—	1.00	1.25	3.00	—
1971D Proof	8,000	Value: 5.00				
1971F	10,017,000	—	1.00	1.25	3.00	—
1971F Proof	8,000	Value: 5.00				
1971G	5,631,000	—	1.00	1.25	3.00	—
1971G Proof	10,000	Value: 5.00				
1971J	8,786,000	—	1.00	1.25	3.00	—
1971J Proof	8,000	Value: 6.00				

KM# 124 2 MARK
7.0000 g., Copper-Nickel Clad Nickel, 26.75 mm.
Subject: Konrad Adenauer **Obv:** Eagle above denomination
Rev: Head left, dates below

Date	Mintage	F	VF	XF	Unc	BU
1969D	7,001,000	—	—	1.50	3.00	—
1969F	7,006,000	—	—	1.50	3.00	—
1969G	7,010,000	—	—	1.50	3.00	—
1969J	7,000,000	—	—	1.50	3.00	—
1970D	7,318,000	—	—	1.50	3.00	—
1970F	8,422,000	—	—	1.50	3.00	—
1970G	4,844,000	—	—	1.50	3.00	—
1970J	7,476,000	—	—	1.50	3.00	—
1971D	7,287,000	—	—	1.50	3.00	—
1971F	8,400,000	—	—	1.50	3.00	—
1971G	4,848,000	—	—	1.50	3.00	—
1971J	7,476,000	—	—	1.50	3.00	—
1972D	7,286,000	—	—	1.50	3.00	—
1972D Proof	8,000	Value: 4.50				
1972F	8,392,000	—	—	1.50	3.00	—
1972F Proof	8,000	Value: 4.50				
1972G	4,848,000	—	—	1.50	3.00	—
1972G Proof	10,000	Value: 4.50				
1972J	7,476,000	—	—	1.50	3.00	—
1972J Proof	8,000	Value: 4.50				
1973D	10,393,000	—	—	1.50	3.00	—
1973D Proof	9,000	Value: 4.50				
1973F	11,015,000	—	—	1.50	3.00	—

Note: Errors exist without edge inscription

Date	Mintage	F	VF	XF	Unc	BU
1973F Proof	9,000	Value: 4.50				
1973G	9,022,000	—	—	1.50	3.00	—
1973G Proof	9,000	Value: 4.50				
1973J	12,272,000	—	—	1.50	3.00	—

Note: Errors with coin alignment exist

Date	Mintage	F	VF	XF	Unc	BU
1973J Proof	9,000	Value: 4.50				
1974D	5,151,000	—	—	1.50	3.00	—
1974D Proof	35,000	Value: 2.25				
1974F	5,894,000	—	—	1.50	3.00	—
1974F Proof	35,000	Value: 2.25				
1974G	3,790,000	—	—	1.50	3.00	—
1974G Proof	35,000	Value: 2.25				
1974J	5,282,000	—	—	1.50	3.00	—
1974J Proof	35,000	Value: 2.25				
1975D	4,553,000	—	—	1.50	2.50	—
1975D Proof	43,000	Value: 2.25				
1975F	5,270,000	—	—	1.50	2.50	—
1975F Proof	43,000	Value: 2.25				
1975G	3,035,000	—	—	1.50	2.50	—
1975G Proof	43,000	Value: 2.25				
1975J	4,673,000	—	—	1.50	2.50	—
1975J Proof	43,000	Value: 2.25				
1976D	4,576,000	—	—	1.50	2.50	—
1976D Proof	43,000	Value: 2.25				
1976F	5,257,000	—	—	1.50	2.50	—
1976F Proof	43,000	Value: 2.25				
1976G	3,028,000	—	—	1.50	2.50	—
1976G Proof	43,000	Value: 2.25				
1976J	4,673,000	—	—	1.50	2.50	—
1976J Proof	43,000	Value: 2.25				
1977D	5,906,000	—	—	1.50	2.50	—
1977D Proof	51,000	Value: 2.00				

Date	Mintage	F	VF	XF	Unc	BU
1977F	6,765,000	—	—	1.50	2.50	—
1977F Proof	51,000	Value: 2.00				
1977G	3,892,000	—	—	1.50	2.50	—
1977G Proof	51,000	Value: 2.00				
1977J	6,007,000	—	—	1.50	2.50	—
1977J Proof	51,000	Value: 2.00				
1978D	3,304,000	—	—	1.50	2.50	—
1978D Proof	54,000	Value: 2.00				
1978F	3,804	—	—	—	—	—
1978F Proof	54,000	Value: 2.00				
1978G	2,217,000	—	—	1.50	2.50	—
1978G Proof	54,000	Value: 2.00				
1978J	3,392,000	—	—	1.50	2.50	—
1978J Proof	54,000	Value: 2.00				
1979D	3,209,000	—	—	1.50	2.50	—
1979D Proof	89,000	Value: 2.00				
1979F	3,689,000	—	—	1.50	2.50	—
1979F Proof	89,000	Value: 2.00				
1979G	2,165,000	—	—	1.50	2.50	—
1979G Proof	89,000	Value: 2.00				
1979J	3,293,000	—	*	1.50	2.50	—
1979J Proof	89,000	Value: 2.00				
1980D	10,810,000	—	—	1.50	2.00	—
1980D Proof	110,000	Value: 2.00				
1980F	8,910,000	—	—	1.50	2.00	—
1980F Proof	110,000	Value: 2.00				
1980G	1,170,000	—	—	1.50	2.00	—
1980G Proof	110,000	Value: 2.00				
1980J	4,670,000	—	—	1.50	2.00	—
1980J Proof	110,000	Value: 2.00				
1981D	8,180,000	—	—	1.50	2.00	—
1981D Proof	91,000	Value: 2.00				
1981F	7,690,000	—	—	1.50	2.00	—
1981F Proof	91,000	Value: 2.00				
1981G	7,070,000	—	—	1.50	2.00	—
1981G Proof	91,000	Value: 2.00				
1981J	8,289,999	—	—	1.50	2.00	—
1981J Proof	91,000	Value: 2.00				
1982D	9,220,000	—	—	1.50	2.00	—
1982D Proof	78,000	Value: 2.00				
1982F	11,260,000	—	—	1.50	2.00	—
1982F Proof	78,000	Value: 2.00				
1982G	6,640,000	—	—	1.50	2.00	—
1982G Proof	78,000	Value: 2.00				
1982J	9,790,000	—	—	1.50	2.00	—
1982J Proof	78,000	Value: 2.00				
1983D	1,560,000	—	—	1.50	2.00	—
1983D Proof	75,000	Value: 2.00				
1983F	1,800,000	—	—	1.50	2.00	—
1983F Proof	75,000	Value: 2.00				
1983G	1,030,000	—	—	1.50	2.00	—
1983G Proof	75,000	Value: 2.00				
1983J	1,600,000	—	—	1.50	2.00	—
1983J Proof	75,000	Value: 2.00				
1984D	52,000	—	2.00	4.50	8.50	—
1984D Proof	64,000	Value: 2.00				
1984F	60,000	—	2.00	4.50	8.50	—
1984F Proof	64,000	Value: 2.00				
1984G	35,000	—	3.00	6.00	11.50	—
1984G Proof	64,000	Value: 2.00				
1984J	53,000	—	2.00	4.50	8.50	—
1984J Proof	64,000	Value: 2.00				
1985D	2,600,000	—	—	—	2.00	—
1985D Proof	56,000	Value: 2.25				
1985F	3,000,000	—	—	—	1.75	—
1985F Proof	54,000	Value: 2.25				
1985G	1,730,000	—	—	—	1.75	—
1985G Proof	55,000	Value: 2.25				
1985J	2,670,000	—	—	—	1.75	—
1985J Proof	54,000	Value: 2.25				
1986D	2,600,000	—	—	—	1.75	—
1986D Proof	44,000	Value: 2.25				
1986F	3,000,000	—	—	—	1.75	—
1986F Proof	44,000	Value: 2.25				
1986G	1,730,000	—	—	—	1.75	—
1986G Proof	44,000	Value: 2.25				
1986J	2,670,000	—	—	—	1.75	—
1986J Proof	44,000	Value: 2.25				
1987D	4,420,000	—	—	—	1.75	—
1987D Proof	45,000	Value: 2.25				
1987F	5,100,000	—	—	—	1.75	—
1987F Proof	45,000	Value: 2.25				
1987G	2,940,000	—	—	—	1.75	—
1987G Proof	45,000	Value: 2.25				
1987J	4,540,000	—	—	—	1.75	—
1987J Proof	45,000	Value: 2.25				

KM# A127 2 MARK
7.0000 g., Copper-Nickel Clad Nickel, 26.75 mm.
Subject: Theodor Heuss **Obv:** Eagle above denomination
Rev: Head left, dates below

Date	Mintage	F	VF	XF	Unc	BU
1970D	7,317,000	—	—	1.50	3.00	—
1970F	8,426,000	—	—	1.50	3.00	—
1970G	4,844,000	—	—	1.50	3.00	—
1970J	7,476,000	—	—	1.50	3.00	—
1971D	7,280,000	—	—	1.50	3.00	—
1971F	8,403,000	—	—	1.50	3.00	—
1971G	4,841,000	—	—	1.50	3.00	—
1971J	7,476,000	—	—	1.50	3.00	—
1972D	7,288,000	—	—	1.50	3.00	—
1972D Proof	8,000	Value: 4.50				
1972F	8,401,000	—	—	1.50	3.00	—
1972F Proof	8,000	Value: 4.50				
1972G	4,859,000	—	—	1.50	3.00	—
1972G Proof	10,000	Value: 4.50				
1972J	7,476,000	—	—	1.50	3.00	—
1972J Proof	8,000	Value: 4.50				
1973D	10,379,000	—	—	1.50	3.00	—
1973D Proof	9,000	Value: 4.50				
1973F	11,018,000	—	—	1.50	3.00	—
1973F Proof	9,000	Value: 4.50				
1973G	8,975,000	—	—	1.50	3.00	—
1973G Proof	9,000	Value: 4.50				
1973J	12,360,000	—	—	1.50	3.00	—
1973J Proof	9,000	Value: 4.50				
1974D	5,147,000	—	—	1.50	3.00	—
1974D Proof	35,000	Value: 2.00				
1974F	5,899,000	—	—	1.50	3.00	—
1974F Proof	35,000	Value: 2.00				
1974G	3,820,000	—	—	1.50	3.00	—
1974G Proof	35,000	Value: 2.00				
1974J	5,280,000	—	—	1.50	3.00	—
1974J Proof	35,000	Value: 2.00				
1975D	4,623,000	—	—	1.50	3.00	—
1975D Proof	43,000	Value: 2.00				
1975F	5,251,000	—	—	1.50	2.00	—
1975F Proof	43,000	Value: 2.00				
1975G	3,034,000	—	—	1.50	2.00	—
1975G Proof	43,000	Value: 2.00				
1975J	4,675,000	—	—	1.50	2.00	—
1975J Proof	43,000	Value: 2.00				
1976D	4,546,000	—	—	1.50	2.00	—
1976D Proof	43,000	Value: 2.00				
1976F	5,259,000	—	—	1.50	2.00	—
1976F Proof	43,000	Value: 2.00				
1976G	3,028,000	—	—	1.50	2.00	—
1976G Proof	43,000	Value: 2.00				
1976J	4,681,000	—	—	1.50	2.00	—
1976J Proof	43,000	Value: 2.00				
1977D	5,857,000	—	—	1.50	2.00	—
1977D Proof	51,000	Value: 1.75				
1977F	6,752,000	—	—	1.50	2.00	—
1977F Proof	51,000	Value: 1.75				
1977G	3,892,000	—	—	1.50	2.00	—
1977G Proof	51,000	Value: 1.75				
1977J	6,009,000	—	—	1.50	2.00	—
1977J Proof	51,000	Value: 1.75				
1978D	3,804,000	—	—	1.50	2.00	—

Note: Errors without edge inscription exist

Date	Mintage	F	VF	XF	Unc	BU
1978D Proof	54,000	Value: 1.75				
1978F	3,804,000	—	—	1.50	2.00	—
1978F Proof	54,000	Value: 1.75				
1978G	2,217,000	—	—	1.50	2.00	—
1978G Proof	54,000	Value: 1.75				
1978J	3,392,000	—	—	1.50	2.00	—
1978J Proof	54,000	Value: 1.75				
1979D	3,209,000	—	—	1.50	2.00	—
1979D Proof	89,000	Value: 1.75				
1979F	3,689,000	—	—	1.50	2.00	—
1979F Proof	89,000	Value: 1.75				
1979G	2,165,000	—	—	1.50	2.00	—
1979G Proof	89,000	Value: 1.75				
1979J	3,293,000	—	—	1.50	2.00	—
1979J Proof	89,000	Value: 1.75				
1980D	2,000,000	—	—	1.50	1.75	—
1980D Proof	110,000	Value: 1.75				
1980F	2,300,000	—	—	1.50	1.75	—
1980F Proof	110,000	Value: 1.75				
1980G	1,300,000	—	—	1.50	1.75	—
1980G Proof	110,000	Value: 1.75				
1980J	2,000,000	—	—	1.50	1.75	—
1980J Proof	110,000	Value: 1.75				
1981D	2,000,000	—	—	1.50	1.75	—
1981D Proof	91,000	Value: 1.75				
1981F	2,300,000	—	—	1.50	1.75	—
1981F Proof	91,000	Value: 1.75				
1981G	1,300,000	—	—	1.50	1.75	—
1981G Proof	91,000	Value: 1.75				
1981J	2,000,000	—	—	1.50	1.75	—
1981J Proof	91,000	Value: 1.75				
1982D	3,100,000	—	—	1.50	1.75	—
1982D Proof	78,000	Value: 1.75				
1982F	3,600,000	—	—	1.50	1.75	—
1982F Proof	78,000	Value: 1.75				
1982G	2,100,000	—	—	1.50	1.75	—
1982G Proof	78,000	Value: 1.75				
1982J	3,200,000	—	—	1.50	1.75	—
1982J Proof	78,000	Value: 1.75				
1983D	1,560,000	—	—	1.50	1.75	—
1983D Proof	75,000	Value: 1.75				
1983F	1,800,000	—	—	1.50	1.75	—
1983F Proof	75,000	Value: 1.75				
1983G	1,030,000	—	—	1.50	1.75	—

Date	Mintage	F	VF	XF	Unc	BU
1983G Proof	75,000	Value: 1.75				
1983J	1,600,000	—	—	1.50	1.75	—
1983J Proof	75,000	Value: 1.75				
1984D	52,000	—	2.00	4.50	8.50	—
1984D Proof	64,000	Value: 2.00				
1984F	60,000	—	2.00	4.50	8.50	—
1984F Proof	64,000	Value: 2.00				
1984G	35,000	—	3.00	6.00	11.50	—
1984G Proof	64,000	Value: 2.00				
1984J	53,000	—	2.00	4.50	8.50	—
1984J Proof	64,000	Value: 2.00				
1985D	2,600,000	—	—	—	1.75	—
1985D Proof	56,000	Value: 2.25				
1985F	3,000,000	—	—	—	1.75	—
1985F Proof	54,000	Value: 2.25				
1985G	1,730,000	—	—	—	1.75	—
1985G Proof	55,000	Value: 2.25				
1985J	2,670,000	—	—	—	1.75	—
1985J Proof	54,000	Value: 2.25				
1986D	2,600,000	—	—	—	1.75	—
1986D Proof	44,000	Value: 2.25				
1986F	3,000,000	—	—	—	1.75	—
1986F Proof	44,000	Value: 2.25				
1986G	1,730,000	—	—	—	1.75	—
1986G Proof	44,000	Value: 2.25				
1986J	2,670,000	—	—	—	1.75	—
1986J Proof	44,000	Value: 2.25				
1987D	4,420,000	—	—	—	1.75	—
1987D Proof	45,000	Value: 2.25				
1987F	5,100,000	—	—	—	1.75	—
1987F Proof	45,000	Value: 2.25				
1987G	2,940,000	—	—	—	1.75	—
1987G Proof	45,000	Value: 2.25				
1987J	4,540,000	—	—	—	1.75	—
1987J Proof	45,000	Value: 2.25				

KM# 149 2 MARK

7.0000 g., Copper-Nickel Clad Nickel, 26.75 mm. **Subject:** Dr. Kurt Schumacher **Obv:** Eagle above denomination **Rev:** Head 3/4 left divides dates

Date	Mintage	F	VF	XF	Unc	BU
1979D	3,209,000	—	—	1.50	2.00	—
1979D Proof	89,000	Value: 1.75				
1979F	3,689,000	—	—	1.50	2.00	—
1979F Proof	89,000	Value: 1.75				
1979G	2,165,000	—	—	1.50	2.00	—
1979G Proof	89,000	Value: 1.75				
1979J	3,293,000	—	—	1.50	2.00	—
1979J Proof	89,000	Value: 1.75				
1980D	2,000,000	—	—	1.50	2.00	—
1980D Proof	110,000	Value: 1.75				
1980F	2,300,000	—	—	1.50	2.00	—
1980F Proof	110,000	Value: 1.75				
1980G	1,300,000	—	—	1.50	2.00	—
1980G Proof	110,000	Value: 1.75				
1980J	2,000,000	—	—	1.50	2.00	—
1980J Proof	110,000	Value: 1.75				
1981D	2,000,000	—	—	1.50	2.00	—
1981D Proof	91,000	Value: 1.75				
1981F	2,000,000	—	—	1.50	2.00	—

Note: Errors without edge inscription exist

Date	Mintage	F	VF	XF	Unc	BU
1981F Proof	91,000	Value: 1.75				
1981G	1,300,000	—	—	1.50	2.00	—
1981G Proof	91,000	Value: 1.75				
1981J	2,000,000	—	—	1.50	2.00	—
1981J Proof	91,000	Value: 1.75				
1982D	3,100,000	—	—	1.50	2.00	—
1982D Proof	78,000	Value: 1.75				
1982F	3,600,000	—	—	1.50	2.00	—
1982F Proof	78,000	Value: 1.75				
1982G	2,100,000	—	—	1.50	2.00	—
1982G Proof	78,000	Value: 1.75				
1982J	3,200,000	—	—	1.50	2.00	—
1982J Proof	78,000	Value: 1.75				
1983D	1,560,000	—	—	1.50	2.00	—
1983D Proof	75,000	Value: 1.75				
1983F	1,800,000	—	—	1.50	2.00	—
1983F Proof	75,000	Value: 1.75				
1983G	1,030,000	—	—	1.50	2.00	—
1983G Proof	75,000	Value: 1.75				
1983J	1,600,000	—	—	1.50	2.00	—
1983J Proof	75,000	Value: 1.75				
1984D	52,000	—	2.00	4.50	8.50	—
1984D Proof	64,000	Value: 1.75				
1984F	60,000	—	2.00	4.50	8.50	—
1984F Proof	64,000	Value: 1.75				
1984G	35,000	—	3.00	6.00	11.50	—
1984G Proof	64,000	Value: 1.75				
1984J	53,000	—	2.00	4.50	8.50	—
1984J Proof	64,000	Value: 1.75				

Date	Mintage	F	VF	XF	Unc	BU
1985D	2,600,000	—	—	—	1.75	—
1985D Proof	56,000	Value: 2.25				
1985F	3,000,000	—	—	—	1.75	—
1985F Proof	54,000	Value: 2.25				
1985G	1,730,000	—	—	—	1.75	—
1985G Proof	55,000	Value: 2.25				
1985J	2,670,000	—	—	—	1.75	—
1985J Proof	54,000	Value: 2.25				
1986D	2,600,000	—	—	—	1.75	—
1986D Proof	44,000	Value: 2.25				
1986F	3,000,000	—	—	—	1.75	—
1986F Proof	44,000	Value: 2.25				
1986G	1,730,000	—	—	—	1.75	—
1986G Proof	44,000	Value: 2.25				
1986J	2,670,000	—	—	—	1.75	—
1986J Proof	44,000	Value: 2.25				
1987D	4,420,000	—	—	—	1.75	—
1987D Proof	45,000	Value: 2.25				
1987F	5,100,000	—	—	—	1.75	—
1987F Proof	45,000	Value: 2.25				
1987G	2,940,000	—	—	—	1.75	—
1987G Proof	45,000	Value: 2.25				
1987J	4,540,000	—	—	—	1.75	—
1987J Proof	45,000	Value: 2.25				
1988D	5,850,000	—	—	—	1.75	—
1988D Proof	45,000	Value: 2.25				
1988F	6,750,000	—	—	—	1.75	—
1988F Proof	45,000	Value: 2.25				
1988G	3,890,000	—	—	—	1.75	—
1988G Proof	45,000	Value: 2.25				
1988J	6,010,000	—	—	—	1.75	—
1988J Proof	45,000	Value: 2.25				
1989D	10,400,000	—	—	—	1.75	—
1989D Proof	45,000	Value: 2.25				
1989F	12,000,000	—	—	—	1.75	—
1989F Proof	45,000	Value: 2.25				
1989G	6,920,000	—	—	—	1.75	—
1989G Proof	45,000	Value: 2.25				
1989J	10,680,000	—	—	—	1.75	—
1989J Proof	45,000	Value: 2.25				
1990D	18,370,000	—	—	—	1.75	—
1990D Proof	45,000	Value: 2.25				
1990F	21,200,000	—	—	—	1.75	—
1990F Proof	45,000	Value: 2.25				
1990G	12,220,000	—	—	—	1.75	—
1990G Proof	45,000	Value: 2.25				
1990J	18,870,000	—	—	—	1.75	—
1990J Proof	45,000	Value: 2.25				
1991A	4,000,000	—	—	—	1.75	—
1991A Proof	45,000	Value: 2.25				
1991D	4,200,000	—	—	—	1.75	—
1991D Proof	45,000	Value: 2.25				
1991F	4,800,000	—	—	—	1.75	—
1991F Proof	45,000	Value: 2.25				
1991G	2,800,000	—	—	—	1.75	—
1991G Proof	45,000	Value: 2.25				
1991J	4,200,000	—	—	—	1.75	—
1991J Proof	45,000	Value: 2.25				
1992A	7,330,000	—	—	—	1.75	—
1992A Proof	45,000	Value: 2.25				
1992D	7,700,000	—	—	—	1.75	—
1992D Proof	45,000	Value: 2.25				
1992F	8,800,000	—	—	—	1.75	—
1992F Proof	45,000	Value: 2.25				
1992G	5,130,000	—	—	—	1.75	—
1992G Proof	45,000	Value: 2.25				
1992J	7,700,000	—	—	—	1.75	—
1992J Proof	45,000	Value: 2.25				
1993A	600,000	—	—	3.00	7.00	—
1993A Proof	45,000	Value: 2.25				
1993D	630,000	—	—	3.00	7.00	—
1993D Proof	45,000	Value: 2.25				
1993F	720,000	—	—	3.00	7.00	—
1993F Proof	45,000	Value: 2.25				
1993G	420,000	—	—	4.00	10.00	—
1993G Proof	45,000	Value: 2.25				
1993J	630,000	—	—	3.00	7.00	—
1993J Proof	45,000	Value: 2.25				

KM# 170 2 MARK

7.0000 g., Copper-Nickel Clad Nickel, 26.75 mm. **Subject:** Ludwig Erhard **Obv:** Eagle above denomination **Rev:** Head facing divides dates

Date	Mintage	F	VF	XF	Unc	BU
1988D	5,850,000	—	—	—	1.65	—
1988D Proof	45,000	Value: 2.00				
1988F	6,750,000	—	—	—	1.65	—
1988F Proof	45,000	Value: 2.00				
1988G	3,890,000	—	—	—	1.65	—
1988G Proof	45,000	Value: 2.00				

Date	Mintage	F	VF	XF	Unc	BU
1988J	6,010,000	—	—	—	1.65	—
1988J Proof	45,000	Value: 2.00				
1989D	10,400,000	—	—	—	1.65	—
1989D Proof	45,000	Value: 2.00				
1989F	12,000,000	—	—	—	1.65	—
1989F Proof	45,000	Value: 2.00				
1989G	6,920,000	—	—	—	1.65	—
1989G Proof	45,000	Value: 2.00				
1989J	10,680,000	—	—	—	1.65	—
1989J Proof	45,000	Value: 2.00				
1990D	18,370,000	—	—	—	1.65	—
1990D Proof	45,000	Value: 2.00				
1990F	21,200,000	—	—	—	1.65	—
1990F Proof	45,000	Value: 2.00				
1990G	12,220,000	—	—	—	1.65	—
1990G Proof	45,000	Value: 2.00				
1990J	18,870,000	—	—	—	1.65	—
1990J Proof	45,000	Value: 2.00				
1991A	4,000,000	—	—	—	1.65	—
1991A Proof	45,000	Value: 2.00				
1991D	4,200,000	—	—	—	1.65	—
1991D Proof	45,000	Value: 2.00				
1991F	4,800,000	—	—	—	1.65	—
1991F Proof	45,000	Value: 2.00				
1991G	2,800,000	—	—	—	1.65	—

Note: Errors without edge inscription exist

Date	Mintage	F	VF	XF	Unc	BU
1991G Proof	45,000	Value: 2.00				
1991J	4,200,000	—	—	—	1.65	—
1991J Proof	45,000	Value: 2.00				
1992A	7,330,000	—	—	—	1.75	—
1992A Proof	45,000	Value: 2.25				
1992D	7,700,000	—	—	—	1.75	—
1992D Proof	45,000	Value: 2.25				
1992F	8,800,000	—	—	—	1.75	—
1992F Proof	45,000	Value: 2.25				
1992G	5,130,000	—	—	—	1.75	—
1992G Proof	45,000	Value: 2.25				
1992J	7,700,000	—	—	—	1.75	—
1992J Proof	45,000	Value: 2.25				
1993A	600,000	—	—	3.00	7.00	—
1993A Proof	45,000	Value: 2.25				
1993D	630,000	—	—	3.00	7.00	—
1993D Proof	45,000	Value: 2.25				
1993F	720,000	—	—	3.00	7.00	—
1993F Proof	45,000	Value: 2.25				
1993G	420,000	—	—	4.00	10.00	—
1993G Proof	45,000	Value: 2.25				
1993J	630,000	—	—	3.00	7.00	—
1993J Proof	45,000	Value: 2.25				
1994A	5,000,000	—	—	—	1.75	—
1994A Proof	45,000	Value: 2.25				
1994D	5,250,000	—	—	—	1.75	—
1994D Proof	45,000	Value: 2.25				
1994F	6,000,000	—	—	—	1.75	—
1994F Proof	45,000	Value: 2.25				
1994G	3,500,000	—	—	—	1.75	—
1994G Proof	45,000	Value: 2.25				
1994J	5,250,000	—	—	—	1.75	—
1994J Proof	45,000	Value: 2.25				
1995A	1,595,000	—	—	—	3.50	—
1995A Proof	45,000	Value: 17.50				
1995D In sets only	20,000	—	—	—	60.00	—
1995D Proof	45,000	Value: 17.50				
1995F In sets only	20,000	—	—	—	60.00	—
1995F Proof	45,000	Value: 17.50				
1995G	920,000	—	—	—	6.00	—
1995G Proof	45,000	Value: 17.50				
1995J In sets only	20,000	—	—	—	60.00	—
1995J Proof	45,000	Value: 17.50				
1996A	—	—	—	—	5.00	—
1996A Proof	45,000	Value: 6.00				
1996D	—	—	—	—	5.00	—
1996D Proof	45,000	Value: 6.00				
1996F	—	—	—	—	5.00	—
1996F Proof	45,000	Value: 6.00				
1996G	—	—	—	—	5.00	—
1996G Proof	45,000	Value: 6.00				
1996J	—	—	—	—	5.00	—
1996J Proof	45,000	Value: 6.00				
1997A In sets only	70,000	—	—	—	4.25	—
1997A Proof	45,000	Value: 5.00				
1997D In sets only	70,000	—	—	—	4.25	—
1997D Proof	45,000	Value: 5.00				
1997F In sets only	70,000	—	—	—	4.25	—
1997F Proof	45,000	Value: 5.00				
1997G In sets only	70,000	—	—	—	4.25	—
1997G Proof	45,000	Value: 5.00				
1997J In sets only	70,000	—	—	—	4.25	—
1997J Proof	45,000	Value: 5.00				
1998A In sets only	70,000	—	—	—	4.25	—
1998A Proof	45,000	Value: 5.00				
1998D In sets only	70,000	—	—	—	4.25	—
1998D Proof	45,000	Value: 5.00				
1998F In sets only	70,000	—	—	—	4.25	—
1998F Proof	45,000	Value: 5.00				
1998G In sets only	70,000	—	—	—	4.25	—
1998G Proof	45,000	Value: 5.00				
1998J In sets only	70,000	—	—	—	4.25	—
1998J Proof	45,000	Value: 5.00				
1999A In sets only	70,000	—	—	—	4.25	—
1999A Proof	45,000	Value: 5.00				
1999D In sets only	70,000	—	—	—	4.25	—

Date	Mintage	F	VF	XF	Unc	BU
1999D Proof	45,000	Value: 5.00				
1999F In sets only	70,000	—	—	—	4.25	—
1999F Proof	45,000	Value: 5.00				
1999G In sets only	70,000	—	—	—	4.75	—
1999G Proof	45,000	Value: 5.00				
1999J In sets only	70,000	—	—	—	4.75	—
1999J Proof	45,000	Value: 5.00				
2000A In sets only	70,000	—	—	—	5.00	—
2000A Proof	45,000	Value: 5.00				
2000D In sets only	70,000	—	—	—	5.00	—
2000D Proof	45,000	Value: 5.00				
2000F In sets only	70,000	—	—	—	5.00	—
2000F Proof	45,000	Value: 5.00				
2000G In sets only	70,000	—	—	—	5.00	—
2000G Proof	45,000	Value: 5.00				
2000J In sets only	70,000	—	—	—	5.00	—
2000J Proof	45,000	Value: 5.00				

KM# 175   2 MARK
7.0000 g., Copper-Nickel Clad Nickel, 26.75 mm.
Subject: Franz Joseph Strauss **Obv:** Eagle above denomination
Rev: Head left divides dates

Date	Mintage	F	VF	XF	Unc	BU
1990D	18,370,000	—	—	—	1.75	—
1990D Proof	45,000	Value: 2.25				
1990F	21,200,000	—	—	—	1.75	—
1990F Proof	45,000	Value: 2.25				
1990G	12,220,000	—	—	—	1.75	—
1990G Proof	45,000	Value: 2.25				
1990J	18,870,000	—	—	—	1.75	—
1990J Proof	45,000	Value: 2.25				
1991A	4,000,000	—	—	—	1.75	—
1991A Proof	45,000	Value: 2.25				
1991D	4,200,000	—	—	—	1.75	—
1991D Proof	45,000	Value: 2.25				
1991F	4,800,000	—	—	—	1.75	—
1991F Proof	45,000	Value: 2.25				
1991G	2,800,000	—	—	—	1.75	—
1991G Proof	45,000	Value: 2.25				
1991J	4,200,000	—	—	—	1.75	—
1991J Proof	45,000	Value: 2.25				
1992A	7,330,000	—	—	—	1.75	—
1992A Proof	45,000	Value: 2.25				
1992D	7,700,000	—	—	—	1.75	—
1992D Proof	45,000	Value: 2.25				
1992F	8,800,000	—	—	—	1.75	—
1992F Proof	45,000	Value: 2.25				
1992G	5,130,000	—	—	—	1.75	—
1992G Proof	45,000	Value: 2.25				
1992J	7,700,000	—	—	—	1.75	—
1992J Proof	45,000	Value: 2.25				
1993A	600,000	—	—	3.00	7.00	—
1993A Proof	45,000	Value: 2.25				
1993D	630,000	—	—	3.00	7.00	—
1993D Proof	45,000	Value: 2.25				
1993F	720,000	—	—	3.00	7.00	—
1993F Proof	45,000	Value: 2.25				
1993G	420,000	—	—	4:00	10.00	—
1993G Proof	45,000	Value: 2.25				
1993J	630,000	—	—	3.00	7.00	—
1993J Proof	45,000	Value: 2.25				
1994A	5,000,000	—	—	—	1.75	—
1994A Proof	45,000	Value: 2.25				
1994D	5,250,000	—	—	—	1.75	—
1994D Proof	45,000	Value: 2.25				
1994F	6,000,000	—	—	—	1.75	—
1994F Proof	45,000	Value: 2.25				
1994G	3,500,000	—	—	—	1.75	—
1994G Proof	45,000	Value: 2.25				
1994J	5,250,000	—	—	—	1.75	—
1994J Proof	45,000	Value: 2.25				
1995A	1,595,000	—	—	—	3.50	—
1995A Proof	45,000	Value: 17.50				
1995D In sets only	20,000	—	—	—	60.00	—
1995D Proof	45,000	Value: 17.50				
1995F In sets only	20,000	—	—	—	60.00	—
1995F Proof	45,000	Value: 17.50				
1995G	620,000	—	—	—	7.00	—
1995G Proof	45,000	Value: 17.50				
1995J In sets only	20,000	—	—	—	60.00	—
1995J Proof	45,000	Value: 17.50				
1996A	—	—	—	—	5.00	—
1996A Proof	45,000	Value: 6.00				
1996D	—	—	—	—	5.00	—
1996D Proof	45,000	Value: 6.00				
1996F	—	—	—	—	5.00	—
1996F Proof	45,000	Value: 6.00				
1996G	—	—	—	—	5.00	—
1996G Proof	45,000	Value: 6.00				
1996J	—	—	—	—	5.00	—

Date	Mintage	F	VF	XF	Unc	BU
1996J Proof	45,000	Value: 6.00				
1997A In sets only	70,000	—	—	—	4.25	—
1997A Proof	45,000	Value: 5.00				
1997D In sets only	70,000	—	—	—	4.25	—
1997D Proof	45,000	Value: 5.00				
1997F In sets only	70,000	—	—	—	4.25	—
1997F Proof	45,000	Value: 5.00				
1997G In sets only	70,000	—	—	—	4.25	—
1997G Proof	45,000	Value: 5.00				
1997J In sets only	70,000	—	—	—	4.25	—
1997J Proof	45,000	Value: 5.00				
1998A In sets only	70,000	—	—	—	4.25	—
1998A Proof	45,000	Value: 5.00				
1998D In sets only	70,000	—	—	—	4.25	—
1998D Proof	45,000	Value: 5.00				
1998F In sets only	70,000	—	—	—	4.25	—
1998F Proof	45,000	Value: 5.00				
1998G In sets only	70,000	—	—	—	4.25	—
1998G Proof	45,000	Value: 5.00				
1998J In sets only	70,000	—	—	—	4.25	—
1998J Proof	45,000	Value: 5.00				
1999A In sets only	70,000	—	—	—	4.25	—
1999A Proof	45,000	Value: 5.00				
1999D In sets only	70,000	—	—	—	4.25	—
1999D Proof	45,000	Value: 5.00				
1999F In sets only	70,000	—	—	—	4.25	—
1999F Proof	45,000	Value: 5.00				
1999G In sets only	70,000	—	—	—	4.25	—
1999G Proof	45,000	Value: 5.00				
1999J In sets only	70,000	—	—	—	4.25	—
1999J Proof	45,000	Value: 5.00				
2000A In sets only	70,000	—	—	—	5.00	—
2000A Proof	45,000	Value: 5.00				
2000D In sets only	70,000	—	—	—	5.00	—
2000D Proof	45,000	Value: 5.00				
2000F In sets only	70,000	—	—	—	5.00	—
2000F Proof	45,000	Value: 5.00				
2000G In sets only	70,000	—	—	—	5.00	—
2000G Proof	45,000	Value: 5.00				
2000J In sets only	70,000	—	—	—	5.00	—
2000J Proof	45,000	Value: 5.00				

KM# 183   2 MARK
7.0000 g., Copper-Nickel Clad Nickel, 26.75 mm. **Subject:** Willy Brandt **Obv:** Eagle above denomination **Rev:** Head facing divides dates

Date	Mintage	F	VF	XF	Unc	BU
1994A	5,000,000	—	—	—	2.00	—
1994A Proof	45,000	Value: 2.50				
1994D	5,250,000	—	—	—	2.00	—
1994D Proof	45,000	Value: 2.50				
1994F	6,000,000	—	—	—	2.00	—
1994F Proof	45,000	Value: 2.50				
1994G	3,600,000	—	—	—	2.00	—
1994G Proof	45,000	Value: 2.50				
1994J	5,250,000	—	—	—	2.00	—
1994J Proof	45,000	Value: 2.50				
1995A	1,595,000	—	—	—	3.50	—
1995A Proof	45,000	Value: 17.50				
1995D	20,000	—	—	—	65.00	—
		Note: In sets only				
1995D Proof	45,000	Value: 17.50				
1995F	20,000	—	—	—	65.00	—
		Note: In sets only				
1995F Proof	45,000	Value: 17.50				
1995G	1,220,000	—	—	—	4.50	—
1995G Proof	45,000	Value: 17.50				
1995J	75,000	—	—	—	30.00	—
1995J Proof	45,000	Value: 17.50				
1996A	—	—	—	—	5.50	—
1996A Proof	45,000	Value: 6.50				
1996D	—	—	—	—	5.50	—
1996D Proof	45,000	Value: 6.50				
1996F	—	—	—	—	5.50	—
1996F Proof	45,000	Value: 6.50				
1996G	—	—	—	—	5.50	—
1996G Proof	45,000	Value: 6.50				
1996J	—	—	—	—	5.50	—
1996J Proof	45,000	Value: 6.50				
1997A In sets only	70,000	—	—	—	4.25	—
1997A Proof	45,000	Value: 5.00				
1997D In sets only	70,000	—	—	—	4.25	—
1997D Proof	45,000	Value: 5.00				
1997F In sets only	70,000	—	—	—	4.25	—
1997F Proof	45,000	Value: 5.00				
1997G In sets only	70,000	—	—	—	4.25	—
1997G Proof	45,000	Value: 5.00				
1997J In sets only	70,000	—	—	—	4.25	—
1997J Proof	45,000	Value: 5.00				
1998A In sets only	70,000	—	—	—	4.25	—

Date	Mintage	F	VF	XF	Unc	BU
1998A Proof	45,000	Value: 5.00				
1998D In sets only	70,000	—	—	—	4.25	—
1998D Proof	45,000	Value: 5.00				
1998F In sets only	70,000	—	—	—	4.25	—
1998F Proof	45,000	Value: 5.00				
1998G In sets only	70,000	—	—	—	4.25	—
1998G Proof	45,000	Value: 5.00				
1998J In sets only	70,000	—	—	—	4.25	—
1998J Proof	45,000	Value: 5.00				
1999A In sets only	70,000	—	—	—	4.25	—
1999A Proof	45,000	Value: 5.00				
1999D In sets only	70,000	—	—	—	4.25	—
1999D Proof	45,000	Value: 5.00				
1999F In sets only	70,000	—	—	—	4.25	—
1999F Proof	45,000	Value: 5.00				
1999G In sets only	70,000	—	—	—	4.25	—
1999G Proof	45,000	Value: 5.00				
1999J In sets only	70,000	—	—	—	4.25	—
1999J Proof	45,000	Value: 5.00				
2000A In sets only	70,000	—	—	—	5.00	—
2000A Proof	45,000	Value: 5.00				
2000D In sets only	70,000	—	—	—	5.00	—
2000D Proof	45,000	Value: 5.00				
2000F In sets only	70,000	—	—	—	5.00	—
2000F Proof	45,000	Value: 5.00				
2000G In sets only	70,000	—	—	—	5.00	—
2000G Proof	45,000	Value: 5.00				
2000J In sets only	70,000	—	—	—	5.00	—
2000J Proof	45,000	Value: 5.00				

KM# 112.1   5 MARK
11.2000 g., 0.6250 Silver 0.2250 oz. ASW, 29 mm.
Obv: Denomination above date **Rev:** Large eagle
Edge: EINIGKEIT UND RECHT UND FREIHEIT

Date	Mintage	F	VF	XF	Unc	BU
1951D	20,600,000	—	4.00	15.00	65.00	—
1951D Proof	—	Value: 425				
1951F	24,000,000	—	4.00	15.00	75.00	—
1951F Proof	280	Value: 350				
1951G	13,840,000	—	4.00	20.00	125	—
1951G Proof	—	Value: 950				
1951J	21,360,000	—	4.00	15.00	60.00	—
1951J Proof	—	Value: 245				
1956D	1,092,000	2.00	15.00	60.00	275	—
1956D Proof	—	Value: 1,500				
1956F	1,200,000	—	10.00	75.00	475	—
1956F Proof	23	Value: 2,500				
1956J	1,068,000	—	10.00	50.00	250	—
1956J Proof	—	Value: 2,750				
1957D	566,000	—	10.00	65.00	300	—
1957D Proof	—	—	—	—	—	—
1957F	2,100,000	—	7.50	50.00	300	—
1957F Proof	—	Value: 2,500				
1957G	692,000	—	10.00	75.00	650	—
1957G Proof	—	Value: 3,500				
1957J	1,630,000	—	7.50	35.00	225	—
1957J Proof	—	—	—	—	—	—
1958D	1,226,000	—	7.50	30.00	150	—
1958D Proof	—	—	—	—	—	—
1958F	600,000	2.00	20.00	145	800	—
1958F Proof	100	Value: 1,350				
1958G	1,557,000	—	7.50	28.00	140	—
1958G Proof	—	—	—	—	—	—
1958J	60,000	—	1,100	2,500	4,250	—
1958J Proof	—	Value: 7,000				
1959D	496,000	—	10.00	45.00	325	—
1959D Proof	—	Value: 1,250				
1959G	692,000	—	15.00	45.00	285	—
1959G Proof	—	Value: 1,500				
1959J	713,000	—	8.00	40.00	300	—
1959J Proof	—	Value: 2,000				
1960D	1,040,000	—	7.00	20.00	110	—
1960D Proof	—	Value: 1,250				
1960F	1,576,000	—	7.00	20.00	135	—
1960F Proof	50	Value: 1,250				
1960G	692,000	—	7.00	22.00	125	—
1960G Proof	—	Value: 750				
1960J	1,618,000	—	7.00	18.00	90.00	—
1960J Proof	—	—	—	—	—	—
1961D	1,040,000	—	4.50	20.00	100	—
1961D Proof	—	Value: 450				
1961F	824,000	—	4.50	22.00	200	—
1961F Proof	—	Value: 2,200				
1961J	518,000	—	6.00	28.00	165	—
1961J Proof	—	Value: 3,000				
1963D	2,080,000	—	4.50	15.00	60.00	—
1963D Proof	—	—	—	—	—	—
1963F	1,254,000	—	4.50	18.00	75.00	—
1963F Proof	—	Value: 2,500				
1963G	600,000	—	7.50	20.00	90.00	—

Date	Mintage	F	VF	XF	Unc	BU
1963G Proof	Est. 100	Value: 500				
1963J	2,136,000	—	4.50	15.00	60.00	—
1963J Proof	—	Value: 3,000				
1964D	456,000	—	15.00	50.00	175	—
1964D Proof	—	Value: 3,250				
1964F	2,646,000	—	4.50	15.00	60.00	—
1964F Proof	—	Value: 2,500				
1964G	1,649,000	—	4.50	15.00	60.00	—
1964G Proof	Est. 600	Value: 450				
1964J	1,335,000	—	4.00	15.00	65.00	—
1964J Proof	—	Value: 2,750				
1965D	4,354,000	—	4.00	12.50	30.00	—
1965D Proof	—	Value: 4,000				
1965F	4,050,000	—	4.00	8.00	30.00	—
1965F Proof	Est. 80	Value: 1,000				
1965G	2,335,000	—	4.00	7.00	25.00	—
1965G Proof	8,233	Value: 50.00				
1965J	3,605,000	—	4.00	7.00	25.00	—
1965J Proof	—	Value: 3,250				
1966D	5,200,000	—	4.00	7.00	22.50	—
1966D Proof	—	Value: 4,000				
1966F	6,000,000	—	4.00	7.00	22.50	—
1966F Proof	100	Value: 1,000				
1966G	3,460,000	—	4.00	7.00	22.50	—
1966G Proof	3,070	Value: 50.00				
1966J	5,340,000	—	4.00	7.00	22.50	—
1966J Proof	1,000	Value: 125				
1967D	3,120,000	—	4.00	7.00	22.50	—
1967D Proof	—	Value: 4,000				
1967F	3,598,000	—	4.00	7.00	22.50	—
1967F Proof	1,500	Value: 110				
1967G	1,406,000	—	4.00	7.00	25.00	—
1967G Proof	4,500	Value: 40.00				
1967J	3,204,000	—	4.00	7.00	22.50	—

Note: Errors exist with coin alignment

Date	Mintage	F	VF	XF	Unc	BU
1967J Proof	1,500	Value: 100				
1968D	1,300,000	—	4.00	10.00	35.00	—
1968D Proof	—	Value: 4,000				
1968F	1,497,000	—	4.00	10.00	35.00	—
1968F Proof	3,000	Value: 125				
1968G	1,535,000	—	4.00	10.00	35.00	—
1968G Proof	6,023	Value: 50.00				
1968J	1,335,000	—	4.00	10.00	35.00	—
1968J Proof	2,000	Value: 125				
1969D	2,080,000	—	4.00	7.00	20.00	—
1969D Proof	—	Value: 35.00				
1969F	2,395,000	—	4.00	7.00	20.00	—
1969F Proof	5,000	Value: 35.00				
1969G	3,484,000	—	4.00	7.00	20.00	—
1969G Proof	8,700	Value: 30.00				
1969J	2,136,000	—	4.00	7.00	20.00	—
1969J Proof	5,000	Value: 30.00				
1970D	2,000,000	—	4.00	7.00	20.00	—
1970D Proof	—	Value: 30.00				
1970F	1,995,000	—	4.00	7.00	20.00	—
1970F Proof	5,140	Value: 25.00				
1970G	6,000,000	—	3.50	4.50	10.00	—
1970G Proof	10,200	Value: 22.00				
1970J	4,000,000	—	3.50	4.50	10.00	—
1970J Proof	5,000	Value: 25.00				
1971D	4,000,000	—	3.50	4.50	10.00	—
1971D Proof	8,000	Value: 22.00				
1971F	3,993,000	—	3.50	4.50	10.00	—
1971F Proof	8,000	Value: 22.00				
1971G	6,010,000	—	3.50	4.50	10.00	—
1971G Proof	10,000	Value: 22.00				
1971J	6,000,000	—	3.50	4.50	10.00	—
1971J Proof	8,000	Value: 22.00				
1972D	3,000,000	—	3.50	4.50	12.00	—
1972D Proof	8,000	Value: 22.00				
1972F	8,992,000	—	3.50	4.50	10.00	—
1972F Proof	8,100	Value: 22.00				
1972G	4,999,000	—	3.50	4.50	10.00	—
1972G Proof	10,000	Value: 22.00				
1972J	6,000,000	—	3.50	4.50	10.00	—
1972J Proof	8,000	Value: 22.00				
1973D	3,380,000	—	3.50	4.50	10.00	—
1973D Proof	9,000	Value: 22.00				
1973F	3,891,000	—	3.50	4.50	8.50	—
1973F Proof	9,100	Value: 22.00				
1973G	2,240,000	—	3.50	4.50	8.50	—
1973G Proof	9,000	Value: 22.00				
1973J	5,571,000	—	3.50	4.50	8.50	—
1973J Proof	9,000	Value: 22.00				
1974D	4,594,000	—	3.50	4.50	8.50	—
1974D Proof	35,000	Value: 22.00				
1974F	6,514,000	—	3.50	4.50	8.50	—
1974F Proof	35,000	Value: 22.00				
1974G	3,708,000	—	3.50	4.50	8.50	—
1974G Proof	35,000	Value: 22.00				
1974J	2,968,000	—	3.50	4.50	8.50	—
1974J Proof	35,000	Value: 22.00				

KM# 112.3 5 MARK

11.2000 g., 0.6250 Silver 0.2250 oz. ASW, 29 mm. Obv: Denomination Rev: Large eagle Note: Error. With edge lettering: GRUSS DICH DEUTSCHLAND AUS HERZENSGRUND.

Date	Mintage	F	VF	XF	Unc	BU
1957J	Inc. above	—	1,250	1,650	2,400	—

KM# 112.2 5 MARK

11.2000 g., 0.6250 Silver 0.2250 oz. ASW, 29 mm. Obv: Denomination Rev: Large eagle Note: Uninscribed plain edge errors. Mintages are included with same dates of KM #112.1.

Date	Mintage	F	VF	XF	Unc	BU
1959D	Inc. above	—	65.00	125	200	—
1959J	Inc. above	—	65.00	125	200	—
1963J	Inc. above	—	65.00	125	200	—
1964G	Inc. above	—	—	—	—	—
1964F	Inc. above	—	65.00	125	200	—
1965J	Inc. above	—	—	—	—	—
1965F	Inc. above	—	65.00	125	200	—
1965G	Inc. above	—	65.00	125	200	—
1966F	Inc. above	—	125	250	350	—
1966G	Inc. above	—	65.00	125	200	—

Note: Errors without edge inscription exist with coin alignment

Date	Mintage	F	VF	XF	Unc	BU
1967D	Inc. above	—	125	250	350	—
1967G	Inc. above	—	65.00	125	200	—
1969F	Inc. above	—	—	—	—	—
1970F	Inc. above	—	—	—	—	—
1970G	Inc. above	—	—	—	—	—
1971F	Inc. above	—	—	—	—	—
1972F	Inc. above	—	—	—	—	—
1973F	Inc. above	—	—	—	—	—
1974F	Inc. above	—	—	—	—	—

KM# 112.4 5 MARK

11.2000 g., 0.6250 Silver 0.2250 oz. ASW, 29 mm. Obv: Denomination Rev: Large eagle Note: Error. With edge lettering: ALLE MENSCHEN WERDEN BRUDER.

Date	Mintage	F	VF	XF	Unc	BU
1970F	—	—	1,250	1,650	2,400	—

KM# 140.1 5 MARK

10.0000 g., Copper-Nickel Clad Nickel, 29 mm. Obv: Denomination within rounded square Rev: Eagle above date

Date	Mintage	F	VF	XF	Unc	BU
1975D	65,663,000	—	—	3.50	4.50	—
Note: Error strikes exist without edge inscription						
1975D Proof	43,000	Value: 7.00				
1975F	75,002,000	—	—	3.50	4.50	—
Note: Error strikes exist without edge inscription						
1975F Proof	43,000	Value: 7.00				
1975G	43,297,000	—	—	3.50	4.50	—
1975G Proof	43,000	Value: 7.00				
1975J	67,372,000	—	—	3.50	4.50	—
1975J Proof	43,000	Value: 7.00				
1976D	7,821,000	—	—	3.50	5.00	—
1976D Proof	43,000	Value: 7.00				
1976F	9,072,000	—	—	3.50	5.00	—
1976F Proof	43,000	Value: 7.00				
1976G	5,784,000	—	—	3.50	5.00	—
1976G Proof	43,000	Value: 7.00				
1976J	8,068,000	—	—	3.50	5.00	—
1976J Proof	43,000	Value: 7.00				
1977D	8,321,000	—	—	3.50	5.00	—
1977D Proof	51,000	Value: 6.00				
1977F	9,612,000	—	—	3.50	5.00	—
1977F Proof	51,000	Value: 6.00				
1977G	5,746,000	—	—	3.50	5.00	—
1977G Proof	51,000	Value: 6.00				
1977J	8,577,000	—	—	3.50	5.00	—
1977J Proof	51,000	Value: 6.00				
1978D	7,854,000	—	—	3.50	5.00	—
1978D Proof	54,000	Value: 6.00				
1978F	9,054,000	—	—	3.50	5.00	—
1978F Proof	54,000	Value: 6.00				
1978G	5,244,000	—	—	3.50	5.00	—
1978G Proof	54,000	Value: 6.00				
1978J	8,064,000	—	—	3.50	5.00	—
1978J Proof	54,000	Value: 6.00				
1979D	7,889,000	—	—	3.50	5.00	—
1979D Proof	89,000	Value: 6.00				
1979F	9,089,000	—	—	3.50	5.00	—
1979F Proof	89,000	Value: 6.00				
1979G	5,279,000	—	—	3.50	5.00	—
1979G Proof	89,000	Value: 6.00				
1979J	8,099,000	—	—	3.50	5.00	—
1979J Proof	89,000	Value: 6.00				
1980D	8,300,000	—	—	3.50	5.00	—
1980D Proof	110,000	Value: 6.00				
1980F	9,640,000	—	—	3.50	5.00	—
1980F Proof	110,000	Value: 6.00				
1980G	5,500,000	—	—	3.50	5.00	—
1980G Proof	110,000	Value: 6.00				
1980J	8,500,000	—	—	3.50	5.00	—
1980J Proof	110,000	Value: 6.00				
1981D	8,300,000	—	—	3.50	5.00	—
1981D Proof	91,000	Value: 7.00				
1981F	9,600,000	—	—	3.50	5.00	—
1981F Proof	91,000	Value: 7.00				
1981G	5,500,000	—	—	3.50	5.00	—
1981G Proof	91,000	Value: 7.00				
1981J	8,500,000	—	—	3.50	5.00	—
1981J Proof	91,000	Value: 7.00				
1982D	8,900,000	—	—	3.50	5.00	—

Date	Mintage	F	VF	XF	Unc	BU
1982D Proof	78,000	Value: 7.00				
1982F	10,300,000	—	—	3.50	5.00	—
1982F Proof	78,000	Value: 7.00				
1982G	5,990,000	—	—	3.50	5.00	—
1982G Proof	78,000	Value: 7.00				
1982J	9,100,000	—	—	3.50	5.00	—
1982J Proof	78,000	Value: 7.00				
1983D	6,240,000	—	—	3.50	5.00	—
1983D Proof	75,000	Value: 9.00				
1983F	7,200,000	—	—	3.50	5.00	—
1983F Proof	75,000	Value: 9.00				
1983G	4,152,000	—	—	3.50	5.00	—
1983G Proof	75,000	Value: 9.00				
1983J	6,408,000	—	—	3.50	5.00	—
1983J Proof	75,000	Value: 9.00				
1984D	6,000,000	—	—	3.50	5.00	—
1984D Proof	64,000	Value: 9.00				
1984F	6,900,000	—	—	3.50	5.00	—
1984F Proof	64,000	Value: 9.00				
1984G	4,000,000	—	—	3.50	5.00	—
1984G Proof	64,000	Value: 9.00				
1984J	6,100,000	—	—	3.50	6.00	—
1984J Proof	64,000	Value: 9.00				
1985D	4,900,000	—	—	3.50	6.00	—
1985D Proof	56,000	Value: 10.00				
1985F	5,700,000	—	—	3.50	6.00	—
1985F Proof	54,000	Value: 10.00				
1985G	3,300,000	—	—	3.50	6.00	—
1985G Proof	55,000	Value: 10.00				
1985J	5,100,000	—	—	3.50	6.00	—
1985J Proof	54,000	Value: 10.00				
1986D	4,900,000	—	—	3.50	7.00	—
1986D Proof	44,000	Value: 20.00				
1986F	5,700,000	—	—	3.50	7.00	—
1986F Proof	44,000	Value: 20.00				
1986G	3,300,000	—	—	3.50	7.00	—
1986G Proof	44,000	Value: 25.00				
1986J	5,100,000	—	—	3.50	7.00	—
1986J Proof	44,000	Value: 20.00				
1987D	6,760,000	—	—	3.50	6.00	—
1987D Proof	45,000	Value: 10.00				
1987F	7,800,000	—	—	3.50	6.00	—
1987F Proof	45,000	Value: 10.00				
1987G	4,500,000	—	—	3.50	6.00	—
1987G Proof	45,000	Value: 10.00				
1987J	6,940,000	—	—	3.50	6.00	—
1987J Proof	45,000	Value: 10.00				
1988D	11,960,000	—	—	—	5.00	—
1988D Proof	45,000	Value: 12.00				
1988F	13,800,000	—	—	—	5.00	—
1988F Proof	45,000	Value: 12.00				
1988G	7,960,000	—	—	—	5.00	—
1988G Proof	45,000	Value: 12.00				
1988J	12,280,000	—	—	—	5.00	—
1988J Proof	45,000	Value: 12.00				
1989D	17,160,000	—	—	—	5.00	—
1989D Proof	45,000	Value: 12.00				
1989F	19,800,000	—	—	—	5.00	—
1989F Proof	45,000	Value: 12.00				
1989G	11,420,000	—	—	—	5.00	—
1989G Proof	45,000	Value: 12.00				
1989J	17,620,000	—	—	—	5.00	—
1989J Proof	45,000	Value: 12.00				
1990D	20,900,000	—	—	—	5.00	—
1990D Proof	45,000	Value: 10.00				
1990F	24,120,000	—	—	—	5.00	—
1990F Proof	45,000	Value: 10.00				
1990G	13,910,000	—	—	—	5.00	—
1990G Proof	45,000	Value: 10.00				
1990J	21,470,000	—	—	—	5.00	—
1990J Proof	45,000	Value: 10.00				
1991A	18,000,000	—	—	—	5.00	—
1991A Proof	45,000	Value: 7.00				
1991D	18,900,000	—	—	—	5.00	—
1991D Proof	45,000	Value: 7.00				
1991F	21,600,000	—	—	—	5.00	—
1991F Proof	45,000	Value: 7.00				
1991G	12,600,000	—	—	—	5.00	—
1991G Proof	45,000	Value: 7.00				
1991J	18,900,000	—	—	—	5.00	—
1991J Proof	45,000	Value: 7.00				
1992A	16,000,000	—	—	—	5.00	—
1992A Proof	45,000	Value: 7.00				
1992D	16,800,000	—	—	—	5.00	—
1992D Proof	45,000	Value: 7.00				
1992F	19,200,000	—	—	—	5.00	—
1992F Proof	45,000	Value: 7.00				
1992G	11,200,000	—	—	—	5.00	—
1992G Proof	45,000	Value: 7.00				
1992J	16,800,000	—	—	—	5.00	—
1992J Proof	45,000	Value: 7.00				
1993A	3,200,000	—	—	—	6.00	—
1993A Proof	45,000	Value: 10.00				
1993D	3,380,000	—	—	—	6.00	—
1993D Proof	45,000	Value: 10.00				
1993F	3,840,000	—	—	—	6.00	—
1993F Proof	45,000	Value: 10.00				
1993G	2,240,000	—	—	—	6.00	—
1993G Proof	45,000	Value: 10.00				
1993J	3,360,000	—	—	—	6.00	—
1993J Proof	45,000	Value: 10.00				
1994A	4,000,000	—	—	—	5.00	—

Date	Mintage	F	VF	XF	Unc	BU
1994A Proof	45,000	Value: 10.00				
1994D	4,200,000	—	—	—	5.00	—
1994D Proof	45,000	Value: 10.00				
1994F	4,800,000	—	—	—	5.00	—
1994F Proof	45,000	Value: 10.00				
1994G	2,800,000	—	—	—	5.00	—
1994G Proof	45,000	Value: 10.00				
1994J	4,200,000	—	—	—	5.00	—
1994J Proof	45,000	Value: 10.00				
1995A In sets only	20,000	—	—	—	80.00	—
1995A Proof	45,000	Value: 30.00				
1995D In sets only	20,000	—	—	—	80.00	—
1995D Proof	45,000	Value: 30.00				
1995F In sets only	20,000	—	—	—	80.00	—
1995F Proof	45,000	Value: 30.00				
1995G In sets only	20,000	—	—	—	80.00	—
1995G Proof	45,000	Value: 30.00				
1995J In sets only	20,000	—	—	—	80.00	—
1995J Proof	45,000	Value: 30.00				
1996A In sets only	50,000	—	—	—	15.00	—
1996A Proof	45,000	Value: 17.50				
1996D In sets only	50,000	—	—	—	15.00	—
1996D Proof	45,000	Value: 17.50				
1996F In sets only	50,000	—	—	—	15.00	—
1996F Proof	45,000	Value: 17.50				
1996G In sets only	50,000	—	—	—	15.00	—
1996G Proof	45,000	Value: 17.50				
1996J In sets only	50,000	—	—	—	15.00	—
1996J Proof	45,000	Value: 17.50				
1997A In sets only	70,000	—	—	—	6.00	—
1997A Proof	45,000	Value: 7.00				
1997D In sets only	70,000	—	—	—	6.00	—
1997D Proof	45,000	Value: 7.00				
1997F In sets only	70,000	—	—	—	6.00	—
1997F Proof	45,000	Value: 7.00				
1997G In sets only	70,000	—	—	—	6.00	—
1997G Proof	45,000	Value: 7.00				
1997J In sets only	70,000	—	—	—	6.00	—
1997J Proof	45,000	Value: 7.00				
1998A In sets only	70,000	—	—	—	6.00	—
1998A Proof	45,000	Value: 7.00				
1998D In sets only	70,000	—	—	—	6.00	—
1998D Proof	45,000	Value: 7.00				
1998F In sets only	70,000	—	—	—	6.00	—
1998F Proof	45,000	Value: 7.00				
1998G In sets only	70,000	—	—	—	6.00	—
1998G Proof	45,000	Value: 7.00				
1998J In sets only	70,000	—	—	—	6.00	—
1998J Proof	45,000	Value: 7.00				
1999A In sets only	70,000	—	—	—	6.00	—
1999A Proof	45,000	Value: 7.00				
1999D In sets only	70,000	—	—	—	6.00	—
1999D Proof	45,000	Value: 7.00				
1999F In sets only	70,000	—	—	—	6.00	—
1999F Proof	45,000	Value: 7.00				
1999G In sets only	70,000	—	—	—	6.00	—
1999G Proof	45,000	Value: 7.00				
1999J In sets only	70,000	—	—	—	6.00	—
1999J Proof	45,000	Value: 7.00				
2000A In sets only	70,000	—	—	—	15.00	—
2000A Proof	45,000	Value: 15.00				
2000D In sets only	70,000	—	—	—	15.00	—
2000D Proof	45,000	Value: 15.00				
2000F In sets only	70,000	—	—	—	15.00	—
2000F Proof	45,000	Value: 15.00				
2000G In sets only	70,000	—	—	—	15.00	—
2000G Proof	45,000	Value: 15.00				
2000J In sets only	70,000	—	—	—	15.00	—
2000J Proof	45,000	Value: 15.00				

KM# 140.2   5 MARK
5.4400 g., Copper-Nickel Clad Nickel, 29 mm. **Obv:** Denomination within rounded square **Rev:** Eagle **Note:** Thin variety.

Date	Mintage	F	VF	XF	Unc	BU
1975J	—	—	—	90.00	150	—

Note: Illegally produced by a German Mint official

KM# 140.3   5 MARK
10.0000 g., Copper-Nickel Clad Nickel, 29 mm.
Obv: Denomination within rounded square **Rev:** Eagle
Note: Errors without edge inscription.

Date	Mintage	F	VF	XF	Unc	BU
1975D	—	—	—	—	—	—
1975F	—	—	—	—	—	—

COMMEMORATIVE COINAGE

KM# 113   5 MARK
11.2000 g., 0.6250 Silver 0.2250 oz. ASW, 29 mm. **Subject:** Centenary - Nurnberg Museum **Obv:** Eagle below legend **Rev:** East-Gothic eagle-booch from the 5th Century AD, between museum dates **Edge:** EINIGKEIT UND RECHT UND FREIHEIT

Date	Mintage	F	VF	XF	Unc	BU
1952D	199,000	—	500	700	800	1,200
1952D Proof	1,240	Value: 4,000				

KM# 114   5 MARK
11.2000 g., 0.6250 Silver 0.2250 oz. ASW, 29 mm.
Subject: 150th Anniversary - Death of Friedrich von Schiller
Obv: Eagle above denomination **Rev:** Head with high collar right
Edge: SEID EINIG EINIG EINIG

Date	Mintage	F	VF	XF	Unc	BU
1955F	199,000	—	260	400	700	800
1955F Proof	1,217	Value: 1,950				

KM# 115   5 MARK
11.2000 g., 0.6250 Silver 0.2250 oz. ASW, 29 mm.
Subject: 300th Anniversary - Birth of Ludwig von Baden **Obv:** In front of palace, eagle above denomination, date below **Rev:** Bust, right **Edge:** SCHILD DES REICHES

Date	Mintage	F	VF	XF	Unc	BU
1955G	198,000	—	260	400	600	750
1955G Proof	Est. 2,000	Value: 1,850				

Note: This coin was restruck without authorization by a mint official using genuine dies - quantity unknown

KM# 117   5 MARK
11.2000 g., 0.6250 Silver 0.2250 oz. ASW, 29 mm.
Subject: Centenary - Death of Joseph Freiherr von Eichendorff **Obv:** Eagle divides date at top, denomination below **Rev:** Head with high collar left, dates below **Edge:** GRÜS . DICH . DEUTSCHLAND . AUS . HERZENSGRUND .

Date	Mintage	F	VF	XF	Unc	BU
1957J	198,000	—	200	380	500	650
1957J Proof	2,000	Value: 1,850				

KM# 118.1   5 MARK
11.2000 g., 0.6250 Silver 0.2250 oz. ASW, 29 mm.
Subject: 150th Anniversary - Death of Johann Gottlieb Fichte, philosopher **Obv:** Eagle divides date above denomination **Rev:** Head with high collar left, dates below **Edge:** NUR DAS MACHT GLÜKSELIG WAS GUT IST

Date	Mintage	F	VF	XF	Unc	BU
1964J	495,000	—	50.00	75.00	125	150
1964J Proof	5,000	Value: 800				

KM# 118.2   5 MARK
11.2000 g., 0.6250 Silver 0.2250 oz. ASW, 29 mm. **Obv:** Eagle above denomination **Rev:** Head with high collar left **Note:** Error. Plain edge.

Date	Mintage	F	VF	XF	Unc	BU
1964J	—	—	250	500	900	975

KM# 119.1   5 MARK
11.2000 g., 0.6250 Silver 0.2250 oz. ASW, 29 mm.
Subject: 250th Anniversary - Death of Gottfried Wilhelm Leibniz, philosopher **Obv:** Eagle divides date above, denomination below **Rev:** Head 3/4 facing, dates below **Edge:** MAGNUM TOTUS GERMANIAE DECUS

Date	Mintage	F	VF	XF	Unc	BU
1966D	1,940,000	—	7.00	12.00	15.00	20.00
1966D Proof	60,000	Value: 110				

KM# 119.2   5 MARK
11.2000 g., 0.6250 Silver 0.2250 oz. ASW, 29 mm. **Obv:** Eagle divides date, denomination below **Rev:** Head 3/4 facing, dates **Note:** Error. Plain edge.

Date	Mintage	F	VF	XF	Unc	BU
1966D	—	—	225	425	700	—

KM# 120.1   5 MARK
11.2000 g., 0.6250 Silver 0.2250 oz. ASW, 29 mm.
Subject: Wilhelm and Alexander von Humboldt **Obv:** Eagle above denomination dividing date **Rev:** Conjoined heads; one left and one facing **Edge:** FREIHEIT ERHÖHT, ZWANG ERSTICKT UNSERE KRAFT

Date	Mintage	F	VF	XF	Unc	BU
1967F	2,000,000	—	9.00	12.00	15.00	20.00
1967F Proof	60,000	Value: 150				

KM# 120.2   5 MARK
11.2000 g., 0.6250 Silver 0.2250 oz. ASW, 29 mm. **Obv:** Eagle **Rev:** Conjoined heads; one left and one facing **Note:** Error. Plain edge.

Date	Mintage	F	VF	XF	Unc	BU
1967F	—	—	225	425	700	—

KM# 121   5 MARK
11.2000 g., 0.6250 Silver 0.2250 oz. ASW, 29 mm.
Subject: 150th Anniversary - Birth of Friedrich Raiffeisen **Obv:** Eagle above denomination and date **Rev:** Bust 3/4 facing, dates below **Edge:** EINER FÜR ALLE - ALLE FÜR EINEN

Date	Mintage	F	VF	XF	Unc	BU
1968J	3,860,000	—	3.00	4.50	6.00	8.00
1968J Proof	140,000	Value: 45.00				

KM# 122   5 MARK
11.2000 g., 0.6250 Silver 0.2250 oz. ASW, 29 mm. **Subject:** 500th Anniversary - Death of Johannes Gutenberg **Obv:** Denomination divides date, eagle above **Rev:** Bust 3/4 right, dates below **Edge:** GESEGNET SEI WER DIE SCHRIFT ERFAND

Date	Mintage	F	VF	XF	Unc	BU
1968G	2,900,000	—	3.50	7.00	9.00	11.00
1968G Proof	100,000	Value: 65.00				

KM# 123.1   5 MARK

11.2000 g., 0.6250 Silver 0.2250 oz. ASW, 29 mm. **Subject:** 150th Anniversary - Birth of Max von Pettenkofer **Obv:** Stylized eagle, denomination above **Rev:** Face 3/4 left, dates below **Edge:** HYGIENE STREBT DER ÜBEL WURZEL AUSZUROTTEN

Date	Mintage	F	VF	XF	Unc	BU
1968D	2,900,000	—	3.50	7.00	9.00	11.00
1968D Proof	100,000	Value: 50.00				

KM# 123.2   5 MARK

11.2000 g., 0.6250 Silver 0.2250 oz. ASW, 29 mm. **Obv:** Stylized eagle, denomination above **Rev:** Face 3/4 left **Note:** Polished devices.

Date	Mintage	F	VF	XF	Unc	BU
1968D Proof	—	Value: 300				

KM# 125.1   5 MARK

11.2000 g., 0.6250 Silver 0.2250 oz. ASW, 29 mm. **Subject:** 150th Anniversary - Birth of Theodor Fontane, writer, poet **Obv:** Eagle divides date, denomination below **Rev:** Head left **Edge:** DER FREIE NUR IST TREU

Date	Mintage	F	VF	XF	Unc	BU
1969G	2,830,000	—	3.50	7.00	9.00	11.00
1969G Proof	170,000	Value: 35.00				

KM# 125.2   5 MARK

11.2000 g., 0.6250 Silver 0.2250 oz. ASW, 29 mm. **Obv:** Eagle divides date, denomination below **Rev:** Head left **Note:** Error. Incomplete nose and hair.

Date	Mintage	F	VF	XF	Unc	BU
1969G Proof	—	Value: 140				

KM# 126.1   5 MARK

11.2000 g., 0.6250 Silver 0.2250 oz. ASW, 29 mm. **Subject:** 375th Anniversary - Death of Gerhard Mercator **Obv:** Eagle, denomination divides date below **Rev:** Bust with long beard 3/4 right **Edge:** TERRAE DESCIPTIO AD USUM NAVIGANTIUM

Date	Mintage	F	VF	XF	Unc	BU
1969F	5,004,000	—	—	—	5.00	6.00
1969F Proof	200,000	Value: 20.00				

KM# 126.2   5 MARK

11.2000 g., 0.6250 Silver 0.2250 oz. ASW, 29 mm. **Obv:** Eagle, denomination divides date below **Rev:** Bust with long beard 3/4 right **Note:** Error. Plain edge.

Date	Mintage	F	VF	XF	Unc	BU
1969F	—	—	250	450	750	—

KM# 126.3   5 MARK

11.2000 g., 0.6250 Silver 0.2250 oz. ASW, 29 mm. **Obv:** Eagle, denomination divides date below **Rev:** Bust with long beard 3/4 right **Note:** Error. With edge lettering: Einigkeit und Recht und Freiheit.

Date	Mintage	F	VF	XF	Unc	BU
1969F	—	—	600	1,000	1,600	—

KM# 126.4   5 MARK

11.2000 g., 0.6250 Silver 0.2250 oz. ASW, 29 mm. **Obv:** Eagle, denomination divides date below **Rev:** Bust with long beard 3/4 right **Note:** Error. With long "R" in "MERCATOR".

Date	Mintage	F	VF	XF	Unc	BU
1969F	—	—	25.00	55.00	100	—

KM# 127   5 MARK

11.2000 g., 0.6250 Silver 0.2250 oz. ASW, 29 mm. **Subject:** 200th Anniversary - Birth of Ludwig van Beethoven, composer **Obv:** Eagle, denomination divides date below **Rev:** Head left, dates below **Edge:** ALLE MENSCHEN WERDEN BRÜDER

Date	Mintage	F	VF	XF	Unc	BU
1970F	5,000,000	—	—	3.50	6.00	7.00
1970F Proof	200,000	Value: 18.00				

KM# 128.1   5 MARK

11.2000 g., 0.6250 Silver 0.2250 oz. ASW, 29 mm. **Subject:** Foundation of German Empire, 1871 **Obv:** Eagle divides date above legend, denomination below **Rev:** Reichstag building, in Berlin **Edge:** EINIGKEIT UND RECHT UND FREIHEIT

Date	Mintage	F	VF	XF	Unc	BU
1971G	5,000,000	—	3.50	5.00	6.00	7.00
1971G Proof	200,000	Value: 20.00				

KM# 128.2   5 MARK

11.2000 g., 0.6250 Silver 0.2250 oz. ASW, 29 mm. **Obv:** Eagle divides date above legend **Rev:** Reichstag building **Note:** Error. With weak window details.

Date	Mintage	F	VF	XF	Unc	BU
1971F Proof	—	Value: 100				

KM# 129   5 MARK

11.2000 g., 0.6250 Silver 0.2250 oz. ASW, 29 mm. **Subject:** 500th Anniversary - Birth of Albrecht Durer **Obv:** Eagle above inscription, date and denomination below **Rev:** Initials above name and dates **Edge:** DER ALLER EDELST SINN DER MENSCHEN IST SEHEN

Date	Mintage	F	VF	XF	Unc	BU
1971D	8,000,000	—	—	—	4.00	6.00
1971D Proof	200,000	Value: 27.50				

KM# 136   5 MARK

11.2000 g., 0.6250 Silver 0.2250 oz. ASW, 29 mm. **Subject:** 500th Anniversary - Birth of Nicholas Copernicus **Obv:** Eagle in grid form, denomination divides date below **Rev:** Sun at center of rings, planet names descend from top towards center **Edge:** IN MEDIO OMNIUM RESIDET SOL

Date	Mintage	F	VF	XF	Unc	BU
1973J	8,000,000	—	—	—	6.00	7.00
1973J Proof	250,000	Value: 12.00				

KM# 137   5 MARK

11.2000 g., 0.6250 Silver 0.2250 oz. ASW, 29 mm. **Subject:** 125th Anniversary - Frankfurt Parliament **Obv:** Denomination below stylized eagle divides date **Rev:** Date at center of Parliament building **Edge:** EINIGKEIT RECHT FREIHEIT

Date	Mintage	F	VF	XF	Unc	BU
1973G	8,000,000	—	—	—	6.00	7.00
1973G Proof	250,000	Value: 12.00				

KM# 138   5 MARK

11.2000 g., 0.6250 Silver 0.2250 oz. ASW, 29 mm. **Subject:** 25th Anniversary - Constitutional Law **Obv:** Fat eagle above date divided by denomination **Rev:** Symbol of the 11 countries forming the Federal Republic **Edge:** DIE MENSCHENWÜRDE IST UNANTASTBAR

Date	Mintage	F	VF	XF	Unc	BU
1974F	8,000,000	—	—	—	6.00	7.00
1974F Proof	250,000	Value: 12.00				

KM# 139   5 MARK

11.2000 g., 0.6250 Silver 0.2250 oz. ASW, 29 mm. **Subject:** 250th Anniversary - Birth of Immanuel Kant, philosopher **Obv:** Legend divides eagle and denomination **Rev:** Bust at left facing right, name and dates at right **Edge:** ACHTUNG FUERS MORALISCHE GESETZ

Date	Mintage	F	VF	XF	Unc	BU
1974D	8,000,000	—	—	—	6.00	7.00
1974D Proof	250,000	Value: 14.00				

KM# 141   5 MARK

11.2000 g., 0.6250 Silver 0.2250 oz. ASW, 29 mm. **Subject:** 50th Anniversary - Death of Friedrich Ebert **Obv:** Eagle above denomination, date at right **Rev:** Head left, dates at left **Edge:** DES VOLKES WOHL IST MEINER ARBEIT ZIER

Date	Mintage	F	VF	XF	Unc	BU
1975J	8,000,000	—	—	—	6.00	7.00
1975J Proof	250,000	Value: 14.00				

KM# 142.1   5 MARK

11.2000 g., 0.6250 Silver 0.2250 oz. ASW, 29 mm. **Subject:** European Monument Protection Year **Obv:** Eagle divides date at top, denomination below **Rev:** Patterned designs and two line inscription with date **Edge:** ZUKUNFT FÜR UNSERE VERGANGENHEIT **Note:** 2.1 mm thick.

Date	Mintage	F	VF	XF	Unc	BU
1975F	8,000,000	—	—	—	6.00	7.00
1975F Proof	250,000	Value: 12.00				

KM# 142.2   5 MARK
5.3000 g., 0.6250 Silver 0.1065 oz. ASW, 29 mm. **Obv:** Eagle divides date at top **Rev:** Patterned design **Note:** 1.4 mm thick.

Date	Mintage	F	VF	XF	Unc	BU
1975F	Inc. above	—	—	—	10.00	11.00

KM# 143   5 MARK
11.2000 g., 0.6250 Silver 0.2250 oz. ASW, 29 mm.
Subject: Centenary - Birth of Albert Schweitzer **Obv:** Eagle above denomination **Rev:** Head facing, dates at right **Edge:** EHRFURCHT VOR DEM LEBEN

Date	Mintage	F	VF	XF	Unc	BU
1975G	8,000,000	—	—	—	6.00	7.00
1975G Proof	250,000	Value: 14.00				

KM# 144   5 MARK
11.2000 g., 0.6250 Silver 0.2250 oz. ASW, 29 mm.
Subject: 300th Anniversary - Death of von Grimmelshausen **Obv:** Eagle above denomination, date at left **Rev:** Mythic figure with book left, dates divided above **Edge:** DER ABENTHEURLICHE SIMPLICISSIMUS

Date	Mintage	F	VF	XF	Unc	BU
1976D	8,000,000	—	—	—	6.00	7.00
1976D Proof	250,000	Value: 18.00				

KM# 145   5 MARK
11.2000 g., 0.6250 Silver 0.2250 oz. ASW, 29 mm.
Subject: 200th Anniversary - Birth of Carl Friedrich Gauss **Obv:** Eagle above date and denomination **Rev:** Head 3/4 facing, dates at right **Edge:** PAUCA SED NATURA

Date	Mintage	F	VF	XF	Unc	BU
1977J	8,000,000	—	—	—	6.00	7.00
1977J Proof	250,000	Value: 18.00				

KM# 146   5 MARK
11.2000 g., 0.6250 Silver 0.2250 oz. ASW, 29 mm. **Subject:** 200th Anniversary - Birth of Heinrich von Kleist **Obv:** Eagle above denomination **Rev:** Bust 3/4 left, dates below **Edge:** FRIEDEN IST DIE BEDINGUNG DOCH VON ALLEM

Date	Mintage	F	VF	XF	Unc	BU
1977G	8,000,000	—	—	—	6.00	7.00
1977G Proof	250,000	Value: 16.00				

KM# 147   5 MARK
11.2000 g., 0.6250 Silver 0.2250 oz. ASW, 29 mm.
Subject: 100th Anniversary - Birth of Gustav Stresemann **Obv:** Eagle above denomination **Rev:** Head left, dates at left **Edge:** DURCH FRIEDEN UND VERSTÄNDIGUNG SIEGEN

Date	Mintage	F	VF	XF	Unc	BU
1978D	8,000,000	—	—	—	6.00	7.00
1978D Proof	250,000	Value: 14.00				

KM# 148   5 MARK
11.2000 g., 0.6250 Silver 0.2250 oz. ASW, 29 mm. **Subject:** 225th Anniversary - Death of Balthasar Neumann **Obv:** Eagle above denomination **Rev:** Interior of Vierzehnheiligen **Edge:** WALLFAHRTSKIRCHE VIERZEHENHEILIGEN 1743 - 1772

Date	Mintage	F	VF	XF	Unc	BU
1978F	8,000,000	—	—	—	6.00	7.00
1978F Proof	259,000	Value: 12.00				

KM# 150   5 MARK
11.2000 g., 0.6250 Silver 0.2250 oz. ASW, 29 mm. **Subject:** 150th Anniversary - German Archaeological Institute **Obv:** Denomination divides date, eagle above **Edge:** MONUMENTIS AC LITTERIS

Date	Mintage	F	VF	XF	Unc	BU
1979J	8,000,000	—	—	—	6.00	7.00
1979J Proof	250,000	Value: 14.00				

KM# 151   5 MARK
10.0000 g., Copper-Nickel Clad Nickel, 29 mm. **Subject:** 100th Anniversary - Birth of Otto Hahn **Obv:** Stylized eagle above legend **Rev:** Symbols of Hahn's studies in chemistry, name and dates below **Edge:** 1938 ERSTE SPALTUNG DES URANKERNS

Date	Mintage	F	VF	XF	Unc	BU
1979G	5,000,000	—	—	3.50	5.00	6.00
1979G Proof	350,000	Value: 11.00				

KM# 151a   5 MARK
11.2000 g., 0.6250 Silver 0.2250 oz. ASW, 29 mm. **Obv:** Stylized eagle above legend **Rev:** Chemistry symbols, name and date below **Edge:** 1938 ERSTE SPALTUNG DES URANKERNS

Date	Mintage	F	VF	XF	Unc	BU
1979G	18	—	—	—	22,500	

KM# 152   5 MARK
10.0000 g., Copper-Nickel Clad Nickel, 29 mm. **Subject:** 750th

Anniversary - Death of von der Vogelweide **Obv:** Eagle above date divided by denomination **Rev:** Reading half figure with paper, dates below **Edge:** WOL VIERZEG JAR HAB ICH GUSUNGEN ODER ME

Date	Mintage	F	VF	XF	Unc	BU
1980D	5,000,000	—	—	3.50	5.00	6.00
1980D Proof	350,000	Value: 11.50				

KM# 153   5 MARK
10.0000 g., Copper-Nickel Clad Nickel, 29 mm. **Subject:** 100th Anniversary - Cologne Cathedral **Obv:** Eagle, narrow design **Rev:** Cathedral **Edge:** ZEUGNIS DES GLAUBENS - ZEICHEN DER EINHEIT

Date	Mintage	F	VF	XF	Unc	BU
1980F	5,000,000	—	—	4.00	5.00	6.00
1980F Proof	350,000	Value: 13.50				

KM# 154   5 MARK
10.0000 g., Copper-Nickel Clad Nickel, 29 mm. **Subject:** 200th Anniversary - Death of Gotthold Ephraim Lessing **Obv:** Denomination divides date below eagle **Rev:** Bust in silhouette left **Edge:** SIEH ÜBERALL MIT DEINEN EIGENEN AUGEN

Date	Mintage	F	VF	XF	Unc	BU
1981J	6,500,000	—	—	4.00	5.00	
1981J Proof	350,000	Value: 10.00				

KM# 155   5 MARK
10.0000 g., Copper-Nickel Clad Nickel, 29 mm. **Subject:** 150th Anniversary - Death of Carl vom Stein **Obv:** Eagle in relief, denomination divides date below **Rev:** Bust 3/4 facing, dates at right **Edge:** ICH HABE NUR EIN VATERLAND - DEUTSCHLAND

Date	Mintage	F	VF	XF	Unc	BU
1981G	6,500,000	—	—	4.00	5.00	
1981G Proof	350,000	Value: 10.00				

KM# 156   5 MARK
10.0000 g., Copper-Nickel Clad Nickel, 29 mm. **Subject:** 150th Anniversary - Death of Johann Wolfgang von Goethe **Obv:** Eagle above denomination, date at right **Rev:** Head right, dates below **Edge:** ZWISCHEN UNS SEI WAHRHEIT

Date	Mintage	F	VF	XF	Unc	BU
1982D	8,000,000	—	—	4.00	5.00	
1982D Proof	350,000	Value: 11.50				

KM# 157   5 MARK

10.0000 g., Copper-Nickel Clad Nickel, 29 mm. **Subject:** 10th Anniversary - U.N. Environmental Conference **Obv:** Eagle above denomination **Rev:** Stylized figure in center of design, date above **Edge:** DIE EINE ERDE SCHUETZEN

Date	Mintage	F	VF	XF	Unc	BU
1982F	8,000,000	—	—	—	4.00	5.00
1982F Proof	350,000	Value: 10.00				

KM# 158   5 MARK

10.0000 g., Copper-Nickel Clad Nickel, 29 mm. **Subject:** 100th Anniversary - Death of Karl Marx **Obv:** Eagle in relief above denomination **Rev:** Head 3/4 facing, dates below **Edge:** WAHRHEIT ALS WIRKLICHKEIT UND MACHT

Date	Mintage	F	VF	XF	Unc	BU
1983J	8,000,000	—	—	—	4.00	5.00
1983J Proof	350,000	Value: 10.00				

KM# 159   5 MARK

10.0000 g., Copper-Nickel Clad Nickel, 29 mm. **Subject:** 500th Anniversary - Birth of Martin Luther **Obv:** Eagle, denomination below divides date **Rev:** Inscription covers head 3/4 right **Edge:** GOTTES WORK BLEIBT IN EWIGKEIT

Date	Mintage	F	VF	XF	Unc	BU
1983G	8,000,000	—	—	—	4.00	5.00
1983G Proof	350,000	Value: 12.00				

KM# 160   5 MARK

10.0000 g., Copper-Nickel Clad Nickel, 29 mm. **Subject:** 150th Anniversary - German Customs Union **Obv:** Eagle, denomination divides date below **Rev:** Horses and carriage passing under open customs barrier **Edge:** ZOLLVEREIN DEUTSCHLAND - EWG EUROPA

Date	Mintage	F	VF	XF	Unc	BU
1984D	8,000,000	—	—	—	4.00	5.00
1984D Proof	350,000	Value: 11.50				

KM# 161   5 MARK

10.0000 g., Copper-Nickel Clad Nickel, 29 mm. **Subject:** 175th Anniversary - Birth of Felix Bartholdy **Obv:** Eagle above denomination **Rev:** 3/4 figure looking left, left hand on hip, music

score in background **Edge:** IHR TÖNE SCHWINGT EUCH FREUDIG DURCH DIE SAITEN

Date	Mintage	F	VF	XF	Unc	BU
1984J	8,000,000	—	—	—	4.00	5.00
1984J Proof	350,000	Value: 12.50				

KM# 162   5 MARK

10.0000 g., Copper-Nickel Clad Nickel, 29 mm. **Subject:** European Year of Music **Obv:** Stylized eagle in circle at left, denomination at right, date above **Rev:** Circle at left holds stars and outline of face in harp, music notes at right **Edge:** SCHÜTZ BACH HÄNDEL SCARLATTI BERG

Date	Mintage	F	VF	XF	Unc	BU
1985F	8,000,000	—	—	—	4.00	5.00
1985F Proof	350,000	Value: 11.50				

KM# 163   5 MARK

10.0000 g., Copper-Nickel Clad Nickel, 29 mm. **Subject:** 150th Anniversary - German Railroad **Obv:** Stylized eagle above denomination **Rev:** Spoked wheel design **Edge:** EISENBAHN NÜRNBERG - FÜHRT 7. DEZEMBER 1835

Date	Mintage	F	VF	XF	Unc	BU
1985G	8,000,000	—	—	—	4.00	5.00
1985G Proof	350,000	Value: 10.00				

KM# 164   5 MARK

10.0000 g., Copper-Nickel Clad Nickel, 29 mm. **Subject:** 600th Anniversary - Heidelberg University **Obv:** Denomination divides date below eagle **Rev:** Crowned rampant lion left within legend **Edge:** AUS TRADITION IN DIE ZUKUNFT

Date	Mintage	F	VF	XF	Unc	BU
1986D	8,000,000	—	—	—	4.00	5.00
1986D Proof	350,000	Value: 10.00				

KM# 165   5 MARK

10.0000 g., Copper-Nickel Clad Nickel, 29 mm. **Subject:** 200th Anniversary - Death of Frederick the Great **Obv:** Eagle above denomination **Rev:** Uniformed bust left, dates below **Edge:** ICH BIN DER ERSTE DIENER MEINES STAATES

Date	Mintage	F	VF	XF	Unc	BU
1986F	8,000,000	—	—	—	4.00	5.00
1986F Proof	350,000	Value: 12.50				

KM# 130   10 MARK

15.5000 g., 0.6250 Silver 0.3114 oz. ASW, 33 mm. **Series:** Munich Olympics **Obv:** Artistic eagle, denomination below **Rev:** "In Deutschland" with spiraling symbol **Edge:** FORTIVS CITIVS ALTIVS

Date	Mintage	F	VF	XF	Unc	BU
1972D	2,500,000	—	—	—	7.50	11.50
1972D Proof	125,000	Value: 26.00				
1972F	2,375,000	—	—	—	7.50	11.50
1972F Proof	125,000	Value: 26.00				
1972G	2,500,000	—	—	—	7.50	11.50
1972G Proof	125,000	Value: 26.00				
1972J	2,500,000	•	—	—	7.50	11.50
1972J Proof	125,000	Value: 26.00				

KM# 131   10 MARK

15.5000 g., 0.6250 Silver 0.3114 oz. ASW, 33 mm. **Series:** Munich Olympics **Obv:** Eagle above denomination **Rev:** Schleife (knot) **Edge:** FORTIVS CITIVS ALTIVS

Date	Mintage	F	VF	XF	Unc	BU
1972D	5,000,000	—	—	—	7.50	11.50
1972D Proof	125,000	Value: 20.00				
1972F	4,875,000	—	—	—	7.50	11.50
1972F Proof	125,000	Value: 20.00				
1972G	5,000,000	—	—	—	7.50	11.50
1972G Proof	125,000	Value: 20.00				
1972J	5,000,000	—	—	—	7.50	11.50
1972J Proof	125,000	Value: 20.00				

KM# 132   10 MARK

15.5000 g., 0.6250 Silver 0.3114 oz. ASW, 33 mm. **Series:** Munich Olympics **Obv:** Eagle above denomination **Rev:** Athletes kneeling **Edge:** FORTIVS CITIVS ALTIVS

Date	Mintage	F	VF	XF	Unc	BU
1972D	5,000,000	—	—	—	7.00	10.00
1972D Proof	150,000	Value: 16.50				
1972F	4,850,000	—	—	—	7.00	10.00
1972F Proof	150,000	Value: 16.50				
1972G	5,000,000	—	—	—	7.00	10.00
1972G Proof	150,000	Value: 16.50				
1972J	5,000,000	—	—	—	7.00	10.00
1972J Proof	150,000	Value: 16.50				

KM# 133   10 MARK

15.5000 g., 0.6250 Silver 0.3114 oz. ASW, 33 mm. **Series:** Munich Olympics **Obv:** Eagle above denomination **Rev:** Stadium - aerial view **Edge:** FORTIVS CITIVS ALTIVS

Date	Mintage	F	VF	XF	Unc	BU
1972D	5,000,000	—	—	—	7.00	10.00
1972D Proof	150,000	Value: 16.50				

Date	F	Mintage	F	VF	XF	Unc	BU
1972F		4,850,000	—	—	—	7.00	10.00
1972F Proof		150,000	Value: 16.50				
1972G		5,000,000	—	—	—	7.00	10.00
1972G Proof		150,000	Value: 16.50				
1972J		5,000,000	—	—	—	7.00	10.00
1972J Proof		150,000	Value: 16.50				

KM# 134.1   10 MARK
15.5000 g., 0.6250 Silver 0.3114 oz. ASW, 33 mm. **Series:** Munich Olympics **Obv:** Eagle above denomination **Rev:** "In Munchen" - with spiral symbol **Edge:** Lettering separated by periods **Edge:** FORTIVS CITIVS ALTIVS

Date	Mintage	F	VF	XF	Unc	BU
1972D	2,500,000	—	—	—	7.50	11.50
1972D Proof	150,000	Value: 20.00				
1972F	2,350,000	—	—	—	7.50	11.50
1972F Proof	150,000	Value: 20.00				
1972G	2,500,000	—	—	—	7.50	11.50
1972G Proof	150,000	Value: 20.00				
1972J	2,500,000	—	—	—	7.50	11.50
1972J Proof	150,000	Value: 20.00				

KM# 134.2   10 MARK
15.5000 g., 0.6250 Silver 0.3114 oz. ASW, 33 mm. **Obv:** Eagle above denomination **Rev:** Spiral design **Edge:** Lettering separated by arabesques **Edge:** FORTIVS CITIVS ALTIVS **Note:** Error.

Date	Mintage	F	VF	XF	Unc	BU
1972D	—	—	—	—	2,760	—
1972F	—	—	—	—	2,760	—
1972G	—	—	—	—	2,760	—
1972J	600	—	200	300	550	—

KM# 135   10 MARK
15.5000 g., 0.6250 Silver 0.3114 oz. ASW, 33 mm. **Series:** Munich Olympics **Obv:** Eagle above denomination **Rev:** Olympic Flame, spiral symbol above, rings divide date below **Edge:** FORTIVS CITIVS ALTIVS

Date	Mintage	F	VF	XF	Unc	BU
1972D	5,000,000	—	—	—	7.00	9.00
1972D Proof	150,000	Value: 16.00				
1972F	4,850,000	—	—	—	7.00	9.00
1972F Proof	150,000	Value: 16.00				
1972G	5,000,000	—	—	—	7.00	9.00
1972G Proof	150,000	Value: 16.00				
1972J	5,000,000	—	—	—	7.00	9.00
1972J Proof	150,000	Value: 16.00				

KM# 166   10 MARK
15.5000 g., 0.6250 Silver 0.3114 oz. ASW, 33 mm. **Subject:** 750th Anniversary - Berlin **Obv:** Eagle above denomination **Rev:** Bear at right holding circular shield **Edge:** EINIGKEIT UND RECHT UND FREIHEIT

Date	Mintage	F	VF	XF	Unc	BU
1987J	8,000,000	—	—	—	9.00	11.00
1987J Proof	350,000	Value: 50.00				

KM# 167   10 MARK
15.5000 g., 0.6250 Silver 0.3114 oz. ASW, 33 mm. **Subject:** 30 Years of European Unity **Obv:** Eagle above denomination **Rev:** Horses pulling 30 year symbol, dates at right **Edge:** ADENAUER . BECH . DE GASPERI . LUNS . SCHUMANN . SPAAK .

Date	Mintage	F	VF	XF	Unc	BU
1987G	8,000,000	—	—	—	7.00	9.00
1987G Proof	350,000	Value: 30.00				

KM# 168   10 MARK
15.5000 g., 0.6250 Silver 0.3114 oz. ASW, 33 mm. **Subject:** 200th Anniversary - Birth of Arthur Schopenhauer **Obv:** Eagle above denomination **Rev:** Head facing, dates below left **Edge:** DIE WELT ALS WILLE UND VORSTELLUNG

Date	Mintage	F	VF	XF	Unc	BU
1988D	8,000,000	—	—	—	7.00	9.00
1988D Proof	350,000	Value: 27.50				

KM# 169   10 MARK
15.5000 g., 0.6250 Silver 0.3114 oz. ASW, 33 mm. **Subject:** 100th Anniversary - Death of Carl Zeiss **Obv:** Eagle above denomination **Rev:** Head at left, looking right **Edge:** OPTIK FÜR WISSENSCHAFT UND TECHNIK

Date	Mintage	F	VF	XF	Unc	BU
1988F	8,000,000	—	—	—	7.00	9.00
1988F Proof	350,000	Value: 25.00				

KM# 171   10 MARK
15.5000 g., 0.6250 Silver 0.3114 oz. ASW, 33 mm. **Subject:** 800th Year - Port of Hamburg **Obv:** Small eagle above denomination **Rev:** Three towered city gate, waves below **Edge:** HAMBURG TOR ZUR WELT

Date	Mintage	F	VF	XF	Unc	BU
1989J	8,000,000	—	—	—	7.00	9.00
1989J Proof	350,000	Value: 25.00				

KM# 172   10 MARK
15.5000 g., 0.6250 Silver 0.3114 oz. ASW, 33 mm. **Subject:** 2000th Anniversary - City of Bonn **Obv:** Eagle above denomination **Rev:** Building left of sun design

Date	Mintage	F	VF	XF	Unc	BU
1989D	8,000,000	—	—	—	7.00	9.00
1989D Proof	350,000	Value: 25.00				

KM# 173   10 MARK
15.5000 g., 0.6250 Silver 0.3114 oz. ASW, 33 mm. **Subject:** 40th Anniversary - Republic **Obv:** Linear eagle above date and denomination **Rev:** Eleven shields form a circle

Date	Mintage	F	VF	XF	Unc	BU
1989G	8,000,000	—	—	—	7.00	9.00
1989G Proof	350,000	Value: 28.00				

KM# 174   10 MARK
15.5000 g., 0.6250 Silver 0.3114 oz. ASW, 33 mm. **Subject:** 800th Anniversary - Death of Kaiser Friedrich Barbarossa **Obv:** Eagle above denomination **Rev:** Crowned figure with royal orb and scepter rising above castle walls, dates below

Date	Mintage	F	VF	XF	Unc	BU
1990F	7,850,000	—	—	—	7.00	9.00
1990F Proof	400,000	Value: 18.00				

KM# 176   10 MARK
15.5000 g., 0.6250 Silver 0.3114 oz. ASW, 33 mm. **Subject:** 800th Anniversary - The Teutonic Order **Obv:** Eagle above denomination **Rev:** Wrinkled page with Madonna and child pictured, shield upper left

Date	Mintage	F	VF	XF	Unc	BU
1990J	8,850,000	—	—	—	7.00	9.00
1990J Proof	450,000	Value: 12.50				

KM# 177   10 MARK
15.5000 g., 0.6250 Silver 0.3114 oz. ASW, 33 mm.
Subject: German Unity **Obv:** Eagle above denomination
Rev: Brandenburg Gate in Berlin

Date	Mintage	F	VF	XF	Unc	BU
1991A	8,850,000	—	—	—	7.00	9.00
1991A Proof	450,000	Value: 17.50				

KM# 178   10 MARK
15.5000 g., 0.6250 Silver 0.3114 oz. ASW, 33 mm.
Subject: 125th Anniversary - Birth of Kathe Kollwitz - Artist and
Sculptor **Obv:** Denomination divides date below eagle
Rev: Figure at easel drawing, dates below

Date	Mintage	F	VF	XF	Unc	BU
1992G	8,450,000	—	—	—	7.00	9.00
1992G Proof	450,000	Value: 12.00				

KM# 179   10 MARK
15.5000 g., 0.6250 Silver 0.3114 oz. ASW, 33 mm.
Subject: 150th Anniversary - Civil Pour-le-Merite Order
Obv: Eagle above denomination, date at left **Rev:** Alexander von
Humbolt, 1st chancellor of the Order

Date	Mintage	F	VF	XF	Unc	BU
1992D	8,450,000	—	—	—	7.00	9.00
1992D Proof	450,000	Value: 12.00				

KM# 180   10 MARK
15.5000 g., 0.6250 Silver 0.3114 oz. ASW, 33 mm.
Subject: 1000th Anniversary - Potsdam **Obv:** Eagle above
denomination, date at left **Rev:** Palace of Sanssouci and
Nicolai Church

Date	Mintage	F	VF	XF	Unc	BU
1993F	7,950,000	—	—	—	7.00	9.00
1993F Proof	450,000	Value: 12.00				

KM# 181   10 MARK
15.5000 g., 0.6250 Silver 0.3114 oz. ASW, 33 mm.
Subject: 150th Birth Anniversary of Robert Koch **Obv:** Eagle
above denomination **Rev:** Head 3/4 facing

Date	Mintage	F	VF	XF	Unc	BU
1993J	7,450,000	—	—	—	7.00	9.00
1993J Proof	450,000	Value: 12.00				

KM# 182   10 MARK
15.5000 g., 0.6250 Silver 0.3114 oz. ASW, 33 mm. **Subject:**
Attempt on Hitler's Life, July 20, 1944 **Obv:** Eagle above
denomination **Rev:** Wing with chain surrounding, date below
Edge: WIDERSTAND GEGEN DEV NATIONALS OZIALIMUS

Date	Mintage	F	VF	XF	Unc	BU
1994A	7,450,000	—	—	—	7.00	9.00
1994A Proof	450,000	Value: 20.00				

KM# 184   10 MARK
15.5000 g., 0.6250 Silver 0.3114 oz. ASW, 33 mm.
Subject: 250th Birth Anniversary- Johann Gottfried Herder
Obv: Eagle, denomination at left and below **Rev:** Head looking
right, shadow head behind

Date	Mintage	F	VF	XF	Unc	BU
1994G	7,450,000	—	—	—	7.00	9.00
1994G Proof	450,000	Value: 12.00				

KM# 185   10 MARK
15.5000 g., 0.6250 Silver 0.3114 oz. ASW, 33 mm.
Subject: 50th Anniversary of Peace and Reconciliation
Obv: Eagle above denomination and date **Rev:** Ruins of Frauen
Kirche in Dresden **Edge:** STEINERNE GLOCKE SYMBOL FUER
TOLERANZ

Date	Mintage	F	VF	XF	Unc	BU
1995J	7,450,000	—	—	—	7.00	9.00
1995J Proof	450,000	Value: 12.00				

KM# 186   10 MARK
15.5000 g., 0.6250 Silver 0.3114 oz. ASW, 33 mm. **Subject:**
500th Anniversary of death - Henry the Lion **Obv:** Thin eagle
divides date and denomination **Rev:** Artistic rampant lion, left
Edge: HEINRICH DER LOEWE AUS KAISERLICHEM STAMM

Date	Mintage	F	VF	XF	Unc	BU
1995F	7,450,000	—	—	—	7.00	9.00
1995F Proof	450,000	Value: 12.00				

KM# 187   10 MARK
15.5000 g., 0.6250 Silver 0.3114 oz. ASW, 33 mm. **Subject:** 150th
Birth Anniversary - Wilhelm Conrad Rontgen; 100th Anniversary of
x-ray **Obv:** Eagle divides date and denomination **Rev:** Hand and X-
rayed hand **Edge:** ERSTER NOBEL PREIS FUER PHYSIK

Date	Mintage	F	VF	XF	Unc	BU
1995D	6,900,000	—	—	—	7.00	9.00
1995D Proof	450,000	Value: 12.00				

KM# 188   10 MARK
15.5000 g., 0.6250 Silver 0.3114 oz. ASW, 33 mm.
Subject: 150th Anniversary of founding - Kolpingwerk
Obv: Eagle, denomination at left and below **Rev:** Globe in
background, face in triangle at right, three pictures in rectangle
at left **Edge:** TAETIGE LIEBE HEILT ALLE WUNDEN

Date	Mintage	F	VF	XF	Unc	BU
1996A	5,600,000	—	—	—	7.00	9.00
1996A Proof	400,000	Value: 12.00				

KM# 189.1   10 MARK
15.5000 g., 0.6250 Silver 0.3114 oz. ASW, 33 mm.
Subject: 500th Birth Anniversary - Philipp Melanchthon **Obv:**
Stylized eagle above denomination **Rev:** Bust left, dates at right

Date	Mintage	F	VF	XF	Unc	BU
1997A Proof	150,000	Value: 17.50				
1997D Proof	150,000	Value: 17.50				
1997F Proof	150,000	Value: 17.50				
1997G Proof	150,000	Value: 17.50				
1997J	3,000,000	—	—	—	9.00	11.00
1997J Proof	150,000	Value: 17.50				

KM# 189.2   10 MARK
15.5000 g., 0.6250 Silver 0.3114 oz. ASW, 33 mm. **Subject:**
500th Birth Anniversary - Philipp Melanchthon **Obv:** Stylized
eagle, denomination **Rev:** Different forelock on portrait

Date	Mintage	F	VF	XF	Unc	BU
1997J	—	—	—	—	9.00	11.00
1997J Proof	—	Value: 20.00				

KM# 190   10 MARK
15.5000 g., 0.6250 Silver 0.3114 oz. ASW, 33 mm. **Subject:**
200th Birth Anniversary - Heinrich Heine **Obv:** Stylized eagle,
denomination below **Rev:** Half figure 3/4 left with handwritten text
in background **Edge:** DEUTSCHLAND DAS SIND WIR SELBER

Date	Mintage	F	VF	XF	Unc	BU
1997A Proof	150,000	Value: 22.50				
1997D	3,000,000	—	—	—	9.00	—
1997D Proof	750,000	Value: 22.50				
1997F Proof	150,000	Value: 22.50				
1997G Proof	150,000	Value: 22.50				
1997J Proof	150,000	Value: 22.50				

KM# 192   10 MARK
15.5000 g., 0.6250 Silver 0.3114 oz. ASW, 33 mm.
Subject: Diesel Engine Centennial **Obv:** Stylized eagle above
denomination **Rev:** First diesel engine

Date	Mintage	F	VF	XF	Unc	BU
1997A Proof	150,000	Value: 16.00				
1997D Proof	150,000	Value: 16.00				
1997F	3,000,000	—	—	—	9.00	11.00
1997F Proof	150,000	Value: 16.00				
1997G Proof	150,000	Value: 16.00				
1997J Proof	150,000	Value: 16.00				

KM# 191   10 MARK
15.5000 g., 0.9250 Silver 0.4609 oz. ASW, 33 mm.
Subject: 300th Anniversary end of 30 Years War - Peace of
Westphalia **Obv:** Stylized eagle above denomination
Rev: Clasped hands, dove and quill

Date	Mintage	F	VF	XF	Unc	BU
1998A Proof	200,000	Value: 16.00				
1998D Proof	200,000	Value: 16.00				
1998F Proof	200,000	Value: 16.00				
1998G Proof	200,000	Value: 16.00				
1998J	3,500,000	—	—	—	9.00	11.00
1998J Proof	200,000	Value: 16.00				

Note: A 1997 strike of this coin does not exist

KM# 193   10 MARK
0.9250 Silver, 33 mm. **Subject:** 900th Anniversary - Birth of
Hildegard von Bingen (1098-1178AD), abbess and scholar **Obv:**
Stylized eagle above denomination **Rev:** Seated figure writing,
small hand above left **Edge:** WISSE DIE WEGE DES HERRN

Date	Mintage	F	VF	XF	Unc	BU
1998A Proof	200,000	Value: 16.00				
1998D Proof	200,000	Value: 16.00				
1998F Proof	200,000	Value: 16.00				
1998G	3,500,000	—	—	—	9.00	11.00
1998G Proof	200,000	Value: 16.00				
1998J Proof	200,000	Value: 16.00				

KM# 194   10 MARK
15.5000 g., 0.9000 Silver 0.4485 oz. ASW, 33 mm.
Subject: 300th Anniversary Franckesche Charitable Endowment

Date	Mintage	F	VF	XF	Unc	BU
1998A	—	—	—	—	9.00	11.00
1998A Proof	—	Value: 16.00				
1998D Proof	—	Value: 16.00				
1998F Proof	—	Value: 16.00				
1998G Proof	—	Value: 16.00				
1998J Proof	—	Value: 16.00				

KM# 195   10 MARK
15.5000 g., 0.9250 Silver 0.4609 oz. ASW, 33 mm. **Subject:** 50
Years of the Deutsch Mark **Obv:** Denomination above eagle
Rev: Seven coin designs **Edge:** EINIGKEIT UND RECHT UND
FREIHEIT

Date	Mintage	F	VF	XF	Unc	BU
1998A Proof	—	Value: 17.50				
1998D Proof	—	Value: 17.50				
1998F	—	—	—	—	9.00	11.00
1998F Proof	—	Value: 17.50				
1998G Proof	—	Value: 17.50				
1998J Proof	—	Value: 17.50				

KM# 196   10 MARK
15.5000 g., 0.9250 Silver 0.4609 oz. ASW, 33 mm.
Subject: 50th Anniversary - Bundes Republic Constitution
Obv: Small eagle above denomination **Rev:** German constitution
Edge: FUR DAS GESAMTE DEUTSCH VOLK

Date	Mintage	F	VF	XF	Unc	BU
1999A Proof	—	Value: 16.00				
1999D	—	—	—	—	9.00	11.00
1999D Proof	—	Value: 16.00				
1999F Proof	—	Value: 16.00				
1999G Proof	—	Value: 16.00				
1999J Proof	—	Value: 16.00				

KM# 197   10 MARK
15.5000 g., 0.9250 Silver 0.4609 oz. ASW, 33 mm.
Subject: 250th Anniversary - Birth of J.W. von Goethe
Obv: Eagle above denomination **Rev:** Bust at left facing inscribed
field right **Edge:** WIRKE GUT SO WIRKST DU LANGER

Date	Mintage	F	VF	XF	Unc	BU
1999A Proof	—	Value: 16.00				
1999D Proof	—	Value: 16.00				
1999F	—	—	—	—	9.00	11.00
1999F Proof	—	Value: 16.00				
1999G Proof	—	Value: 16.00				
1999J Proof	—	Value: 16.00				

KM# 198   10 MARK
15.5000 g., 0.9250 Silver 0.4609 oz. ASW, 33 mm. **Subject:**
Charity for children without parents all over the world **Obv:**
Stylized eagle, denomination divides date below **Rev:** Stylized
globe, children playing **Edge:** SOS - KINDERDORFER - EINE
IDEE FUR DIE WELT

Date	Mintage	F	VF	XF	Unc	BU
1999A Proof	—	Value: 16.00				
1999D Proof	—	Value: 16.00				

Date	Mintage	F	VF	XF	Unc	BU
1999F Proof	—	Value: 16.00				
1999G Proof	—	Value: 16.00				
1999J	—	—	—	—	9.00	11.00
1999J Proof	—	Value: 16.00				

Note: NOTE: A 1997 strike of this coin does not exist.

KM# 199   10 MARK
15.5000 g., 0.9250 Silver 0.4609 oz. ASW, 33 mm. **Subject:** Expo
2000 **Obv:** Stylized eagle **Rev:** Childlike drawing of human balance
scale **Edge:** WELTAUSSTELLUNG EXPO 2000 HANNOVER

Date	Mintage	F	VF	XF	Unc	BU
2000A	3,000,000	—	—	—	9.00	11.00
2000A Proof	160,000	Value: 16.00				
2000D Proof	160,000	Value: 16.00				
2000F Proof	160,000	Value: 16.00				
2000G Proof	160,000	Value: 16.00				
2000J Proof	160,000	Value: 16.00				

KM# 200   10 MARK
15.5000 g., 0.9250 Silver 0.4609 oz. ASW, 33 mm.
Subject: 1200th Anniversary - Founding of the Church in Aachen
by Charlemagne **Obv:** Stylized eagle **Rev:** Charlemagne handing
church model to Madonna and child **Edge:** URBS AQUENSIS -
URBS REGALIS

Date	Mintage	F	VF	XF	Unc	BU
2000A Proof	160,000	Value: 16.00				
2000D Proof	160,000	Value: 16.00				
2000F Proof	160,000	Value: 16.00				
2000G	3,000,000	—	—	—	9.00	11.00
2000G Proof	160,000	Value: 16.00				
2000J Proof	160,000	Value: 16.00				

KM# 201   10 MARK
15.5000 g., 0.9250 Silver 0.4609 oz. ASW, 33 mm.
Subject: 10th Anniversary of Reunification **Obv:** Eagle and
denomination **Rev:** Parliament building **Edge:** "WIR SIND DAS
VOLK WIR SIND EIN VOLK"

Date	Mintage	F	VF	XF	Unc	BU
2000A Proof	—	Value: 16.00				
2000D	—	—	—	—	9.00	11.00
2000D Proof	—	Value: 16.00				
2000F Proof	—	Value: 16.00				
2000G Proof	—	Value: 16.00				
2000J Proof	—	Value: 16.00				

KM# 202   10 MARK
15.5000 g., 0.9250 Silver 0.4609 oz. ASW, 33 mm. **Obv:** Eagle
above denomination **Rev:** Face on inscribed background, dates
below **Edge:** "JOHANN SEBASTIAN BACH 250 TODESTAG"

Date	Mintage	F	VF	XF	Unc	BU
2000A Proof	—	Value: 16.00				
2000D Proof	—	Value: 16.00				
2000F	—	—	—	—	9.00	11.00
2000F Proof	—	Value: 16.00				
2000G Proof	—	Value: 16.00				
2000J Proof	—	Value: 16.00				

PATTERNS
Including off metal strikes

KM#	Date	Mintage	Identification	Mkt Val
Pn397	1950D	—	2 Mark. Copper-Nickel. With Hole. PN#400.	—
Pn398	1951D	—	2 Mark. Copper-Nickel. Max Planck.	—
Pn399	1951F	—	2 Mark. Copper-Nickel. Max Planck.	—
Pn400	1955J	—	2 Mark.	—
Pn401	1959F	—	2 Pfennig. Brass.	—
Pn402	1960F	—	2 Pfennig. Zinc.	—

TRIAL STRIKES

KM#	Date	Mintage	Identification	Mkt Val
TS1	NDJ	—	10 Pfennig. KM#4. Uniface.	—
TS2	NDJ	—	2 Mark. Silver. Pn400. Uniface.	—
TS3	1950J	—	2 Mark. Silver. Pn400. Uniface.	—
TS4	NDJ	—	2 Mark. Lead. Pn400. Uniface.	—
TS5	1950J	—	2 Mark. Lead. Pn400. Uniface.	—
TS6	1951F	—	2 Mark. Lead. Max Planck. Uniface.	—

KM#	Date	Mintage	Identification	Mkt Val
TS7	NDF	—	2 Mark. Lead. Max Planck. Uniface.	—
TS8	1951J	—	2 Mark. Iron. Max Planck. Uniface.	—
TS9	NDJ	—	2 Mark. Iron. Max Planck. Uniface.	—
TS10	1951J	—	2 Mark. Lead. Max Planck. Uniface.	—
TS11	NDJ	—	2 Mark. Lead. Max Planck. Uniface.	—

MINT SETS

KM#	Date	Mintage	Identification	Issue Price	Mkt Val
MS1	1974D (9)	20,000	KM#105, 106a, 107-108, 109.2, 110, 112.1, 124, A127	—	45.00
MS2	1974F (9)	20,000	KM#105, 106a, 107-108, 109.2, 110, 112.1, 124, A127	—	45.00
MS3	1974G (9)	20,000	KM#105, 106a, 107-108, 109.2, 110, 112.1, 124, A127	—	45.00
MS4	1974J (9)	20,000	KM#105, 106a, 107-108, 109.2, 110, 112.1, 124, A127	—	45.00
MS5	1975D (9)	26,000	KM#105, 106a, 107-108, 109.2, 110, 124, A127, 140.1	—	28.00
MS6	1975F (9)	26,000	KM#105, 106a, 107-108, 109.2, 110, 124, A127, 140.1	—	28.00
MS7	1975G (9)	26,000	KM#105, 106a, 107-108, 109.2, 110, 124, A127, 140.1	—	28.00
MS8	1975J (9)	26,000	KM#105, 106a, 107-108, 109.2, 110, 124, A127, 140.1	—	28.00
MS9	1976D (9)	26,000	KM#105, 106a, 107-108, 109.2, 110, 124, A127, 140.1	—	28.00
MS10	1976F (9)	26,000	KM#105, 106a, 107-108, 1092., 110, 124, A127, 140.1	—	28.00
MS11	1976G (9)	26,000	KM#105, 106a, 107-108, 109.2, 110, 124, A127, 140.1	—	28.00
MS12	1976J (9)	26,000	KM#105, 106a, 107-108, 109.2, 110, 124, A127, 140.1	—	28.00
MS13	1977D (9)	29,000	KM#105, 106a, 107-108, 109.2, 110, 124, A127, 140.1	—	20.00
MS14	1977F (9)	29,000	KM#105, 106a, 107-108, 109.2, 110, 124, A127, 140.1	—	20.00
MS15	1977G (9)	29,000	KM#105, 106a, 107-108, 109.2, 110, 124, A127, 140.1	—	20.00
MS16	1977J (9)	29,000	KM#105, 106a, 107-108, 109.2, 110, 124, A127, 140.1	—	20.00
MS17	1978D (9)	30,000	KM#105, 106a, 107-108, 109.2, 110, 124, A127, 140.1	—	20.00
MS18	1978F (9)	30,000	KM#105, 106a, 107-108, 109.2, 110, 124, A127, 140.1	—	20.00
MS19	1978g (9)	30,000	KM#105, 106a, 107-108, 109.2, 110, 124, A127, 140.1	—	20.00
MS20	1978J (9)	30,000	KM#105, 106a, 107-108, 109.2, 110, 124, A127, 140.1	—	20.00
MS21	1979D (10)	34,000	KM105, 106a, 107-108, 109.2, 110, 124, A127, 140.1, 149	11.00	20.00
MS22	1979F (10)	34,000	KM105, 106a, 107-108, 109.2, 110, 124, A127, 140.1, 149	11.00	20.00
MS23	1979G (10)	34,000	KM105, 106a, 107-108, 109.2, 110, 124, A127, 140.1, 149	11.00	20.00
MS24	1979J (10)	34,000	KM105, 106a, 107-108, 109.2, 110, 124, A127, 140.1, 149	11.00	20.00
MS25	1980D (10)	36,000	KM105, 106a, 107-108, 109.2, 110, 124, A127, 140.1, 149	11.00	20.00
MS26	1980F (10)	36,000	KM105, 106a, 107-108, 109.2, 110, 124, A127, 140.1, 149	11.00	20.00
MS27	1980G (10)	36,000	KM105, 106a, 107-108, 109.2, 110, 124, A127, 140.1, 149	11.00	20.00
MS28	1980J (10)	36,000	KM105, 106a, 107-108, 109.2, 110, 124, A127, 140.1, 149	11.00	20.00
MS29	1981D (10)	38,000	KM105, 106a, 107-108, 109.2, 110, 124, A127, 140.1, 149	11.00	20.00
MS30	1981F (10)	38,000	KM105, 106a, 107-108, 109.2, 110, 124, A127, 140.1, 149	11.00	20.00
MS31	1981G (10)	38,000	KM105, 106a, 107-108, 109.2, 110, 124, A127, 140.1, 149	11.00	20.00
MS32	1981J (10)	38,000	KM105, 106a, 107-108, 109.2, 110, 124, A127, 140.1, 149	11.00	20.00
MS33	1982D (10)	33,000	KM105, 106a, 107-108, 109.2, 110, 124, A127, 140.1, 149	11.00	20.00
MS34	1982F (10)	33,000	KM105, 106a, 107-108, 109.2, 110, 124, A127, 140.1, 149	11.00	20.00
MS35	1982G (10)	33,000	KM105, 106a, 107-108, 109.2, 110, 124, A127, 140.1, 149	11.00	20.00
MS36	1982J (10)	33,000	KM105, 106a, 107-108, 109.2, 110, 124, A127, 140.1, 149	11.00	20.00
MS37	1983D (10)	31,000	KM105, 106a, 107-108, 109.2, 110, 124, A127, 140.1, 149	11.00	20.00
MS38	1983F (10)	31,000	KM105, 106a, 107-108, 109.2, 110, 124, A127, 140.1, 149	11.00	20.00
MS39	1983G (10)	31,000	KM105, 106a, 107-108, 109.2, 110, 124, A127, 140.1, 149	11.00	20.00
MS40	1983J (10)	31,000	KM105, 106a, 107-108, 109.2, 110, 124, A127, 140.1, 149	11.00	20.00
MS41	1984D (10)	25,000	KM105, 106a, 107-108, 109.2, 110, 124, A127, 140.1, 149	11.00	50.00
MS42	1984F (10)	25,000	KM105, 106a, 107-108, 109.2, 110, 124, A127, 140.1, 149	11.00	50.00
MS43	1984G (10)	25,000	KM105, 106a, 107-108, 109.2, 110, 124, A127, 140.1, 149	11.00	50.00
MS44	1984J (10)	25,000	KM105, 106a, 107-108, 109.2, 110, 124, A127, 140.1, 149	11.00	50.00
MS45	1985D (10)	23,000	KM105, 106a, 107-108, 109.2, 110, 124, A127, 140.1, 149	11.00	20.00
MS46	1985F (10)	23,000	KM105, 106a, 107-108, 109.2, 110, 124, A127, 140.1, 149	11.00	20.00
MS47	1985G (10)	23,000	KM105, 106a, 107-108, 109.2, 110, 124, A127, 140.1, 149	11.00	20.00
MS48	1985J (10)	23,000	KM105, 106a, 107-108, 109.2, 110, 124, A127, 140.1, 149	11.00	20.00
MS49	1986D (10)	15,000	KM105, 106a, 107-108, 109.2, 110, 124, A127, 140.1, 149	11.00	100
MS50	1986F (10)	15,000	KM105, 106a, 107-108, 109.2, 110, 124, A127, 140.1, 149	11.00	100

KM#	Date	Mintage	Identification	Issue Price	Mkt Val
MS51	1986G (10)	15,000	KM105, 106a, 107-108, 109.2, 110, 124, A127, 140.1, 149	11.00	100
MS52	1986J (10)	15,000	KM105, 106a, 107-108, 109.2, 110, 124, A127, 140.1, 149	11.00	100
MS53	1987D (10)	18,000	KM105, 106a, 107-108, 109.2, 110, 124, A127, 140.1, 149	11.00	45.00
MS54	1987F (10)	18,000	KM105, 106a, 107-108, 109.2, 110, 124, A127, 140.1, 149	11.00	45.00
MS55	1987G (10)	18,000	KM105, 106a, 107-108, 109.2, 110, 124, A127, 140.1, 149	11.00	45.00
MS56	1987J (10)	18,000	KM105, 106a, 107-108, 109.2, 110, 124, A127, 140.1, 149	11.00	45.00
MS57	1988D (9)	18,000	KM105, 106a, 107-108, 109.2, 110, 140.1, 149, 170	—	27.50
MS58	1988F (9)	18,000	KM105, 106a, 107-108, 109.2, 110, 140.1, 149, 170	—	27.50
MS59	1988G (9)	18,000	KM105, 106a, 107-108, 109.2, 110, 140.1, 149, 170	—	27.50
MS60	1988J (9)	18,000	KM105, 106a, 107-108, 109.2, 110, 140.1, 149, 170	—	27.50
MS61	1989D (9)	18,000	KM105, 106a, 107-108, 109.2, 110, 140.1, 149, 170	—	27.50
MS62	1989F (9)	18,000	KM105, 106a, 107-108, 109.2, 110, 140.1, 149, 170	—	27.50
MS63	1989G (9)	18,000	KM105, 106a, 107-108, 109.2, 110, 140.1, 149, 170	—	27.50
MS64	1989J (9)	18,000	KM105, 106a, 107-108, 109.2, 110, 140.1, 149, 170	—	27.50
MS65	1990D (10)	20,000	KM105, 106a, 107-108, 109.2, 110, 140.1, 149, 170, 175	—	25.00
MS66	1990F (10)	20,000	KM105, 106a, 107-108, 109.2, 110, 140.1, 149, 170, 175	—	25.00
MS67	1990G (10)	20,000	KM105, 106a, 107-108, 109.2, 110, 140.1, 149, 170, 175	—	25.00
MS68	1990J (10)	20,000	KM105, 106a, 107-108, 109.2, 110, 140.1, 149, 170, 175	—	25.00
MS69	1991A (10)	20,000	KM105, 106a, 107-108, 109.2, 110, 140.1, 149, 170, 175	—	30.00
MS70	1991D (10)	20,000	KM105, 106a, 107-108, 109.2, 110, 140.1, 149, 170, 175	—	30.00
MS71	1991F (10)	20,000	KM105, 106a, 107-108, 109.2, 110, 140.1, 149, 170, 175	—	30.00
MS72	1991G (10)	20,000	KM105, 106a, 107-108, 109.2, 110, 140.1, 149, 170, 175	—	30.00
MS73	1991J (10)	20,000	KM105, 106a, 107-108, 109.2, 110, 140.1, 149, 170, 175	—	30.00
MS74	1992A (10)	20,000	KM105, 106a, 107-108, 109.2, 110, 140.1, 149, 170, 175	—	30.00
MS75	1992D (10)	20,000	KM105, 106a, 107-108, 109.2, 110, 140.1, 149, 170, 175	—	30.00
MS76	1992F (10)	20,000	KM105, 106a, 107-108, 109.2, 110, 140.1, 149, 170, 175	—	30.00
MS77	1992G (10)	20,000	KM105, 106a, 107-108, 109.2, 110, 140.1, 149, 170, 175	—	30.00
MS78	1992J (10)	20,000	KM105, 106a, 107-108, 109.2, 110, 140.1, 149, 170, 175	—	30.00
MS79	1993A (10)	20,000	KM105, 106a, 107-108, 109.2, 110, 140.1, 149, 170, 175	—	40.00
MS80	1993D (10)	20,000	KM105, 106a, 107-108, 109.2, 110, 140.1, 149, 170, 175	—	40.00
MS81	1993F (10)	20,000	KM105, 106a, 107-108, 109.2, 110, 140.1, 149, 170, 175	—	40.00
MS82	1993G (10)	20,000	KM105, 106a, 107-108, 109.2, 110, 140.1, 149, 170, 175	—	40.00
MS83	1993J (10)	20,000	KM105, 106a, 107-108, 109.2, 110, 140.1, 149, 170, 175	—	40.00
MS84	1994A (10)	10,000	KM105, 106A, 107-108, 109.2, 110, 140.1, 170, 175, 183	—	30.00
MS85	1994D (10)	20,000	KM105, 106a, 107-108, 109.2, 110, 140.1, 170, 175, 183	—	30.00
MS86	1994F (10)	20,000	KM105, 106a, 107-108, 109.2, 110, 140.1, 170, 175, 183	—	30.00
MS87	1994G (10)	20,000	KM105, 106a, 107-108, 109.2, 110, 140.1, 170, 175, 183	—	30.00
MS88	1994J (10)	20,000	KM105, 106a, 107-108, 109.2, 110, 140.1, 170, 175, 183	—	30.00
MS89	1995A (10)	20,000	KM105, 106a, 107-108, 109.2, 110, 140.1, 170, 175, 183	—	300
MS90	1995D (10)	20,000	KM105, 106a, 107-108, 109.2, 110, 140.1, 170, 175, 183	—	300
MS91	1995F (10)	20,000	KM105, 106a, 107-108, 109.2, 110, 140.1, 170, 175, 183	—	300
MS92	1995G (10)	20,000	KM105, 106a, 107-108, 109.2, 110, 140.1, 170, 175, 183	—	300
MS93	1995J (10)	20,000	KM105, 106A, 107-108, 109.2, 110, 140.1, 170, 175, 183	—	300
MS94	1996A (10)	50,000	KM105, 106a, 107-108, 109.2, 110, 140.1, 170, 175, 183	—	50.00
MS95	1996D (10)	50,000	KM105, 106a, 107-108, 109.2, 110, 140.1, 170, 175, 183	—	50.00
MS96	1996F (10)	50,000	KM105, 106a, 107-108, 109.2, 110, 140.1, 170, 175, 183	—	50.00
MS97	1996G (10)	50,000	KM105, 106a, 107-108, 109.2, 110, 140.1, 170, 175, 183	—	50.00
MS98	1996J (10)	50,000	KM105, 106a, 107-108, 109.2, 110, 140.1, 170, 175, 183	—	50.00
MS99	1997A (10)	70,000	KM105, 106a, 108, 109.2, 110, 140.1, 170, 175, 183	—	30.00
MS100	1997D (10)	70,000	KM105, 106a, 107-108, 109.2, 110, 140.1, 170, 175, 183	—	30.00
MS101	1997F (10)	70,000	KM105, 106a, 107-108, 109.2, 110, 140.1, 170, 175, 183	—	30.00
MS102	1997G (10)	70,000	KM105, 106a, 107-108, 109.2, 110, 140.1, 170, 175, 183	—	30.00
MS103	1997J (10)	70,000	KM105, 106a, 107-108, 109.2, 110, 140.1, 170, 175, 183	—	30.00
MS104	1998A (10)	70,000	KM105, 106a, 107-108, 109.2, 110, 140.1, 170, 175, 183	—	30.00

KM#	Date	Mintage	Identification	Issue Price	Mkt Val
MS105	1998D (10)	70,000	KM105, 106a, 107-108, 109.2, 110, 140.1, 170, 175, 183	—	30.00
MS106	1998F (10)	70,000	KM105, 106a, 107-108, 109.2, 110, 140.1, 170, 175, 183	—	30.00
MS107	1998G (10)	70,000	KM105, 106a, 107-108, 109.2, 110, 140.1, 170, 175, 183	—	30.00
MS108	1998J (10)	70,000	KM105, 106a, 107-108, 109.2, 110, 140.1, 170, 175, 183	—	30.00
MS109	1999A (10)	70,000	KM105, 106a, 107-108, 109.2, 110, 140.1, 170, 175, 183	—	30.00
MS110	1999D (10)	70,000	km105, 106A, 107-108, 109.2, 110, 140.1, 170, 175, 183	—	30.00
MS112	1999G (10)	70,000	KM105, 106a, 107-108, 109.2, 110, 140.1, 170, 175, 183	—	30.00
MS114	1999J (10)	70,000	KM105, 106a, 107-108, 109.2, 110, 140.1, 170, 175, 183	—	30.00
MS115	2000D (10)	20,000	KM105, 106a, 107-108, 109.2, 110, 140.1, 170, 175, 183	—	45.00
MS116	2000F (10)	20,000	KM105, 160a, 107-108, 109.2, 110, 140.1, 170, 175, 183	—	45.00
MS117	2000G (10)	20,000	KM105, 106a, 107-108, 109.2, 110, 140.1, 170, 175, 183	—	45.00
MS118	2000J (10)	20,000	KM105, 106a, 107-108, 109.2, 110, 140.1, 170, 175, 183	—	45.00

PROOF SETS

KM#	Date	Mintage	Identification	Issue Price	Mkt Val
PS1	1950-64G (8)	600	KM105-108, 109.1, 110, 112.1, 116	—	1,500
PS2	1950-65F (8)	300	KM105-108, 109.1, 110, 112.1, 116	—	3,500
PS3	1950-65G (8)	8,233	KM105-108, 109.1, 110, 112.1, 116	—	200
PS76	1985D	56,000	MK#105, 106a, 107-108, 109.2, 110, 124, A127, 140.1, 149	15.00	25.00
PS4	1966F (8)	450	KM105-108, 109.1, 110, 112.1, 116	—	3,500
PS5	1966G (8)	3,070	KM105-108, 109.1, 110, 112.1, 116	—	550
PS6	1966J (8)	1,000	KM105-108, 109.1, 110, 112.1, 116	—	900
PS7	1967F (8)	1,600	KM105-108, 109.1, 110, 112.1, 116	—	600
PS8	1967G (8)	3,630	KM105-108, 109.1, 110, 112.1, 116	—	400
PS9	1967G (8)	520	KM105, 106a*, 107-108, 109.1, 110, 112.1, 116	—	3,500
PS10	1967J (8)	1,500	KM105, 106a, 107-108, 109.1, 110, 112.1, 116	—	800
PS11	1968F (8)	3,000	KM105, 106a, 107-108, 109.1, 110, 112.1, 116	—	550
PS12	1968G (8)	3,651	KM105, 106, 107-108, 109.1, 110, 112.1, 116	—	325
PS12a	1968G (8)	2,372	KM105, 106a, 107-108, 109.1, 110, 112.1, 116	—	400
PS13	1968J (8)	2,000	KM105, 106a, 107-108, 109.1, 110, 112.1, 116	—	550
PS14	1969F (8)	5,000	KM105, 106a, 107-108, 109.1, 110, 112.1, 116	—	100
PS15	1969G (8)	8,700	KM105, 106a, 107-108, 109.1, 110, 112.1, 116	—	100
PS16	1969J (8)	5,000	KM105, 106a, 107-108, 109.1, 110, 112.1, 116	—	100
PS17	1970F (8)	5,140	KM105, 106a, 107-108, 109.1, 110, 112.1, 116	—	140
PS18	1970G (8)	10,200	KM105, 106a, 107-108, 109.1, 110, 112.1, 116	—	100
PS19	1970J (8)	5,000	KM105, 106a, 107-108, 109.1, 110, 112.1, 116	—	100
PS20	1971D (8)	8,000	KM105, 106a, 107-108, 109.1, 110, 112.1, 116	—	95.00
PS21	1971F (8)	8,000	KM105, 106a, 107-108, 109.1, 110, 112.1, 116	—	95.00
PS22	1971G (8)	10,200	KM105, 106a, 107-108, 109.1, 110, 112.1, 116	—	95.00
PS23	1971J (8)	8,000	KM105, 106a, 107-108, 109.1, 110, 112.1, 116	—	95.00
PS24	1972D (9)	8,000	KM105, 106a, 107-108, 109.2, 110, 112.1, 124, A127	—	95.00
PS25	1972F (9)	8,000	KM105, 106a, 107-108, 109.2, 110, 112.1, 124, A127	—	95.00
PS26	1972G (9)	10,000	KM105, 106a, 107-108, 109.2, 110, 112.1, 124, A127	—	95.00
PS27	1972J (9)	8,000	KM105, 106a, 107-108, 109.2, 110, 112.1, 124, A127	—	95.00
PS28	1973D (9)	9,000	KM105, 106a, 107-108, 109.2, 110, 112.1, 124, A127	—	95.00
PS29	1973F (9)	9,000	KM105, 106a, 107-108, 109.2, 110, 112.1, 124, A127	—	95.00
PS30	1973G (9)	9,000	KM105, 106a, 107-108, 109.2, 110, 112.1, 124, A127	—	95.00
PS31	1973J (9)	9,000	KM105, 106a, 107-108, 109.2, 110, 112.1, 124, A127	—	95.00
PS32	1974D (9)	35,000	KM105, 106a, 107-108, 109.2, 110,112.1, 124, A127	10.00	40.00
PS33	1974F (9)	35,000	KM105, 106a, 107-108, 109.2, 110, 112.1, 124, A127	10.00	40.00
PS34	1974G (9)	35,000	KM105, 106a, 107-108, 109.2, 110, 112.1, 124, A127	10.00	40.00
PS35	1974J (9)	35,000	KM105, 106a, 107-108, 109.2, 110, 112.1, 124, A127	10.00	40.00
PS36	1975D (9)	43,120	KM105, 106a, 107-108, 109.2, 110, 124, A127, 140.1	10.00	22.00
PS37	1975F (9)	43,100	KM105, 106a, 107-108, 109.2, 110, 124, A127, 140.1	10.00	22.00
PS38	1975G (9)	43,100	KM105, 106a, 107-108, 109.2, 110, 124, A127, 140.1	10.00	22.00

KM#	Date	Mintage	Identification	Issue Price	Mkt Val
PS39	1975J (9)	43,120	KM105,106a, 107-108, 109.2, 110, 124, A127, 140.1	10.00	22.00
PS40	1976D (9)	43,120	KM105, 106a, 107-108, 109.2, 110, 124, A127,140.1	10.00	22.00
PS41	1976F (9)	43,100	KM105, 106a, 107-108, 109.2, 110, 124, A127, 140.1	10.00	22.00
PS42	1976G (9)	43,100	KM105, 106a, 107-108, 109.2, 110, 124, A127, 140.1	10.00	22.00
PS43	1976J (9)	43,120	KM105, 106a, 107-108, 109.2, 110, 124, A127, 140.1	10.00	22.00
PS44	1977D (9)	50,620	KM105, 106a, 107-108, 109.2, 110, 124, A127, 140.1	12.50	22.00
PS45	1977F (9)	50,600	KM105, 106a, 107-108, 109.2, 110, 124, A127, 140.1	12.50	22.00
PS46	1977G (9)	50,600	KM105, 106a, 107-108, 109.2, 110, 124, A127, 140.1	12.50	22.00
PS47	1977J (9)	50,620	KM105, 106a, 107-108, 109.2, 110, 124, A127, 140.1	12.50	22.00
PS48	1978D (9)	54,000	KM105, 106a, 107-108, 109.2, 110, 124, A127, 140.1	13.00	22.00
PS49	1978F (9)	54,000	KM105, 106a, 107-108, 109.2, 110, 124, A127, 140.1	13.00	22.00
PS50	1978G (9)	54,000	KM105, 106a, 107-108, 109.2, 110, 124, A127, 140.1	13.00	22.00
PS51	1978J (9)	54,000	KM105, 106a, 107-108, 109.2, 110, 124, A127, 140.1	13.00	22.00
PS52	1979D (10)	89,000	KM105, 106a, 107-108, 109.2, 110, 124, A127, 140.1, 149	15.00	22.00
PS53	1979F (10)	89,000	KM105, 106a, 107-108, 109.2, 110, 124, A127, 140.1, 149	15.00	22.00
PS54	1979G (10)	89,000	KM105, 106a, 107-108, 109.2, 110, 124, A127, 140.1, 149	15.00	22.00
PS55	1979J (10)	89,000	KM105, 106a, 107-108, 109.2, 110, 124, A127, 140.1, 149	15.00	22.00
PS56	1980D (10)	60,000	KM105, 106a, 107-108, 109.2, 110, 124, A127, 140.1, 149	15.00	22.00
PS57	1980F (10)	60,000	KM105, 106a, 107-108, 109.2, 110, 124, A127, 140.1, 149	15.00	22.00
PS58	1980G (10)	60,000	KM105, 106a, 107-108, 109.2, 110, 124, A127, 140.1, 149	15.00	22.00
PS59	1980J (10)	60,000	KM105, 106a, 107-108, 109.2, 110, 124, A127, 140.1, 149	15.00	22.00
PS60	1981D (10)	60,000	KM105, 106a, 107-108, 109.2, 110, 124, A127, 140.1, 149	15.00	22.00
PS61	1981F (10)	91,000	KM105, 106a, 107-108, 109.2, 110, 124, A127, 140.1, 149	15.00	22.00
PS62	1981G (10)	91,000	KM105, 106a, 107-108, 109.2, 110, 124, A127, 140.1, 149	15.00	22.00
PS63	1981J (10)	78,000	KM105, 106a, 107-108, 109.2, 110, 124, A127, 140.1, 149	15.00	22.00
PS64	1982D (10)	78,000	KM105, 106a, 107-108, 109.2, 110, 124, A127, 140.1, 149	15.00	22.00
PS65	1982F (10)	78,000	KM105, 106a,107-108, 109.2, 110, 124, A127, 140.1, 149	15.00	22.00
PS66	1982G (10)	78,000	KM105, 106a, 107-108, 109.2, 110, 124, A127, 140.1, 149	15.00	22.00
PS67	1982J (10)	78,000	KM105, 106a, 107-108, 109.2, 110, 124, A127, 140.1, 149	15.00	22.00
PS68	1983D (10)	75,000	KM105, 106a, 107-108, 109.2, 110, 124, A127, 140.1, 149	15.00	22.00
PS69	1983F (10)	75,000	KM105, 106a, 107-108, 109.2, 110, 124, A127, 140.1, 149	15.00	22.00
PS70	1983G (10)	75,000	KM105, 106a, 107-108, 109.2, 110, 124, A127, 140.1, 149	15.00	22.00
PS71	1983J (10)	75,000	KM105, 106a, 107-108, 109.2, 110, 124, A127, 140.1, 149	15.00	22.00
PS72	1984D (10)	64,100	KM105, 106a, 107-108, 109.2, 110, 124, A127, 140.1, 149	15.00	26.50
PS73	1984F (10)	64,100	KM105, 106a, 107-108, 109.2, 110, 124, A127, 140.1, 149	15.00	26.50
PS74	1984G (10)	64,100	KM105, 106a, 107-108, 109.2, 110, 124, A127, 140.1, 149	15.00	26.50
PS75	1985D (10)	56,000	KM105, 106a, 107-108, 109.2, 110, 124, A127, 140.1, 149	15.00	26.50
PS77	1985F (10)	54,000	KM105, 106a, 107-108, 109.2, 110, 124, A127, 140.1, 149	15.00	25.00
PS78	1985G (10)	54,000	KM105, 106a, 107-108, 109.2, 110, 124, A127, 140.1, 149	15.00	25.00
PS79	1985J (10)	54,000	KM105, 106a, 107-108, 109.2, 110, 124, A127, 140.1, 149	15.00	25.00
PS80	1986D (10)	44,000	KM105, 106a, 107-108, 109.2, 110, 124, A127, 140.1, 149	15.00	27.50
PS81	1986F (10)	44,000	KM105, 106a, 107-108, 109.2, 110, 124, A127, 140.1, 149	15.00	27.50
PS82	1986G (10)	44,000	KM105, 106a, 107-108, 109.2, 110, 124, A127, 140.1, 149	15.00	27.50
PS83	1986J (10)	44,000	KM105, 106a, 107-108, 109.2, 110, 124, A127, 140.1, 149	15.00	27.50
PS84	1987D (10)	45,000	KM105, 106a, 107-108, 109.2, 110, 124, A127, 140.1, 149	15.00	35.00
PS85	1987F (10)	45,000	KM105, 106a, 107-108, 109.2, 110, 124, A127, 140.1, 149	15.00	35.00
PS86	1987G (10)	45,000	KM105, 106a, 107-108, 109.2, 110, 124, A127, 140.1, 149	15.00	35.00
PS87	1987J (10)	45,000	KM105, 106a, 107-108, 109.2, 110, 124, A127, 140.1, 149	15.00	35.00
PS88	1988D (9)	45,000	KM105, 106a, 107-108, 109.2, 110, 140.1, 149, 170	—	25.00
PS89	1988F (9)	45,000	KM105, 106a, 107-108, 109.2, 110, 140.1, 149, 170	—	25.00
PS90	1988G (9)	45,000	KM105, 106a, 107-108, 109.2, 110, 140.1, 149, 170	—	25.00
PS91	1988J (9)	45,000	KM105, 106a, 107-108, 109.2, 110, 140.1, 149, 170	—	25.00
PS92	1989D (9)	45,000	KM105, 106a, 107-108, 109.2, 110, 140.1, 149, 170	—	25.00
PS93	1989F (9)	45,000	KM105, 106a, 107-108, 109.2, 110, 140.1, 149, 170	—	25.00
PS94	1989G (9)	45,000	KM105-106a, 107-108, 109.2, 110, 140.1, 149, 170	—	25.00
PS95	1989J (9)	45,000	KM105-106a, 107-108, 109.2, 110, 140.1, 149, 170	—	25.00
PS96	1990D (10)	45,000	KM105, 106a, 107-108, 109.2, 110, 140.1, 149, 170, 175	—	25.00
PS97	1990F (10)	45,000	KM105, 106a, 107-108, 109.2, 110, 140.1, 149, 170, 175	—	25.00
PS98	1990G (10)	45,000	KM105,106a,107-180,109.2,110,140.1,149,170,175	—	25.00
PS99	1990J (10)	45,000	KM105,106a,107-108,109.2,110,140.1,149,170,175	—	25.00
PS100	1991A (10)	45,000	KM105,106a,107-108,109.2,110,140.1,149,170,175	—	27.50
PS101	1991D (10)	45,000	KM105,106a,107-108,109.2,110,140.1,149,170,175	—	27.50
PS102	1991F (10)	45,000	KM105,106a,107-108,109.2,110,140.1,149,170,175	—	27.50
PS103	1991G (10)	45,000	KM105,106a,107-108,109.2,110,140.1,149,170,175	—	27.50
PS104	1991J (10)	45,000	KM105,106a,107-108,109.2,110,140.1,149,170,175	—	27.50
PS105	1992A (10)	45,000	KM105,106a,107-108,109.2,110,140.1,149,170,175	—	27.50
PS106	1992D (10)	45,000	KM105,106a,107-108,109.2,110,140.1,149,170,175	—	27.50
PS107	1992F (10)	45,000	KM105,106a,107-108,109.2,110,140.1,149,170,175	—	27.50
PS108	1992G (10)	45,000	KM105,106a,107,108,109.2,110,140.1,149,170,175	—	27.50
PS109	1992J (10)	45,000	KM105,106a,107-108,109.2,110,140.1,149,170,175	—	27.50
PS110	1993A (10)	45,000	KM105,106a,107-108,109.2,110,140.1,149,170,175	—	35.00
PS111	1993D (10)	45,000	KM105,106a,107-108,109.2,110,140.1,149,170,175	—	35.00
PS112	1993F (10)	45,000	KM105,106a,107-108,109.2,110,140.1,149,170,175	—	35.00
PS113	1993J (10)	45,000	KM105,106a,107-108,109.2,110,140.1,149,170,175	—	35.00
PS114	1993J	45,000	KM105,106a,107-108,109.2,110,140.1,149,170,175	—	35.00
PS115	1994A (10)	45,000	KM105,106a,107-108,109.2,110,140.1,170,175,183	—	25.00
PS116	1994D (10)	45,000	KM105,106a,107-108,109.2,110,140.1,170,175,183	—	25.00
PS117	1994F (10)	45,000	KM105,106a,107-108,109.2,110,140.1,170,175,183	—	25.00
PS118	1994G (10)	45,000	KM105,106a,107-108,109.2,110,140.1,170,175,183	—	25.00
PS119	1994J (10)	45,000	KM105,106a,107-108,109.2,110,140.1,170,175,183	—	25.00
PS120	1995A (10)	45,000	KM105,106a,107-108,109.2,110,140.1,170,175,183	—	225
PS121	1995D (10)	45,000	KM105,106a,107-108,109.2,110,140.1,170,175,183	—	225
PS123	1995G (10)	45,000	KM105,106a,107-108,109.2,110,140.1,170,175,183	—	225
PS122	1995F (10)	45,000	KM105,106a,107-108,109.2,110,140.1,170,175,183	—	225
PS124	1995J (10)	45,000	KM105,106a,107-108,109.2,110,140.1,170,175,183	—	225
PS125	1996A (10)	45,000	KM105,106a,107-108,109.2,110,140.1,170,175,183	—	50.00
PS126	1996D (10)	45,000	KM105,106a,107-108,109.2,110,140.1,170,175,183	—	50.00
PS127	1996F (10)	45,000	KM105,106a,107-108,109.2,110,140.1,170,175,183	—	50.00
PS128	1996G (10)	45,000	KM105,106a,107-108,109.2,110,140.1,170,175,183	—	50.00
PS129	1996J (10)	45,000	KM105,106a,107-108,109.2,110,140.1,170,175,183	—	50.00
PS130	1997A (10)	45,000	KM105,106a,107-108,109.2,110,140.1,170,175,183	—	30.00
PS131	1997D (10)	45,000	KM105,106a,107-108,109.2,110,140.1,170,175,183	—	30.00
PS132	1997F (10)	45,000	KM105,106a,107-108,109.2,11o,140.1,170,175,183	—	30.00
PS133	1997G (10)	45,000	KM105,106a,107-108,109.2,110,140.1,170,175,183	—	30.00
PS134	1997J (10)	45,000	KM105,106a,107-108,109.2,110,140.1,170,175,183	—	30.00
PS135	1998A (10)	45,000	KM105,106a,107-108,109.2,110,140.1,170,175,183	—	30.00
PS136	1998D (10)	45,000	KM105,106a,107-108,109.2,110,140.1,170,175,183	—	37.50
PS137	1998F (10)	45,000	KM105,106a,107-108,109.2,110,140.1,170,175,183	—	37.50
PS142	1999F (10)	45,000	KM105,106a,107-108,109.2,110,140.1,170,175,183	—	30.00
PS138	1998G (10)	45,000	KM105,106a,107-108,109.2,110,140.1,170,175,183	—	37.50
PS139	1998J (10)	45,000	KM105,106a,107-108,109.2,110,140.1,170,175,183	—	30.00
PS144	1999J (10)	45,000	KM105,106a,107-108,109.2,110,140.1,170,175,183	—	30.00
PS140	1999A (10)	45,000	KM105,106a,107-108,109.2,110,140.1,170,175,183	—	30.00
PS141	1999D (10)	45,000	KM105,106a,107-108,109.2,110,140.1,170,175,183	—	30.00
PS143	1999G (10)	45,000	KM105,106a,107-108,109.2,110,140.1,170,175,183	—	30.00
PS145	2000A (10)	45,000	KM105,106a,107-108,109.2,110,140.1,170,175,183	—	55.00
PS146	2000D (10)	45,000	KM105,106a,107-108,109.2,110,140.1,170,175,183	—	55.00
PS147	2000F (10)	45,000	KM105,106a,107,108,109.2,110,140.1,170,175,183	—	55.00
PS148	2000G (10)	45,000	KM105,106a,107-108,109.2,110,140.1,170,175,183	—	55.00
PS149	2000J (10)	45,000	KM105,106a,107-108,109.2,110,140.1,170,175,183	—	55.00

GERMANY-DEMOCRATIC REP.

1949-1990

The German Democratic Republic, formerly East Germany, was located on the great north European plain, had an area of 41,768 sq. mi. (108,330 sq. km.) and a population of 16.6 million. The figures included East Berlin, which had been incorporated into the G.D.R. Capital: East Berlin. The economy was highly industrialized. Machinery, transport equipment chemicals, and lignite were exported.

During the closing days of World War II in Europe, Soviet troops advancing into Germany from the east occupied the German provinces of Mecklenburg, Brandenburg, Lusatia, Saxony and Thuringia. These five provinces comprised the occupation zone administered by the Soviet Union after the cessation of hostilities. The other three zones were administered by the U.S., Great Britain and France. Under the Potsdam agreement, questions affecting Germany as a whole were to be settled by the commanders of the occupation zones acting jointly and by unanimous decision. When Soviet intransigence rendered the quadripartite commission inoperable, the three western zones were united to form the Federal Republic of Germany, May 23, 1949. Thereupon the Soviet Union dissolved its occupation zone and established it as the Democratic Republic of Germany, Oct. 7, 1949.

The post-WW II division of Germany was ended Oct. 3, 1990, when the German Democratic Republic (East Germany) ceased to exist and its five constituent provinces were formally admitted to the Federal Republic of Germany. An election Dec. 2, 1990, chose representatives to the united federal parliament (Bundestag), which then conducted its opening session in Berlin in the old Reichstag building.

MARKS
A - Berlin
E - Muldenhutten

MONETARY SYSTEM
100 Pfennig = 1 Mark

DEMOCRATIC REPUBLIC

STANDARD COINAGE

KM# 1 PFENNIG
Aluminum **Obv:** Denomination **Rev:** Cogwheel back of grain sprig

Date	Mintage	F	VF	XF	Unc	BU
1948A	243,000,000	—	1.00	9.00	40.00	70.00
1949E	55,200,000	—	11.50	50.00	250	400
1949A	Inc. above	—	8.00	35.00	45.00	
1950A	—	—	1.00	8.00	35.00	45.00
1950E	—	—	6.00	20.00	75.00	125

KM# 5 PFENNIG
Aluminum **Obv:** Denomination **Rev:** Grain sprigs back of hammer and protractor

Date	Mintage	F	VF	XF	Unc	BU
1952A	297,213,000	—	0.50	3.00	7.00	9.00
1952E	49,296,000	—	5.00	10.00	40.00	55.00
1953E	50,876,000	—	4.00	15.00	55.00	75.00
1953A	114,002,000	—	1.00	3.00	8.00	12.00

KM# 8.1 PFENNIG
Aluminum, 17 mm. **Obv:** State emblem **Rev:** Denomination flanked by oak leaves, date below

Date	Mintage	F	VF	XF	Unc	BU
1960A	101,808,000	—	0.25	0.75	3.00	4.00
1961A	101,776,000	—	0.25	0.75	3.00	4.00
1962A	81,459,000	—	0.25	0.75	3.00	4.00
1963A	101,402,000	—	0.25	0.75	3.00	4.00
1964A	98,967,000	—	0.25	0.75	3.00	4.00
1965A	38,585,000	—	3.00	15.00	45.00	65.00
1968A	813,680,000	—	0.25	0.80	2.50	3.00
1972A	4,801,000	—	3.00	10.00	20.00	25.00
1973A	5,518,000	—	3.00	8.00	20.00	25.00
1975A	202,752,000	—	0.25	0.75	2.50	3.00

KM# 8.2 PFENNIG
0.7000 g., Aluminum, 17 mm. **Obv:** State emblem, smaller design features **Rev:** Denomination flanked by leaves, smaller design features

Date	Mintage	F	VF	XF	Unc	BU
1977A	61,560,000	—	0.10	0.25	2.00	3.00
1978A	200,050,000	—	0.10	0.20	1.00	2.00
1979A	100,640,000	—	0.10	0.20	1.00	2.00
1979A Proof	—	Value: 45.00				
1980A	153,000,000	—	0.10	0.20	1.00	2.00
1980A Proof	—	Value: 45.00				
1981A	200,436,000	—	0.10	0.20	1.00	2.00
1981A Proof	40	—	—	—	1.00	2.00
1982A	99,200,000	—	0.10	0.20	1.00	2.00
1982A Proof	2,500	Value: 10.00				
1983A	150,000,000	—	0.10	0.20	1.00	2.00
1983A Proof	2,550	Value: 18.00				
1984A	137,600,000	—	0.10	0.20	1.00	2.00
1984A Proof	3,015	Value: 4.50				
1985A	125,060,000	—	0.10	0.20	1.00	2.00
1986A	73,900,000	—	0.10	0.20	1.00	2.00
1986A Proof	2,800	Value: 4.50				
1987A	50,015,000	—	0.10	0.20	1.00	2.00
1987A Proof	2,345	Value: 4.50				

Date	Mintage	F	VF	XF	Unc	BU
1988A	75,450,000	—	0.10	0.20	1.00	2.00
1988A Proof	2,300	Value: 4.50				
1989A	84,410,000	—	0.10	0.20	1.00	2.00
1989A Proof	2,300	Value: 4.50				
1990A	15,670,000	—	0.50	1.00	10.00	15.00

KM# 2 5 PFENNIG
Aluminum **Obv:** Denomination **Rev:** Cogwheel back of grain sprig

Date	Mintage	F	VF	XF	Unc	BU
1948A	205,072,000	—	2.50	6.00	65.00	120
1949A	Inc. above	—	2.50	6.00	75.00	140
1950A	Inc. above	—	2.50	6.00	55.00	110

KM# 6 5 PFENNIG
Aluminum **Obv:** Denomination **Rev:** Grain sprigs flank hammer and protractor, date below

Date	Mintage	F	VF	XF	Unc	BU
1952E	24,024,000	—	3.50	9.00	35.00	45.00
1952A	113,397,000	—	2.00	5.00	10.00	15.00
1953A	40,994,000	—	2.00	6.50	15.00	25.00
1953E	28,665,000	—	6.00	20.00	100	150

KM# 9.1 5 PFENNIG
Aluminum, 19 mm. **Obv:** State emblem **Rev:** Denomination flanked by oak leaves, date below

Date	Mintage	F	VF	XF	Unc	BU
1968A	282,303,000	—	0.50	1.00	2.50	3.00
1972A	51,462,000	—	0.50	1.00	2.00	3.00
1975A	84,710,000	—	0.50	1.00	2.00	3.00

KM# 9.2 5 PFENNIG
1.0000 g., Aluminum, 19 mm. **Obv:** State emblem, smaller design features **Rev:** Denomination flanked by oak leaves, smaller design features **Note:** Varieties exist.

Date	Mintage	F	VF	XF	Unc	BU
1976A 2 known	—	—	—	—	—	—
1978A	43,257,000	—	0.15	0.25	1.00	2.00
1979A	46,194,000	—	0.15	0.25	1.00	2.00
1979A Proof	—	Value: 45.00				
1980A	31,977,000	—	0.15	0.25	1.00	2.00
1980A Proof	—	Value: 45.00				
1981A	33,101,999	—	0.15	0.25	1.00	2.00
1981A Proof	40	—	—	—	—	—
1982A	916,000	—	15.00	45.00	100	175
1982A Proof	2,500	Value: 10.00				
1983A	100,890,000	—	0.15	0.25	1.00	2.00
1983A Proof	2,550	Value: 18.00				
1984A	Est. 6,000	—	—	—	35.00	50.00
1984A Proof	3,015	Value: 4.50				
1985A	1,000,000	—	—	1.50	6.50	15.00	18.00
1985A Proof	2,816	Value: 4.50				
1986A	1,000,000	—	—	1.50	6.50	10.00	15.00
1986A Proof	2,800	Value: 4.50				
1987A	Est. 20,000	—	—	—	12.50	16.00
1987A Proof	2,345	Value: 4.50				
1988A	35,930,000	—	0.15	0.25	1.00	2.00
1988A Proof	2,300	Value: 4.50				
1989A	21,550,000	—	0.15	0.25	1.00	2.00
1989A Proof	2,300	Value: 4.50				
1990A	50,640,000	—	0.15	0.25	1.00	2.00

KM# 3 10 PFENNIG
Aluminum **Obv:** Denomination **Rev:** Cogwheel back of grain sprigs **Note:** Also exists with medallic die rotation (1950E).

Date	Mintage	F	VF	XF	Unc	BU
1948A	216,537,000	—	2.50	19.00	75.00	120
1949A	Inc. above	—	2.50	15.00	70.00	100
1950A	Inc. above	—	1.00	70.00	100	
1950E	16,000,000	—	15.00	150	800	1,000

KM# 7 10 PFENNIG
Aluminum **Obv:** Denomination **Rev:** Grain sprigs flank hammer and protractor, date below

Date	Mintage	F	VF	XF	Unc	BU
1952A	70,427,000	—	2.00	12.00	65.00	90.00
1952E	21,498,000	—	10.00	30.00	350	550
1953E	11,500,000	—	15.00	70.00	400	600
1953A	18,611,000	—	3.50	18.00	75.00	100

KM# 10 10 PFENNIG
1.5000 g., Aluminum, 21 mm. **Obv:** State emblem **Rev:** Denomination divides leaf and date

Date	Mintage	F	VF	XF	Unc	BU
1963A	21,063,000	—	7.00	30.00	60.00	85.00
1965A	55,313,000	—	1.00	2.00	3.00	4.00
1967A	96,955,000	—	0.15	1.00	2.00	4.00
1968A	207,461,000	—	0.15	1.00	2.00	3.00
1970A	13,387,000	—	0.15	1.00	3.00	5.00
1971A	66,617,999	—	0.15	1.00	2.00	3.00
1972A	5,702,000	—	0.50	3.00	8.00	10.00
1973A	11,257,000	—	0.15	1.00	3.00	4.00
1978A	40,000,000	—	0.15	1.00	2.00	3.00
1979A	54,665,000	—	0.15	1.00	2.00	3.00
1979A Proof	—	Value: 45.00				
1980A	20,664,000	—	0.15	1.00	3.00	4.00
1980A Proof	—	Value: 45.00				
1981A	40,704,000	—	0.15	1.00	2.00	3.00
1981A Proof	40	—	—	—	—	—
1982A	40,212,000	—	0.15	1.00	3.00	4.00
1982A Proof	2,500	Value: 10.00				
1983A	40,699,000	—	0.15	1.00	3.00	5.00
1983A Proof	2,550	Value: 20.00				
1984A	Est. 12,000	—	—	10.00	25.00	35.00

Note: Issued in sets only, remainder unaccountable

Date	Mintage	F	VF	XF	Unc	BU
1984A Proof	3,015	Value: 4.50				
1985A	1,010,000	—	0.35	4.50	12.00	15.00
1985A Proof	2,816	Value: 4.50				
1986A	1,000,000	—	0.35	4.50	12.00	15.00
1986A Proof	2,800	Value: 4.50				
1987A	Est. 20,000	—	—	7.00	14.00	17.50

Note: Issued in sets only, remainder unaccountable

Date	Mintage	F	VF	XF	Unc	BU
1987A Proof	2,345	Value: 4.50				
1988A	10,705,000	—	0.15	1.00	2.00	3.00
1988A Proof	2,300	Value: 4.50				
1989A	37,640,000	—	0.15	1.00	2.00	3.00
1989A Proof	2,300	Value: 4.50				
1990A	Est. 14,000	—	—	—	17.00	25.00

Note: Issued in sets only, remainder unaccountable

KM# 11 20 PFENNIG
5.4000 g., Brass, 22.3 mm. **Obv:** State emblem **Rev:** Denomination above date **Note:** Ribbon width varieties exist.

Date	Mintage	F	VF	XF	Unc	BU
1969	167,168,000	—	0.25	2.00	5.00	7.00
1971	24,563,000	—	0.25	3.00	6.00	7.00
1972A	5,007,000	—	1.00	4.00	10.00	12.00
1973A	2,524,000	—	1.00	4.50	10.00	12.00
1974A	7,458,000	—	1.00	2.50	8.00	10.00
1979A	293,000	—	1.00	3.00	7.50	9.00
1979A Proof	—	Value: 50.00				
1980A	2,190,000	—	1.00	2.50	8.00	10.00
1980A Proof	—	Value: 50.00				
1981A	983,000	—	1.00	4.00	9.00	12.00
1981A Proof	40	—	—	—	—	—
1982A	10,458,000	—	1.00	4.00	9.00	12.00
1982A Proof	2,500	Value: 12.50				
1983A	25,809,000	—	1.00	2.00	3.00	5.00
1983A Proof	2,550	Value: 25.00				
1984A	25,009,000	—	1.00	2.00	3.00	5.00

Date	Mintage	F	VF	XF	Unc	BU
1984A Proof	3,015	Value: 5.50				
1985A	1,559,000	—	1.00	3.00	8.00	12.00
1985A Proof	2,816	Value: 5.50				
1986A	1,147,000	—	1.00	4.00	10.00	15.00
1986A Proof	2,800	Value: 5.50				
1987A	Est. 20,000	—	4.00	6.00	10.00	25.00

Note: Issued in sets only, remainder unaccountable

Date	Mintage	F	VF	XF	Unc	BU
1987A Proof	2,345	Value: 5.50				
1988A	Est. 15,000	—	4.00	7.00	12.00	30.00

Note: Issued in sets only, remainder unaccountable

Date	Mintage	F	VF	XF	Unc	BU
1988A Proof	2,300	Value: 5.50				
1989A	14,690,000	—	0.20	1.00	2.00	3.00
1989A Proof	2,300	Value: 5.50				
1990A	Est. 14,000	—	—	—	15.00	20.00

Note: Issued in sets only, remainder unaccountable

KM# 4　50 PFENNIG
3.3800 g., Aluminum-Bronze **Obv:** Denomination above date **Rev:** Man and cart in front of buildings with tall smokestacks

Date	Mintage	F	VF	XF	Unc	BU
1949A	Inc. below	—	—	7,500	8,000	10,000
1950A	67,703,000	3.50	10.00	25.00	150	300

Note: Some authorities believe the 1949-dated piece is a pattern

KM# 12.1　50 PFENNIG
Aluminum, 23 mm. **Obv:** Small state emblem

Date	Mintage	F	VF	XF	Unc	BU
1958A	101,606,000	—	1.00	3.00	8.00	10.00

KM# 12.2　50 PFENNIG
1.9000 g., Aluminum, 23 mm. **Obv:** State emblem **Rev:** Denomination divides date and leaf **Note:** Inscription varieties exist.

Date	Mintage	F	VF	XF	Unc	BU
1968A	19,860,000	—	1.00	2.00	4.00	5.00
1971A	35,829,000	—	1.00	2.00	3.00	4.00
1972A	8,117,000	—	1.00	2.00	4.50	5.50
1973A	6,530,000	—	1.00	2.00	6.00	8.00
1979A	1,026,999	—	1.00	2.00	6.00	8.00
1979A Proof	—	—	—	—	—	
1980A	1,118,000	—	5.00	10.00	15.00	20.00
1980A Proof	—	—	—	—	—	
1981A	10,546,000	—	1.00	3.00	5.00	7.00
1981A Proof	40	—	—	—	—	
1982A	79,832,000	—	0.35	0.75	2.50	3.00
1982A Proof	2,500	Value: 12.50				
1983A	1,309,000	—	1.00	3.00	8.00	12.00
1983A Proof	2,550	Value: 25.00				
1984A	Est. 5,000	—	—	—	30.00	40.00
1984A Proof	3,015	Value: 5.50				
1985A	1,565,000	—	1.00		10.00	15.00
1985A Proof	2,816	Value: 5.50				
1986A	776,000	—	1.00	3.00	10.00	15.00
1986A Proof	2,800	Value: 5.50				
1987A	Est. 21,000	—	4.00	9.00	12.50	18.00

Note: Issued in sets only, remainder unaccountable

Date	Mintage	F	VF	XF	Unc	BU
1987A Proof	2,345	Value: 5.50				
1988A	Est. 15,000	—	5.00	10.00	14.00	20.00

Note: Issued in sets only, remainder unaccountable

Date	Mintage	F	VF	XF	Unc	BU
1988A Proof	2,300	Value: 5.50				
1989A	31,000	—	1.00	3.00	10.00	15.00
1989A Proof	2,300	Value: 5.50				
1990A	Est. 14,000	—	—	—	16.00	22.00

Note: Issued in sets only, remainder unaccountable

KM# 13　MARK
Aluminum **Obv:** State emblem **Rev:** Large, thick denomination flanked by leaves, date below

Date	Mintage	F	VF	XF	Unc	BU
1956A	112,108,000	—	1.00	3.00	9.00	14.00
1962A	45,920,000	—	1.00	4.00	8.00	12.00
1963A	31,910,000	—	1.00	2.50	8.00	12.00

KM# 35.1　MARK
Aluminum **Obv:** State emblem **Rev:** Large 1 flanked by oak leaves

Date	Mintage	F	VF	XF	Unc	BU
1972A	30,288,000	—	1.00	4.00	5.00	8.00

KM# 35.2　MARK
2.4000 g., Aluminum, 25 mm. **Obv:** State emblem **Rev:** Large, thick denomination flanked by leaves, small date below

Date	Mintage	F	VF	XF	Unc	BU
1973A	6,972,000	—	1.00	4.00	10.00	12.00
1975A	32,094,000	—	1.00	2.00	5.00	7.00
1977A	119,813,000	—	0.50	1.00	2.00	3.00
1978A	18,824,000	—	0.50	1.00	2.00	3.00
1979A	1,002,999	—	1.00	2.00	7.50	10.00
1979A Proof	—	—	—	—	—	
1980A	1,069,000	—	5.00	10.00	15.00	20.00
1980A Proof	—	—	—	—	—	
1981A	1,006,000	—	1.00	3.00	10.00	15.00
1981A Proof	40	—	—	—	—	
1982A	51,619,000	—	0.50	1.00	2.00	3.00
1982A Proof	2,500	Value: 25.00				
1983A	1,065,000	—	1.00	2.00	7.50	10.00
1983A Proof	2,550	Value: 30.00				
1984A	Est. 5,000	—	—	—	40.00	50.00
1984A Proof	3,015	Value: 7.50				
1985A	1,128,000	—	1.00	2.00	7.50	10.00
1985A Proof	2,816	Value: 7.50				
1986A	1,000,000	—	1.00	2.00	7.50	10.00
1986A Proof	2,800	Value: 7.50				
1987A	Est. 21,000	—	4.00	8.00	12.50	18.00

Note: Issued in sets only, remainder unaccountable

Date	Mintage	F	VF	XF	Unc	BU
1987A Proof	2,345	Value: 7.50				
1988A	Est. 15,000	—	—	—	15.00	20.00

Note: Issued in sets only, remainder unaccountable

Date	Mintage	F	VF	XF	Unc	BU
1988A Proof	2,300	Value: 7.50				
1989A	33,000	—	2.00	10.00	15.00	20.00
1989A Proof	2,300	Value: 7.50				
1990A	Est. 14,000	—	—	—	20.00	25.00

Note: Issued in sets only, remainder unaccountable

KM# 14　2 MARK
Aluminum **Obv:** State emblem **Rev:** Large denomination flanked by leaves, date below

Date	Mintage	F	VF	XF	Unc	BU
1957A	77,961,000	—	2.00	4.00	9.00	12.00

KM# 48　2 MARK
3.0000 g., Aluminum, 27 mm. **Obv:** State emblem **Rev:** Large denomination flanked by leaves, date below

Date	Mintage	F	VF	XF	Unc	BU
1972A	—	—	—	—	—	—

Note: 3 pieces known

Date	Mintage	F	VF	XF	Unc	BU
1974A	5,790,000	—	2.00	9.00	15.00	20.00
1975A	32,464,000	—	2.00	4.00	9.00	10.00
1977A	27,859,000	—	2.00	5.00	8.00	10.00
1978A	23,415,000	—	2.00	5.00	8.00	10.00
1979A	985,000	—	2.00	5.00	8.00	10.00
1979A Proof	—	—	—	—	—	
1980A	1,018,999	—	2.00	5.00	9.00	15.00
1980A Proof	—	—	—	—	—	
1981A	939,000	—	2.00	5.00	8.00	12.00
1981A Proof	40	—	—	—	—	
1982A	60,488,000	—	1.00	2.00	3.00	4.00
1982A Proof	2,500	Value: 55.00				
1983A	1,030,000	—	1.00	2.00	6.00	8.00
1983A Proof	2,550	Value: 75.00				
1984A	Est. 6,000	—	—	—	30.00	40.00
1984A Proof	3,015	Value: 20.00				
1985A	1,310,000	—	3.00	6.00	10.00	15.00

Date	Mintage	F	VF	XF	Unc	BU
1985A Proof	2,816	Value: 20.00				
1986A	1,000,000	—	3.00	6.00	10.00	15.00
1986A Proof	2,800	Value: 20.00				
1987A	Est. 30,000	—	5.00	10.00	15.00	20.00

Note: Issued in sets only, remainder unaccountable

Date	Mintage	F	VF	XF	Unc	BU
1987A Proof	2,345	Value: 20.00				
1988A	Est. 15,000	—	7.00	12.00	18.00	22.00

Note: Issued in sets only, remainder unaccountable

Date	Mintage	F	VF	XF	Unc	BU
1988A Proof	2,300	Value: 20.00				
1989A	46,000	—	5.00	10.00	15.00	20.00
1989A Proof	2,300	Value: 20.00				
1990A	Est. 14,000	—	—	—	30.00	40.00

Note: Issued in sets only, remainder unaccountable

KM# 19.1　5 MARK
9.7000 g., Copper-Nickel, 29 mm. **Subject:** 125th Anniversary of Birth of Robert Koch, doctor **Obv:** State emblem **Rev:** Head left **Edge:** 5 MARK 5 MARK 5 MARK

Date	Mintage	F	VF	XF	Unc	BU
1968	100,000	—	—	10.00	20.00	30.00

KM# 19.2　5 MARK
9.7000 g., Copper-Nickel, 29 mm. **Obv:** State emblem **Rev:** Head left **Note:** Error: plain edge.

Date	Mintage	F	VF	XF	Unc	BU
1968	—	—	—	—	400	500

KM# 23　5 MARK
9.7000 g., Copper-Nickel, 29 mm. **Subject:** Heinrich Hertz, physicist **Obv:** State emblem, denomination **Rev:** Head right, dates below

Date	Mintage	F	VF	XF	Unc	BU
1969	100,000	—	—	20.00	35.00	50.00

KM# 22.1　5 MARK
Nickel-Bronze, 29 mm. **Subject:** 20th Anniversary D.D.R **Obv:** State emblem **Rev:** Denomination, date at left

Date	Mintage	F	VF	XF	Unc	BU
1969	50,222,000	—	—	3.00	4.50	7.50

Note: 10% nickel and 90% copper

KM# 22.1a　5 MARK
Copper-Nickel, 29 mm. **Obv:** State emblem **Rev:** Denomination, date at left

Date	Mintage	F	VF	XF	Unc	BU
1969	12,741	—	50.00	60.00	70.00	80.00

Note: 25% nickel and 75% copper

KM# 22.2　5 MARK
Nickel-Bronze, 29 mm. **Obv:** State emblem **Rev:** Denomination, date at left **Note:** Error: plain edge.

Date	Mintage	F	VF	XF	Unc	BU
1969	—	—	—	—	120	150

KM# 22.3　5 MARK
Nickel-Bronze, 29 mm. **Obv:** State emblem **Rev:** Denomination, date at left **Note:** Error: Mongolian inscription and dates on edge.

Date	Mintage	F	VF	XF	Unc	BU
1969						

KM# 26　5 MARK
9.7000 g., Copper-Nickel, 29 mm. **Subject:** Wilhelm Conrad Rontgen, physicist

Date	Mintage	F	VF	XF	Unc	BU
1970	100,000	—	—	15.00	20.00	25.00

KM# 29   5 MARK
9.7000 g., Copper-Nickel, 29 mm.   **Subject:** Brandenburg Gate

Date	Mintage	F	VF	XF	Unc	BU
1971A	4,000,000	—	—	3.00	10.00	20.00
1979A	32,000	—	—	10.00	25.00	35.00
1979A Proof	2,500	—	—	—	—	—
1980A	30,000	—	—	10.00	15.00	20.00
1980A Proof	2,500	—	—	—	—	—
1981A	30,000	—	—	10.00	15.00	20.00
1981A Proof	2,500	—	—	—	—	—
1982A	28,000	—	—	10.00	15.00	25.00
1982A Proof	2,500	Value: 200				
1983A	3,000	—	—	—	900	1,100
1984A	28,000	—	—	25.00	40.00	60.00
1984A Proof	3,015	Value: 120				
1985A	3,000	—	—	—	900	1,100
1986A	28,000	—	—	50.00	110	125
1986A Proof	2,800	Value: 140				
1987A	220,000	—	—	10.00	15.00	20.00
1987A Proof	6,424	Value: 80.00				
1988A	28,000	—	—	12.00	15.00	35.00
1988A Proof	2,300	Value: 125				
1989A	28,000	—	—	121	25.00	40.00
1989A Proof	2,405	Value: 125				
1990A	50,000	—	—	12.00	25.00	35.00

KM# 30   5 MARK
9.7000 g., Copper-Nickel, 29 mm.   **Subject:** Johannes Kepler, scientist

Date	Mintage	F	VF	XF	Unc	BU
1971	100,000	—	—	15.00	20.00	25.00

KM# 37   5 MARK
9.7000 g., Copper-Nickel, 29 mm.   **Subject:** City of Meissen **Obv:** State emblem, denomination **Rev:** City scene

Date	Mintage	F	VF	XF	Unc	BU
1972A	3,500,000	—	—	4.00	10.00	12.00
1981A Proof	40	Value: 2,750				
1983A	28,000	—	—	150	200	220
1983A Proof	2,550	Value: 400				

KM# 36.1   5 MARK
9.7000 g., Copper-Nickel, 29 mm.   **Subject:** 75th Anniversary - Death of Johannes Brahms **Obv:** State emblem, denomination **Rev:** Name, musical score, dates **Edge:** 5 Mark 5 Mark 5 Mark 5 Mark

Date	Mintage	F	VF	XF	Unc	BU
1972	55,000	—	—	15.00	20.00	25.00

KM# 36.2   5 MARK
9.7000 g., Copper-Nickel, 29 mm.   **Obv:** State emblem, denomination **Rev:** Musical score, name and dates **Note:** Error: Double edge inscription.

Date	Mintage	F	VF	XF	Unc	BU
1972	—	—	—	—	475	575

KM# 43   5 MARK
9.7000 g., Copper-Nickel, 29 mm.   **Subject:** 125th Anniversary - Birth of Otto Lilienthal, aviation pioneer **Obv:** State emblem, denomination **Rev:** Plane divides dates

Date	Mintage	F	VF	XF	Unc	BU
1973	100,000	—	—	40.00	55.00	65.00

KM# 49   5 MARK
9.7000 g., Copper-Nickel, 29 mm.   **Subject:** Centenary - Death of Philipp Reis, physicist, telephone inventor **Obv:** State emblem, denomination **Rev:** Telephone and telegraph divided by name, dates at bottom

Date	Mintage	F	VF	XF	Unc	BU
1974	100,000	—	—	—	20.00	32.00

KM# 54   5 MARK
9.7000 g., Copper-Nickel, 29 mm.   **Subject:** 100th Anniversary - Birth of Thomas Mann, writer **Obv:** State emblem, denomination **Rev:** Head left, dates below

Date	Mintage	F	VF	XF	Unc	BU
1975	100,000	—	—	15.00	22.00	27.00

KM# 55   5 MARK
9.7000 g., Copper-Nickel, 29 mm.   **Subject:** International Women's Year **Obv:** State emblem, denomination **Rev:** Profiles of three women right

Date	Mintage	F	VF	XF	Unc	BU
1975	250,000	—	—	15.00	20.00	25.00

KM# 60   5 MARK
9.7000 g., Copper-Nickel, 29 mm.   **Subject:** 200th Anniversary - Birth of Ferdinand von Schill, military officer **Obv:** State emblem, denomination **Rev:** Hat divides dates above sword and name

Date	Mintage	F	VF	XF	Unc	BU
1976	100,000	—	—	20.00	28.00	35.00

KM# 64   5 MARK
9.7000 g., Copper-Nickel, 29 mm.   **Subject:** 125th Anniversary - Death of Friedrich Ludwig Jahn, father of German gymnastics **Obv:** State emblem, denomination **Rev:** Bust 3/4 facing, dates below

Date	Mintage	F	VF	XF	Unc	BU
1977 Proof	10,000	Value: 75.00				
1977	90,000	—	—	30.00	40.00	50.00

KM# 67   5 MARK
9.7000 g., Copper-Nickel, 29 mm.   **Subject:** 175th Anniversary - Death of Friedrich Klopstock, poet **Obv:** State emblem, denomination **Rev:** Bust left

Date	Mintage	F	VF	XF	Unc	BU
1978 Proof	4,500	Value: 110				
1978	96,000	—	—	30.00	45.00	55.00

KM# 68   5 MARK
9.7000 g., Copper-Nickel, 29 mm.   **Subject:** Anti-Apartheid Year **Obv:** Denomination, date below small state emblem at left **Rev:** Raised clenched fist

Date	Mintage	F	VF	XF	Unc	BU
1978A Proof	4,000	Value: 120				
1978A	196,000	—	—	20.00	25.00	30.00

KM# 72   5 MARK
9.7000 g., Copper-Nickel, 29 mm.   **Subject:** 100th Anniversary - Birth of Albert Einstein, physicist **Obv:** State emblem, denomination **Rev:** Head 3/4 right

Date	Mintage	F	VF	XF	Unc	BU
1979	56,000	—	—	55.00	75.00	90.00
1979 Proof	4,500	Value: 115				

KM# 76   5 MARK
9.7000 g., Copper-Nickel, 29 mm.   **Subject:** 75th Anniversary - Death of Adolph von Menzel **Obv:** State emblem, denomination **Rev:** Bust left divides dates

Date	Mintage	F	VF	XF	Unc	BU
1980 Proof	5,500	Value: 110				
1980	55,000	—	—	35.00	50.00	60.00

KM# 79   5 MARK
9.7000 g., Copper-Nickel, 29 mm.   **Subject:** 450th Anniversary - Death of Tilman Riemenschneider, sculptor **Obv:** State emblem, denomination **Rev:** Bust 3/4 facing, divides dates

Date	Mintage	F	VF	XF	Unc	BU
1981	55,000	—	—	40.00	60.00	70.00
1981 Proof	5,500	Value: 120				

KM# 84   5 MARK
9.7000 g., Copper-Nickel, 29 mm.   **Subject:** 200th Anniversary
- Birth of Friedrich Frobel   **Obv:** State emblem, denomination
Rev: Three children with building blocks, dates below

Date	Mintage	F	VF	XF	Unc	BU
1982	55,000	—	—	40.00	60.00	75.00
1982 Proof	5,500	Value: 120				

KM# 85   5 MARK
9.7000 g., Copper-Nickel-Zinc, 29 mm.   **Subject:** Goethe's Weimar
Cottage   **Obv:** Small state emblem, denomination   **Rev:** Cottage

Date	Mintage	F	VF	XF	Unc	BU
1982A	245,000	—	—	25.00	35.00	42.00
1982A Proof	5,500	Value: 95.00				
Note: House and trees frosted						
1982A Proof	210	Value: 3,000				
Note: House only frosted						

KM# 86   5 MARK
9.7000 g., Copper-Nickel-Zinc, 29 mm.   **Subject:** Wartburg
Castle   **Obv:** State emblem, denomination   **Rev:** Castle

Date	Mintage	F	VF	XF	Unc	BU
1982A	245,000	—	—	25.00	40.00	45.00
1982A Proof	5,500	Value: 100				
1983A	10,000	—	—	—	425	475

KM# 89   5 MARK
9.7000 g., Copper-Nickel, 29 mm.   **Subject:** Wittenberg Church
Obv: Small state emblem, denomination   **Rev:** Church

Date	Mintage	F	VF	XF	Unc	BU
1983A Proof	5,500	Value: 100				
1983A	245,000	—	—	25.00	40.00	55.00

KM# 90   5 MARK
9.7000 g., Copper-Nickel, 29 mm.   **Subject:** Martin Luther's
birthplace   **Obv:** State emblem, denomination   **Rev:** House

Date	Mintage	F	VF	XF	Unc	BU
1983A Proof	5,500	Value: 95.00				
1983A	245,000	—	—	25.00	40.00	55.00

KM# 91   5 MARK
Copper-Nickel-Zinc, 29 mm.   **Subject:** 125th Anniversary - Birth
of Max Planck   **Obv:** State emblem, denomination   **Rev:** Head
right, dates below

Date	Mintage	F	VF	XF	Unc	BU
1983	56,000	—	—	32.00	50.00	60.00
1983 Proof	4,200	Value: 110				

KM# 96   5 MARK
9.7000 g., Copper-Nickel-Zinc, 29 mm.   **Subject:** Leipzig Old City Hall
Obv: State emblem, denomination   **Rev:** City hall building

Date	Mintage	F	VF	XF	Unc	BU
1984A	245,000	—	—	25.00	40.00	50.00
1984A Proof	5,500	Value: 70.00				

KM# 97   5 MARK
9.7000 g., Copper-Nickel, 29 mm.   **Subject:** Thomas Church of
Leipzig   **Obv:** State emblem, denomination   **Rev:** Church

Date	Mintage	F	VF	XF	Unc	BU
1984A	245,000	—	—	25.00	40.00	50.00
1984A Proof	5,500	Value: 70.00				

KM# 98   5 MARK
9.7000 g., Copper-Nickel, 29 mm.   **Subject:** 150th Anniversary
- Death of Adolf Freiherr von Lützow   **Obv:** State emblem,
denomination   **Rev:** Three uniformed figures on horses

Date	Mintage	F	VF	XF	Unc	BU
1984A	55,000	—	—	55.00	70.00	80.00
1984A Proof	5,000	Value: 115				

KM# 102   5 MARK
9.7000 g., Copper-Nickel, 29 mm.   **Subject:** Restoration of
Dresden Women's Church   **Obv:** State emblem divides date
above six line inscription, denomination below   **Rev:** Church
buildings, date above

Date	Mintage	F	VF	XF	Unc	BU
1985A	245,000	—	—	25.00	35.00	40.00
1985A Proof	8,476	Value: 70.00				

KM# 103   5 MARK
9.7000 g., Copper-Nickel, 29 mm.   **Subject:** Restoration of Dresden
Zwinger   **Obv:** State emblem, denomination   **Rev:** Building

Date	Mintage	F	VF	XF	Unc	BU
1985A	245,000	—	—	25.00	35.00	45.00
1985A Proof	5,500	Value: 70.00				

KM# 104   5 MARK
9.7000 g., Copper-Nickel, 29 mm.   **Subject:** 225th Anniversary
- Death of Caroline Neuber   **Obv:** State emblem, denomination
Rev: Caroline on stage, 1697-1760

Date	Mintage	F	VF	XF	Unc	BU
1985A	56,000	—	—	75.00	90.00	100
1985A Proof	4,000	Value: 150				

KM# 110   5 MARK
9.7000 g., Copper-Nickel, 29 mm.   **Subject:** Potsdam - Sanssouci
Palace   **Obv:** State emblem, denomination   **Rev:** Palace

Date	Mintage	F	VF	XF	Unc	BU
1986A	296,000	—	—	9.00	12.00	17.50
1986A Proof	4,200	Value: 115				

KM# 111   5 MARK
9.7000 g., Copper-Nickel, 29 mm.   **Subject:** Potsdam - New
Palace   **Obv:** State emblem, denomination   **Rev:** Palace buildings

Date	Mintage	F	VF	XF	Unc	BU
1986A	296,000	—	—	9.00	12.00	17.50
1986A Proof	4,200	Value: 115				

KM# 112   5 MARK
9.7000 g., Copper-Nickel, 29 mm.   **Subject:** 175th Anniversary
- Death of Heinrich von Kleist   **Obv:** State emblem, denomination
Rev: Bust left looking forward divides dates

Date	Mintage	F	VF	XF	Unc	BU
1986A	56,000	—	—	130	150	180
1986A Proof	4,000	Value: 200				

KM# 114 5 MARK
9.7000 g., Copper-Zinc-Nickel, 29 mm. **Subject:** Berlin - Nikolai Quarter **Obv:** State emblem, denomination **Rev:** Buildings with two towers

Date	Mintage	F	VF	XF	Unc	BU
1987A	496,000	—	—	8.00	12.00	15.00
1987A Proof	4,200	Value: 70.00				

KM# 122 5 MARK
9.7000 g., Copper-Nickel, 29 mm. **Subject:** 50th Anniversary - Death of Ernst Barlach **Obv:** State emblem, denomination **Rev:** Full-length figure playing horn, dates at right

Date	Mintage	F	VF	XF	Unc	BU
1988A	56,000	—	—	50.00	65.00	80.00
1988A Proof	4,000	Value: 200				

KM# 133 5 MARK
9.7000 g., Copper-Zinc-Nickel, 29 mm. **Subject:** 100th Anniversary - Birth of Kurt Tucholsky **Obv:** State emblem, denomination **Rev:** Head facing, dates below

Date	Mintage	F	VF	XF	Unc	BU
1990A	51,000	—	—	40.00	60.00	70.00
1990A Proof	4,000	Value: 165				

KM# 115 5 MARK
9.7000 g., Copper-Zinc-Nickel, 29 mm. **Subject:** Berlin - Red City Hall **Obv:** State emblem, denomination **Rev:** City hall building

Date	Mintage	F	VF	XF	Unc	BU
1987A	496,000	—	—	8.00	12.00	15.00
1987A Proof	4,200	Value: 70.00				

KM# 129 5 MARK
9.7000 g., Copper-Zinc-Nickel, 29 mm. **Subject:** Katharinen Kirche in Zwickau **Obv:** State emblem, denomination **Rev:** Church

Date	Mintage	F	VF	XF	Unc	BU
1989A	496,000	—	—	7.00	9.00	11.50
1989A Proof	4,200	Value: 125				

KM# 134 5 MARK
9.7000 g., Copper-Zinc-Nickel, 29 mm. **Subject:** 500 Years of Postal Service **Obv:** State emblem, denomination **Rev:** Antique car

Date	Mintage	F	VF	XF	Unc	BU
1990A	496,000	—	—	7.00	9.00	11.00
1990A Proof	4,200	Value: 100				

KM# 116 5 MARK
9.7000 g., Copper-Zinc-Nickel, 29 mm. **Subject:** Berlin - Universal Time Clock **Obv:** State emblem, denomination **Rev:** Universal clock

Date	Mintage	F	VF	XF	Unc	BU
1987A	496,000	—	—	8.00	12.00	15.00
1987A Proof	4,200	Value: 70.00				

KM# 130 5 MARK
9.7000 g., Copper-Zinc-Nickel, 29 mm. **Subject:** Marien Kirche in Muhlhausen **Obv:** State emblem, denomination **Rev:** Church and city scene

Date	Mintage	F	VF	XF	Unc	BU
1989A	496,000	—	—	7.00	9.00	11.50
1989A Proof	4,200	Value: 125				

KM# 15.1 10 MARK
17.0000 g., 0.8000 Silver 0.4372 oz. ASW, 31 mm. **Subject:** 125th Anniversary - Death of Karl Friedrich Schinkel, artist, painter **Obv:** State emblem, denomination **Rev:** Head right, dates below **Edge:** 10 MARK DER DEUTSCHEN NOTEN BANK

Date	Mintage	F	VF	XF	Unc	BU
1966	50,000	—	—	350	450	475
1966 Proof, extremely rare						

KM# 15.2 10 MARK
17.0000 g., 0.8000 Silver 0.4372 oz. ASW, 31 mm. **Obv:** State emblem, denomination **Rev:** Head right, dates below **Note:** Error: Plain edge.

Date	Mintage	F	VF	XF	Unc	BU
1966						

KM# 120 5 MARK
9.7000 g., Copper-Nickel, 29 mm. **Subject:** Germany's First Railroad **Obv:** State emblem, denomination **Rev:** Train engine, tower in background

Date	Mintage	F	VF	XF	Unc	BU
1988A	496,000	—	—	8.00	9.00	12.50
1988A Proof	4,200	Value: 160				

KM# 131 5 MARK
9.7000 g., Copper-Zinc-Nickel, 29 mm. **Subject:** 100th Anniversary - Birth of Carl von Ossietzky **Obv:** State emblem, denomination **Rev:** Bust left, dates at right

Date	Mintage	F	VF	XF	Unc	BU
1989A	56,000	—	—	60.00	75.00	90.00
1989A Proof	4,000	Value: 220				

KM# 17.1 10 MARK
17.0000 g., 0.8000 Silver 0.4372 oz. ASW, 31 mm. **Subject:** 100th Anniversary - Birth of Kathe Kollwitz, artist **Obv:** State emblem, denomination **Rev:** Head left, dates below **Edge:** 10 MARK DER DEUTSCHEN NOTENBANK

Date	Mintage	F	VF	XF	Unc	BU
1967	97,000	—	—	60.00	75.00	95.00
1967 Proof, extrememly rare						

KM# 17.2 10 MARK
17.0000 g., 0.8000 Silver 0.4372 oz. ASW, 31 mm. **Subject:** 100th Anniversary - Birth of Kathe Kollwitz **Obv:** State emblem, denomination **Rev:** Head left, dates below **Note:** Error, edge: 10 MARK*10 MARK*10 MARK*

Date	Mintage	F	VF	XF	Unc	BU
1967	3,000	—	—	—	250	300

KM# 20.1 10 MARK
17.0000 g., 0.6250 Silver 0.3416 oz. ASW, 31 mm. **Subject:** 500th Anniversary - Death of Johann Gutenberg

Date	Mintage	F	VF	XF	Unc	BU
1968	100,000	—	—	55.00	70.00	85.00

KM# 121 5 MARK
9.7000 g., Copper-Nickel, 29 mm. **Subject:** Port City of Rostock **Obv:** State emblem, denomination **Rev:** Ships in port

Date	Mintage	F	VF	XF	Unc	BU
1988A	496,000	—	—	8.00	9.00	12.50
1988A Proof	4,200	Value: 145				

KM# 135 5 MARK
9.7000 g., Copper-Zinc-Nickel, 29 mm. **Subject:** Zeughaus Museum **Obv:** State emblem, denomination **Rev:** Museum

Date	Mintage	F	VF	XF	Unc	BU
1990A	496,000	—	—	7.00	8.00	10.00
1990A Proof	4,200	Value: 100				

KM# 20.2   10 MARK
17.0000 g., 0.6250 Silver 0.3416 oz. ASW, 31 mm.
Subject: 500th Anniversary - Death of Johann Gutenberg
Note: Error: Plain edge.

Date	Mintage	F	VF	XF	Unc	BU
1968	—				700	800

KM# 24   10 MARK
17.0000 g., 0.6250 Silver 0.3416 oz. ASW, 31 mm. **Subject:**
250th Anniversary - Death of Johann Friedrich Bottger **Obv:** State emblem, denomination **Rev:** Pitcher, dates divided above

Date	Mintage	F	VF	XF	Unc	BU
1969	100,000			50.00	65.00	80.00

KM# 27.1   10 MARK
17.0000 g., 0.6250 Silver 0.3416 oz. ASW, 31 mm.
Subject: Ludwig Van Beethoven, composer **Obv:** State emblem, denomination **Rev:** Head left, dates below

Date	Mintage	F	VF	XF	Unc	BU
1970	100,000			50.00	60.00	75.00
1970 Proof, extremely rare						

KM# 27.2   10 MARK
17.0000 g., 0.6250 Silver 0.3416 oz. ASW, 31 mm. **Obv:** State emblem, denomination **Rev:** Head left **Note:** Error: Plain edge.

Date	Mintage	F	VF	XF	Unc	BU
1970	—					600

KM# 31   10 MARK
17.0000 g., 0.6250 Silver 0.3416 oz. ASW, 31 mm.
Subject: Albrecht Durer, artist **Obv:** State emblem, denomination **Rev:** Durer's monogram

Date	Mintage	F	VF	XF	Unc	BU
1971	100,000			50.00	60.00	75.00
1971 Proof, extremely rare						

KM# 39   10 MARK
17.0000 g., 0.6250 Silver 0.3416 oz. ASW, 31 mm.
Subject: 175th Anniversary - Birth of Heinrich Heine, poet
Obv: Hammer and protractor within wreath, (state emblem), denomination and date below **Rev:** Bust 3/4 left, divides dates

Date	Mintage	F	VF	XF	Unc	BU
1972	100,000			55.00	65.00	85.00

KM# 38   10 MARK
Copper-Nickel, 31 mm. **Subject:** Buchenwald Memorial
Obv: State emblem, denomination **Rev:** Monument

Date	Mintage	F	VF	XF	Unc	BU
1972A	2,500,000				8.00	10.00
1972A Prooflike	—				20.00	30.00

KM# 44   10 MARK
Copper-Nickel, 31 mm. **Subject:** 10th Youth Festival Games **Obv:** State emblem below date and denomination **Rev:** Games symbol

Date	Mintage	F	VF	XF	Unc	BU
1973A	1,500,000				5.00	12.00
1973A Prooflike	—				15.00	20.00

KM# 45   10 MARK
17.0000 g., 0.6250 Silver 0.3416 oz. ASW, 31 mm. **Subject:**
75th Anniversary - Birth of Bertolt Brecht, poet **Obv:** State emblem, denomination **Rev:** Head left, dates below

Date	Mintage	F	VF	XF	Unc	BU
1973	100,000			50.00	60.00	80.00
1973 Proof, extremely rare						

KM# 51   10 MARK
17.0000 g., 0.6250 Silver 0.3416 oz. ASW, 31 mm.
Subject: 25th Anniversary D.D.R. **Obv:** State emblem, denomination **Rev:** City scene

Date	Mintage	F	VF	XF	Unc	BU
1974	70,000			50.00	60.00	80.00
1974 Proof	200	Value: 5,500				

KM# 52   10 MARK
17.0000 g., 0.6250 Silver 0.3416 oz. ASW, 31 mm.
Subject: 200th Anniversary - Birth of Caspar David Friedrich, painter **Obv:** State emblem, denomination **Rev:** Bust right within inner circle, dates below

Date	Mintage	F	VF	XF	Unc	BU
1974	75,000			50.00	60.00	75.00
1974 Proof	—	Value: 8,000				

KM# 50   10 MARK
Copper-Nickel, 31 mm. **Subject:** 25th Anniversary (with state motto) **Obv:** Date and denomination below legend **Rev:** Dates above state emblem

Date	Mintage	F	VF	XF	Unc	BU
1974A	3,000,000				6.00	14.00
1974A Prooflike	—				15.00	20.00

KM# 56   10 MARK
17.0000 g., 0.6250 Silver 0.3416 oz. ASW, 31 mm. **Subject:**
Centenary - Birth of Albert Schweitzer, doctor and philosopher
Obv: State emblem, denomination **Rev:** Head left, dates below

Date	Mintage	F	VF	XF	Unc	BU
1975	99,000			50.00	60.00	80.00
1975 Proof	1,040	Value: 1,850				

KM# 57   10 MARK
17.0000 g., 0.5000 Silver 0.2733 oz. ASW, 31 mm.
Subject: Mule **Obv:** State emblem below denomination, date
Rev: Head left, dates below **Edge:** Plain

Date	Mintage	F	VF	XF	Unc	BU
1975A	6,700				—	180

KM# 58   10 MARK
Copper-Nickel, 31 mm. **Subject:** 20th Anniversary - Warsaw Pact **Obv:** State emblem below denomination, date **Rev:** Roman numerals, 'XX' divide seven shields

Date	Mintage	F	VF	XF	Unc	BU
1975A	2,500,000			7.00	10.00	15.00
1975A Prooflike	—				20.00	30.00

KM# 62   10 MARK
17.0000 g., 0.5000 Silver 0.2733 oz. ASW, 31 mm. **Subject:**
150th Anniversary - Death of Carl Maria von Weber, composer
Obv: State emblem, denomination **Rev:** Bust right divides dates

Date	Mintage	F	VF	XF	Unc	BU
1976	94,000			70.00	80.00	95.00
1976 Proof	6,037	Value: 125				

KM# 61   10 MARK
Copper-Nickel, 31 mm. **Subject:** 20th Anniversary - National People's Army **Obv:** State emblem below denomination, date **Rev:** Bust of soldier 3/4 facing

Date	Mintage	F	VF	XF	Unc	BU
1976A	750,000	—	—	10.00	15.00	20.00
1976A Prooflike				30.00	40.00	

KM# 65   10 MARK
17.0000 g., 0.5000 Silver 0.2733 oz. ASW, 31 mm. **Subject:** 375th Anniversary - Birth of Otto von Guericke **Obv:** State emblem, denomination **Rev:** Vacuum pump below and castle above divide dates

Date	Mintage	F	VF	XF	Unc	BU
1977	69,000	—	—	100	115	125
1977 Proof	6,000	Value: 160				

KM# 69   10 MARK
17.0000 g., 0.5000 Silver 0.2733 oz. ASW, 31 mm. **Subject:** 175th Anniversary - Birth of Justus von Liebig, chemist **Obv:** State emblem, denomination **Rev:** Bust 3/4 facing, dates at left

Date	Mintage	F	VF	XF	Unc	BU
1978	71,000	—	—	80.00	115	130
1978 Proof	4,500	Value: 150				

KM# 70   10 MARK
Copper-Nickel, 31 mm. **Subject:** Joint USSR-DDR Orbital Flight **Obv:** State emblem below denomination, date

Date	Mintage	F	VF	XF	Unc	BU
1978A	748,000	—	—	20.00	30.00	45.00
1978A Proof	2,200	Value: 650				

KM# 73   10 MARK
17.0000 g., 0.5000 Silver 0.2733 oz. ASW, 31 mm. **Subject:** 175th Anniversary - Birth of Ludwig Feuerbach, philosopher **Obv:** State emblem below denomination, date **Rev:** Bust 3/4 right, dates and name below

Date	Mintage	F	VF	XF	Unc	BU
1979	51,000	—	—	150	175	190
1979 Proof	4,500	Value: 245				

KM# 77   10 MARK
17.0000 g., 0.5000 Silver 0.2733 oz. ASW, 31 mm. **Subject:** 225th Anniversary - Birth of Gerhard von Scharnhorst **Obv:** State emblem below denomination, date **Rev:** Bust left divides dates

Date	Mintage	F	VF	XF	Unc	BU
1980	55,000	—	—	40.00	50.00	60.00
1980 Proof	5,500	Value: 100				

KM# 80   10 MARK
Copper-Nickel, 31 mm. **Subject:** 25th Anniversary - National People's Army **Obv:** State emblem and denomination divide date **Rev:** Plane above ship at center, tank below, dates at sides

Date	Mintage	F	VF	XF	Unc	BU
1981A	745,000	—	—	12.00	22.00	25.00
1981A Proof	5,500	Value: 80.00				

KM# 81   10 MARK
17.0000 g., 0.5000 Silver 0.2733 oz. ASW, 31 mm. **Subject:** 150th Anniversary - Death of Georg Hegel, philosopher **Obv:** Date and denomination above legend, state emblem below **Rev:** Head right divides dates

Date	Mintage	F	VF	XF	Unc	BU
1981	50,000	—	—	45.00	55.00	65.00
1981 Proof	5,500	Value: 95.00				

KM# 82   10 MARK
Copper-Nickel, 31 mm. **Subject:** 700th Anniversary - Berlin Mint **Obv:** State emblem and denomination divide date **Rev:** Ancient coin at center

Date	Mintage	F	VF	XF	Unc	BU
1981	55,000	—	—	40.00	45.00	55.00
1981 Proof	5,500	Value: 95.00				

KM# 87   10 MARK
17.0000 g., 0.5000 Silver 0.2733 oz. ASW, 31 mm. **Subject:** Leipzig Gewandhaus **Obv:** Legend divides denomination and state emblem **Rev:** Design above building

Date	Mintage	F	VF	XF	Unc	BU
1982	50,000	—	—	50.00	60.00	70.00
1982 Proof	5,500	Value: 95.00				

KM# 92   10 MARK
17.1100 g., 0.5000 Silver 0.2750 oz. ASW, 31 mm. **Subject:** 100th Anniversary - Death of Richard Wagner **Obv:** Legend divides state emblem and denomination **Rev:** Group of people, dates below

Date	Mintage	F	VF	XF	Unc	BU
1983	44,000	—	—	50.00	60.00	70.00
1983 Proof	5,500	Value: 95.00				

KM# 93   10 MARK
Copper-Nickel-Zinc, 31 mm. **Subject:** 30th Anniversary - Worker's Militia **Obv:** Legend divides state emblem and denomination **Rev:** Worker and soldier facing left

Date	Mintage	F	VF	XF	Unc	BU
1983A	495,000	—	—	12.00	20.00	30.00
1983A Proof	5,000	Value: 90.00				

KM# 99   10 MARK
17.0000 g., 0.5000 Silver 0.2733 oz. ASW, 31 mm. **Subject:** 100th Anniversary - Death of Alfred Brehm **Obv:** State emblem, denomination **Rev:** Marabou stork left

Date	Mintage	F	VF	XF	Unc	BU
1984A	50,000	—	—	65.00	85.00	100
1984A Proof	5,000	Value: 150				

KM# 101   10 MARK
17.0000 g., 0.5000 Silver 0.2733 oz. ASW, 31 mm. **Subject:** Restoration of Semper Opera in Dresden **Obv:** Legend divides state emblem and denomination **Rev:** Opera House

Date	Mintage	F	VF	XF	Unc	BU
1985A	50,000	—	—	60.00	70.00	85.00
1985A Proof	5,000	Value: 120				

Date	Mintage	F	VF	XF	Unc	BU
1987A	51,000	—	—	60.00	70.00	85.00
1987A Proof	4,000	Value: 125				

Date	Mintage	F	VF	XF	Unc	BU
1989A	746,000	—	—	12.00	15.00	20.00
1989A Proof	3,080	Value: 275				

KM# 106   10 MARK
Copper-Nickel-Zinc, 31 mm.   **Subject:** 40th Anniversary - Liberation from Fascism   **Obv:** State emblem, denomination   **Rev:** Statue divides inscription

Date	Mintage	F	VF	XF	Unc	BU
1985A	745,000	—	—	10.00	20.00	25.00
1985A Proof	5,500	Value: 100				

KM# 107   10 MARK
17.0000 g., 0.5000 Silver 0.2733 oz. ASW, 31 mm.   **Subject:** 175th Anniversary - Humboldt University   **Obv:** Legend divides state emblem and denomination   **Rev:** Seated statues in front of building

Date	Mintage	F	VF	XF	Unc	BU
1985A	51,000	—	—	75.00	90.00	100
1985A Proof	4,000	Value: 125				

KM# 109   10 MARK
Copper-Nickel, 31 mm.   **Subject:** 100th Anniversary - Birth of Ernst Thalmann   **Obv:** State emblem below denomination, date   **Rev:** People behind front figure with right fist raised

Date	Mintage	F	VF	XF	Unc	BU
1986A	746,000	—	—	10.00	17.50	25.00
1986A Proof	4,000	Value: 110*				

KM# 113   10 MARK
17.0000 g., 0.5000 Silver 0.2733 oz. ASW, 31 mm.   **Subject:** Charite - Berlin   **Obv:** State emblem divides date below legend, denomination above   **Rev:** Building

Date	Mintage	F	VF	XF	Unc	BU
1986A	51,000	—	—	70.00	80.00	90.00
1986A Proof	4,000	Value: 125				

KM# 118   10 MARK
17.0000 g., 0.5000 Silver 0.2733 oz. ASW, 31 mm.   **Subject:** Berlin - Theater   **Obv:** State emblem and denomination divide date   **Rev:** Theater building

KM# 123   10 MARK
17.0000 g., 0.5000 Silver 0.2733 oz. ASW, 31 mm.   **Subject:** 500th Anniversary - Birth of Ulrich von Hutten   **Obv:** State emblem, denomination   **Rev:** Half figure left divides dates

Date	Mintage	F	VF	XF	Unc	BU
1988A	52,000	—	—	70.00	90.00	110
1988A Proof	3,500	Value: 300				

KM# 125   10 MARK
Copper-Nickel, 31 mm.   **Subject:** East German Sports   **Obv:** State emblem, denomination   **Rev:** Three women running left, dates below

Date	Mintage	F	VF	XF	Unc	BU
1988A	747,000	—	—	10.00	20.00	28.00
1988A Proof	3,200	Value: 185				

KM# 126   10 MARK
Copper-Nickel, 31 mm.   **Subject:** Council of Mutual Economic Aid   **Obv:** State emblem, denomination   **Rev:** Tall building, dates at right

Date	Mintage	F	VF	XF	Unc	BU
1989A	—	—	—	30.00	50.00	60.00
1989A Proof	4,000	Value: 325				

KM# 128   10 MARK
17.0000 g., 0.5000 Silver 0.2733 oz. ASW, 31 mm.   **Subject:** 225th Anniversary - Birth of Johann Gottfried Schadow   **Obv:** State emblem, denomination   **Rev:** Winged figure in chariot, dates below

Date	Mintage	F	VF	XF	Unc	BU
1989A	51,000	—	—	95.00	120	150
1989A Proof	4,000	Value: 375				

KM# 132   10 MARK
Copper-Nickel-Zinc, 31 mm.   **Subject:** 40th Anniversary - East German Government   **Obv:** State emblem divides dates above inscription, denomination below   **Rev:** Fifteen shields on right, legend at left   **Edge:** 10 MARK (repeated)

KM# 136   10 MARK
Copper-Nickel-Zinc, 31 mm.   **Subject:** International Labor Day   **Obv:** State emblem below date and denomination   **Rev:** Stylized lettering divides dates   **Edge:** 10 MARK (repeated)

Date	Mintage	F	VF	XF	Unc	BU
1990A	747,000	—	—	4.00	7.00	10.00
1990A Proof	4,367	Value: 120				

KM# 137   10 MARK
17.0000 g., 0.5000 Silver 0.2733 oz. ASW, 31 mm.   **Subject:** Johann Gottlieb Fichte   **Obv:** State emblem, denomination   **Rev:** Figure at lectern facing left

Date	Mintage	F	VF	XF	Unc	BU
1990A	37,000	—	—	70.00	90.00	110
1990A Proof	4,900	Value: 185				

KM# 16.2   20 MARK
20.9000 g., 0.8000 Silver 0.5375 oz. ASW, 33 mm.   **Obv:** State emblem, denomination   **Rev:** Bust right **Edge:** Error: In inscription   **Edge:** 10 MARK DER DEUTSCHEN NOTEN BANK

Date	Mintage	F	VF	XF	Unc	BU
1966	—	—	—	—	—	—

KM# 16.1   20 MARK
20.9000 g., 0.8000 Silver 0.5375 oz. ASW, 33 mm.   **Subject:** 250th Anniversary - Death of Gottfried Wilhelm Leibniz   **Obv:** State emblem, denomination   **Rev:** Bust right, dates below   **Edge:** 20 MARK DER DEUTSCHEN NOTEN BANK

Date	Mintage	F	VF	XF	Unc	BU
1966	50,000	—	—	175	225	275
1966 Proof, extremely rare	—	—	—	—	—	—

KM# 18.1   20 MARK
20.9000 g., 0.8000 Silver 0.5375 oz. ASW, 33 mm.   **Subject:** 200th Anniversary - Birth of Wilhelm von Humboldt   **Obv:** State emblem, denomination   **Rev:** Head with high collar left, dates below   **Edge:** 20 MARK DER DEUTSCHEN NOTENBANK

Date	Mintage	F	VF	XF	Unc	BU
1967	97,000	—	—	160	180	210
1967 Proof, extremely rare	—	—	—	—	—	—

KM# 18.2   20 MARK

20.9000 g., 0.8000 Silver 0.5375 oz. ASW, 33 mm. **Obv:** State emblem, denomination **Rev:** Head with high collar left, dates below **Edge:** Error: In inscription **Edge:** 20 MARK*20 MARK*20 MARK*20 MARK

Date	Mintage	F	VF	XF	Unc	BU
1967	3,000	—	—	—	—	275

KM# 21   20 MARK

20.9000 g., 0.8000 Silver 0.5375 oz. ASW, 33 mm. **Subject:** 150th Anniversary - Birth of Karl Marx **Obv:** State emblem, denomination **Rev:** Head left, dates below

Date	Mintage	F	VF	XF	Unc	BU
1968	100,000	—	—	80.00	100	120
1968 Proof, extremely rare	—	—	—	—	—	—

KM# 25   20 MARK

20.9000 g., 0.6250 Silver 0.4200 oz. ASW, 33 mm. **Subject:** 240th Birth Anniversary - Johann Wolfgang von Goethe, poet **Obv:** State emblem, denomination **Rev:** Head left, dates below

Date	Mintage	F	VF	XF	Unc	BU
1969	100,000	—	—	150	170	190
1969 Proof, extremely rare	—	—	—	—	—	—

KM# 28   20 MARK

20.9000 g., 0.6250 Silver 0.4200 oz. ASW, 33 mm. **Subject:** 150th Anniversary - Birth of Friedrich Engels **Obv:** State emblem, denomination **Rev:** Head left, dates at right

Date	Mintage	F	VF	XF	Unc	BU
1970	100,000	—	—	85.00	115	135
1970 Proof, extremely rare	—	—	—	—	—	—

KM# 32   20 MARK

20.9000 g., 0.6250 Silver 0.4200 oz. ASW, 33 mm. **Subject:** Karl Kiebknecht - Rosa Luxemburg **Obv:** State emblem, denomination **Rev:** Jugate busts left, dates below **Edge:** 20 MARK (repeated)

Date	Mintage	F	VF	XF	Unc	BU
1971	100,000	—	—	75.00	90.00	100
1971 Proof, extremely rare	—	—	—	—	—	—

KM# 33   20 MARK

Copper-Nickel, 33 mm. **Subject:** 100th Anniversary - Birth of Heinrich Mann, writer **Obv:** State emblem, denomination **Rev:** Head left, dates below **Edge:** 20 MARK (repeated)

Date	Mintage	F	VF	XF	Unc	BU
1971	2,000,000	—	—	4.00	6.50	28.00
Prooflike	—	—	—	—	30.00	40.00

KM# 34   20 MARK

Copper-Nickel, 33 mm. **Subject:** 85th Birthday of Ernst Thalmann **Obv:** State emblem, denomination **Rev:** Head left, dates below **Edge:** 20 MARK (repeated) **Note:** Edge varieties exist.

Date	Mintage	F	VF	XF	Unc	BU
1971A	2,500,000	—	—	4.00	5.50	20.00
1971A Prooflike	—	—	—	—	25.00	35.00

KM# 40   20 MARK

Copper-Nickel, 33 mm. **Subject:** Friedrich von Schiller, poet **Obv:** State emblem, denomination **Rev:** Head right divides dates

Date	Mintage	F	VF	XF	Unc	BU
1972A	3,000,000	—	—	4.00	15.00	18.00
1972A Prooflike	—	—	—	—	35.00	45.00

KM# 41   20 MARK

20.9000 g., 0.6250 Silver 0.4200 oz. ASW, 33 mm. **Subject:** 500th Anniversary - Birth of Lucas Cranach, painter **Obv:** State emblem, denomination **Rev:** Crowned snake with ring and wings, wings divide dates above **Edge:** 20 MARK (repeated)

Date	Mintage	F	VF	XF	Unc	BU
1972	100,000	—	—	60.00	90.00	110
1972 Proof, extremely rare	—	—	—	—	—	—

KM# 42   20 MARK

Copper-Nickel, 33 mm. **Subject:** Wilhelm Pieck **Obv:** State emblem, denomination **Rev:** Head left, dates below

Date	Mintage	F	VF	XF	Unc	BU
1972A	2,500,000	—	—	4.00	15.00	20.00
1972A Prooflike	—	—	—	—	35.00	45.00

KM# 46   20 MARK

20.9000 g., 0.6250 Silver 0.4200 oz. ASW, 33 mm. **Subject:** 60th Anniversary - Death of August Bebel **Obv:** State emblem, denomination **Rev:** Bust half facing, dates at left

Date	Mintage	F	VF	XF	Unc	BU
1973	100,000	—	—	60.00	70.00	90.00
1973 Proof, extremely rare	—	—	—	—	—	—

KM# 47   20 MARK

Copper-Nickel, 33 mm. **Subject:** Otto Grotewohl **Obv:** State emblem, denomination **Rev:** Head left, dates below **Edge:** 20 MARK (repeated)

Date	Mintage	F	VF	XF	Unc	BU
1973A	2,500,000	—	—	5.00	10.00	15.00
1973A Prooflike	—	—	—	—	20.00	30.00

KM# 53   20 MARK

20.9000 g., 0.6250 Silver 0.4200 oz. ASW, 33 mm. **Subject:** 250th Anniversary - Death of Immanuel Kant, philosopher **Obv:** State emblem, denomination **Rev:** Bust 3/4 facing, dates at left

Date	Mintage	F	VF	XF	Unc	BU
1974	96,000	—	—	60.00	85.00	110
1974 Proof	4,221	Value: 225				

KM# 59   20 MARK

20.9000 g., 0.6250 Silver 0.4200 oz. ASW, 33 mm. **Subject:** 225th

Anniversary - Death of Johann Sebastian Bach, composer **Obv:** State emblem, denomination **Rev:** Musical score, dates upper left

Date	Mintage	F	VF	XF	Unc	BU
1975	100,000	—	—	110	140	160
1975 Proof	Inc. above	Value: 3,500				

KM# 63   20 MARK

20.9000 g., 0.6250 Silver 0.4200 oz. ASW, 33 mm. **Subject:** 150th Anniversary - Birth of Wilhelm Liebknecht (socialist member of Reichstag Parliament) **Obv:** State emblem, denomination **Rev:** Bust 3/4 left divides dates

Date	Mintage	F	VF	XF	Unc	BU
1976	96,000	—	—	60.00	70.00	90.00
1976 Proof	4,000	Value: 220				

KM# 66   20 MARK

20.9000 g., 0.5000 Silver 0.3360 oz. ASW, 33 mm. **Subject:** 200th Anniversary - Birth of Carl Friedrich Gauss, scientist **Obv:** State emblem, denomination **Rev:** Lines and arrows form graph, dates below

Date	Mintage	F	VF	XF	Unc	BU
1977	55,000	—	—	90.00	110	125

KM# 71   20 MARK

20.9000 g., 0.5000 Silver 0.3360 oz. ASW, 33 mm. **Subject:** 175th Anniversary - Death of Johann von Herder, philosopher **Obv:** State emblem, denomination **Rev:** Head 3/4 left, dates at right

Date	Mintage	F	VF	XF	Unc	BU
1978	51,000	—	—	90.00	100	120
1978 Proof	4,500	Value: 185				

KM# 74   20 MARK

20.9000 g., 0.5000 Silver 0.3360 oz. ASW, 33 mm. **Subject:** 250th Anniversary - Birth of Gotthold Ephraim Lessing, poet **Obv:** State emblem, denomination **Rev:** Three figures and two palm trees, dates above

Date	Mintage	F	VF	XF	Unc	BU
1979	41,000	—	—	100	130	150
1979 Proof	4,500	Value: 220				

KM# 75   20 MARK

Copper-Nickel, 33 mm. **Subject:** 30th Anniversary - East German Regime **Obv:** Large denomination above date, state emblem below **Rev:** Two jugate heads; front head facing, back head left, chemical factory at left

Date	Mintage	F	VF	XF	Unc	BU
1979A	1,000,000	—	—	—	15.00	25.00
1979A Prooflike				—	20.00	30.00

KM# 78   20 MARK

20.9200 g., 0.5000 Silver 0.3363 oz. ASW, 33 mm. **Subject:** 75th Anniversary - Death of Ernst Abbe, physicist **Obv:** Legend divides state emblem and denomination **Rev:** Early optical instrument, dates below

Date	Mintage	F	VF	XF	Unc	BU
1980	40,000	—	—	70.00	90.00	110
1980 Proof	5,500	Value: 145				

KM# 83   20 MARK

20.9200 g., 0.5000 Silver 0.3363 oz. ASW, 33 mm. **Subject:** 150th Anniversary - Death of vom Stein **Obv:** Legend divides state emblem and denomination **Rev:** Small bust half left below name

Date	Mintage	F	VF	XF	Unc	BU
1981	40,000	—	—	60.00	70.00	90.00
1981 Proof	5,500	Value: 145				

KM# 88   20 MARK

20.9200 g., 0.5000 Silver 0.3363 oz. ASW, 33 mm. **Subject:** 125th Anniversary - Birth of Clara Zetkin **Obv:** State emblem, denomination **Rev:** Bust 3/4 left, dates at left

Date	Mintage	F	VF	XF	Unc	BU
1982	40,000	—	—	65.00	80.00	100
1982 Proof	5,500	Value: 135				

KM# 94   20 MARK

20.9200 g., 0.5000 Silver 0.3363 oz. ASW, 33 mm. **Subject:** 500th Anniversary - Birth of Martin Luther **Obv:** State emblem divides date, denomination below **Rev:** Bust holding bible looking left

Date	Mintage	F	VF	XF	Unc	BU
1983	45,000	—	—	625	750	825
1983 Proof	5,000	Value: 850				

KM# 95   20 MARK

Copper-Nickel, 33 mm. **Subject:** 100th Anniversary - Death of Karl Marx **Obv:** State emblem above inscription, date and denomination below **Rev:** Head 3/4 facing, name and dates below

Date	Mintage	F	VF	XF	Unc	BU
1983A	995,000	—	—	12.00	20.00	30.00
1983A Proof	5,000	Value: 75.00				

KM# 100   20 MARK

20.9200 g., 0.5000 Silver 0.3363 oz. ASW, 33 mm. **Subject:** 225th Anniversary - Death of Georg Friedrich Handel **Obv:** State emblem, denomination **Rev:** Bust looking right, dates below

Date	Mintage	F	VF	XF	Unc	BU
1984A	41,000	—	—	160	190	220
1984A Proof	4,500	Value: 250				

KM# 105   20 MARK

20.9200 g., 0.5000 Silver 0.3363 oz. ASW, 33 mm. **Subject:** 125th Anniversary - Death of Ernst Moritz Arndt **Obv:** State emblem, denomination **Rev:** Bust 3/4 right divides dates

Date	Mintage	F	VF	XF	Unc	BU
1985A	41,000	—	—	130	160	180
1985A Proof	4,000	Value: 235				

KM# 108   20 MARK
20.9000 g., 0.6250 Silver 0.4200 oz. ASW, 33 mm.
Subject: 200th Anniversary - Birth of Jacob and Wilhelm Grimm
Obv: State emblem, denomination **Rev:** "Puss 'n Boots" divides dates

Date	Mintage	F	VF	XF	Unc	BU
1986A	37,000	—	—	245	300	350
1986A Proof	3,500	Value: 525				

KM# 119.1   20 MARK
20.9000 g., 0.6250 Silver 0.4200 oz. ASW, 33 mm.
Subject: Berlin - City Seal **Obv:** State emblem, denomination
Rev: Helmeted shield with supporters within circle

Date	Mintage	F	VF	XF	Unc	BU
1987A	42,000	—	—	525	600	650
1987A Proof	2,100	Value: 2,500				

Note: Seal on reverse totally frosted on proof coins

KM# 119.2   20 MARK
20.9000 g., 0.6250 Silver 0.4200 oz. ASW, 33 mm. **Obv:** State emblem, denomination **Rev:** Fields in seal polished

Date	Mintage	F	VF	XF	Unc	BU
1987A Proof	2,100	Value: 2,500				

KM# 124   20 MARK
20.9000 g., 0.6250 Silver 0.4200 oz. ASW, 33 mm.
Subject: 100th Anniversary - Death of Carl Zeiss **Obv:** State emblem, denomination **Rev:** Microscope, dates at left

Date	Mintage	F	VF	XF	Unc	BU
1988A	37,000	—	—	225	250	300
1988A Proof	3,500	Value: 500				

KM# 127   20 MARK
20.9000 g., 0.6250 Silver 0.4200 oz. ASW, 33 mm.
Subject: 500th Anniversary - Birth of Thomas Muntzer
Obv: State emblem, denomination **Rev:** Head left divides dates

Date	Mintage	F	VF	XF	Unc	BU
1989A	37,000	—	—	80.00	100	120
1989A Proof	3,500	Value: 325				

KM# 138   20 MARK
20.9000 g., 0.6250 Silver 0.4200 oz. ASW, 33 mm.
Subject: Andreas Schluter **Obv:** State emblem, denomination
Rev: Head right on decorative shield divides dates

Date	Mintage	F	VF	XF	Unc	BU
1990A	37,000	—	—	90.00	120	140
1990A Proof	3,500	Value: 320				

KM# 139   20 MARK
Copper-Nickel, 33 mm. **Subject:** Opening of Brandenburg Gate
Obv: State emblem, denomination **Rev:** Brandenburg Gate

Date	Mintage	F	VF	XF	Unc	BU
1990A	300,000	—	—	7.00	10.00	15.00

KM# 139a   20 MARK
18.2000 g., 0.9990 Silver 0.5845 oz. ASW, 33 mm. **Subject:** Opening of Brandenburg Gate **Obv:** State emblem, denomination

Date	Mintage	F	VF	XF	Unc	BU
1990A	145,000	—	—	18.00	30.00	35.00
1990A Proof	5,000	Value: 175				

PIEFORTS

KM#	Date	Mintage	Identification	Mkt Val
P1	ND(1985)	—	5 Mark. Copper-Zinc-Nickel. KM#110, Unc.	—

PROBAS

KM#	Date	Mintage	Identification	Mkt Val
PR1	1948A	—	Pfennig. Zinc.	1,750
PR2	ND	—	Pfennig. Aluminum. Mule - obv: obv. of KM#8.1, rev: obverse of KM#5.	—
PR3	ND(1967)	—	10 Mark. Silver. Neubauer.	3,750
PR4	1968A	—	5 Pfennig. Brass. KM#9.1.	—
PR5	1968A	—	10 Pfennig. Brass Plated Steel. KM#10.1.	375
PR6	1968A	—	50 Pfennig. Brass. KM#12.	450
PR7	1968	—	20 Mark. 0.9990 Gold. KM#21.	—
	1968	—	20 Mark. 0.9990 Gold. KM#21.	—
PR8	ND(1969)	—	20 Pfennig. Brass. Mule - 2 obverses of KM#11.	—
PR9	1969	—	20 Pfennig. Nickel. KM#11.	—
PR10	1969	12,741	5 Mark. Copper-Nickel-Zinc. PROBE.	500
PR11	1972A	—	10 Pfennig. Steel. KM#10.1.	—
PRA12	1972A	—	2 Mark. Aluminum. KM#48.	—
PR12	1973A	—	10 Mark. Copper-Nickel. Edge: 10 MARK* 10 MARK * 10 MARK *, KM#44	700
PR13	1974A	1,500	10 Mark. 0.5000 Silver. KM#50.	1,500
PR14	1974A	100	10 Mark. 0.6250 Silver. Mintage numbered on lead seal, PROBE, KM#52.	7,500
PR15	1975A	—	5 Pfennig. Nickel. KM#9.1,	—
PR16	1975	10,261	20 Mark. Silver. Incuse notes, Unc, KM#59.	300
PR17	1975	I.A.	20 Mark. Silver. Incuse notes, matte fields, proof, KM#59.	4,500
PR18	1975	8,810	10 Mark. Silver. PROBE, KM#57.	160
PRA19	1976A	—	5 Pfennig. Aluminum. KM#9.2.	—
PR19	ND(1977)	6,000	10 Mark. Silver. State emblem, denomination. Ancient vacuum pump above horses, dates below. Guericke.	500
PR20	1978A	100	10 Mark. Silver. KM#70.	—
PR21	1979A	—	20 Mark. Copper-Nickel-Zinc. Obverse: PROBA instead of date, KM#75.	—
PR22	1979A	10,000	20 Mark. Copper-Nickel-Zinc. Large denomination above state emblem. Dates above split leaf design.	150
PR23	1981	—	10 Mark. 0.5000 Silver. State emblem divides date, denomination below. Shields within inner circle form cross. PROBE on obverse, Unc.	2,000
PR24	1981	2,250	10 Mark. 0.5000 Silver. PROBE on obverse, Proof.	1,300
PR25	1982A	—	5 Pfennig. Aluminum. Reeded edge, PROBA, KM#9.2.	350
PR26	1982A	—	20 Pfennig. Brass Plated Steel. KM#11.	500
PR27	1982A	210	5 Mark. Copper-Zinc-Nickel. House frosted on reverse, K#85, Proof.	6,000

KM#	Date	Mintage	Identification	Mkt Val
PR28	1982	90	20 Mark. Silver. State emblem, denomination. Head 1/4 right, dates at right. Countermark number of issue right of date, KM#88, Unc.	8,500
PRA29	1983A	—	5 Pfennig. Nickel. KM#9.2.	—
PR29	1983A	100	10 Mark. Copper-Zinc-Nickel. Countermark PROBE and number on obverse, KM#93, Unc.	2,000
PR30	1983	100	10 Mark. Copper-Zinc-Nickel: PROBE and number below date, KM#94, Unc.	3,500
PR31	1983	100	20 Mark. Copper-Zinc-Nickel. PROBE and issue number left and right of denomination, KM#95, Unc.	3,250
PR32	ND(1985)	300	5 Mark. Copper-Zinc-Nickel. Incusely numbered, PROBA, Unc.	—
PR33	1985A	112	10 Mark. Silver. Denomination above state emblem. Building within circle.	8,000
PR34	1985A	50	10 Mark. Copper-Zinc-Nickel. Reverse large design size, KM#106, Unc.	5,000
PR35	1985A	—	10 Mark. 0.5000 Silver. KM#106, Unc.	—
PR36	1985A	—	10 Mark. 0.5000 Silver. KM#106, Proof.	12,500
PR37	1985A	266	10 Mark. 0.3330 Gold. Alloyed with silver, KM#16, Proof.	5,500
PR38	1986A	—	Mark. Copper-Zinc-Nickel. PROBE, KM#35.	—
PR39	1986A	—	2 Mark. Copper-Zinc-Nickel. PROBE, KM#48.	—
PR40	1986A	110	5 Mark. Copper-Zinc-Nickel. P below tower, Unc.	—
PR41	1986A	107	10 Mark. 0.5000 Silver. P next to state emblem, KM#109, Unc.	3,000
PR42	1988A	1,000	10 Mark. 0.5000 Silver. P below value, KM#125, Proof.	1,200
PR43	1988A	15	20 Mark. Silver. PROBE, large inscription, KM#124, Unc.	9,500
PR44	1989A	—	10 Mark. 0.5000 Silver. KM#132, Proof.	11,500

TRIAL STRIKES

KM#	Date	Mintage	Identification	Mkt Val
TS1	ND(1966)	300	10 Mark. Aluminum. Uniface, Reverse of KM#15.	230
TS2	ND(1966)	300	20 Mark. Aluminum. Uniface, Reverse of KM#16.	270
TS3	ND(1967)	400	10 Mark. Aluminum. Uniface, Reverse of KM#17.	230
TS4	ND(1967)	400	20 Mark. Aluminum. Uniface, Reverse of KM#18.	270
TS5	1968A	350	5 Mark. Aluminum. Uniface, Reverse of KM#19.	235
TS6	ND(1968)	300	10 Mark. Aluminum. Uniface, Reverse of KM#20.	250
TS7	ND(1968)	300	20 Mark. Aluminum. Uniface, Reverse of KM#21.	270
TS8	ND(1969)	—	5 Mark. Nickel-Bronze. Uniface, obverse of KM#14, edge 5 MARK * 5 MARK * 5 MARK *	—
TS9	ND(1969)	350	5 Mark. Aluminum. Uniface, reverse of KM#23.	235
TS10	ND(1969)	300	10 Mark. Aluminum. Uniface, reverse of KM#24.	250
TS11	ND(1969)	300	20 Mark. Aluminum. Uniface, reverse of KM#25.	260
TS12	ND(1970)	350	5 Mark. Aluminum. Uniface, reverse of KM#26.	235
TS13	ND(1970)	300	10 Mark. Aluminum. Uniface, reverse of KM#27.	250
TS14	ND(1970)	330	20 Mark. Aluminum. Uniface, reverse of KM#28.	260
TS15	ND(1971)	450	5 Mark. Aluminum. Uniface, reverse of KM#30.	235
TS16	ND(1971)	300	10 Mark. Aluminum. Uniface, reverse of KM#31.	250
TS17	ND(1971)	410	20 Mark. Aluminum. Uniface, reverse of KM#32.	250
TS18	ND(1972)	300	5 Mark. Aluminum. Uniface, reverse of KM#36.	235
TS19	ND(1972)	300	10 Mark. Aluminum. Uniface, reverse of KM#39.	250
TS20	ND(1972)	300	20 Mark. Aluminum. Uniface, reverse of KM#41.	260
TS21	ND(1973)	300	5 Mark. Aluminum. Uniface, reverse of KM#43.	235
TS22	ND(1973)	—	20 Mark. Copper-Zinc-Nickel. Uniface, reverse of KM#47.	—
TS23	ND(1973)	—	20 Mark. Copper-Zinc-Nickel. Uniface, reverse with portrait within circular legend, KM#47.	—
TS24	ND(1975)	306	10 Mark. Aluminum. Uniface, reverse of KM#56.	220
TS25	1979	—	20 Mark. Copper-Zinc-Nickel. Uniface, reverse of PR22.	—

MINT SETS

KM#	Date	Mintage	Identification	Issue Price	Mkt Val
MS1	1979A (8)	26,000	KM#8.2-10, 11-12.2, 29, 35.2, 48	—	80.00
MS2	1980A (8)	25,000	KM#8.2-10, 11-12.2, 35.2, 48	—	100
MS3	1981 (8)	25,000	KM#8.2-10, 11-12.2, 29, 35.2, 48	—	70.00
MS4	1982 (8)	21,000	KM#8.2-10, 11-12.2, 29, 35.2, 48	—	100
MS5	1982 (7)	4,500	KM#8.2-10, 11-12.2, 35.2, 48	—	150

KM#	Date	Mintage	Identification	Issue Price	Mkt Val
MS6	1983 (8)	19,000	KM#8.2-10, 11-12.2, 35.2, 37, 48	—	225
MS7	1983 (7)	4,500	KM#8.2-10, 11-12.2, 35.2, 48	—	200
MS8	1984 (8)	19,000	KM#8.2-10, 11-12.2, 29, 35.2, 48	—	175
MS9	1984 (7)	4,500	KM#8.2-10, 11-12.2, 35.2, 48	—	150
MS10	1985 (8)	6,000	KM#8.2-10, 11-12.2, 35.2, 48, 102	—	70.00
MS11	1985 (7)	4,500	KM#8.2-10, 11-12.2, 35.2, 48	—	70.00
MS12	1986 (8)	7,000	KM#8.2-10, 11-12, 29, 35.2, 48	—	130
MS13	1986 (7)	4,500	KM#8.2-10, 11-12.2, 35.2, 48	—	85.00
MS14	1987 (8)	8,000	KM#8.2-10, 11-12.2, 29, 35.2, 48	—	75.00
MS15	1987 (7)	4,500	KM#8.2-10, 11-12.2, 35.2, 48	—	85.00
MSA16	1987 (4)	—	KM#29, 114-116	—	60.00
MS16	1988 (8)	11,000	KM#8.2-10, 11-12.2, 29, 35.2, 48	—	75.00
MS17	1988 (7)	4,500	KM#8.2-10, 11-12.2, 35.2, 48	—	85.00
MS18	1989 (8)	11,000	KM8.2-10, 11-12.2, 29, 35.2, 48	—	75.00
MS19	1989 (7)	4,500	KM#8.2-10, 11-12.2, 35.2, 48	—	85.00
MS20	1990 (8)	11,000	KM#8.2-10, 11-12.2, 29, 35.2, 48	—	180
MS21	1990 (7)	4,500	KM#8.2-10, 11-12.2, 35.2, 48	—	180

PROOF SETS

KM#	Date	Mintage	Identification	Issue Price	Mkt Val
PS1	1981 (8)	20	KM#8.2-10, 11-12.2, 35.2, 48, 79	—	—
PS2	1981 (8)	20	KM#8.2-10, 11-12.2, 35.2, 37, 48	—	—
PS3	1982 (8)	2,500	KM#8.2-10, 11-12.2, 29, 35.2, 48	—	500
PS4	1983 (8)	2,550	KM#8.2-10, 11-12.2, 35.2, 37, 48	—	450
PS5	1984 (8)	3,015	KM#8.2-10, 11-12.2, 29, 35.2, 48	—	200
PS6	1985 (8)	2,816	KM#8.2-10, 11-12.2, 35.2, 48, 102	—	125
PS7	1986 (8)	2,800	KM#8.2-10, 11-12.2, 29, 35.2, 48	—	200
PS8	1987 (8)	2,345	KM#8.2-10, 11-12.2, 35.2, 48	—	150
PS9	1988 (8)	2,300	KM#8.2-10, 11-12.2, 28, 35.2, 48	—	180
PS10	1989 (8)	2,300	KM#8.2-10, 11-12.2, 28, 35.2, 48	—	250

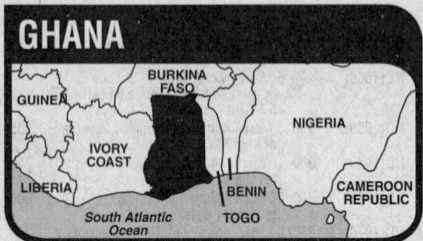

GHANA

The Republic of Ghana, a member of the Commonwealth of Nations situated on the West Coast of Africa between Ivory Coast and Togo, has an area of 92,100 sq. mi. (238,540 sq. km.) and a population of 14 million, almost entirely African. Capital: Accra. Cocoa (the major crop), coconuts, palm kernels and coffee are exported. Mining, second in importance to agriculture, is concentrated on gold, manganese and industrial diamonds.

The state of Ghana, comprising the Gold Coast and British Togoland, obtained independence on March 6, 1957, becoming the first Negro African colony to do so. On July I, 1960, Ghana adopted a republican constitution, changing from a ministerial to a presidential form of government. The government was overthrown, the constitution suspended and the National Assembly dissolved by the Ghanaian army and police on Feb. 24, 1966. The government was returned to civilian authority in Oct. 1969, but was again seized by military officers in a bloodless coup on Jan. 13, 1972, but 3 further coups occurred in 1978, 1979 and 1981. The latter 2 coups were followed by suspension of the constitution and banning of political parties. A new constitution, which allowed multiparty politics, was approved in April 1992.

Ghana's monetary denomination of Cedi' is derived from the word 'sedie' meaning cowrie, a shell money commonly employed by coastal tribes.

MONETARY SYSTEM
12 Pence = 1 Shilling

REPUBLIC
STANDARD COINAGE

KM# 1   1/2 PENNY
Bronze **Obv:** Dr. Kwame Nkrumah head right **Rev:** Date divided by star, denomination below

Date	Mintage	F	VF	XF	Unc	BU
1958	32,200,000	—	0.10	0.25	0.50	1.50
1958 Proof	20,000	Value: 0.75				

KM# 2   PENNY
Bronze **Obv:** Dr. Kwame Nkrumah head right **Rev:** Date divided by star, denomination below

Date	Mintage	F	VF	XF	Unc	BU
1958	60,000,000	—	0.15	0.35	0.75	1.75
1958 Proof	20,000	Value: 1.00				

KM# 3   3 PENCE
Copper Nickel, 19.5 mm. **Obv:** Dr. Kwame Nkrumah head right **Rev:** Date divided by star, denomination below

Date	Mintage	F	VF	XF	Unc	BU
1958	25,200,000	—	0.20	0.45	1.00	2.00
1958 Proof	20,000	Value: 1.50				

KM# 4   6 PENCE
2.2600 g., Copper Nickel **Obv:** Head of Dr. Kwame Nkrumah right **Rev:** Date divided by star, denomination below

Date	Mintage	F	VF	XF	Unc	BU
1958	15,200,000	—	0.20	0.45	1.00	2.00
1958 Proof	—	Value: 1.50				

KM# 5   SHILLING
Copper Nickel, 21 mm. **Obv:** Dr. Kwame Nkrumah head right **Rev:** Date divided by star, denomination below

Date	Mintage	F	VF	XF	Unc	BU
1958	34,400,000	—	0.25	0.50	1.75	3.50
1958 Proof	20,000	Value: 2.50				

KM# 6   2 SHILLING
Copper Nickel, 26.5 mm. **Obv:** Dr. Kwame Nkrumah head right **Rev:** Date divided by star, denomination below

Date	Mintage	F	VF	XF	Unc	BU
1958	72,700,000	—	0.35	0.75	2.25	4.50
1958 Proof	20,000	Value: 3.50				

KM# 7   10 SHILLING
28.2800 g., 0.9250 Silver 0.8410 oz. ASW, 38 mm. **Obv:** Dr. Kwame Nkrumah head right **Rev:** Date divided by star, denomination below **Edge:** 6 MARCH 1957 - INDEPENDENCE OF GHANA

Date	Mintage	F	VF	XF	Unc	BU
1958 Proof	11,000	Value: 17.50				

DECIMAL COINAGE

KM# 12   1/2 PESEWA
Bronze, 20.3 mm. **Obv:** Bush drums **Rev:** Star divides date and denomination

Date	Mintage	F	VF	XF	Unc	BU
1967	30,000,000	—	0.10	0.20	0.50	0.75
1967 Proof	2,000	Value: 1.00				

KM# 13   PESEWA
Bronze, 25.5 mm. **Obv:** Bush drums **Rev:** Star divides date and denomination

Date	Mintage	F	VF	XF	Unc	BU
1967	30,000,000	—	0.15	0.25	0.60	0.85
1967 Proof	2,000	Value: 1.25				
1975	50,250,000	—	0.10	0.20	0.50	0.75
1979	50,000,000	—	0.10	0.20	0.50	0.75

KM# 14   2-1/2 PESEWAS
3.2000 g., Copper-Nickel, 19.5 mm. **Obv:** Cocoa beans within circle **Rev:** Rampant lion at center of quartered shield dividing date and denomination

Date	Mintage	F	VF	XF	Unc	BU
1967	6,000,000	—	0.10	0.20	0.75	1.25
1967 Proof	2,000	Value: 1.50				

KM# 8   5 PESEWAS
Copper-Nickel **Obv:** Dr. Kwame Nkrumah head right **Rev:** Star divides date and denomination

Date	Mintage	F	VF	XF	Unc	BU
1965	30,000,000	—	0.20	0.35	1.25	2.25

KM# 15   5 PESEWAS
Copper-Nickel, 19.5 mm. **Obv:** Cocoa beans within circle **Rev:** Rampant lion at center of quartered shield dividing date and denomination

Date	Mintage	F	VF	XF	Unc	BU
1967	30,000,000	—	0.15	0.25	0.75	1.25
1967 Proof	2,000	Value: 2.00				
1973	8,000,000	—	0.15	0.25	0.75	1.25
1975	20,000,000	—	0.15	0.25	0.75	1.25

KM# 9   10 PESEWAS
Copper-Nickel **Obv:** Dr. Kwame Nkrumah head right **Rev:** Star divides date and denomination

Date	Mintage	F	VF	XF	Unc	BU
1965	50,000,000	—	0.25	0.50	1.25	2.00

KM# 16   10 PESEWAS
5.5700 g., Copper-Nickel, 13.5 mm. **Obv:** Cocoa beans within circle **Rev:** Rampant lion at center of quartered shield dividing date and denomination

Date	Mintage	F	VF	XF	Unc	BU
1967	13,200,000	—	0.20	0.40	1.50	2.00
1967 Proof	2,000	Value: 2.50				
1975	20,000,000	—	0.20	0.40	1.25	1.75
1979	5,500,000	—	0.20	0.40	1.25	1.75

KM# 17   20 PESEWAS
Copper-Nickel, 28.5 mm. **Obv:** Cocoa beans within circle **Rev:** Rampant lion at center of quartered shield dividing date and denomination

Date	Mintage	F	VF	XF	Unc	BU
1967	25,800,000	—	0.25	0.50	1.75	2.50
1967 Proof	2,000	Value: 3.00				
1979	5,000,000	—	0.25	0.50	1.75	2.50

KM# 10   25 PESEWAS
8.6500 g., Copper-Nickel **Obv:** Head of Dr. Kwame Nkrumah right **Rev:** Star divides date and denomination

Date	Mintage	F	VF	XF	Unc	BU
1965	60,100,000	—	0.35	0.75	2.00	3.50

KM# 11   50 PESEWAS
Copper-Nickel **Obv:** Dr. Kwame Nkrumah head right **Rev:** Star divides date and denomination

Date	Mintage	F	VF	XF	Unc	BU
1965	18,200,000	—	0.75	1.50	3.50	5.00

KM# 18   50 PESEWAS
12.3600 g., Brass **Series:** F.A.O. **Obv:** Cocoa beans within circle **Rev:** Rampant lion at center of quartered shield dividing date and denomination

Date	Mintage	F	VF	XF	Unc	BU
1979	60,000,000	—	0.45	0.75	2.25	3.50

KM# 24   50 PESEWAS
Brass **Obv:** Cocoa beans within circle **Rev:** Rampant lion at center of quartered shield dividing date and denomination

Date	Mintage	F	VF	XF	Unc	BU
1984	10,000,000	—	0.10	0.25	0.60	1.00

KM# 19   CEDI
11.9000 g., Brass, 30 mm. **Series:** F.A.O. **Obv:** Cowrie shell **Rev:** Rampant lion at center of quartered shield dividing date and denomination

Date	Mintage	F	VF	XF	Unc	BU
1979	160,000,000	—	0.35	0.85	3.00	8.00

KM# 25   CEDI
2.2400 g., Brass, 19.2 mm. **Obv:** Cowrie shell **Rev:** Rampant lion at center of quartered shield dividing date and denomination

Date	Mintage	F	VF	XF	Unc	BU
1984	40,000,000	—	0.10	0.25	1.50	4.00

KM# 26   5 CEDIS
Brass **Obv:** Bush drums **Rev:** Rampant lion at center of quartered shield dividing date and denomination

Date	Mintage	F	VF	XF	Unc	BU
1984	88,920,000	—	0.10	0.20	0.50	0.75

KM# 33   5 CEDIS
Brass Plated Steel **Obv:** Bush drums **Rev:** Rampant lion at center of quartered shield dividing date and denomination

Date	Mintage	F	VF	XF	Unc	BU
1991	—	—	0.10	0.20	0.50	0.75

KM# 29   10 CEDIS
3.5000 g., Nickel Clad Steel, 21.8 mm. **Obv:** Cocoa beans within circle **Rev:** Rampant lion at center of quartered shield dividing date and denomination

Date	Mintage	F	VF	XF	Unc	BU
1991	—	—	0.35	0.75	1.25

KM# 30   20 CEDIS
5.4000 g., Nickel Clad Steel, 24.5 mm. **Obv:** Cowrie shell **Rev:** Rampant lion at center of quartered shield dividing date and denomination

Date	Mintage	F	VF	XF	Unc	BU
1991	—	—	—	0.35	1.50	3.00
1995	—	—	—	0.35	1.50	3.00

KM# 20   50 CEDIS
28.2800 g., 0.9250 Silver 0.8410 oz. ASW
Subject: International Year of Disabled Persons **Obv:** Triangular symbol within wreath, date above **Rev:** Person in wheelchair divides dates, denomination below

Date	Mintage	F	VF	XF	Unc	BU
1981	10,000	—	—	—	25.00	28.00
1981 Proof	10,000	Value: 35.00				

KM# 21   50 CEDIS
Copper Nickel **Series:** F.A.O. **Subject:** World Fisheries Conference **Obv:** Bush drums **Rev:** People in boat on water, denomination

Date	Mintage	F	VF	XF	Unc	BU
ND(1984)	100,000	—	—	—	6.50	8.50

KM# 21a   50 CEDIS
28.2800 g., 0.9250 Silver 0.8410 oz. ASW **Series:** F.A.O.
Subject: World Fisheries Conference **Obv:** Bust drums
Rev: People in boat on water, denomination

Date	Mintage	F	VF	XF	Unc	BU
ND(1984) Proof	21,000				Value: 55.00	

KM# 21b   50 CEDIS
47.5400 g., 0.9170 Gold 1.4015 oz. AGW **Series:** F.A.O.
Subject: World Fisheries Conference **Obv:** Bush drums
Rev: People in boat on water, denomination

Date	Mintage	F	VF	XF	Unc	BU
ND(1984) Proof	105				Value: 2,000	

KM# 22   50 CEDIS
28.2800 g., 0.9250 Silver 0.8410 oz. ASW **Subject:** Year of the
Scout **Obv:** Rampant lion at center of quartered shield, denomination
below, rope encircles **Rev:** Two scouts planting trees, dates at left

Date	Mintage	F	VF	XF	Unc	BU
ND(1984)	10,000	—	—	—	40.00	—
ND(1984) Proof	Inc. above				Value: 85.00	

KM# 31   50 CEDIS
Copper-Nickel, 27.4 mm. **Obv:** Bush drums **Rev:** Rampant lion
at center of quartered shield dividing date and denomination

Date	Mintage	F	VF	XF	Unc	BU
1991	—	—	—	1.00	2.25	3.50

KM# 31a   50 CEDIS
7.4000 g., Nickel Plated Steel, 27.4 mm. **Obv:** Bush drums
Rev: Rampant lion at center of quartered shield dividing date and
denomination

Date	Mintage	F	VF	XF	Unc	BU
1995	—	—	—	1.00	2.25	3.50
1997	—	—	—	1.00	2.25	3.50
1999	—	—	—	1.00	2.25	3.50

KM# 27   100 CEDIS
28.2800 g., 0.5000 Silver 0.4546 oz. ASW **Subject:**
Commonwealth Games **Obv:** Bush drums **Rev:** Game design,
denomination and date within ring of boxers

Date	Mintage	F	VF	XF	Unc	BU
1986	50,000	—	—	—	16.50	20.00

KM# 27a   100 CEDIS
28.2800 g., 0.9250 Silver 0.8410 oz. ASW **Subject:**
Commonwealth Games **Obv:** Bush drums **Rev:** Game design,
denomination and date within ring of boxers

Date	Mintage	F	VF	XF	Unc	BU
1986 Proof	20,000				Value: 28.00	

KM# 32   100 CEDIS
6.9000 g., Bi-Metallic Brass center in Copper-Nickel ring, 25 mm.
Obv: Cocoa beans within circle **Rev:** Rampant lion at center of
quartered shield dividing date and denomination, circle surrounds

Date	Mintage	F	VF	XF	Unc	BU
1991	—	—	—	1.75	3.50	4.75
1997	—	—	—	1.50	3.25	4.50
1999	—	—	—	1.50	3.25	4.50

KM# 35   200 CEDIS
Nickel Plated Steel **Obv:** Cowrie shell **Rev:** Rampant lion at
center of quartered shield dividing date and denomination

Date	Mintage	F	VF	XF	Unc	BU
1996	—	—	—	—	4.00	6.00
1998	—	—	—	—	4.00	6.00

Note: Fields frosted but not center design

KM# 28   500 CEDIS
15.9800 g., 0.9170 Gold 0.4711 oz. AGW **Subject:** International
Year of Disabled Persons **Obv:** Triangular symbol within wreath,
date above **Rev:** Bust 3/4 left divides dates, denomination below

Date	Mintage	F	VF	XF	Unc	BU
1981	—	—	—	—	465	485
1981 Proof	—				Value: 525	

KM# 23   500 CEDIS
15.9800 g., 0.9170 Gold 0.4711 oz. AGW **Subject:** Year of the
Scout **Obv:** Rampant lion at center of quartered shield, denomination
below, rope encircles **Rev:** Scouting symbol within rope, dates below

Date	Mintage	F	VF	XF	Unc	BU
ND(1984)	2,000	—	—	—	450	465
ND(1984) Proof	2,000				Value: 500	

KM# 34   500 CEDIS
9.1700 g., Nickel-Brass **Obv:** Bush drums **Rev:** Rampant lion
at center of quartered shield dividing date and denomination

Date	Mintage	F	VF	XF	Unc	BU
1996	—	—	—	—	4.75	5.50
1998	—	—	—	—	4.75	5.50

PIEFORTS

KM#	Date	Mintage	Identification	Issue Price	Mkt Val
P1	1981	1,050	50 Cedis. Silver. KM20.	—	65.00
P2	1981	—	500 Cedis. Gold. KM28.	—	850
P2	1981	—	500 Cedis. Gold. KM28.	—	850
P3	ND(1984)	520	50 Cedis. Silver. KM21a.	—	80.00

PROOF SETS

KM#	Date	Mintage	Identification	Issue Price	Mkt Val
PS1	1958 (7)	6,431	KM1-7	—	23.50
PS2	1967 (6)	100	KM12-17	8.53	11.50

GIBRALTAR

The British Colony of Gibraltar, located at the southernmost
point of the Iberian Peninsula, has an area of 2.25 sq. mi. (6.5 sq.
km.) and a population of 29,651. Capital (and only town): Gibraltar. Aside from its strategic importance as guardian of the western
entrance to the Mediterranean Sea, Gibraltar is also a free port
and a British naval base.

Gibraltar, rooted in Greek mythology as one of the Pillars of
Hercules, has long been a coveted stronghold. Moslems took it
from Spain and fortified it in 711. Spain retook it in 1309, lost it
again to the Moors in 1333 and retook it in 1462. After 1540 Spain
strengthened its defenses and held it until the War of the Spanish
Succession when it was captured by a combined British and
Dutch force in 1704. Britain held it against the Franco-Spanish
attacks of 1704-05 and through the historic Great Siege of 1779-
83. Recently Spain has attempted to discourage British occupancy by harassment and economic devices. In 1967, Gibraltar's
inhabitants voted 12,138 to 44 to remain under British rule.

Gibraltar's celebrated Barbary Ape, the last monkey to be
found in a wild state in Europe, is featured on the colony's first
decimal crown, released in 1971.

RULERS
British

MINT MARKS
PM - Pobjoy Mint
PMM – Pobjoy Mint (only appears on coins dated 2000)

**NOTE: ALL coins for 1988 –2003 include the PM mint mark
except the 2000 dated circulation pieces which instead
have PMM.**

MINT PRIVY MARKS
U - Unc finish

DIE MARKS
1988: AA-AE
1989: AA-AF
1990: AA-AB
1991: AA
1992: AA-BB
1993: AA-BB
1994-1999: AA

MONETARY SYSTEM
4 Farthings = 1 Penny
12 Pence = 1 Shilling
2 Shillings = 1 Florin
5 Shillings = 1 Crown
20 Shillings = 1 Pound

BRITISH COLONY

CROWN COINAGE
1967-1970

KM# 4   CROWN
Copper-Nickel, 38.5 mm. **Ruler:** Elizabeth II **Obv:** Young bust
right **Rev:** Key below castle divides date, denomination below

Date	Mintage	F	VF	XF	Unc	BU
1967	125,000	—	1.50	2.50	6.00	—
1968	40,000	—	1.75	2.75	7.00	—

Date	Mintage	F	VF	XF	Unc	BU
1969	40,000	—	1.75	2.75	7.00	—
1970	45,000	—	1.75	2.75	7.00	—

KM# 4a CROWN
28.2800 g., 0.5000 Silver 0.4546 oz. ASW, 38.5 mm.
Ruler: Elizabeth II **Obv:** Young bust right **Rev:** Key below castle divides date

Date	Mintage	F	VF	XF	Unc	BU
1967 Frosted Proof	50	Value: 200				
1967 Proof	10,000	Value: 13.50				

DECIMAL COINAGE
100 Pence = 1 Pound

KM# 20 PENNY
3.5700 g., Bronze, 20.5 mm. **Ruler:** Elizabeth II **Obv:** Crowned head right **Rev:** Barbary partridge divides denomination

Date	Mintage	F	VF	XF	Unc	BU
1988 AA	—	—	—	—	0.35	0.75
1988 AB	—	—	—	—	0.35	0.75
1988 AC	—	—	—	—	0.35	0.75
1988 AD	—	—	—	—	0.35	0.75
1988 AE	—	—	—	—	0.35	0.75
1989 AA	—	—	—	—	0.35	0.75
1989 AB	—	—	—	—	0.35	0.75
1989 AC	—	—	—	—	0.35	0.75
1989 AD	—	—	—	—	0.35	0.75
1989 AE	—	—	—	—	0.35	0.75
1989 AF	—	—	—	—	0.35	0.75
1990 AA	—	—	—	—	0.35	0.75
1990 AB	—	—	—	—	0.35	0.75
1991 AA	—	—	—	—	0.35	0.75
1992 AA	—	—	—	—	0.35	0.75
1992 BB	—	—	—	—	0.35	0.75
1993 AA	—	—	—	—	0.35	0.75
1993 BB	—	—	—	—	0.35	0.75
1994 AA	—	—	—	—	0.35	0.75
1995 AA	—	—	—	—	0.35	0.75
1995 AB	—	—	—	—	0.35	0.75

KM# 20a PENNY
3.5600 g., Bronze Plated Steel, 20.29 mm. **Ruler:** Elizabeth II **Obv:** Crowned head right **Rev:** Barbary partridge left divides denomination **Edge:** Plain

Date	Mintage	F	VF	XF	Unc	BU
1995 AA	—	—	—	—	0.35	0.50
1995PM AB	—	—	—	—	0.35	0.50
1996 AA	—	—	—	—	0.35	0.50
1997 AA	—	—	—	—	0.35	0.50

KM# 773 PENNY
3.5200 g., Bronze Plated Steel, 20.4 mm. **Ruler:** Elizabeth II **Obv:** Head with tiara right **Rev:** Barbary partridge left divides denomination

Date	Mintage	F	VF	XF	Unc	BU
1998 AA	—	—	—	—	0.35	0.50
1999 AA	—	—	—	—	0.35	0.50
2000PMM AA	—	—	—	—	0.35	0.50

KM# 21 2 PENCE
7.1500 g., Bronze, 25.83 mm. **Ruler:** Elizabeth II **Obv:** Crowned head right **Rev:** Lighthouse on Europa Point, denomination **Edge:** Plain

Date	Mintage	F	VF	XF	Unc	BU
1988 AA	—	—	—	—	0.50	0.75
1988 AB	—	—	—	—	0.50	0.75
1988 AC	—	—	—	—	0.50	0.75
1988 AD	—	—	—	—	0.50	0.75
1988 AE	—	—	—	—	0.50	0.75
1989 AA	—	—	—	—	0.50	0.75
1989 AB	—	—	—	—	0.50	0.75
1989 AC	—	—	—	—	0.50	0.75
1989 AD	—	—	—	—	0.50	0.75
1989 AE	—	—	—	—	0.50	0.75
1989 AF	—	—	—	—	0.50	0.75

Date	Mintage	F	VF	XF	Unc	BU
1990 AA	—	—	—	—	0.50	0.75
1990 AB	—	—	—	—	0.50	0.75
1991 AA	—	—	—	—	0.50	0.75
1991 AB	—	—	—	—	0.50	0.75
1992 AA	—	—	—	—	0.50	0.75
1992 BB	—	—	—	—	0.50	0.75
1993 AA	—	—	—	—	0.50	0.75
1993 BB	—	—	—	—	0.50	0.75
1994 AA	—	—	—	—	0.50	0.75
1995 AA	—	—	—	—	0.50	0.75

KM# 21a 2 PENCE
Bronze Plated Steel, 26 mm. **Ruler:** Elizabeth II **Obv:** Crowned head right **Rev:** Lighthouse on Europa Point, denomination

Date	Mintage	F	VF	XF	Unc	BU
1995 AB	—	—	—	—	0.50	0.65
1995 AA	—	—	—	—	0.50	0.75
1996 AA	—	—	—	—	0.50	0.75
1997 AA	—	—	—	—	0.50	0.75

KM# 774 2 PENCE
Bronze Plated Steel, 20.4 mm. **Ruler:** Elizabeth II **Obv:** Head with tiara right

Date	Mintage	F	VF	XF	Unc	BU
1998 AA	—	—	—	—	0.50	0.85
1999 AA	—	—	—	—	0.50	0.85
2000 AA	—	—	—	—	0.50	0.85

KM# 22 5 PENCE
3.2400 g., Copper-Nickel, 23.6 mm. **Ruler:** Elizabeth II **Obv:** Crowned head right **Rev:** Barbary ape divides denomination

Date	Mintage	F	VF	XF	Unc	BU
1988 AA	—	—	—	—	0.85	1.50
1989 AA	—	—	—	—	0.85	1.50
1989 AB	—	—	—	—	0.85	1.50
1989PM AC	—	—	—	—	0.85	1.50
1990 AA	—	—	—	—	0.85	1.50
1990 AB	—	—	—	—	0.85	1.50

KM# 22a 5 PENCE
3.1000 g., Copper-Nickel, 18 mm. **Ruler:** Elizabeth II **Obv:** Crowned head right **Rev:** Barbary ape divides denomination **Note:** Reduced size.

Date	Mintage	F	VF	XF	Unc	BU
1990 AA	—	—	—	—	0.60	1.00
1990 AB	—	—	—	—	0.60	1.00
1991 AA	—	—	—	—	0.60	1.00
1992 AA	—	—	—	—	0.60	1.00
1992 BB	—	—	—	—	0.60	1.00
1993 AA	—	—	—	—	0.60	1.00
1993 BB	—	—	—	—	0.60	1.00
1994 AA	—	—	—	—	0.60	1.00
1995 AA	—	—	—	—	0.60	1.00
1996 AA	—	—	—	—	0.60	1.00
1997 AA	—	—	—	—	0.60	1.00

KM# 22b 5 PENCE
3.2500 g., 0.9250 Silver 0.0966 oz. ASW, 18 mm. **Ruler:** Elizabeth II **Obv:** Crowned head right **Rev:** Barbary ape left divides denomination

Date	Mintage	F	VF	XF	Unc	BU
1990 Proof	5,000	Value: 25.00				

KM# 22c 5 PENCE
3.2500 g., 0.9170 Gold 0.0958 oz. AGW, 18 mm. **Ruler:** Elizabeth II **Obv:** Crowned head right **Rev:** Barbary ape left divides denomination

Date	Mintage	F	VF	XF	Unc	BU
1990 Proof	1,000	Value: 125				

KM# 775 5 PENCE
3.1000 g., Copper-Nickel, 18 mm. **Ruler:** Elizabeth II **Obv:** Head with tiara right **Rev:** Barbary Ape left divides denomination

Date	Mintage	F	VF	XF	Unc	BU
1998 AA	—	—	—	—	0.60	0.75
1999 AA	—	—	—	—	0.60	0.75
2000	—	—	—	—	0.60	0.75

KM# 23.1 10 PENCE
11.5000 g., Copper-Nickel, 28.5 mm. **Ruler:** Elizabeth II **Obv:** Crowned head right **Rev:** Moorish castle, denomination

Date	Mintage	F	VF	XF	Unc	BU
1988 AA	—	—	—	—	1.00	1.25
1988 AB	—	—	—	—	1.00	1.25
1989 AA	—	—	—	—	1.00	1.25
1989PM AB	—	—	—	—	1.00	1.25
1989PM AC	—	—	—	—	1.00	1.25
1989PM AD	—	—	—	—	1.00	1.25
1990 AA	—	—	—	—	1.00	1.25
1990 AB	—	—	—	—	1.00	1.25
1990 AC	—	—	—	—	1.00	1.25
1991 AA	—	—	—	—	1.00	1.25
1991 AB	—	—	—	—	1.00	1.25

KM# 112 10 PENCE
6.5000 g., Copper-Nickel, 24.5 mm. **Ruler:** Elizabeth II **Obv:** Crowned head right **Rev:** Europort

Date	Mintage	F	VF	XF	Unc	BU
1992 AA	—	—	—	—	0.75	1.00
1993 AA	—	—	—	—	0.75	1.00
1995 AA	—	—	—	—	0.75	1.00
1996 AA	—	—	—	—	0.75	1.00
1996PM BB	—	—	—	—	0.75	1.00
1997 AA	—	—	—	—	0.75	1.00

KM# 112a 10 PENCE
6.5000 g., 0.9250 Silver 0.1933 oz. ASW, 24.5 mm. **Ruler:** Elizabeth II **Obv:** Crowned head right **Rev:** Europort

Date	Mintage	F	VF	XF	Unc	BU
1992 Proof	25,000	Value: 25.00				

KM# 112b 10 PENCE
6.5000 g., 0.9170 Gold 0.1916 oz. AGW **Ruler:** Elizabeth II **Obv:** Crowned head right **Rev:** Europort

Date	Mintage	F	VF	XF	Unc	BU
1992 Proof	3,500	Value: 180				

KM# 112c 10 PENCE
6.5000 g., 0.9500 Platinum 0.1985 oz. APW **Ruler:** Elizabeth II **Obv:** Crowned head right **Rev:** Europort

Date	Mintage	F	VF	XF	Unc	BU
1992 Proof	3,500	Value: 340				

KM# 23.2 10 PENCE
6.5000 g., Copper-Nickel, 24.5 mm. **Ruler:** Elizabeth II **Obv:** Crowned head right **Rev:** Moorish castle, denomination **Edge:** Reeded **Note:** Reduced size.

Date	Mintage	F	VF	XF	Unc	BU
1994 AA	—	—	—	—	1.00	1.25

KM# 776 10 PENCE
6.5000 g., Copper-Nickel, 24.5 mm. **Ruler:** Elizabeth II **Obv:** Head with tiara right, date below **Rev:** Denomination below building

Date	Mintage	F	VF	XF	Unc	BU
1998 AA	—	—	—	—	1.00	1.25
1999 AA	—	—	—	—	1.00	1.25
2000	—	—	—	—	1.00	1.25

KM# 16 20 PENCE
5.0000 g., Copper-Nickel, 21.4 mm. **Ruler:** Elizabeth II **Obv:** Crowned head right **Rev:** Our Lady of Europa, a polychrome wood statue, two-feet tall, from the 16th century

Date	Mintage	F	VF	XF	Unc	BU
1988 AA	—	—	—	—	1.50	2.00
1988 AB	—	—	—	—	1.50	2.00
1988 AC	—	—	—	—	1.50	2.00
1988 AA Proof	—	—	—	—	—	—
1989 AA	—	—	—	—	1.50	2.00
1990 AA	—	—	—	—	1.50	2.00
1991 AA	—	—	—	—	1.50	2.00
1992 AA	—	—	—	—	1.50	2.00
1993 AA	—	—	—	—	1.50	2.00
1994 AA	—	—	—	—	1.50	2.00
1995 AA	—	—	—	—	1.50	2.00
1995 AA Proof	—	—	—	—	—	—
1996 AA	—	—	—	—	1.50	2.00
1997 AA	—	—	—	—	1.50	2.00

KM# 777   20 PENCE
5.0000 g., Copper-Nickel, 21.4 mm. **Ruler:** Elizabeth II
Obv: Head with tiara right, date below **Rev:** Our Lady of Europa,
denomination below and right

Date	Mintage	F	VF	XF	Unc	BU
1998 AA	—	—	—	—	1.50	2.00
1999 AA	—	—	—	—	1.50	2.00
2000 AA	—	—	—	—	1.50	2.00

KM# 5   25 NEW PENCE
Copper-Nickel, 38.5 mm. **Ruler:** Elizabeth II **Obv:** Young bust
right, date below **Rev:** Barbary ape left, denomination below

Date	Mintage	F	VF	XF	Unc	BU
1971	75,000	—	—	3.00	9.00	14.00

KM# 5a   25 NEW PENCE
28.2800 g., 0.5000 Silver 0.4546 oz. ASW, 38.5 mm.
Ruler: Elizabeth II **Obv:** Young bust right, date below
Rev: Barbary ape left, denomination

Date	Mintage	F	VF	XF	Unc	BU
1971 Frosted Proof	50	Value: 200				
1971 Proof	20,000	Value: 18.00				

KM# 6   25 NEW PENCE
Copper-Nickel, 38.5 mm. **Ruler:** Elizabeth II **Subject:** 25th
Wedding Anniversary **Obv:** Young bust right **Rev:** Arms of Queen
Elizabeth II and Prince Philip, date and denomination below

Date	Mintage	F	VF	XF	Unc	BU
1972	70,000	—	—	2.00	4.00	6.00

KM# 6a   25 NEW PENCE
28.2800 g., 0.9250 Silver 0.8410 oz. ASW, 38.5 mm.
Ruler: Elizabeth II **Subject:** 25th Wedding Anniversary
Obv: Young bust right

Date	Mintage	F	VF	XF	Unc	BU
1972 Proof	15,000	Value: 18.50				

KM# 10   25 NEW PENCE
Copper-Nickel, 38.5 mm. **Ruler:** Elizabeth II **Subject:** Queen's
Silver Jubilee **Obv:** Young bust right **Rev:** Shield within wreath
of apes and laurel, denomination below

Date	Mintage	F	VF	XF	Unc	BU
1977	65,000	—	—	2.50	5.00	7.00

KM# 10a   25 NEW PENCE
28.2800 g., 0.9250 Silver 0.8410 oz. ASW, 38.5 mm.
Ruler: Elizabeth II **Subject:** Queen's Silver Jubilee **Obv:** Young
bust right

Date	Mintage	F	VF	XF	Unc	BU
1977 Proof	24,000	Value: 18.50				

KM# 17   50 PENCE
13.4000 g., Copper-Nickel, 30 mm. **Ruler:** Elizabeth II
Obv: Crowned head right **Rev:** Denomination in wreath of
Candytuft flowers (Iberis Gibraltarica)

Date	Mintage	F	VF	XF	Unc	BU
1988 AA	30,000	—	—	—	2.00	2.50
1988 AB	—	—	—	—	2.00	2.50
1989 AA	—	—	—	—	2.00	2.50
1989 AB	—	—	—	—	2.00	2.50

KM# 19   50 PENCE
13.4000 g., Copper-Nickel, 30 mm. **Ruler:** Elizabeth II **Subject:**
Christmas **Obv:** Crowned head right **Rev:** The Three Wise Men

Date	Mintage	F	VF	XF	Unc	BU
1988	—	—	—	—	4.00	5.00
1988 Proof	Est. 30,000	Value: 15.00				

KM# 19a   50 PENCE
15.5000 g., 0.9250 Silver 0.4609 oz. ASW, 30 mm.
Ruler: Elizabeth II **Subject:** Christmas **Obv:** Crowned head right
Rev: The Three Wise Men

Date	Mintage	F	VF	XF	Unc	BU
1988 Proof	Est. 5,000	Value: 15.00				

KM# 19b   50 PENCE
26.0000 g., 0.9170 Gold 0.7665 oz. AGW, 30 mm.
Ruler: Elizabeth II **Subject:** Christmas **Obv:** Crowned head right
Rev: The Three Wise Men

Date	Mintage	F	VF	XF	Unc	BU
1988 Proof	250	Value: 735				

KM# 19c   50 PENCE
30.4000 g., 0.9950 Platinum 0.9725 oz. APW, 30 mm.
Ruler: Elizabeth II **Subject:** Christmas **Obv:** Crowned head right
Rev: The Three Wise Men

Date	Mintage	F	VF	XF	Unc	BU
1988 Proof	50	Value: 1,850				

KM# 31   50 PENCE
13.4000 g., Copper-Nickel, 30 mm. **Ruler:** Elizabeth II
Subject: Christmas **Obv:** Crowned head right **Rev:** Choir boy,
denomination below

Date	Mintage	F	VF	XF	Unc	BU
1989 AA	—	—	—	—	4.00	5.00
1989 AA Proof	Est. 30,000	Value: 7.50				

KM# 31a   50 PENCE
15.5000 g., 0.9250 Silver 0.4609 oz. ASW, 30 mm.
Ruler: Elizabeth II **Subject:** Christmas **Obv:** Crowned head right
Rev: Choir boy

Date	Mintage	F	VF	XF	Unc	BU
1989 Proof	Est. 5,000	Value: 45.00				

KM# 31b   50 PENCE
26.0000 g., 0.9170 Gold 0.7665 oz. AGW, 30 mm.
Ruler: Elizabeth II **Subject:** Christmas **Obv:** Crowned head right
Rev: Choir boy

Date	Mintage	F	VF	XF	Unc	BU
1989 Proof	Est. 250	Value: 750				

KM# 31c   50 PENCE
30.4000 g., 0.9950 Platinum 0.9725 oz. APW, 30 mm.
Ruler: Elizabeth II **Subject:** Christmas **Obv:** Crowned head right
Rev: Choir boy

Date	Mintage	F	VF	XF	Unc	BU
1989 Proof	Est. 50	Value: 1,850				

KM# 39   50 PENCE
13.4000 g., Copper-Nickel, 30 mm. **Ruler:** Elizabeth II
Obv: Crowned head right **Rev:** Dolphins surround denomination

Date	Mintage	F	VF	XF	Unc	BU
1990 AA	—	—	—	—	4.50	7.00
1991 AA	—	—	—	—	4.50	7.00
1992 AA	—	—	—	—	4.50	7.00
1993 AA	—	—	—	—	4.50	7.00
1994 AA	—	—	—	—	4.50	7.00
1995 AA	—	—	—	—	4.50	7.00
1996 AA	—	—	—	—	4.50	7.00
1997	—	—	—	—	4.00	7.00

KM# 39a   50 PENCE
15.5000 g., 0.9250 Silver 0.4609 oz. ASW **Ruler:** Elizabeth II
Obv: Crowned head right **Rev:** Dolphins

Date	Mintage	F	VF	XF	Unc	BU
1990 Proof	2,500	Value: 47.50				
1993 Proof	—	Value: 50.00				

KM# 39b   50 PENCE
26.0000 g., 0.9170 Gold 0.7665 oz. AGW, 30 mm.
Ruler: Elizabeth II **Obv:** Crowned head right **Rev:** Dolphins

Date	Mintage	F	VF	XF	Unc	BU
1990 Proof	250	Value: 800				

KM# 47   50 PENCE
13.4000 g., Copper-Nickel, 30 mm. **Ruler:** Elizabeth II
Subject: Christmas **Obv:** Crowned head right **Rev:** Mary and
Joseph with child, denomination below

Date	Mintage	F	VF	XF	Unc	BU
1990 AA	—	—	—	—	—	4.00
1990 Proof	Est. 30,000	Value: 8.00				

KM# 47a   50 PENCE
15.5000 g., 0.9250 Silver 0.4609 oz. ASW, 30 mm.
Ruler: Elizabeth II **Subject:** Christmas **Obv:** Crowned head right
Rev: Mary and Joseph with child

Date	Mintage	F	VF	XF	Unc	BU
1990 Proof	5,000	Value: 45.00				

KM# 47b 50 PENCE
26.0000 g., 0.9170 Gold 0.7665 oz. AGW, 30 mm.
Ruler: Elizabeth II **Subject:** Christmas **Obv:** Crowned head right
Rev: Mary and Joseph with child

Date	Mintage	F	VF	XF	Unc	BU
1990 Proof	250	Value: 730				

KM# 47c 50 PENCE
30.4000 g., 0.9950 Platinum 0.9725 oz. APW, 30 mm.
Ruler: Elizabeth II **Subject:** Christmas **Obv:** Crowned head right
Rev: Mary and Joseph with child

Date	Mintage	F	VF	XF	Unc	BU
1990 Proof	50	Value: 1,850				

KM# 83 50 PENCE
13.4000 g., Copper-Nickel, 30 mm. **Ruler:** Elizabeth II
Subject: Christmas **Obv:** Crowned head right **Rev:** Family
caroling, denomination below

Date	Mintage	F	VF	XF	Unc	BU
1991 AA	—	—	—	—	4.00	5.00
1991 AA Proof	Est. 30,000	Value: 7.50				

KM# 83a 50 PENCE
15.5000 g., 0.9250 Silver 0.4609 oz. ASW, 30 mm.
Ruler: Elizabeth II **Subject:** Christmas **Obv:** Crowned head right
Rev: Family caroling

Date	Mintage	F	VF	XF	Unc	BU
1991 Proof	Est. 5,000	Value: 40.00				

KM# 83b 50 PENCE
26.0000 g., 0.9170 Gold 0.7665 oz. AGW, 30 mm.
Ruler: Elizabeth II **Subject:** Christmas **Obv:** Crowned head right
Rev: Family caroling

Date	Mintage	F	VF	XF	Unc	BU
1991 Proof	250	Value: 730				

KM# 83c 50 PENCE
30.4000 g., 0.9950 Platinum 0.9725 oz. APW, 30 mm.
Ruler: Elizabeth II **Subject:** Christmas **Obv:** Crowned head right
Rev: Family caroling

Date	Mintage	F	VF	XF	Unc	BU
1991 Proof	50	Value: 1,850				

KM# 108 50 PENCE
13.4000 g., Copper-Nickel, 30 mm. **Ruler:** Elizabeth II
Subject: Christmas **Obv:** Crowned head right **Rev:** Bust of Santa
facing, denomination below

Date	Mintage	F	VF	XF	Unc	BU
1992 AA	Est. 30,000	—	—	—	3.50	4.50
1992 AA Proof	—	Value: 6.50				

KM# 108a 50 PENCE
15.5000 g., 0.9250 Silver 0.4609 oz. ASW, 30 mm.
Ruler: Elizabeth II **Subject:** Christmas **Obv:** Crowned head right
Rev: Bust of Santa facing

Date	Mintage	F	VF	XF	Unc	BU
1992 Proof	Est. 5,000	Value: 40.00				

KM# 108b 50 PENCE
26.0000 g., 0.9170 Gold 0.7665 oz. AGW, 30 mm.
Ruler: Elizabeth II **Subject:** Christmas **Obv:** Crowned head right
Rev: Bust of Santa facing

Date	Mintage	F	VF	XF	Unc	BU
1992 Proof	250	Value: 730				

KM# 108c 50 PENCE
30.4000 g., 0.9950 Platinum 0.9725 oz. APW, 30 mm.
Ruler: Elizabeth II **Subject:** Christmas **Obv:** Crowned head right
Rev: Bust of Santa facing

Date	Mintage	F	VF	XF	Unc	BU
1992 Proof	50	Value: 1,850				

KM# 190 50 PENCE
13.4000 g., Copper-Nickel, 30 mm. **Ruler:** Elizabeth II
Subject: Christmas **Obv:** Crowned head right **Rev:** Santa in
automobile, denomination below

Date	Mintage	F	VF	XF	Unc	BU
1993 AA	30,000	—	—	—	3.50	4.50

KM# 190a 50 PENCE
15.5000 g., 0.9250 Silver 0.4609 oz. ASW, 30 mm.
Ruler: Elizabeth II **Subject:** Christmas **Obv:** Crowned head right
Rev: Santa in automobile

Date	Mintage	F	VF	XF	Unc	BU
1993 Proof	Est. 5,000	Value: 40.00				

KM# 190b 50 PENCE
26.0000 g., 0.9170 Gold 0.7665 oz. AGW, 30 mm.
Ruler: Elizabeth II **Subject:** Christmas **Obv:** Crowned head right
Rev: Santa in automobile

Date	Mintage	F	VF	XF	Unc	BU
1993 Proof	Est. 250	Value: 730				

KM# 190c 50 PENCE
30.4000 g., 0.9950 Platinum 0.9725 oz. APW, 30 mm.
Ruler: Elizabeth II **Subject:** Christmas **Obv:** Crowned head right
Rev: Santa in automobile

Date	Mintage	F	VF	XF	Unc	BU
1993 Proof	Est. 50	Value: 1,850				

KM# 294 50 PENCE
13.4000 g., Copper-Nickel, 30 mm. **Ruler:** Elizabeth II
Subject: Christmas **Obv:** Crowned head right **Rev:** Santa with
sack and hot air balloon

Date	Mintage	F	VF	XF	Unc	BU
1994 AA	30,000	—	—	—	3.50	4.50
1994PM Prooflike	—	—	—	—	—	6.00

KM# 294a 50 PENCE
15.5000 g., 0.9250 Silver 0.4609 oz. ASW **Ruler:** Elizabeth II
Subject: Christmas **Obv:** Crowned head right **Rev:** Santa with
sack and hot air balloon

Date	Mintage	F	VF	XF	Unc	BU
1994 Proof	Est. 5,000	Value: 40.00				

KM# 294b 50 PENCE
26.0000 g., 0.9170 Gold 0.7665 oz. AGW, 30 mm.
Ruler: Elizabeth II **Subject:** Christmas **Obv:** Crowned head right
Rev: Santa with sack and hot air balloon

Date	Mintage	F	VF	XF	Unc	BU
1994 Proof	Est. 250	Value: 730				

KM# 294c 50 PENCE
30.4000 g., 0.9950 Platinum 0.9725 oz. APW, 30 mm.
Ruler: Elizabeth II **Subject:** Christmas **Obv:** Crowned head right
Rev: Santa with sack and hot air balloon

Date	Mintage	F	VF	XF	Unc	BU
1994 Proof	Est. 50	Value: 1,850				

KM# 336 50 PENCE
13.4000 g., Copper-Nickel, 30 mm. **Ruler:** Elizabeth II
Subject: Christmas **Obv:** Crowned head right **Rev:** Penguins
parading, denomination below

Date	Mintage	F	VF	XF	Unc	BU
1995 AA	Est. 30,000	—	—	—	4.00	5.00

KM# 336a 50 PENCE
15.5000 g., 0.9250 Silver 0.4609 oz. ASW, 30 mm.
Ruler: Elizabeth II **Subject:** Christmas **Obv:** Crowned head right
Rev: Penguins parading

Date	Mintage	F	VF	XF	Unc	BU
1995 Proof	Est. 5,000	Value: 40.00				

KM# 336b 50 PENCE
26.0000 g., 0.9170 Gold 0.7665 oz. AGW, 30 mm.
Ruler: Elizabeth II **Subject:** Christmas **Obv:** Crowned head right
Rev: Penguins parading

Date	Mintage	F	VF	XF	Unc	BU
1995 Proof	250	Value: 730				

KM# 336c 50 PENCE
30.4000 g., 0.9950 Platinum 0.9725 oz. APW, 30 mm.
Ruler: Elizabeth II **Subject:** Christmas **Obv:** Crowned head right
Rev: Penguins parading

Date	Mintage	F	VF	XF	Unc	BU
1995 Proof	50	Value: 1,850				

KM# 453 50 PENCE
Copper-Nickel, 30 mm. **Ruler:** Elizabeth II **Subject:** Christmas
Obv: Crowned head right **Rev:** Santa Claus and biplane

Date	Mintage	F	VF	XF	Unc	BU
1996 No die letters						
1996 AA	Est. 30,000	—	—	—	4.00	5.00

KM# 453a 50 PENCE
15.0000 g., 0.9250 Silver 0.4461 oz. ASW, 30 mm.
Ruler: Elizabeth II **Subject:** Christmas **Obv:** Crowned head right
Rev: Santa Claus and biplane

Date	Mintage	F	VF	XF	Unc	BU
1996 Proof	Est. 5,000	Value: 35.00				

KM# 453b 50 PENCE
26.0000 g., 0.9170 Gold 0.7665 oz. AGW, 30 mm.
Ruler: Elizabeth II **Subject:** Christmas **Obv:** Crowned head right
Rev: Santa Claus and biplane

Date	Mintage	F	VF	XF	Unc	BU
1996 Proof	Est. 250	Value: 730				

KM# 606 50 PENCE
Copper-Nickel, 27.3 mm. **Ruler:** Elizabeth II **Subject:**
Christmas **Obv:** Crowned head right **Rev:** Santa Claus in sleigh

Date	Mintage	F	VF	XF	Unc	BU
1997	Est. 30,000	—	—	—	4.00	5.00

KM# 606a 50 PENCE
8.0000 g., 0.9250 Silver 0.2379 oz. ASW, 27.3 mm.
Ruler: Elizabeth II **Subject:** Christmas **Obv:** Crowned head right
Rev: Santa Claus in sleigh

Date	Mintage	F	VF	XF	Unc	BU
1997 Proof	Est. 5,000	Value: 35.00				

KM# 606b 50 PENCE
8.0000 g., 0.9170 Gold 0.2358 oz. AGW, 27.3 mm.
Ruler: Elizabeth II **Subject:** Christmas **Obv:** Crowned head right
Rev: Santa in sleigh

Date	Mintage	F	VF	XF	Unc	BU
1997 Proof	Est. 250	Value: 550				

KM# 39.1 50 PENCE
8.0000 g., Copper-Nickel, 27.3 mm. **Ruler:** Elizabeth II
Obv: Crowned head right **Rev:** Dolphins surround denomination

Date	Mintage	F	VF	XF	Unc	BU
1997 AA	—	—	—	—	4.50	5.00

KM# 39.1a 50 PENCE
8.0000 g., 0.9250 Silver 0.2379 oz. ASW, 27.3 mm.
Ruler: Elizabeth II **Obv:** Crowned head right **Rev:** Dolphins
surround denomination

Date	Mintage	F	VF	XF	Unc	BU
1997 Proof	Est. 5,000	Value: 35.00				

KM# 39.1b 50 PENCE
8.0000 g., 0.9999 Gold 0.2572 oz. AGW, 27.3 mm.
Ruler: Elizabeth II **Obv:** Crowned head right **Rev:** Dolphins
surround denomination

Date	Mintage	F	VF	XF	Unc	BU
1997 Proof	Est. 250	Value: 400				

KM# 778   50 PENCE
8.0000 g., Copper-Nickel, 27.3 mm. **Ruler:** Elizabeth II **Obv:** Head with tiara right **Rev:** Dolphins surround denomination **Edge:** Plain

Date	Mintage	F	VF	XF	Unc	BU
1998PM AA	—	—	—	—	4.50	5.50
1999PM AA	—	—	—	—	4.50	5.50
2000PM AA	—	—	—	—	4.50	5.50

KM# 769   50 PENCE
Copper-Nickel, 27.3 mm. **Ruler:** Elizabeth II **Obv:** Head with tiara right, date below **Rev:** Santa Claus in chimney

Date	Mintage	F	VF	XF	Unc	BU
1998	Est. 30,000	—	—	—	4.00	5.00

KM# 769a   50 PENCE
8.0000 g., 0.9250 Silver 0.2379 oz. ASW, 27.3 mm. **Ruler:** Elizabeth II **Obv:** Head with tiara right **Rev:** Santa Claus in chimney

Date	Mintage	F	VF	XF	Unc	BU
1998 Proof	Est. 5,000	Value: 35.00				

KM# 769b   50 PENCE
8.0000 g., 0.9170 Gold 0.2358 oz. AGW, 27.3 mm. **Ruler:** Elizabeth II **Obv:** Head with tiara right **Rev:** Santa Claus in chimney

Date	Mintage	F	VF	XF	Unc	BU
1998 Proof	Est. 250	Value: 550				

KM# 866   50 PENCE
Copper-Nickel, 27.3 mm. **Ruler:** Elizabeth II **Obv:** Head with tiara right, date below **Rev:** Santa with pair of monkeys

Date	Mintage	F	VF	XF	Unc	BU
1999 BB Prooflike	Est. 30,000	—	—	—	4.00	5.00

KM# 866a   50 PENCE
8.0000 g., 0.9250 Silver 0.2379 oz. ASW, 27.3 mm. **Ruler:** Elizabeth II **Obv:** Head with tiara right **Rev:** Santa with pair of monkeys

Date	Mintage	F	VF	XF	Unc	BU
1999 Proof	Est. 5,000	Value: 35.00				

KM# 866b   50 PENCE
8.0000 g., 0.9170 Gold 0.2358 oz. AGW, 27.3 mm. **Ruler:** Elizabeth II **Obv:** Head with tiara right **Rev:** Santa with pair of monkeys

Date	Mintage	F	VF	XF	Unc	BU
1999 Proof	Est. 250	Value: 550				

KM# 887   50 PENCE
8.0000 g., Copper-Nickel, 27.3 mm. **Ruler:** Elizabeth II **Subject:** Christmas **Obv:** Head with tiara right, date below **Rev:** Madonna and child with angels **Edge:** Plain

Date	Mintage	F	VF	XF	Unc	BU
2000 AA	30,000	—	—	—	4.00	5.00

KM# 887a   50 PENCE
8.0000 g., 0.9250 Silver 0.2379 oz. ASW, 27.3 mm. **Ruler:** Elizabeth II **Subject:** Christmas **Obv:** Head with tiara right **Rev:** Madonna and child with angels

Date	Mintage	F	VF	XF	Unc	BU
2000 Proof	5,000	Value: 35.00				

KM# 887b   50 PENCE
8.0000 g., 0.9160 Gold 0.2356 oz. AGW, 27.3 mm. **Ruler:** Elizabeth II **Subject:** Christmas **Obv:** Head with tiara **Rev:** Madonna and child with angels **Note:** KM#310-317 previously listed here do not exist and have been removed.

Date	Mintage	F	VF	XF	Unc	BU
2000 Proof	250	Value: 550				

KM# 310   1/25 CROWN
1.2440 g., 0.9990 Gold 0.0400 oz. AGW, 13.9 mm. **Ruler:** Elizabeth II **Subject:** Barcelona Olympics **Obv:** Crowned bust right **Rev:** Ancient discus thrower within circle, denomination below **Edge:** Reeded

Date	Mintage	F	VF	XF	Unc	BU
1991 Proof	—	Value: 45.00				

KM# 311   1/25 CROWN
1.2440 g., 0.9990 Gold 0.0400 oz. AGW, 13.9 mm. **Ruler:** Elizabeth II **Subject:** Barcelona Olympics **Obv:** Crowned bust right **Rev:** Ancient chariot racers within circle, denomination below **Edge:** Reeded

Date	Mintage	F	VF	XF	Unc	BU
1991 Proof	—	Value: 45.00				

KM# 312   1/25 CROWN
1.2440 g., 0.9990 Gold 0.0400 oz. AGW, 13.9 mm. **Ruler:** Elizabeth II **Subject:** Barcelona Olympics **Obv:** Crowned bust right **Rev:** Ancient runners within circle, denomination below **Edge:** Reeded

Date	Mintage	F	VF	XF	Unc	BU
1991 Proof	—	Value: 45.00				

KM# 313   1/25 CROWN
1.2440 g., 0.9990 Gold 0.0400 oz. AGW, 13.9 mm. **Ruler:** Elizabeth II **Subject:** Barcelona Olympics **Obv:** Crowned bust right **Rev:** Ancient javelin thrower within circle, denomination below **Edge:** Reeded

Date	Mintage	F	VF	XF	Unc	BU
1991 Proof	—	Value: 45.00				

KM# 314   1/25 CROWN
1.2440 g., 0.9990 Gold 0.0400 oz. AGW, 13.9 mm. **Ruler:** Elizabeth II **Subject:** Barcelona Olympics **Obv:** Crowned bust right **Rev:** Ancient wrestlers, head at left looking right, circle surrounds **Edge:** Reeded

Date	Mintage	F	VF	XF	Unc	BU
1991 Proof	—	Value: 45.00				

KM# 315   1/25 CROWN
1.2440 g., 0.9990 Gold 0.0400 oz. AGW, 13.9 mm. **Ruler:** Elizabeth II **Subject:** Barcelona Olympics **Obv:** Crowned bust right **Rev:** Ancient boxer within circle, denomination below **Edge:** Reeded

Date	Mintage	F	VF	XF	Unc	BU
1991 Proof	—	Value: 45.00				

KM# 316   1/25 CROWN
1.2440 g., 0.9990 Gold 0.0400 oz. AGW, 13.9 mm. **Ruler:** Elizabeth II **Subject:** Barcelona Olympics **Obv:** Crowned bust right **Rev:** Long jumper within circle, denomination below **Edge:** Reeded

Date	Mintage	F	VF	XF	Unc	BU
1991 Proof	—	Value: 45.00				

KM# 317   1/25 CROWN
1.2440 g., 0.9990 Gold 0.0400 oz. AGW, 13.9 mm. **Ruler:** Elizabeth II **Subject:** Barcelona Olympics **Obv:** Crowned bust right **Rev:** Ancient victor wearing laurels, denomination below **Edge:** Reeded

Date	Mintage	F	VF	XF	Unc	BU
1991 Proof	—	Value: 45.00				

KM# 124   1/25 CROWN
1.2440 g., 0.9999 Gold 0.0400 oz. AGW, 13.9 mm. **Ruler:** Elizabeth II **Rev:** Japanese Royal Wedding

Date	Mintage	F	VF	XF	Unc	BU
1993 Proof	Est. 25,000	Value: 50.00				

KM# 183   1/25 CROWN
1.2440 g., 0.9990 Gold 0.0400 oz. AGW, 13.9 mm. **Ruler:** Elizabeth II **Obv:** Crowned bust right **Rev:** Stylized panda **Edge:** Reeded

Date	Mintage	F	VF	XF	Unc	BU
1993 Proof	—	Value: 50.00				

KM# 187   1/25 CROWN
1.2440 g., 0.9990 Gold 0.0400 oz. AGW, 13.9 mm. **Ruler:** Elizabeth II **Obv:** Crowned bust right **Rev:** Natural panda amongst bamboo shoots **Edge:** Reeded

Date	Mintage	F	VF	XF	Unc	BU
1993 Proof	—	Value: 50.00				

KM# 202   1/25 CROWN
1.2440 g., 0.9999 Gold 0.0400 oz. AGW, 13.9 mm. **Ruler:** Elizabeth II **Series:** Peter Rabbit Centennial **Subject:** The Tale of Peter Rabbit **Obv:** Crowned bust right **Rev:** Peter Rabbit eating carrots

Date	Mintage	F	VF	XF	Unc	BU
1993 Proof	Est. 25,000	Value: 45.00				

KM# 202a   1/25 CROWN
1.2440 g., 0.9950 Platinum 0.0398 oz. APW, 13.9 mm. **Ruler:** Elizabeth II **Series:** Peter Rabbit Centennial **Subject:** The Tale of Peter Rabbit **Obv:** Crowned bust right **Rev:** Peter Rabbit eating carrots

Date	Mintage	F	VF	XF	Unc	BU
1993 Proof	7,500	Value: 70.00				

KM# 206   1/25 CROWN
1.2440 g., 0.9999 Gold 0.0400 oz. AGW, 13.9 mm. **Ruler:** Elizabeth II **Series:** Peter Rabbit Centennial **Subject:** The Tale of Peter Rabbit **Obv:** Crowned bust right **Rev:** Mrs. Tiggy-Winkel ironing

Date	Mintage	F	VF	XF	Unc	BU
1993 Proof	Est. 25,000	Value: 45.00				

KM# 210   1/25 CROWN
1.2440 g., 0.9999 Gold 0.0400 oz. AGW, 13.9 mm. **Ruler:** Elizabeth II **Series:** Peter Rabbit Centennial **Subject:** The Tale of Peter Rabbit **Obv:** Crowned bust right **Rev:** Jeremy Fisher fishing

Date	Mintage	F	VF	XF	Unc	BU
1993 Proof	Est. 25,000	Value: 45.00				

KM# 214   1/25 CROWN
1.2440 g., 0.9999 Gold 0.0400 oz. AGW, 13.9 mm. **Ruler:** Elizabeth II **Series:** Peter Rabbit Centennial **Subject:** The Tale of Peter Rabbit **Obv:** Crowned bust right **Rev:** Tom Kitten with mother cat

Date	Mintage	F	VF	XF	Unc	BU
1993 Proof	Est. 25,000	Value: 45.00				

KM# 218   1/25 CROWN
1.2440 g., 0.9999 Gold 0.0400 oz. AGW, 13.9 mm. **Ruler:** Elizabeth II **Series:** Peter Rabbit Centennial **Subject:** The Tale of Peter Rabbit **Obv:** Crowned bust right **Rev:** Benjamin Bunny wearing hat and holding coat

Date	Mintage	F	VF	XF	Unc	BU
1993 Proof	Est. 25,000	Value: 45.00				

KM# 222   1/25 CROWN
1.2440 g., 0.9999 Gold 0.0400 oz. AGW, 13.9 mm. **Ruler:** Elizabeth II **Series:** Peter Rabbit Centennial **Subject:** The Tale of Peter Rabbit **Obv:** Crowned bust right **Rev:** Jemima Puddle Duck talking with fox

Date	Mintage	F	VF	XF	Unc	BU
1993 Proof	Est. 25,000	Value: 45.00				

KM# 437   1/25 CROWN
1.2440 g., 0.9999 Gold 0.0400 oz. AGW, 13.9 mm. **Ruler:** Elizabeth II **Series:** Peter Rabbit Centennial **Subject:** The Tale of Peter Rabbit **Obv:** Crowned bust right **Rev:** Mother and bunnies

Date	Mintage	F	VF	XF	Unc	BU
1994 Proof	25,000	Value: 45.00				

KM# 437a   1/25 CROWN
1.2440 g., 0.9950 Platinum 0.0398 oz. APW, 13.9 mm. **Ruler:** Elizabeth II **Series:** Peter Rabbit Centennial **Subject:** The Tale of Peter Rabbit **Obv:** Crowned bust right **Rev:** Mother and bunnies

Date	Mintage	F	VF	XF	Unc	BU
1994 Proof	Est. 7,500	Value: 70.00				

KM# 368   1/25 CROWN
1.2440 g., 0.9999 Gold 0.0400 oz. AGW, 13.9 mm. **Ruler:** Elizabeth II **Obv:** Crowned bust right **Rev:** Roses

Date	Mintage	F	VF	XF	Unc	BU
1996 Proof	Est. 25,000	Value: 45.00				

KM# 375   1/25 CROWN
1.2441 g., 0.9999 Gold 0.0400 oz. AGW, 13.9 mm.
Ruler: Elizabeth II **Series:** Peter Rabbit Centennial **Subject:** The Tale of Peter Rabbit **Obv:** Crowned bust right **Rev:** Rabbit escaping the garden

Date	Mintage	F	VF	XF	Unc	BU
1996 Proof	Est. 25,000		Value: 45.00			

KM# 375a   1/25 CROWN
1.2500 g., 0.9950 Platinum 0.0400 oz. APW, 13.9 mm.
Ruler: Elizabeth II **Series:** Peter Rabbit Centennial **Subject:** The Tale of Peter Rabbit **Obv:** Crowned bust right **Rev:** Rabbit escaping the garden

Date	Mintage	F	VF	XF	Unc	BU
1996 Proof	Est. 7,500		Value: 70.00			

KM# 390   1/25 CROWN
1.2441 g., 0.9999 Gold 0.0400 oz. AGW, 13.9 mm.
Ruler: Elizabeth II **Series:** Centenary of the Cinema **Subject:** Grace Kelly - actress, 1929-82 **Obv:** Crowned bust right **Rev:** Bust 3/4 facing, denomination

Date	Mintage	F	VF	XF	Unc	BU
1996 Proof	Est. 25,000		Value: 45.00			

KM# 395   1/25 CROWN
1.2441 g., 0.9999 Gold 0.0400 oz. AGW, 13.9 mm.
Ruler: Elizabeth II **Series:** Centenary of the Cinema **Subject:** James Dean **Obv:** Crowned bust right **Rev:** Standing central figure, dates at right

Date	Mintage	F	VF	XF	Unc	BU
1996 Proof	Est. 25,000		Value: 45.00			

KM# 400   1/25 CROWN
1.2441 g., 0.9999 Gold 0.0400 oz. AGW, 13.9 mm.
Ruler: Elizabeth II **Series:** Centenary of the Cinema **Subject:** Marilyn Monroe - actress, 1926-62 **Obv:** Crowned bust right **Rev:** Bust looking back over shoulder

Date	Mintage	F	VF	XF	Unc	BU
1996 Proof	Est. 25,000		Value: 45.00			

KM# 405   1/25 CROWN
1.2441 g., 0.9999 Gold 0.0400 oz. AGW, 13.9 mm.
Ruler: Elizabeth II **Series:** Centenary of the Cinema **Subject:** Audrey Hepburn - actress, 1929-93 **Obv:** Crowned bust right **Rev:** Head 3/4 facing

Date	Mintage	F	VF	XF	Unc	BU
1996 Proof	25,000		Value: 45.00			

KM# 405a   1/25 CROWN
1.2500 g., 0.9950 Platinum 0.0400 oz. APW, 13.9 mm.
Ruler: Elizabeth II **Series:** Centenary of the Cinema **Subject:** Audrey Hepburn - actress, 1929-93 **Obv:** Crowned bust right **Rev:** Head 3/4 facing

Date	Mintage	F	VF	XF	Unc	BU
1996 Proof	Est. 1,000		Value: 75.00			

KM# 410   1/25 CROWN
1.2441 g., 0.9999 Gold 0.0400 oz. AGW, 13.9 mm.
Ruler: Elizabeth II **Series:** Centenary of the Cinema **Subject:** Bruce Lee - actor, 1940-73 **Obv:** Crowned bust right **Rev:** Kickboxer and chinese dragon

Date	Mintage	F	VF	XF	Unc	BU
1996 Proof	Est. 25,000		Value: 55.00			

KM# 415   1/25 CROWN
1.2441 g., 0.9999 Gold 0.0400 oz. AGW, 13.9 mm.
Ruler: Elizabeth II **Series:** Centenary of the Cinema **Subject:** Charlie Chaplan - actor, 1889-1977 **Obv:** Crowned bust right **Rev:** Standing central figure with cane, dates

Date	Mintage	F	VF	XF	Unc	BU
1996 Proof	Est. 25,000		Value: 55.00			

KM# 420   1/25 CROWN
1.2441 g., 0.9999 Gold 0.0400 oz. AGW, 13.9 mm. **Ruler:** Elizabeth II **Series:** Centenary of the Cinema **Subject:** Gone With The Wind **Obv:** Crowned bust right **Rev:** Rhett Butler and Scarlett O'Hara

Date	Mintage	F	VF	XF	Unc	BU
1996 Proof	Est. 25,000		Value: 55.00			

KM# 425   1/25 CROWN
1.2441 g., 0.9999 Gold 0.0400 oz. AGW, 13.9 mm. **Ruler:** Elizabeth II **Series:** Centenary of the Cinema **Obv:** Crowned bust right **Rev:** The Flintstones

Date	Mintage	F	VF	XF	Unc	BU
1996 Proof	Est. 25,000		Value: 55.00			

KM# 452   1/25 CROWN
1.2441 g., 0.9999 Gold 0.0400 oz. AGW, 13.9 mm. **Ruler:** Elizabeth II **Series:** Centenary of the Cinema **Subject:** James Dean - actor, 1931-55 **Obv:** Crowned bust right **Rev:** Standing central figure, dates

Date	Mintage	F	VF	XF	Unc	BU
1996 Proof	Est. 25,000		Value: 60.00			

KM# 454   1/25 CROWN
1.2441 g., 0.9999 Gold 0.0400 oz. AGW, 13.9 mm. **Ruler:** Elizabeth II **Series:** Centenary of the Cinema **Subject:** Wizard of Oz **Obv:** Crowned bust right **Rev:** Characters of Oz

Date	Mintage	F	VF	XF	Unc	BU
1996 Proof	Est. 25,000		Value: 45.00			

KM# 458   1/25 CROWN
1.2441 g., 0.9999 Gold 0.0400 oz. AGW, 13.9 mm. **Ruler:** Elizabeth II **Series:** Centenary of the Cinema **Subject:** The Marx Brothers - actors **Obv:** Crowned bust right **Rev:** Three busts 3/4 left

Date	Mintage	F	VF	XF	Unc	BU
1996 Proof	Est. 25,000		Value: 45.00			

KM# 462   1/25 CROWN
1.2441 g., 0.9999 Gold 0.0400 oz. AGW, 13.9 mm. **Ruler:** Elizabeth II **Series:** Centenary of the Cinema **Subject:** Elvis Presley - actor/entertainer, 1935-77 **Obv:** Crowned bust right **Rev:** Guitar beneath and behind bust 3/4 left

Date	Mintage	F	VF	XF	Unc	BU
1996 Proof	Est. 25,000		Value: 45.00			

KM# 466   1/25 CROWN
1.2441 g., 0.9999 Gold 0.0400 oz. AGW, 13.9 mm. **Ruler:** Elizabeth II **Series:** Centenary of the Cinema **Subject:** Casablanca **Obv:** Crowned bust right **Rev:** Bogart and Bergman

Date	Mintage	F	VF	XF	Unc	BU
1996 Proof	Est. 25,000		Value: 45.00			

KM# 470   1/25 CROWN
1.2441 g., 0.9999 Gold 0.0400 oz. AGW, 13.9 mm. **Ruler:** Elizabeth II **Series:** Centenary of the Cinema **Obv:** Crowned bust right **Rev:** E.T.

Date	Mintage	F	VF	XF	Unc	BU
1996 Proof	Est. 25,000		Value: 45.00			

KM# 474   1/25 CROWN
1.2441 g., 0.9999 Gold 0.0400 oz. AGW, 13.9 mm. **Ruler:** Elizabeth II **Series:** Centenary of the Cinema **Subject:** Alfred Hitchcock - Producer/Director, 1899-1980 **Obv:** Crowned bust right **Rev:** Bust facing looking at bird on left shoulder

Date	Mintage	F	VF	XF	Unc	BU
1996 Proof	Est. 25,000		Value: 45.00			

KM# 518   1/25 CROWN
1.2441 g., 0.9999 Gold 0.0400 oz. AGW, 13.9 mm. **Ruler:** Elizabeth II **Subject:** The Tale of Peter Rabbit **Obv:** Crowned bust right **Rev:** Standing rabbit

Date	Mintage	F	VF	XF	Unc	BU
1997 Proof	Est. 25,000		Value: 45.00			

KM# 518a   1/25 CROWN
1.2504 g., 0.9950 Platinum 0.0400 oz. APW, 13.9 mm. **Ruler:** Elizabeth II **Subject:** The Tale of Peter Rabbit **Obv:** Crowned bust right **Rev:** Standing rabbit

Date	Mintage	F	VF	XF	Unc	BU
1997 Proof	Est. 7,500		Value: 70.00			

KM# 537   1/25 CROWN
1.2440 g., 0.9999 Gold 0.0400 oz. AGW, 13.9 mm. **Ruler:** Elizabeth II **Obv:** Crowned bust right **Rev:** Peonies

Date	Mintage	F	VF	XF	Unc	BU
1997 Proof	Est. 25,000		Value: 45.00			

KM# 541   1/25 CROWN
1.2440 g., 0.9999 Gold 0.0400 oz. AGW, 13.9 mm. **Ruler:** Elizabeth II **Subject:** Nefertiti **Obv:** Crowned bust right **Rev:** Head right

Date	Mintage	F	VF	XF	Unc	BU
1997 Proof	Est. 10,000		Value: 45.00			

KM# 545   1/25 CROWN
1.2440 g., 0.9999 Gold 0.0400 oz. AGW, 13.9 mm. **Ruler:** Elizabeth II **Subject:** Cleopatra **Obv:** Crowned bust right **Rev:** Head facing

Date	Mintage	F	VF	XF	Unc	BU
1997 Proof	Est. 10,000		Value: 45.00			

KM# 549   1/25 CROWN
1.2440 g., 0.9999 Gold 0.0400 oz. AGW, 13.9 mm. **Ruler:** Elizabeth II **Subject:** Europa **Obv:** Crowned bust right **Rev:** Head 1/4 left

Date	Mintage	F	VF	XF	Unc	BU
1997 Proof	Est. 10,000		Value: 45.00			

KM# 553   1/25 CROWN
1.2440 g., 0.9999 Gold 0.0400 oz. AGW, 13.9 mm. **Ruler:** Elizabeth II **Subject:** Liberty **Obv:** Crowned bust right **Rev:** Laureate head right

Date	Mintage	F	VF	XF	Unc	BU
1997 Proof	Est. 10,000		Value: 45.00			

KM# 581   1/25 CROWN
1.2440 g., 0.9999 Gold 0.0400 oz. AGW, 13.9 mm. **Ruler:** Elizabeth II **Series:** Evolution of Mankind **Subject:** Egypt **Obv:** Crowned bust right **Rev:** Three ancient Egyptians, pyramids, hieroglyphics

Date	Mintage	F	VF	XF	Unc	BU
1997 Proof	Est. 15,000		Value: 45.00			

KM# 583   1/25 CROWN
1.2440 g., 0.9999 Gold 0.0400 oz. AGW, 13.9 mm. **Ruler:** Elizabeth II **Series:** Evolution of Mankind **Subject:** Israel **Obv:** Crowned bust right **Rev:** Star of David, Moses and Temple of Solomon

Date	Mintage	F	VF	XF	Unc	BU
1997 Proof	Est. 15,000		Value: 45.00			

KM# 585   1/25 CROWN
1.2440 g., 0.9999 Gold 0.0400 oz. AGW, 13.9 mm. **Ruler:** Elizabeth II **Series:** Evolution of Mankind **Subject:** China **Obv:** Crowned bust right **Rev:** Emperor and the Great Wall

Date	Mintage	F	VF	XF	Unc	BU
1997 Proof	Est. 15,000		Value: 45.00			

KM# 587   1/25 CROWN
1.2440 g., 0.9999 Gold 0.0400 oz. AGW, 13.9 mm. **Ruler:** Elizabeth II **Series:** Evolution of Mankind **Subject:** Greece **Obv:** Crowned bust right **Rev:** Aristotle, classic Greek building

Date	Mintage	F	VF	XF	Unc	BU
1997 Proof	Est. 15,000		Value: 45.00			

KM# 589   1/25 CROWN
1.2440 g., 0.9999 Gold 0.0400 oz. AGW, 13.9 mm. **Ruler:** Elizabeth II **Series:** Evolution of Mankind **Subject:** Rome **Obv:** Crowned bust right **Rev:** Julius Caesar and Stonehenge

Date	Mintage	F	VF	XF	Unc	BU
1997 Proof	Est. 15,000		Value: 45.00			

KM# 591   1/25 CROWN
1.2440 g., 0.9999 Gold 0.0400 oz. AGW, 13.9 mm. **Ruler:** Elizabeth II **Series:** Evolution of Mankind **Subject:** India **Obv:** Crowned bust right **Rev:** Krishna playing flute by a temple

Date	Mintage	F	VF	XF	Unc	BU
1997 Proof	Est. 15,000		Value: 45.00			

KM# 593   1/25 CROWN
1.2440 g., 0.9999 Gold 0.0400 oz. AGW, 13.9 mm. **Ruler:** Elizabeth II **Series:** Evolution of Mankind **Subject:** Holy Roman Empire **Obv:** Crowned bust right **Rev:** Charlemagne and soldiers on horseback

Date	Mintage	F	VF	XF	Unc	BU
1997 Proof	Est. 15,000		Value: 45.00			

KM# 595   1/25 CROWN
1.2440 g., 0.9999 Gold 0.0400 oz. AGW, 13.9 mm. **Ruler:** Elizabeth II **Series:** Evolution of Mankind **Subject:** Macedonia **Obv:** Crowned bust right **Rev:** Alexander the Great on horseback

Date	Mintage	F	VF	XF	Unc	BU
1997 Proof	Est. 15,000		Value: 45.00			

KM# 597   1/25 CROWN
1.2440 g., 0.9999 Gold 0.0400 oz. AGW, 13.9 mm. **Ruler:** Elizabeth II **Series:** Evolution of Mankind **Subject:** Native America **Obv:** Crowned bust right **Rev:** Native american on horseback, totem pole at left

Date	Mintage	F	VF	XF	Unc	BU
1997 Proof	Est. 15,000		Value: 45.00			

KM# 599   1/25 CROWN
1.2440 g., 0.9999 Gold 0.0400 oz. AGW, 13.9 mm. **Ruler:** Elizabeth II **Series:** Evolution of Mankind **Subject:** Asia **Obv:** Crowned bust right **Rev:** Buddha and temple

Date	Mintage	F	VF	XF	Unc	BU
1997 Proof	Est. 15,000		Value: 45.00			

KM# 601   1/25 CROWN
1.2440 g., 0.9999 Gold 0.0400 oz. AGW, 13.9 mm. **Ruler:** Elizabeth II **Series:** Evolution of Mankind **Subject:** Inca Empire **Obv:** Crowned bust right **Rev:** Incan Emperor and Machu Picchu

Date	Mintage	F	VF	XF	Unc	BU
1997 Proof	Est. 15,000		Value: 45.00			

KM# 603   1/25 CROWN
1.2440 g., 0.9999 Gold 0.0400 oz. AGW, 13.9 mm. **Ruler:** Elizabeth II **Series:** Evolution of Mankind **Subject:** Islamic Civilization **Obv:** Crowned bust right **Rev:** General Tariq Ibn Ziyad and building

Date	Mintage	F	VF	XF	Unc	BU
1997 Proof	Est. 15,000		Value: 45.00			

KM# 608   1/25 CROWN
1.2440 g., 0.9999 Gold 0.0400 oz. AGW, 13.9 mm. **Ruler:** Elizabeth II **Series:** Traders of the World **Subject:** Sir Francis Drake **Obv:** Crowned bust right **Rev:** Bust at right, ship and beach

Date	Mintage	F	VF	XF	Unc	BU
1997 Proof	Est. 15,000		Value: 45.00			

KM# 610   1/25 CROWN
1.2440 g., 0.9999 Gold 0.0400 oz. AGW, 13.9 mm. **Ruler:** Elizabeth II **Series:** Traders of the World **Subject:** Romans **Obv:** Crowned bust right **Rev:** Lion, lioness, ship, map

Date	Mintage	F	VF	XF	Unc	BU
1997 Proof	Est. 15,000		Value: 45.00			

KM# 612   1/25 CROWN
1.2440 g., 0.9999 Gold 0.0400 oz. AGW, 13.9 mm. **Ruler:** Elizabeth II **Series:** Traders of the World **Subject:** Venetians **Obv:** Crowned bust right **Rev:** Pair of oysters with pearls, Venetian canal scene

Date	Mintage	F	VF	XF	Unc	BU
1997 Proof	Est. 15,000		Value: 45.00			

KM# 614   1/25 CROWN
1.2440 g., 0.9999 Gold 0.0400 oz. AGW, 13.9 mm. **Ruler:** Elizabeth II **Series:** Traders of the World **Subject:** Portuguese **Obv:** Crowned bust right **Rev:** Gold ingots and Portuguese ship

Date	Mintage	F	VF	XF	Unc	BU
1997 Proof	Est. 15,000		Value: 45.00			

KM# 616   1/25 CROWN
1.2440 g., 0.9999 Gold 0.0400 oz. AGW, 13.9 mm. **Ruler:** Elizabeth II **Series:** Traders of the World **Subject:** Spanish **Obv:** Crowned bust right **Rev:** Tobacco leaves, ship, map and gems

Date	Mintage	F	VF	XF	Unc	BU
1997 Proof	Est. 15,000		Value: 45.00			

KM# 618   1/25 CROWN
1.2440 g., 0.9999 Gold 0.0400 oz. AGW, 13.9 mm. **Ruler:** Elizabeth II **Series:** Traders of the World **Subject:** English **Obv:** Crowned bust right **Rev:** Profile of Queen above fighting ships

Date	Mintage	F	VF	XF	Unc	BU
1997 Proof	Est. 15,000		Value: 45.00			

KM# 620   1/25 CROWN
1.2440 g., 0.9999 Gold 0.0400 oz. AGW, 13.9 mm. **Ruler:** Elizabeth II **Series:** Traders of the World **Subject:** Captain Bligh **Obv:** Crowned bust right **Rev:** Figure sitting on rock on beach, ship in background

Date	Mintage	F	VF	XF	Unc	BU
1997 Proof	Est. 15,000		Value: 45.00			

KM# 622 1/25 CROWN
1.2440 g., 0.9999 Gold 0.0400 oz. AGW **Series:** Traders of the World **Subject:** Captain Cook **Obv:** Crowned bust right **Rev:** Beaver on rock, ship in background

Date	Mintage	F	VF	XF	Unc	BU
1997 Proof	Est. 15,000				Value: 45.00	

KM# 649 1/25 CROWN
1.2440 g., 0.9999 Gold 0.0400 oz. AGW, 13.9 mm. **Ruler:** Elizabeth II **Subject:** The Tale of Peter Rabbit **Obv:** Crowned bust right **Rev:** Standing rabbit facing

Date	Mintage	F	VF	XF	Unc	BU
1998 Proof	Est. 25,000				Value: 45.00	

KM# 649a 1/25 CROWN
1.2441 g., 0.9950 Platinum 0.0398 oz. APW, 13.9 mm. **Ruler:** Elizabeth II **Subject:** The Tale of Peter Rabbit **Obv:** Crowned bust right **Rev:** Standing rabbit facing

Date	Mintage	F	VF	XF	Unc	BU
1998 Proof	Est. 7,500				Value: 70.00	

KM# 657 1/25 CROWN
1.2441 g., 0.9999 Gold 0.0400 oz. AGW, 13.9 mm. **Ruler:** Elizabeth II **Subject:** Chrysanthemum **Obv:** Crowned bust right **Rev:** Three blossoms

Date	Mintage	F	VF	XF	Unc	BU
1998 Proof	Est. 25,000				Value: 45.00	

KM# 662 1/25 CROWN
1.2441 g., 0.9999 Gold 0.0400 oz. AGW, 13.9 mm. **Ruler:** Elizabeth II **Subject:** Britannia **Obv:** Crowned bust right **Rev:** Helmeted head right

Date	Mintage	F	VF	XF	Unc	BU
1998 Proof	Est. 10,000				Value: 45.00	

KM# 663 1/25 CROWN
1.2441 g., 0.9999 Gold 0.0400 oz. AGW, 13.9 mm. **Ruler:** Elizabeth II **Subject:** Juno **Obv:** Crowned bust right **Rev:** Head facing

Date	Mintage	F	VF	XF	Unc	BU
1998 Proof	Est. 10,000				Value: 45.00	

KM# 664 1/25 CROWN
1.2441 g., 0.9999 Gold 0.0400 oz. AGW, 13.9 mm. **Ruler:** Elizabeth II **Subject:** Athena **Obv:** Crowned bust right **Rev:** Helmeted head right

Date	Mintage	F	VF	XF	Unc	BU
1998 Proof	Est. 10,000				Value: 45.00	

KM# 665 1/25 CROWN
1.2441 g., 0.9999 Gold 0.0400 oz. AGW, 13.9 mm. **Subject:** Arethusa **Obv:** Crowned bust right **Rev:** Head left with dolphins

Date	Mintage	F	VF	XF	Unc	BU
1998 Proof	Est. 10,000				Value: 45.00	

KM# 678 1/25 CROWN
1.2441 g., 0.9999 Gold 0.0400 oz. AGW, 13.9 mm. **Ruler:** Elizabeth II **Obv:** Crowned bust right **Rev:** Paddington with suitcase

Date	Mintage	F	VF	XF	Unc	BU
1998 Proof	Est. 7,500				Value: 45.00	

KM# 678a 1/25 CROWN
1.2440 g., 0.9950 Platinum 0.0398 oz. APW, 13.9 mm. **Ruler:** Elizabeth II **Obv:** Crowned bust right **Rev:** Paddington with suitcase

Date	Mintage	F	VF	XF	Unc	BU
1998 Proof	Est. 5,000				Value: 70.00	

KM# 691 1/25 CROWN
1.2440 g., 0.9999 Gold 0.0400 oz. AGW, 13.9 mm. **Ruler:** Elizabeth II **Series:** Traders of the World **Subject:** Phoenecians, 200BC-600AD **Obv:** Crowned bust right **Rev:** Phoenician Galley, shells below

Date	Mintage	F	VF	XF	Unc	BU
1998 Proof	Est. 10,000				Value: 45.00	

KM# 693 1/25 CROWN
1.2440 g., 0.9999 Gold 0.0400 oz. AGW, 13.9 mm. **Ruler:** Elizabeth II **Series:** Traders of the World **Subject:** Vikings **Obv:** Crowned bust right **Rev:** Viking ship (900 AD), pair of fish

Date	Mintage	F	VF	XF	Unc	BU
1998 Proof	Est. 10,000				Value: 45.00	

KM# 695 1/25 CROWN
1.2440 g., 0.9999 Gold 0.0400 oz. AGW, 13.9 mm. **Ruler:** Elizabeth II **Series:** Traders of the World **Subject:** Marco Polo, 1254-1324 **Obv:** Crowned bust right **Rev:** Bust at right facing, ship at left

Date	Mintage	F	VF	XF	Unc	BU
1998 Proof	Est. 10,000				Value: 45.00	

KM# 697 1/25 CROWN
1.2440 g., 0.9999 Gold 0.0400 oz. AGW, 13.9 mm. **Ruler:** Elizabeth II **Series:** Traders of the World **Subject:** Hanseatic League Nations **Obv:** Crowned bust right **Rev:** Hanseatic Kogge (circa 1350), coins above ship

Date	Mintage	F	VF	XF	Unc	BU
1998 Proof	Est. 10,000				Value: 45.00	

KM# 699 1/25 CROWN
1.2440 g., 0.9999 Gold 0.0400 oz. AGW, 13.9 mm. **Ruler:** Elizabeth II **Series:** Traders of the World **Subject:** Chinese **Obv:** Crowned bust right **Rev:** Chinese Junk (1400s)

Date	Mintage	F	VF	XF	Unc	BU
1998 Proof	Est. 10,000				Value: 45.00	

KM# 701 1/25 CROWN
1.2440 g., 0.9999 Gold 0.0400 oz. AGW, 13.9 mm. **Ruler:** Elizabeth II **Series:** Traders of the World **Subject:** Christopher Columbus, 1451-1506 **Obv:** Crowned bust right **Rev:** Bust at left looking right and ship

Date	Mintage	F	VF	XF	Unc	BU
1998 Proof	Est. 10,000				Value: 45.00	

KM# 703 1/25 CROWN
1.2440 g., 0.9999 Gold 0.0400 oz. AGW, 13.9 mm. **Ruler:** Elizabeth II **Series:** Traders of the World **Subject:** Sir Walter Raleigh, 1552-1618 **Obv:** Crowned bust right **Rev:** Figure standing on beach, ship in background

Date	Mintage	F	VF	XF	Unc	BU
1998 Proof	Est. 10,000				Value: 45.00	

KM# 705 1/25 CROWN
1.2440 g., 0.9999 Gold 0.0400 oz. AGW, 13.9 mm. **Ruler:** Elizabeth II **Series:** Traders of the World **Obv:** Crowned bust right **Rev:** Sinking ships at the Boston Tea Party (1773), tea leaf

Date	Mintage	F	VF	XF	Unc	BU
1998 Proof	Est. 10,000				Value: 45.00	

KM# 707 1/25 CROWN
1.2440 g., 0.9999 Gold 0.0400 oz. AGW **Ruler:** Elizabeth II **Series:** Evolution of Mankind **Subject:** Australopithecus - Lucy **Obv:** Crowned head right **Rev:** Upright figure left, brain depiction at left

Date	Mintage	F	VF	XF	Unc	BU
1998 Proof	Est. 15,000				Value: 45.00	

KM# 709 1/25 CROWN
1.2440 g., 0.9999 Gold 0.0400 oz. AGW, 13.9 mm. **Ruler:** Elizabeth II **Series:** Traders of the World **Subject:** Homo Habilis **Obv:** Crowned head right **Rev:** Squatting figure using tools

Date	Mintage	F	VF	XF	Unc	BU
1998 Proof	Est. 15,000				Value: 45.00	

KM# 711 1/25 CROWN
1.2440 g., 0.9999 Gold 0.0400 oz. AGW, 13.9 mm. **Ruler:** Elizabeth II **Series:** Traders of the World **Subject:** Homo Erectus **Obv:** Crowned bust right **Rev:** Cave people using fire

Date	Mintage	F	VF	XF	Unc	BU
1998 Proof	Est. 15,000				Value: 45.00	

KM# 713 1/25 CROWN
1.2440 g., 0.9999 Gold 0.0400 oz. AGW, 13.9 mm. **Ruler:** Elizabeth II **Series:** Evolution of Mankind **Subject:** Gibraltar Skull **Obv:** Crowned bust right **Rev:** Caveman, skull and 'the rock'

Date	Mintage	F	VF	XF	Unc	BU
1998 Proof	Est. 15,000				Value: 45.00	

KM# 715 1/25 CROWN
1.2440 g., 0.9999 Gold 0.0400 oz. AGW, 13.9 mm. **Ruler:** Elizabeth II **Series:** Evolution of Mankind **Subject:** Neanderthal Man **Obv:** Crowned bust right **Rev:** Early man at burial scene, skull

Date	Mintage	F	VF	XF	Unc	BU
1998 Proof	Est. 15,000				Value: 45.00	

KM# 717 1/25 CROWN
1.2440 g., 0.9999 Gold 0.0400 oz. AGW, 13.9 mm. **Ruler:** Elizabeth II **Series:** Evolution of Mankind **Subject:** Homo Sapiens **Obv:** Crowned bust right **Rev:** Early man doing cave painting

Date	Mintage	F	VF	XF	Unc	BU
1998 Proof	Est. 15,000				Value: 45.00	

KM# 719 1/25 CROWN
1.2440 g., 0.9999 Gold 0.0400 oz. AGW, 13.9 mm. **Ruler:** Elizabeth II **Series:** Evolution of Mankind **Subject:** Homo Sapiens Hunting Mammoth **Obv:** Crowhed bust right **Rev:** Figures spearing mammoth

Date	Mintage	F	VF	XF	Unc	BU
1998 Proof	Est. 15,000				Value: 45.00	

KM# 722 1/25 CROWN
1.2440 g., 0.9999 Gold 0.0400 oz. AGW, 13.9 mm. **Ruler:** Elizabeth II **Series:** Evolution of Mankind **Subject:** Theory of Evolution **Obv:** Crowned bust right **Rev:** Illustrated theory of evolution

Date	Mintage	F	VF	XF	Unc	BU
1998 Proof	Est. 15,000				Value: 45.00	

KM# 723 1/25 CROWN
1.2440 g., 0.9999 Gold 0.0400 oz. AGW, 13.9 mm. **Ruler:** Elizabeth II **Series:** Evolution of Mankind **Subject:** The Common Ancestry of Man and Ape **Obv:** Crowned bust right **Rev:** Human and primate mothers with young

Date	Mintage	F	VF	XF	Unc	BU
1998 Proof	Est. 15,000				Value: 45.00	

KM# 725 1/25 CROWN
1.2440 g., 0.9999 Gold 0.0400 oz. AGW, 13.9 mm. **Ruler:** Elizabeth II **Series:** Evolution of Mankind **Subject:** Charles Darwin **Obv:** Crowned bust right **Rev:** Bust facing, neanderthal and space shuttle

Date	Mintage	F	VF	XF	Unc	BU
1998 Proof	Est. 15,000				Value: 45.00	

KM# 727 1/25 CROWN
1.2440 g., 0.9999 Gold 0.0400 oz. AGW, 13.9 mm. **Ruler:** Elizabeth II **Series:** Evolution of Mankind **Subject:** Raymond Dart **Obv:** Crowned bust right **Rev:** Bust at left looking at skull on right

Date	Mintage	F	VF	XF	Unc	BU
1998 Proof	Est. 15,000				Value: 45.00	

KM# 729 1/25 CROWN
1.2440 g., 0.9999 Gold 0.0400 oz. AGW, 13.9 mm. **Ruler:** Elizabeth II **Series:** Evolution of Mankind **Subject:** 20th Century Homo Sapiens **Obv:** Crowned bust right **Rev:** Five depictions of evolution

Date	Mintage	F	VF	XF	Unc	BU
1998 Proof	Est. 15,000				Value: 45.00	

KM# 779.1 1/25 CROWN
1.2440 g., 0.9999 Gold 0.0400 oz. AGW, 13.9 mm. **Ruler:** Elizabeth II **Subject:** 1999 The Year of the Rabbit **Obv:** Crowned bust right **Rev:** Rabbit reading, sparrow and chinese characters

Date	Mintage	F	VF	XF	Unc	BU
1999 Proof	Est. 5,000				Value: 45.00	

KM# 779.1a 1/25 CROWN
1.2400 g., 0.9950 Platinum 0.0397 oz. APW, 13.9 mm. **Ruler:** Elizabeth II **Subject:** 1999 The Year of the Rabbit **Obv:** Crowned bust right **Rev:** Rabbit reading, sparrow and chinese characters

Date	Mintage	F	VF	XF	Unc	BU
1999 Proof	Est. 3,000				Value: 70.00	

KM# 779.2 1/25 CROWN
1.2440 g., 0.9999 Gold 0.0400 oz. AGW, 13.9 mm. **Ruler:** Elizabeth II **Subject:** The Year of the Rabbit **Obv:** Crowned bust right **Rev:** Rabbit reading, sparrow; without Chinese characters

Date	Mintage	F	VF	XF	Unc	BU
1999 Proof	Inc. above				Value: 45.00	

KM# 779.2a 1/25 CROWN
1.2400 g., 0.9950 Platinum 0.0397 oz. APW **Ruler:** Elizabeth II **Subject:** The Year of the Rabbit **Obv:** Crowned bust right **Rev:** Rabbit reading, sparrow; without Chinese characters

Date	Mintage	F	VF	XF	Unc	BU
1999 Proof	Inc. above				Value: 70.00	

KM# 50 1/10 CROWN
3.1100 g., 0.9999 Gold 0.1000 oz. AGW, 17.95 mm. **Ruler:** Elizabeth II **Series:** Barcelona Olympics **Obv:** Crowned bust right **Rev:** Discus thrower

Date	Mintage	F	VF	XF	Unc	BU
1991 Proof	Est. 20,000				Value: 95.00	
1992 Proof	Est. 20,000				Value: 95.00	

KM# 51 1/10 CROWN
3.1100 g., 0.9999 Gold 0.1000 oz. AGW, 17.95 mm. **Ruler:** Elizabeth II **Series:** Barcelona Olympics **Obv:** Crowned bust right **Rev:** Chariot racing

Date	Mintage	F	VF	XF	Unc	BU
1991 Proof	Est. 20,000				Value: 95.00	
1992 Proof	Est. 20,000				Value: 95.00	

KM# 52 1/10 CROWN
3.1100 g., 0.9999 Gold 0.1000 oz. AGW, 17.95 mm. **Ruler:** Elizabeth II **Series:** Barcelona Olympics **Obv:** Crowned bust right **Rev:** Runners

Date	Mintage	F	VF	XF	Unc	BU
1991 Proof	Est. 20,000				Value: 95.00	
1992 Proof	Est. 20,000				Value: 95.00	

KM# 53 1/10 CROWN
3.1100 g., 0.9999 Gold 0.1000 oz. AGW, 17.95 mm. **Ruler:** Elizabeth II **Series:** Barcelona Olympics **Obv:** Crowned bust right **Rev:** Javelin thrower

Date	Mintage	F	VF	XF	Unc	BU
1991 Proof	Est. 20,000				Value: 95.00	
1992 Proof	Est. 20,000				Value: 95.00	

KM# 54 1/10 CROWN
3.1100 g., 0.9999 Gold 0.1000 oz. AGW, 17.95 mm. **Ruler:** Elizabeth II **Series:** Barcelona Olympics **Obv:** Crowned bust right **Rev:** Wrestlers

Date	Mintage	F	VF	XF	Unc	BU
1991 Proof	Est. 20,000				Value: 95.00	
1992 Proof	Est. 20,000				Value: 95.00	

KM# 55 1/10 CROWN
3.1100 g., 0.9999 Gold 0.1000 oz. AGW, 17.95 mm. **Ruler:** Elizabeth II **Series:** Barcelona Olympics **Obv:** Crowned bust right **Rev:** Boxers

Date	Mintage	F	VF	XF	Unc	BU
1991 Proof	Est. 20,000				Value: 95.00	
1992 Proof	Est. 20,000				Value: 95.00	

KM# 56 1/10 CROWN
3.1100 g., 0.9999 Gold 0.1000 oz. AGW, 17.95 mm. **Ruler:** Elizabeth II **Series:** Barcelona Olympics **Obv:** Crowned bust right **Rev:** Long jumper

Date	Mintage	F	VF	XF	Unc	BU
1991 Proof	Est. 20,000				Value: 95.00	
1992 Proof	Est. 20,000				Value: 95.00	

KM# 57 1/10 CROWN
3.1100 g., 0.9999 Gold 0.1000 oz. AGW, 17.95 mm. **Ruler:** Elizabeth II **Series:** Barcelona Olympics **Obv:** Crowned bust right **Rev:** Olympic victor

Date	Mintage	F	VF	XF	Unc	BU
1991 Proof	Est. 20,000				Value: 95.00	
1992 Proof	Est. 20,000				Value: 95.00	

KM# 125 1/10 CROWN
3.1100 g., 0.9999 Gold 0.1000 oz. AGW, 17.95 mm. **Ruler:** Elizabeth II **Subject:** Japanese Royal Wedding

Date	Mintage	F	VF	XF	Unc	BU
1993 Proof	Est. 10,000				Value: 95.00	

KM# 203 1/10 CROWN
3.1100 g., 0.9999 Gold 0.1000 oz. AGW, 17.95 mm. **Ruler:** Elizabeth II **Series:** Peter Rabbit Centennial **Subject:** The Tale of Peter Rabbit **Obv:** Crowned bust right **Rev:** Rabbit eating carrots, sparrow on handle

Date	Mintage	F	VF	XF	Unc	BU
1993 Proof	Est. 20,000				Value: 95.00	

KM# 203a 1/10 CROWN
3.1100 g., 0.9990 Platinum 0.0999 oz. APW **Ruler:** Elizabeth II **Series:** Peter Rabbit Centennial **Subject:** The Tale of Peter Rabbit **Obv:** Crowned bust right **Rev:** Rabbit eating carrots, sparrow on handle

Date	Mintage	F	VF	XF	Unc	BU
1993 Proof	Est. 5,000				Value: 200	

KM# 207 1/10 CROWN
3.1100 g., 0.9990 Platinum 0.0999 oz. APW **Ruler:** Elizabeth II **Series:** Peter Rabbit Centennial **Subject:** The Tale of Peter Rabbit **Obv:** Crowned bust right **Rev:** Mrs. Tiggy-Winkel ironing

Date	Mintage	F	VF	XF	Unc	BU
1993 Proof	Est. 20,000				Value: 200	

KM# 211 1/10 CROWN
3.1100 g., 0.9990 Platinum 0.0999 oz. APW **Ruler:** Elizabeth II
Series: Peter Rabbit Centennial **Subject:** The Tale of Peter
Rabbit **Obv:** Crowned bust right **Rev:** Jeremy Fisher fishing

Date	Mintage	F	VF	XF	Unc	BU
1993 Proof	Est. 20,000		Value: 200			

KM# 215 1/10 CROWN
3.1100 g., 0.9990 Platinum 0.0999 oz. APW **Ruler:** Elizabeth II
Series: Peter Rabbit Centennial **Subject:** The Tale of Peter
Rabbit **Obv:** Crowned bust right **Rev:** Tom Kitten with mother cat

Date	Mintage	F	VF	XF	Unc	BU
1993 Proof	Est. 20,000		Value: 200			

KM# 219 1/10 CROWN
3.1100 g., 0.9990 Platinum 0.0999 oz. APW **Ruler:** Elizabeth II
Series: Peter Rabbit Centennial **Subject:** The Tale of Peter
Rabbit **Obv:** Crowned bust right **Rev:** Benjamin Bunny wearing
hat and holding coat

Date	Mintage	F	VF	XF	Unc	BU
1993 Proof	Est. 20,000		Value: 200			

KM# 223 1/10 CROWN
3.1100 g., 0.9990 Platinum 0.0999 oz. APW **Ruler:** Elizabeth II
Series: Peter Rabbit Centennial **Subject:** The Tale of Peter
Rabbit **Obv:** Crowned bust right **Rev:** Jemima Puddle Duck
talking with fox

Date	Mintage	F	VF	XF	Unc	BU
1993 Proof	Est. 20,000		Value: 200			

KM# 439 1/10 CROWN
3.1100 g., 0.9990 Platinum 0.0999 oz. APW **Ruler:** Elizabeth II
Series: Peter Rabbit Centennial **Subject:** The Tale of Peter
Rabbit **Obv:** Crowned bust right **Rev:** Mother Rabbit and bunnies

Date	Mintage	F	VF	XF	Unc	BU
1994 Proof	Est. 20,000		Value: 200			

KM# 439a 1/10 CROWN
3.1103 g., 0.9950 Platinum 0.0995 oz. APW **Ruler:** Elizabeth II
Series: Peter Rabbit Centennial **Obv:** Crowned bust right
Rev: Mother Rabbit and bunnies

Date	Mintage	F	VF	XF	Unc	BU
1994 Proof	Est. 5,000		Value: 200			

KM# 369 1/10 CROWN
3.1103 g., 0.9999 Gold 0.1000 oz. AGW, 17.95 mm.
Ruler: Elizabeth II **Subject:** Roses **Obv:** Crowned bust right

Date	Mintage	F	VF	XF	Unc	BU
1996 Proof	Est. 20,000		Value: 95.00			

KM# 377 1/10 CROWN
3.1103 g., 0.9999 Gold 0.1000 oz. AGW, 17.95 mm.
Ruler: Elizabeth II **Series:** Peter Rabbit Centennial **Subject:** The
Tale of Peter Rabbit **Obv:** Crowned bust right **Rev:** Rabbit
escaping the garden

Date	Mintage	F	VF	XF	Unc	BU
1996 Proof	Est. 20,000		Value: 95.00			

KM# 377a 1/10 CROWN
3.1259 g., 0.9950 Platinum 0.1000 oz. APW **Ruler:** Elizabeth II
Series: Peter Rabbit Centennial **Subject:** The Tale of Peter
Rabbit **Obv:** Crowned bust right **Rev:** Rabbit escaping the garden

Date	Mintage	F	VF	XF	Unc	BU
1996 Proof	Est. 10,000		Value: 200			

KM# 391 1/10 CROWN
3.1103 g., 0.9999 Gold 0.1000 oz. AGW, 17.95 mm.
Ruler: Elizabeth II **Series:** Centenary of the Cinema
Subject: Grace Kelly - actress, 1929-82 **Obv:** Crowned bust right
Rev: Bust 3/4 facing, dates

Date	Mintage	F	VF	XF	Unc	BU
1996 Proof	Est. 20,000		Value: 95.00			

KM# 396 1/10 CROWN
3.1103 g., 0.9999 Gold 0.1000 oz. AGW, 17.95 mm. **Ruler:**
Elizabeth II **Series:** Centenary of the Cinema **Subject:** James Dean
- actor, 1931-55 **Obv:** Crowned bust right **Rev:** Bust facing, dates

Date	Mintage	F	VF	XF	Unc	BU
1996 Proof	20,000		Value: 95.00			

KM# 401 1/10 CROWN
3.1103 g., 0.9999 Gold 0.1000 oz. AGW, 17.95 mm. **Ruler:**
Elizabeth II **Series:** Centenary of the Cinema **Subject:** Marilyn
Monroe - actress, 1926-62 **Obv:** Crowned bust right **Rev:** Bust
looking back over shoulder, dates

Date	Mintage	F	VF	XF	Unc	BU
1996 Proof	Est. 20,000		Value: 95.00			

KM# 406 1/10 CROWN
3.1103 g., 0.9999 Gold 0.1000 oz. AGW, 17.95 mm.
Ruler: Elizabeth II **Series:** Centenary of the Cinema
Subject: Audrey Hepburn - actress, 1929-93 **Obv:** Crowned bust
right **Rev:** Bust facing, dates

Date	Mintage	F	VF	XF	Unc	BU
1996 Proof	Est. 20,000		Value: 95.00			

KM# 406a 1/10 CROWN
3.1103 g., 0.9950 Platinum 0.0995 oz. APW **Ruler:** Elizabeth II
Series: Centenary of the Cinema **Subject:** Audrey Hepburn -
actress, 1929-93 **Obv:** Crowned bust right **Rev:** Bust facing, dates

Date	Mintage	F	VF	XF	Unc	BU
1996 Proof	Est. 1,000		Value: 200			

KM# 411 1/10 CROWN
3.1103 g., 0.9999 Gold 0.1000 oz. AGW, 17.95 mm. **Ruler:**
Elizabeth II **Series:** Centenary of the Cinema **Subject:** Bruce
Lee **Obv:** Crowned bust right **Rev:** Kickboxer and chinese dragon

Date	Mintage	F	VF	XF	Unc	BU
1996 Proof	Est. 20,000		Value: 95.00			

KM# 416 1/10 CROWN
3.1103 g., 0.9999 Gold 0.1000 oz. AGW, 17.95 mm.
Ruler: Elizabeth II **Series:** Centenary of the Cinema
Subject: Charlie Chaplan - actor, 1889-1977 **Obv:** Crowned bust
right **Rev:** Standing central figure with cane, dates

Date	Mintage	F	VF	XF	Unc	BU
1996 Proof	Est. 20,000		Value: 95.00			

KM# 421 1/10 CROWN
3.1103 g., 0.9999 Gold 0.1000 oz. AGW, 17.95 mm.
Ruler: Elizabeth II **Series:** Centenary of the Cinema
Subject: Gone With The Wind **Obv:** Crowned bust right
Rev: Rhett Butler and Scarlett O'Hara

Date	Mintage	F	VF	XF	Unc	BU
1996 Proof	Est. 20,000		Value: 95.00			

KM# 426 1/10 CROWN
3.1103 g., 0.9999 Gold 0.1000 oz. AGW, 17.95 mm.
Ruler: Elizabeth II **Series:** Centenary of the Cinema
Obv: Crowned bust right **Rev:** The Flintstones

Date	Mintage	F	VF	XF	Unc	BU
1996 Proof	Est. 20,000		Value: 95.00			

KM# 446 1/10 CROWN
3.1103 g., 0.9999 Gold 0.1000 oz. AGW, 17.95 mm. **Ruler:**
Elizabeth II **Subject:** Lord Buddha **Rev:** Seated figure facing

Date	Mintage	F	VF	XF	Unc	BU
1996 Proof	Est. 10,000		Value: 95.00			

KM# 455 1/10 CROWN
3.1103 g., 0.9999 Gold 0.1000 oz. AGW, 17.95 mm. **Ruler:**
Elizabeth II **Series:** Centenary of the Cinema **Subject:** Wizard
of Oz **Obv:** Crowned bust right **Rev:** Wizard of Oz characters

Date	Mintage	F	VF	XF	Unc	BU
1996 Proof	Est. 20,000		Value: 95.00			

KM# 459 1/10 CROWN
3.1103 g., 0.9999 Gold 0.1000 oz. AGW, 17.95 mm.
Ruler: Elizabeth II **Series:** Centenary of the Cinema **Subject:**
Marx Brothers **Obv:** Crowned bust right **Rev:** Three busts left

Date	Mintage	F	VF	XF	Unc	BU
1996 Proof	Est. 20,000		Value: 95.00			

KM# 463 1/10 CROWN
3.1103 g., 0.9999 Gold 0.1000 oz. AGW, 17.95 mm.
Ruler: Elizabeth II **Series:** Centenary of the Cinema
Subject: Elvis Presley **Obv:** Crowned bust right **Rev:** Guitar
beneath and behind bust 3/4 left

Date	Mintage	F	VF	XF	Unc	BU
1996 Proof	Est. 20,000		Value: 95.00			

KM# 467 1/10 CROWN
3.1103 g., 0.9999 Gold 0.1000 oz. AGW, 17.95 mm.
Ruler: Elizabeth II **Series:** Centenary of the Cinema **Subject:**
Casablanca **Obv:** Crowned bust right **Rev:** Bogart and Bergman

Date	Mintage	F	VF	XF	Unc	BU
1996 Proof	Est. 20,000		Value: 95.00			

KM# 471 1/10 CROWN
3.1103 g., 0.9999 Gold 0.1000 oz. AGW, 17.95 mm.
Ruler: Elizabeth II **Series:** Centenary of the Cinema
Obv: Crowned bust right **Rev:** E.T.

Date	Mintage	F	VF	XF	Unc	BU
1996 Proof	Est. 20,000		Value: 95.00			

KM# 475 1/10 CROWN
3.1103 g., 0.9999 Gold 0.1000 oz. AGW, 17.95 mm.
Ruler: Elizabeth II **Series:** Centenary of the Cinema **Subject:**
Alfred Hitchcock - Producer/Director, 1899-1980 **Obv:** Crowned
bust right **Rev:** Bust facing looking at bird on left shoulder

Date	Mintage	F	VF	XF	Unc	BU
1996 Proof	Est. 20,000		Value: 95.00			

KM# 520 1/10 CROWN
3.1103 g., 0.9999 Gold 0.1000 oz. AGW, 17.95 mm.
Ruler: Elizabeth II **Subject:** Tale of Peter Rabbit **Obv:** Crowned
bust right **Rev:** Standing rabbit facing

Date	Mintage	F	VF	XF	Unc	BU
1997 Proof	Est. 20,000		Value: 95.00			

KM# 520a 1/10 CROWN
3.1259 g., 0.9950 Platinum 0.1000 oz. APW **Ruler:** Elizabeth II
Subject: Tale of Peter Rabbit **Obv:** Crowned bust right
Rev: Standing rabbit facing

Date	Mintage	F	VF	XF	Unc	BU
1997 Proof	Est. 5,000		Value: 200			

KM# 538 1/10 CROWN
3.1100 g., 0.9999 Gold 0.1000 oz. AGW, 17.95 mm.
Ruler: Elizabeth II **Obv:** Crowned bust right **Rev:** Peonies

Date	Mintage	F	VF	XF	Unc	BU
1997 Proof	Est. 20,000		Value: 95.00			

KM# 542 1/10 CROWN
3.1100 g., 0.9999 Gold 0.1000 oz. AGW, 17.95 mm.
Ruler: Elizabeth II **Subject:** Nefertiti **Obv:** Crowned bust right
Rev: Head right

Date	Mintage	F	VF	XF	Unc	BU
1997 Proof	Est. 7,500		Value: 95.00			

KM# 546 1/10 CROWN
3.1100 g., 0.9999 Gold 0.1000 oz. AGW, 17.95 mm.
Ruler: Elizabeth II **Subject:** Cleopatra **Obv:** Crowned bust right
Rev: Head facing

Date	Mintage	F	VF	XF	Unc	BU
1997 Proof	Est. 7,500		Value: 95.00			

KM# 550 1/10 CROWN
3.1100 g., 0.9999 Gold 0.1000 oz. AGW, 17.95 mm.
Ruler: Elizabeth II **Subject:** Europa **Obv:** Crowned bust right
Rev: Head 3/4 left

Date	Mintage	F	VF	XF	Unc	BU
1997 Proof	Est. 7,500		Value: 95.00			

KM# 554 1/10 CROWN
3.1100 g., 0.9999 Gold 0.1000 oz. AGW, 17.95 mm.
Ruler: Elizabeth II **Subject:** Liberty **Obv:** Crowned bust right
Rev: Laureate head right

Date	Mintage	F	VF	XF	Unc	BU
1997 Proof	Est. 7,500		Value: 95.00			

KM# 651 1/10 CROWN
3.1100 g., 0.9999 Gold 0.1000 oz. AGW, 17.95 mm.
Ruler: Elizabeth II **Subject:** Tale of Peter Rabbit **Obv:** Crowned
bust right **Rev:** Standing rabbit facing, sparrow

Date	Mintage	F	VF	XF	Unc	BU
1998 Proof	Est. 20,000		Value: 95.00			

KM# 651a 1/10 CROWN
3.1103 g., 0.9950 Platinum 0.0995 oz. APW **Ruler:** Elizabeth II
Subject: Tale of Peter Rabbit **Obv:** Crowned bust right
Rev: Standing rabbit facing, sparrow

Date	Mintage	F	VF	XF	Unc	BU
1998 Proof	Est. 5,000		Value: 200			

KM# 658 1/10 CROWN
3.1100 g., 0.9999 Gold 0.1000 oz. AGW, 17.95 mm.
Ruler: Elizabeth II **Subject:** Chrysanthemum **Obv:** Crowned
bust right **Rev:** Three blossoms

Date	Mintage	F	VF	XF	Unc	BU
1998 Proof	Est. 20,000		Value: 95.00			

KM# 666 1/10 CROWN
3.1100 g., 0.9999 Gold 0.1000 oz. AGW, 17.95 mm.
Ruler: Elizabeth II **Subject:** Brittania **Obv:** Crowned bust right
Rev: Helmeted head right

Date	Mintage	F	VF	XF	Unc	BU
1998 Proof	Est. 7,500		Value: 95.00			

KM# 667 1/10 CROWN
3.1100 g., 0.9999 Gold 0.1000 oz. AGW, 17.95 mm.
Ruler: Elizabeth II **Subject:** Juno **Obv:** Crowned bust right
Rev: Head 3/4 facing

Date	Mintage	F	VF	XF	Unc	BU
1998 Proof	Est. 7,500		Value: 95.00			

KM# 668 1/10 CROWN
3.1100 g., 0.9999 Gold 0.1000 oz. AGW, 17.95 mm.
Ruler: Elizabeth II **Subject:** Athena **Obv:** Crowned bust right
Rev: Helmeted head right

Date	Mintage	F	VF	XF	Unc	BU
1998 Proof	Est. 7,500		Value: 95.00			

KM# 669 1/10 CROWN
3.1100 g., 0.9999 Gold 0.1000 oz. AGW, 17.95 mm.
Ruler: Elizabeth II **Subject:** Arethusa **Obv:** Crowned bust right
Rev: Head left with dolphins

Date	Mintage	F	VF	XF	Unc	BU
1998 Proof	Est. 7,500		Value: 95.00			

KM# 679 1/10 CROWN
3.1100 g., 0.9999 Gold 0.1000 oz. AGW, 17.95 mm.
Ruler: Elizabeth II **Subject:** Paddington Bear **Obv:** Crowned
bust right **Rev:** Bear with suitcase

Date	Mintage	F	VF	XF	Unc	BU
1998 Proof	Est. 7,500		Value: 95.00			

KM# 679a 1/10 CROWN
3.1103 g., 0.9950 Platinum 0.0995 oz. APW **Ruler:** Elizabeth II
Subject: Paddington Bear **Obv:** Crowned bust right **Rev:** Bear
with suitcase

Date	Mintage	F	VF	XF	Unc	BU
1998 Proof	Est. 5,000		Value: 200			

KM# 48 1/5 CROWN
6.2200 g., 0.9990 Gold 0.1998 oz. AGW, 22 mm.
Ruler: Elizabeth II **Series:** 150th Anniversary of the First
Adhesive Postage Stamp **Subject:** Penny Black Stamp
Obv: Crowned bust right **Rev:** Heads flank stamp design

Date	Mintage	F	VF	XF	Unc	BU
1990 Proof	Est. 5,000		Value: 215			

KM# 76 1/5 CROWN
6.2200 g., 0.9990 Gold 0.1998 oz. AGW, 22 mm.
Ruler: Elizabeth II **Series:** World Cup Soccer **Obv:** Crowned bust
right **Rev:** Italian flag

Date	Mintage	F	VF	XF	Unc	BU
1990 Proof	Est. 5,000		Value: 215			

KM# 76a   1/5 CROWN
6.2200 g., 0.9950 Platinum 0.1990 oz. APW. **Ruler:** Elizabeth II
Series: World Cup Soccer **Obv:** Crowned bust right **Rev:** Italian flag

Date	Mintage	F	VF	XF	Unc	BU
1990 Proof	Est. 1,000 Value: 400					

KM# 77   1/5 CROWN
6.2200 g., 0.9999 Gold 0.1999 oz. AGW, 22 mm.
Ruler: Elizabeth II **Series:** World Cup Soccer **Obv:** Crowned bust right **Rev:** Map of Italy

Date	Mintage	F	VF	XF	Unc	BU
1990 Proof	Est. 5,000 Value: 215					

KM# 77a   1/5 CROWN
6.2200 g., 0.9950 Platinum 0.1990 oz. APW, 22 mm.
Ruler: Elizabeth II **Series:** World Cup Soccer **Obv:** Crowned bust right **Rev:** Map of Italy

Date	Mintage	F	VF	XF	Unc	BU
1990 Proof	Est. 1,000 Value: 400					

KM# 78   1/5 CROWN
6.2200 g., 0.9999 Gold 0.1999 oz. AGW, 22 mm.
Ruler: Elizabeth II **Series:** World Cup Soccer **Obv:** Crowned bust right **Rev:** Goalie catching ball

Date	Mintage	F	VF	XF	Unc	BU
1990 Proof	Est. 5,000 Value: 215					

KM# 78a   1/5 CROWN
6.2200 g., 0.9950 Platinum 0.1990 oz. APW **Ruler:** Elizabeth II
Series: World Cup Soccer **Obv:** Crowned bust right **Rev:** Goalie catching ball

Date	Mintage	F	VF	XF	Unc	BU
1990 Proof	Est. 1,000 Value: 400					

KM# 79   1/5 CROWN
6.2200 g., 0.9999 Gold 0.1999 oz. AGW, 22 mm.
Ruler: Elizabeth II **Series:** World Cup Soccer **Obv:** Crowned bust right **Rev:** One player

Date	Mintage	F	VF	XF	Unc	BU
1990 Proof	Est. 5,000 Value: 215					

KM# 79a   1/5 CROWN
6.2200 g., 0.9950 Platinum 0.1990 oz. APW **Ruler:** Elizabeth II
Series: World Cup Soccer **Obv:** Crowned bust right **Rev:** One player

Date	Mintage	F	VF	XF	Unc	BU
1990 Proof	Est. 1,000 Value: 400					

KM# 80   1/5 CROWN
6.2200 g., 0.9999 Gold 0.1999 oz. AGW, 22 mm.
Ruler: Elizabeth II **Series:** World Cup Soccer **Obv:** Crowned bust right **Rev:** Two players

Date	Mintage	F	VF	XF	Unc	BU
1990 Proof	Est. 5,000 Value: 215					

KM# 80a   1/5 CROWN
6.2200 g., 0.9950 Platinum 0.1990 oz. APW **Ruler:** Elizabeth II
Series: World Cup Soccer **Obv:** Crowned bust right **Rev:** Two players

Date	Mintage	F	VF	XF	Unc	BU
1990 Proof	Est. 1,000 Value: 400					

KM# 81   1/5 CROWN
6.2200 g., 0.9999 Gold 0.1999 oz. AGW, 22 mm.
Ruler: Elizabeth II **Series:** World Cup Soccer **Obv:** Crowned bust right **Rev:** Three players

Date	Mintage	F	VF	XF	Unc	BU
1990 Proof	Est. 5,000 Value: 215					

KM# 81a   1/5 CROWN
6.2200 g., 0.9950 Platinum 0.1990 oz. APW **Ruler:** Elizabeth II
Series: World Cup Soccer **Obv:** Crowned bust right **Rev:** Three players

Date	Mintage	F	VF	XF	Unc	BU
1990 Proof	Est. 1,000 Value: 400					

KM# 58   1/5 CROWN
6.2200 g., 0.9999 Gold 0.1999 oz. AGW, 22 mm.
Ruler: Elizabeth II **Series:** Barcelona Olympics **Obv:** Crowned bust right **Rev:** Discus thrower

Date	Mintage	F	VF	XF	Unc	BU
1991 Proof	Est. 5,000 Value: 200					
1992 Proof	Est. 5,000 Value: 200					

KM# 58a   1/5 CROWN
6.2200 g., 0.9950 Platinum 0.1990 oz. APW **Ruler:** Elizabeth II
Series: Barcelona Olympics **Obv:** Crowned bust right **Rev:** Discus thrower

Date	Mintage	F	VF	XF	Unc	BU
1991 Proof	Est. 1,000 Value: 400					

KM# 59   1/5 CROWN
6.2200 g., 0.9999 Gold 0.1999 oz. AGW, 22 mm.
Ruler: Elizabeth II **Series:** Barcelona Olympics **Obv:** Crowned bust right **Rev:** Chariot racing

Date	Mintage	F	VF	XF	Unc	BU
1991 Proof	Est. 5,000 Value: 200					
1992 Proof	Est. 5,000 Value: 200					

KM# 59a   1/5 CROWN
6.2200 g., 0.9950 Platinum 0.1990 oz. APW **Ruler:** Elizabeth II
Series: Barcelona Olympics **Obv:** Crowned bust right **Rev:** Chariot racing

Date	Mintage	F	VF	XF	Unc	BU
1991 Proof	Est. 1,000 Value: 400					

KM# 60   1/5 CROWN
6.2200 g., 0.9999 Gold 0.1999 oz. AGW, 22 mm.
Ruler: Elizabeth II **Series:** Barcelona Olympics **Obv:** Crowned bust right **Rev:** Runners

Date	Mintage	F	VF	XF	Unc	BU
1991 Proof	Est. 5,000 Value: 200					
1992 Proof	Est. 5,000 Value: 200					

KM# 60a   1/5 CROWN
6.2200 g., 0.9950 Platinum 0.1990 oz. APW **Ruler:** Elizabeth II
Series: Barcelona Olympics **Obv:** Crowned bust right **Rev:** Runners

Date	Mintage	F	VF	XF	Unc	BU
1991 Proof	Est. 1,000 Value: 400					

KM# 61   1/5 CROWN
6.2200 g., 0.9999 Gold 0.1999 oz. AGW, 22 mm.
Ruler: Elizabeth II **Series:** Barcelona Olympics **Obv:** Crowned bust right **Rev:** Javelin thrower

Date	Mintage	F	VF	XF	Unc	BU
1991 Proof	Est. 5,000 Value: 200					
1992 Proof	Est. 5,000 Value: 200					

KM# 61a   1/5 CROWN
6.2200 g., 0.9950 Platinum 0.1990 oz. APW **Ruler:** Elizabeth II
Series: Barcelona Olympics **Obv:** Crowned bust right **Rev:** Javelin thrower

Date	Mintage	F	VF	XF	Unc	BU
1991 Proof	Est. 1,000 Value: 400					

KM# 62   1/5 CROWN
6.2200 g., 0.9999 Gold 0.1999 oz. AGW, 22 mm.
Ruler: Elizabeth II **Series:** Barcelona Olympics **Obv:** Crowned bust right **Rev:** Wrestlers

Date	Mintage	F	VF	XF	Unc	BU
1991 Proof	Est. 5,000 Value: 200					
1992 Proof	Est. 5,000 Value: 200					

KM# 62a   1/5 CROWN
6.2200 g., 0.9950 Platinum 0.1990 oz. APW **Ruler:** Elizabeth II
Series: Barcelona Olympics **Obv:** Crowned bust right **Rev:** Wrestlers

Date	Mintage	F	VF	XF	Unc	BU
1991 Proof	Est. 1,000 Value: 400					

KM# 63   1/5 CROWN
6.2200 g., 0.9999 Gold 0.1999 oz. AGW, 22 mm.
Ruler: Elizabeth II **Series:** Barcelona Olympics **Obv:** Crowned bust right **Rev:** Boxers

Date	Mintage	F	VF	XF	Unc	BU
1991 Proof	Est. 5,000 Value: 200					
1992 Proof	Est. 5,000 Value: 200					

KM# 63a   1/5 CROWN
6.2200 g., 0.9950 Platinum 0.1990 oz. APW **Ruler:** Elizabeth II
Series: Barcelona Olympics **Obv:** Crowned bust right **Rev:** Boxers

Date	Mintage	F	VF	XF	Unc	BU
1991 Proof	Est. 1,000 Value: 400					

KM# 64   1/5 CROWN
6.2200 g., 0.9999 Gold 0.1999 oz. AGW, 22 mm. **Ruler:** Elizabeth II **Series:** Barcelona Olympics **Obv:** Crowned bust right **Rev:** Long jumper

Date	Mintage	F	VF	XF	Unc	BU
1991 Proof	Est. 5,000 Value: 200					
1992 Proof	Est. 5,000 Value: 200					

KM# 64a   1/5 CROWN
6.2200 g., 0.9950 Platinum 0.1990 oz. APW **Ruler:** Elizabeth II
Series: Barcelona Olympics **Obv:** Crowned bust right **Rev:** Long jumper

Date	Mintage	F	VF	XF	Unc	BU
1991 Proof	Est. 1,000 Value: 400					

KM# 65   1/5 CROWN
6.2200 g., 0.9999 Gold 0.1999 oz. AGW, 22 mm.
Ruler: Elizabeth II **Series:** Barcelona Olympics **Obv:** Crowned bust right **Rev:** Olympic victor

Date	Mintage	F	VF	XF	Unc	BU
1991 Proof	Est. 5,000 Value: 200					
1992 Proof	— Value: 200					

KM# 65a   1/5 CROWN
6.2200 g., 0.9950 Platinum 0.1990 oz. APW **Ruler:** Elizabeth II
Series: Barcelona Olympics **Obv:** Crowned bust right **Rev:** Olympic victor

Date	Mintage	F	VF	XF	Unc	BU
1991 Proof	Est. 1,000 Value: 400					

KM# 126   1/5 CROWN
6.2200 g., 0.9999 Gold 0.1999 oz. AGW, 22 mm.
Ruler: Elizabeth II **Rev:** Japanese Royal Wedding **Note:** Similar to 1/2 Crown, KM#127.

Date	Mintage	F	VF	XF	Unc	BU
1993 Proof	Est. 10,000 Value: 200					

KM# 150   1/5 CROWN
6.2200 g., 0.9999 Gold 0.1999 oz. AGW **Ruler:** Elizabeth II
Series: Preserve Planet Earth **Subject:** Cetiosaurus
Obv: Crowned bust right **Rev:** Long-necked dinosaur

Date	Mintage	F	VF	XF	Unc	BU
1993 Proof	Est. 5,000 Value: 200					

KM# 152   1/5 CROWN
6.2200 g., 0.9999 Gold 0.1999 oz. AGW, 22 mm. **Ruler:** Elizabeth II
Series: Preserve Planet Earth **Subject:** Stegosaurus **Obv:** Crowned bust right **Rev:** Dinosaur with pointed plates along spine

Date	Mintage	F	VF	XF	Unc	BU
1993 Proof	Est. 5,000 Value: 200					

KM# 153   1/5 CROWN
6.2200 g., 0.9999 Gold 0.1999 oz. AGW, 22 mm.
Ruler: Elizabeth II **Series:** WWII Warships **Obv:** Crowned bust right **Rev:** USS Philadelphia

Date	Mintage	F	VF	XF	Unc	BU
1993 Proof	Est. 5,000 Value: 200					

KM# 154   1/5 CROWN
6.2200 g., 0.9999 Gold 0.1999 oz. AGW, 22 mm.
Ruler: Elizabeth II **Series:** WWII Warships **Obv:** Crowned bust right **Rev:** USS McLanahan

Date	Mintage	F	VF	XF	Unc	BU
1993 Proof	Est. 5,000 Value: 200					

KM# 155   1/5 CROWN
6.2200 g., 0.9999 Gold 0.1999 oz. AGW, 22 mm.
Ruler: Elizabeth II **Series:** WWII Warships **Obv:** Crowned bust right **Rev:** HNLMS Isaac Sweers

Date	Mintage	F	VF	XF	Unc	BU
1993 Proof	Est. 5,000 Value: 200					

KM# 156   1/5 CROWN
6.2200 g., 0.9999 Gold 0.1999 oz. AGW, 22 mm.
Ruler: Elizabeth II **Series:** WWII Warships **Obv:** Crowned bust right **Rev:** USS Weehawken

Date	Mintage	F	VF	XF	Unc	BU
1993 Proof	Est. 5,000 Value: 200					

KM# 157   1/5 CROWN
6.2200 g., 0.9999 Gold 0.1999 oz. AGW, 22 mm.
Ruler: Elizabeth II **Series:** WWII Warships **Obv:** Crowned bust right **Rev:** HMS Warspite

Date	Mintage	F	VF	XF	Unc	BU
1993 Proof	Est. 5,000 Value: 200					

KM# 158   1/5 CROWN
6.2200 g., 0.9999 Gold 0.1999 oz. AGW, 22 mm.
Ruler: Elizabeth II **Series:** WWII Warships **Obv:** Crowned bust right **Rev:** HMS Hood

Date	Mintage	F	VF	XF	Unc	BU
1993 Proof	Est. 5,000 Value: 200					

KM# 159   1/5 CROWN
6.2200 g., 0.9999 Gold 0.1999 oz. AGW, 22 mm.
Ruler: Elizabeth II **Series:** WWII Warships **Obv:** Crowned bust right **Rev:** HMS Penelope

Date	Mintage	F	VF	XF	Unc	BU
1993 Proof	Est. 5,000 Value: 200					

KM# 160 1/5 CROWN
6.2200 g., 0.9999 Gold 0.1999 oz. AGW, 22 mm.
Ruler: Elizabeth II **Series:** WWII Warships **Obv:** Crowned bust right **Rev:** HMCS Prescott

Date	Mintage	F	VF	XF	Unc	BU
1993 Proof	Est. 5,000				Value: 200	

KM# 161 1/5 CROWN
6.2200 g., 0.9999 Gold 0.1999 oz. AGW, 22 mm.
Ruler: Elizabeth II **Series:** WWII Warships **Obv:** Crowned bust right **Rev:** HMS Ark Royal

Date	Mintage	F	VF	XF	Unc	BU
1993 Proof	Est. 5,000				Value: 200	

KM# 162 1/5 CROWN
6.2200 g., 0.9999 Gold 0.1999 oz. AGW, 22 mm.
Ruler: Elizabeth II **Series:** WWII Warships **Obv:** Crowned bust right **Rev:** USS Gleaves

Date	Mintage	F	VF	XF	Unc	BU
1993 Proof	Est. 5,000				Value: 200	

KM# 163 1/5 CROWN
6.2200 g., 0.9999 Gold 0.1999 oz. AGW, 22 mm.
Ruler: Elizabeth II **Series:** WWII Warships **Obv:** Crowned bust right **Rev:** HMAS Waterhen

Date	Mintage	F	VF	XF	Unc	BU
1993 Proof	Est. 5,000				Value: 200	

KM# 164 1/5 CROWN
6.2200 g., 0.9999 Gold 0.1999 oz. AGW, 22 mm.
Ruler: Elizabeth II **Series:** WWII Warships **Obv:** Crowned bust right **Rev:** FSS Savorgnan de Brazza

Date	Mintage	F	VF	XF	Unc	BU
1993 Proof	Est. 5,000				Value: 200	

KM# 165 1/5 CROWN
6.2200 g., 0.9999 Gold 0.1999 oz. AGW, 22 mm.
Ruler: Elizabeth II **Series:** House of Stuart **Subject:** Queen Anne, 1702-1714 **Obv:** Young bust right **Rev:** Bust left

Date	Mintage	F	VF	XF	Unc	BU
1993 Proof	Est. 5,000				Value: 200	

KM# 166 1/5 CROWN
6.2200 g., 0.9999 Gold 0.1999 oz. AGW, 22 mm.
Ruler: Elizabeth II **Series:** House of Hanover **Subject:** King George I, 1714-1727 **Obv:** Young bust right **Rev:** Laureate bust right

Date	Mintage	F	VF	XF	Unc	BU
1993 Proof	Est. 5,000				Value: 200	

KM# 167 1/5 CROWN
6.2200 g., 0.9999 Gold 0.1999 oz. AGW, 22 mm.
Ruler: Elizabeth II **Series:** House of Hanover **Subject:** King George II, 1727-1760 **Obv:** Young bust right **Rev:** Bust left

Date	Mintage	F	VF	XF	Unc	BU
1993 Proof	Est. 5,000				Value: 200	

KM# 168 1/5 CROWN
6.2200 g., 0.9999 Gold 0.1999 oz. AGW, 22 mm.
Ruler: Elizabeth II **Series:** House of Hanover **Subject:** King George III, 1760-1820 **Obv:** Young bust right **Rev:** Bust right

Date	Mintage	F	VF	XF	Unc	BU
1993 Proof	Est. 5,000				Value: 200	

KM# 169 1/5 CROWN
6.2200 g., 0.9999 Gold 0.1999 oz. AGW, 22 mm.
Ruler: Elizabeth II **Series:** House of Hanover **Subject:** King George IV, 1820-1830 **Obv:** Young bust right **Rev:** Bust left

Date	Mintage	F	VF	XF	Unc	BU
1993 Proof	Est. 5,000				Value: 200	

KM# 170 1/5 CROWN
6.2200 g., 0.9999 Gold 0.1999 oz. AGW, 22 mm.
Ruler: Elizabeth II **Series:** House of Hanover **Subject:** King William IV, 1830-1837 **Obv:** Young bust right **Rev:** Bust right

Date	Mintage	F	VF	XF	Unc	BU
1993 Proof	Est. 5,000				Value: 200	

KM# 171 1/5 CROWN
6.2200 g., 0.9999 Gold 0.1999 oz. AGW, 22 mm.
Ruler: Elizabeth II **Series:** House of Hanover **Subject:** Queen Victoria, 1837-1901 **Obv:** Young bust right **Rev:** Bust left

Date	Mintage	F	VF	XF	Unc	BU
1993 Proof	Est. 5,000				Value: 200	

KM# 172 1/5 CROWN
6.2200 g., 0.9999 Gold 0.1999 oz. AGW, 22 mm. **Ruler:** Elizabeth II **Series:** House of Saxe-Coburg **Subject:** King Edward VII, 1901-1910 **Obv:** Young bust right **Rev:** Uniformed bust right

Date	Mintage	F	VF	XF	Unc	BU
1993 Proof	Est. 5,000				Value: 200	

KM# 173 1/5 CROWN
6.2200 g., 0.9999 Gold 0.1999 oz. AGW, 22 mm.
Ruler: Elizabeth II **Series:** House of Windsor **Subject:** King George V, 1910-1936 **Obv:** Young bust right **Rev:** Uniformed bust left

Date	Mintage	F	VF	XF	Unc	BU
1993 Proof	Est. 5,000				Value: 200	

KM# 174 1/5 CROWN
6.2200 g., 0.9999 Gold 0.1999 oz. AGW, 22 mm.
Ruler: Elizabeth II **Series:** House of Windsor **Subject:** King Edward VIII, 1936 **Obv:** Young bust right **Rev:** Bust left

Date	Mintage	F	VF	XF	Unc	BU
1993 Proof	Est. 5,000				Value: 200	

KM# 175 1/5 CROWN
6.2200 g., 0.9999 Gold 0.1999 oz. AGW, 22 mm.
Ruler: Elizabeth II **Series:** House of Windsor **Subject:** King George VI, 1936-1952 **Obv:** Young bust right **Rev:** Bust left

Date	Mintage	F	VF	XF	Unc	BU
1993 Proof	Est. 5,000				Value: 200	

KM# 176 1/5 CROWN
6.2200 g., 0.9999 Gold 0.1999 oz. AGW, 22 mm.
Ruler: Elizabeth II **Subject:** 40th Anniversary of Coronation **Obv:** Crowned bust right **Rev:** Queen Elizabeth II bust left

Date	Mintage	F	VF	XF	Unc	BU
1993 Proof	Est. 5,000				Value: 200	

KM# 181 1/5 CROWN
6.2200 g., 0.9999 Gold 0.1999 oz. AGW, 22 mm.
Ruler: Elizabeth II **Series:** International Friendship **Obv:** Crowned bust right **Rev:** Stylized panda

Date	Mintage	F	VF	XF	Unc	BU
1993 Proof	Est. 5,000				Value: 200	

KM# 185 1/5 CROWN
6.2200 g., 0.9999 Gold 0.1999 oz. AGW, 22 mm.
Ruler: Elizabeth II **Series:** International Friendship **Obv:** Crowned bust right **Rev:** Natural panda

Date	Mintage	F	VF	XF	Unc	BU
1993 Proof	Est. 5,000				Value: 200	

KM# 189 1/5 CROWN
6.2200 g., 0.9999 Gold 0.1999 oz. AGW **Ruler:** Elizabeth II **Series:** International Friendship **Obv:** Crowned bust right **Rev:** General Sikarski portrait above B-24 bomber with Rock of Gibraltar in background

Date	Mintage	F	VF	XF	Unc	BU
1993 Proof	Est. 5,000				Value: 200	

KM# 199 1/5 CROWN
6.2143 g., 0.9999 Gold 0.1998 oz. AGW **Ruler:** Elizabeth II **Subject:** Dependent Territories Conference **Obv:** Crowned bust right **Rev:** 7 shields, 2 in center, 5 around with rope loops

Date	Mintage	F	VF	XF	Unc	BU
1993 Proof	Est. 5,000				Value: 200	

KM# 204 1/5 CROWN
6.2200 g., 0.9999 Gold 0.1999 oz. AGW, 22 mm.
Ruler: Elizabeth II **Series:** Peter Rabbit Centennial **Subject:** The Tale of Peter Rabbit **Obv:** Crowned bust right **Rev:** Rabbit eating carrots, sparrow on handle

Date	Mintage	F	VF	XF	Unc	BU
1993 Proof	Est. 5,000				Value: 200	

KM# 204a 1/5 CROWN
6.2200 g., 0.9950 Platinum 0.1990 oz. APW **Ruler:** Elizabeth II **Series:** Peter Rabbit Centennial **Subject:** The Tale of Peter Rabbit **Obv:** Crowned bust right **Rev:** Rabbit eating carrots, sparrow on handle

Date	Mintage	F	VF	XF	Unc	BU
1993 Proof	Est. 5,000				Value: 340	

KM# 208 1/5 CROWN
6.2200 g., 0.9999 Gold 0.1999 oz. AGW, 22 mm. **Ruler:** Elizabeth II **Series:** Peter Rabbit Centennial **Subject:** The Tale of Peter Rabbit **Obv:** Crowned bust right **Rev:** Mrs. Tiggy-Winkel ironing

Date	Mintage	F	VF	XF	Unc	BU
1993 Proof	Est. 5,000				Value: 200	

KM# 212 1/5 CROWN
6.2200 g., 0.9999 Gold 0.1999 oz. AGW, 22 mm. **Ruler:** Elizabeth II **Series:** Peter Rabbit Centennial **Subject:** The Tale of Peter Rabbit **Obv:** Crowned bust right **Rev:** Jeremy Fisher fishing

Date	Mintage	F	VF	XF	Unc	BU
1993 Proof	Est. 5,000				Value: 200	

KM# 216   1/5 CROWN
6.2200 g., 0.9999 Gold 0.1999 oz. AGW, 22 mm. **Ruler:** Elizabeth II **Series:** Peter Rabbit Centennial **Subject:** The Tale of Peter Rabbit **Obv:** Crowned bust right **Rev:** Tom Kitten with mother cat

Date	Mintage	F	VF	XF	Unc	BU
1993 Proof	Est. 5,000			Value: 200		

KM# 220   1/5 CROWN
6.2200 g., 0.9999 Gold 0.1999 oz. AGW, 22 mm. **Ruler:** Elizabeth II **Series:** Peter Rabbit Centennial **Subject:** The Tale of Peter Rabbit **Obv:** Crowned bust right **Rev:** Benjamin Bunny wearing hat and holding coat

Date	Mintage	F	VF	XF	Unc	BU
1993 Proof	Est. 5,000			Value: 200		

KM# 224   1/5 CROWN
6.2200 g., 0.9999 Gold 0.1999 oz. AGW, 22 mm. **Ruler:** Elizabeth II **Series:** Peter Rabbit Centennial **Subject:** The Tale of Peter Rabbit **Obv:** Crowned bust right **Rev:** Jemima Puddle-Duck talking with fox

Date	Mintage	F	VF	XF	Unc	BU
1993 Proof	Est. 5,000			Value: 200		

KM# 643   1/5 CROWN
6.2200 g., 0.9999 Gold 0.1999 oz. AGW, 22 mm. **Ruler:** Elizabeth II **Series:** XVII Winter Olympics **Obv:** Crowned bust right **Rev:** Figure skaters

Date	Mintage	F	VF	XF	Unc	BU
1993 Proof	Est. 5,000			Value: 200		

KM# 644   1/5 CROWN
6.2200 g., 0.9999 Gold 0.1999 oz. AGW, 22 mm. **Ruler:** Elizabeth II **Series:** XVII Winter Olympics **Obv:** Crowned bust right **Rev:** Ice hockey

Date	Mintage	F	VF	XF	Unc	BU
1993 Proof	Est. 5,000			Value: 200		

KM# 645   1/5 CROWN
6.2200 g., 0.9999 Gold 0.1999 oz. AGW, 22 mm. **Ruler:** Elizabeth II **Series:** XVII Winter Olympics **Obv:** Crowned bust right **Rev:** Bobsledding

Date	Mintage	F	VF	XF	Unc	BU
1993 Proof	Est. 5,000			Value: 200		

KM# 646   1/5 CROWN
6.2200 g., 0.9999 Gold 0.1999 oz. AGW, 22 mm. **Ruler:** Elizabeth II **Series:** XVII Winter Olympics **Obv:** Crowned bust right **Rev:** Skiers

Date	Mintage	F	VF	XF	Unc	BU
1993 Proof	Est. 5,000			Value: 200		

KM# 226   1/5 CROWN
6.2200 g., 0.9999 Gold 0.1999 oz. AGW, 22 mm. **Ruler:** Elizabeth II **Series:** World Cup Soccer **Obv:** Crowned bust right **Rev:** 3 players kicking ball up field

Date	Mintage	F	VF	XF	Unc	BU
1994 Proof	Est. 5,000			Value: 200		

KM# 228   1/5 CROWN
6.2200 g., 0.9999 Gold 0.1999 oz. AGW, 22 mm. **Ruler:** Elizabeth II **Series:** World Cup Soccer **Obv:** Crowned bust right **Rev:** 2 players facing; 1 kicking and 1 defending

Date	Mintage	F	VF	XF	Unc	BU
1994 Proof	Est. 5,000			Value: 200		

KM# 230   1/5 CROWN
6.2200 g., 0.9999 Gold 0.1999 oz. AGW, 22 mm. **Ruler:** Elizabeth II **Series:** World Cup Soccer **Obv:** Crowned bust right **Rev:** 2 players; 1 goalie and 1 player trying to score

Date	Mintage	F	VF	XF	Unc	BU
1994 Proof	Est. 5,000			Value: 200		

KM# 232   1/5 CROWN
6.2200 g., 0.9999 Gold 0.1999 oz. AGW, 22 mm. **Ruler:** Elizabeth II **Series:** World Cup Soccer **Obv:** Crowned bust right **Rev:** 1 player looking up

Date	Mintage	F	VF	XF	Unc	BU
1994 Proof	Est. 5,000			Value: 200		

KM# 234   1/5 CROWN
6.2200 g., 0.9999 Gold 0.1999 oz. AGW, 22 mm. **Ruler:** Elizabeth II **Series:** World Cup Soccer **Obv:** Crowned bust right **Rev:** 1 player kicking, 1 player running forward

Date	Mintage	F	VF	XF	Unc	BU
1994 Proof	Est. 5,000			Value: 200		

KM# 236   1/5 CROWN
6.2200 g., 0.9999 Gold 0.1999 oz. AGW, 22 mm. **Ruler:** Elizabeth II **Series:** World Cup Soccer **Obv:** Crowned bust right **Rev:** Player in foreground heading ball to player

Date	Mintage	F	VF	XF	Unc	BU
1994 Proof	Est. 5,000			Value: 200		

KM# 238   1/5 CROWN
6.2200 g., 0.9999 Gold 0.1999 oz. AGW, 22 mm. **Ruler:** Elizabeth II **Series:** Preserve Planet Earth **Obv:** Crowned bust right **Rev:** Sabre Tooth Tiger

Date	Mintage	F	VF	XF	Unc	BU
1994 Proof	Est. 5,000			Value: 200		

KM# 240   1/5 CROWN
6.2200 g., 0.9999 Gold 0.1999 oz. AGW, 22 mm. **Ruler:** Elizabeth II **Series:** Preserve Planet Earth **Obv:** Crowned bust right **Rev:** Spanish Eagle flying above island

Date	Mintage	F	VF	XF	Unc	BU
1994 Proof	Est. 5,000			Value: 200		

KM# 242   1/5 CROWN
6.2200 g., 0.9999 Gold 0.1999 oz. AGW, 22 mm. **Ruler:** Elizabeth II **Series:** Preserve Planet Earth **Obv:** Crowned bust right **Rev:** Three Striped Dolphins

Date	Mintage	F	VF	XF	Unc	BU
1994 Proof	Est. 5,000			Value: 200		

KM# 244   1/5 CROWN
6.2200 g., 0.9999 Gold 0.1999 oz. AGW, 22 mm. **Ruler:** Elizabeth II **Series:** Preserve Planet Earth **Obv:** Crowned bust right **Rev:** Mother and baby elephants

Date	Mintage	F	VF	XF	Unc	BU
1994 Proof	Est. 5,000			Value: 200		

KM# 253   1/5 CROWN
6.2200 g., 0.9999 Gold 0.1999 oz. AGW, 22 mm. **Ruler:** Elizabeth II **Series:** World War II **Obv:** Crowned bust right **Rev:** Maltese convoy of ships

Date	Mintage	F	VF	XF	Unc	BU
1994 Proof	Est. 5,000			Value: 200		

KM# 254   1/5 CROWN
6.2200 g., 0.9999 Gold 0.1999 oz. AGW, 22 mm. **Ruler:** Elizabeth II **Series:** World War II **Obv:** Crowned bust right **Rev:** Squadron 202 flying, Rock of Gibraltar in background

Date	Mintage	F	VF	XF	Unc	BU
1994 Proof	Est. 5,000			Value: 200		

KM# 255   1/5 CROWN
6.2200 g., 0.9999 Gold 0.1999 oz. AGW, 22 mm. **Ruler:** Elizabeth II **Series:** World War II **Obv:** Crowned bust right **Rev:** Admiral Somerville, ship in background

Date	Mintage	F	VF	XF	Unc	BU
1994 Proof	Est. 5,000			Value: 200		

KM# 256   1/5 CROWN
6.2200 g., 0.9999 Gold 0.1999 oz. AGW, 22 mm. **Ruler:** Elizabeth II **Series:** World War II **Obv:** Crowned bust right **Rev:** Glen Miller and band

Date	Mintage	F	VF	XF	Unc	BU
1994 Proof	Est. 5,000			Value: 200		

KM# 257   1/5 CROWN
6.2200 g., 0.9999 Gold 0.1999 oz. AGW, 22 mm. **Ruler:** Elizabeth II **Series:** World War II **Obv:** Crowned bust right **Rev:** King George VI congratulating pilots

Date	Mintage	F	VF	XF	Unc	BU
1994 Proof	Est. 5,000			Value: 200		

KM# 258   1/5 CROWN
6.2200 g., 0.9999 Gold 0.1999 oz. AGW, 22 mm. **Ruler:** Elizabeth II **Series:** World War II **Obv:** Crowned bust right **Rev:** General Eisenhower, planes and ships in background

Date	Mintage	F	VF	XF	Unc	BU
1994 Proof	Est. 5,000			Value: 200		

KM# 265   1/5 CROWN
6.2200 g., 0.9999 Gold 0.1999 oz. AGW, 22 mm. **Ruler:** Elizabeth II **Series:** First Man on Moon **Obv:** Crowned bust right **Rev:** Dr. Wernher von Braun with replica of rocket

Date	Mintage	F	VF	XF	Unc	BU
1994 Proof	Est. 5,000			Value: 200		

KM# 266   1/5 CROWN
6.2200 g., 0.9999 Gold 0.1999 oz. AGW, 22 mm. **Ruler:** Elizabeth II **Series:** First Man on Moon **Obv:** Crowned bust right **Rev:** Rocket on pad before lift-off

Date	Mintage	F	VF	XF	Unc	BU
1994 Proof	Est. 5,000			Value: 200		

KM# 267   1/5 CROWN
6.2200 g., 0.9999 Gold 0.1999 oz. AGW, 22 mm. **Ruler:** Elizabeth II **Series:** First Man on Moon **Obv:** Crowned bust right **Rev:** Recovering space capsule after splashdown

Date	Mintage	F	VF	XF	Unc	BU
1994 Proof	Est. 5,000			Value: 200		

KM# 268   1/5 CROWN
6.2200 g., 0.9999 Gold 0.1999 oz. AGW, 22 mm. **Ruler:** Elizabeth II **Series:** First Man on Moon **Obv:** Crowned bust right **Rev:** Lunar Module landing on the moon

Date	Mintage	F	VF	XF	Unc	BU
1994 Proof	Est. 5,000			Value: 200		

KM# 269   1/5 CROWN
6.2200 g., 0.9999 Gold 0.1999 oz. AGW, 22 mm. **Ruler:** Elizabeth II **Series:** First Man on Moon **Obv:** Crowned bust right **Rev:** Astronaut stepping on the moon

Date	Mintage	F	VF	XF	Unc	BU
1994 Proof	Est. 5,000			Value: 200		

KM# 270   1/5 CROWN
6.2200 g., 0.9999 Gold 0.1999 oz. AGW, 22 mm. **Ruler:** Elizabeth II **Series:** First Man on Moon **Obv:** Crowned bust right **Rev:** Astronaut setting up flag on the moon

Date	Mintage	F	VF	XF	Unc	BU
1994 Proof	Est. 5,000			Value: 200		

KM# 277   1/5 CROWN
6.2200 g., 0.9999 Gold 0.1999 oz. AGW, 22 mm. **Ruler:** Elizabeth II **Series:** Sherlock Holmes **Obv:** Crowned bust right **Rev:** Holmes sitting with pipe in hand

Date	Mintage	F	VF	XF	Unc	BU
1994 Proof	Est. 5,000			Value: 200		

KM# 278   1/5 CROWN
6.2200 g., 0.9999 Gold 0.1999 oz. AGW, 22 mm. **Ruler:** Elizabeth II **Series:** Sherlock Holmes **Obv:** Crowned bust right **Rev:** Holmes playing violin, Dr. Watson watching

Date	Mintage	F	VF	XF	Unc	BU
1994 Proof	Est. 5,000			Value: 200		

KM# 279   1/5 CROWN
6.2200 g., 0.9999 Gold 0.1999 oz. AGW, 22 mm. **Ruler:** Elizabeth II **Series:** Sherlock Holmes **Obv:** Crowned bust right **Rev:** People talking before 221 B Baker St.

Date	Mintage	F	VF	XF	Unc	BU
1994 Proof	Est. 5,000			Value: 200		

KM# 280   1/5 CROWN
6.2200 g., 0.9999 Gold 0.1999 oz. AGW, 22 mm. **Ruler:** Elizabeth II **Series:** Sherlock Holmes **Obv:** Crowned bust right **Rev:** Scene from book "The Empty House"

Date	Mintage	F	VF	XF	Unc	BU
1994 Proof	Est. 5,000			Value: 200		

KM# 281   1/5 CROWN
6.2200 g., 0.9999 Gold 0.1999 oz. AGW, 22 mm. **Ruler:** Elizabeth II **Series:** Sherlock Holmes **Obv:** Crowned bust right **Rev:** Sailing ship "Mary Celeste"

Date	Mintage	F	VF	XF	Unc	BU
1994 Proof	Est. 5,000			Value: 200		

KM# 282   1/5 CROWN
6.2200 g., 0.9999 Gold 0.1999 oz. AGW, 22 mm. uler: Elizabeth II **Series:** Sherlock Holmes **Obv:** Crowned bust right **Rev:** Scene from the "Hound of the Baskervilles"

Date	Mintage	F	VF	XF	Unc	BU
1994 Proof	Est. 5,000			Value: 200		

KM# 283   1/5 CROWN
6.2200 g., 0.9999 Gold 0.1999 oz. AGW, 22 mm. **Ruler:** Elizabeth II **Series:** Sherlock Holmes **Obv:** Crowned bust right **Rev:** Scene from the "Three Garriders"

Date	Mintage	F	VF	XF	Unc	BU
1994 Proof	Est. 5,000			Value: 200		

KM# 284   1/5 CROWN
6.2200 g., 0.9999 Gold 0.1999 oz. AGW, 22 mm. **Ruler:** Elizabeth II **Series:** Sherlock Holmes **Obv:** Crowned bust right **Rev:** Scene from the "Final Problem"

Date	Mintage	F	VF	XF	Unc	BU
1994 Proof	Est. 5,000			Value: 200		

KM# 441   1/5 CROWN
6.2200 g., 0.9999 Gold 0.1999 oz. AGW, 22 mm. **Ruler:** Elizabeth II **Subject:** The Tale of Peter Rabbit **Obv:** Crowned bust right **Rev:** Peter rabbit with four little bunnies

Date	Mintage	F	VF	XF	Unc	BU
1994 Proof	Est. 10,000			Value: 200		

KM# 442   1/5 CROWN
6.2200 g., 0.9950 Platinum 0.1990 oz. APW, 22 mm. **Ruler:** Elizabeth II

Date	Mintage	F	VF	XF	Unc	BU
1994 Proof	Est. 2,500			Value: 400		

KM# 295   1/5 CROWN
6.2200 g., 0.9999 Gold 0.1999 oz. AGW, 22 mm. **Ruler:** Elizabeth II **Series:** Atlanta Olympics **Obv:** Crowned bust right **Rev:** Long jumpers

Date	Mintage	F	VF	XF	Unc	BU
1995 Proof	Est. 5,000			Value: 200		

KM# 296   1/5 CROWN
6.2200 g., 0.9999 Gold 0.1999 oz. AGW, 22 mm. **Ruler:** Elizabeth II **Series:** Atlanta Olympics **Obv:** Crowned bust right **Rev:** Discus throwers

Date	Mintage	F	VF	XF	Unc	BU
1995 Proof	Est. 5,000			Value: 200		

KM# 297   1/5 CROWN
6.2200 g., 0.9999 Gold 0.1999 oz. AGW, 22 mm. **Ruler:** Elizabeth II **Series:** Atlanta Olympics **Obv:** Crowned bust right **Rev:** Relay racers

Date	Mintage	F	VF	XF	Unc	BU
1995 Proof	Est. 5,000			Value: 200		

KM# 298 1/5 CROWN
6.2200 g., 0.9999 Gold 0.1999 oz. AGW, 22 mm.
Ruler: Elizabeth II **Series:** Atlanta Olympics **Obv:** Crowned bust
right **Rev:** Javelin throwers

Date	Mintage	F	VF	XF	Unc	BU
1995 Proof	Est. 5,000				Value: 200	

KM# 303 1/5 CROWN
6.2200 g., 0.9999 Gold 0.1999 oz. AGW, 22 mm.
Ruler: Elizabeth II **Obv:** Crowned bust right **Rev:** Rock of
Gibraltar and rising sun

Date	Mintage	F	VF	XF	Unc	BU
1995 Proof	Est. 5,000				Value: 200	

KM# 326 1/5 CROWN
6.2200 g., 0.9999 Gold 0.1999 oz. AGW, 22 mm.
Ruler: Elizabeth II **Subject:** The Tale of Peter Rabbit
Obv: Crowned bust right **Rev:** Peter Rabbit running right

Date	Mintage	F	VF	XF	Unc	BU
1995 Proof	Est. 5,000				Value: 200	

KM# 326a 1/5 CROWN
6.2200 g., 0.9950 Platinum 0.1990 oz. APW **Ruler:** Elizabeth II
Subject: The Tale of Peter Rabbit **Obv:** Crowned bust right
Rev: Peter Rabbit running right

Date	Mintage	F	VF	XF	Unc	BU
1995 Proof	Est. 2,500				Value: 400	

KM# 328 1/5 CROWN
6.2200 g., 0.9999 Gold 0.1999 oz. AGW, 22 mm.
Ruler: Elizabeth II **Series:** Island Games **Obv:** Crowned bust
right **Rev:** Circle of athletes with shield at center

Date	Mintage	F	VF	XF	Unc	BU
1995 Proof	Est. 5,000				Value: 200	

KM# 330 1/5 CROWN
6.2200 g., 0.9999 Gold 0.1999 oz. AGW, 22 mm.
Ruler: Elizabeth II **Series:** Island Games **Obv:** Crowned bust
right **Rev:** Circle of athletes with shield at center

Date	Mintage	F	VF	XF	Unc	BU
1995 Proof	Est. 5,000				Value: 200	

KM# 342 1/5 CROWN
6.2200 g., 0.9999 Gold 0.1999 oz. AGW, 22 mm.
Ruler: Elizabeth II **Series:** Olympics **Obv:** Crowned bust right
Rev: Tennis player

Date	Mintage	F	VF	XF	Unc	BU
1996 Proof	Est. 5,000				Value: 200	

KM# 343 1/5 CROWN
6.2200 g., 0.9999 Gold 0.1999 oz. AGW, 22 mm.
Ruler: Elizabeth II **Series:** Olympics **Obv:** Crowned bust right
Rev: Wrestlers

Date	Mintage	F	VF	XF	Unc	BU
1996 Proof	Est. 5,000				Value: 200	

KM# 344 1/5 CROWN
6.2200 g., 0.9999 Gold 0.1999 oz. AGW, 22 mm.
Ruler: Elizabeth II **Series:** Olympics **Obv:** Crowned bust right
Rev: Baseball players

Date	Mintage	F	VF	XF	Unc	BU
1996 Proof	Est. 5,000				Value: 200	

KM# 345 1/5 CROWN
6.2200 g., 0.9999 Gold 0.1999 oz. AGW, 22 mm. **Ruler:** Elizabeth II
Series: Olympics **Obv:** Crowned bust right **Rev:** Flame

Date	Mintage	F	VF	XF	Unc	BU
1996 Proof	Est. 5,000				Value: 200	

KM# 346 1/5 CROWN
6.2200 g., 0.9999 Gold 0.1999 oz. AGW, 22 mm.
Ruler: Elizabeth II **Series:** Olympics **Obv:** Crowned bust right
Rev: Volleyball game

Date	Mintage	F	VF	XF	Unc	BU
1996 Proof	Est. 5,000				Value: 200	

KM# 347 1/5 CROWN
6.2200 g., 0.9999 Gold 0.1999 oz. AGW, 22 mm.
Ruler: Elizabeth II **Series:** Olympics **Obv:** Crowned bust right
Rev: Basketball game

Date	Mintage	F	VF	XF	Unc	BU
1996 Proof	Est. 5,000				Value: 200	

KM# 357 1/5 CROWN
6.2200 g., 0.9999 Gold 0.1999 oz. AGW, 22 mm.
Ruler: Elizabeth II **Subject:** Nefusat Yehuda Synagogue
Renovation **Obv:** Crowned bust right **Rev:** Hebrew symbol, rock,
arms and building

Date	Mintage	F	VF	XF	Unc	BU
1996 Proof	Est. 5,000				Value: 200	

KM# 360 1/5 CROWN
6.2200 g., 0.9999 Gold 0.1999 oz. AGW, 22 mm.
Ruler: Elizabeth II **Series:** Euro 96 **Rev:** England

Date	Mintage	F	VF	XF	Unc	BU
1996 Proof	Est. 5,000				Value: 200	

KM# 370 1/5 CROWN
6.2200 g., 0.9999 Gold 0.1999 oz. AGW, 22 mm.
Ruler: Elizabeth II **Obv:** Crowned bust right **Rev:** Roses

Date	Mintage	F	VF	XF	Unc	BU
1996 Proof	Est. 5,000				Value: 200	

KM# 370a 1/5 CROWN
6.2518 g., 0.9950 Platinum 0.2000 oz. APW **Ruler:** Elizabeth II
Obv: Crowned bust right **Rev:** Roses

Date	Mintage	F	VF	XF	Unc	BU
1996 Proof	Est. 1,000				Value: 400	

KM# 379 1/5 CROWN
6.2207 g., 0.9999 Gold 0.2000 oz. AGW, 22 mm. **Ruler:** Elizabeth II
Series: Peter Rabbit Centennial **Subject:** The Tale of Peter Rabbit
Obv: Crowned bust right **Rev:** Peter Rabbit escaping garden

Date	Mintage	F	VF	XF	Unc	BU
1996 Proof	Est. 7,500				Value: 200	

KM# 379a 1/5 CROWN
6.2200 g., 0.9950 Platinum 0.1990 oz. APW **Ruler:** Elizabeth II
Series: Peter Rabbit Centennial **Subject:** The Tale of Peter Rabbit
Obv: Crowned bust right **Rev:** Peter Rabbit escaping garden

Date	Mintage	F	VF	XF	Unc	BU
1996 Proof	Est. 5,000				Value: 400	

KM# 384 1/5 CROWN
6.2207 g., 0.9999 Gold 0.2000 oz. AGW, 22 mm.
Ruler: Elizabeth II **Series:** Preserve Planet Earth **Obv:** Crowned
bust right **Rev:** Shag Birds

Date	Mintage	F	VF	XF	Unc	BU
1996 Proof	Est. 5,000				Value: 200	

KM# 385 1/5 CROWN
6.2207 g., 0.9999 Gold 0.2000 oz. AGW, 22 mm.
Ruler: Elizabeth II **Series:** Preserve Planet Earth **Obv:** Crowned
bust right **Rev:** Puffins

Date	Mintage	F	VF	XF	Unc	BU
1996 Proof	Est. 5,000				Value: 200	

KM# 392 1/5 CROWN
6.2207 g., 0.9999 Gold 0.2000 oz. AGW, 22 mm. **Ruler:** Elizabeth II
Series: Cinema Centennial **Subject:** Grace Kelly - actress, 1929-
82 **Obv:** Crowned bust right **Rev:** Bust 3/4 facing, dates

Date	Mintage	F	VF	XF	Unc	BU
1996 Proof	Est. 5,000				Value: 200	

KM# 392a 1/5 CROWN
6.2200 g., 0.9950 Platinum 0.1990 oz. APW **Ruler:** Elizabeth II
Series: Cinema Centennial **Subject:** Grace Kelly - actress, 1929-
82 **Obv:** Crowned bust right **Rev:** Bust 3/4 facing

Date	Mintage	F	VF	XF	Unc	BU
1996 Proof	Est. 1,000				Value: 400	

KM# 397 1/5 CROWN
6.2207 g., 0.9999 Gold 0.2000 oz. AGW, 22 mm.
Ruler: Elizabeth II **Series:** Centenary of the Cinema
Subject: James Dean - actor, 1931-55 **Obv:** Crowned bust right
Rev: Standing central figure, dates

Date	Mintage	F	VF	XF	Unc	BU
1996 Proof	Est. 5,000				Value: 200	

KM# 397a 1/5 CROWN
6.2200 g., 0.9950 Platinum 0.1990 oz. APW **Ruler:** Elizabeth II
Series: Centenary of the Cinema **Subject:** James Dean - actor,
1931-55 **Obv:** Crowned bust right **Rev:** Standing central figure,
dates

Date	Mintage	F	VF	XF	Unc	BU
1996 Proof	Est. 1,000				Value: 400	

KM# 402 1/5 CROWN
6.2207 g., 0.9999 Gold 0.2000 oz. AGW, 22 mm.
Ruler: Elizabeth II **Series:** Centenary of the Cinema
Subject: Marilyn Monroe - actress, 1926-62 **Obv:** Crowned bust
right **Rev:** Bust looking back over shoulder

Date	Mintage	F	VF	XF	Unc	BU
1996 Proof	Est. 5,000				Value: 200	

KM# 402a 1/5 CROWN
6.2200 g., 0.9950 Platinum 0.1990 oz. APW **Ruler:** Elizabeth II
Series: Centenary of the Cinema **Subject:** Marilyn Monroe -
actress, 1926-62 **Obv:** Crowned bust right **Rev:** Bust looking back
over shoulder

Date	Mintage	F	VF	XF	Unc	BU
1996 Proof	Est. 1,000				Value: 400	

KM# 407 1/5 CROWN
6.2207 g., 0.9999 Gold 0.2000 oz. AGW, 22 mm.
Ruler: Elizabeth II **Series:** Centenary of the Cinema
Subject: Audrey Hepburn - actress, 1929-93 **Obv:** Crowned bust
right **Rev:** Bust 3/4 facing, dates

Date	Mintage	F	VF	XF	Unc	BU
1996 Proof	Est. 5,000				Value: 200	

KM# 407a 1/5 CROWN
6.2200 g., 0.9950 Platinum 0.1990 oz. APW **Ruler:** Elizabeth II
Series: Centenary of the Cinema **Subject:** Audrey Hepburn -
actress, 1929-93 **Obv:** Crowned bust right **Rev:** Bust 3/4 facing,
dates

Date	Mintage	F	VF	XF	Unc	BU
1996 Proof	Est. 1,000				Value: 400	

KM# 412 1/5 CROWN
6.2207 g., 0.9999 Gold 0.2000 oz. AGW, 22 mm.
Ruler: Elizabeth II **Series:** Centenary of the Cinema
Subject: Bruce Lee - actor, 1940-73 **Obv:** Crowned bust right
Rev: Kickboxer and chinese dragon, dates

Date	Mintage	F	VF	XF	Unc	BU
1996 Proof	Est. 5,000				Value: 200	

KM# 417 1/5 CROWN
6.2207 g., 0.9999 Gold 0.2000 oz. AGW, 22 mm.
Ruler: Elizabeth II **Series:** Centenary of the Cinema
Subject: Charlie Chaplan - actor, 1889-1977 **Obv:** Crowned bust
right **Rev:** Standing central figure with cane, dates

Date	Mintage	F	VF	XF	Unc	BU
1996 Proof	Est. 5,000				Value: 200	

KM# 422 1/5 CROWN
6.2207 g., 0.9999 Gold 0.2000 oz. AGW, 22 mm. **Ruler:** Elizabeth II
Series: Centenary of the Cinema **Subject:** Gone With the Wind
Obv: Crowned bust right **Rev:** Rhett Butler and Scarlett O'Hara

Date	Mintage	F	VF	XF	Unc	BU
1996 Proof	Est. 5,000				Value: 200	

KM# 427 1/5 CROWN
6.2207 g., 0.9999 Gold 0.2000 oz. AGW, 22 mm.
Ruler: Elizabeth II **Series:** Centenary of the Cinema
Obv: Crowned bust right **Rev:** The Flintstones

Date	Mintage	F	VF	XF	Unc	BU
1996 Proof	Est. 5,000				Value: 200	

KM# 431 1/5 CROWN
6.2207 g., 0.9999 Gold 0.2000 oz. AGW, 22 mm. **Ruler:**
Elizabeth II **Series:** Duke of Edinburgh Awards Scheme **Obv:**
Crowned bust right **Rev:** 7 Events surround central crowned arms

Date	Mintage	F	VF	XF	Unc	BU
1996 Proof	Est. 5,000				Value: 200	

KM# 434 1/5 CROWN
6.2207 g., 0.9999 Gold 0.2000 oz. AGW, 22 mm. **Ruler:** Elizabeth II
Series: Duke of Edinburgh Awards Scheme **Obv:** Crowned bust
right **Rev:** Cameo above team of horses pulling wagon

Date	Mintage	F	VF	XF	Unc	BU
1996 Proof	Est. 5,000				Value: 200	

KM# 447 1/5 CROWN
6.2207 g., 0.9999 Gold 0.2000 oz. AGW, 22 mm.
Ruler: Elizabeth II **Subject:** Lord Buddha **Obv:** Crowned bust
right **Rev:** Seated facing figure

Date	Mintage	F	VF	XF	Unc	BU
1996 Proof	Est. 8,000				Value: 200	

KM# 456 1/5 CROWN
6.2207 g., 0.9999 Gold 0.2000 oz. AGW, 22 mm. **Ruler:**
Elizabeth II **Series:** Centenary of the Cinema **Subject:** Wizard
of Oz **Obv:** Crowned bust right **Rev:** Wizard of Oz characters

Date	Mintage	F	VF	XF	Unc	BU
1996 Proof	Est. 5,000				Value: 200	

KM# 460 1/5 CROWN
6.2207 g., 0.9999 Gold 0.2000 oz. AGW, 22 mm.
Ruler: Elizabeth II **Series:** Centenary of the Cinema **Subject:**
Marx Brothers **Obv:** Crowned bust right **Rev:** Three busts 3/4 left

Date	Mintage	F	VF	XF	Unc	BU
1996 Proof	Est. 5,000				Value: 200	

KM# 464 1/5 CROWN
6.2207 g., 0.9999 Gold 0.2000 oz. AGW, 22 mm.
Ruler: Elizabeth II **Series:** Centenary of the Cinema **Subject:**
Elvis Presley - actor/entertainer, 1935-77 **Obv:** Crowned bust
right **Rev:** Guitar below and behind bust 3/4 left, dates

Date	Mintage	F	VF	XF	Unc	BU
1996 Proof	Est. 5,000				Value: 200	

KM# 468 1/5 CROWN
6.2207 g., 0.9999 Gold 0.2000 oz. AGW, 22 mm.
Ruler: Elizabeth II **Series:** Centenary of the Cinema **Subject:**
Casablanca **Obv:** Crowned bust right **Rev:** Bogart and Bergman

Date	Mintage	F	VF	XF	Unc	BU
1996 Proof	Est. 5,000				Value: 200	

KM# 472 1/5 CROWN
6.2207 g., 0.9999 Gold 0.2000 oz. AGW, 22 mm.
Ruler: Elizabeth II **Series:** Centenary of the Cinema
Obv: Crowned bust right **Rev:** E.T.

Date	Mintage	F	VF	XF	Unc	BU
1996 Proof	Est. 5,000				Value: 200	

KM# 476 1/5 CROWN
6.2207 g., 0.9999 Gold 0.2000 oz. AGW, 22 mm.
Ruler: Elizabeth II **Series:** Centenary of the Cinema **Subject:**
Alfred Hitchcock - Producer/Director, 1899-1980 **Obv:** Crowned
bust right **Rev:** Bust facing looking at bird on left shoulder

Date	Mintage	F	VF	XF	Unc	BU
1996 Proof	Est. 5,000				Value: 200	

KM# 513 1/5 CROWN
6.2207 g., 0.9999 Gold 0.2000 oz. AGW, 22 mm.
Ruler: Elizabeth II **Obv:** Crowned bust right **Rev:** Peacocks, one
with tail spread

Date	Mintage	F	VF	XF	Unc	BU
1997 Proof	Est. 5,000				Value: 200	

KM# 522   1/5 CROWN
6.2207 g., 0.9999 Gold 0.2000 oz. AGW, 22 mm.
Ruler: Elizabeth II **Subject:** The Tale of Peter Rabbit
Obv: Crowned bust right **Rev:** Standing rabbit 3/4 right

Date	Mintage	F	VF	XF	Unc	BU
1997 Proof	Est. 10,000				Value: 200	

KM# 522a   1/5 CROWN
6.2518 g., 0.9950 Platinum 0.2000 oz. APW **Ruler:** Elizabeth II
Subject: The Tale of Peter Rabbit **Obv:** Crowned bust right
Rev: Standing rabbit 3/4 right

Date	Mintage	F	VF	XF	Unc	BU
1997 Proof	Est. 2,500				Value: 400	

KM# 529   1/5 CROWN
6.2207 g., 0.9999 Gold 0.2000 oz. AGW, 22 mm.
Ruler: Elizabeth II **Series:** Golden Wedding Anniversary
Subject: Queen Elizabeth and Prince Philip **Obv:** Crowned bust
right **Rev:** Engagement portrait

Date	Mintage	F	VF	XF	Unc	BU
1997 Proof	Est. 3,500				Value: 200	

KM# 531   1/5 CROWN
6.2207 g., 0.9999 Gold 0.2000 oz. AGW, 22 mm.
Ruler: Elizabeth II **Series:** Golden Wedding Anniversary
Subject: Queen Elizabeth and Prince Philip **Obv:** Crowned bust
right **Rev:** Queen with her first born, Prince Charles

Date	Mintage	F	VF	XF	Unc	BU
1997 Proof	Est. 3,500				Value: 200	

KM# 533   1/5 CROWN
6.2207 g., 0.9999 Gold 0.2000 oz. AGW, 22 mm.
Ruler: Elizabeth II **Series:** Golden Wedding Anniversary
Subject: Queen Elizabeth and Prince Philip **Obv:** Crowned bust
right **Rev:** the Queen, two children and a monkey

Date	Mintage	F	VF	XF	Unc	BU
1997 Proof	Est. 3,500				Value: 200	

KM# 535   1/5 CROWN
6.2207 g., 0.9999 Gold 0.2000 oz. AGW, 22 mm.
Ruler: Elizabeth II **Series:** Golden Wedding Anniversary
Subject: Queen Elizabeth and Prince Philip **Obv:** Crowned bust
right **Rev:** Queen and adoring crowd

Date	Mintage	F	VF	XF	Unc	BU
1997 Proof	Est. 3,500				Value: 200	

KM# 539   1/5 CROWN
6.2207 g., 0.9999 Gold 0.2000 oz. AGW, 22 mm.
Ruler: Elizabeth II **Obv:** Crowned bust right **Rev:** Peonies

Date	Mintage	F	VF	XF	Unc	BU
1997 Proof	Est. 5,000				Value: 200	

KM# 539a   1/5 CROWN
6.2200 g., 0.9950 Platinum 0.1990 oz. APW **Ruler:** Elizabeth II
Obv: Crowned bust right **Rev:** Peonies

Date	Mintage	F	VF	XF	Unc	BU
1997 Proof	Est. 1,000				Value: 400	

KM# 543   1/5 CROWN
6.2200 g., 0.9999 Gold 0.1999 oz. AGW, 22 mm.
Ruler: Elizabeth II **Subject:** Nefertiti **Obv:** Crowned bust right
Rev: Head right

Date	Mintage	F	VF	XF	Unc	BU
1997 Proof	Est. 5,000				Value: 200	

KM# 543a   1/5 CROWN
6.2200 g., 0.9950 Platinum 0.1990 oz. APW **Ruler:** Elizabeth II
Subject: Nefertiti **Obv:** Crowned bust right **Rev:** Head right

Date	Mintage	F	VF	XF	Unc	BU
1997 Proof	Est. 1,000				Value: 400	

KM# 547   1/5 CROWN
6.2200 g., 0.9999 Gold 0.1999 oz. AGW, 22 mm.
Ruler: Elizabeth II **Subject:** Cleopatra **Obv:** Crowned bust right
Rev: Head facing

Date	Mintage	F	VF	XF	Unc	BU
1997 Proof	Est. 5,000				Value: 200	

KM# 547a   1/5 CROWN
6.2200 g., 0.9950 Platinum 0.1990 oz. APW **Ruler:** Elizabeth II
Subject: Cleopatra **Obv:** Crowned bust right **Rev:** Head facing

Date	Mintage	F	VF	XF	Unc	BU
1997 Proof	Est. 1,000				Value: 400	

KM# 551   1/5 CROWN
6.2200 g., 0.9999 Gold 0.1999 oz. AGW, 22 mm. **Ruler:** Elizabeth II
Subject: Europa **Obv:** Crowned bust right **Rev:** Head 3/4 left

Date	Mintage	F	VF	XF	Unc	BU
1997 Proof	Est. 5,000				Value: 200	

KM# 551a   1/5 CROWN
6.2200 g., 0.9950 Platinum 0.1990 oz. APW **Ruler:** Elizabeth II
Subject: Europa **Obv:** Crowned bust right **Rev:** Head 3/4 left

Date	Mintage	F	VF	XF	Unc	BU
1997 Proof	Est. 1,000				Value: 400	

KM# 555   1/5 CROWN
6.2200 g., 0.9999 Gold 0.1999 oz. AGW, 22 mm.
Ruler: Elizabeth II **Subject:** Liberty **Obv:** Crowned bust right **Rev:**
Laureate head right

Date	Mintage	F	VF	XF	Unc	BU
1997 Proof	Est. 5,000				Value: 200	

KM# 555a   1/5 CROWN
6.2200 g., 0.9950 Platinum 0.1990 oz. APW **Ruler:** Elizabeth II
Subject: Liberty **Obv:** Crowned bust right **Rev:** Laureate head right

Date	Mintage	F	VF	XF	Unc	BU
1997 Proof	Est. 1,000				Value: 400	

KM# 562   1/5 CROWN
6.2200 g., 0.9999 Gold 0.1999 oz. AGW, 22 mm.
Ruler: Elizabeth II **Series:** Queen's Birthday **Obv:** Crowned bust
right **Rev:** Queen on horseback left

Date	Mintage	F	VF	XF	Unc	BU
1997 Proof	Est. 5,000				Value: 200	

KM# 563   1/5 CROWN
6.2200 g., 0.9999 Gold 0.1999 oz. AGW, 22 mm.
Ruler: Elizabeth II **Series:** Queen's Birthday **Obv:** Crowned bust
right **Rev:** Queen on horseback returning salute

Date	Mintage	F	VF	XF	Unc	BU
1997 Proof	Est. 5,000				Value: 200	

KM# 564   1/5 CROWN
6.2200 g., 0.9999 Gold 0.1999 oz. AGW, 22 mm.
Ruler: Elizabeth II **Series:** Queen's Birthday **Obv:** Crowned bust
right **Rev:** Trooping the Colors scene, cameo above

Date	Mintage	F	VF	XF	Unc	BU
1997 Proof	Est. 5,000				Value: 200	

KM# 565   1/5 CROWN
6.2200 g., 0.9999 Gold 0.1999 oz. AGW, 22 mm.
Ruler: Elizabeth II **Series:** Queen's Birthday **Obv:** Crowned bust
right **Rev:** Gurkha troops with dragons

Date	Mintage	F	VF	XF	Unc	BU
1997 Proof	Est. 5,000				Value: 200	

KM# 570   1/5 CROWN
6.2200 g., 0.9999 Gold 0.1999 oz. AGW, 22 mm.
Ruler: Elizabeth II **Subject:** The New Mosque **Obv:** Crowned
bust right **Rev:** Two cavalry riders with mosque in background

Date	Mintage	F	VF	XF	Unc	BU
1997 Proof	Est. 5,000				Value: 200	

KM# 635   1/5 CROWN
6.2200 g., 0.9999 Gold 0.1999 oz. AGW, 22 mm.
Ruler: Elizabeth II **Subject:** Winter Olympics Japan
Obv: Crowned bust right **Rev:** Speed skater and "Bullet Train"

Date	Mintage	F	VF	XF	Unc	BU
1998 Proof	Est. 5,000				Value: 200	

KM# 637   1/5 CROWN
6.2200 g., 0.9999 Gold 0.1999 oz. AGW, 22 mm.
Ruler: Elizabeth II **Series:** Winter Olympics Japan
Obv: Crowned bust right **Rev:** Ski jumper and Buddha

Date	Mintage	F	VF	XF	Unc	BU
1998 Proof	Est. 5,000				Value: 200	

KM# 639   1/5 CROWN
6.2200 g., 0.9999 Gold 0.1999 oz. AGW, 22 mm.
Ruler: Elizabeth II **Series:** Winter Olympics Japan
Obv: Crowned bust right **Rev:** Cross-country skiers

Date	Mintage	F	VF	XF	Unc	BU
1998 Proof	Est. 5,000				Value: 200	

KM# 641   1/5 CROWN
6.2200 g., 0.9999 Gold 0.1999 oz. AGW, 22 mm.
Ruler: Elizabeth II **Series:** Winter Olympics Japan
Obv: Crowned bust right **Rev:** Slalom skier and Zenkoji temple

Date	Mintage	F	VF	XF	Unc	BU
1998 Proof	Est. 5,000				Value: 200	

KM# 653   1/5 CROWN
6.2200 g., 0.9999 Gold 0.1999 oz. AGW, 22 mm.
Ruler: Elizabeth II **Subject:** The Tale of Peter Rabbit **Obv:**
Crowned bust right **Rev:** Standing rabbit facing with sparrow at left

Date	Mintage	F	VF	XF	Unc	BU
1998 Proof	Est. 10,000				Value: 200	

KM# 653a   1/5 CROWN
6.2200 g., 0.9950 Platinum 0.1990 oz. APW **Ruler:** Elizabeth II
Subject: The Tale of Peter Rabbit **Obv:** Crowned bust right
Rev: Standing rabbit facing with sparrow at left

Date	Mintage	F	VF	XF	Unc	BU
1998 Proof	Est. 2,500				Value: 400	

KM# 659   1/5 CROWN
6.2200 g., 0.9999 Gold 0.1999 oz. AGW, 22 mm. **Ruler:**
Elizabeth II **Obv:** Crowned bust right **Rev:** Chrysanthemum

Date	Mintage	F	VF	XF	Unc	BU
1998 Proof	Est. 5,000				Value: 200	

KM# 659a   1/5 CROWN
6.2200 g., 0.9950 Platinum 0.1990 oz. APW **Ruler:** Elizabeth II
Obv: Crowned bust right **Rev:** Chrysanthemum

Date	Mintage	F	VF	XF	Unc	BU
1998 Proof	Est. 1,000				Value: 400	

KM# 671   1/5 CROWN
6.2200 g., 0.9999 Gold 0.1999 oz. AGW, 22 mm. **Ruler:** Elizabeth II
Subject: Juno **Obv:** Crowned bust right **Rev:** Head 3/4 facing

Date	Mintage	F	VF	XF	Unc	BU
1998 Proof	Est. 5,000				Value: 200	

KM# 671a   1/5 CROWN
6.2200 g., 0.9950 Platinum 0.1990 oz. APW **Ruler:** Elizabeth II
Subject: Juno **Obv:** Crowned bust right **Rev:** Head 3/4 facing

Date	Mintage	F	VF	XF	Unc	BU
1998 Proof	Est. 1,000				Value: 400	

KM# 672   1/5 CROWN
6.2200 g., 0.9999 Gold 0.1999 oz. AGW, 22 mm.
Ruler: Elizabeth II **Subject:** Athena **Obv:** Crowned bust right
Rev: Helmeted head right

Date	Mintage	F	VF	XF	Unc	BU
1998 Proof	Est. 5,000				Value: 200	

KM# 672a   1/5 CROWN
6.2200 g., 0.9950 Platinum 0.1990 oz. APW **Ruler:** Elizabeth II
Subject: Athena **Obv:** Crowned bust right **Rev:** Helmeted head
right

Date	Mintage	F	VF	XF	Unc	BU
1998 Proof	Est. 1,000				Value: 400	

KM# 673   1/5 CROWN
6.2200 g., 0.9999 Gold 0.1999 oz. AGW, 22 mm.
Ruler: Elizabeth II **Subject:** Arethusa **Obv:** Crowned bust right
Rev: Head left with dolphins

Date	Mintage	F	VF	XF	Unc	BU
1998 Proof	Est. 5,000				Value: 200	

KM# 673a   1/5 CROWN
6.2200 g., 0.9950 Platinum 0.1990 oz. APW **Ruler:** Elizabeth II
Subject: Arethusa **Obv:** Crowned bust right **Rev:** Head left with
dolphins

Date	Mintage	F	VF	XF	Unc	BU
1998 Proof	Est. 1,000				Value: 400	

KM# 680   1/5 CROWN
6.2200 g., 0.9999 Gold 0.1999 oz. AGW, 22 mm.
Ruler: Elizabeth II **Subject:** Paddington Bear **Obv:** Crowned
bust right **Rev:** Bear with suitcase

Date	Mintage	F	VF	XF	Unc	BU
1998 Proof	Est. 5,000				Value: 200	

KM# 680a   1/5 CROWN
6.2200 g., 0.9950 Platinum 0.1990 oz. APW **Ruler:** Elizabeth II
Subject: Paddington Bear **Obv:** Crowned bust right
Rev: Bear with suitcase

Date	Mintage	F	VF	XF	Unc	BU
1998 Proof	Est. 2,000				Value: 400	

KM# 683   1/5 CROWN
6.2200 g., 0.9999 Gold 0.1999 oz. AGW, 22 mm.
Ruler: Elizabeth II **Subject:** World Cup France 1998
Obv: Crowned bust right **Rev:** Goalie, map of Europe

Date	Mintage	F	VF	XF	Unc	BU
1998 Proof	Est. 5,000				Value: 200	

KM# 684   1/5 CROWN
6.2200 g., 0.9999 Gold 0.1999 oz. AGW, 22 mm.
Ruler: Elizabeth II **Subject:** World Cup France 1998
Obv: Crowned bust right **Rev:** Player kicking to left

Date	Mintage	F	VF	XF	Unc	BU
1998 Proof	Est. 5,000				Value: 200	

KM# 685   1/5 CROWN
6.2200 g., 0.9999 Gold 0.1999 oz. AGW, 22 mm.
Ruler: Elizabeth II **Subject:** World Cup France 1998
Obv: Crowned bust right **Rev:** Player dribbling ball

Date	Mintage	F	VF	XF	Unc	BU
1998 Proof	Est. 5,000				Value: 200	

KM# 686   1/5 CROWN
6.2200 g., 0.9999 Gold 0.1999 oz. AGW, 22 mm.
Ruler: Elizabeth II **Subject:** World Cup France 1998
Obv: Crowned bust right **Rev:** Two players, map of Europe

Date	Mintage	F	VF	XF	Unc	BU
1998 Proof	Est. 5,000				Value: 200	

KM# 731   1/5 CROWN
6.2200 g., 0.9999 Gold 0.1999 oz. AGW, 22 mm. **Ruler:** Elizabeth II
Obv: Crowned bust right **Rev:** Cupid with hologram heart

Date	Mintage	F	VF	XF	Unc	BU
1998 Proof	Est. 5,000				Value: 200	

KM# 741   1/5 CROWN
6.2200 g., 0.9999 Gold 0.1999 oz. AGW, 22 mm.
Ruler: Elizabeth II **Subject:** Year of the Ocean **Obv:** Crowned
bust right **Rev:** Polar bear and walrus

Date	Mintage	F	VF	XF	Unc	BU
1998 Proof	Est. 5,000				Value: 200	

KM# 742   1/5 CROWN
6.2200 g., 0.9999 Gold 0.1999 oz. AGW, 22 mm.
Ruler: Elizabeth II **Subject:** Year of the Ocean **Obv:** Crowned
bust right **Rev:** Seals and penguins

Date	Mintage	F	VF	XF	Unc	BU
1998 Proof	Est. 5,000				Value: 200	

KM# 743   1/5 CROWN
6.2200 g., 0.9999 Gold 0.1999 oz. AGW, 22 mm.
Ruler: Elizabeth II **Subject:** Year of the Ocean **Obv:** Crowned
bust right **Rev:** Sea cow with calf

Date	Mintage	F	VF	XF	Unc	BU
1998 Proof	Est. 5,000				Value: 200	

KM# 744 1/5 CROWN
6.2200 g., 0.9999 Gold 0.1999 oz. AGW, 22 mm.
Ruler: Elizabeth II **Subject:** Year of the Ocean **Obv:** Crowned bust right **Rev:** Surfer

Date	Mintage	F	VF	XF	Unc	BU
1998 Proof	Est. 5,000				Value: 200	

KM# 767 1/5 CROWN
6.2200 g., 0.9999 Gold 0.1999 oz. AGW, 22 mm.
Ruler: Elizabeth II **Subject:** Gibraltar Regiment New Colours **Obv:** Crowned bust right **Rev:** Soldiers presenting keys

Date	Mintage	F	VF	XF	Unc	BU
1998 Proof	Est. 5,000				Value: 200	

KM# 798 1/5 CROWN
6.2200 g., 0.9999 Gold 0.1999 oz. AGW, 22 mm.
Ruler: Elizabeth II **Series:** The World At War **Subject:** General D.D. Eisenhower **Obv:** Crowned bust right **Rev:** Bust facing and North African invasion scene

Date	Mintage	F	VF	XF	Unc	BU
1998 Proof	Est. 5,000				Value: 200	

KM# 781.1 1/5 CROWN
6.2200 g., 0.9999 Gold 0.1999 oz. AGW, 22 mm. **Ruler:** Elizabeth II **Subject:** 1999 Year of the Rabbit **Obv:** Crowned bust right **Rev:** Rabbit reading, sparrow, Chinese characters

Date	Mintage	F	VF	XF	Unc	BU
1999 Proof	Est. 3,500				Value: 200	

KM# 781.1a 1/5 CROWN
6.2200 g., 0.9950 Platinum 0.1990 oz. APW **Ruler:** Elizabeth II **Subject:** 1999 Year of the Rabbit **Obv:** Crowned bust right **Rev:** Rabbit reading, sparrow, Chinese characters

Date	Mintage	F	VF	XF	Unc	BU
1999 Proof	Est. 1,500				Value: 400	

KM# 781.2 1/5 CROWN
6.2200 g., 0.9999 Gold 0.1999 oz. AGW, 22 mm.
Ruler: Elizabeth II **Obv:** Crowned bust right **Rev:** Rabbit reading, sparrow, without Chinese characters

Date	Mintage	F	VF	XF	Unc	BU
1999 Proof	Inc. above				Value: 200	

KM# 781.2a 1/5 CROWN
6.2200 g., 0.9950 Platinum 0.1990 oz. APW **Ruler:** Elizabeth II **Obv:** Crowned bust right **Rev:** Rabbit reading, sparrow; without Chinese characters

Date	Mintage	F	VF	XF	Unc	BU
1999 Proof	Inc. above				Value: 400	

KM# 784 1/5 CROWN
6.2200 g., 0.9999 Gold 0.1999 oz. AGW, 22 mm.
Ruler: Elizabeth II **Series:** Summer Olympics - Sydney **Obv:** Crowned bust right **Rev:** Broad jumper with kangaroo

Date	Mintage	F	VF	XF	Unc	BU
1999 Proof	Est. 5,000				Value: 200	

KM# 786 1/5 CROWN
6.2200 g., 0.9999 Gold 0.1999 oz. AGW, 22 mm.
Ruler: Elizabeth II **Series:** Summer Olympics - Sydney **Obv:** Crowned bust right **Rev:** Sailboats and platypus

Date	Mintage	F	VF	XF	Unc	BU
1999 Proof	Est. 5,000				Value: 200	

KM# 788 1/5 CROWN
6.2200 g., 0.9999 Gold 0.1999 oz. AGW, 22 mm.
Ruler: Elizabeth II **Series:** Summer Olympics - Sydney **Obv:** Crowned bust right **Rev:** Swimmer and koala bear

Date	Mintage	F	VF	XF	Unc	BU
1999 Proof	Est. 5,000				Value: 200	

KM# 790 1/5 CROWN
6.2200 g., 0.9999 Gold 0.1999 oz. AGW, 22 mm.
Ruler: Elizabeth II **Series:** Summer Olympics - Sydney **Obv:** Crowned bust right **Rev:** Two oarsmen and cockatoos

Date	Mintage	F	VF	XF	Unc	BU
1999 Proof	Est. 5,000				Value: 200	

KM# 792 1/5 CROWN
6.2200 g., 0.9999 Gold 0.1999 oz. AGW, 22 mm.
Ruler: Elizabeth II **Series:** Summer Olympics - Sydney **Obv:** Crowned bust right **Rev:** Man with torch and dog

Date	Mintage	F	VF	XF	Unc	BU
1999 Proof	Est. 5,000				Value: 200	

KM# 794 1/5 CROWN
6.2200 g., 0.9999 Gold 0.1999 oz. AGW, 22 mm. **Ruler:** Elizabeth II **Series:** Summer Olympics - Sydney **Obv:** Crowned bust right **Rev:** Torch runner, portrait of Aborigini and Ayers Rock

Date	Mintage	F	VF	XF	Unc	BU
1999 Proof	Est. 5,000				Value: 200	

KM# 796 1/5 CROWN
6.2200 g., 0.9999 Gold 0.1999 oz. AGW, 22 mm. **Ruler:** Elizabeth II **Subject:** Millennium 2000 **Obv:** Head with tiara right **Rev:** Sundial, digital clock face, candle and traditional clock face

Date	Mintage	F	VF	XF	Unc	BU
1999 Proof	Est. 5,000				Value: 200	

KM# 800 1/5 CROWN
6.2200 g., 0.9999 Gold 0.1999 oz. AGW, 22 mm.
Ruler: Elizabeth II **Subject:** King Alfred the Great, 871-899 **Obv:** Crowned bust right **Rev:** Crowned bust left

Date	Mintage	F	VF	XF	Unc	BU
1999 Proof	Est. 5,000				Value: 200	

KM# 802 1/5 CROWN
6.2200 g., 0.9999 Gold 0.1999 oz. AGW, 22 mm.
Ruler: Elizabeth II **Subject:** King Canute, 1016-1035 **Obv:** Crowned bust right **Rev:** Crowned bust left

Date	Mintage	F	VF	XF	Unc	BU
1999 Proof	Est. 5,000				Value: 200	

KM# 804 1/5 CROWN
6.2200 g., 0.9999 Gold 0.1999 oz. AGW, 22 mm.
Ruler: Elizabeth II **Subject:** King Edward the Confessor, 1042-1066 **Obv:** Crowned bust right **Rev:** Crowned bust left

Date	Mintage	F	VF	XF	Unc	BU
1999 Proof	Est. 5,000				Value: 200	

KM# 806 1/5 CROWN
6.2200 g., 0.9999 Gold 0.1999 oz. AGW, 22 mm. **Ruler:** Elizabeth II **Series:** House of Normandy **Subject:** King William I, 1066-1087 **Obv:** Crowned bust right **Rev:** Crowned bust left

Date	Mintage	F	VF	XF	Unc	BU
1999 Proof	Est. 5,000				Value: 200	

KM# 808 1/5 CROWN
6.2200 g., 0.9999 Gold 0.1999 oz. AGW, 22 mm. **Ruler:** Elizabeth II **Series:** House of Plantagenet **Subject:** King Richard I, 1189-1199 **Obv:** Crowned bust right **Rev:** Crowned bust right

Date	Mintage	F	VF	XF	Unc	BU
1999 Proof	Est. 5,000				Value: 200	

KM# 810 1/5 CROWN
6.2200 g., 0.9999 Gold 0.1999 oz. AGW, 22 mm.
Ruler: Elizabeth II **Series:** House of Plantagenet **Subject:** King John, 1199-1216 **Obv:** Crowned bust right **Rev:** Crowned bust left

Date	Mintage	F	VF	XF	Unc	BU
1999 Proof	Est. 5,000				Value: 200	

KM# 812 1/5 CROWN
6.2200 g., 0.9999 Gold 0.1999 oz. AGW, 22 mm.
Ruler: Elizabeth II **Series:** House of Lancaster **Subject:** King Henry V, 1413-1422 **Obv:** Crowned bust right **Rev:** Bust right

Date	Mintage	F	VF	XF	Unc	BU
1999 Proof	Est. 5,000				Value: 200	

KM# 814 1/5 CROWN
6.2200 g., 0.9999 Gold 0.1999 oz. AGW, 22 mm. **Ruler:** Elizabeth II **Series:** House of York **Subject:** King Richard III, 1483-1485 **Obv:** Crowned bust right **Rev:** Bust with hat right

Date	Mintage	F	VF	XF	Unc	BU
1999 Proof	Est. 5,000				Value: 200	

KM# 816 1/5 CROWN
6.2200 g., 0.9999 Gold 0.1999 oz. AGW, 22 mm.
Ruler: Elizabeth II **Series:** House of Tudor **Subject:** King Henry VIII, 1509-1547 **Obv:** Crowned bust right **Rev:** Bust with hat right

Date	Mintage	F	VF	XF	Unc	BU
1999 Proof	Est. 5,000				Value: 200	

KM# 818 1/5 CROWN
6.2200 g., 0.9999 Gold 0.1999 oz. AGW, 22 mm.
Ruler: Elizabeth II **Series:** House of Tudor **Subject:** Queen Elizabeth, 1558-1603 **Obv:** Crowned bust right **Rev:** Crowned bust with high ruffled collar left

Date	Mintage	F	VF	XF	Unc	BU
1999 Proof	Est. 5,000				Value: 200	

KM# 820 1/5 CROWN
6.2200 g., 0.9999 Gold 0.1999 oz. AGW, 22 mm.
Ruler: Elizabeth II **Series:** House of Stuart **Subject:** King Charles I, 1625-1649 **Obv:** Crowned bust right **Rev:** Bust right

Date	Mintage	F	VF	XF	Unc	BU
1999 Proof	Est. 5,000				Value: 200	

KM# 822 1/5 CROWN
6.2200 g., 0.9999 Gold 0.1999 oz. AGW, 22 mm. **Ruler:** Elizabeth II **Series:** House of Stuart **Subject:** King Charles II, 1660-1685 **Obv:** Crowned bust right **Rev:** Laureate bust right

Date	Mintage	F	VF	XF	Unc	BU
1999 Proof	Est. 5,000				Value: 200	

KM# 824 1/5 CROWN
6.2200 g., 0.9999 Gold 0.1999 oz. AGW, 22 mm.
Ruler: Elizabeth II **Subject:** The Wedding of Prince Edward and Miss Sophie Rhys-Jones **Obv:** Crowned bust right **Rev:** Heads facing above banner and wedding bells

Date	Mintage	F	VF	XF	Unc	BU
1999 Proof	Est. 5,000				Value: 200	

KM# A826 1/5 CROWN
6.2200 g., 0.9999 Gold 0.1999 oz. AGW, 22 mm. **Ruler:** Elizabeth II **Subject:** The Wedding of Prince Edward and Miss Sophie Rhys-Jones **Obv:** Crowned bust right **Rev:** St. George's Chapel

Date	Mintage	F	VF	XF	Unc	BU
1999 Proof	Est. 5,000				Value: 200	

KM# 834 1/5 CROWN
6.2200 g., 0.9999 Gold 0.1999 oz. AGW, 22 mm. **Ruler:** Elizabeth II **Subject:** The Life of Queen Elizabeth **Obv:** Crowned bust right **Rev:** 1905 portrait of Queen Mother as a girl

Date	Mintage	F	VF	XF	Unc	BU
1999 Proof	Est. 5,000				Value: 200	

KM# 836 1/5 CROWN
6.2200 g., 0.9999 Gold 0.1999 oz. AGW, 22 mm. **Ruler:** Elizabeth II **Subject:** The Life of Queen Elizabeth **Obv:** Crowned bust right **Rev:** 1918 portrait of Queen Mother with wounded veteran

Date	Mintage	F	VF	XF	Unc	BU
1999 Proof	Est. 5,000				Value: 200	

KM# 838 1/5 CROWN
6.2200 g., 0.9999 Gold 0.1999 oz. AGW, 22 mm.
Ruler: Elizabeth II **Subject:** The Life of Queen Elizabeth **Obv:** Crowned bust right **Rev:** 1923 wedding portrait

Date	Mintage	F	VF	XF	Unc	BU
1999 Proof	Est. 5,000				Value: 200	

KM# 840 1/5 CROWN
6.2200 g., 0.9999 Gold 0.1999 oz. AGW, 22 mm.
Ruler: Elizabeth II **Subject:** The Life of Queen Elizabeth **Obv:** Crowned bust right **Rev:** 1936 family portrait

Date	Mintage	F	VF	XF	Unc	BU
1999 Proof	Est. 5,000				Value: 200	

KM# 843 1/5 CROWN
6.2200 g., 0.9999 Gold 0.1999 oz. AGW, 22 mm.
Ruler: Elizabeth II **Series:** The World At War **Subject:** Franklin D. Roosevelt **Obv:** Crowned bust right **Rev:** Bust writing at left, Zero fighter at right

Date	Mintage	F	VF	XF	Unc	BU
1999 Proof	—				Value: 200	

KM# 844 1/5 CROWN
6.2200 g., 0.9999 Gold 0.1999 oz. AGW, 22 mm.
Ruler: Elizabeth II **Subject:** Operation Manna **Obv:** Crowned bust right **Rev:** Bomber dropping food packets

Date	Mintage	F	VF	XF	Unc	BU
1999 Proof	Est. 5,000				Value: 200	

KM# 847 1/5 CROWN
6.2200 g., 0.9999 Gold 0.1999 oz. AGW, 22 mm.
Ruler: Elizabeth II **Subject:** The World At War **Obv:** Crowned bust right **Rev:** B-29, mushroom cloud and bust at right

Date	Mintage	F	VF	XF	Unc	BU
1999 Proof	Est. 5,000				Value: 200	

KM# 848 1/5 CROWN
6.2200 g., 0.9999 Gold 0.1999 oz. AGW, 22 mm.
Ruler: Elizabeth II **Subject:** Barnes Wallis **Obv:** Crowned bust right **Rev:** Bust at left reading, bomber above dam

Date	Mintage	F	VF	XF	Unc	BU
1999 Proof	Est. 5,000				Value: 200	

KM# 850 1/5 CROWN
6.2200 g., 0.9999 Gold 0.1999 oz. AGW, 22 mm.
Ruler: Elizabeth II **Subject:** The World At War **Obv:** Crowned bust right **Rev:** Bust at left facing, planes in combat

Date	Mintage	F	VF	XF	Unc	BU
1999 Proof	Est. 5,000				Value: 200	

KM# 852 1/5 CROWN
6.2200 g., 0.9999 Gold 0.1999 oz. AGW, 22 mm. **Ruler:** Elizabeth II **Subject:** Winston Churchill **Obv:** Crowned bust right **Rev:** Bust with hand showing 'V' sign, crowd in background

Date	Mintage	F	VF	XF	Unc	BU
1999 Proof	Est. 5,000				Value: 200	

KM# 854 1/5 CROWN
6.2200 g., 0.9999 Gold 0.1999 oz. AGW, 22 mm.
Ruler: Elizabeth II **Subject:** The World At War **Obv:** Crowned bust right **Rev:** Battleship and sailor

Date	Mintage	F	VF	XF	Unc	BU
1999 Proof	Est. 5,000				Value: 200	

KM# 856 1/5 CROWN
6.2200 g., 0.9999 Gold 0.1999 oz. AGW, 22 mm.
Ruler: Elizabeth II **Subject:** War Babies **Obv:** Crowned bust right **Rev:** Soldier kissing child

Date	Mintage	F	VF	XF	Unc	BU
1999 Proof	Est. 5,000				Value: 200	

KM# 858 1/5 CROWN
6.2200 g., 0.9999 Gold 0.1999 oz. AGW, 22 mm.
Ruler: Elizabeth II **Subject:** The World At War **Obv:** Crowned bust right **Rev:** 2 firemen in action after air raid

Date	Mintage	F	VF	XF	Unc	BU
1999 Proof	Est. 5,000				Value: 200	

KM# 860   1/5 CROWN
6.2200 g., 0.9999 Gold 0.1999 oz. AGW, 22 mm.
Ruler: Elizabeth II **Subject:** The World At War **Obv:** Crowned bust right **Rev:** Landing scene

Date	Mintage	F	VF	XF	Unc	BU
1999 Proof	Est. 5,000				Value: 200	

KM# 862   1/5 CROWN
6.2200 g., 0.9999 Gold 0.1999 oz. AGW, 22 mm.
Ruler: Elizabeth II **Subject:** Operation Heavywater **Obv:** Crowned bust right **Rev:** Military skier

Date	Mintage	F	VF	XF	Unc	BU
1999 Proof	Est. 5,000				Value: 200	

KM# 864   1/5 CROWN
6.2200 g., 0.9999 Gold 0.1999 oz. AGW, 22 mm.
Ruler: Elizabeth II **Subject:** The World At War **Obv:** Crowned bust right **Rev:** German tanks in Russia

Date	Mintage	F	VF	XF	Unc	BU
1999 Proof	Est. 5,000				Value: 200	

KM# 870   1/5 CROWN
6.2200 g., 0.9999 Gold 0.1999 oz. AGW, 22 mm.
Ruler: Elizabeth II **Series:** Queen Mother **Obv:** Head with tiara right **Rev:** 1937 Coronation scene

Date	Mintage	F	VF	XF	Unc	BU
2000 Proof	5,000				Value: 870	

KM# 872   1/5 CROWN
6.2200 g., 0.9999 Gold 0.1999 oz. AGW, 22 mm.
Ruler: Elizabeth II **Series:** Queen Mother **Obv:** Crowned bust right **Rev:** 1938 Visit to France

Date	Mintage	F	VF	XF	Unc	BU
2000 Proof	5,000				Value: 200	

KM# 874   1/5 CROWN
6.2200 g., 0.9999 Gold 0.1999 oz. AGW, 22 mm.
Ruler: Elizabeth II **Series:** Queen Mother **Obv:** Crowned bust right **Rev:** 1940 Bomb damage

Date	Mintage	F	VF	XF	Unc	BU
2000 Proof	5,000				Value: 200	

KM# 876   1/5 CROWN
6.2200 g., 0.9999 Gold 0.1999 oz. AGW, 22 mm. **Ruler:** Elizabeth II **Series:** Queen Mother **Obv:** Crowned bust right

Date	Mintage	F	VF	XF	Unc	BU
2000 Proof	5,000				Value: 200	

KM# 879   1/5 CROWN
6.2200 g., 0.9999 Gold 0.1999 oz. AGW, 22 mm.
Ruler: Elizabeth II **Subject:** 18th Birthday of Prince William **Obv:** Crowned bust right **Rev:** Bust facing **Edge:** Reeded

Date	Mintage	F	VF	XF	Unc	BU
2000 Proof	5,000				Value: 200	

KM# 881   1/5 CROWN
6.2200 g., 0.9999 Gold 0.1999 oz. AGW, 22 mm.
Ruler: Elizabeth II **Series:** 100th Birthday of the Queen Mother **Obv:** Crowned bust right **Rev:** Bust facing **Note:** Queen Mother's portrait has a real diamond chip (.015) set in her crown.

Date	Mintage	F	VF	XF	Unc	BU
2000 Proof	2,000				Value: 200	

KM# 868.1   1/4 CROWN
7.7800 g., 0.9250 Silver 0.2314 oz. ASW **Ruler:** Elizabeth II **Subject:** 1999 The Year of the Rabbit **Obv:** Crowned bust right **Rev:** Peter Rabbit reading, sparrow, Chinese characters

Date	Mintage	F	VF	XF	Unc	BU
1999 Proof	Est. 25,000			Value: 35.00		

KM# 868.2   1/4 CROWN
7.7800 g., 0.9250 Silver 0.2314 oz. ASW **Ruler:** Elizabeth II **Obv:** Crowned bust right **Rev:** Rabbit reading, sparrow; without Chinese characters

Date	Mintage	F	VF	XF	Unc	BU
1999 Proof	Inc. above			Value: 35.00		

KM# 886   1/2 CROWN
15.5500 g., 0.9999 Gold 0.4999 oz. AGW, 30 mm. **Ruler:** Elizabeth II **Subject:** Rotary Club of Gibraltar

Date	Mintage	F	VF	XF	Unc	BU
1991 Proof	5,000				Value: 500	

KM# 127   1/2 CROWN
15.5500 g., 0.9999 Gold 0.4999 oz. AGW, 30 mm.
Ruler: Elizabeth II **Subject:** Japanese Royal Wedding **Obv:** Crowned bust right **Rev:** Peacocks

Date	Mintage	F	VF	XF	Unc	BU
1993 Proof	5,000				Value: 470	

KM# 177   1/2 CROWN
15.5500 g., 0.9990 Silver 0.4994 oz. ASW **Ruler:** Elizabeth II **Series:** WWII Warships **Obv:** Crowned bust right **Rev:** HMS Hood

Date	Mintage	F	VF	XF	Unc	BU
1993	Est. 30,000	—	—	—	35.00	—

KM# 198   1/2 CROWN
15.5500 g., 0.9990 Silver 0.4994 oz. ASW **Ruler:** Elizabeth II **Subject:** King Edward VIII, House of Windsor **Obv:** Young bust right **Rev:** Bust left

Date	Mintage	F	VF	XF	Unc	BU
1993 Proof	Est. 30,000			Value: 27.50		

KM# 443   1/2 CROWN
15.5500 g., 0.9999 Gold 0.4999 oz. AGW, 30 mm. **Ruler:** Elizabeth II **Series:** Peter Rabbit Centennial **Subject:** The Tale of Peter Rabbit **Obv:** Crowned bust right **Rev:** Mother and bunnies

Date	Mintage	F	VF	XF	Unc	BU
1994 Proof	Est. 5,000				Value: 470	

KM# 572   1/2 CROWN
15.5500 g., 0.9990 Silver 0.4994 oz. ASW **Ruler:** Elizabeth II **Obv:** Crowned bust right **Rev:** Sherlock Holmes smoking pipe left

Date	Mintage	F	VF	XF	Unc	BU
1994 Proof	Est. 30,000			Value: 22.50		

KM# 372   1/2 CROWN
15.5500 g., 0.9999 Gold 0.4999 oz. AGW, 30 mm.
Ruler: Elizabeth II **Obv:** Crowned bust right **Rev:** Roses

Date	Mintage	F	VF	XF	Unc	BU
1996 Proof	Est. 3,000				Value: 470	

KM# 381   1/2 CROWN
15.5500 g., 0.9999 Gold 0.4999 oz. AGW, 30 mm.
Ruler: Elizabeth II **Series:** Peter Rabbit Centennial **Subject:** The Tale of Peter Rabbit **Obv:** Crowned bust right **Rev:** Peter Rabbit escaping garden

Date	Mintage	F	VF	XF	Unc	BU
1996 Proof	Est. 5,000				Value: 470	

KM# 448   1/2 CROWN
15.5500 g., 0.9999 Gold 0.4999 oz. AGW, 30 mm.
Ruler: Elizabeth II **Subject:** Lord Buddha **Obv:** Crowned bust right **Rev:** Seated figure facing

Date	Mintage	F	VF	XF	Unc	BU
1996 Proof	Est. 5,000				Value: 470	

KM# 524   1/2 CROWN
15.5500 g., 0.9999 Gold 0.4999 oz. AGW, 30 mm.
Ruler: Elizabeth II **Subject:** The Tale of Peter Rabbit **Obv:** Crowned bust right **Rev:** Standing rabbit 3/4 right

Date	Mintage	F	VF	XF	Unc	BU
1997 Proof	Est. 2,500				Value: 470	

KM# 647   1/2 CROWN
15.5500 g., 0.9999 Gold 0.4999 oz. AGW, 30 mm. **Ruler:** Elizabeth II **Obv:** Crowned bust right **Rev:** Cupid with hologram heart

Date	Mintage	F	VF	XF	Unc	BU
1998 Proof	Est. 3,500				Value: 470	

KM# 655   1/2 CROWN
15.5500 g., 0.9999 Gold 0.4999 oz. AGW, 30 mm.
Ruler: Elizabeth II **Subject:** The Tale of Peter Rabbit **Obv:** Crowned bust right **Rev:** Standing rabbit facing, sparrow at left

Date	Mintage	F	VF	XF	Unc	BU
1998 Proof	Est. 2,500				Value: 470	

KM# 681   1/2 CROWN
15.5500 g., 0.9999 Gold 0.4999 oz. AGW, 30 mm.
Ruler: Elizabeth II **Subject:** Paddington Bear **Obv:** Crowned bust right **Rev:** Bear with suitcase

Date	Mintage	F	VF	XF	Unc	BU
1998 Proof	Est. 2,500				Value: 470	

KM# 732   1/2 CROWN
15.5500 g., 0.9999 Gold 0.4999 oz. AGW, 30 mm.
Ruler: Elizabeth II **Subject:** Peacocks **Obv:** Crowned bust right **Rev:** Pair of peacocks, one with full display in hologram, denomination below

Date	Mintage	F	VF	XF	Unc	BU
1998 Proof	Est. 3,500				Value: 470	

KM# 895   1/2 CROWN
15.7800 g., 0.9991 Silver 0.5068 oz. ASW, 32.25 mm.
Ruler: Elizabeth II **Subject:** Cupid **Obv:** Crowned bust right **Rev:** Cupid with multicolor holographic heart similar to 1/2 crown KM#-647 but without the metal content statement, denomination below **Edge:** Reeded

Date	Mintage	F	VF	XF	Unc	BU
1998 Proof	10,000			Value: 50.00		

KM# 782.1   1/2 CROWN
15.5500 g., 0.9999 Gold 0.4999 oz. AGW, 30 mm. **Ruler:** Elizabeth II **Subject:** 1999 The Year of the Rabbit **Obv:** Crowned bust right **Rev:** Rabbit reading, sparrow, Chinese characters

Date	Mintage	F	VF	XF	Unc	BU
1999 Proof	Est. 1,000				Value: 470	

KM# 782.2   1/2 CROWN
15.5500 g., 0.9999 Gold 0.4999 oz. AGW, 30 mm.
Ruler: Elizabeth II **Obv:** Crowned bust right **Rev:** Rabbit reading, sparrow; without Chinese characters

Date	Mintage	F	VF	XF	Unc	BU
1999 Proof	Inc. above				Value: 470	

KM# 883   1/2 CROWN
Ring Weight: 9.0000 g. **Ring:** 0.9990 Gold 0.2891 oz. AGW **Center:** Titanium **Ruler:** Elizabeth II **Subject:** 160th Anniversary of the Uniform Penny Post **Obv:** Crowned bust right **Rev:** Postage stamp design **Edge:** Reeded

Date	Mintage	F	VF	XF	Unc	BU
2000 Proof	5,000	Value: 275				

KM# 894 1/2 CROWN
15.5517 g., 0.9990 Gold 0.4995 oz. AGW, 30 mm.
Ruler: Elizabeth II **Obv:** Crowned bust right **Rev:** Postage stamp design **Edge:** Reeded

Date	Mintage	F	VF	XF	Unc	BU
2000 Proof	999	Value: 470				

KM# 11 CROWN
Copper-Nickel, 38.8 mm. **Ruler:** Elizabeth II **Subject:** 80th Birthday of Queen Mother **Rev:** Bust left, mountain and water in background

Date	Mintage	F	VF	XF	Unc	BU
1980	—	—	—	1.50	3.00	4.00

KM# 11a CROWN
28.2800 g., 0.9250 Silver 0.8410 oz. ASW, 38.8 mm.
Ruler: Elizabeth II **Subject:** 80th Birthday of Queen Mother **Rev:** Bust left, mountains and water in background

Date	Mintage	F	VF	XF	Unc	BU
1980 Proof	Est. 25,000	Value: 35.00				

KM# 12 CROWN
Copper-Nickel, 38.8 mm. **Ruler:** Elizabeth II **Subject:** 175th Anniversary - Death of Nelson **Obv:** Young bust right **Rev:** Head at right looking left, ship in background

Date	Mintage	F	VF	XF	Unc	BU
1980	Est. 100,000	—	—	2.00	4.00	6.50

KM# 12a CROWN
28.2800 g., 0.9250 Silver 0.8410 oz. ASW, 38.8 mm.
Ruler: Elizabeth II **Subject:** 175th Anniversary - Death of Nelson **Obv:** Bust right

Date	Mintage	F	VF	XF	Unc	BU
1980 Proof	Est. 15,000	Value: 40.00				

KM# 14 CROWN
Copper-Nickel, 38.8 mm. **Ruler:** Elizabeth II **Subject:** Wedding of Prince Charles and Lady Diana **Rev:** The royal couple facing

Date	Mintage	F	VF	XF	Unc	BU
1981	—	—	—	1.00	2.50	3.50

KM# 14a CROWN
28.2800 g., 0.9250 Silver 0.8410 oz. ASW, 38.8 mm.
Ruler: Elizabeth II **Subject:** The Wedding of Prince Charles and Lady Diana **Rev:** The royal couple facing

Date	Mintage	F	VF	XF	Unc	BU
1981 Proof	Est. 30,000	Value: 30.00				

KM# 49 CROWN
Copper-Nickel, 38.8 mm. **Ruler:** Elizabeth II **Series:** 150th Anniversary of the First Adhesive Postage Stamp **Subject:** Penny Black Stamp **Obv:** Crowned bust right **Rev:** Heads flank stamp design

Date	Mintage	F	VF	XF	Unc	BU
1990 Proof	Est. 50,000	Value: 18.00				
1990	—	—	—	—	7.50	9.00

KM# 33 CROWN
Copper-Nickel, 38.8 mm. **Ruler:** Elizabeth II **Series:** World Cup Soccer **Obv:** Crowned bust right **Rev:** Italian flag, soccer player and globe

Date	Mintage	F	VF	XF	Unc	BU
1990	—	—	—	—	3.50	5.00

KM# 33a CROWN
28.2800 g., 0.9250 Silver 0.8410 oz. ASW, 38.8 mm. **Ruler:** Elizabeth II **Series:** World Cup Soccer **Obv:** Crowned bust right **Rev:** Italian flag, soccer player and globe

Date	Mintage	F	VF	XF	Unc	BU
1990 Proof	Est. 30,000	Value: 37.50				

KM# 34 CROWN
Copper-Nickel, 38.8 mm. **Ruler:** Elizabeth II **Series:** World Cup Soccer **Obv:** Crowned bust right **Rev:** Map of Italy on soccer ball background

Date	Mintage	F	VF	XF	Unc	BU
1990	—	—	—	—	3.50	5.00

KM# 34a CROWN
28.2800 g., 0.9250 Silver 0.8410 oz. ASW, 38.8 mm.
Ruler: Elizabeth II **Series:** World Cup Soccer **Obv:** Crowned bust right **Rev:** Map of Italy on soccer ball background

Date	Mintage	F	VF	XF	Unc	BU
1990 Proof	Est. 30,000	Value: 32.50				

KM# 35 CROWN
Copper-Nickel, 38.8 mm. **Ruler:** Elizabeth II **Series:** World Cup Soccer **Obv:** Crowned bust right **Rev:** Goalie catching ball

Date	Mintage	F	VF	XF	Unc	BU
1990	—	—	—	—	3.50	5.00

KM# 35a CROWN
28.2800 g., 0.9250 Silver 0.8410 oz. ASW, 38.8 mm.
Ruler: Elizabeth II **Series:** World Cup Soccer **Obv:** Crowned bust right **Rev:** Goalie catching ball

Date	Mintage	F	VF	XF	Unc	BU
1990 Proof	Est. 30,000	Value: 32.50				

KM# 36 CROWN
Copper-Nickel, 38.8 mm. **Ruler:** Elizabeth II **Series:** World Cup Soccer **Obv:** Crowned bust right **Rev:** Ball at head

Date	Mintage	F	VF	XF	Unc	BU
1990	—	—	—	—	3.50	5.00

KM# 36a CROWN
28.2800 g., 0.9250 Silver 0.8410 oz. ASW, 38.8 mm. **Ruler:** Elizabeth II **Series:** World Cup Soccer **Obv:** Crowned bust right **Rev:** Ball at head

Date	Mintage	F	VF	XF	Unc	BU
1990 Proof	Est. 30,000	Value: 32.50				

KM# 37 CROWN
Copper-Nickel, 38.8 mm. **Ruler:** Elizabeth II **Series:** World Cup Soccer **Obv:** Crowned bust right **Rev:** Ball at feet

Date	Mintage	F	VF	XF	Unc	BU
1990	—	—	—	—	3.50	5.00

KM# 37a CROWN
28.2800 g., 0.9250 Silver 0.8410 oz. ASW, 38.8 mm.
Ruler: Elizabeth II **Series:** World Cup Soccer **Obv:** Crowned bust right **Rev:** Ball at feet

Date	Mintage	F	VF	XF	Unc	BU
1990 Proof	Est. 30,000	Value: 32.50				

KM# 38 CROWN
Copper-Nickel, 38.8 mm.. **Ruler:** Elizabeth II **Series:** World Cup Soccer **Obv:** Crowned bust right **Rev:** Three players

Date	Mintage	F	VF	XF	Unc	BU
1990	—	—	—	—	3.50	5.00

KM# 38a CROWN
28.2800 g., 0.9250 Silver 0.8410 oz. ASW, 38.8 mm. **Ruler:** Elizabeth II **Series:** World Cup Soccer **Obv:** Crowned bust right **Rev:** Three players

Date	Mintage	F	VF	XF	Unc	BU
1990 Proof	Est. 30,000	Value: 32.50				

KM# 40 CROWN
Copper-Nickel, 38.8 mm. **Ruler:** Elizabeth II **Subject:** 21st Anniversary - Constitution **Obv:** Crowned bust right **Rev:** Standing figure with key, shield and spear

Date	Mintage	F	VF	XF	Unc	BU
1990	—	—	—	—	6.50	8.50

KM# 40a CROWN
28.2800 g., 0.9250 Silver 0.8410 oz. ASW, 38.8 mm. **Ruler:** Elizabeth II **Subject:** 21st Anniversary - Constitution **Obv:** Crowned bust right **Rev:** Standing figure with key, spear and shield

Date	Mintage	F	VF	XF	Unc	BU
1990 Proof	Est. 30,000	Value: 50.00				

KM# 46 CROWN
Copper-Nickel, 38.6 mm. **Ruler:** Elizabeth II **Obv:** Crowned bust right **Rev:** Head 3/4 left divides dates

Date	Mintage	F	VF	XF	Unc	BU
1990	—	—	—	—	4.50	6.00

KM# 46a CROWN
28.2800 g., 0.9250 Silver 0.8410 oz. ASW, 38.6 mm. **Ruler:** Elizabeth II **Obv:** Crowned bust right **Rev:** Head 3/4 left divides dates

Date	Mintage	F	VF	XF	Unc	BU
1990 Proof	Est. 30,000	Value: 17.50				

KM# 46b CROWN
6.2200 g., 0.9999 Gold 0.1999 oz. AGW **Ruler:** Elizabeth II **Obv:** Crowned bust right **Rev:** Head 3/4 left divides date

Date	Mintage	F	VF	XF	Unc	BU
1990 Proof	Est. 5,000	Value: 200				

KM# 46c CROWN
6.2200 g., 0.9950 Platinum 0.1990 oz. APW **Ruler:** Elizabeth II **Obv:** Crowned bust right **Rev:** Head 3/4 left divides dates

Date	Mintage	F	VF	XF	Unc	BU
1990 Proof	Est. 1,000	Value: 400				

KM# 49a CROWN
28.2800 g., 0.9250 Silver 0.8410 oz. ASW **Ruler:** Elizabeth II **Series:** 150th Anniversary of the First Adhesive Postage Stamp **Subject:** Penny Black Stamp **Obv:** Crowned bust right **Rev:** Heads flank stamp design

Date	Mintage	F	VF	XF	Unc	BU
1990 Proof	Est. 30,000	Value: 45.00				

KM# 49b CROWN
31.1000 g., 0.9999 Gold 0.9997 oz. AGW **Ruler:** Elizabeth II **Series:** 150th Anniversary of the First Adhesive Postage Stamp **Subject:** Penny Black Stamp **Obv:** Crowned bust right **Rev:** Heads flank stamp design

Date	Mintage	F	VF	XF	Unc	BU
1990 Proof	Est. 1,000	Value: 1,100				

KM# 49c CROWN
15.5500 g., 0.9999 Gold 0.4999 oz. AGW **Ruler:** Elizabeth II **Series:** 150th Anniversary of the First Adhesive Postage Stamp **Subject:** Penny Black Stamp **Obv:** Crowned bust right **Rev:** Heads flank stamp design

Date	Mintage	F	VF	XF	Unc	BU
1990 Proof	Est. 2,500	Value: 500				

KM# 66 CROWN
Copper-Nickel, 38.8 mm. **Ruler:** Elizabeth II **Series:** Barcelona Olympics **Obv:** Crowned bust right **Rev:** Discus thrower

Date	Mintage	F	VF	XF	Unc	BU
1991	—	—	—	—	4.50	5.50
1991 Proof	Est. 8,000	Value: 22.50				
1992	—	—	—	—	5.00	6.00

KM# 67 CROWN
Copper-Nickel, 38.8 mm. **Ruler:** Elizabeth II **Series:** Barcelona Olympics **Obv:** Crowned bust right **Rev:** Chariot racing

Date	Mintage	F	VF	XF	Unc	BU
1991	—	—	—	—	5.00	6.00
1991 Proof	Est. 8,000	Value: 22.50				
1992	—	—	—	—	5.00	6.00

KM# 68 CROWN
Copper-Nickel, 38.8 mm. **Ruler:** Elizabeth II **Series:** Barcelona Olympics **Obv:** Crowned bust right **Rev:** Runners

Date	Mintage	F	VF	XF	Unc	BU
1991	—	—	—	—	4.50	5.50
1991 Proof	Est. 8,000	Value: 22.50				
1992	—	—	—	—	5.00	6.00

KM# 69 CROWN
Copper-Nickel, 38.8 mm. **Ruler:** Elizabeth II **Series:** Barcelona Olympics **Obv:** Crowned bust right **Rev:** Javelin thrower

Date	Mintage	F	VF	XF	Unc	BU
1991	—	—	—	—	4.50	5.50
1991 Proof	Est. 8,000	Value: 22.50				
1992	—	—	—	—	5.00	6.00

KM# 70 CROWN
Copper-Nickel, 38.8 mm. **Ruler:** Elizabeth II **Series:** Barcelona Olympics **Obv:** Crowned bust right **Rev:** Head facing at left, wrestlers at right

Date	Mintage	F	VF	XF	Unc	BU
1991	—	—	—	—	4.50	5.50
1991 Proof	Est. 8,000	Value: 22.50				
1992	—	—	—	—	5.00	6.00

KM# 71 CROWN
Copper-Nickel, 38.8 mm. **Ruler:** Elizabeth II **Series:** Barcelona Olympics **Obv:** Crowned bust right **Rev:** Seated figure at left, boxers at right

Date	Mintage	F	VF	XF	Unc	BU
1991	—	—	—	—	4.50	5.50
1991 Proof	Est. 8,000	Value: 22.50				
1992	—	—	—	—	5.00	6.00

KM# 72 CROWN
Copper-Nickel, 38.8 mm. **Ruler:** Elizabeth II **Series:** Barcelona
Olympics **Obv:** Crowned bust right **Rev:** Long jumper

Date	Mintage	F	VF	XF	Unc	BU
1991	—	—	—	—	4.50	5.50
1991 Proof	Est. 8,000	Value: 22.50				
1992	—	—	—	—	5.00	6.00

KM# 73 CROWN
Copper-Nickel **Ruler:** Elizabeth II **Series:** Barcelona Olympics
Obv: Crowned bust right **Rev:** Olympic victor

Date	Mintage	F	VF	XF	Unc	BU
1991	—	—	—	—	4.50	5.50
1991 Proof	Est. 8,000	Value: 22.50				
1992	—	—	—	—	5.00	6.00

KM# 66a CROWN
28.2800 g., 0.9250 Silver 0.8410 oz. ASW **Ruler:** Elizabeth II
Series: Barcelona Olympics **Obv:** Crowned bust right
Rev: Discus thrower

Date	Mintage	F	VF	XF	Unc	BU
1991 Proof	Est. 30,000	Value: 27.50				
1992 Proof	—	Value: 100				

KM# 67a CROWN
28.2800 g., 0.9250 Silver 0.8410 oz. ASW, 38.8 mm.
Ruler: Elizabeth II **Series:** Barcelona Olympics **Obv:** Crowned
bust right **Rev:** Chariot racing

Date	Mintage	F	VF	XF	Unc	BU
1991 Proof	Est. 30,000	Value: 27.50				

KM# 68a CROWN
28.2800 g., 0.9250 Silver 0.8410 oz. ASW, 38.8 mm.
Ruler: Elizabeth II **Series:** Barcelona Olympics **Obv:** Crowned
bust right **Rev:** Runners

Date	Mintage	F	VF	XF	Unc	BU
1991 Proof	Est. 30,000	Value: 27.50				

KM# 69a CROWN
28.2800 g., 0.9250 Silver 0.8410 oz. ASW, 38.8 mm.
Ruler: Elizabeth II **Series:** Barcelona Olympics **Obv:** Crowned
bust right **Rev:** Javelin thrower

Date	Mintage	F	VF	XF	Unc	BU
1991 Proof	Est. 30,000	Value: 27.50				
1992 Proof	—	Value: 65.00				

KM# 70a CROWN
28.2800 g., 0.9250 Silver 0.8410 oz. ASW, 38.8 mm.
Ruler: Elizabeth II **Series:** Barcelona Olympics **Obv:** Crowned
bust right **Rev:** Head facing at left, wrestlers at right

Date	Mintage	F	VF	XF	Unc	BU
1991 Proof	Est. 30,000	Value: 27.50				

KM# 71a CROWN
28.2800 g., 0.9250 Silver 0.8410 oz. ASW, 38.8 mm.
Ruler: Elizabeth II **Series:** Barcelona Olympics **Obv:** Crowned
bust right **Rev:** Seated figure at left, boxers at right

Date	Mintage	F	VF	XF	Unc	BU
1991 Proof	Est. 30,000	Value: 27.50				

KM# 72a CROWN
28.2800 g., 0.9250 Silver 0.8410 oz. ASW, 38.8 mm.
Ruler: Elizabeth II **Series:** Barcelona Olympics **Obv:** Crowned
bust right **Rev:** Long jumper

Date	Mintage	F	VF	XF	Unc	BU
1991 Proof	Est. 30,000	Value: 27.50				

KM# 73a CROWN
28.2800 g., 0.9250 Silver 0.8410 oz. ASW, 38.8 mm.
Ruler: Elizabeth II **Series:** Barcelona Olympics **Obv:** Crowned
bust right **Rev:** Olympic victor

Date	Mintage	F	VF	XF	Unc	BU
1991 Proof	Est. 30,000	Value: 30.00				

KM# 74 CROWN
Copper-Nickel, 38.8 mm. **Ruler:** Elizabeth II **Subject:** Rotary
Club of Gibraltar **Obv:** Crowned bust right **Rev:** Cogwheel design
on globe

Date	Mintage	F	VF	XF	Unc	BU
1991	—	—	—	—	5.00	7.00

KM# 74a CROWN
28.2800 g., 0.9250 Silver 0.8410 oz. ASW, 38.8 mm.
Ruler: Elizabeth II **Subject:** Rotary Club of Gibraltar
Obv: Crowned bust right **Rev:** Cogwheel design on globe

Date	Mintage	F	VF	XF	Unc	BU
1991 Proof	Est. 30,000	Value: 22.50				

KM# 74b CROWN
15.5500 g., 0.9990 Gold 0.4994 oz. AGW, 32.25 mm.
Ruler: Elizabeth II **Subject:** Rotary Club of Gibraltar **Obv:**
Crowned bust right **Rev:** Cogwheel design (Rotary logo) on globe

Date	Mintage	F	VF	XF	Unc	BU
1991 Proof	5,000	Value: 650				

KM# 84 CROWN
Copper-Nickel, 38.5 mm. **Ruler:** Elizabeth II **Series:** 10th
Wedding Anniversary **Subject:** Prince Charles **Rev:** Head 3/4 left

Date	Mintage	F	VF	XF	Unc	BU
1991	—	—	—	—	4.00	5.00

KM# 84a CROWN
28.2800 g., 0.9250 Silver 0.8410 oz. ASW, 38.5 mm.
Ruler: Elizabeth II **Series:** 10th Wedding Anniversary
Subject: Prince Charles **Rev:** Head 3/4 left

Date	Mintage	F	VF	XF	Unc	BU
1991 Proof	Est. 30,000	Value: 35.00				

KM# 84b CROWN
6.2200 g., 0.9999 Gold 0.1999 oz. AGW **Ruler:** Elizabeth II
Series: 10th Wedding Anniversary **Subject:** Prince Charles **Rev:**
Head 3/4 left

Date	Mintage	F	VF	XF	Unc	BU
1991 Proof	Est. 5,000	Value: 200				

KM# 85 CROWN
Copper-Nickel, 38.5 mm. **Ruler:** Elizabeth II **Series:** 10th Wedding
Anniversary **Subject:** Princess Diana **Rev:** Head 3/4 right

Date	Mintage	F	VF	XF	Unc	BU
1991	—	—	—	—	4.00	5.00

KM# 85a CROWN
28.2800 g., 0.9250 Silver 0.8410 oz. ASW, 38.5 mm.
Ruler: Elizabeth II **Series:** 10th Wedding Anniversary
Subject: Princess Diana **Rev:** Head 3/4 right

Date	Mintage	F	VF	XF	Unc	BU
1991 Proof	—	Value: 37.50				

KM# 85b CROWN
6.2200 g., 0.9999 Gold 0.1999 oz. AGW **Ruler:** Elizabeth II
Series: 10th Wedding Anniversary **Subject:** Princess Diana
Rev: Head 3/4 right

Date	Mintage	F	VF	XF	Unc	BU
1991 Proof	—	Value: 200				

KM# 86 CROWN
Copper-Nickel, 38.5 mm. **Ruler:** Elizabeth II **Series:** 10th
Wedding Anniversary **Subject:** Royal Yacht 'Brittannia'
Rev: Luxury liner at sea

Date	Mintage	F	VF	XF	Unc	BU
1991	—	—	—	—	4.00	5.00

KM# 86a CROWN
28.2800 g., 0.9250 Silver 0.8410 oz. ASW, 38.5 mm.
Ruler: Elizabeth II **Series:** 10th Wedding Anniversary
Subject: Royal Yacht 'Britannia' **Rev:** Luxury liner at sea

Date	Mintage	F	VF	XF	Unc	BU
1991 Proof	Est. 30,000	Value: 35.00				

KM# 86b CROWN
6.2200 g., 0.9999 Gold 0.1999 oz. AGW **Ruler:** Elizabeth II
Series: 10th Wedding Anniversary **Subject:** Royal Yacht
'Britannia' **Rev:** Liner at sea

Date	Mintage	F	VF	XF	Unc	BU
1991 Proof	Est. 5,000	Value: 200				

KM# 95 CROWN
Copper-Nickel, 38.8 mm. **Ruler:** Elizabeth II **Obv:** Crowned bust
right **Rev:** Corgi

Date	Mintage	F	VF	XF	Unc	BU
1991	—	—	—	—	12.50	20.00

KM# 95a CROWN
31.1030 g., 0.9990 Silver 0.9989 oz. ASW, 38.8 mm.
Ruler: Elizabeth II **Obv:** Crowned bust right **Rev:** Corgi

Date	Mintage	F	VF	XF	Unc	BU
1991 Proof	Est. 50,000	Value: 35.00				

KM# 103 CROWN
Copper-Nickel, 38.8 mm. **Ruler:** Elizabeth II **Obv:** Crowned bust
right **Rev:** Cocker Spaniel

Date	Mintage	F	VF	XF	Unc	BU
1992	—	—	—	—	12.50	20.00

KM# 103a CROWN
28.2800 g., 0.9250 Silver 0.8410 oz. ASW, 38.8 mm.
Ruler: Elizabeth II **Obv:** Crowned bust right **Rev:** Cocker Spaniel

Date	Mintage	F	VF	XF	Unc	BU
1992 Proof	—	Value: 35.00				

KM# 178 CROWN
Copper-Nickel, 38.8 mm. **Ruler:** Elizabeth II **Subject:** Gibraltar
City Charter **Obv:** Crowned bust right **Rev:** Bust left at right,
building at left

Date	Mintage	F	VF	XF	Unc	BU
1992	—	—	—	—	5.00	6.50

KM# 178a CROWN
28.2800 g., 0.9250 Silver 0.8410 oz. ASW, 38.8 mm.
Ruler: Elizabeth II **Subject:** Gibraltar City Charter **Obv:** Crowned
bust right **Rev:** Bust left at right, building at left

Date	Mintage	F	VF	XF	Unc	BU
1992 Proof	Est. 30,000	Value: 35.00				

KM# 192.2 CROWN
Copper-Nickel, 38.8 mm. **Ruler:** Elizabeth II **Obv:** Crowned bust
right **Rev:** Long-haired Dachshund, mint mark left of dog

Date	Mintage	F	VF	XF	Unc	BU
1993(c)	—	—	—	—	10.00	15.00
1993 Proof	—	Value: 20.00				

KM# 113 CROWN
Copper-Nickel, 38.8 mm. **Ruler:** Elizabeth II **Series:** WWII
Warships **Obv:** Crowned bust right **Rev:** USS Philadelphia

Date	Mintage	F	VF	XF	Unc	BU
1993	—	—	—	—	4.00	5.00

KM# 113a CROWN
28.2800 g., 0.9250 Silver 0.8410 oz. ASW, 38.8 mm.
Ruler: Elizabeth II **Series:** WWII Warships **Obv:** Crowned bust
right **Rev:** USS Philadelphia

Date	Mintage	F	VF	XF	Unc	BU
1993 Proof	Est. 30,000	Value: 26.50				

KM# 114 CROWN
Copper-Nickel, 38.8 mm. **Ruler:** Elizabeth II **Series:** WWII
Warships **Obv:** Crowned bust right **Rev:** USS McLanahan

Date	Mintage	F	VF	XF	Unc	BU
1993	—	—	—	—	4.00	5.00

KM# 114a CROWN
28.2800 g., 0.9250 Silver 0.8410 oz. ASW, 38.8 mm.
Ruler: Elizabeth II **Series:** WWII Warships **Obv:** Crowned bust
right **Rev:** USS McLanahan

Date	Mintage	F	VF	XF	Unc	BU
1993 Proof	Est. 30,000	Value: 26.50				

KM# 115 CROWN
Copper-Nickel, 38.8 mm. **Ruler:** Elizabeth II **Series:** WWII
Warships **Obv:** Crowned bust right **Rev:** HNLMS Isaac Sweers

Date	Mintage	F	VF	XF	Unc	BU
1993	—	—	—	—	4.00	5.00

KM# 115a CROWN
28.2800 g., 0.9250 Silver 0.8410 oz. ASW, 38.8 mm.
Ruler: Elizabeth II **Series:** WWII Warships **Obv:** Crowned bust
right **Rev:** HNLMS Isaac Sweers

Date	Mintage	F	VF	XF	Unc	BU
1993 Proof	Est. 30,000	Value: 26.50				

KM# 116 CROWN
Copper-Nickel, 38.8 mm. **Ruler:** Elizabeth II **Series:** WWII
Warships **Obv:** Crowned bust right **Rev:** USS Weehawken

Date	Mintage	F	VF	XF	Unc	BU
1993	—	—	—	—	4.00	5.00

KM# 116a CROWN
28.2800 g., 0.9250 Silver 0.8410 oz. ASW, 38.8 mm.
Ruler: Elizabeth II **Series:** WWII Warships **Obv:** Crowned bust
right **Rev:** USS Weehawken

Date	Mintage	F	VF	XF	Unc	BU
1993 Proof	Est. 30,000	Value: 26.50				

KM# 117 CROWN
Copper-Nickel, 38.8 mm. **Ruler:** Elizabeth II **Series:** WWII
Warships **Obv:** Crowned bust right **Rev:** HMS Warspite

Date	Mintage	F	VF	XF	Unc	BU
1993	—	—	—	—	4.00	5.00

KM# 117a CROWN
28.2800 g., 0.9250 Silver 0.8410 oz. ASW, 38.8 mm.
Ruler: Elizabeth II **Series:** WWII Warships **Obv:** Crowned bust
right **Rev:** HMS Warspite

Date	Mintage	F	VF	XF	Unc	BU
1993 Proof	Est. 30,000	Value: 26.50				

KM# 118 CROWN
Copper-Nickel, 38.8 mm. **Ruler:** Elizabeth II **Series:** WWII
Warships **Obv:** Crowned bust right **Rev:** HMS Hood

Date	Mintage	F	VF	XF	Unc	BU
1993	—	—	—	—	4.00	5.00

KM# 118a CROWN
28.2800 g., 0.9250 Silver 0.8410 oz. ASW, 38.8 mm. **Ruler:**
Elizabeth II **Series:** WWII Warships **Obv:** Crowned bus
t right **Rev:** HMS Hood

Date	Mintage	F	VF	XF	Unc	BU
1993 Proof	Est. 30,000	Value: 26.50				

KM# 119 CROWN
Copper-Nickel, 38.8 mm. **Ruler:** Elizabeth II **Series:** WWII
Warships **Obv:** Crowned bust right **Rev:** HMS Penelope

Date	Mintage	F	VF	XF	Unc	BU
1993	—	—	—	—	4.00	5.00

KM# 119a CROWN
28.2800 g., 0.9250 Silver 0.8410 oz. ASW, 38.8 mm.
Ruler: Elizabeth II **Series:** WWII Warships **Obv:** Crowned bust
right **Rev:** HMS Penelope

Date	Mintage	F	VF	XF	Unc	BU
1993 Proof	Est. 30,000	Value: 26.50				

KM# 120 CROWN
Copper-Nickel, 38.8 mm. **Ruler:** Elizabeth II **Series:** WWII
Warships **Obv:** Crowned bust right **Rev:** HMCS Prescott

Date	Mintage	F	VF	XF	Unc	BU
1993	—	—	—	—	4.00	5.00

KM# 120a CROWN
28.2800 g., 0.9250 Silver 0.8410 oz. ASW, 38.8 mm.
Ruler: Elizabeth II **Series:** WWII Warships **Obv:** Crowned bust
right **Rev:** HMCS Prescott

Date	Mintage	F	VF	XF	Unc	BU
1993 Proof	Est. 30,000	Value: 26.50				

KM# 121 CROWN
Copper-Nickel, 38.8 mm. **Ruler:** Elizabeth II **Series:** WWII
Warships **Obv:** Crowned bust right **Rev:** HMS Ark Royal

Date	Mintage	F	VF	XF	Unc	BU
1993	—	—	—	—	4.00	5.00

KM# 121a CROWN
28.2800 g., 0.9250 Silver 0.8410 oz. ASW, 38.8 mm.
Ruler: Elizabeth II **Series:** WWII Warships **Obv:** Crowned bust
right **Rev:** HMS Ark Royal

Date	Mintage	F	VF	XF	Unc	BU
1993 Proof	Est. 30,000	Value: 26.50				

KM# 122 CROWN
Copper-Nickel, 38.8 mm. **Ruler:** Elizabeth II **Series:** WWII
Warships **Obv:** Crowned bust right **Rev:** USS Gleaves

Date	Mintage	F	VF	XF	Unc	BU
1993	—	—	—	—	4.00	5.00

KM# 122a CROWN
28.2800 g., 0.9250 Silver 0.8410 oz. ASW, 38.8 mm.
Ruler: Elizabeth II **Series:** WWII Warships **Obv:** Crowned bust right **Rev:** USS Gleaves

Date	Mintage	F	VF	XF	Unc	BU
1993 Proof	Est. 30,000				Value: 26.50	

KM# 123 CROWN
Copper-Nickel, 38.8 mm. **Ruler:** Elizabeth II **Series:** WWII Warships **Obv:** Crowned bust right **Rev:** HMAS Waterhen

Date	Mintage	F	VF	XF	Unc	BU
1993	—	—	—	—	4.00	5.00

KM# 123a CROWN
28.2800 g., 0.9250 Silver 0.8410 oz. ASW, 38.8 mm.
Ruler: Elizabeth II **Series:** WWII Warships **Obv:** Crowned bust right **Rev:** HMAS Waterhen

Date	Mintage	F	VF	XF	Unc	BU
1993 Proof	Est. 30,000				Value: 26.50	

KM# 132 CROWN
Copper-Nickel, 38.8 mm. **Ruler:** Elizabeth II **Series:** House of - Stuart **Subject:** Queen Anne, 1702-1714 **Obv:** Young bust right **Rev:** Bust left

Date	Mintage	F	VF	XF	Unc	BU
1993 Prooflike	—	—	—	—	4.00	5.00

KM# 132a CROWN
28.2800 g., 0.9250 Silver 0.8410 oz. ASW, 38.8 mm.
Ruler: Elizabeth II **Series:** House of - Stuart **Subject:** Queen Anne, 1702-1714 **Obv:** Young bust right **Rev:** Bust left

Date	Mintage	F	VF	XF	Unc	BU
1993 Proof	Est. 30,000				Value: 35.00	

KM# 133 CROWN
Copper-Nickel, 38.8 mm. **Ruler:** Elizabeth II **Series:** House of - Hanover **Subject:** King GeorgeI, 1714-1727 **Obv:** Young bust right **Rev:** Laureate bust right

Date	Mintage	F	VF	XF	Unc	BU
1993 Prooflike	—	—	—	—	4.00	5.00

KM# 133a CROWN
28.2800 g., 0.9250 Silver 0.8410 oz. ASW, 38.8 mm. **Ruler:** Elizabeth II **Series:** House of - Hanover **Subject:** King George I, 1714-1727 **Obv:** Young bust right **Rev:** Laureate bust right

Date	Mintage	F	VF	XF	Unc	BU
1993 Proof	Est. 30,000				Value: 35.00	

KM# 134 CROWN
Copper-Nickel, 38.8 mm. **Ruler:** Elizabeth II **Series:** House of - Hanover **Subject:** King George II, 1727-1760 **Obv:** Young bust right **Rev:** Uniformed bust left

Date	Mintage	F	VF	XF	Unc	BU
1993 Prooflike	—	—	—	—	4.00	5.00

KM# 134a CROWN
28.2800 g., 0.9250 Silver 0.8410 oz. ASW, 38.8 mm. **Ruler:** Elizabeth II **Series:** House of - Hanover **Subject:** King George II, 1727-1760 **Obv:** Young bust right **Rev:** Uniformed bust left

Date	Mintage	F	VF	XF	Unc	BU
1993 Proof	Est. 30,000				Value: 32.50	

KM# 135 CROWN
Copper-Nickel, 38.8 mm. **Ruler:** Elizabeth II **Series:** House of - Hanover **Subject:** King George III, 1760-1820 **Obv:** Young bust right **Rev:** Bust right

Date	Mintage	F	VF	XF	Unc	BU
1993 Prooflike	—	—	—	—	4.00	5.00

KM# 135a CROWN
28.2800 g., 0.9250 Silver 0.8410 oz. ASW, 38.8 mm.
Ruler: Elizabeth II **Series:** House of - Hanover **Subject:** King George III, 1760-1820 **Obv:** Young bust right **Rev:** Bust right

Date	Mintage	F	VF	XF	Unc	BU
1993 Proof	Est. 30,000				Value: 32.50	

KM# 136 CROWN
Copper-Nickel, 38.8 mm. **Ruler:** Elizabeth II **Series:** House of - Hanover **Subject:** King George IV, 1820-1830 **Obv:** Young bust right **Rev:** Bust left

Date	Mintage	F	VF	XF	Unc	BU
1993 Prooflike	—	—	—	—	4.00	5.00

KM# 136a CROWN
28.2800 g., 0.9250 Silver 0.8410 oz. ASW, 38.8 mm.
Ruler: Elizabeth II **Series:** House of - Hanover **Subject:** King George IV, 1820-1830 **Obv:** Young bust right **Rev:** Bust left

Date	Mintage	F	VF	XF	Unc	BU
1993 Proof	Est. 30,000				Value: 35.00	

KM# 137 CROWN
Copper-Nickel, 38.8 mm. **Ruler:** Elizabeth II **Series:** House of - Hanover **Subject:** King William IV, 1830-1837 **Obv:** Young bust right **Rev:** Bust right

Date	Mintage	F	VF	XF	Unc	BU
1993 Prooflike	—	—	—	—	4.00	5.00

KM# 137a CROWN
28.2800 g., 0.9250 Silver 0.8410 oz. ASW, 38.8 mm.
Ruler: Elizabeth II **Series:** House of - Hanover **Subject:** King William IV, 1830-1837 **Obv:** Young bust right **Rev:** Bust right

Date	Mintage	F	VF	XF	Unc	BU
1993 Proof	Est. 30,000				Value: 35.00	

KM# 138 CROWN
Copper-Nickel, 38.8 mm. **Ruler:** Elizabeth II **Series:** House of - Hanover **Subject:** Queen Victoria, 1837-1901 **Obv:** Young bust right **Rev:** Bust left

Date	Mintage	F	VF	XF	Unc	BU
1993 Prooflike	—	—	—	—	4.00	5.00

KM# 138a CROWN
28.2800 g., 0.9250 Silver 0.8410 oz. ASW, 38.8 mm.
Ruler: Elizabeth II **Series:** House of - Hanover **Subject:** Queen Victoria, 1837-1901 **Obv:** Young bust right **Rev:** Bust left

Date	Mintage	F	VF	XF	Unc	BU
1993 Proof	Est. 30,000				Value: 35.00	

KM# 139 CROWN
Copper-Nickel, 38.8 mm. **Ruler:** Elizabeth II **Series:** House of - Saxe-Coburg **Subject:** King Edward VII, 1901-1910 **Obv:** Young bust right **Rev:** Uniformed bust right

Date	Mintage	F	VF	XF	Unc	BU
1993 Prooflike	—	—	—	—	4.00	5.00

KM# 139a CROWN
28.2800 g., 0.9250 Silver 0.8410 oz. ASW, 38.8 mm. **Ruler:** Elizabeth II **Series:** House of - Saxe-Coburg **Subject:** King Edward VII, 1901-1910 **Obv:** Young bust right **Rev:** Uniformed bust right

Date	Mintage	F	VF	XF	Unc	BU
1993 Proof	Est. 30,000				Value: 37.50	

KM# 140 CROWN
Copper-Nickel, 38.8 mm. **Ruler:** Elizabeth II **Series:** House of
- Windsor **Subject:** King George V, 1910-1936 **Obv:** Young bust
right **Rev:** Uniformed bust left

Date	Mintage	F	VF	XF	Unc	BU
1993 Prooflike	—	—	—	—	4.00	5.00

KM# 140a CROWN
28.2800 g., 0.9250 Silver 0.8410 oz. ASW, 38.8 mm. **Ruler:**
Elizabeth II **Series:** House of - Windsor **Subject:** King George
V, 1910-1936 **Obv:** Young bust right **Rev:** Uniformed bust left

Date	Mintage	F	VF	XF	Unc	BU
1993 Proof	Est. 30,000	Value: 35.00				

KM# 141 CROWN
Copper-Nickel, 38.8 mm. **Ruler:** Elizabeth II **Series:** House of
- Windsor **Subject:** King Edward VIII, 1936 **Obv:** Young bust right
Rev: Bust left

Date	Mintage	F	VF	XF	Unc	BU
1993 Prooflike	—	—	—	—	4.00	5.00

KM# 141a CROWN
28.2800 g., 0.9250 Silver 0.8410 oz. ASW, 38.8 mm.
Ruler: Elizabeth II **Series:** House of - Windsor **Subject:** King
Edward VIII, 1936 **Obv:** Young bust right **Rev:** Bust left

Date	Mintage	F	VF	XF	Unc	BU
1993 Proof	Est. 30,000	Value: 35.00				

KM# 142 CROWN
Copper-Nickel, 38.8 mm. **Ruler:** Elizabeth II **Series:** House of
- Windsor **Subject:** King George VI, 1936-1952 **Obv:** Young bust
right **Rev:** Bust left

Date	Mintage	F	VF	XF	Unc	BU
1993 Prooflike	—	—	—	—	4.00	5.00

KM# 142a CROWN
28.2800 g., 0.9250 Silver 0.8410 oz. ASW, 38.8 mm.
Ruler: Elizabeth II **Series:** House of - Windsor **Subject:** King
George VI, 1936-1952 **Obv:** Young bust right **Rev:** Bust left

Date	Mintage	F	VF	XF	Unc	BU
1993 Proof	Est. 30,000	Value: 35.00				

KM# 143 CROWN
Copper-Nickel, 38.8 mm. **Ruler:** Elizabeth II
Subject: Coronation of Queen Elizabeth II **Rev:** Crowned half
figure left with scepter divides dates

Date	Mintage	F	VF	XF	Unc	BU
1993	—				4.00	5.00

KM# 143a CROWN
28.2800 g., 0.9250 Silver 0.8410 oz. ASW **Subject:** Coronation
of Queen Elizabeth II **Rev:** Crowned half figure left with scepter
divides dates

Date	Mintage	F	VF	XF	Unc	BU
1993 Proof	Est. 30,000	Value: 35.00				

KM# 144 CROWN
Copper-Nickel, 38.8 mm. **Ruler:** Elizabeth II **Series:** WWII
Warships **Obv:** Crowned bust right **Rev:** FSS Savorgnan de Brazza

Date	Mintage	F	VF	XF	Unc	BU
1993	—				4.00	5.00

KM# 144a CROWN
28.2800 g., 0.9250 Silver 0.8410 oz. ASW, 38.8 mm.
Ruler: Elizabeth II **Subject:** WWII Warships **Obv:** Crowned bust
right **Rev:** FSS Savorgnan de Brazza

Date	Mintage	F	VF	XF	Unc	BU
1993 Proof	Est. 30,000	Value: 26.50				

KM# 145 CROWN
Copper-Nickel, 38.8 mm. **Ruler:** Elizabeth II **Series:** XVII Winter
Olympics **Rev:** Skaters

Date	Mintage	F	VF	XF	Unc	BU
1993 Proof	—			Value: 5.00		

KM# 145a CROWN
28.2800 g., 0.9250 Silver 0.8410 oz. ASW, 38.8 mm.
Ruler: Elizabeth II **Series:** XVII Winter Olympics **Rev:** Skaters

Date	Mintage	F	VF	XF	Unc	BU
1993 Proof	Est. 30,000	Value: 35.00				

KM# 145b CROWN
6.2200 g., 0.9999 Gold 0.1999 oz. AGW **Ruler:** Elizabeth II
Series: XVII Winter Olympics **Rev:** Skaters

Date	Mintage	F	VF	XF	Unc	BU
1993 Proof	Est. 5,000	Value: 200				

KM# 146 CROWN
Copper-Nickel, 38.8 mm. **Ruler:** Elizabeth II **Series:** XVII Winter
Olympics **Rev:** Ice hockey

Date	Mintage	F	VF	XF	Unc	BU
1993 Proof	—			Value: 5.00		

KM# 146a CROWN
28.2800 g., 0.9250 Silver 0.8410 oz. ASW, 38.8 mm.
Ruler: Elizabeth II **Series:** XVII Winter Olympics **Rev:** Ice hockey

Date	Mintage	F	VF	XF	Unc	BU
1993 Proof	Est. 30,000	Value: 35.00				

KM# 146b CROWN
6.2200 g., 0.9999 Gold 0.1999 oz. AGW **Ruler:** Elizabeth II
Series: XVII Winter Olympics **Rev:** Ice hockey

Date	Mintage	F	VF	XF	Unc	BU
1993 Proof	Est. 5,000	Value: 200				

KM# 147 CROWN
Copper-Nickel, 38.8 mm. **Ruler:** Elizabeth II **Series:** XVII Winter
Olympics **Rev:** Bobsledding

Date	Mintage	F	VF	XF	Unc	BU
1993 Proof	—			Value: 5.00		

KM# 147a CROWN
28.2800 g., 0.9250 Silver 0.8410 oz. ASW, 38.8 mm. **Ruler:**
Elizabeth II **Series:** XVII Winter Olympics **Rev:** Bobsledding

Date	Mintage	F	VF	XF	Unc	BU
1993 Proof	Est. 30,000	Value: 35.00				

KM# 147b CROWN
6.2200 g., 0.9999 Gold 0.1999 oz. AGW **Ruler:** Elizabeth II
Series: XVII Winter Olympics **Rev:** Bobsledding

Date	Mintage	F	VF	XF	Unc	BU
1993 Proof	Est. 5,000	Value: 200				

KM# 148 CROWN
Copper-Nickel, 38.8 mm. **Ruler:** Elizabeth II **Series:** XVII Winter
Olympics **Rev:** Skiers

Date	Mintage	F	VF	XF	Unc	BU
1993 Proof	—			Value: 5.00		

KM# 148a CROWN
28.2800 g., 0.9250 Silver 0.8410 oz. ASW, 38.8 mm.
Ruler: Elizabeth II **Series:** XVII Winter Olympics **Rev:** Skiers

Date	Mintage	F	VF	XF	Unc	BU
1993 Proof	Est. 30,000	Value: 35.00				

KM# 148b CROWN
6.2200 g., 0.9999 Gold 0.1999 oz. AGW **Ruler:** Elizabeth II
Rev: XVII Winter Olympics

Date	Mintage	F	VF	XF	Unc	BU
1993 Proof	Est. 5,000	Value: 200				

KM# 149 CROWN
Copper-Nickel, 38.8 mm. **Ruler:** Elizabeth II **Series:** Preserve Planet Earth **Obv:** Crowned bust right **Rev:** Cetiosaurus

Date	Mintage	F	VF	XF	Unc	BU
1993	—	—	—	—	10.00	14.00

KM# 149a CROWN
28.2800 g., 0.9250 Silver 0.8410 oz. ASW, 38.8 mm. **Ruler:** Elizabeth II **Series:** Preserve Planet Earth **Obv:** Crowned bust right **Rev:** Cetiosaurus

Date	Mintage	F	VF	XF	Unc	BU
1993 Proof	Est. 30,000	Value: 35.00				

KM# 151 CROWN
Copper-Nickel, 38.8 mm. **Ruler:** Elizabeth II **Series:** Preserve Planet Earth **Obv:** Crowned bust right **Rev:** Stegosaurus

Date	Mintage	F	VF	XF	Unc	BU
1993	—	—	—	—	10.00	14.00

KM# 151a CROWN
28.2800 g., 0.9250 Silver 0.8410 oz. ASW, 38.8 mm. **Ruler:** Elizabeth II **Series:** Preserve Planet Earth **Obv:** Crowned bust right **Rev:** Stegosaurus

Date	Mintage	F	VF	XF	Unc	BU
1993 Proof	Est. 30,000	Value: 35.00				

KM# 180 CROWN
Copper-Nickel, 38.8 mm. **Ruler:** Elizabeth II **Series:** International Friendship **Obv:** Crowned bust right **Rev:** Stylized panda

Date	Mintage	F	VF	XF	Unc	BU
1993	—	—	—	—	8.50	15.00

KM# 180a CROWN
28.2800 g., 0.9250 Silver 0.8410 oz. ASW, 38.8 mm. **Ruler:** Elizabeth II **Series:** International Friendship **Obv:** Crowned bust right **Rev:** Stylized panda

Date	Mintage	F	VF	XF	Unc	BU
1993 Proof	Est. 30,000	Value: 35.00				

KM# 184 CROWN
Copper-Nickel, 38.8 mm. **Ruler:** Elizabeth II **Series:** International Friendship **Obv:** Crowned bust right **Rev:** Natural panda

Date	Mintage	F	VF	XF	Unc	BU
1993	—	—	—	—	8.50	15.00

KM# 184a CROWN
28.2800 g., 0.9250 Silver 0.8410 oz. ASW, 38.8 mm. **Ruler:** Elizabeth II **Series:** International Friendship **Obv:** Crowned bust right **Rev:** Natural panda

Date	Mintage	F	VF	XF	Unc	BU
1993 Proof	Est. 30,000	Value: 35.00				

KM# 188 CROWN
Copper-Nickel, 38.8 mm. **Ruler:** Elizabeth II **Series:** International Friendship **Subject:** General Sikorski **Obv:** Crowned bust right **Rev:** Uniformed bust above plane, mountains in background

Date	Mintage	F	VF	XF	Unc	BU
1993	—	—	—	—	5.00	6.50

KM# 188a CROWN
28.2800 g., 0.9250 Silver 0.8410 oz. ASW, 38.8 mm. **Ruler:** Elizabeth II **Series:** International Friendship **Subject:** General Sikorski **Obv:** Crowned bust right **Rev:** Uniformed bust above plane, mountains in background

Date	Mintage	F	VF	XF	Unc	BU
1993 Proof	Est. 30,000	Value: 35.00				

KM# 192.1 CROWN
Copper-Nickel, 38.8 mm. **Ruler:** Elizabeth II **Obv:** Crowned bust right **Rev:** Long-haired Dachshund

Date	Mintage	F	VF	XF	Unc	BU
1993	—	—	—	—	10.00	15.00
1993	Est. 250	Value: 25.00				

KM# 192.1a CROWN
31.1030 g., 0.9250 Silver 0.9249 oz. ASW **Ruler:** Elizabeth II **Obv:** Crowned bust right **Rev:** Long-haired Dachshund

Date	Mintage	F	VF	XF	Unc	BU
1993 Proof	Est. 50,000	Value: 32.00				

KM# 192.2a CROWN
28.2800 g., 0.9250 Silver 0.8410 oz. ASW **Ruler:** Elizabeth II **Obv:** Crowned bust right **Rev:** Mint mark left of dog

Date	Mintage	F	VF	XF	Unc	BU
1993	—	—	—	—	27.50	32.00

KM# 200 CROWN
Copper-Nickel, 38.8 mm. **Ruler:** Elizabeth II **Subject:** Dependent Territories Conference **Obv:** Crowned bust right **Rev:** Two shields at center surrounded by five shields

Date	Mintage	F	VF	XF	Unc	BU
1993	—	—	—	—	5.50	7.00

KM# 200a CROWN
28.2800 g., 0.9250 Silver 0.8410 oz. ASW, 38.8 mm. **Ruler:** Elizabeth II **Subject:** Dependent Territories Conference **Obv:** Crowned bust right **Rev:** Two center shields surrounded by five shields

Date	Mintage	F	VF	XF	Unc	BU
1993 Proof	Est. 30,000	Value: 35.00				

KM# 201 CROWN
Copper-Nickel, 38.8 mm. **Ruler:** Elizabeth II **Series:** Peter Rabbit Centennial **Subject:** The Tale of Peter Rabbit **Obv:** Crowned bust right **Rev:** Peter Rabbit, sparrow on handle

Date	Mintage	F	VF	XF	Unc	BU
1993	—	—	—	—	7.50	9.00

KM# 201a CROWN
28.2800 g., 0.9250 Silver 0.8410 oz. ASW, 38.8 mm. **Ruler:** Elizabeth II **Series:** Peter Rabbit Centennial **Subject:** The Tale of Peter Rabbit **Obv:** Crowned bust right **Rev:** Peter Rabbit, sparrow on handle

Date	Mintage	F	VF	XF	Unc	BU
1993 Proof	Est. 30,000	Value: 37.50				

KM# 205 CROWN
Copper-Nickel, 38.8 mm. **Ruler:** Elizabeth II **Series:** Peter Rabbit Centennial **Subject:** The Tale of Peter Rabbit **Obv:** Crowned bust right **Rev:** Mrs. Tiggy-Winkel ironing

Date	Mintage	F	VF	XF	Unc	BU
1993	—	—	—	—	7.50	9.00

KM# 205a CROWN
28.2800 g., 0.9250 Silver 0.8410 oz. ASW, 38.8 mm. **Ruler:** Elizabeth II **Series:** Peter Rabbit Centennial **Subject:** The Tale of Peter Rabbit **Obv:** Crowned bust right **Rev:** Mrs. Tiggy-Winkel ironing

Date	Mintage	F	VF	XF	Unc	BU
1993 Proof	Est. 30,000	Value: 25.00				

KM# 209 CROWN
Copper-Nickel, 38.8 mm. **Ruler:** Elizabeth II **Series:** Peter Rabbit Centennial **Subject:** The Tale of Peter Rabbit **Obv:** Crowned bust right **Rev:** Jeremy Fisher fishing

Date	Mintage	F	VF	XF	Unc	BU
1993	—	—	—	—	7.50	9.00

KM# 209a CROWN
28.2800 g., 0.9250 Silver 0.8410 oz. ASW, 38.8 mm. **Ruler:** Elizabeth II **Series:** Peter Rabbit Centennial **Subject:** The Tale of Peter Rabbit **Obv:** Crowned bust right **Rev:** Jeremy Fisher fishing

Date	Mintage	F	VF	XF	Unc	BU
1993 Proof	Est. 30,000			Value: 25.00		

KM# 213 CROWN
Copper-Nickel, 38.8 mm. **Ruler:** Elizabeth II **Series:** Peter Rabbit Centennial **Subject:** The Tale of Peter Rabbit **Obv:** Crowned bust right **Rev:** Tom Kitten with mother cat

Date	Mintage	F	VF	XF	Unc	BU
1993	—	—	—	—	7.50	9.00

KM# 213a CROWN
28.2800 g., 0.9250 Silver 0.8410 oz. ASW, 38.8 mm. **Ruler:** Elizabeth II **Series:** Peter Rabbit Centennial **Subject:** The Tale of Peter Rabbit **Obv:** Crowned bust right **Rev:** Tom Kitten with mother cat

Date	Mintage	F	VF	XF	Unc	BU
1993 Proof	Est. 30,000			Value: 25.00		

KM# 217 CROWN
Copper-Nickel, 38.8 mm. **Ruler:** Elizabeth II **Series:** Peter Rabbit Centennial **Subject:** The Tale of Peter Rabbit **Obv:** Crowned bust right **Rev:** Benjamin Bunny with hat, holding coat

Date	Mintage	F	VF	XF	Unc	BU
1993	—	—	—	—	7.50	9.00

KM# 217a CROWN
28.2800 g., 0.9250 Silver 0.8410 oz. ASW, 38.8 mm. **Ruler:** Elizabeth II **Series:** Peter Rabbit Centennial **Subject:** The Tale of Peter Rabbit **Obv:** Crowned bust right **Rev:** Benjamin Bunny with hat holding coat

Date	Mintage	F	VF	XF	Unc	BU
1993 Proof	Est. 30,000			Value: 25.00		

KM# 221 CROWN
Copper-Nickel, 38.8 mm. **Ruler:** Elizabeth II **Series:** Peter Rabbit Centennial **Subject:** The Tale of Peter Rabbit **Obv:** Crowned bust right **Rev:** Jemima Puddle-Duck talking to fox

Date	Mintage	F	VF	XF	Unc	BU
1993	—	—	—	—	7.50	9.00

KM# 221a CROWN
28.2800 g., 0.9250 Silver 0.8410 oz. ASW, 38.8 mm. **Ruler:** Elizabeth II **Series:** Peter Rabbit Centennial **Subject:** The Tale of Peter Rabbit **Obv:** Crowned bust right **Rev:** Jemima Puddle-Duck talking to fox

Date	Mintage	F	VF	XF	Unc	BU
1993 Proof	Est. 30,000			Value: 25.00		

KM# 342C CROWN
Copper-Nickel, 38.8 mm. **Ruler:** Elizabeth II **Subject:** Year of the Cockerel **Obv:** Crowned bust right **Rev:** Cockerel (rooster)

Date	Mintage	F	VF	XF	Unc	BU
1993	—	—	—	—	9.00	—

KM# 225 CROWN
Copper-Nickel, 38.8 mm. **Ruler:** Elizabeth II **Subject:** World Cup Soccer **Obv:** Crowned bust right **Rev:** Three players

Date	Mintage	F	VF	XF	Unc	BU
1994	—	—	—	—	4.75	6.00

KM# 225a CROWN
28.2800 g., 0.9250 Silver 0.8410 oz. ASW, 38.8 mm. **Ruler:** Elizabeth II **Subject:** World Cup Soccer **Obv:** Crowned bust right **Rev:** Three players

Date	Mintage	F	VF	XF	Unc	BU
1994 Proof	Est. 30,000			Value: 30.00		

KM# 227 CROWN
Copper-Nickel, 38.8 mm. **Ruler:** Elizabeth II **Subject:** World Cup Soccer **Obv:** Crowned bust right **Rev:** Two players

Date	Mintage	F	VF	XF	Unc	BU
1994	—	—	—	—	4.75	6.00

KM# 227a CROWN
28.2800 g., 0.9250 Silver 0.8410 oz. ASW, 38.8 mm. **Ruler:** Elizabeth II **Subject:** World Cup Soccer **Obv:** Crowned bust right **Rev:** Two players facing

Date	Mintage	F	VF	XF	Unc	BU
1994 Proof	Est. 30,000			Value: 30.00		

KM# 229 CROWN
Copper-Nickel, 38.8 mm. **Ruler:** Elizabeth II **Subject:** World Cup Soccer **Obv:** Crowned bust right **Rev:** Goalie and scorer

Date	Mintage	F	VF	XF	Unc	BU
1994	—	—	—	—	4.75	6.00

KM# 229a CROWN
28.2800 g., 0.9250 Silver 0.8410 oz. ASW, 38.8 mm. **Ruler:** Elizabeth II **Subject:** World Cup Soccer **Obv:** Crowned bust right **Rev:** Goalie and scorer

Date	Mintage	F	VF	XF	Unc	BU
1994 Proof	Est. 30,000			Value: 30.00		

KM# 231 CROWN
Copper-Nickel, 38.8 mm. **Ruler:** Elizabeth II **Subject:** World Cup Soccer **Obv:** Crowned bust right **Rev:** One player

Date	Mintage	F	VF	XF	Unc	BU
1994	—	—	—	—	4.75	6.00

KM# 231a CROWN
28.2800 g., 0.9250 Silver 0.8410 oz. ASW, 38.8 mm. **Ruler:** Elizabeth II **Subject:** World Cup Soccer **Obv:** Crowned bust right **Rev:** One player

Date	Mintage	F	VF	XF	Unc	BU
1994	Est. 30,000			Value: 30.00		

KM# 233 CROWN
Copper-Nickel, 38.8 mm. **Ruler:** Elizabeth II **Subject:** World Cup Soccer **Obv:** Crowned bust right **Rev:** Two players, one kicking

Date	Mintage	F	VF	XF	Unc	BU
1994	—	—	—	—	4.75	6.00

KM# 233a CROWN
28.2800 g., 0.9250 Silver 0.8410 oz. ASW, 38.8 mm. **Ruler:** Elizabeth II **Subject:** World Cup Soccer **Obv:** Crowned bust right **Rev:** Two players, one kicking

Date	Mintage	F	VF	XF	Unc	BU
1994 Proof	Est. 30,000			Value: 30.00		

KM# 235 CROWN
Copper-Nickel, 38.8 mm. **Ruler:** Elizabeth II **Subject:** World Cup Soccer **Obv:** Crowned bust right **Rev:** Two players sideways

Date	Mintage	F	VF	XF	Unc	BU
1994	—	—	—	—	4.75	6.00

KM# 235a CROWN
28.2800 g., 0.9250 Silver 0.8410 oz. ASW, 38.8 mm.
Ruler: Elizabeth II **Subject:** World Cup Soccer **Obv:** Crowned bust right **Rev:** Two players sideways

Date	Mintage	F	VF	XF	Unc	BU
1994 Proof	Est. 30,000	Value: 30.00				

KM# 239 CROWN
Copper-Nickel, 38.8 mm. **Ruler:** Elizabeth II **Series:** Preserve Planet Earth **Obv:** Crowned bust right **Rev:** Sabre-tooth Tiger

Date	Mintage	F	VF	XF	Unc	BU
1994	—	—	—	—	7.00	15.00

KM# 239a CROWN
28.2800 g., 0.9250 Silver 0.8410 oz. ASW, 38.8 mm.
Ruler: Elizabeth II **Series:** Preserve Planet Earth **Obv:** Crowned bust right **Rev:** Sabre-tooth Tiger

Date	Mintage	F	VF	XF	Unc	BU
1994 Proof	Est. 30,000	Value: 37.50				

KM# 241 CROWN
Copper-Nickel, 38.8 mm. **Ruler:** Elizabeth II **Series:** Preserve Planet Earth **Obv:** Crowned bust right **Rev:** Spanish Eagle

Date	Mintage	F	VF	XF	Unc	BU
1994	—	—	—	—	9.00	14.00

KM# 241a CROWN
28.2800 g., 0.9250 Silver 0.8410 oz. ASW **Series:** Preserve Planet Earth **Obv:** Crowned bust right **Rev:** Spanish Eagle

Date	Mintage	F	VF	XF	Unc	BU
1994 Proof	Est. 30,000	Value: 37.50				

KM# 243 CROWN
Copper-Nickel, 38.8 mm. **Ruler:** Elizabeth II **Series:** Preserve Planet Earth **Obv:** Crowned bust right **Rev:** Striped Dolphins

Date	Mintage	F	VF	XF	Unc	BU
1994	—	—	—	—	9.00	14.00

KM# 243a CROWN
28.2800 g., 0.9250 Silver 0.8410 oz. ASW, 38.8 mm.
Ruler: Elizabeth II **Series:** Preserve Planet Earth **Obv:** Crowned bust right **Rev:** Striped Dolphins

Date	Mintage	F	VF	XF	Unc	BU
1994 Proof	Est. 30,000	Value: 37.50				

KM# 245 CROWN
Copper-Nickel, 38.8 mm. **Ruler:** Elizabeth II **Series:** Preserve Planet Earth **Obv:** Crowned bust right **Rev:** African Elephants

Date	Mintage	F	VF	XF	Unc	BU
1994	—	—	—	—	9.00	14.00

KM# 245a CROWN
28.2800 g., 0.9250 Silver 0.8410 oz. ASW, 38.8 mm.
Ruler: Elizabeth II **Series:** Preserve Planet Earth **Obv:** Crowned bust right **Rev:** African Elephants

Date	Mintage	F	VF	XF	Unc	BU
1994 Proof	Est. 30,000	Value: 37.50				

KM# 259 CROWN
Copper-Nickel, 38.8 mm. **Ruler:** Elizabeth II **Series:** World War II **Obv:** Crowned bust right **Rev:** Maltese convoy

Date	Mintage	F	VF	XF	Unc	BU
1994	—	—	—	—	6.00	8.00

KM# 259a CROWN
28.2800 g., 0.9250 Silver 0.8410 oz. ASW, 38.8 mm.
Ruler: Elizabeth II **Series:** World War II **Obv:** Crowned bust right **Rev:** Maltese convoy

Date	Mintage	F	VF	XF	Unc	BU
1994 Proof	Est. 30,000	Value: 32.50				

KM# 260 CROWN
Copper-Nickel, 38.8 mm. **Ruler:** Elizabeth II **Series:** World War II **Obv:** Crowned bust right **Rev:** Squadron 202 in Gibraltar

Date	Mintage	F	VF	XF	Unc	BU
1994	—	—	—	—	6.00	8.00

KM# 260a CROWN
28.2800 g., 0.9250 Silver 0.8410 oz. ASW, 38.8 mm.
Ruler: Elizabeth II **Series:** World War II **Obv:** Crowned bust right **Rev:** Squadron 202 in Gibraltar

Date	Mintage	F	VF	XF	Unc	BU
1994 Proof	Est. 30,000	Value: 32.50				

KM# 261 CROWN
Copper-Nickel, 38.8 mm. **Ruler:** Elizabeth II **Series:** World War II **Obv:** Crowned bust right **Rev:** Admiral Somerville

Date	Mintage	F	VF	XF	Unc	BU
1994	—	—	—	—	6.00	8.00

KM# 261a CROWN
28.2800 g., 0.9250 Silver 0.8410 oz. ASW, 38.8 mm.
Ruler: Elizabeth II **Series:** World War II **Obv:** Crowned bust right **Rev:** Admiral Somerville

Date	Mintage	F	VF	XF	Unc	BU
1994 Proof	Est. 30,000	Value: 32.50				

KM# 262 CROWN
Copper-Nickel, 38.8 mm. **Ruler:** Elizabeth II **Series:** World War II **Obv:** Crowned bust right **Rev:** Glen Miller and band

Date	Mintage	F	VF	XF	Unc	BU
1994	—	—	—	—	6.00	8.00

KM# 262a CROWN
28.2800 g., 0.9250 Silver 0.8410 oz. ASW, 38.8 mm.
Ruler: Elizabeth II **Series:** World War II **Obv:** Crowned bust right **Rev:** Glen Miller and band

Date	Mintage	F	VF	XF	Unc	BU
1994 Proof	Est. 30,000	Value: 30.00				

KM# 263 CROWN
Copper-Nickel, 38.8 mm. **Ruler:** Elizabeth II **Series:** World War II **Obv:** Crowned bust right **Rev:** King George VI and pilots

Date	Mintage	F	VF	XF	Unc	BU
1994	—	—	—	—	6.00	8.00

KM# 263a CROWN
28.2800 g., 0.9250 Silver 0.8410 oz. ASW, 38.8 mm.
Ruler: Elizabeth II **Series:** World War II **Obv:** Crowned bust right **Rev:** King George VI and pilots

Date	Mintage	F	VF	XF	Unc	BU
1994 Proof	Est. 30,000	Value: 35.00				

KM# 264 CROWN
Copper-Nickel, 38.8 mm. **Ruler:** Elizabeth II **Series:** World War II **Obv:** Crowned bust right **Rev:** General Eisenhower

Date	Mintage	F	VF	XF	Unc	BU
1994	—	—	—	—	6.00	8.00

KM# 264a CROWN
28.2800 g., 0.9250 Silver 0.8410 oz. ASW, 38.8 mm.
Ruler: Elizabeth II **Series:** World War II **Obv:** Crowned bust right **Rev:** General Eisenhower

Date	Mintage	F	VF	XF	Unc	BU
1994 Proof	—	Value: 35.00				

KM# 273 CROWN
Copper-Nickel, 38.8 mm. **Ruler:** Elizabeth II **Series:** First Man on Moon **Obv:** Crowned bust right **Rev:** Space capsule recovery

Date	Mintage	F	VF	XF	Unc	BU
1994	—	—	—	—	5.75	6.50

KM# 273a CROWN
28.2800 g., 0.9250 Silver 0.8410 oz. ASW, 38.8 mm.
Ruler: Elizabeth II **Series:** First Man on Moon **Obv:** Crowned bust right **Rev:** Space capsule recovery

Date	Mintage	F	VF	XF	Unc	BU
1994 Proof	Est. 30,000	Value: 20.00				

KM# 276 CROWN
Copper-Nickel, 38.8 mm. **Ruler:** Elizabeth II **Series:** First Man on Moon **Obv:** Crowned bust right **Rev:** First flag planted on moon

Date	Mintage	F	VF	XF	Unc	BU
1994	—	—	—	—	5.75	6.50

KM# 276a CROWN
28.2800 g., 0.9250 Silver 0.8410 oz. ASW, 38.8 mm.
Ruler: Elizabeth II **Series:** First Man on Moon **Obv:** Crowned bust right **Rev:** First flag planted on moon

Date	Mintage	F	VF	XF	Unc	BU
1994 Proof	Est. 30,000	Value: 20.00				

KM# 271 CROWN
Copper-Nickel, 38.8 mm. **Ruler:** Elizabeth II **Series:** First Man on Moon **Obv:** Crowned bust right **Rev:** Dr. Wernher von Braun with model of shuttle

Date	Mintage	F	VF	XF	Unc	BU
1994	—	—	—	—	5.75	6.50

KM# 271a CROWN
28.2800 g., 0.9250 Silver 0.8410 oz. ASW, 38.8 mm.
Ruler: Elizabeth II **Series:** First Man on Moon **Obv:** Crowned bust right **Rev:** Dr. Wernher von Braun with model of shuttle

Date	Mintage	F	VF	XF	Unc	BU
1994 Proof	Est. 30,000	Value: 22.00				

KM# 274 CROWN
Copper-Nickel, 38.8 mm. **Ruler:** Elizabeth II **Series:** First Man on Moon **Obv:** Crowned bust right **Rev:** First manned lunar landing

Date	Mintage	F	VF	XF	Unc	BU
1994	—	—	—	—	5.75	6.50

KM# 274a CROWN
28.2800 g., 0.9250 Silver 0.8410 oz. ASW, 38.8 mm.
Ruler: Elizabeth II **Series:** First Man on Moon **Obv:** Crowned bust right **Rev:** First manned lunar landing

Date	Mintage	F	VF	XF	Unc	BU
1994 Proof	Est. 30,000	Value: 22.00				

KM# 285 CROWN
Copper-Nickel, 38.8 mm. **Ruler:** Elizabeth II **Series:** 100th Anniversary of The Return of Sherlock Holmes **Subject:** Sherlock Holmes **Obv:** Crowned bust right **Rev:** Bust with pipe left

Date	Mintage	F	VF	XF	Unc	BU
1994	—	—	—	—	8.00	9.00

KM# 285a CROWN
28.2800 g., 0.9250 Silver 0.8410 oz. ASW, 38.8 mm.
Ruler: Elizabeth II **Series:** 100th Anniversary of The Return of Sherlock Holmes **Subject:** Sherlock Holmes **Obv:** Crowned bust right **Rev:** Bust with pipe left

Date	Mintage	F	VF	XF	Unc	BU
1994 Proof	Est. 30,000	Value: 27.50				

KM# 272 CROWN
Copper-Nickel, 38.8 mm. **Ruler:** Elizabeth II **Series:** First Man on Moon **Obv:** Crowned bust right **Rev:** Rocket launching

Date	Mintage	F	VF	XF	Unc	BU
1994	—	—	—	—	5.75	6.50

KM# 272a CROWN
28.2800 g., 0.9250 Silver 0.8410 oz. ASW, 38.8 mm.
Ruler: Elizabeth II **Series:** First Man on Moon **Obv:** Crowned bust right **Rev:** Rocket launching

Date	Mintage	F	VF	XF	Unc	BU
1994 Proof	Est. 30,000	Value: 22.00				

KM# 275 CROWN
Copper-Nickel, 38.8 mm. **Ruler:** Elizabeth II **Series:** First Man on Moon **Obv:** Crowned bust right **Rev:** First step on moon

Date	Mintage	F	VF	XF	Unc	BU
1994	—	—	—	—	5.75	6.50

KM# 275a CROWN
28.2800 g., 0.9250 Silver 0.8410 oz. ASW, 38.8 mm.
Ruler: Elizabeth II **Series:** First Man on Moon **Obv:** Crowned bust right **Rev:** First step on moon

Date	Mintage	F	VF	XF	Unc	BU
1994 Proof	Est. 30,000	Value: 20.00				

KM# 286 CROWN
Copper-Nickel, 38.8 mm. **Ruler:** Elizabeth II **Series:** 100th Anniversary of The Return of Sherlock Holmes **Obv:** Crowned bust right **Rev:** Sherlock Holmes playing violin for Dr. Watson

Date	Mintage	F	VF	XF	Unc	BU
1994	—	—	—	—	8.00	9.00

KM# 286a CROWN
28.2800 g., 0.9250 Silver 0.8410 oz. ASW, 38.8 mm.
Ruler: Elizabeth II **Series:** 100th Anniversary of The Return of Sherlock Holmes **Obv:** Crowned bust right **Rev:** Sherlock Holmes playing violin for Dr. Watson.

Date	Mintage	F	VF	XF	Unc	BU
1994 Proof	Est. 30,000	Value: 27.50				

KM# 287 CROWN
Copper-Nickel, 38.8 mm. **Ruler:** Elizabeth II **Series:** 100th Anniversary of The Return of Sherlock Holmes **Subject:** 221 B Baker Street **Obv:** Crowned bust right **Rev:** Figures in front of building

Date	Mintage	F	VF	XF	Unc	BU
1994	—	—	—	—	8.00	9.00

KM# 287a CROWN
28.2800 g., 0.9250 Silver 0.8410 oz. ASW, 38.8 mm. **Ruler:** Elizabeth II **Series:** 100th Anniversary of The Return of Sherlock Holmes **Subject:** 221 B Baker Street **Obv:** Crowned bust right **Rev:** Figures in front of building

Date	Mintage	F	VF	XF	Unc	BU
1994 Proof	Est. 30,000	Value: 22.50				

KM# 290 CROWN
Copper-Nickel, 38.8 mm. **Ruler:** Elizabeth II **Series:** 100th Anniversary of The Return of Sherlock Holmes **Subject:** The Hound of the Baskervilles **Obv:** Crowned bust right **Rev:** Two figures back and right of large dog at front

Date	Mintage	F	VF	XF	Unc	BU
1994	—	—	—	—	8.00	9.00

KM# 290a CROWN
28.2800 g., 0.9250 Silver 0.8410 oz. ASW, 38.8 mm. **Ruler:** Elizabeth II **Series:** 100th Anniversary of The Return of Sherlock Holmes **Subject:** The Hound of the Baskervilles **Obv:** Crowned bust right **Rev:** Two figures back and right of large dog at front

Date	Mintage	F	VF	XF	Unc	BU
1994 Proof	Est. 30,000	Value: 35.00				

KM# 444 CROWN
Copper-Nickel, 38.8 mm. **Ruler:** Elizabeth II **Subject:** The Tale of Peter Rabbit **Obv:** Crowned bust right **Rev:** Mother rabbit with bunnies

Date	Mintage	F	VF	XF	Unc	BU
1994	—	—	—	—	7.50	10.00

KM# 444a CROWN
28.2800 g., 0.9250 Silver 0.8410 oz. ASW, 38.8 mm. **Ruler:** Elizabeth II **Subject:** The Tale of Peter Rabbit **Obv:** Crowned bust right **Rev:** Mother rabbit with bunnies

Date	Mintage	F	VF	XF	Unc	BU
1994 Proof	Est. 30,000	Value: 40.00				

KM# 288 CROWN
Copper-Nickel, 38.8 mm. **Ruler:** Elizabeth II **Series:** 100th Anniversary of The Return of Sherlock Holmes **Subject:** The Empty House **Obv:** Crowned bust right **Rev:** Three figures

Date	Mintage	F	VF	XF	Unc	BU
1994	—	—	—	—	8.00	9.00

KM# 288a CROWN
28.2800 g., 0.9250 Silver 0.8410 oz. ASW, 38.8 mm. **Ruler:** Elizabeth II **Series:** 100th Anniversary of The Return of Sherlock Holmes **Subject:** The Empty House **Obv:** Crowned bust right **Rev:** Three figures

Date	Mintage	F	VF	XF	Unc	BU
1994 Proof	Est. 30,000	Value: 22.50				

KM# 291 CROWN
Copper-Nickel, 38.8 mm. **Ruler:** Elizabeth II **Series:** 100th Anniversary of The Return of Sherlock Holmes **Subject:** The Three Garriders **Obv:** Crowned bust right **Rev:** Two seated figures **Note:** Variety exists with spelling error: GARRIDEBS.

Date	Mintage	F	VF	XF	Unc	BU
1994	—	—	—	—	8.00	9.00

KM# 291a CROWN
28.2800 g., 0.9250 Silver 0.8410 oz. ASW, 38.8 mm. **Ruler:** Elizabeth II **Series:** 100th Anniversary of The Return of Sherlock Holmes **Subject:** The Three Garriders **Obv:** Crowned bust right **Rev:** Two seated figures

Date	Mintage	F	VF	XF	Unc	BU
1994 Proof	Est. 30,000	Value: 20.00				

KM# 299 CROWN
Copper-Nickel, 38.8 mm. **Ruler:** Elizabeth II **Series:** Atlanta Olympics **Obv:** Crowned bust right **Rev:** Long jumper

Date	Mintage	F	VF	XF	Unc	BU
1995 Proof	—	Value: 6.00				

KM# 299a CROWN
28.2800 g., 0.9250 Silver 0.8410 oz. ASW, 38.8 mm. **Ruler:** Elizabeth II **Series:** Atlanta Olympics **Obv:** Crowned bust right **Rev:** Long jumper

Date	Mintage	F	VF	XF	Unc	BU
1995 Proof	Est. 30,000	Value: 27.50				

KM# 289 CROWN
Copper-Nickel, 38.8 mm. **Ruler:** Elizabeth II **Series:** 100th Anniversary of The Return of Sherlock Holmes **Subject:** The Mary Celeste **Obv:** Crowned bust right **Rev:** Cameo left of masted ship at sea

Date	Mintage	F	VF	XF	Unc	BU
1994	—	—	—	—	8.00	9.00

KM# 289a CROWN
28.2800 g., 0.9250 Silver 0.8410 oz. ASW, 38.8 mm. **Ruler:** Elizabeth II **Series:** 100th Anniversary of The Return of Sherlock Holmes **Subject:** The Mary Celeste **Obv:** Crowned bust right **Rev:** Cameo left of masted ship at sea

Date	Mintage	F	VF	XF	Unc	BU
1994 Proof	Est. 30,000	Value: 37.50				

KM# 292 CROWN
Copper-Nickel, 38.8 mm. **Ruler:** Elizabeth II **Series:** 100th Anniversary of The Return of Sherlock Holmes **Subject:** The Final Problem **Obv:** Crowned bust right **Rev:** Two figures and waterfall

Date	Mintage	F	VF	XF	Unc	BU
1994	—	—	—	—	8.00	9.00

KM# 292a CROWN
28.2800 g., 0.9250 Silver 0.8410 oz. ASW, 38.8 mm. **Ruler:** Elizabeth II **Series:** 100th Anniversary of The Return of Sherlock Holmes **Subject:** The Final Problem **Obv:** Crowned bust right **Rev:** Two figures and waterfall

Date	Mintage	F	VF	XF	Unc	BU
1994 Proof	Est. 30,000	Value: 20.00				

KM# 300 CROWN
Copper-Nickel, 38.8 mm. **Ruler:** Elizabeth II **Series:** Atlanta Olympics **Obv:** Crowned bust right **Rev:** Discus thrower

Date	Mintage	F	VF	XF	Unc	BU
1995	—	—	—	—	5.50	6.00

KM# 300a CROWN
28.2800 g., 0.9250 Silver 0.8410 oz. ASW, 38.8 mm. **Ruler:** Elizabeth II **Series:** Atlanta Olympics **Obv:** Crowned bust right **Rev:** Discus thrower

Date	Mintage	F	VF	XF	Unc	BU
1995 Proof	Est. 30,000	Value: 27.50				

KM# 301 CROWN
Copper-Nickel, 38.8 mm. **Ruler:** Elizabeth II **Obv:** Crowned bust right **Rev:** Relay runners

Date	Mintage	F	VF	XF	Unc	BU
1995	—	—	—	—	5.50	6.00

KM# 301a CROWN
28.2800 g., 0.9250 Silver 0.8410 oz. ASW, 38.8 mm.
Ruler: Elizabeth II **Obv:** Crowned bust right **Rev:** Relay runners

Date	Mintage	F	VF	XF	Unc	BU
1995 Proof	Est. 30,000	Value: 27.50				

KM# 302 CROWN
Copper-Nickel, 38.8 mm. **Ruler:** Elizabeth II **Series:** Atlanta Olympics **Obv:** Crowned bust right **Rev:** Javelin throwers

Date	Mintage	F	VF	XF	Unc	BU
1995	—	—	—	—	5.50	6.00

KM# 302a CROWN
28.2800 g., 0.9250 Silver 0.8410 oz. ASW, 38.8 mm.
Ruler: Elizabeth II **Series:** Atlanta Olympics **Obv:** Crowned bust right **Rev:** Javelin throwers

Date	Mintage	F	VF	XF	Unc	BU
1995 Proof	Est. 30,000	Value: 27.50				

KM# 304 CROWN
Copper-Nickel, 38.8 mm. **Ruler:** Elizabeth II **Obv:** Crowned bust right **Rev:** Sun rising over Rock of Gibraltar

Date	Mintage	F	VF	XF	Unc	BU
1995	—	—	—	—	6.50	7.50

KM# 304a CROWN
28.2800 g., 0.9250 Silver 0.8410 oz. ASW, 38.8 mm.
Ruler: Elizabeth II **Obv:** Crowned bust right **Rev:** Sun rising over Rock of Gibraltar

Date	Mintage	F	VF	XF	Unc	BU
1995 Proof	Est. 30,000	Value: 40.00				

KM# 306 CROWN
Copper-Nickel, 38.8 mm. **Ruler:** Elizabeth II **Series:** Preserve Planet Earth **Obv:** Crowned bust right **Rev:** Monkeys

Date	Mintage	F	VF	XF	Unc	BU
1995	—	—	—	—	10.00	14.00

KM# 306a CROWN
28.2800 g., 0.9250 Silver 0.8410 oz. ASW, 38.8 mm. **Series:** Preserve Planet Earth **Obv:** Crowned bust right **Rev:** Monkeys

Date	Mintage	F	VF	XF	Unc	BU
1995 Proof	Est. 30,000	Value: 40.00				

KM# 308 CROWN
Copper-Nickel, 38.8 mm. **Ruler:** Elizabeth II **Series:** Preserve Planet Earth **Obv:** Crowned bust right **Rev:** Sperm whale

Date	Mintage	F	VF	XF	Unc	BU
1995	—	—	—	—	10.00	14.00

KM# 308a CROWN
28.2800 g., 0.9250 Silver 0.8410 oz. ASW, 38.8 mm.
Ruler: Elizabeth II **Series:** Preserve Planet Earth **Obv:** Crowned bust right **Rev:** Sperm whale

Date	Mintage	F	VF	XF	Unc	BU
1995 Proof	Est. 30,000	Value: 42.50				

KM# 327 CROWN
Copper-Nickel, 38.8 mm. **Ruler:** Elizabeth II **Subject:** The Tale of Peter Rabbit **Obv:** Crowned bust right **Rev:** Rabbit running right

Date	Mintage	F	VF	XF	Unc	BU
1995	—	—	—	—	6.50	8.00

KM# 327a CROWN
28.2800 g., 0.9250 Silver 0.8410 oz. ASW, 38.8 mm.
Ruler: Elizabeth II **Subject:** The Tale of Peter Rabbit **Obv:** Crowned bust right **Rev:** Rabbit running right

Date	Mintage	F	VF	XF	Unc	BU
1995 Proof	Est. 30,000	Value: 37.50				

KM# 329 CROWN
Copper-Nickel, 38.8 mm. **Ruler:** Elizabeth II **Series:** Island Games **Obv:** Crowned bust right **Rev:** Various athletes around shield

Date	Mintage	F	VF	XF	Unc	BU
1995	—	—	—	—	6.00	7.50

KM# 329a CROWN
28.2800 g., 0.9250 Silver 0.8410 oz. ASW, 38.8 mm. **Ruler:** Elizabeth II **Series:** Island Games **Obv:** Crowned bust right **Rev:** Various athletes around shield

Date	Mintage	F	VF	XF	Unc	BU
1995 Proof	Est. 30,000	Value: 35.00				

KM# 331 CROWN
Copper-Nickel, 38.8 mm. **Ruler:** Elizabeth II **Series:** Island Games **Obv:** Crowned bust right **Rev:** Various athletes around shield

Date	Mintage	F	VF	XF	Unc	BU
1995	—	—	—	—	6.00	7.50

KM# 331a CROWN
28.2800 g., 0.9250 Silver 0.8410 oz. ASW, 38.8 mm.
Ruler: Elizabeth II **Series:** Island Games **Obv:** Crowned bust right **Rev:** Various athletes around shield

Date	Mintage	F	VF	XF	Unc	BU
1995 Proof	Est. 30,000	Value: 35.00				

KM# 408a CROWN
28.2800 g., 0.9250 Silver 0.8410 oz. ASW, 38.8 mm.
Ruler: Elizabeth II **Series:** Centenary of the Cinema
Subject: Audrey Hepburn - actress, 1929-93 **Obv:** Crowned bust right **Rev:** Bust 3/4 facing, dates

Date	Mintage	F	VF	XF	Unc	BU
1996 Proof	Est. 30,000	Value: 37.50				

KM# 348 CROWN
Copper-Nickel, 38.8 mm. **Ruler:** Elizabeth II **Series:** Atlanta Olympics **Obv:** Crowned bust right **Rev:** Tennis player

Date	Mintage	F	VF	XF	Unc	BU
1996	—	—	—	—	6.00	7.50

KM# 348a CROWN
28.2800 g., 0.9250 Silver 0.8410 oz. ASW, 38.8 mm.
u**ler:** Elizabeth II **Series:** Atlanta Olympics **Obv:** Crowned bust right **Rev:** Tennis player

Date	Mintage	F	VF	XF	Unc	BU
1996 Proof	Est. 30,000	Value: 42.50				

KM# 349 CROWN
28.2800 g., 0.9250 Silver 0.8410 oz. ASW, 38.8 mm.
Ruler: Elizabeth II **Series:** 1996 Atlanta Olympics **Obv:** Crowned bust right **Rev:** Wrestlers

Date	Mintage	F	VF	XF	Unc	BU
1996	—	—	—	—	6.00	7.50

KM# 349a CROWN
28.2800 g., 0.9250 Silver 0.8410 oz. ASW, 38.8 mm.
Ruler: Elizabeth II **Series:** 1996 Atlanta Olympics **Obv:** Crowned bust right **Rev:** Wrestlers

Date	Mintage	F	VF	XF	Unc	BU
1996 Proof	Est. 30,000	Value: 42.50				

KM# 350 CROWN
Copper-Nickel, 38.8 mm. **Ruler:** Elizabeth II **Series:** 1996 Atlanta Olympics **Obv:** Crowned bust right **Rev:** Flag at center of baseball game

Date	Mintage	F	VF	XF	Unc	BU
1996	—	—	—	—	6.00	7.50

KM# 350a CROWN
28.2800 g., 0.9250 Silver 0.8410 oz. ASW, 38.8 mm.
Ruler: Elizabeth II **Series:** 1996 Atlanta Olympics **Obv:** Crowned bust right **Rev:** Flag at center of baseball game

Date	Mintage	F	VF	XF	Unc	BU
1996 Proof	Est. 30,000	Value: 42.50				

KM# 351 CROWN
Copper-Nickel, 38.8 mm. **Ruler:** Elizabeth II **Series:** 1996
Atlanta Olympics **Obv:** Crowned bust right **Rev:** Olympic Flame

Date	Mintage	F	VF	XF	Unc	BU
1996	—	—	—	—	6.00	7.50

KM# 351a CROWN
28.2800 g., 0.9250 Silver 0.8410 oz. ASW, 38.8 mm.
Ruler: Elizabeth II **Series:** 1996 Atlanta Olympics **Obv:** Crowned
bust right **Rev:** Olympic Flame

Date	Mintage	F	VF	XF	Unc	BU
1996 Proof	Est. 30,000	Value: 42.50				

KM# 352 CROWN
Copper-Nickel, 38.8 mm. **Ruler:** Elizabeth II **Series:** 1996
Atlanta Olympics **Obv:** Crowned bust right **Rev:** Volleyball game

Date	Mintage	F	VF	XF	Unc	BU
1996	—	—	—	—	6.00	7.50

KM# 352a CROWN
28.2800 g., 0.9250 Silver 0.8410 oz. ASW, 38.8 mm.
Ruler: Elizabeth II **Series:** 1996 Atlanta Olympics **Obv:** Crowned
bust right **Rev:** Volleyball game

Date	Mintage	F	VF	XF	Unc	BU
1996 Proof	Est. 30,000	Value: 42.50				

KM# 353 CROWN
Copper-Nickel, 38.8 mm. **Ruler:** Elizabeth II **Series:** 1996
Atlanta Olympics **Obv:** Crowned bust right **Rev:** Basketball game

Date	Mintage	F	VF	XF	Unc	BU
1996	—	—	—	—	6.00	7.50

KM# 353a CROWN
28.2800 g., 0.9250 Silver 0.8410 oz. ASW, 38.8 mm.
Ruler: Elizabeth II **Series:** 1996 Atlanta Olympics **Obv:** Crowned
bust right **Rev:** Basketball game

Date	Mintage	F	VF	XF	Unc	BU
1996 Proof	Est. 30,000	Value: 42.50				

KM# 358 CROWN
Copper-Nickel, 38.8 mm. **Ruler:** Elizabeth II **Obv:** Crowned bust
right **Rev:** Nefusot Yehuda Synagogue Renovation,
denomination below

Date	Mintage	F	VF	XF	Unc	BU
1996					7.00	9.00

KM# 358a CROWN
28.2800 g., 0.9250 Silver 0.8410 oz. ASW, 38.8 mm.
Ruler: Elizabeth II **Obv:** Crowned bust right **Rev:** Nefusot
Yehuda Synagogue Renovation

Date	Mintage	F	VF	XF	Unc	BU
1996 Proof	Est. 30,000	Value: 40.00				

KM# 359 CROWN
Copper-Nickel, 38.8 mm. **Ruler:** Elizabeth II **Subject:** Euro
Soccer 96 **Obv:** Crowned bust right **Rev:** Net and soccer player

Date	Mintage	F	VF	XF	Unc	BU
1996	—	—	—	—	8.00	9.50

KM# 359a CROWN
28.2800 g., 0.9250 Silver 0.8410 oz. ASW, 38.8 mm.
Ruler: Elizabeth II **Subject:** Euro Soccer 96 **Obv:** Crowned bust
right **Rev:** Soccer player and net

Date	Mintage	F	VF	XF	Unc	BU
1996 Proof	Est. 30,000	Value: 45.00				

KM# 373 CROWN
Copper-Nickel, 38.8 mm. **Ruler:** Elizabeth II **Obv:** Crowned bust
right **Rev:** Roses

Date	Mintage	F	VF	XF	Unc	BU
1996	—	—	—	—	8.00	9.50

KM# 373a CROWN
28.2800 g., 0.9250 Silver 0.8410 oz. ASW, 38.8 mm.
Ruler: Elizabeth II **Obv:** Crowned bust right **Rev:** Roses

Date	Mintage	F	VF	XF	Unc	BU
1996 Proof	Est. 30,000	Value: 40.00				

KM# 382 CROWN
Copper-Nickel, 38.8 mm. **Ruler:** Elizabeth II **Subject:** The Tale
of Peter Rabbit **Obv:** Crowned bust right **Rev:** Rabbit escaping
the garden

Date	Mintage	F	VF	XF	Unc	BU
1996	—	—	—	—	6.50	8.00

KM# 382a CROWN
28.2800 g., 0.9250 Silver 0.8410 oz. ASW, 38.8 mm. **Ruler:**
Elizabeth II **Subject:** The Tale of Peter Rabbit **Obv:** Crowned
bust right **Rev:** Rabbit escaping the garden

Date	Mintage	F	VF	XF	Unc	BU
1996 Proof	Est. 30,000	Value: 40.00				

KM# 386 CROWN
Copper-Nickel, 38.8 mm. **Ruler:** Elizabeth II **Series:** Preserve
Planet Earth **Obv:** Crowned bust right **Rev:** Shag Birds

Date	Mintage	F	VF	XF	Unc	BU
1996	—	—	—	—	10.00	14.00

KM# 386a CROWN
28.2800 g., 0.9250 Silver 0.8410 oz. ASW, 38.8 mm.
Ruler: Elizabeth II **Series:** Preserve Planet Earth **Obv:** Crowned
bust right **Rev:** Shag Birds

Date	Mintage	F	VF	XF	Unc	BU
1996 Proof	Est. 30,000	Value: 40.00				

KM# 387 CROWN
Copper-Nickel, 38.8 mm. **Ruler:** Elizabeth II **Series:** Preserve
Planet Earth **Obv:** Crowned bust right **Rev:** Atlantic Puffins

Date	Mintage	F	VF	XF	Unc	BU
1996	—	—	—	—	9.00	14.00

KM# 387a CROWN
28.2800 g., 0.9250 Silver 0.8410 oz. ASW, 38.8 mm.
Ruler: Elizabeth II **Series:** Preserve Planet Earth **Obv:** Crowned
bust right **Rev:** Atlantic Puffins

Date	Mintage	F	VF	XF	Unc	BU
1996 Proof	Est. 30,000	Value: 40.00				

KM# 393 CROWN
Copper-Nickel, 38.8 mm. **Ruler:** Elizabeth II **Series:** Centenary
of the Cinema **Subject:** Grace Kelly - actress, 1929-82
Obv: Crowned bust right **Rev:** Bust 3/4 facing, dates

Date	Mintage	F	VF	XF	Unc	BU
1996	—	—	—	—	8.00	9.50

KM# 393a CROWN
28.2800 g., 0.9250 Silver 0.8410 oz. ASW, 38.8 mm.
Ruler: Elizabeth II **Series:** Centenary of the Cinema
Subject: Grace Kelly - actress, 1929-82 **Obv:** Crowned bust right
Rev: Bust 3/4 facing, dates

Date	Mintage	F	VF	XF	Unc	BU
1996 Proof	Est. 30,000	Value: 37.50				

KM# 398 CROWN
Copper-Nickel, 38.8 mm. **Ruler:** Elizabeth II **Series:** Centenary of the Cinema **Subject:** James Dean - actor, 1931-55 **Obv:** Crowned bust right **Rev:** Standing central figure, dates

Date	Mintage	F	VF	XF	Unc	BU
1996	—	—	—	—	8.00	9.50

KM# 398a CROWN
28.2800 g., 0.9250 Silver 0.8410 oz. ASW, 38.8 mm. **Ruler:** Elizabeth II **Series:** Centenary of the Cinema **Subject:** James Dean - actor, 1931-55 **Obv:** Crowned bust right **Rev:** Standing central figure, dates

Date	Mintage	F	VF	XF	Unc	BU
1996 Proof	Est. 30,000	Value: 40.00				

KM# 403 CROWN
Copper-Nickel, 38.8 mm. **Ruler:** Elizabeth II **Series:** Centenary of the Cinema **Subject:** Marilyn Monroe - actress, 1926-62 **Obv:** Crowned bust right **Rev:** Bust looking back over shoulder, dates

Date	Mintage	F	VF	XF	Unc	BU
1996	—	—	—	—	8.00	9.50

KM# 403a CROWN
28.2800 g., 0.9250 Silver 0.8410 oz. ASW, 38.8 mm. **Ruler:** Elizabeth II **Series:** Centenary of the Cinema **Subject:** Marilyn Monroe - actress, 1926-62 **Obv:** Crowned bust right **Rev:** Bust looking back over shoulder, dates

Date	Mintage	F	VF	XF	Unc	BU
1996 Proof	—	Value: 40.00				

KM# 408 CROWN
Copper-Nickel, 38.8 mm. **Ruler:** Elizabeth II **Series:** Centenary of the Cinema **Subject:** Audrey Hepburn - actress, 1929-93 **Obv:** Crowned bust right **Rev:** Bust 3/4 facing, dates

Date	Mintage	F	VF	XF	Unc	BU
1996	—	—	—	—	8.00	9.50

KM# 413 CROWN
Copper-Nickel, 38.8 mm. **Ruler:** Elizabeth II **Series:** Centenary of the Cinema **Subject:** Bruce Lee - actor, 1940-73 **Obv:** Crowned bust right **Rev:** Kickboxer and chinese dragon

Date	Mintage	F	VF	XF	Unc	BU
1996	—	—	—	—	8.00	9.50

KM# 413a CROWN
28.2800 g., 0.9250 Silver 0.8410 oz. ASW, 38.8 mm. **Ruler:** Elizabeth II **Series:** Centenary of the Cinema **Subject:** Bruce Lee - actor, 1940-73 **Obv:** Crowned bust right **Rev:** Kickboxer and chinese dragon

Date	Mintage	F	VF	XF	Unc	BU
1996 Proof	Est. 30,000	Value: 40.00				

KM# 418 CROWN
Copper-Nickel, 38.8 mm. **Ruler:** Elizabeth II **Series:** Centenary of the Cinema **Subject:** Charlie Chaplin - actor, 1889-1977 **Obv:** Crowned bust right **Rev:** Standing central figure with cane, dates

Date	Mintage	F	VF	XF	Unc	BU
1996	—	—	—	—	8.00	9.50

KM# 418a CROWN
28.2800 g., 0.9250 Silver 0.8410 oz. ASW, 38.8 mm. **Ruler:** Elizabeth II **Series:** Centenary of the Cinema **Subject:** Charlie Chaplan - actor, 1889-1977 **Obv:** Crowned bust right **Rev:** Standing central figure with cane, dates

Date	Mintage	F	VF	XF	Unc	BU
1996 Proof	Est. 30,000	Value: 37.50				

KM# 423 CROWN
Copper-Nickel, 38.8 mm. **Ruler:** Elizabeth II **Series:** Centenary of the Cinema **Subject:** Gone With The Wind **Obv:** Crowned bust right **Rev:** Rhett Butler and Scarlett O'Hara

Date	Mintage	F	VF	XF	Unc	BU
1996	—	—	—	—	8.00	9.50

KM# 423a CROWN
28.2800 g., 0.9250 Silver 0.8410 oz. ASW, 38.8 mm. **Ruler:** Elizabeth II **Series:** Centenary of the Cinema **Subject:** Gone With The Wind **Obv:** Crowned bust right **Rev:** Rhett Butler and Scarlett O'Hara

Date	Mintage	F	VF	XF	Unc	BU
1996 Proof	Est. 30,000	Value: 40.00				

KM# 428 CROWN
Copper-Nickel, 38.8 mm. **Ruler:** Elizabeth II **Series:** Centenary of the Cinema **Obv:** Crowned bust right **Rev:** The Flintstones

Date	Mintage	F	VF	XF	Unc	BU
1996	—	—	—	—	8.00	9.50

KM# 428a CROWN
28.2800 g., 0.9250 Silver 0.8410 oz. ASW, 38.8 mm. **Ruler:** Elizabeth II **Series:** Centenary of the Cinema **Obv:** Crowned bust right **Rev:** The Flintstones

Date	Mintage	F	VF	XF	Unc	BU
1996 Proof	Est. 30,000	Value: 40.00				

KM# 430 CROWN
28.2800 g., 0.9250 Silver 0.8410 oz. ASW, 38.8 mm. **Ruler:** Elizabeth II **Series:** European Football Championship **Subject:** Goliath **Obv:** Crowned bust right **Rev:** Cartoon lion with football

Date	Mintage	F	VF	XF	Unc	BU
1996 Proof	Est. 10,000	Value: 32.50				

KM# 432 CROWN
Copper-Nickel, 38.8 mm. **Ruler:** Elizabeth II **Series:** Duke of Edinburgh Awards Scheme **Obv:** Crowned bust right **Rev:** 7 scenes surround center crowned arms

Date	Mintage	F	VF	XF	Unc	BU
1996	—	—	—	—	8.00	9.00

KM# 432a CROWN
28.2800 g., 0.9250 Silver 0.8410 oz. ASW, 38.8 mm. **Ruler:** Elizabeth II **Series:** Duke of Edinburgh Awards Scheme **Obv:** Crowned bust right **Rev:** 7 scenes surround center crowned arms

Date	Mintage	F	VF	XF	Unc	BU
1996 Proof	Est. 30,000	Value: 40.00				

KM# 435 CROWN
Copper-Nickel, 38.8 mm. **Ruler:** Elizabeth II **Series:** Duke of Edinburgh Awards Scheme **Obv:** Crowned bust right **Rev:** Cameo above team of horses pulling wagon

Date	Mintage	F	VF	XF	Unc	BU
1996	—	—	—	—	8.00	9.00

KM# 435a CROWN
28.2800 g., 0.9250 Silver 0.8410 oz. ASW, 38.8 mm. **Ruler:** Elizabeth II **Series:** Duke of Edinburgh Awards Scheme **Obv:** Duke of Edinburgh Awards Scheme **Rev:** Cameo above team of horses pulling wagon

Date	Mintage	F	VF	XF	Unc	BU
1996 Proof	Est. 30,000	Value: 40.00				

KM# 449 CROWN
Copper-Nickel, 38.8 mm. **Ruler:** Elizabeth II **Subject:** Lord Buddha **Obv:** Crowned bust right **Rev:** Seated figure facing

Date	Mintage	F	VF	XF	Unc	BU
1996	—	—	—	—	7.50	8.50

KM# 449a CROWN
28.2800 g., 0.9250 Silver 0.8410 oz. ASW, 38.8 mm.
Ruler: Elizabeth II **Subject:** Lord Buddha **Obv:** Crowned bust
right **Rev:** Seated figure facing

Date	Mintage	F	VF	XF	Unc	BU
1996 Proof	Est. 15,000				Value: 25.00	

KM# 457 CROWN
Copper-Nickel, 38.8 mm. **Ruler:** Elizabeth II **Series:** Centenary
of the Cinema **Subject:** Wizard of Oz **Obv:** Crowned bust right
Rev: Characters of Oz

Date	Mintage	F	VF	XF	Unc	BU
1996	—	—	—	—	7.75	9.00

KM# 457a CROWN
28.2800 g., 0.9250 Silver 0.8410 oz. ASW, 38.8 mm.
Ruler: Elizabeth II **Series:** Centenary of the Cinema **Subject:**
Wizard of Oz **Obv:** Crowned bust right **Rev:** Characters of Oz

Date	Mintage	F	VF	XF	Unc	BU
1996 Proof	Est. 30,000				Value: 40.00	

KM# 461 CROWN
Copper-Nickel, 38.8 mm. **Ruler:** Elizabeth II **Series:** Centenary
of the Cinema **Subject:** The Marx Brothers **Obv:** Crowned bust
right **Rev:** Three busts 3/4 left

Date	Mintage	F	VF	XF	Unc	BU
1996	—	—	—	—	7.75	9.00

KM# 461a CROWN
28.2800 g., 0.9250 Silver 0.8410 oz. ASW, 38.8 mm.
Ruler: Elizabeth II **Series:** Centenary of the Cinema
Subject: The Marx Brothers **Obv:** Crowned bust right **Rev:** Three
busts 3/4 left

Date	Mintage	F	VF	XF	Unc	BU
1996 Proof	Est. 30,000				Value: 37.50	

KM# 465 CROWN
Copper-Nickel, 38.8 mm. **Ruler:** Elizabeth II **Series:** Centenary of
the Cinema **Subject:** Elvis Presley - actor/entertainer, 1935-77
Obv: Crowned bust right **Rev:** Guitar beneath and behind bust 3/4
left

Date	Mintage	F	VF	XF	Unc	BU
1996	—	—	—	—	7.75	9.00

KM# 465a CROWN
28.0000 g., 0.9250 Silver 0.8327 oz. ASW, 38.8 mm.
Ruler: Elizabeth II **Series:** Centenary of the Cinema
Subject: Elvis Presley - actor/entertainer, 1935-77
Obv: Crowned bust right **Rev:** Guitar beneath and behind bust
3/4 left

Date	Mintage	F	VF	XF	Unc	BU
1996 Proof	Est. 30,000				Value: 40.00	

KM# 469 CROWN
Copper-Nickel, 38.8 mm. **Ruler:** Elizabeth II **Series:** Centenary
of the Cinema **Subject:** Casablanca **Obv:** Crowned bust right
Rev: Bogart and Bergman

Date	Mintage	F	VF	XF	Unc	BU
1996	—	—	—	—	7.75	9.00

KM# 469a CROWN
28.0000 g., 0.9250 Silver 0.8327 oz. ASW, 38.8 mm.
Ruler: Elizabeth II **Series:** Centenary of the Cinema **Subject:**
Casablanca **Obv:** Crowned bust right **Rev:** Bogart and Bergman

Date	Mintage	F	VF	XF	Unc	BU
1996 Proof	Est. 30,000				Value: 37.50	

KM# 473 CROWN
Copper-Nickel, 38.8 mm. **Ruler:** Elizabeth II **Series:** Centenary
of the Cinema **Obv:** Crowned bust right **Rev:** E.T.

Date	Mintage	F	VF	XF	Unc	BU
1996	—	—	—	—	7.75	9.00

KM# 473a CROWN
28.0000 g., 0.9250 Silver 0.8327 oz. ASW, 38.8 mm.
Ruler: Elizabeth II **Series:** Centenary of the Cinema
Obv: Crowned bust right **Rev:** E.T.

Date	Mintage	F	VF	XF	Unc	BU
1996 Proof	Est. 30,000				Value: 37.50	

KM# 477 CROWN
Copper-Nickel, 38.8 mm. **Ruler:** Elizabeth II **Series:** Centenary
of the Cinema **Subject:** Alfred Hitchcock - Director/Producer,
1899-1980 **Obv:** Crowned bust right **Rev:** Bust facing looking at
bird on left shoulder

Date	Mintage	F	VF	XF	Unc	BU
1996	—	—	—	—	7.75	9.00

KM# 477a CROWN
28.0000 g., 0.9250 Silver 0.8327 oz. ASW, 38.8 mm.
Ruler: Elizabeth II **Series:** Centenary of the Cinema
Subject: Alfred Hitchcock - Director/Producer, 1899-1980
Obv: Crowned bust right **Rev:** Bust facing looking at bird on left
shoulder

Date	Mintage	F	VF	XF	Unc	BU
1996 Proof	Est. 30,000				Value: 37.50	

KM# 586a CROWN
28.3400 g., Copper-Nickel, 38.5 mm. **Ruler:** Elizabeth II
Obv: Crowned bust right **Rev:** Chinese Emperor Shih Huang Ti
and Great Wall **Edge:** Reeded

Date	Mintage	F	VF	XF	Unc	BU
1997	—	—	—	—	10.00	14.00

KM# 514 CROWN
Copper-Nickel, 38.8 mm. **Ruler:** Elizabeth II **Obv:** Crowned bust
right **Rev:** Two peacocks, one with tail spread

Date	Mintage	F	VF	XF	Unc	BU
1997	—	—	—	—	12.00	17.50

KM# 514a CROWN
28.2800 g., 0.9250 Silver 0.8410 oz. ASW, 38.8 mm.
Ruler: Elizabeth II **Obv:** Crowned bust right **Rev:** Two peacocks,
one with tail spread

Date	Mintage	F	VF	XF	Unc	BU
1997	Est. 30,000				Value: 45.00	

KM# 525 CROWN
Copper-Nickel, 38.8 mm. **Ruler:** Elizabeth II **Subject:** The Tale of
Peter Rabbit **Obv:** Crowned bust right **Rev:** Rabbit standing 3/4 right

Date	Mintage	F	VF	XF	Unc	BU
1997	—	—	—	—	10.00	15.00

KM# 526 CROWN
28.2800 g., 0.9250 Silver 0.8410 oz. ASW, 38.8 mm.
Ruler: Elizabeth II

Date	Mintage	F	VF	XF	Unc	BU
1997 Proof	Est. 30,000				Value: 40.00	

KM# 530 CROWN
Copper-Nickel, 38.8 mm. **Ruler:** Elizabeth II **Series:** Golden
Wedding Anniversary **Subject:** Queen Elizabeth and Prince
Phillip **Obv:** Crowned bust right **Rev:** Royal couple facing

Date	Mintage	F	VF	XF	Unc	BU
1997	—	—	—	—	7.50	9.00

KM# 530a CROWN
28.2800 g., 0.9250 Gold Clad Silver 0.8410 oz., 38.8 mm.
Ruler: Elizabeth II **Series:** Golden Wedding Anniversary
Subject: Queen Elizabeth and Prince Phillip **Obv:** Crowned bust
right **Rev:** Royal couple facing

Date	Mintage	F	VF	XF	Unc	BU
1997 Proof	Est. 10,000	Value: 45.00				

KM# 536 CROWN
Copper-Nickel, 38.8 mm. **Ruler:** Elizabeth II **Series:** Golden
Wedding Anniversary **Subject:** Queen Elizabeth and Prince Philip
Obv: Crowned bust right **Rev:** The Queen and adoring crowd

Date	Mintage	F	VF	XF	Unc	BU
1997	—	—	—	—	7.50	9.00

KM# 536a CROWN
28.2800 g., 0.9250 Gold Clad Silver 0.8410 oz., 38.8 mm.
Ruler: Elizabeth II **Series:** Golden Wedding Anniversary
Subject: Queen Elizabeth and Prince Philip **Obv:** Crowned bust
right **Rev:** The Queen and adoring crowd

Date	Mintage	F	VF	XF	Unc	BU
1997 Proof	Est. 10,000	Value: 45.00				

KM# 552 CROWN
28.2800 g., 0.9250 Silver 0.8410 oz. ASW, 38.8 mm.
Ruler: Elizabeth II **Subject:** Europa **Obv:** Crowned bust right
Rev: Head 3/4 left

Date	Mintage	F	VF	XF	Unc	BU
1997 Proof	Est. 10,000	Value: 40.00				

KM# 532 CROWN
Copper-Nickel, 38.8 mm. **Ruler:** Elizabeth II **Series:** Golden
Wedding Anniversary **Subject:** Queen Elizabeth and Prince
Philip **Obv:** Crowned bust right **Rev:** The Queen with her first-
born, Prince Charles

Date	Mintage	F	VF	XF	Unc	BU
1997	—	—	—	—	7.50	9.00

KM# 532a CROWN
28.2800 g., 0.9250 Gold Clad Silver 0.8410 oz., 38.8 mm.
Ruler: Elizabeth II **Series:** Golden Wedding Anniversary
Subject: Queen Elizabeth and Prince Philip **Obv:** Crowned
bust right **Rev:** The Queen with her first-born, Prince Charles

Date	Mintage	F	VF	XF	Unc	BU
1997 Proof	Est. 10,000	Value: 45.00				

KM# 540 CROWN
Copper-Nickel, 38.8 mm. **Ruler:** Elizabeth II **Obv:** Crowned bust
right **Rev:** Peonies

Date	Mintage	F	VF	XF	Unc	BU
1997	—	—	—	—	8.00	9.00

KM# 540a CROWN
28.2800 g., 0.9250 Silver 0.8410 oz. ASW, 38.8 mm.
Ruler: Elizabeth II **Obv:** Crowned bust right **Rev:** Peonies

Date	Mintage	F	VF	XF	Unc	BU
1997 Proof	Est. 30,000	Value: 40.00				

KM# 556 CROWN
28.2800 g., 0.9250 Silver 0.8410 oz. ASW, 38.8 mm.
Ruler: Elizabeth II **Subject:** Liberty **Obv:** Crowned bust right
Rev: Laureate head right

Date	Mintage	F	VF	XF	Unc	BU
1997 Proof	Est. 10,000	Value: 40.00				

KM# 561 CROWN
Copper-Nickel, 38.8 mm. **Ruler:** Elizabeth II **Subject:** Yorkshire
Terrier **Obv:** Crowned bust right

Date	Mintage	F	VF	XF	Unc	BU
1997	—	—	—	—	10.00	12.00

KM# 534 CROWN
Copper-Nickel, 38.8 mm. **Ruler:** Elizabeth II **Series:** Golden
Wedding Anniversary **Subject:** Queen Elizabeth and Prince
Philip **Obv:** Crowned bust right **Rev:** The Queen, two children
and a monkey

Date	Mintage	F	VF	XF	Unc	BU
1997	—	—	—	—	7.50	9.00

KM# 534a CROWN
28.2800 g., 0.9250 Gold Clad Silver 0.8410 oz., 38.8 mm.
Ruler: Elizabeth II **Series:** Golden Wedding Anniversary
Subject: Queen Elizabeth and Prince Philip **Obv:** Crowned
bust right **Rev:** The Queen, two children and a monkey

Date	Mintage	F	VF	XF	Unc	BU
1997 Proof	Est. 10,000	Value: 45.00				

KM# 544 CROWN
28.2800 g., 0.9250 Silver 0.8410 oz. ASW, 38.8 mm.
Ruler: Elizabeth II **Subject:** Nefertiti **Obv:** Crowned bust right
Rev: Head right

Date	Mintage	F	VF	XF	Unc	BU
1997 Proof	Est. 10,000	Value: 40.00				

KM# 566 CROWN
Copper-Nickel, 38.8 mm. **Ruler:** Elizabeth II **Series:** Queen's
Birthday **Obv:** Crowned bust right **Rev:** Queen on horseback,
Rock of Gibraltar in background

Date	Mintage	F	VF	XF	Unc	BU
1997	—	—	—	—	8.50	9.50

KM# 566a CROWN
28.2800 g., 0.9250 Silver 0.8410 oz. ASW, 38.8 mm. **Ruler:**
Elizabeth II **Series:** Queen's Birthday **Obv:** Crowned bust right
Rev: Queen on horseback, Rock of Gibraltar in background

Date	Mintage	F	VF	XF	Unc	BU
1997 Proof	Est. 30,000	Value: 40.00				

KM# 548 CROWN
28.2800 g., 0.9250 Silver 0.8410 oz. ASW, 38.8 mm.
Ruler: Elizabeth II **Subject:** Cleopatra **Obv:** Crowned bust right
Rev: Head facing

Date	Mintage	F	VF	XF	Unc	BU
1997 Proof	Est. 10,000	Value: 40.00				

KM# 567 CROWN
Copper-Nickel, 38.8 mm. **Ruler:** Elizabeth II **Series:** Queen's
Birthday **Obv:** Crowned bust right **Rev:** Queen on horseback
returning salute

Date	Mintage	F	VF	XF	Unc	BU
1997	—	—	—	—	8.50	9.50

KM# 567a CROWN
28.2800 g., 0.9250 Silver 0.8410 oz. ASW, 38.8 mm.
Ruler: Elizabeth II **Series:** Queen's Birthday **Obv:** Crowned bust right **Rev:** Queen on horseback returning salute

Date	Mintage	VF	XF	Unc	BU
1997 Proof	Est. 30,000			Value: 40.00	

KM# 568 CROWN
Copper-Nickel, 38.8 mm. **Ruler:** Elizabeth II **Series:** Queen's Birthday **Obv:** Crowned bust right **Rev:** Cameo above Trooping the Colors scene

Date	Mintage	F	VF	XF	Unc	BU
1997	—	—	—	—	8.50	9.50

KM# 568a CROWN
28.2800 g., 0.9250 Silver 0.8410 oz. ASW, 38.8 mm.
Ruler: Elizabeth II **Series:** Queen's Birthday **Obv:** Crowned bust right **Rev:** Cameo above Trooping the Colors scene

Date	Mintage	F	VF	XF	Unc	BU
1997 Proof	Est. 30,000				Value: 40.00	

KM# 569 CROWN
Copper-Nickel, 38.8 mm. **Ruler:** Elizabeth II **Series:** Queen's Birthday **Obv:** Crowned bust right **Rev:** Gurkha troops with dragons

Date	Mintage	F	VF	XF	Unc	BU
1997	—	—	—	—	8.50	9.50

KM# 569a CROWN
28.2800 g., 0.9250 Silver 0.8410 oz. ASW, 38.8 mm.
Ruler: Elizabeth II **Series:** Queen's Birthday **Obv:** Crowned bust right **Rev:** Gurkha troops with dragons

Date	Mintage	F	VF	XF	Unc	BU
1997 Proof	—				Value: 40.00	

KM# 571 CROWN
Copper-Nickel, 38.8 mm. **Ruler:** Elizabeth II **Subject:** The New Mosque **Obv:** Crowned bust right **Rev:** Two Moorish cavalry riders with mosque in background

Date	Mintage	F	VF	XF	Unc	BU
1997	—	—	—	—	8.00	9.00

KM# 571a CROWN
28.2800 g., 0.9250 Silver 0.8410 oz. ASW, 38.8 mm.
Ruler: Elizabeth II **Subject:** The New Mosque **Obv:** Crowned bust right **Rev:** Two Moorish cavalry riders with mosque in background

Date	Mintage	F	VF	XF	Unc	BU
1997 Proof	Est. 30,000				Value: 40.00	

KM# 573 CROWN
28.2800 g., 0.9250 Silver 0.8410 oz. ASW, 38.8 mm.
Ruler: Elizabeth II **Series:** Wonders of the World **Subject:** Mausoleum at Halicarnassus **Obv:** Crowned bust right **Rev:** Gold coin design inset on mausoleum

Date	Mintage	F	VF	XF	Unc	BU
1997 Proof	Est. 7,500				Value: 50.00	

KM# 574 CROWN
28.2800 g., 0.9250 Silver 0.8410 oz. ASW, 38.8 mm.
Ruler: Elizabeth II **Series:** Wonders of the World **Subject:** Statue of Zeus at Olympia **Obv:** Crowned bust right **Rev:** Gold coin design inset on statue of Zeus

Date	Mintage	F	VF	XF	Unc	BU
1997 Proof	Est. 7,500				Value: 50.00	

KM# 575 CROWN
28.2800 g., 0.9250 Silver 0.8410 oz. ASW, 38.8 mm.
Ruler: Elizabeth II **Series:** Wonders of the World **Subject:** The Pharos of Alexandria **Obv:** Crowned bust right **Rev:** Gold coin design inset on lighthouse

Date	Mintage	F	VF	XF	Unc	BU
1997 Proof	Est. 7,500				Value: 50.00	

KM# 576 CROWN
28.2800 g., 0.9250 Silver 0.8410 oz. ASW, 38.8 mm.
Ruler: Elizabeth II **Series:** Wonders of the World **Subject:** The Pillars of Hercules **Obv:** Crowned bust right **Rev:** Gold coin design inset on the Rock of Gibraltar

Date	Mintage	F	VF	XF	Unc	BU
1997 Proof	Est. 7,500				Value: 50.00	

KM# 577 CROWN
28.2800 g., 0.9250 Silver 0.8410 oz. ASW, 38.8 mm.
Ruler: Elizabeth II **Series:** Wonders of the World **Subject:** The Colossus of Rhodes **Obv:** Crowned bust right **Rev:** Gold coin design inset on large statue

Date	Mintage	F	VF	XF	Unc	BU
1997 Proof	Est. 7,500				Value: 50.00	

KM# 578 CROWN
28.2800 g., 0.9250 Silver 0.8410 oz. ASW, 38.8 mm.
Ruler: Elizabeth II **Series:** Wonders of the World **Subject:** The Pyramids of Egypt **Obv:** Crowned bust right **Rev:** Gold coin design inset on pyramids

Date	Mintage	F	VF	XF	Unc	BU
1997 Proof	Est. 7,500				Value: 50.00	

KM# 579 CROWN
28.2800 g., 0.9250 Silver 0.8410 oz. ASW, 38.8 mm.
Ruler: Elizabeth II **Series:** Wonders of the World **Subject:** The Hanging Gardens of Babylon **Obv:** Crowned bust right **Rev:** Gold coin design inset on an overgrown building

Date	Mintage	F	VF	XF	Unc	BU
1997 Proof	Est. 7,500				Value: 50.00	

KM# 580 CROWN
28.2800 g., 0.9250 Silver 0.8410 oz. ASW, 38.8 mm.
Ruler: Elizabeth II **Series:** Wonders of the World **Subject:** The Temple of Artemis at Ephesus **Obv:** Crowned bust right **Rev:** Gold coin design inset on classic Greek building

Date	Mintage	F	VF	XF	Unc	BU
1997		Est. 7,500			Value: 50.00	

KM# 582 CROWN
28.2800 g., 0.9250 Silver 0.8410 oz. ASW, 38.8 mm.
Ruler: Elizabeth II **Series:** Evolution of Mankind **Subject:** Egypt
Obv: Crowned bust right **Rev:** Three ancient Egyptians,
pyramids, hieroglyphics

Date	Mintage	F	VF	XF	Unc	BU
1997 Proof	Est. 10,000	Value: 40.00				

KM# 590 CROWN
28.2800 g., 0.9250 Silver 0.8410 oz. ASW, 38.8 mm.
Ruler: Elizabeth II **Series:** Evolution of Mankind **Subject:** Rome
Obv: Crowned bust right **Rev:** Julius Caesar and Stonehenge

Date	Mintage	F	VF	XF	Unc	BU
1997 Proof	Est. 10,000	Value: 40.00				

KM# 598 CROWN
28.2800 g., 0.9250 Silver 0.8410 oz. ASW, 38.8 mm.
Ruler: Elizabeth II **Series:** Evolution of Mankind **Subject:** Native
America **Obv:** Crowned bust right **Rev:** North American native
on horseback and totem pole

Date	Mintage	F	VF	XF	Unc	BU
1997 Proof	Est. 10,000	Value: 40.00				

KM# 584 CROWN
28.2800 g., 0.9250 Silver 0.8410 oz. ASW, 38.8 mm.
Ruler: Elizabeth II **Series:** Evolution of Mankind **Subject:** Israel
Obv: Crowned bust right **Rev:** Star of David, Moses and Temple
of Solomon

Date	Mintage	F	VF	XF	Unc	BU
1997 Proof	Est. 10,000	Value: 40.00				

KM# 592 CROWN
28.2800 g., 0.9250 Silver 0.8410 oz. ASW, 38.8 mm.
Ruler: Elizabeth II **Series:** Evolution of Mankind **Subject:** India
Obv: Crowned bust right **Rev:** Krishna playing flute by a temple

Date	Mintage	F	VF	XF	Unc	BU
1997 Proof	Est. 10,000	Value: 40.00				

KM# 600 CROWN
28.2800 g., 0.9250 Silver 0.8410 oz. ASW, 38.8 mm.
Ruler: Elizabeth II **Series:** Evolution of Mankind **Subject:** Asia
Obv: Crowned bust right **Rev:** Buddha and temple

Date	Mintage	F	VF	XF	Unc	BU
1997 Proof	Est. 10,000	Value: 40.00				

KM# 586 CROWN
28.2800 g., 0.9250 Copper-Nickel 0.8410 oz., 38.8 mm.
Ruler: Elizabeth II **Series:** Evolution of Mankind **Subject:** China
Obv: Crowned bust right **Rev:** Emperor and the Great Wall

Date	Mintage	F	VF	XF	Unc	BU
1997 Proof	Est. 10,000	Value: 40.00				

KM# 594 CROWN
28.2800 g., 0.9250 Silver 0.8410 oz. ASW, 38.8 mm.
Ruler: Elizabeth II **Series:** Evolution of Mankind **Subject:** Holy
Roman Empire **Obv:** Crowned bust right **Rev:** Charlemagne and
soldiers on horseback

Date	Mintage	F	VF	XF	Unc	BU
1997 Proof	Est. 10,000	Value: 40.00				

KM# 602 CROWN
28.2800 g., 0.9250 Silver 0.8410 oz. ASW, 38.8 mm.
Ruler: Elizabeth II **Series:** Evolution of Mankind **Subject:** Inca
Empire **Obv:** Crowned bust right **Rev:** Incan Emperor and Machu
Picchu

Date	Mintage	F	VF	XF	Unc	BU
1997 Proof	Est. 10,000	Value: 40.00				

KM# 588 CROWN
28.2800 g., 0.9250 Silver 0.8410 oz. ASW, 38.8 mm.
Ruler: Elizabeth II **Series:** Evolution of Mankind **Subject:**
Greece **Obv:** Crowned bust right **Rev:** Aristotle, classic Greek
building

Date	Mintage	F	VF	XF	Unc	BU
1997 Proof	Est. 10,000	Value: 40.00				

KM# 596 CROWN
28.2800 g., 0.9250 Silver 0.8410 oz. ASW, 38.8 mm.
Ruler: Elizabeth II **Series:** Evolution of Mankind
Subject: Macedonia **Obv:** Crowned bust right **Rev:** Alexander
the Great on horseback

Date	Mintage	F	VF	XF	Unc	BU
1997 Proof	Est. 10,000	Value: 40.00				

KM# 604 CROWN
28.2800 g., 0.9250 Silver 0.8410 oz. ASW, 38.8 mm.
Ruler: Elizabeth II **Series:** Evolution of Mankind **Subject:** Islamic
Civilization **Obv:** Crowned bust right **Rev:** General Tariq Ibn Ziyad
and building

Date	Mintage	F	VF	XF	Unc	BU
1997 Proof	Est. 10,000	Value: 40.00				

KM# 609 CROWN
28.2800 g., 0.9250 Silver 0.8410 oz. ASW, 38.8 mm. **Ruler:**
Elizabeth II **Series:** Traders of the World **Subject:** Sir Francis Drake
Obv: Crowned bust right **Rev:** Sir Francis Drake, ship and beach

Date	Mintage	F	VF	XF	Unc	BU
1997 Proof	Est. 10,000	Value: 47.50				

KM# 611 CROWN
28.2800 g., 0.9250 Silver 0.8410 oz. ASW, 38.8 mm.
Ruler: Elizabeth II **Series:** Traders of the World **Subject:**
Romans **Obv:** Crowned bust right **Rev:** Lion, lioness, ship
and map

Date	Mintage	F	VF	XF	Unc	BU
1997 Proof	Est. 10,000	Value: 47.50				

KM# 613 CROWN
28.2800 g., 0.9250 Silver 0.8410 oz. ASW, 38.8 mm.
Ruler: Elizabeth II **Series:** Traders of the World **Subject:**
Venetians **Obv:** Crowned bust right **Rev:** Pair of oysters with
pearls, Venetian canal scene

Date	Mintage	F	VF	XF	Unc	BU
1997 Proof	Est. 10,000	Value: 47.50				

KM# 615 CROWN
28.2800 g., 0.9250 Silver 0.8410 oz. ASW, 38.8 mm.
Ruler: Elizabeth II **Series:** Traders of the World
Subject: Portuguese **Obv:** Crowned bust right **Rev:** Gold ingots
and Portuguese ship

Date	Mintage	F	VF	XF	Unc	BU
1997 Proof	Est. 10,000	Value: 47.50				

KM# 617 CROWN
28.2800 g., 0.9250 Silver 0.8410 oz. ASW, 38.8 mm.
Ruler: Elizabeth II **Series:** Traders of the World **Subject:**
Spanish **Obv:** Crowned bust right **Rev:** Tobacco leaves, ship,
map, gems

Date	Mintage	F	VF	XF	Unc	BU
1997 Proof	Est. 10,000	Value: 47.50				

KM# 619 CROWN
28.2800 g., 0.9250 Silver 0.8410 oz. ASW, 38.8 mm.
Ruler: Elizabeth II **Series:** Traders of the World **Subject:** English
Obv: Crowned bust right **Rev:** Profile of Queen Elizabeth I above
fighting ships

Date	Mintage	F	VF	XF	Unc	BU
1997 Proof	Est. 10,000	Value: 47.50				

KM# 621 CROWN
28.2800 g., 0.9250 Silver 0.8410 oz. ASW, 38.8 mm.
Ruler: Elizabeth II **Series:** Traders of the World **Subject:** Captain
Bligh **Obv:** Queen's portrait **Rev:** Figure seated on rock, ship
at right

Date	Mintage	F	VF	XF	Unc	BU
1997 Proof	Est. 10,000	Value: 47.50				

KM# 623 CROWN
28.2800 g., 0.9250 Silver 0.8410 oz. ASW, 38.8 mm.
Ruler: Elizabeth II **Series:** Traders of the World **Subject:** Captain
Cook **Obv:** Crowned bust right **Rev:** Beaver on rock, ship at right,
bust facing in background

Date	Mintage	F	VF	XF	Unc	BU
1997 Proof	Est. 10,000	Value: 47.50				

KM# 720 CROWN
Copper-Nickel, 38.8 mm. **Ruler:** Elizabeth II **Series:** Evolution
of Mankind **Subject:** Homo Sapiens Hunting Mammoth
Obv: Crowned bust right **Rev:** Figures spearing mammoth

Date	Mintage	F	VF	XF	Unc	BU
1998	—	—	—	—	12.00	20.00

KM# 636 CROWN
Copper-Nickel, 38.8 mm. **Ruler:** Elizabeth II **Series:** Winter
Olympics - Japan **Obv:** Crowned bust right **Rev:** Speed skater
and Bullet Train

Date	Mintage	F	VF	XF	Unc	BU
1998	—	—	—	—	8.00	10.00

KM# 636a CROWN
28.2800 g., 0.9250 Silver 0.8410 oz. ASW, 38.8 mm.
Ruler: Elizabeth II **Series:** Winter Olympics - Japan
Obv: Crowned bust right **Rev:** Speed skater and Bullet Train

Date	Mintage	F	VF	XF	Unc	BU
1998 Proof	Est. 30,000	Value: 45.00				

KM# 638 CROWN
Copper-Nickel, 38.8 mm. **Ruler:** Elizabeth II **Series:** Winter
Olympics - Japan **Obv:** Crowned bust right **Rev:** Ski jumper and
Buddha

Date	Mintage	F	VF	XF	Unc	BU
1998	—	—	—	—	8.00	10.00

KM# 638a CROWN
28.2800 g., 0.9250 Silver 0.8410 oz. ASW, 38.8 mm.
Ruler: Elizabeth II **Subject:** Winter Olympics - Japan
Obv: Crowned bust right **Rev:** Ski jumper and Buddha

Date	Mintage	F	VF	XF	Unc	BU
1998 Proof	Est. 30,000	Value: 45.00				

KM# 640 CROWN
Copper-Nickel, 38.8 mm. **Ruler:** Elizabeth II **Series:** Winter
Olympics - Japan **Obv:** Crowned bust right **Rev:** Cross-country
skiers

Date	Mintage	F	VF	XF	Unc	BU
1998	—	—	—	—	8.00	10.00

KM# 640a   CROWN
28.2800 g., 0.9250 Silver 0.8410 oz. ASW, 38.8 mm.
Ruler: Elizabeth II **Subject:** Winter Olympics - Japan
Obv: Crowned bust right **Rev:** Cross-country skiers

Date	Mintage	F	VF	XF	Unc	BU
1998 Proof	Est. 30,000	Value: 45.00				

KM# 642   CROWN
Copper-Nickel, 38.8 mm. **Ruler:** Elizabeth II **Series:** Winter
Olympics - Japan **Obv:** Crowned bust right **Rev:** Slalom skier,
Zenkoji temple

Date	Mintage	F	VF	XF	Unc	BU
1998	—	—	—	—	8.00	10.00

KM# 642a   CROWN
28.2800 g., 0.9250 Silver 0.8410 oz. ASW, 38.8 mm.
Ruler: Elizabeth II **Series:** Winter Olympics - Japan
Obv: Crowned bust right **Rev:** Slalom skier, Zenkoji temple

Date	Mintage	F	VF	XF	Unc	BU
1998 Proof	Est. 30,000	Value: 45.00				

KM# 656   CROWN
Copper-Nickel, 38.8 mm. **Ruler:** Elizabeth II **Subject:** The Tale
of Peter Rabbit **Obv:** Crowned bust right **Rev:** Standing rabbit
facing, sparrow at left

Date	Mintage	F	VF	XF	Unc	BU
1998	—	—	—	—	10.00	12.00

KM# 656a   CROWN
28.2800 g., 0.9250 Silver 0.8410 oz. ASW, 38.8 mm. **Ruler:**
Elizabeth II **Subject:** The Tale of Peter Rabbit **Obv:** Crowned
bust right **Rev:** Standing rabbit facing, sparrow at left

Date	Mintage	F	VF	XF	Unc	BU
1998 Proof	Est. 30,000	Value: 50.00				

KM# 661   CROWN
Copper-Nickel, 38.8 mm. **Ruler:** Elizabeth II **Subject:**
Chrysanthemum **Obv:** Crowned bust right **Rev:** Three blossoms

Date	Mintage	F	VF	XF	Unc	BU
1998	—	—	—	—	8.50	9.50

KM# 661a   CROWN
28.2800 g., 0.9250 Silver 0.8410 oz. ASW, 38.8 mm.
Ruler: Elizabeth II **Subject:** Chrysanthemum **Obv:** Crowned
bust right **Rev:** Three blossoms

Date	Mintage	F	VF	XF	Unc	BU
1998 Proof	Est. 30,000	Value: 50.00				

KM# 674   CROWN
28.2800 g., 0.9250 Silver 0.8410 oz. ASW, 38.8 mm.
Ruler: Elizabeth II **Subject:** Britannia **Obv:** Crowned bust right
Rev: Helmeted head right

Date	Mintage	F	VF	XF	Unc	BU
1998 Proof	Est. 10,000	Value: 55.00				

KM# 675   CROWN
28.2800 g., 0.9250 Silver 0.8410 oz. ASW, 38.8 mm.
Ruler: Elizabeth II **Subject:** Juno **Obv:** Crowned bust right
Rev: Head 3/4 facing

Date	Mintage	F	VF	XF	Unc	BU
1998 Proof	Est. 10,000	Value: 55.00				

KM# 676   CROWN
28.2800 g., 0.9250 Silver 0.8410 oz. ASW, 38.8 mm.
Ruler: Elizabeth II **Subject:** Athena **Obv:** Crowned bust right
Rev: Helmeted head right

Date	Mintage	F	VF	XF	Unc	BU
1998 Proof	Est. 10,000	Value: 55.00				

KM# 677   CROWN
28.2800 g., 0.9250 Silver 0.8410 oz. ASW, 38.8 mm.
Ruler: Elizabeth II **Subject:** Arethusa **Obv:** Crowned bust right
Rev: Head left with dolphins

Date	Mintage	F	VF	XF	Unc	BU
1998 Proof	Est. 10,000	Value: 55.00				

KM# 682   CROWN
Copper-Nickel, 38.8 mm. **Ruler:** Elizabeth II **Subject:** Paddington
Bear **Obv:** Crowned bust right **Rev:** Bear with suitcase

Date	Mintage	F	VF	XF	Unc	BU
1998	—	—	—	—	10.00	15.00

KM# 682a   CROWN
28.2800 g., 0.9250 Silver 0.8410 oz. ASW, 38.8 mm.
Ruler: Elizabeth II **Subject:** Paddington Bear **Obv:** Crowned
bust right **Rev:** Bear with suitcase

Date	Mintage	F	VF	XF	Unc	BU
1998 Proof	Est. 30,000	Value: 50.00				

KM# 687   CROWN
Copper-Nickel, 38.8 mm. **Ruler:** Elizabeth II **Series:** World Cup
France 1998 **Obv:** Crowned bust right **Rev:** Goalie

Date	Mintage	F	VF	XF	Unc	BU
1998	—	—	—	—	8.00	9.00

KM# 687a   CROWN
28.2800 g., 0.9250 Silver 0.8410 oz. ASW, 38.8 mm.
Ruler: Elizabeth II **Series:** World Cup France 1998
Obv: Crowned bust right **Rev:** Goalie

Date	Mintage	F	VF	XF	Unc	BU
1998 Proof	Est. 30,000	Value: 50.00				

KM# 688   CROWN
Copper-Nickel, 38.8 mm. **Ruler:** Elizabeth II **Series:** World Cup
France 1998 **Obv:** Crowned bust right **Rev:** Player kicking to the left

Date	Mintage	F	VF	XF	Unc	BU
1998	—	—	—	—	8.00	9.00

KM# 688a   CROWN
28.2800 g., 0.9250 Silver 0.8410 oz. ASW, 38.8 mm.
Ruler: Elizabeth II **Series:** World Cup France 1998
Obv. Insc.: Crowned bust right **Rev:** Player kicking to the left

Date	Mintage	F	VF	XF	Unc	BU
1998 Proof	Est. 30,000	Value: 50.00				

KM# 689 CROWN
Copper-Nickel, 38.8 mm. **Ruler:** Elizabeth II **Series:** World Cup France 1998 **Obv:** Crowned bust right **Rev:** Player advancing ball

Date	Mintage	F	VF	XF	Unc	BU
1998	—	—	—	—	8.00	9.00

KM# 689a CROWN
28.2800 g., 0.9250 Silver 0.8410 oz. ASW, 38.8 mm. **Ruler:** Elizabeth II **Series:** World Cup France 1998 **Obv:** Crowned bust right **Rev:** Player advancing ball

Date	Mintage	F	VF	XF	Unc	BU
1998 Proof	Est. 30,000	Value: 50.00				

KM# 690 CROWN
Copper-Nickel, 38.8 mm. **Ruler:** Elizabeth II **Series:** World Cup France 1998 **Obv:** Crowned bust right **Rev:** Two players

Date	Mintage	F	VF	XF	Unc	BU
1998	—	—	—	—	8.00	9.00

KM# 690a CROWN
28.2800 g., 0.9250 Silver 0.8410 oz. ASW, 38.8 mm. **Ruler:** Elizabeth II **Series:** World Cup France 1998 **Obv:** Crowned bust right **Rev:** Two players

Date	Mintage	F	VF	XF	Unc	BU
1998 Proof	Est. 30,000	Value: 50.00				

KM# 692 CROWN
28.2800 g., 0.9250 Silver 0.8410 oz. ASW, 38.8 mm. **Ruler:** Elizabeth II **Series:** Traders of the World **Subject:** Phoenecians **Obv:** Crowned bust right **Rev:** Galley (200BC-600AD) above shells

Date	Mintage	F	VF	XF	Unc	BU
1998 Proof	Est. 10,000	Value: 50.00				

KM# 694 CROWN
28.2800 g., 0.9250 Silver 0.8410 oz. ASW, 38.8 mm. **Ruler:** Elizabeth II **Series:** Traders of the World **Subject:** Vikings, 900AD **Obv:** Crowned bust right **Rev:** Ship (900AD), pair of fish and walrus tusks

Date	Mintage	F	VF	XF	Unc	BU
1998 Proof	Est. 10,000	Value: 50.00				

KM# 696 CROWN
28.2800 g., 0.9250 Silver 0.8410 oz. ASW, 38.8 mm. **Ruler:** Elizabeth II **Series:** Traders of the World **Subject:** Marco Polo, 1254-1324 **Obv:** Crowned bust right **Rev:** Chopsticks with noodles below bust at right, ship at left

Date	Mintage	F	VF	XF	Unc	BU
1998 Proof	Est. 10,000	Value: 50.00				

KM# 698 CROWN
28.2800 g., 0.9250 Silver 0.8410 oz. ASW, 38.8 mm. **Ruler:** Elizabeth II **Series:** Traders of the World **Subject:** Hanseatic League Nations **Obv:** Queen's portrait **Rev:** Coins of the nations above Hanseatic Kogge (circa 1350), map at right

Date	Mintage	F	VF	XF	Unc	BU
1998 Proof	Est. 10,000	Value: 50.00				

KM# 700 CROWN
28.2800 g., 0.9250 Silver 0.8410 oz. ASW, 38.8 mm. **Ruler:** Elizabeth II **Series:** Traders of the World **Subject:** Chinese **Obv:** Crowned bust right **Rev:** Chinese Junk (1400s), silk worm and pottery

Date	Mintage	F	VF	XF	Unc	BU
1998 Proof	Est. 10,000	Value: 50.00				

KM# 702 CROWN
28.2800 g., 0.9250 Silver 0.8410 oz. ASW, 38.8 mm. **Ruler:** Elizabeth II **Series:** Traders of the World **Subject:** Christopher Columbus, 1451-1506 **Obv:** Crowned bust right **Rev:** Bust at left looking right, ship at right

Date	Mintage	F	VF	XF	Unc	BU
1998 Proof	Est. 10,000	Value: 50.00				

KM# 704 CROWN
Copper-Nickel, 38.8 mm. **Ruler:** Elizabeth II **Series:** Traders of the World **Subject:** Sir Walter Raleigh, 1552-1618 **Obv:** Crowned bust right **Rev:** Standing figure, ship in background

Date	Mintage	F	VF	XF	Unc	BU
1998	—	—	—	—	10.00	14.00

KM# 704a CROWN
28.2800 g., 0.9250 Silver 0.8410 oz. ASW, 38.8 mm. **Ruler:** Elizabeth II **Series:** Traders of the World **Subject:** Sir Walter Raleigh, 1552-1618 **Obv:** Crowned bust right **Rev:** Standing figure, ship in background

Date	Mintage	F	VF	XF	Unc	BU
1998 Proof	Est. 10,000	Value: 50.00				

KM# 706 CROWN
28.2800 g., 0.9250 Silver 0.8410 oz. ASW, 38.8 mm. **Ruler:** Elizabeth II **Series:** Traders of the World **Obv:** Crowned bust right **Rev:** Boston Tea Party (1773) scene, tea leaf above

Date	Mintage	F	VF	XF	Unc	BU
1998 Proof	Est. 10,000	Value: 50.00				

KM# 708 CROWN
Copper-Nickel, 38.8 mm. **Ruler:** Elizabeth II **Series:** Evolution of Mankind **Subject:** Australopithecus, Lucy **Obv:** Crowned bust right **Rev:** Upright figure left, brain depiction at left

Date	Mintage	F	VF	XF	Unc	BU
1998	—	—	—	—	12.00	15.00

KM# 708a CROWN
28.2800 g., 0.9250 Silver 0.8410 oz. ASW, 38.8 mm. **Ruler:** Elizabeth II **Series:** Evolution of Mankind **Subject:** Australopithecus, Lucy **Obv:** Crowned bust right **Rev:** Upright figure left, brain depiction at left

Date	Mintage	F	VF	XF	Unc	BU
1998 Proof	Est. 10,000	Value: 50.00				

KM# 710 CROWN
Copper-Nickel, 38.8 mm. **Ruler:** Elizabeth II **Series:** Evolution of Mankind **Subject:** Homo Habilis **Obv:** Crowned bust right **Rev:** Squatted figure right using tools

Date	Mintage	F	VF	XF	Unc	BU
1998	—	—	—	—	12.00	15.00

KM# 710a CROWN
28.2800 g., 0.9250 Silver 0.8410 oz. ASW, 38.8 mm. **Ruler:** Elizabeth II **Series:** Evolution of Mankind **Subject:** Homo Habilis **Obv:** Crowned bust right **Rev:** Squatted figure right using tools

Date	Mintage	F	VF	XF	Unc	BU
1998 Proof	Est. 10,000		Value: 50.00			

KM# 716 CROWN
Copper-Nickel, 38.8 mm. **Ruler:** Elizabeth II **Series:** Evolution of Mankind **Subject:** Neanderthal Man **Obv:** Crowned bust right **Rev:** Skull left of burial scene

Date	Mintage	F	VF	XF	Unc	BU
1998	—	—	—	—	12.00	15.00

KM# 716a CROWN
28.2800 g., 0.9250 Silver 0.8410 oz. ASW, 38.8 mm. **Ruler:** Elizabeth II **Series:** Evolution of Mankind **Subject:** Neanderthal Man **Obv:** Crowned bust right **Rev:** Skull left of burial scene

Date	Mintage	F	VF	XF	Unc	BU
1998 Proof	Est. 10,000		Value: 50.00			

KM# 724 CROWN
Copper-Nickel, 38.8 mm. **Ruler:** Elizabeth II **Series:** Evolution of Mankind **Subject:** The Common Ancestry of Ape and Man **Obv:** Crowned bust right **Rev:** Human and primate mothers with young

Date	Mintage	F	VF	XF	Unc	BU
1998	—	—	—	—	12.00	15.00

KM# 724a CROWN
28.2800 g., 0.9250 Silver 0.8410 oz. ASW, 38.8 mm. **Ruler:** Elizabeth II **Series:** Evolution of Mankind **Subject:** The Common Ancestry of Ape and Man **Obv:** Crowned bust right **Rev:** Human and primate mothers with young

Date	Mintage	F	VF	XF	Unc	BU
1998 Proof	Est. 10,000		Value: 50.00			

KM# 712 CROWN
Copper-Nickel, 38.8 mm. **Ruler:** Elizabeth II **Series:** Evolution of Mankind **Subject:** Homo Erectus **Obv:** Crowned bust right **Rev:** Three figures with fire

Date	Mintage	F	VF	XF	Unc	BU
1998	—	—	—	—	12.00	15.00

KM# 712a CROWN
28.2800 g., 0.9250 Silver 0.8410 oz. ASW, 38.8 mm. **Ruler:** Elizabeth II **Series:** Evolution of Mankind **Subject:** Homo Erectus **Obv:** Crowned bust right **Rev:** Three figures with fire

Date	Mintage	F	VF	XF	Unc	BU
1998 Proof	Est. 10,000		Value: 50.00			

KM# 718 CROWN
Copper-Nickel, 38.8 mm. **Ruler:** Elizabeth II **Series:** Evolution of Mankind **Subject:** Homo Sapiens **Obv:** Crowned bust right **Rev:** Figure doing cave painting

Date	Mintage	F	VF	XF	Unc	BU
1998	—	—	—	—	12.00	15.00

KM# 718a CROWN
28.2800 g., 0.9250 Silver 0.8410 oz. ASW, 38.8 mm. **Ruler:** Elizabeth II **Series:** Evolution of Mankind **Subject:** Homo Sapiens **Obv:** Crowned bust right **Rev:** Figure doing cave painting

Date	Mintage	F	VF	XF	Unc	BU
1998 Proof	Est. 10,000		Value: 50.00			

KM# 720a CROWN
28.2800 g., 0.9250 Silver 0.8410 oz. ASW, 38.8 mm. **Ruler:** Elizabeth II **Series:** Evolution of Mankind **Subject:** Homo Sapiens Hunting Mammoth **Obv:** Crowned bust right **Rev:** Figures spearing mammoth

Date	Mintage	F	VF	XF	Unc	BU
1998 Proof	Est. 10,000		Value: 50.00			

KM# 722a CROWN
28.2800 g., 0.9250 Silver 0.8410 oz. ASW, 38.8 mm. **Ruler:** Elizabeth II **Series:** Evolution of Mankind **Obv:** Queen's portrait **Rev:** Illustrated theory of evolution

Date	Mintage	F	VF	XF	Unc	BU
1998 Proof	Est. 10,000		Value: 50.00			

KM# 726 CROWN
Copper-Nickel, 38.8 mm. **Ruler:** Elizabeth II **Series:** Evolution of Mankind **Subject:** Charles Darwin, 1809-1882 **Obv:** Homo Sapiens Hunting Mammoth **Rev:** Bust facing, caveman and space shuttle at right

Date	Mintage	F	VF	XF	Unc	BU
1998	—	—	—	—	12.00	15.00

KM# 726a CROWN
28.2800 g., 0.9250 Silver 0.8410 oz. ASW, 38.8 mm. **Ruler:** Elizabeth II **Series:** Evolution of Mankind **Subject:** Charles Darwin, 1809-1882 **Obv:** Crowned bust right **Rev:** Bust facing, caveman and space shuttle at right

Date	Mintage	F	VF	XF	Unc	BU
1998 Proof	Est. 10,000		Value: 50.00			

KM# 714 CROWN
Copper-Nickel, 38.8 mm. **Ruler:** Elizabeth II **Series:** Evolution of Mankind **Subject:** Gibraltar Skull **Obv:** Crowned bust right **Rev:** Skull, rock and caveman

Date	Mintage	F	VF	XF	Unc	BU
1998	—	—	—	—	12.00	15.00

KM# 714a CROWN
28.2800 g., 0.9250 Silver 0.8410 oz. ASW, 38.8 mm. **Ruler:** Elizabeth II **Series:** Evolution of Mankind **Subject:** Gibraltar Skull **Obv:** Crowned bust right **Rev:** Skull, rock and caveman

Date	Mintage	F	VF	XF	Unc	BU
1998 Proof	Est. 10,000		Value: 50.00			

KM# 722.1 CROWN
Copper-Nickel, 38.8 mm. **Ruler:** Elizabeth II **Series:** Evolution of Mankind **Obv:** Queen's portrait **Rev:** Pictorial representation of theory of evolution, denomination below

Date	Mintage	F	VF	XF	Unc	BU
1998	—	—	—	—	12.00	15.00

KM# 728 CROWN
Copper-Nickel, 38.8 mm. **Ruler:** Elizabeth II **Series:** Evolution of Mankind **Subject:** Raymond Dart **Obv:** Crowned bust right **Rev:** Bust at left looking at skull

Date	Mintage	F	VF	XF	Unc	BU
1998	—	—	—	—	12.00	15.00

KM# 728a CROWN
28.2800 g., 0.9250 Silver 0.8410 oz. ASW, 38.8 mm. **Ruler:** Elizabeth II **Series:** Evolution of Mankind **Subject:** Raymond Dart **Obv:** Crowned bust right **Rev:** Bust at left looking at skull on right

Date	Mintage	F	VF	XF	Unc	BU
1998 Proof	Est. 10,000		Value: 50.00			

KM# 730 CROWN
Copper-Nickel, 38.8 mm. **Ruler:** Elizabeth II **Series:** Evolution of Mankind **Subject:** 20th Century Homo Sapiens **Obv:** Crowned bust right **Rev:** Five depictions of evolution

Date	Mintage	F	VF	XF	Unc	BU
1998	—	—	—	—	12.00	15.00

KM# 730a CROWN
28.2800 g., 0.9250 Silver 0.8410 oz. ASW, 38.8 mm. **Ruler:** Elizabeth II **Series:** Evolution of Mankind **Subject:** 20th Century Homo Sapiens **Obv:** Crowned bust right **Rev:** Five depictions of evolution

Date	Mintage	F	VF	XF	Unc	BU
1998 Proof	Est. 10,000	Value: 50.00				

KM# 733 CROWN
28.2800 g., 0.9250 Silver 0.8410 oz. ASW, 38.8 mm. **Ruler:** Elizabeth II **Series:** Wonders of the World **Subject:** Guilin Hills, China **Obv:** Crowned bust right **Rev:** Chinese coin design inlay below hill scene

Date	Mintage	F	VF	XF	Unc	BU
1998 Proof	Est. 7,500	Value: 60.00				

KM# 734 CROWN
28.2800 g., 0.9250 Silver 0.8410 oz. ASW, 38.8 mm. **Ruler:** Elizabeth II **Series:** Wonders of the World **Subject:** Victoria Falls, Africa **Obv:** Crowned bust right **Rev:** South African coin design inlay below falls scene

Date	Mintage	F	VF	XF	Unc	BU
1998 Proof	Est. 7,500	Value: 60.00				

KM# 735 CROWN
28.2800 g., 0.9250 Silver 0.8410 oz. ASW, 38.8 mm. **Ruler:** Elizabeth II **Series:** Wonders of the World **Subject:** The Materhorn, Switzerland, Italy **Obv:** Crowned bust right **Rev:** Swiss coin design inlay below mountain

Date	Mintage	F	VF	XF	Unc	BU
1998 Proof	Est. 7,500	Value: 60.00				

KM# 736 CROWN
28.2800 g., 0.9250 Silver 0.8410 oz. ASW, 38.8 mm. **Ruler:** Elizabeth II **Series:** Wonders of the World **Subject:** Taroko Gorge, Taiwan **Obv:** Crowned bust right **Rev:** Taiwanese coin design inlay below gorge scene

Date	Mintage	F	VF	XF	Unc	BU
1998 Proof	Est. 7,500	Value: 60.00				

KM# 737 CROWN
28.2800 g., 0.9250 Silver 0.8410 oz. ASW, 38.8 mm. **Ruler:** Elizabeth II **Series:** Wonders of the World **Subject:** Niagara Falls, Canada, USA **Obv:** Crowned bust right **Rev:** American coin design inlay below falls scene

Date	Mintage	F	VF	XF	Unc	BU
1998 Proof	Est. 7,500	Value: 60.00				

KM# 738 CROWN
28.2800 g., 0.9250 Silver 0.8410 oz. ASW, 38.8 mm. **Ruler:** Elizabeth II **Series:** Wonders of the World **Subject:** Mount Fuji, Japan **Obv:** Crowned bust right **Rev:** Japanese coin design inlay below plants and mountain

Date	Mintage	F	VF	XF	Unc	BU
1998 Proof	Est. 7,500	Value: 60.00				

KM# 739 CROWN
28.2800 g., 0.9250 Silver 0.8410 oz. ASW, 38.8 mm. **Ruler:** Elizabeth II **Series:** Wonders of the World **Subject:** Uluru, Australia **Obv:** Crowned bust right **Rev:** Australian coin design inlay below mountain

Date	Mintage	F	VF	XF	Unc	BU
1998 Proof	Est. 7,500	Value: 60.00				

KM# 745 CROWN
Copper-Nickel, 38.8 mm. **Ruler:** Elizabeth II **Series:** Year of the Ocean **Obv:** Crowned bust right **Rev:** Mermaid and dolphin

Date	Mintage	F	VF	XF	Unc	BU
1998	—	—	—	—	10.00	12.50

KM# 745a CROWN
28.2800 g., 0.9250 Silver 0.8410 oz. ASW, 38.8 mm. **Ruler:** Elizabeth II **Series:** Year of the Ocean **Obv:** Crowned bust right **Rev:** Mermaid and dolphin

Date	Mintage	F	VF	XF	Unc	BU
1998 Proof	Est. 30,000	Value: 50.00				

KM# 746 CROWN
Copper-Nickel, 38.8 mm. **Ruler:** Elizabeth II **Series:** Year of the Ocean **Obv:** Crowned bust right **Rev:** Octopus, fish and coral

Date	Mintage	F	VF	XF	Unc	BU
1998	—	—	—	—	10.00	12.50

KM# 746a CROWN
28.2800 g., 0.9250 Silver 0.8410 oz. ASW, 38.8 mm. **Ruler:** Elizabeth II **Series:** Year of the Ocean **Obv:** Crowned bust right **Rev:** Octopus, fish and coral

Date	Mintage	F	VF	XF	Unc	BU
1998 Proof	Est. 30,000	Value: 50.00				

KM# 747 CROWN
Copper-Nickel, 38.8 mm. **Ruler:** Elizabeth II **Series:** Year of the Ocean **Obv:** Crowned bust right **Rev:** Jellyfish, stingray and fish

Date	Mintage	F	VF	XF	Unc	BU
1998	—	—	—	—	10.00	12.50

KM# 747a CROWN
28.2800 g., 0.9250 Silver 0.8410 oz. ASW, 38.8 mm. **Ruler:** Elizabeth II **Series:** Year of the Ocean **Obv:** Crowned bust right **Rev:** Jellyfish, stingray and fish

Date	Mintage	F	VF	XF	Unc	BU
1998 Proof	Est. 30,000	Value: 60.00				

KM# 748 CROWN
Copper-Nickel, 38.8 mm. **Ruler:** Elizabeth II **Series:** Year of the Ocean **Obv:** Crowned bust right **Rev:** Two wind surfers

Date	Mintage	F	VF	XF	Unc	BU
1998	—	—	—	—	9.50	12.00

KM# 748a CROWN
28.2800 g., 0.9250 Silver 0.8410 oz. ASW, 38.8 mm.
Ruler: Elizabeth II **Series:** Year of the Ocean **Obv:** Crowned bust right **Rev:** Two wind surfers

Date	Mintage	F	VF	XF	Unc	BU
1998 Proof	Est. 30,000	Value: 60.00				

KM# 768 CROWN
Copper-Nickel, 38.8 mm. **Ruler:** Elizabeth II **Subject:** The Gibraltar Regiment New Colors **Obv:** Crowned bust right **Rev:** Soldier presenting keys, flags and crowned arms

Date	Mintage	F	VF	XF	Unc	BU
1998	—	—	—	—	10.00	12.50

KM# 768a CROWN
28.2800 g., 0.9250 Silver 0.8410 oz. ASW, 38.8 mm.
Ruler: Elizabeth II **Subject:** The Gibraltar Regiment New Colors **Obv:** Crowned bust right **Rev:** Soldier presenting keys, flags and crowned arms

Date	Mintage	F	VF	XF	Unc	BU
1998 Proof	Est. 30,000	Value: 50.00				

KM# 799 CROWN
Copper-Nickel, 38.8 mm. **Ruler:** Elizabeth II **Series:** The World At War **Subject:** General D.D. Eisenhower **Obv:** Crowned bust right **Rev:** North African invasion scene

Date	Mintage	F	VF	XF	Unc	BU
1998	—	—	—	—	8.00	10.00

KM# 799a CROWN
28.2800 g., 0.9250 Silver 0.8410 oz. ASW, 38.8 mm.
Ruler: Elizabeth II **Series:** The World At War **Subject:** General D.D. Eisenhower **Obv:** Crowned bust right **Rev:** North African invasion scene

Date	Mintage	F	VF	XF	Unc	BU
1998 Proof	Est. 10,000	Value: 50.00				

KM# 785 CROWN
28.2800 g., Copper-Nickel, 38.8 mm. **Ruler:** Elizabeth II **Series:** Summer Olympics - Sydney **Obv:** Crowned bust right **Rev:** Broad jumper and kangaroo

Date	Mintage	F	VF	XF	Unc	BU
1999	—	—	—	—	8.00	10.00
2000PM	—	—	—	—	8.00	10.00

KM# 787 CROWN
28.2800 g., Copper-Nickel, 38.8 mm. **Ruler:** Elizabeth II **Series:** Summer Olympics - Sydney **Obv:** Crowned bust right **Rev:** Sailboats and platypus

Date	Mintage	F	VF	XF	Unc	BU
1999	—	—	—	—	8.00	10.00
2000PM	—	—	—	—	8.00	10.00

KM# 789 CROWN
28.2800 g., Copper-Nickel, 38.8 mm. **Ruler:** Elizabeth II **Series:** Summer Olympics - Sydney **Obv:** Crowned bust right **Rev:** Swimmer and koala bear

Date	Mintage	F	VF	XF	Unc	BU
1999	—	—	—	—	8.00	10.00
2000PM	—	—	—	—	8.00	10.00

KM# 793 CROWN
28.2800 g., Copper-Nickel, 38.8 mm. **Ruler:** Elizabeth II **Series:** Summer Olympics - Sydney **Obv:** Crowned bust right **Rev:** Man with torch and dingo, denomination below

Date	Mintage	F	VF	XF	Unc	BU
1999	—	—	—	—	8.00	10.00
2000PM	—	—	—	—	8.00	10.00

KM# 795 CROWN
28.2800 g., Copper-Nickel, 38.8 mm. **Ruler:** Elizabeth II **Series:** Summer Olympics - Sydney **Obv:** Crowned bust right **Rev:** Runner with torch, Aboriginal portrait and Ayer's Rock

Date	Mintage	F	VF	XF	Unc	BU
1999	—	—	—	—	8.00	10.00
2000PM	—	—	—	—	8.00	10.00

KM# 859 CROWN
Copper-Nickel, 38.8 mm. **Ruler:** Elizabeth II **Series:** The World At War **Subject:** The Blitz **Obv:** Crowned bust right **Rev:** Firefighters in action after air raid

Date	Mintage	F	VF	XF	Unc	BU
1999	—	—	—	—	10.00	12.00

KM# 791 CROWN
28.2800 g., Copper-Nickel, 38.8 mm. **Ruler:** Elizabeth II **Series:** Summer Olympics - Sydney **Obv:** Crowned bust right **Rev:** Two oarsmen below cockatoos

Date	Mintage	F	VF	XF	Unc	BU
1999	—	—	—	—	8.00	10.00
2000PM	—	—	—	—	8.00	10.00

KM# 783.1 CROWN
Copper-Nickel, 38.8 mm. **Ruler:** Elizabeth II **Subject:** 1999 The Year of the Rabbit **Obv:** Cronwned bust right **Rev:** Rabbit reading, sparrow, Chinese characters

Date	Mintage	F	VF	XF	Unc	BU
1999	—	—	—	—	10.00	12.00

KM# 783.1a CROWN
28.2800 g., 0.9250 Silver 0.8410 oz. ASW, 38.8 mm. **Ruler:**
Elizabeth II **Subject:** 1999 The Year of the Rabbit **Obv:** Crowned
bust right **Rev:** Rabbit reading, sparrow, Chinese characters

Date	Mintage	F	VF	XF	Unc	BU
1999 Proof	Est. 10,000			Value: 50.00		

KM# 783.2 CROWN
Copper-Nickel, 38.8 mm. **Ruler:** Elizabeth II **Obv:** Crowned bust
right **Rev:** Rabbit reading, sparrow; without Chinese characters

Date	Mintage	F	VF	XF	Unc	BU
1999	Inc. above	—	—	—	10.00	12.00

KM# 783.2a CROWN
28.2800 g., 0.9250 Silver 0.8410 oz. ASW, 38.8 mm.
Ruler: Elizabeth II **Obv:** Crowned bust right **Rev:** Rabbit reading,
sparrow; without Chinese characters

Date	Mintage	F	VF	XF	Unc	BU
1999 Proof	Inc. above			Value: 50.00		

KM# 785a CROWN
28.2800 g., 0.9250 Silver 0.8410 oz. ASW, 38.8 mm.
Ruler: Elizabeth II **Series:** Summer Olympics - Sydney
Obv: Crowned bust right **Rev:** Broad jumper and kangaroo

Date	Mintage	F	VF	XF	Unc	BU
1999 Proof	Est. 30,000			Value: 50.00		

KM# 787a CROWN
28.2800 g., 0.9250 Silver 0.8410 oz. ASW, 38.8 mm.
Ruler: Elizabeth II **Series:** Summer Olympics - Sydney
Obv: Crowned bust right **Rev:** Sailboats and platypus

Date	Mintage	F	VF	XF	Unc	BU
1999 Proof	Est. 30,000			Value: 50.00		

KM# 789a CROWN
28.2800 g., 0.9250 Silver 0.8410 oz. ASW, 38.8 mm.
Ruler: Elizabeth II **Series:** Summer Olympics - Sydney
Obv: Crowned bust right **Rev:** Swimmer and koala bear

Date	Mintage	F	VF	XF	Unc	BU
1999 Proof	Est. 30,000			Value: 50.00		

KM# 791a CROWN
28.2800 g., 0.9250 Silver 0.8410 oz. ASW, 38.8 mm. **Ruler:**
Elizabeth II **Series:** Summer Olympics - Sydney **Obv:** Crowned bust
right **Rev:** Two oarsmen below cockatoos **Note:** Prev. KM791.1

Date	Mintage	F	VF	XF	Unc	BU
1999 Proof	Est. 30,000			Value: 50.00		

KM# 793a CROWN
28.2800 g., 0.9250 Silver 0.8410 oz. ASW, 38.8 mm.
Ruler: Elizabeth II **Series:** Summer Olympics - Sydney
Obv: Crowned bust right **Rev:** Man with torch and dingo

Date	Mintage	F	VF	XF	Unc	BU
1999 Proof	Est. 30,000			Value: 50.00		

KM# 795a CROWN
28.2800 g., 0.9250 Silver 0.8410 oz. ASW, 38.8 mm.
Ruler: Elizabeth II **Series:** Summer Olympics - Sydney
Obv: Crowned bust right **Rev:** Runner with torch, Aboriginal portrait
and Ayer's Rock

Date	Mintage	F	VF	XF	Unc	BU
1999 Proof	Est. 30,000			Value: 50.00		

KM# 796.1 CROWN
6.2200 g., 0.9999 Gold 0.1999 oz. AGW **Ruler:** Elizabeth II
Subject: Millennium 2000 **Obv:** Head with tiara right
Rev: Sundial, digital clock face, candle and traditional clock face

Date	Mintage	F	VF	XF	Unc	BU
1999 Proof	5,000			Value: 200		

KM# 801 CROWN
Copper-Nickel, 38.8 mm. **Ruler:** Elizabeth II **Subject:** King
Alfred the Great, 871-899 **Obv:** Crowned bust right **Rev:** Crowned
bust left, dates

Date	Mintage	F	VF	XF	Unc	BU
1999	—	—	—	—	7.50	9.00

KM# 801a CROWN
28.2800 g., 0.9250 Silver 0.8410 oz. ASW, 38.8 mm.
Ruler: Elizabeth II **Subject:** King Alfred the Great, 871-899
Obv: Crowned bust right **Rev:** Crowned bust left, dates

Date	Mintage	F	VF	XF	Unc	BU
1999 Proof	Est. 10,000			Value: 47.50		

KM# 803 CROWN
Copper-Nickel, 38.8 mm. **Ruler:** Elizabeth II **Subject:** King
Canute, 1016-1035 **Obv:** Crowned bust right **Rev:** Crowned bust
left, dates

Date	Mintage	F	VF	XF	Unc	BU
1999	—	—	—	7.50	9.00	

KM# 803a CROWN
28.2800 g., 0.9250 Silver 0.8410 oz. ASW, 38.8 mm.
Ruler: Elizabeth II **Subject:** King Canute, 1016-1035
Obv: Crowned bust right **Rev:** Crowned bust left, dates

Date	Mintage	F	VF	XF	Unc	BU
1999 Proof	Est. 10,000			Value: 47.50		

KM# 805 CROWN
Copper-Nickel, 38.8 mm. **Ruler:** Elizabeth II **Subject:** King
Edward the Confessor, 1042-1066 **Obv:** Crowned bust right
Rev: Crowned bust left, dates

Date	Mintage	F	VF	XF	Unc	BU
1999	—	—	—	7.50	9.00	

KM# 805a CROWN
28.2800 g., 0.9250 Silver 0.8410 oz. ASW, 38.8 mm.
Ruler: Elizabeth II **Subject:** King Edward the Confessor, 1042-
1066 **Obv:** Crowned bust right **Rev:** Crowned bust left, dates

Date	Mintage	F	VF	XF	Unc	BU
1999 Proof	Est. 10,000			Value: 47.50		

KM# 809 CROWN
Copper-Nickel, 38.8 mm. **Ruler:** Elizabeth II **Series:** House of
- Plantagenet **Subject:** King Richard I, 1189-1199 **Obv:** Crowned
bust right **Rev:** Crowned bust right, dates

Date	Mintage	F	VF	XF	Unc	BU
1999	—	—	—	—	7.50	9.00

KM# 809a CROWN
28.2800 g., 0.9250 Silver 0.8410 oz. ASW, 38.8 mm.
Ruler: Elizabeth II **Series:** House of - Plantagenet **Subject:** King
Richard I, 1189-1199 **Obv:** Crowned bust right **Rev:** Crowned
bust right, dates

Date	Mintage	F	VF	XF	Unc	BU
1999 Proof	Est. 10,000			Value: 47.50		

KM# 811 CROWN
Copper-Nickel, 38.8 mm. **Ruler:** Elizabeth II **Series:** House of
- Plantagenet **Subject:** King John, 1199-1216 **Obv:** Crowned
bust right **Rev:** Crowned bust left, dates

Date	Mintage	F	VF	XF	Unc	BU
1999	—	—	—	—	7.50	9.00

KM# 811a CROWN
28.2800 g., 0.9250 Silver 0.8410 oz. ASW, 38.8 mm. **Ruler:**
Elizabeth II **Series:** House of - Plantagenet **Subject:** King John,
1199-1216 **Obv:** Crowned bust right **Rev:** Crowned bust left, dates

Date	Mintage	F	VF	XF	Unc	BU
1999 Proof	Est. 10,000			Value: 47.50		

KM# 813 CROWN
Copper-Nickel, 38.8 mm. **Ruler:** Elizabeth II **Series:** House of
- Lancaster **Subject:** King Henry V, 1413-1422 **Obv:** Crowned
bust right **Rev:** Bust right, dates

Date	Mintage	F	VF	XF	Unc	BU
1999	—	—	—	—	7.50	9.00

KM# 813a CROWN
28.2800 g., 0.9250 Silver 0.8410 oz. ASW, 38.8 mm.
Ruler: Elizabeth II **Series:** House of - Lancaster **Subject:** King
Henry V, 1413-1422 **Obv:** Crowned bust right **Rev:** Bust right,
dates

Date	Mintage	F	VF	XF	Unc	BU
1999 Proof	Est. 10,000			Value: 47.50		

KM# 815   CROWN

Copper-Nickel, 38.8 mm.   **Ruler:** Elizabeth II **Series:** House of
- York **Subject:** King Richard III, 1483-1485 **Obv:** Crowned bust
right **Rev:** Bust with hat right, dates

Date	Mintage	F	VF	XF	Unc	BU
1999	—	—	—	—	7.50	9.00

KM# 815a   CROWN

28.2800 g., 0.9250 Silver 0.8410 oz. ASW, 38.8 mm.
Ruler: Elizabeth II **Series:** House of - York **Subject:** King Richard
III, 1483-1485 **Obv:** Crowned bust right **Rev:** Bust with hat right,
dates

Date	Mintage	F	VF	XF	Unc	BU
1999 Proof	Est. 10,000	Value: 47.50				

KM# 821   CROWN

Copper-Nickel, 38.8 mm.   **Ruler:** Elizabeth II **Series:** House of
- Stuart **Subject:** King Charles I, 1625-1649 **Obv:** Crowned bust
right **Rev:** Bust right, dates

Date	Mintage	F	VF	XF	Unc	BU
1999	—	—	—	—	7.50	9.00

KM# 821a   CROWN

28.2800 g., 0.9250 Silver 0.8410 oz. ASW, 38.8 mm.
Ruler: Elizabeth II **Series:** House of - Stuart **Subject:** King
Charles I, 1625-1649 **Obv:** Crowned bust right **Rev:** Bust right,
dates

Date	Mintage	F	VF	XF	Unc	BU
1999 Proof	Est. 10,000	Value: 47.50				

KM# 827   CROWN

Copper-Nickel, 38.8 mm.   **Ruler:** Elizabeth II **Subject:** The
Wedding of Prince Edward and Miss Sophie Rhys-Jones
Obv: Crowned bust right **Rev:** St. George's Chapel

Date	Mintage	F	VF	XF	Unc	BU
1999	—	—	—	—	8.00	9.50

KM# 827a   CROWN

28.2800 g., 0.9250 Silver 0.8410 oz. ASW, 38.8 mm.
Ruler: Elizabeth II **Subject:** The Wedding of Prince Edward and
Miss Sophie Rhys-Jones **Obv:** Crowned bust right **Rev:** St.
George's Chapel

Date	Mintage	F	VF	XF	Unc	BU
1999 Proof	Est. 10,000	Value: 50.00				

KM# 817   CROWN

Copper-Nickel, 38.8 mm.   **Ruler:** Elizabeth II **Series:** House of
- Tudor **Subject:** King Henry VIII, 1509-1547 **Obv:** Crowned bust
right **Rev:** Bust with flat hat right, dates

Date	Mintage	F	VF	XF	Unc	BU
1999	—	—	—	—	7.50	9.00

KM# 817a   CROWN

28.2800 g., 0.9250 Silver 0.8410 oz. ASW, 38.8 mm.
Ruler: Elizabeth II **Series:** House of - Tudor **Subject:** King Henry
VIII, 1509-1547 **Obv:** Crowned bust right **Rev:** Bust with flat hat
right, dates

Date	Mintage	F	VF	XF	Unc	BU
1999 Proof	Est. 10,000	Value: 47.50				

KM# 823   CROWN

Copper-Nickel, 38.8 mm.   **Ruler:** Elizabeth II **Series:** House of
- Stuart **Subject:** King Charles II, 1660-1685 **Obv:** Crowned bust
right **Rev:** Laureate bust right, dates

Date	Mintage	F	VF	XF	Unc	BU
1999	—	—	—	—	7.50	9.00

KM# 823a   CROWN

28.2800 g., 0.9250 Silver 0.8410 oz. ASW, 38.8 mm.   **Ruler:**
Elizabeth II **Series:** House of -Stuart **Subject:** King Charles II, 1660-
1685 **Obv:** Crowned bust right **Rev:** Laureate bust right, dates

Date	Mintage	F	VF	XF	Unc	BU
1999 Proof	Est. 10,000	Value: 45.00				

KM# 826a   CROWN

28.2800 g., 0.9250 Silver 0.8410 oz. ASW, 38.8 mm.
Ruler: Elizabeth II **Subject:** The Wedding of Prince Edward and
Miss Sophie Rhys-Jones **Obv:** Crowned bust right **Rev:** St.
George's Chapel

Date	Mintage	F	VF	XF	Unc	BU
1999 Proof	10,000	Value: 47.50				

KM# 835   CROWN

Copper-Nickel, 38.8 mm.   **Ruler:** Elizabeth II **Series:** The Life
Of Queen Elizabeth The Queen Mother **Subject:** Queen's
childhood **Obv:** Crowned bust right **Rev:** 1903 portrait of Queen
Mother as a girl

Date	Mintage	F	VF	XF	Unc	BU
1999	—	—	—	—	8.00	9.50

KM# 835a   CROWN

28.2800 g., 0.9250 Silver 0.8410 oz. ASW, 38.8 mm.
Ruler: Elizabeth II **Series:** The Life Of Queen Elizabeth The
Queen Mother **Subject:** Queen's childhood **Obv:** Crowned bust
right **Rev:** 1903 portrait of Queen Mother as a girl

Date	Mintage	F	VF	XF	Unc	BU
1999 Proof	Est. 10,000	Value: 50.00				

KM# 819   CROWN

Copper-Nickel, 38.8 mm.   **Ruler:** Elizabeth II **Series:** Tudor
Subject: Queen Elizabeth I, 1558-1603 **Obv:** Crowned bust right
Rev: Crowned bust with high ruffled collar left, dates

Date	Mintage	F	VF	XF	Unc	BU
1999	—	—	—	—	7.50	9.00

KM# 819a   CROWN

28.2800 g., 0.9250 Silver 0.8410 oz. ASW, 38.8 mm.
Ruler: Elizabeth II **Series:** House of - Tudor **Subject:** Queen
Elizabeth I, 1558-1603 **Obv:** Crowned bust right **Rev:** Crowned
bust with high ruffled collar left, dates

Date	Mintage	F	VF	XF	Unc	BU
1999 Proof	Est. 10,000	Value: 47.50				

KM# 826   CROWN

Copper-Nickel, 38.8 mm.   **Ruler:** Elizabeth II **Subject:** The
Wedding of Prince Edward and Miss Sophie Rhys-Jones
Obv: Crowned bust right **Rev:** Two heads facing above banner
and wedding bells **Note:** Prev. KM#826.1.

Date	Mintage	F	VF	XF	Unc	BU
1999	—	—	—	—	8.00	9.50

KM# 835b   CROWN

28.4600 g., 0.9250 Gilt Silver 0.8463 oz., 38.5 mm.
Ruler: Elizabeth II **Series:** The Life Of Queen Elizabeth The
Queen Mother **Subject:** Queen's childhood **Obv:** Crowned bust
right **Rev:** Queen Mother as a young girl **Edge:** Reeded

Date	Mintage	F	VF	XF	Unc	BU
1999PM Proof	—	Value: 50.00				

KM# 837 CROWN
Copper-Nickel, 38.8 mm. **Ruler:** Elizabeth II **Series:** The Life Of Queen Elizabeth The Queen Mother **Subject:** World War I - Glamis **Obv:** Crowned bust right **Rev:** 1918 portrait with wounded soldier

Date	Mintage	F	VF	XF	Unc	BU
1999	—	—	—	—	8.00	9.50

KM# 837a CROWN
28.2800 g., 0.9250 Silver 0.8410 oz. ASW, 38.8 mm. **Ruler:** Elizabeth II **Series:** The Life Of Queen Elizabeth The Queen Mother **Subject:** World War I - Glamis **Obv:** Crowned bust right **Rev:** 1918 portrait with wounded soldier

Date	Mintage	F	VF	XF	Unc	BU
1999 Proof	Est. 10,000	Value: 50.00				

KM# 837b CROWN
28.4600 g., 0.9250 Gilt Silver 0.8463 oz., 38.5 mm. **Ruler:** Elizabeth II **Series:** The Life Of Queen Elizabeth The Queen Mother **Subject:** World War I - Glamis **Obv:** Crowned bust right **Rev:** Queen Mother with wounded soldier in 1918 **Edge:** Reeded

Date	Mintage	F	VF	XF	Unc	BU
1999PM Proof	—	Value: 50.00				

KM# 839 CROWN
Copper-Nickel, 38.8 mm. **Ruler:** Elizabeth II **Series:** The Life Of Queen Elizabeth The Queen Mother **Subject:** A Royal Marriage **Obv:** Crowned bust right **Rev:** 1923 wedding portrait

Date	Mintage	F	VF	XF	Unc	BU
1999	—	—	—	—	8.00	9.50

KM# 839a CROWN
28.2800 g., 0.9250 Silver 0.8410 oz. ASW, 38.8 mm. **Ruler:** Elizabeth II **Series:** The Life Of Queen Elizabeth The Queen Mother **Subject:** A Royal Marriage **Obv:** Crowned bust right **Rev:** 1923 wedding portrait

Date	Mintage	F	VF	XF	Unc	BU
1999 Proof	Est. 10,000	Value: 50.00				

KM# 839b CROWN
28.4600 g., 0.9250 Gilt Silver 0.8463 oz., 38.5 mm. **Ruler:** Elizabeth II **Series:** The Life Of Queen Elizabeth The Queen Mother **Subject:** A Royal Marriage **Obv:** Crowned bust right **Rev:** Queen Mother's 1923 wedding portrait **Edge:** Reeded

Date	Mintage	F	VF	XF	Unc	BU
1999PM Proof	—	Value: 50.00				

KM# 841 CROWN
Copper-Nickel, 38.8 mm. **Ruler:** Elizabeth II **Series:** The Life Of Queen Elizabeth The Queen Mother **Subject:** A Royal Family **Obv:** Crowned bust right **Rev:** 1936 family portrait

Date	Mintage	F	VF	XF	Unc	BU
1999	—	—	—	—	8.00	9.50

KM# 841a CROWN
28.2800 g., 0.9250 Silver 0.8410 oz. ASW, 38.8 mm. **Ruler:** Elizabeth II **Series:** The Life Of Queen Elizabeth The Queen Mother **Subject:** A Royal Family **Obv:** Crowned bust right **Rev:** 1936 family portrait

Date	Mintage	F	VF	XF	Unc	BU
1999 Proof	Est. 10,000	Value: 50.00				

KM# 841b CROWN
28.4600 g., 0.9250 Gilt Silver 0.8463 oz., 38.5 mm. **Ruler:** Elizabeth II **Series:** The Life Of Queen Elizabeth The Queen Mother **Subject:** A Royal Family **Obv:** Crowned bust right **Rev:** 1936 Queen Mother's family portrait **Edge:** Reeded

Date	Mintage	F	VF	XF	Unc	BU
1999PM Proof	—	Value: 50.00				

KM# 843.1 CROWN
28.2800 g., 0.9250 Silver 0.8410 oz. ASW **Subject:** The World at War **Obv:** Queen's portrait **Rev:** Franklin Roosevelt and Zero fighter

Date	Mintage	F	VF	XF	Unc	BU
1999	—	—	—	—	10.00	12.00

KM# 843a CROWN
28.2800 g., 0.9250 Silver 0.8410 oz. ASW, 38.8 mm. **Ruler:** Elizabeth II **Series:** The World At War **Subject:** Franklin D. Roosevelt **Obv:** Crowned bust right **Rev:** Bust writing at left, Zero fighter plane at right

Date	Mintage	F	VF	XF	Unc	BU
1999 Proof	Est. 10,000	Value: 50.00				

KM# 845 CROWN
Copper-Nickel, 38.8 mm. **Ruler:** Elizabeth II **Series:** The World At War **Subject:** Operation Manna **Obv:** Crowned bust right **Rev:** Bomber dropping food packets

Date	Mintage	F	VF	XF	Unc	BU
1999	—	—	—	—	10.00	12.00

KM# 845a CROWN
28.2800 g., 0.9250 Silver 0.8410 oz. ASW, 38.8 mm. **Ruler:** Elizabeth II **Series:** The World At War **Subject:** Operation Manna **Obv:** Crowned bust right **Rev:** Bomber dropping food packets

Date	Mintage	F	VF	XF	Unc	BU
1999 Proof	Est. 10,000	Value: 50.00				

KM# 847.1 CROWN
Copper-Nickel, 38.8 mm. **Ruler:** Elizabeth II **Series:** The World At War **Subject:** J. Robert Oppenheimer **Obv:** Crowned bust right **Rev:** Bust at right looking left, B-29 and mushroom cloud

Date	Mintage	F	VF	XF	Unc	BU
1999	—	—	—	—	10.00	12.00

KM# 847a CROWN
28.2800 g., 0.9250 Silver 0.8410 oz. ASW, 38.8 mm. **Ruler:** Elizabeth II **Series:** The World At War **Subject:** J. Robert Oppenheimer **Obv:** Crowned bust right **Rev:** Bust at right looking left, B-29 and mushroom cloud

Date	Mintage	F	VF	XF	Unc	BU
1999 Proof	Est. 10,000	Value: 50.00				

KM# 849 CROWN
Copper-Nickel, 38.8 mm. **Ruler:** Elizabeth II **Series:** The World At War **Subject:** Barnes Wallis **Obv:** Crowned bust right **Rev:** Seated figure at left reading, bomber above dam at right

Date	Mintage	F	VF	XF	Unc	BU
1999	—	—	—	—	10.00	12.00

KM# 849a CROWN
28.2800 g., 0.9250 Silver 0.8410 oz. ASW, 38.8 mm. **Ruler:** Elizabeth II **Series:** The World At War **Subject:** Barnes Wallis **Obv:** Crowned bust right **Rev:** Seated figure at left reading, bomber above dam at right

Date	Mintage	F	VF	XF	Unc	BU
1999 Proof	Est. 10,000	Value: 50.00				

KM# 851 CROWN
Copper-Nickel, 38.8 mm. **Ruler:** Elizabeth II **Series:** The World At War **Subject:** Douglas Bader **Obv:** Crowned bust right **Rev:** Bust facing at left, planes in combat

Date	Mintage	F	VF	XF	Unc	BU
1999	—	—	—	—	10.00	12.00

KM# 851a CROWN
28.2800 g., 0.9250 Silver 0.8410 oz. ASW, 38.8 mm. **Ruler:** Elizabeth II **Series:** The World At War **Subject:** Douglas Bader **Obv:** Crowned bust right **Rev:** Bust facing at left, planes in combat

Date	Mintage	F	VF	XF	Unc	BU
1999 Proof	Est. 10,000	Value: 50.00				

KM# 857 CROWN
Copper-Nickel, 38.8 mm. **Ruler:** Elizabeth II **Series:** The World At War **Subject:** War Babies **Obv:** Crowned bust right **Rev:** Soldier kissing child

Date	Mintage	F	VF	XF	Unc	BU
1999	—	—	—	—	10.00	12.00

KM# 857a CROWN
28.2800 g., 0.9250 Silver 0.8410 oz. ASW, 38.8 mm. **Ruler:** Elizabeth II **Series:** The World At War **Subject:** War Babies **Obv:** Crowned bust right **Rev:** Soldier kissing child

Date	Mintage	F	VF	XF	Unc	BU
1999 Proof	Est. 10,000	Value: 50.00				

KM# 859a CROWN
28.2800 g., 0.9250 Silver 0.8410 oz. ASW, 38.8 mm. **Ruler:** Elizabeth II **Series:** The World At War **Subject:** The Blitz **Obv:** Crowned bust right **Rev:** Firefighters in action after air raid

Date	Mintage	F	VF	XF	Unc	BU
1999 Proof	Est. 10,000	Value: 50.00				

KM# 865 CROWN
Copper-Nickel, 38.8 mm. **Ruler:** Elizabeth II **Series:** The World At War **Subject:** Barbarossa **Obv:** Crowned bust right **Rev:** German tanks in Russia

Date	Mintage	F	VF	XF	Unc	BU
1999	—	—	—	—	10.00	12.00

KM# 865a CROWN
28.2800 g., 0.9250 Silver 0.8410 oz. ASW, 38.8 mm. **Ruler:** Elizabeth II **Series:** The World At War **Subject:** Barbarossa **Obv:** Crowned bust right **Rev:** German tanks in Russia

Date	Mintage	F	VF	XF	Unc	BU
1999 Proof	Est. 10,000	Value: 50.00				

KM# 853 CROWN
Copper-Nickel, 38.8 mm. **Ruler:** Elizabeth II **Series:** The World At War **Subject:** Winston Churchill **Obv:** Crowned bust right **Rev:** Bust facing with hand raised in "V" sign and crowd

Date	Mintage	F	VF	XF	Unc	BU
1999	—	—	—	—	10.00	12.00

KM# 853a CROWN
28.2800 g., 0.9250 Silver 0.8410 oz. ASW, 38.8 mm. **Ruler:** Elizabeth II **Series:** The World At War **Subject:** Winston Churchill **Obv:** Crowned bust right **Rev:** Bust facing with hand raised in "V" sign and crowd

Date	Mintage	F	VF	XF	Unc	BU
1999 Proof	Est. 10,000	Value: 50.00				

KM# 861 CROWN
Copper-Nickel, 38.8 mm. **Ruler:** Elizabeth II **Series:** The World At War **Subject:** D-Day **Obv:** Crowned bust right **Rev:** D-Day landing scene

Date	Mintage	F	VF	XF	Unc	BU
1999	—	—	—	—	10.00	12.00

KM# 861a CROWN
28.2800 g., 0.9250 Silver 0.8410 oz. ASW, 38.8 mm. **Ruler:** Elizabeth II **Series:** The World At War **Subject:** D-Day **Obv:** Crowned bust right **Rev:** D-Day landing scene

Date	Mintage	F	VF	XF	Unc	BU
1999 Proof	Est. 10,000	Value: 50.00				

KM# 871 CROWN
28.2800 g., Copper-Nickel, 38.8 mm. **Ruler:** Elizabeth II **Series:** The Life Of Queen Elizabeth The Queen Mother **Subject:** Crowned Queen Consort **Obv:** Head with tiara right **Rev:** 1937 crowning of the Queen consort

Date	Mintage	F	VF	XF	Unc	BU
2000	—	—	—	—	10.00	12.00

KM# 871a CROWN
28.2800 g., 0.9250 Silver 0.8410 oz. ASW, 38.8 mm. **Ruler:** Elizabeth II **Series:** The Life Of Queen Elizabeth The Queen Mother **Subject:** Crowned Queen Consort **Obv:** Head with tiara right **Rev:** 1937 coronation scene

Date	Mintage	F	VF	XF	Unc	BU
2000 Proof	10,000	Value: 50.00				

KM# 855 CROWN
Copper-Nickel, 38.8 mm. **Ruler:** Elizabeth II **Series:** The World At War **Subject:** Tirpitz **Obv:** Crowned bust right **Rev:** Battleship and sailor

Date	Mintage	F	VF	XF	Unc	BU
1999	—	—	—	—	10.00	12.00

KM# 855a CROWN
28.2800 g., 0.9250 Silver 0.8410 oz. ASW, 38.8 mm. **Ruler:** Elizabeth II **Series:** The World At War **Subject:** Tirpitz **Obv:** Crowned bust right **Rev:** Battleship and sailor

Date	Mintage	F	VF	XF	Unc	BU
1999 Proof	Est. 10,000	Value: 50.00				

KM# 863 CROWN
Copper-Nickel, 38.8 mm. **Ruler:** Elizabeth II **Series:** The World At War **Subject:** Operation Heavywater **Obv:** Crowned bust right **Rev:** Military skier

Date	Mintage	F	VF	XF	Unc	BU
1999	—	—	—	—	10.00	12.00

KM# 863a CROWN
28.2800 g., 0.9250 Silver 0.8410 oz. ASW, 38.8 mm. **Ruler:** Elizabeth II **Series:** The World At War **Subject:** Operation Heavywater **Obv:** Crowned bust right **Rev:** Military skier

Date	Mintage	F	VF	XF	Unc	BU
1999 Proof	Est. 10,000	Value: 50.00				

KM# 873 CROWN
Copper-Nickel, 38.8 mm. **Ruler:** Elizabeth II **Series:** The Life Of Queen Elizabeth The Queen Mother **Subject:** State Visit To France **Obv:** Crowned bust right **Rev:** Seated figure looking left

Date	Mintage	F	VF	XF	Unc	BU
2000	—	—	—	—	10.00	12.00

KM# 873a CROWN
28.2800 g., 0.9250 Silver 0.8410 oz. ASW, 38.8 mm. **Ruler:** Elizabeth II **Series:** The Life Of Queen Elizabeth The Queen Mother **Subject:** State Visit To France **Obv:** Crowned bust right **Rev:** Seated figure looking left

Date	Mintage	F	VF	XF	Unc	BU
2000 Proof	10,000	Value: 50.00				

KM# 875 CROWN
Copper-Nickel, 38.8 mm. **Ruler:** Elizabeth II **Series:** The Life Of Queen Elizabeth The Queen Mother **Subject:** London Bombings **Obv:** Crowned bust right **Rev:** Royals looking at bomb damage

Date	Mintage	F	VF	XF	Unc	BU
2000	—	—	—	—	10.00	12.00

KM# 875a CROWN
28.2800 g., 0.9250 Silver 0.8410 oz. ASW, 38.8 mm. **Ruler:** Elizabeth II **Series:** The Life Of Queen Elizabeth The Queen Mother **Subject:** London Bombings **Obv:** Crowned bust right **Rev:** Royals looking at bomb damage

Date	Mintage	F	VF	XF	Unc	BU
2000 Proof	10,000	Value: 50.00				

KM# 877 CROWN
Copper-Nickel, 38.8 mm. **Ruler:** Elizabeth II **Series:** The Life Of Queen Elizabeth The Queen Mother **Subject:** Victory **Obv:** Crowned bust right **Rev:** Portrait of royal family

Date	Mintage	F	VF	XF	Unc	BU
2000	—	—	—	—	10.00	12.00

KM# 877a CROWN
28.2800 g., 0.9250 Silver 0.8410 oz. ASW, 38.8 mm. **Ruler:** Elizabeth II **Series:** The Life Of Queen Elizabeth The Queen Mother **Subject:** Victory **Obv:** Crowned bust right **Rev:** Portrait of royal family

Date	Mintage	F	VF	XF	Unc	BU
2000 Proof	10,000	Value: 50.00				

KM# 880 CROWN
28.2800 g., Copper-Nickel, 38.8 mm. **Ruler:** Elizabeth II **Subject:** 18th Birthday - H.R.H. The Prince William **Obv:** Crowned bust right **Rev:** Bust 3/4 right

Date	Mintage	F	VF	XF	Unc	BU
2000	—	—	—	—	10.00	12.00

KM# 880a CROWN
28.2800 g., 0.9250 Silver 0.8410 oz. ASW, 38.8 mm. **Ruler:** Elizabeth II **Subject:** 18th Birthday - H.R.H. The Prince William **Obv:** Crowned bust right **Rev:** Bust 3/4 right

Date	Mintage	F	VF	XF	Unc	BU
2000 Proof	10,000	Value: 50.00				

KM# 882 CROWN
Copper-Nickel, 38.8 mm. **Ruler:** Elizabeth II **Subject:** Queen Mother **Obv:** Queen's portrait **Rev:** Queen Mother's portrait

Date	Mintage	F	VF	XF	Unc	BU
2000	—	—	—	—	10.00	12.00

KM# 882a CROWN
28.2800 g., 0.9250 Silver 0.8410 oz. ASW, 38.8 mm. **Ruler:** Elizabeth II **Obv:** Queen's portrait

Date	Mintage	F	VF	XF	Unc	BU
2000 Proof	10,000	Value: 50.00				

KM# 884 CROWN
Bi-Metallic Titanium center in Gold ring, 38.8 mm. **Ruler:** Elizabeth II **Subject:** 160th Anniversary - Uniform Penny Post **Obv:** Queen's portrait **Rev:** Postage stamp design **Edge:** Reeded

Date	Mintage	F	VF	XF	Unc	BU
2000 Proof	999	Value: 650				

KM# 128 2 CROWN
62.2070 g., 0.9990 Silver 1.9979 oz. ASW **Ruler:** Elizabeth II **Subject:** Japanese Royal Wedding **Obv:** Crowned bust right **Rev:** Pair of peacocks

Date	Mintage	F	VF	XF	Unc	BU
1993 Proof	Est. 20,000	Value: 60.00				

KM# 128a 2 CROWN
62.2070 g., 0.9999 Gold 1.9997 oz. AGW **Ruler:** Elizabeth II **Subject:** Japanese Royal Wedding **Obv:** Crowned bust right **Rev:** Pair of peacocks

Date	Mintage	F	VF	XF	Unc	BU
1993 Proof	Est. 2,500	Value: 2,000				

KM# 129 2 CROWN
62.2070 g., 0.9990 Silver 1.9979 oz. ASW **Ruler:** Elizabeth II **Subject:** Japanese Royal Wedding **Obv:** Crowned bust right **Rev:** Two peacocks, one in full display

Date	Mintage	F	VF	XF	Unc	BU
1993 Proof	Est. 20,000	Value: 45.00				

KM# 129a 2 CROWN
62.2070 g., 0.9999 Gold 1.9997 oz. AGW **Ruler:** Elizabeth II **Subject:** Japanese Royal Wedding **Obv:** Crowned bust right **Rev:** Two peacocks, one in full display

Date	Mintage	F	VF	XF	Unc	BU
1993 Proof	Est. 2,500	Value: 2,000				

KM# 106 5 CROWN
155.9230 g., 0.9990 Silver 5.0078 oz. ASW, 65 mm. **Ruler:** Elizabeth II **Subject:** Olympics - Barcelona **Obv:** Crowned bust right **Rev:** Discus thrower **Note:** Illustration reduced.

Date	Mintage	F	VF	XF	Unc	BU
1991 Proof	Est. 1,000	Value: 225				

KM# 451 5 CROWN
155.5175 g., 0.9999 Gold 4.9993 oz. AGW **Ruler:** Elizabeth II **Subject:** Lord Buddha **Rev:** Seated figure facing

Date	Mintage	F	VF	XF	Unc	BU
1996 Proof	Est. 250	Value: 5,000				

KM# 107 10 CROWN
311.8460 g., 0.9990 Silver 10.015 oz. ASW, 73 mm. **Ruler:** Elizabeth II **Series:** Olympics - Barcelona **Obv:** Crowned bust right **Rev:** Ancient runners **Note:** Illustration reduced.

Date	Mintage	F	VF	XF	Unc	BU
1991 Proof	Est. 1,000	Value: 300				

KM# 130 10 CROWN
311.8460 g., 0.9990 Silver 10.015 oz. ASW, 73 mm. **Ruler:** Elizabeth II **Subject:** Japanese Royal Wedding **Obv:** Crowned bust right **Rev:** Pair of peacocks

Date	Mintage	F	VF	XF	Unc	BU
1993 Proof	Est. 5,000	Value: 285				

KM# 131 32 CROWNS
1000.0000 g., 0.9990 Silver 32.117 oz. ASW, 85 mm. **Ruler:** Elizabeth II **Subject:** Japanese Royal Wedding **Obv:** Crowned bust right **Rev:** Two peacocks, one in full display

Date	Mintage	F	VF	XF	Unc	BU
1993 Proof	Est. 1,000	Value: 900				

KM# 333 40 CROWN
1244.1400 g., 0.9990 Silver 39.958 oz. ASW, 100 mm. **Ruler:** Elizabeth II **Rev:** Rock of Gibraltar and rising sun **Note:** Illustration reduced.

Date	Mintage	F	VF	XF	Unc	BU
1994 Proof	Est. 1,500	Value: 800				

KM# 18 POUND
9.5000 g., Nickel-Brass, 22.5 mm. **Ruler:** Elizabeth II **Obv:** Crowned head right **Rev:** Gibraltar castle and key

Date	Mintage	F	VF	XF	Unc	BU
1988 AA	—	—	—	—	3.50	4.50
1988PM AB	—	—	—	—	3.50	4.50
1990 AA	—	—	—	—	3.50	4.50
1991 AA	—	—	—	—	3.50	4.50
1991 AC	—	—	—	—	3.50	4.50
1992 AA	—	—	—	—	3.50	4.50
1993 AA	—	—	—	—	3.50	4.50
1996 AA	—	—	—	—	3.50	4.50
1997 AA	—	—	—	—	3.50	4.50

KM# 18a POUND
9.5000 g., 0.9250 Silver 0.2825 oz. ASW, 22.5 mm. **Ruler:** Elizabeth II **Obv:** Crowned head right **Rev:** Gibraltar castle and key

Date	Mintage	F	VF	XF	Unc	BU
1988 Proof	—	Value: 15.00				

KM# 18b POUND
9.5000 g., 0.9170 Gold 0.2801 oz. AGW, 22.5 mm. **Ruler:** Elizabeth II **Obv:** Crowned head right **Rev:** Gibraltar castle and key

Date	Mintage	F	VF	XF	Unc	BU
1988 Proof	—	Value: 350				

KM# 32 POUND
9.5000 g., Nickel-Brass, 22.5 mm. **Ruler:** Elizabeth II **Subject:** 150th Anniversary of Gibraltar Coinage **Obv:** Crowned head right **Rev:** Gibraltar castle and key within circle

Date	Mintage	F	VF	XF	Unc	BU
1989 AA	—	—	—	—	4.00	5.00

KM# 32a POUND
9.5000 g., 0.9250 Silver 0.2825 oz. ASW, 22.5 mm. **Ruler:** Elizabeth II **Subject:** 150th Anniversary of Gibraltar Coinage **Obv:** Crowned head right **Rev:** Gibraltar castle and key

Date	Mintage	F	VF	XF	Unc	BU
1989 Proof	Est. 2,500	Value: 35.00				

KM# 32b POUND
9.5000 g., 0.9170 Gold 0.2801 oz. AGW, 22.5 mm.
Ruler: Elizabeth II **Subject:** 150th Anniversary of Gibraltar
Coinage **Obv:** Crowned head right **Rev:** Gibraltar castle and key

Date	Mintage	F	VF	XF	Unc	BU
1989 Proof	150	Value: 350				

KM# 32c POUND
9.0000 g., 0.9500 Platinum 0.2749 oz. APW, 22.5 mm. **Ruler:**
Elizabeth II **Obv:** Crowned head right **Rev:** Gibraltar castle and key

Date	Mintage	F	VF	XF	Unc	BU
1989 Proof	100	Value: 550				

KM# 191 POUND
Nickel-Brass, 22.5 mm. **Ruler:** Elizabeth II **Subject:**
Referendum of 1967 **Obv:** Crowned head right **Rev:** Gibraltar
arms above Rock of Gibraltar with Union Jack background

Date	Mintage	F	VF	XF	Unc	BU
1993 AA	—	—	—	—	4.50	5.50

KM# 191a POUND
9.5000 g., 0.9250 Silver 0.2825 oz. ASW, 22.5 mm.
Ruler: Elizabeth II **Subject:** Referendum of 1967 **Obv:** Crowned
head right **Rev:** Gibraltar arms above Rock of Gibraltar with Union
Jack background

Date	Mintage	F	VF	XF	Unc	BU
1993 Proof	Est. 5,000	Value: 35.00				

KM# 191b POUND
9.5000 g., 0.9170 Gold 0.2801 oz. AGW, 22.5 mm.
Ruler: Elizabeth II **Subject:** Referendum of 1967 **Obv:** Crowned
head right **Rev:** Gibraltar arms above Rock of Gibraltar with Union
Jack background

Date	Mintage	F	VF	XF	Unc	BU
1993 Proof	Est. 3,500	Value: 350				

KM# 324 POUND
9.5000 g., Nickel-Brass, 22.5 mm. **Ruler:** Elizabeth II
Subject: 40th Anniversary - Queen Elizabeth II's 1st Royal Visit
to Gibraltar **Obv:** Crowned head right **Rev:** Luxury liner at sea

Date	Mintage	F	VF	XF	Unc	BU
1994 AA	—	—	—	—	7.50	9.00

KM# 340 POUND
9.5000 g., Nickel-Brass, 22.5 mm. **Ruler:** Elizabeth II
Subject: National Day, 50th Anniversary of the U.N.
Obv: Crowned head right **Rev:** Rock of Gibraltar

Date	Mintage	F	VF	XF	Unc	BU
1995 AA	—	—	—	—	3.50	5.00

KM# 340a POUND
9.5000 g., 0.9250 Silver 0.2825 oz. ASW, 22.5 mm. **Ruler:**
Elizabeth II **Obv:** Crowned head right **Rev:** Rock of Gibraltar

Date	Mintage	F	VF	XF	Unc	BU
1995 Proof	3,500	Value: 35.00				

KM# 869 POUND
9.5000 g., Nickel-Brass, 22.5 mm. **Ruler:** Elizabeth II
Obv: Head with tiara right **Rev:** Gibraltar castle and key

Date	Mintage	F	VF	XF	Unc	BU
1998 AA	—	—	—	—	3.50	4.50
1999 AA	—	—	—	—	3.50	4.50
2000PMM AA	—	—	—	—	3.50	4.50

KM# 24 2 POUNDS
Virenium **Ruler:** Elizabeth II **Obv:** Crowned head right
Rev: Cannon in fortress tunnel

Date	Mintage	F	VF	XF	Unc	BU
1988 AA	—	—	—	—	7.50	8.50
1989 AA	—	—	—	—	7.50	8.50
1990 AA	—	—	—	—	7.50	8.50
1991 AA	—	—	—	—	7.50	8.50
1993 AA	—	—	—	—	7.50	8.50
1995 AA	—	—	—	—	7.50	8.50
1995 AB	—	—	—	—	7.50	8.50
1995 AC	—	—	—	—	7.50	8.50
1996 AA	—	—	—	—	7.50	8.50

KM# 98 2 POUNDS
Virenium **Ruler:** Elizabeth II **Obv:** Crowned head right
Rev: Columbus and ship

Date	Mintage	F	VF	XF	Unc	BU
1992 AA	—	—	—	—	6.50	7.50

KM# 98a 2 POUNDS
9.3000 g., 0.9250 Silver 0.2766 oz. ASW **Ruler:** Elizabeth II
Obv: Crowned head right **Rev:** Columbus and ship

Date	Mintage	F	VF	XF	Unc	BU
1992 Proof	Est. 5,000	Value: 40.00				

KM# 98b 2 POUNDS
15.9400 g., 0.9170 Gold 0.4699 oz. AGW **Ruler:** Elizabeth II
Obv: Crowned head right **Rev:** Columbus and ship

Date	Mintage	F	VF	XF	Unc	BU
1992 Proof	Est. 5,000	Value: 450				

KM# 98c 2 POUNDS
18.0000 g., 0.9500 Platinum 0.5498 oz. APW **Ruler:** Elizabeth II
Obv: Crowned head right **Rev:** Columbus and ship

Date	Mintage	F	VF	XF	Unc	BU
1992 Proof	Est. 1,000	Value: 1,150				

KM# 325 2 POUNDS
Virenium **Ruler:** Elizabeth II **Subject:** 40th Anniversary - Queen
Elizabeth II's 1st Royal Visit to Gibraltar **Obv:** Crowned head right
Rev: Luxury liner at sea

Date	Mintage	F	VF	XF	Unc	BU
1994 AA	Est. 5,000	—	—	—	6.50	7.50

KM# 755 2 POUNDS
Ring: Brass **Center:** Copper-Nickel, 28.4 mm.
Ruler: Elizabeth II **Subject:** The Labours of Hercules **Obv:**
Crowned head right **Rev:** Hercules wrestling the Nimean Lion

Date	Mintage	F	VF	XF	Unc	BU
1997	—	—	—	—	7.50	9.00
1997 AA	—	—	—	—	7.50	9.00

KM# 755a 2 POUNDS
12.0000 g., 0.9990 Gold Plated Silver 0.3854 oz. ASW AGW
Ruler: Elizabeth II **Subject:** The Labours of Hercules
Obv: Crowned head right **Rev:** Hercules wrestling the
Nimean Lion

Date	Mintage	F	VF	XF	Unc	BU
1997 Proof	Est. 7,500	Value: 60.00				

KM# 756a 2 POUNDS
12.0000 g., 0.9990 Gold Plated Silver 0.3854 oz. ASW AGW
Ruler: Elizabeth II **Subject:** The Labours of Hercules
Obv: Crowned head right **Rev:** Hercules fighting the Hydra

Date	Mintage	F	VF	XF	Unc	BU
1997 Proof	Est. 7,500	Value: 60.00				

KM# 757a 2 POUNDS
12.0000 g., 0.9990 Gold Plated Silver 0.3854 oz. ASW AGW
Ruler: Elizabeth II **Subject:** The Labours of Hercules
Obv: Crowned head right **Rev:** Hercules and the Ceryneian Hind

Date	Mintage	F	VF	XF	Unc	BU
1997 Proof	Est. 7,500	Value: 60.00				

KM# 758a 2 POUNDS
0.9990 Gold Plated Silver **Ruler:** Elizabeth II **Subject:** The
Labours of Hercules **Obv:** Crowned head right **Rev:** Hercules
wrestles the Erymanthian Boar

Date	Mintage	F	VF	XF	Unc	BU
1997 Proof	7,500	Value: 60.00				

KM# 758 2 POUNDS
Bi-Metallic Copper-nickel center in Brass ring, 28.4 mm.
Ruler: Elizabeth II **Subject:** The Labours of Hercules
Obv: Crowned head right **Rev:** Hercules wrestles the
Erymanthian Boar

Date	Mintage	F	VF	XF	Unc	BU
1998 AA	—	—	—	—	7.50	9.00

KM# 757 2 POUNDS
Bi-Metallic Copper-nickel center in Brass ring, 28.4 mm.
Ruler: Elizabeth II **Subject:** The Labours of Hercules
Obv: Crowned head right **Rev:** Hercules and the Ceryneian Hind

Date	Mintage	F	VF	XF	Unc	BU
1998 AA	—	—	—	—	7.50	9.00

KM# 756 2 POUNDS
Bi-Metallic Copper-nickel center in Brass ring, 28.4 mm.
Ruler: Elizabeth II **Subject:** The Labours of Hercules
Obv: Crowned head right **Rev:** Hercules fighting the Hydra

Date	Mintage	F	VF	XF	Unc	BU
1998 AA	—	—	—	—	7.50	9.00

KM# 760 2 POUNDS
Copper-Nickel, 28.4 mm. **Ruler:** Elizabeth II **Subject:** The
Labours of Hercules **Obv:** Crowned head right **Rev:** Hercules
and the Cretan Bull

Date	Mintage	F	VF	XF	Unc	BU
1999 AA	—	—	—	—	7.50	9.00
1999 No die letters	—	—	—	—	7.50	9.00

KM# 760a 2 POUNDS
10.0000 g., 0.9990 Gold Plated Silver 0.3212 oz. ASW AGW
Subject: The Labours of Hercules **Obv:** Crowned head right
Rev: Hercules and the Cretan Bull

Date	Mintage	F	VF	XF	Unc	BU
1999 Proof	Est. 25,000	Value: 60.00				

KM# 761 2 POUNDS
Bi-Metallic Copper-nickel center in Brass ring, 28.4 mm. **Ruler:** Elizabeth II **Subject:** The Labours of Hercules **Obv:** Crowned head right **Rev:** Hercules and the Stymphalian Birds

Date	Mintage	F	VF	XF	Unc	BU
1999 AA	—	—	—	—	8.00	10.00

KM# 761a 2 POUNDS
10.0000 g., 0.9990 Gold Plated Silver 0.3212 oz. ASW AGW **Ruler:** Elizabeth II **Subject:** The Labours of Hercules **Obv:** Crowned head right **Rev:** Hercules and the Stymphalian Birds

Date	Mintage	F	VF	XF	Unc	BU
1999 Proof	Est. 25,000	Value: 60.00				

KM# 762 2 POUNDS
Bi-Metallic Copper-nickel center in Brass ring, 28.4 mm. **Ruler:** Elizabeth II **Subject:** The Labours of Hercules **Obv:** Crowned head right **Rev:** Hercules and the Mares of Diomedes

Date	Mintage	F	VF	XF	Unc	BU
1999 AA	—	—	—	—	8.00	10.00
1999 No die letters	—	—	—	—	7.50	9.00

KM# 762a 2 POUNDS
10.0000 g., 0.9990 Gold Plated Silver 0.3212 oz. ASW AGW **Ruler:** Elizabeth II **Subject:** The Labours of Hercules **Obv:** Crowned head right **Rev:** Hercules and the Mares of Diomedes

Date	Mintage	F	VF	XF	Unc	BU
1999 Proof	Est. 25,000	Value: 60.00				

KM# 759 2 POUNDS
12.0000 g., Bi-Metallic Copper-Nickel center in Brass ring, 28.4 mm. **Ruler:** Elizabeth II **Subject:** The Labours of Hercules **Obv:** Crowned head right **Rev:** Hercules and the Augean Stables

Date	Mintage	F	VF	XF	Unc	BU
1999 AA	—	—	—	—	7.50	9.00

KM# 759a 2 POUNDS
10.0000 g., 0.9990 Gold Plated Silver 0.3212 oz. ASW AGW **Ruler:** Elizabeth II **Subject:** The Labours of Hercules **Obv:** Crowned head right **Rev:** Hercules and the Augean Stables

Date	Mintage	F	VF	XF	Unc	BU
1999 Proof	Est. 25,000	Value: 60.00				

KM# 765 2 POUNDS
Bi-Metallic Copper-nickel center in Brass ring, 28.4 mm. **Ruler:** Elizabeth II **Subject:** The Labours of Hercules **Obv:** Head with tiara right **Rev:** Hercules carrying the world while facing a man with a bushel of apples **Edge:** Reeded

Date	Mintage	F	VF	XF	Unc	BU
2000 AA	—	—	—	—	7.50	9.00
2000 No die letters	—	—	—	—	7.50	9.00
2000 AA	—	—	—	—	7.50	9.00

KM# 766 2 POUNDS
Bi-Metallic Copper-nickel center in Brass ring, 28.4 mm. **Ruler:** Elizabeth II **Subject:** The Labours of Hercules **Obv:** Head with tiara right **Rev:** Hercules chaining Cerberus

Date	Mintage	F	VF	XF	Unc	BU
2000 AA	—	—	—	—	7.50	9.00
2000 No die letters	—	—	—	—	7.50	9.00
2000 AA	—	—	—	—	8.00	10.00

KM# 763 2 POUNDS
Bi-Metallic Copper-nickel center in Brass ring, 28.4 mm. **Ruler:** Elizabeth II **Subject:** The Labours of Hercules **Obv:** Head with tiara right **Rev:** Hercules and Hippolyta's Girdle **Edge:** Reeded

Date	Mintage	F	VF	XF	Unc	BU
2000 AA	Est. 2,000	—	—	—	7.50	9.00
2000 No die letters	—	—	—	—	7.50	9.00

KM# 764 2 POUNDS
12.0000 g., Bi-Metallic Copper-nickel center in Brass ring, 28.4 mm. **Ruler:** Elizabeth II **Subject:** The Labours of Hercules - Geryon's Cattle **Obv:** Head with tiara right **Rev:** Hercules with cow and three devils shot by one arrow **Edge:** Reeded

Date	Mintage	F	VF	XF	Unc	BU
2000 No die letters	—	—	—	—	7.50	9.00
2000 AA	—	—	—	—	8.00	10.00

KM# 763a 2 POUNDS
12.0000 g., 0.9990 Silver 0.3854 oz. ASW, 28.4 mm. **Ruler:** Elizabeth II **Subject:** The Labours of Hercules **Obv:** Crowned head right **Rev:** Hercules and Hippolyta's Girdle **Edge:** Reeded **Note:** Partially gold plated.

Date	Mintage	F	VF	XF	Unc	BU
2000 Proof	7,500	Value: 60.00				

KM# 764a 2 POUNDS
12.0000 g., 0.9990 Silver 0.3854 oz. ASW, 28.4 mm. **Ruler:** Elizabeth II **Subject:** The Labours of Hercules **Obv:** Head with tiara right **Rev:** Hercules with cow and three devils shot by one arrow **Edge:** Reeded **Note:** Partially gold plated.

Date	Mintage	F	VF	XF	Unc	BU
2000 Proof	7,500	Value: 60.00				

KM# 765a 2 POUNDS
12.0000 g., 0.9990 Silver 0.3854 oz. ASW, 28.4 mm. **Ruler:** Elizabeth II **Subject:** The Labours of Hercules **Obv:** Head with tiara right **Rev:** Hercules carrying the world while facing a man with a bushel of apples **Edge:** Reeded **Note:** Partially gold plated.

Date	Mintage	F	VF	XF	Unc	BU
2000 Proof	7,500	Value: 60.00				

KM# 766a 2 POUNDS
12.0000 g., 0.9990 Silver 0.3854 oz. ASW, 28.4 mm. **Ruler:** Elizabeth II **Subject:** The Labours of Hercules **Obv:** Head with tiara right **Rev:** Hercules chaining Cerberus **Note:** Partially gold plated.

Date	Mintage	F	VF	XF	Unc	BU
2000 Proof	7,500	Value: 60.00				

KM# 25 5 POUNDS
Virenium, 36 mm. **Ruler:** Elizabeth II **Obv:** Crowned head right **Rev:** Hercules statue standing

Date	Mintage	F	VF	XF	Unc	BU
1988 AA	—	—	—	—	14.00	16.00
1989 AA	—	—	—	—	14.00	16.00
1989 No die letters	—	—	—	—	14.00	16.00
1990 AA	—	—	—	—	14.00	16.00
1991 AA	—	—	—	—	14.00	16.00
1992 AA	—	—	—	—	14.00	16.00
1993 AA	—	—	—	—	14.00	16.00

KM# 309 5 POUNDS
Virenium, 36 mm. **Ruler:** Elizabeth II **Obv:** Crowned bust right **Rev:** D-Day - Soldier, sailor and pilot above tank, plane, and ship

Date	Mintage	F	VF	XF	Unc	BU
1994 AA	—	—	—	—	16.50	18.00
1994 AA Proof	Est. 5,000	Value: 20.00				

KM# 309a 5 POUNDS
23.5000 g., 0.9250 Silver 0.6988 oz. ASW, 36 mm. **Ruler:** Elizabeth II **Obv:** Crowned bust right **Rev:** D-Day - Soldier, sailor and pilot above tank, plane, and ship

Date	Mintage	F	VF	XF	Unc	BU
1994 Proof	Est. 5,000	Value: 40.00				

KM# 309b 5 POUNDS
39.8300 g., 0.9170 Gold 1.1742 oz. AGW, 36 mm. **Ruler:** Elizabeth II **Obv:** Crowned bust right **Rev:** D-Day - Soldier, sailor and pilot above tank, plane, and ship

Date	Mintage	F	VF	XF	Unc	BU
1994 Proof	Est. 850	Value: 1,150				

KM# 332 5 POUNDS
Virenium, 36 mm. **Ruler:** Elizabeth II **Obv:** Crowned head right **Rev:** 50th Anniversary - VE Day

Date	Mintage	F	VF	XF	Unc	BU
1995	—	—	—	—	16.50	18.50
1995 Proof	Est. 5,000	Value: 22.00				

KM# 332a 5 POUNDS
23.5000 g., 0.9250 Silver 0.6988 oz. ASW, 36 mm. **Ruler:** Elizabeth II **Obv:** Crowned head right **Rev:** 50th Anniversary - VE Day

Date	Mintage	F	VF	XF	Unc	BU
1995 Proof	Est. 5,000	Value: 40.00				

KM# 332b 5 POUNDS
39.8300 g., 0.9170 Gold 1.1742 oz. AGW, 36 mm. **Ruler:** Elizabeth II **Obv:** Crowned head right **Rev:** 50th Anniversary - VE Day

Date	Mintage	F	VF	XF	Unc	BU
1995 Proof	Est. 850	Value: 1,150				

KM# 334 5 POUNDS
Virenium, 36 mm. **Ruler:** Elizabeth II **Obv:** Crowned head right
Rev: Queen Mother viewing bomb-damaged Buckingham Palace

Date	Mintage	F	VF	XF	Unc	BU
1995	—	—	—	—	15.00	17.00

KM# 334a 5 POUNDS
25.5000 g., 0.9250 Silver 0.7583 oz. ASW, 36 mm.
Ruler: Elizabeth II **Obv:** Crowned head right **Rev:** Queen Mother viewing bomb-damaged Buckingham Palace

Date	Mintage	F	VF	XF	Unc	BU
1995 Proof	Est. 5,000	Value: 40.00				

KM# 334b 5 POUNDS
39.8300 g., 0.9170 Gold 1.1742 oz. AGW, 36 mm.
Ruler: Elizabeth II **Obv:** Crowned head right **Rev:** Queen Mother viewing bomb-damaged Buckingham Palace

Date	Mintage	F	VF	XF	Unc	BU
1995 Proof	Est. 850	Value: 1,150				

KM# 335 5 POUNDS
Virenium, 36 mm. **Ruler:** Elizabeth II **Obv:** Crowned head right
Rev: VJ Day - Flag Raising

Date	Mintage	F	VF	XF	Unc	BU
1995 AA	—	—	—	—	16.50	18.50
1995 Proof	Est. 5,000	Value: 22.00				

KM# 335a 5 POUNDS
23.5000 g., 0.9250 Silver 0.6988 oz. ASW, 36 mm. **Ruler:** Elizabeth II **Obv:** Crowned head right **Rev:** VJ Day - Flag Raising

Date	Mintage	F	VF	XF	Unc	BU
1995 Proof	Est. 5,000	Value: 40.00				

KM# 335b 5 POUNDS
39.8300 g., 0.9170 Gold 1.1742 oz. AGW, 36 mm. **Ruler:** Elizabeth II **Obv:** Crowned head right **Rev:** VJ Day - Flag Raising

Date	Mintage	F	VF	XF	Unc	BU
1995 Proof	Est. 850	Value: 1,150				

KM# 341 5 POUNDS
Virenium, 36 mm. **Ruler:** Elizabeth II **Subject:** 190th
Anniversary - Death Of Admiral Nelson **Obv:** Crowned head right
Rev: Bust at right facing left, ship at left

Date	Mintage	F	VF	XF	Unc	BU
1995 AA	—	—	—	—	15.00	17.00

KM# 341a 5 POUNDS
23.5000 g., 0.9250 Silver 0.6988 oz. ASW, 36 mm.
Ruler: Elizabeth II **Subject:** 190th Anniversary - Death of Admiral Nelson **Obv:** Crowned head right **Rev:** Bust at right facing left, ship at left

Date	Mintage	F	VF	XF	Unc	BU
1995 Proof	Est. 5,000	Value: 40.00				

KM# 341b 5 POUNDS
39.8300 g., 0.9170 Gold 1.1742 oz. AGW, 36 mm.
Ruler: Elizabeth II **Subject:** 190th Anniversary - Death of Admiral Nelson **Obv:** Crowned head right **Rev:** Bust at right facing left, ship at left

Date	Mintage	F	VF	XF	Unc	BU
1995 Proof	Est. 850	Value: 1,150				

KM# 354 5 POUNDS
Virenium, 36 mm. **Ruler:** Elizabeth II **Subject:** 70th Birthday of
Queen Elizabeth II **Obv:** Crowned head right **Rev:** Monogram
and castle within ribbon

Date	Mintage	F	VF	XF	Unc	BU
1996 AA	—	—	—	—	16.50	18.50

KM# 354a 5 POUNDS
23.5000 g., 0.9250 Silver 0.6988 oz. ASW, 36 mm. **Ruler:**
Elizabeth II **Subject:** 70th Birthday of Queen Elizabeth II **Obv:**
Crowned head right **Rev:** Monogram and castle within ribbon

Date	Mintage	F	VF	XF	Unc	BU
1996 Proof	Est. 5,000	Value: 40.00				

KM# 354b 5 POUNDS
39.8300 g., 0.9170 Gold 1.1742 oz. AGW, 36 mm. **Ruler:**
Elizabeth II **Subject:** 70th Birthday of Queen Elizabeth II **Obv:**
Crowned head right **Rev:** Monogram and castle within ribbon

Date	Mintage	F	VF	XF	Unc	BU
1996 Proof	Est. 850	Value: 1,150				

KM# 355 5 POUNDS
Virenium, 36 mm. **Ruler:** Elizabeth II **Subject:** Centennial
Olympics **Obv:** Crowned head right **Rev:** Zeus on Throne, various
athletes flank

Date	Mintage	F	VF	XF	Unc	BU
1996	—	—	—	—	16.50	18.50

KM# 355a 5 POUNDS
23.5000 g., 0.9250 Silver 0.6988 oz. ASW, 36 mm.
Ruler: Elizabeth II **Subject:** Centennial Olympics **Obv:** Crowned
head right **Rev:** Zeus on Throne, various athletes flank

Date	Mintage	F	VF	XF	Unc	BU
1996 Proof	Est. 5,000	Value: 40.00				

KM# 355b 5 POUNDS
39.8300 g., 0.9170 Gold 1.1742 oz. AGW, 36 mm.
Ruler: Elizabeth II **Subject:** Centennial Olympics **Obv:** Crowned
head right **Rev:** Zeus on Throne, various athletes flank

Date	Mintage	F	VF	XF	Unc	BU
1996 Proof	850	Value: 1,150				

KM# 527 5 POUNDS
Virenium, 36 mm. **Ruler:** Elizabeth II **Subject:** Queen Elizabeth
II's Golden Wedding Anniversary **Obv:** Crowned head right
Rev: Two hands within wreath of ribbon

Date	Mintage	F	VF	XF	Unc	BU
1997 AA	—	—	—	—	17.50	20.00

KM# 527a 5 POUNDS
25.5000 g., 0.9250 Silver 0.7583 oz. ASW, 36 mm.
Ruler: Elizabeth II **Subject:** Queen Elizabeth II's Golden
Wedding Anniversary **Obv:** Crowned head right **Rev:** Two hands
within wreath of ribbon

Date	Mintage	F	VF	XF	Unc	BU
1997 Proof	Est. 10,000	Value: 40.00				

KM# 527b 5 POUNDS
39.8300 g., 0.9170 Gold 1.1742 oz. AGW, 36 mm.
Ruler: Elizabeth II **Subject:** Queen Elizabeth II's Golden
Wedding Anniversary **Obv:** Crowned head right **Rev:** Two hands
within wreath of ribbon

Date	Mintage	F	VF	XF	Unc	BU
1997 Proof	Est. 850	Value: 1,150				

KM# 605 5 POUNDS
Virenium, 36 mm. **Ruler:** Elizabeth II **Subject:** Bicentennial -
Arrival of Commodore Nelson **Obv:** Crowned head right
Rev: Cameo left of full masted ship

Date	Mintage	F	VF	XF	Unc	BU
1997 AA	—	—	—	—	16.50	18.50

KM# 605a 5 POUNDS
23.5000 g., 0.9250 Silver 0.6988 oz. ASW, 36 mm. **Ruler:**
Elizabeth II **Subject:** Bicentennial - Arrival of Commodore Nelson
Obv: Crowned head right **Rev:** Cameo left of full masted ship

Date	Mintage	F	VF	XF	Unc	BU
1997 Proof	Est. 10,000	Value: 40.00				

KM# 605b 5 POUNDS
39.8300 g., 0.9170 Gold 1.1742 oz. AGW, 36 mm. **Ruler:**
Elizabeth II **Subject:** Bicentennial - Arrival of Commodore Nelson
Obv: Crowned head right **Rev:** Cameo left of full masted ship

Date	Mintage	F	VF	XF	Unc	BU
1997 Proof	Est. 850	Value: 1,150				

KM# 607 5 POUNDS
Virenium, 36 mm. **Ruler:** Elizabeth II **Subject:** Last Voyage of
Britannia **Obv:** Crowned head right **Rev:** Ship sailing past Gibraltar

Date	Mintage	F	VF	XF	Unc	BU
1997 AA	—	—	—	—	16.50	18.50

KM# 607a 5 POUNDS
23.5000 g., 0.9250 Silver 0.6988 oz. ASW, 36 mm.
Ruler: Elizabeth II **Subject:** Last Voyage of Britannia
Obv: Crowned head right **Rev:** Ship sailing past Gibraltar

Date	Mintage	F	VF	XF	Unc	BU
1997 Proof	Est. 5,000	Value: 50.00				

KM# 607b 5 POUNDS
39.8300 g., 0.9170 Gold 1.1742 oz. AGW, 36 mm.
Ruler: Elizabeth II **Subject:** Last Voyage of Britannia
Obv: Crowned head right **Rev:** Ship sailing past Gibraltar

Date	Mintage	F	VF	XF	Unc	BU
1997 Proof	Est. 850	Value: 1,150				

KM# 740 5 POUNDS
Virenium, 36 mm. **Ruler:** Elizabeth II **Subject:** 40th Anniversary
of Radio Gibraltar **Obv:** Head with tiara right **Rev:** Radio
broadcaster, rock in background

Date	Mintage	F	VF	XF	Unc	BU
1998 AA	—	—	—	—	16.00	18.00

KM# 740a 5 POUNDS
23.5000 g., 0.9250 Silver 0.6988 oz. ASW, 36 mm.
Ruler: Elizabeth II **Subject:** 40th Anniversary of Radio Gibraltar
Obv: Head with tiara right **Rev:** Radio broadcaster, rock in background

Date	Mintage	F	VF	XF	Unc	BU
1998 Proof	Est. 5,000	Value: 40.00				

KM# 740b 5 POUNDS
39.8300 g., 0.9170 Gold 1.1742 oz. AGW, 36 mm. **Ruler:** Elizabeth II **Subject:** 40th Anniversary of Radio Gibraltar **Obv:** Head with tiara right **Rev:** Radio broadcaster, rock in background

Date	Mintage	F	VF	XF	Unc	BU
1998 Proof	Est. 850	Value: 1,150				

KM# 770 5 POUNDS
Virenium, 36 mm. **Ruler:** Elizabeth II **Subject:** 80th Anniversary of the RAF **Obv:** Crowned head right **Rev:** Eurofighter over map

Date	Mintage	F	VF	XF	Unc	BU
1998	—	—	—	—	16.00	18.00

KM# 770a 5 POUNDS
23.5000 g., 0.9250 Silver 0.6988 oz. ASW, 36 mm.
Ruler: Elizabeth II **Subject:** 80th Anniversary of the RAF
Obv: Crowned head right **Rev:** Eurofighter over map

Date	Mintage	F	VF	XF	Unc	BU
1998 Proof	Est. 5,000	Value: 50.00				

KM# 770b 5 POUNDS
39.8300 g., 0.9170 Gold 1.1742 oz. AGW, 36 mm.
Ruler: Elizabeth II **Subject:** 80th Anniversary of the RAF
Obv: Crowned head right **Rev:** Eurofighter over map

Date	Mintage	F	VF	XF	Unc	BU
1998 Proof	Est. 850	Value: 1,150				

KM# 771 5 POUNDS
Virenium, 36 mm. **Ruler:** Elizabeth II **Subject:** Millennium 2000 **Obv:** Head with tiara right **Rev:** Landmarks of London

Date	Mintage	F	VF	XF	Unc	BU
1998 AA	—	—	—	—	16.00	18.00

KM# 771a 5 POUNDS
23.5000 g., 0.9250 Silver 0.6988 oz. ASW, 36 mm.
Ruler: Elizabeth II **Subject:** Millennium 2000 **Obv:** Head with tiara right **Rev:** Landmarks of London

Date	Mintage	F	VF	XF	Unc	BU
1998 Proof	Est. 5,000	Value: 50.00				

KM# 771b 5 POUNDS
39.8300 g., 0.9170 Gold 1.1742 oz. AGW, 36 mm. **Ruler:** Elizabeth II **Obv:** Head with tiara right **Rev:** Landmarks of London

Date	Mintage	F	VF	XF	Unc	BU
1998 Proof	850	Value: 1,150				

KM# 772 5 POUNDS
Virenium, 36 mm. **Ruler:** Elizabeth II **Subject:** 50th Birthday of Prince Charles **Obv:** Crowned head right **Rev:** Heads of Prince Charles and sons William and Harry left

Date	Mintage	F	VF	XF	Unc	BU
1998 AA	—	—	—	—	16.00	18.00

KM# 772a 5 POUNDS
23.5000 g., 0.9250 Silver 0.6988 oz. ASW, 36 mm.
Ruler: Elizabeth II **Subject:** 50th Birthday of Prince Charles
Obv: Crowned head right **Rev:** Heads of Prince Charles and sons William and Harry

Date	Mintage	F	VF	XF	Unc	BU
1998 Proof	5,000	Value: 50.00				

KM# 772b 5 POUNDS
39.8300 g., 0.9170 Gold 1.1742 oz. AGW, 36 mm.
Ruler: Elizabeth II **Subject:** 50th Birthday of Prince Charles
Obv: Crowned head right **Rev:** Heads of Prince Charles and sons William and Harry

Date	Mintage	F	VF	XF	Unc	BU
1998 Proof	850	Value: 1,150				

KM# 797 5 POUNDS
Virenium, 36 mm. **Ruler:** Elizabeth II **Subject:** Millennium 2000 **Obv:** Head with tiara right **Rev:** Sundial, digital clock face, candle and traditional clock face

Date	Mintage	F	VF	XF	Unc	BU
1999	—	—	—	—	16.00	18.00

KM# 797a 5 POUNDS
Titanium **Ruler:** Elizabeth II **Subject:** Millennium 2000 **Obv:** Head with tiara right **Rev:** Sundial, digital clock face, candle and traditional clock face

Date	Mintage	F	VF	XF	Unc	BU
1999	Est. 25,000	—	—	—	35.00	40.00

KM# 797b 5 POUNDS
28.2800 g., 0.9250 Silver 0.8410 oz. ASW, 36 mm. **Ruler:** Elizabeth II **Subject:** Millennium 2000 **Obv:** Head with tiara right **Rev:** Sundial, digital clock face, candle and traditional clock face

Date	Mintage	F	VF	XF	Unc	BU
1999 Proof	Est. 5,000	Value: 65.00				

KM# 867 5 POUNDS
Virenium, 36 mm. **Ruler:** Elizabeth II **Subject:** Mediterranean Rowing Club **Obv:** Head with tiara right **Rev:** A one-man and a four-man row boat

Date	Mintage	F	VF	XF	Unc	BU
1999	—	—	—	—	16.00	18.00

KM# 867a 5 POUNDS
23.5000 g., 0.9250 Silver 0.6988 oz. ASW, 36 mm. **Ruler:** Elizabeth II **Subject:** Mediterranean Rowing Club **Obv:** Head with tiara right **Rev:** A one-man and a four-man row boat

Date	Mintage	F	VF	XF	Unc	BU
1999 Proof	Est. 5,000	Value: 65.00				

KM# 867b 5 POUNDS
39.8300 g., 0.9170 Gold 1.1742 oz. AGW, 36 mm.
Ruler: Elizabeth II **Subject:** Mediterranean Rowing Club **Obv:** Head with tiara right **Rev:** A one-man and a four-man row boat

Date	Mintage	F	VF	XF	Unc	BU
1999 Proof	Est. 850	Value: 1,150				

KM# 878 5 POUNDS
Virenium, 36 mm. **Ruler:** Elizabeth II **Subject:** Battle of Britain **Obv:** Head with tiara right **Rev:** Spitfire in flight

Date	Mintage	F	VF	XF	Unc	BU
2000 AA	—	—	—	—	15.00	17.00

KM# 878a 5 POUNDS
23.5000 g., 0.9250 Silver 0.6988 oz. ASW, 36 mm.
Ruler: Elizabeth II **Subject:** Battle of Britain **Obv:** Head with tiara right **Rev:** Spitfire in flight

Date	Mintage	F	VF	XF	Unc	BU
2000 Proof	Est. 10,000	Value: 50.00				

KM# 878b 5 POUNDS
39.8300 g., 0.9160 Gold 1.1729 oz. AGW, 36 mm.
Ruler: Elizabeth II **Subject:** Battle of Britain **Obv:** Head with tiara right **Rev:** Spitfire in flight

Date	Mintage	F	VF	XF	Unc	BU
2000 Proof	Est. 850	Value: 1,150				

KM# 885 5 POUNDS
10.0000 g., Titanium **Ruler:** Elizabeth II **Subject:** 160th Anniversary - Uniform Penny Post **Obv:** Head with tiara right **Rev:** Postage stamp design **Edge:** Reeded

Date	Mintage	F	VF	XF	Unc	BU
2000 Proof	15,000	Value: 50.00				

KM# 7 25 POUNDS
7.7700 g., 0.9170 Gold 0.2291 oz. AGW **Ruler:** Elizabeth II **Subject:** 250th Anniversary - Introduction of British Sterling **Obv:** Young bust right **Rev:** Lion and key

Date	Mintage	F	VF	XF	Unc	BU
1975	2,395	—	—	—	—	225
1975 Proof	750	Value: 240				

KM# 8 50 POUNDS
15.5500 g., 0.9170 Gold 0.4584 oz. AGW **Ruler:** Elizabeth II **Subject:** 250th Anniversary - Introduction of British Sterling **Obv:** Young bust right **Rev:** Our Lady of Europa

Date	Mintage	F	VF	XF	Unc	BU
1975	1,625	—	—	—	—	435
1975 Proof	750	Value: 450				

KM# 13 50 POUNDS
15.9760 g., 0.9170 Gold 0.4710 oz. AGW **Ruler:** Elizabeth II **Subject:** 175th Anniversary - Death of Admiral Nelson **Obv:** Young bust right **Rev:** Bust right of ship at left looking left

Date	Mintage	F	VF	XF	Unc	BU
1980	Est. 7,500	—	—	—	—	450
1980 Proof	Est. 5,000	Value: 465				

KM# 15 50 POUNDS
15.9760 g., 0.9170 Gold 0.4710 oz. AGW **Ruler:** Elizabeth II **Subject:** Wedding of Prince Charles and Lady Diana **Rev:** The royal couple

Date	Mintage	F	VF	XF	Unc	BU
1981		—	—	—	—	450
1981 Proof	Est. 2,500	Value: 465				

KM# 9 100 POUNDS
31.1000 g., 0.9170 Gold 0.9169 oz. AGW **Ruler:** Elizabeth II **Subject:** 250th Anniversary - Introduction of British Sterling **Rev:** Coat of arms

Date	Mintage	F	VF	XF	Unc	BU
1975	1,625	—	—	—	—	900
1975 Proof	750	Value: 950				

SOVEREIGN COINAGE

KM# 26 1/4 SOVEREIGN
1.9900 g., 0.9170 Gold 0.0587 oz. AGW **Ruler:** Elizabeth II **Subject:** 150th Anniversary of Regal Coinage **Obv:** Crowned bust right **Rev:** Queen and lion left

Date	Mintage	F	VF	XF	Unc	BU
1989 U		—	—	—	—	65.00
1989 Proof	Est. 1,989	Value: 70.00				

KM# 41 1/4 SOVEREIGN
1.9900 g., 0.9170 Gold 0.0587 oz. AGW **Ruler:** Elizabeth II **Subject:** 21st Anniversary - Constitution **Obv:** Crowned bust right **Rev:** Standing figure with key and trident, shield lower right

Date	Mintage	F	VF	XF	Unc	BU
1990 Proof	Est. 1,000	Value: 65.00				

KM# 515 1/4 SOVEREIGN
1.2241 g., 0.9999 Gold 0.0394 oz. AGW **Ruler:** Elizabeth II **Obv:** Crowned bust right **Rev:** Queen and lion left

Date	Mintage	F	VF	XF	Unc	BU
1997 Proof		—	Value: 65.00			

KM# 27   1/2 SOVEREIGN
3.9800 g., 0.9170 Gold 0.1173 oz. AGW   **Ruler:** Elizabeth II
Subject: 150th Anniversary of Regal Coinage **Obv:** Crowned
bust right **Rev:** Queen and lion left

Date	Mintage	F	VF	XF	Unc	BU
1989 U	—	—	—	—	—	125
1989 Proof	Est. 1,989	Value: 135				

KM# 42   1/2 SOVEREIGN
3.9800 g., 0.9170 Gold 0.1173 oz. AGW   **Ruler:** Elizabeth II
Subject: 21st Anniversary - Constitution **Obv:** Crowned bust right
Rev: Standing figure with key and trident, shield lower right

Date	Mintage	F	VF	XF	Unc	BU
1990 Proof	1,000	Value: 125				

KM# 516   1/2 SOVEREIGN
3.1103 g., 0.9999 Gold 0.1000 oz. AGW   **Ruler:** Elizabeth II
Obv: Crowned bust right **Rev:** Queen and lion left

Date	Mintage	F	VF	XF	Unc	BU
1997 Proof	—	Value: 100				

KM# 28   SOVEREIGN
7.9600 g., 0.9170 Gold 0.2347 oz. AGW   **Ruler:** Elizabeth II
Subject: 150th Anniversary of Regal Coinage **Obv:** Crowned
bust right **Rev:** Queen and lion left

Date	Mintage	F	VF	XF	Unc	BU
1989 U	—	—	—	—	—	235
1989 Proof	Est. 1,989	Value: 265				

KM# 43   SOVEREIGN
7.9600 g., 0.9170 Gold 0.2347 oz. AGW   **Ruler:** Elizabeth II
Subject: 21st Anniversary - Constitution **Obv:** Crowned bust right
Rev: Standing figure with key and trident, shield at lower right

Date	Mintage	F	VF	XF	Unc	BU
1990 Proof	Est. 1,000	Value: 250				

KM# 517   SOVEREIGN
6.2207 g., 0.9999 Gold 0.2000 oz. AGW   **Ruler:** Elizabeth II
Obv: Crowned bust right **Rev:** Queen and lion left

Date	Mintage	F	VF	XF	Unc	BU
1997 Proof	—	Value: 200				

KM# 29   2 SOVEREIGNS
15.9400 g., 0.9170 Gold 0.4699 oz. AGW   **Ruler:** Elizabeth II
Subject: 150th Anniversary of Regal Coinage **Obv:** Crowned
bust right **Rev:** Queen and lion left

Date	Mintage	F	VF	XF	Unc	BU
1989 Proof	1,989	Value: 550				

KM# 44   2 SOVEREIGNS
15.9400 g., 0.9170 Gold 0.4699 oz. AGW   **Ruler:** Elizabeth II
Subject: 21st Anniversary - Constitution **Obv:** Crowned bust right
Rev: Standing figure with key and trident, shield lower right

Date	Mintage	F	VF	XF	Unc	BU
1990 Proof	1,000	Value: 525				

KM# 30   5 SOVEREIGNS
39.8300 g., 0.9170 Gold 1.1742 oz. AGW   **Ruler:** Elizabeth II
Subject: 150th Anniversary of Regal Coinage **Obv:** Crowned
bust right **Rev:** Queen and lion left

Date	Mintage	F	VF	XF	Unc	BU
1989 Proof	1,989	Value: 1,150				

KM# 45   5 SOVEREIGNS
39.8300 g., 0.9170 Gold 1.1742 oz. AGW   **Ruler:** Elizabeth II
Subject: 21st Anniversary - Constitution **Obv:** Crowned bust right
Rev: Standing figure with key and trident, shield lower right

Date	Mintage	F	VF	XF	Unc	BU
1990 Proof	Est. 1,000	Value: 1,150				

ROYAL COINAGE

KM# 91   1/25 ROYAL
1.2400 g., 0.9999 Gold 0.0399 oz. AGW   **Ruler:** Elizabeth II
Subject: Dogs **Obv:** Crowned bust right **Rev:** Corgi

Date	Mintage	F	VF	XF	Unc	BU
1991	—	—	—	—	—	75.00
1991 Proof	Est. 1,000	Value: 76.50				

KM# 99   1/25 ROYAL
1.2400 g., 0.9999 Gold 0.0399 oz. AGW   **Ruler:** Elizabeth II
Subject: Dogs **Obv:** Crowned bust right **Rev:** Cocker Spaniel

Date	Mintage	F	VF	XF	Unc	BU
1992	—	—	—	—	—	40.00
1992 Proof	Est. 1,000	Value: 42.50				

KM# 193   1/25 ROYAL
1.2400 g., 0.9999 Gold 0.0399 oz. AGW   **Ruler:** Elizabeth II
Subject: Dogs **Obv:** Crowned bust right **Rev:** Long-haired
Dachshund

Date	Mintage	F	VF	XF	Unc	BU
1993	—	—	—	—	—	40.00
1993 Proof	Est. 1,000	Value: 42.50				

KM# 248   1/25 ROYAL
1.2400 g., 0.9999 Gold 0.0399 oz. AGW   **Ruler:** Elizabeth II
Subject: Dogs **Obv:** Crowned bust right **Rev:** Pekingese

Date	Mintage	F	VF	XF	Unc	BU
1994	—	—	—	—	—	40.00
1994 Proof	Est. 1,000	Value: 42.50				

KM# 319   1/25 ROYAL
1.2400 g., 0.9999 Gold 0.0399 oz. AGW   **Ruler:** Elizabeth II
Subject: Crowned bust right **Obv:** Crowned bust right **Rev:** Collie

Date	Mintage	F	VF	XF	Unc	BU
1995	—	—	—	—	—	40.00
1995 Proof	Est. 1,000	Value: 42.50				

KM# 361   1/25 ROYAL
1.2400 g., 0.9999 Gold 0.0399 oz. AGW   **Ruler:** Elizabeth II
Subject: Dogs **Obv:** Crowned bust right **Rev:** Bulldog

Date	Mintage	F	VF	XF	Unc	BU
1996	—	—	—	—	—	40.00
1996 Proof	Est. 1,000	Value: 42.50				

KM# 557   1/25 ROYAL
1.2400 g., 0.9999 Gold 0.0399 oz. AGW   **Ruler:** Elizabeth II
Subject: Dogs **Obv:** Crowned bust right **Rev:** Yorkshire Terrier

Date	Mintage	F	VF	XF	Unc	BU
1997	—	—	—	—	—	50.00
1997 Proof	Est. 1,000	Value: 52.00				

KM# 749   1/25 ROYAL
1.2400 g., 0.9999 Gold 0.0399 oz. AGW   **Ruler:** Elizabeth II
Obv: Crowned bust right **Rev:** Kissing cherubs

Date	Mintage	F	VF	XF	Unc	BU
1998	—	—	—	—	—	50.00
1998 Proof	Est. 1,000	Value: 52.00				

KM# 749a   1/25 ROYAL
1.2400 g., 0.9950 Platinum 0.0397 oz. APW   **Ruler:** Elizabeth II
Obv: Crowned bust right **Rev:** Kissing cherubs

Date	Mintage	F	VF	XF	Unc	BU
1998 Proof	—	Value: 75.00				

KM# 828   1/25 ROYAL
1.2400 g., 0.9990 Gold 0.0398 oz. AGW   **Ruler:** Elizabeth II
Obv: Crowned bust right **Rev:** Cherub

Date	Mintage	F	VF	XF	Unc	BU
1999 U	—	—	—	—	—	40.00
1999 U Y2K	Est. 20,000	—	—	—	—	40.00
1999 Proof	Est. 1,000	Value: 42.50				

KM# 828a   1/25 ROYAL
1.2400 g., 0.9950 Platinum 0.0397 oz. APW   **Ruler:** Elizabeth II
Obv: Crowned bust right **Rev:** One cherub

Date	Mintage	F	VF	XF	Unc	BU
1999 Proof	—	Value: 75.00				

KM# 888   1/25 ROYAL
1.2441 g., 0.9990 Gold 0.0400 oz. AGW, 13.92 mm.   **Ruler:**
Elizabeth II **Subject:** Bullion **Obv:** Crowned bust right **Rev:** 2
cherubs **Edge:** Reeded

Date	Mintage	F	VF	XF	Unc	BU
2000	—	—	—	—	—	40.00
2000	1,000	Value: 42.50				
	Note: In proof sets only					

KM# 92   1/10 ROYAL
3.1100 g., 0.9999 Gold 0.1000 oz. AGW   **Ruler:** Elizabeth II
Subject: Dogs **Obv:** Crowned bust right **Rev:** Corgi

Date	Mintage	F	VF	XF	Unc	BU
1991	—	—	—	—	—	95.00
1991 Proof	Est. 1,000	Value: 100				

KM# 100   1/10 ROYAL
3.1100 g., 0.9999 Gold 0.1000 oz. AGW   **Ruler:** Elizabeth II
Subject: Dogs **Obv:** Crowned bust right **Rev:** Cocker Spaniel

Date	Mintage	F	VF	XF	Unc	BU
1992	—	—	—	—	—	95.00
1992 Proof	Est. 1,000	Value: 100				

KM# 194   1/10 ROYAL
3.1100 g., 0.9999 Gold 0.1000 oz. AGW   **Ruler:** Elizabeth II
Obv: Crowned bust right **Rev:** Long-haired Dachshund

Date	Mintage	F	VF	XF	Unc	BU
1993	—	—	—	—	—	95.00
1993 Proof	Est. 1,000	Value: 100				

KM# 249   1/10 ROYAL
3.1100 g., 0.9999 Gold 0.1000 oz. AGW   **Ruler:** Elizabeth II
Subject: Dogs **Obv:** Crowned bust right **Rev:** Pekingese

Date	Mintage	F	VF	XF	Unc	BU
1994	—	—	—	—	—	95.00
1994 Proof	Est. 1,000	Value: 100				

KM# 320   1/10 ROYAL
3.1100 g., 0.9999 Gold 0.1000 oz. AGW   **Ruler:** Elizabeth II
Subject: Dogs **Obv:** Crowned bust right **Rev:** Collie

Date	Mintage	F	VF	XF	Unc	BU
1995	—	—	—	—	—	95.00
1995 Proof	Est. 1,000	Value: 100				

KM# 362   1/10 ROYAL
3.1100 g., 0.9999 Gold 0.1000 oz. AGW   **Ruler:** Elizabeth II
Subject: Dogs **Obv:** Crowned bust right **Rev:** Bulldog

Date	Mintage	F	VF	XF	Unc	BU
1996	—	—	—	—	—	95.00
1996 Proof	Est. 1,000	Value: 100				

KM# 558   1/10 ROYAL
3.1100 g., 0.9999 Gold 0.1000 oz. AGW   **Ruler:** Elizabeth II
Subject: Dogs **Obv:** Crowned bust right **Rev:** Yorkshire Terrier

Date	Mintage	F	VF	XF	Unc	BU
1997	—	—	—	—	—	95.00
1997 Proof	Est. 1,000	Value: 100				

KM# 750   1/10 ROYAL
3.1100 g., 0.9999 Gold 0.1000 oz. AGW   **Ruler:** Elizabeth II
Obv: Crowned bust right **Rev:** Kissing cherubs

Date	Mintage	F	VF	XF	Unc	BU
1998	—	—	—	—	—	95.00
1998 Proof	Est. 1,000	Value: 100				

KM# 829   1/10 ROYAL
3.1100 g., 0.9999 Gold 0.1000 oz. AGW   **Ruler:** Elizabeth II
Obv: Crowned bust right **Rev:** Cherub

Date	Mintage	F	VF	XF	Unc	BU
1999 U	—	—	—	—	—	95.00
1999 Proof	—	Value: 100				
1999 U Y2K	Est. 10,000	—	—	—	—	95.00

KM# 829a   1/10 ROYAL
3.1100 g., 0.9950 Platinum 0.0995 oz. APW   **Ruler:** Elizabeth II
Obv: Crowned bust right **Rev:** Cherub

Date	Mintage	F	VF	XF	Unc	BU
1999 Proof	Est. 1,000	Value: 175				

KM# 889   1/10 ROYAL
3.1100 g., 0.9990 Gold 0.0999 oz. AGW   **Ruler:** Elizabeth II
Obv: Crowned bust right **Rev:** Two cherubs **Edge:** Reeded

Date	Mintage	F	VF	XF	Unc	BU
2000	—	—	—	—	95.00	
2000 Proof	1,000	Value: 100				

KM# 93   1/5 ROYAL
6.2200 g., 0.9999 Gold 0.1999 oz. AGW   **Ruler:** Elizabeth II
Subject: Dogs **Obv:** Crowned bust right **Rev:** Corgi

Date	Mintage	F	VF	XF	Unc	BU
1991	—	—	—	—	—	195
1991 Proof	Est. 1,000	Value: 200				

KM# 101   1/5 ROYAL
6.2200 g., 0.9999 Gold 0.1999 oz. AGW   **Ruler:** Elizabeth II
Subject: Dogs **Obv:** Crowned bust right **Rev:** Cocker Spaniel

Date	Mintage	F	VF	XF	Unc	BU
1992	—	—	—	—	—	195
1992 Proof	Est. 1,000	Value: 200				

KM# 195 1/5 ROYAL
6.2200 g., 0.9999 Gold 0.1999 oz. AGW **Ruler:** Elizabeth II
Subject: Dogs **Obv:** Crowned bust right **Rev:** Long-haired Dachshund

Date	Mintage	F	VF	XF	Unc	BU
1993	—	—	—	—	—	195
1993 Proof	Est. 1,000	Value: 200				

KM# 250 1/5 ROYAL
6.2200 g., 0.9999 Gold 0.1999 oz. AGW **Ruler:** Elizabeth II
Subject: Dogs **Obv:** Crowned bust right **Rev:** Pekingese

Date	Mintage	F	VF	XF	Unc	BU
1994	—	—	—	—	—	195
1994 Proof	Est. 1,000	Value: 200				

KM# 321 1/5 ROYAL
6.2200 g., 0.9999 Gold 0.1999 oz. AGW **Ruler:** Elizabeth II
Subject: Dogs **Obv:** Crowned bust right **Rev:** Collie

Date	Mintage	F	VF	XF	Unc	BU
1995	—	—	—	—	—	195
1995 Proof	Est. 1,000	Value: 200				

KM# 363 1/5 ROYAL
6.2200 g., 0.9999 Gold 0.1999 oz. AGW **Ruler:** Elizabeth II
Subject: Dogs **Obv:** Crowned bust right **Rev:** Bulldog

Date	Mintage	F	VF	XF	Unc	BU
1996	—	—	—	—	—	195
1996 Proof	Est. 1,000	Value: 200				

KM# 559 1/5 ROYAL
6.2200 g., 0.9999 Gold 0.1999 oz. AGW **Ruler:** Elizabeth II
Subject: Dogs **Obv:** Crowned bust right **Rev:** Yorkshire Terrier

Date	Mintage	F	VF	XF	Unc	BU
1997	—	—	—	—	—	195
1997 Proof	Est. 1,000	Value: 200				

KM# 751 1/5 ROYAL
6.2200 g., 0.9999 Gold 0.1999 oz. AGW **Ruler:** Elizabeth II
Obv: Crowned bust right **Rev:** Kissing cherubs

Date	Mintage	F	VF	XF	Unc	BU
1998	—	—	—	—	—	195
1998 Proof	Est. 1,000	Value: 200				

KM# 830 1/5 ROYAL
6.2200 g., 0.9999 Gold 0.1999 oz. AGW **Ruler:** Elizabeth II
Obv: Crowned bust right **Rev:** Four cherubs

Date	Mintage	F	VF	XF	Unc	BU
1999 U	—	—	—	—	—	195
1999 Proof	—	Value: 200				
1999 U Y2K	Est. 5,000	—	—	—	—	195

KM# 830a 1/5 ROYAL
6.2200 g., 0.9950 Platinum 0.1990 oz. APW **Ruler:** Elizabeth II
Obv: Crowned bust right **Rev:** Four cherubs

Date	Mintage	F	VF	XF	Unc	BU
1999 Proof	Est. 1,000	Value: 340				

KM# 890 1/5 ROYAL
6.2200 g., 0.9990 Gold 0.1998 oz. AGW **Ruler:** Elizabeth II
Obv: Crowned bust right **Rev:** 2 cherubs **Edge:** Reeded

Date	Mintage	F	VF	XF	Unc	BU
2000	—	—	—	—	—	195
2000 Proof	1,000	Value: 200				

KM# 94 1/2 ROYAL
15.5500 g., 0.9999 Gold 0.4999 oz. AGW **Ruler:** Elizabeth II
Subject: Dogs **Obv:** Crowned bust right **Rev:** Corgi

Date	Mintage	F	VF	XF	Unc	BU
1991	—	—	—	—	—	470
1991 Proof	Est. 1,000	Value: 475				

KM# 102 1/2 ROYAL
15.5500 g., 0.9999 Gold 0.4999 oz. AGW **Ruler:** Elizabeth II
Subject: Dogs **Obv:** Crowned bust right **Rev:** Cocker Spaniel

Date	Mintage	F	VF	XF	Unc	BU
1992	—	—	—	—	—	470
1992 Proof	Est. 1,000	Value: 475				

KM# 196 1/2 ROYAL
15.5500 g., 0.9999 Gold 0.4999 oz. AGW **Ruler:** Elizabeth II
Subject: Dogs **Obv:** Crowned bust right **Rev:** Long-haired Dachshund

Date	Mintage	F	VF	XF	Unc	BU
1993	—	—	—	—	—	470
1993 Proof	Est. 1,000	Value: 475				

KM# 251 1/2 ROYAL
15.5500 g., 0.9999 Gold 0.4999 oz. AGW **Ruler:** Elizabeth II
Subject: Dogs **Obv:** Crowned bust right **Rev:** Pekingese

Date	Mintage	F	VF	XF	Unc	BU
1994	—	—	—	—	—	470
1994 Proof	Est. 1,000	Value: 475				

KM# 322 1/2 ROYAL
15.5500 g., 0.9999 Gold 0.4999 oz. AGW **Ruler:** Elizabeth II
Subject: Dogs **Obv:** Crowned bust right **Rev:** Collie

Date	Mintage	F	VF	XF	Unc	BU
1995	—	—	—	—	—	470
1995 Proof	Est. 1,000	Value: 475				

KM# 364 1/2 ROYAL
15.5500 g., 0.9999 Gold 0.4999 oz. AGW **Ruler:** Elizabeth II
Subject: Dogs **Obv:** Crowned bust right **Rev:** Bulldog

Date	Mintage	F	VF	XF	Unc	BU
1996	—	—	—	—	—	470
1996 Proof	Est. 1,000	Value: 475				

KM# 560 1/2 ROYAL
15.5500 g., 0.9999 Gold 0.4999 oz. AGW **Ruler:** Elizabeth II
Subject: Dogs **Obv:** Crowned bust right **Rev:** Yorkshire Terrier

Date	Mintage	F	VF	XF	Unc	BU
1997	—	—	—	—	—	470
1997 Proof	Est. 1,000	Value: 475				

KM# 752 1/2 ROYAL
15.5500 g., 0.9999 Gold 0.4999 oz. AGW **Ruler:** Elizabeth II
Obv: Crowned bust right **Rev:** Kissing cherubs

Date	Mintage	F	VF	XF	Unc	BU
1998	—	—	—	—	—	470
1998 Proof	Est. 1,000	Value: 475				

KM# 831 1/2 ROYAL
15.5500 g., 0.9999 Gold 0.4999 oz. AGW **Ruler:** Elizabeth II
Obv: Crowned bust right **Rev:** Four cherubs

Date	Mintage	F	VF	XF	Unc	BU
1999	—	—	—	—	—	470
1999 Proof	—	Value: 475				

KM# 891 1/2 ROYAL
15.5500 g., 0.9999 Gold 0.4999 oz. AGW **Ruler:** Elizabeth II
Obv: Crowned bust right **Rev:** Two cherubs **Edge:** Reeded

Date	Mintage	F	VF	XF	Unc	BU
2000	—	—	—	—	—	470
2000 Proof	1,000	Value: 475				

KM# 97 ROYAL
31.1030 g., 0.9999 Gold 0.9998 oz. AGW **Ruler:** Elizabeth II
Obv: Crowned bust right **Rev:** Corgi

Date	Mintage	F	VF	XF	Unc	BU
1991	—	—	—	—	—	940
1991 Proof	Est. 1,000	Value: 950				

KM# 105 ROYAL
31.1030 g., 0.9999 Gold 0.9998 oz. AGW **Ruler:** Elizabeth II
Obv: Crowned bust right **Rev:** Cocker Spaniel

Date	Mintage	F	VF	XF	Unc	BU
1992	—	—	—	—	—	940
1992 Proof	Est. 1,000	Value: 950				

KM# 197 ROYAL
31.1030 g., 0.9999 Gold 0.9998 oz. AGW **Ruler:** Elizabeth II
Obv: Crowned bust right **Rev:** Long-haired Dachshund

Date	Mintage	F	VF	XF	Unc	BU
1993	—	—	—	—	—	940
1993 Proof	Est. 1,000	Value: 950				

KM# 252 ROYAL
31.1000 g., 0.9990 Silver 0.9988 oz. ASW **Ruler:** Elizabeth II
Subject: Dogs **Obv:** Crowned bust right **Rev:** Pekingese

Date	Mintage	F	VF	XF	Unc	BU
1994 Proof	Est. 50,000	Value: 35.00				

KM# 252a ROYAL
31.1030 g., 0.9999 Gold 0.9998 oz. AGW **Ruler:** Elizabeth II
Subject: Dogs **Obv:** Crowned bust right **Rev:** Pekingese

Date	Mintage	F	VF	XF	Unc	BU
1994	—	—	—	—	—	940
1994 Proof	Est. 1,000	Value: 950				

KM# 246 ROYAL
Copper-Nickel **Ruler:** Elizabeth II **Subject:** Dogs **Obv:** Crowned bust right **Rev:** Pekingese Dog

Date	Mintage	F	VF	XF	Unc	BU
1994	—	—	—	—	7.00	14.00
1994PM Proof	250	Value: 25.00				

KM# 318 ROYAL
28.6200 g., Copper-Nickel, 38.8 mm. **Ruler:** Elizabeth II
Subject: Collie **Obv:** Crowned bust right **Rev:** Collie **Edge:** Reeded

Date	Mintage	F	VF	XF	Unc	BU
1995	—	—	—	—	12.00	15.00
1995 Proof	Est. 250	Value: 25.00				

KM# 318b ROYAL
31.1030 g., 0.9999 Gold 0.9998 oz. AGW **Ruler:** Elizabeth II
Subject: Dogs **Obv:** Crowned bust right **Rev:** Collie

Date	Mintage	F	VF	XF	Unc	BU
1995	—	—	—	—	—	940
1995 Proof	Est. 1,000	Value: 950				

KM# 318a ROYAL
31.1030 g., 0.9990 Silver 0.9989 oz. ASW **Ruler:** Elizabeth II
Subject: Dogs **Obv:** Crowned bust right **Rev:** Collie

Date	Mintage	F	VF	XF	Unc	BU
1995 Proof	Est. 50,000				Value: 40.00	

KM# 365a ROYAL
31.1030 g., 0.9990 Silver 0.9989 oz. ASW **Ruler:** Elizabeth II
Subject: Dogs **Obv:** Crowned bust right **Rev:** Bulldog

Date	Mintage	F	VF	XF	Unc	BU
1996 Proof	Est. 50,000				Value: 45.00	

KM# 365b ROYAL
31.1030 g., 0.9999 Gold 0.9998 oz. AGW **Ruler:** Elizabeth II
Subject: Dogs **Obv:** Crowned bust right **Rev:** Bulldog

Date	Mintage	F	VF	XF	Unc	BU
1996	—	—	—	—	—	940
1996 Proof	Est. 1,000				Value: 950	

KM# 365 ROYAL
Copper Nickel **Ruler:** Elizabeth II **Subject:** Dogs **Obv:** Crowned bust right **Rev:** Bulldog

Date	Mintage	F	VF	XF	Unc	BU
1996 Prooflike	—	—	—	—	—	15.00

KM# 561a.1 ROYAL
31.3000 g., 0.9990 Silver 1.0053 oz. ASW, 38.5 mm. **Ruler:** Elizabeth II **Subject:** Dogs **Obv:** Crowned bust right **Rev:** Gold-plated Yorkshire Terrier **Edge:** Reeded

Date	Mintage	F	VF	XF	Unc	BU
1997 Proof	—	—	—	—	—	55.00

KM# 561a ROYAL
31.1035 g., 0.9990 Silver 0.9990 oz. ASW **Ruler:** Elizabeth II
Subject: Dogs **Obv:** Crowned bust right **Rev:** Yorkshire terrier

Date	Mintage	F	VF	XF	Unc	BU
1997 Proof	Est. 50,000				Value: 35.00	

KM# 561b ROYAL
31.1035 g., 0.9999 Gold 0.9999 oz. AGW **Ruler:** Elizabeth II
Subject: Dogs **Obv:** Crowned bust right **Rev:** Yorkshire terrier

Date	Mintage	F	VF	XF	Unc	BU
1997	—	—	—	—	—	940
1997 Proof	Est. 1,000				Value: 950	

KM# 753 ROYAL
Copper-Nickel **Ruler:** Elizabeth II **Obv:** Crowned bust right
Rev: Kissing cherubs

Date	Mintage	F	VF	XF	Unc	BU
1998	—	—	—	—	10.00	12.00

KM# 753a ROYAL
28.2800 g., 0.9990 Silver 0.9083 oz. ASW **Ruler:** Elizabeth II
Obv: Crowned bust right **Rev:** Kissing cherubs

Date	Mintage	F	VF	XF	Unc	BU
1998 Proof	Est. 20,000				Value: 45.00	

KM# 754 ROYAL
31.1030 g., 0.9999 Gold 0.9998 oz. AGW **Ruler:** Elizabeth II
Obv: Crowned bust right **Rev:** Kissing cherubs

Date	Mintage	F	VF	XF	Unc	BU
1998	—	—	—	—	—	940
1998 Proof	Est. 1,000				Value: 950	

KM# 832 ROYAL
Copper-Nickel **Ruler:** Elizabeth II **Obv:** Crowned bust right
Rev: Four cherubs

Date	Mintage	F	VF	XF	Unc	BU
1999	—	—	—	—	10.00	12.00

KM# 832a ROYAL
31.1035 g., 0.9990 Silver 0.9990 oz. ASW **Ruler:** Elizabeth II
Obv: Crowned bust right **Rev:** Four cherubs

Date	Mintage	F	VF	XF	Unc	BU
1999 Proof	Est. 50,000				Value: 50.00	

KM# 833 ROYAL
31.1030 g., 0.9999 Gold 0.9998 oz. AGW **Ruler:** Elizabeth II
Obv: Crowned bust right **Rev:** Four cherubs

Date	Mintage	F	VF	XF	Unc	BU
1999 U	—	—	—	—	—	940
1999 Proof	—				Value: 950	

KM# 892 ROYAL
28.2800 g., Copper-Nickel **Ruler:** Elizabeth II **Obv:** Crowned bust right **Rev:** 2 cherubs **Edge:** Reeded

Date	Mintage	F	VF	XF	Unc	BU
2000	—	—	—	—	10.00	12.00

KM# 892a ROYAL
31.1035 g., 0.9990 Silver 0.9990 oz. ASW **Ruler:** Elizabeth II
Obv: Crowned bust right **Rev:** 2 cherubs **Edge:** Reeded

Date	Mintage	F	VF	XF	Unc	BU
2000 Proof	10,000				Value: 50.00	

KM# 893 ROYAL
31.1035 g., 0.9990 Gold 0.9990 oz. AGW **Ruler:** Elizabeth II
Obv: Crowned bust right **Rev:** Two cherubs **Edge:** Reeded

Date	Mintage	F	VF	XF	Unc	BU
2000	—	—	—	—	—	940
2000 Proof	1,000				Value: 950	

Note: In proof sets only

EUROPEAN CURRENCY UNITS
Dual Denomination Coinage

KM# 293 2.8 ECUS-2 POUNDS
Copper-Nickel **Ruler:** Elizabeth II **Obv:** Crowned bust right
Rev: Knight on horseback jumping left, stars encircle

Date	Mintage	F	VF	XF	Unc	BU
1992	—	—	—	—	12.50	14.50

KM# 87 14 ECUS-10 POUNDS
10.0000 g., 0.9250 Silver 0.2974 oz. ASW **Ruler:** Elizabeth II
Subject: European Currency Unit **Obv:** Crowned bust right
Rev: Knight on horseback jumping left, stars encircle

Date	Mintage	F	VF	XF	Unc	BU
1991 Proof	Est. 10,000				Value: 20.00	
1992 Proof	Est. 5,000				Value: 30.00	
1993	—	—	—	—	75.00	80.00
1994	—	—	—	—	75.00	80.00

KM# 109 14 ECUS-10 POUNDS
10.0000 g., 0.9250 Silver 0.2974 oz. ASW **Ruler:** Elizabeth II
Obv: Uncouped portrait **Rev:** Mounted rider right

Date	Mintage	F	VF	XF	Unc	BU
1992	—	—	—	—	15.00	17.50
1992 Proof	—				Value: 30.00	
1993 Proof	—				Value: 35.00	

KM# 624 14 ECUS-10 POUNDS
10.0000 g., 0.9250 Silver 0.2974 oz. ASW **Ruler:** Elizabeth II
Obv: Crowned bust right **Rev:** Knight on horseback jumping left, stars encircle

Date	Mintage	F	VF	XF	Unc	BU
1992 Proof	Est. 2,500				Value: 25.00	

KM# 89 14 ECUS-10 POUNDS
10.0000 g., 0.9250 Silver 0.2974 oz. ASW **Ruler:** Elizabeth II
Obv: Crowned bust right **Rev:** Knight on horse jumping right

Date	Mintage	F	VF	XF	Unc	BU
1992A Matte	—	—	—	—	20.00	22.50

KM# 337 14 ECUS-10 POUNDS
10.0000 g., 0.9250 Silver 0.2974 oz. ASW **Ruler:** Elizabeth II
Obv: Crowned bust right **Rev:** Torch shield

Date	Mintage	F	VF	XF	Unc	BU
1992 Proof	2,500				Value: 25.00	

KM# 627 14 ECUS-10 POUNDS
10.0000 g., 0.9250 Silver 0.2974 oz. ASW **Ruler:** Elizabeth II
Obv: Crowned bust right **Rev:** Knight on horseback jumping right, stars encircle

Date	Mintage	F	VF	XF	Unc	BU
1993 Proof	Est. 2,500				Value: 25.00	

KM# 88 35 ECUS-25 POUNDS
28.2800 g., 0.9250 Silver 0.8410 oz. ASW **Ruler:** Elizabeth II
Obv: Crowned bust right **Rev:** Knight on horseback jumping left, stars encircle

Date	Mintage	F	VF	XF	Unc	BU
1991 Proof	Est. 10,000				Value: 60.00	
1992	—	—	—	—	40.00	45.00
1992 Proof	Est. 15,000				Value: 60.00	

KM# 110   35 ECUS-25 POUNDS
28.2800 g., 0.9250 Silver 0.8410 oz. ASW   **Ruler:** Elizabeth II
Obv: Crowned bust right **Rev:** Knight on horseback jumping right,
stars encircle

Date	Mintage	F	VF	XF	Unc	BU
1992 Proof	Est. 15,000	Value: 50.00				
1993 Proof	—	Value: 70.00				

KM# 338   35 ECUS-25 POUNDS
28.2800 g., 0.9250 Silver 0.8410 oz. ASW   **Ruler:** Elizabeth II
Obv: Crowned bust right **Rev:** Knight on horseback jumping left,
stars encircle

Date	Mintage	F	VF	XF	Unc	BU
1992 Proof	Est. 2,000	Value: 85.00				

KM# 625   35 ECUS-25 POUNDS
28.2800 g., 0.9250 Silver 0.8410 oz. ASW   **Ruler:** Elizabeth II
Obv: Crowned bust right **Rev:** Knight on horseback jumping left,
stars encircle

Date	Mintage	F	VF	XF	Unc	BU
1992 Proof	Est. 2,000	Value: 100				

KM# 628   35 ECUS-25 POUNDS
28.2800 g., 0.9250 Silver 0.8410 oz. ASW   **Ruler:** Elizabeth II
Obv: Crowned bust right **Rev:** Knight on horseback jumping right,
three lions on shield

Date	Mintage	F	VF	XF	Unc	BU
1993 Proof	Est. 2,000	Value: 75.00				

KM# 75   70 ECUS-50 POUNDS
6.1200 g., 0.5000 Gold 0.0984 oz. AGW   **Ruler:** Elizabeth II
Obv: Crowned bust right **Rev:** Knight on horseback jumping left,
stars encircle

Date	Mintage	F	VF	XF	Unc	BU
1991 Proof	Est. 5,000	Value: 200				
1991	—	—	—	—	—	100
1992	—	—	—	—	—	100
1992 Proof	Est. 2,000	Value: 225				
1994	—	—	—	—	250	270

KM# 111   70 ECUS-50 POUNDS
6.1200 g., 0.5000 Gold 0.0984 oz. AGW   **Ruler:** Elizabeth II
Obv: Crowned bust right **Rev:** Knight on horseback jumping right,
stars encircle

Date	Mintage	F	VF	XF	Unc	BU
1992 Proof	Est. 2,000	Value: 175				
1993 Proof	Est. 1,000	Value: 200				

KM# 339   70 ECUS-50 POUNDS
6.1200 g., 0.5000 Gold 0.0984 oz. AGW   **Ruler:** Elizabeth II
Obv: Crowned bust right **Rev:** Knight on horseback jumping left,
stars encircle

Date	Mintage	F	VF	XF	Unc	BU
1992 Proof	Est. 1,000	Value: 200				

KM# 626   70 ECUS-50 POUNDS
6.1200 g., 0.5000 Gold 0.0984 oz. AGW   **Ruler:** Elizabeth II
Obv: Crowned bust right **Rev:** Knight on horseback jumping left,
stars encircle

Date	Mintage	F	VF	XF	Unc	BU
1992 Proof	Est. 1,000	Value: 200				

KM# 629   70 ECUS-50 POUNDS
6.1200 g., 0.5000 Gold 0.0984 oz. AGW   **Ruler:** Elizabeth II
Obv: Crowned bust right **Rev:** Knight on horseback jumping right,
stars encircle

Date	Mintage	F	VF	XF	Unc	BU
1993 Proof	Est. 1,000	Value: 150				

STERLING ECU

KM# 478   2.8 ECU
Copper-Nickel   **Ruler:** Elizabeth II **Subject:** Euro Tunnel
Obv: Crowned bust right **Rev:** Train exiting tunnel

Date	Mintage	F	VF	XF	Unc	BU
1993	—	—	—	—	9.50	11.50

KM# 630   2.8 ECU
Copper-Nickel   **Ruler:** Elizabeth II **Subject:** A'riane - European
Space Programme **Obv:** Crowned bust right **Rev:** Rocket orbiting
earth

Date	Mintage	F	VF	XF	Unc	BU
1993	—	—	—	—	7.50	9.00

KM# 1062   2.8 ECU
28.1000 g., Copper-Nickel, 38.47 mm.   **Ruler:** Elizabeth II
Subject: Euro Tunnel **Obv:** Crowned bust right **Rev:** Partial
tunnels connecting England and France, Euro train emerging,
Gibraltar below **Edge:** Reeded

Date	Mintage	F	VF	XF	Unc	BU
1993PM	—	—	—	—	10.00	12.50

KM# 1022   2.8 ECU
Copper Nickel   **Ruler:** Elizabeth II **Obv:** Crowned bust right
Rev: Europa sowing seeds

Date	Mintage	F	VF	XF	Unc	BU
1994	—	—	—	—	9.00	11.00

KM# 484   2.8 ECU
Copper-Nickel   **Ruler:** Elizabeth II **Subject:** Euro Tunnel
Obv: Crowned bust right **Rev:** Clasping hands

Date	Mintage	F	VF	XF	Unc	BU
1994	—	—	—	—	9.00	11.00

KM# 489   2.8 ECU
Copper-Nickel   **Ruler:** Elizabeth II **Subject:** Mythology
Obv: Crowned bust right **Rev:** Winged Victory above chariot

Date	Mintage	F	VF	XF	Unc	BU
1994	—	—	—	—	8.50	10.00

KM# 494   2.8 ECU
Copper-Nickel   **Ruler:** Elizabeth II **Subject:** 190th Anniversary
of Admiral Nelson's Death **Obv:** Crowned bust right **Rev:** Bust
at right of ship looking left

Date	Mintage	F	VF	XF	Unc	BU
1995	—	—	—	—	8.50	10.00

KM# 508   2.8 ECU
Copper-Nickel   **Ruler:** Elizabeth II **Obv:** Crowned bust right **Rev:**
Austrian knight on rearing horse within circle of shields and stars

Date	Mintage	F	VF	XF	Unc	BU
1996	—	—	—	—	8.50	10.00

KM# 1033   4.2 ECUS
7.4440 g., Bi-Metallic Brass center in Copper-Nickel ring,
26.25 mm.   **Ruler:** Elizabeth II **Obv:** Crowned bust right
Rev: Knight on horseback jumping left, stars encircle
Edge: Segmented reeding

Date	Mintage	F	VF	XF	Unc	BU
1994PM Prooflike	10,000	—	—	—	11.50	14.50

KM# 479   14 ECUS
10.0000 g., 0.9250 Silver 0.2974 oz. ASW   **Ruler:** Elizabeth II
Subject: Euro Tunnel **Obv:** Crowned bust right **Rev:** Train exiting
tunnel

Date	Mintage	F	VF	XF	Unc	BU
1993 Proof	30,000	Value: 13.50				

KM# 631   14 ECUS
10.0000 g., 0.9250 Silver 0.2974 oz. ASW   **Ruler:** Elizabeth II
Subject: Sir Winston Churchill **Obv:** Crowned bust right
Rev: Uniformed bust at left looking right

Date	Mintage	F	VF	XF	Unc	BU
1993 Proof	Est. 20,000	Value: 15.00				

KM# 483   14 ECUS
10.0000 g., 0.9250 Silver 0.2974 oz. ASW   **Ruler:** Elizabeth II
Subject: International Aid for Europe **Obv:** Crowned bust right
Rev: Two faces facing each other

Date	Mintage	F	VF	XF	Unc	BU
1994 Proof	Est. 30,000	Value: 18.50				

KM# 485   14 ECUS
10.0000 g., 0.9250 Silver 0.2974 oz. ASW   **Ruler:** Elizabeth II
Subject: Euro Tunnel **Obv:** Crowned bust right **Rev:** Train exiting
tunnel

Date	Mintage	F	VF	XF	Unc	BU
1994 Proof	Est. 30,000	Value: 20.00				

KM# 490   14 ECUS
10.0000 g., 0.9250 Silver 0.2974 oz. ASW   **Ruler:** Elizabeth II
Obv: Crowned bust right **Rev:** Parthenon and Brandenburg Gate

Date	Mintage	F	VF	XF	Unc	BU
1994 Proof	Est. 30,000	Value: 14.50				

KM# 495   14 ECUS
10.0000 g., 0.9250 Silver 0.2974 oz. ASW   **Ruler:** Elizabeth II
Obv: Crowned bust right **Rev:** L'Arc de Triumph, Ceres

Date	Mintage	F	VF	XF	Unc	BU
1995 Proof	Est. 30,000				Value: 17.50	

KM# 496   14 ECUS
10.0000 g., 0.9250 Silver 0.2974 oz. ASW   **Ruler:** Elizabeth II
Obv: Crowned bust right **Rev:** Richard the Lionheart

Date	Mintage	F	VF	XF	Unc	BU
1995 Proof	Est. 30,000				Value: 17.50	

KM# 509   14 ECUS
10.0000 g., 0.9250 Silver 0.2974 oz. ASW   **Ruler:** Elizabeth II
Obv: Crowned bust right **Rev:** Napoleon Above European Battle Site

Date	Mintage	F	VF	XF	Unc	BU
1996 Proof	Est. 30,000				Value: 16.50	

KM# 510   14 ECUS
10.0000 g., 0.9250 Silver 0.2974 oz. ASW   **Ruler:** Elizabeth II
Obv: Crowned bust right **Rev:** Leaning Tower of Pisa, Irish Harp

Date	Mintage	F	VF	XF	Unc	BU
1996 Proof	Est. 30,000				Value: 16.50	

KM# 497   15 ECUS
1.2400 g., 0.9999 Gold 0.0399 oz. AGW   **Ruler:** Elizabeth II
Obv: Crowned bust right **Rev:** Knight with shield and banner

Date	Mintage	F	VF	XF	Unc	BU
1995 Proof	15,000				Value: 40.00	

KM# 504   15 ECUS
1.2400 g., 0.9999 Gold 0.0399 oz. AGW   **Ruler:** Elizabeth II
Obv: Crowned bust right **Rev:** Sir Francis Drake's ship "Golden Hind"

Date	Mintage	F	VF	XF	Unc	BU
1996 Proof	Est. 1,500				Value: 40.00	

KM# 480   21 ECUS
19.2000 g., 0.9250 Silver 0.5710 oz. ASW   **Ruler:** Elizabeth II
Subject: Euro Tunnel **Obv:** Crowned bust right **Rev:** Trains exiting tunnel

Date	Mintage	F	VF	XF	Unc	BU
1993 Proof	Est. 15,000				Value: 35.00	

KM# 482   21 ECUS
19.2000 g., 0.9250 Silver 0.5710 oz. ASW   **Ruler:** Elizabeth II
Subject: Euro Tunnel **Obv:** Crowned bust right **Rev:** Tunnel view and Napoleon

Date	Mintage	F	VF	XF	Unc	BU
1993 Proof	Est. 15,000				Value: 22.50	

KM# 632   21 ECUS
19.2000 g., 0.9250 Silver 0.5710 oz. ASW   **Ruler:** Elizabeth II
Subject: European Economic Community **Obv:** Crowned bust right **Rev:** European coins within circle

Date	Mintage	F	VF	XF	Unc	BU
1993 Proof	Est. 15,000				Value: 27.50	

KM# 486   21 ECUS
19.2000 g., 0.9250 Silver 0.5710 oz. ASW   **Ruler:** Elizabeth II
Subject: Euro Tunnel **Obv:** Crowned bust right **Rev:** Two trains and motor vehicle

Date	Mintage	F	VF	XF	Unc	BU
1994 Proof	Est. 15,000				Value: 27.50	

KM# 491   21 ECUS
19.2000 g., 0.9250 Silver 0.5710 oz. ASW   **Ruler:** Elizabeth II
Subject: 21 Years - European Community Membership **Obv:** Crowned bust right **Rev:** Europa on bull holding starred rope

Date	Mintage	F	VF	XF	Unc	BU
1994 Proof	Est. 15,000				Value: 35.00	

KM# 498   21 ECUS
19.2000 g., 0.9250 Silver 0.5710 oz. ASW   **Ruler:** Elizabeth II
Obv: Crowned bust right **Rev:** Europa with Shields of Austria, Sweden and Finland

Date	Mintage	F	VF	XF	Unc	BU
1995 Proof	Est. 15,000				Value: 37.50	

KM# 499   21 ECUS
19.2000 g., 0.9250 Silver 0.5710 oz. ASW   **Ruler:** Elizabeth II
Subject: Agreement of Cooperation between Russia and the European Union **Obv:** Crowned bust right **Rev:** European landmark buildings and arrows

Date	Mintage	F	VF	XF	Unc	BU
1995 Proof	Est. 15,000				Value: 35.00	

KM# 505   35 ECUS
3.1100 g., 0.9999 Gold 0.1000 oz. AGW   **Ruler:** Elizabeth II
Obv: Crowned bust right **Rev:** Ship "Hanseatic Kogge"

Date	Mintage	F	VF	XF	Unc	BU
1996 Proof	Est. 1,500				Value: 100	

KM# 633   70 ECUS
155.5175 g., 0.9990 Silver 4.9948 oz. ASW   **Ruler:** Elizabeth II
Subject: Ariane - European Space Programme **Obv:** Crowned bust right **Rev:** Rocket orbiting Earth

Date	Mintage	F	VF	XF	Unc	BU
1993 Proof	Est. 2,000				Value: 175	

KM# 634 70 ECUS

6.2200 g., 0.9999 Gold 0.1999 oz. AGW **Ruler:** Elizabeth II
Subject: Ariane - European Space Programme **Obv:** Crowned
bust right **Rev:** Rocket orbiting Earth, stars encircle

Date	Mintage	F	VF	XF	Unc	BU
1993 Proof	Est. 2,000		Value: 200			
1994 Proof	Est. 1,000		Value: 220			

KM# 1023 70 ECUS

155.5175 g., 0.9990 Silver 4.9948 oz. ASW **Ruler:** Elizabeth II
Obv: Crowned bust right **Rev:** European coins

Date	Mintage	F	VF	XF	Unc	BU
1993 Proof	Est. 2,000		Value: 150			

KM# 1024 70 ECUS

155.5175 g., 0.9990 Silver 4.9948 oz. ASW **Ruler:** Elizabeth II
Obv: Crowned bust right **Rev:** Train exiting tunnel

Date	Mintage	F	VF	XF	Unc	BU
1994 Proof	—		Value: 175			

KM# 487 70 ECUS

155.5175 g., 0.9990 Silver 4.9948 oz. ASW, 65 mm. **Ruler:**
Elizabeth II **Subject:** Euro Tunnel **Obv:** Crowned bust right
Rev: Tunnel view and Napoleon bust **Note:** Illustration reduced.

Date	Mintage	F	VF	XF	Unc	BU
1994 Proof	Est. 2,000		Value: 145			

KM# 492 70 ECUS

155.5175 g., 0.9990 Silver 4.9948 oz. ASW, 65 mm.
Ruler: Elizabeth II **Subject:** European Unity **Obv:** Crowned bust
right **Rev:** Goddess with quadriga **Note:** Illustration reduced.

Date	Mintage	F	VF	XF	Unc	BU
1994 Proof	Est. 2,000		Value: 145			

KM# 488 70 ECUS

6.2200 g., 0.9999 Gold 0.1999 oz. AGW **Ruler:** Elizabeth II
Subject: Euro Tunnel **Obv:** Crowned bust right **Rev:** Outreached
hands above English Channel

Date	Mintage	F	VF	XF	Unc	BU
1994 Proof	Est. 2,000		Value: 200			

KM# 493 70 ECUS

6.2200 g., 0.9999 Gold 0.1999 oz. AGW **Ruler:** Elizabeth II
Subject: Mythology **Obv:** Crowned bust right **Rev:** Europa
sowing seeds

Date	Mintage	F	VF	XF	Unc	BU
1994 Proof	Est. 2,000		Value: 200			

KM# 501 70 ECUS

155.9200 g., 0.9990 Silver 5.0077 oz. ASW **Ruler:** Elizabeth II
Obv: Crowned bust right **Rev:** Liberty and Brittania seated above
Euro Tunnel

Date	Mintage	F	VF	XF	Unc	BU
1995 Proof	Est. 2,000		Value: 175			

KM# 502 70 ECUS

6.2200 g., 0.9999 Gold 0.1999 oz. AGW **Ruler:** Elizabeth II
Obv: Crowned bust right **Rev:** Mercury above ship

Date	Mintage	F	VF	XF	Unc	BU
1995 Proof	Est. 2,000		Value: 200			

KM# 503 70 ECUS

6.2200 g., 0.9999 Gold 0.1999 oz. AGW **Ruler:** Elizabeth II
Obv: Crowned bust right **Rev:** Richard the Lionheart

Date	Mintage	F	VF	XF	Unc	BU
1995 Proof	Est. 2,000		Value: 200			

KM# 500 70 ECUS

155.9200 g., 0.9990 Silver 5.0077 oz. ASW, 65 mm.
Ruler: Elizabeth II **Subject:** 190th Anniversary of Admiral
Nelson's Death **Obv:** Crowned bust right **Rev:** Admiral Nelson
and HMS Victory **Note:** Illustration reduced.

Date	Mintage	F	VF	XF	Unc	BU
1995 Proof	2,000		Value: 175			

KM# 506 70 ECUS

6.2200 g., 0.9999 Gold 0.1999 oz. AGW **Ruler:** Elizabeth II
Obv: Crowned bust right **Rev:** HMS Victory

Date	Mintage	F	VF	XF	Unc	BU
1996 Proof	Est. 1,500		Value: 200			

KM# 511 70 ECUS

155.5175 g., 0.9990 Silver 4.9948 oz. ASW **Ruler:** Elizabeth II
Obv: Crowned bust right **Rev:** Sir Francis Drake and "Golden Hind"

Date	Mintage	F	VF	XF	Unc	BU
1996 Proof	Est. 2,000		Value: 175			

KM# 512 70 ECUS

6.2200 g., 0.9999 Gold 0.1999 oz. AGW **Ruler:** Elizabeth II
Obv: Crowned bust right **Rev:** Austrian Knight within circle of
stars and shields

Date	Mintage	F	VF	XF	Unc	BU
1996 Proof	2,000		Value: 200			

KM# 528 75 ECUS

3.8880 g., 0.9995 Bi-Metallic Platinum center in Gold ring 0.1249 oz..
Ruler: Elizabeth II **Subject:** Austrian Centennial **Obv:** Crowned
bust right **Rev:** Standing allegorical figure with shield and trident

Date	Mintage	F	VF	XF	Unc	BU
1996 Proof	1,500		Value: 350			

KM# 507   140 ECUS
15.5500 g., 0.9999 Gold 0.4999 oz. AGW **Ruler:** Elizabeth II
Obv: Crowned bust right **Rev:** Viking Longship

Date	Mintage	F	VF	XF	Unc	BU
1996	Est. 1,500	—	—	—	—	475

PATTERNS
Including off metal strikes

KM#	Date	Mintage	Identification	Mkt Val
Pn4	1989	—	1/4 Sovereign. Gold. Similar to Pn8.	—
Pn5	1989	—	1/2 Sovereign. Gold. Similar to Pn8.	—
Pn6	1989	—	Sovereign. Gold. Similar to Pn8.	—
Pn7	1989	—	2 Sovereigns. Gold. Similar to Pn8.	—
Pn8	1989	—	5 Sovereigns. Gold. Una and the lion with the Rock of Gibraltar in background.	—

PIEFORTS

KM#	Date	Mintage	Identification	Mkt Val
P1	1990	5,000	5 Pence. 0.9250 Silver. 6.0000 g. KM#22b.	70.00
P2	1990	1,000	5 Pence. 0.9160 Silver. 6.0000 g. KM#22c.	—
P3	1993	5,000	14 Ecus. 0.9250 Silver. KM#631.	60.00

MINT SETS

KM#	Date	Mintage	Identification	Issue Price	Mkt Val
MS1	1975 (3)	1,625	KM#7-9		1,150
MS2	1988 (9)	—	KM#16-18, 20-25	21.00	32.00
MS3	1989 (9)	—	KM#16-17, 20-25, 32	—	35.00
MS4	1990 (9)	—	km#16, 18, 20-21, 22A, 23-25, 39	25.00	35.00
MS5	1991 (9)	—	KM#16, 18, 20-21, 22a, 23-25, 39	25.00	35.00
MS6	1993-1998 (6)	5,000	KM#201, 327, 382, 444, 525, 656, mixed dates	—	45.00
MS7	1995 (9)	—	KM#16, 20-21, 22A, 24, 39, 112, 334, 340	—	35.00
MS8	1996 (9)	—	KM#16, 18, 20-21, 22, 24, 39, 112, 355	—	35.00
MS9	1997 (9)	—	KM#16, 18, 20-21, 22a, 24, 39, 113, 355	—	35.00
MS10	1998 (9)	—	KM#777, 869, 773-75, 778, 776, 758 & 340	—	35.00
MS11	1999 (9)	—	KM#777, 869, 773-75, 778, 776, 759 & 797	—	35.00

PROOF SETS

KM#	Date	Mintage	Identification	Issue Price	Mkt Val
PS1	1975 (3)	750	KM#7-9	875	1,150
PS2	1989 (5)	—	KM#26-30	—	2,250
PS3	1989 (2)	—	KM#29-30	—	1,700
PS4	1990 (6)	500	KM#76-81	—	1,500
PS5	1990 (6)	250	KM#76a-81a	—	2,100
PS6	1990 (5)	1,000	KM#41-45	1,800	1,975
PS7	1991 (8)	20,000	KM#50-57	—	650
PS8	1991 (8)	5,000	KM#58-65	—	1,350
PS9	1991 (8)	1,000	KM#58a-65a	—	2,300
PS10	1991 (8)	50	KM#66-73	120	120
PS11	1991 (5)	1,000	KM#91-94, 97	—	1,450
PS12	1992 (5)	1,000	KM#99-102, 105	—	1,250
PS13	1993 (5)	1,000	KM#193-197	—	1,200
PS14	1993 (5)	300	KM#124-128	—	675
PS15	1994 (5)	1,000	KM#248-251, 252a	—	1,200
PS16	1994-95 (3)	5,000	KM#309, 332, 335	—	60.00
PS17	1994-95 (3)	3,000	KM#309a, 332a, 335a	—	120
PS18	1994-95 (3)	3,000	KM#309, 332, 335	—	120
PS19	1995 (5)	1,000	KM#319-323	—	1,200
PS21	1996 (5)	1,000	KM#361-364, 365b	—	1,200
PS22	1996 (4)	1,500	KM#504-507	—	650
PS23	1997 (5)	1,000	KM#557-560, 561b	—	1,200
PS24	1998 (5)	1,000	KM#749-752, 754	1,310	1,200
PS25	1999 (5)	1,000	KM#828-831, 833	1,310	1,200
PS26	2000 (5)	1,000	KM#888-891, 893	—	1,200

PROOF-LIKE SETS (PL)

KM#	Date	Mintage	Identification	Issue Price	Mkt Val
PL1	1992 (8)	—	KM#66-73	—	100

GREAT BRITAIN

The United Kingdom of Great Britain and Northern Ireland, located off the northwest coast of the European continent, has an area of 94,227 sq. mi. (244,820 sq. km.) and a population of 54 million. Capital: London. The economy is based on industrial activity and trading. Machinery, motor vehicles, chemicals, and textile yarns and fabrics are exported.

After the departure of the Romans, who brought Britain into a more active relationship with Europe, it fell prey to invaders from Scandinavia and the Low Countries who drove the original Britons into Scotland and Wales, and established a profusion of kingdoms that finally united in the 11th century under the Danish King Canute. Norman rule, following the conquest of 1066, stimulated the development of those institutions, which have since distinguished British life. Henry VIII (1509-47) turned Britain from continental adventuring and faced it to the sea - a decision that made Britain a world power during the reign of Elizabeth I (1558-1603). Strengthened by the Industrial Revolution and the defeat of Napoleon, 19th century Britain turned to the remote parts of the world and established a colonial empire of such extent and prosperity that the world has never seen its like. World Wars I and II sealed the fate of the Empire and relegated Britain to a lesser role in world affairs by draining her resources and inaugurating a worldwide movement toward national self-determination in her former colonies.

By the mid-20th century, most of the territories formerly comprising the British Empire had gained independence, and the empire had evolved into the Commonwealth of Nations, an association of equal and autonomous states, which enjoy special trade interests. The Commonwealth is presently composed of 54 member nations, including the United Kingdom. All recognize the British monarch as head of the Commonwealth. Sixteen continue to recognize the British monarch as Head of State. They are: United Kingdom, Antigua and Barbuda, Australia, Bahamas, Barbados, Belize, Canada, Grenada, Jamaica, New Zealand, Papua New Guinea, St. Christopher & Nevis, Saint Lucia, Saint Vincent and the Grenadines, Solomon Islands, and Tuvalu. Elizabeth II is personally, and separately, the Queen of the sovereign, independent countries just mentioned. There is no other British connection between the several individual, national sovereignties, except that High Commissioners represent them each instead of ambassadors in each others' countries.

RULERS
Victoria, 1837-1901
Edward VII, 1901-1910
George V, 1910-1936
Edward VIII, 1936
George VI, 1936-1952
Elizabeth II, 1952--

MINT MARKS
H - Heaton
KN - King's Norton

MONETARY SYSTEM
Colloquial Denomination Terms

Ha'penny = 1/2 Penny
Tanner = 6 Pence
Bob = 1 Shilling
Half a Crown (Half a Dollar) = 2 Shillings 6 Pence
Dollar = 5 Shillings
Half a quid = 10 Shillings
Quid = 1 Pound
Tenner = 10 Pounds
Pony = 20 Pounds

(Until 1970)

4 Farthings = 1 Penny
12 Pence = 1 Shilling
2 Shillings = 1 Florin
5 Shillings = 1 Crown
20 Shillings = 1 Pound (Sovereign)
21 Shillings = 1 Guinea
½ Sovereign = 10 Shillings (i.e. ½ Pound)
1 Sovereign = 1 Pound

NOTE: Proofs exist for many dates of British coins in the 19th and early 20th centuries and for virtually all coins between 1926 and 1964. Those not specifically listed here are extremely rare.

NOTE: Pound Coinage - Strictly red, original mint luster coins in the copper series command premiums.

KINGDOM
PRE-DECIMAL COINAGE

KM# 791   1/3 FARTHING
0.9500 g., Bronze **Ruler:** Edward VII **Obv:** Head right
Rev: Denomination and date within crowned oak wreath
Note: Homeland style struck for Malta.

Date	Mintage	F	VF	XF	Unc	BU
1902	288,000	2.50	5.00	10.00	35.00	—

KM# 823   1/3 FARTHING
0.9500 g., Bronze **Ruler:** George V **Obv:** Head left **Rev:** Crowned value within oak wreath **Note:** Homeland style struck for Malta.

Date	Mintage	F	VF	XF	Unc	BU
1913	288,000	2.50	5.00	10.00	35.00	—

KM# 788.2   FARTHING
2.8000 g., Bronze, 20 mm. **Ruler:** Victoria **Obv:** Mature draped bust right **Obv. Leg.:** VICTORIA • DEI • GRA • BRITT • REGINA • FID • DEF • IND • IMP • **Rev:** Britannia seated right
Note: Blackened finish.

Date	Mintage	F	VF	XF	Unc	BU
1901	8,016,000	0.45	0.75	3.00	17.00	—

KM# 792   FARTHING
2.8000 g., Bronze, 20 mm. **Ruler:** Edward VII **Obv:** Head right **Rev:** Britannia seated right

Date	Mintage	F	VF	XF	Unc	BU
1902	5,125,000	0.50	1.50	5.00	25.00	—
1903	5,331,000	0.50	1.50	5.50	25.00	—
1903 Proof	—	Value: 1,800				

Note: Shield heraldically colored

1904	3,629,000	1.50	2.50	8.00	30.00	—
1905	4,077,000	0.50	1.25	5.50	25.00	—
1906	5,340,000	0.50	1.25	5.50	25.00	—
1907	4,399,000	0.50	1.25	5.50	25.00	—
1908	4,265,000	0.50	1.25	5.50	25.00	—
1909	8,852,000	0.50	1.25	5.50	25.00	—
1910	2,598,000	1.00	3.00	8.00	35.00	—

KM# 808.1   FARTHING
2.8000 g., Bronze, 20 mm. **Ruler:** George V **Obv:** Head left **Rev:** Britannia seated right

Date	Mintage	F	VF	XF	Unc	BU
1911	5,197,000	0.60	1.00	3.00	21.00	—
1912	7,670,000	0.35	0.75	2.25	20.00	—
1913	4,184,000	0.50	0.75	2.25	20.00	—
1914	6,127,000	0.35	0.75	2.25	20.00	—
1915	7,129,000	0.50	0.75	4.50	22.00	—
1916	10,993,000	0.35	0.75	2.00	20.00	—
1917	21,435,000	0.15	0.35	1.50	20.00	—
1918	19,363,000	0.75	1.50	9.50	27.00	—

KM# 808.2   FARTHING
2.8000 g., Bronze, 20 mm. **Ruler:** George V **Obv:** Head left **Rev:** Britannia seated right **Note:** Bright finish.

Date	Mintage	F	VF	XF	Unc	BU
1918	Inc. above	0.20	0.40	1.00	12.50	—
1919	15,089,000	0.20	0.40	1.00	12.50	—
1920	11,481,000	0.20	0.40	1.00	13.50	—
1921	9,469,000	0.20	0.40	1.00	14.00	—

Date	Mintage	F	VF	XF	Unc	BU
1922	9,957,000	0.20	0.40	1.00	14.00	—
1923	8,034,000	0.20	0.40	1.00	14.00	—
1924	8,733,000	0.20	0.40	1.00	14.00	—
1924 Specimen	2	—	—	—	—	2,000
1925	12,635,000	0.20	0.40	1.00	14.00	—

KM# 825 FARTHING
2.8000 g., Bronze, 20 mm. **Ruler:** George V **Obv:** Head left, modified effigy **Rev:** Britannia seated right

Date	Mintage	F	VF	XF	Unc	BU
1926	9,792,000	0.15	0.40	1.00	8.00	—
1926 Proof	—	Value: 1,000				
1927	7,868,000	0.15	0.40	1.00	8.00	—
1927 Proof	—	Value: 850				
1928	11,626,000	0.15	0.35	1.00	8.00	—
1928 Proof	—	Value: 700				
1929	8,419,000	0.15	0.35	1.00	8.00	—
1929 Proof	—	Value: 700				
1930	4,195,000	0.25	0.50	1.00	8.00	—
1930 Proof	—	Value: 700				
1931	6,595,000	0.15	0.35	1.00	8.00	—
1931 Proof	—	Value: 700				
1932	9,293,000	0.15	0.35	1.00	8.00	—
1932 Proof	—	Value: 700				
1933	4,560,000	0.15	0.35	1.00	8.00	—
1933 Proof	—	Value: 700				
1934	3,053,000	0.35	0.75	2.00	12.00	—
1934 Proof	—	Value: 700				
1935	2,227,000	1.00	2.00	3.00	10.00	—
1935 Proof	—	Value: 725				
1936	9,734,000	0.15	0.35	1.00	8.00	—
1936 Proof	—	Value: 700				

KM# 843 FARTHING
2.8000 g., Bronze, 20 mm. **Ruler:** George VI **Obv:** Head left **Rev:** Wren left

Date	Mintage	F	VF	XF	Unc	BU
1937	8,131,000	0.15	0.25	0.50	6.00	—
1937 Matte Proof	—	Value: 1,800				

Note: There are reportedly 3-4 pieces known of this variety struck specifically for use in photographs

1937 Proof	26,000	Value: 11.00				
1938	7,450,000	0.15	0.30	0.60	8.00	—
1938 Proof	—	Value: 600				
1939	31,440,000	0.10	0.25	0.50	7.00	—
1939 Proof	—	Value: 600				
1940	18,360,000	0.10	0.25	0.50	7.00	—
1940 Proof	—	Value: 600				
1941	27,312,000	0.10	0.25	0.50	6.00	—
1941 Proof	—	Value: 600				
1942	28,858,000	0.10	0.20	0.50	6.00	—
1942 Proof	—	Value: 600				
1943	33,345,999	0.10	0.15	0.50	6.00	—
1943 Proof	—	Value: 700				
1944	25,138,000	0.10	0.15	0.50	6.00	—
1944 Proof	—	Value: 700				
1945	23,736,000	0.10	0.20	0.50	6.00	—
1945 Proof	—	Value: 700				
1946	24,365,000	0.10	0.20	0.50	6.00	—
1946 Proof	—	Value: 700				
1947	14,746,000	0.10	0.20	0.50	6.00	—
1947 Proof	—	Value: 750				
1948	16,622,000	0.10	0.20	0.50	6.00	—
1948 Proof	—	Value: 750				

KM# 867 FARTHING
Bronze, 20 mm. **Ruler:** George VI **Obv:** Head left **Obv. Leg.:** Without IND IMP **Rev:** Wren left

Date	Mintage	F	VF	XF	Unc	BU
1949	8,424,000	0.10	0.20	0.50	6.50	—
1949 Proof	—	Value: 700				
1950	10,325,000	0.10	0.20	0.50	6.50	—
1950 Matte Proof	—	Value: 1,800				

Note: There are reportedly 3-4 known of this variety, struck specifically for use in photographs

| 1950 Proof | 18,000 | Value: 13.00 | | | | |

Date	Mintage	F	VF	XF	Unc	BU
1951	14,016,000	0.10	0.20	0.50	7.00	—
1951 Matte Proof	—	Value: 1,800				

Note: There are reportedly 3-4 known of this variety, struck specifically for use in photographs

1951 Proof	20,000	Value: 20.00				
1952	5,251,000	0.10	0.20	0.50	6.00	—
1952 Proof	—	Value: 650				

KM# 881 FARTHING
Bronze, 20 mm. **Ruler:** Elizabeth II **Obv:** Laureate bust right **Rev:** Wren left

Date	Mintage	F	VF	XF	Unc	BU
1953	6,131,000	0.15	0.25	0.50	3.00	—
1953 Proof	40,000	Value: 8.00				
1953 Matte Proof	—	Value: 1,800				

Note: There are reportedly 1-2 known of this variety, struck specifically for use in photographs

KM# 895 FARTHING
Bronze, 20 mm. **Ruler:** Elizabeth II **Obv:** Laureate bust right **Obv. Leg.:** Without BRITT OMN **Rev:** Wren left

Date	Mintage	F	VF	XF	Unc	BU
1954	6,566,000	0.10	0.15	0.50	5.00	—
1954 Proof	—	Value: 600				
1955	5,779,000	0.10	0.15	0.50	5.00	—
1955 Proof	—	Value: 600				
1956	1,997,000	0.25	0.50	3.00	7.50	—
1956 Proof	—	Value: 600				

KM# 789 1/2 PENNY
5.7000 g., Bronze, 25.5 mm. **Ruler:** Victoria **Obv:** Mature draped bust left **Obv. Leg.:** VICTORIA • DEI • GRA • BRITT • REGINA • FID • DEF • IND • IMP • **Rev:** Britannia seated right

Date	Mintage	F	VF	XF	Unc	BU
1901	11,127,000	2.25	4.50	18.00	30.00	—
1901 Proof	—	Value: 900				

KM# 793.1 1/2 PENNY
Bronze, 25.5 mm. **Ruler:** Edward VII **Obv:** Head right **Rev:** Britannia seated right, low horizon line

Date	Mintage	F	VF	XF	Unc	BU
1902	13,673,000	6.50	20.00	75.00	200	—

KM# 793.2 1/2 PENNY
5.2000 g., Bronze, 25.5 mm. **Ruler:** Edward VII **Obv:** Head right **Rev:** Britannia seated right, high horizon line

Date	Mintage	F	VF	XF	Unc	BU
1902	Inc. above	0.95	2.50	10.00	40.00	—
1903	11,451,000	0.95	2.50	10.00	45.00	—
1904	8,131,000	1.50	4.50	16.50	60.00	—
1905	10,125,000	0.95	2.50	10.00	45.00	—
1906	11,101,000	0.95	2.50	10.00	40.00	—
1907	16,849,000	0.95	2.50	10.00	40.00	—
1908	16,620,999	0.95	2.50	10.00	40.00	—
1909	8,279,000	0.95	2.50	10.00	50.00	—
1910	10,770,000	0.95	2.50	10.00	45.00	—

KM# 809 1/2 PENNY
5.4000 g., Bronze, 25.5 mm. **Ruler:** George V **Obv:** Head left **Rev:** Britannia seated right

Date	Mintage	F	VF	XF	Unc	BU
1911	12,571,000	0.75	1.50	9.00	35.00	—
1912	21,186,000	0.75	1.25	9.00	35.00	—
1913	17,476,000	0.75	1.75	12.00	35.00	—
1914	20,289,000	0.75	1.50	9.00	35.00	—
1915	21,563,000	0.75	1.50	9.00	35.00	—
1916	39,386,000	0.75	1.50	5.00	35.00	—
1917	38,245,000	0.75	1.50	5.00	35.00	—
1918	22,321,000	0.75	1.50	5.00	35.00	—
1919	28,104,000	0.75	1.50	5.00	35.00	—
1920	35,147,000	0.75	1.50	5.00	35.00	—
1921	28,027,000	0.75	1.50	5.00	35.00	—
1922	10,735,000	1.00	2.00	7.00	35.00	—
1923	12,266,000	0.75	1.50	5.00	35.00	—
1924	13,971,000	1.00	2.00	7.00	35.00	—
1924 Specimen	2	—	—	—	—	1,800
1925	12,216,000	1.00	2.00	7.00	35.00	—

KM# 824 1/2 PENNY
Bronze, 25.5 mm. **Ruler:** George V **Obv:** Head left, modified effigy **Rev:** Britannia seated right

Date	Mintage	F	VF	XF	Unc	BU
1925	Inc. above	1.50	4.00	8.00	60.00	—
1926	6,712,000	1.50	4.00	8.00	35.00	—
1926 Proof	—	Value: 1,000				
1927	15,590,000	0.75	1.50	5.00	35.00	—
1927 Proof	—	Value: 850				

KM# 837 1/2 PENNY
Bronze, 25.5 mm. **Ruler:** George V **Obv:** Smaller head left **Rev:** Britannia seated right

Date	Mintage	F	VF	XF	Unc	BU
1928	20,935,000	0.25	0.50	2.50	25.00	—
1928 Proof	—	Value: 650				
1929	25,680,000	0.25	0.50	2.50	25.00	—
1929 Proof	—	Value: 650				
1930	12,533,000	0.25	0.50	2.50	25.00	—
1930 Proof	—	Value: 650				
1931	16,138,000	0.25	0.50	2.50	25.00	—
1931 Proof	—	Value: 650				
1932	14,448,000	0.25	0.50	2.50	25.00	—
1932 Proof	—	Value: 650				
1933	10,560,000	0.25	0.50	2.50	25.00	—
1933 Proof	—	Value: 750				
1934	7,704,000	0.50	1.00	4.00	25.00	—
1934 Proof	—	Value: 800				
1935	12,180,000	0.25	0.50	2.50	25.00	—
1935 Proof	—	Value: 650				
1936	23,009,000	0.25	0.50	2.50	19.00	—
1936 Proof	—	Value: 650				

KM# 844 1/2 PENNY
Bronze, 25.5 mm. **Ruler:** George VI **Obv:** Head left **Rev:** The Golden Hind

Date	Mintage	F	VF	XF	Unc	BU
1937	24,504,000	0.25	0.35	0.50	7.00	—
1937 Proof	26,000	Value: 11.00				

Date	Mintage	F	VF	XF	Unc	BU
1937 Matte Proof	Est. 4	Value: 1,800				
1938	40,320,000	0.25	0.50	1.00	10.00	—
1938 Proof	—	Value: 650				
1939	28,925,000	0.25	0.50	2.00	12.00	—
1939 Proof	—	Value: 650				
1940	32,162,000	0.25	0.50	3.00	14.00	—
1940 Proof	—	Value: 650				
1941	45,120,000	0.20	0.50	1.00	7.50	—
1941 Proof	—	Value: 650				
1942	71,909,000	0.10	0.20	0.60	7.50	—
1942 Proof	—	Value: 650				
1943	76,200,000	0.10	0.25	0.75	7.50	—
1943 Proof	—	Value: 700				
1944	81,840,000	0.10	0.25	0.75	7.50	—
1944 Proof	—	Value: 700				
1945	57,000,000	0.10	0.25	1.00	9.00	—
1945 Proof	—	Value: 700				
1946	22,726,000	0.20	0.50	2.50	12.00	—
1946 Proof	—	Value: 700				
1947	21,266,000	0.10	0.25	1.50	10.00	—
1947 Proof	—	Value: 800				
1948	26,947,000	0.10	0.25	0.90	7.50	—
1948 Proof	—	Value: 800				

KM# 868   1/2 PENNY
Bronze, 25.5 mm.   **Ruler:** George VI **Obv:** Head left
Obv. Leg.: Without IND IMP **Rev:** The Golden Hind

Date	Mintage	F	VF	XF	Unc	BU
1949	24,744,000	0.10	0.25	4.00	15.00	—
1949 Proof	—	Value: 900				
1950	24,154,000	0.10	0.25	3.00	12.00	—
1950 Proof	18,000	Value: 12.00				
1950 Matte Proof	—	Value: 1,600				

Note: There are reportedly 1-2 known of this variety, struck specifically for use in photographs

1951	14,868,000	0.25	0.50	5.00	24.00	—
1951 Proof	20,000	Value: 15.00				
1951 Matte Proof	—	Value: 1,600				

Note: There are reportedly 1-2 known of this variety, struck specifically for use in photographs

| 1952 | 33,278,000 | 0.10 | 0.25 | 1.00 | 10.00 | — |
| 1952 Proof | — | Value: 850 | | | | |

KM# 882   1/2 PENNY
Bronze, 25.5 mm.   **Ruler:** Elizabeth II **Obv:** Laureate bust right
Rev: The Golden Hind

Date	Mintage	F	VF	XF	Unc	BU
1953	8,926,000	0.20	0.40	1.00	5.00	—
1953 Proof	40,000	Value: 13.00				
1953 Matte Proof	—	Value: 1,600				

Note: There are reportedly 1-2 known of this variety, struck specifically for use in photographs

KM# 896   1/2 PENNY
5.6000 g., Bronze, 25.44 mm.   **Ruler:** Elizabeth II **Obv:** Laureate bust right **Obv. Leg.:** Without BRITT OMN **Rev:** The Golden Hind
Edge: Plain

Date	Mintage	F	VF	XF	Unc	BU
1954	19,375,000	0.10	0.25	1.50	4.00	—
1954 Proof	—	Value: 600				
1955	18,799,000	0.10	0.25	1.25	3.50	—
1955 Proof	—	Value: 600				
1956	21,799,000	0.15	0.50	1.25	3.50	—
1956 Proof	—	Value: 600				
1957	43,684,000	0.10	0.25	0.50	3.50	—
1957 Proof	—	Value: 550				
1958	62,318,000	—	—	0.20	2.00	—
1958 Proof	—	Value: 500				
1959	79,176,000	—	0.10	0.15	1.50	—
1959 Proof	—	Value: 550				

Date	Mintage	F	VF	XF	Unc	BU
1960	41,340,000	—	0.10	0.15	1.50	—
1960 Proof	—	Value: 550				
1962	41,779,000	—	—	0.10	1.00	—
1962 Proof	—	Value: 600				
1963	45,036,000	—	—	0.10	1.00	—
1963 Proof	—	Value: 600				
1964	78,583,000	—	—	0.10	1.00	—
1964 Proof	—	Value: 600				
1965	98,083,000	—	—	—	1.00	—
1965 Proof	**Note:** Reported, not confirmed					
1966	95,289,000	—	—	—	0.55	—
1966 Proof	**Note:** Reported, not confirmed					
1967	146,491,000	—	—	—	0.55	—
1967 Proof	**Note:** Reported, not confirmed					
1970 Proof	750,000	Value: 3.50				

KM# 775   PENNY
0.4713 g., 0.9250 Silver 0.0140 oz. ASW   **Ruler:** Victoria
Obv: Mature draped bust left **Rev:** Crowned denomination divides date within oak wreath

Date	Mintage	F	VF	XF	Unc	BU
1901 Prooflike	18,000	—	—	20.00	35.00	

KM# 790   PENNY
9.4500 g., Bronze, 30.8 mm.   **Ruler:** Victoria **Obv:** Mature draped bust left **Obv. Leg.:** VICTORIA • DEI • GRA • BRITT • REGINA • FID • DEF • IND • IMP • **Rev:** Britannia seated right

Date	Mintage	F	VF	XF	Unc	BU
1901	22,206,000	0.45	1.50	15.00	35.00	—
1901 Proof	—	—	—	—	—	—

KM# 794.1   PENNY
9.4500 g., Bronze, 30.8 mm.   **Ruler:** Edward VII **Obv:** Head right
Rev: Britannia seated right, low sea level

Date	Mintage	F	VF	XF	Unc	BU
1902	26,977,000	8.00	25.00	100	200	—

KM# 794.2   PENNY
Bronze, 30.8 mm.   **Ruler:** Edward VII **Obv:** Head right
Rev: Britannia seated right, high sea level

Date	Mintage	F	VF	XF	Unc	BU
1902	Inc. above	1.25	3.50	12.50	60.00	—
1903	21,415,000	1.25	5.00	26.00	80.00	—
1904	12,913,000	1.25	7.00	50.00	120	—
1905	17,784,000	1.25	7.00	40.00	100	—
1906	37,990,000	1.25	5.00	26.00	100	—
1907	47,322,000	1.25	5.00	27.00	100	—
1908	31,506,000	0.95	5.00	23.00	100	—
1908 Matte Proof; Rare	3	—	—	—	—	—
1909	19,617,000	1.25	5.00	27.00	90.00	—
1910	29,549,000	0.75	4.50	22.00	90.00	—

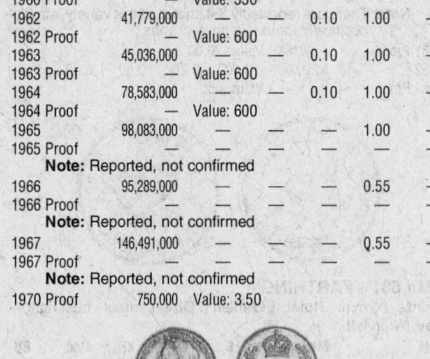

KM# 795   PENNY
0.4713 g., 0.9250 Silver 0.0140 oz. ASW   **Ruler:** Edward VII
Obv: Head right **Rev:** Crowned denomination divides date within oak wreath

Date	Mintage	F	VF	XF	Unc	BU
1902 Prooflike	21,000	—	—	—	25.00	40.00
1903 Prooflike	17,000	—	—	—	25.00	40.00
1904 Prooflike	19,000	—	—	—	25.00	40.00
1905 Prooflike	18,000	—	—	—	25.00	40.00
1906 Prooflike	19,000	—	—	—	25.00	40.00
1907 Prooflike	18,000	—	—	—	25.00	40.00
1908 Prooflike	18,000	—	—	—	25.00	40.00
1909 Prooflike	2,948	—	—	—	35.00	60.00
1910 Prooflike	3,392	—	—	—	40.00	65.00

KM# 811   PENNY
0.4713 g., 0.9250 Silver 0.0140 oz. ASW   **Ruler:** George V **Obv:** Head left **Rev:** Crowned denomination divides date within oak wreath

Date	Mintage	F	VF	XF	Unc	BU
1911 Prooflike	1,913	—	—	—	35.00	45.00
1912 Prooflike	1,616	—	—	—	35.00	45.00
1913 Prooflike	1,590	—	—	—	35.00	45.00
1914 Prooflike	1,818	—	—	—	35.00	45.00
1915 Prooflike	2,072	—	—	—	35.00	45.00
1916 Prooflike	1,647	—	—	—	35.00	45.00
1917 Prooflike	1,820	—	—	—	35.00	45.00
1918 Prooflike	1,911	—	—	—	35.00	45.00
1919 Prooflike	1,699	—	—	—	35.00	45.00
1920 Prooflike	1,715	—	—	—	35.00	45.00

KM# 810   PENNY
9.4500 g., Bronze, 30.8 mm.   **Ruler:** George V **Obv:** Head left
Obv. Leg.: GEORGIVS V DEI GRA: BRITT: OMN: REX FID: DEF: IND: IMP: **Rev:** Britannia seated right **Note:** Fully struck and orginal mint lustre coins command a premium.

Date	Mintage	F	VF	XF	Unc	BU
1911	23,079,000	0.80	2.50	16.00	50.00	—
1912	48,306,000	0.80	2.50	17.00	50.00	—
1912H	16,800,000	1.00	8.00	75.00	250	—
1913	65,497,000	0.80	3.00	22.00	75.00	—
1914	50,821,000	0.80	2.50	17.00	50.00	—
1915	47,311,000	0.80	2.50	17.00	50.00	—
1916	86,411,000	0.80	2.50	17.00	50.00	—
1917	107,905,000	0.80	2.50	17.00	50.00	—
1918	84,227,000	0.80	2.50	17.00	50.00	—
1918H	2,573,000	4.00	30.00	250	800	—
1918KN	Inc. above	4.50	40.00	375	1,600	—
1919	113,761,000	0.80	2.50	17.00	50.00	—
1919H	4,526,000	1.25	13.00	275	1,000	—
1919KN	Inc. above	4.00	25.00	400	2,200	—
1920	124,693,000	0.80	2.50	17.00	50.00	—
1921	129,717,999	0.80	2.50	17.00	50.00	—
1922	16,347,000	0.80	4.00	20.00	60.00	—
1922	—	—	2,500	—	10,000	—

Note: Reverse of 1927

| 1922 Specimen | 2 | — | — | — | — | 25,000 |

Note: Reverse of 1927

| 1926 | 4,499,000 | 2.50 | 7.00 | 30.00 | 100 | — |
| 1926 Proof | — | Value: 2,000 | | | | |

KM# 811a   PENNY
0.4713 g., 0.5000 Silver 0.0076 oz. ASW   **Ruler:** George V
Obv: Head left **Rev:** Crowned denomination divides date within oak wreath

Date	Mintage	F	VF	XF	Unc	BU
1921 Prooflike	1,847	—	—	—	35.00	45.00
1922 Prooflike	1,758	—	—	—	35.00	45.00
1923 Prooflike	1,840	—	—	—	35.00	45.00
1924 Prooflike	1,619	—	—	—	35.00	45.00
1925 Prooflike	1,890	—	—	—	35.00	45.00
1926 Prooflike	2,180	—	—	—	35.00	45.00
1927 Prooflike	1,647	—	—	—	35.00	45.00

KM# 826 PENNY
Bronze, 30.8 mm. **Ruler:** George V **Obv:** Modified head left
Rev: Britannia seated right

Date	Mintage	F	VF	XF	Unc	BU
1926	—	20.00	125	1,200	2,500	—
1926 Proof	—	—	—	—	—	—
Note: Reported, not confirmed						
1927	60,990,000	0.35	0.75	8.00	30.00	—
1927 Proof	—	Value: 1,800				

KM# 838 PENNY
Bronze, 30.8 mm. **Ruler:** George V **Obv:** Smaller head left
Rev: Britannia seated right

Date	Mintage	F	VF	XF	Unc	BU
1928	50,178,000	0.25	0.50	8.00	30.00	—
1928 Proof	—	Value: 1,800				
1929	49,133,000	0.25	0.50	8.00	30.00	—
1929 Proof	—	Value: 1,800				
1930	29,098,000	0.35	1.50	15.00	35.00	—
1930 Proof	—	Value: 1,800				
1931	19,843,000	0.35	1.50	15.00	35.00	—
1931 Proof	—	Value: 1,800				
1932	8,278,000	1.00	4.50	20.00	70.00	—
1932 Proof	—	Value: 2,250				
1933 Rare	Est. 7	—	—	—	100,000	—
1933 Proof	—	—	—	—	—	—
Note: Reported, not confirmed, probably prooflike, early strike						
1934	13,966,000	0.50	4.00	20.00	60.00	—
1934 Proof	—	Value: 2,000				
1935	56,070,000	0.25	0.50	5.00	30.00	—
1935 Proof	—	Value: 1,750				
1936	154,296,000	0.25	0.40	5.00	25.00	—
1936 Proof	—	Value: 1,750				

KM# 839 PENNY
0.4713 g., 0.5000 Silver 0.0076 oz. ASW **Ruler:** George V
Obv: Modified head left **Rev:** Crowned denomination divides date
within oak wreath

Date	Mintage	F	VF	XF	Unc	BU
1928 Prooflike	1,846	—	—	—	45.00	50.00
1929 Prooflike	1,837	—	—	—	45.00	50.00
1930 Prooflike	1,724	—	—	—	45.00	50.00
1931 Prooflike	1,759	—	—	—	45.00	50.00
1932 Prooflike	1,835	—	—	—	45.00	50.00
1933 Prooflike	1,872	—	—	—	45.00	50.00
1934 Prooflike	1,919	—	—	—	45.00	50.00
1935 Prooflike	1,975	—	—	—	45.00	50.00
1936 Prooflike	1,329	—	—	—	50.00	55.00

KM# 845 PENNY
9.4500 g., Bronze, 30.8 mm. **Ruler:** George VI **Obv:** Head left
Rev: Britannia seated right

Date	Mintage	F	VF	XF	Unc	BU
1937	88,896,000	0.20	0.35	1.00	7.50	—
1937 Proof	26,000	Value: 19.00				
1937 Matte Proof	Est. 4	Value: 4,000				
1938	121,560,000	0.20	0.35	1.00	10.00	—
1938 Proof	—	Value: 1,600				

Date	Mintage	F	VF	XF	Unc	BU
1939	55,560,000	0.25	0.50	4.00	15.00	—
1939 Proof	—	Value: 1,600				
1940	42,284,000	0.25	0.50	7.50	30.00	—
1940 Proof	—	Value: 1,800				
1944	42,600,000	0.25	0.50	6.00	20.00	—
1944 Proof	—	Value: 1,700				
1945	79,531,000	0.20	0.35	5.00	19.00	—
1945 Proof	—	Value: 1,700				
1946	66,855,999	0.20	0.35	5.00	19.00	—
1946 Proof	—	Value: 1,700				
1947	52,220,000	0.15	0.25	0.75	7.50	—
1947 Proof	—	Value: 2,250				
1948	63,961,000	0.15	0.25	0.75	7.50	—
1948 Proof	—	Value: 2,250				

KM# 846 PENNY
0.4713 g., 0.5000 Silver 0.0076 oz. ASW **Ruler:** George VI **Obv:**
Head left **Rev:** Crowned denomination divides date within oak wreath

Date	Mintage	F	VF	XF	Unc	BU
1937 Prooflike	1,329	—	—	—	35.00	40.00
1938 Prooflike	1,275	—	—	—	40.00	45.00
1939 Prooflike	1,253	—	—	—	40.00	45.00
1940 Prooflike	1,375	—	—	—	40.00	45.00
1941 Prooflike	1,255	—	—	—	40.00	45.00
1942 Prooflike	1,243	—	—	—	40.00	45.00
1943 Prooflike	1,347	—	—	—	40.00	45.00
1944 Prooflike	1,259	—	—	—	40.00	45.00
1945 Prooflike	1,367	—	—	—	40.00	45.00
1946 Prooflike	1,479	—	—	—	40.00	45.00

KM# 846a PENNY
0.4713 g., 0.9250 Silver 0.0140 oz. ASW **Ruler:** George VI **Obv:**
Head left **Rev:** Crowned denomination divides date within oak wreath

Date	Mintage	F	VF	XF	Unc	BU
1947 Prooflike	1,387	—	—	—	40.00	45.00
1948 Prooflike	1,397	—	—	—	40.00	45.00

KM# 869 PENNY
Bronze, 30.8 mm. **Ruler:** George VI **Obv:** Head left
Obv. Leg.: without IND: IMP: **Rev:** Britannia seated right

Date	Mintage	F	VF	XF	Unc	BU
1949	14,324,000	0.20	0.35	0.75	7.50	—
1949 Proof	—	Value: 2,000				
1950	240,000	3.00	6.00	20.00	55.00	—
1950 Matte Proof	—	Value: 3,000				
Note: There are reportedly 1-2 known of this variety, struck specifically for use in photography						
1950 Proof	18,000	Value: 40.00				
1951	120,000	3.00	13.00	35.00	60.00	—
1951 Matte Proof	—	Value: 3,000				
Note: There are reportedly 1-2 known of this variety, struck specifically for use in photography						
1951 Proof	20,000	Value: 50.00				
1952 Proof, Unique	—	Value: 100,000				

KM# 870 PENNY
0.4713 g., 0.9250 Silver 0.0140 oz. ASW **Ruler:** George VI
Obv: Head left **Obv. Leg.:** without IND: IMP: **Rev:** Crowned
denomination divides date within oak wreath

Date	Mintage	F	VF	XF	Unc	BU
1949 Prooflike	1,407	—	—	—	40.00	45.00
1950 Prooflike	1,527	—	—	—	40.00	45.00
1951 Prooflike	1,480	—	—	—	40.00	45.00
1952 Prooflike	1,024	—	—	—	50.00	55.00

KM# 883 PENNY
9.4400 g., Bronze, 30.8 mm. **Ruler:** Elizabeth II **Obv:** Laureate
bust right **Rev:** Britannia seated right

Date	Mintage	F	VF	XF	Unc	BU
1953	1,308,000	0.75	1.25	5.00	14.00	—
1953 Proof	40,000	Value: 20.00				
1953 Matte Proof; Rare	—	Value: 3,500				
Note: There are reportedly 1-2 known of this variety, struck specifically for use in photography						

KM# 884 PENNY
0.4713 g., 0.9250 Silver 0.0140 oz. ASW **Ruler:** Elizabeth II
Obv: Laureate bust right **Rev:** Britannia seated right

Date	Mintage	F	VF	XF	Unc	BU
1953 Prooflike	1,050	—	—	—	170	185

KM# 897 PENNY
9.4000 g., Bronze, 30.72 mm. **Ruler:** Elizabeth II **Obv:** Laureate
bust right **Obv. Leg.:** without BRITT: OMN: **Rev:** Britannia seated
right **Edge:** Plain

Date	Mintage	F	VF	XF	Unc	BU
1954 1 Known	—	—	—	—	—	—
1961	48,313,000	—	0.10	0.15	1.50	—
1961 Proof	—	Value: 1,500				
1962	143,309,000	—	—	0.10	1.00	—
1962 Proof	—	Value: 1,500				
1963	125,236,000	—	—	0.10	1.00	—
1963 Proof	—	Value: 1,500				
1964	153,294,000	—	—	—	0.55	—
1964 Proof	—	Value: 2,000				
1965	121,310,000	—	—	—	0.55	—
1966	165,739,000	—	—	—	0.55	—
1967	654,564,000	—	—	—	0.30	—
1970 Proof	750,000	Value: 5.00				

KM# 898 PENNY
0.4713 g., 0.9250 Silver 0.0140 oz. ASW, 11 mm.
Ruler: Elizabeth II **Series:** Maundy **Obv:** Laureate bust right **Rev:**
Crowned value in sprays divides date within wreath **Edge:** Reeded

Date	Mintage	F	VF	XF	Unc	BU
1954 Prooflike	1,088	—	—	—	35.00	40.00
1955 Prooflike	1,036	—	—	—	35.00	40.00
1955 Matte	—	—	—	—	—	—
1956 Prooflike	1,100	—	—	—	35.00	40.00
1957 Prooflike	1,168	—	—	—	35.00	40.00
1958 Prooflike	1,112	—	—	—	35.00	40.00
1959 Prooflike	1,118	—	—	—	35.00	40.00
1960 Prooflike	1,124	—	—	—	35.00	40.00
1961 Prooflike	1,200	—	—	—	35.00	40.00
1962 Prooflike	1,127	—	—	—	35.00	40.00
1963 Prooflike	1,133	—	—	—	35.00	40.00
1964 Prooflike	1,215	—	—	—	35.00	40.00
1965 Prooflike	1,143	—	—	—	35.00	40.00
1966 Prooflike	1,206	—	—	—	35.00	40.00
1967 Prooflike	1,068	—	—	—	38.00	45.00
1968 Prooflike	964	—	—	—	38.00	45.00
1969 Prooflike	1,002	—	—	—	38.00	45.00
1970 Prooflike	980	—	—	—	38.00	45.00
1971 Prooflike	1,108	—	—	—	38.00	45.00
1972 Prooflike	1,026	—	—	—	38.00	45.00
1973 Prooflike	1,004	—	—	—	38.00	45.00
1974 Prooflike	1,138	—	—	—	38.00	45.00
1975 Prooflike	1,050	—	—	—	38.00	45.00
1976 Prooflike	1,158	—	—	—	38.00	45.00
1977 Prooflike	1,240	—	—	—	38.00	45.00
1978 Prooflike	1,178	—	—	—	38.00	45.00
1979 Prooflike	1,188	—	—	—	38.00	45.00
1980 Prooflike	1,198	—	—	—	38.00	45.00
1981 Prooflike	1,288	—	—	—	38.00	45.00
1982 Prooflike	1,218	—	—	—	38.00	45.00
1983 Prooflike	1,228	—	—	—	38.00	45.00
1984 Prooflike	1,354	—	—	—	38.00	45.00
1985 Prooflike	1,248	—	—	—	38.00	45.00
1986 Prooflike	1,378	—	—	—	38.00	45.00
1987 Prooflike	1,512	—	—	—	38.00	45.00
1988 Prooflike	1,402	—	—	—	38.00	45.00
1989 Prooflike	1,353	—	—	—	38.00	45.00
1990 Prooflike	1,523	—	—	—	40.00	45.00
1991 Prooflike	1,514	—	—	—	40.00	45.00
1992 Prooflike	1,556	—	—	—	40.00	45.00
1993 Prooflike	1,440	—	—	—	40.00	45.00
1994 Prooflike	1,443	—	—	—	40.00	45.00
1995 Prooflike	1,466	—	—	—	40.00	45.00
1996 Prooflike	1,629	—	—	—	42.00	48.00
1997 Prooflike	1,786	—	—	—	42.00	48.00
1998 Prooflike	1,654	—	—	—	42.00	48.00
1999 Prooflike	1,676	—	—	—	42.00	48.00
2000 Prooflike	1,686	—	—	—	50.00	55.00

KM# 776   2 PENCE
0.9426 g., 0.9250 Silver 0.0280 oz. ASW   **Ruler:** Victoria **Obv:** Mature draped bust left **Rev:** Crowned denomination divides date within oak wreath

Date	Mintage	F	VF	XF	Unc	BU
1901 Prooflike	14,000	—	—	—	20.00	35.00

KM# 796   2 PENCE
0.9426 g., 0.9250 Silver 0.0280 oz. ASW   **Ruler:** Edward VZwithin oak wreath

Date	Mintage	F	VF	XF	Unc	BU
1902 Prooflike	14,000	—	—	—	25.00	40.00
1903 Prooflike	13,000	—	—	—	25.00	40.00
1904 Prooflike	14,000	—	—	—	25.00	40.00
1905 Prooflike	11,000	—	—	—	25.00	40.00
1906 Prooflike	11,000	—	—	—	25.00	40.00
1907 Prooflike	8,760	—	—	—	25.00	40.00
1908 Prooflike	15,000	—	—	—	25.00	40.00
1909 Prooflike	2,695	—	—	—	35.00	60.00
1910 Prooflike	2,998	—	—	—	40.00	65.00

KM# 812   2 PENCE
0.9426 g., 0.9250 Silver 0.0280 oz. ASW   **Ruler:** George V **Obv:** Head left **Rev:** Crowned denomination divides date within oak wreath

Date	Mintage	F	VF	XF	Unc	BU
1911 Prooflike	1,635	—	—	—	45.00	50.00
1912 Prooflike	1,678	—	—	—	45.00	50.00
1913 Prooflike	1,880	—	—	—	45.00	50.00
1914 Prooflike	1,659	—	—	—	45.00	50.00
1915 Prooflike	1,465	—	—	—	45.00	50.00
1916 Prooflike	1,509	—	—	—	45.00	50.00
1917 Prooflike	1,506	—	—	—	45.00	50.00
1918 Prooflike	1,547	—	—	—	45.00	50.00
1919 Prooflike	1,567	—	—	—	45.00	50.00
1920 Prooflike	1,630	—	—	—	45.00	50.00

KM# 812a   2 PENCE
0.9426 g., 0.5000 Silver 0.0152 oz. ASW   **Ruler:** George V **Obv:** Head left **Rev:** Crowned denomination divides date within oak wreath

Date	Mintage	F	VF	XF	Unc	BU
1921 Prooflike	1,794	—	—	—	45.00	50.00
1922 Prooflike	3,074	—	—	—	45.00	50.00
1923 Prooflike	1,527	—	—	—	45.00	50.00
1924 Prooflike	1,602	—	—	—	45.00	50.00
1925 Prooflike	1,670	—	—	—	45.00	50.00
1926 Prooflike	1,902	—	—	—	45.00	50.00
1927 Prooflike	1,766	—	—	—	45.00	50.00

KM# 840   2 PENCE
0.9426 g., 0.5000 Silver 0.0152 oz. ASW   **Ruler:** George V **Obv:** Modified head left **Rev:** Crowned denomination divides date within oak wreath

Date	Mintage	F	VF	XF	Unc	BU
1928 Prooflike	1,706	—	—	—	50.00	60.00
1929 Prooflike	1,862	—	—	—	50.00	60.00
1930 Prooflike	1,901	—	—	—	50.00	60.00
1931 Prooflike	1,897	—	—	—	50.00	60.00
1932 Prooflike	1,960	—	—	—	50.00	60.00
1933 Prooflike	2,066	—	—	—	50.00	60.00
1934 Prooflike	1,927	—	—	—	50.00	60.00
1935 Prooflike	1,928	—	—	—	50.00	60.00
1936 Prooflike	1,365	—	—	—	55.00	65.00

KM# 847   2 PENCE
0.9426 g., 0.5000 Silver 0.0152 oz. ASW   **Ruler:** George VI **Obv:** Head left **Rev:** Crowned denomination divides date within oak wreath

Date	Mintage	F	VF	XF	Unc	BU
1937 Prooflike	1,472	—	—	—	35.00	40.00
1938 Prooflike	1,374	—	—	—	40.00	45.00
1939 Prooflike	1,436	—	—	—	40.00	45.00
1940 Prooflike	1,277	—	—	—	40.00	45.00
1941 Prooflike	1,345	—	—	—	40.00	45.00
1942 Prooflike	1,231	—	—	—	40.00	45.00
1943 Prooflike	1,239	—	—	—	40.00	45.00
1944 Prooflike	1,345	—	—	—	40.00	45.00
1945 Prooflike	1,355	—	—	—	40.00	45.00
1946 Prooflike	1,365	—	—	—	40.00	45.00

KM# 847a   2 PENCE
0.9426 g., 0.9250 Silver 0.0280 oz. ASW   **Ruler:** George VI **Obv:** Head left **Rev:** Crowned denomination divides date within oak wreath

Date	Mintage	F	VF	XF	Unc	BU
1947 Prooflike	1,479	—	—	—	40.00	45.00
1948 Prooflike	1,385	—	—	—	40.00	45.00

KM# 871   2 PENCE
0.9426 g., 0.9250 Silver 0.0280 oz. ASW   **Ruler:** George VI **Obv:** Head left **Obv. Leg.:** without IND IMP **Rev:** Crowned denomination divides date within oak wreath

Date	Mintage	F	VF	XF	Unc	BU
1949 Prooflike	1,395	—	—	—	40.00	45.00
1950 Prooflike	1,405	—	—	—	40.00	45.00
1951 Prooflike	1,580	—	—	—	40.00	45.00
1952 Prooflike	1,064	—	—	—	50.00	55.00

KM# 885   2 PENCE
0.9426 g., 0.9250 Silver 0.0280 oz. ASW   **Ruler:** Elizabeth II **Obv:** Laureate bust right **Rev:** Crowned denomination divides date within oak wreath

Date	Mintage	F	VF	XF	Unc	BU
1953 Prooflike	1,025	—	—	—	170	185

KM# 899   2 PENCE
0.9426 g., 0.9250 Silver 0.0280 oz. ASW, 13 mm. **Ruler:** Elizabeth II **Series:** Maundy **Obv:** Laureate bust right **Obv. Leg.:** Without BRITT OMN **Rev:** Crowned value in sprays divides date within wreath **Edge:** Reeded

Date	Mintage	F	VF	XF	Unc	BU
1954 Prooflike	1,020	—	—	—	35.00	40.00
1955 Prooflike	1,082	—	—	—	35.00	40.00
1955 Matte	—	—	—	—	—	—
1956 Prooflike	1,088	—	—	—	35.00	40.00
1957 Prooflike	1,094	—	—	—	35.00	40.00
1958 Prooflike	1,164	—	—	—	35.00	40.00
1959 Prooflike	1,106	—	—	—	35.00	40.00
1960 Prooflike	1,112	—	—	—	35.00	40.00
1961 Prooflike	1,118	—	—	—	35.00	40.00
1962 Prooflike	1,197	—	—	—	35.00	40.00
1963 Prooflike	1,131	—	—	—	35.00	40.00
1964 Prooflike	1,137	—	—	—	35.00	40.00
1965 Prooflike	1,221	—	—	—	35.00	40.00
1966 Prooflike	1,206	—	—	—	35.00	40.00
1967 Prooflike	986	—	—	—	38.00	45.00
1968 Prooflike	1,048	—	—	—	38.00	45.00
1969 Prooflike	1,002	—	—	—	38.00	45.00
1970 Prooflike	980	—	—	—	38.00	45.00
1971 Prooflike	1,018	—	—	—	38.00	45.00
1972 Prooflike	1,026	—	—	—	38.00	45.00
1973 Prooflike	1,004	—	—	—	38.00	45.00
1974 Prooflike	1,042	—	—	—	38.00	45.00
1975 Prooflike	1,148	—	—	—	38.00	45.00
1976 Prooflike	1,158	—	—	—	38.00	45.00
1977 Prooflike	1,138	—	—	—	38.00	45.00
1978 Prooflike	1,282	—	—	—	38.00	45.00
1979 Prooflike	1,188	—	—	—	38.00	45.00
1980 Prooflike	1,198	—	—	—	38.00	45.00
1981 Prooflike	1,178	—	—	—	38.00	45.00
1982 Prooflike	1,330	—	—	—	38.00	45.00
1983 Prooflike	1,228	—	—	—	38.00	45.00
1984 Prooflike	1,238	—	—	—	38.00	45.00
1985 Prooflike	1,366	—	—	—	38.00	45.00
1986 Prooflike	1,378	—	—	—	38.00	45.00
1987 Prooflike	1,390	—	—	—	38.00	45.00
1988 Prooflike	1,526	—	—	—	38.00	45.00
1989 Prooflike	1,353	—	—	—	38.00	45.00
1990 Prooflike	1,523	—	—	—	40.00	45.00
1991 Prooflike	1,384	—	—	—	40.00	45.00
1992 Prooflike	1,424	—	—	—	40.00	45.00
1993 Prooflike	1,440	—	—	—	40.00	45.00
1994 Prooflike	1,443	—	—	—	40.00	45.00
1995 Prooflike	1,466	—	—	—	40.00	45.00
1996 Prooflike	1,629	—	—	—	42.00	48.00
1997 Prooflike	1,786	—	—	—	42.00	48.00
1998 Prooflike	1,654	—	—	—	42.00	48.00
1999 Prooflike	1,676	—	—	—	42.00	48.00
2000 Prooflike	1,686	—	—	—	55.00	60.00

KM# 777   3 PENCE
1.4138 g., 0.9250 Silver 0.0420 oz. ASW, 16 mm. **Ruler:** Victoria **Obv:** Mature draped bust left **Rev:** Crowned denomination divides date within oak wreath

Date	Mintage	F	VF	XF	Unc	BU
1901	6,100,000	1.00	2.00	6.00	25.00	—
1901 Prooflike	8,976	—	—	—	50.00	60.00

KM# 797.1   3 PENCE
1.4138 g., 0.9250 Silver 0.0420 oz. ASW, 16 mm. **Ruler:** Edward VII **Obv:** Head right **Rev:** Crowned denomination divides date within oak wreath **Note:** The prooflike coins come with a mirror or satin finish.

Date	Mintage	F	VF	XF	Unc	BU
1902	8,287,000	1.00	4.00	8.00	25.00	—
1902 Prooflike	8,976	—	—	—	35.00	50.00
1902 Matte Proof	15,000	Value: 40.00				
1903	5,235,000	2.00	5.00	25.00	75.00	—
1903 Prooflike	8,976	—	—	—	35.00	50.00
1904	3,630,000	5.00	12.00	50.00	200	—
1904 Prooflike	8,876	—	—	—	35.00	50.00

KM# 797.2   3 PENCE
1.4138 g., 0.9250 Silver 0.0420 oz. ASW, 16 mm.   **Ruler:** Edward VII **Obv:** Head right **Rev:** Crowned denomination divides date within oak wreath **Note:** The below Prooflike listings can be of mirror or satin-like finish, which are more difficult to separate from the currency strikes, especially for the years 1903-1906.

Date	Mintage	F	VF	XF	Unc	BU
1904	Inc. above	4.00	8.50	35.00	125	—
1905	3,563,000	2.50	7.50	28.00	75.00	—
1905 Prooflike	8,976	—	—	—	35.00	50.00
1906	3,174,000	3.00	8.50	35.00	100	—
1906 Prooflike	8,800	—	—	—	35.00	50.00
1907	4,841,000	1.50	5.00	28.00	50.00	—
1907 Prooflike	11,000	—	—	—	35.00	50.00
1908	8,176,000	1.50	3.00	15.00	50.00	—
1908 Prooflike	8,760	—	—	—	35.00	50.00
1909	4,054,999	1.50	5.50	27.00	70.00	—
1909 Prooflike	1,983	—	—	—	45.00	75.00
1910	4,565,000	0.75	1.50	15.00	30.00	—
1910 Prooflike	1,140	—	—	—	50.00	80.00

KM# 813   3 PENCE
1.4138 g., 0.9250 Silver 0.0420 oz. ASW, 16 mm. **Ruler:** George V **Obv:** Head left **Rev:** Crowned denomination divides date within oak wreath

Date	Mintage	F	VF	XF	Unc	BU
1911	5,843,000	0.75	1.25	5.00	24.00	—
1911 Prooflike	1,991	—	—	—	60.00	70.00
1911 Proof	6,007	Value: 65.00				
1912	8,934,000	0.75	1.25	5.00	24.00	—
1912 Prooflike	1,246	—	—	—	60.00	70.00
1913	7,144,000	0.75	1.25	5.00	24.00	—
1913 Prooflike	1,228	—	—	—	60.00	70.00
1914	6,735,000	0.75	1.25	5.00	22.00	—
1914 Prooflike	982	—	—	—	60.00	70.00
1915	5,452,000	0.75	1.25	5.00	22.00	—
1915 Prooflike	1,293	—	—	—	60.00	70.00
1916	18,556,000	0.65	1.00	3.00	15.00	—
1916 Prooflike	1,128	—	—	—	60.00	70.00
1917	21,664,000	0.65	1.00	4.50	15.00	—
1917 Prooflike	1,237	—	—	—	60.00	70.00
1918	20,632,000	0.65	1.00	4.50	15.00	—
1918 Prooflike	1,375	—	—	—	60.00	70.00
1919	16,846,000	0.65	1.00	3.00	20.00	—
1919 Prooflike	1,258	—	—	—	60.00	70.00
1920	16,704,999	0.65	1.00	3.00	20.00	—
1920 Prooflike	1,399	—	—	—	60.00	70.00

KM# 813a   3 PENCE
1.4138 g., 0.5000 Silver 0.0227 oz. ASW, 16 mm. **Ruler:** George V **Obv:** Head left **Rev:** Crowned denomination divides date within oak wreath

Date	Mintage	F	VF	XF	Unc	BU
1920	Inc. above	—	1.00	3.00	18.00	—
1921	8,751,000	—	1.00	3.00	30.00	—
1921 Prooflike	1,386	—	—	—	50.00	60.00
1922	7,981,000	—	1.00	7.00	30.00	—
1922 Prooflike	1,373	—	—	—	50.00	60.00
1923 Prooflike	1,430	—	—	—	50.00	60.00
1924 Prooflike	1,515	—	—	—	50.00	60.00
1924 Satin specimen	2	—	—	—	—	2,500
1925	3,733,000	0.75	2.00	14.00	40.00	—
1925 Prooflike	1,438	—	—	—	50.00	60.00
1926	4,109,000	1.25	4.00	16.50	50.00	—
1926 Prooflike	1,504	—	—	—	50.00	60.00
1927 Prooflike	1,690	—	—	—	50.00	60.00

KM# 827 3 PENCE
1.4138 g., 0.5000 Silver 0.0227 oz. ASW, 16 mm.
Ruler: George V **Obv:** Modified head left **Rev:** Crowned denomination divides date within oak wreath

Date	Mintage	F	VF	XF	Unc	BU
1926	Inc. above	0.75	1.75	8.00	50.00	—
1928 Prooflike	1,835	—	—	—	45.00	50.00
1929 Prooflike	1,761	—	—	—	45.00	50.00
1930 Prooflike	1,948	—	—	—	45.00	50.00
1931 Prooflike	1,818	—	—	—	45.00	50.00
1932 Prooflike	2,042	—	—	—	45.00	50.00
1933 Prooflike	1,920	—	—	—	45.00	50.00
1934 Prooflike	1,887	—	—	—	45.00	50.00
1935 Prooflike	2,007	—	—	—	45.00	50.00
1936 Prooflike	1,307	—	—	—	50.00	55.00

KM# 831 3 PENCE
1.4138 g., 0.5000 Silver 0.0227 oz. ASW, 16 mm. **Ruler:** George V **Obv:** Head left **Rev:** Three oak leaves and acorns divided

Date	Mintage	F	VF	XF	Unc	BU
1927 Proof	15,000	Value: 60.00				
1927 Matte Proof	—	Value: 2,000				

Note: There are reportedly 3-4 known of this variety, struck specifically for use in photographs

Date	Mintage	F	VF	XF	Unc	BU
1928	1,302,000	1.75	3.50	14.50	45.00	—
1928 Proof	—	Value: 700				
1930	1,319,000	1.50	3.00	14.00	40.00	—
1930 Proof	—	Value: 700				
1931	6,252,000	BV	0.50	1.25	12.00	—
1931 Proof	—	Value: 700				
1932	5,887,000	BV	0.60	1.75	12.50	—
1932 Proof	—	Value: 700				
1933	5,579,000	BV	0.60	1.75	12.50	—
1933 Proof	—	Value: 700				
1934	7,406,000	BV	0.60	1.75	12.00	—
1934 Proof	—	Value: 700				
1935	7,028,000	BV	0.50	1.25	12.00	—
1935 Proof	—	Value: 700				
1936	3,239,000	BV	0.60	1.75	13.00	—
1936 Proof	—	Value: 700				

KM# 848 3 PENCE
1.4138 g., 0.5000 Silver 0.0227 oz. ASW, 16 mm.
Ruler: George VI **Obv:** Head left **Rev:** St. George shield on Tudor rose divides date

Date	Mintage	F	VF	XF	Unc	BU
1937	8,148,000	BV	0.50	1.25	7.00	—
1937 Proof	26,000	Value: 15.00				
1937 Matte Proof; Rare	—					

Note: There are reportedly 2-4 known of this variety, struck specifically for use in photography

Date	Mintage	F	VF	XF	Unc	BU
1938	6,402,000	BV	0.50	1.25	10.00	—
1938 Proof	—	Value: 600				
1939	1,356,000	BV	1.50	8.50	25.00	—
1939 Proof	—	Value: 600				
1940	7,914,000	BV	0.60	2.50	18.00	—
1940 Proof	—	Value: 600				
1941	7,979,000	BV	0.60	4.00	20.00	—
1941 Proof	—	Value: 600				
1942	4,144,000	1.00	5.00	15.00	50.00	—
1942 Proof	—	Value: 600				
1943	1,379,000	1.00	5.00	24.00	60.00	—
1943 Proof	—	Value: 600				
1944	2,005,999	2.25	10.00	40.00	100	—
1944 Proof	—	Value: 700				
1945 Rare	320,000	—	—	—	—	—

Note: Issue melted, only one known

KM# 849 3 PENCE
Nickel-Brass **Ruler:** George VI **Obv:** Head left **Rev:** Thrift plant (allium porrum)

Date	Mintage	F	VF	XF	Unc	BU
1937	45,708,000	0.25	0.40	2.00	10.00	—
1937 Proof	26,000	Value: 17.50				

Date	Mintage	F	VF	XF	Unc	BU
1937 Matte Proof ; Rare	—					

Note: There are reportedly 2-4 known of this variety, struck specifically for use in photography

Date	Mintage	F	VF	XF	Unc	BU
1938	14,532,000	0.40	0.80	6.00	25.00	—
1938 Proof	—	Value: 500				
1939	5,603,000	0.40	1.50	10.00	50.00	—
1939 Proof	—	Value: 500				
1940	12,636,000	0.25	0.50	5.00	20.00	—
1940 Proof	—	Value: 500				
1941	60,239,000	0.25	0.40	2.50	14.00	—
1941 Proof	—	Value: 500				
1942	103,214,000	0.25	0.40	2.50	12.00	—
1942 Proof	—					
1943	101,702,000	0.25	0.40	2.50	12.00	—
1943 Proof	—					
1944	69,760,000	0.25	0.40	2.50	12.00	—
1944 Proof	—					
1945	33,942,000	0.25	0.50	2.50	18.00	—
1945 Proof	—					
1946	621,000	4.00	17.50	125	600	—
1946 Proof	—	Value: 1,000				
1948	4,230,000	0.60	1.50	8.00	55.00	—
1948 Proof	—	Value: 850				

KM# 850 3 PENCE
1.4138 g., 0.5000 Silver 0.0227 oz. ASW, 16 mm.
Ruler: George VI **Obv:** Head left **Rev:** Crowned denomination divides date within oak wreath

Date	Mintage	F	VF	XF	Unc	BU
1937 Prooflike	1,351	—	—	—	45.00	50.00
1938 Prooflike	1,350	—	—	—	50.00	55.00
1939 Prooflike	1,234	—	—	L	50.00	55.00
1940 Prooflike	1,290	—	—	—	50.00	55.00
1941 Prooflike	1,253	—	—	—	50.00	55.00
1942 Prooflike	1,325	—	—	—	50.00	55.00
1943 Prooflike	1,335	—	—	—	50.00	55.00
1944 Prooflike	1,345	—	—	—	50.00	55.00
1945 Prooflike	1,355	—	—	—	50.00	55.00
1946 Prooflike	1,365	—	—	—	50.00	55.00

KM# 850a 3 PENCE
1.4138 g., 0.9250 Silver 0.0420 oz. ASW, 16 mm.
Ruler: George VI **Obv:** Head left **Rev:** Crowned denomination divides date within oak wreath

Date	Mintage	F	VF	XF	Unc	BU
1947 Prooflike	1,375	—	—	—	50.00	55.00
1948 Prooflike	1,491	—	—	—	50.00	55.00

KM# 872 3 PENCE
1.4138 g., 0.9250 Silver 0.0420 oz. ASW, 16 mm.
Ruler: George VI **Obv:** Head left **Obv. Leg.:** without IND IMP **Rev:** Crowned denomination divides date within oak wreath

Date	Mintage	F	VF	XF	Unc	BU
1949 Prooflike	1,395	—	—	—	50.00	55.00
1950 Prooflike	1,405	—	—	—	50.00	55.00
1951 Prooflike	1,468	—	—	—	50.00	55.00
1952 Prooflike	1,012	—	—	—	55.00	60.00

KM# 873 3 PENCE
6.8000 g., Nickel-Brass **Ruler:** George VI **Obv:** Head left **Obv. Leg.:** without IND IMP **Rev:** Thrift plant (allium porrum)

Date	Mintage	F	VF	XF	Unc	BU
1949	464,000	4.00	17.50	125	550	—
1949 Proof	—	Value: 950				
1950	1,600,000	1.00	3.00	15.00	85.00	—
1950 Proof	18,000	Value: 50.00				
1950 Matte Proof; Rare	—					

Note: There are reportedly 2-4 known of this variety, struck specifically for use in photography

Date	Mintage	F	VF	XF	Unc	BU
1951	1,184,000	1.00	3.00	20.00	110	—
1951 Proof	20,000	Value: 50.00				
1951 Matte Proof; Rare	—	Value: 1,800				

Note: There are reportedly 2-4 known of this variety, struck specifically for use in photography

Date	Mintage	F	VF	XF	Unc	BU
1952	25,494,000	0.25	0.50	5.00	19.00	—
1952 Proof	—	Value: 800				

KM# 886 3 PENCE
Nickel-Brass **Ruler:** Elizabeth II **Obv:** Laureate bust right **Rev:** Crowned portcullis

Date	Mintage	F	VF	XF	Unc	BU
1953	30,618,000	0.25	0.50	0.75	6.00	—
1953 Proof	40,000	Value: 12.00				
1953 Matte Proof; Rare	—	Value: 1,800				

Note: There are reportedly 2-4 known of this variety, struck specifically for use in photography

KM# 887 3 PENCE
1.4138 g., 0.9250 Silver 0.0420 oz. ASW **Ruler:** Elizabeth II **Obv:** Laureate bust right **Rev:** Crowned portcullis

Date	Mintage	F	VF	XF	Unc	BU
1953 Prooflike	1,078	—	—	—	180	200

KM# 900 3 PENCE
Nickel-Brass **Ruler:** Elizabeth II **Obv:** Laureate bust right **Obv. Leg.:** without BRITT OMN **Rev:** Crowned portcullis

Date	Mintage	F	VF	XF	Unc	BU
1954	41,720,000	—	0.25	0.50	10.00	—
1954 Proof	—	Value: 500				
1955	41,075,000	—	—	0.75	10.00	—
1955 Proof	—	Value: 500				
1956	36,902,000	—	—	1.25	10.00	—
1956 Proof	—	Value: 500				
1957	24,294,000	—	—	0.50	5.00	—
1957 Proof	—	Value: 500				
1958	20,504,000	—	1.00	2.25	8.00	—
1958 Proof	—	Value: 500				
1959	28,499,000	—	—	0.50	6.50	—
1959 Proof	—	Value: 500				
1960	83,078,000	—	—	0.40	6.50	—
1960 Proof	—	Value: 500				
1961	41,102,000	—	—	0.25	2.50	—
1961 Proof	—	Value: 500				
1962	47,242,000	—	—	0.25	1.50	—
1962 Proof	—	Value: 500				
1963	35,280,000	—	—	0.25	1.50	—
1963 Proof	—	Value: 500				
1964	47,440,000	—	—	0.25	1.50	—
1964 Proof	—					
1965	23,907,000	—	—	0.25	1.50	—
1965 Proof	—					
1966	55,320,000	—	—	0.25	0.50	—
1966 Proof	—					
1967	49,000,000	—	—	0.15	0.50	—
1967 Proof	—					
1970 Proof	750,000	Value: 3.50				

KM# 901 3 PENCE
1.4138 g., 0.9250 Silver 0.0420 oz. ASW, 16 mm.
Ruler: Elizabeth II **Series:** Maundy **Obv:** Laureate bust right **Obv. Leg.:** without BRITT OMN **Rev:** Crowned value in sprays divides date within wreath **Edge:** Reeded

Date	Mintage	F	VF	XF	Unc	BU
1954 Prooflike	1,076	—	—	—	45.00	50.00
1955 Prooflike	1,082	—	—	—	45.00	50.00
1956 Prooflike	1,088	—	—	—	45.00	50.00
1957 Prooflike	1,094	—	—	—	45.00	50.00
1958 Prooflike	1,100	—	—	—	45.00	50.00
1959 Prooflike	1,172	—	—	—	45.00	50.00
1960 Prooflike	1,112	—	—	—	45.00	50.00
1961 Prooflike	1,118	—	—	—	45.00	50.00
1962 Prooflike	1,125	—	—	—	45.00	50.00
1963 Prooflike	1,205	—	—	—	45.00	50.00
1964 Prooflike	1,213	—	—	—	45.00	50.00
1965 Prooflike	1,221	—	—	—	45.00	50.00
1966 Prooflike	1,206	—	—	—	45.00	50.00
1967 Prooflike	986	—	—	—	48.00	55.00
1968 Prooflike	964	—	—	—	48.00	55.00
1969 Prooflike	1,088	—	—	—	48.00	55.00
1970 Prooflike	980	—	—	—	48.00	55.00
1971 Prooflike	1,018	—	—	—	48.00	55.00
1972 Prooflike	1,026	—	—	—	48.00	55.00
1973 Prooflike	1,098	—	—	—	48.00	55.00
1974 Prooflike	1,138	—	—	—	48.00	55.00

Date	Mintage	F	VF	XF	Unc	BU
1975 Prooflike	1,148	—	—	—	48.00	55.00
1976 Prooflike	1,158	—	—	—	48.00	55.00
1977 Prooflike	1,138	—	—	—	48.00	55.00
1978 Prooflike	1,178	—	—	—	48.00	55.00
1979 Prooflike	1,294	—	—	—	48.00	55.00
1980 Prooflike	1,198	—	—	—	48.00	55.00
1981 Prooflike	1,178	—	—	—	48.00	55.00
1982 Prooflike	1,218	—	—	—	48.00	55.00
1983 Prooflike	1,342	—	—	—	48.00	55.00
1984 Prooflike	1,354	—	—	—	48.00	55.00
1985 Prooflike	1,366	—	—	—	48.00	55.00
1986 Prooflike	1,378	—	—	—	48.00	55.00
1987 Prooflike	1,390	—	—	—	48.00	55.00
1988 Prooflike	1,528	—	—	—	48.00	55.00
1989 Prooflike	1,353	—	—	—	48.00	55.00
1990 Prooflike	1,523	—	—	—	50.00	55.00
1991 Prooflike	1,384	—	—	—	50.00	55.00
1992 Prooflike	1,424	—	—	—	50.00	55.00
1993 Prooflike	1,440	—	—	—	50.00	55.00
1994 Prooflike	1,433	—	—	—	50.00	55.00
1995 Prooflike	1,466	—	—	—	50.00	55.00
1996 Prooflike	1,629	—	—	—	55.00	60.00
1997 Prooflike	1,786	—	—	—	55.00	60.00
1998 Prooflike	1,654	—	—	—	55.00	60.00
1999 Prooflike	1,676	—	—	—	55.00	60.00
2000 Prooflike	1,686	—	—	—	58.00	62.00

KM# 778   4 PENCE (Groat)
1.8851 g., 0.9250 Silver 0.0561 oz. ASW **Ruler:** Victoria
Obv: Mature draped bust left **Obv. Leg.:** VICTORIA • DEI • GRA • BRITT • REGINA • FID • DEF • IND • IMP • **Rev:** Crowned denomination divides date within oak wreath

Date	Mintage	F	VF	XF	Unc	BU
1901 Prooflike	12,000	—	—	—	30.00	50.00

KM# 798   4 PENCE (Groat)
1.8851 g., 0.9250 Silver 0.0561 oz. ASW **Ruler:** Edward VII **Obv:** Head left **Rev:** Crowned denomination divides date within oak wreath

Date	Mintage	F	VF	XF	Unc	BU
1902 Prooflike	10,000	—	—	—	30.00	45.00
1903 Prooflike	9,729	—	—	—	30.00	45.00
1904 Prooflike	12,000	—	—	—	30.00	45.00
1905 Prooflike	11,000	—	—	—	30.00	45.00
1906 Prooflike	11,000	—	—	—	30.00	45.00
1907 Prooflike	11,000	—	—	—	30.00	45.00
1908 Prooflike	9,929	—	—	—	30.00	45.00
1909 Prooflike	2,428	—	—	—	40.00	70.00
1910 Prooflike	2,755	—	—	—	45.00	75.00

KM# 814   4 PENCE (Groat)
1.8851 g., 0.9250 Silver 0.0561 oz. ASW **Ruler:** George V
Obv: Head left **Rev:** Crowned denomination divides date within oak wreath

Date	Mintage	F	VF	XF	Unc	BU
1911 Prooflike	1,768	—	—	—	45.00	50.00
1912 Prooflike	1,700	—	—	—	45.00	50.00
1913 Prooflike	1,798	—	—	—	45.00	50.00
1914 Prooflike	1,651	—	—	—	45.00	50.00
1915 Prooflike	1,441	—	—	—	45.00	50.00
1916 Prooflike	1,499	—	—	—	45.00	50.00
1917 Prooflike	1,478	—	—	—	45.00	50.00
1918 Prooflike	1,479	—	—	—	45.00	50.00
1919 Prooflike	1,524	—	—	—	45.00	50.00
1920 Prooflike	1,460	—	—	—	45.00	50.00

KM# 814a   4 PENCE (Groat)
1.8851 g., 0.5000 Silver 0.0303 oz. ASW **Ruler:** George V
Obv: Head left **Rev:** Crowned denomination divides date within oak wreath

Date	Mintage	F	VF	XF	Unc	BU
1921 Prooflike	1,542	—	—	—	45.00	50.00
1922 Prooflike	1,609	—	—	—	45.00	50.00
1923 Prooflike	1,635	—	—	—	45.00	50.00
1924 Prooflike	1,665	—	—	—	45.00	50.00
1925 Prooflike	1,786	—	—	—	45.00	50.00
1926 Prooflike	1,762	—	—	—	45.00	50.00
1927 Prooflike	1,681	—	—	—	45.00	50.00

KM# 841   4 PENCE (Groat)
1.8851 g., 0.5000 Silver 0.0303 oz. ASW **Ruler:** George V
Obv: Modified head left **Rev:** Crowned denomination divides date within oak wreath

Date	Mintage	F	VF	XF	Unc	BU
1928 Prooflike	1,642	—	—	—	45.00	50.00
1929 Prooflike	1,969	—	—	—	45.00	50.00
1930 Prooflike	1,744	—	—	—	45.00	50.00
1931 Prooflike	1,915	—	—	—	45.00	50.00
1932 Prooflike	1,937	—	—	—	45.00	50.00
1933 Prooflike	1,931	—	—	—	45.00	50.00
1934 Prooflike	1,893	—	—	—	45.00	50.00
1935 Prooflike	1,995	—	—	—	45.00	50.00
1936 Prooflike	1,323	—	—	—	50.00	55.00

KM# 851   4 PENCE (Groat)
1.8851 g., 0.5000 Silver 0.0303 oz. ASW **Ruler:** George VI **Obv:** Head left **Rev:** Crowned denomination divides date within oak wreath

Date	Mintage	F	VF	XF	Unc	BU
1937 Prooflike	1,325	—	—	—	45.00	50.00
1938 Prooflike	1,424	—	—	—	50.00	55.00
1939 Prooflike	1,332	—	—	—	50.00	55.00
1940 Prooflike	1,367	—	—	—	50.00	55.00
1941 Prooflike	1,345	—	—	—	50.00	55.00
1942 Prooflike	1,325	—	—	—	50.00	55.00
1943 Prooflike	1,335	—	—	—	50.00	55.00
1944 Prooflike	1,345	—	—	—	50.00	55.00
1945 Prooflike	1,355	—	—	—	50.00	55.00
1946 Prooflike	1,365	—	—	—	50.00	55.00

KM# 851a   4 PENCE (Groat)
1.8851 g., 0.9250 Silver 0.0561 oz. ASW **Ruler:** George VI **Obv:** Head left **Rev:** Crowned denomination divides date within oak wreath

Date	Mintage	F	VF	XF	Unc	BU
1947 Prooflike	1,375	—	—	—	50.00	55.00
1948 Prooflike	1,385	—	—	—	50.00	55.00

KM# 874   4 PENCE (Groat)
1.8851 g., 0.9250 Silver 0.0561 oz. ASW **Ruler:** George VI **Obv:** Head left **Obv. Leg.:** without IND IMP **Rev:** Crowned denomination divides date within oak wreath

Date	Mintage	F	VF	XF	Unc	BU
1949 Prooflike	1,503	—	—	—	50.00	55.00
1950 Prooflike	1,515	—	—	—	50.00	55.00
1951 Prooflike	1,580	—	—	—	50.00	55.00
1952 Prooflike	1,064	—	—	—	55.00	60.00

KM# 888   4 PENCE (Groat)
1.8851 g., 0.9250 Silver 0.0561 oz. ASW **Ruler:** Elizabeth II **Obv:** Bust right **Rev:** Crowned denomination divides date within oak wreath

Date	Mintage	F	VF	XF	Unc	BU
1953 Prooflike	1,078	—	—	—	180	200

KM# 902   4 PENCE (Groat)
1.8851 g., 0.9250 Silver 0.0561 oz. ASW, 18 mm.
Ruler: Elizabeth II **Obv:** Laureate bust right **Obv. Insc.:** without BRITT OMN **Rev:** Crowned denomination divides date within wreath **Edge:** Reeded

Date	Mintage	F	VF	XF	Unc	BU
1954 Prooflike	1,076	—	—	—	45.00	50.00
1955 Prooflike	1,082	—	—	—	45.00	50.00
1955 Matte	—	—	—	—	—	—
1956 Prooflike	1,088	—	—	—	45.00	50.00
1957 Prooflike	1,094	—	—	—	45.00	50.00
1958 Prooflike	1,100	—	—	—	45.00	50.00
1959 Prooflike	1,106	—	—	—	45.00	50.00
1960 Prooflike	1,180	—	—	—	45.00	50.00
1961 Prooflike	1,118	—	—	—	45.00	50.00
1962 Prooflike	1,197	—	—	—	45.00	50.00
1963 Prooflike	1,205	—	—	—	45.00	50.00
1964 Prooflike	1,213	—	—	—	45.00	50.00
1965 Prooflike	1,221	—	—	—	45.00	50.00

Date	Mintage	F	VF	XF	Unc	BU
1966 Prooflike	1,206	—	—	—	45.00	50.00
1967 Prooflike	986	—	—	—	48.00	55.00
1968 Prooflike	964	—	—	—	48.00	55.00
1969 Prooflike	1,002	—	—	—	48.00	55.00
1970 Prooflike	1,068	—	—	—	48.00	55.00
1971 Prooflike	1,108	—	—	—	48.00	55.00
1972 Prooflike	1,118	—	—	—	48.00	55.00
1973 Prooflike	1,098	—	—	—	48.00	55.00
1974 Prooflike	1,138	—	—	—	48.00	55.00
1975 Prooflike	1,148	—	—	—	48.00	55.00
1976 Prooflike	1,158	—	—	—	48.00	55.00
1977 Prooflike	1,138	—	—	—	48.00	55.00
1978 Prooflike	1,178	—	—	—	48.00	55.00
1979 Prooflike	1,188	—	—	—	48.00	55.00
1980 Prooflike	1,306	—	—	—	48.00	55.00
1981 Prooflike	1,288	—	—	—	48.00	55.00
1982 Prooflike	1,330	—	—	—	48.00	55.00
1983 Prooflike	1,342	—	—	—	48.00	55.00
1984 Prooflike	1,354	—	—	—	48.00	55.00
1985 Prooflike	1,366	—	—	—	48.00	55.00
1986 Prooflike	1,378	—	—	—	48.00	55.00
1987 Prooflike	1,390	—	—	—	48.00	55.00
1988 Prooflike	1,402	—	—	—	48.00	55.00
1989 Prooflike	1,353	—	—	—	48.00	55.00
1990 Prooflike	1,523	—	—	—	50.00	55.00
1991 Prooflike	1,514	—	—	—	50.00	55.00
1992 Prooflike	1,556	—	—	—	50.00	55.00
1993 Prooflike	1,440	—	—	—	50.00	55.00
1994 Prooflike	1,433	—	—	—	50.00	55.00
1995 Prooflike	1,466	—	—	—	50.00	55.00
1996 Prooflike	1,629	—	—	—	55.00	60.00
1997 Prooflike	1,786	—	—	—	55.00	60.00
1998 Prooflike	1,654	—	—	—	55.00	60.00
1999 Prooflike	1,676	—	—	—	55.00	60.00
2000 Prooflike	1,686	—	—	—	58.00	62.00

KM# 779   6 PENCE
3.0100 g., 0.9250 Silver 0.0895 oz. ASW, 19.5 mm.
Ruler: Victoria **Obv:** Mature draped bust left **Obv. Leg.:** VICTORIA • DEI • GRA • BRITT • REGINA • FID • DEF • IND • IMP • **Rev:** Crowned denomination within oak wreath

Date	Mintage	F	VF	XF	Unc	BU
1901	5,109,000	4.00	8.00	25.00	50.00	—

KM# 799   6 PENCE
3.0100 g., 0.9250 Silver 0.0895 oz. ASW, 19.5 mm.
Ruler: Edward VII **Obv:** Head right **Rev:** Crowned denomination within oak wreath, date below

Date	Mintage	F	VF	XF	Unc	BU
1902	6,356,000	5.00	10.00	30.00	65.00	—
1902 Matte Proof	15,000	Value: 50.00				
1903	5,411,000	5.00	10.00	30.00	110	—
1904	4,487,000	6.00	15.00	65.00	200	—
1905	4,236,000	5.00	12.00	35.00	140	—
1906	7,641,000	4.00	10.00	30.00	110	—
1907	8,734,000	5.00	10.00	35.00	110	—
1908	6,739,000	5.00	12.00	40.00	160	—
1909	6,584,000	5.00	10.00	35.00	110	—
1910	12,491,000	5.00	8.50	25.00	80.00	—

KM# 815   6 PENCE
3.0100 g., 0.9250 Silver 0.0895 oz. ASW, 19.5 mm. **Ruler:** George V **Obv:** Head left **Rev:** Lion atop crown dividing date

Date	Mintage	F	VF	XF	Unc	BU
1911	9,165,000	2.00	8.00	18.00	50.00	—
1911 Proof	6,007	Value: 55.00				
1912	10,984,000	4.00	10.00	25.00	75.00	—
1913	7,500,000	5.00	12.00	45.00	80.00	—
1914	22,715,000	2.00	8.00	18.00	40.00	—
1915	15,695,000	2.00	8.00	18.00	40.00	—
1916	22,207,000	2.00	8.00	18.00	40.00	—
1917	7,725,000	5.00	15.00	30.00	85.00	—
1918	27,559,000	2.00	8.00	18.00	40.00	—
1919	13,375,000	4.00	10.00	20.00	45.00	—
1920	14,136,000	4.00	10.00	25.00	60.00	—

KM# 815a.1 6 PENCE
2.8276 g., 0.5000 Silver 0.0455 oz. ASW, 19.5 mm.
Ruler: George V **Obv:** Head left **Rev:** Lion atop crown dividing date **Note:** Narrow rim.

Date	Mintage	F	VF	XF	Unc	BU
1920	Inc. above	2.00	4.00	18.00	55.00	—
1921	30,340,000	2.00	4.00	12.00	35.00	—
1922	16,879,000	2.00	5.00	15.00	38.00	—
1923	6,383,000	3.00	6.00	20.00	90.00	—
1924	17,444,000	2.00	4.00	12.00	35.00	—
1924 Satin specimen	2					1,800
1925	12,721,000	2.00	4.00	15.00	40.00	—

KM# 815a.2 6 PENCE
2.8276 g., 0.5000 Silver 0.0455 oz. ASW, 19.5 mm.
Ruler: George V **Obv:** Head left **Rev:** Lion atop crown dividing date **Note:** Wide rim.

Date	Mintage	F	VF	XF	Unc	BU
1925	Inc. above	2.00	4.00	18.00	40.00	—
1926	21,810,000	2.00	4.00	18.00	35.00	—

KM# 828 6 PENCE
2.8276 g., 0.5000 Silver 0.0455 oz. ASW, 19.5 mm. **Ruler:** George V **Obv:** Modified head left **Rev:** Lion atop crown divides date

Date	Mintage	F	VF	XF	Unc	BU
1926	Inc. above	BV	3.00	10.00	35.00	—
1927	8,925,000	2.00	4.00	15.00	40.00	—
1927 Proof	—	Value: 1,000				

KM# 832 6 PENCE
2.8276 g., 0.5000 Silver 0.0455 oz. ASW, 19.5 mm.
Ruler: George V **Obv:** Head left **Rev:** Six oak leaves and acorns divided **Note:** Varieties in edge milling exist.

Date	Mintage	F	VF	XF	Unc	BU
1927 Proof	15,000	Value: 35.00				
1927 Matte Proof; Rare	—	—	—	—	2,000	—

Note: There are reportedly 3-4 known of this variety, struck specifically for use in photographs

1928	23,123,000	BV	2.00	7.50	22.00	—
1928 Proof	—	Value: 600				
1929	28,319,000	BV	2.00	7.00	22.00	—
1929 Proof	—	Value: 600				
1930	16,990,000	BV	2.00	7.00	25.00	—
1930 Proof	—	Value: 600				
1931	16,873,000	2.00	3.00	8.00	30.00	—
1931 Proof	—	Value: 600				
1932	9,406,000	2.00	4.00	17.00	50.00	—
1932 Proof	—	Value: 650				
1933	22,185,000	2.00	3.00	8.00	25.00	—
1933 Proof	—	Value: 600				
1934	9,304,000	2.00	3.00	10.00	35.00	—
1934 Proof	—	Value: 600				
1935	13,996,000	BV	2.00	7.50	22.00	—
1935 Proof	—	Value: 600				
1936	24,380,000	BV	2.00	7.50	22.00	—
1936 Proof	—	Value: 600				

KM# 852 6 PENCE
2.8276 g., 0.5000 Silver 0.0455 oz. ASW, 19.5 mm. **Ruler:** George VI **Obv:** Head left **Rev:** Crowned monogram divides date

Date	Mintage	F	VF	XF	Unc	BU
1937	22,303,000	—	BV	1.50	10.00	—
1937 Proof	26,000	Value: 18.00				
1937 Matte Proof; Rare	—	—	—	—	—	—

Note: There are reportedly 3-4 known of this variety, struck specifically for use in photographs

1938	13,403,000	BV	1.25	7.00	23.00	—
1938 Proof	—	Value: 500				
1939	28,670,000	—	BV	3.00	15.00	—
1939 Proof	—	Value: 500				
1940	20,875,000	—	BV	3.00	15.00	—
1940 Proof	—	Value: 500				
1941	23,087,000	—	BV	3.00	10.00	—
1941 Proof	—	Value: 500				
1942	44,943,000	—	BV	1.50	10.00	—
1942 Proof	—	Value: 500				
1943	46,927,000	—	BV	1.50	10.00	—

Date	Mintage	F	VF	XF	Unc	BU
1943 Proof	—	Value: 500				
1944	36,953,000	—	BV	1.50	10.00	—
1944 Proof	—	Value: 500				
1945	39,939,000	—	BV	1.50	10.00	—
1945 Proof	—	Value: 650				
1946	43,466,000	—	BV	1.50	10.00	—
1946 Proof	—	Value: 650				

KM# 862 6 PENCE
Copper-Nickel, 19.5 mm. **Ruler:** George VI **Obv:** Head left **Rev:** Crowned monogram divides date

Date	Mintage	F	VF	XF	Unc	BU
1947	29,993,000	—	0.20	0.50	10.00	—
1947 Proof	—	Value: 500				
1948	88,324,000	—	0.20	1.50	7.50	—
1948 Proof	—	Value: 750				

KM# 875 6 PENCE
Copper-Nickel, 19.5 mm. **Ruler:** George VI **Obv:** Head left **Rev:** Crowned monogram divides date **Rev. Leg.:** without IND IMP

Date	Mintage	F	VF	XF	Unc	BU
1949	41,336,000	—	0.20	1.50	10.00	—
1949 Proof	—	Value: 600				
1950	32,741,999	—	0.20	1.50	10.00	—
1950 Proof	18,000	Value: 15.00				
1950 Matte Proof; Rare	—					

Note: There are reportedly 3-4 known of this variety, struck specifically for use in photographs

1951	40,399,000	—	0	3.50	19.00	—
1951 Proof	20,000	Value: 16.00				
1951 Matte Proof; Rare	—					

Note: There are reportedly 3-4 known of this variety, struck specifically for use in photographs

1952	1,012,999	1.25	7.50	30.00	75.00	—
1952 Proof	—	Value: 1,500				

KM# 889 6 PENCE
Copper-Nickel, 19.5 mm. **Ruler:** Elizabeth II **Obv:** Laureate bust right **Rev:** Flora; leek, rose, thistle and shamrock

Date	Mintage	F	VF	XF	Unc	BU
1953	70,324,000	—	0.15	0.50	4.00	—
1953 Proof	40,000	Value: 7.50				
1953 Matte Proof; Rare	—	—	—	—	—	—

Note: There are reportedly 3-4 known of this variety, struck specifically for use in photographs

KM# 903 6 PENCE
Copper-Nickel, 19.5 mm. **Ruler:** Elizabeth II **Obv:** Laureate bust right **Obv. Leg.:** Without BRITT OMN **Rev:** Flora; leek, rose, thistle and shamrock

Date	Mintage	F	VF	XF	Unc	BU
1954	105,241,000	—	0.15	0.50	6.00	—
1954 Proof	—	Value: 500				
1955	109,930,000	—	0.15	0.35	4.00	—
1955 Proof	—	Value: 500				
1956	109,842,000	—	0.15	0.35	4.00	—
1956 Proof	—	Value: 500				
1957	105,654,000	—	0.15	0.35	3.50	—
1957 Proof	—	Value: 500				
1958	123,519,000	—	0.15	0.35	3.00	—
1958 Proof	—	Value: 500				
1959	93,089,000	—	0.15	0.35	3.00	—
1959 Proof	—	Value: 500				
1960	103,283,000	—	0.15	0.35	3.00	—
1960 Proof	—	Value: 500				
1961	115,052,000	—	0.15	0.35	3.00	—

Date	Mintage	F	VF	XF	Unc	BU
1961 Proof	—	Value: 500				
1962	166,484,000	—	0.15	0.35	1.75	—
1962 Proof	—	Value: 500				
1963	120,056,000	—	0.15	0.30	1.50	—
1963 Proof	—	Value: 500				
1964	152,336,000	—	0.15	0.25	1.50	—
1964 Proof	—	Note: Reported, not confirmed				
1965	129,644,000	—	0.10	0.20	1.50	—
1965 Proof	—	Note: Reported, not confirmed				
1966	175,676,000	—	0.10	0.20	1.50	—
1966 Proof	—	Note: Reported, not confirmed				
1967 Proof	—	Note: Reported, not confirmed				
1967	240,788,000	—	0.10	0.20	1.50	—
1970 Proof	750,000	Value: 3.50				

KM# 780 SHILLING
5.6552 g., 0.9250 Silver 0.1682 oz. ASW, 23.5 mm.
Ruler: Victoria **Obv:** Mature draped bust left **Obv. Leg.:** VICTORIA • DEI • GRA • BRITT • REGINA • FID • DEF • IND • IMP • **Rev:** Crowned shields of England, Scotland and Ireland

Date	Mintage	F	VF	XF	Unc	BU
1901	3,426,000	4.00	10.00	55.00	75.00	—

KM# 800 SHILLING
5.6552 g., 0.9250 Silver 0.1682 oz. ASW, 23.5 mm. **Ruler:** Edward VII **Obv:** Head right **Rev:** Lion atop crown dividing date

Date	Mintage	F	VF	XF	Unc	BU
1902	7,890,000	5.00	15.00	50.00	80.00	—
1902 Matte Proof	15,000	Value: 90.00				
1903	2,061,999	10.00	25.00	140	550	—
1904	2,040,000	10.00	20.00	140	450	—
1905	488,000	100	300	1,500	6,000	—
1906	10,791,000	5.00	11.00	60.00	225	—
1907	14,083,000	5.00	11.00	90.00	250	—
1908	3,807,000	10.00	21.00	150	750	—
1909	5,665,000	10.00	21.00	175	700	—
1910	26,547,000	3.00	10.00	65.00	150	—

KM# 816 SHILLING
5.6552 g., 0.9250 Silver 0.1682 oz. ASW, 23.5 mm. **Ruler:** George V **Obv:** Head left **Rev:** Lion atop crown dividing date **Note:** Fully struck 1914-1918 pieces command a premium.

Date	Mintage	F	VF	XF	Unc	BU
1911	20,066,000	2.50	4.50	20.00	75.00	—
1911 Proof	6,007	Value: 90.00				
1912	15,594,000	3.00	6.00	30.00	120	—
1913	9,002,000	4.00	8.00	45.00	140	—
1914	23,416,000	2.50	4.00	25.00	45.00	—
1915	39,279,000	2.50	3.50	20.00	45.00	—
1916	35,862,000	2.50	3.50	20.00	40.00	—
1917	22,203,000	2.50	4.00	25.00	50.00	—
1918	34,916,000	2.50	3.50	20.00	40.00	—
1919	10,824,000	3.00	6.00	30.00	65.00	—

KM# 816a SHILLING
5.6552 g., 0.5000 Silver 0.0909 oz. ASW, 23.5 mm. **Ruler:** George V **Obv:** Head left **Rev:** Lion atop crown dividing date

Date	Mintage	F	VF	XF	Unc	BU
1920	22,825,000	2.00	4.00	27.00	50.00	—
1921	22,649,000	2.50	6.00	30.00	50.00	—
1922	27,216,000	2.00	4.00	27.00	60.00	—
1923	14,575,000	2.00	3.50	27.00	50.00	—
1924	2	—	—	—	—	2,500

Note: Satin specimen

1924	9,250,000	2.00	5.00	30.00	70.00	—
1925	5,419,000	4.00	8.00	45.00	125	—
1926	22,516,000	2.00	5.00	27.00	85.00	—

KM# 829 SHILLING
5.6552 g., 0.5000 Silver 0.0909 oz. ASW, 23.5 mm. **Ruler:** George V **Obv:** Modified head left **Rev:** Lion atop crown dividing date

Date	Mintage	F	VF	XF	Unc	BU
1926	Inc. above	1.50	3.50	27.00	50.00	—
1927	9,262,000	1.50	4.00	25.00	50.00	—

KM# 833 SHILLING
5.6552 g., 0.5000 Silver 0.0909 oz. ASW, 23.5 mm. **Ruler:** George V **Obv:** Head left **Rev:** Lion atop crown

Date	Mintage	F	VF	XF	Unc	BU
1927	Inc. above	1.50	3.00	15.00	50.00	—
1927 Proof	15,000	Value: 50.00				
1927 Matte Proof	—	Value: 3,000				

Note: There are reportedly 1-2 of this variety, struck specifically for use in photographs

Date	Mintage	F	VF	XF	Unc	BU
1928	18,137,000	BV	2.00	11.00	30.00	—
1928 Proof	—	Value: 1,000				
1929	19,343,000	BV	2.00	10.00	30.00	—
1929 Proof	—	Value: 1,000				
1930	3,137,000	2.50	6.00	25.00	75.00	—
1930 Proof	—	Value: 1,000				
1931	6,994,000	2.00	3.50	11.00	25.00	—
1931 Proof	—	Value: 1,000				
1932	12,168,000	2.00	3.50	11.00	25.00	—
1932 Proof	—	Value: 1,000				
1933	11,512,000	1.50	3.00	10.00	25.00	—
1933 Proof	—	Value: 1,000				
1934	6,138,000	2.00	5.50	18.00	65.00	—
1934 Proof	—	Value: 1,000				
1935	9,183,000	1.50	3.00	10.00	25.00	—
1935 Proof	—	Value: 1,000				
1936	11,911,000	1.50	2.50	8.00	25.00	—
1936 Proof	—	Value: 1,000				

KM# 853 SHILLING
5.6552 g., 0.5000 Silver 0.0909 oz. ASW, 23.5 mm. **Ruler:** George VI **Obv:** Head left **Rev:** Lion atop crown dividing date

Date	Mintage	F	VF	XF	Unc	BU
1937	8,359,000	—	BV	2.50	10.00	—
1937 Proof	26,000	Value: 15.00				
1937 Matte Proof	—	Value: 2,500				

Note: There are reportedly 1-2 known of this variety, struck specifically for use in photographs

Date	Mintage	F	VF	XF	Unc	BU
1938	4,833,000	—	BV	7.50	35.00	—
1938 Proof	—	Value: 850				
1939	11,053,000	—	BV	3.00	17.50	—
1939 Proof	—	Value: 800				
1940	11,099,000	—	BV	2.50	13.00	—
1940 Proof	—	Value: 800				
1941	11,392,000	—	BV	2.00	13.00	—
1941 Proof	—	Value: 800				
1942	17,454,000	—	BV	2.00	13.00	—
1942 Proof	—	Value: 800				
1943	11,404,000	—	BV	2.00	13.00	—
1943 Proof	—	Value: 800				
1944	11,587,000	—	BV	2.00	13.00	—
1944 Proof	—	Value: 850				
1945	15,143,000	—	BV	1.50	10.00	—
1945 Proof	—	Value: 1,000				
1946	18,664,000	—	BV	1.50	6.00	—
1946 Proof	—	Value: 1,000				

KM# 854 SHILLING
5.6552 g., 0.5000 Silver 0.0909 oz. ASW, 23.5 mm. **Ruler:** George VI **Obv:** Head left **Rev:** Scottish crest; lion seated atop crown holding sword and scepter divides date, shields flank

Date	Mintage	F	VF	XF	Unc	BU
1937	6,749,000	—	BV	1.75	10.00	—
1937 Proof	26,000	Value: 15.00				
1937 Matte Proof	—	Value: 2,500				

Note: There are reportedly 1-2 known of this variety, struck specifically for use in photographs

Date	Mintage	F	VF	XF	Unc	BU
1938	4,798,000	—	BV	6.00	35.00	—
1938 Proof	—	Value: 850				
1939	10,264,000	—	BV	3.00	17.00	—
1939 Proof	—	Value: 800				
1940	9,913,000	—	BV	2.50	13.00	—
1940 Proof	—	Value: 800				
1941	8,086,000	—	BV	2.00	13.00	—
1941 Proof	—	Value: 800				
1942	13,677,000	—	BV	2.00	13.00	—
1942 Proof	—	Value: 800				
1943	9,824,000	—	BV	2.00	13.00	—
1943 Proof	—	Value: 800				
1944	10,990,000	—	BV	2.00	13.00	—
1944 Proof	—	Value: 850				
1945	15,106,000	—	BV	1.50	10.00	—
1945 Proof	—	Value: 1,000				
1946	16,382,000	—	BV	1.50	10.00	—
1946 Proof	—	Value: 1,000				

KM# 863 SHILLING
Copper-Nickel, 23.5 mm. **Ruler:** George VI **Obv:** Head left **Rev:** English crest; lion atop crown dividing date

Date	Mintage	F	VF	XF	Unc	BU
1947	12,121,000	0.10	0.25	1.00	10.00	—
1947 Proof	—	Value: 750				
1948	45,577,000	0.10	0.20	1.00	10.00	—
1948 Proof	—	Value: 1,000				

KM# 864 SHILLING
Copper-Nickel, 23.5 mm. **Ruler:** George VI **Obv:** Head left **Rev:** Scottish crest; lion seated atop crown holding sword and scepter divides date, shields flank

Date	Mintage	F	VF	XF	Unc	BU
1947	12,283,000	0.10	0.25	1.00	10.00	—
1947 Proof	—	Value: 750				
1948	45,352,000	0.10	0.20	1.00	10.00	—
1948 Proof	—	Value: 1,000				

KM# 876 SHILLING
Copper-Nickel, 23.5 mm. **Ruler:** George VI **Obv:** Head left **Rev:** English crest; lion atop crown dividing date

Date	Mintage	F	VF	XF	Unc	BU
1949	19,328,000	0.10	0.25	1.50	22.00	—
1949 Proof	—	Value: 850				
1950	19,244,000	0.10	0.25	1.50	22.00	—
1950 Proof	18,000	Value: 22.00				
1950 Matte Proof	—	Value: 1,800				

Note: There are reportedly 1-2 known of this variety, struck specifically for use in photographs

Date	Mintage	F	VF	XF	Unc	BU
1951	9,957,000	0.10	0.25	3.50	24.00	—
1951 Proof	20,000	Value: 22.00				
1951 Matte Proof	—	Value: 1,800				

Note: There are reportedly 1-2 known of this variety, struck specifically for use in photographs

Date	Mintage	F	VF	XF	Unc	BU
1952 Proof; Rare	—	—	—	—	—	—

Note: There are reportedly 1-2 known of this variety.

KM# 877 SHILLING
Copper-Nickel, 23.5 mm. **Ruler:** George VI **Obv:** Head left **Rev:** Scottish crest; lion seated atop crown holding sword and scepter divides date, shields flank

Date	Mintage	F	VF	XF	Unc	BU
1949	21,243,000	0.10	0.25	1.50	22.00	—
1949 Proof	—	Value: 850				
1950	14,300,000	0.10	0.25	1.50	22.00	—
1950 Proof	18,000	Value: 22.00				
1950 Matte Proof	—	Value: 1,800				

Note: There are reportedly 1-2 known of this variety, struck specifically for use in photographs

Date	Mintage	F	VF	XF	Unc	BU
1951	10,961,000	0.10	0.25	3.50	24.00	—
1951 Proof	20,000	Value: 22.00				
1951 Matte Proof	—	Value: 1,600				

Note: There are reportedly 1-2 known of this variety, struck specifically for use in photographs

KM# 890 SHILLING
Copper-Nickel, 23.5 mm. **Ruler:** Elizabeth II **Obv:** Laureate bust right **Rev:** Crowned English shield divides date

Date	Mintage	F	VF	XF	Unc	BU
1953	41,943,000	—	0.15	0.50	7.00	—
1953 Proof	40,000	Value: 14.00				
1953 Matte Proof	—	Value: 1,800				

Note: There are reportedly 1-2 known of this variety, struck specifically for use in photographs

KM# 891 SHILLING
Copper-Nickel, 23.5 mm. **Ruler:** Elizabeth II **Obv:** Laureate bust right **Rev:** Crowned Scottish shield divides date

Date	Mintage	F	VF	XF	Unc	BU
1953	20,664,000	—	0.15	0.50	7.50	—
1953 Proof	40,000	Value: 14.00				
1953 Matte Proof	—	Value: 1,800				

Note: There are reportedly 1-2 known of this variety, struck specifically for use in photographs

KM# 904 SHILLING
Copper-Nickel, 23.5 mm. **Ruler:** Elizabeth II **Obv:** Laureate bust right **Obv. Leg.:** without BRITT OMN **Rev:** Crowned English shield divides date

Date	Mintage	F	VF	XF	Unc	BU
1954	30,162,000	—	0.15	0.50	6.50	—
1954 Proof	—	Value: 650				
1955	45,260,000	—	0.15	0.50	6.50	—
1955 Proof	—	Value: 650				
1956	44,970,000	—	0.15	0.50	10.00	—
1956 Proof	—	Value: 650				
1957	42,774,000	—	0.15	0.50	6.00	—
1957 Proof	—	Value: 650				
1958	14,392,000	0.25	0.50	3.00	30.00	—
1958 Proof	—	Value: 700				
1959	19,443,000	—	0.15	0.40	6.00	—
1959 Proof	—	Value: 650				
1960	27,028,000	—	0.15	0.35	4.00	—
1960 Proof	—	Value: 650				
1961	39,817,000	—	0.15	0.35	2.50	—

Date	Mintage	F	VF	XF	Unc	BU
1961 Proof	—	Value: 650				
1962	36,704,000	—	0.15	0.25	1.75	—
1962 Proof	—	Value: 650				
1963	49,434,000	—	—	0.25	1.25	—
1963 Proof	—	Value: 650				
1964	8,591,000	—	—	0.25	1.25	—
1964 Proof	—	—	—	—	—	—
Note: Reported, not confirmed						
1965	9,216,000	—	—	0.25	1.25	—
1965 Proof	—	—	—	—	—	—
Note: Reported, not confirmed						
1966	15,002,000	—	—	0.25	1.25	—
1966 Proof	—	—	—	—	—	—
Note: Reported, not confirmed						
1970 Proof	750,000	Value: 5.00				

KM# 905 SHILLING

5.6000 g., Copper-Nickel, 23.5 mm. **Ruler:** Elizabeth II
Obv: Laureate bust right **Rev:** Crowned Scottish shield divides date

Date	Mintage	F	VF	XF	Unc	BU
1954	26,772,000	—	0.15	0.25	6.50	—
1954 Proof	—	Value: 650				
1954 Matte Proof; Rare	Est. 2	—	—	—	—	—
1955	27,951,000	—	0.15	0.35	8.00	—
1955 Proof	—	Value: 650				
1956	42,854,000	—	0.15	1.00	12.00	—
1956 Proof	—	Value: 650				
1957	17,960,000	—	0.25	3.50	30.00	—
1957 Proof	—	Value: 700				
1958	40,823,000	—	0.15	0.50	6.00	—
1958 Proof	—	Value: 650				
1959	1,012,999	0.50	1.00	3.50	35.00	—
1959 Proof	—	Value: 700				
1960	14,376,000	—	0.15	0.50	5.00	—
1960 Proof	—	Value: 650				
1961	2,763,000	—	0.20	1.00	14.00	—
1961 Proof	—	Value: 650				
1962	17,475,000	—	0.15	0.25	3.50	—
1962 Proof	—	Value: 650				
1963	32,299,999	—	0.15	0.25	1.25	—
1963 Proof	—	Value: 650				
1964	5,239,000	—	0.15	0.25	2.00	—
1964 Proof	—	—	—	—	—	—
Note: Reported, not confirmed						
1965	2,774,000	—	0.15	0.25	1.75	—
1965 Proof	—	—	—	—	—	—
Note: Reported, not confirmed						
1966	15,604,000	—	0.15	0.25	1.25	—
1966 Proof	—	—	—	—	—	—
Note: Reported, not confirmed						
1970 Proof	750,000	Value: 3.00				

KM# 781 FLORIN (Two Shillings)

11.3104 g., 0.9250 Silver 0.3364 oz. ASW, 28.3 mm.
Ruler: Victoria **Obv:** Mature draped bust left **Obv. Leg.:** VICTORIA • DEI • GRA • BRITT • REGINA • FID • DEF • IND • IMP • **Rev:** Crowned shields of England, Scotland and Ireland

Date	Mintage	F	VF	XF	Unc	BU
1901	2,649,000	6.00	12.00	60.00	125	—

KM# 801 FLORIN (Two Shillings)

11.3104 g., 0.9250 Silver 0.3364 oz. ASW, 28.3 mm.
Ruler: Edward VII **Obv:** Head right **Rev:** Britannia standing looking right

Date	Mintage	F	VF	XF	Unc	BU
1902	2,190,000	8.00	20.00	60.00	120	—
1902 Matte Proof	15,000	Value: 120				
1903	995,000	18.00	40.00	125	425	—
1904	2,770,000	18.00	40.00	175	475	—
1905	1,188,000	100	225	750	1,500	—
1906	6,910,000	10.00	25.00	100	425	—
1907	5,948,000	10.00	30.00	125	450	—
1908	3,280,000	18.00	50.00	225	650	—
1909	3,483,000	18.00	50.00	225	650	—
1910	5,651,000	10.00	20.00	90.00	300	—

KM# 817 FLORIN (Two Shillings)

11.3104 g., 0.9250 Silver 0.3364 oz. ASW, 28.3 mm.
Ruler: George V **Obv:** Head left **Rev:** Cross of crowned shield, sceptres in angles **Note:** Fully struck examples are scarce

Date	Mintage	F	VF	XF	Unc	BU
1911	5,951,000	5.00	10.00	40.00	100	—
1911 Proof	6,007	Value: 110				
1912	8,572,000	5.00	12.00	55.00	110	—
1913	4,545,000	6.50	15.00	75.00	150	—
1914	21,253,000	BV	6.00	35.00	60.00	—
1915	12,358,000	4.75	8.00	45.00	110	—
1916	21,064,000	BV	6.00	28.00	70.00	—
1917	11,182,000	4.75	7.00	30.00	85.00	—
1918	29,212,000	BV	6.00	28.00	65.00	—
1919	9,469,000	5.00	12.00	30.00	100	—

KM# 817a FLORIN (Two Shillings)

11.3104 g., 0.5000 Silver 0.1818 oz. ASW, 28.3 mm.
Ruler: George V **Obv:** Head left **Rev:** Cross of crowned shields, sceptres in angles

Date	Mintage	F	VF	XF	Unc	BU
1920	15,388,000	2.75	6.00	35.00	110	—
1921	34,864,000	2.75	5.50	30.00	100	—
1922	23,861,000	2.65	4.50	28.00	55.00	—
1923	21,547,000	2.50	4.00	23.00	45.00	—
1924	4,582,000	3.50	7.00	45.00	100	—
1924 Satin specimen	2	—	—	—	—	2,500
1925	1,404,000	25.00	50.00	175	425	—
1926	5,125,000	3.00	8.50	40.00	110	—

KM# 834 FLORIN (Two Shillings)

11.3104 g., 0.5000 Silver 0.1818 oz. ASW, 28.3 mm.
Ruler: George V **Obv:** Head left **Rev:** Cross of crowned sceptres, shields in angles

Date	Mintage	F	VF	XF	Unc	BU
1927 Proof	15,000	Value: 75.00				
1927 Matte Proof	—	Value: 3,500				
Note: There are reportedly 3-4 known of this variety, struck specifically for use in photographs						
1928	11,088,000	BV	3.00	11.50	25.00	—
1928 Proof	—	Value: 900				
1929	16,397,000	BV	3.00	11.50	25.00	—
1929 Proof	—	Value: 950				
1930	5,734,000	BV	5.00	12.50	37.50	—
1930 Proof	—	Value: 1,350				
1931	6,556,000	BV	5.00	11.50	45.00	—
1931 Proof	—	Value: 900				
1932	717,000	20.00	85.00	225	700	—
1932 Proof	—	Value: 2,500				
1933	8,685,000	BV	3.00	11.50	30.00	—
1933 Proof	—	Value: 900				
1935	7,541,000	BV	3.00	11.50	25.00	—
1935 Proof	—	Value: 900				
1936	9,897,000	BV	2.75	11.50	25.00	—
1936 Proof	—	Value: 900				

KM# 855 FLORIN (Two Shillings)

11.3104 g., 0.5000 Silver 0.1818 oz. ASW, 28.3 mm.
Ruler: George VI **Obv:** Head left **Rev:** Crowned tudor rose, thistle, letter 'G', and shamrock, letter 'R' flanking

Date	Mintage	F	VF	XF	Unc	BU
1937	13,007,000	—	BV	3.00	13.00	—
1937 Proof	26,000	Value: 18.00				
1937 Matte Proof; Rare	—	—	—	—	—	—
Note: There are reportedly 1-2 known of this variety, struck specifically for use in photographs						
1938	7,909,000	BV	2.75	10.00	30.00	—
1938 Proof	—	Value: 850				
1939	20,851,000	—	BV	4.50	18.00	—
1939 Proof	—	Value: 800				
1940	18,700,000	—	BV	4.50	12.00	—
1940 Proof	—	Value: 800				
1941	24,451,000	—	BV	4.50	12.00	—
1941 Proof	—	Value: 800				
1942	39,895,000	—	BV	3.00	10.00	—
1942 Proof	—	Value: 750				
1943	26,712,000	—	BV	3.00	10.00	—
1943 Proof	—	Value: 500				
1944	27,560,000	—	BV	3.00	10.00	—

Date	Mintage	F	VF	XF	Unc	BU
1944 Proof	—	Value: 600				
1945	25,858,000	—	BV	3.00	10.00	—
1945 Proof	—	Value: 1,000				
1946	22,300,000	—	BV	3.00	10.00	—
1946 Proof	—	Value: 1,000				

KM# 865 FLORIN (Two Shillings)

Copper-Nickel, 28.3 mm. **Ruler:** George VI **Obv:** Head left **Rev:** Crowned tudor rose, thistle, letter 'G', and shamrock, letter 'R' flanking

Date	Mintage	F	VF	XF	Unc	BU
1947	22,910,000	0.20	0.35	1.00	10.00	—
1947 Proof	—	Value: 700				
1948	67,554,000	0.20	0.35	1.00	10.00	—
1948 Proof	—	Value: 850				

KM# 878 FLORIN (Two Shillings)

Copper-Nickel, 28.3 mm. **Ruler:** George VI **Obv:** Head left **Obv. Leg.:** without IND IMP **Rev:** Crowned tudor rose, thistle, letter 'G', and shamrock, letter 'R' flanking

Date	Mintage	F	VF	XF	Unc	BU
1949	28,615,000	0.20	0.35	1.00	18.00	—
1949 Proof	—	Value: 800				
1950	24,357,000	0.20	0.35	1.00	20.00	—
1950 Proof	18,000	Value: 25.00				
1950 Matte Proof; Rare	—	—	—	—	—	—
Note: There are reportedly 1-2 known of this variety, struck specifically for use in photographs						
1951	27,412,000	0.20	0.75	4.00	25.00	—
1951 Proof	20,000	Value: 30.00				
1951 Matte Proof; Rare	—	—	—	—	—	—
Note: There are reportedly 1-2 known of this variety, struck specifically for use in photographs						

KM# 892 FLORIN (Two Shillings)

Copper-Nickel, 28.3 mm. **Ruler:** Elizabeth II **Obv:** Laureate bust right **Rev:** Tudor rose at center, thistle and shamrock wreath surround

Date	Mintage	F	VF	XF	Unc	BU
1953	11,959,000	0.25	0.50	1.00	8.00	—
1953 Proof	40,000	Value: 15.00				
1953 Matte Proof; Rare	—	—	—	—	—	—
Note: There are reportedly 1-2 known of this variety, struck specifically for use in photographs						

KM# 906 FLORIN (Two Shillings)

Copper-Nickel, 28.3 mm. **Ruler:** Elizabeth II **Obv:** Laureate bust right **Obv. Leg.:** without BRITT OMN **Rev:** Tudor rose at center, thistle and shamrock wreath surround

Date	Mintage	F	VF	XF	Unc	BU
1954	13,085,000	0.20	0.50	5.50	65.00	—
1954 Proof	—	Value: 600				
1955	25,887,000	0.20	0.50	2.00	6.00	—
1955 Proof	—	Value: 600				
1956	47,824,000	0.20	0.30	1.00	6.00	—
1956 Proof	—	Value: 600				
1957	33,070,999	0.20	0.40	5.00	65.00	—
1957 Proof	—	Value: 700				
1958	9,565,000	0.25	1.25	5.00	30.00	—
1958 Proof	—	Value: 700				
1959	14,080,000	0.25	0.50	9.00	40.00	—
1959 Proof	—	Value: 650				
1960	13,832,000	—	0.20	1.25	6.00	—
1960 Proof	—	Value: 600				
1961	37,735,000	—	0.20	1.00	5.00	—
1961 Proof	—	Value: 600				
1962	35,148,000	—	0.20	0.75	5.00	—
1962 Proof	—	Value: 600				
1963	26,471,000	—	0.20	0.75	5.00	—
1963 Proof	—	Value: 600				
1964	16,539,000	—	0.20	0.50	5.00	—
1965	48,163,000	—	0.20	0.50	4.50	—
1966	83,999,000	—	0.20	0.30	2.50	—
1967	39,718,000	—	0.20	0.30	2.00	—
1970 Proof	750,000	Value: 6.50				

KM# 782   1/2 CROWN
14.1380 g., 0.9250 Silver 0.4204 oz. ASW, 32.3 mm.
Ruler: Victoria **Obv:** Mature draped bust left **Rev:** Crowned and quartered spade shield within wreath **Rev. Leg.:** FID • DEF • IND • IMP • around top, HALF date CROWN below

Date	Mintage	F	VF	XF	Unc	BU
1901	1,577,000	16.00	27.00	65.00	150	—

KM# 802   1/2 CROWN
14.1380 g., 0.9250 Silver 0.4204 oz. ASW, 32.3 mm.
Ruler: Edward VII **Obv:** Head right **Rev:** Crowned and quartered shield within Garter band **Note:** Particular attention should be given to quality of detail in hair and beard on obverse.

Date	Mintage	F	VF	XF	Unc	BU
1902	1,316,000	15.00	40.00	70.00	225	—
1902 Matte Proof	15,000	Value: 185				
1903	275,000	100	275	850	3,500	—
1904	710,000	50.00	200	700	2,000	—
1905	166,000	250	800	4,000	10,500	—
1906	2,886,000	20.00	45.00	200	750	—
1907	3,694,000	20.00	45.00	200	800	—
1908	1,759,000	25.00	50.00	500	1,250	—
1909	3,052,000	20.00	45.00	400	1,000	—
1910	2,558,000	15.00	35.00	175	650	—

KM# 818.1   1/2 CROWN
14.1380 g., 0.9250 Silver 0.4204 oz. ASW, 32.3 mm.
Ruler: George V **Obv:** Head left **Rev:** Crowned and quartered shield within Garter band **Note:** Fully struck World War I (1914-1918) specimens command a premium.

Date	Mintage	F	VF	XF	Unc	BU
1911	2,915,000	8.00	18.00	60.00	135	—
1911 Proof	6,007	Value: 150				
1912	4,701,000	9.00	25.00	65.00	240	—
1913	4,090,000	10.00	30.00	75.00	240	—
1914	18,333,000	BV	10.00	28.00	100	—
1915	32,433,000	BV	10.00	28.00	95.00	—
1916	29,530,000	BV	10.00	28.00	95.00	—
1917	11,172,000	8.00	15.00	45.00	95.00	—
1918	29,080,000	BV	10.00	28.00	65.00	—
1919	10,267,000	8.00	15.00	45.00	85.00	—

KM# 818.1a   1/2 CROWN
14.1380 g., 0.5000 Silver 0.2273 oz. ASW, 32.3 mm. **Ruler:** George V **Obv:** Head left **Rev:** Crowned shield within Garter rose, crown touches shield **Note:** Fully struck coins command a premium.

Date	Mintage	F	VF	XF	Unc	BU
1920	17,983,000	5.00	8.00	25.00	75.00	—
1921	23,678,000	6.00	10.00	30.00	85.00	—
1922	16,396,999	5.50	8.00	35.00	100	—

KM# 818.2   1/2 CROWN
14.1380 g., 0.5000 Silver 0.2273 oz. ASW, 32.3 mm.
Ruler: George V **Obv:** Head left **Rev:** Crowned shield within Garter band, groove between crown and shield **Note:** Fully struck coins command a premium.

Date	Mintage	F	VF	XF	Unc	BU
1922	Inc. above	5.00	8.00	25.00	100	—
1923	26,309,000	BV	6.00	15.00	50.00	—
1924	5,866,000	6.00	10.00	35.00	100	—
1924 Satin specimen	Est. 2	—	—	—	—	3,500
1925	1,413,000	23.00	50.00	300	600	—
1926	4,474,000	6.00	10.00	35.00	150	—

KM# 830   1/2 CROWN
14.1380 g., 0.5000 Silver 0.2273 oz. ASW, 32.3 mm.
Ruler: Modified head left, larger beads
Rev: Crowned shield within Garter band

Date	Mintage	F	VF	XF	Unc	BU
1926	Inc. above	6.00	10.00	45.00	125	—
1927	6,838,000	5.00	7.00	28.00	70.00	—

KM# 835   1/2 CROWN
14.1380 g., 0.5000 Silver 0.2273 oz. ASW, 32.3 mm.
Ruler: George V **Obv:** Head left **Rev:** Quartered shield flanked by crowned monograms

Date	Mintage	F	VF	XF	Unc	BU
1927 Proof	15,000	Value: 60.00				
1927 Matte Proof; Rare	—	—	—	—	—	—
		Note: There are reportedly 1-2 known of this variety, struck specifically for use in photographs				
1928	18,763,000	BV	5.00	11.00	35.00	—
1928 Proof	—	Value: 1,250				
1929	17,633,000	BV	5.00	11.00	35.00	—
1929 Proof	—	Value: 1,250				
1930	810,000	10.00	45.00	175	550	—
1930 Proof	—	Value: 1,500				
1931	11,264,000	BV	5.00	11.00	35.00	—
1931 Proof	—	Value: 1,250				
1932	4,794,000	4.00	8.00	17.50	75.00	—
1932 Proof	—	Value: 1,350				
1933	10,311,000	BV	5.00	11.00	35.00	—
1933 Proof	—	Value: 2,150				
1934	2,422,000	4.50	10.00	25.00	100	—
1934 Proof	—	Value: 1,350				
1935	7,022,000	BV	5.00	11.00	28.00	—
1935 Proof	—	Value: 1,200				
1936	7,039,000	BV	4.00	9.00	25.00	—
1936 Proof	—	Value: 1,200				

KM# 856   1/2 CROWN
14.1380 g., 0.5000 Silver 0.2273 oz. ASW, 32.3 mm.
Ruler: George VI **Obv:** Head left **Rev:** Quartered shield flanked by crowned monograms

Date	Mintage	F	VF	XF	Unc	BU
1937	9,106,000	—	BV	5.00	19.00	—
1937 Proof	26,000	Value: 2,500				
1937 Matte Proof; Rare	—	—	—	—	—	—
		Note: There are reportedly 1-2 known of this variety, struck specifically for use in photographs				
1938	6,426,000	—	BV	10.00	35.00	—
1938 Proof	—	Value: 1,250				
1939	15,479,000	—	BV	5.50	19.00	—
1939 Proof	—	Value: 1,000				
1940	17,948,000	—	BV	5.50	19.00	—
1940 Proof	—	Value: 1,000				
1941	15,774,000	—	BV	5.50	19.00	—
1941 Proof	—	Value: 1,000				
1942	31,220,000	—	BV	4.50	10.00	—
1942 Proof	—	Value: 1,000				
1943	15,463,000	—	BV	4.50	19.00	—
1943 Proof	—	Value: 850				
1944	15,255,000	—	BV	4.50	10.00	—
1944 Proof	—	Value: 900				
1945	19,849,000	—	BV	4.50	10.00	—
1945 Proof	—	Value: 1,000				
1946	22,725,000	—	BV	4.50	10.00	—
1946 Proof	—	Value: 1,000				

KM# 866   1/2 CROWN
Copper-Nickel, 32.3 mm. **Ruler:** George VI **Obv:** Head left **Rev:** Quartered shield flanked by crowned monograms

Date	Mintage	F	VF	XF	Unc	BU
1947	21,910,000	0.25	0.50	1.00	10.00	—
1947 Proof	—	Value: 900				
1948	71,165,000	0.25	0.50	1.00	10.00	—
1948 Proof	—	Value: 1,350				

KM# 879   1/2 CROWN
Copper-Nickel, 32.3 mm. **Ruler:** George VI **Obv:** Head left **Rev:** Quartered shield flanked by crowned monograms
Rev. Leg.: without IND IMP

Date	Mintage	F	VF	XF	Unc	BU
1949	28,273,000	0.25	0.50	1.25	16.00	—
1949 Proof	—	Value: 1,200				
1950	28,336,000	0.25	0.50	3.00	22.50	—
1950 Proof	18,000	Value: 25.00				
1950 Matte Proof; Rare	—	—	—	—	—	—
		Note: There are reportedly 1-2 known of this variety, struck specifically for use in photographs				
1951	9,004,000	0.50	0.75	1.50	35.00	—
1951 Proof	20,000	Value: 30.00				
1951 Matte Proof; Rare	—	—	—	—	—	—
		Note: There are reportedly 1-2 known of this variety, struck specifically for use in photographs				
1952	Est. 1	—	—	—	80,000	—
1952 Proof	Est. 1	Value: 100,000				

KM# 893   1/2 CROWN
Copper-Nickel, 32.3 mm. **Ruler:** Elizabeth II **Obv:** Laureate bust right **Rev:** Crowned quartered shield flanked by initials, 'ER'

Date	Mintage	F	VF	XF	Unc	BU
1953	4,333,000	0.50	0.75	1.75	10.50	—
1953 Proof	40,000	Value: 15.00				
1953 Matte Proof; Rare	—	—	—	—	—	—
		Note: There are reportedly 1-2 known of this variety, struck specifically for use in photographs				

KM# 907   1/2 CROWN
14.0000 g., Copper-Nickel, 32.3 mm. **Ruler:** Elizabeth II **Obv:** Laureate bust right **Obv. Leg.:** with BRITT OMN **Rev:** Crowned quartered shield flanked by initials, 'ER'

Date	Mintage	F	VF	XF	Unc	BU
1954	11,615,000	0.50	0.75	4.00	50.00	—
1954 Proof	—	Value: 850				
1955	23,629,000	0.25	0.50	1.00	10.00	—

Date	Mintage	F	VF	XF	Unc	BU
1955 Proof	—	Value: 800				
1956	33,935,000	0.25	0.50	0.75	13.00	—
1956 Proof	—	Value: 800				
1957	34,201,000	0.25	0.50	0.75	8.50	—
1957 Proof	—	Value: 800				
1958	15,746,000	0.25	0.75	3.50	30.00	—
1958 Proof	—	Value: 900				
1959	9,029,000	0.75	1.25	6.00	60.00	—
1959 Proof	—	Value: 900				
1960	19,929,000	0.25	0.50	0.75	7.00	—
1960 Proof	—	Value: 800				
1961	25,888,000	0.25	0.50	0.75	5.00	—
1961 Prooflike	—	—	—	—	15.00	—
1961 Proof	—	Value: 900				
1962	24,013,000	0.25	0.50	0.75	5.00	—
1962 Proof	—	—				
1963	17,625,000	0.25	0.50	0.75	5.00	—
1963 Proof	—	—				
1964	5,974,000	0.25	0.50	0.75	6.00	—
1965	9,778,000	0.20	0.30	0.50	5.00	—
1966	13,375,000	0.20	0.30	0.50	1.50	—
1967	33,058,000	0.20	0.30	0.50	1.50	—
1970 Proof	750,000	Value: 6.50				

KM# 803 CROWN
28.2759 g., 0.9250 Silver 0.8409 oz. ASW, 38.61 mm. **Ruler:** Edward VII **Obv:** Head right **Rev:** St. George slaying the dragon

Date	Mintage	F	VF	XF	Unc	BU
1902	256,000	50.00	75.00	125	250	—
1902 Matte Proof	15,000	Value: 250				

KM# 836 CROWN
28.2759 g., 0.5000 Silver 0.4545 oz. ASW, 38.61 mm. **Ruler:** George V **Obv:** Head left **Rev:** Date divided above crown within wreath

Date	Mintage	F	VF	XF	Unc	BU
1927 Proof	15,000	Value: 275				
1927 Matte Proof; Rare	—	Value: 12,500				

Note: There are reportedly 1-2 known of this variety, struck specifically for use in photographs

1928	9,034	100	150	225	450	—
1928 Proof	—	Value: 2,800				
1929	4,994	100	160	250	475	—
1929 Proof	—	Value: 2,800				
1930	4,847	100	160	250	475	—
1930 Proof	—	Value: 2,800				
1931	4,056	110	170	280	500	—
1931 Proof	—	Value: 2,800				
1932	2,395	180	275	450	1,100	—
1932 Proof	—	Value: 3,500				
1933	7,132	100	150	225	475	—
1933 Proof	—	Value: 2,500				
1934	932	1,650	2,400	4,000	8,500	—
1934 Proof	—	Value: 10,000				
1936	2,473	180	275	450	1,100	—
1936 Proof	—	Value: 4,000				

KM# 842 CROWN
28.2759 g., 0.5000 Silver 0.4545 oz. ASW, 38.61 mm. **Ruler:** George V **Subject:** Silver Jubilee **Obv:** Head left **Rev:** St. George slaying the dragon

Date	Mintage	F	VF	XF	Unc	BU
1935	715,000	10.00	15.00	20.00	60.00	—

Note: Incused edge lettering

| 1935 Proof | — | Value: 550 | | | | |

Note: Raised edge lettering

| 1935 | — | — | — | — | 125 | |

Note: Specimen in box of issue

| 1935 | Inc. above | — | 250 | 500 | 1,000 | |

Note: (Error) Edge lettering: MEN.ANNO-REGNIXXV

KM# 842a CROWN
0.9250 Silver, 38.61 mm. **Ruler:** George V **Subject:** Silver Jubilee **Obv:** Head left **Rev:** St. George slaying the dragon

Date	Mintage	F	VF	XF	Unc	BU
1935	2,500	Value: 2,500				

Note: Raised edge lettering

| 1935 Proof | — | Value: 1,750 | | | | |

Note: (Error) Edge lettering: DECUS ANNO REGNI TUTA-MEN•XXV•

KM# 842b CROWN
47.8300 g., 0.9170 Gold 1.4101 oz. AGW, 38.61 mm. **Ruler:** George V **Subject:** Silver Jubilee **Obv:** Head left **Rev:** St. George slaying the dragon

Date	Mintage	F	VF	XF	Unc	BU
1935 Proof	28	Value: 25,000				

KM# 857 CROWN
0.5000 Silver, 38.61 mm. **Ruler:** George VI **Obv:** Head left **Rev:** Crowned, quartered shield with supporters

Date	Mintage	F	VF	XF	Unc	BU
1937	419,000	8.00	12.00	25.00	50.00	—
1937 Proof	26,000	Value: 60.00				

Date	Mintage	F	VF	XF	Unc	BU
1937 Proof, VIP accentuated device cameo	—	Value: 1,100				

Note: Frosted cameo relief; V.I.P. issue

| 1937 Matte Proof; Rare | | | | | | |

Note: 1-2 pieces known

KM# 880 CROWN
Copper-Nickel, 38.61 mm. **Ruler:** George VI **Subject:** Festival of Britain **Obv:** Head left **Rev:** St. George slaying the dragon

Date	Mintage	F	VF	XF	Unc	BU
1951 Prooflike	2,004,000	—	—	—	22.50	—
1951 Proof	—	Value: 25.00				
1951 Proof	—	Value: 800				

Note: Frosted cameo relief; V.I.P. issue; 30-50 pieces known

| 1951 Matte Proof | — | Value: 3,500 | | | | |

Note: 1-2 pieces known

KM# 894 CROWN
Copper-Nickel, 38.61 mm. **Ruler:** Elizabeth II **Subject:** Coronation of Queen Elizabeth II **Obv:** Queen on horseback left, crowned monograms flank **Rev:** Crown at center of cross formed by rose, shamrock, leek and thistle, shields in angles **Edge:** FAITH AND TRUTH I WILL BEAR UNTO YOU

Date	Mintage	F	VF	XF	Unc	BU
1953	5,963,000	—	—	7.50	15.00	—
1953 Proof	40,000	Value: 45.00				
1953 Proof	—	Value: 800				

Note: 20-30 pieces; V.I.P. issue

| 1953 Matte Proof | — | Value: 3,500 | | | | |

Note: 1-2 pieces

KM# 909 CROWN
Copper-Nickel, 38.61 mm. **Ruler:** Elizabeth II **Subject:** British Exhibition in New York **Obv:** Laureate bust right **Rev:** Crown at center of cross formed by rose, shamrock, leek and thistle, shields in angles

Date	Mintage	F	VF	XF	Unc	BU
1960	1,024,000	—	—	6.00	12.00	—
1960 Prooflike	70,000	—	—	—	35.00	—
1960 Proof	—	Value: 750				

Note: V.I.P. issue; 30-50 pieces

KM# 910   CROWN
Copper-Nickel, 38.61 mm.   **Ruler:** Elizabeth II **Obv:** Laureate bust right **Rev:** Sir. Winston Churchill head right **Rev. Leg.:** CHURCHILL

Date	Mintage	F	VF	XF	Unc	BU
1965	9,640,000	—	—	0.65	2.00	—
1965 Specimen	—	—	—	—	2,000	—
Note: Satin finish						

DECIMAL COINAGE

1971-1981, 100 New Pence = 1 Pound;
1982, 100 Pence = 1 Pound

KM# 914   1/2 NEW PENNY
1.7820 g., Bronze, 17.14 mm.   **Ruler:** Elizabeth II **Obv:** Young bust right **Rev:** Crown

Date	Mintage	F	VF	XF	Unc	BU
1971	1,394,188,000	—	—	0.10	0.20	—
1971 Proof	350,000	Value: 1.00				
1972 Proof	150,000	Value: 3.00				
1973	365,680,000	—	—	0.15	0.40	—
1973 Proof	100,000	Value: 1.00				
1974	365,448,000	—	—	0.15	0.35	—
1974 Proof	100,000	Value: 1.00				
1975	197,600,000	—	—	0.15	0.45	—
1975 Proof	100,000	Value: 1.00				
1976	412,172,000	—	—	0.15	0.35	—
1976 Proof	100,000	Value: 1.00				
1977	66,368,000	—	—	0.15	0.20	—
1977 Proof	194,000	Value: 1.00				
1978	59,532,000	—	—	0.15	0.20	—
1978 Proof	88,000	Value: 1.00				
1979	219,132,000	—	—	0.15	0.20	—
1979 Proof	81,000	Value: 1.00				
1980	202,788,000	—	—	0.15	0.20	—
1980 Proof	143,000	Value: 1.00				
1981	46,748,000	—	—	0.15	0.40	—
1981 Proof	100,000	Value: 1.00				

KM# 926   1/2 PENNY
1.7820 g., Bronze, 17.14 mm.   **Ruler:** Elizabeth II **Obv:** Bust right **Rev:** HALF PENNY above crown and fraction **Note:** Denomination now demonetized.

Date	Mintage	F	VF	XF	Unc	BU
1982	190,752,000	—	—	0.15	0.20	—
1982 Proof	107,000	Value: 1.00				
1983	7,600,000	—	—	0.25	0.55	—
1983 Proof	108,000	Value: 1.50				
1984 In sets only	Est. 159,000	—	—	—	2.00	—
1984 Proof	107,000	Value: 2.50				

KM# 915   NEW PENNY
3.5600 g., Bronze, 20.32 mm.   **Ruler:** Elizabeth II **Obv:** Young bust right **Rev:** Crowned portocullis

Date	Mintage	F	VF	XF	Unc	BU
1971	1,521,666,000	—	—	0.15	0.20	—
1971 Proof	350,000	Value: 1.25				
1972 Proof	150,000	Value: 3.00				
1973	280,196,000	—	—	0.15	0.40	—
1973 Proof	100,000	Value: 1.25				
1974	330,892,000	—	—	0.15	0.40	—
1974 Proof	100,000	Value: 1.25				
1975	221,604,000	—	—	0.15	0.50	—
1975 Proof	100,000	Value: 1.25				
1976	300,160,000	—	—	0.15	0.30	—
1976 Proof	100,000	Value: 1.25				
1977	285,430,000	—	—	0.15	0.20	—

Date	Mintage	F	VF	XF	Unc	BU
1977 Proof	194,000	Value: 1.25				
1978	292,770,000	—	—	0.15	0.45	—
1978 Proof	88,000	Value: 1.25				
1979	459,000,000	—	—	0.15	0.20	—
1979 Proof	81,000	Value: 1.25				
1980	416,304,000	—	—	0.15	0.20	—
1980 Proof	143,000	Value: 1.25				
1981	301,800,000	—	—	0.15	0.25	—
1981 Proof	100,000	Value: 1.25				

KM# 927   PENNY
3.5600 g., Bronze, 20.32 mm.   **Ruler:** Elizabeth II **Obv:** Young bust right **Rev:** Crowned portcullis

Date	Mintage	F	VF	XF	Unc	BU
1982	100,292,000	—	—	0.15	0.20	—
1982 Proof	107,000	Value: 1.25				
1983	243,002,000	—	—	0.15	0.40	—
1983 Proof	108,000	Value: 1.25				
1984	154,760,000	—	—	0.20	1.25	—
1984 Proof	107,000	Value: 1.25				

KM# 935   PENNY
3.5600 g., Bronze, 20.32 mm.   **Ruler:** Elizabeth II **Obv:** Crowned head right **Rev:** Crowned portcullis

Date	Mintage	F	VF	XF	Unc	BU
1985	200,605,000	—	—	0.15	0.35	—
1985 Proof	102,000	Value: 1.25				
1986	369,989,000	—	—	0.15	0.35	—
1986 Proof	125,000	Value: 1.25				
1987	499,946,000	—	—	0.15	0.25	—
1987 Proof	89,000	Value: 1.25				
1988	793,492,000	—	—	0.15	0.25	—
1988 Proof	125,000	Value: 1.25				
1989	658,142,000	—	—	0.15	0.25	—
1989 Proof	100,000	Value: 1.25				
1990	529,048,000	—	—	0.15	0.25	—
1990 Proof	100,000	Value: 1.25				
1991	206,458,000	—	—	0.15	0.25	—
1991 Proof	—	Value: 1.25				
1992 In sets only	—	—	—	—	0.50	—
1992 Proof	—	Value: 1.75				

KM# 935a   PENNY
Copper Plated Steel, 20.32 mm.   **Ruler:** Elizabeth II **Obv:** Crowned head right **Rev:** Crowned portcullis

Date	Mintage	F	VF	XF	Unc	BU
1992	253,867,000	—	—	0.15	0.25	—
1993	602,590,000	—	—	0.15	0.25	—
1993 Proof	—	Value: 1.25				
1994	843,834,000	—	—	0.15	0.25	—
1994 Proof	—	Value: 1.25				
1995	303,314,000	—	—	0.15	0.25	—
1995 Proof	—	Value: 1.25				
1996	723,840,000	—	—	—	0.25	—
1996 Proof	—	Value: 1.25				
1997	396,874,000	—	—	—	0.25	—
1997 Proof	—	Value: 1.25				

KM# 935b   PENNY
3.5600 g., 0.9250 Silver 0.1059 oz. ASW, 20.32 mm.   **Ruler:** Elizabeth II **Obv:** Crowned head right **Rev:** Crowned portcullis

Date	Mintage	F	VF	XF	Unc	BU
1996 Proof	—	Value: 16.50				

KM# 986   PENNY
3.5900 g., Copper Plated Steel, 20.34 mm.   **Ruler:** Elizabeth II **Obv:** Head with tiara right **Rev:** Crowned portcullis **Edge:** Plain

Date	Mintage	F	VF	XF	Unc	BU
1998	739,770,000	—	—	—	0.20	—
1998 Proof	Est. 100,000	Value: 3.25				
1999	891,392,000	—	—	—	0.20	—
2000	1,060,364,000	—	—	—	0.20	—

KM# 986a   PENNY
3.5000 g., Bronze, 20.3 mm.   **Ruler:** Elizabeth II **Obv:** Head with tiara right **Rev:** Crowned portcullis **Edge:** Plain **Note:** Issued in sets only

Date	Mintage	F	VF	XF	Unc	BU
1999 Proof	79,401	Value: 2.50				
1999	916,000,000	—	—	—	0.20	—

KM# 986b   PENNY
3.5600 g., 0.9250 Silver 0.1059 oz. ASW, 20.3 mm.   **Ruler:** Elizabeth II **Obv:** Head with tiara right **Rev:** Crowned portcullis **Edge:** Plain

Date	Mintage	F	VF	XF	Unc	BU
2000 Proof	15,000	Value: 16.50				

KM# 916   2 NEW PENCE
7.1200 g., Bronze, 25.91 mm.   **Ruler:** Elizabeth II **Obv:** Young bust right **Rev:** Welsh plumes and crown

Date	Mintage	F	VF	XF	Unc	BU
1971	1,454,856,000	—	—	0.10	0.20	—
1971 Proof	350,000	Value: 1.50				
1972 Proof	150,000	Value: 3.50				
1973 Proof	100,000	Value: 3.50				
1974 Proof	100,000	Value: 3.50				
1975	145,545,000	—	—	0.15	0.40	—
1975 Proof	100,000	Value: 1.50				
1976	181,379,000	—	—	0.15	0.30	—
1976 Proof	100,000	Value: 1.50				
1977	109,281,000	—	—	0.15	0.20	—
1977 Proof	194,000	Value: 1.50				
1978	189,658,000	—	—	0.15	0.40	—
1978 Proof	88,000	Value: 1.50				
1979	260,200,000	—	—	0.15	0.25	—
1979 Proof	81,000	Value: 1.50				
1980	408,527,000	—	—	0.15	0.25	—
1980 Proof	143,000	Value: 1.50				
1981	353,191,000	—	—	0.15	0.25	—
1981 Proof	100,000	Value: 1.50				

KM# 928   2 PENCE
7.1200 g., Bronze, 25.91 mm.   **Ruler:** Elizabeth II **Obv:** Young bust right **Rev:** Welsh plumes and crown **Note:** In sets only

Date	Mintage	F	VF	XF	Unc	BU
1982	205,000	—	—	—	1.00	—
1982 Proof	107,000	Value: 1.50				
1983	631,000	—	—	—	1.00	—
1983 Proof	108,000	Value: 1.50				
1984	159,000	—	—	—	1.50	—
1984 Proof	107,000	Value: 1.50				

KM# 936   2 PENCE
7.1200 g., Bronze, 25.91 mm.   **Ruler:** Elizabeth II **Obv:** Crowned head right **Rev:** Welsh plumes and crown

Date	Mintage	F	VF	XF	Unc	BU
1985	107,113,000	—	—	0.15	0.25	—
1985 Proof	102,000	Value: 1.50				
1986	168,968,000	—	—	0.15	0.50	—
1986 Proof	125,000	Value: 1.50				
1987	218,101,000	—	—	0.15	0.25	—
1987 Proof	89,000	Value: 1.50				
1988	419,889,000	—	—	0.15	0.25	—
1988 Proof	125,000	Value: 1.50				
1989	359,226,000	—	—	0.15	0.25	—
1989 Proof	100,000	Value: 1.50				
1990	204,500,000	—	—	0.15	0.25	—
1990 Proof	100,000	Value: 1.50				
1991	86,625,000	—	—	0.15	0.25	—
1991 Proof	—	Value: 1.50				
1992 In sets only	—	—	—	—	0.50	—
1992 Proof	—	Value: 2.00				

KM# 936a 2 PENCE
Copper Plated Steel, 25.91 mm. **Ruler:** Elizabeth II
Obv: Crowned head right **Rev:** Welsh plumes and crown

Date	Mintage	F	VF	XF	Unc	BU
1992	102,247,000	—	—	0.15	0.25	—
1993	235,674,000	—	—	0.15	0.25	—
1993 Proof	—	Value: 1.50				
1994	531,628,000	—	—	0.10	0.25	—
1994 Proof	—	Value: 1.50				
1995	124,482,000	—	—	0.10	0.25	—
1995 Proof	—	Value: 1.50				
1996	296,278,000	—	—	0.10	0.25	—
1996 Proof	—	Value: 1.50				
1997	496,116,000	—	—	0.10	0.25	—
1997 Proof	—	Value: 1.50				

KM# 936b 2 PENCE
7.1200 g., 0.9250 oz. ASW, 25.91 mm. **Ruler:** Elizabeth II **Obv:** Crowned head right **Rev:** Welsh plumes and crown

Date	Mintage	F	VF	XF	Unc	BU
1996 Proof	—	Value: 17.50				

KM# 987 2 PENCE
7.1400 g., Copper Plated Steel, 25.86 mm. **Ruler:** Elizabeth II **Obv:** Head with tiara right **Rev:** Welsh plumes and crown **Edge:** Plain

Date	Mintage	F	VF	XF	Unc	BU
1998	115,154,000	—	—	—	0.25	—
1998 Proof	Est. 100,000	Value: 3.25				
1999	353,816,000	—	—	—	0.25	—
1999 Proof	—	Value: 3.25				
2000	536,643,000	—	—	—	0.25	—

KM# 987a 2 PENCE
Bronze, 25.91 mm. **Ruler:** Elizabeth II **Obv:** Head with tiara right **Rev:** Welsh plumes and crown

Date	Mintage	F	VF	XF	Unc	BU
1998	98,676,000	—	—	—	0.25	—
1999	460,000,000	—	—	—	0.25	—
1999 Proof	79,401	Value: 2.50				
2000 Proof	—	Value: 2.50				

KM# 987b 2 PENCE
7.1200 g., 0.9250 oz. ASW, 25.9 mm. **Ruler:** Elizabeth II **Obv:** Head with tiara right **Rev:** Welsh plumes and crown **Edge:** Plain

Date	Mintage	F	VF	XF	Unc	BU
2000 Proof	15,000	Value: 17.50				

KM# 911 5 NEW PENCE
5.6500 g., Copper-Nickel, 23.59 mm. **Ruler:** Elizabeth II **Obv:** Young bust right **Rev:** Crowned thistle

Date	Mintage	F	VF	XF	Unc	BU
1968	98,868,000	—	—	0.15	0.30	—
1969	120,270,000	—	—	0.15	0.40	—
1970	225,949,000	—	—	0.15	0.40	—
1971	81,783,000	—	—	0.15	0.45	—
1971 Proof	350,000	Value: 1.75				
1972 Proof	150,000	Value: 3.50				
1973 Proof	100,000	Value: 3.50				
1974 Proof	100,000	Value: 3.50				
1975	141,539,000	—	—	0.15	0.30	—
1975 Proof	100,000	Value: 1.50				
1976 Proof	100,000	Value: 3.50				
1977	24,308,000	—	—	0.15	0.35	—
1977 Proof	194,000	Value: 1.50				
1978	61,094,000	—	—	0.15	0.50	—
1978 Proof	88,000	Value: 1.50				
1979	155,456,000	—	—	0.15	0.30	—
1979 Proof	81,000	Value: 1.50				
1980	220,566,000	—	—	0.15	0.30	—
1980 Proof	143,000	Value: 1.50				
1981 Proof	100,000	Value: 1.75				

KM# 929 5 PENCE
5.6500 g., Copper-Nickel, 23.59 mm. **Ruler:** Elizabeth II **Obv:** Young bust right **Rev:** Crowned thistle **Note:** In sets only

Date	Mintage	F	VF	XF	Unc	BU
1982	205,000	—	—	—	2.25	—
1982 Proof	107,000	Value: 1.75				
1983	637,000	—	—	—	1.75	—
1983 Proof	108,000	Value: 1.75				
1984	159,000	—	—	—	1.75	—
1984 Proof	107,000	Value: 1.50				

KM# 937 5 PENCE
5.6500 g., Copper-Nickel, 23.59 mm. **Ruler:** Elizabeth II **Obv:** Crowned head right **Rev:** Modified design, Five Pence is away from the edge

Date	Mintage	F	VF	XF	Unc	BU
1985 In sets only	178,000	—	—	—	2.00	—
1985 Proof	102,000	Value: 1.50				
1986 In sets only	167,000	—	—	—	1.00	—
1986 Proof	125,000	Value: 1.50				
1987	48,220,000	—	—	0.15	0.30	—
1987 Proof	89,000	Value: 1.75				
1988	120,745,000	—	—	0.15	0.30	—
1988 Proof	125,000	Value: 1.75				
1989	101,406,000	—	—	0.15	0.30	—
1989 Proof	100,000	Value: 1.75				
1990 In sets only	—	—	—	—	2.50	—
1990 Proof	—	Value: 2.75				

KM# 937a 5 PENCE
5.6000 g., 0.9250 Silver 0.1665 oz. ASW, 23.59 mm. **Ruler:** Elizabeth II **Obv:** Crowned head right **Rev:** Crowned thistle

Date	Mintage	F	VF	XF	Unc	BU
1990 Proof	35,000	Value: 22.00				

KM# 937b 5 PENCE
3.2500 g., Copper-Nickel, 18 mm. **Ruler:** Elizabeth II **Obv:** Crowned head right **Rev:** Crowned thistle **Note:** Reduced size. Varieties in thickness and edge milling exist.

Date	Mintage	F	VF	XF	Unc	BU
1990	1,634,976,000	—	—	—	0.35	—
1990 Proof	—	Value: 2.00				
1991	724,979,000	—	—	—	0.35	—
1991 Proof	—	Value: 2.00				
1992	453,174,000	—	—	—	0.35	—
1992 Proof	—	Value: 2.00				
1993 In sets only	56,945	—	—	—	1.25	—
1993 Proof	—	Value: 2.00				
1994	93,602,000	—	—	—	0.35	—
1994 Proof	—	Value: 2.00				
1995	183,384,000	—	—	—	0.35	—
1995 Proof	—	Value: 2.00				
1996	302,902,000	—	—	—	0.35	—
1996 Proof	—	Value: 2.00				
1997	236,596,000	—	—	—	0.35	—
1997 Proof	—	Value: 2.00				

KM# 937c 5 PENCE
3.2500 g., 0.9250 Silver 0.0966 oz. ASW, 18 mm. **Ruler:** Elizabeth II **Obv:** Crowned head right **Rev:** Crowned thistle

Date	Mintage	F	VF	XF	Unc	BU
1990 Proof	35,000	Value: 20.00				
1996 Proof	—	Value: 20.00				

KM# 988 5 PENCE
3.2500 g., Copper-Nickel, 18 mm. **Ruler:** Elizabeth II **Obv:** Head with tiara right **Rev:** Crowned thistle

Date	Mintage	F	VF	XF	Unc	BU
1998	217,376,000	—	—	—	0.30	—
1998 Proof	Est. 100,000	Value: 3.25				

Date	Mintage	F	VF	XF	Unc	BU
1999	195,490,000	—	—	—	0.30	—
1999 Proof	79,401	Value: 3.00				
2000	388,506,000	—	—	—	0.30	—
2000 Proof	Est. 100,000	Value: 3.00				

KM# 988a 5 PENCE
3.2500 g., 0.9250 Silver 0.0966 oz. ASW, 18 mm. **Ruler:** Elizabeth II **Obv:** Head with tiara right **Rev:** Crowned thistle **Edge:** Reeded

Date	Mintage	F	VF	XF	Unc	BU
2000 Proof	15,000	Value: 20.00				

KM# 912 10 NEW PENCE
11.3100 g., Copper-Nickel, 28.5 mm. **Ruler:** Elizabeth II **Obv:** Young bust right **Rev:** Crowned lion prancing left

Date	Mintage	F	VF	XF	Unc	BU
1968	336,143,000	—	—	0.25	0.50	—
1969	314,008,000	—	—	0.25	0.55	—
1970	133,571,000	—	—	0.25	0.65	—
1971	63,205,000	—	—	0.25	0.90	—
1971 Proof	350,000	Value: 1.75				
1972 Proof	150,000	Value: 3.75				
1973	152,174,000	—	—	0.25	0.50	—
1973 Proof	100,000	Value: 1.75				
1974	92,741,000	—	—	0.25	0.50	—
1974 Proof	100,000	Value: 1.75				
1975	181,559,000	—	—	0.25	0.50	—
1975 Proof	100,000	Value: 1.75				
1976	228,220,000	—	—	0.25	0.50	—
1976 Proof	100,000	Value: 1.75				
1977	59,323,000	—	—	0.25	0.60	—
1977 Proof	194,000	Value: 1.75				
1978 Proof	88,000	Value: 5.25				
1979	115,457,000	—	—	0.25	0.60	—
1979 Proof	81,000	Value: 1.75				
1980	88,650,000	—	—	0.25	0.65	—
1980 Proof	143,000	Value: 1.75				
1981	3,487,000	—	0.25	0.50	1.75	—
1981 Proof	100,000	Value: 1.75				

KM# 930 10 PENCE
11.3100 g., Copper-Nickel, 28.5 mm. **Ruler:** Elizabeth II **Obv:** Young bust right **Rev:** Crowned lion prancing left **Note:** In sets only

Date	Mintage	F	VF	XF	Unc	BU
1982	205,000	—	—	—	2.75	—
1982 Proof	107,000	Value: 1.75				
1983	637,000	—	—	—	2.75	—
1983 Proof	108,000	Value: 1.75				
1984	159,000	—	—	—	2.00	—
1984 Proof	107,000	Value: 1.75				

KM# 938 10 PENCE
11.3100 g., Copper-Nickel, 28.5 mm. **Ruler:** Elizabeth II **Obv:** Crowned head right **Rev:** Modified design, TEN PENCE is away from the edge **Note:** In sets only

Date	Mintage	F	VF	XF	Unc	BU
1985	178,000	—	—	—	2.75	—
1985 Proof	102,000	Value: 1.75				
1986	167,000	—	—	—	1.75	—
1986 Proof	125,000	Value: 1.75				
1987	172,000	—	—	—	2.75	—
1987 Proof	89,000	Value: 2.75				
1988	134,000	—	—	—	2.75	—
1988 Proof	125,000	Value: 2.75				
1989	78,000	—	—	—	3.50	—
1989 Proof	100,000	Value: 2.75				
1990	—	—	—	—	3.50	—
1990 Proof	100,000	Value: 2.75				
1991	—	—	—	—	3.50	—
1991 Proof	—	Value: 2.75				

Date	Mintage	F	VF	XF	Unc	BU
1992	—			—	2.75	—
1992 Proof	—	Value: 3.50				

KM# 938a   10 PENCE
11.3100 g., 0.9250 Silver 0.3363 oz. ASW, 28.5 mm.
Ruler: Elizabeth II **Obv:** Crowned head right **Rev:** Crowned lion prancing left **Note:** Date varieties exist.

Date	Mintage	F	VF	XF	Unc	BU
1992 Proof	35,000	Value: 25.00				

KM# 938b   10 PENCE
6.5000 g., Copper-Nickel, 24.5 mm. **Ruler:** Elizabeth II
Obv: Crowned head right **Rev:** Crowned lion prancing left
Note: Reduced size. Varieties in thickness and edge milling exist.

Date	Mintage	F	VF	XF	Unc	BU
1992	1,413,455,000	—	—	0.25	0.50	—
1992 Proof	—	Value: 2.75				
1993 In sets only	—	—	—	—	1.00	—
1993 Proof	—	Value: 1.75				
1994 In sets only	—	—	—	—	1.00	—
1994 Proof	—	Value: 1.75				
1995	43,259,000	—	—	—	1.00	—
1995 Proof	—	Value: 1.75				
1996	118,738,000	—	—	—	1.00	—
1996 Proof	—	Value: 1.75				
1997	99,196,000	—	—	—	1.00	—
1997 Proof	—	Value: 1.75				

KM# 938c   10 PENCE
6.5000 g., 0.9250 Silver 0.1933 oz. ASW, 28.5 mm.
Ruler: Elizabeth II **Obv:** Crowned head right **Rev:** Crowned lion prancing left

Date	Mintage	F	VF	XF	Unc	BU
1992 Proof	35,000	Value: 17.50				
1996 Proof	—	Value: 17.50				

KM# 989   10 PENCE
6.5000 g., Copper-Nickel, 24.5 mm. **Ruler:** Elizabeth II
Obv: Head with tiara right **Rev:** Crowned lion prancing left

Date	Mintage	F	VF	XF	Unc	BU
1998 In sets only	—	—	—	—	1.25	—
1998 Proof	—	Value: 4.50				
1999 In sets only	136,492	—	—	—	1.25	—
1999 Proof	79,401	Value: 3.25				
2000 In sets only	134,727,000	—	—	—	0.40	—
2000 Proof	Est. 100,000	Value: 3.25				

KM# 989a   10 PENCE
6.5000 g., 0.9250 Silver 0.1933 oz. ASW, 24.5 mm.
Ruler: Elizabeth II **Obv:** Head with tiara right **Rev:** Crowned lion prancing left **Edge:** Reeded

Date	Mintage	F	VF	XF	Unc	BU
2000 Proof	15,000	Value: 17.50				

KM# 931   20 PENCE
5.0000 g., Copper-Nickel, 21.4 mm. **Ruler:** Elizabeth II
Obv: Young bust right **Rev:** Crowned rose

Date	Mintage	F	VF	XF	Unc	BU
1982	740,815,000	—	—	0.45	0.65	—
1982 Proof	107,000	Value: 4.50				
1983	158,463,000	—	—	0.45	0.65	—
1983 Proof	108,000	Value: 2.25				
1984	65,351,000	—	—	0.45	0.65	—
1984 Proof	107,000	Value: 2.25				

KM# 939   20 PENCE
5.0000 g., Copper-Nickel, 21.4 mm. **Ruler:** Elizabeth II
Obv: Crowned head right **Rev:** Crowned rose

Date	Mintage	F	VF	XF	Unc	BU
1985	74,274,000	—	—	0.45	0.75	—
1985 Proof	102,000	Value: 4.50				
1986 In sets only	167,000	—	—	—	1.00	—
1986 Proof	125,000	Value: 4.50				
1987	137,450,000	—	—	0.45	0.75	—
1987 Proof	89,000	Value: 4.50				
1988	38,038,000	—	—	0.45	0.75	—
1988 Proof	125,000	Value: 5.00				
1989	132,014,000	—	—	0.45	0.75	—
1989 Proof	100,000	Value: 5.00				
1990	88,098,000	—	—	0.45	0.75	—
1990 Proof	100,000	Value: 5.00				
1991	35,901,000	—	—	0.45	1.00	—
1991 Proof	—	Value: 5.00				
1992	31,205,000	—	—	0.45	1.00	—
1992 Proof	—	Value: 5.00				
1993	123,124,000	—	—	0.45	0.75	—
1993 Proof	—	Value: 5.00				
1994	67,131,000	—	—	0.45	1.00	—
1994 Proof	—	Value: 5.00				
1995	102,005,000	—	—	0.45	0.75	—
1995 Proof	—	Value: 5.00				
1996	83,164,000	—	—	0.45	0.75	—
1996 Proof	—	Value: 5.00				
1997	89,519,000	—	—	0.45	0.75	—

Note: Variations in portrait exist

Date	Mintage	F	VF	XF	Unc	BU
1997 Proof	—	Value: 5.00				

KM# 939a   20 PENCE
5.0000 g., 0.9250 Silver 0.1487 oz. ASW, 21.4 mm.
Ruler: Elizabeth II **Obv:** Crowned head right **Rev:** Crowned rose

Date	Mintage	F	VF	XF	Unc	BU
1996 Proof	—	Value: 18.50				

KM# 990   20 PENCE
5.0000 g., Copper-Nickel, 21.4 mm. **Ruler:** Elizabeth II
Obv: Head with tiara right **Rev:** Crowned rose

Date	Mintage	F	VF	XF	Unc	BU
1998	76,965,000	—	—	—	0.60	—
1998 Proof	Est. 100,000	Value: 3.50				
1999	73,478,750	—	—	—	0.60	—
1999 Proof	79,401	Value: 3.00				
2000	136,418,750	—	—	—	0.60	—
2000 Proof	Est. 100,000	Value: 3.25				

KM# 990a   20 PENCE
5.0000 g., 0.9250 Silver 0.1487 oz. ASW, 21.4 mm.
Ruler: Elizabeth II **Obv:** Head with tiara right **Rev:** Crowned rose **Edge:** Plain

Date	Mintage	F	VF	XF	Unc	BU
2000 Proof	15,000	Value: 18.50				

KM# 917   25 NEW PENCE
Copper-Nickel, 38.61 mm. **Ruler:** Elizabeth II **Subject:** Royal Silver Wedding Anniversary **Obv:** Young bust right **Rev:** Crowned EP monogram

Date	Mintage	F	VF	XF	Unc	BU
ND(1972)	7,452,000	—	—	0.65	2.50	—
ND(1972) Proof	150,000	Value: 7.50				

KM# 917a   25 NEW PENCE
28.2759 g., 0.9250 Silver 0.8409 oz. ASW, 38.61 mm. **Ruler:** Elizabeth II **Obv:** Young bust right **Rev:** Crowned EP monogram

Date	Mintage	F	VF	XF	Unc	BU
ND(1972) Proof	100,000	Value: 25.00				

KM# 920   25 NEW PENCE
Copper-Nickel, 38.61 mm. **Ruler:** Elizabeth II **Subject:** Silver Jubilee of Reign **Obv:** Queen on horseback left **Rev:** Eagle over spoon within circle, crown above

Date	Mintage	F	VF	XF	Unc	BU
1977	37,061,000	—	—	0.65	1.50	—
1977 Proof	194,000	Value: 6.00				
1977 (RMF)	—	—	—	—	—	4.00

Note: Seated in Royal Mint Folder and First Day Covers

1981 (RMF)						

Note: Reported, not confirmed

KM# 920a   25 NEW PENCE
28.2759 g., 0.9250 Silver 0.8409 oz. ASW, 38.61 mm.
Ruler: Elizabeth II **Obv:** Queen on horseback left **Rev:** Eagle over spoon within circle, crown above

Date	Mintage	F	VF	XF	Unc	BU
1977 Proof	377,000	Value: 20.00				

KM# 921   25 NEW PENCE
Copper-Nickel, 38.61 mm. **Ruler:** Elizabeth II **Subject:** 80th Birthday of Queen Mother **Obv:** Young bust right **Rev:** Queen Mother's profile left within circle of rampant lions and banners

Date	Mintage	F	VF	XF	Unc	BU
ND(1980)	9,306,000	—	—	0.65	2.50	—

KM# 921a   25 NEW PENCE

28.2759 g., 0.9250 Silver 0.8409 oz. ASW, 38.61 mm.
Ruler: Elizabeth II **Obv:** Young bust right **Rev:** Queen Mother's profile left in circle of rampant lions and banners

Date	Mintage	F	VF	XF	Unc	BU
ND(1980) Proof	84,000		Value: 55.00			

KM# 925   25 NEW PENCE

Copper-Nickel, 38.61 mm. **Ruler:** Elizabeth II
Subject: Wedding of Prince Charles and Lady Diana **Obv:** Young bust right **Rev:** Jugate heads left

Date	Mintage	F	VF	XF	Unc	BU
1981	26,773,000	—	—	0.65	2.50	—

KM# 925a   25 NEW PENCE

28.2759 g., 0.9250 Silver 0.8409 oz. ASW, 38.61 mm.
Ruler: Elizabeth II **Subject:** Wedding of Prince Charles and Lady Diana **Obv:** Young bust right **Rev:** Conjoined busts left

Date	Mintage	F	VF	XF	Unc	BU
1981 Proof	218,000		Value: 27.50			

KM# 913   50 NEW PENCE

13.5000 g., Copper-Nickel, 30 mm. **Ruler:** Elizabeth II
Obv: Young bust right **Rev:** Britannia seated right

Date	Mintage	F	VF	XF	Unc	BU
1969	188,400,000	—	—	1.25	2.50	—
1970	19,461,000	—	—	1.25	3.50	—
1971 Proof	350,000		Value: 3.50			
1972 Proof	150,000		Value: 6.50			
1974 Proof	100,000		Value: 3.00			
1975 Proof	100,000		Value: 3.00			
1976	43,747,000	—	—	1.75	3.50	—
1976 Proof	100,000		Value: 2.50			
1977	49,536,000	—	—	1.75	3.50	—
1977 Proof	194,000		Value: 2.50			
1978	72,005,000	—	—	1.75	3.50	—
1978 Proof	88,000		Value: 2.75			
1979	58,680,000	—	—	1.75	2.25	—
1979 Proof	81,000		Value: 2.75			
1980	89,086,000	—	—	1.75	2.25	—
1980 Proof	143,000		Value: 2.50			
1981	74,003,000	—	—	1.75	2.25	—
1981 Proof	100,000		Value: 2.50			

KM# 918   50 PENCE

13.5000 g., Copper-Nickel, 30 mm. **Ruler:** Elizabeth II
Subject: Britain's entry into E.E.C **Obv:** Young bust right
Rev: Denomination and date at center of nine clasped hands

Date	Mintage	F	VF	XF	Unc	BU
1973	89,775,000	—	—	1.25	2.00	—
1973 Proof	357,000		Value: 5.50			

KM# 932   50 PENCE

13.5000 g., Copper-Nickel, 30 mm. **Ruler:** Elizabeth II
Obv: Young bust right **Rev:** Britannia seated right

Date	Mintage	F	VF	XF	Unc	BU
1982	51,312,000	—	—	1.25	1.75	—
1982 Proof	107,000		Value: 2.50			
1983	62,825,000	—	—	1.25	2.00	—
1983 Proof	125,000		Value: 2.50			
1984 In sets only	Est. 107,000	—	—	—	2.75	—
1984 Proof	125,000		Value: 2.50			

KM# 940.1   50 PENCE

13.5000 g., Copper-Nickel, 30 mm. **Ruler:** Elizabeth II
Obv: Crowned head right **Rev:** Britannia seated right

Date	Mintage	F	VF	XF	Unc	BU
1985	682,100	—	—	1.25	5.50	—
1985 Proof	102,000		Value: 2.75			
1986 In sets only	167,000	—	—	—	2.75	—
1986 Proof	125,000		Value: 2.75			
1987 In sets only	172,000	—	—	—	2.75	—
1987 Proof	89,000		Value: 2.75			
1988 In sets only	134,000	—	—	—	2.75	—
1988 Proof	125,000		Value: 3.50			
1989 In sets only	78,000	—	—	—	3.50	—
1989 Proof	100,000		Value: 2.75			
1990 In sets only		—	—	—	3.50	—
1990 Proof	100,000		Value: 6.00			
1991 In sets only		—	—	—	3.50	—
1991 Proof		Value: 6.50				
1992 In sets only		—	—	—	3.50	—
1992 Proof		Value: 6.50				
1993 In sets only		—	—	—	3.50	—
1993 Proof		Value: 3.50				
1995 In sets only		—	—	—	2.75	—
1995 Proof		Value: 3.50				
1996 In sets only		—	—	—	2.75	—
1996 Proof		Value: 3.50				
1997 In sets only		—	—	—	2.75	—
1997 Proof		Value: 3.50				

KM# 963   50 PENCE

13.5000 g., Copper-Nickel, 30 mm. **Ruler:** Elizabeth II
Subject: British Presidency of European Council of Ministers
Obv: Crowned head right **Rev:** Stars on conference table

Date	Mintage	F	VF	XF	Unc	BU
ND(1992)	109,000	—	—	—	5.75	—
ND(1992) Proof	Est. 100,000		Value: 13.50			

KM# 963a   50 PENCE

13.5000 g., 0.9250 Silver 0.4015 oz. ASW, 30 mm. **Ruler:** Elizabeth II **Obv:** Crowned head right **Rev:** Stars on conference table

Date	Mintage	F	VF	XF	Unc	BU
ND(1992) Proof	Est. 35,000		Value: 30.00			

KM# 963b   50 PENCE

26.3200 g., 0.9170 Gold 0.7759 oz. AGW, 30 mm. **Ruler:** Elizabeth II **Subject:** British Presidency of European Council of Ministers **Obv:** Crowned head right **Rev:** Stars on conference table

Date	Mintage	F	VF	XF	Unc	BU
ND(1992) Proof	Est. 2,500		Value: 750			

KM# 966   50 PENCE

13.5000 g., Copper-Nickel, 30 mm. **Ruler:** Elizabeth II **Subject:** 50th Anniversary of Normandy Invasion **Obv:** Crowned head right **Rev:** Boats and planes

Date	Mintage	F	VF	XF	Unc	BU
1994	6,706,000	—	—	—	2.50	—
1994 Proof		Value: 11.50				

KM# 966a   50 PENCE

13.5000 g., 0.9250 Silver 0.4015 oz. ASW, 30 mm.
Ruler: Elizabeth II **Obv:** Crowned head right **Rev:** Boats and planes

Date	Mintage	F	VF	XF	Unc	BU
1994 Proof		Value: 45.00				

KM# 966b   50 PENCE

26.3200 g., 0.9170 Gold 0.7759 oz. AGW, 30 mm. **Ruler:** Elizabeth II **Obv:** Crowned head right **Rev:** Boats and planes

Date	Mintage	F	VF	XF	Unc	BU
1994 Proof		Value: 775				

KM# 940.1a   50 PENCE

13.5000 g., 0.9250 Silver 0.4015 oz. ASW, 30 mm. **Ruler:** Elizabeth II **Obv:** Crowned head right **Rev:** Britannia seated

Date	Mintage	F	VF	XF	Unc	BU
1996 Proof		Value: 30.00				

KM# 940.2a   50 PENCE

8.0000 g., 0.9250 Silver 0.2379 oz. ASW **Ruler:** Elizabeth II **Obv:** Crowned head right **Rev:** Britannia seated right

Date	Mintage	F	VF	XF	Unc	BU
1997 Proof		Value: 6.50				

KM# 940.2   50 PENCE

8.0000 g., Copper-Nickel, 27.3 mm. **Ruler:** Elizabeth II **Obv:** Crowned head right **Rev:** Britannia seated right **Note:** Reduced size.

Date	Mintage	F	VF	XF	Unc	BU
1997 Proof		Value: 3.50				
1997	456,364,000	—	—	—	2.50	—

KM# 991   50 PENCE

8.0000 g., Copper-Nickel, 27.3 mm. **Ruler:** Elizabeth II
Obv: Head with tiara right **Rev:** Britannia seated right

Date	Mintage	F	VF	XF	Unc	BU
1998	74,350,500	—	—	—	1.75	—
1998 Proof	Est. 100,000		Value: 2.50			
1999	29,905,000	—	—	—	1.75	—
1999 Proof	79,401		Value: 2.50			
2000	39,172,000	—	—	—	1.75	—
2000 Proof	Est. 100,000		Value: 2.50			

KM# 992   50 PENCE

8.0000 g., Copper-Nickel, 27.3 mm. **Ruler:** Elizabeth II
Subject: 25th Anniversary - Britain in the Common Market
Obv: Head with tiara right **Rev:** Bouquet of stars

Date	Mintage	F	VF	XF	Unc	BU
1998	4,967,000	—	—	—	2.75	—
1998 Proof	Est. 100,000		Value: 9.50			

KM# 992a   50 PENCE

8.0000 g., 0.9250 Silver 0.2379 oz. ASW, 27.3 mm. **Ruler:** Elizabeth II **Obv:** Head with tiara right **Rev:** Bouquet of stars

Date	Mintage	F	VF	XF	Unc	BU
1998 Proof		Value: 45.00				

KM# 996   50 PENCE

8.0000 g., Copper-Nickel, 27.3 mm. **Ruler:** Elizabeth II
Subject: National Health Service **Obv:** Head with tiara right
Rev: Radiant hands within circle

Date	Mintage	F	VF	XF	Unc	BU
1998	5,001,000	—	—	—	2.75	—
1998		—	—	—	7.00	—

Date	Mintage	F	VF	XF	Unc	BU

Note: In folder

1998 Proof — Value: 12.00

KM# 996a 50 PENCE

8.0000 g., 0.9250 Silver 0.2379 oz. ASW, 27.3 mm.
Ruler: Elizabeth II **Subject:** National Health Service **Obv:** Head with tiara right **Rev:** Radiant hands

Date	Mintage	F	VF	XF	Unc	BU

1998 Proof   Est. 25,000   Value: 45.00

KM# 996b 50 PENCE

15.5000 g., 0.9167 Gold 0.4568 oz. AGW, 27.3 mm.
Ruler: Elizabeth II **Subject:** National Health Service **Obv:** Head with tiara right **Rev:** Radiant hands

Date	Mintage	F	VF	XF	Unc	BU

1998 Proof   Est. 1,500   Value: 475

KM# 1083 50 PENCE

8.1100 g., 0.9854 Silver 0.2569 oz. ASW, 22 mm.
Ruler: Elizabeth II **Obv:** Head with tiara right **Rev:** Britannia in chariot right **Edge:** Reeded

Date	Mintage	F	VF	XF	Unc	BU

1999 Proof   — Value: 35.00

KM# 991a 50 PENCE

8.0000 g., 0.9250 Silver 0.2379 oz. ASW, 27.3 mm.
Ruler: Elizabeth II **Obv:** Head with tiara right **Rev:** Britannia seated **Edge:** Plain

Date	Mintage	F	VF	XF	Unc	BU

2000 Proof   15,000   Value: 25.00

KM# 1004 50 PENCE

8.0000 g., Copper-Nickel, 27.3 mm. **Ruler:** Elizabeth II
Subject: Public Library **Obv:** Head with tiara right **Rev:** Open book above building, CDs in pediment **Edge:** Plain edge

Date	Mintage	F	VF	XF	Unc	BU
2000	Est. 5,000,000				2.75	—
2000 Proof	100,000	Value: 12.50				

KM# 1004a 50 PENCE

Silver **Ruler:** Elizabeth II **Subject:** Public Library **Obv:** Queen Elizabeth II right **Rev:** Open book above building, CDs in pediment **Edge:** Plain

Date	Mintage	F	VF	XF	Unc	BU

2000 Proof   — —

KM# 933 POUND

9.5000 g., Nickel-Brass, 22.5 mm. **Ruler:** Elizabeth II
Obv: Young bust right **Rev:** Shield of Great Britain within the Garter, crowned and supported **Edge:** DECUS ET TUTAMEN

Date	Mintage	F	VF	XF	Unc	BU
1983	443,054,000	—		2.25	4.00	5.50
1983 Proof	108,000	Value: 6.00				

KM# 933a POUND

9.5000 g., 0.9250 Silver 0.2825 oz. ASW, 22.5 mm.
Ruler: Elizabeth II **Obv:** Young bust right **Rev:** Shield of Great Britain within the Garter, crowned and supported

Date	Mintage	F	VF	XF	Unc	BU

1983 Proof   50,000   Value: 27.50

KM# 934 POUND

9.5000 g., Nickel-Brass, 22.5 mm. **Ruler:** Elizabeth II
Obv: Young bust right **Rev:** Scottish thistle **Edge:** NEMO ME IMPUNE LACESSIT

Date	Mintage	F	VF	XF	Unc	BU
1984	146,257,000	—		2.25	4.00	5.50
1984 Proof	107,000	Value: 6.00				

KM# 934a POUND

9.5000 g., 0.9250 Silver 0.2825 oz. ASW, 22.5 mm.
Ruler: Elizabeth II **Obv:** Young bust right **Rev:** Scottish thistle

Date	Mintage	F	VF	XF	Unc	BU

1984 Proof   45,000   Value: 27.50

KM# 941 POUND

9.5000 g., Nickel-Brass, 22.5 mm. **Ruler:** Elizabeth II
Obv: Crowned head right **Rev:** Welsh leek, crown encircles **Edge:** PLEIDIOL WYF I'M GWLAD

Date	Mintage	F	VF	XF	Unc	BU
1985	228,431,000	—		2.00	3.50	5.00
1985 Proof	102,000	Value: 6.00				
1990	97,269,000	—		2.00	4.00	5.50
1990 Proof	100,000	Value: 6.00				

KM# 941a POUND

9.5000 g., 0.9250 Silver 0.2825 oz. ASW, 22.5 mm.
Ruler: Elizabeth II **Obv:** Crowned head right **Rev:** Welsh leek, crown encircles

Date	Mintage	F	VF	XF	Unc	BU
1985 Proof	50,000	Value: 27.50				
1990 Proof	Est. 25,000	Value: 36.50				

KM# 946 POUND

9.5000 g., Nickel-Brass, 22.5 mm. **Ruler:** Elizabeth II
Obv: Crowned head right **Rev:** Northern Ireland - Blooming flax, crown encircles **Edge:** DECUS ET TUTAMEN

Date	Mintage	F	VF	XF	Unc	BU
1986	10,410,000	—		2.00	4.00	5.50
1986 Proof	125,000	Value: 6.00				
1991	38,444,000	—		2.00	4.00	5.50
1991 Proof		Value: 6.00				

KM# 946a POUND

9.5000 g., 0.9250 Silver 0.2825 oz. ASW, 22.5 mm.
Ruler: Elizabeth II **Obv:** Crowned head right **Rev:** Northern Ireland - Blooming flax, crown encircles

Date	Mintage	F	VF	XF	Unc	BU
1986 Proof	50,000	Value: 27.50				
1991 Proof	Est. 25,000	Value: 35.00				

KM# 948 POUND

9.5000 g., Nickel-Brass, 22.5 mm. **Ruler:** Elizabeth II
Obv: Crowned head right **Rev:** Oak tree, crown encircles **Edge:** DECUS ET TUTAMEN

Date	Mintage	F	VF	XF	Unc	BU
1987	39,299,000	—		—	3.50	5.00
1987 Proof	125,000	Value: 6.00				
1992	36,320,000	—			4.00	5.50
1992 Proof		Value: 6.00				

KM# 948a POUND

9.5000 g., 0.9250 Silver 0.2825 oz. ASW, 22.5 mm. **Ruler:** Elizabeth II **Obv:** Crowned head right **Rev:** Oak tree, crown encircles

Date	Mintage	F	VF	XF	Unc	BU
1987 Proof	50,000	Value: 27.50				
1992 Proof	Est. 25,000	Value: 36.50				

KM# 954 POUND

9.5000 g., Nickel-Brass, 22.5 mm. **Ruler:** Elizabeth II
Obv: Crowned head right **Rev:** Crowned shield of the United Kingdom **Edge:** DECUS ET TUTAMEN

Date	Mintage	F	VF	XF	Unc	BU
1988	7,119,000	—			4.00	5.50
1988 Proof	Est. 125,000	Value: 7.00				

KM# 954a POUND

9.5000 g., 0.9250 Silver 0.2825 oz. ASW, 22.5 mm.
Ruler: Elizabeth II **Obv:** Crowned head right **Rev:** Crowned shield of the United Kingdom

Date	Mintage	F	VF	XF	Unc	BU

1988 Proof   Est. 50,000   Value: 40.00

KM# 959 POUND

9.5000 g., Nickel-Brass, 22.5 mm. **Ruler:** Elizabeth II
Obv: Crowned head right **Rev:** Scottish thistle, crown encircles **Edge:** NEMO ME IMPUNE LACESSIT

Date	Mintage	F	VF	XF	Unc	BU
1989	70,581,000	—		—	4.00	5.50
1989 Proof	100,000	Value: 6.00				

KM# 959a POUND

9.5000 g., 0.9250 Silver 0.2825 oz. ASW, 22.5 mm.
Ruler: Elizabeth II **Obv:** Crowned head right **Rev:** Scottish thistle, crown encircles

Date	Mintage	F	VF	XF	Unc	BU

1989 Proof   Est. 25,000   Value: 32.50

KM# 964 POUND

9.5000 g., Nickel-Brass, 22.5 mm. **Ruler:** Elizabeth II
Obv: Crowned head right **Rev:** Shield of Great Britain with Garter, crowned and supported **Edge:** DECUS ET TUTAMEN

Date	Mintage	F	VF	XF	Unc	BU
1993	114,745,000	—		—	4.00	5.50
1993 Proof	—	Value: 6.00				

KM# 964a POUND

9.5000 g., 0.9250 Silver 0.2825 oz. ASW, 22.5 mm.
Ruler: Elizabeth II **Obv:** Crowned head right **Rev:** Shield of Great Britain within Garter, crowned and supported

Date	Mintage	F	VF	XF	Unc	BU

1993 Proof   Est. 25,000   Value: 40.00

KM# 967 POUND

9.5000 g., Nickel-Brass, 22.5 mm. **Ruler:** Elizabeth II
Obv: Crowned head right **Rev:** Scottish arms; rampant lion left within circle **Edge:** NEMO ME IMPUNE LACESSIT

Date	Mintage	F	VF	XF	Unc	BU
1994	29,753,000	—		2.00	3.50	6.00
1994 Proof	—	Value: 6.00				

KM# 967a POUND

9.5000 g., 0.9250 Silver 0.2825 oz. ASW, 22.5 mm.
Ruler: Elizabeth II **Obv:** Crowned head right **Rev:** Scottish arms; rampant lion left within circle

Date	Mintage	F	VF	XF	Unc	BU

1994 Proof   Est. 25,000   Value: 60.00

KM# 969 POUND

9.5000 g., Nickel-Brass, 22.5 mm. **Ruler:** Elizabeth II
Obv: Crowned head right **Rev:** Welsh Dragon left **Edge:** PLEIDIOL WYF I'M GWLAD

Date	Mintage	F	VF	XF	Unc	BU
1995	34,504,000	—		2.50	5.50	8.00
1995 Proof	100,000	Value: 7.00				

KM# 969a POUND

9.5000 g., 0.9250 Silver 0.2825 oz. ASW, 22.5 mm.
Ruler: Elizabeth II **Obv:** Crowned head right **Rev:** Welsh dragon left

Date	Mintage	F	VF	XF	Unc	BU

1995 Proof   27,000   Value: 37.50

KM# 972 POUND
9.5000 g., Nickel-Brass, 22.5 mm. **Ruler:** Elizabeth II
Obv: Crowned head right **Rev:** Celtic Cross **Edge:** DECUS ET
TUTAMEN

Date	Mintage	F	VF	XF	Unc	BU
1996	89,886,000	—	—	—	3.50	5.00
1996 Proof	Est. 100,000	Value: 6.00				

KM# 972a POUND
9.5000 g., 0.9250 Silver 0.2825 oz. ASW, 22.5 mm.
Ruler: Elizabeth II **Obv:** Crowned head right **Rev:** Celtic cross

Date	Mintage	F	VF	XF	Unc	BU
1996 Proof	40,000	Value: 37.50				

KM# 975 POUND
9.5000 g., Nickel-Brass, 22.5 mm. **Ruler:** Elizabeth II
Obv: Crowned head right **Rev:** Plantagenet lions **Edge:** DECUS
ET TUTAMEN

Date	Mintage	F	VF	XF	Unc	BU
1996						
	Note: Counterfeit date					
1997	57,117,450	—	—	—	3.50	6.00
1997 Proof	Est. 100,000	Value: 6.00				

KM# 975a POUND
9.5000 g., 0.9250 Silver 0.2825 oz. ASW, 22.5 mm.
Ruler: Elizabeth II **Obv:** Crowned head right **Rev:** Plantagenet
lions **Edge:** DECUS ET TUTAMEN

Date	Mintage	F	VF	XF	Unc	BU
1997 Proof	30,000	Value: 40.00				

KM# 993 POUND
9.5000 g., Nickel-Brass, 22.5 mm. **Ruler:** Elizabeth II
Obv: Head with tiara right **Rev:** Shield of Great Britain within
Garter, crowned and supported **Edge:** DECUS ET TUTAMEN

Date	Mintage	F	VF	XF	Unc	BU
1998	Est. 100,000	—	—	—	8.50	10.00
	Note: In sets only					

KM# 993a POUND
9.5000 g., 0.9250 Silver 0.2825 oz. ASW, 22.5 mm.
Ruler: Elizabeth II **Obv:** Head with tiara right **Rev:** Shield of Great
Britain within Garter, crowned and supported

Date	Mintage	F	VF	XF	Unc	BU
1998	13,863	—	—	—	40.00	—

KM# 998 POUND
9.5000 g., Nickel-Brass, 22.5 mm. **Ruler:** Elizabeth II
Obv: Head with tiara right **Rev:** Scottish lion within circle
Edge: NEMO ME IMPUNE LACESSTT

Date	Mintage	F	VF	XF	Unc	BU
1999		—	—	2.00	3.50	7.50
1999 Proof	Est. 100,000	Value: 6.00				

KM# 998a POUND
9.5000 g., 0.9250 Silver 0.2825 oz. ASW, 22.5 mm. **Ruler:**
Elizabeth II **Obv:** Head with tiara right **Rev:** Scottish lion within circle

Date	Mintage	F	VF	XF	Unc	BU
1999 Proof	Est. 2,000					
	Note: Frosted reverse					
1999 Proof	23,000	Value: 40.00				

KM# 1005 POUND
9.5000 g., Nickel-Brass, 22.5 mm. **Ruler:** Elizabeth II
Obv: Head with tiara right **Rev:** Welsh dragon left **Edge:** Reeded
and lettered **Edge:** PLEIDIOL WYF I'M GWLAD

Date	Mintage	F	VF	XF	Unc	BU
2000	109,496,500	—	—	—	3.50	7.00
2000 Proof	Est. 100,000	Value: 6.00				

KM# 1005a POUND
9.5000 g., 0.9250 Silver 0.2825 oz. ASW, 22.5 mm.
Ruler: Elizabeth II **Subject:** Wales **Obv:** Head with tiara right
Rev: Welsh dragon left **Edge:** Reeded **Edge:** PLEIDIOL WYF
I'M GWLAD

Date	Mintage	F	VF	XF	Unc	BU
2000 Proof	15,865	Value: 40.00				

KM# 947 2 POUNDS
15.9800 g., Nickel-Brass, 28.4 mm. **Ruler:** Elizabeth II
Subject: Commonwealth Games **Obv:** Crowned head right
Rev: Thistle on St. Andrew's Cross **Edge:** XIII
COMMONWEALTH GAMES SCOTLAND 1986

Date	Mintage	F	VF	XF	Unc	BU
1986	8,212,000	—	—	4.50	6.50	10.00
1986 Proof	125,000	Value: 11.50				

KM# 947a 2 POUNDS
15.9800 g., 0.5000 Silver 0.2569 oz. ASW, 28.4 mm.
Ruler: Elizabeth II **Subject:** Commonwealth Games
Obv: Crowned head right **Rev:** Thistle on St. Andrew's cross

Date	Mintage	F	VF	XF	Unc	BU
1986	125,000	—	—	—	15.00	20.00

KM# 947b 2 POUNDS
15.9800 g., 0.9250 Silver 0.4752 oz. ASW, 28.4 mm.
Ruler: Elizabeth II **Subject:** Commonwealth Games
Obv: Crowned head right **Rev:** Thistle on St. Andrew's Cross

Date	Mintage	F	VF	XF	Unc	BU
1986 Proof	75,000	Value: 25.00				

KM# 947c 2 POUNDS
15.9800 g., 0.9170 Gold 0.4711 oz. AGW, 28.4 mm.
Ruler: Elizabeth II **Subject:** Commonwealth Games
Obv: Crowned head right **Rev:** Thistle on St. Andrew's Cross

Date	Mintage	F	VF	XF	Unc	BU
1986 Proof	18,000	Value: 450				

KM# 960 2 POUNDS
15.9800 g., Nickel-Brass, 28.4 mm. **Ruler:** Elizabeth II
Subject: Tercentenary - Bill of Rights **Obv:** Crowned head right
Rev: St. Edward's crown above sceptre and WM monogram

Date	Mintage	F	VF	XF	Unc	BU
ND(1989)	4,397,000	—	—	—	6.50	10.00
ND(1989) Proof	100,000	Value: 11.50				

KM# 960a 2 POUNDS
15.9800 g., 0.9250 Silver 0.4752 oz. ASW, 28.4 mm. **Ruler:**
Elizabeth II **Subject:** Tercentenary - Bill of Rights **Obv:** Crowned
head right **Rev:** St. Edward's crowned above sceptre and WM
monogram

Date	Mintage	F	VF	XF	Unc	BU
ND(1989) Proof	25,000	Value: 25.00				

KM# 961 2 POUNDS
15.9800 g., Nickel-Brass, 28.4 mm. **Ruler:** Elizabeth II
Subject: Tercentenary - Bill of Rights **Obv:** Crowned head right
Rev: Crown of Scotland above sceptre and WM monogram

Date	Mintage	F	VF	XF	Unc	BU
ND(1989)	346,000	—	—	—	9.00	15.00
ND(1989) Proof	100,000	Value: 17.50				

KM# 961a 2 POUNDS
15.9800 g., 0.9250 Silver 0.4752 oz. ASW, 28.4 mm.
Ruler: Elizabeth II **Subject:** Tercentenary - Bill of Rights
Obv: Crowned head right **Rev:** Crown of Scotland above sceptre
and WM monogram

Date	Mintage	F	VF	XF	Unc	BU
ND(1989) Proof	25,000	Value: 25.00				

KM# 968 2 POUNDS
15.9800 g., Nickel-Brass, 28.4 mm. **Ruler:** Elizabeth II
Subject: 300th Anniversary - Bank of England **Obv:** Crowned
head right **Rev:** Britiannia seated within oval divides dates,
crowned WM monogram above **Edge:** SIC VOS NON VOBIS

Date	Mintage	F	VF	XF	Unc	BU
ND(1994)	1,443,000	—	—	—	5.50	9.00
ND(1994) Proof	—	Value: 10.00				

KM# 968a 2 POUNDS
15.9800 g., 0.9250 Silver 0.4752 oz. ASW, 28.4 mm.
Ruler: Elizabeth II **Subject:** 300th Anniversary - Bank of England
Obv: Crowned head right **Rev:** Britiannia seated within oval,
Crowned WM monogram above

Date	Mintage	F	VF	XF	Unc	BU
ND(1994) Proof	Est. 40,000	Value: 40.00				

KM# 968c 2 POUNDS
15.9800 g., 0.9170 Gold 0.4711 oz. AGW, 28.4 mm.
Ruler: Elizabeth II **Subject:** 300th Anniversary - Bank of England
Obv: Crowned head right **Rev:** Britiannia seated within oval,
Crowned WM monogram above

Date	Mintage	F	VF	XF	Unc	BU
ND(1994) Proof	Est. 3,500	Value: 470				

KM# 1012 2 POUNDS
15.9800 g., 0.9170 Gold 0.4711 oz. AGW, 28.4 mm. **Ruler:**
Elizabeth II **Obv:** Crowned head right **Rev:** Britiannia seated
within oval, crowned WM monogram above **Note:** Muled die error.

Date	Mintage	F	VF	XF	Unc	BU
ND(1994)	—	—	—	—	600	—

KM# 970 2 POUNDS
15.9800 g., Nickel-Brass, 28.4 mm. **Ruler:** Elizabeth II
Subject: 50th Anniversary - End of World War II **Obv:** Crowned
head right **Rev:** Large dove with laurel branch **Edge:** 1945 IN
PEACE GOODWILL 1995

Date	Mintage	F	VF	XF	Unc	BU
ND(1995)	6,057,000	—	—	—	6.00	10.00
ND(1995) Proof	100,000	Value: 12.00				

KM# 970a 2 POUNDS
15.9800 g., 0.9250 Silver 0.4752 oz. ASW, 28.4 mm.
Ruler: Elizabeth II **Subject:** 50th Anniversary - End of World War
II **Obv:** Crowned head right **Rev:** Dove with laurel branch

Date	Mintage	F	VF	XF	Unc	BU
ND(1995) Proof	50,000	Value: 40.00				

KM# 970c 2 POUNDS
15.9800 g., 0.9170 Gold 0.4711 oz. AGW, 28.4 mm.
Ruler: Elizabeth II **Subject:** 50th Anniversary - End of World War
II **Obv:** Crowned head right **Rev:** Dove with laurel branch

Date	Mintage	F	VF	XF	Unc	BU
ND(1995) Proof	2,500	Value: 475				

KM# 971 2 POUNDS
15.9800 g., Nickel-Brass, 28.4 mm. **Ruler:** Elizabeth II **Subject:**
50th Anniversary - United Nations **Obv:** Crowned head right
Rev: Flags and UN Logo **Note:** Mintage included with KM#970.

Date	Mintage	F	VF	XF	Unc	BU
ND(1995)	Inc. above	—	—	—	6.00	9.00

KM# 971a   2 POUNDS
15.9760 g., 0.9250 Silver 0.4751 oz. ASW, 28.4 mm.
Ruler: Elizabeth II **Subject:** 50th Anniversary - United Nations
Obv: Crowned head right **Rev:** Flags and UN Logo

Date	Mintage	F	VF	XF	Unc	BU
ND(1995) Proof	Est. 175,000		Value: 40.00			

KM# 971c   2 POUNDS
15.9760 g., 0.9170 Gold 0.4710 oz. AGW, 28.4 mm.
Ruler: Elizabeth II **Subject:** 50th Anniversary - United Nations
Obv: Crowned head right **Rev:** Flags and UN Logo

Date	Mintage	F	VF	XF	Unc	BU
ND(1995) Proof	Est. 5,000		Value: 450			

KM# 973   2 POUNDS
15.9800 g., Nickel-Brass, 28.4 mm. **Ruler:** Elizabeth II
Obv: Crowned head right **Rev:** Soccer ball, date in center
Edge: 10th European Championship of Football (Soccer)

Date	Mintage	F	VF	XF	Unc	BU
1996	5,141,000	—	—	—	6.50	10.00
1996 Proof	Est. 100,000		Value: 11.50			

KM# 973a   2 POUNDS
15.9760 g., 0.9250 Silver 0.4751 oz. ASW, 28.4 mm.
Ruler: Elizabeth II **Obv:** Crowned head right **Rev:** Soccer ball,
date at center

Date	Mintage	F	VF	XF	Unc	BU
1996 Proof	—		Value: 40.00			

KM# 976   2 POUNDS
12.0000 g., Bi-Metallic Copper-Nickel center in Nickel-Brass ring,
28.35 mm. **Ruler:** Elizabeth II **Obv:** Crowned head right
Rev: Celtic designs within circle **Edge:** STANDING ON THE
SHOULDERS OF GIANTS

Date	Mintage	F	VF	XF	Unc	BU
1997	13,735,000	—	—	—	7.50	12.50
1997 Proof	Est. 100,000		Value: 13.00			

KM# 976a   2 POUNDS
12.0000 g., 0.9250 Silver 0.3569 oz. ASW, 28.35 mm.
Ruler: Elizabeth II **Obv:** Crowned head right **Rev:** Celtic designs
within circle **Note:** Gold plated silver ring, silver center.

Date	Mintage	F	VF	XF	Unc	BU
1997 Proof	Est. 40,000		Value: 45.00			

KM# 976b   2 POUNDS
15.9800 g., 0.9170 Gold 0.4711 oz. AGW, 28.35 mm.
Ruler: Elizabeth II **Obv:** Crowned head right **Rev:** Celtic design
within circle **Note:** Red gold ring, yellow gold center.

Date	Mintage	F	VF	XF	Unc	BU
1997 Proof	Est. 2,500		Value: 600			

KM# 994a   2 POUNDS
12.0000 g., 0.9250 Silver 0.3569 oz. ASW, 28.35 mm.
Ruler: Elizabeth II **Obv:** Head with tiara right within circle
Rev: Celtic design within circle **Note:** Gold plated silver ring, silver
center.

Date	Mintage	F	VF	XF	Unc	BU
1998 Proof	7,646		Value: 50.00			
2000 Proof	15,000	—	—	—	—	—

KM# 994   2 POUNDS
12.0000 g., Bi-Metallic Copper-Nickel center in Nickel-Brass ring,
28.35 mm. **Ruler:** Elizabeth II **Obv:** Head with tiara right within
circle **Rev:** Celtic design within circle **Edge:** STANDING ON THE
SHOULDERS OF GIANTS

Date	Mintage	F	VF	XF	Unc	BU
1998	91,110,375	—	—	—	6.00	8.50
1998 Proof	Est. 100,000		Value: 10.00			
1999	38,652,000	—	—	—	6.00	8.50
1999 Proof		Value: 10.00				
2000	25,770,000	—	—	—	6.00	8.50
2000 Proof		Value: 10.00				

KM# 994b   2 POUNDS
12.0000 g., 0.9250 Silver 0.3569 oz. ASW, 28.35 mm.
Ruler: Elizabeth II **Obv:** Head with tiara right within circle
Rev: Celtic design within circle **Note:** Without gold plating.

Date	Mintage	F	VF	XF	Unc	BU
1998 Proof	19,978		Value: 40.00			

KM# 999   2 POUNDS
12.0000 g., Bi-Metallic Copper-Nickel center in Nickel-Brass ring,
28.35 mm. **Ruler:** Elizabeth II **Subject:** Rugby World Cup
Obv: Head with tiara right **Rev:** 2-tone rugby design
Edge: RUGBY WORLD CUP 1999 **Note:** Varieties exist.

Date	Mintage	F	VF	XF	Unc	BU
1999	5,000,000	—	—	—	7.00	9.00
1999 Proof	Est. 100,000		Value: 11.50			

KM# 999a   2 POUNDS
12.0000 g., 0.9250 Silver 0.3569 oz. ASW, 28.35 mm.
Ruler: Elizabeth II **Subject:** Rugby World Cup **Obv:** Head with
tiara right **Rev:** 2-tone rugby design **Edge:** Reeded, lettered edge
Note: Gold plated ring.

Date	Mintage	F	VF	XF	Unc	BU
1999 Proof	Est. 25,000		Value: 47.50			

KM# 999b   2 POUNDS
15.9800 g., 0.9170 Gold 0.4711 oz. AGW, 28.35 mm.
Ruler: Elizabeth II **Subject:** Rugby World Cup **Obv:** Head with
tiara right **Rev:** 2-tone rugby design

Date	Mintage	F	VF	XF	Unc	BU
1999 Proof	4,250		Value: 500			

KM# 999c   2 POUNDS
24.0000 g., 0.9250 Silver 0.7137 oz. ASW, 28.35 mm.
Ruler: Elizabeth II **Obv:** Head with tiara right within gold-plated
ring **Rev:** Multicolor hologram center within gold-plated ring
Edge: Reeded, lettered edge

Date	Mintage	F	VF	XF	Unc	BU
1999 Proof	10,000		Value: 75.00			

KM# 994c   2 POUNDS
15.9800 g., 0.9167 Gold 0.4710 oz. AGW, 28.35 mm.
Ruler: Elizabeth II **Obv:** Head with tiara right within circle
Rev: Celtic design within circle

Date	Mintage	F	VF	XF	Unc	BU
2000 Proof	1,250		Value: 550			

KM# 962   5 POUNDS
28.2800 g., Copper-Nickel, 38.61 mm. **Ruler:** Elizabeth II
Subject: 90th Birthday of Queen Mother **Obv:** Crowned head
right **Rev:** Crowned monogram with rose and thistle flanking

Date	Mintage	F	VF	XF	Unc	BU
ND(1990)	2,761,000	—	—	—	15.00	17.00

KM# 962a   5 POUNDS
28.2800 g., 0.9250 Silver 0.8410 oz. ASW, 38.61 mm.
Ruler: Elizabeth II **Subject:** 90th Birthday of Queen Mother
Obv: Crowned head right **Rev:** Crowned monogram with rose
and thistle flanking

Date	Mintage	F	VF	XF	Unc	BU
ND(1990) Proof	Est. 150,000		Value: 40.00			

KM# 962b   5 POUNDS
39.9400 g., 0.9170 Gold 1.1775 oz. AGW, 38.61 mm.
Ruler: Elizabeth II **Subject:** 90th Birthday of Queen Mother
Obv: Crowned head right **Rev:** Crowned monogram with rose
and thistle flanking

Date	Mintage	F	VF	XF	Unc	BU
ND(1990) Proof	Est. 2,500		Value: 1,150			

KM# 965   5 POUNDS
28.2800 g., Copper-Nickel, 38.61 mm. **Ruler:** Elizabeth II
Subject: 40th Anniversary of Reign **Obv:** Laureate head, right
within circle of bugling horsemen **Rev:** Crown within circle

Date	Mintage	F	VF	XF	Unc	BU
ND(1993)	1,835,000	—	—	—	13.50	15.00
ND(1993) Proof	Est. 100,000		Value: 18.50			

KM# 965a   5 POUNDS
28.2800 g., 0.9250 Silver 0.8410 oz. ASW, 38.61 mm. **Ruler:**
Elizabeth II **Subject:** 40th Anniversary of Reign **Obv:** Laureate head
right within circle of bugling horsemen **Rev:** Crown within circle

Date	Mintage	F	VF	XF	Unc	BU
ND(1993) Proof	Est. 100,000		Value: 45.00			

KM# 965b   5 POUNDS
39.9400 g., 0.9170 Gold 1.1775 oz. AGW, 38.61 mm. **Ruler:**
Elizabeth II **Subject:** 40th Anniversary of Reign **Obv:** Laureate head
right with circle of bugling horsemen **Rev:** Crown within circle

Date	Mintage	F	VF	XF	Unc	BU
ND(1993) Proof	Est. 2,500		Value: 1,400			

KM# 974   5 POUNDS
28.2800 g., Copper-Nickel, 38.61 mm. **Ruler:** Elizabeth II
Subject: 70th Birthday of Queen Elizabeth II **Obv:** Crowned head
right **Rev:** Five banners above Windsor Castle **Edge:** VIVAT
REGINA ELIZABETHA

Date	Mintage	F	VF	XF	Unc	BU
ND(1996)	2,936,000	—	—	—	14.00	16.00
ND(1996) Proof		Value: 22.00				

KM# 974a   5 POUNDS
28.2800 g., 0.9250 Silver 0.8410 oz. ASW, 38.61 mm.
Ruler: Elizabeth II **Subject:** 70th Birthday of Queen Elizabeth II
Obv: Crowned head right **Rev:** Five banners above Windsor
Castle

Date	Mintage	F	VF	XF	Unc	BU
ND(1996) Proof	Est. 70,000	Value: 45.00				

KM# 974b   5 POUNDS
39.9400 g., 0.9170 Gold 1.1775 oz. AGW, 38.61 mm.
Ruler: Elizabeth II **Subject:** 70th Birthday of Queen Elizabeth II
Obv: Crowned head right **Rev:** Five banners above Windsor
Castle

Date	Mintage	F	VF	XF	Unc	BU
ND(1996) Proof	Est. 2,750	Value: 1,150				

KM# 977   5 POUNDS
28.2800 g., Copper-Nickel, 38.61 mm.   **Ruler:** Elizabeth II
Subject: Queen Elizabeth II and Prince Philip - Golden Wedding
Anniversary **Obv:** Jugate busts right **Rev:** Crown above two
shields, anchor below

Date	Mintage	F	VF	XF	Unc	BU
ND(1997)	1,733,000	—	—	—	15.00	17.00
ND(1997) Proof	—	Value: 22.00				

KM# 977a   5 POUNDS
28.2800 g., 0.9250 Silver 0.8410 oz. ASW, 38.61 mm.
Ruler: Elizabeth II **Subject:** Queen Elizabeth II and Prince Philip
- Golden Wedding Anniversary **Obv:** Jugate busts right
Rev: Crown above two shields, anchor below

Date	Mintage	F	VF	XF	Unc	BU
ND(1997) Proof	Est. 70,000	Value: 50.00				

KM# 977b   5 POUNDS
39.9400 g., 0.9170 Gold 1.1775 oz. AGW, 38.61 mm.
Ruler: Elizabeth II **Subject:** Queen Elizabeth II and Prince Philip
- Golden Wedding Anniversary **Obv:** Jugate busts right
Rev: Crown above two shields, anchor below

Date	Mintage	F	VF	XF	Unc	BU
ND(1997) Proof	Est. 2,750	Value: 1,150				

KM# 995   5 POUNDS
28.2800 g., Copper-Nickel, 38.61 mm.   **Ruler:** Elizabeth II
Subject: 50th Birthday - Prince Charles **Obv:** Head with tiara
right **Rev:** Portrait of Prince Charles

Date	Mintage	F	VF	XF	Unc	BU
1998	1,407,000	—	—	—	15.00	—
1998 Proof	Est. 100,000	Value: 20.00				

KM# 995a   5 POUNDS
28.2800 g., 0.9250 Silver 0.8410 oz. ASW, 38.61 mm.
Ruler: Elizabeth II **Subject:** 50th Birthday - Prince Charles
Obv: Head right **Rev:** Portrait of Prince Charles

Date	Mintage	F	VF	XF	Unc	BU
1998 Proof	13,379	Value: 50.00				

KM# 995b   5 POUNDS
39.9400 g., 0.9167 Gold 1.1771 oz. AGW, 38.61 mm.
Ruler: Elizabeth II **Subject:** 50th Birthday - Prince Charles
Obv: Head with tiara right **Rev:** Portrait of Prince Charles

Date	Mintage	F	VF	XF	Unc	BU
1998 Proof	773	Value: 1,150				

KM# 997   5 POUNDS
Copper-Nickel, 38.61 mm.   **Ruler:** Elizabeth II **Subject:** In
Memory of Diana - Princess of Wales **Obv:** Head with tiara right
Rev: Head right, dates

Date	Mintage	F	VF	XF	Unc	BU
1999	5,000,000	—	—	—	16.00	18.00
1999 Proof	Est. 100,000	Value: 22.00				

KM# 997a   5 POUNDS
28.2800 g., 0.9250 Silver 0.8410 oz. ASW, 38.61 mm.
Ruler: Elizabeth II **Subject:** In Memory of Diana - Princess of
Wales **Obv:** Head with tiara right **Rev:** Head right, dates

Date	Mintage	F	VF	XF	Unc	BU
1999 Proof	Est. 49,545	Value: 50.00				

KM# 997b   5 POUNDS
39.9400 g., 0.9170 Gold 1.1775 oz. AGW, 38.61 mm.
Ruler: Elizabeth II **Subject:** In Memory of Diana - Princess of
Wales **Obv:** Head with tiara right **Rev:** Head right, dates

Date	Mintage	F	VF	XF	Unc	BU
1999 Proof	Est. 7,500	Value: 1,150				

KM# 1006   5 POUNDS
28.2800 g., Copper-Nickel, 38.61 mm.   **Ruler:** Elizabeth II
Obv: Head with tiara right **Rev:** Map with Greenwich Meridian
Edge: WHAT'S PAST IS PROLOGUE

Date	Mintage	F	VF	XF	Unc	BU
1999 Proof	—	Value: 20.00				
1999	5,396,300	—	—	—	14.00	16.00
2000	3,147,010	—	—	—	14.00	16.00
2000 Proof	Est. 100,000	Value: 20.00				

Note: Gold overlay on the British Isles

KM# 1006a   5 POUNDS
28.2800 g., 0.9250 Silver 0.8410 oz. ASW, 38.61 mm.
Ruler: Elizabeth II **Obv:** Head with tiara right **Rev:** Map with
Greenwich Meridian

Date	Mintage	F	VF	XF	Unc	BU
1999 Proof	75,000	Value: 55.00				
2000 Proof	50,000	Value: 55.00				

KM# 1006b   5 POUNDS
39.9400 g., 0.9170 Gold 1.1775 oz. AGW, 38.61 mm.
Ruler: Elizabeth II **Obv:** Head with tiara right **Rev:** Map with
Greenwich Meridian

Date	Mintage	F	VF	XF	Unc	BU
1999 Proof	2,500	Value: 1,400				
2000 Proof	2,500	Value: 1,400				

KM# 1006c   5 POUNDS
28.2800 g., 0.9990 Silver 0.9083 oz. ASW, 38.61 mm.
Ruler: Elizabeth II **Obv:** Head with tiara right **Rev:** Map with
Greenwich Meridian **Note:** With gold-plated British map.

Date	Mintage	F	VF	XF	Unc	BU
2000 Proof	15,000	Value: 65.00				

KM# 1006.1   5 POUNDS
28.2800 g., Copper-Nickel, 38.61 mm.   **Ruler:** Elizabeth II
Obv: Head with tiara right **Rev:** Map with Greenwich Meridian,
world globe at 3 o'clock in inner circle

Date	Mintage	F	VF	XF	Unc	BU
2000	—	—	—	—	20.00	22.00

KM# 1007   5 POUNDS
Copper-Nickel   **Ruler:** Elizabeth II **Subject:** 100th Birthday -
Queen Elizabeth, The Queen Mother **Obv:** Head with tiara right
Rev: Head left, signature below **Edge:** Reeded

Date	Mintage	F	VF	XF	Unc	BU
2000	3,147,092	—	—	—	15.00	17.00

KM# 1007a   5 POUNDS
28.2800 g., 0.9250 Silver 0.8410 oz. ASW, 38.61 mm.
Ruler: Elizabeth II **Subject:** Queen Mother's Centennial
Obv: Head with tiara right **Rev:** Head left with signature below
Edge: Reeded

Date	Mintage	F	VF	XF	Unc	BU
2000 Proof	100,000	Value: 55.00				

KM# 1007b   5 POUNDS
39.9400 g., 0.9167 Gold 1.1771 oz. AGW, 38.61 mm.
Ruler: Elizabeth II **Subject:** Queen Mother's Centennial
Obv: Head with tiara right **Rev:** Head left with signature below

Date	Mintage	F	VF	XF	Unc	BU
2000 Proof	3,000	Value: 1,350				

SOVEREIGN COINAGE

KM# 784   1/2 SOVEREIGN
3.9940 g., 0.9170 Gold 0.1177 oz. AGW   **Ruler:** Victoria
Obv: Mature draped bust left **Obv. Leg.:** VICTORIA • DEI • GRA
• BRITT • REGINA • FID • DEF • IND • IMP • **Rev:** St. George
slaying the dragon right

Date	Mintage	F	VF	XF	Unc	BU
1901	2,037,999	BV	BV	125	175	—

KM# 804 1/2 SOVEREIGN
3.9940 g., 0.9170 Gold 0.1177 oz. AGW **Ruler:** Edward VII
Obv: Head right **Rev:** St. George slaying the dragon

Date	Mintage	F	VF	XF	Unc	BU
1902	4,244,000	—	BV	BV	140	—
1902 Proof	15,000	Value: 225				
1903	2,522,000	—	BV	BV	140	—
1904	1,717,000	—	BV	BV	140	—
1905	3,024,000	—	BV	BV	140	—
1906	4,245,000	—	BV	BV	140	—
1907	4,233,000	—	BV	BV	140	—
1908	3,997,000	—	BV	BV	140	—
1909	4,011,000	—	BV	BV	140	—
1910	5,024,000	—	BV	BV	140	—

KM# 819 1/2 SOVEREIGN
3.9940 g., 0.9170 Gold 0.1177 oz. AGW **Ruler:** George V
Obv: Head left **Rev:** St. George slaying the dragon

Date	Mintage	F	VF	XF	Unc	BU
1911	6,104,000	—	BV	110	140	—
1911 Proof	3,764	Value: 350				
1912	6,224,000	—	BV	110	140	—
1913	6,094,000	—	BV	110	140	—
1914	7,251,000	—	BV	110	140	—
1915	2,043,000	—	BV	110	140	—

KM# 858 1/2 SOVEREIGN
3.9940 g., 0.9170 Gold 0.1177 oz. AGW **Ruler:** George VI
Obv: Head left **Rev:** St. George slaying the dragon

Date	Mintage	F	VF	XF	Unc	BU
1937 Proof	5,500	Value: 400				
1937 Matte Proof; Unique						

KM# 922 1/2 SOVEREIGN
3.9900 g., 0.9170 Gold 0.1176 oz. AGW **Ruler:** Elizabeth II
Obv: Young bust right **Rev:** St. George slaying the dragon

Date	Mintage	F	VF	XF	Unc	BU
1980 Proof	10,000	Value: 140				
1982 Proof	23,000	Value: 120				
1982	2,500,000	—	—	—	—	140
1983 Proof	22,000	Value: 140				
1984 Proof	22,000	Value: 140				

KM# 942 1/2 SOVEREIGN
3.9900 g., 0.9170 Gold 0.1176 oz. AGW **Ruler:** Elizabeth II
Obv: Crowned head right **Rev:** St. George slaying the dragon

Date	Mintage	F	VF	XF	Unc	BU
1985 Proof	25,000	Value: 140				
1986 Proof	25,000	Value: 140				
1987 Proof	23,000	Value: 140				
1988 Proof	Est. 23,000	Value: 140				
1990 Proof	Est. 20,000	Value: 150				
1991 Proof	Est. 9,000	Value: 150				
1992 Proof	7,500	Value: 160				
1993 Proof	7,500	Value: 160				
1994 Proof	Est. 7,500	Value: 160				
1995 Proof	4,900	Value: 170				
1996 Proof	5,730	Value: 160				
1997 Proof	7,500	Value: 160				

KM# 955 1/2 SOVEREIGN
3.9900 g., 0.9170 Gold 0.1176 oz. AGW **Ruler:** Elizabeth II
Subject: 500th Anniversary of the Gold Sovereign
Obv: Elizabeth II seated on the Coronation throne **Rev:** Crowned and quartered shield on tudor rose

Date	Mintage	F	VF	XF	Unc	BU
ND(1989) Proof	Est. 25,000	Value: 450				

KM# 1001 1/2 SOVEREIGN
3.9900 g., 0.9170 Gold 0.1176 oz. AGW **Ruler:** Elizabeth II
Obv: Head with tiara right **Rev:** St. George slaying the dragon

Date	Mintage	F	VF	XF	Unc	BU
1998 Proof	6,144	Value: 150				
1999 Proof	7,500	Value: 175				
2000	146,542	—	—	—	—	120
2000 Proof	7,500	Value: 150				

KM# 785 SOVEREIGN
7.9881 g., 0.9170 Gold 0.2355 oz. AGW **Ruler:** Victoria
Obv: Mature draped bust left **Obv. Leg.:** VICTORIA • DEI • GRA • BRITT • REGINA • FID • DEF • IND • IMP • **Rev:** St. George slaying the dragon

Date	Mintage	F	VF	XF	Unc	BU
1901	1,579,000	—	—	BV	250	—

KM# 805 SOVEREIGN
7.9881 g., 0.9170 Gold 0.2355 oz. AGW **Ruler:** Edward VII
Obv: Head right **Rev:** St. George slaying the dragon

Date	Mintage	F	VF	XF	Unc	BU
1902	4,738,000	—	—	BV	235	—
1902 Proof	15,000	Value: 350				
1903	8,889,000	—	—	BV	235	—
1904	10,041,000	—	—	BV	235	—
1905	5,910,000	—	—	BV	235	—
1906	10,467,000	—	—	BV	235	—
1907	18,459,000	—	—	BV	235	—
1908	11,729,000	—	—	BV	235	—
1909	12,157,000	—	—	BV	235	—
1910	22,380,000	—	—	BV	235	—

KM# 820 SOVEREIGN
7.9881 g., 0.9170 Gold 0.2355 oz. AGW **Ruler:** George V
Obv: Head left **Rev:** St. George slaying the dragon

Date	Mintage	F	VF	XF	Unc	BU
1911	30,044,000	—	—	BV	245	—
1911 Proof	3,764	Value: 800				
1912	30,318,000	—	—	BV	245	—
1913	24,540,000	—	—	BV	245	—
1914	11,501,000	—	—	BV	245	—
1915	20,295,000	—	—	BV	245	—
1916	1,554,000	—	—	BV	270	—
1917	1,014,999	3,000	3,500	6,500	12,000	—
1925	4,406,000	—	—	BV	245	—

KM# 859 SOVEREIGN
7.9881 g., 0.9170 Gold 0.2355 oz. AGW **Ruler:** George VI
Obv: Head left **Rev:** St. George slaying the dragon

Date	Mintage	F	VF	XF	Unc	BU
1937 Proof	5,500	Value: 2,000				
1937 Matte Proof; Unique						

KM# 908 SOVEREIGN
7.9881 g., 0.9170 Gold 0.2355 oz. AGW **Ruler:** Elizabeth II
Obv: Laureate bust right **Rev:** St. George slaying the dragon

Date	Mintage	F	VF	XF	Unc	BU
1957	2,072,000	—	—	—	BV	245	—
1957 Proof	—	—	—	—	—	—
1958	8,700,000	—	—	—	BV	245	—
1958 Proof	—	—	—	—	—	—
1959	1,358,000	—	—	—	BV	245	—
1959 Proof	—	—	—	—	—	—
1962	3,000,000	—	—	—	BV	245	—
1962 Proof	—	—	—	—	—	—
1963	7,400,000	—	—	—	BV	245	—
1963 Proof	—	—	—	—	—	—
1964	3,000,000	—	—	—	BV	245	—
1965	3,800,000	—	—	—	BV	245	—
1966	7,050,000	—	—	—	BV	245	—
1967	5,000,000	—	—	—	BV	245	—
1968	4,203,000	—	—	—	BV	245	—

KM# 919 SOVEREIGN
7.9881 g., 0.9170 Gold 0.2355 oz. AGW **Ruler:** Elizabeth II
Obv: Young bust right **Rev:** St. George slaying the dragon

Date	Mintage	F	VF	XF	Unc	BU
1974	5,003,000	—	—	—	BV	245
1976	4,150,000	—	—	—	BV	245
1978	6,550,000	—	—	—	BV	245
1979	9,100,000	—	—	—	BV	245
1979 Proof	50,000	Value: 240				
1980	5,100,000	—	—	—	BV	245
1980 Proof	91,000	Value: 240				
1981	5,000,000	—	—	—	BV	245
1981 Proof	33,000	Value: 240				
1982	2,950,000	—	—	—	BV	245
1982 Proof	23,000	Value: 240				
1983 Proof	21,000	Value: 240				
1984 Proof	20,000	Value: 240				

KM# 943 SOVEREIGN
7.9881 g., 0.9170 Gold 0.2355 oz. AGW **Ruler:** Elizabeth II
Obv: Crowned head right **Rev:** St. George slaying the dragon

Date	Mintage	F	VF	XF	Unc	BU
1985 Proof	17,000	Value: 240				
1986 Proof	25,000	Value: 240				
1987 Proof	22,000	Value: 240				
1988 Proof	Est. 25,000	Value: 240				
1990 Proof	Est. 20,000	Value: 240				
1991 Proof	Est. 9,000	Value: 260				
1992 Proof	7,500	Value: 260				
1993 Proof	7,500	Value: 260				
1994 Proof	Est. 7,500	Value: 260				
1995 Proof	7,500	Value: 260				
1996 Proof	7,500	Value: 260				
1997 Proof	7,500	Value: 260				

KM# 956 SOVEREIGN
7.9881 g., 0.9170 Gold 0.2355 oz. AGW **Ruler:** Elizabeth II
Subject: 500th Anniversary of the Gold Sovereign
Obv: Elizabeth II seated on coronation throne **Rev:** Crowned and quartered shield on tudor rose

Date	Mintage	F	VF	XF	Unc	BU
ND(1989) Proof	Est. 28,000	Value: 1,250				

KM# 1002 SOVEREIGN
7.9881 g., 0.9170 Gold 0.2355 oz. AGW **Ruler:** Elizabeth II
Obv: Head with tiara right **Rev:** St. George slaying the dragon

Date	Mintage	F	VF	XF	Unc	BU
1998 Proof	10,000	Value: 260				
1999 Proof	10,000	Value: 350				
2000	129,069	—	—	—	—	245
2000 Proof	10,000	Value: 250				

KM# 806 2 POUNDS
15.9761 g., 0.9170 Gold 0.4710 oz. AGW **Ruler:** Edward VII
Obv: Head right **Rev:** St. George slaying the dragon

Date	Mintage	F	VF	XF	Unc	BU
1902	46,000	—	BV	475	700	—
1902 Proof	8,066	Value: 750				

Note: Proof issues with mint mark S below right rear hoof of horse were struck at Sydney, refer to Australia listings

KM# 821 2 POUNDS
15.9761 g., 0.9170 Gold 0.4710 oz. AGW **Ruler:** George V
Obv: Head left **Rev:** St. George slaying the dragon

Date	Mintage	F	VF	XF	Unc	BU
1911 Proof	2,812	Value: 1,100				

KM# 860 2 POUNDS
15.9761 g., 0.9170 Gold 0.4710 oz. AGW **Ruler:** George VI
Obv: Head left **Rev:** St. George slaying the dragon

Date	Mintage	F	VF	XF	Unc	BU
1937 Proof	5,500	Value: 1,100				
1937 Matte Proof; Unique	—	—	—	—	—	—

KM# 923 2 POUNDS
15.9200 g., 0.9170 Gold 0.4693 oz. AGW **Ruler:** Elizabeth II
Obv: Young bust right

Date	Mintage	F	VF	XF	Unc	BU
1980 Proof	10,000	Value: 450				
1982 Proof	2,500	Value: 450				
1983 Proof	13,000	Value: 450				

KM# 944 2 POUNDS
15.9200 g., 0.9170 Gold 0.4693 oz. AGW **Ruler:** Elizabeth II
Obv: Crowned head right **Rev:** St. George slaying the dragon

Date	Mintage	F	VF	XF	Unc	BU
1985 Proof	5,849	Value: 465				
1987 Proof	14,000	Value: 465				
1988 Proof	15,000	Value: 465				
1990 Proof	Est. 12,000	Value: 465				
1991 Proof	Est. 5,000	Value: 465				
1992 Proof	3,000	Value: 465				

Date	Mintage	F	VF	XF	Unc	BU
1993 Proof	3,000	Value: 465				
1999 Proof	—	Value: 500				

KM# 957 2 POUNDS
15.9800 g., 0.9170 Gold 0.4711 oz. AGW **Ruler:** Elizabeth II
Subject: 500th Anniversary of the Gold Sovereign
Obv: Elizabeth II seated on Coronation throne **Rev:** Crowned and quartered shield on tudor rose

Date	Mintage	F	VF	XF	Unc	BU
ND(1989) Proof	Est. 17,000	Value: 1,350				

KM# 807 5 POUNDS
39.9403 g., 0.9170 Gold 1.1775 oz. AGW **Ruler:** Edward VII
Obv: Head right **Rev:** St. George slaying the dragon

Date	Mintage	F	VF	XF	Unc	BU
1902	Est. 35,000	—	BV	1,200	1,600	—

Note: 27,000 pieces were melted

1902 Proof	8,066	Value: 1,400				

Note: Proof issues with mint mark S below right rear hoof of horse were struck at Sydney, refer to Australia listings

KM# 822 5 POUNDS
39.9403 g., 0.9170 Gold 1.1775 oz. AGW **Ruler:** George V
Obv: Head left **Rev:** St. George slaying the dragon

Date	Mintage	F	VF	XF	Unc	BU
1911 Proof	2,812	Value: 2,750				

KM# 861 5 POUNDS
39.9403 g., 0.9170 Gold 1.1775 oz. AGW **Ruler:** George VI
Obv: Head left **Rev:** St. George slaying the dragon

Date	Mintage	F	VF	XF	Unc	BU
1937 Proof	5,500	Value: 1,750				

Note: Impaired and blemished proofs of the 1937 issue are common and trade at much lower values; The value listed here is for blemish-free examples

1937 Matte Proof; Unique	—	—	—	—	—	—

KM# 924 5 POUNDS
39.9400 g., 0.9170 Gold 1.1775 oz. AGW **Ruler:** Elizabeth II
Obv: Young bust right **Rev:** St. George slaying the dragon

Date	Mintage	F	VF	XF	Unc	BU
1980 Proof	10,000	Value: 1,200				
1981 Proof	5,400	Value: 1,200				
1982 Proof	2,500	Value: 1,200				
1984 Proof	8,000	Value: 1,200				
1984	25,000	—	—	—	—	1,250

KM# 945 5 POUNDS
39.9400 g., 0.9170 Gold 1.1775 oz. AGW **Ruler:** Elizabeth II
Obv: Crowned head right **Rev:** St. George slaying the dragon

Date	Mintage	F	VF	XF	Unc	BU
1985	14,000	—	—	—	—	1,250
1985 Proof	13,000	Value: 1,200				
1986	7,723	—	—	—	—	1,250
1990	1,226	—	—	—	—	1,250
1990 Proof	Est. 2,500	Value: 1,200				
1991	976	—	—	—	—	1,300
1991 Proof	Est. 1,500	Value: 1,200				
1992	797	—	—	—	—	1,300
1992 Proof	1,250	Value: 1,200				
1993	906	—	—	—	—	1,300
1994 Proof	Est. 1,250	Value: 1,200				
1995	Est. 1,000	—	—	—	—	1,300
1995 Proof	Est. 1,250	Value: 1,200				
1996	901	—	—	—	—	1,300
1997	802	—	—	—	—	1,300

KM# 949 5 POUNDS
39.9400 g., 0.9170 Gold 1.1775 oz. AGW **Ruler:** Elizabeth II
Obv: Crowned head right **Rev:** St. George slaying the dragon

Date	Mintage	F	VF	XF	Unc	BU
1987	10,000	—	—	—	—	1,150
1988	Est. 10,000	—	—	—	—	1,150

KM# 958 5 POUNDS
39.9400 g., 0.9170 Gold 1.1775 oz. AGW **Ruler:** Elizabeth II
Subject: 500th Anniversary of the Gold Sovereign
Obv: Elizabeth II seated on Coronation throne **Rev:** Crowned and quartered shield on tudor rose

Date	Mintage	F	VF	XF	Unc	BU
1989	10,000	—	—	—	—	1,500
1989 Proof	Est. 5,000	Value: 1,600				

KM# 1003   5 POUNDS
39.9400 g., 0.9170 Gold 1.1775 oz. AGW, 36 mm.
Ruler: Elizabeth II **Obv:** Head with tiara right **Rev:** St. George slaying dragon **Edge:** Reeded

Date	Mintage	F	VF	XF	Unc	BU
1999 Proof	—	Value: 1,200				
2000	10,000	—	—	—	—	1,150

BULLION COINAGE

Until 1990, .917 Gold was commonly alloyed with copper by the British Royal Mint.

All proof issues have designers name as P. Nathan. The uncirculated issues use only Nathan.

KM# 978   20 PENCE
3.2400 g., 0.9580 Silver 0.0998 oz. ASW, 16.5 mm.
Ruler: Elizabeth II **Obv:** Crowned head right **Rev:** Britannia in chariot **Edge:** Reeded

Date	Mintage	F	VF	XF	Unc	BU
1997 Proof	8,686	Value: 25.00				

KM# 1079   20 PENCE
3.2400 g., 0.9584 Silver 0.0998 oz. ASW, 16.5 mm.
Ruler: Elizabeth II **Obv:** Head with tiara right **Rev:** Britannia standing **Edge:** Reeded

Date	Mintage	F	VF	XF	Unc	BU
1998 Proof	—	Value: 25.00				
2000 Proof	—	Value: 25.00				

KM# 1082   20 PENCE
3.2400 g., 0.9584 Silver 0.0998 oz. ASW, 16.5 mm.
Ruler: Elizabeth II **Obv:** Head with tiara right **Rev:** Britannia in chariot right **Edge:** Reeded

Date	Mintage	F	VF	XF	Unc	BU
1999 Proof	—	Value: 25.00				

KM# 979   50 PENCE
8.1100 g., 0.9580 Silver 0.2498 oz. ASW, 27.3 mm.
Ruler: Elizabeth II **Obv:** Crowned head right **Rev:** Britannia in chariot

Date	Mintage	F	VF	XF	Unc	BU
1997	Est. 15,000	Value: 25.00				

Note: In proof sets only

KM# 1080   50 PENCE
8.1100 g., 0.9584 Silver 0.2499 oz. ASW, 22 mm. **Obv:** Head with tiara right **Rev:** Britannia standing **Edge:** Reeded

Date	Mintage	F	VF	XF	Unc	BU
1998 Proof	—	Value: 35.00				
2000 Proof	—	Value: 35.00				

KM# 980   POUND
16.2200 g., 0.9580 Silver 0.4996 oz. ASW   **Ruler:** Elizabeth II **Obv:** Crowned head right **Rev:** Britannia in chariot

Date	Mintage	F	VF	XF	Unc	BU
1997 Proof	Est. 15,000	Value: 40.00				

KM# 1081   POUND
16.2200 g., 0.9584 Silver 0.4998 oz. ASW, 27 mm.
Ruler: Elizabeth II **Obv:** Head with tiara right **Rev:** Britannia standing **Edge:** Reeded

Date	Mintage	F	VF	XF	Unc	BU
1998 Proof	—	Value: 50.00				
2000 Proof	—	Value: 50.00				

KM# 1084   POUND
16.2200 g., 0.9584 Silver 0.4998 oz. ASW, 27 mm.
Ruler: Elizabeth II **Obv:** Head with tiara right **Rev:** Britannia in chariot right **Edge:** Reeded

Date	Mintage	F	VF	XF	Unc	BU
1999 Proof	—	Value: 50.00				

KM# 981   2 POUNDS
32.5400 g., 0.9580 Silver 1.0022 oz. ASW   **Ruler:** Elizabeth II **Obv:** Crowned head right **Rev:** Britannia in chariot

Date	Mintage	F	VF	XF	Unc	BU
1997 Proof	Est. 35,000	Value: 50.00				

KM# 1029   2 POUNDS
32.5400 g., 0.9580 Silver 1.0022 oz. ASW, 40 mm.
Ruler: Elizabeth II **Obv:** Head with tiara right **Rev:** Standing Britannia **Edge:** Reeded

Date	Mintage	F	VF	XF	Unc	BU
1998	88,909	—	—	—	—	25.00
1998 Proof	2,168	Value: 50.00				
2000	81,301	—	—	—	—	27.50
2000 Proof	—	Value: 50.00				

KM# 1000   2 POUNDS
32.5400 g., 0.9580 Silver 1.0022 oz. ASW   **Ruler:** Elizabeth II **Obv:** Head with tiara right **Rev:** Britannia in chariot

Date	Mintage	F	VF	XF	Unc	BU
1999 Proof	Est. 100,000	Value: 45.00				

KM# 950   10 POUNDS (1/10 Ounce - Britannia)
3.4120 g., 0.9170 Gold 0.1006 oz. AGW   **Ruler:** Elizabeth II **Obv:** Crowned head right **Rev:** Britannia standing **Note:** Copper alloy.

Date	Mintage	F	VF	XF	Unc	BU
1987	—	—	—	—	BV+16%	
1987 Proof	3,500	Value: 115				
1988	—	—	—	—	BV+16%	
1988 Proof	2,694	Value: 115				
1989	—	—	—	—	BV+16%	
1989 Proof	1,609	Value: 115				

KM# 950a   10 POUNDS (1/10 Ounce - Britannia)
3.4120 g., 0.9170 Gold 0.1006 oz. AGW, 16.5 mm.
Ruler: Elizabeth II **Obv:** Crowned head right **Rev:** Britannia standing **Edge:** Reeded **Note:** Silver alloy.

Date	Mintage	F	VF	XF	Unc	BU
1990 Proof	1,571	Value: 120				
1991 Proof	954	Value: 135				
1992 Proof	1,000	Value: 135				
1993 Proof	997	Value: 135				
1994 Proof	994	Value: 120				
1995 Proof	1,500	Value: 120				
1996 Proof	2,379	Value: 120				

KM# 982   10 POUNDS (1/10 Ounce - Britannia)
3.4100 g., 0.9167 Gold 0.1005 oz. AGW   **Ruler:** Elizabeth II **Obv:** Crowned head right **Rev:** Britannia in chariot

Date	Mintage	F	VF	XF	Unc	BU
1997 Proof	11,821	Value: 130				

KM# 1008   10 POUNDS (1/10 Ounce - Britannia)
3.4100 g., 0.9167 Gold 0.1005 oz. AGW, 16.5 mm.
Ruler: Elizabeth II **Obv:** Head with tiara right **Rev:** Britannia standing **Edge:** Reeded

Date	Mintage	F	VF	XF	Unc	BU
1998 Proof	—	Value: 125				
1999 Proof	1,058	Value: 125				
2000 Proof	659	Value: 200				

KM# 951   25 POUNDS (1/4 Ounce - Britannia)
8.5130 g., 0.9170 Gold 0.2510 oz. AGW   **Ruler:** Elizabeth II **Obv:** Crowned head right **Rev:** Britannia standing **Note:** Copper alloy.

Date	Mintage	F	VF	XF	Unc	BU
1987	—	—	—	—	BV+10%	
1987 Proof	3,500	Value: 275				
1988	—	—	—	—	BV+10%	
1988 Proof	Est. 14,000	Value: 275				
1989	—	—	—	—	BV+10%	
1989 Proof	Est. 4,000	Value: 275				

KM# 951a   25 POUNDS (1/4 Ounce - Britannia)
8.5130 g., 0.9170 Gold 0.2510 oz. AGW, 22 mm.
Ruler: Elizabeth II **Obv:** Head with tiara right **Rev:** Britannia standing **Edge:** Reeded **Note:** Silver alloy.

Date	Mintage	F	VF	XF	Unc	BU
1990 Proof	Est. 2,500	Value: 275				
1991 Proof	750	Value: 275				
1992 Proof	500	Value: 275				
1993 Proof	Est. 500	Value: 275				
1994 Proof	500	Value: 275				
1995 Proof	500	Value: 275				
1996 Proof	2,500	Value: 275				

KM# 983   25 POUNDS (1/4 Ounce - Britannia)
8.5100 g., 0.9167 Gold 0.2508 oz. AGW   **Ruler:** Elizabeth II **Obv:** Crowned head right **Rev:** Britannia in chariot

Date	Mintage	F	VF	XF	Unc	BU
1997 Proof	Est. 4,000	Value: 240				

KM# 1009   25 POUNDS (1/4 Ounce - Britannia)
8.5100 g., 0.9167 Gold 0.2508 oz. AGW, 22 mm.
Ruler: Elizabeth II **Obv:** Head with tiara right **Rev:** Britannia standing **Edge:** Reeded

Date	Mintage	F	VF	XF	Unc	BU
1998 Proof	—	Value: 350				
1999 Proof	1,000	Value: 275				
2000 Proof	Est. 500	Value: 275				

KM# 952   50 POUNDS (1/2 Ounce - Britannia)
17.0250 g., 0.9170 Gold 0.5019 oz. AGW   **Ruler:** Elizabeth II **Obv:** Crowned head right **Rev:** Britannia standing **Note:** Copper alloy.

Date	Mintage	F	VF	XF	Unc	BU
1987	—	—	—	—	BV+10%	
1987 Proof	2,486	Value: 535				
1988	—	—	—	—	BV+10%	
1988 Proof	626	Value: 535				
1989	—	—	—	—	BV+10%	
1989 Proof	338	Value: 535				

KM# 952a   50 POUNDS (1/2 Ounce - Britannia)
17.0250 g., 0.9170 Gold 0.5019 oz. AGW, 27 mm.
Ruler: Elizabeth II **Obv:** Crowned head right **Rev:** Britannia standing **Edge:** Reeded **Note:** Silver alloy.

Date	Mintage	F	VF	XF	Unc	BU
1990 Proof	527	Value: 535				
1991 Proof	509	Value: 535				
1992 Proof	500	Value: 535				
1993 Proof	462	Value: 535				
1994 Proof	435	Value: 535				
1995 Proof	500	Value: 535				
1996 Proof	483	Value: 535				

KM# 984   50 POUNDS (1/2 Ounce - Britannia)
17.0300 g., 0.9167 Gold 0.5019 oz. AGW   **Ruler:** Elizabeth II **Obv:** Crowned head right **Rev:** Britannia in chariot

Date	Mintage	F	VF	XF	Unc	BU
1997 Proof	Est. 1,500	Value: 470				

KM# 1010   50 POUNDS (1/2 Ounce - Britannia)
17.0300 g., 0.9167 Gold 0.5019 oz. AGW, 27 mm.
Ruler: Elizabeth II **Obv:** Head with tiara right **Rev:** Britannia standing **Edge:** Reeded

Date	Mintage	F	VF	XF	Unc	BU
1998 Proof	—	Value: 600				
1999 Proof	—	Value: 550				
2000 Proof	750	Value: 550				

KM# 953   100 POUNDS (1 Ounce - Britannia)
34.0500 g., 0.9170 Gold 1.0038 oz. AGW **Ruler:** Elizabeth II **Obv:** Crowned head right **Rev:** Britannia standing **Note:** Copper alloy.

Date	Mintage	F	VF	XF	Unc	BU
1987	—	—	—	—	—BV+12%	—
1987 Proof	13,000	Value: 1,100				
1988	—	—	—	—	—BV+12%	—
1988 Proof	Est. 8,500	Value: 1,100				
1989	—	—	—	—	—BV+12%	—
1989 Proof	Est. 2,600	Value: 1,100				

KM# 953a   100 POUNDS (1 Ounce - Britannia)
34.0500 g., 0.9170 Gold 1.0038 oz. AGW, 32.7 mm.
Ruler: Elizabeth II **Obv:** Crowned head right **Rev:** Britannia standing **Edge:** Reeded **Note:** Silver alloy.

Date	Mintage	F	VF	XF	Unc	BU
1990 Proof	262	Value: 1,100				
1991 Proof	143	Value: 1,100				
1992 Proof	500	Value: 1,100				
1993 Proof	Est. 500	Value: 1,100				
1994 Proof	Est. 500	Value: 1,100				
1995 Proof	Est. 500	Value: 1,100				
1996 Proof	2,500	Value: 1,100				

KM# 985   100 POUNDS (1 Ounce - Britannia)
34.0500 g., 0.9167 Gold 1.0035 oz. AGW **Ruler:** Elizabeth II **Obv:** Crowned head right **Rev:** Britannia in chariot

Date	Mintage	F	VF	XF	Unc	BU
1997	—	—	—	—	—BV+15%	—
1997 Proof	164	Value: 950				

KM# 1011   100 POUNDS (1 Ounce - Britannia)
34.0500 g., 0.9167 Gold 1.0035 oz. AGW, 32.7 mm.
Ruler: Elizabeth II **Obv:** Head with tiara right **Rev:** Britannia standing **Edge:** Reeded

Date	Mintage	F	VF	XF	Unc	BU
1998	—	—	—	—	—	—BV+15%
1998 Proof	—	Value: 1,150				
1999	—	—	—	—	—	—BV+15%
1999 Proof	—	Value: 1,150				
2000	—	—	—	—	—	—BV+15%
2000 Proof	750	Value: 1,150				

TRADE COINAGE
Britannia Issues

Issued to facilitate British trade in the Orient, the reverse design incorporated the denomination in Chinese characters and Malay script.

This issue was struck at the Bombay (B) and Calcutta (C) Mints in India, except for 1925 and 1930 issues which were struck at London. Through error the mint marks did not appear on some early (1895-1900) issues as indicated.

KM# T5   DOLLAR
26.9568 g., 0.9000 Silver 0.7800 oz. ASW **Obv:** Britannia standing **Rev:** Oriental designs on cross **Note:** Miltmark is located within the top of the trident held by Britannia.

Date	Mintage	F	VF	XF	Unc	BU
1901/0B	25,680,000	40.00	60.00	100	200	—
1901B	Inc. above	20.00	25.00	30.00	70.00	—
1901C	1,514,000	25.00	45.00	100	200	—
1901B Proof	Inc. above	Value: 800				
1902B	30,404,000	20.00	25.00	30.00	70.00	—
1902C	1,267,000	25.00	45.00	80.00	175	—
1902B Proof	Inc. above	Value: 800				
1902C Proof	Inc. above	Value: 800				
1903/2B	3,956,000	20.00	25.00	40.00	75.00	—
1903B	Inc. above	20.00	25.00	—	70.00	—
1903B Proof	Inc. above	Value: 800				
1904/898B	649,000	50.00	80.00	125	200	—
1904/3B	Inc. above	30.00	50.00	100	225	—
1904/0B	Inc. above	80.00	125	175	300	—
1904B	Inc. above	40.00	60.00	100	250	—
1904B Proof	Inc. above	Value: 700				
1907B	1,946,000	20.00	25.00	30.00	70.00	—

Date	Mintage	F	VF	XF	Unc	BU
1908/3B	6,871,000	40.00	60.00	100	175	—
1908/7B	Inc. above	35.00	50.00	90.00	125	—
1908B	Inc. above	20.00	25.00	30.00	70.00	—
1908B Proof	Inc. above	Value: 700				
1909/8B	5,954,000	30.00	45.00	80.00	125	—
1909B	Inc. above	20.00	25.00	30.00	70.00	—
1910/00B	553,000	40.00	60.00	100	175	—
1910B	Inc. above	20.00	25.00	30.00	70.00	—
1911/00B	—	30.00	50.00	100	150	—
1911B	37,471,000	20.00	25.00	30.00	60.00	—
1912B	5,672,000	20.00	25.00	30.00	60.00	—
1912B Proof	Inc. above	Value: 800				
1913/2B	—	100	150	250	700	—
1913B	1,567,000	40.00	60.00	125	300	—
1913B Proof	Inc. above	Value: 800				
1921B	5	—	—	—	15,000	—

Note: Original mintage 50,211.

Date	Mintage	F	VF	XF	Unc	BU
1921B Proof; restrike	—	Value: 4,500				
1925	6,870,000	22.00	28.00	32.00	80.00	—
1929/1B	5,100,000	30.00	50.00	80.00	200	—
1929B	Inc. above	20.00	25.00	30.00	60.00	—
1929B Proof	Inc. above	Value: 800				
1930B	10,400,000	20.00	25.00	30.00	60.00	—
1930B Proof	Inc. above	Value: 800				
1930	6,660,000	20.00	25.00	30.00	60.00	—
1934B	17,335,000	80.00	150	200	550	—
1934B Proof	Inc. above	Value: 3,500				
1934B Proof; restrike	20	Value: 3,000				
1935B	Est. 25	1,000	1,500	2,500	15,000	—

Note: Original mintage 6,811,995.

Date	Mintage	F	VF	XF	Unc	BU
1935B Proof	20	Value: 7,500				
1935B Proof; restrike	20	Value: 4,000				

KM# T5a   DOLLAR
Gold **Obv:** Britannia standing **Rev:** Oriental design on cross

Date	Mintage	F	VF	XF	Unc	BU
1901B Proof; restrike	—	Value: 7,500				
1902B Proof; restrike	—	Value: 7,500				

PIEFORTS

KM#	Date	Mintage	Identification	Mkt Val
P1	1973	—	50 Pence. 0.9250 Silver.	1,250
P2	1982	—	20 Pence. 0.9250 Silver.	50.00
P3	1983	10,000	Pound. 0.9250 Silver. KM#933.	125
P4	1984	15,000	Pound. 0.9250 Silver. KM#934.	50.00
P5	1985	15,000	Pound. 0.9250 Silver. KM#941.	45.00
P6	1986	15,000	Pound. 0.9250 Silver. KM#946.	45.00
P7	1987	15,000	Pound. 0.9250 Silver. KM#948.	45.00
P8	1988	15,000	Pound. 0.9250 Silver. KM#954.	45.00
P9	1989	15,000	Pound. 0.9250 Silver. KM#959.	45.00
P10	1989	25,000	2 Pounds. 0.9250 Silver. KM#960a.	47.50
P11	1989	10,000	2 Pounds. 0.9250 Silver. KM#961a.	47.50
P12	1990	20,000	5 Pence. 0.9250 Silver. KM#937c.	25.00
P13	1992	15,000	10 Pence. 0.9250 Silver. KM#938b.	50.00
P15	1992	—	50 Pence. 0.9250 Silver. KM#963a.	70.00
P16	1993	—	Pound. 0.9250 Silver. KM#964.	47.50
P17	1994	—	50 Pence. 0.9250 Silver. KM#966b.	65.00
P18	1994	—	Pound. 0.9250 Silver. KM#967.	70.00
P19	1994	—	2 Pounds. 0.9250 Silver. KM#968a.	80.00
P20	1995	8,458	Pound. 0.9250 Silver. KM#969.	65.00
P21	1995	—	2 Pounds. 0.9250 Silver. KM#970a.	70.00
P22	1995	—	2 Pounds. 0.9250 Silver. KM#971a.	70.00
P23	1996	10,000	Pound. 0.9250 Silver. KM#972.	60.00
	1996	—	25 Euro. 0.9990 Silver. 41.7100 g. X#M31.	85.00
P24	1997	—	50 Pence. 0.9250 Silver. KM#963.	70.00
P25	1997	—	Pound. 0.9250 Silver. KM#975.	70.00
P26	1998	—	Pound. 0.9250 Silver. KM#993a.	—
P27	1997	—	2 Pounds. 0.9250 Silver. KM#976a.	75.00
P28	1998	—	50 Pence. 0.9250 Silver. KM#992a.	70.00
P29	1998	—	50 Pence. 0.9250 Silver. KM#996a.	70.00
P30	1998	—	2 Pounds. 0.9250 Silver. KM#994a.	75.00
P31	1999	—	Pound. 0.9250 Silver. KM998a	—

TRIAL STRIKES

KM#	Date	Mintage	Identification	Mkt Val
TS1	1926	—	3 Pence. Silver. MODEL. Thistle.	1,500
TS2	1926	—	6 Pence. Silver. MODEL.	1,200
TS3	1926	—	Shilling. Silver. MODEL. Lion on crown.	1,500
TS4	1926	—	2 Shilling. Silver. MODEL. Stemmed rose.	1,750
TS5	1926	—	1/2 Crown. Silver. MODEL. Crown over heraldic shield.	4,000
TSA6	1926	—	Crown. Silver. MODEL, Britannia reclining. 2-3 pieces	10,000

Note: A complete set of silver plated copper electro types officially prepared for the designer has been recorded; Market value $2,000

KM#	Date	Mintage	Identification	Mkt Val
TS6	1926	—	Crown. Silver. Britannia reclining. Blank. (MCMXXVI) Unique	15,000
TS7	1963	—	1/4 New Penny. Aluminum. Rose. Uniface.	—
TS8	1963	—	1/2 New Penny. Bronze. Winged animal. Uniface.	—
TS9	1963	—	New Penny. Bronze. Uniface.	—
TS10	1963	—	2 New Pence. Bronze. Britannia seated right. Uniface.	—
TS11	1963	—	5 New Pence. Copper-Nickel. Three crowns. Uniface.	—
TS12	1963	—	10 New Pence. Silver. Uniface.	—
TS13	1963	—	20 New Pence. Silver. Uniface.	—
TS14	1963	—	20 New Pence. Silver. Helmeted and supported arms. Uniface.	—

PATTERNS
Including off metal strikes

KM#	Date	Mintage	Identification	Mkt Val
PnA121	1922	—	Florin. Gold. KM817a	2,500
PnC121	1923	—	Shilling. Nickel. KM816a	1,400
PnB121	1923	—	3 Pence. Nickel. KM#813a.	3,500
Pn121	1924	—	Shilling. Nickel. KM816a	1,400
PnFJ121	1924	—	Shilling. Nickel. 5.0000 g. KM816a	1,400
PnD121	1924	1	3 Pence. Gold. KM813a	10,000
pnE121	1924	3	6 Pence. Gold. KM#815a.1	10,000
PnA122	1925	—	3 Pence. Nickel. Modified effigy. KM#831.	2,500
PnB122	1925	—	3 Pence. Silver. MODEL. Matte proof; KM#831.	2,500
PnC122	1925	—	6 Pence. Nickel. Modified effigy. KM#832.	1,850
PnD122	1925	—	6 Pence. Silver. MODEL. Matte proof; KM#832.	1,850
PnE122	1925	—	Shilling. Nickel. Modified effigy. KM#833.	2,500
PnF122	1925	—	Shilling. Silver. MODEL. Matte proof; Reverse of KM#833.	2,500
PnG122	1926	—	1/2 Crown. Silver. MODEL. 1-2 pieces, Matte proof; KM#835.	5,000
PnH122	1926	—	Crown. Silver. MODEL. Matte proof; KM#836.	—
PnK122	1927	—	1/2 Crown. Nickel. Modified effigy. KM830	—
PnL122	1927	—	1/2 Crown. Gold. Modified Effigy. KM830	—
PnJ122	1927	—	Florin. Silver. MODEL. Matte proof, KM#834.	2,500
PnI122	1927	—	6 Pence. Nickel. KM#828	1,200
PnJ122A	1927	—	Shilling. Silver. MODEL. Unique. Reverse of KM#833	—
PnM122	1935	—	Crown. Gold. Similar to KM842.	35,000
Pn123	1937	18,000	1/2 Penny. Bronze. Edward VIII.	3,000
Pn125	1937	—	3 Pence. Nickel-Brass. Edward VIII.	25,000
Pn126	1937	—	3 Pence. Nickel-Brass. Head left. Thrift Plant. Edward VIII.	45,000
Pn128	1937	25,000	Shilling. 0.5000 Silver. Head left. Scottish Crest. Edward VIII.	37,000
Pn131	1937	120,000	Crown. 0.5000 Silver. Head left. Crowned and quartered shield with supporters. Edward VIII.	150,000
Pn132	1937	6	Sovereign. 0.9160 Gold. Head left. St. George slaying the dragon. Edward VIII.	300,000
Pn130a	1937	—	1/2 Crown. 0.5000 Silver. Head left. Rev Model. Edward III	12,000
Pn124	1937	25,000	Penny. Bronze. Head left. Edward VIII.	—
Pn127	1937	18,000	6 Pence. 0.5000 Silver. Head left. Six joined rings form design. Edward VIII.	—
Pn129	1937	35,000	Florin. 0.5000 Silver. Edward VIII.	—
Pn130	1937	60,000	1/2 Crown. 0.5000 Silver. Head left. Quartered flag divides crowned monograms. Edward VIII.	—
Pn122	1937	18,000	Farthing. Bronze. Head left. Wren left. Edward VIII.	—
Pn133	1946	—	6 Pence. Copper-Nickel. KM# 852.	—
PnA133	1946	—	Shilling. Copper-Nickel. KM# 853.	2,000
PnB133	1946	—	2 Shilling. Copper-Nickel. KM# 855.	2,000
PnC133	1946	—	1/2 Crown. Copper-Nickel. KM# 856.	—
PnA134	1950	—	4 Shilling. Copper-Nickel.	—
PnA134a	1950	—	Farthing. Copper-Nickel.	1,500
PnB134	1952	—	Shilling. Nickel. KM#876.	—
Pn134	1953	—	Penny. Bronze. Dentilated border.	—
PnA135	1953	—	Crown. Copper-Nickel. Matte, KM#894.	—
Pn135	1953	—	1/2 Sovereign. 0.9160 Gold.	—
Pn137	1953	—	2 Pounds. 0.9160 Gold.	—
Pn138	1953	—	5 Pounds. 0.9160 Gold.	—
Pn136	1953	—	Sovereign. 0.9160 Gold. Y#137.	40,000
Pn139	1961	—	Cent. Bronze.	—
Pn140	1961	—	2 Cents. Bronze.	—
Pn141	1961	—	5 Cents. Copper-Nickel. Lion on crown.	—
Pn142	1961	—	10 Cents. Copper-Nickel.	—
Pn143	1961	—	20 Cents. Copper-Nickel. Britannia, standing facing.	—
Pn144	1961	—	50 Cents. Silver. Una and lion.	—
Pn145	1963	—	1/2 Penny. Bronze. Decimal.	—
Pn146	1963	—	Penny. Bronze. Decimal.	—

MAUNDY SETS

KM#	Date	Mintage	Identification	Issue Price	Mkt Val
MDS157	1901 (4)	8,976	KM#775-778	—	150
MDS158	1902 (4)	8,976	KM#795-796, 797.1-798	—	125
MDS159	1902 (4)	—	KM#795-796, 797.1-798 Proof	—	150
MDS160	1903 (4)	8,976	KM#795-796; 797.1-798	—	125
MDS161	1904 (4)	8,976	KM#795-796, 797.1-798	—	150
MDS162	1905 (4)	8,976	KM#795-796, 797.2-798	—	150
MDS163	1906 (4)	8,800	KM#795-796, 797.2-798	—	125
MDS164	1907 (4)	8,760	KM#795-796, 797.2-798	—	125
MDS165	1908 (4)	8,760	KM#795-796, 797.2-798	—	125
MDS166	1909 (4)	1,983	KM#795-796, 797.2-798	—	225
MDS167	1910 (4)	1,440	KM#795-796, 797.2-798	—	245
MDS168	1911 (4)	1,768	KM#811-814	—	195
MDS169	1911 (4)	6,007	KM#811-814 Proof	—	195
MDS170	1912 (4)	1,246	KM#811-814	—	195
MDS171	1913 (4)	1,228	KM#811-814	—	195
MDS172	1914 (4)	982	KM#811-814	—	215
MDS173	1915 (4)	1,293	KM#811-814	—	195
MDS174	1916 (4)	1,128	KM#811-814	—	185

KM#	Date	Mintage	Identification	Issue Price	Mkt Val
MDS175	1917 (4)	1,237	KM#811-814	—	195
MDS176	1918 (4)	1,375	KM#811-814	—	185
MDS177	1919 (4)	1,258	KM#811-814	—	195
MDS178	1920 (4)	1,399	KM#811-814	—	195
MDS179	1921 (4)	1,386	KM#811a-814a	—	200
MDS180	1922 (4)	1,373	KM#811a-814a	—	195
MDS181	1923 (4)	1,430	KM#811a-814a	—	200
MDS182	1924 (4)	1,515	KM#811a-814a	—	200
MDS183	1925 (4)	1,438	KM#811a-814a	—	185
MDS184	1926 (4)	1,504	KM#811a-814a	—	185
MDS185	1927 (4)	1,647	KM#811a-814a	—	195
MDS186	1928 (4)	1,642	KM#827, 839-841	—	195
MDS187	1929 (4)	1,761	KM#827, 839-841	—	200
MDS188	1930 (4)	1,724	KM#827, 839-841	—	185
MDS189	1931 (4)	1,759	KM#827, 839-841	—	185
MDS190	1932 (4)	1,835	KM#827, 839-841	—	185
MDS191	1933 (4)	1,872	KM#827, 839-841	—	185
MDS192	1934 (4)	1,887	KM#827, 839-841	—	185
MDS193	1935 (4)	1,926	KM#827, 839-841	—	210
MDS194	1936 (4)	1,323	KM#827, 839-841	—	225
MDS195	1937 (4)	1,325	KM#846-847, 850-851	—	160
MDS196	1937 (4)	26,000	KM#846-847, 850-851 Proof	—	160
MDS197	1938 (4)	1,275	KM#846-847, 850-851	—	185
MDS198	1939 (4)	1,234	KM#846-847, 850-851	—	185
MDS199	1940 (4)	1,277	KM#846-847, 850-851	—	185
MDS200	1941 (4)	1,253	KM#846-847, 850-851	—	195
MDS201	1942 (4)	1,231	KM#846-847, 850-851	—	185
MDS202	1943 (4)	1,239	KM#846-847, 850-851	—	185
MDS203	1944 (4)	1,259	KM#846-847, 850-851	—	185
MDS204	1945 (4)	1,355	KM#846-847, 850-851	—	185
MDS205	1946 (4)	1,365	KM#846-847, 850-851	—	185
MDS206	1947 (4)	1,375	KM#846a-847a, 850a-851a	—	195
MDS207	1948 (4)	1,385	KM#846a-847a, 850a-851a	—	195
MDS208	1949 (4)	1,395	KM#870-872, 874	—	195
MDS209	1950 (4)	1,405	KM#870-872, 874	—	195
MDS210	1951 (4)	1,468	KM#870-872, 874, also struck in matte proof	—	195
MDS211	1952 (4)	1,012	KM#870-872, 874	—	225
MDS212	1953 (4)	1,025	KM#884-885, 887-888, also struck in gold $30,000.00	—	750
MDS213	1954 (4)	1,020	KM#898-899, 901-902	—	165
MDS214	1955 (4)	1,036	KM#898-899, 901-902, also struck in matte proof	—	165
MDS215	1956 (4)	1,088	KM#898-899, 901-902	—	165
MDS216	1957 (4)	1,094	KM#898-899, 901-902	—	165
MDS217	1958 (4)	1,100	KM#898-899, 901-902	—	165
MDS218	1959 (4)	1,106	KM#898-899, 901-902	—	165
MDS219	1960 (4)	1,112	KM#898-899, 901-902	—	165
MDS220	1961 (4)	—	KM#898-899, 901-902	—	165
MDS221	1962 (4)	1,125	KM#898-899, 901-902	—	165
MDS222	1963 (4)	1,131	KM#898-899, 901-902	—	165
MDS223	1964 (4)	1,137	KM#898-899, 901-902	—	165
MDS224	1965 (4)	1,143	KM#898-899, 901-902	—	165
MDS225	1966 (4)	1,206	KM#898-899, 901-902	—	165
MDS226	1967 (4)	986	KM#898-899, 901-902	—	175
MDS227	1968 (4)	964	KM#898-899, 901-902	—	175
MDS228	1969 (4)	1,002	KM#898-899, 901-902	—	175
MDS229	1970 (4)	980	KM#898-899, 901-902	—	175
MDS230	1971 (4)	1,018	KM#898-899, 901-902 Tewkesbury Abbey	—	175
MDS231	1972 (4)	1,026	KM#898-899, 901-902 York Minster Abbey	—	185
MDS232	1973 (4)	1,004	KM#898-899, 901-902 Westminster Abbey	—	175
MDS233	1974 (4)	1,042	KM#898-899, 901-902 Salisbury Cathedral	—	175
MDS234	1975 (4)	1,050	KM#898-899, 901-902 Peterborough Cathedral	—	175
MDS235	1976 (4)	1,257	KM#898-899, 901-902 Hereford Cathedral	—	175
MDS236	1977 (4)	1,248	KM#898-899, 901-902 Westminster Abbey	—	185
MDS237	1978 (4)	1,179	KM#898-899, 901-902 Carlisle Cathedral	—	175
MDS238	1979 (4)	1,180	KM#898-899, 901-902 Winchester Cathedral	—	175
MDS239	1980 (4)	1,148	KM#898-899, 901-902 Worcester Cathedral	—	175
MDS240	1981 (4)	1,398	KM#898-899, 901-902 Westminster Abbey	—	175
MDS241	1982 (4)	1,220	KM#898-899, 901-902 St. David's Cathedral	—	175
MDS242	1983 (4)	1,228	KM#898-899, 901-902 Exeter Cathedral	—	175
MDS243	1984 (4)	1,238	KM#898-899, 901-902 Southwell Minster	—	175
MDS244	1985 (4)	1,248	KM#898-899, 901-902 Ripon Cathedral	—	175
MDS245	1986 (4)	1,378	KM#898-899, 901-902 Chichester Cathedral	—	175
MDS246	1987 (4)	1,390	KM#898-899, 901-902 Ely Cathedral	—	185
MDS247	1988 (4)	1,402	KM#898-899, 901-902 Lichfield Cathedral	—	185
MDS248	1989 (4)	1,353	KM#898-899, 901-902 Birmingham Cathedral	—	185
MDS249	1990 (4)	1,523	KM#898-899, 901-902 Newcastle Cathedral	—	190
MDS250	1991 (4)	1,384	KM#898-899, 901-902 Westminster Abbey	—	190
MDS251	1992 (4)	1,424	KM#898-899, 901-902 Chester Cathedral	—	190

KM#	Date	Mintage	Identification	Issue Price	Mkt Val
MDS252	1993 (4)	1,440	KM#898-899, 901-902 Wells Cathedral	—	190
MDS253	1994 (4)	1,433	KM#898-899, 901-902 Truro Cathedral	—	190
MDS254	1995 (4)	1,466	KM#898-899, 901-902 Coventry Cathedral	—	195
MDS255	1996 (4)	1,629	KM#898-899, 901-902 Norwich Cathedral	—	200
MDS256	1997 (4)	1,786	KM#898-899, 901-902 Birmingham Cathedral	—	200
MDS257	1998 (4)	1,654	KM#898-899, 901-902 Portsmouth Cathedral	—	200
MDS258	1999 (4)	1,676	KM#898-899, 901-902 Bristol Cathedral	—	200
MDS259	2000 (4)	1,686	KM#898-899, 901-902 Lincoln Cathedral	—	225

MINT SETS

KM#	Date	Mintage	Identification	Issue Price	Mkt Val
MS101	1953 (9)	—	KM#881-883, 886, 889-893	1.25	30.00
MS102	1968/71 (5)	—	KM#911-912 (1968), 914-916 (1971), blue wallet	0.50	2.00
MS103	1982 (7)	205,000	KM#926-932	6.00	12.50
MS104	1983 (8)	637,100	KM#926-933	8.75	22.00
MS105	1984 (8)	158,820	KM#926-932, 934	8.75	19.00
MS106	1985 (7)	178,375	KM#935-940.1, 941	8.75	15.00
MS107	1986 (8)	167,224	KM#935-940.1, 946-947	9.75	20.00
MS108	1987 (7)	172,425	KM#935-940.1, 948	9.00	21.50
MS109	1988 (7)	134,067	KM#935-940.1, 954	9.00	17.50
MS110	1989 (7)	77,569	KM#935-940.1, 959	10.00	30.00
MS111	1989 (2)	—	KM#960-961	11.00	17.00
MS112	1990 (7)	102,606	KM#935-936, 937, 936b, 938-940.1, 941	15.00	30.00
MS113	1991 (7)	74,975	KM#935-936, 937b, 938-940.1, 946	15.00	30.00
MS114	1991 (7)	—	KM#935-936, 937b, 938-940.1, 946 Baby Pack	18.50	30.00
MS115	1992 (10)	78,421	KM#935-936, 937b, 938, 938b, 939-940.1, 948, 963	17.50	30.00
MS116	1992 (9)	—	KM#935-936, 937b, 938, 938b, 939-940.1, 948, 963 Baby Pack	22.50	30.00
MS117	1993 (8)	56,945	KM#935a-936a, 937b, 938b, 939-940.1, 963-964	22.50	35.00
MS118	1994 (8)	177,971	KM#935a-936a, 937b, 938b, 939, 966-968	22.50	20.00
MS119	1995 (8)	105,647	KM#935a-936a, 937b-938b, 939-940.1, 969-970	—	20.00
MS120	1996 (8)	86,501	KM#935a-936a, 937b-938b, 939-940.1, 972-973	18.50	20.00
MS121	1997 (9)	109,557	KM#935a, 936a, 937b, 938b, 939-940.1, 940.2, 975-976	—	20.00
MS122	1998 (9)	16,192	KM#986-994	25.00	22.00
MS124	1998 (2)	96,149	KM#991-992	15.00	9.50
MS125	1999 (10)	136,492	KM#986a-987a, 988-991, 998-999	20.00	22.00
MS126	2000 (9)	—	KM#986-991, 994, 1004, 1005 Wedding Collection	20.00	20.00
MS127	2000 (9)	117,750	KM#986-991, 994, 1004, 1005	25.00	25.00
MS128	2000 (9)	—	M#986-991, 994, 1004, 1005 Baby Gift Set	25.00	25.00

PROOF SETS

KM#	Date	Mintage	Identification	Issue Price	Mkt Val
PS15	1902 (13)	8,066	KM#795-797.1, 798-807	—	3,000
PS16	1902 (11)	7,057	KM#795-797.1, 798-805	—	900
PS17	1911 (12)	2,812	KM#811-818.1, 819-822	—	4,000
PS18	1911 (10)	952	KM#811-818.1, 819-820	—	1,150
PS19	1911 (8)	2,241	KM#811-818.1	—	600
PS20	1927 (6)	15,030	KM#831-836	—	375
PSA20	1927 (6)	—	KM#831-836 Matte Proof; Rare	—	15,000
PS21	1937 (15)	26,402	KM#843-857	—	350
PSA21	1937 (15)	—	KM#843-857 Matte Proof; Rare	—	—
PS22	1937 (4)	5,500	KM#858-861	—	4,500
PSA22	1937 (4)	1	KM#858-861 Matte Proof; Unique	—	25,000
PS23	1950 (9)	17,513	KM#867-869, 873, 875-879	2.50	125
PSA23	1950 (9)	3	KM#867-869, 873, 875-879; Rare, matte proof	—	10,000
PS24	1951 (10)	20,000	KM#867-869, 873, 875-880	2.80	150
PSA24	1951 (10)	3	KM#867-869, 873, 875-880; Rare, matte proof	—	10,000
PS25	1953 (10)	40,000	KM#881-883, 886, 889-894	3.50	100
PSA25	1953 (10)	3	KM#881-883, 886, 889-894; Rare, matte proof	—	10,000
PS26	1970 (8)	750,000	KM#896-897, 900, 903-907	8.75	24.00
PS27	1971 (6)	350,000	KM#911-916 (Issued 1973)	8.85	22.00
PS28	1972 (7)	150,000	KM#911-917 (Issued 1976)	13.00	29.00
PS29	1973 (6)	100,000	KM#911-912, 914-916, 918 (Issued 1976)	13.00	17.50

KM#	Date	Mintage	Identification	Issue Price	Mkt Val
PS30	1974 (6)	100,000	KM#911-916 (Issued 1976)	13.00	13.50
PS31	1975 (6)	100,000	KM#911-916 (Issued 1976)	13.00	13.50
PS32	1976 (6)	100,000	KM#911-916	13.00	14.00
PS33	1977 (7)	193,800	KM#911-916, 920	17.00	17.50
PS34	1978 (6)	88,100	KM#911-916	15.00	19.50
PS35	1979 (6)	81,000	KM#911-916	15.00	16.00
PS37	1980 (4)	10,000	KM#919, 922-924	2,650	1,150
PS36	1980 (6)	143,400	KM#911-916	23.00	15.50
PS38	1981 (2)	2,500	KM#919, 925a	—	160
PS39	1981 (6)	—	KM#911-916	26.00	15.50
PS40	1981 (9)	5,000	KM#911-916, 919, 924, 925a	—	935
PS42	1982 (4)	2,500	KM#919, 922-924	—	1,350
PS41	1982 (7)	—	KM#926-932	21.60	24.00
PS44	1983 (3)	—	KM#919, 922-923	775	535
PS43	1983 (8)	125,000	KM#926-933	29.95	25.00
PS46	1984 (3)	—	KM#919, 922, 924	1,275	910
PS45	1984 (8)	125,000	KM#926-932, 934	29.95	23.50
PS48	1985 (4)	12,500	KM#942-945	1,395	1,175
PS47	1985 (8)	125,000	KM#935-940.1, 941	29.75	23.50
PS50	1986 (3)	12,500	KM#942-943, 947c	675	535
PS49	1986 (8)	125,000	KM#935-940.1, 946-947	29.75	28.50
PS53	1987 (3)	12,500	KM#942-944	675	535
PS51	1987 (7)	125,000	KM#935-940.1, 948	29.75	25.00
PS52	1987 (4)	10,000	KM#950-953	1,595	1,000
PS54	1987 (2)	12,500	KM#950-951	325	190
PS57	1988 (3)	—	KM#942-944	775	510
PS55	1988 (7)	125,000	KM#935-940.1, 954	29.75	27.50
PS56	1988 (4)	6,500	KM#950-953	1,595	1,000
PS58	1988 (2)	7,500	KM#950-951	340	190
PS61	1989 (4)	5,000	KM#955-958	1,595	1,600
PS62	1989 (3)	15,000	KM#955-957	775	675
PS64	1989 (2)	—	KM#960a-961a	—	55.00
PS59	1989 (9)	100,000	KM#935-940.1, 959-961	34.95	46.00
PS60	1989 (4)	2,500	KM#950-953	1,595	1,000
PS63	1989 (2)	1,500	KM#950-951	340	200
PS68	1990 (4)	2,500	KM#942-944, 949	1,595	1,400
PS69	1990 (4)	2,500	KM#950a-953a	1,595	1,000
PS70	1990 (3)	7,500	KM#942-944	775	570
PS71	1990 (2)	35,000	KM#937a-937c	47.50	39.00
PS65	1989	—	KM#960b-961b	—	65.00
PS66	1990 (8)	100,000	KM#935-937, 937b, 938-940.1, 941 Leatherette Case	35.00	36.00
PS67	1990 (8)	I.A.	KM#935-937, 937b, 938-940.1, 941 Leather Case	45.00	35.00
PS74	1991 (4)	1,500	KM#942-944, 949	1,750	1,500
PS75	1991 (4)	750	KM#950a-953a	1,750	1,500
PS76	1991 (3)	2,500	KM#942-944	895	665
PS72	1991 (7)	10,000	KM#935-936, 937b, 938-940.1, 946 Leatherette Case	38.50	35.00
PS73	1991 (7)	10,000	KM#935-936, 937b, 938-940.1, 946 Leather Case	48.50	40.00
PS79	1992 (4)	1,250	KM#942-945	1,750	1,450
PS80	1992 (4)	1,000	KM#938b, 938c, 948a, 963a	122	125
PS81	1992 (3)	1,250	KM#942-944	895	710
PS82	1992 (2)	—	KM#938a-938c	59.45	46.00
PS77	1992 (9)	100,000	KM#935-936, 937b, 938, 938b, 939-94.1, 948, 963 Leatherette Case	44.50	46.00
PS78	1992 (9)	100,000	KM#935-936, 937b, 938, 938b, 939-940.1, 948, 963 Leather Case	44.50	40.00
PS85	1993 (4)	500	KM#950a-953a	1,755	1,600
PS86	1993 (4)	1,250	KM#942-945	1,560	1,530
PS87	1993 (3)	1,250	KM#942-944	800	670
PS83	1993 (8)	100,000	KM#935a-936a, 937b, 938b, 939-940.1, 964-965 Standard Case	50.00	47.00
PS84	1993 (8)	I.A.	KM#935a-936a, 937b, 938b, 939-940.1, 964-965 Deluxe Case	60.00	55.00
PS90	1994 (4)	500	KM#950a-953a	1,499	1,500
PS91	1994 (4)	1,250	KM#942-943, 945, 968c	—	1,550
PS92	1994 (3)	1,250	KM#942-943, 968c	—	760
PS88	1994 (8)	100,000	KM#935a-936a, 937b, 938b, 939, 966-968 Standard Case	45.00	34.00
PS89	1994 (8)	I.A.	KM#935a-936a, 937b, 938b, 939, 966-968 Deluxe Case	55.00	50.00
PS93	1995 (8)	42,842	KM#935a-936a, 937b-938b, 939-940.1, 969-970	—	41.50
PS94	1995 (8)	17,797	KM#935a-936a, 937b-938b, 939-940.1, 969-970 Deluxe Case	—	60.00
PS95	1995 (4)	1,250	KM#942-943, 945, 971c	—	1,675
PS96	1995 (4)	500	KM#950a-953a	1,500	1,500
PS97	1995 (3)	1,250	KM#942-943, 945	—	860
PS100	1996 (4)	2,500,000	KM#950a-953a	1,600	1,500
PS101	1996 (7)	—	KM#935b, 936b, 937c, 938c, 939a, 940.1a, 972a	—	155
PS98	1996 (9)	100,000	KM#935a-936a, 937b-938b, 939-940.1, 972-973	44.75	42.50
PS99	1996 (9)	—	KM#935a-936a, 937b-938b, 939-940.1, 972-973 Deluxe Case	56.00	55.00

KM#	Date	Mintage	Identification	Issue Price	Mkt Val
PS102	1997 (10)	70,000	KM#935a, 936a, 937b, 938b, 939, 940.1, 940.2, 975-976, 977a	—	50.00
PS103	1997 (4)	15,000	KM#978-981	145	135
PS104	1997 (4)	1,500	KM#982-985	1,600	1,650
PS105	1998 (10)	100,000	KM#986,987a, 988-995	55.00	50.00
PS157	1998 (4)	—	KM#1029, 1079-1081	—	175
PSA105	1998 (2)	10,000	Piefort versions of KM#992a, 996a	—	140
PS107	1999 (4)	1,000	KM#999a, 1001-1003	1,725	1,725
PS108	1999 (3)	1,250	KM#1001-1003	—	955
PS109	1999 (4)	750	KM#950a-953a	1,495	1,500
PS110	1999 (4)	—	KM#1008-1011	1,595	—
PS115	2000 (13)	15,000	KM#898, 899, 901, 902, 986b, 987b, 988a, 989a, 990a, 991a, 994a, 1005a, 1006a	—	375
PS158	1999 (4)	—	KM#1000, 1082-1084	—	175
PS106	1999 (9)	100,000	KM#986a-987a, 988-991, 997-999	50.00	50.00
PS111	2000 (10)	90,000	KM#986-991, 994, 1004-1006 Standard Set	50.00	50.00
PS112	2000 (10)	10,000	KM#986-991, 994, 1004-1006 Deluxe Set	65.00	65.00
PS114	2000 (4)	750	KM#1008-1011	1,495	1,498
PS159	2000 (4)	—	KM#1029, 1079-1081	—	175
PSA115	2000 (3)	1,250	KM#994c, 1001, 1002	—	—
PS113	2000 (10)	15,000	KM#986-991, 994, 1004-1006 Executive Set	115	115

GREECE

The Hellenic (Greek) Republic is situated in southeastern Europe on the southern tip of the Balkan Peninsula. The republic includes many islands, the most important of which are Crete and the Ionian Islands. Greece (including islands) has an area of 50,944 sq. mi. (131,940 sq. km.) and a population of 10.3 million. Capital: Athens. Greece is still largely agricultural. Tobacco, cotton, fruit and wool are exported.

Greece, the Mother of Western civilization, attained the peak of its culture in the 5th century B.C., when it contributed more to government, drama, art and architecture than any other people to this time. Greece fell under Roman domination in the 2nd and 1st centuries B.C., becoming part of the Byzantine Empire until Constantinople fell to the Crusaders in 1202. With the fall of Constantinople to the Turks in 1453, Greece became part of the Ottoman Empire. Independence from Turkey was won with the revolution of 1821-27. In 1833, Greece was established as a monarchy, with sovereignty guaranteed by Britain, France and Russia. After a lengthy power struggle between the monarchist forces and democratic factions, Greece was proclaimed a republic in 1925. The monarchy was restored in 1935 and reconfirmed by a plebiscite in 1946. The Italians invaded Greece via Albania on Oct. 28, 1940 but were driven back well within the Albanian border. Germany began their invasion in April 1941 and quickly overran the entire country and drove off a British Expeditionary force by the end of April. King George II and his new government went into exile. The German-Italian occupation of Greece lasted until Oct. 1944 after which only German troops remained until the end of the occupation. On April 21, 1967, a military junta took control of the government and suspended the constitution. King Constantine II made an unsuccessful attempt against the junta in the fall of 1968 and consequently fled to Italy. The monarchy was formally abolished by plebiscite, Dec. 8, 1974, and Greece was established as the Hellenic Republic, the third republic in Greek history.

RULERS
George I, 1863-1913
Constantine I, 1913-1917, 1920-1922
Alexander I, 1917-1920
George II, 1922-1923, 1935-1947
Paul I, 1947-1964
Constantine II, 1964-1973

MINT MARKS
(a) - Paris, privy marks only
A - Paris
B - Vienna
BB - Strassburg
H - Heaton, Birmingham
K - Bordeaux
KN - King's Norton
(p) - Poissy – Thunderbolt
Anthemion – Greek National Mint, Athens

MONETARY SYSTEM
Commencing 1831
100 Lepta = 1 Drachma

KINGDOM
DECIMAL COINAGE

KM# 62 5 LEPTA
Nickel Ruler: George I Obv: Crown right of center hole Rev: Owl on amphora left of center hole

Date	Mintage	F	VF	XF	Unc	BU
1912(a)	25,053,000	0.75	3.00	7.50	75.00	125

KM# 63 10 LEPTA
Nickel, 21 mm. Ruler: George I Obv: Crown right of center hole Rev: Owl on amphora left of center hole

Date	Mintage	F	VF	XF	Unc	BU
1912(a)	28,973,000	0.75	3.00	7.50	75.00	125

KM# 66.1 10 LEPTA
1.5200 g., Aluminum Ruler: George II Obv: Crown above date Rev: Olive branch, denomination Note: 1.77mm thick.

Date	Mintage	F	VF	XF	Unc	BU
1922(p)	120,000,000	1.00	2.00	9.00	40.00	60.00

KM# 66.2 10 LEPTA
1.6500 g., Aluminum Ruler: Constantine I Obv: Crown above date Rev: Olive branch, denomination Note: 2.2mm thick.

Date	Mintage	F	VF	XF	Unc	BU
1922(p)	—	3.00	10.00	20.00	100	250

KM# 64 20 LEPTA
Nickel Ruler: George I Obv: Crowned, mantled shield right of center hole Rev: Athena standing at left of center hole, olive branch at right

Date	Mintage	F	VF	XF	Unc	BU
1912(a)	10,145,000	0.75	3.00	8.50	100	150

KM# 65 50 LEPTA
Copper-Nickel Ruler: Constantine I Obv: Crowned, mantled shield right of center hole Rev: Olive branch below center hole Note: Most of these were melted and only 30 - 40 of each piece are known to exist.

Date	Mintage	F	VF	XF	Unc	BU
1921H	1,000,000	—	1,500	3,500	8,000	13,000
1921KN	1,524,000	—	4,000	7,000	11,000	18,000

KM# 60 DRACHMA
5.0000 g., 0.8350 Silver 0.1342 oz. ASW Ruler: George I Obv: Head left Rev: Mythological figure Thetis with shield of Achilles, seated on sea horse

Date	Mintage	F	VF	XF	Unc	BU
1910(a)	4,570,000	7.50	15.00	45.00	250	400
1911(a)	1,881,000	9.00	20.00	60.00	470	800

KM# 61 2 DRACHMAI
10.0000 g., 0.8350 Silver 0.2684 oz. ASW Ruler: George I Obv: Head left Rev: Mythological figure Thetis with shield of Achilles seated on sea horse

Date	Mintage	F	VF	XF	Unc	BU
1911(a)	1,500,000	10.00	30.00	100	1,520	2,500

REPUBLIC
DECIMAL COINAGE

KM# 67 20 LEPTA
1.7300 g., Copper-Nickel Obv: Denomination above date Rev: Athena head left

Date	Mintage	F	VF	XF	Unc	BU
1926	20,000,000	0.75	1.50	5.00	25.00	60.00

KM# 68 50 LEPTA
2.8900 g., Copper-Nickel Obv: Denomination above date Rev: Athena head left

Date	Mintage	F	VF	XF	Unc	BU
1926B (1930)	20,000,000	0.45	1.00	4.50	30.00	75.00
1926	20,000,000	0.45	1.00	4.50	25.00	60.00

KM# 69 DRACHMA
5.0300 g., Copper-Nickel, 23 mm. Obv: Denomination above date Rev: Athena head left

Date	Mintage	F	VF	XF	Unc	BU
1926B	20,000,000	0.45	1.00	5.00	50.00	100
1926	15,000,000	0.45	1.00	5.00	35.00	75.00

KM# 70 2 DRACHMAI
Copper-Nickel, 27 mm. Obv: Denomination above date Rev: Athena head left

Date	Mintage	F	VF	XF	Unc	BU
1926	22,000,000	1.00	2.00	9.00	50.00	100

KM# 71.1 5 DRACHMAI
Nickel Obv: Phoenix and flames Rev: Denomination within wreath Note: LONDON MINT: In second set of berries on left only 1 berry will have a dot on it.

Date	Mintage	F	VF	XF	Unc	BU
1930	23,500,000	0.75	1.50	8.00	80.00	250
1930 Proof	—	Value: 2,500				

KM# 71.2 5 DRACHMAI
Nickel **Obv:** Phoenix and flames **Rev:** Denomination within wreath **Note:** BRUSSELLS MINT: 2 berries will have dots.

Date	Mintage	F	VF	XF	Unc	BU
1930	1,500,000	1.50	3.50	15.00	200	400

KM# 72 10 DRACHMAI
7.0000 g., 0.5000 Silver 0.1125 oz. ASW, 25 mm. **Obv:** Grain sprig divides denomination **Rev:** Demeter head left

Date	Mintage	F	VF	XF	Unc	BU
1930	7,500,000	5.00	10.00	25.00	400	800
1930 Proof	—	Value: 3,000				

KM# 73 20 DRACHMAI
11.3100 g., 0.5000 Silver 0.1818 oz. ASW, 28.43 mm.
Obv: Prow of ancient ship **Rev:** Neptune head right

Date	Mintage	F	VF	XF	Unc	BU
1930	11,500,000	6.00	12.50	28.00	250	550
1930 Proof	—	Value: 3,000				

KINGDOM

DECIMAL COINAGE

KM# 77 5 LEPTA
0.8500 g., Aluminum, 20.5 mm. **Obv:** Center hole within crowned wreath **Rev:** Grain sprigs left of center hole

Date	Mintage	F	VF	XF	Unc	BU
1954	15,000,000	—	0.20	0.50	4.00	10.00
1971	1,002,000	0.20	0.50	1.00	5.00	10.00

Note: 1971 dated coins have smaller hole at center

KM# 78 10 LEPTA
Aluminum **Obv:** Center hole within crowned wreath **Rev:** Olives above center hole, double denomination below

Date	Mintage	F	VF	XF	Unc	BU
1954	48,000,000	—	0.15	0.45	4.00	10.00
1959	20,000,000	—	0.15	0.45	4.00	10.00
1964	12,000,000	—	0.15	0.45	7.00	18.00
1965 In sets only	—				6.50	—
1965 Proof	4,987	Value: 10.00				
1966	20,000,000	—	0.15	0.45	4.00	7.00
1969	20,000,000	—	0.15	0.45	4.00	7.00
1971	5,922,000	—	0.35	1.00	5.00	8.00

Note: Small center hole

KM# 102 10 LEPTA
Aluminum **Obv:** Soldier and Phoenix **Rev:** Trident between two dolphins

Date	Mintage	F	VF	XF	Unc	BU
1973	2,742,000	—	0.20	1.00	5.00	7.00

KM# 79 20 LEPTA
Aluminum, 24 mm. **Obv:** Center hole within crowned wreath **Rev:** Olive branch left of center hole

Date	Mintage	F	VF	XF	Unc	BU
1954	24,000,000	—	0.15	0.50	4.00	10.00
1959	20,000,000	—	0.15	0.50	4.00	10.00
1964	8,000,000	—	0.15	0.50	8.00	18.00
1966	15,000,000	—	0.15	0.50	3.50	6.50
1969	20,000,000	—	0.15	0.50	3.50	6.50
1971	4,108,000	—	0.35	1.00	4.00	7.00

Note: Small center hole

KM# 104 20 LEPTA
Aluminum **Obv:** Soldier in front of phoenix, anniversary date below **Rev:** Olive branch, denomination

Date	Mintage	F	VF	XF	Unc	BU
1973	2,718,000	—	0.20	0.60	5.00	7.00

KM# 80 50 LEPTA
Copper-Nickel, 18 mm. **Ruler:** Paul I **Obv:** Head left **Rev:** Crowned arms with supporters

Date	Mintage	F	VF	XF	Unc	BU
1954	37,228,000	0.15	0.25	1.25	50.00	100
1957	5,108,000	1.00	5.00	40.00	210	450
1957 Proof	—	Value: 2,000				
1959	10,160,000	0.15	0.25	5.00	60.00	150
1962	Inc. above	0.15	0.25	1.50	8.00	75.00
	Note: Serrated edge					
1962	20,500,000	0.15	0.25	1.50	8.00	75.00
	Note: Plain edge by error					
1964	20,000,000	0.15	0.25	1.50	8.00	75.00
1965 In sets only	—	—	—	—	6.50	—
1965 Proof	4,987	Value: 12.50				

KM# 88 50 LEPTA
Copper-Nickel, 18 mm. **Ruler:** Constantine II **Obv:** Head left **Rev:** Crowned arms with supporters

Date	Mintage	F	VF	XF	Unc	BU
1966	30,000,000	0.20	0.50	1.00	5.50	25.00
1966 Proof	—	Value: 1,500				
1970	10,160,000	0.30	0.60	1.50	6.00	27.50

KM# 97.1 50 LEPTA
Copper-Nickel **Ruler:** Constantine II **Obv:** Small head left **Rev:** Soldier in front of Phoenix

Date	Mintage	F	VF	XF	Unc	BU
1971	10,999,000	—	0.10	0.15	4.00	20.00
1973	9,342,000	—	0.20	0.50	5.00	22.00

KM# 97.2 50 LEPTA
Copper-Nickel **Ruler:** Constantine II **Obv:** Large head left **Rev:** Soldier in front of Phoenix

Date	Mintage	F	VF	XF	Unc	BU
1973	Inc. above	—	0.20	0.50	5.00	15.00

KM# 81 DRACHMA
Copper-Nickel, 20.8 mm. **Ruler:** Paul I **Obv:** Head left **Rev:** Crowned arms with supporters

Date	Mintage	F	VF	XF	Unc	BU
1954	24,091,000	0.15	0.25	0.75	75.00	125
1957	8,151,000	1.00	5.00	50.00	160	400
1957 Proof	—	Value: 2,500				
1959	10,180,000	0.15	0.25	2.00	65.00	200
1962	20,060,000	0.25	1.00	2.00	8.00	50.00
1965 In sets only	—	—	—	—	6.50	—
1965 Proof	4,987	Value: 12.50				

KM# 89 DRACHMA
Copper-Nickel **Ruler:** Constantine II **Obv:** Head left **Rev:** Crowned arms with supporters

Date	Mintage	F	VF	XF	Unc	BU
1966	20,000,000	—	0.15	0.45	5.00	15.00
1966 Proof	—	Value: 1,250				
1967	20,000,000	—	0.15	0.45	5.00	15.00
1970	7,001,000	—	0.50	1.00	7.00	16.00
1970 Proof	—	Value: 1,500				

KM# 98 DRACHMA
Copper-Nickel **Ruler:** Constantine II **Obv:** Head left **Rev:** Soldier in front of Phoenix

Date	Mintage	F	VF	XF	Unc	BU
1971	11,985,000	—	0.20	0.75	4.50	13.00
1973	8,196,000	—	0.25	1.00	5.50	14.00

KM# 82 2 DRACHMAI
Copper-Nickel **Ruler:** Paul I **Obv:** Head left **Rev:** Crowned arms with supporters

Date	Mintage	F	VF	XF	Unc	BU
1954	12,609,000	0.50	0.75	1.50	50.00	125
1957	10,171,000	1.00	5.00	50.00	150	400
1957 Proof	—	Value: 3,000				
1959	5,000,000	1.00	2.00	25.00	230	650
1962	10,096,000	0.50	0.75	2.50	10.00	50.00
1965 In sets only	—	—	—	—	5.50	—
1965 Proof	4,987	Value: 12.50				

KM# 90 2 DRACHMAI
Copper-Nickel **Ruler:** Constantine II **Obv:** Head left **Rev:** Crowned arms with supporters

Date	Mintage	F	VF	XF	Unc	BU
1966	10,000,000	0.15	0.25	0.50	4.50	15.00
1966 Proof	—	Value: 1,400				
	Note: NGSA Auction 12/08 $1105					
1967	10,000,000	0.15	0.25	0.50	5.00	15.00
1970	7,000,000	0.50	1.00	2.00	8.00	30.00
1970 Proof	—	Value: 2,000				

KM# 99   2 DRACHMAI
Copper-Nickel, 22.9 mm. **Ruler:** Constantine II **Obv:** Head left
Rev: Soldier in front of Phoenix

Date	Mintage	F	VF	XF	Unc	BU
1971	9,998,000	0.15	0.25	0.75	4.50	12.00
1973	7,972,000	0.20	0.50	1.50	5.50	14.00

KM# 83   5 DRACHMAI
Copper-Nickel **Ruler:** Paul I

Date	Mintage	F	VF	XF	Unc	BU
1954	21,000,000	0.25	0.50	1.50	35.00	60.00
1965 In sets only	—	—	—	—	5.50	—
1965 Proof	4,987	Value: 15.00				

KM# 91   5 DRACHMAI
Copper-Nickel, 27.5 mm. **Ruler:** Constantine II **Obv:** Head left
Rev: Crowned arms with supporters

Date	Mintage	F	VF	XF	Unc	BU
1966	12,000,000	0.15	0.25	1.00	6.00	25.00
1966 Proof	—	Value: 1,250				
Note: NGSA Auction 12/08 $1100						
1970	5,000,000	0.50	1.00	3.00	10.00	30.00

KM# 100   5 DRACHMAI
Copper-Nickel **Ruler:** Constantine II **Obv:** Head left **Rev:** Soldier in front of Phoenix

Date	Mintage	F	VF	XF	Unc	BU
1971	4,014,000	0.25	0.50	2.00	6.00	15.00
1973	3,166,000	0.25	0.50	1.50	5.50	15.00

KM# 84   10 DRACHMAI
Nickel, 30 mm. **Ruler:** Paul I **Obv:** Head left **Rev:** Crowned arms
with supporters

Date	Mintage	F	VF	XF	Unc	BU
1959	20,000,000	0.30	0.50	2.00	16.00	50.00
1959 Proof	—	Value: 2,000				
1965 In sets only	—	—	—	—	5.50	—
1965 Proof	4,987	Value: 15.00				

KM# 96   10 DRACHMAI
Copper-Nickel **Ruler:** Constantine II **Obv:** Head left
Rev: Crowned arms with supporters

Date	Mintage	F	VF	XF	Unc	BU
1968	40,000,000	0.25	0.50	0.75	7.00	15.00

KM# 101   10 DRACHMAI
7.5400 g., Copper-Nickel, 29.9 mm. **Ruler:** Constantine II
Obv: Head left **Rev:** Soldier in front of Phoenix

Date	Mintage	F	VF	XF	Unc	BU
1971	502,000	0.25	0.50	1.00	7.50	16.00
1973	541,000	0.50	1.00	2.50	8.00	18.00

KM# 74   20 DRACHMAI
6.4516 g., 0.9000 Gold 0.1867 oz. AGW, 22 mm.
Ruler: George II **Subject:** 5th Anniversary - Restoration of
Monarchy **Obv:** Head left **Rev:** Denomination within crowned
wreath

Date	Mintage	F	VF	XF	Unc	BU
ND(1940) Proof	200	Value: 18,000				

KM# 85   20 DRACHMAI
7.5000 g., 0.8350 Silver 0.2013 oz. ASW, 26.2 mm.
Ruler: Paul I **Obv:** Head left **Rev:** Selene, moon goddess

Date	Mintage	F	VF	XF	Unc	BU
1960	20,000,000	—	—	BV	7.00	25.00
1960 Proof	—	Value: 2,000				
1965	—	—	—	—	8.00	18.00
1965 Proof	4,987	Value: 18.00				

KM# 92   20 DRACHMAI
6.4516 g., 0.9000 Gold 0.1867 oz. AGW **Ruler:** Constantine II
Subject: Commemorative of the April 21, 1967 revolution
Obv: Crowned shield with supporters **Rev:** Soldier in front of
Phoenix

Date	Mintage	F	VF	XF	Unc	BU
ND (1970)	20,000	—	—	—	400	600

KM# 111.3   20 DRACHMAI
Copper-Nickel **Ruler:** Constantine II **Obv:** Soldier in front of
Phoenix **Rev:** Selene, wide rim with continuous wave design at
rear hoof

Date	Mintage	F	VF	XF	Unc	BU
1973	Inc. above	0.50	1.00	2.00	10.00	15.00

KM# 111   20 DRACHMAI
Copper-Nickel **Ruler:** Constantine II **Obv:** Soldier in front of
Phoenix **Rev:** Selene, narrow rim with faint veil or no veil
Note: Possible varieties exist; narrow rim with faint veil or no veil
/ wide rim with heavy veil and broken wave design at rear hoof.

Date	Mintage	F	VF	XF	Unc	BU
1973	3,092,000	0.50	1.00	2.00	8.50	11.50

KM# 86   30 DRACHMAI
18.0000 g., 0.8350 Silver 0.4832 oz. ASW, 34 mm. **Ruler:** Paul I
Subject: Centennial - Five Greek Kings **Edge:** Greek text

Date	Mintage	F	VF	XF	Unc	BU
ND(1963)	3,000,000	—	BV	7.50	10.00	18.00

KM# 87   30 DRACHMAI
12.0000 g., 0.8350 Silver 0.3221 oz. ASW, 30.3 mm.
Ruler: Constantine II **Subject:** Constantine and Anne-Marie
Wedding **Edge:** Greek text

Date	Mintage	F	VF	XF	Unc	BU
1964	1,000,000	—	BV	5.00	9.00	12.00
Note: Berne: small edge lettering, BØ below epaulette						
1964	1,000,000	—	BV	5.00	8.00	12.00
Note: Kongsberg: large edge lettering, BØ on top of shoulder						
1964 Proof	—	Value: 3,500				

KM# 93   50 DRACHMAI
12.5000 g., 0.8350 Silver 0.3356 oz. ASW **Ruler:** Constantine II
Subject: April 21, 1967 Revolution **Obv:** Crowned shield with
supporters **Rev:** Soldier in front of Phoenix

Date	Mintage	F	VF	XF	Unc	BU
1967(1970)	100,000	—	—	25.00	75.00	100

KM# 75   100 DRACHMAI
25.0000 g., 0.9000 Silver 0.7234 oz. ASW, 38 mm.
Ruler: George II **Subject:** 5th Anniversary - Restoration of
Monarchy **Obv:** Head left **Rev:** Crowned and mantled arms

Date	Mintage	F	VF	XF	Unc	BU
ND (1940) Proof	500	Value: 2,500				

KM# 76   100 DRACHMAI
32.2580 g., 0.9000 Gold 0.9334 oz. AGW, 38 mm. Ruler: George II
Obv: Head left Rev: Denomination within crowned wreath

Date	Mintage	F	VF	XF	Unc	BU
ND (1940) Proof	140	Value: 25,000				

KM# 94   100 DRACHMAI
25.0000 g., 0.8350 Silver 0.6711 oz. ASW Ruler: Constantine II
Subject: April 21, 1967 Revolution

Date	Mintage	F	VF	XF	Unc	BU
ND (1970)	30,000	—	—	35.00	100	150

KM# 95   100 DRACHMAI
32.2580 g., 0.9000 Gold 0.9334 oz. AGW Ruler: Constantine II
Subject: April 21, 1967 Revolution Obv: Crowned arms with
supporters Rev: Soldier in front of Phoenix

Date	Mintage	F	VF	XF	Unc	BU
ND (1970)	10,000	—	—	—	1,150	1,600

REPUBLIC

DECIMAL COINAGE

KM# 103   10 LEPTA
1.0900 g., Aluminum Obv: Phoenix above flame Rev: Pair of
dolphins flank trident

Date	Mintage	F	VF	XF	Unc	BU
1973	15,134,472	—	0.10	0.50	2.00	5.00

KM# 113   10 LEPTA
Aluminum Obv: Arms within wreath Rev: Charging bull right

Date	Mintage	F	VF	XF	Unc	BU
1976	2,043,000	—	0.10	0.30	2.00	5.00
1978	791,000	0.50	1.00	2.50	5.00	10.00
1978 Proof	20,000	Value: 5.00				

KM# 105   20 LEPTA
Aluminum Obv: Phoenix with date below Rev: Olive branch,
denomination

Date	Mintage	F	VF	XF	Unc	BU
1973	15,265,797	—	0.20	0.50	2.50	5.00

KM# 114   20 LEPTA
Aluminum Obv: Arms within wreath Rev: Stallion's head left

Date	Mintage	F	VF	XF	Unc	BU
1976	2,506,000	—	0.15	0.40	2.50	5.00
1978	803,000	0.45	0.50	2.50	5.00	10.00
1978 Proof	20,000	Value: 5.00				

KM# 106   50 LEPTA
Nickel-Brass, 18 mm. Obv: Phoenix and flame Rev: Ornamental
plume

Date	Mintage	F	VF	XF	Unc	BU
1973	55,231,898	—	—	0.15	1.00	3.00

KM# 115   50 LEPTA
2.5200 g., Nickel-Brass, 18 mm. Subject: Markos Botsaris
Obv: Denomination Rev: Bust left

Date	Mintage	F	VF	XF	Unc	BU
1976	51,016,000	—	—	0.15	1.00	—
1978	12,010,000	—	—	0.15	1.00	—
1978 Proof	20,000	Value: 8.00				
1980	6,682,000	—	—	0.15	1.25	—
1982	3,365,000	—	—	0.15	1.25	—
1984	1,208,000	—	—	0.15	1.25	—
1986		—	—	0.15	1.25	—

KM# 107   DRACHMA
Nickel-Brass, 21 mm. Obv: Phoenix and flame Rev: Owl left of
denomination

Date	Mintage	F	VF	XF	Unc	BU
1973	45,218,431	—	0.75	1.50	3.00	6.00

KM# 116   DRACHMA
Nickel-Brass, 21 mm. Subject: Konstantinos Kanaris Obv: Full
masted ship at sea Rev: Bust left

Date	Mintage	F	VF	XF	Unc	BU
1976	102,060,000	—	—	0.15	1.00	3.00
Note: Varieties exist						
1978	21,200,000	—	—	0.15	1.00	2.00
1978 Proof	20,000	Value: 8.00				
1980	52,503,000	—	—	0.15	1.00	2.00
1982	54,186,000	—	—	0.15	1.00	2.00
1984	33,665,000	—	—	0.15	1.00	2.00
1986	17,901,000	—	—	0.15	1.00	3.00

KM# 150   DRACHMA
2.8000 g., Copper, 18 mm. Subject: Lascarina Bouboulina,
1783-1825 Obv: Full masted ship at sea Rev: Bust left

Date	Mintage	F	VF	XF	Unc	BU
1988(an)	36,707,000	—	—	—	0.50	1.00
1990(an)		—	—	—	0.50	1.00
1992		—	—	—	0.50	1.00
1993 In sets only		—	—	—	10.00	15.00
1993 Proof		Value: 45.00				

Date	Mintage	F	VF	XF	Unc	BU
1994	—			—	0.50	1.00
1998	—			—	0.50	1.00
2000	—			—	0.50	1.00

KM# 189   DRACHMA
8.5000 g., 0.9167 Gold 0.2505 oz. AGW Obv: Sailing ship
Rev: Bouboulina, heroine, bust left

Date	Mintage	F	VF	XF	Unc	BU
2000 Proof	—	Value: 400				

KM# 108   2 DRACHMAI
Nickel-Brass Obv: Phoenix and flame Rev: Owl left of
denomination

Date	Mintage	F	VF	XF	Unc	BU
1973	51,163,812	—	0.75	1.50	4.00	7.00

KM# 117   2 DRACHMAI
Nickel-Brass, 24 mm. Subject: Georgios Karaiskakis
Obv: Crossed rifles with branch Rev: Bust left

Date	Mintage	F	VF	XF	Unc	BU
1976	92,401,000	—	—	0.25	1.00	2.00
1978	16,772,000	—	—	0.25	1.00	2.00
1978 Proof	20,000	Value: 8.00				
1980	45,955,000	—	—	0.25	1.00	2.00

KM# 130   2 DRACHMES
Nickel-Brass, 24 mm. Subject: Georgios Karaiskakis
Obv: Crossed rifles and branch Rev: Bust left

Date	Mintage	F	VF	XF	Unc	BU
1982	64,414,000	—	—	0.20	1.00	2.00
1984	37,861,000	—	—	0.20	1.00	2.00
1986	21,019,000	—	—	0.20	1.00	2.00

KM# 151   2 DRACHMES
3.8000 g., Copper, 21 mm. Subject: Manto Mavrogenous,
1797-1840 - independence hero Obv: Ship's wheel, scope and
anchor Rev: Bust facing looking right

Date	Mintage	F	VF	XF	Unc	BU
1988(an)	36,707,000	—	—	—	0.50	1.00
1990	—			—	0.50	1.00
1992	—			—	0.50	1.00
1993 In sets only	—			—	10.00	15.00
1993 Proof	—	Value: 45.00				
1994	—			—	0.50	1.00
1998	—			—	0.50	1.00
2000	—			—	0.50	1.00

KM# 109.1   5 DRACHMAI
Copper-Nickel, 25 mm. Obv: Phoenix and flame Rev: Pegasus
rearing right Note: Denomination spelling ends with I.

Date	Mintage	F	VF	XF	Unc	BU
1973	33,957,473	0.75	1.25	2.00	4.00	10.00

KM# 109.2 5 DRACHMAI
Copper-Nickel, 25 mm. **Obv:** Phoenix and flame **Rev:** Pegasus rearing right **Note:** Denomination spelling ends with A.

Date	Mintage	F	VF	XF	Unc	BU
1973	Inc. above	1.00	2.00	4.00	70.00	200

KM# 118 5 DRACHMAI
Copper-Nickel, 22.5 mm. **Subject:** Aristotle **Obv:** Denomination **Rev:** Head left

Date	Mintage	F	VF	XF	Unc	BU
1976	85,187,000	—	0.20	0.35	1.00	2.00
1978 In sets only	17,404,000	—	0.20	0.35	1.00	3.00
1978 Proof	20,000	Value: 8.00				
1980	33,701,000	—	0.20	0.35	1.00	2.00

KM# 131 5 DRACHMES
5.5500 g., Copper-Nickel, 22.46 mm. **Subject:** Aristotle **Obv:** Denomination **Rev:** Head left **Edge:** Plain

Date	Mintage	F	VF	XF	Unc	BU
1982	42,647,000	—	0.20	0.35	1.00	2.00
1984	29,778,000	—	0.20	0.35	1.00	2.00
1986	16,730,000	—	0.20	0.35	1.00	2.00
1988	30,273,000	—	—	0.30	0.75	1.50
1990	—	—	—	0.30	0.75	1.50
1992	—	—	—	0.30	0.75	1.50
1993 In sets only	—	—	—	—	10.00	15.00
1993 Proof	—	Value: 50.00				
1994	—	—	—	—	0.75	1.50
1998	—	—	—	—	0.75	1.50
1999	—	—	—	—	0.75	1.50
2000	—	—	—	—	0.75	1.50

KM# 110 10 DRACHMAI
7.5500 g., Copper-Nickel **Obv:** Phoenix and flame **Rev:** Pegasus rearing right

Date	Mintage	F	VF	XF	Unc	BU
1973	22,599,848	1.00	1.50	2.50	6.00	10.00

KM# 119 10 DRACHMAI
7.5400 g., Copper-Nickel, 25.95 mm. **Subject:** Democritus **Obv:** Atom design **Rev:** Head left **Edge:** Plain

Date	Mintage	F	VF	XF	Unc	BU
1976	76,816,000	—	0.25	0.50	1.00	5.00
1978	14,637,000	—	0.25	0.50	1.00	5.00
1978 Proof	20,000	Value: 10.00				
1980	28,733,000	—	0.25	0.50	1.00	5.00

KM# 132 10 DRACHMES
7.6000 g., Copper-Nickel, 26 mm. **Obv:** Atom design **Rev:** Head of Democritus left

Date	Mintage	F	VF	XF	Unc	BU
1982	35,539,000	—	0.25	0.50	1.00	2.00
1984	23,802,000	—	0.25	0.50	1.00	2.00

Date	Mintage	F	VF	XF	Unc	BU
1986	24,441,000	—	0.25	0.50	1.00	2.00
1988	16,869,000	—	0.20	0.45	1.00	2.00
1990	—	—	0.20	0.45	1.00	2.00
1992	—	—	0.20	0.45	1.00	2.00
1993 In sets only	—	—	—	—	15.00	20.00
1993 Proof	—	Value: 60.00				
1994	—	—	0.20	0.45	1.00	2.00
1998	—	—	0.20	0.45	1.00	2.00
2000	—	—	—	—	1.00	2.00

KM# 112 20 DRACHMAI
Copper-Nickel, 29 mm. **Subject:** Athena **Obv:** Phoenix and flame **Rev:** Helmeted head left

Date	Mintage	F	VF	XF	Unc	BU
1973	20,650,087	0.35	0.50	1.00	2.00	5.00

KM# 120 20 DRACHMAI
Copper-Nickel, 29 mm. **Subject:** Pericles **Obv:** The Parthenon **Rev:** Helmeted head left **Edge:** In Greek

Date	Mintage	F	VF	XF	Unc	BU
1976	53,167,500	—	0.30	0.50	1.25	5.00
1978	65,353,000	—	0.30	0.50	1.50	5.00
1978 Proof	20,000	Value: 10.00				
1980	17,562,000	—	0.30	0.50	5.00	12.00

KM# 133 20 DRACHMES
Copper-Nickel, 28.8 mm. **Subject:** Pericles **Obv:** The Parthenon **Rev:** Helmeted head left **Edge:** In Greek

Date	Mintage	F	VF	XF	Unc	BU
1982	24,299,000	—	0.30	0.50	1.00	3.00
1984	13,412,000	—	0.30	0.50	1.25	3.50
1986	10,553,000	—	0.30	0.50	1.00	3.00
1988	16,196,000	—	—	0.50	1.00	3.00

KM# 154 20 DRACHMES
7.0000 g., Nickel-Bronze, 24.5 mm. **Subject:** Dionysios Solomos, composer of National Anthem **Obv:** Olive branch right of lined field **Rev:** Bust looking right

Date	Mintage	F	VF	XF	Unc	BU
1990(an)	—	—	—	—	1.25	2.50
1992	—	—	—	—	1.25	2.50
1993 In sets only	—	—	—	—	15.00	20.00
1993 Proof	—	Value: 85.00				
1994	—	—	—	—	1.25	2.50
1998(an)	—	—	—	—	1.25	2.50
2000	—	—	—	—	1.25	2.50

KM# 124 50 DRACHMAI
Copper-Nickel **Subject:** Solon the Archon of Athens **Obv:** Denomination above waves and date **Rev:** Head left

Date	Mintage	F	VF	XF	Unc	BU
1980(an)	32,250,999	0.50	0.75	1.50	3.50	6.00

KM# 134 50 DRACHMES
11.9600 g., Copper-Nickel, 31 mm. **Subject:** Solon the Archon of Athens **Obv:** Denomination above waves and date **Rev:** Head left **Note:** Obv: Denomination in modern Greek

Date	Mintage	F	VF	XF	Unc	BU
1982(an)	18,899,000	0.40	0.60	1.00	1.50	3.00
1984(an)	11,411,000	0.40	0.60	1.00	1.50	3.00

KM# 147 50 DRACHMES
9.2000 g., Nickel-Brass, 27.6 mm. **Subject:** Homer **Obv:** Ancient sailing boat **Rev:** Head left

Date	Mintage	F	VF	XF	Unc	BU
1986(an)	12,078,000	—	0.50	1.00	2.50	5.00
1988(an)	23,589,000	—	—	0.75	1.50	3.00
1990(an)	—	—	—	0.75	1.75	3.50
1992	—	—	—	0.75	1.75	3.50
1993 In sets only	—	—	—	—	20.00	25.00
1993 Proof	—	Value: 70.00				
1994	—	—	—	0.75	1.75	3.50
1998	—	—	—	—	1.75	3.50
1999	—	—	—	—	1.75	3.50
2000	—	—	—	—	1.75	3.50

KM# 164 50 DRACHMES
Brass, 27 mm. **Series:** 150th Anniversary of the Constitution **Subject:** Dimitrios Kallergis **Obv:** Bust 3/4 left **Rev:** Center of Parliament Building

Date	Mintage	F	VF	XF	Unc	BU
ND(1994)(an)	7,500,000	—	—	—	3.00	5.00

KM# 168 50 DRACHMES
Brass, 27 mm. **Series:** 150th Anniversary of the Constitution **Subject:** Makrygiannis **Obv:** Bust 3/4 left **Rev:** Center of Parliament Building

Date	Mintage	F	VF	XF	Unc	BU
ND(1994)(an)	7,500,000	—	—	—	3.00	5.00

KM# 171   50 DRACHMES
Brass   **Subject:** Rigas Feraios **Obv:** Arms within wreath **Rev:** Bust 3/4 right divides dates

Date	Mintage	F	VF	XF	Unc	BU
ND (1998)	—	—	—	—	3.50	5.50

KM# 172   50 DRACHMES
Brass   **Subject:** Dionysios Solomos **Obv:** Arms within wreath **Rev:** Bust 3/4 facing divides dates

Date	Mintage	F	VF	XF	Unc	BU
ND (1998)	—	—	—	—	3.50	5.50

KM# 121   100 DRACHMAI
13.0000 g., 0.6500 Silver 0.2717 oz. ASW   **Subject:** 50th Anniversary - Bank of Greece **Obv:** Denomination **Rev:** Athena seated right

Date	Mintage	F	VF	XF	Unc	BU
1978 Proof	25,000	Value: 150				

KM# 125   100 DRACHMAI
5.7800 g., 0.9000 Silver 0.1672 oz. ASW   **Subject:** Pan-European Games **Obv:** Arms within wreath **Rev:** Ancient olympic broad jump

Date	Mintage	F	VF	XF	Unc	BU
1981	150,000	—	—	—	8.00	10.00
1981 Proof	150,000	Value: 15.00				

KM# 135   100 DRACHMAI
5.7800 g., 0.9000 Silver 0.1672 oz. ASW   **Subject:** Pan-European Games **Obv:** Arms within wreath **Rev:** Olympic high jump

Date	Mintage	F	VF	XF	Unc	BU
1982	150,000	—	—	—	8.00	10.00
1982 Proof	Inc. above	Value: 15.00				

KM# 136   100 DRACHMAI
5.7800 g., 0.9000 Silver 0.1672 oz. ASW   **Subject:** Pan-European Games **Obv:** Arms within wreath **Rev:** Pole vault

Date	Mintage	F	VF	XF	Unc	BU
1982	150,000	—	—	—	8.00	10.00
1982 Proof	Inc. above	Value: 15.00				

KM# 152   100 DRACHMES
Copper-Nickel   **Subject:** 28th Chess Olympics **Obv:** Castle towers and stylized chessboard **Rev:** Legend divides block design, shield at left and owl at right

Date	Mintage	F	VF	XF	Unc	BU
1988(an)	30,000	—	—	—	12.00	15.00

KM# 159   100 DRACHMES
10.2000 g., Brass, 29.3 mm.   **Subject:** Macedonia - Alexander the Great **Obv:** Radiant design within circle **Rev:** Head right

Date	Mintage	F	VF	XF	Unc	BU
1990(an)	—	—	—	—	2.35	4.50
Note: Varieties exist						
1992	—	—	—	—	2.35	4.50
1993 Proof	—	Value: 85.00				
1993 In sets only	—	—	—	—	20.00	25.00
1994	—	—	—	—	2.35	4.50
1998	—	—	—	—	2.35	4.50
2000	—	—	—	—	2.35	4.50

KM# 169   100 DRACHMES
9.8700 g., Brass, 29.48 mm.   **Subject:** VI Universal Track Championship Games **Obv:** Ancient city view and track **Rev:** Runner and track **Edge:** Alternating reeded and smooth sections

Date	Mintage	F	VF	XF	Unc	BU
1997(an)	5,000,000	—	—	—	2.75	5.00

KM# 170   100 DRACHMES
9.8500 g., Brass, 29.45 mm.   **Subject:** 13th World Basketball Championships **Obv:** Cup in ball design **Rev:** Four basketball players in action **Edge:** Segmented reeding

Date	Mintage	F	VF	XF	Unc	BU
1998(an)	—	—	—	—	4.50	6.50

KM# 173   100 DRACHMES
10.0000 g., Brass, 29.4 mm.   **Obv:** Ancient wrestlers **Rev:** Modern wrestlers **Edge:** Reeded and plain sections

Date	Mintage	F	VF	XF	Unc	BU
1999	—	—	—	—	3.50	5.50

KM# 174   100 DRACHMES
10.0000 g., Brass, 29.4 mm.   **Obv:** Statue of Atlas **Rev:** Weight lifter **Edge:** Reeded and plain sections

Date	Mintage	F	VF	XF	Unc	BU
1999	—	—	—	—	3.50	5.50

KM# 126   250 DRACHMAI
14.4400 g., 0.9000 Silver 0.4178 oz. ASW   **Subject:** Pan-European Games **Obv:** Arms within wreath **Rev:** Ancient Olympic javelin throwing

Date	Mintage	F	VF	XF	Unc	BU
1981	150,000	—	—	—	12.50	14.50
1981 Proof	150,000	Value: 20.00				

KM# 137   250 DRACHMAI
14.4400 g., 0.9000 Silver 0.4178 oz. ASW   **Subject:** Pan-European Games **Obv:** Arms within wreath **Rev:** 1896 Olympic discus throwing

Date	Mintage	F	VF	XF	Unc	BU
1982	150,000	—	—	—	12.50	14.50
1982 Proof	Inc. above	Value: 20.00				

KM# 138   250 DRACHMAI
14.4400 g., 0.9000 Silver 0.4178 oz. ASW   **Subject:** Pan-European Games **Obv:** Arms within wreath **Rev:** Shot put

Date	Mintage	F	VF	XF	Unc	BU
1982	150,000	—	—	—	12.50	14.50
1982 Proof	Inc. above	Value: 20.00				

KM# 127   500 DRACHMAI
28.8800 g., 0.9000 Silver 0.8356 oz. ASW   **Subject:** Pan-European Games **Obv:** Arms within wreath **Rev:** Ancient Olympic relay race

Date	Mintage	F	VF	XF	Unc	BU
1981	150,000	—	—	—	20.00	22.50
1981 Proof	150,000	Value: 27.50				

KM# 139   500 DRACHMAI
28.8800 g., 0.9000 Silver 0.8356 oz. ASW **Subject:** Pan-European Games **Obv:** Arms within wreath **Rev:** 1896 Olympic racers at starting blocks

Date	Mintage	F	VF	XF	Unc	BU
1982	150,000	—	—	—	20.00	22.50
1982 Proof	Inc. above	Value: 27.50				

KM# 140   500 DRACHMAI
28.8800 g., 0.9000 Silver 0.8356 oz. ASW **Subject:** Pan-European Games **Obv:** Arms within wreath **Rev:** Racers

Date	Mintage	F	VF	XF	Unc	BU
1982	150,000	—	—	—	20.00	22.50
1982 Proof	Inc. above	Value: 27.50				

KM# 122   500 DRACHMES
13.0000 g., 0.9000 Silver 0.3761 oz. ASW **Subject:** Common Market Membership **Obv:** Inscription above denomination **Rev:** Figure in tree

Date	Mintage	F	VF	XF	Unc	BU
ND (1979)	—					
ND (1979) Proof	18,000	Value: 200				

KM# 145   500 DRACHMES
18.0000 g., 0.9000 Silver 0.5208 oz. ASW **Subject:** Olympics **Obv:** Arms within wreath, torch at right **Rev:** Runner with torch

Date	Mintage	F	VF	XF	Unc	BU
1984	25,000	—	—	—	80.00	100
1984 Proof	25,000	Value: 150				

KM# 153   500 DRACHMES
18.1100 g., 0.9000 Silver 0.5240 oz. ASW **Subject:** 28th Chess Olympics **Obv:** Ancient figures playing chess **Rev:** Legend divides block design, shield at left and owl at right

Date	Mintage	F	VF	XF	Unc	BU
1988 Proof	3,000	Value: 300				

KM# 157   500 DRACHMES
18.0000 g., 0.9000 Silver 0.5208 oz. ASW **Subject:** XI Mediterranean Games **Obv:** Design and denomination **Rev:** Fish wearing hat, logo at right

Date	Mintage	F	VF	XF	Unc	BU
1991 Proof	10,000	Value: 75.00				

KM# 160   500 DRACHMES
17.0000 g., 0.9250 Silver 0.5055 oz. ASW **Subject:** 2500th Anniversary of Democracy **Obv:** Head on old coin right **Rev:** One seated and one standing figure within square

Date	Mintage	F	VF	XF	Unc	BU
1993 Proof	Est. 30,000	Value: 300				

KM# 162   500 DRACHMES
17.0000 g., 0.9250 Silver 0.5055 oz. ASW **Subject:** Volleyball Centennial **Rev:** Players in rectangle, date at corners

Date	Mintage	F	VF	XF	Unc	BU
1994 Proof	1,750	Value: 150				

KM# 175   500 DRACHMES
9.5400 g., Copper-Nickel, 28 mm. **Series:** 2004 Olympics **Obv:** Laurel wreath within square, games logo below **Rev:** Arched entry to ancient Olympic stadium **Edge:** Plain

Date	Mintage	F	VF	XF	Unc	BU
2000	—	—	—	—	4.50	6.00

KM# 176   500 DRACHMES
9.5400 g., Copper-Nickel, 28 mm. **Series:** 2004 Olympics **Obv:** Laurel wreath within square, games logo below **Rev:** Runner receiving Olympic torch **Edge:** Plain

Date	Mintage	F	VF	XF	Unc	BU
2000	—	—	—	—	4.50	6.00

KM# 177   500 DRACHMES
9.5400 g., Copper-Nickel, 28 mm. **Series:** 2004 Olympics **Obv:** Laurel wreath within square, games logo below **Rev:** Ancient winner Diagoras being carried **Edge:** Plain

Date	Mintage	F	VF	XF	Unc	BU
2000	—	—	—	—	4.50	6.00

KM# 178   500 DRACHMES
9.5400 g., Copper-Nickel, 28 mm. **Series:** 2004 Olympics **Subject:** President Vikelas and Baron Couberten **Obv:** Laurel wreath within square, games logo below **Rev:** Jugate busts; one left and one facing **Edge:** Plain

Date	Mintage	F	VF	XF	Unc	BU
2000	—	—	—	—	4.50	6.00

KM# 179   500 DRACHMES
9.5400 g., Copper-Nickel, 28 mm. **Series:** 2004 Olympics **Subject:** Spyros Louis, 1896 marathon winner **Obv:** Laurel wreath within square **Rev:** Standing figure **Edge:** Plain

Date	Mintage	F	VF	XF	Unc	BU
2000	—	—	—	—	4.50	6.00

KM# 180   500 DRACHMES
9.5400 g., Copper-Nickel, 28 mm. **Series:** 2004 Olympics **Obv:** Laurel wreath within square, games logo below **Rev:** 1896 Olympic gold medal design **Edge:** Plain

Date	Mintage	F	VF	XF	Unc	BU
2000	—	—	—	—	4.50	6.00

KM# 148   1000 DRACHMES
23.3300 g., 0.9250 Silver 0.6938 oz. ASW **Subject:** Decade For Women **Rev:** Statue of women figures with arms raised

Date	Mintage	F	VF	XF	Unc	BU
1985 Proof	3,660	Value: 150				

KM# 155   1000 DRACHMES
18.0000 g., 0.9000 Silver 0.5208 oz. ASW   **Subject:** 50th Anniversary - Italian Invasion of Greece **Obv:** Arms within wreath **Rev:** Soldiers and horse

Date	Mintage	F	VF	XF	Unc	BU
1990 Proof	7,000	Value: 170				

KM# 165   1000 DRACHMES
33.6300 g., 0.9250 Silver 1.0000 oz. ASW   **Subject:** Olympics **Obv:** Track field **Rev:** 4 ancient runners **Edge:** CITIUS ALTIUS FORTIUS

Date	Mintage	F	VF	XF	Unc	BU
1996 Proof	100,000	Value: 50.00				

KM# 166   1000 DRACHMES
33.6300 g., 0.9250 Silver 1.0000 oz. ASW   **Subject:** Olympics **Rev:** 2 ancient wrestlers **Edge:** CITIUS ALTIUS FORTIUS

Date	Mintage	F	VF	XF	Unc	BU
1996 Proof	100,000	Value: 50.00				

KM# 128   2500 DRACHMAI
6.4500 g., 0.9000 Gold 0.1866 oz. AGW   **Series:** Pan-European Games **Subject:** Ancient Olympics, Agon **Obv:** Arms within wreath **Rev:** Winged figure holding rings

Date	Mintage	F	VF	XF	Unc	BU
1981 Proof	75,000	Value: 225				

KM# 141   2500 DRACHMAI
6.4500 g., 0.9000 Gold 0.1866 oz. AGW   **Series:** Pan-European Games **Subject:** 1896 Olympics, Spiros **Obv:** Arms within wreath **Rev:** Half figure holding wreath

Date	Mintage	F	VF	XF	Unc	BU
1982 Proof	50,000	Value: 225				

KM# 142   2500 DRACHMAI
6.4500 g., 0.9000 Gold 0.1866 oz. AGW   **Series:** Pan-European Games **Obv:** Arms within wreath **Rev:** Winged statue

Date	Mintage	F	VF	XF	Unc	BU
1982 Proof	50,000	Value: 225				

KM# 129   5000 DRACHMAI
12.5000 g., 0.9000 Gold 0.3617 oz. AGW   **Series:** Pan-European Games **Subject:** Ancient Olympics, Zeus **Obv:** Arms within wreath **Rev:** Laureate head left

Date	Mintage	F	VF	XF	Unc	BU
1981 Proof	75,000	Value: 360				

KM# 143   5000 DRACHMAI
12.5000 g., 0.9000 Gold 0.3617 oz. AGW   **Series:** Pan-European Games **Subject:** 1896 Olympics, Pierre de Coubertin **Obv:** Arms within wreath **Rev:** Head 3/4 facing

Date	Mintage	F	VF	XF	Unc	BU
1982 Proof	50,000	Value: 360				

KM# 144   5000 DRACHMAI
12.5000 g., 0.9000 Gold 0.3617 oz. AGW   **Series:** Pan-European Games **Obv:** Arms within wreath **Rev:** Birds flying

Date	Mintage	F	VF	XF	Unc	BU
1982 Proof	50,000	Value: 380				

KM# 146   5000 DRACHMAI
8.0000 g., 0.9000 Gold 0.2315 oz. AGW   **Subject:** Olympics **Obv:** Arms at left, torch at right **Rev:** Apollo

Date	Mintage	F	VF	XF	Unc	BU
1984 Proof	15,000	Value: 500				

KM# 123   10000 DRACHMES
20.0000 g., 0.9000 Gold 0.5787 oz. AGW   **Subject:** Common Market Membership **Obv:** Inscription above denomination **Rev:** Seated figure left

Date	Mintage	F	VF	XF	Unc	BU
ND (1979) Proof	—	Value: 700				

KM# 149   10000 DRACHMES
7.1300 g., 0.9000 Gold 0.2063 oz. AGW   **Subject:** Decade For Women **Obv:** Arms within wreath **Rev:** Standing figure

Date	Mintage	F	VF	XF	Unc	BU
1985 Proof	2,835	Value: 850				

KM# 158   10000 DRACHMES
8.0000 g., 0.9000 Gold 0.2315 oz. AGW   **Subject:** XI Mediterranean Games **Obv:** Design, denomination **Rev:** Fish wearing hat, logo at right

Date	Mintage	F	VF	XF	Unc	BU
1991 Proof	2,000	Value: 430				

KM# 161   10000 DRACHMES
8.5000 g., 0.9170 Gold 0.2506 oz. AGW   **Subject:** 2500th Anniversary of Democracy **Obv:** Statue **Rev:** Head left

Date	Mintage	F	VF	XF	Unc	BU
1993 Proof	Est. 10,000	Value: 500				

KM# 163   10000 DRACHMES
8.5000 g., 0.9170 Gold 0.2506 oz. AGW   **Subject:** Volleyball Centennial **Obv:** Ancient coin divides date

Date	Mintage	F	VF	XF	Unc	BU
1994 Proof	669	Value: 2,200				

KM# 156   20000 DRACHMES
8.0000 g., 0.9000 Gold 0.2315 oz. AGW   **Subject:** 50th Anniversary - Italian Invasion of Greece **Rev:** Soldiers and horse

Date	Mintage	F	VF	XF	Unc	BU
1990 Proof	1,000	Value: 2,700				

KM# 167   20000 DRACHMES
16.9700 g., 0.9170 Gold 0.5003 oz. AGW   **Subject:** Olympics **Obv:** Track field **Rev:** Ancient javelin throwers **Edge:** CITIUS ALTIUS FORTIUS

Date	Mintage	F	VF	XF	Unc	BU
1996 Proof	60,000	Value: 500				

ESSAIS

KM#	Date	Mintage	Identification	Mkt Val
E23	1911	4	2 Drachmai. Silver. 1868 2 Drachmai. ESSAI to right of denomination.	8,600
EA23	1911	2	2 Drachmai. Silver. Without mintmark, ESSAI to right of sea-horse.	10,250
E24	1912	—	5 Lepta. Nickel. Crown right of center hole. Owl left of center hole. ESSAI, plain edge, without mintmark	2,500
E25	1912	—	5 Lepta. Zinc. ESSAI	3,000
E26	1912	—	10 Lepta. Nickel. Crown right of center hole. Owl left of center hole. ESSAI, plain edge, without mintmark	2,500
E27	1912	—	10 Lepta. Zinc. ESSAI.	3,000
E28	1912	—	10 Lepta. Nickel. ESSAI, with mintmark	4,000
E29	1912	—	20 Lepta. Nickel. Crowned arms right of center hole. Center hole divides statue and branch. ESSAI.	2,500
E30	1912	—	20 Lepta. Zinc. ESSAI.	3,200
E31	1913	—	Drachma. Silver. ESSAI.	40,000
E32	1915	—	Drachma. Copper-Nickel. ESSAI.	18,000

Note: NGSA 12/08 $18,000

KM#	Date	Mintage	Identification	Mkt Val
E33	1915	—	Drachma. Silver. Head left. Crowned and mantled shield. ESSAI.	40,000
E34	1915	—	Drachma. Gold. 9.2000 g. ESSAI.	—
	1915	—	Drachma. Gold. 9.2000 g. ESSAI.	—
E35	1915	—	2 Drachmai. Silver. ESSAI.	60,000
E36	1915	—	2 Drachmai. Gold. 15.9000 g. ESSAI.	—
E37	1922	—	10 Lepta. Aluminum. Crown above date. Olive branch left of denomination. ESSAI.	2,500

Note: NGSA 12/08 $2,800

PATTERNS
Including off metal strikes

KM#	Date	Mintage	Identification	Mkt Val
Pn40	1910	—	Drachma. Silver. Value in lower case letters.	8,000
Pn41	1910	—	Drachma. Silver. Without mintmark.	8,000
Pn42	1911	—	2 Drachmai. Silver. Seahorse. Without mintmark.	10,000
PnA44	1922	3	10 Lepta. Nickel. With (IAKOBIAHS) engraver's name.	10,000
PnB44	1922	2	10 Lepta. Aluminum. With (IAKOBIAHS) engraver's name.	10,500
PnC44	1926	—	20 Lepta. Copper Nickel. Large letters.	5,000
Pn44	1926	—	Drachma. Nickel. Large letters.	5,000
Pn54	1926	—	2 Drachmai. Nickel. Large letters.	3,000
Pn55	1930	—	5 Drachmai. Nickel. With "MODEL" on reverse.	5,000
Pn59	ND	—	20 Drachmai. Copper. 21mm, KM74.	5,000
Pn60	ND	—	20 Drachmai. Gold. Without "20", KM74.	50,000
Pn61	ND	—	100 Drachmai. Copper. KM75.	7,150
Pn62	ND	—	100 Drachmai. Copper. KM76.	7,150
Pn63	1954	50	50 Lepta. Copper-Nickel. "ANAMNHETIKON" above date.	2,500
Pn64	1954	10	50 Lepta. Gold.	6,000
Pn65	1954	—	50 Lepta. Copper-Nickel. "hollow cheek" variety, not approved, die use discontinued.	750
Pn66	1954	50	Drachma. Copper Nickel. "ANAMNHETIKON" above date.	3,000
Pn67	1954	10	Drachma. Gold.	6,000
Pn68	1954	—	Drachma. Copper-Nickel. "hollow cheek" variety, not approved, die use discontinued.	600
Pn69	1954	50	2 Drachmai. Copper-Nickel. "ANAMNHETIKON" above date.	3,000
Pn70	1954	10	2 Drachmai. Gold.	6,000
Pn71	1954	—	2 Drachmai. Copper-Nickel. "hollow cheek" variety, not approved, die use discontinued.	1,500
Pn72	1954	50	5 Drachmai. Copper-Nickel. "ANAMNHETIKON" above date.	2,000
Pn73	1954	10	5 Drachmai. Gold.	6,000
Pn74	1954	—	5 Drachmai. Copper-Nickel. "hollow cheek" variety, not approved, die use discontinued.	50.00
PnA75	1959	—	10 Drachmai. Silver. KM#84	6,000
Pn75	1959	10	10 Drachmai. Gold.	20,000
Pn77	1960	—	20 Drachmai. Gold.	20,000
Pn78	1963	—	30 Drachmai. Gold. With "ANAMNHETIKON".	7,000
Pn79	1964	—	30 Drachmai. Gold.	15,000
Pn80	1966	—	50 Lepta. Gold.	—

Note: NGSA Auction 12/08 $4,500

KM#	Date	Mintage	Identification	Mkt Val
PnA81	1966	—	2 Drachmai. Silver.	2,400
PnB81	1966	—	2 Drachmai. Copper-Nickel.	1,100
Pn81	1966	—	50 Lepta. Silver.	5,250

Note: Platinum strikes have been reported, but not confirmed

Pn82	1967	—	Drachma. Gold.	6,500

Note: NGSA 12/08 $5,000

Pn83	1967	—	Drachma. Silver.	4,500

Note: Platinum strikes have been reported, but not confirmed. NGSA 12/08 $1,200

Pn84	1967	—	2 Drachmai. Gold.	6,500

Note: NGSA 12/08 $6,000

Pn85	1967	—	2 Drachmai. Silver.	5,250

Note: Platinum strikes have been reported, but not confirmed. NGSA 12/08 $1,400

Pn86	1967	—	5 Drachmai. Gold.	6,500

Note: NGSA 12/08 $10,000

Pn87	1967	—	5 Drachmai. Silver.	8,250

Note: Platinum strikes have been reported, but not confirmed. NGSA Auction 12/08 $1,200

KM#	Date	Mintage	Identification	Mkt Val
Pn88	1973	—	20 Drachmai. Bronze-Nickel. Low relief and date, without veil.	75.00
Pn89	1976	—	Drachma. Nickel. 4 sails and 2 waves.	2,000
Pn90	1986	4	Drachma. Aluminum.	2,500
Pn91	1986	4	2 Drachmai. Aluminum.	2,500
Pn92	1987	—	Drachma. Copper.	2,500

Note: Off metal strike resulting from wrong planchet error

Pn93	1987	—	2 Drachmes. Nickel-Brass.	—

Note: Off metal strike resulting from wrong planchet error

PIEFORTS

KM#	Date	Mintage	Identification	Mkt Val
P1	1922	—	10 Lepta. Copper. With ESSAI.	3,000
P3	ND	2	20 Drachmai. Lead. KM74.	3,500

TRIAL STRIKES

KM#	Date	Mintage	Identification	Mkt Val
TSA22	1921	—	50 Lepta. Brass. Uniface	2,500
TS19	1921	—	5 Lepta. Aluminum. Reverse uniface.	—
TS20	1921	—	5 Lepta. Aluminum. Obverse uniface.	—
TS21	1921	—	50 Lepta. Aluminum. Uniface.	2,000
TS22	1926	—	2 Drachmai. Copper. Uniface.	1,000
TS23	1930	—	5 Drachmai. Copper. Uniface.	1,500
TS24	1930	—	20 Drachmai. Brass. Test marks.	500
TS25	1960	—	20 Drachmai. Copper.	5,000
TS26	1969/70	—	10 Lepta. Base Metal. 3.6000 g. Uniface pattern of obverse	3,500
TS27	ND(1969)	—	10 Lepta. Base Metal. 3.6100 g. Uniface pattern of reverse	3,500
TS28	1969/70	—	10 Lepta. Silver. 4.7200 g. Uniface pattern of obverse	4,000
TS29	ND(1969)	—	10 Lepta. Silver. 4.7500 g. Uniface pattern of reverse	4,000
TS30	1969/70	—	10 Lepta. Gold. 8.9300 g. Uniface pattern of obverse	5,000
TS31	ND(1969)	—	10 Lepta. Gold. 8.9300 g. Uniface pattern of reverse	5,000
TS32	1969/4	—	20 Lepta. Base Metal. 4.3400 g. Uniface pattern of obverse	3,500
TS33	ND(1969)	—	20 Lepta. Base Metal. 4.3400 g. Uniface pattern of reverse	3,500
TS34	ND1969/4	—	20 Lepta. Silver. 5.7200 g. Uniface pattern of obverse	4,000
TS35	ND(1969)	—	20 Lepta. Silver. 5.7200 g. Uniface pattern of reverse	4,000
TS36	1969/4	—	20 Lepta. Gold. 10.7400 g. Uniface pattern of obverse	5,000
TS37	ND(1969)	—	20 Lepta. Gold. 10.6900 g. Uniface pattern of reverse	5,000
TSA34	1969/4	—	20 Lepta. Aluminum. Obverse uniface.	3,000

MINT SETS

KM#	Date	Mintage	Identification	Issue Price	Mkt Val
MS1	1965 (7)	—	KM78, 80-85	—	55.00
MS2	1978 (8)	50,000	KM#113, 114, 115, 116, 117, 118, 119, 120	—	60.00
MS3	1982 (7)	—	KM115-116, 130-134	—	20.00
MS4	1993 (7)	—	KM#131-132, 147, 150-151, 154, 159	—	270
MS5	2000 (7)	—	KM#131-132, 147, 150-151, 154, 159	—	20.00

PROOF SETS

KM#	Date	Mintage	Identification	Issue Price	Mkt Val
PS1	1965 (7)	4,987	KM78, 80-85	10.25	85.00
PS2	1978 (8)	20,000	KM113-120	—	65.00
PS3	1993 (8)	—	KM131-132, 147, 150-151, 154, 159-160	65.00	825
PS4	1994 (2)	—	KM162-163	—	2,650

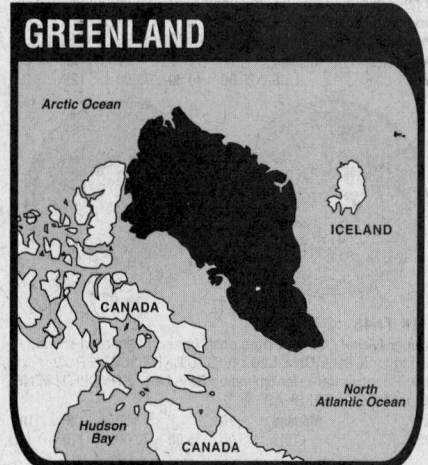

Greenland, an integral part of the Danish realm is situated between the North Atlantic Ocean and the Polar Sea, almost entirely within the Arctic Circle. An island nation, it has an area of 840,000 sq. mi. (2,175,600 sq. km.) and a population of 57,000. Capital: Nuuk (formerly Godthaab). Greenland is the world's only

source of natural cryolite, a fluoride of sodium and aluminum important in making aluminum. Fish products and minerals are exported.

Eric the Red discovered Greenland in 982 and established the first settlement in 986. Greenland was a republic until 1261, when the sovereignty of Norway was extended to the island. The original colony was abandoned about 1400 when increasing cold interfered with the breeding of cattle. Successful recolonization was undertaken by Denmark in 1721. In 1921 Denmark extended its claim to include the entire island, and made it a colony of the crown in 1924. The island's colonial status was abolished by amendment to the Danish constitution on June 5, 1953, and Greenland became an integral part of the Kingdom of Denmark. The last Greenlandic coins were withdrawn on July 1, 1967, and since then, Danish coins have been used. Greenland has had home rule since May 1, 1979.

RULERS
Danish

MINT MARKS
Heart (h). Copenhagen (Kobenhavn)

MINTMASTERS' INITIALS
HCN - Hans Christian Nielsen, 1919-1927
C - Alfred Kristian Frederik Christiansen, 1956-1971
GJ - Knud Gunnar Jensen, 1901-1933
S - Harald Salomon, 1933-1968

MONETARY SYSTEM
(Since 1824)
100 Øre = 1 Krone

DANISH COLONY

TOKEN ISSUES - GREENLAND MINING LTD.
Josva (Innatsiaq)

A place in southwest Greenland, where the Grønlandsk Minedrifts Aktieselskab ran a copper mine from 1907-1914 yielding little more than 60 tons of copper, as a minor bonus, over 50 kg of silver and half a kg of gold.

KM# Tn1 10 ORE
Nickel Plated Zinc **Obv:** Date within legend **Obv. Leg.:** GRØNLANDSK MINEDRIFTS-AKTIESELSKAB **Rev:** Crossed hammers over denomination **Note:** Struck at L. Chr. Lauer, Nürnberg, Germany.

Date	Mintage	VG	F	VF	XF	Unc
1911	5,000	—	12.50	20.00	40.00	75.00

KM# Tn2 25 ORE
Nickel Plated Zinc **Obv:** Date within legend **Obv. Leg.:** GRØNLANDSK MINEDRIFTS-AKTIESELSKAB **Rev:** Crossed hammers over denomination **Note:** Struck at L. Chr. Lauer, Nürnberg, Germany.

Date	Mintage	VG	F	VF	XF	Unc
1911	5,000	—	12.50	20.00	40.00	75.00

KM# Tn3 100 ORE
Nickel Plated Zinc **Obv:** Date within legend **Obv. Leg.:** GRØNLANDSK MINEDRIFTS-AKTIESELSKAB **Rev:** Crossed hammers over denomination **Note:** Struck at L. Chr. Lauer, Nürnberg, Germany.

Date	Mintage	VG	F	VF	XF	Unc
1911	5,000	—	12.50	20.00	40.00	75.00

TOKEN ISSUES - ROYAL GREENLAND TRADE (COMPANY)
(Den Kongelige Grønlandske Handel)

Ammassalik is a municipality in East Greenland with a population of 3100.

KM# Tn25   500 ORE
Aluminum **Note:** Uniface

Date	Mintage	VG	F	VF	XF	Unc
ND(1905)	200	50.00	100	210	350	—

DANISH COLONY

MILLED COINAGE

KM# 6   25 ORE
Copper-Nickel **Obv:** Crowned arms of Denmark **Rev:** Hole at center of polar bear walking, left, denomination above, date below divided by 'GS' **Note:** Center hole added to KM#5.

Date	Mintage	F	VF	XF	Unc	BU
1926(h) HCN GJ	60,000	20.00	40.00	90.00	150	—

Note: The hole was added 1940/41 in New York to avoid confusion with the 1 Krone coins of Denmark

KM# 5   25 ORE
Copper-Nickel **Obv:** Crowned arms of Denmark **Obv. Leg.:** GRØNLANDS STYRELSE **Rev:** Polar bear walking left, denomination above, date below divided by 'GS'

Date	Mintage	F	VF	XF	Unc	BU
1926(h) HCN GJ	310,000	4.00	7.00	15.00	40.00	60.00

Note: This coin was withdrawn from circulation during 1940 and sent to the United States to be holed to avoid confusion with the Danish 1 Krone coin

KM# 7   50 ORE
Aluminum-Bronze **Obv:** Crowned arms of Denmark **Obv. Leg.:** GRØNLANDS STYRELSE **Rev:** Polar bear walking left, denomination above, date below divided by 'GS'

Date	Mintage	F	VF	XF	Unc	BU
1926(h) HCN CJ	195,837	6.00	9.50	15.00	45.00	70.00

KM# 8   KRONE
Aluminum-Bronze **Obv:** Crowned arms of Denmark **Obv. Leg.:** GRØNLANDS STYRELSE **Rev:** Polar bear walking left, denomination above, date below divided by 'GS'

Date	Mintage	F	VF	XF	Unc	BU
1926(h) HCN CJ	286,982	4.50	10.00	20.00	60.00	75.00

KM# 9   5 KRONER
Brass **Obv:** Crowned arms of Denmark **Obv. Leg.:** GRØNLANDS STYRELSE **Rev:** Polar bear walking left, denomination above, date below divided by "GS" **Note:** Mainly struck for use by American forces in Greenland during WWII, when 5 Kroner was equal to one U.S. dollar.

Date	Mintage	F	VF	XF	Unc	BU
1944	100,000	40.00	60.00	100	160	190

Note: Struck at the Philadelphia Mint; without mintmark

TOKEN ISSUES - IVIGTUT CRYOLITE MINING & TRADING CO.
Series IV, 1922

KM# Tn46   10 ORE
Copper-Nickel **Obv:** Seated polar bear on helmeted shield, mining tools flank **Obv. Leg.:** IVIGTUT KRYOLITHBRUD **Rev:** Denomination at center **Rev. Leg.:** KRYOLITH MINE OG HANDELS SELSKABET

Date	Mintage	VG	F	VF	XF	Unc
1922	10,018	5.00	12.00	15.00	32.50	53.50

KM# Tn47   50 ORE
Copper-Nickel **Obv:** Seated polar bear on helmeted shield, mining tools flank **Obv. Leg.:** IVIGTUT KRYOLITHBRUD **Rev. Leg.:** KRYOLITH MINE OG HANDELS SELSKABET

Date	Mintage	F	VF	XF	Unc
1922	4,018	20.00	40.00	75.00	125	180

KM# Tn48   2 KRONER
Copper-Nickel **Obv:** Seated polar bear on helmeted shield, mining tools flank **Obv. Leg.:** IVIGTUT KRYOLITHBRUD **Rev:** Rosettes flank denomination **Rev. Leg.:** KRYOLITH MINE OG HANDELS SELSKABET

Date	Mintage	VG	F	VF	XF	Unc
1922	4,018	15.00	35.00	70.00	110	180

KM# Tn49   10 KRONER
Copper-Nickel **Obv:** Seated polar bear on shield **Obv. Leg.:** IVIGTUT KRYOLITHBRUD **Rev. Leg.:** KRYOLITH MINE OG HANDELS SELSKABET **Edge:** Reeded

Date	Mintage	VG	F	VF	XF	Unc
1922	10,706	20.00	45.00	70.00	140	200

Note: Struck in 1926 using 1922 dies. Many new coins have appeared on the market lately.

KM# Tn49a   10 KRONER
Aluminum-Bronze **Obv:** Polar bear on shield **Edge:** Plain

Date	Mintage	VG	F	VF	XF	Unc
1922	7,018	—	—	1,000	1,500	2,000

Note: This token was removed from circulation because it had the same size, weight and color as Denmark's 2 Kroner, issued in 1924.

DANISH STATE
1953-1979

MILLED COINAGE

KM# 10   KRONE
Aluminum-Bronze, 27.3 mm. **Issuer:** Royal Greenland Trade Company **Obv:** Crowned arms of Denmark and Greenland, date below **Obv. Leg.:** DEN KONGELIGE GRØNLANDSKE HANDEL **Rev:** Denomination within floral wreath

Date	Mintage	F	VF	XF	Unc	BU
1957(h) C S	100,209	8.00	12.50	22.50	62.00	80.00

KM# 10a   KRONE
Copper-Nickel, 27.3 mm. **Issuer:** Royal Greenland Trade Company **Obv:** Crowned arms of Denmark and Greenland **Rev:** Denomination within floral wreath

Date	Mintage	F	VF	XF	Unc	BU
1960(h) C S	108,500	3.75	7.50	12.50	22.50	—
1964(h) C S	110,000	8.00	15.00	20.00	30.00	—

TRIAL STRIKES
Angmagssalik - Royal Greenland Trade (Company)

KM#	Date	Mintage Identification	Mkt Val
TS1	ND(1905)	— Ore. Aluminum. 27 mm.	

Note: Similar to the zinc-tokens ND (1894)

TS2	ND(1905)	— 5 Ore. Aluminum. 30 mm.	

Note: Similar to the zinc-tokens ND (1894)

TS3	ND(1905)	— 10 Ore. Aluminum. 34 mm.	

Note: Similar to the zinc-tokens ND (1894)

TS4	ND(1905)	— 25 Ore. Aluminum. 34 mm.	

Note: Similar to the zinc-tokens ND (1894)

TS5	ND(1905)	— 50 Ore. Aluminum. 38 mm.	

Note: Similar to the zinc-tokens ND (1894)

TS6	ND(1905)	— 100 Ore. Aluminum. 39 mm.	

Note: Similar to the zinc-tokens ND (1894)

THULE-KAP YORK

Trading station founded by Knud Rasmussen in 1910. The money circulated from 1914 to 1937, but they bear the date of the founding year. They were produced by the date of the founding year. They were produced by L. Chr. Lauer, Nürnberg, Germany in 1913.

TOKEN COINAGE

KM# Tn5.1   5 ORE
Aluminum **Obv:** Legend, center hole **Obv. Leg.:** THULE *KAP YORK* **Rev:** Center hole divides denomination and date

Date	Mintage	F	VF	XF	Unc	BU
1910	5,000	4.00	8.00	14.00	25.00	—

KM# Tn5.2   5 ORE
Aluminum **Obv:** Legend **Obv. Leg.:** THULE *KAP YORK* **Rev:** Denomination above date **Note:** Error - struck without center hole.

Date	Mintage	F	VF	XF	Unc	BU
1910 Rare						

KM# Tn6 25 ORE
Aluminum **Obv:** Legend, center hole **Obv. Leg.:** THULE *KAP YORK* **Rev:** Center hole divides date and denomination

Date	Mintage	F	VF	XF	Unc	BU
1910	5,000	4.00	8.00	14.00	25.00	—

KM# Tn7 100 ORE
Aluminum **Obv:** Legend, center hole **Obv. Leg.:** THULE *KAP YORK* **Rev:** Center hole divides date and denomination

Date	Mintage	F	VF	XF	Unc	BU
1910	2,000	8.00	15.00	25.00	50.00	—

KM# Tn8 500 ORE
Aluminum **Obv:** Legend, center hole **Obv. Leg.:** THULE *KAP YORK* **Rev:** Center hole divides date and denomination

Date	Mintage	F	VF	XF	Unc	BU
1910	2,000	10.00	22.50	30.00	55.00	—

Note: Tn5-8 were struck at L. Chr. Lauer, Nürnberg, Germany, in 1913

KM# Tn9 5 KRONER
Aluminum **Obv:** Legend, center hole **Obv. Leg.:** THULE *KAP YORK* **Rev:** Center hole divides date and denomination

Date	Mintage	F	VF	XF	Unc	BU
1932	500	15.00	30.00	80.00	125	—

KM# Tn10 10 KRONER
Aluminum **Obv. Leg.:** THULE *KAP YORK* **Rev:** Center hole divides date and denomination

Date	Mintage	F	VF	XF	Unc	BU
1932	500	40.00	100	200	250	—

Note: Tn9-10 were struck at H. Th. Neergaard Gravør-og Stempelfabrik, engraving and stamp factory.

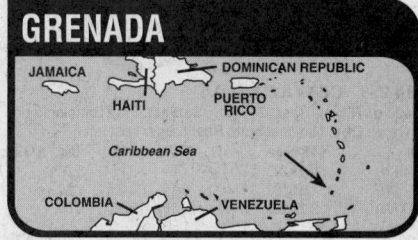

Columbus discovered Grenada in 1498 during his third voyage to the Americas. Spain failed to colonize the island, and in 1627 granted it to the British who sold it to the French who colonized it in 1650. Grenada was captured by the British in 1763, retaken by the French in 1779, and finally ceded to the British in 1783. In 1958 Grenada joined the Federation of the West Indies, which was dissolved in 1962. In 1967 it became an internally self-governing British associated state. Full independence was attained on Feb. 4, 1974. Grenada is a member of the Commonwealth of Nations. The prime minister is the Head of Government. Elizabeth II is Head of State as Queen of Grenada.

The early coinage of Grenada consists of cut and countermarked pieces of Spanish or Spanish Colonial Reales, which were valued at 11 Bits. In 1787 8 Reales coins were cut into 11 triangular pieces and countermarked with an incuse G. Later in 1814 large denomination cut pieces were issued being 1/2, 1/3 or 1/6 cuts and countermarked with a TR, incuse G and a number 6, 4,2, or 1 indicating the value in bitts.

RULERS
British

INDEPENDENT STATE
Commonwealth of Nations
MODERN COINAGE

KM# 15 4 DOLLARS
Copper-Nickel, 38.5 mm. **Series:** F.A.O. **Obv:** Cocoa beans within oval **Rev:** Sugar cane and banana tree branch

Date	Mintage	F	VF	XF	Unc	BU
1970	13,000	—	6.00	10.00	20.00	30.00
1970 Proof	2,000	Value: 35.00				

KM# 16 10 DOLLARS
Copper-Nickel **Subject:** Royal Visit **Obv:** Crowned bust right **Rev:** Arms with supporters within circle

Date	Mintage	F	VF	XF	Unc	BU
1985	Est. 100,000			4.50	9.00	—

KM# 16a 10 DOLLARS
28.2800 g., 0.9250 Silver 0.8410 oz. ASW **Subject:** Royal Visit **Obv:** Crowned bust right **Rev:** Arms with supporters within circle

Date	Mintage	F	VF	XF	Unc	BU
1985 Proof	Est. 5,000	Value: 55.00				

KM# 16b 10 DOLLARS
47.5400 g., 0.9170 Gold 1.4015 oz. AGW **Subject:** Royal Visit **Obv:** Crowned bust right **Rev:** Arms with supporters within circle

Date	Mintage	F	VF	XF	Unc	BU
1985 Proof	Est. 250	Value: 1,400				

KM# 17 100 DOLLARS
129.5900 g., 0.9250 Silver 3.8538 oz. ASW, 63 mm. **Subject:** Tropical Birds - Grenada Dove **Obv:** Arms within in circle, country name above **Note:** Illustration reduced.

Date	Mintage	F	VF	XF	Unc	BU
1988 Proof	Est. 10,000	Value: 125				

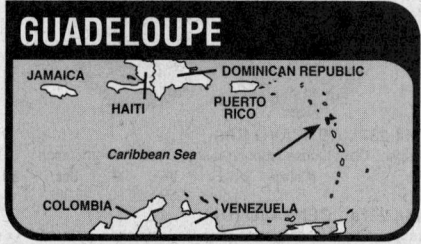

Guadeloupe was discovered by Columbus in 1493 and settled in 1635 by two Frenchmen, L'Olive and Duplessis, who took possession in the name of the French Company of the Islands of America. When repeated efforts by private companies to colonize the island failed, it was relinquished to the French crown in 1674, and established as a dependency of Martinique. The British occupied the island on two occasions, 1759-63 and 1810-16, before it passed permanently to France. A colony until 1946 Guadeloupe was then made an overseas territory of the French Union. In 1958 it voted to become an Overseas Department within the new French Community.

The well-known R.F. in garland oval countermark of the French Government is only legitimate if on a French Colonies 12 deniers 1767 C#4. Two other similar but incuse RF countermarks are on cut pieces in the values of 1 and 4 escalins. Contemporary and modern counterfeits are known of both these types.

RULER
French 1816-

MONETARY SYSTEM
100 Centimes = 1 Franc

FRENCH COLONY
MODERN COINAGE

KM# 45 50 CENTIMES
Copper-Nickel **Obv:** Armored head left within circle **Rev:** Sugar cane stalk divides date and denomination

Date	Mintage	F	VF	XF	Unc	BU
1903	600,000	16.00	35.00	85.00	240	500
1921	600,000	12.00	30.00	75.00	185	400

KM# 46 FRANC
Copper-Nickel **Obv:** Armored head left within circle **Rev:** Sugar cane stalk divides date and denomination **Note:** 20-sided.

Date	Mintage	F	VF	XF	Unc	BU
1903	700,000	20.00	40.00	90.00	250	550
1921	700,000	15.00	30.00	80.00	200	450

ESSAIS

KM#	Date	Mintage	Identification	Mkt Val
E1	1903	—	50 Centimes. Copper-Nickel.	200
E2	1903	—	50 Centimes. Silver.	450
E3	1903	—	Franc. Copper-Nickel.	250
E4	1903	—	Franc. Silver.	600
E5	19(21)	—	Franc. Bronze.	180

PIEFORTS

KM#	Date	Mintage	Identification	Mkt Val
P1	1903	—	50 Centimes. Copper-Nickel. Armored head left within circle. Sugar cane stalk divides date and denomination.	600
P2	1903	—	Franc. Copper-Nickel.	650

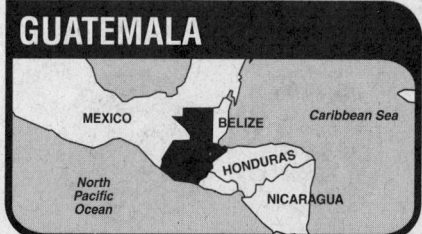

GUATEMALA

The Republic of Guatemala, the northernmost of the five Central American republics, has an area of 42,042 sq. mi. (108,890 sq. km.) and a population of 10.7 million. Capital: Guatemala City. The economy of Guatemala is heavily dependent on agriculture, however, the country is rich in nickel resources which are being developed. Coffee, cotton and bananas are exported.

Guatemala, once the site of an ancient Mayan civilization, was conquered by Pedro de Alvarado, the resourceful lieutenant of Cortes who undertook the conquest from Mexico. Cruel but strategically skillful, he progressed rapidly along the Pacific coastal lowlands to the highland plain of Quetzaltenango where the decisive battle for Guatemala was fought. After routing the Indian forces, he established the city of Guatemala in 1524. The

Spanish Captaincy-General of Guatemala included all Central America but Panama. Guatemala declared its independence of Spain in 1821 and was absorbed into the Mexican empire of Augustin Iturbide (1822-23). From 1823 to 1839 Guatemala was a constituent state of the Central American Republic. Upon dissolution of that confederation, Guatemala proclaimed itself an independent republic. Like El Salvador, Guatemala suffered from internal strife between right-wing, US-backed military government and leftist indigenous peoples from ca. 1954 to ca. 1997.

MINT MARKS
H, (H) - Heaton, Birmingham
(KN) – Birmingham, King's Norton Mint
(L) – London, Royal Mint
(P) – Philadelphia, USA
NG - ??? 1992
(S) – San Francisco, USA

STANDARD COINAGE
8 Reales = 1 Peso

KM# 175 1/4 REAL
Copper-Nickel **Obv:** Sun above three mountains **Rev:** Denomination within wreath, 5 stars below **Note:** Medal rotation.

Date	Mintage	F	VF	XF	Unc	BU
1901H	5,056,000	0.25	0.45	1.00	2.50	—

KM# 176 1/2 REAL (Medio)
Copper-Nickel **Obv:** Justice seated left **Rev:** Quetzal with scroll and weapons within thick wreath **Note:** Medal rotation.

Date	Mintage	F	VF	XF	Unc	BU
1901(H)	6,652,000	0.35	0.65	1.25	3.50	—

KM# 177 REAL
Copper-Nickel, 21 mm. **Obv:** Justice seated left **Rev:** National arms, thick wreath **Note:** Medal rotation.

Date	Mintage	F	VF	XF	Unc	BU
1901(H)	7,388,000	0.20	0.35	1.20	4.00	—
1910(H)	4,000,000	0.25	0.40	1.25	5.00	—
1911(H)	2,000,000	0.25	0.45	1.35	5.00	—
1912(H)	8,000,000	0.20	0.35	1.00	3.00	—

PROVISIONAL COINAGE
1915-1923

KM# 230 12-1/2 CENTAVOS
Copper **Obv:** Word at center divides flower **Rev:** Denomination within circle

Date	Mintage	F	VF	XF	Unc	BU
1915	6,000,000	0.75	1.25	3.50	15.00	—

KM# 231 25 CENTAVOS
Copper **Obv:** Word at center divides flower **Rev:** Denomination within circle

Date	Mintage	F	VF	XF	Unc	BU
1915	4,000,000	0.75	1.25	5.00	16.50	—

KM# 232.1 50 CENTAVOS
Aluminum-Bronze **Obv:** Flower design **Rev:** Denomination within circle **Note:** Thin numerals in denomination.

Date	Mintage	F	VF	XF	Unc	BU
1922	3,803,000	0.80	1.50	5.50	18.50	—

KM# 232.2 50 CENTAVOS
Aluminum-Bronze **Obv:** Flower design **Rev:** Denomination within circle **Note:** Thick numerals in denomination.

Date	Mintage	F	VF	XF	Unc	BU
1922	Inc. above	0.80	1.50	5.50	18.50	—

KM# 233 PESO
Aluminum-Bronze **Subject:** Miguel Garcia Granados **Obv:** Bust left **Rev:** Denomination

Date	Mintage	F	VF	XF	Unc	BU
1923	1,477,000	1.50	3.00	10.00	30.00	—

KM# 234 5 PESOS
Aluminum-Bronze **Subject:** Justo Rufino Barrios **Obv:** Bust right **Rev:** Denomination

Date	Mintage	F	VF	XF	Unc	BU
1923	440,000	2.00	5.00	20.00	50.00	—

KM# 234a 5 PESOS
Copper **Subject:** Justo Rufino Barrios **Obv:** Bust right **Rev:** Denomination

Date	Mintage	F	VF	XF	Unc	BU
1923	Inc. above	2.00	4.00	16.00	48.00	—

REFORM COINAGE
100 Centavos = 1 Quetzal

KM# 248.1 1/2 CENTAVO (Medio)
Brass **Obv:** National arms **Rev:** Denomination

Date	Mintage	F	VF	XF	Unc	BU
1932(L)	6,000,000	0.15	0.50	2.00	5.00	—
1932(L) Proof	—	Value: 200				

KM# 248.2 1/2 CENTAVO (Medio)
Brass **Obv:** National arms **Rev:** Denomination, center dot

Date	Mintage	F	VF	XF	Unc	BU
1946	640,000	0.75	1.75	3.75	15.00	—

KM# 237 CENTAVO (Un)
Copper **Obv:** Incuse legend on scroll **Rev:** Denomination

Date	Mintage	F	VF	XF	Unc	BU
1925	357,000	4.50	7.50	20.00	40.00	—

KM# 237a CENTAVO (Un)
Bronze **Obv:** National arms **Rev:** Denomination

Date	Mintage	F	VF	XF	Unc	BU
1925	Inc. above	5.00	8.00	15.00	40.00	—

KM# 247 CENTAVO (Un)
Copper **Obv:** National arms **Rev:** Denomination

Date	Mintage	F	VF	XF	Unc	BU
1929(L)	500,000	2.00	3.00	8.00	25.00	—
1929(L) Proof	—	—	—	—	—	—

KM# 249 CENTAVO (Un)
Brass, 20.3 mm. **Obv:** National arms **Rev:** Denomination

Date	Mintage	F	VF	XF	Unc	BU
1932(L)	3,000,000	0.40	1.00	350	11.50	—
1932(L) Proof	—	—	—	—	—	—
1933(L)	1,500,000	0.60	1.50	4.50	12.50	—
1933(L) Proof	—	—	—	—	—	—
1934(L)	1,000,000	0.50	1.25	4.50	12.50	—
1934(L) Proof	—	—	—	—	—	—
1936(L)	1,500,000	0.40	1.00	4.50	10.50	—
1936(L) Proof	—	—	—	—	—	—
1938/7(L)	1,000,000	0.40	1.00	5.00	14.00	—
1938(L)	inc. above	0.40	1.00	4.50	12.50	—
1938(L) Proof	—	—	—	—	—	—
1939(L)	1,500,000	0.50	1.25	4.50	10.00	—
1939(L) Proof	—	—	—	—	—	—
1946	539,000	—	0.15	0.75	6.00	—
1947	1,121,000	—	0.15	0.35	3.50	—
1948	1,651,000	—	0.15	0.35	4.50	—
1949	1,022,000	—	0.15	0.45	5.00	—

KM# 251 CENTAVO (Un)
3.0000 g., Brass, 20 mm. **Obv:** Bird with shield above date **Rev:** Branch right of denomination

Date	Mintage	F	VF	XF	Unc	BU
1943(P)	450,000	3.00	6.00	10.00	30.00	—
1944(S)	2,049,999	0.50	1.25	2.50	8.00	—

KM# 254 CENTAVO (Un)
Brass, 22 mm. **Subject:** Fray Bartolome de las Casas **Obv:** National arms **Rev:** Bust left

Date	Mintage	F	VF	XF	Unc	BU
1949	1,091,000	—	0.15	0.35	5.00	—
1950	3,663,000	—	0.15	0.25	1.75	—
1951	3,586,000	—	0.25	5.00	25.00	—
1952	1,445,000	—	0.15	0.30	20.00	—
1953	2,214,000	—	0.15	0.25	5.00	—
1954	1,455,000	—	0.15	0.30	2.25	—

KM# 259 CENTAVO (Un)
2.9400 g., Nickel-Brass, 21 mm. **Subject:** Fray Bartolome de las Casas **Obv:** National arms **Rev:** Larger bust left

Date	Mintage	F	VF	XF	Unc	BU
1954(KN)	10,000,000	—	—	0.15	3.00	—
1957(KN)	1,600,000	—	0.15	0.25	1.00	—
1958(KN)	2,000,000	—	0.15	0.25	2.00	—

KM# 260 CENTAVO (Un)
2.9900 g., Brass, 21 mm. **Subject:** Fray Bartolome de las Casas **Obv:** National arms **Rev:** Bust left **Note:** Larger obverse lettering

Date	Mintage	F	VF	XF	Unc	BU
1958	10,001,000	—	—	0.15	2.00	—
1961	1,826,000	—	—	0.15	1.00	—
1963	4,926,000	—	—	0.15	1.00	—
1964	4,280,000	—	—	0.15	1.00	—

KM# 265 CENTAVO (Un)
2.4500 g., Brass, 19 mm. **Subject:** Fray Bartolome de las Casas **Obv:** National arms **Rev:** Bust left **Note:** Size reduced. Varieties in size and style of date exist.

Date	Mintage	F	VF	XF	Unc	BU
1965	3,845,000	—	—	0.15	1.00	—
1966	6,100,000	—	—	0.15	1.00	—
1967	6,400,000	—	—	0.15	1.00	—
1968	2,590,000	—	—	0.15	1.00	—
1969	13,780,000	—	—	0.15	1.00	—
1970	10,511,000	—	—	0.15	1.00	—

KM# 273 CENTAVO (Un)
2.4400 g., Brass **Subject:** Fray Bartolome de las Casas **Obv:** National arms **Rev:** Bust left **Note:** Smaller date and lettering.

Date	Mintage	F	VF	XF	Unc	BU
1972	11,500,000	—	—	0.15	0.25	—
1973	12,000,000	—	—	0.15	0.25	—

KM# 275.1 CENTAVO (Un)
2.4700 g., Brass, 19.1 mm. **Subject:** Fray Bartolome de las Casas **Obv:** National arms **Rev:** Bust left, larger head **Note:** Larger date and lettering; no dots left and right of date.

Date	Mintage	F	VF	XF	Unc	BU
1974	10,000,000	—	—	0.15	0.25	—
1975	15,000,000	—	—	0.15	0.25	—
1976	15,230,000	—	—	0.15	0.25	—
1977	30,000,000	—	—	0.15	0.25	—
1978	30,000,000	—	—	0.15	0.25	—
1979	30,000,000	—	—	0.15	0.25	—

KM# 275.2 CENTAVO (Un)
2.5500 g., Brass, 18 mm. **Obv:** National arms **Rev:** Bust left, smaller head **Note:** Smaller legend and date. Dots left and right of date

Date	Mintage	F	VF	XF	Unc	BU
1979	Inc. above	—	—	0.15	0.25	—
1980	20,000,000	—	—	0.15	0.25	—
1984	20,000,000	—	—	0.15	0.25	—

KM# 275.4 CENTAVO (Un)
Brass **Obv:** National arms, legend on scroll in relief **Rev:** Bust left **Note:** Varieties exist.

Date	Mintage	F	VF	XF	Unc	BU
1981	30,000,000	—	—	0.15	0.25	—
1982	30,000,000	—	—	0.15	0.25	—

KM# 275.3 CENTAVO (Un)
2.5600 g., Brass, 18.97 mm. **Rev:** Fray Bartolome de las Casas, smaller head **Edge:** Plain **Note:** Smaller legend and date. Dots left and right of date.

Date	Mintage	F	VF	XF	Unc	BU
1985	—	—	—	0.15	0.25	—
1986	—	—	—	0.15	0.25	—
1987	50,000,000	—	—	0.15	0.25	—
1988	51,400,000	—	—	0.15	0.25	—
1989	—	—	—	0.15	0.25	—
1990	—	—	—	0.15	0.25	—
1991	—	—	—	0.15	0.25	—
1992	—	—	—	0.15	0.25	—

KM# 275.5 CENTAVO (Un)
2.5500 g., Brass **Subject:** Fray Bartolome de las Casas **Obv:** National arms **Rev:** Head left, modified portrait

Date	Mintage	F	VF	XF	Unc	BU
1993	—	—	—	0.15	0.25	—
1994	—	—	—	0.15	0.25	—
1995	—	—	—	0.15	0.25	—

KM# 282 CENTAVO (Un)
0.8000 g., Aluminum, 18.92 mm. **Subject:** Fray Bartolome de las Casas **Obv:** National arms **Rev:** Bust left **Edge:** Plain

Date	Mintage	F	VF	XF	Unc	BU
1999	—	—	—	0.15	0.25	—

KM# 250 2 CENTAVOS (Dos)
Brass **Obv:** National arms **Rev:** Denomination

Date	Mintage	F	VF	XF	Unc	BU
1932(L)	3,000,000	0.50	1.25	10.00	35.00	—
1932(L) Proof	—					—

KM# 252 2 CENTAVOS (Dos)
6.0000 g., Brass **Obv:** Bird with shield above date **Rev:** Branch right of denomination

Date	Mintage	F	VF	XF	Unc	BU
1943(P)	150,000	3.50	7.50	15.00	45.00	—
1944(S)	1,100,000	0.60	2.00	8.00	28.00	—

KM# 238.1 5 CENTAVOS
1.6667 g., 0.7200 Silver 0.0386 oz. ASW **Obv:** National arms **Rev:** Bird on pillar, engraver's initials 'JAC' below "Centavos"

Date	Mintage	F	VF	XF	Unc	BU
1925	573,000	3.00	5.75	15.00	35.00	—
1944	1,026,000	BV	1.25	5.00	15.00	—
1945	4,026,000	BV	0.75	4.00	10.00	—
1947	1,834,000	BV	1.00	4.00	10.00	—

Date	Mintage	F	VF	XF	Unc	BU
1948	1,103,000	BV	1.00	5.00	12.00	—
1949	551,000	0.65	1.50	10.00	25.00	—

KM# 238.1a 5 CENTAVOS
2.5000 g., 0.9000 Gold 0.0723 oz. AGW **Obv:** National arms **Rev:** Bird on pillar

Date	Mintage	F	VF	XF	Unc	BU
1925	8	—	—	750	950	—

KM# 238.2 5 CENTAVOS
1.6667 g., 0.7200 Silver 0.0386 oz. ASW **Obv:** National arms, short-tailed quetzal **Rev:** Bird on pillar, without engraver's initials

Date	Mintage	F	VF	XF	Unc	BU
1928(L)	1,000,000	BV	1.00	10.00	35.00	—
1928(L) Proof	—	Value: 400				
1929(L)	1,000,000	BV	1.00	4.00	12.00	—
1929(L) Proof	—					—
1932(L)	2,000,000	BV	1.00	4.00	10.00	—
1932(L) Proof	—					—
1933(L)	600,000	BV	1.00	5.00	15.00	—
1933(L) Proof	—					—
1934(L)	1,200,000	BV	1.00	4.00	10.00	—
1934(L) Proof	—					—
1937(L)	400,000	BV	1.00	4.00	10.00	—
1937(L) Proof	—					—
1938(L)	300,000	0.65	1.50	5.00	15.00	—
1938(L) Proof	—					—
1943(P)	900,000	BV	0.75	4.00	10.00	—

KM# 255 5 CENTAVOS
1.6667 g., 0.7200 Silver 0.0386 oz. ASW **Obv:** National arms **Rev:** Kapok tree **Note:** Varieties exist with and without dashes.

Date	Mintage	F	VF	XF	Unc	BU
1949	305,000	0.65	1.50	7.00	15.00	—

KM# 257.1 5 CENTAVOS
1.6667 g., 0.7200 Silver 0.0386 oz. ASW **Obv:** National arms **Rev:** Kapok tree

Date	Mintage	F	VF	XF	Unc	BU
1950	453,000	BV	1.00	4.00	10.00	—
1951	1,032,000	BV	1.00	2.00	8.00	—
1952	913,000	BV	1.00	2.00	7.00	—
1953	447,000	BV	1.00	2.00	7.00	—
1954	520,000	BV	1.00	3.00	9.00	—
1955	2,061,999	BV	1.00	1.50	3.00	—
1956	1,301,000	BV	1.00	1.50	3.00	—
1957	2,941,000	BV	1.00	1.50	2.50	—

KM# 257.1a 5 CENTAVOS
2.7300 g., 0.6200 Gold 0.0544 oz. AGW **Obv:** National arms **Rev:** Kapok tree **Note:** Distributed among delegates.

Date	Mintage	F	VF	XF	Unc	BU
1953	25	—	—	—	550	—

KM# 257.2 5 CENTAVOS
1.6670 g., 0.7200 Silver 0.0386 oz. ASW **Obv:** National arms **Rev:** Kapok tree **Note:** Small crude date and large crude dates.

Date	Mintage	F	VF	XF	Unc	BU
1958 Small date	3,025,000	BV	0.75	1.00	2.50	—
1958 Large date	Inc. above	BV	1.00	1.75	3.50	—
1959	232,000	BV	1.00	1.50	2.00	—

KM# 257.3 5 CENTAVOS
1.6670 g., 0.7200 Silver 0.0386 oz. ASW **Obv:** National arm, short-tailed quetzal **Obv. Leg.:** Kapok tree

Date	Mintage	F	VF	XF	Unc	BU
1958 Small date	—	BV	1.00	1.75	3.50	—
1958 Large date	—	BV	1.00	1.75	3.50	—

KM# 261   5 CENTAVOS
1.6670 g., 0.7200 Silver 0.0386 oz. ASW   **Obv:** National arms
Rev: Kapok tree, level ground

Date	Mintage	F	VF	XF	Unc	BU
1960	4,770,000	—	BV	0.65	1.25	—
1961	6,756,000	—	BV	0.65	1.25	—
1964	1,529,000	—	BV	0.65	1.25	—

KM# 266.1   5 CENTAVOS
Copper-Nickel, 16 mm.   **Obv:** National arms **Rev:** Kapok tree
Note: Coins Dated 1965 are smaller with curved tails in the "9"
& "6", while dates for 1967-1970 have straight tails in the "9" & "6".

Date	Mintage	F	VF	XF	Unc	BU
1965 Small date	1,642,000	—	0.15	0.50	4.00	—
1967 Large date	2,800,000	—	—	0.15	0.35	—
1968 Large date	4,030,000	—	—	0.15	0.35	—
1969 Large date	7,210,000	—	—	0.15	0.35	—
1970 Large date	8,121,000	—	—	0.15	0.35	—

KM# 266.2   5 CENTAVOS
Copper-Nickel, 16 mm.   **Obv:** National arms, dashes before and
after legend **Rev:** Kapok tree **Note:** Coins dates 1966 are smaller
with curved tails in the "9" & "6".

Date	Mintage	F	VF	XF	Unc	BU
1966 Small date	3,600,000	—	—	0.15	0.35	—

KM# 270   5 CENTAVOS
1.6000 g., Copper-Nickel, 16 mm.   **Obv:** Legend on scroll incuse,
small shield and quetzal **Obv. Leg.:** Kapok tree

Date	Mintage	F	VF	XF	Unc	BU
1971	8,270,000	—	—	0.15	0.35	—
1974	10,575,000	—	—	0.15	0.35	—
1975	10,000,000	—	—	0.15	0.35	—
1976	6,000,000	—	—	0.15	0.35	—
1977	20,000,000	—	—	0.15	0.35	—

KM# 276.1   5 CENTAVOS
Copper-Nickel, 16 mm.   **Obv:** National arms, large shield and
quetzal **Rev:** Kapok tree

Date	Mintage	F	VF	XF	Unc	BU
1977	Inc. above	—	—	0.15	0.35	—
1978	15,000,000	—	—	0.15	0.30	—
1979	12,000,000	—	—	0.15	0.30	—

KM# 276.2   5 CENTAVOS
Copper-Nickel, 16 mm.   **Obv:** Legend on scroll in relief
Rev: Kapok tree

Date	Mintage	F	VF	XF	Unc	BU
1980	8,000,000	—	—	0.15	0.30	—

KM# 276.3   5 CENTAVOS
Copper-Nickel, 16 mm.   **Obv:** National arms **Rev:** Kapok tee
modified

Date	Mintage	F	VF	XF	Unc	BU
1981	8,000,000	—	—	0.15	0.30	—
1985	—	—	—	0.15	0.30	—

KM# 276.4   5 CENTAVOS
2.6900 g., Copper-Nickel, 16 mm.   **Obv:** National arms, legend
on scroll incuse **Obv. Leg.:** REPUBLICA DE GUATEMALA • 1986
• **Rev:** Kapok tree smaller, less ground below **Edge:** Reeded
Note: Varieties exist.

Date	Mintage	F	VF	XF	Unc	BU
1985	—	—	—	0.15	0.30	—
1986 Large date	—	—	—	0.15	0.30	—
1986 Small date	—	—	—	—	—	—
1987	25,000,000	—	—	0.15	0.30	—
1988	21,800,000	—	—	0.15	0.30	—
1989	—	—	—	0.15	0.30	—
1990	—	—	—	0.15	0.30	—

Date	Mintage	F	VF	XF	Unc	BU
1991	—	—	—	0.15	0.30	—
1992	—	—	—	0.15	0.30	—
1993	—	—	—	0.15	0.30	—
1994	—	—	—	0.15	0.30	—
1996	—	—	—	0.15	0.30	—
1998	—	—	—	0.15	0.30	—

KM# 276.5   5 CENTAVOS
Copper-Nickel, 16 mm.   **Obv:** National arms, smaller lettering
Rev: Kapok tree

Date	Mintage	F	VF	XF	Unc	BU
1995	—	—	—	0.15	0.30	—

KM# 276.6   5 CENTAVOS
1.6000 g., Copper-Nickel, 16 mm.   **Obv:** National arms, smaller
sized emblem, no dots by date **Obv. Leg.:** REPUBLICA DE
GUATEMALA 1997 **Rev:** Kapok tree center, value at right, ground
below **Note:** Varieties exist.

Date	Mintage	F	VF	XF	Unc	BU
1997	—	—	—	0.15	0.30	—
1998	—	—	—	0.15	0.30	—
2000	—	—	—	0.15	0.30	—

KM# 239.1a   10 CENTAVOS
5.0000 g., 0.9000 Gold 0.1447 oz. AGW   **Obv:** National arms
Rev: Long-tailed quetzal on pillar

Date	Mintage	F	VF	XF	Unc	BU
1925 Rare	8	—	—	—	—	—

KM# 239.1   10 CENTAVOS
3.3333 g., 0.7200 Silver 0.0772 oz. ASW   **Obv:** National arms
Rev: Bird on engraved pillar, engraver's initials below
"CENTAVOS" **Note:** Varieties exist.

Date	Mintage	F	VF	XF	Unc	BU
1925	573,000	3.50	6.50	15.00	35.00	—
1944	155,000	1.25	3.50	10.00	20.00	—
1945	1,499,000	BV	1.25	2.00	5.00	—
1947	471,000	BV	1.50	3.00	10.00	—
1948	324,000	BV	1.50	2.00	7.00	—
1949	145,000	BV	2.00	4.50	10.00	—

KM# 239.2   10 CENTAVOS
3.3333 g., 0.7200 Silver 0.0772 oz. ASW   **Obv:** National arms,
short-tailed quetzal **Rev:** Bird on engraved pillar, without
engraver's initials

Date	Mintage	F	VF	XF	Unc	BU
1928(L)	500,000	BV	2.50	5.00	30.00	—
1928(L) Proof	—	Value: 250				
1929(L)	500,000	BV	2.00	3.50	25.00	—
1929(L) Proof	—	—	—	—	—	—
1932(L)	500,000	BV	2.00	3.50	15.00	—
1932(L) Proof	—	—	—	—	—	—
1933(L)	650,000	BV	1.75	3.00	18.00	—
1933(L) Proof	—	—	—	—	—	—
1934(L)	300,000	BV	1.75	3.00	18.00	—
1934(L) Proof	—	—	—	—	—	—
1936(L)	200,000	BV	2.50	6.00	20.00	—
1936(L) Proof	—	—	—	—	—	—
1938(L)	150,000	1.25	3.00	6.00	18.00	—
1938(L) Proof	—	—	—	—	—	—
1943(P)	600,000	BV	1.25	3.00	10.00	—

KM# 239.3   10 CENTAVOS
3.3333 g., 0.7200 Silver 0.0772 oz. ASW   **Obv:** National arms
Rev: Quetzal on pillar, with engraver's initials **Note:** Mintage
included above, in KM#239.1. Varieties exist.

Date	Mintage	F	VF	XF	Unc	BU
1947	—	BV	3.00	4.00	10.00	—

KM# 256.1   10 CENTAVOS
3.3333 g., 0.7200 Silver 0.0772 oz. ASW   **Obv:** National arms
Rev: Small monolith

Date	Mintage	F	VF	XF	Unc	BU
1949	281,000	BV	2.50	5.00	15.00	—
1950	550,000	BV	1.50	3.00	7.00	—
1951	263,000	BV	2.50	5.00	15.00	—
1952	307,000	BV	1.50	3.00	7.00	—
1953	388,000	BV	1.50	3.00	7.00	—
1955	896,000	BV	1.50	3.00	7.00	—
1956	501,000	BV	1.50	5.00	15.00	—
1958	1,528,000	BV	1.50	3.00	8.00	—

KM# 256.2   10 CENTAVOS
3.3333 g., 0.7200 Silver 0.0772 oz. ASW   **Obv:** National arms
Rev: Larger monolith

Date	Mintage	F	VF	XF	Unc	BU
1957	1,123,000	BV	1.25	2.00	3.00	—
1958	Inc. above	6.00	12.00	22.50	40.00	—
	Note: Medallic die alignment					
1958	Inc. above	BV	1.50	2.50	5.00	—

KM# 256.3   10 CENTAVOS
3.3333 g., 0.7200 Silver 0.0772 oz. ASW   **Obv:** National arms
Rev: Small monolith

Date	Mintage	F	VF	XF	Unc	BU
1958	Inc. above	BV	1.25	2.00	3.00	—
1959	Inc. above	6.00	12.00	22.50	37.50	—
	Note: Medallic die alignment					
1959	461,000	BV	1.25	2.00	3.00	—

KM# 262   10 CENTAVOS
3.3333 g., 0.7200 Silver 0.0772 oz. ASW   **Obv:** National arms
Rev: Monolith

Date	Mintage	F	VF	XF	Unc	BU
1960	1,743,000	BV	1.50	2.00	2.50	—
1961	2,647,000	BV	1.50	2.00	2.50	—
1964	965,000	BV	1.50	2.00	2.50	—

KM# 267   10 CENTAVOS
2.8500 g., Copper-Nickel, 21 mm.   **Obv:** National arms **Rev:**
Monolith **Note:** Varieties of curved and straight "9" in date exist.

Date	Mintage	F	VF	XF	Unc	BU
1965	2,227,000	—	0.15	0.25	0.75	—
1966	1,550,000	—	0.15	0.35	0.85	—
1967	3,120,000	—	0.15	0.25	0.75	—
1968	3,220,000	—	0.15	0.25	0.75	—
1969	3,530,000	—	0.15	0.25	0.75	—
1970	4,153,000	—	0.15	0.25	0.75	—

KM# 271.1   10 CENTAVOS
Copper-Nickel, 21 mm.   **Obv:** National arms, small wreath
Rev: Monolith

Date	Mintage	F	VF	XF	Unc	BU
1971	4,580,000	—	0.15	0.25	0.75	—

KM# 271.2   10 CENTAVOS
Copper-Nickel, 21 mm.   **Obv:** National arms, large wreath
Rev: Monolith

Date	Mintage	F	VF	XF	Unc	BU
1971	Inc. above	—	0.15	0.25	0.75	—
1973	—	—	0.15	0.25	0.75	—

KM# 274 10 CENTAVOS
3.1700 g., Copper-Nickel, 21 mm. **Obv:** National arms
Rev: Monolith

Date	Mintage	F	VF	XF	Unc	BU
1974	3,500,000	—	0.15	0.25	0.75	—
1975 Dots flank date	6,000,000	—	0.15	0.25	0.75	—

KM# 277.1 10 CENTAVOS
Copper-Nickel, 21 mm. **Obv:** National arms **Rev:** Monolith
Note: Wide rim toothed border.

Date	Mintage	F	VF	XF	Unc	BU
1976	2,000,000	—	0.15	0.25	0.75	—
1977	5,000,000	—	0.15	0.25	0.75	—

KM# 277.2 10 CENTAVOS
Copper-Nickel, 21 mm. **Obv:** National arms **Rev:** Monolith
Note: Round beads instead of toothed border.

Date	Mintage	F	VF	XF	Unc	BU
1978	8,500,000	—	0.15	0.25	0.75	—
1979	11,000,000	—	0.15	0.25	0.75	—

KM# 277.3 10 CENTAVOS
Copper-Nickel, 21 mm. **Obv:** Legend on scroll in relief, quetzal
in silhouette **Rev:** Monolith, front view

Date	Mintage	F	VF	XF	Unc	BU
1980	5,000,000	—	0.15	0.25	0.75	—
1981	4,000,000	—	0.15	0.25	0.75	—

KM# 277.4 10 CENTAVOS
3.1400 g., Copper-Nickel, 21 mm. **Obv:** Quetzal is solid
Rev: Monolith, larger

Date	Mintage	F	VF	XF	Unc	BU
1983	20,000,000	—	0.15	0.25	0.75	—
1986	—	—	0.15	0.25	0.75	—

KM# 277.5 10 CENTAVOS
3.2000 g., Copper-Nickel, 21 mm. **Obv:** National arms
Rev: Monolith, larger **Note:** Varieties exist with fine and coarse
characters.

Date	Mintage	F	VF	XF	Unc	BU
1986	—	—	0.15	0.25	0.75	—
1987	17,000,000	—	0.15	0.25	0.75	—
1988	13,250,000	—	0.15	0.25	0.75	—
1989	—	—	0.15	0.25	0.75	—
1990	—	—	0.15	0.25	0.75	—
1991	—	—	0.15	0.25	0.75	—
1992	—	—	0.15	0.25	0.75	—
1993	—	—	0.15	0.25	0.75	—
1994	—	—	0.15	0.25	0.75	—

KM# 277.6 10 CENTAVOS
3.2000 g., Copper-Nickel, 21 mm. **Obv:** National arms, small
letters in legend **Obv. Leg.:** REPUBLICA DE GUATEMALA
Rev: Monolith **Note:** Varieties exist.

Date	Mintage	F	VF	XF	Unc	BU
1995	—	—	0.15	0.25	0.75	—
1996	—	—	0.15	0.25	0.75	—
1997	—	—	0.15	0.25	0.75	—

Date	Mintage	F	VF	XF	Unc	BU
1998	—	—	0.15	0.25	0.75	—
2000	—	—	0.15	0.25	0.75	—

KM# 240.1 1/4 QUETZAL
8.3333 g., 0.7200 Silver 0.1929 oz. ASW **Obv:** National arms
Rev: Quetzal on pillar **Edge:** Lettered

Date	Mintage	F	VF	XF	Unc	BU
1925(P)	1,160,000	4.50	9.00	25.00	50.00	75.00

KM# 240.2 1/4 QUETZAL
8.3333 g., 0.7200 Silver 0.1929 oz. ASW **Obv:** National arms,
without NOBLES below scroll **Rev:** Quetzal atop engraved pillar

Date	Mintage	F	VF	XF	Unc	BU
1925 (P)	Inc. above	37.50	75.00	175	400	—

KM# 240a 1/4 QUETZAL
0.9000 Gold **Obv:** National arms **Rev:** Quetzal on pillar

Date	Mintage	F	VF	XF	Unc	BU
1925 (P) Rare	8					

KM# 243.1 1/4 QUETZAL
8.3333 g., 0.7200 Silver 0.1929 oz. ASW, 27 mm. **Obv:** National
arms **Rev:** Quetzal on pillar, larger design **Edge:** REPUBLICA
DE GUATEMALA AMERICA CENTRAL

Date	Mintage	F	VF	XF	Unc	BU
1926(L)	2,000,000	3.00	6.00	15.00	65.00	—
1926(L) Proof	—	—	—	—	—	—
1928(L)	400,000	3.50	5.50	10.00	55.00	70.00
1928(L) Proof	—	—	—	—	—	—
1929(L)	400,000	3.50	6.00	12.50	45.00	55.00
1929(L) Proof	—	—	—	—	—	—

KM# 243.2 1/4 QUETZAL
8.3333 g., 0.7200 Silver 0.1929 oz. ASW, 27 mm. **Obv:** National
arms **Rev:** Quetzal atop engraved pillar **Edge:** Reeded

Date	Mintage	F	VF	XF	Unc	BU
1946	203,000	3.50	6.50	13.50	22.00	30.00
1947	134,000	4.00	8.00	12.50	20.00	30.00
1948	129,000	4.00	7.50	12.00	20.00	30.00
1949/8	25,000	5.25	10.00	16.50	30.00	40.00
1949	Inc. above	12.50	27.50	55.00	100	—

KM# 253 25 CENTAVOS
8.3333 g., 0.7200 Silver 0.1929 oz. ASW, 27 mm. **Obv:** Quetzal
and map of the state **Rev:** Government buildings

Date	Mintage	F	VF	XF	Unc	BU
1943(P)	900,000	3.00	6.00	12.00	45.00	55.00

Note: 150,000 of total mintage struck in 1943, remainder
struck in 1944

KM# 258 25 CENTAVOS
8.3333 g., 0.7200 Silver 0.1929 oz. ASW, 27 mm. **Obv:** National
arms **Rev:** Head left **Note:** Denticulated rims.

Date	Mintage	F	VF	XF	Unc	BU
1950	81,000	3.50	6.00	12.00	30.00	45.00
1951	11,000	8.50	17.50	27.50	70.00	85.00
1952	112,000	BV	3.50	7.00	15.00	25.00
1954	246,000	BV	3.50	6.00	12.00	17.50
1955	409,000	BV	3.50	6.00	12.00	17.50
1956	342,000	BV	3.50	6.00	12.00	17.50
1957	257,000	BV	3.25	5.50	10.00	14.00
1958	394,000	BV	3.25	5.50	10.00	14.00
1959/8	277,000	BV	3.25	5.50	10.00	14.00
1959	Inc. above	BV	3.50	6.50	12.50	20.00

KM# 263 25 CENTAVOS
8.3333 g., 0.7200 Silver 0.1929 oz. ASW, 27 mm.

Date	Mintage	F	VF	XF	Unc	BU
1960	560,000	BV	3.50	4.00	6.00	—
1960	Inc. above	20.00	50.00	100	175	—

Note: Planchet size and weight vary in 1960 type as well
as density of reeding; Medallic die alignment

Date	Mintage	F	VF	XF	Unc	BU
1961	750,000	BV	3.50	4.00	6.00	—
1962	—	—	BV	4.00	6.00	—
1963	1,100,000	—	BV	3.25	5.50	—
1964	299,000	BV	3.50	4.00	6.00	—

KM# 268 25 CENTAVOS
8.0500 g., Copper-Nickel, 27 mm. **Obv:** National arms
Rev: Head left **Edge:** REPUBLICA DE GUATEMALA C. A.

Date	Mintage	F	VF	XF	Unc	BU
1965	1,178,000	0.15	0.25	0.60	1.75	—
1966	910,000	0.15	0.25	0.60	1.75	—

KM# 269 25 CENTAVOS
Copper-Nickel, 27 mm. **Obv:** National arms **Rev:** Head left,
modified design **Edge:** REPUBLICA DE GUATEMALA C. A.

Date	Mintage	F	VF	XF	Unc	BU
1967 Small date	1,140,000	0.15	0.25	0.60	1.75	—
1968 Medium date	1,540,000	0.15	0.25	0.60	1.50	—
1969 Large date	2,069,000	0.15	0.25	0.60	1.50	—
1970 Large date	2,501,000	0.15	0.25	0.60	1.50	—

KM# 272 25 CENTAVOS
Copper-Nickel, 27 mm. **Obv:** Smaller arms, legend on scroll
incuse **Rev:** Head left

Date	Mintage	F	VF	XF	Unc	BU
1971	2,850,000	0.15	0.25	0.50	1.00	—

Date	Mintage	F	VF	XF	Unc	BU
1975	1,592,000	0.15	0.25	0.50	1.00	—
1976	2,000,000	0.15	0.25	0.50	1.00	—

KM# 278.1   25 CENTAVOS
7.9000 g., Copper-Nickel, 27 mm.   **Obv:** National arms
Rev: Large head left

Date	Mintage	F	VF	XF	Unc	BU
1977	2,000,000	0.15	0.25	0.65	1.25	—
1978	4,400,000	0.15	0.25	0.45	1.00	—
1979	5,400,000	0.15	0.25	0.45	1.00	—

KM# 278.2   25 CENTAVOS
Copper-Nickel, 27 mm.   **Obv:** National arms, legend on scroll in relief **Rev:** Small head left **Note:** Wide rim

Date	Mintage	F	VF	XF	Unc	BU
1981	1,600,000	0.15	0.25	0.50	1.00	—

KM# 278.4   25 CENTAVOS
Copper-Nickel, 27 mm.   **Obv:** National arms, quetzal is solid **Rev:** Head left **Note:** Narrow rim.

Date	Mintage	F	VF	XF	Unc	BU
1982	2,000,000	0.15	0.25	0.50	1.00	—

KM# 278.3   25 CENTAVOS
Copper-Nickel, 27 mm.   **Obv:** National arms, legend on scroll incuse **Rev:** Small head left

Date	Mintage	F	VF	XF	Unc	BU
1984	2,000,000	.0.15	0.25	0.50	1.00	—

KM# 278.5   25 CENTAVOS
8.0300 g., Copper-Nickel, 27 mm.   **Obv:** National arms
Rev: Large head left **Edge:** REPUBLICA DE GUATEMALA C. A. **Note:** Varieties exist in number of wing feathers and details on head.

Date	Mintage	F	VF	XF	Unc	BU
1985	—	0.15	0.25	0.35	0.85	—
1986	—	0.15	0.25	0.35	0.85	—
1987	13,316,000	0.15	0.25	0.35	0.85	—
1988	6,600,000	0.15	0.25	0.35	0.85	—
1989	—	0.15	0.25	0.35	0.85	—
1990	—	0.15	0.25	0.35	0.85	—
1991	—	0.15	0.25	0.35	0.85	—
1992	—	0.15	0.25	0.35	0.85	—
1993	—	0.15	0.25	0.35	0.85	—
1994	—	0.15	0.25	0.35	0.85	—
1995	—	0.15	0.25	0.35	0.85	—

KM# 278.6   25 CENTAVOS
8.0900 g., Copper-Nickel, 27 mm.   **Obv:** Smaller design with wider rims **Rev:** Head left, smaller design with wider rims
Edge: REPUBLICA DE GUATEMALA CA **Note:** Varieties exist.

Date	Mintage	F	VF	XF	Unc	BU
1996	—	0.15	0.25	0.35	0.85	—
1997	—	0.15	0.25	0.35	0.85	—
1998	—	0.15	0.25	0.35	0.85	—
2000	—	0.15	0.25	0.35	0.85	—

KM# 264   50 CENTAVOS
12.0000 g., 0.7200 Silver 0.2778 oz. ASW, 30.95 mm.   **Obv:** National arms **Rev:** Whitenun orchid (lycaste skinneri var. alba)
Rev. Leg.: MONJA BLANCA FLOR NACIONAL **Edge:** Reeded

Date	Mintage	F	VF	XF	Unc	BU
1962	1,983,000	—	BV	4.00	6.00	9.00
1963/2	350,000	4.00	8.00	12.50	20.00	25.00
1963	Inc. above	—	—	4.00	6.00	9.00

KM# 283   50 CENTAVOS
5.5400 g., Brass, 24.2 mm.   **Obv:** National arms **Rev:** Whitenun orchid (lycaste skinneri var. alba orchidaceae) **Edge:** Reeded

Date	Mintage	F	VF	XF	Unc	BU
1998	—	—	—	0.50	1.25	1.75

KM# 241.1   1/2 QUETZAL
16.6667 g., 0.7200 Silver 0.3858 oz. ASW   **Obv:** National arms
Rev: Quetzal on engraved pillar

Date	Mintage	F	VF	XF	Unc	BU
1925(P)	400,000	18.50	30.00	65.00	225	300

KM# 241.2   1/2 QUETZAL
16.6667 g., 0.7200 Silver 0.3858 oz. ASW   **Obv:** Without NOBLES below scroll **Rev:** Quetzal on pillar

Date	Mintage	F	VF	XF	Unc	BU
1925 (P)	Inc. above	70.00	120	250	550	

KM# 242   QUETZAL
33.3333 g., 0.7200 Silver 0.7716 oz. ASW   **Obv:** National arms
Rev: Quetzal on engraved pillar

Date	Mintage	F	VF	XF	Unc	BU
1925(P)	Est. 10,000	475	675	1,150	2,250	

Note: 7,000 pieces were withdrawn and remelted in 1927 and 1928. Of those remaining, an additonal unknown quantity was melted in 1932, leaving somewhat less than 3000 survivors of this type.

KM# 279   QUETZAL
27.0000 g., 0.9250 Silver 0.8029 oz. ASW   **Subject:** Carlos Merida **Obv:** National arms **Rev:** Heads facing and right

Date	Mintage	F	VF	XF	Unc	BU
1992NG Proof	—	Value: 50.00				

KM# 280   QUETZAL
27.0000 g., 0.9250 Silver 0.8029 oz. ASW
Subject: Environmental Protection **Rev:** Horned Guan

Date	Mintage	F	VF	XF	Unc	BU
1994 Proof	20,000	Value: 45.00				

KM# 281   QUETZAL
27.0000 g., 0.9250 Silver 0.8029 oz. ASW   **Subject:** 50th Anniversary - National Bank of Guatemala **Obv:** Coin designs around national emblem **Rev:** Pre-Columbian artisans

Date	Mintage	F	VF	XF	Unc	BU
1996 Proof	—	Value: 55.00				

KM# 284   QUETZAL
11.1000 g., Brass, 28.9 mm.   **Obv:** National arms **Rev:** PAZ above stylized dove **Edge:** Reeded

Date	Mintage	F	VF	XF	Unc	BU
1999	—	—	—	1.00	2.50	3.00
2000 Small letters		—	—	1.00	2.50	3.00

KM# 286   QUETZAL
27.0000 g., 0.9250 Silver 0.8029 oz. ASW, 40 mm.
Subject: Ibero-America Series **Obv:** National arms in circle of arms **Rev:** Horse pulling a walk-behind plow **Edge:** Reeded

Date	Mintage	F	VF	XF	Unc	BU
2000 Proof	—	Value: 100				

KM# 244 5 QUETZALES
8.3592 g., 0.9000 Gold 0.2419 oz. AGW **Obv:** National arms
Rev: Quetzal atop engraved pillar

Date	Mintage	F	VF	XF	Unc	BU
1926(P)	48,000	BV	225	275	350	—

KM# 245 10 QUETZALES
16.7185 g., 0.9000 Gold 0.4837 oz. AGW **Obv:** National arms
Rev: Quetzal atop engraved pillar

Date	Mintage	F	VF	XF	Unc	BU
1926(P)	18,000	BV	460	500	750	—

KM# 246 20 QUETZALES
33.4370 g., 0.9000 Gold 0.9675 oz. AGW **Obv:** National arms
Rev: Quetzal atop engraved pillar

Date	Mintage	F	VF	XF	Unc	BU
1926(P)	49,000		BV	950	1,100	—

TRIAL STRIKES

KM#	Date	Mintage	Identification	Mkt Val
TS1	1945	—	10 Centavos. Copper Nickel.	150

PATTERNS
Including off metal strikes

KM#	Date	Mintage	Identification	Mkt Val
Pn17	ND(ca.1920-22)	—	2 Pesos. Porcelain. 25.26 mm. QUATEMALA/*PESOS*/large 2 in center. Arms of Quatemala within triangle; coffee tree leaf to each side; below: Meissen mint mark (crossed swords) separates two stars. Arms in triangle; made at state porcelain works, Meissen, Germany.	2,000
Pn18	1921	—	Peso. Copper-Nickel. 5.1000 g. 25 mm. Plain edge. MONEDA NACIONAL NIQUEL.	—
Pn19	1922	—	5 Pesos. Silver. 3/4 facing bust of Barrios.	—
Pn20	1922	—	5 Pesos. Aluminum-Brass. 3/4 facing bust of Barrios.	—
Pn21	1923	—	5 Pesos. Gold. KM234	—
Pn22	1949	20	Centavo. Brass. large bust.	450
Pn23	1949	20	5 Centavos. 0.7200 Silver.	475
Pn24	1949	20	10 Centavos. 0.7200 Silver.	525
Pn25	1949	20	25 Centavos. 0.7200 Silver.	575
Pn26	1960	—	25 Centavos. Aluminum. Plain edge. KM#263.	—
Pn27	1995	100	Quetzal. Brass center. Silver ring. 22.4300 g. 38 mm. Humming bird flying above lake. Reeded edge. Brass center in Silver ring within Brass ring.	100
Pn28	1995	100	50 Quetzales. Brass center. Silver ring. 22.2400 g. 38 mm. National arms. Parrot on branch, buildings in back. Reeded edge. Brass center in Silver ring within Brass ring.	100

GUERNSEY

The Bailiwick of Guernsey, a British crown dependency located in the English Channel 30 miles (48 km.) west of Normandy, France, has an area of 30 sq. mi. (194 sq. km.)(including the isles of Alderney, Jethou, Herm, Brechou, and Sark), and a population of 54,000. Capital: St. Peter Port. Agriculture and cattle breeding are the main occupations.

Militant monks from the duchy of Normandy established the first permanent settlements on Guernsey prior to the Norman invasion of England, but the prevalence of prehistoric monuments suggests an earlier occupancy. The island, the only part of the duchy of Normandy belonging to the British crown, has been a possession of Britain since the Norman Conquest of 1066. During the Anglo-French wars, the harbors of Guernsey were employed in the building and out-fitting of ships for the English privateers preying on French shipping. Guernsey is administered by its own laws and customs. Unless the island is mentioned specifically, acts passed by the British Parliament are not applicable to Guernsey. During World War II, German troops occupied the island from June 30, 1940 till May 9,1945.

RULERS
British

MINT MARKS
H - Heaton, Birmingham

MONETARY SYSTEM
8 Doubles = 1 Penny
12 Pence = 1 Shilling
5 Shillings = 1 Crown
20 Shillings = 1 Pound

1 Stem	3 Stems

BRITISH DEPENDENCY
STANDARD COINAGE

KM# 10 DOUBLE
Bronze **Obv:** National arms **Rev:** Value, date

Date	Mintage	F	VF	XF	Unc	BU
1902H	84,000	0.25	0.60	2.50	6.00	—
1902H Proof	—	Value: 250				
1903H	112,000	0.25	0.50	2.25	5.00	—
1911H	45,000	0.50	1.50	4.00	12.00	—

KM# 11 DOUBLE
Bronze **Obv:** Arms **Rev:** Denomination above date

Date	Mintage	F	VF	XF	Unc	BU
1911H	90,000	0.30	1.20	3.00	10.00	—
1914H	45,000	1.50	3.00	6.00	12.00	—
1929H	79,000	0.30	0.85	2.50	5.50	—
1933H	96,000	0.30	0.85	2.50	5.50	—
1938H	96,000	0.30	0.85	2.50	5.50	—

KM# 9 2 DOUBLES
3.6200 g., Bronze, 22 mm. **Obv:** National arms **Rev:** Value, date

Date	Mintage	F	VF	XF	Unc	BU
1902H	18,000	4.50	9.00	18.00	30.00	—
1902H Proof	—	Value: 250				
1903H	18,000	6.00	12.50	22.00	35.00	—
1906H	18,000	6.00	12.50	22.00	35.00	—
1908H	18,000	6.00	12.50	22.00	35.00	—
1911H	29,000	4.50	9.00	15.00	27.50	—

KM# 12 2 DOUBLES
Bronzed Copper **Obv:** Arms **Rev:** Denomination above date

Date	Mintage	F	VF	XF	Unc	BU
1914H	29,000	4.50	9.00	18.50	30.00	—
1914H Proof	—	Value: 125				
1917H	15,000	20.00	35.00	70.00	155	—
1918H	57,000	1.25	2.50	9.00	15.00	—
1920H	57,000	1.25	2.50	9.00	15.00	—
1929H	79,000	0.35	1.25	6.00	10.00	—

KM# 5 4 DOUBLES
4.8400 g., Bronze, 26.10 mm. **Obv:** National arms **Rev:** Value, date **Note:** Varieties exist.

Date	Mintage	F	VF	XF	Unc	BU
1902H	105,000	1.50	3.00	5.00	22.00	—
1902H Proof	—	Value: 250				
1903H	52,000	1.50	3.00	9.00	25.00	—
1906H	52,000	1.50	3.00	9.00	25.00	—
1908H	26,000	3.00	7.50	15.00	30.00	—
1910H	52,000	1.50	3.00	9.00	25.00	—
1910H Proof	—	Value: 250				
1911H	52,000	2.25	4.50	13.50	27.50	—

KM# 13 4 DOUBLES
4.7600 g., Bronze **Obv:** Arms **Rev:** Denomination above date

Date	Mintage	F	VF	XF	Unc	BU
1914H	209,000	0.75	1.50	4.50	24.00	—
1918H	157,000	0.75	1.50	6.00	27.00	—
1920H	157,000	0.45	1.25	4.50	18.00	—
1945H	96,000	0.45	1.25	4.50	10.00	—
1949H	19,000	1.50	3.00	12.00	20.00	—

KM# 15 4 DOUBLES
4.8200 g., Bronze **Obv:** Arms **Rev:** Guernsey lily

Date	Mintage	F	VF	XF	Unc	BU
1956	240,000	0.25	0.45	0.75	2.00	3.50
1956 Proof	2,100	Value: 4.00				
1966 Proof	10,000	Value: 2.00				

KM# 7   8 DOUBLES
8.3400 g., Bronze, 31.13 mm.   **Obv:** National arms within 3/4 wreath **Rev:** Value, date within wreath

Date	Mintage	F	VF	XF	Unc	BU
1902H	235,000	2.50	4.50	12.00	30.00	—
1902H Proof	—	Value: 250				
1903H	118,000	1.00	4.00	11.00	28.00	—
1910H	91,000	1.25	4.00	12.50	35.00	—
1910H Proof	—	Value: 250				
1911H	78,000	6.00	17.00	40.00	80.00	—

KM# 14   8 DOUBLES
10.1400 g., Bronze **Obv:** Arms within wreath **Rev:** Denomination and date within wreath

Date	Mintage	F	VF	XF	Unc	BU
1914H	157,000	1.00	3.00	8.00	25.00	—
1914H Proof	—	Value: 150				
1918H	157,000	1.50	4.00	11.00	28.00	—
1920H	157,000	1.00	2.00	6.00	15.00	—
1920H Proof	—	Value: 150				
1934H	124,000	1.00	2.00	6.00	18.00	—
1934H Proof	500	Value: 175				
1938H	120,000	0.50	1.50	4.00	9.00	—
1938H Proof	—	Value: 250				
1945H	192,000	0.40	0.85	2.00	5.50	—
1947H	240,000	0.30	0.60	2.25	5.00	—
1949H	230,000	0.30	0.60	2.25	5.00	—

KM# 16   8 DOUBLES
Bronze   **Ruler:** Elizabeth II **Obv:** Arms **Rev:** Three flowered lily

Date	Mintage	F	VF	XF	Unc	BU
1956	500,000	0.10	0.20	0.50	1.25	2.50
1956 Proof	2,100	Value: 4.00				
1959	500,000	0.10	0.20	0.50	1.25	2.50
1959 Proof	—					
1966 Proof	10,000	Value: 3.50				

KM# 17   3 PENCE
Copper Nickel, 21 mm.   **Ruler:** Elizabeth II **Obv:** Arms **Rev:** Guernsey cow (bos primigenius taurus) right **Note:** Thin flan.

Date	Mintage	F	VF	XF	Unc	BU
1956	500,000	0.10	0.20	0.50	1.50	2.00
1956 Proof	2,100	Value: 4.00				

KM# 18   3 PENCE
Copper Nickel, 21 mm.   **Ruler:** Elizabeth II **Obv:** Arms **Rev:** Guernsey cow (bos primigenius taurus) right **Note:** Thick flan.

Date	Mintage	F	VF	XF	Unc	BU
1959	500,000	0.10	0.20	0.50	1.50	2.00
1959 Proof	—	Value: 150				
1966 Proof	10,000	Value: 2.00				

KM# 19   10 SHILLING
Copper Nickel   **Ruler:** Elizabeth II **Series:** 90th Anniversary - Norman Conquest **Subject:** William I **Obv:** Young bust right **Rev:** Crowned bust left

Date	Mintage	F	VF	XF	Unc	BU
1966	300,000	—	1.25	1.50	2.00	—
1966 Proof	10,000	Value: 3.50				

DECIMAL COINAGE
100 Pence = 1 Pound

KM# 20   1/2 NEW PENNY
Bronze, 17.14 mm.   **Ruler:** Elizabeth II **Obv:** Arms **Rev:** Denomination and date

Date	Mintage	F	VF	XF	Unc	BU
1971	2,066,000	—	—	0.15	0.30	0.50
1971 Proof	—	Value: 1.00				

KM# 33   1/2 PENNY
Bronze, 17.14 mm.   **Ruler:** Elizabeth II **Obv:** Arms **Rev:** Denomination and date

Date	Mintage	F	VF	XF	Unc	BU
1979 Proof	20,000	Value: 1.00				

KM# 21   NEW PENNY
3.5500 g., Bronze, 20.3 mm.   **Ruler:** Elizabeth II **Obv:** Arms **Rev:** Gannet in flight

Date	Mintage	F	VF	XF	Unc	BU
1971	1,922,000	—	—	0.15	0.45	1.00
1971 Proof	10,000	Value: 1.00				

KM# 27   PENNY
3.5500 g., Bronze, 20.3 mm.   **Ruler:** Elizabeth II **Obv:** Arms **Rev:** Gannet in flight

Date	Mintage	F	VF	XF	Unc	BU
1977	640,000	—	—	0.15	0.45	1.00
1979	2,400,000	—	—	0.15	0.45	1.00
1979 Proof	20,000	Value: 1.00				
1981 Proof	10,000	Value: 2.00				

KM# 40   PENNY
3.6500 g., Bronze, 20.3 mm.   **Ruler:** Elizabeth II **Obv:** Crowned head right, small arms at left **Rev:** Edible crab **Edge:** Plain

Date	Mintage	F	VF	XF	Unc	BU
1985	60,000	—	—	0.15	0.50	1.00
1985 Proof	2,500	Value: 2.00				
1986	1,010,000	—	—	0.15	0.50	1.00
1986 Proof	2,500	Value: 2.00				
1987	5,000	—	—	0.15	0.50	1.00

Date	Mintage	F	VF	XF	Unc	BU
1987 Proof	2,500	Value: 2.00				
1988	500,000	—	—	0.15	0.50	1.00
1988 Proof	2,500	Value: 2.00				
1989	1,000,000	—	—	0.15	0.50	1.00
1989 Proof	2,500	Value: 2.00				
1990	5,000	—	—	0.15	0.50	1.00
1990 Proof	700	Value: 4.00				

KM# 40a   PENNY
3.5500 g., Copper Plated Steel, 20.3 mm.   **Ruler:** Elizabeth II **Obv:** Crowned head right, small arms at left **Rev:** Chancre crab

Date	Mintage	F	VF	XF	Unc	BU
1992 In sets only	—	—	—	—	0.35	1.00
1992 Proof	—	Value: 5.00				
1994	750,000	—	—	—	0.35	1.00
1997	2,000,000	—	—	—	0.35	1.00
1997 Proof	—	Value: 5.00				

KM# 89   PENNY
3.5300 g., Copper Plated Steel, 20.3 mm.   **Ruler:** Elizabeth II **Obv:** Head with tiara right **Rev:** Edible crab **Edge:** Plain

Date	Mintage	F	VF	XF	Unc	BU
1998	—	—	—	—	0.50	0.75

KM# 22   2 NEW PENCE
7.1000 g., Bronze, 25.9 mm.   **Ruler:** Elizabeth II **Obv:** Arms **Rev:** Windmill from Sark

Date	Mintage	F	VF	XF	Unc	BU
1971	1,680,000	—	—	0.15	0.35	0.50
1971 Proof	10,000	Value: 1.00				

KM# 28   2 PENCE
7.1000 g., Bronze, 25.9 mm.   **Ruler:** Elizabeth II **Obv:** Arms **Rev:** Windmill from Sark

Date	Mintage	F	VF	XF	Unc	BU
1977	700,000	—	—	0.15	0.25	0.45
1979	2,400,000	—	—	0.15	0.25	0.45
1979 Proof	20,000	Value: 1.00				
1981 Proof	10,000	Value: 2.00				

KM# 41   2 PENCE
7.2000 g., Bronze, 25.80 mm.   **Ruler:** Elizabeth II **Obv:** Crowned head right, small arms at left **Rev:** Guernsey cows **Edge:** Plain

Date	Mintage	F	VF	XF	Unc	BU
1985	60,000	—	—	0.20	0.75	2.00
1985 Proof	2,500	Value: 50.00				
1986	510,000	—	—	0.20	0.75	2.00
1986 Proof	2,500	Value: 2.00				
1987	5,000	—	—	0.20	0.75	2.00
1987 Proof	2,500	Value: 2.00				
1988	500,000	—	—	0.20	0.75	2.00
1988 Proof	2,500	Value: 2.00				
1989	500,000	—	—	0.20	0.75	2.00
1989 Proof	2,500	Value: 2.00				
1990	380,000	—	—	0.20	0.75	2.00
1990 Proof	700	Value: 4.00				

KM# 41a 2 PENCE
7.2000 g., Copper Plated Steel, 25.9 mm. **Ruler:** Elizabeth II
Obv: Crowned head right, small arms at left **Rev:** Guernsey cows
Edge: Plain

Date	Mintage	F	VF	XF	Unc	BU
1992 In sets only	—			—	0.30	1.00
1992 Proof	—	Value: 5.00				
1996	500,000			—	0.30	1.00
1997 In sets only	—			—	0.30	1.00
1997 Proof	—	Value: 5.00				

KM# 96 2 PENCE
7.2000 g., Copper Plated Steel, 25.9 mm. **Ruler:** Elizabeth II
Obv: Head with tiara, shield at left **Rev:** Guernsey cows **Edge:** Plain

Date	Mintage	F	VF	XF	Unc	BU
1999	600,000			—	0.50	1.10

KM# 23 5 NEW PENCE
5.6500 g., Copper-Nickel, 23.6 mm. **Ruler:** Elizabeth II
Obv: Arms **Rev:** Guernsey lily

Date	Mintage	F	VF	XF	Unc	BU
1968	800,000	—	0.15	0.25	0.45	0.65
1971 Proof	10,000	Value: 1.00				

KM# 29 5 PENCE
5.6500 g., Copper-Nickel, 23.6 mm. **Ruler:** Elizabeth II
Obv: Arms **Rev:** Guernsey lily

Date	Mintage	F	VF	XF	Unc	BU
1977	250,000	—		0.20	0.45	0.65
1979	200,000	—		0.20	0.45	0.65
1979 Proof	20,000	Value: 2.00				
1981 Proof	10,000	Value: 3.00				
1982	200,000	—		0.20	0.45	0.65

KM# 42.1 5 PENCE
5.6500 g., Copper-Nickel, 23.6 mm. **Ruler:** Elizabeth II
Obv: Crowned head right, small arms at left **Rev:** Sailboats

Date	Mintage	F	VF	XF	Unc	BU
1985	35,000	—		0.20	0.45	0.65
1985 Proof	2,500	Value: 2.50				
1986	100,000	—		0.20	0.45	0.65
1986 Proof	2,500	Value: 2.50				
1987	300,000	—		0.20	0.45	0.65
1987 Proof	2,500	Value: 2.50				
1988	405,000	—		0.20	0.45	0.65
1988 Proof	2,500	Value: 2.50				
1989	5,000	—		0.20	0.50	0.75
1989 Proof	2,500	Value: 2.50				
1990 In sets only	Est. 2,520	—		—	0.60	0.85
1990 Proof	700	Value: 5.00				

KM# 42.2 5 PENCE
3.2600 g., Copper-Nickel, 18 mm. **Obv:** Crowned head right,
small arms at left **Rev:** Sailboats **Note:** Reduced size

Date	Mintage	F	VF	XF	Unc	BU
1990	2,400,000	—		0.20	0.45	0.65
1990 Proof	700	Value: 5.00				
1992	1,300,000			—	0.50	0.75
1992 Proof	—	Value: 6.00				
1997	—			—	0.50	0.75
1997 Proof	—	Value: 5.00				

KM# 97 5 PENCE
3.2200 g., Copper-Nickel, 18 mm. **Ruler:** Elizabeth II **Obv:** Head
with tiara right **Rev:** Sailboat **Edge:** Reeded

Date	Mintage	F	VF	XF	Unc	BU
1999	1,700,000			—	0.45	0.65

KM# 24 10 NEW PENCE
11.3000 g., Copper-Nickel, 28.5 mm. **Ruler:** Elizabeth II
Obv: Arms **Rev:** Guernsey cow

Date	Mintage	F	VF	XF	Unc	BU
1968	600,000	—	0.20	0.40	1.50	2.50
1970	300,000	—	0.20	0.40	1.50	2.50
1971 Proof	10,000	Value: 2.00				

KM# 30 10 PENCE
11.3000 g., Copper-Nickel, 28.5 mm. **Ruler:** Elizabeth II
Obv: Arms **Rev:** Guernsey cow

Date	Mintage	F	VF	XF	Unc	BU
1977	480,000	—		0.25	1.00	2.00
1979	659,000	—		0.25	1.00	2.00
1979 Proof	20,000	Value: 2.00				
1981 Proof	10,000	Value: 3.00				
1982	200,000	—		0.35	1.25	2.00
1984	400,000	—		0.25	1.00	2.00

KM# 43.1 10 PENCE
11.3000 g., Copper-Nickel, 28.5 mm. **Ruler:** Elizabeth II
Obv: Crowned head right, small arms at left **Rev:** Tomato plant

Date	Mintage	F	VF	XF	Unc	BU
1985	110,000	—		0.25	0.60	0.85
1985 Proof	2,500	Value: 2.50				
1986	300,000	—		0.25	0.60	0.85
1986 Proof	2,500	Value: 6.00				
1987	250,000	—		0.25	0.60	0.85
1987 Proof	2,500	Value: 2.50				
1988	300,000	—		0.25	0.60	0.85
1988 Proof	2,500	Value: 2.50				
1989	200,000	—		0.25	0.60	0.85
1989 Proof	2,500	Value: 2.50				
1990	3,500	—		0.25	0.60	0.85
1990 Proof	700	Value: 5.00				

KM# 43.2 10 PENCE
Copper-Nickel, 24.5 mm. **Obv:** Crowned head right, small arms
at left **Rev:** Tomato plant **Note:** Reduced size.

Date	Mintage	F	VF	XF	Unc	BU
1992	3,500,000			—	0.60	0.85
1992 Proof	—	Value: 6.00				
1997 In sets only	—			—	0.60	0.85
1997 Proof	—	Value: 6.00				

KM# 38 20 PENCE
5.1000 g., Copper-Nickel, 21.4 mm. **Ruler:** Elizabeth II
Obv: Arms **Rev:** Guernsey milk can

Date	Mintage	F	VF	XF	Unc	BU
1982	500,000	—		0.45	0.90	1.25
1983	500,000	—		0.45	0.90	1.25

KM# 44 20 PENCE
5.1000 g., Copper-Nickel, 21.4 mm. **Ruler:** Elizabeth II
Obv: Crowned head right, small arms at left **Rev:** Island map
within cogwheel

Date	Mintage	F	VF	XF	Unc	BU
1985	35,000			0.45	0.85	1.20
1985 Proof	2,500	Value: 3.00				
1986	10,000			0.45	0.85	1.20
1986 Proof	2,500	Value: 3.00				
1987	5,000			0.45	0.85	1.20
1987 Proof	2,500	Value: 3.00				
1988	5,000			0.45	0.85	1.20
1988 Proof	2,500	Value: 3.00				
1989	93,000			0.45	0.85	1.20
1989 Proof	2,500	Value: 3.00				
1990	113,000			0.45	0.85	1.20
1990 Proof	700	Value: 6.00				
1992	800,000			—	1.00	1.50
1992 Proof	—	Value: 7.00				
1997	—			—	1.00	1.50
1997 Proof	—	Value: 3.00				

KM# 90 20 PENCE
5.1000 g., Copper-Nickel, 21.4 mm. **Ruler:** Elizabeth II
Obv: Head with tiara right, small arms at left **Rev:** Island map
within cogwheel

Date	Mintage	F	VF	XF	Unc	BU
1999	800,000			—	0.90	1.25
1999 Proof	—	Value: 3.00				

KM# 26 25 PENCE
Copper-Nickel, 38.5 mm. **Ruler:** Elizabeth II **Subject:** 25th
Wedding Anniversary - Elizabeth and Philip **Obv:** Arms
Rev: Standing cupid right

Date	Mintage	F	VF	XF	Unc	BU
1972	56,000	—	—	3.00	6.00	8.00

KM# 26a 25 PENCE
28.2759 g., 0.9250 Silver 0.8409 oz. ASW, 38.5 mm.
Ruler: Elizabeth II **Subject:** 25th Wedding Anniversary -
Elizabeth and Philip **Obv:** Arms **Rev:** Standing cupid right

Date	Mintage	F	VF	XF	Unc	BU
1972 Proof	15,000	Value: 18.00				

KM# 31   25 PENCE
Copper-Nickel, 38.5 mm. **Ruler:** Elizabeth II **Subject:** Queen's Silver Jubilee **Obv:** Young bust right **Rev:** Scene from above

Date	Mintage	F	VF	XF	Unc	BU
ND(1977)	207,000	—	—	1.25	2.25	3.50

KM# 31a   25 PENCE
28.2759 g., 0.9250 Silver 0.8409 oz. ASW, 38.5 mm. **Ruler:** Elizabeth II **Subject:** Queen's Silver Jubilee **Obv:** Young bust right **Rev:** Scene from above

Date	Mintage	F	VF	XF	Unc	BU
ND(1977) Proof	25,000	Value: 17.00				

KM# 32   25 PENCE
Copper-Nickel, 38.5 mm. **Ruler:** Elizabeth II **Subject:** Royal Visit **Obv:** Young bust right **Rev:** Arms

Date	Mintage	F	VF	XF	Unc	BU
1978	105,000	—	—	1.25	2.50	3.75

KM# 32a   25 PENCE
28.2759 g., 0.9250 Silver 0.8409 oz. ASW, 38.5 mm. **Ruler:** Elizabeth II **Subject:** Royal Visit **Obv:** Young bust right **Rev:** Arms

Date	Mintage	F	VF	XF	Unc	BU
1978 Proof	25,000	Value: 18.00				

KM# 35   25 PENCE
13.5500 g., Copper-Nickel, 38.5 mm. **Ruler:** Elizabeth II **Subject:** Queen Mother's 80th Birthday **Obv:** Young bust right **Rev:** Bust left

Date	Mintage	F	VF	XF	Unc	BU
ND(1980)	150,000	—	—	1.25	2.50	3.75

KM# 35a   25 PENCE
28.2759 g., 0.9250 Silver 0.8409 oz. ASW, 38.5 mm. **Ruler:** Elizabeth II **Subject:** Queen Mother's 80th Birthday **Obv:** Young bust right **Rev:** Bust left

Date	Mintage	F	VF	XF	Unc	BU
ND(1980) Proof	25,000	Value: 18.00				

KM# 36   25 PENCE
Copper-Nickel, 38.5 mm. **Ruler:** Elizabeth II **Subject:** Wedding of Prince Charles and Lady Diana **Obv:** Young bust right **Rev:** Arms divided by royal couple

Date	Mintage	F	VF	XF	Unc	BU
1981	114,000	—	—	1.50	2.75	4.00

KM# 36a   25 PENCE
28.2759 g., 0.9250 Silver 0.8409 oz. ASW, 38.5 mm. **Ruler:** Elizabeth II **Subject:** Wedding of Prince Charles and Lady Diana **Obv:** Young bust right **Rev:** Royal couple divide arms

Date	Mintage	F	VF	XF	Unc	BU
1981 Proof	12,000	Value: 20.00				

KM# 25   50 NEW PENCE
13.5000 g., Copper-Nickel, 30 mm. **Obv:** Arms **Rev:** Ducal cap of the Duke of Normandy

Date	Mintage	F	VF	XF	Unc	BU
1969	200,000	—	1.00	1.50	2.50	3.50
1970	200,000	—	1.00	1.50	2.50	3.50
1971 Proof	10,000	Value: 4.00				

KM# 34   50 PENCE
13.5000 g., Copper-Nickel, 30 mm. **Ruler:** Elizabeth II **Obv:** Arms **Rev:** Ducal cap of the Duke of Normandy

Date	Mintage	F	VF	XF	Unc	BU
1979 Proof	20,000	Value: 4.50				
1981	200,000	—	—	0.90	1.45	2.25
1981 Proof	10,000	Value: 5.50				
1982	150,000	—	—	0.90	1.45	2.25
1983	200,000	—	—	0.90	1.45	2.25
1984	200,000	—	—	0.90	1.45	2.25

KM# 45.1   50 PENCE
13.5000 g., Copper-Nickel, 30 mm. **Ruler:** Elizabeth II **Obv:** Crowned head right, small shield at left **Rev:** Freesia flowers

Date	Mintage	F	VF	XF	Unc	BU
1985	35,000	—	—	0.90	1.45	2.25
1985 Proof	2,500	Value: 4.00				
1986	10,000	—	—	0.90	1.45	2.25
1986 Proof	2,500	Value: 4.00				
1987	5,000	—	—	0.90	1.45	2.25
1987 Proof	2,500	Value: 4.50				
1988	6,000	—	—	0.90	1.45	2.25
1988 Proof	2,500	Value: 4.50				
1989	55,000	—	—	0.90	1.45	2.25
1989 Proof	2,500	Value: 4.50				
1990	80,000	—	—	0.90	1.45	2.25

Date	Mintage	F	VF	XF	Unc	BU
1990 Proof	700	Value: 7.50				
1992	65,000	—	—	—	2.00	3.00
1992 Proof	—	Value: 7.50				
1997 Proof	—	Value: 7.50				

KM# 45.2   50 PENCE
Copper-Nickel, 27.3 mm. **Ruler:** Elizabeth II **Obv:** Crowned head right, small shield at left **Rev:** Freesia flowers

Date	Mintage	F	VF	XF	Unc	BU
1997 Proof	—	Value: 8.50				
1997	1,000,000	—	—	—	1.75	2.75

KM# 105   50 PENCE
7.9700 g., Copper-Nickel, 27.3 mm. **Ruler:** Elizabeth II **Subject:** 60th Anniversary - Battle of Britain **Obv:** Head with tiara right **Rev:** Pilot and fighter plane **Edge:** Plain

Date	Mintage	F	VF	XF	Unc	BU
2000	10,000	—	—	—	2.00	3.00

KM# 105a   50 PENCE
8.1000 g., 0.9250 Silver 0.2409 oz. ASW, 27.3 mm. **Ruler:** Elizabeth II **Obv:** Head with tiara right **Rev:** Pilot and fighter plane

Date	Mintage	F	VF	XF	Unc	BU
2000 Proof	15,000	Value: 25.00				

KM# 105b   50 PENCE
15.5000 g., 0.9170 Gold 0.4570 oz. AGW, 27.3 mm. **Ruler:** Elizabeth II **Obv:** Head with tiara right **Rev:** Pilot and fighter plane **Edge:** Plain

Date	Mintage	F	VF	XF	Unc	BU
2000 Proof	1,500	Value: 465				

KM# 37   POUND
7.9000 g., Nickel-Brass, 22 mm. **Ruler:** Elizabeth II **Obv:** Arms **Rev:** Guernsey lily

Date	Mintage	F	VF	XF	Unc	BU
1981	200,000	—	1.80	2.00	3.50	4.50
1981 Proof	10,000	Value: 5:00				

KM# 37a   POUND
8.0000 g., 0.9170 Gold 0.2358 oz. AGW, 22 mm. **Ruler:** Elizabeth II **Obv:** Arms **Rev:** Guernsey lily

Date	Mintage	F	VF	XF	Unc	BU
1981 Proof	4,500	Value: 245				

KM# 39   POUND
Nickel-Brass, 22.5 mm. **Ruler:** Elizabeth II **Obv:** Arms **Rev:** H.M.S. Crescent

Date	Mintage	F	VF	XF	Unc	BU
1983	269,000	—	1.80	2.00	3.50	4.50

KM# 46 POUND
Nickel-Brass, 22.5 mm. **Ruler:** Elizabeth II **Obv:** Crowned head right, small shield at left **Rev:** Design divides denomination

Date	Mintage	F	VF	XF	Unc	BU
1985	35,000	—	—	1.75	2.50	3.50
1985 Proof	2,500	Value: 6.50				
1986	10,000	—	—	1.75	2.50	3.50
1986 Proof	2,500	Value: 6.50				
1987	5,000	—	—	1.75	2.50	3.50
1987 Proof	2,500	Value: 6.50				
1988	5,000	—	—	1.75	2.50	3.50
1988 Proof	2,500	Value: 6.50				
1989	5,000	—	—	1.75	2.50	3.50
1989 Proof	2,500	Value: 6.50				
1990	3,500	—	—	1.75	2.50	3.50
1990 Proof	700	Value: 10.00				
1992 In sets only	—	—	—	—	3.50	5.00
1992 Proof	—	Value: 12.50				
1997 In sets only	—	—	—	—	3.50	5.00
1997 Proof	—	Value: 12.50				

KM# 77 POUND
9.5000 g., 0.9250 Silver 0.2825 oz. ASW, 22.5 mm. **Ruler:** Elizabeth II **Subject:** Queen Elizabeth the Queen Mother **Rev:** Bust facing, flowers flank

Date	Mintage	F	VF	XF	Unc	BU
1995 Proof	—	Value: 27.50				

KM# 78 POUND
9.5000 g., 0.9250 Silver 0.2825 oz. ASW, 22.5 mm. **Ruler:** Elizabeth II **Subject:** 70th Birthday of Queen Elizabeth II **Obv:** Crowned head right **Rev:** Queen Mother at left, arms above rock at right

Date	Mintage	F	VF	XF	Unc	BU
1996 Proof	—	Value: 20.00				

KM# 70 POUND
9.5000 g., 0.9250 Silver 0.2825 oz. ASW, 22.5 mm. **Ruler:** Elizabeth II **Subject:** Golden Wedding Anniversary **Obv:** Crowned head right **Rev:** Queen Elizabeth II and Prince Philip, monogrammed shield, Westminster Abbey

Date	Mintage	F	VF	XF	Unc	BU
1997 Proof	Est. 50,000	Value: 20.00				

KM# 73 POUND
9.5000 g., 0.9250 Silver 0.2825 oz. ASW, 22.5 mm. **Ruler:** Elizabeth II **Series:** Castle **Subject:** Tower of London

Date	Mintage	F	VF	XF	Unc	BU
1997 Proof	15,000	Value: 32.50				

KM# 84 POUND
9.5000 g., 0.9250 Silver 0.2825 oz. ASW, 22.5 mm. **Ruler:** Elizabeth II **Subject:** 80th Anniversary - Royal Air Force **Obv:** Head with tiara right **Rev:** Three Spitfires and RAF Benevolent Fund Crest

Date	Mintage	F	VF	XF	Unc	BU
1998 Proof	Est. 30,000	Value: 45.00				

KM# 95 POUND
9.5000 g., 0.9250 Silver 0.2825 oz. ASW, 22.5 mm. **Ruler:** Elizabeth II **Subject:** Prince Edward's Wedding **Obv:** Queen's portrait **Rev:** Portraits of Edward and Sophie **Edge:** Reeded

Date	Mintage	F	VF	XF	Unc	BU
1999 Proof	50,000	Value: 30.00				

KM# 109 POUND
9.5000 g., 0.9250 Silver 0.2825 oz. ASW, 22.5 mm. **Ruler:** Elizabeth II **Subject:** Winston Churchill **Obv:** Queen's portrait **Rev:** Churchill's portrait **Edge:** Reeded

Date	Mintage	F	VF	XF	Unc	BU
1999 Proof	30,000	Value: 25.00				

KM# 120 POUND
9.5000 g., 0.9250 Silver 0.2825 oz. ASW, 22.4 mm. **Ruler:** Elizabeth II **Subject:** Queen Mother **Obv:** Head with tiara right **Rev:** Bust 3/4 right **Edge:** Reeded

Date	Mintage	F	VF	XF	Unc	BU
1999 Proof	—	Value: 35.00				

KM# 133 POUND
9.5000 g., 0.9250 Silver 0.2825 oz. ASW, 22.5 mm. **Ruler:** Elizabeth II **Subject:** Queen Mother **Obv:** Head with tiara right **Rev:** Bust 3/4 right **Edge:** Reeded

Date	Mintage	F	VF	XF	Unc	BU
1999 Proof	50,000	Value: 30.00				

KM# 87 POUND
9.5000 g., 0.9250 Gold Plated Silver 0.2825 oz. ASW AGW, 22.5 mm. **Ruler:** Elizabeth II **Subject:** Year 2000 **Obv:** Head with tiara right **Rev:** Hands holding planet Earth, **Note:** Millennium insert for 5 pounds, KM#86.

Date	Mintage	F	VF	XF	Unc	BU
2000 Proof	Est. 50,000	Value: 45.00				

KM# 99 POUND
9.5000 g., 0.9250 Silver 0.2825 oz. ASW, 22.5 mm. **Ruler:** Elizabeth II **Subject:** Queen Mother's 100th Birthday **Obv:** Head with tiara right **Rev:** Head facing, flowers and age at right **Edge:** Reeded

Date	Mintage	F	VF	XF	Unc	BU
2000 Proof	50,000	Value: 25.00				

KM# 47 2 POUNDS
Copper-Nickel, 38.61 mm. **Ruler:** Elizabeth II **Subject:** 40th Anniversary - Liberation from Germany **Obv:** Crowned head right, small arms at left **Rev:** Pair of doves sharing laurel branch

Date	Mintage	F	VF	XF	Unc	BU
ND(1985)	75,000	—	—	3.50	6.00	7.50
ND(1985) Proof	2,500	Value: 9.00				

KM# 47a 2 POUNDS
28.2800 g., 0.9250 Silver 0.8410 oz. ASW, 38.61 mm. **Ruler:** Elizabeth II **Subject:** 40th Anniversary - Liberation from Germany **Obv:** Crowned head right, small arms at left **Rev:** Pair of doves sharing laurel branch

Date	Mintage	F	VF	XF	Unc	BU
ND (1985) Proof	2,500	Value: 30.00				

KM# 48 2 POUNDS
Copper-Nickel, 38.61 mm. **Ruler:** Elizabeth II **Subject:** Commonwealth Games **Rev:** Eight shields of athletes surround arms

Date	Mintage	F	VF	XF	Unc	BU
1986	18,000	—	—	—	6.00	7.00
1986 Proof	Est. 2,500	Value: 10.00				

KM# 48a 2 POUNDS
28.2800 g., 0.5000 Silver 0.4546 oz. ASW, 38.61 mm. **Ruler:** Elizabeth II **Subject:** Commonwealth Games **Rev:** Eight shields of athletes surround arms

Date	Mintage	F	VF	XF	Unc	BU
1986	Est. 50,000	—	—	—	13.50	15.00

KM# 48b 2 POUNDS
28.2800 g., 0.9250 Silver 0.8410 oz. ASW, 38.61 mm. **Ruler:** Elizabeth II **Subject:** Commonwealth Games **Rev:** Eight shields of athletes surround arms

Date	Mintage	F	VF	XF	Unc	BU
1986 Proof	Est. 20,000	Value: 22.50				

KM# 49 2 POUNDS
Copper-Nickel, 38.5 mm. **Ruler:** Elizabeth II **Subject:** 900th Anniversary - Death of William the Conqueror **Obv:** Crowned head right, small arms at left **Rev:** Crowned bust left

Date	Mintage	F	VF	XF	Unc	BU
ND(1987)	18,000	—	—	—	6.50	7.50
ND(1987) Proof	Est. 2,500	Value: 10.00				

KM# 49a 2 POUNDS
28.2800 g., 0.9250 Silver 0.8410 oz. ASW, 38.5 mm.
Ruler: Elizabeth II **Subject:** 900th Anniversary - Death of William
the Conqueror **Obv:** Crowned head right, small arms at left
Rev: Crowned bust left

Date	Mintage	F	VF	XF	Unc	BU
ND(1987) Proof	2,500	Value: 30.00				

KM# 49b 2 POUNDS
47.5400 g., 0.9170 Gold 1.4015 oz. AGW, 38.5 mm.
Ruler: Elizabeth II **Subject:** 900th Anniversary - Death of William
the Conqueror **Obv:** Crowned head right, small arms at left
Rev: Crowned bust left

Date	Mintage	F	VF	XF	Unc	BU
ND(1987) Proof	90	Value: 1,350				

KM# 50 2 POUNDS
Copper-Nickel, 38.5 mm. **Ruler:** Elizabeth II **Subject:** William
II, 1087-1100 **Obv:** Crowned head right, small arms at left
Rev: Bust facing

Date	Mintage	F	VF	XF	Unc	BU
1988	7,500	—	—	—	6.50	7.50
1988 Proof	2,500	Value: 10.00				

KM# 50a 2 POUNDS
28.2800 g., 0.9250 Silver 0.8410 oz. ASW, 38.5 mm.
Ruler: Elizabeth II **Subject:** William II, 1087-1100 **Obv:** Crowned
head right, small arms at left **Rev:** Bust facing

Date	Mintage	F	VF	XF	Unc	BU
1988 Proof	2,500	Value: 28.00				

KM# 51 2 POUNDS
Copper-Nickel, 38.5 mm. **Ruler:** Elizabeth II **Subject:** Henry I,
1100-1135 **Obv:** Crowned head right, small arms at left
Rev: Crowned bust right

Date	Mintage	F	VF	XF	Unc	BU
1989	10,000	—	—	—	6.50	7.50
1989 Proof	Est. 2,500	Value: 10.00				

KM# 51a 2 POUNDS
28.2800 g., 0.9250 Silver 0.8410 oz. ASW, 38.5 mm.
Ruler: Elizabeth II **Subject:** Henry I, 1100-1135 **Obv:** Crowned
head right, small arms at left **Rev:** Crowned bust right

Date	Mintage	F	VF	XF	Unc	BU
1989 Proof	Est. 2,500	Value: 28.00				

KM# 52 2 POUNDS
Copper-Nickel, 38.5 mm. **Ruler:** Elizabeth II **Subject:** Royal
Visit **Obv:** Crowned bust right **Rev:** Royal Yacht "Britannia"

Date	Mintage	F	VF	XF	Unc	BU
1989	5,000	—	—	—	8.00	10.00

KM# 52a 2 POUNDS
28.2800 g., 0.9250 Silver 0.8410 oz. ASW, 38.5 mm.
Ruler: Elizabeth II **Subject:** Royal Visit **Obv:** Crowned bust right
Rev: Royal yacht, "Britannia"

Date	Mintage	F	VF	XF	Unc	BU
1989 Proof	5,000	Value: 35.00				

KM# 53 2 POUNDS
Copper-Nickel, 38.5 mm. **Ruler:** Elizabeth II **Subject:** 90th
Birthday of Queen Mother **Obv:** Crowned bust right
Rev: Crowned monogram flanked by flowers

Date	Mintage	F	VF	XF	Unc	BU
ND(1990)	9,000	—	—	—	7.00	8.00

KM# 53a 2 POUNDS
28.2800 g., 0.9250 Silver 0.8410 oz. ASW, 38.5 mm.
Ruler: Elizabeth II **Subject:** 90th Birthday of Queen Mother **Obv:**
Crowned bust right **Rev:** Crowned monogram flanked by flowers

Date	Mintage	F	VF	XF	Unc	BU
ND(1990) Proof	1,302	Value: 50.00				

KM# 54 2 POUNDS
Copper-Nickel, 38.5 mm. **Ruler:** Elizabeth II **Subject:** Henry II,
1154-1189 **Obv:** Crowned head right, small arms at left
Rev: Crowned bust half left

Date	Mintage	F	VF	XF	Unc	BU
1991	1,200	—	—	—	6.50	7.50

KM# 54a 2 POUNDS
28.2800 g., 0.9250 Silver 0.8410 oz. ASW, 38.5 mm.
Ruler: Elizabeth II **Subject:** Henry II, 1154-1189 **Obv:** Crowned
head right, small arms at left **Rev:** Crowned half left

Date	Mintage	F	VF	XF	Unc	BU
1991 Proof	Est. 2,500	Value: 50.00				

KM# 55 2 POUNDS
Copper-Nickel, 38.5 mm. **Ruler:** Elizabeth II **Subject:** 40th
Anniversary of Coronation **Obv:** Crowned bust right **Rev:**
Crowned, ribbon monogram with date on field of vines and flowers

Date	Mintage	F	VF	XF	Unc	BU
ND(1993)	13,000	—	—	—	6.50	7.50

KM# 55a 2 POUNDS
28.2800 g., 0.9250 Silver 0.8410 oz. ASW, 38.5 mm.
Ruler: Elizabeth II **Subject:** 40th Anniversary of Coronation
Obv: Crowned bust right **Rev:** Crowned, ribbon monogram with
date on field of vines and flowers

Date	Mintage	F	VF	XF	Unc	BU
ND(1993) Proof	Est. 10,000	Value: 45.00				

KM# 56 2 POUNDS
Copper-Nickel, 38.5 mm. **Ruler:** Elizabeth II **Subject:** 50th
Anniversary - Normandy Landing **Obv:** Crowned head right, small
arms at left **Rev:** Cameo portrait above invasion scene

Date	Mintage	F	VF	XF	Unc	BU
ND(1994)	49,000	—	—	—	7.50	9.00

KM# 56a 2 POUNDS
28.2800 g., 0.9250 Silver 0.8410 oz. ASW, 38.5 mm.
Ruler: Elizabeth II **Subject:** 50th Anniversary - Normandy
Landing **Obv:** Crowned head right, small arms at left **Rev:** Cameo
portrait above invasion scene

Date	Mintage	F	VF	XF	Unc	BU
ND(1994) Proof	Est. 10,000	Value: 35.00				

KM# 61 2 POUNDS
Copper-Nickel, 38.5 mm. **Ruler:** Elizabeth II **Subject:** 50th
Anniversary of Liberation **Obv:** Crowned head right, small arms
at left **Rev:** Soldiers and ship

Date	Mintage	F	VF	XF	Unc	BU
ND(1995)	42,000	—	—	—	7.50	9.00

KM# 61a 2 POUNDS
28.2800 g., 0.9250 Silver 0.8410 oz. ASW, 38.5 mm.
Ruler: Elizabeth II **Subject:** 50th Anniversary of Liberation **Obv:**
Crowned head right, small arms at left **Rev:** Soldiers and ship

Date	Mintage	F	VF	XF	Unc	BU
ND(1995) Proof	7,000	Value: 45.00				

KM# 61b 2 POUNDS
56.5600 g., 0.9250 Silver 1.6820 oz. ASW, 38.5 mm.
Ruler: Elizabeth II **Subject:** 50th Anniversary of Liberation **Obv:**
Crowned head right, small arms at left **Rev:** Soldiers and ship

Date	Mintage	F	VF	XF	Unc	BU
ND(1995) Proof	800	Value: 95.00				

KM# 80 2 POUNDS
Copper-Nickel, 38.5 mm. **Ruler:** Elizabeth II **Subject:** WWF
Conserving Nature **Obv:** Crowned head right **Rev:** Emperor Moth

Date	Mintage	F	VF	XF	Unc	BU
1997	—	—	—	—	9.00	14.00

KM# 80a 2 POUNDS
28.2800 g., 0.9250 Silver 0.8410 oz. ASW, 38.5 mm.
Ruler: Elizabeth II **Subject:** WWF Conserving Nature
Obv: Crowned head right **Rev:** Emperor moth

Date	Mintage	F	VF	XF	Unc	BU
1997 Proof	Est. 15,000	Value: 50.00				

KM# 88 2 POUNDS
12.0000 g., Bi-Metallic Copper-Nickel center in Nickel-Brass ring, 28.35 mm. **Ruler:** Elizabeth II **Obv:** Crowned head right **Rev:** Latent image arms on cross design **Edge:** BAILIWICK OF GUERNSEY

Date	Mintage	F	VF	XF	Unc	BU
1997	—	—	—	—	8.50	10.00
1997 Proof	—	Value: 12.00				

KM# 81 2 POUNDS
Copper-Nickel, 38.5 mm. **Ruler:** Elizabeth II **Subject:** WWF Conserving Nature **Obv:** Crowned head right **Rev:** Brimstone butterfly

Date	Mintage	F	VF	XF	Unc	BU
1998	—	—	—	—	8.00	14.00

KM# 83 2 POUNDS
12.0000 g., Bi-Metallic Copper-Nickel center in Nickel-Brass ring, 28.35 mm. **Ruler:** Elizabeth II **Obv:** Head with tiara right **Rev:** Latent image arms on cross **Edge:** BAILIWICK OF GUERNSEY

Date	Mintage	F	VF	XF	Unc	BU
1998	Est. 150,000	—	—	—	8.50	10.00

KM# 66 5 POUNDS
Copper-Nickel, 38.5 mm. **Ruler:** Elizabeth II **Subject:** Queen Elizabeth the Queen Mother **Obv:** Crowned head right **Rev:** Bust facing, flowers flank

Date	Mintage	F	VF	XF	Unc	BU
1995	56,000	—	—	—	15.00	16.50

KM# 66a 5 POUNDS
28.2800 g., 0.9250 Silver 0.8410 oz. ASW, 38.5 mm. **Ruler:** Elizabeth II **Subject:** Queen Elizabeth The Queen Mother **Obv:** Crowned head right **Rev:** Bust facing, flowers flank

Date	Mintage	F	VF	XF	Unc	BU
1995 Proof	Est. 40,000	Value: 50.00				

KM# 67 5 POUNDS
7.8100 g., 0.9990 Gold 0.2508 oz. AGW. **Ruler:** Elizabeth II **Obv:** Crowned head right **Rev:** Queen Mother

Date	Mintage	F	VF	XF	Unc	BU
1995 Proof	Est. 2,500	Value: 250				

KM# 68 5 POUNDS
Copper-Nickel, 38.5 mm. **Ruler:** Elizabeth II **Subject:** European Football **Rev:** Soccer ball and European map

Date	Mintage	F	VF	XF	Unc	BU
1996	—	—	—	—	15.00	16.50

KM# 68a 5 POUNDS
28.2800 g., 0.9250 Silver 0.8410 oz. ASW, 38.5 mm. **Ruler:** Elizabeth II **Subject:** European Football **Rev:** Soccer ball and European map

Date	Mintage	F	VF	XF	Unc	BU
1996 Proof	Est. 20,000	Value: 65.00				

KM# 79 5 POUNDS
Copper-Nickel, 38.5 mm. **Ruler:** Elizabeth II **Subject:** 70th Birthday of Queen Elizabeth II **Obv:** Crowned head right **Rev:** Bust at left looking right, ship and arms at right

Date	Mintage	F	VF	XF	Unc	BU
1996	—	—	—	—	15.00	16.50

KM# 79a 5 POUNDS
28.2800 g., 0.9250 Silver 0.8410 oz. ASW, 38.5 mm. **Ruler:** Elizabeth II **Subject:** 70th Birthday of Queen Elizabeth II **Obv:** Crowned head right **Rev:** Bust at left looking right, arms and ship at right

Date	Mintage	F	VF	XF	Unc	BU
1996 Proof	—	Value: 45.00				

KM# 71 5 POUNDS
Copper-Nickel, 38.5 mm. **Ruler:** Elizabeth II **Subject:** Queen Elizabeth II's Golden Wedding Anniversary **Obv:** Crowned head right **Rev:** Queen Elizabeth II and Prince Philip, monogrammed shield and Westminster Abbey

Date	Mintage	F	VF	XF	Unc	BU
1997	22,000	—	—	—	12.50	14.00

KM# 71a 5 POUNDS
28.2800 g., 0.9250 Silver 0.8410 oz. ASW, 38.5 mm. **Ruler:** Elizabeth II **Subject:** Queen Elizabeth II's Golden Wedding Anniversary **Obv:** Crowned head right **Rev:** Queen Elizabeth II and Prince Philip, monogrammed shield and Westminster Abbey

Date	Mintage	F	VF	XF	Unc	BU
1997 Proof	Est. 20,000	Value: 65.00				

KM# 74 5 POUNDS
Copper-Nickel, 38.5 mm. **Ruler:** Elizabeth II **Subject:** Castle Cornet **Obv:** Crowned head right **Rev:** Castle

Date	Mintage	F	VF	XF	Unc	BU
1997	—	—	—	—	10.00	12.00

KM# 74a 5 POUNDS
28.2800 g., 0.9250 Silver 0.8410 oz. ASW, 38.5 mm. **Ruler:** Elizabeth II **Subject:** Castle Cornet **Obv:** Crowned head right **Rev:** Castle

Date	Mintage	F	VF	XF	Unc	BU
1997 Proof	Est. 10,000	Value: 60.00				

KM# 75 5 POUNDS
28.2800 g., 0.9250 Silver 0.8410 oz. ASW, 38.5 mm. **Ruler:** Elizabeth II **Subject:** Castle Caernarfon **Obv:** Crowned head right **Rev:** Castle

Date	Mintage	F	VF	XF	Unc	BU
1997 Proof	Est. 10,000	Value: 60.00				

KM# 76 5 POUNDS
28.2800 g., 0.9250 Silver 0.8410 oz. ASW, 38.5 mm. **Ruler:** Elizabeth II **Subject:** Castle Leeds **Obv:** Crowned head right **Rev:** Castle

Date	Mintage	F	VF	XF	Unc	BU
1997 Proof	Est. 10,000	Value: 60.00				

KM# 98 5 POUNDS
1.2000 g., 0.9167 Gold 0.0354 oz. AGW, 9 mm. **Ruler:** Elizabeth II **Subject:** Queen's 50th Wedding Anniversary **Rev:** Royal couple, shield and church **Edge:** Reeded

Date	Mintage	F	VF	XF	Unc	BU
1997 Proof	—	Value: 50.00				

KM# 82 5 POUNDS
Copper-Nickel, 38.5 mm. **Ruler:** Elizabeth II **Subject:** 80th Anniversary of the Royal Air Force **Obv:** Head with tiara right **Rev:** Three Spitfires and an oval crest

Date	Mintage	F	VF	XF	Unc	BU
1998	—	—	—	—	12.50	14.50

KM# 82a 5 POUNDS
28.2800 g., 0.9250 Silver 0.8410 oz. ASW, 38.5 mm. **Ruler:** Elizabeth II **Subject:** 80th Anniversary of the Royal Air Force **Obv:** Head with tiara right **Rev:** Three Spitfires and an oval crest

Date	Mintage	F	VF	XF	Unc	BU
1998 Proof	15,000	Value: 55.00				

KM# 86 5 POUNDS
28.2800 g., 0.9250 Silver 0.8410 oz. ASW, 38.5 mm. **Ruler:** Elizabeth II **Subject:** Millennium 2000 **Obv:** Head with tiara right below center hole **Rev:** Rising sun design surrounds center hole

Date	Mintage	F	VF	XF	Unc	BU
1999 Proof	Est. 50,000	Value: 40.00				

KM# 91 5 POUNDS
Bi-Metallic Brass center in Copper-Nickel ring, 38.5 mm. **Ruler:** Elizabeth II **Subject:** Millennium 2000 **Obv:** Head with tiara right at center and below **Rev:** Hands holding planet earth in center, rising sun design surrounds

Date	Mintage	F	VF	XF	Unc	BU
1999	22,000	—	—	—	18.00	20.00

KM# 92   5 POUNDS
27.7100 g., Copper Nickel, 38.6 mm. **Ruler:** Elizabeth II
Subject: Prince Edward's Marriage **Obv:** Head with tiara right
Rev: Conjoined heads of Edward and Sophie left **Edge:** Reeded

Date	Mintage	F	VF	XF	Unc	BU
1999	19,000	—	—	—	15.00	16.50

KM# 92a   5 POUNDS
28.2800 g., 0.9250 Silver 0.8410 oz. ASW, 38.6 mm.
Ruler: Elizabeth II **Subject:** Prince Edward's Marriage
Obv: Head with tiara right **Rev:** Conjoined heads left of Edward
and Sophie left

Date	Mintage	F	VF	XF	Unc	BU
1999 Proof	—	Value: 37.50				

KM# 93   5 POUNDS
27.7100 g., Copper-Nickel, 38.5 mm. **Ruler:** Elizabeth II **Subject:**
Queen Mother **Obv:** Head with tiara right **Rev:** Bust 3/4 right

Date	Mintage	F	VF	XF	Unc	BU
1999	5,000	—	—	—	16.50	18.00

KM# 94   5 POUNDS
27.7100 g., Copper-Nickel, 38.5 mm. **Ruler:** Elizabeth II
Subject: Winston Churchill **Obv:** Head with tiara right **Rev:** Head
right **Edge:** Reeded

Date	Mintage	F	VF	XF	Unc	BU
1999	5,000	—	—	—	16.50	18.00

KM# 94a   5 POUNDS
28.2800 g., 0.9250 Silver 0.8410 oz. ASW, 38.5 mm.
Ruler: Elizabeth II **Obv:** Head with tiara right **Rev:** Head right
Rev. Insc.: Winston Spencer Churchill

Date	Mintage	F	VF	XF	Unc	BU
1999 Proof	—	Value: 47.50				

KM# 94b   5 POUNDS
47.5400 g., 0.9166 Gold 1.4009 oz. AGW, 38.5 mm.
Ruler: Elizabeth II **Subject:** Winston Churchill **Obv:** Head with
tiara right **Rev:** Head right **Edge:** Reeded

Date	Mintage	F	VF	XF	Unc	BU
1999 Proof	125,000	Value: 1,325				

KM# 134   5 POUNDS
1.2440 g., 0.9990 Gold 0.0400 oz. AGW, 13.9 mm.
Ruler: Elizabeth II **Subject:** Queen Mother **Obv:** Head with tiara
right **Rev:** Queen Mother's portrait **Edge:** Reeded

Date	Mintage	F	VF	XF	Unc	BU
1999	20,000	—	—	—	—	75.00

KM# 100   5 POUNDS
28.2800 g., Copper-Nickel, 38.6 mm. **Ruler:** Elizabeth II
Obv: Head with tiara right **Rev:** Queen Mother's portrait
Edge: Reeded

Date	Mintage	F	VF	XF	Unc	BU
2000	2,000	—	—	—	7.50	8.50

KM# 100a   5 POUNDS
28.2800 g., 0.9250 Silver 0.8410 oz. ASW, 38.6 mm.
Ruler: Elizabeth II **Subject:** Queen Mother's 100th Birthday
Obv: Head with tiara right with gold-plated "100" **Rev:** Queen
Mother's portrait **Edge:** Reeded

Date	Mintage	F	VF	XF	Unc	BU
2000 Proof	20,000	Value: 47.50				

KM# 101   5 POUNDS
1.1300 g., 0.9170 Gold 0.0333 oz. AGW, 13.9 mm.
Ruler: Elizabeth II **Subject:** Queen Mother's 100th Birthday
Obv: Head with tiara right **Rev:** Queen Mother's portrait
Edge: Reeded

Date	Mintage	F	VF	XF	Unc	BU
2000 Proof	20,000	Value: 65.00				

KM# 102   5 POUNDS
27.9500 g., Copper-Nickel, 38.4 mm. **Ruler:** Elizabeth II
Subject: Century of Monarchy **Obv:** Head with tiara right
Rev: Portraits of past five sovereigns **Edge:** Reeded

Date	Mintage	F	VF	XF	Unc	BU
2000	10,246	—	—	—	11.00	12.50

KM# 102a   5 POUNDS
28.2800 g., 0.9250 Silver 0.8410 oz. ASW, 38.6 mm.
Ruler: Elizabeth II **Subject:** Century of Monarchy **Obv:** Head
with tiara right **Rev:** Portraits of past five sovereigns
Edge: Reeded

Date	Mintage	F	VF	XF	Unc	BU
2000 Proof	10,000	Value: 47.50				

KM# 113   5 POUNDS
1.1300 g., 0.9170 Gold 0.0333 oz. AGW, 13.9 mm.
Ruler: Elizabeth II **Subject:** 20th Century Monarchy **Obv:** Head
with tiara right **Rev:** Portraits of past five sovereigns
Edge: Reeded

Date	Mintage	F	VF	XF	Unc	BU
2000 Proof	—	Value: 65.00				

KM# 102b   5 POUNDS
39.9400 g., 0.9166 Gold 1.1770 oz. AGW, 38.6 mm.
Ruler: Elizabeth II **Subject:** Century of Monarchy **Obv:** Head
with tiara right **Rev:** Portraits of past five sovereigns
Edge: Reeded

Date	Mintage	F	VF	XF	Unc	BU
2000 Proof	200	Value: 1,150				

KM# 57   10 POUNDS
3.1300 g., 0.9990 Gold 0.1005 oz. AGW **Ruler:** Elizabeth II
Subject: 50th Anniversary - Normandy Invasion **Rev:** Soldiers
and tank

Date	Mintage	F	VF	XF	Unc	BU
ND(1994) Proof	Est. 500	Value: 100				

KM# 62   10 POUNDS
3.1300 g., 0.9990 Gold 0.1005 oz. AGW **Ruler:** Elizabeth II
Subject: 50th Anniversary of Liberation **Rev:** Uniformed figure
giving speech

Date	Mintage	F	VF	XF	Unc	BU
ND(1995) Proof	Est. 500	Value: 100				

KM# 157   10 POUNDS
163.2000 g., 0.9250 Silver with Gold insert 4.8533 oz. ASW,
64.9 mm. **Ruler:** Elizabeth II **Subject:** Queen's Golden Wedding
Anniversary **Obv:** Crowned head right **Rev:** Elizabeth and Philip,
gold insert shield and cathedral **Edge:** Reeded **Note:** Illustration
reduced.

Date	Mintage	F	VF	XF	Unc	BU
1997 Proof	—	Value: 250				

KM# 171   10 POUNDS
155.5170 g., 0.9250 Silver 4.6248 oz. ASW, 65 mm.
Ruler: Elizabeth II **Subject:** Queen Mother Elizabeth
Edge: Reeded

Date	Mintage	F	VF	XF	Unc	BU
1998 Proof	—	Value: 185				

KM# 104   10 POUNDS
141.7500 g., 0.9990 Silver 4.5526 oz. ASW, 65 mm.
Ruler: Elizabeth II **Subject:** Century of Monarchy **Obv:** Head
with tiara right **Rev:** Portraits of past five sovereigns
Edge: Reeded

Date	Mintage	F	VF	XF	Unc	BU
2000 Proof	950	Value: 200				

KM# 138   10 POUNDS
13.6600 g., 0.9990 Gold 0.4387 oz. AGW, 19.35 mm.
Ruler: Elizabeth II **Subject:** Millennium **Obv:** Head with tiara right
Rev: Hands holding planet **Edge:** Reeded

Date	Mintage	F	VF	XF	Unc	BU
2000	7,500	—	—	—	550	—

KM# 58   25 POUNDS
7.8100 g., 0.9990 Gold 0.2508 oz. AGW **Ruler:** Elizabeth II
Subject: 50th Anniversary - Normandy Invasion **Rev:** Uniformed
figure standing at right, invasion scene in background

Date	Mintage	F	VF	XF	Unc	BU
ND(1994)	Est. 500	—	—	—	—	245
ND(1994) Proof	Est. 500	Value: 250				

KM# 63   25 POUNDS
7.8100 g., 0.9990 Gold 0.2508 oz. AGW **Ruler:** Elizabeth II
Subject: 50th Anniversary of Liberation **Obv:** Crowned head
right, small arms at left **Rev:** Supply worker and ship

Date	Mintage	F	VF	XF	Unc	BU
ND(1995)	Est. 500				Value: 250	

KM# 69   25 POUNDS
7.8100 g., 0.9990 Gold 0.2508 oz. AGW **Ruler:** Elizabeth II
Subject: European Football **Rev:** Soccer ball and European map

Date	Mintage	F	VF	XF	Unc	BU
1996 Proof	1,500				Value: 250	

KM# 72   25 POUNDS
7.8100 g., 0.9990 Gold 0.2508 oz. AGW **Ruler:** Elizabeth II
Subject: Queen Elizabeth II's Golden Wedding Anniversary
Obv: Crowned head right **Rev:** Queen Elizabeth II and Prince
Philip, monogrammed shield and Westminster Abbey

Date	Mintage	F	VF	XF	Unc	BU
1997 Proof	Est. 5,000				Value: 275	

KM# 85   25 POUNDS
7.8100 g., 0.9990 Gold 0.2508 oz. AGW **Ruler:** Elizabeth II
Subject: 80th Anniversary - Royal Air Force **Obv:** Head with tiara
right **Rev:** Three Spitfires and RAF Benevolent Fund Crest

Date	Mintage	F	VF	XF	Unc	BU
1998 Proof	Est. 2,500				Value: 245	

KM# 132   25 POUNDS
7.8100 g., 0.9990 Gold 0.2508 oz. AGW, 22 mm.
Ruler: Elizabeth II **Subject:** Winston Churchill **Obv:** Head with
tiara right **Rev:** Head right **Edge:** Reeded

Date	Mintage	F	VF	XF	Unc	BU
1999 Proof	2,500				Value: 250	

KM# 135   25 POUNDS
7.8100 g., 0.9990 Gold 0.2508 oz. AGW, 22 mm.
Ruler: Elizabeth II **Subject:** Queen Mother **Obv:** Head with tiara
right **Rev:** Queen Mother's portrait **Edge:** Reeded

Date	Mintage	F	VF	XF	Unc	BU
1999 Proof	5,000				Value: 250	

KM# 137   25 POUNDS
7.8100 g., 0.9990 Gold 0.2508 oz. AGW, 22 mm. **Ruler:** Elizabeth II
Subject: Prince Edward's Marriage **Obv:** Head with tiara right
Rev: Jugate heads left of Edward and Sophie left **Edge:** Reeded

Date	Mintage	F	VF	XF	Unc	BU
1999 Proof	5,000				Value: 250	

KM# 103   25 POUNDS
7.8100 g., 0.9170 Gold 0.2302 oz. AGW, 22 mm.
Ruler: Elizabeth II **Subject:** Queen Mother's 100th Birthday
Obv: Head with tiara right **Rev:** Queen Mother's portrait
Edge: Reeded

Date	Mintage	F	VF	XF	Unc	BU
2000 Proof	5,000				Value: 240	

KM# 59   50 POUNDS
15.6100 g., 0.9990 Gold 0.5014 oz. AGW **Ruler:** Elizabeth II
Subject: 50th Anniversary - Normandy Invasion **Rev:** Paratroopers

Date	Mintage	F	VF	XF	Unc	BU
ND(1994) Proof	Est. 500				Value: 485	

KM# 64   50 POUNDS
15.6100 g., 0.9990 Gold 0.5014 oz. AGW **Ruler:** Elizabeth II
Subject: 50th Anniversary of Liberation **Rev:** Uniformed figure
signing document, ship in background

Date	Mintage	F	VF	XF	Unc	BU
ND(1995) Proof	Est. 500				Value: 485	

KM# 136   50 POUNDS
15.5517 g., 0.9990 Gold 0.4995 oz. AGW, 27 mm.
Ruler: Elizabeth II **Subject:** Queen Mother **Obv:** Head with tiara
right **Rev:** Queen Mother's portrait **Edge:** Reeded

Date	Mintage	F	VF	XF	Unc	BU
1999 Proof	1,250				Value: 575	

KM# 60   100 POUNDS
31.2100 g., 0.9990 Gold 1.0024 oz. AGW **Ruler:** Elizabeth II
Subject: 50th Anniversary - Normandy Invasion **Obv:** Crowned
head right, small arms at left **Rev:** Cameo portrait of Winston
Churchill above invasion scene

Date	Mintage	F	VF	XF	Unc	BU
ND(1994) Proof	Est. 500				Value: 975	

KM# 65   100 POUNDS
31.2100 g., 0.9990 Gold 1.0024 oz. AGW **Ruler:** Elizabeth II
Subject: 50th Anniversary of Liberation **Rev:** Soldiers and ship

Date	Mintage	F	VF	XF	Unc	BU
ND(1995) Proof	Est. 500				Value: 975	

PIEFORTS

KM#	Date	Mintage	Identification	Mkt Val
P1	1981	500	Pound. 16.0000 g. KM#37a.	265
P2	2000	10,000	50 Pence. 0.9250 Silver. 16.2000 g. KM#105a.	55.00

MINT SETS

KM#	Date	Mintage	Identification	Issue Price	Mkt Val
MS1	1985 (8)	10,000	KM40-41, 42.1, 43-47	8.75	12.50
MS2	1985 (7)	—	KM40-41, 42.1, 43-46		6.50
MS3	1986 (7)	5,000	KM40-46	8.75	6.50
MS4	1987 (7)	7,500	KM40-46	11.00	6.50
MS5	1988 (7)	5,000	KM40-46	13.00	15.00
MS6	1989 (7)	5,000	KM40-46	17.00	16.50
MS7	1990 (8)	2,520	KM40-41, 42.1-42.2, 43-46	16.00	20.00
MS8	1992 (7)	1,500	KM40-41, 42.2, 43-46	22.50	25.00
MS9	1997 (9)	—	KM 40a, 41a, 42.2, 43.2, 44, 45.2, 46, 88	—	25.00

PROOF SETS

KM#	Date	Mintage	Identification	Issue Price	Mkt Val
PS3	1902H (4)	—	KM5, 7-8, 10	—	1,000
PS4	1910H (2)	—	KM5, 7	—	500
PS5	1956 (6)	1,050	KM15-17 double set	—	22.50
PS6	1966 (4)	10,000	KM15-16, 18, 19	—	8.50
PS7	1971 (6)	10,000	KM20-25	16.00	9.50
PS8	1979 (6)	4,963	KM27-30, 33-34	25.00	11.50
PS9	1981 (6)	10,000	KM27-30, 34, 37	29.00	20.00
PS10	1985 (8)	2,500	KM40-47	29.75	30.00
PS11	1986 (8)	2,500	KM40-46, 48	35.00	32.00
PS12	1987 (8)	2,500	KM40-46, 49	33.00	32.00
PS13	1988 (8)	2,500	KM40-46, 50	45.00	32.00
PS14	1989 (8)	2,500	KM40-46, 51	45.00	32.00
PS15	1990 (9)	700	KM40-41, 42.1-42.2, 43-46	46.00	46.00
PS16	1992 (7)	500	KM40-41, 42.2, 43.2, 44-46	52.50	55.00
PS17	1994 (4)	500	KM57-60	1,595	1,400
PS18	ND (1995) (4)	500	KM62-65	1,600	1,400
PS19	1996 (2)	1,500	KM68a, 69	—	275
PS20	1997 (3)	—	KM70, 71a, 72	—	420
PS22	1997 (9)	—	KM#40a, 41a, 42.2, 43.2, 44, 45.1, 45.2, 46, 88	—	—
PS21	1997 (4)	—	KM73, 74a, 75-76	181	215

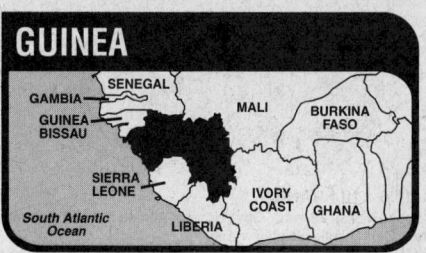

GUINEA

GAMBIA
SENEGAL
GUINEA
BISSAU
MALI
BURKINA
FASO
SIERRA
LEONE
IVORY
COAST
GHANA
South Atlantic Ocean
LIBERIA

The Republic of Guinea, situated on the Atlantic Coast of
Africa between Sierra Leone and Guinea-Bissau, has an area of
94,964 sq. mi. (245,860 sq. km.) and a population of 6.4 million.
Capital: Conakry. Although Guinea contains one-third of the
world's reserves of bauxite and significant deposits of iron ore,
gold and diamonds, the economy is still dependent on agriculture, aluminum, bananas, copra and coffee are exported.

The coast of Guinea was known to Portuguese navigators of
the 15th century but was seldom visited by European traders of
the 16th-18th centuries because of its dangerous coastal waters.
French penetration of the area began in the mid-19th century with
the entering into of protectorate treaties with several of the coastal
chiefs. After a long struggle with Guinea's native leader Samory
Toure, France secured the area and until 1890 administered it as
a part of Senegal. In 1895 the colony (Guinee Francais) became
an autonomous part of the federation of French West Africa. The
inhabitants were extended French citizenship in 1946 when the
colony became an overseas territory of the French Union. Guinea
became an independent republic on Oct. 2, 1958, when it declined
to enter the new French Community.

MONETARY SYSTEM
100 Centimes = 1 Franc

REPUBLIC
DECIMAL COINAGE

KM# 4   FRANC
Copper-Nickel **Obv:** Head of Ahmed Sekou Toure left
Rev: Feathers flank denomination within wreath

Date	Mintage	F	VF	XF	Unc	BU
1962	—	1.25	2.00	3.50	7.00	15.00
1962 Proof	—				Value: 50.00	

KM# 1   5 FRANCS
Aluminum-Bronze **Obv:** Head of Ahmed Sekou Toure right
Rev: Palm trees flank denomination

Date	Mintage	F	VF	XF	Unc	BU
1959	—	2.75	4.75	12.00	22.50	—

KM# 5   5 FRANCS
Copper-Nickel, 20 mm. **Obv:** Head right **Rev:** Denomination within
wreath, coconuts below **Note:** Mules with two obverses exist.

Date	Mintage	F	VF	XF	Unc	BU
1962	—	1.25	2.00	3.00	6.50	12.50
1962 Proof	—				Value: 70.00	

KM# 2   10 FRANCS
Aluminum-Bronze **Obv:** Head of Ahmed Sekou Toure left
Rev: Denomination above spray

Date	Mintage	F	VF	XF	Unc	BU
1959	—	5.00	20.00	50.00	90.00	—

KM# 6   10 FRANCS
Copper-Nickel, 22 mm.   **Obv:** Head of Ahmed Sekou Toure left
Rev: Denomination within wreath

Date	Mintage	F	VF	XF	Unc	BU
1962	—	1.75	2.75	6.00	12.00	25.00
1962 Proof	—	Value: 85.00				

KM# 3   25 FRANCS
Aluminum-Bronze   **Obv:** Head of Ahmed Sekou Toure right
Rev: Palm trees flank denomination

Date	Mintage	F	VF	XF	Unc	BU
1959	—	10.00	50.00	110	200	—

KM# 7   25 FRANCS
Copper-Nickel   **Obv:** Head of Ahmed Sekou Toure right
Rev: Denomination within wreath

Date	Mintage	F	VF	XF	Unc	BU
1962	—	2.50	4.00	7.50	15.00	30.00
1962 Proof	—	Value: 120				

KM# 8   50 FRANCS
Copper-Nickel   **Obv:** Head of Ahmed Sekou Toure left **Rev:**
Denomination within wreath **Note:** Not released into circulation.

Date	Mintage	F	VF	XF	Unc	BU
1969	4,000	—	—	35.00	55.00	85.00

KM# 9   100 FRANCS
5.6500 g., 0.9990 Silver 0.1815 oz. ASW   **Series:** 10th Anniversary
of Independence **Subject:** Martin Luther King **Obv:** Head right
Rev: National arms and "1000" in an oval c/m at 4 oclock

Date	Mintage	F	VF	XF	Unc	BU
1969 Proof	9,700	Value: 10.00				
1970	Inc. above	—	—	—	—	—

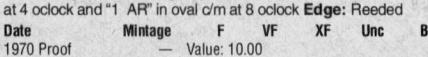

KM# 9.1   100 FRANCS
5.6500 g., 0.9990 Silver 0.1815 oz. ASW, 21 mm.   **Subject:** Martin
Luther King **Obv:** Head right **Rev:** National arms "1000" in oval c/m
at 4 oclock and "1 AR" in oval c/m at 8 oclock **Edge:** Reeded

Date	Mintage	F	VF	XF	Unc	BU
1970 Proof	—	Value: 10.00				

KM# 9.2   100 FRANCS
5.6500 g., 0.9990 Silver 0.1815 oz. ASW, 21 mm.
Subject: Martin Luther King **Obv:** Head right **Rev:** National arms
and "999.9" in oval c/m at 4 oclock **Edge:** Reeded

Date	Mintage	F	VF	XF	Unc	BU
1970 Proof	—	Value: 10.00				

KM# 41   100 FRANCS
Copper-Nickel   **Obv:** Head of Ahmed Sekou Toure right **Rev:**
Denomination within wreath **Note:** Not released into circulation.

Date	Mintage	F	VF	XF	Unc	BU
1971	2,585,000	—	—	22.50	45.00	75.00

KM# 10   200 FRANCS
11.7000 g., 0.9990 Silver 0.3758 oz. ASW   **Series:** 10th
Anniversary of Independence **Subject:** John and Robert
Kennedy **Obv:** Conjoined heads right **Rev:** National arms

Date	Mintage	F	VF	XF	Unc	BU
1969 Proof	10,000	Value: 20.00				
1970 Proof	Inc. above	Value: 20.00				

KM# 11   200 FRANCS
11.7000 g., 0.9990 Silver 0.3758 oz. ASW   **Series:** 10th
Anniversary of Independence **Subject:** Almamy Samory Toure
Obv: Bust facing divides dates **Rev:** National arms

Date	Mintage	F	VF	XF	Unc	BU
1969 Proof	6,100	Value: 25.00				
1970 Proof	Inc. above	Value: 25.00				

KM# 12   250 FRANCS
14.5300 g., 0.9990 Silver 0.4667 oz. ASW **Series:** 10th Anniversary
of Independence **Subject:** Lunar Landing **Obv:** Planets bound
together, astronaut and space shuttle **Rev:** National arms

Date	Mintage	F	VF	XF	Unc	BU
1969 Proof	26,000	Value: 22.00				
1970 Proof	Inc. above	Value: 22.00				

KM# 13   250 FRANCS
14.5300 g., 0.9990 Silver 0.4667 oz. ASW **Series:** 10th
Anniversary of Independence **Subject:** Alpha Yaya Diallo
Obv: Bust with spear facing **Rev:** National arms

Date	Mintage	F	VF	XF	Unc	BU
1969 Proof	6,100	Value: 32.50				
1970 Proof	Inc. above	Value: 32.50				

KM# 14   250 FRANCS
14.5300 g., 0.9990 Silver 0.4667 oz. ASW   **Series:** 10th
Anniversary of Independence **Subject:** Apollo XIII **Obv:** Radiant
planet back of three charging horses **Rev:** National arms

Date	Mintage	F	VF	XF	Unc	BU
1969 Proof	4,450	Value: 32.00				
1970 Proof	Inc. above	Value: 32.00				

KM# 21   250 FRANCS
14.5300 g., 0.9990 Silver 0.4667 oz. ASW   **Series:** 10th
Anniversary of Independence **Subject:** Spacecraft Soyuz
Obv: Spacecraft in flight **Rev:** National arms

Date	Mintage	F	VF	XF	Unc	BU
1970 Proof	3,500	Value: 35.00				

KM# 15   500 FRANCS
29.0800 g., 0.9990 Silver 0.9340 oz. ASW   **Series:** 10th
Anniversary of Independence **Subject:** Munich Olympics
Obv: Medals of the Olympics in Helsinki 1952; Melbourne 1956;
Rome 1968; Tokyo 1964; Mexico City 1968 **Rev:** National arms

Date	Mintage	F	VF	XF	Unc	BU
1969 Proof	7,200	Value: 35.00				
1970 Proof	1,900	Value: 45.00				

KM# 16   500 FRANCS
29.0800 g., 0.9990 Silver 0.9340 oz. ASW **Series:** 10th
Anniversary of Independence **Subject:** Oiseaux Dancers
Obv: Dancers and hut **Rev:** National arms

Date	Mintage	F	VF	XF	Unc	BU
1969 Proof	7,150	Value: 37.50				
1970 Proof	—	Value: 47.50				

KM# 22   500 FRANCS
29.0800 g., 0.9990 Silver 0.9340 oz. ASW **Series:** 10th
Anniversary of Independence **Subject:** Ikhnaton **Obv:** Head 3/4
facing **Rev:** National arms

Date	Mintage	F	VF	XF	Unc	BU
1970 Proof	4,180	Value: 32.50				

KM# 23   500 FRANCS
29.0800 g., 0.9990 Silver 0.9340 oz. ASW **Series:** 10th
Anniversary of Independence **Subject:** Chephren **Obv:** Head
with parrot right **Rev:** National arms

Date	Mintage	F	VF	XF	Unc	BU
1970 Proof	4,600	Value: 32.50				

KM# 24   500 FRANCS
29.0800 g., 0.9990 Silver 0.9340 oz. ASW **Series:** 10th
Anniversary of Independence **Subject:** Cleopatra **Obv:** Head left
Rev: National arms

Date	Mintage	F	VF	XF	Unc	BU
1970 Proof	5,250	Value: 35.00				

KM# 25   500 FRANCS
29.0800 g., 0.9990 Silver 0.9340 oz. ASW **Series:** 10th
Anniversary of Independence **Subject:** Nefertiti, 1372-1350BC
Obv: Head left **Rev:** National arms

Date	Mintage	F	VF	XF	Unc	BU
1970 Proof	4,610	Value: 35.00				

KM# 26   500 FRANCS
29.0800 g., 0.9990 Silver 0.9340 oz. ASW **Series:** 10th
Anniversary of Independence **Subject:** Ramses III **Obv:** Head
right **Rev:** National arms

Date	Mintage	F	VF	XF	Unc	BU
1970 Proof	4,330	Value: 35.00				

KM# 27   500 FRANCS
29.0800 g., 0.9990 Silver 0.9340 oz. ASW **Series:** 10th
Anniversary of Independence **Subject:** Tutankhamen **Obv:** Bust
facing **Rev:** National arms

Date	Mintage	F	VF	XF	Unc	BU
1970 Proof	4,280	Value: 40.00				

KM# 28   500 FRANCS
29.0800 g., 0.9990 Silver 0.9340 oz. ASW **Series:** 10th
Anniversary of Independence **Subject:** Queen Teyi, mother of
Pharoah Amenophis IV (Ichnation), reigned 1352-1336BC
Obv: Head right **Rev:** National arms

Date	Mintage	F	VF	XF	Unc	BU
1970 Proof	4,120	Value: 32.50				

KM# 29   500 FRANCS
29.0800 g., 0.9990 Silver 0.9340 oz. ASW **Series:** 10th
Anniversary of Independence **Subject:** Gamal Abdel Nasser
Obv: Head right **Rev:** National arms

Date	Mintage	F	VF	XF	Unc	BU
1970 Proof	950	Value: 125				

KM# 17   1000 FRANCS
4.0000 g., 0.9000 Gold 0.1157 oz. AGW **Series:** 10th
Anniversary of Independence **Subject:** John and Robert
Kennedy **Obv:** Jugate heads right **Rev:** National arms

Date	Mintage	F	VF	XF	Unc	BU
1969 Proof	6,600	Value: 125				
1970 Proof	Inc. above	Value: 125				

KM# 18   2000 FRANCS
8.0000 g., 0.9000 Gold 0.2315 oz. AGW **Series:** 10th Anniversary
of Independence **Subject:** Lunar Landing **Obv:** Planets bound
together, space shuttle and astronaut **Rev:** National arms

Date	Mintage	F	VF	XF	Unc	BU
1969 Proof	15,000	Value: 245				

KM# 30   2000 FRANCS
8.0000 g., 0.9000 Gold 0.2315 oz. AGW **Series:** 10th
Anniversary of Independence **Subject:** Apollo XIII **Obv:** Radiant
planet back of three charging horses **Rev:** National arms

Date	Mintage	F	VF	XF	Unc	BU
1970 Proof	1,775	Value: 245				

KM# 31   2000 FRANCS
8.0000 g., 0.9000 Gold 0.2315 oz. AGW **Series:** 10th
Anniversary of Independence **Subject:** Spacecraft Soyuz
Obv: Spacecraft in flight **Rev:** National arms

Date	Mintage	F	VF	XF	Unc	BU
1970 Proof	2,840	Value: 245				

KM# 32   5000 FRANCS
20.0000 g., 0.9000 Gold 0.5787 oz. AGW **Series:** 10th
Anniversary of Independence **Subject:** Munich Olympics
Obv: Medals of the Olympics in Helsinki 1952; Melbourne 1956;
Rome 1968; Tokyo 1964; Mexico City 1968 **Rev:** National arms

Date	Mintage	F	VF	XF	Unc	BU
1969 Proof	2,740	Value: 575				
1970 Proof	500	Value: 575				

KM# 19   5000 FRANCS
20.0000 g., 0.9000 Gold 0.5787 oz. AGW **Series:** 10th
Anniversary of Independence **Subject:** Gamel Abdel Nasser
Obv: Head right **Rev:** National arms

Date	Mintage	F	VF	XF	Unc	BU
1970 Proof	4,000	Value: 575				

KM# 33   5000 FRANCS

20.0000 g., 0.9000 Gold 0.5787 oz. AGW **Series:** 10th Anniversary of Independence **Subject:** Ikhnaton **Obv:** Head 3/4 facing **Rev:** National arms

Date	Mintage	F	VF	XF	Unc	BU
1970 Proof	685	Value: 575				

KM# 34   5000 FRANCS

20.0000 g., 0.9000 Gold 0.5787 oz. AGW **Series:** 10th Anniversary of Independence **Subject:** Chephren **Obv:** Head with parrot right **Rev:** National arms

Date	Mintage	F	VF	XF	Unc	BU
1970 Proof	675	Value: 575				

KM# 35   5000 FRANCS

20.0000 g., 0.9000 Gold 0.5787 oz. AGW **Series:** 10th Anniversary of Independence **Subject:** Cleopatra **Obv:** Head left **Rev:** National arms

Date	Mintage	F	VF	XF	Unc	BU
1970 Proof	789	Value: 575				

KM# 36   5000 FRANCS

20.0000 g., 0.9000 Gold 0.5787 oz. AGW **Series:** 10th Anniversary of Independence **Subject:** Queen Nefertiti, 1372-1350BC **Obv:** Head left **Rev:** National arms

Date	Mintage	F	VF	XF	Unc	BU
1970 Proof	774	Value: 575				

KM# 37   5000 FRANCS

20.0000 g., 0.9000 Gold 0.5787 oz. AGW **Series:** 10th Anniversary of Independence **Subject:** Ramses III **Obv:** Head right **Rev:** National arms

Date	Mintage	F	VF	XF	Unc	BU
1970 Proof	695	Value: 575				

KM# 38   5000 FRANCS

20.0000 g., 0.9000 Gold 0.5787 oz. AGW **Series:** 10th Anniversary of Independence **Subject:** Tutankhamen **Obv:** Bust facing **Rev:** National arms

Date	Mintage	F	VF	XF	Unc	BU
1970 Proof	675	Value: 575				

KM# 39   5000 FRANCS

20.0000 g., 0.9000 Gold 0.5787 oz. AGW **Series:** 10th Anniversary of Independence **Subject:** Queen Teyi, mother of Pharoah Amenophis IV (Ichnaton), reigned 1352-1336BC **Obv:** Head right **Rev:** National arms

Date	Mintage	F	VF	XF	Unc	BU
1970 Proof	685	Value: 575				

KM# 20   10000 FRANCS

40.0000 g., 0.9000 Gold 1.1574 oz. AGW **Series:** 10th Anniversary of Independence **Subject:** Ahmed Sekou Toure **Obv:** Head left **Rev:** National arms

Date	Mintage	F	VF	XF	Unc	BU
1969 Proof	2,300	Value: 1,150				
1970 Proof	—	Value: 1,150				

DECIMAL COINAGE
100 Cauris = 1 Syli

KM# 42   50 CAURIS

Aluminum **Obv:** Cowrie shell **Rev:** Denomination within wreath
Note: Nkrumah

Date	Mintage	F	VF	XF	Unc	BU
1971	—	1.00	2.00	3.50	6.00	—

KM# 43   SYLI

Aluminum **Obv:** Bust facing **Rev:** Denomination within wreath

Date	Mintage	F	VF	XF	Unc	BU
1971	—	2.00	3.00	5.50	12.50	—

KM# 44   2 SYLIS

Aluminum **Obv:** Head left **Rev:** Denomination within wreath

Date	Mintage	F	VF	XF	Unc	BU
1971	—	1.00	2.00	5.00	10.00	

KM# 45   5 SYLIS

2.2700 g., Aluminum **Obv:** Head left **Rev:** Denomination within wreath

Date	Mintage	F	VF	XF	Unc	BU
1971	—	1.25	2.25	5.50	11.50	

KM# 46   500 SYLI

40.0000 g., 0.9250 Silver 1.1895 oz. ASW **Subject:** Miriam Makeba, South African singer in exile **Obv:** Bust right divides people at lower right and left **Rev:** National arms

Date	Mintage	F	VF	XF	Unc	BU
1977	500	—	—	—	175	—
1977 Proof	500	Value: 210				

KM# 47   500 SYLI

40.0000 g., 0.9250 Silver 1.1895 oz. ASW **Subject:** Patrice Lumumba **Obv:** Bust facing **Rev:** National arms

Date	Mintage	F	VF	XF	Unc	BU
1977	250	—	—	—	180	—
1977 Proof	150	Value: 275				

KM# 48   1000 SYLI

2.9300 g., 0.9000 Gold 0.0848 oz. AGW **Subject:** Miriam Makeba, South African singer in exile **Obv:** Bust right divides people at lower right and left **Rev:** National arms

Date	Mintage	F	VF	XF	Unc	BU
1977	300	—	—	—	—	100
1977 Proof	250	Value: 125				

KM# 49   1000 SYLI

2.9300 g., 0.9000 Gold 0.0848 oz. AGW **Subject:** Nkrumah **Obv:** Bust right **Rev:** National arms

Date	Mintage	F	VF	XF	Unc	BU
1977	150	—	—	—	—	125
1977 Proof	150	Value: 135				

KM# 50   2000 SYLI

5.8700 g., 0.9000 Gold 0.1698 oz. AGW **Subject:** Mao Tse Tung **Obv:** Bust facing **Rev:** National arms

Date	Mintage	F	VF	XF	Unc	BU
1977 Proof	200	Value: 250				
1977	200	—	—	—	—	225

KM# 51   2000 SYLI

5.8700 g., 0.9000 Gold 0.1698 oz. AGW **Subject:** Ahmen Sekou Toure **Obv:** Bust left **Rev:** National arms

Date	Mintage	F	VF	XF	Unc	BU
1977	100	—	—	—	—	250
1977 Proof	50	Value: 325				

REFORM COINAGE

KM# 56   FRANC

1.4400 g., Brass Clad Steel, 15.50 mm. **Obv:** Shield with rifle and sword crossed on branch held by bird above **Rev:** Palm branch right of denomination **Edge:** Plain

Date	Mintage	F	VF	XF	Unc	BU
1985	—	0.10	0.20	0.40	1.00	—

KM# 53   5 FRANCS

2.0000 g., Brass Clad Steel, 17.5 mm. **Obv:** Shield with rifle and sword crossed on branch held by bird above **Rev:** Palm branch right of denomination

Date	Mintage	F	VF	XF	Unc	BU
1985	—	0.10	0.20	0.40	1.00	—

KM# 52   10 FRANCS

2.9500 g., Brass Clad Steel, 20.4 mm. **Obv:** Shield with rifle and sword crossed on branch held by bird above **Rev:** Palm branch right of denomination

Date	Mintage	F	VF	XF	Unc	BU
1985	—	0.20	0.40	0.80	1.25	—

KM# 60   25 FRANCS
4.9500 g., Brass, 22.5 mm. **Obv:** Shield with rifle and sword crossed on branch held by bird above **Rev:** Palm branch right of denomination

Date	Mintage	F	VF	XF	Unc	BU
1987	—	0.20	0.40	0.85	1.75	—

KM# 63   50 FRANCS
Copper-Nickel **Obv:** Without sword and rifle **Rev:** Leaves right of denomination

Date	Mintage	F	VF	XF	Unc	BU
1994	—	0.30	0.60	1.25	2.75	—

KM# 57   100 FRANCS
16.0000 g., 0.9990 Silver 0.5139 oz. ASW **Subject:** 1992 Olympics **Obv:** Shield with rifle and sword crossed on branch held by bird above **Rev:** Discus thrower, lady with parasol and shield at left

Date	Mintage	F	VF	XF	Unc	BU
1988 Matte	Est. 5,000	—	—	—	75.00	—

KM# 58   200 FRANCS
16.0000 g., 0.9990 Silver 0.5139 oz. ASW **Subject:** 1992 Olympics **Obv:** Shield with rifle and sword crossed on branch held by bird above **Rev:** Basketball players, lady with parasol and shield at left

Date	Mintage	F	VF	XF	Unc	BU
1988 Matte	Est. 5,000	—	—	—	85.00	—

KM# 59   300 FRANCS
16.0000 g., 0.9990 Silver 0.5139 oz. ASW **Subject:** 1992 Olympics **Obv:** Shield with rifle and sword crossed on branch held by bird above **Rev:** Stadium, lady with parasol and shield above

Date	Mintage	F	VF	XF	Unc	BU
1988	Est. 5,000	—	—	—	95.00	—

KM# 61   10000 FRANCS
25.0000 g., 0.9990 Silver 0.8029 oz. ASW **Subject:** 30th Anniversary of Currency **Obv:** Shield with rifle and sword crossed on branch held by bird above **Rev:** Palm branch and denomination

Date	Mintage	F	VF	XF	Unc	BU
ND(1990) Proof	1,000	Value: 75.00				

KM# 62   10000 FRANCS
15.9760 g., 0.9170 Gold 0.4710 oz. AGW **Subject:** 30th Anniversary of Currency **Obv:** Arms with dates on each side **Rev:** Palm branches and denomination

Date	Mintage	F	VF	XF	Unc	BU
1990 Proof	Est. 200	Value: 500				

KM# 64   20000 FRANCS
31.4700 g., 0.9250 Silver 0.9359 oz. ASW **Subject:** 35th Anniversary of Guinea Franc **Obv:** Without sword and rifle **Rev:** Woman planting palm tree

Date	Mintage	F	VF	XF	Unc	BU
ND(1995) Proof	Est. 5,000	Value: 40.00				

TRIAL STRIKES

KM#	Date	Mintage	Identification	Mkt Val
TS1	ND(1969)	—	100 Francs. KM#9.	45.00
TS2	ND(1969)	—	200 Francs. KM#11.	45.00
TS3	ND(1969)	—	250 Francs. KM#13.	50.00
TS4	ND(1969)	—	500 Francs. KM#16.	60.00
TS5	ND(1969)	—	1000 Francs. Goldine. Jugate heads right.	100

MINT SETS

KM#	Date	Mintage	Identification	Issue Price	Mkt Val
MS1	1977 (6)	—	KM46-51	—	830
MS2	1988 (3)	5,000	KM57-59	150	250

PROOF SETS

KM#	Date	Mintage	Identification	Issue Price	Mkt Val
PS1	1969 (7)	5,000	KM#9-13, 15-16	62.50	145
PS2	1969 (8)	—	KM9, 11, 13, 16-18, 20, 32	—	1,825
PS3	1969 (4)	—	KM#17-20	—	1,310
PS4	1969 (4)	4,000	KM#17, 18, 20, 32	223	1,235
PS5	1969-70 (17)	—	KM#9-21, 29-32	1,326	2,192
PS6	1969-70 (6)	—	KM#12, 14, 18, 21, 30-31	318	530
PS7	1970 (3)	900	KM12, 14, 21	30.00	60.00
PS8	1970 (7)	300	KM#9-13, 15-16	62.50	165
PS9	1970 (7)	750	KM#22-28	201	245
PS10	1970 (7)	—	KM#33-39	440	3,325
PS11	1970 (10)	—	KM#9-16, 21, 29	220	292
PS12	1970 (14)	—	KM#22-28, 33-39	1,650	3,570

GUINEA-BISSAU

The Republic of Guinea-Bissau, formerly Portuguese Guinea, an overseas province on the west coast of Africa between Senegal and Guinea, has an area of 13,948 sq. mi. (36,120 sq. km.) and a population of 1.1 million. Capital: Bissau. The country has undeveloped deposits of oil and bauxite. Peanuts, oil-palm kernels and hides are exported.

Portuguese Guinea was discovered by Portuguese navigator, Nuno Tristao, in 1446. Trading rights in the area were granted to Cape Verde islanders but few prominent posts were established before 1851, and they were principally coastal installations. The chief export of this colony's early period was slaves for South America, a practice that adversely affected trade with the native people and retarded subjection of the interior. Territorial disputes with France delayed final demarcation of the colony's frontiers until 1905.

The African Party for the Independence of Guinea-Bissau was founded in 1956, and several years later began a guerrilla warfare that grew in effectiveness until 1974, when the rebels controlled most of the colony. Portugal's costly overseas wars in her African territories resulted in a military coup in Portugal in April 1974, which appreciably brightened the prospects for freedom for Guinea-Bissau. In August 1974, the Lisbon government signed an agreement granting independence to Portuguese Guinea effective Sept. 10, 1974. The new republic took the name of Guinea-Bissau.

RULER
Portuguese until 1974

PORTUGUESE GUINEA
DECIMAL COINAGE

KM# 1   5 CENTAVOS
Bronze **Obv:** Denomination above date **Rev:** Liberty head left

Date	Mintage	F	VF	XF	Unc	BU
1933	100,000	30.00	60.00	90.00	165	—

KM# 2   10 CENTAVOS
Bronze **Obv:** Denomination above date **Rev:** Liberty head left

Date	Mintage	F	VF	XF	Unc	BU
1933	250,000	28.00	85.00	500	1,000	—

KM# 12   10 CENTAVOS
Aluminum **Obv:** Denomination above date **Rev:** Divided shield with crowned towers and small shields above on lined circle

Date	Mintage	F	VF	XF	Unc	BU
1973	100,000	3.00	6.00	12.00	25.00	30.00

KM# 3   20 CENTAVOS
Bronze **Obv:** Denomination above date **Rev:** Liberty head left

Date	Mintage	F	VF	XF	Unc	BU
1933	350,000	4.00	8.50	35.00	65.00	100

KM# 13   20 CENTAVOS
Bronze **Obv:** Denomination above date **Rev:** Crowned towers and small shields above divided shield on lined circle

Date	Mintage	F	VF	XF	Unc	BU
1973	100,000	3.00	6.00	15.00	30.00	40.00

KM# 4   50 CENTAVOS
Nickel-Bronze **Obv:** Laureate head right **Rev:** Shield on lined circle within wreath

Date	Mintage	F	VF	XF	Unc	BU
1933	600,000	15.00	50.00	200	450	—

KM# 6   50 CENTAVOS
Bronze, 23 mm. **Subject:** 500th Anniversary of Discovery **Obv:** Denomination within circle, dates below **Rev:** Crowned towers above divided shield on lined circle

Date	Mintage	F	VF	XF	Unc	BU
ND(1946)	2,000,000	1.00	3.00	15.00	30.00	40.00

KM# 8   50 CENTAVOS
Bronze **Obv:** Denomination **Rev:** Towers above divided shield on lined circle

Date	Mintage	F	VF	XF	Unc	BU
1952	10,000,000	0.35	0.75	2.00	5.00	8.00

KM# 5   ESCUDO
Nickel-Bronze **Obv:** Laureate head right **Rev:** Shield on lined circle within wreath

Date	Mintage	F	VF	XF	Unc	BU
1933	800,000	7.50	22.50	200	450	—

KM# 7   ESCUDO
Bronze, 27 mm. **Subject:** 500th Anniversary of Discovery **Obv:** Denomination within circle **Rev:** Crowned towers and small shields above divided shield on lined circle

Date	Mintage	F	VF	XF	Unc	BU
ND(1946)	2,000,000	0.75	2.00	6.00	16.00	28.00

KM# 14   ESCUDO
Bronze **Obv:** Denomination **Rev:** Crowned towers and small shields above divided shield on lined circle

Date	Mintage	F	VF	XF	Unc	BU
1973	250,000	6.50	12.50	22.50	40.00	55.00

KM# 9   2-1/2 ESCUDOS
3.4100 g., Copper-Nickel **Obv:** Shield on lined circle at center of cross **Rev:** Crowned towers and small shields above divided shield on lined circle

Date	Mintage	F	VF	XF	Unc	BU
1952	3,010,000	0.50	1.50	3.00	7.00	10.00

KM# 15   5 ESCUDOS
Copper-Nickel **Obv:** Shield on lined circle at center of cross **Rev:** Crowned towers and small shields above divided shield on lined circle

Date	Mintage	F	VF	XF	Unc	BU
1973	800,000	2.50	5.00	10.00	20.00	28.00

KM# 10   10 ESCUDOS
5.0000 g., 0.7200 Silver 0.1157 oz. ASW **Obv:** Shield on lined circle at center of cross **Rev:** Crowned towers and small shields above divided shield on lined circle

Date	Mintage	F	VF	XF	Unc	BU
1952	1,200,000	4.00	18.00	70.00	140	180

KM# 16   10 ESCUDOS
Copper-Nickel **Obv:** Shield on lined circle at center of cross **Rev:** Crowned towers and small shields above divided shield on lined circle

Date	Mintage	F	VF	XF	Unc	BU
1973	1,700,000	3.00	10.00	20.00	40.00	55.00

KM# 11   20 ESCUDOS
10.0000 g., 0.7200 Silver 0.2315 oz. ASW **Obv:** Shield on lined circle at center of cross, date below **Rev:** Crowned towers and small shields above divided shield on lined circle

Date	Mintage	F	VF	XF	Unc	BU
1952	750,000	6.00	15.00	45.00	90.00	—

REPUBLIC
DECIMAL COINAGE

KM# 17   50 CENTAVOS
2.2000 g., Aluminum **Series:** F.A.O. **Obv:** National arms **Rev:** Palm tree left of denomination

Date	Mintage	F	VF	XF	Unc	BU
1977	6,000,000	2.00	3.00	4.50	8.00	10.00

KM# 17a   50 CENTAVOS
6.0000 g., Aluminum-Bronze, 25 mm. **Obv:** National arms **Rev:** Palm tree left of denomination **Note:** Struck on KM#19 planchet.

Date	Mintage	F	VF	XF	Unc	BU
1977	—	—	—	—	—	—

KM# 18   PESO
4.0200 g., Aluminum-Bronze **Series:** F.A.O. **Obv:** National arms **Rev:** Denomination below bouquet

Date	Mintage	F	VF	XF	Unc	BU
1977	7,000,000	2.25	3.50	5.50	9.00	12.00

KM# 19   2-1/2 PESOS
6.0400 g., Aluminum-Bronze **Series:** F.A.O. **Obv:** National arms **Rev:** Tree divides denomination

Date	Mintage	F	VF	XF	Unc	BU
1977	4,000,000	2.25	4.50	6.50	10.00	15.00

KM# 20   5 PESOS
8.0000 g., Copper-Nickel **Series:** F.A.O. **Obv:** National arms **Rev:** Denomination above bouquet

Date	Mintage	F	VF	XF	Unc	BU
1977	6,000,000	2.50	5.00	7.00	11.50	16.00

KM# 21   20 PESOS
12.6500 g., Copper-Nickel **Series:** F.A.O. **Obv:** National arms **Rev:** Plants left of denomination

Date	Mintage	F	VF	XF	Unc	BU
1977	2,500,000	4.00	6.50	11.50	18.00	25.00

KM# 28   2000 PESOS
Nickel Plated Steel **Subject:** Olympics **Obv:** National arms
Rev: Handball player, stylized date in background

Date	Mintage	F	VF	XF	Unc	BU
1991	5,000	—	—	—	17.50	20.00

KM# 38   2000 PESOS
Nickel Plated Steel **Subject:** 50th Anniversary - FAO
Obv: National arms **Rev:** Pineapple harvest

Date	Mintage	F	VF	XF	Unc	BU
ND(1995)	—	—	—	—	17.50	20.00

KM# 27   10000 PESOS
16.0000 g., 0.9990 Silver 0.5139 oz. ASW **Subject:** Nuno
Tristao - Discovery of Guinea-Bissau **Obv:** National arms
Rev: Ships landing

Date	Mintage	F	VF	XF	Unc	BU
1991 Proof	—	Value: 35.00				

KM# 29   10000 PESOS
11.9700 g., 0.9990 Silver 0.3844 oz. ASW **Obv:** National arms
Rev: Soccer player

Date	Mintage	F	VF	XF	Unc	BU
1991	—	—	—	—	30.00	32.00

KM# 30   10000 PESOS
19.6700 g., 0.9990 Silver 0.6317 oz. ASW **Subject:** XXV
Olympics **Obv:** National arms **Rev:** Floor exercise, date below

Date	Mintage	F	VF	XF	Unc	BU
1992 Proof	Est. 10,000	Value: 25.00				

KM# 39   10000 PESOS
20.0000 g., 0.9990 Silver 0.6423 oz. ASW **Subject:** European
Soccer '94

Date	Mintage	F	VF	XF	Unc	BU
1992 Proof	—	Value: 27.50				

KM# 31   10000 PESOS
15.0000 g., 0.9990 Silver 0.4818 oz. ASW **Obv:** National arms
Rev: Elephant standing on Africa

Date	Mintage	F	VF	XF	Unc	BU
1993 Proof	—	Value: 25.00				

KM# 32   10000 PESOS
15.0000 g., 0.9990 Silver 0.4818 oz. ASW **Subject:** Prehistoric
Life **Obv:** National arms **Rev:** Stegosaurus

Date	Mintage	F	VF	XF	Unc	BU
1993 Proof	—	Value: 35.00				

KM# 35   10000 PESOS
16.1000 g., 0.9990 Silver 0.5171 oz. ASW **Subject:** Prehistoric
Life **Obv:** National arms **Rev:** Vulcanodon

Date	Mintage	F	VF	XF	Unc	BU
1994 Proof	—	Value: 40.00				

KM# 25   20000 PESOS
25.0000 g., 0.9990 Silver 0.8029 oz. ASW **Obv:** Stylized
national arms **Rev:** Bust 3/4 right **Rev. Leg.:** II CONGRESSO
EXTRAORDINARIO

Date	Mintage	F	VF	XF	Unc	BU
ND(1990)	2,000	—	—	—	45.00	—

KM# 26   20000 PESOS
25.0000 g., 0.9990 Silver 0.8029 oz. ASW **Subject:** 10th
Anniversary - L. Cabral Deposed **Obv:** National arms **Rev:** Figure
giving speech, soldiers in background

Date	Mintage	F	VF	XF	Unc	BU
1990 Proof	Est. 2,500	Value: 47.50				

KM# 33   20000 PESOS
20.0000 g., 0.9990 Silver 0.6423 oz. ASW **Subject:** Defense of
Nature **Obv:** National arms **Rev:** Elephant

Date	Mintage	F	VF	XF	Unc	BU
1993 Proof	—	Value: 37.50				

KM# 34   20000 PESOS
20.1000 g., 0.9990 Silver 0.6456 oz. ASW **Obv:** National arms
Rev: Sailing ship - Passat

Date	Mintage	F	VF	XF	Unc	BU
1993	100	—	—	—	—	275
1993 Proof	—	Value: 37.50				

KM# 41   20000 PESOS
25.0000 g., 0.9990 Silver 0.8029 oz. ASW **Subject:** 50 Years -
FAO **Obv:** National arms, value below **Rev:** Woman with basket of
pineapples lower right, FAO emblem at left, 2 farm workers above

Date	Mintage	F	VF	XF	Unc	BU
1995 Proof						

KM# 36   50000 PESOS
31.4700 g., 0.9250 Silver 0.9359 oz. ASW **Obv:** National arms
Rev: Female hippopotamus and calf

Date	Mintage	F	VF	XF	Unc	BU
1996 Proof	Est. 15,000	Value: 60.00				

KM# 37 50000 PESOS
31.4700 g., 0.9250 Silver 0.9359 oz. ASW **Obv:** National arms
Rev: Sailing ship - Alvise Da Cadamosto

Date	Mintage	F	VF	XF	Unc	BU
1996 Proof	Est. 10,000	Value: 50.00				

PATTERNS

KM#	Date	Mintage	Identification	Mkt Val
Pn1	1977	—	2-1/2 Pesos. Aluminum. KM#19.	—

PROVAS
Standard metals; stamped

KM#	Date	Mintage	Identification	Issue Price	Mkt Val
Pr1	1933	—	5 Centavos. Bronze. KM#1.	—	30.00
Pr2	1933	—	10 Centavos. Bronze. KM#2.	—	30.00
Pr3	1933	—	20 Centavos. Bronze. KM#3.	—	30.00
Pr4	1933	—	50 Centavos. Nickel-Bronze. KM#4.	—	40.00
Pr5	1933	—	Escudo. Nickel-Bronze. KM#5.	—	45.00
Pr6	1946	—	50 Centavos. Bronze. KM#6.	—	15.00
Pr7	1946	—	Escudo. Bronze. KM#7.	—	15.00
Pr8	1952	—	50 Centavos. Bronze. KM#8.	—	15.00
Pr9	1952	—	2-1/2 Escudos. Copper-Nickel. KM#9.	—	20.00
Pr10	1952	—	10 Escudos. Silver center. KM#10.	—	45.00
Pr11	1952	—	20 Escudos. Silver. KM#11.	—	50.00
Pr12	1973	—	Escudo. Bronze. KM#14.	—	20.00
Pr13	1973	—	10 Escudos. Copper-Nickel. KM#16.	—	25.00

GUYANA

The Cooperative Republic of Guyana, is situated on the northeast coast of South America, has an area of 83,000 sq. mi. (214,970 sq. km.) and a population of 729,000. Capital: Georgetown. The economy is basically agrarian. Sugar, rice and bauxite are exported.

The original area of Essequibo and Demerary, which included present-day Suriname, French Guiana, and parts of Brazil and Venezuela was sighted by Columbus in 1498. The first European settlement was made late in the 16th century by the Dutch, however, the region was claimed for the British by Sir Walter Raleigh during the reign of Elizabeth I. For the next 150 years, possession alternated between the Dutch and the British, with a short interval of French control. The British exercised de facto control after 1796 over the Dutch colonies of Essequibo, Demerary and Berbice. They were not ceded to them by the Dutch until 1814. From 1803 to 1831, Essequibo and Demerary were administered separately from Berbice. The three colonies were united in the British Crown Colony of British Guiana in 1831. British Guiana won internal self-government in 1952 and full independence, under the traditional name of Guyana, on May 26,1966. Guyana became a republic on Feb. 23, 1970. It is a member of the Commonwealth of Nations. The president is the Chief of State. The prime minister is the Head of Government. Guyana is a member of the Caribbean Community and Common Market (CARICOM).

RULER
British, until 1966

*NOTE: From 1975-1985 the Franklin Mint produced coinage in up to 3 different qualities. Qualities of issue are designated in ( ) after each date and are defined as follows:

(**M**) **MATTE** - Normal circulation strike or a dull finish produced by sandblasting special uncirculated (polish finish) or proof quality dies.

(**U**) **SPECIAL UNCIRCULATED** - Polished or proof-like in appearance without any frosted features.

(**P**) **PROOF** - The highest quality obtainable having mirror-like fields and frosted features.

BRITISH GUIANA AND WEST INDIES
STERLING COINAGE

KM# 26 4 PENCE
1.8851 g., 0.9250 Silver 0.0561 oz. ASW **Obv:** Head left
Rev: Crowned denomination within wreath

Date	Mintage	F	VF	XF	Unc	BU
1901	60,000	5.00	10.00	22.50	55.00	70.00

KM# 27 4 PENCE
1.8851 g., 0.9250 Silver 0.0561 oz. ASW **Obv:** Crowned bust right **Rev:** Crowned denomination within wreath

Date	Mintage	F	VF	XF	Unc	BU
1903	60,000	5.00	10.00	22.50	55.00	70.00
1903 Matte proof	—	Value: 450				
1908	30,000	5.00	12.50	40.00	90.00	100
1909	36,000	5.00	12.50	40.00	90.00	100
1910	66,000	5.00	10.00	40.00	85.00	100

KM# 28 4 PENCE
1.8851 g., 0.9250 Silver 0.0561 oz. ASW **Obv:** Crowned bust left **Rev:** Crowned denomination within wreath

Date	Mintage	F	VF	XF	Unc	BU
1911	30,000	8.00	25.00	70.00	115	130
1913	30,000	8.00	25.00	70.00	115	130
1916	30,000	8.00	25.00	70.00	115	130

BRITISH GUIANA
STERLING COINAGE

KM# 29 4 PENCE
1.8851 g., 0.9250 Silver 0.0561 oz. ASW **Obv:** Crowned bust left **Rev:** Crowned denomination within wreath

Date	Mintage	F	VF	XF	Unc	BU
1917	72,000	5.00	12.50	40.00	90.00	100
1917 Matte proof	—	Value: 450				
1918	210,000	1.25	3.50	15.00	55.00	65.00
1921	90,000	5.00	10.00	27.50	70.00	85.00
1923	12,000	20.00	45.00	85.00	160	180
1925	30,000	8.00	20.00	50.00	100	125
1926	30,000	8.00	20.00	50.00	100	125
1931	15,000	10.00	25.00	60.00	120	140
1931 Proof	—	Value: 175				
1935	36,000	3.00	12.50	50.00	175	200
1935 Proof	—	Value: 175				
1936	63,000	1.75	2.50	10.00	30.00	45.00
1936 Proof	—	Value: 225				

KM# 30 4 PENCE
1.8851 g., 0.9250 Silver 0.0561 oz. ASW **Obv:** Crowned head left **Rev:** Crowned denomination within wreath

Date	Mintage	F	VF	XF	Unc	BU
1938	30,000	8.00	20.00	50.00	100	125
1938 Proof	—	Value: 175				
1939	48,000	1.75	2.50	7.50	20.00	30.00
1939 Proof	—	Value: 175				
1940	90,000	1.25	2.00	6.50	18.50	25.00
1940 Proof	—	Value: 175				
1941	120,000	1.25	1.75	3.00	12.50	17.50
1941 Proof	—	Value: 175				
1942	180,000	1.25	1.75	3.00	12.50	17.50
1942 Proof	—	Value: 175				
1943	240,000	1.25	1.75	2.50	8.00	12.00
1943 Proof	—	Value: 400				

KM# 30a 4 PENCE
1.8851 g., 0.5000 Silver 0.0303 oz. ASW **Obv:** Head left
Rev: Crowned denomination within wreath

Date	Mintage	F	VF	XF	Unc	BU
1944	90,000	1.25	2.00	6.50	18.50	25.00
1945	120,000	1.85	1.75	3.00	12.50	17.50
1945 Proof	—	Value: 200				

REPUBLIC
DECIMAL COINAGE

KM# 31 CENT
1.5300 g., Nickel-Brass, 15.99 mm. **Obv:** Denomination within circle **Rev:** Stylized lotus flower **Edge:** Plain

Date	Mintage	F	VF	XF	Unc	BU
1967	6,000,000	—	—	0.10	0.25	0.35
1967 Proof	5,100	Value: 2.00				
1969	4,000,000	—	—	0.10	0.25	0.35
1970	6,000,000	—	—	0.10	0.25	0.35
1971	4,000,000	—	—	0.10	0.25	0.35
1972	4,000,000	—	—	0.10	0.25	0.35
1973	4,000,000	—	—	0.10	0.25	0.35
1974	11,000,000	—	—	0.10	0.20	0.30
1975	—	—	—	0.10	0.25	0.35
1976	—	—	—	0.10	0.25	0.35
1977	16,000,000	—	—	0.10	0.20	0.30
1978	10,450,000	—	—	0.10	0.20	0.30
1979	—	—	—	0.10	0.20	0.30
1980	12,000,000	—	—	0.10	0.20	0.30
1981	10,000,000	—	—	0.10	0.20	0.30
1982	8,000,000	—	—	0.10	0.20	0.30
1983	12,000,000	—	—	0.10	0.20	0.30
1985	8,000,000	—	—	0.10	0.20	0.30
1987	6,000,000	—	—	0.10	0.20	0.30
1988	80,000	—	—	0.15	0.50	0.75
1989	—	—	—	0.10	0.20	0.30
1991	—	—	—	0.10	0.20	0.30
1992	—	—	—	0.10	0.20	0.30

KM# 37 CENT
Nickel-Brass, 16 mm. **Subject:** 10th Anniversary of Independence **Obv:** Helmeted and supported arms **Rev:** Manatee

Date	Mintage	F	VF	XF	Unc	BU
1976FM (M)	15,000	—	—	0.15	1.00	4.00
1976FM (U)	50	—	—	—	—	—
1976FM (P)	28,000	Value: 3.00				
1977FM (M)	—	—	—	1.50	3.00	4.50
1977FM (U)	15,000	—	—	0.20	1.00	3.00
1977FM (P)	7,215	Value: 3.00				
1978FM (M)	—	—	—	1.50	3.00	4.50
1978FM (U)	15,000	—	—	0.20	1.00	3.00
1978FM (P)	5,044	Value: 3.00				
1979FM (U)	15,000	—	—	0.20	1.00	3.00
1979FM (P)	3,547	Value: 3.00				
1980FM (U)	30,000	—	—	0.20	1.00	3.00
1980FM (P)	2,763	Value: 3.00				

KM# 32 5 CENTS
Nickel-Brass, 19.5 mm. **Obv:** Denomination within circle
Rev: Stylized lotus flower **Note:** Varieties exist.

Date	Mintage	F	VF	XF	Unc	BU
1967	4,600,000	—	—	0.10	0.30	0.40
1967 Proof	5,100	Value: 2.00				
1972	1,200,000	—	—	0.10	0.35	0.45
1974	3,000,000	—	—	0.10	0.35	0.45
1975	—	—	—	0.10	0.35	0.45
1976	—	—	—	0.10	0.35	0.45
1977	1,500,000	—	—	0.10	0.35	0.45
1978	2,000	—	—	1.25	4.00	6.00
1979	—	—	—	0.30	1.00	1.50
1980	1,000,000	—	—	0.10	0.35	0.45
1981	1,000,000	—	—	0.10	0.35	0.45

Date	Mintage	F	VF	XF	Unc	BU
1982	2,000,000	—	—	0.10	0.30	0.40
1985	3,000,000	—	—	0.10	0.30	0.40
1986	4,000,000	—	—	0.10	0.30	0.40
1987	3,000,000	—	—	0.10	0.30	0.40
1988	2,000,000	—	—	0.10	0.30	0.40
1989	—	—	—	0.10	0.30	0.40
1990	—	—	—	0.10	0.30	0.40
1991	—	—	—	0.10	0.30	0.40
1992	—	—	—	0.10	0.30	0.40

KM# 38 5 CENTS
Nickel-Brass, 19.5 mm. **Subject:** 10th Anniversary of Independence **Obv:** Helmeted and supported arms **Rev:** Jaguar (panthera onca)

Date	Mintage	F	VF	XF	Unc	BU
1976FM (M)	15,000	—	—	0.20	1.75	5.00
1976FM (U)	50	—	—	—	—	—
1976FM (P)	28,000	Value: 2.00				
1977FM (M)	—	—	—	1.50	3.00	5.00
1977FM (U)	15,000	—	—	0.20	1.75	5.00
1977FM (P)	7,215	Value: 2.00				
1978FM (M)	—	—	—	2.50	5.00	6.50
1978FM (U)	15,000	—	—	0.50	1.75	5.00
1978FM (P)	5,044	Value: 2.00				
1979FM (U)	15,000	—	—	0.50	1.75	5.00
1979FM (P)	3,547	Value: 2.25				
1980FM (U)	30,000	—	—	0.50	1.75	5.00
1980FM (P)	2,763	Value: 2.50				

KM# 33 10 CENTS
2.7500 g., Copper-Nickel, 18 mm. **Obv:** Denomination within circle **Rev:** Helmeted and supported arms **Edge:** Reeded

Date	Mintage	F	VF	XF	Unc	BU
1967	4,000,000	—	0.10	0.20	0.35	0.50
1967 Proof	5,100	Value: 2.50				
1973	1,500,000	—	0.10	0.20	0.40	0.60
1974	1,700,000	—	0.10	0.20	0.40	0.60
1976	—	—	0.10	0.20	0.40	0.60
1977	4,000,000	—	0.10	0.20	0.40	0.60
1978	2,010,000	—	0.10	0.20	0.40	0.60
1979	—	—	0.10	0.20	0.40	0.60
1980	1,000,000	—	0.10	0.20	0.40	0.60
1981	1,000,000	—	0.10	0.20	0.40	0.60
1982	2,000,000	—	0.10	0.20	0.40	0.60
1985	3,000,000	—	0.10	0.20	0.35	0.50
1986	4,000,000	—	0.10	0.20	0.35	0.50
1987	3,000,000	—	0.10	0.20	0.35	0.50
1988	2,000,000	—	0.10	0.20	0.35	0.50
1989	—	—	0.10	0.20	0.35	0.50
1990	—	—	0.10	0.20	0.35	0.50
1991	—	—	0.10	0.20	0.35	0.50
1992	—	—	0.10	0.20	0.35	0.50

KM# 39 10 CENTS
Copper-Nickel, 18 mm. **Subject:** 10th Anniversary of Independence **Obv:** Helmeted and supported arms **Rev:** Squirrel Monkey

Date	Mintage	F	VF	XF	Unc	BU
1976	2,006,000	—	—	0.25	1.50	3.00
1976FM (M)	10,000	—	—	1.00	2.50	5.00
1976FM (U)	50	—	—	—	—	—
1976FM (P)	28,000	Value: 3.00				
1977	1,500,000	—	—	0.25	1.50	3.00
1977FM (M)	—	—	—	4.00	8.00	10.00
1977FM (U)	10,000	—	—	0.25	1.50	3.00
1977FM (P)	7,215	Value: 3.00				
1978FM (M)	—	—	—	4.00	8.00	10.00
1978FM (U)	10,000	—	—	0.25	1.50	3.00
1978FM (P)	5,044	Value: 3.00				
1979FM (U)	10,000	—	—	0.25	1.50	3.00
1979FM (P)	3,547	Value: 3.00				
1980FM (U)	20,000	—	—	0.25	1.50	3.00
1980FM (P)	2,763	Value: 4.00				

KM# 34 25 CENTS
4.2900 g., Copper-Nickel, 20.42 mm. **Obv:** Denomination within circle **Rev:** Helmeted and supported arms **Edge:** Plain

Date	Mintage	F	VF	XF	Unc	BU
1967	3,500,000	—	0.15	0.25	0.60	0.75
1967 Proof	5,100	Value: 2.50				
1972	1,000,000	—	0.15	0.25	0.65	0.85
1974	4,000,000	—	0.15	0.25	0.65	0.85
1975	—	—	0.15	0.25	0.65	0.85
1976	—	—	0.15	0.25	0.65	0.85
1977	4,000,000	—	0.15	0.25	0.65	0.85
1978	2,006,000	—	0.15	0.25	0.65	0.85
1981	1,000,000	—	0.15	0.25	0.65	0.85
1982	1,500,000	—	0.15	0.25	0.65	0.85
1984	1,000,000	—	0.15	0.25	0.65	0.85
1985	2,000,000	—	0.15	0.25	0.60	0.75
1986	4,000,000	—	0.15	0.25	0.60	0.75
1987	3,000,000	—	0.15	0.25	0.60	0.75
1988	4,000,000	—	0.15	0.25	0.60	0.75
1989	—	—	0.15	0.25	0.60	0.75
1990	—	—	0.15	0.25	0.60	0.75
1991	—	—	0.15	0.25	0.60	0.75
1992	—	—	0.15	0.25	0.60	0.75

KM# 40 25 CENTS
Copper-Nickel, 21.5 mm. **Subject:** 10th Anniversary of Independence **Obv:** Helmeted and supported arms **Rev:** Harpy Eagle

Date	Mintage	F	VF	XF	Unc	BU
1976FM (M)	4,000	—	—	0.30	2.50	3.50
1976FM (U)	50	—	—	—	—	—
1976FM (P)	28,000	Value: 3.00				
1977	2,000,000	—	0.15	0.25	2.00	3.50
1977FM (M)	—	—	—	5.00	10.00	12.00
1977FM (U)	4,000	—	—	2.50	4.00	5.00
1977FM (P)	7,215	Value: 3.00				
1978FM (M)	—	—	—	3.00	10.00	12.00
1978FM (U)	4,000	—	—	0.30	4.00	5.00
1978FM (P)	5,044	Value: 3.50				
1979FM (U)	4,000	—	—	1.00	4.00	5.00
1979FM (P)	3,547	Value: 3.50				
1980FM (U)	8,437	—	—	1.00	4.00	5.00
1980FM (P)	2,763	Value: 4.50				

KM# 35 50 CENTS
Copper-Nickel **Obv:** Denomination within circle **Rev:** Helmeted and supported arms

Date	Mintage	F	VF	XF	Unc	BU
1967	1,000,000	—	0.25	0.35	0.75	1.25
1967 Proof	5,100	Value: 3.50				

KM# 41 50 CENTS
Copper-Nickel, 25 mm. **Subject:** 10th Anniversary of Independence **Obv:** Helmeted and supported arms **Rev:** Hoatzin

Date	Mintage	F	VF	XF	Unc	BU
1976FM (M)	2,000	—	—	0.40	5.00	6.00
1976FM (U)	50	—	—	—	—	—
1976FM (P)	28,000	Value: 4.00				
1977FM (M)	—	—	—	—	20.00	22.50
1977FM (U)	2,000	—	—	0.40	5.00	6.00
1977FM (P)	7,215	Value: 4.00				
1978FM (M)	—	—	—	10.00	20.00	22.50

Date	Mintage	F	VF	XF	Unc	BU
1978FM (U)	2,000	—	—	0.40	5.00	6.00
1978FM (P)	5,044	Value: 4.50				
1979FM (U)	2,000	—	—	0.40	5.00	6.00
1979FM (P)	3,547	Value: 4.50				
1980FM (U)	4,437	—	—	0.40	3.50	5.00
1980FM (P)	2,763	Value: 5.50				

KM# 36 DOLLAR
Copper-Nickel, 35.5 mm. **Series:** F.A.O. **Obv:** Bulls head left of denomination **Rev:** Head left **Note:** Cuffy, slave who organized a revolt on 23 Feb. 1763, which was the first step towards independence.

Date	Mintage	F	VF	XF	Unc	BU
1970	500,000	—	0.50	1.75	4.00	5.00
1970 Proof	5,000	Value: 6.00				

KM# 42 DOLLAR
Copper-Nickel, 35.5 mm. **Series:** F.A.O. **Subject:** 10th Anniversary of Independence **Obv:** Helmeted and supported arms **Rev:** Common Caiman

Date	Mintage	F	VF	XF	Unc	BU
1976FM (M)	600	—	—	0.50	6.00	7.00
1976FM (U)	50	—	—	—	—	—
1976FM (P)	28,000	Value: 7.00				
1977FM (M)	—	—	—	12.50	30.00	32.50
1977FM (U)	500	—	—	0.50	6.00	7.00
1977FM (P)	7,215	Value: 7.50				
1978FM (M)	—	—	—	12.50	30.00	32.50
1978FM (U)	500	—	—	0.50	6.00	7.00
1978FM (P)	5,044	Value: 8.00				
1979FM (U)	500	—	—	0.50	6.00	7.00
1979FM (P)	3,547	Value: 8.00				
1980FM (U)	1,437	—	—	0.50	6.00	7.00
1980FM (P)	2,763	Value: 8.50				

KM# 50 DOLLAR
2.4000 g., Copper Plated Steel, 16.96 mm. **Obv:** Helmeted and supported arms **Rev:** Hand gathering rice **Edge:** Reeded

Date	Mintage	F	VF	XF	Unc	BU
1996	—	—	—	—	0.50	0.65

KM# 43 5 DOLLARS
Copper-Nickel **Subject:** 10th Anniversary of Independence **Obv:** Helmeted and supported arms **Rev:** Head at right facing

Date	Mintage	F	VF	XF	Unc	BU
1976FM (M)	400	—	—	7.50	15.00	17.50
1976FM (U)	150	—	—	8.00	17.50	20.00
1977FM (M)	—	—	—	15.00	45.00	50.00

Date	Mintage	F	VF	XF	Unc	BU
1977FM (U)	100	—	—	20.00	25.00	27.50
1978FM (M)	—	—	—	30.00	45.00	50.00
1978FM (U)	100	—	—	12.50	25.00	27.50
1979FM (U)	100	—	—	12.50	25.00	27.50
1980FM (U)	200	—	—	12.50	15.00	17.50

KM# 43a 5 DOLLARS
37.3000 g., 0.5000 Silver 0.5996 oz. ASW **Obv:** Helmeted and supported arms **Rev:** Head at right facing

Date	Mintage	F	VF	XF	Unc	BU
1976FM (P)	18,000	Value: 11.00				
1977FM (P)	5,685	Value: 12.00				
1978FM (P)	3,825	Value: 13.00				
1979FM (P)	2,665	Value: 15.00				
1980FM (P)	2,763	Value: 15.00				

KM# 51 5 DOLLARS
3.7800 g., Copper Plated Steel, 20.5 mm. **Obv:** Helmeted and supported arms **Rev:** Sugar cane **Edge:** Reeded

Date	Mintage	F	VF	XF	Unc	BU
1996	—	—	—	—	0.75	1.00

KM# 44 10 DOLLARS
Copper-Nickel **Subject:** 10th Anniversary of Independence **Obv:** Helmeted and supported arms **Rev:** Head at left looking right

Date	Mintage	F	VF	XF	Unc	BU
1976FM (M)	300	—	—	15.00	30.00	40.00
1976FM (U)	300	—	—	15.00	30.00	40.00
1977FM (M)	—	—	—	40.00	80.00	100
1977FM (U)	100	—	—	25.00	50.00	60.00
1978FM (M)	—	—	—	40.00	80.00	90.00
1978FM (U)	100	—	—	25.00	50.00	60.00
1979FM (U)	100	—	—	25.00	50.00	60.00
1980FM (U)	200	—	—	25.00	40.00	50.00

KM# 44a 10 DOLLARS
43.2300 g., 0.9250 Silver 1.2856 oz. ASW **Subject:** 10th Anniversary of Independence **Obv:** Helmeted and supported arms **Rev:** Head at left looking right

Date	Mintage	F	VF	XF	Unc	BU
1976FM (P)	18,000	Value: 22.50				
1977FM (P)	5,685	Value: 24.00				
1978FM (P)	3,825	Value: 26.00				
1979FM (P)	2,665	Value: 28.00				
1980FM (P)	2,763	Value: 28.00				

KM# 52 10 DOLLARS
5.0000 g., Nickel Plated Steel, 23 mm. **Obv:** Helmeted and supported arms **Rev:** Gold mining scene **Edge:** Reeded

Date	Mintage	F	VF	XF	Unc	BU
1996	—	—	—	—	0.75	1.25	1.50

KM# 45 50 DOLLARS
48.3000 g., 0.9250 Silver 1.4364 oz. ASW **Subject:** 10th Anniversary of Independence **Rev:** Enmoe Martyrs

Date	Mintage	F	VF	XF	Unc	BU
1976FM (U)	100	—	—	50.00	100	120
1976FM (P)	1,001	Value: 70.00				

KM# 48 50 DOLLARS
28.2800 g., 0.9250 Silver 0.8410 oz. ASW **Subject:** Royal Visit **Rev:** Small portraits of royals above people welcoming the royal ship

Date	Mintage	F	VF	XF	Unc	BU
1994 Proof	—	Value: 50.00				

KM# 46 100 DOLLARS
5.7400 g., 0.5000 Gold 0.0923 oz. AGW **Subject:** 10th Anniversary of Independence **Obv:** Helmeted and supported arms **Rev:** Arawak Indian

Date	Mintage	F	VF	XF	Unc	BU
1976FM (U)	100	—	—	50.00	100	120
1976FM (P)	21,000	Value: 95.00				

KM# 47 100 DOLLARS
5.5800 g., 0.5000 Gold 0.0897 oz. AGW **Obv:** Helmeted and supported arms **Rev:** Legendary Golden Man

Date	Mintage	F	VF	XF	Unc	BU
1977FM (U)	100	—	—	50.00	100	120
1977FM (P)	7,635	Value: 95.00				

KM# 49 500 DOLLARS
47.5400 g., 0.9170 Gold 1.4015 oz. AGW **Subject:** Royal Visit **Obv:** Small portraits left of royals above people welcoming the royal ship

Date	Mintage	F	VF	XF	Unc	BU
1994 Proof	100	Value: 1,450				

KM# 53 2000 DOLLARS
28.5000 g., 0.9250 Silver 0.8475 oz. ASW, 38.6 mm. **Subject:** Millennium **Obv:** Helmeted and supported arms **Rev:** World globe and radiant sun within circle **Edge:** Plain

Date	Mintage	F	VF	XF	Unc	BU
ND(1999) Proof	Est. 30,000	Value: 45.00				

KM# 53a 2000 DOLLARS
28.5000 g., Copper-Nickel, 38.6 mm. **Subject:** Millennium **Obv:** National arms **Rev:** World globe and radiant sun **Edge:** Plain

Date	Mintage	F	VF	XF	Unc	BU
ND(1999)	—	—	—	—	15.00	—

PATTERNS
Including off metal strikes

KM#	Date	Mintage Identification	Mkt Val
Pn1	1967	— 5 Cents. Silver. KM#32.	—

MINT SETS

KM#	Date	Mintage Identification	Issue Price	Mkt Val
MS1	1977 (8)	— KM#37-44	—	150
MS2	1978 (8)	— KM#37-44	—	150

PROOF SETS

KM#	Date	Mintage	Identification	Issue Price	Mkt Val
PS1	1967 (5)	5,100	KM#31-35	10.50	9.00
PS2	1976 (8)	17,536	KM#37-42, 43a, 44a	45.00	37.50
PS3	1976 (6)	10,302	KM#37-42	15.00	17.00
PS4	1977 (8)	5,685	KM#37-42, 43a, 44a	45.00	42.00
PS5	1977 (6)	1,530	KM#37-42	15.00	20.00
PS6	1978 (8)	3,825	KM#37-42, 43a, 44a	47.50	47.50
PS7	1978 (6)	1,219	KM#37-42	16.00	20.00
PS8	1979 (8)	2,665	KM#37-42, 43a, 44a	47.50	52.00
PS9	1979 (6)	882	KM#37-42	16.00	20.00
PS10	1980 (8)	1,900	KM#37-42, 43a, 44a	100	58.00
PS11	1980 (6)	863	KM#37-42	19.00	22.50

HAITI

Caribbean Sea

The Republic of Haiti, which occupies the western one-third of the island of Hispaniola in the Caribbean Sea between Puerto Rico and Cuba, has an area of 10,714 sq. mi. (27,750 sq. km.) and a population of 6.5 million. Capital: Port-au-Prince. The economy is based on agriculture; but light manufacturing and tourism are increasingly important. Coffee, bauxite, sugar, essential oils and handicrafts are exported.

Columbus discovered Hispaniola in 1492. Spain colonized the island, making Santo Domingo the base for exploration of the Western Hemisphere. The area that is now Haiti was ceded to France by Spain in 1697. Slaves brought from Africa to work the coffee and sugar cane plantations made it one of the richest colonies of the French Empire. A slave revolt in the 1790's led to the establishment of the Republic of Haiti in 1804, making it the oldest Black republic in the world and the second oldest republic (after the United States) in the Western Hemisphere.

The French language is used on Haitian coins although it is spoken by only about 10% of the populace. A form of Creole is the language of the Haitians.

MINT MARKS
A - Paris
(a) - Paris, privy marks only
HEATON - Birmingham
R - Rome
(w) = Waterbury (Connecticut, USA) (Scoville Mfg. Co.)
(p) – Philadelphia (U.S.A. mint)

MONETARY SYSTEM
100 Centimes = 1 Gourde

REPUBLIC
1863 -
DECIMAL COINAGE

100 Centimes = 1 Gourde

KM# 53 5 CENTIMES
Copper-Nickel **Obv:** President Pierre Nord Alexis left **Rev:** National arms

Date	Mintage	F	VF	XF	Unc	BU
1904(w)	2,000,000	1.00	5.00	15.00	30.00	40.00
1904(w) Proof	—	Value: 90.00				
1905(w)	20,000,000	0.75	3.00	10.00	25.00	30.00
1905(w) Proof	—	Value: 100				

KM# 52 5 CENTIMES
Copper-Nickel **Obv:** National arms **Rev:** Denomination above date **Note:** Struck at the Scovill Mfg. Co., Waterbury, Connecticut; design incorporates Paris privy and mint director's marks.

Date	Mintage	F	VF	XF	Unc	BU
1904(w)	—	3.00	10.00	20.00	55.00	65.00
1904(w) Proof	—	Value: 120				

KM# 57 5 CENTIMES
Copper-Nickel **Obv:** President Dumarsais Estime left
Rev: National arms

Date	Mintage	F	VF	XF	Unc	BU
1949(p)	10,000,000	0.25	0.75	2.00	6.00	7.50

KM# 59 5 CENTIMES
Copper-Zinc-Nickel **Obv:** President Paul Eugene Magloire left

Date	Mintage	F	VF	XF	Unc	BU
1953(p)	3,000,000	0.25	0.35	0.65	1.50	2.00

KM# 62 5 CENTIMES
Copper-Nickel, 20 mm. **Obv:** President Francois Duvalier left
Rev: National arms

Date	Mintage	F	VF	XF	Unc	BU
1958(p)	15,000,000	—	—	0.10	0.25	0.50
1970	5,000,000	—	—	0.10	0.20	0.45

KM# 119 5 CENTIMES
2.7000 g., Copper-Nickel, 20 mm. **Series:** F.A.O.
Obv: President Jean-Claude Duvalier left **Rev:** National arms

Date	Mintage	F	VF	XF	Unc	BU
1975	16,000,000	—	—	0.10	0.20	0.45

KM# 145 5 CENTIMES
Copper-Nickel **Series:** F.A.O. **Obv:** Head right, small logo at
left **Rev:** Woman and child **Note:** Denomination as 0.05 Gourdes.

Date	Mintage	F	VF	XF	Unc	BU
1981R	15,000	—	0.10	0.75	1.00	1.50

KM# 154 5 CENTIMES
3.1000 g., Copper-Nickel-Zinc, 19.9 mm. **Subject:** Charlemagne
Peralte, national hero **Obv:** Bust facing **Rev:** National arms

Date	Mintage	F	VF	XF	Unc	BU
1986	—	—	—	—	0.25	0.40

KM# 154a 5 CENTIMES
Nickel Plated Steel, 19.9 mm. **Subject:** Charlemagne Peralte,
national hero **Obv:** Bust facing **Rev:** National arms

Date	Mintage	F	VF	XF	Unc	BU
1995	—	—	—	—	0.25	0.40
1997	—	—	—	—	0.25	0.40

KM# 54 10 CENTIMES
Copper-Nickel **Obv:** President Pierre Nord Alexis left
Rev: National arms

Date	Mintage	F	VF	XF	Unc	BU
1906(w)	10,000,000	1.00	3.00	7.00	20.00	25.00
1906(w) Proof	—	Value: 100				

KM# 58 10 CENTIMES
3.7800 g., Copper-Nickel, 22.70 mm. **Obv:** President
Dumarsais Estime left **Rev:** National arms

Date	Mintage	F	VF	XF	Unc	BU
1949(p)	5,000,000	0.50	2.00	6.00	15.00	17.50

KM# 60 10 CENTIMES
Copper-Zinc-Nickel **Obv:** President Paul Eugene Magloire left
Rev: National arms

Date	Mintage	F	VF	XF	Unc	BU
1953(p)	1,500,000	—	0.25	1.00	5.00	7.50

KM# 63 10 CENTIMES
Copper-Zinc-Nickel, 22.5 mm. **Obv:** President Francois Duvalier
left **Rev:** National arms

Date	Mintage	F	VF	XF	Unc	BU
1958(p)	7,500,000	—	0.10	0.15	0.35	0.50
1970	2,500,000	—	—	0.10	0.20	0.40

KM# 120 10 CENTIMES
Copper-Nickel, 23 mm. **Series:** F.A.O. **Obv:** President Jean-
Claude Duvalier left **Rev:** National arms

Date	Mintage	F	VF	XF	Unc	BU
1975	12,000,000	—	—	0.10	0.20	0.40
1983	2,000,000	—	—	0.10	0.30	0.50

KM# 146 10 CENTIMES
Copper-Nickel **Series:** F.A.O. **Obv:** Head right, small logo at
left **Rev:** Sun above farmer in field on tractor **Note:** Denomination
as 0.10 Gourdes.

Date	Mintage	F	VF	XF	Unc	BU
1981R	15,000	—	0.10	0.35	1.00	1.25

KM# 55 20 CENTIMES
Copper-Nickel **Obv:** President Pierre Nord Alexis left
Rev: National arms

Date	Mintage	F	VF	XF	Unc	BU
1907(w)	5,000,000	2.00	6.00	15.00	35.00	40.00
1907(w) Proof	—	Value: 125				
1908(w)	—	—	—	—	—	—

Note: Reported, not confirmed

KM# 61 20 CENTIMES
Nickel-Silver **Obv:** President Paul Eugene Magliore left
Rev: National arms

Date	Mintage	F	VF	XF	Unc	BU
1956(p)	2,500,000	0.60	1.00	2.00	5.00	6.50

KM# 77 20 CENTIMES
Nickel-Silver **Obv:** President Francois Duvalier left **Rev:** National
arms

Date	Mintage	F	VF	XF	Unc	BU
1970	1,000,000	—	0.25	0.35	0.85	1.00

KM# 100 20 CENTIMES
Copper-Nickel, 26 mm. **Series:** F.A.O. **Obv:** President Jean-
Claude Duvalier left **Rev:** National arms

Date	Mintage	F	VF	XF	Unc	BU
1972	1,500,000	—	0.10	0.25	1.00	1.25
1975	4,000,000	—	0.10	0.20	0.85	1.00
1983	1,500,000	—	0.10	0.20	0.85	1.00

KM# 147 20 CENTIMES
Copper-Nickel, 26.2 mm. **Series:** F.A.O. **Obv:** Head right, small
logo at left **Rev:** Harvesters **Note:** Denomination as 0.20 Gourdes.

Date	Mintage	F	VF	XF	Unc	BU
1981R	15,000	—	0.10	0.45	1.25	1.40

KM# 152 20 CENTIMES
7.5400 g., Copper-Nickel, 26.15 mm. **Subject:** Charlemagne
Peralte, national hero **Obv:** Bust facing **Rev:** National arms
Edge: Plain **Note:** No accent marks on obverse legend.

Date	Mintage	F	VF	XF	Unc	BU
1986	2,500,000	—	0.10	0.20	0.65	0.95
1989	—	—	0.10	0.20	0.65	0.95
1991	—	—	0.10	0.20	0.65	0.95

KM# 152a   20 CENTIMES
Nickel Plated Steel, 26.2 mm.   **Subject:** Charlemagne Peralte, national hero **Obv:** Bust facing **Rev:** National arms **Note:** Accent marks on E and Is in obverse legend.

Date	Mintage	F	VF	XF	Unc	BU
1995	—	—	—	—	0.75	1.00
2000	—	—	—	—	0.75	1.00

KM# 56   50 CENTIMES
9.7300 g., Copper-Nickel, 29 mm.   **Obv:** President Pierre Nord Alexis left **Rev:** National arms

Date	Mintage	F	VF	XF	Unc	BU
1907(w)	2,000,000	1.00	5.50	15.00	45.00	50.00
1907(w) Proof	—	Value: 250				
1908(w)	800,000	1.25	10.00	30.00	55.00	60.00
1908(w) Proof	—	Value: 300				

KM# 101   50 CENTIMES
Copper-Nickel   **Series:** F.A.O. **Obv:** President Jean-Claude Duvalier left **Rev:** National arms

Date	Mintage	F	VF	XF	Unc	BU
1972	600,000	—	0.10	0.25	1.50	2.00

KM# 101a   50 CENTIMES
Copper-Nickel-Zinc   **Obv:** Head left **Rev:** National arms **Note:** Varieties exist.

Date	Mintage	F	VF	XF	Unc	BU
1975	1,200,000	—	0.10	0.20	1.00	1.50
1979	2,000,000	—	0.10	0.20	1.00	1.50
1983	1,000,000	—	0.10	0.20	1.00	1.50
1985	—	—	—	—	0.75	1.00

KM# 148   50 CENTIMES
Copper-Nickel   **Series:** F.A.O. **Obv:** Head right, small logo at left **Rev:** Plants **Note:** Denomination as 0.50 Gourdes.

Date	Mintage	F	VF	XF	Unc	BU
1981R	15,000	—	0.15	0.65	1.75	2.00

KM# 153   50 CENTIMES
9.8500 g., Copper-Nickel, 28.97 mm.   **Subject:** Charlemagne Peralte, national hero **Obv:** Bust facing **Rev:** National arms **Edge:** Plain **Note:** No accent marks on obverse legend.

Date	Mintage	F	VF	XF	Unc	BU
1986	2,000,000	—	0.10	0.25	1.00	1.50
1989	—	—	0.10	0.25	1.00	1.50
1991	—	—	0.10	0.25	1.00	1.50

KM# 153a   50 CENTIMES
Nickel Plated Steel, 29 mm.   **Subject:** Charlemagne Peralte, national hero **Obv:** Bust facing **Rev:** National arms **Note:** Accent marks on obverse legend.

Date	Mintage	F	VF	XF	Unc	BU
1995	—	—	0.10	0.25	1.25	1.50
1999	—	—	0.10	0.25	1.25	1.50

KM# 155   GOURDE
6.3000 g., Brass Plated Steel, 23 mm.   **Obv:** Citadelle de Roi Christophe

Date	Mintage	F	VF	XF	Unc	BU
1995	—	—	—	—	1.75	2.00
2000	—	—	—	—	1.75	2.00

KM# 64.1   5 GOURDES
23.5200 g., 0.9990 Silver 0.7554 oz. ASW   **Series:** 10th Anniversary of Revolution **Subject:** Columbus Discovers America **Obv:** Three ships and map **Rev:** National arms

Date	Mintage	F	VF	XF	Unc	BU
1967 IC Proof	4,650	Value: 15.00				
1968 IC Proof	5,750	Value: 15.00				
1969 IC Proof	1,175	Value: 20.00				
1970 IC Proof	2,060	Value: 18.00				

KM# 64.2   5 GOURDES
23.5200 g., 0.9990 Silver 0.7554 oz. ASW   **Series:** 10th Anniversary of the Revolution **Subject:** Columbus Discovers America **Obv:** Three ships and map **Rev:** Additional "1 AR" countermark at 8 o'clock

Date	Mintage	F	VF	XF	Unc	BU
1970 Proof	—	Value: 25.00				

KM# 78   5 GOURDES
23.5200 g., 0.9990 Silver 0.7554 oz. ASW   **Rev:** Haitienne paradise

Date	Mintage	F	VF	XF	Unc	BU
1971 IC Proof	1,585	Value: 60.00				

KM# 156   5 GOURDES
9.2000 g., Brass Plated Steel, 28 mm.   **Obv:** Four portraits in circle of Haitian statesmen top: Gen. Tonsaint Louverture, Left: Henri Christophe, Right: Jean Jacques Dessalines, Bottom: Alexandre Petion, date below **Rev:** National arms

Date	Mintage	F	VF	XF	Unc	BU
1995	—	—	—	—	2.75	3.00
1998	—	—	—	—	2.75	3.00

KM# 65.1   10 GOURDES
47.0500 g., 0.9990 Silver 1.5111 oz. ASW   **Series:** 10th Anniversary of Revolution **Subject:** General Toussaint L'Overture **Obv:** Figure on rearing horse left **Rev:** National arms

Date	Mintage	F	VF	XF	Unc	BU
1967 IC Proof	6,750	Value: 32.00				
1968 IC Proof	5,725	Value: 32.00				
1969 IC Proof	1,100	Value: 40.00				
1970 IC Proof	1,500	Value: 40.00				

KM# 65.2   10 GOURDES
47.0500 g., 0.9990 Silver 1.5111 oz. ASW   **Series:** 10th Anniversary of the Revolution **Subject:** General Toussaint L'Overture **Obv:** Figure on rearing horse left **Rev:** National arms **Note:** Rev; Additional "1 AR" countermark left of the initials "IC"

Date	Mintage	F	VF	XF	Unc	BU
1970 IC Proof	—	Value: 65.50				

KM# 79 10 GOURDES
47.0500 g., 0.9990 Silver 1.5111 oz. ASW **Obv:** Seminole Chief
- Osceola facing **Rev:** National arms

Date	Mintage	F	VF	XF	Unc	BU
1971 IC Proof	3,535	Value: 37.50				

KM# 80 10 GOURDES
47.0500 g., 0.9990 Silver 1.5111 oz. ASW **Obv:** Sioux Chief -
Sitting Bull **Rev:** National arms

Date	Mintage	F	VF	XF	Unc	BU
1971 IC Proof	3,185	Value: 37.50				

KM# 81 10 GOURDES
47.0500 g., 0.9990 Silver 1.5111 oz. ASW **Obv:** Fox Chief -
Playing Fox **Rev:** National arms

Date	Mintage	F	VF	XF	Unc	BU
1971 IC Proof	3,035	Value: 35.00				

KM# 82 10 GOURDES
47.0500 g., 0.9990 Silver 1.5111 oz. ASW **Obv:** Chiricahua
Chief - Geronimo **Rev:** National arms

Date	Mintage	F	VF	XF	Unc	BU
1971 IC Proof	3,285	Value: 35.00				

KM# 83 10 GOURDES
47.0500 g., 0.9990 Silver 1.5111 oz. ASW **Obv:** Seminole Chief
- Billy Bowlegs **Rev:** National arms

Date	Mintage	F	VF	XF	Unc	BU
1971 IC Proof	3,735	Value: 37.50				

KM# 84 10 GOURDES
47.0500 g., 0.9990 Silver 1.5111 oz. ASW **Obv:** Nez Perce Chief
- Joseph **Rev:** National arms

Date	Mintage	F	VF	XF	Unc	BU
1971 IC Proof	3,235	Value: 37.50				

KM# 85 10 GOURDES
47.0500 g., 0.9990 Silver 1.5111 oz. ASW **Obv:** Yankton Sioux
Chief - War Eagle **Rev:** National arms

Date	Mintage	F	VF	XF	Unc	BU
1971 IC Proof	3,135	Value: 37.50				

KM# 86 10 GOURDES
47.0500 g., 0.9990 Silver 1.5111 oz. ASW **Obv:** Oglala Sioux
Chief - Red Cloud **Rev:** National arms

Date	Mintage	F	VF	XF	Unc	BU
1971 IC Proof	3,235	Value: 35.00				

KM# 87 10 GOURDES
47.0500 g., 0.9990 Silver 1.5111 oz. ASW **Obv:** Cherokee Chief
- Stalking Turkey **Rev:** National arms

Date	Mintage	F	VF	XF	Unc	BU
1971 IC Proof	3,185	Value: 37.50				

KM# 66 20 GOURDES
3.9500 g., 0.9000 Gold 0.1143 oz. AGW **Series:** 10th
Anniversary of Revolution **Obv:** Native left with knife in left hand
Rev: National arms **Note:** Mackandal

Date	Mintage	F	VF	XF	Unc	BU
1967 IC Proof	10,351	Value: 120				
1968 IC Proof	—	Value: 120				
1969 IC Proof	—	Value: 120				
1970 IC Proof	—	Value: 120				

KM# 67.1 25 GOURDES
117.6000 g., 0.9990 Silver 3.7770 oz. ASW, 60 mm. **Subject:** 10th
Anniversary of Revolution **Obv:** Art objects **Rev:** National arms

Date	Mintage	F	VF	XF	Unc	BU
1967 IC Proof	4,650	Value: 75.00				
1968 IC Proof	5,810	Value: 75.00				
1969 IC Proof	1,115	Value: 95.00				
1970 IC Proof	1,000	Value: 95.00				

KM# 67.2   25 GOURDES
117.6000 g., 0.9990 Silver 3.7770 oz. ASW, 60 mm. **Obv:** Art objects **Rev:** National arms with additional "1 AR" countermark at 8 o'clock

Date	Mintage	F	VF	XF	Unc	BU
1970 Proof	—	Value: 165				

KM# 88   25 GOURDES
117.6000 g., 0.9990 Silver 3.7770 oz. ASW, 60 mm. **Obv:** International airport **Rev:** National arms

Date	Mintage	F	VF	XF	Unc	BU
1971 IC Proof	1,935	Value: 100				

KM# 102   25 GOURDES
10.0000 g., 0.9250 Silver 0.2974 oz. ASW **Obv:** Bust facing **Rev:** National arms

Date	Mintage	F	VF	XF	Unc	BU
1973	6,100	—	—	—	6.50	8.00
1973 Proof	5,470	Value: 9.00				
1974 Proof	—	Value: 30.00				

KM# 103   25 GOURDES
10.0000 g., 0.9250 Silver 0.2974 oz. ASW **Subject:** World Soccer Championship Games **Obv:** Games logo **Rev:** National arms

Date	Mintage	F	VF	XF	Unc	BU
1973	57,000	—	—	—	6.00	7.50
1973 Proof	6,430	Value: 9.00				
1974 Proof	—	Value: 30.00				

KM# 112.1   25 GOURDES
8.3750 g., 0.9250 Silver 0.2491 oz. ASW **Series:** United States Bicentennial **Obv:** Soldiers with cannon **Rev:** National arms

Date	Mintage	F	VF	XF	Unc	BU
1974	25,000	—	—	—	6.50	8.00
1974 Proof	600	Value: 20.00				
1975 Proof	—	Value: 35.00				
1976 Proof	10,000	Value: 12.50				

KM# 112.2   25 GOURDES
8.3750 g., 0.9250 Silver 0.2491 oz. ASW **Obv:** Soldiers with cannon, error; without country name at top **Rev:** National arms

Date	Mintage	F	VF	XF	Unc	BU
1974	25,000	—	—	—	40.00	45.00

KM# 121   25 GOURDES
8.3750 g., 0.9250 Silver 0.2491 oz. ASW **Series:** International Women's Year **Obv:** Women with raised arms, inscription **Rev:** National arms

Date	Mintage	F	VF	XF	Unc	BU
1975	7,180	—	—	—	20.00	30.00
1975 Proof	1,440	Value: 40.00				

KM# 72   30 GOURDES
9.1100 g., 0.8580 Gold 0.2513 oz. AGW **Series:** 10th Anniversary of Revolution **Obv:** Citadel of Saint Christopher **Rev:** National arms

Date	Mintage	F	VF	XF	Unc	BU
1969 IC Proof	1,185	Value: 250				
1970 IC Proof	Inc. above	Value: 250				

KM# 73   40 GOURDES
12.1500 g., 0.5850 Gold 0.2285 oz. AGW **Series:** 10th Anniversary of Revolution **Subject:** J.J. Dessalines **Obv:** Uniformed bust facing divides dates **Rev:** National arms

Date	Mintage	F	VF	XF	Unc	BU
1969 Proof	1,005	Value: 240				
1970 Proof	Inc. above	Value: 240				

KM# 68   50 GOURDES
9.8700 g., 0.9000 Gold 0.2856 oz. AGW **Series:** 10th Anniversary of Revolution **Obv:** Dancer **Rev:** National arms

Date	Mintage	F	VF	XF	Unc	BU
1967 IC Proof	8,681	Value: 280				
1968 IC Proof	—	Value: 280				
1969 IC Proof	—	Value: 280				
1970 IC Proof	—	Value: 280				

KM# 89   50 GOURDES
9.8700 g., 0.9000 Gold 0.2856 oz. AGW **Series:** 10th Anniversary of Revolution **Obv:** Soldiers **Rev:** National arms **Note:** Heros de Vertieres

Date	Mintage	F	VF	XF	Unc	BU
1971 IC Proof	485	Value: 300				

KM# 104.1   50 GOURDES
20.0000 g., 0.9250 Silver 0.5948 oz. ASW **Obv:** Woman on the beach **Rev:** National arms, fineness mark left of value

Date	Mintage	F	VF	XF	Unc	BU
1973	8,685	—	—	—	17.50	20.00
1973 Proof	5,973	Value: 25.00				
1974 Proof	—	Value: 45.00				

KM# 104.2   50 GOURDES
16.4500 g., 0.9250 Silver 0.4892 oz. ASW, 37.9 mm. **Obv:** Woman on beach **Rev:** National arms, fineness stamp right of value **Edge:** Reeded

Date	Mintage	F	VF	XF	Unc	BU
1973 Proof	—	Value: 50.00				

KM# 105   50 GOURDES
20.0000 g., 0.9250 Silver 0.5948 oz. ASW **Obv:** Woman and child **Rev:** National arms

Date	Mintage	F	VF	XF	Unc	BU
1973	7,300	—	—	—	13.50	15.00
1973 Proof	5,853	Value: 16.50				

Date	Mintage	F	VF	XF	Unc	BU
1974	—			—	37.50	40.00
1974 Proof	—	Value: 45.00				

KM# 106   50 GOURDES
16.7500 g., 0.9250 Silver 0.4981 oz. ASW **Series:** World Soccer Championship Games **Obv:** Games logo **Rev:** National arms

Date	Mintage	F	VF	XF	Unc	BU
1973 Proof	12,000	Value: 15.00				

KM# 113.1   50 GOURDES
16.7500 g., 0.9250 Silver 0.4981 oz. ASW **Series:** 1976 Montreal Olympiad **Obv:** Half-figure with torch above Olympic flame flanked by athletes **Rev:** National arms **Note:** Prev. KM#113.

Date	Mintage	F	VF	XF	Unc	BU
1974	21,000			—	15.00	20.00
1974 Proof	2,358	Value: 22.00				
1975 Proof	—	Value: 27.50				
1976						
1976 Thin 6; Proof	8,000	Value: 25.00				
1976 Thick 6; Proof	Inc. above	Value: 30.00				

KM# 113.2   50 GOURDES
16.7500 g., 0.9250 Silver 0.4981 oz. ASW **Series:** 1976 Montreal Olympiad **Obv:** Half-figure with torch above Olympic flame, athletes flank **Rev:** National arms, smaller 4 in date **Note:** Prev. KM#114.

Date	Mintage	F	VF	XF	Unc	BU
1974	—			—	20.00	25.00
1974 Proof	—	Value: 30.00				

KM# 123   50 GOURDES
16.7500 g., 0.9250 Silver 0.4981 oz. ASW, 38.14 mm. **Subject:** Holy Year **Obv:** Pope Paul and Praying hands above St. Peter's Square **Rev:** National arms **Edge:** Reeded

Date	Mintage	F	VF	XF	Unc	BU
1974	—			—	12.50	15.00
1974 Proof	960	Value: 25.00				
1975	—			—	35.00	40.00
1975 Proof	—	Value: 40.00				
1976 Proof	6,000	Value: 25.00				

KM# 129   50 GOURDES
21.3000 g., 0.9250 Silver 0.6334 oz. ASW **Series:** 1980 Moscow Olympics **Obv:** Olympic flame above date, athletes flank **Rev:** National arms

Date	Mintage	F	VF	XF	Unc	BU
1977	3,969	—	—	—	22.50	25.00
1977 Proof	3,720	Value: 27.50				
1978 Proof	Est. 350	Value: 225				

KM# 130.1   50 GOURDES
21.3000 g., 0.9250 Silver 0.6334 oz. ASW **Series:** 20th Anniversary of European Market **Obv:** Map of Europe on globe design **Rev:** National arms

Date	Mintage	F	VF	XF	Unc	BU
1977	421	—	—	—	65.00	70.00
1977 Proof	364	Value: 80.00				
1978	—	—	—	—	65.00	70.00

KM# 130.2   50 GOURDES
21.3000 g., 0.9250 Silver 0.6334 oz. ASW **Obv:** Map of Europe on globe design, entire area within circle frosted **Rev:** National arms

Date	Mintage	F	VF	XF	Unc	BU
1978	—			—	75.00	80.00
1978 Proof	—	Value: 90.00				

KM# 127   50 GOURDES
21.3000 g., 0.9250 Silver 0.6334 oz. ASW **Series:** World Soccer Championship Games **Obv:** Soccer ball with date at center **Rev:** National arms

Date	Mintage	F	VF	XF	Unc	BU
1977	11,000	—	—	—	22.50	25.00
1977 Proof	9,000	Value: 28.00				

KM# 128   50 GOURDES
21.3000 g., 0.9250 Silver 0.6334 oz. ASW **Subject:** Human Rights **Obv:** Kneeling figure with broken chains **Rev:** National arms

Date	Mintage	F	VF	XF	Unc	BU
1977	800	—	—	—	27.50	30.00
1977 Proof	545	Value: 35.00				

KM# 131   50 GOURDES
21.3000 g., 0.9250 Silver 0.6334 oz. ASW **Obv:** Queen of the Sugar left **Rev:** National arms

Date	Mintage	F	VF	XF	Unc	BU
1977	321	—	—	—	30.00	35.00
1977 Proof	602	Value: 37.50				

KM# 149   50 GOURDES
20.0000 g., 0.9250 Silver 0.5948 oz. ASW **Series:** F.A.O. **Obv:** Head left **Rev:** Plants

Date	Mintage	F	VF	XF	Unc	BU
1981R	Est. 14,000	—	—	—	30.00	35.00
1981R Proof	—	Value: 55.00				

KM# 150   50 GOURDES
20.0000 g., 0.9250 Silver 0.5948 oz. ASW **Subject:** Holy Year **Obv:** National arms **Rev:** Buildings

Date	Mintage	F	VF	XF	Unc	BU
1983R Proof	1,000	Value: 85.00				

KM# 74   60 GOURDES
18.2200 g., 0.5850 Gold 0.3427 oz. AGW **Series:** 10th Anniversary of the Revolution **Obv:** Alexandre Petion **Rev:** National arms

Date	Mintage	F	VF	XF	Unc	BU
1969 IC Proof	935	Value: 360				
1970 IC Proof	Inc. above	Value: 385				

KM# 69   100 GOURDES
19.7500 g., 0.9000 Gold 0.5715 oz. AGW **Series:** 10th Anniversary of the Revolution **Subject:** Marie Jeanne **Obv:** Half-figure left with knife in right hand **Rev:** National arms

Date	Mintage	F	VF	XF	Unc	BU
1967 IC Proof	Est. 8,682	Value: 575				
1968 IC Proof	—	Value: 575				
1969 IC Proof	—	Value: 575				
1970 IC Proof	—	Value: 575				

KM# 90   100 GOURDES
19.7500 g., 0.9000 Gold 0.5715 oz. AGW **Obv:** Seminole Tribal Chief - Osceola **Rev:** National arms

Date	Mintage	F	VF	XF	Unc	BU
1971 IC Proof	435	Value: 560				

KM# 91   100 GOURDES
19.7500 g., 0.9000 Gold 0.5715 oz. AGW **Obv:** Sioux Chief - Sitting Bull **Rev:** National arms

Date	Mintage	F	VF	XF	Unc	BU
1971 IC Proof	475	Value: 560				

KM# 92   100 GOURDES
19.7500 g., 0.9000 Gold 0.5715 oz. AGW **Obv:** Fox Chief - Playing Fox **Rev:** National arms

Date	Mintage	F	VF	XF	Unc	BU
1971 IC Proof	425	Value: 560				

KM# 93   100 GOURDES
19.7500 g., 0.9000 Gold 0.5715 oz. AGW **Obv:** Chiricahua Chief - Geronimo **Rev:** National arms

Date	Mintage	F	VF	XF	Unc	BU
1971 IC Proof	520	Value: 560				

KM# 94   100 GOURDES
19.7500 g., 0.9000 Gold 0.5715 oz. AGW **Obv:** Seminole Chief - Billy Bowlegs **Rev:** National arms

Date	Mintage	F	VF	XF	Unc	BU
1971 IC Proof	425	Value: 560				

KM# 95   100 GOURDES
19.7500 g., 0.9000 Gold 0.5715 oz. AGW **Obv:** Nez Perce Chief - Joseph **Rev:** National arms

Date	Mintage	F	VF	XF	Unc	BU
1971 IC Proof	455	Value: 550				

KM# 96   100 GOURDES
19.7500 g., 0.9000 Gold 0.5715 oz. AGW **Obv:** Yankton Sioux Chief - War Eagle **Rev:** National arms

Date	Mintage	F	VF	XF	Unc	BU
1971 IC Proof	455	Value: 560				

KM# 97   100 GOURDES
19.7500 g., 0.9000 Gold 0.5715 oz. AGW **Obv:** Oglala Sioux Chief - Red Cloud **Rev:** National arms

Date	Mintage	F	VF	XF	Unc	BU
1971 IC Proof	455	Value: 560				

KM# 98   100 GOURDES
19.7500 g., 0.9000 Gold 0.5715 oz. AGW **Obv:** Cherokee Chief - Stalking Turkey **Rev:** National arms

Date	Mintage	F	VF	XF	Unc	BU
1971 IC Proof	425	Value: 560				

KM# 107   100 GOURDES
1.4500 g., 0.9000 Gold 0.0420 oz. AGW **Subject:** Christopher Columbus **Obv:** Bust facing **Rev:** National arms

Date	Mintage	F	VF	XF	Unc	BU
1973	3,233	—	—	—	—	45.00
1973 Proof	915	Value: 55.00				

KM# 132   100 GOURDES
43.0000 g., 0.9250 Silver 1.2787 oz. ASW **Subject:** Presidents Sadat and Begin **Obv:** Profiles facing each other, Dove of Peace above **Rev:** National arms

Date	Mintage	F	VF	XF	Unc	BU
1977	550	—	—	—	55.00	60.00
1977 Proof	500	Value: 80.00				

KM# 133   100 GOURDES
43.0000 g., 0.9250 Silver 1.2787 oz. ASW **Subject:** 20th Anniversary of European Market **Obv:** Ships wheel and sailboat **Rev:** National arms

Date	Mintage	F	VF	XF	Unc	BU
1977	321	—	—	—	85.00	90.00
1977 Proof	214	Value: 100				

KM# 134   100 GOURDES
43.0000 g., 0.9250 Silver 1.2787 oz. ASW **Subject:** 50th Anniversary of Lindbergh's New York to Paris Flight **Obv:** Portrait of Lindbergh in flier's cap above "Spirit of St. Louis" **Rev:** National arms

Date	Mintage	F	VF	XF	Unc	BU
1977	321	—	—	—	80.00	85.00
1977 Proof	214	Value: 125				

KM# 135 100 GOURDES
43.0000 g., 0.9250 Silver 1.2787 oz. ASW **Obv:** Statue of Liberty
Rev: National arms

Date	Mintage	F	VF	XF	Unc	BU
1977	321	—	—	—	80.00	85.00
1977 Proof	214	Value: 125				

KM# 158 100 GOURDES
40.0000 g., 0.9250 Silver 1.1895 oz. ASW **Subject:** 10th
Anniversary of the Presidency of Jean Claude Duvalier
Obv: Head right without FAO **Rev:** Woman and child

Date	Mintage	F	VF	XF	Unc	BU
1981R Proof	—	Value: 150				

KM# 159 100 GOURDES
40.0000 g., 0.9250 Silver 1.1895 oz. ASW **Subject:** 10th
Anniversary of the Presidency of Jean Claude Duvalier
Obv: Head right without FAO **Rev:** Infants on open book

Date	Mintage	F	VF	XF	Unc	BU
1981R Proof	—	Value: 150				

KM# 160 100 GOURDES
40.0000 g., 0.9250 Silver 1.1895 oz. ASW **Subject:** 10th
Anniversary of the Presidency of Jean Claude Duvalier **Obv:**
Head right without FAO **Rev:** Nude woman and man

Date	Mintage	F	VF	XF	Unc	BU
1981R Proof	—	Value: 175				

KM# 70 200 GOURDES
39.4900 g., 0.9000 Gold 1.1426 oz. AGW **Subject:** Revolt of
Santo Domingo **Obv:** Native running with weapons **Rev:** National
arms

Date	Mintage	F	VF	XF	Unc	BU
1967 IC Proof	Est. 4,199	Value: 1,150				
1968 IC Proof	—	Value: 1,150				
1969 IC Proof	—	Value: 1,150				
1970 IC Proof	—	Value: 1,150				

KM# 99 200 GOURDES
39.4900 g., 0.9000 Gold 1.1426 oz. AGW **Obv:** Revolutionist
from Santo Domingo **Rev:** National arms

Date	Mintage	F	VF	XF	Unc	BU
1971 IC Proof	235	Value: 1,150				

KM# 108 200 GOURDES
2.9100 g., 0.9000 Gold 0.0842 oz. AGW **Series:** World Soccer
Championship Games **Obv:** Games logo **Rev:** National arms

Date	Mintage	F	VF	XF	Unc	BU
1973	5,167	—	—	—	—	90.00
1973 Proof	915	Value: 95.00				

KM# 115 200 GOURDES
2.9100 g., 0.9000 Gold 0.0842 oz. AGW **Subject:** Holy Year
Obv: Pope Paul and Praying hands above St. Peter's Square
Rev: National arms, fineness stamped on hexagonal mound

Date	Mintage	F	VF	XF	Unc	BU
1974	4,965	—	—	—	—	90.00
1974 Proof	660	Value: 100				

KM# 124 200 GOURDES
2.9100 g., 0.9000 Gold 0.0842 oz. AGW **Subject:** Holy Year
Obv: Pope Paul and Praying hands above St. Peter's Square
Rev: National arms, fineness stamped on oval mound

Date	Mintage	F	VF	XF	Unc	BU
1975 Proof	—	Value: 95.00				

KM# 125 200 GOURDES
2.9100 g., 0.9000 Gold 0.0842 oz. AGW **Series:** International
Women's Year **Obv:** Two women with arms upraised
Rev: National arms

Date	Mintage	F	VF	XF	Unc	BU
1975	2,260	—	—	—	—	90.00
1975 Proof	840	Value: 125				

KM# 75 250 GOURDES
75.9500 g., 0.5850 Gold 1.4284 oz. AGW **Series:** 10th Anniversary
of Revolution **Obv:** King H. Christophe **Rev:** National arms

Date	Mintage	F	VF	XF	Unc	BU
1969 IC Proof	470	Value: 1,400				
1970 IC Proof	—	Value: 1,400				

KM# 136 250 GOURDES
4.2500 g., 0.9000 Gold 0.1230 oz. AGW **Subject:** Human Rights
Obv: Kneeling figure with broken chains **Rev:** National arms

Date	Mintage	F	VF	XF	Unc	BU
1977	282	—	—	—	—	140
1977 Proof	288	Value: 145				

KM# 137 250 GOURDES
4.2500 g., 0.9000 Gold 0.1230 oz. AGW **Subject:** Presidents
Sadat and Begin **Obv:** Profiles facing each other, Dove of Peace
above **Rev:** National arms

Date	Mintage	F	VF	XF	Unc	BU
1977	270	—	—	—	—	125
1977 Proof	520	Value: 120				

KM# 138 250 GOURDES
4.2500 g., 0.9000 Gold 0.1230 oz. AGW **Subject:** 20th
Anniversary of European Market **Obv:** Ships wheel and sailboat
Rev: National arms

Date	Mintage	F	VF	XF	Unc	BU
1977	107	—	—	—	—	200
1977 Proof	107	Value: 210				

KM# 139 250 GOURDES
4.2500 g., 0.9000 Gold 0.1230 oz. AGW **Subject:** 50th Anniversary
of Lindbergh's New York to Paris Flight **Obv:** Portrait of Lindbergh
in flier's cap above "Spirit of St. Louis" **Rev:** National arms

Date	Mintage	F	VF	XF	Unc	BU
1977	107	—	—	—	—	245
1977 Proof	107	Value: 250				

KM# 76   500 GOURDES
151.9000 g., 0.5850 Gold 2.8568 oz. AGW, 68 mm.
Series: 10th Anniversary of Revolution **Obv:** Haitian native art
Rev: National arms **Note:** Illustration reduced.

Date	Mintage	F	VF	XF	Unc	BU
1969 IC Proof	435	Value: 2,750				
1970 IC Proof	—	Value: 2,750				

KM# 109   500 GOURDES
7.2800 g., 0.9000 Gold 0.2106 oz. AGW **Obv:** Woman with shell right **Rev:** National arms

Date	Mintage	F	VF	XF	Unc	BU
1973	2,380	—	—	—	—	210
1973 Proof	915	Value: 220				

KM# 110   500 GOURDES
7.2800 g., 0.9000 Gold 0.2106 oz. AGW **Obv:** Woman with child **Rev:** National arms

Date	Mintage	F	VF	XF	Unc	BU
1973	2,265	—	—	—	—	210
1973 Proof	915	Value: 220				

KM# 116   500 GOURDES
6.5000 g., 0.9000 Gold 0.1881 oz. AGW **Obv:** Battle scene **Rev:** National arms

Date	Mintage	F	VF	XF	Unc	BU
1974 Proof	—	Value: 190				

KM# 117   500 GOURDES
6.5000 g., 0.9000 Gold 0.1881 oz. AGW **Series:** 1976 Montreal & Insbruck Olympics **Obv:** Half-figure with torch above Olympic flame, athletes flank **Rev:** National arms, fineness stamped on hexagonal mound

Date	Mintage	F	VF	XF	Unc	BU
1974	3,489	—	—	—	—	185
1974 Proof	1,140	Value: 190				

KM# 126   500 GOURDES
6.5000 g., 0.9000 Gold 0.1881 oz. AGW **Series:** 1976 Montreal & Insbruck Olympics **Obv:** Half-figure with torch above Olympic flame, athletes flank **Rev:** National arms, fineness stamped on oval mound

Date	Mintage	F	VF	XF	Unc	BU
1975	120	—	—	—	450	500

KM# 140   500 GOURDES
8.5000 g., 0.9000 Gold 0.2459 oz. AGW **Series:** World Soccer Championship Games **Obv:** Soccer ball with date in center **Rev:** National arms

Date	Mintage	F	VF	XF	Unc	BU
1977	450	—	—	—	—	240
1977 Proof	200	Value: 250				

KM# 141   500 GOURDES
8.5000 g., 0.9000 Gold 0.2459 oz. AGW **Series:** 1980 Moscow Olympics **Rev:** National arms

Date	Mintage	F	VF	XF	Unc	BU
1977	695	—	—	—	—	240
1977 Proof	504	Value: 250				
1978 Proof	Est. 350	Value: 350				

KM# 142   500 GOURDES
8.5000 g., 0.9000 Gold 0.2459 oz. AGW **Subject:** 20th Anniversary of European Common Market **Obv:** Map of Europe **Rev:** National arms

Date	Mintage	F	VF	XF	Unc	BU
1977	207	—	—	—	—	250
1977 Proof	257	Value: 265				
1978		—	—	—	—	300
1978 Proof	150	Value: 350				

KM# 143   500 GOURDES
8.5000 g., 0.9000 Gold 0.2459 oz. AGW **Subject:** Economic Connections **Rev:** National arms

Date	Mintage	F	VF	XF	Unc	BU
1977	107	—	—	—	—	260
1977 Proof	107	Value: 300				

KM# 144   500 GOURDES
8.5000 g., 0.9000 Gold 0.2459 oz. AGW **Obv:** Jean-Claude Duvalier **Rev:** National arms

Date	Mintage	F	VF	XF	Unc	BU
1977	107	—	—	—	—	250
1977 Proof	328	Value: 240				

KM# 161   500 GOURDES
7.0000 g., 0.9000 Gold 0.2025 oz. AGW **Subject:** 10th Anniversary of the Presidency of Jean Claude Duvalier **Obv:** Head right without FAO **Rev:** Sun above farmer on tractor in field

Date	Mintage	F	VF	XF	Unc	BU
1981R Proof	—	Value: 650				

KM# 162   500 GOURDES
7.0000 g., 0.9000 Gold 0.2025 oz. AGW **Subject:** 10th Anniversary of the Presidency of Jean Claude Duvalier **Obv:** Head right without FAO **Rev:** Plants

Date	Mintage	F	VF	XF	Unc	BU
1981R Proof	—	Value: 650				

KM# 163   500 GOURDES
7.0000 g., 0.9000 Gold 0.2025 oz. AGW **Subject:** 10th Anniversary of the Presidency of Jean Claude Duvalier **Obv:** Head right without FAO **Rev:** Harvesters

Date	Mintage	F	VF	XF	Unc	BU
1981R Proof	—	Value: 650				

KM# 151   500 GOURDES
10.5000 g., 0.9000 Gold 0.3038 oz. AGW **Subject:** Papal Visit **Obv:** National arms **Rev:** Bust left above people

Date	Mintage	F	VF	XF	Unc	BU
1983R Proof	1,000	Value: 295				

KM# 165   500 GOURDES
28.2300 g., 0.9250 Silver 0.8395 oz. ASW, 38.5 mm.
Subject: Millennium **Obv:** Multicolor and gold-plated national arms **Rev:** Dove and partially gold-plated sun rays **Edge:** Reeded

Date	Mintage	F	VF	XF	Unc	BU
ND(1999) Proof	—	Value: 100				

KM# 71   1000 GOURDES
197.4800 g., 0.9000 Gold 5.7140 oz. AGW **Series:** 10th Anniversary of Revolution **Obv:** Dr. Francois Duvalier **Rev:** National arms

Date	Mintage	F	VF	XF	Unc	BU
1967 IC Proof	Est. 2,950	Value: 5,500				
1968 IC Proof	—	Value: 5,500				

Date	Mintage	F	VF	XF	Unc	BU
1969 IC Proof	—	Value: 5,500				
1970 IC Proof	—	Value: 5,500				

KM# 111   1000 GOURDES
14.5600 g., 0.9000 Gold 0.4213 oz. AGW **Obv:** President Jean Claude Duvalier left **Rev:** National arms

Date	Mintage	F	VF	XF	Unc	BU
1973	—	—	—	—	—	415
1973 Proof	915	Value: 425				

KM# 118.1   1000 GOURDES
13.0000 g., 0.9000 Gold 0.3761 oz. AGW **Series:** United States Bicentennial **Obv:** Battle scene **Rev:** National arms

Date	Mintage	F	VF	XF	Unc	BU
1974	3,040	—	—	—	—	360
1974 Proof	480	Value: 375				
1975 Proof	—	Value: 600				

KM# 118.2   1000 GOURDES
13.0000 g., 0.9000 Gold 0.3761 oz. AGW **Obv:** Error; without country name at top **Rev:** National arms

Date	Mintage	F	VF	XF	Unc	BU
1974	—	—	—	—	650	700

KM# 164   1000 GOURDES
14.0000 g., 0.9000 Gold 0.4051 oz. AGW **Subject:** 10th Anniversary of the Presidency of Jean Claude Duvalier **Obv:** Head right without FAO **Rev:** Three nudes and flag

Date	Mintage	F	VF	XF	Unc	BU
1981R Proof	—	Value: 1,150				

PATTERNS
Including off metal strikes

KM#	Date	Mintage Identification	Mkt Val
Pn87	1974	— 25 Gourdes. 0.9250 Silver, KM#112	

TRIAL STRIKES

KM#	Date	Mintage Identification	Mkt Val
TS1	ND(1971)	— 100 Gourdes. Gilt Bronze. Bust in headdress facing. Blank. KM#93	100

MINT SETS

KM#	Date	Mintage Identification	Issue Price	Mkt Val
MS1	1973 (8)	8,000 KM#102, 104-105, 107-111	490	600
MS2	1973 (8)	— KM#102, 104, 105, 107-111	60.00	37.50
MS3	1974 (2)	— KM#115, 123	—	70.00
MS4	1975 (2)	— KM#121, 125	50.25	65.00
MS5	1976 (2)	— KM#113, 117	—	
MS6	1995 (5)	— KM#152a-156a	—	10.00

PROOF SETS

KM#	Date	Mintage Identification	Issue Price	Mkt Val
PSA1	1967 (8)	— KM#64.1, 65-71	—	3,500
PS1	1967 (5)	2,525 KM#66, 68-71	722	3,900
PS2	1967 (5)	4,650 KM#64.1, 65.1, 67.1	47.00	90.00
PS3	1968 (5)	475 KM#66, 68-71	823	4,200
PS4	1968 (5)	5,725 KM#64, 65, 67	53.50	100
PS5	1969 (5)	435 KM#72-76	475	3,750
PS6	1969 (5)	140 KM#66, 68-71	823	4,650
PS7	1969 (3)	1,100 KM#64, 65, 67	53.50	145
PS8	1970 (5)	— KM#66, 68-71	823	5,000

KM#	Date	Mintage	Identification	Issue Price	Mkt Val
PSA9	1970 (3)	1,000	KM#64, 65, 67	53.50	145
PS9	1970 (3)	—	KM#64.2, 65.2, 67.2	—	265
PSA10	1970-71 (5)	—	KM#64.1, 65.1, 67.1, 78, 88	265	—
PS10	1971 (9)	—	KM#79-87	135	325
PSA11	1971 (18)	—	KM#79-87, 90-98	—	3,900
PS11	1971 (9)	—	KM#90-98	—	3,500
PS12	1973 (8)	1,250	KM#102-105, 107-109, 111	830	600
PS13	1973 (4)	3,500	KM#102-105	60.00	50.00
PS14	1974 (4)	—	KM#102-105	—	145
PS15	1975 (2)	—	KM#121, 125	67.25	160
PS17	1976 (3)	—	KM#112, 113, 123 Although the insert information card in #PS17 state B.U., this issue is considered to be of proof quality.	—	65.00
PS18	1978 (2)	350	KM#129, 141	—	475
PS19	1978 (2)	—	KM#130.2, 142	—	450
PS20	1981R (7)	10	KM#158-164	—	3,650

HEJAZ

Hejaz, a province of Saudi Arabia and a former vilayet of the Ottoman Empire, occupies an 800-mile long (1,287km.) coastal strip between Nejd and the Red Sea. The province was a Turkish dependency until freed in World War I. Husain Ibn Ali, Amir of Mecca, opposed the Turkish control and, with the aid of Lawrence of Arabia, wrested much of Hejaz from the Turks and in 1916 assumed the title of King of Hejaz. Abd Al-Aziz Bin Sa'ud, of Nejd conquered Hejaz in 1925, and in 1926 combined it and Nejd into a single kingdom.

TITLES

الحجاز

Hal-Hejaz

RULERS
al Husain Ibn Ali, AH1334-42/1916-24AD
Abd Al-Aziz Bin Sa'ud, AH1343-1373/1925-1953AD

MONETARY SYSTEM
40 Para = 1 Piastre (Ghirsh)
20 Piastres = 1 Riyal
100 Piastres = 1 Dinar

KINGDOM

COUNTERMARKED COINAGE
Minor Coins

Following the defeat of the Ottomans in 1916, Turkish 10, 20 and 40 Para coins of Muhammed V and 40 Para coins of Muhammed VI were countermarked al-Hejaz in Arabic. The countermark was applied to the obverse side effacing the Ottoman Sultan's toughra, and thus refuting Turkish rule in Hejaz.

Countermarks on the reverse are rare errors. The 10 Para of Muhammed V and 10 and 20 Para (billon) of Abdul Mejid and Mahmud II exist with a smaller, 6-millimeter countermark. These are probably unofficial. Other host coins are considered controversial.

KM# 2   10 PARA
Nickel **Countermark:** Hejaz **Obv:** Reshat **Note:** Large countermark on Turkey 10 Para, KM#760. Accession date: 1327.

CM Date	Host Date	Good	VG	F	VF	XF
ND(1327)	AH1327//2-7 Rare					
ND(AH1327)	AH1327//7 Rare					

KM# 3   20 PARA
Nickel **Countermark:** "Hejaz" **Note:** Countermark on Turkey 20 Para, KM#761. Accession date: 1327.

CM Date	Host Date	Good	VG	F	VF	XF
ND(1327)	AH1327//2	5.00	9.00	20.00	40.00	—
ND(1327)	AH1327//3	4.00	7.00	15.00	30.00	—
ND(1327)	AH1327//4	3.00	6.00	12.00	25.00	—
ND(1327)	AH1327//5	3.00	6.00	12.00	25.00	—

CM Date	Host Date	Good	VG	F	VF	XF
ND(1327)	AH1327//6	3.00	6.00	12.00	25.00	—
ND(1327)	AH1327//x p.y. obliterated	2.00	5.00	10.00	20.00	—

KM# 4   40 PARA
Nickel **Countermark:** "Hejaz" **Obv:** El Ghazi **Note:** Countermark on Turkey 40 Para, KM#766. Accession date: 1327.

CM Date	Host Date	Good	VG	F	VF	XF
ND(1327)	AH1327//3	6.00	10.00	20.00	40.00	—
ND(1327)	AH1327//4	3.00	6.00	12.00	25.00	—
ND(1327)	AH1327//5	3.00	6.00	12.00	25.00	—
ND(1327)	AH1327//x p.y. obliterated	2.00	5.00	10.00	20.00	—

KM# 5   40 PARA
Copper-Nickel **Countermark:** "Hejaz" **Note:** Countermark on Turkey 40 Para, KM#779. Accession date: 1327.

CM Date	Host Date	Good	VG	F	VF	XF
ND(1327)	AH1327//8	4.00	6.00	12.00	25.00	—
ND(1327)	AH1327//9	20.00	30.00	75.00	150	—
ND(1327)	AH1327//x p.y. obliterated	3.00	6.00	10.00	20.00	—

KM# 6   40 PARA
Copper-Nickel **Countermark:** "Hejaz" **Note:** Countermark on Turkey 40 Para, KM#828. Accession date: 1336.

CM Date	Host Date	Good	VG	F	VF	XF
ND(1326)	AH1336//4	50.00	75.00	150	250	—
ND(1326)	AH1336//x	40.00	50.00	100	200	—

COUNTERMARKED COINAGE
Silver Coins

Silver coins of various sizes were also countermarked al-Hejaz. The most common host coins include the Maria Theresa Thaler of Austria, and 5, 10, and 20 Kurush or Qirsh of Turkey and Egypt. The countermark occurs in various sizes and styles of script. These countermarks may have been applied by local silversmiths to discourage re-exportation of the badly needed hard currency and silver of known fineness.

Some crown-sized examples exist with both the al-Hejaz and Nejd countermarks. The authenticity of the silver countermarked coins has long been discussed, and it is likely that most were privately produced. Other host coins are considered controversial.

KM# 10   5 PIASTRES
Silver **Countermark:** "Hejaz" **Note:** Countermark on Turkey 5 Kurush, KM#750. Accession date: 1327.

CM Date	Host Date	Good	VG	F	VF	XF
(1916-20)	ND(AH1327//1-7)	100	125	200	400	—

KM# 11   5 PIASTRES
Silver **Countermark:** "Hejaz" **Note:** Countermark on Turkey 5 Kurush, KM#771. Accession date: 1327.

CM Date	Host Date	Good	VG	F	VF	XF
(1916-20)	ND(AH1327//7-9)	100	125	200	400	—

KM# 12   5 PIASTRES
Silver **Countermark:** "Hejaz" **Note:** Countermark on Egypt 5 Qirsh, KM#308. Accession date: 1327.

CM Date	Host Date	Good	VG	F	VF	XF
(1916-20)	ND(AH1327// 2H-4H, 6H)	100	125	200	400	—

KM# 13   10 PIASTRES
Silver **Countermark:** "Hejaz" **Note:** Countermark on Turkey 10 Kurush, KM#751. Accession date: 1327.

CM Date	Host Date	Good	VG	F	VF	XF
(1916-20)	ND(AH1327//1-7)	125	200	300	500	—

KM# 14   10 PIASTRES
Silver **Countermark:** "Hejaz" **Note:** Countermark on Turkey 10 Kurush, KM#772. Accession date: 1327.

CM Date	Host Date	Good	VG	F	VF	XF
(1916-20)	ND(AH1327// 7-10)	125	200	300	500	—

KM# 15   10 PIASTRES
Silver **Countermark:** "Hejaz" **Note:** Countermark on Egypt 10 Qirsh, KM#309. Accession date: 1327.

CM Date	Host Date	Good	VG	F	VF	XF
(1916-20)	ND(AH1327// 2H-4H, 6H)	125	200	300	500	—

KM# 16 20 PIASTRES
Silver **Countermark:** "Hejaz" **Note:** Countermark on Egypt 20 Qirsh, KM#310. Accession date: 1327.

CM Date	Host Date	Good	VG	F	VF	XF
(1916-20)	ND(AH1327// 2H-4H, 6H)	125	200	300	500	—

KM# 17 20 PIASTRES
Silver **Countermark:** "Hejaz" **Note:** Countermark on Turkey 20 Kurush, KM#780. Accession date: 1327.

CM Date	Host Date	Good	VG	F	VF	XF
(1916-20)	ND(AH1327//8-10)	125	200	300	500	—

KM# 18 20 PIASTRES
Silver **Countermark:** "Hejaz" **Note:** Countermark on Austria Maria Theresa Thaler, KM#T1. Accession date: 1327.

CM Date	Host Date	Good	VG	F	VF	XF
ND(1916-20)	1780	100	150	250	400	—

REGULAR COINAGE

All the regular coins of Hejaz bear the accessional date AH1334 of Al-Husain Ibn Ali, plus the regnal year. Many of the bronze coins occur with a light silver wash mostly on thicker specimens. A variety of planchet thicknesses exist.

KM# 21 1/8 PIASTRE
Bronze, 12-13 mm. **Note:** Reeded and plain edge varieties exist. Size varies.

Date	Mintage	Good	VG	F	VF	XF
AH1334//5	—	—	125	200	300	600

KM# 22 1/4 PIASTRE
1.1400 g., Bronze, 16 mm. **Note:** Reeded and plain edge varieties exist.

Date	Mintage	Good	VG	F	VF	XF
AH1334//5	—	—	8.00	15.00	35.00	65.00
AH1334//6/5	—	—	75.00	300	600	1,200
AH1334//6	—	—	400	750	1,500	2,500

KM# 25 1/4 PIASTRE
Bronze, 17 mm. **Edge:** Plain

Date	Mintage	Good	VG	F	VF	XF
AH1334//8	—	—	10.00	20.00	40.00	75.00

KM# 23 1/2 PIASTRE
Bronze, 18-19 mm. **Note:** Reeded and plain edge varieties exist. Size varies.

Date	Mintage	Good	VG	F	VF	XF
AH1334//5	—	—	10.00	20.00	35.00	75.00

KM# 26 1/2 PIASTRE
3.1400 g., Bronze, 19 mm. **Note:** Similar to 1/4 Piastre, KM#25. Most known specimens were overstruck as "Hejaz & Nejd" KM#1.

Date	Mintage	Good	VG	F	VF	XF
AH1334//8 Rare	—					

KM# 24 PIASTRE
Bronze, 21-22 mm. **Edge:** Reeded **Note:** Size varies.

Date	Mintage	Good	VG	F	VF	XF
AH1334//5	—	—	10.00	20.00	40.00	75.00
AH1334//6/5	—	—	100	200	400	750

KM# 27 PIASTRE
Bronze, 21 mm. **Edge:** Plain

Date	Mintage	Good	VG	F	VF	XF
AH1334//8	—	—	60.00	125	200	325

KM# 28 5 PIASTRES
6.1000 g., 0.9170 Silver 0.1798 oz. ASW, 24 mm.

Date	Mintage	Good	VG	F	VF	XF
AH1334//8	—	—	50.00	90.00	175	300

KM# 29 10 PIASTRES
12.0500 g., 0.9170 Silver 0.3552 oz. ASW, 28 mm.

Date	Mintage	Good	VG	F	VF	XF
AH1334//8	—	—	250	400	750	1,200

KM# 30 20 PIASTRES (1 Riyal)
24.1000 g., 0.9170 Silver 0.7105 oz. ASW, 37 mm.

Date	Mintage	Good	VG	F	VF	XF
AH1334//8	—	—	40.00	75.00	125	200
AH1334//9	—	—	125	200	300	500

KM# 31 DINAR HASHIMI
Gold

Date	Mintage	VG	F	VF	XF	Unc
AH1334-8	—	—	300	450	650	1,000

PATTERNS
Including off metal strikes

KM#	Date	Mintage	Identification	Mkt Val
Pn1	AH1340//1	—	20 Piastres. Bronze. Struck at the Heaton Mint (not to be confused with the modern copies listed in Unusual World Coins; struck in various metals, including bronze, nickel and silver).	
pnA1	AH1340/1	—	10 Piastres. Bronze. Struck at the Heaton Mint.	

HONDURAS

The Republic of Honduras, situated in Central America alongside El Salvador, between Nicaragua and Guatemala, has an area of 43,277sq. mi. (112,090 sq. km.) and a population of 5.6 million. Capital: Tegucigalpa. Agriculture, mining (gold and silver), and logging are the major economic activities, with increasing tourism and emerging petroleum resource discoveries. Precious metals, bananas, timber and coffee are exported.

After declaring its independence from Spain on September 15, 1821, Honduras fell under the Mexican empire of Augustin de Iturbide, and then joined the Central American Republic (1823-39). Upon the effective dissolution of that federation (ca. 1840), Honduras reclaimed its independence as a self-standing republic. Honduras forces played a major part in permanently ending the threat of William Walker to establish a slave holding empire in Central America based on his self engineered elections to the Presidency of Nicaragua. Thrice expelled from Central America, Walker was shot by a Honduran firing squad in 1860. 1876 to 1933 saw a period of instability and for some months were under U.S. Marine Corp military occupation. From 1933 to 1940 General Tiburcio Carias Andino was dictator president of the Republic. Since 1990 democratic practices have become more consistent.

MINT MARKS
T.G. - Yoro
T.L. – Comayagua

MONETARY SYSTEM
100 Centavos = 1 Lempira

REPUBLIC

DECIMAL COINAGE
100 Centavos = 1 Peso

KM# 46 CENTAVO
4.5000 g., Bronze **Obv:** Arms within circle **Rev:** Value, date within wreath **Edge:** Plain, reeded, and plain and reeded **Note:** Varieties exist.

Date	Mintage	VG	F	VF	XF	Unc
1901/0	98,000	6.50	20.00	42.50	60.00	—
1901	Inc. above	6.50	20.00	42.50	60.00	—
1902 large 0	—	5.00	15.00	27.50	50.00	150
1902 small 0	—	5.00	15.00	27.50	50.00	150
1903/2/1/0	—	40.00	80.00	145	200	—
Note: 5 known						
1904	—	5.00	15.00	32.50	70.00	—
1907	Inc. above	6.50	16.50	30.00	65.00	—
1907/4	234,000	8.00	20.00	35.00	60.00	—

KM# 59 CENTAVO
4.5000 g., Bronze **Obv:** Arms within circle **Rev:** Value within circle, date below **Note:** Varieties exist.

Date	Mintage	VG	F	VF	XF	Unc
1907 large UN	—	0.80	2.00	4.00	10.00	25.00
Note: Mintage included in KM#46						
1907 small UN	—	0.80	2.00	4.00	10.00	25.00
Note: Mintage included in KM#46						
1908/7	263,000	9.00	16.50	35.00	80.00	—
1908	—	9.00	16.50	35.00	80.00	—

KM# 61 CENTAVO
4.5000 g., Bronze **Obv:** Arms within circle and wreath **Rev:** Value within circle **Note:** The 1890, 1891 and 1908 dates are found with a die-cutting error or broken die that reads REPLBLICA. Other differences exist.

Date	Mintage	VG	F	VF	XF	Unc
1908	—	6.50	15.00	40.00	80.00	—

KM# 65 CENTAVO

2.1200 g., Bronze **Obv:** Towers front pyramid within circle
Rev: Denomination and date within wreath **Note:** Obverse and reverse are altered dies of KM45, 1/2 centavo (1881-1891). Numerous reverse varieties exist.

Date	Mintage	VG	F	VF	XF	Unc
1910/1884	—	12.50	25.00	40.00	70.00	—
1910/5	410,000	10.00	22.00	35.00	60.00	—
1910 large 0	410,000	8.50	20.00	32.50	50.00	—
1911/811	62,000	6.00	18.00	28.00	45.00	—
1911/885	Inc. above	6.00	18.00	28.00	45.00	—
1911/886	Inc. above	6.00	18.00	28.00	45.00	—
1911 CENTAVO	Inc. above	6.00	15.00	25.00	40.00	—
1911 CENTAVOS	Inc. above	100	165	280	450	750

KM# 66 CENTAVO

2.1200 g., Bronze **Obv:** Towers front pyramid within circle, obverse of 5 centavos, KM48 (1884-1902) **Rev:** Altered KM#45, 1/2 centavo.

Date	Mintage	VG	F	VF	XF	Unc
1910	Inc. above	9.00	25.00	45.00	90.00	—
1610 error, inverted 9	Inc. above	65.00	125	225	350	—
1910 error, second 1 inverted	Inc. above	12.00	27.50	50.00	100	—
1911 Reported, not confirmed	—	—	—	—	—	—

KM# 67 CENTAVO

2.1200 g., Bronze **Obv:** Towers front pyramid within inner circle, wreath surrounds outer circle, obverse of 5 centavos, KM48 (1884-1902) **Rev:** Denomination within wreath, altered dies of KM48

Date	Mintage	VG	F	VF	XF	Unc
1910	Inc. above	6.50	10.00	22.50	50.00	—
1911 Reported, not confirmed	—	—	—	—	—	—

KM# 68 CENTAVO

2.1200 g., Bronze **Obv:** Towers front pyramid within inner circle, obverse of centavo KM45 (1881-1891) **Rev:** Denomination within wreath, altered reverse of die of 5 centavos KM48 (1884-1902)

Date	Mintage	VG	F	VF	XF	Unc
1910	Inc. above	25.00	55.00	115	225	—

KM# 70 CENTAVO

2.1200 g., Bronze **Obv:** Towers front pyramid within circle **Rev:** Denomination and date within wreath, CENTAVO omitted

Date	Mintage	VG	F	VF	XF	Unc
1919	168,000	1.50	3.00	8.00	28.50	—
1920	30,000	3.00	6.50	16.50	42.50	—

KM# 64 2 CENTAVOS

4.2500 g., Bronze **Obv:** Towers front pyramid within circle, obverse of KM46, 1 centavo (1881-1907) **Rev:** Denomination within thick circle, altered reverse of KM49, 10 centavos (1884-1900)

Date	Mintage	VG	F	VF	XF	Unc
1907 Rare	Inc. below	—	—	—	—	—
1908/7	Inc. below	50.00	100	250	500	—
1908	Inc. below	50.00	100	250	500	—

KM# 69 2 CENTAVOS

Bronze **Obv:** Towers front pyramid within circle, obverse of KM46, 1 centavo (1881-1907) **Rev:** Denomination and date within wreath **Note:** Reverse dies often very crudely recut of KM46, especially 1910 and 1911. Some coins of 1910 appear to be struck over earlier 1 or 2 Centavos, probably 1907 or 1908. 1912 and 1913 reverse appear newly made.

Date	Mintage	VG	F	VF	XF	Unc
1910	435,000	1.25	4.00	10.00	20.00	45.00
1911	68,000	6.50	18.50	40.00	85.00	—
1912 CENTAVOS	88,000	1.00	4.50	15.00	35.00	—

Date	Mintage	VG	F	VF	XF	Unc
1912 CENTAVO	Inc. above	3.00	6.00	14.50	35.00	—
1913	258,000	1.00	2.50	6.00	18.50	—

KM# 71 2 CENTAVOS

4.2500 g., Bronze **Obv:** Towers front pyramid within circle **Rev:** Denomination and date within wreath, CENTAVOS omitted **Note:** Varieties exist.

Date	Mintage	VG	F	VF	XF	Unc
1919	117,000	2.50	9.00	20.00	55.00	—
1920	283,000	0.65	275	15.00	40.00	125
1920 Dot divides date	Inc. above	5.00	10.00	20.00	60.00	—

KM# 48 5 CENTAVOS

1.2500 g., 0.8350 Silver 0.0336 oz. ASW **Obv:** Arms within circle and wreath **Rev:** Value within wreath

Date	Mintage	VG	F	VF	XF	Unc
1902	—	50.00	100	175	300	500

KM# 50a 25 CENTAVOS

6.2500 g., 0.8350 Silver 0.1678 oz. ASW **Obv:** Flags sourround arms within circle **Rev:** Standing Liberty **Note:** Varieties exist.

Date	Mintage	VG	F	VF	XF	Unc
1901/801	54,000	4.00	8.00	15.00	45.00	—
1901/11	Inc. above	6.00	12.50	30.00	60.00	—
1901/0	—	7.00	15.00	35.00	65.00	200
1901 Large first 1	Inc. above	3.00	5.00	9.00	20.00	—
1902/801	—	10.00	17.50	25.00	50.00	—
1902/802	—	10.00	17.50	25.00	50.00	—
1902/812	—	10.00	17.50	25.00	50.00	—
1902/891	—	10.00	17.50	25.00	50.00	200
1902/1 F	—	3.75	6.00	10.00	20.00	200
1902 F	—	4.00	7.50	13.50	25.00	—
1904	—	20.00	40.00	75.00	150	400
1907/4	14,000	7.00	20.00	40.00	75.00	—
1907	—	7.50	20.00	40.00	75.00	—
1912 .835/.900	7,168	12.50	22.50	65.00	125	—
1913/0	52,000	25.00	50.00	100	215	—
1913/2	Inc. above	—	—	—	—	—
1913	Inc. above	12.50	25.00	45.00	75.00	—

KM# 51a 50 CENTAVOS

12.5000 g., Silver **Obv:** Towers front pyramid within inner circle, crowned and flagged decorative mantle behind **Rev:** Seated Liberty figure with flag and tablet, Neptunes symbols flank **Note:** Fineness can be .835 or .900.

Date	Mintage	VG	F	VF	XF	Unc
1908/897	447	35.00	65.00	165	300	500
1908	Inc. above	30.00	55.00	125	235	600

KM# 51 50 CENTAVOS

12.5000 g., 0.9000 Silver 0.3617 oz. ASW **Obv:** Flags sourround arms within circle **Rev:** Standing Liberty

Date	Mintage	VG	F	VF	XF	Unc
1910	602	500	1,000	—	—	—

KM# 56 PESO

1.6120 g., 0.9000 Gold 0.0466 oz. AGW **Obv:** Arms within circle, bouquets flanking, banner and stars above **Rev:** Liberty head left

Date	Mintage	F	VF	XF	Unc	BU
1901	—	150	300	600	1,150	—
1902	—	140	300	500	1,000	—
1907	—	140	250	450	900	—
1914/882	—	275	450	750	1,500	—
1914/03	—	275	450	750	1,500	—
1919	—	150	300	550	1,100	—
1920	—	150	300	550	1,100	—
1922	—	140	250	450	900	—
ND(ca.1922-25)	—	140	250	—	—	—

Note: These are marriage pieces.

KM# 52 PESO

25.0000 g., 0.9000 Silver 0.7234 oz. ASW **Obv:** Flags sourround arms within circle **Rev:** Standing Liberty **Note:** Overdates and recut dies are prevalent.

Date	Mintage	VG	F	VF	XF	Unc
1902	—	27.50	50.00	80.00	150	—
1903 flat-top 3	—	27.50	45.00	70.00	150	250
1903 round-top 3	—	30.00	55.00	100	200	400
1904	20,000	30.00	55.00	100	200	400
1914	—	200	500	900	1,500	2,500

KM# 53 5 PESOS

8.0645 g., 0.9000 Gold 0.2333 oz. AGW **Obv:** Arms within circle, bouquets flank outer circle **Rev:** Liberty head left

Date	Mintage	F	VF	XF	Unc	BU
1902	—	700	1,250	2,500	4,000	—
1908/888	—	600	1,000	2,000	3,000	—
1913	1,200	700	1,250	2,500	5,000	—

KM# 57 20 PESOS

32.2580 g., 0.9000 Gold 0.9334 oz. AGW **Obv:** Arms within inner circle, bouquets flank outer circle **Rev:** Liberty head left

Date	Mintage	F	VF	XF	Unc	BU
1908/888	—	—	20,000	30,000	—	—
1908/897 Rare	—	—	—	—	—	—

Note: Stack's Hammel sale 9-82 VF 1908/897 realized $12,000. Ponterio & Associates NYINC. sale 12-86 choice XF realized $30,800. Superior Casterline sale 5-89 choice XF realized $28,600.

1908 Rare	—	—	—	—	—	—

REFORM COINAGE

KM# 77.1 CENTAVO

2.0000 g., Bronze, 15 mm. **Obv:** National arms **Rev:** Denomination within circle, wreath surrounds **Note:** Thick planchet.

Date	Mintage	F	VF	XF	Unc	BU
1935(P)	2,000,000	0.25	1.00	5.00	15.00	—
1939(P)	2,000,000	0.25	0.75	3.00	10.00	—
1949(P)	4,000,000	0.10	0.50	2.00	4.00	—

KM# 77.2 CENTAVO

1.5000 g., Bronze, 15 mm. **Obv:** National arms **Rev:** Denomination within circle, wreath surrounds **Note:** Thin planchet.

Date	Mintage	F	VF	XF	Unc	BU
1954	3,500,000	0.10	0.15	1.00	3.00	—
1956	2,000,000	0.10	0.15	0.75	2.00	—
1957/6	28,000,000	—	—	—	—	—
1957	Inc. above	—	0.10	0.15	0.30	—

KM# 77a CENTAVO
1.3700 g., Copper Clad Steel, 15 mm. **Obv:** National arms, without clouds behind pyramids **Rev:** Denomination within circle, wreath surrounds

Date	Mintage	F	VF	XF	Unc	BU
1974	—	—	0.10	0.15	0.25	—
1985	—	—	0.10	0.15	0.25	—
1992	—	—	0.10	0.15	0.25	—
1994	—	—	0.10	0.15	0.25	—
1998	—	—	0.10	0.15	0.25	—

KM# 77b CENTAVO
Copper Plated Steel, 15 mm. **Obv:** National arms, clouds behind pyramids **Rev:** Denomination within circle, wreath surrounds

Date	Mintage	F	VF	XF	Unc	BU
1988	50,000,000	—	0.10	0.15	0.25	—

KM# 78 2 CENTAVOS
3.0000 g., Bronze, 21 mm. **Obv:** National arms **Rev:** Denomination within circle, wreath surrounds

Date	Mintage	F	VF	XF	Unc	BU
1939(P)	2,000,000	0.25	1.00	3.00	9.00	—
1949(P)	3,000,000	0.10	0.50	2.00	6.00	—
1954	2,000,000	0.10	0.25	1.00	3.00	—
1956	20,000,000	—	0.10	0.25	1.00	—

KM# 78a 2 CENTAVOS
2.7000 g., Bronze Clad Steel, 21 mm. **Obv:** National arms **Rev:** Denomination within circle, wreath surrounds

Date	Mintage	F	VF	XF	Unc	BU
1974	—	—	0.10	0.15	0.25	—

KM# 72.1 5 CENTAVOS
5.0000 g., Copper-Nickel, 21 mm. **Obv:** National arms **Rev:** Denomination within circle, wreath surrounds **Note:** Dentilated border.

Date	Mintage	F	VF	XF	Unc	BU
1931(P)	2,000,000	0.50	2.00	7.00	20.00	—
1932(P)	1,000,000	0.35	0.75	4.00	14.00	—
1949(P)	2,000,000	0.20	0.50	3.00	9.00	—
1956(P)	10,070,000	—	0.15	0.25	0.60	—
1972	5,000,000	—	0.10	0.15	0.35	—

KM# 72.2 5 CENTAVOS
5.0000 g., Copper-Nickel, 21 mm. **Obv:** National arms **Rev:** Denomination within circle, wreath surrounds **Note:** Beaded border.

Date	Mintage	F	VF	XF	Unc	BU
1954	1,400,000	0.15	0.25	1.00	3.00	—
1980	20,000,000	—	0.10	0.50	1.00	—

KM# 72.2a 5 CENTAVOS
Brass, 21 mm. **Obv:** National arms, without clouds behind pyramids **Rev:** Denomination within circle, wreath surrounds

Date	Mintage	F	VF	XF	Unc	BU
1975	20,000,000	—	0.10	0.15	0.35	—
1989	—	—	0.10	0.15	0.35	—

KM# 72.3 5 CENTAVOS
Brass, 21 mm. **Obv:** National arms, with clouds behind pyramids **Rev:** Denomination within circle, wreath surrounds

Date	Mintage	F	VF	XF	Unc	BU
1993	—	—	0.10	0.15	0.35	—
1994	—	—	0.10	0.15	0.35	—

KM# 72.4 5 CENTAVOS
3.2500 g., Brass, 20.96 mm. **Obv:** National arms **Rev:** Value in circle within sprays **Edge:** Plain

Date	Mintage	F	VF	XF	Unc	BU
1995	—	—	—	0.10	0.25	0.35
1998	—	—	—	0.10	0.25	0.35
1999	—	—	—	0.10	0.25	0.35

KM# 76.1 10 CENTAVOS
7.0000 g., Copper-Nickel, 26 mm. **Obv:** National arms **Rev:** Denomination within circle, wreath surrounds **Note:** Dentilated border.

Date	Mintage	F	VF	XF	Unc	BU
1932(P)	1,500,000	1.00	2.50	10.00	35.00	50.00
1951(P)	1,000,000	0.50	1.00	4.00	12.00	20.00
1956(P)	7,560,000	0.10	0.25	0.50	1.00	3.00

KM# 76.2 10 CENTAVOS
7.0000 g., Copper-Nickel, 26 mm. **Obv:** National arms **Rev:** Denomination within circle, wreath surrounds **Note:** Beaded border.

Date	Mintage	F	VF	XF	Unc	BU
1954	1,200,000	0.10	0.25	1.00	7.00	—
1967	—	0.10	0.25	0.50	2.00	—
1980	15,000,000	0.10	0.25	0.50	2.00	—
1993	—	0.10	0.25	0.50	2.00	—

KM# 76.1a 10 CENTAVOS
Brass, 26 mm. **Obv:** Large letters and national arms **Rev:** Denomination within circle, wreath surrounds

Date	Mintage	F	VF	XF	Unc	BU
1976	—	0.10	0.15	0.25	0.60	—
1989	—	0.10	0.15	0.25	0.60	—

KM# 76.2a 10 CENTAVOS
6.0300 g., Brass, 26 mm. **Obv:** Small letters and national arms, with clouds behind pyramids **Rev:** Denomination within circle, wreath surrounds **Edge:** Plain **Note:** Beaded border.

Date	Mintage	F	VF	XF	Unc	BU
1993	—	—	0.10	0.20	0.45	—
1994	—	—	0.10	0.20	0.45	—
1995	—	—	0.10	0.20	0.45	—
1995 Small date	—	—	0.10	0.20	0.45	—

KM# 76.3 10 CENTAVOS
5.9700 g., Brass, 26 mm. **Obv:** National arms, without clouds behind pyramid **Rev:** Denomination within circle, wreath surrounds

Date	Mintage	F	VF	XF	Unc	BU
1995	—	—	0.10	0.20	0.45	—
1995 Small date	—	—	—	—	—	—
1998	—	—	0.10	0.20	0.45	—

KM# 73 20 CENTAVOS
2.5000 g., 0.9000 Silver 0.0723 oz. ASW, 18 mm. **Obv:** National arms **Rev:** Chief Lempira left within circle

Date	Mintage	F	VF	XF	Unc	BU
1931(P)	1,000,000	1.25	3.50	9.00	30.00	—
1932(P)	750,000	1.25	3.50	8.00	22.50	—
1951(P)	1,500,000	BV	1.25	3.00	8.00	—
1952	2,500,000	BV	1.25	2.50	7.00	—
1958	2,000,000	BV	1.25	2.00	6.00	—

KM# 79 20 CENTAVOS
2.2000 g., Copper-Nickel, 18 mm. **Obv:** National arms **Rev:** Chief Lempira left within circle

Date	Mintage	F	VF	XF	Unc	BU
1967	12,000,000	—	0.10	0.35	1.00	1.50

KM# 81 20 CENTAVOS
2.2000 g., Copper-Nickel, 18 mm. **Obv:** National arms, date below **Rev:** Chief Lempira left within circle **Note:** Different style lettering.

Date	Mintage	F	VF	XF	Unc	BU
1973	15,000,000	—	0.10	0.20	0.60	1.00

KM# 83.1 20 CENTAVOS
2.2000 g., Copper-Nickel, 18 mm. **Obv:** National arms **Rev:** Head left within circle

Date	Mintage	F	VF	XF	Unc	BU
1978	30,000,000	—	0.10	0.20	0.60	1.00
1990	—	—	0.10	0.20	0.60	1.00

KM# 83.1a 20 CENTAVOS
2.0000 g., Nickel Plated Steel, 17.93 mm. **Obv:** Small arms and legend, with clouds behind pyramid **Rev:** Head left within circle **Edge:** Reeded

Date	Mintage	F	VF	XF	Unc	BU
1991	—	—	0.10	0.20	0.60	1.00
1993	—	—	0.10	0.20	0.60	1.00
1994	—	—	0.10	0.20	0.60	1.00

KM# 83.2a 20 CENTAVOS
2.0000 g., Nickel Plated Steel, 17.94 mm. **Obv:** National arms, without clouds **Rev:** Head of Chief Lempira left within circle **Edge:** Reeded

Date	Mintage	F	VF	XF	Unc	BU
1995	—	—	0.10	0.20	0.60	1.00
1996	—	—	0.10	0.20	0.60	1.00
1999	—	—	0.10	0.20	0.60	1.00

KM# 74 50 CENTAVOS
6.2500 g., 0.9000 Silver 0.1808 oz. ASW, 23.8 mm.
Obv: National arms **Rev:** Chiefs head left within circle

Date	Mintage	F	VF	XF	Unc	BU
1931(P)	500,000	5.00	7.00	15.00	40.00	—
1932(P)	1,100,000	3.75	5.00	10.00	35.00	—
1937(P)	1,000,000	3.75	5.00	10.00	35.00	50.00
1951(P)	500,000	3.75	5.00	9.00	30.00	60.00

KM# 80 50 CENTAVOS
5.7000 g., Copper-Nickel, 24 mm. **Obv:** National arms
Rev: Chief Lempira left within circle

Date	Mintage	F	VF	XF	Unc	BU
1967	4,800,000	—	0.25	0.35	1.25	2.00

KM# 82 50 CENTAVOS
5.7000 g., Copper-Nickel, 24 mm. **Series:** F.A.O. **Obv:** National arms **Rev:** Chief Lempira left within circle

Date	Mintage	F	VF	XF	Unc	BU
1973	4,400,000	—	0.25	0.35	1.25	2.00

KM# 84 50 CENTAVOS
5.7000 g., Copper-Nickel, 24 mm. **Obv:** National arms, with clouds behind pyramid **Rev:** Head left within circle

Date	Mintage	F	VF	XF	Unc	BU
1978	12,000,000	—	0.25	0.35	1.00	1.50
1990	—	—	0.25	0.35	1.00	1.50

KM# 84.a1 50 CENTAVOS
Nickel Plated Steel, 24 mm. **Obv:** National arms **Rev:** Head left within circle

Date	Mintage	F	VF	XF	Unc	BU
1991	—	—	0.25	0.35	1.00	1.50
1994	—	—	0.25	0.35	1.00	1.50

KM# 88 50 CENTAVOS
Nickel Plated Steel, 24 mm. **Subject:** 50th Anniversary F.A.O. **Obv:** National arms **Rev:** Head left within circle, logo below

Date	Mintage	F	VF	XF	Unc	BU
1994	2,000,000	—	—	—	1.50	2.00

KM# 84a.2 50 CENTAVOS
5.1800 g., Nickel Plated Steel, 24 mm. **Obv:** National arms **Rev:** Head of Chief Lempira left within circle **Edge:** Reeded

Date	Mintage	F	VF	XF	Unc	BU
1995	—	—	0.15	0.45	1.10	1.50
1996	—	—	0.15	0.45	1.10	1.50

KM# 75 LEMPIRA
12.5000 g., 0.9000 Silver 0.3617 oz. ASW, 31 mm.
Obv: National arms **Rev:** Chiefs head left within circle

Date	Mintage	F	VF	XF	Unc	BU
1931(P)	550,000	7.50	10.00	20.00	75.00	125
1932(P)	1,000,000	BV	9.00	16.00	65.00	100
1933(P)	400,000	BV	8.00	10.00	45.00	75.00
1934(P)	600,000	BV	7.50	9.00	40.00	100
1935(P)	1,000,000		BV	9.00	40.00	60.00
1937(P)	4,000,000		BV	8.00	25.00	50.00

KM# 89 LEMPIRA
33.6250 g., 0.9250 Silver 0.9999 oz. ASW, 38 mm.
Subject: Central Bank's 50th Anniversary **Obv:** National arms within beaded circle **Rev:** Bank building within beaded circle, wreath surrounds **Edge:** Plain

Date	Mintage	F	VF	XF	Unc	BU
ND(2000) Proof	3,000	Value: 65.00				

KM# 85 100 LEMPIRAS
27.0000 g., 0.9250 Silver 0.8029 oz. ASW **Subject:** 500th Anniversary - Discovery of America **Obv:** National arms in inner circle, legend at top, date below **Rev:** Ship approaching curved wall

Date	Mintage	F	VF	XF	Unc	BU
1992 Proof	5,000	Value: 60.00				

KM# 86 200 LEMPIRAS
6.5000 g., 0.9000 Gold 0.1881 oz. AGW, 20 mm.
Subject: Bicentenary of Birth - Gen. Francisco Morazan
Obv: Emblem within legend **Rev:** Head left

Date	Mintage	F	VF	XF	Unc	BU
1992 Proof	1,500	Value: 180				

KM# 87 500 LEMPIRAS
12.5000 g., 0.9000 Gold 0.3617 oz. AGW, 26 mm.
Subject: Bicentenary of Birth - Gen. Francisco Morazan

Date	Mintage	F	VF	XF	Unc	BU
1992	1,500	Value: 340				

PATTERNS
Including off metal strikes

Rosettes separate legends on Pn1-Pn5a.

KM#	Date	Mintage	Identification	Mkt Val
Pn22	1909	—	Centavo. Copper.	150
Pn23	1919	—	Peso. Copper. KM#56.	100

HONG KONG

CHINA TAIWAN

Hong Kong, a former British colony, reverted to control of the People's Republic of China on July 1, 1997 as a Special Administrative Region. It is situated at the mouth of the Canton or Pearl River 90 miles (145 km.) southeast of Canton, has an area of 403 sq. mi. (1,040 sq. km.) and an estimated population of 6.3 million. Capital: Victoria. The free port of Hong Kong, the commercial center of the Far East, is a trans-shipment point for goods destined for China and the countries of the Pacific Rim. Light manufacturing and tourism are important components of the economy.

Long a haven for fishermen-pirates and opium smugglers, the island of Hong Kong was ceded to Britain at the conclusion of the first Opium War, 1839-1842. The acquisition of a 'barren rock' was ridiculed by London and English merchants operating in the Far East. The Kowloon Peninsula and Stonecutter's Island were ceded in 1860, and the so-called New Territories, comprising most of the mainland of the colony, were leased to Britain for 99 years in 1898.

The legends on Hong Kong coinage are bilingual: English and Chinese. The rare 1941 cent was dispatched to Hong Kong in several shipments. One fell into Japanese hands, while another was melted down by the British and a third was sunk during enemy action.

RULER
British 1842-1997

MINT MARKS
H - Heaton
KN - King's Norton

MONETARY SYSTEM
10 Mils (Wen, Ch'ien) = 1 Cent (Hsien)
10 Cents = 1 Chiao
100 Cents = 10 Chiao = 1 Dollar (Yuan)

BRITISH COLONY

DECIMAL COINAGE

KM# 4.3 CENT
Bronze, 27.6 mm. **Ruler:** Victoria **Obv:** Crowned bust left
Rev: Chinese value within beaded circle

Date	Mintage	F	VF	XF	Unc	BU
1901	5,000,000	2.50	5.50	16.00	85.00	—
1901H	10,000,000	2.50	5.50	16.00	75.00	—

KM# 11 CENT
7.1700 g., Bronze, 27.6 mm. **Ruler:** Edward VII **Obv:** Crowned
bust right **Rev:** English around central Chinese legend

Date	Mintage	F	VF	XF	Unc	BU
1902	5,000,000	2.50	4.50	10.00	80.00	—
1903	5,000,000	2.50	4.50	10.00	85.00	—
1904H	10,000,000	1.75	3.50	10.00	65.00	—
1905H	12,500,000	2.50	4.50	10.00	130	—
1905	2,500,000	3.75	7.50	15.00	125	—

KM# 16 CENT
Bronze, 27.6 mm. **Ruler:** George V **Obv:** Crowned bust left
Rev: English around central Chinese legend

Date	Mintage	F	VF	XF	Unc	BU
1919H	2,500,000	2.00	4.00	10.00	50.00	—
1923	2,500,000	1.50	3.00	7.50	40.00	—
1924	5,000,000	1.25	2.50	4.50	20.00	—
1925	2,500,000	1.25	2.50	4.50	20.00	—
1926	2,500,000	1.25	2.50	4.50	20.00	—
1926 Proof	—	Value: 350				

KM# 17 CENT
3.9400 g., Bronze, 22 mm. **Ruler:** George V **Obv:** Crowned bust
left **Rev:** English around central Chinese legend

Date	Mintage	F	VF	XF	Unc	BU
1931	5,000,000	0.75	1.00	2.00	5.50	—
1931 Proof	—	Value: 250				
1933	6,500,000	0.75	1.00	2.00	5.50	—
1933 Proof	—	Value: 250				
1934	5,000,000	0.75	1.00	2.00	5.50	—
1934 Proof	—	Value: 250				

KM# 24 CENT
Bronze **Ruler:** George VI **Obv:** Crowned head left **Rev:** English
around central Chinese legend

Date	Mintage	F	VF	XF	Unc	BU
1941	5,000,000	1,500	2,500	5,000	8,500	—
1941 Proof	—	Value: 10,000				

KM# 5 5 CENTS
1.3577 g., 0.8000 Silver 0.0349 oz. ASW, 15.53 mm.
Ruler: Victoria **Obv:** Crowned head left **Rev:** Chinese value
within beaded circle **Note:** Coins dated 1866-1868 struck at the
Hong Kong Mint; coins without mintmarks dated 1872-1901, were
struck at the British Royal Mint.

Date	Mintage	F	VF	XF	Unc	BU
1901	10,000,000	1.25	2.50	5.00	25.00	—

KM# 12 5 CENTS
1.3577 g., 0.8000 Silver 0.0349 oz. ASW **Ruler:** Edward VII
Obv: Crowned bust right **Rev:** English around central Chinese
legend

Date	Mintage	F	VF	XF	Unc	BU
1903	6,000,000	1.00	2.00	4.00	25.00	—
1903 Proof	—	Value: 225				
1904	8,000,000	1.00	2.00	4.00	25.00	—
1904 Proof	—	Value: 200				
1905	1,000,000	1.25	3.00	6.50	35.00	—
1905H	7,000,000	1.00	2.00	4.00	25.00	—

KM# 18 5 CENTS
1.3577 g., 0.8000 Silver 0.0349 oz. ASW **Ruler:** George V
Obv: Crowned bust left **Rev:** English around central Chinese
legend

Date	Mintage	F	VF	XF	Unc	BU
1932	3,000,000	1.00	1.50	4.00	10.00	—
1932 Proof	—	Value: 165				
1933	2,000,000	1.00	1.50	3.25	10.00	—
1933 Proof	—	Value: 165				

KM# 18a 5 CENTS
Copper-Nickel **Ruler:** George V **Obv:** Crowned bust left
Rev: English around central Chinese legend

Date	Mintage	F	VF	XF	Unc	BU
1935	1,000,000	1.00	2.00	4.50	16.50	—
1935 Proof	—	Value: 115				

KM# 20 5 CENTS
Nickel **Ruler:** George VI **Obv:** Crowned head left **Rev:** English
around central Chinese legend **Edge:** Reeded with security

Date	Mintage	F	VF	XF	Unc	BU
1937	3,000,000	0.75	1.25	2.25	7.50	—
1937 Proof	—	Value: 85.00				

KM# 22 5 CENTS
Nickel **Ruler:** George VI **Obv:** Crowned head left
Rev: English around central Chinese legend **Edge:** Reeded with
security

Date	Mintage	F	VF	XF	Unc	BU
1938	3,000,000	0.50	1.00	2.00	6.50	—
1938 Proof	—	Value: 125				
1939H	3,090,000	0.50	1.00	2.00	6.50	—
1939H Proof	—	Value: 125				
1939KN	4,710,000	0.50	1.00	2.00	6.50	—
1941H	777,000	350	750	1,400	3,150	—
1941KN	1,075,000	150	300	600	1,200	—

KM# 26 5 CENTS
Nickel-Brass, 16.5 mm. **Ruler:** George VI **Obv:** Crowned head
left **Rev:** English around central Chinese legend

Date	Mintage	F	VF	XF	Unc	BU
1949	15,000,000	0.25	0.50	1.25	7.50	—
1949 Proof	—	Value: 125				
1950	20,400,000	0.25	0.50	1.25	7.50	—
1950 Proof	—	Value: 125				

KM# 29.1 5 CENTS
Nickel-Brass, 16.5 mm. **Ruler:** Elizabeth II **Obv:** Crowned head
right **Rev:** English around central Chinese legend **Edge:** Reeded
and security

Date	Mintage	F	VF	XF	Unc	BU
1958H	5,000,000	—	0.25	0.75	4.50	—
1960	5,000,000	—	0.15	0.50	3.50	—
1960 Proof	—	Value: 65.00				
1963	7,000,000	—	0.15	0.50	3.50	—
1963 Proof	—	Value: 65.00				
1964H		50.00	85.00	150	550	—
1965	18,000,000	—	0.10	0.40	2.00	—
1967	10,000,000	—	0.10	0.40	2.00	—

KM# 29.2 5 CENTS
Nickel-Brass, 16.5 mm. **Ruler:** Elizabeth II **Obv:** Crowned head
right **Rev:** English around central Chinese legend **Edge:** Reeded
Note: Error.

Date	Mintage	F	VF	XF	Unc	BU
1958H	Inc. above	2.50	5.00	9.00	20.00	—
1960	Inc. above	2.50	5.00	9.00	20.00	—

KM# 29.3 5 CENTS
2.6000 g., Nickel-Brass, 16.5 mm. **Ruler:** Elizabeth II
Obv: Crowned head right **Rev:** English around central Chinese
legend **Edge:** Reeded

Date	Mintage	F	VF	XF	Unc	BU
1971KN	14,000,000	—	—	0.25	0.50	—
1971H	6,000,000	—	—	0.25	0.50	—
1972H	14,000,000	—	—	0.25	0.50	—
1977	6,000,000	—	—	0.25	0.50	—
1978	10,000,000	—	—	0.25	0.50	—
1979	4,000,000	—	—	0.25	0.50	—
1980 Not issued	50,000,000					

KM# 61 5 CENTS
2.6000 g., Nickel-Brass, 16.5 mm. **Ruler:** Elizabeth II **Obv:**
Crowned head right **Rev:** English around central Chinese legend

Date	Mintage	F	VF	XF	Unc	BU
1988	50,000				4.00	—
1988 Proof	25,000	Value: 5.00				

KM# 6.3 10 CENTS
2.7154 g., 0.8000 Silver 0.0698 oz. ASW, 17.84 mm.
Ruler: Victoria **Obv:** Crowned bust left **Rev:** Chinese value within
beaded circle **Note:** Coins dated 1866-1868 struck at the Hong
Kong Mint; coins without mintmarks dated 1869-1901, struck at
the British Royal Mint.

Date	Mintage	F	VF	XF	Unc	BU
1901	25,000,000	1.25	2.25	4.50	20.00	—

KM# 13 10 CENTS
2.7154 g., 0.8000 Silver 0.0698 oz. ASW **Ruler:** Edward VII **Obv:**
Crowned bust right **Rev:** English around central Chinese legend

Date	Mintage	F	VF	XF	Unc	BU
1902	18,000,000	1.25	2.25	4.50	32.00	—
1902 Proof	—	Value: 200				
1903	25,000,000	1.25	2.25	4.50	32.00	—

Date	Mintage	F	VF	XF	Unc	BU
1903 Proof	—	Value: 200				
1904	30,000,000	1.25	2.25	4.50	32.00	—
1904 Proof	—	Value: 165				
1905	33,487,000	225	400	650	2,150	—
1905 Proof	—	Value: 2,500				

KM# 19 10 CENTS
Copper-Nickel, 20.5 mm. **Ruler:** George V **Obv:** Crowned bust left **Rev:** English around central Chinese legend

Date	Mintage	F	VF	XF	Unc	BU
1935	10,000,000	0.50	1.00	3.50	15.00	—
1935 Proof	—	Value: 75.00				
1936	5,000,000	0.50	1.00	3.50	15.00	—
1936 Proof	—	Value: 75.00				

KM# 21 10 CENTS
Nickel, 20.5 mm. **Ruler:** George VI **Obv:** Crowned head left **Rev:** English around central Chinese legend **Edge:** Reeded with security

Date	Mintage	F	VF	XF	Unc	BU
1937	17,500,000	0.50	0.80	1.50	6.50	—
1937 Proof	—	Value: 85.00				

KM# 23 10 CENTS
Nickel, 20.5 mm. **Ruler:** George VI **Obv:** Crowned head left **Rev:** English around central Chinese legend **Edge:** Reeded with security

Date	Mintage	F	VF	XF	Unc	BU
1938	7,500,000	0.65	1.00	2.25	7.50	—
1938 Proof	—	Value: 85.00				
1939H	5,000,000	0.65	1.00	2.25	7.50	—
1939KN	5,000,000	0.65	1.00	2.25	7.50	—
1939KN Proof	—	Value: 85.00				

KM# 25 10 CENTS
Nickel-Brass, 20.5 mm. **Ruler:** George VI **Obv:** Crowned head left **Rev:** English around central Chinese legend **Edge:** Reeded and security

Date	Mintage	F	VF	XF	Unc	BU
1948	30,000,000	0.25	0.50	1.25	6.50	—
1948 Proof	—	Value: 65.00				
1949	35,000,000	0.25	0.50	1.25	6.50	—
1949 Proof	—	Value: 65.00				
1950	20,000,000	0.25	0.50	1.25	6.50	—
1950 Proof	—	Value: 65.00				
1951	5,000,000	0.50	1.00	3.00	22.50	—
1951 Proof	—	Value: 85.00				

KM# 25a 10 CENTS
Nickel-Brass, 20.5 mm. **Ruler:** George VI **Obv:** Crowned head left **Rev:** English around central Chinese legend **Edge:** Reeded **Note:** Error.

Date	Mintage	F	VF	XF	Unc	BU
1950	Inc. above	3.50	6.50	12.50	25.00	—

KM# 28.1 10 CENTS
4.4600 g., Nickel-Brass, 20.5 mm. **Ruler:** Elizabeth II **Obv:** Crowned head right **Rev:** English around central Chinese legend **Edge:** Reeded with security

Date	Mintage	F	VF	XF	Unc	BU
1955	10,000,000	0.15	0.25	0.50	5.50	—
1955 Proof	—	Value: 50.00				

Date	Mintage	F	VF	XF	Unc	BU
1956	3,110,000	0.25	0.50	1.25	15.00	—
1956 Proof	—	Value: 50.00				
1956H	4,488,000	0.15	0.25	1.00	10.00	—
1956KN	2,500,000	0.25	0.50	2.00	16.50	—
1957H	5,250,000	0.15	0.25	0.50	10.00	—
1957KN	2,800,000	0.15	0.25	1.00	10.00	—
1958KN	10,000,000	0.15	0.25	0.50	10.00	—
1959H	20,000,000	0.10	0.15	0.25	6.00	—
1960	12,500,000	0.10	0.15	0.25	6.00	—
1960 Proof	—	Value: 50.00				
1960H	10,000,000	0.10	0.15	0.25	6.00	—
1961	20,000,000	0.10	0.15	0.25	4.00	—
1961 Proof	—	Value: 50.00				
1961H	5,000,000	0.15	0.25	0.50	5.00	—
1961KN	5,000,000	0.15	0.25	0.50	5.00	—
1963	27,000,000	0.10	0.15	0.25	4.00	—
1963 Proof	—	Value: 50.00				
1963H	3,000,000	0.20	0.30	0.50	4.00	—
1963KN	Inc. above	0.10	0.15	0.25	3.50	—
1964	9,000,000	0.10	0.15	0.25	2.00	—
1964H	21,000,000	0.10	0.15	0.25	2.00	—
1965	40,000,000	0.10	0.15	0.25	2.00	—
1965H	8,000,000	0.10	0.15	0.25	2.50	—
1965KN	Inc. above	0.10	0.15	0.25	2.50	—
1967	10,000,000	0.10	0.15	0.25	2.00	—
1968H	15,000,000	0.10	0.15	0.25	2.00	—

KM# 28.2 10 CENTS
Nickel-Brass, 20.5 mm. **Ruler:** Elizabeth II **Obv:** Crowned head right **Rev:** English around central Chinese legend **Edge:** Reeded **Note:** Error.

Date	Mintage	F	VF	XF	Unc	BU
1956	Inc. above	2.25	4.50	8.50	25.00	—
1963	—	2.25	4.50	8.50	25.00	—

KM# 28.3 10 CENTS
Nickel-Brass, 20.5 mm. **Ruler:** Elizabeth II **Obv:** Crowned head right **Rev:** English around central Chinese legend **Edge:** Reeded

Date	Mintage	F	VF	XF	Unc	BU
1971H	22,000,000	—	0.10	0.15	0.65	—
1972KN	20,000,000	—	0.10	0.15	0.65	—
1973	2,250,000	0.15	0.25	0.65	3.50	—
1974	4,600,000	—	0.10	0.15	0.65	—
1975	44,840,000	—	0.10	0.15	0.65	—
1978	57,500,000	—	0.10	0.15	0.65	—
1979	101,500,000	—	0.10	0.15	0.65	—
1980	24,000,000	—	7.00	15.00	35.00	—

Note: Few pieces were released for circulation in 1980, but large numbers have found their way onto the market in subsequent years. About 3,500 are known to exist.

KM# 49 10 CENTS
2.0000 g., Nickel-Brass, 17.55 mm. **Ruler:** Elizabeth II **Obv:** Young bust right **Rev:** Denomination

Date	Mintage	F	VF	XF	Unc	BU
1982	—	—	0.10	0.15	0.25	—
1983	110,016,000	—	0.10	0.15	0.25	—
1984	30,016,000	—	0.10	0.15	0.25	—

KM# 55 10 CENTS
Nickel-Brass, 17.55 mm. **Ruler:** Elizabeth II **Obv:** Crowned head right **Rev:** Denomination

Date	Mintage	F	VF	XF	Unc	BU
1985	34,016,000	—	0.10	0.15	0.25	—
1986	40,000,000	—	0.10	0.15	0.25	—
1987	—	—	0.10	0.15	0.25	—
1988	30,000,000	—	0.10	0.15	0.25	—
1988 Proof	20,000	Value: 5.00				
1989	40,000,000	—	0.10	0.15	0.25	—
1990	—	—	0.10	0.15	0.25	—
1991	—	—	0.10	0.15	0.25	—
1992	24,000,000	—	0.10	0.15	0.25	—

KM# 66 10 CENTS
1.8400 g., Brass Plated Steel, 16.54 mm. **Ruler:** Elizabeth II **Obv:** Bauhinia flower **Rev:** Denomination **Edge:** Plain

Date	Mintage	F	VF	XF	Unc	BU
1993	—	—	0.10	0.15	0.30	—
1993 Proof	—	Value: 2.50				
1994	—	—	0.10	0.15	0.30	—

Date	Mintage	F	VF	XF	Unc	BU
1995	—	—	0.10	0.15	0.30	—
1996	—	—	0.10	0.15	0.30	—
1997	—	—	0.10	0.15	0.30	—
1998	—	—	0.10	0.15	0.30	—

KM# 14 20 CENTS
5.4308 g., 0.8000 Silver 0.1397 oz. ASW **Ruler:** Edward VII **Obv:** Crowned bust right **Rev:** English around central Chinese legend

Date	Mintage	F	VF	XF	Unc	BU
1902	250,000	20.00	40.00	110	600	—
1902 Proof	—	Value: 1,200				
1904	250,000	20.00	40.00	120	650	—
1905	750,000	300	600	1,200	4,000	—
1905 Proof	—	Value: 7,000				

KM# 36 20 CENTS
2.6000 g., Nickel-Brass, 19 mm. **Ruler:** Elizabeth II **Obv:** Young bust right **Rev:** English around central Chinese legend **Edge:** Scalloped

Date	Mintage	F	VF	XF	Unc	BU
1975	71,000,000	—	0.10	0.20	0.35	—
1976	42,000,000	—	0.10	0.20	0.35	—
1977	Inc. above	—	0.10	0.20	0.35	—
1978	86,000,000	—	0.10	0.20	0.35	—
1979	94,500,000	—	0.10	0.20	0.35	—
1980	65,000,000	—	0.10	0.20	0.35	—
1982	30,000,000	—	0.10	0.20	0.35	—
1983	15,000,000	—	0.10	0.20	0.35	—

KM# 59 20 CENTS
2.6000 g., Brass, 19 mm. **Ruler:** Elizabeth II **Obv:** Crowned head right **Rev:** English around central Chinese legend **Edge:** Scalloped

Date	Mintage	F	VF	XF	Unc	BU
1985	10,000,000	—	0.10	0.20	0.35	—
1988	Est. 40,000	—	0.10	0.20	0.35	—
1988 Proof	Est. 20,000	Value: 5.00				
1989	17,000,000	—	0.10	0.20	0.35	—
1990	—	—	0.10	0.20	0.35	—
1991	131,000,000	—	0.10	0.20	0.35	—

KM# 67 20 CENTS
2.6200 g., Nickel-Brass, 18.95 mm. **Ruler:** Elizabeth II **Obv:** Bauhinia flower **Rev:** Denomination **Edge:** Scalloped

Date	Mintage	F	VF	XF	Unc	BU
1993	—	—	0.10	0.20	0.40	—
1993 Proof	—	Value: 2.50				
1994	—	—	0.10	0.20	0.40	—
1995	—	—	0.10	0.20	0.40	—
1997	—	—	0.10	0.20	0.40	—
1998	—	—	0.10	0.20	0.40	—

KM# 15 50 CENTS
13.5769 g., 0.8000 Silver 0.3492 oz. ASW **Ruler:** Edward VII **Obv:** Crowned bust right **Rev:** English and Chinese legend, denomination at center

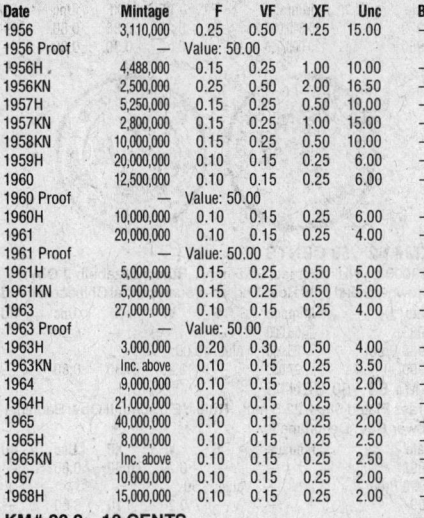

Date	Mintage	F	VF	XF	Unc	BU
1902	100,000	25.00	35.00	55.00	320	—
1902 Proof	—	Value: 650				
1904	100,000	25.00	35.00	60.00	360	—
1904 Proof	—	Value: 650				
1905	300,000	20.00	25.00	50.00	225	—
1905 Proof	—	Value: 650				

KM# 27.1   50 CENTS
Copper-Nickel, 23.5 mm. **Ruler:** George VI **Obv:** Crowned head left **Rev:** English around central Chinese legend **Edge:** Reeded and security

Date	Mintage	F	VF	XF	Unc	BU
1951	15,000,000	1.00	2.00	3.50	12.00	—
1951 Proof	—	Value: 250				

KM# 27.2   50 CENTS
Copper-Nickel, 23.5 mm. **Ruler:** George VI **Obv:** Crowned head left **Rev:** English around central Chinese legend **Edge:** Reeded **Note:** Error.

Date	Mintage	F	VF	XF	Unc	BU
1951	Inc. above	3.00	5.00	10.00	22.00	—

KM# 30.1   50 CENTS
5.8500 g., Copper-Nickel, 23.5 mm. **Ruler:** Elizabeth II **Obv:** Crowned head right **Rev:** English around central Chinese legend **Edge:** Reeded and security

Date	Mintage	F	VF	XF	Unc	BU
1958H	4,000,000	—	0.50	1.25	4.50	—
1960	4,000,000	—	0.40	1.00	4.00	—
1960 Proof	—	Value: 100				
1961	6,000,000	—	0.40	1.00	3.50	—
1961 Proof	—	Value: 100				
1963H	10,000,000	—	0.40	1.00	3.50	—
1964	5,000,000	—	0.40	1.00	3.50	—
1965KN	8,000,000	—	0.40	1.00	3.00	—
1966	5,000,000	—	0.40	1.00	3.50	—
1967	12,000,000	—	0.40	1.00	3.00	—
1968H	12,000,000	—	0.40	1.00	3.00	—
1970H	4,600,000	—	0.40	1.00	3.00	—

KM# 30.2   50 CENTS
Copper-Nickel, 23.5 mm. **Ruler:** Elizabeth II **Obv:** Crowned head right **Rev:** English around central Chinese legend **Edge:** Reeded **Note:** Error.

Date	Mintage	F	VF	XF	Unc	BU
1958H	Inc. above	2.00	4.00	8.00	20.00	—

KM# 34   50 CENTS
Copper-Nickel, 23.5 mm. **Ruler:** Victoria **Obv:** Crowned head right **Rev:** English around central Chinese legend **Edge:** Reeded

Date	Mintage	F	VF	XF	Unc	BU
1971KN	—	—	0.20	0.40	1.50	—
1972	30,000,000	—	0.20	0.40	1.50	—
1973	36,800,000	—	0.20	0.40	1.50	—
1974	6,000,000	—	0.20	0.40	1.50	—
1975	8,000,000	—	0.20	0.40	1.50	—

KM# 41   50 CENTS
4.9000 g., Nickel-Brass, 22.5 mm. **Ruler:** Elizabeth II **Obv:** Young bust right **Rev:** English around central Chinese legend

Date	Mintage	F	VF	XF	Unc	BU
1977	60,001,000	—	0.20	0.30	0.80	—
1978	70,000,000	—	0.20	0.30	0.80	—

Date	Mintage	F	VF	XF	Unc	BU
1979	60,640,000	—	0.20	0.30	0.80	—
1980	120,000,000	—	0.20	0.30	0.80	—

KM# 62   50 CENTS
4.9000 g., Nickel-Brass, 22.5 mm. **Ruler:** Elizabeth II **Obv:** Crowned head right **Rev:** English around central Chinese legend

Date	Mintage	F	VF	XF	Unc	BU
1988	50,000				8.00	—
1988 Proof	25,000	Value: 10.00				
1990	27,000	—	0.20	0.30	0.80	—

KM# 68   50 CENTS
Brass Plated Steel, 22.5 mm. **Ruler:** Elizabeth II **Obv:** Bauhinia flower **Rev:** Denomination

Date	Mintage	F	VF	XF	Unc	BU
1993	—	—	0.20	0.30	0.80	—
1993 Proof	—	Value: 5.50				
1994	—	—	0.20	0.30	0.80	—
1995	—	—	0.20	0.30	0.80	—
1997	—	—	0.20	0.30	0.80	—
1998	—	—	0.20	0.30	0.80	—

KM# 31.1   DOLLAR
Copper-Nickel, 29.8 mm. **Ruler:** Elizabeth II **Obv:** Crowned head right **Rev:** Upright crowned 3/4 lion with orb left **Edge:** Security **Note:** Mint mark is below "LL" of "DOLLAR".

Date	Mintage	F	VF	XF	Unc	BU
1960H	40,000,000	—	0.60	1.75	5.50	—
1960H Proof	—	Value: 3,350				
1960KN	40,000,000	—	0.60	1.75	5.50	—
1970H	15,000,000	—	0.60	1.25	4.50	—

KM# 31.2   DOLLAR
Copper-Nickel, 29.8 mm. **Ruler:** Elizabeth II **Obv:** Crowned head right **Rev:** Upright crowned 3/4 lion with orb left **Edge:** Reeded **Note:** Error. Mint mark is below "LL" of "DOLLAR"

Date	Mintage	F	VF	XF	Unc	BU
1960H	Inc. above	4.00	7.00	15.00	30.00	—

KM# 35   DOLLAR
Copper-Nickel, 29.8 mm. **Ruler:** Elizabeth II **Obv:** Crowned head right **Rev:** Upright crowned 3/4 lion with orb left **Edge:** Reeded

Date	Mintage	F	VF	XF	Unc	BU
1971H	8,000,000	—	0.60	1.25	4.50	—
1972	20,000,000	—	0.60	1.25	3.50	—
1973	8,125,000	—	0.60	1.25	3.50	—
1974	26,000,000	—	0.60	1.25	3.50	—
1975	22,500,000	—	0.60	1.25	3.50	—

KM# 43   DOLLAR
7.1000 g., Copper-Nickel, 25.5 mm. **Ruler:** Elizabeth II **Obv:** Young bust right **Rev:** Upright crowned 3/4 lion with orb left

Date	Mintage	F	VF	XF	Unc	BU
1978	120,000,000	—	0.40	0.70	1.50	—
1979	104,908,000	—	0.40	0.70	1.50	—
1980	100,000,000	—	0.40	0.70	1.50	—

KM# 63   DOLLAR
7.1000 g., Copper-Nickel, 25.5 mm. **Ruler:** Elizabeth II **Obv:** Crowned head right **Rev:** Upright crowned 3/4 lion with orb left

Date	Mintage	F	VF	XF	Unc	BU
1987	—	—	0.30	0.50	1.00	—
1988	20,000,000	—	0.30	0.50	1.00	—
1988 Proof	20,000	Value: 20.00				
1989	20,000,000	—	0.30	0.50	1.00	—
1990	—	—	0.30	0.50	1.00	—
1991	—	—	0.30	0.50	1.00	—
1992	25,000,000	—	0.30	0.50	1.00	—

KM# 69   DOLLAR
7.1000 g., Nickel Plated Steel, 25.5 mm. **Ruler:** Elizabeth II **Obv:** Bauhinia flower **Rev:** Denomination, large numeral

Date	Mintage	F	VF	XF	Unc	BU
1993	—	—	0.30	0.50	1.00	—
1993 Proof	—	Value: 10.00				

KM# 69a   DOLLAR
7.1000 g., Copper-Nickel, 25.5 mm. **Ruler:** Elizabeth II **Obv:** Bauhinia flower **Rev:** Denomination, large numeral

Date	Mintage	F	VF	XF	Unc	BU
1994	—	—	0.30	0.50	1.00	—
1995	—	—	0.30	0.50	1.00	—
1996	—	—	0.30	0.50	1.00	—
1997	—	—	0.30	0.50	1.00	—
1998	—	—	0.30	0.50	1.00	—

KM# 37   2 DOLLARS
8.4000 g., Copper-Nickel, 28 mm. **Ruler:** Elizabeth II **Obv:** Young bust right **Rev:** Upright crowned 3/4 lion with orb left **Edge:** Scalloped

Date	Mintage	F	VF	XF	Unc	BU
1975	60,000,000	—	0.45	0.85	1.75	—
1978	504,000	—	0.45	1.00	10.00	—
1979	9,032,000	—	0.45	0.85	1.75	—
1980	30,000,000	—	0.45	0.85	1.75	—
1981	30,000,000	—	0.45	0.85	1.75	—
1982	30,000,000	—	0.45	0.85	1.75	—
1983	7,002,000	—	0.45	0.85	1.75	—
1984	22,002,000	—	0.45	0.85	1.75	—

KM# 60   2 DOLLARS
8.4000 g., Copper-Nickel, 28 mm. **Ruler:** Elizabeth II **Obv:** Crowned head right **Rev:** Upright crowned 3/4 lion with orb left **Edge:** Scalloped

Date	Mintage	F	VF	XF	Unc	BU
1985	10,002,000	—	0.45	0.65	1.25	—
1986	15,000,000	—	0.45	0.65	1.25	—

Date	Mintage	F	VF	XF	Unc	BU
1987	—		0.45	2.00	10.00	—
1988	5,000,000		0.45	0.65	1.25	—
1988 Proof	20,000	Value: 35.00				
1989	33,000,000		0.45	0.65	1.25	—
1990	—		0.45	0.65	1.25	—
1992	4,370,000		0.45	2.00	10.00	—

KM# 64   2 DOLLARS
8.4000 g., Copper-Nickel, 28 mm.   **Ruler:** Elizabeth II **Obv:** Bauhinia flower **Rev:** Denomination, large numeral **Edge:** Scalloped

Date	Mintage	F	VF	XF	Unc	BU
1993	—		0.45	0.65	1.25	—
1993 Proof	—	Value: 12.50				
1994	—		0.45	0.65	1.25	—
1995	—		0.45	0.65	1.25	—
1997	—		0.45	0.65	1.25	—
1998	—		0.45	0.65	1.25	—

KM# 39   5 DOLLARS
10.8500 g., Copper-Nickel, 30.8 mm.   **Ruler:** Elizabeth II **Obv:** Young bust right **Rev:** Upright crowned 3/4 lion with orb left

Date	Mintage	F	VF	XF	Unc	BU
1976	30,000,000	—	1.00	3.00	10.00	—
1978	10,000,000	—	1.00	3.00	15.00	—
1979	12,000,000	—	1.00	3.00	12.00	—

KM# 46   5 DOLLARS
13.4000 g., Copper-Nickel, 27 mm.   **Ruler:** Elizabeth II **Obv:** Young bust right **Rev:** Denomination, large numeral

Date	Mintage	F	VF	XF	Unc	BU
1980	40,000,000	—	1.00	1.50	6.00	—
1981	20,000,000	—	1.00	1.50	6.00	—
1982	10,000,000	—	1.00	1.50	6.00	—
1983	4,000,000	—	1.00	1.50	10.00	—
1984	4,500,000	—	1.00	1.50	10.00	—

KM# 56   5 DOLLARS
13.4000 g., Copper-Nickel, 27 mm.   **Ruler:** Elizabeth II **Obv:** Crowned head right **Rev:** Denomination, large numeral

Date	Mintage	F	VF	XF	Unc	BU
1985	6,000,000	—	0.75	1.25	6.00	—
1986	8,000,000	—	0.75	1.25	6.00	—
1987	—	—	0.75	1.25	6.00	—
1988	16,000,000	—	0.75	1.25	6.00	—
1988 Proof	25,000	Value: 45.00				
1989	37,000,000	—	0.75	1.25	6.00	—

KM# 65   5 DOLLARS
13.4000 g., Copper-Nickel, 27 mm.   **Ruler:** Elizabeth II **Obv:** Bauhinia flower **Rev:** Denomination, large numeral **Edge:** in Chinese: HONG KONG FIVE DOLLARS

Date	Mintage	F	VF	XF	Unc	BU
1993	—		0.75	1.25	2.25	—
1993 Proof	—	Value: 20.00				
1995	—		0.75	1.25	2.25	—
1997	—		0.75	1.25	2.25	—
1998	—		0.75	1.25	2.25	—

KM# 70   10 DOLLARS
Bi-Metallic Nickel-Brass center in Copper-Nickel ring, 24 mm.   **Ruler:** Elizabeth II **Obv:** Bauhinia flower **Rev:** Numerals 10 and denomination in Chinese and English

Date	Mintage	F	VF	XF	Unc	BU
1993	—		2.50	4.50	10.00	—
1993 Proof	Est. 30,000	Value: 20.00				
1994	—	—	1.50	2.50	5.00	—
1995	—	—	1.50	2.50	5.00	—

KM# 70a   10 DOLLARS
Ring: 0.3750 Gold **Center Weight:** 18.3000 g. **Center:** 0.9170 Gold 0.5395 oz. AGW , 24 mm.   **Ruler:** Elizabeth II **Obv:** Bauhinia flower **Rev:** Numerals 10 and denomination in Chinese and English

Date	Mintage	F	VF	XF	Unc	BU
1994	20,000	—	—	—	465	480

KM# 38   1000 DOLLARS
15.9700 g., 0.9170 Gold 0.4708 oz. AGW   **Ruler:** Elizabeth II **Subject:** Visit of Queen Elizabeth **Obv:** Young bust right **Rev:** Arms with supporters

Date	Mintage	F	VF	XF	Unc	BU
1975	15,000	—	—	—	—	495
1975 Proof	5,005	Value: 1,150				

KM# 40   1000 DOLLARS
15.9700 g., 0.9170 Gold 0.4708 oz. AGW   **Ruler:** Elizabeth II **Subject:** Year of the Dragon **Obv:** Young bust right **Rev:** Dragon left

Date	Mintage	F	VF	XF	Unc	BU
1976	20,000	—	—	—	—	550
1976 Proof	6,911	Value: 1,000				

KM# 42   1000 DOLLARS
15.9700 g., 0.9170 Gold 0.4708 oz. AGW   **Ruler:** Elizabeth II **Subject:** Year of the Snake **Obv:** Young bust right **Rev:** Snake

Date	Mintage	F	VF	XF	Unc	BU
1977	20,000				—	475
1977 Proof	10,000	Value: 500				

KM# 44   1000 DOLLARS
15.9700 g., 0.9170 Gold 0.4708 oz. AGW   **Ruler:** Elizabeth II **Subject:** Year of the Horse **Obv:** Young bust right **Rev:** Horse left

Date	Mintage	F	VF	XF	Unc	BU
1978	20,000				—	475
1978 Proof	10,000	Value: 500				

KM# 45   1000 DOLLARS
15.9700 g., 0.9170 Gold 0.4708 oz. AGW   **Ruler:** Elizabeth II **Subject:** Year of the Goat **Obv:** Young bust right **Rev:** Ram left

Date	Mintage	F	VF	XF	Unc	BU
1979	30,000				—	475
1979 Proof	15,000	Value: 500				

KM# 47   1000 DOLLARS
15.9700 g., 0.9170 Gold 0.4708 oz. AGW   **Ruler:** Elizabeth II **Subject:** Year of the Monkey **Obv:** Young bust right **Rev:** Monkey seated right

Date	Mintage	F	VF	XF	Unc	BU
1980	31,000				—	475
1980 Proof	18,000	Value: 500				

KM# 48   1000 DOLLARS
15.9700 g., 0.9170 Gold 0.4708 oz. AGW   **Ruler:** Elizabeth II **Subject:** Year of the Cockerel **Obv:** Young bust right **Rev:** Rooster right

Date	Mintage	F	VF	XF	Unc	BU
1981	33,000				—	475
1981 Proof	22,000	Value: 500				

KM# 50   1000 DOLLARS
15.9700 g., 0.9170 Gold 0.4708 oz. AGW   **Ruler:** Elizabeth II **Subject:** Year of the Dog **Obv:** Young bust right **Rev:** Dog right

Date	Mintage	F	VF	XF	Unc	BU
1982	33,000				—	475
1982 Proof	22,000	Value: 500				

KM# 51   1000 DOLLARS
15.9700 g., 0.9170 Gold 0.4708 oz. AGW **Ruler:** Elizabeth II
Subject: Year of the Pig **Obv:** Young bust right **Rev:** Pig right

Date	Mintage	F	VF	XF	Unc	BU
1983	33,000	—	—	—	—	475
1983 Proof	22,000	Value: 675				

KM# 52   1000 DOLLARS
15.9700 g., 0.9170 Gold 0.4708 oz. AGW **Ruler:** Elizabeth II
Subject: Year of the Rat **Obv:** Young bust right **Rev:** Rat left

Date	Mintage	F	VF	XF	Unc	BU
1984	20,000	—	—	—	—	475
1984 Proof	10,000	Value: 550				

KM# 53   1000 DOLLARS
15.9700 g., 0.9170 Gold 0.4708 oz. AGW **Ruler:** Elizabeth II
Subject: Year of the Ox **Obv:** Young bust right **Rev:** Ox left

Date	Mintage	F	VF	XF	Unc	BU
1985	30,000	—	—	—	—	475
1985 Proof	10,000	Value: 550				

KM# 54   1000 DOLLARS
15.9700 g., 0.9170 Gold 0.4708 oz. AGW **Ruler:** Elizabeth II
Subject: Year of the Tiger **Obv:** Young bust right **Rev:** Tiger

Date	Mintage	F	VF	XF	Unc	BU
1986	20,000	—	—	—	—	450
1986 Proof	10,000	Value: 475				

KM# 57   1000 DOLLARS
15.9700 g., 0.9170 Gold 0.4708 oz. AGW **Ruler:** Elizabeth II
Subject: Royal visit of Queen Elizabeth II **Obv:** Crowned head
right **Rev:** Arms with supporters

Date	Mintage	F	VF	XF	Unc	BU
1986	20,000	—	—	—	—	475
1986 Proof	12,000	Value: 500				

KM# 58   1000 DOLLARS
15.9700 g., 0.9170 Gold 0.4708 oz. AGW **Ruler:** Elizabeth II
Subject: Year of the Rabbit **Obv:** Young bust right **Rev:** Rabbit left

Date	Mintage	F	VF	XF	Unc	BU
1987	20,000	—	—	—	—	475
1987 Proof	12,000	Value: 500				

SPECIAL ADMINISTRATION REGION (S.A.R.)
DECIMAL COINAGE

KM# 72   10 CENTS
Brass Plated Steel, 17.55 mm. **Obv:** Bauhinia flower
Rev: Sailing junk

Date	Mintage	F	VF	XF	Unc	BU
1997	—	—	0.10	0.15	0.30	0.45
1997 Proof	Est. 97,000	Value: 1.50				

KM# 73   20 CENTS
Nickel-Brass, 19 mm. **Obv:** Bauhinia flower **Rev:** Butterfly kites

Date	Mintage	F	VF	XF	Unc	BU
1997	—	—	0.10	0.20	0.40	0.60
1997 Proof	—	Value: 1.50				

KM# 74   50 CENTS
Brass Plated Steel, 22.5 mm. **Obv:** Bauhinia flower **Rev:** Ox left
divides date

Date	Mintage	F	VF	XF	Unc	BU
1997	—	—	0.20	0.30	0.80	1.25
1997 Proof	Est. 97,000	Value: 2.50				

KM# 75   DOLLAR
7.1000 g., Copper-Nickel, 25.5 mm. **Obv:** Bauhinia flower
Rev: Chinese unicorn divides date

Date	Mintage	F	VF	XF	Unc	BU
1997	—	—	0.30	0.50	1.00	1.25
1997 Proof	—	Value: 5.50				

KM# 76   2 DOLLARS
8.4000 g., Copper-Nickel, 28 mm. **Obv:** Bauhinia flower
Rev: Ho Ho brothers divide date

Date	Mintage	F	VF	XF	Unc	BU
1997	—	—	0.45	0.65	1.25	1.50
1997 Proof	Est. 97,000	Value: 8.00				

KM# 77   5 DOLLARS
13.4000 g., Copper-Nickel, 27 mm. **Obv:** Bauhinia flower
Rev: Shou character divides date **Edge:** in Chinese: HONG
KONG FIVE DOLLARS

Date	Mintage	F	VF	XF	Unc	BU
1997	—	—	0.75	1.25	2.25	2.50
1997 Proof	Est. 97,000	Value: 12.50				

KM# 78   10 DOLLARS
Bi-Metallic Nickel-Brass center in Copper-Nickel ring, 24 mm.
Obv: Bauhinia flower **Rev:** Suspension bridge

Date	Mintage	F	VF	XF	Unc	BU
1997	—	—	1.75	3.50	6.50	7.00
1997 Proof	Est. 97,000	Value: 13.50				

KM# 71   1000 DOLLARS
15.9700 g., 0.9170 Gold 0.4708 oz. AGW **Subject:** Return of
Hong Kong to China **Obv:** Bauhinia flower **Rev:** Skyline view

Date	Mintage	F	VF	XF	Unc	BU
1997 Proof	97,000	Value: 465				

KM# 79   1000 DOLLARS
15.9700 g., 0.9170 Gold 0.4708 oz. AGW **Subject:** Hong Kong
International Airport **Obv:** Bauhinia flower **Rev:** Stylized airplane
lifting off from runway

Date	Mintage	F	VF	XF	Unc	BU
1998 Proof	15,000	Value: 485				

MINT SETS

KM#	Date	Mintage	Identification	Issue Price	Mkt Val
MS1	1988 (7)	50,000	KM55-56, 59-63	13.00	30.00
MS2	1993 (7)	—	KM64-70	20.00	20.00
MS3	1997 (7)	—	KM72-78	30.00	12.50

PROOF SETS

KM#	Date	Mintage	Identification	Issue Price	Mkt Val
PS5	1988 (7)	25,000	KM55-56, 59-63	39.75	125
PS6	1993 (7)	30,000	KM64-70	50.00	75.00
PS7	1997 (7)	97,000	KM72-78	—	40.00

HUNGARY

The Republic of Hungary, located in central Europe, has an area of 35,929 sq. mi. (93,030 sq. km.) and a population of 10.7 million. Capital: Budapest. The economy is based on agriculture, bauxite and a rapidly expanding industrial sector. Machinery, chemicals, iron and steel, and fruits and vegetables are exported.

The ancient kingdom of Hungary, founded by the Magyars in the 9th century, achieved its greatest extension in the mid-14th century when its dominions touched the Baltic, Black and Mediterranean Seas. After suffering repeated Turkish invasions, Hungary accepted Habsburg rule to escape Turkish occupation, regaining independence in 1867 with the Emperor of Austria as king of a dual Austro-Hungarian monarchy.

After World War I, Hungary lost 2/3 of its territory and 1/2 of its population and underwent a period of drastic political revision. The short-lived republic of 1918 was followed by a chaotic interval of communist rule, 1919, and the restoration of the monarchy in 1920 with Admiral Horthy as regent of the kingdom. Although a German ally in World War II, Hungary was occupied by German troops who imposed a pro-Nazi dictatorship, 1944. Soviet armies drove out the Germans in 1945 and assisted the communist minority in seizing power. A revised constitution published on Aug. 20, 1949, established Hungary as a People's Republic' of the Soviet type. On October 23, 1989, Hungary was pro-claimed the Republic of Hungary.

RULERS
Franz Joseph I, 1848-1916
Karl I, 1916-1918

MINT MARKS
B, K, KB - Kremnitz (Kormoczbanya)
BP - Budapest

MONETARY SYSTEM
	1892-1925
100 Filler = 1 Korona	
	1926-1945
100 Filler = 1 Pengo	
	Commencing 1946
100 Filler = 1 Forint	

NOTE: Many coins of Hungary through 1948, especially 1925-1945, have been restruck in recent times. These may be identified by a rosette in the vicinity of the mintmark. Restrike mintages for KM#440-449, 451-458, 468-469,475-477, 480-483, 494, 496-498 are usually about 1000 pieces, later date mintages are not known.

KINGDOM

REFORM COINAGE
100 Filler = 1 Korona

KM# 480   FILLER
Bronze **Ruler:** Franz Joseph I **Obv:** Crown above date **Rev:** Value within wreath

Date	Mintage	F	VF	XF	Unc	BU
1901KB	5,994,000	4.00	8.00	17.00	32.50	—
1902KB	16,299,000	0.20	0.50	1.25	4.00	—
1903KB	2,291,000	12.00	25.00	65.00	120	—
1906KB	61,000	65.00	160	350	600	—
1914KB	—	65.00	130	280	400	—
1914KB Proof	—	Value: 350				

KM# 481   2 FILLER
3.2800 g., Bronze **Ruler:** Franz Joseph I **Obv:** Crown above date **Rev:** Value within wreath

Date	Mintage	F	VF	XF	Unc	BU
1901KB	25,805,000	0.50	1.00	2.50	5.00	—
1902KB	6,937,000	5.50	8.50	13.50	20.00	—
1903KB	4,052,000	12.00	20.00	65.00	130	—
1904KB	4,203,000	6.00	12.00	25.00	70.00	—
1905KB	9,335,000	0.70	1.75	3.00	6.00	—
1906KB	3,140,000	1.75	2.50	5.00	7.50	—
1907KB	9,943,000	5.50	9.00	12.00	17.50	—
1908KB	16,486,000	0.50	1.00	2.50	5.00	—

Date	Mintage	F	VF	XF	Unc	BU
1909KB	19,075,000	0.50	1.00	2.50	5.00	—
1910KB	5,338,000	4.50	7.50	10.00	15.00	—
1910KB Proof, restrike with rosette	—	Value: 10.00				
1914KB	4,106,000	0.50	1.00	2.50	5.00	—
1915KB	1,294,000	1.50	2.00	4.00	7.00	—

KM# 497   2 FILLER
Iron **Ruler:** Karl I **Obv:** Crown of St. Stephen **Rev:** Denomination above sprays **Note:** Varieties in planchet thickness exist for 1917.

Date	Mintage	F	VF	XF	Unc	BU
1916	—	6.00	10.00	15.00	35.00	—
1917	—	1.00	2.50	7.00	15.00	—
1918	—	2.00	4.50	9.00	18.00	—

KM# 482   10 FILLER
Nickel **Ruler:** Franz Joseph I **Obv:** Crown above date **Rev:** Value within wreath **Note:** Edge varieties exist.

Date	Mintage	F	VF	XF	Unc	BU
1906KB	56,000	75.00	175	250	325	—
1908KB	6,819,000	0.25	0.50	1.50	4.00	—
1909KB	17,204,000	0.30	0.60	2.00	4.00	—
1914KB	—	200	300	650	1,100	

KM# 494   10 FILLER
Copper-Nickel-Zinc **Ruler:** Franz Joseph I **Obv:** Crown of St. Stephen **Rev:** Denomination above sprays **Note:** Varieties exist.

Date	Mintage	F	VF	XF	Unc	BU
1914	4,400,000	—	200	300	600	1,000
1915	Inc. above	0.30	0.60	1.50	4.00	—
1915 Proof	Inc. above	Value: 4.00				
	Note: Restrike with rosette					
1916	Inc. above	0.50	1.25	2.50	5.00	—

KM# 496   10 FILLER
Iron **Ruler:** Karl I **Obv:** Crown of St. Stephen **Rev:** Denomination above sprays **Note:** Varieties exist.

Date	Mintage	F	VF	XF	Unc	BU
1915	11,500,000	9.00	20.00	80.00	140	—
1916 Rare	Inc. above					
1918	Inc. above	15.00	30.00	55.00	85.00	—
1918 Proof, restrike	—	Value: 18.00				
1920	3,275,000	4.50	19.00	50.00	85.00	—
1920 Proof, restrike	—	Value: 18.00				

KM# 483   20 FILLER
Nickel **Ruler:** Franz Joseph I **Obv:** Crown above date **Rev:** Value within wreath **Note:** Edge varieties exist.

Date	Mintage	F	VF	XF	Unc	BU
1906KB	67,000	300	500	950	2,000	—
1907KB	1,248,000	3.00	6.00	12.00	24.00	—
1908KB	10,770,000	0.75	1.75	3.75	7.50	—
1914KB	5,387,000	3.75	6.50	10.00	15.00	—
1914KB Restrike; proof	—	Value: 12.50				

KM# 498   20 FILLER
Iron **Obv:** Crown of St. Stephen **Rev:** Denomination within wreath **Note:** Edge varieties exist.

Date	Mintage	F	VF	XF	Unc	BU
1914	18,826,000	18.00	32.50	45.00	70.00	—
1916	Inc. above	0.50	1.25	2.50	7.00	—
1917	Inc. above	0.75	1.75	3.50	8.00	—
1918	Inc. above	0.75	1.75	3.50	8.00	—
1918 Proof, restrike	—	Value: 6.00				
1920	12,000,000	2.50	5.00	9.00	18.00	—
1921	Inc. above	18.00	32.50	45.00	70.00	—
1921 Proof, restrike	—	Value: 12.00				
1922 Rare	—					
1922 Proof, restrike	—	Value: 12.00				

KM# 498a   20 FILLER
Brass **Obv:** Crown of St. Stephen **Rev:** Denomination above sprays

Date	Mintage	F	VF	XF	Unc	BU
1922	400					—
1922 Proof, restrike	—	Value: 30.00				

KM# 484   KORONA
5.0000 g., 0.8350 Silver 0.1342 oz. ASW **Ruler:** Franz Joseph I **Obv:** Laureate head, right **Rev:** Crown, value within wreath **Note:** Obverse varieties exist.

Date	Mintage	F	VF	XF	Unc	BU
1906KB	24,000	175	275	400	700	—

KM# 492   KORONA
5.0000 g., 0.8350 Silver 0.1342 oz. ASW **Ruler:** Franz Joseph I **Obv:** Laureate head right **Obv. Leg.:** Crown of St. Stephen within wreath

Date	Mintage	F	VF	XF	Unc	BU
1912	4,004,000	2.50	5.00	10.00	18.00	—
1913	5,214	50.00	100	200	350	—
1914	5,886,000	BV	3.75	6.50	12.00	—
1915	3,934,000	BV	3.00	4.50	6.00	—
1916	—	BV	3.50	6.00	8.00	—

KM# 493   2 KORONA
10.0000 g., 0.8350 Silver 0.2684 oz. ASW **Ruler:** Franz Joseph I **Obv:** Laureate head right **Rev:** Crown of St. Stephen supported by two angels, spray below

Date	Mintage	F	VF	XF	Unc	BU
1912KB	4,000,000	BV	4.50	6.50	13.50	—
1913KB	3,000,000	BV	4.50	7.50	15.00	—
1914KB	500,000	20.00	30.00	50.00	80.00	—

KM# 488 5 KORONA

24.0000 g., 0.9000 Silver 0.6944 oz. ASW **Ruler:** Franz Joseph I
Obv: Laureate head, right **Rev:** Angels holding crown above value and date within sprigs

Date	Mintage	F	VF	XF	Unc	BU
1906KB	1,263	1,250	2,750	5,000	9,000	—
1907KB	500,000	14.00	20.00	50.00	150	—
1908KB	1,742,000	12.00	18.00	45.00	120	—
1909KB	1,299,000	12.00	20.00	50.00	150	—
1909KB U.P. Proof, restrike	—	Value: 35.00				

KM# 489 5 KORONA

24.0000 g., 0.9000 Silver 0.6944 oz. ASW, 36 mm.
Ruler: Franz Joseph I **Subject:** 40th Anniversary - Coronation of Franz Josef **Obv:** Laureate head right **Rev:** Coronation scene **Edge:** BIZALMAM AZ OSI ERÈNYBEN

Date	Mintage	F	VF	XF	Unc	BU
1907	300,000	15.00	22.00	55.00	.100	—
1907 Proof, restrike	—	Value: 30.00				
1907 U.P. Proof, restrike	—	Value: 30.00				

KM# 485 10 KORONA

3.3875 g., 0.9000 Gold 0.0980 oz. AGW **Ruler:** Franz Joseph I
Obv: Emperor standing **Rev:** Crowned shield with angel supporters

Date	Mintage	F	VF	XF	Unc	BU
1901KB	230,000	—	BV	100	120	—
1902KB	243,000	—	BV	110	125	—
1903KB	228,000	—	BV	110	125	—
1904KB	1,531,000	—	BV	110	125	—
1905KB	869,000	—	BV	110	125	—
1906KB	748,000	—	BV	110	125	—
1907KB	752,000	—	BV	110	125	—
1908KB	509,000	—	BV	110	125	—
1909KB	574,000	—	BV	110	125	—
1910KB	1,362,000	—	BV	110	125	—
1911KB	1,828,000	—	BV	110	125	—
1912KB	739,000	BV	110	130	220	—
1913KB	137,000	BV	120	220	300	—
1914KB	115,000	BV	200	450	600	—
1915KB	54,000	1,250	2,750	4,000	6,500	—

KM# 486 20 KORONA

6.7750 g., 0.9000 Gold 0.1960 oz. AGW **Ruler:** Franz Joseph I
Obv: Emperor standing **Rev:** Crowned shield with angel supporters

Date	Mintage	F	VF	XF	Unc	BU
1901KB	510,000	—	BV	195	210	—
1901KB	510,000	—	BV	195	210	—
1902KB	523,000	—	BV	195	210	—
1903KB	505,000	—	BV	195	210	—
1904KB	572,000	—	BV	195	210	—
1905KB	526,000	—	BV	195	210	—
1906KB	353,000	—	BV	195	210	—

Date	Mintage	F	VF	XF	Unc	BU
1907KB	194,000	—	BV	200	225	—
1908KB	138,000	—	BV	195	210	—
1909KB	459,000	—	BV	195	210	—
1910KB	85,000	—	200	250	300	—
1911KB	63,000	—	BV	195	210	—
1912KB	211,000	—	BV	195	210	—
1913KB	320,000	—	195	200	225	—
1914KB	176,000	—	BV	195	210	—
1915KB	690,000	—	195	200	225	—

KM# 495 20 KORONA

6.7750 g., 0.9000 Gold 0.1960 oz. AGW **Ruler:** Franz Joseph I
Obv: Emperor standing **Rev:** Crowned shield (Bosnian arms added) with angel supporters

Date	Mintage	F	VF	XF	Unc	BU
1914	—	—	—	200	250	—
1915	—	—	—	—	—	—
1916	—	—	225	350	500	—

KM# 500 20 KORONA

6.7750 g., 0.9000 Gold 0.1960 oz. AGW **Ruler:** Karl I
Obv. Leg.: KAROLY...

Date	Mintage	F	VF	XF	Unc	BU
1918 Rare	—	—	—	—	—	—

KM# 490 100 KORONA

33.8753 g., 0.9000 Gold 0.9802 oz. AGW, 36 mm.
Ruler: Franz Joseph I **Subject:** 40th Anniversary - Coronation of Franz Josef **Obv:** Laureate head right **Rev:** Coronation scene **Edge:** BIZALMAM AZ ÖSI ERÈNYBEN

Date	Mintage	F	VF	XF	Unc	BU
1907KB	11,000	—	BV	1,000	1,500	—
1907KB U.P. Restrike	—	—	—	—	950	—

KM# 491 100 KORONA

33.8753 g., 0.9000 Gold 0.9802 oz. AGW **Ruler:** Franz Joseph I
Obv: Emperor standing **Rev:** Crowned shield with angel supporters

Date	Mintage	F	VF	XF	Unc	BU
1907	1,088	BV	1,100	1,550	2,500	—
1907 U.P. Restrike	—	—	—	—	950	—
1908	4,038	—	1,000	1,350	2,200	—
1908 U.P Restrike	—	—	—	—	950	—

REGENCY COINAGE

1926 - 1945

KM# 505 FILLER

1.6800 g., Bronze **Obv:** Crown of St. Stephen **Rev:** Denomination

Date	Mintage	F	VF	XF	Unc	BU
1926BP	6,471,000	0.50	1.00	2.00	4.00	—
1927BP	16,529,000	0.10	0.20	0.50	3.00	—
1928BP	7,000,000	0.25	0.50	1.00	3.75	—
1929BP	418,000	5.00	10.00	20.00	35.00	—
1930BP	3,734,000	0.30	0.60	1.50	5.00	—

Date	Mintage	F	VF	XF	Unc	BU
1931BP	10,849,000	0.10	0.20	0.60	3.00	—
1932BP	5,000,000	0.25	0.50	1.00	4.00	—
1932BP Proof, restrike	—	Value: 3.75				
1933BP	5,000,000	0.25	0.50	1.00	4.00	—
1934BP	3,111,000	0.30	0.60	1.20	4.50	—
1935BP	6,889,000	0.25	0.50	1.00	4.00	—
1936BP	10,000,000	0.10	0.20	0.60	2.50	—
1938BP	10,575,000	0.10	0.20	0.60	2.50	—
1939BP	10,425,000	0.10	0.20	0.60	2.50	—

KM# 506 2 FILLER

3.2300 g., Bronze **Obv:** Crown of St. Stephen **Rev:** Denomination

Date	Mintage	F	VF	XF	Unc	BU
1926BP	17,777,000	0.10	0.20	0.40	2.00	—
1927BP	44,836,000	0.10	0.20	0.40	2.00	—
1928BP	11,448,000	0.10	0.20	0.40	2.00	—
1929BP	8,995,000	0.10	0.25	0.50	2.50	—
1930BP	6,943,000	0.10	0.25	0.50	2.50	—
1931BP	826,000	0.40	0.90	2.50	6.50	—
1932BP	4,174,000	4.00	8.00	15.00	28.00	—
1933BP	501,000	3.00	6.00	10.00	20.00	—
1934BP	9,499,000	0.10	0.20	0.40	2.00	—
1935BP	10,000,000	0.10	0.20	0.40	2.00	—
1936BP	2,049,000	0.15	0.30	0.75	4.00	—
1937BP	7,951,000	0.10	0.20	0.40	1.50	—
1938BP	14,125,000	0.10	0.20	0.40	1.50	—
1939BP	16,875,000	0.10	0.20	0.40	1.50	—
1940BP	7,000,000	0.10	0.20	0.50	1.50	—

KM# 518.1 2 FILLER

Steel **Obv:** Crown of St. Stephen **Rev:** Denomination

Date	Mintage	F	VF	XF	Unc	BU
1940	64,500,000	1.00	2.00	5.00	12.00	—

KM# 518.2 2 FILLER

3.3000 g., Steel **Obv:** Crown of St. Stephen **Rev:** Denomination

Date	Mintage	F	VF	XF	Unc	BU
1940	78,000,000	0.50	1.00	2.00	4.50	—
1941	12,000,000	30.00	65.00	125	220	—
1942	13,000,000	0.50	1.00	2.00	4.50	—
1942 Proof, restrike	—	Value: 6.50				

KM# 519 2 FILLER

Zinc, 17 mm. **Obv:** Crown of St. Stephen **Rev:** Denomination
Note: Variations in planchets exist.

Date	Mintage	F	VF	XF	Unc	BU
1943	37,000,000	0.10	0.20	0.70	3.00	—
1943 Proof, restrike	—	Value: 6.50				
1944	55,159,000	0.10	0.20	0.70	2.50	—

KM# 507 10 FILLER

Copper-Nickel **Obv:** Crown of St. Stephen within small circle on radiant background **Rev:** Denomination

Date	Mintage	F	VF	XF	Unc	BU
1926BP	20,001,000	0.50	1.50	3.00	10.00	—
1927BP	12,255,000	0.50	1.50	3.00	7.00	—
1935BP	4,740,000	0.50	1.50	3.00	4.50	—
1936BP	3,005,000	0.50	1.50	3.00	4.50	—
1938BP	6,700,000	0.50	1.50	3.00	4.50	—
1939BP	4,460,000	3.00	5.00	10.00	20.00	—
1940BP	960,000	15.00	30.00	50.00	85.00	—

KM# 507a   10 FILLER
3.0800 g., Steel **Obv:** Crown of St. Stephen within small circle
on radiant background **Rev:** Denomination

Date	Mintage	F	VF	XF	Unc	BU
1940	45,927,000	0.10	0.20	0.80	3.50	—
1941	24,963,000	0.10	0.20	0.80	3.50	—
1942	44,110,000	0.10	0.20	0.80	3.50	—

KM# 508   20 FILLER
Copper-Nickel **Obv:** Crown of St. Stephen within small circle on
radiant background **Rev:** Denomination

Date	Mintage	F	VF	XF	Unc	BU
1926BP	25,000,000	1.50	3.50	10.00	15.00	—
1927BP	830,000	10.00	30.00	60.00	110	—
1938BP	20,150,000	0.10	0.25	1.00	2.50	—
1939BP	2,020,000	6.50	10.00	20.00	35.00	—
1940BP	2,470,000	4.00	7.50	18.00	30.00	—

KM# 520   20 FILLER
3.5600 g., Steel, 21 mm. **Obv:** Crown of St. Stephen above
center hole **Rev:** Center hole divides denomination

Date	Mintage	F	VF	XF	Unc	BU
1941	75,007,000	0.10	0.20	0.90	4.00	—
1943	7,500,000	0.10	0.20	0.90	4.00	—
1944	25,000,000	0.10	0.20	0.90	4.00	—
1944 Proof, restrike	—	Value: 7.00				

KM# 509   50 FILLER
Copper-Nickel **Obv:** Crown of St. Stephen **Rev:** Denomination

Date	Mintage	F	VF	XF	Unc	BU
1926BP	14,921,000	0.75	2.00	3.50	6.00	—
1938BP	20,079,000	0.20	0.40	1.00	3.00	—
1939BP	2,770,000	6.50	15.00	30.00	55.00	—
1939BP Proof, restrike	—	Value: 20.00				
1940BP	6,230,000	4.00	7.50	18.00	35.00	—

KM# 510   PENGO
5.0000 g., 0.6400 Silver 0.1029 oz. ASW, 22.88 mm. **Obv:**
Crowned shield within branches **Rev:** Denomination within wreath

Date	Mintage	F	VF	XF	Unc	BU
1926BP	15,000,000	BV	2.50	6.50	20.00	—
1927BP	18,000,000	BV	175	4.50	12.00	—
1937BP	4,000,000	—	BV	2.50	6.00	—
1938BP	5,000,000	—	BV	2.50	6.00	—
1939BP	13,000,000	—	BV	2.00	5.00	—

KM# 521   PENGO
1.5000 g., Aluminum **Obv:** Crowned shield **Rev:** Denomination
and date divide wreath

Date	Mintage	F	VF	XF	Unc	BU
1941	80,000,000	0.10	0.20	0.50	1.00	—
1942	19,000,000	0.10	0.20	0.50	1.00	—
1943	2,000,000	1.00	4.00	8.00	16.00	—
1944	16,000,000	0.10	0.20	0.50	1.00	—

KM# 511   2 PENGO
10.0000 g., 0.6400 Silver 0.2058 oz. ASW, 27 mm. **Obv:** Angels
flank crowned shield above spray **Rev:** Hungarian Madonna

Date	Mintage	F	VF	XF	Unc	BU
1929BP	5,000,000	BV	4.00	6.50	12.50	—
1931BP	110,000	10.00	25.00	45.00	90.00	—
1932BP	602,000	BV	5.00	8.00	16.00	—
1933BP	1,051,000	BV	4.00	6.00	12.50	—
1935BP	50,000	25.00	65.00	120	250	—
1936BP	711,000	BV	6.00	10.00	20.00	—
1937BP	1,500,000	BV	3.75	4.75	9.00	—
1938BP	6,417,000	BV	3.75	5.00	10.00	—
1939BP	2,103,000	BV	3.75	5.00	10.00	—

KM# 513   2 PENGO
10.0000 g., 0.6400 Silver 0.2058 oz. ASW, 27 mm. **Subject:**
Tercentenary - Founding of Pazmany University **Obv:** Crowned,
ornate shield **Rev:** Cardinal Peter Pazmany with two others

Date	Mintage	F	VF	XF	Unc	BU
1935	50,000	4.00	6.50	10.00	20.00	—
1935 Proof	—	Value: 22.50				

Note: Restrike not marked

KM# 514   2 PENGO
10.0000 g., 0.6400 Silver 0.2058 oz. ASW, 27 mm. **Subject:**
Bicentennial - Death of Rakoczi, Prince of Hungary and Transylvania
Obv: Ornaments surround crowned shield **Rev:** Bust right

Date	Mintage	F	VF	XF	Unc	BU
1935	100,000	BV	4.50	6.50	11.50	—
1935 Proof	—	Value: 22.50				

Note: Restrike not marked

KM# 515   2 PENGO
10.0000 g., 0.6400 Silver 0.2058 oz. ASW, 27 mm. **Subject:**
50th Anniversary - Death of Franz von Liszt **Obv:** Crowned shield
within wreath **Rev:** Head right

Date	Mintage	F	VF	XF	Unc	BU
1936	200,000	—	BV	4.50	8.00	—

Date	Mintage	F	VF	XF	Unc	BU
1936 Proof	—	Value: 18.00				

Note: Restrike not marked

KM# 522.1   2 PENGO
2.8000 g., Aluminum, 27 mm. **Obv:** Crowned shield within circle
Rev: Denomination within circle, wreath surrounds

Date	Mintage	F	VF	XF	Unc	BU
1941	24,000,000	0.15	0.30	0.50	1.00	—
1942	8,000,000	0.15	0.30	0.50	1.00	—
1943	10,000,000	0.15	0.30	0.50	1.00	—

KM# 522.2   2 PENGO
Aluminum, 27 mm. **Obv:** Crowned shield within circle **Rev:**
Denomination within circle, wreath surrounds, base of 2 is wavy

Date	Mintage	F	VF	XF	Unc	BU
1941	40,000	10.00	20.00	35.00	65.00	—
1941 Restrike, rose	—	—	—	—	—	—

KM# 512.1   5 PENGO
25.0000 g., 0.6400 Silver 0.5144 oz. ASW, 36 mm.
Subject: 10th Anniversary - Regency of Admiral Horthy
Obv: Bust right **Rev:** Crowned shield with standing angel
supporters **Edge:** Raised, sharp reeding

Date	Mintage	F	VF	XF	Unc	BU
1930BP	3,650,000	BV	10.00	12.00	17.50	—

KM# 512.2   5 PENGO
25.3300 g., 0.6400 Silver 0.5212 oz. ASW, 36 mm.
Subject: 10th Anniversary - Regency of Admiral Horthy **Obv:** Bust
right **Rev:** Crowned shield with standing angel supporters

Date	Mintage	F	VF	XF	Unc	BU
1930 Proof, restrike	—	Value: 18.50				

KM# 516   5 PENGO
25.0000 g., 0.6400 Silver 0.5144 oz. ASW, 36 mm. **Subject:** 900th
Anniversary - Death of St. Stephan **Obv:** Sword and scepter between
crown and shield **Rev:** Crowned bust right

Date	Mintage	F	VF	XF	Unc	BU
1938	600,000	BV	10.00	12.50	25.00	—
1938 Proof, restrike not marked	—	Value: 28.50				

KM# 517   5 PENGO
25.0000 g., 0.6400 Silver 0.5144 oz. ASW, 36 mm. **Subject:**
Admiral Miklos Horthy **Obv:** Uniformed bust left **Rev:** Crowned
shield with standing angel supporters **Edge:** Smooth, ornamented

Date	Mintage	F	VF	XF	Unc	BU
1938	60				800	—
1939	408,000	BV	10.00	12.50	25.00	—

KM# 523 5 PENGO
Aluminum, 36 mm. **Subject:** 75th Birthday of Admiral Horthy **Obv:** Uniformed bust left **Rev:** Crowned shield with standing angel supporters

Date	Mintage	F	VF	XF	Unc	BU
1943	2,000,000	0.50	1.00	2.00	4.50	—
1943 Proof, restrike			Value: 6.00			

PROVISIONAL GOVERNMENT
1944-1946
DECIMAL COINAGE

KM# 525 5 PENGO
Aluminum **Obv:** Parliament Building **Rev:** Crowned shield flanked by grain, fruit and leaves

Date	Mintage	F	VF	XF	Unc	BU
1945BP	5,002,000	0.50	1.00	3.00	6.50	—
1945BP PROBAVERET Proof, restrike			Value: 17.50			

FIRST REPUBLIC
1946-1949
DECIMAL COINAGE

KM# 529 2 FILLER
3.0000 g., Bronze **Obv:** Arms of the Republic **Rev:** Grain stalk divides denomination

Date	Mintage	F	VF	XF	Unc	BU
1946BP	13,665,000	0.25	0.50	1.00	2.00	—
1947BP	23,865,000	0.25	0.50	1.00	2.50	—
1947BP Proof, restrike			Value: 6.50			

KM# 535 5 FILLER
6.0000 g., Aluminum **Obv:** Head left **Rev:** Denomination within wreath

Date	Mintage	F	VF	XF	Unc	BU
1948BP	24,000,000	0.40	1.00	2.00	6.00	—
1951BP	15,000,000	0.40	0.75	1.75	5.00	—

KM# 530 10 FILLER
3.0000 g., Aluminum-Bronze **Obv:** Dove with branch **Rev:** Denomination

Date	Mintage	F	VF	XF	Unc	BU
1946BP	23,565,000	0.15	0.30	0.70	2.00	—
1947BP	29,580,000	0.15	0.30	0.70	2.00	—
1947BP Proof, restrike	—		Value: 7.50			
1948BP	4,885,000	2.00	3.00	4.00	8.00	—
1950BP	8,000,000	1.00	2.00	3.50	7.50	—

KM# 530a 10 FILLER
1.0000 g., Aluminum **Obv:** Dove with branch **Rev:** Denomination

Date	Mintage	F	VF	XF	Unc	BU
1950	—	20.00	30.00	40.00	60.00	—

KM# 531 20 FILLER
4.0000 g., Aluminum-Bronze **Obv:** Three wheat ears divide date **Rev:** Denomination

Date	Mintage	F	VF	XF	Unc	BU
1946BP	16,560,000	0.40	0.80	1.50	3.00	—
1946BP Proof, restrike	—		Value: 8.00			
1947BP	18,260,000	0.50	1.00	2.00	4.00	—
1948BP	5,180,000	2.00	4.00	8.00	12.00	—
1950BP	6,000,000	1.00	2.00	4.00	10.00	—

KM# 536 50 FILLER
1.4000 g., Aluminum **Obv:** Blacksmith sitting on anvil **Rev:** Denomination within wreath

Date	Mintage	F	VF	XF	Unc	BU
1948BP	15,000,000	65.00	90.00	175		—
1948BP Proof, restrike						

KM# 532 FORINT
1.5000 g., Aluminum **Obv:** Arms of the Republic **Rev:** Denomination flanked by leaves

Date	Mintage	F	VF	XF	Unc	BU
1946BP	38,900,000	1.00	2.00	4.00	10.00	—
1947BP	2,600,000	4.00	8.00	15.00	25.00	—
1949BP	17,000,000	2.50	5.00	10.00	20.00	—

KM# 533 2 FORINT
2.8000 g., Aluminum **Obv:** Shield within wreath, star at top **Rev:** Denomination, large numeral

Date	Mintage	F	VF	XF	Unc	BU
1946BP	10,000,000	2.00	5.00	10.00	20.00	—
1947BP	3,500,000	3.00	7.50	15.00	30.00	—

KM# 534 5 FORINT
20.0000 g., 0.8350 Silver 0.5369 oz. ASW **Subject:** Lajos Kossuth **Obv:** Arms of the Republic **Rev:** Head right **Edge:** MUNKA A NEMZETI **Note:** Thick planchet.

Date	Mintage	F	VF	XF	Unc	BU
1946BP	39,802	BV	10.00	15.00	30.00	—

KM# 534a 5 FORINT
12.0000 g., 0.5000 Silver 0.1929 oz. ASW, 32 mm. **Subject:** Lajos Kossuth **Obv:** Arms of the Republic **Rev:** Head right **Note:** 1.7mm thin planchet.

Date	Mintage	F	VF	XF	Unc	BU
1947	10,004,252		BV	4.00	6.00	—
1947 Proof, restrike	—		Value: 12.00			

KM# 537 5 FORINT
12.0000 g., 0.5000 Silver 0.1929 oz. ASW, 32 mm. **Subject:** Centenary of 1848 Revolution - Sandor Petofi **Obv:** Denomination above date **Rev:** Head left

Date	Mintage	F	VF	XF	Unc	BU
1948	100,000	BV	4.00	6.00	10.00	—
1948 Proof, restrike	—		Value: 15.00			

KM# 538 10 FORINT
20.0000 g., 0.5000 Silver 0.3215 oz. ASW, 36 mm. **Subject:** Centenary of 1848 Revolution **Obv:** Denomination **Rev:** Istvan Szechenyi

Date	Mintage	F	VF	XF	Unc	BU
1948BP	100,000	BV	7.00	9.00	15.00	—
1948BP Proof, restrike	—		Value: 22.50			

KM# 539 20 FORINT
28.0000 g., 0.5000 Silver 0.4501 oz. ASW, 40 mm.
Subject: Centenary of 1848 Revolution **Obv:** Arms of the Republic **Rev:** Mihaly Tancsics

Date	Mintage	F	VF	XF	Unc	BU
1948BP	50,000	9.00	12.00	17.50	30.00	—
1948BP Proof, restrike	—	Value: 40.00				

PEOPLES REPUBLIC
1949-1989
DECIMAL COINAGE

KM# 546 2 FILLER
0.6900 g., Aluminum, 17.88 mm. **Obv:** Legend and wreath surround center hole **Rev:** Center hole divides denomination within wreath **Edge:** Plain

Date	Mintage	F	VF	XF	Unc	BU
1950BP	24,990,000	—	0.10	0.20	0.50	—
1952BP	5,600,000	—	0.10	0.30	1.00	—
1953BP	9,400,000	—	0.10	0.20	0.50	—
1954BP	10,000,000	—	0.10	0.20	0.50	—
1955BP	6,029,000	—	0.10	0.25	0.75	—
1956BP	4,000,000	—	0.15	0.30	1.00	—
1957BP	5,000,000	—	0.10	0.25	0.50	—
1960BP	3,000,000	0.10	0.15	0.30	0.60	—
1961BP	2,000,000	0.20	0.40	0.60	1.00	—
1962BP	3,000,000	0.10	0.15	0.30	0.60	—
1963BP	2,082,000	0.10	0.20	0.35	0.70	—
1965BP	540,000	—	4.00	8.00	16.00	—
1971BP	1,041,000	0.10	0.15	0.30	0.60	—
1972BP	1,000,000	0.10	0.15	0.30	0.60	—
1973BP	2,820,000	0.10	0.15	0.30	0.60	—
1974BP	50,000	—	0.40	0.80	1.50	—
1975BP	50,000	—	0.40	0.80	1.50	—
1976BP	50,000	—	0.40	0.80	1.50	—
1977BP	60,000	—	0.40	0.80	1.50	—
1978BP	50,000	—	0.40	0.80	1.50	—
1979BP	30,000	—	0.75	1.25	2.50	—
1980BP	30,000	—	0.75	1.25	2.50	—
1981BP	30,000	—	0.75	1.25	2.50	—
1982BP	30,000	—	0.75	1.25	2.50	—
1983BP	30,000	—	0.75	1.25	2.50	—
1984BP	30,000	—	0.75	1.25	2.50	—
1985BP	30,000	—	0.75	1.25	2.50	—
1986BP	30,000	—	0.75	1.25	2.50	—
1987BP	30,000	—	0.75	1.25	2.50	—
1988BP	30,000	—	0.75	1.25	2.50	—
1989BP	30,000	—	0.75	1.25	2.50	—

KM# 546a 2 FILLER
0.6500 g., Copper-Nickel, 17 mm. **Obv:** Legend and wreath surround center hole **Rev:** Center hole divides denomination within wreath

Date	Mintage	F	VF	XF	Unc	BU
1966 Proof	5,000	Value: 4.00				
1967 Proof	5,000	Value: 4.00				

KM# 549 5 FILLER
0.6000 g., Aluminum, 17 mm. **Obv:** Head left
Rev: Denomination within wreath

Date	Mintage	F	VF	XF	Unc	BU
1953BP	10,000,000	0.10	0.15	0.30	0.50	—
1955BP	6,005,000	0.15	0.20	0.50	1.00	—
1956BP	6,012,000	0.15	0.20	0.50	1.00	—
1957BP	5,000,000	0.20	0.30	0.60	1.20	—
1959BP	8,000,000	0.15	0.20	0.50	1.00	—
1960BP	7,000,000	0.15	0.20	0.50	1.00	—
1961BP	4,410,000	0.20	0.30	0.60	1.20	—
1962BP	5,590,000	0.20	0.30	0.60	1.20	—
1963BP	4,020,000	0.20	0.30	0.60	1.20	—
1964BP	3,600,000	0.20	0.30	0.60	1.20	—
1965BP	6,000,000	0.20	0.30	0.60	1.20	—
1970BP	3,900,000	—	2.50	5.00	10.00	—
1971BP	100,000	—	0.25	0.50	1.00	—
1972BP	50,000	—	0.25	0.50	1.00	—
1973BP	105,000	—	0.25	0.50	1.00	—
1974BP	60,000	—	0.25	0.50	1.00	—
1975BP	60,000	—	0.25	0.50	1.00	—
1976BP	50,000	—	0.25	0.50	1.00	—
1977BP	60,000	—	0.25	0.50	1.00	—
1978BP	50,000	—	0.25	0.50	1.00	—
1979BP	30,000	—	0.50	1.00	2.00	—
1980BP	30,000	—	0.50	1.00	2.00	—
1981BP	30,000	—	0.50	1.00	2.00	—
1982BP	30,000	—	0.50	1.00	2.00	—
1983BP	30,000	—	0.50	1.00	2.00	—
1984BP	30,000	—	0.50	1.00	2.00	—
1985BP	30,000	—	0.50	1.00	2.00	—
1986BP	30,000	—	0.50	1.00	2.00	—
1987BP	30,000	—	0.50	1.00	2.00	—
1988BP	30,000	—	0.50	1.00	2.00	—
1989BP	30,000	—	0.50	1.00	2.00	—

KM# 549a 5 FILLER
Copper-Nickel, 17 mm. **Obv:** Head left **Rev:** Denomination within wreath

Date	Mintage	F	VF	XF	Unc	BU
1966 Proof	5,000	Value: 5.00				
1967 Proof	5,000	Value: 5.00				

KM# 547 10 FILLER
0.8600 g., Aluminum **Obv:** Dove with branch **Rev:** Denomination

Date	Mintage	F	VF	XF	Unc	BU
1950BP	5,040,000	10.00	20.00	30.00	50.00	—
1951BP	80,950,000	1.50	3.00	5.00	10.00	—
1955BP	10,019,000	2.00	4.00	7.00	15.00	—
1957BP	13,000,000	2.00	4.00	7.00	15.00	—
1958BP	12,015,000	2.00	4.00	7.00	15.00	—
1959BP	15,000,000	2.00	4.00	7.00	15.00	—
1960BP	5,000,000	2.50	5.00	8.00	17.00	—
1961BP	13,000,000	2.00	4.00	7.00	15.00	—
1962BP	4,000,000	2.50	5.00	9.00	18.00	—
1963BP	8,000,000	2.50	5.00	8.00	17.00	—
1964BP	17,008,000	2.00	4.00	7.00	15.00	—
1965BP	21,880,000	2.00	4.00	7.00	15.00	—
1966BP	8,120,000	2.50	5.00	8.00	17.00	—

KM# 547a 10 FILLER
Copper-Nickel **Obv:** Dove with branch **Rev:** Denomination

Date	Mintage	F	VF	XF	Unc	BU
1966 Proof	5,000	Value: 6.00				
1967 Proof	5,000	Value: 6.00				

KM# 572 10 FILLER
0.6000 g., Aluminum, 18.5 mm. **Obv:** Dove with branch **Rev:** Denomination **Note:** Reduced size.

Date	Mintage	F	VF	XF	Unc	BU
1967	5,000	5.00	10.00	20.00	45.00	—
1968	16,000,000	0.50	1.00	2.50	5.00	—
1969	50,760,000	0.50	1.00	2.50	5.00	—
1970	28,470,000	0.50	1.00	2.50	5.00	—
1971	28,800,000	—	0.50	1.25	2.50	—
1972	17,220,000	—	0.50	1.25	2.50	—
1973	33,720,000	—	0.50	1.25	2.50	—
1974	24,930,000	—	0.50	1.25	2.50	—
1975	30,000,000	—	0.50	1.25	2.50	—
1976	20,025,000	—	0.50	1.25	2.50	—

Date	Mintage	F	VF	XF	Unc	BU
1977	30,075,000	—	0.50	1.25	2.50	—
1978	36,005,000	—	0.40	1.00	2.00	—
1979	36,060,000	—	0.40	1.00	2.00	—
1980	36,010,000	—	0.40	1.00	2.00	—
1981	36,000,000	—	0.40	1.00	2.00	—
1982	45,015,000	—	0.30	0.75	1.50	—
1983	45,030,000	—	0.30	0.75	1.50	—
1984	42,075,000	—	0.30	0.75	1.50	—
1985	40,035,000	—	0.30	0.75	1.50	—
1986	48,075,000	—	0.30	0.75	1.50	—
1987	45,000,000	—	0.30	0.75	1.50	—
1988	48,015,000	—	0.30	0.75	1.50	—
1989	55,515,000	—	0.25	0.65	1.50	—

KM# 550 20 FILLER
1.2000 g., Aluminum, 21 mm. **Obv:** Three wheat ears divide date **Rev:** Lines divide denomination

Date	Mintage	F	VF	XF	Unc	BU
1953BP	45,000,000	1.00	2.00	4.00	8.00	—
1955BP	10,023,000	1.25	2.50	5.00	10.00	—
1957BP	5,000,000	1.75	3.50	7.00	15.00	—
1958BP	10,000,000	1.25	*2.50	5.00	10.00	—
1959BP	13,000,000	1.25	2.50	5.00	10.00	—
1961BP	9,000,000	1.25	2.50	5.00	10.00	—
1963BP	7,000,000	1.50	3.00	6.00	12.00	—
1964BP	10,400,000	1.25	2.50	5.00	10.00	—
1965BP	15,000,000	1.25	2.50	5.00	10.00	—
1966BP	5,000,000	1.50	3.00	6.50	12.50	—

KM# 550a 20 FILLER
Copper-Nickel **Obv:** Three wheat ears divide date **Rev:** Lines divide denomination

Date	Mintage	F	VF	XF	Unc	BU
1966 Proof	5,000	Value: 8.00				
1967 Proof	5,000	Value: 8.00				

KM# 573 20 FILLER
0.9000 g., Aluminum, 20.4 mm. **Obv:** Three wheat ears divide date **Rev:** Lines divide denomination **Note:** Reduced size.

Date	Mintage	F	VF	XF	Unc	BU
1967	10,000,000	0.25	0.75	2.50	6.00	—
1968	56,500,000	0.10	0.40	1.25	3.00	—
1969	28,550,000	0.15	0.45	1.50	4.00	—
1970	19,960,000	0.20	0.60	2.00	5.00	—
1971	31,090,000	0.10	0.20	0.75	2.00	—
7971 Error	11,000	3.50	7.50	15.00	30.00	—
1972	21,070,000	0.15	0.30	0.75	1.50	—
1973	22,970,000	0.15	0.30	0.75	1.50	—
1974	35,010,000	0.15	0.30	0.75	1.50	—
1975	30,010,000	0.15	0.30	0.75	1.50	—
1976	30,010,000	0.15	0.30	0.75	1.50	—
1977	30,050,000	0.15	0.30	0.75	1.50	—
1978	30,140,000	0.15	0.30	0.75	1.50	—
1979	32,010,000	0.15	0.30	0.75	1.50	—
1980	45,010,000	0.10	0.20	0.50	1.00	—
1981	34,030,000	0.10	0.20	0.50	1.00	—
1982	35,010,000	0.10	0.20	0.50	1.00	—
1983	43,210,000	0.10	0.20	0.50	1.00	—
1984	42,270,000	0.10	0.20	0.50	1.00	—
1985	40,440,000	0.10	0.20	0.50	1.00	—
1986	48,000,000	0.10	0.20	0.50	1.00	—
1987	55,000,000	0.10	0.20	0.50	1.00	—
1988	48,010,000	0.10	0.20	0.50	1.00	—
1989	64,660,000	—	—	0.10	0.50	—

KM# 627 20 FILLER
0.9000 g., Aluminum, 20.4 mm. **Series:** F.A.O. **Obv:** Three wheat ears above banner **Rev:** Lines divide denomination

Date	Mintage	F	VF	XF	Unc	BU
1983	50,000	—	0.50	1.00	2.50	—

KM# 551   50 FILLER
1.4000 g., Aluminum   **Obv:** Blacksmith seated on anvil
Rev: Denomination within wreath

Date	Mintage	F	VF	XF	Unc	BU
1953BP	10,017,000	1.50	3.00	6.00	12.00	—
1965BP	3,005,000	1.25	2.50	5.00	10.00	—
1966BP	1,500,000	1.75	3.50	7.00	15.00	—

KM# 551a   50 FILLER
Copper-Nickel   **Obv:** Blacksmith seated on anvil
Rev: Denomination within wreath

Date	Mintage	F	VF	XF	Unc	BU
1966 Proof	5,000	Value: 10.00				
1967 Proof	5,000	Value: 10.00				

KM# 574   50 FILLER
1.2000 g., Aluminum, 21.5 mm.   **Subject:** Elizabeth Bridge in Budapest   **Obv:** Bridge   **Rev:** Denomination above date

Date	Mintage	F	VF	XF	Unc	BU
1967	20,000,000	0.50	1.00	2.00	4.00	—
1968	13,861,000	0.60	1.25	2.50	5.00	—
1969	10,085,000	0.60	1.25	2.50	5.00	—
1971	50,000	0.30	0.60	1.25	2.50	—
1972	470,000	0.20	0.50	1.00	2.00	—
1973	7,600,000	0.20	0.50	1.00	2.00	—
1974	5,000,000	0.20	0.50	1.00	2.00	—
1975	10,160,000	0.10	0.30	0.75	1.50	—
1976	15,130,000	0.10	0.30	0.75	1.50	—
1977	10,050,000	0.10	0.30	0.75	1.50	—
1978	10,110,000	0.10	0.30	0.75	1.50	—
1979	10,070,000	0.10	0.30	0.75	1.50	—
1980	15,000,000	0.10	0.30	0.75	1.50	—
1981	10,030,000	0.10	0.30	0.75	1.50	—
1982	10,000,000	0.10	0.30	0.75	1.50	—
1983	10,070,000	0.10	0.30	0.75	1.50	—
1984	14,060,000	0.10	0.30	0.75	1.50	—
1985	12,020,000	0.10	0.30	0.75	1.50	—
1986	17,140,000	0.10	0.30	0.75	1.50	—
1987	23,000,000	—	0.10	0.50	1.00	—
1988	18,050,000	—	0.10	0.50	1.00	—
1989	18,200,000	—	0.10	0.50	1.00	—

KM# 545   FORINT
1.4600 g., Aluminum   **Obv:** Wreath surrounds wheat ear and hammer on radiant background below star   **Rev:** Leaves flank denomination

Date	Mintage	F	VF	XF	Unc	BU
1949BP	19,440,000	1.50	3.00	6.00	12.00	—
1950BP	39,060,000	2.25	4.50	9.00	18.00	—
1952BP	63,018,000	2.00	4.00	8.00	16.00	—

KM# 555   FORINT
1.5000 g., Aluminum, 22.8 mm.   **Obv:** Star above shield within wreath   **Rev:** Leaves flank denomination

Date	Mintage	F	VF	XF	Unc	BU
1957	7,500,000	2.00	4.00	8.00	16.00	—
1958	5,070,000	1.50	3.00	6.00	12.00	—
1960	5,000,000	1.25	2.50	5.00	10.00	—
1961	5,000,000	1.25	2.50	5.00	10.00	—
1963	3,000,000	1.50	3.00	6.50	12.50	—
1964	6,080,000	1.00	2.00	4.00	8.00	—
1965	9,810,000	1.00	2.00	4.00	8.00	—
1966	5,680,000	1.75	3.50	7.50	15.00	—

KM# 555a   FORINT
5.8500 g., 0.8350 Silver 0.1570 oz. ASW, 22.8 mm.   **Obv:** Star above shield within wreath   **Rev:** Leaves flank denomination

Date	Mintage	F	VF	XF	Unc	BU
1966 Proof	5,000	Value: 12.00				
1967 Proof	5,000	Value: 12.00				

KM# 575   FORINT
1.4000 g., Aluminum, 22.8 mm.   **Obv:** Star above shield within wreath   **Rev:** Leaves flank denomination

Date	Mintage	F	VF	XF	Unc	BU
1967	60,000,000	0.65	1.25	2.50	5.00	—
1968	53,230,000	0.65	1.25	2.50	6.00	—
1969	27,664,000	1.00	2.00	4.00	8.00	—
1970	11,290,000	1.00	2.00	4.00	10.00	—
1971	100,000	0.10	0.20	0.50	1.00	—
1972	110,000	0.25	0.50	1.00	2.00	—
1973	1,990,000	0.10	0.20	0.50	1.00	—
1974	4,990,000	0.10	0.20	0.50	1.00	—
1975	10,000,000	0.10	0.20	0.40	0.80	—
1976	15,000,000	0.10	0.20	0.40	0.80	—
1977	10,050,000	0.10	0.20	0.40	0.80	—
1978	50,000	0.20	0.40	0.85	1.75	—
1979	10,070,000	0.10	0.20	0.35	0.70	—
1980	20,040,000	0.10	0.20	0.35	0.70	—
1981	25,040,000	0.10	0.20	0.35	0.70	—
1982	10,000,000	0.10	0.20	0.35	0.70	—
1983	20,140,000	0.10	0.20	0.35	0.70	—
1984	6,010,000	0.15	0.30	0.60	1.20	—
1985	30,000	0.25	0.50	1.00	2.00	—
1986	30,000	0.25	0.50	1.00	2.00	—
1987	13,000,000	0.10	0.20	0.50	1.00	—
1988	20,080,000	0.10	0.20	0.35	0.75	—
1989	115,920,000	—	0.15	0.30	0.60	—

KM# 548   2 FORINT
Copper-Nickel   **Obv:** Wreath surrounds hammer and wheat ear on radiant background with star above   **Rev:** Denomination within 3/4 wreath

Date	Mintage	F	VF	XF	Unc	BU
1950BP	18,500,000	1.75	3.50	7.00	15.00	—
1951BP	4,000,000	2.00	4.00	8.00	16.00	—
1952BP	4,530,000	2.00	4.00	8.00	16.00	—

KM# 556   2 FORINT
4.9500 g., Copper-Nickel, 25 mm.   **Obv:** Star above shield within wreath   **Rev:** Denomination within 3/4 wreath   **Edge:** Flora vines

Date	Mintage	F	VF	XF	Unc	BU
1957	5,000,000	1.50	3.00	6.00	12.50	—
1958	1,033,000	1.75	3.50	7.00	15.00	—
1960	4,000,000	1.50	3.00	6.00	12.50	—
1961	690,000	2.00	4.00	8.00	16.00	—
1962	1,190,000	1.50	3.00	6.00	12.50	—

KM# 556a   2 FORINT
5.1200 g., Copper-Nickel-Zinc   **Obv:** Star above shield within wreath   **Rev:** Denomination within 3/4 wreath

Date	Mintage	F	VF	XF	Unc	BU
1962	1,210,000	1.25	2.50	5.00	10.00	—
1963	3,100,000	1.25	2.50	5.00	10.00	—
1964	3,250,000	1.25	2.50	5.00	10.00	—
1965	4,395,000	1.25	2.50	5.00	10.00	—
1966	6,630,000	1.25	2.50	5.00	10.00	—

KM# 556b   2 FORINT
6.1200 g., 0.8350 Silver 0.1643 oz. ASW   **Obv:** Star above shield within wreath   **Rev:** Denomination within 3/4 wreath

Date	Mintage	F	VF	XF	Unc	BU
1966 Proof	5,000	Value: 14.00				
1967 Proof	5,000	Value: 14.00				

KM# 591   2 FORINT
4.4400 g., Brass, 22.4 mm.   **Rev:** Denomination divides date

Date	Mintage	F	VF	XF	Unc	BU
1970	49,195,000	0.50	1.00	2.00	4.00	—
1971	10,830,000	0.10	0.50	1.00	2.00	—
1972	10,015,000	0.10	0.50	1.00	2.00	—
1973	820,000	1.00	2.00	4.00	8.00	—
1974	10,000,000	0.25	0.75	1.50	3.00	—
1975	20,030,000	0.25	0.75	1.50	3.00	—
1976	15,000,000	0.25	0.75	1.50	3.00	—
1977	10,115,000	0.25	0.75	1.50	3.00	—
1978	12,000,000	0.25	0.75	1.50	3.00	—
1979	12,107,000	0.25	0.75	1.50	3.00	—
1980	12,005,000	0.25	0.75	1.50	3.00	—
1981	10,010,000	0.25	0.75	1.50	3.00	—
1982	10,005,000	0.25	0.75	1.50	3.00	—
1983	20,160,000	0.25	0.75	1.50	3.00	—
1984	5,000,000	0.75	1.50	3.00	6.00	—
1985	10,675,000	0.25	0.75	1.50	3.00	—
1986	30,000	1.50	3.00	6.00	12.00	—
1987	5,030,000	0.50	1.00	2.00	4.00	—
1988	5,035,000	0.50	1.00	2.00	4.00	—
1989	79,223,000	0.10	0.25	0.50	1.00	—

KM# 576   5 FORINT
7.2100 g., Copper-Nickel, 27 mm.   **Subject:** Lajos Kossuth   **Obv:** Star above shield within wreath   **Rev:** Head right

Date	Mintage	F	VF	XF	Unc	BU
1967BP	20,000,000	0.50	1.00	2.50	5.00	—
1968BP	29,000	5.00	10.00	20.00	35.00	—

KM# 594   5 FORINT
5.7300 g., Nickel, 24.3 mm.   **Obv:** Head right   **Rev:** Small shield above denomination

Date	Mintage	F	VF	XF	Unc	BU
1971	20,004,000	0.20	0.35	0.75	1.50	—
1972	5,000,000	0.25	0.50	1.00	2.00	—
1973	100,000	0.35	0.75	1.50	3.00	—
1974	50,000	0.35	0.75	1.50	3.00	—
1975	50,000	0.35	0.75	1.50	3.00	—
1976	5,090,000	0.25	0.50	1.00	2.00	—
1977	50,000	0.35	0.75	1.50	3.00	—
1978	6,000,000	0.25	0.50	1.00	2.00	—
1979	10,000,000	0.25	0.50	1.00	2.00	—
1980	6,002,000	0.25	0.50	1.00	2.00	—
1981	5,002,000	0.25	0.50	1.00	2.00	—
1982	936,000	0.30	0.60	1.25	2.50	—

KM# 628   5 FORINT
Nickel   **Series:** F.A.O.   **Obv:** Flower holds logo within circle   **Rev:** Small shield above denomination

Date	Mintage	F	VF	XF	Unc	BU
1983	50,000	—	1.00	2.00	3.50	—

KM# 635   5 FORINT
Copper-Nickel   **Subject:** Lajos Kossuth **Obv:** Head right
Rev: Small shield above denomination

Date	Mintage	F	VF	XF	Unc	BU
1983	15,240,000	0.15	0.25	0.50	1.00	—
1984	25,018,000	0.15	0.25	0.50	1.00	—
1985	25,286,000	0.15	0.25	0.50	1.00	—
1986	1,030,000	0.20	0.35	0.75	1.50	—
1987	30,000	0.30	0.60	1.25	2.50	—
1988	4,050,000	0.20	0.35	0.75	1.50	—
1989	39,014,000	0.15	0.25	0.50	1.00	—

KM# 552   10 FORINT
12.5000 g., 0.8000 Silver 0.3215 oz. ASW, 30 mm.   **Subject:**
10th Anniversary of Forint **Obv:** National Museum in Budapest
Rev: Leaves back of denomination, small shield above

Date	Mintage	F	VF	XF	Unc	BU
1956BP	22,000	BV	5.50	8.00	16.00	—

KM# 595   10 FORINT
8.8300 g., Nickel, 28 mm.   **Obv:** Strobl Monument **Rev:** Small
shield below denomination

Date	Mintage	F	VF	XF	Unc	BU
1971	24,998,000	0.35	0.75	1.50	3.00	4.50
1972	25,078,000	0.35	0.75	1.50	3.00	4.50
1973	78,000	0.60	1.25	2.50	5.00	7.50
1974	50,000	0.60	1.25	2.50	5.00	7.50
1975	50,000	0.60	1.25	2.50	5.00	7.50
1976	3,568,000	0.50	1.00	2.00	4.00	5.50
1977	4,618,000	0.50	1.00	2.00	4.00	5.50
1978	50,000	0.60	1.25	2.50	5.00	7.50
1979	5,000,000	0.50	1.00	2.00	4.00	5.50
1980	2,550,000	0.50	1.00	2.00	4.00	5.50
1982	30,000	0.60	1.25	2.50	5.00	7.50

KM# 620   10 FORINT
8.8300 g., Nickel, 28 mm.   **Series:** F.A.O. **Obv:** Strobl Monument
Rev: Small shield below denomination

Date	Mintage	F	VF	XF	Unc	BU
1981	60,000	—	—	2.50	5.00	7.50

KM# 629   10 FORINT
8.8300 g., Nickel, 28 mm.   **Series:** F.A.O. **Obv:** Logo at right of
figure with large jar and bowl **Rev:** Small shield below denomination

Date	Mintage	F	VF	XF	Unc	BU
1983	50,000	—	—	2.50	5.00	—

KM# 636   10 FORINT
6.0100 g., Aluminum-Bronze, 28 mm.   **Obv:** Strobl Monument
Rev: Small shield below denomination **Note:** Circulation coinage.

Date	Mintage	F	VF	XF	Unc	BU
1983	11,004,000	0.25	0.50	1.00	2.00	3.00
1984	7,578,000	0.25	0.50	1.00	2.00	3.00
1985	27,648,000	0.25	0.50	1.00	2.00	3.00
1986	15,006,000	0.25	0.50	1.00	2.00	3.00
1987	10,000,000	0.25	0.50	1.00	2.00	3.00
1988	5,000,000	0.25	0.50	1.00	2.00	3.00
1989	37,094,000	0.25	0.50	1.00	2.00	3.00

KM# 553   20 FORINT
17.5000 g., 0.8000 Silver 0.4501 oz. ASW, 32 mm.   **Subject:**
10th Anniversary of Forint **Obv:** Szechenyi suspension bridge in
Budapest **Rev:** Shield on ornamental background

Date	Mintage	F	VF	XF	Unc	BU
1956BP	22,000	8.00	10.00	12.00	20.00	—

KM# 630   20 FORINT
Copper-Nickel, 26.5 mm.   **Subject:** György Dózsa **Obv:** Head
looking left **Rev:** Small shield above denomination

Date	Mintage	F	VF	XF	Unc	BU
1982	13,404,000	0.25	0.50	0.80	1.60	—
1983	18,006,000	0.25	0.50	0.80	1.60	—
1984	31,016,000	0.25	0.50	0.80	1.60	—
1985	20,122,000	0.25	0.50	0.80	1.60	—
1986	6,000,000	0.35	0.65	1.25	2.25	—
1987	30,000	0.40	0.75	1.50	3.00	—
1988	30,000	0.40	0.75	1.50	3.00	—
1989	31,890,000	0.25	0.50	0.80	1.60	—

KM# 637   20 FORINT
Copper-Nickel   **Subject:** Forestry for Development **Obv:** Leaf
within globe above denomination **Rev:** Stylized tree within
patterned archway

Date	Mintage	F	VF	XF	Unc	BU
1984	15,000	—	—	—	3.00	—
1984 Proof	5,000	Value: 7.00				

KM# 653   20 FORINT
Copper-Nickel   **Series:** F.A.O. **Obv:** Logos with dates within box
above stylized denomination **Rev:** Wheat ear divides fish and
leaf, lined background

Date	Mintage	F	VF	XF	Unc	BU
1985	25,000	—	—	—	4.00	—

KM# 554   25 FORINT (Huszonot)
20.0000 g., 0.8000 Silver 0.5144 oz. ASW, 34 mm.
Subject: 10th Anniversary Forint **Obv:** Parliament Building in
Budapest **Rev:** Leaves within cogwheel, arms above

Date	Mintage	F	VF	XF	Unc	BU
1956BP	22,000	9.00	12.00	15.00	20.00	—

KM# 557   25 FORINT (Huszonot)
17.5000 g., 0.7500 Silver 0.4220 oz. ASW   **Subject:** 150th
Anniversary - Birth of Liszt, Musician **Obv:** Harp **Rev:** Head right

Date	Mintage	F	VF	XF	Unc	BU
1961 Proof	15,000	Value: 15.50				

KM# 558   25 FORINT (Huszonot)
17.5000 g., 0.7500 Silver 0.4220 oz. ASW   **Subject:** 80th
Anniversary - Birth of Bartok, Composer **Obv:** Small harp above
denomination **Rev:** Head left

Date	Mintage	F	VF	XF	Unc	BU
1961 Proof	15,000	Value: 16.50				

KM# 567   25 FORINT (Huszonot)
12.0000 g., 0.6400 Silver 0.2469 oz. ASW   **Subject:** 40th
Anniversary - Death of Zrinyi **Obv:** Monument **Rev:** Head 3/4 right

Date	Mintage	F	VF	XF	Unc	BU
1966 Proof	11,000	Value: 20.00				

KM# 577   25 FORINT (Huszonot)
12.0000 g., 0.7500 Silver 0.2893 oz. ASW   **Subject:** 85th
Birthday of Kodaly, Composer **Obv:** Peacock above
denomination **Rev:** Bust 3/4 left

Date	Mintage	F	VF	XF	Unc	BU
1967	15,000	—	—	—	10.00	—
1967 Proof	—	Value: 12.50				

KM# 559   50 FORINT (Otven)
20.0000 g., 0.7500 Silver 0.4822 oz. ASW **Subject:** 150th
Anniversary - Birth of Liszt, Musician **Obv:** Harp below
denomination **Rev:** Head right

Date	Mintage	F	VF	XF	Unc	BU
1961BP Proof	15,000			Value: 20.00		

KM# 560   50 FORINT (Otven)
3.8380 g., 0.9860 Gold 0.1217 oz. AGW **Subject:** 150th
Anniversary - Birth of Liszt, Musician **Obv:** Harp below
denomination **Rev:** Head right

Date	Mintage	F	VF	XF	Unc	BU
1961 Proof	2,503			Value: 125		

KM# 561   50 FORINT (Otven)
20.0000 g., 0.7500 Silver 0.4822 oz. ASW **Subject:** 80th
Anniversary - Birth of Bartok, Composer **Obv:** Small harp above
denomination **Rev:** Head left

Date	Mintage	F	VF	XF	Unc	BU
1961 Proof	15,000			Value: 20.00		

KM# 562   50 FORINT (Otven)
3.8380 g., 0.9860 Gold 0.1217 oz. AGW **Subject:** 80th
Anniversary - Birth of Bartok, Composer **Obv:** Small harp above
denomination **Rev:** Head left

Date	Mintage	F	VF	XF	Unc	BU
1961 Proof	2,503			Value: 130		

KM# 568   50 FORINT (Otven)
20.0000 g., 0.6400 Silver 0.4115 oz. ASW **Subject:** 400th
Anniversary - Death of Zrinyi **Obv:** Monument **Rev:** Head 3/4 right

Date	Mintage	F	VF	XF	Unc	BU
1966BP Proof	11,000			Value: 25.00		

KM# 578   50 FORINT (Otven)
20.0000 g., 0.7500 Silver 0.4822 oz. ASW **Subject:** 85th
Birthday of Kodaly, Composer **Obv:** Peacock above
denomination **Rev:** Bust 3/4 left

Date	Mintage	F	VF	XF	Unc	BU
1967	15,000	—	—	—	10.00	11.50

KM# 582   50 FORINT (Otven)
20.0000 g., 0.6400 Silver 0.4115 oz. ASW **Subject:** 150th
Anniversary - Birth of Semmelweis **Obv:** Head right **Rev:** Star
above shield on radiant background, wreath surrounds

Date	Mintage	F	VF	XF	Unc	BU
1968	20,250	—	—	—	10.00	11.50
1968 Proof	4,750			Value: 12.50		

KM# 583   50 FORINT (Otven)
4.2050 g., 0.9000 Gold 0.1217 oz. AGW **Subject:** 150th
Anniversary - Birth of Semmelweis **Obv:** Head right **Rev:** Star
above shield within wreath

Date	Mintage	F	VF	XF	Unc	BU
1968 Proof	25,000			Value: 120		

KM# 589   50 FORINT (Otven)
16.0000 g., 0.6400 Silver 0.3292 oz. ASW **Subject:** 50th
Anniversary - Republic of Councils **Obv:** Small arms above
denomination **Rev:** Half figure with arms spread

Date	Mintage	F	VF	XF	Unc	BU
1969	12,000	—	—	—	8.00	10.00
1969 Proof	3,000			Value: 15.00		

KM# 592   50 FORINT (Otven)
16.0000 g., 0.6400 Silver 0.3292 oz. ASW **Subject:** 25th
Anniversary of Liberation **Obv:** Strobl monument **Rev:** Small
shield below denomination

Date	Mintage	F	VF	XF	Unc	BU
1970	20,000	—	—	—	7.00	9.00
1970 Proof	5,000			Value: 12.50		

KM# 596   50 FORINT (Otven)
16.0000 g., 0.6400 Silver 0.3292 oz. ASW **Subject:** 1000th
Anniversary of St. Stephen **Obv:** Denomination below
central design **Rev:** St. Stephan on horseback

Date	Mintage	F	VF	XF	Unc	BU
1972	24,000	—	—	—	10.00	12.00
1972 Proof	6,000			Value: 15.00		

KM# 599   50 FORINT (Otven)
16.0000 g., 0.6400 Silver 0.3292 oz. ASW **Subject:** 150th
Anniversary - Birth of Sandor Petofi, Poet **Obv:** Ribbon above
denomination **Rev:** Bust 3/4 facing, upper right

Date	Mintage	F	VF	XF	Unc	BU
1973	24,000	—	—	—	8.00	10.00
1973 Proof	6,000			Value: 12.00		

KM# 601   50 FORINT (Otven)
16.0000 g., 0.6400 Silver 0.3292 oz. ASW **Subject:** 50th
Anniversary of National Bank **Obv:** Small shield left of
denomination **Rev:** Bank building

Date	Mintage	F	VF	XF	Unc	BU
1974	24,000	—	—	—	7.00	8.50
1974 Proof	6,000			Value: 10.00		

KM# 663   50 FORINT (Otven)
Copper-Nickel **Subject:** 25th Anniversary of World Wildlife
Foundation **Obv:** Star above shield within wreath **Rev:** Red-
footed Falcon

Date	Mintage	F	VF	XF	Unc	BU
1988	45,000	—	—	—	6.50	8.00

KM# 563   100 FORINT (Szaz)
7.6760 g., 0.9860 Gold 0.2433 oz. AGW **Subject:** 150th
Anniversary - Birth of Liszt, Musician **Obv:** Head right **Rev:** Harp
below denomination

Date	Mintage	F	VF	XF	Unc	BU
1961BP Proof	2,500			Value: 245		

KM# 564   100 FORINT (Szaz)
7.6760 g., 0.9860 Gold 0.2433 oz. AGW **Subject:** 80th Anniversary - Birth of Bartok, Composer **Obv:** Head left **Rev:** Small harp above denomination

Date	Mintage	F	VF	XF	Unc	BU
1961 Proof	2,500	Value: 245				

KM# 569   100 FORINT (Szaz)
8.4100 g., 0.9000 Gold 0.2433 oz. AGW **Subject:** 400th Anniversary - Death of Zrinyi **Obv:** Monument **Rev:** Head 3/4 right

Date	Mintage	F	VF	XF	Unc	BU
1966 Proof	3,300	Value: 245				

KM# 579   100 FORINT (Szaz)
28.0000 g., 0.7500 Silver 0.6751 oz. ASW **Subject:** 85th Birthday of Kodaly, Composer **Obv:** Peacock above denomination **Rev:** Bust 3/4 left

Date	Mintage	F	VF	XF	Unc	BU
1967BP	10,000	—	—	—	25.00	28.00

KM# 584   100 FORINT (Szaz)
28.0000 g., 0.6400 Silver 0.5761 oz. ASW **Subject:** 150th Anniversary - Birth of Semmelweis **Obv:** Head right **Rev:** Star above shield within wreath

Date	Mintage	F	VF	XF	Unc	BU
1968	20,250	—	—	—	10.00	12.00
1968 Proof	4,750	Value: 17.50				

KM# 585   100 FORINT (Szaz)
8.4100 g., 0.9000 Gold 0.2433 oz. AGW **Subject:** 150th Anniversary - Birth of Semmelweis **Obv:** Head right **Rev:** Star above shield within wreath

Date	Mintage	F	VF	XF	Unc	BU
1968 Proof	23,000	Value: 235				

KM# 590   100 FORINT (Szaz)
22.0000 g., 0.6400 Silver 0.4527 oz. ASW **Subject:** 50th Anniversary - Republic of Councils **Obv:** Denomination below small arms flanked by clovers **Rev:** Half figure with arms spread

Date	Mintage	F	VF	XF	Unc	BU
1969	12,000	—	—	—	10.00	12.00
1969 Proof	3,000	Value: 15.00				

KM# 593   100 FORINT (Szaz)
22.0000 g., 0.6400 Silver 0.4527 oz. ASW **Subject:** 25th Anniversary of Liberation **Obv:** Strobl monument **Rev:** Star above shield within wreath

Date	Mintage	F	VF	XF	Unc	BU
1970	20,000	—	—	—	10.00	12.00
1970 Proof	5,000	Value: 16.00				

KM# 597   100 FORINT (Szaz)
22.0000 g., 0.6400 Silver 0.4527 oz. ASW **Subject:** 1000th Anniversary - Birth of St. Stephen **Obv:** St. Stephen's monogram **Rev:** Crowned bust facing

Date	Mintage	F	VF	XF	Unc	BU
1972	24,000	—	—	—	10.00	12.00
1972 Proof	6,000	Value: 15.00				

KM# 598   100 FORINT (Szaz)
22.0000 g., 0.6400 Silver 0.4527 oz. ASW **Subject:** Buda and Pest Union Centennial **Obv:** Star above shield within wreath **Rev:** Design depicting union, roman numerals below

Date	Mintage	F	VF	XF	Unc	BU
1972	25,000	—	—	—	10.00	12.00

KM# 600   100 FORINT (Szaz)
22.0000 g., 0.6400 Silver 0.4527 oz. ASW **Subject:** 150th Anniversary - Birth of Sandor Petofi, Poet **Obv:** Star above shield within wreath divides date **Rev:** Head 3/4 facing below inscription

Date	Mintage	F	VF	XF	Unc	BU
1973	24,000	—	—	—	8.50	10.00
1973 Proof	6,000	Value: 12.50				

KM# 602   100 FORINT (Szaz)
22.0000 g., 0.6400 Silver 0.4527 oz. ASW **Subject:** 25th Anniversary of KGST **Obv:** Star above shield within wreath **Rev:** Coins of Hungary, Russia, Romania, East Germany, Mongolia, Poland, Cuba, Czechoslovakia and Bulgaria

Date	Mintage	F	VF	XF	Unc	BU
1974	20,000	—	—	—	8.50	9.50
1974 Proof	5,000	Value: 11.50				

KM# 603   100 FORINT (Szaz)
22.0000 g., 0.6400 Silver 0.4527 oz. ASW **Subject:** 50th Anniversary of National Bank **Obv:** Small shield at upper left **Rev:** Depictions of symbols of various professions

Date	Mintage	F	VF	XF	Unc	BU
1974	24,000	—	—	—	8.00	9.00
1974 Proof	6,000	Value: 10.00				

KM# 617   100 FORINT (Szaz)
Nickel, 32 mm. **Subject:** 1st Soviet-Hungarian Space Flight
Obv: Star above shield within wreath **Rev:** Astronauts above globe, shuttle lower right

Date	Mintage	F	VF	XF	Unc	BU
1980	180,000	—	—	—	4.00	6.00
1980 Proof	20,000	Value: 8.00				

KM# 621   100 FORINT (Szaz)
Nickel, 32 mm. **Subject:** World Food Day **Obv:** Grain stalks
Rev: Kneeling figure

Date	Mintage	F	VF	XF	Unc	BU
1981	80,000	—	—	—	9.00	—
1981 Proof	20,000	Value: 11.00				

KM# 622   100 FORINT (Szaz)
Copper-Nickel-Zinc, 32 mm. **Subject:** 1300th Anniversary of Bulgarian Statehood **Obv:** Star above shield within wreath, grain stalks flank **Rev:** Sword handle and feather divide heads of Sàndor Petofi and Khristro Botev

Date	Mintage	F	VF	XF	Unc	BU
1981 Proof	50,000	Value: 8.00				

KM# 626   100 FORINT (Szaz)
Copper-Nickel, 38.5 mm. **Subject:** World Football Championship
Obv: Star above shield within wreath **Rev:** Soccer players

Date	Mintage	F	VF	XF	Unc	BU
1982	150,000	—	—	—	2.50	4.00

KM# 631   100 FORINT (Szaz)
Copper-Nickel, 38.5 mm. **Series:** F.A.O. **Obv:** Denomination and date right of logo on lined background **Rev:** Small hearts below stylized design

Date	Mintage	F	VF	XF	Unc	BU
1983	50,000	—	—	—	3.50	4.50
1983 Proof	10,000	Value: 5.50				

KM# 632   100 FORINT (Szaz)
Copper-Nickel-Zinc, 32 mm. **Subject:** 200th Anniversary - Birth of Simon Bolivar **Obv:** Andean Condor **Rev:** Grain sprigs form collar below head 3/4 left, map at left

Date	Mintage	F	VF	XF	Unc	BU
1983	20,000	—	—	—	6.50	7.50
1983 Proof	10,000	Value: 9.50				

KM# 633   100 FORINT (Szaz)
Copper-Nickel-Zinc, 32 mm. **Subject:** Count Istvàn Szèchenyi
Obv: Small shield above denomination **Rev:** Bust at left, three shields at right

Date	Mintage	F	VF	XF	Unc	BU
1983	30,000	—	—	—	6.00	7.00
1983 Proof	20,000	Value: 9.00				

KM# 634   100 FORINT (Szaz)
Copper-Nickel-Zinc, 32 mm. **Subject:** 100th Anniversary - Birth of Bèla Czobel, Painter **Obv:** Denomination within wreath
Rev: Head 3/4 facing

Date	Mintage	F	VF	XF	Unc	BU
1983	20,000	—	—	—	6.00	7.00
1983 Proof	10,000	Value: 10.00				

KM# 638   100 FORINT (Szaz)
Copper-Nickel-Zinc **Subject:** 200th Anniversary - Birth of Sàndor Kórósicsoma **Obv:** Design divides date and denomination
Rev: Half figure and dates left

Date	Mintage	F	VF	XF	Unc	BU
1984	20,000	—	—	—	6.00	7.00
1984 Proof	10,000	Value: 10.00				

KM# 639   100 FORINT (Szaz)
Copper-Nickel-Zinc, 32 mm. **Subject:** Forestry for Development
Obv: Tree at center of globe **Rev:** Stumps and seedlings

Date	Mintage	F	VF	XF	Unc	BU
1984	15,000	—	—	—	6.00	7.00
1984 Proof	5,000	Value: 10.00				

KM# 644   100 FORINT (Szaz)
Copper-Nickel-Zinc, 32 mm. **Subject:** Wildlife Preservation
Obv: Dates within side circles, divided by artistic denomination and legend within box **Rev:** Pond Turtle within square

Date	Mintage	F	VF	XF	Unc	BU
1985	20,000	—	—	—	10.00	14.00

KM# 645   100 FORINT (Szaz)
Copper-Nickel-Zinc, 32 mm. **Subject:** Wildlife Preservation
Obv: Dates within side circles, divided by artistic denomination and legend within box **Rev:** European Otter

Date	Mintage	F	VF	XF	Unc	BU
1985	20,000	—	—	—	10.00	14.00

KM# 646   100 FORINT (Szaz)
Copper-Nickel-Zinc, 32 mm. **Subject:** Wildlife Preservation
Obv: Dates within side circles, divided by artistic denomination and legend within box **Rev:** Wildcat

Date	Mintage	F	VF	XF	Unc	BU
1985	20,000	—	—	—	10.00	14.00

KM# 647   100 FORINT (Szaz)

Copper-Nickel-Zinc, 38.5 mm.   **Subject:** World Football
Obv: Soccer ball and globe form zeros of denomination
Rev: Map of Mexico

Date	Mintage	F	VF	XF	Unc	BU
1985	30,000	—	—	—	7.50	9.00

KM# 648   100 FORINT (Szaz)

Copper-Nickel-Zinc, 38.5 mm.   **Subject:** World Football
Obv: Soccer ball and globe form zeros of denomination
Rev: Native Mexican artifacts

Date	Mintage	F	VF	XF	Unc	BU
1985	30,000	—	—	—	7.50	9.00

KM# 651   100 FORINT (Szaz)

Copper-Nickel-Zinc, 32 mm.   **Subject:** Budapest Cultural Forum
Obv: Denomination **Rev:** Inscription within window, plant on sill

Date	Mintage	F	VF	XF	Unc	BU
1985	40,000	—	—	—	5.00	6.00

KM# 654   100 FORINT (Szaz)

Copper-Nickel-Zinc, 32 mm.   **Series:** F.A.O. **Obv:** Logo and
dates within box above denomination **Rev:** Grain sprigs divide
fish in water and tree

Date	Mintage	F	VF	XF	Unc	BU
1985	20,000	—	—	—	6.00	7.00
1985 Proof	5,000	Value: 8.00				

KM# 655   100 FORINT (Szaz)

Copper-Nickel-Zinc, 32 mm.   **Subject:** 200th Anniversary - Birth
of Andras Fay **Obv:** Denomination and date above legend, fly
below **Rev:** Bust at right looking left **Note:** See also KM#678 for
similar design.

Date	Mintage	F	VF	XF	Unc	BU
1986	42,000	—	—	—	5.00	6.00
1986 Proof	8,000	Value: 8.00				

KM# 664   100 FORINT (Szaz)

Copper-Nickel, 38.5 mm.   **Subject:** 1990 World Cup Soccer
Obv: Denomination **Rev:** Soccer players

Date	Mintage	F	VF	XF	Unc	BU
1988	23,000	—	—	—	9.00	10.00

KM# 665   100 FORINT (Szaz)

Copper-Nickel-Zinc, 38.5 mm.   **Subject:** Europe Football
Championship **Obv:** Flag and maps on globes make up
denomination numerals **Rev:** Soccer player and net within
television screen

Date	Mintage	F	VF	XF	Unc	BU
1988	20,000	—	—	—	9.00	10.00

KM# 668   100 FORINT (Szaz)

Copper-Nickel, 38.5 mm.   **Subject:** 1990 World Cup Soccer
Obv: Denomination **Rev:** Players with pennants shaking hands

Date	Mintage	F	VF	XF	Unc	BU
1989	23,000	—	—	—	9.00	10.00

KM# 586   200 FORINT (Ketszaz)

16.8210 g., 0.9000 Gold 0.4867 oz. AGW, 34 mm.
Subject: 150th Anniversary - Birth of Ignac Semmelweis
Obv: Head right **Rev:** Star above shield within wreath

Date	Mintage	F	VF	XF	Unc	BU
1968BP Proof	13,500	Value: 475				

KM# 604   200 FORINT (Ketszaz)

28.0000 g., 0.6400 Silver 0.5761 oz. ASW **Subject:** 30th
Anniversary of Liberation **Obv:** Small shield divides date,
denomination below **Rev:** Dove above legend and bridge

Date	Mintage	F	VF	XF	Unc	BU
1975BP	20,000	—	—	—	10.00	12.00
1975BP Proof	10,000	Value: 15.00				

KM# 605   200 FORINT (Ketszaz)

28.0000 g., 0.6400 Silver 0.5761 oz. ASW **Subject:** 150th
Anniversary - Academy of Science **Obv:** Denomination, legend
Rev: Legend on building at center divides dates

Date	Mintage	F	VF	XF	Unc	BU
1975	20,000	—	—	—	10.00	12.00
1975 Proof	10,000	Value: 15.00				

KM# 606   200 FORINT (Ketszaz)

28.0000 g., 0.6400 Silver 0.5761 oz. ASW **Subject:** 300th
Anniversary - Birth of Ferencz Rakoczi II **Obv:** Shield within
wreath divides denomination and date **Rev:** Figure on horseback
and soldiers

Date	Mintage	F	VF	XF	Unc	BU
1976	25,000	—	—	—	10.00	12.00
1976 Proof	5,000	Value: 15.00				

KM# 607   200 FORINT (Ketszaz)
28.0000 g., 0.6400 Silver 0.5761 oz. ASW   **Obv:** Quartered design with arms and denomination opposite each other   **Rev:** Mihaly Munkacsy, painter

Date	Mintage	F	VF	XF	Unc	BU
1976	25,000	—	—	—	10.00	12.00
1976 Proof	5,000	Value: 15.00				

KM# 608   200 FORINT (Ketszaz)
28.0000 g., 0.6400 Silver 0.5761 oz. ASW   **Obv:** Quartered design with arms and denomination opposite each other   **Rev:** Pal Szinyei Merse, painter

Date	Mintage	F	VF	XF	Unc	BU
1976	25,000	—	—	—	10.00	12.00
1976 Proof	5,000	Value: 15.00				

KM# 609   200 FORINT (Ketszaz)
28.0000 g., 0.6400 Silver 0.5761 oz. ASW   **Obv:** Quartered design with arms and denomination opposite each other   **Rev:** Gyula Derkovits, painter

Date	Mintage	F	VF	XF	Unc	BU
1976	25,000	—	—	—	10.00	12.00
1976 Proof	5,000	Value: 15.00				

KM# 610   200 FORINT (Ketszaz)
28.0000 g., 0.6400 Silver 0.5761 oz. ASW   **Obv:** Quartered design with arms and denomination opposite each other **Rev:** Adam Manyoki, painter

Date	Mintage	F	VF	XF	Unc	BU
1977	25,000	—	—	—	10.00	12.00
1977 Proof	5,000	Value: 15.00				

KM# 611   200 FORINT (Ketszaz)
28.0000 g., 0.6400 Silver 0.5761 oz. ASW   **Obv:** Quartered design with arms and denomination opposite each other   **Rev:** Tivadar CS. Kosztka, painter

Date	Mintage	F	VF	XF	Unc	BU
1977	25,000	—	—	—	10.00	12.00
1977 Proof	5,000	Value: 15.00				

KM# 612   200 FORINT (Ketszaz)
28.0000 g., 0.6400 Silver 0.5761 oz. ASW   **Obv:** Quartered design with arms and denomination opposite each other   **Rev:** Jozsef Rippl-Ronai, painter

Date	Mintage	F	VF	XF	Unc	BU
1977	25,000	—	—	—	10.00	12.00
1977 Proof	5,000	Value: 15.00				

KM# 613   200 FORINT (Ketszaz)
28.0000 g., 0.6400 Silver 0.5761 oz. ASW   **Subject:** 175th Anniversary of National Museum **Obv:** Denomination within building, date below **Rev:** Stylized bird with condors flanking

Date	Mintage	F	VF	XF	Unc	BU
1977	25,000	—	—	—	10.00	12.00
1977 Proof	5,000	Value: 16.00				

KM# 614   200 FORINT (Ketszaz)
28.0000 g., 0.6400 Silver 0.5761 oz. ASW   **Subject:** First Hungarian Gold Forint **Obv:** Artistic fleur design **Rev:** Figure and shield within design

Date	Mintage	F	VF	XF	Unc	BU
1978	25,000	—	—	—	10.00	12.00
1978 Proof	5,000	Value: 16.00				

KM# 615   200 FORINT (Ketszaz)
28.0000 g., 0.6400 Silver 0.5761 oz. ASW, 37 mm.
Subject: International Year of the Child **Obv:** Logo
Rev: Depictions of childrens artwork

Date	Mintage	F	VF	XF	Unc	BU
1979	9,000	—	—	—	10.00	12.00
1979 Proof	21,000	Value: 14.00				

KM# 616   200 FORINT (Ketszaz)
22.0000 g., 0.6400 Silver 0.4527 oz. ASW, 37 mm.
Subject: 350th Anniversary - Death of Gabor Bethlen
Obv: Crowned shield at center, legend within circle surrounds
Rev: Half-figure at left looking right

Date	Mintage	F	VF	XF	Unc	BU
1979	15,000	—	—	—	13.50	16.00
1979 Proof	5,000	Value: 18.50				

KM# 618   200 FORINT (Ketszaz)
16.0000 g., 0.6400 Silver 0.3292 oz. ASW, 36 mm. **Series:** XIII Winter Olympics - Lake Placid **Obv:** Two figure skaters and denomination **Rev:** Olympic logo

Date	Mintage	F	VF	XF	Unc	BU
1980 Proof	15,000	Value: 10.00				

KM# 643   200 FORINT (Ketszaz)
16.0000 g., 0.6400 Silver 0.3292 oz. ASW   **Subject:** Wildlife Preservation **Obv:** Dates within side circles, divided by artistic denomination and legend within box **Rev:** Otter within square

Date	Mintage	F	VF	XF	Unc	BU
1985	13,000	—	—	—	12.50	17.00
1985 Proof	2,000	Value: 20.00				

KM# 649   200 FORINT (Ketszaz)
16.0000 g., 0.6400 Silver 0.3292 oz. ASW **Subject:** Wildlife
Preservation **Obv:** Date within side circles divided by artistic
denomination and legend within box **Rev:** Pond turtle within square

Date	Mintage	F	VF	XF	Unc	BU
1985	13,000	—	—	—	12.50	17.00
1985 Proof	2,000	Value: 20.00				

KM# 650   200 FORINT (Ketszaz)
16.0000 g., 0.6400 Silver 0.3292 oz. ASW **Subject:** Wildlife
Preservation **Obv:** Date within side circles, divided by artistic
denomination and legend within box **Rev:** Wildcat within square

Date	Mintage	F	VF	XF	Unc	BU
1985	13,000	—	—	—	12.50	17.00
1985 Proof	2,000	Value: 20.00				

KM# 565   500 FORINT (Otszaz)
38.3800 g., 0.9860 Gold 1.2166 oz. AGW, 40 mm.
Subject: 150th Anniversary - Birth of Ferenc Liszt **Obv:** Harp
below denomination **Rev:** Head right

Date	Mintage	F	VF	XF	Unc	BU
1961BP	2,503	Value: 1,200				

KM# 566   500 FORINT (Otszaz)
38.3800 g., 0.9860 Gold 1.2166 oz. AGW, 40 mm. **Subject:**
80th Anniversary - Birth of Bela Bartok, Composer **Obv:** Small
harp above denomination **Rev:** Head left

Date	Mintage	F	VF	XF	Unc	BU
1961	2,503	Value: 1,200				

KM# 570   500 FORINT (Otszaz)
42.0522 g., 0.9000 Gold 1.2168 oz. AGW, 40 mm.
Subject: 400th Anniversary - Death of Miklos Zrinyi **Obv:**
Monument **Rev:** Head right

Date	Mintage	F	VF	XF	Unc	BU
1966 Proof	1,100	Value: 1,250				

KM# 580   500 FORINT (Otszaz)
42.0522 g., 0.9000 Gold 1.2168 oz. AGW, 40 mm.
Subject: 85th Birthday of Zoltan Kodaly, Composer
Obv: Peacock above denomination **Rev:** Bust 3/4 left

Date	Mintage	F	VF	XF	Unc	BU
1967	1,000	Value: 1,250				

KM# 587   500 FORINT (Otszaz)
42.0522 g., 0.9000 Gold 1.2168 oz. AGW, 46 mm.
Subject: 150th Anniversary - Birth of Ignacz Semmelweis
Obv: Head right **Rev:** Star above shield within wreath

Date	Mintage	F	VF	XF	Unc	BU
1968 Proof	9,000	Value: 1,200				

KM# 619   500 FORINT (Otszaz)
39.0000 g., 0.6400 Silver 0.8024 oz. ASW, 46 mm. **Series:** XIII
Winter Olympics - Lake Placid **Obv:** Two figure skaters
Rev: Olympic logo

Date	Mintage	F	VF	XF	Unc	BU
1980BP Proof	12,500	Value: 55.00				

KM# 623   500 FORINT (Otszaz)
25.0000 g., 0.6400 Silver 0.5144 oz. ASW **Subject:** Centennial
- Birth of Bela Bartok, Composer **Obv:** Musical score, statue and
denomination **Rev:** Head left, map in background

Date	Mintage	F	VF	XF	Unc	BU
1981	12,500	—	—	—	16.50	18.00
1981 Proof	12,500	Value: 20.00				

KM# 624   500 FORINT (Otszaz)
28.0000 g., 0.6400 Silver 0.5761 oz. ASW **Subject:** World
Football Championship **Obv:** Soccer player **Rev:** Soccer field,
soccer ball on shield at lower left

Date	Mintage	F	VF	XF	Unc	BU
1981	6,000	—	—	—	20.00	25.00
1981 Proof	40,000	Value: 16.50				

KM# 625   500 FORINT (Otszaz)
28.0000 g., 0.6400 Silver 0.5761 oz. ASW **Subject:** World
Football Championship **Obv:** Soccer ball on shield within lined
design **Rev:** Soccer players

Date	Mintage	F	VF	XF	Unc	BU
1981	6,000	—	—	—	20.00	25.00
1981 Proof	40,000	Value: 16.50				

KM# 642   500 FORINT (Otszaz)
28.0000 g., 0.6400 Silver 0.5761 oz. ASW **Subject:** Los Angeles
Olympics **Obv:** Denomination, torch at left **Rev:** Gymnast

Date	Mintage	F	VF	XF	Unc	BU
1984	8,000	—	—	—	10.00	11.50
1984 Proof	12,000	Value: 12.50				

KM# 657   500 FORINT (Otszaz)
28.0000 g., 0.6400 Silver 0.5761 oz. ASW **Subject:** World
Football Championship **Obv:** Denomination **Rev:** Stadium

Date	Mintage	F	VF	XF	Unc	BU
1986	8,000	—	—	—	14.00	16.00
1986 Proof	17,000	Value: 12.50				

KM# 640   500 FORINT (Otszaz)
28.0000 g., 0.6400 Silver 0.5761 oz. ASW **Subject:** Decade for
Women **Obv:** Ankh on shaded stylized dove **Rev:** Kneeling woman

Date	Mintage	F	VF	XF	Unc	BU
1984	8,000	—	—	—	18.50	20.00
1984 Proof	20,000	Value: 22.50				

KM# 652   500 FORINT (Otszaz)
28.0000 g., 0.6400 Silver 0.5761 oz. ASW **Subject:** Budapest
Cultural Forum **Obv:** Denomination **Rev:** Bird, right of shield
within ornamental design, legend within column below

Date	Mintage	F	VF	XF	Unc	BU
1985	15,000	—	—	—	10.00	11.50
1985 Proof	10,000	Value: 17.50				

KM# 658   500 FORINT (Otszaz)
28.0000 g., 0.9000 Silver 0.8102 oz. ASW **Subject:** 300th
Anniversary - Repossession of Buda from the Turks **Obv:** Sword
crosses top of denomination **Rev:** Village scene

Date	Mintage	F	VF	XF	Unc	BU
1986	20,000	—	—	—	20.00	22.00
1986 Proof	10,000	Value: 25.00				

KM# 641   500 FORINT (Otszaz)
28.0000 g., 0.6400 Silver 0.5761 oz. ASW **Series:** Winter
Olympics - Sarajevo **Obv:** Olympic flame, snowflakes and
denomination **Rev:** Cross-country skiers

Date	Mintage	F	VF	XF	Unc	BU
1984	8,000	—	—	—	10.00	11.50
1984 Proof	12,000	Value: 12.50				

KM# 656   500 FORINT (Otszaz)
28.0000 g., 0.6400 Silver 0.5761 oz. ASW **Subject:** World
Football Championship **Obv:** Soccer ball and globe make up
zeros of denomination **Rev:** Football players

Date	Mintage	F	VF	XF	Unc	BU
1986	8,000	—	—	—	14.00	16.00
1986 Proof	17,000	Value: 12.50				

KM# 659   500 FORINT (Otszaz)
28.0000 g., 0.9000 Silver 0.8102 oz. ASW **Series:** Winter
Olympics - Calgary 1988 **Obv:** Snowflake designs on flames
Rev: Speed skater

Date	Mintage	F	VF	XF	Unc	BU
1986	15,000	—	—	—	12.50	14.00
1986 Proof	15,000	Value: 15.00				

KM# 660 500 FORINT (Otszaz)
28.0000 g., 0.9000 Silver 0.8102 oz. ASW **Subject:** Seoul
Olympics **Obv:** Denomination **Rev:** Wrestlers

Date	Mintage	F	VF	XF	Unc	BU
1987	15,000			—	14.50	16.50
1987 Proof	15,000	Value: 22.50				

KM# 661 500 FORINT (Otszaz)
28.0000 g., 0.9000 Silver 0.8102 oz. ASW **Subject:** World
Wildlife Fund **Obv:** Denomination **Rev:** Montagu's Harrier

Date	Mintage	F	VF	XF	Unc	BU
1988	10,000			—	22.50	25.00
1988 Proof	25,000	Value: 27.00				

KM# 662 500 FORINT (Otszaz)
28.0000 g., 0.9000 Silver 0.8102 oz. ASW **Subject:** 950th
Anniversary - Death of St. Stephan **Obv:** Ancient coin designs
above denomination **Rev:** Figure of King Stephen at left and
Queen Gisela of Bavaria at right

Date	Mintage	F	VF	XF	Unc	BU
1988	5,000			—	38.00	42.00
1988 Proof	15,000	Value: 25.00				

KM# 666 500 FORINT (Otszaz)
28.0000 g., 0.9000 Silver 0.8102 oz. ASW **Subject:** Europe
Football Championship **Obv:** Stenciled denomination
Rev: Soccer player behind net

Date	Mintage	F	VF	XF	Unc	BU
1988	8,000			—	17.50	18.50
1988 Proof	12,000	Value: 16.50				

KM# 667 500 FORINT (Otszaz)
28.0000 g., 0.9000 Silver 0.8102 oz. ASW **Subject:** World
Football Championship **Obv:** Denomination **Rev:** Soccer players

Date	Mintage	F	VF	XF	Unc	BU
1988	7,000			—	18.50	20.00
1988 Proof	14,500	Value: 17.50				

KM# 669 500 FORINT (Otszaz)
28.0000 g., 0.9000 Silver 0.8102 oz. ASW **Subject:** World
Football Championship **Obv:** Denomination **Rev:** Two players

Date	Mintage	F	VF	XF	Unc	BU
1989	7,000			—	18.50	20.00
1989 Proof	14,500	Value: 17.50				

KM# 670 500 FORINT (Otszaz)
28.0000 g., 0.9000 Silver 0.8102 oz. ASW **Subject:** Save the
Children Fund **Obv:** Denomination below figure and lined design
Rev: Seedling within outline of child

Date	Mintage	F	VF	XF	Unc	BU
1989	10,000			—	22.50	25.00
1989 Proof	20,000	Value: 22.50				

KM# 671 500 FORINT (Otszaz)
28.0000 g., 0.9000 Silver 0.8102 oz. ASW **Series:** 1992
Barcelona Olympics **Obv:** Denomination within lined design
Rev: Torch bearer lighting the flame

Date	Mintage	F	VF	XF	Unc	BU
1989	15,000	—	—	—	22.50	25.00
1989 Proof	15,000	Value: 27.50				

KM# 571 1000 FORINT (Ezer)
84.1040 g., 0.9000 Gold 2.4335 oz. AGW **Subject:** 400th
Anniversary - Death of Miklos Zrinyi **Obv:** Monument **Rev:** Head
3/4 right

Date	Mintage	F	VF	XF	Unc	BU
1966 Proof	330	Value: 2,500				

KM# 581 1000 FORINT (Ezer)
84.1040 g., 0.9000 Gold 2.4335 oz. AGW **Subject:** 85th Birthday of Zoltan Kodaly, Composer **Obv:** Peacock above denomination **Rev:** Bust 3/4 left

Date	Mintage	F	VF	XF	Unc	BU
1967	500	Value: 2,500				

KM# 588 1000 FORINT (Ezer)
84.1040 g., 0.9000 Gold 2.4335 oz. AGW **Subject:** 150th Anniversary - Birth of Ignacz Semmelweis **Rev:** Star above shield within wreath

Date	Mintage	F	VF	XF	Unc	BU
1968 Proof	7,000	Value: 2,350				

TRANSITIONAL COINAGE

KM# 736 FORINT
Aluminum **Obv:** Star above shield within wreath **Rev:** Leaves flank denomination **Note:** Communist design type with New Republic legends

Date	Mintage	F	VF	XF	Unc	BU
1990	10,000	—	—	—	10.00	12.00

KM# 737 2 FORINT
Brass **Obv:** Star above shield within wreath **Rev:** Large denomination divides date **Note:** Communist design type with New Republic legends

Date	Mintage	F	VF	XF	Unc	BU
1990	10,000	—	—	—	15.00	17.00

KM# 738 5 FORINT
Copper-Nickel **Subject:** Lajos Kossuth **Obv. Insc.:** Head right **Rev:** Small shield divides date above denomination **Note:** Communist design with New Republic legends

Date	Mintage	F	VF	XF	Unc	BU
1990	10,000	—	—	—	20.00	25.00

KM# 739 10 FORINT
Aluminum-Bronze **Obv:** Strobl Monument **Rev:** Small shield below denomination

Date	Mintage	F	VF	XF	Unc	BU
1990	10,000	—	—	—	25.00	30.00

KM# 740 20 FORINT
Copper-Nickel **Subject:** György Dózsa **Obv:** Head looking left **Rev:** Grain sprigs flank denomination, small shield above

Date	Mintage	F	VF	XF	Unc	BU
1990	—	—	—	—	30.00	35.00

SECOND REPUBLIC
1989-present
DECIMAL COINAGE

KM# 673 2 FILLER
6.5000 g., Aluminum **Obv:** Wreath surrounds center hole **Rev:** Center hole divides denomination within wreath

Date	Mintage	F	VF	XF	Unc	BU
1990BP	10,000	—	—	—	2.00	—
1991BP	10,000	—	—	—	3.00	—
1992BP	30,000	—	—	—	3.00	—

KM# 674 5 FILLER
6.0000 g., Aluminum **Obv:** Head left **Rev:** Denomination within wreath

Date	Mintage	F	VF	XF	Unc	BU
1990BP	10,000	—	—	—	2.00	—
1991BP	10,000	—	—	—	3.00	—
1992BP	30,000	—	—	—	3.00	—

KM# 675 10 FILLER
6.0000 g., Aluminum **Obv:** Dove with branch **Rev:** Denomination

Date	Mintage	F	VF	XF	Unc	BU
1990BP	46,515,000	0.10	0.15	0.20	0.50	—
1991BP	2,370,000	0.25	0.40	0.55	0.50	—
1992BP	15,828,000	0.15	0.25	0.35	0.50	—
1993BP	30,000	—	—	—	0.50	—
1994BP	30,000	—	—	—	0.50	—
1995BP	30,000	—	—	—	0.50	—
1996BP	20,000	—	—	—	0.50	—
1996 Proof	—	—	—	—	—	—

KM# 676 20 FILLER
1.0000 g., Aluminum, 20.21 mm. **Obv:** Three wheat ears divide date **Rev:** Lines divide denomination **Edge:** Reeded

Date	Mintage	F	VF	XF	Unc	BU
1990BP	59,360,000	0.10	0.15	0.20	0.35	—
1991BP	20,210,000	0.20	0.35	0.50	0.75	—
1992BP	30,000	—	—	—	1.00	—
1993BP	30,000	—	—	—	1.00	—
1994BP	30,000	—	—	—	1.00	—
1995BP	30,000	—	—	—	1.00	—
1996BP	20,000	—	—	—	1.25	—
1996 Proof	—	—	—	—	—	—

KM# 677 50 FILLER
1.2700 g., Aluminum, 19.78 mm. **Obv:** Erzsebet Bridge **Rev:** Denomination **Edge:** Plain

Date	Mintage	F	VF	XF	Unc	BU
1990BP	20,550,000	—	0.10	0.20	0.30	—
1991BP	31,250,000	—	—	0.10	0.25	—
1992BP	440,000	—	—	—	0.85	—
1993BP	30,000	—	—	—	1.20	—
1994BP	30,000	—	—	—	1.20	—
1995BP	30,000	—	—	—	1.20	—
1996BP	20,000	—	—	—	1.60	—
1996 Proof	—	—	—	—	—	—
1997BP	10,000	—	—	—	2.50	—
1998BP	10,000	—	—	—	2.50	—
1999BP	10,000	—	—	—	2.50	—

KM# 692 FORINT
2.0500 g., Brass, 16.5 mm. **Obv:** Crowned shield **Rev:** Denomination

Date	Mintage	F	VF	XF	Unc	BU
1992BP	23,890,100	—	0.10	0.25	0.35	—
1992BP Proof	1,000	Value: 6.00				
1993BP	75,100,000	—	—	0.10	0.25	—
1993BP Proof	30,000	Value: 1.00				
1994BP	66,605,005	—	—	0.10	0.25	—
1994BP Proof	15,000	Value: 1.20				
1995BP	50,535,000	—	—	0.10	0.25	—
1995BP Proof	15,000	Value: 1.20				
1996BP	67,000,010	—	—	0.10	0.25	—
1996BP Proof	10,000	Value: 1.40				
1997BP	—	—	—	—	—	—
1997BP Proof	3,000	Value: 3.75				
1998BP	—	—	—	0.10	0.25	—
1998BP Proof	3,000	Value: 3.75				
1999BP	—	—	—	0.10	0.25	—
1999BP Proof	3,000	Value: 3.75				
2000BP	—	—	—	0.10	0.25	—
2000BP Proof	3,000	Value: 3.75				

KM# 693 2 FORINT
3.1000 g., Copper-Nickel, 19 mm. **Obv:** Native flower: Colchicum Hungaricum **Rev:** Denomination

Date	Mintage	F	VF	XF	Unc	BU
1992BP	10,380,100	0.10	0.25	0.35	0.50	—
1992BP Proof	1,000	Value: 6.00				
1993BP	82,915,000	—	0.10	0.25	0.35	—
1993BP Proof	30,000	Value: 1.50				
1994BP	68,370,005	—	0.10	0.25	0.35	—
1994BP Proof	15,000	Value: 1.75				
1995BP	60,945,000	—	0.10	0.25	0.35	—
1995BP Proof	15,000	Value: 1.75				
1996BP	50,010,000	—	0.10	0.25	0.35	—
1996BP Proof	10,000	Value: 1.95				
1997BP	70,007,000	—	0.10	0.20	0.35	—
1997BP Proof	3,000	Value: 4.25				
1998BP	20,007,000	—	—	—	0.35	—
1998BP Proof	3,000	Value: 4.25				
1999BP	50,007,000	—	—	—	0.35	—
1999BP Proof	3,000	Value: 4.25				
2000BP	55,007,000	—	—	—	0.20	0.35
2000BP Proof	3,000	Value: 4.25				

KM# 694 5 FORINT
4.2000 g., Brass, 21.5 mm. **Obv:** Great White Egret **Rev:** Denomination

Date	Mintage	F	VF	XF	Unc	BU
1992BP	1,145,300	0.15	0.30	0.60	1.00	1.50
1992BP Proof	1,000	Value: 7.00				
1993BP	37,180,000	0.10	0.25	0.45	1.00	1.50
1993BP Proof	30,000	Value: 2.00				
1994BP	53,615,000	0.10	0.20	0.30	1.00	1.50
1994BP Proof	15,000	Value: 2.50				
1995BP	24,670,000	0.15	0.30	0.40	1.00	1.50
1995BP Proof	15,000	Value: 2.50				
1996BP	6,010,000	0.25	0.50	0.65	1.00	1.50
1996BP Proof	10,000	Value: 3.00				
1997BP	20,007,000	0.15	0.30	0.40	1.00	1.50
1997BP Proof	3,000	Value: 5.00				
1998BP	7,000	0.15	0.30	0.40	1.00	1.50
1998BP Proof	3,000	Value: 5.00				
1999BP	25,007,000	0.15	0.30	0.40	1.00	1.50
1999BP Proof	3,000	Value: 5.00				
2000BP	30,007,000	0.10	0.25	0.35	1.00	1.50
2000BP Proof	3,000	Value: 5.00				

KM# 695 10 FORINT
6.1000 g., Copper-Nickel Clad Brass, 25 mm. **Obv:** Crowned shield **Rev:** Denomination

Date	Mintage	F	VF	XF	Unc	BU
1992BP	2,000	—	—	—	6.00	—
1992BP Proof	1,000	Value: 8.00				
1993BP	35,565,000	0.10	0.25	0.45	1.00	2.00
1993BP Proof	30,000	Value: 2.50				
1994BP	69,078,000	—	0.15	0.35	0.85	2.00
1994BP Proof	15,000	Value: 3.00				
1995BP	40,910,000	0.10	0.25	0.45	1.00	2.00
1995BP Proof	15,000	Value: 3.00				
1996BP	13,010,000	0.15	0.30	0.50	1.00	2.00
1996BP Proof	10,000	Value: 3.50				
1997BP	8,007,000	0.20	0.35	0.55	1.00	2.00
1997BP Proof	3,000	Value: 5.50				
1998BP	7,000	—	—	—	1.00	2.50
1998BP Proof	3,000	Value: 5.50				
1999BP	7,000	—	—	—	1.00	2.50
1999BP Proof	3,000	Value: 5.50				
2000BP	7,000	—	—	—	1.00	2.50
2000BP Proof	3,000	Value: 5.50				

KM# 696 20 FORINT
6.9000 g., Nickel-Brass, 26.3 mm. **Obv:** Hungarian Iris
Rev: Denomination

Date	Mintage	F	VF	XF	Unc	BU
1992BP	2,000	—	—	—	7.00	—
1992BP Proof	1,000	Value: 9.00				
1993BP	42,965,000	0.20	0.30	0.60	1.50	2.00
1993BP Proof	30,000	Value: 3.50				
1994BP	68,965,005	0.15	0.25	0.50	1.25	1.75
1994BP Proof	15,000	Value: 4.00				
1995BP	53,395,000	0.15	0.25	0.50	1.25	1.75
1995BP Proof	15,000	Value: 4.00				
1996BP	6,010,000	0.20	0.35	0.70	1.50	—
1996BP Proof	10,000	Value: 4.00				
1997BP	7,000	—	—	—	5.00	6.00
1997BP Proof	3,000	Value: 6.00				
1998BP	7,000	—	—	—	3.50	4.00
1998BP Proof	3,000	Value: 6.00				
1999BP	7,000	—	—	—	3.50	4.00
1999BP Proof	3,000	Value: 6.00				
2000BP	7,000	—	—	—	3.50	4.00
2000BP Proof	3,000	Value: 6.00				

KM# 697 50 FORINT
7.7000 g., Copper-Nickel Clad Brass, 27.5 mm. **Obv:** Saker
falcon **Rev:** Denomination

Date	Mintage	F	VF	XF	Unc	BU
1992BP	2,000	—	—	—	10.00	—
1992BP Proof	1,000	Value: 12.00				
1993BP	860,500	0.50	0.65	1.25	3.00	3.50
1993BP Proof	30,000	Value: 5.00				
1994BP	8,397,005	0.25	0.45	0.85	3.00	3.50
1994BP Proof	15,000	Value: 5.00				
1995BP	36,985,000	—	0.25	0.50	2.50	3.00
1995BP Proof	15,000	Value: 5.00				
1996BP	7,010,000	0.30	0.50	1.00	3.00	3.50
1996BP Proof	10,000	Value: 5.00				
1997BP	12,007,000	—	—	—	3.00	3.50
1997BP Proof	3,000	Value: 6.50				
1998BP	7,000	—	—	—	5.50	6.50
1998BP Proof	3,000	Value: 6.50				
1999BP	7,000	—	—	—	5.50	6.50
1999BP Proof	3,000	Value: 6.50				
2000BP	7,000	—	—	—	5.50	6.50
2000BP Proof	3,000	Value: 6.50				

KM# 734 75 FORINT
31.4600 g., 0.9250 Silver 0.9356 oz. ASW, 38.6 mm. **Subject:**
75th Anniversary - Hungarian National Bank **Obv:** Crowned
shield above denomination **Rev:** Goddess Juno **Edge:** Reeded

Date	Mintage	F	VF	XF	Unc	BU
1999BP	3,000	—	—	—	32.50	35.00
1999BP Proof	4,500	Value: 40.00				

KM# 700 100 FORINT (Szaz)
12.0000 g., Copper-Nickel **Subject:** S.O.S. Gyermekfalu,
Children's Village **Obv:** Children and flower within box divide date
above denomination **Rev:** Mother protecting child

Date	Mintage	F	VF	XF	Unc	BU
1990BP Proof	50,000	Value: 12.00				

KM# 701 100 FORINT (Szaz)
12.0000 g., Copper-Nickel **Subject:** Hungarian Theatre
Obv: Denomination divides date within wreath **Rev:** Theatre
scene

Date	Mintage	F	VF	XF	Unc	BU
1990BP	5,000	—	—	—	10.00	—
1990BP Proof	5,000	Value: 12.00				

KM# 678 100 FORINT (Szaz)
12.0000 g., Copper-Nickel-Zinc, 32 mm. **Subject:** Adreas Fay
- 150th Anniversary of Savings Bank **Obv:** Fly below legend,
denomination and date above **Rev:** Bust 3/4 left **Edge:** Reeded
Note: See also #655 for similar type

Date	Mintage	F	VF	XF	Unc	BU
1990BP	20,000	—	—	—	—	5.00
1990BP Proof	10,000	Value: 7.00				

KM# 682 100 FORINT (Szaz)
12.0000 g., Copper-Nickel-Zinc **Subject:** Papal Visit **Obv:** Arms
of the Republic **Rev:** Pope John Paul II

Date	Mintage	F	VF	XF	Unc	BU
1991BP	30,000	—	—	—	3.00	—
1991BP Proof	30,000	Value: 6.00				

KM# 698 100 FORINT (Szaz)
9.4000 g., Brass **Obv:** Crowned shield **Rev:** Denomination

Date	Mintage	F	VF	XF	Unc	BU
1992BP	2,000	—	—	—	12.00	—
1992BP Proof	1,000	Value: 15.00				
1993BP	924,500	—	—	—	3.00	—
1993BP Proof	30,000	Value: 6.00				
1994BP	7,861,005	—	—	—	2.50	—
1994BP Proof	15,000	Value: 6.00				
1995BP	27,485,000	—	—	—	2.50	—
1995BP Proof	15,000	Value: 6.00				
1996BP	6,210,000	—	—	—	2.50	—
1996BP Proof	10,000	Value: 6.00				
1997BP	7,000	—	—	—	6.00	—
1997BP Proof	3,000	Value: 8.00				
1998BP	7,000	—	—	—	6.00	—
1998BP Proof	3,000	Value: 8.00				

KM# 721 100 FORINT (Szaz)
Bi-Metallic Brass plated Steel center in Stainless Steel ring,
23.6 mm. **Obv:** Crowned shield **Rev:** Denomination

Date	Mintage	F	VF	XF	Unc	BU
1996BP	35,001,000	—	—	—	3.00	4.50
1996BP Proof	1,000	Value: 12.00				
1997BP	60,007,000	—	—	—	3.00	4.50
1997BP Proof	3,000	Value: 8.00				
1998BP	60,007,000	—	—	—	3.00	4.50
1998BP Proof	3,000	Value: 8.00				
1999BP	7,000	—	—	—	3.00	4.50
1999BP Proof	3,000	Value: 8.00				
2000BP	7,000	—	—	—	4.00	6.50
2000BP Proof	3,000	Value: 8.00				

KM# 726 100 FORINT (Szaz)
9.4000 g., Bronze **Subject:** Revolution of 1848 **Obv:** Hungarian
Order of Military Merit (1848-1849) II Class **Rev:** Revolutionary
ribbon badge above poetry verse

Date	Mintage	F	VF	XF	Unc	BU
1998BP	15,000	—	—	—	7.00	—
1998BP Proof	15,000	Value: 9.00				

KM# 688 200 FORINT
10.0000 g., 0.5000 Silver 0.1607 oz. ASW **Obv:** Crowned shield
below globe **Rev:** White storks

Date	Mintage	F	VF	XF	Unc	BU
1992BP	20,000	—	—	—	10.00	15.00
1992BP Proof	80,000	Value: 20.00				

KM# 689 200 FORINT
12.0000 g., 0.5000 Silver 0.1929 oz. ASW **Obv:** Erzsebet
Bridge, crowned shield divides date above **Rev:** National Bank

Date	Mintage	F	VF	XF	Unc	BU
1992BP	3,514,023	—	—	—	6.00	7.00
1992BP Proof	29,998	Value: 9.00				
1993BP	2,540,993	—	—	—	6.00	7.00
1993BP Proof	30,000	Value: 9.00				

KM# 707 200 FORINT

12.0000 g., 0.5000 Silver 0.1929 oz. ASW **Obv:** Erzsebet Bridge
Rev: Ferenc Deak

Date	Mintage	F	VF	XF	Unc	BU
1994BP	5,000,000	—	—	—	6.50	—
1994BP Proof	15,000	Value: 10.00				
1995BP	85,000	—	—	—	7.50	—
1995BP Proof	15,000	Value: 10.00				
1997BP	7,000	—	—	—	10.00	—
1997BP Proof	3,000	Value: 12.00				
1998BP	7,000	—	—	—	10.00	—
1998BP Proof	3,000	Value: 12.00				

KM# 745 200 FORINT

9.5600 g., Brass **Subject:** Millennium **Obv:** Crowned shield above denomination **Rev:** Rodin's "The Thinker" statue and solar system **Edge:** Plain

Date	Mintage	F	VF	XF	Unc	BU
2000BP	15,000	—	—	—	5.50	—
2000BP Proof	10,000	Value: 7.00				

KM# 672 500 FORINT (Otszaz)

28.0000 g., 0.9000 Silver 0.8102 oz. ASW **Series:** Albertville Olympics 1992 **Obv:** Denomination, date below **Rev:** Hockey players

Date	Mintage	F	VF	XF	Unc	BU
1989BP	15,000	—	—	—	27.50	30.00
1989BP Proof	15,000	Value: 32.50				

KM# 679 500 FORINT (Otszaz)

28.0000 g., 0.9000 Silver 0.8102 oz. ASW **Obv:** King Mathias on horse left **Rev:** Busts of King Mathias and Queen Beatrix facing each other

Date	Mintage	F	VF	XF	Unc	BU
1990BP	15,000	—	—	—	32.50	35.00
1990BP Proof	15,000	Value: 37.50				

KM# 680 500 FORINT (Otszaz)

28.0000 g., 0.9000 Silver 0.8102 oz. ASW **Obv:** Denomination, legend and date within decorative outline **Rev:** Two capital cities of King Mathias

Date	Mintage	F	VF	XF	Unc	BU
1990BP	15,000	—	—	—	32.50	35.00
1990BP Proof	15,000	Value: 37.50				

KM# 699 500 FORINT (Otszaz)

28.0000 g., 0.9000 Silver 0.8102 oz. ASW **Subject:** 200th Anniversary - Birth of Ferenc Kolcsey **Obv:** Crowned arms and denomination **Rev:** Ferenc Kölcsey

Date	Mintage	F	VF	XF	Unc	BU
1990BP	10,000	—	—	—	40.00	42.50
1990BP Proof	5,000	Value: 50.00				

KM# 683 500 FORINT (Otszaz)

28.0000 g., 0.9000 Silver 0.8102 oz. ASW **Subject:** Papal Visit **Obv:** Arms of the Republic **Rev:** Pope John Paul II

Date	Mintage	F	VF	XF	Unc	BU
1991BP	10,000	—	—	—	22.50	25.00
1991BP Proof	20,000	Value: 28.50				

KM# 685 500 FORINT (Otszaz)

28.0000 g., 0.9000 Silver 0.8102 oz. ASW **Subject:** 200th Anniversary - Birth of Count Szechenyi **Obv:** Locomotive and value **Rev:** Istvan Szechenyi

Date	Mintage	F	VF	XF	Unc	BU
1991BP	15,000	—	—	—	25.00	27.50
1991BP Proof	15,000	Value: 32.50				

KM# 686 500 FORINT (Otszaz)

28.0000 g., 0.9000 Silver 0.8102 oz. ASW **Obv:** Denomination **Rev:** Anjou Liliom **Rev. Leg.:** Karoly Robert Emlekere

Date	Mintage	F	VF	XF	Unc	BU
1992BP	10,000	—	—	—	22.50	25.00
1992BP Proof	20,000	Value: 30.00				

KM# 687 500 FORINT (Otszaz)

28.0000 g., 0.9000 Silver 0.8102 oz. ASW **Subject:** Canonization of King Ladislaus **Obv:** Ladislaus Denar (obv. and rev.) and denomination **Rev:** King Ladislaus

Date	Mintage	F	VF	XF	Unc	BU
1992BP	10,000	—	—	—	25.00	27.50
1992BP Proof	20,000	Value: 32.50				

KM# 690 500 FORINT (Otszaz)
31.4600 g., 0.9250 Silver 0.9356 oz. ASW **Obv:** Crowned shield and denomination **Rev:** Telstar I satellite above globe

Date	Mintage	F	VF	XF	Unc	BU
1992BP	Est. 5,000	—	—	—	22.50	25.00
1992BP Proof	Est. 15,000	Value: 27.50				

KM# 702 500 FORINT (Otszaz)
31.4600 g., 0.9250 Silver 0.9356 oz. ASW **Obv:** Denomination above crowned arms **Rev:** Old Danube Ship "Arpad"

Date	Mintage	F	VF	XF	Unc	BU
1993BP	10,000	—	—	—	17.50	18.50
1993BP Proof	15,000	Value: 20.00				

KM# 704 500 FORINT (Otszaz)
31.4600 g., 0.9250 Silver 0.9356 oz. ASW **Obv:** Crowned arms divide date above denomination **Rev:** European Currency Union

Date	Mintage	F	VF	XF	Unc	BU
1993BP	10,000	—	—	—	18.50	20.00
1993BP Proof	30,000	Value: 22.00				

KM# 705 500 FORINT (Otszaz)
31.4600 g., 0.9250 Silver 0.9356 oz. ASW **Subject:** Expo '96 **Obv:** Logo above denomination **Rev:** Ship sailing on sea of letters

Date	Mintage	F	VF	XF	Unc	BU
1993BP	20,000	—	—	—	17.50	20.00
1993BP Proof	80,000	Value: 20.00				

KM# 708 500 FORINT (Otszaz)
31.4600 g., 0.9250 Silver 0.9356 oz. ASW **Obv:** Denomination above crowned arms **Rev:** Old Danube Ship "Carolina"

Date	Mintage	F	VF	XF	Unc	BU
1994BP	10,000	—	—	—	18.00	20.00
1994BP Proof	15,000	Value: 22.00				

KM# 709 500 FORINT (Otszaz)
31.4600 g., 0.9250 Silver 0.9356 oz. ASW **Subject:** Death of Lajos Kossuth **Obv:** Denomination within shield outline **Rev:** Bust 3/4 right

Date	Mintage	F	VF	XF	Unc	BU
1994BP	10,000	—	—	—	23.50	25.00
1994BP Proof	10,000	Value: 28.50				

KM# 710 500 FORINT (Otszaz)
31.4600 g., 0.9250 Silver 0.9356 oz. ASW **Subject:** International European Union **Obv:** Crowned arms divide date above denomination **Rev:** St. Istvan and Halaszbastya

Date	Mintage	F	VF	XF	Unc	BU
1994BP	10,000	—	—	—	22.50	25.00
1994BP Proof	30,000	Value: 27.50				

KM# 723 750 FORINT
10.0000 g., 0.5000 Silver 0.1607 oz. ASW **Subject:** Soccer **Obv:** Denomination in goal **Rev:** Ball in net above the Eiffel Tower

Date	Mintage	F	VF	XF	Unc	BU
1997BP	3,000	—	—	—	25.00	30.00
1997BP Proof	17,000	Value: 20.00				

KM# 725 750 FORINT
10.0000 g., 0.5000 Silver 0.1607 oz. ASW **Subject:** 125th Anniversary - Budapest **Obv:** Lanc Bridge **Rev:** City map and arms

Date	Mintage	F	VF	XF	Unc	BU
1998BP	3,000	—	—	—	30.00	35.00
1998BP Proof	12,000	Value: 20.00				

KM# 706 1000 FORINT
31.4600 g., 0.9250 Silver 0.9356 oz. ASW **Subject:** World Cup Soccer **Obv:** Small crowned arms above denomination **Rev:** Goalie

Date	Mintage	F	VF	XF	Unc	BU
1993BP	10,000	—	—	—	23.50	25.00
1993BP Proof	15,000	Value: 27.50				

KM# 712 1000 FORINT
31.4600 g., 0.9250 Silver 0.9356 oz. ASW **Series:** Atlanta Olympics **Obv:** Olympic flame in bowl above denomination **Rev:** Swimmers

Date	Mintage	F	VF	XF	Unc	BU
1994BP	10,000	—	—	—	20.00	22.50
1994BP Proof	40,000	Value: 24.00				

KM# 713   1000 FORINT
31.4600 g., 0.9250 Silver 0.9356 oz. ASW **Subject:** Protect Our World **Obv:** Stylized bird right below denomination **Rev:** Globe in trunk

Date	Mintage	F	VF	XF	Unc	BU
1994BP	10,000	—	—	—	25.00	27.50
1994BP Proof	10,000	Value: 30.00				

KM# 720   1000 FORINT
31.4600 g., 0.9250 Silver 0.9356 oz. ASW **Subject:** European Union **Obv:** Crowned arms divide date **Rev:** Hungarian Parliament building, "ecu"

Date	Mintage	F	VF	XF	Unc	BU
1995BP	5,000	—	—	—	32.50	37.50
1995BP Proof	18,000	Value: 30.00				

KM# 722   2000 FORINT
31.4600 g., 0.9250 Silver 0.9356 oz. ASW **Obv:** Lake Balaton view above denomination **Rev:** Steam ships "Helka" and "Kelen"

Date	Mintage	F	VF	XF	Unc	BU
1997BP	5,000	—	—	—	38.00	42.00
1997BP Proof	15,000	Value: 35.00				

KM# 714   1000 FORINT
31.4600 g., 0.9250 Silver 0.9356 oz. ASW **Obv:** Crowned shield below denomination **Rev:** Old Danube Ship "Hableany"

Date	Mintage	F	VF	XF	Unc	BU
1995BP	10,000	—	—	—	25.00	27.50
1995BP Proof	20,000	Value: 28.00				

KM# 715   1000 FORINT
31.4600 g., 0.9250 Silver 0.9356 oz. ASW **Obv:** Abbot's seal impression and value **Rev:** Pannonhalma ruins

Date	Mintage	F	VF	XF	Unc	BU
1995BP	10,000	—	—	—	28.00	30.00
1995BP Proof	10,000	Value: 32.50				

KM# 717   2000 FORINT
31.4600 g., 0.9250 Silver 0.9356 oz. ASW **Subject:** 50th Anniversary Forint Rebirth **Obv:** Anjou Lilium below fold of material, crowned arms above **Rev:** 13 coin designs

Date	Mintage	F	VF	XF	Unc	BU
1996BP	5,000	—	—	—	35.00	40.00
1996BP Proof	5,000	Value: 45.00				

KM# 724   2000 FORINT
31.1035 g., 0.9250 Silver 0.9250 oz. ASW **Subject:** European Union **Obv:** Crowned shield divides date above denomination **Rev:** Royal Palace of Budapest

Date	Mintage	F	VF	XF	Unc	BU
1997BP	3,000	—	—	—	38.00	42.00
1997BP Proof	27,000	Value: 35.00				

KM# 716   1000 FORINT
31.4600 g., 0.9250 Silver 0.9356 oz. ASW **Series:** Atlanta Olympics **Obv:** Denomination **Rev:** Fencing match

Date	Mintage	F	VF	XF	Unc	BU
1995BP	5,000	—	—	—	30.00	35.00
1995BP Proof	25,000	Value: 27.50				

KM# 718   2000 FORINT
31.4600 g., 0.9250 Silver 0.9356 oz. ASW **Subject:** 1100th Anniversary of Hungarian Nationhood **Obv:** Date and denomination below shield of designs **Rev:** Three equestrian archers above old shield

Date	Mintage	F	VF	XF	Unc	BU
1996BP	10,000	—	—	—	35.00	40.00
1996BP Proof	10,000	Value: 45.00				

KM# 727   2000 FORINT
31.4600 g., 0.9250 Silver 0.9356 oz. ASW **Subject:** Revolution of 1848 **Obv:** Hungarian Order of Military Merit (1848-1849) I Class **Rev:** Hungarian military flag over European map

Date	Mintage	F	VF	XF	Unc	BU
1998BP	5,000	—	—	—	38.00	42.00
1998BP Proof	10,000	Value: 35.00				

KM# 729   2000 FORINT
31.4600 g., 0.9250 Silver 0.9356 oz. ASW   **Subject:** UNICEF - For the Children of the World **Obv:** UNICEF logo above denomination **Rev:** Child's drawing of a princess

Date	Mintage	F	VF	XF	Unc	BU
1998BP Proof	28,000	Value: 47.50				

KM# 730   2000 FORINT
31.4600 g., 0.9250 Silver 0.9356 oz. ASW   **Subject:** World Wildlife Fund **Obv:** World Wildlife Fund logo above arms **Rev:** Fork-tailed barn swallows

Date	Mintage	F	VF	XF	Unc	BU
1998BP Proof	18,000	Value: 45.00				

KM# 731   2000 FORINT
31.4600 g., 0.9250 Silver 0.9356 oz. ASW   **Obv:** Sailboats on Lake Balaton **Rev:** The "Phoenix" under full sail

Date	Mintage	F	VF	XF	Unc	BU
1998BP	5,000	—	—	—	37.50	40.00
1998BP Proof	10,000	Value: 32.50				

KM# 732   2000 FORINT
31.4600 g., 0.9250 Silver 0.9356 oz. ASW, 38.6 mm.   **Subject:** 150th Birthday - Lorand Eotvos **Obv:** Denomination **Rev:** Framed portrait at right, scientific instrument on fancy table edge at left **Edge:** Reeded

Date	Mintage	F	VF	XF	Unc	BU
1998BP	3,000	—	—	—	40.00	42.50
1998BP Proof	3,000	Value: 45.00				

KM# 733   2000 FORINT
31.4600 g., 0.9250 Silver 0.9356 oz. ASW, 38.6 mm.   **Subject:** European Union **Obv:** National arms **Rev:** Monuments, Euro logo **Edge:** Reeded

Date	Mintage	F	VF	XF	Unc	BU
1998BP	3,000	—	—	—	40.00	45.00
1998BP Proof	12,000	Value: 50.00				

KM# 743   2000 FORINT
20.0000 g., 0.9250 Silver 0.5948 oz. ASW, 33.17 mm.   **Subject:** Millennium **Obv:** Crowned shield divides date, denomination below **Rev:** Rodin's "The Thinker" and solar system **Edge:** Plain

Date	Mintage	F	VF	XF	Unc	BU
1999BP	5,000	—	—	—	35.00	40.00
1999BP Proof	15,000	Value: 37.50				

KM# 744   2000 FORINT
19.9800 g., 0.9250 Silver 0.5942 oz. ASW, 33.91 mm.   **Subject:** Olympics **Obv:** Crowned shield above denomination **Rev:** Hammer throw **Edge:** Reeded

Date	Mintage	F	VF	XF	Unc	BU
1999BP	4,000	—	—	—	27.50	30.00
1999BP Proof	14,000	Value: 32.50				

KM# 748   2000 FORINT
15.7240 g., 0.9250 Silver 0.4676 oz. ASW   **Obv:** Country name, denomination and date **Rev:** Seal and dates **Rev. Insc.:** Lorántffy/ Zsuzsanna/ 1600-1660

Date	Mintage	F	VF	XF	Unc	BU
2000BP	3,000	—	—	—	20.00	22.50
2000BP Proof	3,000	Value: 25.00				

KM# 747   2000 FORINT
15.7240 g., 0.9250 Silver 0.4676 oz. ASW   **Obv:** Denomination and date **Rev:** Angel in wreath **Rev. Insc.:** Koll./ Sàrospatak/ • 1531 • **Edge:** Reeded and plain section **Note:** 19.3 x 38.4

Date	Mintage	F	VF	XF	Unc	BU
2000BP	3,000	—	—	—	20.00	22.50
2000BP Proof	3,000	Value: 25.00				

KM# 735   3000 FORINT
31.4600 g., 0.9250 Silver 0.9356 oz. ASW, 38.6 mm.   **Subject:** European Union **Obv:** Crowned arms above denomination **Rev:** Statue and Euro logo **Edge:** Reeded

Date	Mintage	F	VF	XF	Unc	BU
1999BP	3,000	—	—	—	35.00	40.00
1999BP Proof	17,000	Value: 42.50				

KM# 741   3000 FORINT
31.4600 g., 0.9250 Silver 0.9356 oz. ASW   **Subject:** Hungarian Millennium **Obv:** Crown above denomination within circle, date below **Rev:** Round window design **Edge:** Plain **Note:** Gold-plated center.

Date	Mintage	F	VF	XF	Unc	BU
1999BP	5,000	—	—	—	40.00	42.50
1999BP Proof	5,000	Value: 50.00				

KM# 746   3000 FORINT
31.4600 g., 0.9250 Silver 0.9356 oz. ASW, 38.55 mm.
Obv: Denomination **Rev:** Beaver **Edge:** Reeded

Date	Mintage	F	VF	XF	Unc	BU
2000BP	3,000	—	—	—	42.50	45.00
2000BP Proof	7,000	Value: 60.00				

KM# 749   3000 FORINT
31.4600 g., 0.9250 Silver 0.9356 oz. ASW   **Subject:** Hologram inventor - Denes Gabor **Obv:** Hologram initials in center **Rev:** Bust right **Edge:** Reeded

Date	Mintage	F	VF	XF	Unc	BU
2000BP	3,000	—	—	—	47.50	50.00
2000BP Proof	3,000	Value: 57.50				

KM# 750   3000 FORINT
31.4600 g., 0.9250 Silver 0.9356 oz. ASW, 38.57 mm.   **Subject:** 125th Anniversary - Franz Liszt Music Academy **Obv:** Half-length Franz Liszt right **Rev:** Academy entrance **Edge:** Reeded

Date	Mintage	F	VF	XF	Unc	BU
2000BP	3,000	—	—	—	47.50	50.00
2000BP Proof	3,000	Value: 57.50				

KM# 681   5000 FORINT
6.9820 g., 0.9860 Gold 0.2213 oz. AGW   **Subject:** 500th Anniversary - Death of Mathias I **Obv:** Hunyadi coat of arms **Rev:** Seated King Mathias with scepter and orb

Date	Mintage	F	VF	XF	Unc	BU
1990BP Proof	10,000	Value: 220				

KM# 711   5000 FORINT
7.7700 g., 0.5840 Gold 0.1459 oz. AGW   **Obv:** Denomination and date **Rev:** Great Bustard Bird

Date	Mintage	F	VF	XF	Unc	BU
1994BP Proof	5,000	Value: 155				

KM# 684   10000 FORINT (Tizezer)
6.9820 g., 0.9860 Gold 0.2213 oz. AGW   **Subject:** Papal Visit **Obv:** Crowned shield within beaded circle **Rev:** Madonna and child

Date	Mintage	F	VF	XF	Unc	BU
1991BP Proof	10,000	Value: 225				

KM# 691   10000 FORINT (Tizezer)
6.9820 g., 0.9860 Gold 0.2213 oz. AGW   **Subject:** 650th Anniversary - Death of King Karoly Robert **Obv:** Denomination **Rev:** Crowned head 3/4 right

Date	Mintage	F	VF	XF	Unc	BU
1992BP Proof	10,000	Value: 220				

KM# 703   10000 FORINT (Tizezer)
6.9820 g., 0.9860 Gold 0.2213 oz. AGW   **Subject:** Centennial - Death of Ferenc Erkel **Obv:** Denomination and date **Rev:** Bust 3/4 left

Date	Mintage	F	VF	XF	Unc	BU
1993BP Proof	5,000	Value: 225				

KM# 719   20000 FORINT
6.9820 g., 0.9860 Gold 0.2213 oz. AGW   **Subject:** 1100th Anniversary of Hungarian Nationhood **Obv:** Denomination and date above designs at bottom **Rev:** Two equestrian archers right

Date	Mintage	F	VF	XF	Unc	BU
1996BP Proof	5,000	Value: 225				

KM# 728   20000 FORINT
6.9820 g., 0.9860 Gold 0.2213 oz. AGW   **Subject:** Revolution of 1848 **Obv:** Hungarian Order of Military Merit III Class **Rev:** Portrait of Lajos Batthyany

Date	Mintage	F	VF	XF	Unc	BU
1998BP Proof	5,000	Value: 225				

KM# 742   20000 FORINT
6.9820 g., 0.9860 Gold 0.2213 oz. AGW   **Subject:** Hungarian State Millennium **Obv:** Portrait of St. Michael the Archangel **Rev:** Crown of St. Stephen **Edge:** Plain

Date	Mintage	F	VF	XF	Unc	BU
1999BP Proof	3,000	Value: 250				

PATTERNS
Including off metal strikes

KM#	Date	Mintage	Identification	Mkt Val
Pn126	1910	—	2 Korona. Lead. KM#493.	—
Pn127	1913	—	2 Korona. Aluminum. KM#493.	—
Pn128	1914	—	Filler. Steel. KM#480.	—
Pn130	1914	—	2 Korona. Aluminum. KM#493.	—
Pn129	1914	—	10 Filler. Silver. KM#482.	800
Pn131	1915	—	2 Filler. New Silver. KM#481	130
Pn132	1915	—	10 Filler. Nickel. KM#494.	—
Pn133	1915	—	10 Filler. Nickel. KM#496.	—
Pn134	1915	—	20 Filler. Iron. KM#498.	250
Pn135	1915	—	20 Filler. Iron. Circle around crown.	—
Pn136	1915	—	20 Filler. Silver. KM#483.	1,000
Pn137	1915	—	1/2 Korona. Silver. Franz Joseph I bust right. Value in wreath.	1,000
Pn138	1916	—	2 Heller. Lead. One side.	—
Pn139	1916	—	2 Filler. Iron. KM#481	350
Pn140	1916	—	2 Filler. Iron. 2 in square.	—
Pn141	1916	—	2 Filler. Iron. Circle around crown.	—
Pn142	ND(1916)	—	2 Filler. Lead. Ornaments around 2, without legend.	—
Pn143	1916KB	—	10 Filler. Iron. KM#496	—
Pn144	1916	—	20 Filler. Lead. KM#498.	—
Pn145	1917	—	20 Filler. Zinc.	—
Pn146	1917	—	2 Filler. Steel. With rosette.	—
Pn147	1917	—	10 Filler. Iron. Crown above sceptor and sword. Value between wheat.	—
Pn148	1917	—	10 Filler. Zinc.	—
Pn149	1917	—	10 Filler. New Silver.	—
Pn150	1918	—	2 Filler. Aluminum. KM#497.	—
Pn151	1918	—	50 Filler. Iron. Large crown.	—
Pn152	1918	—	50 Filler. Lead.	—
Pn153	NDBP	—	10 Korona. Silver.	—
Pn154	NDBP	3	10 Korona. Bronze.	—
Pn155	1922	—	20 Filler. Bronze.	—
Pn156	1922	—	20 Filler. New Silver.	—
Pn157	1922	—	20 Filler. Nickel.	—
Pn158	1922	—	5 Korona. Aluminum.	—
Pn159	1922	—	5 Korona. Brass.	—
Pn160	1926	—	10 Filler. Lead. KM#507.	—
Pn161	1927	—	10 Pengo. Brass. Fr#100	—
Pn162	1927	—	10 Pengo. Gold.	—
Pn163	1927	—	20 Pengo. Brass. Denomination in grape-wheat ear wreath. Fr#99.	—
Pn164	1927	—	20 Pengo. Brass. Denomination in wreath. Fr#99.	—

KM#	Date	Mintage	Identification	Mkt Val
Pn165	1927	—	20 Pengo. Gold. Denomination in grape-wheat ear wreath.	—
Pn166	1927	—	20 Pengo. Gold. Denomination in laurel wreath.	2,700
Pn167	1928BP	—	10 Pengo. Gold. Fr#100	2,700
Pn168	1928	—	20 Pengo. Brass. Smaller arms. Fr#99a.	—
Pn169	1928BP	—	20 Pengo. Gold. Fr#99.	2,700
Pn170	1929	—	5 Pengo. Lead.	—
Pn171	1929	—	5 Pengo. Silver.	—
Pn172	1929BP	—	20 Pengo. Gold. Fr#99a.	2,700
Pn173	1930	—	5 Pengo. Y#44	—
Pn174	1935	—	2 Filler. Nickel. KM#506.	—
Pn175	1935BP	—	2 Pengo.	—
Pn176	1938	—	50 Filler. Aluminum. KM#509.	—
Pn177	1939	—	Filler. Aluminum. KM#505.	—
Pn178	1940	—	Filler. Iron. KM#505.	—
Pn179	1940	—	10 Filler. Lead. KM#507.	—
Pn180	1941	—	50 Filler. Iron. KM#509.	—
Pn181	1943	—	2 Filler. Aluminum. KM#519.	—

PIEFORTS

KM#	Date	Mintage	Identification	Mkt Val
P22	1979	2,500	200 Forint. Silver. 0.6400 g. KM#615	100
P23	1979	2,500	200 Forint. Silver. 0.6400 g. KM#616	40.00
P24	1980	3,000	100 Forint. Nickel. KM#617	30.00
P25	1980	3,000	200 Forint. Silver. 0.6400 g. KM#618	27.50
P26	1980	1,500	500 Forint. Silver. 0.6400 g. KM#619	125

PROBA

KM#	Date	Mintage	Identification	Mkt Val
Pr1	1986	—	500 Forint. Silver. KM#656. Soccer players.	325
Pr2	1986	—	500 Forint. Silver. KM#657. Stadium.	325
Pr3	1988	—	100 Forint. Copper-Nickel. KM#664. Soccer players.	—
Pr4	1988	—	100 Forint. Copper-Nickel. KM#665. Soccer goalie in net.	—
Pr5	1989	—	100 Forint. Copper-Nickel. KM#668. Soccer players shaking hands.	—

TRIAL STRIKES

KM#	Date	Mintage	Identification	Mkt Val
TS39	1907	—	100 Korona. Bronze. KM#491.	—
TS40	1907	—	100 Korona. Bronze. KM#490. Without legend.	—
TS41	1910	—	2 Korona. Lead. KM#493.	—
TS42	1913	—	2 Korona. Aluminum. KM#493.	—
TS43	1914KB	—	Filler. Iron. KM#480.	—
TS44	1914KB	—	2 Filler. Nickel. KM#481.	—
TS45	1914KB	—	10 Filler. Copper-Zinc. KM#482.	—
TS46	1914	—	10 Filler. Silver-Plated Copper-Nickel-Zinc.	—
TS47	1914KB	—	10 Filler. Silver. KM#482.	—
TS48	1914KB	—	20 Filler. Iron. KM#483.	—
TS49	1914	—	2 Korona. Aluminum. KM#493.	—
TS50	1914	—	2 Korona. Bronze. KM#486.	—
TS51	1915KB	—	2 Filler. Iron. KM#481.	—
TS52	1915KB	—	10 Filler. Nickel. KM#496.	—
TS53	1915KB	—	20 Filler. Silver. KM#483.	1,200
TS55	1916KB	—	1/2 Korona. Silver.	1,200
TS54	1916	—	20 Filler. Lead. KM#498.	—
TS56	1917KB	—	10 Filler. Lead.	—
TS57	1917KB	—	10 Filler. Zinc.	—
TS58	1917KB	—	10 Filler. Copper-Nickel-Zinc.	—
TS59	1918KB	—	50 Filler. Lead.	—
TS60	1918	—	20 Korona. Lead. KM#486.	—
TS61	1920	—	10 Filler. Copper-Nickel-Zinc. KM#496.	—
TS62	1922	—	20 Filler. Nickel. KM#498.	—
TS63	1922	—	20 Filler. Bronze. KM#498.	—
TS64	1922	—	20 Filler. Brass. KM#498.	—
TS65	1922	—	20 Filler. Copper-Nickel-Zinc. KM#498.	—
TS66	1930	—	5 Pengo. Lead. Obverse only. KM#512.	—
TS67	1930	—	5 Pengo. Lead. Reverse only. KM#512.	—
TS68	1935	—	2 Filler. Nickel. KM#506	—
TS69	1935	—	2 Pengo. Lead. Reverse only. KM#514.	—
TS70	1936	—	2 Pengo. Lead. Obverse only. KM#515.	—
TS71	1938	—	5 Pengo. Copper-Zinc. KM#517.	—
TS72	1938	—	5 Pengo. Copper-Zinc. KM#516.	—
TS73	1938	—	5 Pengo. Lead. Obverse only. KM#516.	—
TS74	1938	—	5 Pengo. Lead. Reverse only. KM#516.	—
TS75	1939	—	Filler. Aluminum. KM#505.	—
TS76	1939	—	50 Filler. Aluminum. KM#509.	—
TS77	1941	—	50 Filler. Iron. KM#509.	—
TS78	1943	—	2 Filler. Aluminum. KM#519.	—
TS79	1943	—	5 Pengo. Copper-Zinc. KM#523.	—

MINT SETS

KM#	Date	Mintage	Identification	Issue Price	Mkt Val
MS-A1	1956 (3)	—	KM#552, 553, 554	—	55.00
MS1	1971 (9)	—	KM#546, 549, 572-575, 591, 594, 595	—	20.00
MS2	1972 (9)	—	KM#546, 549, 572-575, 591, 594, 595	—	20.00
MS3	1973 (9)	—	KM#546, 549, 572-575, 591, 594, 595	—	20.00
MS4	1974 (9)	—	KM#546, 549, 572-575, 591, 594, 595	—	20.00
MS5	1975 (9)	—	KM#546, 549, 572-575, 591, 594, 595	—	20.00
MS6	1976 (9)	—	KM#546, 549, 572-575, 591, 594, 595	—	20.00
MS7	1977 (9)	—	KM#546, 549, 572-575, 591, 594, 595	—	20.00

KM#	Date	Mintage	Identification	Issue Price	Mkt Val
MSA7	1977 (3)	—	KM#610-612	—	35.00
MS8	1978 (9)	—	KM#546, 549, 572-575, 591, 594, 595	—	20.00
MS9	1979 (9)	—	KM#546, 549, 572-575, 591, 594, 595	—	20.00
MS10	1980 (9)	—	KM#546, 549, 572-575, 591, 594, 595	—	20.00
MS11	1981 (9)	—	KM#546, 549, 572-575, 591, 594, 620	—	20.00
MS12	1982 (9)	—	KM#546, 549, 572-575, 591, 594, 595	—	20.00
MS13	1983 (10)	—	KM#546, 549, 572-575, 591, 630, 635, 636	—	22.00
MSA13	1983 (3)	—	KM#627, 628, 629	—	15.00
MS14	1984 (10)	—	KM#546, 549, 572-575, 591, 630, 635, 636	—	22.00
MS15	1985 (10)	—	KM#546, 549, 572-575, 591, 630, 635, 636	—	22.00
MS16	1986 (10)	—	KM#546, 549, 572-575, 591, 630, 635, 636	—	22.00
MS17	1987 (10)	—	KM#546, 549, 572-575, 591, 630, 635, 636	—	22.00
MS18	1988 (10)	—	KM#546, 549, 572-575, 591, 630, 635, 636	—	22.00
MS19	1989 (10)	—	KM#546, 549, 572-575, 591, 630, 635, 636	—	22.00
MS20	1990 (5)	—	KM673-677	—	15.00
MS21	1991 (5)	—	KM673-677	—	18.00
MS22	1992 (8)	—	KM689, 692-698	—	30.00
MSA22	1992 (5)	—	KM673-677	—	20.00
MS23	1993 (11)	—	KM675-677, 689, 692-698	—	25.00
MS24	1994 (11)	—	KM675-677, 692-698, 707	—	22.00
MS25	1995 (10)	—	KM675-677, 692-698	—	15.00
MS26	1995 (11)	—	KM675-677, 692-698, 707	17.50	25.00
MS27	1996 (10)	—	KM675-677, 692-698	—	15.00
MS28	1997 (10)	7,000	KM677, 692-698, 707, 721	18.50	22.00
MS29	1998 (11)	—	KM677, 692-698, 707, 721, 726	22.50	30.00
MS30	1999 (8)	—	KM677, 692-697, 721	—	17.50
MS31	2000 (8)	—	KM692-697, 721, 745	—	16.50

PROOF SETS

KM#	Date	Mintage	Identification	Issue Price	Mkt Val
PSA1	1948 (3)	—	KM537-539	70.00	70.00
PS1	1961 (6)	2,500	KM560, 562-566	—	2,200
PS2	1961 (4)	—	KM557-559, 561	—	80.00
PS3	1966 (8)	2,000	KM534b, 546a, 547a, 549a-551a, 555a, 556b	15.00	48.00
PS4	1966 (3)	330	KM569-571	430	2,850
PS5	1966 (2)	11,000	KM567-568	7.50	45.00
PS6	1967 (8)	5,000	KM534b, 546a, 547a, 549a-551a, 555a, 556b	15.00	55.00
PS7	1967 (2)	500	KM580, 581	—	2,450
PS8	1968 (5)	7,000	KM583, 585-588	—	2,850
PS9	1968 (2)	4,750	KM582, 584	35.00	90.00
PS10	1969 (2)	3,000	KM589, 590	35.00	30.00
PS11	1970 (2)	4,000	KM592, 593	25.00	25.00
PS12	1972 (2)	6,000	KM596, 597	25.00	32.50
PS13	1973 (2)	6,000	KM599, 600	—	27.50
PS14	1974 (2)	—	KM601, 603	—	25.00
PS15	1976 (3)	5,000	KM607-609	—	50.00
PS16	1977 (3)	—	KM610-612	—	50.00
PS17	1992 (8)	1,000	KM689, 692-698	—	80.00
PS18	1993 (8)	—	KM 689, 692-698	—	47.50
PSA19	1993/4 (2)	—	KM704, 710	—	52.50
PS19	1994 (8)	—	KM692-698, 707	—	47.50
PS20	1995 (8)	—	KM692-698, 707	24.50	47.50
PS34	1996 (10)	—	KM#675-677, 692-698	—	—
PS21	1997 (8)	3,000	KM692-698, 707, 721	29.50	50.00
PS22	1998 (3)	5,000	KM726-728	268	275
PS35	1998 (10)	—	KM#692-698, 707, 721, 726	—	—
PS24	1999 (2)	—	KM741, 742	240	310
PS23	1999 (7)	—	KM692-697, 721	—	32.50
PS25	2000 (8)	—	KM692-697, 721, 745	—	40.00

SPECIMEN SETS (SS)

KM#	Date	Mintage	Identification	Issue Price	Mkt Val
SS1	1977 (9)	—	KM546, 549, 572-575, 591, 594-595	—	10.00
SS2	1978 (9)	—	KM546, 549, 572-575, 591, 594-595	—	10.00
SS3	1979 (9)	—	KM546, 549, 572-575, 591, 594-595	—	10.00
SS4	1981 (9)	—	KM546, 549, 572-575, 591, 594, 620	—	10.00
SS5	1989 (10)	—	KM546, 549, 572-575, 591, 630, 635, 636	—	9.00

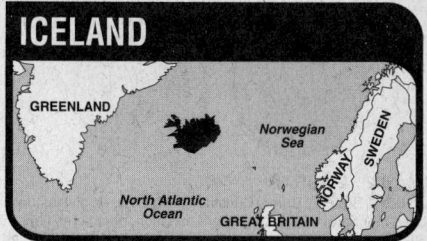

The Republic of Iceland, an island of recent volcanic origin in the North Atlantic east of Greenland and immediately south of the Arctic Circle, has an area of 39,768sq. mi. (103,000 sq. km.) and a population of just over 300,000. Capital: Reykjavik. Fishing is the chief industry and accounts for a little less than 60 percent of the exports.

Iceland was settled by Norwegians in the 9th century and established as an independent republic in 930. The Icelandic assembly called the Althingi, also established in 930, is the oldest parliament in the world. Iceland came under Norwegian sovereignty in 1262, and passed to Denmark when Norway and Denmark were united under the Danish crown in 1380. In 1918 it was established as a virtually independent kingdom in union with Denmark. On June 17, 1944, while Denmark was still under occupation by troops of the Third Reich, Iceland was established by plebiscite as an independent republic.

RULER
Christian X, 1912-1944

MINT MARK
Heart (h) - Copenhagen

MINTMASTERS' INITIALS
HCN - Hans Christian Nielsen, 1919-1927 (for Iceland, 1922-1926)
N - Niels Peter Nielsen, 1927-1955 (for Iceland, 1929-1940)

MONEYERS' INITIALS
GJ - Knud Gunnar Jensen, 1901-1933

MONETARY SYSTEM
100 Aurar = 1 Krona

KINGDOM

DECIMAL COINAGE

KM# 5.1 EYRIR
Bronze **Ruler:** Christian X **Obv:** Crown divides date above monogram **Rev:** Large denomination

Date	Mintage	F	VF	XF	Unc	BU
1926(h) HCN-GJ	405,000	1.50	3.00	7.50	33.50	—
1931(h) N-GJ	462,000	1.00	2.50	6.00	32.00	—
1937(h) N-GJ Wide date	211,000	2.00	4.00	8.00	38.00	—
1937(h) N-GJ Narrow date	Inc. above	2.00	4.00	8.00	38.00	—
1938(h) N-GJ	279,000	1.00	2.00	4.00	15.00	—
1939(h) N-GJ Large 3	305,000	1.00	2.00	3.50	13.00	—
1939(h) N-GJ Small 3	Inc. above	1.00	2.00	3.50	13.00	—

KM# 5.2 EYRIR
1.5700 g., Bronze, 15 mm. **Ruler:** Christian X **Obv:** Crown divides date above monogram **Rev:** Large denomination, ornaments flank

Date	Mintage	F	VF	XF	Unc	BU
1940	1,000,000	0.25	0.50	1.00	2.50	—
1940 Proof	—	Value: 250				
1942	2,000,000	0.25	0.40	0.75	2.00	—

KM# 6.1 2 AURAR
Bronze **Ruler:** Christian X **Obv:** Crown divides date above monogram **Rev:** Large denomination, ornaments flank
Note: Varieties exist in the appearance of the numeral 8 in 1938 dated coins. As the die slowly deteriorated, "globs" were added to the upper loop and later to the lower loop.

Date	Mintage	F	VF	XF	Unc	BU
1926(h) HCN-GJ	498,000	1.50	3.00	8.00	43.50	—
1931(h) N-GJ	446,000	1.00	2.50	7.00	33.50	—
1938(h) N-GJ	206,000	6.00	12.00	17.50	60.00	—
1940(h) N-GJ	257,000	5.00	10.00	15.00	40.00	—

KM# 6.2 2 AURAR
3.0100 g., Bronze **Ruler:** Christian X **Obv:** Crown divides date above monogram **Rev:** Large denomination, ornaments flank

Date	Mintage	F	VF	XF	Unc	BU
1940	1,000,000	0.40	0.75	1.50	3.00	—
1940 Proof	—	Value: 280				
1942	2,000,000	0.20	0.50	1.00	2.00	—

KM# 7.1 5 AURAR
Bronze **Ruler:** Christian X **Obv:** Crown divides date above monogram **Rev:** Large denomination, ornaments flank

Date	Mintage	F	VF	XF	Unc	BU
1926(h) HCN-GJ	355,000	5.00	10.00	25.00	95.00	—
1931(h) N-GJ	311,000	5.00	10.00	25.00	95.00	—

KM# 7.2 5 AURAR
6.0200 g., Bronze **Ruler:** Christian X **Obv:** Crown divides date above monogram **Rev:** Large denomination, ornaments flank

Date	Mintage	F	VF	XF	Unc	BU
1940	1,000,000	0.60	1.25	2.50	5.00	—
1940 Proof	—	Value: 300				
1942	2,000,000	0.35	0.85	1.50	3.00	—

KM# 1.1 10 AURAR
Copper-Nickel **Ruler:** Christian X **Obv:** Ornaments flank denomination **Rev:** Crowned arms divide monogram

Date	Mintage	F	VF	XF	Unc	BU
1922(h) HCN GJ	300,000	2.00	3.50	7.00	43.50	—
1923(h) HCN GJ	302,000	3.00	4.50	9.00	50.00	—
1925(h) HCN GJ	321,000	15.00	25.00	40.00	118	—
1929(h) N-GJ	176,000	15.00	25.00	45.00	133	—
1933(h) N-GJ	157,000	10.00	20.00	30.00	95.00	—
1936(h) N-GJ	213,000	3.00	6.00	10.00	37.50	—
1939/6(h) N-GJ	208,000	5.00	10.00	15.00	46.50	—
1939(h) N-GJ	Inc. above	4.00	8.00	12.00	35.00	—

KM# 1.2 10 AURAR
1.4800 g., Copper-Nickel **Ruler:** Christian X **Obv:** Ornaments flank denomination **Rev:** Crowned arms divide monogram

Date	Mintage	F	VF	XF	Unc	BU
1940	1,500,000	0.35	0.75	1.50	4.50	—
1940 Proof	—	Value: 250				

KM# 1a 10 AURAR
1.2800 g., Zinc **Ruler:** Christian X **Obv:** Ornaments flank denomination **Rev:** Crowned arms divide monogram

Date	Mintage	F	VF	XF	Unc	BU
1942	2,000,000	1.50	3.00	6.00	32.50	—
1942 Prooflike	—	—	—	—	—	—

KM# 2.1 25 AURAR
Copper-Nickel **Ruler:** Christian X **Obv:** Ornaments flank denomination **Rev:** Crowned arms divide monogram

Date	Mintage	F	VF	XF	Unc	BU
1922(h) HCN GJ	300,000	1.00	2.50	4.00	38.00	—
1923(h) HCN GJ	304,000	1.00	2.50	4.00	38.00	—
1925(h) HCN GJ	207,000	2.50	4.50	10.00	58.50	—
1933(h) N-GJ	104,000	10.00	15.00	25.00	110	—
1937(h) N-GJ Near 7	201,000	3.00	5.00	9.00	45.00	—
1937(h) N-GJ Far 7	Inc. above	3.00	5.00	9.00	43.50	—

KM# 2.2 25 AURAR
2.4000 g., Copper-Nickel **Ruler:** Christian X **Obv:** Ornaments flank denomination **Rev:** Crowned arms divide monogram

Date	Mintage	F	VF	XF	Unc	BU
1940	1,500,000	0.25	0.50	1.00	2.50	—
1940 Proof	—	Value: 270				

KM# 2a 25 AURAR
2.0000 g., Zinc **Ruler:** Christian X **Obv:** Ornaments flank denomination **Rev:** Crowned arms divide monogram

Date	Mintage	F	VF	XF	Unc	BU
1942	2,000,000	1.00	2.50	5.50	30.00	—
1942 Prooflike	—	—	—	—	—	—

KM# 3.1 KRONA
Aluminum-Bronze **Ruler:** Christian X **Obv:** Ornaments flank denomination **Rev:** Crowned arms divide monogram

Date	Mintage	F	VF	XF	Unc	BU
1925(h) HCN GJ	252,000	3.00	6.00	25.00	195	—
1929(h) N-GJ	154,000	5.00	10.00	32.00	230	—
1940(h) N-GJ	209,000	1.50	2.50	5.00	15.00	—

KM# 3.2 KRONA
4.7400 g., Aluminum-Bronze **Ruler:** Christian X **Obv:** Ornaments flank denomination **Rev:** Crowned arms divide monogram

Date	Mintage	F	VF	XF	Unc	BU
1940	715,000	1.00	2.00	4.00	10.00	—
1940 Proof; rare	—	—	—	—	—	—

KM# 4.1 2 KRONUR
Aluminum-Bronze **Ruler:** Christian X **Obv:** Ornaments flank denomination **Rev:** Crowned arms divide monogram

Date	Mintage	F	VF	XF	Unc	BU
1925(h) HCN GJ	126,000	7.50	12.50	41.50	250	—
1929(h) N-GJ	77,000	10.00	20.00	70.00	270	—

KM# 4.2 2 KRONUR
Aluminum-Bronze **Ruler:** Christian X **Obv:** Ornaments flank denomination **Rev:** Crowned arms divide monogram

Date	Mintage	F	VF	XF	Unc	BU
1940	546,000	0.75	1.50	3.50	10.00	—
1940 Proof; rare	—	—	—	—	—	—

TOKEN COINAGE
N. Chr. Gram.

Thingeyri

KM# Tn3 10 ORE
Bronze **Issuer:** N. Chr. Gram., Thingeyri **Note:** Similar to 25 Ore, KM#Tn4.

Date	Mintage	VG	F	VF	XF	Unc
ND(1902) Rare	—	—	—	—	—	—

KM# Tn4 25 ORE
Bronze **Issuer:** N. Chr. Gram., Thingeyri

Date	Mintage	VG	F	VF	XF	Unc
ND(1902) Rare	—	—	—	—	—	—

KM# Tn23 50 ORE
Bronze **Issuer:** N. Chr. Gram., Thingeyri **Note:** Similar to 25 Ore, KM#Tn4.

Date	Mintage	VG	F	VF	XF	Unc
ND(1902) Rare	—	—	—	—	—	—

P.J. Thorsteinsson
Bildudal

KM# Tn12 10 AURAR
1.7000 g., Brass **Issuer:** P.J. Thorsteinsson, Bildudal **Note:** Similar to 100 Aurar, KM#Tn21. Struck by L. Chr. Lauer of Nurnberg.

Date	Mintage	VG	F	VF	XF	Unc
ND(1901)	—	12.00	25.00	52.50	145	—

KM# Tn15 25 AURAR
1.7000 g., Brass **Issuer:** P.J. Thorsteinsson, Bildudal **Note:** Similar to 100 Aurar, KM#Tn21. Struck by L. Chr. Lauer of Nurnberg.

Date	Mintage	VG	F	VF	XF	Unc
ND(1901)	—	6.00	12.00	25.00	65.00	—

KM# Tn18 50 AURAR
2.2000 g., Brass **Issuer:** P.J. Thorsteinsson, Bildudal **Note:** Similar to 100 Aurar, KM#Tn21. Struck by L. Chr. Lauer of Nurnberg.

Date	Mintage	VG	F	VF	XF	Unc
ND(1901)	—	6.00	12.00	25.00	65.00	—

KM# Tn21 100 AURAR
1.1000 g., Aluminum **Issuer:** P.J. Thorsteinsson, Bildudal **Note:** Struck by L. Chr. Lauer of Nurnberg.

Date	Mintage	VG	F	VF	XF	Unc
ND(1901) Rare	—	—	—	—	—	—

KM# Tn22 500 AURAR
1.1000 g., Aluminum **Issuer:** P.J. Thorsteinsson, Bildudal **Note:** Similar to 100 Aurar, KM#Tn21. Struck by L. Chr. Lauer of Nurnberg.

Date	Mintage	VG	F	VF	XF	Unc
ND(1901)	—	7.00	15.00	30.00	80.00	—

REPUBLIC
DECIMAL COINAGE

KM# 8 EYRIR
1.6200 g., Bronze, 15.10 mm. **Obv:** Leaves flank denomination **Rev:** Arms within wreath **Note:** Values for the 1953-59 proof issues are for impaired proofs. Brilliant proofs may bring 3 to 4 times these figures.

Date	Mintage	F	VF	XF	Unc	BU
1946	4,000,000	0.10	0.15	0.50	1.00	—
1946 Proof	—	Value: 280				
1953	4,000,000	0.10	0.15	0.40	0.75	—
1953 Proof	—	Value: 75.00				
1956	2,000,000	0.10	0.15	0.40	0.75	—
1956 Proof	—	Value: 75.00				
1957	2,000,000	0.10	0.15	0.40	0.75	—
1957 Proof	—	Value: 75.00				
1958	2,000,000	0.10	0.15	0.40	0.75	—
1958 Proof	—	Value: 75.00				
1959	1,600,000	0.10	0.15	0.40	0.75	—
1959 Proof	—	Value: 75.00				
1966	1,000,000	0.10	0.15	0.40	0.75	—
1966 Proof	15,000	Value: 3.25				

KM# 9 5 AURAR
6.0600 g., Bronze **Obv:** Leaves flank denomination **Rev:** Arms within wreath **Note:** Values for the 1958-63 proof issues are for impaired proofs. Brilliant proofs may bring 3 to 4 times these figures.

Date	Mintage	F	VF	XF	Unc	BU
1946	4,000,000	0.10	0.25	0.50	1.25	—
1946 Proof	—	Value: 435				
1958	400,000	0.50	2.00	3.50	5.00	—
1958 Proof	—	Value: 105				
1959	600,000	0.50	2.00	3.00	4.50	—
1959 Proof	—	Value: 105				
1960	1,200,000	0.15	0.40	1.00	1.75	—
1960 Proof	—	Value: 105				
1961	1,200,000	0.15	0.40	1.00	1.75	—
1961 Proof	—	Value: 105				
1963	1,200,000	0.10	0.30	0.75	1.50	—
1963 Proof	—	Value: 105				
1965	800,000	0.10	0.20	0.50	1.00	—
1966	1,000,000	0.10	0.20	0.50	1.00	—
1966 Proof	15,000	Value: 3.25				

KM# 10 10 AURAR
1.5200 g., Copper-Nickel, 14.98 mm. **Obv:** Leaves flank denomination **Rev:** Arms within wreath **Edge:** Plain **Note:** Values for the 1953-63 proof issues are for impaired proofs. Brilliant proofs may bring 3 to 4 times these figures.

Date	Mintage	F	VF	XF	Unc	BU
1946	4,000,000	—	0.10	0.20	0.60	
1946 Proof	—	Value: 450				
1953	4,000,000	—	0.10	0.20	0.50	
1953 Proof	—	Value: 72.50				
1957	1,200,000	0.25	0.75	2.00	5.00	
1957 Proof	—	Value: 72.50				
1958	500,000	0.20	0.50	1.00	2.00	
1958 Proof	—	Value: 72.50				
1959	3,000,000	0.20	0.50	1.50	4.00	
1959 Proof	—	Value: 72.50				
1960	1,000,000	0.10	0.20	0.40	1.00	
1960 Proof	—	Value: 72.50				
1961	2,000,000	—	—	0.10	0.30	
1961 Proof	—	Value: 72.50				
1962	3,000,000	—	—	0.10	0.20	
1962 Proof	—	Value: 72.50				
1963	4,000,000	—	—	0.10	0.20	
1963 Proof	—	Value: 72.50				
1965	2,000,000	—	—	0.10	0.20	
1966	4,000,000	—	—	0.10	0.20	
1967	2,000,000	—	—	0.10	0.20	
1969	3,200,000	—	—	0.10	0.20	

Note: Coarse edge reeding

Date	Mintage	F	VF	XF	Unc	BU
1969	Inc. above	—	—	0.10	0.20	

Note: Fine edge reeding

KM# 10a 10 AURAR
0.4800 g., Aluminum, 14.64 mm. **Obv:** Leaves flank denomination **Rev:** Arms within wreath **Edge:** Reeded

Date	Mintage	F	VF	XF	Unc	BU
1970	4,800,000	—	—	0.10	0.20	—
1971	11,200,000	—	—	0.10	0.20	—
1973	4,800,000	—	—	0.10	0.20	—
1974	4,800,000	—	—	0.10	0.20	—
1974 Proof	15,000	Value: 3.25				

KM# 11 25 AURAR
2.4400 g., Copper-Nickel, 16.06 mm. **Obv:** Leaves flank denomination **Rev:** Arms within wreath **Edge:** Reeded
Note: Values for the 1951-63 proof issues are for impaired proofs. Brilliant proofs may bring 3 to 4 times these figures.

Date	Mintage	F	VF	XF	Unc	BU
1946	2,000,000	0.10	0.15	0.35	1.25	—
1946 Proof	—	Value: 450				
1951	2,000,000	0.10	0.15	0.35	0.75	—
1951 Proof	—	Value: 82.50				
1954	2,000,000	0.10	0.15	0.35	0.75	—
1954 Proof	—	Value: 82.50				
1957	1,000,000	0.20	0.50	1.50	3.50	—
1957 Proof	—	Value: 82.50				
1958	500,000	0.20	0.40	0.60	1.00	—
1958 Proof	—	Value: 82.50				
1959	2,000,000	0.20	0.50	1.50	3.00	—
1959 Proof	—	Value: 82.50				
1960	1,000,000	—	—	—	0.30	—
1960 Proof	—	Value: 82.50				
1961	1,200,000	—	—	—	0.30	—
1961 Proof	—	Value: 82.50				
1962	2,000,000	—	—	0.10	0.25	—
1962 Proof	—	Value: 82.50				
1963	3,000,000	—	—	0.10	0.25	—
1963 Proof	—	Value: 82.50				
1965	4,000,000	—	—	0.10	0.25	—
1966	2,000,000	—	—	0.10	0.25	—
1967	3,000,000	—	—	0.10	0.25	—
1967 Proof	15,000	Value: 3.25				

KM# 17 50 AURAR
2.4000 g., Nickel-Brass, 19.04 mm. **Obv:** Leaves flank denomination **Rev:** Arms within wreath **Edge:** Reeded

Date	Mintage	F	VF	XF	Unc	BU
1969	2,000,000	—	—	0.10	0.30	—
1970	2,000,000	—	—	0.10	0.30	—
1971	2,000,000	—	—	0.10	0.30	—
1973	1,000,000	—	—	0.10	0.30	—
1974	2,000,000	—	—	0.10	0.30	—
1974 Proof	15,000	Value: 3.25				

KM# 12 KRONA
4.7800 g., Aluminum-Bronze **Obv:** Leaves flank denomination **Rev:** Arms with supporters

Date	Mintage	F	VF	XF	Unc	BU
1946	2,175,000	—	0.10	0.40	1.50	
1946 Proof	—	Value: 450				

KM# 12a KRONA
4.8000 g., Nickel-Brass, 22.3 mm. **Obv:** Denomination, leaves flank **Rev:** Shield with supporters, date below **Note:** Values for the 1957-63 proof issues are for impaired proofs. Brilliant proofs may bring 3 to 4 times these figures.

Date	Mintage	F	VF	XF	Unc	BU
1957	1,000,000	0.10	0.15	0.40	1.50	—
1957 Proof	—	Value: 100				
1959	500,000	0.10	0.20	0.75	2.00	—
1959 Proof	—	Value: 100				
1961	500,000	0.10	0.20	0.75	2.00	—
1961 Proof	—	Value: 100				
1962	1,000,000	0.10	0.15	0.20	0.60	—
1962 Proof	—	Value: 100				
1963	1,500,000	—	0.10	0.15	0.50	—
1963 Proof	—	Value: 100				
1965	2,000,000	—	—	0.10	0.50	—
1966	2,000,000	—	—	0.10	0.50	—
1969	2,000,000	—	—	0.10	0.25	—
1970	3,000,000	—	—	0.10	0.25	—
1971	2,500,000	—	—	0.10	0.25	—
1973 Large round-knob 3	2,500,000	—	—	0.10	0.50	—
1973 Thin, sharp-end 3	3,500,000	—	—	0.10	0.25	—
1974	5,000,000	—	—	0.10	0.25	—
1975	10,500,000	—	—	0.10	0.25	—
1975 Proof	15,000	Value: 3.25				

KM# 23 KRONA
0.5650 g., Aluminum, 16.01 mm. **Obv:** Leaves flank denomination **Rev:** Arms with supporters **Edge:** Reeded

Date	Mintage	F	VF	XF	Unc	BU
1976	10,000,000	—	—	0.10	0.20	—
1977	10,000,000	—	—	0.10	0.20	—
1978	13,000,000	—	—	0.10	0.20	—
1980	7,225,000	—	—	0.10	0.20	—
1980 Proof	15,000	Value: 3.25				

KM# 13 2 KRONUR
Aluminum-Bronze **Obv:** Leaves flank denomination **Rev:** Arms with supporters

Date	Mintage	F	VF	XF	Unc	BU
1946	1,086,000	0.20	0.40	0.80	3.50	—
1946 Proof	—	Value: 500				

KM# 13a.1 2 KRONUR
9.5000 g., Nickel-Brass, 28 mm. **Obv:** Leaves flank denomination **Rev:** Arms with supporters **Note:** Values for the 1958-63 proof issues are for impaired proofs. Brilliant proofs may bring 3 to 4 times these figures.

Date	Mintage	F	VF	XF	Unc	BU
1958	500,000	0.20	0.50	1.00	3.00	—
1958 Proof	—	Value: 130				
1962	500,000	0.20	0.50	1.00	3.00	—
1962 Proof	—	Value: 130				
1963	750,000	0.15	0.30	0.60	2.00	—
1963 Proof	—	Value: 130				
1966	1,000,000	0.10	0.20	0.40	1.50	—
1966 Proof	15,000	Value: 3.25				

KM# 13a.2 2 KRONUR
11.5000 g., Nickel-Brass **Obv:** Leaves flank denomination **Rev:** Arms with supporters **Note:** Thick planchet.

Date	Mintage	F	VF	XF	Unc	BU
1966	300	—	—	400	525	—

KM# 18 5 KRONUR
4.0000 g., Copper-Nickel **Obv:** Leaves flank denomination **Rev:** Arms with supporters

Date	Mintage	F	VF	XF	Unc	BU
1969	2,000,000	—	0.15	0.25	0.50	—
1970	1,000,000	—	0.15	0.25	0.50	—
1971	500,000	0.10	0.20	0.50	1.00	—
1973	1,100,000	—	0.10	0.20	0.40	—
1974	1,200,000	—	0.10	0.15	0.25	—
1975	1,500,000	—	0.10	0.15	0.25	—
1976	500,000	—	0.10	0.20	0.40	—
1977	1,000,000	—	0.10	0.15	0.25	—
1978	4,672,000	—	0.10	0.15	0.25	—
1980	2,400,000	—	0.10	0.15	0.25	—
1980 Proof	15,000	Value: 3.25				

KM# 15 10 KRONUR
6.5200 g., Copper-Nickel, 25 mm. **Obv:** Leaves flank denomination **Rev:** Arms with supporters

Date	Mintage	F	VF	XF	Unc	BU
1967	1,000,000	0.15	0.25	0.50	1.50	—
1969	500,000	0.15	0.30	0.75	2.00	—
1970	1,500,000	—	0.15	0.30	0.75	—
1971	1,500,000	—	0.15	0.30	0.75	—
1973	1,500,000	—	0.15	0.30	0.75	—
1974	2,000,000	—	0.10	0.25	0.60	—
1975	2,500,000	—	0.10	0.25	0.60	—
1976	2,500,000	—	0.10	0.25	0.60	—
1977	2,000,000	—	0.10	0.25	0.60	—
1978	10,500,000	—	0.10	0.25	0.60	—
1980	4,600,000	—	0.10	0.25	0.60	—
1980 Proof	15,000	Value: 3.25				

KM# 16 50 KRONUR
Nickel **Subject:** 50th Anniversary of Sovereignty **Obv:** Denomination **Rev:** Parliament Building in Reikjavik

Date	Mintage	F	VF	XF	Unc	BU
1968	100,000	1.50	2.50	4.00	7.00	—

KM# 19 50 KRONUR
12.3800 g., Copper-Nickel, 30 mm. **Obv:** Denomination **Rev:** Parliament Building in Reykjavic

Date	Mintage	F	VF	XF	Unc	BU
1970	800,000	0.25	0.50	1.00	2.00	—
1971	500,000	0.25	0.50	1.00	2.50	—
1973	50,000	1.00	1.50	2.50	4.00	—
1974	200,000	0.25	0.50	1.00	2.00	—
1975	500,000	0.20	0.35	0.75	1.50	—
1976	500,000	0.20	0.35	0.75	1.50	—
1977	200,000	0.20	0.35	0.75	1.50	—
1978	2,040,000	0.20	0.35	0.50	1.00	—
1980	1,500,000	0.20	0.35	0.50	1.00	—
1980 Proof	15,000	Value: 3.25				

KM# 14 500 KRONUR
8.9604 g., 0.9000 Gold 0.2593 oz. AGW **Subject:** Jon Sigurdsson Sesquicentennial **Obv:** Arms with supporters **Rev:** Head right

Date	Mintage	F	VF	XF	Unc	BU
ND(1961)	10,000	—	—	—	285	—
ND(1961) Proof	—	Value: 875				

KM# 20 500 KRONUR
20.0000 g., 0.9250 Silver 0.5948 oz. ASW **Subject:** 1100th Anniversary - 1st Settlement **Obv:** Quartered design of eagle, dragon, bull and giant **Rev:** Female and cow

Date	Mintage	F	VF	XF	Unc	BU
ND(1974)	70,000	—	—	—	14.00	16.00
ND(1974) Proof	Est. 58,000	Value: 20.00				

Note: 17,000 proof coins were remelted

KM# 21 1000 KRONUR
30.0000 g., 0.9250 Silver 0.8921 oz. ASW **Subject:** 1100th Anniversary - 1st Settlement **Obv:** Quartered design of eagle, dragon, bull and giant **Rev:** Two Vikings and fire

Date	Mintage	F	VF	XF	Unc	BU
ND(1974)	70,000	—	—	—	18.00	22.00
ND(1974) Proof	Est. 58,000	Value: 27.00				

Note: 17,000 proof coins were remelted

KM# 22 10000 KRONUR
15.5000 g., 0.9000 Gold 0.4485 oz. AGW **Subject:** 1100th Anniversary - 1st Settlement **Obv:** Quartered design of eagle, dragon, bull, giant **Rev:** Ingulfur Arnason getting ready to throw his home posts on the beach

Date	Mintage	F	VF	XF	Unc	BU
ND(1974)	12,000	—	—	—	—	435
ND(1974) Proof	8,000	Value: 450				

REFORM COINAGE
100 Old Kronur = 1 New Krona

KM# 24 5 AURAR
1.5000 g., Bronze, 14.58 mm. **Obv:** Eagle with upraised wing **Rev:** Denomination on Skate **Edge:** Plain

Date	Mintage	F	VF	XF	Unc	BU
1981	15,000,000	—	—	—	0.35	1.00
1981 Proof	15,000	Value: 3.50				

KM# 25 10 AURAR
2.0000 g., Bronze, 16.95 mm. **Obv:** Bulls head facing **Rev:** Flying squid **Edge:** Plain

Date	Mintage	F	VF	XF	Unc	BU
1981	50,000,000	—	—	—	0.45	1.00
1981 Proof	15,000	Value: 5.00				

KM# 26 50 AURAR
Bronze, 20 mm. **Obv:** Dragons head right **Rev:** Northern shrimp

Date	Mintage	F	VF	XF	Unc	BU
1981	10,000,000	—	—	0.10	0.50	1.00
1981 Proof	15,000	Value: 6.00				

KM# 26a 50 AURAR
2.6600 g., Bronze Coated Steel, 20 mm. **Obv:** Dragons head right **Rev:** Northern shrimp

Date	Mintage	F	VF	XF	Unc	BU
1986	2,144,000	—	—	—	0.50	1.00

KM# 27 KRONA
4.5000 g., Copper-Nickel, 21.5 mm. **Obv:** Giant facing **Rev:** Cod **Edge:** Reeded

Date	Mintage	F	VF	XF	Unc	BU
1981	18,000,000	—	—	0.15	0.75	1.50
1981 Proof	15,000	Value: 8.00				
1984	7,000,000	—	—	0.15	0.75	1.50
1987	7,500,000	—	—	0.15	0.75	1.50

KM# 27a KRONA
4.0000 g., Nickel Plated Steel, 19.79 mm. **Obv:** Giant facing **Rev:** Cod **Edge:** Reeded

Date	Mintage	F	VF	XF	Unc	BU
1989	5,000,000	—	—	—	0.75	1.50
1991	5,180,000	—	—	—	0.75	1.50
1992	5,000,000	—	—	—	0.75	1.50
1994	5,000,000	—	—	—	0.75	1.50
1996	6,000,000	—	—	—	0.75	1.50
1999	10,000,000	—	—	—	0.75	1.50
2000	10,000	—	—	—	1.50	2.00

KM# 28 5 KRONUR
6.5000 g., Copper-Nickel, 24.5 mm. **Obv:** Quartered design of Eagle, dragon, bull and giant **Rev:** Two dolphins leaping left **Edge:** Reeded

Date	Mintage	F	VF	XF	Unc	BU
1981	-4,350,000	—	—	0.25	1.50	2.50
1981 Proof	15,000	Value: 10.00				
1984	1,000,000	—	—	0.25	1.50	2.50
1987	3,000,000	—	—	0.25	1.50	2.50
1992	2,000,000	—	—	0.25	1.50	2.50

KM# 28a 5 KRONUR
5.6000 g., Nickel Clad Steel, 24.5 mm. **Obv:** Quartered design of Eagle, dragon, bull and giant **Rev:** Two dolphins leaping left **Edge:** Reeded

Date	Mintage	F	VF	XF	Unc	BU
1996	1,500,000	—	—	—	1.50	2.00
1999	2,000,000	—	—	—	1.50	2.00
2000	10,000	—	—	—	2.00	3.00

KM# 29.1 10 KRONUR
Copper-Nickel, 27.5 mm. **Obv:** Quartered design of Eagle, dragon, bull and giant **Rev:** Four capelins left **Edge:** Reeded

Date	Mintage	F	VF	XF	Unc	BU
1984	10,000,000	—	—	0.35	1.75	3.00
1987	7,500,000	—	—	0.35	1.75	3.00
1994	2,500,000	—	—	0.35	1.75	3.00

KM# 29.2 10 KRONUR
8.0000 g., Copper-Nickel, 24.5 mm. **Obv:** Quartered design of Eagle, dragon, bull and giant **Rev:** Four capelins left **Edge:** Reeded **Note:** Struck on flan of Indian Rupee in error.

Date	Mintage	F	VF	XF	Unc	BU
1984	Inc. above	—	—	150	225	—

KM# 29.1a 10 KRONUR
8.0000 g., Nickel Clad Steel, 27.5 mm. **Obv:** Quartered design of Eagle, dragon, bull and giant **Rev:** Four capelins left **Edge:** Reeded

Date	Mintage	F	VF	XF	Unc	BU
1996	4,000,000	—	—	—	1.75	2.50
2000	10,000	—	—	—	2.50	3.50

KM# 31 50 KRONUR
8.2500 g., Nickel-Brass, 23 mm. **Obv:** Quartered design of eagle, dragon, bull and giant **Rev:** Crab **Edge:** Reeded

Date	Mintage	F	VF	XF	Unc	BU
1987	4,000,000	—	—	—	4.00	6.00
1992	2,000,000	—	—	—	4.00	6.00
2000	10,000	—	—	—	5.00	7.00

KM# 35   100 KRONUR
8.5000 g., Nickel-Brass, 25.5 mm. **Obv:** Quartered design of Eagle, dragon, bull and giant **Rev:** Lumpfish left **Edge:** Reeded

Date	Mintage	F	VF	XF	Unc	BU
1995	6,000,000	—	—	—	6.00	12.00
2000	10,000	—	—	—	7.00	12.00

KM# 30   500 KRONUR
20.0000 g., 0.5000 Silver 0.3215 oz. ASW **Subject:** 100th Anniversary of Icelandic Banknotes **Obv:** Fishing vessel **Rev:** Seated figure with sword and shield

Date	Mintage	F	VF	XF	Unc	BU
ND(1986)	20,000	—	—	—	60.00	75.00

KM# 30a   500 KRONUR
20.0000 g., 0.9250 Silver 0.5948 oz. ASW **Subject:** 100th Anniversary of Icelandic Banknotes **Obv:** Fishing vessel **Rev:** Seated figure with sword and shield

Date	Mintage	F	VF	XF	Unc	BU
ND(1986) Proof	5,000	Value: 77.50				

KM# 32   1000 KRONUR
30.0000 g., 0.9250 Silver 0.8921 oz. ASW **Subject:** 50th Anniversary of Icelandic Republic - Sveinn Bjornsson **Obv:** Arms with supporters **Rev:** Head left **Note:** In sets only.

Date	Mintage	F	VF	XF	Unc	BU
ND(1994)	6,000	—	—	—	60.00	70.00
ND(1994) Proof	3,000	Value: 110				

KM# 33   1000 KRONUR
30.0000 g., 0.9250 Silver 0.8921 oz. ASW **Subject:** Asgeir Asgeirsson **Obv:** Arms with supporters **Rev:** Head left **Note:** In sets only.

Date	Mintage	F	VF	XF	Unc	BU
ND(1994)	6,000	—	—	—	60.00	70.00
ND(1994) Proof	3,000	Value: 110				

KM# 34   1000 KRONUR
30.0000 g., 0.9250 Silver 0.8921 oz. ASW **Subject:** Kristjan Eldjarn **Obv:** Arms with supporters **Rev:** Head left **Note:** In sets only.

Date	Mintage	F	VF	XF	Unc	BU
ND(1994)	6,000	—	—	—	60.00	70.00
ND(1994) Proof	3,000	Value: 110				

KM# 37   1000 KRONUR
27.7300 g., 0.9000 Silver 0.8024 oz. ASW **Subject:** Leif Ericsson Millennium **Note:** Struck in the U.S. at the Philadelphia Mint.

Date	Mintage	F	VF	XF	Unc	BU
ND(2000) Proof	150,000	Value: 73.50				

KM# 36   10000 KRONUR
8.6500 g., 0.9000 Gold 0.2503 oz. AGW **Subject:** 1000 Years of Christianity **Obv:** Arms with supporters **Rev:** Old crosier top

Date	Mintage	F	VF	XF	Unc	BU
ND(2000) Proof	3,000	Value: 300				

MINT SETS

KM#	Date	Mintage	Identification	Issue Price	Mkt Val
MS1	1930 (3)	10,000	KM#M1-M3	—	400
MS2	1970 (6)	—	KM#10a, 12a, 15, 17-19	—	12.00
MS3	1971 (6)	—	KM#10a, 12a, 15, 17-19	—	10.00
MS4	1973 (6)	—	KM#10a, 12a (knob 3), 15, 17-19	3.25	9.00
MS5	1974 (6)	—	KM#10a, 12a, 15, 17-19	3.25	7.50
MS6	1974 (2)	70,000	KM#20-21	30.00	26.50
MS7	1975 (4)	—	KM#12a, 15, 18-19	—	5.50
MS8	1976 (4)	—	KM#15, 18-19, 23	—	5.50
MS9	1977 (4)	—	KM#15, 18-19, 23	—	5.50
MS10	1978 (4)	—	KM#15, 18-19, 23	—	5.50
MS11	1980 (4)	—	KM#15, 18-19, 23	—	5.50
MS12	1981 (5)	—	KM#24-28	—	5.50
MS13	1981-1996 (8)	—	1981: KM#24-25; 1986: KM#26a; 1992: KM#31; 1995: KM#35; 1996: KM#27a, 28a, 29.1a	—	12.50
MS14	1994 (3)	6,000	KM#32-34	110	190
MS15	2000 (5)	10,000	KM#27a, 28a, 29.1a, 31, 35	—	18.50

PROOF SETS

KM#	Date	Mintage	Identification	Issue Price	Mkt Val
PS3	1966-1980 (11)	15,000	1966: KM#8-9, 13a.1; 1967: KM#11; 1974: KM#10a, 17; 1975: KM#12a; 1980: KM#15, 18-19, 23	40.00	38.50
PS1	1974 (3)	8,000	KM#20-22	272	365
PS2	1974 (2)	58,000	KM#20-21	38.00	40.00
PS4	1981 (5)	15,000	KM#24-28	32.00	45.00
PS5	1994 (3)	3,000	KM#32-34	155	330
PS6	2000 (1)	150,000	KM#37 and US Ericson Dollar	68.00	130

a map of the
INDIA NATIVE STATES
1822-1824 A.D.

Inset C

Nagod
Maihar
Ajaigarh
Chhatarpur
Panna
Bijawar
Panna
Orchha

Inset B

Raigarh
13
Narsinghgarh
13
Jhabua
Gwalior
Indore
Indore
Gwalior
Dhar
12
Indore
Jhabua
Jaora
Ratlam
Gwalior
Dhar
Pratapgarh
Banswara
Jhabua
Gwalior
Barwani
13
Indore
Dungarpur
3
Alirajpur
Lunaveda
Baria
Udaipur
Chhota
Udaipur

KEY

1 Bela
2 Nawanagar
3 Porbandar
4 Junagadh
5 Bhaunagar
6 Cambay
7 Broach
8 Baroda
9 Radhanpur
10 Tonk (5 parts)
11 Dewas, Junior
12 Dewas, Senior
13 Indore (7 parts)
14 Kishangarh
15 Bundi
16 Jhansi
17 Datia
18 Farrukhabad
19 Karauli
20 Dholpur
21 Narwar
22 Bharatpur
23 Alwar
24 Nabha
25 Jind (2 parts)
26 Patiala (2 parts)
27 Jammu
28 Chamba
29 Sirmur
30 Almora
31 Cooch Bihar
32 Jaintiapur
33 Hasanabad
34 Tripura
35 Janjira
36 Satara
37 Kolhapur
38 Coorg
39 Cochin
40 Travancore
41 Makrai
42 Sind
43 Arcot
44 Cannanore
45 Bijawar

Assam
Chhota Nagpur
Sirguja
Rewah
Awadh
Bastar
Nagpur
Bhopal
Hyderabad
Gwalior
Kotah
Jaipur
Bikanir
Bahawalpur
Jaisalmir
Jodhpur
Mewar
Khairpur
Kutch
Punjab
Kalat
Mysore

See Inset C
See Inset B
See Inset A

East India Company

Inset A

KEY

B Baroda
Ba Bajana
Bh Bhavnagar
D Dhrol
G Gondal
Ja Jasdan
La Lakhtar
L Limbdi
Ma Manavadar
M Morvi
N Nawanagar
P Palitana
R Rajkot
S Sayla
V Vala
Va Vadia
W Wedhwan

1 Baroda
2 Nawanagar
3 Porbandar
4 Junagadh

Little Rann
Malia
Morvi
Dhrangadhra
Dhol
British India
Limbdi
Bajana
Jasdan
Bhagwa
Palitana
Baroda
Bhavnagar
Gondal
Junagadh
Baroda

INDIA-PRINCELY STATES

MONETARY SYSTEMS

In each state, local rates of exchange prevailed. There was no fixed rate between copper, silver or gold coin, but the rates varied in accordance with the values of the metal and by the edict of the local authority.

Within the subcontinent, different regions used distinctive coinage standards. In North India and the Deccan, the silver rupee (11.6 g) and gold mohur (11.0 g) predominated. In Gujarat, the silver kori (4.7 g) and gold kori (6.4 g) were the main currency. In South India the silver fanam (0.7-1.0 g) and gold hun or Pagoda (3.4 g) were current. Copper coins in all parts of India were produced to a myriad of local metrologies with seemingly endless varieties.

NAZARANA ISSUES

Throughout the Indian Princely States listings are Nazarana designations for special full flan strikings of copper, silver and some gold coinage. The purpose of these issues was for presentation to the local monarch to gain favor. For example if one had an audience with one's ruler he would exchange goods, currency notes or the cruder struck circulating coinage for Nazarana pieces which he would present to the ruler as a gift. The borderline between true Nazarana pieces and well struck regular issues is often indistinct. The Nazaranas sometimes circulated alongside the cruder "dump" issues.

PRICING

As the demand for Indian Princely coinage develops, and more dealers handle the material, sale records and price lists enable a firmer basis for pricing most series. For scarcer types adequate sale records are often not available, and prices must be regarded as tentative. Inasmuch as date collectors of Princely States series are few, dates known to be scarce are usually worth little more than common ones. Coins of a dated type, which do not show the full date on their flans should be valued at about 70 per cent of the prices indicated.

DATING

Coins are dated in several eras. Arabic and Devanagari numerals are used in conjunction with the Hejira era (AH), the Vikrama Samvat (VS), Saka Samvat (Saka), Fasli era (FE) Mauludi era (AM), and Malabar era (ME), as well as the Christian era (AD).

GRADING

Copper coins are rarely found in high grade, as they were the workhorse of coinage circulation, and were everywhere used for day-to-day transactions. Moreover, they were carelessly struck and even when 'new', can often only be distinguished from VF coins with difficulty, if at all.

Silver coins were often hoarded and not infrequently, turn up in nearly as-struck condition. The silver coins of Hyderabad (dump coins) are common in high grades, and the rupees of some states are scarcer 'used' than 'new'. Great caution must be exercised in determining the value or scarcity of high grade dump coins.

Dump gold was rarely circulated, and usually occurs in high grades, or is found made into jewelry.

BAHAWALPUR

The Amirs of Bahawalpur established their independence from Afghan control towards the close of the 18th century. In the 1830's the state's independence under British suzerainty became guaranteed by treaty. With the creation of Pakistan in 1947 Bahawalpur, with an area of almost 17,500 square miles, became its premier Princely State. Bahawalpur State, named after its capital, stretched for almost three hundred miles along the left bank of the Sutlej, Panjnad and Indus rivers.

For earlier issues in the names of the Durrani rulers, see Afghanistan.

RULERS
Amirs
Alhaj Muhammad Bahawal Khan V, AH1317-1325/1899-1907AD
Sir Sadiq Muhammad Khan V, AH1325-1365/1907-1947AD

MINT
Bahawalpur

Alhaj Muhammad Bahawal Khan V
AH1317-1325 / 1899-1907AD
HAMMERED COINAGE

Y# 6 PAISA
Copper **Obv:** Legend in Persian **Obv. Leg.:** Muhammad Bahawal ... **Mint:** Bahawalpur **Note:** For anonymous Paisas struck during the years of his reign, see Y#2.1, 2.2.

Date	Mintage	Good	VG	F	VF	XF
AH1324	—	—	3.00	8.00	15.00	25.00
AH1325	—	—	3.00	8.00	15.00	25.00

Anonymous
(Alhaj Muhammad Bahawal Khan V) 1899-1907
ANONYMOUS HAMMERED COINAGE

Y# 2.1 PAISA
Copper **Obv:** Star above cresent, flanked by sprigs **Rev:** Inscription divides date above **Mint:** Bahawalpur

Date	Mintage	Good	VG	F	VF	XF
AH1321	—	—	3.50	8.00	15.00	25.00
AH1325	—	—	3.50	8.00	15.00	25.00

Y# 2.2 PAISA
Copper **Mint:** Bahawalpur **Note:** Contemporary ND imitations exist.

Date	Mintage	Good	VG	F	VF	XF
ND(ca. 1909)	—	—	5.00	12.00	20.00	32.50

Y# 2.2a PAISA
Brass **Mint:** Bahawalpur **Note:** These may be modern counterfeits.

Date	Mintage	Good	VG	F	VF	XF
ND(ca.1909)	—	—	8.00	17.50	25.00	—

Sir Sadiq Muhammad Khan V
AH1325-1365 / 1907-1947AD
HAMMERED COINAGE

Y# 7.1 PAISA
Copper **Obv:** Legend in Persian **Obv. Leg.:** Sadiq Muhammad ... **Mint:** Bahawalpur

Date	Mintage	Good	VG	F	VF	XF
AH1326	—	—	3.00	7.50	12.50	20.00
AH1327	—	—	3.00	7.50	12.50	20.00
AH1328	—	—	3.50	9.00	15.00	25.00

Y# 7.2 PAISA
Copper **Obv:** Legend in Persian **Obv. Leg.:** Sadiq Muhammad ... **Rev:** Without date **Mint:** Bahawalpur

Date	Mintage	Good	VG	F	VF	XF
ND(c. 1910)	—	—	5.00	12.50	20.00	32.50

Y# 7.3 PAISA
Copper **Obv:** Legend in Persian **Obv. Leg.:** Sadiq Muhammad ... **Rev:** Without date or star **Mint:** Bahawalpur

Date	Mintage	Good	VG	F	VF	XF
ND(c. 1910)	—	—	6.00	15.00	25.00	50.00

Y# 8 PAISA
Copper **Obv:** Toughra **Mint:** Bahawalpur

Date	Mintage	Good	VG	F	VF	XF
AH1342	—	—	5.00	12.00	20.00	35.00
AH1343	—	—	5.00	12.00	20.00	35.00

MILLED COINAGE

Y# 12 1/2 PICE
Copper **Obv:** Bust of Muhammad Bahawal Khan V left **Rev:** Toughra **Mint:** Bahawalpur

Date	Mintage	VG	F	VF	XF	Unc
AH1359	—	—	0.25	0.50	3.00	
AH1359 Proof	—					

Y# 9 PAISA (1/4 Anna)
Copper Or Bronze **Obv:** Toughra **Rev:** Three branches in square **Mint:** Bahawalpur

Date	Mintage	VG	F	VF	XF	Unc
AH1343	—	5.00	12.00	25.00	50.00	

Y# 9a PAISA (1/4 Anna)
Brass **Obv:** Toughra **Rev:** Three branches in square **Mint:** Bahawalpur

Date	Mintage	VG	F	VF	XF	Unc
AH1343	—	5.00	12.00	25.00	50.00	

Y# 13 1/4 ANNA (Paisa)
Copper **Obv:** Bust of Muhammad Bahawal Khan V left **Rev:** Toughra **Mint:** Bahawalpur

Date	Mintage	VG	F	VF	XF	Unc
AH1359	—	—	0.25	0.50	3.00	
AH1359 Proof	—					

Y# 14 RUPEE
6.5000 g., Silver **Obv:** Toughra **Mint:** Bahawalpur **Note:** Experts believe this issue is a modern concoction.

Date	Mintage	VG	F	VF	XF	Unc
AH1343	—	BV	5.00	10.00	20.00	50.00

BARODA

Maratha state located in western India. The ruling line was descended from Damaji, a Maratha soldier, who received the title of "Distinguished Swordsman" in 1721 (hence the scimitar on most Baroda coins). The Baroda title "Gaikwara" comes from "gaikwar" or cow herd, Damaji's father's occupation.

The Maratha rulers of Baroda, the Gaekwar family rose to prominence in the mid-18th century by carving out for themselves a dominion from territories, which were previously under the control of the Poona Marathas, and to a lesser extent, of the Raja of Jodhpur. Chronic internal disputes regarding the succession to the masnad culminated in the intervention of British troops in support of one candidate, Anand Rao Gaekwar, in 1800. Then, in 1802, an agreement with the East India Company released the Baroda princes from their fear of domination by the Maratha Peshwa of Poona but subordinated them to Company interests. Nevertheless, for almost the next century and a half Baroda maintained a good relationship with the British and continued as a major Princely State right up to 1947, when it acceded to the Indian Union.

RULERS
Gaekwars
Sayaji Rao III, AH1292-1357/VS1932-1995/1875-1938AD
Pratap Singh, VS1995-2008/1938-1951AD

Sayaji Rao III
AH1292-1357 / VS1932-95 / 1875-1938AD
MILLED COINAGE

Y# 37 1/6 MOHUR
Gold, 14.5 mm. **Obv:** Crowned bust, right **Rev:** Inscription, scimitar, date within wreath **Mint:** Baroda **Note:** 1.04-1.18 grams.

Date	Mintage	VG	F	VF	XF	Unc
VS1959 (1902)	—	—	175	225	275	350

Y# 38 1/3 MOHUR
Gold, 16 mm. **Obv:** Bust of Sayaji Rao III right **Mint:** Baroda **Note:** Weight varies: 2.07-2.39 grams.

Date	Mintage	VG	F	VF	XF	Unc
VS1959 (1902)	—	—	225	275	350	450

Y# 39 MOHUR
Gold, 21 mm. **Obv:** Crowned bust, right **Rev:** Inscription, scimitar, date within wreath **Mint:** Baroda **Note:** Weight varies: 6.20-6.40 grams.

Date	Mintage	VG	F	VF	XF	Unc
VS1959 (1902)	—		265	350	475	650

BHAUNAGAR

State located in northwest India on the west shore of the Gulf of Cambay.

The Thakurs of Bhaunagar, as the rulers were titled, were Gohel Rajputs. They traced their control of the area back to the 13th century. Under the umbrella of British paramountcy, the Thakurs of Bhaunagar were regarded as relatively enlightened rulers. The State was absorbed into Saurashtra in February 1948.

Anonymous Types: Bearing the distinguishing Nagari legend *Bahadur* in addition to the Mughal legends.

MONETARY SYSTEM
2 Trambiyo = 1 Dokda
1-1/2 Dokda = 1 Dhingla

Thakurs of Bhaunagar
Gohel Rajputs

ANONYMOUS HAMMERED COINAGE

KM# 1 DOKDA
Copper

Date	Mintage	Good	VG	F	VF	XF
VS2004(1947)	—	2.50	6.50	15.00	20.00	35.00

BUNDI

State in Rajputana in northwest India.

Bundi was founded in 1342 by a Chauhan Rajput, Rao Dewa (Deoraj). Until the Maratha defeat early in the 19th century, Bundi was greatly harassed by the forces of Holkar and Sindhia. In 1818 it came under British protection and control and remained so until 1947.In 1948 the State was absorbed into Rajasthan.

RULERS
Raghubir Singh VS1946-1984/1889-1927AD
Ishwari Singh VS1984-2004/1927-1947AD

MINT

	PERSO-ARABIC	DEVANAGARI
Bundi	بندي	बु ndी

بوندي

Mint name: Bundi

Victoria
1837-1901AD

HAMMERED COINAGE
Regal Style

Y# 10 NAZARANA RUPEE
Silver **Obv:** Seated figure holding katar **Obv. Leg.:** VICTORIA QUEEN **Note:** Weight varies: 10.60-11.00 grams.

Date	Mintage	Good	VG	F	VF	XF
VS1958 (1901)	—	45.00	90.00	125	175	

Edward VII
1901-1910AD

HAMMERED COINAGE
Regal Style

Y# A12 1/2 PAISA
Copper **Obv:** Katar **Obv. Leg.:** EDWARD VII EMPEROR **Note:** Weight varies: 4.70-5.10 grams.

Date	Mintage	Good	VG	F	VF	XF
NDVS1963 (1906)	—	1.00	2.00	5.00	12.00	20.00
VS1965 (1908)	—	1.00	2.00	5.00	12.00	20.00
VS1966 (1909)	—	1.00	2.00	5.00	12.00	20.00
VS1967 (1910)	—	1.00	2.00	5.00	12.00	20.00
VS1973 (1916)	—	1.00	2.00	5.00	12.00	20.00
VS1974 (1917)	—	1.00	2.00	5.00	12.00	20.00
VS1976 (1918)	—	1.00	2.00	5.00	12.00	20.00

Y# B11 1/4 RUPEE
Silver **Obv:** Seated figure holding katar **Obv. Leg.:** EMPEROR-EDWARD VII **Note:** Weight varies: 2.65-2.70 grams.

Date	Mintage	Good	VG	F	VF	XF
VS1958 (1901)	—	—	6.50	15.00	30.00	75.00
VS1959 (1902)	—	—	6.50	15.00	30.00	75.00
VS1961 (1904)	—	—	6.50	15.00	30.00	75.00
VS1962 (1905)	—	—	6.50	15.00	30.00	75.00

Y# 12 1/4 RUPEE
Silver **Obv:** Katar **Obv. Leg.:** EDWARD VII EMPEROR **Note:** Weight varies: 2.65-2.70 grams.

Date	Mintage	Good	VG	F	VF	XF
VS1963 (1906)	—		2.50	5.00	10.00	15.00
VS1964 (1907)	—		2.50	5.00	10.00	15.00
VS1965 (1908)	—		2.50	5.00	10.00	15.00
VS1966 (1909)	—		2.50	5.00	10.00	15.00

Y# A11 1/2 RUPEE
Silver, 16-18 mm. **Obv:** Seated figure holding katar **Obv. Leg.:** EMPEROR-EDWARD VII **Note:** Weight varies: 5.30-5.40 grams.

Date	Mintage	Good	VG	F	VF	XF
VS1958 (1901)	—	—	12.00	25.00	45.00	75.00

Y# 13 1/2 RUPEE
Silver, 16-18 mm. **Obv:** Katar **Obv. Leg.:** EDWARD VII EMPEROR **Note:** Weight varies: 5.30-5.40 grams.

Date	Mintage	Good	VG	F	VF	XF
VS1963 (1906)	—		2.50	5.00	10.00	15.00
VS1964 (1907)	—		2.50	5.00	10.00	15.00
VS1965 (1908)	—		2.50	5.00	10.00	15.00
VS1966 (1909)	—		2.50	5.00	10.00	15.00

Y# 11 RUPEE
Silver, 21-25 mm. **Obv:** Seated figure holding katar **Obv. Leg.:** EMPEROR-EDWARD VII **Note:** Weight varies: 10.60-10.70 grams. Size varies.

Date	Mintage	Good	VG	F	VF	XF
VS1958 (1901)	—	—	2.50	5.00	10.00	15.00
VS1959 (1902)	—	—	2.50	5.00	10.00	15.00
VS1960 (1903)	—	—	2.50	5.00	10.00	15.00
VS1961 (1904)	—	—	2.50	5.00	10.00	15.00
VS1962 (1905)	—	—	2.50	5.00	10.00	15.00
VS1963 (1906)	—	—	2.50	5.00	10.00	15.00

Y# 14 RUPEE
Silver, 18-21 mm. **Obv:** Katar **Obv. Leg.:** EDWARD VII EMPEROR **Note:** Weight varies: 10.60-10.70 grams. Size varies.

Date	Mintage	Good	VG	F	VF	XF
VS1963 (1906)	—		2.50	5.00	10.00	15.00
VS1964 (1907)	—		2.50	5.00	10.00	15.00
VS1965 (1908)	—		2.50	5.00	10.00	15.00
VS1966 (1909)	—		2.50	5.00	10.00	15.00
VS1967 (1910)	—		2.50	5.00	10.00	15.00
VS1968 (1911)	—		2.50	5.00	10.00	15.00
VS1969 (1912)	—		2.50	5.00	10.00	15.00

Y# 11a NAZARANA RUPEE
Silver **Obv:** Seated figure holding katar **Obv. Leg.:** EMPEROR-EDWARD VII **Note:** Weight varies: 10.60-10.70 grams.

Date	Mintage	Good	VG	F	VF	XF
VS1962 (1906)	—		40.00	100	175	250

Y# 14a NAZARANA RUPEE
Silver **Obv:** Katar **Obv. Leg.:** EDWARD VII EMPEROR **Note:** Weight varies: 10.60-10.70 grams. Struck on square flan.

Date	Mintage	Good	VG	F	VF	XF
VS1965 (1908)	—		30.00	75.00	100	200
VS1966 (1909)	—		30.00	75.00	100	200
VS1967 (1910)	—		30.00	75.00	100	200
VS1968 (1911)	—		30.00	75.00	125	200
VS1969 (1912)	—		30.00	75.00	125	200
VS1970 (1913)	—		30.00	75.00	125	200

Y# 14b NAZARANA RUPEE
Silver, 26 mm. **Obv:** Katar **Obv. Leg.:** EDWARD VII EMPEROR **Note:** Weight varies: 10.60-10.70 grams.

Date	Mintage	Good	VG	F	VF	XF
VS1966 (1909)	—		40.00	100	150	250
VS1967 (1910)	—		40.00	100	150	250
VS1968 (1911)	—		40.00	100	150	250
VS1969 (1912)	—		40.00	100	150	250
VS1970 (1913)	—		40.00	100	150	250

George V
1910-1936AD

HAMMERED COINAGE
Regal Style

Y# 15.1 1/2 PAISA
Copper **Obv:** Katar **Obv. Leg.:** EMPEROR-GEORGE V **Note:** Weight varies: 5.00-5.35 grams.

Date	Mintage	Good	VG	F	VF	XF
VS1973 (1916)	—	—	1.25	3.00	4.00	—
VS1974 (1917)	—	—	1.25	3.00	4.00	—

Date	Mintage	Good	VG	F	VF	XF
VS1976 (1919)	—	—	1.25	3.00	4.00	—
VS1977 (1920)	—	—	1.25	3.00	4.00	—

Y# 15.2 1/2 PAISA
Copper **Obv:** Katar **Obv. Leg.:** GEORGE V EMPEROR
Note: Weight varies: 5.00-5.35 grams. Size varies.

Date	Mintage	Good	VG	F	VF	XF
VS1980 (1923)	—	—	1.25	3.00	4.00	—
VS1981 (1924)	—	—	1.25	3.00	4.00	—
VS1982 (1925)	—	—	1.25	3.00	4.00	—
VS1983 (1926)	—	—	1.25	3.00	4.00	—
VS1984 (1927)	—	—	1.25	3.00	4.00	—
VS1986 (1929)	—	—	1.25	3.00	4.00	—
VS1987 (1930)	—	—	1.25	3.00	4.00	—
VS1988 (1931)	—	—	1.25	3.00	4.00	—
VS1990 (1933)	—	—	1.25	3.00	4.00	—
VS1991 (1934)	—	—	1.25	3.00	4.00	—
VS1992 (1935)	—	—	1.25	3.00	4.00	—

Y# 16.1 1/4 RUPEE
Silver **Obv:** Katar **Obv. Leg.:** EMPEROR-GEORGE V
Note: Weight varies: 2.60-2.70 grams.

Date	Mintage	Good	VG	F	VF	XF
VS1972 (1915)	—	—	1.50	3.00	5.00	9.00
VS1973 (1916)	—	—	1.50	3.00	5.00	9.00
VS1974 (1917)	—	—	1.50	3.00	5.00	9.00

Y# 16.2 1/4 RUPEE
Silver **Obv:** Katar **Obv. Leg.:** GEORGE V EMPEROR
Note: Weight varies: 2.60-2.70 grams.

Date	Mintage	Good	VG	F	VF	XF
VS1980 (1923)	—	—	2.00	5.00	7.50	12.00
VS1981 (1924)	—	—	2.00	5.00	7.50	12.00
VS1982 (1925)	—	—	2.00	5.00	7.50	12.00

Y# A19 1/4 RUPEE
Silver, 13 mm. **Obv:** Date 1925 at center **Obv. Leg.:** EMPEROR
GEORGE V **Note:** Weight varies: 2.60-2.70 grams.

Date	Mintage	Good	VG	F	VF	XF
VS1915 (1925)	—	—	75.00	150	200	275

Y# 17.1 1/2 RUPEE
Silver **Note:** Weight varies: 5.30-5.40 grams.

Date	Mintage	Good	VG	F	VF	XF
VS1972 (1915)	—	—	1.50	3.00	7.00	10.00
VS1973 (1916)	—	—	1.50	3.00	7.00	10.00
VS1974 (1917)	—	—	1.50	3.00	7.00	10.00
VS1979 (1922)	—	—	1.50	3.00	7.00	10.00

Y# 17.2 1/2 RUPEE
Silver **Obv:** Legend arranged differently **Note:** Weight varies:
5.30-5.40 grams.

Date	Mintage	Good	VG	F	VF	XF
VS1979 (1922)	—	—	1.50	3.00	7.00	10.00
VS1980 (1923)	—	—	1.50	3.00	7.00	10.00
VS1981 (1924)	—	—	1.50	3.00	7.00	10.00
VS1982 (1925)	—	—	1.50	3.00	7.00	10.00
VS1983 (1926)	—	—	1.50	3.00	7.00	10.00
VS1984 (1927)	—	—	1.50	3.00	7.00	10.00

Y# 19 1/2 RUPEE
Silver **Obv:** Date 1925 at center **Obv. Leg.:** EMPEROR
GEORGE V **Note:** Weight varies: 5.30-5.40 grams.

Date	Mintage	Good	VG	F	VF	XF
VS1915 (1925)	—	—	65.00	125	175	250

Y# 18.1 RUPEE
Silver **Obv:** Katar **Obv. Leg.:** EMPEROR GEORGE V
Note: Weight varies: 10.60-10.70 grams.

Date	Mintage	Good	VG	F	VF	XF
VS1972 (1915)	—	—	2.50	5.00	10.00	15.00
VS1973 (1916)	—	—	2.50	5.00	10.00	15.00
VS1974 (1917)	—	—	2.50	5.00	10.00	15.00
VS1975 (1918)	—	—	2.50	5.00	10.00	15.00
VS1979 (1922)	—	—	2.50	5.00	10.00	15.00

Y# 18.2 RUPEE
Silver **Obv:** Katar **Obv. Leg.:** GEORGE V EMPEROR
Note: Weight varies: 10.60-10.70 grams.

Date	Mintage	Good	VG	F	VF	XF
VS1979 (1922)	—	—	2.50	5.00	10.00	15.00
VS1980 (1923)	—	—	2.50	5.00	10.00	15.00
VS1981 (1924)	—	—	2.50	5.00	10.00	15.00
VS1982 (1925)	—	—	2.50	5.00	10.00	15.00
VS1983 (1926)	—	—	2.50	5.00	10.00	15.00
VS1984 (1927)	—	—	2.50	5.00	10.00	15.00
VS1985 (1928)	—	—	2.50	5.00	10.00	15.00
VS1987 (1930)	—	—	2.50	5.00	10.00	15.00
VS1989 (1932)	—	—	2.50	5.00	10.00	15.00

Y# 20 RUPEE
Silver **Obv:** Date "1925" at center **Obv. Leg.:** EMPEROR
GEORGE V **Note:** Weight varies: 10.60-10.70 grams.

Date	Mintage	Good	VG	F	VF	XF
VS1915 (1925)	—	—	45.00	90.00	150	225

Y# 18a.1 NAZARANA RUPEE
Silver **Obv:** Katar **Obv. Leg.:** EMPEROR GEORGE V
Note: Weight varies: 10.55-10.80 grams.

Date	Mintage	Good	VG	F	VF	XF
VS1965 (1908)	—	—	35.00	75.00	125	200
VS1971 (1914)	—	—	35.00	75.00	125	200
VS1974 (1917)	—	—	35.00	75.00	125	200
VS1975 (1918)	—	—	35.00	75.00	125	200
VS1977 (1920)	—	—	35.00	75.00	125	200

Y# 18a.2 NAZARANA RUPEE
Silver **Obv:** Katar **Obv. Leg.:** GEORGE V **Note:** Weight varies:
10.55-10.80 grams.

Date	Mintage	Good	VG	F	VF	XF
VS1979 (1922)	—	—	35.00	75.00	125	200
VS1980 (1923)	—	—	35.00	75.00	125	200
VS1981 (1924)	—	—	35.00	75.00	125	200
VS1983 (1926)	—	—	35.00	75.00	125	200
VS1984 (1927)	—	—	35.00	75.00	125	200
VS1987 (1930)	—	—	35.00	75.00	125	200

Y# 20a NAZARANA RUPEE
Silver **Obv:** Date "1925" at center **Obv. Leg.:** EMPEROR
GEORGE V **Note:** Weight varies: 10.55-10.80 grams.

Date	Mintage	Good	VG	F	VF	XF
VS1915 (1925)	—	—	65.00	125	175	250

CAMBAY

Khanbayat
Although of very ancient origins as a port, located at the head
of the Gulf of Cambay in West India, Cambay did not come into
existence as a separate state until about 1730 after the breakdown of Mughal authority in Delhi. The nawabs of Cambay traced
their ancestry to Momin Khan II, the last of the Muslim governors
of Gujerat. The State came under British control after two decades
of Maratha rule.

RULER
Ja'far Ali Khan, AH1297-1333/VS1937-1972/1880-1915AD

MINT
Khanbayat

Jafar Ali Khan
1880-1915AD

ANONYMOUS HAMMERED COINAGE

Y# 5 1/2 PAISA
Copper **Obv:** Persian inscription **Obv. Insc.:** Cambay **Rev:**
Denomination in words **Note:** Varieties in countermark exist.

Date	Mintage	Good	VG	F	VF	XF
VS1963(1906)	—	—	2.25	5.00	9.00	—
VS1964(1907)	—	—	2.25	5.00	9.00	—

Y# 5a 1/2 PAISA
Copper **Obv:** Persian inscription **Obv. Insc.:** Cambay
Rev: Denomination in numerals

Date	Mintage	Good	VG	F	VF	XF
VS1964(1907)	—	—	2.00	4.00	8.00	—
VS1965(1908)	—	—	2.00	4.00	8.00	—
VS1966(1909)	—	—	2.00	4.00	8.00	—

Y# 6 PAISA
Copper **Obv:** Persian inscription **Obv. Insc.:** Cambay
Note: Varieties exist.

Date	Mintage	Good	VG	F	VF	XF
VS1962(1905)	—	—	0.75	2.00	3.50	—
VS1963(1906)	—	—	0.75	2.00	3.50	—
VS1964(1907)	—	—	0.75	2.00	3.50	—
VS1965(1908)	—	—	0.75	2.00	3.50	—
VS1966(1909)	—	—	0.75	2.00	3.50	—
VS1967 (1910)	—	—	0.75	2.00	3.50	—
VS1968(1911)	—	—	0.75	2.00	3.50	—
VS1970(1913)	—	—	0.75	2.00	3.50	—

HAMMERED COINAGE

Y# 10 RUPEE
Silver, 19-20 mm. **Obv:** Inscription **Obv. Insc.:** Ja'afar Ali Khan
Rev: Mint name **Mint:** Cambay **Note:** Weight varies, 10.70-11.60
grams. Size varies.

Date	Mintage	Good	VG	F	VF	XF
AH1319//23(1901 -1902)	—	—	25.00	50.00	80.00	125

COUNTERMARKED COINAGE

Y# 2   1/4 PAISA
Copper **Countermark:** Persian "Shah" **Note:** Varieties in countermark exist.

CM Date	Host Date	Good	VG	F	VF	XF
ND	ND	—	3.00	7.50	10.00	—

Y# 3   1/2 PAISA
Copper **Countermark:** Persian "Shah" **Note:** Varieties in countermark exist.

CM Date	Host Date	Good	VG	F	VF	XF
ND	ND	—	3.00	7.50	10.00	—

DATIA

State located in north-central India, governed by Maharajas. Datia was founded in 1735 by Bhagwan Das, son of Narsingh Dev of the Orchha royal house. In 1804 the State concluded its first treaty with the East India Company and thereafter came under British protection and control.

RULERS
Bhawani Singh, AH1274-1325/1857-1907AD
Govind Singh, AH1325-1368/1907-1948AD

MINT

Dalipnagar

Gaja Shahi Series
Struck for more than 100 years, with the AH date on the obverse and the regnal year on the reverse bearing little relationship to each other. These are close copies of Orchha C#24-32 and can only be distinguished by the symbols, which are always different from those of Orchha, except for the Gaja (mace):

Gaja always on reverse

On obverse (Datia Mint Symbol)

On reverse

BRITISH PROTECTORATE

Bhawani Singh
AH1274-1325 / 1857-1907AD

HAMMERED COINAGE
Gaja Shahi Series

C# 22   1/2 PAISA
6.0000 g., Copper **Obv:** Inscription **Rev:** Inscription
Note: Weight varies 6.00-6.50 grams. Posthumous regnal years of Muhammad Akbar II.

Date	Mintage	Good	VG	F	VF	XF
AH1320(1902)	—	—	6.00	15.00	30.00	—

DEWAS

A Maratha state located in west-central India. The raja, the brother of the raja of Dewas Senior Branch had a palace in Dewas City. They descended from two brothers, Tukoji and Jiwaji who were given Dewas City in 1726 by Peshwa Baji Rao as a reward for army services.

Largely due to its geographical location Dewas suffered much at the hands of the armies of Holkar and Sindhia, and from Pindari incursions. In 1818 the State came under British protection.

LOCAL RULER
Vikrama Simha Rao, 1937-1948AD

BRITISH PROTECTORATE
Senior Branch

Vikrama Simha Rao
VS1994-2005 / 1937-1948AD

MILLED COINAGE
Regal Style

KM# 13   PAISA
Copper **Obv:** Bust of Vikrama Simha Rao right **Rev:** Arms
Mint: Allote

Date	Mintage	VG	F	VF	XF	Unc
2000/1944	—	—	30.00	75.00	125	200
2001/1944	—	—	30.00	75.00	125	200

DUNGARPUR

A district in northwest India which became part of Rajasthan in 1948.

The maharawals of Dungarpur were descended from the Mewar chieftains of the 12th century. In 1527 the upper Mahi basin was bifurcated to form the Princely States of Dungarpur and Banswara. Thereafter Dungarpur came successively under Mughal and Maratha control until in 1818 it came under British protection.

RULERS
Bijey Singh, VS1955-1975/1898-1918AD
Lakshman Singh, VS1975-2005/1918-1948AD

INSCRIPTION
Rajya Dungarpur

BRITISH PROTECTORATE

Lakshman Singh
VS1975-2005 / 1918-1948AD

HAMMERED COINAGE

KM# 9   NAZARANA MOHUR
11.0000 g., Gold **Obv:** Sword and "jhar" to right
Rev. Insc.: Rajya/Dungarpur

Date	Mintage	Good	VG	F	VF	XF
VS1996 (1939)	—	—	1,000	1,500	2,000	3,500

WW II EMERGENCY COINAGE

KM# 7   PAISA
Copper **Rev:** 2 bars above 'P' in "Paisa"

Date	Mintage	Good	VG	F	VF	XF
VS2001(1944)	—	—	12.00	30.00	50.00	75.00

KM# 8   PAISA
Copper **Rev:** One bar above 'P' in "Paisa"

Date	Mintage	Good	VG	F	VF	XF
VS2001(1944)	—	—	6.00	15.00	25.00	37.50

GWALIOR
Sindhia

State located in central India. Capital originally was Ujjain (= Daru-I-fath), but was later transferred to Gwalior in 1810. The Gwalior ruling family, the Sindhias, were descendants of the Maratha chief Ranoji Sindhia (d.1750). His youngest son, Mahadji

Sindhia (d.1794) was anxious to establish his independence from the overlordship of the Peshwas of Poona. Unable to achieve this alone, it was the Peshwa's crushing defeat by Ahmad Shah Durrani at Panipat in 1761, which helped realize his ambitions. Largely in the interests of sustaining this autonomy, but partly as a result of a defeat at East India Company hands in 1781, Mahadji concluded an alliance with the British in 1782. In 1785, he reinstalled the fallen Mughal Emperor, Shah Alam, on the throne at Dehli. Very early in the 19th century, Gwalior's relationship with the British began to deteriorate, a situation which culminated in the Anglo-Maratha War of 1803. Gwalior's forces under Daulat Rao were defeated. In consequence, and by the terms of the peace treaty which followed, his territory was truncated. In 1818, Gwalior suffered a further loss of land at British hands. In the years that ensued, as the East India Company's possessions became transformed into empire and as the Pax Britannica swept across the subcontinent, the Sindhia family's relationship with their British overlords steadily improved.

RULERS
Madho Rao, VS1943-1982/1886-1925AD
Jivaji Rao, VS1982-2005/1925-1948AD

MINT

Gwalior Fort

KINGDOM

Madho Rao
VS1943-1982 / 1886-1925AD

MILLED COINAGE

KM# 164   1/2 PICE
Copper, 20 mm. **Obv:** Cobra above crossed spear and trident
Mint: Gwalior Fort

Date	Mintage	Good	VG	F	VF	XF
VS1958 (1901)	—	—	—	0.65	2.00	4.00

KM# 169   1/4 ANNA
Copper **Obv:** Cobra above crossed spear and trident

Date	Mintage	VG	F	VF	XF	Unc
VS1958 (1901)	—	—	0.75	2.00	4.00	9.00

KM# 170   1/4 ANNA
6.6000 g., Copper **Obv:** Bust of Madho Rao right **Rev:** Arms
Note: Thick planchet, 2.2mm.

Date	Mintage	VG	F	VF	XF	Unc
VS1970 (1913)	—	—	0.25	0.75	1.50	3.00

KM# 171   1/4 ANNA
5.1000 g., Copper **Obv:** Bust of Madho Rao right **Rev:** Arms
Note: Thin planchet, 1.6mm.

Date	Mintage	VG	F	VF	XF	Unc
VS1970 (1913)	—	—	1.25	3.50	5.00	7.00
VS1974 (1917)	—	—	0.25	0.75	1.50	3.00

گوالیار

KM# 172 1/4 ANNA
Copper **Obv:** Bust of Madho Rao right, continuous legend around portrait **Rev:** Arms

Date	Mintage	VG	F	VF	XF	Unc
VS1974 (1917)	—	0.75	2.00	4.00	9.00

KM# 175 1/3 MOHUR
3.4500 g., Gold **Obv:** Bust of Madho Rao right **Rev:** Arms

Date	Mintage	VG	F	VF	XF	Unc
VS1959 (1902)	—	—	275	550	1,150	2,000

Jivaji Rao
VS1985-2005 / 1925-1948AD
MILLED COINAGE

KM# 177 1/4 ANNA
Copper **Obv:** Crude style bust of Jivaji Rao left **Rev:** Arms
Note: Thin planchet. 3.00-3.15 grams.

Date	Mintage	VG	F	VF	XF	Unc
VS1986 (1929)	—	—	0.75	2.00	3.00	6.00
VS1999 (1942)	—	—	0.75	2.00	3.00	6.00

KM# 176.1 1/4 ANNA
Copper **Obv:** Fine style bust of Jivaji Rao left **Rev:** Arms
Note: Thick planchet. 4.65-5.15 grams.

Date	Mintage	VG	F	VF	XF	Unc
VS1986 (1929)	—	—	0.25	0.75	1.50	3.00

KM# 176.2 1/4 ANNA
Copper **Obv:** Crude style "pug-nose" bust of Jivaji Rao left **Rev:** Arms

Date	Mintage	VG	F	VF	XF	Unc
VS1986 (1929)	—	—	0.25	0.75	1.50	3.00

KM# 178.1 1/4 ANNA
Copper **Obv:** Facing coiled cobras below bust of Jivaji Rao left **Rev:** Arms, without inscription on side

Date	Mintage	VG	F	VF	XF	Unc
VS1999 (1942)	—	—	0.20	0.60	1.00	2.00

KM# 178.2 1/4 ANNA
Copper **Obv:** Without facing coiled cobras below bust of Jivaji Rao left **Rev:** Arms

Date	Mintage	VG	F	VF	XF	Unc
VS1999 (1942)	—	—	0.20	0.60	1.00	2.00

KM# 179 1/2 ANNA
Brass **Obv:** Bust of Jivaji Rao left **Rev:** Arms

Date	Mintage	VG	F	VF	XF	Unc
VS1999 (1942)	—	—	0.20	0.60	1.00	2.00
VS1999 (1942) Proof	—	Value: 50.00				

PATTERNS
Including off metal strikes

KM#	Date	Mintage	Identification	Mkt Val
Pn1	VS1977(1920)	—	4 Anna. Silver.	—

HYDERABAD
Haidarabad

Hyderabad State, the largest Indian State and the last remnant of Mughal suzerainty in South or Central India, traced its foundation to Nizam-ul Mulk, the Mughal viceroy in the Deccan. From about 1724 the first nizam, as the rulers of Hyderabad came to be called, took advantage of Mughal decline in the North to assert an all but ceremonial independence of the emperor. The East India Company defeated Hyderabad's natural enemies, the Muslim rulers of Mysore and the Marathas, with the help of troops furnished under alliances between them and the Nizam. This formed the beginning of a relationship, which persisted for a century and a half until India's Independence. Hyderabad was the premier Princely State, with a population (in 1935) of fourteen and a half million. It was not absorbed into the Indian Union until 1948. Hyderabad City is located beside Golkonda, the citadel of the Qutb Shahi sultans until they were overthrown by Aurangzeb in 1687. A beautifully located city on the bank of the Musi river, the mint epithet was appropriately Farkhanda Bunyad, "of happy foundation".

Hyderabad exercised authority over a number of feudatories or samasthans. Some of these, such as Gadwal and Shorapur, paid tribute to both the Nizam and the Marathas. These feudatories were generally in the hands of local rajas whose ancestry predated the establishment of Hyderabad State. There were also many mints in the State, both private and government. There was little or no standardization of the purity of silver coinage until the 20th century. At least one banker, Pestonji Meherji by name, was distinguished by minting his own coins.

RULERS
Mir Mahbub Ali Khan II, AH1285-1329/1869-1911AD
Mir Usman Ali Khan, AH1329-1367/1911-1948AD

MINT

فرخنده بنياد حيدراباد

Haidarabad
Mintname: Farkhanda Bunyad Haidarabad

NIZAMATE
Mir Mahbub Ali Khan II
AH1285-1329 / 1869-1911AD
HAMMERED COINAGE

Y# 13 1/16 RUPEE
0.6980 g., 0.8180 Silver 0.0184 oz. ASW **Obv:** Persian letter "M" for Mahbub above "k" of "Mulk" **Obv. Insc.:** "Asaf Jah, Nizam al-Mulk" **Mint:** Haidarabad (Farkhanda Bunyad)

Date	Mintage	Good	VG	F	VF	XF
AH1321//37	—	BV	0.85	1.75	2.50	4.00

Y# 14 1/8 RUPEE
1.3970 g., 0.8180 Silver 0.0367 oz. ASW **Obv:** Persian letter "M" for Mahbub above "k" of "Mulk" **Obv. Insc.:** "Asaf Jah, Nizam al-Mulk" **Mint:** Haidarabad (Farkhanda Bunyad)

Date	Mintage	Good	VG	F	VF	XF
AH1321//37	—	BV	1.20	2.25	3.00	4.50

Y# 15 1/4 RUPEE
2.7940 g., 0.8180 Silver 0.0735 oz. ASW **Obv:** Persian letter "M" for Mahbub above "k" of "Mulk" **Obv. Insc.:** "Asaf Jah, Nizam al-Mulk" **Mint:** Haidarabad (Farkhanda Bunyad)

Date	Mintage	Good	VG	F	VF	XF
AH1321//37	—	BV	1.25	2.75	4.50	7.00

Y# 18 1/16 ASHRAFI
0.6980 g., 0.9100 Gold 0.0204 oz. AGW **Obv:** Persian letter "M" for Mahbub above "k" of "Mulk" **Obv. Insc.:** "Asaf Jah, Nizam al-Mulk" **Mint:** Haidarabad (Farkhanda Bunyad)

Date	Mintage	Good	VG	F	VF	XF
AH1321//37	—	15.00	22.00	32.00	40.00	60.00

Y# 19 1/8 ASHRAFI
1.3970 g., 0.9100 Gold 0.0409 oz. AGW **Obv:** Persian letter "M" for Mahbub above "k" of "Mulk" **Obv. Insc.:** "Asaf Jah, Nizam al-Mulk" **Mint:** Haidarabad (Farkhanda Bunyad)

Date	Mintage	Good	VG	F	VF	XF
AH1320	—	—	BV	45.00	60.00	80.00
AH1321	—	—	BV	45.00	60.00	80.00

Y# 20 1/4 ASHRAFI
2.7940 g., 0.9100 Gold 0.0817 oz. AGW **Obv:** Persian letter "M" for Mahbub above "k" of "Mulk" **Obv. Insc.:** "Asaf Jah, Nizam al-Mulk" **Mint:** Haidarabad (Farkhanda Bunyad)

Date	Mintage	Good	VG	F	VF	XF
AH1318//35 (sic)	—	—	BV	70.00	85.00	110
AH1319//35	—	—	BV	70.00	85.00	110

Y# 21 1/2 ASHRAFI
5.5890 g., 0.9100 Gold 0.1635 oz. AGW **Obv:** Persian letter "M" for Mahbub above "k" of "Mulk" **Obv. Insc.:** "Asaf Jah, Nizam al-Mulk" **Mint:** Haidarabad (Farkhanda Bunyad)

Date	Mintage	Good	VG	F	VF	XF
AH1320	—	—	BV	150	175	225
AH1321	—	—	BV	150	175	225

Y# 22 ASHRAFI
11.1780 g., 0.9100 Gold 0.3270 oz. AGW **Obv:** Persian letter "M" for Mahbub above "k" of "Mulk" **Obv. Insc.:** "Asaf Jah, Nizam al-Mulk" **Mint:** Haidarabad (Farkhanda Bunyad)

Date	Mintage	Good	VG	F	VF	XF
AH1319	—	—	BV	275	300	325
AH1320	—	—	BV	275	300	325
AH1321	—	—	BV	275	300	325

MILLED COINAGE
Provisional Series

Y# 29 2 ANNAS
1.3970 g., 0.8180 Silver 0.0367 oz. ASW **Obv:** Persian letter "M" for Mahbub above "k" of "Mulk" **Obv. Insc.:** "Asaf Jah, Nizam al-Mulk", (Founder of the Nizami line) **Mint:** Haidarabad (Farkhanda Bunyad)

Date	Mintage	VG	F	VF	XF	Unc
AH1318//35 (sic)	—	/	13.50	27.50	37.50	75.00

Y# 30 4 ANNAS
2.7940 g., 0.8180 Silver 0.0735 oz. ASW **Obv:** Persian letter "M" for Mahbub above "k" of "Mulk" **Obv. Insc.:** "Asaf Jah, Nizam al-Mulk" **Mint:** Haidarabad (Farkhanda Bunyad)

Date	Mintage	VG	F	VF	XF	Unc
AH1318//35 (sic)	—	—	12.50	25.00	35.00	75.00

Y# 31 8 ANNAS
5.5890 g., 0.8180 Silver 0.1470 oz. ASW **Obv:** Persian letter "M" for Mahbub above "k" of "Mulk" **Obv. Insc.:** "Asaf Jah, Nizam al-Mulk" **Mint:** Haidarabad (Farkhanda Bunyad)

Date	Mintage	VG	F	VF	XF	Unc
AH1318//34	—	10.00	20.00	30.00	40.00	85.00

MILLED COINAGE
Standard Series

Year 25

Note: The AH date exists with two different regnal years in many cases.

Type I   Type II

The early renditions of the name of Asaf Jah in Type I included an accent bar at lower right. This was removed for Type II during the production year of AH 1328. Numerals for 92 appear above similar to earlier coinage not to be confused with regnal years or date.

Y# 34 PAI
Copper **Obv:** Toughra **Mint:** Haidarabad (Farkhanda Bunyad)

Date	Mintage	VG	F	VF	XF	Unc
AH1326//42	—	—	2.50	6.00	15.00	25.00
AH1327//42	—	—	2.50	6.00	15.00	25.00

Y# 35 2 PAI
Copper **Obv:** Toughra **Mint:** Haidarabad (Farkhanda Bunyad)

Date	Mintage	VG	F	VF	XF	Unc
AH1322//37	—	—	0.20	0.50	1.00	3.00
AH1322//38	—	—	0.20	0.50	1.00	3.00
AH1322//39 (sic)	—	—	0.20	0.50	1.00	3.00
AH1323//38	—	—	0.20	0.50	1.00	3.00
AH1323//39	—	—	0.20	0.50	1.00	3.00
AH1323//40 (sic)	—	—	0.20	0.50	1.00	3.00
AH1323//41 (sic)	—	—	0.20	0.50	1.00	3.00
AH1324//39	—	—	0.20	0.50	1.00	3.00
AH1324//40	—	—	0.20	0.50	1.00	3.00
AH1324//41 (sic)	—	—	0.20	0.50	1.00	3.00
AH1325//40	—	—	0.20	0.50	1.00	3.00
AH1325//41	—	—	0.20	0.50	1.00	3.00
AH1328//42	—	—	0.20	0.50	1.00	3.00
AH1329//43 (sic)	—	—	0.20	0.50	1.00	3.00
AH1329//44	—	—	0.20	0.50	1.00	3.00
AH1329//45 (sic)	—	—	0.20	0.50	1.00	3.00

Y# 36 1/2 ANNA
Copper **Obv:** Toughra **Mint:** Haidarabad (Farkhanda Bunyad)

Date	Mintage	VG	F	VF	XF	Unc
AH1324//38 (sic)	—	—	1.50	4.00	7.00	12.00
AH1324//40	—	—	0.75	2.00	4.00	9.00
AH1325//40	—	—	0.75	2.00	4.00	9.00
AH1325//41 (sic)	—	—	0.75	2.00	4.00	9.00
AH1324//41	—	—	0.75	2.00	4.00	9.00
AH1326//41	—	—	0.75	2.00	4.00	9.00
AH1329//44	—	—	0.75	2.00	4.00	9.00

Y# 37 2 ANNAS
1.3900 g., 0.8180 Silver 0.0366 oz. ASW, 15 mm. **Obv:** Chahar Minar gateway **Mint:** Haidarabad (Farkhanda Bunyad)

Date	Mintage	VG	F	VF	XF	Unc
AH1323//34	—	—	1.75	3.50	6.00	10.00

Note: R.Y. '34' error for '39'

| AH1323//39 | — | — | 1.00 | 1.85 | 3.00 | 6.00 |

Y# 38.1 4 ANNAS
2.7940 g., 0.8180 Silver 0.0735 oz. ASW, 20 mm. **Obv:** Chahar Minar gateway, signature variety Type I between minarets **Mint:** Haidarabad (Farkhanda Bunyad)

Date	Mintage	VG	F	VF	XF	Unc
AH1323//39	—	—	2.75	5.50	7.50	12.50
AH1326//43 (sic)	—	—	8.00	16.50	25.00	40.00

Y# 38.2 4 ANNAS
2.7940 g., 0.8180 Silver 0.0735 oz. ASW, 20 mm. **Obv:** Chahar Minar gateway, signature variety Type I between minarets **Mint:** Haidarabad (Farkhanda Bunyad) **Note:** Struck with dies of 1/2 Ashrafi.

Date	Mintage	VG	F	VF	XF	Unc
AH1324//40 Rare	—	—	—	—	—	—

Y# 38.3 4 ANNAS
2.7940 g., 0.8180 Silver 0.0735 oz. ASW, 20 mm. **Obv:** Chahar Minar gateway, signature variety Type II between minarets **Mint:** Haidarabad (Farkhanda Bunyad)

Date	Mintage	VG	F	VF	XF	Unc
AH1328//43	—	—	2.50	5.00	6.50	11.50
AH1329//44	—	—	2.50	5.00	6.00	10.00

Y# 39.1 8 ANNAS
5.5890 g., 0.8180 Silver 0.1470 oz. ASW, 24 mm. **Obv:** Chahar Minar gateway, signature variety Type I **Mint:** Haidarabad (Farkhanda Bunyad)

Date	Mintage	VG	F	VF	XF	Unc
AH1322//38	—	—	—	—	—	—

Y# 39.2 8 ANNAS
5.5890 g., 0.8180 Silver 0.1470 oz. ASW, 24 mm. **Obv:** Chahar Minar gateway, signature variety Type II between minarets **Mint:** Haidarabad (Farkhanda Bunyad)

Date	Mintage	VG	F	VF	XF	Unc
AH1328//43	—	—	3.75	7.50	10.00	16.50
AH1329//44	—	—	3.75	7.50	10.00	16.50

Y# 40.1 RUPEE
11.1780 g., 0.8180 Silver 0.2940 oz. ASW, 30 mm. **Obv:** Chahar Minar gateway, signature variety Type I between minarets **Mint:** Haidarabad (Farkhanda Bunyad)

Date	Mintage	VG	F	VF	XF	Unc
AH1319//35	—	—	6.50	13.50	18.50	30.00
AH1321//37	—	—	6.50	13.50	18.50	30.00
AH1322//38 (sic)	—	—	6.00	12.50	15.00	25.00
AH1321//38	—	—	6.00	12.50	15.00	25.00
AH1323//39 (sic)	—	—	6.00	12.50	15.00	25.00
AH1322//39	—	—	6.00	12.50	15.00	25.00
AH1324//40	—	—	6.00	12.50	15.00	25.00
AH1325//41	—	—	6.00	12.50	15.00	25.00
AH1326//41	—	—	6.00	12.50	15.00	25.00

Y# 40.2 RUPEE
11.1780 g., 0.8180 Silver 0.2940 oz. ASW, 30 mm. **Obv:** Chahar Minar gateway, signature variety Type II between minarets **Mint:** Haidarabad (Farkhanda Bunyad)

Date	Mintage	VG	F	VF	XF	Unc
AH1328//43	—	—	6.00	12.50	15.00	25.00
AH1329//44	—	—	6.00	12.50	15.00	25.00

Y# 41.1 1/8 ASHRAFI
1.3940 g., 0.9100 Gold 0.0408 oz. AGW **Obv:** Chahar Minar gateway, signature variety Type I between minarets **Mint:** Haidarabad (Farkhanda Bunyad)

Date	Mintage	VG	F	VF	XF	Unc
AH1325//41	—	BV	40.00	55.00	75.00	100

Y# 41.2 1/8 ASHRAFI
1.3940 g., 0.9100 Gold 0.0408 oz. AGW **Obv:** Chahar Minar gateway, signature variety Type II between minarets **Mint:** Haidarabad (Farkhanda Bunyad)

Date	Mintage	VG	F	VF	XF	Unc
AH1329//44	—	BV	40.00	55.00	75.00	100

Y# 42.1 1/4 ASHRAFI
2.7940 g., 0.9100 Gold 0.0817 oz. AGW **Obv:** Chahar Minar gateway, signature variety Type I between minarets **Mint:** Haidarabad (Farkhanda Bunyad)

Date	Mintage	VG	F	VF	XF	Unc
AH1325//41	—	BV	70.00	85.00	110	150

Y# 42.2 1/4 ASHRAFI
2.7940 g., 0.9100 Gold 0.0817 oz. AGW **Obv:** Chahar Minar gateway, signature variety Type II between minarets **Mint:** Haidarabad (Farkhanda Bunyad)

Date	Mintage	VG	F	VF	XF	Unc
AH1327//42	—	BV	70.00	85.00	100	150
AH1328//43	—	BV	70.00	85.00	100	150
AH1329//44	—	BV	70.00	85.00	100	150

Y# 43.1 1/2 ASHRAFI
5.5890 g., 0.9100 Gold 0.1635 oz. AGW **Obv:** Chahar Minar gateway, signature variety Type I between minarets **Mint:** Haidarabad (Farkhanda Bunyad)

Date	Mintage	VG	F	VF	XF	Unc
AH1325//41	—	BV	140	160	185	275
AH1326//41	—	BV	140	160	185	275

Y# 43.2 1/2 ASHRAFI
5.5890 g., 0.9100 Gold 0.1635 oz. AGW **Obv:** Chahar Minar gateway, signature variety Type II between minarets **Mint:** Haidarabad (Farkhanda Bunyad)

Date	Mintage	VG	F	VF	XF	Unc
AH1328//43	—	BV	140	160	185	275
AH1329//44	—	BV	140	160	185	275

Y# 44.1 ASHRAFI
11.1780 g., 0.9100 Gold 0.3270 oz. AGW **Obv:** Chahar Minar gateway, signature variety Type I between minarets **Mint:** Haidarabad (Farkhanda Bunyad)

Date	Mintage	VG	F	VF	XF	Unc
AH1325//41	—	—	BV	280	325	400

Y# 44.2 ASHRAFI
11.1780 g., 0.9100 Gold 0.3270 oz. AGW **Obv:** Chahar Minar gateway, signature variety Type II between minarets **Mint:** Haidarabad (Farkhanda Bunyad)

Date	Mintage	VG	F	VF	XF	Unc
AH1328//43	—	—	BV	280	325	400
AH1329//44	—	—	BV	280	325	400

Mir Usman Ali Khan
AH1329-1367 / 1911-1948AD

MILLED COINAGE
First Series

Y# 45 PAI
Bronze **Obv:** Toughra **Mint:** Haidarabad (Farkhanda Bunyad)

Date	Mintage	VG	F	VF	XF	Unc
AH1338	—	—	0.20	0.50	1.00	3.00
AH1344//15	—	—	0.20	0.50	1.00	3.00
AH1349//20	—	—	0.20	0.50	1.00	3.00
AH1352//23	—	—	0.20	0.50	1.00	3.00
AH1352//24	—	—	0.20	0.50	1.00	3.00
AH1353//23 (sic)	—	—	0.20	0.50	1.00	3.00
AH1353//24	—	—	0.20	0.50	1.00	3.00

Y# 46a 2 PAI
3.9000 g., Bronze **Obv:** Full "Ain" in toughra **Mint:** Haidarabad (Farkhanda Bunyad)

Date	Mintage	VG	F	VF	XF	Unc
AH1330//1	—	—	0.20	0.50	1.00	2.00
AH1330//2	—	—	0.20	0.50	1.00	2.00
AH1331//2	—	—	0.20	0.50	1.00	2.00
AH1331//3	—	—	0.20	0.50	1.00	2.00
AH1332//3	—	—	0.20	0.50	1.00	2.00
AH1333//3 (sic)	—	—	0.20	0.50	1.00	2.00
AH1332//4	—	—	0.20	0.50	1.00	2.00
AH1333//4	—	—	0.20	0.50	1.00	2.00
AH1334//3 (sic)	—	—	0.20	0.50	1.00	2.00
AH1333//5	—	—	0.20	0.50	1.00	2.00
AH1335//6	—	—	0.20	0.50	1.00	2.00
AH1336//7	—	—	0.20	0.50	1.00	2.00
AH1335//7	—	—	0.20	0.50	1.00	2.00
AH1337//7	—	—	0.20	0.50	1.00	2.00
AH1337//8	—	—	0.20	0.50	1.00	2.00
AH1336//8	—	—	0.20	0.50	1.00	2.00
AH1338//8	—	—	0.20	0.50	1.00	2.00
AH1338//9	—	—	0.20	0.50	1.00	2.00
AH1339//10	—	—	0.20	0.50	1.00	2.00
AH1338//11 (sic)	—	—	0.20	0.50	1.00	2.00
AH1339//11	—	—	0.20	0.50	1.00	2.00
AH1342//13	—	—	0.20	0.50	1.00	2.00
AH1342//14	—	—	0.20	0.50	1.00	2.00
AH1343//14	—	—	0.20	0.50	1.00	2.00
AH1343//15	—	—	0.20	0.50	1.00	2.00
AH1344//15	—	—	0.20	0.50	1.00	2.00
AH1345//16	—	—	0.20	0.50	1.00	2.00
AH1347//18	—	—	0.20	0.50	1.00	2.00
AH1347//19	—	—	0.20	0.50	1.00	2.00
AH1348//19	—	—	0.20	0.50	1.00	2.00
AH1348//20	—	—	0.20	0.50	1.00	2.00
AH1349//20	—	—	0.20	0.50	1.00	2.00

Y# 46 2 PAI
Bronze **Obv:** Short "Ain" in toughra **Mint:** Haidarabad (Farkhanda Bunyad) **Note:** See also 1 Rupee, Y#53 and Y#53a.

Date	Mintage	VG	F	VF	XF	Unc
AH1329//1	—	—	6.00	15.00	25.00	50.00
AH1330//1	—	—	6.00	15.00	25.00	50.00

Y# 47 1/2 ANNA
Bronze **Obv:** Toughra **Mint:** Haidarabad (Farkhanda Bunyad)

Date	Mintage	VG	F	VF	XF	Unc
AH1332//2 (sic)	—	—	0.40	1.00	2.00	5.00
AH1332//3	—	—	0.40	1.00	2.00	5.00
AH1334//4 (sic)	—	—	0.40	1.00	2.00	5.00
AH1344//15	—	—	0.40	1.00	2.00	5.00
AH1348//20	—	—	0.40	1.00	2.00	5.00

Y# 48 ANNA
Copper-Nickel **Obv:** Toughra **Mint:** Haidarabad (Farkhanda Bunyad) **Note:** Round flan.

Date	Mintage	VG	F	VF	XF	Unc
AH1338	—	—	0.20	0.50	1.00	2.00
AH1339	—	—	0.20	0.50	1.00	2.00
AH1340	—	—	0.20	0.50	1.00	2.00
AH1341	—	—	0.20	0.50	1.00	2.00
AH1344	—	—	0.20	0.50	1.00	2.00
AH1347	—	—	0.20	0.50	1.00	2.00
AH1348	—	—	0.20	0.50	1.00	2.00
AH1349	—	—	0.20	0.50	1.00	2.00
AH1351	—	—	0.20	0.50	1.00	2.00
AH1352	—	—	0.20	0.50	1.00	2.00
AH1353	—	—	0.20	0.50	1.00	2.00
AH1354	—	—	0.20	0.50	1.00	2.00

Y# 49 ANNA
Copper-Nickel **Obv:** Toughra **Mint:** Haidarabad (Farkhanda Bunyad) **Note:** Square flan.

Date	Mintage	VG	F	VF	XF	Unc
AH1356	—	—	0.20	0.50	1.00	2.00
AH1357	—	—	0.20	0.50	1.00	2.00
AH1358	—	—	0.20	0.50	1.00	2.00
AH1359	—	—	0.20	0.50	1.00	2.00
AH1360	—	—	0.20	0.50	1.00	2.00
AH1361	—	—	0.20	0.50	1.00	2.00

Y# 50 2 ANNAS
1.3970 g., 0.8180 Silver 0.0367 oz. ASW **Obv:** Chahar Minar gateway **Mint:** Haidarabad (Farkhanda Bunyad)

Date	Mintage	VG	F	VF	XF	Unc
AH1335//6	—	—	BV	1.00	2.00	5.00
AH1337//9	—	—	BV	1.00	2.00	5.00
AH1338//10	—	—	BV	1.00	2.00	5.00
AH1340//11	—	—	BV	1.00	2.00	5.00
AH1341//13	—	—	BV	1.00	2.00	5.00
AH1342//13	—	—	BV	1.00	2.00	5.00
AH1341//14 (sic)	—	—	BV	1.00	2.00	5.00
AH1343//14	—	—	BV	1.00	2.00	5.00
AH1343//15	—	—	BV	1.00	2.00	5.00
AH1347//18	—	—	BV	1.00	2.00	5.00
AH1348//19	—	—	BV	1.00	2.00	5.00
AH1351//22	—	—	BV	1.00	2.00	5.00
AH1355//26	—	—	BV	1.00	2.00	5.00

Y# 51 4 ANNAS
2.7940 g., 0.8180 Silver 0.0735 oz. ASW **Obv:** Chahar Minar gateway **Mint:** Haidarabad (Farkhanda Bunyad)

Date	Mintage	VG	F	VF	XF	Unc
AH1337//9	—	—	BV	2.00	3.00	5.00
AH1340//11	—	—	BV	2.00	3.00	5.00
AH1342//13	—	—	BV	2.00	3.00	5.00
AH1342//14	—	—	BV	2.00	3.00	5.00
AH1348//19	—	—	BV	2.00	3.00	5.00
AH1351//22	—	—	BV	2.00	3.00	5.00
AH1354//25	—	—	BV	2.00	3.00	5.00
AH1358//30	—	—	BV	2.00	3.00	5.00

Y# 52 8 ANNAS
5.5890 g., 0.8180 Silver 0.1470 oz. ASW **Obv:** Chahar Minar gateway **Mint:** Haidarabad (Farkhanda Bunyad)

Date	Mintage	VG	F	VF	XF	Unc
AH1337//9	—	—	BV	3.00	4.00	9.00
AH1342//13	—	—	BV	3.00	4.00	9.00
AH1343//13 (sic)	—	—	BV	3.00	4.00	9.00
AH1354//25	—	—	BV	3.00	4.00	9.00

Y# 53 RUPEE
11.1780 g., 0.8180 Silver 0.2940 oz. ASW **Obv:** Chahar Minar gateway with short initials "Ain" in doorway **Mint:** Haidarabad (Farkhanda Bunyad)

Date	Mintage	VG	F	VF	XF	Unc
AH1330//1	—	BV	5.00	10.00	20.00	30.00

Y# 53a RUPEE
11.1780 g., 0.8180 Silver 0.2940 oz. ASW **Obv:** Chahar Minar gateway with full "Ain" in doorway **Mint:** Haidarabad (Farkhanda Bunyad)

Date	Mintage	VG	F	VF	XF	Unc
AH1330//1	—	—	BV	5.00	8.00	15.00
AH1330//2	—	—	BV	5.00	8.00	15.00
AH1331//2	—	—	BV	5.00	8.00	15.00
AH1331//3	—	—	BV	5.00	8.00	15.00
AH1332//3	—	—	BV	5.00	8.00	15.00
AH1334//6	—	—	BV	5.00	8.00	15.00
AH1335//6	—	—	BV	5.00	8.00	15.00
AH1335//7	—	—	BV	5.00	8.00	15.00
AH1336//7	—	—	BV	5.00	8.00	15.00
AH1337//8	—	—	BV	5.00	8.00	15.00
AH1337//9	—	—	BV	5.00	8.00	15.00
AH1338//9	—	—	BV	5.00	8.00	15.00
AH1339//9 (sic)	—	—	BV	5.00	8.00	15.00
AH1340//11	—	—	BV	5.00	8.00	15.00
AH1341//12	—	—	BV	5.00	8.00	15.00
AH1342//13	—	—	BV	5.00	8.00	15.00
AH1343//14	—	—	BV	5.00	8.00	15.00

Y# 54.1 1/8 ASHRAFI
1.3940 g., 0.9100 Gold 0.0408 oz. AGW **Obv:** Chahar Minar gateway with short "Ain" in doorway **Mint:** Haidarabad (Farkhanda Bunyad)

Date	Mintage	VG	F	VF	XF	Unc
AH1329//1 Rare						

Y# 54.2 1/8 ASHRAFI
1.3940 g., 0.9100 Gold 0.0408 oz. AGW **Obv:** Chahar Minar gateway with full "Ain" in doorway **Mint:** Haidarabad (Farkhanda Bunyad)

Date	Mintage	VG	F	VF	XF	Unc
AH1337//8	—	—	BV	42.50	50.00	80.00
AH1340//11	—	—	BV	42.50	50.00	80.00
AH1343//14	—	—	BV	42.50	50.00	80.00

Date	Mintage	VG	F	VF	XF	Unc
AH1344//15	—	—	BV	42.50	50.00	80.00
AH1353//24	—	—	BV	42.50	50.00	80.00
AH1354//25	—	—	BV	42.50	50.00	80.00
AH1356//27	—	—	BV	42.50	50.00	80.00
AH1360//31	—	—	BV	42.50	50.00	80.00
AH1366//37	—	—	BV	42.50	50.00	80.00
AH1368//39	—	—	BV	42.50	50.00	80.00

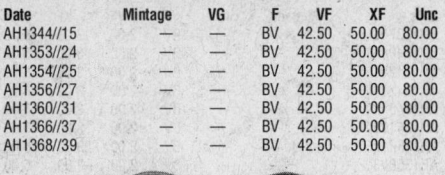

Y# 55   1/4 ASHRAFI
2.7940 g., 0.9100 Gold 0.0817 oz. AGW **Obv:** Chahar Minar gateway **Mint:** Haidarabad (Farkhanda Bunyad)

Date	Mintage	VG	F	VF	XF	Unc
AH1337//8	—	—	BV	75.00	90.00	135
AH1342//13	—	—	BV	75.00	90.00	135
AH1342//14	—	—	BV	75.00	90.00	135
AH1349//20	—	—	BV	75.00	90.00	135
AH1353//23 (sic)	—	—	BV	75.00	90.00	135
AH1354//25	—	—	BV	75.00	90.00	135
AH1357//29	—	—	BV	75.00	90.00	135
AH1360//31	—	—	BV	75.00	90.00	135
AH1367//38	—	—	BV	75.00	90.00	135

Y# 56.1   1/2 ASHRAFI
5.5890 g., 0.9100 Gold 0.1635 oz. AGW **Obv:** Chahar Minar gateway with short "Ain" in doorway **Mint:** Haidarabad (Farkhanda Bunyad)

Date	Mintage	VG	F	VF	XF	Unc
AH1329//1	—	—	BV	145	185	300

Y# 56.2   1/2 ASHRAFI
5.5890 g., 0.9100 Gold 0.1635 oz. AGW **Obv:** Chahar Minar gateway with full "Ain" in doorway **Mint:** Haidarabad (Farkhanda Bunyad)

Date	Mintage	VG	F	VF	XF	Unc
AH1337//8	—	—	BV	150	175	250
AH1341//12	—	—	BV	150	175	250
AH1342//14	—	—	BV	150	175	250
AH1343//14	—	—	BV	150	175	250
AH1344//14 (sic)	—	—	BV	150	175	250
AH1345//16	—	—	BV	150	175	250
AH1349//20	—	—	BV	150	175	250
AH1354//25	—	—	BV	150	175	250
AH1357//29	—	—	BV	150	175	250
AH1366//37	—	—	BV	150	175	250
AH1367//38	—	—	BV	150	175	250

Y# 57   ASHRAFI
11.1780 g., 0.9100 Gold 0.3270 oz. AGW **Obv:** Chahar Minar gateway with short initial "Ain" in doorway **Mint:** Haidarabad (Farkhanda Bunyad)

Date	Mintage	VG	F	VF	XF	Unc
AH1329//1	—	—	BV	300	350	500
AH1330//1	—	—	BV	300	350	500

Y# 57a   ASHRAFI
11.1780 g., 0.9100 Gold 0.3270 oz. AGW **Obv:** Chahar Minar gateway with full initial "Ain" in doorway **Mint:** Haidarabad (Farkhanda Bunyad)

Date	Mintage	VG	F	VF	XF	Unc
AH1331//3	—	—	BV	285	325	450
AH1332//4	—	—	BV	285	325	450
AH1333//4	—	—	BV	285	325	450
AH1337//8	—	—	BV	285	325	450
AH1337//9	—	—	BV	285	325	450
AH1338//9	—	—	BV	285	325	450
AH1340//11	—	—	BV	285	325	450

Date	Mintage	VG	F	VF	XF	Unc
AH1342//14	—	—	BV	285	325	450
AH1343//14	—	—	BV	285	325	450
AH1344//15	—	—	BV	285	325	450
AH1348//19	—	—	BV	285	325	450
AH1349//20	—	—	BV	285	325	450
AH1354//25	—	—	BV	285	325	450
AH1358//30	—	—	BV	285	325	450
AH1360//31	—	—	BV	285	325	450
AH1362//34	—	—	BV	285	325	450
AH1364//35	—	—	BV	285	325	450

MILLED COINAGE
Second Series

Y# 58   2 PAI
Bronze **Mint:** Haidarabad (Farkhanda Bunyad)

Date	Mintage	VG	F	VF	XF	Unc
AH1362//33	—	—	0.25	0.35	0.50	1.00
AH1363//34	—	—	0.25	0.35	0.50	1.00
AH1363//35	—	—	—	0.25	0.50	1.00
AH1364//35	—	—	—	0.25	0.50	1.00
AH1365//36	—	—	—	0.25	0.50	1.00
AH1366//37	—	—	—	0.25	0.50	1.00
AH1368//39	—	—	—	0.25	0.50	1.00

Y# 59   ANNA
Bronze **Obv:** Toughra **Mint:** Haidarabad (Farkhanda Bunyad) **Note:** Square flan.

Date	Mintage	VG	F	VF	XF	Unc
AH1361	—	—	0.25	0.50	0.75	1.50
AH1362	—	—	0.25	0.50	0.75	1.50
AH1364	—	—	0.25	0.50	0.75	1.50
AH1365	—	—	0.25	0.50	0.75	1.50
AH1366	—	—	0.25	0.50	0.75	1.50
AH1368	—	—	0.25	0.50	0.75	1.50

Y# 60   2 ANNAS
1.3970 g., 0.8180 Silver 0.0367 oz. ASW, 15 mm. **Mint:** Haidarabad (Farkhanda Bunyad)

Date	Mintage	VG	F	VF	XF	Unc
AH1362//33	—	—	BV	0.60	1.00	2.00

Y# 64   2 ANNAS
Nickel **Mint:** Haidarabad (Farkhanda Bunyad)

Date	Mintage	VG	F	VF	XF	Unc
AH1366//37	—	—	—	0.25	0.50	1.00
AH1368//39	—	—	—	0.35	0.50	1.00

Y# 61   4 ANNAS
2.7940 g., 0.8180 Silver 0.0735 oz. ASW, 20 mm. **Mint:** Haidarabad (Farkhanda Bunyad)

Date	Mintage	VG	F	VF	XF	Unc
AH1362//33	—	—	BV	1.20	2.00	3.00
AH1362//34	—	—	BV	1.20	2.00	3.00
AH1364//33 (sic)	—	—	BV	1.20	2.00	3.00
AH1364//35	—	—	BV	1.20	2.00	3.00
AH1364//36	—	—	BV	1.20	2.00	3.00
AH1365//36	—	—	BV	1.20	2.00	3.00

Y# 65   4 ANNAS
Nickel **Mint:** Haidarabad (Farkhanda Bunyad)

Date	Mintage	VG	F	VF	XF	Unc
AH1366//37	—	—	0.25	0.50	0.75	1.50
AH1368//37	—	—	—	—	—	—
AH1368//39	—	—	0.25	0.50	0.75	1.50

Y# 62   8 ANNAS
5.5890 g., 0.8180 Silver 0.1470 oz. ASW, 24 mm. **Mint:** Haidarabad (Farkhanda Bunyad)

Date	Mintage	VG	F	VF	XF	Unc
AH1363//34	—	—	2.00	5.00	8.00	15.00

Y# 66   8 ANNAS
Nickel **Mint:** Haidarabad (Farkhanda Bunyad)

Date	Mintage	VG	F	VF	XF	Unc
AH1366//37	—	—	0.25	0.50	1.00	2.00

Y# 63   RUPEE
11.1780 g., Silver, 30 mm. **Mint:** Haidarabad (Farkhanda Bunyad)

Date	Mintage	VG	F	VF	XF	Unc
AH1361//31	—	—	BV	5.00	8.00	15.00
AH1361//32	—	—	BV	5.00	8.00	15.00
AH1362//34	—	—	BV	5.00	8.00	15.00
AH1364//35	—	—	BV	5.00	8.00	15.00
AH1364//36	—	—	BV	5.00	8.00	15.00
AH1365//36	—	—	BV	5.00	8.00	15.00

Y# 67   ASHRAFI
11.1780 g., 0.9100 Gold 0.3270 oz. AGW **Mint:** Haidarabad (Farkhanda Bunyad)

Date	Mintage	VG	F	VF	XF	Unc
AH1368//39	—	—	—	—	—	—

PATTERNS
Including off metal strikes

KM#	Date	Mintage	Identification	Mkt Val
Pn10	AH1319//35	—	Rupee. Silver. Y#53a.	—
Pn11	AH1324//40	—	1/2 Ashrafi. Silver. Y#43.	500
Pn12	AH1324//40	—	Ashrafi. Silver. Y#44.	500
Pn13	AH1362/33	—	2 Annas. Copper. 1.3800 g. Copper, Y#60.	—
Pn14	AH1366/37	—	2 Pai. Bronze. 0.8100 g. Small, thin flan, larger hole, Y#58.	—

INDORE

The Holkars were one of the three dominant Maratha powers (with the Peshwas and Sindhias), with major landholdings in Central India.

Indore State originated in 1728 with a grant of land north of the Narbada river by the Maratha Peshwa of Poona to Malhar Rao Holkar, a cavalry commander in his service. After Holkar's death (ca.1765) his daughter-in-law, Ahalya Bai, assumed the position of Queen Regent. Together with Tukoji Rao she effectively ruled the State until her death thirty years later. But it was left to Tukoji's son, Jaswant Rao, to challenge the dominance of the Poona Marathas in the Maratha Confederacy, eventually defeating the Peshwa's army in 1802. But at this point the fortunes of the Holkars suffered a serious reverse. Although Jaswant Rao had initially defeated a small British force under Col. William Monson, he was badly beaten by a contingent under Lord Lake. As a result Holkar was forced to cede a considerable portion of his territory and from this time until India's independence in 1947, the residual State of Indore was obliged to accept British protection.

For more detailed data on the Indore series, see *A Study of Holkar State Coinage*, by P.K.Sethi, S.K. Bhatt and R. Holkar (1976).

HOLKAR RULERS
Shivaji Rao, VS1943-1960/FE1296-1313/1886-1903AD
Tukoji Rao III, VS1960-1983/1903-1926AD
Yashwant Rao, VS1983-2005/1926-1948AD

HONORIFIC TITLE
Bahadur

MINT

اندور or इंदोर

Indore

INDORE MINT
Coins issued intermittently from 1772-1935AD.

BRITISH PROTECTORATE

Shivaji Rao
VS1943-1960 / FE1296-1313 / 1886-1903AD

MILLED COINAGE

KM# 33.3   1/4 ANNA
Copper, 27 mm.   **Obv:** Continuous legend around reclining bull **Obv. Leg.:** Shivaji Rao...Bahadur **Rev:** "Indore" above denomination and date **Mint:** Indore **Note:** Floral border varieties exist. Weight varies 6.026-6.674 grams.

Date	Mintage	Good	VG	F	VF	XF
VS1958(1901)	—	—	0.50	1.00	3.00	6.00
VS1959(1902)	—	—	0.50	1.00	3.00	6.00

KM# 35.3   1/2 ANNA
Copper, 31 mm.   **Obv:** Continuous legend around reclining bull **Obv. Leg.:** Shivaji Rao **Rev:** "Indore" above denomination and date **Mint:** Indore

Date	Mintage	Good	VG	F	VF	XF
VS1958(1901)	—	—	1.00	2.00	4.00	9.00
VS1959(1902)	—	—	1.00	2.00	4.00	9.00

MILLED COINAGE
Third Series

This series was introduced in 1898 to counteract counterfeiting of the second series which had begun to proliferate as a result of a sharp fall in the price of silver. Idle minting machines were reactivated for this purpose, but the series was short-lived.

KM# 47.2   RUPEE
11.2000 g., Silver **Obv:** Bust facing; continuous legend **Rev:** Arms **Mint:** Indore

Date	Mintage	VG	F	VF	XF	Unc
VS1958(1901)	—	—	75.00	150	225	375

Yashwant Rao II
VS1983-2005 / 1926-1948AD

MILLED COINAGE
Fourth Series

KM# 49   1/4 ANNA
Copper   **Obv:** Bust facing 3/4 right **Mint:** Indore

Date	Mintage	VG	F	VF	XF	Unc
VS1992 - 1935	—	—	0.50	1.00	3.50	7.00

KM# 50   1/2 ANNA
Copper   **Obv:** Bust facing **Mint:** Indore

Date	Mintage	VG	F	VF	XF	Unc
VS1992 - 1935	—	—	0.60	1.25	4.00	8.00

JAIPUR

Tradition has it that the region of Jaipur, located in northwest India, once belonged to an ancient Kachwaha Rajput dynasty which claimed descent from Kush, one of the sons of Rama, King of Ayodhya. But the Princely State of Jaipur originated in the 12th century. Comparatively small in size, the State remained largely unnoticed until after the 16th century when the Jaipur royal house became famous for its military skills and thereafter supplied the Mughals with some of their more distinguished generals. The city of Jaipur was founded about 1728 by Maharaja Jai Singh II who was well known for his knowledge of mathematics and astronomy. The late 18th and early 19th centuries were difficult times for Jaipur. They were marked by internal rivalry, exacerbated by Maratha or Pindari incursions. In 1818 this culminated with a treaty whereby Jaipur came under British protection and oversight.

RULERS
Madho Singh II, 1880-1922AD
Man Singh II, 1922-1949AD

MINT NAMES
Coins were struck at two mints, which bear the following characteristic marks on the reverse:
Sawai Jaipur
Sawai Madhopur

JAIPUR MINT
In the names of Queen Victoria

كوين وكتوريا

ماد هو سنگه

And Madho Singh II

Years 1-43/1880-1922AD
NOTE: Queen Victoria's name was retained on Madho Singh II's coinage until 1922AD. No coins were struck with Edward VII's name by Madho Singh II.

Madho Singh II
AH1298-1341 / 1880-1922AD

HAMMERED COINAGE
Regal Style

To distinguish coins between Ram Singh and his son/successor Madho Singh II, note that the coins of Ram Singh have a small slanting cross or dagger between the Ram and Singh symbols, whereas the coins of Singh II do not.

KM# 130   PAISA
Copper **Obv:** Inscription: Queen Victoria... **Rev:** Jhar, inscription **Rev. Insc.:** "Madho Singh II" **Mint:** Sawai Jaipur **Note:** Weight varies 6.15-6.30g.

Date	Mintage	Good	VG	F	VF	XF
ND//22 (1901)	—	—	0.45	1.00	2.00	—
ND//23 (1902)	—	—	0.45	1.00	2.00	—
ND//24 (1903)	—	—	0.45	1.00	2.00	—
ND//25 (1904)	—	—	0.45	1.00	2.00	—
ND//25 (1904)	—	—	0.45	1.00	2.00	—
ND//27 (1906)	—	—	0.45	1.00	2.00	—
ND//28 (1907)	—	—	0.45	1.00	2.00	—
ND//29 (1908)	—	—	0.45	1.00	2.00	—
ND//37 (1916)	—	—	0.45	1.00	2.00	—
ND//38 (1917)	—	—	0.45	1.00	2.00	—
ND//39 (1918)	—	—	0.45	1.00	2.00	—
ND//41 (1920)	—	—	0.45	1.00	2.00	—

KM# 135   1/16 RUPEE
Silver **Obv. Insc.:** Victoria... **Rev:** Jhar **Rev. Insc.:** "Madho Singh II" **Mint:** Sawai Jaipur **Note:** Weight varies 0.67-0.72g.

Date	Mintage	Good	VG	F	VF	XF
ND//33 (1912)	—	2.00	5.00	7.00	10.00	15.00

KM# 137   1/8 RUPEE
Silver **Obv. Insc.:** Victoria... **Rev:** Jhar **Rev. Insc.:** "Madho Singh II" **Mint:** Sawai Jaipur **Note:** Weight varies 1.34-1.45g.

Date	Mintage	Good	VG	F	VF	XF
ND//22 (1901)	—	—	BV	1.00	2.00	5.00
ND//23 (1902)	—	—	BV	1.00	2.00	5.00
ND//26 (1905)	—	—	BV	1.00	2.00	5.00
ND//27 (1906)	—	—	BV	1.00	2.00	5.00
ND//28 (1907)	—	—	BV	1.00	2.00	5.00
ND//29 (1908)	—	—	BV	1.00	2.00	5.00
ND//41 (1920)	—	—	BV	1.00	2.00	5.00
ND//42 (1921)	—	—	BV	1.00	2.00	5.00

KM# 139   1/4 RUPEE
Silver **Obv. Insc.:** Victoria... **Rev:** Jhar **Rev. Insc.:** "Madho Singh II" **Mint:** Sawai Jaipur **Note:** Weight varies 2.68-2.90g.

Date	Mintage	Good	VG	F	VF	XF
ND//22 (1901)	—	—	BV	1.00	3.00	7.00
ND//23 (1902)	—	—	BV	1.00	3.00	7.00
ND//24 (1903)	—	—	BV	1.00	3.00	7.00
ND//26 (1905)	—	—	BV	1.00	3.00	7.00
ND//27 (1906)	—	—	BV	1.00	3.00	7.00
ND//28 (1907)	—	—	BV	1.00	3.00	7.00
ND//29 (1908)	—	—	BV	1.00	3.00	7.00
ND//30 (1909)	—	—	BV	1.00	3.00	7.00
ND//34 (1913)	—	—	BV	1.00	3.00	7.00
ND//37 (1916)	—	—	BV	1.00	3.00	7.00
ND//38 (1917)	—	—	BV	1.00	3.00	7.00
ND//42 (1921)	—	—	BV	1.00	3.00	7.00

KM# 142   1/2 RUPEE
Silver **Obv. Insc.:** Victoria... **Rev:** Jhar **Rev. Insc.:** "Madho Singh II" **Mint:** Sawai Jaipur **Note:** Weight varies 5.35-5.80g.

Date	Mintage	Good	VG	F	VF	XF
ND//22 (1901)	—	—	BV	2.00	4.00	8.00
ND//23 (1902)	—	—	BV	2.00	4.00	8.00
ND//25 (1904)	—	—	BV	2.00	4.00	8.00
ND//26 (1905)	—	—	BV	2.00	4.00	8.00
ND//27 (1906)	—	—	BV	2.00	4.00	8.00
ND//28 (1907)	—	—	BV	2.00	4.00	8.00
ND//29 (1908)	—	—	BV	2.00	4.00	8.00
ND//30 (1909)	—	—	BV	2.00	4.00	8.00
ND//34 (1913)	—	—	BV	2.00	4.00	8.00
ND//37 (1916)	—	—	BV	2.00	4.00	8.00

KM# 145 RUPEE
Silver **Obv. Insc.:** Victoria... **Rev:** Jhar **Rev. Insc.:** "Madho Singh II" **Mint:** Sawai Jaipur **Note:** Weight varies 10.70-11.60g.

Date	Mintage	Good	VG	F	VF	XF
ND//23 (1902)	—	—	BV	3.00	5.00	10.00
ND//24 (1903)	—	—	BV	3.00	5.00	10.00
ND//25 (1904)	—	—	BV	3.00	5.00	10.00
ND//26 (1905)	—	—	BV	3.00	5.00	10.00
ND//27 (1906)	—	—	BV	3.00	5.00	10.00
ND//29 (1908)	—	—	BV	3.00	5.00	10.00
ND//30 (1909)	—	—	BV	3.00	5.00	10.00
ND//31 (1910)	—	—	BV	3.00	5.00	10.00
ND//33 (1912)	—	—	BV	3.00	5.00	10.00
ND//37 (1916)	—	—	BV	3.00	5.00	10.00
191(8)//39	—	—	BV	3.00	5.00	10.00
ND//40 (1919)	—	—	BV	3.00	5.00	10.00
ND//42 (1921)	—	—	BV	3.00	5.00	10.00
ND//43 (1922)	—	—	BV	3.00	5.00	10.00

KM# 150 MOHUR
Gold **Obv. Insc.:** Victoria.... **Rev:** Jhar **Rev. Insc.:** "Madho Singh II" **Mint:** Sawai Jaipur **Note:** Weight varies 10.70-11.40 g.

Date	Mintage	Good	VG	F	VF	XF
ND//25 (1904)	—	—	BV	250	275	325
ND//37 (1916)	—	—	BV	250	275	325
ND//40 (1919)	—	—	BV	250	275	325
ND//41 (1920)	—	—	BV	250	275	325

MILLED COINAGE

KM# 132 NAZARANA NEW PAISA
Copper, 32-36 mm. **Obv. Insc.:** Victoria... **Rev:** Jhar **Rev. Insc.:** "Madho Singh II" **Mint:** Sawai Jaipur **Note:** Size varies. Well-centered issues on thin planchets may be restrikes.

Date	Mintage	Good	VG	F	VF	XF
1901//22	—	—	7.00	17.50	25.00	40.00
1902//23	—	—	7.00	17.50	25.00	40.00
1903//24	—	—	7.00	17.50	25.00	40.00
1904//25	—	—	7.00	17.50	25.00	40.00
1905//26	—	—	7.00	17.50	25.00	40.00
1906//27	—	—	7.00	17.50	25.00	40.00
1907//28	—	—	7.00	17.50	25.00	40.00
1908//29	—	—	7.00	17.50	25.00	40.00
1909//30	—	—	7.00	17.50	25.00	40.00
1910//31	—	—	7.00	17.50	25.00	40.00
1911//32	—	—	7.00	17.50	25.00	40.00
1912//33	—	—	7.00	17.50	25.00	40.00
1913//34	—	—	7.00	17.50	25.00	40.00
1914//35	—	—	7.00	17.50	25.00	40.00
1915//36	—	—	7.00	17.50	25.00	40.00
1916//37	—	—	7.00	17.50	25.00	40.00
1917//38	—	—	7.00	17.50	25.00	40.00

KM# 147 NAZARANA RUPEE
Silver **Obv. Insc.:** Victoria... **Rev:** Jhar **Rev. Insc.:** "Madho Singh II" **Mint:** Sawai Jaipur **Note:** Size varies 36-37mm.

Date	Mintage	Good	VG	F	VF	XF
1901//22	—	—	20.00	40.00	52.50	75.00
1903//24	—	—	20.00	40.00	52.50	75.00
1904//25	—	—	20.00	40.00	52.50	75.00
1906//27	—	—	20.00	40.00	52.50	75.00
1908//29	—	—	20.00	40.00	52.50	75.00
1909//30	—	—	20.00	40.00	52.50	75.00
1910//31	—	—	20.00	40.00	52.50	75.00
1911//32	—	—	20.00	40.00	52.50	75.00

(continued)

Date	Mintage	Good	VG	F	VF	XF
1912//33	—	—	20.00	40.00	52.50	75.00
1913//34	—	—	20.00	40.00	52.50	75.00
1914//35	—	—	20.00	40.00	52.50	75.00
1915//36	—	—	20.00	40.00	52.50	75.00
1916//37	—	—	20.00	40.00	52.50	75.00
1917//38	—	—	20.00	40.00	52.50	75.00
1918/39	—	—	20.00	40.00	52.50	75.00
1919/39	—	—	20.00	40.00	52.50	75.00
1920//41	—	—	20.00	40.00	52.50	75.00
1921//42	—	—	20.00	40.00	52.50	75.00

Man Singh II
AH1341-1369 / 1922-1949AD

HAMMERED COINAGE
Regal Style

To distinguish coins between Ram Singh and his son/successor Madho Singh II, note that the coins of Ram Singh have a small slanting cross or dagger between the Ram and Singh symbols, whereas the coins of Singh II do not.

KM# 175 1/2 PAISA
Copper, 21-23 mm. **Obv. Insc.:** George VI... **Rev:** Jhar **Rev. Insc.:** Man Singh (II)... **Mint:** Sawai Jaipur **Note:** Size varies.

Date	Mintage	Good	VG	F	VF	XF
ND//21 (1942)	—	—	0.80	2.00	5.00	12.00

KM# 158 RUPEE
10.7000 g., Silver **Obv. Insc.:** George V... **Rev:** Jhar **Rev. Insc.:** Man Singh II... **Mint:** Sawai Jaipur

Date	Mintage	Good	VG	F	VF	XF
1922//1	—	—	BV	50.00	90.00	150

KM# 163 MOHUR
Gold **Obv. Insc.:** George V... **Rev:** Jhar **Rev. Insc.:** Man Singh II... **Mint:** Sawai Jaipur **Note:** Weight varies 10.70-11.40 g.

Date	Mintage	Good	VG	F	VF	XF
ND//2 (1923)	—	—	BV	275	300	425
1(924)//3	—	—	BV	275	300	425
1925//4	—	—	BV	275	300	425
19(28)//7	—	—	BV	275	300	425

KM# 200 MOHUR
Gold **Obv. Insc.:** George (VI)... **Rev. Insc.:** Man Singh (II)... **Mint:** Sawai Jaipur **Note:** Weight varies 10.70-11.40 g.

Date	Mintage	Good	VG	F	VF	XF
ND//20 (1941)	—	—	BV	260	275	325
ND//22 (1943)	—	—	BV	260	275	325
ND//26 (1947)	—	—	BV	260	275	325
ND//27 (1948)	—	—	BV	260	275	325
1949//28	—	—	BV	260	275	325

MILLED COINAGE

KM# 185 ANNA
Brass **Obv:** Jhar **Mint:** Sawai Jaipur

Date	Mintage	Good	VG	F	VF	XF
1943	—	—	—	0.25	0.50	1.00

Note: Lg. and sm. denomination

1944/3	—	—	—	0.25	0.50	1.00
1944	—	—	—	0.25	0.50	1.00

KM# 186 ANNA
5.1700 g., Brass **Obv:** Jhar **Mint:** Sawai Jaipur **Note:** Thick planchet; weight varies.

Date	Mintage	Good	VG	F	VF	XF
1943	—	—	—	0.25	0.50	1.50

KM# 187 ANNA
2.7800 g., Brass **Obv:** Jhar **Mint:** Sawai Jaipur **Note:** Thin planchet.

Date	Mintage	Good	VG	F	VF	XF
1943	—	—	—	0.25	0.50	1.00

KM# 188 ANNA
Brass **Obv:** Bust of Man Singh II right **Rev:** Jhar **Mint:** Sawai Jaipur

Date	Mintage	Good	VG	F	VF	XF
1944	—	—	—	0.25	0.50	1.00
1944 Proof; Restrike	—	Value: 100				

KM# 190 2 ANNA
Brass **Rev:** Jhar **Mint:** Sawai Jaipur **Note:** Square flan.

Date	Mintage	Good	VG	F	VF	XF
1942//21	—	—	2.00	5.00	7.00	15.00

KM# 176 1/2 PAISA
Copper, 21-23 mm. **Obv:** George VI **Rev:** Jhar **Rev. Insc.:** Man Singh (II)... **Mint:** Sawai Jaipur **Note:** Crude struck in collar. Size varies.

Date	Mintage	Good	VG	F	VF	XF
ND//22 (1943)	—	—	0.50	1.00	2.00	5.00
ND//23 (1944)	—	—	0.50	1.00	2.00	5.00

KM# 155 NAZARANA PAISA
Copper **Obv. Insc.:** George V... **Rev:** Jhar **Rev. Insc.:** Man Singh II... **Mint:** Sawai Jaipur

Date	Mintage	Good	VG	F	VF	XF
1922//1	—	—	10.00	25.00	40.00	60.00
1923//2	—	—	10.00	25.00	40.00	60.00
1924//3	—	—	10.00	25.00	40.00	60.00
1924//4	—	—	10.00	25.00	40.00	60.00
1925//4	—	—	10.00	25.00	40.00	60.00
1926//5	—	—	10.00	25.00	40.00	60.00
1927//5	—	—	10.00	25.00	40.00	60.00
1927//6	—	—	10.00	25.00	40.00	60.00
1928//7	—	—	10.00	25.00	40.00	60.00
1929//8	—	—	10.00	25.00	40.00	60.00
1930//9	—	—	10.00	25.00	40.00	60.00
1931//10	—	—	10.00	25.00	40.00	60.00
1932//11	—	—	10.00	25.00	40.00	60.00
1933//12	—	—	10.00	25.00	40.00	60.00
1934//13	—	—	10.00	25.00	40.00	60.00
1935//14	—	—	10.00	25.00	40.00	60.00

KM# 167 NAZARANA PAISA
6.4400 g., Copper **Obv. Insc.:** Edward (VIII)... **Rev:** Jhar **Rev. Insc.:** Man Singh (II)... **Mint:** Sawai Jaipur

Date	Mintage	Good	VG	F	VF	XF
1936//15	—	—	60.00	150	225	375

KM# 180 NAZARANA PAISA
Copper **Obv. Insc.:** George VI... **Rev:** Jhar **Rev. Insc.:** Man Singh (II)... **Mint:** Sawai Jaipur

Date	Mintage	Good	VG	F	VF	XF
1937//16	—	—	7.00	17.50	25.00	40.00
1938//17	—	—	7.00	17.50	25.00	40.00
1939//18	—	—	7.00	17.50	25.00	40.00
1940//19	—	—	7.00	17.50	25.00	40.00
1941//19	—	—	7.00	17.50	25.00	40.00
1941//20	—	—	7.00	17.50	25.00	40.00
1942//21	—	—	7.00	17.50	25.00	40.00
1943//22	—	—	7.00	17.50	25.00	40.00
1944//23	—	—	7.00	17.50	25.00	40.00
1945//24	—	—	7.00	17.50	25.00	40.00
1946//25	—	—	7.00	17.50	25.00	40.00
1947//26	—	—	7.00	17.50	25.00	40.00
1947//27	—	—	7.00	17.50	25.00	40.00
1948//27	—	—	7.00	17.50	25.00	40.00
1949//28	—	—	7.00	17.50	25.00	40.00

KM# 159 NAZARANA RUPEE
10.7000 g., Silver **Obv. Insc.:** George V... **Rev:** Jhar **Rev. Insc.:** Man Singh II... **Mint:** Sawai Jaipur

Date	Mintage	Good	VG	F	VF	XF
1924//3	—	—	35.00	75.00	100	150
1928//7	—	—	35.00	75.00	100	150
1932//11	—	—	35.00	75.00	100	150

KM# 170 NAZARANA RUPEE
10.7000 g., Silver **Obv. Insc.:** Edward (VIII)... **Rev:** Jhar **Rev. Insc.:** Man Singh (II)... **Mint:** Sawai Jaipur

Date	Mintage	VG	F	VF	XF	Unc
1936//15 Rare	—	—	—	—	—	—

KM# 196 NAZARANA RUPEE
Silver, 37-38 mm. **Obv. Insc.:** George (VI)... **Rev. Insc.:** Man Singh (II)... **Mint:** Sawai Jaipur

Date	Mintage	Good	VG	F	VF	XF
1938//20	—	—	22.50	42.50	70.00	100
1939//18	—	—	8.50	16.50	28.50	40.00
1941//20	—	—	8.50	16.50	28.50	40.00
1943//22	—	—	8.50	16.50	28.50	40.00
1945//24	—	—	8.50	16.50	28.50	40.00
1948//27	—	—	8.50	16.50	28.50	40.00
1949//28	—	—	8.50	16.50	28.50	40.00

KM# A196 NAZARANA RUPEE
Silver, 30 mm. **Obv. Insc.:** George (V)... **Rev. Insc.:** Man Singh (II)...

Date	Mintage	Good	VG	F	VF	XF
1941//20	—	—	75.00	150	225	375

KM# 195 NAZARANA RUPEE
Silver **Obv:** Similar to KM#196 **Obv. Insc.:** George (VI)... **Rev:** Similar to KM#147 **Rev. Insc.:** Madho Singh (II)... **Mint:** Sawai Jaipur **Note:** Weight varies 10.70-11.60 g.; possibly modern forgeries.

Date	Mintage	Good	VG	F	VF	XF
1949//3	—	—	—	—	—	—

KM# 201 NAZARANA MOHUR
Gold **Obv. Insc.:** George (VI)... **Rev. Insc.:** Man Singh (II)... **Mint:** Sawai Jaipur

Date	Mintage	Good	VG	F	VF	XF
ND1949//28 Rare	—	—	—	—	—	—

JODHPUR

Jodhpur, also known as Marwar, located in northwest India, was the largest Princely State in the Rajputana Agency. Its population in 1941 exceeded two and a half million. The "Maharajadhirajas" ("Great Kings of Kings") of Jodhpur were Rathor Rajputs who claimed an extremely ancient ancestry from Rama, king of Ayodhya. With the collapse of the Rathor rulers of Kanauj in 1194 the family entered Marwar where they laid the foundation of the new state. The city of Jodhpur was built by Rao Jodha in 1459, and the city and the state were named after him. In 1561 the Mughal Emperor Akbar invaded Jodhpur, forcing its submission. In 1679 Emperor Aurangzeb sacked the city, an experience which stimulated the Rajput royal house to forge a new unity among themselves in order to extricate themselves from Mughal hegemony. Internal dissension once again asserted itself and Rajput unity, which had both benefited from and accelerated Mughal decline, fell apart before the Marathas. In 1818 Jodhpur came under British protection and control and after Indian independence in 1947 the State was merged into Rajasthan. Jodhpur is best known for its particular style of riding breeches (jodhpurs) which became very popular in the West in the late 19th century.

RULERS
Sardar Singh, VS1952-1968/1895-1911AD
Sumer Singh, VS1968-1975/1911-1918AD
Umaid Singh, VS1975-2004/1918-1947AD
Hanwant Singh, as Titular Ruler, VS2004-2009/1947-1949AD

MINTS

جودهپور
Jodhpur

جودپور
Jodpur

دارالمنصور
Dar-al-Mansur

Issues of Edward VII and George V and Sardar Singh and Sumer Singh

م
Jodhpur (KM#91-95, 98-100, 109, 113-115)
Jodhpur (KM#120)

Issues of George V and Sumer Singh

د
Jodhpur (KM#111-112)

Issues of George V and Umaid Singh

ॲ
Jodhpur (KM#128 & 129)

श्री
Jodhpur (KM#129)

Issues of Edward VIII and Umaid Singh

रं
Jodhpur all

Issues of George VI and Umaid Singh

रं
Jodhpur (KM#141-143)

गो
Jodhpur (KM#144- 147, 150-151)

Issues of George VI and Hanwant Singh

गो
Jodhpur all

The Daroga's marks generally consist of a symbol or a single Nagari letter, sometimes inverted, and even lying on its side. Some letters are found on more than one series, so that the mark is not a positive identification, but taken together with the city mark and the style of the coin, will provide a correct attribution.

JODHPUR MINT
Operative between 1761AD (AH1175) and 1945AD (VS2002). There are a number of mules of late Jodhpur types struck in 1945 and later for collectors.

KINGDOM

Sardar Singh
VS1952-1968 / 1895-1911AD

HAMMERED COINAGE

KM# 91.1 1/4 ANNA
10.5000 g., Copper, 18 mm. **Obv. Insc.:** Edward (VII)... **Rev:** Inscription; date at top **Rev. Insc.:** Sardar Singh... **Mint:** Jodhpur **Note:** Other blundered dates may exist. Y#20.

Date	Mintage	Good	VG	F	VF	XF
1901	—	—	0.50	1.00	2.00	—
1902	—	—	0.50	1.00	2.00	—
1903	—	—	0.50	1.00	2.00	—
1904	—	—	0.50	1.00	2.00	—
1905	—	—	0.50	1.00	2.00	—
1906	—	—	0.50	1.00	2.00	—
1609 Error	—	—	0.50	1.00	2.00	—
1907	—	—	0.50	1.00	2.00	—
1908	—	—	0.50	1.00	2.00	—
1909	—	—	0.50	1.00	2.00	—
1910	—	—	0.50	1.00	2.00	—
1290(1910) Error	—	—	0.50	1.00	2.00	—
1291(1910) Error	—	—	0.50	1.00	2.00	—
1292(1910) Error	—	—	—	—	—	—
1967(1910) Error	—	—	0.50	1.00	2.00	—
2091(1910) Error	—	—	0.50	1.00	2.00	—
5201(1910) Error	—	—	0.50	1.00	2.00	—
5291(1910) Error	—	—	—	—	—	—
0292 (1910) Error	—	—	—	—	—	—
192 (1910) Error	—	—	—	—	—	—
0192 (1910) Error	—	—	—	—	—	—
1091 (1910) Error	—	—	—	—	—	—
0196 (1910) Error	—	—	—	—	—	—
1291 (1910) Retrograde 9	—	—	—	—	—	—
1067 (1910) Error	—	—	—	—	—	—
1291 (1910) 2 engraved over 1	—	—	—	—	—	—

KM# 91.2 1/4 ANNA
10.5000 g., Copper, 16 mm. **Obv. Insc.:** Edward (VII)... **Rev:** Inscription; date at bottom **Rev. Insc.:** Sardar Singh... **Mint:** Jodhpur **Note:** Y#20.

Date	Mintage	Good	VG	F	VF	XF
1906						

KM# 92.1   1/2 ANNA
Copper Obv. Insc.: Edward (VII)... Rev. Insc.: Sardar Singh...
Mint: Jodhpur Note: 20.00-21.00 grams. Y#21.

Date	Mintage	Good	VG	F	VF	XF
1906	—	—	3.00	7.50	11.50	18.00
1908	—	—	3.00	7.50	11.50	18.00

KM# 92.2   1/2 ANNA
Copper Obv. Insc.: Edward (VII)... Rev: Legend without
Bahadur Rev. Insc.: Sardar Singh... Mint: Jodhpur Note: Y#21.

Date	Mintage	Good	VG	F	VF	XF
1906	—	—	3.00	7.50	11.50	—
1908	—	—	3.00	7.50	11.50	—

KM# 93   1/8 RUPEE
1.4000 g., Silver Obv. Insc.: Edward (VII)... Rev. Insc.: Sardar
Singh... Mint: Jodhpur

Date	Mintage	Good	VG	F	VF	XF
ND(1908)	—	—	35.00	75.00	100	125

KM# 94   1/4 RUPEE
2.8000 g., Silver, 19 mm. Obv. Insc.: Edward (VII)...
Rev. Insc.: Sardar Singh... Mint: Jodhpur Note: Y#22.

Date	Mintage	Good	VG	F	VF	XF
VS1965	—	—	25.00	50.00	75.00	100

KM# 95   1/2 RUPEE
5.6000 g., Silver, 13 mm. Obv. Insc.: Edward (VII)...
Rev. Insc.: Sardar Singh... Mint: Jodhpur

Date	Mintage	Good	VG	F	VF	XF
1906	—	—	55.00	100	125	150
ND(1908)	—	—	55.00	100	125	150

KM# 98   1/4 MOHUR
2.8000 g., Gold Obv. Insc.: Edward (VII)... Rev. Insc.: Sardar
Singh... Mint: Jodhpur Note: Y#23.

Date	Mintage	Good	VG	F	VF	XF
ND(1906)	—	—	BV	85.00	110	165

KM# 99   1/2 MOHUR
5.5000 g., Gold, 18 mm. Obv. Insc.: Edward (VII)...
Rev. Insc.: Sardar Singh... Mint: Jodhpur Note: Y#24.

Date	Mintage	Good	VG	F	VF	XF
ND(1906)	—	—	BV	165	225	300

KM# 100.1   MOHUR
11.0000 g., Gold, 20 mm. Obv: "Ma." Obv. Insc.: Edward (VII)...
Rev. Insc.: Sardar Singh... Mint: Jodhpur Note: Y#25.

Date	Mintage	Good	VG	F	VF	XF
1906	—	—	BV	285	375	550

KM# 100.2   MOHUR
11.0000 g., Gold, 20 mm. Obv: "Sa." Obv. Insc.: Edward (VII)...
Rev. Insc.: Sardar Singh... Mint: Jodhpur Note: Y#25.

Date	Mintage	Good	VG	F	VF	XF
1906	—	—	BV	285	375	550

Sumar Singh
HAMMERED COINAGE

KM# 110   1/4 ANNA
10.5000 g., Copper, 16-18 mm. Obv. Insc.: George V, "Emperor"...
Rev. Insc.: Sumar Singh... Mint: Jodhpur Note: Y#27. Size varies.

Date	Mintage	Good	VG	F	VF	XF
1914	—	—	5.00	12.50	17.50	—

KM# 111   1/4 ANNA
10.5000 g., Copper, 16-18 mm. Obv. Insc.: George V, "Shah"...
Rev. Insc.: Sumar Singh... Mint: Jodhpur Note: Y#27. Size varies.

Date	Mintage	Good	VG	F	VF	XF
1914	—	—	—	—	—	—

KM# 112.1   1/2 ANNA
21.0000 g., Copper, 25 mm. Obv. Insc.: George V, "Emperor"...
Rev. Insc.: Sumar Singh... Mint: Jodhpur Note: Y#28.

Date	Mintage	Good	VG	F	VF	XF
1914	—	—	8.50	12.50	20.00	—

KM# 112.2   1/2 ANNA
21.0000 g., Copper, 25 mm. Obv. Insc.: George V, "Shah"...
Rev. Insc.: Sumar Singh... Mint: Jodhpur Note: Y#28.

Date	Mintage	Good	VG	F	VF	XF
1914	—	—	8.50	12.50	20.00	—

KM# 113   1/8 RUPEE
1.4000 g., Silver, 13 mm. Obv. Insc.: George V, "Shah"...
Rev. Insc.: Sumar Singh... Mint: Jodhpur Note: Y#29.

Date	Mintage	Good	VG	F	VF	XF
ND(1911-18)	—	—	35.00	75.00	100	125

KM# 114   1/4 RUPEE
2.8000 g., Silver, 14 mm. Mint: Jodhpur Note: Y#30.

Date	Mintage	Good	VG	F	VF	XF
ND(1911-18)	—	—	35.00	75.00	100	125

KM# 115   1/2 RUPEE
5.6000 g., Silver, 18 mm. Mint: Jodhpur Note: Y#31.

Date	Mintage	Good	VG	F	VF	XF
ND(1911-18)	—	—	35.00	75.00	100	125

KM# 116   RUPEE
11.2000 g., Silver, 21 mm. Mint: Jodhpur Note: Y#32.

Date	Mintage	Good	VG	F	VF	XF
ND(1911-18)	—	—	50.00	100	150	200

KM# 119   1/2 MOHUR
5.5000 g., Gold, 19 mm. Obv. Insc.: "Ha" Mint: Jodhpur
Note: Y#26.

Date	Mintage	Good	VG	F	VF	XF
ND(1911-18)	—	—	BV	150	190	250

KM# 120.1   MOHUR
11.0000 g., Gold, 18 mm. Obv: "Ma. " Mint: Jodhpur Note: Y#33.

Date	Mintage	Good	VG	F	VF	XF
ND(1911-18)	—	—	BV	285	375	550

KM# 120.2   MOHUR
11.0000 g., Gold, 18 mm. Obv. Insc.: "Ha" Mint: Jodhpur
Note: Y#33.

Date	Mintage	Good	VG	F	VF	XF
ND(1911-18)	—	—	BV	300	400	600

Umaid Singh
HAMMERED COINAGE

KM# 132   1/4 ANNA
10.5000 g., Copper Obv: Large Persian "8" left of Daroga's mark
Obv. Insc.: Edward (VIII)... Rev. Insc.: Umaid Singh...
Mint: Jodhpur Note: Varieties include 2 dots replacing the
Persian "8" in the inscription and are quite common.

Date	Mintage	Good	VG	F	VF	XF
1936	—	—	2.00	4.00	6.50	—

Note: Blundered legend varieties also exist

KM# 133   1/4 ANNA
10.5000 g., Copper Obv: Small Persian "8" left of Daroga's mark
Obv. Insc.: Edward (VIII)... Rev. Insc.: Umaid Singh...
Mint: Jodhpur Note: Varieties include 2 dots replacing the
Persian "8" in the inscription and are quite common.

Date	Mintage	Good	VG	F	VF	XF
1936	—	—	2.00	4.00	6.50	—

KM# 131   1/4 ANNA
10.5000 g., Copper Obv: Without Persian "8" left of Daroga's
mark Obv. Insc.: Edward (VIII)... Rev. Insc.: Umaid Singh...
Mint: Jodhpur Note: Y#39.

Date	Mintage	Good	VG	F	VF	XF
1936	—	—	2.00	4.00	6.50	—

KM# 141   1/4 ANNA
Copper Obv. Insc.: George (VI)... Rev: Inscription; date at top
Rev. Insc.: Umaid Singh... Mint: Jodhpur Note: Thick, 10.50-
10.70 grams. Y#40.

Date	Mintage	Good	VG	F	VF	XF
1937	—	—	1.00	2.50	3.50	—
1938	—	—	1.00	2.50	3.50	—
1939	—	—	1.00	2.50	3.50	—

KM# 142   1/4 ANNA
Copper Obv. Insc.: George (VI)... Rev. Insc.: Umaid Singh...
Mint: Jodhpur

Date	Mintage	Good	VG	F	VF	XF
VS1996	—	—	1.75	4.00	6.00	—

KM# 143   1/4 ANNA
Copper, 19-20 mm. Obv. Insc.: George (VI)... Rev. Insc.: Umaid
Singh... Mint: Jodhpur Note: Size varies.

Date	Mintage	Good	VG	F	VF	XF
ND	—	—	2.00	6.50	10.00	—

KM# 124   1/4 RUPEE
3.1000 g., Silver Obv. Insc.: George (V)... Rev. Insc.: Umaid
Singh... Mint: Jodhpur Note: Y#35.

Date	Mintage	Good	VG	F	VF	XF
ND(1918-35)	—	—	15.00	30.00	60.00	90.00

KM# 125   1/2 RUPEE
Silver Obv. Insc.: George (V)... Rev. Insc.: Umaid Singh...
Mint: Jodhpur

Date	Mintage	Good	VG	F	VF	XF
ND(1918-35)	—	—	25.00	50.00	75.00	125

KM# 125a   1/2 RUPEE
Silver Obv. Insc.: George (V)... Rev. Insc.: Umaid Singh...
Mint: Jodhpur Note: Square flan.

Date	Mintage	Good	VG	F	VF	XF
ND(1918-35)	—	—	30.00	60.00	90.00	150

KM# 126   RUPEE
Silver Obv. Insc.: George (V)... Rev. Insc.: Umaid Singh...
Mint: Jodhpur

Date	Mintage	Good	VG	F	VF	XF
ND(1918-35)	—	—	35.00	75.00	125	200

KM# 127.1   1/4 MOHUR
2.7000 g., Gold, 16 mm. Obv: "OM" Obv. Insc.: George (V)...
Rev. Insc.: Umaid Singh... Mint: Jodhpur Note: Y#36.

Date	Mintage	Good	VG	F	VF	XF
ND(1918-35)	—	—	BV	70.00	90.00	120	175

KM# 127.2 1/4 MOHUR
2.7000 g., Gold, 16 mm. **Obv:** "Shri" **Obv. Insc.:** George (V)...
Rev. Insc.: Umaid Singh... **Mint:** Jodhpur **Note:** Y#36.

Date	Mintage	Good	VG	F	VF	XF
ND(1918-35)	—	BV	70.00	90.00	120	175

KM# 128 1/2 MOHUR
5.5000 g., Gold, 18 mm. **Obv. Insc.:** "George (V)..."
Rev. Insc.: "Umaid Singh..." **Mint:** Jodhpur **Note:** Y#37.

Date	Mintage	Good	VG	F	VF	XF
ND(1918-35)	—	BV	165	220	300	

KM# 129 MOHUR
11.0000 g., Gold, 18-20 mm. **Obv:** "Om" **Obv. Insc.:** "George (V)..."
Rev. Insc.: "Umaid Singh..." **Mint:** Jodhpur **Note:** Y#38. Size varies.

Date	Mintage	Good	VG	F	VF	XF
19x8	—	BV	285	375	550	

KM# 130 MOHUR
11.0000 g., Gold, 18-20 mm. **Obv:** "Shri" **Obv. Insc.:** "George (V)..." **Rev. Insc.:** "Umaid Singh..." **Mint:** Jodhpur **Note:** Y#38. Size varies.

Date	Mintage	Good	VG	F	VF	XF
ND(1918-35)	—	BV	265	325	450	

KM# 140 MOHUR
11.0100 g., Gold **Obv. Insc.:** Edward VIII **Mint:** Jodhpur

Date	Mintage	Good	VG	F	VF	XF
1936	—	—	—	—	—	—

KM# 150 MOHUR
11.0000 g., Gold, 18 mm. **Obv:** Large legend, Persian "6" after "George" **Obv. Insc.:** "George (VI)..." **Rev:** Large legend, Persian "6" after "George" **Rev. Insc.:** "Umaid Singh..." **Mint:** Jodhpur **Note:** Y#42.

Date	Mintage	Good	VG	F	VF	XF
VS1997 (1940)	—	—	—	—	—	—
ND(1943)	—	—	BV	325	450	650

KM# 151.1 MOHUR
11.0200 g., Gold **Obv:** Small legend, without Persian "6" **Obv. Insc.:** "George (VI)..." **Rev:** Small legend, without Persian "6" **Rev. Insc.:** "Umaid Singh..." **Mint:** Jodhpur

Date	Mintage	Good	VG	F	VF	XF
VS1999	—	—	BV	325	450	650
ND(1942)	—	—	BV	325	450	650
VS2000	—	—	BV	325	450	650

KM# 151.2 MOHUR
11.0200 g., Gold **Obv:** With Persian "6" below Daroga's mark **Obv. Insc.:** George (VI)... **Rev. Insc.:** Umaid Singh ... **Mint:** Jodhpur **Note:** Varieties exist.

Date	Mintage	Good	VG	F	VF	XF
VS2001 (1944)	—	—	BV	325	450	650

MILLED COINAGE

KM# 144 1/4 ANNA
3.0000 g., Copper **Obv:** Without Persian "6" below Daroga's mark **Obv. Insc.:** George (VI)... **Rev. Insc.:** Umaid Singh... **Mint:** Jodhpur **Note:** Thin flan. Y#41.

Date	Mintage	Good	VG	F	VF	XF
ND Date off flan	—	—	0.25	0.50	1.00	—
VS2000	—	—	1.75	3.75	5.50	—

KM# 147 1/4 ANNA
2.6000 g., Copper **Obv:** Cock with wings raised facing left, legend around **Obv. Insc.:** George (VI)... **Rev:** Date and "Rajya Marwar" **Rev. Insc.:** Umaid Singh... **Mint:** Jodhpur

Date	Mintage	Good	VG	F	VF	XF
VS2000 Rare	—	—	—	—	—	—

KM# 145 1/4 ANNA
2.6000 g., Copper **Obv:** Persian "6" below Daroga's mark **Obv. Insc.:** George (VI)... **Rev. Insc.:** Umaid Singh... **Mint:** Jodhpur **Note:** Varieties exist.

Date	Mintage	Good	VG	F	VF	XF
VS2001	—	—	1.75	3.75	5.50	—
VS2002	—	—	1.75	3.75	5.50	—

KM# 146 1/4 ANNA
2.6000 g., Copper **Obv:** Persian 2 (error for 6) below Daroga's mark **Obv. Insc.:** George (VI)... **Rev. Insc.:** Umaid Singh... **Mint:** Jodhpur

Date	Mintage	Good	VG	F	VF	XF
	—	—	—	—	—	—

Hanwant Singh
as Titular Ruler

HAMMERED COINAGE

KM# 152 1/4 ANNA
4.2000 g., Copper **Obv. Insc.:** George (VI)... **Rev. Insc.:** Hanwant Singh... **Mint:** Jodhpur **Note:** Y#43.

Date	Mintage	Good	VG	F	VF	XF
VS(2004)	—	—	25.00	50.00	90.00	—

KM# 158 1/4 MOHUR
2.7000 g., Gold **Obv. Insc.:** "George (VI)..." **Rev. Insc.:** "Hanwant Singh..." **Mint:** Jodhpur

Date	Mintage	Good	VG	F	VF	XF
VS(2004) Rare	—	—	—	—	—	—

KM# 160 MOHUR
11.0000 g., Gold **Obv. Insc.:** "George (VI)..." **Rev. Insc.:** "Hanwant Singh..." **Mint:** Jodhpur

Date	Mintage	Good	VG	F	VF	XF
VS(2004)	—	—	275	350	500	650

JUNAGADH

A state located in the Kathiawar peninsula of Western India was originally a petty Rajput kingdom until conquered by the Sultan of Ahmadabad in 1472. It became a Mughal dependency under the Emperor Akbar, administered by the Ahmadabad Subah. In 1735, when the empire began to disintegrate, a Mughal officer and military adventurer, Sher Khan Babi, expelled the Mughal governor and asserted his independence. From that time until Indian independence his descendents ruled the state as nawabs. In 1947 the Nawab of Junagadh tried to accede to the new nation of Pakistan but the Hindu majority in the state objected and Junagadh was absorbed by the Republic of India.

Junagadh first entered into treaty relations with the British in 1807 and maintained a close and friendly association with the Raj. In 1924 this relationship was formalized when Junagadh was placed under an Agent to the Governor General in the western India States. In 1935 the state comprised 3,337 square miles with a population of 545,152, four-fifths of whom were Hindus.

RULERS
Rasul Muhammad Khan, AH1309-1329/VS1948-1968/1891-1911AD
Mahabat Khan III, AH1329-1368/VS1968-2005/1911-1948AD

KINGDOM

Rasul Muhammad Khan
AH1309-1329 / VS1948-1968 / 1891-1911AD

MILLED COINAGE

KM# 43 DOKDO
Copper **Obv. Insc.:** Perso-Arabic "Ek paisa Junagadh Riiyaasat (government)" **Rev. Insc.:** "Devanagari-Shri Sorath Sarkaar" **Mint:** Junagadh

Date	Mintage	Good	VG	F	VF	XF
AH1325/VS1963	—	—	4.00	10.00	15.00	—

KM# 44.1 DOKDO
Copper **Obv. Insc.:** Perso-Arabic Ek paisa Junagadh Riiyaasat (government) **Rev:** Inscription; date without rosettes **Rev. Insc.:** Devanagari-Shri Sorath Sarkaar **Mint:** Junagadh

Date	Mintage	Good	VG	F	VF	XF
VS1963(1906)	—	—	1.25	3.00	4.50	—
VS1964(1907)	—	—	—	—	—	—

KM# 44.2 DOKDO
Copper **Obv. Insc.:** Perso-Arabic Ek paisa Junagadh Riiyaasat (government) **Rev:** Inscription; date with annulets **Rev. Insc.:** Devanagari-Shri Sorath Sarkaar **Mint:** Junagadh

Date	Mintage	Good	VG	F	VF	XF
VS1964(1907)	—	—	1.25	3.00	4.50	—

KM# 44.3 DOKDO
Copper **Obv. Insc.:** Perso-Arabic Ek paisa Junagadh Riiyaasat (government); date between solid stars **Rev. Insc.:** Devanagari-Shri Sorath Sarkaar **Mint:** Junagadh

Date	Mintage	Good	VG	F	VF	XF
VS1964(1907)	—	—	1.25	3.00	4.50	—

KM# 44.5 DOKDO
Copper **Obv. Insc.:** Perso-Arabic Ek paisa Junagadh Riiyaasat (government) **Rev:** Inscription; solid star only to left of date **Rev. Insc.:** Devanagari-Shri Sorath Sarkaar **Mint:** Junagadh **Note:** Prev. KM#44.3a.

Date	Mintage	Good	VG	F	VF	XF
VS1964(1907)	—	—	2.50	6.00	10.00	—

KM# 44.4 DOKDO
Copper **Obv. Insc.:** Perso-Arabic Ek paisa Junagadh Riiyaasat (government) **Rev:** Date with outlined stars **Rev. Insc.:** Devanagari-Shri Sorath Sarkaar **Mint:** Junagadh

Date	Mintage	Good	VG	F	VF	XF
VS1964(1907)	—	—	1.25	3.00	4.50	7.50

KM# 45.1 DOKDO
3.9300 g., Copper **Obv. Insc.:** Perso-Arabic Ek paisa Junagadh Riiyaasat (government) **Rev:** Date between rosettes **Rev. Insc.:** Devanagari-Shri Sorath Sarkaar **Mint:** Junagadh

Date	Mintage	Good	VG	F	VF	XF
VS1964(1907)	—	—	0.50	1.00	2.00	—
VS1965(1908)	—	—	0.50	1.00	2.00	—
VS1966(1909)	—	—	0.50	1.00	2.00	—
VS1967(1910)	—	—	0.50	1.00	2.00	—

KM# 45.2 DOKDO
Copper **Obv. Insc.:** Perso-Arabic Ek paisa Junagadh Riiyaasat (government) **Rev:** Date divided by space in legend **Rev. Insc.:** Devanagari-Shri Sorath Sarkaar **Mint:** Junagadh

Date	Mintage	Good	VG	F	VF	XF
VS1966(1909)	—	—	0.50	1.00	2.00	—

KM# 45.3 DOKDO
Copper **Obv. Insc.:** Perso-Arabic Ek paisa Junagadh Riiyaasat (government) **Rev:** Date at top in legend **Rev. Insc.:** Devanagari-Shri Sorath Sarkaar **Mint:** Junagadh

Date	Mintage	Good	VG	F	VF	XF
VS1966(1909)	—	—	1.00	2.00	5.00	—

KM# 46.1 DOKDO
Copper **Obv. Insc.:** Perso-Arabic Ek paisa Junagadh Riiyaasat (government) **Rev. Insc.:** Devanagari-Shri Sorath Sarkaar **Mint:** Junagadh

Date	Mintage	Good	VG	F	VF	XF
ND(1909)	—	—	1.00	2.00	5.00	—

KM# 46.2 DOKDO
Copper **Obv. Insc.:** Perso-Arabic Ek paisa Junagadh Riiyaasat (government) **Rev:** Stars between inscriptions **Rev. Insc.:** Devanagari-Shri Sorath Sarkaar **Mint:** Junagadh

Date	Mintage	Good	VG	F	VF	XF
ND(1909)	—	—	1.00	2.00	5.00	—

KM# 48 2 DOKDA
Copper **Obv. Insc.:** Perso-Arabic Ek paisa Junagadh Riiyaasat (government) **Rev. Insc.:** Devanagari-Shri Sorath Sarkaar **Mint:** Junagadh

Date	Mintage	Good	VG	F	VF	XF
VS1964(1907)	—	—	7.00	15.00	25.00	—

KM# 52 KORI
4.6000 g., Silver, 15 mm. **Mint:** Junagadh

Date	Mintage	VG	F	VF	XF	Unc
VS1966(1909)	—	—	25.00	35.00	50.00	—

KM# 58 GOLD KORI
Gold **Obv:** Perso-Arabic inscription **Obv. Insc.:** "Nawab Bahadur Muhammad Khanji" **Rev:** Date, mint name **Mint:** Junagadh **Note:** Weight varies: 4.02-4.77 grams.

Date	Mintage	VG	F	VF	XF	Unc
AH1325/VS1963 (1908)	—	—	—	500	850	1,250

KM# 60 MOHUR
11.5400 g., Gold **Obv:** Perso-Arabic inscription **Obv. Insc.:** "Nawab Bahadur Muhammad Khanji" **Rev:** Date, mint name **Mint:** Junagadh

Date	Mintage	VG	F	VF	XF	Unc
AH1325/VS1963 (1908)	—	—	—	2,000	2,800	

KM# 61 MOHUR
11.5400 g., Gold **Obv:** "Shri Divan" in Devanagari below **Mint:** Junagadh

Date	Mintage	Good	VG	F	VF	XF
AH1325(1907) Rare	—	—	—	—	—	—

Mahabat Khan III
AH1329-1368 / VS1968-2005 / 1911-1948AD
MILLED COINAGE

KM# 63 DOKDO
Copper

Date	Mintage	Good	VG	F	VF	XF
VS1985(1928)	—	—	20.00	50.00	75.00	—
VS1990(1933)	—	—	20.00	50.00	75.00	—

KISHANGARH

The maharajas of Kishangarh, a small state in northwest India, in the vicinity of Ajmer, belonged to the Rathor Rajputs. The town of Kishangarh, which gave its name to the state, was founded in 1611 and was itself named after Kishen Singh, the first ruler. The maharajas succeeded in reaching terms with Akbar in the late 16th century, and again in 1818 with the British. In 1949 the state was merged into Rajasthan.

RULERS
Sardul Singh, VS1936-1957/1879-1900AD
Madan Singh, VS1957-1983/1900-1926AD
Yaghyanarayan Singh, VS1983-1995/1926-1938AD
Sumer Singh, VS1995-2000/1938-1949AD

MINT

Kishangarh

MINT MARK

Symbol on reverse: Jhar

KINGDOM
HAMMERED COINAGE
Regal Style
1900-1926

Y# B3 1/4 RUPEE
2.7000 g., Silver **Obv. Insc.:** Edward (VII)... **Rev:** Jhar **Rev. Insc.:** Madan Singh...

Date	Mintage	Good	VG	F	VF	XF
ND//24 (sic) (1902)	—	—	15.00	30.00	60.00	9.00

Y# 3 1/2 RUPEE
5.4000 g., Silver **Obv. Insc.:** Edward (VII)... **Rev:** Jhar **Rev. Insc.:** Madan Singh...

Date	Mintage	Good	VG	F	VF	XF
1902//24	—	—	12.50	25.00	50.00	75.00

HAMMERED COINAGE
1926-1938

Y# 4 1/4 RUPEE
2.7000 g., Silver **Obv. Insc.:** George (V)... **Rev:** Jhar **Rev. Insc.:** Yaghyanarayan...

Date	Mintage	Good	VG	F	VF	XF
ND//24 (sic) (1926-38)	—	—	15.00	30.00	60.00	90.00

Y# 5 1/2 RUPEE
5.4000 g., Silver **Obv. Insc.:** George (V)... **Rev:** Jhar **Rev. Insc.:** Yaghyanarayan...

Date	Mintage	Good	VG	F	VF	XF
ND//24 (sic) (1926-38)	—	—	12.50	25.00	50.00	75.00

Y# 6 RUPEE
10.8000 g., Silver **Obv. Insc.:** George (V)... **Rev:** Jhar **Rev. Insc.:** Yaghyanarayan...

Date	Mintage	Good	VG	F	VF	XF
ND//24 (sic) (1926-38)	—	—	12.50	25.00	40.00	60.00

Y# 6a NAZARANA RUPEE
Silver **Obv. Insc.:** George (V)... **Rev:** Jhar **Rev. Insc.:** Yaghyanarayan... **Note:** Weight varies: 10.70-10.80 grams.

Date	Mintage	Good	VG	F	VF	XF
ND(1926-38)	—	—	100	200	350	500

Y# 7 1/2 MOHUR
Gold, 18 mm. **Obv. Insc.:** George (V)... **Rev:** Jhar **Rev. Insc.:** Yaghyanarayan... **Note:** Approximately 5.50 grams.

Date	Mintage	Good	VG	F	VF	XF
ND//24 (sic) (1926-38)	—	—	BV	225	550	850

Y# 8 MOHUR
Gold, 19 mm. **Obv. Insc.:** George (V)... **Rev:** Jhar **Rev. Insc.:** Yaghyanarayan... **Note:** Approximately 11.00 grams.

Date	Mintage	Good	VG	F	VF	XF
ND//24 (sic) (1926-38)	—	—	245	300	500	800

ANONYMOUS HAMMERED COINAGE
First Series

Y# 9   1/8 RUPEE
1.3500 g., Silver, 12 mm. **Obv. Insc.:** Nagari "Chadi" (silver)
Rev: Jhar

Date	Mintage	Good	VG	F	VF	XF
ND//24 (sic) (ca.1902-38)	—	—	30.00	65.00	100	150

Y# 10   1/4 RUPEE
2.7000 g., Silver, 15 mm. **Obv. Insc.:** Nagari "Chadi" (silver)
Rev: Jhar

Date	Mintage	Good	VG	F	VF	XF
ND//24 (sic) (ca.1902-38)	—	—	30.00	65.00	100	150

Y# A11   1/2 RUPEE
Obv: As #Y11. **Obv. Insc.:** Nagari "Chadi" (Silver) **Rev:** As #Y5. **Rev. Insc.:** Maharajah Yaghyanarayan... **Note:** Mule.

Date	Mintage	VG	F	VF	XF	Unc
ND(1902-38) Rare	—	—	—	—	—	—

Y# 11   1/2 RUPEE
5.4000 g., Silver, 17-18 mm. **Obv. Insc.:** Nagari "Chadi" (silver)
Rev: Jhar **Note:** Size varies.

Date	Mintage	VG	F	VF	XF	Unc
ND(ca.1902-38)	—	30.00	65.00	100	150	—

KM# 12.1   RUPEE
Silver, 20-24 mm. **Obv. Insc.:** Nagari "Chadi" (silver) **Rev:** Jhar
Note: Weight varies: 10.85-11.05 grams. Small flan, thick.

Date	Mintage	Good	VG	F	VF	XF
ND//24 (sic) (ca.1902-38)	—	—	20.00	40.00	65.00	100

KM# 12.2   RUPEE
Silver, 20-24 mm. **Obv. Insc.:** Nagari "Chadi" (silver) **Rev:** Jhar
Note: Weight varies: 10.85-11.05 g. Large flan, thin.

Date	Mintage	Good	VG	F	VF	XF
ND//24 (sic) (ca.1902-38)	—	—	20.00	40.00	65.00	100

ANONYMOUS HAMMERED COINAGE
Second Series

Denominations in Nagari, Persian and 'merchants numerals', in Annas on obverse.

Y# 13   2 ANNAS
1.3200 g., Silver, 11 mm. **Rev:** Jhar

Date	Mintage	Good	VG	F	VF	XF
ND//24 (sic) (ca.1902-38)	—	—	25.00	50.00	85.00	125

Y# 14   4 ANNAS
2.6200 g., Silver, 12-13 mm. **Rev:** Jhar **Note:** Size varies.

Date	Mintage	Good	VG	F	VF	XF
ND//24 (sic) (ca.1902-38)	—	—	15.00	30.00	50.00	85.00

Y# 15   8 ANNAS
5.3500 g., Silver, 16 mm. **Rev:** Jhar

Date	Mintage	Good	VG	F	VF	XF
ND//24 (sic) (ca.1902-38)	—	—	12.50	25.00	40.00	75.00

KOTAH

Kotah State, located in northwest India was subdivided out of Bundi early in the 17th century when it was given to a younger son of the Bundi raja by the Mughal emperor. The ruler, or maharao, was a Chauhan Rajput. During the years of Maratha ascendancy Kotah fell on hard times, especially from the depredations of Holkar. In 1817 the State came under treaty with the British.

RULERS
Ram Singh II,
   VS1885-1923/1828-1866AD
Chattar Singh,
   VS1923-1946/1866-1889AD
Umed Singh II,
   VS1946-1992/1889-1935AD

MINT

Mint name: *Nandgaon*

Kotah urf Nandgaon
or *Nandgaon urf Kotah* on earliest issues.

MINT MARKS

	1.	2.	3.	4.	5.

Mint mark #1 appears beneath #4 on most Kotah coins, and serves to distinguish coins of Kotah from similar issues of Bundi in the pre-Victoria period.
   C#28 has mint mark #2 on obv., #1, 3 and 4 on rev. All later issues have #1 on obv., #1, 5 and 4 on rev.

BRITISH PROTECTORATE
HAMMERED COINAGE
Regal Style

Y# 6   RUPEE
11.2000 g., Silver, 18-20 mm. **Obv. Insc.:** "Badshah Zaman Inglistan... (Victoria)" **Note:** Size varies.

Date	Mintage	Good	VG	F	VF	XF
ND//44 (1901)	—	6.00	9.00	15.00	25.00	—

Y# 6a   NAZARANA RUPEE
11.2000 g., Silver, 26-30 mm. **Obv. Insc.:** "Badshah Zaman Inglistan... (Victoria)" **Note:** Size varies.

Date	Mintage	Good	VG	F	VF	XF
ND//44 (1901)	—	17.50	32.50	45.00	75.00	125

Y# 8   MOHUR
10.7000 g., Gold, 18 mm. **Obv. Insc.:** "Badshah Zaman Inglistan... (Victoria)"

Date	Mintage	Good	VG	F	VF	XF
ND//44 (1901)	—	250	300	400	600	—

KUTCH

State located in northwest India, consisting of a peninsula north of the Gulf of Kutch.
   The rulers of Kutch were Jareja Rajputs who, coming from Tatta in Sind, conquered Kutch in the 14th or 15th centuries. The capital city of Bhuj is thought to date from the mid-16th century. In 1617, after Akbar's conquest of Gujerat and the fall of the Gujerat sultans, the Kutch ruler, Rao Bharmal I (1586-1632) visited Jahangir and established a relationship which was sufficiently warm to leave Kutch virtually independent throughout the Mughal period. Early in the 19th century internal disorder and the existence of rival claimants to the throne resulted in British intrusion into the state's affairs. Rao Bharmalji II was deposed in favor of Rao Desalji II who proved much more amenable to the

Government of India's wishes. He and his successors continued to rule in a manner considered by the British to be most enlightened and, as a result, Maharao Khengarji III was created a Knight Grand Commander of the Indian Empire. In view of its geographical isolation Kutch came under the direct control of the Central Government at India's independence.
   First coinage was struck in 1617AD.

RULERS
Khengarji III, VS1932-1999/1875-1942AD

M(a)-ha-ra-o Sri Khen-ga-r-ji

मादारउ खेंगरजी

Ma-ha-ra-o Khen-ga-r-ji

मादाराजादेराजमेरजमदारात्रे

Ma-ha-ra-ja Dhi-ra-j Mi-r-ja M(a)-ha-ra-o Sri

खेंगरजीढदारकढनुज

Khen-ga-r-ji B(a)-ha-du-r K(a)-chh-bhu-j

मेरजामदाराओश्री खेंगरजी

Mi-r-jan M(a)-ha-ra-o Sri Khen-ga-r-ji

मदारात्रे श्री खेंगरजी

M(a)-ha-ra-o Sri Khen-ga-r-ji

मदाराजादे राजामेरज मदारात

M(a)-ha-ra-ja Dhi-ra-j Mi-r-jan M(a)-ha-ra-o

श्री खेंगरजीढदार

Sri-Khen-ga-r-ji B(a)-ha-du-r

श्री खेंगरजीसबाडॅ ढदार

Sri Khen-ga-r-ji Sa-va-i B(a)-ha-du-r

मदारउश्री खेंगरजी क ढनुज

M(a)-ha-ra-o Sri Khen-ga-r-ji K(a)-chchh-bhu-j
Vijayarajji, VS1999-2004/1942-1947AD

विज यराजी

Vi-j(a)-y(a)-ra-j-ji

मदाराओश्री विज य राजी

M(a)-ha-ra-o Sri Vi-j(a)-y(a)-ra-j-ji K(a)-chchh 2000
Madanasinhji, VS2004-- /1947-1948AD

मदन सेंदजी

M(a)-d(a)-n(a)-sin-h-ji
Pragmalji III & Maharani Pritidevi, VS2048-/1991AD-

MINT

 or

Bhuj   (Devanagari)   (Persian)

KINGDOM

Khengarji III
VS1932-98/1985-1942AD

MILLED COINAGE
Regal Issues - Second Series

Y# 35.1   KORI
4.7000 g., 0.6100 Silver 0.0922 oz. ASW   **Ruler:** Khengarji III
VS1932-98 / 1875-1942AD **Obv. Insc.:** "Victoria, Empress of
India" **Rev:** Open crescent

Date	Mintage	Good	VG	F	VF	XF
1901//VS1957	—	1.50	3.00	4.50	6.50	10.00

Y# 37.6   5 KORI
13.8700 g., 0.9370 Silver 0.4178 oz. ASW   **Ruler:** Khengarji III
VS1932-98 / 1875-1942AD **Obv. Insc.:** "Victoria, Empress of India"

Date	Mintage	Good	VG	F	VF	XF
1901//VS1957	—	7.00	17.50	25.00	35.00	50.00

MILLED COINAGE
Regal Issues - Third Series

Y# 38   TRAMBIYO
4.0000 g., Copper, 16 mm.   **Ruler:** Khengarji III VS1932-98 /
1875-1942AD **Obv. Leg.:** Edward VII...

Date	Mintage	Good	VG	F	VF	XF
1908/VS1965	—	0.60	1.50	2.50	3.50	4.50
1909/VS1965	—	0.25	0.60	1.00	1.50	2.50
1909/VS1966	—	0.25	0.60	1.00	1.50	2.00
1910/VS1966	—	0.85	1.65	2.75	4.25	6.00

Y# 39   DOKDO
8.0000 g., Copper, 20.5 mm.   **Ruler:** Khengarji III VS1932-98 /
1875-1942AD **Obv. Leg.:** Edward VII...

Date	Mintage	Good	VG	F	VF	XF
1909/VS1965	—	0.30	0.75	1.25	1.50	2.00
1909/VS1966	—	0.30	0.75	1.25	1.50	2.00

Y# 40   1-1/2 DOKDA
12.0000 g., Copper, 23 mm.   **Ruler:** Khengarji III VS1932-98 /
1875-1942AD **Obv. Leg.:** Edward VII...

Date	Mintage	Good	VG	F	VF	XF
1909/VS1965	—	30.00	60.00	100	115	150

Y# 41   3 DOKDA
24.0000 g., Copper   **Ruler:** Khengarji III VS1932-98 / 1875-
1942AD **Obv. Leg.:** Edward VII...

Date	Mintage	Good	VG	F	VF	XF
1909/VS1965	—	30.00	60.00	100	120	150

Y# 45   5 KORI
13.8700 g., 0.9370 Silver 0.4178 oz. ASW   **Ruler:** Khengarji III
VS1932-98 / 1875-1942AD **Obv. Leg.:** Edward VII...

Date	Mintage	Good	VG	F	VF	XF
1902/VS1959	—	60.00	120	185	250	375
1903/VS1960	—	60.00	120	185	250	375
1904/VS1961	—	60.00	120	185	250	375
1905/VS1962	—	60.00	120	185	250	375
1906/VS1963	—	60.00	120	185	250	375
1907VS1964	—	60.00	120	185	250	375
1908/VS1965	—	50.00	100	150	235	350
1909/VS1966	—	50.00	100	150	235	350

MILLED COINAGE
Regal Issues - Fourth Series

Y# 46   TRAMBIYO
4.0000 g., Copper, 16 mm.   **Ruler:** Khengarji III VS1932-98 /
1875-1942AD **Obv. Insc.:** George V...

Date	Mintage	Good	VG	F	VF	XF
1919/VS1976	—	0.10	0.30	0.50	0.75	1.00
1920/VS1976	—	0.10	0.30	0.50	0.75	1.50
1920/VS1977	—	0.10	0.30	0.50	0.75	1.50

Y# 54   TRAMBIYO
4.0000 g., Copper, 16 mm.   **Ruler:** Khengarji III VS1932-98 /
1875-1942AD **Obv. Insc.:** George V...

Date	Mintage	Good	VG	F	VF	XF
1928/VS1984	—	0.25	0.60	1.00	2.00	3.00
1928/VS1985	—	0.10	0.30	0.50	0.75	1.00

Y# 47   DOKDO
8.0000 g., Copper, 21 mm.   **Ruler:** Khengarji III VS1932-98 /
1875-1942AD **Obv. Insc.:** George V...

Date	Mintage	Good	VG	F	VF	XF
1920/VS1976	—	0.25	0.60	1.00	1.25	2.00
1920/VS1977	—	0.25	0.60	1.00	1.25	2.00

Y# 55   DOKDO
8.0000 g., Copper, 21 mm.   **Ruler:** Khengarji III VS1932-98 /
1875-1942AD **Obv. Insc.:** George V...

Date	Mintage	Good	VG	F	VF	XF
1922/VS1982 (sic)	—	0.50	1.25	1.75	2.50	3.50
1928/VS1984	—	0.25	0.60	1.00	1.25	1.50
1929/VS1985	—	0.25	0.60	1.00	1.25	1.50

Y# 48   1-1/2 DOKDA
12.0000 g., Copper, 23.5 mm.   **Ruler:** Khengarji III VS1932-98
/ 1875-1942AD **Obv. Insc.:** George V...

Date	Mintage	Good	VG	F	VF	XF
1926/VS1982	—	0.35	0.90	1.50	2.50	3.00

Y# 56   1-1/2 DOKDA
12.0000 g., Copper, 23 mm.   **Ruler:** Khengarji III VS1932-98 /
1875-1942AD **Obv. Insc.:** George V...

Date	Mintage	Good	VG	F	VF	XF
1928/VS1985	—	0.20	0.50	0.75	1.00	1.50
1929/VS1985	—	0.20	0.50	0.75	1.00	1.50
1929/VS1986	—	0.20	0.50	0.75	1.00	1.50
1931/VS1987	—	0.20	0.50	0.75	1.00	1.50
1931/VS1988	—	0.20	0.50	0.75	1.00	1.50
1932/VS1988	—	0.40	1.00	1.50	2.50	4.00
1932/VS1989	—	0.20	0.50	0.75	1.00	1.50

Y# 49   3 DOKDA
24.0000 g., Copper, 33 mm.   **Ruler:** Khengarji III VS1932-98 /
1875-1942AD **Obv. Insc.:** George V...

Date	Mintage	Good	VG	F	VF	XF
1926/VS1982	—	0.60	1.50	2.50	3.50	5.00

Y# 57   3 DOKDA
24.0000 g., Copper, 33 mm.   **Ruler:** Khengarji III VS1932-98 /
1875-1942AD **Obv. Insc.:** George V...

Date	Mintage	Good	VG	F	VF	XF
1928/VS1985	—	0.25	0.60	1.00	1.50	2.50
1929/VS1985	—	0.25	0.60	1.00	1.50	2.50
1929/VS1986	—	0.25	0.60	1.00	1.50	2.50
1930/VS1987	—	0.25	0.60	1.00	1.50	2.50
1931/VS1987	—	0.25	0.60	1.00	1.50	2.50
1934/VS1990	—	0.25	0.60	1.00	1.50	2.50
1934/VS1991	—	0.25	0.60	1.00	1.50	2.50
1935/VS1992	—	0.25	0.60	1.00	1.50	2.50

Y# 58   1/2 KORI
2.3500 g., 0.6010 Silver 0.0454 oz. ASW, 14 mm.   **Ruler:**
Khengarji III VS1932-98 / 1875-1942AD **Obv. Insc.:** George V...

Date	Mintage	Good	VG	F	VF	XF
1928/VS1985	—	BV	2.00	3.00	4.00	7.00

Y# 51   KORI
4.7000 g., 0.6010 Silver 0.0908 oz. ASW   **Ruler:** Khengarji III
VS1932-98 / 1875-1942AD **Obv. Insc.:** George V...

Date	Mintage	VG	F	VF	XF	Unc
1913/VS1970	—	BV	2.00	3.00	4.00	7.00
1923/VS1979	—	BV	2.00	3.00	4.00	7.00
1923/VS1980	—	BV	2.00	3.00	4.00	7.00
1927/VS1984	—	BV	2.50	3.50	5.00	8.00

Y# 59 KORI

4.7000 g., 0.6010 Silver 0.0908 oz. ASW, 17 mm. **Ruler:** Khengarji III VS1932-98 / 1875-1942AD **Obv. Leg.:** George V...

Date	Mintage	VG	F	VF	XF	Unc
1928/VS1985	—	BV	2.50	3.50	5.00	8.00
1929/VS1985	—	BV	2.50	3.50	5.00	8.00
1931/VS1987	—	2.75	6.50	10.00	15.00	22.50
1931/VS1988	—	BV	2.50	3.00	5.00	8.00
1932/VS1988	—	BV	2.50	3.00	5.00	8.00
1932/VS1989	—	BV	2.50	3.00	5.00	8.00
1933/VS1989	—	BV	2.50	3.00	5.00	8.00
1933/VS1990	—	BV	2.50	3.00	5.00	8.00
1934/VS1990	—	BV	2.50	3.00	5.00	8.00
1934/VS1991	—	BV	2.50	3.00	5.00	8.00
1935/VS1991	—	BV	2.50	3.00	5.00	8.00
1935/VS1992	—	BV	2.50	3.00	5.00	8.00
1936/VS1992	—	BV	3.00	4.50	6.50	10.00

Y# 52 2-1/2 KORI

6.9350 g., 0.9370 Silver 0.2089 oz. ASW **Ruler:** Khengarji III VS1932-98 / 1875-1942AD **Obv. Insc.:** George V...

Date	Mintage	VG	F	VF	XF	Unc
1916/VS1973	—	BV	4.00	6.00	9.00	13.50
1917/VS1973	—	BV	4.00	6.00	9.00	13.50
1917/VS1974	—	BV	4.00	6.00	9.00	13.50
1918/VS1974	—	BV	4.00	6.00	9.00	13.50
1919/VS1975	—	BV	4.00	6.00	9.00	13.50
1922/VS1978	—	BV	4.00	6.00	9.00	13.50
1922/VS1979	—	BV	4.00	6.00	9.00	13.50
1924/VS1981	—	BV	4.00	6.00	9.00	13.50
1926/VS1983	—	BV	4.00	6.00	9.00	13.50

Y# 52a 2-1/2 KORI

6.9350 g., 0.9370 Silver 0.2089 oz. ASW **Ruler:** Khengarji III VS1932-98 / 1875-1942AD **Obv. Insc.:** George V... **Rev:** Smaller legend

Date	Mintage	VG	F	VF	XF	Unc
1927/VS1984	—	BV	5.00	7.00	10.00	15.00
1928/VS1985	—	BV	4.00	6.00	9.00	13.50
1930/VS1986	—	BV	4.00	6.00	9.00	13.50
1930/VS1987	—	BV	4.00	6.00	9.00	13.50
1932/VS1988	—	BV	4.00	6.00	9.00	13.50
1932/VS1989	—	BV	4.00	6.00	9.00	13.50
1933/VS1989	—	BV	4.00	6.00	9.00	13.50
1933/VS1990	—	BV	4.00	6.00	9.00	13.50
1934/VS1990	—	BV	4.00	6.00	9.00	13.50
1934/VS1991	—	BV	4.00	6.00	9.00	13.50
1935/VS1991	—	BV	4.00	6.00	9.00	13.50
1935/VS1992	—	BV	4.00	6.00	9.00	13.50

Y# 53 5 KORI

13.8700 g., 0.9370 Silver 0.4178 oz. ASW **Ruler:** Khengarji III VS1932-98 / 1875-1942AD **Obv. Insc.:** George V... **Note:** 5 Kori coins were issued with reeded edges until 1928AD, which is when the security edge was introduced. Due to counterfeiting, the government recalled pieces and added lettering as a mark of authentication.

Date	Mintage	VG	F	VF	XF	Unc
1913/VS1970	—	BV	7.50	10.00	15.00	22.50
1915/VS1972	—	BV	7.50	10.00	15.00	22.50
1916/VS1973	—	BV	7.50	10.00	15.00	22.50
1916/VS1975 (Sic)	—	BV	12.50	18.50	25.00	35.00
1917/VS1973	—	BV	7.50	10.00	15.00	22.50
1917/VS1974	—	BV	7.50	10.00	15.00	22.50

Date	Mintage	VG	F	VF	XF	Unc
1918/VS1974	—	BV	7.50	10.00	15.00	22.50
1918/VS1975	—	BV	7.50	10.00	15.00	22.50
1919/VS1975	—	BV	7.50	10.00	15.00	22.50
1919/VS1976	—	12.50	25.00	37.50	50.00	70.00
1920/VS1977	—	BV	8.00	11.50	16.50	25.00
1921/VS1977	—	BV	7.50	10.00	15.00	22.50
1921/VS1978	—	BV	7.50	10.00	15.00	22.50
1922/VS1974 (Sic)	—	—	—	—	—	—
1922/VS1978	—	BV	7.50	10.00	15.00	22.50
1922/VS1979	—	BV	7.50	10.00	15.00	22.50
1922/VS1982 (Sic)	—	BV	7.50	12.50	18.50	27.50
1923/VS1979	—	BV	7.50	10.00	15.00	22.50
1924/VS1978 (Sic)	—	10.00	20.00	31.50	42.50	60.00
1924/VS1980	—	BV	7.50	10.00	15.00	22.50
1924/VS1981	—	BV	7.50	10.00	15.00	22.50
1925/VS1982	—	BV	7.50	10.00	15.00	22.50
1926/VS1978 (Sic)	—	BV	12.50	18.50	25.00	35.00
1926/VS1982	—	BV	7.50	10.00	15.00	22.50
1926/VS1893	—	BV	7.50	10.00	15.00	22.50
1927/VS1984	—	BV	17.50	25.00	35.00	50.00
1927/VS1984 Proof	—	Value: 275				

Y# 53a 5 KORI

13.8700 g., 0.9370 Silver 0.4178 oz. ASW **Ruler:** Khengarji III VS1932-98 / 1875-1942AD **Obv:** Smaller legend **Obv. Insc.:** George V... **Rev:** Smaller legend

Date	Mintage	VG	F	VF	XF	Unc
1928/VS1985	—	BV	15.00	21.50	30.00	40.00
1929/VS1986	—	BV	7.50	10.00	15.00	22.50
1930/VS1986	—	BV	7.50	10.00	15.00	22.50
1930/VS1987	—	BV	7.50	10.00	15.00	22.50
1931/VS1987	—	BV	7.50	10.00	15.00	22.50
1931/VS1988	—	BV	7.50	10.00	15.00	22.50
1932/VS1988	—	BV	7.50	10.00	15.00	22.50
1932/VS1989	—	BV	7.50	10.00	15.00	22.50
1933/VS1989	—	BV	7.50	10.00	15.00	22.50
1933/VS1990	—	BV	7.50	10.00	15.00	22.50
1934/VS1990	—	BV	7.50	10.00	15.00	22.50
1934/VS1991	—	BV	7.50	10.00	15.00	22.50
1935/VS1991	—	BV	7.50	10.00	15.00	22.50
1935/VS1992	—	BV	7.50	10.00	15.00	22.50
1936/VS1992	—	BV	7.50	10.00	15.00	22.50

MILLED COINAGE
Regal Issues - Fifth Series

Y# 63 3 DOKDA

24.0000 g., Copper **Ruler:** Khengarji III VS1932-98 / 1875-1942AD **Obv. Leg.:** Edward VIII...

Date	Mintage	Good	VG	F	VF	XF
1936/VS1993	—	1.25	3.00	5.00	7.50	10.00

Y# 65 KORI

4.7000 g., 0.6010 Silver 0.0908 oz. ASW **Ruler:** Khengarji III VS1932-98 / 1875-1942AD **Obv. Leg.:** Edward VIII...

Date	Mintage	VG	F	VF	XF	Unc
1936/VS1992	—	BV	3.00	4.50	6.50	10.00
1936/VS1993	—	BV	3.00	4.50	6.50	10.00

Y# 66 2-1/2 KORI

6.9350 g., 0.9370 Silver 0.2089 oz. ASW **Ruler:** Khengarji III VS1932-98 / 1875-1942AD **Obv. Insc.:** Edward VIII...

Date	Mintage	VG	F	VF	XF	Unc
1936/VS1992	—	BV	11.50	17.50	23.50	32.50
1936/VS1993	—	BV	11.50	17.50	23.50	32.50

Y# 67 5 KORI

13.8700 g., 0.9370 Silver 0.4178 oz. ASW **Ruler:** Khengarji III VS1932-98 / 1875-1942AD **Obv. Insc.:** Edward VIII...

Date	Mintage	VG	F	VF	XF	Unc
1936/VS1992	—	BV	7.00	8.00	11.50	17.50
1936/VS1993	—	BV	7.00	8.00	11.50	17.50

Vijayarajji
VS1996-2004/1942-1947AD

MILLED COINAGE
Regal Issues - Sixth Series

Y# 76 TRAMBIYO

Copper **Ruler:** Vijayarajji VS1998-2004 / 1942-1947AD **Obv. Leg.:** George VI

Date	Mintage	VG	F	VF	XF	Unc
1943/VS2000	—	0.10	0.25	0.50	1.00	1.50
1944/VS2000	—	0.10	0.25	0.50	1.00	1.50

Y# 77 DHINGLO (1/16 Kori = 1-1/2 Dokda)

4.1100 g., Copper, 21 mm. **Ruler:** Vijayarajji VS1998-2004 / 1942-1947AD **Obv. Leg.:** George VI

Date	Mintage	VG	F	VF	XF	Unc
1943/VS2000	—	0.10	0.25	0.40	0.65	1.00
1944/VS2000	—	0.10	0.25	0.40	0.65	1.00
1947/VS2004	—	0.10	0.25	0.40	0.65	1.00
1948/VS2004	—	0.20	0.50	1.00	2.00	3.50

Madanasinghji
VS2004-2005/1947-1948AD

MILLED COINAGE
Regal Issues - Sixth Series

Y# 83 DHABU (1/8 Kori)

Copper **Ruler:** Madanasinghji VS2004-2005 / 1947-1948AD **Subject:** Victory for Indian Independence

Date	Mintage	VG	F	VF	XF	Unc
VS2004/1947	—	0.30	0.75	1.25	1.75	3.00

Y# 78   DHABU (1/8 Kori = 3 Dokda)
Copper, 23 mm. **Ruler:** Vijayarajji VS1998-2004 / 1942-1947AD
Obv. Leg.: George VI

Date	Mintage	VG	F	VF	XF	Unc
1943/VS1999	—	0.10	0.25	0.40	0.65	1.00
1943/VS1999	—	0.10	0.25	0.40	0.65	1.00
1944/VS2000	—	0.10	0.25	0.40	0.65	1.00
1947/VS2004	—	0.10	0.25	0.40	0.65	1.00

Y# 71   3 DOKDA
24.0000 g., Copper **Ruler:** Khengarji III VS1932-98 / 1875-1942AD **Obv. Leg.:** George VI

Date	Mintage	VG	F	VF	XF	Unc
1937/VS1993	—	0.90	1.50	2.00	3.00	5.50

Y# 79   PAYALO (1/4 Kori)
Copper, 27 mm. **Ruler:** Vijayarajji VS1998-2004 / 1942-1947AD
Obv. Leg.: George VI

Date	Mintage	VG	F	VF	XF	Unc
1943/VS1999	—	0.30	0.75	1.00	1.50	2.50
1943/VS2000	—	0.30	0.75	1.00	1.50	2.50
1944/VS2000	—	0.30	0.75	1.00	1.50	2.50
1944/VS2001	—	0.30	0.75	1.00	1.50	2.50
1945/VS2001	—	0.15	0.35	0.50	0.75	1.25
1945/VS2002	—	0.15	0.35	0.50	0.75	1.25
1946/VS2002	—	0.15	0.35	0.50	0.75	1.25
1946/VS2003	—	0.15	0.35	0.50	0.75	1.25
1947/VS2003	—	0.30	0.75	1.00	1.50	2.50

Y# 80   ADHIO (1/2 Kori)
Copper, 36 mm. **Ruler:** Vijayarajji VS1998-2004 / 1942-1947AD
Obv. Leg.: George VI

Date	Mintage	VG	F	VF	XF	Unc
1943/VS1999	—	0.60	1.50	1.75	2.00	3.50
1943/VS2000	—	0.60	1.50	1.75	2.00	3.50
1944/VS2001	—	0.60	1.25	1.50	1.75	3.00
1945/VS2001	—	0.60	1.50	1.75	2.00	3.50
1945/VS2002	—	0.60	1.50	1.75	2.00	3.50
1946/VS2002	—	0.60	1.50	1.75	2.00	3.50

Y# 73   KORI
4.7000 g., 0.6010 Silver 0.0908 oz. ASW **Ruler:** Khengarji III VS1932-98 / 1875-1942AD **Obv. Leg.:** George VI

Date	Mintage	VG	F	VF	XF	Unc
1937/VS1993	—	BV	3.00	4.50	6.50	10.00
1937/VS1994	—	BV	3.00	4.50	6.50	10.00
1938/VS1995	—	BV	3.00	4.50	6.50	10.00
1939/VS1995	—	BV	3.00	4.50	6.50	10.00
1939/VS1996	—	BV	3.00	4.50	6.50	10.00
1940/VS1996	—	BV	3.00	4.50	6.50	10.00

Y# 81   KORI
4.7000 g., 0.6010 Silver 0.0908 oz. ASW **Ruler:** Vijayarajji VS1998-2004 / 1942-1947AD **Obv. Leg.:** George VI

Date	Mintage	VG	F	VF	XF	Unc
1942/VS1999	—	BV	2.50	3.50	5.00	8.00
1943/VS1999	—	BV	2.50	3.50	5.00	8.00
1943/VS2000	—	BV	2.50	3.50	5.00	8.00
1944/VS2000	—	BV	2.50	3.50	5.00	8.00
1944/VS2001	—	BV	2.50	3.50	5.00	8.00

Y# A81   KORI
4.6600 g., Silver **Ruler:** Vijayarajji VS1998-2004 / 1942-1947AD
Obv. Leg.: George VI **Note:** Similar to Y#51.

Date	Mintage	VG	F	VF	XF	Unc
1942/VS1998 Rare	—	—	—	—	—	—

Y# 84   KORI
4.7000 g., 0.6010 Silver 0.0908 oz. ASW **Ruler:** Madanasinghji VS2004-2005 / 1947-1948AD **Subject:** Victory for Indian Independence

Date	Mintage	VG	F	VF	XF	Unc
VS2004/1947	—	BV	5.00	7.00	10.00	15.00

Y# 74   2-1/2 KORI
6.9350 g., 0.9370 Silver 0.2089 oz. ASW **Ruler:** Khengarji III VS1932-98 / 1875-1942AD **Obv. Insc.:** George VI

Date	Mintage	VG	F	VF	XF	Unc
1937/VS1993	—	BV	5.00	7.00	10.00	15.00

Y# 75   5 KORI
13.8700 g., 0.9370 Silver 0.4178 oz. ASW **Ruler:** Khengarji III VS1932-98 / 1875-1942AD **Obv. Insc.:** George VI

Date	Mintage	VG	F	VF	XF	Unc
1936/VS1993	—	BV	8.50	11.50	16.50	25.00
1937/VS1993	—	BV	7.50	10.00	15.00	22.50
1937/VS1994	—	BV	7.50	10.00	15.00	22.50
1938/VS1994	—	BV	7.50	10.00	15.00	22.50
1938/VS1995	—	BV	7.50	10.00	15.00	22.50
1941/VS1997	—	BV	10.00	15.00	21.50	30.00
1941/VS1998	—	BV	10.00	15.00	15.00	22.50

Y# 82   5 KORI
13.8700 g., 0.9370 Silver 0.4178 oz. ASW **Ruler:** Vijayarajji VS1998-2004 / 1942-1947AD **Obv. Insc.:** George VI

Date	Mintage	VG	F	VF	XF	Unc
1942/VS1998	—	BV	7.50	10.00	15.00	22.50

Date	Mintage	VG	F	VF	XF	Unc
1942/VS1999	—	BV	7.50	10.00	15.00	22.50
1943/VS1998 Reported, not confirmed						

Y# 85   5 KORI
13.8700 g., 0.9370 Silver 0.4178 oz. ASW **Ruler:** Madanasinghji VS2004-2005 / 1947-1948AD **Subject:** Victory for Indian Independence

Date	Mintage	VG	F	VF	XF	Unc
VS2004/1947	—	35.00	80.00	125	185	275

Y# 82A   10 KORI
17.3900 g., Silver **Ruler:** Vijayarajji VS1998-2004 / 1942-1947AD **Obv. Insc.:** George VI

Date	Mintage	VG	F	VF	XF	Unc
1943/VS1999 Rare	—	—	—	—	—	—

LUNAVADA

This small state in the Panch Mahal district of western India was ruled by Solanki Rajputs who claimed descent from Sidraj Jaisingh, the ruler of Anhalwara Patan and Gujerat. The rulers, or maharanas, traced their sovereignty to the early decades of the 15th century. At different times the State was feudatory to either Baroda or Sindhia.

Wakhat Singhji
VS1924-1986/1867-1929AD
HAMMERED COINAGE

KM# 12   PAISA
Copper **Obv:** Lotus Blossom **Rev:** Persian legend **Note:** Weight varies: 6.50-8.30 grams.

Date	Mintage	Good	VG	F	VF	XF
ND(ca.1911)	—	2.75	4.50	6.00	9.00	—
VS1968(1911)	—	2.75	4.50	6.00	9.00	—

MALER KOTLA

State located in the Punjab in northwest India, founded by the Maler Kotla family who were Sherwani Afghans who had travelled to India from Kabul in 1467 as officials of the Delhi emperors.

Coins are rupees of Ahmad Shah Durrani, and except for the last ruler, contain the chief's initial on the reverse. The chiefs were called Ra'is until 1821, Nawabs thereafter.

For similar issues see Jind, Nabha and Patiala.

RULERS
Ibrahim Ali Khan, AH1288-1326/1871-1908AD
Ahmad ali Khan, AH1326/1908AD

Ibrahim Ali Khan
AH1288-1326 / 1871-1908AD
HAMMERED COINAGE

Y# 4   1/4 RUPEE
Silver **Note:** 2.68-2.90 grams.

Date	Mintage	Good	VG	F	VF	XF
ND(1871-1908)	—	16.00	40.00	65.00	100	150

Y# 5   1/2 RUPEE
Silver, 16 mm. **Note:** 5.35-5.80 grams.

Date	Mintage	Good	VG	F	VF	XF
ND(1871-1908)	—	18.00	45.00	75.00	120	170

Y# 6 RUPEE
Silver **Note:** 10-70.11.60 grams.

Date	Mintage	Good	VG	F	VF	XF
ND(1871-1908)	—	4.25	7.00	9.00	13.50	20.00
AH1292	—	5.00	12.50	15.00	20.00	35.00
AH1311	—	5.00	12.50	15.00	20.00	35.00

Ahmad Ali Khan
AH1326- / 1908- AD
HAMMERED COINAGE

Y# 7 1/2 PAISA
Copper **Obv:** Persian inscription **Obv. Insc.:** Ahmad Ali Khan ...

Date	Mintage	Good	VG	F	VF	XF
AH1326 (1908)	—	7.00	11.00	16.50	25.00	—

Y# 8 PAISA
Copper **Obv:** Persian inscription **Obv. Insc.:** Ahmad Ali Khan ...

Date	Mintage	Good	VG	F	VF	XF
AH1326(1908-09)	—	17.50	25.00	35.00	50.00	—

Y# A9 RUPEE
10.7700 g., Silver, 18.5 mm. **Obv. Insc.:** Persian "Ahmad Ali Kahn..." **Rev. Insc.:** "Nawab" to left of "S" in "Julus" **Edge:** Plain

Date	Mintage	F	VF	XF	Unc	BU
ND(1908)	-	-	-	-	-	-

Y# 9 RUPEE
Silver **Obv:** Persian inscription **Obv. Insc.:** Ahmad Ali Khan ...
Note: Weight varies: 10.70-11.60 grams.

Date	Mintage	Good	VG	F	VF	XF
ND(1908-09)	—	4.50	6.50	10.00	15.00	25.00

Y# 10 NAZARANA 2 RUPEE
22.0000 g., Silver **Obv:** Persian inscription **Obv. Insc.:** Ahmad Ali Khan ...

Date	Mintage	Good	VG	F	VF	XF
AH1326(1908-09) Rare	—	—	—	—	—	—

Y# 11 1/2 MOHUR
5.9400 g., Gold **Obv:** Persian inscription **Obv. Insc.:** Ahmad Ali Khan ...

Date	Mintage	F	VF	XF	Unc	BU
AH1326 (1908-09)	—					

MEWAR

State located in Rajputana, northwest India. Capital: Udaipur.
The rulers of Mewar were universally regarded as the highest ranking Rajput house in India. The maharana of Mewar was looked upon as the representative of Rama, the ancient king of Ayodhya - and the family who were Sesodia Rajputs of the Gehlot clan, traced its descent through Rama to Kanak Sen who ruled in the 2nd century. The clan is believed to have migrated to Chitor from Gujarat sometime in the 8th century.

None of the indigenous rulers of India resisted the Muslim invasions into India with greater tenacity than the Rajputs of Mewar. It was their proud boast that they had never permitted a daughter to go into the Mughal harem. Three times the fortress and town of Chitor had fallen to Muslim invaders, to Alauddin Khilji (1303), to Bahadur Shah of Gujarat (1534) and to Akbar (1568). Each time Chitor gradually recovered but the last was the most traumatic experience of all. Rather than to submit to the Mughal onslaught, the women burned themselves on funeral pyres in a fearful rite called jauhar, and the men fell on the swords of the invaders.

After the sacking of Chitor the rana, Udai Singh, retired to the Aravali hills where he founded Udaipur, the capital after 1570. Udai Singh's son, Partab, refused to submit to the Mughal and recovered most of the territory lost in 1568. In the early 19th century Mewar suffered much at the hands of Marathas - Holkar, Sindhia and the Pindaris - until, in 1818, the State came under British supervision. In April 1948 Mewar was merged into Rajasthan and the maharana became governor Maharaj pramukh of the new province.

RULERS
Fatteh Singh, VS1941-1986/1884-1929AD
Bhupal Singh, VS1987-2005/1930-1948AD

MINTS

بهيلوارا
Bhilwara

चितोड़
Chitor

चित्रकूट
Chitarkot

उदयपुर
Udaipur

NOTE: All Mewar coinage is struck without ruler's name, and is largely undated. Certain types were generally struck over several reigns.

BRITISH PROTECTORATE

Fatteh Singh
VS1941-1986 / 1884-1929AD
MILLED COINAGE

VS1985 ie. 1928AD, but actually struck at the Alipore Mint in Calcutta between 1931-1932AD, the Y#22 rupee in 1931, the rest in 1932

Y# 13 PIE
2.5000 g., Copper, 16 mm. **Obv:** Inscription and date
Obv. Insc.: Chitor, date **Rev. Insc.:** Udaipur **Mint:** Udaipur

Date	Mintage	Good	VG	F	VF	XF
VS1975(1918)	—	—	12.50	25.00	50.00	—

Y# 14 PIE
2.1000 g., Copper **Obv:** Inscription and date **Obv. Insc.:** Chitor, date **Rev. Insc.:** Udaipur **Mint:** Udaipur

Date	Mintage	Good	VG	F	VF	XF
VS1978(1921)	—	—	7.00	15.00	22.50	—

Y# 18 1/16 RUPEE
0.9500 g., Silver, 12 mm. **Obv. Insc.:** Chitarkot / Udaipur **Rev. Insc.:** Dosti Lundhun (Friendship with London)

Date	Mintage	VG	F	VF	XF	Unc
VS1985(1928)	3,262,000	—	1.50	3.00	5.00	7.00

Y# 18a 1/16 RUPEE
Gold **Obv. Insc.:** Chitarkot / Udaipur **Rev. Insc.:** Dosti Lundhun (Friendship with London)

Date	Mintage	VG	F	VF	XF	Unc
VS1985 (1928) Proof	—					

Y# 19 1/8 RUPEE
1.3600 g., Silver, 15 mm. **Obv. Insc.:** "Chitarkot/Udaipur" **Rev. Insc.:** "Dosti Lundhun (Friendship with London)"

Date	Mintage	VG	F	VF	XF	Unc
VS1985(1928)	800,000	—	1.25	3.50	6.00	8.00

Y# 19a 1/8 RUPEE
Gold **Obv. Insc.:** Chitarkot / Udaipur **Rev. Insc.:** Dosti Lundhun (Friendship with London)

Date	Mintage	VG	F	VF	XF	Unc
VS1985 (1928) Proof	—					

Y# 20 1/4 RUPEE
2.7200 g., Silver, 19 mm. **Obv. Insc.:** "Chitarkot/Udaipur" **Rev. Insc.:** "Dosti Lundhun (Friendship with London)"

Date	Mintage	VG	F	VF	XF	Unc
VS1985(1928)	839,000	—	2.00	4.00	7.50	10.00

Y# 20a 1/4 RUPEE
Gold **Obv. Insc.:** Chitarkot / Udaipur **Rev. Insc.:** Dosti Lundhun (Friendship with London)

Date	Mintage	VG	F	VF	XF	Unc
VS1985 (1928) Proof	—					

Y# 21 1/2 RUPEE
5.4600 g., Silver, 24 mm. **Obv. Insc.:** "Chitarkot/Udaipur" **Rev. Insc.:** "Dosti Lundhun (Friendship with London)"

Date	Mintage	VG	F	VF	XF	Unc
VS1985(1928)	648,000	—	3.00	6.00	9.00	15.00

Y# 21a 1/2 RUPEE
Gold, 24 mm. **Obv. Insc.:** "Chitarkot/Udaipur" **Rev. Insc.:** "Dosti Lundhun (Friendship with London)" **Note:** Weight varies: 5.35-5.70 grams.

Date	Mintage	VG	F	VF	XF	Unc
VS1985(1928) Proof	—	Value: 1,500				

Y# 22.1 RUPEE
10.8600 g., Silver, 30 mm. **Obv. Insc.:** Thin characters, Chitarkot/Udaipur **Rev. Insc.:** Dosti Lundhun (Friendship with London)

Date	Mintage	VG	F	VF	XF	Unc
VS1985(1928)	14,906,000	—	BV	7.50	10.00	15.00

Y# 22.2 RUPEE
10.8600 g., Silver, 30 mm. **Obv. Insc.:** Thick characters, Chitarkot/Udaipur **Rev. Insc.:** Dosti Lundhun (Friendship with London)

Date	Mintage	VG	F	VF	XF	Unc
VS1985(1928)	Inc. above	—	BV	10.00	15.00	25.00

Y# 22a RUPEE
Gold, 30 mm. **Obv. Insc.:** Chitarkot/Udaipur **Rev. Insc.:** Dosti Lundhun (Friendship with London)

Date	Mintage	VG	F	VF	XF	Unc
VS1985(1928) Proof	—	Value: 2,500				

Bhupal Singh
VS1987-2005 / 1930-1948AD

HAMMERED COINAGE
Umarda Local Issues

Y# 24 1/2 PAISA
Copper **Note:** Varieties exist.

Date	Mintage	Good	VG	F	VF	XF
ND(1938-1941)	—	—	1.00	2.00	3.00	—

MILLED COINAGE
VS1985 ie. 1928AD, but actually struck at the Alipore Mint in Calcutta between 1931-1932AD, the Y#22 rupee in 1931, the rest in 1932

Y# 15 1/4 ANNA
2.2000 g., Copper **Obv. Insc.:** "Chitarkot/Udaipur"

Date	Mintage	VG	F	VF	XF	Unc
VS1999 (1942)	—	—	0.25	0.50	1.00	2.00

Y# 16.1 1/2 ANNA
3.5000 g., Copper **Obv:** Large character inscription **Obv. Insc.:** Chitarkot/Udaipur

Date	Mintage	VG	F	VF	XF	Unc
VS1999 (1942)	—	—	0.25	0.50	1.00	2.00

Y# 16.3 1/2 ANNA
Copper **Obv. Insc.:** Chitarkot / Udaipur **Note:** Octagonal flan.

Date	Mintage	VG	F	VF	XF	Unc
VS1999 (1942) Rare	—	—	—	—	—	—

Y# 16.2 1/2 ANNA
3.5000 g., Copper **Obv:** Small characters inscription **Obv. Insc.:** Chitarkot/Udaipur

Date	Mintage	VG	F	VF	XF	Unc
VS1999 (1942)	—	—	0.25	0.50	1.00	2.00

Y# 17 ANNA
4.3000 g., Copper **Obv. Insc.:** "Chitarkot/Udaipur" **Note:** Variations with 3 or 4 brushes exist.

Date	Mintage	VG	F	VF	XF	Unc
VS2000	—	—	0.25	0.50	1.00	2.00

PATTERNS
Including off metal strikes

KM#	Date	Mintage	Identification	Mkt Val
Pn1	VS1985 (1928)	—	1/16 Rupee. Silver.	—
Pn2	VS1985 (1928)	—	1/16 Rupee. Gold. Y18a.	—
Pn3	VS1985 (1928)	—	1/8 Rupee. Silver.	—
Pn4	VS1985 (1928)	—	1/8 Rupee. Gold. Y19a.	—
Pn5	VS1985 (1928)	—	1/4 Rupee. Silver.	—
Pn6	VS1985 (1928)	—	1/4 Rupee. Gold. KM20a.	850
Pn7	VS1985 (1928)	—	1/2 Rupee. Silver.	—
Pn8	VS1985 (1928)	—	1/2 Rupee. Gold. Y21a.	—
Pn9	VS1985 (1928)	—	Rupee. Silver. Y22a.	—
Pn10	VS1985 (1928)	—	Rupee. Gold.	—

PATIALA

State located in the Punjab in northwest India. In the mid-18th century the Raja was given his title and mint right by Ahmad Shah Durrani of Afghanistan, whose coin he copied.

The rulers became Maharajas in 1810AD. The maharaja of Patiala was also recognized as the leader of the Phulkean tribe. Unlike others, Patiala's Sikh rulers had never hesitated to seek British assistance at those times when they felt threatened by their co-religionist neighbors. In 1857, Patiala's forces were immediately made available on the side of the British.

RULERS
Bhupindar Singh, VS1958-1994/1900-1937AD
Yadvindar Singh, VS1994-2005/1937-1948AD

Bhupindar Singh
VS1958-1994 / 1900-1937AD

HAMMERED COINAGE

KM# 28 RUPEE
Silver **Obv:** Persian inscription **Obv. Insc.:** Guru Govind Singh **Rev:** Dagger at left **Note:** Weight varies: 11.10-11.20 grams. Prev. Y#A3.

Date	Mintage	VG	F	VF	XF	Unc
VS1958 (1901)	—	—	—	—	—	—

Y# 14 1/6 MOHUR
1.7500 g., Gold **Obv:** Persian inscription **Obv. Insc.:** "Ahmad Shah Durrani" **Rev:** Dagger at left

Date	Mintage	VG	F	VF	XF	Unc
VS(19)58	—	—	85.00	100	125	175
VS(19)90	—	—	—	—	—	—

KM# 15 1/3 MOHUR
3.5000 g., Gold **Obv:** Persian inscription **Obv. Insc.:** "Ahmad Shah Durrani" **Rev:** Dagger at left

Date	Mintage	VG	F	VF	XF	Unc
VS(19)58	—	—	100	120	140	200

Y# 16 2/3 MOHUR
7.0000 g., Gold **Obv:** Persian inscription **Obv. Insc.:** "Ahmad Shah Durrani" **Rev:** Dagger at left

Date	Mintage	VG	F	VF	XF	Unc
VS(19)58	—	—	175	200	250	325

Y# 17 MOHUR
10.5000 g., Gold **Obv:** Persian inscription **Obv. Insc.:** "Ahmad Shah Durrani" **Rev:** Dagger at left

Date	Mintage	VG	F	VF	XF	Unc
VS(19)58	—	—	BV	265	325	400

Yadvindar Singh
VS1994-2005 / 1937-1948AD

HAMMERED COINAGE

KM# 27 1/4 RUPEE
Silver **Obv:** Persian inscription **Obv. Insc.:** Guru Govind Singh **Rev:** Bayoneted rifle at left **Note:** Weight varies: 11.10-11.20 grams. Prev. Y#A1.

Date	Mintage	VG	F	VF	XF	Unc
VS1994 (1937)	—	—	—	—	—	—

KM# 29 1/6 MOHUR
1.7500 g., Gold **Obv:** Persian inscription **Obv. Insc.:** "Ahmad Shah Durrani" **Rev:** Bayoneted rifle at left **Note:** Prev. Y#19.

Date	Mintage	VG	F	VF	XF	Unc
VS(19)94 /(1937)	—	—	80.00	100	125	175

KM# 30 1/3 MOHUR
3.5000 g., Gold **Obv:** Persian inscription **Obv. Insc.:** "Ahmad Shah Durrani" **Rev:** Bayoneted rifle at left **Note:** Prev. KM#20.

Date	Mintage	VG	F	VF	XF	Unc
VS(19)94 /(1937AD)	—	—	100	120	140	200

KM# 31 2/3 MOHUR
7.0000 g., Gold **Obv:** Persian inscription **Obv. Insc.:** "Ahmad Shah Durrani" **Rev:** Bayoneted rifle at left **Note:** Prev. Y#21.

Date	Mintage	VG	F	VF	XF	Unc
VS(19)94/(1937 AD)	—	—	75.00	200	250	325

SAILANA

This small state in west-central India, of slightly over one hundred square miles had once been part of Ratlam, but about 1709 it asserted its independence under the leadership of Pratab Singh, the second son of Chhatrasal. The town of Sailana was founded in 1730 by Jai Singh's successor, and from that date the state was named after it. Due to its small size and vulnerability, Sailana was obliged to become tributary to Sindhia to ensure its survival. In 1819 this payment was limited to one-third of the state's revenues. Later, under agreements of 1840 and 1860, the tribute went to the British for the support of British Indian troops in the region. Barmawal was feudatory to Sailana.

LOCAL RULERS
Jaswant Singh, 1895-1919AD
Dilip Singh Bahadur, 1919-1948

Jaswant Singh
1890-1919AD

MILLED COINAGE
Regal Series

KM# 15 1/4 ANNA
Copper **Obv:** Bust of King Edward VII right

Date	Mintage	VG	F	VF	XF	Unc
1908	224,000	—	15.00	30.00	75.00	200
1908 Proof	—	Value: 350				

KM# 16 1/4 ANNA
Copper **Obv:** Crowned bust of King George V left

Date	Mintage	VG	F	VF	XF	Unc
1912	224,000	—	2.50	5.00	10.00	25.00
1912 Proof	—	Value: 175				

TONK

Tonk

State located partially in Rajputana and in central India. Tonk was founded in 1806 by Amir Khan (d. 1834), the Pathan Pindari leader who received the territory from Holkar. Amir Khan caused great havoc in Central India by his lightning raids into neighboring states. In 1817 he was forced into submission by the East India Company and remained under British control until India's independence. In March 1948 Tonk was incorporated into Rajasthan.

RULERS

Muhammad Ibrahim Ali Khan, AH1284-1349/1868-1930AD
Muhammad Sa'adat Ali Khan, AH1349-1368/1930-1949AD

MINT MARKS

Sironj

Tonk

Flower (on all)

Leaf (several forms)

Beginning with the reign of Muhammad Ibrahim Ali Khan, most coins have both AD and AH dates. Coins with both dates fully legible are worth about 20% more than listed prices. Coins with one date fully legible are worth prices shown. Coins with both dates off are of little value.

There are many minor and major variations of type, varying with location of date, orientation of leaf, arrangement of legend. Although these fall into easily distinguished patterns, they are strictly for the specialist and are omitted here.

The Tonk rupee was known as the "Chanwarshahi".

BRITISH PROTECTORATE

Muhammad Ibrahim Ali Khan
AH1284-1349 / 1868-1930AD

HAMMERED COINAGE

Y# A24 1/2 PAISA
5.4000 g., Copper Obv. Insc.: George V...
Rev. Insc.: Muhammad Ibrahim Ali Khan... Mint: Tonk

Date	Mintage	Good	VG	F	VF	XF
AH13(46)//1928	—	—	7.00	15.00	25.00	—

Y# 24.1 PAISA
7.3000 g., Copper Obv. Insc.: George V...
Rev. Insc.: Muhammad Ibrahim Ali Khan... Mint: Tonk

Date	Mintage	Good	VG	F	VF	XF
AH1329//1911	—	—	0.50	1.00	3.00	—
AH1329(sic)//1329	—	—	0.50	1.00	3.00	—
1911(sic)	—	—	0.50	1.00	3.00	—
AH1330//1911	—	—	0.50	1.00	3.00	—

Y# 24.2 PAISA
5.0000 g., Copper Obv. Insc.: George V... Rev. Insc.: Muhammad Ibrahim Ali Khan... Mint: Tonk Note: Reduced weight.

Date	Mintage	Good	VG	F	VF	XF
AH1335//1917	—	—	0.50	1.00	3.00	—
AH(13)38//1924	—	—	0.50	1.00	3.00	—
AH1342//1924	—	—	0.50	1.00	3.00	—
AH1344//1925	—	—	0.50	1.00	3.00	—
AH1344//1926	—	—	0.50	1.00	3.00	—
AH1345//1927	—	—	0.50	1.00	3.00	—
AH134x//1928	—	—	0.50	1.00	3.00	—

Y# A25.1 1/4 ANNA
8.3000 g., Copper Obv. Insc.: George V...
Rev. Insc.: Muhammad Ibrahim Ali Khan... Mint: Tonk

Date	Mintage	Good	VG	F	VF	XF
AH1335//1917	—	—	1.50	3.00	5.00	—
AH1336//1917	—	—	1.50	3.00	5.00	—

Y# A25.2 1/4 ANNA
5.4000 g., Copper Obv. Insc.: George V... Rev. Insc.: Muhammad Ibrahim Ali Khan... Mint: Tonk Note: Reduced weight.

Date	Mintage	Good	VG	F	VF	XF
AH1336//1917	—	—	1.50	3.00	5.00	—

Y# 25 1/8 RUPEE
Silver Obv. Insc.: George V... Rev. Insc.: Muhammad Ibrahim Ali Khan... Mint: Tonk Note: Weight varies: 1.34-1.45 grams.

Date	Mintage	Good	VG	F	VF	XF
AH1340//1922	—	—	10.00	20.00	30.00	50.00
AH-//1927	—	—	10.00	20.00	30.00	50.00
AH1346//1928	—	—	10.00	20.00	30.00	50.00

Y# 26 1/4 RUPEE
Silver Obv. Insc.: George V... Rev. Insc.: Muhammad Ibrahim Ali Khan... Mint: Tonk Note: Weight varies: 2.68-2.90 grams.

Date	Mintage	Good	VG	F	VF	XF
AH1346//1928	—	—	7.50	15.00	25.00	40.00

Y# 27 1/2 RUPEE
Silver Obv. Insc.: George V... Rev. Insc.: Muhammad Ibrahim Ali Khan... Mint: Tonk Note: Weight varies: 5.35-5.80 grams.

Date	Mintage	Good	VG	F	VF	XF
AH1346//1928	—	—	7.50	15.00	25.00	40.00

Y# 28 RUPEE
Silver Obv. Insc.: George V... Rev. Insc.: Muhammad Ibrahim Ali Khan... Mint: Tonk Note: Weight varies: 10.70-11.60 grams.

Date	Mintage	Good	VG	F	VF	XF
AH1329//1911	—	—	4.00	8.00	12.00	20.00
AH1330//1912	—	—	4.00	8.00	12.00	20.00
AH1341//1923	—	—	4.00	8.00	12.00	20.00
AH1342//1923	—	—	4.00	8.00	12.00	20.00
AH1342//1924	—	—	4.00	8.00	12.00	20.00
AH1343//1924	—	—	4.00	8.00	12.00	20.00
AH1343//1925	—	—	4.00	8.00	12.00	20.00
AH1344//1925	—	—	4.00	8.00	12.00	20.00
AH1344//1926	—	—	4.00	8.00	12.00	20.00
AH1345//1926	—	—	4.00	8.00	12.00	20.00
AH1346//1926	—	—	4.00	8.00	12.00	20.00
AH1346//1927	—	—	4.00	8.00	12.00	20.00
AH1347//1928	—	—	4.00	8.00	12.00	20.00
AH1348//1928	—	—	4.00	8.00	12.00	20.00
AH1348//1929	—	—	4.00	8.00	12.00	20.00
AH134x//1930	—	—	4.00	8.00	12.00	20.00

Muhammad Sa'adat Ali Khan
AH1349-1368 / 1930-1949AD

HAMMERED COINAGE

Y# 30 1/8 RUPEE
Silver Obv. Insc.: George V... Rev. Insc.: Muhammad Sa'adat Ali Khan... Mint: Tonk Note: Weight varies: 1.34-1.45 grams.

Date	Mintage	Good	VG	F	VF	XF
AH1351//1932	—	—	3.50	7.00	15.00	25.00
AH1352//1933	—	—	3.50	7.00	15.00	25.00
AH1353//1934	—	—	3.50	7.00	15.00	25.00

MILLED COINAGE

KM# 29 PICE (Paisa)
Copper, 26 mm. Obv: Arms Rev: Leaf

Date	Mintage	VG	F	VF	XF	Unc
AH1350//1932	640,000	—	0.25	1.00	3.00	

KM# 29a PICE (Paisa)
Copper, 21 mm. Obv: Arms Rev: Leaf

Date	Mintage	VG	F	VF	XF	Unc
AH1350//1932	640,000	—	0.25	0.50	2.00	

TRAVANCORE

State located in extreme southwest India. A mint was established in ME965/1789-1790AD.

The region of Travancore had a lengthy history before being annexed by the Vijayanagar kingdom. With Vijayanagar's defeat at the battle of Talikota in 1565, Travancore passed under Muslim control until the late 18th century, when it merged as a state in its own right under Raja Martanda Varma. At this time the raja allied himself with British interests as a protection against the Muslim dynasty of Mysore. In 1795 the raja of Travancore officially accepted a subsidiary alliance with the East India Company, and remained within the orbit of British influence from then until India's independence.

RULERS
Rama Varma VI, ME1062-1101/1885-1924AD
Bala Rama Varma II, ME1101-1126/1924-1949AD

DATING
ME dates are of the Malabar Era. Add 824 or 825 to the ME date for the AD date. (i.e., ME1112 plus 824-825 = 1936-1937AD).

KINGDOM

Rama Varma VI
ME1062-1101 / 1885-1924AD

MILLED COINAGE

KM# 40 CASH
0.6500 g., Copper Obv. Leg.: CASH 1

Date	Mintage	VG	F	VF	XF	Unc
ND(1901)	—	4.00	9.00	15.00	22.50	35.00

KM# 46 CASH
0.6500 g., Copper Obv: Sankha (conch shell) in 8-pointed star
Note: Thick

Date	Mintage	VG	F	VF	XF	Unc
ND(1901-10)	—	—	0.25	0.50	1.00	

Note: Refer to Bala Rama Varma II listings for thin variety, KM#57

KM# 41 4 CASH
Copper Obv: RV monogram Obv. Leg.: CASH FOUR
Rev: Sankha (conch shell) in sprays

Date	Mintage	VG	F	VF	XF	Unc
ND(1901-10)	—	—	1.50	3.00	5.00	15.00

KM# 47   4 CASH
Copper **Obv:** RV monogram **Obv. Leg.:** FOUR CASH
Rev: Malayalam "Oru Kasu" (One Cash)

Date	Mintage	VG	F	VF	XF	Unc
ND(1906-35)	—	—	0.80	1.00	3.00	5.00
ND(1906-35) Proof	—	Value: 65.00				

KM# 42   8 CASH
Copper **Obv:** RV monogram **Obv. Leg.:** CASH EIGHT
Rev: Sankha (conch shell) in sprays

Date	Mintage	VG	F	VF	XF	Unc
ND(1901-10)	—	—	1.50	3.00	8.00	25.00

KM# 48   8 CASH
Copper **Obv:** RV monogram **Obv. Leg.:** EIGHT CASH
Rev: Sankha (conch shell) in sprays

Date	Mintage	VG	F	VF	XF	Unc
ND(1906-35)	—	—	0.50	1.00	3.00	5.00
ND(1906-35) Proof	—	Value: 75.00				

KM# 43   CHUCKRAM
Copper **Obv:** RV monogram **Obv. Leg.:** CHUCKRAM ONE
Rev: Sankha (conch shell) in sprays

Date	Mintage	VG	F	VF	XF	Unc
ND(1901-10)	—	—	3.50	7.00	10.00	17.50

KM# 49   CHUCKRAM
Copper **Obv:** RV monogram **Obv. Leg.:** ONE CHUCKRAM
Rev: Sankha (conch shell) in sprays

Date	Mintage	VG	F	VF	XF	Unc
ND(1906-35)	—	—	0.50	1.00	3.00	5.00

KM# 44   2 CHUCKRAMS
Silver, 10 mm. **Obv:** RV monogram **Obv. Leg.:** CHS. 2 **Rev:** Sankha (conch shell) in sprays

Date	Mintage	VG	F	VF	XF	Unc
ND(1901)	—	—	2.50	5.00	10.00	25.00

KM# 50   2 CHUCKRAMS
Silver **Obv:** RV monogram **Obv. Leg.:** 2 CHS. **Rev:** Sankha (conch shell) in sprays

Date	Mintage	VG	F	VF	XF	Unc
ND(1906-28)	—	—	1.00	2.00	3.00	10.00

KM# 45   FANAM
Silver **Obv:** RV monogram **Obv. Leg.:** FANAM ONE
Rev: Sankha (conch shell) in sprays **Edge:** Plain

Date	Mintage	VG	F	VF	XF	Unc
ND(1901)	—	—	2.50	5.00	10.00	25.00

KM# 54   FANAM
Silver **Obv:** RV monogram **Obv. Leg.:** ONE FANAM
Rev: Sankha (conch shell) in sprays **Edge:** Plain

Date	Mintage	VG	F	VF	XF	Unc
ND(1911)	—	—	7.50	15.00	25.00	50.00

KM# 55   FANAM
Silver **Obv:** RV monogram **Obv. Leg.:** FANAM ONE
Rev: Sankha (conch shell) in sprays **Edge:** Reeded

Date	Mintage	VG	F	VF	XF	Unc
ND(1911)	—	1.50	3.00	5.00	7.00	12.50

KM# 51   FANAM
0.9500 Silver **Rev:** Sankha (conch shell) in sprays

Date	Mintage	VG	F	VF	XF	Unc
ME1087(1911-12)	1,100,000	—	1.50	2.00	5.00	12.00
ME1096 (1920-21)	350,000	—	1.50	2.00	5.00	12.00
ME1099 (1923-24)	350,000	—	1.50	2.00	5.00	12.00
ME1100 (1924-25)	700,000	—	1.50	2.00	5.00	12.00
ME1103 (1927-28)	700,000	—	1.50	2.00	5.00	12.00
ME1106 (1930-31)	—	—	1.50	2.00	5.00	12.00

KM# 52   1/4 RUPEE
2.7200 g., 0.9500 Silver 0.0831 oz. ASW **Obv. Leg.:** RAMA VURMA-TRAVENCORE **Rev:** Sankha (conch shell) in sprays

Date	Mintage	VG	F	VF	XF	Unc
ME1082 (1906-07)	—	—	1.50	3.00	5.00	12.00
ME1083 (1907-08)	—	—	1.50	3.00	5.00	12.00
ME1085 (1909-10)	—	—	1.50	3.00	5.00	12.00
ME1086 (1910-11)	—	—	1.50	3.00	5.00	12.00
ME1087 (1911-12)	400,000	—	1.50	3.00	5.00	12.00
ME1096 (1920-21)	—	—	1.50	3.00	5.00	12.00
ME1099 (1923-24)	—	—	1.50	3.00	5.00	12.00
ME1100 (1924-25)	—	—	1.50	3.00	5.00	12.00
ME1103 (1927-28)	200,000	—	1.50	3.00	5.00	12.00
ME1106 (1930-31)	200,000	—	1.50	3.00	5.00	12.00

KM# 53   1/2 RUPEE
5.4400 g., 0.9500 Silver 0.1661 oz. ASW **Rev:** Legend shorter on bottom

Date	Mintage	VG	F	VF	XF	Unc
ME1084 (1908-09)	—	—	4.50	9.00	15.00	25.00
ME1085 (1909-10)	—	—	4.50	9.00	15.00	25.00
ME1086 (1910-11)	—	—	4.50	9.00	15.00	25.00
ME1087 (1911-12)	300,000	—	4.50	9.00	15.00	25.00
ME1103 (1927-28)	100,000	—	4.50	9.00	15.00	25.00
ME1106 (1930-31)	100,000	—	4.50	9.00	15.00	25.00
ME1106 (1930-31) Proof; Rare	—	—	—	—	—	—
ME1107 (1931-32)	800,000	—	4.50	9.00	15.00	25.00

Bala Rama Varma II
ME1101-1126 / 1924-1949AD
MILLED COINAGE

KM# 57   CASH
0.4800 g., Copper **Obv:** Sankha (conch shell) in 8-pointed star
Rev: Malayalam "Oru Kasu" (one cash) **Note:** Thin .8mm planchet.

Date	Mintage	VG	F	VF	XF	Unc
ND(1928-49)	—	—	—	0.10	0.25	0.50

Note: Refer to Rama Varma VI listings for thick variety, KM#46

KM# 58   4 CASH
1.9400 g., Bronze, 17.5 mm. **Obv:** RV monogram **Rev:** Sankha (conch shell) in sprays **Edge:** Plain

Date	Mintage	VG	F	VF	XF	Unc
ND(1938-49)	—	—	—	0.25	0.50	2.00
ND(1938-49) Proof, Rare	—	Value: 75.00				

KM# 59   8 CASH
Bronze **Obv:** BRV monogram **Rev:** Sankha (conch shell) in sprays

Date	Mintage	VG	F	VF	XF	Unc
ND(1938-49)	—	—	0.50	1.00	2.00	4.00

KM# 60   CHUCKRAM
Bronze **Obv:** Bust of Bala Rama Barma II right **Rev:** Sankha (conch shell) in sprays

Date	Mintage	VG	F	VF	XF	Unc
ME1114(1938-39)	—	—	0.50	1.00	2.00	5.00
ND(1939-40)	—	—	0.50	1.00	1.50	2.50
ND(1939-40) Proof	—	Value: 150				

KM# 60a   CHUCKRAM
Gold **Obv:** Bust of Bala Rama Barma II right **Rev:** Sankha (conch shell) in sprays

Date	Mintage	VG	F	VF	XF	Unc
ND(1939-40) Prooflike; restrike	—	—	—	—	—	5,000

KM# 61   FANAM
0.9500 g., Silver **Obv. Leg.:** BALA RAMA VARMA-TRAVANCORE **Rev:** Sankha (conch shell) in sprays

Date	Mintage	VG	F	VF	XF	Unc
ME1112(1936-37)	350,000	BV	2.50	5.00	7.00	12.50

KM# 65   FANAM
1.5100 g., 0.5000 Silver 0.0243 oz. ASW **Obv. Leg.:** BALA RAMA VARMA-TRAVANCORE **Rev:** Sankha (conch shell) in sprays

Date	Mintage	VG	F	VF	XF	Unc
ME1116(1940-41)	2,096,000	BV	0.25	0.50	1.00	3.00
ME1118(1942-43)	4,157,000	BV	0.25	0.50	1.00	3.00
ME1121(1945-46)	1,925,000	BV	0.25	0.50	1.00	3.00

KM# 62   1/4 RUPEE
0.9500 g., Silver **Obv. Leg.:** BALA RAMA VARMA-TRAVANCORE

Date	Mintage	VG	F	VF	XF	Unc
ME1112(1936-37)	200,000	BV	2.50	5.00	10.00	25.00

KM# 66   1/4 RUPEE

2.6600 g., 0.5000 Silver 0.0428 oz. ASW **Obv. Leg.:** BALA RAMA VARMA-TRAVANCORE

Date	Mintage	VG	F	VF	XF	Unc
ME1116(1940-41)	126,000	BV	1.75	3.75	5.50	9.00
ME1116(1940-41) Proof	—	Value: 125				
ME1118(1942-43)		BV	3.00	7.00	10.00	17.50

KM# 63   1/2 RUPEE

0.9500 g., Silver **Obv. Leg.:** BALA RAMA VARMA-TRAVENCORE

Date	Mintage	VG	F	VF	XF	Unc
ME1112(1936-37)	200,000	BV	10.00	20.00	50.00	75.00

KM# 64   1/2 CHITRA RUPEE

Silver **Obv. Leg.:** BALA RAMA VARMA-TRAVENCORE **Edge:** Reeded

Date	Mintage	VG	F	VF	XF	Unc
ME1114 (1938-39)	—	BV	2.50	5.00	10.00	25.00

KM# 67   1/2 CHITRA RUPEE

5.3100 g., 0.5000 Silver 0.0854 oz. ASW **Obv. Leg.:** BALA RAMA VARMA-TRAVENCORE **Edge:** Security

Date	Mintage	VG	F	VF	XF	Unc
ME1116(1940-41)	1,600,000	BV	1.75	3.00	5.00	10.00
ME1118/6(1942-43)	1,111,000	BV	1.75	3.00	5.00	10.00
ME1118(1942-43)	Inc. above	BV	1.75	3.00	5.00	10.00
ME1118(1942-43) Proof	—	Value: 150				
ME1121(1945-46)	200,000	BV	1.75	3.00	5.00	10.00

PATTERNS
Including off metal strikes

KM#	Date	Mintage	Identification	Mkt Val
Pn3	ME1086(1910)	—	1/4 Rupee. Bronze. KM#52	90.00

EUROPEAN INFLUENCES IN INDIA

Vasco da Gama, the Portuguese explorer, first visited India in 1498. Portugal seized control of a number of islands and small enclaves on the west coast of India, and for the next hundred years enjoyed a monopoly on trade. With the arrival of powerful Dutch and English fleets in the first half of the 17th century, Portuguese power in the area declined until virtually all of India that remained under Portuguese control were the west coast enclaves of Goa, Damao and Diu. They were forcibly annexed by India in 1962.

RULER
Portuguese, until 1961

DENOMINATION
The denomination of most copper coins appears in numerals on the reverse, though 30 Reis is often given as "1/2 T," and 60 Reis as "T" (T = Tanga). The silver coins have the denomination in words, usually on the obverse until 1850, then on the reverse.

MONETARY SYSTEM
960 Reis = 16 Tanga = 1 Rupia

PORTUGUESE ADMINISTRATION
Kingdom of Portugal
MILLED COINAGE

KM# 13   1/12 TANGA

Bronze **Obv:** Head of Carlos I right **Rev:** Crowned shield **Note:** Roman numeral dating.

Date	Mintage	F	VF	XF	Unc	BU
1901	960,000	6.00	12.00	28.00	55.00	—
1901 Prooflike	—	—	—	—	—	—
1903	960,000	6.00	12.00	28.00	55.00	—

KM# 14   1/8 TANGA

Bronze **Obv:** Head of Carlos I right **Rev:** Crowned shield **Note:** Roman numeral dating

Date	Mintage	F	VF	XF	Unc	BU
1901	960,000	7.00	15.00	32.00	70.00	—
1901 Prooflike	—	—	—	—	—	—
1903	960,000	7.00	15.00	32.00	70.00	—

KM# 15   1/4 TANGA (15 Reis)

Bronze **Obv:** Head of Carlos I right **Rev:** Crowned shield **Note:** Roman numeral dating.

Date	Mintage	F	VF	XF	Unc	BU
1901	800,000	7.50	16.00	35.00	75.00	—
1901 Prooflike	—	—	—	—	200	—
1903	800,000	7.50	16.00	35.00	75.00	—

KM# 16   1/2 TANGA (30 Reis)

Bronze **Obv:** Head of Carlos I right **Note:** Roman numeral dating.

Date	Mintage	F	VF	XF	Unc	BU
1901	800,000	8.00	17.50	37.50	80.00	—
1901 Prooflike	—	—	—	—	225	—
1903	800,000	8.00	17.50	37.50	80.00	—

KM# 17   RUPIA

11.6600 g., 0.9170 Silver 0.3437 oz. ASW **Obv:** Head of Carlos I right **Rev:** Crowned shield within wreath

Date	Mintage	F	VF	XF	Unc	BU
1903	200,000	8.00	16.00	32.00	65.00	—
1904	100,000	9.00	18.00	35.00	70.00	—

PORTUGUESE ADMINISTRATION
Republic of Portugal
MILLED COINAGE

KM# 19 TANGA (60 Reis)
Bronze **Obv:** Divided shield **Rev:** Five shields on shield

Date	Mintage	F	VF	XF	Unc	BU
1934	100,000	25.00	70.00	245	500	—

KM# 24 TANGA (60 Reis)
Bronze, 25 mm. **Obv:** Denomination **Rev:** Tiny towers and shields above divided shield on lined circle

Date	Mintage	F	VF	XF	Unc	BU
1947	1,000,000	2.00	7.00	15.00	30.00	—

KM# 28 TANGA (60 Reis)
Bronze, 20 mm. **Obv:** Denomination **Rev:** Tiny towers and shields above divided shield on lined circle

Date	Mintage	F	VF	XF	Unc	BU
1952	9,600,000	1.00	4.00	9.00	20.00	—

KM# 20 2 TANGAS
Copper-Nickel

Date	Mintage	F	VF	XF	Unc	BU
1934	150,000	10.00	20.00	185	400	—

KM# 21 4 TANGAS
Copper-Nickel **Obv:** Divided shield **Rev:** Five shields on shield

Date	Mintage	F	VF	XF	Unc	BU
1934	100,000	20.00	60.00	210	450	—

KM# 25 1/4 RUPIA
Copper-Nickel **Obv:** Denomination **Rev:** Tiny towers and shields above divided shield on lined circle

Date	Mintage	F	VF	XF	Unc	BU
1947	800,000	5.00	10.00	20.00	40.00	—
1952	4,000,000	2.00	4.00	12.00	25.00	—

KM# 23 1/2 RUPIA
6.0000 g., 0.9170 Silver 0.1769 oz. ASW, 25 mm. **Obv:** Shield on lined circle at center of Maltese cross **Rev:** Divided shield

Date	Mintage	F	VF	XF	Unc	BU
1936	100,000	16.00	28.00	45.00	90.00	—

KM# 26 1/2 RUPIA
Copper-Nickel **Obv:** Denomination **Rev:** Tiny towers and shields above divided shield on lined circle

Date	Mintage	F	VF	XF	Unc	BU
1947	600,000	7.00	15.00	30.00	60.00	—
1952	2,000,000	2.00	5.00	12.00	25.00	—

1912/1

KM# 18 RUPIA
11.6600 g., 0.9170 Silver 0.3437 oz. ASW **Obv:** Liberty head left **Rev:** Denomination within wreath

Date	Mintage	F	VF	XF	Unc	BU
1912/1	300,000	75.00	150	285	500	—
1912/1 Proof	—	Value: 1,250				
1912	Inc. above	35.00	75.00	150	285	—

KM# 22 RUPIA
12.0000 g., 0.9170 Silver 0.3538 oz. ASW **Obv:** Shield on lined circle at center of Maltese Cross **Rev:** Divided shield

Date	Mintage	F	VF	XF	Unc	BU
1935	300,000	7.50	15.00	30.00	55.00	—

KM# 27 RUPIA
12.0000 g., 0.5000 Silver 0.1929 oz. ASW **Obv:** Shield on lined circle at center of Maltese Cross **Rev:** Tiny towers and shields above divided shield on lined circle

Date	Mintage	F	VF	XF	Unc	BU
1947	900,000	7.50	15.00	30.00	60.00	—

KM# 29 RUPIA
Copper-Nickel **Obv:** Shield on lined circle at center of Maltese cross **Rev:** Tiny towers and shields above divided shield on lined circle

Date	Mintage	F	VF	XF	Unc	BU
1952	1,000,000	7.50	15.00	30.00	60.00	—

DECIMAL COINAGE
100 Centavos = 1 Escudo

KM# 30 10 CENTAVOS
2.0000 g., Bronze, 18 mm. **Obv:** Denomination **Rev:** Tiny towers and shields above divided shield on lined circle

Date	Mintage	F	VF	XF	Unc	BU
1958	5,000,000	1.00	3.00	7.00	16.00	—
1959	Inc. above	1.00	3.00	7.00	16.00	—
1961	1,000,000	0.50	1.00	1.50	3.00	—

KM# 31 30 CENTAVOS
Bronze **Obv:** Denomination **Rev:** Tiny towers and shields above divided shield on lined circle

Date	Mintage	F	VF	XF	Unc	BU
1958	5,000,000	0.75	2.50	7.00	16.00	—
1959	Inc. above	2.50	7.00	15.00	30.00	—

KM# 32 60 CENTAVOS
Copper-Nickel **Obv:** Shield on lined circle at center of Maltese Cross **Rev:** Tiny towers and shields above divided shield on lined circle

Date	Mintage	F	VF	XF	Unc	BU
1958	5,000,000	2.00	4.00	10.00	20.00	—
1959	Inc. above	1.25	2.50	6.50	13.50	—

KM# 33 ESCUDO
Copper-Nickel **Obv:** Shield on lined circle at center of Maltese Cross **Rev:** Tiny towers and shields above divided shield on lined circle

Date	Mintage	F	VF	XF	Unc	BU
1958	6,000,000	1.25	2.50	7.50	16.00	—
1959	Inc. above	1.25	2.50	6.50	13.50	—

KM# 34 3 ESCUDOS
Copper-Nickel **Obv:** Shield on lined circle at center of Maltese Cross **Rev:** Tiny towers and shields above divided shield on lined circle

Date	Mintage	F	VF	XF	Unc	BU
1958	5,000,000	2.50	5.00	12.00	22.00	—
1959	Inc. above	2.50	4.50	9.00	18.00	—

KM# 35 6 ESCUDOS
Copper-Nickel **Obv:** Shield on lined circle at center of Maltese Cross **Rev:** Tiny towers and shields above divided shield on lined circle

Date	Mintage	F	VF	XF	Unc	BU
1959	4,000,000	2.50	4.50	9.00	20.00	—

PATTERNS
Including off metal strikes

KM#	Date	Mintage	Identification	Mkt Val
Pn28	1901	—	1/2 Tanga. Aluminum. KM#13	150
Pn29	1901	—	1/8 Tanga. Aluminum. KM#14	150
Pn30	1901	—	1/4 Tanga. Aluminum. KM#15	150
Pn31	1911	—	Rupia. Silver. KM#18	—
Pn32	1911	—	Rupia. Copper. KM#18	750

PROVAS
Standard metals unless otherwise noted; Stamped

KM#	Date	Mintage	Identification	Issue Price	Mkt Val
Pr1	1934	—	Tanga. Bronze. KM#19	—	325
Pr2	1934	—	2 Tangas. Copper-Nickel. KM#20	—	335
Pr3	1934	—	4 Tangas. Copper-Nickel. KM#21	—	340
Pr4	1935	—	Rupia. Silver. KM#22	—	140
Pr5	1936	—	1/2 Rupia. Silver. KM#23	—	95.00
Pr6	1947	—	1/4 Rupia. Copper-Nickel. KM#25	—	50.00
Pr7	1947	—	1/2 Rupia. Copper-Nickel. KM#26	—	50.00
Pr8	1947	—	Tanga. Bronze. KM#24	—	50.00
Pr9	1947	—	Rupia. Silver. KM#27	—	85.00
Pr10	1952	—	1/4 Rupia. Copper-Nickel. KM#25	—	50.00
Pr11	1952	—	1/2 Rupia. Copper-Nickel. KM#26	—	40.00
Pr12	1952	—	Tanga. Bronze. KM#28	—	40.00
Pr13	1952	—	Rupia. Copper-Nickel. KM#29	—	50.00
Pr14	1954	—	Rupia. Copper-Nickel. KM#29	—	250
Pr15	1958	—	10 Centavos. Bronze. KM#30	—	30.00
Pr16	1958	—	30 Centavos. Bronze. KM#31	—	40.00
Pr17	1958	—	60 Centavos. Copper-Nickel. KM#32	—	40.00
Pr18	1958	—	Escudo. Copper-Nickel. KM#33	—	45.00
Pr19	1958	—	3 Escudos. Copper-Nickel. KM#34	—	45.00
Pr20	1959	—	10 Centavos. Bronze. KM#30	—	40.00
Pr21	1959	—	30 Centavos. Bronze. KM#31	—	40.00
Pr22	1959	—	60 Centavos. Copper-Nickel. KM#32	—	40.00
Pr23	1959	—	Escudo. Copper-Nickel. KM#33	—	40.00
Pr24	1959	—	3 Escudos. Copper-Nickel. KM#34	—	40.00
Pr25	1959	—	6 Escudos. Copper-Nickel. KM#35	—	40.00
Pr26	1961	—	10 Centavos. Bronze. KM#30	—	35.00
Pr27	1961	—	10 Centavos. Nickel-Brass. Incuse N; KM#30	—	45.00

INDIA - BRITISH

The civilization of India, which began about 2500 B.C., flourished under a succession of empires - notably those of the Mauryas, the Kushans, the Guptas, the Delhi Sultans and the Mughals – until undermined in the 18th and 19th centuries by European colonial powers.

The Portuguese were the first to arrive, off Calicut in May 1498. It wasn't until 1612, after the Portuguese and Spanish power had begun to wane, that the British East India Company established its initial settlement at Surat. Britain could not have chosen a more propitious time as the central girdle of petty states, and the southern Vijayanagar Empire were crumbling and ripe for foreign exploitation. By the end of the century, English traders were firmly established in Bombay, Madras, Calcutta and lesser places elsewhere, and Britain was implementing its announced policy to create such civil and military institutions as may be the foundation of secure English domination for all time'. By 1757, following the successful conclusion of a war of colonial rivalry with France during which the military victories of Robert Clive, a young officer with the British East India Company, made him a powerful man in India, the British were firmly settled in India not only as traders but as conquerors. During the next 60 years, the British East India Company acquired dominion over most of India by bribery and force, and governed it directly or through puppet princelings.

As a result of the Sepoy Mutiny of 1857-58, a large-scale mutiny among Indian soldiers of the Bengal army, control of the government of India was transferred from the East India Company to the British Crown. At this point in world history, India was the brightest jewel in the British imperial diadem, but even then a movement for greater Indian representation in government presaged the Indian Empire's twilight hour less than a century later-it would pass into history on Aug. 15, 1947.

COLONIAL COINAGE
This section lists the coins of British India from the reign of William IV (1835) to the reign of George VI (1947). The issues are divided into two main parts:

Coins struck under the authority of the East India Company (E.I.C.) from 1835 until the trading monopoly of the E.I.C. was abolished in 1853. From August 2, 1858 the property and powers of the Company were transferred to the British Crown. From November 1, 1858 to November 1, 1862 the coins continued to bear the design and inscription of the Company.

Coins struck under the authority of the Crown (Regal issues) from 1862 until 1947.

The first regal issues bear the date 1862 and were struck with the date 1862 unchanged until 1874. From then onward all coins bear the year date.

The copper coins dated 1862 have been tentatively attributed by their size to the mint of issue. The silver coins dated 1862

have been attributed to various years of issue by their characteristic marks according to mint records.

In 1877 Queen Victoria was proclaimed Empress of India and the title of the obverse legend was changed accordingly.

For a detailed account of the work of the various mints and the numerous die varieties the general collector and specialist should refer to *The Coins of the British Commonwealth of Nations*, to the end of the reign of King George VI – 1952, Part 4, India, Vol. 1 and 2, by F. Pridmore, Spink, 1980.

RULERS
British until 1947

MINT MARKS
The coins of British India were struck at the following mints, indicated in the catalogue by either capital letters after the date when the actual letter appears on the coins or small letters in ( ) designating the mint of issue. Plain dates indicate Royal Mint strikes.
B – Mumbai (Bombay), 1835-1947, (dot on coin)
C or CM – Calcutta, 1835-1947, (no mint mark on coin)
I – Mumbai (Bombay), 1918-1919
L – Lahore, 1943-1945
P – Pretoria, South Africa, 1943-1944

In 1947 British rule came to an end and India was divided into two self-governing countries, India and Pakistan. In 1971 Bangladash seceded from Pakistan. All are now independent republics and although they are still members of the British Commonwealth of Nations, their coinages do not belong to the British India series.

MONETARY SYSTEM
3 Pies = 1 Pice (Paisa)
4 Pice = 1 Anna
16 Annas = 1 Rupee
15 Rupees = 1 Mohur

The transition from the coins of the Moslem monetary system began with the silver pattern Rupees of William IV, 1834, issued by the East India Company, with the value on the reverse, given in English, Bengali, Persian and Nagari characters. This coinage was struck for several years, as dated, except for the currency, Rupee, which was struck from 1835-1840, all dated 1835.

The portrait coins issued by the East India Company for Victoria show two different head designs on the obverse, which are called Type I and Type II. The coins with Type I head have a continuous obverse legend and were struck from 1840 to 1851. The coins with the Type II head have a divided obverse legend and were struck from 1850 (Calcutta) until 1862. The date on the coins remained unchanged: The Rupee, 1/2 Rupee and 1/4 Rupee are dated 1840. Noticeable differences in the ribbon designs of the English vs. Indian obverses exist.

Type I coins have on the reverse a dot after the date those of Type II have no dot, except for some rare 1/4 Rupees and 2 Annas. The latter are mules, struck from reverse dies of the preceding issue.

KING GEORGE VI: First and Second Heads
While King George VI's First Head is engraved in somewhat higher relief than his second head on all denominations from the 1/12 Anna to the Rupee, an easier way of distinguishing between the two types is that on the First Head the two *fleurs de lis* on the royal crown are larger and extend upward to touch the beaded crest at the top of the crown, while the two *fleurs de lis* on the crown of the Second Head are smaller and extend upward to touch only the line on the crown below the beaded crest.

ENGRAVER INITIALS
The following initials appear on the obverse on the truncation:
S incuse (Type I).
WW raised or incuse (Type II).
WWS or SWW (Type II).
WWB raised (Type II).

Proof and Prooflike restrikes
Original proofs are similar to early English Specimen strikes with wire edges and matte finish busts, arms, etc. Restrikes of most of the coins minted from the period 1835 were regularly supplied until this practice was discontinued on July 1, 1970.

Early proof restrikes are found with slight hairlines from polishing of the old dies. Bust, field, arms, etc. are of even smoothness.

Modern proof-like (P/L) restrikes usually have many hairlines from excessive polishing of the old dies and have a glassy, varnished or proof-like appearance. Many are common while some are quite scarce including some unusual mulings. These listings are indicated by **P/L-R** after the date and mint mark, for example; "1907(s) P/L R".

DISTINGUISHING FEATURES
Pice
NOTE: There are three types of the crown, which is on the obverse at the top. These are shown below and are designated as (RC) Round Crown, (HC) High Crown, and (FC) Flat Crown. Calcutta Mint issues have no mint mark. The issues from the other mints have the mint mark below the date as following: Lahore, raised "L"; Pretoria, small round dot; Mumbai (Bombay), diamond dot or "large" round dot. On the Mumbai (Bombay) issues dated 1944 the mint mark appears to be a large dot over a diamond.

Round Crown (RC)

High Crown (HC)

Flat Crown (FC)

1/2 Anna
The Calcutta Mint continued to issue this denomination with the dot before and after INDIA in 1946 and 1947. Mumbai (Bombay) also struck in 1946 and 1947, the 1946 issue denoted by a small dot in the center of the dashes before and after the date on the reverse (as well as a dot before and after INDIA, like Calcutta); the characteristics of the 1947 Bombay issue have not been determined but are thought also to resemble the 1946 issue. This denomination is also reported to have been struck in a quantity of 50,829,000 pieces in 1946 at the new Lahore Mint but no way of distinguishing this issue has been found. The proof issue in 1946 was struck by Mumbai (Bombay), not Calcutta. Source: Pridmore.

1/4 Rupee
BUST A - Front of dress has 4 panels. The bottom panel has 3 leaves at left and a small flower at upper right.
BUST B - Front of dress has 3-1/2 panels. The bottom incomplete panel has only 3 leaf tops.
REVERSE I - Large top flower; 2 large petals above the base of the top flower are long and curved downward.
REVERSE II - Small top flower; 2 large petals above the base of the top flower are short and horizontal.

First Head
Small head, high relief, small denticles

Second Head
Small head, low relief, large denticles

Second Head
Large head, low relief, small denticles
From 1942 to 1945 the reverse designs of the silver coins change slightly every year. However, a distinct reverse variety occurs on Rupees and 1/4 Rupees dated 1943-44 and on the half Rupee dated 1944, all struck at Mumbai (Bombay). This variety may be distinguished from the other coins by the design of the center bottom flower as illustrated, and is designated as Reverse B.

On the normal common varieties dated 1943-44 the three "scalloped circles" are not connected to each other and the bead in the center is not attached to the nearest circle.

Obv: First head, reeded edge

Calcutta Mint issues have no mint mark. Mumbai (Bombay) coins have a small bead below the lotus flower at the bottom on the reverse, except those dated 1943-1944 with reverse B which has a diamond. Lahore Mint issues have a small "L" in the same position. The nickel coins have a diamond below the date on the reverse.

Rupee
Obverse Dies

Type I	Type II

Type I - Obv. die w/elephant with pig-like feet and short tail. Nicknamed "pig rupee".

Type II - Obv. die w/redesigned elephant with outlined ear, heavy feet and long tail.

The Rupees, dated 1911, were rejected by the public because the elephant, on the Order of the Indian Empire shown on the King's robe, was thought to resemble a pig, an animal considered unclean by most Indians. Out of a total of 9.4 million pieces struck at both mints, only 700,000 were issued, and many of these were withdrawn and melted with un-issued pieces. The issues dated 1912 and later have a re-designed elephant.

COLONY

MILLED COINAGE
Regal Style

KM# 483 1/12 ANNA (1 Pie)
2.0700 g., Copper, 17.5 mm. **Ruler:** Victoria **Obv:** Crowned bust left **Obv. Leg.:** VICTORIA EMPRESS **Rev:** Value and date within beaded circle and wreath

Date	Mintage	F	VF	XF	Unc	BU
1901(c)	21,345,000	0.35	0.75	1.75	4.00	—
1901(c) Proof	—	Value: 175				
1901(c) P/L; Restrike	—	—	—	—	90.00	

KM# 483b 1/12 ANNA (1 Pie)
Silver **Ruler:** Victoria **Obv:** Crowned bust left **Rev:** Value and date within beaded circle and wreath

Date	Mintage	F	VF	XF	Unc	BU
1901(c) P/L; Restrike	—	—	—	—	250	—

KM# 483c 1/12 ANNA (1 Pie)
Gold **Ruler:** Victoria **Obv:** Crowned bust left **Rev:** Value and date within beaded circle and wreath **Note:** All dates of this type are prooflike restrikes.

Date	Mintage	F	VF	XF	Unc	BU
1901(c)	—	—	—	—	750	—

KM# 497 1/12 ANNA (1 Pie)
Copper, 17.5 mm. **Ruler:** Edward VII **Obv:** Head right **Obv. Leg.:** EDWARD VII KING & EMPEROR **Rev:** Date and denomination within circle, wreath surrounds **Note:** Thick planchet.

Date	Mintage	F	VF	XF	Unc	BU
1903(c)	7,883,000	0.35	1.25	6.00	15.00	—
1903(c) Proof	—	Value: 180				
1903(c) P/L; Restrike	—	—	—	—	80.00	
1904(c)	16,506,000	0.25	1.00	4.00	12.00	—
1904(c) Proof	—	Value: 180				
1904(c) P/L; Restrike	—	—	—	—	80.00	

Date	Mintage	F	VF	XF	Unc	BU
1905(c)	13,060,000	0.25	1.00	4.00	12.00	—
1905(c) P/L; Restrike	—	—	—	—	80.00	
1906(c)	9,072,000	0.25	1.00	4.00	12.00	—
1906(c) Proof	—	Value: 180				
1906(c) P/L; Restrike	—	—	—	—	80.00	

KM# 497a 1/12 ANNA (1 Pie)
Silver **Ruler:** Edward VII **Obv:** Head right **Rev:** Date and denomination within circle, wreath surrounds

Date	Mintage	F	VF	XF	Unc	BU
1904(c) P/L; Restrike	—	—	—	—	200	
1905(c) P/L; Restrike	—	—	—	—	200	

KM# 498 1/12 ANNA (1 Pie)
Bronze, 17.5 mm. **Ruler:** Edward VII **Obv:** Head right **Obv. Leg.:** EDWARD VII KING & EMPEROR **Rev:** Date and denomination within circle, wreath surrounds **Note:** Thin planchet.

Date	Mintage	F	VF	XF	Unc	BU
1906(c)	2,184,000	0.35	0.75	5.00	15.00	—
1906(c) Proof	—	Value: 150				
1907(c)	20,985,000	0.25	0.50	3.00	9.00	—
1907(c) Proof	—	Value: 150				
1907(c) P/L; Restrike	—	—	—	—	80.00	
1908(c)	22,036,000	0.25	0.50	3.00	9.00	—
1908(c) Proof	—	Value: 150				
1908(c) P/L; Restrike	—	—	—	—	80.00	
1909(c)	12,316,000	0.25	0.50	3.00	9.00	—
1909(c) P/L; Restrike	—	—	—	—	80.00	
1910(c)	23,520,000	0.25	0.50	3.00	9.00	—
1910(c) P/L; Restrike	—	—	—	—	80.00	

KM# 498a 1/12 ANNA (1 Pie)
Aluminum, 17.5 mm. **Ruler:** Edward VII **Obv:** Head right **Rev:** Date and denomination within circle, wreath surrounds

Date	Mintage	F	VF	XF	Unc	BU
1909(c) Proof	—	Value: 200				

KM# 509 1/12 ANNA (1 Pie)
1.6400 g., Bronze, 17.5 mm. **Ruler:** George V **Obv:** Crowned bust left **Obv. Leg.:** GEORGE V KING EMPEROR **Rev:** Date and denomination within circle, wreath surrounds

Date	Mintage	F	VF	XF	Unc	BU
1912(c)	25,938,000	0.50	0.75	1.50	4.50	—
1912(c) Proof	—	Value: 150				
1912(c) P/L; Restrike	—	—	—	—	80.00	
1913(c)	16,149,000	0.25	0.50	1.00	3.00	—
1913(c) Proof	—	Value: 120				
1913(c) P/L; Restrike	—	—	—	—	80.00	
1914(c)	19,814,000	0.25	0.50	0.75	2.00	—
1914(c) Proof	—	Value: 120				
1914(c) P/L; Restrike	—	—	—	—	80.00	
1915(c)	20,563,000	0.25	0.50	0.75	2.00	—
1915(c) Proof	—	Value: 120				
1915(c) P/L; Restrike	—	—	—	—	80.00	
1916(c)	14,438,000	0.25	0.50	0.75	2.00	—
1916(c) Proof	—	Value: 120				
1916(c) P/L; Restrike	—	—	—	—	80.00	
1917(c)	35,174,000	0.25	0.50	0.75	2.00	—
1917(c) Proof	—	Value: 120				
1917(c) P/L; Restrike	—	—	—	—	80.00	
1918(c)	24,192,000	0.25	0.50	0.75	2.00	—
1918(c) Proof	—	Value: 120				
1918(c) P/L; Restrike	—	—	—	—	80.00	
1919(c)	17,472,000	0.25	0.50	0.75	2.00	—
1919(c) Proof	—	Value: 120				
1919(c) P/L; Restrike	—	—	—	—	80.00	
1920(c)	39,878,000	0.25	0.50	0.75	2.00	—
1920(c) Proof	—	Value: 120				
1920(c) P/L; Restrike	—	—	—	—	80.00	
1921(c)	19,334,000	0.25	0.50	0.75	2.00	—
1921(c) P/L; Restrike	—	—	—	—	80.00	
1921(c) Proof	—	Value: 120				
1923(c)	8,429,000	0.25	0.50	0.75	2.00	—
1923(c) Proof	—	Value: 120				
1923(b)	8,717,000	0.25	0.50	0.75	2.00	—
1923(b) Proof	—	Value: 120				
1923(b) P/L; Restrike	—	—	—	—	80.00	
1924(c)	7,200,000	0.50	0.75	1.50	4.50	—
1924(c) Proof	—	Value: 120				
1924(b)	9,869,000	0.25	0.50	0.75	2.00	—
1924(b) Proof	—	Value: 120				
1924(b) P/L; Restrike	—	—	—	—	80.00	
1925(c)	5,818,000	0.50	0.75	1.50	4.50	—
1925(c) Proof	—	Value: 120				
1925(b)	6,415,000	0.50	0.75	1.50	4.50	—
1925(b) Proof	—	Value: 120				
1925(b) P/L; Restrike	—	—	—	—	80.00	
1926(c)	4,147,000	0.50	0.75	1.50	4.50	—

Date	Mintage	F	VF	XF	Unc	BU
1926(c) Proof	—	Value: 120				
1926(b)	15,464,000	0.25	0.50	0.75	2.00	—
1926(b) Proof	—	Value: 120				
1926(b) P/L; Restrike	—	—	—	—	80.00	
1927(c)	6,662,000	0.50	0.75	1.50	4.50	—
1927(c) Proof	—	Value: 120				
1927(b)	6,788,000	0.50	0.75	1.50	4.50	—
1927(b) Proof	—	Value: 120				
1927(b) P/L; Restrike	—	—	—	—	80.00	
1928(c)	8,064,000	0.25	0.50	0.75	2.00	—
1928(c) Proof	—	Value: 120				
1928(b)	6,135,000	0.50	0.75	1.50	4.50	—
1928(b) Proof	—	Value: 120				
1928(b) P/L; Restrike	—	—	—	—	80.00	
1929(c)	15,130,000	0.25	0.50	0.75	2.00	—
1929(c) Proof	—	Value: 120				
1929(c) P/L; Restrike	—	—	—	—	80.00	
1930(c)	13,498,000	0.25	0.50	0.75	2.00	—
1930(c) Proof	—	Value: 120				
1930(c) P/L; Restrike	—	—	—	—	80.00	
1931(c)	18,278,000	0.25	0.50	0.75	2.00	—
1931(c) Proof	—	Value: 120				
1931(c) P/L; Restrike	—	—	—	—	80.00	
1932(c)	23,213,000	0.25	0.50	0.75	2.00	—
1932(c) Proof	—	Value: 120				
1932(c) P/L; Restrike	—	—	—	—	80.00	
1933(c)	16,896,000	0.25	0.50	0.75	2.00	—
1933(c) Proof	—	Value: 120				
1933(c) P/L; Restrike	—	—	—	—	80.00	
1934(c)	17,146,000	0.25	0.50	0.75	2.00	—
1934(c) Proof	—	Value: 120				
1934(c) P/L; Restrike	—	—	—	—	80.00	
1935(c)	19,142,000	0.25	0.50	0.75	2.00	—
1935(c) Proof	—	Value: 120				
1935(c) P/L; Restrike	—	—	—	—	80.00	
1936(c)	23,213,000	0.25	0.50	0.75	2.00	—
1936(b)	12,887,000	0.25	0.50	0.75	2.00	—
1936(b) P/L; Restrike	—	—	—	—	80.00	

KM# 526 1/12 ANNA (1 Pie)
Bronze, 17.5 mm. **Ruler:** George VI **Obv:** Crowned head left **Obv. Leg.:** GEORGE VI KING EMPEROR **Rev:** Date and denomination within circle, wreath surrounds **Note:** First head.

Date	Mintage	F	VF	XF	Unc	BU
1938(c) Proof	—	Value: 120				
1939(c)	3,571,000	0.50	0.75	1.50	4.50	—
1939(b)	17,407,000	0.25	0.50	1.00	2.50	—

KM# 527 1/12 ANNA (1 Pie)
Bronze, 17.5 mm. **Ruler:** George VI **Obv:** Crowned head left **Obv. Leg.:** GEORGE VI KING EMPEROR **Rev:** Date and denomination within circle, wreath surrounds **Note:** Second head.

Date	Mintage	F	VF	XF	Unc	BU
1938(c) P/L; Restrike	—	—	—	—	80.00	—
1939(c)	5,245,000	0.25	0.50	1.00	2.50	—
1939(c) Proof	—	Value: 120				
1939(b)	31,306,000	0.25	0.50	0.75	2.00	—
1939(b) Proof	—	Value: 120				
1939(b) P/L; Restrike	—	—	—	—	80.00	—
1941(b)	6,137,000	0.25	0.50	0.75	2.00	—
1942(b)	6,124,000	0.50	0.75	1.50	4.50	—
1942(b) Proof	—	Value: 120				
1942(b) P/L; Restrike	—	—	—	—	80.00	—

KM# 484 1/2 PICE
Copper **Ruler:** Victoria **Obv:** Crowned bust left **Obv. Leg.:** VICTORIA EMPRESS **Rev:** Value and date within beaded circle and wreath

Date	Mintage	F	VF	XF	Unc	BU
1901	16,057,000	1.00	1.75	3.50	8.50	—
1901 Proof	—	Value: 175				
1901(c) P/L; Restrike	—	—	—	—	90.00	—

KM# 484b 1/2 PICE
Silver **Ruler:** Victoria **Obv:** Crowned bust left **Rev:** Value and date within beaded circle and wreath

Date	Mintage	F	VF	XF	Unc	BU
1901(c) P/L; Restrike	—	—	—	—	250	—

KM# 484c 1/2 PICE
Gold **Ruler:** Victoria **Obv:** Crowned bust left **Rev:** Value and date within beaded circle and wreath **Note:** All dates of this type are prooflike restrikes.

Date	Mintage	F	VF	XF	Unc	BU
1901(c)	—	—	—	—	950	

KM# 500c 1/2 PICE
Silver **Ruler:** Edward VII

Date	Mintage	F	VF	XF	Unc	BU
1903(c) P/L; Restrike	—	—	—	—	200	
1904(c) P/L; Restrike	—	—	—	—	200	
1905(c) P/L; Restrike	—	—	—	—	200	

KM# 499 1/2 PICE
Copper **Ruler:** Edward VII **Obv:** Head right **Obv. Leg.:** EDWARD VII KING & EMPEROR **Rev:** Date and denomination within circle, wreath surrounds

Date	Mintage	F	VF	XF	Unc	BU
1903(c)	5,376,000	0.75	1.50	5.00	15.00	—
1903(c) Proof	— Value: 135					
1903(c) P/L; Restrike	—	—	—	—	80.00	
1904(c)	8,464,000	0.75	1.50	5.00	15.00	—
1904(c) Proof	— Value: 135					
1904(c) P/L; Restrike	—	—	—	—	80.00	
1905(c)	8,922,000	0.75	1.50	5.00	15.00	—
1905(c) P/L; Restrike	—	—	—	—	80.00	
1906(c)	6,346,000	0.75	1.50	5.00	15.00	—
1906(c) Proof	— Value: 135					
1906(c) P/L; Restrike	—	—	—	—	80.00	

KM# 500 1/2 PICE
Bronze **Ruler:** Edward VII **Obv. Leg.:** EDWARD VII KING & EMPEROR **Note:** Thinner planchets.

Date	Mintage	F	VF	XF	Unc	BU
1904(c) Proof	— Value: 135					
1906(c)	5,860,000	0.75	1.50	4.50	12.50	—
1906(c) Proof	— Value: 135					
1907(c)	8,060,000	0.75	1.50	4.50	12.50	—
1907(c) Proof	— Value: 135					
1907(c) P/L; Restrike	—	—	—	—	80.00	
1908(c)	10,035,000	0.75	1.50	4.50	12.50	—
1908(c) Proof	— Value: 135					
1908(c) P/L; Restrike	—	—	—	—	80.00	
1909(c)	8,493,000	0.75	1.50	4.50	12.50	—
1909(c) P/L; Restrike	—	—	—	—	80.00	
1910(c)	17,408,000	0.75	1.50	4.50	12.50	—

KM# 500a 1/2 PICE
Aluminum **Ruler:** Edward VII

Date	Mintage	F	VF	XF	Unc	BU
1909(c) Proof	— Value: 300					

KM# 500b 1/2 PICE
Nickel **Ruler:** Edward VII

Date	Mintage	F	VF	XF	Unc	BU
1904(c) Proof	— Value: 300					

KM# 510 1/2 PICE
Bronze **Ruler:** George V **Obv:** Crowned bust left **Obv. Leg.:** GEORGE V KING EMPEROR **Rev:** Date and denomination within circle, wreath surrounds

Date	Mintage	F	VF	XF	Unc	BU
1912(c)	12,911,000	0.25	0.50	0.75	3.00	—
1912(c) Proof	— Value: 120					
1912(c) P/L; Restrike	—	—	—	—	80.00	—
1913(c)	10,897,000	0.25	0.50	0.75	3.00	—
1913(c) Proof	— Value: 120					
1913(c) P/L; Restrike	—	—	—	—	80.00	—
1914(c)	4,877,000	0.15	0.30	0.50	2.50	—
1914(c) Proof	— Value: 120					
1914(c) P/L; Restrike	—	—	—	—	80.00	—
1915(c)	9,830,000	0.15	0.30	0.50	2.50	—
1915(c) Proof	— Value: 120					
1915(c) P/L; Restrike	—	—	—	—	80.00	—
1916(c)	5,734,000	0.15	0.30	0.50	2.50	—
1916(c) Proof	— Value: 120					
1916(c) P/L; Restrike	—	—	—	—	80.00	—
1917(c)	15,296,000	0.15	0.30	0.50	2.50	—
1917(c) Proof	— Value: 120					
1917(c) P/L; Restrike	—	—	—	—	80.00	
1918(c)	6,244,000	0.15	0.30	0.50	2.50	—
1918(c) Proof	— Value: 120					
1918(c) P/L; Restrike	—	—	—	—	80.00	
1919(c)	11,162,000	0.15	0.30	0.50	2.50	—
1919(c) Proof	— Value: 120					
1919(c) P/L; Restrike	—	—	—	—	80.00	
1920(c)	4,493,000	0.15	0.30	0.50	2.50	—
1920(c) Proof	— Value: 120					
1920(c) P/L; Restrike	—	—	—	—	80.00	
1921(c)	6,234,000	0.15	0.30	0.50	2.50	—
1921(c) Proof	— Value: 120					
1921(c) P/L; Restrike	—	—	—	—	80.00	
1922(c)	6,336,000	0.15	0.30	0.50	2.50	—
1922(c) Proof	— Value: 120					
1922(c) P/L; Restrike	—	—	—	—	80.00	
1923(c)	7,411,000	0.15	0.30	0.50	2.50	—
1923(c) Proof	— Value: 120					
1923(c) P/L; Restrike	—	—	—	—	80.00	
1924(c)	9,523,000	0.15	0.30	0.50	2.50	—
1924(c) Proof	— Value: 120					
1924(c) P/L; Restrike	—	—	—	—	80.00	
1925(c)	3,981,000	0.50	0.75	1.50	4.50	—
1925(c) Proof	— Value: 120					
1925(c) P/L; Restrike	—	—	—	—	80.00	
1926(c)	7,885,000	0.15	0.30	0.50	2.50	—
1926(c) Proof	— Value: 120					
1926(c) P/L; Restrike	—	—	—	—	80.00	
1927(c)	5,888,000	0.15	0.30	0.50	2.50	—
1927(c) Proof	— Value: 120					
1927(c) P/L; Restrike	—	—	—	—	80.00	
1928(c)	5,456,000	0.15	0.30	0.50	2.50	—
1928(c) Proof	— Value: 120					
1928(c) P/L; Restrike	—	—	—	—	80.00	
1929(c)	7,654,000	0.15	0.30	0.50	2.50	—
1929(c) Proof	— Value: 120					
1929(c) P/L; Restrike	—	—	—	—	80.00	
1930(c)	7,181,000	0.15	0.30	0.50	2.50	—
1930(c) Proof	— Value: 120					
1930(c) P/L; Restrike	—	—	—	—	80.00	
1931(c)	8,794,000	0.15	0.30	0.50	2.50	—
1931(c) Proof	— Value: 120					
1931(c) P/L; Restrike	—	—	—	—	80.00	
1932(c)	5,440,000	0.15	0.30	0.50	2.50	—
1932(c) Proof	— Value: 120					
1932(c) P/L; Restrike	—	—	—	—	80.00	
1933(c)	9,242,000	0.15	0.30	0.50	2.50	—
1933(c) Proof	— Value: 120					
1933(c) P/L; Restrike	—	—	—	—	80.00	
1934(c)	8,947,000	0.15	0.30	0.50	2.50	—
1934(c) Proof	— Value: 120					
1934(c) P/L; Restrike	—	—	—	—	80.00	
1935(c)	15,501,000	0.15	0.30	0.50	2.50	—
1935(c) Proof	— Value: 120					
1935(c) P/L; Restrike	—	—	—	—	80.00	
1936(c)	26,726,000	0.10	0.25	0.40	1.25	—
1936(c) P/L; Restrike	—	—	—	—	80.00	

KM# 528 1/2 PICE
Bronze **Ruler:** George VI **Obv:** First head; high relief **Obv. Leg.:** GEORGE VI KING EMPEROR **Rev:** Date and denomination within circle, wreath surrounds **Note:** Calcutta Mint issues have no mint mark. Mumbai (Bombay) Mint issues have a small dot below the date.

Date	Mintage	F	VF	XF	Unc	BU
1938(c) Proof	— Value: 100					
1938(c) P/L; Restrike	—	—	—	—	80.00	

Note: Calcutta Mint reported 11,161,000 mintage for 1938 but only proof and modern prooflike restrikes are known

Date	Mintage	F	VF	XF	Unc	BU
1939(c)	17,357,000	0.15	0.40	0.60	1.75	—
1939(c) Proof	— Value: 100					
1939(b)	9,343,000	0.20	0.45	0.85	3.50	—
1939(b) Proof	— Value: 100					
1939(b) P/L; Restrike	—	—	—	—	80.00	
1940(c)	23,770,000	0.15	0.40	0.65	1.75	—
1940(c) Proof	— Value: 100					
1940(c) P/L; Restrike	—	—	—	—	80.00	

KM# 529 1/2 PICE
Bronze **Ruler:** George VI **Obv:** Second head; low relief **Obv. Leg.:** GEORGE VI KING EMPEROR **Rev:** Date and denomination within circle, wreath surrounds

Date	Mintage	F	VF	XF	Unc	BU
1942(b) Proof	— Value: 150					
1942(b) P/L; Restrike	—	—	—	—	100	

KM# 532 PICE
Bronze **Ruler:** George VI **Obv:** Small date, small legends

Date	Mintage	F	VF	XF	Unc	BU
1943(b) (RC) diamond	164,659	0.30	0.50	1.00	3.50	

KM# 533 PICE
2.0000 g., Bronze, 21.32 mm. **Ruler:** George VI **Obv:** Center hole, large date, large legends **Rev:** Wreath surrounds center hole

Date	Mintage	F	VF	XF	Unc	BU
1943(b) (HC) large dot	—	0.15	0.35	0.65	1.25	—
1943(p) (HC) small dot	98,997,000	0.15	0.35	0.65	1.25	—
1944(c) (HC)	—	0.15	0.35	0.65	1.25	—
1944(c) (HC) Proof	— Value: 100					
1944(b) (HC) large dot	195,354,000	0.15	0.35	0.65	1.25	—
1944(b) (HC) diamond	—	0.20	0.40	0.75	2.00	—
1944(b) (HC) large dot	—	0.20	0.40	0.75	2.00	—
1944(b) P/L; Restrike	—	—	—	—	80.00	
1944(p) (HC) small dot	141,003,000	0.20	0.40	0.75	2.00	—
1944L (HC)	29,802,000	0.20	0.40	0.80	3.50	—
1945(c) (FC)	156,322,000	0.15	0.35	0.65	1.25	—
1945(b) (FC) diamond	237,197,000	0.15	0.35	0.65	1.25	—
1945(b) (FC) large dot	Inc. above	0.15	0.35	0.65	1.25	—
1945(b) P/L; Restrike	—	—	—	—	80.00	
1945L (FC)	238,825,000	0.15	0.35	0.65	1.25	—
1947(c) (HC)	153,702,000	0.15	0.35	0.65	1.25	—
1947(b) (HC) diamond	43,654,000	0.20	0.40	0.80	3.50	—
1947(b) Proof	— Value: 100					
1947 P/L; Restrike	—	—	—	—	80.00	

KM# 486 1/4 ANNA
6.4000 g., Copper **Ruler:** Victoria **Obv:** Crowned bust left **Obv. Leg.:** VICTORIA EMPRESS **Rev:** Value and date within beaded circle and wreath

Date	Mintage	F	VF	XF	Unc	BU
1901(c)	136,091,000	0.35	0.75	1.50	4.50	—
1901(c) Proof	— Value: 250					
1901(c) P/L; Restrike	—	—	—	—	125	

KM# 486b 1/4 ANNA
Silver **Ruler:** Victoria **Obv:** Crowned bust left **Rev:** Value and date within beaded circle and wreath

Date	Mintage	F	VF	XF	Unc	BU
1901(c) P/L; Restrike	—	—	—	—	275	

KM# 486c 1/4 ANNA
Gold **Ruler:** Victoria **Obv:** Crowned bust left **Rev:** Value and date within beaded circle and wreath **Note:** All dates of this type are Prooflike Restrikes.

Date	Mintage	F	VF	XF	Unc	BU
1901(c) P/L; Restrike	—	—	—	—	1,200	

KM# 501 1/4 ANNA
6.4800 g., Copper **Ruler:** Edward VII **Obv. Leg.:** EDWARD VII KING & EMPEROR

Date	Mintage	F	VF	XF	Unc	BU
1903(c)	105,974,000	0.35	1.75	7.50	35.00	—
1903(c) Proof	— Value: 150					
1903(c) P/L; Restrike	—	—	—	—	85.00	
1904(c)	104,595,000	0.35	1.75	7.50	35.00	—
1904(c) Proof	— Value: 150					
1904(c) P/L; Restrike	—	—	—	—	85.00	
1905(c)	130,058,000	0.35	1.75	7.50	35.00	—
1905(c) Proof	— Value: 150					
1905(c) P/L; Restrike	—	—	—	—	85.00	
1906(c)	47,229,000	0.35	1.75	7.50	35.00	—
1906(c) Proof	— Value: 150					

KM# 501b 1/4 ANNA
Silver **Ruler:** Edward VII **Obv. Leg.:** EDWARD VII KING & EMPEROR

Date	Mintage	F	VF	XF	Unc	BU
1903(c) P/L; Restrike	—	—	—	—	300	
1904(c) P/L; Restrike	—	—	—	—	300	
1905(c) P/L; Restrike	—	—	—	—	300	

KM# 501a 1/4 ANNA
Nickel **Ruler:** Edward VII **Obv. Leg.:** EDWARD VII KING & EMPEROR

Date	Mintage	F	VF	XF	Unc	BU
1906(c) Proof	— Value: 450					

KM# 502   1/4 ANNA
Bronze, 25.5 mm. **Ruler:** Edward VII **Obv:** Head right **Obv. Leg.:** EDWARD VII KING & EMPEROR **Rev:** Date and denomination within circle, wreath surrounds **Note:** Thinner planchet.

Date	Mintage	F	VF	XF	Unc	BU
1906(c)	115,786,000	0.35	1.25	6.50	30.00	—
1906(c) Proof	—	Value: 120				
1907(c)	234,682,000	0.35	1.25	6.50	30.00	—
1907(c) Proof	—	Value: 120				
1907(c) P/L; Restrike	—	—	—	—	80.00	—
1908(c)	58,066,000	0.35	1.25	6.50	30.00	—
1908(c) Proof	—	Value: 120				
1908(c) P/L; Restrike	—	—	—	—	80.00	—
1909(c)	29,966,000	0.35	1.25	6.50	30.00	—
1909(c) Proof	—	Value: 120				
1909(c) P/L; Restrike	—	—	—	—	80.00	—
1910(c)	47,265,000	0.35	1.25	6.50	30.00	—
1910(c) P/L; Restrike	—	—	—	—	80.00	—

KM# 502a   1/4 ANNA
Aluminum **Ruler:** Edward VII **Obv:** Head right
Obv. Leg.: EDWARD VII KING & EMPEROR **Rev:** Date and denomination within circle, wreath surrounds

Date	Mintage	VG	F	VF	XF	Unc
1908(c) Proof	—	Value: 450				

KM# 511   1/4 ANNA
Bronze **Ruler:** George V **Obv:** Type I **Obv. Leg.:** GEORGE V KING EMPEROR **Note:** Calcutta Mint issues have no mint mark. Mumbai (Bombay) Mint issues have a small dot below the date. The pieces dated 1911, like the other coins with that date, show the "Pig" elephant.

Date	Mintage	F	VF	XF	Unc	BU
1911(c)	55,918,000	0.75	2.00	5.00	20.00	—
1911(c) Proof	—	Value: 175				
1911(c) P/L; Restrike	—	—	—	—	80.00	—

KM# 512   1/4 ANNA
4.8600 g., Bronze **Ruler:** George V **Obv:** Crowned bust left, type II **Obv. Leg.:** GEORGE V KING EMPEROR **Rev:** Date and denomination within circle, wreath surrounds

Date	Mintage	F	VF	XF	Unc	BU
1912(c)	107,456,000	0.20	0.40	1.00	4.00	—
1912(c) Proof	—	Value: 120				
1912(c) P/L; Restrike	—	—	—	—	80.00	—
1913(c)	82,061,000	0.25	0.50	1.25	4.50	—
1913(c) Proof	—	Value: 120				
1913(c) P/L; Restrike	—	—	—	—	80.00	—
1914(c)	40,576,000	0.50	0.75	1.50	3.50	—
1914(c) Proof	—	Value: 120				
1914(c) P/L; Restrike	—	—	—	—	80.00	—
1916(c)	1,632,000	3.50	7.00	12.00	25.00	—
1916(c) Proof	—	Value: 150				
1917(c)	69,370,000	0.20	0.40	0.80	3.50	—
1917(c) Proof	—	Value: 120				
1917(c) P/L; Restrike	—	—	—	—	80.00	—
1918(c)	84,045,000	0.20	0.40	0.80	3.50	—
1918(c) Proof	—	Value: 120				
1918(c) P/L; Restrike	—	—	—	—	80.00	—
1919(c)	212,467,000	0.20	0.40	0.80	3.50	—
1919(c) Proof	—	Value: 120				
1919(c) P/L; Restrike	—	—	—	—	80.00	—
1920(c)	96,019,000	0.20	0.40	0.80	3.50	—
1920(c) Proof	—	Value: 120				
1920(c) P/L; Restrike	—	—	—	—	80.00	—
1921(c) Proof	—	Value: 120				
1924(b)	16,322,000	0.20	0.40	0.80	3.50	—
1924(b) Proof	—	Value: 120				
1925(c)	14,598,000	0.20	0.40	0.80	3.50	—
1925(b)	14,588,000	0.20	0.40	0.80	3.50	—
1925(b) Proof	—	Value: 120				
1926(c)	17,389,000	0.20	0.40	0.80	3.50	—
1926(c) Proof	—	Value: 120				
1926(b)	16,073,000	0.20	0.40	0.80	3.50	—
1926(b) Proof	—	Value: 120				
1926(b) P/L; Restrike	—	—	—	—	80.00	—
1927(c)	6,925,000	0.50	0.75	1.50	4.50	—
1927(c) Proof	—	Value: 120				
1927(b)	12,440,000	0.20	0.40	0.80	3.50	—
1927(b) Proof	—	Value: 120				
1927(b) P/L; Restrike	—	—	—	—	80.00	—
1928(c)	257,779,000	0.20	0.40	0.80	3.50	—

Date	Mintage	F	VF	XF	Unc	BU
1928(c) Proof	—	Value: 120				
1928(b)	10,057,000	0.20	0.40	0.80	3.50	—
1928(b) Proof	—	Value: 120				
1928(b) P/L; Restrike	—	—	—	—	80.00	—
1929(c)	61,542,000	0.20	0.40	0.80	3.50	—
1929(c) Proof	—	Value: 120				
1929(c) P/L; Restrike	—	—	—	—	80.00	—
1930(c)	40,698,000	0.20	0.40	0.80	3.50	—
1930(c) Proof	—	Value: 120				
1930(b)	9,646,000	0.50	0.75	1.50	4.50	—
1930(b) Proof	—	Value: 120				
1930(b) P/L; Restrike	—	—	—	—	80.00	—
1931(c)	6,835,000	0.50	0.75	1.50	4.50	—
1931(c) Proof	—	Value: 120				
1931(c) P/L; Restrike	—	—	—	—	80.00	—
1933(c)	40,230,000	0.20	0.40	0.80	3.50	—
1933(c) Proof	—	Value: 120				
1933(c) P/L; Restrike	—	—	—	—	80.00	—
1934(c)	80,506,000	0.20	0.40	0.80	3.50	—
1934(c) Proof	—	Value: 120				
1934(c) P/L; Restrike	—	—	—	—	80.00	—
1935(c)	92,595,000	0.20	0.40	0.80	3.50	—
1935(c) Proof	—	Value: 120				
1935(c) P/L; Restrike	—	—	—	—	80.00	—
1936(c)	227,501,000	0.20	0.40	0.80	3.50	—
1936(c)	61,926,000	0.20	0.40	0.80	3.50	—
1936(b) Proof	—	Value: 120				
1936(b) P/L; Restrike	—	—	—	—	80.00	—

KM# 530   1/4 ANNA
4.8600 g., Bronze **Ruler:** George VI **Obv:** First head; high relief **Obv. Leg.:** GEORGE VI KING EMPEROR **Rev:** Date and denomination within circle, wreath surrounds

Date	Mintage	F	VF	XF	Unc	BU
1938(c)	33,792,000	0.25	0.40	0.75	2.00	—
1938(c) Proof	—	Value: 120				
1938(b)	16,796,000	0.50	0.75	1.50	4.50	—
1938(b) P/L; Restrike	—	—	—	—	100	—
1939(c)	78,279,000	0.30	0.50	1.00	2.50	—
1939(c) Proof	—	Value: 120				
1939(b)	60,171,000	0.30	0.50	1.00	3.50	—
1939(b) Proof	—	Value: 120				
1939(b) P/L; Restrike	—	—	—	—	100	—
1940(b)	116,721,000	0.35	0.75	1.50	3.50	—

KM# 531   1/4 ANNA
4.6000 g., Bronze, 25.33 mm. **Ruler:** George VI **Obv:** Second head; low relief **Obv. Leg.:** GEORGE VI KING EMPEROR **Rev:** Denomination and date within wreath

Date	Mintage	F	VF	XF	Unc	BU
1940(c)	140,410,000	0.30	0.50	1.00	3.50	—
1940(c) Proof	—	Value: 120				
1940(b)	—	0.30	0.50	1.00	3.50	—
1940(b)	**Note:** Mintage included in KM#530					
1940(b) P/L; Restrike	—	—	—	—	100	—
1941(c)	121,107,000	0.30	0.50	1.00	3.50	—
1941(c) P/L; Restrike	—	—	—	—	100	—
1941(b)	1,446,000	0.40	0.90	2.00	6.00	—
1942(c)	34,298,000	0.30	0.50	1.00	3.50	—
1942(b)	8,768,000	0.30	0.50	1.00	3.50	—
1942(b) P/L; Restrike	—	—	—	—	100	—

KM# 503   1/2 ANNA
Copper **Ruler:** Edward VII **Obv:** Head of Edward VII **Rev:** Value and date within beaded circle and wreath

Date	Mintage	F	VF	XF	Unc	BU
1904(c) Proof	—	Value: 2,200				

KM# 534   1/2 ANNA
Copper-Nickel **Ruler:** George VI **Obv:** Crowned head left **Obv. Leg.:** GEORGE VI KING EMPEROR **Rev:** Denomination and date within decorative outline **Rev. Leg.:** • INDIA •

Date	Mintage	F	VF	XF	Unc	BU
1940(c) Proof	—	Value: 650				
1940(c) P/L; Restrike	—	—	—	—	150	—

KM# 534a   1/2 ANNA
Gold **Ruler:** George VI **Obv:** Crowned head left
Rev: Denomination and date within decorative outline

Date	Mintage	F	VF	XF	Unc	BU
1940(c)	—	—	—	—	600	—
	Note: Prooflike; Restrike					

KM# 534b.2   1/2 ANNA
2.8700 g., Nickel-Brass, 17.3 mm. **Ruler:** George VI **Obv:** Crowned head left **Rev:** Denomination and date within decorative outline **Rev. Leg.:** • INDIA •

Date	Mintage	F	VF	XF	Unc	BU
1942(c)	159,000,000	0.10	0.25	0.50	2.00	—
1942(c) Proof	—	Value: 100				
1943(c)	437,760,000	0.10	0.25	0.50	2.00	—
1943(c) Proof	—	Value: 120				
1944(c)	514,800,000	0.10	0.25	0.50	2.00	—
1944(c) Proof	—	Value: 120				
1945(c)	215,732,000	0.10	0.25	0.50	2.00	—
1945(c) Proof	—	Value: 120				

KM# 534b.1   1/2 ANNA
2.9200 g., Nickel-Brass **Ruler:** George VI **Obv:** Crowned head left, second head **Obv. Leg.:** GEORGE VI KING EMPEROR **Rev:** Denomination and date within decorative outline **Rev. Leg.:** INDIA (without dots) **Note:** Bombay Mint issues dated 1942-1945 are without a dot before and after India.

Date	Mintage	F	VF	XF	Unc	BU
1942(b)	7,945,000	0.30	0.50	1.00	3.50	—
1942(b) P/L; Restrike	—	—	—	—	120	—
1943(b) P/L; Restrike	—	—	—	—	120	—
1944(b) P/L; Restrike	—	—	—	—	120	—
1945(b) P/L; Restrike	—	—	—	—	100	—

KM# 535.1   1/2 ANNA
2.8700 g., Copper-Nickel **Ruler:** George VI **Obv:** Crowned head left **Rev:** Denomination and date within decorative outline

Date	Mintage	F	VF	XF	Unc	BU
1946(b)	48,744,000	0.10	0.25	0.50	2.00	—
1946(b) Proof	—	Value: 120				
1946(b) P/L; Restrike	—	—	—	—	100	—
1947(b) P/L; Restrike	—	—	—	—	150	—

KM# 535.2   1/2 ANNA
2.9000 g., Copper-Nickel **Ruler:** George VI **Obv:** Crowned head left **Rev:** Denomination and date within decorative outline

Date	Mintage	F	VF	XF	Unc	BU
1946(c)	75,159,000	0.15	0.30	0.50	2.50	—
1947(c)	126,392,000	0.10	0.25	0.45	1.25	—
1947(c) Proof	—	Value: 120				
1947(c) P/L; Restrike	—	—	—	—	100	—

KM# 504   ANNA
Copper-Nickel **Ruler:** Edward VII **Obv:** Crowned bust right **Obv. Leg.:** EDWARD VII KING & EMPEROR **Rev:** Denomination and date within decorative outline **Note:** Struck only at the Mumbai (Bombay) Mint. Small incuse "B" mint mark in the space below the cross pattee of the crown on the obverse.

Date	Mintage	F	VF	XF	Unc	BU
1906B	200,000	20.00	50.00	125	300	—
1907B	37,256,000	0.50	1.25	2.00	5.00	—

Date	Mintage	F	VF	XF	Unc	BU
1907B Proof	—	Value: 60.00				
1908B	22,536,000	0.50	1.25	2.00	5.00	—
1908B Proof	—	Value: 60.00				
1909B	24,800,000	0.50	1.25	2.00	5.00	—
1909B Proof	—	Value: 60.00				
1910B	40,200,000	0.50	1.25	2.00	5.00	—
1910B Proof	—	Value: 60.00				

KM# 513 ANNA

3.8100 g., Copper-Nickel **Ruler:** George VI **Obv:** Crowned bust left **Obv. Leg.:** GEORGE VI KING EMPEROR **Rev:** Denomination and date within decorative outline **Note:** Until 1920, all were struck at the Mumbai (Bombay) Mint without mint mark. From 1923 on, the Mumbai (Bombay) Mint issues have a small, raised bead or dot below the date. Calcutta Mint issues have no mint mark.

Date	Mintage	F	VF	XF	Unc	BU
1912(b)	39,400,000	0.40	1.00	2.50	6.00	—
1912 Proof	—	Value: 150				
1913(b)	39,776,000	0.40	1.00	2.50	6.00	—
1913 Proof	—	Value: 150				
1914(b)	48,000,000	0.25	0.50	1.75	4.00	—
1914 Proof	—	Value: 150				
1915(b)	7,670,000	0.40	1.00	2.50	6.00	—
1915 Proof	—	Value: 150				
1916(b)	39,087,000	0.25	0.50	1.75	4.00	—
1917(b)	58,067,000	0.25	0.50	1.75	4.00	—
1917 Proof	—	Value: 150				
1918(b)	80,692,000	0.25	0.50	1.75	4.00	—
1918(b) Proof	—	Value: 150				
1919(b)	122,795,000	0.25	0.50	1.75	4.00	—
1919(b) Proof	—	Value: 150				
1919(c) Proof	—	Value: 150				
1920(b)	9,264,000	0.25	0.50	1.75	4.50	—
1920(b) Proof	—	Value: 150				
1923(b)	7,125,000	0.25	0.50	1.75	4.50	—
1923(b) Proof	—	Value: 150				
1924(c)	16,640,000	0.25	0.50	1.75	4.00	—
1924(c) Proof	—	Value: 150				
1924(b)	17,285,000	0.25	0.50	2.00	5.00	—
1924(b) Proof	—	Value: 150				
1924(b) P/L; Restrike	—	—	—	—	80.00	—
1925(b)	22,388,000	0.25	0.50	2.00	5.00	—
1925(c) Proof	—	Value: 150				
1925(b)	11,763,000	0.25	0.50	2.00	5.00	—
1925(b) Proof	—	Value: 150				
1925(b) P/L; Restrike	—	—	—	—	80.00	—
1926(c)	13,440,000	0.25	0.50	2.00	5.00	—
1926(c) Proof	—	Value: 150				
1926(b)	8,088,000	0.25	0.50	2.00	5.00	—
1926(b) Proof	—	Value: 150				
1926(b) P/L; Restrike	—	—	—	—	80.00	—
1927(c)	6,296,000	0.40	1.00	2.50	6.00	—
1927(c) Proof	—	Value: 150				
1927(b)	12,953,000	0.25	0.50	2.00	5.00	—
1927(b) Proof	—	Value: 150				
1927(b) P/L; Restrike	—	—	—	—	80.00	—
1928(c)	29,568,000	1.00	1.75	3.50	8.50	—
1928(c) Proof	—	Value: 150				
1928(b)	4,832,000	0.25	0.50	2.00	5.00	—
1928(b) Proof	—	Value: 150				
1928(b) P/L; Restrike	—	—	—	—	80.00	—
1929(c)	42,200,000	0.25	0.50	2.00	5.00	—
1929(c) Proof	—	Value: 150				
1929(c) P/L; Restrike	—	—	—	—	80.00	—
1930(c)	22,816,000	0.25	0.50	2.00	5.00	—
1930(c) Proof	—	Value: 150				
1930(c) P/L; Restrike	—	—	—	—	80.00	—
1933(c)	17,432,000	0.25	0.50	2.00	5.00	—
1933(c) Proof	—	Value: 150				
1933(c) P/L; Restrike	—	—	—	—	80.00	—
1934(c)	34,216,000	0.25	0.40	1.50	4.00	—
1934(c) Proof	—	Value: 150				
1934(c) P/L; Restrike	—	—	—	—	80.00	—
1935(c)	12,952,000	0.25	0.40	1.50	4.00	—
1935(c) Proof	—	Value: 150				
1935(b)	41,112,000	0.25	0.40	1.50	4.00	—
1935(b) Proof	—	Value: 150				
1935(b) P/L; Restrike	—	—	—	—	80.00	—
1936(c)	21,592,000	0.25	0.40	1.50	4.00	—
1936(b)	107,136,000	0.20	0.35	1.25	3.00	—
1936(b) Proof	—	Value: 150				

KM# 536 ANNA

3.7000 g., Copper-Nickel **Ruler:** George VI **Obv:** First head, high relief **Obv. Leg.:** GEORGE VI KING EMPEROR **Rev:** Denomination and date within decorative outline **Note:** Calcutta Mint issues have no mint mark. Bombay Mint issues have a small dot below the date.

Date	Mintage	VG	F	VF	XF	Unc
1938(c)	7,128,000	—	0.30	0.75	1.50	5.00
1938(c) Proof	—	Value: 120				
1938(b)	3,126,000	—	0.40	1.00	2.00	5.00
1938(b) P/L; Restrike	—	—	—	—	—	80.00
1939(c)	18,192,000	—	0.30	0.75	1.50	3.00
1939(b)	36,157,000	—	0.30	0.75	1.50	3.00
1939(b) P/L; Restrike	—	—	—	—	—	80.00
1940(c)	60,945,000	—	0.30	0.75	1.50	3.00
1940(c) P/L; Restrike	—	—	—	—	—	80.00
1940(b)	—	—	1.00	2.00	4.00	10.00

KM# 537 ANNA

Copper-Nickel **Ruler:** George VI **Obv:** Second head, low relief, large crown **Obv. Leg.:** GEORGE VI KING EMPEROR **Rev:** Large denomination and date within decorative outline

Date	Mintage	VG	F	VF	XF	Unc
1940(c)	76,392,000	—	0.10	0.25	0.50	2.00
1940(c) P/L; Restrike	—	—	—	—	—	100
1940(b)	144,712,000	—	0.10	0.25	0.50	2.00
1940(b) P/L; Restrike	—	—	—	—	—	80.00
1941(c)	62,480,000	—	0.10	0.25	0.50	2.00
1941(b)	40,170,000	—	0.15	0.40	1.00	1.50
1941(b) P/L; Restrike	—	—	—	—	—	100

KM# 537a ANNA

3.8900 g., Nickel-Brass, 20.50 mm. **Ruler:** George VI **Obv:** Second head, low relief, large crown **Obv. Leg.:** GEORGE VI KING EMPEROR **Rev:** Large denomination and date within decorative outline

Date	Mintage	VG	F	VF	XF	Unc
1942(c)	194,056,000	—	0.10	0.25	0.50	2.00
1942(c) Proof	—	Value: 120				
1942(b)	103,240,000	—	0.15	0.40	1.00	2.50
1942(b) P/L; Restrike	—	—	—	—	—	80.00
1943(c)	352,256,000	—	0.10	0.25	0.50	2.00
1943(c) Proof	—	Value: 120				
1943(b)	134,500,000	—	0.10	0.25	0.50	2.00
1943(b) P/L; Restrike	—	—	—	—	—	80.00
1944(c)	457,608,000	—	0.10	0.25	0.50	2.00
1944(c) Proof	—	Value: 120				
1944(b)	175,208,000	—	0.10	0.25	0.50	2.00
1944(b) P/L; Restrike	—	—	—	—	—	80.00
1945(c)	278,360,000	—	0.10	0.25	0.50	2.00
1945(b)	61,228,000	—	0.20	0.40	0.80	3.50

KM# 539 ANNA

Nickel-Brass, 21 mm. **Ruler:** George VI **Obv:** Second head, low relief, small crown **Obv. Leg.:** GEORGE VI KING EMPEROR **Rev:** Denomination and date within decorative outline

Date	Mintage	VG	F	VF	XF	Unc
1945(c)	278,360,000	—	0.10	0.25	0.75	2.00
1945(c) Proof	—	Value: 120				
1945(b)	61,228,000	—	0.10	0.25	0.75	2.00
1945(b) P/L; Restrike	—	—	—	—	—	100

KM# 538 ANNA

3.8700 g., Copper-Nickel **Ruler:** George VI **Obv:** Second head, low relief, small crown **Obv. Leg.:** GEORGE VI KING EMPEROR **Rev:** Denomination and date within decorative outline

Date	Mintage	F	VF	XF	Unc	BU
1946(c)	100,820,000	0.10	0.15	0.35	1.50	—
1946(b)	82,052,000	0.10	0.15	0.35	1.50	—

Date	Mintage	F	VF	XF	Unc	BU
1946(b) Proof	—	Value: 120				
1946(b) P/L; Restrike	—	—	—	—	100	—
1947(c)	148,656,000	0.10	0.25	0.35	1.50	—
1947(c) Proof	—	Value: 120				
1947(b)	50,096,000	0.10	0.25	0.50	2.00	—
1947(b) Proof	—	Value: 120				

KM# 488 2 ANNAS

1.4600 g., 0.9170 Silver 0.0430 oz. ASW **Ruler:** Victoria **Obv:** Crowned bust left **Obv. Leg.:** VICTORIA EMPRESS **Rev:** Value and date within wreath

Date	Mintage	F	VF	XF	Unc	BU
1901C Incuse	8,944,000	1.25	2.50	5.00	10.00	—
	Note: Type B Bust, Type II Reverse					
1901C Proof	Inc. above	Value: 35.00				
1901B Incuse	—	2.50	5.00	10.00	20.00	—
	Note: Type B Bust, Type I Reverse					
1901B Incuse	1,706,000	1.25	2.50	5.00	10.00	—
	Note: Type B Bust, Type II Reverse					
1901B Proof	—	Value: 125				
1901B P/L; Restrike	—	—	—	—	30.00	—
1901B Raised	—	2.50	5.00	10.00	20.00	—
	Note: Type B Bust, Type I Reverse					
1901B Raised	Inc. above	1.25	2.50	5.00	10.00	—
	Note: Type B Bust, Type II Reverse					

KM# 505 2 ANNAS

1.4600 g., 0.9170 Silver 0.0430 oz. ASW **Ruler:** Edward VII **Obv:** Head right **Obv. Leg.:** EDWARD VII KING AND EMPEROR **Rev:** Crown above denomination, sprays flank **Note:** Mule.

Date	Mintage	F	VF	XF	Unc	BU
1903(c)	4,434,000	1.75	3.50	7.00	14.00	—
1903(c) Proof	—	Value: 200				
1903(c) P/L; Restrike	—	—	—	—	100	—
1904(c)	14,632,000	1.50	3.00	6.00	12.00	—
1904(c) Proof	—	Value: 200				
1904(c) P/L; Restrike	—	—	—	—	100	—
1905(c)	19,303,000	1.50	3.00	6.00	12.00	—
1905(c) P/L; Restrike	—	—	—	—	100	—
1906(c)	13,031,000	1.50	3.00	6.00	12.00	—
1906(c) P/L; Restrike	—	—	—	—	100	—
1907(c)	22,145,000	1.50	3.00	6.00	12.00	—
1907(c) Proof	—	Value: 200				
1908(c)	21,600,000	1.50	3.00	6.00	12.00	—
1908(c) Proof	—	Value: 200				
1908(c) P/L; Restrike	—	—	—	—	100	—
1909(c)	6,769,000	1.75	3.50	7.00	14.00	—
1909(c) Proof	—	Value: 200				
1909(c) P/L; Restrike	—	—	—	—	100	—
1910(c)	1,604,000	1.75	3.50	7.00	14.00	—
1910(c) Proof	—	Value: 200				
1910(c) P/L; Restrike	—	—	—	—	100	—

KM# 505a 2 ANNAS

Gold **Ruler:** Edward VII **Obv:** Head right **Obv. Leg.:** EDWARD VII KING AND EMPEROR **Rev:** Crown above denomination, sprays flank **Note:** All dates of this type are prooflike restrikes.

Date	Mintage	F	VF	XF	Unc	BU
1904(c)	—	—	—	—	950	—
1906(c)	—	—	—	—	950	—
1910(c)	—	—	—	—	950	—

KM# 514 2 ANNAS

1.4600 g., 0.9170 Silver 0.0430 oz. ASW **Ruler:** George V **Obv:** Crowned bust left, type I **Obv. Leg.:** GEORGE V KING EMPEROR **Rev:** Denomination within wreath

Date	Mintage	F	VF	XF	Unc	BU
1911(c)	16,760,000	1.50	3.00	6.00	12.00	—
1911(c) Proof	—	Value: 200				
1911(c) P/L; Restrike	—	—	—	—	150	—

KM# 515 2 ANNAS

1.4600 g., 0.9170 Silver 0.0430 oz. ASW **Ruler:** George V **Obv:** Crowned bust left, type II **Obv. Leg.:** GEORGE V KING EMPEROR **Rev:** Denomination within wreath

Date	Mintage	F	VF	XF	Unc	BU
1912(c)	7,724,000	1.25	2.50	5.00	10.00	—
1912(c) Proof	—	Value: 150				
1912(b)	2,462,000	1.50	3.00	6.00	12.00	—
1912(b) Proof	—	Value: 150				
1912(b) P/L; Restrike	—	—	—	—	100	—
1913(c)	13,959,000	1.25	2.50	5.00	10.00	—
1913(c) Proof	—	Value: 150				
1913(b)	5,461,000	1.25	2.50	5.00	10.00	—
1913(b) Proof	—	Value: 150				
1913(b) P/L; Restrike	—	—	—	—	100	—
1914(c)	13,622,000	1.25	2.50	5.00	10.00	—
1914(c) Proof	—	Value: 150				
1914(b)	8,579,000	1.25	2.50	5.00	10.00	—
1914(b) P/L; Restrike	—	—	—	—	100	—
1915(c)	5,892,000	1.25	2.50	5.00	10.00	—
1915(c) Proof	—	Value: 150				
1915(b)	5,943,000	1.25	2.50	5.00	10.00	—
1915(b) P/L; Restrike	—	—	—	—	100	—
1916(c)	197,878,000	1.25	2.00	4.00	8.00	—
1916(c) Proof	—	Value: 150				
1916(c) P/L; Restrike	—	—	—	—	100	—
1917(c)	25,560,000	1.25	2.00	4.00	8.00	—
1917(c) Proof	—	Value: 150				
1917(c) P/L; Restrike	—	—	—	—	100	—

KM# 516 2 ANNAS

5.6200 g., Copper-Nickel **Ruler:** George V **Obv:** Crowned bust left within circle **Obv. Leg.:** GEORGE V KING EMPEROR **Rev:** Large denomination within square **Note:** Calcutta Mint issues have no mint mark. Bombay Mint issues have a small raised dot on the reverse at the bottom near the rim.

Date	Mintage	F	VF	XF	Unc	BU
1918(c)	53,412,000	1.25	1.75	4.00	10.00	—
1918(c) Proof	—	Value: 250				
1918(b)	9,191,000	1.25	1.75	4.00	10.00	—
1918(b) Proof	—	Value: 250				
1918(b) P/L; Restrike	—	—	—	—	150	—
1919(c)	89,040,000	1.25	1.75	4.00	10.00	—
1919(c) Proof	—	Value: 250				
1919(b) P/L; Restrike	—	—	—	—	150	—
1920(b) Proof	—	Value: 350				
1920(c)	13,520,000	1.25	1.75	4.00	10.00	—
1920(c) Proof	—	Value: 250				
1921(c) P/L; Restrike	—	1.25	1.75	4.00	10.00	—
1923(c)	7,656,000	1.25	1.75	4.00	10.00	—
1923(c) Proof	—	Value: 250				
1923(b)	6,431,000	1.25	1.75	4.00	10.00	—
1923(b) Proof	—	Value: 250				
1923(b) P/L; Restrike	—	—	—	—	150	—
1924(c)	8,384,000	1.25	1.75	4.00	10.00	—
1924(c) Proof	—	Value: 250				
1924(b)	4,818,000	1.50	3.00	6.00	12.00	—
1924(b) Proof	—	Value: 250				
1924(b) P/L; Restrike	—	—	—	—	150	—
1925(c)	10,848,000	1.25	1.75	4.00	10.00	—
1925(c) Proof	—	Value: 250				
1925(b)	8,348,000	1.25	1.75	4.00	10.00	—
1925(b) Proof	—	Value: 250				
1925(b) P/L; Restrike	—	—	—	—	150	—
1926(c)	8,352,000	1.25	1.75	4.00	10.00	—
1926(c) Proof	—	Value: 250				
1926(b)	2,927,000	1.75	3.50	7.00	14.00	—
1926(b) Proof	—	Value: 250				
1926(b) P/L; Restrike	—	—	—	—	150	—
1927(c)	6,424,000	1.25	1.375	4.00	10.00	—
1927(c) Proof	—	Value: 250				
1927(b)	4,835,000	1.50	3.00	6.00	12.00	—
1927(b) Proof	—	Value: 250				
1927(b) P/L; Restrike	—	—	—	—	150	—
1928(c)	7,352,000	1.25	1.75	4.00	10.00	—
1928(c) Proof	—	Value: 250				
1928(b)	4,876,000	1.50	3.00	6.00	12.00	—
1928(b) Proof	—	Value: 250				
1928(b) P/L; Restrike	—	—	—	—	150	—
1929(c)	13,408,000	1.25	1.75	4.00	10.00	—
1929(c) Proof	—	Value: 250				
1929(c) P/L; Restrike	—	—	—	—	150	—
1930(c)	8,888,000	1.25	1.75	4.00	10.00	—
1930(c) Proof	—	Value: 250				
1930(c) P/L; Restrike	—	—	—	—	150	—
1930(b)	—	1.25	1.75	4.00	10.00	—
1933	4,300,000	1.50	3.00	6.00	12.00	—
1933(c)	—					—
1933(c) Proof	—					—
1933(c) P/L; Restrike	—	—	—	—	150	—
1934(c)	7,016,000	1.25	1.75	4.00	10.00	—
1934(c) Proof	—	Value: 250				
1934(c) P/L; Restrike	—	—	—	—	150	—
1935(c)	12,344,000	1.25	1.75	4.00	10.00	—
1935(b)	21,017,000	1.00	1.50	3.00	8.00	—
1935(b) Proof	—	Value: 250				
1935(b) P/L; Restrike	—	—	—	—	150	—

Date	Mintage	F	VF	XF	Unc	BU
1936(b)	36,295,000	1.00	1.50	3.00	8.00	—
1936(b) Proof	—	Value: 250				

KM# 540 2 ANNAS

Copper-Nickel, 25 mm. **Ruler:** George VI **Obv:** First head, high relief **Obv. Leg.:** GEORGE VI KING EMPEROR **Rev:** Denomination and date within decorative outlines **Note:** Calcutta Mint issues have no mint mark. Mumbai (Bombay) Mint issues have a small dot before and after the date.

Date	Mintage	F	VF	XF	Unc	BU
1939(c)	4,148,000	1.25	3.00	6.00	15.00	—
1939(b)	3,392,000	2.00	5.00	10.00	25.00	—

KM# 541 2 ANNAS

5.8400 g., Copper-Nickel, 25 mm. **Ruler:** George VI **Obv:** Second head, low relief, large crown **Obv. Leg.:** GEORGE VI KING EMPEROR **Rev:** Denomination and date within decorative outlines

Date	Mintage	F	VF	XF	Unc	BU
1939(c)	Inc. above	1.25	2.00	2.50	4.00	—
1939(c) Proof	—	Value: 185				
1939(b)	Inc. above	0.20	0.30	0.50	1.50	—
1939(b) Proof	—	Value: 185				
1939(b) P/L; Restrike	—	—	—	—	125	—
1940(c)	37,636,000	0.20	0.30	0.50	2.00	—
1940(c) Proof	—	Value: 185				
1940(b)	50,599,000	0.20	0.30	0.50	2.00	—
1940(b) P/L; Restrike	—	—	—	—	125	—
1941(c)	63,456,000	0.20	0.30	0.50	1.50	—
1941(b)	10,760,000	1.25	2.00	2.50	4.00	—
1941(b) Proof	—	Value: 185				
1941(b) P/L; Restrike	—	—	—	—	125	—

KM# 541a 2 ANNAS

5.7400 g., Nickel-Brass, 25 mm. **Ruler:** George VI **Obv:** Second head, low relief, large crown **Obv. Leg.:** GEORGE VI KING EMPEROR **Rev:** Denomination and date within decorative outlines

Date	Mintage	F	VF	XF	Unc	BU
1942(b) Small 4	133,000,000	0.25	0.35	0.50	2.25	—
1942(b) Large 4	Inc. above	0.20	0.35	0.50	2.25	—
1943(b)	343,680,000	0.25	0.35	0.50	2.25	—
1944L	6,352,000	0.50	1.25	2.00	5.00	—
	Note: On 1944 Lahore issues, a tiny L replaces the decorative stroke in the four quatrefoil angles.					
1944(b) Small 4	219,700,000	0.25	0.35	0.50	2.25	—
1944(b) Large 4	Inc. above	0.25	0.35	0.50	2.25	—

KM# 543 2 ANNAS

Nickel-Brass **Ruler:** George VI **Obv:** Second head, low relief, large crown **Obv. Leg.:** GEORGE VI KING EMPEROR **Rev:** Small "2"

Date	Mintage	F	VF	XF	Unc	BU
1945(c)	24,260,000	0.25	0.75	1.25	2.75	—
1945(c) Proof	—	Value: 185				
1945(b)	136,688,000	0.25	0.35	0.50	1.50	—
1945(b) P/L; Restrike	—	—	—	—	125	—

KM# 542 2 ANNAS

5.9000 g., Copper-Nickel **Ruler:** George VI **Obv:** Second head, low relief, small crown **Obv. Leg.:** GEORGE VI KING EMPEROR **Rev:** Denomination and date within decorative outlines

Date	Mintage	F	VF	XF	Unc	BU
1946(c)	67,267,000	0.20	0.30	0.50	2.25	—
1946(b)	52,500,000	0.20	0.30	0.50	2.25	—

Date	Mintage	F	VF	XF	Unc	BU
1946(b) Proof	—	Value: 185				
1946(b) P/L; Restrike	—	—	—	—	125	—
1946(l)	25,480,000	0.20	0.30	0.50	2.25	—
	Note: Without "L" mintmark but with small diamond-shaped mark left of "I" on reverse					
1947(c)	57,428,000	0.20	0.30	0.50	2.25	—
1947(b)	38,908,000	0.20	0.30	0.50	2.25	—
1947(b) Proof	—	Value: 185				
1947(b) P/L; Restrike	—	—	—	—	125	—

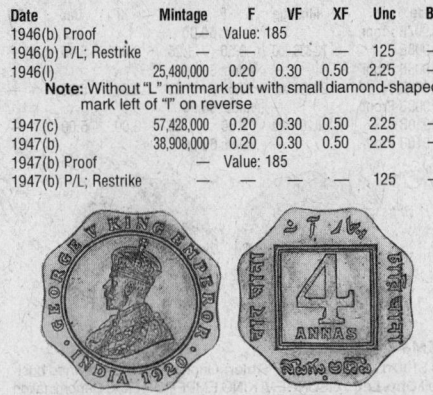

KM# 519 4 ANNAS

6.5000 g., Copper-Nickel **Ruler:** George V **Obv:** Crowned bust left within circle **Obv. Leg.:** GEORGE V KING EMPEROR • INDIA • **Rev:** Denomination within square **Note:** Calcutta Mint issues have no mint mark. Bombay Mint issues have a small raised dot on the reverse at the bottom near the rim.

Date	Mintage	F	VF	XF	Unc	BU
1919(c)	18,632,000	2.50	5.00	10.00	20.00	—
1919(c) Proof	—	Value: 550				
1919(b)	7,672,000	3.25	6.50	12.50	25.00	—
1919 P/L; Restrike	—	—	—	—	125	—
1920(c)	18,191,000	2.50	5.00	10.00	20.00	—
1920(c) Proof	—	Value: 550				
1920(b)	1,666,000	3.25	6.50	12.50	25.00	—
1920(b) Proof	—	Value: 550				
1920(b) P/L; Restrike	—	—	—	—	125	—
1921(c) Proof	—	Value: 550				
1921(c) P/L; Restrike	—	—	—	—	125	—
1921(b)	1,219,000	3.75	7.50	15.00	30.00	—
1921(b) Proof	—	Value: 550				

KM# 520 8 ANNAS

Copper-Nickel **Ruler:** George V **Obv:** Crowned bust left **Obv. Leg.:** GEORGE V KING EMPEROR **Rev:** Denomination and date within scallop, square surrounds **Note:** Calcutta Mint issues have no mint mark. Mumbai (Bombay) Mint issues have a small raised dot on the reverse at the bottom near the rim.

Date	Mintage	F	VF	XF	Unc	BU
1919(c)	2,980,000	3.75	7.50	15.00	30.00	—
1919(c) Proof	—	Value: 550				
1919(b)	1,400,000	4.00	8.50	17.50	35.00	—
1919(b) P/L; Restrike	—	—	—	—	150	—
1920(c) Proof	—	Value: 550				
1920(c) P/L; Restrike	—	—	—	—	350	—
1920(b)	1,000,000	12.50	25.00	50.00	100	—
1920(b) Proof	—	Value: 550				
1920(b) P/L; Restrike	—	—	—	—	150	—

KM# 490 1/4 RUPEE

2.9200 g., 0.9170 Silver 0.0861 oz. ASW **Ruler:** Victoria **Obv:** Crowned bust left **Obv. Leg.:** VICTORIA EMPRESS **Rev:** Value and date within wreath **Note:** Mule.

Date	Mintage	F	VF	XF	Unc	BU
1901C Incuse	4,476,000	2.00	3.00	6.00	15.00	—
	Note: Type C Bust, Type II Reverse					
1901C Proof	—	Value: 600				
1901C P/L; Restrike	—	—	—	—	175	—

KM# 506 1/4 RUPEE

2.9200 g., 0.9170 Silver 0.0861 oz. ASW **Ruler:** Edward VII **Obv:** Head right **Obv. Leg.:** EDWARD VII KING AND EMPEROR **Rev:** Crown above denomination, sprays flank

Date	Mintage	F	VF	XF	Unc	BU
1903(c)	7,060,000	1.75	3.50	8.00	20.00	—
1903(c) Proof	—	Value: 400				

Date	Mintage	F	VF	XF	Unc	BU
1903(c) P/L; Restrike	—	—	—	—	150	—
1904(c)	10,026,000	1.75	3.50	8.00	20.00	—
1904(c) Proof	—	Value: 400				
1904(c) P/L; Restrike	—	—	—	—	150	—
1905(c)	6,300,000	1.75	3.50	8.00	20.00	—
1905(c) Proof	—	Value: 400				
1905(c) P/L; Restrike	—	—	—	—	150	—
1906(c)	10,672,000	1.75	3.50	8.00	20.00	—
1906(c) P/L; Restrike	—	—	—	—	150	—
1907(c)	11,464,000	1.75	3.50	8.00	20.00	—
1907(c) Proof	—	Value: 400				
1907(c) P/L; Restrike	—	—	—	—	150	—
1908(c)	7,084,000	1.75	3.50	8.00	20.00	—
1908(c) Proof	—	Value: 400				
1908(c) P/L; Restrike	—	—	—	—	150	—
1909(c) Proof	—	Value: 500				
1909(c) P/L; Restrike	—	—	—	—	150	—
1910(c)	8,024,000	1.75	3.50	8.00	20.00	—
1910(c) Proof	—	Value: 400				
1910(c) P/L; Restrike	—	—	—	—	150	—

KM# 506a 1/4 RUPEE
Gold **Ruler:** Edward VII **Obv:** Head right **Rev:** Crown above denomination, sprays flank

Date	Mintage	F	VF	XF	Unc	BU
1910(c)	—	—	—	—	1,100	—

Note: Prooflike; Restrike

KM# 517 1/4 RUPEE
2.9200 g., 0.9170 Silver 0.0861 oz. ASW **Ruler:** George V **Obv:** Type I **Obv. Leg.:** GEORGE V KING EMPEROR

Date	Mintage	F	VF	XF	Unc	BU
1911(c)	2,245,000	2.00	4.00	8.00	8.00	—
1911(c) Proof	—	Value: 350				
1911(c) P/L; Restrike	—	—	—	—	300	—

KM# 518 1/4 RUPEE
2.9200 g., 0.9170 Silver 0.0861 oz. ASW **Ruler:** George V **Obv:** Crowned bust left, type II **Obv. Leg.:** GEORGE V KING EMPEROR **Rev:** Denomination and date within circle, wreath surrounds

Date	Mintage	F	VF	XF	Unc	BU
1912(c)	9,587,000	2.00	3.00	5.00	12.00	—
1912(c) Proof	—	Value: 250				
1912(b)	2,200,000	2.00	3.00	5.00	12.00	—
1912(b) Proof	—	Value: 250				
1912(b) P/L; Restrike	—	—	—	—	120	—
1913(c)	12,686,000	2.00	3.00	5.00	12.00	—
1913(c) Proof	—	Value: 250				
1913(b)	2,276,000	2.00	3.00	5.00	12.00	—
1913(b) Proof	—	Value: 250				
1913(b) P/L; Restrike	—	—	—	—	120	—
1914(c)	1,423,000	2.00	3.00	5.00	12.00	—
1914(c) Proof	—	Value: 250				
1914(b)	7,949,000	2.00	3.00	5.00	10.00	—
1914(b) P/L; Restrike	—	—	—	—	120	—
1915(c)	851,000	2.25	4.00	10.00	35.00	—
1915(c) Proof	—	Value: 250				
1915(b)	2,096,000	2.00	3.00	5.00	12.00	—
1915(c) P/L; Restrike	—	—	—	—	120	—
1915(b) P/L; Restrike	—	—	—	—	120	—
1916(c)	13,178,000	2.00	3.00	5.00	12.00	—
1916(c) Proof	—	Value: 250				
1916(c) P/L; Restrike	—	—	—	—	120	—
1917(c)	21,072,000	2.00	3.00	5.00	12.00	—
1917(c) Proof	—	Value: 250				
1917(c) P/L; Restrike	—	—	—	—	120	—
1918(c)	50,575,000	2.00	3.00	5.00	12.00	—
1918(c) Proof	—	Value: 250				
1919(b)	—	3.50	7.50	15.00	30.00	—
1919(b)	26,135,000	2.00	3.00	5.00	12.00	—
1919(c) Proof	—	Value: 250				
1920(b)	—	3.25	6.50	12.50	25.00	—
1925(b)	4,007,000	2.00	3.00	5.00	12.00	—
1925(b) Proof	—	Value: 250				
1925(b) P/L; Restrike	—	—	—	—	120	—
1926(c)	8,169,000	2.00	3.00	5.00	12.00	—
1926(c) Proof	—	Value: 250				
1926(c) P/L; Restrike	—	—	—	—	120	—
1928(b)	4,023,000	2.00	3.00	5.00	12.00	—
1928(b) Proof	—	Value: 250				
1929(c)	4,013,000	2.00	3.00	5.00	12.00	—
1929(c) Proof	—	Value: 250				
1929(c) P/L; Restrike	—	—	—	—	120	—
1930(c)	3,222,000	2.00	3.00	5.00	12.00	—
1930(c) Proof	—	Value: 250				
1930(c) P/L; Restrike	—	—	—	—	120	—
1934(c)	3,946,000	2.00	3.00	5.00	10.00	—
1936(c)	25,744,000	1.50	2.50	4.00	8.00	—
1936(b)	9,864,000	1.50	2.50	4.00	8.00	—
1936(b) P/L; Restrike	—	—	—	—	120	—

KM# 544 1/4 RUPEE
2.9200 g., 0.9170 Silver 0.0861 oz. ASW **Ruler:** George VI **Obv:** Crowned head left **Obv. Leg.:** GEORGE VI KING EMPEROR **Rev:** Denomination and date within circle, wreath surrounds

Date	Mintage	F	VF	XF	Unc	BU
1938(c) Proof	—	Value: 250				
1938(c) P/L; Restrike	—	—	—	—	125	—
1939(c)	3,072,000	2.00	3.50	6.00	12.00	—
1939(c) Proof	—	Value: 250				
1939(b)	6,770,000	2.00	3.50	5.00	10.00	—
1939(b) P/L; Restrike	—	—	—	—	125	—

KM# 544a 1/4 RUPEE
2.9200 g., 0.5000 Silver 0.0469 oz. ASW **Ruler:** George VI **Obv:** Crowned head left **Obv. Leg.:** GEORGE VI KING EMPEROR **Rev:** Denomination and date within circle, wreath surrounds

Date	Mintage	F	VF	XF	Unc	BU
1940(b)	24,635,000	2.00	3.50	5.00	10.00	—

KM# 545 1/4 RUPEE
2.9200 g., 0.5000 Silver 0.0469 oz. ASW **Ruler:** George VI **Obv:** Large second head, small rim decoration **Obv. Leg.:** GEORGE VI KING EMPEROR **Rev:** Denomination and date within circle, wreath surrounds **Edge:** Reeded

Date	Mintage	VG	F	VF	XF	Unc
1940(c)	68,675,000	—	BV	1.50	2.50	6.00
1940(c) Proof	—	Value: 250				
1940(b)	28,947,000	—	BV	1.50	2.50	6.00

KM# 546 1/4 RUPEE
2.9200 g., 0.5000 Silver 0.0469 oz. ASW **Ruler:** George VI **Obv:** Small second head, large rim decoration **Obv. Leg.:** GEORGE VI KING EMPEROR **Rev:** Denomination and date within circle, wreath surrounds **Edge:** Reeded

Date	Mintage	F	VF	XF	Unc	BU
1942(c)	88,096,000	BV	1.50	2.25	4.50	—
1943(c)	90,994,000	BV	1.50	2.25	4.50	—

KM# 547 1/4 RUPEE
2.9200 g., 0.5000 Silver 0.0469 oz. ASW **Ruler:** George VI **Obv:** Small second head, large rim decoration **Obv. Leg.:** GEORGE VI KING EMPEROR **Rev:** Denomination and date within circle, wreath surrounds **Edge:** Security

Date	Mintage	F	VF	XF	Unc	BU
1943B	95,200,000	BV	1.50	2.25	4.50	—
1943B Proof	—	Value: 250				
1943B Reverse B	Inc. above	BV	1.50	2.25	4.50	—
1943L	23,700,000	BV	1.50	2.25	4.50	—
1944B	170,504,000	BV	1.50	2.25	4.50	—
1944B Reverse B	Inc. above	BV	1.50	2.25	4.50	—
1944L	86,400,000	BV	1.50	2.25	4.50	—
1945(b) Small 5	181,648,000	BV	1.50	2.25	4.50	—
1945(b) Large 5	Inc. above	10.00	15.00	25.00	40.00	—
1945L Small 5	29,751,000	BV	1.50	2.25	4.50	—
1945L Large 5	Inc. above	BV	1.00	2.00	5.00	—

KM# 548 1/4 RUPEE
2.9000 g., Nickel **Ruler:** George VI **Obv:** Crowned head left **Obv. Leg.:** GEORGE VI KING EMPEROR **Rev:** Indian tiger (panthera tigris) **Edge:** Reeded

Date	Mintage	F	VF	XF	Unc	BU
1946(b)	83,600,000	0.40	0.75	2.50	7.50	12.00
1947(b)	109,948,000	0.40	0.75	2.50	7.50	12.00
1947(b) Proof	—	Value: 200				

KM# 507 1/2 RUPEE
5.8300 g., 0.9170 Silver 0.1719 oz. ASW **Ruler:** Edward VII **Obv:** Head right **Obv. Leg.:** EDWARD VII KING AND EMPEROR **Rev:** Crown above denomination, sprays flank **Note:** Calcutta Mint issues have no mint mark. Mumbai (Bombay) Mint issues have a small incuse "B" in the space below the cross pattee of the crown on the reverse.

Date	Mintage	F	VF	XF	Unc	BU
1904(c) Proof	—	Value: 500				
1904(c) P/L; Restrike	—	—	—	—	175	—
1905(c)	823,000	5.00	10.00	25.00	50.00	—
1905(c) P/L; Restrike	—	—	—	—	175	—
1906(c)	3,036,000	5.00	10.00	25.00	50.00	—
1906B	400,000	5.00	12.50	30.00	60.00	—
1906B P/L; Restrike	—	—	—	—	175	—
1907(c)	2,786,000	5.00	10.00	25.00	50.00	—
1907(c) Proof	—	Value: 450				
1907B	1,856,000	5.00	10.00	25.00	50.00	—
1907B Proof	—	Value: 450				
1907B P/L; Restrike	—	—	—	—	175	—
1908(c)	1,577,000	5.00	10.00	25.00	50.00	—
1908(c) Proof	—	Value: 450				
1908(c) P/L; Restrike	—	—	—	—	175	—
1909(c)	1,569,000	5.00	10.00	25.00	50.00	—
1909(c) P/L; Restrike	—	—	—	—	175	—
1909(c) Proof	—	Value: 450				
1909B Proof	—	Value: 750				
1909B P/L; Restrike	—	—	—	—	350	—
1910(c)	3,413,000	5.00	10.00	25.00	50.00	—
1910(c) Proof	—	Value: 450				
1910B	809,000	5.00	10.00	25.00	50.00	—
1910B "B" raised	—	10.00	15.00	30.00	55.00	—
1910B Proof	—	Value: 450				
1910B P/L; Restrike	—	—	—	—	175	—

KM# 521 1/2 RUPEE
5.8300 g., 0.9170 Silver 0.1719 oz. ASW **Ruler:** George V **Obv:** Crowned bust left, type I **Obv. Leg.:** GEORGE V KING EMPEROR **Rev:** Denomination and date within circle, wreath surrounds **Note:** Calcutta Mint issues have no mint mark. Mumbai (Bombay) Mint issues have a small raised bead or dot in the space below the lotus flower at the bottom of the reverse. The half Rupee dated 1911 like the Rupee and all the other issues of that year has the "Pig" elephant. It was struck only at the Calcutta Mint.

Date	Mintage	F	VF	XF	Unc	BU
1911(c)	2,293,000	3.50	6.00	12.50	30.00	—
1911(c) Proof	—	Value: 500				
1911(c) P/L; Restrike	—	—	—	—	250	—

KM# 522 1/2 RUPEE
5.8300 g., 0.9170 Silver 0.1719 oz. ASW **Ruler:** George V **Obv:** Crowned bust left, type II **Obv. Leg.:** GEORGE V KING EMPEROR **Rev:** Denomination and date within circle, wreath surrounds

Date	Mintage	F	VF	XF	Unc	BU
1912(c)	3,390,000	5.00	6.00	12.00	28.00	—
1912(c) Proof	—	Value: 500				
1912(b)	1,505,000	5.00	6.00	12.00	28.00	—
1912(b) Proof	—	Value: 500				
1912(b) P/L; Restrike	—	—	—	—	150	—
1913(c)	2,723,000	5.00	6.00	12.00	28.00	—
1913(c) Proof	—	Value: 500				
1913(b)	1,825,000	5.00	6.00	12.00	28.00	—
1913(b) Proof	—	Value: 500				
1913(b) P/L; Restrike	—	—	—	—	150	—
1914(c)	1,400,000	5.00	6.00	12.00	28.00	—
1914(c) Proof	—	Value: 500				
1914(b)	903,000	5.00	6.00	12.50	30.00	—
1914(b) P/L; Restrike	—	—	—	—	150	—
1915(c)	2,804,000	5.00	6.00	12.00	28.00	—
1915(c) Proof	—	Value: 500				
1915(c) P/L; Restrike	—	5.00	6.00	12.00	28.00	—
1916(c)	3,644,000	5.00	6.00	12.00	28.00	—
1916(c) Proof	—	Value: 500				
1916(b)	5,880,000	5.00	6.00	12.00	28.00	—
1917(c) Proof	—	Value: 500				
1917(b)	8,822,000	5.00	6.00	12.00	28.00	—
1917(b) Proof	—	Value: 500				
1918(b) P/L; Restrike	—	—	—	—	150	—
1918(c) P/L; Restrike	—	—	—	—	150	—
1918(b)	10,325,000	5.00	6.00	12.00	28.00	—
1919(b)	8,958,000	5.00	6.00	12.00	28.00	—
1919(b) Proof	—	Value: 500				
1919(b) P/L; Restrike	—	—	—	—	150	—
1919(c) P/L; Restrike	—	—	—	—	150	—
1921(c)	5,804,000	5.00	6.00	12.00	28.00	—
1921(c) Proof	—	Value: 500				
1921(c) P/L; Restrike	—	—	—	—	150	—
1922(c)	5,551,000	5.00	6.00	12.00	28.00	—
1922(c) Proof	—	Value: 500				
1922(b)	1,037,000	5.00	6.00	12.00	28.00	—
1922(b) Proof	—	Value: 500				
1922(b) P/L; Restrike	—	—	—	—	150	—
1923(c)	3,925,000	5.00	6.00	12.00	28.00	—
1923(c) P/L; Restrike	—	—	—	—	150	—
1923(b)	2,076,000	5.00	6.00	12.00	28.00	—
1923(b) Proof	—	Value: 500				
1923(b) P/L; Restrike	—	—	—	—	150	—
1924(c)	4,007,000	5.00	6.00	12.00	28.00	—
1924(c) Proof	—	Value: 500				
1924(b)	2,664,000	5.00	6.00	12.00	28.00	—
1924(b) Proof	—	Value: 500				
1924(b) P/L; Restrike	—	—	—	—	150	—
1925(c)	4,119,000	5.00	6.00	12.00	28.00	—
1925(c) Proof	—	Value: 500				
1925(b)	1,627,000	5.00	6.00	12.00	28.00	—
1925(b) Proof	—	Value: 500				
1925(b) P/L; Restrike	—	—	—	—	150	—
1926(c)	4,027,000	5.00	6.00	12.00	28.00	—
1926(c) Proof	—	Value: 500				
1926(b)	2,011,000	5.00	6.00	12.00	28.00	—
1926(b) Proof	—	Value: 500				
1926(b) P/L; Restrike	—	—	—	—	150	—
1927(c)	2,032,000	5.00	6.00	12.00	28.00	—
1927(c) Proof	—	Value: 500				
1927(c) P/L; Restrike	—	—	—	—	150	—
1928(b)	2,466,000	5.00	6.00	12.00	28.00	—
1928(b) Proof	—	Value: 500				
1929(c)	4,050,000	5.00	6.00	12.00	28.00	—
1929(c) Proof	—	Value: 500				
1929(c) P/L; Restrike	—	—	—	—	150	—
1930(c)	2,036,000	5.00	6.00	12.00	28.00	—
1930(c) Proof	—	Value: 500				
1930(c) P/L; Restrike	—	—	—	—	150	—
1933/2(c)	4,056,000	5.00	10.00	25.00	50.00	—
1933(c)	Inc. above	5.00	6.00	12.00	28.00	—
1933(c) Proof	—	Value: 300				
1933(c) P/L; Restrike	—	—	—	—	150	—
1934(c)	4,056,000	5.00	6.00	12.00	28.00	—
1934(c) Proof	—	Value: 500				
1934(c) P/L; Restrike	—	—	—	—	150	—
1936(c)	16,919,000	5.00	6.00	12.00	28.00	—
1936(b)	6,693,000	5.00	6.00	12.00	28.00	—
1936(b) P/L; Restrike	—	—	—	—	150	—

KM# 549 1/2 RUPEE
5.8300 g., 0.9170 Silver 0.1719 oz. ASW **Ruler:** George VI
Obv: Crowned head left, first head **Obv. Leg.:** GEORGE VI KING EMPEROR **Rev:** Denomination and date within circle, wreath surrounds **Edge:** Reeded

Date	Mintage	F	VF	XF	Unc	BU
1938(c) Proof	—	Value: 400				
1938(b)	2,200,000	BV	4.00	7.50	15.00	—
1938(b) P/L; Restrike	—	—	—	—	150	—
1939(c)	3,300,000	BV	4.00	7.50	15.00	—
1939(c) Proof	—	Value: 300				
1939(b)	10,096,000	BV	4.00	7.50	15.00	—

Date	Mintage	F	VF	XF	Unc	BU
1939(b) Proof	—	Value: 300				
1939(b) P/L; Restrike	—	—	—	150		—

KM# A553 1/2 RUPEE
Copper-Nickel **Ruler:** George VI **Obv:** Crowned head left
Obv. Leg.: GEORGE VI KING EMPEROR **Rev:** Denomination and date within circle, wreath surrounds **Note:** Mule.

Date	Mintage	F	VF	XF	Unc	BU
1938(c) P/L; Restrike	—					

KM# 550 1/2 RUPEE
5.8300 g., 0.9170 Silver 0.1719 oz. ASW **Ruler:** George VI
Obv: Large second head, small rim decoration
Obv. Leg.: GEORGE VI KING EMPEROR **Rev:** Denomination and date within circle, wreath surrounds **Edge:** Reeded

Date	Mintage	VG	F	VF	XF	Unc
1939(c)	Inc. above	—	BV	4.00	6.50	15.00
1939(b)	Inc. above	—	BV	4.00	6.50	13.50

KM# 550a 1/2 RUPEE
5.8300 g., 0.5000 Silver 0.0937 oz. ASW **Ruler:** George VI
Obv: Large second head, small rim decoration **Obv. Leg.:** GEORGE VI KING EMPEROR **Rev:** Denomination and date within circle, wreath surrounds

Date	Mintage	F	VF	XF	Unc	BU
1940(c)	32,898,000	BV	4.00	6.00	12.00	—
1940(c) Proof	—	Value: 300				
1940(b)	17,811,000	BV	4.00	6.50	13.50	—
1940(b) P/L; Restrike	—	—	—	—	150	—

KM# 551 1/2 RUPEE
5.8300 g., 0.5000 Silver 0.0937 oz. ASW **Ruler:** George VI
Obv: Large second head, small rim decoration
Obv. Leg.: GEORGE VI KING EMPEROR **Rev:** Denomination and date within circle, wreath surrounds **Edge:** Security

Date	Mintage	VG	F	VF	XF	Unc
1941(b)	26,100,000	—	BV	2.00	5.00	12.50
1942(b)	61,600,000	—	BV	2.00	5.00	12.50

NOTE: Example of large 5 in date 1945.

KM# 552 1/2 RUPEE
5.8300 g., 0.5000 Silver 0.0937 oz. ASW **Ruler:** George VI
Obv: Small second head, large rim decoration
Obv. Leg.: GEORGE VI KING EMPEROR **Rev:** Denomination and inner circle smaller **Edge:** Security

Date	Mintage	F	VF	XF	Unc	BU
1942(b)	Inc. above	BV	2.00	4.50	9.00	—
1943(b) Dot	90,400,000	BV	2.00	4.50	9.00	—
1943(b) Proof	—	Value: 300				
1943(b) Diamond	—	BV	2.00	4.50	9.00	—
1943L	9,000,000	BV	2.00	4.50	9.00	—
1943L Proof	—	Value: 300				
1944(b) Dot	46,200,000	BV	2.00	4.50	9.00	—
1944(b) Diamond	Inc. above	BV	2.00	4.50	9.00	—
1944L	79,100,000	BV	2.00	4.50	9.00	—
1944L Proof	—	Value: 300				
1945(b) Small 5	32,722,000	BV	2.00	4.50	9.00	—
1945(b) Large 5	—	20.00	25.00	35.00	50.00	—
1945L Small dot	79,192,000	BV	2.00	4.50	9.00	—
1945L Proof	—	Value: 300				
1945L Large dot	Inc. above	2.50	5.00	10.00	20.00	—

KM# 553 1/2 RUPEE
5.8000 g., Nickel **Ruler:** George VI **Obv:** Crowned head left
Obv. Leg.: GEORGE VI KING EMPEROR **Rev:** Indian tiger (panthera tigris) **Edge:** Reeded

Date	Mintage	F	VF	XF	Unc	BU
1946(b)	47,500,000	0.50	1.00	2.50	7.50	15.00
1947(b)	62,724,000	0.50	1.00	2.50	7.50	15.00
1947(b) Proof	—	Value: 275				

KM# 492 RUPEE
11.6600 g., 0.9170 Silver 0.3437 oz. ASW, 30.79 mm.
Ruler: Victoria **Obv:** Crowned bust left **Obv. Leg.:** VICTORIA EMPRESS **Rev:** Value and date within wreath **Edge:** Reeded

Date	Mintage	F	VF	XF	Unc	BU
1901C C/I, "C" incuse	72,017,000	6.50	8.00	12.00	25.00	—
1901C Proof	Inc. above	Value: 725				
1901B A/I, "B" incuse	130,258,000	6.50	8.00	12.00	25.00	—
1901B Proof	—	Value: 725				
1901B P/L; Restrike	—	—	—	—	250	—
1901B C/I, "B" incuse	Inc. above	6.50	8.00	12.00	25.00	—

KM# 508 RUPEE
11.6600 g., 0.9170 Silver 0.3437 oz. ASW **Ruler:** Edward VII
Obv: Head right **Obv. Leg.:** EDWARD VII KING & EMPEROR **Rev:** Crown above denomination, sprays flank **Note:** Calcutta Mint issues have no mint mark. Mumbai (Bombay) Mint issues have a small incuse "B" in the space below the cross pattee of the crown on the reverse.

Date	Mintage	F	VF	XF	Unc	BU
1903(c)	49,403,000	7.00	9.00	13.50	28.00	—
1903(c) Proof	—	Value: 700				
1903B In relief	52,969	7.00	9.00	13.50	28.00	—
1903B Proof	—	Value: 700				
1903B Incuse	Inc. above	7.00	9.00	13.50	28.00	—
1903B P/L; Restrike	—	—	—	—	200	—
1904(c)	58,339,000	7.00	9.00	13.50	28.00	—
1904(c) Proof	—	Value: 700				
1904B	101,949,000	7.00	9.00	13.50	28.00	—
1904B Proof	—	Value: 700				
1904B P/L; Restrike	—	—	—	—	200	—
1905(c)	51,258,000	7.00	9.00	13.50	28.00	—
1905(c) Proof	—	Value: 700				
1905B	76,202,000	7.00	9.00	13.50	28.00	—
1905B Proof	—	Value: 700				
1905B P/L; Restrike	—	—	—	—	200	—
1906(c)	104,797,000	7.00	9.00	15.00	30.00	—
1906B	158,953,000	7.00	9.00	15.00	30.00	—
1906B Proof	—	Value: 700				
1906B P/L; Restrike	—	—	—	—	200	—
1907(c)	81,338,000	7.00	9.00	15.00	30.00	—
1907(c) Proof	—	Value: 700				
1907B	170,912,000	7.00	9.00	15.00	30.00	—
1907B Proof	—	Value: 700				
1907B P/L; Restrike	—	—	—	—	200	—
1908(c)	20,218,000	7.00	9.00	15.00	30.00	—
1908(c) Proof	—	Value: 700				
1908B	10,715,000	8.50	15.00	30.00	60.00	—
1908B Proof	—	Value: 700				
1908B P/L; Restrike	—	—	—	—	200	—
1909(c)	12,759,000	7.00	9.00	15.00	30.00	—
1909(c) Proof	—	Value: 700				
1909B	9,539,000	8.50	15.00	30.00	60.00	—
1909B Proof	—	Value: 700				
1909B P/L; Restrike	—	—	—	—	200	—
1910(c)	12,627,000	7.00	9.00	15.00	30.00	—
1910(c) Proof	—	Value: 700				
1910B	10,885,000	7.00	9.00	15.00	30.00	—

Date	Mintage	F	VF	XF	Unc	BU
1910B Proof	—	Value: 700				
1910B P/L; Restrike	—	—	—	—	200	—

KM# 523 RUPEE
11.6600 g., 0.9170 Silver 0.3437 oz. ASW **Ruler:** George V **Obv:** Type I **Obv. Leg.:** GEORGE V KING EMPEROR

Date	Mintage	F	VF	XF	Unc	BU
1911(c)	4,300,000	10.00	20.00	40.00	100	—
1911(c) Proof	—	Value: 1,200				
1911(b)	5,143,000	10.00	20.00	40.00	100	—
1911(b) P/L; Restrike	—	—	—	—	350	—

KM# 524 RUPEE
11.6600 g., 0.9170 Silver 0.3437 oz. ASW **Ruler:** George V **Obv:** Crowned bust left, type II **Obv. Leg.:** GEORGE V KING EMPEROR **Rev:** Denomination and date within circle, wreath surrounds

Date	Mintage	F	VF	XF	Unc	BU
1912(c)	45,122,000	6.00	9.50	15.00	35.00	—
1912(c) Proof	—	Value: 1,000				
1912(b)	79,067,000	5.50	8.00	12.50	25.00	—
1912(b) Proof	—	Value: 1,000				
1912B P/L; Restrike	—	—	—	—	225	—
1913(c)	75,800,000	5.50	8.00	12.50	25.00	—
1913(c) Proof	—	Value: 1,000				
1913(b)	87,466,000	5.50	8.00	12.50	25.00	—
1913(b) Proof	—	Value: 1,000				
1913(b) P/L; Restrike	—	—	—	—	225	—
1914(c)	33,100,000	5.50	8.00	12.50	25.00	—
1914(c) Proof	—	Value: 1,000				
1914(b)	15,270,000	5.50	8.00	12.50	25.00	—
1914(b) Proof	—	Value: 1,000				
1914(b) P/L; Restrike	—	—	—	—	225	—
1915(c)	9,900,000	8.50	15.00	30.00	60.00	—
1915(c) Proof	—	Value: 1,000				
1915(b)	5,372,000	10.00	20.00	40.00	80.00	—
1915(b) Proof	—	Value: 1,000				
1915(b) P/L; Restrike	—	—	—	—	225	—
1916(c)	115,000,000	5.50	8.00	12.50	20.00	—
1916(c) Proof	—	Value: 1,000				
1916(b)	97,900,000	5.50	8.00	12.50	20.00	—
1916(b) Proof	—	Value: 1,000				
1916(b) P/L; Restrike	—	—	—	—	225	—
1917(c)	114,974,000	5.50	8.00	12.50	20.00	—
1917(c) Proof	—	Value: 1,000				
1917(b)	151,583,000	5.50	8.00	12.50	20.00	—
1917(b) Proof	—	Value: 1,000				
1917(b) P/L; Restrike	—	—	—	—	225	—
1918(c)	205,420,000	5.50	8.00	12.50	20.00	—
1918(c) Proof	—	Value: 1,000				
1918(b)	210,550,000	5.50	8.00	12.50	20.00	—
1918(b) Proof	—	Value: 1,000				
1918(b) P/L; Restrike	—	—	—	—	225	—
1919(c)	211,206,000	5.50	8.00	12.50	20.00	—
1919(c) Proof	—	Value: 1,000				
1919(b)	226,706,000	5.50	8.00	12.50	20.00	—
1919(b) Proof	—	Value: 1,000				
1919(b) P/L; Restrike	—	—	—	—	225	—
1920(c)	50,500,000	5.50	8.00	12.50	20.00	—
1920(c) Proof	—	Value: 1,000				
1920(b)	55,937,000	5.50	8.00	12.50	20.00	—
1920(b) Proof	—	Value: 1,000				
1921(b)	5,115,000	10.00	20.00	40.00	85.00	—
1921(b) Proof	—	Value: 1,000				
1922(b)	2,051,000	10.00	20.00	40.00	85.00	—
1922(b) Proof	—	Value: 1,000				
1935(c) Proof	—	Value: 1,000				
1935(c) P/L; Restrike	—	—	—	—	225	—
1936(c) Proof	—	Value: 1,000				

KM# 554 RUPEE
11.6600 g., 0.9170 Silver 0.3437 oz. ASW **Ruler:** George VI **Obv:** Crowned head left, first head **Obv. Leg.:** GEORGE VI KING EMPEROR **Rev:** Denomination and date within circle, wreath surrounds **Edge:** Reeded

Date	Mintage	F	VF	XF	Unc	BU
1938(c) Proof	—	Value: 600				
1939(c) Proof	—	Value: 750				

KM# 555 RUPEE
11.6600 g., 0.9170 Silver 0.3437 oz. ASW **Ruler:** George VI **Obv:** Second head, small rim decoration **Obv. Leg.:** GEORGE VI KING EMPEROR **Rev:** Denomination and date within circle, wreath surrounds **Edge:** Reeded

Date	Mintage	F	VF	XF	Unc	BU
1938(b) Without dot	7,352,000	7.50	11.50	16.50	27.50	—
1938(b) Dot	Inc. above	7.50	11.50	16.50	27.50	—
1938(b) P/L; Restrike	—	—	—	—	375	—
1939(b) Dot	2,450,000	150	300	600	1,200	—

KM# A559 RUPEE
Copper-Nickel **Ruler:** George VI **Obv:** Small second head, large rim decoration **Obv. Leg.:** GEORGE VI KING EMPEROR **Rev:** Denomination and date within circle, wreath surrounds **Note:** Mule

Date	Mintage	F	VF	XF	Unc	BU
1938(c) P/L; Restrike	—	—	—	—	750	—

KM# A556 RUPEE
Copper-Nickel **Ruler:** George VI **Obv:** Small second head, large rim decoration **Obv. Leg.:** GEORGE VI KING EMPEROR **Rev:** Denomination and date within circle, wreath surrounds **Note:** Mule.

Date	Mintage	F	VF	XF	Unc	BU
1938(c) P/L; Restrike	—	—	—	—	150	—

KM# 556 RUPEE
11.6600 g., 0.5000 Silver 0.1874 oz. ASW **Ruler:** George VI **Obv:** Crowned head left **Obv. Leg.:** GEORGE VI KING EMPEROR **Rev:** Denomination and date within circle, wreath surrounds **Edge:** Security

Date	Mintage	F	VF	XF	Unc	BU
1939(b)	—	200	400	800	1,500	—
1940(b)	153,120,000	BV	6.00	10.00	20.00	—
1941(b)	111,480,000	BV	6.00	10.00	20.00	—
1943(b)	—	BV	6.00	10.00	20.00	—

Note: 1943(b) mintage included with KM#557.1.

KM# 557.1 RUPEE
11.6600 g., 0.5000 Silver 0.1874 oz. ASW, 30.5 mm. **Ruler:** George VI **Obv:** Small second head, large rim decoration **Obv. Leg.:** GEORGE VI KING EMPEROR **Rev:** Denomination and date within circle, wreath surrounds **Edge:** Security

Date	Mintage	F	VF	XF	Unc	BU
1942(b) Without dot	7,352,000	BV	4.50	10.00	20.00	—
1943(b)	65,995,000	BV	4.50	10.00	20.00	—
1943(b) Reverse B	Inc. above	BV	4.50	10.00	20.00	—
1944(b) Reverse B	146,206,000	BV	4.50	10.00	20.00	—
1944(b)	Inc. above	BV	4.50	10.00	20.00	—
1944L Small L	91,400,000	BV	4.50	10.00	20.00	—
1944L Large L	Inc. above	BV	4.50	10.00	20.00	—
1945(b) Small 5	142,666,000	BV	3.50	6.00	12.50	—
1945(b) Large 5	Inc. above	30.00	35.00	45.00	60.00	—
1945(b) Proof	—	—	—	—	—	—
1945L	118,126,000	BV	3.50	6.00	12.50	—

KM# 557a RUPEE
Copper-Nickel, 30.5 mm. **Ruler:** George VI **Obv:** Crowned head left **Obv. Leg.:** GEORGE VI KING EMPEROR **Rev:** Denomination and date within circle, wreath surrounds

Date	Mintage	F	VF	XF	Unc	BU
1943(b) P/L; Restrike	—	—	—	—	700	—

KM# 557.2 RUPEE
11.6600 g., 0.9170 Silver 0.3437 oz. ASW **Ruler:** George VI **Obv:** Crowned head left **Rev:** Denomination and date within circle, wreath surrounds **Note:** Reeded edge (error). Prev. KM#558.

Date	Mintage	F	VF	XF	Unc	BU
1944(b)	—	—	—	—	—	—
1945(b)	—	—	—	—	—	—

KM# 559 RUPEE
Nickel **Ruler:** George VI **Obv:** Crowned head left **Rev:** Indian tiger (panthera tigris) **Edge:** Security

Date	Mintage	F	VF	XF	Unc	BU
1947(b)	118,028,000	1.50	2.50	5.00	12.00	17.50
1947B Proof	—	Value: 375				

Note: Mumbai (Bombay) issue has diamond mark below date

Date	Mintage	F	VF	XF	Unc	BU
1947(I)	41,911,000	1.50	3.00	6.00	15.00	20.00

Note: Lahore issue without privy mark

KM# 525 15 RUPEES
7.9881 g., 0.9170 Gold 0.2355 oz. AGW **Ruler:** George V **Obv:** Crowned bust left **Obv. Leg.:** GEORGE V KING EMPEROR **Rev:** Denomination and date within circle, wreath surrounds **Note:** This issue is equal in weight and fineness to the British sovereign.

Date	Mintage	F	VF	XF	Unc	BU
1918(b)	2,110,000	275	350	550	800	—
1918(b) Proof	12	Value: 7,000				
1918(b) P/L; Restrike	—	—	—	—	850	—

TRADE COINAGE

The Mansfield Commission of 1868 allowed for the admission of British and Australian sovereigns (see Australian section; sovereigns with shield reverse were struck for export to India) as payment for sums due.

The fifth branch of the Royal Mint was established in a section of the Mumbai (Bombay) Mint as of December 21, 1917. This was a war-time measure, its purpose being to strike into sovereigns the gold blanks supplied by the Mumbai and other Indian mints. The Mumbai sovereigns bear the mint mark 'I' and were struck from August 15, 1918, to April 22, 1919. The branch mint was closed in May 1919.

KM# 525A SOVEREIGN
7.9881 g., 0.9170 Gold 0.2355 oz. AGW **Ruler:** George V **Obv:** Head left **Rev:** St. George slaying the dragon **Note:** Mint mark "I".

Date	Mintage	F	VF	XF	Unc	BU
1918	1,295,000	—	BV	235	275	—
1918 Proof	—	—	—	—	—	—
1918 P/L; Restrike	—	—	—	—	850	—

PATTERNS
Including off metal strikes

P# are in reference to The Coins of the British Commonwealth of Nations Part 4, India, Vol. 1 and 2 by F. Pridmore (Spink and Son Ltd., London 1980).

KM#	Date	Mintage	Identification	Issue Price	Mkt Val
Pn66	1901(c)	—	Rupee. Silver. Prid.#1045	—	1,850
Pn67	1901(c)	—	Rupee. Silver. Prid.#1046	—	1,850
PnA68	1903(c)	—	Rupee. Gold. 19.5900 g. Proof, Rare.	—	—
Pn68	1903(c)	—	1/4 Rupee. Silver. With "718.93" countermark. Prid.#1074	—	—
Pn69	1903(c)	—	Anna. Nickel. Prid.#1053	—	500
Pn70	1904(c)	—	1/4 Anna. Copper. Prid.#1051	—	850
Pn80a	1904C	—	1/4 Rupee. Bronze. 3.8600 g. 21.2 mm. Edward VII. Denom. Scalloped edge.	—	—
PnA80	1904(c)	—	1/4 Rupee. Copper. 3.9000 g. as Prid.#1075	—	400
Pn71	1904(c)	—	Anna. Copper-Nickel. Prid.#1054.	—	400
Pn72	1904(c)	—	Anna. Tin. 22 mm. Prid.#1055	—	500
Pn73	1904(c)	—	Anna. Copper-Nickel. 21 mm. Prid.#1056	—	350
Pn74	1904(c)	—	Anna. Copper-Nickel. Prid.#1058	—	400
Pn75	1904(c)	—	Anna. Copper-Nickel. Prid.#1059	—	400
Pn76	1904(c)	—	Anna. Copper-Nickel. Prid.#1060	—	400
Pn77	1904(c)	—	Anna. White Metal. Prid.#1061	—	400
Pn78	1904(c)	—	Anna. Copper-Nickel. Prid.#1062	—	400
Pn79	1904(c)	—	Anna. Copper-Nickel. Prid.#1063	—	400
Pn80	1904(c)	—	1/4 Rupee. Nickel. Prid.#1075	—	400
Pn81	1905(c)	—	Anna. Copper-Nickel. Prid.#924	—	—
Pn82	1905(c)	—	Anna. White Metal. Prid.#1057	—	400
Pn83	1905(c)	—	Anna.	—	400
Pn84	1905(c)	—	Anna. White Metal. Low relief bust; Prid.#1066	—	400
Pn85	1905(c)	—	Anna. White Metal. High relief bust; Prid.#1067	—	400
Pn86	1905(c)	—	Anna. White Metal. High relief bust; Prid.#1069	—	400
Pn87	1905(c)	—	Anna. Silver. High relief bust; Prid.#1068	—	400
Pn88	1905(c)	—	Anna. White Metal. Without dot border. Prid.#1070A	—	400
Pn89	1905	—	Anna. Copper-Nickel.	—	—
Pn90	1905(c)	—	Anna. Silver. Without dot border. Prid.#1070B	—	400
Pn91	1906(c)	—	Anna. White Metal. Raised bar edge. Prid.#1064	—	400
Pn92	1906(c)	—	Anna. White Metal. Double raised bar edge. Prid.#1065	—	400
Pn93	1906(c)	—	Anna. Copper-Nickel. Scalloped planchet; Prid.#1071	—	400
Pn94	1906(c)	—	Rupee. Copper-Nickel. "SPEC-IMEN" divided by crown. Lettered edge. Prid.#1047	—	1,150
Pn95	1907(b)	—	Rupee. Silver. Prid.#1048	—	—
Pn96	1908	—	1/2 Anna. Copper-Nickel.	—	400
Pn97	1908(c)	—	1/2 Anna. White Metal. Prid.#1073	—	550
Pn98	1909	—	1/2 Pice. Aluminum.	—	200
Pn99	1910(c)	—	Rupee. Silver. Prid.#1049	—	1,850
Pn100	1910(c)	—	Rupee. Gold. Prid.#1050	—	—
Pn100	1910(c)	—	Rupee. Gold. Prid.#1050	—	—
Pn101	ND(c)	—	2 Annas. Tin. Prid.#1052	—	—
Pn102	1917(c)	—	2 Annas. Copper-Nickel. Round; Prid.#1078	—	—
Pn103	1917(c)	—	2 Annas. Copper-Nickel. Square; Prid.#1079	—	—
Pn104	1918(c)	—	4 Annas. Copper-Nickel. Round with center hole; Prid.#1076	—	—
Pn105	1919(c)	—	2 Annas. Copper-Nickel. Eight-lobed planchet; Prid.#1087	—	—
Pn106	1919(c)	—	4 Annas. Copper-Nickel. Triangle; Prid.#1077	—	—
Pn107	1921(c)	—	Anna. Copper-Nickel. Prid.#1080	—	275
Pn108	1921(c)	—	Anna. Copper. Prid.#1081	—	275
Pn109	1921(c)	—	Anna. Gold. Prid.#1082	—	—
Pn109	1921(c)	—	Anna. Gold. Prid.#1082	—	450
Pn110	1929(c)	—	Anna. Copper-Nickel. Prid.#1083	—	—
Pn111	1929(c)	—	Anna. Copper-Nickel. Wide border; Prid.#1084	—	850
Pn112	1937(c)	—	2 Annas. Copper-Nickel. Prid.#1093	—	850
Pn113	1937(c)	—	2 Annas. Copper-Nickel. Serrated circular border. Prid.#1094	—	850
Pn114	1938(b)	—	1/4 Anna. Bronze. Head of George V	—	—
Pn115	1938(c)	—	1/2 Anna. Nickel. Prid.#1095	—	—
Pn116	1938(b)	—	Rupee. Silver. Head of George V	—	—
Pn117	1941(c)	—	Dollar. Silver. Prid.#1088A	—	2,700
Pn118	1941(c)	—	Dollar. Silver. Fine milled edge.	—	775

KM#	Date	Mintage	Identification	Issue Price	Mkt Val
Pn119	1941(b)	—	Dollar. Silver. "S" in "RUPEES" 1/2 to left of large "1"; Prid.#1088B	—	—
Pn120	1941(c)	—	Dollar. Silver. Prid.#1089	—	2,700
Pn121	1943(c)	—	Pice. Bronze. Prid.#1091	—	475
Pn122	1945(c)	—	Pie. Bronze. Prid.#1092	—	—
Pn123	1946(c)	—	Pie. Bronze. Tiger left. Prid.#1090.	—	—

PROOF SETS

KM#	Date	Mintage	Identification	Issue Price	Mkt Val
PS3	1904 (5)	—	KM#497, 499, 503, Pn70(2)	—	3,000
PS4	1904 (3)	—	KM#497, 499, 501(bronze) with "1" countermark on reverse	—	3,000
PS5	1911(c) (4)	—	KM#514, 517, 521, 523	—	400
PS6	1919(c) (8)	—	KM#513, 516, 519-520 (2 each - V.I.P.)	—	1,500
PS7	1938(c) (6)	—	KM#527-528, 530, 536, 544, 555	—	350
PS8	1947(b) (7)	—	KM#533, 535, 538, 542, 548, 553, 559	—	300

INDIA

The Republic of India, a subcontinent jutting southward from the mainland of Asia, has an area of 1,269,346 sq. mi. (3,287,590 sq. km.) and a population of over 1.1 billion, second only to that of the People's Republic of China. Capital: New Delhi. India's economy is based on agriculture and industrial activity. Engineering goods, cotton apparel and fabrics, handicrafts, tea, iron and steel are exported.

The Indian Mutiny (called the first War of Independence by Indian Nationalists) of 1857-58, begun by Indian troops in the service of the British East India Company, revealed the intensity of the growing resentment against British domination. The widespread rebellion against British rule was unsuccessful, but resulted in the transfer of government from the company to the British crown, and was a source of inspiration, to later Indian nationalists. Agitation for representation in the government continued.

Following World War I, in which India sent six million troops to fight at the side of the Allies, Indian nationalism intensified under the banner of the Indian National Congress and the leadership of Mohandas Karamchand Gandhi, who called for non-violent revolt against British authority. The Government of India Act of 1935 proposed a federal status linking the British Indian provinces with the many princely states; in addition, provincial legislatures were to be created. The federal status was never implemented, but the legislatures were created after the election of 1937, with the National Congress winning majorities in most of the provinces.

When Britain declared war on Germany in Sept. 1939, the Viceroy declared India also to be at war with a common enemy. The Congress, however, demanded independence as a condition for cooperation; Britain refused. But as the Japanese advanced into Asia, Britain offered to transfer to Indians power over all but military affairs during the war, and set forth a plan for postwar independence. Congress was willing to accept the wartime transfer of power, but both Congress and the Muslim League rejected Britain's plan for independence; Congress because it did not sufficiently safeguard Indian unity, the Muslims (who wanted a separate Muslim state) because of fears of what would happen to Muslims within a united India.

Early in 1947, Prime Minister Clement Attlee announced that Britain would leave India "by a date not later than June 1948," even though the Hindus and Muslims could not agree among themselves on a plan for self-government. The National Congress, aware that the Muslim League would revolt rather than accept an all-India government, reluctantly agreed to the formation of a separate Muslim state. The Muslim-majority provinces of the North West Frontier, Sindh and West Punjab in the west, and East Bengal in the east were separated from India to form the Muslim state of Pakistan, which became independent on Aug. 14, 1947. India became independent on the following day. Because British India coins dated 1947 were struck until 1950, they can be considered the first coins of Independent India. India became a republic on Jan. 26, 1950.

The Republic of India is a member of the Commonwealth of Nations. The president is the Chief of State. The prime minister is the Head of Government.

MINT MARKS
(Mint marks usually appear directly below the date.)
B - Mumbai (Bombay), proof issues only (1969 until 1995)
(B) - Mumbai (Bombay), diamond
C – Ottawa (1985 25 Paise; 1988 10, 25 & 50 Paise)
(C) – Kolkata (Calcutta) no mint mark
H - Birmingham (1985 Rupee only)
(H) - Hyderabad, star (1963)
(Hd) - Hyderabad, diamond split vertically (1953-1960)
(Hy) - Hyderabad, incuse dot in diamond (1960-1968)
(K) - Kremnica, Slovakia, MK in circle
(L) - British Royal Mint, Llantrisant (1985 rupee only), diamond below first date digit
(Ld) – British Royal Mint Llantrisant, tower, looks like a bridge
M - Mumbai (Bombay), proof only starting 1996
(M) - Mexico City, M beneath O
(N) - Noida, dot
(P) - Pretoria, M in oval
(R) – Moscow, MMD in oval
(T) - Taegu (Korea), star below first or last date (1997 and 98 2 Rupees only)

From 1950 through 1964 the Republic of India proof coins carry the regular diamond mint mark and can be distinguished from circulation issues only by their proof-like finish. From 1969 proofs carry the capital "B" mint mark. Some Bombay issues after 1969 have a "proof-like" appearance although bearing the diamond mint mark of circulation issues. Beginning in 1972 proofs of the larger denominations - 10, 20 and 100 rupees - were partly frosted on their main features, including numerals. From 1975 all proofs were similarly frosted, from the 1 paisa to 100 rupees. Proof-like issues are often erroneously offered as proofs.

MONETARY SYSTEM
(Until 1957)
4 Pice = 1 Anna
16 Annas = 1 Rupee

In addition to the denomination, the value as fraction of the Rupee is added in words above the denomination numeral for educational purposes on all 1, 2, 5, 10, 25, and 50 Naya Paisa on the first 1, 2, 5, 10, 25, and 50 Paisa types (i.e. Naya Paisa – 1/100 Rupee).

REPUBLIC
STANDARD COINAGE

KM# 1.1 PICE
Bronze **Obv:** Asoka lion pedestal **Rev:** Horse (equus caballus equidae) **Note:** 1.6mm thick, 0.3mm edge rim.

Date	Mintage	F	VF	XF	Unc	BU
1950(B)	32,080,000	—	1.00	2.00	3.00	5.00

KM# 1.2 PICE
Bronze **Obv:** Asoka lion pedestal **Rev:** Horse left **Note:** 1.6mm thick, 1.0mm edge rim.

Date	Mintage	F	VF	XF	Unc	BU
1950(B)	Inc. above	—	0.40	0.80	1.50	2.00
1950(B) Proof	—	Value: 2.50				
1950C	14,000,000	—	0.50	1.00	1.75	2.25

KM# 1.3 PICE
Bronze **Obv:** Asoka lion pedestal **Rev:** Horse left **Note:** 1.2mm thick, 0.8mm edge rim.

Date	Mintage	F	VF	XF	Unc	BU
1951(B)	104,626,000	—	0.20	0.40	0.75	1.50
1951(C)	127,300,000	—	0.20	0.40	0.75	1.50

KM# 1.4 PICE
2.9500 g., Bronze, 21 mm. **Obv:** Asoka lion pedestal **Rev:** Horse left **Note:** Larger date, 2mm thick, 0.8mm edge rim.

Date	Mintage	F	VF	XF	Unc	BU
1952(B)	213,830,000	—	0.25	0.40	0.80	1.50
1953(B)	242,358,000	—	0.25	0.50	1.50	
1953(C)	111,000,000	—	—	—	—	—
1953(Hd)	Inc. above	—	15.00	20.00	—	—
1954(B)	136,758,000	—	0.25	0.50	1.00	1.50
1954(C)	52,600,000	—	0.35	0.70	1.25	2.00
1954(Hd)	Inc. above	—	10.00	15.00	—	—
1954(B) Proof	Inc. above	Value: 5.00				
1955(B)	24,423,000	—	0.50	1.25	2.00	2.50
1955(Hd)	Inc. above	—	15.00	20.00	—	—

KM# 2.1 1/2 ANNA
2.8900 g., Copper-Nickel **Obv:** Asoka lion pedestal **Rev:** Zebu

Date	Mintage	F	VF	XF	Unc	BU
1950(B)	26,076,000	—	0.20	0.40	1.00	—
1950(B) Proof		—	Value: 3.00			
1950(C)	3,100,000	—	1.25	2.00	3.25	—

KM# 2.2 1/2 ANNA
2.8500 g., Copper-Nickel **Obv:** Asoka lion pedestal **Rev:** Zebu, larger date

Date	Mintage	F	VF	XF	Unc	BU
1954(B)	14,000,000	—	0.40	0.65	1.25	—
1954(B) Proof		—	Value: 5.00			
1954(C)	20,800,000	—	0.30	0.50	1.00	—
1955(B)	22,488,000	—	0.40	0.65	1.25	—

KM# 3.1 ANNA
Copper-Nickel **Obv:** Asoka lion pedestal **Rev:** Zebu **Note:** A similar shaped Independence commemorative token issued in 1947, bearing a map of India, circulated to some degree as an Anna coin.

Date	Mintage	F	VF	XF	Unc	BU
1950(B)	9,944,000	—	0.45	0.75	1.50	—
1950(B) Proof		—	Value: 4.00			

KM# 3.2 ANNA
Copper-Nickel **Obv:** Asoka lion pedestal **Rev:** Zebu, larger date, first Hindi letter varieties

Date	Mintage	F	VF	XF	Unc	BU
1954(B)	20,388,000	—	0.35	0.60	1.25	—
1954(B) Proof		—	Value: 6.50			
1955(B)	—	—	15.00	20.00	30.00	—

KM# 4.1 2 ANNAS
5.7800 g., Copper-Nickel **Obv:** Asoka lion pedestal **Rev:** Zebu **Note:** A similar shaped Independence commemorative token issued in 1947, bearing a map of India, circulated to some degree as a 2 Anna coin. (Refer to 5th edition of Unusual World Coins, X#104.)

Date	Mintage	F	VF	XF	Unc	BU
1950(B)	7,536,000	—	0.75	1.50	2.50	—
1950(B) Proof		—	Value: 5.00			

KM# 4.2 2 ANNAS
Copper-Nickel **Obv:** Asoka lion pedestal **Rev:** Zebu **Note:** Larger date.

Date	Mintage	F	VF	XF	Unc	BU
1954(B)	10,548,000	—	0.75	1.50	2.50	—
1954(B) Proof		—	Value: 8.00			
1955(B)	—	—	15.00	20.00	30.00	—

KM# 5.1 1/4 RUPEE
2.8600 g., Nickel **Obv:** Asoka lion pedestal **Rev:** Grain sprigs flank denomination **Note:** Large lion.

Date	Mintage	F	VF	XF	Unc	BU
1950(B)	7,650,000	—	0.60	1.50	2.50	—
1950(B) Proof		—	Value: 5.00			
1950(C)	7,800,000	—	0.60	1.50	2.50	—

Date	Mintage	F	VF	XF	Unc	BU
1951(B)	41,439,000	—	0.45	1.00	2.00	—
1951(C)	13,500,000	—	0.55	1.00	2.00	—

KM# 5.2 1/4 RUPEE
Nickel **Obv:** Asoka lion pedestal **Rev:** Grain sprigs flank denomination **Note:** Larger date, large lion.

Date	Mintage	F	VF	XF	Unc	BU
1954(C)	58,300,000	—	0.65	1.50	2.50	—
1954(B) Proof	Inc. above		Value: 6.00			
1955(B)	57,936,000	—	2.00	4.00	6.00	—

KM# 5.3 1/4 RUPEE
2.7300 g., Nickel **Obv:** Asoka lion pedestal **Rev:** Grain sprigs flank denomination **Note:** Small lion.

Date	Mintage	F	VF	XF	Unc	BU
1954(C)	Inc. above	—	0.40	1.00	1.75	—
1955(C)	28,900,000	—	0.40	1.00	1.75	—
1956(C)	22,000,000	—	0.70	1.25	2.00	—

KM# 6.1 1/2 RUPEE
Nickel **Obv:** Asoka lion pedestal **Rev:** Grain sprigs flank denomination **Note:** Large lion.

Date	Mintage	F	VF	XF	Unc	BU
1950(B)	12,352,000	—	0.75	1.25	2.50	—
1950(B) Proof		—	Value: 5.50			
1950(C)	1,100,000	—	1.25	2.00	5.00	—
1951(B)	9,239,000	—	1.00	1.50	3.50	—

KM# 6.2 1/2 RUPEE
5.7800 g., Nickel **Obv:** Asoka lion pedestal **Rev:** Grain sprigs flank denomination **Note:** Larger date, large lion.

Date	Mintage	F	VF	XF	Unc	BU
1954(C)	36,300,000	—	0.50	1.00	2.50	—
1954(B) Proof		—	Value: 8.00			
1955(B)	18,977,000	—	0.75	1.50	4.50	—

KM# 6.3 1/2 RUPEE
Nickel **Obv:** Asoka lion pedestal within circle, dots missing between words **Rev:** Grain sprigs flank denomination

Date	Mintage	F	VF	XF	Unc	BU
1956(C)	24,900,000	—	0.50	1.00	2.50	—

KM# 7.1 RUPEE
Nickel **Obv:** Asoka lion pedestal **Rev:** Grain sprigs flank denomination, thick numeral

Date	Mintage	F	VF	XF	Unc	BU
1950(B)	19,412,000	—	1.50	2.50	4.50	—
1950(B) Proof		—	Value: 7.00			

KM# 7.2 RUPEE
Nickel **Obv:** Asoka lion pedestal **Rev:** Thick numeral, first Hindi letter varieties, larger date

Date	Mintage	F	VF	XF	Unc	BU
1954(B)	Inc. above	—	2.00	3.00	5.50	—
1954(B) Proof		—	Value: 10.00			

DECIMAL COINAGE
100 Naye Paise = 1 Rupee (1957-63);
100 Paise = 1 Rupee (1964-)

NOTE: The Paisa was at first called Naya Paisa (= New Paisa), so that people would distinguish from the old non-decimal Paisa (or Pice, equal to 1/64 Rupee).

After 7 years, the word new was dropped, and the coin was simply called a Paisa.

NOTE: Many of the Paisa standard types come with three obverse varieties.

1957-1989

TYPE 1: Side lions toothless with 2 to 3 fur rows, short squat D in INDIA.

1967-1994

TYPE 2: Asoka lion pedestal more imposing. Side lions with 3 or 4 fur rows, more elegant D in INDIA. The shape of the D in INDIA is the easiest way to distinguish this obverse.

1979-

TYPE 3: Similar to Type I but 2 teeth, 4 to 5 fur rows, smaller lion head.

NOTE: Paisa standard pieces with mint mark B, 1969 to date, were struck only in proof.

KM# 8 NAYA PAISA
1.5000 g., Bronze, 16.04 mm. **Obv:** Asoka lion pedestal **Rev:** Denomination and date

Date	Mintage	F	VF	XF	Unc	BU
1957(B)	618,630,000	—	0.30	0.50	0.85	—
1957(C)	Inc. above	—	0.30	0.50	0.85	—
1957(Hd)	Inc. above	—	0.30	0.50	0.85	—
1958(B)	468,630,000	—	0.45	0.75	1.50	—
1958(Hd)	Inc. above	—	0.45	0.75	1.50	—
1959(B)	351,120,000	—	0.30	0.50	0.85	—
1959(C)	Inc. above	—	0.30	0.50	0.85	—
1959(Hd)	Inc. above	—	0.30	0.50	0.85	—
1960(B)	357,940,000	—	0.30	0.50	0.85	—
1960(B) Proof		—	Value: 2.00			
1960(C)	Inc. above	—	2.25	3.50	5.00	—
1960(Hd)	Inc. above	—	3.25	4.00	5.00	—
1961(B)	573,170,000	—	0.30	0.50	0.85	—

Date	Mintage	F	VF	XF	Unc	BU
1961(B) Proof	—	Value: 2.00				
1961(C)	Inc. above	—	0.30	0.50	0.85	—
1961(Hy)	Inc. above	—	0.50	0.75	1.25	—
1962(B)	—	—	—	—	—	—

Note: 1962(B) has only been found in some of the 1962 uncirculated mint sets; varieties of the split diamond have been reported.

KM# 8a NAYA PAISA
1.5100 g., Nickel-Brass, 16 mm. **Obv:** Asoka lion pedestal
Rev: Denomination and date

Date	Mintage	F	VF	XF	Unc	BU
1962(B)	235,103,000	—	0.20	0.35	0.70	—
1962(B) Proof	—	Value: 1.50				
1962(C)	Inc. above	—	0.20	0.35	0.70	—
1962(Hy)	Inc. above	—	0.50	0.75	1.25	—
1963(B)	343,313,000	—	0.20	0.35	0.70	—
1963(B) Proof	—	Value: 1.50				
1963(C)	Inc. above	—	0.25	0.50	1.00	—
1963(H)	Inc. above	—	0.25	0.40	0.80	—

KM# 9 PAISA
1.4800 g., Nickel-Brass **Obv:** Asoka lion pedestal
Rev: Denomination and date **Note:** Type I.

Date	Mintage	F	VF	XF	Unc	BU
1964(B)	539,068,000	—	0.20	0.45	1.00	—
1964(C)	Inc. above	—	0.20	0.45	1.00	—
1964(H)	Inc. above	—	0.20	0.45	1.00	—

KM# 9a PAISA
Nickel-Brass **Obv:** Asoka lion pedestal **Rev:** Denomination and date **Note:** Included in mintage of KM#9. Type 1.

Date	Mintage	F	VF	XF	Unc	BU
1964(H)	Inc. above	—	0.20	0.45	1.00	—

KM# 10.1 PAISA
0.7500 g., Aluminum **Obv:** Asoka lion pedestal **Rev:** Denomination and date **Edge:** Plain **Note:** Type 1. 14.67mm x 14.67mm.

Date	Mintage	F	VF	XF	Unc	BU
1965(B)	223,480,000	—	0.40	0.65	1.00	—
1965(Hy)	Inc. above	—	0.40	0.65	1.00	—
1966(B)	404,200,000	—	0.20	0.30	0.50	—
1966(C)	Inc. above	—	0.30	0.50	1.00	—
1966(Hy)	Inc. above	—	0.20	0.30	0.50	—
1967(B)	450,433,000	—	0.20	0.30	0.50	—
1967(C)	Inc. above	—	0.20	0.30	0.50	—
1967(Hy)	Inc. above	—	0.20	0.30	0.50	—
1968(B)	302,720,000	—	0.20	0.30	0.50	—
1968(C)	Inc. above	—	0.20	0.30	0.50	—
1968(Hy)	Inc. above	—	0.20	0.30	0.50	—
1969(B)	125,930,000	—	1.50	2.25	3.00	—
1969B Proof	9,147	Value: 1.50				
1969(H)	Inc. above	—	3.00	4.00	5.00	—
1970(H)	15,800,000	—	2.00	2.50	5.00	—

Note: 1970(B) is found only in the uncirculated sets of that year. It has a mirror-like surface.

Date	Mintage	F	VF	XF	Unc	BU
1970B Proof	3,046	Value: 1.00				
1971B Proof	4,375	Value: 1.00				
1971(H)	112,100,000	—	0.20	0.30	0.50	—
1972(B)	62,090,000	—	0.20	0.30	0.50	—
1972B Proof	7,895	Value: 1.00				
1972(H)	Inc. above	—	0.20	0.30	0.50	—
1973B Proof	7,562	Value: 1.00				
1974B Proof	—	Value: 1.00				
1975B Proof	—	Value: 1.00				
1976B Proof	—	Value: 1.00				
1977B Proof	—	Value: 1.00				
1978B Proof	—	Value: 1.00				
1979B Proof	—	Value: 1.00				
1980B Proof	—	Value: 1.00				
1981B Proof	—	Value: 1.00				

KM# 10.2 PAISA
Aluminum **Obv:** Asoka lion pedestal **Rev:** Denomination and date **Note:** Type 2.

Date	Mintage	F	VF	XF	Unc	BU
1969(C)	Inc. above	—	2.50	3.00	4.00	—
1970(C)	Inc. above	—	0.40	0.65	1.00	—

KM# 11 2 NAYE PAISE
2.9500 g., Copper-Nickel **Obv:** Asoka lion pedestal
Rev: Denomination and date

Date	Mintage	F	VF	XF	Unc	BU
1957(B)	406,230,000	—	0.15	0.40	0.80	—
1957(C)	Inc. above	—	0.15	0.40	0.80	—
1958(B)	245,660,000	—	0.15	0.40	0.80	—
1958(C)	Inc. above	—	0.15	0.40	0.80	—
1959(B)	171,445,000	—	0.15	0.40	0.80	—
1959(C)	Inc. above	—	0.15	0.40	0.80	—
1960(B)	121,820,000	—	0.15	0.40	0.80	—
1960(B) Proof	—	Value: 2.00				
1960(C)	Inc. above	—	0.20	0.40	0.80	—
1961(B)	190,610,000	—	0.20	0.40	0.80	—
1961(B) Proof	—	Value: 2.00				
1961(C)	Inc. above	—	0.20	0.40	0.80	—
1962(B)	318,181,000	—	0.20	0.40	0.80	—
1962(B) Proof	—	Value: 1.50				
1962(C)	Inc. above	—	0.20	0.40	0.80	—
1963(B)	372,380,000	—	0.20	0.40	0.80	—
1963(B) Proof	—	Value: 1.50				
1963(C)	Inc. above	—	0.20	0.40	0.80	—

KM# 12 2 PAISE
Copper-Nickel **Obv:** Asoka lion pedestal **Rev:** Denomination and date **Note:** Type 1.

Date	Mintage	F	VF	XF	Unc	BU
1964(B)	323,504,000	—	0.20	0.40	0.80	—
1964(C)	Inc. above	—	0.20	0.40	0.80	—

KM# 13.1 2 PAISE
1.0200 g., Aluminum **Obv:** Asoka lion pedestal
Rev: Denomination and date, 10mm "2" **Note:** Type 1.

Date	Mintage	F	VF	XF	Unc	BU
1965(B)	175,770,000	—	0.20	0.40	0.80	—
1965(C)	Inc. above	—	0.40	0.65	1.00	—
1966(B)	386,795,000	—	0.20	0.30	0.50	—
1966(C)	Inc. above	—	0.20	0.30	0.50	—
1967(B)	454,593,000	—	0.20	0.30	0.50	—

KM# 13.2 2 PAISE
Aluminum **Obv:** Asoka lion pedestal **Rev:** Denomination and date, 10-1/2mm "2" **Note:** Type 1.

Date	Mintage	F	VF	XF	Unc	BU
1967(C)	Inc. above	—	0.40	0.65	1.25	—

KM# 13.3 2 PAISE
Aluminum **Obv:** Asoka lion pedestal **Rev:** Denomination and date, 10mm "2" **Note:** Type 2.

Date	Mintage	F	VF	XF	Unc	BU
1967(B)	—	—	3.00	5.00	8.00	—

KM# 13.5 2 PAISE
1.0000 g., Aluminum **Obv:** Asoka lion pedestal
Rev: Denomination and date, 11mm "2" **Note:** Type 2.

Date	Mintage	F	VF	XF	Unc	BU
1968(C)	Inc. above	—	0.20	0.30	0.50	—
1968(B)	305,205,000	—	0.10	0.25	0.50	—
1969(B)	5,335,000	—	2.00	3.00	5.00	—
1969B Proof	9,147	Value: 1.00				
1970(B)	—	—	—	—	5.00	—

Note: 1970(B) is found only in the uncirculated sets of that year; It has a mirror-like surface.

Date	Mintage	F	VF	XF	Unc	BU
1970B Proof	3,046	Value: 1.00				
1970(H)	79,100,000	—	0.20	0.30	0.50	—
1971B Proof	4,375	Value: 1.00				
1971(C)	207,900,000	—	0.20	0.30	0.50	—

KM# 13.4 2 PAISE
Aluminum **Obv:** Asoka lion pedestal **Rev:** Denomination and date, 11mm "2" **Note:** Type 1.

Date	Mintage	F	VF	XF	Unc	BU
1968(C)	—	—	6.00	8.00	10.00	—

Date	Mintage	F	VF	XF	Unc	BU
1977(B)	—	—	0.60	1.00	1.50	—
1978(B)	—	—	0.40	0.65	1.00	—

KM# 13.6 2 PAISE
Aluminum, 19.84 mm. **Obv:** Asoka lion pedestal
Rev: Denomination and small date **Edge:** Plain scalloped
Note: Varieties of date size exist. Type 2.

Date	Mintage	F	VF	XF	Unc	BU
1972B Proof	7,895	Value: 1.00				
1972(C)	261,270,000	—	0.20	0.30	0.50	—
1972(H)	Inc. above	—	0.20	0.30	0.50	—
1973B Proof	7,562	Value: 1.00				
1973(C)	—	—	0.15	0.25	0.50	—
1973(H)	—	—	0.15	0.25	0.50	—
1974B Proof	—	Value: 1.00				
1974(C)	—	—	0.15	0.25	0.50	—
1974(H)	—	—	0.15	0.25	0.50	—
1975B Proof	—	Value: 1.00				
1975(C)	184,500,000	—	0.40	0.65	1.00	—
1975(H)	Inc. above	—	0.15	0.25	0.50	—
1976(C)	68,140,000	—	0.15	0.25	0.50	—
1976B Proof	—	Value: 1.00				
1976(H)	—	—	1.50	2.25	3.00	—
1977(B)	251,955,000	—	0.25	0.40	0.70	—
1977B Proof	—	Value: 1.00				
1977(H)	Inc. above	—	0.15	0.25	0.50	—
1978B Proof	—	Value: 1.00				
1978(H)	144,010,000	—	0.15	0.25	0.50	—
1979B Proof	—	Value: 1.00				
1979(H)	—	—	0.65	1.00	1.50	—
1980B Proof	—	Value: 1.00				
1981B Proof	—	Value: 1.00				

KM# 14.1 3 PAISE
1.2100 g., Aluminum **Obv:** Asoka lion pedestal
Rev: Denomination and date **Note:** Type 1.

Date	Mintage	F	VF	XF	Unc	BU
1964(B)	138,890,000	—	0.20	0.40	0.70	—
1964(C)	Inc. above	—	0.20	0.40	0.70	—
1965(B)	459,825,000	—	0.20	0.30	0.60	—
1965(C)	Inc. above	—	0.20	0.30	0.60	—
1966(B)	390,440,000	—	0.20	0.30	0.60	—
1966(C)	Inc. above	—	0.20	0.30	0.60	—
1966(Hy)	Inc. above	—	0.20	0.30	0.60	—
1967(B)	167,018,000	—	0.20	0.30	0.60	—
1967(C)	Inc. above	—	0.20	0.30	0.60	—
1967(H)	Inc. above	—	0.75	1.25	2.00	—
1968(B)	—	—	3.00	4.00	6.00	—
1968(H)	—	—	5.00	15.00	30.00	—

KM# 14.2 3 PAISE
1.2300 g., Aluminum **Obv:** Asoka lion pedestal
Rev: Denomination and date **Note:** Type 2.

Date	Mintage	F	VF	XF	Unc	BU
1967(C)	—	—	4.00	6.00	8.00	—
1967(H)	Inc. above	—	4.00	6.00	8.00	—
1968(B)	246,390,000	—	—	0.25	0.50	—
1968(C)	Inc. above	—	0.10	0.25	0.50	—
1968(H)	Inc. above	—	0.20	0.35	0.60	—
1969(B)	—	—	0.10	0.25	0.50	—
1969B Proof	9,147	Value: 1.00				
1969(C)	7,025,000	—	0.20	0.30	0.50	—
1969(H)	Inc. above	—	1.75	2.50	4.00	—
1970(B)	—	—	—	—	5.00	—

Note: 1970(B) is found only in the uncirculated sets of that year; It has a mirror-like surface.

Date	Mintage	F	VF	XF	Unc	BU
1970B Proof	3,046	Value: 1.00				
1970(H)	15,300,000	—	0.10	0.25	0.50	—
1971B Proof	4,375	Value: 1.00				
1971(C)	203,100,000	—	—	0.25	0.50	—
1971(H)	Inc. above	—	—	0.25	0.50	—

KM# 15 3 PAISE
Aluminum **Obv:** Asoka lion pedestal **Rev:** Denomination and date **Note:** Type 2.

Date	Mintage	F	VF	XF	Unc	BU
1972B Proof	.7,895	Value: 1.00				
1973B Proof	7,562	Value: 1.00				
1974B Proof	—	Value: 1.00				
1975B Proof	—	Value: 1.00				
1976B Proof	—	Value: 1.00				
1977B Proof	—	Value: 1.00				
1978B Proof	—	Value: 1.00				
1979B Proof	—	Value: 1.00				
1980B Proof	—	Value: 1.00				
1981B Proof	—	Value: 1.00				

KM# 16 5 NAYE PAISE
4.0500 g., Copper-Nickel, 22 mm. **Obv:** Asoka lion pedestal **Rev:** Denomination and date

Date	Mintage	F	VF	XF	Unc	BU
1957(B)	227,210,000	—	0.25	0.45	1.00	—
1957(C)	Inc. above	—	0.25	0.45	1.00	—
1958(B)	214,320,000	—	0.25	0.45	1.00	—
1958(C)	Inc. above	—	0.25	0.45	1.00	—
1959(B)	137,105,000	—	0.25	0.45	1.00	—
1959(C)	Inc. above	—	2.50	4.00	7.00	—
1960(B)	93,345,000	—	0.25	0.45	1.00	—
1960(B) Proof	—	Value: 2.00				
1960(C)	Inc. above	—	0.25	0.45	1.00	—
1960(Hy)	Inc. above	—	6.00	10.00	—	—
1961(B)	197,620,000	—	0.25	0.45	1.00	—
1961(B) Proof	—	Value: 2.00				
1961(C)	Inc. above	—	0.35	0.60	1.00	—
1961(Hy)	Inc. above	—	6.00	10.00	—	—
1962(B)	224,277,000	—	0.25	0.45	1.00	—
1962(B) Proof	—	Value: 1.50				
1962(C)	Inc. above	—	0.25	0.45	1.00	—
1962(Hy)	Inc. above	—	2.00	3.25	7.00	—
1963(B)	332,600,000	—	0.20	0.35	0.80	—
1963(B) Proof	—	Value: 1.50				
1963(C)	Inc. above	—	2.00	3.00	6.00	—
1963(H)	Inc. above	—	2.00	3.25	7.00	—

KM# 17 5 PAISE
4.0500 g., Copper-Nickel **Obv:** Asoka lion pedestal **Rev:** Denomination and date **Note:** Type 1.

Date	Mintage	F	VF	XF	Unc	BU
1964(B)	156,000,000	—	0.40	0.60	1.00	—
1964(C)	Inc. above	—	0.40	0.60	1.00	—
1964(H)	Inc. above	—	6.00	10.00	—	—
1965(B)	203,855,000	—	0.25	0.45	0.75	—
1965(C)	Inc. above	—	0.40	0.60	1.00	—
1965(H)	Inc. above	—	6.00	10.00	—	—
1966(B)	101,395,000	—	0.75	1.25	2.00	—
1966(C)	Inc. above	—	0.40	0.60	1.00	—

KM# 18.1 5 PAISE
Aluminum **Obv:** Asoka lion pedestal **Rev:** Denomination and date, 6mm "5" **Note:** Type 1.

Date	Mintage	F	VF	XF	Unc	BU
1967(C)	—	—	0.35	0.60	1.00	—
1967(B)	608,533,000	—	0.35	0.60	1.00	—

KM# 18.2 5 PAISE
Aluminum **Obv:** Asoka lion pedestal **Rev:** Denomination and date, 7mm "5". **Note:** Type 1.

Date	Mintage	F	VF	XF	Unc	BU
1967(B)	Inc. above	—	0.15	0.25	0.50	—
1967(H)	Inc. above	—	0.15	0.25	0.50	—
1967(C)	Inc. above	—	0.15	0.25	0.50	—
1968(B)	—	—	3.50	5.00	8.50	—
1968(C)	—	—	3.50	5.00	8.50	—
1968(H)	666,750,000	—	0.75	1.25	2.00	—
1971(H)	499,200,000	—	0.10	0.25	0.50	—

KM# 18.5 5 PAISE
Aluminum **Obv:** Asoka lion pedestal **Rev:** Larger 11mm "5", date **Note:** Type 1. Varieties in Hindi style exist.

Date	Mintage	F	VF	XF	Unc	BU
1973(H)	—	—	2.50	3.50	5.50	—
1977(B)	—	—	2.00	3.00	5.00	—
1978(B)	—	—	0.75	1.25	2.00	—

KM# 18.3 5 PAISE
1.5000 g., Aluminum **Obv:** Asoka lion pedestal **Rev:** Denomination and date, 7mm "5" **Note:** Type 2.

Date	Mintage	F	VF	XF	Unc	BU
1967(H)	—	—	4.50	7.00	10.00	—
1968(B)	—	—	0.15	0.25	0.50	—
		Note: Mintage included in KM18.2				
1968(C)	—	—	0.15	0.25	0.50	—
		Note: Mintage included in KM18.2				
1968(H)	—	—	0.40	0.60	1.00	—
		Note: Mintage included in KM18.2				
1969(B)	3,740,000	—	2.00	3.50	5.00	—
1969B Proof	9,147	Value: 1.00				
1970(B)	39,900,000	—	1.25	2.00	3.50	—
1970B Proof	3,046	Value: 1.00				
1970(C)	Inc. above	—	0.25	0.35	0.60	—
1970(H)	Inc. above	—	0.25	0.40	0.75	—
1971(B)	—	—	0.10	0.15	0.50	—
		Note: Included with 1971(H) of KM18.2				
1971B Proof	4,375	Value: 1.00				
1971(C)	Inc. above	—	0.10	0.15	0.50	—
1971(H)	—	—	0.25	0.45	0.75	—

KM# 18.6 5 PAISE
1.5300 g., Aluminum **Obv:** Asoka lion pedestal **Rev:** Denomination and date **Note:** Type 2.

Date	Mintage	F	VF	XF	Unc	BU
1972(B)	—	—	0.10	0.15	0.50	—
		Note: Mintage included in KM18.4				
1972B Proof	7,895	Value: 1.00				
1972(C)	—	—	0.10	0.15	0.50	—
		Note: Mintage included in KM18.4				
1972(H)	—	—	3.50	5.00	7.00	—
1973(B)	—	—	0.10	0.15	0.50	—
1973B Proof	7,562	Value: 1.00				
1973(C)	—	—	0.20	0.30	0.60	—
1973(H)	—	—	0.10	0.15	0.50	—
1974B Proof	—	Value: 1.00				
1974(B)	—	—	0.10	0.15	0.50	—
1974(C)	—	—	0.10	0.15	0.50	—
1974(H)	—	—	0.10	0.15	0.50	—
1975(B)	—	—	0.10	0.15	0.50	—
1975B Proof	—	Value: 1.00				
1975(C)	289,080,000	—	0.20	0.30	0.60	—
1975(H)	Inc. above	—	0.10	0.15	0.50	—
1976(B)	53,205,000	—	0.10	0.15	0.50	—
1976(C)	—	—	0.10	0.20		—
1976(H)	—	—	0.10	0.15	0.50	—
1977(B)	257,899,999	—	0.10	0.15	0.50	—
1977(C)	Inc. above	—	0.10	0.15	0.50	—
1977(H)	Inc. above	—	0.10	0.15	0.50	—
1978(C)	—	—	0.10	0.15	0.50	—
1978(H)	—	—	0.10	0.15	0.50	—
1979(B)	—	—	0.10	0.15	0.50	—
1979(C)	—	—	0.20	0.35	0.80	—

Date	Mintage	F	VF	XF	Unc	BU
1979(H)	—	—	0.10	0.15	0.50	—
1980(B)	21,440,000	—	0.10	0.15	0.50	—
1980B Proof	—	Value: 1.00				
1980(C)	Inc. above	—	0.20	0.30	0.60	—
1980(H)	Inc. above	—	0.10	0.15	0.50	—
1981B Proof	—	Value: 1.00				
1981(C)	4,365,000	—	0.10	0.15	0.50	—
1981(H)	Inc. above	—	0.10	0.15	0.50	—
		Note: Due to faulty dies, 1981(H) often resembles the non-existent 1981(B).				
1982B Proof	3,499,000	Value: 1.00				
1982(C)	Inc. above	—	0.10	0.15	0.50	—
1982(H)	Inc. above	—	0.10	0.15	0.50	—
1983(C)	3,110,000	—	0.25	0.50	1.00	—
1983(H)	Inc. above	—	0.10	0.15	0.50	—
1984(C)	—	—	0.25	0.50	1.00	—
1984(H)	Inc. above	—	0.10	0.15	0.50	—

KM# 18.4 5 PAISE
Aluminum **Obv:** Asoka lion pedestal **Rev:** Larger 11mm "5", date **Note:** Type 1.

Date	Mintage	F	VF	XF	Unc	BU
1972(H)	512,430,000	—	0.35	0.60	1.00	—

KM# 19 5 PAISE
1.5100 g., Aluminum, 22 mm. **Series:** F.A.O. **Subject:** Food and Work For All **Obv:** Asoka lion pedestal **Rev:** Figure on tractor, utility pole and buildings in background **Edge:** Plain **Note:** 18.95mm x 18.95mm.

Date	Mintage	F	VF	XF	Unc	BU
1976(B)	34,680,000	—	0.35	0.50	1.00	—
1976B Proof	—	Value: 1.00				
1976(C)	60,040,000	—	0.35	0.50	1.00	—
1976(H)	60,290,000	—	0.35	1.00	2.00	—

KM# 20 5 PAISE
1.5000 g., Aluminum **Series:** F.A.O. **Subject:** Save For Development **Obv:** Asoka lion pedestal **Rev:** Symbols and date

Date	Mintage	F	VF	XF	Unc	BU
1977(B)	20,100,000	—	0.30	0.50	1.00	—
1977B Proof	2,224	Value: 1.25				
1977(C)	40,470,000	—	0.30	0.50	1.00	—
1977(H)	20,380,000	—	2.25	3.50	5.00	—

KM# 21 5 PAISE
Aluminum **Series:** F.A.O. **Subject:** Food and Shelter For All **Obv:** Asoka lion pedestal **Rev:** Building, grain sprig and road within circle

Date	Mintage	F	VF	XF	Unc	BU
1978(B)	28,440,000	—	0.35	0.50	1.00	—
1978B Proof	—	Value: 1.25				
1978(C)	30,870,000	—	0.50	1.00	2.00	—
1978(H)	21,100,000	—	1.00	1.50	2.25	—

KM# 22 5 PAISE
1.5200 g., Aluminum **Series:** International Year of the Child **Obv:** Asoka lion pedestal **Rev:** Logo within circle, wreath surrounds

Date	Mintage	F	VF	XF	Unc	BU
1979(B)	39,860,000	—	0.35	0.50	1.00	—
1979B Proof	—	Value: 1.25				
1979(C)	80,370,000	—	0.35	0.50	1.00	—
1979(H)	1,100,000	—	1.50	2.00	2.50	—

KM# 23   5 PAISE
1.0300 g., Aluminum **Obv:** Asoka lion pedestal **Rev:** Denomination and date **Edge:** Plain **Note:** Weight reduced. 19mm x 19mm.

Date	Mintage	F	VF	XF	Unc	BU
1984(C)	—	—	6.00	8.00	10.00	—
1985(B)	54,860,000	—	6.00	8.00	10.00	—
1985(C)	Inc. above	—	10.00	15.00	20.00	—
1985(H)	Inc. above	—	0.50	0.75	1.00	—
1986(C)	—	—	0.50	0.75	1.00	—
1986(H)	—	—	0.50	0.75	1.00	—
1987(C)	—	—	0.50	0.75	1.00	—
1987(H)	—	—	0.75	1.00	2.00	—
1988(C)	—	—	0.25	0.50	1.00	—
1988(H)	—	—	0.50	1.00	2.00	—
1989(C)	—	—	0.50	1.00	2.00	—
1989(H)	—	—	0.50	1.00	2.00	—
1990(B)	—	—	2.00	4.00	6.00	—
1990(H)	—	—	1.00	1.50	2.50	—
1990(H)	—	—	1.00	1.50	2.50	—
1991(C)	—	—	0.50	0.75	1.25	—
1991(H)	—	—	0.25	0.50	1.00	—
1992(B)	—	—	1.00	1.50	2.50	—
1992(H)	—	—	0.25	0.50	1.00	—
1993(C)	—	—	1.00	1.50	2.50	—
1993(H)	—	—	0.25	0.50	1.00	—
1994(H)	—	—	0.25	0.50	1.00	—

KM# 24.1   10 NAYE PAISE
4.8500 g., Copper-Nickel, 23 mm. **Obv:** Asoka lion pedestal **Rev:** Denomination and date, 6.5mm "10"

Date	Mintage	F	VF	XF	Unc	BU
1957(B)	139,655,000	—	0.25	0.50	1.00	—
1957(C)	Inc. above	—	0.25	0.50	1.00	—

KM# 24.2   10 NAYE PAISE
5.0000 g., Copper-Nickel, 23 mm. **Obv:** Asoka lion pedestal **Rev:** Denomination and date, 7mm "10"

Date	Mintage	F	VF	XF	Unc	BU
1958(B)	123,160,000	—	0.25	0.50	1.00	—
1958(C)	Inc. above	—	0.25	0.50	1.00	—
1959(B)	148,570,000	—	0.25	0.50	1.00	—
1959(C)	Inc. above	—	0.25	0.50	1.00	—
1960(B)	52,335,000	—	0.35	0.75	2.00	—
1960(B) Proof	—	Value: 2.00				
1961(B)	172,545,000	—	0.25	0.50	1.00	—
1961(C)	Inc. above	—	0.25	0.50	1.00	—
1961(Hy)	Inc. above	—	3.50	6.50	11.50	—
1961(B) Proof	—	Value: 2.00				
1962(B)	172,777,000	—	0.25	0.50	1.00	—
1962(C)	Inc. above	—	0.25	0.50	1.00	—
1962(Hy)	Inc. above	—	3.25	5.00	9.00	—
1962(B) Proof	—	Value: 1.50				
1963(B)	182,834,000	—	0.25	0.50	1.00	—
1963(H)	Inc. above	—	1.00	2.50	5.00	—
1963(C)	Inc. above	—	0.25	0.50	1.00	—
1963(B) Proof	—	Value: 1.50				

KM# 25   10 PAISE
Copper-Nickel, 23 mm. **Obv:** Asoka lion pedestal **Rev:** Denomination and date, 6.5mm "10" **Note:** Type 1.

Date	Mintage	F	VF	XF	Unc	BU
1964(B) Open 4	84,112,000	—	0.20	0.50	1.00	—
1964(B) Closed 4	Inc. above	—	5.00	7.00	10.00	—
1964(C)	Inc. above	—	0.20	0.50	1.00	—
1964(H)	Inc. above	—	3.00	5.00	7.00	—
1965(B)	253,430,000	—	0.20	0.50	1.00	—
1965(C)	Inc. above	—	0.20	0.50	1.00	—
1965(Hy)	Inc. above	—	4.00	6.00	8.00	—
1965(H)	Inc. above	—	3.00	5.00	7.00	—
1966(B)	326,990,000	—	0.20	0.50	1.00	—
1966(C)	Inc. above	—	0.20	1.00	1.00	—
1966(Hy)	Inc. above	—	0.40	0.75	1.25	—
1967(B)	59,443,000	—	0.40	0.75	1.25	—
1967(C)	Inc. above	—	0.40	0.75	1.25	—
1967(H)	Inc. above	—	3.00	5.00	7.00	—

KM# 26.1   10 PAISE
Nickel-Brass, 23 mm. **Obv:** Asoka lion pedestal **Rev:** Denomination and date **Note:** Type 1.

Date	Mintage	F	VF	XF	Unc	BU
1968(H)	55,940,000	—	30.00	50.00	80.00	—

KM# 26.2   10 PAISE
4.2400 g., Nickel-Brass, 23 mm. **Obv:** Asoka lion pedestal **Rev:** 6.5mm "10", date **Note:** Type 2. Mintage included in KM26.1. Some, not all, have die damage in 9 of 1968.

Date	Mintage	F	VF	XF	Unc	BU
1968(B)	—	—	0.20	0.50	1.00	—
1968(C)	—	—	0.20	0.50	1.00	—
1968(H)	—	—	0.20	0.50	1.00	—

KM# 26.3   10 PAISE
4.1800 g., Nickel-Brass, 23 mm. **Obv:** Asoka lion pedestal **Rev:** Denomination and date, 7mm "10" **Note:** Type 2.

Date	Mintage	F	VF	XF	Unc	BU
1969(B)	65,405,000	—	0.20	0.50	1.00	—
1969B Proof	9,147	Value: 1.50				
1969(C)	Inc. above	—	0.20	0.50	1.00	—
1969(H)	Inc. above	—	0.20	0.50	1.00	—
1970(B)	48,400,000	—	0.20	0.50	1.00	—
1970B Proof	3,046	Value: 1.50				
1970(C)	Inc. above	—	0.20	0.50	1.00	—
1971(B)	88,800,000	—	0.20	0.50	1.00	—
1971B Proof	4,375	Value: 1.30				

KM# 27.1   10 PAISE
2.3000 g., Aluminum, 26 mm. **Obv:** Asoka lion pedestal within beaded circle, wreath surrounds **Rev:** Denomination and date within beaded circle, wreath surrounds, 9mm "10" **Note:** Type 2.

Date	Mintage	F	VF	XF	Unc	BU
1971(B)	146,100,000	—	0.20	0.50	1.00	—
1971(C)	—	—	0.20	0.50	1.00	—
1971(H)	Inc. above	—	0.50	1.00	2.00	—
1972(B)	735,090,000	—	0.20	0.35	1.00	—
1972B Proof	7,895	Value: 1.30				
1972(C)	Inc. above	—	0.20	0.50	1.00	—
1973(B)	—	—	0.20	0.50	1.00	—
1973B Proof	7,567	Value: 1.30				
1973(C)	—	—	0.20	0.50	1.00	—
1973(H)	—	—	0.20	0.50	1.00	—
1974(B)	—	—	0.20	0.50	1.00	—
1974(C)	—	—	0.20	0.50	1.00	—
1974(H)	—	—	2.00	3.00	5.00	—
1975(B)	—	—	1.00	2.00	3.00	—
1975(C)	298,830,000	—	1.00	2.00	3.00	—
1976(B)	Inc. above	—	2.00	3.00	5.00	—
1977(B)	25,288,000	—	1.00	2.00	5.00	—
1977(C)	Inc. above	—	0.25	0.50	1.00	—
1978(B)	48,215,000	—	0.15	0.30	1.00	—
1978(C)	Inc. above	—	0.15	0.30	1.00	—
1978(H)	Inc. above	—	0.15	0.30	1.00	—

KM# 27.2   10 PAISE
Aluminum, 26 mm. **Obv:** Asoka lion pedestal within beaded circle, wreath surrounds **Rev:** Denomination and date within beaded circle, wreath surrounds, 8mm "10" **Note:** Type 2.

Date	Mintage	F	VF	XF	Unc	BU
1979(B)	—	—	0.50	1.00	2.00	—
1979(C)	—	—	0.50	1.50	3.00	—
1979(H)	—	—	0.50	1.00	2.00	—
1980(C)	—	—	10.00	12.00	15.00	—

KM# 27.3   10 PAISE
2.3100 g., Aluminum, 26 mm. **Obv:** Asoka lion pedestal within beaded circle, wreath surrounds **Rev:** Denomination and date within beaded circle, wreath surrounds **Note:** Type 3.

Date	Mintage	F	VF	XF	Unc	BU
1980(B)	—	—	0.20	0.50	1.00	—
1980(C)	—	—	0.20	0.50	1.00	—
1980(C)	—	—	0.20	0.50	1.00	—
1981(B)	—	—	0.20	0.50	1.00	—
1981(C)	—	—	0.20	0.50	1.00	—
1982(C)	—	—	0.20	0.50	1.00	—
1982(H)	—	—	0.20	0.50	1.00	—

KM# 28   10 PAISE
Aluminum, 26 mm. **Series:** F.A.O. **Obv:** Asoka lion pedestal **Rev:** Family above date within triangle, grain sprigs flank

Date	Mintage	F	VF	XF	Unc	BU
1974(B)	146,070,000	—	0.30	0.50	1.00	—
1974B Proof	—	Value: 1.00				
1974(C)	168,500,000	—	0.50	1.00	2.00	—
1974(H)	10,010,000	—	3.00	4.00	6.00	—

KM# 29   10 PAISE
2.2800 g., Aluminum, 26 mm. **Series:** F.A.O. **Subject:** Women's Year **Obv:** Asoka lion pedestal **Rev:** Bust at left looking right, grain sprig at right **Note:** Mint mark is below wheat stalk.

Date	Mintage	F	VF	XF	Unc	BU
1975(B)	69,160,000	—	0.30	0.50	1.00	—
1975B Proof	—	Value: 1.00				
1975(C)	84,820,000	—	0.30	0.60	1.00	—
1975(H)	—	—	0.30	0.60	1.00	—

KM# 30   10 PAISE
Aluminum, 26 mm. **Series:** F.A.O. **Subject:** Food and Work For All **Obv:** Asoka lion pedestal **Rev:** Figure on tractor, utility pole and buildings in background

Date	Mintage	F	VF	XF	Unc	BU
1976(B)	36,040,000	—	1.00	1.50	2.00	—
1976B Proof	—	Value: 3.00				
1976(C)	26,180,000	—	2.00	3.00	5.00	—

KM# 31   10 PAISE
Aluminum, 26 mm. **Series:** F.A.O. **Subject:** Save For Development **Obv:** Asoka lion pedestal **Rev:** Symbols and date

Date	Mintage	F	VF	XF	Unc	BU
1977(B)	17,040,000	—	0.25	0.50	1.00	—

Date   Mintage   F   VF   XF   Unc   BU
1979(H)   —   —   0.50   1.00   2.00   —

Date	Mintage	F	VF	XF	Unc	BU
1977B Proof	2,224	Value: 1.00				
1977(C)	8,020,000	—	2.00	3.00	5.00	—

KM# 32 10 PAISE
Aluminum, 26 mm. **Series:** F.A.O. **Subject:** Food and Shelter For All **Obv:** Asoka lion pedestal **Rev:** Building, grain sprig and road within circle

Date	Mintage	F	VF	XF	Unc	BU
1978(B)	24,470,000	—	0.25	0.50	1.00	—
1978B Proof	—	Value: 1.00				
1978(C)	26,160,000	—	1.00	1.50	2.00	—
1978(H)	12,100,000	—	1.00	1.50	2.00	—

KM# 33 10 PAISE
2.2900 g., Aluminum, 26 mm. **Series:** International Year of the Child **Obv:** Asoka lion pedestal **Rev:** Logo on square within circle, wreath surrounds

Date	Mintage	F	VF	XF	Unc	BU
1979(B)	39,270,000	—	0.25	0.50	1.00	—
1979B Proof	—	Value: 1.00				
1979(C)	61,700,000	—	0.50	1.00	2.50	—
1979(H)	2,250,000	—	0.60	1.00	2.50	—

KM# 34 10 PAISE
Aluminum, 26 mm. **Obv:** Asoka lion pedestal, denomination below **Rev:** Emblem on square, within circle, wreath surrounds, date below **Note:** Mule.

Date	Mintage	F	VF	XF	Unc	BU
1979(B)	—	—	5.00	7.50	10.00	—

KM# 35 10 PAISE
Aluminum, 26 mm. **Subject:** Rural Women's Advancement **Obv:** Asoka lion pedestal **Rev:** Woman grinding wheat within circle

Date	Mintage	F	VF	XF	Unc	BU
1980(B)	38,080,000	—	0.25	0.40	1.00	—
1980B Proof	—	Value: 1.00				
1980(C)	42,830,000	—	0.25	0.50	1.00	—
1980(H)	11,070,000	—	0.50	1.00	1.50	—

KM# 36 10 PAISE
2.3000 g., Aluminum, 26 mm. **Subject:** World Food Day **Obv:** Asoka lion pedestal **Rev:** Man and woman, man carrying sheaf

Date	Mintage	F	VF	XF	Unc	BU
1981(B)	83,280,000	—	0.25	0.40	1.00	—
1981B Proof	—	Value: 1.00				
1981(C)	33,930,000	—	0.25	0.50	1.00	—

KM# 37 10 PAISE
2.3000 g., Aluminum, 26 mm. **Subject:** IX Asian Games **Obv:** Asoka lion pedestal **Rev:** Sun above symbol

Date	Mintage	F	VF	XF	Unc	BU
1982(B)	—	—	0.25	0.45	0.75	—
1982B Proof	—	Value: 1.00				
1982(C)	30,560,000	—	0.25	0.45	0.75	—
1982(H)	17,080,000	—	0.25	0.50	1.00	—

KM# 38 10 PAISE
2.3000 g., Aluminum, 26 mm. **Subject:** World Food Day **Obv:** Asoka lion pedestal **Rev:** Grain sprig within stylized sun design

Date	Mintage	F	VF	XF	Unc	BU
1982(C)	2,970,000	—	2.50	3.50	5.00	—
1982(B)	—	—	—	—	—	—
1982(H)	11,690,000	—	0.50	1.00	2.00	—

KM# 39 10 PAISE
2.3000 g., Aluminum, 26 mm. **Obv:** Asoka lion pedestal **Rev:** Denomination and date

Date	Mintage	F	VF	XF	Unc	BU
1983(B)	—	—	0.10	0.25	0.50	—
1983(C)	—	—	0.10	0.25	0.50	—
1983(H)	—	—	0.10	0.25	0.50	—
1984(B)	112,050,000	—	0.10	0.25	0.50	—
1984(C)	Inc. above	—	0.25	0.50	1.00	—
1984(H)	Inc. above	—	0.10	0.25	0.50	—
1985(B)	184,655,000	—	0.20	0.30	0.50	—
1985(C)	Inc. above	—	0.20	0.30	0.50	—
1985(H)	Inc. above	—	0.20	0.30	0.50	—
1986(B)	298,525,000	—	0.10	0.15	0.30	—
1986(C)	Inc. above	—	0.20	0.30	0.50	—
1986(H)	Inc. above	—	0.50	1.00	1.50	—
1987(C)	299,460,000	—	0.15	0.25	0.45	—
1987(H)	Inc. above	—	0.15	0.25	0.45	—
1988(B)	264,510,000	—	0.10	0.15	0.30	—
1988(C)	Inc. above	—	0.10	0.15	0.30	—
1988(H)	Inc. above	—	1.00	1.50	2.00	—
1989(B)	—	—	0.15	0.25	0.45	—
1989(C)	—	—	0.15	0.25	0.45	—
1989(H)	—	—	0.15	0.25	0.45	—
1990(B)	—	—	0.50	0.75	1.25	—
1991(B)	—	—	0.15	0.25	0.45	—
1991(C)	—	—	0.15	0.25	0.45	—
1991(H)	—	—	0.15	0.25	0.45	—
1993(C)	—	—	0.15	0.30	0.60	—
1993(H)	—	—	0.30	0.50	0.75	—

KM# 40.1 10 PAISE
2.0000 g., Stainless Steel, 16 mm. **Obv:** Asoka lion pedestal **Obv. Leg.:** BHARAT **Rev:** Denomination and date

Date	Mintage	F	VF	XF	Unc	BU
1988C	183,040,000	—	0.10	0.15	0.25	—
1988(B)	4,040,000	—	0.25	0.40	0.75	—
1988(C)	—	—	5.00	7.00	10.00	—
1988(H)	Inc. above	—	3.00	5.00	8.00	—
1988	—	—	0.15	0.25	0.40	—
1989(B)	—	—	0.60	1.00	1.50	—
1989(C)	—	—	0.40	0.70	1.00	—
1989(H)	—	—	0.20	0.30	0.50	—
1989	—	—	0.25	0.40	0.75	—
1990(B)	—	—	0.15	0.30	0.50	—
1990(C)	—	—	0.40	0.70	1.00	—
1990(H)	—	—	0.20	0.30	0.50	—
1990 Small mm	—	—	0.15	0.30	0.50	—
1990 Large mm	—	—	1.25	1.75	2.50	—
1991(C)	—	—	0.15	0.30	0.50	—
1991(H)	—	—	0.15	0.30	0.50	—
1991	—	—	0.15	0.30	0.50	—
1992	—	—	0.30	0.60	1.00	—
1992(B)	—	—	1.00	1.50	2.50	—
1993(H)	—	—	0.15	0.30	0.50	—
1996(C)	—	—	0.15	0.30	0.50	—
1996(B)	—	—	1.50	2.50	5.00	—
1996	—	—	0.15	0.30	0.50	—
1997(C)	—	—	0.15	0.30	0.50	—
1997(B)	—	—	1.50	2.50	5.00	—
1997(H)	—	—	0.20	0.30	0.50	—
1998(B)	—	—	0.25	0.40	0.70	—
1998(C)	—	—	0.25	0.40	0.70	—

KM# 40.2 10 PAISE
2.0300 g., Stainless Steel, 15.95 mm. **Obv:** Error: MARAT for BHARAT **Rev:** Denomination and date **Edge:** Plain

Date	Mintage	F	VF	XF	Unc	BU
1988C	—	—	1.25	2.00	3.00	—
1989C	—	—	7.00	10.00	15.00	—

KM# 41 20 PAISE
Nickel-Brass **Obv:** Asoka lion pedestal **Rev:** Lotus blossom **Note:** Varieties of high and low date exist.

Date	Mintage	F	VF	XF	Unc	BU
1968(B)	10,585,000	—	0.50	1.00	1.50	—
1968(C)	Inc. above	—	0.50	1.00	1.50	—
1969(B)	197,940,000	—	0.40	0.85	1.50	—
1969(C)	—	—	0.40	0.85	1.50	—
1970(B)	Inc. above	—	0.30	0.60	1.00	—
1970(C)	Inc. above	—	0.30	0.60	1.00	—
1970(H)	Inc. above	—	0.30	0.60	1.00	—
1971(B)	124,200,000	—	0.30	0.60	1.00	—

KM# 42.1 20 PAISE
4.4500 g., Aluminum-Bronze **Subject:** Centennial - Birth of Mahatma Gandhi **Obv:** Asoka lion pedestal **Obv. Leg.:** .7-.9 from rims **Rev:** Head left

Date	Mintage	F	VF	XF	Unc	BU
ND(1969)(B)	45,010	—	0.40	0.65	1.00	—
ND(1969)B Proof	9,147	Value: 2.00				
ND(1969)(C)	45,070,000	—	0.50	0.80	1.50	—
ND(1969)(H)	3,000,000	—	0.75	1.50	2.50	—

KM# 42.2 20 PAISE
Aluminum-Bronze **Obv:** Asoka lion pedestal **Obv. Leg.:** 1.2mm from rim **Rev:** Head left

Date	Mintage	F	VF	XF	Unc	BU
ND(1969)(B)	—	—	2.00	3.00	5.00	—
ND(1969)(C)	—	—	3.00	5.00	8.00	—

KM# 42.3 20 PAISE
Aluminum-Bronze **Obv:** Asoka lion pedestal **Rev:** Head left **Note:** Eyes, mustache recut, legends 1.2mm from rim.

Date	Mintage	F	VF	XF	Unc	BU
ND(1969)(B)	—	—	0.60	1.00	1.50	—

Note: The KM 42 subtypes were struck during 1969 and 1970

KM# 43.1 20 PAISE
Aluminum-Bronze **Series:** F.A.O. **Subject:** Food For All **Obv:** Asoka lion pedestal **Rev:** Sun above floating lotus **Note:** Wide rims.

Date	Mintage	F	VF	XF	Unc	BU
1970(B)	5,160,000	—	0.75	1.25	2.00	—
1970B Proof	3,046	Value: 2.00				
1970(C)	5,010,000	—	0.75	1.25	2.00	—

KM# 43.2 20 PAISE
Aluminum-Bronze **Obv:** Asoka lion pedestal **Rev:** Sun above floating lotus **Note:** Narrow rims.

Date	Mintage	F	VF	XF	Unc	BU
1971(B)	60,000	—	0.70	0.90	1.25	—
1971B Proof	4,375	Value: 2.00				

KM# 44 20 PAISE
2.1500 g., Aluminum, 26 mm. **Obv:** Asoka lion pedestal **Rev:** Denomination and date within decorative wreath

Date	Mintage	F	VF	XF	Unc	BU
1982(B)	—	—	0.25	0.40	1.00	—
1982(H)	—	—	0.25	0.40	1.00	—
1982(H) Without mm	—	—	0.25	0.40	1.00	—
1983(C)	28,505,000	—	0.25	0.40	1.00	—
1983(H)	Inc. above	—	0.25	0.40	1.00	—
1984(B)	—	—	0.25	0.40	1.00	—
1984(C)	Inc. above	—	0.25	0.40	1.00	—
1984(H)	Inc. above	—	0.25	0.40	1.00	—
1985(B)	84,495,000	—	0.25	0.40	1.00	—
1985(C)	Inc. above	—	0.25	0.40	1.00	—
1985(H)	Inc. above	—	0.25	0.40	1.00	—
1986(B)	155,610,000	—	0.25	0.40	0.75	—
1986(C)	Inc. above	—	0.15	0.30	0.75	—
1986(H)	Inc. above	—	0.15	0.30	0.75	—
1987(C)	—	—	0.15	0.30	0.75	—
1987(H)	153,073,000	—	0.15	0.30	0.75	—
1988(B)	125,048,000	—	0.15	0.30	0.75	—
1988(C)	Inc. above	—	0.35	0.60	1.00	—
1989(C)	—	—	0.35	0.60	1.00	—
1989(H)	—	—	0.15	0.25	0.75	—
1990(C)	—	—	0.35	0.60	1.00	—
1990(H)	—	—	0.15	0.25	0.75	—
1991(C)	—	—	0.15	0.25	0.75	—
1991(H)	—	—	0.15	0.25	0.75	—
1992(H)	—	—	0.15	0.25	0.75	—
1994(H)	—	—	0.15	0.25	0.75	—
1996(H)	—	—	1.00	2.00	4.00	—
1997(H)	—	—	3.00	5.00	10.00	—

KM# 45 20 PAISE
Aluminum **Series:** F.A.O. **Obv:** Asoka lion pedestal **Rev:** Grain sprig within stylized sun design

Date	Mintage	F	VF	XF	Unc	BU
1982(C)	—	—	2.00	3.25	5.00	—
1982(H)	—	—	1.00	1.50	2.50	—

KM# 46 20 PAISE
2.1500 g., Aluminum, 26 mm. **Series:** F.A.O. **Subject:** Fisheries **Obv:** Asoka lion pedestal **Rev:** People with fishing nets

Date	Mintage	F	VF	XF	Unc	BU
1983(C)	—	—	1.00	1.50	2.50	—
Note: Mintage included in KM44						
1983(H)	—	—	1.00	1.50	2.50	—
Note: Mintage included in KM44						

KM# 47.1 25 NAYE PAISE
2.4200 g., Nickel **Obv:** Asoka lion pedestal **Rev:** Denomination and date

Date	Mintage	F	VF	XF	Unc	BU
1957(B)	5,640,000	—	0.75	1.25	2.00	—
1957(C)	Inc. above	—	0.75	1.25	2.00	—
1959(B)	43,080,000	—	0.45	0.75	1.25	—
1959(C)	Inc. above	—	0.45	0.75	1.25	—
1960(B)	115,320,000	—	0.30	0.60	1.00	—
1960(B) Proof	—	Value: 2.00				
1960(C)	Inc. above	—	0.30	0.60	1.00	—

KM# 47.2 25 NAYE PAISE
2.5000 g., Nickel, 19 mm. **Obv:** Asoka lion pedestal **Rev:** Denomination and date, large 25

Date	Mintage	F	VF	XF	Unc	BU
1961(B)	109,008,000	—	0.30	0.60	1.00	—
1961(B) Proof	—	Value: 2.00				
1961(C)	Inc. above	—	0.30	0.60	1.00	—
1962(B)	79,242,000	—	0.30	0.60	1.00	—
1962(B) Proof	—	Value: 2.00				
1962(C)	Inc. above	—	0.30	0.60	1.00	—
1963(B)	101,565,000	—	0.30	0.60	1.00	—
1963(B) Proof	—	Value: 2.00				
1963(C)	Inc. above	—	0.30	0.60	1.00	—

KM# 48.1 25 PAISE
Nickel, 19 mm. **Obv:** Asoka lion pedestal **Rev:** Denomination and date **Note:** Type 1.

Date	Mintage	F	VF	XF	Unc	BU
1964(B)	85,321,000	—	0.30	0.60	1.25	—
1964(C)	Inc. above	—	0.30	0.60	1.25	—

KM# 48.2 25 PAISE
2.5500 g., Nickel, 19 mm. **Obv:** Asoka lion pedestal **Rev:** Smaller date and denomination **Note:** Type 1.

Date	Mintage	F	VF	XF	Unc	BU
1965(B)	143,662,000	—	0.30	0.60	1.00	—
1965(C)	Inc. above	—	0.30	0.60	1.00	—
1966(B)	59,040,000	—	0.30	0.60	1.00	—
1966(C)	Inc. above	—	0.30	0.60	1.00	—
1967(B)	30,027,000	—	4.50	6.00	8.00	—

KM# 48.3 25 PAISE
Nickel, 19 mm. **Obv:** Asoka lion pedestal **Rev:** Denomination and date **Note:** Type 2. Mintage included in KM48.2.

Date	Mintage	F	VF	XF	Unc	BU
1967(C)	—	—	0.30	0.70	1.50	—
1968(C)	—	—	1.50	2.25	3.50	—

KM# 49.3 25 PAISE
2.4000 g., Copper-Nickel, 19 mm. **Obv:** Asoka lion pedestal **Rev:** Denomination and date **Note:** Type 2, 10mm between lion nosetips, 16-16.3mm across field. Bull has three legs.

Date	Mintage	F	VF	XF	Unc	BU
1972(C)	—	—	2.50	3.50	5.00	—
Note: Mintage included in KM49.1						
1973(C)	—	—	0.85	1.25	2.00	—
1974(C)	—	—	0.85	1.25	2.00	—

KM# 49.2 25 PAISE
Copper-Nickel, 19 mm. **Obv:** Asoka lion pedestal **Rev:** Denomination and date **Note:** Type 2, 9mm between lions' nose tips, 15mm across field.

Date	Mintage	F	VF	XF	Unc	BU
1972(C)	—	—	0.35	0.60	1.00	—
1977(B)	—	—	0.35	0.60	1.00	—
Note: Mintage included in KM49.1						
1977B Proof	—	Value: 1.50				
Note: Mintage included in KM49.1						
1978(B)	—	—	3.25	5.00	7.00	—
Note: Mintage included in KM49.1						
1979B Proof	—	Value: 1.50				

KM# 49.7 25 PAISE
Nickel **Obv:** KM#48.2. **Rev:** KM#49.1. **Note:** Mule. Type 1, lion without whiskers.

Date	Mintage	F	VF	XF	Unc	BU
1972(B)	—	—	8.00	12.00	18.00	—

KM# 49.1 25 PAISE
2.5000 g., Copper-Nickel, 19 mm. **Obv:** Asoka lion pedestal **Rev:** Denomination and date **Note:** Type 1, but with lion with whiskers and faces and wheel redesigned. 1984-86 have edges rounded (local blanks) or flat (Korean blanks).

Date	Mintage	F	VF	XF	Unc	BU
1972(B)	367,640,000	—	0.20	0.40	0.70	—
1972B Proof	7,895	Value: 1.00				

Date	Mintage	F	VF	XF	Unc	BU
1972(H)	Inc. above	—	0.45	1.00	2.00	—
1973(B)	—	—	0.20	0.40	0.70	—
1973B Proof	7,567	Value: 1.00				
1973(H)	—	—	0.35	0.60	1.00	—
1974(B)	—	—	0.20	0.40	0.70	—
1974B Proof	—	Value: 1.00				
1974(H)	—	—	0.45	0.75	1.25	—
1975(B)	559,980,000	—	0.20	0.40	0.70	—
1975B Proof	—	Value: 1.00				
1975(H)	Inc. above	—	3.00	4.00	5.00	—
1976(B)	30,016,000	—	0.60	1.00	1.50	—
1976B Proof	Inc. above	Value: 1.00				
1976(H)	Inc. above	—	0.60	1.00	1.50	—
1977(B)	270,520,000	—	0.20	0.40	0.70	—
1977(C)	Inc. above	—	0.35	0.60	1.00	—
1977(H)	Inc. above	—	0.35	0.60	1.00	—
1978B Proof	—	Value: 1.00				
1978(C)	131,632,000	—	0.25	0.40	0.70	—
1978(H)	—	—	0.25	0.40	0.70	—
1979(C)	—	—	0.50	1.00	1.50	—
1979(H)	—	—	0.50	1.00	1.50	—
1980(C)	6,175,000	—	0.25	0.40	0.70	—
1980(H)	Inc. above	—	0.25	0.40	0.70	—
1981(B)	11,048,000	—	0.25	0.40	0.70	—
1981(C)	Inc. above	—	1.50	2.00	2.50	—
1981(H)	Inc. above	—	0.45	0.75	1.25	—
1982(C)	38,288,000	—	0.45	0.75	1.25	—
1983(C)	137,488,000	—	0.45	0.75	1.25	—
1984(B)	98,740,000	—	0.45	0.75	1.25	—
1984(C)	Inc. above	—	0.45	0.75	1.25	—
1985(B)	113,872,000	—	0.45	0.75	1.25	—
1985C	Inc. above	—	0.15	0.25	0.50	—
1985(C)	Inc. above	—	0.45	0.75	1.25	—
1985(H)	Inc. above	—	0.45	0.75	1.25	—
1986(B)	362,624,000	—	0.60	0.90	1.50	—
1986(C)	Inc. above	—	0.60	0.90	1.50	—
1986(H)	Inc. above	—	0.60	0.90	1.50	—
1987(C)	341,160,000	—	0.60	0.90	1.50	—
1987(H)	Inc. above	—	0.60	0.90	1.50	—
1988(H)	303,252,000	—	0.60	0.90	1.50	—

KM# 49.4 25 PAISE
Copper-Nickel, 19 mm. **Obv:** Asoka lion pedestal **Rev:** Denomination and date **Note:** Type 1, central lion with bull and horse re-engraved.

Date	Mintage	F	VF	XF	Unc	BU
1974(B)	—	—	2.00	5.00	6.50	—
1975(B)	—	—	5.00	7.00	12.00	—
1975(H)	—	—	1.00	3.00	5.00	—
1976(H)	—	—	6.00	8.00	15.00	—
1977(B)	—	—	2.00	4.00	8.00	—
1978(B)	—	—	2.00	3.00	5.00	—
1979(B)	—	—	2.50	5.00	7.00	—
1981(B)	—	—	4.00	6.00	8.00	—

KM# 49.6 25 PAISE
2.6100 g., Copper-Nickel, 19 mm. **Obv:** Asoka lion pedestal **Rev:** Denomination and date **Note:** 9-1/2mm between lions' nose tips. Bull has four legs. Type 2.

Date	Mintage	F	VF	XF	Unc	BU
1974(C)	—	—	0.85	1.25	2.00	—
1975(C)	—	—	0.85	1.25	2.00	—
1976(C)	—	—	2.00	3.50	5.00	—

KM# 49.5 25 PAISE
2.5000 g., Copper-Nickel, 19 mm. **Obv:** Asoka lion pedestal **Rev:** Denomination and date **Note:** Type 3.

Date	Mintage	F	VF	XF	Unc	BU
1986(B)	—	—	0.15	0.30	1.00	—
1986(C)	—	—	0.45	0.75	1.25	—
1986(H)	—	—	0.45	0.75	1.25	—
1987(B)	—	—	0.15	0.30	1.00	—
1987(C)	—	—	0.25	0.40	1.50	—
1987(C) Long 7	—	—	0.25	0.40	1.50	—
1988(C)	—	—	0.20	0.35	1.25	—
1988(C) 8's 1.3mm tall	—	—	0.45	0.75	2.00	—
1988(C) 8's 1.8mm tall	—	—	0.45	0.75	2.00	—
1988(H)	—	—	0.45	1.00	1.75	—
1989(B)	—	—	0.45	1.00	1.75	—
1989(C)	—	—	2.00	2.50	3.00	—
1990(B)	—	—	2.00	3.50	7.00	—
1990(C)	—	—	2.00	3.50	7.00	—

KM# 48.4 25 PAISE
Nickel, 19 mm. **Obv:** Asoka lion pedestal **Rev:** Denomination and date **Note:** Type 1, lion without whiskers. Mule = Obv. of KM#48.2; Rev. of KM#49.1. Prev. KM#49.7.

Date	Mintage	F	VF	XF	Unc	BU
1972(B)	—	—	8.00	14.00	20.00	—

KM# 50   25 PAISE
Copper-Nickel, 19 mm. **Subject:** Rural Women's Advancement
Obv: Asoka lion pedestal **Rev:** Woman grinding wheat

Date	Mintage	F	VF	XF	Unc	BU
1980(B)	15,050,000	—	0.30	0.50	1.00	—
1980B Proof		Value: 1.00				
1980(C)	8,520,000	—	0.50	1.00	1.50	—
1980(H)	10,380,000	—	1.00	1.50	2.00	—

KM# 51   25 PAISE
Copper-Nickel, 19 mm. **Subject:** World Food Day **Obv:** Asoka
lion pedestal **Rev:** Man and woman, man carrying sheaf

Date	Mintage	F	VF	XF	Unc	BU
1981(B)	2,170,000	—	1.00	1.50	2.00	—
1981B Proof		Value: 2.00				
1981(C)	4,500,000	—	1.00	1.50	2.00	—
1981(H)	9,340,000	—	1.50	2.00	3.00	—

KM# 52   25 PAISE
Copper-Nickel, 19 mm. **Subject:** IX Asian Games **Obv:** Asoka
lion pedestal **Rev:** Sun above symbol

Date	Mintage	F	VF	XF	Unc	BU
1982(B)	12,000,000	—	0.30	0.50	1.00	—
1982B Proof		Value: 1.00				
1982(C)	12,000,000	—	0.30	0.50	1.00	—
1982(H)	330,000	—	2.50	3.50	5.00	—

KM# 53   25 PAISE
2.5000 g., Copper-Nickel, 19 mm. **Subject:** Forestry
Obv: Asoka lion pedestal **Rev:** Central tree divides squatting
figure and stag **Edge:** Rounded

Date	Mintage	F	VF	XF	Unc	BU
1985(C)	—	—	3.00	5.00	7.00	—
1985(B)	—	—	1.50	2.00	2.75	—

Note: Mintage included in KM49.1. 1985 (B) have rounded or flat edge.

1985(H)	—	—	5.00	7.00	10.00	—

Note: Mintage included in KM49.1

KM# 54   25 PAISE
2.8200 g., Stainless Steel, 19 mm. **Obv:** Small Asoka lion
pedestal **Rev:** Rhinoceros left **Edge:** Plain **Note:** Varieties of date
size exist.

Date	Mintage	F	VF	XF	Unc	BU
1988C	305,280,000	—	0.10	0.20	1.00	—
1988(B)	—	—	0.45	0.75	1.25	—
1988(C)	18,920,000	—	3.50	5.00	8.00	—
1988(H)	—	—	6.00	8.00	10.00	—
1988	Inc. above	—	0.45	0.75	1.25	—
1989(B)	—	—	0.65	1.00	1.50	—
1989(C) fine grass below rhino	—	—	0.65	1.00	1.50	—
1989(C) bold grass below rhino	—	—	0.65	1.00	1.50	—
1989(H)	—	—	1.00	2.00	3.00	—
1989	—	—	0.15	0.30	1.00	—
1990(B)	—	—	0.25	0.50	1.00	—
1990(C)	—	—	0.25	0.50	1.00	—
1990(H)	—	—	0.25	0.40	1.00	—
1990 Small mm	—	—	0.40	0.65	1.00	—
1991(B)	—	—	0.25	0.40	1.00	—
1991(C)	—	—	0.25	0.40	1.00	—

Date	Mintage	F	VF	XF	Unc	BU
1991(H)	—	—	0.25	0.40	1.00	—
1991	—	—	0.25	0.40	1.00	—
1992(B)	—	—	0.25	0.40	1.00	—
1992(C)	—	—	1.00	2.00	3.00	—
1992(H)	—	—	1.00	2.00	3.00	—
1992	—	—	0.50	1.00	2.00	—
1993(B)	—	—	0.50	1.00	2.00	—
1993(C)	—	—	0.50	1.00	2.00	—
1993(H)	—	—	2.00	3.00	5.00	—
1993	—	—	0.50	0.70	1.00	—
1994(B)	—	—	0.15	0.30	1.00	—
1994(C)	—	—	0.10	0.20	1.00	—
1994(H)	—	—	0.10	0.20	1.00	—
1994	—	—	0.10	0.20	1.00	—
1995(B)	—	—	0.10	0.20	1.00	—
1995(C)	—	—	0.25	0.50	1.00	—
1995(H)	—	—	0.10	0.20	1.00	—
1995	—	—	0.10	0.20	1.00	—
1996(B)	—	—	0.10	0.20	1.00	—
1996(C)	—	—	0.10	0.20	1.00	—
1996(H)	—	—	0.10	0.20	1.00	—
1996	—	—	0.10	0.20	1.00	—
1997(B)	—	—	0.10	0.20	1.00	—
1997(C)	—	—	0.10	0.20	1.00	—
1997(H)	—	—	0.50	1.00	2.00	—
1997	—	—	0.10	0.20	1.00	—
1998(B)	—	—	0.10	0.20	1.00	—
1998(C)	—	—	0.10	0.20	1.00	—
1998(H)	—	—	0.10	0.20	1.00	—
1998	—	—	0.10	0.20	1.00	—
1999(B)	—	—	0.10	0.20	1.00	—
1999(C)	—	—	0.10	0.20	1.00	—
1999(H)	—	—	0.10	0.20	1.00	—
1999	—	—	0.10	0.20	1.00	—
2000(B)	—	—	0.10	0.20	1.00	—
2000(C)	—	—	0.10	0.20	1.00	—
2000(H)	—	—	0.10	0.20	1.00	—
2000	—	—	0.10	0.20	1.00	—

KM# 55   50 NAYE PAISE
5.0000 g., Nickel, 24 mm. **Obv:** Asoka lion pedestal
Rev: Denomination and date

Date	Mintage	F	VF	XF	Unc	BU
1960(B)	11,224,000	—	1.00	1.50	2.50	—
1960(B) Proof		Value: 3.00				
1960(C)	Inc. above	—	0.50	1.25	2.00	—
1961(B)	45,992,000	—	0.25	0.60	1.25	—
1961(B) Proof		Value: 3.00				
1961(C)	Inc. above	—	0.25	0.60	1.25	—
1962(B)	64,227,999	—	0.25	0.60	1.25	—
1962(B) Proof		Value: 3.00				
1962(C)	Inc. above	—	0.25	0.60	1.25	—
1963(B)	58,168,000	—	0.25	0.60	1.25	—
1963(B) Proof		Value: 3.00				
1963(C)	Inc. above	—	1.00	1.50	2.50	—

KM# 56   50 PAISE
Nickel   **Subject:** Death of Jawaharlal Nehru **Obv:** Asoka lion
pedestal **Rev:** Head left **Rev. Leg.:** English **Note:** Struck from
1964 until 1967.

Date	Mintage	F	VF	XF	Unc	BU
ND(1964)(B)	21,900,000	—	0.40	0.65	1.00	—
ND(1964)B Proof		Value: 2.50				
ND(1964)(C)	7,160,000	—	0.75	1.50	2.75	—

KM# 57   50 PAISE
Nickel   **Subject:** Death of Jawaharlal Nehru **Obv:** Asoka lion
pedestal **Rev:** Head left **Rev. Leg.:** Hindi **Note:** Struck from 1964
until 1967.

Date	Mintage	F	VF	XF	Unc	BU
ND(1964)(B)	36,190,000	—	0.40	0.65	1.00	—
ND(1964)(C)	28,350,000	—	0.40	0.65	1.00	—

KM# 58.1   50 PAISE
Nickel **Obv:** Asoka lion pedestal **Rev:** 7mm "50", date **Note:** Type 1.

Date	Mintage	F	VF	XF	Unc	BU
1964(C)	23,361,000	—	0.50	1.00	1.75	—
1967(B)	19,267,000	—	0.50	1.00	1.75	—

Note: Varieties of 1967(B) reverse edges exist, half teeth and the scarce full teeth

KM# 58.3   50 PAISE
Nickel   **Obv:** Asoka lion pedestal **Rev:** 6.5mm "50", date
Note: Type 1.

Date	Mintage	F	VF	XF	Unc	BU
1970(B)	—	—	1.00	2.00	3.00	—

Note: Mintage included with 1969

1970B Proof	3,046	Value: 2.00				
1971B Proof	4,375	Value: 2.00				

KM# 58.2   50 PAISE
5.0500 g., Nickel, 24.03 mm.   **Obv:** Asoka lion pedestal
Rev: 6.5mm "50", date **Note:** Type 2.

Date	Mintage	F	VF	XF	Unc	BU
1967(C)	—	—	0.60	1.00	1.50	—
1968(B)	28,076,000	—	0.25	0.60	1.00	—

Note: A scarce 1968(B) variety exists with crude obverse, no whiskers, thick horsetail

1968(C)	Inc. above	—	0.25	0.60	1.00	—
1969(B)	59,388,000	—	0.25	0.60	1.00	—
1969(C)	Inc. above	—	0.35	0.75	1.25	—
1970(B)	Inc. above	—	0.35	0.75	1.25	—
1970(C)	Inc. above	—	0.25	0.60	1.00	—
1971(C)	57,900,000	—	0.25	0.50	0.85	—

KM# 59   50 PAISE
5.0300 g., Nickel, 24 mm.   **Subject:** Centennial - Birth of
Mahatma Gandhi **Obv:** Asoka lion pedestal **Rev:** Head left
Note: Struck during 1969 and 1970.

Date	Mintage	F	VF	XF	Unc	BU
ND(1969)(B)	10,260,000	—	0.25	0.50	1.00	—
ND(1969)B Proof	9,147	Value: 2.00				
ND(1969)(C)	12,100,000	—	0.25	0.50	1.00	—

KM# 61   50 PAISE
4.9500 g., Copper-Nickel, 24 mm.   **Obv:** Asoka lion pedestal
Rev: Denomination above date, lettering spaced out **Note:** Type
2. Wide and narrow security edge varieties exist.

Date	Mintage	F	VF	XF	Unc	BU
1972(C)	—	—	0.35	0.60	1.00	—
1972(B)	—	—	0.35	0.60	1.00	—
1973(B)	—	—	0.35	0.60	1.00	—
1973(C)	—	—	2.00	3.50	6.00	—

KM# 60   50 PAISE
Copper-Nickel, 24 mm.   **Subject:** 25th Anniversary of Independence **Obv:** Asoka lion pedestal **Rev:** Figures with flag, building in background

Date	Mintage	F	VF	XF	Unc	BU
ND(1972)(B)	43,800,000	—	0.30	0.50	1.00	—
ND(1972)B Proof	7,895	Value: 2.00				
ND(1972)(C)	40,080,000	—	0.45	0.75	1.50	—

KM# 62   50 PAISE
Copper-Nickel, 24 mm.   **Series:** F.A.O. **Subject:** Grow More Food **Obv:** Asoka lion pedestal **Rev:** Inscription on shield within grain sprigs

Date	Mintage	F	VF	XF	Unc	BU
1973(B)	28,720,000	—	0.30	0.50	1.00	—
1973B Proof	11,000	Value: 2.00				
1973(C)	40,100,000	—	0.30	0.50	1.00	—

KM# 63   50 PAISE
4.9700 g., Copper-Nickel, 24 mm.   **Obv:** Asoka lion pedestal **Rev:** Denomination above date, lettering close **Note:** Type 2.

Date	Mintage	F	VF	XF	Unc	BU
1974(B)	—	—	0.25	0.50	1.00	—
1974B Proof	—	Value: 2.00				
1974(C)	—	—	0.35	0.75	1.50	—
1975(B)	225,880,000	—	0.25	0.50	1.00	—
1975B Proof	—	Value: 2.00				
1975(C)	Inc. above	—	0.25	0.50	1.00	—
1975(H)	—	—	0.75	1.25	2.00	—
1976(B)	99,564,000	—	0.25	0.50	1.00	—
1976B Proof	Inc. above	Value: 2.00				
1976(C)	Inc. above	—	0.35	0.75	1.50	—
1976(H)	Inc. above	—	0.75	1.25	2.00	—
1977(B)	97,272,000	—	0.25	0.50	1.00	—
1977B Proof	Inc. above	Value: 2.00				
1977(C)	Inc. above	—	0.40	0.75	1.50	—
1977(H)	Inc. above	—	0.40	0.75	1.50	—
1978B Proof	25,648,000	Value: 2.00				
1978(C)	—	—	0.25	0.50	1.00	—
1979B Proof	—	Value: 2.00				
1980(B)	—	—	0.25	0.50	1.00	—
1980B Proof	—	Value: 2.00				
1980(C)	—	—	5.00	8.00	12.00	—
1981B Proof	—	Value: 2.00				
1983(C)	62,634,000	—	5.00	8.00	12.00	—

KM# 64   50 PAISE
Copper-Nickel, 24 mm.   **Subject:** National Integration **Obv:** Asoka lion pedestal **Rev:** Flag on map

Date	Mintage	F	VF	XF	Unc	BU
1982(B)	9,804,000	—	0.40	0.75	1.25	—
1982B Proof	—	Value: 3.00				
1982(C)	Inc. above	—	10.00	15.00	20.00	—

KM# 65   50 PAISE
5.0900 g., Copper-Nickel, 24 mm.   **Obv:** Asoka lion pedestal, ornaments surround **Rev:** Denomination and date, ornaments surround **Note:** Type 3.

Date	Mintage	F	VF	XF	Unc	BU
1984(B)	61,548,000	—	0.25	0.50	0.85	—
1984(C)	Inc. above	—	1.00	1.50	2.50	—
1984(H)	—	—	2.00	3.00	5.00	—
1985(B)	210,964,000	—	0.25	0.50	0.85	—
1985(C)	Inc. above	—	0.25	0.50	0.85	—
1985(H)	—	—	1.00	1.50	3.00	—
1985(T)	—	—	0.20	0.30	0.65	—
1986(C)	117,576,000	—	0.50	1.00	2.00	—
1987(B)	—	—	0.25	0.50	0.85	—
1987(C)	145,140,000	—	0.25	0.50	0.85	—
1987(H)	Inc. above	—	0.40	0.75	1.50	—
1988(B)	149,092,000	—	0.25	0.50	0.85	—
1988(C)	Inc. above	—	1.00	1.50	3.00	—
1988(H)	Inc. above	—	1.00	1.50	2.50	—
1989(B)	—	—	0.50	1.00	2.00	—
1989(C)	—	—	0.50	1.00	2.00	—
1990(B)	—	—	2.00	4.00	7.00	—

KM# 66   50 PAISE
Copper-Nickel, 24 mm.   **Subject:** Golden Jubilee of Reserve Bank of India **Obv:** Asoka lion pedestal **Rev:** Lion beneath trees

Date	Mintage	F	VF	XF	Unc	BU
ND(1985)(B)	—	—	0.50	1.00	4.50	—
Note: Mintage included in KM65						
ND(1985)B Proof	—	Value: 15.00				
Note: Mintage included in KM#65						
ND(1985)(C)	—	—	2.00	3.00	6.00	—
ND(1985)(H)	—	—	0.75	1.25	4.00	—
Note: Mintage included in KM65						

KM# 67.1   50 PAISE
Copper-Nickel, 24 mm.   **Subject:** Death of Indira Gandhi - statesperson, 1917-1984 **Obv:** Asoka lion pedestal **Rev:** Head right

Date	Mintage	F	VF	XF	Unc	BU
ND(1985)(B)	—	—	0.20	0.40	1.00	—
ND(1985)B Proof	—	Value: 17.50				
Note: Mintage included in KM65						
ND(1985)(C)	—	—	0.20	0.40	1.00	—
Note: Mintage included in KM65						
ND(1985)(H)	—	—	0.65	1.00	1.50	—
Note: Mintage included in KM65						

KM# 67.2   50 PAISE
Copper-Nickel, 24 mm.   **Subject:** Death of Indira Gandhi, 1917-84 statesperson **Obv:** Asoka lion pedestal **Rev:** Head right **Note:** Mule.

Date	Mintage	F	VF	XF	Unc	BU
ND(1985)(C)	—	—	35.00	50.00	80.00	—

KM# 68.1   50 PAISE
4.9700 g., Copper-Nickel, 24 mm.   **Series:** F.A.O. **Subject:** Fisheries **Obv:** Asoka lion pedestal **Rev:** People with fishing nets

Date	Mintage	F	VF	XF	Unc	BU
1986(B)	—	—	0.30	0.75	1.50	—
Note: Mintage included in KM65						
1986B Proof	—	Value: 15.00				

Date	Mintage	F	VF	XF	Unc	BU
Note: Mintage included in KM65						
1986(C)	—	—	2.00	3.00	5.00	—
1986(H)	—	—	2.00	3.00	5.00	—
Note: Mintage included in KM65						

KM# 68.2   50 PAISE
Copper-Nickel, 24 mm.   **Obv:** Asoka lion pedestal **Rev:** People with fishing nets **Note:** Mule.

Date	Mintage	F	VF	XF	Unc	BU
1986(C)	—	—	50.00	70.00	100	—

KM# 69   50 PAISE
3.8000 g., Stainless Steel, 22 mm.   **Subject:** Parliament Building in New Delhi **Obv:** Denomination **Rev:** Building

Date	Mintage	F	VF	XF	Unc	BU
1988C	272,160,000	—	0.20	0.30	0.50	—
1988(B)	—	—	0.20	0.40	0.75	—
1988(C)	2,195,000	—	6.00	9.00	14.00	—
1988(H)	Inc. above	—	6.00	9.00	14.00	—
1988(N)	—	—	0.20	0.40	0.75	—
1989(B)	—	—	0.20	0.40	0.75	—
1989(C)	—	—	1.50	3.00	5.00	—
1989(H)	—	—	0.50	1.00	2.00	—
1989(N)	—	—	0.15	0.50	1.00	—
1990(B)	—	—	0.15	0.50	1.00	—
1990(C)	—	—	0.50	1.00	2.00	—
1990(N)	—	—	0.15	0.50	1.00	—
1990(N) Small mm	—	—	0.15	0.50	1.00	—
1990(N) Large mm	—	—	0.15	0.50	1.00	—
1991(B)	—	—	0.15	0.50	1.00	—
1991(C)	—	—	0.15	0.50	1.00	—
1991(H)	—	—	0.15	0.25	0.50	—
1991(N)	—	—	0.10	0.35	0.60	—
1992(B)	—	—	0.10	0.35	0.60	—
1992(C)	—	—	0.50	1.00	2.00	—
1992(H)	—	—	0.10	0.35	0.60	—
1992(N)	—	—	0.10	0.35	0.60	—
1993(C)	—	—	0.50	1.00	2.00	—
1993(N)	—	—	0.10	0.35	0.60	—
1994(B)	—	—	0.10	0.35	0.60	—
1994(C)	—	—	0.50	1.00	2.00	—
1994(H)	—	—	0.10	0.35	0.60	—
1994(N)	—	—	0.10	0.35	0.60	—
1995(B)	—	—	0.10	0.20	0.35	—
1995(C)	—	—	0.50	1.00	2.00	—
1995(N)	—	—	0.20	0.30	0.50	—
1995(N)	—	—	0.10	0.20	0.35	—
1996(B)	—	—	0.10	0.20	0.35	—
1996(C)	—	—	0.10	0.20	0.35	—
1996(N)	—	—	0.10	0.20	0.35	—
1997(B)	—	—	0.10	0.20	0.35	—
1997(C)	—	—	0.10	0.20	0.35	—
1997	—	—	2.00	3.00	5.00	—
1997(N)	—	—	0.10	0.20	0.35	—
1998(B)	—	—	0.10	0.20	0.35	—
1998(C)	—	—	0.10	0.20	0.35	—
1998(H)	—	—	1.00	1.50	3.00	—
1998(N)	—	—	0.10	0.20	0.35	—
1999(B)	—	—	0.15	0.25	0.50	—
1999(C)	—	—	0.15	0.25	0.50	—
1999(H)	—	—	0.15	0.25	0.50	—
2000(B)	—	—	0.15	0.25	0.50	—
2000(C)	—	—	0.15	0.25	0.50	—
2000(H)	—	—	0.15	0.25	0.50	—

KM# 70   50 PAISE
Stainless Steel   **Subject:** 50th Anniversary of Independence **Obv:** Small Asoka lion pedestal above denomination **Rev:** Line of people

Date	Mintage	F	VF	XF	Unc	BU
1997(B)	—	—	0.25	0.40	0.75	—
1997(C)	—	—	0.25	0.40	0.75	—
1997(H)	—	—	0.25	0.40	0.75	—
1997(M) Proof	—	Value: 15.00				
1997	—	—	0.25	0.40	0.75	—

KM# 75.1   RUPEE
10.0000 g., Nickel, 28 mm.   **Obv:** Asoka lion pedestal **Rev:** Denomination and date, grain ears flank **Note:** Type 1.

Date	Mintage	F	VF	XF	Unc	BU
1962(B) Proof	—					
1962(C)	3,689,000	—	1.00	2.00	3.00	—

Top-right partial table (above KM# 68.2):

Date	Mintage	F	VF	XF	Unc	BU
Note: Mintage included in KM65						
1986(C)	—	—	2.00	3.00	5.00	—
1986(H)	—	—	2.00	3.00	5.00	—
Note: Mintage included in KM65						

KM# 75.2 RUPEE
10.0000 g., Nickel, 28 mm. **Obv:** Asoka lion pedestal
Rev: Smaller date and denomination **Note:** Type 1.

Date	Mintage	F	VF	XF	Unc	BU
1970(B)	Inc. above	—	3.50	5.00	7.00	—
1970B Proof	3,046	Value: 3.00				
1971B Proof	4,375	Value: 3.00				
1972B Proof	7,895,000	Value: 2.50				
1973B Proof	7,567	Value: 2.50				
1974B Proof		Value: 2.50				

KM# 76 RUPEE
9.9300 g., Nickel, 27 mm. **Subject:** Death of Jawaharlal Nehru
Obv: Small Asoka lion pedestal **Rev:** Head left **Note:** Type II.
Struck from 1964 until 1967.

Date	Mintage	F	VF	XF	Unc	BU
ND(1964)(B)	10,010,000	—	0.65	1.00	2.00	—
ND(1964)B Proof		Value: 5.00				
ND(1964)(C)	10,020,000	—	0.65	1.00	2.00	—

KM# 77 RUPEE
10.0000 g., Nickel, 28 mm. **Subject:** Centennial - Birth of
Mahatma Gandhi **Obv:** Asoka lion pedestal **Rev:** Head left
Note: Struck during 1969 and 1970.

Date	Mintage	F	VF	XF	Unc	BU
ND(1969)(B)	5,180,000	—	0.70	1.25	2.00	—
ND(1969)B Proof	9,147	Value: 3.00				
ND(1969)(C)	6,690,000	—	1.00	1.50	2.50	—

KM# 78.1 RUPEE
8.0000 g., Copper-Nickel, 28 mm. **Obv:** Asoka lion pedestal
Rev: Denomination and date, grain ears flank **Note:** Type 1.

Date	Mintage	F	VF	XF	Unc	BU
1975(B)	98,850,000	—	0.40	0.85	1.50	—
1975B Proof		Value: 2.50				
1975(C)		—	6.50	8.00	10.00	—
1976(B)	161,895,000	—	0.35	0.75	1.50	—
1976B Proof	Inc. above	Value: 2.50				
1977(B)	177,105,000	—	0.35	0.75	1.50	—
1977B Proof	Inc. above	Value: 2.50				
1978(B)	127,348,000	—	0.40	0.80	1.50	—
1978B Proof	Inc. above	Value: 2.50				
1978(C)	Inc. above	—	0.50	1.00	1.75	—
1979(C)		—	8.00	11.00	15.00	—
1979(B)		—	8.00	11.00	15.00	—

KM# 78.2 RUPEE
8.0000 g., Copper-Nickel, 28 mm. **Obv:** Asoka lion pedestal
Rev: Denomination and date, grain ears flank **Note:** Type 2.

Date	Mintage	F	VF	XF	Unc	BU
1975(C)		—	0.40	0.85	1.50	—
Note: Mintage included in KM78.1						
1976(C)		—	0.50	1.25	2.25	—
Note: Mintage included in KM78.1						

KM# 78.3 RUPEE
8.0000 g., Copper-Nickel, 28 mm. **Obv:** Asoka lion pedestal
Rev: Denomination and date, grain ears flank **Note:** Type 3.
Border varieties of long vs. short teeth on 1981 reverse and 1982
obverse. Wide and narrow security edge varieties exist.

Date	Mintage	F	VF	XF	Unc	BU
1979(B)	—	—	0.35	0.60	1.00	—
1979B Proof	—	Value: 2.50				
1979(C)	—	—	0.40	0.75	1.50	—
1980(B)	84,768,000	—	0.35	0.60	1.00	—
1980B Proof	—	Value: 2.50				
1980(C)	Inc. above	—	0.40	0.75	1.25	—
1981(B)	82,458,000	—	0.35	0.60	1.00	—
1981B Proof	—	Value: 2.50				
1981(C)	Inc. above	—	0.40	0.75	1.25	—
1982(B)	116,811,000	—	0.40	0.75	1.25	—

KM# 79.1 RUPEE
6.0000 g., Copper-Nickel, 26 mm. **Obv:** Asoka lion pedestal within
seven sided beaded outline **Rev:** Denomination and date, grain ears
flank, seven-sided outline surrounds **Edge:** Security **Note:** Type 3.
Lions' hair and ears on 1984(B)-1989(B) issues vary from others.

Date	Mintage	F	VF	XF	Unc	BU
1983(B)	32,490,000	—	0.30	0.50	1.00	—
1983(C)	Inc. above	—	0.30	0.50	1.00	—
1984(B)	152,378,000	—	0.25	0.40	0.75	—
1984(C)	Inc. above	—	0.25	0.40	0.75	—
1984(H)	Inc. above	—	1.50	2.25	3.00	—
1985(B)	444,516,000	—	0.25	0.40	0.75	—
1985(C)	Inc. above	—	0.25	0.40	0.75	—
1985H	Inc. above	—	0.25	0.40	0.75	—
1985(L)	Inc. above	—	0.25	0.40	0.75	—
1986(B)	1,396,074,000	—	0.25	0.40	0.75	—
1986(C)	Inc. above	—	0.25	0.40	0.75	—
1986(H)	Inc. above	—	1.50	2.25	3.00	—
1987(B)	685,502,000	—	0.25	0.40	0.75	—
1987(C)	Inc. above	—	0.25	0.40	0.75	—
1987(H)	Inc. above	—	0.25	0.40	0.75	—
1988(B)	240,447,000	—	0.75	1.25	2.00	—
1988(C)	Inc. above	—	0.25	0.40	0.75	—
1988(H)	Inc. above	—	0.40	0.75	1.25	—
1989(B)	—	—	1.50	2.25	3.00	—
1989(C)	—	—	0.25	0.45	0.75	—
1989(H)	—	—	0.25	0.45	0.75	—
1990(C)	—	—	1.50	2.25	3.00	—
1990(H)	—	—	0.25	0.45	0.75	—

KM# 80 RUPEE
6.0000 g., Copper-Nickel, 26 mm. **Subject:** Youth Year
Obv: Small asoka lion pedestal above denomination **Rev:** Three
outlined profiles between dove and laurel branch **Edge:** Security

Date	Mintage	F	VF	XF	Unc	BU
1985(B)	—	—	0.35	0.60	1.25	2.00
Note: Mintage included in KM79.1						
1985(C)	—	—	0.50	1.00	1.50	2.00
Note: Mintage included in KM79.1						
1985(C) Proof	—	Value: 10.00				
Note: Mintage included in KM79.1						
1985(H)	—	—	2.00	3.00	5.00	—

KM# 81 RUPEE
6.0000 g., Copper-Nickel, 26 mm. **Series:** F.A.O. **Obv:** Asoka
lion pedestal **Rev:** Two figures working in field

Date	Mintage	F	VF	XF	Unc	BU
1987(B)	234,223,000	—	0.35	0.60	1.25	—
1987B Proof	—	Value: 5.00				
1987(C)	Inc. above	—	0.50	1.00	2.00	—
1987(H)	191,120,000	—	1.50	3.00	4.00	—

KM# 82 RUPEE
6.0000 g., Copper-Nickel, 26 mm. **Series:** F.A.O.
Subject: Rainfed farming **Obv:** Asoka lion pedestal **Rev:** Figure
with flowers, rain cloud in background

Date	Mintage	F	VF	XF	Unc	BU
1988(B)	—	—	1.00	1.50	3.00	—
Note: Mintage included in KM79.1						
1988(C)	—	—	1.00	2.00	4.00	—
1988(H)	—	—	3.00	5.00	8.00	—

KM# 79.2 RUPEE
6.0000 g., Copper-Nickel, 26 mm. **Obv:** Horse on pedestal
different, more detailed, 7-sided beaded outline surrounds
Rev: Denomination and date, grain ears flank, within 7-sided
beaded outline **Note:** Type 3.

Date	Mintage	F	VF	XF	Unc	BU
1988(B)	—	—	1.00	1.50	2.50	—
1989	—	—	1.00	1.50	2.50	—
1990	—	—	1.00	1.50	2.50	—

KM# 79.3 RUPEE
6.0000 g., Copper-Nickel, 26 mm. **Obv:** Lions' chest hairs restyled,
7-sided beaded outline surrounds **Rev:** Denomination and date,
grain ears flank, 7-sided beaded outline surrounds **Note:** Type 3.

Date	Mintage	F	VF	XF	Unc	BU
1988(B)	—	—	0.25	0.50	1.00	—
1989(B)	—	—	0.25	0.50	1.00	—
1990(B)	—	—	0.25	0.50	1.00	—

KM# 79.4 RUPEE
6.0000 g., Copper-Nickel, 26 mm. **Obv:** Asoka lion pedestal, within
7-sided beaded outline, similar to 79.1 **Rev:** Denomination and date,
grain ears flank, 7-sided beaded outline surrounds **Edge:** Milled
Note: Traces of security edge and/or mostly smooth edges are
encountered, especially for 1989. 1989-1991(C) is a variety with
bulging eyes on side lions and irregular straight hair on central lion.

Date	Mintage	F	VF	XF	Unc	BU
1988(C)	—	—	5.00	7.00	11.00	—
1989(B)	—	—	10.00	15.00	20.00	—
1989(C)	—	—	5.00	7.00	11.00	—
1989(H)	—	—	10.00	15.00	20.00	—
1990(C)	—	—	0.35	0.50	1.00	—
1990(H)	—	—	0.50	0.75	1.50	—
1991(C)	—	—	0.35	0.50	1.00	—

KM# 79.5 RUPEE
6.0000 g., Copper-Nickel, 26 mm. **Obv:** Lions' chest hairs restyled,
7-sided beaded outline surrounds **Rev:** Denomination and date,
grain ears flank, 7-sided beaded outline surrounds **Note:** Type 3.

Date	Mintage	F	VF	XF	Unc	BU
1990(C)	—	—	0.50	1.00	2.00	—
1990(B)	—	—	0.35	0.60	1.00	—
1991(B)	—	—	0.20	0.35	0.85	—
1991(H)	—	—	0.35	0.60	1.00	—

KM# 84 RUPEE
6.0000 g., Copper-Nickel, 26 mm. **Series:** F.A.O. **Subject:** Food and Environment **Obv:** Asoka lion pedestal **Rev:** Sun above wheat stalks

Date	Mintage	F	VF	XF	Unc	BU
1989	—	—	1.00	2.00	3.50	—
1989(H)	—	—	5.00	8.00	10.00	—
1989(B)	—	—	1.00	2.00	3.50	—

KM# 83.1 RUPEE
6.0000 g., Copper-Nickel, 26 mm. **Subject:** 100th Anniversary of Nehru's Birth **Obv:** Asoka lion pedestal **Rev:** Head right

Date	Mintage	F	VF	XF	Unc	BU
1989B Proof	—	Value: 5.00				
1989(C)	—	—	1.00	2.00	3.00	—
1989(H)	—	—	1.00	2.00	3.00	—
1989(B)	—	—	0.25	0.50	1.00	—

KM# 83.2 RUPEE
Copper-Nickel, 26 mm. **Obv:** Asoka lion pedestal, similar to KM#90. **Rev:** Head right

Date	Mintage	F	VF	XF	Unc	BU
1989(B)	—	—	20.00	50.00	80.00	—

KM# 88.2 RUPEE
6.0000 g., Copper-Nickel, 26 mm. **Series:** F.A.O. **Obv:** Asoka lion pedestal **Rev:** Farming scene **Edge:** Plain

Date	Mintage	F	VF	XF	Unc	BU
1990(H)	—	—	5.00	12.00	15.00	—

KM# 87.1 RUPEE
6.0000 g., Copper-Nickel, 26 mm. **Subject:** SAARC Year - Care for the Girl Child **Obv:** Asoka lion pedestal **Rev:** Girl cutout below sun, symbol at left **Edge:** Security

Date	Mintage	F	VF	XF	Unc	BU
1990(B)	—	—	0.40	0.80	2.00	—

KM# 87.2 RUPEE
6.0000 g., Copper-Nickel, 26 mm. **Subject:** SAARC Year - Care for the Girl Child **Obv:** Asoka lion pedestal, denomination below **Rev:** Girl cutout below sun, symbol at left **Edge:** Milled **Note:** Edge varieties exist.

Date	Mintage	F	VF	XF	Unc	BU
1990(B)	—	—	0.50	1.25	3.00	—
1990(H)	—	—	0.50	1.25	3.00	—

KM# 85 RUPEE
6.0000 g., Copper-Nickel, 26 mm. **Subject:** Dr. Ambedkar **Obv:** Asoka lion pedestal, denomination below **Rev:** Bust looking right

Date	Mintage	F	VF	XF	Unc	BU
1990(B)	—	—	0.20	0.75	1.50	—
1990(H)	—	—	0.40	1.25	2.50	—

KM# 86 RUPEE
6.0000 g., Copper-Nickel, 26 mm. **Subject:** 15th Anniversary of I.C.D.S. **Obv:** Asoka lion pedestal, denomination below **Rev:** Seated figure holding child, radiant design surrounds **Edge:** Narrow and wide reeded **Note:** Varieties exist.

Date	Mintage	F	VF	XF	Unc	BU
ND(1990)(B)	—	—	0.20	0.75	1.50	—
ND(1990)(H)	—	—	0.40	1.25	2.50	—

KM# 88.1 RUPEE
6.0000 g., Copper-Nickel, 26 mm. **Series:** F.A.O. **Obv:** Asoka lion pedestal, denomination below **Rev:** Farming scene **Edge:** Reeded

Date	Mintage	F	VF	XF	Unc	BU
1990(C)	—	—	3.00	5.00	8.00	—
Note: 1990(C) is seldom well struck						
1990(H)	—	—	5.00	7.00	10.00	—

KM# 89 RUPEE
6.0000 g., Copper-Nickel, 26 mm. **Subject:** Rajiv Gandhi **Obv:** Asoka lion pedestal, denomination below **Rev:** Head looking left **Note:** Edge varieties exist.

Date	Mintage	F	VF	XF	Unc	BU
ND(1991)(B)	—	—	0.35	0.75	1.50	—
Note: The Mumbai (Bombay) mint mark occasionally resembles the Noida mintmark						
ND(1991)(H)	—	—	0.40	1.00	2.00	—

KM# 90 RUPEE
6.0000 g., Copper-Nickel, 26 mm. **Subject:** Commonwealth Parliamentary Conference **Obv:** Asoka lion pedestal, denomination below **Rev:** Building **Note:** Variety of breast with flat details exist (worn dies).

Date	Mintage	F	VF	XF	Unc	BU
1991(B)	—	—	0.35	0.75	1.50	—
1991(B) Prooflike	—	—	—	—	3.00	—
1991B Proof	—	Value: 5.00				

KM# 91 RUPEE
6.0000 g., Copper-Nickel, 26 mm. **Subject:** Tourism Year **Obv:** Asoka lion pedestal above denomination **Rev:** Stylized peacock

Date	Mintage	F	VF	XF	Unc	BU
1991(B)	—	—	0.35	0.75	1.50	—
1991(H)	—	—	0.60	1.25	2.50	—
1991(B) Prooflike	—	—	—	—	3.00	—
1991B Proof	—	Value: 5.00				

KM# 92.1 RUPEE
4.8500 g., Stainless Steel, 25 mm. **Obv:** Asoka lion pedestal **Rev:** Denomination and date, grain ears flank **Edge:** Milled **Note:** Edge sometimes faint, mintmark varieties exist.

Date	Mintage	F	VF	XF	Unc	BU
1992(H)	—	—	0.20	0.30	0.60	—
1992(B)	—	—	0.20	0.30	0.60	—
1993(B)	—	—	0.20	0.30	0.60	—
Note: Two mintmark shapes exist						
1993(C)	—	—	0.20	0.30	0.60	—
1993(H)	—	—	0.20	0.30	0.60	—
1993	—	—	0.20	0.30	0.60	—
1994(B)	—	—	0.15	0.25	0.50	—
Note: Two mintmark shapes exist						
1994(C)	—	—	0.15	0.25	0.50	—
1994(H)	—	—	0.15	0.25	0.50	—
1994	—	—	0.15	0.25	0.50	—
1995(B)	—	—	0.15	0.25	0.50	—
1995(C)	—	—	0.15	0.25	0.50	—
1995(H)	—	—	0.15	0.25	0.50	—
1995	—	—	0.15	0.25	0.50	—
1996(H)	—	—	1.00	1.50	2.50	—

KM# 93 RUPEE
Copper-Nickel **Subject:** Quit India **Obv:** Asoka lion pedestal, denomination below **Rev:** Monument **Edge:** Milled

Date	Mintage	F	VF	XF	Unc	BU
ND(1992)(C)	—	—	1.00	3.00	6.00	—
ND(1992)(H)	—	—	2.00	3.50	8.00	—
ND(1992)(B)	—	—	0.50	1.00	2.00	—

KM# 94 RUPEE
Copper-Nickel **Series:** World Food Day **Obv:** Asoka lion pedestal, denomination below **Rev:** Food items left of grain stalks **Edge:** Milled

Date	Mintage	F	VF	XF	Unc	BU
1992(C)	—	—	1.50	2.50	4.50	—

KM# 95 RUPEE
Copper-Nickel **Subject:** Inter Parliamentary Union Conference **Obv:** Asoka lion pedestal, denomination below **Rev:** Small building and date within wreath below curved building

Date	Mintage	F	VF	XF	Unc	BU
1993(B)	—	—	0.50	1.25	3.00	—

KM# 96.1 RUPEE
Stainless Steel **Subject:** International Year of the Family **Obv:** Asoka lion pedestal, denomination below **Rev:** Family group forms circular design at center **Edge:** Reeded

Date	Mintage	F	VF	XF	Unc	BU
1994(B)	—	—	0.40	0.75	2.00	—
1994	—	—	1.00	1.50	2.50	—

KM# 96.2   RUPEE
Stainless Steel **Subject:** International Year of the Family
Obv: Arms **Rev:** Family inside inner circle **Edge:** Plain

Date	Mintage	F	VF	XF	Unc	BU
1994(B)	—	—	5.00	12.00	15.00	—

KM# 97.1   RUPEE
Stainless Steel **Subject:** Eighth World Tamil Conference
Obv: Asoka lion pedestal, denomination below **Rev:** St.
Thiruvalluvar **Edge:** Milled

Date	Mintage	F	VF	XF	Unc	BU
1995(B)	—	—	0.50	1.00	1.50	—
1995(H)	—	—	0.70	1.25	2.00	—
1995	—	—	0.50	1.00	1.75	—

KM# 97.2   RUPEE
Stainless Steel **Subject:** Eighth World Tamil Conference
Obv: Asoka lion pedestal, denomination below **Rev:** St.
Thiruvalluvar **Edge:** Plain

Date	Mintage	F	VF	XF	Unc	BU
1995(H)	—	—	4.00	7.00	10.00	—
1995	—	—	4.00	7.00	10.00	—

KM# 92.2   RUPEE
4.8500 g., Stainless Steel, 25 mm. **Obv:** Asoka lion pedestal
Rev: Denomination and date, grain ears flank **Edge:** Plain
Note: Mint mark varieties exist.

Date	Mintage	F	VF	XF	Unc	BU
1995(B)	—	—	1.00	1.50	2.50	—
1995(H)	—	—	1.00	1.50	2.50	—
1995	—	—	1.00	1.50	2.50	—
1996(B)	—	—	0.15	0.35	0.60	—
1996(C)	—	—	0.15	0.35	0.60	—
1996(H)	—	—	0.15	0.35	0.60	—
1996	—	—	0.15	0.35	0.60	—
1997(B)	—	—	0.15	0.35	0.60	—
1997(C)	—	—	0.15	0.35	0.60	—
1997(H)	—	—	1.50	2.00	3.00	—
1997(M)	—	—	0.15	0.35	0.50	—
1997	—	—	0.15	0.35	0.50	—
1998(P)	—	—	0.15	0.30	0.45	—
1998(B)	—	—	0.15	0.35	0.50	—
1998(C)	—	—	0.15	0.35	0.50	—
1998(H)	—	—	0.15	0.35	0.50	—
1998(K)	—	—	0.15	0.35	0.50	—
1998	—	—	0.15	0.35	0.50	—
1999(B)	—	—	0.15	0.35	0.50	—
1999(K)	—	—	0.15	0.30	0.45	—
1999(P)	—	—	0.15	0.30	0.45	—
1999	—	—	0.15	0.30	0.45	—
1999(C)	—	—	0.15	0.35	0.50	—
1999(H)	—	—	0.15	0.35	0.50	—
2000(K)	—	—	0.15	0.30	0.45	—
2000(B)	—	—	0.15	0.30	0.45	—
2000(C)	—	—	0.15	0.30	0.45	—
2000(H)	—	—	0.15	0.30	0.45	—
2000	—	—	0.15	0.30	0.45	—

KM# 98   RUPEE
Stainless Steel **Obv:** Asoka lion pedestal, denomination below
Rev: Cellular jail, Port Blair **Note:** Varieties exist.

Date	Mintage	F	VF	XF	Unc	BU
1997(B)	—	—	0.30	0.50	0.80	—
1997(C)	—	—	0.30	0.50	0.80	—
1997(H)	—	—	0.30	0.50	0.80	—
1997	—	—	0.40	0.60	1.00	—

KM# 295.1   RUPEE
4.8500 g., Stainless Steel **Subject:** St. Dnyaneshwar
Obv: Asoka lion pedestal, denomination below **Rev:** Seated
figure **Note:** Asoka column 13.2mm tall.

Date	Mintage	F	VF	XF	Unc	BU
1999(B)	—	—	1.75	3.00	5.00	—
1999(C)	—	—	0.60	0.90	1.50	—
1999(C) Proof	—	Value: 5.00				

KM# 295.2   RUPEE
4.8500 g., Stainless Steel **Subject:** St. Dnyaneshwar
Obv: Asoka lion pedestal, denomination below **Rev:** Seated
figure **Note:** Asoka column 13.8mm tall.

Date	Mintage	F	VF	XF	Unc	BU
1999(B)	—	—	0.40	0.60	1.00	—

KM# 295.3   RUPEE
4.8500 g., Stainless Steel **Subject:** St. Dnyaneshwar
Obv: Asoka lion pedestal, denomination below **Rev:** Seated figure
Note: Asoka column 14.5mm tall.

Date	Mintage	F	VF	XF	Unc	BU
1999	—	—	1.50	2.50	4.00	—

2 RUPEES
2 Rupee Obverses

Type A. Asoka column 15mm tall. 5 fur rows on right
lion. No lion whiskers.

Type B. Asoka column 14mm tall. 3 fur rows on right
lion. 5 lion whiskers.

Type C. Asoka column 13mm tall. 4 fur rows on right
lion.

Type D. Asoka column 13mm tall. 4 fur rows.
Recut chest on central lion.

Type E. Asoka column 13mm tall. No fur rows on
right lion. 2 whiskers on central lion

NOTE: Obverses C and D include both 4.5 x 5mm
and 5 x 5.5mm numeral 2 varieties.

KM# 120   2 RUPEES
Copper-Nickel, 28 mm. **Subject:** IX Asian Games **Obv:** Asoka
lion pedestal, denomination below **Rev:** Sun above logo
Note: Incomplete security edge known.

Date	Mintage	F	VF	XF	Unc	BU
1982(B)	12,720,000	—	0.35	0.50	1.25	—
1982B Proof	Inc. above	Value: 2.50				
1982(C)	Inc. above	—	0.35	0.50	1.25	—

KM# 121.1   2 RUPEES
7.9500 g., Copper-Nickel, 28 mm. **Subject:** National Integration
Rev: Flag on map **Note:** Security edge, small date.

Date	Mintage	F	VF	XF	Unc	BU
1982B Proof	—	Value: 3.50				
1982(C)	—	—	0.30	1.00	2.25	—
	Note: Mintage included in KM120					
1982(B)	—	—	0.30	1.00	1.75	—
	Note: Mintage included in KM120					

KM# 122   2 RUPEES
Copper-Nickel **Subject:** Golden Jubilee of Reserve Bank of
India **Obv:** Asoka lion pedestal, denomination below **Rev:** Lion
in front of tree

Date	Mintage	F	VF	XF	Unc	BU
ND(1985)(B) Proof	—	Value: 100				
	Note: In sets only					

KM# 121.2   2 RUPEES
8.0200 g., Copper-Nickel, 28 mm. **Subject:** National Integration
Rev: Flag on map **Note:** Incomplete security edges known, lg. date.

Date	Mintage	F	VF	XF	Unc	BU
1990(C) Plain edge	—	—	10.00	30.00	50.00	—
1990(H) Reeded edge	—	—	20.00	40.00	80.00	—
1990(C)	—	—	0.40	1.00	2.25	—
1990(H)	—	—	0.80	3.00	5.00	—
1990(B)	—	—	0.40	1.00	2.25	—

KM# 121.3   2 RUPEES
6.0000 g., Copper-Nickel, 26 mm. **Subject:** National Integration
Obv: Type A **Rev:** Flag on map **Edge:** Plain **Note:** Reduced size,
non magnetic.

Date	Mintage	F	VF	XF	Unc	BU
1992(B)	—	—	2.50	4.00	7.00	—
1992(C)	—	—	0.30	0.50	1.00	—
1992(C)	—	—	0.40	1.00	1.50	—
1993(C)	—	—	0.40	1.25	2.00	—
1993(H)	—	—	0.35	0.60	1.25	—
1994(C)	—	—	0.40	1.25	2.00	—
1994(H)	—	—	0.35	0.80	1.50	—
1995(B)	—	—	2.50	4.00	7.00	—
1995(C)	—	—	0.30	0.50	1.00	—
1995(H)	—	—	0.30	0.50	1.00	—
1996(C)	—	—	0.30	0.50	1.00	—
1996(H)	—	—	0.30	0.50	1.00	—
1997(C)	—	—	0.30	0.50	1.00	—
1997(H)	—	—	0.30	0.50	1.00	—
1998(C)	—	—	0.30	0.50	1.00	—
1999(C)	—	—	0.30	0.50	1.00	—
2000(C)	—	—	0.30	0.50	1.00	—
2000(R)	—	—	0.30	0.50	1.00	—

KM# 123   2 RUPEES
Copper-Nickel **Subject:** Tourism Year **Obv:** Asoka lion pedestal
above denomination **Rev:** Stylized design

Date	Mintage	F	VF	XF	Unc	BU
1991 Prooflike	—	—	—	—	8.00	—
1991 Proof	—	Value: 12.00				

KM# 121.4 2 RUPEES
5.0000 g., Copper-Nickel, 26 mm. **Subject:** National Integration **Obv:** Type B **Rev:** Flag on map **Edge:** Plain

Date	Mintage	F	VF	XF	Unc	BU
1992(B)	—	—	0.30	0.50	1.00	—
1993(B)	—	—	0.30	0.50	1.00	—
1994(B)	—	—	0.30	0.50	1.00	—
1994(C)	—	—	0.30	0.50	1.00	—
1994(H)	—	—	2.75	5.00	6.50	—
1994	—	—	2.75	5.00	6.50	—
1995(B)	—	—	0.30	0.50	1.00	—
1995(H)	—	—	3.00	5.50	8.00	—
1995	—	—	0.30	0.50	1.00	—
1996(B)	—	—	2.50	4.00	6.00	—
1996(B-H)	—	—	5.00	10.00	15.00	—
1996	—	—	0.30	0.50	1.00	—
1997(B)	—	—	0.30	0.50	1.00	—
1998	—	—	0.30	0.50	1.00	—
1999(N)	—	—	0.30	0.50	1.00	—

KM# 121.5 2 RUPEES
6.0600 g., Copper-Nickel, 26 mm. **Subject:** National Integration **Obv:** Type C **Rev:** Flag on map **Edge:** Plain **Note:** 11-sided

Date	Mintage	F	VF	XF	Unc	BU
1995(B)	—	—	2.50	4.00	6.00	—
1996(B)	—	—	0.30	0.50	1.00	—
1996(H)	—	—	0.30	0.50	1.00	—
1997(B)	—	—	0.30	0.50	1.00	—
1997(H)	—	—	0.30	0.50	1.00	—
1997(T)	—	—	0.30	0.50	1.00	—
1998(B)	—	—	0.30	0.50	1.00	—
1998(H)	—	—	0.30	0.50	1.00	—
1998(P)	—	—	0.30	0.50	1.00	—
1998(T)	—	—	0.30	0.50	1.00	—
1999(B)	—	—	0.30	0.50	1.00	—
1999(H)	—	—	0.30	0.50	1.00	—
1999(Ld)	—	—	0.30	0.50	1.00	—
1999	—	—	0.30	0.50	1.00	—
1999(C)	—	—	0.30	0.50	1.00	—
2000(B)	—	—	0.30	0.50	1.00	—
2000(C)	—	—	0.30	0.50	1.00	—
2000(H)	—	—	0.30	0.50	1.00	—
2000(R)	—	—	0.30	0.50	1.00	—

KM# A128 2 RUPEES
Copper-Nickel **Subject:** National Land Conservation Week

Date	Mintage	F	VF	XF	Unc	BU
1992(C)	—	—	—	—	—	—

Note: Not released for general circulation

KM# 323 2 RUPEES
5.7500 g., Copper-Nickel, 26.4 mm. **Subject:** National Land Conservation **Obv:** Asoka lion pedestal above denomination **Rev:** Tree above wavy lines **Edge:** Plain

Date	Mintage	F	VF	XF	Unc	BU
1992 (1993)	—	—	—	—	—	—

KM# 124.1 2 RUPEES
Copper-Nickel **Subject:** Small Family Happy Family **Obv:** Type B **Rev:** Family scene

Date	Mintage	F	VF	XF	Unc	BU
1993(B)	—	—	0.50	0.90	1.50	—

KM# 124.2 2 RUPEES
Copper-Nickel **Subject:** Small Family Happy Family **Obv:** Type A **Rev:** Family scene

Date	Mintage	F	VF	XF	Unc	BU
1993(H)	—	—	2.00	3.00	5.00	—

KM# 125.1 2 RUPEES
Copper-Nickel **Series:** World Food Day **Subject:** Bio Diversity **Obv:** Type B **Rev:** Mountains, trees and fish

Date	Mintage	F	VF	XF	Unc	BU
1993(B)	—	—	0.50	0.90	1.50	—

KM# 125.2 2 RUPEES
Copper-Nickel **Subject:** Bio Diversity **Obv:** Type A **Rev:** Mountains, trees and fish

Date	Mintage	F	VF	XF	Unc	BU
1993(H)	—	—	2.00	3.00	5.00	—

KM# 126.1 2 RUPEES
Copper-Nickel **Series:** F.A.O. **Subject:** Water For Life **Obv:** Type A **Rev:** Large teardrop above water

Date	Mintage	F	VF	XF	Unc	BU
1994(B)	—	—	0.60	1.10	2.00	—
1994(C)	—	—	1.00	2.00	4.00	—
1994(H)	—	—	2.00	4.50	11.00	—

KM# 126.2 2 RUPEES
Copper-Nickel **Subject:** Water for Life **Obv:** Type B **Rev:** Large teardrop above water

Date	Mintage	F	VF	XF	Unc	BU
1994(B)	—	20.00	35.00	50.00	75.00	—

KM# 127.1 2 RUPEES
Copper-Nickel **Subject:** Globalizing Indian Agriculture - Agriexpo 95 **Obv:** Type A **Rev:** Steer head within wreath of two stalks of wheat

Date	Mintage	F	VF	XF	Unc	BU
1995(B)	—	—	0.60	1.25	2.00	—
1995(C)	—	—	1.00	3.00	6.00	—

KM# 127.2 2 RUPEES
Copper-Nickel **Subject:** Globalizing Indian Agriculture - Agriexpo 55 **Obv:** Type B **Rev:** Steer head within wreath of two stalks of wheat

Date	Mintage	F	VF	XF	Unc	BU
1995(B)	—	20.00	30.00	50.00	75.00	—

KM# 127.3 2 RUPEES
Copper-Nickel **Obv:** Type C **Rev:** Steer head within wreath of two stalks of wheat

Date	Mintage	F	VF	XF	Unc	BU
1995(B)	—	30.00	50.00	75.00	100	—

KM# 128.1 2 RUPEES
Copper-Nickel **Subject:** Eighth World Tamil Conference **Obv:** Type C, Asoka column 13mm tall **Rev:** St. Thiruvalluvar

Date	Mintage	F	VF	XF	Unc	BU
1995(B)	—	—	0.60	1.00	1.75	—

KM# 128.2 2 RUPEES
Copper-Nickel **Subject:** 8th World Tamil Conference **Obv:** Type B **Rev:** St. Thiruvalluvar

Date	Mintage	F	VF	XF	Unc	BU
1995(B)	—	—	1.00	2.00	3.00	—

KM# 129.1 2 RUPEES
Copper-Nickel **Subject:** Sardar Vallabhbhai Patel **Obv:** Type A **Rev:** Bust right

Date	Mintage	F	VF	XF	Unc	BU
1996(C)	—	—	2.50	4.00	7.00	—

KM# 129.2 2 RUPEES
Copper-Nickel **Subject:** Sardar Vallabhbhai Patel **Obv:** Type B **Rev:** Bust right

Date	Mintage	F	VF	XF	Unc	BU
1996	—	—	1.00	1.50	3.00	—

KM# 129.3 2 RUPEES
Copper-Nickel **Subject:** Sardar Vallabhbhai Patel **Obv:** Type C **Rev:** Bust right

Date	Mintage	F	VF	XF	Unc	BU
1996(B)	—	—	2.00	3.00	5.00	—
1996(H)	—	—	0.40	0.70	1.25	—
1996M Proof	—	Value: 8.00				

KM# 129.4 2 RUPEES
Copper-Nickel **Subject:** Sardar Vallabhbhai Patel **Obv:** Type D **Rev:** Bust right

Date	Mintage	F	VF	XF	Unc	BU
1996(B)	—	—	0.40	0.70	1.25	—
1996(C)	—	—	0.30	0.60	1.00	—

KM# 129.5 2 RUPEES
Copper-Nickel **Subject:** Sardar Vallabhbhai Patel **Obv:** Type E **Rev:** Bust right

Date	Mintage	F	VF	XF	Unc	BU
1996(B)	—	30.00	40.00	55.00	80.00	—
1996(H)	—	30.00	40.00	55.00	80.00	—

KM# 130.1 2 RUPEES
6.0000 g., Copper-Nickel **Subject:** Subhas Chandra Bose **Obv:** Type C **Rev:** Bust left

Date	Mintage	F	VF	XF	Unc	BU
1996(C)	—	—	10.00	12.00	15.00	—
1997(B)	—	—	0.60	0.90	1.25	—
1997(C)	—	—	0.60	0.90	1.25	—
1997(H)	—	—	1.50	2.50	4.00	—
1997(C) Proof	—	Value: 3.25				

KM# 130.2 2 RUPEES
6.0000 g., Copper-Nickel **Subject:** Subhas Chandra Bose **Obv:** Type B **Rev:** Bust left

Date	Mintage	F	VF	XF	Unc	BU
1997	—	—	1.00	2.00	3.50	—
1997(H)	—	—	0.60	0.90	1.25	—

KM# 131.1 2 RUPEES
6.0000 g., Copper-Nickel **Subject:** Sri Aurobindo **Obv:** Type C **Rev:** Head 3/4 facing

Date	Mintage	F	VF	XF	Unc	BU
1998(B)	—	—	0.60	0.90	1.50	—
1998	—	—	1.00	1.50	3.00	—
1998(C)	—	—	1.00	1.50	3.00	—
1998M Proof	—	Value: 3.50				

KM# 131.3 2 RUPEES
Copper-Nickel **Subject:** Sri Aurobindo **Obv:** Type A **Rev:** Bust facing

Date	Mintage	F	VF	XF	Unc	BU
1998(C)	—	—	—	—	—	5.00

KM# 121.3a   2 RUPEES
Nickel magnetic   Obv: Type A   Edge: Plain

Date	Mintage	F	VF	XF	Unc	BU
1998(C)	—	—	30.00	60.00	100	—

KM# 121.6   2 RUPEES
Copper-Nickel, 26 mm.   Subject: National Integration   Obv: Type D   Rev: Flag on map   Edge: Plain

Date	Mintage	F	VF	XF	Unc	BU
1998(B)	—	—	0.30	0.50	1.00	—
1998(H)	—	—	0.30	0.50	1.00	—
1999(B)	—	—	0.75	1.00	1.50	—
2000(B)	—	—	0.75	1.00	1.50	—

KM# 296.5   2 RUPEES
6.0000 g., Copper-Nickel   Subject: Deshbandhu Chittaranjan Das   Obv: Type C   Rev: Head facing   Note: 3-5mm, edge flat.

Date	Mintage	F	VF	XF	Unc	BU
1998	—	—	2.00	3.00	5.00	—
1998(C)	—	—	3.00	4.00	6.00	—

KM# 131.2   2 RUPEES
Copper-Nickel   Subject: Sri Aurobindo   Obv: Type D   Rev: Head 3/4 facing

Date	Mintage	F	VF	XF	Unc	BU
1998(B)	—	—	3.00	5.00	8.00	—

KM# 296.1   2 RUPEES
6.0000 g., Copper-Nickel   Subject: Deshbandhu Chittaranjan Das   Obv: Type A   Rev: Head facing

Date	Mintage	F	VF	XF	Unc	BU
1998(C)	—	—	10.00	15.00	25.00	—

KM# 296.2   2 RUPEES
Copper-Nickel   Subject: Deshbandhu Chittaranjan Das   Obv: Type B   Rev: Head facing

Date	Mintage	F	VF	XF	Unc	BU
1998	—	—	3.00	4.00	6.00	—

KM# 296.3   2 RUPEES
Copper-Nickel   Subject: Deshbandhu Chittaranjan Das   Obv: Type C   Rev: Head facing   Note: 7mm, edge flat.

Date	Mintage	F	VF	XF	Unc	BU
1998(C)	—	—	4.00	6.00	8.00	—
1998(C) Proof	—	—	—	—	—	—

KM# 296.4   2 RUPEES
6.0000 g., Copper-Nickel   Subject: Deshbandhu Chittaranjan Das   Obv: Type C   Rev: Head facing   Note: 5-6mm, edge flat.

Date	Mintage	F	VF	XF	Unc	BU
1998(C)	—	—	6.00	8.00	12.00	—

KM# 296.6   2 RUPEES
Copper-Nickel   Subject: Deshbandhu Chittaranjan Das   Obv: Type D   Rev: Head facing   Note: 3-5mm, edge flat.

Date	Mintage	F	VF	XF	Unc	BU
1998(C)	—	—	0.75	1.25	2.00	—

KM# 290   2 RUPEES
6.0000 g., Copper-Nickel   Subject: Chhatrapati Shivaji   Obv: Type C   Rev: Turbaned bust right

Date	Mintage	F	VF	XF	Unc	BU
1999(B)	—	—	0.75	1.25	2.00	—
1999	—	—	0.75	1.25	2.00	—
1999M Proof	—	Value: 3.50				
1999(C)	—	—	0.75	1.25	2.00	—
1999(H)	—	—	1.00	1.75	3.00	—

KM# 291   2 RUPEES
6.0000 g., Copper-Nickel   Subject: Supreme Court: 50 Years   Obv: Type C   Rev: Wheel above asoka lion pedestal   Edge: Plain

Date	Mintage	F	VF	XF	Unc	BU
2000(B)	—	—	0.75	1.25	2.00	—
2000(C)	—	—	0.75	1.25	2.00	—

KM# 150   5 RUPEES
Copper-Nickel   Subject: Death of Indira Gandi - statesperson, 1917-1984   Obv: Asoka lion pedestal, denomination below   Rev: Bust right

Date	Mintage	F	VF	XF	Unc	BU
ND(1985)(B)	59,288,000	—	0.75	1.50	3.00	—
ND(1985)B Proof	Inc. above	Value: 27.50				
ND(1985)(H)	Inc. above	—	3.50	6.00	15.00	—

KM# 151   5 RUPEES
Copper-Nickel   Subject: 100th Anniversary - Nehru's Birth   Obv: Asoka lion pedestal, denomination below   Rev: Head right

Date	Mintage	F	VF	XF	Unc	BU
1989(B)	—	—	1.00	2.00	3.00	—
Note: Short rim teeth.						
1989(B)	—	—	2.00	3.00	4.50	—
Note: Long rim teeth.						
1989B Proof	—	Value: 25.00				
1989(H)	—	—	3.50	6.00	15.00	—

KM# 152   5 RUPEES
Copper-Nickel   Subject: Commonwealth Parliamentary Conference   Obv: Asoka lion pedestal, denomination below   Rev: Building

Date	Mintage	F	VF	XF	Unc	BU
1991(B) Prooflike	—	—	—	—	10.00	—
1991B Proof	—	Value: 20.00				

KM# 153   5 RUPEES
Copper-Nickel   Subject: Tourism Year   Obv: Asoka lion pedestal, denomination below   Rev: Stylized design

Date	Mintage	F	VF	XF	Unc	BU
1991(B) Prooflike	—	—	—	—	10.00	—
1991B Proof	—	Value: 20.00				

KM# 154.2   5 RUPEES
8.9100 g., Copper-Nickel, 23 mm.   Obv: Asoka lion pedestal   Rev: Denomination flanked by flowers   Edge: Milled

Date	Mintage	F	VF	XF	Unc	BU
1992(C)	—	—	8.00	10.00	15.00	—
1992(C) Milled edge	—	—	8.00	10.00	15.00	—
1992(H)	—	—	8.00	10.00	15.00	—
1993(B)	—	—	8.00	10.00	15.00	—
1993(C)	—	—	8.00	10.00	15.00	—
1994(B)	—	—	8.00	10.00	15.00	—
1994(C)	—	—	8.00	10.00	15.00	—
1994(H)	—	—	8.00	10.00	15.00	—
1995(B)	—	—	8.00	10.00	15.00	—
1995(C)	—	—	8.00	10.00	15.00	—
1995(H)	—	—	8.00	10.00	15.00	—
1996(B)	—	—	8.00	10.00	15.00	—
1996(C)	—	—	8.00	10.00	15.00	—
1996(H)	—	—	8.00	10.00	15.00	—
1997(B)	—	—	8.00	10.00	15.00	—
1997(C)	—	—	8.00	10.00	15.00	—
1998(C)	—	—	8.00	10.00	15.00	—
1998(B)	—	—	8.00	10.00	15.00	—
1998(H)	—	—	8.00	10.00	15.00	—
1999(B)	—	—	8.00	10.00	15.00	—
1999(C)	—	—	8.00	10.00	15.00	—
1999(H)	—	—	8.00	10.00	15.00	—
2000(C)	—	—	8.00	10.00	15.00	—
2000(B)	—	—	8.00	10.00	15.00	—
2000(H)	—	—	8.00	10.00	15.00	—

KM# 154.1   5 RUPEES
9.0000 g., Copper-Nickel, 23.10 mm.   Obv: Asoka lion pedestal   Rev: Denomination flanked by flowers   Edge: Security   Note: (C) - Calcutta mint has issued 2 distinctly different security edge varieties every year 1992-2003 with large dots and thick center line, w/small dots and narrow center line.

Date	Mintage	F	VF	XF	Unc	BU
1992(B)	—	—	0.20	0.75	1.50	—
1992(C)	—	—	0.20	0.75	1.50	—
1992(H)	—	—	0.20	0.75	1.50	—
1993(B)	—	—	0.20	0.75	1.50	—
1993(C)	—	—	0.20	0.75	1.50	—
1994(B)	—	—	0.20	0.75	1.50	—
1994(C)	—	—	0.20	0.75	1.50	—
1994(H)	—	—	0.20	0.75	1.50	—
1995(B)	—	—	0.20	0.75	1.50	—
1995(C)	—	—	0.20	0.75	1.50	—
1995(H)	—	—	0.20	0.75	1.50	—
1995	—	—	0.20	0.75	1.50	—
1996(B)	—	—	0.20	0.50	1.00	—
1996(C)	—	—	0.20	0.50	1.00	—
1996(H)	—	—	0.20	0.50	1.00	—
1996	—	—	0.20	0.50	1.00	—
1997(B)	—	—	0.20	0.50	1.00	—
1997(C)	—	—	0.20	0.50	1.00	—
1997(H)	—	—	0.20	0.50	1.00	—
1997	—	—	0.20	0.50	1.00	—
1998(B)	—	—	0.20	0.50	1.00	—
1998(C)	—	—	0.20	0.50	1.00	—
1998(H)	—	—	0.25	0.50	1.00	—
1998	—	—	0.25	0.50	1.00	—
1999(B)	—	—	0.50	0.25	1.00	—
1999M	—	—	0.25	0.50	1.00	—
1999(H)	—	—	0.25	0.50	1.00	—
1999	—	—	0.25	0.50	1.00	—
1999(R)	—	—	0.25	0.50	1.00	—
2000(B)	—	—	0.50	0.25	1.00	—
2000(C)	—	—	0.25	0.50	1.00	—
2000(H)	—	—	0.50	1.00	2.00	—
2000	—	—	0.30	0.60	1.50	—
2000(R)	—	—	0.25	0.50	1.00	—

KM# 155.1   5 RUPEES
Copper-Nickel, 23 mm.   Subject: World of Work   Obv: Asoka lion pedestal, denomination below   Rev: Denomination within broken dentil circle, wreath surrounds   Edge: Security

Date	Mintage	F	VF	XF	Unc	BU
ND(1994)(B)	—	—	0.75	1.00	1.75	—
ND(1994)B Proof	—	Value: 5.00				
ND(1994)(H)	—	—	1.50	2.25	4.00	—
ND(1994)	—	—	1.00	1.50	3.00	—

KM# 155.2   5 RUPEES
Copper-Nickel, 23 mm.   Subject: World of Work   Obv: Asoka lion pedestal, denomination below   Rev: Denomination within broken dentil circle, wreath surrounds   Edge: Milled

Date	Mintage	F	VF	XF	Unc	BU
1994(B)	—	—	8.00	10.00	15.00	—
1994(H)	—	—	8.00	10.00	15.00	—

KM# 157   5 RUPEES
Copper-Nickel, 23 mm.   Series: 50th Anniversary - F.A.O.   Obv: Asoka lion pedestal, denomination below   Rev: Hand clutching stalks of wheat   Edge: Milled or security

Date	Mintage	F	VF	XF	Unc	BU
1995(B)	—	—	0.75	1.00	1.75	—
1995(H)	—	—	1.50	3.00	5.00	—
1995	—	—	1.00	1.50	3.00	—

KM# 158   5 RUPEES
Copper-Nickel, 23 mm.   **Subject:** Eighth World Tamil
Conference **Obv:** Asoka lion pedestal, denomination below
Rev: St. Thiruvalluvar **Edge:** Milled or security

Date	Mintage	F	VF	XF	Unc	BU
1995(B)	—	—	0.75	1.00	1.75	—

KM# 156.1   5 RUPEES
Copper-Nickel, 23 mm.   **Series:** 50 Years - United Nations
Obv: Asoka lion pedestal, denomination below **Rev:** Date above
UN logo **Edge:** Security or plain **Note:** Tall and short letters

Date	Mintage	F	VF	XF	Unc	BU
1995(B)	—	—	0.75	1.00	1.75	—
1995	—	—	1.00	1.50	3.00	—

KM# 156.2   5 RUPEES
Copper-Nickel, 23 mm.   **Subject:** 50 Years United Nations
Obv: Asoka lion pedestal similar to 2 Rupees, KM#121.3
Rev: Date above UN logo

Date	Mintage	F	VF	XF	Unc	BU
1995(B)	—	—	10.00	—	—	—

KM# 160   5 RUPEES
Copper-Nickel, 23 mm.   **Subject:** 2nd International Crop Science
Conference **Obv:** Asoka lion pedestal, denomination below
Rev: Plants on globe, spray below, braid above **Edge:** Security
Note: This conference was never held.

Date	Mintage	F	VF	XF	Unc	BU
1996(C)	11,000	—	20.00	30.00	40.00	—

KM# 159   5 RUPEES
Copper-Nickel, 23 mm.   **Subject:** Mother's Health is Child's
Health **Edge:** Milled or security

Date	Mintage	F	VF	XF	Unc	BU
1996(B)	—	—	0.75	1.00	1.50	—
1996(H)	—	—	0.75	1.00	1.50	—
1996	—	—	1.00	1.50	2.25	—

KM# 154.4   5 RUPEES
Copper-Nickel, 23 mm.   **Obv:** Asoka lion pedestal as seen on 2
Rupees, KM#121.5 **Rev:** Denomination flanked by flowers

Date	Mintage	F	VF	XF	Unc	BU
1998(B)	—	—	0.25	0.50	1.00	—
1999(B)	—	—	0.25	0.50	1.00	—
2000(B)	—	—	0.25	0.50	1.00	—

KM# 154.3   5 RUPEES
Copper-Nickel, 23 mm.   **Obv:** Asoka lion pedestal
Rev: Denomination flanked by flowers **Edge:** Plain

Date	Mintage	F	VF	XF	Unc	BU
1998(H)	—	—	5.00	10.00	15.00	—
1999(H)	—	—	5.00	10.00	15.00	—

KM# 185   10 RUPEES
15.0000 g., 0.8000 Silver 0.3858 oz. ASW   **Subject:** Centennial -
Mahatma Gandhi's Birth **Obv:** Asoka lion pedestal, denomination
below **Rev:** Head left **Note:** Struck during 1969 and 1970.

Date	Mintage	F	VF	XF	Unc	BU
ND(1969)(B)	3,160,000	—	—	7.00	10.00	—
ND(1969)B Proof	9,147	Value: 12.00				
ND(1969)(C)	100,000	—	—	8.00	12.00	—

KM# 186   10 RUPEES
15.0000 g., 0.8000 Silver 0.3858 oz. ASW   **Series:** F.A.O.
Obv: Asoka lion pedestal **Rev:** Floating lotus flower below sun

Date	Mintage	F	VF	XF	Unc	BU
1970(B)	300,000	—	—	7.00	10.00	—
1970B Proof	3,046	Value: 10.00				
1970(C)	100,000	—	—	8.00	12.00	—
1971(B)	—	—	—	8.00	12.00	—
1971B Proof	1,594	Value: 12.00				

KM# 187.1   10 RUPEES
22.5000 g., 0.5000 Silver 0.3617 oz. ASW   **Subject:** 25th
Anniversary of Independence **Obv:** Asoka lion pedestal
Rev: Figures holding flag, building in background **Note:** Inner
flag circle complete.

Date	Mintage	F	VF	XF	Unc	BU
ND(1972)(B)	1,000,000	—	—	—	8.00	—
ND(1972)B Proof	7,895	Value: 10.00				

KM# 187.2   10 RUPEES
22.5000 g., 0.5000 Silver 0.3617 oz. ASW   **Subject:** 25th
Anniversary of Independence **Obv:** Aslka lion pedestal
Rev: Figures holding flag, building in background **Note:** Rim
thinner, inner flag circle missing on Calcutta issues.

Date	Mintage	F	VF	XF	Unc	BU
ND(1972)(C)	—	—	—	—	7.00	—

KM# 188   10 RUPEES
22.3000 g., 0.5000 Silver 0.3585 oz. ASW   **Series:** F.A.O.
Obv: Asoka lion pedestal **Rev:** Inscription on shield within grain
stalks

Date	Mintage	F	VF	XF	Unc	BU
1973(B)	64,000	—	—	—	8.00	—
1973B Proof	15,000	Value: 10.00				

KM# 189   10 RUPEES
Copper-Nickel   **Series:** F.A.O. **Obv:** Asoka lion pedestal
Rev: Family within triangle, grain ears flank

Date	Mintage	F	VF	XF	Unc	BU
1974(B)	65,000	—	—	2.00	4.50	—
1974B Proof	12,000	Value: 7.00				

KM# 190   10 RUPEES
Copper-Nickel   **Series:** F.A.O. **Subject:** Women's Year
Obv: Asoka lion pedestal **Rev:** Bust at left looking right,
grain ear at right

Date	Mintage	F	VF	XF	Unc	BU
1975(B)	49,000	—	—	2.00	4.50	—
1975B Proof	2,531	Value: 8.50				

KM# 191   10 RUPEES
Copper-Nickel   **Series:** F.A.O. **Subject:** Food and Work For All
Obv: Asoka lion pedestal **Rev:** Figure on tractor, utility pole and
buildings in background

Date	Mintage	F	VF	XF	Unc	BU
1976(B)	49,000	—	—	2.00	4.50	—
1976B Proof	3,400	Value: 8.50				

KM# 192   10 RUPEES
Copper-Nickel   **Series:** F.A.O. **Subject:** Save For Development
Obv: Asoka lion pedestal **Rev:** Symbols of development

Date	Mintage	F	VF	XF	Unc	BU
1977(B)	20,000	—	—	2.00	4.50	—
1977B Proof	5,969	Value: 8.50				

KM# 193   10 RUPEES
Copper-Nickel   **Series:** F.A.O. **Subject:** Food and Shelter For
All **Obv:** Asoka lion pedestal **Rev:** Grain sprig, house and road
within circle

Date	Mintage	F	VF	XF	Unc	BU
1978(B)	25,000	—	—	2.00	4.50	—
1978B Proof	—	Value: 8.50				

KM# 194   10 RUPEES
Copper-Nickel   **Series:** International Year of the Child
Obv: Asoka lion pedestal, denomination below **Rev:** Logo on
square within circle, wreath surrounds

Date	Mintage	F	VF	XF	Unc	BU
1979(B)	—	—	—	2.50	5.00	—
1979B Proof	—	Value: 9.50				

KM# 195   10 RUPEES
Copper-Nickel   **Subject:** Rural Women's Advancement
Obv: Asoka lion pedestal, denomination below **Rev:** Woman
grinding wheat

Date	Mintage	F	VF	XF	Unc	BU
1980(B)	—	—	—	2.50	5.00	—
1980B Proof	—	Value: 9.50				

KM# 196   10 RUPEES
Copper-Nickel   **Series:** World Food Day **Obv:** Asoka lion
pedestal **Rev:** Man and woman, man carrying sheaf

Date	Mintage	F	VF	XF	Unc	BU
1981(B)	—	—	—	2.50	5.00	—
1981B Proof	—	Value: 9.50				

KM# 197   10 RUPEES
Copper-Nickel   **Subject:** IX Asian Games

Date	Mintage	F	VF	XF	Unc	BU
1982(B)	—	—	—	2.50	5.00	—
1982B Proof	—	Value: 9.50				

KM# 198   10 RUPEES
Copper-Nickel   **Subject:** National Integration **Obv:** Asoka lion
pedestal **Rev:** Flag on map

Date	Mintage	F	VF	XF	Unc	BU
1982(B)	—	—	—	—	6.00	—
1982B Proof	—	Value: 10.00				

KM# 199   10 RUPEES
Copper-Nickel   **Subject:** Golden Jubilee - Reserve Bank of India
Obv: Asoka lion pedestal **Rev:** Lion in front of tree

Date	Mintage	F	VF	XF	Unc	BU
ND(1985)(B)	—	—	—	—	75.00	—
ND(1985)B Proof	—	Value: 85.00				
Note: In sets only						

KM# 200   10 RUPEES
Copper-Nickel   **Subject:** Youth Year **Obv:** Small asoka pedestal
above denomination **Rev:** Three outlined profiles between dove
and laurel branch

Date	Mintage	F	VF	XF	Unc	BU
1985(C)	—	—	—	—	10.00	—
1985(C) Proof	—	Value: 30.00				

KM# 201   10 RUPEES
Copper-Nickel   **Subject:** Commonwealth Parliamentary
Conference **Obv:** Asoka lion pedestal above denomination
Rev: Building

Date	Mintage	F	VF	XF	Unc	BU
1991B Proof	—	Value: 20.00				
1991(B) Prooflike	—	—	—	—	10.00	—

KM# 202   10 RUPEES
Copper-Nickel   **Subject:** India **Obv:** Asoka lion pedestal above
denomination **Rev:** Monument

Date	Mintage	F	VF	XF	Unc	BU
1992B Proof	—	Value: 10.00				

KM# 203   10 RUPEES
Copper-Nickel   **Subject:** 100th Anniversary - Birth of Patel
Obv: Type A **Rev:** Head right

Date	Mintage	F	VF	XF	Unc	BU
1996(B)	—	—	—	—	8.00	—
1996M Proof	—	Value: 12.00				

KM# 204   10 RUPEES
12.5000 g., Copper-Nickel, 31 mm.   **Subject:** Subhas Chandra
Bose **Obv:** Type C **Rev:** Bust left

Date	Mintage	F	VF	XF	Unc	BU
1997(C)	—	—	—	—	8.00	—
1997(C) Proof	—	Value: 12.00				

KM# 205   10 RUPEES
12.5000 g., Copper-Nickel, 31 mm.   **Subject:** Sri Aurobindo
Obv: Type C **Rev:** Head 3/4 facing **Edge:** Reeded

Date	Mintage	F	VF	XF	Unc	BU
1998(B)	—	—	—	—	8.00	—
1998M Proof	—	Value: 12.00				

KM# 297   10 RUPEES
12.5000 g., Copper-Nickel, 31 mm.   **Subject:** Deshbandhu
Chittaranjan Das **Obv:** Asoka lion pedestal above denomination
Rev: Bust facing **Edge:** Reeded

Date	Mintage	F	VF	XF	Unc	BU
1998(C)	—	—	—	—	—	7.50
1998(C) Proof	—	Value: 12.00				

KM# 240   20 RUPEES
30.0000 g., 0.5000 Silver 0.4822 oz. ASW   **Series:** F.A.O.
Obv: Asoka lion pedestal, denomination below **Rev:** Inscription
on shield, grain stalks flank

Date	Mintage	F	VF	XF	Unc	BU
1973(B)	64,000	—	—	—	8.50	—
1973B Proof	12,000	Value: 12.50				

KM# 241   20 RUPEES
Copper-Nickel **Subject:** Death of Indira Gandhi - statesperson,
1917-1984 **Rev:** Head right

Date	Mintage	F	VF	XF	Unc	BU
ND(1985)(B)	—	—	—	—	12.50	—
ND(1985)B Proof	—	Value: 50.00				

KM# 242   20 RUPEES
Copper-Nickel **Series:** F.A.O. **Subject:** Fisheries **Obv:** Asoka
lion pedestal, denomination below **Rev:** People with fishing nets

Date	Mintage	F	VF	XF	Unc	BU
1986(B)	—	—	—	—	12.00	—
1986B Proof	—	Value: 22.00				

KM# 243   20 RUPEES
Copper-Nickel **Series:** F.A.O. **Subject:** Small Farmers
Obv: Asoka lion pedestal, denomination below **Rev:** Farmers
planting

Date	Mintage	F	VF	XF	Unc	BU
1987(B)	—	—	—	—	12.00	—
1987B Proof	—	Value: 22.00				

KM# 244   20 RUPEES
Copper-Nickel **Subject:** 100th Anniversary of Nehru's Birth
Obv: Asoka lion pedestal, denomination below **Rev:** Head right

Date	Mintage	F	VF	XF	Unc	BU
1989(B)	—	—	—	—	10.00	—
1989B Proof	—	Value: 20.00				

KM# 255   50 RUPEES
34.7000 g., 0.5000 Silver 0.5578 oz. ASW **Series:** F.A.O.
Obv: Asoka lion pedestal, denomination below **Rev:** Family
within triangle, grain ears flank

Date	Mintage	F	VF	XF	Unc	BU
1974(B)	82,000	—	—	—	12.00	—
1974B Proof	13,000	Value: 14.00				

KM# 256   50 RUPEES
34.7000 g., 0.5000 Silver 0.5578 oz. ASW **Series:** F.A.O.
Subject: Women's Year **Obv:** Asoka lion pedestal, denomination
below **Rev:** Bust at left looking right, grain sprig at right

Date	Mintage	F	VF	XF	Unc	BU
1975(B)	65,000	—	—	—	14.00	—
1975B Proof	2,691	Value: 22.50				

KM# 257   50 RUPEES
34.7000 g., 0.5000 Silver 0.5578 oz. ASW **Series:** F.A.O.
Subject: Food and Work For All **Obv:** Asoka lion pedestal,
denomination below **Rev:** Figure on tractor, utility pole and
buildings in background

Date	Mintage	F	VF	XF	Unc	BU
1976(B)	42,000	—	—	—	14.00	—
1976B Proof	3,385	Value: 22.50				

KM# 258   50 RUPEES
34.7000 g., 0.5000 Silver 0.5578 oz. ASW **Series:** F.A.O.
Subject: Save For Development **Obv:** Asoka lion pedestal,
denomination below **Rev:** Symbols of development

Date	Mintage	F	VF	XF	Unc	BU
1977(B)	26,000	—	—	—	14.00	—
1977B Proof	2,544	Value: 22.50				

KM# 259   50 RUPEES
34.7000 g., 0.5000 Silver 0.5578 oz. ASW **Series:** F.A.O.
Subject: Food and Shelter For All **Obv:** Asoka lion pedestal,
denomination below **Rev:** Grain stalk, house and road within circle

Date	Mintage	F	VF	XF	Unc	BU
1978(B)	25,000	—	—	—	14.00	—
1978B Proof	—	Value: 22.50				

KM# 260   50 RUPEES
34.7000 g., 0.5000 Silver 0.5578 oz. ASW **Series:** International
Year of the Child **Obv:** Asoka lion pedestal, denomination below
Rev: Emblem on square within circle, wreath surrounds

Date	Mintage	F	VF	XF	Unc	BU
1979(B)	—	—	—	—	14.00	—
1979B Proof	—	Value: 22.50				

KM# 261   50 RUPEES
Copper-Nickel **Subject:** India **Obv:** Asoka lion pedestal,
denomination below **Rev:** Monument

Date	Mintage	F	VF	XF	Unc	BU
1992(B)	—	—	—	—	12.50	—
1992(B) Proof	—	Value: 22.50				

KM# 262   50 RUPEES
Copper-Nickel **Subject:** International Labor Organizations
Obv: Asoka lion pedestal, denomination below **Rev:**
Denomination within broken dentil circle, wreath surrounds

Date	Mintage	F	VF	XF	Unc	BU
ND(1994)	—	—	—	—	15.00	—
ND(1994) Proof	—	Value: 22.50				

KM# 263   50 RUPEES
Copper-Nickel **Subject:** 100th Anniversary - Birth of Patel
Obv: Type A **Rev:** Head right

Date	Mintage	F	VF	XF	Unc	BU
1996(B)	—	—	—	—	15.00	—
1996M Proof	—	Value: 30.00				

KM# 264   50 RUPEES
30.0000 g., Copper-Nickel, 39 mm. **Subject:** Subhas Chandra
Bose **Obv:** Type C **Rev:** Bust left

Date	Mintage	F	VF	XF	Unc	BU
1997(C)	—	—	—	—	15.00	—
1997(C) Proof	—	Value: 45.00				

KM# 265 50 RUPEES
22.5000 g., 0.5000 Silver 0.3617 oz. ASW **Subject:** 50th Anniversary of Independence **Obv:** Small Asoka lion pedestal above large denomination **Rev:** Line of people

Date	Mintage	F	VF	XF	Unc	BU
1997(B)	—	—	—	—	35.00	—
1997M Proof	—	Value: 60.00				

KM# 266 50 RUPEES
30.0000 g., Copper-Nickel, 39 mm. **Subject:** Sri Aurobindo **Obv:** Type C **Rev:** Head 3/4 facing

Date	Mintage	F	VF	XF	Unc	BU
1998(B)	—	—	—	—	15.00	—
1998M Proof	—	Value: 30.00				

KM# 298 50 RUPEES
30.0000 g., Copper-Nickel, 39 mm. **Subject:** Deshbandhu Chittaranjan Das **Obv:** Type C **Rev:** Bust facing **Edge:** Reeded

Date	Mintage	F	VF	XF	Unc	BU
1998(C)	—	—	—	—	15.00	—
1998(C) Proof	—	Value: 30.00				

KM# 300 50 RUPEES
30.0000 g., Copper-Nickel, 39 mm. **Subject:** Chhatrapati Shivaji **Obv:** Asoka lion pedestal above denomination **Rev:** Turbaned bust right **Edge:** Reeded

Date	Mintage	F	VF	XF	Unc	BU
1999(B)	—	—	—	—	16.50	—
1999M Proof	—	Value: 30.00				

KM# 293 50 RUPEES
22.5000 g., 0.5000 Silver 0.3617 oz. ASW, 39 mm. **Subject:** Supreme Court - 50 Years **Obv:** Type C **Rev:** Wheel above asoka lion pedestal **Edge:** Reeded

Date	Mintage	F	VF	XF	Unc	BU
2000(C)	—	—	—	—	15.00	—
2000(C) Proof	—	Value: 30.00				

KM# 275 100 RUPEES
35.0000 g., 0.5000 Silver 0.5626 oz. ASW **Subject:** Rural Women's Advancement **Obv:** Asoka lion pedestal above denomination **Rev:** Woman grinding wheat

Date	Mintage	F	VF	XF	Unc	BU
1980(B)	21,000	—	—	—	18.50	—
1980B Proof	5,811	Value: 27.50				

KM# 276 100 RUPEES
35.0000 g., 0.5000 Silver 0.5626 oz. ASW **Series:** World Food Day

Date	Mintage	F	VF	XF	Unc	BU
1981(B)	22,000	—	—	—	18.50	—
1981B Proof	2,950	Value: 28.50				

KM# 277 100 RUPEES
29.1600 g., 0.9250 Silver 0.8672 oz. ASW **Series:** International Year of the Child **Obv:** Asoka lion pedestal, denomination below **Rev:** Native musicians and dancer

Date	Mintage	F	VF	XF	Unc	BU
1981B Proof	—	Value: 25.00				

KM# 278 100 RUPEES
35.0000 g., 0.5000 Silver 0.5626 oz. ASW **Subject:** IX Asian Games

Date	Mintage	F	VF	XF	Unc	BU
1982(B)	—	—	—	—	17.50	—
1982B Proof	—	Value: 27.50				

KM# 279 100 RUPEES
35.0000 g., 0.5000 Silver 0.5626 oz. ASW **Subject:** National Integration **Obv:** Asoka lion pedestal above denomination **Rev:** Flag on map

Date	Mintage	F	VF	XF	Unc	BU
1982(B)	—	—	—	—	25.00	—
1982B Proof	—	Value: 35.00				

KM# 280 100 RUPEES
35.0000 g., 0.5000 Silver 0.5626 oz. ASW **Subject:** Golden Jubilee - Reserve Bank of India

Date	Mintage	F	VF	XF	Unc	BU
1985(B)	—	—	—	—	75.00	—
1985B Proof	—	Value: 85.00				

KM# 281 100 RUPEES
35.0000 g., 0.5000 Silver 0.5626 oz. ASW **Subject:** Death of Indira Gandhi - statesperson, 1917-1984 **Obv:** Asoka lion pedestal above denomination **Rev:** Bust right

Date	Mintage	F	VF	XF	Unc	BU
ND(1985)(B)	—	—	—	—	30.00	—
ND(1985)B Proof	—	Value: 70.00				

KM# 282 100 RUPEES
35.0000 g., 0.5000 Silver 0.5626 oz. ASW **Subject:** Youth Year **Obv:** Small Asoka lion pedestal, denomination below **Rev:** Three outlined profiles between dove and laurel branch

Date	Mintage	F	VF	XF	Unc	BU
1985(C)	16,000	—	—	—	30.00	—
1985(C) Proof	6,267	Value: 50.00				

KM# 283 100 RUPEES
35.0000 g., 0.5000 Silver 0.5626 oz. ASW **Series:** F.A.O. **Subject:** Fisheries **Obv:** Asoka lion pedestal, denomination below **Rev:** People with fishing nets

Date	Mintage	F	VF	XF	Unc	BU
1986(B)	—	—	—	—	30.00	—
1986B Proof	—	Value: 50.00				

KM# 284 100 RUPEES
35.0000 g., 0.5000 Silver 0.5626 oz. ASW **Series:** F.A.O. **Subject:** Small Farmers **Obv:** Asoka lion pedestal, denomination below **Rev:** Farmers planting

Date	Mintage	F	VF	XF	Unc	BU
1987(B)	—	—	—	—	30.00	—
1987B Proof	—	Value: 50.00				

KM# 285 100 RUPEES
35.0000 g., 0.5000 Silver 0.5626 oz. ASW **Subject:** 100th Anniversary of Nehru's Birth **Obv:** Asoka lion pedestal, denomination below **Rev:** Head right

Date	Mintage	F	VF	XF	Unc	BU
1989(B)	—	—	—	—	30.00	—
1989B Proof	—	Value: 50.00				

KM# 286 100 RUPEES
35.0000 g., 0.5000 Silver 0.5626 oz. ASW **Subject:** India **Obv:** Asoka lion pedestal, denomination below **Rev:** Monument

Date	Mintage	F	VF	XF	Unc	BU
1992(B)	—	—	—	—	25.00	—
1992(B) Proof	—	Value: 40.00				

KM#	Date	Mintage	Identification	Issue Price	Mkt Val
MS36	1996(M) (2)	—	KM#263, 288	65.00	45.00
MS37	1997(C) (3)	—	KM#204, 264, 289	—	50.00
MS38	1997(B) (2)	—	KM#70, 265	50.00	40.00
MS39	1998(B) (4)	—	KM#131.1, 205, 266, 292	—	55.00
MS40	1998(C) (3)	—	KM#297, 298, 299	—	50.00
MS41	1999(C) (2)	—	KM#295, 302	—	50.00
MS42	1999(B) (3)	—	KM#290, 300, 301	—	50.00
MS43	2000(B) (2)	—	KM#291, 293	—	40.00

PROOF SETS

KM#	Date	Mintage	Identification	Issue Price	Mkt Val
PS1	1950(B) (7)	—	KM#1.2, 2.1, 3.1, 4, 5.1, 6.1, 7.1	8.40	30.00
PS2	1954(B) (7)	—	KM#1.3, 2.2, 3.2, 4, 5.1, 6.1, 7.2	8.40	50.00
PS3	1960(B) (6)	—	KM#8, 11, 16, 24.2, 47.1, 55	7.00	30.00
PS4	1961(B) (6)	—	KM#8, 11, 16, 24.2, 47.2, 55	7.00	40.00
PS5	1962(B) (7)	—	KM#8, 11, 16, 24.2, 47.2, 55, 75.1	8.40	40.00
PS7	1963(B) (6)	—	KM#8a, 11, 16, 24.2, 47.2, 55, 75.1	7.00	30.00
PS8	1963(B) (7)	—	KM#8a, 11, 16, 24.2, 47.2, 55, 75.1	8.40	25.00
PS6	1962(B) (7)	—	KM#8a, 11, 16, 24.1, 47.2, 55, 75.1	8.40	35.00
PS9	ND(1964)(B) (2)	—	KM#56, 76	5.00	7.50
PS10	1969B (9)	9,097	KM#10.1, 13.5, 14.2, 18.3, 26.3, 42.1, 59, 77, 185	15.25	15.00
PS12	1971B (9)	4,161	KM#10.1, 13.5, 14.2, 18.3, 26.3, 43.2, 58.3, 75.2, 186	15.25	15.00
PS11	1970B (9)	2,900	KM#10.1, 13.5, 14.2, 18.3, 26.3, 43.1, 58.3, 75.2, 186	15.25	15.00
PS13	1972B (9)	7,701	KM#10.1, 13.6, 15, 18.6, 27.1, 49.1, 60, 75.2, 187	15.25	15.00
PS14	1973B (10)	7,563	KM#10.1, 13.5, 15, 18.6, 27.1, 49.1, 62, 75.1, 188, 240	26.00	25.00
PS15	1973B (9)	3,326	KM#10.1, 13.6, 15, 18.6, 27.1, 49.1, 62, 75.2, 188	15.25	15.00
PS17	1974B (10)	9,138	KM#10.1, 13.6, 15, 18.6, 28, 49.1, 63, 75.2, 189, 255	29.00	22.00
PS16	1973B (2)	2,408	KM#188, 240	17.50	22.00
PS18	1974B (2)	1,712	KM#189, 255	7.50	20.00
PS19	1975B (10)	2,370	KM#10.1, 13.6, 15, 18.6, 29, 49.1, 63, 78.1	35.00	30.00
PS20	1975B (2)	160	KM#190, 256	22.00	27.50
PS21	1976B (10)	3,209	KM#10.1, 13.6, 15, 19, 30, 49.1, 63, 78.1, 191, 257	35.00	30.00
PS22	1976B (2)	190	KM#191, 257	22.00	27.50
PS23	1977B (10)	2,222	KM#10.1, 13.6, 15, 20, 31, 63, 78.1, 192, 258	35.00	30.00
PS24	1977B (2)	—	KM#192, 258	—	27.50
PS25	1978B (10)	1,390	KM#10.1, 13.6, 15, 21, 32, 49.1, 63, 78.1, 193, 259	35.00	30.00
PS26	1978B (2)	—	KM#193, 259	—	27.50
PS27	1979B (10)	—	KM#10.1, 13.6, 15, 22, 33, 49.2, 63, 78.3, 194, 260	—	35.00
PS28	1979B (2)	—	KM#194, 260	—	28.00
PS29	1980B (4)	—	KM#35, 50, 195, 275	—	40.00
PS30	1980B (2)	—	KM#195, 275	—	35.00
PS31	1981B (4)	—	KM#36, 51, 196, 276	—	40.00
PS32	1981B (2)	—	KM#196, 276	—	35.00
PS-A33	1982B (4)	—	KM#64, 121.1, 198, 279	—	52.50
PS-A34	1982B (2)	—	KM#198, 279	—	45.00
PS33	1982B (4)	—	KM#52, 120, 197, 278	48.00	40.00
PS34	1982B (2)	—	KM#197, 278	38.00	35.00
PS35	1985B (4)	—	KM#66, 122, 199, 280	98.00	235
PS37	ND(1985)B (4)	—	KM#67.1, 150, 241, 281	88.00	150
PS36	1985B (2)	—	KM#199, 280	58.00	160
PS38	ND(1985)B (2)	—	KM#241, 281	48.00	120
PS39	1985(C) (3)	—	KM#80, 200, 282	—	70.00
PS40	1986B (3)	—	KM#68.1, 242, 283	70.00	130
PS41	1986B (2)	—	KM#242, 283	50.00	120
PS42	1987B (3)	—	KM#81, 243, 284	65.00	75.00
PS43	1987B (2)	—	KM#243, 284	60.00	70.00
PS44	1989B (4)	—	KM#83, 151, 244, 285	90.00	100
PS45	1989B (2)	—	KM#244, 285	65.00	70.00
PS46	1991(B) (3)	—	KM#90, 152, 201	—	45.00
PS47	1991(B) (3)	—	KM#91, 123, 153	—	35.00
PS48	ND(1994) (3)	—	KM#155, 262, 287	18.75	55.00
PS49	ND(1994) (2)	—	KM#262, 287	18.05	50.00
PS50	1996M (4)	—	KM#129, 203, 263, 288	110	85.00
PS51	1996M (2)	—	KM#263, 288	100	75.00
PS52	1997(C) (3)	—	KM#24, 264, 289	—	75.00
PS53	1997M (2)	—	KM#70, 265	75.00	60.00
PS55	1998(C) (4)	—	KM#296.3, 298, 299, 297	—	85.00
PS54	1998M (4)	—	KM#131.1, 205, 266, 290	—	85.00

KM# 287   100 RUPEES
35.0000 g., 0.5000 Silver 0.5626 oz. ASW **Subject:** World of Work **Obv:** Asoka lion pedestal, denomination below **Rev:** Denomination within broken dentil circle, wreath surrounds

Date	Mintage	F	VF	XF	Unc	BU
ND(1994)(B)	—	—	—	25.00	—	
ND(1994)M Proof	—	Value: 40.00				

KM# 288   100 RUPEES
35.0000 g., 0.5000 Silver 0.5626 oz. ASW **Subject:** 100th Anniversary - Birth of Patel **Obv:** Type A **Rev:** Head right

Date	Mintage	F	VF	XF	Unc	BU
1996(B)	—	—	—	50.00	—	
1996M Proof	—	Value: 70.00				

KM# 289   100 RUPEES
35.0000 g., 0.5000 Silver 0.5626 oz. ASW **Subject:** Subhas Chandra Bose **Obv:** Type C **Rev:** Bust left

Date	Mintage	F	VF	XF	Unc	BU
1997(C)	—	—	—	35.00	—	
1997(C) Proof	—	Value: 50.00				

KM# 299   100 RUPEES
35.0000 g., 0.5000 Silver 0.5626 oz. ASW, 44 mm. **Subject:** Deshbandhu Chittaranjan Das **Obv:** Asoka lion pedestal, denomination below **Rev:** Bust facing **Edge:** Reeded

Date	Mintage	F	VF	XF	Unc	BU
1998(C)	—	—	—	30.00	—	
1998(C) Proof	—	Value: 50.00				

KM# 292   100 RUPEES
35.0000 g., 0.5000 Silver 0.5626 oz. ASW, 44 mm. **Subject:** Sri Aurobindo **Obv:** Type C **Rev:** Head 3/4 facing **Edge:** Reeded

Date	Mintage	F	VF	XF	Unc	BU
1998(B)	—	—	—	30.00	—	
1998M Proof	—	Value: 50.00				

KM# 301   100 RUPEES
35.0000 g., 0.5000 Silver 0.5626 oz. ASW, 44 mm. **Subject:** Chhatrapati Shivaji **Obv:** Asoka lion pedestal, denomination below **Rev:** Turbaned bust right **Edge:** Reeded

Date	Mintage	F	VF	XF	Unc	BU
1999(B)	—	—	—	30.00	—	
1999M Proof	—	Value: 50.00				

KM# 302   100 RUPEES
35.0000 g., 0.5000 Silver 0.5626 oz. ASW, 44 mm. **Subject:** St. Dnyanneshwar **Obv:** Asoka lion pedestal, denomination below **Rev:** Seated figure **Edge:** Reeded

Date	Mintage	F	VF	XF	Unc	BU
1999(C)	—	—	—	—	30.00	—
1999(C) Proof	—	Value: 50.00				

PATTERNS
Including off metal strikes

KM#	Date	Mintage	Identification	Mkt Val
Pn1	1946(B)	—	1/4 Rupee. Nickel. KM#548.	—
Pn2	1946(B)	—	1/2 Rupee. Nickel. KM#553.	—
Pn3	1946(B)	—	Rupee. Nickel. KM#559.	—
Pn4	1947(B)	—	1/4 Rupee. Copper-Nickel.	—
Pn5	1947(B)	—	1/2 Rupee. Copper-Nickel.	—
Pn6	1947(B)	—	Rupee. Copper-Nickel.	—
Pn7	1947(B)	—	Rupee. Nickel. Set of Pn1-3.	1,500
Pn8	1949	—	Pice. Bronze.	—
Pn9	1949	—	Anna. Copper-Nickel.	—
Pn10	1949	—	2 Annas. Copper-Nickel. Profile peacock left.	—
Pn11	1949	—	2 Annas. Copper-Nickel. Facing displayed peacock.	—
PnA12	1949	—	2 Annas. Brass. Proof	—
Pn12	1949	—	1/4 Rupee. Nickel.	—
Pn13	1949	—	1/2 Rupee. Nickel. Worker with finished background.	—
Pn14	1949	—	1/2 Rupee. Nickel. Worker with plain background.	—
Pn15	1949	—	Rupee. Nickel. Standing figure.	—
Pn16	1949	—	Rupee. Nickel. Similar to Pn9.	—
Pn17	1964(C)	—	Paisa. Copper. Half thickness and weight.	—
Pn18	1992(C)	—	2 Rupees.	—

PIEFORTS

KM#	Date	Mintage	Identification	Mkt Val
P1	1981	—	100 Rupees. Silver. KM#277	250

MINT SETS

KM#	Date	Mintage	Identification	Issue Price	Mkt Val
MS3	1962(B) (6)	—	KM#8a, 11, 16, 24.2, 47.2, 55	1.50	5.00
MS4	1962(B) (7)	—	KM#8a, 11, 16, 24.2, 47.2, 55, 75.1(C)	3.60	8.00
MS6	1967(B) (8)	—	KM#10.1, 13.1, 14.1, 18.1, 25, 48.2, 58.1, 75.1 (1962 dated Rupee)	1.00	15.00
MS8	1970(B) (8)	—	KM#10.1, 13.5, 14.2, 18.3, 26.3, 41, 58.2, 75.2 Brown vinyl case	1.00	18.00
MS5	ND(1964)(B) (2)	—	KM#56, 76	1.00	3.75
MS7	ND(1969)(B) (4)	25,281	KM#42.1, 59, 77, 185 Blue plastic case	2.50	10.00
MS9	1970(B) (2)	22,999	KM#43.1, 186	2.00	9.00
MS10	1971(B) (2)	9,987	KM#43.2, 186	—	8.50
MS11	1972(B) (2)	43,121	KM#60, 187	2.00	7.00
MS11a	1972(B) (2)	—	KM#60, 187a	2.00	7.50
MS12	1973(B) (2)	48,670	KM#188, 240	—	15.00
MS13	1974(B) (2)	50,219	KM#189, 255	10.00	12.50
MS14	1975(B) (2)	40,279	KM#190, 256	12.00	13.50
MS15	1976(B) (2)	25,105	KM#191, 257	12.00	16.00
MS16	1977(B) (2)	17,071	KM#192, 258	12.00	16.00
MS17	1978(B) (2)	15,041	KM#193, 259	10.00	16.00
MS18	1979(B) (2)	—	KM#194, 260	—	16.50
MS19	1980(B) (2)	—	KM#195, 275	—	21.50
MS20	1981(B) (2)	—	KM#196, 276	—	21.50
MS21	1982(B) (2)	—	KM#197, 278	—	21.50
MS22	1985(B) (2)	—	KM#199, 280	48.00	140
MS23	ND(1985)(B) (2)	—	KM#241, 281	43.00	100
MS24	ND(1985)(C) (2)	—	KM#200, 282	—	40.00
MS25	1986 (2)	—	KM#242, 283	45.00	100
MS26	1987(B) (2)	—	KM#243, 284	45.00	40.00
MS27	1989(B) (2)	—	KM#244, 285	40.00	40.00
MS28	1989(B) (2)	—	KM#83, 285	50.00	45.00
MS29	1991(B) (2)	—	KM#152, 201	—	18.00
MS30	1991(B) (3)	—	KM#90, 152, 201	—	20.00
MS31	1991(B) (2)	—	KM#123, 153	—	20.00
MS32	1991(B) (3)	—	KM#91, 123, 153	—	22.00
MS33	1992(B) (4)	—	KM#92.1, 202, 261, 286	—	45.00
MS34	1994(B) (3)	—	KM#155, 262, 287	—	45.00
MS35	1996(M) (3)	—	KM#203, 263, 288	—	50.00

INDONESIA

The Republic of Indonesia, the world's largest archipelago, extends for more than 3,000 miles (4,827 km.) along the equator from the mainland of southeast Asia to Australia. The 17,508 islands comprising the archipelago have a combined area of 788,425 sq. mi. (1,919,440 sq.km.) and a population of 205 million, including East Timor. On August 30, 1999, the Timorese majority voted for independence. The Inter FET (International Forces for East Timor) is now in charge of controlling the chaotic situation. Capitol: Jakarta. Petroleum, timber, rubber, and coffee are exported.

Had Columbus succeeded in reaching the fabled Spice Islands, he would have found advanced civilizations a millennium old, and temples still ranking among the finest examples of ancient art. During the opening centuries of the Christian era, the islands were influenced by Hindu priests and traders who spread their culture and religion. Moslem invasions began in the 13th century, fragmenting the island kingdoms into small states which were unable to resist Western colonial infiltration. Portuguese traders established posts in the 16th century, but they were soon outnumbered by the Dutch who arrived in 1596 and gradually asserted control over the islands comprising present-day Indonesia. Dutch dominance, interrupted by British incursions during the Napoleonic Wars, established the Netherlands East Indies as one of the richest colonial possessions in the world.

The Indonesian independence movement, which began between the two world wars, was encouraged by the Japanese during their 3 1/2-year occupation during World War II. Indonesia proclaimed its independence on Aug. 17, 1945, three days after the surrender of Japan and full sovereignty. On Dec. 27, 1949, after four years of guerilla warfare including two large-scale campaigns by the Dutch in an effort to reassert control, complete independence was established. Rebellions in Bandung and on the Molluccan Islands occurred in 1950. During the reign of President Mohammad Achmad Sukarno (1950-67) the new Republic not only held together but started to develop. West Irian, formerly Netherlands New Guinea, came under the administration of Indonesia on May 1, 1963. In 1965, the army staged an anti-communist coup in which thousands perished.

On November 28, 1975, the Portuguese Province of Timor, an overseas province occupying the eastern half of the East Indian island of Timor, attained independence as the People's Democratic Republic of East Timor. On December 5, 1975, the government of the People's Democratic Republic was seized by a guerrilla faction sympathetic to the Indonesian territorial claim to East Timor which ousted the constitutional government and replaced it with the Provisional Government of East Timor. On July 17, 1976, the Provisional Government enacted a law that dissolved the free republic and made East Timor the 27th province of Indonesia.

The VOC (United East India Company) struck coins and emergency issues for the Indonesian Archipelago and for the islands at various mints in the Netherlands and the islands. In 1798 the VOC was subsumed by the Dutch government, which issued VOC type transitional and regal types during the Batavian Republic and the Kingdom of the Netherlands until independence. The British issued a coinage during the various occupations by the British East Indian Company, 1811-24. Modern coinage issued by the Republic of Indonesia includes separate series for West Irian and for the Riau Archipelago, an area of small islands between Singapore and Sumatra.

MONETARY SYSTEM
100 Sen = 1 Rupiah

REPUBLIC

STANDARD COINAGE

100 Sen = 1 Rupiah

KM# 7 SEN
0.7500 g., Aluminum **Obv:** Rice stalk surrounds center hole
Rev: Text around center hole

Date	Mintage	F	VF	XF	Unc	BU
1952	100,000	—	0.20	0.40	0.85	1.65

KM# 5 5 SEN
1.3000 g., Aluminum, 22 mm. **Obv:** Rice stalk surrounds center hole **Rev:** Text around center hole

Date	Mintage	F	VF	XF	Unc	BU
1951	—	—	0.10	0.25	0.60	1.25
1954	—	—	0.10	0.25	0.60	1.25

KM# 6 10 SEN
1.7200 g., Aluminum **Obv:** Denomination within scalloped design, ornaments flank date below **Rev:** National emblem

Date	Mintage	F	VF	XF	Unc	BU
1951(u)	—	—	0.10	0.20	0.35	0.65
1954	50,000,000	—	0.10	0.20	0.35	0.75

KM# 12 10 SEN
Aluminum **Obv:** Denomination within scalloped design, ornaments flank date below **Rev:** National emblem

Date	Mintage	F	VF	XF	Unc	BU
1957	50,224,000	—	0.20	0.40	0.75	1.25

KM# 8 25 SEN
2.2000 g., Aluminum, 27.7 mm. **Obv:** Denomination within scalloped design, ornaments flank date below **Rev:** National emblem

Date	Mintage	F	VF	XF	Unc	BU
1952(u)	200,000,000	—	0.10	0.20	0.25	0.45

KM# 11 25 SEN
Aluminum **Obv:** Denomination within scalloped design, ornaments flank date below **Rev:** National emblem

Date	Mintage	F	VF	XF	Unc	BU
1955	25,767,000	—	0.10	0.20	0.35	0.65
1957	99,752,926	—	0.10	0.20	0.35	0.50

KM# 9 50 SEN
Copper-Nickel **Obv:** Denomination within scalloped design, ornaments flank date below **Rev:** Turbaned head left

Date	Mintage	F	VF	XF	Unc	BU
1952(u)	100,000,000	—	0.10	0.20	0.35	0.50

KM# 10.1 50 SEN
3.2400 g., Copper-Nickel **Obv:** Denomination within scalloped design, ornaments flank date below **Rev:** Turbaned head left

Date	Mintage	F	VF	XF	Unc	BU
1954	1,290,000	—	1.00	2.25	4.50	—
1955	15,000,000	—	0.10	0.20	0.35	0.75

KM# 10.2 50 SEN
Copper-Nickel **Obv:** Denomination within scalloped design, ornaments flank date below **Rev:** Different head, larger lettering

Date	Mintage	F	VF	XF	Unc	BU
1957	26,267,313	—	0.10	0.20	0.35	0.65

KM# 13 50 SEN
Aluminum **Obv:** Denomination within inner circle, ornaments flank date below **Rev:** National emblem

Date	Mintage	F	VF	XF	Unc	BU
1958	33,740,000	—	0.10	0.20	0.40	0.75

KM# 14 50 SEN
3.0200 g., Aluminum, 29 mm. **Obv:** Denomination within inner circle, ornaments flank date below **Rev:** National emblem, modified eagle

Date	Mintage	F	VF	XF	Unc	BU
1959	100,009,000	—	0.10	0.20	0.40	0.65
1961	150,000,000	—	0.10	0.20	0.40	0.65

KM# 20 RUPIAH
1.4400 g., Aluminum, 20.36 mm. **Rev:** Fantail flycatcher
Edge: Plain

Date	Mintage	F	VF	XF	Unc	BU
1970	136,010,000	—	—	0.15	0.50	0.75

KM# 21 2 RUPIAH
2.3000 g., Aluminum, 26 mm. **Obv:** Stars flank date below denomination **Rev:** Rice and cotton stalks

Date	Mintage	F	VF	XF	Unc	BU
1970	139,230,000	—	—	0.15	0.25	0.40

KM# 22 5 RUPIAH
Aluminum **Obv:** Stars flank date below denomination **Rev:** Black drongo

Date	Mintage	F	VF	XF	Unc	BU
1970	448,000,000	—	0.15	0.30	0.75	1.00

KM# 37   5 RUPIAH
Aluminum, 28.6 mm.   **Subject:** Family Planning Program
Obv: Stars flank date below denomination **Rev:** The ideal family within rice and cotton stalk wreath

Date	Mintage	F	VF	XF	Unc	BU
1974	447,910,000	—	0.10	0.15	0.25	0.35

KM# 43   5 RUPIAH
1.4000 g., Aluminum, 23 mm.   **Subject:** Family Planning Program **Obv:** Stars flank date below denomination, inner circle surrounds **Rev:** The ideal family within rice and cotton stalk wreath, inner circle surrounds

Date	Mintage	F	VF	XF	Unc	BU
1979	413,200,000	—	0.10	0.15	0.25	0.35
1995	6,420,000	—	0.20	0.30	0.60	1.00
1996	—	—	0.20	0.30	0.60	1.00

KM# 33   10 RUPIAH
1.7700 g., Copper-Nickel, 15.6 mm.   **Series:** F.A.O. **Rev:** Rice and cotton stalks

Date	Mintage	F	VF	XF	Unc	BU
1971	286,360,000	—	0.10	0.25	0.50	0.75

KM# 38   10 RUPIAH
Brass-Clad Steel, 22 mm.   **Subject:** National Saving Program **Obv:** Stars flank date below denomination **Rev:** Rice and cotton stalks form wreath around teapot design

Date	Mintage	F	VF	XF	Unc	BU
1974	222,910,000	—	0.10	0.25	0.75	1.25

KM# 44   10 RUPIAH
1.9000 g., Aluminum, 25 mm.   **Series:** F.A.O. **Obv:** Stars flank date below denomination **Rev:** Rice and cotton stalks form wreath around teapot design

Date	Mintage	F	VF	XF	Unc	BU
1979	285,670,000	—	0.10	0.20	0.40	0.65

KM# 34   25 RUPIAH
3.5000 g., Copper-Nickel, 28 mm.   **Obv:** Stars flank date below denomination **Rev:** Victoria crowned pigeon

Date	Mintage	F	VF	XF	Unc	BU
1971	1,221,610,000	—	0.10	0.25	0.80	1.00

KM# 55   25 RUPIAH
1.2500 g., Aluminum, 18.01 mm.   **Obv:** National emblem **Rev:** Nutmeg plant **Edge:** Plain

Date	Mintage	F	VF	XF	Unc	BU
1991	30,000,000	—	—	0.40	0.75	1.25
1992	64,000,000	—	—	0.40	0.75	1.25

Date	Mintage	F	VF	XF	Unc	BU
1993	20,000,000	—	—	0.40	0.75	1.25
1994	250,000,000	—	—	0.25	0.50	0.75
1995	184,480,000	—	—	0.25	0.50	0.75
1996	—	—	—	0.25	0.50	0.75

KM# 35   50 RUPIAH
6.0000 g., Copper-Nickel, 24 mm.   **Obv:** Stars flank date below denomination **Rev:** Greater Bird of Paradise

Date	Mintage	F	VF	XF	Unc	BU
1971	1,035,435,000	—	0.25	0.80	1.00	1.50

KM# 52   50 RUPIAH
3.2000 g., Aluminum-Bronze, 19.94 mm.   **Obv:** National emblem **Rev:** Komodo dragon lizard **Edge:** Reeded

Date	Mintage	F	VF	XF	Unc	BU
1991	67,000,000	—	0.10	0.30	0.75	1.50
1992	70,000,000	—	0.10	0.30	0.75	1.50
1993	120,000,000	—	0.10	0.30	0.75	1.50
1994	300,000,000	—	0.10	0.30	0.75	1.50
1995	591,880,000	—	0.10	0.30	0.75	1.50
1996	—	—	0.10	0.30	0.75	1.50
1997	150,000	—	0.10	0.30	0.75	1.50
1998	150,000	—	0.10	0.30	0.75	1.50

KM# 60   50 RUPIAH
1.3600 g., Aluminum, 19.95 mm.   **Obv:** National emblem **Rev:** Black-naped Oriole **Edge:** Plain

Date	Mintage	F	VF	XF	Unc	BU
1999	—	—	—	—	0.40	0.75

KM# 36   100 RUPIAH
Copper-Nickel   **Obv:** Stars flank date below denomination **Rev:** Minangkabu house

Date	Mintage	F	VF	XF	Unc	BU
1973	252,868,000	—	0.35	0.75	1.50	3.00

KM# 42   100 RUPIAH
7.0000 g., Copper-Nickel, 28.5 mm.   **Subject:** Forestry for prosperity **Obv:** Minangkabu house **Rev:** Legendary tree of life

Date	Mintage	F	VF	XF	Unc	BU
1978	907,773,000	—	0.25	0.50	1.50	3.00

KM# 53   100 RUPIAH
4.0600 g., Aluminum-Bronze, 22 mm.   **Subject:** Buffalo racing **Obv:** National emblem **Rev:** Buffalo racers **Edge:** Reeded

Date	Mintage	F	VF	XF	Unc	BU
1991	94,000,000	—	0.15	0.30	0.60	1.00
1992	120,000,000	—	0.15	0.30	0.60	1.00
1993	300,000,000	—	0.15	0.30	0.60	1.00
1994	550,000,000	—	0.15	0.30	0.60	1.00
1995	798,100,000	—	0.15	0.30	0.60	1.00
1996	41,000,000	—	0.15	0.30	0.65	1.00
1997	150,000,000	—	0.15	0.30	0.65	1.00
1998	59,000,000	—	0.15	0.30	0.65	1.00

KM# 61   100 RUPIAH
1.7900 g., Aluminum, 23 mm.   **Obv:** National emblem **Rev:** Palm Cockatoo **Edge:** Plain

Date	Mintage	F	VF	XF	Unc	BU
1999	—	—	—	—	0.75	1.50
2000	—	—	—	—	0.75	1.50

KM# 23   200 RUPIAH
8.0000 g., 0.9990 Silver 0.2569 oz. ASW   **Subject:** 25th anniversary of independence **Obv:** Great Bird of Paradise (paradisea apoda- Paradiseaidae) **Rev:** National emblem

Date	Mintage	F	VF	XF	Unc	BU
1970 Proof	5,100		Value: 30.00			

KM# 24   250 RUPIAH
10.0000 g., 0.9990 Silver 0.3212 oz. ASW   **Subject:** 25th anniversary of independence **Obv:** Manjusri statue from Temple of Tumpang **Rev:** National emblem

Date	Mintage	F	VF	XF	Unc	BU
1970 Proof	5,000		Value: 18.50			

KM# 25   500 RUPIAH
20.0000 g., 0.9990 Silver 0.6423 oz. ASW   **Subject:** 25th Anniversary of Independence **Obv:** Wayang dancer **Rev:** National emblem

Date	Mintage	F	VF	XF	Unc	BU
1970 Proof	4,800		Value: 30.00			

KM# 54   500 RUPIAH
Aluminum-Bronze, 24 mm. **Obv:** National emblem
Rev: Jasmine **Edge:** Plain

Date	Mintage	F	VF	XF	Unc	BU
1991	71,000,000	—	—	1.25	2.50	3.00
1992	100,000,000	—	—	1.25	2.50	3.00
1993	—	—	—	1.25	2.50	3.00
1994	—	—	—	1.25	2.50	3.00

KM# 59   500 RUPIAH
5.3200 g., Aluminum-Bronze, 24 mm. **Obv:** National emblem
Rev: Denomination

Date	Mintage	F	VF	XF	Unc	BU
1997	—	—	—	—	2.00	2.50
1999	—	—	—	—	2.00	2.50
2000	—	—	—	—	2.00	2.50

KM# 26   750 RUPIAH
30.0000 g., 0.9990 Silver 0.9635 oz. ASW **Subject:** 25th
Anniversary of Independence **Obv:** Garuda bird **Rev:** National
emblem

Date	Mintage	F	VF	XF	Unc	BU
1970 Proof	4,950	Value: 45.00				

KM# 27   1000 RUPIAH
40.0000 g., 0.9990 Silver 1.2847 oz. ASW **Subject:** 25th
Anniversary of Independence - Gen. Sudirman **Obv:** Bust 3/4
facing **Rev:** National emblem

Date	Mintage	F	VF	XF	Unc	BU
1970 Proof	4,250	Value: 60.00				

KM# 56   1000 RUPIAH
8.6100 g., Bi-Metallic Brass center in Copper-Nickel ring
Obv: National emblem within inner circle **Rev:** Palm tree within
inner circle

Date	Mintage	F	VF	XF	Unc	BU
1993	5,000,000	—	—	—	3.50	5.00
1994	6,000,000	—	—	—	3.50	5.00
1995	19,900,000	—	—	—	3.50	5.00
1996	—	—	—	—	3.50	5.00
1997	—	—	—	—	3.50	5.00
2000	—	—	—	—	3.50	5.00

KM# 28   2000 RUPIAH
4.9300 g., 0.9000 Gold 0.1426 oz. AGW **Subject:** 25th
Anniversary of Independence **Obv:** Great Bird of Paradise
Rev: National emblem

Date	Mintage	F	VF	XF	Unc	BU
1970 Proof	2,970	Value: 140				

KM# 39   2000 RUPIAH
25.6500 g., 0.5000 Silver 0.4123 oz. ASW **Subject:** Conservation
series **Obv:** National emblem **Rev:** Javan tiger (panthera tigris-
felidae)

Date	Mintage	F	VF	XF	Unc	BU
1974	43,000	—	—	—	17.50	24.00

KM# 39a   2000 RUPIAH
28.2800 g., 0.9250 Silver 0.8410 oz. ASW **Subject:** Conservation
series **Obv:** National emblem **Rev:** Javan tiger (panthera tigris-
felidae)

Date	Mintage	F	VF	XF	Unc	BU
1974 Proof	18,000	Value: 27.50				

KM# 29   5000 RUPIAH
12.3400 g., 0.9000 Gold 0.3571 oz. AGW **Subject:** 25th
Anniversary of Independence **Obv:** Manjusri statue from Temple
of Tumpang **Rev:** National emblem

Date	Mintage	F	VF	XF	Unc	BU
1970 Proof	2,150	Value: 350				

KM# 40   5000 RUPIAH
32.0000 g., 0.5000 Silver 0.5144 oz. ASW **Series:** Conservation
Obv: National emblem **Rev:** Orangutan (pongo pygmaeus
Pongidae)

Date	Mintage	F	VF	XF	Unc	BU
1974	43,000	—	—	—	20.00	24.00

KM# 40a   5000 RUPIAH
35.0000 g., 0.9250 Silver 1.0408 oz. ASW **Series:** Conservation
Obv: National emblem **Rev:** Orangutan

Date	Mintage	F	VF	XF	Unc	BU
1974 Proof	17,000	Value: 27.50				

KM# 30   10000 RUPIAH
24.6800 g., 0.9000 Gold 0.7141 oz. AGW **Subject:** 25th
Anniversary of Independence **Obv:** Wayang dancer
Rev: National emblem

Date	Mintage	F	VF	XF	Unc	BU
1970 Proof	1,440	Value: 675				

KM# 45   10000 RUPIAH
19.4400 g., 0.9250 Silver 0.5781 oz. ASW **Subject:** Wildlife
Obv: National emblem **Rev:** Babi rusa (wild pig)

Date	Mintage	F	VF	XF	Unc	BU
1987 Proof	25,000	Value: 35.00				

KM# 50   10000 RUPIAH
19.4400 g., 0.9250 Silver 0.5781 oz. ASW **Series:** Save the
Child **Obv:** National emblem **Rev:** Playing badminton

Date	Mintage	F	VF	XF	Unc	BU
1990 Proof	20,000	Value: 50.00				

KM# 62   10000 RUPIAH
28.2800 g., 0.9250 Silver 0.8410 oz. ASW, 38.61 mm.
Obv: National emblem; UNICEF logo at left **Rev:** Two girl scouts planting a tree **Edge:** Milled **Note:** Struck at Hungarian Mint.

Date	Mintage	F	VF	XF	Unc	BU
1999 Proof	—	Value: 40.00				

KM# 31   20000 RUPIAH
49.3700 g., 0.9000 Gold 1.4285 oz. AGW **Subject:** 25th Anniversary of Independence **Obv:** Garuda bird **Rev:** National emblem

Date	Mintage	F	VF	XF	Unc	BU
1970 Proof	1,285	—	—	—	1,400	—

KM# 32   25000 RUPIAH
61.7100 g., 0.9000 Gold 1.7855 oz. AGW **Subject:** 25th Anniversary of Independence - Gen. Sudirman **Obv:** Bust facing **Rev:** National Emblem

Date	Mintage	F	VF	XF	Unc	BU
1970 Proof	970	Value: 1,700				

KM# 41   100000 RUPIAH
33.4370 g., 0.9000 Gold 0.9675 oz. AGW **Series:** Conservation **Obv:** National emblem **Rev:** Komodo dragon lizard (varanus komodensis)

Date	Mintage	F	VF	XF	Unc	BU
1974	5,333	—	—	—	925	—
1974 Proof	1,369	Value: 1,000				

KM# 47   125000 RUPIAH
8.0000 g., 0.9580 Gold 0.2464 oz. AGW **Subject:** Museum of Struggle '45 **Obv:** National emblem **Rev:** Museum

Date	Mintage	F	VF	XF	Unc	BU
1990 Proof	16,000	Value: 250				

KM# 63   150000 RUPIAH
6.2200 g., 0.9990 Gold 0.1998 oz. AGW, 22 mm. **Subject:** UNICEF - For the Children of the World **Obv:** National emblem; UNICEF logo at left **Rev:** Young boy riding a horse **Edge:** Milled.

Date	Mintage	F	VF	XF	Unc	BU
1999 Proof	—	Value: 220				

KM# 46   200000 RUPIAH
10.0000 g., 0.9170 Gold 0.2948 oz. AGW **Subject:** Wildlife **Obv:** National emblem **Rev:** Javan rhinoceros right

Date	Mintage	F	VF	XF	Unc	BU
1987 Proof	5,000	Value: 300				

KM# 51   200000 RUPIAH
10.0000 g., 0.9170 Gold 0.2948 oz. AGW **Series:** Save the Children **Obv:** National emblem **Rev:** Balinese dancer

Date	Mintage	F	VF	XF	Unc	BU
1990 Proof	3,000	Value: 300				

KM# 48   250000 RUPIAH
17.0000 g., 0.9580 Gold 0.5236 oz. AGW **Subject:** 45 years - Indonesian Independence **Obv:** National emblem **Rev:** Map, dates and denomination below

Date	Mintage	F	VF	XF	Unc	BU
1990 Proof	16,000	Value: 485				

KM# 57   300000 RUPIAH
17.0000 g., 0.9583 Gold 0.5237 oz. AGW **Subject:** 50th Anniversary of Independence **Obv:** National emblem **Rev:** Presidential talk show

Date	Mintage	F	VF	XF	Unc	BU
1995 Sets only	3,000	—	—	—	800	—

KM# 49   750000 RUPIAH
45.0000 g., 0.9580 Gold 1.3860 oz. AGW **Subject:** 45 Years - Arms of Generation 1945 **Obv:** National emblem **Rev:** National emblem within wreath of rice and cotton stalks

Date	Mintage	F	VF	XF	Unc	BU
1990 Proof	16,000	—	—	—	1,350	—

KM# 58   850000 RUPIAH
50.0000 g., 0.9583 Gold 1.5404 oz. AGW **Subject:** 50th Anniversary of Independence - President Soeharto **Obv:** National emblem **Rev:** Bust facing

Date	Mintage	F	VF	XF	Unc	BU
1995 Sets only	3,000	—	—	—	2,200	—

PATTERNS
Including off metal strikes

KM#	Date	Mintage	Identification	Mkt Val
Pn1	1951	—	25 Sen. Aluminum.	275
Pn2	1955	—	50 Sen. Raised SPECIMEN.	325
Pn3	1963	—	2-1/2 Rupiah. Aluminum.	185
PnA4	1965	—	50 Sen. Aluminum. Sukarno. Arms.	185
Pn4	1970	—	Rupiah. Bronze. KM20.	160
Pn5	1970	—	2 Rupiah. Copper. KM21.	160
Pn6	1970	—	2 Rupiah. Bronze. KM20.	160
Pn7	1970	—	25 Rupiah. Bronze.	—
Pn8	1973	—	100 Rupiah. Aluminum.	250
Pn9	1979	—	10 Rupiah. Copper-Nickel.	—
Pn10	1990	—	125000 Rupiah. Gold. Gold-plated base metal. KM#47.	—
Pn11	1990	—	250000 Rupiah. Gold. Gold-plated base metal. KM#48.	—
Pn12	1990	—	750000 Rupiah. Gold. Gold-plated base metal. KM#49.	—
Pn13	1991	—	500 Rupiah. Copper-Nickel.	—
Pn14	1992	—	500 Rupiah. Bronze.	—
Pn15	1993	—	50 Rupiah. Copper-Nickel.	—
Pn16	1993	—	100 Rupiah. Copper-Nickel.	—

MINT SETS

KM#	Date	Mintage	Identification	Issue Price	Mkt Val
MS1	Mixed dates (14)	—	KM5-6 (1951, 1954), 7-9 (1952), 10.1 (1955), 10.2 (1957), 11 (1955, 1957), 12 (1957), 14 (1961)	—	18.00
MS2	Mixed dates (9)	—	KM20-21 (1970), 33-35 (1971), 36 (1973), 37-38 (1974), 42 (1978)	2.40	6.50
MS3	1970 (3)	—	KM20-22	—	1.50
MS4	1971 (3)	—	KM33-35	—	1.50

PROOF SETS

KM#	Date	Mintage	Identification	Issue Price	Mkt Val
PS1	1970 (10)	970	KM23-32	490	3,400
PS2	1970 (5)	4,250	KM23-27	50.00	170
PS3	1974 (2)	30,000	KM39a-40a	50.00	36.00
PS4	1990 (3)	15,750	KM47-49	755	1,525
PS5	1990 (2)	—	KM50-51	—	350
PS6	1995 (2)	3,000	KM57-58	2,975	3,000

IRIAN BARAT
(West Irian, Irian Jaya,
Netherlands New Guinea)
A province of Indonesia comprising the western half of the island of New Guinea. A special set of coins dated 1962 were issued in 1964, were recalled December 31, 1971, and are no longer legal tender.

INDONESIAN PROVINCE

STANDARD COINAGE

No inscription on edge

KM# 5 SEN
Aluminum **Subject:** Mohammed Ahmad Sukarno **Obv:** Head left **Rev:** Denomination within wreath of cotton and rice stalks **Edge:** Plain

Date	Mintage	F	VF	XF	Unc	BU
1962	—	0.25	0.50	1.00	2.00	—

KM# 6 5 SEN
Aluminum **Subject:** Mohammed Ahmad Sukarno **Obv:** Head left **Rev:** Denomination within wreath of cotton and rice stalks **Edge:** Plain

Date	Mintage	F	VF	XF	Unc	BU
1962	—	0.25	0.50	1.25	2.00	—

KM# 7 10 SEN
Aluminum **Subject:** Mohammed Ahmad Sukarno **Obv:** Head left **Rev:** Denomination within rice and cotton stalks **Edge:** Plain

Date	Mintage	F	VF	XF	Unc	BU
1962	—	0.25	0.50	1.25	2.50	—

KM# 8.1 25 SEN
Aluminum **Subject:** Mohammed Ahmad Sukarno **Obv:** Head left **Rev:** Denomination within wreath of cotton and rice stalks **Edge:** Reeded

Date	Mintage	F	VF	XF	Unc	BU
1962	—					

KM# 8.2 25 SEN
Aluminum **Obv:** Head left **Rev:** Denomination within wreath of cotton and rice stalks

Date	Mintage	F	VF	XF	Unc	BU
1962	—	0.75	1.50	2.50	4.00	—

KM# 9 50 SEN
Aluminum **Subject:** Mohammed Ahmad Sukarno **Obv:** Head left **Rev:** Denomination within wreath of cotton and rice stalks **Edge:** Reeded

Date	Mintage	F	VF	XF	Unc	BU
1962	—	0.85	1.60	3.00	5.00	—

PATTERNS

Including off metal strikes

KM#	Date	Mintage	Identification	Mkt Val
Pn1	1962	—	50 Sen. Aluminum. Double reverse as KM#9	125
Pn2	1963	—	2-1/2 Rupiah.	100
Pn3	1965	—	25 Sen. Aluminum. Plain edge. KM#8.2	100
Pn4	1965	—	50 Sen. Aluminum center. Reeded edge. KM#9	100
Pn5	1965	—	50 Sen. Aluminum. Plain edge. KM#9	100
Pn6	1965//1962	—	50 Sen. Aluminum. As KM#9.	150

RIAU ARCHIPELAGO

A group of 3,214 islands off the tip of the Malay Peninsula. Coins were issued near the end of 1963 (although dated 1962) and recalled as worthless on Sept. 30, 1964. They were legal tender from Oct. 15, 1963 to July 1, 1964.

INSCRIPTION ON EDGE
KEPULAUAN RIAU

INDONESIAN PROVINCE

STANDARD COINAGE

Inscription on edge: "Kepulauan Riau"

KM# 5 SEN
Aluminum **Obv:** Head left **Rev:** Denomination within wreath of cotton and rice stalks

Date	Mintage	F	VF	XF	Unc	BU
1962	—	0.35	0.75	1.25	2.00	—

KM# 6 5 SEN
Aluminum **Obv:** Head left **Rev:** Denomination within wreath of cotton and rice stalks

Date	Mintage	F	VF	XF	Unc	BU
1962	—	0.30	0.60	1.50	2.00	—

KM# 7 10 SEN
Aluminum **Subject:** Mohammed Ahmad Sukarno **Obv:** Head left **Rev:** Denomination within wreath of cotton and rice stalks

Date	Mintage	F	VF	XF	Unc	BU
1962	—	0.35	0.70	1.75	2.75	—

KM# 8.1 25 SEN
Aluminum **Obv:** Head left **Rev:** Denomination within wreath of cotton and rice stalks

Date	Mintage	F	VF	XF	Unc	BU
1962	—					

KM# 8.2 25 SEN
Aluminum **Subject:** Mohammed Ahmad Sukarno **Obv:** Head left **Rev:** Denomination within wreath of cotton and rice stalks

Date	Mintage	F	VF	XF	Unc	BU
1962	—	0.85	1.60	2.75	4.50	—

KM# 9 50 SEN
Aluminum **Subject:** Mohammed Ahmad Sukarno **Obv:** Bust left **Rev:** Denomination within wreath of cotton and rice stalks

Date	Mintage	F	VF	XF	Unc	BU
1962	—	1.00	2.00	3.50	5.50	—

IRAN

The Islamic Republic of Iran, located between the Caspian Sea and the Persian Gulf in southwestern Asia, has an area of 636,296 sq. mi. (1,648,000 sq. km.) and a population of 40 million. Capital: Tehran. Although predominantly an agricultural state, Iran depends heavily on oil for foreign exchange. Crude oil, carpets and agricultural products are exported.

Iran (historically known as Persia until 1931AD) is one of the world's most ancient and resilient nations. Strategically astride the lower land gate to Asia, it has been conqueror and conquered, sovereign nation and vassal state, ever emerging from its periods of glory or travail with its culture and political individuality intact. Iran (Persia) was a powerful empire under Cyrus the Great (600-529 B.C.), its borders extending from the Indus to the Nile. It has also been conquered by the predatory empires of antique and recent times - Assyrian, Medean, Macedonian, Seljuq, Turk, Mongol - and more recently been coveted by Russia, the Third Reich and Great Britain. Revolts against the absolute power of the Persian shahs resulted in the establishment of a constitutional monarchy in 1906.

With 4,000 troops, Reza Khan marched on the capital arriving in Tehran in the early morning of Feb. 22, 1921. The government was taken over with hardly a shot and Zia ad-Din was set up as premier, but the real power was with Reza Khan, although he was officially only the minister of war. In 1923, Reza Khan appointed himself prime minister and summoned the "majlis." Who eventually gave him military powers and he became independent of the shah's authority. In 1925 Reza Khan Pahlavi was elected Shah of Persia. A few weeks later his eldest son, Shahpur Mohammed Reza was appointed Crown Prince and was crowned on April 25, 1926.

In 1931 the Kingdom of Persia became known as the Kingdom of Iran. In 1979 the monarchy was toppled and an Islamic Republic proclaimed.

TITLES

دار الخلافة

Dar al-Khilafat

RULERS

Qajar Dynasty

مظفر الدين

Muzaffar al-Din Shah, AH1313-1324/1896-1907AD

محمد علي

Muhammad Ali Shah, AH1324-1327/1907-1909AD

سلطان احمد

Sultan Ahmad Shah, AH1327-1344/1909-1925AD

Pahlavi Dynasty

رضا

Reza Shah, as prime minister, SH1302-1304/1923-1925AD
as Shah, SH1304-1320/1925-1941AD

محمد رضا

Mohammad Reza Pahlavi, Shah SH1320-1358/1941-1979AD

جمهوری اسلامی ایران

Islamic Republic, SH1358-/1979-AD

MINT NAMES

طهران

Tehran

تفلیس

Tiflis

MINT MARKS

H - Heaton (Birmingham)
L - Leningrad (St. Petersburg)

COIN DATING

Iranian coins were dated according to the Moslem lunar calendar until March 21, 1925 (AD), when dating was switched to a new calendar based on the solar year, indicated by the notation SH. The monarchial calendar system was adopted in 1976 = MS2535 and was abandoned in 1978 = MS2537. The previously used solar year calendar was restored at that time.

MONETARY SYSTEM

1825-1931
(AH1241-1344, SH1304-09)

50 Dinars = 1 Shahi
20 Shahis = 1 Kran (Qiran)
10 Krans = 1 Toman

NOTE: From AD1830-34 (AH1245-50) the gold Toman was known as a 'Keshwarsetan.'

1932-Date (SH1310-Date)

5 Dinars = 1 Shahi
20 Shahis = 1 Rial (100 Dinars)
10 Rials = 1 Toman

NOTE: The Toman ceased to be an official unit in 1932, but continues to be applied in popular usage. Thus, 135 Rials' is always expressed as 13 Toman, 5 Rials'. The term Rial' is often used in conversation, as well as either Kran' or Ezar' (short for Hazar = 1000) is used.

NOTE: The Law of 18 March 1930 fixed the gold Pahlavi at 20 Rials. No gold coins were struck. The Law of 13 March1932 divided the Pahlavi into 100 Rials, instead of 20. The Rial's weight was reduced from 0.3661 grams of pure gold to 0.0732. Since 1937 gold has been allowed to float and the Pahlavi is quoted daily in Rials in the marketplaces.

KINGDOM

NOTE: Other mints also produced local Falus, for which examples were not available to illustrate. Still other mints operated only or largely at earlier dates. These include Damavand, Damghan, Darabjird, Fa'Farafad, Kangan, Ra', Semnan, Tus, Tuy and others.

SILVER AND GOLD COINAGE

The precious metal monetary system of Qajar Persia prior to the reforms of 1878 was the direct descendant of the Mongol system introduced by Ghazan Mahmud in 1297AD, and was the last example of a medieval islamic coinage. It is not a modern system, and cannot be understood as such. It is not possible to list types, dates, and mints as for other countries, both because of the nature of the coinage, and because very little research has been done on the series. The following comments should help elucidate its nature.

STANDARDS: The weight of the primary silver and gold coins was set by law and was expressed in terms of the Mesqal (about 4.61 g) and the Nokhod (24 Nokhod = 1 Mesqal). The primary silver coin was the Rupee from AH1211-1212, the Riyal from AH1212-1241, and the Gheran from AH1241-1344. The standard gold coin was the Toman. Currently the price of gold is quoted in Mesqals.

DENOMINATIONS: In addition to the primary denominations, noted in the last paragraph, fractional pieces were coined, valued at one-eighth, one-fourth, and one-half the primary denomination, usually in much smaller quantities. These were ordinarily struck from the same dies as the larger pieces, sometimes on broad, thin flans, sometimes on thick, dumpy flans. On the smaller coins, the denomination can best be determined only by weighing the coin. The denomination is almost never expressed on the coin!

DEVALUATIONS: From time to time, the standard for silver and gold was reduced, and the old coin recalled and replaced with lighter coin, the difference going to the government coffers. The effect was that of a devaluation of the primary silver and gold coins, or inversely regarded, an increase in the price of silver and gold. The durations of each standard varied from about 2 to 20 years. The standards are given for each ruler, as the denomination can only be determined when the standard is known.

LIGHTWEIGHT AND ALLOYED PIECES: Most of the smaller denomination coins were issued at lighter weights than those prescribed by law, with the difference going to the pockets of the mintmasters. Other mints, notably Hamadan, added excessive amounts of alloy to the coins, and some mintmasters lost their heads as a result. Discrepancies in weight of as much as 15 percent and more are observed, with the result that it is often quite impossible to determine the denomination of a coin!

OVERSIZE COINS: Occasionally, multiples of the primary denominations were produced, usually on special occasions for presentation by the Shah to his favorites. These 'coins' did not circulate (except as bullion), and were usually worn as ornaments. They were the 'NCLT's' of their day.

MINTS & EPITHETS: Qajar coinage was struck at 34 mints (plus at least a dozen others striking only copper Falus), which are listed previously, with drawings of the mintnames in Persian, as they appear on the coins. However, the Persian script admits of infinite variation and stylistic whimsy, so the forms given are only guides, and not absolute. Only a knowledge of the script will assure correct reading. In addition to the city name, most mintnames were given identifying epithets, which occasionally appear in lieu of the mintname, particularly at Iravan and Mashhad.

TYPES: There were no types in the modern sense, but the arrangement of the legends and the ornamental borders were frequently changed. These changes do not coincide with changes in standards, and cannot be used to determine the mint, which must be found by actually reading the reverse inscriptions.

ARRANGEMENT

The following listings are arranged first by ruler, with various standards explained. Then, the coins are listed by denomination within each reign. For each denomination, one or more pieces, when available, are illustrated, with the mint and date noted beneath each photo. For each type, a date range is given, but this range indicates the years during which the particular type was current, and does not imply that every year of the interval is known on actual coins. Because dates were carelessly engraved, and old dies were used until they wore out or broke, we occasionally find coins of a particular type dated before or after the indicated interval. Such coins command no premium. No attempt has been made to determine which mints actually exist for which types.

KRAN STANDARD

AH1293-1344, SH1304-1309,
1876-1931AD
50 Dinars = 1 Shahi
1000 Dinars = 20 Shahis = 1 Kran (Qiron)
10 Krans = 1 Toman

Special Gold Issue

AH1337/1918-1919AD
1 Ashrafi (= 1 Toman)
SH1305-1309/1927-1931AD

Toman replaced by Pahlavi (light standard). Relationship of Pahlavi to Kran not known.

NOTE: Dated reverse dies lacking the ruler's name were not discarded at the end of a reign (especially from Nasir al-Din to Muzaffar al-Din), but remained in use until broken or worn out. Sometimes the old date was scratched out or changed, but often the die was used with the old date unaltered. Some dies with date below wreath retained the old date but had the new date engraved among the lion's legs.

SHAHI SEFID
(White Shahi)

Called the White (i.e. silver) Shahi to distinguish it from the Black or Copper Shahi, the Shahi Sefid was actually worth 3 Shahis (150 Dinars) or 3 1/8 Shahis (156 ¼ Dinars). It was used primarily for distribution on New Year's Day (now RUZ) as good-luck gifts. Since 1926 special privately struck tokens, having no monetary value, have been used instead of coins. The Shahi Sefid was broader, but much thinner than the ¼ Kran (Rob'l), worth 250 Dinars.

Milled Gold Coinage:

Numerous imitations exist of many types, particularly the small 1/5, 1/2, and 1 Toman coins. These are usually underweight (or rarely overweight), and are sold in the bazaars at a small premium over bullion. They are usually crude and probably not intended to deceive collectors, but some are sold for jewelry and some are dated outside the reign of the ruler whose name or portrait they bear. A few deceptive counterfeits are known of the large 10 Toman pieces.

KINGDOM

Anonymous

Muzaffar al-Din Shah
AH1313-1324 / 1896-1907AD

MILLED COINAGE

KM# 961   50 DINARS

Copper-Nickel **Obv:** Legend within beaded circle with crown on top **Rev:** Radiant lion holding sword within wreath **Mint:** Tehran

Date	Mintage	F	VF	XF	Unc	BU
AH1319	12,000,000	1.00	3.50	7.00	10.00	—
AH1321	10,000,000	0.75	1.50	4.00	8.00	—
AH1326	8,000,000	4.00	10.00	20.00	30.00	—
AH1332	6,000,000	1.00	2.00	5.00	12.50	—
AH1337	7,000,000	1.50	4.00	8.00	12.00	—

KM# 965   SHAHI SEFID (White Shahi)

0.8000 g., 0.9000 Silver 0.0231 oz. ASW **Obv:** Legend and value within circle and wreath **Obv. Leg.:** "Muzaffar al-Din Shah" **Rev:** Crown above lion and sun within wreath **Mint:** Tehran

Date	Mintage	F	VF	XF	Unc	BU
AH1319	—	15.00	30.00	60.00	120	—
AH1039	—	25.00	50.00	100	200	—
Note: Error for 1319						
AH1320	150,000	15.00	30.00	60.00	120	—

KM# 966   SHAHI SEFID (White Shahi)

0.8000 g., 0.9000 Silver 0.0231 oz. ASW **Obv:** Legend within circle and wreath **Rev:** Radiant lion holding sword within crowned wreath **Mint:** Tehran

Date	Mintage	F	VF	XF	Unc	BU
ND (1901)	—	50.00	80.00	165	300	—
AH1319 (1901) Rare						

Note: A number of varieties and mulings of KM#965 and KM#966 with other denominations, especially 1/4 Krans and 500 Dinar pieces, are reported; these command a premium over others of the same types; a total of 58,000 pieces were reported struck in AH1322, 1323 and 1324, but none are known with those dates; the specimens were either struck from old dies or were undated types.

KM# 967   SHAHI SEFID (White Shahi)

0.8000 g., 0.9000 Silver 0.0231 oz. ASW **Obv. Leg.:** "Muzaffar al-Din Shah" **Rev:** Legend within center circle of wreath **Rev. Leg.:** "Sahib al-Zaman" **Mint:** Tehran **Note:** Thick and thin lettering varieties exist.

Date	Mintage	F	VF	XF	Unc	BU
ND (1903)	—	50.00	85.00	165	300	—

KM# 962   100 DINARS (2 Shahi)

4.4000 g., Copper-Nickel **Obv:** Legend within beaded circle and crowned wreath **Rev:** Radiant lion holding sword within crowned wreath

Date	Mintage	F	VF	XF	Unc	BU
AH1319	9,000,000	2.50	5.00	10.00	20.00	—
AH1321/19	5,000,000	6.00	12.00	30.00	50.00	—
AH1321	Inc. above	0.75	1.50	4.00	8.00	—
AH1326	6,000,000	1.50	2.50	6.00	15.00	—
AH1332	5,000,000	1.00	2.00	5.00	12.50	—
AH1337	6,500,000	2.00	5.00	10.00	15.00	—

KM# 968   1/4 KRAN (Robi = 5 Shahis)

1.1513 g., 0.9000 Silver 0.0333 oz. ASW **Obv:** Legend and value within circle and wreath **Obv. Leg.:** "Muzaffar al-din Shah" **Rev:** Crown above lion and sun within wreath **Mint:** Tehran **Note:** 300 specimens reportedly struck in AH1322, but none known to exist.

Date	Mintage	F	VF	XF	Unc	BU
AH1319	—	20.00	35.00	65.00	130	—

KM# 969   500 DINARS (10 Shahis = 1/2 Kran)

2.3025 g., 0.9000 Silver 0.0666 oz. ASW **Obv:** Legend and value within circle and wreath **Obv. Leg.:** "Muzaffar al-din", 500 Dinars **Rev:** Crown above lion and sun within wreath **Mint:** Tehran **Note:** Some reverse dies were previously used under Nasir al-Din and show traces of old date beneath wreath on reverse.

Date	Mintage	F	VF	XF	Unc	BU
AH1319	—	20.00	40.00	100	200	—
AH1322	—	20.00	30.00	50.00	100	—

KM# 977 500 DINARS (10 Shahis = 1/2 Kran)
2.3025 g., 0.9000 Silver 0.0666 oz. ASW Obv: Uniformed bust 1/4 right Rev: Radiant lion holding sword within crowned wreath Mint: Tehran

Date	Mintage	F	VF	XF	Unc	BU
AH1323 (1905)	130,000	20.00	35.00	80.00	160	—

1000 DINARS:
یکهزاردینار

1 KRAN:
یک قران

KM# 972 1000 DINARS (Kran, Qiran)
4.6050 g., 0.9000 Silver 0.1332 oz. ASW Obv: Legend and value within circle and wreath Rev: Crown above lion and sun within wreath Mint: Tehran

Date	Mintage	F	VF	XF	Unc	BU
AH1319	—	150	225	350	500	—
AH1322	—	100	175	250	350	—

KM# 978 1000 DINARS (Kran, Qiran)
4.6050 g., 0.9000 Silver 0.1332 oz. ASW Obv: Uniformed bust 1/4 right Rev: Radiant lion holding sword within crowned wreath Mint: Tehran

Date	Mintage	F	VF	XF	Unc	BU
AH1323 (1905)	125,000	20.00	30.00	65.00	125	—

KM# 974 2000 DINARS (2 Kran)
9.2100 g., 0.9000 Silver 0.2665 oz. ASW Obv: Legend and value within wreath, star above Rev: Crown above lion and sun within wreath Mint: Tehran Note: Blundered dates exist.

Date	Mintage	F	VF	XF	Unc	BU
AH1319	—	10.00	20.00	35.00	90.00	—
AH1320	13,959,000	10.00	20.00	35.00	75.00	—

KM# 975 2000 DINARS (2 Kran)
9.2100 g., 0.9000 Silver 0.2665 oz. ASW Obv: Legend within circle and wreath Rev: Radiant lion holding sword within crowned wreath Rev. Leg.: 2 Krans Mint: Tehran

Date	Mintage	F	VF	XF	Unc	BU
AH1320 (1902)	Inc. above	12.50	20.00	40.00	100	—
AH1321 (1903)	18,108,000	15.00	22.50	45.00	100	—
Note: In blundered form as 13201						
AH1322 (1904)	8,640,000	8.00	15.00	30.00	80.00	—

KM# 979 2000 DINARS (2 Kran)
9.2100 g., 0.9000 Silver 0.2665 oz. ASW Obv: Uniformed bust 1/4 right within wreath Rev: Radiant lion holding sword within crowned wreath Mint: Tehran

Date	Mintage	F	VF	XF	Unc	BU
AH1323 (1905)	—	15.00	30.00	60.00	120	—
Note: Mintage inluded in AH1323 above						
AH'13' (1905)	—	60.00	100	200	400	—
Note: 23 of 1323 filled in or never punched						
AH13233 (1905)	—	45.00	85.00	190	380	—
Note: Error						

KM# 976 5000 DINARS (5 Kran)
23.0251 g., 0.9000 Silver 0.6662 oz. ASW Obv: Legend within crowned wreath Obv. Leg.: "Muzaffar al-din Shah" Rev: Radiant lion holding sword within crowned wreath Note: Dav.#288.

Date	Mintage	F	VF	XF	Unc	BU
AH1320 (1902)	250,000	12.00	16.00	32.00	60.00	—
Note: Actual mintage must be considerably greater						

KM# 980 5000 DINARS (5 Kran)
23.0251 g., 0.9000 Silver 0.6662 oz. ASW, 36 mm. Subject: Royal Birthday Obv: Uniformed bust 1/4 right within wreath Rev: Radiant lion holding sword within crowned wreath Note: Dav.#287.

Date	Mintage	F	VF	XF	Unc	BU
AH1322 (1904)	—	400	550	800	1,200	—

KM# 981 5000 DINARS (5 Kran)
23.0251 g., 0.9000 Silver 0.6662 oz. ASW, 36 mm. Obv: Uniformed bust 1/4 right within wreath Rev: Radiant lion holding sword within crowned wreath Note: Dav.#289. Without additional inscription flanking head

Date	Mintage	F	VF	XF	Unc	BU
AH1324 (1906)	3,040	1,000	2,000	3,000	4,000	—

KM# 986 2000 DINARS (1/5 Toman)
0.6520 g., 0.9000 Gold 0.0189 oz. AGW Obv. Leg.: "Mazaffar-al-Din Shah" Rev: Crown above lion and sun within wreath

Date	Mintage	F	VF	XF	Unc	BU
AH9301 Error for 1319	—	200	300	500	750	—

KM# 922 2000 DINARS (1/5 Toman)
0.6520 g., 0.9000 Gold 0.0189 oz. AGW Rev: Legend and value within wreath Note: Mule. Reverse: KM#923, reverse: KM#991.

Date	Mintage	VG	F	VF	XF	Unc
AH1295 (sic)						

KM# 991 2000 DINARS (1/5 Toman)
0.5749 g., 0.9000 Gold 0.0166 oz. AGW Obv: Uniformed bust left Rev: Legend and value within circle and wreath

Date	Mintage	F	VF	XF	Unc	BU
AH1319 (1901)	—	200	300	400	500	—

KM# 992 2000 DINARS (1/5 Toman)
0.5749 g., 0.9000 Gold 0.0166 oz. AGW Obv: Date and denomination added

Date	Mintage	F	VF	XF	Unc	BU
AH1319 (1901)	—	50.00	100	150	250	—
AH1322 (1904)	—	50.00	100	150	250	—
AH1323 (1905)	—	100	200	300	400	—
AH1324 (1906)	—	100	200	300	400	—

KM# 994.1 5000 DINARS (1/2 Toman)
1.4372 g., 0.9000 Gold 0.0416 oz. AGW Obv: Uniformed bust 3/4 right Rev: Legend and value within cirlce and wreath Note: Prev. KM#994.

Date	Mintage	F	VF	XF	Unc	BU
AH1319	—	100	200	300	400	—
AH1320	—	35.00	60.00	100	200	—
AH1321	—	35.00	60.00	100	200	—
AH1322	—	35.00	60.00	100	200	—
AH1324	—	100	200	300	400	—

KM# 994.2 5000 DINARS (1/2 Toman)
1.4372 g., 0.9000 Gold 0.0416 oz. AGW Obv: Bust with headdress 3/4 right divides date Rev: Legend within circle and wreath

Date	Mintage	F	VF	XF	Unc	BU
AH1323	—	100	200	300	400	—

KM# 995 TOMAN
2.8744 g., 0.9000 Gold 0.0832 oz. AGW, 19 mm. Obv: Uniformed bust 3/4 right, accession date, AH1314 above left Rev: Legend and value within circle and wreath

Date	Mintage	F	VF	XF	Unc	BU
AH1319	—	60.00	100	160	250	—
AH1321	—	100	200	300	400	—

KM# 996 2 TOMAN
5.7488 g., 0.9000 Gold 0.1663 oz. AGW, 19 mm. Obv: Uniformed bust 3/4 left, date at left Rev: Legend within circle and wreath Rev. Leg.: "Muzaffer al-Din Shah"

Date	Mintage	F	VF	XF	Unc	BU
AH1322 (1904)	—	250	400	750	1,500	—

KM# 997 2 TOMAN
5.7488 g., 0.9000 Gold 0.1663 oz. AGW, 19 mm. Subject: Royal Birthday Obv: Uniformed bust 3/4 left divides legend Rev: Legend within circle and wreath Rev. Leg.: "Muzaffer al-Din Shah"

Date	Mintage	F	VF	XF	Unc	BU
AH1322 (1904)	—	250	500	1,000	1,500	—

Muhammad Ali Shah
AH1324-1327 / 1907-1909AD
MILLED COINAGE

KM# 1006 SHAHI SEFID (White Shahi)
0.0691 g., 0.9000 Silver 0.0020 oz. ASW, 17 mm. Obv: Legend within circle and wreath Obv. Leg.: "Muhammad Ali Shah" Rev: Radiant lion holding sword within crowned wreath Mint: Tehran

Date	Mintage	F	VF	XF	Unc	BU
AH1325 (1907)	—	30.00	60.00	110	200	—

Date	Mintage	F	VF	XF	Unc	BU
AH1326 (1908)	—	25.00	40.00	90.00	180	—
AH1327 (1909)	—	20.00	40.00	80.00	160	—

KM# 1007   SHAHI SEFID (White Shahi)
0.0691 g., 0.9000 Silver 0.0020 oz. ASW **Obv:** Legend within circle and wreath **Obv. Leg.:** "Sahib al-Zaman" **Rev:** Radiant lion holding sword within crowned wreath **Mint:** Tehran

Date	Mintage	F	VF	XF	Unc	BU
AH1326 (1908)	—	60.00	125	175	325	—

KM# 1008   SHAHI SEFID (White Shahi)
0.0691 g., 0.9000 Silver 0.0020 oz. ASW **Obv:** Legend within circle and wreath **Rev:** Radiant lion holding sword within crowned wreath **Mint:** Tehran

Date	Mintage	F	VF	XF	Unc	BU
ND (1909)	—	50.00	80.00	150	300	—

KM# 1009   1/4 KRAN (Robi = 5 Shahis)
1.1513 g., 0.9000 Silver 0.0333 oz. ASW, 15 mm. **Obv:** Legend within circle and wreath **Obv. Leg.:** "Muhammad Ali Shah" **Rev:** Radiant lion holding sword within crowned wreath **Mint:** Tehran

Date	Mintage	F	VF	XF	Unc	BU
AH1325 (1907)	—	30.00	50.00	100	200	—
AH1326 (1908)	—	15.00	27.50	40.00	80.00	—
AH1327 (1909)	—	10.00	20.00	35.00	70.00	—

KM# 1010   500 DINARS (10 Shahis = 1/2 Kran)
2.3025 g., 0.9000 Silver 0.0666 oz. ASW, 18 mm. **Obv:** Legend within circle and wreath **Obv. Leg.:** "Muhammad Ali Shah" **Rev:** Radiant lion holding sword within crowned wreath **Mint:** Tehran

Date	Mintage	F	VF	XF	Unc	BU
AH1325 (1907)	218,000	40.00	75.00	160	300	—
AH1335 (1907) Error for 1325	—	50.00	85.00	175	325	—
AH1326 (1908)	218,000	25.00	50.00	110	225	—
AH1336 (1908) Error for 1326	Inc. above	35.00	60.00	125	250	—

KM# 1014   500 DINARS (10 Shahis = 1/2 Kran)
2.3025 g., 0.9000 Silver 0.0666 oz. ASW **Obv:** Uniformed bust 3/4 left within wreath, date **Rev:** Crown above lion and sun within wreath, date **Mint:** Tehran

Date	Mintage	F	VF	XF	Unc	BU
AH1325 (1907)	—	125	175	320	500	—
AH1326 (1908)	—	100	150	240	400	—

KM# 1013   500 DINARS (10 Shahis = 1/2 Kran)
2.3025 g., 0.9000 Silver 0.0666 oz. ASW **Obv:** Uniformed bust 1/4 left within sprigs **Rev:** Radiant lion holding sword within crowned wreath **Mint:** Tehran

Date	Mintage	F	VF	XF	Unc	BU
AH1326 (1908)	—	40.00	85.00	150	300	—
Note: Mintage included in KM#1010						
AH1327 (1909)	—	40.00	85.00	150	300	—

KM# 1011   1000 DINARS (Kran, Qiran)
4.6050 g., 0.9000 Silver 0.1332 oz. ASW **Obv:** Legend within circle and crowned wreath **Obv. Leg.:** "Muhammad Ali Shah" **Rev:** Radiant lion holding sword within crowned wreath **Mint:** Tehran

Date	Mintage	F	VF	XF	Unc	BU
AH1325 (1907)	289,000	150	300	600	800	—
AH1326 (1908)	289,000	150	300	600	800	—

KM# 1015   1000 DINARS (Kran, Qiran)
4.6050 g., 0.9000 Silver 0.1332 oz. ASW **Obv:** Uniformed bust 3/4 left within wreath, date below **Rev:** Radiant lion holding sword within crowned wreath **Mint:** Tehran

Date	Mintage	F	VF	XF	Unc	BU
AH1326 (1908)	—	45.00	70.00	150	375	—
Note: Mintage included in KM#1011						
AH1327/6 (1909)	—	40.00	60.00	125	350	—
AH1327 (1909)	—	40.00	60.00	125	350	—

KM# 1016   1000 DINARS (Kran, Qiran)
4.6050 g., 0.9000 Silver 0.1332 oz. ASW **Obv:** Uniformed bust 3/4 left within wreath, date **Rev:** Radiant lion holding sword within crowned wreath, date **Mint:** Tehran

Date	Mintage	F	VF	XF	Unc	BU
AH1326 (1908)	—	125	200	350	500	—
Note: Mintage included in KM#1011						

KM# 1012   2000 DINARS (2 Kran)
9.2100 g., 0.9000 Silver 0.2665 oz. ASW, 28 mm. **Obv:** Legend within circle and crowned wreath **Obv. Leg.:** "Muhammad Ali Shah" **Rev:** Radiant lion holding sword within crowned wreath **Mint:** Tehran

Date	Mintage	F	VF	XF	Unc	BU
AH1325 (1907)	3,076,000	15.00	25.00	50.00	100	—
AH1326 (1908)	3,069,000	7.50	11.50	20.00	50.00	—
AH1327 (1909)	—	7.50	11.50	20.00	50.00	—

KM# 1017   2000 DINARS (2 Kran)
9.2100 g., 0.9000 Silver 0.2665 oz. ASW **Obv:** Uniformed bust 3/4 left within wreath, date below **Rev:** Radiant lion holding sword within crowned wreath **Mint:** Tehran

Date	Mintage	F	VF	XF	Unc	BU
AH1326 (1908)	—	500	1,000	1,500	2,500	—
Note: Mintage included in KM#1012						

KM# 1018   5000 DINARS (5 Kran)
23.0251 g., 0.9000 Silver 0.6662 oz. ASW **Obv:** Uniformed bust 3/4 left within wreath **Rev:** Crown above lion and sun within wreath **Note:** Dav.#290.

Date	Mintage	F	VF	XF	Unc	BU
AH1327 (1909)	—	250	500	1,000	1,500	—
Note: Obverse always weakly struck with little detail in head and face						

KM# 1024   2000 DINARS (1/5 Toman)
0.5749 g., 0.9000 Gold 0.0166 oz. AGW **Obv:** Uniformed bust 3/4 left within wreath **Rev:** Legend in wreath

Date	Mintage	F	VF	XF	Unc	BU
AH1326 (1908)	—	75.00	100	150	275	—
AH1327 (1909)	—	75.00	100	150	275	—

KM# 1021   5000 DINARS (1/2 Toman)
1.4372 g., 0.9000 Gold 0.0416 oz. AGW, 17 mm. **Obv:** Legend within circle and wreath **Obv. Leg.:** Muhammad Ali Shah **Rev:** Radiant lion holding sword within crowned wreath

Date	Mintage	F	VF	XF	Unc	BU
AH1324 (1906)	—	75.00	100	150	275	—
AH1325 (1907)	—	75.00	100	150	275	—

KM# 1025   5000 DINARS (1/2 Toman)
1.4372 g., 0.9000 Gold 0.0416 oz. AGW, 17 mm. **Obv:** Uniformed bust 3/4 left divides date **Rev:** Legend within circle and wreath **Rev. Leg.:** "Muhammad Ali Shah"

Date	Mintage	F	VF	XF	Unc	BU
AH1326 (1908)	—	75.00	100	150	275	—
AH1362 (1908) Error for 1326	—	75.00	100	150	275	—
AH1327 (1909)	—	75.00	100	150	275	—

KM# 1022   TOMAN
2.8744 g., 0.9000 Gold 0.0832 oz. AGW, 19 mm. **Obv:** Legend within circle and wreath **Obv. Leg.:** "Muhammad Ali Shah" **Rev:** Radiant lion holding sword within crowned wreath

Date	Mintage	F	VF	XF	Unc	BU
AH1324 (1906)	—	90.00	150	300	500	—

KM# 1026   TOMAN
2.8744 g., 0.9000 Gold 0.0832 oz. AGW **Obv:** Uniformed bust 3/4 left divides date **Rev:** Legend within circle and closed wreath **Rev. Leg.:** "Muhammad Ali Shah"

Date	Mintage	F	VF	XF	Unc	BU
AH1327 (1909)	—	90.00	150	300	500	—

MILLED COINAGE
Silver Kran Standard

KM# 891   SHAHI SEFID (White Shahi)
Copper-Nickel Clad Brass **Obv. Leg.:** "Nasir al-Din" (KM#889) **Rev. Leg.:** "Shahib al-zaman" (obverse of KM#1007) **Mint:** Tehran **Note:** Mule using old obverse die.

Date	Mintage	F	VF	XF	Unc	BU
ND	—	50.00	75.00	125	250	—

Sultan Ahmad Shah
AH1327-1344 / 1909-1925AD

MILLED COINAGE

KM# 1031   SHAHI SEFID (White Shahi)
0.0691 g., 0.9000 Silver 0.0020 oz. ASW **Obv:** Legend within circle and wreath **Obv. Leg.:** "Ahmad Shah" **Rev:** Radiant lion holding sword within crowned wreath **Mint:** Tehran

Date	Mintage	F	VF	XF	Unc	BU
AH1328 (1910)	—	5.00	10.00	20.00	40.00	—
AH1329 (1911)	—	6.00	12.00	25.00	50.00	—
AH1330 (1911)	189,000	4.00	10.00	20.00	40.00	—

KM# 1032 SHAHI SEFID (White Shahi)
0.0691 g., 0.9000 Silver 0.0020 oz. ASW **Obv:** Legend within circle and wreath **Rev:** Radiant lion holding sword within crowned wreath **Mint:** Tehran

Date	Mintage	F	VF	XF	Unc	BU
AH1332 (1913)	10,000	30.00	50.00	85.00	150	—

KM# 1033 SHAHI SEFID (White Shahi)
0.0691 g., 0.9000 Silver 0.0020 oz. ASW **Obv:** Legend within circle and wreath **Obv. Leg.:** "Ahmad Shah" **Rev:** Legend within circle and wreath **Rev. Leg.:** "Sahib-al-Zaman" **Mint:** Tehran

Date	Mintage	F	VF	XF	Unc	BU
ND (1913)	—	60.00	125	200	400	—

KM# 1049 SHAHI SEFID (White Shahi)
0.0691 g., 0.9000 Silver 0.0020 oz. ASW **Obv:** Legend within circle and wreath **Rev:** Radiant lion holding sword within crowned wreath **Rev. Leg.:** "Sahib-al-Zaman" **Mint:** Tehran

Date	Mintage	F	VF	XF	Unc	BU
ND (1913)	—	10.00	20.00	40.00	75.00	—
AH1332 (1913)	—	10.00	18.00	35.00	80.00	—
Note: Included in KM#1032						
AH1333 (1914)	—	10.00	20.00	40.00	80.00	—
Note: Included in KM#1047						
AH1337 (1918)	—	10.00	20.00	40.00	80.00	—
Note: Included in KM#1047						
AH1341 (1922)	3,000	15.00	25.00	50.00	100	—
AH1342 (1923)	—	15.00	25.00	50.00	100	—
Note: Included in KM#1047						

KM# 1047 SHAHI SEFID (White Shahi)
0.0691 g., 0.9000 Silver 0.0020 oz. ASW **Obv:** Legend within circle and wreath, date below **Rev:** Radiant lion holding sword within crowned wreath **Mint:** Tehran **Note:** Varieties exist.

Date	Mintage	F	VF	XF	Unc	BU
AH1333 (1914)	78,000	5.00	10.00	20.00	40.00	—
AH1334 (1915)	6,000	12.00	20.00	40.00	80.00	—
AH1335 (1916)	73,000	8.00	15.00	30.00	60.00	—
AH1335//1337 (1918)	Inc. above	40.00	80.00	165	250	—
AH1337 (1918)	76,000	8.00	15.00	30.00	60.00	—
AH1337//1337 (1918)	—	40.00	75.00	150	280	—
AH1339 (1920)	10,000	12.00	20.00	40.00	80.00	—
AH1342 (1923)	20,000	12.00	20.00	40.00	80.00	—

KM# 1048 SHAHI SEFID (White Shahi)
0.0691 g., 0.9000 Silver 0.0020 oz. ASW **Obv:** Legend within circle and wreath **Rev:** Legend within circle and wreath, date below **Rev. Leg.:** "Sahib-al-Zaman" **Mint:** Tehran

Date	Mintage	F	VF	XF	Unc	BU
AH1335 (1916)	—	50.00	80.00	150	300	—
Note: Mintage included in KM#1047 of AH1335						

KM# 1050 SHAHI SEFID (White Shahi)
0.6908 g., 0.9000 Silver 0.0200 oz. ASW **Obv:** Legend within circle and wreath, dated AH1339 **Rev:** Radiant lion with sword within crowned wreath with AH1341 between lion's legs, AH1327 below wreath **Mint:** Tehran

Date	Mintage	F	VF	XF	Unc	BU
AH1339//1341 & 1327 (1922)	—	50.00	80.00	150	300	—
Note: Numerous silver Nouruz tokens, some with dates SH1328-1346, are available in Tehran for a fraction of the price of true Shahis						

KM# 1035 1/4 KRAN (Robi = 5 Shahis)
1.1513 g., 0.9000 Silver 0.0333 oz. ASW, 15 mm. **Obv:** Legend within circle and wreath **Obv. Leg.:** "Ahmad Shah" **Rev:** Radiant lion holding sword within crowned wreath **Mint:** Tehran

Date	Mintage	F	VF	XF	Unc	BU
AH1327 (1909)	—	5.00	10.00	20.00	40.00	—
AH1328 (1910)	—	4.00	7.50	15.00	30.00	—
AH1329 (1911)	130,000	12.50	20.00	40.00	80.00	—
AH1330 (1911)	156,000	4.00	7.50	15.00	30.00	—
AH1331 (1912)	30,000					
Note: Reported, not confirmed.						
AH1313 (1912) Error for 1331	Inc. above	—	—	—	—	—
Note: Reported, not confirmed.						

KM# 1052 1/4 KRAN (Robi = 5 Shahis)
1.1513 g., 0.9000 Silver 0.0333 oz. ASW **Obv:** Legend within circle and wreath, date below **Obv. Leg.:** "Ahmad Shah" **Rev:** Radiant lion holding sword within crowned wreath **Mint:** Tehran **Note:** Mule.

Date	Mintage	F	VF	XF	Unc	BU
ND (1909)	—	45.00	65.00	125	200	—
AH1327 (1909)	—	65.00	135	185	300	—

KM# 1051 1/4 KRAN (Robi = 5 Shahis)
1.1513 g., 0.9000 Silver 0.0333 oz. ASW **Obv:** Legend within circle and wreath **Obv. Leg.:** "Ahmad Shah" **Rev:** Radiant lion holding sword within crowned wreath **Mint:** Tehran

Date	Mintage	F	VF	XF	Unc	BU
AH1332 (1913)	252,000	5.00	10.00	20.00	40.00	—
AH1333 (1914)	Inc. above	6.00	12.00	25.00	50.00	—
AH1334 (1915)	70,000	10.00	20.00	50.00	100	—
AH1335 (1916)	260,000	4.00	8.00	15.00	30.00	—
AH1336 (1917)	160,000	4.00	8.00	15.00	30.00	—
AH1337 (1918)	80,000	6.00	12.00	25.00	50.00	—
AH1339 (1920)	28,000	9.00	15.00	30.00	60.00	—
AH1341 (1922)	22,000	12.00	20.00	40.00	80.00	—
AH1342 (1923)	110,000	6.00	12.00	25.00	50.00	—
AH1343 (1924)	186,000	4.00	8.00	15.00	30.00	—

KM# 1053 1/4 KRAN (Robi = 5 Shahis)
1.1513 g., 0.9000 Silver 0.0333 oz. ASW **Obv:** Legend within circle and wreath **Rev:** Radiant lion holding sword within crowned wreath **Mint:** Tehran

Date	Mintage	F	VF	XF	Unc	BU
AH1334 (1915)	—	35.00	75.00	150	250	—
Note: Mintage included with KM#1051						

KM# 1036 500 DINARS (10 Shahis = 1/2 Kran)
2.3025 g., 0.9000 Silver 0.0666 oz. ASW, 18 mm. **Obv:** Legend within circle and wreath **Obv. Leg.:** "Ahmad Shah" **Rev:** Radiant lion holding sword within crowned wreath **Mint:** Tehran

Date	Mintage	F	VF	XF	Unc	BU
AH1327 (1909)	—	8.00	15.00	30.00	50.00	—
AH1328 (1910)	—	5.00	12.50	20.00	40.00	—
AH1329 (1911)	44,000	10.00	20.00	40.00	80.00	—
AH1330 (1911)	627,000	8.00	15.00	30.00	50.00	—

KM# 1054 500 DINARS (10 Shahis = 1/2 Kran)
2.3025 g., 0.9000 Silver 0.0666 oz. ASW **Obv:** Uniformed bust 1/4 left within wreath, date below **Rev:** Radiant lion holding sword within crowned wreath **Mint:** Tehran

Date	Mintage	F	VF	XF	Unc	BU
AH1331 (1912)	—	8.00	15.00	30.00	50.00	—
Note: Mintage included in AH1330 above						
AH1332 (1913)	560,000	8.00	15.00	30.00	50.00	—
AH1333 (1914)	292,000	5.00	10.00	15.00	30.00	—
AH1334 (1915)	65,000	5.00	10.00	15.00	30.00	—
AH1335 (1916)	150,000	8.00	15.00	30.00	60.00	—
AH1336 (1917)	240,000	4.00	8.00	20.00	40.00	—
AH1339 (1920)	—	17.50	25.00	40.00	80.00	—
AH1343 (1924)	160,000	6.00	15.00	30.00	50.00	—
Note: 10,000 reported struck in AH1337 probably dated AH1336						

KM# 1055 500 DINARS (10 Shahis = 1/2 Kran)
2.3025 g., 0.9000 Silver 0.0666 oz. ASW **Obv:** Uniformed bust 1/4 left within wreath, date below **Rev:** Radiant lion holding sword within crowned wreath **Mint:** Tehran

Date	Mintage	F	VF	XF	Unc	BU
AH1332 (1913)	—	30.00	50.00	90.00	200	—
Note: Mintage included in KM#1054						

KM# 1038 1000 DINARS (Kran, Qiran)
4.6050 g., 0.9000 Silver 0.1332 oz. ASW, 23 mm. **Obv:** Legend within circle and wreath **Obv. Leg.:** "Sultan Ahmad Shah" **Rev:** Radiant lion holding sword within crowned wreath **Mint:** Tehran

Date	Mintage	F	VF	XF	Unc	BU
AH1327 (1909)	—	7.50	15.00	30.00	60.00	—
AH1328 (1910)	—	6.50	12.50	25.00	50.00	—
AH1329 (1911)	3,000,000	6.50	12.50	25.00	50.00	—
AH1330 (1911)	—	6.50	12.50	25.00	50.00	—

KM# 1037 1000 DINARS (Kran, Qiran)
4.6050 g., 0.9000 Silver 0.1332 oz. ASW **Obv:** Legend within circle and wreath **Rev:** Radiant lion holding sword within crowned wreath **Mint:** Tehran **Note:** Mule.

Date	Mintage	F	VF	XF	Unc	BU
AH1336 (1909)	—	—	—	100	200	—

KM# 1056 1000 DINARS (Kran, Qiran)
4.6050 g., 0.9000 Silver 0.1332 oz. ASW **Obv:** Uniformed bust 1/4 left within wreath, date below **Rev:** Radiant lion holding sword within crowned wreath **Mint:** Tehran

Date	Mintage	F	VF	XF	Unc	BU
AH1331 (1912)	1,310,000	5.00	8.00	25.00	40.00	—
AH1332 (1913)	1,891,000	3.00	5.00	12.50	30.00	—
AH1333 (1914)	2,179,000	7.50	12.00	25.00	40.00	—
AH1334 (1915)	1,273,000	3.00	5.00	12.50	25.00	—
AH1335 (1916)	2,162,000	3.00	5.00	12.50	25.00	—
AH1336 (1917)	1,412,000	3.50	6.00	15.00	30.00	—
AH1337 (1918)	3,330,000	3.00	5.00	12.50	25.00	—
AH1339 (1920)	35,000	12.50	25.00	55.00	90.00	—
AH1330 (1921) Error for 1340	—	30.00	65.00	125	175	—
AH1340 (1921)	28,000	15.00	30.00	60.00	100	—
AH1341 (1922)	170,000	8.00	15.00	35.00	60.00	—

Date	Mintage	F	VF	XF	Unc	BU
AH1342 (1923)	255,000	3.00	6.00	20.00	30.00	—
AH1343 (1924)	1,345,000	3.00	6.00	20.00	30.00	—
AH1344 (1925)	2,978,000	4.00	6.00	20.00	35.00	—

KM# 1059   1000 DINARS (Kran, Qiran)
4.6050 g., 0.9000 Silver 0.1332 oz. ASW, 23 mm. **Subject:** 10th Year of Reign **Obv:** Uniformed bust 1/4 left within wreath, date below **Rev:** Radiant lion holding sword within crowned wreath **Mint:** Tehran

Date	Mintage	F	VF	XF	Unc	BU
AH1337 (1918)	975,000	35.00	75.00	125	250	—

KM# 1040   2000 DINARS (2 Kran)
9.2100 g., 0.9000 Silver 0.2665 oz. ASW, 28 mm. **Obv:** Legend within circle and crowned wreath **Obv. Leg.:** "Ahmad Shah" **Rev:** Radiant lion holding sword within crowned wreath **Mint:** Tehran

Date	Mintage	F	VF	XF	Unc	BU
AH1327 (1909)	—	7.50	15.00	30.00	50.00	—
Note: Mintage included in KM#1328
AH1328 (1910)	30,000,000	5.00	10.00	20.00	40.00	—
AH1329 (1911)	29,250,000	5.00	10.00	20.00	40.00	—

KM# 1041   2000 DINARS (2 Kran)
9.2100 g., 0.9000 Silver 0.2665 oz. ASW **Obv:** Legend within circle and crowned wreath **Rev:** Radiant lion holding sword within crowned wreath **Mint:** Tehran

Date	Mintage	F	VF	XF	Unc	BU
AH1330 (1911)	2,901,000	7.50	15.00	30.00	60.00	—

KM# 1043   2000 DINARS (2 Kran)
9.2100 g., 0.9000 Silver 0.2665 oz. ASW **Obv:** Legend within circle and crowned wreath **Obv. Leg.:** "Ahmad Shah" **Rev:** Radiant lion holding sword within crowned wreath **Mint:** Tehran

Date	Mintage	F	VF	XF	Unc	BU
AH1330 (1911)	—	7.50	15.00	30.00	60.00	—
Note: Mintage included in KM#1041
AH1331 (1912)	13,412,000	7.50	15.00	30.00	60.00	—

KM# 1057   2000 DINARS (2 Kran)
9.2100 g., 0.9000 Silver 0.2665 oz. ASW **Obv:** Uniformed bust 1/4 left within wreath, date below **Rev:** Radiant lion holding sword within crowned wreath **Mint:** Tehran

Date	Mintage	F	VF	XF	Unc	BU
AH1331 (1912)	—	6.00	12.50	25.00	50.00	—
Note: Mintage included in KM#1043
AH1332 (1913)	12,926,000	5.00	7.50	15.00	30.00	—
AH1333 (1914)	Inc. above	5.00	7.50	15.00	30.00	—
AH1334 (1915)	4,299,000	5.00	7.50	15.00	30.00	—
AH1335 (1916)	9,777,000	5.00	7.50	15.00	30.00	—
AH1336 (1917)	5,401,000	5.00	7.50	15.00	30.00	—

Date	Mintage	F	VF	XF	Unc	BU
AH1337 (1918)	2,951,000	5.00	7.50	15.00	30.00	—
AH1339 (1920)	1,085,000	6.00	12.50	25.00	50.00	—
AH1330 (1921)	—	50.00	100	150	250	—
Error for 1340
Note: Mintage included in KM#1043
AH1340 (1921)	254,000	9.00	15.00	30.00	65.00	—
AH1341 (1922)	4,460,000	5.00	7.50	15.00	30.00	—
AH1342 (1923)	2,245,000	5.00	8.00	20.00	35.00	—
AH1343 (1924)	5,205,000	5.00	8.00	20.00	35.00	—
AH1344/34 (1925)	12,354	7.00	12.00	25.00	55.00	—
AH1344 (1925)	Inc. above	6.00	10.00	20.00	40.00	—

KM# 1060   2000 DINARS (2 Kran)
9.2100 g., 0.9000 Silver 0.2665 oz. ASW, 28 mm. **Subject:** 10th Anniversary of Reign **Obv:** Uniformed bust 1/4 left within wreath **Rev:** Radiant lion with sword within crowned wreath **Mint:** Tehran

Date	Mintage	F	VF	XF	Unc	BU
AH1337 (1918)	3,503,000	60.00	100	150	300	—

KM# 1058   5000 DINARS (5 Kran)
23.0251 g., 0.9000 Silver 0.6662 oz. ASW **Obv:** Uniformed bust 1/4 left within wreath, date below **Rev:** Radiant lion holding sword within crowned wreath **Note:** Dav.#291.

Date	Mintage	F	VF	XF	Unc	BU
AH1331 (1912)	—	60.00	150	250	500	—
AH1332 (1913)	3,000,000	10.00	14.00	30.00	85.00	—
AH1333 (1914)	667,000	12.00	16.00	35.00	90.00	—
AH1334 (1915)	443,000	12.00	16.00	35.00	90.00	—
AH1335 (1916)	1,884,000	12.00	16.00	35.00	90.00	—
AH1337 (1918)	165,000	14.00	25.00	55.00	110	—
AH1339 (1920)	90,000	20.00	30.00	65.00	125	—
AH1340 (1921)	303,000	14.00	25.00	55.00	110	—
AH1341 (1922)	757,000	12.00	16.00	35.00	90.00	—
AH1342/32 (1923)	546,000	12.00	16.00	35.00	90.00	—
AH1342 (1923)	Inc. above	12.00	16.00	35.00	90.00	—
AH1343/33 (1924)	935,000	12.00	16.00	35.00	90.00	—
AH1343 (1924)	Inc. above	12.00	16.00	35.00	90.00	—
AH1344/34 (1925)	2,284,000	12.00	16.00	30.00	85.00	—
AH1344 (1925)	Inc. above	15.00	20.00	40.00	95.00	—

Note: Beware of altered date AH1331 specimens. 9,000 reported minted in AH1336, probably dated earlier

KM# 1066   2000 DINARS (1/5 Toman)
0.5749 g., 0.9000 Gold 0.0166 oz. AGW, 14 mm. **Obv:** Legend within circle and wreath **Obv. Leg.:** "Ahmad Shah" **Rev:** Radiant lion holding sword within crowned wreath

Date	Mintage	F	VF	XF	Unc	BU
AH1328 (1910)	—	100	175	250	500	—
AH1329 (1911)	—	250	550	750	900	—
AH1330 (1911)	—	100	175	250	500	—

KM# 1070   2000 DINARS (1/5 Toman)
0.5749 g., 0.9000 Gold 0.0166 oz. AGW, 14 mm. **Obv:** Uniformed bust 1/4 left divides date **Rev:** Legend within circle and wreath **Rev. Leg.:** "Ahmad Shah"

Date	Mintage	F	VF	XF	Unc	BU
AH1332 (1913)	—	22.50	40.00	60.00	130	—
AH1333 (1914)	—	18.50	35.00	60.00	125	—
AH1334 (1915)	—	25.00	50.00	100	200	—
AH1335 (1916)	—	16.50	30.00	40.00	60.00	—
AH1337 (1918)	—	16.50	30.00	40.00	100	—
AH1339 (1920)	—	18.50	35.00	50.00	100	—
AH1340 (1921)	—	18.50	40.00	60.00	120	—
AH1341 (1922)	—	18.50	35.00	50.00	100	—
AH1342 (1923)	—	18.50	35.00	50.00	100	—
AH1343/33 (1924)	—	50.00	100	200	400	—
AH1343 (1924)	—	25.00	50.00	100	200	—

KM# 1067   5000 DINARS (1/2 Toman)
1.4372 g., 0.9000 Gold 0.0416 oz. AGW **Obv:** Legend within circle and wreath **Obv. Leg.:** "Ahmad Shah" **Rev:** Radiant lion holding sword within crowned wreath

Date	Mintage	F	VF	XF	Unc	BU
AH1328 (1910)	—	60.00	125	200	275	—
AH1329 (1911)	—	175	400	600	750	—
AH1330 (1911)	—	175	400	600	750	—

KM# 1071   5000 DINARS (1/2 Toman)
1.4372 g., 0.9000 Gold 0.0416 oz. AGW, 17 mm. **Obv:** Uniformed bust 1/4 left divides date **Rev:** Legend within circle and wreath **Rev. Leg.:** "Ahmad Shah"

Date	Mintage	F	VF	XF	Unc	BU
AH1331 (1912)	—	50.00	100	150	300	—
AH1332 (1913)	—	40.00	60.00	100	150	—
AH1333 (1914)	—	50.00	100	200	300	—
AH1334 (1915)	—	50.00	100	200	300	—
AH1335 (1916)	—	50.00	100	200	300	—
AH1336 (1917)	—	40.00	45.00	60.00	90.00	—
AH1337 (1918)	—	50.00	100	200	300	—
AH1339 (1920)	—	60.00	125	250	350	—
AH1340 (1921)	—	40.00	45.00	60.00	110	—
AH1341 (1922)	—	40.00	45.00	60.00	90.00	—
AH1342 (1923)	—	40.00	45.00	60.00	90.00	—
AH1343/33 (1924)	—	100	200	400	600	—
AH1343 (1924)	—	50.00	100	200	300	—

KM# 1072   5000 DINARS (1/2 Toman)
1.4372 g., 0.9000 Gold 0.0416 oz. AGW **Obv:** Bust with headdress 1/4 left within sprigs **Rev. Leg.:** "Sahib al-Zaman"

Date	Mintage	F	VF	XF	Unc	BU
AH1339 (1920)	—	100	150	250	600	—
AH1340 (1921)	—	100	150	250	600	—

KM# 1068   TOMAN
2.8744 g., 0.9000 Gold 0.0832 oz. AGW, 19 mm. **Obv. Leg.:** "Ahmad Shah", AH1328-1332 **Rev:** Lion and sun

Date	Mintage	F	VF	XF	Unc	BU
AH1329 (1911)	Rare	—	—	—	—	—
Note: Only two examples are known

KM# 1074   TOMAN
2.8744 g., 0.9000 Gold 0.0832 oz. AGW, 19 mm. **Obv:** Uniformed bust 1/4 left divides date **Rev:** Legend within circle and wreath **Rev. Leg.:** "Ahmad Shah"

Date	Mintage	F	VF	XF	Unc	BU
AH1332 (1913)	—	80.00	150	250	500	—
AH1333 (1914)	—	500	750	1,000	1,250	—
AH1334 (1915)	—	80.00	125	175	300	—
AH1335 (1916)	—	80.00	125	175	300	—
AH1337 (1918)	—	BV	80.00	100	175	—
AH1339 (1920)	—	BV	80.00	100	175	—
AH1340 (1921)	—	100	200	300	400	—
AH1341 (1922)	—	BV	80.00	100	150	—
AH1342 (1923)	—	BV	80.00	100	150	—
AH1343 (1924)	—	BV	80.00	100	150	—

KM# 1073   TOMAN
2.8744 g., 0.9000 Gold 0.0832 oz. AGW, 19 mm. **Obv:** Bust with headdress 1/4 left **Rev:** Ahmad Shah Pattern 2 Toman **Note:** The reverse die used was of an unadopted pattern.

Date	Mintage	F	VF	XF	Unc	BU
AH1332 (1913)	—	300	600	900	1,500	—
AH1333 (1914)	—	350	650	1,000	1,750	—

KM# 1075 5 TOMAN
14.3720 g., 0.9000 Gold 0.4158 oz. AGW, 30 mm. **Obv:** Legend within beaded circle and wreath **Obv. Leg.:** "Ahmad Shah" **Rev:** Radiant lion holding sword within wreath

Date	Mintage	F	VF	XF	Unc	BU
AH1332/1 (1913)	—	3,500	4,500	6,000	8,000	—
AH1334/2/1 (1915)	—	1,100	1,600	2,000	2,700	—

Note: A number of gold medals of 5 Toman weight were struck between 1297 and 1326; These bear a couplet which clearly indicates that they are medals awarded by the Shah for bravery

KM# 1076 10 TOMAN
28.7440 g., 0.9000 Gold 0.8317 oz. AGW, 37 mm.
Obv: Uniformed bust 1/4 left within wreath, date below
Obv. Leg.: "Ahmad Shah" **Rev:** Legend within circle and wreath

Date	Mintage	F	VF	XF	Unc	BU
AH1331 (1912)	—	2,400	4,350	6,500	8,500	—
AH1334 (1915) Rare	—	—	—	—	—	—
AH1337//1334 (1918)	—	—	—	6,500	8,500	—

Note: The date on the AH1334 reverse die was not changed for use as the reverse to the 1337 issue

KM# 1077 10 TOMAN
28.7440 g., 0.9000 Gold 0.8317 oz. AGW **Obv:** Uniformed bust 1/4 left within wreath, date **Rev:** Radiant lion holding sword within wreath

Date	Mintage	F	VF	XF	Unc	BU
AH1337 (1918)	—	1,850	3,000	4,500	5,500	—

KM# 1080 ASHRAFI
Gold **Obv:** Bust of Ahmad Shah **Rev:** Lion and sun within crowned wreath

Date	Mintage	F	VF	XF	Unc	BU
AH1337 (1918)	—	—	150	275	400	—

KM# A1081 2 ASHRAFI
Gold **Obv:** Uniformed bust 1/4 left within wreath **Rev:** Crown above lion and sun within wreath

Date	Mintage	F	VF	XF	Unc	BU
AH1337 (1918)	—	—	275	500	750	—

KM# 1081 5 ASHRAFI
Gold **Obv:** Uniformed bust 1/4 left within wreath **Rev:** Lion and sun within crowned wreath

Date	Mintage	F	VF	XF	Unc	BU
AH1337 (1918)	—	—	500	750	1,000	—

KM# 1082 10 ASHRAFI
Gold **Obv:** Uniformed bust 1/4 left within wreath **Rev:** Lion and sun within crowned wreath

Date	Mintage	F	VF	XF	Unc	BU
AH1337 (1918)	—	—	500	1,000	1,500	2,000	—

CLANDESTINE COINAGE

KM# 1039 1000 DINARS (Kran, Qiran)
Silver **Obv:** Legend within beaded circle and wreath **Rev:** Radiant lion holding sword within crowned wreath **Mint:** Tehran

Date	Mintage	F	VF	XF	Unc	BU
AH1330 (sic) (1915)	—	12.00	25.00	50.00	75.00	—
AH1330 (sic) (1915) Proof, rare	—	—	—	—	—	—

Note: KM#1039 differs from KM#1038 in that it is about 1 millimeter broader and has a much thicker rim and more clearly defined denticles. Struck in Germany, without Iranian authorization, for circulation in western Iran during World War I. Also, the lion lacks the triangular face and fierce expression of KM#1038 and the point of the Talwar (scimitar) does not touch the sunburst as it does on Tehran issues.

KM# 1042 2000 DINARS (2 Kran)
Silver **Rev:** Lion's face has friendly expression **Mint:** Tehran

Date	Mintage	F	VF	XF	Unc	BU
AH1330 (sic) (1915)	—	12.00	25.00	50.00	75.00	—

Note: See general note for KM#1039

Reza Shah
AH1344-1360 / 1925-1941AD
MILLED COINAGE

KM# 1091 50 DINARS
19.0000 g., Copper-Nickel, 19 mm. **Obv:** Legend within circle and crowned wreath **Rev:** Radiant lion holding sword within crowned wreath, date **Edge:** Plain **Mint:** Tehran

Date	Mintage	F	VF	XF	Unc	BU
SH1305 (1926)	11,000,000	2.50	5.00	10.00	20.00	—
SH1307 (1928)	2,500,000	2.50	5.00	10.00	20.00	—

KM# 1092 100 DINARS (2 Shahi)
4.5000 g., Copper-Nickel, 21 mm. **Obv:** Legend within circle and crowned wreath **Rev:** Radiant lion holding sword within crowned wreath, 1305 **Edge:** Plain

Date	Mintage	F	VF	XF	Unc	BU
SH1305 (1926)	4,500,000	2.50	5.00	10.00	20.00	—
SH1307 (1928)	3,750,000	2.50	5.00	10.00	20.00	—

KM# 1093 1/4 KRAN (Robi = 5 Shahis)
1.1513 g., 0.9000 Silver 0.0333 oz. ASW **Obv:** Legend within circle and wreath **Rev:** Crown above lion and sun within wreath **Mint:** Tehran **Note:** 8,000 reported struck in SH1305, but that year not yet found and presumed not to exist.

Date	Mintage	F	VF	XF	Unc	BU
SH1304 (1925)	Est. 24,000	20.00	50.00	85.00	160	—

Note: For similar looking coins dated SH1315, see 1/4 Rial, KM#1127.

KM# 1094 500 DINARS (10 Shahis = 1/2 Kran)
2.3025 g., 0.9000 Silver 0.0666 oz. ASW **Obv:** Legend within circle and wreath **Rev:** Radiant lion holding sword within crowned wreath **Mint:** Tehran

Date	Mintage	F	VF	XF	Unc	BU
SH1304 (1925) Rare	—	—	—	—	—	—

KM# 1098 500 DINARS (10 Shahis = 1/2 Kran)
2.3025 g., 0.9000 Silver 0.0666 oz. ASW **Obv:** Legend within wreath **Obv. Leg.:** "Reza Shah" **Rev:** Lion and sun within wreath **Mint:** Tehran

Date	Mintage	F	VF	XF	Unc	BU
SH1305 (1926)	10,000	150	250	500	750	—

KM# 1102 500 DINARS (10 Shahis = 1/2 Kran)
2.3025 g., 0.9000 Silver 0.0666 oz. ASW **Obv:** Uniformed bust 3/4 right within wreath divides date **Rev:** Radiant lion holding sword within crowned wreath **Mint:** Tehran

Date	Mintage	F	VF	XF	Unc	BU
SH1306 (1927)	5,000	50.00	100	150	250	—
SH1307 (1928)	46,000	10.00	15.00	30.00	60.00	—
SH1308 (1929)	464,000	10.00	15.00	30.00	60.00	—

Note: Some of the coins reported in SH1308 were dated 1307

KM# 1095 1000 DINARS (Kran, Qiran)
4.6050 g., 0.9000 Silver 0.1332 oz. ASW **Obv:** Legend within circle and wreath **Rev:** Radiant lion holding sword within crowned wreath **Mint:** Tehran

Date	Mintage	F	VF	XF	Unc	BU
SH1304 (1925)	2,573,000	10.00	20.00	30.00	50.00	—
SH1305 (1926)	2,265,000	10.00	20.00	30.00	50.00	—

KM# 1099 1000 DINARS (Kran, Qiran)
4.6050 g., 0.9000 Silver 0.1332 oz. ASW **Obv:** Legend within circle and wreath **Obv. Leg.:** "Reza Shah" **Rev:** Radiant lion holding sword within crowned wreath **Mint:** Tehran

Date	Mintage	F	VF	XF	Unc	BU
SH1305 (1926)	—	10.00	20.00	30.00	50.00	—

Note: Mintage included in KM#1095

| SH1306/5 (1927) | 3,130,000 | 5.00 | 8.00 | 15.00 | 25.00 | — |
| SH1306 (1927) | Inc. above | 10.00 | 20.00 | 30.00 | 50.00 | — |

KM# 1103 1000 DINARS (Kran, Qiran)
4.6050 g., 0.9000 Silver 0.1332 oz. ASW **Obv:** Uniformed bust 3/4 right within wreath divides date of Ascession in SH1304 **Rev:** Lion and sun within crowned wreath **Mint:** Tehran

Date	Mintage	F	VF	XF	Unc	BU
SH1306 (1927)	—	10.00	20.00	30.00	60.00	—

Note: Mintage included in KM#1099

| SH1307 (1928) | 4,300,000 | 10.00 | 20.00 | 30.00 | 50.00 | — |
| SH1308 (1929) | 603,000 | 10.00 | 20.00 | 30.00 | 50.00 | — |

KM# 1096 2000 DINARS (2 Kran)
9.2100 g., 0.9000 Silver 0.2665 oz. ASW **Obv:** Legend within circle and wreath **Rev:** Date below lion **Mint:** Tehran

Date	Mintage	F	VF	XF	Unc	BU
SH1304 (1925)	11,920,000	15.00	30.00	50.00	75.00	—
SH1305 (1926)	9,785,000	15.00	30.00	50.00	75.00	—

KM# 1100   2000 DINARS (2 Kran)
9.2100 g., 0.9000 Silver 0.2665 oz. ASW **Obv:** Legend within circle and wreath **Obv. Leg.:** "Reza Shah" **Rev:** Radiant lion holding sword within crowned wreath **Mint:** Tehran

Date	Mintage		VF	XF	Unc	BU
SH1305 (1926)	—	15.00	30.00	50.00	75.00	—
SH1306 (1927)	9,380,000	4.50	7.50	12.50	25.00	—

KM# 1104   2000 DINARS (2 Kran)
9.2100 g., 0.9000 Silver 0.2665 oz. ASW **Obv:** Uniformed bust 3/4 right within wreath divides date of Ascension in SH1304 **Rev:** Radiant lion holding sword within crowned wreath

Date	Mintage	F	VF	XF	Unc	BU
SH1306 (1927)	—	5.00	10.00	25.00	50.00	—
Note: Mintage included in KM#1100						
SH1306 (1927) H	11,714,000	5.00	10.00	25.00	50.00	—
SH1306 (1927) L	7,500,000	5.00	10.00	25.00	50.00	—
SH1306 (1927) H Proof	—	Value: 375				
SH1307 (1928)	11,146,000	5.00	10.00	25.00	50.00	—
SH1308 (1929)	1,611,000	5.00	10.00	25.00	50.00	—

KM# 1105   2000 DINARS (2 Kran)
9.2100 g., 0.9000 Silver 0.2665 oz. ASW **Obv:** Uniformed bust 3/4 right within wreath **Rev:** Crown above lion and sun within wreath **Mint:** Tehran **Note:** Mule.

Date	Mintage	F	VF	XF	Unc	BU
SH1306 (1927)	—	—	—	50.00	100	—

KM# 1097   5000 DINARS (5 Kran)
23.0251 g., 0.9000 Silver 0.6662 oz. ASW **Obv:** Legend within crowned wreath **Rev:** Radiant lion holding sword within wreath **Note:** Dav.#292.

Date	Mintage	F	VF	XF	Unc	BU
SH1304 (1925)	500,000	16.00	40.00	75.00	150	—
SH1305 (1926)	1,363,000	16.00	40.00	75.00	150	—

KM# 1101   5000 DINARS (5 Kran)
23.0251 g., 0.9000 Silver 0.6662 oz. ASW **Obv:** Legend within crowned wreath **Obv. Leg.:** "Reza Shah" **Rev:** Radiant lion holding sword within wreath **Note:** Dav.#293.

Date	Mintage	F	VF	XF	Unc	BU
SH1305 (1926)	—	35.00	70.00	100	150	—
Note: Mintage included in KM#1097						
SH1306 (1927)	3,186,000	35.00	70.00	100	150	—

KM# 1106   5000 DINARS (5 Kran)
23.0251 g., 0.9000 Silver 0.6662 oz. ASW **Obv:** Uniformed bust 3/4 right within divides date of Ascension in SH1304 **Rev:** Crown above lion and sun within wreath **Note:** Dav.#294. Mint marks located as on 2000 Dinars, KM#1104.

Date	Mintage	F	VF	XF	Unc	BU
SH1306 (1927)	—	12.00	25.00	50.00	100	
Note: Mintage including in KM#1101						
SH1306 (1927) Proof	—	Value: 400				
SH1306 (1927) H	4,711,000	12.00	25.00	50.00	100	—
SH1306 (1927) L	3,000,000	12.00	25.00	50.00	100	—
SH1307 (1928)	3,928,000	15.00	35.00	75.00	150	—
SH1308 (1929)	584,000	15.00	35.00	75.00	150	—

KM# 1107   5000 DINARS (5 Kran)
23.0251 g., 0.9000 Silver 0.6662 oz. ASW **Obv:** Uniformed bust 3/4 right within wreath **Rev:** Crown above lion and sun within wreath **Note:** Mule.

Date	Mintage	F	VF	XF	Unc	BU
SH1306 (1927)	—	—	75.00	150	—	

KM# 1108   TOMAN
2.8744 g., Gold, 19 mm. **Subject:** Reza's First New Year Celebration **Obv:** Reza type legend **Rev:** Radiant lion holding sword within crowned wreath

Date	Mintage	F	VF	XF	Unc	BU
SH1305 (1926)	—	200	300	500	750	—

KM# 1111   PAHLAVI
1.9180 g., Gold **Obv:** Legend within crowned wreath **Rev:** Radiant lion holding sword within crowned wreath

Date	Mintage	F	VF	XF	Unc	BU
SH1305 (1926)	5,000	125	250	400	600	—

KM# 1114   PAHLAVI
2.8744 g., Gold **Obv:** Uniformed bust right above sprays **Rev:** Value and legend within beaded circle and crowned wreath

Date	Mintage	F	VF	XF	Unc	BU
SH1306 (1927)	21,000	BV	65.00	85.00	125	—
SH1307 (1928)	5,000	65.00	90.00	125	185	—
SH1308 (1929)	989	80.00	100	160	275	—

KM# 1112   2 PAHLAVI
3.8360 g., Gold **Obv:** Legend within crowned wreath **Rev:** Radiant lion holding sword within crowned wreath

Date	Mintage	F	VF	XF	Unc	BU
SH1305 (1926)	1,134	250	400	750	1,250	—

KM# 1115   2 PAHLAVI
3.8360 g., Gold **Obv:** Uniformed bust right above sprays **Rev:** Value and legend within beaded circle and crowned wreath

Date	Mintage	F	VF	XF	Unc	BU
SH1306 (1927)	2,494	80.00	100	150	250	—
SH1307 (1928)	7,000	80.00	100	150	230	—
SH1308 (1929)	789	90.00	115	200	285	—

KM# 1113   5 PAHLAVI
9.5900 g., Gold **Obv:** Legend within crowned wreath **Rev:** Radiant lion holding sword within crowned wreath

Date	Mintage	F	VF	XF	Unc	BU
SH1305 (1926)	271	500	700	950	2,000	—

KM# 1116   5 PAHLAVI
9.5900 g., Gold **Obv:** Uniformed bust right above sprays **Rev:** Legend and value within beaded circle and crowned wreath

Date	Mintage	F	VF	XF	Unc	BU
SH1306 (1927)	909	600	1,000	1,500	2,000	—
SH1307 (1928)	785	600	1,000	1,500	2,000	—
SH1308 (1929)	121	750	1,250	2,000	2,500	—

REFORM COINAGE

KM# 1126.2   2-1/2 ABBASI (10 Shahi)
4.4500 g., Copper, 24.7 mm. **Obv:** Radiant lion holding sword within crowned wreath **Rev:** Legend within beaded heart-shaped circle within designed crowned wreath **Edge:** Reeded

Date	Mintage	F	VF	XF	Unc	BU
SH1314 (1935) Large date	Inc. above	3.00	4.00	12.50	30.00	—
SH1314 (1935) Small date	20,000,000	3.00	4.00	12.50	30.00	—

KM# 1126.1   2-1/2 ABBASI (10 Shahi)
4.4500 g., Copper, 24.7 mm. **Obv:** Radiant lion holding sword within crowned wreath **Rev:** Legend within beaded heart-shaped circle within designed crowned wreath **Edge:** Plain

Date	Mintage	F	VF	XF	Unc	BU
SH1314 (1935)	Inc. below	5.00	7.00	15.00	40.00	—

KM# 1121   DINAR
1.7000 g., Bronze, 16 mm. **Obv:** Radiant lion holding sword within crowned wreath **Rev:** Value within large flowered wreath **Edge:** Plain

Date	Mintage	F	VF	XF	Unc	BU
SH1310 (1931)	10,000,000	30.00	50.00	75.00	175	—

KM# 1122 2 DINARS
1.8000 g., Bronze, 26.5 mm. **Obv:** Radiant lion holding sword within crowned wreath **Rev:** Value within large flowered wreath **Edge:** Plain

Date	Mintage	F	VF	XF	Unc	BU
SH1310 (1931)	5,000,000	30.00	50.00	75.00	175	—

KM# 1123 5 DINARS
1.9500 g., Copper-Nickel, 18.5 mm. **Obv:** Radiant lion holding sword within crowned wreath **Rev:** Value within beaded circle and designed crowned wreath **Edge:** Plain

Date	Mintage	F	VF	XF	Unc	BU
SH1310 (1931)	3,750,000	20.00	40.00	100	275	—

KM# 1123a 5 DINARS
2.1500 g., Copper, 18.2 mm. **Obv:** Radiant lion holding sword within crowned wreath **Rev:** Value within beaded circle and crowned designed wreath **Edge:** Plain

Date	Mintage	F	VF	XF	Unc	BU
SH1314	480,000	200	400	750	—	—

KM# 1138 5 DINARS
Aluminum-Bronze, 16 mm. **Obv:** Radiant lion holding sword within crowned wreath **Rev:** Value within large flowered wreath

Date	Mintage	F	VF	XF	Unc	BU
SH1315 (1936)	5,665,000	2.50	4.00	10.00	20.00	—
SH1316 (1937)	Inc. above	0.40	0.75	1.50	5.00	—
SH1317 (1938)	13,025,000	0.40	0.75	1.50	5.00	—
SH1318 (1939)	—	0.40	0.75	1.50	5.00	—
SH1319 (1940)	—	0.40	0.75	1.50	5.00	—
SH1320 (1941)	—	0.40	0.75	1.50	4.00	—
SH1321 (1942)	—	0.40	0.75	1.50	5.00	—

KM# 1124 10 DINARS
3.8000 g., Copper-Nickel, 21 mm. **Obv:** Radiant lion holding sword within crowned wreath **Rev:** Value within beaded circle and crowned designed wreath **Edge:** Plain **Note:** Struck at Berlin.

Date	Mintage	F	VF	XF	Unc	BU
SH1310 (1931)	3,750,000	15.00	40.00	100	350	—

KM# 1124a 10 DINARS
3.2000 g., Copper, 21 mm. **Obv:** Radiant lion holding sword within crowned wreath **Rev:** Value within beaded circle and crowned designed wreath **Edge:** Plain **Mint:** Tehran **Note:** Struck at Tehran.

Date	Mintage	F	VF	XF	Unc	BU
SH1314 (1935)	11,350,000	11.50	20.00	45.00	125	—

KM# 1139 10 DINARS
2.6500 g., Aluminum-Bronze, 18 mm. **Obv:** Radiant lion holding sword within crowned wreath **Rev:** Value within wreath

Date	Mintage	F	VF	XF	Unc	BU
SH1315 (1936)	6,195,000	2.00	5.00	15.00	25.00	—
SH1316 (1937)	Inc. above	0.80	1.50	4.00	10.00	—
SH1317 (1938)	17,120,000	0.40	0.80	2.00	6.00	—
SH1318 (1939)	—	0.40	0.80	2.00	6.00	—
SH1319 (1940)	—	0.40	0.80	2.00	6.00	—
SH1320 (1941)	—	0.40	0.80	2.00	6.00	—
SH1321 (1942)	—	0.45	1.00	2.50	6.00	—

KM# 1125 25 DINARS
4.8500 g., Copper-Nickel, 24 mm. **Obv:** Radiant lion holding sword within crowned wreath **Rev:** Value within beaded circle and crowned designed wreath **Edge:** Plain

Date	Mintage	F	VF	XF	Unc	BU
SH1310 (1931)	750,000	25.00	60.00	150	300	—

KM# 1125a 25 DINARS
4.2000 g., Copper, 24.2 mm. **Obv:** Radiant lion holding sword within crowned wreath **Rev:** Value within beaded circle and crowned designed wreath **Edge:** Plain

Date	Mintage	F	VF	XF	Unc	BU
SH1314 (1935)	1,152,000	25.00	50.00	75.00	125	—

KM# 1142 50 DINARS
3.4700 g., Aluminum-Bronze, 20 mm. **Obv:** Radiant lion holding sword within crowned wreath **Rev:** Value within wreath

Date	Mintage	F	VF	XF	Unc	BU
SH1315 (1936)	15,968,000	3.00	4.50	10.00	35.00	—
SH1316 (1937)	34,200,000	1.25	2.50	6.00	20.00	—
SH1317 (1938)	17,314,000	0.60	1.50	4.00	15.00	—
SH1318 (1939)	—	0.60	1.50	4.00	15.00	—
SH1319 (1940)	—	1.50	2.50	6.00	20.00	—
SH1320 (1941)	—	0.75	1.50	3.00	10.00	—
SH1321/0 (1942)	—	0.75	1.50	3.00	15.00	—
SH1322/10 (1943)	—	0.75	1.50	3.00	15.00	—
SH1322/12 (1943)	—	0.75	1.50	3.00	10.00	—
SH1322/0 (1943)	—	0.75	1.50	3.00	10.00	—
SH1322/1 (1943)	—	0.75	1.50	3.00	10.00	—
SH1331 (1952)	8,162,000	3.50	4.50	10.00	25.00	—
SH1332 (1953)	22,892,000	2.00	3.00	5.00	10.00	—

KM# 1142a 50 DINARS
Copper **Obv:** Radiant lion holding sword within crowned wreath **Rev:** Value within wreath

Date	Mintage	F	VF	XF	Unc	BU
SH1322 (1943)	—	2.00	4.00	7.00	12.00	—
SH1322/0 (1943)	—	2.00	6.00	9.00	15.00	—

KM# 1127 1/4 RIAL
1.2500 g., 0.8280 Silver 0.0333 oz. ASW **Obv:** Value within circle and wreath **Rev:** Radiant lion holding sword within crowned wreath

Date	Mintage	F	VF	XF	Unc	BU
SH1315	600,000	1.50	2.50	5.00	10.00	—

Note: The second "1" is often short, so that the date looks like 1305

KM# 1128 1/2 RIAL
2.5000 g., 0.8280 Silver 0.0665 oz. ASW, 18 mm. **Obv:** Value within crowned wreath **Obv. Leg.:** "Reza Shah" **Rev:** Radiant lion holding sword within crowned wreath **Note:** All 1/2 Rials dated SH1311-1315 are recut dies, usually from SH1310.

Date	Mintage	F	VF	XF	Unc	BU
SH1310 (1931)	2,000,000	2.50	5.00	10.00	20.00	—
SH1311 (1932)	—	50.00	100	150	200	—
SH1312 (1933)	—	2.50	5.00	10.00	20.00	—
SH1313 (1934)	1,945,000	2.50	5.00	10.00	20.00	—
SH1314 (1935)	100,000	2.50	5.00	10.00	20.00	—
SH1315 (1936)	800,000	5.00	10.00	20.00	30.00	—

KM# 1129 RIAL
5.0000 g., 0.8280 Silver 0.1331 oz. ASW, 22.5 mm. **Obv:** Value within crowned wreath **Rev:** Radiant lion holding sword within crowned wreath

Date	Mintage	F	VF	XF	Unc	BU
SH1310	2,190,000	10.00	20.00	25.00	35.00	—
AH1311	10,256,000	20.00	30.00	50.00	75.00	—
AH1312	25,768,000	20.00	30.00	50.00	75.00	—
AH1313	6,670,000	20.00	30.00	50.00	75.00	—

KM# 1130 2 RIALS
10.0000 g., 0.8280 Silver 0.2662 oz. ASW, 26 mm. **Obv:** Value within crowned wreath **Obv. Leg.:** "Reza Shah" **Rev:** Radiant lion holding sword within crowned wreath **Note:** All coins dated SH1311-13 cut or punched over SH1310.

Date	Mintage	F	VF	XF	Unc	BU
SH1310 (1931)	6,145,000	10.00	20.00	25.00	35.00	—
SH1311 (1932)	8,838,000	20.00	30.00	50.00	75.00	—
SH1312 (1933)	19,175,000	10.00	15.00	25.00	35.00	—
SH1313 (1934)	4,015,000	20.00	30.00	50.00	75.00	—

KM# 1131 5 RIALS
25.0000 g., 0.8280 Silver 0.6655 oz. ASW, 37 mm. **Obv:** Value within crowned wreath **Obv. Leg.:** "Reza Shah" **Rev:** Radiant lion holding sword within crowned wreath **Note:** Most coins dated SH1311-13 are cut or punched over SH1310.

Date	Mintage	F	VF	XF	Unc	BU
SH1310 (1931)	5,471,000	12.00	18.00	25.00	50.00	—
SH1311 (1932)	4,527,000	12.00	18.00	25.00	50.00	—
SH1312/0 (1933)	5,502,000	15.00	20.00	30.00	60.00	—
SH1312 (1933)	Inc. above	12.00	18.00	25.00	50.00	—
SH1313 (1934)	1,208,000	15.00	20.00	30.00	60.00	—

KM# 1132 1/2 PAHLAVI
4.0680 g., 0.9000 Gold 0.1177 oz. AGW **Obv:** Uniformed bust left **Rev:** Radiant lion holding sword within crowned wreath

Date	Mintage	F	VF	XF	Unc	BU
SH1310 (1931)	696	BV	150	275	375	—
SH1311 (1932)	286	BV	175	300	400	—
SH1312 (1933)	892	BV	150	250	350	—
SH1313 (1934)	531	BV	175	300	400	—
SH1314 (1935)	—	BV	175	300	400	—
SH1315 (1936)	1,042	BV	175	275	375	—

KM# 1133 PAHLAVI
8.1360 g., 0.9000 Gold 0.2354 oz. AGW **Obv:** Uniformed bust left **Rev:** Radiant lion holding sword within crowned wreath

Date	Mintage	F	VF	XF	Unc	BU
SH1310 (1931)	304	1,500	3,000	4,000	5,000	—

Muhammad Reza Pahlavi Shah
SH1320-1358 / 1941-1979AD

REFORM COINAGE

KM# 1140 25 DINARS
Aluminum-Bronze, 19 mm. **Obv:** Radiant lion holding sword within crowned wreath **Rev:** Value within wreath

Date	Mintage	F	VF	XF	Unc	BU
SH1326 (1947)	—	20.00	30.00	60.00	125	—
SH1327 (1948)	—	25.00	50.00	100	150	—
SH1329 (1950)	—	25.00	50.00	100	150	—

KM# 1141 25 DINARS
Aluminum-Bronze **Obv:** Value within wreath **Rev:** Radiant lion holding sword within crowned wreath **Note:** Mule

Date	Mintage	F	VF	XF	Unc	BU
SH1329 (1950)	—	500	750	1,000	1,500	—

KM# 1156 50 DINARS
2.9100 g., Aluminum-Bronze **Obv:** Radiant lion holding sword within crowned wreath **Rev:** Value within wreath **Note:** Reduced thickness = 1mm; wide and narrow rim varieties exist for some dates.

Date	Mintage	F	VF	XF	Unc	BU
SH1332 (1953)	—	25.00	30.00	40.00	50.00	—
SH1333 (1954)	4,036,000	0.75	1.50	2.50	8.00	—
SH1334 (1955)	1,370,000	0.75	1.50	4.00	10.00	—
SH1335 (1956)	926,000	0.75	1.50	2.50	8.00	—
SH1336 (1957)	—	1.00	1.25	2.00	8.00	—

Note: Mint reports record 126,500 in SH1337 and 20,000 in SH1338; these were probably dated SH1336

Date	Mintage	F	VF	XF	Unc	BU
SH1342 (1963)	800,000	0.60	1.00	1.75	6.00	—
SH1343 (1964)	1,400,000	0.60	1.00	1.75	6.00	—
SH1344 (1965)	1,600,000	0.35	0.65	1.25	5.00	—
SH1345 (1966)	1,690,000	0.35	0.65	1.25	5.00	—
SH1346 (1967)	—	0.20	0.25	0.50	2.00	—

Note: Mintage report seems excessive for this and all SH1346 coinage

Date	Mintage	F	VF	XF	Unc	BU
SH1347 (1968)	2,000,000	0.20	0.25	0.50	2.00	—
SH1348 (1969)	1,500,000	0.20	0.25	0.50	2.00	—
SH1349 (1970)	360,000	2.00	3.00	4.50	12.50	—
SH1350 (1971)	—	0.30	0.50	0.75	2.00	—
SH1351 (1972)	—	0.30	0.50	0.75	2.00	—
SH1353 (1974)	60,000	0.30	0.50	0.75	2.00	—
SH1354 (1975)	16,000	0.75	1.25	2.00	5.00	—

KM# 1156a 50 DINARS
Brass-Coated Steel **Obv:** Radiant lion holding sword within crowned wreath **Rev:** Value within wreath

Date	Mintage	F	VF	XF	Unc	BU
MS2535 (1976)	27,000	5.00	10.00	20.00	30.00	—
MS2536 (1977)	—	5.00	10.00	20.00	30.00	—
MS2537 (1978)	—	5.00	10.00	20.00	30.00	—
SH1357 (1978)	—	5.00	10.00	20.00	30.00	—
SH1358 (1979)	—					—

Note: Reported, not confirmed

KM# 1143 RIAL
1.6000 g., 0.6000 Silver 0.0309 oz. ASW, 18 mm. **Obv:** Value within crowned wreath **Obv. Leg.:** "Muhammad Reza Shah Pahlavi" **Rev:** Radiant lion holding sword within crowned wreath

Date	Mintage	F	VF	XF	Unc	BU
SH1322 (1943)	—	0.60	1.00	2.00	5.00	—
SH1323/3 (1944)	—					—
SH1323 (1944)	—	0.60	1.00	2.00	5.00	—
SH1324/3 (1945)	—					—
SH1324 (1945)	—	0.60	1.00	2.00	5.00	—
SH1424 (1945) Error for 1324	—					—
SH1325 (1946)	—	0.75	1.50	2.00	5.00	—
SH1326 (1947)	567,000	35.00	40.00	50.00	100	—
SH1327 (1948)	5,795,000	1.50	2.50	4.00	8.00	—
SH1328 (1949)	1,565,000	1.50	2.50	4.00	8.00	—
SH1329 (1950)	144,000	50.00	100	150	200	—
SH1330 (1951)	—	2.00	3.00	5.00	15.00	—

KM# 1157 RIAL
Copper-Nickel, 18.5 mm. **Obv:** Value within wreath **Obv. Leg.:** "Muhammad Reza Shah Pahlavi" **Rev:** Radiant lion holding sword within crowned wreath

Date	Mintage	F	VF	XF	Unc	BU
SH(13)31 (1952)	4,735,000	1.00	2.00	5.00	15.00	—
SH(13)32 (1953)	3	4.00	8.00	15.00	30.00	—
SH(13)33 (1954)	16,405,000	0.60	1.00	2.00	5.00	—
SH(13)34 (1955)	8,980,000	0.60	1.00	2.00	5.00	—
SH(13)35 (1956)	8,910,000	0.50	1.00	1.00	5.00	—
SH(13)36 (1957)	4,450,000	1.00	2.00	8.00	20.00	—

KM# 1171 RIAL
2.0000 g., Copper-Nickel **Obv:** Value within crowned wreath **Obv. Leg.:** "Muhammad Reza Pahlavi" **Rev:** Radiant lion holding sword within crowned wreath

Date	Mintage	F	VF	XF	Unc	BU
SH1337 (1958)	8,005,000	0.50	1.00	2.00	5.00	—

KM# 1171a RIAL
1.7500 g., Copper-Nickel, 18.3 mm. **Obv:** Value within crowned wreath **Rev:** Radiant lion holding sword within crowned wreath **Note:** Date varieties exist.

Date	Mintage	F	VF	XF	Unc	BU
SH1338 (1959)	14,940,000	0.10	0.20	0.40	3.00	—
SH1339 (1960)	8,400,000	0.25	0.50	1.00	4.00	—
SH1340 (1961)	8,490,000	0.25	0.50	1.00	4.00	—
SH1341 (1962)	8,680,000	0.25	0.50	1.00	4.00	—
SH1342 (1963)	13,332,000	0.10	0.20	0.40	3.00	—
SH1343 (1964)	14,746,000	0.10	0.15	0.25	2.00	—
SH1344 (1965)	12,050,000	0.10	0.20	0.50	3.50	—
SH1345 (1966)	13,786,000	0.10	0.15	0.20	2.00	—
SH1346 (1967)	155,321,000	0.10	0.15	0.20	2.00	—
SH1347 (1968)	20,664,000	0.10	0.15	0.25	3.00	—
SH1348 (1969)	22,960,000	0.10	0.15	0.20	2.00	—
SH1349 (1970)	19,918,000	0.10	0.15	0.20	2.00	—
SH1350 (1971)	24,248,000	0.10	0.20	0.65	2.00	—
SH1351/0 (1972)	21,825,000	0.10	0.25	0.40	3.00	—
SH1351 (1972)	Inc. above	0.10	0.15	0.20	2.00	—
SH1352 (1973)	31,449,000	0.10	0.15	0.20	2.00	—
SH1353 (1974) Large date	33,700,000	0.10	0.20	0.25	3.00	—
SH1353 (1974) Small date	Inc. above	0.10	0.15	0.20	2.00	—
SH1354 (1975)	—	3.00	6.00	8.00	10.00	—
MS2536 (1977)	—	3.00	6.00	8.00	10.00	—

KM# 1183 RIAL
1.7600 g., Copper-Nickel, 18.5 mm. **Series:** F.A.O. **Obv:** Head left divides date **Obv. Leg.:** "Muhammad Reza Shah Pahlavi" **Rev:** Crown above lion and sun within wreath

Date	Mintage	F	VF	XF	Unc	BU
SH1350 (1971)	2,770,000	3.00	6.00	8.00	10.00	—
SH1351 (1972)	8,605,000	3.00	6.00	8.00	10.00	—

Date	Mintage	F	VF	XF	Unc	BU
SH1353 (1974)	2,000,000	3.00	6.00	8.00	10.00	—
SH1354 (1975)	1,000,000	3.00	6.00	8.00	10.00	—

KM# 1205 RIAL
Copper-Nickel, 18.3 mm. **Subject:** 50th Anniversary of Pahlavi Rule **Obv:** Value within crowned wreath **Rev:** Radiant lion holding sword within crowned wreath

Date	Mintage	F	VF	XF	Unc	BU
MS2535 (1976)	61,945,000	3.00	6.00	8.00	10.00	—

KM# 1172 RIAL
1.7500 g., Copper-Nickel **Obv:** Value within crowned wreath, "Aryamehr" added to legend **Rev:** Radiant lion holding sword within crowned wreath

Date	Mintage	F	VF	XF	Unc	BU
MS2536 (1977)	71,150,000	3.00	6.00	8.00	10.00	—
MS2537 (1978)	—	3.00	6.00	8.00	10.00	—
MS2537/6537 (1978) Error 2/6	—	—	—	—	6.00	—
SH1357/6 (1978)	—	3.00	6.00	8.00	10.00	—
SH1357 (1978)	—	2.50	5.00	10.00	15.00	—

KM# 1144 2 RIALS
3.2000 g., 0.6000 Silver 0.0617 oz. ASW, 22 mm. **Obv:** Value within crowned wreath **Obv. Leg.:** "Muhammad Reza Shah Pahlavi" **Rev:** Radiant lion holding sword within crowned wreath

Date	Mintage	F	VF	XF	Unc	BU
SH1322 (1943)	—	1.00	1.50	3.50	7.00	—
SH1323/2 (1944)	—	10.00	20.00	30.00	50.00	—
SH1323 (1944)	—	1.00	1.50	3.00	6.00	—
SH1324 (1945)	—	2.50	5.00	10.00	15.00	—
SH1325 (1946)	—	5.00	10.00	15.00	25.00	—
SH1326 (1947)	187,000	5.00	10.00	25.00	50.00	—
SH1327 (1948)	3,140,000	1.50	3.00	5.00	12.50	—
SH1328 (1949)	1,198,000	2.50	4.50	7.50	16.00	—
SH1329 (1950)	—	100	200	300	400	—
SH1330 (1951)	—	5.00	8.00	12.50	30.00	—

KM# 1158 2 RIALS
Copper-Nickel, 22.5 mm. **Obv:** Value above sprigs **Obv. Leg.:** "Muhammad Reza Shah Pahlavi" **Rev:** Crown above radiant lion holding sword within wreath

Date	Mintage	F	VF	XF	Unc	BU
SH1331 (1952)	5,335,000	1.25	3.00	7.00	20.00	—
SH1332 (1953)	6,870,000	1.00	2.00	4.00	8.00	—
SH1333 (1954)	13,668,000	0.15	0.75	2.00	7.00	—
SH1334 (1955)	7,185,000	0.15	0.75	2.00	7.00	—
SH1335 (1956)	2,400,000	0.15	0.75	3.00	12.50	—
SH1336 (1957)	325,000	25.00	50.00	75.00	100	—

KM# 1173 2 RIALS
3.0000 g., Copper-Nickel **Obv:** Value within crowned wreath **Obv. Leg.:** "Muhammad Reza Pahlavi" **Rev:** Radiant lion holding sword within crowned wreath

Date	Mintage	F	VF	XF	Unc	BU
SH1338 (1959)	17,610,000	0.10	0.25	0.75	4.00	—
SH1339 (1960)	8,575,000	0.10	0.25	0.50	4.00	—
SH1340 (1961)	5,668,000	0.10	0.25	0.50	4.00	—

Date	Mintage	F	VF	XF	Unc	BU
SH1341 (1962)	5,820,000	0.10	0.25	0.75	4.00	—
SH1342 (1963)	8,570,000	0.10	0.25	0.50	4.00	—
SH1343 (1964)	11,250,000	0.10	0.25	0.50	3.00	—
SH1344 (1965)	5,155,000	0.10	0.25	0.50	4.00	—
SH1345 (1966)	2,267,000	0.15	0.30	1.00	5.00	—
SH1346 (1967)	92,792,000	—	0.10	0.20	4.00	—
SH1347 (1968)	10,300,000	—	0.10	1.00	6.00	—
SH1348 (1969)	9,319,000	0.20	0.45	1.10	4.00	—
SH1349 (1970)	9,895,000	0.20	0.40	1.00	4.00	—
SH1350 (1971)	9,545,000	0.15	0.35	1.00	4.00	—
SH1351 (1972)	13,305,000	0.15	0.35	1.00	3.00	—
SH1352 (1973)	15,910,000	—	0.10	0.20	3.00	—
SH1353 (1974)	28,477,000	—	0.10	0.20	3.00	—
SH1354/3 (1975)	—	0.20	0.40	1.00	5.00	—
SH1354 (1975)	41,700,000	—	0.10	0.20	3.00	—
MS2536 (1977)	54,725,000	—	0.10	0.20	3.00	—

KM# 1206   2 RIALS
Copper-Nickel   **Subject:** 50th Anniversary of Pahlavi Rule
Obv: Value within crowned wreath **Rev:** Radiant lion holding
sword within crowned wreath

Date	Mintage	F	VF	XF	Unc	BU
MS2535 (1976)	59,568,000	2.50	5.00	10.00	15.00	—

KM# 1174   2 RIALS
3.0400 g., Copper-Nickel   **Obv:** Value within crowned wreath
Obv. Leg.: "Muhammad Reza Pahlavi","Aryamehr" added
Rev: Radiant lion holding sword within crowned wreath

Date	Mintage	F	VF	XF	Unc	BU
MS2536 (1977)	Inc. above	0.50	1.00	2.50	5.00	—
MS2537 (1978)	—	0.50	1.00	2.50	5.00	—
SH1357 (1978)	—	2.50	5.00	10.00	20.00	—

KM# 1145   5 RIALS
8.0000 g., 0.6000 Silver 0.1543 oz. ASW, 26 mm. **Obv:** Value
within crowned wreath **Obv. Leg.:** "Muhammad Reza
Pahlavi" **Rev:** Radiant lion holding sword within crowned wreath

Date	Mintage	F	VF	XF	Unc	BU
SH1322 (1943)	—	BV	2.50	3.50	6.00	—
SH1323 (1944)	—	BV	2.50	3.50	6.00	—
SH1324 (1945)	—	BV	2.75	4.50	10.00	—
SH1325 (1946)	—	BV	2.50	3.50	6.00	—
SH1326 (1947)	61,000	5.00	10.00	25.00	50.00	—
SH1327 (1948)	836,000	2.50	5.00	7.50	20.00	—
SH1328 (1949)	282,000	3.50	10.00	20.00	40.00	—
SH1329 (1950)	—	85.00	125	200	350	—

KM# 1159   5 RIALS
Copper-Nickel, 26 mm.   **Obv:** Value above sprigs, date below
Obv. Leg.: "Muhammad Reza Shah Pahlavi" **Rev:** Crown above
radiant lion holding sword within crowned wreath

Date	Mintage	F	VF	XF	Unc	BU
SH1331 (1952)	3,660,000	2.50	5.00	10.00	20.00	—
SH1332 (1953)	16,350,000	1.00	2.50	5.00	10.00	—
SH1333 (1954)	6,582,000	1.00	2.50	5.00	10.00	—
SH1334 (1955)	300,000	15.00	25.00	50.00	75.00	—
SH1336 (1957)	1,410,000	15.00	25.00	50.00	75.00	—

KM# 1175   5 RIALS
7.0000 g., Copper-Nickel, 25.5 mm. **Obv:** Value within crowned
wreath **Obv. Leg.:** "Muhammad Reza Shah Pahlavi"
Rev: Radiant lion holding sword within crowned wreath

Date	Mintage	F	VF	XF	Unc	BU
SH1337 (1958)	3,660,000	1.00	2.50	7.50	22.50	—
SH1338 (1959)	10,467,000	0.50	2.50	8.00	20.00	—

KM# 1175a   5 RIALS
5.0000 g., Copper-Nickel, 25.6 mm. **Obv:** Value within crowned
wreath **Rev:** Radiant lion holding sword within crowned wreath

Date	Mintage	F	VF	XF	Unc	BU
SH1338 (1959)	Inc. above	0.25	0.40	1.50	5.00	—
SH1339 (1960)	3,980,000	0.25	0.40	1.50	5.00	—
SH1340 (1961)	3,814,000	0.25	0.40	1.50	5.00	—
SH1341 (1962)	2,332,000	0.25	0.40	1.50	5.00	—
SH1342 (1963)	7,838,000	0.25	0.40	1.00	4.00	—
SH1343 (1964)	9,484,000	0.25	0.40	1.00	4.00	—
SH1344 (1965)	3,468,000	0.25	0.40	1.00	4.00	—
SH1345 (1966)	6,092,000	0.25	0.40	1.00	4.00	—
SH1346/36 (1967)	74,781,000	0.25	0.40	1.50	5.00	—
SH1346 (1967)	Inc. above	0.25	0.40	1.00	4.00	—

KM# 1176   5 RIALS
4.6000 g., Copper-Nickel **Obv:** Value and legend within crowned
wreath, "Aryamehr" added to legend **Rev:** Radiant lion holding
sword within crowned wreath

Date	Mintage	F	VF	XF	Unc	BU
SH1347 (1968)	7,745,000	0.50	0.85	1.50	4.00	—
SH1348 (1969)	9,193,000	0.50	0.75	1.25	4.00	—
SH1349 (1970)	7,300,000	0.50	0.75	1.25	4.00	—
SH1350 (1971)	10,160,000	0.35	0.75	1.25	3.50	—
SH1351 (1972)	20,582,000	0.25	0.75	1.25	3.50	—
SH1352 (1973)	23,590,000	0.25	0.75	1.25	3.50	—
SH1353 (1974)	28,367,000	0.25	0.75	1.25	3.50	—
SH1353 (1974) Large date	Inc. above	0.25	0.75	1.25	3.50	—
SH1354 (1975)	27,294,000	0.25	0.75	1.25	3.50	—
MS2536 (1977)	47,906,000	0.20	0.50	1.25	3.50	—
MS2537 (1978)	—	0.35	0.65	1.25	3.50	—
SH1357 (1978)	—	2.50	5.00	10.00	20.00	—

KM# 1207   5 RIALS
Copper-Nickel, 24 mm. **Subject:** 50th Anniversary of Pahlavi Rule

Date	Mintage	F	VF	XF	Unc	BU
MS2535 (1976)	37,144,000	1.00	2.50	5.00	10.00	—

KM# 1146   10 RIALS
16.0000 g., 0.6000 Silver 0.3086 oz. ASW, 32 mm. **Obv:** Value
and legend within crowned wreath **Obv. Leg.:** "Muhammad Reza
Shah Pahlavi" **Rev:** Radiant lion holding sword within crowned
wreath **Note:** Counterfeits are known dated SH1322.

Date	Mintage	F	VF	XF	Unc	BU
SH1323/2 (1944)	—	—	4.50	7.50	20.00	—
SH1323 (1944)	—	—	BV	5.00	12.00	—
SH1324 (1945)	—	—	BV	5.50	15.00	—
SH1325 (1946)	—	—	BV	6.00	17.50	—
SH1326 (1947)	—	5.50	15.00	35.00	75.00	—

KM# 1177   10 RIALS
12.0000 g., Copper-Nickel **Obv:** Crown above value and legend
within wreath **Obv. Leg.:** "Muhammad Reza Shah Pahlavi"
Rev: Crown above lion and sun within wreath

Date	Mintage	F	VF	XF	Unc	BU
SH1333 (1954)	—	—	—	—	—	—
SH1335 (1956)	6,225,000	0.50	2.00	4.00	9.00	—
SH1336 (1957)	4,415,000	5.00	10.00	15.00	25.00	—
SH1337 (1958)	715,000	3.00	6.00	9.00	20.00	—
SH1338 (1959)	1,210,000	0.50	2.00	6.00	14.00	—
SH1339 (1960)	2,775,000	0.50	2.00	4.00	9.00	—
SH1340 (1961)	3,660,000	0.50	2.00	4.00	9.00	—
SH1341 (1962)	744,000	20.00	35.00	50.00	75.00	—
SH1343 (1963)	6,874,000	0.50	2.00	4.00	9.00	—

KM# 1177a   10 RIALS
9.0000 g., Copper-Nickel **Obv:** Crown above value and legend
wtihin wreath **Rev:** Crown above radiant lion holding sword within
wreath **Note:** Thin flan.

Date	Mintage	F	VF	XF	Unc	BU
SH1341 (1962)	—	0.35	1.00	2.50	5.00	—
	Note: Mintage included in KM#1177					
SH1342 (1963)	3,763,000	0.35	1.00	2.00	4.00	—
SH1343 (1964)	—	0.35	0.75	1.50	2.50	—
	Note: Mintage included in KM#1177					
SH1344 (1965)	1,627,000	0.35	0.75	1.50	2.50	—

KM# 1178   10 RIALS
6.8000 g., Copper-Nickel, 28 mm. **Obv:** Head left, legend above,
date below **Obv. Leg.:** "Muhammad Reza Shah Pahlavi"
Rev: Crown above radiant lion holding sword within wreath

Date	Mintage	F	VF	XF	Unc	BU
SH1345 (1966)	1,699,000	0.50	0.60	2.00	5.00	—
SH1346 (1967)	38,897,000	0.40	0.50	1.00	4.00	—
SH1347 (1968)	8,220,000	0.40	0.65	1.50	8.00	—
SH1348 (1969)	7,156,000	0.40	0.50	1.00	4.00	—
SH1349 (1970)	7,397,000	0.40	0.50	1.00	4.00	—
SH1350 (1971)	8,972,000	0.40	0.50	1.00	4.00	—
SH1351 (1972)	9,912,000	0.40	0.50	1.00	4.00	—
SH1352 (1973)	28,776,000	0.50	0.50	4.50	7.00	—

KM# 1182 10 RIALS
Copper-Nickel **Series:** F.A.O. **Obv:** Head left, legend above **Rev:** Crown above radiant lion holding sword within wreath, dates and F.A.O

Date	Mintage	F	VF	XF	Unc	BU
SH1348 (1969)	150,000	1.00	2.50	5.00	10.00	—

KM# 1179 10 RIALS
Copper-Nickel **Obv:** Head left, legend above, date below **Rev:** Crown above lion, sun and numeral value within wreath

Date	Mintage	F	VF	XF	Unc	BU
SH1352 (1973)	Inc. above	0.30	0.60	1.00	4.00	—
SH1353 (1974)	22,234,000	0.30	0.60	1.00	3.00	—
SH1354 (1975)	23,482,000	0.30	0.60	1.00	4.00	—
MS2536 (1977)	24,324,000	0.30	0.60	1.00	4.00	—
MS2537 (1978)	—	0.30	0.60	1.00	4.00	—
SH1357 (1978)	—	10.00	15.00	20.00	25.00	—

KM# 1208 10 RIALS
Copper-Nickel **Subject:** 50th Anniversary of Pahlavi Rule **Obv:** Head left, legend above, date below **Rev:** Crown above lion, sun and numeral value within wreath

Date	Mintage	F	VF	XF	Unc	BU
MS2535 (1976)	29,859,000	0.50	1.00	2.50	5.00	—

KM# 1180 20 RIALS
Copper-Nickel **Obv:** Head left, legend above, date below **Obv. Leg.:** "Muhammad Reza Shah Pahlavi" **Rev:** Crown above lion, sun and written value within wreath

Date	Mintage	F	VF	XF	Unc	BU
SH1350 (1971)	2,349,000	0.25	1.00	3.00	6.00	—
SH1351 (1972)	11,416,000	0.25	0.85	1.00	3.00	—
SH1352 (1973)	7,172,000	0.25	0.85	1.25	5.00	—

KM# 1181 20 RIALS
Copper-Nickel, 30 mm. **Obv:** Head left, legend above, date below **Rev:** Crown above lion, sun and numeral value within wreath **Note:** Varieties exist in date size.

Date	Mintage	F	VF	XF	Unc	BU
SH1352 (1973)		0.25	0.75	1.00	3.50	—
Note: Mintage included in KM#1180						
SH1353 (1974)	12,601,000	0.25	0.75	1.00	3.75	—

Date	Mintage	F	VF	XF	Unc	BU
SH1354 (1975)	16,246,000	0.25	0.75	1.00	4.00	—
MS2536 (1977)	—	0.40	0.75	1.00	4.00	—
MS2537 (1978)	—	0.50	0.75	1.00	4.00	—
SH1357 (1978)	—	5.00	10.00	15.00	25.00	—

KM# 1196 20 RIALS
Copper-Nickel **Subject:** 7th Asian Games **Obv:** Head left, legend above **Rev:** Star design within entwined circles and written words

Date	Mintage	F	VF	XF	Unc	BU
SH1353 (1974)	Inc. above	5.00	10.00	15.00	25.00	—

KM# 1209 20 RIALS
Copper-Nickel **Subject:** 50th Anniversary of Pahlavi Rule **Obv:** Head left, legend above, date below **Rev:** Crown above lion, sun and numeral value within wreath

Date	Mintage	F	VF	XF	Unc	BU
MS2535 (1976)		3.00	7.50	12.00	15.00	—

KM# 1211 20 RIALS
Copper-Nickel **Series:** F.A.O. **Obv:** Head left, legend above **Rev:** Crown above lion, sun and numeral value within wreath

Date	Mintage	F	VF	XF	Unc	BU
MS2535-1976	10,000,000	3.00	7.50	12.00	15.00	—
MS2536-1977	23,370,000	3.00	7.50	12.00	15.00	—

KM# 1215 20 RIALS
Copper-Nickel **Series:** F.A.O. **Obv:** Head left, legend above **Rev:** Crown above lion, sun, numeral value, dates and F.A.O. within wreath

Date	Mintage	F	VF	XF	Unc	BU
SH1357-1978	5,000,000	3.00	7.50	12.00	15.00	—

KM# 1214 20 RIALS
Copper-Nickel **Subject:** 50th Anniversary of Bank Melli **Obv:** Head left, legend above and below **Rev:** Head left, legend above and below

Date	Mintage	F	VF	XF	Unc	BU
SH1357 (1978)	—	5.00	10.00	20.00	30.00	—

KM# 1184 25 RIALS
7.5000 g., 0.9990 Silver 0.2409 oz. ASW **Subject:** 2500th Anniversary of Persian Empire **Obv:** Small crown over lion and sun above value within circle of crowns **Rev:** Conjoined column heads **Note:** Column head from Artaxerxes' Palace in Susa. With "1 AR" and 1000 assayer's marks

Date	Mintage	F	VF	XF	Unc	BU
SH1350-1971 Proof	18,000	Value: 12.00				

KM# 1185 50 RIALS
15.0000 g., 0.9990 Silver 0.4818 oz. ASW **Subject:** 2500th Anniversary of Persian Empire **Obv:** Small crown over lion and sun above value and dates within circle of crowns **Rev:** Winged griffin with ram antlers **Note:** With "1 AR" and 1000 assayer's marks

Date	Mintage	F	VF	XF	Unc	BU
SH1350-1971 Proof	18,000	Value: 16.50				

KM# 1186 75 RIALS
22.5000 g., 0.9990 Silver 0.7226 oz. ASW **Subject:** 2500th Anniversary of Persian Empire **Obv:** Small crown above radiant lion holding sword above value and dates within circle of crowns **Rev:** Arms above Stone of Cyrus II and inscription, wreath of crowns surrounds **Note:** With "1 AR" and 1000 assayer's marks

Date	Mintage	F	VF	XF	Unc	BU
SH1350-1971 Proof	18,000	Value: 18.50				

KM# 1187.1 100 RIALS
30.0000 g., 0.9990 Silver 0.9635 oz. ASW **Subject:** 2500th Anniversary of Persian Empire **Obv:** Small crown over lion and sun, value and date below **Rev:** Polished field below pillared palace

Date	Mintage	F	VF	XF	Unc	BU
SH1350-1971 Proof	18,000	Value: 27.50				

KM# 1187.2 100 RIALS
30.0000 g., 0.9990 Silver 0.9635 oz. ASW **Obv:** Small crown over lion and sun above value and dates within circle of crowns **Rev:** Frosted field below pillared palace **Note:** Countermarked with "1 AR" and "1000" on reverse.

Date	Mintage	F	VF	XF	Unc	BU
SH1350-1971 Proof	Inc. above				Value: 27.50	

KM# 1188 200 RIALS
60.0000 g., 0.9990 Silver 1.9270 oz. ASW **Subject:** 2500th Anniversary of Persian Empire **Obv:** Conjoined busts left **Rev:** Small crown over lion and sun above value and dates within circle of crowns **Note:** Countermarked with "1 AR" and "1000" on reverse.

Date	Mintage	F	VF	XF	Unc	BU
SH1350-1971 Proof	23,000				Value: 45.00	

KM# 1189 500 RIALS
6.5100 g., 0.9000 Gold 0.1884 oz. AGW **Subject:** 2500th Anniversary of Persian Empire **Obv:** Small crown over lion and sun above value and dates within circle of crowns **Rev:** Walking griffin with ram antlers

Date	Mintage	F	VF	XF	Unc	BU
SH1350-1971 Proof	11,000				Value: 185	

KM# 1190 750 RIALS
9.7700 g., 0.9000 Gold 0.2827 oz. AGW **Subject:** 2500th Anniversary of Persian Empire **Obv:** Small crown above lion and sun, value and date below **Rev:** Arms above Stone of Cyrus II and inscription within wreath of crowns

Date	Mintage	F	VF	XF	Unc	BU
SH1350-1971 Proof	10,000				Value: 275	

KM# 1191.1 1000 RIALS
13.0300 g., 0.9000 Gold 0.3770 oz. AGW **Subject:** 2500th Anniversary of Persian Empire **Obv:** Small crown over lion and sun above value and dates within circle of crowns **Rev:** Polished fields below pillared palace

Date	Mintage	F	VF	XF	Unc	BU
SH1350-1971 Proof	10,000				Value: 365	

KM# 1191.2 1000 RIALS
13.0300 g., 0.9000 Gold 0.3770 oz. AGW **Subject:** 2500th Anniversary of Persian Empire **Obv:** Small crown over lion and sun above value and dates within circle of crowns **Rev:** Polished fields below pillared palace

Date	Mintage	F	VF	XF	Unc	BU
SH1350-1971 Proof	Inc. above				Value: 365	

KM# 1192 2000 RIALS
26.0600 g., 0.9000 Gold 0.7540 oz. AGW **Subject:** 2500th Anniversary of Persian Empire **Obv:** Conjoined busts left **Rev:** Small crown over lion and sun above value and dates within circle of crowns

Date	Mintage	F	VF	XF	Unc	BU
SH1350-1971 Proof	9,805				Value: 700	

KM# 1160 1/4 PAHLAVI
2.0340 g., 0.9000 Gold 0.0589 oz. AGW, 14 mm. **Obv:** Head left, legend above, date below **Rev:** Crown over lion and sun above value within wreath

Date	Mintage	F	VF	XF	Unc	BU
SH1332 (1953)	41,000	BV	60.00	100	125	—
SH1333 (1954)	7,000	60.00	70.00	125	175	—
SH1334 (1955)	—		BV	60.00	70.00	—
SH1335 (1956)	41,000	BV	60.00	100	125	—
SH1336 (1957)	—	BV	60.00	100	175	—

KM# 1160a 1/4 PAHLAVI
2.0340 g., 0.9000 Gold 0.0589 oz. AGW, 16 mm. **Obv:** Head left, legend above, date below **Rev:** Crown above lion holding sword within wreath **Note:** Thinner and broader.

Date	Mintage	F	VF	XF	Unc	BU
SH1336 (1957)	7,000	—	60.00	75.00	125	—
SH1337 (1958)	33,000	—	—	BV	60.00	—
SH1338 (1959)	136,000	—	—	BV	60.00	—
SH1339 (1960)	156,000	—	—	BV	60.00	—
SH1340 (1961)	60,000	—	—	BV	60.00	—
SH1342 (1963)	80,000	—	—	BV	60.00	—
SH1344 (1965)	30,000	—	60.00	90.00	125	—
SH1345 (1966)	40,000	—	—	BV	60.00	—
SH1346 (1967)	30,000	—	—	BV	60.00	—
SH1347 (1968)	60,000	—	—	BV	60.00	—
SH1348 (1969)	60,000	—	—	BV	60.00	—

Date	Mintage	F	VF	XF	Unc	BU
SH1349 (1970)	80,000	—	—	BV	60.00	—
SH1350 (1971)	80,000	—	—	BV	60.00	—
SH1351 (1972)	103,000	—	—	BV	60.00	—
SH1352 (1973)	—	—	—	BV	60.00	—

KM# 1198 1/4 PAHLAVI
2.0340 g., 0.9000 Gold 0.0589 oz. AGW **Obv:** Head left, legend above, date below, "Aryamehr" added to legend **Rev:** Crown above lion and sun within wreath

Date	Mintage	F	VF	XF	Unc	BU
SH1353 (1974)	—	—	—	BV	60.00	—
SH1354 (1975)	106,000	—	—	BV	60.00	—
SH1355 (1976)	186,000	—	—	BV	60.00	—
MS2536 (1977)	—	—	—	BV	60.00	—
MS2537 (1978)	—	—	—	BV	60.00	—
SH1358 (1979)	—	200	300	400	500	—

KM# 1147 1/2 PAHLAVI
4.0680 g., 0.9000 Gold 0.1177 oz. AGW **Obv:** Legend **Obv. Leg.:** "Muhammad Reza Shah" **Rev:** Crown above radiant lion holding sword within wreath

Date	Mintage	F	VF	XF	Unc	BU
SH1320 (1941)	—	1,000	2,000	2,500	3,000	—
SH1321 (1942)	—	—	115	200	300	—
SH1322 (1943)	—	—	—	BV	115	—
SH1323 (1944)	76,000	—	—	BV	115	—

KM# 1149 1/2 PAHLAVI
4.0680 g., 0.9000 Gold 0.1177 oz. AGW **Obv:** High relief head left, legend above and date below **Rev:** Crown above radiant lion holding sword within wreath

Date	Mintage	F	VF	XF	Unc	BU
SH1324 (1945)	—	—	—	BV	115	—
SH1325 (1946)	—	—	—	BV	115	—
SH1326 (1947)	36,000	—	BV	115	125	—
SH1327 (1948)	36,000	—	BV	115	125	—
SH1328 (1949)	—	—	BV	115	130	—
SH1329 (1950)	75	—	275	475	750	—
SH1330 (1951)	98,000	—	175	300	500	—

KM# 1161 1/2 PAHLAVI
4.0680 g., 0.9000 Gold 0.1177 oz. AGW **Obv:** Low relief head left, legend above with date below **Rev:** Crown above radiant lion holding sword within wreath

Date	Mintage	F	VF	XF	Unc	BU
SH1330 (1951)	—	—	—	BV	115	—
Note: Mintage included in KM#1149						
SH1332 (1952)	—	—	1,250	2,000	2,500	—
SH1333 (1954)	—	BV	200	250	300	—
SH1334 (1955)	—	BV	200	250	300	—
SH1335 (1956)	—	—	—	BV	115	—
SH1336 (1957)	132,000	—	—	BV	115	—
SH1337 (1958)	102,000	—	—	BV	115	—
SH1338 (1959)	140,000	—	—	BV	115	—
SH1339 (1960)	142,000	—	—	BV	115	—
SH1340 (1961)	439,000	—	—	BV	115	—
SH1342 (1963)	40,000	—	—	BV	115	—
SH1344 (1965)	30,000	BV	200	250	300	—
SH1345 (1966)	40,000	—	—	BV	115	—
SH1346 (1967)	40,000	—	—	BV	115	—
SH1347 (1968)	50,000	—	—	BV	115	—
SH1348 (1969)	40,000	—	—	BV	115	—
SH1349 (1970)	80,000	—	—	BV	115	—
SH1350 (1971)	80,000	—	—	BV	115	—
SH1351 (1972)	103,000	—	—	BV	115	—
SH1352 (1973)	67,000	—	—	BV	115	—
SH1353 (1974)	—	—	—	BV	115	—

KM# 1199 1/2 PAHLAVI
4.0680 g., 0.9000 Gold 0.1177 oz. AGW **Obv:** Head left, legend above and date below, "Aryamehr" added to legend **Rev:** Crown above radiant lion holding sword within wreath

Date	Mintage	F	VF	XF	Unc	BU
SH1354 (1975)	37,000	—	—	BV	115	—
SH1355 (1976)	153,000	—	—	BV	115	—
MS2536 (1977)	—	—	—	BV	115	—
MS2537 (1978)	—	—	—	BV	115	—
SH1358 (1979)	—	—	700	1,000	1,500	—

KM# 1148 PAHLAVI
8.1360 g., 0.9000 Gold 0.2354 oz. AGW **Obv:** Legend and date **Obv. Leg.:** "Muhammad Reza Shah" **Rev:** Crown above radiant lion holding sword within wreath

Date	Mintage	F	VF	XF	Unc	BU
SH1320 (1941)	—	—	—	3,000	4,000	—
Note: Possibly a pattern						
SH1321 (1942)	—	—	—	3,000	4,000	—
Note: Possibly a pattern						
SH1322 (1943)	—	—	—	BV	220	—
SH1323 (1944)	311,000	—	—	BV	220	—
SH1324 (1945)	—	—	—	BV	220	—

KM# 1150 PAHLAVI
8.1360 g., 0.9000 Gold 0.2354 oz. AGW **Obv:** High relief head left, legend above and date below **Rev:** Crown above radiant lion holding sword within wreath

Date	Mintage	F	VF	XF	Unc	BU
SH1324 (1945)	—	—	—	BV	225	—
SH1325 (1946)	—	—	—	BV	225	—
SH1326 (1947)	151,000	—	—	BV	225	—
SH1327 (1948)	20,000	—	—	BV	225	—
SH1328 (1949)	4,000	—	BV	240	260	—
SH1329 (1950)	4,000	—	300	500	750	—
SH1330 (1951)	48,000	—	250	300	400	—

KM# 1162 PAHLAVI
8.1360 g., 0.9000 Gold 0.2354 oz. AGW **Obv:** Low relief head left, legend above and date below **Rev:** Crown above radiant lion holding sword within wreath

Date	Mintage	F	VF	XF	Unc	BU
SH1330 (1951)	—	—	—	BV	225	—
SH1331 (1952)	—	2,000	3,000	3,500	3,750	—
SH1332 (1953)	—	2,000	3,000	3,500	3,750	—
SH1333 (1954)	—	BV	240	275	350	—
SH1334 (1955)	—	BV	240	275	350	—
SH1335 (1956)	—	—	—	BV	225	—
SH1336 (1957)	453,000	—	—	BV	225	—
SH1337 (1958)	665,000	—	—	BV	225	—
SH1338 (1959)	776,000	—	—	BV	225	—
SH1339 (1960)	847,000	—	—	BV	225	—
SH1340 (1961)	528,000	—	—	BV	225	—
SH1342 (1963)	20,000	—	—	BV	225	—
SH1344 (1965)	—	BV	240	275	350	—
SH1345 (1966)	20,000	—	—	BV	225	—
SH1346 (1967)	30,000	—	—	BV	225	—
SH1347 (1968)	40,000	—	—	BV	225	—
SH1348 (1969)	70,000	—	—	BV	225	—
SH1349 (1970)	70,000	—	—	BV	225	—
SH1350 (1971)	60,000	—	—	BV	225	—
SH1351 (1972)	100,000	—	—	BV	225	—
SH1352 (1973)	320,000	—	—	BV	225	—
SH1353 (1974)	—	—	—	BV	225	—

KM# 1200 PAHLAVI
8.1360 g., 0.9000 Gold 0.2354 oz. AGW **Obv:** Head left, legend above, date below, "Aryamehr" added to legend **Rev:** Crown above radiant lion holding sword within wreath

Date	Mintage	F	VF	XF	Unc	BU
SH1354 (1975)	21,000	—	—	BV	225	—
SH1355 (1976)	203,000	—	—	BV	225	—
MS2536 (1977)	—	—	—	BV	225	—
MS2537 (1978)	—	—	—	BV	225	—
SH1358 (1979)	—	—	700	1,000	1,500	—

KM# A1163 2-1/2 PAHLAVI
20.3400 g., 0.9000 Gold 0.5885 oz. AGW **Obv:** Head left, legend above **Rev:** Inscription and date

Date	Mintage	F	VF	XF	Unc	BU
SH1338 (1959)	—	—	BV	550	580	—

KM# 1163 2-1/2 PAHLAVI
20.3400 g., 0.9000 Gold 0.5885 oz. AGW **Obv:** Head left, legend above **Rev:** Crown above lion, sun and value within wreath

Date	Mintage	F	VF	XF	Unc	BU
SH1339 (1960)	1,682	—	—	BV	575	—
SH1340 (1961)	2,788	—	—	BV	575	—
SH1342 (1963)	30	—	—	—	—	—
SH1348 (1969)	3,000	—	—	BV	575	—
SH1350 (1971)	2,000	—	—	BV	575	—
SH1351 (1972)	2,500	—	—	BV	575	—
SH1352 (1973)	3,000	—	—	BV	575	—
SH1353 (1974)	—	—	—	BV	575	—

KM# 1201 2-1/2 PAHLAVI
20.3400 g., 0.9000 Gold 0.5885 oz. AGW, 30 mm. **Obv:** Head left, legend above, date below, "Aryamehr" added to legend **Rev:** Crown above radiant lion holding sword within wreath **Edge:** Reeded

Date	Mintage	F	VF	XF	Unc	BU
SH1354 (1975)	18,000	—	—	BV	575	—
SH1355 (1976)	16,000	—	—	BV	575	—
MS2536 (1977)	—	—	—	BV	575	—
MS2537 (1978)	—	—	—	BV	575	—
SH1358 (1979)	Rare					

KM# 1164 5 PAHLAVI
40.6799 g., 0.9000 Gold 1.1771 oz. AGW **Obv:** Head left, legend above **Rev:** Crown above lion and sun within wreath

Date	Mintage	F	VF	XF	Unc	BU
SH1339 (1960)	2,225	—	—	BV	1,150	—
SH1340 (1961)	2,430	—	—	BV	1,150	—
SH1342 (1963)	20	—	—	2,500	4,000	—
SH1348 (1969)	2,000	—	—	BV	1,150	—
SH1350 (1971)	2,000	—	—	BV	1,150	—
SH1351 (1972)	2,500	—	—	BV	1,150	—
SH1352 (1973)	2,100	—	—	BV	1,150	—
SH1353 (1974)	—	—	—	BV	1,150	—

KM# 1202 5 PAHLAVI
40.6799 g., 0.9000 Gold 1.1771 oz. AGW **Obv:** Head left, legend above, date below, "Aryamehr" added to legend **Rev:** Crown above radiant lion holding sword within wreath

Date	Mintage	F	VF	XF	Unc	BU
SH1354 (1975)	10,000	—	—	BV	1,150	—
SH1355 (1976)	17,000	—	—	BV	1,150	—
MS2536 (1977)	—	—	—	BV	1,150	—
MS2537 (1978)	—	—	—	BV	1,150	—
SH1358 (1979)	—	—	1,250	1,500	1,750	—

KM# 1210 10 PAHLAVI
81.3598 g., 0.9000 Gold 2.3541 oz. AGW **Subject:** 50th Anniversary of Pahlavi Rule **Obv:** Conjoined busts left **Rev:** Crown, inscription and date at center circle of circle wreaths

Date	Mintage	F	VF	XF	Unc	BU
MS2535 (1976)	—	—	—	BV	2,250	—

KM# 1212 10 PAHLAVI

81.3598 g., 0.9000 Gold 2.3541 oz. AGW **Subject:** Centenary of Reza Shah's Birth **Obv:** Conjoined busts left **Rev:** Crown above inscription and date within wreath

Date	Mintage	F	VF	XF	Unc	BU
MS2536 (1977)	—	—	—	BV	2,250	—

KM# 1213 10 PAHLAVI

81.3598 g., 0.9000 Gold 2.3541 oz. AGW **Obv:** Head left, legend above, date below, "Aryamehr" added to legend **Rev:** Crown above radiant lion holding sword within wreath

Date	Mintage	F	VF	XF	Unc	BU
MS2537 (1978)	—	—	—	BV	2,250	—
SH1358 (1979)	—	—	—	4,000	5,000	—

ISLAMIC REPUBLIC

MILLED COINAGE

KM# 1231 50 DINARS

Brass Clad Steel **Obv:** Radiant lion holding sword within wreath **Rev:** Value within flowered wreath

Date	Mintage	F	VF	XF	Unc	BU
SH1358 (1979)	—	10.00	20.00	30.00	40.00	—

KM# 1232 RIAL

1.8000 g., Copper-Nickel **Obv:** Inscription within wreath **Rev:** Value and date within wreath

Date	Mintage	F	VF	XF	Unc	BU
SH1358 (1979)	—	—	0.25	0.75	1.75	—
SH1359 (1980)	—	—	0.25	0.75	1.75	—

Date	Mintage	F	VF	XF	Unc	BU
SH1360 (1981)	—	—	0.25	0.75	1.75	—
SH1361 (1982)	—	—	0.25	0.75	1.75	—
SH1362 (1983)	—	—	0.25	0.75	1.75	—
SH1363 (1984)	—	—	0.25	0.75	1.75	—
SH1364 (1985)	—	—	0.25	0.75	1.75	—
SH1365 (1986)	—	—	0.15	0.65	1.25	—
SH1366 (1987)	—	—	0.15	0.65	1.25	—
SH1367 (1988)	—	—	0.15	0.65	1.25	—

KM# 1245 RIAL

Brass Clad Steel, 20 mm. **Subject:** World Jerusalem Day **Obv:** Value flanked by tulips **Rev:** Mosque above date

Date	Mintage	F	VF	XF	Unc	BU
SH1359 (1980)	—	—	1.00	2.50	5.00	—

KM# 1263 RIAL

Brass **Obv:** Value and date divides inscription and flower sprig within beaded circle **Rev:** Mountain within beaded circle

Date	Mintage	F	VF	XF	Unc	BU
SH1371 (1992)	—	—	10.00	20.00	30.00	—
SH1372 (1993)	—	—	10.00	10.00	15.00	—
SH1373 (1994)	—	—	10.00	20.00	30.00	—
SH1374 (1995)	—	—	10.00	20.00	30.00	—

KM# 1233 2 RIALS

3.0100 g., Copper-Nickel **Obv:** Inscription within tulip wreath **Rev:** Value and date within wreath

Date	Mintage	F	VF	XF	Unc	BU
SH1358 (1979)	—	—	0.60	1.25	3.50	—
SH1359 (1980)	—	—	0.50	1.25	3.50	—
SH1360 (1981)	—	—	0.50	1.25	3.50	—
SH1361 (1982)	—	—	0.50	1.00	3.00	—
SH1362 (1983)	—	—	0.35	0.75	2.75	—
SH1363 (1984)	—	—	0.50	1.00	3.00	—
SH1364 (1985)	—	—	0.35	0.75	2.75	—
SH1365 (1986)	—	—	0.25	0.75	2.50	—
SH1366 (1987)	—	—	0.25	0.75	2.50	—
SH1367 (1988)	—	—	0.25	0.75	2.50	—

KM# 1234 5 RIALS

5.0000 g., Copper-Nickel, 25 mm. **Obv:** Inscription within tulip wreath **Rev:** Value and date within wreath **Note:** Date varieties exist.

Date	Mintage	F	VF	XF	Unc	BU
SH1358 (1979)	—	—	0.75	1.25	3.50	—
SH1359 (1980)	—	—	0.75	1.25	3.50	—
SH1360 (1981)	—	—	0.75	1.25	3.50	—
SH1361 (1982)	—	—	0.75	1.25	3.50	—
SH1362 (1983)	—	—	0.75	1.25	3.50	—
SH1363 (1984)	—	—	0.75	1.25	3.50	—
SH1364 (1985)	—	—	0.75	1.25	3.50	—
SH1365 (1986)	—	—	0.75	1.25	3.50	—
SH1366 (1987)	—	—	0.75	1.25	3.50	—
SH1367 (1988)	—	—	0.75	1.25	3.50	—
SH1368 (1989)	—	—	0.75	1.25	3.50	—

Date	Mintage	F	VF	XF	Unc	BU
SH1373 (1994)	—	—	0.50	1.25	3.00	—
SH1375 (1996)	—	—	0.50	1.25	3.00	—
SH1376 (1997)	—	—	0.50	1.25	3.00	—
SH1378 (1999)	—	—	—	2.00	5.00	—

KM# 1235.1 10 RIALS

Copper-Nickel, 28 mm. **Obv:** Inscription and value within tulip wreath **Rev:** Value and date within wreath

Date	Mintage	F	VF	XF	Unc	BU
SH1358 (1979)	—	—	1.00	2.50	4.50	—
SH1358 (1979) Large date	—	—	1.00	2.50	4.50	—
SH1359 (1980)	—	—	1.00	2.50	4.50	—
SH1360 (1981)	—	—	1.00	2.50	4.50	—
SH1361 (1982)	—	—	1.00	2.00	4.00	—

KM# 1243 10 RIALS

Copper-Nickel, 28 mm. **Subject:** 1st Anniversary of Revolution **Obv:** Value and inscription within wreath **Rev:** Tulips in center of inscription, dates and value

Date	Mintage	F	VF	XF	Unc	BU
SH1358 (1979)	—	—	5.00	10.00	15.00	—

KM# 1249 10 RIALS

6.9700 g., Copper-Nickel, 28 mm. **Subject:** Moslem Unity **Obv:** Capitol building flanked by dates **Rev:** Kaaba at Mecca, date with value below **Edge:** Reeded

Date	Mintage	F	VF	XF	Unc	BU
SH1361-AH1402 (1982)	—	—	5.00	10.00	15.00	—

KM# 1235.2 10 RIALS

Copper-Nickel, 28 mm. **Obv:** Inscription and value within tulip wreath **Rev:** Value and date within wreath **Note:** Date varieties exist.

Date	Mintage	F	VF	XF	Unc	BU
SH1361 (1982)	—	—	1.00	2.00	4.00	—
SH1362 (1983)	—	—	1.00	2.00	4.00	—
SH1363 (1984)	—	—	1.00	2.00	4.00	—
SH1364 (1985)	—	—	0.90	1.50	4.00	—
SH1365 (1986)	—	—	0.90	1.50	4.00	—
SH1366 (1987)	—	—	0.90	1.50	4.00	—
SH1366 (1987) Small date	—	—	0.90	1.50	4.00	—
SH1367 (1988)	—	—	0.65	1.50	3.00	—

KM# 1258 5 RIALS

Brass, 19.5 mm. **Obv:** Value and date divides inscription and flower sprig within beaded circle **Rev:** Tomb within beaded circle

Date	Mintage	F	VF	XF	Unc	BU
SH1371 (1992)	—	—	0.50	1.25	3.00	—
SH1372 (1993)	—	—	0.50	1.25	3.00	—

KM# 1253.1   10 RIALS

3.0200 g., Copper-Nickel, 21.2 mm. **Subject:** World Jerusalem Day **Obv:** Capitol building divides date **Rev:** Kaaba at Mecca divides date with value below **Edge:** Plain

Date	Mintage	F	VF	XF	Unc	BU
SH1368 (1989)	—	—	1.50	3.00	6.00	—

KM# 1253.2   10 RIALS

3.0200 g., Copper-Nickel, 21.2 mm. **Obv:** Capitol building divides dates **Rev:** Kaaba at Mecca divides dates with value below

Date	Mintage	F	VF	XF	Unc	BU
SH1368 (1989)	—	—	1.50	3.00	6.00	—

KM# 1259   10 RIALS

Aluminum-Bronze, 21 mm. **Subject:** Tomb of Ferdousi **Obv:** Value and date divides inscription and flower sprig within beaded circle **Rev:** Tomb within beaded circle

Date	Mintage	F	VF	XF	Unc	BU
SH1371 (1992)	—	—	1.00	2.00	3.75	—
SH1372 (1993)	—	—	1.00	2.00	3.75	—
SH1373 (1994)	—	—	1.00	2.00	3.75	—
SH1374 (1995)	—	—	1.00	2.00	3.75	—
SH1375 (1996)	—	—	1.00	2.00	3.75	—
SH1376 (1997)	—	—	1.00	2.00	3.75	—

KM# 1244   20 RIALS

Copper-Nickel, 31 mm. **Subject:** 1400th Anniversary of Mohammed's Flight **Obv:** Value and inscription within wreath **Rev:** Inscription within banner on top of world globe under radiant sun

Date	Mintage	F	VF	XF	Unc	BU
SH1358-AH1400 (1979)	—	—	5.00	10.00	15.00	—

KM# 1236   20 RIALS

Copper-Nickel, 31 mm. **Obv:** Inscription within tulip wreath **Rev:** Value and date within wreath **Note:** Date varieties exist.

Date	Mintage	F	VF	XF	Unc	BU
SH1358 (1979)	—	—	1.00	1.75	4.50	—
SH1359 (1980)	—	—	1.00	1.75	4.50	—
SH1360 (1981)	—	—	1.00	1.75	4.50	—
SH1361 (1982)	—	—	1.00	1.75	4.50	—
SH1362 (1983)	—	—	1.00	1.75	4.50	—
SH1363 (1984)	—	—	1.00	1.75	4.50	—
SH1364 (1985)	—	—	1.00	1.75	4.50	—
SH1365 (1986)	—	—	1.00	1.75	4.50	—
SH1366 (1987)	—	—	1.00	1.75	4.50	—
SH1367 (1988)	—	—	1.00	1.75	4.50	—

KM# 1246   20 RIALS

Copper-Nickel, 31 mm. **Subject:** 2nd Anniversary of Islamic Revolution **Obv:** Value flanked by tulips and inscription with date below **Rev:** Legend

Date	Mintage	F	VF	XF	Unc	BU
SH1359 (1980)	—	—	5.00	10.00	15.00	—

KM# 1247   20 RIALS

Copper-Nickel, 31 mm. **Subject:** 3rd Anniversary of Islamic Revolution **Obv:** Artistic tulip design within circle **Rev:** Inscription within artistic design

Date	Mintage	F	VF	XF	Unc	BU
SH1360 (1981)	—	—	5.00	10.00	15.00	—

KM# 1251   20 RIALS

Copper-Nickel, 31 mm. **Subject:** Islamic Banking Week **Obv:** Inscription within tulip wreath **Rev:** Building within 1/2 wreath and gear design

Date	Mintage	F	VF	XF	Unc	BU
SH1367 (1988)	—	—	5.00	10.00	15.00	—

KM# 1254.1   20 RIALS

Copper-Nickel, 24 mm. **Subject:** 8 Years of Sacred Defense **Obv:** Value and date within circle of 22 small ornaments **Rev:** Shield divides dates and inscription within wreath **Note:** 1.48 mm thick.

Date	Mintage	F	VF	XF	Unc	BU
SH1368 (1989)	—	—	3.00	5.00	10.00	—

KM# 1254.2   20 RIALS

4.6400 g., Copper-Nickel, 24 mm. **Obv:** Value, date and inscription within circle of 20 small ornaments **Rev:** Shield divides inscription and dates within wreath **Note:** 1.46 mm thick.

Date	Mintage	F	VF	XF	Unc	BU
SH1368 (1989)	—	—	3.00	5.00	10.00	—

KM# 1254.3   20 RIALS

Copper-Nickel, 24 mm. **Obv:** Inscription, value and date within circle of 20 small ornaments **Rev:** Shield divides inscription and dates within wreath

Date	Mintage	F	VF	XF	Unc	BU
SH1368 (1989)	—	—	3.00	5.00	10.00	—

KM# 1237.1   50 RIALS

Aluminum-Bronze, 26 mm. **Subject:** Oil and Agriculture **Obv:** Value at upper left of towers within 1/2 gear and oat sprigs **Rev:** Map in relief **Edge:** Lettered in Arabic **Note:** Two varieties of edge lettering exist.

Date	Mintage	F	VF	XF	Unc	BU
SH1359 (1980)	—	—	2.00	3.50	8.00	—
SH1360 (1981)	—	—	2.00	3.50	8.00	—
SH1361 (1982)	—	—	2.00	3.50	8.00	—
SH1362 (1983)	—	—	2.00	3.50	8.00	—
SH1364 (1985)	—	—	2.00	3.50	8.00	—
SH1365 (1986)	—	—	2.00	3.50	8.00	—

KM# 1237.2   50 RIALS

Aluminum-Bronze, 26 mm. **Obv:** Value at upper left of towers within 1/2 gear and oat sprigs **Rev:** Map incuse **Edge:** Lettered in Arabic

Date	Mintage	F	VF	XF	Unc	BU
SH1366 (1987)	—	—	4.00	6.00	9.00	—
SH1367 (1988)	—	—	—	4.50	7.00	—
SH1368 (1989)	—	—	—	4.50	7.00	—

KM# 1252   50 RIALS

Copper-Nickel **Subject:** 10th Anniversary of Revolution **Obv:** Value at upper left of towers within 1/2 gear and oat sprigs **Rev:** Flower-like design above inscription and date within designed border

Date	Mintage	F	VF	XF	Unc	BU
SH1367 (1988)	—	—	5.00	10.00	15.00	—

KM# 1237.1a   50 RIALS

Copper-Nickel **Obv:** Value at upper left of towers within 1/2 gear and oat sprigs **Rev:** Map in relief **Edge:** Lettered in Arabic

Date	Mintage	F	VF	XF	Unc	BU
SH1368 (1989)	—	—	2.00	3.50	7.50	—
SH1369 (1990)	—	—	2.00	3.50	7.50	—
SH1370 (1991)	—	—	2.00	3.50	7.50	—

KM# 1260   50 RIALS

Copper-Nickel, 26 mm. **Subject:** Shrine of Hazrat Masumah **Obv:** Value and date **Rev:** Shrine within beaded circle **Edge:** Reeded

Date	Mintage	F	VF	XF	Unc	BU
SH1371 (1992)	—	—	2.50	3.50	5.00	—
SH1372 (1993)	—	—	2.50	3.50	5.00	—
SH1373 (1994)	—	—	2.50	3.50	5.00	—
SH1374 (1995)	—	—	2.50	3.50	5.00	—
SH1375 (1996)	—	—	2.50	3.50	5.00	—
SH1376 (1997)	—	—	2.50	3.50	5.00	—
SH1377 (1998)	—	—	2.50	3.50	5.00	—
SH1378 (1999)	—	—	2.50	3.50	5.00	—
SH1379 (2000)	—	—	2.50	3.50	5.00	—

KM# 1261.1 100 RIALS
8.7800 g., Copper-Nickel **Subject:** Shrine of Imam Reza
Obv: Value and date divides inscription and flower sprig within beaded border **Rev:** Shrine within designed border **Note:** Thin denomination and numerals

Date	Mintage	F	VF	XF	Unc	BU
SH1371 (1992)	—				6.50	—

KM# 1261.2 100 RIALS
Copper-Nickel, 29 mm. **Obv:** Value and date **Rev:** Shrine within designed border **Note:** Thick denomination and numerals

Date	Mintage	F	VF	XF	Unc	BU
SH1372 (1993)	—				6.50	—
SH1373 (1994)	—				6.50	—
SH1375 (1996)	—				6.50	—
SH1376 (1997)	—				6.50	—
SH1377 (1998)	—				6.50	—
SH1378 (1999)	—				6.50	—
SH1379 (2000)	—				6.50	—

KM# 1262 250 RIALS
Bi-Metallic Copper-Nickel center in Brass ring, 28 mm.
Obv: Value within circle, inscription and date divide wreath
Rev: Stylized flower within circle and wreath

Date	Mintage	F	VF	XF	Unc	BU
SH1371 (1993)	—			—	7.50	—
SH1372 (1993)	—			—	7.50	—
SH1373 (1994)	—			—	7.50	—
SH1374 (1995)	—			—	7.50	—
SH1375 (1996)	—			—	7.50	—
SH1376 (1997)	—			—	7.50	—
SH1377 (1998)	—			—	7.50	—
SH1378 (1999)	—			—	7.50	—
SH1379 (2000)	—			—	7.50	—

BULLION COINAGE

Issued by the National Bank of Iran

KM# 1238 1/4 AZADI
2.0339 g., 0.9000 Gold 0.0588 oz. AGW **Obv:** Mosque within circle **Obv. Leg.:** "1st Spring of Freedom" **Rev:** Artistic design within hexagon and designed border

Date	Mintage	F	VF	XF	Unc	BU
SH1358 (1979)	—	—	—	—	300	—

KM# 1265 1/4 AZADI
2.0339 g., 0.9000 Gold 0.0588 oz. AGW **Obv. Leg.:** "Spring of Freedom"

Date	Mintage	F	VF	XF	Unc	BU
SH1366 (1987)	—	—	—	—	300	—
SH1368 (1989)	—	—	—	—	300	—
SH1369 (1990)	—	—	—	—	300	—
SH1370 (1991)	—	—	—	—	300	—

KM# 1239 1/2 AZADI
4.0680 g., 0.9000 Gold 0.1177 oz. AGW **Obv:** Mosque within circle **Obv. Leg.:** "1st Spring of Freedom" **Rev:** Artistic design within hexagon and designed border

Date	Mintage	F	VF	XF	Unc	BU
SH1358 (1979)	—				120	

KM# 1250.1 1/2 AZADI
4.0680 g., 0.9000 Gold 0.1177 oz. AGW **Obv:** Legend shortened **Obv. Leg.:** "Spring of Freedom"

Date	Mintage	F	VF	XF	Unc	BU
SH1363 (1984)	—				200	

KM# 1250.2 1/2 AZADI
4.0680 g., 0.9000 Gold 0.1177 oz. AGW **Obv:** Legend larger **Obv. Leg.:** "Spring of Freedom"

Date	Mintage	F	VF	XF	Unc	BU
SH1366 (1987)	—				200	
SH1368 (1989)	—				200	
SH1370 (1991)	—				150	

KM# 1240 AZADI
8.1360 g., 0.9000 Gold 0.2354 oz. AGW **Obv:** Mosque within circle **Obv. Leg.:** "1st Spring of Freedom" **Rev:** Artistic design within hexagon and designed border

Date	Mintage	F	VF	XF	Unc	BU
SH1358 (1979)	—			BV	240	

KM# 1248.1 AZADI
8.1360 g., 0.9000 Gold 0.2354 oz. AGW **Obv:** Mosque within circle **Obv. Leg.:** "Spring of Freedom" **Rev:** Artistic design within hexagon and designed border **Note:** Legend shortened

Date	Mintage	F	VF	XF	Unc	BU
SH1363 (1984)	—			BV	240	

KM# 1248.2 AZADI
8.1360 g., 0.9000 Gold 0.2354 oz. AGW **Obv:** Mosque within circle **Obv. Leg.:** "Spring of Freedom" **Rev:** Artistic design within hexagon and designed border **Note:** Larger legend

Date	Mintage	F	VF	XF	Unc	BU
SH1364 (1985)	—	—	—	BV	240	—
SH1365 (1986)	—	—	—	BV	240	—
SH1366 (1987)	—	—	—	BV	240	—
SH1367 (1988)	—	—	—	BV	240	—
SH1368 (1989)	—	—	—	BV	240	—
SH1369 (1990)	—	—	—	BV	240	—
SH1370 (1991)	—	—	—	BV	240	—

KM# 1264 AZADI
8.1360 g., 0.9000 Gold 0.2354 oz. AGW **Subject:** Central Bank of Islamic Republic of Iran **Obv:** Bank within circle **Rev:** Head 3/4 right above date

Date	Mintage	F	VF	XF	Unc	BU
SH1370 (1991)	—			BV	240	—
SH1373 (1994)	—			BV	240	—
SH1374 (1995)	—			BV	240	—
SH1375 (1996)	—			BV	240	—

KM# A1264 AZADI
8.1360 g., 0.9000 Gold 0.2354 oz. AGW, 23.7 mm.
Obv: Mosque within circle **Rev:** Head left above date
Edge: Reeded **Mint:** Tehran

Date	Mintage	F	VF	XF	Unc	BU
SH1370 (1991)	—			BV	240	—

KM# 1241 2-1/2 AZADI
20.3400 g., 0.9000 Gold 0.5885 oz. AGW **Obv:** Mosque within circle **Obv. Leg.:** "1st Spring of Freedom" **Rev:** Artistic design within hexagon in designed border

Date	Mintage	F	VF	XF	Unc	BU
SH1358 (1979)	6	—	—	—	1,500	—

Note: A mintage of 6 pieces is reported, but more exist

KM# 1242 5 AZADI
40.6800 g., 0.9000 Gold 1.1771 oz. AGW **Obv:** Mosque within circle **Obv. Leg.:** "1st Spring of Freedom" **Rev:** Artistic design within hexagon within designed border

Date	Mintage	F	VF	XF	Unc	BU
SH1358 (1979)	—	—	—	—	3,500	—

PATTERNS
Including off metal strikes

KM#	Date	Mintage	Identification	Mkt Val
Pn26	AH1319H	—	1/4 Kran.	
Pn27	AH1319	—	250 Dinars. Silver. Plain edge. Mouzaffer profile.	550
Pn28	AH1319	—	500 Dinars. Silver. Plain edge.	700
Pn29	AH1319	—	1000 Dinars. Silver. Plain edge.	700
Pn30	AH1319	—	2000 Dinars. Silver. Plain edge.	800
Pn31	AH1319	—	5000 Dinars. Silver. Plain edge.	1,750
Pn32	AH1319	—	1/4 Toman.	300
Pn33	AH1326	—	2000 Dinars. Gold. KM#1024	1,000
Pn33a	AH1326	—	2000 Dinars. Gold. Mule. Obv. KM#1024, Rev. KM#1070.	2,500
Pn34	AH1326	—	5000 Dinars. Gold. Legend in open wreath. KM#1025	1,500
Pn34a	AH1326	—	5000 Dinars. Gold. Mule. Obv. KM#1025, Rev. KM#1071.	3,000
Pn35	AH1326	—	Toman. Gold. Legend in open wreath. KM#1026	375
Pn36	AH1326	—	2 Ashrafi. Legend in open wreath.	2,500
PnA37	AH1330	—	2000 Dinars. Nickel. Struck at Berlin.	
Pn37	AH1331	—	Toman. Gilt Bronze.	1,000
Pn37a	AH1331	—	5000 Dinars. Gold. Mule. Obv. KM#1070, Rev. KM#1024.	2,500
Pn38	AH1331	—	2 Toman. Gilt Bronze. Portrait of Ahmed Shah.	1,000
Pn40a	AH1331	—	2000 Dinars. Gold. Mule. Obv. KM#1071, Rev. KM#1025.	3,000
Pn39	AH1332	—	5 Krans. Silver. Plain edge.	1,000
Pn40	AH1332	—	2000 Dinars. Gold.	
Pn41	AH1337	—	2 Toman. Gold. KM#1080; "2 Ashrafi"	

KM#	Date	Mintage	Identification	Mkt Val
Pn42	AH1337	—	2000 Dinars. Gold. 14.0000 g.	2,000
Pn43	AH1337	—	2000 Dinars. Gold. 14.0000 g.	2,000
Pn44	AH1337	—	5 Toman. Gold. KM#1081; "5 Ashrafi"	3,500
Pn45	AH1337	—	10 Toman. Gold. KM#1082	
Pn46	SH1305	—	2000 Dinars. Silver. Reeded edge.	6,500
Pn47	SH1305	—	5000 Dinars. Silver. Reeded edge.	9,500
Pn49	SH1354 (1974)	—	2-1/2 Pahlavi. 0.9160 Silver. KM#1201.	50.00
Pn50	MS2537 (1978)	—	5 Pahlavi. 0.9167 Silver. KM#1202.	75.00
Pn48	MS2537 (1978)	—	10 Pahlavi. Silver. 51.5100 g. 48.95 mm. Reeded edge. KM#1213.	—

MINT SETS

KM#	Date	Mintage	Identification	Issue Price	Mkt Val
MS1	SH1342(1963) (4)	—	KM#1171a, 1173, 1175a, 1177a	2.00	20.00
MS2	SH1342-1343 (1963-64) (4)	—	KM#1171a, 1173, 1175a, 1177a	2.00	20.00
MS4	SH1343-44 (1964-65) (4)	—	KM#1171a, 1173, 1175a, 1177a	2.00	20.00
MS3	SH1343(1964) (4)	—	KM#1171a, 1173, 1175a, 1177a	2.00	20.00
MS5	SH1344(1965) (4)	—	KM#1171a, 1173, 1175a, 1177a	2.00	20.00
MS6	SH1344-45 (1965-66) (4)	—	KM#1171a, 1173, 1175a, 1177a	2.00	20.00
MS7	SH1348(1969) (5)	—	KM#1156, 1171a, 1173, 1176, 1178	2.00	17.00
MS8	SH1350(1971) (5)	—	KM#1156, 1171a, 1173, 1176, 1178	2.00	17.00
MS9	SH1353(1974) (6)	—	KM#1156, 1171a, 1173, 1176, 1179, 1181	2.00	19.00
MS10	SH1354(1975) (6)	—	KM#1156, 1171a, 1173, 1176, 1179, 1181	2.00	22.00
MS11	MS2535(1976) (6)	—	KM#1156a, 1205-1209	2.50	21.50
MS12	MS2536(1977) (6)	—	KM#1156a, 1172-1173, 1176, 1179, 1181	2.50	20.00
MS13	SH1358(1989) (8)	—	KM#1243-1244 dated 1358; 1246 dated 1359; 1247 dated 1360; 1252 dated 1367; 1253.1, 1253.2, 1254.1 dated 1368	—	40.00
MS14	SH1366(1989) (7)	—	KM#1232-1234, 1236 dated 1366; 1235.2, 1237.2 dated 1367; 1237.1a dated 1368	—	60.00
MS15	SH1371(1993) (5)	—	KM#1258-1262	—	60.00
MS16	SH1372, 1375, 1378 (1993, 1996, 1999) (6)	—	KM#1258-1260, 1261.2, 1262, 1263	—	100
MS17	SH1373, 1375, 1378 (1994, 1996, 1999) (6)	—	KM#1258-1260, 1261.2, 1262, 1263	—	100

PROOF SETS

KM#	Date	Mintage	Identification	Issue Price	Mkt Val
PS1	SH1306(1927) (2)	20	KM#1104, 1106	—	1,700
PS2	SH1350(1971) (9)	9,805	KM#1184-1192	262	825
PS3	SH1350(1971) (5)	18,100	KM#1184-1188	59.50	85.00

The Republic of Iraq, historically known as Mesopotamia, is located in the Near East and is bordered by Kuwait, Iran, Turkey, Syria, Jordan and Saudi Arabia. It has area of 167,925 sq. mi. (434,920 sq. km.) and a population of 14 million. Capital: Baghdad. The economy of Iraq is based on agriculture and petroleum. Crude oil accounted for 94 percent of the exports before the war with Iran began in 1980.

Mesopotamia was the site of a number of flourishing civilizations of antiquity - Sumeria, Assyria, Babylonia, Parthia, Persia and the Biblical cities of Ur, Ninevehand and Babylon. Desired because of its favored location, which embraced the fertile alluvial plains of the Tigris and Euphrates Rivers, Mesopotamia - 'land between the rivers'- was conquered by Cyrus the Great of Persia, Alexander of Macedonia and by Arabs who made the legendary city of Baghdad the capital of the ruling caliphate. Suleiman the Magnificent conquered Mesopotamia for Turkey in1534, and it formed part of the Ottoman Empire until 1623, and from 1638 to 1917. Great Britain, given a League of Nations mandate over the territory in 1920, recognized Iraq as a kingdom in 1922. Iraq became an independent constitutional monarchy presided over by the Hashemite family, direct descendants of the prophet Mohammed, in 1932. In 1958, the army-led revolution of July 14 overthrew the monarchy and proclaimed a republic.

NOTE: The 'I' mintmark on 1938 and 1943 issues appears on the obverse near the point of the bust. Some of the issues of 1938 have a dot to denote a composition change from nickel to copper-nickel.

RULERS
Ottoman, until 1917
British, 1921-1922
Faisal I, 1921-1933
Ghazi I, 1933-1939
Faisal II, Regency, 1939-1953
 As King, 1953-1958

MINT MARK
I — Bombay

MONETARY SYSTEM

Falus, Fulus   Fals, Fils   Falsan

50 Fils = 1 Dirham
200 Fils = 1 Riyal
1000 Fils = 1 Dinar (Pound)

TITLES

العراق

Al-Iraq

المملكة العراقية

SAI-Mamlaka(t) al-Iraqiya(t)

الجمهورية العرقية

Al-Jumhuriya(t) al-Iraqiya(t)

KINGDOM OF IRAQ

Faisal I
1921-1933AD
DECIMAL COINAGE

KM# 95   FILS
2.5000 g., Bronze, 19.5 mm. Obv: Head right Rev: Value in center circle flanked by dates

Date	Mintage	F	VF	XF	Unc	BU
1931	4,000,000	1.00	3.00	10.00	25.00	—
1931 Proof	—					—
1933	6,000,000	1.00	3.00	10.00	25.00	—
1933 Proof	—					—

KM# 96   2 FILS
5.0000 g., Bronze, 24 mm. Obv: Head right Rev: Value in center circle flanked by dates

Date	Mintage	F	VF	XF	Unc	BU
1931	2,500,000	1.25	3.50	10.00	25.00	—
1931 Proof	—					—
1933	1,000,000	1.50	4.00	15.00	35.00	—
1933 Proof	—					—

KM# 97   4 FILS
4.0000 g., Nickel, 21 mm. Obv: Head right Rev: Value in center circle flanked by dates

Date	Mintage	F	VF	XF	Unc	BU
1931	4,500,000	1.50	4.00	15.00	50.00	—
1931 Proof	—					—

Date	Mintage	F	VF	XF	Unc	BU
1933	6,500,000	1.50	4.00	15.00	50.00	—
1933 Proof	—					—

KM# 98   10 FILS
6.7500 g., Nickel, 25 mm. Obv: Head right Rev: Value within center circle flanked by dates

Date	Mintage	F	VF	XF	Unc	BU
1931	2,400,000	2.00	5.00	16.50	50.00	—
1931 Proof	—					—
1933	2,200,000	2.00	5.00	16.50	50.00	—
1933 Proof	—					—

KM# 99   20 FILS
3.6000 g., 0.5000 Silver 0.0579 oz. ASW, 20.5 mm. Obv: Head right Rev: Value in center circle flanked by dates

Date	Mintage	F	VF	XF	Unc	BU
1931	1,500,000	2.50	9.00	25.00	75.00	—
1931 Proof	—					—
1933	1,100,000	2.50	9.00	25.00	75.00	—
1933 Proof	—					—
1933 (error) 1252	Inc. above	20.00	60.00	100	200	—

KM# 100   50 FILS
9.0000 g., 0.5000 Silver 0.1447 oz. ASW, 26.5 mm. Obv: Head right Rev: Value in center circle flanked by dates

Date	Mintage	F	VF	XF	Unc	BU
1931	8,800,000	3.50	10.00	28.00	80.00	—
1931 Proof	—					—
1933	800,000	6.00	15.00	35.00	100	—
1933 Proof	—					—

KM# 101   RIYAL (200 Fils)
20.0000 g., 0.5000 Silver 0.3215 oz. ASW, 34 mm. Obv: Head right Rev: Value in center circle flanked by dates Note: Dav. #255.

Date	Mintage	F	VF	XF	Unc	BU
1932	500,000	7.50	15.00	35.00	350	—
1932 Proof	Est. 20	Value: 1,600				

Ghazi I
1933-1939AD
DECIMAL COINAGE

KM# 102   FILS
2.5000 g., Bronze, 19.5 mm. Obv: Head left Rev: Value in center circle flanked by dates Note: Struck at Royal and Bombay Mint.

Date	Mintage	F	VF	XF	Unc	BU
1936	3,000,000	1.25	4.00	10.00	25.00	—
1936 Proof	—					—

Date	Mintage	F	VF	XF	Unc	BU
1938	36,000,000	0.25	0.50	1.00	3.00	—
1938 Proof	—	—	—	—	—	—
1938 -I	3,000,000	0.50	2.00	5.00	15.00	—

KM# 105 4 FILS
4.0000 g., Nickel, 21 mm. **Obv:** Head left **Rev:** Value within center circle flanked by dates

Date	Mintage	F	VF	XF	Unc	BU
1938	1,000,000	1.00	2.00	6.00	15.00	—
1938 Proof	—	—	—	—	—	—
1939	1,000,000	1.25	2.50	10.00	30.00	—
1939 Proof	—	—	—	—	—	—

KM# 105a 4 FILS
21.0000 g., Copper-Nickel, 21 mm. **Obv:** Head left **Rev:** Value within center circle flanked by dates **Note:** Struck at Royal and Bombay Mint.

Date	Mintage	F	VF	XF	Unc	BU
1938	2,750,000	0.75	1.00	2.00	6.00	—
1938 Proof	—	—	—	—	—	—
1938 -I	2,500,000	1.00	2.00	7.50	15.00	—

KM# 105b 4 FILS
4.0000 g., Bronze, 21 mm. **Obv:** Head left **Rev:** Value in center circle flanked by dates

Date	Mintage	F	VF	XF	Unc	BU
1938	8,000,000	0.50	1.00	2.00	6.00	—
1938 Proof	—	—	—	—	—	—

KM# 103 10 FILS
6.7500 g., Nickel, 25 mm. **Obv:** Head left **Rev:** Value in center circle flanked by dates

Date	Mintage	F	VF	XF	Unc	BU
1937	400,000	3.00	5.00	16.50	50.00	—
1937 Proof	—	—	—	—	—	—
1938	600,000	2.50	4.00	10.00	35.00	—
1938 Proof	—	—	—	—	—	—

KM# 103a 10 FILS
6.7500 g., Copper-Nickel, 25 mm. **Obv:** Head left **Rev:** Value within center circle flanked by dates **Note:** Struck at Royal and Bombay Mint.

Date	Mintage	F	VF	XF	Unc	BU
1938	1,100,000	1.00	2.00	4.00	10.00	—
1938 Proof	—	—	—	—	—	—
1938 -I	1,500,000	1.50	2.50	6.00	15.00	—

KM# 103b 10 FILS
6.7500 g., Bronze, 25 mm. **Obv:** Head left **Rev:** Value within center circle flanked by dates

Date	Mintage	F	VF	XF	Unc	BU
1938	8,250,000	0.50	1.00	2.50	6.50	—
1938 Proof	—	—	—	—	—	—

KM# 106 20 FILS
3.6000 g., 0.5000 Silver 0.0579 oz. ASW, 20.5 mm. **Obv:** Head left **Rev:** Value in center circle flanked by dates

Date	Mintage	F	VF	XF	Unc	BU
1938	1,200,000	2.00	3.50	8.00	22.00	—
1938 -I	1,350,000	2.00	4.00	9.00	26.00	—

KM# 104 50 FILS
9.0000 g., 0.5000 Silver 0.1447 oz. ASW, 26.5 mm. **Obv:** Head left **Rev:** Value in center circle flanked by dates **Note:** Struck at Royal and Bombay Mint.

Date	Mintage	F	VF	XF	Unc	BU
1937	1,200,000	3.00	7.00	10.00	30.00	—
1937 Proof	—	—	—	—	—	—

Date	Mintage	F	VF	XF	Unc	BU
1938	5,300,000	2.50	4.00	8.00	25.00	—
1938 Proof	—	—	—	—	—	—
1938 -I	7,500,000	2.50	4.00	8.00	25.00	—

Faisal II - Regency
1939-1953AD
DECIMAL COINAGE

KM# 107 4 FILS
4.0000 g., Bronze, 21 mm. **Obv:** Head right **Rev:** Value in center circle flanked by dates

Date	Mintage	F	VF	XF	Unc	BU
1943 -I	1,500,000	2.00	3.00	7.00	15.00	—

KM# 108 10 FILS
6.7500 g., Bronze, 25 mm. **Obv:** Head right **Rev:** Value in center circle flanked by dates

Date	Mintage	F	VF	XF	Unc	BU
1943 -I	1,500,000	3.00	7.00	20.00	50.00	—

Faisal II - King
1953-1958AD
DECIMAL COINAGE

KM# 109 FILS
Bronze **Obv:** Head right **Rev:** Value in center circle flanked by dates

Date	Mintage	F	VF	XF	Unc	BU
1953	41,000,000	0.25	0.40	0.60	1.00	—
1953 Proof	200	Value: 75.00				

KM# 110 2 FILS
Bronze **Obv:** Head right **Rev:** Value in center circle flanked by dates

Date	Mintage	F	VF	XF	Unc	BU
1953	500,000	0.50	1.00	3.00	12.50	—
1953 Proof	200	Value: 100				

KM# 111 4 FILS
4.0000 g., Copper-Nickel, 21 mm. **Obv:** Head right **Rev:** Value in center circle flanked by dates

Date	Mintage	F	VF	XF	Unc	BU
1953	20,750,000	0.50	0.75	1.00	2.50	—
1953 Proof	200	Value: 75.00				

KM# 112 10 FILS
6.7500 g., Copper-Nickel, 25 mm. **Obv:** Head right **Rev:** Value in center circle flanked by dates

Date	Mintage	F	VF	XF	Unc	BU
1953	11,400,000	0.50	0.75	1.00	2.50	—
1953 Proof	200	Value: 75.00				

KM# 113 20 FILS
3.6000 g., 0.5000 Silver 0.0579 oz. ASW, 20.5 mm. **Obv:** Head right **Rev:** Value in center circle flanked by dates

Date	Mintage	F	VF	XF	Unc	BU
1953	250,000	25.00	45.00	70.00	140	—
1953 Proof	200	Value: 300				

KM# 116 20 FILS
2.8000 g., 0.5000 Silver 0.0450 oz. ASW, 19 mm. **Obv:** Head right **Rev:** Value in center circle, date above sprigs, legend above

Date	Mintage	F	VF	XF	Unc	BU
1955	4,000,000	1.50	3.00	10.00	—	—
1955 Proof	—	Value: 80.00				

KM# 114 50 FILS
9.0000 g., 0.5000 Silver 0.1447 oz. ASW, 26.5 mm. **Obv:** Head right **Rev:** Value in center circle flanked by dates

Date	Mintage	F	VF	XF	Unc	BU
1953	560,000	50.00	100	150	250	—
1953 Proof	200	Value: 450				

KM# 117 50 FILS
7.0000 g., 0.5000 Silver 0.1125 oz. ASW, 26 mm. **Obv:** Head right **Rev:** Value in center circle, date above sprigs, legend above

Date	Mintage	F	VF	XF	Unc	BU
1955	12,000,000	2.50	4.00	6.00	11.50	—
1955 Proof	—	Value: 80.00				

KM# 115 100 FILS
10.0000 g., 0.9000 Silver 0.2893 oz. ASW, 29 mm. **Obv:** Head right **Rev:** Value in center circle flanked by dates

Date	Mintage	F	VF	XF	Unc	BU
1953	1,200,000	5.00	7.50	20.00	50.00	—
1953 Proof	200	Value: 250				

KM# 118 100 FILS
10.0000 g., 0.5000 Silver 0.1607 oz. ASW, 29 mm. **Obv:** Head right **Rev:** Value in center circle flanked by dates

Date	Mintage	F	VF	XF	Unc	BU
1955	1,000,000	—	700	1,000	1,500	—
1955 Proof	—	Value: 300				

REPUBLIC

DECIMAL COINAGE

KM# 119 FILS
2.5000 g., Bronze, 19 mm. **Obv:** Value in center circle, dates above sprig, legend above **Rev:** Oat sprig within center circle of star design

Date	Mintage	F	VF	XF	Unc	BU
1959	72,000,000	0.15	0.25	0.50	1.00	—
1959 Proof	400	Value: 30.00				

KM# 120 5 FILS
5.0000 g., Copper-Nickel, 22 mm. **Obv:** Value in center circle above dates and sprigs, legend above **Rev:** Oat sprig within center circle of star design

Date	Mintage	F	VF	XF	Unc	BU
1959	30,000,000	0.15	0.25	0.50	1.00	—
1959 Proof	400	Value: 30.00				

KM# 125 5 FILS
Copper-Nickel **Obv:** Value in center circle above oat sprigs, legend above **Rev:** Palm trees divide dates

Date	Mintage	F	VF	XF	Unc	BU
1967	17,000,000	0.15	0.25	0.35	0.50	—
1971	15,000,000	0.15	0.25	0.35	0.50	—

KM# 125a 5 FILS
3.9000 g., Stainless Steel, 22 mm. **Obv:** Value in center circle above oat sprigs, legend above **Rev:** Palm trees divide dates

Date	Mintage	F	VF	XF	Unc	BU
1971	2,000,000	0.20	0.30	0.50	0.75	—
1974	15,000,000	0.10	0.15	0.25	0.35	—
1975	94,800,000	0.10	0.15	0.25	0.35	—
1980	20,160,000	0.10	0.15	0.25	0.35	—
1981	29,840,000	0.10	0.15	0.25	0.35	—

Note: Non-magnetic

KM# 141 5 FILS
Stainless Steel **Series:** F.A.O. **Obv:** Value in center circle divides legend **Rev:** Palm trees divide date

Date	Mintage	F	VF	XF	Unc	BU
1975	2,000,000	0.10	0.15	0.25	0.50	—

KM# 159 5 FILS
Stainless Steel **Subject:** Babylon-Ruins **Obv:** Value in center circle divides legend **Rev:** Dates above ruins

Date	Mintage	F	VF	XF	Unc	BU
1982	—	0.10	0.15	0.25	0.50	—

KM# 159a 5 FILS
Copper-Nickel **Subject:** Babylon-Ruins **Obv:** Value in center circle divides legend **Rev:** Dates above ruins

Date	Mintage	F	VF	XF	Unc	BU
1982 Proof	—	Value: 3.00				

KM# 121 10 FILS
6.7500 g., Copper-Nickel, 26 mm. **Obv:** Value in center circle above dates and sprigs, legend above **Rev:** Oat sprig within center circle of star-like design

Date	Mintage	F	VF	XF	Unc	BU
1959	24,000,000	0.25	0.35	0.65	1.50	—
1959 Proof	400	Value: 30.00				

KM# 126 10 FILS
6.8100 g., Copper-Nickel, 26 mm. **Obv:** Value in center circle above oat sprigs, legend above **Rev:** Palm trees divide dates

Date	Mintage	F	VF	XF	Unc	BU
1967	13,400,000	0.20	0.30	0.60	1.25	—
1971	12,000,000	0.20	0.30	0.60	1.25	—

KM# 126a 10 FILS
5.6400 g., Stainless Steel, 27 mm. **Obv:** Value in center circle above sprigs, legend above **Rev:** Palm trees divide dates

Date	Mintage	F	VF	XF	Unc	BU
1971	1,550,000	0.25	0.35	0.65	1.50	—
1974	12,000,000	0.20	0.30	0.50	1.00	—
1975	52,456,000	0.20	0.30	0.50	1.00	—
1979	13,800,000	0.20	0.30	0.50	1.00	—
1980	11,264,000	0.20	0.30	0.50	1.00	—
1981	63,736,000	0.20	0.30	0.50	1.00	—

Note: Non-magnetic

KM# 142 10 FILS
Stainless Steel, 26 mm. **Series:** F.A.O. **Obv:** Value within circle divides legend **Rev:** Palm trees divide dates

Date	Mintage	F	VF	XF	Unc	BU
1975	1,000,000	0.15	0.25	0.50	0.75	—

KM# 160 10 FILS
Stainless Steel, 26 mm. **Obv:** Value within circle divides legends **Rev:** Dates above ruins **Rev. Leg.:** Babylon - Ishtar Gate

Date	Mintage	F	VF	XF	Unc	BU
1982	—	—	—	—	0.75	—

KM# 160a 10 FILS
Copper-Nickel **Obv:** Value within circle divides legends **Rev:** Dates above ruins **Rev. Leg.:** Babylon - Ishtar Gate

Date	Mintage	F	VF	XF	Unc	BU
1982 Proof	—	Value: 3.00				

KM# 122 25 FILS
2.5000 g., 0.5000 Silver 0.0402 oz. ASW, 20 mm. **Obv:** Value within circle above dates and sprigs, legend above **Rev:** Oat sprig within center circle of star-like design

Date	Mintage	F	VF	XF	Unc	BU
1959	12,000,000	0.65	0.85	1.50	3.00	—
1959 Proof	400	Value: 40.00				

KM# 127 25 FILS
2.7900 g., Copper-Nickel, 20 mm. **Obv:** Value in center circle above sprigs, legend above **Rev:** Palm trees divide dates

Date	Mintage	F	VF	XF	Unc	BU
1969	6,000,000	0.20	0.30	0.50	1.00	—
1970	6,000,000	0.20	0.30	0.50	1.00	—
1972	12,000,000	0.20	0.30	0.50	1.00	—
1975	48,000,000	0.20	0.30	0.50	1.00	—
1981	60,000,000	0.20	0.30	0.50	1.00	—

KM# 161 25 FILS
Copper-Nickel, 20 mm. **Obv:** Value in center circle divides legend **Rev:** Dates above lion

Date	Mintage	F	VF	XF	Unc	BU
1982	—	—	—	—	1.25	—
1982 Proof	—	Value: 4.00				

KM# 123 50 FILS
5.0000 g., 0.5000 Silver 0.0804 oz. ASW, 23 mm. **Obv:** Value in center circle above dates and sprigs, legend above **Rev:** Oat sprig within center circle of star-like design

Date	Mintage	F	VF	XF	Unc	BU
1959	24,000,000	1.25	1.50	2.50	5.00	—
1959 Proof	400	Value: 80.00				

KM# 128 50 FILS
5.5400 g., Copper-Nickel, 23 mm. **Obv:** Value within circle above sprigs, legend above **Rev:** Palm trees divide dates

Date	Mintage	F	VF	XF	Unc	BU
1969	12,000,000	0.25	0.35	0.65	1.25	—
1970	12,000,000	0.25	0.35	0.65	1.25	—
1972	12,000,000	0.25	0.35	0.65	1.25	—
1975	36,000,000	0.25	0.35	0.65	1.25	—
1979	1,500,000	0.25	0.35	0.65	1.75	—
1980	23,520,000	0.25	0.35	0.65	1.25	—
1981	138,995,000	0.25	0.35	0.65	1.00	—
1990	—	0.25	0.35	0.65	1.00	—

KM# 162 50 FILS
Copper-Nickel, 23 mm. **Obv:** Value in center circle divides legend **Rev:** Horse right

Date	Mintage	F	VF	XF	Unc	BU
1982	—	0.25	0.50	0.75	2.50	—
1982 Proof	—	Value: 6.00				

KM# 124 100 FILS
10.0000 g., 0.5000 Silver 0.1607 oz. ASW, 29 mm. **Obv:** Value within circle above dates and sprigs, legend above **Rev:** Oat sprig within center circle of star-like design

Date	Mintage	F	VF	XF	Unc	BU
1959	6,000,000	2.75	3.75	6.00	10.00	—
1959 Proof	400	Value: 150				

KM# 129 100 FILS
10.8300 g., Copper-Nickel **Obv:** Value within circle above sprigs, legend above **Rev:** Palm trees divide dates

Date	Mintage	F	VF	XF	Unc	BU
1970	6,000,000	0.35	0.50	0.75	1.50	—
1972	6,000,000	0.35	0.50	0.75	1.50	—
1975	12,000,000	0.35	0.50	0.75	1.50	—
1979	1,000,000	0.35	0.75	1.50	3.00	—

KM# 130 250 FILS
Nickel **Series:** F.A.O. **Subject:** Agrarian Reform Day **Obv:** Value within circle above sprigs, legend above **Rev:** Palm trees divide dates

Date	Mintage	F	VF	XF	Unc	BU
1970	500,000	—	1.50	3.00	6.00	—
1970 Proof	1,000	Value: 14.50				

Note: Varieties exist with edge inscription w/FAO-250-repeated three times in relief

KM# 131 250 FILS
Nickel **Subject:** 1st Anniversary Peace with Kurds **Obv:** Value within circle above dates and sprigs, legend above **Rev:** Value, design and dove within circle, outer circle consists of 1/2 gear and 1/2 sprigs

Date	Mintage	F	VF	XF	Unc	BU
1971	500,000	—	1.50	3.00	6.00	—
1971 Proof	1,000	Value: 14.50				

KM# 135 250 FILS
Nickel **Subject:** Silver Jublilee of Al Baath Party **Obv:** Value within circle above dates, legend above and below **Rev:** Palm trees divide dates

Date	Mintage	F	VF	XF	Unc	BU
1972	250,000	—	1.50	3.00	6.00	—

KM# 136 250 FILS
Nickel **Subject:** 25th Anniversary of Central Bank **Obv:** Value within circle above dates, legend above and below **Rev:** Palm trees divide dates

Date	Mintage	F	VF	XF	Unc	BU
1972	250,000	—	1.50	3.00	6.00	—

KM# 138 250 FILS
Nickel **Subject:** Oil Nationalization **Obv:** Value within circle above dates, legend above and below **Rev:** Torch divides oil rig tower and pump, flanked by dates

Date	Mintage	F	VF	XF	Unc	BU
1973	260,000	—	1.50	3.00	6.50	—
1973 Proof	5,000	Value: 12.00				

KM# 144 250 FILS
Nickel **Subject:** International Year of the Child **Obv:** Value within circle divides legends and emblems **Rev:** Child's laureate head right within circle

Date	Mintage	F	VF	XF	Unc	BU
1979 Proof	10,000	Value: 8.00				

KM# 146 250 FILS
Copper-Nickel **Subject:** 1st Anniversary of Hussein as President **Obv:** Value within center circle flanked by dates, legend above and below **Rev:** Bust 1/4 left

Date	Mintage	F	VF	XF	Unc	BU
1980	—	—	3.00	6.00	12.00	28.00

KM# 147 250 FILS
10.4000 g., Copper-Nickel, 29.8 mm. **Obv:** Value within circle above sprigs, legend above **Rev:** Palm trees divide dates

Date	Mintage	F	VF	XF	Unc	BU
1980	—	—	1.00	2.00	5.00	—
1981	25,568,000	—	1.00	2.00	5.00	—
1990	—	—	1.00	2.00	5.00	—

KM# 152 250 FILS
Copper-Nickel **Subject:** World Food Day **Obv:** F.A.O logo below value flanked by designs, legend above and below **Rev:** Design within circle divides dates

Date	Mintage	F	VF	XF	Unc	BU
1981	46,432,000	—	1.00	2.00	4.00	—

KM# 155 250 FILS
Copper-Nickel **Subject:** Nonaligned Nations Baghdad Conference **Obv:** Value within circle, legend above and below **Rev:** Styilized tree divides dates above legend

Date	Mintage	F	VF	XF	Unc	BU
1982	—	—	1.00	2.00	5.00	—

KM# 163 250 FILS
Copper-Nickel **Obv:** Value within circle, legend above and below **Rev:** Monument flanked by dates

Date	Mintage	F	VF	XF	Unc	BU
1982	—	—	1.00	2.00	4.50	—
1982 Proof	—	Value: 8.00				

KM# 132 500 FILS
Nickel **Subject:** 50th Anniversary of Iraqi Army **Obv:** Value in circle flanked by designs , legend above and below **Rev:** Conjoined armored busts divide dates

Date	Mintage	F	VF	XF	Unc	BU
1971	100,000	—	2.50	4.50	10.00	12.50
1971 Proof	5,000	Value: 15.00				

KM# 139   500 FILS
Nickel   **Subject:** Oil Nationalization **Obv:** Value within circle, date below, legend above and below **Rev:** Oil rig divides dates

Date	Mintage	F	VF	XF	Unc	BU
1973	260,000	—	2.50	4.50	10.00	—
1973 Proof	5,000	Value: 17.50				

KM# 165   500 FILS
9.0800 g., Nickel, 30.1 mm.   **Obv:** Value within circle above sprigs, "500 Fals" **Rev:** Palm trees divide dates

Date	Mintage	F	VF	XF	Unc	BU
1982	—	—	2.50	4.00	7.00	—

KM# 165a   500 FILS
8.9800 g., Nickel, 30.1 mm.   **Obv:** Value within circle above sprigs, "500 Falsan" **Rev:** Palm trees divide dates **Note:** Reduced weight.

Date	Mintage	F	VF	XF	Unc	BU
1982	—	—	20.00	35.00	85.00	—

KM# 168   500 FILS
9.0800 g., Nickel   **Obv:** Value within circle divides legend, "500 Fals" **Rev:** Lion of Babylon flanked by dates

Date	Mintage	F	VF	XF	Unc	BU
1982	—	—	2.00	3.50	8.00	—
1982 Proof	—	Value: 12.50				

KM# 168a   500 FILS
9.0800 g., Nickel   **Obv:** Value within circle divides legend, "500 Falsan" **Rev:** Lion of Babylon flanked by dates

Date	Mintage	F	VF	XF	Unc	BU
1982	—	—	15.00	25.00	75.00	—

KM# 133   DINAR
31.0000 g., 0.9000 Silver 0.8970 oz. ASW   **Subject:** 50th Anniversary of Iraqi Army **Obv:** Value within circle flanked by designs, legend above and below **Rev:** Conjoined armored busts divide dates

Date	Mintage	F	VF	XF	Unc	BU
1971	14,500	—	—	—	22.50	30.00
1971 Proof	5,500	Value: 40.00				

KM# 137   DINAR
31.0000 g., 0.5000 Silver 0.4983 oz. ASW   **Subject:** 25th Anniversary of Central Bank **Obv:** Value within circle flanked by designs, legend above and below **Rev:** Palm trees divide dates

Date	Mintage	F	VF	XF	Unc	BU
1972	50,000	—	—	—	20.00	25.00
1972 Proof	—	Value: 35.00				

KM# 140   DINAR
31.0000 g., 0.5000 Silver 0.4983 oz. ASW   **Subject:** Oil Nationalization **Obv:** Value within circle flanked by designs, legend above and below **Rev:** Half radiant sun divides dates above long ship

Date	Mintage	F	VF	XF	Unc	BU
1973	60,000	—	—	—	20.00	25.00
1973 Proof	5,000	Value: 37.50				

KM# 143   DINAR
31.0000 g., 0.9000 Silver 0.8970 oz. ASW   **Subject:** Inauguaration of Tharthat-Euphrates Canal **Obv:** Value within circle flanked by designs, legend above and below **Rev:** Dam with inscription above and dates below

Date	Mintage	F	VF	XF	Unc	BU
1977 Proof	7,000	Value: 40.00				

KM# 145   DINAR
31.0000 g., 0.9000 Silver 0.8970 oz. ASW   **Subject:** International Year of the Child **Obv:** Value within circle flanked by designs, legend above and below **Rev:** Child's laureate head right within circle **Note:** KM#145 is commonly found impaired. Value listed is for unimpaired Proof.

Date	Mintage	F	VF	XF	Unc	BU
1979 Proof	5,000	Value: 47.50				

KM# 148   DINAR
30.5300 g., 0.9000 Silver 0.8834 oz. ASW   **Subject:** 15th Century of Hegira **Obv:** Value and dates within circle with legend around border **Rev:** Stylized value within Mosque **Note:** KM#148 is commonly found impaired. Value listed is for unimpaired Proof.

Date	Mintage	F	VF	XF	Unc	BU
1980 Proof	25,000	Value: 50.00				

KM# 149   DINAR
Nickel   **Subject:** Battle of Qadissyiat **Obv:** Value within circle flanked by dates, legends and map **Rev:** Bust 1/4 left in front of battle scene

Date	Mintage	F	VF	XF	Unc	BU
1980	—	—	—	7.00	14.00	30.00
1980 Proof	—	Value: 35.00				

KM# 153   DINAR
Nickel   **Subject:** 50th Anniversary of Iraq Air Force **Obv:** Value within circle with legend above and dates and legend below **Rev:** Bust left divides dates, planes above with banner, sprigs below

Date	Mintage	F	VF	XF	Unc	BU
1981	—	—	—	9.00	18.00	35.00

KM# 170 DINAR
Nickel **Subject:** Circulation Coinage **Obv:** Value within circle above sprigs, legend above **Rev:** Palm trees divide dates

Date	Mintage	F	VF	XF	Unc	BU
1981	—	—	—	—	6.50	—

KM# 156 DINAR
Nickel **Subject:** Nonaligned Nations Baghdad Conference **Obv:** Value within circle with legend above and below **Rev:** Stylized tree divides dates within legend

Date	Mintage	F	VF	XF	Unc	BU
1982	—	—	—	3.50	8.00	—

KM# 164 DINAR
Nickel **Obv:** Value within circle divides legend **Rev:** Tower of Babylon flanked by dates

Date	Mintage	F	VF	XF	Unc	BU
1982	—	—	—	3.50	8.00	—
1982 Proof	—	Value: 12.50				

KM# 134 5 DINARS
13.5700 g., 0.9170 Gold 0.4001 oz. AGW **Subject:** 50th Anniversary of Iraqi Army **Obv:** Value within circle flanked by designs with legend above and below **Rev:** Conjoined armored busts divide dates

Date	Mintage	F	VF	XF	Unc	BU
1971	20,000	—	—	—	BV	400
1971 Proof	—	Value: 425				

KM# 171 5 DINARS
Bronze, 28 mm. **Obv:** Denomination and legend **Rev:** Two swords arched above palm tree

Date	Mintage	F	VF	XF	Unc	BU
1990	—	—	—	—	5.00	—

Note: Not released to circulation

KM# 172 10 DINARS
Bronze **Obv:** Denomination and legend **Rev:** Two swords arched above palm tree

Date	Mintage	F	VF	XF	Unc	BU
1990	—	—	—	—	10.00	—

Note: Not released to circulation

KM# 166 50 DINARS
13.7000 g., 0.9170 Gold 0.4039 oz. AGW **Subject:** International Year of the Child **Obv:** Value within circle flanked designs with legend above and below **Rev:** Child's laureate head right within circle

Date	Mintage	F	VF	XF	Unc	BU
1979 Proof	10,000	Value: 450				
1979 Impaired Proof	Inc. above	BV+10%				

KM# 150 50 DINARS
13.0000 g., 0.9170 Gold 0.3833 oz. AGW **Subject:** 15th Century of Hegira **Obv:** Value and inscription within center circle of legend **Rev:** Stylized value within Mosque

Date	Mintage	F	VF	XF	Unc	BU
1980 Proof	13,000	Value: 425				
1980 Impaired Proof	Inc. above	BV+10%				

KM# 173 50 DINARS
16.9650 g., 0.9170 Gold 0.5001 oz. AGW **Subject:** 1st Anniversary of Hussein as President

Date	Mintage	F	VF	XF	Unc	BU
1980 Proof	—	Value: 500				

KM# 157 50 DINARS
13.7000 g., 0.9170 Gold 0.4039 oz. AGW **Subject:** Nonaligned Nations Baghdad Conference

Date	Mintage	F	VF	XF	Unc	BU
1982 Proof	10,000	Value: 400				

KM# 167 100 DINARS
26.0000 g., 0.9170 Gold 0.7665 oz. AGW **Subject:** International Year of the Child **Obv:** Value within circle flanked by designs, legend above and below **Rev:** Child's laureate head right within circle

Date	Mintage	F	VF	XF	Unc	BU
1979 Proof	10,000	Value: 825				
1979 Impaired Proof	Inc. above	BV+10%				

KM# 151 100 DINARS
26.0000 g., 0.9170 Gold 0.7665 oz. AGW **Subject:** 15th Century of Hegira **Obv:** Inscription and value within center circle of legend **Rev:** Stylized value within Mosque

Date	Mintage	F	VF	XF	Unc	BU
1980 Proof	14,000	Value: 825				
1980 Impaired Proof	Inc. above	BV+10%				

KM# 174 100 DINARS
33.9300 g., 0.9170 Gold 1.0003 oz. AGW **Subject:** 1st Anniversary of Hussein as President

Date	Mintage	F	VF	XF	Unc	BU
1980 Proof	—	Value: 1,000				

KM# 158 100 DINARS
33.9300 g., 0.9170 Gold 1.0003 oz. AGW **Subject:** Nonaligned Nations Baghdad Conference **Obv:** Value within circle with legend above and below **Rev:** Stylized tree divides dates

Date	Mintage	F	VF	XF	Unc	BU
1982 Proof	10,000	Value: 1,000				

PATTERNS
Including off metal strikes

KM#	Date	Mintage	Identification	Mkt Val
Pn1	1935	—	20 Fils. Silver center. KM106.	450
Pn2	1935	—	50 Fils. Silver. KM104.	450
Pn3	1936	—	2 Fils. Bronze. KM96.	250
Pn4	1936	—	4 Fils. Nickel. KM105.	275
Pn5	1936	—	10 Fils. Nickel. KM103.	325
Pn6	1936	—	20 Fils. Silver center. KM106.	425
Pn7	1936	—	50 Fils. Silver. KM104.	450

PROOF SETS

KM#	Date	Mintage	Identification	Issue Price	Mkt Val
PS1	1953 (7)	200	KM109-115	—	1,325
PS2	1955 (3)	—	KM116-118	—	500
PS3	1959 (6)	400	KM119-124	—	360
PS4	1959 (7)	—	KM119-124, plus medallic crown (M1)	—	400
PS5	1973 (3)	5,000	KM138-140	—	62.00
PS6	1982 (7)	—	KM159a-160a, 161-164, 168	—	50.00

IRELAND REPUBLIC

The Republic of Ireland, which occupies five-sixths of the island of Ireland located in the Atlantic Ocean west of Great Britain, has an area of 27,136 sq. mi. (70,280 sq. km.) and a population of 4.3 million. Capital: Dublin. Agriculture and dairy farming are the principal industries. Meat, livestock, dairy products and textiles are exported.

A race of tall, red-haired Celts from Gaul arrived in Ireland about 400 B.C., assimilated the native Erainn and Picts, and established a Gaelic civilization. After the arrival of St. Patrick in 432AD, Ireland evolved into a center of Latin learning, which sent missionaries to Europe and possibly North America. In 1154, Pope Adrian IV gave all of Ireland to English King Henry II to administer as a Papal fief. Because of the enactment of anti-Catholic laws and the awarding of vast tracts of Irish land to Protestant absentee landowners, English control did not become reasonably absolute until 1800 when England and Ireland became the 'United Kingdom of Great Britain and Ireland'. Religious freedom was restored to the Irish in 1829, but agitation for political autonomy continued until the Irish Free State was established as a dominion on Dec. 6, 1921 until 1937 when it became Éire. Ireland proclaimed itself a republic on April 18, 1949. The government, however, does not use the term 'Republic of Ireland,' which tacitly acknowledges the partitioning of the island into Ireland and Northern Ireland, but refers to the country simply as 'Ireland.'

RULER
British, until 1921

MONETARY SYSTEM

(1928-1971)
4 Farthings = 1 Penny
12 Pence = 1 Shilling
2 Shillings = 1 Florin
20 Shillings = 1 Pound

NOTE: This section has been renumbered to segregate the coinage of the Irish Free State from the earlier crown coinage of Ireland.

REPUBLIC
STERLING COINAGE

KM# 1   FARTHING
2.8300 g., Bronze, 20.3 mm. **Obv:** Irish harp divides date
Obv. Leg.: SAORSTAT EIREANN (Irish Free State)
Rev: Woodcock below value **Edge:** Plain

Date	Mintage	F	VF	XF	Unc	BU
1928	300,000	0.50	1.50	4.50	10.00	—
1928 Proof; Rare	6,001	Value: 15.00				
1930	288,000	0.75	1.50	4.50	16.50	—
1930 Proof; Rare	—	—	—	—	—	—
1931	192,000	4.50	8.00	15.00	35.00	—
1931 Proof	—	—	—	—	—	—
1932	192,000	5.00	10.00	18.00	45.00	—
1932 Proof; Rare	—	—	—	—	—	—
1933	480,000	0.75	1.50	4.00	16.50	—
1933 Proof; Rare	—	—	—	—	—	—
1935	192,000	5.00	8.00	15.00	35.00	—
1935 Proof; Rare	—	—	—	—	—	—
1936	192,000	5.00	8.00	16.50	37.50	—
1936 Proof; Rare	—	—	—	—	—	—
1937	480,000	0.50	1.50	3.00	14.50	—
1937 Proof; Rare	—	—	—	—	—	—

KM# 9   FARTHING
2.8300 g., Bronze, 20.3 mm. **Obv:** Irish harp divides date **Obv. Leg.:** EIRE (Ireland) **Rev:** Woodcock below value **Edge:** Plain

Date	Mintage	F	VF	XF	Unc	BU
1939	786,000	0.50	1.00	2.00	7.50	—
1939 Proof	—	Value: 815				
1940	192,000	2.00	4.00	8.00	20.00	—
1940 Proof; Rare	—	—	—	—	—	—
1941	480,000	0.50	0.75	2.00	6.50	—
1941 Proof; Rare	—	—	—	—	—	—
1943	480,000	0.50	0.75	2.00	6.50	15.00
1944	480,000	0.75	1.25	3.00	10.00	—
1946	480,000	0.50	0.75	2.00	6.00	12.50
1946 Proof; Rare	—	—	—	—	—	—
1949	192,000	0.75	3.00	6.00	18.00	—
1949 Proof	—	Value: 300				
1953	192,000	0.25	0.50	1.25	3.00	7.50
1953 Proof	—	Value: 300				
1959	192,000	0.25	0.50	1.25	3.00	—
1959 Proof; Rare	—	—	—	—	—	—
1966	96,000	0.35	0.75	1.50	3.50	8.00

KM# 2   1/2 PENNY
5.6700 g., Bronze, 25.5 mm. **Obv:** Irish harp divides date
Obv. Leg.: SAORSTAT EIREANN (Irish Free State) **Rev:** Sow with piglets below value **Edge:** Plain

Date	Mintage	F	VF	XF	Unc	BU
1928	2,880,000	0.75	2.00	5.00	15.00	—
1928 Proof	6,001	Value: 15.00				
1933	720,000	5.00	15.00	80.00	465	—
1933 Proof; Rare	—	—	—	—	—	—
1935	960,000	2.00	6.00	50.00	285	—
1935 Proof; Rare	—	—	—	—	—	—
1937	960,000	1.00	3.00	15.00	37.50	—

KM# 10   1/2 PENNY
5.6700 g., Bronze, 25.5 mm. **Obv:** Irish harp **Obv. Leg.:** EIRE (Ireland) **Rev:** Sow with piglets below value **Edge:** Plain

Date	Mintage	F	VF	XF	Unc	BU
1939	240,000	10.00	17.50	60.00	220	—
1939 Proof	—	Value: 1,000				
1940	1,680,000	1.00	4.50	40.00	175	—
1940 Proof; Rare	—	—	—	—	—	—
1941	2,400,000	0.20	0.50	2.50	22.50	—
1941 Proof; Rare	—	—	—	—	—	—
1942	6,931,000	0.10	0.25	1.50	8.50	—
1943	2,669,000	0.20	0.50	3.00	22.00	37.50

Date	Mintage	F	VF	XF	Unc	BU
1946	720,000	1.00	2.50	15.00	60.00	—
1946 Proof; Rare	—	—	—	—	—	—
1949	1,344,000	0.10	0.25	1.50	12.50	—
1949 Proof; Rare	—	—	—	—	—	—
1953	2,400,000	0.10	0.15	0.25	1.50	5.00
1953 Proof	—	Value: 400				
1964	2,160,000	0.10	0.15	0.25	1.50	3.00
1964 Proof; Rare	—	—	—	—	—	—
1965	1,440,000	0.10	0.15	0.75	2.50	4.00
1966	1,680,000	0.10	0.15	0.25	1.50	3.00
1967	1,200,000	0.10	0.15	0.25	1.50	5.00

KM# 3   PENNY
9.4500 g., Bronze, 30.9 mm. **Obv:** Irish harp divides date
Obv. Leg.: SAORSTAT EIREANN (Irish Free State) **Rev:** Hen with chicks **Edge:** Plain

Date	Mintage	F	VF	XF	Unc	BU
1928	9,000,000	0.50	1.00	4.00	20.00	—
1928 Proof	6,001	Value: 18.50				
1931	2,400,000	1.00	2.00	12.00	50.00	—
1931 Proof	—	Value: 1,500				
1933	1,680,000	1.00	2.50	20.00	125	—
1933 Proof; Rare	—	—	—	—	—	—
1935	5,472,000	0.50	1.00	8.00	32.00	—
1935 Proof; Rare	—	—	—	—	—	—
1937	5,400,000	0.50	1.00	15.00	70.00	—
1937 Proof	—	Value: 1,250				

KM# 11   PENNY
9.4500 g., Bronze, 30.9 mm. **Obv:** Irish harp **Obv. Leg.:** EIRE (Ireland) **Rev:** Hen with chicks **Edge:** Plain **Note:** Varieties exist.

Date	Mintage	F	VF	XF	Unc	BU
1940	312,000	3.00	10.00	65.00	600	—
1940 Proof; Rare	—	—	—	—	—	—
1941	4,680,000	0.25	0.50	8.00	50.00	—
1941 Proof; Rare	—	—	—	—	—	—
1942	17,520,000	0.25	0.50	2.00	12.00	—
1942 Proof; Rare	—	—	—	—	—	—
1943	3,360,000	0.75	1.50	7.50	45.00	—
1946	4,800,000	0.25	0.50	3.00	22.00	35.00
1946 Proof; Rare	—	—	—	—	—	—
1948	4,800,000	0.25	0.50	3.00	9.00	—
1948 Proof; Rare	—	—	—	—	—	—
1949	4,080,000	0.25	0.50	3.00	9.00	—
1949 Proof	—	Value: 600				
1950	2,400,000	0.25	0.50	3.50	15.00	—
1950 Proof	—	Value: 600				
1952	2,400,000	0.25	0.50	2.00	7.00	—
1952 Proof; Rare	—	—	—	—	—	—
1962	1,200,000	0.75	2.50	3.50	15.00	—
1962 Proof	—	Value: 175				
1963	9,600,000	0.20	0.40	0.75	2.00	—
1963 Proof	—	Value: 175				
1964	6,000,000	0.20	0.40	0.75	1.50	3.50
1964 Proof	—	—	—	—	—	—
1965	11,160,000	0.20	0.40	0.75	1.50	3.50
1966	6,000,000	0.20	0.40	0.75	1.50	3.50
1967	2,400,000	0.20	0.40	0.75	1.50	3.50
1968	21,000,000	0.20	0.40	0.75	1.50	3.50
1968 Proof	—	Value: 350				

KM# 4   3 PENCE
3.2400 g., Nickel, 17.6 mm. **Obv:** Irish harp divides date **Obv. Leg.:** SAORSTAT EIREANN (Irish Free State) **Rev:** Hare **Edge:** Plain

Date	Mintage	F	VF	XF	Unc	BU
1928	1,500,000	0.50	1.00	3.50	10.00	—
1928 Proof	6,001	Value: 20.00				
1933	320,000	3.00	10.00	75.00	350	—

Date	Mintage	F	VF	XF	Unc	BU
1933 Proof; Rare	—	—	—	—	—	—
1934	800,000	1.00	2.00	12.50	70.00	—
1934 Proof; Rare	—	—	—	—	—	—
1935	240,000	3.00	8.00	35.00	225	—
1935 Proof; Rare	—	—	—	—	—	—

KM# 12   3 PENCE
3.2400 g., Nickel, 17.6 mm. **Obv:** Irish harp **Obv. Leg.:** EIRE (Ireland) **Rev:** Hare **Edge:** Plain

Date	Mintage	F	VF	XF	Unc	BU
1939	64,000	10.00	20.00	70.00	525	—
1939 Proof	—	Value: 1,725				
1940	720,000	1.50	3.00	12.50	50.00	—
1940 Proof; Rare	—	—	—	—	—	—

KM# 12a   3 PENCE
3.2400 g., Copper-Nickel, 18 mm. **Obv:** Irish harp **Obv. Leg.:** EIRE (Ireland) **Rev:** Hare **Edge:** Plain

Date	Mintage	F	VF	XF	Unc	BU
1942	4,000,000	0.25	0.75	6.00	30.00	—
1942 Proof	—	Value: 350				
1943	1,360,000	0.50	2.00	15.00	80.00	—
1943 Proof; Rare	—	—	—	—	—	—
1946	800,000	1.00	2.00	10.00	45.00	—
1946 Proof	—	Value: 200				
1948	1,600,000	1.00	2.00	35.00	125	—
1948 Proof; Rare	—	—	—	—	—	—
1949	1,200,000	0.25	0.50	3.00	25.00	—
1949 Proof	—	Value: 200				
1950	1,600,000	0.25	0.50	3.00	20.00	—
1950 Proof	—	Value: 400				
1953	1,600,000	0.25	0.50	2.00	10.00	—
1953 Proof; Rare	—	—	—	—	—	—
1956	1,200,000	0.25	0.50	8.00	15.00	—
1956 Proof; Rare	—	—	—	—	—	—
1961	2,400,000	0.15	0.25	0.50	6.00	—
1961 Proof; Rare	—	—	—	—	—	—
1962	3,200,000	0.15	0.25	0.50	8.00	—
1962 Proof; Rare	—	—	—	—	—	—
1963	4,000,000	0.15	0.25	0.50	2.50	—
1963 Proof; Rare	—	—	—	—	—	—
1964	4,000,000	0.10	0.15	0.50	1.50	3.00
1965	3,600,000	0.10	0.15	0.50	1.50	3.00
1966	4,000,000	0.10	0.15	0.50	1.50	3.00
1967	2,400,000	0.10	0.15	0.50	1.50	3.00
1968	4,000,000	0.10	0.15	0.50	1.50	3.00
1968 Proof; Rare	—	—	—	—	—	—

KM# 5   6 PENCE
4.5400 g., Nickel, 20.8 mm. **Obv:** Irish harp divides date **Obv. Leg.:** SAORSTAT EIREANN (Irish Free State) **Rev:** Irish Wolfhound **Edge:** Plain

Date	Mintage	F	VF	XF	Unc	BU
1928	3,201,000	0.50	1.00	5.00	17.50	—
1928 Proof	6,001	Value: 25.00				
1933 Proof; Rare	—	—	—	—	—	—
1934	600,000	1.00	2.00	18.00	120	—
1934 Proof; Rare	—	—	—	—	—	—
1935	520,000	1.00	3.00	30.00	325	—
1935 Proof; Rare	—	—	—	—	—	—

KM# 13   6 PENCE
4.5400 g., Nickel, 20.8 mm. **Obv:** Irish harp **Obv. Leg.:** EIRE (Ireland) **Rev:** Irish Wolfhound **Edge:** Plain

Date	Mintage	F	VF	XF	Unc	BU
1939	876,000	0.75	2.00	8.00	55.00	—
1939 Proof	—	Value: 1,300				
1940	1,120,000	0.75	2.00	6.00	45.00	—
1940 Proof; Rare	—	—	—	—	—	—

KM# 13a   6 PENCE
4.5400 g., Copper-Nickel, 20.8 mm. **Obv:** Irish harp
Obv. Leg.: EIRE (Ireland) **Rev:** Irish Wolfhound **Edge:** Plain

Date	Mintage	F	VF	XF	Unc	BU
1942	1,320,000	0.50	1.00	5.00	40.00	—
1942 Proof; Rare	—	—	—	—	—	—
1945	400,000	2.00	8.00	50.00	170	—
1945 Proof; Rare	—	—	—	—	—	—
1946	720,000	2.00	10.00	75.00	350	—
1946 Proof; Rare	—	—	—	—	—	—
1947	800,000	1.00	12.00	30.00	70.00	—
1947 Proof; Rare	—	—	—	—	—	—
1948	800,000	1.00	1.50	10.00	55.00	—
1948 Proof; Rare	—	—	—	—	—	—
1949	600,000	1.50	3.50	15.00	65.00	—
1949 Proof; Rare	—	—	—	—	—	—
1950	800,000	1.00	3.00	12.00	60.00	—
1950 Proof; Rare	—	—	—	—	—	—
1952	800,000	0.50	1.00	5.00	20.00	—
1952 Proof	—	Value: 175				
1953	800,000	0.50	1.00	5.00	18.00	—
1953 Proof; Rare	—	—	—	—	—	—
1955	600,000	1.00	2.50	8.00	20.00	—
1955 Proof; Rare	—	—	—	—	—	—
1956	600,000	0.75	2.00	4.00	15.00	—
1956 Proof; Rare	—	—	—	—	—	—
1958	—	Value: 350				
1958	600,000	1.00	2.50	6.00	65.00	—
1959	2,000,000	0.25	0.50	3.00	15.00	—
1959 Proof; Rare	—	—	—	—	—	—
1960	2,020,000	0.25	0.50	2.00	12.00	—
1960 Proof; Rare	—	—	—	—	—	—
1961	3,000,000	0.25	0.25	1.00	6.50	—
1961 Proof; Rare	—	—	—	—	—	—
1962	4,000,000	0.25	0.75	4.00	60.00	—
1962 Proof; Rare	—	—	—	—	—	—
1963	4,000,000	0.15	0.25	0.50	3.00	—
1963 Proof; Rare	—	—	—	—	—	—
1964	6,000,000	0.15	0.25	0.50	3.00	—
1966	2,000,000	0.15	0.25	0.50	3.00	—
1967	4,000,000	0.15	0.25	0.50	3.00	—
1968	8,000,000	0.15	0.25	0.50	3.00	—
1969	2,000,000	0.15	0.25	0.50	3.00	—

KM# 6   SHILLING
5.6552 g., 0.7500 Silver 0.1364 oz. ASW, 23.6 mm. **Obv:** Irish harp divides date **Obv. Leg.:** SAORSTAT EIREANN (Irish Free State) **Rev:** Bull **Edge:** Reeded

Date	Mintage	F	VF	XF	Unc	BU
1928	2,700,000	2.00	5.00	10.00	30.00	—
1928 Proof	6,001	Value: 27.50				
1930	460,000	6.00	25.00	100	450	—
1930 Proof	—	Value: 1,200				
1931	400,000	4.50	18.00	90.00	275	—
1931 Proof; Rare	—	—	—	—	—	—
1933	300,000	5.00	20.00	100	325	—
1933 Proof; Rare	—	—	—	—	—	—
1935	400,000	3.00	7.00	25.00	85.00	—
1935 Proof; Rare	—	—	—	—	—	—
1937	100,000	12.00	65.00	500	2,000	—
1937 Proof; Rare	—	—	—	—	—	—

KM# 14   SHILLING
5.6552 g., 0.7500 Silver 0.1364 oz. ASW, 23.6 mm. **Obv:** Irish harp **Obv. Leg.:** EIRE (Ireland) **Rev:** Bull **Edge:** Reeded

Date	Mintage	F	VF	XF	Unc	BU
1939	1,140,000	2.50	4.50	12.50	40.00	—
1939 Proof	—	Value: 900				
1940	580,000	3.00	5.00	15.00	45.00	—
1940 Proof; Rare	—	—	—	—	—	—
1941	300,000	4.00	12.00	22.50	50.00	—
1941 Proof; Rare	—	—	—	—	—	—

Date	Mintage	F	VF	XF	Unc	BU
1942	286,000	4.00	7.50	15.00	40.00	60.00
1942 Proof; Rare	—	—	—	—	—	—

KM# 14a   SHILLING
5.6600 g., Copper-Nickel, 23.6 mm. **Obv:** Irish harp
Obv. Leg.: EIRE (Ireland) **Rev:** Bull **Edge:** Reeded

Date	Mintage	F	VF	XF	Unc	BU
1951	2,000,000	0.25	0.50	2.50	15.00	—
1951 Proof	—	Value: 500				
1954	3,000,000	0.25	0.50	2.50	11.50	—
1954 Proof; Rare	—	—	—	—	—	—
1955	1,000,000	1.00	2.00	5.00	15.00	—
1955 Proof; Rare	—	—	—	—	—	—
1959	2,000,000	0.25	0.50	4.00	35.00	—
1959 Proof; Rare	—	—	—	—	—	—
1962	4,000,000	0.25	0.50	1.00	7.00	—
1962 Proof; Rare	—	—	—	—	—	—
1963	4,000,000	0.25	0.50	1.00	3.00	7.50
1963 Proof; Rare	—	—	—	—	—	—
1964	4,000,000	0.25	0.50	1.00	2.50	3.00
1966	3,000,000	0.25	0.50	1.00	2.50	5.00
1968	4,000,000	0.25	0.50	1.00	2.50	3.00

KM# 7   FLORIN
11.3104 g., 0.7500 Silver 0.2727 oz. ASW, 28.5 mm. **Obv:** Irish harp divides date **Obv. Leg.:** SAORSTAT EIREANN (Irish Free State) **Rev:** Salmon **Edge:** Reeded

Date	Mintage	F	VF	XF	Unc	BU
1928	2,025,000	4.00	7.00	15.00	40.00	—
1928 Proof	6,001	Value: 42.50				
1930	330,000	6.50	25.00	135	400	—
1930 Proof; Rare	—	—	—	—	—	—
1931	200,000	8.00	35.00	175	500	—
1931 Proof; Rare	—	—	—	—	—	—
1933	300,000	6.50	27.50	195	575	—
1933 Proof; Rare	—	—	—	—	—	—
1934	150,000	10.00	60.00	250	750	—
1934 Proof	—	Value: 2,750				
1935	390,000	5.00	17.50	65.00	185	—
1935 Proof; Rare	—	—	—	—	—	—
1937	150,000	10.00	35.00	210	750	—
1937 Proof; Rare	—	—	—	—	—	—

KM# 15   FLORIN
11.3104 g., 0.7500 Silver 0.2727 oz. ASW, 28.5 mm. **Obv:** Irish harp **Obv. Leg.:** EIRE (Ireland) **Rev:** Salmon **Edge:** Reeded

Date	Mintage	F	VF	XF	Unc	BU
1939	1,080,000	4.00	7.00	18.00	45.00	—
1939 Proof	—	Value: 925				
1940	670,000	4.00	7.50	20.00	50.00	—
1940 Proof; Rare	—	—	—	—	—	—
1941	400,000	4.00	8.50	22.50	60.00	—
1941 Proof	—	Value: 800				
1942	109,000	5.00	15.00	25.00	55.00	—
1943	—	1,200	2,000	4,000	8,000	—

Note: Approximately 35 known

KM# 15a   FLORIN
11.3100 g., Copper-Nickel, 28.5 mm. **Obv:** Irish harp
Obv. Leg.: EIRE (Ireland) **Rev:** Salmon **Edge:** Reeded

Date	Mintage	F	VF	XF	Unc	BU
1951	1,000,000	1.00	2.00	6.00	16.00	—
1951 Proof	—	Value: 600				
1954	1,000,000	1.00	2.00	6.00	18.00	—
1954 Proof	—	Value: 900				
1955	1,000,000	1.00	2.00	5.00	15.00	—
1955 Proof	—	Value: 900				
1959	2,000,000	0.50	1.00	2.50	10.00	—
1959 Proof; Rare	—	—	—	—	—	—
1961	2,000,000	0.50	1.00	7.00	22.00	—
1961 Proof; Rare	—	—	—	—	—	—
1962	2,400,000	0.50	1.00	2.00	10.00	—
1962 Proof; Rare	—	—	—	—	—	—
1963	3,000,000	0.25	0.50	0.75	4.00	15.00
1963 Proof; Rare	—	—	—	—	—	—
1964	4,000,000	0.25	0.50	0.75	4.00	8.00
1965	2,000,000	0.25	0.50	0.75	2.00	—
1966	3,625,000	0.25	0.50	0.75	2.00	4.00
1968	1,000,000	0.25	0.35	1.00	4.50	5.00
1969	—	0.25	0.35	1.00	4.50	5.00

KM# 8   1/2 CROWN
14.1380 g., 0.7500 Silver 0.3409 oz. ASW, 32.3 mm. **Obv:** Irish harp divides date **Obv. Leg.:** SAORSTAT EIREANN (Irish Free State) **Rev:** Horse **Edge:** Reeded **Note:** Close O and I in COROIN. 8 tufts in horse's tail, with 156 beads.

Date	Mintage	F	VF	XF	Unc	BU
1928	2,160,000	5.00	10.00	20.00	50.00	—
1928 Proof	6,001	Value: 55.00				
1930	352,000	7.00	20.00	125	400	—
1930 Proof; Rare	—	—	—	—	—	—
1931	160,000	10.00	30.00	250	650	—
1931 Proof; Rare	—	—	—	—	—	—
1933	336,000	7.00	20.00	125	400	—
1933 Proof; Rare	—	—	—	—	—	—
1934	480,000	6.00	15.00	40.00	225	—
1934 Proof; Rare	—	—	—	—	—	—
1937	40,000	65.00	150	750	1,750	—
1937 Proof; Rare	—	—	—	—	—	—

KM# 16   1/2 CROWN
14.1380 g., 0.7500 Silver 0.3409 oz. ASW, 32.3 mm. **Obv:** Irish harp **Obv. Leg.:** EIRE (Ireland) **Rev:** Horse **Edge:** Reeded **Note:** Normal spacing between O and I in COROIN, 7 tufts in horse's tail, with 151 beads in border.

Date	Mintage	F	VF	XF	Unc	BU
1939	888,000	5.00	9.50	17.50	55.00	—
1939 Proof	—	Value: 925				
1940	752,000	5.00	9.00	15.00	50.00	—
1940 Proof; Rare	—	—	—	—	—	—
1941	320,000	5.50	12.50	30.00	75.00	—
1941 Proof; Rare	—	—	—	—	—	—
1942	286,000	5.50	12.50	25.00	50.00	—
1943	Est. 1,000	250	500	1,350	4,000	—

Note: Approximately 500 known

KM# 16a   1/2 CROWN
14.1400 g., Copper-Nickel, 32.3 mm. **Obv:** Irish harp
Obv. Leg.: EIRE (Ireland) **Rev:** Horse **Edge:** Reeded
Note: Normal spacing between O and I on "COROIN", 7 tufts in horse's tail, with 151 beads in border.

Date	Mintage	F	VF	XF	Unc	BU
1951	800,000	1.50	3.00	10.00	35.00	—
1951 Proof	—	Value: 600				
1954	400,000	2.00	4.00	15.00	50.00	—
1954 Proof	—	Value: 500				
1955	1,080,000	1.00	2.00	6.00	25.00	—
1955 Proof	—	Value: 1,000				
1959	1,600,000	1.00	1.75	3.00	12.50	—
1959 Proof; Rare	—	—	—	—	—	—
1961	1,600,000	1.00	1.75	3.50	20.00	—
1961 Proof; Rare	—	—	—	—	—	—
1962	3,200,000	0.50	1.00	2.50	12.50	—
1962 Proof; Rare	—	—	—	—	—	—
1963	2,400,000	0.50	1.00	2.00	8.00	12.00
1963 Proof; Rare	—	—	—	—	—	—
1964	3,200,000	0.50	1.00	2.00	8.00	12.00
1966	700,000	0.75	1.50	3.00	8.00	12.00
1967	2,000,000	0.50	1.00	2.00	8.00	12.00

Note: 1967 exists struck with a polished reverse die; Estimated value is $15.00 in Uncirculated

KM# 17   1/2 CROWN
Copper-Nickel **Obv:** Irish harp **Rev:** Horse **Note:** Mule. Distinguishing characteristics: 2s6d the d is open, PM the P is not under the hoof.

Date	Mintage	VG	F	VF	XF	Unc
1961	Inc. above	—	8.00	25.00	200	—

KM# 18   10 SHILLING
18.1400 g., 0.8333 Silver 0.4860 oz. ASW, 30.5 mm.
Subject: 50th Anniversary - Irish Uprising of Easter, 1916
Obv: Bust right **Rev:** Monument **Edge:** EIRI AMAC NA CASCA 1916 (both normal and inverted)

Date	Mintage	F	VF	XF	Unc	BU
1966	Est. 2,000,000	—	—	22.00	35.00	38.00

Note: Approximately 1,270,000 melted down

| 1966 Proof | 20,000 | Value: 45.00 | | | | |

DECIMAL COINAGE
100 Pence = 1 Pound (Punt)

KM# 19   1/2 PENNY
1.7800 g., Bronze, 17.1 mm. **Subject:** Styilized bird adapted from an illumination in a celtic manuscript from Cologne Cathedral **Obv:** Irish harp **Rev:** Stylized bird and value **Edge:** Plain
Note: This mintage figure represents a surplus of coins minted for Polished Standard Specimen Sets (proof sets) later released into circulation. The entire surplus was presumably remelted due to demonitization of this denomination Jan. 1, 1987

Date	Mintage	F	VF	XF	Unc	BU
1971	100,500,000	—	—	0.10	0.30	0.50
1971 Proof	50,000	Value: 1.00				
1975	10,500,000	—	—	0.10	0.30	0.50
1976	5,464,000	—	—	0.10	0.30	0.50
1978	20,302,000	—	—	0.25	0.50	
1980	20,616,000	—	—	—	0.25	0.50
1982	9,660,000	—	—	—	0.30	0.50
1985	2,784,000	—	—	—	—	—
1986	Est. 12,250	—	—	—	—	—

Note: This mintage figure represents a surplus of coins minted for Polished Standard Specimen Sets (Proof Sets) later released into circulation. The entire surplus was presumably remelted due to demonitization of this denomination Jan. 1, 1987.

| 1986 Proof | 6,750 | Value: 12.50 | | | | |

KM# 20   PENNY
3.5600 g., Bronze, 20.3 mm. **Obv:** Irish harp **Rev:** Stylized bird **Edge:** Plain **Note:** Stylized bird adapted form an ornamental detail in the book of Kells

Date	Mintage	F	VF	XF	Unc	BU
1971	100,500,000	—	—	0.10	0.30	0.75
1971 Proof	50,000	Value: 1.25				
1974	10,000,000	—	—	0.10	0.35	0.75
1975	10,000,000	—	—	0.10	0.35	0.75
1976	38,164,000	—	—	0.10	0.30	0.75
1978	25,746,000	—	—	0.10	0.30	0.75
1979	21,766,000	—	—	0.10	0.30	0.75
1980	86,712,000	—	—	0.10	0.30	0.75
1982	54,189,000	—	—	0.10	0.30	0.75
1985	19,242,000	—	—	0.10	0.30	0.75
1986	36,584,000	—	—	0.10	0.30	0.75
1986 Proof	6,750	Value: 1.25				
1988	56,772,000	—	—	0.10	0.30	0.75

KM# 20a   PENNY
3.5600 g., Copper Plated Steel, 20.3 mm. **Subject:** Stylized bird adapted from an ornamental detail in the book of Kells **Obv:** Irish harp **Rev:** Stylized bird **Edge:** Plain

Date	Mintage	F	VF	XF	Unc	BU
1988	Inc. above	—	—	—	—	—
1990	65,099,000	—	—	0.10	0.15	0.50
1992	25,643,000	—	—	0.10	0.15	0.50
1993	10,000,000	—	—	0.10	0.15	0.50
1994	45,800,000	—	—	0.10	0.15	0.50
1995	70,836,000	—	—	0.10	0.15	0.50
1996	190,092,000	—	—	0.10	0.15	0.50
1998	40,744,000	—	—	0.10	0.15	0.50
2000	133,760,000	—	—	0.10	0.15	0.50

KM# 21   2 PENCE
7.1200 g., Bronze, 25.9 mm. **Subject:** Stylized bird detail from the Second Bible of Charles the Bald **Obv:** Irish harp **Rev:** Stylized bird **Edge:** Plain

Date	Mintage	F	VF	XF	Unc	BU
1971	75,500,000	—	—	0.10	1.00	1.20
1971 Proof	50,000	Value: 1.50				
1975	20,010,000	—	—	0.10	0.50	0.75
1976	5,414,000	—	—	0.10	0.60	0.85
1978	12,000,000	—	—	0.10	0.50	0.75
1979	32,373,000	—	—	0.10	0.50	0.75
1980	59,828,000	—	—	0.10	0.50	0.75
1982	30,435,000	—	—	0.10	0.50	0.75
1985	14,469,000	—	—	0.10	0.50	0.75
1986	23,865,000	—	—	0.10	0.50	0.75
1986 Proof	6,750	Value: 1.50				
1988	35,868,000	—	—	0.10	0.50	0.75

KM# 21a   2 PENCE
7.1200 g., Copper Plated Steel, 25.9 mm. **Subject:** Stylized bird detail from the Second Bible of Charles the Bald **Obv:** Irish harp **Rev:** Stylized bird **Edge:** Plain

Date	Mintage	F	VF	XF	Unc	BU
1988	Inc. above	—	—	—	—	—
1990	34,284,000	—	—	0.10	0.25	0.50
1992	10,215,000	—	—	0.10	0.25	0.50
1995	55,459,000	—	—	0.10	0.25	0.50
1996	69,342,000	—	—	0.10	0.25	0.50
1998	33,688,000	—	—	0.10	0.25	0.50
2000	66,960,000	—	—	0.10	0.25	0.50

KM# 22   5 PENCE
5.6600 g., Copper-Nickel, 23.6 mm. **Obv:** Irish harp **Rev:** Bull right **Edge:** Reeded

Date	Mintage	F	VF	XF	Unc	BU
1969	5,000,000	—	0.10	0.15	1.00	1.25
1970	10,000,000	—	—	0.10	0.75	1.20
1971	8,000,000	—	—	0.10	0.75	1.25
1971 Proof	50,000	Value: 2.00				
1974	7,000,000	—	—	0.10	0.75	1.25
1975	10,000,000	—	—	0.10	0.75	1.25
1976	20,616,000	—	—	0.10	0.75	1.25
1978	28,536,000	—	—	0.10	0.75	1.25
1980	22,190,000	—	—	0.10	0.75	1.25
1982	24,404,000	—	—	0.10	0.75	1.20
1985	4,202,000	—	—	0.10	0.75	1.20
1986	15,298,000	—	0.10	0.15	1.00	1.25
1986 Proof	6,750	Value: 2.00				
1990	7,547,000	—	—	0.10	0.75	1.20

KM# 28   5 PENCE
3.2500 g., Copper-Nickel, 18.5 mm. **Obv:** Irish harp **Rev:** Bull left **Edge:** Reeded **Note:** Reduced size: 18.5mm. Varieties exist.

Date	Mintage	F	VF	XF	Unc	BU
1992	74,526,000	—	—	0.10	0.50	0.75
1993	89,109,000	—	—	0.10	0.50	0.75
1994	31,058,000	—	—	0.10	0.50	0.75
1995	14,667,000	—	—	0.10	0.50	0.75
1996	158,546,000	—	—	0.10	0.50	0.75
1998	63,247,000	—	—	0.10	0.50	0.75
2000	58,000,000	—	—	0.10	0.50	0.75

KM# 23   10 PENCE
11.3200 g., Copper-Nickel, 28.5 mm. **Obv:** Irish harp **Rev:** Salmon **Edge:** Reeded

Date	Mintage	F	VF	XF	Unc	BU
1969	27,000,000	—	—	0.40	1.25	2.00
1971	4,000,000	—	—	0.40	1.25	2.00
1971 Proof	50,000	Value: 2.50				
1973	2,500,000	—	—	0.40	1.50	2.25
1974	7,500,000	—	—	0.35	1.25	2.00
1975	15,000,000	—	—	0.35	1.25	2.00
1976	9,433,000	—	—	0.35	1.25	2.00
1978	30,905,000	—	—	0.25	1.00	1.75
1980	44,605,000	—	—	0.25	1.00	1.75
1982	7,374,000	—	—	0.25	1.00	1.75
1985	4,099,999	—	—	0.25	1.25	2.00
1986	Est. 4,250	—	2.00	5.00	16.50	—

Note: This mintage figure represents a surplus of coins minted for Polished Standard Specimen Sets (Proof Sets), later released into circulation.

| 1986 Proof | 6,750 | Value: 16.50 | | | | |

KM# 29   10 PENCE
5.4500 g., Copper-Nickel, 22 mm. **Obv:** Irish harp **Rev:** Salmon **Edge:** Reeded **Note:** Reduced size.

Date	Mintage	F	VF	XF	Unc	BU
1993	80,061,000	—	—	—	0.75	1.25
1994	58,510,000	—	—	—	0.75	1.25
1995	15,781,000	—	—	—	0.75	1.25
1996	18,402,000	—	—	—	0.75	1.25
1997	10,033,000	—	—	—	0.75	1.25
1998	10,000,000	—	—	—	0.75	1.25

Date	Mintage	F	VF	XF	Unc	BU
1999	24,500,000	—	—	—	0.75	1.25
2000	45,679,000	—	—	—	0.75	1.25

KM# 25 20 PENCE

8.4700 g., Nickel-Bronze, 27.1 mm. **Obv:** Irish harp **Rev:** Horse
Edge: Alternating plain and reeded

Date	Mintage	F	VF	XF	Unc	BU
1986	50,430,000	—	—	0.50	2.00	4.00
1986 Proof	6,750	Value: 3.50				
1988	20,661,000	—	—	0.50	2.00	4.00
1992	14,761,000	—	—	0.50	2.00	4.00
1994	11,086,000	—	—	0.50	2.00	4.00
1995	18,160,000	—	—	0.50	2.00	4.00
1996	29,291,000	—	—	0.50	2.00	4.00
1998	25,024,000	—	—	0.50	2.00	4.00
1999	11,000,000	—	—	0.50	2.00	4.00
2000	28,500,000	—	—	0.50	2.00	4.00

KM# 24 50 PENCE

13.3000 g., Copper-Nickel, 30 mm. **Obv:** Harp **Rev:** Woodcock
Edge: Plain

Date	Mintage	F	VF	XF	Unc	BU
1970	9,000,000	—	—	1.50	4.00	5.00
1971	600,000	—	1.00	2.00	6.00	8.00
1971 Proof	50,000	Value: 3.50				
1974	1,000,000	—	1.00	2.00	7.00	9.00
1975	2,000,000	—	—	1.50	4.00	5.00
1976	3,000,000	—	—	1.25	3.00	4.00
1977	4,800,000	—	—	1.25	3.00	4.00
1978	4,500,000	—	—	1.25	3.00	4.00
1979	4,000,000	—	—	1.25	3.00	4.00
1981	6,000,000	—	—	1.00	2.00	3.50
1982	2,000,000	—	—	1.25	3.00	4.00
1983	7,000,000	—	—	1.00	2.00	3.50
1984						
1986	3,250	—	3.00	6.00	18.50	

Note: This circulation mintage figure represents a surplus
of coins minted for Polished Standard Specimen Sets
(Proof Sets), later released into circulation.

1986 Proof	6,750	Value: 18.50				
1988	Est. 7,000,500	—	—	1.00	2.00	3.50
1996	6,000,000	—	—	1.00	2.00	3.50
1997	6,000,000	—	—	1.00	2.00	3.50
1998	13,825,000	—	—	1.00	2.00	3.50
1999	7,000,000	—	—	1.00	2.00	3.50
2000	15,600,000	—	—	1.00	2.00	3.50

KM# 26 50 PENCE

13.5000 g., Copper-Nickel, 30 mm. **Subject:** Dublin Millennium
Obv: Irish harp **Rev:** Sheild above banner with value above

Date	Mintage	F	VF	XF	Unc	BU
1988	5,000,000	—	—	—	2.50	3.50
1988 Proof	50,000	Value: 15.00				

KM# 27 PUNT (Pound)

10.0000 g., Copper-Nickel, 31.1 mm. **Obv:** Irish harp **Rev:** Irish
Red Deer left **Note:** The normal KM27 was struck with an milled
and engrailed edge. Examples with plain edge, or partial
engrailing command a premium of approximately four times the
values listed here.

Date	Mintage	F	VF	XF	Unc	BU
1990	62,292,000	2.00	3.00	5.50	7.00	8.00
1990 Proof	42,000	Value: 27.50				
1994	14,925,000	2.00	3.00	5.50	7.50	9.00
1995	10,215,000	2.00	3.00	5.50	7.50	9.00
1996	9,230,000	2.00	3.00	5.50	7.50	9.00
1998	22,955,000	2.00	3.00	5.50	7.50	9.00
1999	10,000,000	2.00	3.00	5.50	7.50	9.00
2000	31,913,000	2.00	3.00	5.50	7.50	9.00

KM# 30 PUNT (Pound)

28.2800 g., 0.9250 Silver 0.8410 oz. ASW, 38.6 mm.
Subject: 50th Anniversary - United Nations **Obv:** Irish harp above
dates **Rev:** Dove holding banner with dates to left of U.N. logo
and numeral 50 **Rev. Insc.:** NATIONS UNITED FOR PEACE
Edge: Milled

Date	Mintage	F	VF	XF	Unc	BU
ND(1995) Proof	—	Value: 100				

KM# 31 PUNT (Pound)

10.0000 g., Copper-Nickel **Subject:** Millennium **Obv:** Irish harp
Rev: Cross within stylized ancient ship **Edge:** Milled and
engrailed **Note:** Struck at Sandyford.

Date	Mintage	F	VF	XF	Unc	BU
2000	5,000,000	—	—	—	7.50	9.00

PATTERNS

Including off metal strikes

KM#	Date	Mintage	Identification	Mkt Val
Pn1	1938	—	Penny. Bronze. KM11.	—

Note: One in National Museum and one in private hands

| Pn2 | 1938 | — | 1/2 Crown. 0.7500 Silver. KM16. Unique. | |

Note: In National Museum of Ireland

| Pn3 | 1985 | — | 20 Pence. Nickel-Bronze. KM#25. | |

PROVAS

Publio Morbiducci Series

KM#	Date	Mintage	Identification	Mkt Val
Pr1	1927	—	Farthing.	—
Pr2	1927	—	1/2 Penny.	—
Pr3	1927	—	Penny. Silvered Bronze. Irish harp. Hen with chicks.	8,000
Pr4	1927	4	3 Pence. Nickel. Irish harp. Rabbit.	5,000

KM#	Date	Mintage	Identification	Mkt Val
Pr5	1927	4	6 Pence. Nickel. Irish harp. Irish wolfhound.	5,000
Pr6	1927	5	Shilling. Silver. Irish harp. Bull with head down.	5,000
Pr7	1927	4	Florin. Silver. Irish harp. Fish.	6,500
Pr8	1927	5	1/2 Crown. Silver. Irish harp. Rearing horse.	8,500
Pr9	1927	—	1/2 Crown. Copper. Irish harp. Rearing horse.	

Note: This series exists in other than standard metals

PIEFORTS

KM#	Date	Mintage	Identification	Mkt Val
P1	2000	—	Punt. Silver. 20.0000 g. Stylized ancient ship. as KM#31	35.00

MINT SETS

KM#	Date	Mintage	Identification	Issue Price	Mkt Val
MS1	1928 (8)	—	KM#1-8	—	—
MS2	1966 (8)	96,000	KM9-11, 12a-16a	—	25.00
MS3	1969-1971 (6)	—	KM19-21(1971), 22 (1970), 23(1969), 24(1970), mixed dates	—	6.50
MS4	1971 (6)	—	KM19-24	1.50	9.00
MS5	1978 (6)	—	KM19-24	—	5.00
MS6	1982 (6)	—	KM19-24	—	5.00
MS7	1996 (7)	—	KM20a-21a, 24-25, 27-29	—	30.00
MS8	1998 (7)	—	KM20a-21a, 25-25, 27-29	—	30.00
MS9	2000 (7)	—	KM20a-21a, 24-25, 28-29, 31	—	100

PROOF SETS

KM#	Date	Mintage	Identification	Issue Price	Mkt Val
PS1	1928 (8)	6,001	KM1-8	—	400
PS2	1966 (1)	1,000	KM18(2), normal and inverted edge lettering	—	100
PS3	1971 (6)	50,000	KM19-24	4.40	15.00
PS4	1986 (7)	6,750	KM19-25	—	800
PS5	1990 (3)	—	KMM1-M3	—	500
PS6	2006 (8)	5,000	KM#32-39	125	150
PS7	2006 (2)	—	KM#45-46	—	110

ISLE OF MAN

IRELAND

UNITED KINGDOM

The Isle of Man, a dependency of the British Crown located
in the Irish Sea equidistant from Ireland, Scotland and England,
has an area of 227 sq. mi. (588 sq. km.) and a population of
68,000. Capital: Douglas. Agriculture, dairy farming, fishing and
tourism are the chief industries.

The prevalence of prehistoric artifacts and monuments on
the island give evidence that its' mild, almost sub-tropical climate
was enjoyed by mankind before the dawn of history. Vikings
came to the Isle of Man during the 9th century and remained until
ejected by the Scottish in 1266. The island came under the protection of the British Crown in 1288, and in 1406 was granted, in
perpetuity, to the earls of Derby, from whom it was inherited,
1736, by the Duke of Atholl. The British Crown purchased the
rights and title in 1765; the remaining privileges of the Atholl family were transferred to the crown in 1829. The Isle of Man is ruled
by its own legislative council and the House of Keys, the oldest,
continuous legislative assembly in the world. Acts of Parliament
passed in London do not affect the island unless it is specifically
mentioned.

RULERS

James Murray, Duke of Atholl, 1736-1765
British Commencing 1765

MINT MARK

PM - Pobjoy Mint

PRIVY MARKS

(a) - Big Apple - 1988
(at) - Angel Blowing Trumpet – 1997

(b) - Baby Crib - 1982
(ba) - Basel Bugle - 1990
(bb) - Big Ben - 1987-1988
(br) - Brooklyn Bridge - 1989
(bs) - Teddy Bear in Stocking - 1996
(c) - Chicago Water Tower CICF - 1990-1991
(cc) - Christmas cracker - 1991
(d) - St. Paul's Cathedral - 1989

(f) - FUN logo - 1988
(fl) - Fleur de Lis - 1990
(fr) - Frauenkirche - Munich Numismata - 1990-1991
(fw) - Fairy w/magic wand - 1999
(h) - Horse - Hong Kong Int. - 1990
(l) - Statue of Liberty - 1987
(lc) - Lion crowned - 1989
(m) - Queen mother's portrait - 1980
(ma) - Maple leaf - CNA - 1990
(mt) - Mistletoe - Christmas - 1987, 1989
(ns) - North Star - 1994
(p) - Carrier Pigeon - Basel - 1988-1989
(pi) - Pine tree - 1986
(pt) - Partridge in a pear tree - 1988
(py) - Poppy - 1995
(s) - Bridge - SINPEX - 1987
(sb) - Soccer ball - 1982
(sc) - Santa Claus - 1995
(sg) - Sleigh - Christmas - 1990
(SL) - St. Louis Arch - 1987
(ss) - Sailing Ship - Sydney - 1988
(t) - Stylized triskelion - 1979
(tb) - Tower Bridge - 1990
(ti) - TICC logo - Tokyo - 1990
(v) - Viking ship - 1980
(vw) - Viking ship in wreath - 1986
(w) - Stylized triskelion - 1985
(x) - Snowman - 1998

PRIVY LETTERS
A - ANA - 1985-1992
C - Coinex, London - 1985-1989
D.M.I.H.E. - Ideal Home Exhibit, London, 1980
D.M.I.H.E.N. - Ideal Home Exhibit, Manchester, 1980
F - FUN - 1987
H - Hong Kong Expo - 1985
L - Long Beach - 1985-1987
T - Torex, Toronto - 1986
U - Uncirculated - 1988, 1990, 1994, 1995
X - Ameripex - 1986

BRITISH DEPENDENCY

DECIMAL COINAGE
100 Pence = 1 Pound

KM# 19 1/2 NEW PENNY
1.7700 g., Bronze, 17.14 mm. **Ruler:** Elizabeth II **Obv:** Young bust right **Rev:** Flowered weed

Date	Mintage	F	VF	XF	Unc	BU
1971	495,000	—	—	0.15	0.35	0.75
1971 Proof	10,000	Value: 1.50				
1972	1,000	—	—	—	18.00	20.00
1973	1,000	—	—	—	18.00	20.00
1974	1,000	—	—	—	18.00	20.00
1975	825,000	—	—	0.15	0.25	0.65

KM# 19a 1/2 NEW PENNY
2.1000 g., 0.9250 Silver 0.0625 oz. ASW, 17.4 mm.
Ruler: Elizabeth II **Obv:** Young bust right **Rev:** Flowered weed

Date	Mintage	F	VF	XF	Unc	BU
1975	20,000	—	—	—	2.50	3.00

KM# 19b 1/2 NEW PENNY
4.0000 g., 0.9500 Platinum 0.1222 oz. APW, 17.4 mm.
Ruler: Elizabeth II **Obv:** Young bust right **Rev:** Flowered weed

Date	Mintage	F	VF	XF	Unc	BU
1975 Proof	600	Value: 210				

KM# 32 1/2 PENNY
Bronze, 17.14 mm. **Ruler:** Elizabeth II **Obv:** Young bust right **Rev:** Atlantic herring

Date	Mintage	F	VF	XF	Unc	BU
1976	600,000	—	—	0.20	0.45	1.00
1978		—	—	0.20	0.45	1.00
1978 Proof		—	Value: 1.25			
1979(t) AA		—	—	0.20	0.45	1.00
1979(t) AB		—	—	0.20	0.45	1.00

KM# 32a 1/2 PENNY
2.1000 g., 0.9250 Silver 0.0625 oz. ASW, 17.14 mm.
Ruler: Elizabeth II **Obv:** Young bust right **Rev:** Atlantic herring

Date	Mintage	F	VF	XF	Unc	BU
1976	20,000	—	—	—	2.00	2.50
1978	10,000	—	—	—	2.00	2.50
1979 (t) Proof	10,000	Value: 2.50				

KM# 32b 1/2 PENNY
4.0000 g., 0.9500 Platinum 0.1222 oz. APW, 17.14 mm.
Ruler: Elizabeth II **Obv:** Young bust right **Rev:** Atlantic herring

Date	Mintage	F	VF	XF	Unc	BU
1976 Proof	600	Value: 250				
1978 Proof	600	Value: 250				
1979 (t) Proof	500	Value: 250				

KM# 40 1/2 PENNY
1.7600 g., Bronze, 17.14 mm. **Ruler:** Elizabeth II **Series:** F.A.O. **Obv:** Young bust right **Rev:** Atlantic herring

Date	Mintage	F	VF	XF	Unc	BU
1977	700,000	—	—	0.20	0.45	1.00
	Note: "1977 PM" on both sides					
1977	Inc. above	—	—	—	5.00	6.00
	Note: "1977 PM" on obverse only					

KM# 40a 1/2 PENNY
2.1000 g., 0.9250 Silver 0.0625 oz. ASW, 17.14 mm.
Ruler: Elizabeth II **Obv:** Young bust right **Rev:** Atlantic herring

Date	Mintage	F	VF	XF	Unc	BU
1977 Proof	10,000	Value: 4.00				

KM# 58 1/2 PENNY
1.7700 g., Bronze, 17.14 mm. **Ruler:** Elizabeth II **Obv:** Young bust right **Rev:** Atlantic herring within net

Date	Mintage	F	VF	XF	Unc	BU
1980 AA	—	—	—	0.15	0.35	0.75
1980 AB	—	—	—	0.15	0.35	0.75
1980PM DD Proof	—	Value: 1.00				
1981 AA	—	—	—	0.15	0.35	0.75
1981 DD Proof	—	Value: 1.00				
1982 AA	—	—	—	0.15	0.35	0.75
1982 (b)	—	—	—	0.15	0.35	0.75
1982 (b) Proof	25,000	Value: 1.00				
1983 AA	—	—	—	0.15	0.35	0.75

KM# 58b 1/2 PENNY
2.1000 g., 0.9250 Silver 0.0625 oz. ASW, 17.14 mm. **Ruler:** Elizabeth II **Obv:** Young bust right **Rev:** Atlantic herring within net

Date	Mintage	F	VF	XF	Unc	BU
1982 Proof	10,000	Value: 4.00				
1983 Proof	5,000	Value: 5.00				

KM# 58c 1/2 PENNY
3.5500 g., 0.9170 Gold 0.1047 oz. AGW, 17.14 mm. **Ruler:** Elizabeth II **Obv:** Young bust right **Rev:** Atlantic herring within net

Date	Mintage	F	VF	XF	Unc	BU
1980 Proof	—	Value: 110				
1982 (b) Proof	500	Value: 110				
1983 Proof	—	Value: 110				

KM# 58d 1/2 PENNY
4.0000 g., 0.9500 Platinum 0.1222 oz. APW, 17.14 mm. **Ruler:** Elizabeth II **Obv:** Young bust right **Rev:** Atlantic herring within net

Date	Mintage	F	VF	XF	Unc	BU
1980 Proof	500	Value: 250				
1982 (b) Proof	500	Value: 250				
1983 Proof	—	Value: 250				

KM# 58a 1/2 PENNY
2.1000 g., 0.5000 Silver 0.0338 oz. ASW, 17.14 mm. **Ruler:** Elizabeth II **Obv:** Young bust right **Rev:** Atlantic herring within net

Date	Mintage	F	VF	XF	Unc	BU
1980 Proof	10,000	Value: 4.00				

KM# 72.1 1/2 PENNY
Bronze, 17.14 mm. **Ruler:** Elizabeth II **Series:** F.A.O. **Obv:** Young bust right **Rev:** Atlantic herring

Date	Mintage	F	VF	XF	Unc	BU
1981		—	—	—	0.50	1.00

KM# 72.2 1/2 PENNY
Bronze, 17.14 mm. **Ruler:** Elizabeth II **Obv:** Young bust right **Rev:** Atlantic herring

Date	Mintage	F	VF	XF	Unc	BU
1981	10,000	—	2.00	5.00	10.00	12.50

KM# 111 1/2 PENNY
Bronze, 17.14 mm. **Ruler:** Elizabeth II **Subject:** Quincentenary of the College of Arms **Obv:** Young bust right **Rev:** Fuchsia blossom on garnished and scrolled shield

Date	Mintage	F	VF	XF	Unc	BU
1984 AA	—	—	—	—	0.15	0.25

KM# 111a 1/2 PENNY
2.1000 g., 0.9250 Silver 0.0625 oz. ASW, 17.14 mm. **Ruler:** Elizabeth II **Obv:** Young bust right **Rev:** Fuchsia blossom on garnished and scrolled shield

Date	Mintage	F	VF	XF	Unc	BU
1984 Proof	—	Value: 5.00				

KM# 111b 1/2 PENNY
3.5500 g., 0.9170 Gold 0.1047 oz. AGW, 17.14 mm. **Ruler:** Elizabeth II **Obv:** Young bust right **Rev:** Fuchsia blossom on garnished and scrolled shield

Date	Mintage	F	VF	XF	Unc	BU
1984 Proof	150	Value: 125				

KM# 142 1/2 PENNY
Bronze, 17.14 mm. **Ruler:** Elizabeth II **Obv:** Crowned head right **Rev:** Fuchsia blossom on garnished and scrolled shield

Date	Mintage	F	VF	XF	Unc	BU
1985(w) AA	—	—	—	—	0.15	0.25
1985 Proof	50,000	Value: 2.00				

KM# 142a 1/2 PENNY
2.1000 g., 0.9250 Silver 0.0625 oz. ASW, 17.14 mm. **Ruler:** Elizabeth II **Obv:** Crowned head right **Rev:** Fuchsia blossom on garnished and scrolled shield

Date	Mintage	F	VF	XF	Unc	BU
1985 Proof	10,000	Value: 3.00				

KM# 142b 1/2 PENNY
3.5500 g., 0.9170 Gold 0.1047 oz. AGW, 17.14 mm. **Ruler:** Elizabeth II **Obv:** Crowned head right **Rev:** Fuchsia blossom on garnished and scrolled shield

Date	Mintage	F	VF	XF	Unc	BU
1985 Proof	300	Value: 115				

KM# 142c 1/2 PENNY
4.0000 g., 0.9500 Platinum 0.1222 oz. APW, 17.14 mm. **Ruler:** Elizabeth II **Obv:** Crowned head right **Rev:** Fuchsia blossom on garnished and scrolled shield

Date	Mintage	F	VF	XF	Unc	BU
1985 Proof	200	Value: 250				

KM# 20 NEW PENNY
3.5500 g., Bronze, 20.32 mm. **Ruler:** Elizabeth II **Obv:** Young bust right **Rev:** Celtic cross

Date	Mintage	F	VF	XF	Unc	BU
1971	100,000	—	—	0.10	0.35	0.65
1971 Proof	10,000	Value: 2.00				
1972	1,000	—	—	—	18.00	20.00
1973	1,000	—	—	—	18.00	20.00
1974	1,000	—	—	—	18.00	20.00
1975	855,000	—	—	0.10	0.20	0.40

KM# 20a NEW PENNY
4.2000 g., 0.9250 Silver 0.1249 oz. ASW, 20.32 mm. **Ruler:** Elizabeth II **Obv:** Young bust right **Rev:** Celtic cross

Date	Mintage	F	VF	XF	Unc	BU
1975	20,000	—	—	—	5.00	6.50

KM# 20b NEW PENNY
8.0000 g., 0.9500 Platinum 0.2443 oz. APW, 20.32 mm. **Ruler:** Elizabeth II **Obv:** Young bust right **Rev:** Celtic cross

Date	Mintage	F	VF	XF	Unc	BU
1975 Proof	600	Value: 500				

KM# 33 PENNY
3.5600 g., Bronze, 20.32 mm. **Ruler:** Elizabeth II **Obv:** Young bust right **Rev:** Loaghtyn sheep

Date	Mintage	F	VF	XF	Unc	BU
1976	900,000	—	—	0.25	0.75	1.25
1977	1,000,000	—	—	0.25	0.75	1.25
1978		—	—	0.25	0.75	1.25
1978 Proof	—	Value: 1.50				
1979 AA(t)		—	—	0.25	0.75	1.25
1979 AB(t)		—	—	0.25	0.75	1.25
1979 AC(t)		—	—	0.25	0.75	1.25
1979 AD(t)		—	—	0.25	0.75	1.25
1979 AE(t)		—	—	0.25	0.75	1.25

KM# 33a PENNY
4.2000 g., 0.9250 Silver 0.1249 oz. ASW, 20.32 mm. **Ruler:** Elizabeth II **Obv:** Young bust right **Rev:** Loaghtyn sheep

Date	Mintage	F	VF	XF	Unc	BU
1976	20,000	—	—	—	4.00	4.50
1977 Proof	10,000	Value: 5.00				
1978	10,000	—	—	—	4.00	4.50
1979 (t) Proof	10,000	Value: 5.00				

KM# 33b PENNY
8.0000 g., 0.9500 Platinum 0.2443 oz. APW, 20.32 mm.
Ruler: Elizabeth II **Obv:** Young bust right **Rev:** Loaghtyn sheep

Date	Mintage	F	VF	XF	Unc	BU
1976 Proof	600	Value: 500				
1978 Proof	600	Value: 500				
1979 (t) Proof	500	Value: 500				

KM# 59 PENNY
3.5600 g., Bronze, 20.32 mm. **Ruler:** Elizabeth II **Obv:** Young bust right **Rev:** Manx cat

Date	Mintage	F	VF	XF	Unc	BU
1980 AA	—	—	—	0.25	1.50	3.00
1980 AB	—	—	—	0.25	1.50	3.00
1980 AC	—	—	—	0.25	1.50	3.00
1980PM DD Proof	—	Value: 2.75				
1981 AA	—	—	—		1.50	3.00
1981 DD Proof	—	Value: 2.75				
1982 AA	—	—	—	0.25	1.50	3.00
1982 (b)	—	—	—	0.25	1.50	3.00
1982 (b) Proof	25,000	Value: 2.75				
1983 AA	—	—	—	0.25	1.50	3.00
1983 AC	—	—	—	0.25	1.50	3.00
1983 AB	—	—	—	0.25	1.50	3.00

KM# 59a PENNY
4.2000 g., 0.5000 Silver 0.0675 oz. ASW, 20.32 mm.
Ruler: Elizabeth II **Obv:** Young bust right **Rev:** Manx cat

Date	Mintage	F	VF	XF	Unc	BU
1980 Proof	10,000	Value: 6.00				

KM# 59b PENNY
4.2000 g., 0.9250 Silver 0.1249 oz. ASW, 20.32 mm.
Ruler: Elizabeth II **Obv:** Young bust right **Rev:** Manx cat

Date	Mintage	F	VF	XF	Unc	BU
1981 Proof	—	Value: 6.00				
1982 (b) Proof	10,000	Value: 6.00				
1983 Proof	5,000	Value: 6.00				

KM# 59c PENNY
7.1000 g., 0.9170 Gold 0.2093 oz. AGW, 20.32 mm.
Ruler: Elizabeth II **Obv:** Young bust right **Rev:** Manx cat

Date	Mintage	F	VF	XF	Unc	BU
1980 Proof	300	Value: 220				
1982 (b) Proof	500	Value: 220				
1983 Proof	500	Value: 220				

KM# 59d PENNY
8.0000 g., 0.9500 Platinum 0.2443 oz. APW, 20.32 mm.
Ruler: Elizabeth II **Obv:** Young bust right **Rev:** Manx cat

Date	Mintage	F	VF	XF	Unc	BU
1980 Proof	500	Value: 475				
1982 (b) Proof	500	Value: 475				
1983 Proof	—	Value: 475				

KM# 112 PENNY
3.5600 g., Bronze, 20.32 mm. **Ruler:** Elizabeth II
Subject: Quincentenary of the College of Arms **Obv:** Young bust right **Rev:** Shag bird on tilting shield

Date	Mintage	F	VF	XF	Unc	BU
1984 AA	—	—	—	0.25	0.50	1.50

KM# 112a PENNY
4.2000 g., 0.9250 Silver 0.1249 oz. ASW, 20.32 mm. **Ruler:** Elizabeth II **Obv:** Young bust right **Rev:** Shag bird on tilting shield

Date	Mintage	F	VF	XF	Unc	BU
1984 Proof	—	Value: 5.00				

KM# 112b PENNY
7.1000 g., 0.9170 Gold 0.2093 oz. AGW, 20.32 mm. **Ruler:** Elizabeth II **Obv:** Young bust right **Rev:** Shag bird on tilting shield

Date	Mintage	F	VF	XF	Unc	BU
1984 Proof	150	Value: 250				

KM# 143 PENNY
3.5600 g., Bronze, 20.32 mm. **Ruler:** Elizabeth II **Obv:** Crowned head right **Rev:** Shag bird on tilting shield

Date	Mintage	F	VF	XF	Unc	BU
1985 AA(w)	—	—	—	0.10	0.50	1.50
1985 Proof	50,000	Value: 2.00				

Date	Mintage	F	VF	XF	Unc	BU
1986 AA	—	—	—	0.10	0.50	1.50
1987 AA	—	—	—	0.10	0.50	1.50
1987 AB	—	—	—	0.10	0.50	1.50
1987 AC	—	—	—	0.10	0.50	1.50

KM# 143a PENNY
4.2000 g., 0.9250 Silver 0.1249 oz. ASW, 20.32 mm. **Ruler:** Elizabeth II **Obv:** Crowned head right **Rev:** Shag bird on tilting shield

Date	Mintage	F	VF	XF	Unc	BU
1985 Proof	10,000	Value: 3.00				

KM# 143b PENNY
7.1000 g., 0.9170 Gold 0.2093 oz. AGW, 20.32 mm. **Ruler:** Elizabeth II **Obv:** Crowned head right **Rev:** Shag bird on tilting shield

Date	Mintage	F	VF	XF	Unc	BU
1985 Proof	300	Value: 220				

KM# 143c PENNY
8.0000 g., 0.9500 Platinum 0.2443 oz. APW, 20.32 mm. **Ruler:** Elizabeth II **Obv:** Crowned head right **Rev:** Shag bird on tilting shield

Date	Mintage	F	VF	XF	Unc	BU
1985 Proof	200	Value: 500				

KM# 207 PENNY
3.5600 g., Bronze, 20.32 mm. **Ruler:** Elizabeth II **Obv:** Crowned head right **Rev:** Precision lathe superimposed on a cog wheel

Date	Mintage	F	VF	XF	Unc	BU
1988 AA	—	—	—		0.20	0.35
1988 AB	—	—	—	0.10	0.30	0.50
1988 AC	—	—	—	0.10	0.30	0.50
1988 AD	—	—	—	0.10	0.30	0.50
1989 AA	—	—	—		0.20	0.35
1989 AB	—	—	—	0.10	0.30	0.50
1989 AC	—	—	—	0.10	0.30	0.50
1989 AD	—	—	—	0.10	0.30	0.50
1989 AE	—	—	—	0.10	0.30	0.50
1990 AA	—	—	—		0.20	0.35
1991 AA	—	—	—		0.20	0.35
1991 AB	—	—	—		0.20	0.35
1991 AC	—	—	—		0.20	0.35
1991 AD	—	—	—		0.20	0.35
1991 AE	—	—	—		0.20	0.35
1992 AA	—	—	—		0.20	0.35
1993 AA	—	—	—		0.20	0.35
1994 AA	—	—	—		0.20	0.35
1995 AA	—	—	—		0.20	0.35

KM# 588 PENNY
Bronze-Plated Steel, 20.32 mm. **Ruler:** Elizabeth II
Subject: Sports **Obv:** Crowned head right **Rev:** Rugby ball within 3/4 square and wreath

Date	Mintage	F	VF	XF	Unc	BU
1996 AA	—	—	—		0.20	0.35
1997 AA	—	—	—		0.20	0.35
1998 AA	—	—	—		0.20	0.35

KM# 588a PENNY
4.2000 g., 0.9250 Silver 0.1249 oz. ASW, 20.32 mm.
Ruler: Elizabeth II **Subject:** Sports **Obv:** Crowned head right **Rev:** Rugby ball within 3/4 square and wreath

Date	Mintage	F	VF	XF	Unc	BU
1996 Proof	—	Value: 10.00				

KM# 823.1 PENNY
Bronze-Plated Steel, 20.32 mm. **Ruler:** Elizabeth II **Obv:** Head with tiara right **Rev:** Rugby ball within 3/4 square and wreath

Date	Mintage	F	VF	XF	Unc	BU
1998PM AA	—	—	—		0.20	0.35

KM# 823.2 PENNY
Bronze-Plated Steel, 20.32 mm. **Ruler:** Elizabeth II **Obv:** Head with tiara right with small triskeles dividing legend **Rev:** Rugby ball within 3/4 square and wreath

Date	Mintage	F	VF	XF	Unc	BU
1998PM AA	—	—	—		0.20	0.35
1999PM AA	—	—	—		0.20	0.35
1999PM AB	—	—	—		0.20	0.35

KM# 1036 PENNY
3.5600 g., Bronze-Plated Steel, 20.32 mm. **Ruler:** Elizabeth II **Obv:** Head with tiara right with small triskeles dividing legend **Rev:** Ruins **Edge:** Plain

Date	Mintage	F	VF	XF	Unc	BU
2000PMM AA	—	—	—		0.25	0.45

KM# 21 2 NEW PENCE
7.0000 g., Bronze, 25.91 mm. **Ruler:** Elizabeth II **Obv:** Young bust right **Rev:** Falcons

Date	Mintage	F	VF	XF	Unc	BU
1971	100,000	—	—	0.25	1.00	2.00
1971 Proof	10,000	Value: 2.50				
1972	1,000	—	—	—	18.00	20.00
1973	1,000	—	—	—	18.00	20.00
1974	1,000	—	—	—	18.00	20.00
1975	725,000	—	—	0.25	1.00	1.50

KM# 21a 2 NEW PENCE
8.4000 g., 0.9250 Silver 0.2498 oz. ASW, 25.91 mm.
Ruler: Elizabeth II **Obv:** Young bust right **Rev:** Falcons

Date	Mintage	F	VF	XF	Unc	BU
1975	20,000	—	—	—	7.50	8.50

KM# 21b 2 NEW PENCE
16.0000 g., 0.9500 Platinum 0.4887 oz. APW, 25.91 mm.
Ruler: Elizabeth II **Obv:** Young bust right **Rev:** Falcons

Date	Mintage	F	VF	XF	Unc	BU
1975 Proof	600	Value: 1,000				

KM# 34 2 PENCE
7.1200 g., Bronze, 25.91 mm. **Ruler:** Elizabeth II **Obv:** Young bust right **Rev:** Bird in flight over map

Date	Mintage	F	VF	XF	Unc	BU
1976	800,000	—	—	0.20	0.50	1.00
1977	1,000,000	—	—	0.20	0.50	1.00
1978		—	—	—	0.50	1.00
1978 Proof	—	Value: 1.25				
1979 AA(t)	10,000	—	—	0.20	0.50	1.00
1979 AB(t)	—	—	—	0.20	0.50	1.00
1979 AC(t)	—	—	—	0.20	0.50	1.00
1979 AD(t)	—	—	—	0.20	0.50	1.00
1979 AE(t)	—	—	—	0.20	0.50	1.00
1979 AF(t)	—	—	—	0.20	0.50	1.00
1979 AG(t)	—	—	—	0.20	0.50	1.00
1979 AH(t)	—	—	—	0.20	0.50	1.00

KM# 34a 2 PENCE
8.4000 g., 0.9250 Silver 0.2498 oz. ASW, 25.91 mm. **Ruler:** Elizabeth II **Obv:** Young bust right **Rev:** Bird in flight over map

Date	Mintage	F	VF	XF	Unc	BU
1976	20,000	—	—	—	4.50	5.00
1977 Proof	10,000	Value: 6.00				
1978	10,000	—	—	—	5.50	6.00
1979 (t) Proof	10,000	Value: 6.00				

KM# 34b 2 PENCE
16.0000 g., 0.9500 Platinum 0.4887 oz. APW, 25.91 mm. **Ruler:** Elizabeth II **Obv:** Young bust right **Rev:** Bird in flight over map

Date	Mintage	F	VF	XF	Unc	BU
1976 Proof	600	Value: 1,000				
1977 Proof	600	Value: 1,000				
1978 Proof	—	Value: 1,000				
1979 (t) Proof	500	Value: 1,000				

KM# 60 2 PENCE
7.1200 g., Bronze, 25.91 mm. **Ruler:** Elizabeth II **Obv:** Young bust right **Rev:** Bird in center of design

Date	Mintage	F	VF	XF	Unc	BU
1980 AA	—	—	—	0.25	0.60	1.50
1980 AB	—	—	—	0.25	0.60	1.50
1980 AC	—	—	—	0.25	0.60	1.50
1980 AD	—	—	—	0.25	0.60	1.50
1980PM DD Proof	—	Value: 1.75				

Date	Mintage	F	VF	XF	Unc	BU
1981 AA	—	—	—	0.25	0.60	1.50
1981 AB	—	—	—	0.25	0.60	1.50
1981 DD Proof	—	Value: 1.75				
1982 AA	—	—	—	0.25	0.60	1.50
1982 (b)	—	—	—	0.25	0.60	1.50
1982 (b) Proof	25,000	Value: 1.75				
1983 AA	—	—	—	0.25	0.60	1.50
1983 AB	—	—	—	0.25	0.60	1.50
1983 AC	—	—	—	0.25	0.60	1.50
1983 AD	—	—	—	0.25	0.60	1.50
1983 AE	—	—	—	0.25	0.60	1.50

KM# 60a   2 PENCE
8.4000 g., 0.5000 Silver 0.1350 oz. ASW, 25.91 mm. **Ruler:** Elizabeth II **Obv:** Young bust right **Rev:** Bird in center of design

Date	Mintage	F	VF	XF	Unc	BU
1980 Proof	10,000	Value: 5.00				

KM# 60b   2 PENCE
8.4000 g., 0.9250 Silver 0.2498 oz. ASW, 25.91 mm. **Ruler:** Elizabeth II **Obv:** Young bust right **Rev:** Bird in center of design

Date	Mintage	F	VF	XF	Unc	BU
1981 Proof	—	Value: 5.00				
1982 (b) Proof	10,000	Value: 5.00				
1983 Proof	5,000	Value: 7.00				

KM# 60c   2 PENCE
14.2000 g., 0.9170 Gold 0.4186 oz. AGW, 25.91 mm. **Ruler:** Elizabeth II **Obv:** Young bust right **Rev:** Bird in center of design

Date	Mintage	F	VF	XF	Unc	BU
1980 Proof	300	Value: 425				
1982 (b) Proof	500	Value: 425				
1983 Proof	—	Value: 425				

KM# 60d   2 PENCE
16.0000 g., 0.9500 Platinum 0.4887 oz. APW, 25.91 mm. **Ruler:** Elizabeth II **Obv:** Young bust right **Rev:** Bird in center of design

Date	Mintage	F	VF	XF	Unc	BU
1980 Proof	500	Value: 1,000				
1982 (b) Proof	500	Value: 1,000				
1983 Proof	—	Value: 1,000				

KM# 113   2 PENCE
7.1200 g., Bronze, 25.91 mm. **Ruler:** Elizabeth II **Subject:** Quincentenary of the College of Arms **Obv:** Young bust right **Rev:** Falcon on ornamented shield

Date	Mintage	F	VF	XF	Unc	BU
1984 AA	—	—	—	0.20	1.00	3.00

KM# 113a   2 PENCE
8.4000 g., 0.9250 Silver 0.2498 oz. ASW, 25.91 mm. **Ruler:** Elizabeth II **Obv:** Young bust right **Rev:** Falcon on ornamented shield

Date	Mintage	F	VF	XF	Unc	BU
1984 Proof	—	Value: 9.00				

KM# 113b   2 PENCE
14.2000 g., 0.9170 Gold 0.4186 oz. AGW, 25.91 mm. **Ruler:** Elizabeth II **Obv:** Young bust right **Rev:** Falcon on ornamented shield

Date	Mintage	F	VF	XF	Unc	BU
1984 Proof	150	Value: 450				

KM# 144   2 PENCE
7.1200 g., Bronze, 25.91 mm. **Ruler:** Elizabeth II **Obv:** Crowned head right **Rev:** Falcon on ornamented shield

Date	Mintage	F	VF	XF	Unc	BU
1985(w) AA	—	—	—	0.20	1.25	3.00
1985(w) AB	—	—	—	0.20	1.25	3.00
1985 Proof	50,000	Value: 3.00				
1986 AA	—	—	—	0.20	1.25	3.00
1986 AB	—	—	—	0.20	1.25	3.00
1986 AC	—	—	—	0.20	1.25	3.00
1986 AD	—	—	—	0.20	1.25	3.00
1987 AA	—	—	—	0.20	1.25	3.00
1987 AB	—	—	—	0.20	1.25	3.00
1987 AC	—	—	—	0.20	1.25	3.00
1987 AD	—	—	—	0.20	1.25	3.00

KM# 144a   2 PENCE
8.4000 g., 0.9250 Silver 0.2498 oz. ASW, 25.91 mm. **Ruler:** Elizabeth II **Obv:** Crowned head right **Rev:** Falcon on ornamented shield

Date	Mintage	F	VF	XF	Unc	BU
1985 Proof	10,000	Value: 12.00				

KM# 144b   2 PENCE
14.2000 g., 0.9170 Gold 0.4186 oz. AGW, 25.91 mm. **Ruler:** Elizabeth II **Obv:** Crowned head right **Rev:** Falcon on ornamented shield

Date	Mintage	F	VF	XF	Unc	BU
1985 Proof	300	Value: 425				

KM# 144c   2 PENCE
16.0000 g., 0.9500 Platinum 0.4887 oz. APW, 25.91 mm. **Ruler:** Elizabeth II **Obv:** Crowned head right **Rev:** Falcon on ornamented shield

Date	Mintage	F	VF	XF	Unc	BU
1985 Proof	200	Value: 1,000				

KM# 208   2 PENCE
7.1200 g., Bronze, 25.91 mm. **Ruler:** Elizabeth II **Obv:** Crowned head right **Rev:** Assorted designs within celtic cross within circle

Date	Mintage	F	VF	XF	Unc	BU
1988 AA	—	—	—	—	0.30	0.50
1988 AB	—	—	—	0.10	0.30	0.50
1988 AC	—	—	—	0.10	0.30	0.50
1988 AD	—	—	—	0.10	0.30	0.50
1989 AA	—	—	—	—	0.30	0.50
1989 AB	—	—	—	0.10	0.30	0.50
1989 AC	—	—	—	0.10	0.30	0.50
1989 AD	—	—	—	0.10	0.30	0.50
1989 AE	—	—	—	0.10	0.30	0.50
1990 AA	—	—	—	—	0.30	0.50
1991 AA	—	—	—	—	0.30	0.50
1992 AA	—	—	—	—	0.30	0.50
1993 AA	—	—	—	—	0.30	0.50
1994 AA	—	—	—	—	0.30	0.50
1995 AA	—	—	—	—	0.30	0.50

KM# 589   2 PENCE
Bronze Clad Steel, 25.91 mm. **Ruler:** Elizabeth II **Subject:** Sports **Obv:** Crowned head right **Rev:** Bicyclists within sprigs

Date	Mintage	F	VF	XF	Unc	BU
1996 AA	—	—	—	—	0.20	0.40
1997 AA	—	—	—	—	0.20	0.40

KM# 901.1   2 PENCE
Bronze Clad Steel, 25.91 mm. **Ruler:** Elizabeth II **Obv:** Head with tiara right **Rev:** Two bicyclists within sprigs

Date	Mintage	F	VF	XF	Unc	BU
1998PM AA	—	—	—	—	0.20	0.40

KM# 901.2   2 PENCE
Bronze Plated Steel, 25.91 mm. **Ruler:** Elizabeth II **Obv:** Head with tiara right with small triskeles dividing legend **Rev:** Two bicyclists within sprigs

Date	Mintage	F	VF	XF	Unc	BU
1998PM AA	—	—	—	—	0.20	0.40
1999PM AA	—	—	—	—	0.20	0.40

KM# 1037   2 PENCE
7.1650 g., Brass Plated Steel, 25.86 mm. **Ruler:** Elizabeth II **Obv:** Head with tiara right **Rev:** Sailboat **Edge:** Plain

Date	Mintage	F	VF	XF	Unc	BU
2000PM AA	—	—	—	—	0.40	0.60

KM# 22   5 NEW PENCE
5.6500 g., Copper-Nickel, 23.59 mm. **Ruler:** Elizabeth II **Obv:** Young bust right **Rev:** Towers on hill

Date	Mintage	F	VF	XF	Unc	BU
1971	100,000	—	—	0.10	0.50	1.00
1971 Proof	10,000	Value: 2.50				
1972	1,000	—	—	—	20.00	22.50
1973	1,000	—	—	—	20.00	22.50
1974	1,000	—	—	—	20.00	22.50
1975	1,400,000	—	—	0.10	0.25	0.50

KM# 22a   5 NEW PENCE
6.5000 g., 0.9250 Silver 0.1933 oz. ASW, 23.59 mm. **Ruler:** Elizabeth II **Obv:** Young bust right **Rev:** Towers on hill

Date	Mintage	F	VF	XF	Unc	BU
1975	20,000	—	—	—	5.00	6.00

KM# 22b   5 NEW PENCE
12.5000 g., 0.9500 Platinum 0.3818 oz. APW, 23.59 mm. **Ruler:** Elizabeth II **Obv:** Young bust right **Rev:** Towers on hill

Date	Mintage	F	VF	XF	Unc	BU
1975 Proof	600	Value: 775				

KM# 35.1b   5 PENCE
12.5000 g., 0.9500 Platinum 0.3818 oz. APW, 23.59 mm. **Ruler:** Elizabeth II **Obv:** Young bust right **Rev:** Laxey wheel

Date	Mintage	F	VF	XF	Unc	BU
1976 Proof	600	Value: 800				
1978 Proof	600	Value: 800				
1979 Proof	500	Value: 800				

KM# 35.1a   5 PENCE
6.5000 g., 0.9250 Silver 0.1933 oz. ASW, 23.59 mm. **Ruler:** Elizabeth II **Obv:** Young bust right **Rev:** Laxey wheel

Date	Mintage	F	VF	XF	Unc	BU
1976	20,000	—	—	—	5.00	6.00
1977 Proof	10,000	Value: 7.00				
1978	10,000	—	—	—	5.00	6.00
1979(t) AA Proof	10,000	Value: 7.00				

KM# 35.1   5 PENCE
5.6500 g., Copper-Nickel, 23.59 mm. **Ruler:** Elizabeth II **Obv:** Young bust right **Rev:** Laxey wheel **Note:** Lady Isabella; Mint mark: PM on obverse and reverse.

Date	Mintage	F	VF	XF	Unc	BU
1976	800,000	—	—	0.10	0.60	0.85
1977	—	—	—	0.10	0.60	0.85
1978	—	—	—	0.10	0.60	0.85
1978 Proof	—	Value: 1.50				
1979(t) AA	—	—	—	0.10	0.60	0.85
1979(t) AB	—	—	—	0.10	0.60	0.85

KM# 35.2   5 PENCE
5.6500 g., Copper-Nickel, 23.59 mm. **Ruler:** Elizabeth II **Obv:** Young bust right **Rev:** Laxey wheel **Note:** Mint mark: PM on obverse only.

Date	Mintage	F	VF	XF	Unc	BU
1976	Inc. above	—	—	0.15	0.75	1.00

KM# 61a   5 PENCE
6.5000 g., 0.5000 Silver 0.1045 oz. ASW, 23.59 mm. **Ruler:** Elizabeth II **Obv:** Young bust right **Rev:** Stylized Loagthyn sheep

Date	Mintage	F	VF	XF	Unc	BU
1980 Proof	10,000	Value: 5.00				

KM# 61   5 PENCE
5.6500 g., Copper-Nickel, 23.59 mm. **Ruler:** Elizabeth II **Obv:** Young bust right **Rev:** Stylized Loagthyn sheep

Date	Mintage	F	VF	XF	Unc	BU
1980 AA	—	—	—	0.15	0.75	1.25
1980 AB	—	—	—	0.15	0.75	1.25
1980 AC	—	—	—	0.15	0.75	1.25
1980PM DD Proof	—	Value: 1.50				
1981 AA	—	—	—	0.15	0.75	1.25
1981 DD Proof	—	Value: 1.50				
1982 (b)	—	—	—	0.15	0.75	1.25
1982 AA	—	—	—	0.15	0.75	1.00
1982 (b) Proof	25,000	Value: 1.50				
1983 AA	—	—	—	0.15	0.75	1.25

KM# 61b   5 PENCE
6.5000 g., 0.9250 Silver 0.1933 oz. ASW, 23.59 mm. **Ruler:** Elizabeth II **Obv:** Young bust right **Rev:** Stylized Loagthyn sheep

Date	Mintage	F	VF	XF	Unc	BU
1981 Proof	—	Value: 5.00				
1982 Proof	10,000	Value: 5.00				
1983 Proof	5,000	Value: 5.00				

KM# 61c 5 PENCE
11.0000 g., 0.9170 Gold 0.3243 oz. AGW, 23.59 mm. **Ruler:** Elizabeth II **Obv:** Young bust right **Rev:** Stiylized Loagthyn sheep

Date	Mintage	F	VF	XF	Unc	BU
1980 Proof	300	Value: 325				
1982 (b) Proof	500	Value: 325				
1983 Proof	—	Value: 325				

KM# 61d 5 PENCE
12.5000 g., 0.9500 Platinum 0.3818 oz. APW, 23.59 mm. **Ruler:** Elizabeth II **Obv:** Young bust right **Rev:** Stiylized Loagthyn sheep

Date	Mintage	F	VF	XF	Unc	BU
1980 Proof	500	Value: 800				
1982 Proof	500	Value: 800				
1983 Proof	—	Value: 800				

KM# 114 5 PENCE
5.6500 g., Copper-Nickel, 23.59 mm. **Ruler:** Elizabeth II **Subject:** Quincentenary of the College of Arms **Obv:** Young bust right **Rev:** Cushag within design

Date	Mintage	F	VF	XF	Unc	BU
1984 AA	—	—	—	0.10	0.50	0.75

KM# 114a 5 PENCE
6.5000 g., 0.9250 Silver 0.1933 oz. ASW, 23.59 mm. **Ruler:** Elizabeth II **Obv:** Young bust right **Rev:** Cushag within design

Date	Mintage	F	VF	XF	Unc	BU
1984 Proof	—	Value: 5.00				

KM# 114b 5 PENCE
11.0000 g., 0.9170 Gold 0.3243 oz. AGW, 23.59 mm. **Ruler:** Elizabeth II **Obv:** Young bust right **Rev:** Cushag within design

Date	Mintage	F	VF	XF	Unc	BU
1984 Proof	150	Value: 400				

KM# 145 5 PENCE
5.6500 g., Copper-Nickel, 23.59 mm. **Ruler:** Elizabeth II **Obv:** Crowned head right **Rev:** Cushag within design

Date	Mintage	F	VF	XF	Unc	BU
1985(w) AA	—	—	—	0.10	0.50	0.75
1985 Proof	50,000	Value: 3.00				
1986 AA	—	—	—	0.10	0.50	0.75
1986 AB	—	—	—	0.10	0.50	0.75
1986 AC	—	—	—	0.10	0.50	0.75
1986 AD	—	—	—	0.10	0.50	0.75
1987 AA	—	—	—	0.10	0.50	0.75

KM# 145a 5 PENCE
6.5000 g., 0.9250 Silver 0.1933 oz. ASW, 23.59 mm. **Ruler:** Elizabeth II **Obv:** Crowned head right **Rev:** Cushag within design

Date	Mintage	F	VF	XF	Unc	BU
1985 Proof	10,000	Value: 8.00				

KM# 145b 5 PENCE
11.0000 g., 0.9170 Gold 0.3243 oz. AGW, 23.59 mm. **Ruler:** Elizabeth II **Obv:** Crowned head right **Rev:** Cushag within design

Date	Mintage	F	VF	XF	Unc	BU
1985 Proof	300	Value: 325				

KM# 145c 5 PENCE
12.5000 g., 0.9500 Platinum 0.3818 oz. APW, 23.59 mm. **Ruler:** Elizabeth II **Obv:** Crowned head right **Rev:** Cushag within design

Date	Mintage	F	VF	XF	Unc	BU
1985 Proof	200	Value: 800				

KM# 209.1 5 PENCE
5.6500 g., Copper-Nickel, 23.59 mm. **Ruler:** Elizabeth II **Obv:** Crowned head right **Rev:** Windsurfing

Date	Mintage	F	VF	XF	Unc	BU
1988 AA	—	—	—	—	0.50	0.75
1989 AA	—	—	—	—	0.50	0.75
1990	—	—	—	—	0.50	0.75

KM# 209.2 5 PENCE
Copper-Nickel, 18 mm. **Ruler:** Elizabeth II **Obv:** Crowned head right **Rev:** Windsurfing **Note:** Reduced size.

Date	Mintage	F	VF	XF	Unc	BU
1990 AA	—	—	—	—	0.50	0.75
1991 AA	—	—	—	—	0.50	0.75
1991 AB	—	—	—	—	0.50	0.75
1992 AA	—	—	—	—	0.50	0.75
1993 AA	—	—	—	—	0.50	0.75

KM# 392 5 PENCE
Copper-Nickel, 18 mm. **Ruler:** Elizabeth II **Obv:** Crowned head right **Rev:** Golf clubs and ball

Date	Mintage	F	VF	XF	Unc	BU
1994 AA	—	—	—	—	0.50	0.75
1995 AA	—	—	—	—	0.50	0.75

KM# 392a 5 PENCE
3.2500 g., 0.9250 Silver 0.0966 oz. ASW, 18 mm. **Ruler:** Elizabeth II **Obv:** Crowned head right **Rev:** Golf clubs and ball

Date	Mintage	F	VF	XF	Unc	BU
1994 Proof	Est. 25,000	Value: 10.00				

KM# 392b 5 PENCE
3.2500 g., 0.9170 Gold 0.0958 oz. AGW, 18 mm. **Ruler:** Elizabeth II **Obv:** Crowned head right **Rev:** Golf clubs and ball

Date	Mintage	F	VF	XF	Unc	BU
1994 Proof	10,000	Value: 100				

KM# 392c 5 PENCE
3.2500 g., 0.9500 Platinum 0.0993 oz. APW, 18 mm. **Ruler:** Elizabeth II **Obv:** Crowned head right **Rev:** Golf clubs and ball

Date	Mintage	F	VF	XF	Unc	BU
1994 Proof	3,500	Value: 200				

KM# 590 5 PENCE
Copper-Nickel, 18 mm. **Ruler:** Elizabeth II **Subject:** Sports **Obv:** Crowned head right **Rev:** Golfer within sprigs

Date	Mintage	F	VF	XF	Unc	BU
1996 AA	—	—	—	—	0.50	0.75
1997 AA	—	—	—	—	0.50	0.75

KM# 590a 5 PENCE
3.2500 g., 0.9250 Silver 0.0966 oz. ASW, 18 mm. **Ruler:** Elizabeth II **Subject:** Sports **Obv:** Crowned head right **Rev:** Golfer within sprigs

Date	Mintage	F	VF	XF	Unc	BU
1996 Proof	—	Value: 10.00				

KM# 902.2 5 PENCE
Copper Nickel, 18 mm. **Ruler:** Elizabeth II **Obv:** Head with tiara right with small triskeles dividing legend **Rev:** Golpher within sprigs

Date	Mintage	F	VF	XF	Unc	BU
1998PM AA	—	—	—	—	0.50	0.75
1999PM AA	—	—	—	—	0.50	0.75
1999PM AB	—	—	—	—	0.50	0.75

KM# 902.1 5 PENCE
Copper-Nickel, 18 mm. **Ruler:** Elizabeth II **Obv:** Head with tiara right **Rev:** Golfer within sprigs

Date	Mintage	F	VF	XF	Unc	BU
1998 AA	—	—	—	—	0.50	0.75

KM# 1038 5 PENCE
3.2500 g., Copper-Nickel, 18 mm. **Ruler:** Elizabeth II **Obv:** Head with tiara right **Rev:** Gaut's Cross **Edge:** Reeded

Date	Mintage	F	VF	XF	Unc	BU
2000 AA	—	—	—	—	0.75	1.00
2000PMM AA	—	—	—	—	0.75	1.00
2000 AB	—	—	—	—	0.75	1.00
2000PMM AC	—	—	—	—	0.75	1.00

KM# 23 10 NEW PENCE
11.5000 g., Copper-Nickel, 28.5 mm. **Ruler:** Elizabeth II **Obv:** Young bust right **Rev:** Triskeles

Date	Mintage	F	VF	XF	Unc	BU
1971	100,000	—	—	0.20	0.50	1.00
1971 Proof	10,000	Value: 3.50				
1972	1,000	—	—	—	20.00	22.50
1973	1,000	—	—	—	20.00	22.50
1974	1,000	—	—	—	20.00	22.50
1975	1,500,000	—	—	0.20	0.40	0.75

KM# 23a 10 NEW PENCE
13.0000 g., 0.9250 Silver 0.3866 oz. ASW, 28.5 mm. **Ruler:** Elizabeth II **Obv:** Young bust right **Rev:** Triskeles

Date	Mintage	F	VF	XF	Unc	BU
1975	20,000	—	—	—	9.00	10.00

KM# 23b 10 NEW PENCE
25.0000 g., 0.9500 Platinum 0.7635 oz. APW, 28.5 mm. **Ruler:** Elizabeth II **Obv:** Young bust right **Rev:** Triskeles

Date	Mintage	F	VF	XF	Unc	BU
1975 Proof	600	Value: 1,500				

KM# 36.1a 10 PENCE
13.0000 g., 0.9250 Silver 0.3866 oz. ASW, 28.5 mm. **Ruler:** Elizabeth II **Obv:** Young bust right **Rev:** Triskeles on map

Date	Mintage	F	VF	XF	Unc	BU
1976	20,000	—	—	—	9.00	10.00
1977 Proof	10,000	Value: 10.00				
1978	10,000	—	—	—	9.00	10.00
1979 (t) Proof	10,000	Value: 10.00				

KM# 36.1b 10 PENCE
25.0000 g., 0.9500 Platinum 0.7635 oz. APW, 28.5 mm. **Ruler:** Elizabeth II **Obv:** Young bust right **Rev:** Triskeles on map

Date	Mintage	F	VF	XF	Unc	BU
1976 Proof	600	Value: 1,500				
1978 Proof	600	Value: 1,500				
1979 (t) Proof	500	Value: 1,500				

KM# 36.1 10 PENCE
11.5000 g., Copper-Nickel, 28.5 mm. **Ruler:** Elizabeth II **Obv:** Young bust right **Rev:** Triskeles on map **Note:** Mintmark: PM on obverse and reverse.

Date	Mintage	F	VF	XF	Unc	BU
1976	2,800,000	—	—	0.20	0.80	1.00
1977	—	—	—	0.20	0.80	1.00
1978	—	—	—	0.20	0.80	1.00
1978 Proof	—	Value: 2.00				
1979(t) AA	—	—	—	0.20	0.80	1.00
1979(t) AB	—	—	—	0.20	0.80	1.00

KM# 36.2 10 PENCE
Copper-Nickel, 28.5 mm. **Ruler:** Elizabeth II **Obv:** Young bust right **Rev:** Triskeles on map **Note:** Mintmark: PM on obverse only.

Date	Mintage	F	VF	XF	Unc	BU
1976	Inc. above	—	—	0.20	1.00	1.25
1977	—	—	—	0.20	1.00	1.25

KM# 62 10 PENCE
11.5000 g., Copper-Nickel, 28.5 mm. **Ruler:** Elizabeth II **Obv:** Young bust right **Rev:** Falcon within design

Date	Mintage	F	VF	XF	Unc	BU
1980 AA	—	—	—	0.25	1.00	2.00
1980 AB	—	—	—	0.25	1.00	2.00
1980PM DD Proof	—	Value: 2.50				
1981 AA	—	—	—	0.25	1.00	2.00
1981 DD Proof	—	Value: 2.50				

Date	Mintage	F	VF	XF	Unc	BU
1982 AA	—	—	—	0.25	1.00	2.00
1982 AB	—	—	—	0.25	1.00	2.00
1982 AB(b)	—	—	—	0.25	1.00	2.00
1982 AC	—	—	—	0.25	1.00	2.00
1982 AD	—	—	—	0.25	1.00	2.00
1982 (b) Proof	25,000	Value: 2.50				
1983 AA	—	—	—	0.25	1.00	2.00
1983 AB	—	—	—	0.25	1.00	2.00
1983 AC	—	—	—	0.25	1.00	2.00
1983 AD	—	—	—	0.25	1.00	2.00

KM# 62a   10 PENCE
13.0000 g., 0.5000 Silver 0.2090 oz. ASW, 28.5 mm. **Ruler:** Elizabeth II **Obv:** Young bust right **Rev:** Falcon within design

Date	Mintage	F	VF	XF	Unc	BU
1980 Proof	10,000	Value: 12.00				

KM# 62b   10 PENCE
13.0000 g., 0.9250 Silver 0.3866 oz. ASW, 28.5 mm. **Ruler:** Elizabeth II **Obv:** Young bust right **Rev:** Falcon within design

Date	Mintage	F	VF	XF	Unc	BU
1981 Proof	—	Value: 12.00				
1982 Proof	10,000	Value: 12.00				
1983 Proof	5,000	Value: 12.50				

KM# 62c   10 PENCE
22.0000 g., 0.9170 Gold 0.6486 oz. AGW, 28.5 mm. **Ruler:** Elizabeth II **Obv:** Young bust right **Rev:** Falcon within design

Date	Mintage	F	VF	XF	Unc	BU
1980 Proof	300	Value: 700				
1982 (b) Proof	500	Value: 700				
1983 Proof	—	Value: 700				

KM# 62d   10 PENCE
25.0000 g., 0.9500 Platinum 0.7635 oz. APW, 28.5 mm. **Ruler:** Elizabeth II **Obv:** Young bust right **Rev:** Falcon within design

Date	Mintage	F	VF	XF	Unc	BU
1980 Proof	500	Value: 1,500				
1982 (b) Proof	500	Value: 1,500				
1983 Proof	—	Value: 1,500				

KM# 115   10 PENCE
11.5000 g., Copper-Nickel, 28.5 mm. **Ruler:** Elizabeth II **Subject:** Quincentenary of the College of Arms **Obv:** Young bust right **Rev:** Loagthyn ram within shield

Date	Mintage	F	VF	XF	Unc	BU
1984 AA	—	—	—	0.25	1.00	1.25
1984 AB	—	—	—	0.25	1.00	1.25
1984 AC	—	—	—	0.25	1.00	1.25
1984 AD	—	—	—	0.25	1.00	1.25
1984 AE	—	—	—	0.25	1.00	1.25
1984 AF	—	—	—	0.25	1.00	1.25
1984 AG	—	—	—	0.25	1.00	1.25

KM# 115a   10 PENCE
Silver, 28.5 mm. **Ruler:** Elizabeth II **Obv:** Young bust right **Rev:** Loagthyn ram within shield

Date	Mintage	F	VF	XF	Unc	BU
1984 Proof	—	Value: 10.00				

KM# 115b   10 PENCE
22.0000 g., 0.9170 Gold 0.6486 oz. AGW, 28.5 mm. **Ruler:** Elizabeth II **Obv:** Young bust right **Rev:** Loagthyn ram within shield

Date	Mintage	F	VF	XF	Unc	BU
1984 Proof	150	Value: 750				

KM# 146   10 PENCE
11.5000 g., Copper-Nickel, 28.5 mm. **Ruler:** Elizabeth II **Obv:** Crowned head right **Rev:** Loagthyn ram within designed shield

Date	Mintage	F	VF	XF	Unc	BU
1985(w) AA	—	—	—	0.20	0.80	1.00
1985(w) AB	—	—	—	0.20	0.80	1.00
1985 Proof	50,000	Value: 3.00				
1986 AA	—	—	—	0.20	0.80	1.00
1987 AA	—	—	—	0.20	0.80	1.00

KM# 146a   10 PENCE
13.0000 g., 0.9250 Silver 0.3866 oz. ASW, 28.5 mm. **Ruler:** Elizabeth II **Obv:** Crowned head right **Rev:** Loagthyn ram within designed shield

Date	Mintage	F	VF	XF	Unc	BU
1985 Proof	10,000	Value: 18.00				

KM# 146b   10 PENCE
22.0000 g., 0.9170 Gold 0.6486 oz. AGW, 28.5 mm. **Ruler:** Elizabeth II **Obv:** Crowned head right **Rev:** Loagthyn ram within designed shield

Date	Mintage	F	VF	XF	Unc	BU
1985 Proof	300	Value: 700				

KM# 146c   10 PENCE
25.0000 g., 0.9500 Platinum 0.7635 oz. APW, 28.5 mm. **Ruler:** Elizabeth II **Obv:** Crowned head right **Rev:** Loagthyn ram within designed shield

Date	Mintage	F	VF	XF	Unc	BU
1985 Proof	200	Value: 1,500				

KM# 210   10 PENCE
11.5000 g., Copper-Nickel, 28.5 mm. **Ruler:** Elizabeth II **Obv:** Crowned head right **Rev:** Island and portcullis on globe

Date	Mintage	F	VF	XF	Unc	BU
1988 AA	—	—	—	—	0.75	1.00
1989 AA	—	—	—	—	0.75	1.00
1990 AA	—	—	—	—	0.75	1.00
1991 AA	—	—	—	—	0.75	1.00
1991 AB	—	—	—	—	0.75	1.00
1991 AC	—	—	—	—	0.75	1.00
1992 AA	—	—	—	—	0.75	1.00

KM# 337   10 PENCE
6.5000 g., Copper-Nickel, 24.5 mm. **Ruler:** Elizabeth II **Obv:** Crowned head right **Rev:** Triskeles and value **Note:** Varieties exist.

Date	Mintage	F	VF	XF	Unc	BU
1992PM AA	—	—	—	—	0.75	1.00
1992PM AB	—	—	—	—	0.75	1.00
1992PM AC	—	—	—	—	0.75	1.00
1992PM AD	—	—	—	—	0.75	1.00
1992PM AE	—	—	—	—	1.00	1.25
1993PM AA	—	—	—	—	0.75	1.00
1994PM AA	—	—	—	—	0.75	1.00
1995PM AA	—	—	—	—	0.75	1.00

KM# 337a   10 PENCE
8.0457 g., 0.9250 Silver 0.2393 oz. ASW, 24.5 mm. **Ruler:** Elizabeth II **Obv:** Crowned head right **Rev:** Triskeles and value

Date	Mintage	F	VF	XF	Unc	BU
1992PM D Proof	—	Value: 13.50				

KM# 337b   10 PENCE
13.6158 g., 0.9170 Gold 0.4014 oz. AGW, 24.5 mm. **Ruler:** Elizabeth II **Obv:** Crowned head right **Rev:** Triskeles and value

Date	Mintage	F	VF	XF	Unc	BU
1992 Proof	—	Value: 450				

KM# 337c   10 PENCE
15.4725 g., 0.9500 Platinum 0.4726 oz. APW, 24.5 mm. **Ruler:** Elizabeth II **Obv:** Crowned head right **Rev:** Triskeles and value

Date	Mintage	F	VF	XF	Unc	BU
1992 Proof	—	Value: 950				

KM# 591   10 PENCE
6.5000 g., Copper-Nickel, 24.5 mm. **Ruler:** Elizabeth II **Subject:** Sports **Obv:** Crowned head right **Rev:** Sailboat divides wreath

Date	Mintage	F	VF	XF	Unc	BU
1996 AA	—	—	—	—	1.00	1.50
1997 AA	—	—	—	—	1.00	1.50

KM# 591a   10 PENCE
8.0457 g., 0.9250 Silver 0.2393 oz. ASW, 24.5 mm. **Ruler:** Elizabeth II **Subject:** Sports **Obv:** Crowned head right **Rev:** Sailboat divides wreath

Date	Mintage	F	VF	XF	Unc	BU
1996 Proof	—	Value: 22.50				

KM# 903.2   10 PENCE
6.5000 g., Copper-Nickel, 24.5 mm. **Ruler:** Elizabeth II **Obv:** Head with tiara right with small triskeles dividing legend **Rev:** Sailboat divides wreath

Date	Mintage	F	VF	XF	Unc	BU
1998PM AA	—	—	—	—	1.00	1.50
1999PM AA	—	—	—	—	1.00	1.50

KM# 903.1   10 PENCE
6.5000 g., Copper-Nickel, 24.5 mm. **Ruler:** Elizabeth II **Obv:** Head with tiara right **Rev:** Sailboat divides wreath

Date	Mintage	F	VF	XF	Unc	BU
1998PM AA	—	—	—	—	1.00	1.50

KM# 1039   10 PENCE
6.5000 g., Copper-Nickel, 24.5 mm. **Ruler:** Elizabeth II **Obv:** Head with tiara right **Rev:** Cathedral **Edge:** Reeded

Date	Mintage	F	VF	XF	Unc	BU
2000PM AA	—	—	—	—	1.00	1.50

KM# 90   20 PENCE
5.0000 g., Copper-Nickel, 21.4 mm. **Ruler:** Elizabeth II **Subject:** Medieval Norse History **Obv:** Young bust right **Rev:** Ship within small circle within artistic design with viking helmet above

Date	Mintage	F	VF	XF	Unc	BU
1982 AA	30,000	—	—	0.35	1.00	1.50
1982 AB	—	—	—	0.35	1.00	1.50
1982 AB(b)	—	—	0.50	1.00	5.00	—
1982 AC	—	—	—	0.35	1.00	1.50
1982 AD	—	—	—	0.35	1.00	1.50
1982 (b) Proof	25,000	Value: 6.00				
1982 BB Proof	—	Value: 1.50				
1982 BC Proof	—	Value: 1.50				
1983 AA	—	—	—	0.35	1.00	1.50

KM# 90a   20 PENCE
6.0000 g., 0.9250 Silver 0.1784 oz. ASW, 21.4 mm. **Ruler:** Elizabeth II **Subject:** Medieval Norse History **Obv:** Young bust right **Rev:** Ship within small circle of design with Viking helmet above

Date	Mintage	F	VF	XF	Unc	BU
1982 Proof	15,000	Value: 10.00				
1982 (b) Proof	10,000	Value: 10.00				
1983 Proof	5,000	Value: 15.00				

KM# 90b   20 PENCE
10.0000 g., 0.9170 Gold 0.2948 oz. AGW, 21.4 mm. **Ruler:** Elizabeth II **Subject:** Medieval Norse History **Obv:** Young bust right **Rev:** Ship within small circle of design with Viking helmet above

Date	Mintage	F	VF	XF	Unc	BU
1982 Proof	1,500	Value: 300				
1982 (b) Proof	500	Value: 300				
1983 Proof	—	Value: 300				

KM# 90c   20 PENCE
11.3000 g., 0.9500 Platinum 0.3451 oz. APW, 21.4 mm. **Ruler:** Elizabeth II **Subject:** Medieval Norse History **Obv:** Young bust right **Rev:** Ship within small circle of design with Viking helmet above

Date	Mintage	F	VF	XF	Unc	BU
1982 Proof	250	Value: 700				
1982 (b) Proof	500	Value: 700				
1983 Proof	—	Value: 700				

KM# 116   20 PENCE
5.0000 g., Copper-Nickel, 21.4 mm. **Ruler:** Elizabeth II **Subject:** Quincentenary of the College of Arms **Obv:** Young bust right **Rev:** Atlantic herring within designed shield

Date	Mintage	F	VF	XF	Unc	BU
1984 AA	—	—	—	0.35	1.00	1.50

KM# 116a   20 PENCE
Silver, 21.4 mm. **Ruler:** Elizabeth II **Subject:** Quincentenary of the College of Arms **Obv:** Young bust right **Rev:** Atlantic herring within designed shield

Date	Mintage	F	VF	XF	Unc	BU
1984 Proof	—	Value: 20.00				

KM# 116b   20 PENCE
5.0000 g., 0.9170 Gold 0.1474 oz. AGW, 21.4 mm. **Ruler:** Elizabeth II **Subject:** Quincentenary of the College of Arms **Obv:** Young bust right **Rev:** Atlantic herring within designed shield

Date	Mintage	F	VF	XF	Unc	BU
1984 Proof	150	Value: 175				

KM# 147   20 PENCE
5.0000 g., Copper-Nickel, 21.4 mm. **Ruler:** Elizabeth II **Obv:** Crowned head right **Rev:** Atlantic herring within designed shield

Date	Mintage	F	VF	XF	Unc	BU
1985(w) AA	—	—	—	0.35	1.00	1.50
1985 Proof	50,000	Value: 3.00				
1986 AA	—	—	—	0.35	1.00	1.50
1986 AB	—	—	—	0.35	1.00	1.50
1986 AC	—	—	—	0.35	1.00	1.50
1987 AA	—	—	—	0.35	1.00	1.50

KM# 147a   20 PENCE
5.0000 g., 0.9250 Silver 0.1487 oz. ASW, 21,4 mm. **Ruler:** Elizabeth II **Obv:** Crowned head right **Rev:** Atlantic herring within designed shield

Date	Mintage	F	VF	XF	Unc	BU
1985 Proof	10,000	Value: 8.00				

KM# 147b   20 PENCE
5.0000 g., 0.9170 Gold 0.1474 oz. AGW, 21.4 mm. **Ruler:** Elizabeth II **Obv:** Crowned head right **Rev:** Atlantic herring within designed shield

Date	Mintage	F	VF	XF	Unc	BU
1985 Proof	300	Value: 165				

KM# 147c   20 PENCE
5.0000 g., 0.9500 Platinum 0.1527 oz. APW, 21.4 mm. **Ruler:** Elizabeth II **Obv:** Crowned head right **Rev:** Atlantic herring within designed shield

Date	Mintage	F	VF	XF	Unc	BU
1985 Proof	200	Value: 325				

KM# 211   20 PENCE
5.0000 g., Copper-Nickel, 21.4 mm. **Ruler:** Elizabeth II **Obv:** Crowned head right **Rev:** Combine within sprigs

Date	Mintage	F	VF	XF	Unc	BU
1988 AA	—	—	—	—	1.00	1.50
1989 AA	—	—	—	—	1.00	1.50
1990 AA	—	—	—	—	1.00	1.50
1991 AA	—	—	—	—	1.00	1.50
1992 AA	—	—	—	—	1.00	1.50

KM# 391   20 PENCE
5.0000 g., Copper-Nickel, 21.4 mm. **Ruler:** Elizabeth II **Obv:** Crowned head right **Rev:** Combine within sprigs **Note:** Obverse and reverse design revised with border.

Date	Mintage	F	VF	XF	Unc	BU
1993 AA	—	—	—	—	1.00	1.50

Date	Mintage	F	VF	XF	Unc	BU
1994 AA	—	—	—	—	1.00	1.50
1995 AA	—	—	—	—	1.00	1.50

KM# 592   20 PENCE
5.0000 g., Copper-Nickel, 21.4 mm. **Ruler:** Elizabeth II **Subject:** Sports **Obv:** Crowned head right **Rev:** Race cars within sprigs

Date	Mintage	F	VF	XF	Unc	BU
1996 AA	—	—	—	—	1.25	1.75
1997 AA	—	—	—	—	1.25	1.75

KM# 904.1   20 PENCE
5.0000 g., Copper-Nickel, 21.4 mm. **Ruler:** Elizabeth II **Obv:** Head with tiara right with small triskeles dividing legend **Obv. Leg.:** "ELIZABETH II" **Rev:** Rally cars above sprigs **Note:** Prev. KM#904.

Date	Mintage	F	VF	XF	Unc	BU
1998PM AA	—	—	—	—	1.25	1.75

KM# 904.2   20 PENCE
5.0000 g., Copper Nickel, 21.4 mm. **Ruler:** Elizabeth II **Obv:** Head with tiara right with small triskeles dividing legend **Obv. Leg.:** ISLE OF MAN **Rev:** Rally cars above sprigs

Date	Mintage	F	VF	XF	Unc	BU
1999PM AA	—	—	—	—	1.25	1.75

KM# 1040   20 PENCE
5.0000 g., Copper-Nickel, 21.4 mm. **Ruler:** Elizabeth II **Subject:** Rushen Abbey **Obv:** Head with tiara right **Rev:** Monk writing **Edge:** Plain

Date	Mintage	F	VF	XF	Unc	BU
2000 AA	—	—	—	—	1.50	2.00

KM# 25   25 PENCE
Copper-Nickel, 38.5 mm. **Ruler:** Elizabeth II **Subject:** 25th Wedding Anniversary **Obv:** Young bust right **Rev:** Tilted shields divide date within rope wreath **Note:** Struck at the Royal Canadian Mint.

Date	Mintage	F	VF	XF	Unc	BU
1972	70,000	—	—	—	4.50	5.00

KM# 25a   25 PENCE
28.2800 g., 0.9250 Silver 0.8410 oz. ASW, 38.5 mm. **Ruler:** Elizabeth II **Obv:** Young bust right **Rev:** Tilted shields divide dates within rope wreath **Note:** Struck at the Royal Canadian Mint.

Date	Mintage	F	VF	XF	Unc	BU
1972 Proof	15,000	Value: 17.50				

KM# 31   25 PENCE
Copper-Nickel, 38.5 mm. **Ruler:** Elizabeth II **Obv:** Young bust right **Rev:** Manx cat

Date	Mintage	F	VF	XF	Unc	BU
1975	35,000	—	—	—	6.00	7.50

KM# 31a   25 PENCE
28.2800 g., 0.9250 Silver 0.8410 oz. ASW, 38.5 mm. **Ruler:** Elizabeth II **Obv:** Young bust right **Rev:** Manx cat

Date	Mintage	F	VF	XF	Unc	BU
1975	—	—	—	—	17.50	18.50
1975 Proof	30,000	Value: 20.00				

KM# 24   50 NEW PENCE
13.5000 g., Copper-Nickel, 30 mm. **Ruler:** Elizabeth II **Obv:** Young bust right **Rev:** Sailing Viking ship

Date	Mintage	F	VF	XF	Unc	BU
1971	100,000	—	—	1.00	5.00	7.50
1971 Proof	10,000	Value: 8.00				
1972	1,000	—	—	—	27.50	32.50
1973	1,000	—	—	—	27.50	32.50
1974	1,000	—	—	—	27.50	32.50
1975	227,000	—	—	1.00	5.00	7.50

KM# 24a   50 NEW PENCE
15.5000 g., 0.9250 Silver 0.4609 oz. ASW, 30 mm. **Ruler:** Elizabeth II **Obv:** Young bust right **Rev:** Sailing Viking ship

Date	Mintage	F	VF	XF	Unc	BU
1975	20,000	—	—	—	12.00	13.00

KM# 24b   50 NEW PENCE
30.4000 g., 0.9500 Platinum 0.9285 oz. APW, 30 mm. **Ruler:** Elizabeth II **Obv:** Young bust right **Rev:** Sailing Viking ship

Date	Mintage	F	VF	XF	Unc	BU
1975 Proof	600	Value: 1,750				

KM# 39   50 PENCE
13.5000 g., Copper-Nickel, 30 mm. **Ruler:** Elizabeth II **Obv:** Young bust right **Rev:** Sailing Viking ship

Date	Mintage	F	VF	XF	Unc	BU
1976	250,000	—	—	0.75	2.00	3.00
1977	50,000	—	—	0.75	2.50	3.50
1978	25,000	—	—	0.75	2.50	3.50
1978 Proof	—	Value: 4.50				
1979 (t)AA	—	—	—	0.75	3.00	4.00

KM# 39a   50 PENCE
15.5000 g., 0.9250 Silver 0.4609 oz. ASW, 30 mm. **Ruler:** Elizabeth II **Obv:** Young bust right **Rev:** Sailing Viking ship

Date	Mintage	F	VF	XF	Unc	BU
1976	20,000	—	—	—	12.00	13.00
1977 Proof	10,000	Value: 12.50				
1978	10,000	—	—	—	12.00	13.00
1979 (t) Proof	10,000	Value: 12.50				

KM# 39b   50 PENCE
30.4000 g., 0.9500 Platinum 0.9285 oz. APW, 30 mm. **Ruler:** Elizabeth II **Obv:** Young bust right **Rev:** Sailing Viking ship

Date	Mintage	F	VF	XF	Unc	BU
1976 Proof	600	Value: 1,750				
1978 Proof	600	Value: 1,750				
1979 (t) Proof	500	Value: 1,750				

KM# 51.1   50 PENCE
13.5000 g., Copper-Nickel, 30 mm. **Ruler:** Elizabeth II **Subject:** Manx Day of Tynwald, July 5 **Obv:** Young bust right **Rev:** Viking ship **Edge:** Upright with obverse on top **Edge:** H.M Q.E-II ROYAL VISIT I.O.M. JULY 1979

Date	Mintage	F	VF	XF	Unc	BU
1979 AA	50,000	—	—	—	4.50	5.00
1979 AB	—	—	—	—	4.50	5.00

KM# 51.2   50 PENCE
13.5000 g., Copper-Nickel, 30 mm. **Ruler:** Elizabeth II **Obv:** Young bust right **Rev:** Viking ship **Edge:** Lettering upright with reverse on top

Date	Mintage	F	VF	XF	Unc	BU
1979 AA	—	—	—	—	4.50	5.00
1979 AB	—	—	—	—	4.50	5.00

KM# 51.3   50 PENCE
13.5000 g., Copper-Nickel, 30 mm. **Ruler:** Elizabeth II **Obv:** Young bust right **Rev:** Viking ship **Note:** Inscription not centered in flat sections.

Date	Mintage	F	VF	XF	Unc	BU
1979 AA	—	—	—	—	4.50	5.00
1979 AB	—	—	—	—	4.50	5.00

KM# 51a   50 PENCE
15.5000 g., 0.9250 Silver 0.4609 oz. ASW, 30 mm. **Ruler:** Elizabeth II **Obv:** Young bust right **Rev:** Viking ship

Date	Mintage	F	VF	XF	Unc	BU
1979	10,000	—	—	—	10.00	12.00
1979 D Proof	5,000	Value: 15.00				
1979 E Proof	—	Value: 15.00				
1979 D Proof	5,000	Value: 15.00				

KM# 51b   50 PENCE
30.4000 g., 0.9500 Platinum 0.9285 oz. APW, 30 mm. **Ruler:** Elizabeth II **Subject:** Manx Millennium of Tynwald **Obv:** Young bust right **Rev:** Viking ship **Edge:** H.M.Q.E. II ROYAL VISIT I.O.M. JULY 5, 1979

Date	Mintage	F	VF	XF	Unc	BU
1979 Proof	500	Value: 1,750				

KM# 53   50 PENCE
13.5000 g., Copper-Nickel, 30 mm. **Ruler:** Elizabeth II **Obv:** Young bust right **Rev:** Odin's Raven, Point of Ayre lighthouse **Note:** Same as KM#51.1 with no edge lettering.

Date	Mintage	F	VF	XF	Unc	BU
1979 AA	—	—	—	—	3.00	4.00
1979 AB	—	—	—	—	3.00	4.00

KM# 53a   50 PENCE
15.5000 g., 0.9250 Silver 0.4609 oz. ASW, 30 mm.
Ruler: Elizabeth II **Obv:** Young bust right **Rev:** Odin's Raven,
Point of Ayre lighhouse

Date	Mintage	F	VF	XF	Unc	BU
1979	—	—	—	—	10.00	12.00
1979 Proof		Value: 15.00				

KM# 69   50 PENCE
13.5000 g., Copper-Nickel, 30 mm. **Ruler:** Elizabeth II
Obv: Young bust right **Obv. Leg.:** ELIZABETH THE SECOND
Edge: ODINS RAVEN VIKING EXHIBN NEW YORK 1980
Note: Same as KM#51.1, different edge lettering.

Date	Mintage	F	VF	XF	Unc	BU
1980 AA Prooflike	20,000	—	—	—	4.00	5.00
1980PM AB Prooflike	Inc. above	—	—	—	4.00	5.00
1980PM AC Prooflike	Inc. above	—	—	—	4.00	5.00

KM# 69a   50 PENCE
15.5000 g., 0.9250 Silver 0.4609 oz. ASW, 30 mm.
Ruler: Elizabeth II **Obv:** Young bust right **Obv. Leg.:** ELIZABETH
THE SECOND

Date	Mintage	F	VF	XF	Unc	BU
1980	—	—	—	—	15.00	17.00
1980 Proof	5,000	Value: 20.00				

KM# 69b   50 PENCE
26.0000 g., 0.9170 Gold 0.7665 oz. AGW, 30 mm.
Ruler: Elizabeth II **Obv:** Young bust right **Obv. Leg.:** ELIZABETH
THE SECOND **Edge:** ODINS RAVEN VIKING EXHIBN NEW
YORK 1980

Date	Mintage	F	VF	XF	Unc	BU
1980	250	—	—	—	—	750

KM# 69c   50 PENCE
30.4000 g., 0.9500 Platinum 0.9285 oz. APW, 30 mm.
Ruler: Elizabeth II **Obv:** Young bust right **Obv.Leg.:** ELIZABETH
THE SECOND

Date	Mintage	F	VF	XF	Unc	BU
1980 Proof	50	Value: 1,750				

KM# 70a   50 PENCE
15.5000 g., 0.5000 Silver 0.2492 oz. ASW, 30 mm.
Ruler: Elizabeth II **Obv:** Young bust right **Rev:** Viking longship
within design

Date	Mintage	F	VF	XF	Unc	BU
1980 Proof	10,000	Value: 10.00				
1982 (b) Proof	10,000	Value: 15.00				

KM# 70b   50 PENCE
15.5000 g., 0.9250 Silver 0.4609 oz. ASW, 30 mm.
Ruler: Elizabeth II **Obv:** Young bust right **Rev:** Viking longship
within design

Date	Mintage	F	VF	XF	Unc	BU
1981 Proof	—	Value: 17.50				
1983 Proof	5,000	Value: 17.50				

KM# 70c   50 PENCE
26.0000 g., 0.9170 Gold 0.7665 oz. AGW, 30 mm.
Ruler: Elizabeth II **Obv:** Young bust right **Rev:** Viking longship
within design

Date	Mintage	F	VF	XF	Unc	BU
1980 Proof	300	Value: 800				
1982 (b) Proof	500	Value: 800				
1983 Proof	—	Value: 800				

KM# 70d   50 PENCE
30.4000 g., 0.9500 Platinum 0.9285 oz. APW, 30 mm.
Ruler: Elizabeth II **Obv:** Young bust right **Rev:** Viking longship
within design

Date	Mintage	F	VF	XF	Unc	BU
1980 Proof	500	Value: 1,750				
1982 (b) Proof	500	Value: 1,750				
1983 Proof	—	Value: 1,750				

KM# 70.1   50 PENCE
13.5000 g., Copper-Nickel, 30 mm. **Ruler:** Elizabeth II
Obv: Young bust right **Rev:** Viking longship within design

Date	Mintage	F	VF	XF	Unc	BU
1980 AA	10,000	—	—	1.00	5.00	7.50
1980 AB	—	—	—	1.00	5.00	7.50
1980PM DD Proof		Value: 8.00				

KM# 71   50 PENCE
13.5000 g., Copper-Nickel, 30 mm. **Ruler:** Elizabeth II
Subject: Christmas 1980 **Obv:** Young bust right **Rev:** Carriage
pulled by horses, ship in background

Date	Mintage	F	VF	XF	Unc	BU
1980 AA	30,000	—	—	—	2.50	3.50
1980 AB	—	—	—	—	2.50	3.50
1980 AC	—	—	—	—	2.50	3.50
1980 AD	—	—	—	—	2.50	3.50
1980PM BC	—	—	—	—	2.50	3.50

Note: Pobjoy called this item a "Diamond finish".

KM# 71a   50 PENCE
15.5000 g., 0.9250 Silver 0.4609 oz. ASW, 30 mm.
Ruler: Elizabeth II **Obv:** Young bust right **Rev:** Carriage pulled
by horses, ship in background

Date	Mintage	F	VF	XF	Unc	BU
1980 D Proof	5,000	Value: 12.50				

KM# 71b   50 PENCE
26.0000 g., 0.9170 Gold 0.7665 oz. AGW, 30 mm.
Ruler: Elizabeth II **Subject:** Christmas 1980 **Obv:** Young bust
right **Rev:** Carriage pulled by horses, ship in background

Date	Mintage	F	VF	XF	Unc	BU
1980 Proof	250	Value: 800				

KM# 71c   50 PENCE
30.4000 g., 0.9500 Platinum 0.9285 oz. APW, 30 mm.
Ruler: Elizabeth II **Obv:** Young bust right **Rev:** Carriage pulled
by horses, ship in background

Date	Mintage	F	VF	XF	Unc	BU
1980 Proof	50	Value: 1,750				

KM# 57   50 PENCE
15.5000 g., 0.9250 Silver 0.4609 oz. ASW, 30 mm. **Ruler:**
Elizabeth II **Obv:** Young bust right **Rev:** Christmas scene with
stage coach **Note:** Mule: obverse KM#69 and reverse KM#71.

Date	Mintage	F	VF	XF	Unc	BU
1980	—	—	—	—	—	—

KM# 57a   50 PENCE
13.5000 g., Copper Nickel, 30 mm. **Ruler:** Elizabeth II **Subject:**
Christmas **Obv:** Young bust right **Rev:** Christmas scene with
stagecoach **Note:** Mule: obverse KM#69 and reverse KM#71.

Date	Mintage	F	VF	XF	Unc	BU
1980	—	—	—	—	50.00	55.00

KM# 83   50 PENCE
13.5000 g., Copper-Nickel, 30 mm. **Ruler:** Elizabeth II
Subject: Tourist Trophy Motorcycle Races **Obv:** Young bust right
Rev: Motorcyclist within sprigs

Date	Mintage	F	VF	XF	Unc	BU
1981 AA	30,000	—	—	—	3.00	4.00
1981 AB	Inc. above	—	—	—	3.00	4.00
1981PM BB Proof	Est. 30,000	—	—	—	—	—

KM# 84   50 PENCE
13.5000 g., Copper-Nickel, 30 mm. **Ruler:** Elizabeth II
Subject: Christmas 1981 **Obv:** Young bust right **Rev:** Boat,
standing figures and value

Date	Mintage	F	VF	XF	Unc	BU
1981 AA	30,000	—	—	—	3.00	4.00
1981 AB	Inc. above	—	—	—	3.00	4.00
1981PM BB Proof	30,000	Value: 7.50				
1981PM BC Proof	Inc. above	Value: 7.50				

KM# 70.2   50 PENCE
13.5000 g., Copper-Nickel **Ruler:** Elizabeth II **Obv:** Young bust
right **Rev:** Viking longship within design

Date	Mintage	F	VF	XF	Unc	BU
1981 AA	—	—	—	1.00	5.00	7.50
1982 (b)	—	—	—	1.00	5.00	7.50
1982 (b) Proof	Est. 25,000	Value: 8.00				
1982 AC	—	—	—	1.00	5.00	7.50
1983 AA	—	—	—	1.00	5.00	7.50
1983 AB	—	—	—	1.00	5.00	7.50
1984 AA	—	—	—	1.00	5.00	7.50

KM# 84a   50 PENCE
15.5000 g., 0.9250 Silver 0.4609 oz. ASW, 30 mm.
Ruler: Elizabeth II **Subject:** Christmas 1981 **Obv:** Young bust
right **Rev:** Boat, standing figures and value

Date	Mintage	F	VF	XF	Unc	BU
1981PM D Proof	5,000	Value: 12.50				

KM# 84c   50 PENCE
30.4000 g., 0.9500 Platinum 0.9285 oz. APW, 30 mm.
Ruler: Elizabeth II **Subject:** Christmas 1981 **Obv:** Young bust
right **Rev:** Boat, standing figures and value

Date	Mintage	F	VF	XF	Unc	BU
1981 Proof	—	Value: 1,750				

KM# 83a   50 PENCE
15.5000 g., 0.9250 Silver 0.4609 oz. ASW, 30 mm.
Ruler: Elizabeth II **Subject:** Tourist Trophy Motorcycle Races
Obv: Young bust right **Rev:** Motorcyclist within sprigs

Date	Mintage	F	VF	XF	Unc	BU
1981PM D Proof	5,000	Value: 15.00				

KM# 83b   50 PENCE
26.0000 g., 0.9170 Gold 0.7665 oz. AGW, 30 mm.
Ruler: Elizabeth II **Subject:** Tourist Trophy Motorcycle Races
Obv: Young bust right **Rev:** Motorcyclist within sprigs

Date	Mintage	F	VF	XF	Unc	BU
1981 Proof	250	Value: 800				

KM# 83c   50 PENCE
30.4000 g., 0.9500 Platinum 0.9285 oz. APW, 30 mm.
Ruler: Elizabeth II **Subject:** Tourist Trophy Motorcycle Races
Obv: Young bust right **Rev:** Motorcyclist within sprigs

Date	Mintage	F	VF	XF	Unc	BU
1981 Proof	50	Value: 1,750				

KM# 84b   50 PENCE
26.0000 g., 0.9170 Gold 0.7665 oz. AGW, 30 mm.
Ruler: Elizabeth II **Subject:** Christmas 1981 **Obv:** Young bust
right **Rev:** Boat, standing figures and value

Date	Mintage	F	VF	XF	Unc	BU
1981 Proof	250	Value: 800				

KM# 101   50 PENCE
13.5000 g., Copper-Nickel, 30 mm. **Ruler:** Elizabeth II
Subject: Tourist Trophy Motorcycle Races **Obv:** Young bust right
Rev: Motorcyclist within sprigs

Date	Mintage	F	VF	XF	Unc	BU
1982 AA	30,000	—	—	—	3.00	4.00
1982 Proof	—	Value: 7.50				

KM# 101a   50 PENCE
15.5000 g., 0.9250 Silver 0.4609 oz. ASW, 30 mm.
Ruler: Elizabeth II **Subject:** Tourist Trophy Motorcycle Races
Obv: Young bust right **Rev:** Motorcyclist within sprigs

Date	Mintage	F	VF	XF	Unc	BU
1982 Proof	5,000	Value: 15.00				

KM# 102   50 PENCE
13.5000 g., Copper-Nickel, 30 mm. **Ruler:** Elizabeth II **Subject:**
Christmas 1982 **Obv:** Young bust right **Rev:** Carolers around tree

Date	Mintage	F	VF	XF	Unc	BU
1982 AA	30,000	—	—	—	2.50	3.50
1982 AB	Inc. above	—	—	—	2.50	3.50
1982PM BB Proof	30,000	Value: 7.50				

KM# 102a   50 PENCE
15.5000 g., 0.9250 Silver 0.4609 oz. ASW, 30 mm.
Ruler: Elizabeth II **Subject:** Christmas 1982 **Obv:** Young bust
right **Rev:** Carolers around tree

Date	Mintage	F	VF	XF	Unc	BU
1982PM D Proof	5,000	Value: 12.50				

KM# 102b   50 PENCE
26.0000 g., 0.9170 Gold 0.7665 oz. AGW, 30 mm.
Ruler: Elizabeth II **Subject:** Christmas 1982 **Obv:** Young bust right **Rev:** Carolers around tree

Date	Mintage	F	VF	XF	Unc	BU
1982 Proof	250	Value: 800				

KM# 102c   50 PENCE
30.4000 g., 0.9500 Platinum 0.9285 oz. APW, 30 mm.
Ruler: Elizabeth II **Subject:** Christmas 1982 **Obv:** Young bust right **Rev:** Carolers around tree

Date	Mintage	F	VF	XF	Unc	BU
1982 Proof	50	Value: 1,750				

KM# 101b   50 PENCE
26.0000 g., 0.9170 Gold 0.7665 oz. AGW, 30 mm.
Ruler: Elizabeth II **Subject:** Tourist Trophy Motorcycle Races **Obv:** Young bust right **Rev:** Motorcyclist within sprigs

Date	Mintage	F	VF	XF	Unc	BU
1982 Proof	250	Value: 800				

KM# 101c   50 PENCE
30.4000 g., 0.9500 Platinum 0.9285 oz. APW, 30 mm.
Ruler: Elizabeth II **Subject:** Tourist Trophy Motorcycle Races **Obv:** Young bust right **Rev:** Motorcyclist within sprigs

Date	Mintage	F	VF	XF	Unc	BU
1982 Proof	50	Value: 1,750				

KM# 107   50 PENCE
13.5000 g., Copper-Nickel, 30 mm.   **Ruler:** Elizabeth II **Subject:** Christmas 1983 **Obv:** Young bust right **Rev:** Ford Model T driving left

Date	Mintage	F	VF	XF	Unc	BU
1983 AA	—	—	—	—	4.00	5.00
1983 AA/C	—	—	—	—	4.00	5.00
1983 AB	—	—	—	—	4.00	5.00
1983 AC	30,000	—	—	—	4.00	5.00
1983 BB Proof	—	—	—	—	—	—

KM# 107a   50 PENCE
15.5000 g., 0.9250 Silver 0.4609 oz. ASW, 30 mm.
Ruler: Elizabeth II **Series:** Christmas 1983 **Obv:** Young bust right **Rev:** Ford Model T driving left

Date	Mintage	F	VF	XF	Unc	BU
1983 Proof	5,000	Value: 12.50				

KM# 107b   50 PENCE
26.0000 g., 0.9170 Gold 0.7665 oz. AGW, 30 mm.
Ruler: Elizabeth II **Subject:** Christmas 1983 **Obv:** Young bust right **Rev:** Ford Model T driving left

Date	Mintage	F	VF	XF	Unc	BU
1983 Proof	250	Value: 800				

KM# 107c   50 PENCE
30.4000 g., 0.9500 Platinum 0.9285 oz. APW, 30 mm.
Ruler: Elizabeth II **Subject:** Christmas 1983 **Obv:** Young bust right **Rev:** Ford Model T driving left

Date	Mintage	F	VF	XF	Unc	BU
1983 Proof	50	Value: 1,750				

KM# 108   50 PENCE
13.5000 g., Copper-Nickel, 30 mm.   **Ruler:** Elizabeth II **Subject:** Tourist Trophy Motorcycle Races **Obv:** Young bust right **Rev:** Motorcyclist within sprigs

Date	Mintage	F	VF	XF	Unc	BU
1983 AA	30,000	—	—	—	5.00	6.00
1983 AB	Inc. above	—	—	—	5.00	6.00
1983 AC	Inc. above	—	—	—	5.00	6.00
1983 AD	Inc. above	—	—	—	5.00	6.00

KM# 108a   50 PENCE
15.5000 g., 0.9250 Silver 0.4609 oz. ASW, 30 mm.
Ruler: Elizabeth II **Obv:** Young bust right **Rev:** Motorcyclist within sprigs **Edge:** Tourist Trophy Motorcycle Races

Date	Mintage	F	VF	XF	Unc	BU
1983 Proof	5,000	Value: 15.00				

KM# 108b   50 PENCE
26.0000 g., 0.9170 Gold 0.7665 oz. AGW, 30 mm.
Ruler: Elizabeth II **Subject:** Tourist Trophy Motorcycle Races **Obv:** Young bust right **Rev:** Motorcyclist within sprigs

Date	Mintage	F	VF	XF	Unc	BU
1983 Proof	250	Value: 800				

KM# 108c   50 PENCE
30.4000 g., 0.9500 Platinum 0.9285 oz. APW, 30 mm.
Ruler: Elizabeth II **Subject:** Tourist Trophy Motorcycle Races **Obv:** Young bust right **Rev:** Motorcyclist within sprigs

Date	Mintage	F	VF	XF	Unc	BU
1983 Proof	50	Value: 1,750				

KM# 125   50 PENCE
13.5000 g., Copper-Nickel, 30 mm.   **Ruler:** Elizabeth II **Subject:** Quincentenary of the College of Arms **Obv:** Young bust right **Rev:** Viking longship on shield

Date	Mintage	F	VF	XF	Unc	BU
1984 AA	—	—	—	—	5.00	6.00
1984 AB	—	—	—	—	5.00	6.00

KM# 125a   50 PENCE
15.5000 g., 0.9250 Silver 0.4609 oz. ASW, 30 mm.
Ruler: Elizabeth II **Subject:** Quincentenary of the College of Arms **Obv:** Young bust right **Rev:** Viking longship on shield

Date	Mintage	F	VF	XF	Unc	BU
1984 Proof	—	Value: 15.00				

KM# 125b   50 PENCE
26.0000 g., 0.9170 Gold 0.7665 oz. AGW, 30 mm.
Ruler: Elizabeth II **Subject:** Quincentenary of the College of Arms **Obv:** Young bust right **Rev:** Viking longship on shield

Date	Mintage	F	VF	XF	Unc	BU
1984 Proof	150	Value: 800				

KM# 126   50 PENCE
13.5000 g., Copper-Nickel, 30 mm.   **Ruler:** Elizabeth II **Subject:** Tourist Trophy Motorcycle Races **Obv:** Young bust right **Rev:** Motorcyclists within sprigs

Date	Mintage	F	VF	XF	Unc	BU
1984 AA	30,000	—	—	—	5.00	6.00

KM# 126a   50 PENCE
15.5000 g., 0.9250 Silver 0.4609 oz. ASW, 30 mm.
Ruler: Elizabeth II **Subject:** Tourist Trophy Motorcyle Races **Obv:** Young bust right **Rev:** Motorcyclists within sprigs

Date	Mintage	F	VF	XF	Unc	BU
1984 Proof	5,000	Value: 15.00				

KM# 126b   50 PENCE
26.0000 g., 0.9170 Gold 0.7665 oz. AGW, 30 mm.
Ruler: Elizabeth II **Subject:** Tourist Trophy Motorcycle Races **Obv:** Young bust right **Rev:** Motorcyclists within sprigs

Date	Mintage	F	VF	XF	Unc	BU
1984 Proof	250	Value: 800				

KM# 126c   50 PENCE
30.4000 g., 0.9500 Platinum 0.9285 oz. APW, 30 mm.
Ruler: Elizabeth II **Subject:** Tourist Trophy Motorcycle Races **Obv:** Young bust right **Rev:** Motorcyclists within sprigs

Date	Mintage	F	VF	XF	Unc	BU
1984 Proof	50	Value: 1,750				

KM# 127   50 PENCE
13.5000 g., Copper-Nickel, 30 mm.   **Ruler:** Elizabeth II **Subject:** Christmas 1984 **Obv:** Young bust right **Rev:** Train and standing figures

Date	Mintage	F	VF	XF	Unc	BU
1984 AA	—	—	—	—	5.00	6.00
1984 AB	—	—	—	—	5.00	6.00
1984 AC	—	—	—	—	5.00	6.00
1984 AD	—	—	—	—	5.00	6.00
1984 BB Proof	30,000	Value: 8.00				

KM# 127a   50 PENCE
15.5000 g., 0.9250 Silver 0.4609 oz. ASW, 30 mm.
Ruler: Elizabeth II **Subject:** Christmas 1984 **Obv:** Young bust right **Rev:** Train and standing figures

Date	Mintage	F	VF	XF	Unc	BU
1984 Proof	—	Value: 25.00				

KM# 127b   50 PENCE
26.0000 g., 0.9170 Gold 0.7665 oz. AGW, 30 mm.
Ruler: Elizabeth II **Subject:** Christmas 1984 **Obv:** Young bust right **Rev:** Train and standing figures

Date	Mintage	F	VF	XF	Unc	BU
1984 Proof	250	Value: 800				

KM# 127c   50 PENCE
30.4000 g., 0.9500 Platinum 0.9285 oz. APW, 30 mm. **Ruler:** Elizabeth II **Subject:** Christmas 1984 **Obv:** Young bust right **Rev:** Train and standing figures

Date	Mintage	F	VF	XF	Unc	BU
1984 Proof	—	Value: 1,750				

KM# 148   50 PENCE
13.5000 g., Copper-Nickel, 30 mm.   **Ruler:** Elizabeth II **Obv:** Crowned head right **Rev:** Viking longship on shield

Date	Mintage	F	VF	XF	Unc	BU
1985(w) AA	—	—	—	—	5.00	6.00
1985(w) AB	—	—	—	—	5.00	6.00
1985 (w) Proof	50,000	Value: 8.00				
1986 AA	—	—	—	—	5.00	6.00
1986 AB	—	—	—	—	5.00	6.00
1987 AA	—	—	—	—	5.00	6.00

KM# 148a   50 PENCE
15.5000 g., 0.9250 Silver 0.4609 oz. ASW, 30 mm.
Ruler: Elizabeth II **Obv:** Crowned head right **Rev:** Viking longship on shield

Date	Mintage	F	VF	XF	Unc	BU
1985 Proof	Est. 10,000	Value: 15.00				

KM# 148b   50 PENCE
26.0000 g., 0.9170 Gold 0.7665 oz. AGW, 30 mm.
Ruler: Elizabeth II **Obv:** Crowned head right **Rev:** Viking longship on shield

Date	Mintage	F	VF	XF	Unc	BU
1985 Proof	Est. 300	Value: 800				

KM# 148c   50 PENCE
30.4000 g., 0.9500 Platinum 0.9285 oz. APW, 30 mm.
Ruler: Elizabeth II **Obv:** Crowned head right **Rev:** Viking longship on shield

Date	Mintage	F	VF	XF	Unc	BU
1985 Proof	Est. 200	Value: 1,750				

KM# 158   50 PENCE
13.5000 g., Copper-Nickel, 30 mm.   **Ruler:** Elizabeth II **Subject:** Christmas 1985, commemorates first Christmas air mail of 1935 **Obv:** Crowned head right **Rev:** Airplanes

Date	Mintage	F	VF	XF	Unc	BU
1985 AA	—	—	—	—	3.50	4.50
1985 AB	—	—	—	—	3.50	4.50
1985 BB	—	—	—	—	3.50	4.50
1985 Proof	—	Value: 9.50				

KM# 158a   50 PENCE
15.5000 g., 0.9250 Silver 0.4609 oz. ASW, 30 mm.
Ruler: Elizabeth II **Subject:** Christmas 1985 **Obv:** Crowned head right **Rev:** Airplanes

Date	Mintage	F	VF	XF	Unc	BU
1985 Proof	5,000	Value: 20.00				

KM# 158b   50 PENCE
26.0000 g., 0.9170 Gold 0.7665 oz. AGW, 30 mm.
Ruler: Elizabeth II **Subject:** Christmas 1985 **Obv:** Crowned head right **Rev:** Airplanes

Date	Mintage	F	VF	XF	Unc	BU
1985 Proof	Est. 250	Value: 800				

KM# 158c   50 PENCE
30.4000 g., 0.9500 Platinum 0.9285 oz. APW, 30 mm.
Ruler: Elizabeth II **Subject:** Christmas 1985 **Obv:** Crowned head right **Rev:** Airplanes

Date	Mintage	F	VF	XF	Unc	BU
1985 Proof	—	Value: 1,750				

KM# 172   50 PENCE
13.5000 g., Copper-Nickel, 30 mm. **Ruler:** Elizabeth II
Subject: Christmas 1986 **Obv:** Crowned head right **Rev:** Horse-drawn tram

Date	Mintage	F	VF	XF	Unc	BU
1986 AA	—	—	—	—	3.50	4.50
1986 AB	—	—	—	—	3.50	4.50
1986 Proof	— Value: 9.50					

KM# 172a   50 PENCE
15.5000 g., 0.9250 Silver 0.4609 oz. ASW, 30 mm.
Ruler: Elizabeth II **Subject:** Christmas 1986 **Obv:** Crowned head right **Rev:** Horse-drawn tram

Date	Mintage	F	VF	XF	Unc	BU
1986 Proof	Est. 5,000 Value: 20.00					

KM# 172b   50 PENCE
26.0000 g., 0.9170 Gold 0.7665 oz. AGW, 30 mm.
Ruler: Elizabeth II **Subject:** Christmas 1986 **Obv:** Crowned head right **Rev:** Horse-drawn tram

Date	Mintage	F	VF	XF	Unc	BU
1986 Proof	— Value: 800					

KM# 190   50 PENCE
13.5000 g., Copper-Nickel, 30 mm. **Ruler:** Elizabeth II
Subject: Christmas 1987 **Obv:** Crowned head right **Rev:** Bus and standing figures

Date	Mintage	F	VF	XF	Unc	BU
1987 AA	Est. 30,000	—	—	—	2.50	3.50
1987 D		—	—	—	2.50	3.50
1987 Proof	— Value: 7.50					

KM# 190a   50 PENCE
15.5000 g., 0.9250 Silver 0.4609 oz. ASW, 30 mm.
Ruler: Elizabeth II **Subject:** Christmas 1987 **Obv:** Crowned head right **Rev:** Bus and standing figures

Date	Mintage	F	VF	XF	Unc	BU
1987 Proof	Est. 5,000 Value: 20.00					

KM# 190b   50 PENCE
26.0000 g., 0.9170 Gold 0.7665 oz. AGW, 30 mm.
Ruler: Elizabeth II **Subject:** Christmas 1987 **Obv:** Crowned head right **Rev:** Bus and standing figures

Date	Mintage	F	VF	XF	Unc	BU
1987 Proof	Est. 250 Value: 800					

KM# 190c   50 PENCE
30.4000 g., 0.9500 Platinum 0.9285 oz. APW, 30 mm.
Ruler: Elizabeth II **Subject:** Christmas 1987 **Obv:** Crowned head right **Rev:** Bus and standing figures

Date	Mintage	F	VF	XF	Unc	BU
1987 Proof	Est. 50 Value: 1,750					

KM# 212   50 PENCE
13.5000 g., Copper-Nickel, 30 mm. **Ruler:** Elizabeth II
Obv: Crowned head right **Rev:** Computer

Date	Mintage	F	VF	XF	Unc	BU
1988 AA	—	—	—	—	5.00	6.00
1989 AA	—	—	—	—	5.00	6.00
1990 AA	—	—	—	—	5.00	6.00
1991 AA	—	—	—	—	5.00	6.00
1992 AA	—	—	—	—	5.00	6.00
1993 AA	—	—	—	—	5.00	6.00
1994 AA	—	—	—	—	5.00	6.00
1995 AA	—	—	—	—	5.00	6.00
1997 AA	—	—	—	—	5.00	6.00

KM# 244   50 PENCE
13.5000 g., Copper-Nickel, 30 mm. **Ruler:** Elizabeth II
Subject: Christmas 1988 **Obv:** Crowned head right **Rev:** Motorbike and sidecar

Date	Mintage	F	VF	XF	Unc	BU
1988 AA	—	—	—	—	2.50	3.50
1988 BA	—	—	—	—	2.50	3.50
1988 BB Proof	— Value: 6.50					

KM# 244a   50 PENCE
15.5000 g., 0.9250 Silver 0.4609 oz. ASW, 30 mm.
Ruler: Elizabeth II **Subject:** Christmas 1988 **Obv:** Crowned head right **Rev:** Motorbike and sidecar

Date	Mintage	F	VF	XF	Unc	BU
1988 Proof	— Value: 20.00					

KM# 244b   50 PENCE
26.0000 g., 0.9170 Gold 0.7665 oz. AGW, 30 mm.
Ruler: Elizabeth II **Subject:** Christmas 1988 **Obv:** Crowned head right **Rev:** Motorbike and sidecar

Date	Mintage	F	VF	XF	Unc	BU
1988 Proof	— Value: 800					

KM# 244c   50 PENCE
30.4000 g., 0.9500 Platinum 0.9285 oz. APW, 30 mm.
Ruler: Elizabeth II **Subject:** Christmas 1988 **Obv:** Crowned head right **Rev:** Motorbike and sidecar

Date	Mintage	F	VF	XF	Unc	BU
1988 Proof	— Value: 1,750					

KM# 259   50 PENCE
13.5000 g., Copper-Nickel, 30 mm. **Ruler:** Elizabeth II **Subject:** Christmas 1989 **Obv:** Crowned head right **Rev:** Electric trolley car

Date	Mintage	F	VF	XF	Unc	BU
1989 AA	—	—	—	—	2.50	3.50
1989 BB Proof	— Value: 6.50					

KM# 259a   50 PENCE
15.5000 g., 0.9250 Silver 0.4609 oz. ASW, 30 mm.
Ruler: Elizabeth II **Subject:** Christmas 1989 **Obv:** Crowned head right **Rev:** Electric trolly car

Date	Mintage	F	VF	XF	Unc	BU
1989 Proof	— Value: 40.00					

KM# 259b   50 PENCE
26.0000 g., 0.9170 Gold 0.7665 oz. AGW, 30 mm.
Ruler: Elizabeth II **Subject:** Christmas 1989 **Obv:** Crowned head right **Rev:** Electric trolley car

Date	Mintage	F	VF	XF	Unc	BU
1989 Proof	— Value: 800					

KM# 259c   50 PENCE
30.4000 g., 0.9500 Platinum 0.9285 oz. APW, 30 mm.
Ruler: Elizabeth II **Subject:** Christmas 1989 **Obv:** Crowned head right **Rev:** Electric trolley car

Date	Mintage	F	VF	XF	Unc	BU
1989 Proof	— Value: 1,750					

KM# 282   50 PENCE
13.5000 g., Copper-Nickel, 30 mm. **Ruler:** Elizabeth II
Subject: Christmas 1990 **Obv:** Crowned head right **Rev:** Ship and standing figures

Date	Mintage	F	VF	XF	Unc	BU
1990 AA	—	—	—	—	2.50	3.50
1990 AB	—	—	—	—	2.50	3.50
1990 Proof	30,000 Value: 6.50					

KM# 282a   50 PENCE
15.5000 g., 0.9250 Silver 0.4609 oz. ASW, 30 mm.
Ruler: Elizabeth II **Subject:** Christmas 1990 **Obv:** Crowned head right **Rev:** Ship and standing figures

Date	Mintage	F	VF	XF	Unc	BU
1990 Proof	5,000 Value: 40.00					

KM# 282b   50 PENCE
26.0000 g., 0.9170 Gold 0.7665 oz. AGW, 30 mm.
Ruler: Elizabeth II **Subject:** Christmas 1990 **Obv:** Crowned head right **Rev:** Ship and standing figures

Date	Mintage	F	VF	XF	Unc	BU
1990 Proof	250 Value: 800					

KM# 282c   50 PENCE
30.4000 g., 0.9500 Platinum 0.9285 oz. APW, 30 mm.
Ruler: Elizabeth II **Subject:** Christmas 1990 **Obv:** Crowned head right **Rev:** Ship and standing figures

Date	Mintage	F	VF	XF	Unc	BU
1990 Proof	50 Value: 1,750					

KM# 303   50 PENCE
13.5000 g., Copper-Nickel, 30 mm. **Ruler:** Elizabeth II
Subject: Christmas 1991 **Obv:** Crowned head right **Rev:** Nativity scene

Date	Mintage	F	VF	XF	Unc	BU
1991 AA	—	—	—	—	5.00	6.00
1991 Proof	30,000 Value: 8.00					

KM# 303a   50 PENCE
15.5000 g., 0.9250 Silver 0.4609 oz. ASW, 30 mm.
Ruler: Elizabeth II **Subject:** Christmas 1991 **Obv:** Crowned head right **Rev:** Nativity scene

Date	Mintage	F	VF	XF	Unc	BU
1991 Proof	5,000 Value: 40.00					

KM# 303b   50 PENCE
26.0000 g., 0.9170 Gold 0.7665 oz. AGW, 30 mm.
Ruler: Elizabeth II **Subject:** Christmas 1991 **Obv:** Crowned head right **Rev:** Nativity scene

Date	Mintage	F	VF	XF	Unc	BU
1991 Proof	250 Value: 800					

KM# 303c   50 PENCE
30.4000 g., 0.9500 Platinum 0.9285 oz. APW, 30 mm.
Ruler: Elizabeth II **Subject:** Christmas 1991 **Obv:** Crowned head right **Rev:** Nativity scene

Date	Mintage	F	VF	XF	Unc	BU
1991 Proof	50 Value: 1,750					

KM# 335   50 PENCE
13.5000 g., Copper-Nickel, 30 mm. **Ruler:** Elizabeth II
Subject: Christmas 1992 **Obv:** Crowned head right
Rev: Newspaper boy hawking the Manx Mercury

Date	Mintage	F	VF	XF	Unc	BU
1992 AA	—	—	—	—	2.50	3.50
1992 Proof	— Value: 6.50					

KM# 335a   50 PENCE
15.5000 g., 0.9250 Silver 0.4609 oz. ASW, 30 mm.
Ruler: Elizabeth II **Subject:** Christmas 1992 **Obv:** Crowned head right **Rev:** Newspaper boy hawking the Manx Mercury

Date	Mintage	F	VF	XF	Unc	BU
1992 Proof	5,000 Value: 40.00					

KM# 335b   50 PENCE
26.0000 g., 0.9170 Gold 0.7665 oz. AGW, 30 mm.
Ruler: Elizabeth II **Subject:** Christmas 1992 **Obv:** Crowned head right **Rev:** Newspaper boy hawking the Manx Mercury

Date	Mintage	F	VF	XF	Unc	BU
1992 Proof	250 Value: 800					

KM# 335c   50 PENCE
30.4000 g., 0.9500 Platinum 0.9285 oz. APW, 30 mm.
Ruler: Elizabeth II **Subject:** Christmas 1992 **Obv:** Crowned head right **Rev:** Newspaper boy hawking the Manx Mercury

Date	Mintage	F	VF	XF	Unc	BU
1992 Proof	50 Value: 1,750					

KM# 356 50 PENCE
13.5000 g., Copper-Nickel, 30 mm. **Ruler:** Elizabeth II
Subject: Christmas 1993 **Obv:** Crowned head right **Rev:** Framed
nativity scene

Date	Mintage	F	VF	XF	Unc	BU
1993 AA	—	—	—	—	2.50	3.50
1993 D	—	—	—	—	2.50	3.50
1993 Proof	30,000	Value: 6.50				

KM# 356a 50 PENCE
15.5000 g., 0.9250 Silver 0.4609 oz. ASW, 30 mm.
Ruler: Elizabeth II **Subject:** Christmas 1993 **Obv:** Crowned head
right **Rev:** Framed nativity scene

Date	Mintage	F	VF	XF	Unc	BU
1993 Proof	Est. 5,000	Value: 40.00				

KM# 356b 50 PENCE
26.0000 g., 0.9170 Gold 0.7665 oz. AGW, 30 mm.
Ruler: Elizabeth II **Subject:** Christmas 1993 **Obv:** Crowned head
right **Rev:** Framed nativity scene

Date	Mintage	F	VF	XF	Unc	BU
1993 Proof	Est. 250	Value: 800				

KM# 356c 50 PENCE
30.4000 g., 0.9500 Platinum 0.9285 oz. APW, 30 mm.
Ruler: Elizabeth II **Subject:** Christmas 1993 **Obv:** Crowned head
right **Rev:** Framed nativity scene

Date	Mintage	F	VF	XF	Unc	BU
1993 Proof	Est. 50	Value: 1,750				

KM# 425 50 PENCE
13.5000 g., Copper-Nickel, 30 mm. **Ruler:** Elizabeth II
Subject: Christmas 1994 **Obv:** Crowned head right **Rev:** Two
young boys with pole **Edge:** Smooth

Date	Mintage	F	VF	XF	Unc	BU
1994 AA	—	—	—	—	2.50	3.50

KM# 425a 50 PENCE
15.5000 g., 0.9250 Silver 0.4609 oz. ASW, 30 mm.
Ruler: Elizabeth II **Subject:** Christmas 1994 **Obv:** Crowned head
right **Rev:** Two young boys with pole

Date	Mintage	F	VF	XF	Unc	BU
1994 Proof	—	Value: 40.00				

KM# 456 50 PENCE
13.5000 g., Copper-Nickel, 30 mm. **Ruler:** Elizabeth II
Subject: Legislative Building Centenary **Obv:** Crowned head
right **Rev:** Building **Edge:** Smooth

Date	Mintage	F	VF	XF	Unc	BU
1994 AA	—	—	—	—	3.00	4.00

KM# 456a 50 PENCE
15.5000 g., 0.9250 Silver 0.4609 oz. ASW, 30 mm.
Ruler: Elizabeth II **Subject:** Legislative Building Centenary
Obv: Crowned head right **Rev:** Building

Date	Mintage	F	VF	XF	Unc	BU
1994 Proof	—	Value: 40.00				

KM# 521 50 PENCE
13.5000 g., Copper-Nickel, 30 mm. **Ruler:** Elizabeth II
Subject: Christmas 1995 **Obv:** Crowned head right
Rev: Sledding scene **Edge:** Smooth

Date	Mintage	F	VF	XF	Unc	BU
1995 AA	Est. 30,000	—	—	—	2.50	3.50

KM# 521a 50 PENCE
15.5000 g., 0.9250 Silver 0.4609 oz. ASW, 30 mm.
Ruler: Elizabeth II **Subject:** Christmas 1995 **Obv:** Crowned head
right **Rev:** Sledding scene

Date	Mintage	F	VF	XF	Unc	BU
1995 Proof	Est. 5,000	Value: 40.00				

KM# 521b 50 PENCE
26.0000 g., 0.9170 Gold 0.7665 oz. AGW, 30 mm.
Ruler: Elizabeth II **Subject:** Christmas 1995 **Obv:** Crowned head
right **Rev:** Sledding scene

Date	Mintage	F	VF	XF	Unc	BU
1995 Proof	Est. 250	Value: 800				

KM# 593 50 PENCE
13.5000 g., Copper-Nickel, 30 mm. **Ruler:** Elizabeth II **Subject:**
Sports **Obv:** Crowned head right **Rev:** Motorcyclists **Edge:** Smooth

Date	Mintage	F	VF	XF	Unc	BU
1996 AA	—	—	—	—	3.00	4.00
1997 AA	—	—	—	—	3.00	4.00

KM# 694 50 PENCE
13.5000 g., Copper-Nickel, 30 mm. **Ruler:** Elizabeth II
Subject: Christmas 1996 **Obv:** Crowned head right **Rev:**
Children throwing snowballs in front of church **Edge:** Smooth

Date	Mintage	F	VF	XF	Unc	BU
1996 AA	Est. 30,000	—	—	—	5.00	6.00

KM# 694a 50 PENCE
15.5000 g., 0.9250 Silver 0.4609 oz. ASW, 30 mm.
Ruler: Elizabeth II **Subject:** Christmas 1996 **Obv:** Crowned head
right **Rev:** Children throwing snowballs in front of church

Date	Mintage	F	VF	XF	Unc	BU
1996 Proof	Est. 5,000	Value: 40.00				

KM# 694b 50 PENCE
26.0000 g., 0.9170 Gold 0.7665 oz. AGW, 30 mm.
Ruler: Elizabeth II **Subject:** Christmas 1996 **Obv:** Crowned head
right **Rev:** Children throwing snowballs in front of church

Date	Mintage	F	VF	XF	Unc	BU
1996 Proof	Est. 250	Value: 800				

KM# 794 50 PENCE
8.0000 g., Copper-Nickel, 27.3 mm. **Ruler:** Elizabeth II
Subject: Christmas 1997 **Obv:** Crowned head right **Rev:** Cameo
at lower left of figures on book **Edge:** Smooth

Date	Mintage	F	VF	XF	Unc	BU
1997	Est. 30,000	—	—	—	2.75	3.75

KM# 794a 50 PENCE
8.0000 g., 0.9250 Silver 0.2379 oz. ASW, 27.3 mm.
Ruler: Elizabeth II **Subject:** Christmas 1987 **Obv:** Crowned head
right **Rev:** Cameo at lower left of figures on book

Date	Mintage	F	VF	XF	Unc	BU
1997 Proof	Est. 5,000	Value: 40.00				

KM# 794b 50 PENCE
8.0000 g., 0.9160 Gold 0.2356 oz. AGW, 27.3 mm.
Ruler: Elizabeth II **Subject:** Christmas 1997 **Obv:** Crowned head
right **Rev:** Cameo to lower left of figures on book

Date	Mintage	F	VF	XF	Unc	BU
1997 Proof	250	Value: 500				

KM# 806 50 PENCE
8.0000 g., Copper Nickel, 27.3 mm. **Ruler:** Elizabeth II **Obv:**
Crowned head right **Rev:** Two motorcycle racers **Edge:** Plain

Date	Mintage	F	VF	XF	Unc	BU
1997PM AA	—	—	—	—	3.00	4.00

KM# 806a 50 PENCE
8.0000 g., 0.9250 Silver 0.2379 oz. ASW, 27.3 mm.
Ruler: Elizabeth II **Obv:** Crowned head right **Rev:** Two
motorcycle racers **Edge:** Plain

Date	Mintage	F	VF	XF	Unc	BU
1997PM Proof	5,000	Value: 35.00				

KM# 806b 50 PENCE
8.0000 g., 0.9999 Gold 0.2572 oz. AGW, 27.3 mm.
Ruler: Elizabeth II **Obv:** Crowned head right **Rev:** Two
motorcycle racers **Edge:** Plain

Date	Mintage	F	VF	XF	Unc	BU
1997PM Proof	250	Value: 500				

KM# 905 50 PENCE
8.0000 g., Copper-Nickel, 27.3 mm. **Ruler:** Elizabeth II
Obv: Head with tiara right **Rev:** Motorcyclists **Edge:** Smooth

Date	Mintage	F	VF	XF	Unc	BU
1998PM AA	—	—	—	—	3.00	4.00
1999PM AA	—	—	—	—	3.00	4.00

KM# 905a 50 PENCE
8.0000 g., 0.9250 Silver 0.2379 oz. ASW, 27.3 mm. **Ruler:**
Elizabeth II **Obv:** Head with tiara right **Rev:** Two motorcycle racers

Date	Mintage	F	VF	XF	Unc	BU
1998PM Proof	5,000	Value: 35.00				

KM# 905b 50 PENCE
8.0000 g., 0.9999 Gold 0.2572 oz. AGW, 27.3 mm. **Ruler:**
Elizabeth II **Obv:** Head with tiara right **Rev:** Two motorcycle racers

Date	Mintage	F	VF	XF	Unc	BU
1998PM Proof	Est. 250	Value: 500				

KM# 908 50 PENCE
Copper-Nickel, 27.3 mm. **Ruler:** Elizabeth II **Subject:** Christmas
1998 **Obv:** Head with tiara right **Rev:** Kitchen scene **Edge:** Smooth

Date	Mintage	F	VF	XF	Unc	BU
1998PM	Est. 30,000	—	—	—	3.00	4.00

KM# 908a 50 PENCE
8.0000 g., 0.9250 Silver 0.2379 oz. ASW, 27.3 mm.
Ruler: Elizabeth II **Subject:** Christmas 1998 **Obv:** Head with tiara
right **Rev:** Kitchen scene

Date	Mintage	F	VF	XF	Unc	BU
1998 Proof	5,000	Value: 35.00				

KM# 908b 50 PENCE
8.0000 g., 0.9167 Gold 0.2358 oz. AGW, 27.3 mm.
Ruler: Elizabeth II **Subject:** Christmas 1998 **Obv:** Head with tiara
right **Rev:** Kitchen scene

Date	Mintage	F	VF	XF	Unc	BU
1998 Proof	250	Value: 500				

KM# 993 50 PENCE
Copper-Nickel, 27.3 mm. **Ruler:** Elizabeth II **Obv:** Head with tiara right **Rev:** Motorcyclist within sprigs **Edge:** Smooth

Date	Mintage	F	VF	XF	Unc	BU
1999PM AA	—	—	—	—	3.00	4.00

KM# 993a 50 PENCE
8.0000 g., 0.9250 Silver 0.2379 oz. ASW, 27.3 mm.
Ruler: Elizabeth II **Obv:** Head with tiara right **Rev:** Motorcyclist within sprigs

Date	Mintage	F	VF	XF	Unc	BU
1999 Proof	Est. 5,000	Value: 35.00				

KM# 993b 50 PENCE
8.0000 g., 0.9160 Gold 0.2356 oz. AGW, 27.3 mm.
Ruler: Elizabeth II **Obv:** Head with tiara right **Rev:** Motorcyclist within sprigs

Date	Mintage	F	VF	XF	Unc	BU
1999 Proof	Est. 250	Value: 500				

KM# 1011 50 PENCE
8.0000 g., Copper-Nickel, 27.3 mm. **Ruler:** Elizabeth II **Subject:** Christmas 1999 **Obv:** Head with tiara right **Rev:** Tree decorating scene **Edge:** Smooth

Date	Mintage	F	VF	XF	Unc	BU
1999 AA	Est. 30,000	—	—	—	3.00	4.00

KM# 1011a 50 PENCE
8.0000 g., 0.9250 Silver 0.2379 oz. ASW, 27.3 mm.
Ruler: Elizabeth II **Subject:** Christmas 1999 **Obv:** Head with tiara right **Rev:** Tree decorating scene

Date	Mintage	F	VF	XF	Unc	BU
1999 Proof	Est. 5,000	Value: 35.00				

KM# 1011b 50 PENCE
8.0000 g., 0.9160 Gold 0.2356 oz. AGW, 27.3 mm.
Ruler: Elizabeth II **Subject:** Christmas 1999 **Obv:** Head with tiara right **Rev:** Tree decorating scene

Date	Mintage	F	VF	XF	Unc	BU
1999 Proof	Est. 250	Value: 500				

KM# 1041 50 PENCE
8.0000 g., Copper-Nickel, 27.3 mm. **Ruler:** Elizabeth II **Obv:** Head with tiara right **Rev:** Stylized crucifix **Edge:** Plain

Date	Mintage	F	VF	XF	Unc	BU
2000PM AA	—	—	—	—	2.25	2.75

KM# 1050 50 PENCE
8.0000 g., Copper-Nickel, 27.3 mm. **Ruler:** Elizabeth II **Obv:** Head with tiara right **Rev:** Seated figure at desk **Edge:** Plain

Date	Mintage	F	VF	XF	Unc	BU
2000 BB	30,000	—	—	—	7.00	8.00

KM# 1050a 50 PENCE
8.0000 g., 0.9250 Silver 0.2379 oz. ASW, 27.3 mm.
Ruler: Elizabeth II **Obv:** Head with tiara right **Rev:** Seated figure at desk **Edge:** Plain

Date	Mintage	F	VF	XF	Unc	BU
2000 Proof	5,000	Value: 35.00				

KM# 1050b 50 PENCE
8.0000 g., 0.9160 Gold 0.2356 oz. AGW, 27.3 mm.
Ruler: Elizabeth II **Obv:** Head with tiara right **Rev:** Seated figure at desk **Edge:** Plain

Date	Mintage	F	VF	XF	Unc	BU
2000 Proof	250	Value: 500				

KM# 15 1/2 SOVEREIGN (1/2 Pound)
3.9940 g., 0.9170 Gold 0.1177 oz. AGW **Ruler:** Elizabeth II **Subject:** 200th Anniversary of Acquisition **Obv:** Crowned bust right **Rev:** Triskeles on shield within rope wreath

Date	Mintage	F	VF	XF	Unc	BU
1965	1,500	—	—	—	115	125

KM# 15a 1/2 SOVEREIGN (1/2 Pound)
4.0000 g., 0.9800 Gold 0.1260 oz. AGW **Ruler:** Elizabeth II **Subject:** 200th Anniversary of Acquisition **Obv:** Crowned bust right **Rev:** Triskeles on shield within rope wreath

Date	Mintage	F	VF	XF	Unc	BU
1965 Proof	1,000	Value: 130				

KM# 26 1/2 SOVEREIGN (1/2 Pound)
3.9813 g., 0.9170 Gold 0.1174 oz. AGW **Ruler:** Elizabeth II **Obv:** Young bust right **Rev:** Armored equestrian

Date	Mintage	F	VF	XF	Unc	BU
1973 A	14,000	—	—	—	115	125
1973 Proof	1,250	Value: 135				
1974 A	6,566	—	—	—	115	125
1974 B	Inc. above	—	—	—	115	125
1974 Proof	2,500	Value: 135				
1975 A	1,956	—	—	—	115	125
1975 B	Inc. above	—	—	—	115	125
1975 Proof	—	Value: 135				
1976 A	2,558	—	—	—	115	125
1976 B	Inc. above	—	—	—	115	125
1976 Proof	—	Value: 135				
1977 A	—	—	—	—	115	125
1977 B	—	—	—	—	115	125
1977 Proof	1,250	Value: 135				
1978 Proof	1,250	Value: 135				
1979 (t) A	8,000	—	—	—	115	125
1979 (t) B	Inc. above	—	—	—	115	125
1979 (t) Proof	30,000	Value: 135				
1980 A	—	—	—	—	—	—
1980 B	—	—	—	—	—	—
1980 (m) Proof	7,500	Value: 135				
1980 (v) Proof	—	Value: 135				
1982 (b)	40,000	—	—	—	115	125
1982 (b) Proof	30,000	Value: 135				

KM# 85 1/2 SOVEREIGN (1/2 Pound)
3.9813 g., 0.9170 Gold 0.1174 oz. AGW **Ruler:** Elizabeth II **Subject:** Wedding of Prince Charles and Lady Diana **Obv:** Young bust right **Rev:** Portraits of Royal Couple, joined shields

Date	Mintage	F	VF	XF	Unc	BU
1981 Proof	30,000	Value: 125				

KM# 260 1/2 SOVEREIGN (1/2 Pound)
3.9813 g., 0.9170 Gold 0.1174 oz. AGW **Ruler:** Elizabeth II **Obv:** Young bust right **Rev:** Four crowned shields

Date	Mintage	F	VF	XF	Unc	BU
1984	20	—	—	—	200	210
1984 Proof	20	Value: 220				

KM# 264 1/2 SOVEREIGN (1/2 Pound)
3.9813 g., 0.9170 Gold 0.1174 oz. AGW **Ruler:** Elizabeth II **Obv:** Crowned head right **Rev:** Four crowned shields

Date	Mintage	F	VF	XF	Unc	BU
1988 Proof	5,879	Value: 120				

KM# 16 SOVEREIGN (Pound)
7.9881 g., 0.9170 Gold 0.2355 oz. AGW **Ruler:** Elizabeth II **Subject:** 200th Anniversary of Acquisition **Obv:** Crowned bust right **Rev:** Triskeles on shield within rope wreath

Date	Mintage	F	VF	XF	Unc	BU
1965	2,000	—	—	—	225	235

KM# 16a SOVEREIGN (Pound)
8.0000 g., 0.9800 Gold 0.2521 oz. AGW **Ruler:** Elizabeth II **Subject:** 200th Anniversary of Acquisition **Obv:** Crowned bust right **Rev:** Triskeles on shield within rope wreath

Date	Mintage	F	VF	XF	Unc	BU
1965 Proof	1,000	Value: 250				

KM# 27 SOVEREIGN (Pound)
7.9627 g., 0.9170 Gold 0.2347 oz. AGW **Ruler:** Elizabeth II **Obv:** Young bust right **Rev:** Armored equestrian

Date	Mintage	F	VF	XF	Unc	BU
1973 A	40,000	—	—	—	—	225
1973 B	Inc. above	—	—	—	—	225
1973 C	Inc. above	—	—	—	—	225
1973 Proof	1,250	Value: 235				
1974 A	8,604	—	—	—	—	225
1974 B	Inc. above	—	—	—	—	225
1974 C	Inc. above	—	—	—	—	225
1974 Proof	2,500	Value: 235				
1975 A	956	—	—	—	—	225
1975 B	Inc. above	—	—	—	—	225
1975 C	Inc. above	—	—	—	—	225
1975 Proof	—	Value: 235				
1976 A	1,238	—	—	—	—	225
1976 B	Inc. above	—	—	—	—	225
1976 C	Inc. above	—	—	—	—	225
1976 Proof	—	Value: 235				
1977 A	—	—	—	—	—	225
1977 B	—	—	—	—	—	225
1977 C	—	—	—	—	—	225
1977 Proof	1,250	Value: 235				
1978 Proof	1,250	Value: 235				
1979 B	—	—	—	—	—	225
1979 C	—	—	—	—	—	225
1979 AA (t)	10,000	—	—	—	—	225
1979 D (t)	—	—	—	—	—	225
1979 (t) Proof	30,000	Value: 235				
1980 (v) Proof	—	Value: 235				
1980 D (m) Proof	5,000	Value: 235				
1982 (b)	30,000	—	—	—	—	225
1982 (b) Proof	40,000	Value: 235				

KM# 44 SOVEREIGN (Pound)
Virenium **Ruler:** Elizabeth II **Obv:** Young bust right **Rev:** Triskeles flanked by designs

Date	Mintage	F	VF	XF	Unc	BU
1978 AA	—	—	—	—	3.00	3.50
1978 AB	—	—	—	—	3.00	3.50
1978 AC	—	—	—	—	2.50	3.00
1978 AD	3,780	—	—	—	7.50	8.50
1978 BB Proof	150,000	—	—	—	—	—
1978 BC Proof	Inc. above	Value: 3.50				
1979 AA(t)	—	—	—	—	2.50	3.00
1979 AB(t)	—	—	—	—	2.50	3.00
1979 AC(t)	—	—	—	—	2.50	3.00
1979 BB(t) Proof	—	Value: 3.50				
1979 (t) Crossed oars	—	—	—	—	2.50	3.00
1980 AA DMIHE	30,000	—	—	—	2.50	3.00
1980 AA DMIHEN	—	—	—	—	2.50	3.00
1980 AA TT	—	—	—	—	2.50	3.00
1980 AB DMIHE	—	—	—	—	2.50	3.00
1980 AB DHIHEN	—	—	—	—	2.50	3.00
1980 AB TT	—	—	—	—	5.50	6.50
1980 AC DMIHE	100,000	—	—	—	2.50	3.00
1980PM BB Proof	5,000	Value: 10.00				
1980 AA	—	—	—	—	2.50	3.00
1980 AB	—	—	—	—	2.50	3.00
1980 AC	—	—	—	—	2.50	3.00
1981PM BB Proof	26,000	Value: 10.00				
1981 AA	—	—	—	—	2.50	3.00
1982PM (b) Proof						

KM# 44b SOVEREIGN (Pound)
9.0000 g., 0.9500 Platinum 0.2749 oz. APW **Ruler:** Elizabeth II **Obv:** Young bust right **Rev:** Triskeles flanked by designs

Date	Mintage	F	VF	XF	Unc	BU
1978 Proof	1,000	Value: 550				
1979 Proof	—	Value: 550				
1980 Proof	1,000	Value: 550				
1982 Proof	100	Value: 575				

KM# 44c SOVEREIGN (Pound)
7.9627 g., 0.9170 Gold 0.2347 oz. AGW **Ruler:** Elizabeth II **Obv:** Young bust right **Rev:** Triskeles flanked by designs

Date	Mintage	F	VF	XF	Unc	BU
1980 Proof	5,000	Value: 225				
1980 T.T. Proof	300	Value: 235				
1982 (b)	250	—	—	—	235	—
1982 (b) Proof	750	Value: 225				

KM# 44d SOVEREIGN (Pound)
4.6000 g., 0.5000 Silver 0.0739 oz. ASW **Ruler:** Elizabeth II **Obv:** Young bust right **Rev:** Triskeles flanked by designs

Date	Mintage	F	VF	XF	Unc	BU
1980 Proof	10,000	Value: 15.00				

KM# 44a SOVEREIGN (Pound)
4.6000 g., 0.9250 Silver 0.1368 oz. ASW **Ruler:** Elizabeth II **Obv:** Young bust right **Rev:** Triskeles flanked by designs **Edge:** Smooth, reeded alternating edge

Date	Mintage	F	VF	XF	Unc	BU
1978PM D Proof	100,000	Value: 8.00				
1978PM E Proof	Inc. above	Value: 8.00				

Date	Mintage	F	VF	XF	Unc	BU
1979PM D(t) Proof	75,000	Value: 15.00				
1979PM E(t) Proof	Inc. above	Value: 15.00				
1980PM Proof	75,000	Value: 8.00				
1981PM Proof	—	Value: 8.00				
1982PM (b) Proof	1,000	Value: 35.00				

KM# 86 SOVEREIGN (Pound)
7.9627 g., 0.9170 Gold 0.2347 oz. AGW **Ruler:** Elizabeth II
Subject: Wedding of Prince Charles and Lady Diana **Obv:** Young bust right **Rev:** Portraits of Royal Couple, joined shields

Date	Mintage	F	VF	XF	Unc	BU
1981 Proof	40,000	Value: 225				

KM# 109 SOVEREIGN (Pound)
9.5000 g., Nickel-Brass, 22.5 mm. **Ruler:** Elizabeth II
Obv: Young bust right **Rev:** City view with ships within circle

Date	Mintage	F	VF	XF	Unc	BU
1983 AA	—	—	—	—	3.50	4.00
1983 AB	—	—	—	—	3.50	4.00

KM# 109a SOVEREIGN (Pound)
4.6000 g., 0.9250 Silver 0.1368 oz. ASW, 22.5 mm.
Ruler: Elizabeth II **Obv:** Young bust right **Rev:** City view with ships within cricle **Edge:** Reeded, smooth alternating edge

Date	Mintage	F	VF	XF	Unc	BU
1983 D Proof	—	Value: 20.00				

KM# 109b SOVEREIGN (Pound)
9.5000 g., 0.3740 Gold 0.1142 oz. AGW, 22.5 mm.
Ruler: Elizabeth II **Obv:** Young bust right **Rev:** City view with ships within circle

Date	Mintage	F	VF	XF	Unc	BU
1983 Proof	—	Value: 115				

KM# 109c SOVEREIGN (Pound)
7.9627 g., 0.9170 Gold 0.2347 oz. AGW, 22.5 mm.
Ruler: Elizabeth II **Obv:** Young bust right **Rev:** City view with ships within circle

Date	Mintage	F	VF	XF	Unc	BU
1983 Proof	—	Value: 225				

KM# 109d SOVEREIGN (Pound)
9.0000 g., 0.9500 Platinum 0.2749 oz. APW, 22.5 mm.
Ruler: Elizabeth II **Obv:** Young bust right **Rev:** City view with ships within circle

Date	Mintage	F	VF	XF	Unc	BU
1983 Proof	—	Value: 550				

KM# 128 SOVEREIGN (Pound)
9.5000 g., Nickel-Brass, 22.5 mm. **Ruler:** Elizabeth II
Obv: Young bust right **Rev:** Crown flanked by designs above city view within shield **Edge:** Reeded, smooth alternating edge

Date	Mintage	F	VF	XF	Unc	BU
1984 D	—	—	—	—	4.00	4.50
1984 AA	—	—	—	—	4.00	4.50

KM# 128a SOVEREIGN (Pound)
4.6000 g., 0.9250 Silver 0.1368 oz. ASW, 22.5 mm.
Ruler: Elizabeth II **Obv:** Young bust right **Rev:** Crown flanked by designs above city view within shield **Edge:** Reeded, smooth alternating edge

Date	Mintage	F	VF	XF	Unc	BU
1984	—	—	—	—	10.00	12.00
1984 D Proof	—	Value: 20.00				

KM# 128b SOVEREIGN (Pound)
9.5000 g., 0.3740 Gold 0.1142 oz. AGW, 22.5 mm.
Ruler: Elizabeth II **Obv:** Young bust right **Rev:** Crown flanked by designs above city view within shield

Date	Mintage	F	VF	XF	Unc	BU
1984 Proof	4,950	Value: 115				

KM# 128c SOVEREIGN (Pound)
7.9627 g., 0.9170 Gold 0.2347 oz. AGW, 22.5 mm.
Ruler: Elizabeth II **Obv:** Young bust right **Rev:** Crown flanked by designs above city view within shield

Date	Mintage	F	VF	XF	Unc	BU
1984 Proof	950	Value: 225				

KM# 128d SOVEREIGN (Pound)
9.0000 g., 0.9500 Platinum 0.2749 oz. APW, 22.5 mm.
Ruler: Elizabeth II **Obv:** Young bust right **Rev:** Crown flanked by designs above city view within shield

Date	Mintage	F	VF	XF	Unc	BU
1984 Proof	—	Value: 550				

KM# 261 SOVEREIGN (Pound)
7.9627 g., 0.9170 Gold 0.2347 oz. AGW, 22.5 mm. **Ruler:** Elizabeth II **Obv:** Young bust right **Rev:** Four crowned shields

Date	Mintage	F	VF	XF	Unc	BU
1984	20	—	—	—	350	375
1984 Proof	20	Value: 450				

KM# 151 SOVEREIGN (Pound)
9.5000 g., Nickel-Brass, 22.5 mm. **Ruler:** Elizabeth II
Obv: Crowned head right **Rev:** Shield **Edge:** Smooth, reeded alternating edge

Date	Mintage	F	VF	XF	Unc	BU
1985 AA	—	—	—	—	3.50	4.00
1985 AA Proof	25,000	Value: 6.00				

Date	Mintage	F	VF	XF	Unc	BU
1985(w) AA	—	—	—	—	3.50	4.00
1985 AA Proof	25,000	Value: 6.00				

KM# 135 SOVEREIGN (Pound)
4.6000 g., 0.9250 Silver 0.1368 oz. ASW, 22.5 mm.
Ruler: Elizabeth II **Obv:** Young bust right **Rev:** Shield
Edge: Reeded, smooth alternating edge

Date	Mintage	F	VF	XF	Unc	BU
1985 D	—	—	—	—	10.00	12.00
1985 D Proof	Est. 5,000	Value: 22.50				

KM# 135b SOVEREIGN (Pound)
7.9627 g., 0.9170 Gold 0.2347 oz. AGW, 22.5 mm.
Ruler: Elizabeth II **Obv:** Young bust right **Rev:** Shield

Date	Mintage	F	VF	XF	Unc	BU
1985 Proof	Est. 150	Value: 225				

KM# 135c SOVEREIGN (Pound)
9.0000 g., 0.9500 Platinum 0.2749 oz. APW, 22.5 mm.
Ruler: Elizabeth II **Obv:** Young bust right **Rev:** Shield

Date	Mintage	F	VF	XF	Unc	BU
1985 Proof	Est. 550	Value: 550				

KM# 151a SOVEREIGN (Pound)
4.6000 g., 0.9250 Silver 0.1368 oz. ASW, 22.5 mm.
Ruler: Elizabeth II **Obv:** Crowned head right **Rev:** Shield

Date	Mintage	F	VF	XF	Unc	BU
1985 Proof	—	Value: 35.00				

KM# 136 SOVEREIGN (Pound)
4.6000 g., 0.9250 Silver 0.1368 oz. ASW, 22.5 mm.
Ruler: Elizabeth II **Obv:** Crowned head right **Rev:** Shield

Date	Mintage	F	VF	XF	Unc	BU
1986 AA	—	—	—	—	10.00	12.00
1986 D Proof	—	Value: 25.00				

KM# 136b SOVEREIGN (Pound)
7.9627 g., 0.9170 Gold 0.2347 oz. AGW, 22.5 mm.
Ruler: Elizabeth II **Obv:** Crowned head right **Rev:** Shield

Date	Mintage	F	VF	XF	Unc	BU
1986 Proof	—	Value: 225				

KM# 136c SOVEREIGN (Pound)
9.0000 g., 0.9500 Platinum 0.2749 oz. APW, 22.5 mm.
Ruler: Elizabeth II **Obv:** Crowned head right **Rev:** Shield

Date	Mintage	F	VF	XF	Unc	BU
1986 Proof	—	Value: 550				

KM# 175 SOVEREIGN (Pound)
9.5000 g., Nickel-Brass, 22.5 mm. **Ruler:** Elizabeth II
Obv: Crowned head right **Rev:** Shield

Date	Mintage	F	VF	XF	Unc	BU
1986	—	—	—	—	3.50	4.00
1986 Proof	25,000	Value: 6.00				

KM# 182 SOVEREIGN (Pound)
9.5000 g., Nickel-Brass, 22.5 mm. **Ruler:** Elizabeth II
Obv: Crowned head right **Rev:** Rearing armored equestrian within circle **Edge:** Reeded, smooth alternating edge

Date	Mintage	F	VF	XF	Unc	BU
1987 AA	—	—	—	—	3.50	4.00

KM# 265 SOVEREIGN (Pound)
7.9627 g., 0.9170 Gold 0.2347 oz. AGW, 22.5 mm. **Ruler:** Elizabeth II **Obv:** Crowned head right **Rev:** Four crowned shields

Date	Mintage	F	VF	XF	Unc	BU
1988	5,876	—	—	—	—	225
1988 Proof	1,600	Value: 235				

KM# 213 SOVEREIGN (Pound)
9.5000 g., Nickel-Brass, 22.5 mm. **Ruler:** Elizabeth II
Obv: Crowned head right **Rev:** Cordless phone divides satellite and receiving station **Edge:** Reeded, smooth alternating edge

Date	Mintage	F	VF	XF	Unc	BU
1988 AA	—	—	—	—	2.50	3.00
1988 BB	—	—	—	—	2.50	3.00
1988 D	—	—	—	—	2.50	3.00
1989 AA	—	—	—	—	2.50	3.00
1990 AA	—	—	—	—	2.50	3.00
1991 AA	—	—	—	—	2.50	3.00
1992 AB	—	—	—	—	2.50	3.00
1993 AA	—	—	—	—	2.50	3.00
1994 AA	—	—	—	—	2.50	3.00
1995 AA	—	—	—	—	2.50	3.00

KM# 213a SOVEREIGN (Pound)
4.6000 g., 0.9250 Silver 0.1368 oz. ASW, 22.5 mm.
Ruler: Elizabeth II **Obv:** Crowned head right **Rev:** Cordless phone divides satelite and receiving station

Date	Mintage	F	VF	XF	Unc	BU
1988 Proof	—	Value: 10.00				
1989 Proof	—	Value: 10.00				

Date	Mintage	F	VF	XF	Unc	BU
1990 Proof	—	Value: 10.00				
1991 Proof	—	Value: 10.00				
1992 Proof	—	Value: 10.00				

KM# 594 SOVEREIGN (Pound)
9.5000 g., Nickel-Brass, 22.5 mm. **Ruler:** Elizabeth II **Subject:** Sports **Obv:** Crowned head right **Rev:** Cricket equipment

Date	Mintage	F	VF	XF	Unc	BU
1996 AA	—	—	—	—	4.00	4.50
1997 AA	—	—	—	—	4.00	4.50

KM# 594a SOVEREIGN (Pound)
4.6000 g., 0.9250 Silver 0.1368 oz. ASW, 22.5 mm.
Ruler: Elizabeth II **Subject:** Sports **Obv:** Crowned head right **Rev:** Cricket equipment

Date	Mintage	F	VF	XF	Unc	BU
1996 Proof	—	Value: 25.00				

KM# 655 SOVEREIGN (Pound)
9.5000 g., Nickel-Brass, 22.5 mm. **Ruler:** Elizabeth II **Subject:** Douglas Centenary **Obv:** Crowned head right **Rev:** City arms

Date	Mintage	F	VF	XF	Unc	BU
1996 AA	—	—	—	—	4.00	4.50

KM# 655a SOVEREIGN (Pound)
9.5000 g., 0.9250 Silver 0.2825 oz. ASW, 22.5 mm.
Ruler: Elizabeth II **Subject:** Douglas Centenary **Obv:** Crowned head right **Rev:** City arms

Date	Mintage	F	VF	XF	Unc	BU
1996 Proof	25,000	Value: 15.00				

KM# 655b SOVEREIGN (Pound)
9.5000 g., 0.9160 Gold 0.2798 oz. AGW, 22.5 mm.
Ruler: Elizabeth II **Subject:** Douglas Centenary **Obv:** Crowned head right **Rev:** City arms

Date	Mintage	F	VF	XF	Unc	BU
1996 Proof	Est. 10,000	Value: 275				

KM# 906.1 SOVEREIGN (Pound)
9.5000 g., Nickel-Brass, 22.5 mm. **Ruler:** Elizabeth II **Obv:** Head with tiara right **Rev:** Cricket equipment flanked by sprigs

Date	Mintage	F	VF	XF	Unc	BU
1998 AA	—	—	—	—	4.00	4.50

KM# 906.2 POUND
9.5000 g., Nickel-Brass, 22.5 mm. **Ruler:** Elizabeth II
Obv: Head with tiara right with small triskeles dividing legend **Rev:** Cricket equipment

Date	Mintage	F	VF	XF	Unc	BU
1998PM AA	—	—	—	—	4.00	4.50
1999PM AA	—	—	—	—	4.00	4.50

KM# 1042 POUND
9.5000 g., Brass, 22.5 mm. **Ruler:** Elizabeth II
Subject: Millennium Bells **Obv:** Head with tiara right **Rev:** Triskeles and three bells **Edge:** Reeded and plain sections

Date	Mintage	F	VF	XF	Unc	BU
2000PM AA	—	—	—	—	4.00	5.00

KM# 28 2 POUNDS
15.9253 g., 0.9170 Gold 0.4695 oz. AGW **Ruler:** Elizabeth II
Obv: Young bust right **Rev:** Armored equestrian

Date	Mintage	F	VF	XF	Unc	BU
1973 A	3,612	—	—	—	—	440
1973 Proof	1,250	Value: 450				
1974 A	1,257	—	—	—	—	440
1974 B	Inc. above	—	—	—	—	440
1974 Proof	2,500	Value: 450				
1975 A	456	—	—	—	—	440
1975 B	Inc. above	—	—	—	—	440
1975 Proof	—	Value: 450				
1976 A	578	—	—	—	—	440
1976 B	Inc. above	—	—	—	—	440
1976 Proof	—	Value: 450				
1977 A	—	—	—	—	—	440

Date	Mintage	F	VF	XF	Unc	BU
1977 B	Inc. above	—	—	—	—	440
1977 Proof	1,250	Value: 450				
1978 Proof	1,250	Value: 450				
1979 (t) A	2,000	—	—	—	—	440
1979 (t) B	Inc. above	—	—	—	—	440
1979 (t) Proof	30,000	Value: 450				
1980 (m) Proof	2,000	Value: 450				
1982 (b)	15,000	—	—	—	—	440
1982 (b) Proof	5,000	Value: 450				

KM# 87 2 POUNDS
15.9253 g., 0.9170 Gold 0.4695 oz. AGW **Ruler:** Elizabeth II
Subject: Wedding of Prince Charles and Lady Diana **Obv:** Young
bust right **Rev:** Portraits of Royal Couple, joined shields

Date	Mintage	F	VF	XF	Unc	BU
1981 Proof	5,000	Value: 450				

KM# 129 2 POUNDS
Virenium Ruler: Elizabeth II **Obv:** Young bust right **Rev:** Tower
of Refuge and Manx Shearwater in flight

Date	Mintage	F	VF	XF	Unc	BU
1984PM	—	—	—	—	—	—

Note: Reported, not confirmed

KM# 129a 2 POUNDS
Silver **Ruler:** Elizabeth II **Obv:** Young bust right **Rev:** Tower of
Refuge and Manx Shearwater in flight

Date	Mintage	F	VF	XF	Unc	BU
1984PM	—	—	—	—	—	—

Note: Reported, not confirmed

KM# 262 2 POUNDS
15.9200 g., 0.9170 Gold 0.4693 oz. AGW **Ruler:** Elizabeth II
Obv: Young bust right **Rev:** Four crowned shields

Date	Mintage	F	VF	XF	Unc	BU
1984	20	—	—	—	650	
1984 Proof	20	Value: 800				

KM# 149 2 POUNDS
Virenium Ruler: Elizabeth II **Obv:** Crowned head right
Rev: Tower of Refuge and Manx Shearwater in flight

Date	Mintage	F	VF	XF	Unc	BU
1985	—	—	—	—	—	—

Note: Reported, not confirmed

KM# 149a 2 POUNDS
Silver **Ruler:** Elizabeth II **Obv:** Crowned head right **Rev:** Tower
of Refuge and Manx Shearwater in flight

Date	Mintage	F	VF	XF	Unc	BU
1985	—	—	—	—	—	—

Note: Reported, not confirmed

KM# 167 2 POUNDS
Virenium. Ruler: Elizabeth II **Obv:** Crowned head right **Rev:** Bird
above towered building

Date	Mintage	F	VF	XF	Unc	BU
1986 (vw)	—	—	—	—	7.50	8.50
1986 Proof	—	Value: 10.00				
1987 AA	—	—	—	—	7.50	8.50

KM# 214 2 POUNDS
Virenium Ruler: Elizabeth II **Obv:** Crowned head right **Rev:**
BAC 146-100 jet

Date	Mintage	F	VF	XF	Unc	BU
1988 AA	—	—	—	—	7.50	8.50
1988 D	—	—	—	—	7.50	8.50
1989	—	—	—	—	7.50	8.50
1990 AA	—	—	—	—	7.50	8.50
1991 AA	—	—	—	—	7.50	8.50
1992 AA	—	—	—	—	7.50	8.50
1993 AA	—	—	—	—	7.50	8.50

KM# 257 2 POUNDS
Virenium Ruler: Elizabeth II **Obv:** Crowned head right **Rev:** Blimp

Date	Mintage	F	VF	XF	Unc	BU
1989 AA Rare	—	—	—	—	—	—

Note: Most recalled by government; Few actually issued.

KM# 257a 2 POUNDS
9.3000 g., 0.9250 Silver 0.2766 oz. ASW **Ruler:** Elizabeth II
Obv: Crowned head right **Rev:** Blimp

Date	Mintage	F	VF	XF	Unc	BU
1989	—	—	—	—	—	—

Note: Reported, not confirmed

KM# 257b 2 POUNDS
15.9400 g., 0.9170 Gold 0.4699 oz. AGW **Ruler:** Elizabeth II
Obv: Crowned head right **Rev:** Blimp

Date	Mintage	F	VF	XF	Unc	BU
1989	—	—	—	—	—	—

Note: Reported, not confirmed

KM# 257c 2 POUNDS
18.0000 g., 0.9500 Platinum 0.5498 oz. APW **Ruler:** Elizabeth II
Obv: Crowned head right **Rev:** Blimp **Note:** Reported, not
confirmed; most recalled by government; few actually issued

Date	Mintage	F	VF	XF	Unc	BU
1989	—	—	—	—	—	—

Note: Reported, not confirmed

KM# 344 2 POUNDS
Virenium Ruler: Elizabeth II **Subject:** World Champion - Nigel
Mansell **Obv:** Crowned head right **Rev:** Racecars

Date	Mintage	F	VF	XF	Unc	BU
No die letters	—	—	—	—	8.00	10.00
1993 AA	—	—	—	—	6.50	

KM# 398 2 POUNDS
Virenium Ruler: Elizabeth II **Subject:** Indycar World Series
Champion - Nigel Mansell **Obv:** Crowned head right **Rev:** Racecars

Date	Mintage	F	VF	XF	Unc	BU
1994 AA	—	—	—	—	8.00	10.00

KM# 465 2 POUNDS
Virenium Ruler: Elizabeth II **Subject:** 50th Anniversary - VE
and VJ Day **Obv:** Crowned head right **Rev:** Lion head within
crowned circular design within flowered wreath

Date	Mintage	F	VF	XF	Unc	BU
1995	—	—	—	—	7.00	8.00

KM# 595 2 POUNDS
Virenium Ruler: Elizabeth II **Subject:** Sports **Obv:** Crowned
head right **Rev:** Racecars within sprigs **Edge:** Reeded, smooth
alternating edge

Date	Mintage	F	VF	XF	Unc	BU
1996 ÁA	—	—	—	—	7.50	8.50
1997 AA	—	—	—	—	7.50	8.50

KM# 844 2 POUNDS
Bi-Metallic Copper-Nickel center in Brass ring **Ruler:** Elizabeth II
Obv: Crowned head right within beaded circle **Rev:** Racecars
within beaded circle and sprigs **Edge:** Reeded

Date	Mintage	F	VF	XF	Unc	BU
1997 AA	—	—	—	—	8.00	9.00

KM# 858 2 POUNDS
12.0000 g., Bi-Metallic Copper-Nickel center in Brass ring
Ruler: Elizabeth II **Obv:** Head with tiara right within beaded circle
Rev: Three racecars **Edge:** Reeded

Date	Mintage	F	VF	XF	Unc	BU
1998 AA	—	—	—	—	8.00	9.00
1999 AA	—	—	—	—	8.00	9.00

KM# 1043 2 POUNDS
12.0000 g., Bi-Metallic Copper-Nickel center in Brass ring,
28.4 mm. **Ruler:** Elizabeth II **Subject:** Thorwald's Cross
Obv: Head with tiara right within beaded circle **Rev:** Ancient
drawing within circle **Edge:** Reeded

Date	Mintage	F	VF	XF	Unc	BU
2000PM AA	—	—	—	—	6.50	7.50

KM# 17 5 POUNDS
39.9403 g., 0.9170 Gold 1.1775 oz. AGW **Ruler:** Elizabeth II
Subject: 200th Anniversary of Acquisition **Obv:** Crowned bust
right **Rev:** Triskeles on shield within rope wreath

Date	Mintage	F	VF	XF	Unc	BU
1965	500	—	—	—	—	1,200

KM# 17a 5 POUNDS
39.9500 g., 0.9800 Gold 1.2587 oz. AGW **Ruler:** Elizabeth II
Subject: 200th Anniversary of Acquisition **Obv:** Crowned bust
right **Rev:** Triskeles on shield within rope wreath

Date	Mintage	F	VF	XF	Unc	BU
1965 Proof	1,000	Value: 1,300				

KM# 29 5 POUNDS
39.8134 g., 0.9170 Gold 1.1737 oz. AGW **Ruler:** Elizabeth II
Obv: Young bust right **Rev:** Rearing armored equestrian

Date	Mintage	F	VF	XF	Unc	BU
1973 A	3,035	—	—	—	—	1,150
1973 B	Inc. above	—	—	—	—	1,150
1973 C	Inc. above	—	—	—	—	1,150
1973 D	Inc. above	—	—	—	—	1,150
1973 E	Inc. above	—	—	—	—	1,150
1973 Proof	1,250	Value: 1,250				
1974 A	481	—	—	—	—	1,150
1974 B	Inc. above	—	—	—	—	1,150
1974 Proof	2,500	Value: 1,250				
1975 A	306	—	—	—	—	1,150
1975 B	Inc. above	—	—	—	—	1,150
1975 Proof	—	Value: 1,250				
1976 A	370	—	—	—	—	1,150
1976 B	Inc. above	—	—	—	—	1,150
1976 Proof	—	Value: 1,250				
1977 A	—	—	—	—	—	1,150
1977 B	Inc. above	—	—	—	—	1,150
1977 Proof	1,250	Value: 1,250				
1978 Proof	1,250	Value: 1,250				
1979 (t) A	1,000	—	—	—	—	1,150
1979 (t) B	Inc. above	—	—	—	—	1,150
1979 (t) Proof	1,000	Value: 1,250				
1980 (m)	250	—	—	—	—	1,150
1982 (b)	10,000	—	—	—	—	1,150
1982 (b) Proof	500	Value: 1,250				

KM# 29a 5 POUNDS
23.8400 g., 0.9800 Silver 0.7511 oz. ASW, 36.1 mm.
Ruler: Elizabeth II **Obv:** Young bust right **Rev:** Rearing armored
equestrian **Edge:** Reeded **Note:** Subject is a possible pattern.

Date	Mintage	F	VF	XF	Unc	BU
1980(m)PM Proof	—	—	—	—	—	—

KM# 88 5 POUNDS
Virenium, 36.5 mm. **Ruler:** Elizabeth II **Obv:** Young bust right
Rev: Triskeles on map **Edge:** Reeded, smooth alternating edge

Date	Mintage	F	VF	XF	Unc	BU
1981 AA	—	—	—	—	10.00	12.50
1981 AB	—	—	—	—	10.00	12.50
1981 AC	—	—	—	—	10.00	12.50
1981 AD	—	—	—	—	10.00	12.50
1981PM BB Proof	30,000	Value: 14.00				
1982 Proof	—	Value: 14.00				
1982 (b) Proof	—	—	—	—	—	—
1983 AA	—	—	—	—	20.00	22.00
1984 AA	—	—	—	—	20.00	22.00
1984 AB	—	—	—	—	20.00	22.00
1984 AC	—	—	—	—	10.00	12.50

KM# 88a 5 POUNDS
23.5000 g., 0.9250 Silver 0.6988 oz. ASW, 36.5 mm.
Ruler: Elizabeth II **Obv:** Young bust right **Rev:** Triskeles on map

Date	Mintage	F	VF	XF	Unc	BU
1981 Proof	500	Value: 40.00				
1982 (b) Proof	1,000	Value: 35.00				
1983 Proof	5,000	Value: 25.00				

KM# 88b 5 POUNDS
39.9000 g., 0.9170 Gold 1.1763 oz. AGW, 36.5 mm.
Ruler: Elizabeth II **Obv:** Young bust right **Rev:** Triskeles on map

Date	Mintage	F	VF	XF	Unc	BU
1981 Proof	1,000	Value: 1,150				
1982 (b) Proof	250	Value: 1,150				

Date	Mintage	F	VF	XF	Unc	BU
1982 (b) Proof	750	Value: 1,150				
1983 Proof	—	Value: 1,150				

KM# 88c 5 POUNDS
45.5000 g., 0.9500 Platinum 1.3897 oz. APW, 36.5 mm.
Ruler: Elizabeth II **Obv:** Young bust right **Rev:** Triskeles on map

Date	Mintage	F	VF	XF	Unc	BU
1981 Proof	500	Value: 2,500				
1982 (b) Proof	100	Value: 2,500				
1983 Proof	—	Value: 2,500				

KM# 89 5 POUNDS
39.8134 g., 0.9170 Gold 1.1737 oz. AGW **Ruler:** Elizabeth II
Subject: Wedding of Prince Charles and Lady Diana **Obv:** Young
bust right **Rev:** Portraits of Royal Couple, joined shields

Date	Mintage	F	VF	XF	Unc	BU
1981 Proof	1,000	Value: 1,150				

KM# 134 5 POUNDS
Virenium, 36.5 mm. **Ruler:** Elizabeth II **Subject:** Quincentenary
of the College of Arms **Obv:** Young bust right **Rev:** Mounted
knight in armor with sword facing right within circle

Date	Mintage	F	VF	XF	Unc	BU
1984 AA	—	—	—	—	10.00	12.50
1984 BB	—	—	—	—	10.00	12.50

KM# 134a 5 POUNDS
23.5000 g., 0.9250 Silver 0.6988 oz. ASW, 36.5 mm.
Ruler: Elizabeth II **Subject:** Quincentenery of the College of
Arms **Obv:** Young bust right **Rev:** Mounted knight in armor with
sword, facing right within circle

Date	Mintage	F	VF	XF	Unc	BU
1984 Proof	—	Value: 40.00				

KM# 134b 5 POUNDS
39.9000 g., 0.9170 Gold 1.1763 oz. AGW, 36.5 mm.
Ruler: Elizabeth II **Subject:** Quincentenery of the College of
Arms **Obv:** Young bust right **Rev:** Mounted knight in armor with
sword, facing right within circle

Date	Mintage	F	VF	XF	Unc	BU
1984 Proof	150	Value: 1,150				

KM# 134c 5 POUNDS
45.5000 g., 0.9500 Platinum 1.3897 oz. APW, 36.5 mm.
Ruler: Elizabeth II **Subject:** Quincentenery of the College of
Arms **Obv:** Young bust right **Rev:** Mounted knight in armor with
sword facing right within circle

Date	Mintage	F	VF	XF	Unc	BU
1984 Proof	—	Value: 2,500				

KM# 263 5 POUNDS
39.8300 g., 0.9170 Gold 1.1742 oz. AGW **Ruler:** Elizabeth II
Obv: Young bust right **Rev:** Four crowned shields

Date	Mintage	F	VF	XF	Unc	BU
1984	20	—	—	—	1,250	1,350
1984 Proof	20	Value: 1,650				

KM# 150 5 POUNDS
Virenium, 36.5 mm. **Ruler:** Elizabeth II **Obv:** Crowned head
right **Rev:** Similar to KM#134 with additional sports privy mark
Edge: Reeded, smooth alternating edge

Date	Mintage	F	VF	XF	Unc	BU
1985 AA(w)	—	—	—	—	10.00	12.50
1985 Proof	25,000	Value: 12.50				
1986 AA	—	—	—	—	10.00	12.50
1987 AA	—	—	—	—	10.00	12.50

KM# 150a 5 POUNDS
23.5000 g., 0.9250 Silver 0.6988 oz. ASW, 36.5 mm.
Ruler: Elizabeth II **Obv:** Crowned head right **Rev:** Mounted
knight in armor with sword facing right within circle

Date	Mintage	F	VF	XF	Unc	BU
1985 Proof	Est. 5,000	Value: 40.00				

KM# 150b 5 POUNDS
39.9000 g., 0.9170 Gold 1.1763 oz. AGW, 36.5 mm.
Ruler: Elizabeth II **Obv:** Crowned head right **Rev:** Mounted
knight in armor with sword facing right within circle

Date	Mintage	F	VF	XF	Unc	BU
1985 Proof	Est. 150	Value: 1,150				

KM# 150c 5 POUNDS
45.5000 g., 0.9500 Platinum 1.3897 oz. APW, 36.5 mm.
Ruler: Elizabeth II **Obv:** Crowned head right **Rev:** Mounted
knight in armor with sword facing right within circle

Date	Mintage	F	VF	XF	Unc	BU
1985 Proof	Est. 100	Value: 2,500				

KM# 215 5 POUNDS
Virenium, 36.5 mm. **Ruler:** Elizabeth II **Obv:** Crowned head
right **Rev:** Boat below triskeles within circle **Edge:** Smooth,
reeded alternating edge

Date	Mintage	F	VF	XF	Unc	BU
1988 AA	—	—	—	—	10.00	12.50
1989 AA	—	—	—	—	10.00	12.50
1990 AA	—	—	—	—	10.00	12.50
1991 AA	—	—	—	—	10.00	12.50
1992 AA	—	—	—	—	10.00	12.50

KM# 336 5 POUNDS
Virenium, 36.5 mm. **Ruler:** Elizabeth II **Subject:** World
Champion - Nigel Mansell **Obv:** Crowned head right
Rev: Racecars **Edge:** Reeded, smooth alternating edge

Date	Mintage	F	VF	XF	Unc	BU
1993 AA	—	—	—	—	12.50	16.50

KM# 399 5 POUNDS
Virenium, 36.5 mm. **Ruler:** Elizabeth II **Subject:** Indycar World
Series Champion - Nigel Mansell **Obv:** Crowned head right
Rev: Two racecars

Date	Mintage	F	VF	XF	Unc	BU
1994 AA	—	—	—	—	15.00	18.50

KM# 466 5 POUNDS
Virenium, 36.5 mm. **Ruler:** Elizabeth II **Subject:** 50th
Anniversary - End of World War II **Obv:** Crowned head right
Rev: Bust facing giving peace sign

Date	Mintage	F	VF	XF	Unc	BU
1995	—	—	—	—	14.00	17.50

KM# 466a   5 POUNDS
23.5000 g., 0.9250 Silver 0.6988 oz. ASW, 36.5 mm.
Ruler: Elizabeth II **Subject:** 50th Anniversary - End of World War
II **Obv:** Crowned head right **Rev:** Bust facing giving peace sign

Date	Mintage	F	VF	XF	Unc	BU
1995 Proof	—				Value: 40.00	

KM# 466b   5 POUNDS
39.8300 g., 0.9170 Gold 1.1742 oz. AGW, 36.5 mm.
Ruler: Elizabeth II **Subject:** 50th Anniversary - End of World War
II **Obv:** Crowned head right **Rev:** Bust facing giving peace sign

Date	Mintage	F	VF	XF	Unc	BU
1995 Proof	Est. 850				Value: 1,150	

KM# 587   5 POUNDS
Virenium, 36.5 mm. **Ruler:** Elizabeth II **Subject:** European Soccer
Championships **Obv:** Crowned head right **Rev:** Soccer players

Date	Mintage	F	VF	XF	Unc	BU
1996 AA	—	—	—	—	16.00	—

KM# 587a   5 POUNDS
23.5000 g., 0.9250 Silver 0.6988 oz. ASW, 36.5 mm.
Ruler: Elizabeth II **Subject:** European Soccer Championships
Obv: Crowned head right **Rev:** Soccer players

Date	Mintage	F	VF	XF	Unc	BU
1996 Proof	Est. 5,000				Value: 40.00	

KM# 587b   5 POUNDS
39.8300 g., 0.9160 Gold 1.1729 oz. AGW, 36.5 mm.
Ruler: Elizabeth II **Subject:** European Soccer Championships
Obv: Crowned head right **Rev:** Soccer players

Date	Mintage	F	VF	XF	Unc	BU
1996 Proof	Est. 850				Value: 1,150	

KM# 769   5 POUNDS
Virenium, 36.5 mm. **Ruler:** Elizabeth II **Subject:** 50th
Anniversary - Queen Elizabeth and Prince Philip **Obv:** Crowned
head right **Rev:** Current portrait of Queen Elizabeth and Prince
Philip **Edge:** Reeded, smooth alternating edge

Date	Mintage	F	VF	XF	Unc	BU
1997 AA	—	—	—	—	17.50	—

KM# 769a   5 POUNDS
23.5000 g., 0.9250 Silver 0.6988 oz. ASW, 36.5 mm.
Ruler: Elizabeth II **Subject:** 50th Anniversary - Queen Elizabeth
and Prince Philip **Obv:** Crowned head right **Rev:** Current portrait
of Queen Elizabeth and Prince Philip

Date	Mintage	F	VF	XF	Unc	BU
1997 Proof	Est. 5,000				Value: 40.00	

KM# 769b   5 POUNDS
39.8300 g., 0.9167 Gold 1.1738 oz. AGW, 36.5 mm.
Ruler: Elizabeth II **Subject:** 50th Anniversary - Queen Elizabeth
and Prince Philip **Obv:** Crowned head right **Rev:** Current portrait
of Queen Elizabeth and Prince Philip

Date	Mintage	F	VF	XF	Unc	BU
1997 Proof	Est. 850				Value: 1,150	

KM# 991   5 POUNDS
Virenium, 36.5 mm.   **Ruler:** Elizabeth II **Subject:** Soccer
Obv: Head with tiara right **Rev:** Soccer players flanked by sprigs
Edge: Reeded, smooth alternating edge

Date	Mintage	F	VF	XF	Unc	BU
1998 AA	—	—	—	—	16.50	18.00
1999 AA	—	—	—	—	16.50	18.00

KM# 912   5 POUNDS
Virenium, 36.5 mm.   **Ruler:** Elizabeth II **Subject:** 50th Birthday
- Prince Charles **Obv:** Head with tiara right **Rev:** Portrait of Prince
Charles **Edge:** Reeded, smooth alternating edge

Date	Mintage	F	VF	XF	Unc	BU
1998 AA	—	—	—	—	15.50	17.50

KM# 912a   5 POUNDS
23.5000 g., 0.9250 Silver 0.6988 oz. ASW, 36.5 mm.
Ruler: Elizabeth II **Subject:** 50th Birthday - Prince Charles
Obv: Head with tiara right **Rev:** Portrait of Prince Charles

Date	Mintage	F	VF	XF	Unc	BU
1998 Proof	Est. 5,000				Value: 50.00	

KM# 912b   5 POUNDS
39.8300 g., 0.9167 Gold 1.1738 oz. AGW, 36.5 mm.
Ruler: Elizabeth II **Subject:** 50th Birthday - Prince Charles
Obv: Head with tiara right **Rev:** Portrait of Prince Charles

Date	Mintage	F	VF	XF	Unc	BU
1998 Proof	Est. 850				Value: 1,150	

KM# 943   5 POUNDS
Virenium, 36.5 mm. **Ruler:** Elizabeth II **Subject:** 175th Anniversary
of the RN LI **Obv:** Head with tiara right **Rev:** Lifeboat with flag

Date	Mintage	F	VF	XF	Unc	BU
1999	—	—	—	—	15.50	17.50

KM# 943a   5 POUNDS
23.5000 g., 0.9250 Silver 0.6988 oz. ASW, 36.5 mm.
Ruler: Elizabeth II **Subject:** 175th Anniversary of the RN LI
Obv: Head with tiara right **Rev:** Lifeboat with flag

Date	Mintage	F	VF	XF	Unc	BU
1999 Proof	Est. 10,000				Value: 50.00	

KM# 943b   5 POUNDS
39.8300 g., 0.9167 Gold 1.1738 oz. AGW, 36.5 mm.
Ruler: Elizabeth II **Subject:** 175th Anniversary of the RN LI
Obv: Head with tiara right **Rev:** Lifeboat with flag

Date	Mintage	F	VF	XF	Unc	BU
1999 Proof	850				Value: 1,150	

KM# 1044   5 POUNDS
20.1000 g., Virenium, 36.5 mm. **Ruler:** Elizabeth II **Subject:** St.
Patrick's Hymn **Obv:** Head with tiara right **Rev:** Stylized cross
design **Edge:** Reeded and plain sections

Date	Mintage	F	VF	XF	Unc	BU
2000PM AA	—	—	—	—	15.00	16.50

KM# 345   10 POUNDS
10.0000 g., 0.9250 Silver 0.2974 oz. ASW **Ruler:** Elizabeth II
Subject: Indycar World Series Champion - Nigel Mansell
Obv: Crowned head right **Rev:** Racecar

Date	Mintage	F	VF	XF	Unc	BU
1993 Proof	Est. 20,000				Value: 35.00	

KM# 400   10 POUNDS
10.0000 g., 0.9250 Silver 0.2974 oz. ASW **Ruler:** Elizabeth II
Subject: Indycar World Series Champion - Nigel Mansell
Obv: Crowned head right **Rev:** Two racecars

Date	Mintage	F	VF	XF	Unc	BU
1994 Proof	Est. 20,000				Value: 35.00	

KM# 346   25 POUNDS
28.2800 g., 0.9250 Silver 0.8410 oz. ASW **Ruler:** Elizabeth II
Subject: World Champion - Nigel Mansell **Obv:** Crowned bust
right **Rev:** Two racecars

Date	Mintage	F	VF	XF	Unc	BU
1993 Proof	Est. 15,000				Value: 50.00	

KM# 347   50 POUNDS
6.2200 g., 0.9990 Gold 0.1998 oz. AGW **Ruler:** Elizabeth II
Subject: World Champion - Nigel Mansell **Obv:** Crowned bust
right **Rev:** Two racecars

Date	Mintage	F	VF	XF	Unc	BU
1993 Proof	Est. 5,000				Value: 200	

KM# 401   50 POUNDS
6.2200 g., 0.9990 Gold 0.1998 oz. AGW **Ruler:** Elizabeth II
Subject: Indycar World Series Champion - Nigel Mansell
Obv: Crowned bust right **Rev:** Two racecars

Date	Mintage	F	VF	XF	Unc	BU
1994 Proof	Est. 5,000				Value: 200	

CROWN SERIES
Pobjoy Mint Key

(M) MATTE - Normal circulation strike

(U) SPECIAL UNCIRCULATED - Polished or prooflike
in appearance, slightly frosted features.

(P) PROOF - The highest quality obtainable having mirror-like fields and frosted features.

KM# 235   1/25 CROWN
1.2441 g., 0.9990 Gold 0.0400 oz. AGW, 13.9 mm.
Ruler: Elizabeth II **Obv:** Crowned bust right **Rev:** Manx cat

Date	Mintage	F	VF	XF	Unc	BU
1988	40,000					40.00
1988 Proof	5,000				Value: 45.00	

KM# 252   1/25 CROWN
1.2441 g., 0.9990 Gold 0.0400 oz. AGW, 13.9 mm.
Ruler: Elizabeth II **Obv:** Crowned bust right **Rev:** Persian cat

Date	Mintage	F	VF	XF	Unc	BU
1989	—	—	—	—	—	40.00
1989 Proof	—				Value: 45.00	

KM# 467   1/25 CROWN
1.2441 g., 0.9995 Platinum 0.0400 oz. APW, 13.9 mm.
Ruler: Elizabeth II **Obv:** Crowned bust right **Rev:** Persian cat

Date	Mintage	F	VF	XF	Unc	BU
1989	—	—	—	—	—	70.00
1989 Proof	—				Value: 75.00	

KM# 277 1/25 CROWN
1.2441 g., 0.9990 Gold 0.0400 oz. AGW, 13.9 mm.
Ruler: Elizabeth II **Obv:** Crowned bust right **Rev:** Alley cat

Date	Mintage	F	VF	XF	Unc	BU
1990	—	—	—	—	—	50.00
1990 Proof	—	Value: 55.00				

KM# 294 1/25 CROWN
1.2441 g., 0.9990 Gold 0.0400 oz. AGW, 13.9 mm.
Ruler: Elizabeth II **Obv:** Crowned bust right **Rev:** Norwegian cat

Date	Mintage	F	VF	XF	Unc	BU
1991	—	—	—	—	—	50.00
1991 Proof	—	Value: 55.00				

KM# 322 1/25 CROWN
1.2441 g., 0.9990 Gold 0.0400 oz. AGW, 13.9 mm.
Ruler: Elizabeth II **Subject:** America's Cup **Obv:** Crowned bust right **Rev:** Cameo of "Star of India" above two modern sailboats

Date	Mintage	F	VF	XF	Unc	BU
1992 Prooflike	50,000	—	—	—	—	50.00

KM# 328 1/25 CROWN
1.2441 g., 0.9990 Gold 0.0400 oz. AGW, 13.9 mm.
Ruler: Elizabeth II **Obv:** Crowned bust right **Rev:** Siamese cat

Date	Mintage	F	VF	XF	Unc	BU
1992	—	—	—	—	—	45.00
1992 Proof	—	Value: 50.00				

KM# 338 1/25 CROWN
1.2441 g., 0.9990 Gold 0.0400 oz. AGW, 13.9 mm.
Ruler: Elizabeth II **Subject:** Year of the Cockerel **Obv:** Crowned bust right **Rev:** Cockerel within circle

Date	Mintage	F	VF	XF	Unc	BU
1993 Proof	Est. 25,000	Value: 45.00				

KM# 349 1/25 CROWN
1.2441 g., 0.9990 Gold 0.0400 oz. AGW, 13.9 mm.
Ruler: Elizabeth II **Obv:** Crowned bust right **Rev:** Maine Coon cat

Date	Mintage	F	VF	XF	Unc	BU
1993	—	—	—	—	—	45.00
1993 Proof	—	Value: 50.00				

KM# 376 1/25 CROWN
1.2441 g., 0.9990 Gold 0.0400 oz. AGW, 13.9 mm.
Ruler: Elizabeth II **Obv:** Crowned bust right **Rev:** Japanese Bobtail cat

Date	Mintage	F	VF	XF	Unc	BU
1994	—	—	—	—	—	40.00
1994 Proof	—	Value: 45.00				

KM# 402 1/25 CROWN
1.2441 g., 0.9990 Gold 0.0400 oz. AGW, 13.9 mm.
Ruler: Elizabeth II **Obv:** Crowned bust right **Rev:** Pekingese

Date	Mintage	F	VF	XF	Unc	BU
1994 Proof	Est. 25,000	Value: 50.00				

KM# 473 1/25 CROWN
1.2441 g., 0.9995 Platinum 0.0400 oz. APW, 13.9 mm.
Ruler: Elizabeth II **Obv:** Crowned bust right **Rev:** Japanese Bobtail cat

Date	Mintage	F	VF	XF	Unc	BU
1994	—	—	—	—	—	70.00
1994 Proof	—	Value: 75.00				

KM# 442 1/25 CROWN
1.2441 g., 0.9990 Gold 0.0400 oz. AGW, 13.9 mm.
Ruler: Elizabeth II **Obv:** Crowned bust right **Rev:** Turkish cat

Date	Mintage	F	VF	XF	Unc	BU
1995 U	—	—	—	—	—	40.00
1995 Proof	—	Value: 45.00				

KM# 449 1/25 CROWN
1.2441 g., 0.9990 Gold 0.0400 oz. AGW, 13.9 mm.
Ruler: Elizabeth II **Subject:** Year of the Pig **Obv:** Crowned bust right **Rev:** Sow with piglets

Date	Mintage	F	VF	XF	Unc	BU
1995 Proof	Est. 25,000	Value: 45.00				

KM# 478 1/25 CROWN
1.2441 g., 0.9995 Platinum 0.0400 oz. APW, 13.9 mm.
Ruler: Elizabeth II **Obv:** Crowned bust right **Rev:** Turkish cat

Date	Mintage	F	VF	XF	Unc	BU
1995	—	—	—	—	—	70.00
1995 Proof	—	Value: 75.00				

KM# 597 1/25 CROWN
1.2441 g., 0.9990 Gold 0.0400 oz. AGW, 13.9 mm.
Ruler: Elizabeth II **Series:** Flower Fairies **Obv:** Crowned bust right **Rev:** Orchis

Date	Mintage	F	VF	XF	Unc	BU
1996 Proof	Est. 25,000	Value: 45.00				

KM# 598 1/25 CROWN
1.2441 g., 0.9990 Gold 0.0400 oz. AGW, 13.9 mm.
Ruler: Elizabeth II **Series:** Flower Fairies **Obv:** Crowned bust right **Rev:** Rose

Date	Mintage	F	VF	XF	Unc	BU
1996 Proof	Est. 25,000	Value: 45.00				

KM# 599 1/25 CROWN
1.2441 g., 0.9990 Gold 0.0400 oz. AGW, 13.9 mm.
Ruler: Elizabeth II **Series:** Flower Fairies **Obv:** Crowned bust right **Rev:** Fuchsia

Date	Mintage	F	VF	XF	Unc	BU
1996 Proof	Est. 25,000	Value: 45.00				

KM# 600 1/25 CROWN
1.2441 g., 0.9990 Gold 0.0400 oz. AGW, 13.9 mm.
Ruler: Elizabeth II **Series:** Flower Fairies **Obv:** Crowned bust right **Rev:** Pinks

Date	Mintage	F	VF	XF	Unc	BU
1996 Proof	Est. 25,000	Value: 45.00				

KM# 613 1/25 CROWN
1.2441 g., 0.9990 Gold 0.0400 oz. AGW, 13.9 mm.
Ruler: Elizabeth II **Obv:** Crowned bust right **Rev:** Burmese cat
Note: #621a.

Date	Mintage	F	VF	XF	Unc	BU
1996 U	—	—	—	—	—	40.00
1996 Proof	—	Value: 45.00				

KM# 614 1/25 CROWN
1.2441 g., 0.9995 Platinum 0.0400 oz. APW, 13.9 mm.
Ruler: Elizabeth II **Obv:** Crowned bust right **Rev:** Burmese cat

Date	Mintage	F	VF	XF	Unc	BU
1996	—	—	—	—	—	70.00
1996 Proof	—	Value: 75.00				

KM# 728 1/25 CROWN
1.2441 g., 0.9990 Gold 0.0400 oz. AGW, 13.9 mm.
Ruler: Elizabeth II **Subject:** Year of the Rat **Obv:** Crowned bust right **Rev:** Rat

Date	Mintage	F	VF	XF	Unc	BU
1996 Proof						

Note: Entire series purchased by one buyer; Mintage, disposition, and market value unknown

KM# 721 1/25 CROWN
1.2441 g., 0.9990 Gold 0.0400 oz. AGW, 13.9 mm.
Ruler: Elizabeth II **Subject:** Year of the Ox **Obv:** Crowned bust right **Rev:** Ox laying down

Date	Mintage	F	VF	XF	Unc	BU
1997 Proof	Est. 20,000	Value: 45.00				

KM# 735 1/25 CROWN
1.2441 g., 0.9990 Gold 0.0400 oz. AGW, 13.9 mm.
Ruler: Elizabeth II **Series:** Flower Fairies **Obv:** Crowned bust right **Rev:** Candytuft

Date	Mintage	F	VF	XF	Unc	BU
1997 Proof	Est. 25,000	Value: 45.00				

KM# 735a 1/25 CROWN
1.2504 g., 0.9950 Platinum 0.0400 oz. APW, 13.9 mm.
Ruler: Elizabeth II **Series:** Flower Fairies **Obv:** Crowned bust right **Rev:** Candytuft

Date	Mintage	F	VF	XF	Unc	BU
1997 Proof	Est. 7,500	Value: 75.00				

KM# 736 1/25 CROWN
1.2441 g., 0.9999 Gold 0.0400 oz. AGW, 13.9 mm.
Ruler: Elizabeth II **Series:** Flower Fairies **Obv:** Crowned bust right **Rev:** Snowdrop

Date	Mintage	F	VF	XF	Unc	BU
1997 Proof	Est. 25,000	Value: 45.00				

KM# 736a 1/25 CROWN
1.2504 g., 0.9950 Platinum 0.0400 oz. APW, 13.9 mm.
Ruler: Elizabeth II **Series:** Flower Fairies **Obv:** Crowned bust right **Rev:** Snowdrop

Date	Mintage	F	VF	XF	Unc	BU
1997 Proof	Est. 7,500	Value: 75.00				

KM# 737 1/25 CROWN
1.2441 g., 0.9999 Gold 0.0400 oz. AGW, 13.9 mm.
Ruler: Elizabeth II **Series:** Flower Fairies **Obv:** Crowned bust right **Rev:** Tulip

Date	Mintage	F	VF	XF	Unc	BU
1997 Proof	Est. 25,000	Value: 45.00				

KM# 737a 1/25 CROWN
1.2504 g., 0.9950 Platinum 0.0400 oz. APW, 13.9 mm.
Ruler: Elizabeth II **Series:** Flower Fairies **Obv:** Crowned bust right **Rev:** Tulip

Date	Mintage	F	VF	XF	Unc	BU
1997 Proof	Est. 7,500	Value: 75.00				

KM# 738 1/25 CROWN
1.2441 g., 0.9999 Gold 0.0400 oz. AGW, 13.9 mm.
Ruler: Elizabeth II **Series:** Flower Fairies **Obv:** Crowned bust right **Rev:** Jasmine

Date	Mintage	F	VF	XF	Unc	BU
1997 Proof	Est. 25,000	Value: 75.00				

KM# 738a 1/25 CROWN
1.2504 g., 0.9950 Platinum 0.0400 oz. APW, 13.9 mm.
Ruler: Elizabeth II **Series:** Flower Fairies **Obv:** Crowned bust right **Rev:** Jasmine

Date	Mintage	F	VF	XF	Unc	BU
1997 Proof	Est. 7,500	Value: 85.00				

KM# 770 1/25 CROWN
1.2440 g., 0.9999 Gold 0.0400 oz. AGW, 13.9 mm.
Ruler: Elizabeth II **Obv:** Crowned bust right **Rev:** Long-haired Smoke cat

Date	Mintage	F	VF	XF	Unc	BU
1997	—	—	—	—	—	40.00
1997 Proof	—	Value: 45.00				

KM# 770a 1/25 CROWN
1.2440 g., 0.9999 Platinum 0.0400 oz. APW, 13.9 mm.
Ruler: Elizabeth II **Obv:** Crowned bust right **Rev:** Long-haired Smoke cat

Date	Mintage	F	VF	XF	Unc	BU
1997	—	—	—	—	—	70.00
1997 Proof	—	Value: 75.00				

KM# 789 1/25 CROWN
1.2440 g., 0.9999 Gold 0.0400 oz. AGW, 13.9 mm.
Ruler: Elizabeth II **Subject:** History of the Cat **Obv:** Crowned bust right **Rev:** Cat stalking a spider

Date	Mintage	F	VF	XF	Unc	BU
1997 Proof	Est. 25,000	Value: 45.00				

KM# 812 1/25 CROWN
1.2441 g., 0.9999 Gold 0.0400 oz. AGW, 13.9 mm.
Ruler: Elizabeth II **Subject:** Year of the Tiger **Obv:** Crowned bust right **Rev:** Tiger

Date	Mintage	F	VF	XF	Unc	BU
1998 Proof	Est. 20,000	Value: 45.00				

KM# 828 1/25 CROWN
1.2441 g., 0.9999 Gold 0.0400 oz. AGW, 13.9 mm.
Ruler: Elizabeth II **Series:** Flower Fairies **Obv:** Crowned bust right **Rev:** Fairy standing, lavender

Date	Mintage	F	VF	XF	Unc	BU
1998 Proof	Est. 25,000	Value: 45.00				

KM# 828a 1/25 CROWN
1.2441 g., 0.9995 Platinum 0.0400 oz. APW, 13.9 mm.
Ruler: Elizabeth II **Series:** Flower Fairies **Obv:** Crowned bust right **Rev:** Fairy standing, lavender

Date	Mintage	F	VF	XF	Unc	BU
1998 Proof	Est. 7,500	Value: 75.00				

KM# 829 1/25 CROWN
1.2441 g., 0.9999 Gold 0.0400 oz. AGW, 13.9 mm.
Ruler: Elizabeth II **Series:** Flower Fairies **Obv:** Crowned bust right **Rev:** Two fairies, sweet pea

Date	Mintage	F	VF	XF	Unc	BU
1998 Proof	Est. 25,000	Value: 45.00				

KM# 829a 1/25 CROWN
1.2441 g., 0.9995 Platinum 0.0400 oz. APW, 13.9 mm.
Ruler: Elizabeth II **Series:** Flower Fairies **Obv:** Crowned bust right **Rev:** Two fairies, sweet pea

Date	Mintage	F	VF	XF	Unc	BU
1998 Proof	Est. 7,500	Value: 75.00				

KM# 830 1/25 CROWN
1.2441 g., 0.9999 Gold 0.0400 oz. AGW, 13.9 mm.
Ruler: Elizabeth II **Series:** Flower Fairies **Obv:** Crowned bust right **Rev:** Two fairies, sweet pea

Date	Mintage	F	VF	XF	Unc	BU
1998 Proof	—	Value: 45.00				

KM# 830a 1/25 CROWN
1.2441 g., 0.9995 Platinum 0.0400 oz. APW, 13.9 mm.
Ruler: Elizabeth II **Series:** Flower Fairies **Obv:** Crowned bust right **Rev:** Two fairies, sweet pea

Date	Mintage	F	VF	XF	Unc	BU
1998 Proof	Est. 30,000	Value: 75.00				

KM# 831 1/25 CROWN
1.2441 g., 0.9999 Gold 0.0400 oz. AGW, 13.9 mm.
Ruler: Elizabeth II **Series:** Flower Fairies **Obv:** Crowned bust right **Rev:** Fairy standing, daffodil

Date	Mintage	F	VF	XF	Unc	BU
1998 Proof	Est. 25,000	Value: 45.00				

KM# 831a 1/25 CROWN
1.2441 g., 0.9995 Platinum 0.0400 oz. APW, 13.9 mm.
Ruler: Elizabeth II **Series:** Flower Fairies **Obv:** Crowned bust right **Rev:** Fairy standing, daffodil

Date	Mintage	F	VF	XF	Unc	BU
1998 Proof	Est. 7,500	Value: 75.00				

KM# 853 1/25 CROWN
1.2440 g., 0.9999 Gold 0.0400 oz. AGW, 13.9 mm.
Ruler: Elizabeth II **Obv:** Crowned bust right **Rev:** Birman cat

Date	Mintage	F	VF	XF	Unc	BU
1998	—	—	—	—	—	40.00
1998 Proof	1,000	Value: 45.00				

KM# 853a 1/25 CROWN
1.2440 g., 0.9995 Platinum 0.0400 oz. APW, 13.9 mm.
Ruler: Elizabeth II **Obv:** Crowned bust right **Rev:** Birman cat

Date	Mintage	F	VF	XF	Unc	BU
1998 Proof	— Value: 75.00					

KM# 859 1/25 CROWN
1.2440 g., 0.9999 Gold 0.0400 oz. AGW, 13.9 mm.
Ruler: Elizabeth II **Subject:** History of the Cat **Obv:** Crowned bust right **Rev:** Egyptian Mau cat with earring

Date	Mintage	F	VF	XF	Unc	BU
1998 Proof	Est. 25,000 Value: 45.00					

KM# 948 1/25 CROWN
1.2440 g., 0.9999 Gold 0.0400 oz. AGW, 13.9 mm.
Ruler: Elizabeth II **Subject:** Year of the Rabbit **Obv:** Crowned bust right **Rev:** Two rabbits

Date	Mintage	F	VF	XF	Unc	BU
1999 Proof	Est. 20,000 Value: 45.00					

KM# 958 1/25 CROWN
1.2440 g., 0.9999 Gold 0.0400 oz. AGW, 13.9 mm.
Ruler: Elizabeth II **Obv:** Crowned bust right **Rev:** British Blue cat

Date	Mintage	F	VF	XF	Unc	BU
1999						40.00
1999 Proof	— Value: 45.00					
1999 U Y2K	20,000					40.00

KM# 958a 1/25 CROWN
1.2441 g., 0.9995 Platinum 0.0400 oz. APW, 13.9 mm.
Ruler: Elizabeth II **Obv:** Crowned bust right **Rev:** British Blue cat

Date	Mintage	F	VF	XF	Unc	BU
1999 Proof	— Value: 75.00					

KM# 1052 1/25 CROWN
1.2400 g., 0.9999 Gold 0.0399 oz. AGW, 13.92 mm.
Ruler: Elizabeth II **Obv:** Crowned bust right **Rev:** Scottish fold kitten **Edge:** Reeded

Date	Mintage	F	VF	XF	Unc	BU
2000						40.00
2000 Proof	— Value: 45.00					

KM# 1052a 1/25 CROWN
1.2441 g., 0.9995 Platinum 0.0400 oz. APW, 13.9 mm. **Ruler:** Elizabeth II **Obv:** Crowned bust right **Rev:** Scottish fold kitten

Date	Mintage	F	VF	XF	Unc	BU
2000						70.00

KM# 1012 1/25 CROWN
1.2440 g., 0.9999 Gold 0.0400 oz. AGW, 13.9 mm.
Ruler: Elizabeth II **Subject:** Year of the Dragon **Obv:** Crowned bust right **Rev:** Dragon, Chinese characters

Date	Mintage	F	VF	XF	Unc	BU
2000 Proof	Est. 20,000 Value: 45.00					

KM# 236 1/10 CROWN
3.1100 g., 0.9990 Gold 0.0999 oz. AGW **Ruler:** Elizabeth II **Obv:** Crowned bust right **Rev:** Manx cat

Date	Mintage	F	VF	XF	Unc	BU
1988	12,000					100
1988 Proof	5,000 Value: 105					

KM# 253 1/10 CROWN
3.1100 g., 0.9990 Gold 0.0999 oz. AGW, 17.95 mm.
Ruler: Elizabeth II **Obv:** Crowned bust right **Rev:** Persian cat

Date	Mintage	F	VF	XF	Unc	BU
1989						100
1989 Proof	— Value: 105					

KM# 253a 1/10 CROWN
3.1100 g., 0.9995 Platinum 0.0999 oz. APW, 17.95 mm.
Ruler: Elizabeth II **Obv:** Crowned bust right **Rev:** Persian cat **Note:** Prev. KM#468.

Date	Mintage	F	VF	XF	Unc	BU
1989						180
1989 Proof	— Value: 190					

KM# 278 1/10 CROWN
3.1100 g., 0.9990 Gold 0.0999 oz. AGW, 17.95 mm.
Ruler: Elizabeth II **Obv:** Crowned bust right **Rev:** Alley cat

Date	Mintage	F	VF	XF	Unc	BU
1990						100
1990 Proof	— Value: 105					

KM# 295 1/10 CROWN
3.1100 g., 0.9990 Gold 0.0999 oz. AGW, 17.95 mm.
Ruler: Elizabeth II **Obv:** Crowned bust right **Rev:** Norwegian cat

Date	Mintage	F	VF	XF	Unc	BU
1991						100
1991 Proof	— Value: 105					

KM# 323 1/10 CROWN
3.1100 g., 0.9990 Gold 0.0999 oz. AGW, 17.95 mm.
Ruler: Elizabeth II **Subject:** America's Cup **Obv:** Crowned bust right **Rev:** Cameo of "Star of India" above modern sailboat, Sidney Opera House and Harbor Bridge.

Date	Mintage	F	VF	XF	Unc	BU
1992 Prooflike	25,000					125

KM# 323a 1/10 CROWN
3.1100 g., 0.9995 Platinum 0.0999 oz. APW, 17.95 mm.
Ruler: Elizabeth II **Subject:** America's Cup **Obv:** Crowned bust right **Rev:** Sailboat

Date	Mintage	F	VF	XF	Unc	BU
1992 Prooflike	5,000					180

KM# 329 1/10 CROWN
3.1100 g., 0.9990 Gold 0.0999 oz. AGW, 17.95 mm.
Ruler: Elizabeth II **Obv:** Crowned bust right **Rev:** Siamese cat

Date	Mintage	F	VF	XF	Unc	BU
1992						100
1992 Proof	— Value: 105					

KM# 339 1/10 CROWN
3.1100 g., 0.9990 Gold 0.0999 oz. AGW, 17.95 mm.
Ruler: Elizabeth II **Subject:** Year of the Cockerel **Obv:** Crowned bust right **Rev:** Cockerel in inner circle

Date	Mintage	F	VF	XF	Unc	BU
1993 Proof	Est. 20,000 Value: 105					

KM# 350 1/10 CROWN
3.1100 g., 0.9990 Gold 0.0999 oz. AGW, 17.95 mm.
Ruler: Elizabeth II **Obv:** Crowned bust right **Rev:** Maine Coon cat

Date	Mintage	F	VF	XF	Unc	BU
1993						100
1993 Proof	— Value: 105					

KM# 377 1/10 CROWN
3.1100 g., 0.9990 Gold 0.0999 oz. AGW, 17.95 mm. **Ruler:** Elizabeth II **Obv:** Crowned bust right **Rev:** Japanese Bobtail cat

Date	Mintage	F	VF	XF	Unc	BU
1994						100
1994 Proof	— Value: 105					

KM# 403 1/10 CROWN
3.1100 g., 0.9990 Gold 0.0999 oz. AGW, 17.95 mm.
Ruler: Elizabeth II **Obv:** Crowned bust right **Rev:** Pekingese dog

Date	Mintage	F	VF	XF	Unc	BU
1994 Proof	20,000 Value: 105					

KM# 377a 1/10 CROWN
3.1100 g., 0.9995 Platinum 0.0999 oz. APW, 17.95 mm.
Ruler: Elizabeth II **Obv:** Crowned bust right **Rev:** Japanese Bobtail cat **Note:** Prev. KM#474.

Date	Mintage	F	VF	XF	Unc	BU
1994						180
1994 Proof	— Value: 190					

KM# 443 1/10 CROWN
3.1100 g., 0.9990 Gold 0.0999 oz. AGW, 17.95 mm.
Ruler: Elizabeth II **Obv:** Crowned bust right **Rev:** Turkish cat

Date	Mintage	F	VF	XF	Unc	BU
1995						100
1995 Proof	— Value: 105					

KM# 450 1/10 CROWN
3.1100 g., 0.9990 Gold 0.0999 oz. AGW, 17.95 mm.
Ruler: Elizabeth II **Subject:** Year of the Pig **Obv:** Crowned bust right **Rev:** Sow with piglets

Date	Mintage	F	VF	XF	Unc	BU
1995 Proof	Est. 20,000 Value: 105					

KM# 443a 1/10 CROWN
3.1100 g., 0.9995 Platinum 0.0999 oz. APW, 17.95 mm.
Ruler: Elizabeth II **Obv:** Crowned bust right **Rev:** Turkish cat **Note:** Prev. KM#479.

Date	Mintage	F	VF	XF	Unc	BU
1995						180
1995 Proof	— Value: 190					

KM# 601 1/10 CROWN
3.1100 g., 0.9990 Gold 0.0999 oz. AGW, 17.95 mm.
Ruler: Elizabeth II **Series:** Flower Fairies **Obv:** Crowned bust right **Rev:** Orchis

Date	Mintage	F	VF	XF	Unc	BU
1996 Proof	Est. 20,000 Value: 105					

KM# 602 1/10 CROWN
3.1100 g., 0.9990 Gold 0.0999 oz. AGW, 17.95 mm.
Ruler: Elizabeth II **Series:** Flower Fairies **Obv:** Crowned bust right **Rev:** Rose

Date	Mintage	F	VF	XF	Unc	BU
1996 Proof	Est. 20,000 Value: 105					

KM# 603 1/10 CROWN
3.1100 g., 0.9990 Gold 0.0999 oz. AGW, 17.95 mm.
Ruler: Elizabeth II **Series:** Flower Fairies **Obv:** Crowned bust right **Rev:** Fuchsia

Date	Mintage	F	VF	XF	Unc	BU
1996 Proof	Est. 20,000 Value: 105					

KM# 604 1/10 CROWN
3.1100 g., 0.9990 Gold 0.0999 oz. AGW, 17.95 mm.
Ruler: Elizabeth II **Obv:** Crowned bust right **Rev:** Pinks

Date	Mintage	F	VF	XF	Unc	BU
1996 Proof	Est. 20,000 Value: 105					

KM# 615 1/10 CROWN
3.1100 g., 0.9990 Gold 0.0999 oz. AGW, 17.95 mm.
Ruler: Elizabeth II **Obv:** Crowned bust right **Rev:** Burmese cat

Date	Mintage	F	VF	XF	Unc	BU
1996						100
1996 Proof	— Value: 105					

KM# 615a 1/10 CROWN
3.1100 g., 0.9995 Platinum 0.0999 oz. APW, 17.95 mm.
Ruler: Elizabeth II **Obv:** Crowned bust right **Rev:** Burmese cat **Note:** Prev. KM#616.

Date	Mintage	F	VF	XF	Unc	BU
1996						180
1996 Proof	— Value: 190					

KM# 729 1/10 CROWN
3.1100 g., 0.9990 Gold 0.0999 oz. AGW, 17.95 mm.
Ruler: Elizabeth II **Subject:** Year of the Rat **Obv:** Crowned bust right **Rev:** Rat

Date	Mintage	F	VF	XF	Unc	BU
1996 Proof	— Value: 105					

Note: Entire series purchased by one buyer. Mintage, disposition and market value unknown

KM# 722 1/10 CROWN
3.1100 g., 0.9990 Gold 0.0999 oz. AGW, 17.95 mm.
Ruler: Elizabeth II **Subject:** Year of the Ox **Obv:** Crowned bust right **Rev:** Ox laying down

Date	Mintage	F	VF	XF	Unc	BU
1997 Proof	Est. 15,000 Value: 105					

KM# 743 1/10 CROWN
3.1100 g., 0.9990 Gold 0.0999 oz. AGW, 17.95 mm.
Ruler: Elizabeth II **Series:** Flower Fairies **Obv:** Crowned bust right **Rev:** Candytuft

Date	Mintage	F	VF	XF	Unc	BU
1997 Proof	Est. 20,000 Value: 105					

KM# 743a 1/10 CROWN
3.1259 g., 0.9950 Platinum 0.1000 oz. APW, 17.95 mm.
Ruler: Elizabeth II **Series:** Flower Fairies **Obv:** Crowned bust right **Rev:** Candytuft

Date	Mintage	F	VF	XF	Unc	BU
1997 Proof	Est. 5,000 Value: 190					

KM# 744 1/10 CROWN
3.1103 g., 0.9999 Gold 0.1000 oz. AGW, 17.95 mm.
Ruler: Elizabeth II **Obv:** Crowned bust right **Rev:** Snowdrop

Date	Mintage	F	VF	XF	Unc	BU
1997 Proof	Est. 20,000 Value: 105					

KM# 744a 1/10 CROWN
3.1259 g., 0.9950 Platinum 0.1000 oz. APW, 17.95 mm.
Ruler: Elizabeth II **Series:** Flower Fairies **Obv:** Crowned bust right **Rev:** Snowdrop

Date	Mintage	F	VF	XF	Unc	BU
1997 Proof	Est. 5,000 Value: 190					

KM# 745 1/10 CROWN
3.1103 g., 0.9999 Gold 0.1000 oz. AGW, 17.95 mm.
Ruler: Elizabeth II **Series:** Flower Fairies **Obv:** Crowned bust right **Rev:** Tulip

Date	Mintage	F	VF	XF	Unc	BU
1997 Proof	Est. 20,000 Value: 105					

KM# 745a 1/10 CROWN
3.1259 g., 0.9950 Platinum 0.1000 oz. APW, 17.95 mm.
Ruler: Elizabeth II **Series:** Flower Fairies **Obv:** Crowned bust right **Rev:** Tulip

Date	Mintage	F	VF	XF	Unc	BU
1997 Proof	Est. 5,000 Value: 190					

KM# 746 1/10 CROWN
3.1103 g., 0.9999 Gold 0.1000 oz. AGW, 17.95 mm.
Ruler: Elizabeth II **Series:** Flower Fairies **Obv:** Crowned bust right **Rev:** Jasmine

Date	Mintage	F	VF	XF	Unc	BU
1997 Proof	Est. 20,000 Value: 105					

KM# 746a 1/10 CROWN
3.1259 g., 0.9950 Platinum 0.1000 oz. APW, 17.95 mm.
Ruler: Elizabeth II **Series:** Flower Fairies **Obv:** Crowned bust right **Rev:** Jasmine

Date	Mintage	F	VF	XF	Unc	BU
1997 Proof	Est. 5,000 Value: 190					

KM# 771 1/10 CROWN
3.1100 g., 0.9999 Gold 0.1000 oz. AGW, 17.95 mm. **Ruler:** Elizabeth II **Obv:** Crowned bust right **Rev:** Long-haired Smoke cat

Date	Mintage	F	VF	XF	Unc	BU
1997						100
1997 Proof	— Value: 105					

KM# 771a 1/10 CROWN
3.1100 g., 0.9995 Platinum 0.0999 oz. APW, 17.95 mm.
Ruler: Elizabeth II **Obv:** Crowned bust right **Rev:** Long-haired Smoke cat

Date	Mintage	F	VF	XF	Unc	BU
1997						180
1997 Proof	— Value: 190					

KM# 790 1/10 CROWN
3.1100 g., 0.9999 Gold 0.1000 oz. AGW, 17.95 mm.
Ruler: Elizabeth II **Subject:** History of the Cat **Obv:** Crowned bust right **Rev:** Cat stalking a spider

Date	Mintage	F	VF	XF	Unc	BU
1997 Proof	Est. 20,000 Value: 105					

KM# 813 1/10 CROWN
3.1100 g., 0.9999 Gold 0.1000 oz. AGW, 17.95 mm.
Ruler: Elizabeth II **Subject:** Year of the Tiger **Obv:** Crowned bust right **Rev:** Tiger

Date	Mintage	F	VF	XF	Unc	BU
1998 Proof	Est. 15,000				Value: 105	

KM# 832 1/10 CROWN
3.1100 g., 0.9999 Gold 0.1000 oz. AGW, 17.95 mm.
Ruler: Elizabeth II **Series:** Flower Fairies **Obv:** Crowned bust right **Rev:** Standing fairy, lavender

Date	Mintage	F	VF	XF	Unc	BU
1998 Proof	Est. 20,000				Value: 105	

KM# 832a 1/10 CROWN
3.1100 g., 0.9995 Platinum 0.0999 oz. APW, 17.95 mm.
Ruler: Elizabeth II **Series:** Flower Fairies **Obv:** Crowned bust right **Rev:** Standing fairy, lavender

Date	Mintage	F	VF	XF	Unc	BU
1998 Proof	Est. 5,000				Value: 190	

KM# 833 1/10 CROWN
3.1100 g., 0.9999 Gold 0.1000 oz. AGW, 17.95 mm.
Ruler: Elizabeth II **Series:** Flower Fairies **Obv:** Crowned bust right **Rev:** Two fairies, sweet pea

Date	Mintage	F	VF	XF	Unc	BU
1998 Proof	Est. 20,000				Value: 105	

KM# 833a 1/10 CROWN
3.1100 g., 0.9995 Platinum 0.0999 oz. APW, 17.95 mm.
Ruler: Elizabeth II **Series:** Flower Fairies **Obv:** Crowned bust right **Rev:** Two fairies, sweet pea

Date	Mintage	F	VF	XF	Unc	BU
1998 Proof	Est. 5,000				Value: 190	

KM# 834 1/10 CROWN
3.1100 g., 0.9999 Gold 0.1000 oz. AGW, 17.95 mm.
Ruler: Elizabeth II **Obv:** Crowned bust right **Rev:** Fairy looking into flower, White Bindweed

Date	Mintage	F	VF	XF	Unc	BU
1998 Proof	Est. 20,000				Value: 105	

KM# 834a 1/10 CROWN
3.1100 g., 0.9995 Platinum 0.0999 oz. APW, 17.95 mm.
Ruler: Elizabeth II **Series:** Flower Fairies **Obv:** Crowned bust right **Rev:** Fairy looking into flower, White Bindweed

Date	Mintage	F	VF	XF	Unc	BU
1998 Proof	Est. 5,000				Value: 190	

KM# 835 1/10 CROWN
3.1100 g., 0.9999 Gold 0.1000 oz. AGW, 17.95 mm.
Ruler: Elizabeth II **Series:** Flower Fairies **Obv:** Crowned bust right **Rev:** Fairy standing with flower, daffodil

Date	Mintage	F	VF	XF	Unc	BU
1998 Proof	Est. 20,000				Value: 105	

KM# 835a 1/10 CROWN
3.1100 g., 0.9995 Platinum 0.0999 oz. APW, 17.95 mm.
Ruler: Elizabeth II **Obv:** Crowned bust right **Rev:** Fairy standing with flower, daffodil **Rev. Leg.:** Flower Fairies

Date	Mintage	F	VF	XF	Unc	BU
1998 Proof	Est. 5,000				Value: 190	

KM# 854 1/10 CROWN
3.1100 g., 0.9999 Gold 0.1000 oz. AGW, 17.95 mm.
Ruler: Elizabeth II **Obv:** Crowned bust right **Rev:** Birman cat

Date	Mintage	F	VF	XF	Unc	BU
1998	—	—	—	—	—	100
1998 Proof	1,000				Value: 105	

KM# 854a 1/10 CROWN
3.1100 g., 0.9995 Platinum 0.0999 oz. APW, 17.95 mm.
Ruler: Elizabeth II **Obv:** Crowned bust right **Rev:** Birman cat

Date	Mintage	F	VF	XF	Unc	BU
1998 Proof	—				Value: 190	

KM# 860 1/10 CROWN
3.1100 g., 0.9999 Gold 0.1000 oz. AGW, 17.95 mm.
Ruler: Elizabeth II **Subject:** History of the Cat **Obv:** Crowned bust right **Rev:** Egyptian Mau cat with earring

Date	Mintage	F	VF	XF	Unc	BU
1998 Proof	Est. 20,000				Value: 105	

KM# 949 1/10 CROWN
3.1100 g., 0.9999 Gold 0.1000 oz. AGW, 17.95 mm.
Ruler: Elizabeth II **Subject:** Year of the Rabbit **Obv:** Crowned bust right **Rev:** Two rabbits

Date	Mintage	F	VF	XF	Unc	BU
1999 Proof	—				Value: 105	

KM# 960 1/10 CROWN
3.1100 g., 0.9999 Gold 0.1000 oz. AGW, 17.95 mm.
Ruler: Elizabeth II **Obv:** Crowned bust right **Rev:** British Blue cat cleaning its paw

Date	Mintage	F	VF	XF	Unc	BU
1999	—	—	—	—	—	100
1999 Proof	—				Value: 105	
1999 U Y2K	10,000	—	—	—	—	100

KM# 960a 1/10 CROWN
3.1104 g., 0.9995 Platinum 0.0999 oz. APW, 17.95 mm.
Ruler: Elizabeth II **Obv:** Crowned bust right **Rev:** British Blue cat cleaning its paw

Date	Mintage	F	VF	XF	Unc	BU
1999 Proof	—				Value: 190	

KM# 1053 1/10 CROWN
3.1100 g., 0.9999 Gold 0.1000 oz. AGW, 17.95 mm.
Ruler: Elizabeth II **Obv:** Crowned bust right **Rev:** Scottish kitten playing with the world **Edge:** Reeded

Date	Mintage	F	VF	XF	Unc	BU
2000	—	—	—	—	—	100
2000 Proof	—				Value: 105	

KM# 1053a 1/10 CROWN
3.1104 g., 0.9995 Platinum 0.0999 oz. APW, 17.95 mm.
Ruler: Elizabeth II **Obv:** Crowned bust right **Rev:** Scottish kitten playing with the world

Date	Mintage	F	VF	XF	Unc	BU
2000	—					180

KM# 1013 1/10 CROWN
3.1100 g., 0.9999 Gold 0.1000 oz. AGW, 17.95 mm.
Ruler: Elizabeth II **Subject:** Year of the Dragon **Obv:** Crowned bust right **Rev:** Dragon, Chinese characters

Date	Mintage	F	VF	XF	Unc	BU
2000 Proof	Est. 15,000				Value: 105	

KM# 237 1/5 CROWN
6.2200 g., 0.9990 Gold 0.1998 oz. AGW, 22 mm.
Ruler: Elizabeth II **Obv:** Crowned bust right **Rev:** Manx cat

Date	Mintage	F	VF	XF	Unc	BU
1988	6,750	—	—	—	—	195
1988 Proof	5,000				Value: 200	

KM# 254 1/5 CROWN
6.2200 g., 0.9990 Gold 0.1998 oz. AGW, 22 mm.
Ruler: Elizabeth II **Obv:** Crowned bust right **Rev:** Persian cat

Date	Mintage	F	VF	XF	Unc	BU
1989	—	—	—	—	—	195
1989 Proof	—				Value: 200	

KM# 274 1/5 CROWN
6.2200 g., 0.9990 Gold 0.1998 oz. AGW, 22 mm.
Ruler: Elizabeth II **Obv:** Crowned bust right **Rev:** Cameo head facing within circle

Date	Mintage	F	VF	XF	Unc	BU
1989 Proof	Est. 5,000				Value: 200	

KM# 254a 1/5 CROWN
6.2200 g., 0.9990 Platinum 0.1998 oz. APW, 22 mm.
Ruler: Elizabeth II **Obv:** Crowned bust right **Rev:** Persian cat **Note:** Prev. KM#469.

Date	Mintage	F	VF	XF	Unc	BU
1989	—	—	—	—	—	375
1989 Proof	—				Value: 385	

KM# 268 1/5 CROWN
6.2200 g., 0.9990 Gold 0.1998 oz. AGW, 22 mm.
Ruler: Elizabeth II **Subject:** 150th Anniversary of "Penny Black" Stamp **Obv:** Crowned bust right **Rev:** Penny Black Stamp

Date	Mintage	F	VF	XF	Unc	BU
1990 Proof	Est. 5,000				Value: 210	

KM# 279.1 1/5 CROWN
6.2200 g., 0.9990 Gold 0.1998 oz. AGW, 22 mm.
Ruler: Elizabeth II **Obv:** Crowned bust right **Rev:** Alley cat

Date	Mintage	F	VF	XF	Unc	BU
1990	—	—	—	—	—	195
1990 Proof	—				Value: 200	

KM# 279.2 1/5 CROWN
6.2200 g., 0.9990 Gold 0.1998 oz. AGW, 22 mm.
Ruler: Elizabeth II **Obv:** Crowned bust right **Rev:** Alley cat **Note:** Error.(Rev) Dies claiming platinum metal content

Date	Mintage	F	VF	XF	Unc	BU
1990	467	—	—	—	—	375

KM# 306 1/5 CROWN
6.2200 g., 0.9990 Gold 0.1998 oz. AGW, 22 mm.
Ruler: Elizabeth II **Obv:** Crowned bust right **Rev:** Queen Mother with two daughters

Date	Mintage	F	VF	XF	Unc	BU
1990 Proof	—				Value: 200	

KM# 306a 1/5 CROWN
6.2200 g., 0.9990 Platinum 0.1998 oz. APW, 22 mm.
Ruler: Elizabeth II **Obv:** Crowned bust right **Rev:** Queen Mother with two daughters

Date	Mintage	F	VF	XF	Unc	BU
1990 Proof	—				Value: 385	

KM# 279.1a 1/5 CROWN
6.2200 g., 0.9990 Platinum 0.1998 oz. APW, 22 mm.
Ruler: Elizabeth II **Obv:** Crowned bust right **Rev:** Alley cat **Note:** Prev. KM#472.

Date	Mintage	F	VF	XF	Unc	BU
1990	—	—	—	—	—	375
1990 Proof	—				Value: 385	

KM# 819 1/5 CROWN
6.2200 g., 0.9990 Gold 0.1998 oz. AGW, 22 mm. **Ruler:** Elizabeth II **Subject:** Soccer **Obv:** Crowned bust right **Rev:** Milano

Date	Mintage	F	VF	XF	Unc	BU
1990 Proof	Est. 500				Value: 200	

KM# 819a 1/5 CROWN
6.2200 g., 0.9990 Platinum 0.1998 oz. APW, 22 mm.
Ruler: Elizabeth II **Subject:** Soccer **Obv:** Crowned bust right **Rev:** Milano

Date	Mintage	F	VF	XF	Unc	BU
1990 Proof	Est. 250				Value: 385	

KM# 820 1/5 CROWN
6.2200 g., 0.9990 Gold 0.1998 oz. AGW, 22 mm. **Ruler:** Elizabeth II **Subject:** Soccer **Obv:** Crowned bust right **Rev:** Torino

Date	Mintage	F	VF	XF	Unc	BU
1990 Proof	Est. 500				Value: 200	

KM# 820a 1/5 CROWN
6.2200 g., 0.9990 Platinum 0.1998 oz. APW, 22 mm.
Ruler: Elizabeth II **Subject:** Soccer **Obv:** Crowned bust right **Rev:** Torino

Date	Mintage	F	VF	XF	Unc	BU
1990 Proof	Est. 250				Value: 385	

KM# 821 1/5 CROWN
6.2200 g., 0.9990 Gold 0.1998 oz. AGW, 22 mm. **Ruler:** Elizabeth II **Subject:** Soccer **Obv:** Crowned bust right **Rev:** Bologna

Date	Mintage	F	VF	XF	Unc	BU
1990 Proof	Est. 500				Value: 200	

KM# 821a 1/5 CROWN
6.2200 g., 0.9990 Platinum 0.1998 oz. APW, 22 mm.
Ruler: Elizabeth II **Subject:** Soccer **Obv:** Crowned bust right **Rev:** Bologna

Date	Mintage	F	VF	XF	Unc	BU
1990	Est. 250				Value: 385	

KM# 822 1/5 CROWN
6.2200 g., 0.9990 Gold 0.1998 oz. AGW, 22 mm. **Ruler:** Elizabeth II **Subject:** Soccer **Obv:** Crowned bust right **Rev:** Palermo

Date	Mintage	F	VF	XF	Unc	BU
1990 Proof	Est. 500				Value: 200	

KM# 822a 1/5 CROWN
6.2200 g., 0.9990 Platinum 0.1998 oz. APW, 22 mm.
Ruler: Elizabeth II **Subject:** Soccer **Obv:** Crowned bust right **Rev:** Palermo

Date	Mintage	F	VF	XF	Unc	BU
1990	Est. 250				Value: 385	

KM# 290 1/5 CROWN
6.2200 g., 0.9990 Gold 0.1998 oz. AGW, 22 mm.
Ruler: Elizabeth II **Subject:** 100th Anniversary - American Numismatic Association **Obv:** Crowned bust right **Rev:** Assorted famous world coins

Date	Mintage	F	VF	XF	Unc	BU
1991 Proof	100				Value: 200	

KM# 296 1/5 CROWN
6.2200 g., 0.9990 Gold 0.1998 oz. AGW, 22 mm.
Ruler: Elizabeth II **Obv:** Crowned bust right **Rev:** Norwegian cat

Date	Mintage	F	VF	XF	Unc	BU
1991	—					195
1991 Proof	—				Value: 200	

KM# 302 1/5 CROWN
6.2200 g., 0.9990 Gold 0.1998 oz. AGW, 22 mm.
Ruler: Elizabeth II **Subject:** America's Cup **Obv:** Crowned bust right **Rev:** Cameo above two modern sailboats

Date	Mintage	F	VF	XF	Unc	BU
1991 Proof	Est. 250				Value: 200	

KM# 324 1/5 CROWN
6.2200 g., 0.9990 Gold 0.1998 oz. AGW, 22 mm.
Ruler: Elizabeth II **Subject:** America's Cup **Obv:** Crowned bust right **Rev:** Cameo above modern sailboat, Sidney Opera House and the Harbor bridge.

Date	Mintage	F	VF	XF	Unc	BU
1992 Prooflike	10,000	—	—	—		195

KM# 330 1/5 CROWN
6.2200 g., 0.9990 Gold 0.1998 oz. AGW, 22 mm.
Ruler: Elizabeth II **Obv:** Crowned bust right **Rev:** Siamese cat

Date	Mintage	F	VF	XF	Unc	BU
1992	—	—	—	—	—	195
1992 Proof	—				Value: 200	

KM# 340 1/5 CROWN
6.2200 g., 0.9990 Gold 0.1998 oz. AGW, 22 mm.
Ruler: Elizabeth II **Subject:** Year of the Cockerel **Obv:** Crowned bust right within circle **Rev:** Cockerel within circle

Date	Mintage	F	VF	XF	Unc	BU
1993 Proof	Est. 10,000				Value: 200	

KM# 351 1/5 CROWN
6.2200 g., 0.9990 Gold 0.1998 oz. AGW, 22 mm.
Ruler: Elizabeth II **Obv:** Crowned bust right **Rev:** Maine Coon cat

Date	Mintage	F	VF	XF	Unc	BU
1993	—	—	—	—	—	195
1993 Proof	—				Value: 200	

KM# 365 1/5 CROWN
6.2200 g., 0.9990 Gold 0.1998 oz. AGW, 22 mm.
Ruler: Elizabeth II **Subject:** World Cup Soccer - Type I **Obv:** Crowned bust right **Rev:** Player in foreground kicking ball

Date	Mintage	F	VF	XF	Unc	BU
1994 Proof	Est. 5,000				Value: 200	

KM# 367 1/5 CROWN
6.2200 g., 0.9990 Gold 0.1998 oz. AGW, 22 mm.
Ruler: Elizabeth II **Subject:** World Cup Soccer - Type II **Obv:** Crowned bust right **Rev:** Three players

Date	Mintage	F	VF	XF	Unc	BU
1994 Proof	Est. 5,000				Value: 200	

KM# 369 1/5 CROWN
6.2200 g., 0.9990 Gold 0.1998 oz. AGW, 22 mm.
Ruler: Elizabeth II **Subject:** World Cup Soccer - Type III **Obv:** Crowned bust right **Rev:** Soccer players

Date	Mintage	F	VF	XF	Unc	BU
1994 Proof	Est. 5,000				Value: 200	

KM# 371 1/5 CROWN
6.2200 g., 0.9990 Gold 0.1998 oz. AGW, 22 mm.
Ruler: Elizabeth II **Subject:** World Cup Soccer - Type IV **Obv:** Crowned bust right **Rev:** Soccer players

Date	Mintage	F	VF	XF	Unc	BU
1994 Proof	Est. 5,000				Value: 200	

KM# 373 1/5 CROWN
6.2200 g., 0.9990 Gold 0.1998 oz. AGW, 22 mm.
Ruler: Elizabeth II **Subject:** World Cup Soccer - Type V **Obv:** Crowned bust right **Rev:** Goalie catching ball in hand

Date	Mintage	F	VF	XF	Unc	BU
1994 Proof	Est. 5,000				Value: 200	

KM# 375 1/5 CROWN
6.2200 g., 0.9990 Gold 0.1998 oz. AGW, 22 mm.
Ruler: Elizabeth II **Subject:** World Cup Soccer - Type VI **Obv:** Crowned bust right **Rev:** Soccer players

Date	Mintage	F	VF	XF	Unc	BU
1994 Proof	Est. 5,000				Value: 200	

KM# 378 1/5 CROWN
6.2200 g., 0.9990 Gold 0.1998 oz. AGW, 22 mm. **Ruler:** Elizabeth II **Obv:** Crowned bust right **Rev:** Japanese Bobtail cat

Date	Mintage	F	VF	XF	Unc	BU
1994	—	—	—	—	—	195
1994 Proof	—				Value: 200	

KM# 383 1/5 CROWN
6.2200 g., 0.9990 Gold 0.1998 oz. AGW, 22 mm.
Ruler: Elizabeth II **Series:** Preserve Planet Earth **Obv:** Crowned bust right **Rev:** Woolly mammoth

Date	Mintage	F	VF	XF	Unc	BU
1994 Proof	Est. 5,000				Value: 200	

KM# 388 1/5 CROWN
6.2200 g., 0.9990 Gold 0.1998 oz. AGW, 22 mm.
Ruler: Elizabeth II **Series:** Preserve Planet Earth **Obv:** Crowned bust right **Rev:** Kangaroos

Date	Mintage	F	VF	XF	Unc	BU
1994 Proof	5,000				Value: 200	

KM# 389 1/5 CROWN
6.2200 g., 0.9990 Gold 0.1998 oz. AGW, 22 mm.
Ruler: Elizabeth II **Series:** Preserve Planet Earth **Obv:** Crowned bust right **Rev:** Seals

Date	Mintage	F	VF	XF	Unc	BU
1994 Proof	5,000				Value: 200	

KM# 390 1/5 CROWN
6.2200 g., 0.9990 Gold 0.1998 oz. AGW, 22 mm.
Ruler: Elizabeth II **Series:** Preserve Planet Earth **Obv:** Crowned bust right **Rev:** Deer

Date	Mintage	F	VF	XF	Unc	BU
1994 Proof	5,000				Value: 200	

KM# 404 1/5 CROWN
6.2200 g., 0.9990 Gold 0.1998 oz. AGW, 22 mm.
Ruler: Elizabeth II **Obv:** Crowned bust right **Rev:** Pekingese

Date	Mintage	F	VF	XF	Unc	BU
1994 Proof	10,000				Value: 200	

KM# 409 1/5 CROWN
6.2200 g., 0.9990 Gold 0.1998 oz. AGW, 22 mm.
Ruler: Elizabeth II **Series:** Man in Flight **Obv:** Crowned bust right **Rev:** Manned glider

Date	Mintage	F	VF	XF	Unc	BU
1994 Proof	Est. 5,000				Value: 200	

KM# 410 1/5 CROWN
6.2200 g., 0.9990 Gold 0.1998 oz. AGW, 22 mm.
Ruler: Elizabeth II **Series:** Man in Flight **Obv:** Crowned bust right **Rev:** Dirigible, Ferdinand von Zeppelin

Date	Mintage	F	VF	XF	Unc	BU
1994 Proof	Est. 5,000				Value: 200	

KM# 411 1/5 CROWN
6.2200 g., 0.9990 Gold 0.1998 oz. AGW, 22 mm. **Ruler:** Elizabeth II **Series:** Man in Flight **Obv:** Crowned bust right **Rev:** Bust of Louis Bleriot behind plane flying across channel

Date	Mintage	F	VF	XF	Unc	BU
1994 Proof	Est. 5,000				Value: 200	

KM# 412 1/5 CROWN
6.2200 g., 0.9990 Gold 0.1998 oz. AGW, 22 mm.
Ruler: Elizabeth II **Series:** Man in Flight **Obv:** Crowned bust right **Rev:** Plane in flight above ocean

Date	Mintage	F	VF	XF	Unc	BU
1994 Proof	Est. 5,000				Value: 200	

KM# 413 1/5 CROWN
6.2200 g., 0.9990 Gold 0.1998 oz. AGW, 22 mm. **Ruler:** Elizabeth II **Series:** Man in Flight **Subject:** First England to Australia Flight **Obv:** Crowned bust right **Rev:** Biplane flying

Date	Mintage	F	VF	XF	Unc	BU
1994 Proof	Est. 5,000				Value: 200	

KM# 414 1/5 CROWN
6.2200 g., 0.9990 Gold 0.1998 oz. AGW, 22 mm. **Ruler:** Elizabeth II **Series:** Man in Flight **Subject:** 60th Anniversary of Airmail **Obv:** Crowned bust right **Rev:** Plane flying left above inscription

Date	Mintage	F	VF	XF	Unc	BU
1994 Proof	Est. 5,000				Value: 200	

KM# 415 1/5 CROWN
6.2200 g., 0.9990 Gold 0.1998 oz. AGW, 22 mm.
Ruler: Elizabeth II **Series:** Man in Flight **Subject:** 50th Anniversary of International Civil Aviation Organization **Obv:** Crowned bust right **Rev:** Trademark of ICAO

Date	Mintage	F	VF	XF	Unc	BU
1994 Proof	Est. 5,000				Value: 200	

KM# 416 1/5 CROWN
6.2200 g., 0.9990 Gold 0.1998 oz. AGW, 22 mm. **Ruler:** Elizabeth II **Series:** Man in Flight **Subject:** First Concorde Flight **Obv:** Crowned bust right **Rev:** Concorde waiting at airport

Date	Mintage	F	VF	XF	Unc	BU
1994 Proof	Est. 5,000				Value: 200	

KM# 378a 1/5 CROWN
6.2200 g., 0.9990 Platinum 0.1998 oz. APW, 22 mm.
Ruler: Elizabeth II **Obv:** Crowned bust right **Rev:** Japanese Bobtail cat **Note:** Prev. KM#475.

Date	Mintage	F	VF	XF	Unc	BU
1994	—	—	—	—	—	375
1994 Proof	—				Value: 385	

KM# 429 1/5 CROWN
6.2200 g., 0.9990 Gold 0.1998 oz. AGW, 22 mm.
Ruler: Elizabeth II **Series:** Man in Flight **Obv:** Crowned bust right **Rev:** Airplane in flight

Date	Mintage	F	VF	XF	Unc	BU
1995 Proof	Est. 5,000				Value: 200	

KM# 426 1/5 CROWN
6.2200 g., 0.9990 Gold 0.1998 oz. AGW, 22 mm.
Ruler: Elizabeth II **Series:** Man in Flight **Obv:** Crowned bust right **Rev:** Icarus' wings melting

Date	Mintage	F	VF	XF	Unc	BU
1995 Proof	Est. 5,000				Value: 200	

KM# 427 1/5 CROWN
6.2200 g., 0.9990 Gold 0.1998 oz. AGW, 22 mm.
Ruler: Elizabeth II **Series:** Man in Flight **Obv:** Crowned bust right **Rev:** Leonardo Da Vinci and aircraft design

Date	Mintage	F	VF	XF	Unc	BU
1995 Proof	Est. 5,000				Value: 200	

KM# 428 1/5 CROWN
6.2200 g., 0.9990 Gold 0.1998 oz. AGW, 22 mm.
Ruler: Elizabeth II **Series:** Man in Flight **Obv:** Crowned bust right **Rev:** Balloon in flight

Date	Mintage	F	VF	XF	Unc	BU
1995 Proof	Est. 5,000				Value: 200	

KM# 430 1/5 CROWN
6.2200 g., 0.9990 Gold 0.1998 oz. AGW, 22 mm.
Ruler: Elizabeth II **Series:** Man in Flight **Subject:** 1st Flight Tokyo to Paris by Abe and Kawachi **Obv:** Crowned bust right **Rev:** Busts above airplane

Date	Mintage	F	VF	XF	Unc	BU
1995 Proof	Est. 5,000				Value: 200	

KM# 431 1/5 CROWN
6.2200 g., 0.9990 Gold 0.1998 oz. AGW, 22 mm. **Ruler:** Elizabeth II **Series:** Man in Flight **Subject:** FW109, First Diesel Powered Aircraft **Obv:** Crowned bust right **Rev:** Grounded airplane

Date	Mintage	F	VF	XF	Unc	BU
1995 Proof	Est. 5,000				Value: 200	

KM# 432 1/5 CROWN
6.2200 g., 0.9990 Gold 0.1998 oz. AGW, 22 mm.
Ruler: Elizabeth II **Series:** Man in Flight **Subject:** ME262, First Jet Aircraft **Obv:** Crowned bust right **Rev:** Jet flying into clouds

Date	Mintage	F	VF	XF	Unc	BU
1995 Proof	Est. 5,000				Value: 200	

KM# 433 1/5 CROWN
6.2200 g., 0.9990 Gold 0.1998 oz. AGW, 22 mm.
Ruler: Elizabeth II **Series:** Man in Flight **Subject:** 25th Anniversary of Boeing 747 **Obv:** Crowned bust right **Rev:** Jumbo jet in flight

Date	Mintage	F	VF	XF	Unc	BU
1995 Proof	Est. 5,000				Value: 200	

KM# 444 1/5 CROWN
6.2200 g., 0.9990 Gold 0.1998 oz. AGW, 22 mm.
Ruler: Elizabeth II **Obv:** Crowned bust right **Rev:** Turkish cat

Date	Mintage	F	VF	XF	Unc	BU
1995	—	—	—	—	—	195
1995 Proof	—				Value: 200	

KM# 451 1/5 CROWN
6.2200 g., 0.9990 Gold 0.1998 oz. AGW, 22 mm.
Ruler: Elizabeth II **Subject:** Year of the Pig **Obv:** Crowned bust right **Rev:** Sow and piglets

Date	Mintage	F	VF	XF	Unc	BU
1995 Proof	Est. 10,000				Value: 200	

KM# 457 1/5 CROWN
6.2200 g., 0.9990 Gold 0.1998 oz. AGW, 22 mm.
Ruler: Elizabeth II **Subject:** 95th Birthday of Queen Mother
Obv: Crowned bust right **Rev:** Bust of Queen Mother

Date	Mintage	F	VF	XF	Unc	BU
1995 Proof	Est. 5,000	Value: 200				

KM# 459 1/5 CROWN
6.2200 g., 0.9990 Gold 0.1998 oz. AGW, 22 mm.
Ruler: Elizabeth II **Series:** Preserve Planet Earth **Obv:** Crowned
bust right **Rev:** Otter

Date	Mintage	F	VF	XF	Unc	BU
1995 Proof	Est. 5,000	Value: 200				

KM# 460 1/5 CROWN
6.2200 g., 0.9990 Gold 0.1998 oz. AGW, 22 mm.
Ruler: Elizabeth II **Series:** Preserve Planet Earth **Obv:** Crowned
bust right **Rev:** Egret Birds

Date	Mintage	F	VF	XF	Unc	BU
1995 Proof	Est. 5,000	Value: 200				

KM# 444a 1/5 CROWN
6.2200 g., 0.9990 Platinum 0.1998 oz. APW, 22 mm.
Ruler: Elizabeth II **Obv:** Crowned bust right **Rev:** Turkish cat
Note: Prev. KM#480.

Date	Mintage	F	VF	XF	Unc	BU
1995	—	—	—	—	—	375
1995 Proof	—	Value: 385				

KM# 483 1/5 CROWN
6.2200 g., 0.9990 Gold 0.1998 oz. AGW, 22 mm.
Ruler: Elizabeth II **Series:** Aircraft of World War II **Obv:** Crowned
bust right **Rev:** Hawker Hurricane

Date	Mintage	F	VF	XF	Unc	BU
1995 Proof	Est. 5,000	Value: 200				

KM# 484 1/5 CROWN
6.2200 g., 0.9990 Gold 0.1998 oz. AGW, 22 mm.
Ruler: Elizabeth II **Series:** Aircraft of World War II **Obv:** Crowned
bust right **Rev:** P-51 Mustang

Date	Mintage	F	VF	XF	Unc	BU
1995 Proof	Est. 5,000	Value: 200				

KM# 485 1/5 CROWN
6.2200 g., 0.9990 Gold 0.1998 oz. AGW, 22 mm.
Ruler: Elizabeth II **Series:** Aircraft of World War II **Obv:** Crowned
bust right **Rev:** Letrov S328

Date	Mintage	F	VF	XF	Unc	BU
1995 Proof	Est. 5,000	Value: 200				

KM# 486 1/5 CROWN
6.2200 g., 0.9990 Gold 0.1998 oz. AGW, 22 mm.
Ruler: Elizabeth II **Series:** Aircraft of World War II **Obv:** Crowned
bust right **Rev:** Messerschmitt ME262

Date	Mintage	F	VF	XF	Unc	BU
1995 Proof	Est. 5,000	Value: 200				

KM# 487 1/5 CROWN
6.2200 g., 0.9990 Gold 0.1998 oz. AGW, 22 mm.
Ruler: Elizabeth II **Series:** Aircraft of World War II **Obv:** Crowned
bust right **Rev:** JU87 Stuka

Date	Mintage	F	VF	XF	Unc	BU
1995 Proof	Est. 5,000	Value: 200				

KM# 488 1/5 CROWN
6.2200 g., 0.9990 Gold 0.1998 oz. AGW, 22 mm.
Ruler: Elizabeth II **Series:** Aircraft of World War II **Obv:** Crowned
bust right **Rev:** MIG 3

Date	Mintage	F	VF	XF	Unc	BU
1995 Proof	Est. 5,000	Value: 200				

KM# 489 1/5 CROWN
6.2200 g., 0.9990 Gold 0.1998 oz. AGW, 22 mm.
Ruler: Elizabeth II **Series:** Aircraft of World War II **Obv:** Crowned
bust right **Rev:** Nakajima Ki-49 Donryu

Date	Mintage	F	VF	XF	Unc	BU
1995 Proof	Est. 5,000	Value: 200				

KM# 490 1/5 CROWN
6.2200 g., 0.9990 Gold 0.1998 oz. AGW, 22 mm.
Ruler: Elizabeth II **Series:** Aircraft of World War II **Obv:** Crowned
bust right **Rev:** Vickers Wellington

Date	Mintage	F	VF	XF	Unc	BU
1995 Proof	Est. 5,000	Value: 200				

KM# 491 1/5 CROWN
6.2200 g., 0.9990 Gold 0.1998 oz. AGW, 22 mm.
Ruler: Elizabeth II **Series:** Aircraft of World War II **Obv:** Crowned
bust right **Rev:** Spitfire

Date	Mintage	F	VF	XF	Unc	BU
1995 Proof	Est. 5,000	Value: 200				

KM# 492 1/5 CROWN
6.2200 g., 0.9990 Gold 0.1998 oz. AGW, 22 mm.
Ruler: Elizabeth II **Series:** Aircraft of World War II **Obv:** Crowned
bust right **Rev:** Fokker G. 1a

Date	Mintage	F	VF	XF	Unc	BU
1995 Proof	Est. 5,000	Value: 200				

KM# 493 1/5 CROWN
6.2200 g., 0.9990 Gold 0.1998 oz. AGW, 22 mm.
Ruler: Elizabeth II **Series:** Aircraft of World War II **Obv:** Crowned
bust right **Rev:** Commonwealth Boomerang CA-13

Date	Mintage	F	VF	XF	Unc	BU
1995 Proof	Est. 5,000	Value: 200				

KM# 494 1/5 CROWN
6.2200 g., 0.9990 Gold 0.1998 oz. AGW, 22 mm.
Ruler: Elizabeth II **Series:** Aircraft of World War II **Obv:** Crowned
bust right **Rev:** Briston Blenheim 142M

Date	Mintage	F	VF	XF	Unc	BU
1995 Proof	Est. 5,000	Value: 200				

KM# 495 1/5 CROWN
6.2200 g., 0.9990 Gold 0.1998 oz. AGW, 22 mm.
Ruler: Elizabeth II **Series:** Aircraft of World War II **Obv:** Crowned
bust right **Rev:** Mitsubishi Zero

Date	Mintage	F	VF	XF	Unc	BU
1995 Proof	Est. 5,000	Value: 200				

KM# 496 1/5 CROWN
6.2200 g., 0.9990 Gold 0.1998 oz. AGW, 22 mm.
Ruler: Elizabeth II **Series:** Aircraft of World War II **Obv:** Crowned
bust right **Rev:** Heinkel HE111

Date	Mintage	F	VF	XF	Unc	BU
1995 Proof	Est. 5,000	Value: 200				

KM# 497 1/5 CROWN
6.2200 g., 0.9990 Gold 0.1998 oz. AGW, 22 mm.
Ruler: Elizabeth II **Series:** Aircraft of World War II **Obv:** Crowned
bust right **Rev:** Boulton Paul P82 Defiant

Date	Mintage	F	VF	XF	Unc	BU
1995 Proof	Est. 5,000	Value: 200				

KM# 498 1/5 CROWN
6.2200 g., 0.9990 Gold 0.1998 oz. AGW, 22 mm.
Ruler: Elizabeth II **Series:** Aircraft of World War II **Obv:** Crowned
bust right **Rev:** Boeing B289 - Enola Gay

Date	Mintage	F	VF	XF	Unc	BU
1995 Proof	Est. 5,000	Value: 200				

KM# 499 1/5 CROWN
6.2200 g., 0.9990 Gold 0.1998 oz. AGW, 22 mm.
Ruler: Elizabeth II **Series:** Aircraft of World War II **Obv:** Crowned
bust right **Rev:** Douglas DC-3 (C47)

Date	Mintage	F	VF	XF	Unc	BU
1995 Proof	Est. 5,000	Value: 200				

KM# 500 1/5 CROWN
6.2200 g., 0.9990 Gold 0.1998 oz. AGW, 22 mm.
Ruler: Elizabeth II **Series:** Aircraft of World War II **Obv:** Crowned
bust right **Rev:** Fairey Swordfish

Date	Mintage	F	VF	XF	Unc	BU
1995 Proof	Est. 5,000	Value: 200				

KM# 501 1/5 CROWN
6.2200 g., 0.9990 Gold 0.1998 oz. AGW, 22 mm.
Ruler: Elizabeth II **Series:** Aircraft of World War II **Obv:** Crowned
bust right **Rev:** Curtiss P40

Date	Mintage	F	VF	XF	Unc	BU
1995 Proof	Est. 5,000	Value: 200				

KM# 523 1/5 CROWN
6.2200 g., 0.9990 Gold 0.1998 oz. AGW, 22 mm. **Ruler:** Elizabeth II
Subject: America's Cup **Obv:** Crowned bust right **Rev:** Boats

Date	Mintage	F	VF	XF	Unc	BU
1995 Proof	Est. 5,000	Value: 200				

KM# 525 1/5 CROWN
6.2200 g., 0.9999 Gold 0.1999 oz. AGW, 22 mm.
Ruler: Elizabeth II **Series:** Inventions of the Modern World
Obv: Crowned bust right **Rev:** Cameo of Tsai Lun, paper and tree

Date	Mintage	F	VF	XF	Unc	BU
1995 Proof	Est. 5,000	Value: 200				

KM# 527 1/5 CROWN
6.2200 g., 0.9999 Gold 0.1999 oz. AGW, 22 mm. **Ruler:** Elizabeth II
Series: Inventions of the Modern World **Obv:** Crowned bust right
Rev: Cameo of Chang Heng and Seismograph

Date	Mintage	F	VF	XF	Unc	BU
1995 Proof	Est. 5,000	Value: 200				

KM# 529 1/5 CROWN
6.2200 g., 0.9999 Gold 0.1999 oz. AGW, 22 mm. **Ruler:** Elizabeth II
Series: Inventions of the Modern World **Obv:** Crowned bust right
Rev: Cameo of Tsu Chung Chih and compass cart

Date	Mintage	F	VF	XF	Unc	BU
1995 Proof	Est. 5,000	Value: 200				

KM# 531 1/5 CROWN
6.2200 g., 0.9999 Gold 0.1999 oz. AGW, 22 mm.
Ruler: Elizabeth II **Series:** Inventions of the Modern World
Obv: Crowned bust right **Rev:** Cameo bust facing and movable
type

Date	Mintage	F	VF	XF	Unc	BU
1995 Proof	Est. 5,000	Value: 200				

KM# 533 1/5 CROWN
6.2200 g., 0.9999 Gold 0.1999 oz. AGW, 22 mm. **Ruler:** Elizabeth II
Series: Inventions of the Modern World **Obv:** Crowned bust right
Rev: Cameo of Charles Babbage and first computer

Date	Mintage	F	VF	XF	Unc	BU
1995 Proof	Est. 5,000	Value: 200				

KM# 535 1/5 CROWN
6.2200 g., 0.9999 Gold 0.1999 oz. AGW, 22 mm.
Ruler: Elizabeth II **Series:** Inventions of the Modern World
Obv: Crowned bust right **Rev:** Cameo of Fox Talbot, photography

Date	Mintage	F	VF	XF	Unc	BU
1995 Proof	Est. 5,000	Value: 200				

KM# 537 1/5 CROWN
6.2200 g., 0.9999 Gold 0.1999 oz. AGW, 22 mm.
Ruler: Elizabeth II **Series:** Inventions of the Modern World **Obv:**
Crowned bust right **Rev:** Cameo of Rudolf Diesel, diesel engine

Date	Mintage	F	VF	XF	Unc	BU
1995 Proof	Est. 5,000	Value: 200				

KM# 539 1/5 CROWN
6.2200 g., 0.9999 Gold 0.1999 oz. AGW, 22 mm. **Ruler:** Elizabeth II
Series: Inventions of the Modern World **Obv:** Crowned bust right
Rev: Cameo of Wilhelm K. Roentgen and xray of hand

Date	Mintage	F	VF	XF	Unc	BU
1995 Proof	Est. 5,000	Value: 200				

KM# 541 1/5 CROWN
6.2200 g., 0.9999 Gold 0.1999 oz. AGW, 22 mm.
Ruler: Elizabeth II **Series:** Inventions of the Modern World **Obv:**
Crowned bust right **Rev:** Cameo bust facing and radio equipment

Date	Mintage	F	VF	XF	Unc	BU
1995 Proof	Est. 5,000	Value: 200				

KM# 543 1/5 CROWN
6.2200 g., 0.9999 Gold 0.1999 oz. AGW, 22 mm. **Ruler:** Elizabeth II
Series: Inventions of the Modern World **Obv:** Crowned bust right
Rev: Cameo of John L. Baird and television equipment

Date	Mintage	F	VF	XF	Unc	BU
1995 Proof	Est. 5,000	Value: 200				

KM# 545 1/5 CROWN
6.2200 g., 0.9999 Gold 0.1999 oz. AGW, 22 mm. **Ruler:** Elizabeth II
Series: Inventions of the Modern World **Obv:** Crowned bust right
Rev: Cameo of Alexander Fleming and microscope

Date	Mintage	F	VF	XF	Unc	BU
1995 Proof	Est. 5,000	Value: 200				

KM# 547 1/5 CROWN
6.2200 g., 0.9999 Gold 0.1999 oz. AGW, 22 mm.
Ruler: Elizabeth II **Series:** Inventions of the Modern World **Obv:**
Crowned bust right **Rev:** Cameo of Lazlo Biro and ball-point pen

Date	Mintage	F	VF	XF	Unc	BU
1995 Proof	Est. 5,000	Value: 200				

KM# 549 1/5 CROWN
6.2200 g., 0.9999 Gold 0.1999 oz. AGW, 22 mm.
Ruler: Elizabeth II **Series:** Inventions of the Modern World **Obv:**
Crowned bust right **Rev:** Cameo of Wernher von Braun and rocket

Date	Mintage	F	VF	XF	Unc	BU
1996 Proof	Est. 5,000	Value: 200				

KM# 550 1/5 CROWN
6.2200 g., 0.9999 Gold 0.1999 oz. AGW, 22 mm.
Ruler: Elizabeth II **Series:** Inventions of the Modern World **Obv:**
Crowned bust right **Rev:** Cameo of Thomas Edison, electricity

Date	Mintage	F	VF	XF	Unc	BU
1996 Proof	Est. 5,000	Value: 200				

KM# 551 1/5 CROWN
6.2200 g., 0.9999 Gold 0.1999 oz. AGW, 22 mm.
Ruler: Elizabeth II **Series:** Inventions of the Modern World **Obv:**
Crowned bust right **Rev:** Compass

Date	Mintage	F	VF	XF	Unc	BU
1996 Proof	Est. 5,000	Value: 200				

KM# 552 1/5 CROWN
6.2200 g., 0.9999 Gold 0.1999 oz. AGW, 22 mm.
Ruler: Elizabeth II **Series:** Inventions of the Modern World **Obv:**
Crowned bust right **Rev:** Cameo of Michael Faraday, electricity

Date	Mintage	F	VF	XF	Unc	BU
1996 Proof	Est. 5,000	Value: 200				

KM# 553 1/5 CROWN
6.2200 g., 0.9999 Gold 0.1999 oz. AGW, 22 mm. **Ruler:** Elizabeth II
Series: Inventions of the Modern World **Obv:** Crowned bust right
Rev: Cameo of Emile Berliner and gramophone

Date	Mintage	F	VF	XF	Unc	BU
1996 Proof	Est. 5,000	Value: 200				

KM# 554 1/5 CROWN
6.2200 g., 0.9999 Gold 0.1999 oz. AGW, 22 mm. **Ruler:** Elizabeth II
Series: Inventions of the Modern World **Obv:** Crowned bust right
Rev: Cameo of Alexander Graham Bell, voice transmission

Date	Mintage	F	VF	XF	Unc	BU
1996 Proof	Est. 5,000	Value: 200				

KM# 561 1/5 CROWN
6.2200 g., 0.9999 Gold 0.1999 oz. AGW, 22 mm.
Ruler: Elizabeth II **Series:** 1996 Summer Olympics - Atlanta
Obv: Crowned bust right **Rev:** Hurdler

Date	Mintage	F	VF	XF	Unc	BU
1996 Proof	Est. 5,000	Value: 200				

KM# 562 1/5 CROWN
6.2200 g., 0.9999 Gold 0.1999 oz. AGW, 22 mm.
Ruler: Elizabeth II **Series:** 1996 Summer Olympics - Atlanta
Obv: Crowned bust right **Rev:** Runners

Date	Mintage	F	VF	XF	Unc	BU
1996 Proof	Est. 5,000	Value: 200				

KM# 563 1/5 CROWN
6.2200 g., 0.9999 Gold 0.1999 oz. AGW, 22 mm.
Ruler: Elizabeth II **Series:** 1996 Summer Olympics - Atlanta
Obv: Crowned bust right **Rev:** Sailing

Date	Mintage	F	VF	XF	Unc	BU
1996 Proof	Est. 5,000	Value: 200				

KM# 564 1/5 CROWN
6.2200 g., 0.9999 Gold 0.1999 oz. AGW, 22 mm.
Ruler: Elizabeth II **Series:** 1996 Summer Olympics - Atlanta
Obv: Crowned bust right **Rev:** Swimmers

Date	Mintage	F	VF	XF	Unc	BU
1996 Proof	Est. 5,000	Value: 200				

KM# 565 1/5 CROWN
6.2200 g., 0.9999 Gold 0.1999 oz. AGW, 22 mm.
Ruler: Elizabeth II **Series:** 1996 Summer Olympics - Atlanta
Obv: Crowned bust right **Rev:** Equestrian

Date	Mintage	F	VF	XF	Unc	BU
1996 Proof	Est. 5,000	Value: 200				

KM# 566 1/5 CROWN
6.2200 g., 0.9999 Gold 0.1999 oz. AGW, 22 mm.
Ruler: Elizabeth II **Series:** 1996 Summer Olympics - Atlanta
Obv: Crowned bust right **Rev:** Cyclists and Nike

Date	Mintage	F	VF	XF	Unc	BU
1996 Proof	Est. 5,000	Value: 200				

KM# 573 1/5 CROWN
6.2200 g., 0.9990 Gold 0.1998 oz. AGW, 22 mm.
Ruler: Elizabeth II **Series:** Bicentennial of Robert Burns
Obv: Crowned bust right **Rev:** Seated

Date	Mintage	F	VF	XF	Unc	BU
1996 Proof	Est. 5,000	Value: 200				

KM# 574 1/5 CROWN
6.2200 g., 0.9990 Gold 0.1998 oz. AGW, 22 mm.
Ruler: Elizabeth II **Series:** Bicentennial of Robert Burns
Obv: Crowned bust right **Rev:** Pirate ships

Date	Mintage	F	VF	XF	Unc	BU
1996 Proof	Est. 5,000	Value: 200				

KM# 575 1/5 CROWN
6.2200 g., 0.9990 Gold 0.1998 oz. AGW, 22 mm.
Ruler: Elizabeth II **Series:** Bicentennial of Robert Burns
Obv: Crowned bust right **Rev:** Auld Lang Syne

Date	Mintage	F	VF	XF	Unc	BU
1996 Proof	Est. 5,000	Value: 200				

KM# 576 1/5 CROWN
6.2200 g., 0.9990 Gold 0.1998 oz. AGW, 22 mm.
Ruler: Elizabeth II **Series:** Bicentennial of Robert Burns
Obv: Crowned bust right **Rev:** Edinburgh Castle

Date	Mintage	F	VF	XF	Unc	BU
1996 Proof	Est. 5,000	Value: 200				

KM# 581 1/5 CROWN
6.2200 g., 0.9990 Gold 0.1998 oz. AGW, 22 mm. **Ruler:** Elizabeth II
Subject: Queen's Birthday **Obv:** Crowned bust right **Rev:** Flowers

Date	Mintage	F	VF	XF	Unc	BU
1996 Proof	Est. 5,000	Value: 200				

KM# 583 1/5 CROWN
6.2200 g., 0.9990 Gold 0.1998 oz. AGW, 22 mm.
Ruler: Elizabeth II **Subject:** Preserve Planet Earth
Obv: Crowned bust right **Rev:** Killer whale

Date	Mintage	F	VF	XF	Unc	BU
1996 Proof	Est. 5,000	Value: 200				

KM# 584 1/5 CROWN
6.2200 g., 0.9990 Gold 0.1998 oz. AGW, 22 mm.
Ruler: Elizabeth II **Subject:** Preserve Planet Earth
Obv: Crowned bust right **Rev:** Razorbill feeding chick

Date	Mintage	F	VF	XF	Unc	BU
1996 Proof	Est. 5,000	Value: 200				

KM# 605 1/5 CROWN
6.2200 g., 0.9990 Gold 0.1998 oz. AGW, 22 mm. **Ruler:** Elizabeth II
Series: Flower Fairies **Obv:** Crowned bust right **Rev:** Orchis

Date	Mintage	F	VF	XF	Unc	BU
1996 Proof	Est. 5,000	Value: 200				

KM# 606 1/5 CROWN
6.2200 g., 0.9990 Gold 0.1998 oz. AGW, 22 mm. **Ruler:** Elizabeth II
Series: Flower Fairies **Obv:** Crowned bust right **Rev:** Rose

Date	Mintage	F	VF	XF	Unc	BU
1996 Proof	Est. 5,000	Value: 200				

KM# 607 1/5 CROWN
6.2200 g., 0.9990 Gold 0.1998 oz. AGW, 22 mm. **Ruler:** Elizabeth II
Series: Flower Fairies **Obv:** Crowned bust right **Rev:** Fuchsia

Date	Mintage	F	VF	XF	Unc	BU
1996 Proof	Est. 5,000	Value: 200				

KM# 608 1/5 CROWN
6.2200 g., 0.9990 Gold 0.1998 oz. AGW, 22 mm. **Ruler:** Elizabeth II
Series: Flower Fairies **Obv:** Crowned bust right **Rev:** Pinks

Date	Mintage	F	VF	XF	Unc	BU
1996 Proof	Est. 5,000	Value: 200				

KM# 617 1/5 CROWN
6.2200 g., 0.9990 Gold 0.1998 oz. AGW, 22 mm.
Ruler: Elizabeth II **Obv:** Crowned bust right **Rev:** Burmese cat

Date	Mintage	F	VF	XF	Unc	BU
1996	—	—	—	—	—	195
1996 Proof	—	Value: 200				

KM# 617a 1/5 CROWN
6.2200 g., 0.9990 Platinum 0.1998 oz. APW, 22 mm. **Ruler:**
Elizabeth II **Obv:** Crowned bust right **Rev:** Burmese cat **Note:**
Prev. KM#618.

Date	Mintage	F	VF	XF	Unc	BU
1996	—	—	—	—	—	375
1996 Proof	—	Value: 385				

KM# 625 1/5 CROWN
6.2200 g., 0.9990 Gold 0.1998 oz. AGW, 22 mm. **Ruler:**
Elizabeth II **Obv:** Crowned bust right **Rev:** Portrait of Ferdinand
Magellan, map and ship

Date	Mintage	F	VF	XF	Unc	BU
1996 Proof	Est. 5,000	Value: 200				

KM# 628 1/5 CROWN
6.2200 g., 0.9990 Gold 0.1998 oz. AGW, 22 mm. **Ruler:**
Elizabeth II **Obv:** Crowned bust right **Rev:** Portrait of Sir Francis
Drake, map and ship

Date	Mintage	F	VF	XF	Unc	BU
1996 Proof	Est. 5,000	Value: 200				

KM# 631 1/5 CROWN
6.2200 g., 0.9990 Gold 0.1998 oz. AGW, 22 mm.
Ruler: Elizabeth II **Series:** European Football Championship
Obv: Crowned bust right **Rev:** Romania vs Bulgaria

Date	Mintage	F	VF	XF	Unc	BU
1996 Proof	Est. 5,000	Value: 200				

KM# 634 1/5 CROWN
6.2200 g., 0.9990 Gold 0.1998 oz. AGW, 22 mm.
Ruler: Elizabeth II **Series:** European Football Championship
Obv: Crowned bust right **Rev:** Czech Republic vs Italy

Date	Mintage	F	VF	XF	Unc	BU
1996 Proof	Est. 5,000	Value: 200				

KM# 637 1/5 CROWN
6.2200 g., 0.9990 Gold 0.1998 oz. AGW, 22 mm.
Ruler: Elizabeth II **Series:** European Football Championship
Obv: Crowned bust right **Rev:** Germany vs Russia

Date	Mintage	F	VF	XF	Unc	BU
1996 Proof	Est. 5,000	Value: 200				

KM# 640 1/5 CROWN
6.2200 g., 0.9990 Gold 0.1998 oz. AGW, 22 mm.
Ruler: Elizabeth II **Series:** European Football Championship
Obv: Crowned bust right **Rev:** Spain vs France

Date	Mintage	F	VF	XF	Unc	BU
1996 Proof	Est. 5,000	Value: 200				

KM# 643 1/5 CROWN
6.2200 g., 0.9990 Gold 0.1998 oz. AGW, 22 mm.
Ruler: Elizabeth II **Series:** European Football Championship
Obv: Crowned bust right **Rev:** Turkey vs Croatia

Date	Mintage	F	VF	XF	Unc	BU
1996 Proof	Est. 5,000	Value: 200				

KM# 646 1/5 CROWN
6.2200 g., 0.9990 Gold 0.1998 oz. AGW, 22 mm.
Ruler: Elizabeth II **Series:** European Football Championship
Obv: Crowned bust right **Rev:** Denmark vs Portugal

Date	Mintage	F	VF	XF	Unc	BU
1996 Proof	Est. 5,000	Value: 200				

KM# 649 1/5 CROWN
6.2200 g., 0.9990 Gold 0.1998 oz. AGW, 22 mm.
Ruler: Elizabeth II **Series:** European Football Championship
Obv: Crowned bust right **Rev:** Scotland vs England

Date	Mintage	F	VF	XF	Unc	BU
1996 Proof	Est. 5,000	Value: 200				

KM# 652 1/5 CROWN
6.2200 g., 0.9990 Gold 0.1998 oz. AGW, 22 mm.
Ruler: Elizabeth II **Series:** European Football Championship
Obv: Crowned bust right **Rev:** Holland vs Switzerland

Date	Mintage	F	VF	XF	Unc	BU
1996 Proof	Est. 5,000	Value: 200				

KM# 656 1/5 CROWN
6.2200 g., 0.9990 Gold 0.1998 oz. AGW, 22 mm.
Ruler: Elizabeth II **Series:** European Football Championship
Obv: Crowned bust right **Rev:** Winner, Germany

Date	Mintage	F	VF	XF	Unc	BU
1996 Proof	Est. 5,000	Value: 200				

KM# 659 1/5 CROWN
6.2200 g., 0.9990 Gold 0.1998 oz. AGW, 22 mm.
Ruler: Elizabeth II **Series:** Legend of King Arthur **Obv:** Crowned
bust right **Rev:** King Arthur with sword, orb

Date	Mintage	F	VF	XF	Unc	BU
1996 Proof	Est. 5,000	Value: 200				

KM# 660 1/5 CROWN
6.2200 g., 0.9990 Gold 0.1998 oz. AGW, 22 mm. **Ruler:** Elizabeth II
Series: Legend of King Arthur **Obv:** Crowned bust right **Rev:** 3/4-
length figure of Queen Guinevere coming through archway

Date	Mintage	F	VF	XF	Unc	BU
1996 Proof	Est. 5,000	Value: 200				

KM# 661 1/5 CROWN
6.2200 g., 0.9990 Gold 0.1998 oz. AGW, 22 mm.
Ruler: Elizabeth II **Series:** Legend of King Arthur **Obv:** Crowned
bust right **Rev:** Sir Lancelot

Date	Mintage	F	VF	XF	Unc	BU
1996 Proof	Est. 5,000	Value: 200				

KM# 662 1/5 CROWN
6.2200 g., 0.9990 Gold 0.1998 oz. AGW, 22 mm.
Ruler: Elizabeth II **Series:** Legend of King Arthur **Obv:** Crowned
bust right **Rev:** Merlin

Date	Mintage	F	VF	XF	Unc	BU
1996 Proof	Est. 5,000	Value: 200				

KM# 663 1/5 CROWN
6.2200 g., 0.9990 Gold 0.1998 oz. AGW, 22 mm.
Ruler: Elizabeth II **Series:** Legend of King Arthur **Obv:** Crowned
bust right **Rev:** Camelot Castle within circle

Date	Mintage	F	VF	XF	Unc	BU
1996 Proof	Est. 5,000	Value: 200				

KM# 659a 1/5 CROWN
6.2200 g., 0.9990 Platinum 0.1998 oz. APW, 22 mm.
Ruler: Elizabeth II **Series:** Legend of King Arthur **Obv:** Crowned
bust right **Rev:** King Arthur with sword, orb **Note:** Prev. KM#664.

Date	Mintage	F	VF	XF	Unc	BU
1996 Proof	Est. 5,000	Value: 385				

KM# 660a 1/5 CROWN
6.2200 g., 0.9990 Platinum 0.1998 oz. APW, 22 mm.
Ruler: Elizabeth II **Series:** Legend of King Arthur **Obv:** Crowned
bust right **Rev:** Queen Guinevere **Note:** Prev. KM#665.

Date	Mintage	F	VF	XF	Unc	BU
1996 Proof	Est. 5,000	Value: 385				

KM# 661a 1/5 CROWN
6.2200 g., 0.9990 Platinum 0.1998 oz. APW, 22 mm.
Ruler: Elizabeth II **Series:** Legend of King Arthur **Obv:** Crowned
bust right **Rev:** Sir Lancelot **Note:** Prev. KM#666.

Date	Mintage	F	VF	XF	Unc	BU
1996 Proof	Est. 5,000	Value: 410				

KM# 662a 1/5 CROWN
6.2200 g., 0.9990 Platinum 0.1998 oz. APW, 22 mm.
Ruler: Elizabeth II **Series:** Legend of King Arthur **Obv:** Crowned
bust right **Rev:** Merlin **Note:** Prev. KM#667.

Date	Mintage	F	VF	XF	Unc	BU
1996 Proof	Est. 5,000	Value: 385				

KM# 663a 1/5 CROWN
6.2200 g., 0.9990 Platinum 0.1998 oz. APW, 22 mm.
Ruler: Elizabeth II **Series:** Legend of King Arthur **Obv:** Crowned
bust right **Rev:** Camelot Castle **Note:** Prev. KM#668.

Date	Mintage	F	VF	XF	Unc	BU
1996 Proof	Est. 5,000	Value: 385				

KM# 730 1/5 CROWN
6.2200 g., 0.9990 Gold 0.1998 oz. AGW, 22 mm. **Ruler:** Elizabeth II
Subject: Year of the Rat **Obv:** Crowned bust right **Rev:** Rat

Date	Mintage	F	VF	XF	Unc	BU
1996 Proof	—	—	—	—	—	—

Note: Entire series purchased by one buyer. Mintage, disposition and market value unknown

KM# 766 1/5 CROWN
6.2200 g., 0.9999 Gold 0.1999 oz. AGW, 22 mm.
Ruler: Elizabeth II **Subject:** Fridtjof Nansen 1861-1930
Obv: Crowned bust right **Rev:** Portrait, map and ship "The Fram"

Date	Mintage	F	VF	XF	Unc	BU
1997 Proof	Est. 5,000	Value: 200				

KM# 723 1/5 CROWN
6.2200 g., 0.9990 Gold 0.1998 oz. AGW, 22 mm.
Ruler: Elizabeth II **Subject:** Year of the Ox **Obv:** Crowned bust right **Rev:** Ox laying down

Date	Mintage	F	VF	XF	Unc	BU
1997 Proof	Est. 12,000 Value: 200					

KM# 751 1/5 CROWN
6.2200 g., 0.9990 Gold 0.1998 oz. AGW, 22 mm. **Ruler:** Elizabeth II
Series: Flower Fairies **Obv:** Crowned bust right **Rev:** Candytuft

Date	Mintage	F	VF	XF	Unc	BU
1997 Proof	Est. 5,000 Value: 200					

KM# 751a 1/5 CROWN
6.2518 g., 0.9950 Platinum 0.2000 oz. APW, 22 mm.
Ruler: Elizabeth II **Series:** Flower Fairies **Obv:** Crowned bust right **Rev:** Candytuft

Date	Mintage	F	VF	XF	Unc	BU
1997 Proof	Est. 2,500 Value: 385					

KM# 752 1/5 CROWN
6.2200 g., 0.9999 Gold 0.1999 oz. AGW, 22 mm.
Ruler: Elizabeth II **Series:** Flower Fairies **Obv:** Crowned bust right **Rev:** Snowdrop

Date	Mintage	F	VF	XF	Unc	BU
1997 Proof	Est. 5,000 Value: 200					

KM# 752a 1/5 CROWN
6.2518 g., 0.9950 Platinum 0.2000 oz. APW, 22 mm.
Ruler: Elizabeth II **Series:** Flower Fairies **Obv:** Crowned bust right **Rev:** Snowdrop

Date	Mintage	F	VF	XF	Unc	BU
1997 Proof	Est. 2,500 Value: 385					

KM# 753 1/5 CROWN
6.2200 g., 0.9999 Gold 0.1999 oz. AGW, 22 mm. **Ruler:** Elizabeth II
Series: Flower Fairies **Obv:** Crowned bust right **Rev:** Tulip

Date	Mintage	F	VF	XF	Unc	BU
1997 Proof	Est. 5,000 Value: 200					

KM# 753a 1/5 CROWN
6.2518 g., 0.9950 Platinum 0.2000 oz. APW, 22 mm.
Ruler: Elizabeth II **Series:** Flower Fairies **Obv:** Crowned bust right **Rev:** Tulip

Date	Mintage	F	VF	XF	Unc	BU
1997 Proof	Est. 2,500 Value: 385					

KM# 754 1/5 CROWN
6.2200 g., 0.9999 Gold 0.1999 oz. AGW, 22 mm. **Ruler:** Elizabeth II
Series: Flower Fairies **Obv:** Crowned bust right **Rev:** Jasmine

Date	Mintage	F	VF	XF	Unc	BU
1997 Proof	Est. 5,000 Value: 200					

KM# 754a 1/5 CROWN
6.2518 g., 0.9950 Platinum 0.2000 oz. APW, 22 mm.
Ruler: Elizabeth II **Series:** Flower Fairies **Obv:** Crowned bust right **Rev:** Jasmine

Date	Mintage	F	VF	XF	Unc	BU
1997 Proof	Est. 2,500 Value: 385					

KM# 763 1/5 CROWN
6.2200 g., 0.9999 Gold 0.1999 oz. AGW, 22 mm.
Ruler: Elizabeth II **Subject:** Leif Eriksson 999-1001
Obv: Crowned bust right **Rev:** Portrait and Viking ship with map sail

Date	Mintage	F	VF	XF	Unc	BU
1997 Proof	Est. 5,000 Value: 200					

KM# 772 1/5 CROWN
6.2200 g., 0.9999 Gold 0.1999 oz. AGW, 22 mm. **Ruler:** Elizabeth II
Obv: Crowned bust right **Rev:** Long-haired Smoke cat

Date	Mintage	F	VF	XF	Unc	BU
1997	—	—	—	—	—	195
1997 Proof	— Value: 200					

KM# 772a 1/5 CROWN
6.2200 g., 0.9999 Platinum 0.1999 oz. APW, 22 mm.
Ruler: Elizabeth II **Obv:** Crowned bust right **Rev:** Long-haired Smoke cat

Date	Mintage	F	VF	XF	Unc	BU
1997 Proof	— Value: 385					

KM# 776 1/5 CROWN
6.2200 g., 0.9999 Gold 0.1999 oz. AGW, 22 mm.
Ruler: Elizabeth II **Subject:** History of the Cat **Obv:** Crowned bust right **Rev:** Cat stalking a spider

Date	Mintage	F	VF	XF	Unc	BU
1997 Proof	Est. 7,500 Value: 200					

KM# 781 1/5 CROWN
6.2200 g., 0.9999 Gold 0.1999 oz. AGW, 22 mm.
Ruler: Elizabeth II **Subject:** 90th Anniversary of the TT - 1907
Obv: Crowned bust right **Rev:** 1907 winner Charlie Collier

Date	Mintage	F	VF	XF	Unc	BU
1997 Proof	Est. 5,000 Value: 200					

KM# 783 1/5 CROWN
6.2200 g., 0.9999 Gold 0.1999 oz. AGW, 22 mm.
Ruler: Elizabeth II **Subject:** 90th Anniversary of the TT - 1907
Obv: Crowned bust right **Rev:** 1937 winner Omobono Tenni

Date	Mintage	F	VF	XF	Unc	BU
1997 Proof	Est. 5,000 Value: 200					

KM# 785 1/5 CROWN
6.2200 g., 0.9999 Gold 0.1999 oz. AGW, 22 mm.
Ruler: Elizabeth II **Subject:** 90th Anniversary of the TT - 1907
Obv: Crowned bust right **Rev:** 1957 winner Bob McIntyre

Date	Mintage	F	VF	XF	Unc	BU
1997 Proof	Est. 5,000 Value: 200					

KM# 787 1/5 CROWN
6.2200 g., 0.9999 Gold 0.1999 oz. AGW, 22 mm.
Ruler: Elizabeth II **Subject:** 90th Anniversary of the TT - 1907
Obv: Crowned bust right **Rev:** 1967 winner Mike Hailwood

Date	Mintage	F	VF	XF	Unc	BU
1997 Proof	Est. 5,000 Value: 200					

KM# 792 1/5 CROWN
6.2200 g., 0.9999 Gold 0.1999 oz. AGW, 22 mm.
Ruler: Elizabeth II **Subject:** Golden Wedding Anniversary of Queen Elizabeth II and Prince Philip **Obv:** Crowned bust right **Rev:** Wedding portrait

Date	Mintage	F	VF	XF	Unc	BU
1997 Proof	Est. 3,500 Value: 200					

KM# 798 1/5 CROWN
6.2200 g., 0.9999 Gold 0.1999 oz. AGW, 22 mm.
Ruler: Elizabeth II **Series:** Year 2000 **Subject:** Birth of Christ
Obv: Crowned bust right **Rev:** Madonna and child with angels

Date	Mintage	F	VF	XF	Unc	BU
1997 Proof	Est. 2,000 Value: 200					

KM# 800 1/5 CROWN
6.2200 g., 0.9999 Gold 0.1999 oz. AGW, 22 mm. **Ruler:** Elizabeth II **Series:** Year 2000 **Subject:** Fall of the Roman Empire 476 **Obv:** Crowned bust right **Rev:** Barbarian defeating Roman soldier

Date	Mintage	F	VF	XF	Unc	BU
1997 Proof	Est. 2,000 Value: 200					

KM# 802 1/5 CROWN
6.2200 g., 0.9999 Gold 0.1999 oz. AGW, 22 mm. **Ruler:** Elizabeth II **Series:** Year 2000 **Subject:** Flight of Mohammed 622 **Obv:** Crowned bust right **Rev:** Arabs and camels at an oasis

Date	Mintage	F	VF	XF	Unc	BU
1997 Proof	Est. 2,000 Value: 200					

KM# 804 1/5 CROWN
6.2200 g., 0.9999 Gold 0.1999 oz. AGW, 22 mm. **Ruler:** Elizabeth II **Series:** Year 2000 **Subject:** Norman Conquest 1066 **Obv:** Crowned bust right **Rev:** William the Conqueror rallying his troops

Date	Mintage	F	VF	XF	Unc	BU
1997 Proof	Est. 2,000 Value: 200					

KM# 807 1/5 CROWN
6.2200 g., 0.9999 Gold 0.1999 oz. AGW, 22 mm.
Ruler: Elizabeth II **Series:** World Cup Soccer **Obv:** Crowned bust right **Rev:** Standing figures shaking hands within circle

Date	Mintage	F	VF	XF	Unc	BU
1998 Proof	Est. 5,000 Value: 200					

KM# 814 1/5 CROWN
6.2200 g., 0.9999 Gold 0.1999 oz. AGW, 22 mm.
Ruler: Elizabeth II **Series:** Year of the Tiger **Obv:** Crowned bust right **Rev:** Tiger

Date	Mintage	F	VF	XF	Unc	BU
1998 Proof	Est. 12,000 Value: 200					

KM# 824 1/5 CROWN
6.2200 g., 0.9999 Gold 0.1999 oz. AGW, 22 mm.
Ruler: Elizabeth II **Obv:** Crowned bust right **Rev:** Portrait of Marco Polo, caravan and palace

Date	Mintage	F	VF	XF	Unc	BU
1998 Proof	Est. 5,000 Value: 200					

KM# 826 1/5 CROWN
6.2200 g., 0.9999 Gold 0.1999 oz. AGW, 22 mm.
Ruler: Elizabeth II **Obv:** Crowned bust right **Rev:** Bust with headdress facing, ship and African map

Date	Mintage	F	VF	XF	Unc	BU
1998 Proof	Est. 5,000 Value: 200					

KM# 836 1/5 CROWN
6.2200 g., 0.9999 Gold 0.1999 oz. AGW, 22 mm.
Ruler: Elizabeth II **Series:** Flower Fairies **Obv:** Crowned bust right **Rev:** Fairy standing, lavender

Date	Mintage	F	VF	XF	Unc	BU
1998 Proof	Est. 5,000 Value: 200					

KM# 836a 1/5 CROWN
6.2200 g., 0.9999 Platinum 0.1999 oz. APW, 22 mm.
Ruler: Elizabeth II **Series:** Flower Fairies **Obv:** Crowned bust right **Rev:** Fairy standing, lavender

Date	Mintage	F	VF	XF	Unc	BU
1998 Proof	Est. 2,500 Value: 385					

KM# 837 1/5 CROWN
6.2200 g., 0.9999 Gold 0.1999 oz. AGW, 22 mm.
Ruler: Elizabeth II **Series:** Flower Fairies **Obv:** Crowned bust right **Rev:** Two fairies, sweet pea

Date	Mintage	F	VF	XF	Unc	BU
1998 Proof	Est. 5,000 Value: 200					

KM# 837a 1/5 CROWN
6.2200 g., 0.9999 Platinum 0.1999 oz. APW, 22 mm.
Ruler: Elizabeth II **Series:** Flower Fairies **Obv:** Crowned bust right **Rev:** Two fairies, sweet pea

Date	Mintage	F	VF	XF	Unc	BU
1998 Proof	Est. 2,500 Value: 385					

KM# 838 1/5 CROWN
6.2200 g., 0.9999 Gold 0.1999 oz. AGW, 22 mm.
Ruler: Elizabeth II **Series:** Flower Fairies **Obv:** Crowned bust right **Rev:** Fairy looking into flower, White Bindweed

Date	Mintage	F	VF	XF	Unc	BU
1998 Proof	Est. 5,000 Value: 200					

KM# 838a 1/5 CROWN
6.2200 g., 0.9999 Platinum 0.1999 oz. APW, 22 mm.
Ruler: Elizabeth II **Series:** Flower Fairies **Obv:** Crowned bust right **Rev:** Fairy looking into flower, White Bindweed

Date	Mintage	F	VF	XF	Unc	BU
1998 Proof	Est. 2,500 Value: 385					

KM# 839 1/5 CROWN
6.2200 g., 0.9999 Gold 0.1999 oz. AGW, 22 mm.
Ruler: Elizabeth II **Series:** Flower Fairies **Obv:** Crowned bust right **Rev:** Fairy standing, daffodil

Date	Mintage	F	VF	XF	Unc	BU
1998 Proof	Est. 5,000 Value: 200					

KM# 839a 1/5 CROWN
6.2200 g., 0.9999 Platinum 0.1999 oz. APW, 22 mm.
Ruler: Elizabeth II **Series:** Flower Fairies **Obv:** Crowned bust right **Rev:** Fairy standing, daffodil

Date	Mintage	F	VF	XF	Unc	BU
1998 Proof	Est. 2,500 Value: 385					

KM# 845 1/5 CROWN
6.2200 g., 0.9999 Gold 0.1999 oz. AGW, 22 mm.
Ruler: Elizabeth II **Series:** Winter Olympics - Nagano
Obv: Crowned bust right **Rev:** Ski jumper

Date	Mintage	F	VF	XF	Unc	BU
1998 Proof	Est. 5,000 Value: 200					

KM# 846 1/5 CROWN
6.2200 g., 0.9999 Gold 0.1999 oz. AGW, 22 mm.
Ruler: Elizabeth II **Series:** Winter Olympics - Nagano
Obv: Crowned bust right **Rev:** Slalom skier

Date	Mintage	F	VF	XF	Unc	BU
1998 Proof	Est. 5,000 Value: 200					

KM# 847 1/5 CROWN
6.2200 g., 0.9999 Gold 0.1999 oz. AGW, 22 mm.
Ruler: Elizabeth II **Series:** Winter Olympics - Nagano
Obv: Crowned bust right **Rev:** Figure skaters below flames

Date	Mintage	F	VF	XF	Unc	BU
1998	Est. 5,000 Value: 200					

KM# 848 1/5 CROWN
6.2200 g., 0.9999 Gold 0.1999 oz. AGW, 22 mm.
Ruler: Elizabeth II **Series:** Winter Olympics - Nagano
Obv: Crowned bust right **Rev:** Figure skater, speed skater and skier

Date	Mintage	F	VF	XF	Unc	BU
1998 Proof	Est. 5,000 Value: 200					

KM# 855 1/5 CROWN
6.2200 g., 0.9999 Gold 0.1999 oz. AGW, 22 mm.
Ruler: Elizabeth II **Obv:** Crowned bust right **Rev:** Birman cat

Date	Mintage	F	VF	XF	Unc	BU
1998 Proof	1,000 Value: 200					

KM# 855a 1/5 CROWN
6.2200 g., 0.9995 Platinum 0.1999 oz. APW, 22 mm.
Ruler: Elizabeth II **Obv:** Crowned bust right **Rev:** Birman cat

Date	Mintage	F	VF	XF	Unc	BU
1998 Proof	—	Value: 385				

KM# 861 1/5 CROWN
6.2200 g., 0.9999 Gold 0.1999 oz. AGW, 22 mm.
Ruler: Elizabeth II **Series:** History of the Cat **Obv:** Crowned bust right **Rev:** Egyptian Mau cat with earring

Date	Mintage	F	VF	XF	Unc	BU
1998 Proof	Est. 7,500	Value: 200				

KM# 871 1/5 CROWN
6.2200 g., 0.9999 Gold 0.1999 oz. AGW, 22 mm.
Ruler: Elizabeth II **Subject:** 125th Anniversary of the Steam Railway **Obv:** Crowned bust right **Rev:** "The General" locomotive

Date	Mintage	F	VF	XF	Unc	BU
1998 Proof	Est. 5,000	Value: 200				

KM# 873 1/5 CROWN
6.2200 g., 0.9999 Gold 0.1999 oz. AGW, 22 mm. **Ruler:** Elizabeth II **Subject:** 125th Anniversary of the Steam Railway **Obv:** Crowned bust right **Rev:** "The Rocket" locomotive and portrait

Date	Mintage	F	VF	XF	Unc	BU
1998 Proof	Est. 5,000	Value: 200				

KM# 875 1/5 CROWN
6.2200 g., 0.9999 Gold 0.1999 oz. AGW, 22 mm. **Ruler:** Elizabeth II **Subject:** 125th Anniversary of the Steam Railway **Obv:** Crowned bust right **Rev:** Orient Express parlor car, interior view

Date	Mintage	F	VF	XF	Unc	BU
1998 Proof	Est. 5,000	Value: 200				

KM# 877 1/5 CROWN
6.2200 g., 0.9999 Gold 0.1999 oz. AGW, 22 mm.
Ruler: Elizabeth II **Subject:** 125th Anniversary of the Steam Railway **Obv:** Crowned bust right **Rev:** Mount Pilatus Railway

Date	Mintage	F	VF	XF	Unc	BU
1998 Proof	Est. 5,000	Value: 200				

KM# 879 1/5 CROWN
6.2200 g., 0.9999 Gold 0.1999 oz. AGW, 22 mm.
Ruler: Elizabeth II **Subject:** 125th Anniversary of the Steam Railway **Obv:** Crowned bust right **Rev:** Locomotive No. 1 "Sutherland"

Date	Mintage	F	VF	XF	Unc	BU
1998 Proof	Est. 5,000	Value: 200				

KM# 881 1/5 CROWN
6.2200 g., 0.9999 Gold 0.1999 oz. AGW, 22 mm.
Ruler: Elizabeth II **Subject:** 125th Anniversary of the Steam Railway **Obv:** Crowned bust right **Rev:** The "Flying Scotsman" locomotive

Date	Mintage	F	VF	XF	Unc	BU
1998 Proof	Est. 5,000	Value: 200				

KM# 883 1/5 CROWN
6.2200 g., 0.9999 Gold 0.1999 oz. AGW, 22 mm.
Ruler: Elizabeth II **Subject:** 125th Anniversary of the Steam Railway **Obv:** Crowned bust right **Rev:** A Mallard class locomotive

Date	Mintage	F	VF	XF	Unc	BU
1998 Proof	Est. 5,000	Value: 200				

KM# 885 1/5 CROWN
6.2200 g., 0.9999 Gold 0.1999 oz. AGW, 22 mm.
Ruler: Elizabeth II **Subject:** 125th Anniversary of the Steam Railway **Obv:** Crowned bust right **Rev:** A Big Boy class locomotive

Date	Mintage	F	VF	XF	Unc	BU
1998 Proof	Est. 5,000	Value: 200				

KM# 887 1/5 CROWN
6.2200 g., 0.9999 Gold 0.1999 oz. AGW, 22 mm.
Ruler: Elizabeth II **Series:** Year 2000 **Obv:** Crowned bust right **Rev:** American Independence 1776

Date	Mintage	F	VF	XF	Unc	BU
1998 Proof	Est. 2,000	Value: 200				

KM# 889 1/5 CROWN
6.2200 g., 0.9999 Gold 0.1999 oz. AGW, 22 mm.
Ruler: Elizabeth II **Series:** Year 2000 **Obv:** Crowned bust right **Rev:** French Revolution 1789

Date	Mintage	F	VF	XF	Unc	BU
1998 Proof	Est. 2,000	Value: 200				

KM# 891 1/5 CROWN
6.2200 g., 0.9999 Gold 0.1999 oz. AGW, 22 mm.
Ruler: Elizabeth II **Series:** Year 2000 **Obv:** Crowned bust right **Rev:** Reformation of the Church 1517

Date	Mintage	F	VF	XF	Unc	BU
1998 Proof	Est. 2,000	Value: 200				

KM# 893 1/5 CROWN
6.2200 g., 0.9999 Gold 0.1999 oz. AGW, 22 mm.
Ruler: Elizabeth II **Series:** Year 2000 **Obv:** Crowned bust right **Rev:** 400th Anniversary of the Renaissance

Date	Mintage	F	VF	XF	Unc	BU
1998 Proof	Est. 2,000	Value: 200				

KM# 895 1/5 CROWN
6.2200 g., 0.9999 Gold 0.1999 oz. AGW, 22 mm.
Ruler: Elizabeth II **Subject:** Year of the Ocean **Obv:** Crowned bust right **Rev:** Ocean wave and sea gull

Date	Mintage	F	VF	XF	Unc	BU
1998 Proof	Est. 5,000	Value: 200				

KM# 913 1/5 CROWN
6.2200 g., 0.9999 Gold 0.1999 oz. AGW, 22 mm.
Ruler: Elizabeth II **Subject:** Battle of Waterloo 1815 **Obv:** Crowned bust right **Rev:** Duke of Wellington on horseback

Date	Mintage	F	VF	XF	Unc	BU
1999 Proof	Est. 2,000	Value: 200				

KM# 915 1/5 CROWN
6.2200 g., 0.9999 Gold 0.1999 oz. AGW, 22 mm.
Ruler: Elizabeth II **Subject:** U.S. Civil War **Obv:** Crowned bust right **Rev:** Cameos of General Lee and Grant, flags, sword and drum

Date	Mintage	F	VF	XF	Unc	BU
1999 Proof	Est. 2,000	Value: 200				

KM# 917 1/5 CROWN
6.2200 g., 0.9999 Gold 0.1999 oz. AGW, 22 mm.
Ruler: Elizabeth II **Subject:** Bolshevik Revolution 1917 **Obv:** Crowned bust right **Rev:** V. I. Lenin above the Aurora

Date	Mintage	F	VF	XF	Unc	BU
1999 Proof	Est. 2,000	Value: 200				

KM# 919 1/5 CROWN
6.2200 g., 0.9999 Gold 0.1999 oz. AGW, 22 mm.
Ruler: Elizabeth II **Subject:** Armistice Day 1918 **Obv:** Crowned bust right **Rev:** Biplane above tank

Date	Mintage	F	VF	XF	Unc	BU
1999 Proof	Est. 2,000	Value: 200				

KM# 921 1/5 CROWN
6.2200 g., 0.9999 Gold 0.1999 oz. AGW, 22 mm. **Ruler:** Elizabeth II **Series:** Summer Olympics - Sydney **Obv:** Crowned bust right **Rev:** Three javelin throwers

Date	Mintage	F	VF	XF	Unc	BU
1999 Proof	Est. 5,000	Value: 200				

KM# 923 1/5 CROWN
6.2200 g., 0.9999 Gold 0.1999 oz. AGW, 22 mm.
Ruler: Elizabeth II **Series:** Summer Olympics - Sydney **Obv:** Crowned bust right **Rev:** Female diver

Date	Mintage	F	VF	XF	Unc	BU
1999 Proof	Est. 5,000	Value: 200				

KM# 925 1/5 CROWN
6.2200 g., 0.9999 Gold 0.1999 oz. AGW, 22 mm.
Ruler: Elizabeth II **Series:** Summer Olympics - Sydney **Obv:** Crowned bust right **Rev:** Sailboat, Sydney Opera House and Harbor Bridge

Date	Mintage	F	VF	XF	Unc	BU
1999 Proof	Est. 5,000	Value: 200				

KM# 927 1/5 CROWN
6.2200 g., 0.9999 Gold 0.1999 oz. AGW, 22 mm.
Ruler: Elizabeth II **Series:** Summer Olympics - Sydney **Obv:** Crowned bust right **Rev:** Two runners

Date	Mintage	F	VF	XF	Unc	BU
1999 Proof	Est. 5,000	Value: 200				

KM# 929 1/5 CROWN
6.2200 g., 0.9999 Gold 0.1999 oz. AGW, 22 mm.
Ruler: Elizabeth II **Series:** Summer Olympics - Sydney **Obv:** Crowned bust right **Rev:** Two hurdlers

Date	Mintage	F	VF	XF	Unc	BU
1999 Proof	Est. 5,000	Value: 200				

KM# 931 1/5 CROWN
6.2200 g., 0.9999 Gold 0.1999 oz. AGW, 22 mm.
Ruler: Elizabeth II **Series:** World Cup Rugby 1999 **Obv:** Crowned bust right **Rev:** Bust of William Webb Ellis

Date	Mintage	F	VF	XF	Unc	BU
1999 Proof	Est. 5,000	Value: 200				

KM# 933 1/5 CROWN
6.2200 g., 0.9999 Gold 0.1999 oz. AGW, 22 mm.
Ruler: Elizabeth II **Series:** World Cup Rugby 1999 **Obv:** Crowned bust right **Rev:** Rugby scrum

Date	Mintage	F	VF	XF	Unc	BU
1999 Proof	Est. 5,000	Value: 200				

KM# 935 1/5 CROWN
6.2200 g., 0.9999 Gold 0.1999 oz. AGW, 22 mm.
Ruler: Elizabeth II **Series:** World Cup Rugby 1999 **Obv:** Crowned bust right **Rev:** Player running for catch

Date	Mintage	F	VF	XF	Unc	BU
1999 Proof	Est. 5,000	Value: 200				

KM# 937 1/5 CROWN
6.2200 g., 0.9999 Gold 0.1999 oz. AGW, 22 mm.
Ruler: Elizabeth II **Series:** World Cup Rugby 1999 **Obv:** Crowned bust right **Rev:** Goal kick

Date	Mintage	F	VF	XF	Unc	BU
1999 Proof	Est. 5,000	Value: 200				

KM# 939 1/5 CROWN
6.2200 g., 0.9999 Gold 0.1999 oz. AGW, 22 mm.
Ruler: Elizabeth II **Series:** World Cup Rugby 1999 **Obv:** Crowned bust right **Rev:** Tackled ball carrier

Date	Mintage	F	VF	XF	Unc	BU
1999 Proof	Est. 5,000	Value: 200				

KM# 941 1/5 CROWN
6.2200 g., 0.9999 Gold 0.1999 oz. AGW, 22 mm.
Ruler: Elizabeth II **Series:** World Cup Rugby 1999 **Obv:** Crowned bust right **Rev:** Player leaping for catch

Date	Mintage	F	VF	XF	Unc	BU
1999 Proof	Est. 5,000	Value: 200				

KM# 950 1/5 CROWN
6.2200 g., 0.9999 Gold 0.1999 oz. AGW, 22 mm.
Ruler: Elizabeth II **Subject:** Year of the Rabbit **Obv:** Crowned bust right **Rev:** Two rabbits

Date	Mintage	F	VF	XF	Unc	BU
1999 Proof	Est. 12,000	Value: 200				

KM# 954 1/5 CROWN
6.2200 g., 0.9999 Gold 0.1999 oz. AGW, 22 mm.
Ruler: Elizabeth II **Obv:** Crowned bust right **Rev:** Portrait Sir Walter Raleigh, ship and dates

Date	Mintage	F	VF	XF	Unc	BU
1999 Proof	Est. 5,000	Value: 200				

KM# 956 1/5 CROWN
6.2200 g., 0.9999 Gold 0.1999 oz. AGW, 22 mm.
Ruler: Elizabeth II **Obv:** Crowned bust right **Rev:** Portrait Robert Falcon Scott and compass

Date	Mintage	F	VF	XF	Unc	BU
1999 Proof	Est. 5,000	Value: 200				

KM# 962 1/5 CROWN
6.2200 g., 0.9999 Gold 0.1999 oz. AGW, 22 mm.
Ruler: Elizabeth II **Subject:** British Blue Cat **Obv:** Crowned bust right **Rev:** Cat cleaning paw

Date	Mintage	F	VF	XF	Unc	BU
1999	—	—	—	—	—	195
1999 Proof	—	Value: 200				
1999 U Y2K	Est. 5,000	—	—	—	—	195

KM# 962a 1/5 CROWN
6.2200 g., 0.9995 Platinum 0.1999 oz. APW, 22 mm.
Ruler: Elizabeth II **Subject:** British Blue Cat **Obv:** Crowned bust right **Rev:** Cat cleaning paw

Date	Mintage	F	VF	XF	Unc	BU
1999 Proof	—	Value: 385				

KM# 975 1/5 CROWN
6.2200 g., 0.9999 Gold 0.1999 oz. AGW, 22 mm.
Ruler: Elizabeth II **Series:** The Life and Times of the Queen Mother **Obv:** Crowned bust right **Rev:** Child in chair

Date	Mintage	F	VF	XF	Unc	BU
1999 Proof	Est. 5,000	Value: 200				

KM# 977 1/5 CROWN
6.2200 g., 0.9999 Gold 0.1999 oz. AGW, 22 mm.
Ruler: Elizabeth II **Series:** The Life and Times of the Queen Mother **Obv:** Crowned bust right **Rev:** Engagement portrait

Date	Mintage	F	VF	XF	Unc	BU
1999 Proof	Est. 5,000	Value: 200				

KM# 979 1/5 CROWN
6.2200 g., 0.9999 Gold 0.1999 oz. AGW, 22 mm.
Ruler: Elizabeth II **Series:** The Life and Times of the Queen Mother **Obv:** Crowned bust right **Rev:** Honeymoon departure

Date	Mintage	F	VF	XF	Unc	BU
1999 Proof	Est. 5,000	Value: 200				

KM# 994   1/5 CROWN
6.2200 g., 0.9999 Gold 0.1999 oz. AGW, 22 mm.
Ruler: Elizabeth II **Subject:** The Wedding of HRH Prince Edward
Obv: Crowned bust right **Rev:** Portrait of Prince Edward

Date	Mintage	F	VF	XF	Unc	BU
1999 Proof	Est. 5,000			Value: 200		

KM# 995   1/5 CROWN
6.2200 g., 0.9999 Gold 0.1999 oz. AGW, 22 mm.
Ruler: Elizabeth II **Subject:** The Wedding of HRH Prince Edward
Obv: Crowned bust right **Rev:** Head of Prince Edward

Date	Mintage	F	VF	XF	Unc	BU
1999 Proof	Est. 5,000			Value: 200		

KM# 997   1/5 CROWN
6.2200 g., 0.9999 Gold 0.1999 oz. AGW, 22 mm.
Ruler: Elizabeth II **Subject:** The Wedding of HRH Prince Edward
Obv: Crowned bust right **Rev:** Head of Sophie Rhys-Jones

Date	Mintage	F	VF	XF	Unc	BU
1999 Proof	Est. 5,000			Value: 200		

KM# 999   1/5 CROWN
6.2200 g., 0.9999 Gold 0.1999 oz. AGW, 22 mm.
Ruler: Elizabeth II **Subject:** 30th Anniversary of First Man on the
Moon **Obv:** Crowned bust right **Rev:** Apollo XI, two moon walkers,
date

Date	Mintage	F	VF	XF	Unc	BU
1999 Proof	Est. 2,000			Value: 200		

KM# 1001   1/5 CROWN
6.2200 g., 0.9999 Gold 0.1999 oz. AGW, 22 mm. **Ruler:** Elizabeth II
Subject: 30th Anniversary of First Man on the Moon **Obv:** Crowned
bust right **Rev:** Mariner IX, 1971, space craft orbiting Mars

Date	Mintage	F	VF	XF	Unc	BU
1999 Proof	Est. 2,000			Value: 200		

KM# 1003   1/5 CROWN
6.2200 g., 0.9999 Gold 0.1999 oz. AGW, 22 mm.
Ruler: Elizabeth II **Subject:** 30th Anniversary of First Man on the
Moon **Obv:** Crowned bust right **Rev:** Apollo-Soyuz link-up

Date	Mintage	F	VF	XF	Unc	BU
1999 Proof	Est. 2,000			Value: 200		

KM# 1005   1/5 CROWN
6.2200 g., 0.9999 Gold 0.1999 oz. AGW, 22 mm.
Ruler: Elizabeth II **Subject:** 30th Anniversary of First Man on the
Moon **Obv:** Crowned bust right **Rev:** Viking Mars Lander, 1978

Date	Mintage	F	VF	XF	Unc	BU
1999 Proof	Est. 2,000			Value: 200		

KM# 1007   1/5 CROWN
6.2200 g., 0.9999 Gold 0.1999 oz. AGW, 22 mm.
Ruler: Elizabeth II **Subject:** 30th Anniversary of First Man on the
Moon **Obv:** Crowned bust right **Rev:** Shuttle Columbia, 1981

Date	Mintage	F	VF	XF	Unc	BU
1999 Proof	Est. 2,000			Value: 200		

KM# 1009   1/5 CROWN
6.2200 g., 0.9999 Gold 0.1999 oz. AGW, 22 mm.
Ruler: Elizabeth II **Subject:** 30th Anniversary of First Man on the
Moon **Obv:** Crowned bust right **Rev:** Mars Pathfinder, 1997

Date	Mintage	F	VF	XF	Unc	BU
1999 Proof	Est. 2,000			Value: 200		

KM# 984   1/5 CROWN
6.2200 g., 0.9999 Gold 0.1999 oz. AGW, 22 mm.
Ruler: Elizabeth II **Subject:** Founding of the UN - Millennium
Obv: Crowned bust right **Rev:** UN Building, logo

Date	Mintage	F	VF	XF	Unc	BU
2000 Proof	Est. 2,000			Value: 200		

KM# 984a   1/5 CROWN
28.2800 g., 0.9250 Silver 0.8410 oz. ASW **Ruler:** Elizabeth II
Subject: Founding of the UN 1945 **Obv:** Crowned bust right
Rev: UN building and logo

Date	Mintage	F	VF	XF	Unc	BU
2000 Proof	—			Value: 50.00		

KM# 985   1/5 CROWN
6.2200 g., 0.9999 Gold 0.1999 oz. AGW, 22 mm.
Ruler: Elizabeth II **Subject:** First Man on the Moon - Millennium
Obv: Crowned bust right **Rev:** Landing scene, date

Date	Mintage	F	VF	XF	Unc	BU
2000 Proof	Est. 2,000			Value: 200		

KM# 987   1/5 CROWN
6.2200 g., 0.9999 Gold 0.1999 oz. AGW, 22 mm.
Ruler: Elizabeth II **Subject:** Fall of the Berlin Wall - Millennium
Obv: Crowned bust right **Rev:** Crowds surrounding wall

Date	Mintage	F	VF	XF	Unc	BU
2000 Proof	Est. 2,000			Value: 200		

KM# 989   1/5 CROWN
6.2200 g., 0.9999 Gold 0.1999 oz. AGW, 22 mm.
Ruler: Elizabeth II **Subject:** Millennium 2000 - The Future
Obv: Crowned bust right **Rev:** International space station

Date	Mintage	F	VF	XF	Unc	BU
2000 Proof	Est. 2,000			Value: 200		

KM# 1014   1/5 CROWN
6.2200 g., 0.9999 Gold 0.1999 oz. AGW, 22 mm.
Ruler: Elizabeth II **Subject:** Year of the Dragon **Obv:** Crowned
bust right **Rev:** Dragon, Chinese characters

Date	Mintage	F	VF	XF	Unc	BU
2000 Proof	Est. 12,000			Value: 200		

KM# 1020   1/5 CROWN
6.2200 g., 0.9999 Gold 0.1999 oz. AGW, 22 mm.
Ruler: Elizabeth II **Obv:** Crowned bust right **Rev:** Armored
portrait of Francisco Pizarro, map and ship **Edge:** Reeded

Date	Mintage	F	VF	XF	Unc	BU
2000 Proof	5,000			Value: 200		

KM# 1022   1/5 CROWN
6.2200 g., 0.9999 Gold 0.1999 oz. AGW, 22 mm.
Ruler: Elizabeth II **Obv:** Crowned bust right **Rev:** Portrait, ship
on ice and map, Willem Barents

Date	Mintage	F	VF	XF	Unc	BU
2000 Proof	5,000			Value: 200		

KM# 1024   1/5 CROWN
6.2200 g., 0.9999 Gold 0.1999 oz. AGW, 22 mm.
Ruler: Elizabeth II **Series:** Queen Mother **Obv:** Crowned bust
right **Rev:** 1931 family scene **Edge:** Reeded

Date	Mintage	F	VF	XF	Unc	BU
2000 Proof	5,000			Value: 200		

KM# 1026   1/5 CROWN
6.2200 g., 0.9999 Gold 0.1999 oz. AGW, 22 mm.
Ruler: Elizabeth II **Series:** Queen Mother **Obv:** Crowned bust
right **Rev:** 1937 Coronation scene

Date	Mintage	F	VF	XF	Unc	BU
2000 Proof	5,000			Value: 200		

KM# 1028   1/5 CROWN
6.2200 g., 0.9999 Gold 0.1999 oz. AGW, 22 mm.
Ruler: Elizabeth II **Series:** Queen Mother **Obv:** Crowned bust
right **Rev:** 1945 Victory Visit scene

Date	Mintage	F	VF	XF	Unc	BU
2000 Proof	5,000			Value: 200		

KM# 1030   1/5 CROWN
6.2200 g., 0.9999 Gold 0.1999 oz. AGW, 22 mm.
Ruler: Elizabeth II **Series:** Queen Mother **Obv:** Crowned bust
right **Rev:** 1963 Royal Visit scene

Date	Mintage	F	VF	XF	Unc	BU
2000 Proof	175			Value: 200		

KM# 1032   1/5 CROWN
6.2200 g., 0.9990 Gold 0.1998 oz. AGW, 22 mm.
Ruler: Elizabeth II **Subject:** Battle of Britain **Obv:** Crowned bust
right **Rev:** Aerial battle scene **Edge:** Reeded

Date	Mintage	F	VF	XF	Unc	BU
2000 Proof	5,000			Value: 200		

KM# 1034   1/5 CROWN
6.2200 g., 0.9990 Gold 0.1998 oz. AGW, 22 mm.
Ruler: Elizabeth II **Subject:** Global Challenge Yacht Race
Obv: Crowned bust right **Rev:** Partial view of ship and map

Date	Mintage	F	VF	XF	Unc	BU
2000 Proof	5,000			Value: 200		

KM# 1046   1/5 CROWN
6.2200 g., 0.9999 Gold 0.1999 oz. AGW, 22 mm.
Ruler: Elizabeth II **Obv:** Crowned bust right **Rev:** Prince William's
portrait **Edge:** Reeded

Date	Mintage	F	VF	XF	Unc	BU
2000 Proof	5,000			Value: 200		

KM# 1048   1/5 CROWN
6.2200 g., 0.9999 Gold 0.1999 oz. AGW, 22 mm. **Ruler:**
Elizabeth II **Obv:** Crowned bust right **Rev:** Bust with hat facing

Date	Mintage	F	VF	XF	Unc	BU
2000 Proof	2,000			Value: 200		

KM# 1054   1/5 CROWN
6.2200 g., 0.9999 Gold 0.1999 oz. AGW, 22 mm. **Ruler:** Elizabeth II
Obv: Crowned bust right **Rev:** Scottish kitten **Edge:** Reeded

Date	Mintage	F	VF	XF	Unc	BU
2000	—			Value: 200		195
2000 Proof	—			Value: 200		

KM# 1054a   1/5 CROWN
6.2200 g., 0.9995 Platinum 0.1999 oz. APW, 22 mm.
Ruler: Elizabeth II **Obv:** Crowned bust right **Rev:** Scottish kitten

Date	Mintage	F	VF	XF	Unc	BU
2000	—	—	—	—	—	375

KM# 669   1/4 CROWN
0.9990 Bi-Metallic Gold center in Platinum ring
Ruler: Elizabeth II **Series:** Legend of King Arthur **Obv:** Crowned
bust right **Rev:** King Arthur with sword and orb

Date	Mintage	F	VF	XF	Unc	BU
1996 Proof	Est. 5,000			Value: 400		

KM# 670   1/4 CROWN
0.9990 Bi-Metallic **Ruler:** Elizabeth II **Series:** Legend of King
Arthur **Obv:** Crowned bust right **Rev:** Queen Guinevere

Date	Mintage	F	VF	XF	Unc	BU
1996 Proof	Est. 5,000			Value: 400		

KM# 671   1/4 CROWN
0.9990 Bi-Metallic Gold center in Platinum ring
Ruler: Elizabeth II **Series:** Legend of King Arthur **Obv:** Crowned
bust right **Rev:** Sir Lancelot

Date	Mintage	F	VF	XF	Unc	BU
1996 Proof	Est. 5,000			Value: 400		

KM# 672   1/4 CROWN
0.9990 Bi-Metallic Gold center in Platinum ring
Ruler: Elizabeth II **Series:** Legend of King Arthur **Obv:** Crowned
bust right **Rev:** Merlin

Date	Mintage	F	VF	XF	Unc	BU
1996 Proof	Est. 5,000			Value: 400		

KM# 673   1/4 CROWN
0.9990 Bi-Metallic Gold center in Platinum ring
Ruler: Elizabeth II **Series:** Legend of King Arthur **Obv:** Crowned
bust right **Rev:** Camelot Castle

Date	Mintage	F	VF	XF	Unc	BU
1996 Proof	Est. 5,000			Value: 400		

KM# 669a   1/4 CROWN
3.8880 g., 0.9950 Platinum 0.1244 oz. APW **Ruler:** Elizabeth II
Series: Legend of King Arthur **Obv:** Crowned bust right
Rev: King Arthur with sword and orb **Note:** Prev. KM#674.

Date	Mintage	F	VF	XF	Unc	BU
1996 Proof	Est. 5,000			Value: 275		

KM# 670a   1/4 CROWN
3.8880 g., 0.9950 Platinum 0.1244 oz. APW **Ruler:** Elizabeth II
Series: Legend of King Arthur **Obv:** Crowned bust right
Rev: Queen Guinevere **Note:** Prev. KM#675.

Date	Mintage	F	VF	XF	Unc	BU
1996 Proof	Est. 5,000			Value: 245		

KM# 671a   1/4 CROWN
3.8880 g., 0.9950 Platinum 0.1244 oz. APW **Ruler:** Elizabeth II
Series: Legend of King Arthur **Obv:** Crowned bust right **Rev:** Sir
Lancelot **Note:** Prev. KM#676.

Date	Mintage	F	VF	XF	Unc	BU
1996 Proof	Est. 5,000			Value: 245		

KM# 672a   1/4 CROWN
3.8880 g., 0.9950 Platinum 0.1244 oz. APW **Ruler:** Elizabeth II
Series: Legend of King Arthur **Obv:** Crowned bust right
Rev: Merlin **Note:** Prev. KM#677.

Date	Mintage	F	VF	XF	Unc	BU
1996 Proof	Est. 5,000			Value: 245		

KM# 673a   1/4 CROWN
3.8880 g., 0.9950 Platinum 0.1244 oz. APW **Ruler:** Elizabeth II
Series: Legend of King Arthur **Obv:** Crowned bust right within
circle **Rev:** Castle within circle **Note:** Prev. KM#678.

Date	Mintage	F	VF	XF	Unc	BU
1996 Proof	Est. 5,000			Value: 245		

KM# 187   1/2 CROWN
15.5500 g., 0.9990 Gold 0.4994 oz. AGW **Ruler:** Elizabeth II
Subject: U.S. Constitution **Obv:** Crowned bust right within circle
Rev: Statue of Liberty at center of Presidential busts within circle

Date	Mintage	F	VF	XF	Unc	BU
1987 Proof	12,000			Value: 475		

KM# 187a   1/2 CROWN
15.5500 g., 0.9990 Platinum 0.4994 oz. APW **Ruler:** Elizabeth II
Subject: U.S. Constitution **Obv:** Crowned bust right **Rev:** Busts
of American presidents, Statue of Liberty at center

Date	Mintage	F	VF	XF	Unc	BU
1987 Proof	250			Value: 850		

KM# 238   1/2 CROWN
15.5500 g., 0.9990 Gold 0.4994 oz. AGW **Ruler:** Elizabeth II
Obv: Crowned bust right **Rev:** Manx cat

Date	Mintage	F	VF	XF	Unc	BU
1988	6,375	—		—	—	475
1988 Proof	5,000			Value: 485		

KM# 286   1/2 CROWN
16.4000 g., 0.9480 Gold 0.4998 oz. AGW **Ruler:** Elizabeth II
Subject: Australian Bicentennial **Obv:** Crowned bust right within
circle **Rev:** Cockatoo on branch within circle

Date	Mintage	F	VF	XF	Unc	BU
1988 Proof	Est. 7,500			Value: 475		

KM# 287   1/2 CROWN
16.4000 g., 0.9480 Gold 0.4998 oz. AGW **Ruler:** Elizabeth II
Subject: Australian Bicentennial **Obv:** Crowned bust right
Rev: Koala bear

Date	Mintage	F	VF	XF	Unc	BU
1988 Proof	Est. 7,500	Value: 475				

KM# 288   1/2 CROWN
16.4000 g., 0.9480 Gold 0.4998 oz. AGW **Ruler:** Elizabeth II
Subject: Australian Bicentennial **Obv:** Crowned bust right
Rev: Duckbill platypus

Date	Mintage	F	VF	XF	Unc	BU
1988 Proof	Est. 7,500	Value: 475				

KM# 289   1/2 CROWN
16.4000 g., 0.9480 Gold 0.4998 oz. AGW **Ruler:** Elizabeth II
Subject: Australian Bicentennial **Obv:** Crowned bust right within
circle **Rev:** Kangaroo within circle

Date	Mintage	F	VF	XF	Unc	BU
1988 Proof	Est. 7,500	Value: 475				

KM# 286a   1/2 CROWN
15.5500 g., 0.9990 Platinum 0.4994 oz. APW **Ruler:** Elizabeth II
Subject: Australian Bicentennial **Obv:** Crowned bust right
Rev: Cockatoo **Note:** Prev. KM#359.

Date	Mintage	F	VF	XF	Unc	BU
1988 Proof	—	Value: 850				

KM# 287a   1/2 CROWN
15.5500 g., 0.9990 Platinum 0.4994 oz. APW **Ruler:** Elizabeth II
Subject: Australian Bicentennial **Obv:** Crowned bust right
Rev: Koala bear **Note:** Prev. KM#360.

Date	Mintage	F	VF	XF	Unc	BU
1988 Proof	—	Value: 850				

KM# 288a   1/2 CROWN
15.5500 g., 0.9990 Platinum 0.4994 oz. APW **Ruler:** Elizabeth II
Subject: Australian Bicentennial **Obv:** Crowned bust right
Rev: Duckbill platypus **Note:** Prev. KM#361.

Date	Mintage	F	VF	XF	Unc	BU
1988 Proof	—	Value: 850				

KM# 289a   1/2 CROWN
15.5500 g., 0.9990 Platinum 0.4994 oz. APW **Ruler:** Elizabeth II
Subject: Australian Bicentennial **Obv:** Crowned bust right
Rev: Kangaroo **Note:** Prev. KM#362.

Date	Mintage	F	VF	XF	Unc	BU
1988 Proof	—	Value: 850				

KM# 363   1/2 CROWN
15.5500 g., 0.9990 Platinum 0.4994 oz. APW **Ruler:** Elizabeth II
Subject: Australian Bicentennial **Obv:** Crowned bust right
Rev: Dingo Dog

Date	Mintage	F	VF	XF	Unc	BU
1988 Proof	—	Value: 850				

KM# 255   1/2 CROWN
16.4000 g., 0.9480 Gold 0.4998 oz. AGW **Ruler:** Elizabeth II
Obv: Crowned bust right **Rev:** Persian cat

Date	Mintage	F	VF	XF	Unc	BU
1989	—	—	—	—	—	475
1989 Proof	—	Value: 485				

KM# 255a   1/2 CROWN
15.5500 g., 0.9990 Platinum 0.4994 oz. APW **Ruler:** Elizabeth II
Obv: Crowned bust right **Rev:** Persian cat **Note:** Prev. KM#470.

Date	Mintage	F	VF	XF	Unc	BU
1989	—	—	—	—	—	850
1989 Proof	—	Value: 900				

KM# 1265   1/2 CROWN
15.5500 g., 0.9990 Gold 0.4994 oz. AGW, 30 mm.
Ruler: Elizabeth II **Obv:** Crowned bust right **Rev:** Stamp design
in black center **Edge:** Reeded

Date	Mintage	F	VF	XF	Unc	BU
1990PM	—	—	—	—	—	475

KM# 280   1/2 CROWN
16.4000 g., 0.9480 Gold 0.4998 oz. AGW **Ruler:** Elizabeth II
Obv: Crowned bust right **Rev:** Alley cat

Date	Mintage	F	VF	XF	Unc	BU
1990	—	—	—	—	—	475
1990 Proof	—	Value: 485				

KM# 297   1/2 CROWN
15.5500 g., 0.9990 Gold 0.4994 oz. AGW **Ruler:** Elizabeth II
Obv: Crowned bust right **Rev:** Norwegian cat

Date	Mintage	F	VF	XF	Unc	BU
1991	—	—	—	—	—	475
1991 Proof	—	Value: 485				

KM# 325   1/2 CROWN
15.5500 g., 0.9990 Gold 0.4994 oz. AGW **Ruler:** Elizabeth II
Subject: America's Cup **Obv:** Crowned bust right **Rev:** Cameo
of "Star of India" above two modern sailboats

Date	Mintage	F	VF	XF	Unc	BU
1992 Prooflike	2,000	—	—	—	—	475

KM# 331   1/2 CROWN
15.5500 g., 0.9990 Gold 0.4994 oz. AGW **Ruler:** Elizabeth II
Obv: Crowned bust right **Rev:** Siamese cat

Date	Mintage	F	VF	XF	Unc	BU
1992	—	—	—	—	—	475
1992 Proof	—	Value: 485				

KM# 341   1/2 CROWN
15.5500 g., 0.9990 Gold 0.4994 oz. AGW **Ruler:** Elizabeth II
Subject: Year of the Rooster **Obv:** Crowned bust right
Rev: Cockerel within circle

Date	Mintage	F	VF	XF	Unc	BU
1993 Proof	Est. 5,000	Value: 485				

KM# 352   1/2 CROWN
15.5500 g., 0.9990 Gold 0.4994 oz. AGW **Ruler:** Elizabeth II
Obv: Crowned bust right **Rev:** Maine coon cat

Date	Mintage	F	VF	XF	Unc	BU
1993	—	—	—	—	—	475
1993 Proof	—	Value: 485				

KM# 379   1/2 CROWN
15.5500 g., 0.9990 Gold 0.4994 oz. AGW **Ruler:** Elizabeth II
Obv: Crowned bust right **Rev:** Japanese bobtail cat

Date	Mintage	F	VF	XF	Unc	BU
1994	—	—	—	—	—	475
1994 Proof	—	Value: 485				

KM# 405   1/2 CROWN
15.5500 g., 0.9990 Gold 0.4994 oz. AGW **Ruler:** Elizabeth II
Obv: Crowned bust right **Rev:** Pekingese dog

Date	Mintage	F	VF	XF	Unc	BU
1994 Proof	5,000	Value: 485				

KM# 379a   1/2 CROWN
15.5500 g., 0.9990 Platinum 0.4994 oz. APW **Ruler:** Elizabeth II
Obv: Crowned bust right **Rev:** Japanese bobtail cat **Note:** Prev.
KM#476.

Date	Mintage	F	VF	XF	Unc	BU
1994	—	—	—	—	—BV+20%—	
1994 Proof	—	BV+20%				

KM# 445   1/2 CROWN
15.5500 g., 0.9990 Gold 0.4994 oz. AGW **Ruler:** Elizabeth II
Obv: Crowned bust right **Rev:** Turkish cat looking back

Date	Mintage	F	VF	XF	Unc	BU
1995 U	—	—	—	—	—	475
1995 Proof	—	Value: 485				

KM# 452   1/2 CROWN
15.5500 g., 0.9990 Gold 0.4994 oz. AGW **Ruler:** Elizabeth II
Subject: Year of the Pig **Obv:** Crowned bust right **Rev:** Sow with
piglets

Date	Mintage	F	VF	XF	Unc	BU
1995 Proof	Est. 5,000	Value: 485				

KM# 445a   1/2 CROWN
15.5500 g., 0.9990 Platinum 0.4994 oz. APW **Ruler:** Elizabeth II
Obv: Crowned bust right **Rev:** Turkish cat **Note:** Prev. KM#481.

Date	Mintage	F	VF	XF	Unc	BU
1995	—	—	—	—	—	850
1995 Proof	—	Value: 900				

KM# 731   1/2 CROWN
15.5517 g., 0.9999 Gold 0.4999 oz. AGW **Ruler:** Elizabeth II
Subject: Year of the Rat **Obv:** Crowned bust right **Rev:** Rat

Date	Mintage	F	VF	XF	Unc	BU
1996 Proof	—	Value: 485				

KM# 619   1/2 CROWN
15.5500 g., 0.9990 Gold 0.4994 oz. AGW **Ruler:** Elizabeth II
Obv: Crowned bust right **Rev:** Burmese cat

Date	Mintage	F	VF	XF	Unc	BU
1996 U	—	—	—	—	—	475
1996 Proof	—	Value: 485				

KM# 619a   1/2 CROWN
15.5500 g., 0.9990 Platinum 0.4994 oz. APW **Ruler:** Elizabeth II
Obv: Crowned bust right **Rev:** Burmese cat

Date	Mintage	F	VF	XF	Unc	BU
1996 U	—	—	—	—	—	850
1996 Proof	—	Value: 900				

KM# 724   1/2 CROWN
15.5517 g., 0.9999 Gold 0.4999 oz. AGW **Ruler:** Elizabeth II
Subject: Year of the Ox **Obv:** Crowned bust right **Rev:** Ox laying
down

Date	Mintage	F	VF	XF	Unc	BU
1996 Proof	Est. 6,000	Value: 485				

KM# 764a   1/2 CROWN
15.5500 g., 0.9999 Silver 0.4999 oz. ASW **Ruler:** Elizabeth II
Obv: Crowned bust right **Rev:** Portrait of Leif Eriksson and Viking
ship with map sail

Date	Mintage	F	VF	XF	Unc	BU
1997 Proof	—	Value: 30.00				

KM# 764   1/2 CROWN
15.5517 g., 0.9999 Gold 0.4999 oz. AGW **Ruler:** Elizabeth II
Obv: Crowned bust right **Rev:** Portrait of Leif Eriksson and Viking
ship with map sail

Date	Mintage	F	VF	XF	Unc	BU
1997 Proof	Est. 2,500	Value: 485				

KM# 767   1/2 CROWN
15.5517 g., 0.9999 Gold 0.4999 oz. AGW **Ruler:** Elizabeth II
Obv: Crowned bust right **Rev:** Portrait of Fridtjof Nansen, map
and ship "The Fram"

Date	Mintage	F	VF	XF	Unc	BU
1997 Proof	Est. 2,500	Value: 485				

KM# 767a   1/2 CROWN
15.5500 g., 0.9990 Silver 0.4994 oz. ASW **Ruler:** Elizabeth II
Obv: Crowned bust right **Rev:** Portrait of Fridtjof Nansen, map
and ship "The Fram"

Date	Mintage	F	VF	XF	Unc	BU
1997 Proof	—	Value: 30.00				

KM# 773 1/2 CROWN
15.5517 g., 0.9999 Gold 0.4999 oz. AGW **Ruler:** Elizabeth II
Obv: Crowned bust right **Rev:** Long-haired Smoke cat

Date	Mintage	F	VF	XF	Unc	BU
1997	—	—	—	—	—	475
1997 Proof	—	Value: 485				

KM# 791 1/2 CROWN
15.5517 g., 0.9999 Gold 0.4999 oz. AGW **Ruler:** Elizabeth II
Subject: History of the Cat **Obv:** Crowned bust right **Rev:** Cat
stalking a spider

Date	Mintage	F	VF	XF	Unc	BU
1997 Proof	Est. 2,500	Value: 485				

KM# 815 1/2 CROWN
15.5000 g., 0.9999 Gold 0.4983 oz. AGW **Ruler:** Elizabeth II
Subject: Year of the Tiger **Obv:** Crowned bust right **Rev:** Tiger

Date	Mintage	F	VF	XF	Unc	BU
1998 Proof	Est. 6,000	Value: 485				

KM# 856 1/2 CROWN
15.5517 g., 0.9999 Gold 0.4999 oz. AGW **Ruler:** Elizabeth II
Obv: Crowned bust right **Rev:** Birman cat

Date	Mintage	F	VF	XF	Unc	BU
1998	—	—	—	—	—	475
1998 Proof	1,000	Value: 485				

KM# 856a 1/2 CROWN
15.5517 g., 0.9995 Platinum 0.4997 oz. APW **Ruler:** Elizabeth II
Obv: Crowned bust right **Rev:** Birman cat

Date	Mintage	F	VF	XF	Unc	BU
1998	—	—	—	—	—	—

Note: Reported, not confirmed

KM# 862 1/2 CROWN
15.5517 g., 0.9999 Gold 0.4999 oz. AGW **Ruler:** Elizabeth II
Subject: History of the Cat **Obv:** Crowned bust right
Rev: Egyptain Mau cat with earring

Date	Mintage	F	VF	XF	Unc	BU
1998 Proof	Est. 250	Value: 485				

KM# 951 1/2 CROWN
15.5517 g., 0.9999 Gold 0.4999 oz. AGW **Ruler:** Elizabeth II
Subject: Year of the Rabbit **Obv:** Crowned bust right **Rev:** Two
rabbits

Date	Mintage	F	VF	XF	Unc	BU
1999 Proof	Est. 6,000	Value: 485				

KM# 964 1/2 CROWN
15.5517 g., 0.9999 Gold 0.4999 oz. AGW **Ruler:** Elizabeth II
Subject: British Blue cat **Obv:** Crowned bust right **Rev:** Cat
cleaning paw

Date	Mintage	F	VF	XF	Unc	BU
1999	—	—	—	—	—	475
1999 Proof	—	Value: 485				

KM# 964a 1/2 CROWN
15.5518 g., 0.9995 Platinum 0.4997 oz. APW **Ruler:** Elizabeth II
Subject: British Blue cat **Obv:** Crowned bust right **Rev:** Cat
cleaning paw

Date	Mintage	F	VF	XF	Unc	BU
1999	—	—	—	—	—	—

Note: Reported, not confirmed

KM# 1084 1/2 CROWN
9.0000 g., 0.9990 Bi-Metallic Titanium center in Gold ring 0.2891 oz.,
32.25 mm. **Ruler:** Elizabeth II **Subject:** Greenwich Meridian Time
Clock **Obv:** Head with tiara right within beaded circle
Rev: Greenwich meridian line on map clock face **Edge:** Reeded

Date	Mintage	F	VF	XF	Unc	BU
2000 Proof	10,000	Value: 225				

KM# 1263 1/2 CROWN
15.0400 g., Titanium, 38.5 mm. **Ruler:** Elizabeth II
Obv: Crowned bust right **Rev:** Space station and shuttle
Edge: Reeded

Date	Mintage	F	VF	XF	Unc	BU
2000PM Matte	—	—	—	—	40.00	

KM# 1055 1/2 CROWN
15.5517 g., 0.9999 Gold 0.4999 oz. AGW, 30 mm.
Ruler: Elizabeth II **Subject:** Scottish Fold Kitten **Obv:** Crowned
bust right **Rev:** Kitten playing with world **Edge:** Reeded

Date	Mintage	F	VF	XF	Unc	BU
2000	—	—	—	—	—	475
2000 Proof	—	Value: 485				

KM# 1055a 1/2 CROWN
6.2200 g., 0.9995 Platinum 0.1999 oz. APW **Ruler:** Elizabeth II
Subject: Scottish Fold Kitten **Obv:** Crowned bust right
Rev: Kitten playing with world

Date	Mintage	F	VF	XF	Unc	BU
2000	—	—	—	—	—	375

KM# 1015 1/2 CROWN
15.5517 g., 0.9999 Gold 0.4999 oz. AGW **Ruler:** Elizabeth II
Subject: Year of the Dragon **Obv:** Head with tiara right
Rev: Dragon, Chinese characters

Date	Mintage	F	VF	XF	Unc	BU
2000 Proof	Est. 6,000	Value: 485				

KM# 18 CROWN
Copper-Nickel, 38.5 mm. **Ruler:** Elizabeth II **Obv:** Young bust
right **Rev:** Manx cat **Edge:** Reeded

Date	Mintage	F	VF	XF	Unc	BU
1970	150,000	—	—	—	10.00	14.00

KM# 18a CROWN
28.2800 g., 0.9250 Silver 0.8410 oz. ASW, 38.5 mm.
Ruler: Elizabeth II **Obv:** Young bust right **Rev:** Manx cat

Date	Mintage	F	VF	XF	Unc	BU
1970 Proof	11,000	Value: 17.50				

KM# 30 CROWN
Copper-Nickel, 38.5 mm. **Ruler:** Elizabeth II **Subject:** Centenary
- Birth of Winston Churchill **Obv:** Young bust of Winston Churchill
right **Rev:** Bust facing **Edge:** Reeded **Note:** Most of this issue are
doubled die.

Date	Mintage	F	VF	XF	Unc	BU
1974	45,000	—	—	—	5.00	6.00

KM# 30a CROWN
28.2800 g., 0.9250 Silver 0.8410 oz. ASW **Ruler:** Elizabeth II
Obv: Young bust of Winston Churchill right **Rev:** Bust facing
Edge: Reeded

Date	Mintage	F	VF	XF	Unc	BU
1974	—	—	—	—	16.50	17.50
1974 Proof	30,000	Value: 20.00				

KM# 37 CROWN
Copper-Nickel, 38.5 mm. **Ruler:** Elizabeth II
Subject: Bicentenary of American Independence **Obv:** Young
bust right **Rev:** Bust of George Washington left **Edge:** Reeded
Note: Doubled die strike exists.

Date	Mintage	F	VF	XF	Unc	BU
1976	50,000	—	—	—	6.00	7.00

KM# 37a CROWN
28.2800 g., 0.9250 Silver 0.8410 oz. ASW, 38.5 mm.
Ruler: Elizabeth II **Subject:** Bicentenary of American
Independence **Obv:** Young bust of George Washington right
Rev: Bust left

Date	Mintage	F	VF	XF	Unc	BU
1976	—	—	—	—	16.50	17.50
1976 Proof	30,000	Value: 20.00				

KM# 38 CROWN
Copper-Nickel, 38.5 mm. **Ruler:** Elizabeth II **Obv:** Young bust
right **Rev:** Horse-drawn tram **Edge:** Reeded **Note:** Doubled die
strike exists.

Date	Mintage	F	VF	XF	Unc	BU
1976	50,000	—	—	—	7.50	10.00

KM# 38a CROWN
28.2800 g., 0.9250 Silver 0.8410 oz. ASW, 38.5 mm.
Ruler: Elizabeth II **Obv:** Young bust right **Rev:** Horse-drawn tram

Date	Mintage	F	VF	XF	Unc	BU
1976	—	—	—	—	17.50	18.50
1976 Proof	30,000	Value: 25.00				

KM# 41 CROWN
Copper-Nickel, 38.5 mm. **Ruler:** Elizabeth II **Subject:** Silver
Jubilee **Obv:** Young bust right **Rev:** Triskeles in center of crowns
Edge: Reeded

Date	Mintage	F	VF	XF	Unc	BU
ND(1977)	—	—	—	—	4.50	6.00
ND(1977) Proof	—	Value: 15.00				

KM# 41a CROWN
28.2800 g., 0.9250 Silver 0.8410 oz. ASW, 38.5 mm.
Ruler: Elizabeth II **Subject:** Silver Jubilee **Obv:** Crowned bust
right **Rev:** Triskeles in center of crowns **Edge:** Reeded

Date	Mintage	F	VF	XF	Unc	BU
ND(1977)	—	—	—	—	17.50	18.50
ND(1977) Proof	30,000	Value: 25.00				

KM# 42 CROWN
Copper-Nickel, 38.5 mm. **Ruler:** Elizabeth II **Subject:** Queen's
Jubilee Appeal **Obv:** Young bust right **Rev:** Triskeles on shield
and crown divide wreath with monogram at center **Edge:** Reeded

Date	Mintage	F	VF	XF	Unc	BU
1977	—	—	—	—	6.00	7.00

Note: Wide and narrow rims exist

KM# 42a CROWN

28.2800 g., 0.9250 Silver 0.8410 oz. ASW, 38.5 mm.
Ruler: Elizabeth II **Subject:** Queen's Jubilee Appeal **Obv:** Young bust right **Rev:** Triskeles on shield and crown divide wreath with monogram at center

Date	Mintage	F	VF	XF	Unc	BU
1977	70,000	—	—	—	17.50	18.50
1977 Proof	30,000	Value: 25.00				

KM# 43 CROWN

Copper-Nickel, 38.5 mm. **Ruler:** Elizabeth II **Subject:** 25th Anniversary of Coronation **Obv:** Young bust right **Rev:** Falcons **Edge:** Reeded **Note:** For mule of Isle of Man obverse with Ascension Island KM#1 reverse, refer to Ascension Island listings.

Date	Mintage	F	VF	XF	Unc	BU
1978	—	—	—	—	10.00	15.00
1978 Proof	—	Value: 17.50				

KM# 43a CROWN

28.2800 g., 0.9250 Silver 0.8410 oz. ASW, 38.5 mm.
Ruler: Elizabeth II **Subject:** 25th Anniversary of Coronation **Obv:** Young bust right **Rev:** Falcons

Date	Mintage	F	VF	XF	Unc	BU
1978	70,000	—	—	—	17.50	18.50
1978 Proof	30,000	Value: 25.00				

KM# 45 CROWN

28.4700 g., Copper-Nickel, 38.47 mm. **Ruler:** Elizabeth II **Subject:** 300th Anniversary of Manx Coinage **Obv:** Head with tiara right **Rev:** Triskeles coin at center of 8 assorted coins **Edge:** Reeded

Date	Mintage	F	VF	XF	Unc	BU
1979PM	—	—	—	—	8.00	9.00
1979PM Proof	—	Value: 10.00				

KM# 45a CROWN

28.2800 g., 0.9250 Silver 0.8410 oz. ASW, 38.47 mm.
Ruler: Elizabeth II **Subject:** 300th Anniversary of Manx Coinage **Obv:** Head with tiara right **Rev:** Triskeles coin at center of 8 assorted coins **Edge:** Reeded

Date	Mintage	F	VF	XF	Unc	BU
1979PM	70,000	—	—	—	17.50	18.50
1979PM Proof	30,000	Value: 25.00				

KM# 46 CROWN

Copper-Nickel, 38.5 mm. **Ruler:** Elizabeth II **Subject:** Millennium of Tynwald **Obv:** Young bust right **Rev:** Viking longship, Godred Cravan **Edge:** Reeded

Date	Mintage	F	VF	XF	Unc	BU
1979	100,000	—	—	—	3.50	4.50

KM# 46a CROWN

28.2800 g., 0.9250 Silver 0.8410 oz. ASW, 38.5 mm.
Ruler: Elizabeth II **Subject:** Millennium of Tynwald **Obv:** Young bust right **Rev:** Viking longship, Godred Cravan

Date	Mintage	F	VF	XF	Unc	BU
1979	25,000	—	—	—	17.50	18.50
1979 Proof	10,000	Value: 25.00				

KM# 46b CROWN

43.0000 g., 0.9170 Gold 1.2677 oz. AGW, 38.5 mm.
Ruler: Elizabeth II **Subject:** Millennium of Tynwald **Obv:** Young bust right **Rev:** Viking longship

Date	Mintage	F	VF	XF	Unc	BU
1979 Proof	300	Value: 1,250				

KM# 46c CROWN

52.0000 g., 0.9500 Platinum 1.5882 oz. APW, 38.5 mm.
Ruler: Elizabeth II **Subject:** Millennium of Tynwald **Obv:** Young bust right **Rev:** Viking longship

Date	Mintage	F	VF	XF	Unc	BU
1979 Proof	100	Value: 3,000				

KM# 47 CROWN

Copper-Nickel, 38.5 mm. **Ruler:** Elizabeth II **Subject:** Millennium of Tynwald **Obv:** Young bust right **Rev:** English cog, Castle Rushen **Edge:** Reeded

Date	Mintage	F	VF	XF	Unc	BU
1979	100,000	—	—	—	6.50	7.50
1979 CB		—	—	—	6.50	7.50

KM# 47a CROWN

28.2800 g., 0.9250 Silver 0.8410 oz. ASW, 38.5 mm.
Ruler: Elizabeth II **Subject:** Millennium of Tynwald **Obv:** Young bust right **Rev:** English cog, Castle Rushen

Date	Mintage	F	VF	XF	Unc	BU
1979	25,000	—	—	—	17.50	18.50
1979 Proof	10,000	Value: 25.00				

KM# 47b CROWN

43.0000 g., 0.9170 Gold 1.2677 oz. AGW, 38.5 mm.
Ruler: Elizabeth II **Subject:** Millennium of Tynwald **Obv:** Young bust right **Rev:** English cog, Castle Rushen

Date	Mintage	F	VF	XF	Unc	BU
1979 Proof	300	Value: 1,250				

KM# 47c CROWN

52.0000 g., 0.9500 Platinum 1.5882 oz. APW, 38.5 mm.
Ruler: Elizabeth II **Subject:** Millennium of Tynwald **Obv:** Young bust right **Rev:** English cog, Castle Rushen

Date	Mintage	F	VF	XF	Unc	BU
1979 Proof	100	Value: 3,000				

KM# 48 CROWN

Copper-Nickel, 38.5 mm. **Ruler:** Elizabeth II **Subject:** Millennium of Tynwald **Obv:** Young bust right **Rev:** Ship **Edge:** Reeded

Date	Mintage	F	VF	XF	Unc	BU
1979	100,000	—	—	—	8.00	9.00

KM# 48a CROWN

28.2800 g., 0.9250 Silver 0.8410 oz. ASW, 38.5 mm.
Ruler: Elizabeth II **Subject:** Millennium of Tynwald **Obv:** Young bust right **Rev:** Ship

Date	Mintage	F	VF	XF	Unc	BU
1979	25,000	—	—	—	17.50	18.50
1979 Proof	10,000	Value: 25.00				

KM# 48b CROWN

43.0000 g., 0.9170 Gold 1.2677 oz. AGW, 38.5 mm.
Ruler: Elizabeth II **Subject:** Millennium of Tynwald **Obv:** Young bust right **Rev:** Ship

Date	Mintage	F	VF	XF	Unc	BU
1979 Proof	300	Value: 1,250				

KM# 48c CROWN

52.0000 g., 0.9500 Platinum 1.5882 oz. APW, 38.5 mm.
Ruler: Elizabeth II **Subject:** Millennium of Tynwald **Obv:** Young bust right **Rev:** Ship

Date	Mintage	F	VF	XF	Unc	BU
1979 Proof	100	Value: 3,000				

KM# 49 CROWN

28.2800 g., Copper-Nickel, 38.5 mm. **Ruler:** Elizabeth II **Subject:** Millennium of Tynwald **Obv:** Young bust right **Rev:** Standing figure and ship **Edge:** Reeded

Date	Mintage	F	VF	XF	Unc	BU
1979	100,000	—	—	—	8.00	9.00

KM# 49a CROWN

28.2800 g., 0.9250 Silver 0.8410 oz. ASW, 38.5 mm.
Ruler: Elizabeth II **Subject:** Millennium of Tynwald **Obv:** Young bust right **Rev:** Standing figure and ship

Date	Mintage	F	VF	XF	Unc	BU
1979	25,000	—	—	—	17.50	18.50
1979 Proof	10,000	Value: 25.00				

KM# 49b CROWN

43.0000 g., 0.9170 Gold 1.2677 oz. AGW, 38.5 mm.
Ruler: Elizabeth II **Subject:** Millennium of Tynwald **Obv:** Young bust right **Rev:** Standing figure and ship

Date	Mintage	F	VF	XF	Unc	BU
1979 Proof	300	Value: 1,250				

KM# 49c CROWN

52.0000 g., 0.9500 Platinum 1.5882 oz. APW, 38.5 mm.
Ruler: Elizabeth II **Subject:** Millennium of Tynwald **Obv:** Young bust right **Rev:** Standing figure and ship

Date	Mintage	F	VF	XF	Unc	BU
1979 Proof	100	Value: 3,000				

KM# 50 CROWN

28.2800 g., Copper-Nickel, 38.5 mm. **Ruler:** Elizabeth II **Subject:** Millennium of Tynwald **Obv:** Young bust right **Rev:** Lifeboat and Sir William Hillory portrait **Edge:** Reeded

Date	Mintage	F	VF	XF	Unc	BU
1979	100,000	—	—	—	8.00	9.00

KM# 50a CROWN

28.2800 g., 0.9250 Silver 0.8410 oz. ASW, 38.5 mm.
Ruler: Elizabeth II **Subject:** Millennium of Tynwald **Obv:** Young bust right **Rev:** Lifeboat and Sir William Hillory portrait

Date	Mintage	F	VF	XF	Unc	BU
1979	25,000	—	—	—	17.50	18.50
1979 Proof	10,000	Value: 25.00				

KM# 50b CROWN

43.0000 g., 0.9170 Gold 1.2677 oz. AGW, 38.5 mm.
Ruler: Elizabeth II **Subject:** Millennium of Tynwald **Obv:** Young bust right **Rev:** Lifeboat and Sir William Hillory portrait

Date	Mintage	F	VF	XF	Unc	BU
1979 Proof	300	Value: 1,250				

KM# 50c CROWN

52.0000 g., 0.9500 Platinum 1.5882 oz. APW, 38.5 mm.
Ruler: Elizabeth II **Subject:** Millennium of Tynwald **Obv:** Young bust right **Rev:** Lifeboat and Sir William Hillory portrait

Date	Mintage	F	VF	XF	Unc	BU
1979 Proof	100	Value: 3,000				

KM# 63 CROWN
Copper-Nickel, 38.5 mm. **Ruler:** Elizabeth II **Subject:** Derby Bicentennial **Obv:** Young bust right **Rev:** Men racing horses **Edge:** Reeded

Date	Mintage	F	VF	XF	Unc	BU
1980	100,000	—	—	—	6.00	10.00

KM# 63a CROWN
28.2800 g., 0.9250 Silver 0.8410 oz. ASW, 38.5 mm.
Ruler: Elizabeth II **Subject:** Derby Bicentennial **Obv:** Young bust right **Rev:** Men racing horses

Date	Mintage	F	VF	XF	Unc	BU
1980	35,000	—	—	—	17.50	18.50
1980 Proof	20,000	Value: 25.00				

KM# 63b CROWN
52.0000 g., 0.9500 Platinum 1.5882 oz. APW, 38.5 mm.
Ruler: Elizabeth II **Subject:** Derby Bicentennial **Obv:** Young bust right **Rev:** Men racing horses

Date	Mintage	F	VF	XF	Unc	BU
1980 Proof	500	Value: 3,000				

KM# 63c CROWN
43.0000 g., 0.9170 Gold 1.2677 oz. AGW, 38.5 mm.
Ruler: Elizabeth II **Subject:** Derby Bicentennial **Obv:** Young bust right **Rev:** Men racing horses

Date	Mintage	F	VF	XF	Unc	BU
1980 Proof	—	Value: 1,250				

KM# 64 CROWN
Copper-Nickel, 38.5 mm. **Ruler:** Elizabeth II **Subject:** 1980 Winter Olympics - Lake Placid **Obv:** Young bust right **Rev:** Triskeles at center of assorted olympic figures **Edge:** Reeded

Date	Mintage	F	VF	XF	Unc	BU
1980						

Note: With dot between Olympics and Lake

Date	Mintage	F	VF	XF	Unc	BU
1980	100,000	—	—	—	3.00	4.00

Note: Without dot

Date	Mintage	F	VF	XF	Unc	BU
1980 Prooflike		—	—	—	7.50	9.00

KM# 64a CROWN
28.2800 g., 0.9250 Silver 0.8410 oz. ASW, 38.5 mm.
Ruler: Elizabeth II **Subject:** 1980 Winter Olympics - Lake Placid **Obv:** Young bust right **Rev:** Triskeles at center of assorted olympic figures

Date	Mintage	F	VF	XF	Unc	BU
1980 Matte	—	—	—	—	20.00	22.00
1980 Proof	10,000	Value: 28.00				

KM# 64b CROWN
39.8000 g., 0.9170 Gold 1.1733 oz. AGW, 38.5 mm.
Ruler: Elizabeth II **Subject:** 1980 Winter Olympics - Lake Placid **Obv:** Young bust right **Rev:** Triskeles at center of assorted olympic figures

Date	Mintage	F	VF	XF	Unc	BU
1980	1,500	—	—	—	—	1,200

Note: With dot between Olympics and Lake

Date	Mintage	F	VF	XF	Unc	BU
1980 Proof	500	Value: 1,250				

KM# 64c CROWN
52.0000 g., 0.9500 Platinum 1.5882 oz. APW, 38.5 mm.
Ruler: Elizabeth II **Subject:** 1980 Winter Olympics - Lake Placid **Obv:** Young bust right **Rev:** Triskeles at center of assorted olympic figures

Date	Mintage	F	VF	XF	Unc	BU
1980 Proof	100	Value: 3,000				

Note: With dot between Olympics and Lake

KM# 65 CROWN
Copper-Nickel, 38.5 mm. **Ruler:** Elizabeth II **Subject:** 1980 Summer Olympics - Moscow **Obv:** Young bust right **Rev:** Triskeles at center of assorted olympic figures

Date	Mintage	F	VF	XF	Unc	BU
1980		—	—	—	3.50	4.00

Note: Without dot between Olympiad and Moscow; without dots to right and left of One Crown

Date	Mintage	F	VF	XF	Unc	BU
1980		—	—	—	3.50	4.00

Note: Without dot between Olympiad and Moscow; with dots to right and left of One Crown

Date	Mintage	F	VF	XF	Unc	BU
1980	30,000	—	—	—	3.50	4.00

Note: With dot between Olympiad and Moscow; with dots to right and left of One Crown

Date	Mintage	F	VF	XF	Unc	BU
1980 Prooflike		—	—	—	7.50	9.00

KM# 65a CROWN
28.2800 g., 0.9250 Silver 0.8410 oz. ASW, 38.5 mm.
Ruler: Elizabeth II **Subject:** 1980 Summer Olympics - Moscow **Obv:** Young bust right **Rev:** Triskeles at center of assorted olympic figures

Date	Mintage	F	VF	XF	Unc	BU
1980		—	—	—	20.00	22.00

Note: Without dot between Olympiad and Moscow; without dots to right and left of One Crown

Date	Mintage	F	VF	XF	Unc	BU
1980		—	—	—	20.00	22.00

Note: Without dot between Olympiad and Moscow; with dots to right and left of One Crown

Date	Mintage	F	VF	XF	Unc	BU
1980		—	—	—	20.00	22.00

Note: With dot between Olympiad and Moscow; with dots to right and left of One Crown

Date	Mintage	F	VF	XF	Unc	BU
1980 Proof	10,000	Value: 28.00				

KM# 65b CROWN
39.8000 g., 0.9170 Gold 1.1733 oz. AGW, 38.5 mm.
Ruler: Elizabeth II **Subject:** 1980 Summer Olympics - Moscow **Obv:** Young bust right **Rev:** Triskeles at center of assorted olympic figures

Date	Mintage	F	VF	XF	Unc	BU
1980	1,500	—	—	—	—	1,200

Note: With dot between Olympiad and Moscow; with dots to right and left of One Crown

KM# 65c CROWN
52.0000 g., 0.9500 Platinum 1.5882 oz. APW, 38.5 mm.
Ruler: Elizabeth II **Subject:** 1980 Summer Olympics - Moscow **Obv:** Young bust right **Rev:** Triskeles at center of assorted olympic figures

Date	Mintage	F	VF	XF	Unc	BU
1980 Proof	100	Value: 3,000				

Note: With dot between Olympiad and Moscow; with dots to right and left of One Crown

KM# 66 CROWN
Copper-Nickel, 38.5 mm. **Ruler:** Elizabeth II **Subject:** 1980 Summer Olympics - Moscow **Obv:** Young bust right **Rev:** Triskeles at center of assorted olympic figures **Edge:** Reeded

Date	Mintage	F	VF	XF	Unc	BU
1980	30,000	—	—	—	6.00	7.00
1980 Prooflike		—	—	—	7.50	9.00

KM# 66a CROWN
28.2800 g., 0.9250 Silver 0.8410 oz. ASW, 38.5 mm.
Ruler: Elizabeth II **Subject:** 1980 Summer Olympics - Moscow **Obv:** Young bust right **Rev:** Triskeles at center of assorted olympic figures

Date	Mintage	F	VF	XF	Unc	BU
1980 Matte	—	—	—	—	20.00	22.00
1980 Proof	10,000	Value: 28.00				

KM# 66b CROWN
39.8000 g., 0.9170 Gold 1.1733 oz. AGW, 38.5 mm.
Ruler: Elizabeth II **Subject:** 1980 Summer Olympics - Moscow **Obv:** Young bust right **Rev:** Triskeles at center of assorted olympic figures

Date	Mintage	F	VF	XF	Unc	BU
1980	1,500	—	—	—	—	1,200

KM# 66c CROWN
52.0000 g., 0.9500 Platinum 1.5882 oz. APW, 38.5 mm.
Ruler: Elizabeth II **Subject:** 1980 Summer Olympics - Moscow **Obv:** Young bust right **Rev:** Triskeles at center of assorted olympic figures

Date	Mintage	F	VF	XF	Unc	BU
1980 Proof	100	Value: 3,000				

KM# 67 CROWN
Copper-Lead Alloy, 38.5 mm. **Ruler:** Elizabeth II **Subject:** 1980 Summer Olympics - Moscow **Obv:** Young bust right **Rev:** Triskeles at center of assorted olympic figures **Edge:** Reeded

Date	Mintage	F	VF	XF	Unc	BU
1980	30,000	—	—	—	6.00	7.00
1980 Proof like		—	—	—	7.50	9.00

KM# 67a CROWN
28.2800 g., 0.9250 Silver 0.8410 oz. ASW, 38.5 mm.
Ruler: Elizabeth II **Subject:** 1980 Summer Olympics - Moscow **Obv:** Young bust right **Rev:** Triskeles at center of assorted olympic figures

Date	Mintage	F	VF	XF	Unc	BU
1980 Matte	—	—	—	—	20.00	22.00
1980 Proof	10,000	Value: 28.00				

KM# 67b CROWN
39.8000 g., 0.9170 Gold 1.1733 oz. AGW, 38.5 mm.
Ruler: Elizabeth II **Subject:** 1980 Summer Olympics - Moscow **Obv:** Young bust right **Rev:** Triskeles at center of assorted olympic figures

Date	Mintage	F	VF	XF	Unc	BU
1980	1,500	—	—	—	—	1,200

KM# 67c CROWN
52.0000 g., 0.9500 Platinum 1.5882 oz. APW, 38.5 mm.
uler: Elizabeth II **Subject:** 1980 Summer Olympics - Moscow **Obv:** Young bust right **Rev:** Triskeles at center of assorted olympic figures

Date	Mintage	F	VF	XF	Unc	BU
1980 Proof	100	Value: 3,000				

KM# 68 CROWN
Copper-Nickel, 38.5 mm. **Ruler:** Elizabeth II **Subject:** 80th Birthday of Queen Mother **Obv:** Young bust right **Rev:** Crowned head facing divides dates **Edge:** Reeded

Date	Mintage	F	VF	XF	Unc	BU
1980	100,000	—	—	—	5.00	6.00

KM# 68a CROWN
28.2800 g., 0.5000 Silver 0.4546 oz. ASW, 38.5 mm.
Ruler: Elizabeth II **Subject:** 80th Birthday of Queen Mother **Obv:** Young bust right **Rev:** Crowned head facing divides dates

Date	Mintage	F	VF	XF	Unc	BU
1980	50,000	—	—	—	10.00	11.50

KM# 68b CROWN
28.2800 g., 0.9250 Silver 0.8410 oz. ASW, 38.5 mm.
Ruler: Elizabeth II **Subject:** 80th Birthday of Queen Mother **Obv:** Young bust right **Rev:** Crowned head facing divides dates

Date	Mintage	F	VF	XF	Unc	BU
1980 Proof	30,000	Value: 25.00				

KM# 68c CROWN
5.0000 g., 0.3740 Gold 0.0601 oz. AGW **Ruler:** Elizabeth II
Subject: 80th Birthday of Queen Mother **Obv:** Young bust right
Rev: Crowned head of Queen Mother facing, divides dates

Date	Mintage	F	VF	XF	Unc	BU
1980	50,000	—	—	—	—	75.00

KM# 68d CROWN
7.9600 g., 0.9170 Gold 0.2347 oz. AGW, 38.5 mm. **Ruler:**
Elizabeth II **Subject:** 80th Birthday of Queen Mother **Obv:** Young
bust right **Rev:** Crowned head of Queen Mother facing, divides dates

Date	Mintage	F	VF	XF	Unc	BU
1980	1,000	—	—	—	—	250

KM# 73 CROWN
Copper-Nickel, 38.5 mm. **Ruler:** Elizabeth II **Subject:** Duke of
Edinburgh Award Scheme **Obv:** Young bust right **Rev:** Bust
facing **Edge:** Reeded

Date	Mintage	F	VF	XF	Unc	BU
1981	50,000	—	—	—	2.50	3.50

KM# 73a CROWN
28.2800 g., 0.9250 Silver 0.8410 oz. ASW, 38.5 mm.
Ruler: Elizabeth II **Subject:** Duke of Edinburgh Award Scheme
Obv: Young bust right **Rev:** Bust facing

Date	Mintage	F	VF	XF	Unc	BU
1981	20,000	—	—	—	16.50	17.50
1981 Proof	15,000	Value: 25.00				

KM# 73b CROWN
5.1000 g., 0.3740 Gold 0.0613 oz. AGW **Ruler:** Elizabeth II
Subject: Duke of Edinburgh Award Scheme **Obv:** Young bust
right **Rev:** Bust facing

Date	Mintage	F	VF	XF	Unc	BU
1981 Proof	10,000	Value: 85.00				

KM# 73c CROWN
7.9600 g., 0.9170 Gold 0.2347 oz. AGW **Ruler:** Elizabeth II
Subject: Duke of Edinburgh Award Scheme **Obv:** Young bust
right **Rev:** Bust facing

Date	Mintage	F	VF	XF	Unc	BU
1981 Proof	1,000	Value: 250				

KM# 73d CROWN
52.0000 g., 0.9500 Platinum 1.5882 oz. APW, 38.5 mm.
Ruler: Elizabeth II **Subject:** Duke of Edinburgh Award Scheme
Obv: Young bust right **Rev:** Bust facing

Date	Mintage	F	VF	XF	Unc	BU
1981 Proof	100	Value: 3,000				

KM# 74 CROWN
Copper-Nickel, 38.5 mm. **Ruler:** Elizabeth II **Subject:** Duke of
Edinburgh Award Scheme **Obv:** Young bust right **Rev:**
Monogram within crowned belt within sprigs **Edge:** Reeded

Date	Mintage	F	VF	XF	Unc	BU
1981	50,000	—	—	—	6.00	7.00

KM# 74a CROWN
28.2800 g., 0.9250 Silver 0.8410 oz. ASW, 38.5 mm.
Ruler: Elizabeth II **Subject:** Duke of Edinburgh Award Scheme
Obv: Young bust right **Rev:** Monogram within crowned belt within
sprigs

Date	Mintage	F	VF	XF	Unc	BU
1981	20,000	—	—	—	16.50	17.50
1981 Proof	15,000	Value: 25.00				

KM# 74b CROWN
5.1000 g., 0.3740 Gold 0.0613 oz. AGW **Ruler:** Elizabeth II
Subject: Duke of Edinburgh Award Scheme **Obv:** Young bust
right **Rev:** Monogram within crowned garter within sprigs

Date	Mintage	F	VF	XF	Unc	BU
1981 Proof	10,000	Value: 75.00				

KM# 74c CROWN
7.9600 g., 0.9170 Gold 0.2347 oz. AGW **Ruler:** Elizabeth II
Subject: Duke of Edinburgh Award Scheme **Obv:** Young bust
right **Rev:** Monogram within crowned garter within sprigs

Date	Mintage	F	VF	XF	Unc	BU
1981 Proof	1,000	Value: 250				

KM# 74d CROWN
52.0000 g., 0.9500 Platinum 1.5882 oz. APW, 38.5 mm.
Ruler: Elizabeth II **Subject:** Duke of Edinburgh Award Scheme
Obv: Young bust right **Rev:** Monogram within crowned garter within
sprigs

Date	Mintage	F	VF	XF	Unc	BU
1981 Proof	100	Value: 3,000				

KM# 75 CROWN
Copper-Nickel, 38.5 mm. **Ruler:** Elizabeth II **Subject:** Duke of
Edinburgh Award Scheme **Obv:** Young bust right **Rev:** Nursing,
hiking, swimming **Edge:** Reeded

Date	Mintage	F	VF	XF	Unc	BU
1981	50,000	—	—	—	6.00	7.00

KM# 75a CROWN
28.2800 g., 0.9250 Silver 0.8410 oz. ASW, 38.5 mm.
Ruler: Elizabeth II **Subject:** Duke of Edinburgh Award Scheme
Obv: Young bust right **Rev:** Nursing, hiking, swimming

Date	Mintage	F	VF	XF	Unc	BU
1981	20,000	—	—	—	16.50	17.50
1981 Proof	15,000	Value: 25.00				

KM# 75b CROWN
5.1000 g., 0.3740 Gold 0.0613 oz. AGW **Ruler:** Elizabeth II
Subject: Duke of Edinburgh Award Scheme **Obv:** Young bust
right **Rev:** Nursing, hiking, swimming

Date	Mintage	F	VF	XF	Unc	BU
1981 Proof	10,000	Value: 75.00				

KM# 75c CROWN
7.9600 g., 0.9170 Gold 0.2347 oz. AGW **Ruler:** Elizabeth II
Subject: Duke of Edinburgh Award Scheme **Obv:** Young bust
right **Rev:** Nursing, hiking, swimming

Date	Mintage	F	VF	XF	Unc	BU
1981 Proof	1,000	Value: 250				

KM# 75d CROWN
52.0000 g., 0.9500 Platinum 1.5882 oz. APW, 38.5 mm.
Ruler: Elizabeth II **Subject:** Duke of Edinburgh Award Scheme
Obv: Young bust right **Rev:** Nursing, hiking, swimming

Date	Mintage	F	VF	XF	Unc	BU
1981 Proof	100	Value: 3,000				

KM# 76 CROWN
Copper-Nickel, 38.5 mm. **Ruler:** Elizabeth II **Subject:** Duke of
Edinburgh Award Scheme **Obv:** Young bust right **Rev:** Rock
climbing, sailing, motorcycling **Edge:** Reeded

Date	Mintage	F	VF	XF	Unc	BU
1981	50,000	—	—	—	6.00	7.00

KM# 76a CROWN
28.2800 g., 0.9250 Silver 0.8410 oz. ASW, 38.5 mm.
Ruler: Elizabeth II **Subject:** Duke of Edinburgh Award Scheme
Obv: Young bust right **Rev:** Rock climbing, sailing, motorcycling

Date	Mintage	F	VF	XF	Unc	BU
1981	20,000	—	—	—	16.50	17.50
1981 Proof	15,000	Value: 25.00				

KM# 76b CROWN
5.1000 g., 0.3740 Gold 0.0613 oz. AGW **Ruler:** Elizabeth II
Subject: Duke of Edinburgh Award Scheme **Obv:** Young bust
right **Rev:** Rock climbing, sailing, motorcycling

Date	Mintage	F	VF	XF	Unc	BU
1981 Proof	10,000	Value: 75.00				

KM# 76c CROWN
7.9600 g., 0.9170 Gold 0.2347 oz. AGW **Ruler:** Elizabeth II
Subject: Duke of Edinburgh Award Scheme **Obv:** Young bust
right **Rev:** Rock climbing, sailing, motorcycling

Date	Mintage	F	VF	XF	Unc	BU
1981 Proof	1,000	Value: 250				

KM# 76d CROWN
52.0000 g., 0.9500 Platinum 1.5882 oz. APW, 38.5 mm.
Ruler: Elizabeth II **Subject:** Duke of Edinburgh Award Scheme
Obv: Young bust right **Rev:** Rock climbing, sailing, motorcycling

Date	Mintage	F	VF	XF	Unc	BU
1981 Proof	100	Value: 3,000				

KM# 77 CROWN
Copper-Nickel, 38.5 mm. **Ruler:** Elizabeth II
Subject: International Year of Disabled **Obv:** Young bust right
Rev: Braille and bust 1/4 left **Edge:** Reeded

Date	Mintage	F	VF	XF	Unc	BU
1981	50,000	—	—	—	2.50	3.50
1981 Prooflike	—	—	—	—	5.00	6.00

KM# 77a CROWN
28.2800 g., 0.9250 Silver 0.8410 oz. ASW, 38.5 mm.
Ruler: Elizabeth II **Subject:** International Year of Disabled
Obv: Young bust right **Rev:** Braille and bust 1/4 left

Date	Mintage	F	VF	XF	Unc	BU
1981	20,000	—	—	—	16.50	17.50
1981 Proof	15,000	Value: 25.00				

KM# 77b CROWN
5.1000 g., 0.3740 Gold 0.0613 oz. AGW **Ruler:** Elizabeth II
Subject: International Year of Disabled **Obv:** Young bust right
Rev: Braille and bust 1/4 left

Date	Mintage	F	VF	XF	Unc	BU
1981 Proof	10,000	Value: 75.00				

KM# 77c CROWN
7.9600 g., 0.9170 Gold 0.2347 oz. AGW **Ruler:** Elizabeth II
Subject: International Year of Disabled **Obv:** Young bust right
Rev: Braille and bust 1/4 left

Date	Mintage	F	VF	XF	Unc	BU
1981 Proof	1,000	Value: 250				

KM# 77d CROWN
52.0000 g., 0.9500 Platinum 1.5882 oz. APW, 38.5 mm.
Ruler: Elizabeth II **Subject:** International Year of Disabled
Obv: Young bust right **Rev:** Braille and bust 1/4 left

Date	Mintage	F	VF	XF	Unc	BU
1981 Proof	100	Value: 3,000				

KM# 78 CROWN
Copper-Nickel, 38.5 mm. **Ruler:** Elizabeth II
Subject: International Year of Disabled **Obv:** Young bust right
Rev: Beethoven, violin and music score **Edge:** Reeded

Date	Mintage	F	VF	XF	Unc	BU
1981	50,000	—	—	—	8.00	9.00
1981 Prooflike	—	—	—	—	10.00	12.00

KM# 78a CROWN
28.2800 g., 0.9250 Silver 0.8410 oz. ASW, 38.5 mm.
Ruler: Elizabeth II **Subject:** International Year of Disabled
Obv: Young bust right **Rev:** Beethoven, violin and music score

Date	Mintage	F	VF	XF	Unc	BU
1981	20,000	—	—	—	16.50	17.50
1981 Proof	15,000	Value: 25.00				

KM# 78b CROWN
5.1000 g., 0.3740 Gold 0.0613 oz. AGW **Ruler:** Elizabeth II
Subject: International Year of Disabled **Obv:** Young bust right
Rev: Beethoven, violin and music score

Date	Mintage	F	VF	XF	Unc	BU
1981 Proof	10,000	Value: 75.00				

KM# 78c   CROWN
7.9600 g., 0.9170 Gold 0.2347 oz. AGW **Ruler:** Elizabeth II
Subject: International Year of Disabled **Obv:** Young bust right
Rev: Beethoven, violin and music score

Date	Mintage	F	VF	XF	Unc	BU
1981 Proof	1,000	Value: 250				

KM# 78d   CROWN
52.0000 g., 0.9500 Platinum 1.5882 oz. APW, 38.5 mm.
Ruler: Elizabeth II **Subject:** International Year of Disabled
Obv: Young bust right **Rev:** Beethoven, violin and music score

Date	Mintage	F	VF	XF	Unc	BU
1981 Proof	100	Value: 3,000				

KM# 79   CROWN
Copper-Nickel, 38.5 mm. **Ruler:** Elizabeth II
Subject: International Year of Disabled **Obv:** Young bust right
Rev: Bust facing **Edge:** Reeded

Date	Mintage	F	VF	XF	Unc	BU
1981	50,000	—	—	—	8.00	9.00
1981 Prooflike	—	—	—	—	9.00	10.00

KM# 79a   CROWN
28.2800 g., 0.9250 Silver 0.8410 oz. ASW, 38.5 mm.
Ruler: Elizabeth II **Subject:** International Year of Disabled
Obv: Young bust right **Rev:** Bust facing

Date	Mintage	F	VF	XF	Unc	BU
1981	20,000	—	—	—	16.50	17.50
1981 Proof	15,000	Value: 25.00				

KM# 79b   CROWN
5.1000 g., 0.3740 Gold 0.0613 oz. AGW **Ruler:** Elizabeth II
Subject: International Year of Disabled **Obv:** Young bust right
Rev: Bust facing

Date	Mintage	F	VF	XF	Unc	BU
1981 Proof	10,000	Value: 75.00				

KM# 79c   CROWN
7.9600 g., 0.9170 Gold 0.2347 oz. AGW **Ruler:** Elizabeth II
Subject: International Year of Disabled **Obv:** Young bust right
Rev: Bust facing

Date	Mintage	F	VF	XF	Unc	BU
1981 Proof	1,000	Value: 250				

KM# 79d   CROWN
52.0000 g., 0.9500 Platinum 1.5882 oz. APW, 38.5 mm.
Ruler: Elizabeth II **Subject:** International Year of Disabled
Obv: Young bust right **Rev:** Bust facing

Date	Mintage	F	VF	XF	Unc	BU
1981 Proof	100	Value: 3,000				

KM# 80   CROWN
Copper-Nickel, 38.5 mm. **Ruler:** Elizabeth II
Subject: International Year of Disabled **Obv:** Young bust right
Rev: Uniformed bust 1/4 left and sailboat **Edge:** Reeded

Date	Mintage	F	VF	XF	Unc	BU
1981	50,000	—	—	—	8.00	9.00
1981 Prooflike	—	—	—	—	9.00	10.00

KM# 80a   CROWN
28.2800 g., 0.9250 Silver 0.8410 oz. ASW, 38.5 mm.
Ruler: Elizabeth II **Subject:** International Year of Disabled
Obv: Young bust right **Rev:** Uniformed bust 1/4 left and sailboat

Date	Mintage	F	VF	XF	Unc	BU
1981	20,000	—	—	—	18.00	20.00
1981 Proof	15,000	Value: 30.00				

KM# 80b   CROWN
5.1000 g., 0.3740 Gold 0.0613 oz. AGW **Ruler:** Elizabeth II
Subject: International Year of Disabled **Obv:** Young bust right
Rev: Uniformed bust 1/4 left and sailboat

Date	Mintage	F	VF	XF	Unc	BU
1981 Proof	10,000	Value: 75.00				

KM# 80c   CROWN
7.9600 g., 0.9170 Gold 0.2347 oz. AGW **Ruler:** Elizabeth II
Subject: International Year of Disabled **Obv:** Young bust right
Rev: Uniformed bust 1/4 left and sailboat

Date	Mintage	F	VF	XF	Unc	BU
1981 Proof	1,000	Value: 250				

KM# 80d   CROWN
52.0000 g., 0.9500 Platinum 1.5882 oz. APW, 38.5 mm.
Ruler: Elizabeth II **Subject:** International Year of Disabled
Obv: Young bust right **Rev:** Uniformed bust 1/4 left and sailboat

Date	Mintage	F	VF	XF	Unc	BU
1981 Proof	100	Value: 3,000				

KM# 81   CROWN
Copper-Nickel, 38.5 mm. **Ruler:** Elizabeth II **Subject:** Wedding
of Prince Charles and Lady Diana **Obv:** Young bust right
Rev: Crown above shields

Date	Mintage	F	VF	XF	Unc	BU
1981	50,000	—	—	—	6.00	7.00

KM# 81a   CROWN
28.2800 g., 0.9250 Silver 0.8410 oz. ASW, 38.5 mm.
Ruler: Elizabeth II **Subject:** Wedding of Prince Charles and Lady
Diana **Obv:** Young bust right **Rev:** Crown above shields

Date	Mintage	F	VF	XF	Unc	BU
1981	20,000	—	—	—	16.50	17.50
1981 Proof	15,000	Value: 25.00				

KM# 81b   CROWN
5.1000 g., 0.3740 Gold 0.0613 oz. AGW **Ruler:** Elizabeth II
Subject: Wedding of Prince Charles and Lady Diana **Obv:** Young
bust right **Rev:** Crown above shields **Edge:** Reeded

Date	Mintage	F	VF	XF	Unc	BU
1981 Proof		Value: 75.00				

KM# 81c   CROWN
7.9600 g., 0.9170 Gold 0.2347 oz. AGW **Ruler:** Elizabeth II
Subject: Wedding of Prince Charles and Lady Diana **Obv:** Young
bust right **Rev:** Crown above shields

Date	Mintage	F	VF	XF	Unc	BU
1981 Proof	1,000	Value: 250				

KM# 81d   CROWN
52.0000 g., 0.9500 Platinum 1.5882 oz. APW, 38.5 mm.
Ruler: Elizabeth II **Subject:** Wedding of Prince Charles and Lady
Diana **Obv:** Young bust right **Rev:** Crown above shields

Date	Mintage	F	VF	XF	Unc	BU
1981 Proof	100	Value: 3,000				

KM# 82   CROWN
Copper-Nickel, 38.5 mm. **Ruler:** Elizabeth II **Subject:** Wedding
of Prince Charles and Lady Diana **Obv:** Young bust right
Rev: Conjoined heads right **Edge:** Reeded

Date	Mintage	F	VF	XF	Unc	BU
1981	50,000	—	—	—	6.00	7.00

KM# 82a   CROWN
28.2800 g., 0.9250 Silver 0.8410 oz. ASW, 38.5 mm.
Ruler: Elizabeth II **Subject:** Wedding of Prince Charles and Lady
Diana **Obv:** Young bust right **Rev:** Conjoined heads right

Date	Mintage	F	VF	XF	Unc	BU
1981	20,000	—	—	—	16.50	17.50
1981	15,000	Value: 25.00				

KM# 82b   CROWN
5.1000 g., 0.3740 Gold 0.0613 oz. AGW **Ruler:** Elizabeth II
Subject: Wedding of Prince Charles and Lady Diana **Obv:** Young
bust right **Rev:** Conjoined heads right

Date	Mintage	F	VF	XF	Unc	BU
1981 Proof	10,000	Value: 75.00				

KM# 82c   CROWN
7.9600 g., 0.9170 Gold 0.2347 oz. AGW **Ruler:** Elizabeth II
Subject: Wedding of Prince Charles and Lady Diana **Obv:** Young
bust right **Rev:** Conjoined heads right

Date	Mintage	F	VF	XF	Unc	BU
1981 Proof	1,000	Value: 250				

KM# 82d   CROWN
52.0000 g., 0.9500 Platinum 1.5882 oz. APW, 38.5 mm.
Ruler: Elizabeth II **Subject:** Wedding of Prince Charles and Lady
Diana **Obv:** Young bust right **Rev:** Conjoined heads right

Date	Mintage	F	VF	XF	Unc	BU
1981 Proof	—	Value: 3,000				

KM# 91   CROWN
Copper-Nickel, 38.5 mm. **Ruler:** Elizabeth II **Series:** XII World
Cup - Spain **Obv:** Young bust right **Rev:** Half figure holding World
Cup trophy within map

Date	Mintage	F	VF	XF	Unc	BU
1982	50,000	—	—	—	3.50	4.50

KM# 91a   CROWN
28.2800 g., 0.9250 Silver 0.8410 oz. ASW, 38.5 mm.
Ruler: Elizabeth II **Series:** XII World Cup - Spain **Obv:** Young
bust right **Rev:** Half figure holding World Cup trophy within map

Date	Mintage	F	VF	XF	Unc	BU
1982	20,000	—	—	—	16.50	18.00
1982 Proof	15,000	Value: 25.00				

KM# 91b   CROWN
5.1000 g., 0.3740 Gold 0.0613 oz. AGW **Ruler:** Elizabeth II
Series: XII World Cup - Spain **Obv:** Young bust right **Rev:** Half
figure holding World Cup trophy within map

Date	Mintage	F	VF	XF	Unc	BU
1982 Proof	40,000	Value: 75.00				

KM# 91c   CROWN
7.9600 g., 0.9170 Gold 0.2347 oz. AGW **Ruler:** Elizabeth II
Series: XII World Cup - Spain **Obv:** Young bust right **Rev:** Half
figure holding World Cup trophy within map

Date	Mintage	F	VF	XF	Unc	BU
1982 Proof	4,000	Value: 250				

KM# 91d   CROWN
52.0000 g., 0.9500 Platinum 1.5882 oz. APW, 38.5 mm.
Ruler: Elizabeth II **Series:** XII World Cup - Spain **Obv:** Young
bust right **Rev:** Half figure holding World Cup trophy within map

Date	Mintage	F	VF	XF	Unc	BU
1982 Proof	100	Value: 3,000				

KM# 92   CROWN
Copper-Nickel, 38.5 mm. **Ruler:** Elizabeth II **Series:** XII World
Cup - Spain **Obv:** Young bust right **Rev:** Triskeles at center of
assorted shields

Date	Mintage	F	VF	XF	Unc	BU
1982	50,000	—	—	—	3.50	4.50

KM# 92a   CROWN
28.2800 g., 0.9250 Silver 0.8410 oz. ASW, 38.5 mm.
Ruler: Elizabeth II **Series:** XII World Cup - Spain **Obv:** Young
bust right **Rev:** Triskeles at center of assorted shields

Date	Mintage	F	VF	XF	Unc	BU
1982	20,000	—	—	—	16.50	17.50
1982 Proof	15,000	Value: 28.00				

KM# 92b   CROWN
5.1000 g., 0.3740 Gold 0.0613 oz. AGW **Ruler:** Elizabeth II
Series: XII World Cup - Spain **Obv:** Young bust right
Rev: Triskeles at center of assorted shields

Date	Mintage	F	VF	XF	Unc	BU
1982 Proof	40,000	Value: 75.00				

KM# 92c   CROWN
7.9600 g., 0.9170 Gold 0.2347 oz. AGW **Ruler:** Elizabeth II
Series: XII World Cup - Spain **Obv:** Young bust right
Rev: Triskeles at center of assorted shields

Date	Mintage	F	VF	XF	Unc	BU
1982 Proof	4,000	Value: 250				

KM# 92d   CROWN
52.0000 g., 0.9500 Platinum 1.5882 oz. APW, 38.5 mm.
Ruler: Elizabeth II **Series:** XII World Cup - Spain **Obv:** Young
bust right **Rev:** Triskeles at center of assorted shields

Date	Mintage	F	VF	XF	Unc	BU
1982 Proof	100	Value: 3,000				

KM# 93 CROWN
Copper-Nickel, 38.5 mm. **Ruler:** Elizabeth II **Series:** XII World Cup - Spain **Obv:** Young bust right **Rev:** Soccer scenes

Date	Mintage	F	VF	XF	Unc	BU
1982	50,000	—	—	—	8.00	9.00
1982 (sb)		—	—	—	9.00	10.00

KM# 93a CROWN
28.2800 g., 0.9250 Silver 0.8410 oz. ASW, 38.5 mm.
Ruler: Elizabeth II **Series:** XII World Cup - Spain **Obv:** Young bust right **Rev:** Soccer scenes

Date	Mintage	F	VF	XF	Unc	BU
1982	20,000	—	—	—	16.50	17.50
1982 Proof	15,000	Value: 28.00				

KM# 93b CROWN
5.1000 g., 0.3740 Gold 0.0613 oz. AGW **Ruler:** Elizabeth II **Series:** XII World Cup - Spain **Obv:** Young bust right **Rev:** Soccer scenes

Date	Mintage	F	VF	XF	Unc	BU
1982 Proof	40,000	Value: 75.00				

KM# 93c CROWN
7.9600 g., 0.9170 Gold 0.2347 oz. AGW **Ruler:** Elizabeth II **Series:** XII World Cup - Spain **Obv:** Young bust right **Rev:** Soccer scenes

Date	Mintage	F	VF	XF	Unc	BU
1982 Proof	4,000	Value: 250				

KM# 93d CROWN
52.0000 g., 0.9500 Platinum 1.5882 oz. APW, 38.5 mm.
Ruler: Elizabeth II **Series:** XII World Cup - Spain **Obv:** Young bust right **Rev:** Soccer scenes

Date	Mintage	F	VF	XF	Unc	BU
1982 Proof	100	Value: 3,000				

KM# 94 CROWN
Copper-Nickel, 38.5 mm. **Ruler:** Elizabeth II **Series:** XII World Cup - Spain **Obv:** Young bust right **Rev:** Soccer scenes

Date	Mintage	F	VF	XF	Unc	BU
1982	50,000	—	—	—	8.00	9.00

KM# 94a CROWN
28.2800 g., 0.9250 Silver 0.8410 oz. ASW, 38.5 mm.
Ruler: Elizabeth II **Series:** XII World Cup - Spain **Obv:** Young bust right **Rev:** Soccer scenes

Date	Mintage	F	VF	XF	Unc	BU
1982	20,000	—	—	—	16.50	17.50
1982 Proof	15,000	Value: 28.00				

KM# 94b CROWN
5.1000 g., 0.3740 Gold 0.0613 oz. AGW **Ruler:** Elizabeth II **Series:** XII World Cup - Spain **Obv:** Young bust right **Rev:** Soccer scenes

Date	Mintage	F	VF	XF	Unc	BU
1982 Proof	40,000	Value: 75.00				

KM# 94c CROWN
7.9600 g., 0.9170 Gold 0.2347 oz. AGW **Ruler:** Elizabeth II **Series:** XII World Cup - Spain **Obv:** Young bust right **Rev:** Soccer scenes

Date	Mintage	F	VF	XF	Unc	BU
1982 Proof	4,000	Value: 225				

KM# 94d CROWN
52.0000 g., 0.9500 Platinum 1.5882 oz. APW, 38.5 mm.
Ruler: Elizabeth II **Series:** XII World Cup - Spain **Obv:** Young bust right **Rev:** Soccer scenes

Date	Mintage	F	VF	XF	Unc	BU
1982 Proof	100	Value: 3,000				

KM# 95 CROWN
Copper-Nickel, 38.5 mm. **Ruler:** Elizabeth II **Series:** XII World Cup - Spain **Obv:** Young bust right **Rev:** Assorted shields

Date	Mintage	F	VF	XF	Unc	BU
1982		—	—	—	3.50	4.50

KM# 95a CROWN
28.2800 g., 0.9250 Silver 0.8410 oz. ASW, 38.5 mm.
Ruler: Elizabeth II **Series:** XII World Cup - Spain **Obv:** Young bust right **Rev:** Assorted shields

Date	Mintage	F	VF	XF	Unc	BU
1982	—	Value: 28.00				

KM# 95b CROWN
5.1000 g., 0.3740 Gold 0.0613 oz. AGW **Ruler:** Elizabeth II **Series:** XII World Cup - Spain **Obv:** Young bust right **Rev:** Assorted shields

Date	Mintage	F	VF	XF	Unc	BU
1982 Proof	3,000	Value: 75.00				

KM# 95c CROWN
7.9600 g., 0.9170 Gold 0.2347 oz. AGW **Ruler:** Elizabeth II **Series:** XII World Cup - Spain **Obv:** Young bust right **Rev:** Assorted shields

Date	Mintage	F	VF	XF	Unc	BU
1982 Proof	—	Value: 220				

KM# 95d CROWN
52.0000 g., 0.9500 Platinum 1.5882 oz. APW, 38.5 mm.
Ruler: Elizabeth II **Series:** XII World Cup - Spain **Obv:** Young bust right **Rev:** Assorted shields

Date	Mintage	F	VF	XF	Unc	BU
1982 Proof	—	Value: 3,000				

KM# 96 CROWN
Copper-Nickel, 38.5 mm. **Ruler:** Elizabeth II **Series:** Maritime Heritage **Obv:** Young bust right **Rev:** Ship and cameo

Date	Mintage	F	VF	XF	Unc	BU
1982	Est. 50,000	—	—	—	9.00	10.00
1982 Prooflike	Inc. above	—	—	—	10.00	12.00

KM# 96a CROWN
28.2800 g., 0.9250 Silver 0.8410 oz. ASW, 38.5 mm.
Ruler: Elizabeth II **Series:** Maritime Heritage **Obv:** Young bust right **Rev:** Ship and cameo

Date	Mintage	F	VF	XF	Unc	BU
1982	15,000	—	—	—	20.00	22.50
1982 Proof	10,000	Value: 25.00				

KM# 96b CROWN
5.1000 g., 0.3740 Gold 0.0613 oz. AGW **Ruler:** Elizabeth II **Series:** Maritime Heritage **Obv:** Crowned bust right **Rev:** Ship and cameo

Date	Mintage	F	VF	XF	Unc	BU
1982 Proof	22,000	Value: 75.00				

KM# 96c CROWN
7.9600 g., 0.9170 Gold 0.2347 oz. AGW **Ruler:** Elizabeth II **Series:** Maritime Heritage **Obv:** Young bust right **Rev:** Ship and cameo

Date	Mintage	F	VF	XF	Unc	BU
1982 Proof	2,000	Value: 250				

KM# 96d CROWN
52.0000 g., 0.9500 Platinum 1.5882 oz. APW, 38.5 mm.
Ruler: Elizabeth II **Series:** Maritime Heritage **Obv:** Young bust right **Rev:** Ship and cameo

Date	Mintage	F	VF	XF	Unc	BU
1982 Proof	50	Value: 3,000				

KM# 97 CROWN
Copper-Nickel, 38.5 mm. **Ruler:** Elizabeth II **Series:** Maritime Heritage **Obv:** Young bust right **Rev:** Ship and cameo

Date	Mintage	F	VF	XF	Unc	BU
1982	Est. 50,000	—	—	—	3.00	4.00
1982 Prooflike	Inc. above	—	—	—	5.00	7.00

KM# 97a CROWN
28.2800 g., 0.9250 Silver 0.8410 oz. ASW, 38.5 mm.
Ruler: Elizabeth II **Series:** Maritime Heritage **Obv:** Young bust right **Rev:** Ship and cameo

Date	Mintage	F	VF	XF	Unc	BU
1982	15,000	—	—	—	20.00	22.50
1982 Proof	10,000	Value: 25.00				

KM# 97b CROWN
5.1000 g., 0.3740 Gold 0.0613 oz. AGW **Ruler:** Elizabeth II **Series:** Maritime Heritage **Obv:** Young bust right **Rev:** Ship and cameo

Date	Mintage	F	VF	XF	Unc	BU
1982 Proof	22,000	Value: 75.00				

KM# 97c CROWN
7.9600 g., 0.9170 Gold 0.2347 oz. AGW **Ruler:** Elizabeth II **Series:** Maritime Heritage **Obv:** Young bust right **Rev:** Ship and cameo

Date	Mintage	F	VF	XF	Unc	BU
1982 Proof	2,000	Value: 250				

KM# 97d CROWN
52.0000 g., 0.9500 Platinum 1.5882 oz. APW, 38.5 mm.
Ruler: Elizabeth II **Series:** Maritime Heritage **Obv:** Young bust right **Rev:** Ship and cameo

Date	Mintage	F	VF	XF	Unc	BU
1982 Proof	50	Value: 3,000				

KM# 98 CROWN
Copper-Nickel, 38.5 mm. **Ruler:** Elizabeth II **Series:** Maritime Heritage **Obv:** Young bust right **Rev:** Ship and cameo

Date	Mintage	F	VF	XF	Unc	BU
1982	Est. 50,000	—	—	—	8.00	9.00
1982 Prooflike	Inc. above	—	—	—	9.00	10.00

KM# 98a CROWN
28.2800 g., 0.9250 Silver 0.8410 oz. ASW, 38.5 mm.
Ruler: Elizabeth II **Series:** Maritime Heritage **Obv:** young bust right **Rev:** Ship and cameo

Date	Mintage	F	VF	XF	Unc	BU
1982	15,000	—	—	—	20.00	22.50
1982 Proof	10,000	Value: 25.00				

KM# 98b CROWN
5.1000 g., 0.3740 Gold 0.0613 oz. AGW **Ruler:** Elizabeth II **Series:** Maritime Heritage **Obv:** Young bust right **Rev:** Ship and cameo

Date	Mintage	F	VF	XF	Unc	BU
1982 Proof	22,000	Value: 75.00				

KM# 98c CROWN
7.9600 g., 0.9170 Gold 0.2347 oz. AGW **Ruler:** Elizabeth II **Series:** Maritime Heritage **Obv:** Young bust right **Rev:** Ship and cameo

Date	Mintage	F	VF	XF	Unc	BU
1982 Proof	2,000	Value: 250				

KM# 98d CROWN
52.0000 g., 0.9500 Platinum 1.5882 oz. APW, 38.5 mm.
Ruler: Elizabeth II **Series:** Maritime Heritage **Obv:** Young bust right **Rev:** Ship and cameo

Date	Mintage	F	VF	XF	Unc	BU
1982 Proof	50	Value: 3,000				

KM# 99 CROWN
Copper-Nickel, 38.5 mm. **Ruler:** Elizabeth II **Series:** Maritime Heritage **Obv:** Young bust right **Rev:** Ship and cameo

Date	Mintage	F	VF	XF	Unc	BU
1982	Est. 50,000	—	—	—	3.00	4.00
1982 Prooflike	Inc. above	—	—	—	5.00	7.00

KM# 99a CROWN
28.2800 g., 0.9250 Silver 0.8410 oz. ASW, 38.5 mm.
Ruler: Elizabeth II **Series:** Maritime Heritage **Obv:** Young bust right **Rev:** Ship and cameo

Date	Mintage	F	VF	XF	Unc	BU
1982	15,000	—	—	—	20.00	22.50
1982 Proof	10,000	Value: 25.00				

KM# 99b CROWN
5.1000 g., 0.3740 Gold 0.0613 oz. AGW **Ruler:** Elizabeth II **Series:** Maritime Heritage **Obv:** Young bust right **Rev:** Ship and cameo

Date	Mintage	F	VF	XF	Unc	BU
1982 Proof	22,000	Value: 75.00				

KM# 99c CROWN
7.9600 g., 0.9170 Gold 0.2347 oz. AGW **Ruler:** Elizabeth II **Series:** Maritime Heritage **Obv:** Young bust right **Rev:** Ship and cameo

Date	Mintage	F	VF	XF	Unc	BU
1982 Proof	2,000	Value: 250				

KM# 99d CROWN
52.0000 g., 0.9500 Platinum 1.5882 oz. APW, 38.5 mm.
Ruler: Elizabeth II **Series:** Maritime Heritage **Obv:** Young bust right **Rev:** Ship and cameo

Date	Mintage	F	VF	XF	Unc	BU
1982 Proof	50	Value: 3,000				

KM# 103 CROWN
Copper-Nickel, 38.5 mm. **Ruler:** Elizabeth II **Series:** Manned Flight **Obv:** Young bust right **Rev:** Hot air balloon

Date	Mintage	F	VF	XF	Unc	BU
1983	50,000	—	—	—	8.00	10.00
1983 DMIHE	—	—	—	—	15.00	17.00

KM# 103a CROWN
28.2800 g., 0.9250 Silver 0.8410 oz. ASW, 38.5 mm.
Ruler: Elizabeth II **Series:** Manned Flight **Obv:** Young bust right **Rev:** Hot air balloon

Date	Mintage	F	VF	XF	Unc	BU
1983	15,000	—	—	—	20.00	22.50
1983	11,000	Value: 25.00				

KM# 103b CROWN
5.1000 g., 0.3740 Gold 0.0613 oz. AGW **Ruler:** Elizabeth II **Series:** Manned Flight **Obv:** Young bust right **Rev:** Hot air balloon

Date	Mintage	F	VF	XF	Unc	BU
1983 Proof	5,500	Value: 80.00				

KM# 103c CROWN
7.9600 g., 0.9170 Gold 0.2347 oz. AGW **Ruler:** Elizabeth II **Series:** Manned Flight **Obv:** Young bust right **Rev:** Hot air balloon

Date	Mintage	F	VF	XF	Unc	BU
1983 Proof	500	Value: 250				

KM# 103d CROWN
52.0000 g., 0.9500 Platinum 1.5882 oz. APW, 38.5 mm.
Ruler: Elizabeth II **Series:** Manned Flight **Obv:** Young bust right **Rev:** Hot air balloon

Date	Mintage	F	VF	XF	Unc	BU
1983 Proof	50	Value: 3,000				

KM# 104 CROWN
Copper-Nickel, 38.5 mm. **Ruler:** Elizabeth II **Series:** Manned Flight **Obv:** Young bust right **Rev:** Biplane

Date	Mintage	F	VF	XF	Unc	BU
1983	50,000	—	—	—	8.00	10.00
1983 DMIHE	—	—	—	—	15.00	17.00

KM# 104a CROWN
28.2800 g., 0.9250 Silver 0.8410 oz. ASW, 38.5 mm.
Ruler: Elizabeth II **Series:** Manned Flight **Obv:** Young bust right **Rev:** Biplane

Date	Mintage	F	VF	XF	Unc	BU
1983	15,000	—	—	—	20.00	22.50
1983 Proof	11,000	Value: 25.00				

KM# 104b CROWN
5.1000 g., 0.3740 Gold 0.0613 oz. AGW **Ruler:** Elizabeth II **Series:** Manned Flight **Obv:** Young bust right **Rev:** Biplane

Date	Mintage	F	VF	XF	Unc	BU
1983 Proof	5,500	Value: 80.00				

KM# 104c CROWN
7.9600 g., 0.9170 Gold 0.2347 oz. AGW **Ruler:** Elizabeth II **Series:** Manned Flight **Obv:** Young bust right **Rev:** Biplane

Date	Mintage	F	VF	XF	Unc	BU
1983 Proof	500	Value: 250				

KM# 104d CROWN
52.0000 g., 0.9500 Platinum 1.5882 oz. APW, 38.5 mm.
Ruler: Elizabeth II **Series:** Manned Flight **Obv:** Young bust right **Rev:** Biplane

Date	Mintage	F	VF	XF	Unc	BU
1983 Proof	50	Value: 3,000				

KM# 105 CROWN
Copper-Nickel, 38.5 mm. **Ruler:** Elizabeth II **Series:** Manned Flight **Obv:** Young bust right **Rev:** Jet

Date	Mintage	F	VF	XF	Unc	BU
1983	50,000	—	—	—	8.00	10.00
1983 DMIHE	—	—	—	—	15.00	17.00

KM# 105a CROWN
28.2800 g., 0.9250 Silver 0.8410 oz. ASW, 38.5 mm. **Ruler:** Elizabeth II **Series:** Manned Flight **Obv:** Young bust right **Rev:** Jet

Date	Mintage	F	VF	XF	Unc	BU
1983	15,000	—	—	—	20.00	22.50
1983 Proof	11,000	Value: 25.00				

KM# 105b CROWN
5.1000 g., 0.3740 Gold 0.0613 oz. AGW **Ruler:** Elizabeth II **Series:** Manned Flight **Obv:** Young bust right **Rev:** Jet

Date	Mintage	F	VF	XF	Unc	BU
1983 Proof	5,500	Value: 80.00				

KM# 105c CROWN
7.9600 g., 0.9170 Gold 0.2347 oz. AGW **Ruler:** Elizabeth II **Series:** Manned Flight **Obv:** Young bust right **Rev:** Jet

Date	Mintage	F	VF	XF	Unc	BU
1983 Proof	500	Value: 250				

KM# 105d CROWN
52.0000 g., 0.9500 Platinum 1.5882 oz. APW, 38.5 mm. **Ruler:** Elizabeth II **Series:** Manned Flight **Obv:** Young bust right **Rev:** Jet

Date	Mintage	F	VF	XF	Unc	BU
1983 Proof	50	Value: 3,000				

KM# 106 CROWN
Copper-Nickel, 38.5 mm. **Ruler:** Elizabeth II **Series:** Manned Flight **Obv:** Young bust right **Rev:** Space Shuttle

Date	Mintage	F	VF	XF	Unc	BU
1983	50,000	—	—	—	8.00	10.00
1983 DMIHE	—	—	—	—	15.00	17.00

KM# 106a CROWN
28.2800 g., 0.9250 Silver 0.8410 oz. ASW, 38.5 mm.
Ruler: Elizabeth II **Series:** Manned Flight **Obv:** Young bust right **Rev:** Space shuttle

Date	Mintage	F	VF	XF	Unc	BU
1983	15,000	—	—	—	16.50	17.50
1983 Proof	11,000	Value: 28.00				

KM# 106b CROWN
5.1000 g., 0.3740 Gold 0.0613 oz. AGW **Ruler:** Elizabeth II **Series:** Manned Flight **Obv:** Young bust right **Rev:** Space shuttle

Date	Mintage	F	VF	XF	Unc	BU
1983 Proof	5,500	Value: 80.00				

KM# 106c CROWN
7.9600 g., 0.9170 Gold 0.2347 oz. AGW **Ruler:** Elizabeth II **Series:** Manned Flight **Obv:** Young bust right **Rev:** Space shuttle

Date	Mintage	F	VF	XF	Unc	BU
1983 Proof	500	Value: 250				

KM# 106d CROWN
52.0000 g., 0.9500 Platinum 1.5882 oz. APW, 38.5 mm.
Ruler: Elizabeth II **Series:** Manned Flight **Obv:** Young bust right **Rev:** Space Shuttle

Date	Mintage	F	VF	XF	Unc	BU
1983 Proof	50	Value: 3,000				

KM# 117 CROWN
Copper-Nickel, 38.5 mm. **Ruler:** Elizabeth II **Series:** 1984 Winter Olympics - Sarajevo **Obv:** Young bust right **Rev:** Figure skaters

Date	Mintage	F	VF	XF	Unc	BU
1984	50,000	—	—	—	8.00	9.00
1984 Proof	—	Value: 10.00				

KM# 117a CROWN
28.2800 g., 0.9250 Silver 0.8410 oz. ASW, 38.5 mm.
Ruler: Elizabeth II **Series:** 1984 Winter Olympics - Sarajevo **Obv:** Young bust right **Rev:** Figure Skaters

Date	Mintage	F	VF	XF	Unc	BU
1984 Proof	15,000	Value: 30.00				

KM# 117b CROWN
5.1000 g., 0.3740 Gold 0.0613 oz. AGW **Ruler:** Elizabeth II **Series:** 1984 Winter Olympics - Sarajevo **Obv:** Young bust right **Rev:** Figure skaters

Date	Mintage	F	VF	XF	Unc	BU
1984 Proof	10,000	Value: 75.00				

KM# 117c CROWN
7.9600 g., 0.9170 Gold 0.2347 oz. AGW **Ruler:** Elizabeth II **Series:** 1984 Winter Olympics - Sarajevo **Obv:** Young bust right **Rev:** Figure skaters

Date	Mintage	F	VF	XF	Unc	BU
1984 Proof	1,000	Value: 250				

KM# 117d CROWN
52.0000 g., 0.9500 Platinum 1.5882 oz. APW, 38.5 mm.
Ruler: Elizabeth II **Series:** 1984 Winter Olympics - Sarajevo **Obv:** Young bust right **Rev:** Figure skaters

Date	Mintage	F	VF	XF	Unc	BU
1984 Proof	100	Value: 3,000				

KM# 117e CROWN
Silver Clad Copper-Nickel, 38.5 mm. **Ruler:** Elizabeth II **Series:** 1984 Winter Olympics - Sarajevo **Obv:** Young bust right **Rev:** Figure skaters

Date	Mintage	F	VF	XF	Unc	BU
1984	20,000	—	—	—	20.00	22.50

KM# 118 CROWN
Copper-Nickel, 38.5 mm. **Ruler:** Elizabeth II **Series:** 1984 Olympics - Los Angeles **Obv:** Young bust right **Rev:** Runners

Date	Mintage	F	VF	XF	Unc	BU
1984	50,000	—	—	—	6.00	7.00
1984 Proof	—	Value: 8.50				

KM# 118a CROWN
28.2800 g., 0.9250 Silver 0.8410 oz. ASW, 38.5 mm.
Ruler: Elizabeth II **Series:** 1984 Olympics - Los Angeles **Obv:** Young bust right **Rev:** Runners

Date	Mintage	F	VF	XF	Unc	BU
1984 Proof	15,000	Value: 30.00				

KM# 118b CROWN
5.1000 g., 0.3740 Gold 0.0613 oz. AGW **Ruler:** Elizabeth II **Series:** 1984 Olympics - Los Angeles **Obv:** Young bust right **Rev:** Runners

Date	Mintage	F	VF	XF	Unc	BU
1984 Proof	10,000	Value: 75.00				

KM# 118c CROWN
7.9600 g., 0.9170 Gold 0.2347 oz. AGW **Ruler:** Elizabeth II **Series:** 1984 Olympics - Los Angeles **Obv:** Young bust right **Rev:** Runners

Date	Mintage	F	VF	XF	Unc	BU
1984 Proof	1,000	Value: 250				

KM# 118d CROWN
52.0000 g., 0.9500 Platinum 1.5882 oz. APW, 38.5 mm.
Ruler: Elizabeth II **Series:** 1984 Olympics - Los Angeles **Obv:** Young bust right **Rev:** Runners

Date	Mintage	F	VF	XF	Unc	BU
1984 Proof	100	Value: 3,000				

KM# 118e CROWN
Silver Clad Copper-Nickel, 38.5 mm. **Ruler:** Elizabeth II **Series:** 1984 Olympics - Los Angeles **Obv:** Young bust right **Rev:** Runners

Date	Mintage	F	VF	XF	Unc	BU
1984	20,000	—	—	—	20.00	22.50

KM# 119 CROWN
Copper-Nickel, 38.5 mm. **Series:** 1984 Olympics - Los Angeles **Obv:** Young bust right **Rev:** Gymnastics

Date	Mintage	F	VF	XF	Unc	BU
1984	50,000	—	—	—	3.50	5.00
1984 Proof	—	Value: 8.50				

KM# 119a CROWN
28.2800 g., 0.9250 Silver 0.8410 oz. ASW, 38.5 mm.
Ruler: Elizabeth II **Series:** 1984 Olympics - Los Angeles **Obv:** Young bust right **Rev:** Gymnastics

Date	Mintage	F	VF	XF	Unc	BU
1984 Proof	15,000	Value: 30.00				

KM# 119b CROWN
5.1000 g., 0.3740 Gold 0.0613 oz. AGW **Ruler:** Elizabeth II **Series:** 1984 Olympics - Los Angeles **Obv:** Young bust right **Rev:** Gymnastics

Date	Mintage	F	VF	XF	Unc	BU
1984 Proof	10,000	Value: 75.00				

KM# 119c CROWN
7.9600 g., 0.9170 Gold 0.2347 oz. AGW **Ruler:** Elizabeth II **Series:** 1984 Olympics - Los Angeles **Obv:** Young bust right **Rev:** Gymnastics

Date	Mintage	F	VF	XF	Unc	BU
1984 Proof	1,000	Value: 250				

KM# 119d CROWN
52.0000 g., 0.9500 Platinum 1.5882 oz. APW, 38.5 mm.
Ruler: Elizabeth II **Series:** 1984 Olympics - Los Angeles
Obv: Young bust right **Rev:** Gymnastics

Date	Mintage	F	VF	XF	Unc	BU
1984 Proof	100	Value: 3,000				

KM# 119e CROWN
Silver Clad Copper-Nickel, 38.5 mm. **Ruler:** Elizabeth II
Series: 1984 Olympics - Los Angeles **Obv:** Young bust right
Rev: Gymnastics

Date	Mintage	F	VF	XF	Unc	BU
1984	20,000	—	—	—	20.00	22.50

KM# 120 CROWN
Copper-Nickel, 38.5 mm. **Ruler:** Elizabeth II **Series:** 1984
Olympics - Los Angeles **Obv:** Young bust right **Rev:** Equestrian

Date	Mintage	F	VF	XF	Unc	BU
1984	50,000	—	—	—	6.00	7.00
1984 Proof	—	Value: 8.50				

KM# 120a CROWN
28.2800 g., 0.9250 Silver 0.8410 oz. ASW, 38.5 mm.
Ruler: Elizabeth II **Series:** 1984 Olympics - Los Angeles
Obv: Young bust right **Rev:** Equestrian

Date	Mintage	F	VF	XF	Unc	BU
1984 Proof	15,000	Value: 30.00				

KM# 120b CROWN
5.1000 g., 0.3740 Gold 0.0613 oz. AGW **Ruler:** Elizabeth II
Series: 1984 Olympics - Los Angeles **Obv:** Young bust right
Rev: Equestrian

Date	Mintage	F	VF	XF	Unc	BU
1984 Proof	10,000	Value: 75.00				

KM# 120c CROWN
7.9600 g., 0.9170 Gold 0.2347 oz. AGW **Ruler:** Elizabeth II
Series: 1984 Olympics - Los Angeles **Obv:** Young bust right
Rev: Equestrian

Date	Mintage	F	VF	XF	Unc	BU
1984 Proof	1,000	Value: 250				

KM# 120d CROWN
52.0000 g., 0.9500 Platinum 1.5882 oz. APW, 38.5 mm.
Ruler: Elizabeth II **Series:** 1984 Olympics - Los Angeles
Obv: Young bust right **Rev:** Equestrian

Date	Mintage	F	VF	XF	Unc	BU
1984 Proof	100	Value: 3,000				

KM# 120e CROWN
Silver Clad Copper-Nickel, 38.5 mm. **Ruler:** Elizabeth II
Series: 1984 Olympics - Los Angeles **Obv:** Young bust right
Rev: Equestrian

Date	Mintage	F	VF	XF	Unc	BU
1984	20,000	—	—	—	20.00	22.50

KM# 121 CROWN
Copper-Nickel, 38.5 mm. **Ruler:** Elizabeth II **Subject:**
Quincentenary **Obv:** Young bust right **Rev:** Arms with supporters

Date	Mintage	F	VF	XF	Unc	BU
1984	—	—	—	—	6.00	7.00
1984 Prooflike	—	—	—	—	—	8.50

KM# 121a CROWN
28.2800 g., 0.9250 Silver 0.8410 oz. ASW, 38.5 mm.
Ruler: Elizabeth II **Subject:** Quincentenary **Obv:** Young bust
right **Rev:** Arms with supporters

Date	Mintage	F	VF	XF	Unc	BU
1984	—	—	—	—	16.50	17.50
1984 Proof	—	Value: 25.00				

KM# 121b CROWN
5.1000 g., 0.3740 Gold 0.0613 oz. AGW **Ruler:** Elizabeth II
Subject: Quincentenary **Obv:** Young bust right **Rev:** Arms with
supporters

Date	Mintage	F	VF	XF	Unc	BU
1984 Proof	10,000	Value: 65.00				

KM# 121c CROWN
7.9600 g., 0.9170 Gold 0.2347 oz. AGW **Ruler:** Elizabeth II
Subject: Quincentenary **Obv:** Young bust right **Rev:** Arms with
supporters

Date	Mintage	F	VF	XF	Unc	BU
1984 Proof	1,000	Value: 250				

KM# 121d CROWN
52.0000 g., 0.9500 Platinum 1.5882 oz. APW, 38.5 mm.
Ruler: Elizabeth II **Subject:** Quincentenary **Obv:** Young bust
right **Rev:** Arms with supporters

Date	Mintage	F	VF	XF	Unc	BU
1984 Proof	—	Value: 3,000				

KM# 122 CROWN
Copper-Nickel, 38.5 mm. **Ruler:** Elizabeth II **Subject:**
Quincentenary **Obv:** Young bust right **Rev:** Lion above shields

Date	Mintage	F	VF	XF	Unc	BU
1984	—	—	—	—	6.00	7.00
1984 Prooflike	—	—	—	—	—	8.50

KM# 122a CROWN
28.2800 g., 0.9250 Silver 0.8410 oz. ASW, 38.5 mm.
Ruler: Elizabeth II **Subject:** Quincentenary **Obv:** Young bust
right **Rev:** Lion above shields

Date	Mintage	F	VF	XF	Unc	BU
1984	—	—	—	—	16.50	17.50
1984 Proof	—	Value: 25.00				

KM# 122b CROWN
5.1000 g., 0.3740 Gold 0.0613 oz. AGW **Ruler:** Elizabeth II
Subject: Quincentenary **Obv:** Young bust right **Rev:** Lion above
shields

Date	Mintage	F	VF	XF	Unc	BU
1984 Proof	10,000	Value: 75.00				

KM# 122c CROWN
7.9600 g., 0.9170 Gold 0.2347 oz. AGW **Ruler:** Elizabeth II
Subject: Quincentenary **Obv:** Young bust right **Rev:** Lion above
shields

Date	Mintage	F	VF	XF	Unc	BU
1984 Proof	1,000	Value: 250				

KM# 122d CROWN
52.0000 g., 0.9500 Platinum 1.5882 oz. APW, 38.5 mm.
Ruler: Elizabeth II **Subject:** Quincentenary **Obv:** Young bust
right **Rev:** Lion above shields

Date	Mintage	F	VF	XF	Unc	BU
1984 Proof	—	Value: 3,000				

KM# 123 CROWN
Copper-Nickel, 38.5 mm. **Ruler:** Elizabeth II
Subject: Quincentenary **Obv:** Young bust right **Rev:** Bird above
shields

Date	Mintage	F	VF	XF	Unc	BU
1984	—	—	—	—	6.00	7.00
1984 Prooflike	—	—	—	—	—	8.50

KM# 123a CROWN
28.2800 g., 0.9250 Silver 0.8410 oz. ASW, 38.5 mm.
Ruler: Elizabeth II **Subject:** Quincentenary **Obv:** Young bust
right **Rev:** Bird above shields

Date	Mintage	F	VF	XF	Unc	BU
1984	—	—	—	—	16.50	17.50
1984 Proof	—	Value: 25.00				

KM# 123b CROWN
5.1000 g., 0.3740 Gold 0.0613 oz. AGW **Ruler:** Elizabeth II
Subject: Quincentenary **Obv:** Young bust right **Rev:** Bird above
shields

Date	Mintage	F	VF	XF	Unc	BU
1984 Proof	10,000	Value: 75.00				

KM# 123c CROWN
7.9600 g., 0.9170 Gold 0.2347 oz. AGW **Ruler:** Elizabeth II
Subject: Quincentenary **Obv:** Young bust right **Rev:** Bird above
shields

Date	Mintage	F	VF	XF	Unc	BU
1984 Proof	1,000	Value: 250				

KM# 123d CROWN
52.0000 g., 0.9500 Platinum 1.5882 oz. APW, 38.5 mm.
Ruler: Elizabeth II **Subject:** Quincentenary **Obv:** Young bust
right **Rev:** Bird above shields

Date	Mintage	F	VF	XF	Unc	BU
1984 Proof	—	Value: 3,000				

KM# 124 CROWN
Copper-Nickel, 38.5 mm. **Ruler:** Elizabeth II
Subject: Quincentenary **Obv:** Young bust right **Rev:** Arms with
supporters

Date	Mintage	F	VF	XF	Unc	BU
1984	—	—	—	—	6.00	7.00
1984 Prooflike	—	—	—	—	—	8.50

KM# 124a CROWN
28.2800 g., 0.9250 Silver 0.8410 oz. ASW, 38.5 mm.
Ruler: Elizabeth II **Subject:** Quincentenary **Obv:** Young bust
right **Rev:** Arms with supporters

Date	Mintage	F	VF	XF	Unc	BU
1984	—	—	—	—	16.50	17.50
1984 Proof	—	Value: 25.00				

KM# 124b CROWN
5.1000 g., 0.3740 Gold 0.0613 oz. AGW **Ruler:** Elizabeth II
Subject: Quincentenary **Obv:** Crowned bust right **Rev:** Arms with
supporters

Date	Mintage	F	VF	XF	Unc	BU
1984 Proof	10,000	Value: 75.00				

KM# 124c CROWN
7.9600 g., 0.9170 Gold 0.2347 oz. AGW **Ruler:** Elizabeth II
Subject: Quincentenary **Obv:** Young bust right **Rev:** Arms with
supporters

Date	Mintage	F	VF	XF	Unc	BU
1984 Proof	1,000	Value: 250				

KM# 124d CROWN
52.0000 g., 0.9500 Platinum 1.5882 oz. APW, 38.5 mm.
uler: Elizabeth II **Subject:** Quincentenary **Obv:** Young bust right
Rev: Arms with supporters

Date	Mintage	F	VF	XF	Unc	BU
1984 Proof	—	Value: 3,000				

KM# 130 CROWN
Copper-Nickel, 38.5 mm. **Ruler:** Elizabeth II **Subject:** 30th
Commonwealth Parliamentary Conference **Obv:** Young bust
right **Rev:** Conjoined heads right within circle **Rev. Leg.:** Celtic
uncial script

Date	Mintage	F	VF	XF	Unc	BU
1984	—	—	—	—	3.00	4.00

KM# 130a CROWN
28.2800 g., 0.9250 Silver 0.8410 oz. ASW, 38.5 mm.
Ruler: Elizabeth II **Subject:** 30th Commonwealth Parliamentary
Conference **Obv:** Young bust right **Rev:** Conjoined heads right
within circle **Rev. Leg.:** Celtic uncial script

Date	Mintage	F	VF	XF	Unc	BU
1984	—	—	—	—	15.00	16.50
1984 Proof	—	Value: 20.00				

KM# 130b CROWN
5.1000 g., 0.3740 Gold 0.0613 oz. AGW **Ruler:** Elizabeth II
Subject: 30th Commonwealth Parliamentary Conference
Obv: Young bust right **Rev:** Conjoined heads right within circle
Rev. Leg.: Celtic uncial script

Date	Mintage	F	VF	XF	Unc	BU
1984 Proof	10,000	Value: 75.00				

KM# 130c CROWN
7.9600 g., 0.9170 Gold 0.2347 oz. AGW **Ruler:** Elizabeth II
Subject: 30th Commonwealth Parliamentary Conference
Obv: Young bust right **Rev:** Conjoined heads right within circle
Rev. Leg.: Celtic uncial script

Date	Mintage	F	VF	XF	Unc	BU
1984 Proof	1,000	Value: 250				

KM# 130d CROWN
52.0000 g., 0.9500 Platinum 1.5882 oz. APW, 38.5 mm.
Ruler: Elizabeth II **Subject:** 30th Commonwealth Parliamentary
Conference **Obv:** Young bust right **Rev:** Conjoined heads right
within circle **Rev. Leg.:** Celtic uncial script

Date	Mintage	F	VF	XF	Unc	BU
1984 Proof	—	Value: 3,000				

KM# 131 CROWN
Copper-Nickel, 38.5 mm. **Ruler:** Elizabeth II **Subject:** 30th
Commonwealth Parliamentary Conference **Obv:** Young bust
right **Rev:** Throne, shield and sword **Rev. Leg.:** Celtic uncial script

Date	Mintage	F	VF	XF	Unc	BU
1984	—	—	—	—	3.00	4.00

KM# 131a CROWN
28.2800 g., 0.9250 Silver 0.8410 oz. ASW, 38.5 mm.
Ruler: Elizabeth II **Subject:** 30th Commonwealth Parliamentary Conference **Obv:** Young bust right **Rev:** Throne, sword and shield **Rev. Leg.:** Celtic uncial script

Date	Mintage	F	VF	XF	Unc	BU
1984	—	—	—	15.00	16.50	
1984 Proof	—	Value: 20.00				

KM# 131b CROWN
5.1000 g., 0.3740 Gold 0.0613 oz. AGW **Ruler:** Elizabeth II **Subject:** 30th Commonwealth Parliamentary Conference **Obv:** Young bust right **Rev:** Throne, sword and shield **Rev. Leg.:** Celtic uncial script

Date	Mintage	F	VF	XF	Unc	BU
1984 Proof	10,000	Value: 75.00				

KM# 131c CROWN
7.9600 g., 0.9170 Gold 0.2347 oz. AGW **Ruler:** Elizabeth II **Subject:** 30th Commonwealth Parliamentary Conference **Obv:** Young bust right **Rev:** Throne, sword and shield **Rev. Leg.:** Celtic uncial script

Date	Mintage	F	VF	XF	Unc	BU
1984 Proof	1,000	Value: 250				

KM# 131d CROWN
52.0000 g., 0.9500 Platinum 1.5882 oz. APW, 38.5 mm.
Ruler: Elizabeth II **Subject:** 30th Commonwealth Parliamentary Conference **Obv:** Young bust right **Rev:** Throne, shield and sword **Rev. Leg.:** Celtic uncial script

Date	Mintage	F	VF	XF	Unc	BU
1984 Proof	—	Value: 3,000				

KM# 132 CROWN
Copper-Nickel, 38.5 mm. **Ruler:** Elizabeth II **Subject:** 30th Commonwealth Parliamentary Conference **Obv:** Young bust right **Rev:** Crowned head facing within circle **Rev. Leg.:** Celtic uncial script

Date	Mintage	F	VF	XF	Unc	BU
1984	—	—	—	—	3.00	4.00

KM# 132a CROWN
28.2800 g., 0.9250 Silver 0.8410 oz. ASW, 38.5 mm.
Ruler: Elizabeth II **Subject:** 30th Commonwealth Parliamentary Conference **Obv:** Young bust right **Rev:** Crowned head facing within circle **Rev. Leg.:** Celtic uncial script

Date	Mintage	F	VF	XF	Unc	BU
1984	—	—	—	—	15.00	16.50
1984 Proof	—	Value: 20.00				

KM# 132b CROWN
5.1000 g., 0.3740 Gold 0.0613 oz. AGW **Ruler:** Elizabeth II **Subject:** 30th Commonwealth Parliamentary Conference **Obv:** Young bust right **Rev:** crowned head facing within circle **Rev. Leg.:** Celtic uncial script

Date	Mintage	F	VF	XF	Unc	BU
1984 Proof	10,000	Value: 75.00				

KM# 132c CROWN
7.9600 g., 0.9170 Gold 0.2347 oz. AGW **Ruler:** Elizabeth II **Subject:** 30th Commonwealth Parliamentary Conference **Obv:** Young bust right **Rev:** Crowned head facing within circle **Rev. Leg.:** Celtic uncial script

Date	Mintage	F	VF	XF	Unc	BU
1984 Proof	1,000	Value: 250				

KM# 132d CROWN
52.0000 g., 0.9500 Platinum 1.5882 oz. APW, 38.5 mm.
Ruler: Elizabeth II **Subject:** 30th Commonwealth Parliamentary Conference **Obv:** Young bust right **Rev:** Crowned head facing within circle **Rev. Leg.:** Celtic uncial script

Date	Mintage	F	VF	XF	Unc	BU
1984 Proof	—	Value: 3,000				

KM# 133 CROWN
Copper-Nickel, 38.5 mm. **Ruler:** Elizabeth II **Subject:** 30th Commonwealth Parliamentary Conference **Obv:** Young bust right **Rev:** Conference tent **Rev. Leg.:** Celtic uncial script

Date	Mintage	F	VF	XF	Unc	BU
1984	—	—	—	—	3.00	4.00

KM# 133a CROWN
28.2800 g., 0.9250 Silver 0.8410 oz. ASW, 38.5 mm.
Ruler: Elizabeth II **Subject:** 30th Commonwealth Parliamentary Conference **Obv:** Young bust right **Rev:** Conference tent **Rev. Leg.:** Celtic uncial script

Date	Mintage	F	VF	XF	Unc	BU
1984	—	—	—	—	15.00	16.50
1984 Proof	—	Value: 20.00				

KM# 133b CROWN
5.1000 g., 0.3740 Gold 0.0613 oz. AGW **Ruler:** Elizabeth II **Subject:** 30th Commonwealth Parliamentary Conference **Obv:** Young bust right **Rev:** Conference tent within circle **Rev. Leg.:** Celtic uncial script

Date	Mintage	F	VF	XF	Unc	BU
1984 Proof	10,000	Value: 75.00				

KM# 133c CROWN
7.9600 g., 0.9170 Gold 0.2347 oz. AGW **Ruler:** Elizabeth II **Subject:** 30th Commonwealth Parliamentary Conference **Obv:** Young bust right **Rev:** Conference tent **Rev. Leg.:** Celtic uncial script

Date	Mintage	F	VF	XF	Unc	BU
1984 Proof	1,000	Value: 250				

KM# 133d CROWN
52.0000 g., 0.9500 Platinum 1.5882 oz. APW, 38.5 mm.
Ruler: Elizabeth II **Subject:** 30th Commonwealth Parliamentary Conference **Obv:** Young bust right **Rev:** Conference tent **Rev. Leg.:** Celtic uncial script

Date	Mintage	F	VF	XF	Unc	BU
1984 Proof	—	Value: 3,000				

KM# 216 CROWN
Copper-Nickel, 38.5 mm. **Ruler:** Elizabeth II **Obv:** Crowned bust right **Rev:** Child half figure facing

Date	Mintage	F	VF	XF	Unc	BU
1985	Est. 50,000	—	—	—	2.50	3.50

KM# 220 CROWN
Copper-Nickel, 38.5 mm. **Ruler:** Elizabeth II **Obv:** Crowned bust right **Rev:** Adult and two children facing

Date	Mintage	F	VF	XF	Unc	BU
1985	Est. 50,000	—	—	—	2.50	3.50
1990	—	—	—	—	2.50	3.50
1990PM Proof	—	Value: 10.00				

KM# 220a CROWN
Silver Clad Copper-Nickel, 38.5 mm. **Ruler:** Elizabeth II **Obv:** Crowned bust right **Rev:** Adult and two children facing

Date	Mintage	F	VF	XF	Unc	BU
1985 Proof	Est. 20,000	Value: 15.00				
1990PM Proof	—	Value: 35.00				

KM# 216a CROWN
Silver Clad Copper-Nickel, 38.5 mm. **Ruler:** Elizabeth II **Obv:** Crowned bust right **Rev:** Child half figure facing

Date	Mintage	F	VF	XF	Unc	BU
1985 Proof	Est. 20,000	Value: 10.00				

KM# 216b CROWN
28.2800 g., 0.9250 Silver 0.8410 oz. ASW, 38.5 mm. **Ruler:** Elizabeth II **Obv:** Crowned bust right **Rev:** Child half figure facing

Date	Mintage	F	VF	XF	Unc	BU
1985 Proof	Est. 15,000	Value: 25.00				

KM# 216c CROWN
5.1000 g., 0.3740 Gold 0.0613 oz. AGW **Ruler:** Elizabeth II **Obv:** Crowned bust right **Rev:** Child half figure facing

Date	Mintage	F	VF	XF	Unc	BU
1985 Proof	Est. 10,000	Value: 75.00				

KM# 216d CROWN
7.9600 g., 0.9170 Gold 0.2347 oz. AGW **Ruler:** Elizabeth II **Obv:** Crowned bust right **Rev:** Child half figure facing

Date	Mintage	F	VF	XF	Unc	BU
1985 Proof	Est. 1,000,000	Value: 250				

KM# 216e CROWN
52.0000 g., 0.9500 Platinum 1.5882 oz. APW, 38.5 mm. **Ruler:** Elizabeth II **Obv:** Crowned bust right **Rev:** Child half figure facing

Date	Mintage	F	VF	XF	Unc	BU
1985 Proof	Est. 100	Value: 3,000				

KM# 217 CROWN
Copper-Nickel, 38.5 mm. **Ruler:** Elizabeth II **Obv:** Crowned bust right **Rev:** Conjoined busts facing

Date	Mintage	F	VF	XF	Unc	BU
1985	Est. 50,000	—	—	—	2.50	3.50

KM# 217a CROWN
Silver Clad Copper-Nickel, 38.5 mm. **Ruler:** Elizabeth II **Obv:** Crowned bust right **Rev:** Conjoined busts facing

Date	Mintage	F	VF	XF	Unc	BU
1985 Proof	Est. 20,000	Value: 10.00				

KM# 217b CROWN
28.2800 g., 0.9250 Silver 0.8410 oz. ASW **Ruler:** Elizabeth II **Obv:** Crowned bust right **Rev:** Conjoined busts facing

Date	Mintage	F	VF	XF	Unc	BU
1985 Proof	Est. 15,000	Value: 25.00				

KM# 217c CROWN
5.1000 g., 0.3740 Gold 0.0613 oz. AGW **Ruler:** Elizabeth II **Obv:** Crowned bust right **Rev:** Conjoined busts facing

Date	Mintage	F	VF	XF	Unc	BU
1985 Proof	Est. 10,000	Value: 75.00				

KM# 217d CROWN
7.9600 g., 0.9170 Gold 0.2347 oz. AGW **Ruler:** Elizabeth II **Obv:** Crowned bust right **Rev:** Conjoined busts facing

Date	Mintage	F	VF	XF	Unc	BU
1985 Proof	Est. 1,000	Value: 250				

KM# 217e CROWN
52.0000 g., 0.9500 Platinum 1.5882 oz. APW, 38.5 mm. **Ruler:** Elizabeth II **Obv:** Crowned bust right **Rev:** Conjoined busts facing

Date	Mintage	F	VF	XF	Unc	BU
1985 Proof	Est. 100	Value: 3,000				

KM# 218 CROWN
Copper-Nickel, 38.5 mm. **Ruler:** Elizabeth II **Obv:** Crowned bust right **Rev:** Royal Wedding couple

Date	Mintage	F	VF	XF	Unc	BU
1985	Est. 50,000	—	—	—	2.50	3.50

KM# 218a CROWN
Silver Clad Copper-Nickel, 38.5 mm. **Ruler:** Elizabeth II **Obv:** Crowned bust right **Rev:** 3/4 length figures of Royal couple facing

Date	Mintage	F	VF	XF	Unc	BU
1985 Proof	Est. 20,000	Value: 10.00				

KM# 218c CROWN
5.1000 g., 0.3740 Gold 0.0613 oz. AGW **Ruler:** Elizabeth II **Obv:** Crowned bust right **Rev:** 3/4 length figures of Royal couple facing

Date	Mintage	F	VF	XF	Unc	BU
1985 Proof	Est. 10,000	Value: 75.00				

KM# 218b CROWN
28.2800 g., 0.9250 Silver 0.8410 oz. ASW, 38.5 mm. **Ruler:** Elizabeth II **Obv:** Crowned bust right **Rev:** 3/4 length figures of Royal couple facing

Date	Mintage	F	VF	XF	Unc	BU
1985 Proof	Est. 15,000	Value: 25.00				

KM# 218d CROWN
7.9600 g., 0.9170 Gold 0.2347 oz. AGW **Ruler:** Elizabeth II
Obv: Crowned bust right **Rev:** 3/4 length figures of Royal couple
facing

Date	Mintage	F	VF	XF	Unc	BU
1985 Proof	Est. 1,000	Value: 250				

KM# 218e CROWN
52.0000 g., 0.9500 Platinum 1.5882 oz. APW, 38.5 mm.
Ruler: Elizabeth II **Obv:** Crowned bust right **Rev:** 3/4 length
figures of Royal couple facing

Date	Mintage	F	VF	XF	Unc	BU
1985 Proof	Est. 100	Value: 3,000				

KM# 219 CROWN
Copper-Nickel, 38.5 mm. **Ruler:** Elizabeth II **Obv:** Crowned bust
right **Rev:** Queen Mother and Princess Elizabeth

Date	Mintage	F	VF	XF	Unc	BU
1985	Est. 50,000	—	—	—	2.50	3.50

KM# 219a CROWN
Silver Clad Copper-Nickel, 38.5 mm. **Ruler:** Elizabeth II
Obv: Crowned bust right **Rev:** Queen Mother and Princess
Elizabeth

Date	Mintage	F	VF	XF	Unc	BU
1985 Proof	Est. 20,000	Value: 10.00				

KM# 219b CROWN
28.2800 g., 0.9250 Silver 0.8410 oz. ASW, 38.5 mm.
Ruler: Elizabeth II **Obv:** Crowned bust right **Rev:** Queen Mother
and Princess Elizabeth

Date	Mintage	F	VF	XF	Unc	BU
1985 Proof	Est. 15,000	Value: 25.00				

KM# 219c CROWN
5.1000 g., 0.3740 Gold 0.0613 oz. AGW **Ruler:** Elizabeth II
Obv: Crowned bust right **Rev:** Queen Mother and Princess Elizabeth

Date	Mintage	F	VF	XF	Unc	BU
1985 Proof	Est. 10,000	Value: 75.00				

KM# 219d CROWN
7.9600 g., 0.9170 Gold 0.2347 oz. AGW **Ruler:** Elizabeth II
Obv: Crowned bust right **Rev:** Queen Mother and Princess Elizabeth

Date	Mintage	F	VF	XF	Unc	BU
1985 Proof	Est. 1,000	Value: 250				

KM# 219e CROWN
52.0000 g., 0.9500 Platinum 1.5882 oz. APW, 38.5 mm.
Ruler: Elizabeth II **Obv:** Crowned bust right **Rev:** Queen Mother
and Princess Elizabeth

Date	Mintage	F	VF	XF	Unc	BU
1985 Proof	Est. 100	Value: 3,000				

KM# 220b CROWN
28.2800 g., 0.9250 Silver 0.8410 oz. ASW, 38.5 mm.
Ruler: Elizabeth II **Obv:** Crowned bust right **Rev:** Adult and two
children facing

Date	Mintage	F	VF	XF	Unc	BU
1985 Proof	Est. 15,000	Value: 25.00				
1990 Proof	—	Value: 28.00				

KM# 220c CROWN
5.1000 g., 0.3740 Gold 0.0613 oz. AGW **Ruler:** Elizabeth II
Obv: Crowned bust right **Rev:** Adult and two children facing

Date	Mintage	F	VF	XF	Unc	BU
1985 Proof	Est. 10,000	Value: 75.00				

KM# 220d CROWN
7.9600 g., 0.9170 Gold 0.2347 oz. AGW **Ruler:** Elizabeth II
Obv: Crowned bust right **Rev:** Adult and two children facing

Date	Mintage	F	VF	XF	Unc	BU
1985 Proof	Est. 1,000	Value: 250				

KM# 220e CROWN
52.0000 g., 0.9500 Platinum 1.5882 oz. APW, 38.5 mm.
Ruler: Elizabeth II **Obv:** Crowned bust right **Rev:** Adult and two
children facing

Date	Mintage	F	VF	XF	Unc	BU
1985 Proof	Est. 100	Value: 3,000				

KM# 221 CROWN
Copper-Nickel, 38.5 mm. **Ruler:** Elizabeth II **Subject:** 85th
Birthday of Queen Mother **Obv:** Crowned bust right **Rev:** Queen
Mother

Date	Mintage	F	VF	XF	Unc	BU
1985.	Est. 50,000	—	—	—	2.50	3.50

KM# 221a CROWN
Silver Clad Copper-Nickel, 38.5 mm. **Ruler:** Elizabeth II
Subject: 85th Birthday of Queen Mother **Obv:** Crowned bust right
Rev: Queen Mother

Date	Mintage	F	VF	XF	Unc	BU
1985 Proof	Est. 20,000	Value: 10.00				

KM# 221b CROWN
28.2800 g., 0.9250 Silver 0.8410 oz. ASW, 38.5 mm.
Ruler: Elizabeth II **Subject:** 85th Birthday of Queen Mother
Obv: Crowned bust right **Rev:** Queen Mother

Date	Mintage	F	VF	XF	Unc	BU
1985 Proof	Est. 15,000	Value: 25.00				

KM# 221c CROWN
5.1000 g., 0.3740 Gold 0.0613 oz. AGW **Ruler:** Elizabeth II
Subject: 85th Birthday of Queen Mother **Obv:** Crowned bust right
Rev: Queen Mother

Date	Mintage	F	VF	XF	Unc	BU
1985 Proof	Est. 10,000	Value: 75.00				

KM# 221d CROWN
7.9600 g., 0.9170 Gold 0.2347 oz. AGW **Ruler:** Elizabeth II
Subject: 85th Birthday of Queen Mother **Obv:** Crowned bust right
Rev: Queen Mother

Date	Mintage	F	VF	XF	Unc	BU
1985 Proof	Est. 1,000,000	Value: 250				

KM# 221e CROWN
52.0000 g., 0.9500 Platinum 1.5882 oz. APW, 38.5 mm.
Ruler: Elizabeth II **Subject:** 85th Birthday of Queen Mother
Obv: Crowned bust right **Rev:** Queen Mother

Date	Mintage	F	VF	XF	Unc	BU
1985 Proof	Est. 100	Value: 3,000				

KM# 160 CROWN
Copper-Nickel, 38.5 mm. **Ruler:** Elizabeth II **Series:** World Cup
Soccer - Mexico **Obv:** Crowned bust right **Rev:** Map and soccer
players within circle **Edge:** Reeded

Date	Mintage	F	VF	XF	Unc	BU
1986	Est. 50,000	—	—	—	2.50	3.50

KM# 160a CROWN
Silver Clad Copper-Nickel, 38.5 mm. **Ruler:** Elizabeth II
Series: World Cup Soccer - Mexico **Obv:** Crowned bust right
Rev: Map and soccer players within circle

Date	Mintage	F	VF	XF	Unc	BU
1986 Proof	Est. 20,000	Value: 10.00				

KM# 160b CROWN
28.2800 g., 0.9250 Silver 0.8410 oz. ASW, 38.5 mm.
Ruler: Elizabeth II **Series:** World Cup Soccer - Mexico
Obv: Crowned bust right **Rev:** Map and soccer players within
circle

Date	Mintage	F	VF	XF	Unc	BU
1986 Proof	Est. 15,000	Value: 17.50				

KM# 160c CROWN
5.1000 g., 0.3740 Gold 0.0613 oz. AGW **Ruler:** Elizabeth II
Series: World Cup Soccer - Mexico **Obv:** Crowned bust right
Rev: Map and soccer players within circle

Date	Mintage	F	VF	XF	Unc	BU
1986 Proof	Est. 10,000	Value: 75.00				

KM# 160d CROWN
7.9600 g., 0.9170 Gold 0.2347 oz. AGW **Ruler:** Elizabeth II
Series: World Cup Soccer - Mexico **Obv:** Crowned bust right
Rev: Map and soccer players within circle

Date	Mintage	F	VF	XF	Unc	BU
1986 Proof	Est. 1,000	Value: 250				

KM# 160e CROWN
52.0000 g., 0.9500 Platinum 1.5882 oz. APW, 38.5 mm.
Ruler: Elizabeth II **Series:** World Cup Soccer - Mexico
Obv: Crowned bust right **Rev:** Map and soccer players within
circle

Date	Mintage	F	VF	XF	Unc	BU
1986 Proof	Est. 200	Value: 3,000				

KM# 161 CROWN
Copper-Nickel, 38.5 mm. **Ruler:** Elizabeth II **Series:** World Cup
Soccer - Mexico **Obv:** Crowned bust right **Rev:** Soccer players
within circle

Date	Mintage	F	VF	XF	Unc	BU
1986	Est. 50,000	—	—	—	2.50	3.50

KM# 161a CROWN
Silver Clad Copper-Nickel, 38.5 mm. **Ruler:** Elizabeth II
Series: World Cup Soccer - Mexico **Obv:** Crowned bust right
Rev: Soccer players within circle

Date	Mintage	F	VF	XF	Unc	BU
1986 Proof	Est. 20,000	Value: 10.00				

KM# 161b CROWN
28.2800 g., 0.9250 Silver 0.8410 oz. ASW, 38.5 mm.
Ruler: Elizabeth II **Series:** World Cup Soccer - Mexico
Obv: Crowned bust right **Rev:** Soccer players within circle

Date	Mintage	F	VF	XF	Unc	BU
1986 Proof	Est. 15,000	Value: 17.50				

KM# 161c CROWN
5.1000 g., 0.3740 Gold 0.0613 oz. AGW **Ruler:** Elizabeth II
Series: World Cup Soccer - Mexico **Obv:** Crowned bust right
Rev: Soccer players within circle

Date	Mintage	F	VF	XF	Unc	BU
1986 Proof	Est. 10,000	Value: 75.00				

KM# 161d CROWN
7.9600 g., 0.9170 Gold 0.2347 oz. AGW **Ruler:** Elizabeth II
Series: World Cup Soccer - Mexico **Obv:** Crowned bust right
Rev: Soccer players within circle

Date	Mintage	F	VF	XF	Unc	BU
1986 Proof	Est. 1,000	Value: 220				

KM# 161e CROWN
52.0000 g., 0.9500 Platinum 1.5882 oz. APW, 38.5 mm.
Ruler: Elizabeth II **Series:** World Cup Soccer - Mexico
Obv: Crowned bust right **Rev:** Soccer players within circle

Date	Mintage	F	VF	XF	Unc	BU
1986 Proof	Est. 200	Value: 3,250				

KM# 162 CROWN
Copper-Nickel, 38.5 mm. **Ruler:** Elizabeth II **Series:** World Cup
Soccer - Mexico **Obv:** Crowned bust right **Rev:** Soccer players
within circle **Edge:** Reeded

Date	Mintage	F	VF	XF	Unc	BU
1986	Est. 50,000	—	—	—	2.50	3.50

KM# 162a CROWN
Silver-Clad Copper-Nickel, 38.5 mm. **Ruler:** Elizabeth II
Series: World Cup Soccer - Mexico **Obv:** Crowned bust right
Rev: Soccer players within circle

Date	Mintage	F	VF	XF	Unc	BU
1986 Proof	Est. 20,000	Value: 10.00				

KM# 162b CROWN
28.2800 g., 0.9250 Silver 0.8410 oz. ASW, 38.5 mm.
Ruler: Elizabeth II **Series:** World Cup Soccer - Mexico
Obv: Crowned bust right **Rev:** Soccer players within circle

Date	Mintage	F	VF	XF	Unc	BU
1986 Proof	Est. 15,000	Value: 17.50				

KM# 162c CROWN
5.1000 g., 0.3740 Gold 0.0613 oz. AGW **Ruler:** Elizabeth II **Series:** World Cup Soccer - Mexico **Obv:** Crowned bust right **Rev:** Soccer players within circle

Date	Mintage	F	VF	XF	Unc	BU
1986 Proof	Est. 10,000	Value: 65.00				

KM# 162d CROWN
7.9600 g., 0.9170 Gold 0.2347 oz. AGW **Ruler:** Elizabeth II **Series:** World Cup Soccer - Mexico **Obv:** Crowned bust right **Rev:** Soccer players within circle

Date	Mintage	F	VF	XF	Unc	BU
1986 Proof	Est. 1,000	Value: 250				

KM# 162e CROWN
52.0000 g., 0.9500 Platinum 1.5882 oz. APW, 38.5 mm. **Ruler:** Elizabeth II **Series:** World Cup Soccer - Mexico **Obv:** Crowned bust right **Rev:** Soccer players within circle

Date	Mintage	F	VF	XF	Unc	BU
1986 Proof	Est. 200	Value: 3,000				

KM# 163 CROWN
Copper-Nickel, 38.5 mm. **Ruler:** Elizabeth II **Series:** World Cup Soccer - Mexico **Obv:** Crowned bust right **Rev:** Net and soccer players within circle **Edge:** Reeded

Date	Mintage	F	VF	XF	Unc	BU
1986	Est. 50,000	—	—	—	2.50	3.50

KM# 163a CROWN
Silver-Clad Copper-Nickel **Ruler:** Elizabeth II **Series:** World Cup Soccer - Mexico **Obv:** Crowned bust right **Rev:** Net and soccer players within circle

Date	Mintage	F	VF	XF	Unc	BU
1986 Proof	Est. 20,000	Value: 10.00				

KM# 163b CROWN
28.2800 g., 0.9250 Silver 0.8410 oz. ASW, 38.5 mm. **Ruler:** Elizabeth II **Series:** World Cup Soccer - Mexico **Obv:** Crowned bust right **Rev:** Net and soccer players within circle

Date	Mintage	F	VF	XF	Unc	BU
1986 Proof	Est. 15,000	Value: 17.50				

KM# 163c CROWN
5.1000 g., 0.3740 Gold 0.0613 oz. AGW **Ruler:** Elizabeth II **Series:** World Cup Soccer - Mexico **Obv:** Crowned bust right **Rev:** Net and soccer players within circle

Date	Mintage	F	VF	XF	Unc	BU
1986 Proof	Est. 10,000	Value: 75.00				

KM# 163d CROWN
7.9600 g., 0.9170 Gold 0.2347 oz. AGW **Ruler:** Elizabeth II **Series:** World Cup Soccer - Mexico **Obv:** Crowned bust right **Rev:** Net and soccer players within circle

Date	Mintage	F	VF	XF	Unc	BU
1986 Proof	Est. 1,000	Value: 250				

KM# 163e CROWN
52.0000 g., 0.9500 Platinum 1.5882 oz. APW, 38.5 mm. **Ruler:** Elizabeth II **Series:** World Cup Soccer - Mexico **Obv:** Crowned bust right **Rev:** Net and soccer players within circle

Date	Mintage	F	VF	XF	Unc	BU
1986 Proof	Est. 200	Value: 3,000				

KM# 164 CROWN
Copper-Nickel, 38.5 mm. **Ruler:** Elizabeth II **Series:** World Cup Soccer - Mexico **Obv:** Crowned bust right **Rev:** Globe **Edge:** Reeded

Date	Mintage	F	VF	XF	Unc	BU
1986	Est. 50,000	—	—	—	2.50	3.50

KM# 164a CROWN
Silver-Clad Copper-Nickel, 38.5 mm. **Ruler:** Elizabeth II **Series:** World Cup Soccer - Mexico **Obv:** Crowned bust right **Rev:** Globe

Date	Mintage	F	VF	XF	Unc	BU
1986	Est. 20,000	Value: 10.00				
1989	—	—	—	—	80.00	—

KM# 164b CROWN
28.2800 g., 0.9250 Silver 0.8410 oz. ASW, 38.5 mm. **Ruler:** Elizabeth II **Series:** World Cup Soccer - Mexico **Obv:** Crowned bust right **Rev:** Globe

Date	Mintage	F	VF	XF	Unc	BU
1986 Proof	Est. 15,000	Value: 17.50				

KM# 164c CROWN
5.1000 g., 0.3740 Gold 0.0613 oz. AGW **Ruler:** Elizabeth II **Series:** World Cup Soccer - Mexico **Obv:** Crowned bust right **Rev:** Globe

Date	Mintage	F	VF	XF	Unc	BU
1986 Proof	Est. 10,000	Value: 75.00				

KM# 164d CROWN
7.9600 g., 0.9170 Gold 0.2347 oz. AGW **Ruler:** Elizabeth II **Series:** World Cup Soccer - Mexico **Obv:** Crowned bust right **Rev:** Globe

Date	Mintage	F	VF	XF	Unc	BU
1986 Proof	Est. 1,000	Value: 250				

KM# 164e CROWN
52.0000 g., 0.9500 Platinum 1.5882 oz. APW, 38.5 mm. **Ruler:** Elizabeth II **Series:** World Cup Soccer - Mexico **Obv:** Crowned bust right **Rev:** Globe

Date	Mintage	F	VF	XF	Unc	BU
1986 Proof	Est. 200	Value: 3,000				

KM# 165 CROWN
Copper-Nickel, 38.5 mm. **Ruler:** Elizabeth II **Series:** World Cup Soccer - Mexico **Obv:** Crowned bust right **Rev:** Flags within circle **Edge:** Reeded

Date	Mintage	F	VF	XF	Unc	BU
1986	Est. 50,000	—	—	—	2.50	3.50

KM# 165a CROWN
Silver-Clad Copper-Nickel, 38.5 mm. **Ruler:** Elizabeth II **Series:** World Cup Soccer - Mexico **Obv:** Crowned bust right **Rev:** Flags within circle

Date	Mintage	F	VF	XF	Unc	BU
1986	Est. 20,000	Value: 10.00				
1989	—	—	—	—	80.00	—

KM# 165b CROWN
28.2800 g., 0.9250 Silver 0.8410 oz. ASW, 38.5 mm. **Ruler:** Elizabeth II **Series:** World Cup Soccer - Mexico **Obv:** Crowned bust right **Rev:** Flags within circle

Date	Mintage	F	VF	XF	Unc	BU
1986 Proof	Est. 15,000	Value: 17.50				

KM# 165c CROWN
5.1000 g., 0.3740 Gold 0.0613 oz. AGW **Ruler:** Elizabeth II **Series:** World Cup Soccer - Mexico **Obv:** Crowned bust right **Rev:** Flags within circle

Date	Mintage	F	VF	XF	Unc	BU
1986 Proof	Est. 10,000	Value: 75.00				

KM# 165d CROWN
7.9600 g., 0.9170 Gold 0.2347 oz. AGW **Ruler:** Elizabeth II **Series:** World Cup Soccer - Mexico **Obv:** Crowned bust right **Rev:** Flags within circle

Date	Mintage	F	VF	XF	Unc	BU
1986 Proof	Est. 1,000	Value: 250				

KM# 165e CROWN
52.0000 g., 0.9500 Platinum 1.5882 oz. APW, 38.5 mm. **Ruler:** Elizabeth II **Series:** World Cup Soccer - Mexico **Obv:** Crowned bust right **Rev:** Flags within circle

Date	Mintage	F	VF	XF	Unc	BU
1986 Proof	Est. 200	Value: 3,000				

KM# 173 CROWN
Copper-Nickel, 38.5 mm. **Ruler:** Elizabeth II **Subject:** Prince Andrew's Wedding **Obv:** Crowned bust right **Rev:** Conjoined heads left **Edge:** Reeded

Date	Mintage	F	VF	XF	Unc	BU
1986	Est. 50,000	—	—	—	4.00	5.00
1986 Proof	—	Value: 8.00				

KM# 173a CROWN
Silver-Clad Copper-Nickel, 38.5 mm. **Ruler:** Elizabeth II **Subject:** Prince Andrew's Wedding **Obv:** Crowned bust right **Rev:** Conjoined heads left

Date	Mintage	F	VF	XF	Unc	BU
1986 Proof	Est. 20,000	Value: 12.00				

KM# 173b CROWN
28.2800 g., 0.9250 Silver 0.8410 oz. ASW, 38.5 mm. **Ruler:** Elizabeth II **Subject:** Prince Andrew's Wedding **Obv:** Crowned bust right **Rev:** Conjoined heads left

Date	Mintage	F	VF	XF	Unc	BU
1986	Est. 20,000	—	—	—	15.00	16.00
1986 Proof	Est. 15,000	Value: 18.00				

KM# 173c CROWN
5.1000 g., 0.3740 Gold 0.0613 oz. AGW **Ruler:** Elizabeth II **Subject:** Prince Andrew's Wedding **Obv:** Crowned bust right **Rev:** Conjoined heads left

Date	Mintage	F	VF	XF	Unc	BU
1986 Proof	Est. 10,000	Value: 75.00				

KM# 173d CROWN
7.9600 g., 0.9170 Gold 0.2347 oz. AGW **Ruler:** Elizabeth II **Subject:** Prince Andrew's Wedding **Obv:** Crowned bust right **Rev:** Conjoined heads left

Date	Mintage	F	VF	XF	Unc	BU
1986 Proof	Est. 1,000	Value: 250				

KM# 173e CROWN
52.0000 g., 0.9500 Platinum 1.5882 oz. APW, 38.5 mm. **Ruler:** Elizabeth II **Subject:** Prince Andrew's Wedding **Obv:** Crowned bust right **Rev:** Conjoined heads left

Date	Mintage	F	VF	XF	Unc	BU
1986 Proof	Est. 100	Value: 3,000				

KM# 174 CROWN
Copper-Nickel, 38.5 mm. **Ruler:** Elizabeth II **Subject:** Prince Andrew's Wedding **Obv:** Crowned bust right **Rev:** Two sets of arms **Edge:** Reeded

Date	Mintage	F	VF	XF	Unc	BU
1986	Est. 50,000	—	—	—	4.00	5.00
1986 Proof	—	Value: 8.00				

KM# 174a CROWN
Silver Clad Copper-Nickel, 38.5 mm. **Ruler:** Elizabeth II **Subject:** Prince Andrew's Wedding **Obv:** Crowned bust right **Rev:** Two sets of arms

Date	Mintage	F	VF	XF	Unc	BU
1986 Proof	Est. 20,000	Value: 12.00				

KM# 174b CROWN
28.2800 g., 0.9250 Silver 0.8410 oz. ASW, 38.5 mm. **Ruler:** Elizabeth II **Subject:** Prince Andrew's Wedding **Obv:** Crowned bust right **Rev:** Two sets of arms

Date	Mintage	F	VF	XF	Unc	BU
1986	Est. 20,000	—	—	—	15.00	16.00
1986 Proof	Est. 15,000	Value: 18.00				

KM# 174c CROWN
5.1000 g., 0.3740 Gold 0.0613 oz. AGW **Ruler:** Elizabeth II **Subject:** Prince Andrew's Wedding **Obv:** Crowned bust right **Rev:** Two sets of arms

Date	Mintage	F	VF	XF	Unc	BU
1986 Proof	Est. 10,000	Value: 75.00				

KM# 174d CROWN
7.9600 g., 0.9170 Gold 0.2347 oz. AGW **Ruler:** Elizabeth II **Subject:** Prince Andrew's Wedding **Obv:** Crowned bust right **Rev:** Two sets of arms

Date	Mintage	F	VF	XF	Unc	BU
1986 Proof	Est. 1,000	Value: 250				

KM# 174e CROWN
52.0000 g., 0.9500 Platinum 1.5882 oz. APW, 38.5 mm. **Ruler:** Elizabeth II **Subject:** Prince Andrew's Wedding **Obv:** Crowned bust right **Rev:** Two sets of arms

Date	Mintage	F	VF	XF	Unc	BU
1986 Proof	Est. 100	Value: 3,000				

KM# 179a CROWN
28.2800 g., Silver-Clad Copper-Nickel, 38.5 mm. **Ruler:** Elizabeth II **Obv:** Crowned bust right within circle **Rev:** Sailboats and map within circle **Edge:** Reeded

Date	Mintage	F	VF	XF	Unc	BU
1987PM Proof	20,000	Value: 7.00				

KM# 176 CROWN
Copper-Nickel, 38.5 mm. **Ruler:** Elizabeth II **Subject:** United States Constitution **Obv:** Crowned bust right **Rev:** Statue of Liberty divides dates within circle of Presidential busts **Edge:** Reeded

Date	Mintage	F	VF	XF	Unc	BU
1987	—	—	—	—	5.00	6.00

KM# 176a CROWN
31.1000 g., 0.9990 Palladium 0.9988 oz., 38.5 mm. **Ruler:** Elizabeth II **Subject:** United States Constitution Bicentennial **Obv:** Crowned bust right **Rev:** Statue of Liberty divides dates within circle of Presidential busts

Date	Mintage	F	VF	Unc	BU
1987 Proof	Est. 25,000	Value: 475			

KM# 176b CROWN
31.1000 g., 0.9950 Platinum 0.9948 oz. APW, 38.5 mm. **Ruler:** Elizabeth II **Subject:** United States Constitution Bicentennial **Obv:** Crowned bust right **Rev:** Statue of Liberty divides dates within circle of Presidential busts

Date	Mintage	F	VF	XF	Unc	BU
1987 Proof	Est. 1,000	Value: 1,850				

KM# 179 CROWN
Copper-Nickel, 38.5 mm. **Ruler:** Elizabeth II **Series:** Americ'a Cup **Obv:** Crowned bust right within circle **Rev:** Sailboats and map within circle **Edge:** Reeded

Date	Mintage	F	VF	XF	Unc	BU
1987	50,000	—	—	—	10.00	11.50

KM# 179b CROWN
28.2800 g., 0.9250 Silver 0.8410 oz. ASW, 38.5 mm. **Ruler:** Elizabeth II **Series:** America's Cup **Obv:** Crowned bust right within circle **Rev:** Sailboats and map within circle

Date	Mintage	F	VF	XF	Unc	BU
1987	Est. 20,000	—	—	—	26.50	28.50
1987 Proof	Est. 15,000	Value: 40.00				

KM# 179c CROWN
31.1030 g., 0.9990 Palladium 0.9989 oz. **Ruler:** Elizabeth II **Series:** America's Cup **Obv:** Crowned bust right within circle **Rev:** Sailboats and map within circle

Date	Mintage	F	VF	XF	Unc	BU
1987 Proof	1,000	Value: 475				

KM# 183 CROWN
Copper-Nickel, 38.5 mm. **Ruler:** Elizabeth II **Series:** America's Cup **Obv:** Crowned bust right **Rev:** Sailboats and cup **Edge:** Reeded

Date	Mintage	F	VF	XF	Unc	BU
1987	50,000	—	—	—	10.00	11.50

KM# 183b CROWN
28.2800 g., 0.9250 Silver 0.8410 oz. ASW, 38.5 mm. **Ruler:** Elizabeth II **Series:** America's Cup **Obv:** Crowned bust right **Rev:** Sailboats and cup

Date	Mintage	F	VF	XF	Unc	BU
1987	Est. 20,000	—	—	—	26.50	28.50
1987 Proof	Est. 15,000	Value: 40.00				

KM# 183c CROWN
31.1030 g., 0.9990 Palladium 0.9989 oz. **Ruler:** Elizabeth II **Series:** America's Cup **Obv:** Crowned bust right **Rev:** Sailboats and cup

Date	Mintage	F	VF	XF	Unc	BU
1987 Proof	1,000	Value: 475				

KM# 184 CROWN
Copper-Nickel, 38.5 mm. **Ruler:** Elizabeth II **Series:** America's Cup **Obv:** Crowned bust right **Rev:** Statue of Liberty and sailboats **Edge:** Reeded

Date	Mintage	F	VF	XF	Unc	BU
1987	50,000	—	—	—	10.00	11.50

KM# 184b CROWN
28.2800 g., 0.9250 Silver 0.8410 oz. ASW, 38.5 mm. **Ruler:** Elizabeth II **Series:** Americ'a Cup **Obv:** Crowned bust right **Rev:** Statue of Liberty and sailboats

Date	Mintage	F	VF	XF	Unc	BU
1987	Est. 20,000	—	—	—	26.50	28.50
1987 Proof	Est. 15,000	Value: 40.00				

KM# 184c CROWN
31.1030 g., 0.9990 Palladium 0.9989 oz. **Ruler:** Elizabeth II **Series:** America's Cup **Obv:** Crowned bust right **Rev:** Statue of Liberty and sailboats

Date	Mintage	F	VF	XF	Unc	BU
1987 Proof	1,000	Value: 475				

KM# 185 CROWN
Copper-Nickel, 38.5 mm. **Ruler:** Elizabeth II **Series:** America's Cup **Obv:** Crowned bust right **Rev:** Bust of George Steers and sailboat **Edge:** Reeded

Date	Mintage	F	VF	XF	Unc	BU
1987	50,000	—	—	—	10.00	11.50

KM# 185b CROWN
28.2800 g., 0.9250 Silver 0.8410 oz. ASW, 38.5 mm. **Ruler:** Elizabeth II **Series:** America's Cup **Obv:** Crowned bust right **Rev:** Bust of George Steers and sailboat

Date	Mintage	F	VF	XF	Unc	BU
1987	Est. 20,000	—	—	—	26.50	28.50
1987 Proof	Est. 15,000	Value: 40.00				

KM# 185c CROWN
31.1030 g., 0.9990 Palladium 0.9989 oz. **Ruler:** Elizabeth II **Series:** America's Cup **Obv:** Crowned bust right **Rev:** Bust of George Steers and sailboat

Date	Mintage	F	VF	XF	Unc	BU
1987 Proof	1,000	Value: 475				

KM# 186 CROWN
Copper-Nickel, 38.5 mm. **Ruler:** Elizabeth II **Series:** America's Cup **Obv:** Crowned bust right **Rev:** Bust of Sir Thomas Lipton and sailboat **Edge:** Reeded

Date	Mintage	F	VF	XF	Unc	BU
1987	50,000	—	—	—	10.00	11.50

KM# 186b CROWN
28.2800 g., 0.9250 Silver 0.8410 oz. ASW, 38.5 mm. **Ruler:** Elizabeth II **Series:** America's Cup **Obv:** Crowned bust right **Rev:** Bust of Sir Thomas Lipton and sailboat

Date	Mintage	F	VF	XF	Unc	BU
1987	Est. 20,000	—	—	—	26.50	28.50
1987 Proof	Est. 15,000	Value: 40.00				

KM# 186c CROWN
31.1030 g., 0.9990 Palladium 0.9989 oz. **Ruler:** Elizabeth II **Series:** America's Cup **Obv:** Crowned bust right **Rev:** Bust of Sir Thomas Lipton and sailboat

Date	Mintage	F	VF	XF	Unc	BU
1987 Proof	1,000	Value: 475				

KM# 222 CROWN
Copper-Nickel, 38.5 mm. **Ruler:** Elizabeth II **Subject:** Australian Bicentennial **Obv:** Crowned bust right **Rev:** Cockatoo on branch within circle

Date	Mintage	F	VF	XF	Unc	BU
1988	—	—	—	—	10.00	17.50
1988 Proof	500	Value: 30.00				

KM# 222a CROWN
31.1000 g., 0.9990 Silver 0.9988 oz. ASW, 38.5 mm. **Ruler:** Elizabeth II **Subject:** Australian Bicentennial **Obv:** Crowned bust right **Rev:** Cockatoo on branch within circle

Date	Mintage	F	VF	Unc	BU
1988 Proof	—	Value: 175			

KM# 223 CROWN
Copper-Nickel, 38.5 mm. **Ruler:** Elizabeth II **Subject:** Australian Bicentennial **Obv:** Crowned bust right **Rev:** Koala bear in tree within circle

Date	Mintage	F	VF	XF	Unc	BU
1988	—	—	—	—	10.00	17.50
1988 Proof	500	Value: 30.00				

KM# 223a CROWN
31.1000 g., 0.9990 Silver 0.9988 oz. ASW, 38.5 mm. **Ruler:** Elizabeth II **Subject:** Australian Bicentennial **Obv:** Crowned bust right **Rev:** Koala bear in tree within circle

Date	Mintage	F	VF	Unc	BU
1988 Proof	—	Value: 175			

KM# 224 CROWN

Copper-Nickel, 38.5 mm. **Ruler:** Elizabeth II **Subject:** Australian Bicentennial **Obv:** Crowned bust right **Rev:** Duckbill platypus below two men and tent, all within circle

Date	Mintage	F	VF	XF	Unc	BU
1988	—	—	—	—	12.00	17.50
1988 Proof	500	Value: 30.00				

KM# 224a CROWN

31.1000 g., 0.9990 Silver 0.9988 oz. ASW, 38.5 mm. **Ruler:** Elizabeth II **Subject:** Australian Bicentennial **Obv:** Crowned bust right **Rev:** Duckbill platypus below two men and tent all within circle

Date	Mintage	F	VF	XF	Unc	BU
1988 Proof	—	Value: 175				

KM# 225 CROWN

Copper-Nickel, 38.5 mm. **Ruler:** Elizabeth II **Subject:** Australian Bicentennial **Obv:** Crowned bust right **Rev:** Kangaroo within circle

Date	Mintage	F	VF	XF	Unc	BU
1988	—	—	—	—	12.00	17.50
1988 Proof	500	Value: 30.00				

KM# 225a CROWN

31.1000 g., 0.9999 Silver 0.9997 oz. ASW, 38.5 mm. **Ruler:** Elizabeth II **Subject:** Australian Bicentennial **Obv:** Crowned bust right **Rev:** Kangaroo within circle

Date	Mintage	F	VF	XF	Unc	BU
1988 Proof	—	Value: 175				

KM# 226 CROWN

Copper-Nickel, 38.5 mm. **Ruler:** Elizabeth II **Subject:** Australian Bicentennial **Obv:** Crowned bust right **Rev:** Dingo and train within circle

Date	Mintage	F	VF	XF	Unc	BU
1988	—	—	—	—	12.50	17.50

KM# 226a CROWN

31.1000 g., 0.9999 Silver 0.9997 oz. ASW, 38.5 mm. **Ruler:** Elizabeth II **Subject:** Australian Bicentennial **Obv:** Crowned bust right **Rev:** Dingo and train within circle

Date	Mintage	F	VF	XF	Unc	BU
1988 Proof	—	Value: 175				

KM# 227 CROWN

Copper-Nickel, 38.5 mm. **Ruler:** Elizabeth II **Subject:** Australian Bicentennial **Obv:** Crowned bust right **Rev:** Tasmanian devil and map within circle

Date	Mintage	F	VF	XF	Unc	BU
1988	—	—	—	—	12.00	17.50

KM# 227a CROWN

31.1000 g., 0.9999 Silver 0.9997 oz. ASW, 38.5 mm. **Ruler:** Elizabeth II **Subject:** Australian Bicentennial **Obv:** Crowned bust right **Rev:** Tasmanian devil and map within circle

Date	Mintage	F	VF	XF	Unc	BU
1988 Proof	—	Value: 175				

KM# 228 CROWN

Copper-Nickel, 38.5 mm. **Ruler:** Elizabeth II **Series:** Steam Navigation **Obv:** Crowned bust right **Rev:** Patrick Miller's Number One

Date	Mintage	F	VF	XF	Unc	BU
1988	—	—	—	—	8.00	10.00

KM# 229 CROWN

Copper-Nickel, 38.5 mm. **Ruler:** Elizabeth II **Series:** Steam Navigation **Obv:** Crowned bust right **Rev:** Ship within circle

Date	Mintage	F	VF	XF	Unc	BU
1988	—	—	—	—	8.00	10.00

KM# 230 CROWN

Copper-Nickel, 38.5 mm. **Ruler:** Elizabeth II **Series:** Steam Navigation **Obv:** Crowned bust right **Rev:** Steamship within circle

Date	Mintage	F	VF	XF	Unc	BU
1988	—	—	—	—	8.00	10.00

KM# 231 CROWN

Copper-Nickel, 38.5 mm. **Ruler:** Elizabeth II **Series:** Steam Navigation **Obv:** Crowned bust right **Rev:** Steamship within circle

Date	Mintage	F	VF	XF	Unc	BU
1988	—	—	—	—	8.00	10.00

KM# 232 CROWN

Copper-Nickel, 38.5 mm. **Ruler:** Elizabeth II **Series:** Steam Navigation **Obv:** Crowned bust right **Rev:** Steamship within circle

Date	Mintage	F	VF	XF	Unc	BU
1988	—	—	—	—	8.00	10.00

KM# 233 CROWN

Copper-Nickel, 38.5 mm. **Ruler:** Elizabeth II **Series:** Steam Navigation **Obv:** Crowned bust right **Rev:** Steamship divides circle

Date	Mintage	F	VF	XF	Unc	BU
1988	—	—	—	—	8.00	10.00

KM# 245a CROWN

31.1000 g., 0.9990 Silver 0.9988 oz. ASW, 38.5 mm. **Ruler:** Elizabeth II **Obv:** Crowned bust right **Rev:** Manx cat **Note:** Prev. KM#234.

Date	Mintage	F	VF	XF	Unc	BU
1988 Proof	15,000	Value: 20.00				

KM# 245b CROWN
31.1000 g., 0.9990 Gold 0.9988 oz. AGW **Ruler:** Elizabeth II
Obv: Crowned bust right **Rev:** Manx cat **Note:** Prev. KM#239.

Date	Mintage	F	VF	XF	Unc	BU
1988 U	4,300				—	975
1988 Proof	5,000	Value: 985				

KM# 245 CROWN
Copper-Nickel, 38.5 mm. **Ruler:** Elizabeth II **Obv:** Crowned bust
right **Rev:** Manx cat

Date	Mintage	F	VF	XF	Unc	BU
1988					10.00	15.00
1988 Proof	250	Value: 25.00				

KM# 240 CROWN
Copper-Nickel, 38.5 mm. **Ruler:** Elizabeth II
Series: Bicentenary of the Mutiny on the Bounty **Obv:** Crowned
bust right **Rev:** Standing figures facing within circle

Date	Mintage	F	VF	XF	Unc	BU
1989	—	—	—	—	3.25	4.50
1989 Prooflike	—	—	—	—	—	15.00
1989 Proof	—	Value: 18.50				

KM# 240a CROWN
28.2800 g., 0.9250 Silver 0.8410 oz. ASW, 38.5 mm.
Ruler: Elizabeth II **Series:** Mutiny on the Bounty **Obv:** Crowned
bust right **Rev:** Standing figures facing within circle

Date	Mintage	F	VF	XF	Unc	BU
1989 Proof	—	Value: 45.00				

KM# 241 CROWN
Copper-Nickel, 38.5 mm. **Ruler:** Elizabeth II **Series:** Mutiny on
the Bounty **Obv:** Crowned bust right **Rev:** H.M.S. Bounty

Date	Mintage	F	VF	XF	Unc	BU
1989	—	—	—	—	7.50	9.00
1989 Prooflike	—	—	—	—	—	15.00
1989 Proof	—	Value: 18.50				

KM# 241a CROWN
28.2800 g., 0.9250 Silver 0.8410 oz. ASW, 38.5 mm.
Ruler: Elizabeth II **Series:** Mutiny on the Bounty **Obv:** Crowned
bust right **Rev:** H.M.S. Bounty

Date	Mintage	F	VF	XF	Unc	BU
1989 Proof	—	Value: 45.00				

KM# 242 CROWN
Copper-Nickel, 38.5 mm. **Ruler:** Elizabeth II **Series:** Mutiny on
the Bounty **Obv:** Crowned bust right **Rev:** Captain Bligh and crew
set afloat

Date	Mintage	F	VF	XF	Unc	BU
1989	—	—	—	—	7.50	9.00
1989 Prooflike	—	—	—	—	—	15.00
1989 Proof	—	Value: 18.50				

KM# 242a CROWN
28.2800 g., 0.9250 Silver 0.8410 oz. ASW, 38.5 mm.
Ruler: Elizabeth II **Series:** Mutiny on the Bounty **Obv:** Crowned
bust right **Rev:** Captain Bligh and crew set afloat

Date	Mintage	F	VF	XF	Unc	BU
1989 Proof	—	Value: 45.00				

KM# 243 CROWN
Copper-Nickel, 38.5 mm. **Ruler:** Elizabeth II **Series:** Muntiny
on the Bounty **Obv:** Crowned bust right **Rev:** Pitcairn Island

Date	Mintage	F	VF	XF	Unc	BU
1989	—	—	—	—	7.50	9.00
1989 Prooflike	—	—	—	—	—	15.00
1989 Proof	—	Value: 18.50				

KM# 243a CROWN
28.2800 g., 0.9250 Silver 0.8410 oz. ASW, 38.5 mm.
Ruler: Elizabeth II **Series:** Mutiny on the Bounty **Obv:** Crowned
bust right **Rev:** Pitcairn Island

Date	Mintage	F	VF	XF	Unc	BU
1989 Proof	—	Value: 45.00				

KM# 246 CROWN
Copper-Nickel, 38.5 mm. **Ruler:** Elizabeth II **Obv:** Crowned bust
right **Rev:** Washington crossing the Delaware

Date	Mintage	F	VF	XF	Unc	BU
1989	—	—	—	—	2.75	3.50
1989 Proof	—	Value: 9.00				

KM# 246a CROWN
28.2800 g., 0.9250 Silver 0.8410 oz. ASW, 38.5 mm.
Ruler: Elizabeth II **Obv:** Crowned bust right **Rev:** Washington
crossing the Delaware

Date	Mintage	F	VF	XF	Unc	BU
1989 Proof	—	Value: 22.50				

KM# 247 CROWN
Copper-Nickel, 38.5 mm. **Ruler:** Elizabeth II **Subject:** George
Washington Inauguration **Obv:** Crowned bust right **Rev:** Head of
George Washington **Edge:** Reeded

Date	Mintage	F	VF	XF	Unc	BU
1989	—	—	—	—	2.75	3.50
1989 Proof	—	Value: 9.00				

KM# 247a CROWN
28.2800 g., 0.9250 Silver 0.8410 oz. ASW, 38.5 mm.
Ruler: Elizabeth II **Subject:** George Washington Inauguration
Obv: Crowned bust right **Rev:** Head of George Washington

Date	Mintage	F	VF	XF	Unc	BU
1989 Proof	—	Value: 22.50				

KM# 248 CROWN
Copper-Nickel, 38.5 mm. **Ruler:** Elizabeth II **Subject:** George
Washington Inauguration **Obv:** Crowned bust right **Rev:** Cameo
within eagle **Edge:** Reeded

Date	Mintage	F	VF	XF	Unc	BU
1989	—	—	—	—	7.00	8.00
1989 Proof	—	Value: 9.00				

KM# 248a CROWN
28.2800 g., 0.9250 Silver 0.8410 oz. ASW, 38.5 mm.
Ruler: Elizabeth II **Subject:** George Washington Inauguration
Obv: Crowned bust right **Rev:** Cameo within eagle

Date	Mintage	F	VF	XF	Unc	BU
1989 Proof	—	Value: 22.50				

KM# 249 CROWN
Copper-Nickel, 38.5 mm. **Ruler:** Elizabeth II **Subject:** George
Washington Inauguration **Obv:** Crowned bust right **Rev:** George
Washington taking oath **Edge:** Reeded

Date	Mintage	F	VF	XF	Unc	BU
1989	—	—	—	—	5.00	6.00
1989 Proof	—	Value: 9.00				

KM# 249a CROWN
28.2800 g., 0.9250 Silver 0.8410 oz. ASW, 38.5 mm.
Ruler: Elizabeth II **Subject:** George Washington Inauguration
Obv: Crowned bust right **Rev:** George Washington taking oath

Date	Mintage	F	VF	XF	Unc	BU
1989 Proof	—	Value: 22.50				

KM# 250 CROWN
Copper-Nickel, 38.5 mm. **Ruler:** Elizabeth II **Obv:** Crowned bust right **Rev:** Persian cat **Edge:** Reeded

Date	Mintage	F	VF	XF	Unc	BU
1989	—	—	—	—	10.00	14.00
1989 Proof	250	Value: 35.00				

KM# 250a CROWN
31.1000 g., 0.9990 Silver 0.9988 oz. ASW, 38.5 mm.
Ruler: Elizabeth II **Obv:** Crowned bust right **Rev:** Persian cat **Note:** Prev. KM#251.

Date	Mintage	F	VF	XF	Unc	BU
1989 Proof	—	Value: 30.00				

KM# 250b CROWN
31.1000 g., 0.9990 Gold 0.9988 oz. AGW **Ruler:** Elizabeth II **Obv:** Crowned bust right **Rev:** Persian cat **Note:** Prev. KM#256.

Date	Mintage	F	VF	XF	Unc	BU
1989	—	—	—	—	—	975
1989 Proof	—	Value: 985				

KM# 273 CROWN
Copper-Nickel, 38.5 mm. **Ruler:** Elizabeth II **Subject:** Royal Visit **Obv:** Crowned bust right **Rev:** Three scenes from ship **Edge:** Reeded

Date	Mintage	F	VF	XF	Unc	BU
1989	Est. 50,000	—	—	—	8.00	9.00

KM# 273a CROWN
31.1000 g., 0.9990 Silver 0.9988 oz. ASW, 38.5 mm.
Ruler: Elizabeth II **Subject:** Royal Visit **Obv:** Crowned bust right **Rev:** Three scenes from ship

Date	Mintage	F	VF	XF	Unc	BU
1989 Proof	Est. 20,000	Value: 35.00				

KM# 273b CROWN
31.1000 g., 0.9990 Gold 0.9988 oz. AGW **Ruler:** Elizabeth II **Subject:** Royal Visit **Obv:** Crowned bust right **Rev:** Three scenes from ship

Date	Mintage	F	VF	XF	Unc	BU
1989 Proof	Est. 7,500	Value: 985				

KM# 250c CROWN
31.1035 g., 0.9995 Platinum 0.9995 oz. APW **Ruler:** Elizabeth II **Obv:** Crowned bust right **Rev:** Persian cat **Note:** Prev. KM#471.

Date	Mintage	F	VF	XF	Unc	BU
1989	—	—	—	—	—	1,600
1989 Proof	—	Value: 1,850				

KM# 307 CROWN
28.2800 g., Copper-Nickel, 38.6 mm. **Ruler:** Elizabeth II **Obv:** Crowned bust right **Rev:** Adult and two children facing **Edge:** Reeded

Date	Mintage	F	VF	XF	Unc	BU
1990PM	—	—	—	—	10.00	12.00

KM# 307a CROWN
28.2800 g., 0.9250 Silver 0.8410 oz. ASW, 38.6 mm.
Ruler: Elizabeth II **Obv:** Crowned bust right **Rev:** Adult and two children facing

Date	Mintage	F	VF	XF	Unc	BU
1990PM Proof	—	Value: 50.00				

KM# 267 CROWN
Copper-Nickel, 38.5 mm. **Ruler:** Elizabeth II **Subject:** 150th Anniversary of "Penny Black" Stamp **Obv:** Crowned bust right **Rev:** Crowned head left within stamp **Note:** Struck in "pearl black" Copper-Nickel.

Date	Mintage	F	VF	XF	Unc	BU
1990	—	—	—	—	12.50	13.50
1990 Proof	50,000	Value: 16.50				

KM# 267a CROWN
28.2800 g., 0.9250 Silver 0.8410 oz. ASW, 38.5 mm.
Ruler: Elizabeth II **Subject:** 150th Anniversary of "Penny Black" Stamp **Obv:** Crowned bust right **Rev:** Crowned head left within stamp **Edge:** Reeded

Date	Mintage	F	VF	XF	Unc	BU
1990 Proof	30,000	Value: 30.00				

KM# 267b CROWN
31.1000 g., 0.9990 Gold 0.9988 oz. AGW **Ruler:** Elizabeth II **Subject:** 150th Anniversary of "Penny Black" Stamp **Obv:** Crowned bust right **Rev:** Crowned head of Queen Victoria left within stamp

Date	Mintage	F	VF	XF	Unc	BU
1990 Proof	Est. 1,000	Value: 985				

KM# 267c CROWN
52.0000 g., 0.9500 Platinum 1.5882 oz. APW, 38.5 mm. **Ruler:** Elizabeth II **Subject:** 150th Anniversary of "Penny Black" Stamp **Obv:** Crowned bust right **Rev:** Crowned head left within stamp

Date	Mintage	F	VF	XF	Unc	BU
1990 Proof	Est. 50	Value: 3,000				

KM# 269 CROWN
Copper-Nickel, 38.5 mm. **Ruler:** Elizabeth II **Series:** World Cup - Italy **Obv:** Crowned bust right **Rev:** Soccer players and shield **Edge:** Reeded

Date	Mintage	F	VF	XF	Unc	BU
1990	—	—	—	—	3.25	4.50

KM# 269a CROWN
28.2800 g., 0.9250 Silver 0.8410 oz. ASW, 38.5 mm.
Ruler: Elizabeth II **Series:** World Cup - Italy **Obv:** Crowned bust right **Rev:** Soccer players and shield

Date	Mintage	F	VF	XF	Unc	BU
1990 Proof	Est. 30,000	Value: 20.00				

KM# 269b CROWN
6.2200 g., 0.9990 Gold 0.1998 oz. AGW **Ruler:** Elizabeth II **Series:** World Cup - Italy **Obv:** Crowned bust right **Rev:** Soccer players and shield

Date	Mintage	F	VF	XF	Unc	BU
1990 Proof	Est. 500	Value: 200				

KM# 269c CROWN
6.2230 g., 0.9990 Platinum 0.1999 oz. APW **Ruler:** Elizabeth II **Series:** World Cup - Italy **Obv:** Crowned bust right **Rev:** Soccer players and shield

Date	Mintage	F	VF	XF	Unc	BU
1990 Proof	Est. 100	Value: 375				

KM# 270 CROWN
Copper-Nickel, 38.5 mm. **Ruler:** Elizabeth II **Series:** World Cup - Italy **Obv:** Crowned bust right **Rev:** Soccer player in center of three shields

Date	Mintage	F	VF	XF	Unc	BU
1990	—	—	—	—	6.00	7.00

KM# 270a CROWN
28.2800 g., 0.9250 Silver 0.8410 oz. ASW, 38.5 mm.
Ruler: Elizabeth II **Series:** World Cup - Italy **Obv:** Crowned bust right **Rev:** Soccer player in center of three shields

Date	Mintage	F	VF	XF	Unc	BU
1990 Proof	Est. 30,000	Value: 20.00				

KM# 270b CROWN
6.2200 g., 0.9990 Gold 0.1998 oz. AGW **Ruler:** Elizabeth II **Series:** World Cup - Italy **Obv:** Crowned bust right **Rev:** Soccer player in center of three shields

Date	Mintage	F	VF	XF	Unc	BU
1990 Proof	Est. 500	Value: 200				

KM# 270c CROWN
6.2230 g., 0.9990 Platinum 0.1999 oz. APW **Ruler:** Elizabeth II **Series:** World Cup - Italy **Obv:** Crowned bust right **Rev:** Soccer player in center of three shields

Date	Mintage	F	VF	XF	Unc	BU
1990 Proof	Est. 100	Value: 375				

KM# 271 CROWN
Copper-Nickel, 38.5 mm. **Ruler:** Elizabeth II **Series:** World Cup - Italy **Obv:** Crowned bust right **Rev:** Three shields flanked by emblems with soccer ball below **Edge:** Reeded

Date	Mintage	F	VF	XF	Unc	BU
1990	—	—	—	—	6.00	7.00

KM# 271a CROWN
28.2800 g., 0.9250 Silver 0.8410 oz. ASW, 38.5 mm.
Ruler: Elizabeth II **Series:** World Cup - Italy **Obv:** Crowned bust right **Rev:** Three shields flanked by emblems with soccer ball below

Date	Mintage	F	VF	XF	Unc	BU
1990 Proof	Est. 30,000	Value: 30.00				

KM# 271b CROWN
6.2200 g., 0.9990 Gold 0.1998 oz. AGW **Ruler:** Elizabeth II **Series:** World Cup - Italy **Obv:** Crowned bust right **Rev:** Three shields flanked by emblems with soccer ball below

Date	Mintage	F	VF	XF	Unc	BU
1990 Proof	Est. 500	Value: 200				

KM# 271c CROWN
6.2230 g., 0.9990 Platinum 0.1999 oz. APW **Ruler:** Elizabeth II **Series:** World Cup - Italy **Obv:** Crowned bust right **Rev:** Three shields flanked by emblems with soccer ball below

Date	Mintage	F	VF	XF	Unc	BU
1990 Proof	Est. 100	Value: 375				

KM# 272 CROWN
Copper-Nickel, 38.5 mm. **Ruler:** Elizabeth II **Series:** World Cup - Italy **Obv:** Crowned bust right **Rev:** Three shields flanked by soccer players **Edge:** Reeded

Date	Mintage	F	VF	XF	Unc	BU
1990	—	—	—	—	6.00	7.00

KM# 272a CROWN
28.2800 g., 0.9250 Silver 0.8410 oz. ASW, 38.5 mm.
Ruler: Elizabeth II **Series:** World Cup - Italy **Obv:** Crowned bust right **Rev:** Three shields flanked by soccer players

Date	Mintage	F	VF	XF	Unc	BU
1990 Proof	Est. 30,000	Value: 20.00				

KM# 272b CROWN
6.2200 g., 0.9990 Gold 0.1998 oz. AGW **Ruler:** Elizabeth II
Series: World Cup - Italy **Obv:** Crowned bust right **Rev:** Three
shields flanked by soccer players

Date	Mintage	F	VF	XF	Unc	BU
1990 Proof	Est. 500	Value: 200				

KM# 272c CROWN
6.2230 g., 0.9990 Platinum 0.1999 oz. APW **Ruler:** Elizabeth II
Series: World Cup - Italy **Obv:** Crowned bust right **Rev:** Three
shields flanked by soccer players

Date	Mintage	F	VF	XF	Unc	BU
1990 Proof	Est. 100	Value: 375				

KM# 275 CROWN
Copper-Nickel, 38.5 mm. **Ruler:** Elizabeth II **Obv:** Crowned bust
right **Rev:** Alley cat

Date	Mintage	F	VF	XF	Unc	BU
1990	—	—	—	—	10.00	15.00
1990 Proof	250	Value: 35.00				

KM# 275a CROWN
31.1000 g., 0.9990 Silver 0.9988 oz. ASW, 38.5 mm.
Ruler: Elizabeth II **Obv:** Crowned bust right **Rev:** Alley cat
Note: Prev. KM#276.

Date	Mintage	F	VF	XF	Unc	BU
1990 Proof	—	Value: 32.50				

KM# 275b CROWN
31.1000 g., 0.9990 Gold 0.9988 oz. AGW **Ruler:** Elizabeth II
Obv: Crowned bust right **Rev:** Alley cat **Note:** Prev. KM#281.

Date	Mintage	F	VF	XF	Unc	BU
1990	—	—	—	—	—	975
1990 Proof	—	Value: 985				

KM# 283 CROWN
Copper-Nickel, 38.5 mm. **Ruler:** Elizabeth II **Obv:** Crowned bust
right **Rev:** Winston Churchill right with hat and cigar **Edge:** Reeded

Date	Mintage	F	VF	XF	Unc	BU
1990	—	—	—	—	3.25	4.50

KM# 283a CROWN
28.2800 g., 0.9250 Silver 0.8410 oz. ASW, 38.5 mm.
Ruler: Elizabeth II **Obv:** Crowned bust right **Rev:** Winston
Churchill right with hat and cigar

Date	Mintage	F	VF	XF	Unc	BU
1990 Proof	Est. 25,000	Value: 50.00				

KM# 283b CROWN
6.2230 g., 0.9990 Gold 0.1999 oz. AGW **Ruler:** Elizabeth II
Obv: Crowned bust right **Rev:** Winston Churchill right with hat and
cigar

Date	Mintage	F	VF	XF	Unc	BU
1990 Proof	Est. 500	Value: 200				

KM# 283c CROWN
6.2230 g., 0.9990 Platinum 0.1999 oz. APW **Ruler:** Elizabeth II
Obv: Crowned bust right **Rev:** Winston Churchill right with hat
and cigar

Date	Mintage	F	VF	XF	Unc	BU
1990 Proof	Est. 100	Value: 375				

KM# 284 CROWN
Copper-Nickel, 38.5 mm. **Ruler:** Elizabeth II **Obv:** Crowned bust
right **Rev:** Winston Churchill left **Edge:** Reeded

Date	Mintage	F	VF	XF	Unc	BU
1990	—	—	—	—	3.25	4.50

KM# 284a CROWN
28.2800 g., 0.9250 Silver 0.8410 oz. ASW, 38.5 mm.
Ruler: Elizabeth II **Obv:** Crowned bust right **Rev:** Winston
Churchill left

Date	Mintage	F	VF	XF	Unc	BU
1990 Proof	Est. 25,000	Value: 50.00				

KM# 284b CROWN
6.2230 g., 0.9990 Gold 0.1999 oz. AGW **Ruler:** Elizabeth II
Obv: Crowned bust right **Rev:** Winston Churchill left

Date	Mintage	F	VF	XF	Unc	BU
1990 Proof	Est. 500	Value: 200				

KM# 284c CROWN
6.2230 g., 0.9990 Platinum 0.1999 oz. APW **Ruler:** Elizabeth II
Obv: Crowned bust right **Rev:** Winston Churchill left

Date	Mintage	F	VF	XF	Unc	BU
1990 Proof	Est. 100	Value: 375				

KM# 320 CROWN
28.2800 g., Copper-Nickel, 38.6 mm. **Ruler:** Elizabeth II
Subject: America's Cup **Obv:** Crowned bust right **Rev:** Cameo
of sailboats with no roman numerals in legend **Edge:** Reeded
Note: Officially "sales samples" about 25 pieces were sold or
presented to distributors

Date	Mintage	F	VF	XF	Unc	BU
1991PM	100	—	—	—	35.00	40.00

KM# 320a CROWN
28.2800 g., 0.9250 Silver 0.8410 oz. ASW, 38.6 mm.
Ruler: Elizabeth II **Subject:** America's Cup - San Diego
Obv: Crowned bust right **Rev:** Cameo of sailboats
Rev. Leg.: AMERICA'S CUP CHALLENGE

Date	Mintage	F	VF	XF	Unc	BU
1991 Proof	15	Value: 485				

KM# 291 CROWN
Copper-Nickel, 38.5 mm. **Ruler:** Elizabeth II **Subject:** 100th
Anniversary - American Numismatic Association **Obv:** Crowned
bust right **Rev:** Cat within circle of assorted coins **Edge:** Reeded

Date	Mintage	F	VF	XF	Unc	BU
1991	—	—	—	—	4.50	6.50

KM# 291a CROWN
28.2800 g., 0.9250 Silver 0.8410 oz. ASW, 38.5 mm.
Ruler: Elizabeth II **Subject:** 100th Anniversary - American
Numismatic Association **Obv:** Crowned bust right **Rev:** Cat within
circle of assorted coins

Date	Mintage	F	VF	XF	Unc	BU
1991 Proof	—	Value: 25.00				

KM# 292 CROWN
Copper-Nickel, 38.5 mm. **Ruler:** Elizabeth II **Obv:** Crowned bust
right **Rev:** Norwegian cat **Edge:** Reeded

Date	Mintage	F	VF	XF	Unc	BU
1991	—	—	—	—	10.00	15.00
1991 Proof	25					

KM# 292a CROWN
31.1000 g., 0.9990 Silver 0.9988 oz. ASW, 38.5 mm.
Ruler: Elizabeth II **Obv:** Crowned bust right **Rev:** Norwegian cat
Note: Prev. KM#293.

Date	Mintage	F	VF	XF	Unc	BU
1991 Proof	50,000	Value: 35.00				

KM# 292b CROWN
31.1000 g., 0.9990 Gold 0.9988 oz. AGW **Ruler:** Elizabeth II
Obv: Crowned bust right **Rev:** Norwegian cat **Note:** Prev. KM#298.

Date	Mintage	F	VF	XF	Unc	BU
1991	—	—	—	—	—	975
1991 Proof	—	Value: 985				

KM# 304 CROWN
Copper-Nickel, 38.5 mm. **Ruler:** Elizabeth II **Subject:** 10th
Wedding Anniversary **Obv:** Crowned bust right **Rev:** Head of
Prince Charles

Date	Mintage	F	VF	XF	Unc	BU
1991	—	—	—	—	4.00	6.00

KM# 304a CROWN
28.2800 g., 0.9250 Silver 0.8410 oz. ASW, 38.5 mm.
Ruler: Elizabeth II **Subject:** 10th Wedding Anniversary
Obv: Crowned bust right **Rev:** Head of Prince Charles

Date	Mintage	F	VF	XF	Unc	BU
1991 Proof	—	Value: 40.00				

KM# 304b CROWN
6.2200 g., 0.9990 Gold 0.1998 oz. AGW **Ruler:** Elizabeth II
Subject: 10th Wedding Anniversary **Obv:** Crowned bust right
Rev: Head of Prince Charles

Date	Mintage	F	VF	XF	Unc	BU
1991 Proof	—	Value: 200				

KM# 305 CROWN
Copper-Nickel, 38.5 mm. **Ruler:** Elizabeth II **Subject:** 10th
Wedding Anniversary **Obv:** Crowned bust right **Rev:** Head of
Princess Diana

Date	Mintage	F	VF	XF	Unc	BU
1991	—	—	—	—	4.00	6.00

KM# 305a CROWN
28.2800 g., 0.9250 Silver 0.8410 oz. ASW, 38.5 mm.
Ruler: Elizabeth II **Subject:** 10th Wedding Anniversary
Obv: Crowned bust right **Rev:** Head of Princess Diana

Date	Mintage	F	VF	XF	Unc	BU
1991 Proof	—	Value: 40.00				

KM# 305b CROWN
6.2200 g., 0.9990 Gold 0.1998 oz. AGW **Ruler:** Elizabeth II
Subject: 10th Wedding Anniversary **Obv:** Crowned bust right
Rev: Head of Princess Diana

Date	Mintage	F	VF	XF	Unc	BU
1991 Proof	—	Value: 200				

KM# 326a CROWN
28.2800 g., 0.9250 Silver 0.8410 oz. ASW, 38.5 mm.
Ruler: Elizabeth II **Subject:** America's Cup - San Diego
Obv: Crowned bust right **Rev:** Cameo above sailboats

Date	Mintage	F	VF	XF	Unc	BU
1992 Proof	25,000	—	—	—	60.00	65.00

KM# 310 CROWN
Copper-Nickel, 38.5 mm. **Ruler:** Elizabeth II **Series:** Discovery
of America **Obv:** Crowned bust right **Rev:** Head with hat facing
and train engine within circle

Date	Mintage	F	VF	XF	Unc	BU
1992	—	—	—	—	3.75	4.50
1992 Proof	—	Value: 12.00				

KM# 311 CROWN
Copper-Nickel, 38.5 mm. **Ruler:** Elizabeth II **Series:** Discovery of America **Obv:** Crowned bust right **Rev:** Head facing and train engine within circle

Date	Mintage	F	VF	XF	Unc	BU
1992	—		—	—	3.75	4.50
1992 Proof	—	Value: 12.00				

KM# 311a CROWN
28.2800 g., 0.9250 Silver 0.8410 oz. ASW, 38.5 mm.
Ruler: Elizabeth II **Series:** Discovery of America **Obv:** Crowned bust right **Rev:** Head facing and train engine within circle

Date	Mintage	F	VF	XF	Unc	BU
1992 Proof	—	Value: 45.00				

KM# 310a CROWN
28.2800 g., 0.9250 Silver 0.8410 oz. ASW, 38.5 mm.
Ruler: Elizabeth II **Series:** Discovery of America **Obv:** Crowned bust right **Rev:** Head with hat facing and train engine within circle

Date	Mintage	F	VF	XF	Unc	BU
1992 Proof	—	Value: 45.00				

KM# 313 CROWN
Copper-Nickel, 38.5 mm. **Ruler:** Elizabeth II **Series:** Discovery of America **Obv:** Crowned bust right **Rev:** Triskeles on shield above crossed flags within circle

Date	Mintage	F	VF	XF	Unc	BU
1992	—		—	—	8.00	9.00
1992 Proof	—	Value: 10.00				

KM# 313a CROWN
28.2800 g., 0.9250 Silver 0.8410 oz. ASW, 38.5 mm.
Ruler: Elizabeth II **Series:** Discovery of America **Obv:** Bust of Queen Elizabeth II right **Rev:** Triskeles on shield above crossed flags within circle

Date	Mintage	F	VF	XF	Unc	BU
1992 Proof	—	Value: 25.00				

KM# 332b CROWN
31.1000 g., 0.9990 Gold 0.9988 oz. AGW **Ruler:** Elizabeth II **Obv:** Crowned bust right **Rev:** Seated Siamese cat **Note:** Prev. KM#334.

Date	Mintage	F	VF	XF	Unc	BU
1992	—	—	—	—	—	975
1992 Proof	—	Value: 985				

KM# 326b CROWN
31.0300 g., 0.9990 Gold 0.9966 oz. AGW **Ruler:** Elizabeth II **Subject:** America's Cup - San Diego **Obv:** Crowned bust right **Rev:** Cameo above sailboats

Date	Mintage	F	VF	XF	Unc	BU
1992 Proof	—	Value: 985				

KM# 353 CROWN
Copper-Nickel, 38.5 mm. **Ruler:** Elizabeth II **Obv:** Crowned bust right **Rev:** Maine coon cat

Date	Mintage	F	VF	XF	Unc	BU
1993	—		—	—	10.00	15.00

KM# 353a CROWN
31.1000 g., 0.9990 Silver 0.9988 oz. ASW, 38.5 mm.
Ruler: Elizabeth II **Obv:** Crowned bust right **Rev:** Maine coon cat **Note:** Prev. KM#354.

Date	Mintage	F	VF	XF	Unc	BU
1993 Proof	50,000	Value: 35.00				

KM# 353b CROWN
31.1000 g., 0.9990 Gold 0.9988 oz. AGW **Ruler:** Elizabeth II **Obv:** Crowned bust right **Rev:** Maine coon cat **Note:** Prev. KM#355.

Date	Mintage	F	VF	XF	Unc	BU
1993	—	—	—	—	—	975
1993 Proof	—	Value: 985				

KM# 357 CROWN
Copper-Nickel, 38.5 mm. **Ruler:** Elizabeth II **Series:** Preserve Planet Earth **Obv:** Crowned bust right **Rev:** Dinosaur

Date	Mintage	F	VF	XF	Unc	BU
1993	—		—	—	10.00	14.00

KM# 312 CROWN
Copper-Nickel, 38.5 mm. **Ruler:** Elizabeth II **Series:** Discovery of America **Obv:** Crowned bust right **Rev:** Group of standing figures within circle

Date	Mintage	F	VF	XF	Unc	BU
1992 Proof	—	Value: 10.00				
1992	—		—	—	3.75	4.50

KM# 312a CROWN
28.2800 g., 0.9250 Silver 0.8410 oz. ASW, 38.5 mm.
Ruler: Elizabeth II **Series:** Discovery of America **Obv:** Crowned bust right **Rev:** Group of standing figures within circle

Date	Mintage	F	VF	XF	Unc	BU
1992 Proof	—	Value: 45.00				

KM# 332 CROWN
Copper-Nickel, 38.5 mm. **Ruler:** Elizabeth II **Obv:** Crowned bust right **Rev:** Seated Siamese cat

Date	Mintage	F	VF	XF	Unc	BU
1992	—	—	—	—	10.00	15.00

KM# 332a CROWN
31.1000 g., 0.9990 Silver 0.9988 oz. ASW, 38.5 mm.
Ruler: Elizabeth II **Obv:** Crowned bust right **Rev:** Seated Siamese cat **Note:** Prev. KM#333.

Date	Mintage	F	VF	XF	Unc	BU
1992 Proof	50,000	Value: 30.00				

KM# 357a CROWN
Silver, 38.5 mm. **Ruler:** Elizabeth II **Series:** Preserve Planet Earth **Obv:** Crowned bust right **Rev:** Dinosaur

Date	Mintage	F	VF	XF	Unc	BU
1993	—	—	—	—	—	—

KM# 358 CROWN
Copper-Nickel, 38.5 mm. **Ruler:** Elizabeth II **Series:** Preserve Planet Earth **Obv:** Crowned bust right **Rev:** Diplodocus

Date	Mintage	F	VF	XF	Unc	BU
1993	—		—	—	9.00	14.00

KM# 326 CROWN
Copper-Nickel, 38.5 mm. **Ruler:** Elizabeth II **Subject:** America's Cup - San Diego **Obv:** Crowned bust right **Rev. Leg.:** AMERICA'S CUP • SAN DIEGO • 1992

Date	Mintage	F	VF	XF	Unc	BU
1992	—		—	—	4.75	6.00
1992 Proof	—	Value: 12.50				

KM# 342 CROWN
31.1000 g., 0.9990 Gold 0.9988 oz. AGW **Ruler:** Elizabeth II **Subject:** Year of the Cockerel **Obv:** Crowned bust right **Rev:** Cockerel within circle

Date	Mintage	F	VF	XF	Unc	BU
1993 Proof	Est. 2,500	Value: 985				

KM# 364 CROWN
Copper-Nickel, 38.5 mm. **Ruler:** Elizabeth II **Series:** World Cup Soccer - U.S.A. **Obv:** Crowned bust right **Rev:** Two players

Date	Mintage	F	VF	XF	Unc	BU
1994	—	—	—	—	6.00	7.00

KM# 364a CROWN
28.2800 g., 0.9250 Silver 0.8410 oz. ASW, 38.5 mm. **Ruler:** Elizabeth II **Series:** World Cup Soccer - U.S.A. **Obv:** Crowned bust right **Rev:** Two players

Date	Mintage	F	VF	XF	Unc	BU
1994 Proof	Est. 30,000	Value: 35.00				

KM# 370 CROWN
Copper-Nickel, 38.5 mm. **Ruler:** Elizabeth II **Series:** World Cup Soccer - U.S.A. **Obv:** Crowned bust right **Rev:** Soccer players

Date	Mintage	F	VF	XF	Unc	BU
1994	—	—	—	—	6.00	7.00

KM# 370a CROWN
28.2800 g., 0.9250 Silver 0.8410 oz. ASW, 38.5 mm. **Ruler:** Elizabeth II **Series:** World Cup Soccer - U.S.A. **Obv:** Crowned bust right **Rev:** Soccer players

Date	Mintage	F	VF	XF	Unc	BU
1994 Proof	Est. 30,000	Value: 35.00				

KM# 380b CROWN
31.1000 g., 0.9990 Gold 0.9988 oz. AGW **Ruler:** Elizabeth II **Obv:** Crowned bust right **Rev:** Japanese bobtail cat **Note:** Prev. KM#382.

Date	Mintage	F	VF	XF	Unc	BU
1994	—	—	—	—	—	975
1994 Proof	—	Value: 985				

KM# 380c CROWN
31.1035 g., 0.9995 Platinum 0.9995 oz. APW **Ruler:** Elizabeth II **Obv:** Crowned bust right **Rev:** Japanese bobtail cat **Note:** Prev. KM#477.

Date	Mintage	F	VF	XF	Unc	BU
1994	—	—	—	—BV+20%	—	
1994 Proof	—	BV_25%				

KM# 384 CROWN
Copper-Nickel, 38.5 mm. **Ruler:** Elizabeth II **Series:** Preserve Planet Earth **Obv:** Crowned bust right **Rev:** Woolly mammoth

Date	Mintage	F	VF	XF	Unc	BU
1994	—	—	—	—	10.00	17.50

KM# 384a CROWN
28.2800 g., 0.9250 Silver 0.8410 oz. ASW, 38.5 mm. **Ruler:** Elizabeth II **Series:** Preserve Planet Earth **Obv:** Crowned bust right **Rev:** Woolly mammoth

Date	Mintage	F	VF	XF	Unc	BU
1994 Proof	Est. 30,000	Value: 35.00				

KM# 366 CROWN
Copper-Nickel, 38.5 mm. **Ruler:** Elizabeth II **Series:** World Cup Soccer - U.S.A. **Obv:** Crowned bust right **Rev:** Three players

Date	Mintage	F	VF	XF	Unc	BU
1994	—	—	—	—	6.00	7.00

KM# 366a CROWN
28.2800 g., 0.9250 Silver 0.8410 oz. ASW, 38.5 mm. **Ruler:** Elizabeth II **Series:** World Cup Soccer - U.S.A. **Obv:** Crowned bust right **Rev:** Three players

Date	Mintage	F	VF	XF	Unc	BU
1994 Proof	Est. 30,000	Value: 35.00				

KM# 372 CROWN
Copper-Nickel, 38.5 mm. **Ruler:** Elizabeth II **Series:** World Cup Soccer - U.S.A. **Obv:** Crowned bust right **Rev:** Soccer players

Date	Mintage	F	VF	XF	Unc	BU
1994	—	—	—	—	8.00	9.00

KM# 372a CROWN
28.2800 g., 0.9250 Silver 0.8410 oz. ASW, 38.5 mm. **Ruler:** Elizabeth II **Series:** World Cup Soccer - U.S.A. **Obv:** Crowned bust right **Rev:** Soccer players

Date	Mintage	F	VF	XF	Unc	BU
1994 Proof	Est. 30,000	Value: 35.00				

KM# 385 CROWN
Copper-Nickel, 38.5 mm. **Ruler:** Elizabeth II **Series:** Preserve Planet Earth **Obv:** Crowned bust right **Rev:** Kangaroos

Date	Mintage	F	VF	XF	Unc	BU
1994	—	—	—	—	9.00	14.00

KM# 385a CROWN
28.2800 g., 0.9250 Silver 0.8410 oz. ASW, 38.5 mm. **Ruler:** Elizabeth II **Series:** Preserve Planet Earth **Obv:** Crowned bust right **Rev:** Kangaroos

Date	Mintage	F	VF	XF	Unc	BU
1994 Proof	Est. 30,000	Value: 35.00				

KM# 368 CROWN
Copper-Nickel, 38.5 mm. **Ruler:** Elizabeth II **Series:** World Cup Soccer - U.S.A. **Obv:** Crowned bust right **Rev:** Soccer players

Date	Mintage	F	VF	XF	Unc	BU
1994	—	—	—	—	6.00	7.00

KM# 368a CROWN
28.2800 g., 0.9250 Silver 0.8410 oz. ASW, 38.5 mm. **Ruler:** Elizabeth II **Series:** World Cup Soccer - U.S.A. **Obv:** Crowned bust right **Rev:** Soccer players

Date	Mintage	F	VF	XF	Unc	BU
1994 Proof	Est. 30,000	Value: 35.00				

KM# 374 CROWN
Copper-Nickel, 38.5 mm. **Ruler:** Elizabeth II **Series:** World Cup Soccer - U.S.A. **Obv:** Crowned bust right **Rev:** Soccer players

Date	Mintage	F	VF	XF	Unc	BU
1994	—	—	—	—	6.00	7.00

KM# 374a CROWN
28.2800 g., 0.9250 Silver 0.8410 oz. ASW, 38.5 mm. **Ruler:** Elizabeth II **Series:** World Cup Soccer - U.S.A. **Obv:** Crowned bust right **Rev:** Soccer players

Date	Mintage	F	VF	XF	Unc	BU
1994 Proof	Est. 30,000	Value: 35.00				

KM# 380 CROWN
Copper-Nickel, 38.5 mm. **Ruler:** Elizabeth II **Obv:** Crowned bust right **Rev:** Japanese bobtail cat.

Date	Mintage	F	VF	XF	Unc	BU
1994	—	—	—	—	11.00	15.00

KM# 380a CROWN
31.1000 g., 0.9990 Silver 0.9988 oz. ASW, 38.5 mm. **Ruler:** Elizabeth II **Obv:** Crowned bust right **Rev:** Japanese bobtail cat **Note:** Prev. KM#381.

Date	Mintage	F	VF	XF	Unc	BU
1994 Proof	—	Value: 35.00				

KM# 386 CROWN
Copper-Nickel, 38.5 mm. **Ruler:** Elizabeth II **Series:** Preserve Planet Earth **Obv:** Crowned bust right **Rev:** Seals

Date	Mintage	F	VF	XF	Unc	BU
1994	—	—	—	—	9.00	14.00

KM# 386a CROWN
28.2800 g., 0.9250 Silver 0.8410 oz. ASW, 38.5 mm.
Ruler: Elizabeth II **Series:** Preserve Planet Earth **Obv:** Crowned bust right **Rev:** Seals

Date	Mintage	F	VF	XF	Unc	BU
1994 Proof	Est. 30,000	Value: 35.00				

KM# 387 CROWN
Copper-Nickel, 38.5 mm. **Ruler:** Elizabeth II **Series:** Preserve Planet Earth **Obv:** Crowned bust right **Rev:** Deer

Date	Mintage	F	VF	XF	Unc	BU
1994	—	—	—	—	9.00	14.00

KM# 387a CROWN
28.2800 g., 0.9250 Silver 0.8410 oz. ASW, 38.5 mm.
Ruler: Elizabeth II **Series:** Preserve Planet Earth **Obv:** Crowned bust right **Rev:** Deer

Date	Mintage	F	VF	XF	Unc	BU
1994 Proof	Est. 30,000	Value: 35.00				

KM# 406 CROWN
Copper-Nickel, 38.5 mm. **Ruler:** Elizabeth II **Subject:** Year of the Dog **Obv:** Crowned bust right **Rev:** Pekingese within circle

Date	Mintage	F	VF	XF	Unc	BU
1994	—	—	—	—	10.00	16.00

KM# 407 CROWN
31.1000 g., 0.9990 Silver 0.9988 oz. ASW, 38.5 mm.
Ruler: Elizabeth II **Subject:** Year of the Dog **Obv:** Crowned bust right **Rev:** Pekingese within circle

Date	Mintage	F	VF	XF	Unc	BU
1994 Proof	—	Value: 40.00				

KM# 408 CROWN
31.1000 g., 0.9990 Gold 0.9988 oz. AGW. **Ruler:** Elizabeth II **Subject:** Year of the Dog **Obv:** Crowned bust right **Rev:** Pekingese within circle

Date	Mintage	F	VF	XF	Unc	BU
1994 Proof	Est. 5,000	Value: 985				

KM# 417 CROWN
Copper-Nickel, 38.5 mm. **Ruler:** Elizabeth II **Series:** Man in Flight **Obv:** Crowned bust right **Rev:** Otto Lilienthal

Date	Mintage	F	VF	XF	Unc	BU
1994	—	—	—	—	7.00	8.00

KM# 417a CROWN
28.2800 g., 0.9250 Silver 0.8410 oz. ASW, 38.5 mm.
Ruler: Elizabeth II **Series:** Man in Flight **Obv:** Crowned bust right **Rev:** Otto Lilienthal

Date	Mintage	F	VF	XF	Unc	BU
1994 Proof	Est. 30,000	Value: 40.00				

KM# 418 CROWN
Copper-Nickel, 38.5 mm. **Ruler:** Elizabeth II **Series:** Man in Flight **Obv:** Crowned bust right **Rev:** Ferdinand von Zeppelin

Date	Mintage	F	VF	XF	Unc	BU
1994	—	—	—	—	11.00	13.50

KM# 419 CROWN
Copper-Nickel, 38.5 mm. **Ruler:** Elizabeth II **Series:** Man in Flight **Obv:** Crowned bust right **Rev:** Louis Bleriot

Date	Mintage	F	VF	XF	Unc	BU
1994	—	—	—	—	8.00	9.00

KM# 419a CROWN
28.2800 g., 0.9250 Silver 0.8410 oz. ASW, 38.5 mm.
Ruler: Elizabeth II **Series:** Man in Flight **Subject:** First Channel Crossing - 1909 **Obv:** Crowned bust right **Rev:** Louis Bleriot

Date	Mintage	F	VF	XF	Unc	BU
1994 Proof	Est. 30,000	Value: 40.00				

KM# 420 CROWN
Copper-Nickel, 38.5 mm. **Ruler:** Elizabeth II **Series:** Man in Flight **Subject:** First Atlantic Crossing - 1919 **Obv:** Crowned bust right **Rev:** Alcock and Brown

Date	Mintage	F	VF	XF	Unc	BU
1994	—	—	—	—	10.00	12.00

KM# 420a CROWN
28.2800 g., 0.9250 Silver 0.8410 oz. ASW, 38.5 mm.
Ruler: Elizabeth II **Series:** Man in Flight **Subject:** First Atlantic Crossing - 1919 **Obv:** Crowned bust right **Rev:** Alcock and Brown

Date	Mintage	F	VF	XF	Unc	BU
1994 Proof	Est. 30,000	Value: 40.00				

KM# 421 CROWN
Copper-Nickel, 38.5 mm. **Ruler:** Elizabeth II **Series:** Man in Flight **Subject:** First England to Australia flight **Obv:** Crowned bust right **Rev:** Biplane

Date	Mintage	F	VF	XF	Unc	BU
1994	—	—	—	—	8.00	9.50

KM# 421a CROWN
28.2800 g., 0.9250 Silver 0.8410 oz. ASW, 38.5 mm.
Ruler: Elizabeth II **Series:** Man in Flight **Subject:** First England to Australia flight **Obv:** Crowned bust right **Rev:** Biplane

Date	Mintage	F	VF	XF	Unc	BU
1994 Proof	Est. 30,000	Value: 40.00				

KM# 422 CROWN
Copper-Nickel, 38.5 mm. **Ruler:** Elizabeth II **Series:** Man in Flight **Subject:** 60th Anniversary of Airmail **Obv:** Crowned bust right **Rev:** Airplane

Date	Mintage	F	VF	XF	Unc	BU
1994	—	—	—	—	8.00	9.50

KM# 422a CROWN
28.2800 g., 0.9250 Silver 0.8410 oz. ASW, 38.5 mm.
Ruler: Elizabeth II **Series:** Man in Flight **Subject:** 60th Anniversary of Airmail **Obv:** Crowned bust right **Rev:** Airplane

Date	Mintage	F	VF	XF	Unc	BU
1994 Proof	Est. 30,000	Value: 40.00				

KM# 423 CROWN
Copper-Nickel, 38.5 mm. **Ruler:** Elizabeth II **Series:** Man in Flight **Subject:** 50th Anniversary of International Civil Aviation Organization **Obv:** Crowned bust right **Rev:** Emblem

Date	Mintage	F	VF	XF	Unc	BU
1994	—	—	—	—	8.00	9.50

KM# 423a CROWN
28.2800 g., 0.9250 Silver 0.8410 oz. ASW, 38.5 mm.
Ruler: Elizabeth II **Series:** Man in Flight **Subject:** 50th Anniversary of International Civil Aviation Organization **Obv:** Crowned bust right **Rev:** Emblem

Date	Mintage	F	VF	XF	Unc	BU
1994 Proof	Est. 30,000	Value: 40.00				

KM# 424 CROWN
Copper-Nickel, 38.5 mm. **Ruler:** Elizabeth II **Series:** Man in Flight **Subject:** 25th Anniversary of First Concorde Flight **Obv:** Crowned bust right **Rev:** Concorde

Date	Mintage	F	VF	XF	Unc	BU
1994	—	—	—	—	8.00	9.50

KM# 424a CROWN
28.2800 g., 0.9250 Silver 0.8410 oz. ASW, 38.5 mm.
Ruler: Elizabeth II **Series:** Man in Flight **Subject:** 25th Anniversary of First Concorde Flight **Obv:** Crowned bust right **Rev:** Concorde

Date	Mintage	F	VF	XF	Unc	BU
1994 Proof	Est. 30,000	Value: 40.00				

KM# 697 CROWN
Copper-Nickel, 38.5 mm. **Ruler:** Elizabeth II **Series:** Normandy Invasion **Obv:** Crowned bust right **Rev:** American soldier behind rock

Date	Mintage	F	VF	XF	Unc	BU
1994	—	—	—	—	6.50	7.50

KM# 697a CROWN
28.2800 g., 0.9250 Silver 0.8410 oz. ASW, 38.5 mm.
Ruler: Elizabeth II **Series:** Normandy Invasion **Obv:** Crowned bust right **Rev:** American soldier behind rock

Date	Mintage	F	VF	XF	Unc	BU
1994 Proof	Est. 30,000	Value: 26.50				

KM# 700 CROWN
Copper-Nickel, 38.5 mm. **Ruler:** Elizabeth II **Series:** Normandy Invasion **Obv:** Crowned bust right **Rev:** General Eisenhower left

Date	Mintage	F	VF	XF	Unc	BU
1994	—	—	—	—	6.50	7.50

KM# 700a CROWN
28.2800 g., 0.9250 Silver 0.8410 oz. ASW, 38.5 mm.
Ruler: Elizabeth II **Series:** Normandy Invasion **Obv:** Crowned bust right **Rev:** General Eisenhower left

Date	Mintage	F	VF	XF	Unc	BU
1994 Proof	Est. 30,000	Value: 26.50				

KM# 695 CROWN
Copper-Nickel, 38.5 mm. **Ruler:** Elizabeth II **Series:** Normandy Invasion **Obv:** Crowned bust right **Rev:** Troop ship and landing craft

Date	Mintage	F	VF	XF	Unc	BU
1994	—	—	—	—	6.50	7.50

KM# 695a CROWN
28.2800 g., 0.9250 Silver 0.8410 oz. ASW, 38.5 mm.
Ruler: Elizabeth II **Series:** Normandy Invasion **Obv:** Crowned bust right **Rev:** Troop ship and landing craft

Date	Mintage	F	VF	XF	Unc	BU
1994 Proof	Est. 30,000	Value: 26.50				

KM# 698 CROWN
Copper-Nickel, 38.5 mm. **Ruler:** Elizabeth II **Series:** Normandy Invasion **Obv:** Crowned bust right **Rev:** German machine gun nest

Date	Mintage	F	VF	XF	Unc	BU
1994	—	—	—	—	6.50	7.50

KM# 698a CROWN
28.2800 g., 0.9250 Silver 0.8410 oz. ASW, 38.5 mm.
Ruler: Elizabeth II **Series:** Normandy Invasion **Obv:** Crowned bust right **Rev:** German machine gun nest

Date	Mintage	F	VF	XF	Unc	BU
1994 Proof	Est. 30,000	Value: 26.50				

KM# 701 CROWN
Copper-Nickel, 38.5 mm. **Ruler:** Elizabeth II **Series:** Normandy Invasion **Obv:** Crowned bust right **Rev:** General Omar Bradley looking right

Date	Mintage	F	VF	XF	Unc	BU
1994	—	—	—	—	6.50	7.50

KM# 701a CROWN
28.2800 g., 0.9250 Silver 0.8410 oz. ASW, 38.5 mm.
Ruler: Elizabeth II **Series:** Normandy Invasion **Obv:** Crowned bust right **Rev:** General Omar Bradley looking right

Date	Mintage	F	VF	XF	Unc	BU
1994 Proof	Est. 30,000	Value: 26.50				

KM# 696 CROWN
Copper-Nickel, 38.5 mm. **Ruler:** Elizabeth II **Series:** Normandy Invasion **Obv:** Crowned bust right **Rev:** American troops landing

Date	Mintage	F	VF	XF	Unc	BU
1994	—	—	—	—	6.50	7.50

KM# 696a CROWN
28.2800 g., 0.9250 Silver 0.8410 oz. ASW, 38.5 mm.
Ruler: Elizabeth II **Series:** Normandy Invasion **Obv:** Crowned bust right **Rev:** American troops landing

Date	Mintage	F	VF	XF	Unc	BU
1994 Proof	Est. 30,000	Value: 26.50				

KM# 699 CROWN
Copper-Nickel, 38.5 mm. **Ruler:** Elizabeth II **Series:** Normandy Invasion **Obv:** Crowned bust right **Rev:** British troops landing

Date	Mintage	F	VF	XF	Unc	BU
1994	—	—	—	—	6.50	7.50

KM# 699a CROWN
28.2800 g., 0.9250 Silver 0.8410 oz. ASW, 38.5 mm.
Ruler: Elizabeth II **Series:** Normandy Invasion **Obv:** Crowned bust right **Rev:** British troops landing

Date	Mintage	F	VF	XF	Unc	BU
1994 Proof	Est. 30,000	Value: 26.50				

KM# 702 CROWN
Copper-Nickel, 38.5 mm. **Ruler:** Elizabeth II **Series:** Normandy Invasion **Obv:** Crowned bust right **Rev:** General Montgomery left

Date	Mintage	F	VF	XF	Unc	BU
1994	—	—	—	—	6.50	7.50

KM# 702a CROWN
28.2800 g., 0.9250 Silver 0.8410 oz. ASW, 38.5 mm.
Ruler: Elizabeth II **Series:** Normandy Invasion **Obv:** Crowned bust right **Rev:** General Montgomery left

Date	Mintage	F	VF	XF	Unc	BU
1994 Proof	Est. 30,000	Value: 26.50				

KM# 699b CROWN
6.2200 g., 0.9999 Gold 0.1999 oz. AGW **Ruler:** Elizabeth II **Series:** Normandy Invasion **Obv:** Crowned bust right **Rev:** Troop ship and landing craft **Note:** Prev. KM#703.

Date	Mintage	F	VF	XF	Unc	BU
1994 Proof	Est. 5,000	Value: 200				

KM# 696b CROWN
6.2200 g., 0.9999 Gold 0.1999 oz. AGW **Ruler:** Elizabeth II **Series:** Normandy Invasion **Obv:** Crowned bust right **Rev:** American troops landing **Note:** Prev. KM#704.

Date	Mintage	F	VF	XF	Unc	BU
1994 Proof	Est. 5,000	Value: 200				

KM# 697b CROWN
6.2200 g., 0.9999 Gold 0.1999 oz. AGW. **Ruler:** Elizabeth II
Series: Normandy Invasion **Obv:** Crowned bust right
Rev: American soldier behind rock **Note:** Prev. KM#705.

Date	Mintage	F	VF	XF	Unc	BU
1994 Proof	Est. 5,000	Value: 200				

KM# 698b CROWN
6.2200 g., 0.9999 Gold 0.1999 oz. AGW. **Ruler:** Elizabeth II
Series: Normandy Invasion **Obv:** Crowned bust right **Rev:**
German machine gun nest **Note:** Prev. KM#706.

Date	Mintage	F	VF	XF	Unc	BU
1994 Proof	Est. 5,000	Value: 200				

KM# 707 CROWN
6.2200 g., 0.9999 Gold 0.1999 oz. AGW. **Ruler:** Elizabeth II
Series: Normandy Invasion **Obv:** Crowned bust right **Rev:** British
troops landing

Date	Mintage	F	VF	XF	Unc	BU
1994 Proof	Est. 5,000	Value: 200				

KM# 700b CROWN
6.2200 g., 0.9999 Gold 0.1999 oz. AGW. **Ruler:** Elizabeth II
Series: Normandy Invasion **Obv:** Crowned bust right
Rev: General Eisenhower left **Note:** Prev. KM#708.

Date	Mintage	F	VF	XF	Unc	BU
1994 Proof	Est. 5,000	Value: 200				

KM# 701b CROWN
6.2200 g., 0.9999 Gold 0.1999 oz. AGW. **Ruler:** Elizabeth II
Series: Normandy Invasion **Obv:** Crowned bust right
Rev: General Omar Bradley right **Note:** Prev. KM#709.

Date	Mintage	F	VF	XF	Unc	BU
1994 Proof	Est. 5,000	Value: 200				

KM# 702b CROWN
6.2200 g., 0.9999 Gold 0.1999 oz. AGW. **Ruler:** Elizabeth II
Series: Normandy Invasion **Obv:** Crowned bust right
Rev: General Montgomery left **Note:** Prev. KM#710.

Date	Mintage	F	VF	XF	Unc	BU
1994 Proof	Est. 5,000	Value: 200				

KM# 434 CROWN
Copper-Nickel, 38.5 mm. **Ruler:** Elizabeth II **Series:** Man in
Flight **Obv:** Crowned bust right **Rev:** Icarus' wings melting

Date	Mintage	F	VF	XF	Unc	BU
1995 Proof	—	Value: 7.50				

KM# 434a CROWN
28.2800 g., 0.9250 Silver 0.8410 oz. ASW, 38.5 mm.
Ruler: Elizabeth II **Series:** Man in Flight **Obv:** Crowned bust right
Rev: Icarus' wings melting

Date	Mintage	F	VF	XF	Unc	BU
1995 Proof	Est. 30,000	Value: 37.50				

KM# 435 CROWN
Copper-Nickel, 38.5 mm. **Ruler:** Elizabeth II **Series:** Man in
Flight **Obv:** Crowned bust right **Rev:** Leonardo Da Vinci and
aircraft design

Date	Mintage	F	VF	XF	Unc	BU
1995 Proof	—	Value: 7.50				

KM# 435a CROWN
28.2800 g., 0.9250 Silver 0.8410 oz. ASW, 38.5 mm.
Ruler: Elizabeth II **Series:** Man in Flight **Obv:** Crowned bust right
Rev: Leonardo da Vinci and aircraft design

Date	Mintage	F	VF	XF	Unc	BU
1995 Proof	Est. 30,000	Value: 37.50				

KM# 436 CROWN
Copper-Nickel, 38.5 mm. **Ruler:** Elizabeth II **Series:** Man in
Flight **Obv:** Crowned bust right **Rev:** Montgolfier Brothers' balloon

Date	Mintage	F	VF	XF	Unc	BU
1995 Proof	—	Value: 7.50				

KM# 436a CROWN
28.2800 g., 0.9250 Silver 0.8410 oz. ASW, 38.5 mm.
Ruler: Elizabeth II **Series:** Man in Flight **Obv:** Crowned bust right
Rev: Montgolfier Brothers' balloon

Date	Mintage	F	VF	XF	Unc	BU
1995 Proof	Est. 30,000	Value: 35.00				

KM# 437 CROWN
Copper-Nickel, 38.5 mm. **Ruler:** Elizabeth II **Series:** Man in
Flight **Obv:** Crowned bust right **Rev:** Wright Brothers' airplane

Date	Mintage	F	VF	XF	Unc	BU
1995	—	—	—	7.00	9.00	

KM# 437a CROWN
28.2800 g., 0.9250 Silver 0.8410 oz. ASW, 38.5 mm.
Ruler: Elizabeth II **Series:** Man in Flight **Obv:** Crowned bust right
Rev: Wright brothers' airplane

Date	Mintage	F	VF	XF	Unc	BU
1995 Proof	Est. 30,000	Value: 38.50				

KM# 438 CROWN
Copper-Nickel, 38.5 mm. **Ruler:** Elizabeth II **Series:** Man in
Flight **Subject:** First Flight Toyko to Paris **Obv:** Crowned bust
right **Rev:** Heads of Abe and Kawachi over airplane

Date	Mintage	F	VF	XF	Unc	BU
1995 Proof	—	Value: 6.50				

KM# 438a CROWN
28.2800 g., 0.9250 Silver 0.8410 oz. ASW, 38.5 mm.
Ruler: Elizabeth II **Series:** Man in Flight **Subject:** First Flight
Tokyo to Paris **Obv:** Crowned bust right **Rev:** Heads of Abe and
Kawachi above plane

Date	Mintage	F	VF	XF	Unc	BU
1995 Proof	Est. 30,000	Value: 40.00				

KM# 439.1 CROWN
Copper-Nickel, 38.5 mm. **Ruler:** Elizabeth II **Series:** Man in Flight
Obv: Crowned bust right **Rev:** FW190, first diesel powered aircraft

Date	Mintage	F	VF	XF	Unc	BU
1995 Proof	500	Value: 12.50				

KM# 439.1a CROWN
28.2800 g., 0.9250 Silver 0.8410 oz. ASW, 38.5 mm.
Ruler: Elizabeth II **Series:** Man in Flight **Obv:** Crowned bust right
Rev: First diesel powered aircraft

Date	Mintage	F	VF	XF	Unc	BU
1995 Proof	Est. 30,000	Value: 40.00				

KM# 439.2 CROWN
Copper-Nickel, 38.5 mm. **Ruler:** Elizabeth II **Series:** Man in Flight
Obv: Crowned bust right **Rev:** FW190 BMW injection aero engine

Date	Mintage	F	VF	XF	Unc	BU
1995	—	—	—	6.50	7.50	

KM# 440.1 CROWN
Copper-Nickel, 38.5 mm. **Ruler:** Elizabeth II **Series:** Man in
Flight **Obv:** Crowned bust right **Rev:** ME262, first jet aircraft 1941

Date	Mintage	F	VF	XF	Unc	BU
1995 Proof	500	Value: 12.50				

KM# 440.1a CROWN
28.2800 g., 0.9250 Silver 0.8410 oz. ASW, 38.5 mm.
Ruler: Elizabeth II **Series:** Man in Flight **Obv:** Crowned bust right
Rev: ME262, first jet aircraft 1941

Date	Mintage	F	VF	XF	Unc	BU
1995 Proof	Est. 30,000	Value: 40.00				

KM# 440.2 CROWN
Copper-Nickel, 38.5 mm. **Ruler:** Elizabeth II **Series:** Man in
Flight **Obv:** Crowned bust right **Rev:** Jet powered aircraft 1942

Date	Mintage	F	VF	XF	Unc	BU
1995	—	—	—	6.50	7.50	

KM# 441 CROWN
Copper-Nickel, 38.5 mm. **Ruler:** Elizabeth II **Series:** Man in Flight **Subject:** 25th Anniversary of Boeing 747 **Obv:** Crowned bust right **Rev:** Boeing 747

Date	Mintage	F	VF	XF	Unc	BU
1995 Proof	—	Value: 7.50				

KM# 441a CROWN
28.2800 g., 0.9250 Silver 0.8410 oz. ASW, 38.5 mm. **Ruler:** Elizabeth II **Series:** Man in Flight **Subject:** 25th Anniversary of Boeing 747 **Obv:** Crowned bust right **Rev:** Boeing 747

Date	Mintage	F	VF	XF	Unc	BU
1995 Proof	Est. 30,000	Value: 38.50				

KM# 446 CROWN
Copper-Nickel, 38.5 mm. **Ruler:** Elizabeth II **Obv:** Crowned bust right **Rev:** Turkish cat

Date	Mintage	F	VF	XF	Unc	BU
1995	—	—	—	—	10.00	15.00

KM# 446a CROWN
31.1000 g., 0.9990 Silver 0.9988 oz. ASW, 38.5 mm. **Ruler:** Elizabeth II **Obv:** Crowned bust right **Rev:** Turkish cat **Note:** Prev. KM#447.

Date	Mintage	F	VF	XF	Unc	BU
1995 Proof	—	Value: 35.00				

KM# 446b CROWN
31.1000 g., 0.9990 Gold 0.9988 oz. AGW **Ruler:** Elizabeth II **Obv:** Crowned bust right **Rev:** Turkish cat **Note:** Prev. KM#448.

Date	Mintage	F	VF	XF	Unc	BU
1995 U	—	—	—	—	—	975
1995 Proof	—	Value: 985				

KM# 453 CROWN
Copper-Nickel, 38.5 mm. **Ruler:** Elizabeth II **Subject:** Year of the Pig **Obv:** Crowned bust right **Rev:** Sow with piglets

Date	Mintage	F	VF	XF	Unc	BU
1995	—	—	—	—	10.00	15.00

KM# 453a CROWN
31.1035 g., 0.9990 Silver 0.9990 oz. ASW, 38.5 mm. **Ruler:** Elizabeth II **Subject:** Year of the Pig **Obv:** Crowned bust right **Rev:** Sow with piglets **Note:** Prev. KM#454.

Date	Mintage	F	VF	XF	Unc	BU
1995 Proof	—	Value: 40.00				

KM# 453b CROWN
31.1035 g., 0.9990 Gold 0.9990 oz. AGW **Ruler:** Elizabeth II **Subject:** Year of the Pig **Obv:** Crowned bust right **Rev:** Sow with piglets **Note:** Prev. KM#455.

Date	Mintage	F	VF	XF	Unc	BU
1995 Proof	Est. 2,500	Value: 985				

KM# 458 CROWN
Copper-Nickel, 38.5 mm. **Ruler:** Elizabeth II **Subject:** 95th Birthday of Queen Mother **Obv:** Crowned bust right **Rev:** Crowned bust facing

Date	Mintage	F	VF	XF	Unc	BU
1995	—	—	—	—	6.00	7.00

KM# 458a CROWN
28.2800 g., 0.9250 Silver 0.8410 oz. ASW, 38.5 mm. **Ruler:** Elizabeth II **Subject:** 95th Birthday of Queen Mother **Obv:** Crowned bust right **Rev:** Crowned bust facing

Date	Mintage	F	VF	XF	Unc	BU
1995 Proof	Est. 30,000	Value: 35.00				

KM# 461 CROWN
Copper-Nickel, 38.5 mm. **Ruler:** Elizabeth II **Series:** Preserve Planet Earth **Obv:** Crowned bust right **Rev:** European otter

Date	Mintage	F	VF	XF	Unc	BU
1995	—	—	—	—	12.00	15.00

KM# 461a CROWN
28.2800 g., 0.9250 Silver 0.8410 oz. ASW, 38.5 mm. **Ruler:** Elizabeth II **Series:** Preserve Planet Earth **Obv:** Crowned bust right **Rev:** European otter

Date	Mintage	F	VF	XF	Unc	BU
1995 Proof	Est. 30,000	Value: 40.00				

KM# 462 CROWN
Copper-Nickel, 38.5 mm. **Ruler:** Elizabeth II **Series:** Preserve Planet Earth **Obv:** Crowned bust right **Rev:** Egrets

Date	Mintage	F	VF	XF	Unc	BU
1995	—	—	—	—	11.00	15.00

KM# 462a CROWN
28.2800 g., 0.9250 Silver 0.8410 oz. ASW, 38.5 mm. **Ruler:** Elizabeth II **Series:** Preserve Planet Earth **Obv:** Crowned bust right **Rev:** Egrets

Date	Mintage	F	VF	XF	Unc	BU
1995 Proof	Est. 30,000	Value: 40.00				

KM# 446c CROWN
31.1035 g., 0.9995 Platinum 0.9995 oz. APW **Ruler:** Elizabeth II **Obv:** Crowned bust right **Rev:** Turkish cat **Note:** Prev. KM#482.

Date	Mintage	F	VF	XF	Unc	BU
1995	—	—	—	—	—	2,000
1995 Proof	—	Value: 2,250				

KM# 502 CROWN
Copper-Nickel, 38.5 mm. **Ruler:** Elizabeth II **Series:** Aircraft of World War II **Obv:** Crowned bust right **Rev:** Airplanes

Date	Mintage	F	VF	XF	Unc	BU
1995	—	—	—	—	5.50	7.50

KM# 502a CROWN
28.2800 g., 0.9250 Silver 0.8410 oz. ASW, 38.5 mm. **Ruler:** Elizabeth II **Series:** Aircraft of World War II **Obv:** Crowned bust right **Rev:** Airplanes

Date	Mintage	F	VF	XF	Unc	BU
1995 Proof	Est. 30,000	Value: 30.00				

KM# 503 CROWN
Copper-Nickel, 38.5 mm. **Ruler:** Elizabeth II **Series:** Aircraft of World War II **Obv:** Crowned bust right **Rev:** P-51 Mustang

Date	Mintage	F	VF	XF	Unc	BU
1995	—	—	—	—	5.50	7.50

KM# 503a CROWN
28.2800 g., 0.9250 Silver 0.8410 oz. ASW, 38.5 mm. **Ruler:** Elizabeth II **Series:** Aircraft of World War II **Obv:** Crowned bust right **Rev:** P-51 Mustang

Date	Mintage	F	VF	XF	Unc	BU
1995 Proof	—	Value: 30.00				

KM# 504 CROWN
Copper-Nickel, 38.5 mm. **Ruler:** Elizabeth II **Series:** Aircraft of World War II **Obv:** Crowned bust right **Rev:** Letov 5328 **Edge:** Reeded

Date	Mintage	F	VF	XF	Unc	BU
1995	—	—	—	—	5.50	7.50

KM# 504a CROWN
28.2800 g., 0.9250 Silver 0.8410 oz. ASW, 38.5 mm. **Ruler:** Elizabeth II **Series:** Aircraft of World War II **Obv:** Crowned bust right **Rev:** Letov 5328

Date	Mintage	F	VF	XF	Unc	BU
1995 Proof	Est. 30,000	Value: 30.00				

KM# 505 CROWN
Copper-Nickel, 38.5 mm. **Ruler:** Elizabeth II **Series:** Aircraft of
World War II **Obv:** Crowned bust right **Rev:** Messerschmitt
ME262 **Edge:** Reeded

Date	Mintage	F	VF	XF	Unc	BU
1995	—	—	—	—	5.50	7.50

KM# 505a CROWN
28.2800 g., 0.9250 Silver 0.8410 oz. ASW, 38.5 mm.
Ruler: Elizabeth II **Series:** Aircraft of World War II **Obv:** Crowned
bust right **Rev:** Messerschmitt ME262

Date	Mintage	F	VF	XF	Unc	BU
1995 Proof	Est. 30,000	Value: 30.00				

KM# 506 CROWN
Copper-Nickel, 38.5 mm. **Ruler:** Elizabeth II **Series:** Aircraft of
World War II **Obv:** Crowned bust right **Rev:** JU87 Stuka
Edge: Reeded

Date	Mintage	F	VF	XF	Unc	BU
1995	—	—	—	—	5.50	7.50

KM# 506a CROWN
28.2800 g., 0.9250 Silver 0.8410 oz. ASW, 38.5 mm.
Ruler: Elizabeth II **Series:** Aircraft of World War II **Obv:** Crowned
bust right **Rev:** JU87 Stuka

Date	Mintage	F	VF	XF	Unc	BU
1995 Proof	Est. 30,000	Value: 30.00				

KM# 507 CROWN
Copper-Nickel, 38.5 mm. **Ruler:** Elizabeth II **Series:** Aircraft of
World War II **Obv:** Crowned bust right **Rev:** MIG 3 **Edge:** Reeded

Date	Mintage	F	VF	XF	Unc	BU
1995	—	—	—	—	5.50	7.50

KM# 507a CROWN
28.2800 g., 0.9250 Silver 0.8410 oz. ASW, 38.5 mm.
Ruler: Elizabeth II **Series:** Aircraft of World War II **Obv:** Crowned
bust right **Rev:** MIG 3

Date	Mintage	F	VF	XF	Unc	BU
1995 Proof	Est. 30,000	Value: 30.00				

KM# 508 CROWN
Copper-Nickel, 38.5 mm. **Ruler:** Elizabeth II **Series:** Aircraft of
World War II **Obv:** Crowned bust right **Rev:** Nakajima KI-49
Donryu **Edge:** Reeded

Date	Mintage	F	VF	XF	Unc	BU
1995	—	—	—	—	5.50	7.50

KM# 508a CROWN
28.2800 g., 0.9250 Silver 0.8410 oz. ASW, 38.5 mm.
Ruler: Elizabeth II **Series:** Aircraft of World War II **Obv:** Crowned
bust right **Rev:** Nakajima KI-49 Donryu

Date	Mintage	F	VF	XF	Unc	BU
1995 Proof	Est. 30,000	Value: 30.00				

KM# 509 CROWN
Copper-Nickel, 38.5 mm. **Ruler:** Elizabeth II **Series:** Aircraft of
World War II **Obv:** Crowned bust right **Rev:** Vickers Wellington
Edge: Reeded

Date	Mintage	F	VF	XF	Unc	BU
1995	—	—	—	—	5.50	7.50

KM# 509a CROWN
28.2800 g., 0.9250 Silver 0.8410 oz. ASW, 38.5 mm.
Ruler: Elizabeth II **Series:** Aircraft of World War II **Obv:** Crowned
bust right **Rev:** Vickers Wellington

Date	Mintage	F	VF	XF	Unc	BU
1995 Proof	Est. 30,000	Value: 30.00				

KM# 510 CROWN
Copper-Nickel, 38.5 mm. **Ruler:** Elizabeth II **Series:** Aircraft of
World War II **Obv:** Crowned bust right **Rev:** Supermarine Spitfire
Edge: Reeded

Date	Mintage	F	VF	XF	Unc	BU
1995 (py)	—	—	—	—	6.00	8.00
1995	—	—	—	—	6.00	8.00

KM# 510a CROWN
28.2800 g., 0.9250 Silver 0.8410 oz. ASW, 38.5 mm.
Ruler: Elizabeth II **Series:** Aircraft of World War II **Obv:** Crowned
bust right **Rev:** Supermarine Spitfire

Date	Mintage	F	VF	XF	Unc	BU
1995 Proof	Est. 30,000	Value: 30.00				

KM# 511 CROWN
Copper-Nickel, 38.5 mm. **Ruler:** Elizabeth II **Series:** Aircraft of
World War II **Obv:** Crowned bust right **Rev:** Fokker G.1a
Edge: Reeded

Date	Mintage	F	VF	XF	Unc	BU
1995	—	—	—	—	5.50	7.50

KM# 511a CROWN
28.2800 g., 0.9250 Silver 0.8410 oz. ASW, 38.5 mm.
Ruler: Elizabeth II **Series:** Aircraft of World War II **Obv:** Crowned
bust right **Rev:** Fokker G.1a

Date	Mintage	F	VF	XF	Unc	BU
1995 Proof	Est. 30,000	Value: 30.00				

KM# 512 CROWN
Copper-Nickel, 38.5 mm. **Ruler:** Elizabeth II **Series:** Aircraft of
World War II **Obv:** Crowned bust right **Rev:** Commonwealth
Boomerang CA-13 **Edge:** Reeded

Date	Mintage	F	VF	XF	Unc	BU
1995	—	—	—	—	5.50	7.50

KM# 512a CROWN
28.2800 g., 0.9250 Silver 0.8410 oz. ASW, 38.5 mm.
Ruler: Elizabeth II **Series:** Aircraft of World War II **Obv:** Crowned
bust right **Rev:** Boomerang CA-13

Date	Mintage	F	VF	XF	Unc	BU
1995 Proof	Est. 30,000	Value: 30.00				

KM# 513 CROWN
Copper-Nickel, 38.5 mm. **Ruler:** Elizabeth II **Series:** Aircraft of
World War II **Obv:** Crowned bust right **Rev:** Bristol Blenheim 142
Edge: Reeded

Date	Mintage	F	VF	XF	Unc	BU
1995	—	—	—	—	5.50	7.50

KM# 513a CROWN
28.2800 g., 0.9250 Silver 0.8410 oz. ASW, 38.5 mm.
Ruler: Elizabeth II **Series:** Aircraft of World War II **Obv:** Crowned
bust right **Rev:** Bristol Blenheim 142

Date	Mintage	F	VF	XF	Unc	BU
1995 Proof	Est. 30,000	Value: 30.00				

KM# 514 CROWN
Copper-Nickel, 38.5 mm. **Ruler:** Elizabeth II **Series:** Aircraft of World War II **Obv:** Crowned bust right **Rev:** Mitsubishi Zero **Edge:** Reeded

Date	Mintage	F	VF	XF	Unc	BU
1995	—	—	—	—	5.50	7.50

KM# 514a CROWN
28.2800 g., 0.9250 Silver 0.8410 oz. ASW, 38.5 mm. **Ruler:** Elizabeth II **Series:** Aircraft of World War II **Obv:** Crowned bust right **Rev:** Mitsubishi Zero

Date	Mintage	F	VF	XF	Unc	BU
1995 Proof	Est. 30,000	Value: 30.00				

KM# 517 CROWN
Copper-Nickel, 38.5 mm. **Ruler:** Elizabeth II **Series:** Aircraft of World War II **Obv:** Crowned bust right **Rev:** Boeing B-29 Enola Gay **Edge:** Reeded

Date	Mintage	F	VF	XF	Unc	BU
1995	—	—	—	—	5.50	7.50

KM# 517a CROWN
28.2800 g., 0.9250 Silver 0.8410 oz. ASW, 38.5 mm. **Ruler:** Elizabeth II **Series:** Aircraft of World War II **Obv:** Crowned bust right **Rev:** Boeing B-29 Enola Gay

Date	Mintage	F	VF	XF	Unc	BU
1995 Proof	Est. 30,000	Value: 30.00				

KM# 520 CROWN
Copper-Nickel, 38.5 mm. **Ruler:** Elizabeth II **Series:** Aircraft of WWII **Obv:** Crowned bust right **Rev:** Curtiss P-40 Tomahawk **Edge:** Reeded

Date	Mintage	F	VF	XF	Unc	BU
1995	—	—	—	—	5.50	7.50

KM# 520a CROWN
28.2800 g., 0.9250 Silver 0.8410 oz. ASW, 38.5 mm. **Ruler:** Elizabeth II **Series:** Aircraft of WWII **Obv:** Crowned bust right **Rev:** Curtiss P-40 Tomahawk

Date	Mintage	F	VF	XF	Unc	BU
1995 Proof	Est. 30,000	Value: 30.00				

KM# 515 CROWN
Copper-Nickel, 38.5 mm. **Ruler:** Elizabeth II **Series:** Aircraft of World War II **Obv:** Crowned bust right **Rev:** Heinkel HE 111 **Edge:** Reeded

Date	Mintage	F	VF	XF	Unc	BU
1995	—	—	—	—	5.50	7.50

KM# 515a CROWN
28.2800 g., 0.9250 Silver 0.8410 oz. ASW, 38.5 mm. **Ruler:** Elizabeth II **Series:** Aircraft of World War II **Obv:** Crowned bust right **Rev:** Heinkel HE 111

Date	Mintage	F	VF	XF	Unc	BU
1995 Proof	Est. 30,000	Value: 30.00				

KM# 518 CROWN
Copper-Nickel, 38.5 mm. **Ruler:** Elizabeth II **Series:** Aircraft of World War II **Obv:** Crowned bust right **Rev:** Douglas DC-3 (C-47) Dakota **Edge:** Reeded

Date	Mintage	F	VF	XF	Unc	BU
1995	—	—	—	—	5.50	7.50

KM# 518a CROWN
28.2800 g., 0.9250 Silver 0.8410 oz. ASW, 38.5 mm. **Ruler:** Elizabeth II **Series:** Aircraft of World War II **Obv:** Crowned bust right **Rev:** Douglas DC-3 (C-47) Dakota

Date	Mintage	F	VF	XF	Unc	BU
1995 Proof	Est. 30,000	Value: 30.00				

KM# 524 CROWN
Copper-Nickel, 38.5 mm. **Ruler:** Elizabeth II **Series:** America's Cup **Obv:** Crowned bust right **Rev:** Sailboats **Edge:** Reeded

Date	Mintage	F	VF	XF	Unc	BU
1995	—	—	—	—	5.00	6.50

KM# 524a CROWN
28.2800 g., 0.9250 Silver 0.8410 oz. ASW, 38.5 mm. **Ruler:** Elizabeth II **Series:** America's Cup **Obv:** Crowned bust right **Rev:** Sailboats

Date	Mintage	F	VF	XF	Unc	BU
1995 Proof	Est. 30,000	Value: 50.00				

KM# 516 CROWN
Copper-Nickel, 38.5 mm. **Ruler:** Elizabeth II **Series:** Aircraft of World War II **Obv:** Crowned bust right **Rev:** Boulton Paul P.82 Defiant **Edge:** Reeded

Date	Mintage	F	VF	XF	Unc	BU
1995	—	—	—	—	5.50	7.50

KM# 516a CROWN
28.2800 g., 0.9250 Silver 0.8410 oz. ASW, 38.5 mm. **Ruler:** Elizabeth II **Series:** Aircraft of World War II **Obv:** Crowned bust right **Rev:** Boulton Paul P.82 Defiant

Date	Mintage	F	VF	XF	Unc	BU
1995 Proof	Est. 30,000	Value: 30.00				

KM# 519 CROWN
Copper-Nickel, 38.5 mm. **Ruler:** Elizabeth II **Series:** Aircraft of World War II **Obv:** Crowned bust right **Rev:** Fairey Swordfish **Edge:** Reeded

Date	Mintage	F	VF	XF	Unc	BU
1995	—	—	—	—	5.50	7.50

KM# 519a CROWN
28.2800 g., 0.9250 Silver 0.8410 oz. ASW, 38.5 mm. **Ruler:** Elizabeth II **Series:** Aircraft of World War II **Obv:** Crowned bust right **Rev:** Fairey Swordfish

Date	Mintage	F	VF	XF	Unc	BU
1995 Proof	Est. 30,000	Value: 30.00				

KM# 526 CROWN
Copper-Nickel, 38.5 mm. **Ruler:** Elizabeth II **Series:** Inventions of the Modern World **Obv:** Crowned bust right **Rev:** Cameo Tsai Lun, paper and tree **Edge:** Reeded

Date	Mintage	F	VF	XF	Unc	BU
1995	—	—	—	—	6.00	8.00

KM# 526a CROWN
28.2800 g., 0.9250 Silver 0.8410 oz. ASW, 38.5 mm. **Ruler:** Elizabeth II **Series:** Inventions of the Modern World **Obv:** Crowned bust right **Rev:** Cameo of Tsai Lun, paper and tree

Date	Mintage	F	VF	XF	Unc	BU
1995 Proof	Est. 30,000	Value: 40.00				

KM# 528 CROWN
Copper-Nickel, 38.5 mm. **Ruler:** Elizabeth II **Series:** Inventions of the Modern World **Obv:** Crowned bust right **Rev:** Cameo of Chang Heng and seismograph **Edge:** Reeded

Date	Mintage	F	VF	XF	Unc	BU
1995	—	—	—	—	5.00	6.50

KM# 528a CROWN
28.2800 g., 0.9250 Silver 0.8410 oz. ASW, 38.5 mm.
Ruler: Elizabeth II **Series:** Inventions of the Modern World **Obv:** Crowned bust right **Rev:** Cameo of Chang Heng and seismograph

Date	Mintage	F	VF	XF	Unc	BU
1995 Proof	Est. 30,000	Value: 40.00				

KM# 534 CROWN
Copper-Nickel, 38.5 mm. **Ruler:** Elizabeth II **Series:** Inventions of the Modern World **Obv:** Crowned bust right **Rev:** Cameo of Charles Babbage and first computer **Edge:** Reeded

Date	Mintage	F	VF	XF	Unc	BU
1995	—	—	—	—	6.00	8.00

KM# 534a CROWN
28.2800 g., 0.9250 Silver 0.8410 oz. ASW, 38.5 mm.
Ruler: Elizabeth II **Series:** Inventions of the Modern World **Obv:** Crowned bust right **Rev:** Cameo of Charles Babbage and first computer

Date	Mintage	F	VF	XF	Unc	BU
1995 Proof	Est. 30,000	Value: 40.00				

KM# 540 CROWN
Copper-Nickel, 38.5 mm. **Ruler:** Elizabeth II **Series:** Inventions of the Modern World **Obv:** Crowned bust right **Rev:** Cameo of Wilhelm K. Roentgern, xray **Edge:** Reeded

Date	Mintage	F	VF	XF	Unc	BU
1995	—	—	—	—	5.00	6.50

KM# 540a CROWN
28.2800 g., 0.9250 Silver 0.8410 oz. ASW, 38.5 mm.
Ruler: Elizabeth II **Series:** Inventions of the Modern World **Obv:** Crowned bust right **Rev:** Cameo of Wilhelm K. Roentgen, xray

Date	Mintage	F	VF	XF	Unc	BU
1995 Proof	Est. 30,000	Value: 40.00				

KM# 530 CROWN
Copper-Nickel, 38.5 mm. **Ruler:** Elizabeth II **Series:** Inventions of the Modern World **Obv:** Crowned bust right **Rev:** Cameo of Tsu Chung Chih and compass cart **Edge:** Reeded

Date	Mintage	F	VF	XF	Unc	BU
1995	—	—	—	—	8.00	10.00

KM# 530a CROWN
28.2800 g., 0.9250 Silver 0.8410 oz. ASW, 38.5 mm.
Ruler: Elizabeth II **Series:** Inventions of the Modern World **Obv:** Crowned bust right **Rev:** Cameo of Tsu Chung Chih and compass car

Date	Mintage	F	VF	XF	Unc	BU
1995 Proof	Est. 30,000	Value: 40.00				

KM# 536 CROWN
Copper-Nickel, 38.5 mm. **Ruler:** Elizabeth II **Series:** Inventions of the Modern World **Obv:** Crowned bust right **Rev:** Cameo of Fox Talbot, photography **Edge:** Reeded

Date	Mintage	F	VF	XF	Unc	BU
1995	—	—	—	—	8.00	10.00

KM# 536a CROWN
28.2800 g., 0.9250 Silver 0.8410 oz. ASW, 38.5 mm.
Ruler: Elizabeth II **Series:** Inventions of the Modern World **Obv:** Crowned bust right **Rev:** Cameo of Fox Talbot, photography

Date	Mintage	F	VF	XF	Unc	BU
1995 Proof	Est. 30,000	Value: 40.00				

KM# 542 CROWN
Copper-Nickel, 38.5 mm. **Ruler:** Elizabeth II **Series:** Inventions of the Modern World **Obv:** Crowned bust right **Rev:** Cameo of Guglielmo Marconi, radio equipment **Edge:** Reeded

Date	Mintage	F	VF	XF	Unc	BU
1995	—	—	—	—	5.00	6.50

KM# 542a CROWN
28.2800 g., 0.9250 Silver 0.8410 oz. ASW, 38.5 mm.
Ruler: Elizabeth II **Series:** Inventions of the Modern World **Obv:** Crowned bust right **Rev:** Cameo of Guglielmo Marconi and radio equipment

Date	Mintage	F	VF	XF	Unc	BU
1995 Proof	Est. 30,000	Value: 40.00				

KM# 532 CROWN
Copper-Nickel, 38.5 mm. **Ruler:** Elizabeth II **Series:** Inventions of the Modern World **Obv:** Crowned bust right **Rev:** Cameo of Pi Sheng and movable type **Edge:** Reeded

Date	Mintage	F	VF	XF	Unc	BU
1995	—	—	—	—	5.00	6.50

KM# 532a CROWN
28.2800 g., 0.9250 Silver 0.8410 oz. ASW, 38.5 mm.
Ruler: Elizabeth II **Series:** Inventions of the Modern World **Obv:** Crowned bust right **Rev:** Cameo of Pi Sheng and movable type

Date	Mintage	F	VF	XF	Unc	BU
1995 Proof	Est. 30,000	Value: 40.00				

KM# 538 CROWN
Copper-Nickel, 38.5 mm. **Ruler:** Elizabeth II **Series:** Inventions of the Modern World **Obv:** Crowned bust right **Rev:** Cameo Rudolf Diesel and engine

Date	Mintage	F	VF	XF	Unc	BU
1995	—	—	—	—	5.00	6.50

KM# 538a CROWN
28.2800 g., 0.9250 Silver 0.8410 oz. ASW, 38.5 mm.
Ruler: Elizabeth II **Series:** Inventions of the Modern World **Obv:** Crowned bust right **Rev:** Cameo of Rudolf Diesel and engine

Date	Mintage	F	VF	XF	Unc	BU
1995 Proof	Est. 30,000	Value: 40.00				

KM# 544 CROWN
Copper-Nickel, 38.5 mm. **Ruler:** Elizabeth II **Series:** Inventions of the Modern World **Obv:** Crowned bust right **Rev:** Cameo L. Baird and television equipment **Edge:** Reeded

Date	Mintage	F	VF	XF	Unc	BU
1995	—	—	—	—	5.00	6.50

KM# 544a CROWN
28.2800 g., 0.9250 Silver 0.8410 oz. ASW, 38.5 mm.
Ruler: Elizabeth II **Series:** Inventions of the Modern World **Obv:** Crowned bust right **Rev:** Cameo of John L. Baird and television equipment

Date	Mintage	F	VF	XF	Unc	BU
1995 Proof	Est. 30,000	Value: 40.00				

KM# 546   CROWN
Copper-Nickel, 38.5 mm. **Ruler:** Elizabeth II **Series:** Inventions of the Modern World **Obv:** Crowned bust right **Rev:** Cameo of Alexander Fleming and microscope **Edge:** Reeded

Date	Mintage	F	VF	XF	Unc	BU
1995	—				5.00	6.50

KM# 546a   CROWN
28.2800 g., 0.9250 Silver 0.8410 oz. ASW, 38.5 mm.
Ruler: Elizabeth II **Series:** Inventions of the Modern World
Obv: Crowned bust right **Rev:** Cameo of Alexander Fleming and microscope

Date	Mintage	F	VF	XF	Unc	BU
1995 Proof	Est. 30,000	Value: 40.00				

KM# 548   CROWN
Copper-Nickel, 38.5 mm. **Ruler:** Elizabeth II **Series:** Inventions of the Modern World **Obv:** Crowned bust right **Rev:** Cameo of Lazlo Biro, ball-point pen **Edge:** Reeded

Date	Mintage	F	VF	XF	Unc	BU
1995	—				5.00	6.50

KM# 548a   CROWN
28.2800 g., 0.9250 Silver 0.8410 oz. ASW, 38.5 mm.
Ruler: Elizabeth II **Series:** Inventions of the Modern World
Obv: Crowned bust right **Rev:** Cameo of Lazlo Biro, ball-point pen

Date	Mintage	F	VF	XF	Unc	BU
1995 Proof	Est. 30,000	Value: 40.00				

KM# 555   CROWN
Copper-Nickel, 38.5 mm. **Ruler:** Elizabeth II **Series:** Inventions of the Modern World **Obv:** Crowned bust right **Rev:** Cameo of Wernher von Braun and rocket **Edge:** Reeded

Date	Mintage	F	VF	XF	Unc	BU
1996	—				5.00	6.50

KM# 555a   CROWN
28.2800 g., 0.9250 Silver 0.8410 oz. ASW, 38.5 mm.
Ruler: Elizabeth II **Series:** Inventions of the Modern World
Obv: Crowned bust right **Rev:** Cameo of Wernher von Braun and rocket

Date	Mintage	F	VF	XF	Unc	BU
1996 Proof	Est. 30,000	Value: 40.00				

KM# 556   CROWN
Copper-Nickel, 38.5 mm. **Ruler:** Elizabeth II **Series:** Inventions of the Modern World **Obv:** Crowned bust right **Rev:** Cameo of Thomas Edison, electricity **Edge:** Reeded

Date	Mintage	F	VF	XF	Unc	BU
1996	—				8.00	10.00

KM# 556a   CROWN
28.2800 g., 0.9250 Silver 0.8410 oz. ASW, 38.5 mm. **Ruler:** Elizabeth II **Series:** Inventions of the Modern World **Obv:** Crowned bust right **Rev:** Cameo of Thomas Edison, electricity

Date	Mintage	F	VF	XF	Unc	BU
1996 Proof	—	Value: 40.00				

KM# 557   CROWN
Copper-Nickel, 38.5 mm. **Ruler:** Elizabeth II **Series:** Inventions of the Modern World **Obv:** Crowned bust right **Rev:** Compass

Date	Mintage	F	VF	XF	Unc	BU
1996	—				6.00	8.00

KM# 557a   CROWN
28.2800 g., 0.9250 Silver 0.8410 oz. ASW, 38.5 mm.
Ruler: Elizabeth II **Series:** Inventions of the Modern World
Obv: Crowned bust right **Rev:** Compass

Date	Mintage	F	VF	XF	Unc	BU
1996 Proof	—	Value: 40.00				

KM# 558.1   CROWN
Copper-Nickel, 38.5 mm. **Ruler:** Elizabeth II **Series:** Inventions of the Modern World **Obv:** Crowned bust right **Rev:** Cameo of Michael Faraday, electricity **Edge:** Reeded

Date	Mintage	F	VF	XF	Unc	BU
1996	—				5.00	6.50

KM# 558.2   CROWN
Copper-Nickel, 38.5 mm. **Ruler:** Elizabeth II **Series:** Inventions of the Modern World **Obv:** Crowned bust right **Rev:** Cameo of Michael Faraday, electricity; legend error
Rev. Leg.: EXRERIMENTAL **Edge:** Reeded

Date	Mintage	F	VF	XF	Unc	BU
1996	—				11.50	12.50

KM# 558.2a   CROWN
28.2800 g., 0.9250 Silver 0.8410 oz. ASW, 38.5 mm.
Ruler: Elizabeth II **Series:** Inventions of the Modern World
Obv: Crowned bust right **Rev:** Cameo of Michael Faraday, electricity; legend error **Rev. Leg.:** EXRERIMENTAL

Date	Mintage	F	VF	XF	Unc	BU
1996 Proof	Est. 30,000	Value: 40.00				

KM# 559   CROWN
Copper-Nickel, 38.5 mm. **Ruler:** Elizabeth II **Series:** Inventions of the Modern World **Obv:** Crowned bust right **Rev:** Emile Berliner, gramophone **Edge:** Reeded

Date	Mintage	F	VF	XF	Unc	BU
1996	—				5.00	6.50

KM# 559a   CROWN
28.2800 g., 0.9250 Silver 0.8410 oz. ASW, 38.5 mm.
Ruler: Elizabeth II **Series:** Inventions of the Modern World
Obv: Crowned bust right **Rev:** Cameo of Emile Berliner and gramophone

Date	Mintage	F	VF	XF	Unc	BU
1996 Proof	Est. 30,000	Value: 40.00				

KM# 560   CROWN
Copper-Nickel, 38.5 mm. **Ruler:** Elizabeth II **Series:** Inventions of the Modern World **Obv:** Crowned bust right **Rev:** Cameo of Alexander Graham Bell, voice transmission **Edge:** Reeded

Date	Mintage	F	VF	XF	Unc	BU
1996	—				8.00	10.00

KM# 560a   CROWN
28.2800 g., 0.9250 Silver 0.8410 oz. ASW, 38.5 mm.
Ruler: Elizabeth II **Series:** Inventions of the Modern World
Obv: Crowned bust right **Rev:** Cameo of Alexander Graham Bell, voice transmission

Date	Mintage	F	VF	XF	Unc	BU
1996 Proof	30,000	Value: 40.00				

KM# 567   CROWN
Copper-Nickel, 38.5 mm. **Ruler:** Elizabeth II **Series:** 1996 Summer Olympics - Atlanta **Obv:** Crowned bust right **Rev:** Hurdler within sprigs

Date	Mintage	F	VF	XF	Unc	BU
1996	—				6.00	8.00

KM# 567a   CROWN
28.2800 g., 0.9250 Silver 0.8410 oz. ASW, 38.5 mm.
Ruler: Elizabeth II **Series:** 1996 Summer Olympics - Atlanta
Obv: Crowned bust right **Rev:** Hurdler within sprigs

Date	Mintage	F	VF	XF	Unc	BU
1996 Proof	Est. 30,000	Value: 35.00				

KM# 568   CROWN
Copper-Nickel, 38.5 mm. **Ruler:** Elizabeth II **Series:** 1996 Summer
Olympics - Atlanta **Obv:** Crowned bust right **Rev:** Runners

Date	Mintage	F	VF	XF	Unc	BU
1996	—	—	—	—	6.00	8.00

KM# 568a   CROWN
28.2800 g., 0.9250 Silver 0.8410 oz. ASW, 38.5 mm.
Ruler: Elizabeth II **Series:** 1996 Summer Olympics - Atlanta
Obv: Crowned bust right **Rev:** Runners

Date	Mintage	F	VF	XF	Unc	BU
1996 Proof	Est. 30,000	Value: 35.00				

KM# 571   CROWN
Copper-Nickel, 38.5 mm. **Ruler:** Elizabeth II **Series:** 1996
Summer Olympics - Atlanta **Obv:** Crowned bust right
Rev: Equestrian within wreath

Date	Mintage	F	VF	XF	Unc	BU
1996	—	—	—	—	6.00	8.00

KM# 571a   CROWN
28.2800 g., 0.9250 Silver 0.8410 oz. ASW, 38.5 mm.
Ruler: Elizabeth II **Series:** 1996 Summer Olympics - Atlanta
Obv: Crowned bust right **Rev:** Equestrian within wreath

Date	Mintage	F	VF	XF	Unc	BU
1996 Proof	Est. 30,000	Value: 35.00				

KM# 578   CROWN
Copper-Nickel, 38.5 mm. **Ruler:** Elizabeth II
Series: Bicentenary of Robert Burns **Obv:** Crowned bust right
Rev: Pirate ship **Edge:** Reeded

Date	Mintage	F	VF	XF	Unc	BU
1996	—	—	—	—	5.00	6.50

KM# 578a   CROWN
28.2800 g., 0.9250 Silver 0.8410 oz. ASW, 38.5 mm.
Ruler: Elizabeth II **Series:** Bicentenary of Robert Burns
Obv: Crowned bust right **Rev:** Pirate ship

Date	Mintage	F	VF	XF	Unc	BU
1996 Proof	Est. 30,000	Value: 40.00				

KM# 569   CROWN
Copper-Nickel, 38.5 mm. **Ruler:** Elizabeth II **Series:** 1996
Summer Olympics - Atlanta **Obv:** Crowned bust right **Rev:** Sailing

Date	Mintage	F	VF	XF	Unc	BU
1996	—	—	—	—	6.00	8.00

KM# 569a   CROWN
28.2800 g., 0.9250 Silver 0.8410 oz. ASW, 38.5 mm.
Ruler: Elizabeth II **Series:** 1996 Summer Olympics - Atlanta
Obv: Crowned bust right **Rev:** Sailing

Date	Mintage	F	VF	XF	Unc	BU
1996 Proof	Est. 30,000	Value: 35.00				

KM# 572   CROWN
Copper-Nickel, 38.5 mm. **Ruler:** Elizabeth II **Series:** 1996
Summer Olympics - Atlanta **Obv:** Crowned bust right
Rev: Cyclists and Nike

Date	Mintage	F	VF	XF	Unc	BU
1996	—	—	—	—	6.00	8.00

KM# 572a   CROWN
28.2800 g., 0.9250 Silver 0.8410 oz. ASW, 38.5 mm.
Ruler: Elizabeth II **Series:** 1996 Summer Olympics - Atlanta
Obv: Crowned bust right **Rev:** Cyclists and Nike

Date	Mintage	F	VF	XF	Unc	BU
1996 Proof	Est. 30,000	Value: 35.00				

KM# 579   CROWN
Copper-Nickel, 38.5 mm. **Ruler:** Elizabeth II **Series:** Bicentenary
of Robert Burns **Obv:** Crowned bust right **Rev:** Auld Lang Syne

Date	Mintage	F	VF	XF	Unc	BU
1996	—	—	—	—	5.00	6.50

KM# 579a   CROWN
28.2800 g., 0.9250 Silver 0.8410 oz. ASW, 38.5 mm.
Ruler: Elizabeth II **Series:** Bicentenary of Robert Burns
Obv: Crowned bust right **Rev:** Auld Lang Syne

Date	Mintage	F	VF	XF	Unc	BU
1996 Proof	Est. 30,000	Value: 40.00				

KM# 570   CROWN
Copper-Nickel, 38.5 mm. **Ruler:** Elizabeth II **Series:** 1996 Summer
Olympics - Atlanta **Obv:** Crowned bust right **Rev:** Swimming

Date	Mintage	F	VF	XF	Unc	BU
1996	—	—	—	—	6.00	8.00

KM# 570a   CROWN
28.2800 g., 0.9250 Silver 0.8410 oz. ASW, 38.5 mm.
Ruler: Elizabeth II **Series:** 1996 Summer Olympics - Atlanta
Obv: Crowned bust right **Rev:** Swimming

Date	Mintage	F	VF	XF	Unc	BU
1996 Proof	Est. 30,000	Value: 35.00				

KM# 577   CROWN
Copper-Nickel, 38.5 mm. **Ruler:** Elizabeth II
Series: Bicentenary of Robert Burns **Obv:** Crowned bust right
Rev: Seated figure facing right within circle **Edge:** Reeded

Date	Mintage	F	VF	XF	Unc	BU
1996	—	—	—	—	8.00	10.00

KM# 577a   CROWN
28.2800 g., 0.9250 Silver 0.8410 oz. ASW, 38.5 mm.
Ruler: Elizabeth II **Series:** Bicentenary of Robert Burns
Obv: Crowned bust right **Rev:** Seated figure facing right within
circle

Date	Mintage	F	VF	XF	Unc	BU
1996 Proof	Est. 30,000	Value: 40.00				

KM# 580   CROWN
Copper-Nickel, 38.5 mm. **Ruler:** Elizabeth II **Series:** Bicentenary
of Robert Burns **Obv:** Crowned bust right **Rev:** Edinburgh Castle

Date	Mintage	F	VF	XF	Unc	BU
1996	—	—	—	—	8.00	10.00

KM# 580a   CROWN
28.2800 g., 0.9250 Silver 0.8410 oz. ASW, 38.5 mm.
Ruler: Elizabeth II **Series:** Bicentenary of Robert Burns
Obv: Crowned bust right **Rev:** Edinburgh Castle

Date	Mintage	F	VF	XF	Unc	BU
1996 Proof	Est. 30,000	Value: 40.00				

KM# 582 CROWN
28.2800 g., 0.9250 Silver 0.8410 oz. ASW, 38.5 mm.
Ruler: Elizabeth II **Subject:** 70th Birthday of Queen Elizabeth II
Obv: Crowned bust right **Rev:** Monogram and numeral 70 flanked by flower sprigs

Date	Mintage	F	VF	XF	Unc	BU
1996	—	—	—	—	6.00	8.00

KM# 582a CROWN
28.2800 g., 0.9250 Silver 0.8410 oz. ASW, 38.5 mm.
Ruler: Elizabeth II **Subject:** 70th Birthday of Queen Elizabeth II
Obv: Crowned bust right **Rev:** Monogram and numeral 70 flanked by flower sprigs

Date	Mintage	F	VF	XF	Unc	BU
1996 Proof	Est. 30,000	Value: 40.00				

KM# 585 CROWN
Copper-Nickel, 38.5 mm. **Ruler:** Elizabeth II **Series:** Preserve Planet Earth **Obv:** Crowned bust right **Rev:** Killer whale

Date	Mintage	F	VF	XF	Unc	BU
1996	—	—	—	—	12.00	15.00

KM# 585a CROWN
28.2800 g., 0.9250 Silver 0.8410 oz. ASW, 38.5 mm.
Ruler: Elizabeth II **Series:** Preserve Planet Earth **Obv:** Crowned bust right **Rev:** Killer whale

Date	Mintage	F	VF	XF	Unc	BU
1996 Proof	Est. 30,000	Value: 40.00				

KM# 586 CROWN
Copper-Nickel, 38.5 mm. **Ruler:** Elizabeth II **Series:** Preserve Planet Earth **Obv:** Crowned bust right **Rev:** Razorbill feeding chick

Date	Mintage	F	VF	XF	Unc	BU
1996	—	—	—	—	12.00	14.00

KM# 586a CROWN
28.2800 g., 0.9250 Silver 0.8410 oz. ASW, 38.5 mm.
Ruler: Elizabeth II **Series:** Preserve Planet Earth **Obv:** Crowned bust right **Rev:** Razorbill feeding chick

Date	Mintage	F	VF	XF	Unc	BU
1996 Proof	Est. 30,000	Value: 40.00				

KM# 609 CROWN
Copper-Nickel, 38.5 mm. **Ruler:** Elizabeth II **Series:** Flower Fairies **Obv:** Crowned bust right **Rev:** Orchis

Date	Mintage	F	VF	XF	Unc	BU
1996	—	—	—	—	5.00	6.50

KM# 609a CROWN
28.2800 g., 0.9250 Silver 0.8410 oz. ASW, 38.5 mm.
Ruler: Elizabeth II **Series:** Flower Fairies **Obv:** Crowned bust right **Rev:** Orchis

Date	Mintage	F	VF	XF	Unc	BU
1996 Proof	Est. 30,000	Value: 40.00				

KM# 610 CROWN
Copper-Nickel, 38.5 mm. **Ruler:** Elizabeth II **Series:** Flower Fairies **Obv:** Crowned bust right **Rev:** Rose

Date	Mintage	F	VF	XF	Unc	BU
1996	—	—	—	—	8.00	10.00

KM# 610a CROWN
28.2800 g., 0.9250 Silver 0.8410 oz. ASW, 38.5 mm.
Ruler: Elizabeth II **Series:** Flower Fairies **Obv:** Crowned bust right **Rev:** Rose

Date	Mintage	F	VF	XF	Unc	BU
1996 Proof	Est. 30,000	Value: 40.00				

KM# 611 CROWN
Copper-Nickel, 38.5 mm. **Ruler:** Elizabeth II **Series:** Flower Fairies **Obv:** Crowned bust right **Rev:** Fuchsia

Date	Mintage	F	VF	XF	Unc	BU
1996	—	—	—	—	5.00	6.50

KM# 611a CROWN
28.2800 g., 0.9250 Silver 0.8410 oz. ASW, 38.5 mm.
Ruler: Elizabeth II **Series:** Flower Fairies **Obv:** Crowned bust right **Rev:** Fuchsia

Date	Mintage	F	VF	XF	Unc	BU
1996 Proof	Est. 30,000	Value: 40.00				

KM# 612 CROWN
Copper-Nickel, 38.5 mm. **Ruler:** Elizabeth II **Series:** Flower Fairies **Obv:** Crowned bust right **Rev:** Pinks

Date	Mintage	F	VF	XF	Unc	BU
1996	—	—	—	—	5.00	6.50

KM# 612a CROWN
28.2800 g., 0.9250 Silver 0.8410 oz. ASW, 38.5 mm.
Ruler: Elizabeth II **Series:** Flower Fairies **Obv:** Crowned bust right **Rev:** Pinks

Date	Mintage	F	VF	XF	Unc	BU
1996 Proof	Est. 30,000	Value: 40.00				

KM# 621 CROWN
Copper-Nickel, 38.5 mm. **Ruler:** Elizabeth II **Obv:** Crowned bust right **Rev:** Burmese cat

Date	Mintage	F	VF	XF	Unc	BU
1996	—	—	—	—	12.50	17.50

KM# 621a CROWN
31.1035 g., 0.9990 Silver 0.9990 oz. ASW, 38.5 mm.
Ruler: Elizabeth II **Obv:** Crowned bust right **Rev:** Burmese cat

Date	Mintage	F	VF	XF	Unc	BU
1996 Proof	Est. 50,000	Value: 40.00				

KM# 621b CROWN
31.1000 g., 0.9990 Gold 0.9988 oz. AGW **Ruler:** Elizabeth II **Obv:** Crowned bust right **Rev:** Burmese cat

Date	Mintage	F	VF	XF	Unc	BU
1996 U	—	—	—	—	—	975
1996 Proof	—	Value: 985				

KM# 621c CROWN
31.1035 g., 0.9995 Platinum 0.9995 oz. APW **Ruler:** Elizabeth II **Obv:** Crowned bust right **Rev:** Burmese cat **Note:** Prev. KM#624.

Date	Mintage	F	VF	XF	Unc	BU
1996	—	—	—	—	—	2,000
1996 Proof	—	Value: 2,250				

KM# 626 CROWN
Copper-Nickel, 38.5 mm. **Ruler:** Elizabeth II **Obv:** Crowned bust right **Rev:** Bust within map and ship

Date	Mintage	F	VF	XF	Unc	BU
1996	—	—	—	—	7.50	10.00

KM# 626a CROWN
28.2800 g., 0.9250 Silver 0.8410 oz. ASW, 38.5 mm.
Ruler: Elizabeth II **Obv:** Crowned bust right **Rev:** Bust within map and ship

Date	Mintage	F	VF	XF	Unc	BU
1996 Proof	Est. 30,000	Value: 40.00				

KM# 629 CROWN
Copper-Nickel, 38.5 mm. **Ruler:** Elizabeth II **Obv:** Crowned bust right **Rev:** Bust, map and ship

Date	Mintage	F	VF	XF	Unc	BU
1996	—	—	—	—	7.00	9.00

KM# 629a CROWN
28.2800 g., 0.9250 Silver 0.8410 oz. ASW, 38.5 mm.
Ruler: Elizabeth II **Obv:** Crowned bust right **Rev:** Bust, map and ship

Date	Mintage	F	VF	XF	Unc	BU
1996 Proof	Est. 30,000	Value: 40.00				

KM# 632 CROWN
Copper-Nickel, 38.5 mm. **Ruler:** Elizabeth II **Series:** European Football Championship **Obv:** Crowned bust right **Rev:** Football player flanked by emblems within broken circle

Date	Mintage	F	VF	XF	Unc	BU
1996	—	—	—	—	7.00	9.00

KM# 632a CROWN
28.2800 g., 0.9250 Silver 0.8410 oz. ASW, 38.5 mm.
Ruler: Elizabeth II **Series:** European Football Championship **Obv:** Crowned bust right **Rev:** Football player flanked by emblems within broken circle

Date	Mintage	F	VF	XF	Unc	BU
1996 Proof	Est. 30,000	Value: 40.00				

KM# 635 CROWN
Copper-Nickel, 38.5 mm. **Ruler:** Elizabeth II **Series:** European Football Championship **Obv:** Crowned bust right **Rev:** Czech Republic vs Itay

Date	Mintage	F	VF	XF	Unc	BU
1996	—	—	—	—	7.00	9.00

KM# 635a CROWN
28.2800 g., 0.9250 Silver 0.8410 oz. ASW, 38.5 mm.
Ruler: Elizabeth II **Series:** European Football Championship **Obv:** Crowned bust right **Rev:** Czech Republic vs Italy

Date	Mintage	F	VF	XF	Unc	BU
1996 Proof	Est. 30,000	Value: 40.00				

KM# 638 CROWN
Copper-Nickel, 38.5 mm. **Ruler:** Elizabeth II **Series:** European Football Championship **Obv:** Crowned bust right **Rev:** Germany vs Russia

Date	Mintage	F	VF	XF	Unc	BU
1996	—	—	—	—	7.00	9.00

KM# 638a CROWN
28.2800 g., 0.9250 Silver 0.8410 oz. ASW, 38.5 mm.
Ruler: Elizabeth II **Series:** European Football Championship **Obv:** Crowned bust right **Rev:** Germany vs Russia

Date	Mintage	F	VF	XF	Unc	BU
1996 Proof	Est. 30,000	Value: 40.00				

KM# 641 CROWN
Copper-Nickel, 38.5 mm. **Ruler:** Elizabeth II **Series:** European Football Championship **Obv:** Crowned bust right **Rev:** Spain vs France

Date	Mintage	F	VF	XF	Unc	BU
1996	—	—	—	—	7.00	9.00

KM# 641a CROWN
28.2800 g., 0.9250 Silver 0.8410 oz. ASW, 38.5 mm.
Ruler: Elizabeth II **Series:** European Football Championship **Obv:** Crowned bust right **Rev:** Spain vs France

Date	Mintage	F	VF	XF	Unc	BU
1996 Proof	Est. 30,000	Value: 40.00				

KM# 644 CROWN
Copper-Nickel, 38.5 mm. **Ruler:** Elizabeth II **Series:** European Football Championship **Obv:** Crowned bust right **Rev:** Turkey vs Croatia

Date	Mintage	F	VF	XF	Unc	BU
1996	—	—	—	—	7.00	9.00

KM# 644a CROWN
28.2800 g., 0.9250 Silver 0.8410 oz. ASW, 38.5 mm.
Ruler: Elizabeth II **Series:** European Football Championship **Obv:** Crowned bust right **Rev:** Turkey vs Croatia

Date	Mintage	F	VF	XF	Unc	BU
1996 Proof	Est. 30,000	Value: 40.00				

KM# 647 CROWN
Copper-Nickel, 38.5 mm. **Ruler:** Elizabeth II **Series:** European Football Championship **Obv:** Crowned bust right **Rev:** Denmark vs Portugal

Date	Mintage	F	VF	XF	Unc	BU
1996	—	—	—	—	6.00	8.00

KM# 647a CROWN
28.2800 g., 0.9250 Silver 0.8410 oz. ASW, 38.5 mm.
Ruler: Elizabeth II **Series:** European Football Championship **Obv:** Crowned bust right **Rev:** Denmark vs Portugal

Date	Mintage	F	VF	XF	Unc	BU
1996 Proof	Est. 30,000	Value: 40.00				

KM# 650 CROWN
Copper-Nickel, 38.5 mm. **Ruler:** Elizabeth II **Series:** European Football Championship **Obv:** Crowned bust right **Rev:** Scotland vs England

Date	Mintage	F	VF	XF	Unc	BU
1996	—	—	—	—	7.00	9.00

KM# 650a CROWN
28.2800 g., 0.9250 Silver 0.8410 oz. ASW, 38.5 mm.
Ruler: Elizabeth II **Series:** European Football Championship **Obv:** Crowned bust right **Rev:** Scotland vs England

Date	Mintage	F	VF	XF	Unc	BU
1996 Proof	Est. 30,000	Value: 40.00				

KM# 653 CROWN
Copper-Nickel, 38.5 mm. **Ruler:** Elizabeth II **Series:** European Football Championship **Obv:** Crowned bust right **Rev:** Holland vs Switzerland

Date	Mintage	F	VF	XF	Unc	BU
1996	—	—	—	—	7.00	9.00

KM# 653a CROWN
28.2800 g., 0.9250 Silver 0.8410 oz. ASW, 38.5 mm.
Ruler: Elizabeth II **Series:** European Football Championship **Obv:** Crowned bust right **Rev:** Holland vs Switzerland

Date	Mintage	F	VF	XF	Unc	BU
1996 Proof	Est. 30,000	Value: 40.00				

KM# 657   CROWN
Copper-Nickel, 38.5 mm. **Ruler:** Elizabeth II **Series:** European Football Championship **Obv:** Crowned bust right **Rev:** German shield, winner

Date	Mintage	F	VF	XF	Unc	BU
1996	—	—	—	—	7.00	9.00

KM# 657a   CROWN
28.2800 g., 0.9250 Silver 0.8410 oz. ASW, 38.5 mm.
Ruler: Elizabeth II **Series:** European Football Championship **Obv:** Crowned bust right **Rev:** German shield, winner

Date	Mintage	F	VF	XF	Unc	BU
1996 Proof	Est. 30,000	Value: 40.00				

KM# 679   CROWN
Copper-Nickel, 38.5 mm. **Ruler:** Elizabeth II **Series:** Legend of King Arthur **Obv:** Crowned bust right **Rev:** King Arthur with sword and orb

Date	Mintage	F	VF	XF	Unc	BU
1996	—	—	—	—	10.00	12.50

KM# 679a   CROWN
28.2800 g., 0.9250 Silver 0.8410 oz. ASW, 38.5 mm.
Ruler: Elizabeth II **Series:** Legend of King Arthur **Obv:** Crowned bust right **Rev:** King Arthur with sword and orb

Date	Mintage	F	VF	XF	Unc	BU
1996 Proof	Est. 30,000	Value: 22.50				

KM# 680   CROWN
Copper-Nickel, 38.5 mm. **Ruler:** Elizabeth II **Series:** Legend of King Arthur **Obv:** Crowned bust right **Rev:** Crowned Queen Guinevere facing walking through archway

Date	Mintage	F	VF	XF	Unc	BU
1996	—	—	—	—	10.00	12.50

KM# 680a   CROWN
28.2800 g., 0.9250 Silver 0.8410 oz. ASW, 38.5 mm.
Ruler: Elizabeth II **Series:** Legend of King Arthur **Obv:** Crowned bust right **Rev:** Crowned Queen Guinevere facing walking through archway

Date	Mintage	F	VF	XF	Unc	BU
1996 Proof	Est. 30,000	Value: 22.50				

KM# 681   CROWN
Copper-Nickel, 38.5 mm. **Ruler:** Elizabeth II **Series:** Legend of King Arthur **Obv:** Crowned bust right **Rev:** Sir Lancelot on horse right within inner circle

Date	Mintage	F	VF	XF	Unc	BU
1996	—	—	—	—	10.00	12.50

KM# 681a   CROWN
28.2800 g., 0.9250 Silver 0.8410 oz. ASW, 38.5 mm.
Ruler: Elizabeth II **Series:** Legend of King Arthur **Obv:** Crowned bust right **Rev:** Sir Lancelot on horse right within inner circle

Date	Mintage	F	VF	XF	Unc	BU
1996 Proof	Est. 30,000	Value: 22.50				

KM# 682   CROWN
Copper-Nickel, 38.5 mm. **Ruler:** Elizabeth II **Series:** Legend of King Arthur **Obv:** Crowned bust right **Rev:** Merlin

Date	Mintage	F	VF	XF	Unc	BU
1996	—	—	—	—	10.00	12.50

KM# 682a   CROWN
28.2800 g., 0.9250 Silver 0.8410 oz. ASW, 38.5 mm.
Ruler: Elizabeth II **Series:** Legend of King Arthur **Obv:** Crowned bust right **Rev:** Merlin

Date	Mintage	F	VF	XF	Unc	BU
1996 Proof	Est. 30,000	Value: 22.50				

KM# 683   CROWN
Copper-Nickel, 38.5 mm. **Ruler:** Elizabeth II **Series:** Legend of King Arthur **Obv:** Crowned bust right **Rev:** Camelot Castle

Date	Mintage	F	VF	XF	Unc	BU
1996	—	—	—	—	10.00	12.50

KM# 683a   CROWN
28.2800 g., 0.9250 Silver 0.8410 oz. ASW, 38.5 mm.
Ruler: Elizabeth II **Series:** Legend of King Arthur **Obv:** Crowned bust right **Rev:** Camelot Castle

Date	Mintage	F	VF	XF	Unc	BU
1996 Proof	Est. 30,000	Value: 25.00				

KM# 732   CROWN
Copper-Nickel, 38.5 mm. **Ruler:** Elizabeth II **Subject:** Year of the Rat **Obv:** Crowned bust right within circle **Rev:** Rat within circle

Date	Mintage	F	VF	XF	Unc	BU
1996	—	—	—	—	12.00	15.00

KM# 732a   CROWN
28.2800 g., 0.9250 Silver 0.8410 oz. ASW, 38.5 mm.
Ruler: Elizabeth II **Subject:** Year of the Rat **Obv:** Crowned bust right within circle **Rev:** Rat within circle

Date	Mintage	F	VF	XF	Unc	BU
1996 Proof	—					

Note: Entire silver issue purchased by one buyer. Mintage, disposition and market value unknown

KM# 732b   CROWN
31.1035 g., 0.9999 Gold 0.9999 oz. AGW **Ruler:** Elizabeth II **Subject:** Year of the Rat **Obv:** Crowned bust right **Rev:** Rat **Note:** Prev. KM#733.

Date	Mintage	F	VF	XF	Unc	BU
1996 Proof	—					

Note: Entire gold issue purchased by one buyer. Mintage, disposition and market value unknown

KM# 725   CROWN
Copper-Nickel, 38.5 mm. **Ruler:** Elizabeth II **Subject:** Year of the Ox **Obv:** Crowned bust right **Rev:** Ox laying down

Date	Mintage	F	VF	XF	Unc	BU
1997	—	—	—	—	10.00	14.00

KM# 725a   CROWN
28.2800 g., 0.9250 Silver 0.8410 oz. ASW, 38.5 mm.
Ruler: Elizabeth II **Subject:** Year of the Ox **Obv:** Crowned bust right **Rev:** Ox laying down

Date	Mintage	F	VF	XF	Unc	BU
1997 Proof	Est. 30,000	Value: 35.00				

KM# 725b   CROWN
31.1035 g., 0.9999 Gold 0.9999 oz. AGW **Ruler:** Elizabeth II **Subject:** Year of the Ox **Obv:** Crowned bust right **Rev:** Ox laying down **Note:** Prev. KM#726.

Date	Mintage	F	VF	XF	Unc	BU
1997 Proof	Est. 2,000	Value: 985				

KM# 759   CROWN
Copper-Nickel, 38.5 mm. **Ruler:** Elizabeth II **Series:** Flower Fairies **Obv:** Crowned bust right **Rev:** Fairy sitting on flowers - Candytuft

Date	Mintage	F	VF	XF	Unc	BU
1997	—	—	—	—	8.00	10.00

KM# 759a   CROWN
28.2800 g., 0.9250 Silver 0.8410 oz. ASW, 38.5 mm.
Ruler: Elizabeth II **Series:** Flower Fairies **Obv:** Crowned bust right **Rev:** Fairy sitting on flowers - Candytuft

Date	Mintage	F	VF	XF	Unc	BU
1997 Proof	Est. 30,000	Value: 40.00				

KM# 760   CROWN
Copper-Nickel, 38.5 mm. **Ruler:** Elizabeth II **Series:** Flower Fairies **Obv:** Crowned bust right **Rev:** Snowdrop

Date	Mintage	F	VF	XF	Unc	BU
1997	—	—	—	—	8.00	10.00

KM# 760a   CROWN
28.2800 g., 0.9250 Silver 0.8410 oz. ASW, 38.5 mm.
Ruler: Elizabeth II **Series:** Flower Fairies **Obv:** Crowned bust right **Rev:** Snowdrop

Date	Mintage	F	VF	XF	Unc	BU
1997 Proof	Est. 30,000	Value: 40.00				

KM# 761 CROWN
Copper-Nickel, 38.5 mm. **Ruler:** Elizabeth II **Series:** Flower Fairies **Obv:** Crowned bust right **Rev:** Tulip

Date	Mintage	F	VF	XF	Unc	BU
1997	—	—	—	—	8.00	10.00

KM# 761a CROWN
28.2800 g., 0.9250 Silver 0.8410 oz. ASW, 38.5 mm.
Ruler: Elizabeth II **Series:** Flower Fairies **Obv:** Crowned bust right **Rev:** Tulip

Date	Mintage	F	VF	XF	Unc	BU
1997 Proof	Est. 30,000	Value: 40.00				

KM# 762 CROWN
Copper-Nickel, 38.5 mm. **Ruler:** Elizabeth II **Series:** Flower Fairies **Obv:** Crowned bust right **Rev:** Jasmine

Date	Mintage	F	VF	XF	Unc	BU
1997	—	—	—	—	8.00	10.00

KM# 762a CROWN
28.2800 g., 0.9250 Silver 0.8410 oz. ASW, 38.5 mm.
Ruler: Elizabeth II **Series:** Flower Fairies **Obv:** Crowned bust right **Rev:** Jasmine

Date	Mintage	F	VF	XF	Unc	BU
1997 Proof	Est. 30,000	Value: 40.00				

KM# 765 CROWN
Copper-Nickel, 38.5 mm. **Ruler:** Elizabeth II **Obv:** Crowned bust right **Rev:** Leif Eriksson 999-1001, viking ship with map sail

Date	Mintage	F	VF	XF	Unc	BU
1997	—	—	—	—	8.00	10.00

KM# 765a CROWN
28.2800 g., 0.9250 Silver 0.8410 oz. ASW, 38.5 mm.
Ruler: Elizabeth II **Obv:** Crowned bust right **Rev:** Leif Eriksson 999-1001, viking ship with map sail

Date	Mintage	F	VF	XF	Unc	BU
1997 Proof	Est. 30,000	Value: 40.00				

KM# 768 CROWN
Copper-Nickel, 38.5 mm. **Ruler:** Elizabeth II **Obv:** Crowned bust right **Rev:** Bust of Fridtjof Nansen, map and his ship "The Fram"

Date	Mintage	F	VF	XF	Unc	BU
1997	—	—	—	—	8.00	10.00

KM# 768a CROWN
28.2800 g., 0.9250 Silver 0.8410 oz. ASW, 38.5 mm.
Ruler: Elizabeth II **Obv:** Crowned bust right **Rev:** Bust of Fridtjof Nansen, map and his ship "The Fram"

Date	Mintage	F	VF	XF	Unc	BU
1997 Proof	Est. 30,000	Value: 40.00				

KM# 774 CROWN
Copper-Nickel, 38.5 mm. **Ruler:** Elizabeth II **Obv:** Crowned bust right **Rev:** Long-haired Smoke cat

Date	Mintage	F	VF	XF	Unc	BU
1997	—	—	—	—	10.00	15.00
1997 Proof	—	Value: 20.00				

KM# 774a CROWN
31.1035 g., 0.9999 Silver 0.9999 oz. ASW, 38.5 mm.
Ruler: Elizabeth II **Obv:** Crowned bust right **Rev:** Long-haired Smoke cat

Date	Mintage	F	VF	XF	Unc	BU
1997 Proof	Est. 50,000	Value: 40.00				

KM# 774b CROWN
31.1035 g., 0.9999 Gold 0.9999 oz. AGW. **Ruler:** Elizabeth II **Obv:** Crowned bust right **Rev:** Long-haired Smoke cat

Date	Mintage	F	VF	XF	Unc	BU
1997	—	—	—	—	—	975
1997 Proof	—	Value: 985				

KM# 777 CROWN
28.2800 g., 0.9250 Silver 0.8410 oz. ASW, 38.5 mm.
Ruler: Elizabeth II **Series:** History of the Cat **Obv:** Crowned bust right **Rev:** Ancestry of Felidae, evolution of the cat

Date	Mintage	F	VF	XF	Unc	BU
1997 Proof	Est. 10,000	Value: 45.00				

KM# 778 CROWN
28.2800 g., 0.9250 Silver 0.8410 oz. ASW, 38.5 mm.
Ruler: Elizabeth II **Series:** History of the Cat **Obv:** Crowned bust right **Rev:** Snarling cat

Date	Mintage	F	VF	XF	Unc	BU
1997 Proof	Est. 10,000	Value: 45.00				

KM# 779 CROWN
28.2800 g., 0.9250 Silver 0.8410 oz. ASW, 38.5 mm.
Ruler: Elizabeth II **Series:** History of the Cat **Obv:** Crowned bust right **Rev:** Cat walking left

Date	Mintage	F	VF	XF	Unc	BU
1997 Proof	Est. 10,000	Value: 45.00				

KM# 780 CROWN
28.2800 g., 0.9250 Silver 0.8410 oz. ASW, 38.5 mm.
Ruler: Elizabeth II **Series:** History of the Cat **Obv:** Crowned bust right **Rev:** Ancient Egyptian Goddess Bast and artifacts

Date	Mintage	F	VF	XF	Unc	BU
1997 Proof	Est. 10,000	Value: 45.00				

KM# 782 CROWN
Copper-Nickel, 38.5 mm. **Ruler:** Elizabeth II **Subject:** 90th Anniversary of the TT **Obv:** Crowned bust right **Rev:** Motorcyclist flanked by emblems above sprigs

Date	Mintage	F	VF	XF	Unc	BU
1997	—	—	—	—	8.00	10.00

KM# 782a CROWN
28.2800 g., 0.9250 Silver 0.8410 oz. ASW, 38.5 mm.
Ruler: Elizabeth II **Subject:** 90th Anniversary of the TT **Obv:** Crowned bust right **Rev:** Motorcyclist flanked by emblems above sprigs

Date	Mintage	F	VF	XF	Unc	BU
1997 Proof	Est. 30,000	Value: 42.50				

KM# 784 CROWN
Copper-Nickel, 38.5 mm. **Ruler:** Elizabeth II **Subject:** 90th
Anniversary of the TT **Obv:** Crowned bust right **Rev:** 1937 winner
Omobono Tenni

Date	Mintage	F	VF	XF	Unc	BU
1997	—			—	9.50	11.50

KM# 784a CROWN
28.2800 g., 0.9250 Silver 0.8410 oz. ASW, 38.5 mm.
Ruler: Elizabeth II **Subject:** 90th Anniversary of the TT
Obv: Crowned bust right **Rev:** 1937 winner Omobono Tenni

Date	Mintage	F	VF	XF	Unc	BU
1997 Proof	Est. 30,000		Value: 42.50			

KM# 786 CROWN
Copper-Nickel, 38.5 mm. **Ruler:** Elizabeth II **Subject:** 90th
Anniversary of the TT **Obv:** Crowned bust right **Rev:** 1957 winner
Bob McIntyre

Date	Mintage	F	VF	XF	Unc	BU
1997	—			—	9.50	11.50

KM# 786a CROWN
28.2800 g., 0.9250 Silver 0.8410 oz. ASW, 38.5 mm.
Ruler: Elizabeth II **Subject:** 90th Anniversary of the TT
Obv: Crowned bust right **Rev:** 1957 winner Bob McIntyre

Date	Mintage	F	VF	XF	Unc	BU
1997 Proof	Est. 30,000		Value: 42.50			

KM# 788 CROWN
Copper-Nickel, 38.5 mm. **Ruler:** Elizabeth II **Subject:** 90th
Anniversary of the TT **Obv:** Crowned bust right **Rev:** 1967 winner
Mike Hailwood

Date	Mintage	F	VF	XF	Unc	BU
1997	—			—	9.50	11.50

KM# 788a CROWN
28.2800 g., 0.9250 Silver 0.8410 oz. ASW, 38.5 mm.
Ruler: Elizabeth II **Subject:** 90th Anniversary of the TT
Obv: Crowned bust right **Rev:** 1967 winner Mike Hailwood

Date	Mintage	F	VF	XF	Unc	BU
1997 Proof	Est. 30,000		Value: 42.50			

KM# 793 CROWN
Copper-Nickel, 38.5 mm. **Ruler:** Elizabeth II **Subject:** 50th
Wedding Anniversary of Queen Elizabeth II and Prince Philip
Obv: Crowned bust right **Rev:** Conjoined 3/4 length figures facing

Date	Mintage	F	VF	XF	Unc	BU
1997	—				8.00	10.00

KM# 793a CROWN
28.2800 g., 0.9250 Gold Clad Silver 0.8410 oz., 38.5 mm.
Ruler: Elizabeth II **Subject:** 50th Wedding Anniversary of Queen
Elizabeth II and Prince Philip **Obv:** Crowned bust right
Rev: Conjoined 3/4 length figures facing

Date	Mintage	F	VF	XF	Unc	BU
1997 Proof	Est. 10,000		Value: 40.00			

KM# 799 CROWN
Copper-Nickel, 38.5 mm. **Ruler:** Elizabeth II **Series:** Year 2000
Subject: Birth of Christ **Obv:** Crowned bust right **Rev:** Madonna
and child with angels

Date	Mintage	F	VF	XF	Unc	BU
1997	—				7.50	9.50

KM# 799a CROWN
28.2800 g., 0.9250 Silver 0.8410 oz. ASW, 38.5 mm.
Ruler: Elizabeth II **Series:** Year 2000 **Subject:** Birth of Christ
Obv: Crowned bust right **Rev:** Madonna and child with angels

Date	Mintage	F	VF	XF	Unc	BU
1997 Proof	Est. 10,000		Value: 50.00			

KM# 801 CROWN
Copper-Nickel, 38.5 mm. **Ruler:** Elizabeth II **Series:** Year 2000
Subject: Fall of the Roman Empire 476 **Obv:** Crowned bust right
Rev: Barbarian defeating soldier

Date	Mintage	F	VF	XF	Unc	BU
1997	—				7.50	9.50

KM# 801a CROWN
28.2800 g., 0.9250 Silver 0.8410 oz. ASW, 38.5 mm.
Ruler: Elizabeth II **Series:** Year 2000 **Subject:** Fall of the Roman
Empire 476 **Obv:** Crowned bust right **Rev:** Barbarian defeating
soldier

Date	Mintage	F	VF	XF	Unc	BU
1997 Proof	Est. 10,000		Value: 50.00			

KM# 803 CROWN
Copper-Nickel, 38.5 mm. **Ruler:** Elizabeth II **Series:** Year 2000
Subject: Flight of Mohammed 622 **Obv:** Crowned bust right
Rev: Arabs and camels at oasis

Date	Mintage	F	VF	XF	Unc	BU
1997	—				7.50	12.00

KM# 803a CROWN
28.2800 g., 0.9250 Silver 0.8410 oz. ASW, 38.5 mm.
Ruler: Elizabeth II **Series:** Year 2000 **Subject:** Flight of
Mohammed 622 **Obv:** Crowned bust right **Rev:** Arabs and camels
at oasis

Date	Mintage	F	VF	XF	Unc	BU
1997 Proof	Est. 10,000		Value: 45.00			

KM# 805 CROWN
Copper-Nickel, 38.5 mm. **Ruler:** Elizabeth II **Series:** Year 2000
Subject: Norman Conquest 1066 **Obv:** Crowned bust right
Rev: William the Conqueror rallying his troops

Date	Mintage	F	VF	XF	Unc	BU
1997	—				7.50	9.50

KM# 805a CROWN
28.2800 g., 0.9250 Silver 0.8410 oz. ASW, 38.5 mm.
Ruler: Elizabeth II **Series:** Year 2000 **Subject:** Norman Conquest
1066 **Obv:** Crowned bust right **Rev:** Armored equestrian rallying
his troops

Date	Mintage	F	VF	XF	Unc	BU
1997 Proof	Est. 10,000		Value: 50.00			

KM# 808 CROWN
Copper-Nickel, 38.5 mm. **Ruler:** Elizabeth II **Series:** World Cup
Soccer **Obv:** Crowned bust right **Rev:** Soccer players within ball

Date	Mintage	F	VF	XF	Unc	BU
1998	—				7.50	9.50

KM# 808a CROWN
28.2800 g., 0.9250 Silver 0.8410 oz. ASW, 38.5 mm.
Ruler: Elizabeth II **Series:** World Cup Soccer **Obv:** Crowned bust
right **Rev:** Soccer players within ball

Date	Mintage	F	VF	XF	Unc	BU
1998 Proof	Est. 30,000		Value: 45.00			

KM# 809 CROWN

Copper-Nickel, 38.5 mm. **Ruler:** Elizabeth II **Series:** World Cup Soccer **Obv:** Crowned bust right **Rev:** Soccer players

Date	Mintage	F	VF	XF	Unc	BU
1998	—	—	—	—	7.50	9.50

KM# 809a CROWN

28.2800 g., 0.9250 Silver 0.8410 oz. ASW, 38.5 mm. **Ruler:** Elizabeth II **Series:** World Cup Soccer **Obv:** Crowned bust right **Rev:** Soccer players

Date	Mintage	F	VF	XF	Unc	BU
1998 Proof	Est. 30,000	Value: 45.00				

KM# 810 CROWN

Copper-Nickel, 38.5 mm. **Ruler:** Elizabeth II **Series:** World Cup Soccer **Obv:** Crowned bust right **Rev:** Soccer players

Date	Mintage	F	VF	XF	Unc	BU
1998	—	—	—	—	7.50	9.50

KM# 810a CROWN

28.2800 g., 0.9250 Silver 0.8410 oz. ASW, 38.5 mm. **Ruler:** Elizabeth II **Series:** World Cup Soccer **Obv:** Crowned bust right **Rev:** Soccer players

Date	Mintage	F	VF	XF	Unc	BU
1998 Proof	Est. 30,000	Value: 45.00				

KM# 811 CROWN

Copper-Nickel, 38.5 mm. **Ruler:** Elizabeth II **Series:** World Cup Soccer **Obv:** Crowned bust right **Rev:** Soccer players

Date	Mintage	F	VF	XF	Unc	BU
1998	—	—	—	—	7.50	9.50

KM# 811a CROWN

28.2800 g., 0.9250 Silver 0.8410 oz. ASW, 38.5 mm. **Ruler:** Elizabeth II **Series:** World Cup Soccer **Obv:** Crowned bust right **Rev:** Soccer players

Date	Mintage	F	VF	XF	Unc	BU
1998 Proof	Est. 30,000	Value: 45.00				

KM# 816 CROWN

Copper-Nickel, 38.5 mm. **Ruler:** Elizabeth II **Subject:** Year of the Tiger **Obv:** Crowned bust right within circle **Rev:** Tiger within circle

Date	Mintage	F	VF	XF	Unc	BU
1998	—	—	—	—	12.00	15.00

KM# 816a CROWN

28.2800 g., 0.9250 Silver 0.8410 oz. ASW, 38.5 mm. **Ruler:** Elizabeth II **Subject:** Year of the Tiger **Obv:** Crowned bust right within circle **Rev:** Tiger within circle

Date	Mintage	F	VF	XF	Unc	BU
1998 Proof	Est. 30,000	Value: 45.00				

KM# 817 CROWN

31.1035 g., 0.9999 Gold 0.9999 oz. AGW **Ruler:** Elizabeth II **Subject:** Year of the Tiger **Obv:** Crowned bust right **Rev:** Tiger

Date	Mintage	F	VF	XF	Unc	BU
1998 Proof	Est. 2,000	Value: 985				

KM# 825 CROWN

Copper-Nickel, 38.5 mm. **Ruler:** Elizabeth II **Subject:** Marco Polo **Obv:** Crowned bust right **Rev:** Bust right, caravan and palace

Date	Mintage	F	VF	XF	Unc	BU
1998	—	—	—	—	8.00	10.00

KM# 825a CROWN

28.2800 g., 0.9250 Silver 0.8410 oz. ASW, 38.5 mm. **Ruler:** Elizabeth II **Subject:** Marco Polo **Obv:** Crowned bust right **Rev:** Bust right, caravan and palace

Date	Mintage	F	VF	XF	Unc	BU
1998 Proof	Est. 30,000	Value: 47.50				

KM# 827 CROWN

Copper-Nickel, 38.5 mm. **Ruler:** Elizabeth II **Obv:** Crowned bust right **Rev:** Bust, ship and African map

Date	Mintage	F	VF	XF	Unc	BU
1998	—	—	—	—	8.00	10.00

KM# 827a CROWN

28.2800 g., 0.9250 Silver 0.8410 oz. ASW, 38.5 mm. **Ruler:** Elizabeth II **Obv:** Crowned bust right **Rev:** Bust, ship and African map

Date	Mintage	F	VF	XF	Unc	BU
1998 Proof	Est. 30,000	Value: 47.50				

KM# 840 CROWN

Copper-Nickel, 38.5 mm. **Ruler:** Elizabeth II **Series:** Flower Fairies **Obv:** Crowned bust right **Rev:** Standing fairy - Lavender

Date	Mintage	F	VF	XF	Unc	BU
1998	—	—	—	—	8.00	10.00

KM# 840a CROWN

28.2800 g., 0.9250 Silver 0.8410 oz. ASW, 38.5 mm. **Ruler:** Elizabeth II **Series:** Flower Fairies **Obv:** Crowned bust right **Rev:** Standing fairy - Lavender

Date	Mintage	F	VF	XF	Unc	BU
1998 Proof	Est. 30,000	Value: 47.50				

KM# 841 CROWN

Copper-Nickel, 38.5 mm. **Ruler:** Elizabeth II **Series:** Flower Fairies **Obv:** Crowned bust right **Rev:** Sweet pea, two fairies

Date	Mintage	F	VF	XF	Unc	BU
1998	—	—	—	—	7.50	9.50

KM# 841a CROWN

28.2800 g., 0.9250 Silver 0.8410 oz. ASW, 38.5 mm. **Ruler:** Elizabeth II **Series:** Flower Fairies **Obv:** Crowned bust right **Rev:** Sweet pea, two fairies

Date	Mintage	F	VF	XF	Unc	BU
1998 Proof	Est. 30,000	Value: 47.50				

KM# 842 CROWN

Copper-Nickel, 38.5 mm. **Ruler:** Elizabeth II **Series:** Flower Fairies **Obv:** Crowned bust right **Rev:** Fairy looking into flower - White Bindweed

Date	Mintage	F	VF	XF	Unc	BU
1998	—	—	—	—	7.50	9.50

KM# 842a CROWN

28.2800 g., 0.9250 Silver 0.8410 oz. ASW, 38.5 mm. **Ruler:** Elizabeth II **Series:** Flower Fairies **Obv:** Crowned bust right **Rev:** Fairy looking into flower - White Bindweed

Date	Mintage	F	VF	XF	Unc	BU
1998 Proof	Est. 30,000	Value: 47.50				

KM# 843 CROWN

Copper-Nickel, 38.5 mm. **Ruler:** Elizabeth II **Series:** Flower Fairies **Obv:** Crowned bust right **Rev:** Fairy standing with flower - Daffodil

Date	Mintage	F	VF	XF	Unc	BU
1998	—	—	—	—	8.00	10.00

KM# 843a CROWN

28.2800 g., 0.9250 Silver 0.8410 oz. ASW, 38.5 mm. **Ruler:** Elizabeth II **Series:** Flower Fairies **Obv:** Crowned bust right **Rev:** Fairy standing with flower - Daffodil

Date	Mintage	F	VF	XF	Unc	BU
1998 Proof	Est. 20,000	Value: 47.50				

KM# 849 CROWN
Copper-Nickel, 38.5 mm. **Ruler:** Elizabeth II **Series:** Winter Olympics - Nagano **Obv:** Crowned bust right **Rev:** Bobsled

Date	Mintage	F	VF	XF	Unc	BU
1998	—	—	—	—	7.50	9.50

KM# 849a CROWN
28.2800 g., 0.9250 Silver 0.8410 oz. ASW, 38.5 mm.
Ruler: Elizabeth II **Series:** Winter Olympics - Nagano
Obv: Crowned bust right **Rev:** Bobsled

Date	Mintage	F	VF	XF	Unc	BU
1998 Proof	Est. 30,000	Value: 47.50				

KM# 852 CROWN
Copper-Nickel, 38.5 mm. **Ruler:** Elizabeth II **Series:** Winter Olympics - Nagano **Obv:** Crowned bust right **Rev:** Two speed skaters

Date	Mintage	F	VF	XF	Unc	BU
1998	—	—	—	—	7.50	9.50

KM# 852a CROWN
28.2800 g., 0.9250 Silver 0.8410 oz. ASW, 38.5 mm.
Ruler: Elizabeth II **Series:** Winter Olympics - Nagano
Obv: Crowned bust right **Rev:** Two speed skaters

Date	Mintage	F	VF	XF	Unc	BU
1998 Proof	Est. 30,000	Value: 47.50				

KM# 874 CROWN
28.4000 g., Copper-Nickel, 38.52 mm. **Ruler:** Elizabeth II
Subject: 125th Anniversary of the Steam Railway **Obv:** Crowned bust right **Rev:** English steam locomotive "The Rocket" below bust of George Stephenson **Edge:** Reeded

Date	Mintage	F	VF	XF	Unc	BU
1998PM	—	—	—	—	10.00	12.00

KM# 874a CROWN
28.2800 g., 0.9250 Silver 0.8410 oz. ASW, 38.52 mm.
Ruler: Elizabeth II **Subject:** 125th Anniversary of the Steam Railway **Obv:** Crowned bust right **Rev:** English steam locomotive "The Rocket" below bust of George Stephenson **Edge:** Reeded

Date	Mintage	F	VF	XF	Unc	BU
1998PM Proof	Est. 30,000	Value: 47.50				

KM# 850 CROWN
Copper-Nickel, 38.5 mm. **Ruler:** Elizabeth II **Series:** Winter Olympics - Nagano **Obv:** Crowned bust right **Rev:** Cross-country skier

Date	Mintage	F	VF	XF	Unc	BU
1998	—	—	—	—	7.50	9.50

KM# 850a CROWN
28.2800 g., 0.9250 Silver 0.8410 oz. ASW, 38.5 mm.
Ruler: Elizabeth II **Series:** Winter Olympics - Nagano
Obv: Crowned bust right **Rev:** Cross-country skier

Date	Mintage	F	VF	XF	Unc	BU
1998 Proof	Est. 30,000	Value: 47.50				

KM# 857 CROWN
Copper-Nickel, 38.5 mm. **Ruler:** Elizabeth II **Obv:** Crowned bust right **Rev:** Birman cat

Date	Mintage	F	VF	XF	Unc	BU
1998	—	—	—	—	10.00	15.00
1998 Proof		Value: 17.50				

KM# 857a CROWN
31.1035 g., 0.9999 Silver 0.9999 oz. ASW, 38.5 mm.
Ruler: Elizabeth II **Obv:** Crowned bust right **Rev:** Birman cat

Date	Mintage	F	VF	XF	Unc	BU
1998 Proof	Est. 50,000	Value: 40.00				

KM# 857b CROWN
31.1035 g., 0.9999 Gold 0.9999 oz. AGW **Ruler:** Elizabeth II
Obv: Crowned bust right **Rev:** Birman cat

Date	Mintage	F	VF	XF	Unc	BU
1998	—	—	—	—	—	975
1998 Proof	1,000	Value: 985				

KM# 876 CROWN
Copper-Nickel, 38.5 mm. **Ruler:** Elizabeth II **Subject:** 125th Anniversary of the Steam Railway **Obv:** Crowned bust right **Rev:** View within parlor car

Date	Mintage	F	VF	XF	Unc	BU
1998	—	—	—	—	10.00	12.00

KM# 876a CROWN
28.2800 g., 0.9250 Silver 0.8410 oz. ASW, 38.5 mm.
Ruler: Elizabeth II **Subject:** 125th Anniversary of the Steam Railway **Obv:** Crowned bust right **Rev:** View within parlor car

Date	Mintage	F	VF	XF	Unc	BU
1998 Proof	Est. 30,000	Value: 47.50				

KM# 851 CROWN
Copper-Nickel, 38.5 mm. **Ruler:** Elizabeth II **Series:** Winter Olympics - Nagano **Obv:** Crowned bust right **Rev:** Two hockey players

Date	Mintage	F	VF	XF	Unc	BU
1998	—	—	—	—	7.50	9.50

KM# 851a CROWN
28.2800 g., 0.9250 Silver 0.8410 oz. ASW, 38.5 mm.
Ruler: Elizabeth II **Series:** Winter Olympics - Nagano
Obv: Crowned bust right **Rev:** Two hockey players

Date	Mintage	F	VF	XF	Unc	BU
1998 Proof	Est. 30,000	Value: 47.50				

KM# 872 CROWN
28.4000 g., Copper-Nickel, 38.52 mm. **Ruler:** Elizabeth II
Subject: 125th Anniversary of the Steam Railway **Obv:** Crowned bust right **Rev:** American steam locomotive "The General" **Edge:** Reeded

Date	Mintage	F	VF	XF	Unc	BU
1998PM	—	—	—	—	10.00	12.00

KM# 872a CROWN
28.2800 g., 0.9250 Silver 0.8410 oz. ASW, 38.52 mm.
Ruler: Elizabeth II **Subject:** 125th Anniversary of the Steam Railway **Obv:** Crowned bust right **Rev:** American steam locomotive "The General" **Edge:** Reeded

Date	Mintage	F	VF	XF	Unc	BU
1998PM Proof	Est. 30,000	Value: 47.50				

KM# 878 CROWN
28.4000 g., Copper-Nickel, 38.52 mm. **Ruler:** Elizabeth II
Subject: 125th Anniversary of the Steam Railway **Obv:** Crowned bust right **Rev:** Mount Pilatus Railway **Edge:** Reeded

Date	Mintage	F	VF	XF	Unc	BU
1998PM	—	—	—	—	10.00	12.00

KM# 878a CROWN
28.2800 g., 0.9250 Silver 0.8410 oz. ASW, 38.52 mm.
Ruler: Elizabeth II **Subject:** 125th Anniversary of the Steam Railway **Obv:** Crowned bust right **Rev:** Mount Pilatus Railway **Edge:** Reeded

Date	Mintage	F	VF	XF	Unc	BU
1998PM Proof	Est. 30,000	Value: 47.50				

KM# 880 CROWN
28.4000 g., Copper-Nickel, 38.52 mm. **Ruler:** Elizabeth II
Subject: 125th Anniversary of the Steam Railway **Obv:** Crowned
bust right **Rev:** English steam locomotive "No. 1 Sutherland"
Edge: Reeded

Date	Mintage	F	VF	XF	Unc	BU
1998PM	—	—	—	—	10.00	12.00

KM# 880a CROWN
28.2800 g., 0.9250 Silver 0.8410 oz. ASW, 38.52 mm.
Ruler: Elizabeth II **Subject:** 125th Anniversary of the Steam
Railway **Obv:** Crowned bust right **Rev:** English steam locomotive
"No. 1 Sutherland" **Edge:** Reeded

Date	Mintage	F	VF	XF	Unc	BU
1998PM Proof	Est. 30,000	Value: 47.50				

KM# 882 CROWN
Copper-Nickel, 38.5 mm. **Ruler:** Elizabeth II **Subject:** 125th
Anniversary of the Steam Railway **Obv:** Crowned bust right
Rev: "Flying Scotsman" locomotive

Date	Mintage	F	VF	XF	Unc	BU
1998	—	—	—	—	10.00	12.00

KM# 882a CROWN
28.2800 g., 0.9250 Silver 0.8410 oz. ASW, 38.5 mm.
Ruler: Elizabeth II **Subject:** 125th Anniversary of the Steam
Railway **Obv:** Crowned bust right **Rev:** "Flying Scotsman"
locomotive

Date	Mintage	F	VF	XF	Unc	BU
1998 Proof	Est. 30,000	Value: 47.50				

KM# 884 CROWN
Copper-Nickel, 38.5 mm. **Ruler:** Elizabeth II **Subject:** 125th
Anniversary of the Steam Railway **Obv:** Crowned bust right
Rev: "The Mallard" locomotive

Date	Mintage	F	VF	XF	Unc	BU
1998	—	—	—	—	10.00	12.00

KM# 884a CROWN
28.2800 g., 0.9250 Silver 0.8410 oz. ASW, 38.5 mm.
Ruler: Elizabeth II **Subject:** 125th Anniversary of the Steam
Railway **Obv:** Crowned bust right **Rev:** "The Mallard" locomotive

Date	Mintage	F	VF	XF	Unc	BU
1998 Proof	Est. 30,000	Value: 47.50				

KM# 886 CROWN
Copper-Nickel, 38.5 mm. **Ruler:** Elizabeth II **Subject:** 125th
Anniversary of the Steam Railway **Obv:** Crowned bust right
Rev: "The Big Boy" locomotive

Date	Mintage	F	VF	XF	Unc	BU
1998	—	—	—	—	10.00	12.00

KM# 886a CROWN
28.2800 g., 0.9250 Silver 0.8410 oz. ASW, 38.5 mm.
Ruler: Elizabeth II **Subject:** 125th Anniversary of the Steam
Railway
Obv: Bust of Queen Elizabeth II right **Rev:** "The Big Boy" locomotive

Date	Mintage	F	VF	XF	Unc	BU
1998 Proof	Est. 30,000	Value: 47.50				

KM# 888 CROWN
Copper-Nickel, 38.5 mm. **Ruler:** Elizabeth II **Series:** Year 2000
Obv: Crowned bust right **Rev:** Group of standing figures

Date	Mintage	F	VF	XF	Unc	BU
1998	—	—	—	—	8.00	10.00

KM# 888a CROWN
28.2800 g., 0.9250 Silver 0.8410 oz. ASW, 38.5 mm.
Ruler: Elizabeth II **Series:** Year 2000 **Obv:** Crowned bust right
Rev: Group of standing figures

Date	Mintage	F	VF	XF	Unc	BU
1998 Proof	Est. 30,000	Value: 28.50				

KM# 890 CROWN
Copper-Nickel, 38.5 mm. **Ruler:** Elizabeth II **Series:** Year 2000
Obv: Crowned bust right **Rev:** French Revolution 1789

Date	Mintage	F	VF	XF	Unc	BU
1998	—	—	—	—	7.50	9.50

KM# 890a CROWN
28.2800 g., 0.9250 Silver 0.8410 oz. ASW, 38.5 mm.
Ruler: Elizabeth II **Series:** Year 2000 **Obv:** Crowned bust right
Rev: French Revolution 1789

Date	Mintage	F	VF	XF	Unc	BU
1998 Proof	Est. 30,000	Value: 28.50				

KM# 892 CROWN
Copper-Nickel, 38.5 mm. **Ruler:** Elizabeth II **Series:** Year 2000
Obv: Crowned bust right **Rev:** Reformation of the Church 1517

Date	Mintage	F	VF	XF	Unc	BU
1998	—	—	—	—	7.50	9.50

KM# 892a CROWN
28.2800 g., 0.9250 Silver 0.8410 oz. ASW, 38.5 mm.
Ruler: Elizabeth II **Series:** Year 2000 **Obv:** Crowned bust right
Rev: Reformation of the Church 1517

Date	Mintage	F	VF	XF	Unc	BU
1998 Proof	Est. 30,000	Value: 28.50				

KM# 894 CROWN
Copper-Nickel, 38.5 mm. **Ruler:** Elizabeth II **Series:** Year 2000
Obv: Crowned bust right **Rev:** 400th Anniversary of the
Renaissance

Date	Mintage	F	VF	XF	Unc	BU
1998	—	—	—	—	7.50	9.50

KM# 894a CROWN
28.2800 g., 0.9250 Silver 0.8410 oz. ASW, 38.5 mm.
Ruler: Elizabeth II **Series:** Year 2000 **Obv:** Crowned bust right
Rev: 400th Anniversary of the Renaissance

Date	Mintage	F	VF	XF	Unc	BU
1998 Proof	Est. 30,000	Value: 28.50				

KM# 896 CROWN
Copper-Nickel, 38.5 mm. **Ruler:** Elizabeth II **Series:** Year of the
Ocean **Obv:** Crowned bust right **Rev:** Basking shark

Date	Mintage	F	VF	XF	Unc	BU
1998	—	—	—	—	12.50	17.50

KM# 896a CROWN
28.2800 g., 0.9250 Silver 0.8410 oz. ASW, 38.5 mm.
Ruler: Elizabeth II **Series:** Year of the Ocean **Obv:** Crowned
bust right **Rev:** Basking shark

Date	Mintage	F	VF	XF	Unc	BU
1998 Proof	Est. 30,000	Value: 47.50				

KM# 897 CROWN
Copper-Nickel, 38.5 mm. **Ruler:** Elizabeth II **Series:** Year of the Ocean **Obv:** Crowned bust right **Rev:** Humpback whale

Date	Mintage	F	VF	XF	Unc	BU
1998	—	—	—	—	12.50	15.00

KM# 897a CROWN
28.2800 g., 0.9250 Silver 0.8410 oz. ASW, 38.5 mm.
Ruler: Elizabeth II **Series:** Year of the Ocean **Obv:** Crowned bust right **Rev:** Humpback whale

Date	Mintage	F	VF	XF	Unc	BU
1998 Proof	Est. 30,000	Value: 47.50				

KM# 898 CROWN
Copper-Nickel, 38.5 mm. **Ruler:** Elizabeth II **Series:** Year of the Ocean **Obv:** Crowned bust right **Rev:** Penguins and seals

Date	Mintage	F	VF	XF	Unc	BU
1998	—	—	—	—	12.00	18.00

KM# 898a CROWN
28.2800 g., 0.9250 Silver 0.8410 oz. ASW, 38.5 mm.
Ruler: Elizabeth II **Series:** Year of the Ocean **Obv:** Crowned bust right **Rev:** Penguins and seals

Date	Mintage	F	VF	XF	Unc	BU
1998 Proof	Est. 30,000	Value: 45.00				

KM# 899 CROWN
Copper-Nickel, 38.5 mm. **Ruler:** Elizabeth II **Series:** Year of the Ocean **Obv:** Crowned bust right **Rev:** Sailboats

Date	Mintage	F	VF	XF	Unc	BU
1998	—	—	—	—	10.00	12.00

KM# 899a CROWN
28.2800 g., 0.9250 Silver 0.8410 oz. ASW, 38.5 mm.
Ruler: Elizabeth II **Series:** Year of the Ocean **Obv:** Crowned bust right **Rev:** Sailboats

Date	Mintage	F	VF	XF	Unc	BU
1998 Proof	Est. 30,000	Value: 47.50				

KM# A984 CROWN
Copper-Nickel, 38.5 mm. **Ruler:** Elizabeth II **Subject:** Founding of the UN 1945 **Obv:** Crowned bust right **Rev:** UN Building and logo

Date	Mintage	F	VF	XF	Unc	BU
2000	—	—	—	—	8.00	10.00

KM# 914 CROWN
Copper-Nickel, 38.5 mm. **Ruler:** Elizabeth II **Subject:** Battle of Waterloo 1815 **Obv:** Crowned bust right **Rev:** Napoleon on horse half left

Date	Mintage	F	VF	XF	Unc	BU
1999	—	—	—	—	8.00	10.00

KM# 914a CROWN
28.2800 g., 0.9250 Silver 0.8410 oz. ASW, 38.5 mm.
Ruler: Elizabeth II **Subject:** Battle of Waterloo 1815 **Obv:** Crowned bust right **Rev:** Napoleon on horse half left

Date	Mintage	F	VF	XF	Unc	BU
1999 Proof	Est. 10,000	Value: 50.00				

KM# 918 CROWN
Copper-Nickel, 38.5 mm. **Ruler:** Elizabeth II **Subject:** Russian Revolution 1917 **Obv:** Crowned bust right **Rev:** Lenin above the Aurora

Date	Mintage	F	VF	XF	Unc	BU
1999	—	—	—	—	7.50	9.50

KM# 918a CROWN
28.2800 g., 0.9250 Silver 0.8410 oz. ASW, 38.5 mm.
Ruler: Elizabeth II **Subject:** Russian Revolution 1917 **Obv:** Crowned bust right **Rev:** Lenin above the Aurora

Date	Mintage	F	VF	XF	Unc	BU
1999 Proof	Est. 10,000	Value: 50.00				

KM# 916 CROWN
Copper-Nickel, 38.5 mm. **Ruler:** Elizabeth II **Subject:** American Civil War 1865 **Obv:** Crowned bust right **Rev:** Cameos, swords, flag and drum

Date	Mintage	F	VF	XF	Unc	BU
1999	—	—	—	—	9.50	11.50

KM# 916a CROWN
28.2800 g., 0.9250 Silver 0.8410 oz. ASW, 38.5 mm.
Ruler: Elizabeth II **Subject:** American Civil War 1865 **Obv:** Crowned bust right **Rev:** Cameos, swords, flag and drum

Date	Mintage	F	VF	XF	Unc	BU
1999 Proof	Est. 10,000	Value: 50.00				

KM# 988 CROWN
Copper-Nickel, 38.5 mm. **Ruler:** Elizabeth II **Subject:** Fall of Berlin Wall 1989 **Obv:** Crowned bust right **Rev:** Crowds around wall **Edge:** Reeded

Date	Mintage	F	VF	XF	Unc	BU
2000	—	—	—	—	7.50	9.50

KM# 988a CROWN
28.2800 g., 0.9250 Silver 0.8410 oz. ASW, 38.5 mm.
Ruler: Elizabeth II **Subject:** Fall of Berlin Wall 1989 **Obv:** Crowned bust right **Rev:** Crowds around wall

Date	Mintage	F	VF	XF	Unc	BU
2000 Proof	Est. 10,000	Value: 50.00				

KM# 920 CROWN
Copper-Nickel, 38.5 mm. **Ruler:** Elizabeth II **Subject:** World War I Armistice Day 1918 **Obv:** Crowned bust right **Rev:** Biplane above tank **Edge:** Reeded

Date	Mintage	F	VF	XF	Unc	BU
1999	—	—	—	—	7.50	9.50

KM# 920a CROWN
28.2800 g., 0.9250 Silver 0.8410 oz. ASW, 38.5 mm.
Ruler: Elizabeth II **Subject:** World War I Armistice Day 1918 **Obv:** Crowned bust right **Rev:** Biplane above tank

Date	Mintage	F	VF	XF	Unc	BU
1999 Proof	Est. 10,000	Value: 50.00				

KM# 990 CROWN
Copper-Nickel, 38.5 mm. **Ruler:** Elizabeth II **Subject:** Millennium 2000 - The Future **Obv:** Crowned bust right **Rev:** International Space Station **Edge:** Reeded

Date	Mintage	F	VF	XF	Unc	BU
2000	—	—	—	—	7.50	9.50

KM# 990a CROWN
28.2800 g., 0.9250 Silver 0.8410 oz. ASW, 38.5 mm.
Ruler: Elizabeth II **Subject:** Millennium 2000 - The Future **Obv:** Crowned bust right **Rev:** International Space Station

Date	Mintage	F	VF	XF	Unc	BU
2000 Proof	Est. 10,000	Value: 50.00				

KM# 922 CROWN
Copper-Nickel, 38.5 mm. **Ruler:** Elizabeth II **Series:** Summer Olympics - Sydney **Obv:** Crowned bust right **Rev:** Javelin throwers **Edge:** Reeded

Date	Mintage	F	VF	XF	Unc	BU
1999	—	—	—	—	7.50	9.50

KM# 922a CROWN
28.2800 g., 0.9250 Silver 0.8410 oz. ASW, 38.5 mm.
Ruler: Elizabeth II **Series:** Summer Olympics - Sydney
Obv: Crowned bust right **Rev:** Javelin throwers

Date	Mintage	F	VF	XF	Unc	BU
1999 Proof	Est. 10,000	Value: 50.00				

KM# 924 CROWN
Copper-Nickel, 38.5 mm. **Ruler:** Elizabeth II **Series:** Summer Olympics - Sydney **Obv:** Crowned bust right **Rev:** Diver divides map **Edge:** Reeded

Date	Mintage	F	VF	XF	Unc	BU
1999	—	—	—	—	7.50	9.50

KM# 924a CROWN
28.2800 g., 0.9250 Silver 0.8410 oz. ASW, 38.5 mm.
Ruler: Elizabeth II **Series:** Summer Olympics - Sydney
Obv: Crowned bust right **Rev:** Diver divides map

Date	Mintage	F	VF	XF	Unc	BU
1999 Proof	Est. 10,000	Value: 50.00				

KM# 926 CROWN
Copper-Nickel, 38.5 mm. **Ruler:** Elizabeth II **Series:** Summer Olympics - Sydney **Obv:** Crowned bust right **Rev:** Sailboat and Sydney Opera House **Edge:** Reeded

Date	Mintage	F	VF	XF	Unc	BU
1999	—	—	—	—	7.50	9.50

KM# 926a CROWN
28.2800 g., 0.9250 Silver 0.8410 oz. ASW, 38.5 mm.
Ruler: Elizabeth II **Series:** Summer Olympics - Sydney
Obv: Crowned bust right **Rev:** Sailboat and Sydney Opera House

Date	Mintage	F	VF	XF	Unc	BU
1999 Proof	Est. 10,000	Value: 50.00				

KM# 928 CROWN
Copper-Nickel, 38.5 mm. **Ruler:** Elizabeth II **Series:** Summer Olympics - Sydney **Obv:** Crowned bust right **Rev:** Runners and torch **Edge:** Reeded

Date	Mintage	F	VF	XF	Unc	BU
1999	—	—	—	—	7.50	9.50

KM# 928a CROWN
28.2800 g., 0.9250 Silver 0.8410 oz. ASW, 38.5 mm.
Ruler: Elizabeth II **Series:** Summer Olympics - Sydney
Obv: Crowned bust right **Rev:** Runners and torch

Date	Mintage	F	VF	XF	Unc	BU
1999 Proof	Est. 10,000	Value: 50.00				

KM# 930 CROWN
Copper-Nickel, 38.5 mm. **Ruler:** Elizabeth II **Series:** Summer Olympics - Sydney **Obv:** Crowned bust right **Rev:** Hurdlers and Sydney Opera House **Edge:** Reeded

Date	Mintage	F	VF	XF	Unc	BU
1999	—	—	—	—	7.50	9.50

KM# 930a CROWN
28.2800 g., 0.9250 Silver 0.8410 oz. ASW, 38.5 mm.
Ruler: Elizabeth II **Series:** Summer Olympics - Sydney
Obv: Crowned bust right **Rev:** Hurdlers and Sydney Opera House

Date	Mintage	F	VF	XF	Unc	BU
1999 Proof	Est. 10,000	Value: 50.00				

KM# 932 CROWN
Copper-Nickel, 38.5 mm. **Ruler:** Elizabeth II **Series:** World Cup Rugby 1999 **Obv:** Crowned bust right **Rev:** Bust 1/4 right flanked by players **Edge:** Reeded

Date	Mintage	F	VF	XF	Unc	BU
1999	—	—	—	—	8.00	10.00

KM# 932a CROWN
28.2800 g., 0.9250 Silver 0.8410 oz. ASW, 38.5 mm..
Ruler: Elizabeth II **Series:** World Cup Rugby 1999
Obv: Crowned bust right **Rev:** Bust 1/4 right flanked by players

Date	Mintage	F	VF	XF	Unc	BU
1999 Proof	Est. 10,000	Value: 50.00				

KM# 934 CROWN
Copper-Nickel, 38.5 mm. **Ruler:** Elizabeth II **Series:** World Cup Rugby 1999 **Obv:** Crowned bust right **Rev:** Rugby scrum **Edge:** Reeded

Date	Mintage	F	VF	XF	Unc	BU
1999	—	—	—	—	8.00	10.00

KM# 934a CROWN
28.2800 g., 0.9250 Silver 0.8410 oz. ASW, 38.5 mm.
Ruler: Elizabeth II **Series:** World Cup Rugby 1999
Obv: Crowned bust right **Rev:** Rugby scrum

Date	Mintage	F	VF	XF	Unc	BU
1999 Proof	Est. 10,000	Value: 50.00				

KM# 936 CROWN
Copper-Nickel, 38.5 mm. **Ruler:** Elizabeth II **Series:** World Cup Rugby 1999 **Obv:** Crowned bust right **Rev:** Player catching ball **Edge:** Reeded

Date	Mintage	F	VF	XF	Unc	BU
1999	—	—	—	—	8.00	10.00

KM# 936a CROWN
28.2800 g., 0.9250 Silver 0.8410 oz. ASW, 38.5 mm.
Ruler: Elizabeth II **Series:** World Cup Rugby 1999
Obv: Crowned bust right **Rev:** Player catching ball

Date	Mintage	F	VF	XF	Unc	BU
1999 Proof	Est. 10,000	Value: 50.00				

KM# 938 CROWN
Copper-Nickel, 38.5 mm. **Ruler:** Elizabeth II **Series:** World Cup Rugby 1999 **Obv:** Crowned bust right **Rev:** Goal kick **Edge:** Reeded

Date	Mintage	F	VF	XF	Unc	BU
1999	—	—	—	—	8.00	10.00

KM# 938a CROWN
28.2800 g., 0.9250 Silver 0.8410 oz. ASW, 38.5 mm.
Ruler: Elizabeth II **Series:** World Cup Rugby 1999
Obv: Crowned bust right **Rev:** Goal kick

Date	Mintage	F	VF	XF	Unc	BU
1999 Proof	Est. 10,000	Value: 50.00				

KM# 940 CROWN
Copper-Nickel, 38.5 mm. **Ruler:** Elizabeth II **Series:** World Cup
Rugby 1999 **Obv:** Crowned bust right **Rev:** Ball runner being
tackled **Edge:** Reeded

Date	Mintage	F	VF	XF	Unc	BU
1999	—	—	—	—	8.00	10.00

KM# 940a CROWN
28.2800 g., 0.9250 Silver 0.8410 oz. ASW, 38.5 mm.
Ruler: Elizabeth II **Series:** World Cup Rugby 1999
Obv: Crowned bust right **Rev:** Ball runner being tackled

Date	Mintage	F	VF	XF	Unc	BU
1999 Proof	Est. 10,000	Value: 50.00				

KM# 942 CROWN
Copper-Nickel, 38.5 mm. **Ruler:** Elizabeth II **Series:** World Cup
Rugby 1999 **Obv:** Crowned bust right **Rev:** Player jumping for
catch **Edge:** Reeded

Date	Mintage	F	VF	XF	Unc	BU
1999	—	—	—	—	8.00	10.00

KM# 942a CROWN
28.2800 g., 0.9250 Silver 0.8410 oz. ASW, 38.5 mm.
Ruler: Elizabeth II **Series:** World Cup Rugby 1999
Obv: Crowned bust right **Rev:** Player jumping for catch

Date	Mintage	F	VF	XF	Unc	BU
1999 Proof	Est. 10,000	Value: 50.00				

KM# 952 CROWN
Copper-Nickel, 38.5 mm. **Ruler:** Elizabeth II **Subject:** Year of
the Rabbit **Obv:** Crowned bust right **Rev:** Rabbits **Edge:** Reeded

Date	Mintage	F	VF	XF	Unc	BU
1999	—	—	—	—	12.00	15.00

KM# 952a CROWN
28.2800 g., 0.9250 Silver 0.8410 oz. ASW, 38.5 mm.
Ruler: Elizabeth II **Subject:** Year of the Rabbit **Obv:** Crowned
bust right **Rev:** Rabbits

Date	Mintage	F	VF	XF	Unc	BU
1999 Proof	Est. 10,000	Value: 45.00				

KM# 952b CROWN
31.1035 g., 0.9999 Gold 0.9999 oz. AGW **Ruler:** Elizabeth II
Subject: Year of the Rabbit **Obv:** Crowned bust right **Rev:** Rabbits

Date	Mintage	F	VF	XF	Unc	BU
1999 Proof	Est. 2,000	Value: 985				

KM# 955 CROWN
Copper-Nickel, 38.5 mm. **Ruler:** Elizabeth II **Subject:** Sir Walter
Raleigh **Obv:** Crowned bust right **Rev:** Bust with hat, map of
America and ship **Edge:** Reeded

Date	Mintage	F	VF	XF	Unc	BU
1999	—	—	—	—	8.00	10.00

KM# 955a CROWN
28.2800 g., 0.9250 Silver 0.8410 oz. ASW, 38.5 mm.
Ruler: Elizabeth II **Subject:** Sir Walter Raleigh **Obv:** Crowned
bust right **Rev:** Bust with hat, map of America and ship

Date	Mintage	F	VF	XF	Unc	BU
1999 Proof	Est. 10,000	Value: 50.00				

KM# 957 CROWN
Copper-Nickel, 38.5 mm. **Ruler:** Elizabeth II **Obv:** Crowned bust
right **Rev:** Compass, bust of Robert Falcon Scott and men pulling
sled **Edge:** Reeded

Date	Mintage	F	VF	XF	Unc	BU
1999	—	—	—	—	8.00	10.00

KM# 957a CROWN
28.2800 g., 0.9250 Silver 0.8410 oz. ASW, 38.5 mm.
Ruler: Elizabeth II **Obv:** Crowned bust right **Rev:** Compass, bust
of Robert Falcon Scott and men pulling sled

Date	Mintage	F	VF	XF	Unc	BU
1999 Proof	Est. 10,000	Value: 50.00				

KM# 966 CROWN
Copper-Nickel, 38.5 mm. **Ruler:** Elizabeth II **Obv:** Crowned bust
right **Rev:** British Blue cat cleaning its paws **Edge:** Reeded

Date	Mintage	F	VF	XF	Unc	BU
1999	—	—	—	—	9.00	15.00

KM# 966a CROWN
31.1035 g., 0.9990 Silver 0.9990 oz. ASW, 38.5 mm.
Ruler: Elizabeth II **Obv:** Crowned bust right **Rev:** British Blue cat
cleaning its paws **Note:** Prev. KM#967.

Date	Mintage	F	VF	XF	Unc	BU
1999 Proof	Est. 50,000	Value: 40.00				

KM# 966b CROWN
31.1035 g., 0.9990 Gold 0.9990 oz. AGW **Ruler:** Elizabeth II
Obv: Crowned bust right **Rev:** British Blue cat cleaning its paws
Note: Prev. KM#968.

Date	Mintage	F	VF	XF	Unc	BU
1999	—	—	—	—	—	975
1999 Proof	—	Value: 985				

KM# 976 CROWN
Copper-Nickel, 38.5 mm. **Ruler:** Elizabeth II **Series:** The Life
and Times of the Queen Mother **Obv:** Crowned bust right
Rev: Seated child facing **Edge:** Reeded

Date	Mintage	F	VF	XF	Unc	BU
1999	—	—	—	—	7.50	9.50

KM# 976a CROWN
28.2800 g., 0.9250 Silver 0.8410 oz. ASW, 38.5 mm.
Ruler: Elizabeth II **Series:** The Life and Times of the Queen
Mother **Obv:** Crowned bust right **Rev:** Seated child facing

Date	Mintage	F	VF	XF	Unc	BU
1999 Proof	Est. 10,000	Value: 50.00				

KM# 978 CROWN
Copper-Nickel, 38.5 mm. **Ruler:** Elizabeth II **Series:** The Life
and Times of the Queen Mother **Obv:** Crowned bust right
Rev: Royal engagement portrait **Edge:** Reeded

Date	Mintage	F	VF	XF	Unc	BU
1999	—	—	—	—	7.50	9.50

KM# 978a CROWN
28.2800 g., 0.9250 Silver 0.8410 oz. ASW, 38.5 mm.
Ruler: Elizabeth II **Series:** The Life and Times of the Queen
Mother **Obv:** Crowned bust right **Rev:** Royal engagement portrait

Date	Mintage	F	VF	XF	Unc	BU
1999 Proof	Est. 10,000	Value: 50.00				

KM# 980 CROWN
Copper-Nickel, 38.5 mm. **Ruler:** Elizabeth II **Series:** The Life
and Times of the Queen Mother **Obv:** Crowned bust right
Rev: Wedding portrait **Edge:** Reeded

Date	Mintage	F	VF	XF	Unc	BU
1999	—	—	—	—	7.50	9.50

KM# 980a CROWN
28.2800 g., 0.9250 Silver 0.8410 oz. ASW **Ruler:** Elizabeth II
Series: The Life and Times of the Queen Mother **Obv:** Crowned
bust right **Rev:** Wedding portrait

Date	Mintage	F	VF	XF	Unc	BU
1999 Proof	Est. 10,000	Value: 50.00				

KM# 982 CROWN
Copper-Nickel, 38.5 mm. **Ruler:** Elizabeth II **Subject:** The Life and Times of the Queen Mother **Obv:** Crowned bust right **Rev:** Honeymoon departure **Edge:** Reeded

Date	Mintage	F	VF	XF	Unc	BU
1999	—	—	—	—	7.50	9.50

KM# 982a CROWN
28.2800 g., 0.9250 Silver 0.8410 oz. ASW, 38.5 mm.
Ruler: Elizabeth II **Series:** The Life and Times of the Queen Mother **Obv:** Crowned bust right **Rev:** Honeymoon departure

Date	Mintage	F	VF	XF	Unc	BU
1999 Proof	Est. 10,000	Value: 50.00				

KM# 1000 CROWN
Copper-Nickel, 38.5 mm. **Ruler:** Elizabeth II **Subject:** 30th Anniversary of First Man on the Moon **Obv:** Crowned bust right **Rev:** Apollo XI and moon walkers

Date	Mintage	F	VF	XF	Unc	BU
1999	—	—	—	—	7.50	9.50

KM# 1000a CROWN
28.2800 g., 0.9250 Silver 0.8410 oz. ASW, 38.5 mm.
Ruler: Elizabeth II **Subject:** 30th Anniversary of First Man on the Moon **Obv:** Crowned bust right **Rev:** Apollo XI and two moon walkers

Date	Mintage	F	VF	XF	Unc	BU
1999 Proof	Est. 10,000	Value: 50.00				

KM# 1006 CROWN
Copper-Nickel, 38.5 mm. **Ruler:** Elizabeth II **Subject:** 30th Anniversary of First Man on the Moon **Obv:** Crowned bust right **Rev:** Viking Mars Lander, 1978

Date	Mintage	F	VF	XF	Unc	BU
1999	—	—	—	—	7.50	9.50

KM# 1006a CROWN
28.2800 g., 0.9250 Silver 0.8410 oz. ASW, 38.5 mm.
Ruler: Elizabeth II **Subject:** 30th Anniversary of First Man on the Moon **Obv:** Crowned bust right **Rev:** Viking Mars lander, 1978

Date	Mintage	F	VF	XF	Unc	BU
1999 Proof	Est. 10,000	Value: 50.00				

KM# 996 CROWN
Copper-Nickel, 38.5 mm. **Ruler:** Elizabeth II **Subject:** The Wedding of HRH Prince Edward and Sophie Rhys-Jones **Obv:** Crowned bust right **Rev:** Head right

Date	Mintage	F	VF	XF	Unc	BU
1999	—	—	—	—	7.50	9.50

KM# 996a CROWN
28.2800 g., 0.9250 Silver 0.8410 oz. ASW, 38.5 mm.
Ruler: Elizabeth II **Subject:** The Wedding of HRH Prince Edward and Sophie Rhys-Jones **Obv:** Crowned bust right **Rev:** Head right

Date	Mintage	F	VF	XF	Unc	BU
1999 Proof	Est. 10,000	Value: 50.00				

KM# 1002 CROWN
Copper-Nickel, 38.5 mm. **Ruler:** Elizabeth II **Subject:** 30th Anniversary of First Man on the Moon **Obv:** Crowned bust right **Rev:** Mariner IX, 1971 and orbiting Mars

Date	Mintage	F	VF	XF	Unc	BU
1999	—	—	—	—	7.50	9.50

KM# 1002a CROWN
28.2800 g., 0.9250 Silver 0.8410 oz. ASW, 38.5 mm.
Ruler: Elizabeth II **Subject:** 30th Anniversary of First Man on the Moon **Obv:** Crowned bust right **Rev:** Mariner IX orbiting Mars

Date	Mintage	F	VF	XF	Unc	BU
1999	—	—	—	—	—	—

KM# 1008 CROWN
Copper-Nickel, 38.5 mm. **Ruler:** Elizabeth II **Subject:** 30th Anniversary of First Man on the Moon **Obv:** Crowned bust right **Rev:** Shuttle orbiter Columbia, 1981

Date	Mintage	F	VF	XF	Unc	BU
1999	—	—	—	—	8.00	10.00

KM# 1008a CROWN
28.2800 g., 0.9250 Silver 0.8410 oz. ASW, 38.5 mm.
Ruler: Elizabeth II **Subject:** 30th Anniversary of First Man on the Moon **Obv:** Crowned bust right **Rev:** Shuttle orbiter Columbia, 1981

Date	Mintage	F	VF	XF	Unc	BU
1999 Proof	Est. 10,000	Value: 50.00				

KM# 998 CROWN
Copper-Nickel, 38.5 mm. **Ruler:** Elizabeth II **Subject:** The Wedding of HRH Prince Edward and Sophie Rhys-Jones **Obv:** Crowned bust right **Rev:** Head left

Date	Mintage	F	VF	XF	Unc	BU
1999	—	—	—	—	7.50	9.50

KM# 998a CROWN
28.2800 g., 0.9250 Silver 0.8410 oz. ASW, 38.5 mm.
Ruler: Elizabeth II **Subject:** The Wedding of HRH Prince Edward and Sophie Rhys-Jones **Obv:** Crowned bust right **Rev:** Head left

Date	Mintage	F	VF	XF	Unc	BU
1999 Proof	Est. 10,000	Value: 50.00				

KM# 1004 CROWN
Copper-Nickel, 38.5 mm. **Ruler:** Elizabeth II **Subject:** 30th Anniversary of First Man on the Moon **Obv:** Crowned bust right **Rev:** Apollo-Soyuz link-up, 1975

Date	Mintage	F	VF	XF	Unc	BU
1999	—	—	—	—	7.50	9.50

KM# 1004a CROWN
28.2800 g., 0.9250 Silver 0.8410 oz. ASW, 38.5 mm.
Ruler: Elizabeth II **Subject:** 30th Anniversary of First Man on the Moon **Obv:** Crowned bust right **Rev:** Apollo-Soyuz link-up, 1975

Date	Mintage	F	VF	XF	Unc	BU
1999 Proof	Est. 10,000	Value: 50.00				

KM# 1010 CROWN
Copper-Nickel, 38.5 mm. **Ruler:** Elizabeth II **Subject:** 30th Anniversary of First Man on the Moon **Obv:** Crowned bust right **Rev:** Mars Pathfinder, 1997

Date	Mintage	F	VF	XF	Unc	BU
1999	—	—	—	—	12.00	14.00

KM# 1010a CROWN
28.2800 g., 0.9250 Silver 0.8410 oz. ASW, 38.5 mm.
Ruler: Elizabeth II **Subject:** 30th Anniversary of First Man on the Moon **Obv:** Crowned bust right **Rev:** Mars Pathfinder, 1997

Date	Mintage	F	VF	XF	Unc	BU
1999 Proof	Est. 10,000	Value: 50.00				

KM# 1264 CROWN
28.2800 g., Copper-Nickel, 38.5 mm. **Ruler:** Elizabeth II **Obv:** Crowned bust right **Rev:** Space station and shuttle **Edge:** Reeded

Date	Mintage	F	VF	XF	Unc	BU
2000PM	—	—	—	—	15.00	17.00

KM# 1264a   CROWN
28.2200 g., 0.9250 Silver 0.8392 oz. ASW, 38.5 mm.
Ruler: Elizabeth II **Obv:** Crowned bust right **Rev:** Space station
and shuttle **Edge:** Reeded

Date	Mintage	F	VF	XF	Unc	BU
2000PM Proof	—	Value: 50.00				

KM# 1267   CROWN
28.2500 g., Silver, 38.7 mm.   **Ruler:** Elizabeth II **Subject:** Fall
of the Berlin Wall - 1989 **Obv:** Crowned bust right
Rev: Brandenburg Gate behind crowd holding pennant with
slogan, Love and Peace in West & East **Edge:** Reeded

Date	Mintage	F	VF	XF	Unc	BU
2000	—	—	—	—	12.00	14.00

KM# 986   CROWN
Copper-Nickel, 38.5 mm.   **Ruler:** Elizabeth II **Subject:** First Man
on the Moon **Obv:** Crowned bust right **Rev:** Astronauts on moon
and flag

Date	Mintage	F	VF	XF	Unc	BU
2000	—	—	—	—	7.50	9.50

KM# 986a   CROWN
28.2800 g., 0.9250 Silver 0.8410 oz. ASW, 38.5 mm.
Ruler: Elizabeth II **Subject:** First Man on the Moon
Obv: Crowned bust right **Rev:** Astronauts on moon and flag

Date	Mintage	F	VF	XF	Unc	BU
2000 Proof	Est. 10,000	Value: 50.00				

KM# 1016   CROWN
Copper-Nickel, 38.5 mm.   **Ruler:** Elizabeth II **Subject:** Year of
the Dragon **Obv:** Crowned bust right **Rev:** Dragon

Date	Mintage	F	VF	XF	Unc	BU
2000	—	—	—	—	12.00	15.00

KM# 1016a   CROWN
28.2800 g., 0.9250 Silver 0.8410 oz. ASW, 38.5 mm.
Ruler: Elizabeth II **Subject:** Year of the Dragon **Obv:** Crowned
bust right **Rev:** Dragon

Date	Mintage	F	VF	XF	Unc	BU
2000 Proof	Est. 30,000	Value: 45.00				

KM# 1016b   CROWN
31.1035 g., 0.9999 Gold 0.9999 oz. AGW, 32.7 mm.
Ruler: Elizabeth II **Subject:** Year of the Dragon **Obv:** Crowned
bust right **Rev:** Dragon **Note:** Prev. KM#1017.

Date	Mintage	F	VF	XF	Unc	BU
2000 Proof	Est. 2,000	Value: 985				

KM# 1019   CROWN
28.2800 g., Copper-Nickel, 38.6 mm.   **Ruler:** Elizabeth II
Subject: Millennium **Obv:** Crowned bust right **Rev:** Stylized
monogram **Edge:** Reeded

Date	Mintage	F	VF	XF	Unc	BU
2000	—	—	—	—	8.00	10.00

KM# 1019a   CROWN
28.2800 g., 0.9250 Silver 0.8410 oz. ASW, 38.6 mm.
Ruler: Elizabeth II **Subject:** Millennium **Obv:** Crowned bust right
Rev: Stylized monogram **Edge:** Reeded

Date	Mintage	F	VF	XF	Unc	BU
2000 Proof	10,000	Value: 47.50				

KM# 1021   CROWN
28.2800 g., Copper-Nickel, 38.6 mm.   **Ruler:** Elizabeth II
Obv: Crowned bust right **Rev:** Armored 1/2 bust, map and ship

Date	Mintage	F	VF	XF	Unc	BU
2000	—	—	—	—	8.00	10.00

KM# 1021a   CROWN
28.2800 g., 0.9250 Silver 0.8410 oz. ASW, 38.6 mm.
Ruler: Elizabeth II **Obv:** Crowned bust right **Rev:** Armored 1/2
bust, map and ship

Date	Mintage	F	VF	XF	Unc	BU
2000 Proof	10,000	Value: 47.50				

KM# 1023   CROWN
Copper-Nickel, 38.5 mm.   **Ruler:** Elizabeth II **Obv:** Crowned bust
right **Rev:** Portrait of Willem Barents, ship on ice, map

Date	Mintage	F	VF	XF	Unc	BU
2000	—	—	—	—	8.00	10.00

KM# 1023a   CROWN
28.2800 g., 0.9250 Silver 0.8410 oz. ASW, 38.5 mm.
Ruler: Elizabeth II **Obv:** Crowned bust right **Rev:** Portrait of
Willem Barents, ship on ice, map

Date	Mintage	F	VF	XF	Unc	BU
2000 Proof	10,000	Value: 47.50				

KM# 1025   CROWN
28.2800 g., Copper-Nickel, 38.5 mm.   **Ruler:** Elizabeth II
Series: Queen Mother **Obv:** Crowned bust right **Rev:** 1931
family scene **Edge:** Reeded

Date	Mintage	F	VF	XF	Unc	BU
2000	—	—	—	—	10.00	12.00

KM# 1025a   CROWN
28.2800 g., 0.9250 Silver 0.8410 oz. ASW, 38.5 mm.
Ruler: Elizabeth II **Series:** Queen Mother **Obv:** Crowned bust
right **Rev:** 1931 family scene **Edge:** Reeded

Date	Mintage	F	VF	XF	Unc	BU
2000 Proof	10,000	Value: 47.50				

KM# 1027   CROWN
Copper-Nickel, 38.5 mm.   **Ruler:** Elizabeth II **Obv:** Crowned bust
right **Rev:** 1937 Coronation scene

Date	Mintage	F	VF	XF	Unc	BU
2000	—	—	—	—	10.00	12.00

KM# 1027a   CROWN
28.2800 g., 0.9250 Silver 0.8410 oz. ASW, 38.5 mm.
Ruler: Elizabeth II **Obv:** Crowned bust right **Rev:** Coronation
scene

Date	Mintage	F	VF	XF	Unc	BU
2000 Proof	10,000	Value: 47.50				

KM# 1029   CROWN
Copper-Nickel, 38.5 mm.   **Ruler:** Elizabeth II **Obv:** Crowned bust
right **Rev:** 1945 Victory Visit

Date	Mintage	F	VF	XF	Unc	BU
2000	—	—	—	—	10.00	12.00

KM# 1029a   CROWN
28.2800 g., 0.9250 Silver 0.8410 oz. ASW, 38.5 mm.
Ruler: Elizabeth II **Obv:** Crowned bust right **Rev:** 1945 Victory
Visit

Date	Mintage	F	VF	XF	Unc	BU
2000 Proof	10,000	Value: 47.50				

KM# 1029b   CROWN
28.6500 g., 0.9250 Gilt Silver 0.8520 oz., 38.5 mm.
Ruler: Elizabeth II **Subject:** Queen Mother **Obv:** Crowned bust
right **Rev:** 1945 Royal visit to Isle of Man **Edge:** Reeded

Date	Mintage	F	VF	XF	Unc	BU
2000PM Proof	—	Value: 50.00				

KM# 1031   CROWN
Copper-Nickel, 38.5 mm.   **Ruler:** Elizabeth II **Obv:** Crowned bust
right **Rev:** Queen Mother, coach, and man

Date	Mintage	F	VF	XF	Unc	BU
2000	—	—	—	—	10.00	12.00

KM# 1031a   CROWN
28.2800 g., 0.9250 Silver 0.8410 oz. ASW, 38.5 mm.
Ruler: Elizabeth II **Obv:** Crowned bust right **Rev:** Queen Mother,
coach, and man

Date	Mintage	F	VF	XF	Unc	BU
2000 Proof	10,000	Value: 47.50				

KM# 1031b   CROWN
28.6500 g., 0.9250 Gilt Silver 0.8520 oz., 38.6 mm.
Ruler: Elizabeth II **Subject:** Queen Mother **Obv:** Crowned bust
right **Rev:** 1963 Visit to Isle of Man **Edge:** Reeded

Date	Mintage	F	VF	XF	Unc	BU
2000PM Proof	—	Value: 50.00				

KM# 1033   CROWN
28.2800 g., Copper-Nickel, 38.5 mm.   **Ruler:** Elizabeth II
Subject: Battle of Britain **Obv:** Crowned bust right **Rev:** Aerial
battle scene

Date	Mintage	F	VF	XF	Unc	BU
2000	—	—	—	—	10.00	12.00

KM# 1033a   CROWN
28.2800 g., 0.9250 Silver 0.8410 oz. ASW, 38.5 mm.
Ruler: Elizabeth II **Subject:** Battle of Britain **Obv:** Crowned
bust right **Rev:** Aerial battle scene

Date	Mintage	F	VF	XF	Unc	BU
2000 Proof	10,000	Value: 47.50				

KM# 1035   CROWN
Copper-Nickel, 38.5 mm.   **Ruler:** Elizabeth II **Subject:** Global
Challenge Yacht Race **Obv:** Crowned bust right **Rev:** Partial ship
and map

Date	Mintage	F	VF	XF	Unc	BU
2000	—	—	—	—	10.00	12.00

KM# 1035a CROWN
28.2800 g., 0.9250 Silver 0.8410 oz. ASW, 38.5 mm.
Ruler: Elizabeth II **Subject:** Global Challenge Yacht Race
Obv: Crowned bust right **Rev:** Partial ship and map

Date	Mintage	F	VF	XF	Unc	BU
2000 Proof	10,000				Value: 47.50	

KM# 1047 CROWN
28.2800 g., Copper-Nickel, 38.5 mm. **Ruler:** Elizabeth II
Obv: Crowned bust right **Rev:** Head 3/4 right **Edge:** Reeded

Date	Mintage	F	VF	XF	Unc	BU
2000	—				7.50	9.50

KM# 1047a CROWN
28.2800 g., 0.9250 Silver 0.8410 oz. ASW, 38.5 mm.
Ruler: Elizabeth II **Obv:** Crowned bust right **Rev:** Head 3/4 right
Edge: Reeded

Date	Mintage	F	VF	XF	Unc	BU
2000 Proof	10,000				Value: 47.50	

KM# 1049 CROWN
Copper-Nickel, 38.5 mm. **Ruler:** Elizabeth II **Obv:** Crowned bust
right **Rev:** Queen Mother's portrait

Date	Mintage	F	VF	XF	Unc	BU
2000	—				10.00	12.00

KM# 1049a CROWN
28.2800 g., 0.9250 Silver 0.8410 oz. ASW, 38.5 mm. **Ruler:**
Elizabeth II **Obv:** Crowned bust right **Rev:** Queen Mother's portrait

Date	Mintage	F	VF	XF	Unc	BU
2000 Proof	10,000				Value: 47.50	

KM# 1051 CROWN
28.2800 g., 0.9250 Silver 0.8410 oz. ASW, 38.6 mm.
Ruler: Elizabeth II **Subject:** Millennium-Meridian **Obv:** Crowned
bust right **Rev:** Observatory clock face with an embedded brass
strip **Edge:** Reeded

Date	Mintage	F	VF	XF	Unc	BU
2000 Proof	10,000				Value: 47.50	

KM# 1056 CROWN
Copper-Nickel, 38.6 mm. **Ruler:** Elizabeth II **Subject:** Scottish
Fold Kitten **Obv:** Crowned bust right **Rev:** Kitten playing with
world **Edge:** Reeded

Date	Mintage	F	VF	XF	Unc	BU
2000	—			—	11.00	14.00

KM# 1056a CROWN
31.1035 g., 0.9999 Silver 0.9999 oz. ASW, 38.6 mm.
Ruler: Elizabeth II **Subject:** Scottish Fold Kitten **Obv:** Crowned
bust right **Rev:** Kitten playing with world **Edge:** Reeded

Date	Mintage	F	VF	XF	Unc	BU
2000 Proof	50,000				Value: 40.00	

KM# 1056b CROWN
31.1035 g., 0.9999 Gold 0.9999 oz. AGW, 32.7 mm. **Ruler:**
Elizabeth II **Subject:** Scottish Fold Kitten **Obv:** Crowned bust right
Rev: Kitten playing with world **Edge:** Reeded **Note:** Prev. KM#1057

Date	Mintage	F	VF	XF	Unc	BU
2000	—	—	—	—	—	975
2000 Proof	—				Value: 985	

KM# 177 5 CROWN
155.5500 g., 0.9990 Silver 4.9958 oz. ASW, 65 mm. **Ruler:**
Elizabeth II **Subject:** Bicentennial of U.S. Constitution **Obv:**
Crowned bust right **Rev:** Statue of Liberty divides dates within
circle of assorted Presidential busts **Note:** Illustration reduced.

Date	Mintage	F	VF	XF	Unc	BU
1987 Proof	9,000				Value: 125	

KM# 180 5 CROWN
155.5500 g., 0.9990 Silver 4.9958 oz. ASW, 65 mm.
Ruler: Elizabeth II **Series:** America's Cup **Obv:** Crowned bust
right **Rev:** Sailboats and trophy **Note:** Illustration reduced.

Date	Mintage	F	VF	XF	Unc	BU
1987 Proof	6,000				Value: 135	

KM# 299 5 CROWN
155.5500 g., 0.9990 Silver 4.9958 oz. ASW, 65 mm.
Ruler: Elizabeth II **Series:** America's Cup **Obv:** Crowned bust
right **Rev:** Sailboats and Statue of Liberty **Note:** Illustration
reduced.

Date	Mintage	F	VF	XF	Unc	BU
1987 Proof	200				Value: 220	

KM# 308 5 CROWN
155.5500 g., 0.9990 Silver 4.9958 oz. ASW, 65 mm.
Ruler: Elizabeth II **Series:** America's Cup **Obv:** Crowned bust
right **Rev:** Sailboats and map **Note:** Illustration reduced.

Date	Mintage	F	VF	XF	Unc	BU
1987 Proof	—				Value: 350	

KM# 206 5 CROWN
155.5500 g., 0.9990 Silver 4.9958 oz. ASW, 65 mm.
Ruler: Elizabeth II **Subject:** Steam Navigation **Obv:** Crowned
bust right **Rev:** Ship **Note:** Illustration reduced.

Date	Mintage	F	VF	XF	Unc	BU
1988	—	—	—	—	145	165

KM# 285   5 CROWN
155.5500 g., 0.9990 Silver 4.9958 oz. ASW, 65 mm.
Ruler: Elizabeth II **Subject:** Australian Bicentennial
Obv: Crowned bust right **Rev:** Kangaroo **Note:** Illustration reduced.

Date	Mintage	F	VF	XF	Unc	BU
1988 Proof	—				Value: 160	

KM# 321   5 CROWN
155.5500 g., 0.9990 Silver 4.9958 oz. ASW, 65 mm.
Ruler: Elizabeth II **Series:** America's Cup **Obv:** Crowned bust right **Rev:** Cameo above two modern sailboats **Note:** Officially a "sales sample" about 10 pieces were sold or presented to distributors

Date	Mintage	F	VF	XF	Unc	BU
1991 Proof	Est. 15	—	—	—	—	—

KM# 327   5 CROWN
155.5500 g., 0.9990 Silver 4.9958 oz. ASW, 65 mm.
Ruler: Elizabeth II **Series:** America's Cup **Obv:** Crowned bust right **Rev:** Cameo above two modern sailboats

Date	Mintage	F	VF	XF	Unc	BU
1992	—	—	—	—	145	165

KM# 348   5 CROWN
155.5500 g., 0.9990 Silver 4.9958 oz. ASW, 65 mm.
Ruler: Elizabeth II **Obv:** Crowned bust right **Rev:** Siamese cat **Note:** Illustration reduced.

Date	Mintage	F	VF	XF	Unc	BU
1992 Proof	—				Value: 225	

KM# 689   5 CROWN
155.5175 g., 0.9990 Silver 4.9948 oz. ASW, 65 mm.
Ruler: Elizabeth II **Series:** Legend of King Arthur **Obv:** Crowned bust right **Rev:** King Arthur with sword and orb **Note:** Illustration reduced.

Date	Mintage	F	VF	XF	Unc	BU
1996 Proof	Est. 999				Value: 120	

KM# 690   5 CROWN
155.5175 g., 0.9990 Silver 4.9948 oz. ASW, 65 mm.
Ruler: Elizabeth II **Series:** Legend of King Arthur **Obv:** Crowned bust right **Rev:** Queen Guinevere **Note:** Illustration reduced.

Date	Mintage	F	VF	XF	Unc	BU
1996 Proof	Est. 999				Value: 120	

KM# 691   5 CROWN
155.5175 g., 0.9990 Silver 4.9948 oz. ASW, 65 mm.
Ruler: Elizabeth II **Series:** Legend of King Arthur **Obv:** Crowned bust right **Rev:** Sir Lancelot **Note:** Illustration reduced.

Date	Mintage	F	VF	XF	Unc	BU
1996	Est. 999				Value: 120	

KM# 692   5 CROWN
155.5175 g., 0.9990 Silver 4.9948 oz. ASW, 65 mm.
Ruler: Elizabeth II **Series:** Legend of King Arthur **Obv:** Crowned bust right **Rev:** Merlin **Note:** Illustration reduced.

Date	Mintage	F	VF	XF	Unc	BU
1996	Est. 999				Value: 125	

KM# 693   5 CROWN
155.5175 g., 0.9990 Silver 4.9948 oz. ASW, 65 mm.
Ruler: Elizabeth II **Series:** Legend of King Arthur **Obv:** Crowned bust right **Rev:** Camelot Castle

Date	Mintage	F	VF	XF	Unc	BU
1996	Est. 999				Value: 125	

KM# 734   5 CROWN
155.5175 g., 0.9999 Gold 4.9993 oz. AGW **Ruler:** Elizabeth II **Subject:** Year of the Rat **Obv:** Crowned bust right **Rev:** Rat

Date	Mintage	F	VF	XF	Unc	BU
1996 Proof	—	—	—	—	—	—

Note: Entire series purchased by one buyer. Mintage, disposition, and market value unknown

KM# 727   5 CROWN
155.5175 g., 0.9999 Gold 4.9993 oz. AGW **Ruler:** Elizabeth II **Subject:** Year of the Ox **Obv:** Crowned bust right **Rev:** Ox laying down

Date	Mintage	F	VF	XF	Unc	BU
1997 Proof	Est. 250				Value: 4,800	

KM# 818   5 CROWN
155.5175 g., 0.9999 Gold 4.9993 oz. AGW **Ruler:** Elizabeth II **Subject:** Year of the Tiger **Obv:** Crowned bust right **Rev:** Tiger

Date	Mintage	F	VF	XF	Unc	BU
1998 Proof	Est. 250				Value: 4,800	

KM# 953   5 CROWN
155.5175 g., 0.9999 Gold 4.9993 oz. AGW **Ruler:** Elizabeth II **Subject:** Year of the Rabbit **Obv:** Crowned bust right **Rev:** Two rabbits

Date	Mintage	F	VF	XF	Unc	BU
1999 Proof	Est. 250				Value: 4,800	

KM# 1018   5 CROWN
155.5175 g., 0.9999 Gold 4.9993 oz. AGW **Ruler:** Elizabeth II **Subject:** Year of the Dragon **Obv:** Crowned bust right **Rev:** Dragon

Date	Mintage	F	VF	XF	Unc	BU
2000 Proof	Est. 250				Value: 4,800	

KM# 181   10 CROWN
311.0350 g., 0.9990 Silver 9.9896 oz. ASW, 75 mm.
Ruler: Elizabeth II **Series:** America's Cup **Obv:** Crowned bust right **Rev:** Sailboats and Statue of Liberty **Note:** Similar to 5 Crown, KM#299.

Date	Mintage	F	VF	XF	Unc	BU
1987 Proof	2,000				Value: 225	

KM# 188   10 CROWN
311.0350 g., 0.9990 Silver 9.9896 oz. ASW, 75 mm.
Ruler: Elizabeth II **Subject:** Bicentenary of America's Constitution **Obv:** Crowned bust right **Rev:** Statue of Liberty within circle of assorted Presidential busts **Note:** Similar to 5 Crowns, KM#177.

Date	Mintage	F	VF	XF	Unc	BU
1987 Proof	6,000				Value: 215	

KM# 300   10 CROWN
311.0350 g., 0.9990 Silver 9.9896 oz. ASW, 75 mm.
Ruler: Elizabeth II **Series:** America's Cup **Obv:** Crowned bust right **Rev:** Sailboats and trophy **Note:** Similar to 5 Crowns, KM#180.

Date	Mintage	F	VF	XF	Unc	BU
1987 Proof	69				Value: 350	

KM# 309   10 CROWN
311.0350 g., 0.9990 Silver 9.9896 oz. ASW, 75 mm.
Ruler: Elizabeth II **Series:** America's Cup **Obv:** Crowned bust right **Rev:** Sailboats and map **Note:** Similar to 5 Crowns, KM#308.

Date	Mintage	F	VF	XF	Unc	BU
1987 Proof	—				Value: 525	

KM# 258 10 CROWN
311.0350 g., 0.9990 Silver 9.9896 oz. ASW, 75 mm.
Ruler: Elizabeth II **Subject:** Australian Bicentennial
Obv: Crowned bust right **Rev:** Koala **Note:** Illustration reduced.

Date	Mintage	F	VF	XF	Unc	BU
1988 Proof	Est. 13,000	Value: 215				

KM# 992 10 CROWN
311.0350 g., 0.9990 Silver 9.9896 oz. ASW, 75 mm.
Ruler: Elizabeth II **Obv:** Crowned bust right **Rev:** Siamese cat
Note: Similar to 5 Crowns, KM#348.

Date	Mintage	F	VF	XF	Unc	BU
1992 Proof	—	Value: 300				

KM# 775 10 CROWN
311.0300 g., 0.9250 Silver 9.2495 oz. ASW, 75 mm.
Ruler: Elizabeth II **Subject:** 10th Anniversary of the Manx Cat
Obv: Crowned bust right **Rev:** Cat in center of assorted cat coins
Note: Illustration reduced.

Date	Mintage	F	VF	XF	Unc	BU
1997 Proof	Est. 1,997	Value: 400				

SILVER BULLION ANGEL SERIES

KM# 522 ANGEL
31.1035 g., 0.9999 Silver 0.9999 oz. ASW, 38.5 mm.
Ruler: Elizabeth II **Obv:** Crowned bust right **Rev:** Archangel
Michael slaying dragon right

Date	Mintage	F	VF	XF	Unc	BU
1995 Proof	—	Value: 30.00				

KM# 1326 5 ANGEL
155.5150 g., 0.9999 Silver 4.9992 oz. ASW **Ruler:** Elizabeth II
Obv: Crowned bust right **Rev:** Archangel Michael slaying dragon

Date	Mintage	F	VF	XF	Unc	BU
1995PM Proof	—	Value: 175				

GOLD BULLION COINAGE
Angel Issues

KM# 166 1/20 ANGEL
1.6970 g., 0.9170 Gold 0.0500 oz. AGW **Ruler:** Elizabeth II
Obv: Crowned bust right **Rev:** Archangel Michael slaying dragon

Date	Mintage	F	VF	XF	Unc	BU
1986	—	—	—	—	—	55.00
1986 (pi) Proof	5,000	Value: 65.00				
1987	—	—	—	—	—	55.00
1987 Proof	—	Value: 65.00				

KM# 193 1/20 ANGEL
1.6970 g., 0.9170 Gold 0.0500 oz. AGW **Ruler:** Elizabeth II
Obv: Crowned bust right **Rev:** Archangel Michael slaying dragon

Date	Mintage	F	VF	XF	Unc	BU
1988	—	—	—	—	—	55.00
1988 (pi) Proof	—	Value: 65.00				
1989 (h) Proof	Est. 5,000	Value: 65.00				
1989 (mt) Proof	3,000	Value: 65.00				
1990 (sg) Proof	Est. 3,000	Value: 65.00				
1991 (cc) Proof	1,000	Value: 65.00				
1992 (cb) Proof	1,000	Value: 65.00				
1993 Proof	Est. 1,000	Value: 65.00				

KM# 393 1/20 ANGEL
1.5551 g., 0.9999 Gold 0.0500 oz. AGW **Ruler:** Elizabeth II
Obv: Crowned bust right **Rev:** Archangel Michael slaying dragon right

Date	Mintage	F	VF	XF	Unc	BU
1994	—	—	—	—	—	55.00
1994 Proof	—	Value: 65.00				
1994 (ns) Proof	Est. 1,000	Value: 70.00				
1995	—	—	—	—	—	55.00
1995 Proof	—	Value: 65.00				
1995 (sc) Proof	Est. 1,000					
Note: Privy mark: Santa						
1996	—	—	—	—	—	55.00
1996 Proof	—	Value: 65.00				
1996 (bs) Proof	Est. 1,000	Value: 70.00				
Note: Privy mark: Teddy bear						
1997	—	—	—	—	—	55.00
1997 Proof	—	Value: 65.00				
1997 (at) Proof	Est. 1,000	Value: 70.00				
Note: Privy mark: Angel						
1998	—	—	—	—	—	55.00
1998 Proof	—	Value: 65.00				
1998 (x) Proof	Est. 1,000	Value: 70.00				
Note: Privy mark: Snowman						
1999	—	—	—	—	—	55.00
1999 Proof	—	Value: 65.00				
1999 (fw) Proof	Est. 1,000	Value: 70.00				
Note: Privy mark: Fairy						
2000	—	—	—	—	—	55.00
2000 Proof	—	Value: 65.00				
2000 (ch) Proof	Est. 1,000	Value: 70.00				
Note: Privy mark: Candle						

KM# 138 1/10 ANGEL
3.3900 g., 0.9170 Gold 0.0999 oz. AGW **Ruler:** Elizabeth II
Obv: Crowned bust right **Rev:** Archangel Michael slaying dragon

Date	Mintage	F	VF	XF	Unc	BU
1984 Proof	5,000	Value: 110				

KM# 140 1/10 ANGEL
3.3900 g., 0.9170 Gold 0.0999 oz. AGW **Ruler:** Elizabeth II
Obv: Crowned bust right **Rev:** Archangel Michael slaying dragon left

Date	Mintage	F	VF	XF	Unc	BU
1985	8,000	—	—	—	—	95.00
1985 Proof	3,000	Value: 110				
1986	—	—	—	—	—	95.00
1986 Proof	—	Value: 110				
1987	—	—	—	—	—	95.00
1987 Proof	—	Value: 110				

KM# 159 1/10 ANGEL
3.3900 g., 0.9170 Gold 0.0999 oz. AGW **Ruler:** Elizabeth II
Obv: Crowned bust right **Rev:** Archangel Michael slaying dragon left

Date	Mintage	F	VF	XF	Unc	BU
1985 A	1,000	—	—	—	—	95.00
1985 C	1,000	—	—	—	—	95.00
1985 H	1,000	—	—	—	—	95.00
1985 L	1,000	—	—	—	—	95.00

Date	Mintage	F	VF	XF	Unc	BU
1985	5,000	—	—	—	—	95.00
1986 A	1,000	—	—	—	—	95.00
1986 T	1,000	—	—	—	—	95.00
1986 X	1,000	—	—	—	—	95.00
1987 A	1,000	—	—	—	—	95.00
1987 L	1,000	—	—	—	—	95.00
1987 (mt) Proof	3,000	Value: 110				
1987 F Proof	1,000	Value: 110				
1988 A Proof	1,000	Value: 110				

KM# 194 1/10 ANGEL
3.3900 g., 0.9170 Gold 0.0999 oz. AGW **Ruler:** Elizabeth II
Obv: Crowned bust right **Rev:** Archangel Michael slaying dragon

Date	Mintage	F	VF	XF	Unc	BU
1988	—	—	—	—	—	95.00
1989 A Proof	250	Value: 125				
1990 A Proof	1,000	Value: 110				
1991 A Proof	400	Value: 110				
Note: 299 pieces have been melted						
1992 A	100	—	—	—	—	95.00

KM# 394 1/10 ANGEL
3.1103 g., 0.9999 Gold 0.1000 oz. AGW **Ruler:** Elizabeth II
Obv: Crowned bust right **Rev:** Archangel Michael

Date	Mintage	F	VF	XF	Unc	BU
1994 Proof	—	Value: 110				
1995	—	—	—	—	—	100
1995 Proof	—	Value: 110				
1996	—	—	—	—	—	100
1996 Proof	—	Value: 110				
1997	—	—	—	—	—	100
1997 Proof	—	Value: 110				
1998	—	—	—	—	—	100
1998 Proof	—	Value: 110				
1999	—	—	—	—	—	100
1999 Proof	—	Value: 110				
2000	—	—	—	—	—	100
2000 Proof	—	Value: 110				

KM# 152.1 1/4 ANGEL
8.4830 g., 0.9170 Gold 0.2501 oz. AGW **Ruler:** Elizabeth II
Obv: Crowned bust right **Rev:** Archangel Michael slaying dragon left

Date	Mintage	F	VF	XF	Unc	BU
1985	2,117	—	—	—	—	235
1985 Proof	51	Value: 275				
1986 L	1,000	—	—	—	—	235
1986 Proof	—	Value: 240				

KM# 152.2 1/4 ANGEL
8.4830 g., 0.9170 Gold 0.2501 oz. AGW **Ruler:** Elizabeth II
Obv: Crowned bust right **Rev:** Archangel Michael slaying dragon

Date	Mintage	F	VF	XF	Unc	BU
1987	—	—	—	—	—	235
1987 Proof	—	Value: 240				
1987 (bb) Proof	1,000	Value: 240				
1987 (s) Proof	1,000	Value: 240				
1987 (SL) Proof	568	Value: 240				

KM# 195 1/4 ANGEL
8.4830 g., 0.9170 Gold 0.2501 oz. AGW **Ruler:** Elizabeth II
Obv: Crowned bust right **Rev:** Archangel Michael slaying dragon left

Date	Mintage	F	VF	XF	Unc	BU
1988	—	—	—	—	—	235
1988 (f) Proof	1,000	Value: 240				
1988 (p) Proof	1,000	Value: 240				
1988 (ss) Proof	1,000	Value: 240				
1989 (y)	—	—	—	—	—	235
1989 (hk) Proof	1,000	Value: 240				
1989 (p) Proof	500	Value: 240				
1989 C (d) Proof	1,000	Value: 240				
1990 (tb)	1,000	—	—	—	—	235
Note: 10 pieces melted						
1990 (fl)	1,000	—	—	—	—	235
Note: 9 pieces melted						
1990 (h) Proof	1,000	Value: 240				

Date	Mintage	F	VF	XF	Unc	BU
1990 (c) Proof	250	Value: 250				
1990 (ma) Proof	200	Value: 265				
Note: 40 pieces melted						
1990 (ba) Proof	1,000	Value: 240				
Note: 513 pieces melted						
1991 (fr) Proof	500	Value: 240				
1991 (c) Proof	200	Value: 265				
Note: 57 pieces melted						
1993 Proof	—	Value: 240				

KM# 395   1/4 ANGEL
7.7758 g., 0.9999 Gold 0.2500 oz. AGW   **Ruler:** Elizabeth II
Obv: Crowned bust right **Rev:** Archangel Michael slaying dragon

Date	Mintage	F	VF	XF	Unc	BU
1994 Proof	750	Value: 250				
1995	—	—	—	—	—	240
1995 Proof	—	Value: 250				
1996	—	—	—	—	—	240
1996 Proof	—	Value: 250				
1997	—	—	—	—	—	240
1997 Proof	—	Value: 250				
1998	—	—	—	—	—	240
1998 Proof	—	Value: 250				
1999	—	—	—	—	—	240
1999 Proof	—	Value: 250				
2000	—	—	—	—	—	240
2000 Proof	—	Value: 250				

KM# 155   1/2 ANGEL
16.9380 g., 0.9170 Gold 0.4993 oz. AGW   **Ruler:** Elizabeth II
Obv: Crowned bust right **Rev:** Archangel Michael slaying dragon left

Date	Mintage	F	VF	XF	Unc	BU
1985	1,776	—	—	—	—	460
1985 Proof	51	Value: 485				
1986	—	—	—	—	—	460
1986 Proof	3,000	Value: 470				
1987	—	—	—	—	—	460
1987 Proof	—	Value: 470				

KM# 196   1/2 ANGEL
16.9380 g., 0.9170 Gold 0.4993 oz. AGW   **Ruler:** Elizabeth II
Obv: Crowned bust right **Rev:** Archangel Michael slaying dragon

Date	Mintage	F	VF	XF	Unc	BU
1988	—	—	—	—	—	455

KM# 396   1/2 ANGEL
15.5517 g., 0.9999 Gold 0.4999 oz. AGW   **Ruler:** Elizabeth II
Obv: Crowned bust right **Rev:** Archangel Michael slaying dragon

Date	Mintage	F	VF	XF	Unc	BU
1994	—	—	—	—	—	460
1994 Proof	—	Value: 470				
1995	—	—	—	—	—	460
1995 Proof	—	Value: 470				
1996	—	—	—	—	—	460
1996 Proof	—	Value: 470				
1997	—	—	—	—	—	460
1997 Proof	—	Value: 470				
1998	—	—	—	—	—	460
1998 Proof	—	Value: 470				
1999	—	—	—	—	—	460
1999 Proof	—	Value: 470				

KM# 139   ANGEL
33.9300 g., 0.9170 Gold 1.0003 oz. AGW   **Ruler:** Elizabeth II
Obv: Young bust right **Rev:** Archangel Michael slaying dragon left

Date	Mintage	F	VF	XF	Unc	BU
1984	—	—	—	—	—	925
1984 Proof	3,000	Value: 935				

KM# 141   ANGEL
33.9300 g., 0.9170 Gold 1.0003 oz. AGW   **Ruler:** Elizabeth II
Obv: Crowned bust right **Rev:** Archangel Michael slaying dragon left

Date	Mintage	F	VF	XF	Unc	BU
1985	28,000	—	—	—	—	925
1985 Prooflike	—	—	—	—	—	925
1985 Proof	3,000	Value: 935				
1986	—	—	—	—	—	925
1986 Proof	—	Value: 935				
1987	—	—	—	—	—	925
1987 Proof	—	Value: 935				

KM# 191   ANGEL
33.9300 g., 0.9170 Gold 1.0003 oz. AGW   **Ruler:** Elizabeth II
Subject: Hong Kong Coin Show **Obv:** Crowned bust right
Rev: Archangel Michael slaying dragon left

Date	Mintage	F	VF	XF	Unc	BU
1987	—	—	—	—	—	925
1987 Proof	1,000	Value: 935				

KM# 197   ANGEL
33.9300 g., 0.9170 Gold 1.0003 oz. AGW   **Ruler:** Elizabeth II
Obv: Crowned bust right **Rev:** Archangel Michael slaying dragon left

Date	Mintage	F	VF	XF	Unc	BU
1988	—	—	—	—	—	925
1988 (ss) Proof	1,000	Value: 935				

KM# 397   ANGEL
31.1035 g., 0.9999 Gold 0.9999 oz. AGW   **Ruler:** Elizabeth II
Obv: Crowned bust right **Rev:** Archangel Michael slaying dragon right

Date	Mintage	F	VF	XF	Unc	BU
1994	—	—	—	—	—	985
1994 Proof	—	Value: 1,000				
1995	—	—	—	—	—	985
1995 Proof	—	Value: 1,000				
1996	—	—	—	—	—	985
1996 Proof	—	Value: 1,000				
1997	—	—	—	—	—	985
1997 Proof	—	Value: 1,000				
1998	—	—	—	—	—	985
1998 Proof	—	Value: 1,000				
1999	—	—	—	—	—	985
1999 Proof	—	Value: 1,000				
2000	—	—	—	—	—	985
2000 Proof	—	Value: 1,000				

KM# 156   5 ANGEL
169.6680 g., 0.9170 Gold 5.0020 oz. AGW   **Ruler:** Elizabeth II
Obv: Crowned bust right **Rev:** Archangel Michael slaying dragon left

Date	Mintage	F	VF	XF	Unc	BU
1985	104	—	—	—	—	4,600
1985 Proof	90	Value: 4,650				
1986	89	—	—	—	—	4,600
1986 Proof	250	Value: 4,650				
1987	150	—	—	—	—	4,600
1987 Proof	27	Value: 4,650				

KM# 198   5 ANGEL
169.6680 g., 0.9170 Gold 5.0020 oz. AGW   **Ruler:** Elizabeth II
Obv: Crowned bust right **Rev:** Archangel Michael slaying dragon

Date	Mintage	F	VF	XF	Unc	BU
1988	250	—	—	—	—	4,500

KM# 157   10 ANGEL
339.3350 g., 0.9170 Gold 10.003 oz. AGW   **Ruler:** Elizabeth II
Obv: Crowned bust right **Rev:** Archangel Michael slaying dragon left **Note:** Similar to 5 Angel, KM#156.

Date	Mintage	F	VF	XF.	Unc	BU
1985	79	—	—	—	—	9,150
1985 Proof	68	Value: 9,200				
1986	47	—	—	—	—	9,150
1986 Proof	250	Value: 9,200				
1987	150	—	—	—	—	9,150
1987 Proof	30	Value: 9,200				

KM# 199   10 ANGEL
339.3350 g., 0.9170 Gold 10.003 oz. AGW   **Ruler:** Elizabeth II
Obv: Crowned bust right **Rev:** Archangel Michael slaying dragon

Date	Mintage	F	VF	XF	Unc	BU
1988 Proof	250	Value: 9,000				

KM# 189   15 ANGEL
508.9575 g., 0.9170 Gold 15.004 oz. AGW   **Ruler:** Elizabeth II
Obv: Crowned bust right **Rev:** Archangel Michael slaying dragon left

Date	Mintage	F	VF	XF	Unc	BU
1987	150	—	—	—	—	14,000
1987 Proof	18	Value: 14,500				

KM# 200   15 ANGEL
508.9575 g., 0.9170 Gold 15.004 oz. AGW   **Ruler:** Elizabeth II
Obv: Crowned bust right **Rev:** Archangel Michael slaying dragon left **Note:** Similar to 5 Angel, KM#156.

Date	Mintage	F	VF	XF	Unc	BU
1988 Proof	—	Value: 14,500				

KM# 201 20 ANGEL
678.6720 g., 0.9170 Gold 20.007 oz. AGW, 75.2 mm.
Ruler: Elizabeth II **Obv:** Crowned bust right **Rev:** Archangel
Michael slaying dragon left **Note:** Similar to 5 Angel, KM#156.

Date	Mintage	F	VF	XF	Unc	BU
1988	250	—	—	—	—	18,500
1988 Proof	100	Value: 19,000				

KM# 201a 20 ANGEL
Gilt Silver **Ruler:** Elizabeth II **Obv:** Crowned bust right
Rev: Archangel Michael slaying dragon left

Date	Mintage	F	VF	XF	Unc	BU
1988	—	—	—	—	—	—

KM# 301 25 ANGEL
848.2750 g., 0.9170 Gold 25.008 oz. AGW **Ruler:** Elizabeth II
Obv: Crowned bust right **Rev:** Archangel Michael slaying dragon

Date	Mintage	F	VF	XF	Unc	BU
1989	—	—	—	—	—	23,500

GOLD BULLION COINAGE
Sovereign Issues

KM# 969 1/5 SOVEREIGN
1.0000 g., 0.9999 Gold 0.0321 oz. AGW **Ruler:** Elizabeth II
Obv: Head with tiara right **Rev:** Triskeles

Date	Mintage	F	VF	XF	Unc	BU
1999	—	—	—	—	BV+40%	—

KM# 970 1/2 SOVEREIGN
2.5000 g., 0.9999 Gold 0.0804 oz. AGW **Ruler:** Elizabeth II
Obv: Head with tiara right **Rev:** Triskeles

Date	Mintage	F	VF	XF	Unc	BU
1999	—	—	—	—	BV+30%	—

KM# 971 3/4 SOVEREIGN
3.5000 g., 0.9999 Gold 0.1125 oz. AGW **Ruler:** Elizabeth II
Obv: Head with tiara right **Rev:** Triskeles

Date	Mintage	F	VF	XF	Unc	BU
1999	—	—	—	—	BV+25%	—

KM# 972 SOVEREIGN
5.0000 g., 0.9999 Gold 0.1607 oz. AGW **Ruler:** Elizabeth II
Obv: Head with tiara right **Rev:** Triskeles

Date	Mintage	F	VF	XF	Unc	BU
1999	—	—	—	—	BV+20%	—

KM# 973 2 SOVEREIGNS
10.0000 g., 0.9999 Gold 0.3215 oz. AGW **Ruler:** Elizabeth II
Obv: Head with tiara right **Rev:** Triskeles

Date	Mintage	F	VF	XF	Unc	BU
1999	—	—	—	—	BV+10%	—

KM# 974 5 SOVEREIGNS
31.1035 g., 0.9999 Gold 0.9999 oz. AGW **Ruler:** Elizabeth II
Obv: Head with tiara right **Rev:** Triskeles

Date	Mintage	F	VF	XF	Unc	BU
1999	—	—	—	—	BV+5%	—

GOLD BULLION COINAGE
Platina Issues

KM# 944 1/25 PLATINA
1.2447 g., 0.7500 White Gold 0.0300 oz. AGW **Ruler:** Elizabeth II
Obv: Crowned bust right **Rev:** Crowned arms

Date	Mintage	F	VF	XF	Unc	BU
1999 Proof	Est. 10,000	Value: 45.00				

KM# 945 1/10 PLATINA
3.1103 g., 0.7500 White Gold 0.0750 oz. AGW
Ruler: Elizabeth II **Obv:** Crowned bust right **Rev:** Crowned arms

Date	Mintage	F	VF	XF	Unc	BU
1999 Proof	Est. 7,500	Value: 80.00				

KM# 946 1/5 PLATINA
6.2200 g., 0.7500 White Gold 0.1500 oz. AGW **Ruler:** Elizabeth II
Obv: Crowned bust right **Rev:** Crowned arms flanked by falcons

Date	Mintage	F	VF	XF	Unc	BU
1999 Proof	Est. 5,000	Value: 160				

KM# 947 1/2 PLATINA
15.5517 g., 0.7500 White Gold 0.3750 oz. AGW **Ruler:** Elizabeth II
Obv: Crowned bust right **Rev:** Crowned arms

Date	Mintage	F	VF	XF	Unc	BU
1999 Proof	Est. 3,500	Value: 375				

GOLD & PLATINUM BIMETALLIC BULLION COINAGE

KM# 1065 1/4 ANGEL
Ring Weight: 3.8880 g. **Ring:** 0.9995 Platinum 0.1249 oz. APW
Center Weight: 3.8880 g. **Center:** 0.9999 Gold 0.1250 oz. AGW
, 22 mm. **Ruler:** Elizabeth II **Obv:** Crowned bust right
Rev: Archangel Michael slaying dragon **Edge:** Reeded

Date	Mintage	F	VF	XF	Unc	BU
1995 Proof	—	Value: 265				

KM# 1066 1/4 NOBLE
Bi-Metallic Platinum center in Gold ring, 22 mm. **Ruler:** Elizabeth II
Obv: Crowned bust right **Rev:** Viking ship **Edge:** Reeded

Date	Mintage	F	VF	XF	Unc	BU
1995 Proof	—	Value: 265				

PLATINUM BULLION COINAGE
Noble Series

KM# 266 1/20 NOBLE
1.5551 g., 0.9995 Platinum 0.0500 oz. APW **Ruler:** Elizabeth II
Obv: Crowned bust right **Rev:** Viking ship

Date	Mintage	F	VF	XF	Unc	BU
1989	10,000	Value: 100				
1992	—	—	—	—	—	85.00

KM# 137 1/10 NOBLE
3.1100 g., 0.9995 Platinum 0.0999 oz. APW **Ruler:** Elizabeth II
Obv: Young bust right **Rev:** Viking ship

Date	Mintage	F	VF	XF	Unc	BU
1984	—	—	—	—	—	175
1984 Proof	5,000	Value: 185				

KM# 153 1/10 NOBLE
3.1100 g., 0.9995 Platinum 0.0999 oz. APW **Ruler:** Elizabeth II
Obv: Crowned head right **Rev:** Viking ship

Date	Mintage	F	VF	XF	Unc	BU
1985	99,000	—	—	—	—	175
1985 Proof	5,000	Value: 190				

Date	Mintage	F	VF	XF	Unc	BU
1986	—	—	—	—	—	175
1986 Proof	5,000	Value: 190				
1987	—	—	—	—	—	175
1987 Proof	5,000	Value: 190				

KM# 202 1/10 NOBLE
3.1100 g., 0.9995 Platinum 0.0999 oz. APW **Ruler:** Elizabeth II
Obv: Crowned bust right **Rev:** Viking ship with hologram sail

Date	Mintage	F	VF	XF	Unc	BU
1988	5,000	—	—	—	—	175
1989	5,000	—	—	—	—	175

KM# 168 1/4 NOBLE
7.7757 g., 0.9995 Platinum 0.2499 oz. APW **Ruler:** Elizabeth II
Obv: Crowned bust right **Rev:** Viking ship

Date	Mintage	F	VF	XF	Unc	BU
1986 Proof	2,015	Value: 450				
1987 Proof	3,250	Value: 450				
1987PM Proof	750	Value: 450				

KM# 203 1/4 NOBLE
7.7757 g., 0.9995 Platinum 0.2499 oz. APW **Ruler:** Elizabeth II
Obv: Crowned bust right **Rev:** Viking ship

Date	Mintage	F	VF	XF	Unc	BU
1988	—	—	—	—	—	440
1988 (a)	100	—	—	—	—	440
1988 (bb) Proof	1,000	Value: 450				
1988 (p) Proof	1,000	Value: 450				
1989 (br) Proof	250	Value: 450				
1989 (p) Proof	500	Value: 450				
1990 (ba) Proof	1,000	Value: 450				
1990 (ti) Proof	Est. 1,000	Value: 450				

KM# 717 1/4 NOBLE
7.7757 g., 0.9995 Platinum 0.2499 oz. APW **Ruler:** Elizabeth II
Obv: Crowned bust right **Rev:** Ship with hologram sail

Date	Mintage	F	VF	XF	Unc	BU
1996 Proof	Est. 10,000	Value: 450				

KM# 169 1/2 NOBLE
15.5514 g., 0.9995 Platinum 0.4997 oz. APW **Ruler:** Elizabeth II
Obv: Crowned bust right **Rev:** Ship with hologram sail

Date	Mintage	F	VF	XF	Unc	BU
1986 Proof	15	Value: 1,000				
1987 Proof	3,000	Value: 900				

KM# 204 1/2 NOBLE
15.5514 g., 0.9995 Platinum 0.4997 oz. APW **Ruler:** Elizabeth II
Obv: Crowned bust right **Rev:** Viking ship

Date	Mintage	F	VF	XF	Unc	BU
1988 Proof	3,000	Value: 900				
1989 Proof	3,000	Value: 900				
1994PM Proof	250	Value: 900				

Note: The 1994 date was issued as a 2-piece set with a
rhodium-plated silver medal marking the 10th anniversary of the platinum noble series

KM# 110   NOBLE
31.1030 g., 0.9995 Platinum 0.9994 oz. APW   **Ruler:** Elizabeth II
Obv: Young bust right **Rev:** Viking ship

Date	Mintage	F	VF	XF	Unc	BU
1983	1,700	—	—	—	—	1,750
1983 Proof	94	Value: 1,850				
1984	—	—	—	—	—	1,750
1984 Proof	2,000	Value: 1,850				

KM# 154   NOBLE
31.1030 g., 0.9995 Platinum 0.9994 oz. APW **Ruler:** Elizabeth II
Obv: Crowned bust right **Rev:** Viking ship

Date	Mintage	F	VF	XF	Unc	BU
1985	—	—	—	—	—	1,750
1985 Proof	3,000	Value: 1,800				
1986	—	—	—	—	—	1,750
1986 Proof	3,000	Value: 1,800				
1987	—	—	—	—	—	1,750
1987 Proof	3,000	Value: 1,800				

KM# 205   NOBLE
31.1030 g., 0.9995 Platinum 0.9994 oz. APW **Ruler:** Elizabeth II
Obv: Crowned bust right **Rev:** Viking ship

Date	Mintage	F	VF	XF	Unc	BU
1988 Proof	3,000	Value: 1,800				
1989 Proof	3,000	Value: 1,800				

KM# 170   5 NOBLE
155.5140 g., 0.9995 Platinum 4.9972 oz. APW
Ruler: Elizabeth II **Obv:** Crowned bust right **Rev:** Viking ship

Date	Mintage	F	VF	XF	Unc	BU
1986 Proof	15	Value: 9,000				
1987 Proof	11	Value: 9,000				
1988 Proof	—	Value: 9,000				

KM# 171   10 NOBLE
311.0280 g., 0.9995 Platinum 9.9944 oz. APW, 63 mm.
Ruler: Elizabeth II **Obv:** Crowned bust right **Rev:** Viking ship
Note: Similar to 5 Noble, KM#170.

Date	Mintage	F	VF	XF	Unc	BU
1986 Proof	15	Value: 18,000				

Date	Mintage	F	VF	XF	Unc	BU
1987 Proof	11	Value: 18,000				
1988 Proof	—	Value: 18,000				

TRADE COINAGE
Ecu Series

KM# 711   15 ECUS
10.0000 g., 0.9250 Silver 0.2974 oz. ASW **Ruler:** Elizabeth II
Obv: Crowned bust right **Rev:** Manx cat within shield and wings

Date	Mintage	F	VF	XF	Unc	BU
1994	Est. 30,000	—	—	—	42.50	—

KM# 714   15 ECUS
10.0000 g., 0.9250 Silver 0.2974 oz. ASW **Ruler:** Elizabeth II
Subject: 50th Anniversary of United Nations **Obv:** Crowned bust right **Rev:** Blacksmith

Date	Mintage	F	VF	XF	Unc	BU
1995 Proof	Est. 30,000	Value: 42.50				

KM# 712   25 ECUS
19.2000 g., 0.9250 Silver 0.5710 oz. ASW **Ruler:** Elizabeth II
Subject: 50th Anniversary of United Nations **Obv:** Crowned bust right **Rev:** Viking boat on helmeted shield

Date	Mintage	F	VF	XF	Unc	BU
1994	Est. 15,000	—	—	—	52.50	55.00

KM# 715   25 ECUS
19.2000 g., 0.9250 Silver 0.5710 oz. ASW **Ruler:** Elizabeth II
Subject: 50th Anniversary of United Nations **Obv:** Crowned bust right **Rev:** Ram's head within shield

Date	Mintage	F	VF	XF	Unc	BU
1995 Proof	Est. 15,000	Value: 55.00				

KM# 713   75 ECUS
6.2200 g., 0.9990 Gold 0.1998 oz. AGW   **Ruler:** Elizabeth II
Obv: Crowned bust right **Rev:** Triskeles on crowned shield

Date	Mintage	F	VF	XF	Unc	BU
1994	Est. 2,000	—	—	—	—	200

KM# 716   75 ECUS
6.2200 g., 0.9990 Gold 0.1998 oz. AGW   **Ruler:** Elizabeth II
Obv: Crowned bust right **Rev:** Falcons on shield

Date	Mintage	F	VF	XF	Unc	BU
1995 Proof	Est. 2,000	Value: 200				

TRADE COINAGE
Euro Series

KM# 718   10 EURO
10.0000 g., 0.9250 Silver 0.2974 oz. ASW **Ruler:** Elizabeth II
Subject: Spain - 10 years Membership E.C. **Obv:** Crowned bust right **Rev:** Head facing below standing figures within circle

Date	Mintage	F	VF	XF	Unc	BU
1996 Proof	Est. 30,000	Value: 40.00				

KM# 795   10 EURO
10.0000 g., 0.9250 Silver 0.2974 oz. ASW   **Ruler:** Elizabeth II
Subject: 200th Anniversary - Birth of Franza Schubert
Obv: Crowned bust right **Rev:** Head below piano recital scene

Date	Mintage	F	VF	XF	Unc	BU
1997 Proof	Est. 30,000	Value: 40.00				

KM# 796   10 EURO
10.0000 g., 0.9250 Silver 0.2974 oz. ASW   **Ruler:** Elizabeth II
Obv: Crowned bust right **Rev:** Head below organ player

Date	Mintage	F	VF	XF	Unc	BU
1997 Proof	Est. 30,000	Value: 40.00				

KM# 909   10 EURO
10.0000 g., 0.9250 Silver 0.2974 oz. ASW   **Ruler:** Elizabeth II
Subject: 125th Anniversary of the Isle of Man Railway
Obv: Crowned bust right **Rev:** Old steam train

Date	Mintage	F	VF	XF	Unc	BU
1998 Proof	Est. 30,000	Value: 40.00				

KM# 910   10 EURO
10.0000 g., 0.9250 Silver 0.2974 oz. ASW **Ruler:** Elizabeth II
Subject: Myths and Legends - Manannan **Obv:** Crowned bust right **Rev:** Equestrian

Date	Mintage	F	VF	XF	Unc	BU
1998 Proof	Est. 30,000	Value: 40.00				

KM# 719   15 EURO
19.2000 g., 0.9250 Silver 0.5710 oz. ASW **Ruler:** Elizabeth II
Subject: First Performance - La Boheme **Obv:** Crowned bust right **Rev:** Head below standing figures

Date	Mintage	F	VF	XF	Unc	BU
1996 Proof	Est. 15,000	Value: 75.00				

KM# 720   50 EURO
6.2200 g., 0.9999 Gold 0.1999 oz. AGW **Ruler:** Elizabeth II
Subject: 125th Anniversary of Aida-Verdi **Obv:** Crowned bust right **Rev:** Head below standing figures

Date	Mintage	F	VF	XF	Unc	BU
1996 Proof	Est. 2,000	Value: 200				

KM# 797   50 EURO
6.2200 g., 0.9999 Gold 0.1999 oz. AGW **Ruler:** Elizabeth II
Obv: Crowned bust right **Rev:** Head below harp player

Date	Mintage	F	VF	XF	Unc	BU
1997 Proof	Est. 2,000	Value: 200				

KM# 911   50 EURO
6.2200 g., 0.9999 Gold 0.1999 oz. AGW **Ruler:** Elizabeth II
Subject: St. George **Obv:** Crowned bust right **Rev:** Rider spearing dragon as captive damsel watches

Date	Mintage	F	VF	XF	Unc	BU
1998 Proof	Est. 2,000	Value: 200				

WW II P.O.W TOKEN COINAGE

KM# Tn23   1/2 PENNY
Brass

Date	Mintage	F	VF	XF	Unc	BU
ND	2,000	17.50	35.00	75.00	170	

KM# Tn24   PENNY
Brass

Date	Mintage	F	VF	XF	Unc	BU
ND	20,000	6.00	15.00	35.00	85.00	—

KM# Tn25   6 PENCE
Brass

Date	Mintage	F	VF	XF	Unc	BU
ND	2,500	12.00	28.00	60.00	140	—

PATTERNS
Including off metal strikes

KM#	Date	Mintage	Identification	Mkt Val
Pn20	1987	30	1/2 Crown. Silver.	325
Pn21	1989	—	Crown. Copper-Nickel. Black finish, first penny postage stamp.	—
Pn23	1992	—	5 Pounds. Virenium. Nigell Mansell, KM336.	—

PIEFORTS

KM#	Date	Mintage	Identification	Mkt Val
P4	1983	4,950	Pound. Silver. KM109.	37.50
P5	1983	4,950	Pound. Silver. KM127	37.50
P6	1983	4,950	Pound. Silver. KM130	42.50
P7	1983	4,950	Pound. Silver. KM131	42.50
P8	1984	1,000	Pound. 0.3740 Gold.	150
P9	1984	250	Pound. 0.9170 Gold.	375
P10	1985	4,950	Pound. Silver.	42.50
P11	1985	950	Pound. 0.3740 Gold.	150
P12	1985	250	Pound. 0.9170 Gold.	375
P13	1985	50	Pound. Platinum.	500

MINT SETS

KM#	Date	Mintage	Identification	Issue Price	Mkt Val
MS1	1965 (3)	1,500	KM15-17	—	1,100
MS2	1971 (6)	50,000	KM19-24	3.00	3.00
MS3	1973 (4)	2,500	KM26-29	760	820
MS4	1974 (4)	250	KM26-29	—	1,400
MS5	1975 (6)	20,000	KM19-24	—	3.00
MS6	1975 (6)	20,000	KM19a-24a	56.50	45.00
MS7	1975 (4)	200	KM26-29	—	1,400
MS8	1976 (6)	20,000	KM32-34, 35.1,36.2, 39	—	4.00
MS9	1976 (6)	20,000	KM32a-34a, 35.1a-36.1a, 39a	—	40.00
MS10	1976 (4)	—	KM26-29	—	1,400
MS11	1977 (6)	50,000	KM33-34, 35.1-36.1, 39-40	—	4.00
MS12	1977 (4)	180	KM26-29	—	1,400
MS13	1978 (6)	10,000	KM32a-34a, 35.1a-36.1a, 39a	—	50.00
MS14	1978 (6)	—	KM32-34, 35.1-36.1, 39	—	4.00
MS15	1979 (6)	—	KM32-34, 35.1-36.1, 39	—	5.00
MS16	1979 (4)	—	KM26-29	—	1,400
MS17	1980 (6)	30,000	KM58-62, 70	—	5.00
MS18	1981 (6)	—	KM58-62, 70	—	5.00
MS20	1983 (9)	—	KM58-62, 70, 88, 90, 109	—	30.00
MS21	1983 (6)	—	KM58-62, 70	—	5.00
MS22	1989 (9)	—	KM207-208, 209.1, 210-215	—	28.00
MS23	1990 (9)	—	KM207-208, 209.1, 210-215	25.00	28.00
MS24	1992 (9)	—	KM207-208, 209.2, 210-215	25.00	28.00
MS25	1994 (9)	—	KM207-208, 212-213, 337, 391-392, 398-399	25.00	28.00
MS26	1995 (9)	—	KM207-208, 212-213, 337, 391-392, 465-466	—	
MS27	1996 (9)	—	KM587-595	—	28.00
MS28	1997 (5)	5,000	KM770-773, 774b	—	1,300
MS29	1985 (9)	—	KM142-148, 150-151, plus rectangular medal	—	28.00

PROOF SETS

KM#	Date	Mintage	Identification	Issue Price	Mkt Val
PS1	1965 (3)	1,000	KM15a-17a	—	1,180
PS2	1971 (6)	10,000	KM19-24	20.00	20.00
PS3	1973 (4)	1,250	KM26-29	950	1,500
PS4	1974 (4)	2,500	KM26-29	900	1,500
PS5	1975 (6)	600	KM19b-24b	1,175	4,050
PS6	1975 (4)	—	KM26-29	—	1,500
PS7	1976 (6)	600	KM32b-34b, 35.1b-36.1b, 39b	—	4,050
PS8	1976 (4)	—	KM26-29	—	1,500
PS9	1977 (6)	10,000	KM33a-34a, 35.1a-36.1a, 39a, 40a	—	42.50
PS10	1977 (4)	1,250	KM26-29	—	1,500
PS11	1978 (7)	—	KM32-34, 35.1-36.1, 39, 44	—	15.00
PS12	1978 (7)	600	KM32b-34b, 35.1b-36.1b, 39b, 44b	—	4,425
PS13	1979 (7)	10,000	KM32a-34a, 35.1a-36.1a, 39a, 44a	110	50.00
PS14	1979 (7)	500	KM32b-34b, 35.1b, 36.1b, 39b, 44b	2,765	4,425
PS15	1979 (4)	1,000	KM26-29	—	1,500
PSA16	1980 (7)	—	KM44, 58-62, 70	—	27.50
PS16	1980 (7)	10,000	KM44d, 58a-62a, 70a	—	55.00
PS17	1980 (7)	—	KM44c, 58c-62c, 70c	—	1,960
PS18	1980 (7)	300	KM44b, 58d-62d, 70d	—	4,425
PSA19	1981 (7)	—	KM44a, 59b-62b, 70b, 88a,	—	90.00
PSB19	1982 (9)	—	KM44, 58, 59, 60, 61, 62, 70, 90, 88	—	—
PS19	1982 (9)	1,000	KM44a, 58b-62b, 70a, 88a, 90a	—	130
PS20	1982 (9)	250	KM44c, 58b-62b, 88b, 90b	—	1,295
PS21	1982 (9)	100	KM44b, 58c-62c, 88c, 90c	—	4,000
PSA22	1982 (8)	—	KM44a, 59b-62b, 70a, 88a, 90a	—	95.00
PS22	1982 (7)	25,000	KM58-62, 70, 90	—	22.50
PS23	1982 (7)	9,000	KM58b-62b, 70a, 90a	—	60.00
PS24	1982 (7)	250	KM58c-62c, 70c, 90b	—	2,000
PS25	1982 (7)	400	KM58d-62d, 70d, 90c	—	4,550
PS26	1983 (7)	—	KM58d-62d, 90a, 109a	—	2,550
PS27	1983 (7)	—	KM58b-62b, 90b, 109b	—	345
PS28	1983 (7)	—	KM58c-62c, 90c, 109c	—	1,925
PSA29	1983 (9)	—	KM59b-62b, 70b, 88a, 90a, 109a	—	110
PS29	1985 (9)	25,000	KM142-148, 150-151	36.00	42.50
PS30	1985 (9)	5,000	KM135, 142a-148a, 150a	120	120
PS31	1985 (9)	150	KM135b, 142b-148b, 150b	3,240	3,000
PS32	1985 (9)	100	KM135c, 142c-148c, 150c	3,600	6,550
PS33	1985 (7)	25,000	KM142-148	20.00	24.00
PS34	1985 (7)	5,000	KM142a-148a	72.00	72.00
PS35	1985 (7)	150	KM142b-148b	2,160	2,000
PS36	1985 (7)	100	KM142c-148c	2,400	4,350
PS37	1985 (6)	51	KM140-141, 152.1, 155-157	—	11,850
PS38	1986 (7)	17	KM140-141, 152.1, 155-157, 166	—	12,000
PS39	1986 (6)	15	KM153-154, 168-171	—	21,500
PSA40	1983-1986 (4)	—	KM109a, 128a, 135-136	—	85.00
PS40	1986 (4)	2,000	KM153-154, 168-169	1,950	2,500
PS41	1986 (5)	2,500	KM140-141, 152.1, 155, 166	—	1,400
PS42	1987 (4)	—	KM176a, 177, 187-188	—	1,000
PS43	1987 (6)	30	KM140-141, 152.2, 155-157	—	11,850
PS44	1987 (5)	—	KM140-141, 152.2, 155, 166	—	1,400
PS45	1987 (4)	3,000	KM140-141, 152.2, 155	—	1,350
PS46	1987 (6)	11	KM153-154, 168-169, 170-171	—	21,400
PS47	1987 (4)	2,500	KM153-154, 168-169	—	2,400
PS48	1988 (5)	611	KM235-239	—	1,425
PS49	1988 (4)	500	KM222-225	—	120
PS50	1988 (6)	7,500	KM286-289 Medal	—	1,450
PS53	1989 (4)	—	KM#240-243 Mutiny on the Bounty	—	—
PS54	1994 (1)	250	KM#204 plus Rhodium-plated Silver 31 g medal 10th Anniversary of the Platinum Noble Coin Series	—	1,150
PS55	1996 (5)	500	KM613, 615, 617, 619, 621b	—	1,375
PS56	1997 (5)	1,000	KM853-856, 857b	—	1,385
PS57	1999 (5)	1,000	KM958, 960, 962, 964, 968	1,300	1,385
PS58	2000 (5)	1,000	KM1052-1055, 1057	1,300	1,400

PROOF-LIKE SETS (PL)

KM#	Date	Mintage	Identification	Issue Price	Mkt Val
PL1	1980 (4)	—	KM64-67	—	35.00
PL2	1981 (4)	—	KM77-80	—	38.00
PL3	1982 (4)	50,000	KM96-99	—	35.00
PL4	1984 (4)	—	KM121-124 College of Arms	—	35.00
PL5	1986 (2)	—	KM173-174 Andrew and Sarah Wedding	—	16.00
PL6	1989 (6)	50,000	KM240-243	—	60.00

ISRAEL

The state of Israel, a Middle Eastern republic at the eastern end of the Mediterranean Sea, bounded by Lebanon on the north, Syria on the northeast, Jordan on the east, and Egypt on the southwest, has an area of 9,000sq. mi. (20,770 sq. km.) and a population of 6 million. Capital: Jerusalem. Finished diamonds, chemicals, citrus, textiles, minerals, electronic and transportation equipment are exported.

HEBREW COIN DATING

Modern Israel's coins carry Hebrew dating formed from a combination of the 22 consonant letters of the Hebrew alphabet and read from right to left. The Jewish calendar dates back more than 5700 years; but five millenniums are assumed in the dating of coins (until 1981). Thus, the year 5735 (1975AD) appears as 735, with the first two characters from the right indicating the number of years in hundreds; tav (400), plus shin (300). The next is lamedh (30), followed by a separation mark which has the appearance of double quotation marks, then heh (5).

The separation mark - generally similar to a single quotation mark through 5718 (1958 AD) and, like a double quotation mark thereafter - serves the purpose of indicating that the letters form a number, not a word, and on some issues can be confused with the character yodh (10), which in a stylized rendering can appear similar, although slightly larger and thicker. The separation mark does not appear in either form on a few commemorative issues.

The Jewish New Year falls in September or October by Christian calendar reckoning. Where dual dating is encountered, with but a few exceptions the Hebrew dating on the coins of modern Israel is 3760 years greater than the Christian dating; 5735 is equivalent to 1975AD, with the 5000 assumed until 1981, when full dates appear on the coins. These exceptions are most of the Hanukka coins, (Feast of Lights), the Bank of Israel gold 50 Pound commemorative of 5725 (1964AD) and others. In such special instances the differential from Christian dating is 3761 years, except in the instance of the 5720 Chanuka Pound, which is dated 1960AD, as is the issue of 5721, an arrangement reflecting the fact that the events fall early in the Jewish year and late in the Christian.

The Star of David is not a mintmark. It appears only on some coins sold by the Israel Government Coins and Medals Corporation Ltd., which is owned by the Israel government, and is a division of the Prime Minister's office and sole distributor to collectors. The Star of David was first used in 1971 on the science coin to signify that it was minted in Jerusalem, but was later used by different mint facilities.

AD Date		Jewish Era
1948	תש״ח	5708
1949	תש״ט	5709
1952	תשי״ב	5712
1954	תשי״ד	5714
1955	תשט״ו	5715
1957	תשי״ז	5717
1958	תשי״ח	5718
1959	תשי״ט	5719
1960	תש״ך	5720
1960	תשך	5720
1961	תשכ״א	5721
1962	תשכ״ב	5722
1963	תשכ״ג	5723
1964	תשכ״ד	5724
1965	תשכ״ה	5725
1966	תשכ״ו	5726

1967	תשכ״ז	5727
1968	תשכ״ח	5728
1969	תשכ״ט	5729
1970	תש״ל	5730
1971	תשל״א	5731
1972	תשל״ב	5732
1973	תשל״ג	5733
1974	תשל״ד	5734
1975	תשל״ה	5735
1976	תשל״ו	5736
1977	תשל״ז	5737
1978	תשל״ח	5738
1979	תשל״ט	5739
1980	תש״ם	5740
1981	תשמ״א	5741
1981	התשמ״א	5741
1982	התשמ״ב	5742
1983	התשמ״ג	5743
1984	התשמ״ד	5744
1985	התשמ״ה	5745
1986	התשמ״ו	5746
1987	התשמ״ז	5747
1988	התשמ״ח	5748
1989	התשמ״ט	5749
1990	התש״ן	5750
1991	התשנ״א	5751
1992	התשנ״ב	5752
1993	התשנ״ג	5753
1994	התשנ״ד	5754
1995	התשנ״ה	5755
1996	התשנ״ו	5756
1997	התשנ״ז	5757
1998	התשנ״ח	5758
1999	התשנ״ט	5759
2000	התש״ס	5760

MINT MARKS
(o) - Ottawa
(s) - San Francisco
None – Jerusalem

(M) MATTE - Normal circulation strike or a dull finish produced by sandblasting special uncirculated (polish finish) or proof quality dies.

(U) SPECIAL UNCIRCULATED - Polished or prooflike in appearance without any frosted features.

(P) PROOF - The highest quality obtainable having mirror-like fields and frosted features.

MONETARY SYSTEM
1000 Mils = 1 Pound

NOTE:
All proof commemoratives with the exception of the 1 and 5 Lirot issues of 1958 are distinguished from the uncirculated editions by the presence fo the Hebrew letter "mem".

REPUBLIC
MIL COINAGE

KM# 8   25 MILS
Aluminum, 30 mm. **Obv:** Grape cluster **Rev:** Value within wreath
Note: Released April 6, 1949.

Date	Mintage	F	VF	XF	Unc	BU
JE5708 (1948)(hn)	42,650	35.00	75.00	200	800	1,000
JE5709 (1949) closed link	650,000	5.00	10.00	15.00	50.00	—
JE5709 (1949) open link	Inc. above	15.00	25.00	70.00	150	—

REFORM COINAGE
1000 Pruta (Prutot) = 1 Lira

NOTE: The 1949 Pruta coins, except for the 100 and 500 Pruta values, occur with and without a small pearl under the bar connecting the wreath on the reverse. Only the 50 and 100 Pruta coins were issued in 5709. All later coins were struck with frozen dates.

KM# 9   PRUTA
1.3000 g., Aluminum, 21 mm. **Obv:** Anchor **Rev:** Value within wreath

Date	Mintage	F	VF	XF	Unc	BU
JE5709 (1949)(i) With pearl	2,660,000	—	0.50	1.00	2.00	—
JE5709(1949)(i) With pearl, Prooflike	Inc. above			—	5.00	—
JE5709 (1949)(ht) Without pearl	2,500,000	1.00	2.00	5.00	20.00	—
JE5709 (1949)(i) Proof	20,000	Value: 500				

KM# 10   5 PRUTA
3.2000 g., Bronze, 20 mm. **Obv:** 4-stringed lyre

Date	Mintage	F	VF	XF	Unc	BU
JE5709 (1949)(i) With pearl	5,020,000	—	0.50	1.00	2.50	—
JE5709 (1949)(i) Proof	25,000	Value: 500				
JE5709 (1949)(ht) Without pearl	5,000,000	1.00	3.50	8.00	20.00	—

KM# 11   10 PRUTA
6.1000 g., Bronze, 27 mm. **Obv:** Amphora **Rev:** Value within wreath

Date	Mintage	F	VF	XF	Unc	BU
JE5709 (1949)(i) With pearl	7,428,000	—	0.75	5.00	20.00	—
JE5709 (1949)(i) Proof	20,000	Value: 1,000				
JE5709 (1949)(ht) Without pearl	7,500,000	—	0.50	1.00	3.00	—

KM# 17 10 PRUTA
1.6000 g., Aluminum, 24.5 mm. **Obv:** Ceremonial pitcher flanked by sprigs **Rev:** Value within wreath

Date	Mintage	F	VF	XF	Unc	BU
JE5712 (1952)(i)	26,042,000	—	0.35	0.75	2.00	—

KM# 20 10 PRUTOT
1.6000 g., Aluminum, 24.5 mm. **Obv:** Ceremonial pitcher flanked by sprigs **Rev:** Value within wreath

Date	Mintage	F	VF	XF	Unc	BU
JE5717 (1957)(t)	1,000,000	—	0.35	0.75	2.50	—

KM# 20a 10 PRUTOT
1.6000 g., Copper Electroplated Aluminum, 24.5 mm.
Obv: Ceremonial pitcher flanked by sprigs **Rev:** Value within wreath

Date	Mintage	F	VF	XF	Unc	BU
JE5717 (1957)(t)	1,088,000	—	0.35	0.75	2.00	—

KM# 12 25 PRUTA
2.8000 g., Copper-Nickel, 19.5 mm. **Obv:** Grape cluster
Rev: Value within wreath

Date	Mintage	F	VF	XF	Unc	BU
JE5709 (1949)(i) With pearl	10,500,000	—	0.50	0.75	2.00	—
JE5709 (1949)(ht) Without pearl	2,500,000	—	5.00	10.00	30.00	—
JE5709 (1949)(i) Proof	20,000	Value: 1,000				

KM# 12a 25 PRUTA
2.5000 g., Nickel-Clad Steel, 19.5 mm. **Obv:** Grape cluster
Rev: Value within wreath

Date	Mintage	F	VF	XF	Unc	BU
JE5714 (1954)(t)	3,697,347	—	0.50	1.00	2.50	—

KM# 13.1 50 PRUTA
5.6000 g., Copper-Nickel, 23.5 mm. **Obv:** Grape leaves
Rev: Value within wreath **Edge:** Reeded

Date	Mintage	F	VF	XF	Unc	BU
JE5709 (1949)(i)	6,020,000	—	5.00	10.00	25.00	—
JE5709 (1949)(i) Proof	20,000	Value: 1,000				
JE5709 (1949)(ht) Without pearl	6,000,000	—	0.75	1.50	3.00	—
JE5714 (1954)(t)	250,000	—	2.00	15.00	32.00	—

KM# 13.2 50 PRUTA
5.6000 g., Copper-Nickel, 23.5 mm. **Obv:** Grape leaves
Rev: Value within wreath **Edge:** Plain

Date	Mintage	F	VF	XF	Unc	BU
JE5714 (1954)(t)	4,500,000	—	0.50	1.00	2.00	—

KM# 13.2a 50 PRUTA
5.0000 g., Nickel-Clad Steel, 23.6 mm. **Obv:** Grape leaves
Rev: Value within wreath **Edge:** Plain

Date	Mintage	F	VF	XF	Unc	BU
JE5714 (1954)(t)	17,773,633	—	0.50	1.00	2.00	—

KM# 14 100 PRUTA
11.3000 g., Copper-Nickel, 28.5 mm. **Obv:** Date palm
Rev: Value within wreath

Date	Mintage	F	VF	XF	Unc	BU
JE5709 (1949)	6,042,000	—	0.75	1.25	2.50	—
Note: 3,042,000 minted at (i) and 3,000,000 minted at (ht).						
JE5709 (1949)(i) Proof	20,000	Value: 1,000				
JE5715 (1955)(t)	5,867,674	—	1.00	1.50	2.50	—

KM# 19 100 PRUTA
7.3900 g., Nickel Clad Steel, 25.6 mm. **Obv:** Date palm
Rev: Value within wreath **Note:** Reduced size, greater space between wreath and rim.

Date	Mintage	F	VF	XF	Unc	BU
JE5714 (1954)(u)	20,000	50.00	100	250	1,000	—

KM# 18 100 PRUTA
7.3000 g., Nickel-Clad Steel, 25.6 mm. **Obv:** Date palm
Rev: Value within wreath **Note:** Reduced size.

Date	Mintage	F	VF	XF	Unc	BU
JE5714 (1954)(b)	700,000	—	1.00	1.50	3.00	—

KM# 15 250 PRUTA
14.1000 g., Copper-Nickel, 32.2 mm. **Obv:** Oat sprigs
Rev: Value within wreath

Date	Mintage	F	VF	XF	Unc	BU
JE5709 (1949)(i) With pearl	1,496,000	—	2.50	10.00	20.00	—
JE5709 (1949)(ht) Without pearl	524,000	—	1.00	2.00	5.00	—

KM# 15a 250 PRUTA
14.4000 g., 0.5000 Silver 0.2315 oz. ASW, 32.2 mm. **Obv:** Oat sprigs **Rev:** Value within wreath

Date	Mintage	F	VF	XF	Unc	BU
JE5709 (1949) H	44,125	—	4.50	6.50	12.00	—
Note: Not placed into circulation						

KM# 16 500 PRUTA
25.0000 g., 0.5000 Silver 0.4019 oz. ASW, 38 mm.
Obv: Pomegranates **Rev:** Value within wreath **Note:** Dav. #257.

Date	Mintage	F	VF	XF	Unc	BU
JE5709 (1949)(ht)	33,812	—	8.50	12.50	35.00	50.00
Note: Not placed into circulation						

REFORM COINAGE
100 Agorot = 1 Lira

Commencing January 1, 1960-1980

KM# 24.1 AGORA
1.0300 g., Aluminum, 20 mm. **Obv:** Text to left and below oat sprigs **Rev:** Value

Date	Mintage	F	VF	XF	Unc	BU
JE5720 (1960)(i)	12,768,000	—	4.00	8.00	20.00	—
Note: Letter "Lamed" in Israel with serif						
JE5720 (1960)(i) Inc. above		—	10.00	20.00	100	—
Note: Letter "Lamed" in Israel without lower serif						
JE5720 (1960)(i)	300	—	150	300	750	—
Note: Large date						
JE5721 (1961)(i)	19,262,000	—	0.50	2.00	5.00	—
JE5721 (1961)(i) Inc. above		—	5.00	15.00	100	—
Note: Thick date						
JE5721 (1961)(i) Inc. above		—	5.00	15.00	100	—
Note: Wide date						
JE5722 (1962)	14,500,000	—	0.10	0.40	0.75	—
Note: Large date						
JE5722 (1962) Inc. above		—	5.00	10.00	20.00	—
Note: Small date, small serifs						
JEJE5723 (1963)(t)	8,804,000	—	0.10	0.40	0.75	—
Note: Medal alignment						
JE5723 (1963)(t)	Est. 10,000	—	2.50	4.50	10.00	20.00
Note: Coin alignment						
JE5724 (1964)(i)	4,950,000	—	—	—	0.75	—
JE5724 (1964)(t)	22,604,241	—	—	—	0.75	—
JE5725 (1965)(b)	10,024,000	—	—	—	0.25	—
JE5725 (1965)(t)	10,707,625	—	—	—	0.25	—
JE5726 (1966)(b)	1,680,000	—	—	—	0.25	—
JE5726 (1966)(t)	8,482,502	—	—	—	0.25	—
JE5727 (1967)(t)	6,782,271	—	—	—	0.25	—
JE5728 (1968)(t)	20,899,000	—	—	—	0.25	—
JE5729 (1969)(t)	22,120,000	—	—	—	0.25	—
JE5730 (1970)(t)	17,748,000	—	—	—	0.25	—
JE5731 (1971)(t)	10,290,000	—	—	—	0.25	—
JE5732 (1972)(t)	24,512,000	—	—	—	0.25	—
JE5733 (1973)(t)	20,496,000	—	—	—	0.25	—
JE5734 (1974)(t) Matte	8,080,000	—	—	—	0.75	—
JE5734 (1974)(o) Prooflike	34,000,000	—	—	—	0.25	—
JE5735 (1975)(j)	1,574,000	—	—	—	0.25	—
JE5736 (1976)(j)	4,512,000	—	—	—	0.25	—
JE5737 (1977)(j)	9,680,000	—	—	—	0.25	—
JE5738 (1978)(j)	8,864,000	—	—	—	0.25	—
JE5739 (1979)(j)	4,048,763	—	—	—	0.25	—
JE5740 (1980)(j)	2,599,634	—	—	—	1.00	—

KM# 24.2 AGORA
1.0300 g., Aluminum, 20 mm. **Obv:** Text to left and below oat sprigs, star of David in field **Rev:** Value **Edge:** Plain

Date	Mintage	F	VF	XF	Unc	BU
JE5731 (1971)(j)	125,921	—	—	—	0.75	—
JE5732 (1972)(j)	68,513	—	—	—	0.75	—
JE5734 (1974)(j)	92,868	—	—	—	0.75	—
JE5735 (1975)(j)	61,686	—	—	—	1.00	—
JE5736 (1976)(j)	64,654	—	—	—	0.75	—
JE5737 (1977)(j)	37,208	—	—	—	1.00	—

Date	Mintage	F	VF	XF	Unc	BU
JE5738 (1978)(j)	57,072	—	—	—	0.75	—
JE5739 (1979)(j)	31,590	—	—	—	1.00	—

KM# 63 AGORA
1.0300 g., Aluminum, 20 mm. **Subject:** 25th Anniversary of Independence **Obv:** Text to left and below oat sprigs **Rev:** Value **Note:** Struck for sets only.

Date	Mintage	F	VF	XF	Unc	BU
JE5733 (1973)(j)	98,107	—	—	—	0.75	—

KM# 96 AGORA
Nickel, 20 mm. **Subject:** 25th Anniversary - Bank of Israel **Obv:** Text to left and below oat sprigs **Rev:** Value **Note:** Struck for sets only

Date	Mintage	F	VF	XF	Unc	BU
JE5740 (1980)(b)	35,000	—	—	—	2.00	—

Normal 1961   1961 I.C.I.

KM# 25 5 AGOROT
2.3000 g., Aluminum-Bronze, 17.5 mm. **Obv:** Pomegranates **Rev:** Value **Edge:** Plain

Date	Mintage	F	VF	XF	Unc	BU
JE5720 (1960)(t)	8,019,000	—	5.00	10.00	25.00	—
JE5721 (1961)	15,090,000	—	0.25	0.50	1.50	—
Note: Sharp, flat date						
JE5721 (1961)(i)	5,000,000	—	10.00	20.00	60.00	—
Note: High date with serifs						
JE5722 (1962)(t)	11,198,000	—	0.25	0.50	1.00	—
Large date						
JE5722 (1962)(t)	Inc. above	—	5.00	10.00	25.00	—
Small date						
JE5723 (1963)(t)	1,429,000	—	0.25	0.50	1.25	—
JE5724 (1964)(t)	21,451	—	12.00	120	4,540	600
JE5725 (1965)(t)	201,281	—	—	0.10	0.25	—
JE5726 (1966)(j)	290,866	—	—	0.10	0.25	—
JE5727 (1967)(j)	2,195,114	—	—	0.10	0.25	—
JE5728 (1968)(j)	4,020,000	—	—	0.10	0.25	—
JE5729 (1969)(j)	2,200,103	—	—	0.10	0.25	—
JE5730 (1970)(j)	4,004,000	—	—	0.10	0.25	—
JE5731 (1971)(j)	14,010,000	—	—	0.10	0.25	—
JE5732 (1972)(j)	9,005,000	—	—	0.10	0.25	—
JE5733 (1973)(o)	16,340,000	—	—	0.10	0.25	—
JE5733 (1973)(j)	9,380,000	—	—	0.10	0.25	—
JE5734 (1974)(j)	10,470,000	—	—	0.10	0.25	—
JE5735 (1975)(j)	10,232,000	—	—	0.10	0.25	—

KM# 25a 5 AGOROT
2.3000 g., Aluminum-Bronze, 17.5 mm. **Obv:** Pomegranates, Star of David in field **Rev:** Value

Date	Mintage	F	VF	XF	Unc	BU
JE5731 (1971)(j)	125,921	—	—	—	0.75	—
JE5732 (1972)(j)	68,513	—	—	—	0.75	—

KM# 25b 5 AGOROT
0.7700 g., Aluminum, 17.5 mm. **Obv:** Pomegranates **Rev:** Value

Date	Mintage	F	VF	XF	Unc	BU
JE5736 (1976)(j)	13,156,000	—	—	0.10	0.50	—
JE5737 (1977)(j) Matte	16,800,000	—	—	0.10	0.50	—
JE5737 (1977)(j) Prooflike	15,000,010	—	—	0.10	0.50	—
JE5738 (1978)(j) Matte	21,480,000	—	—	0.10	0.50	—
JE5738 (1978)(o) Prooflike	38,716,000	—	—	0.10	0.50	—
JE5739 (1979)(j)	12,835,709	—	—	0.10	0.50	—

KM# 25c 5 AGOROT
Copper-Nickel, 17.5 mm. **Rev:** Value

Date	Mintage	F	VF	XF	Unc	BU
JE5734 (1974)(j)	92,868	—	—	—	0.75	—
JE5735 (1975)(j)	61,686	—	—	—	1.00	—

Date	Mintage	F	VF	XF	Unc	BU
JE5736 (1976)(j)	64,654	—	—	—	0.75	—
JE5737 (1977)(j)	37,208	—	—	—	1.00	—
JE5738 (1978)(j)	57,072	—	—	—	0.75	—
JE5739 (1979)(j)	31,590	—	—	—	1.00	—

KM# 64 5 AGOROT
Copper-Nickel, 17.5 mm. **Subject:** 25th Anniversary of Independence **Obv:** Pomegranates **Rev:** Value **Note:** In sets only.

Date	Mintage	F	VF	XF	Unc	BU
JE5733 (1973)(j)	98,107	—	—	—	0.75	—

KM# 97 5 AGOROT
Nickel, 17.5 mm. **Subject:** 25th Anniversary - Bank of Israel **Obv:** Pomegranates **Rev:** Value **Note:** Struck for sets only.

Date	Mintage	F	VF	XF	Unc	BU
JE5740 (1980)(b)	35,000	—	—	—	2.00	—

Large date   Small date

KM# 26 10 AGOROT
5.0000 g., Aluminum-Bronze, 21.5 mm. **Obv:** Date palm **Rev:** Value

Date	Mintage	F	VF	XF	Unc	BU
JE5720 (1960)(t)	14,397,000	—	0.50	1.00	10.00	—
JE5721 (1961)	12,821,000	—	0.50	1.00	6.00	—
JE5721 (1961)	Inc. above	—	25.00	60.00	325	—
Note: "Fatha" in Arabic, legend: "Israel"						
JE5722 (1962)(t) Large date, thick letters	8,845,000	—	0.25	0.50	1.00	—
JE5722 (1962)(t) Small date, thin letters	Inc. above	—	5.00	10.00	20.00	—
JE5723 (1963)(t)	3,931,000	—	0.25	0.50	1.00	—
JE5724 (1964)(t) Large date	3,612,000	—	0.25	0.50	1.00	—
Note: Hebrew letter "shin" is rounded						
JE5724 (1964)(t) Small date	Inc. above	—	8.00	15.00	50.00	—
Note: Hebrew letter "shin" is straight and sharp						
JE5725 (1965)(t)	200,561	—	—	0.20	0.25	—
JE5726 (1966)(t)	7,276,610	—	—	0.10	0.25	—
JE5727 (1967)(j)	6,426,438	—	—	0.10	0.25	—
JE5728 (1968)(j)	4,825,000	—	—	0.10	0.25	—
JE5729 (1969)(j)	6,810,000	—	—	0.10	0.25	—
JE5730 (1970)(j)	6,131,000	—	—	0.10	0.25	—
JE5731 (1971)(j)	6,810,000	—	—	0.10	0.25	—
JE5732 (1972)(j)	1,260,000	—	—	0.10	0.25	—
JE5732 (1972)(b)	18,393,112	—	—	0.10	0.25	—
JE5733 (1973)(j)	5,625,000	—	—	0.10	0.25	—
JE5733 (1973)(o)	10,580,000	—	—	0.10	0.25	—
JE5734 (1974)(j)	3,880,000	—	—	0.10	0.25	—
JE5734 (1974)(o)	18,160,000	—	—	0.10	0.25	—
JE5735 (1975)(j)	25,135,000	—	—	0.10	0.25	—
JE5736 (1976)(j)	34,870,000	—	—	0.10	0.25	—
JE5736 (1976)(o)	20,000,000	—	—	0.10	0.25	—
JE5737 (1977)(j)	27,885,863	—	—	0.10	0.25	—

KM# 26a 10 AGOROT
5.0000 g., Aluminum-Bronze, 21.5 mm. **Obv:** Date palm with star of David in field **Rev:** Value

Date	Mintage	F	VF	XF	Unc	BU
JE5731 (1971)(j)	125,921	—	—	—	0.75	—
JE5732 (1972)(j)	68,513	—	—	—	0.75	—

KM# 26b 10 AGOROT
1.6100 g., Aluminum, 21.5 mm. **Obv:** Date palm **Rev:** Value

Date	Mintage	F	VF	XF	Unc	BU
JE5737 (1977)(o) Prooflike	30,000,010	—	—	0.10	0.25	—
JE5738 (1978)(j) Matte	24,050,000	—	—	0.10	0.25	—
JE5738 (1978)(o) Prooflike	104,335,750	—	—	0.10	0.25	—
JE5739 (1979)(j)	22,201,469	—	—	0.10	0.25	—

Date	Mintage	F	VF	XF	Unc	BU
JE5740 (1980)(j)	4,752,333	—	—	0.10	0.50	—

Note: Most of the 5740 dated coins were melted down before being issued.

KM# 26c 10 AGOROT
Copper-Nickel, 21.5 mm. **Obv:** Date palm with star of David in field **Rev:** Value **Note:** In sets only.

Date	Mintage	F	VF	XF	Unc	BU
JE5734 (1974)(j)	92,868	—	—	—	0.75	—
JE5735 (1975)(j)	61,686	—	—	—	1.00	—
JE5736 (1976)(j)	64,654	—	—	—	0.75	—
JE5737 (1977)(j)	37,208	—	—	—	1.00	—
JE5738 (1978)(j)	57,072	—	—	—	0.75	—
JE5739 (1979)(j)	31,590	—	—	—	1.00	—

KM# 65 10 AGOROT
Copper-Nickel, 21.5 mm. **Subject:** 25th Anniversary of Independence **Obv:** Date palm **Rev:** Value **Note:** In sets only.

Date	Mintage	F	VF	XF	Unc	BU
JE5733 (1973)(j)	98,107	—	—	—	0.75	—

KM# 98 10 AGOROT
Nickel, 21.5 mm. **Subject:** 25th Anniversary - Bank of Israel **Obv:** Date palm **Rev:** Value **Note:** Struck for sets only.

Date	Mintage	F	VF	XF	Unc	BU
JE5740 (1980)(b)	35,000	—	—	—	2.00	—

KM# 27 25 AGOROT
6.5000 g., Aluminum-Bronze, 25.5 mm. **Obv:** Three-string lyre **Rev:** Value

Date	Mintage	F	VF	XF	Unc	BU
JE5720 (1960)(u)	40,000	—	0.25	0.50	3.00	—
JE5720 (1960)(t)	4,351,000	—	0.25	0.50	3.00	—
JE5721 (1961)(b)	2,010,000	—	0.10	0.20	1.00	—
JE5721 (1961)(t)	2,994,000	—	0.10	0.20	1.00	—
5721 (1961)(u)	5,000	—	0.10	0.20	1.00	—
JE5722 (1962)(t)	882,000	—	0.15	0.30	1.00	—
JE5723 (1963)(t)	194,000	—	0.50	1.00	5.00	—
JE5724 (1964)	—	—	—	—	—	—
Note: Five trial pieces only						
JE5725 (1965)(t)	186,544	—	0.10	0.20	0.50	—
JE5726 (1966)(j)	320,000	—	—	0.10	0.40	—
JE5727 (1967)(j)	325,041	—	—	0.10	0.40	—
JE5728 (1968)(j)	445,000	—	—	0.10	0.40	—
JE5729 (1969)(j)	432,004	—	—	0.10	0.40	—
JE5730 (1970)(j)	417,000	—	—	0.10	0.40	—
JE5731 (1971)(j)	500,030	—	—	0.10	0.40	—
JE5732 (1972)(j)	1,883,000	—	—	0.10	0.40	—
JE5733 (1973)(j)	3,770,000	—	—	0.10	0.40	—
JE5734 (1974)(j)	2,320,000	—	—	0.10	0.40	—
JE5735 (1975)(j)	3,968,000	—	—	0.10	0.40	—
JE5736 (1976)(j)	3,901,000	—	—	0.10	0.40	—
JE5737 (1977)(j)	1,832,000	—	—	0.10	0.40	—
JE5738 (1978)(j)	12,200,000	—	—	0.10	0.40	—
JE5739 (1979)(j)	10,842,140	—	—	0.10	0.40	—

KM# 27a 25 AGOROT
6.5000 g., Aluminum-Bronze, 25.5 mm. **Obv:** Three stringed lyre with star of David in field **Rev:** Value

Date	Mintage	F	VF	XF	Unc	BU
JE5731 (1971)(j)	125,921	—	—	—	0.75	—
JE5732 (1972)(j)	68,513	—	—	—	0.75	—

KM# 27b 25 AGOROT

Copper-Nickel, 25.5 mm. **Obv:** Three stringed lyre with star of David in field **Rev:** Value **Note:** Struck for sets only.

Date	Mintage	F	VF	XF	Unc	BU
JE5734 (1974)(j)	92,868	—	—	—	0.75	—
JE5735 (1975)(j)	61,686	—	—	—	1.00	—
JE5736 (1976)(j)	64,654	—	—	—	0.75	—
JE5737 (1977)(j)	37,208	—	—	—	1.00	—
JE5738 (1978)(j)	57,072	—	—	—	0.75	—
JE5739 (1979)(j)	31,590	—	—	—	1.00	—

KM# 66 25 AGOROT

Copper-Nickel, 25.5 mm. **Subject:** 25th Anniversary of Independence **Obv:** Three-string lyre **Rev:** Value **Note:** Struck for sets only.

Date	Mintage	F	VF	XF	Unc	BU
JE5733 (1973)(j)	98,107	—	—	—	0.75	—

KM# 99 25 AGOROT

Nickel, 25.5 mm. **Subject:** 25th Anniversary - Bank of Israel **Obv:** Three-string lyre **Rev:** Value **Note:** Struck for sets only.

Date	Mintage	F	VF	XF	Unc	BU
JE5740 (1980)(b)	35,000	—	—	—	2.00	—

KM# 31 1/2 LIRA

Copper-Nickel, 30 mm. **Subject:** Feast of Purim **Obv:** Inscription **Rev:** Chalice within beaded circle

Date	Mintage	F	VF	XF	Unc	BU
JE5721 (1961)(u)	19,939	—	—	—	5.00	—
JE5721 (1961)(u) Proof	4,901	Value: 12.00				
JE5722 (1962)(u)	19,890	—	—	—	6.00	—
JE5722 (1962)(u) Proof	9,894	Value: 9.00				

KM# 36.1 1/2 LIRA

6.8000 g., Copper-Nickel, 24.5 mm. **Obv:** Menorah flanked by sprigs **Rev:** Value **Edge:** Reeded

Date	Mintage	F	VF	XF	Unc	BU
JE5723 (1963)(t) Large animals	5,593,000	—	0.50	2.00	5.00	—
JE5723 (1963)(h) Small animals	14,000	—	3.00	15.00	30.00	—
JE5724 (1964)(t)	3,761,890	—	0.10	0.75	2.00	—
JE5725 (1965)(t)	1,551,167	—	0.10	0.15	1.00	—
JE5726 (1966)(t)	2,139,000	—	0.10	0.15	0.50	—
JE5727 (1967)(t)	1,942,579	—	0.10	0.15	0.50	—
JE5728 (1968)(j)	1,183,000	—	0.10	0.15	0.50	—
JE5729 (1969)(j)	450,000	—	0.10	0.20	0.60	—
JE5730 (1970)(j)	1,001,023	—	0.10	0.20	0.60	—
JE5731 (1971)(j)	500,008	—	0.10	0.20	0.60	—
JE5732 (1972)(j)	421,040	—	0.10	0.20	0.60	—
JE5733 (1973)(b)	3,115,000	—	0.10	0.20	0.50	—
JE5733 (1973)(j)	110,000	—	0.10	0.15	0.50	—
JE5734 (1974)(j)	4,275,015	—	0.10	0.15	0.50	—
JE5735 (1975)(c)	5,000,010	—	0.10	0.15	0.50	—
JE5735 (1975)(j)	6,066,000	—	0.10	0.15	0.50	—
JE5736 (1976)(j)	4,959,000	—	0.10	0.15	0.50	—
JE5737 (1977)(j)	4,983,010	—	0.10	0.15	0.50	—
JE5738 (1978)(j)	14,325,000	—	0.10	0.15	0.50	—
JE5739 (1979)(j)	21,391,170	—	0.10	0.15	0.50	—

KM# 36.2 1/2 LIRA

6.8000 g., Copper-Nickel, 24.5 mm. **Obv:** Menorah with star of David in field flanked by sprigs **Rev:** Value **Note:** Struck for sets only.

Date	Mintage	F	VF	XF	Unc	BU
JE5731 (1971)(j)	125,921	—	—	—	1.00	—
JE5732 (1972)(j)	68,513	—	—	—	1.00	—
JE5734 (1974)(j)	92,868	—	—	—	1.00	—
JE5735 (1975)(j)	61,686	—	—	—	1.00	—
JE5736 (1976)(j)	64,654	—	—	—	1.00	—
JE5737 (1977)(j)	37,208	—	—	—	1.25	—

Date	Mintage	F	VF	XF	Unc	BU
JE5738 (1978)(j)	57,072	—	—	—	1.00	—
JE5739 (1979)(j)	31,590	—	—	—	1.25	—

KM# 67 1/2 LIRA

6.8000 g., Copper-Nickel, 24.5 mm. **Subject:** 25th Anniversary of Independence **Obv:** Menorah flanked by sprigs **Rev:** Value **Edge:** Reeded **Note:** Struck for sets only.

Date	Mintage	F	VF	XF	Unc	BU
JE5733 (1973)(j)	98,107	—	—	—	1.50	—

KM# 100 1/2 LIRA

Nickel, 24.5 mm. **Subject:** 25th Anniversary - Bank of Israel **Obv:** Menorah flanked by sprigs **Rev:** Value **Edge:** Reeded **Note:** Struck for sets only.

Date	Mintage	F	VF	XF	Unc	BU
JE5740 (1980)(b)	35,000	—	—	—	3.00	—

KM# 22 LIRA

Copper-Nickel, 32 mm. **Subject:** Hanukka - Law Is Light **Obv:** Value to upper right of text and date **Rev:** Menorah flanked by stars with text below **Edge:** Smooth

Date	Mintage	F	VF	XF	Unc	BU
JE5719-1958(b)	149,594	—	—	—	2.00	—
JE5719-1958(b) Proof	5,000	Value: 21.00				

KM# 28 LIRA

Copper-Nickel, 32 mm. **Subject:** Hannukah - 50th Anniversary of Deganya, oldest Kibbuto founded in 1909 **Obv:** Text at upper left of desert scene **Rev:** Text at upper and lower left of value

Date	Mintage	F	VF	XF	Unc	BU
JE5720-1960(u)	49,455	—	—	—	4.50	—
JE5720-1960(u) Proof	4,702	Value: 23.00				

KM# 32 LIRA

Copper-Nickel, 32 mm. **Subject:** Hanukka-Henrietta Szold **Obv:** Block-like design **Rev:** Seated hooded figure holding lamb **Edge:** Smooth

Date	Mintage	F	VF	XF	Unc	BU
JE5721-1960(u)	16,781	—	—	—	13.00	—
JE5721-1960(u) Proof	3,000	Value: 85.00				

KM# 34 LIRA

Copper-Nickel, 32 mm. **Subject:** Hanukka-nacabbean hero **Obv:** Large torch flanked by text with small value at upper right **Rev:** Rearing elephant

Date	Mintage	F	VF	XF	Unc	BU
JE5722-1961(u)	18,801	—	—	—	6.00	10.00
JE5722-1961(u) Proof	9,324	Value: 15.00				

KM# 38 LIRA

Copper-Nickel, 32 mm. **Subject:** Hanukka **Obv:** Italian lamp **Rev:** Value above text and date

Date	Mintage	F	VF	XF	Unc	BU
JE5723-1962(b)	9,560	—	—	—	12.00	15.00
JE5723-1962(b) Proof	5,941	Value: 25.00				

KM# 42 LIRA

Copper-Nickel, 32 mm. **Subject:** Hanukka **Obv:** Value above text and date within rectangle **Rev:** 18th Century North African lamp

Date	Mintage	F	VF	XF	Unc	BU
JE5724-1963(u)	9,928	—	—	—	10.00	15.00
JE5724-1963(u) Proof	5,412	Value: 25.00				

KM# 37 LIRA

9.0000 g., Copper-Nickel, 27.5 mm. **Obv:** Menorah flanked by sprigs **Rev:** Value **Edge:** Reeded

Date	Mintage	F	VF	XF	Unc	BU
JE5723 (1963) Large animals	4,212,000	—	0.50	1.50	3.00	—
JE5723 (1963) Small animals	Inc. above	—	1.00	10.00	35.00	—
JE5724 (1964)	—	—	—	—	—	—
Note: Only ten trial pieces struck						
JE5725 (1965)(t)	166,053	—	0.25	0.50	1.25	—
JE5726 (1966)(t)	290,000	—	0.25	0.50	1.25	—
JE5727 (1967)(t)	180,066	—	0.25	0.50	1.25	—

KM# 47.1 LIRA
9.0000 g., Copper-Nickel, 27.5 mm. **Obv:** Pomegranates
Rev: Value flanked by stars above text **Edge:** Reeded, smooth alternating edge

Date	Mintage	F	VF	XF	Unc	BU
JE5727 (1967)(j)	3,830,388	—	0.10	0.25	1.00	—
JE5728 (1968)(j)	3,932,061	—	0.10	0.25	1.00	—
JE5729 (1969)(j)	12,484,016	—	0.10	0.25	0.75	—
JE5730 (1970)(j)	4,793,663	—	0.10	0.25	0.75	—
JE5731 (1971)(j)	2,993,000	—	0.10	0.25	0.75	—
JE5732 (1972)(j)	2,485,041	—	0.10	0.25	0.75	—
JE5733 (1973)(b)	10,115,000	—	0.10	0.25	0.75	—
JE5733 (1973)(b)	150,000	—	0.10	0.25	0.75	—
JE5734 (1974)(j)	2,287,000	—	0.10	0.25	0.75	—
JE5734 (1974)(o)	4,000,000	—	0.10	0.25	0.75	—
JE5735 (1975)(j)	7,225,000	—	0.10	0.25	0.75	—
JE5736 (1976)(j)	4,268,000	—	0.10	0.25	0.75	—
JE5737 (1977)(j)	11,129,000	—	0.10	0.25	0.75	—
5738 (1978)(j)	25,361,000	—	0.10	0.25	0.75	—
JE5738 (1978)(o)	36,391,000	—	0.10	0.25	0.75	—
5739 (1979)	10,615,464	—	0.10	0.25	0.75	—
JE5739 (1979)(o)	24,200,000	—	0.10	0.25	0.75	—
JE5740 (1980)	10,840,424	—	0.10	0.25	0.75	—

Note: Most of the 5740 dated coins were melted down before being issued.

KM# 47.2 LIRA
9.0000 g., Copper-Nickel, 27.5 mm. **Obv:** Pomegranates with star of David in field **Rev:** Value flanked by stars above text **Note:** Struck for sets only.

Date	Mintage	F	VF	XF	Unc	BU
JE5731 (1971)(j)	125,921	—	—	—	1.00	—
JE5732 (1972)(j)	68,513	—	—	—	1.00	—
JE5734 (1974)(j)	92,868	—	—	—	1.00	—
JE5735 (1975)(j)	61,686	—	—	—	1.00	—
JE5736 (1976)(j)	64,654	—	—	—	1.00	—
JE5737 (1977)(j)	37,208	—	—	—	1.50	—
JE5738 (1978)(j)	57,072	—	—	—	1.00	—
JE5739 (1979)(j)	31,590	—	—	—	1.50	—

KM# 68 LIRA
9.0000 g., Copper-Nickel, 27.5 mm. **Subject:** 25th Anniversary of Independence **Obv:** Pomegranates with star of David in field **Rev:** Value flanked by stars above text **Edge:** Smooth, reeded alternating edge **Note:** Struck for sets only.

Date	Mintage	F	VF	XF	Unc	BU
JE5733 (1973)(j)	98,107	—	—	—	1.00	—

KM# 101 LIRA
9.0000 g., Nickel, 27.5 mm. **Subject:** 25th Anniversary - Bank of Israel **Obv:** Pomegranates with star of David in field **Rev:** Value flanked by stars above text **Edge:** Reeded, smooth alternating edge **Note:** Struck for sets only.

Date	Mintage	F	VF	XF	Unc	BU
JE5740 (1980)(b)	35,000	—	—	—	4.00	—

KM# 21 5 LIROT
25.0000 g., 0.9000 Silver 0.7234 oz. ASW, 34 mm.
Subject: 10th Anniversary of Independence **Obv:** Large value at lower right of text **Rev:** Menorah **Note:** Dav. #258

Date	Mintage	F	VF	XF	Unc	BU
JE5718-1958(u)	97,860	—	—	—	15.00	17.50
JE5718-1958(u)	2,000	Value: 280				
Frosted Proof						

KM# 23 5 LIROT
25.0000 g., 0.9000 Silver 0.7234 oz. ASW, 34 mm.
Subject: 11th Anniversary of Independence **Obv:** Value at lower right of text **Rev:** Ingathering of exiles **Note:** Dav. #259.

Date	Mintage	F	VF	XF	Unc	BU
JE5719-1959(b)	27,016	—	—	—	15.00	20.00
JE5719-1959(b)	4,682	Value: 35.00				
Proof						

KM# 29 5 LIROT
25.0000 g., 0.9000 Silver 0.7234 oz. ASW, 34 mm.
Subject: 12th Anniversary of Independence **Obv:** Value at lower right of text **Rev:** Head left within square at upper right **Note:** Dav. #29.

Date	Mintage	F	VF	XF	Unc	BU
JE5720-1960(b)	34,281	—	—	—	12.00	18.00
JE5720-1960(b)	4,827	Value: 35.00				
Proof						

KM# 33 5 LIROT
25.0000 g., 0.9000 Silver 0.7234 oz. ASW, 34 mm. **Subject:** 13th Anniversary of Independence **Obv:** Olive branch with 10 leaves and 3 olives **Rev:** Ark of the law with 6 torah **Note:** Dav. #261

Date	Mintage	F	VF	XF	Unc	BU
JE5721-1961(u)	19,363	—	—	—	35.00	45.00
JE5721-1961(u)	4,455	Value: 60.00				
Proof						

KM# 35 5 LIROT
25.0000 g., 0.9000 Silver 0.7234 oz. ASW, 34 mm.
Subject: 14th Anniversary of Independence **Rev:** Negev Industrialization **Note:** Dav. #262,

Date	Mintage	F	VF	XF	Unc	BU
JE5722-1962(u)	10,380	—	—	—	25.00	35.00
JE5722-1962(u)	4,960	Value: 50.00				
Proof						

KM# 39 5 LIROT
25.0000 g., 0.9000 Silver 0.7234 oz. ASW, 34 mm.
Subject: 15th Anniversary of Independence **Obv:** Value and star within upright design **Rev:** Longship **Note:** Dav. #263.

Date	Mintage	F	VF	XF	Unc	BU
JE5723-1963(r)	5,960	—	—	—	200	225
JE5723-1963(r)	4,495	Value: 225				
Proof						

KM# 43 5 LIROT
25.0000 g., 0.9000 Silver 0.7234 oz. ASW, 34 mm.
Subject: 16th Anniversary of Independence **Obv:** Value at lower right of text **Rev:** Ionic style column with value at upper right **Note:** Dav. #264.

Date	Mintage	F	VF	XF	Unc	BU
JE5724-1964(r)	10,967	—	—	—	30.00	40.00
JE5724-1964(r)	4,421	Value: 55.00				
Proof						

KM# 45 5 LIROT
25.0000 g., 0.9000 Silver 0.7234 oz. ASW, 34 mm.
Subject: 17th Anniversary of Independence **Rev:** Knesset Building **Note:** Dav. #265.

Date	Mintage	F	VF	XF	Unc	BU
JE5725-1965(r)	25,147	—	—	—	11.00	14.00
JE5725-1965(r)	7,537	Value: 15.00				
Proof						

KM# 46 5 LIROT
25.0000 g., 0.9000 Silver 0.7234 oz. ASW, 34 mm.
Subject: 18th Anniversary of Independence **Rev:** Abstract design **Note:** Dav. #266.

Date	Mintage	F	VF	XF	Unc	BU
JE5726-1966(u)	32,356	—	—	—	11.00	14.00
JE5726-1966(u) Proof	10,368	Value: 15.00				

KM# 48 5 LIROT
25.0000 g., 0.9000 Silver 0.7234 oz. ASW, 34 mm.
Subject: 19th Anniversary of Independence **Obv:** Large styilized value **Rev:** Port of Eilat **Note:** Dav. #267.

Date	Mintage	F	VF	XF	Unc	BU
JE5727-1967(u)	30,158	—	—	—	12.00	14.00
JE5727-1967(u) Proof	7,680	Value: 16.00				
JE5727-1967(u) Frosted Proof	Inc. above	Value: 75.00				

KM# 69.1 5 LIROT
20.0000 g., 0.7500 Silver 0.4822 oz. ASW **Subject:** Hanukka **Obv:** Menorah flanked by sprigs to left of value with text around top half **Rev:** Russian lamp **Edge:** Plain

Date	Mintage	F	VF	XF	Unc	BU
JE5733-1972(j)	74,506	—	—	—	10.00	—

KM# 69.2 5 LIROT
20.0000 g., 0.7500 Silver 0.4822 oz. ASW **Subject:** Hanukka **Obv:** Menorah flanked by sprigs to left of value with text arount top half **Rev:** Russian lamp **Edge:** Reeded

Date	Mintage	F	VF	XF	Unc	BU
JE5733-1972(j) Proof	22,336	Value: 12.00				

KM# 75.1 5 LIROT
20.0000 g., 0.5000 Silver 0.3215 oz. ASW **Subject:** Hanukkah **Rev:** Babylonian lamp **Edge:** Plain

Date	Mintage	F	VF	XF	Unc	BU
JE5734-1973(j)	94,686	—	—	—	8.00	10.00

KM# 75.2 5 LIROT
20.0000 g., 0.5000 Silver 0.3215 oz. ASW **Subject:** Hanuka **Rev:** Babylonian lamp **Edge:** Reeded

Date	Mintage	F	VF	XF	Unc	BU
JE5734-1973(j) Proof	44,860	Value: 10.00				

KM# 90 5 LIROT
11.2000 g., Copper-Nickel, 30 mm. **Obv:** Roaring lion left with menorah above **Rev:** Value flanked by stars **Edge:** Smooth

Date	Mintage	F	VF	XF	Unc	BU
JE5738 (1978)(j)	8,350,000	—	0.40	1.00	3.50	6.00
JE5739 (1979)(c)	32,000,000	—	0.40	1.00	3.00	6.00
JE5739 (1979)(j)	5,646,428	—	0.40	1.00	3.00	6.00

KM# 90a 5 LIROT
11.2000 g., Copper-Nickel, 30 mm. **Obv:** Roaring lion left with star of David in field **Rev:** Value flanked by stars **Edge:** Smooth **Note:** Struck for sets only.

Date	Mintage	F	VF	XF	Unc	BU
JE5739 (1979)(j)	31,590	—	—	—	3.00	—

KM# 102 5 LIROT
Nickel, 30 mm. **Subject:** 25th Anniversary - Bank of Israel **Obv:** Roaring lion left with menorah above **Rev:** Value flanked by stars **Edge:** Smooth **Note:** Struck for sets only.

Date	Mintage	F	VF	XF	Unc	BU
JE5740 (1980)(b)	35,000	—	—	—	3.00	7.00

KM# 49 10 LIROT
26.0000 g., 0.9000 Silver 0.7523 oz. ASW, 37 mm. **Subject:** Victory Commemorative **Obv:** Artistic star-like design with a sprig wrapped around the sword with text below **Rev:** Wailing Wall with text around bottom **Edge:** "28 Iyar-2 Sivan 5727" and small stars **Note:** Dav. #268

Date	Mintage	F	VF	XF	Unc	BU
JE5727-1967(b)	234,461	—	—	—	12.00	13.00

KM# 49a 10 LIROT
26.0000 g., 0.9250 Silver 0.7732 oz. ASW, 37 mm. **Subject:** Victory Commemorative **Obv:** Artistic star-like design with sprig wrapped around sword with text below **Edge:** "28 Iyar-2 Sivan 5727" and three small diamonds **Note:** Dav. #268

Date	Mintage	F	VF	XF	Unc	BU
JE5727-1967(b)	50,380	—	—	—	—	20.00

KM# 51 10 LIROT
26.0000 g., 0.9000 Silver 0.7523 oz. ASW, 37 mm. **Subject:** 20th Anniversary of Independence **Obv:** Building with pillars with text and dates below **Rev:** City view to right of menorah flanked by sprigs **Edge:** Hebrew **Note:** Dav. #269.

Date	Mintage	F	VF	XF	Unc	BU
JE5728-1968(b)	49,996	—	—	—	14.00	—
JE5728-1968(b) Proof	20,494	Value: 16.00				

KM# 53 10 LIROT
26.0000 g., 0.9000 Silver 0.7523 oz. ASW **Subject:** 21st Anniversary of Independence **Obv:** Pyramid of block letters **Rev:** Shalom

Date	Mintage	F	VF	XF	Unc	BU
JE5729-1969(s)	39,884	—	—	—	14.00	—
JE5729-1969(s) Proof	19,838	Value: 16.00				
JE5729-1969(k)	20,185	—	—	—	14.00	—

Note: Hebrew letter KOF below helmet

KM# 55 10 LIROT
26.0000 g., 0.9000 Silver 0.7523 oz. ASW, 37.3 mm. **Subject:** 22nd Anniversary of Independence **Obv:** Value and text within artistic design **Rev:** Mikveh Israel Centenary **Edge:** Hebrew

Date	Mintage	F	VF	XF	Unc	BU
JE5730-1970(k)	47,509	—	—	—	13.00	—
JE5730-1970(b) Proof	22,434	Value: 16.00				

KM# 56.1 10 LIROT
26.0000 g., 0.9000 Silver 0.7523 oz. ASW **Subject:** Pidyon Haben **Obv:** Menorah flanked by sprigs at upper left of text **Rev:** Text among the letter M flanked by diamonds **Edge:** Plain

Date	Mintage	F	VF	XF	Unc	BU
JE5730-1970(j)	48,847	—	—	—	14.00	15.00

KM# 56.2 10 LIROT
26.0000 g., 0.9000 Silver 0.7523 oz. ASW **Subject:** Pidyon Haben **Obv:** Menorah flanked by sprigs to upper left of text **Rev:** Text within letter M flanked by diamonds **Edge:** Reeded

Date	Mintage	F	VF	XF	Unc	BU
JE5730-1970(s) Proof	14,719	Value: 15.00				

KM# 57.1 10 LIROT
26.0000 g., 0.9000 Silver 0.7523 oz. ASW **Subject:** Pidyon Haben **Obv:** Menorah flanked by sprigs to upper left of text **Rev:** Text within letter M flanked by diamonds **Edge:** Plain

Date	Mintage	F	VF	XF	Unc	BU
JE5731-1971(j)	30,144	—	—	—	13.00	15.00

KM# 57.2 10 LIROT
26.0000 g., 0.9000 Silver 0.7523 oz. ASW **Subject:** Pidyon Haben **Obv:** Menorah flanked by sprigs to upper left of text **Rev:** Text within letter M flanked by diamonds **Edge:** Reeded

Date	Mintage	F	VF	XF	Unc	BU
JE5731-1971(s)	13,897				Value: 15.00	
Proof						

KM# 58 10 LIROT
26.0000 g., 0.9000 Silver 0.7523 oz. ASW **Subject:** 23rd Anniversary of Independence **Obv:** Stylized atomic reactor **Rev:** Molecule, cog wheel

Date	Mintage	F	VF	XF	Unc	BU
JE5731-1971(u) Without star	29,943	—	—	—	14.00	
JE5731-1971(j) With star	22,697	—	—	—	15.00	
JE5731-1971(u) Proof	17,481				Value: 16.00	

KM# 59.1 10 LIROT
26.0000 g., 0.9000 Silver 0.7523 oz. ASW **Subject:** Let My People Go **Obv:** Menorah flanked by sprigs to upper left of text and date **Rev:** Text within rectangle

Date	Mintage	F	VF	XF	Unc	BU
JE5731-1971(j)	73,444	—	—	—	12.00	
JE5731-1971(j) Proof	20,132				Value: 14.00	

KM# 59.2 10 LIROT
26.0000 g., 0.9000 Silver 0.7523 oz. ASW **Obv:** Menorah flanked by sprigs to upper left of text and date **Rev:** Text within rectangle **Note:** Bern die.

Date	Mintage	F	VF	XF	Unc	BU
JE5731-1971(j) Proof	80				Value: 700	

KM# 61.1 10 LIROT
26.0000 g., 0.9000 Silver 0.7523 oz. ASW **Subject:** Pidyon Haben **Obv:** Menorah flanked by sprigs below value and text **Rev:** Text within the letter M flanked by diamonds **Edge:** Plain

Date	Mintage	F	VF	XF	Unc	BU
JE5732-1972(j) With star	29,744				12.00	—
JE5732-1972(j) Without star	14,944				13.00	15.00

KM# 61.2 10 LIROT
26.0000 g., 0.9000 Silver 0.7523 oz. ASW **Subject:** Pidyon Haben **Obv:** Menorah flanked by sprigs below value and text **Rev:** Text within letter M flanked by diamonds **Edge:** Reeded

Date	Mintage	F	VF	XF	Unc	BU
JE5732-1972(j) Proof	12,443				Value: 15.00	

KM# 62 10 LIROT
26.0000 g., 0.9000 Silver 0.7523 oz. ASW, 37.3 mm. **Subject:** 24th Anniversary of Independence **Obv:** Value as the 1 being a rocket **Rev:** Flying jet **Edge:** Lettered

Date	Mintage	F	VF	XF	Unc	BU
JE5732-1972(j)	49,832	—	—	—	13.00	14.00
JE5732-1972(j) Proof	14,989				Value: 16.00	

KM# 70.1 10 LIROT
26.0000 g., 0.9000 Silver 0.7523 oz. ASW **Subject:** Pidyon Haben **Obv:** Menorah flanked by sprigs above text **Rev:** Artistic design within oblong circle **Edge:** Plain

Date	Mintage	F	VF	XF	Unc	BU
JE5733-1973(j)	100,676	—	—	—	13.00	15.00

KM# 70.2 10 LIROT
26.0000 g., 0.9000 Silver 0.7523 oz. ASW **Subject:** Pidyon Haben **Obv:** Menorah flanked by sprigs above text **Rev:** Artistic designs within oblong circle **Edge:** Reeded

Date	Mintage	F	VF	XF	Unc	BU
JE5733-1973(j)	14,837				Value: 15.00	

KM# 71 10 LIROT
26.0000 g., 0.9000 Silver 0.7523 oz. ASW **Subject:** 25th Anniversary of Independence **Obv:** Menorah flanked by sprigs above text **Rev:** Text on scroll **Edge:** Lettered

Date	Mintage	F	VF	XF	Unc	BU
JE5733-1973(j)	123,953	—	—	—	12.00	14.00
JE5733-1973(j) Proof	41,484				Value: 15.00	

KM# 77 10 LIROT
26.0000 g., 0.9000 Silver 0.7523 oz. ASW **Subject:** 26th Anniversary of Independence **Obv:** Value at upper right of text **Rev:** Text to left of upright design **Edge:** Lettered

Date	Mintage	F	VF	XF	Unc	BU
JE5734-1974(j)	127,195	—	—	—	12.00	14.00
JE5734-1974(j) Proof	49,657				Value: 15.00	

KM# 76.1 10 LIROT
26.0000 g., 0.9000 Silver 0.7523 oz. ASW **Subject:** Pidyon Haben **Obv:** Value above menorah flanked by sprigs **Rev:** Artistic design within oblong circle **Edge:** Plain

Date	Mintage	F	VF	XF	Unc	BU
JE5734-1974(j)	108,547	—	—	—	12.00	15.00

KM# 76.2 10 LIROT
26.0000 g., 0.9000 Silver 0.7523 oz. ASW **Subject:** Pidyon Haben **Obv:** Value above menorah flanked by sprigs **Rev:** Artistic designs within oblong circle **Edge:** Reeded

Date	Mintage	F	VF	XF	Unc	BU
JE5734-1974(j) Proof	44,348				Value: 15.00	

KM# 78.1 10 LIROT
20.0000 g., 0.5000 Silver 0.3215 oz. ASW **Subject:** Hanukka **Obv:** Value and date above text **Rev:** Damascus lamp **Edge:** Plain

Date	Mintage	F	VF	XF	Unc	BU
JE5735-1974(j)	74,112	—	—	—	8.00	10.00

KM# 78.2 10 LIROT
20.0000 g., 0.5000 Silver 0.3215 oz. ASW **Subject:** Hanukka **Obv:** Value and date above text **Rev:** Damascus lamp **Edge:** Reeded

Date	Mintage	F	VF	XF	Unc	BU
JE5735-1974(j) Proof	58,642				Value: 10.00	

KM# 84.1 10 LIROT
20.0000 g., 0.5000 Silver 0.3215 oz. ASW **Subject:** Hanukka **Obv:** Value above text with date below **Rev:** Holland lamp **Edge:** Plain

Date	Mintage	F	VF	XF	Unc	BU
JE5736-1975(j)	44,215	—	—	—	9.00	10.00

KM# 84.2 10 LIROT
20.0000 g., 0.5000 Silver 0.3215 oz. ASW **Subject:** Hanukka
Obv: Value above text with date below **Rev:** Holland lamp
Edge: Reeded

Date	Mintage	F	VF	XF	Unc	BU
JE5736-1975(j)	33,537	Value: 11.00				
Proof						

KM# 87.1 10 LIROT
20.0000 g., 0.5000 Silver 0.3215 oz. ASW **Subject:** Hanukka
Obv: Value within square **Rev:** U.S. lamp **Edge:** Plain

Date	Mintage	F	VF	XF	Unc	BU
JE5737-1976(j)	24,844	—	—	—	13.00	14.00

KM# 87.2 10 LIROT
20.0000 g., 0.5000 Silver 0.3215 oz. ASW **Subject:** Hanukka
Obv: Value within square **Rev:** U.S. lamp **Edge:** Reeded

Date	Mintage	F	VF	XF	Unc	BU
JE5737-1976(j)	19,989	Value: 20.00				
Proof						

KM# 91.1 10 LIROT
Copper-Nickel, 34 mm. **Subject:** Hanukka **Obv:** Text to left and
below value **Rev:** Jerusalem lamp **Edge:** Plain

Date	Mintage	F	VF	XF	Unc	BU
JE5738-1977(j)	46,106	—	—	—	4.00	—

KM# 91.2 10 LIROT
Copper-Nickel, 34 mm. **Subject:** Hanukka **Obv:** Text to left and
below value **Rev:** Jerusalem lamp **Edge:** Reeded **Note:** Open
style "mem."

Date	Mintage	F	VF	XF	Unc	BU
JE5738-1977(j)	29,516	Value: 6.00				
Proof						

KM# 91.3 10 LIROT
Copper-Nickel, 34 mm. **Subject:** Hanukkah **Obv:** Text to left
and below value **Rev:** Jerusalem lamp **Edge:** Reeded
Note: Closed style "mem".

Date	Mintage	F	VF	XF	Unc	BU
JE5738-1977(j)	Inc. above	Value: 10.00				
Proof						

KM# 30 20 LIROT
7.9880 g., 0.9170 Gold 0.2355 oz. AGW, 22 mm. **Subject:** 100th
Anniversary - Birth of Dr. Theodor Herzl **Obv:** Menorah flanked
by sprigs within beaded circle **Rev:** Head left within rectangle

Date	Mintage	F	VF	XF	Unc	BU
JE5720-1960(b)	10,460	—	—	—	240	260

KM# 79.1 25 LIROT
26.0000 g., 0.9350 Silver 0.7816 oz. ASW **Subject:** 1st
Anniversary - Death of David Ben Gurion **Obv:** Menorah flanked
by sprigs **Rev:** Head left within rectangle **Edge:** Plain

Date	Mintage	F	VF	XF	Unc	BU
JE5735-1974(j)	99,291	—	—	—	14.50	—

KM# 79.2 25 LIROT
26.0000 g., 0.9350 Silver 0.7816 oz. ASW **Subject:** 1st
Anniversary - Death of David Ben Gurion **Obv:** Menorah flanked
by sprigs **Rev:** Head left within rectangle **Edge:** Reeded

Date	Mintage	F	VF	XF	Unc	BU
JE5735-1974(b)	64,153	Value: 16.00				
Proof						

KM# 81 25 LIROT
30.0000 g., 0.8000 Silver 0.7716 oz. ASW **Subject:** 25th
Anniversary of Israel Bond Program **Obv:** Large value above
menorah flanked by sprigs **Rev:** Artistic design **Edge:** Lettered

Date	Mintage	F	VF	XF	Unc	BU
JE5735-1975(j)	49,140	—	—	—	13.50	—
JE5735-1975(j)	39,847	Value: 16.00				
Proof						

KM# 80.1 25 LIROT
26.0000 g., 0.9000 Silver 0.7523 oz. ASW **Subject:** Pidyon
Haben **Obv:** Menorah flanked by sprigs above value **Rev:** Artistic
designs within oblong circle **Edge:** Plain

Date	Mintage	F	VF	XF	Unc	BU
JE5735-1975(j)	62,187	—	—	—	13.00	14.00

KM# 80.2 25 LIROT
26.0000 g., 0.9000 Silver 0.7523 oz. ASW **Subject:** Pidyon
Haben **Obv:** Menorah flanked by sprigs above value **Rev:** Artistic
designs within oblong circle **Edge:** Reeded

Date	Mintage	F	VF	XF	Unc	BU
JE5735-1975(j)	49,192	Value: 14.00				
Proof						

KM# 85 25 LIROT
26.0000 g., 0.9000 Silver 0.7523 oz. ASW **Subject:** 28th
Anniversary of Independence **Obv:** Value menorah flanked by
sprigs **Rev:** Block-like text with star to upper left **Edge:** Lettered

Date	Mintage	F	VF	XF	Unc	BU
JE5736-1976(j)	37,813	—	—	—	13.00	—
JE5736-1976(j)	27,471	Value: 15.00				
Proof						

KM# 86.1 25 LIROT
30.0000 g., 0.8000 Silver 0.7716 oz. ASW **Subject:** Pidyon
Haben **Obv:** Menorah flanked by sprigs at upper left above text
Rev: Artistic star-like design **Edge:** Plain

Date	Mintage	F	VF	XF	Unc	BU
JE5736-1976(j)	37,345	—	—	—	12.00	—

KM# 86.2 25 LIROT
30.0000 g., 0.8000 Silver 0.7716 oz. ASW **Subject:** Pidyon
Haben **Obv:** Menorah flanked by sprigs to upper left above text
Rev: Artistic star-like design **Edge:** Reeded

Date	Mintage	F	VF	XF	Unc	BU
JE5736-1976(j)	29,430	Value: 16.00				
Proof						

KM# 88 25 LIROT
20.0000 g., 0.5000 Silver 0.3215 oz. ASW **Subject:** 29th
Anniversary of Independence **Obv:** Large value above menorah
flanked by sprigs **Rev:** Stylized bird below castle **Edge:** Lettered

Date	Mintage	F	VF	XF	Unc	BU
JE5737-1977(j)	36,976	—	—	—	7.00	—
JE5737-1977(j)	26,735	Value: 9.00				
Proof						

KM# 89.1 25 LIROT
26.0000 g., 0.9000 Silver 0.7523 oz. ASW **Subject:** Pidyon
Haben **Obv:** Value above menorah flanked by sprigs **Rev:** Artistic
star-like design **Edge:** Plain

Date	Mintage	F	VF	XF	Unc	BU
JE5737-1977(j)	32,089	—	—	—	13.00	—

KM# 89.2 25 LIROT
26.0000 g., 0.9000 Silver 0.7523 oz. ASW **Subject:** Pidyon
Haben **Obv:** Value above menorah flanked by sprigs **Rev:** Artistic
star-like design **Edge:** Reeded

Date	Mintage	F	VF	XF	Unc	BU
JE5737-1977(j)	18,541	Value: 16.50				
Proof						

KM# 94.1 25 LIROT
Copper-Nickel, 34 mm. **Subject:** Hanukka **Obv:** Value above
text **Rev:** French lamp **Edge:** Plain

Date	Mintage	F	VF	XF	Unc	BU
JE5739-1978(j)	36,200	—	—	—	4.00	—

KM# 94.2 25 LIROT
Copper-Nickel, 34 mm. **Subject:** Hanukka **Rev:** French lamp
Edge: Reeded

Date	Mintage	F	VF	XF	Unc	BU
JE5739-1978(j)	22,300	Value: 6.50				
Proof						

KM# 40 50 LIROT
13.3400 g., 0.9170 Gold 0.3933 oz. AGW, 27 mm.
Subject: 10th Anniversary - Death of Weizmann **Obv:** Menorah
flanked by sprigs within circle **Rev:** Bust left within rectangle

Date	Mintage	F	VF	XF	Unc	BU
JE5723-1962(b)	6,195	Value: 400				
Proof						
Note: With "mem"						
JE5723-1962(b)	10	Value: 2,000				
Proof						
Note: Without "mem"						

KM# 44 50 LIROT
13.3400 g., 0.9170 Gold 0.3933 oz. AGW, 27 mm.
Subject: 10th Anniversary - Bank of Israel **Obv:** Menorah flanked
by sprigs **Rev:** Artistic design to upper right of text

Date	Mintage	F	VF	XF	Unc	BU
JE5725-1964(b)	5,975	—	—	—	—	400
JE5725-1964(b)	1,502	Value: 3,250				
Proof						
Note: Includes 702 used officially by the Bank of Israel						

KM# 72 50 LIROT
7.0000 g., 0.9000 Gold 0.2025 oz. AGW **Subject:** 25th
Anniversary of Independence **Obv:** Menorah flanked by sprigs
above text **Rev:** Text on scroll

Date	Mintage	F	VF	XF	Unc	BU
JE5733-1973(b)	27,724	Value: 225				
Proof						

KM# 92.1 50 LIROT
20.0000 g., 0.5000 Silver 0.3215 oz. ASW, 33 mm.
Subject: 30th Anniversary of Independence **Obv:** Menorah
flanked by sprigs above value **Rev:** Text within tree
Edge: Lettered

Date	Mintage	F	VF	XF	Unc	BU
JE5738-1978(j)	40,402	—	—	—	12.00	—

KM# 92.2 50 LIROT
20.0000 g., 0.5000 Silver 0.3215 oz. ASW **Subject:** 30th
Anniversary of Independence **Obv:** Menorah flanked by sprigs
above value **Rev:** Text within tree **Edge:** Reeded

Date	Mintage	F	VF	XF	Unc	BU
JE5738-1978(b)	21,806	Value: 15.00				
Proof						

KM# 95 50 LIROT
20.0000 g., 0.5000 Silver 0.3215 oz. ASW **Subject:** 31st
Anniversary of Independence **Obv:** Value above menorah flanked
by sprigs **Rev:** Stylized mother and children **Edge:** Lettered

Date	Mintage	F	VF	XF	Unc	BU
JE5739-1979(j)	24,108	—	—	—	12.00	—
JE5739-1979(o)	16,102	Value: 14.00				
Proof						

KM# 41 100 LIROT
26.6800 g., 0.9170 Gold 0.7866 oz. AGW, 33 mm.
Subject: 10th Anniversary - Death of Weizmann **Obv:** Menorah
flanked by sprigs within circle **Rev:** Head left within rectangle

Date	Mintage	F	VF	XF	Unc	BU
JE5723-1962(b)	6,196	Value: 800				
Proof						
Note: With "mem"						
JE5723-1962(b)	10	Value: 2,500				
Proof						
Note: Without "mem"						

KM# 50 100 LIROT
26.6800 g., 0.9170 Gold 0.7866 oz. AGW, 33 mm.
Subject: Victory Commemorative **Obv:** Leafy sprig around sword
within artistic star-like design **Rev:** Western Wall, Temple of
Solomon

Date	Mintage	F	VF	XF	Unc	BU
JE5727-1967(b)	9,004	Value: 800				
Proof						

KM# 52 100 LIROT
25.0000 g., 0.8000 Gold 0.6430 oz. AGW, 33 mm. **Subject:** 20th
Anniversary - Jerusalem Reunification **Obv:** Building pillars, text and
value **Rev:** Menorah flanked by sprigs to upper left of city view

Date	Mintage	F	VF	XF	Unc	BU
JE5728-1968(b)	12,490	Value: 650				

KM# 54 100 LIROT
25.0000 g., 0.8000 Gold 0.6430 oz. AGW, 33 mm.
Subject: 21st Anniversary of Independence **Obv:** Block-like
letters within triangular design **Rev:** Shalom

Date	Mintage	F	VF	XF	Unc	BU
JE5729-1969(u)	12,500	Value: 650				
Proof						

KM# 60 100 LIROT
22.0000 g., 0.9000 Gold 0.6366 oz. AGW, 30 mm. **Subject:** Let
My People Go **Obv:** Menorah flanked by sprigs to upper left of
text **Rev:** Text within rectangle to right of moon within lines

Date	Mintage	F	VF	XF	Unc	BU
JE5731-1971(b)	9,956	Value: 675				
Proof						

KM# 73 100 LIROT
13.5000 g., 0.9000 Gold 0.3906 oz. AGW **Subject:** 25th
Anniversary of Independence **Obv:** Text on scroll **Rev:** Menorah
flanked by sprigs above text

Date	Mintage	F	VF	XF	Unc	BU
JE5733-1973(b)	27,472	Value: 400				
Proof						

KM# 103.1 100 LIROT
20.0000 g., 0.5000 Silver 0.3215 oz. ASW **Subject:** Hanukkah
Obv: Value **Rev:** Egyptian lamp within star design **Edge:** Plain

Date	Mintage	F	VF	XF	Unc	BU
JE5740-1979(b)	31,588	—	—	—	10.00	—

KM# 103.2 100 LIROT
20.0000 g., 0.5000 Silver 0.3215 oz. ASW **Subject:** Hanukkah
Obv: Value **Rev:** Egyptian lamp **Edge:** Reeded

Date	Mintage	F	VF	XF	Unc	BU
JE5740-1979(b)	19,019	Value: 12.00				
Proof						

KM# 74 200 LIROT
27.0000 g., 0.9000 Gold 0.7812 oz. AGW **Subject:** 25th
Anniversary of Independence **Obv:** Menorah flanked by sprigs
above text **Rev:** Text on scroll

Date	Mintage	F	VF	XF	Unc	BU
JE5733-1973(b)	17,889	Value: 775				
Proof						

KM# 104 200 LIROT
26.0000 g., 0.9000 Silver 0.7523 oz. ASW **Subject:** 32nd Anniversary of Independence **Obv:** Menorah flanked by sprigs to upper right of text and value **Rev:** Sprig divides text **Edge:** Lettered

Date	Mintage	F	VF	XF	Unc	BU
JE5740-1980(b)	20,197	—	—	—	13.00	—
JE5740-1980(b) Proof	12,911	Value: 16.00				

KM# 82 500 LIROT
28.0000 g., 0.9000 Gold 0.8102 oz. AGW **Subject:** 1st Anniversary - Death of David Ben Gurion **Obv:** Menorah flanked by sprigs **Rev:** Head left within rectangle

Date	Mintage	F	VF	XF	Unc	BU
JE5735-1974(b) Proof	47,528	Value: 800				

KM# 83 500 LIROT
20.0000 g., 0.9000 Gold 0.5787 oz. AGW **Subject:** 25th Anniversary of Israel Bond Program **Obv:** Large value above menorah flanked by sprigs **Rev:** Artistic design

Date	Mintage	F	VF	XF	Unc	BU
JE5735-1975(u) Proof	31,693	Value: 575				

KM# 93 1000 LIROT
12.0000 g., 0.9000 Gold 0.3472 oz. AGW **Subject:** 30th Anniversary of Independence **Obv:** Text and value above menorah flanked by sprigs **Rev:** Text within tree

Date	Mintage	F	VF	XF	Unc	BU
JE5738-1978(b) Proof	12,043	Value: 350				

KM# 105 5000 LIROT
17.2800 g., 0.9000 Gold 0.5000 oz. AGW **Subject:** 32nd Anniversary of Independence **Obv:** Menorah flanked by sprigs above text and value **Rev:** Sprig divides text

Date	Mintage	F	VF	XF	Unc	BU
JE5740-1980(o) Proof	6,382	Value: 500				

REFORM COINAGE
10 (old) Agorot = 1 New Agora; 100 New Agorot = 1 Sheqel

Commencing February 24, 1980-1985

KM# 106 NEW AGORA
0.6000 g., Aluminum, 15 mm. **Obv:** Date palm **Rev:** Value **Edge:** Plain

Date	Mintage	F	VF	XF	Unc	BU
JE5740 (1980)(o)	200,000,000	—	—	—	0.20	—
Note: 90 million coins were reportedly melted down						
JE5741 (1981)(o)	1,000,000	—	—	0.20	1.00	—
JE5742 (1982)(f)	1,000,000	—	—	0.20	1.00	—

KM# 107 5 NEW AGOROT
0.9000 g., Aluminum, 18.5 mm. **Obv:** Menorah flanked by sprigs **Rev:** Value **Edge:** Reeded

Date	Mintage	F	VF	XF	Unc	BU
JE5740 (1980)(o)	69,532,000	—	—	—	0.25	—
JE5741 (1981)(o)	1,000,000	—	—	0.20	1.00	—
JE5742 (1982)(f)	5,000,000	—	—	—	0.25	—

KM# 108 10 NEW AGOROT
2.1100 g., Bronze, 15.96 mm. **Obv:** Pomegranate **Rev:** Value **Edge:** Reeded

Date	Mintage	F	VF	XF	Unc	BU
JE5740 (1980)(o)	167,932,000	—	—	—	0.20	—
Note: 70.2 million coins were reportedly melted down						
JE5741 (1981)	241,100,000	—	—	—	0.20	—
Note: 123,000,000 were minted at (f); 90,000,000 at (p) and 28,160,000 at (j).						
JE5742 (1982)(f)	23,000,000	—	—	—	0.20	—
JE5743 (1983)(j)	2,500,000	—	—	0.15	0.50	—
JE5744 (1984)(j)	500,000	—	—	0.20	1.00	—

KM# 109 1/2 SHEQEL
3.0000 g., Copper-Nickel, 19.96 mm. **Obv:** Roaring lion left **Rev:** Value flanked by stars **Edge:** Reeded

Date	Mintage	F	VF	XF	Unc	BU
JE5740 (1980)(b)	52,308,000	—	—	0.50	1.00	1.25
JE5741 (1981)	53,272,000	—	—	0.50	1.00	1.25
Note: 37,976,000 minted at (j) and 15,296,000 minted at (p).						
JE5742 (1982)(j)	18,808,484	—	—	0.50	1.00	1.25
JE5743 (1983)(j)	250,000	—	—	0.50	1.00	1.25
JE5744 (1984)(j)	250,000	—	—	0.50	1.00	1.25

KM# 121 1/2 SHEQEL
7.2000 g., 0.8500 Silver 0.1968 oz. ASW **Series:** Holyland Sites **Obv:** Value **Rev:** Qumran Caves

Date	Mintage	F	VF	XF	Unc	BU
JE5743-1982(p)	15,151	—	—	—	12.00	—

KM# 126 1/2 SHEQEL
7.2000 g., 0.8500 Silver 0.1968 oz. ASW **Series:** Holyland Sites **Obv:** Value **Rev:** Herodion Ruins

Date	Mintage	F	VF	XF	Unc	BU
JE5744-1983(d)	11,044	—	—	—	10.00	—

KM# 140 1/2 SHEQEL
7.2000 g., 0.8500 Silver 0.1968 oz. ASW **Series:** Holyland Sites **Obv:** Value **Rev:** Kidron Valley

Date	Mintage	F	VF	XF	Unc	BU
JE5745-1984(p)	7,538	—	—	—	15.00	—

KM# 152 1/2 SHEQEL
7.2000 g., 0.8500 Silver 0.1968 oz. ASW **Series:** Holyland Sites **Obv:** Value **Rev:** Capernaum

Date	Mintage	F	VF	XF	Unc	BU
JE5746-1985(p)	6,010	—	—	—	15.00	—

KM# 110.1 SHEQEL
14.4000 g., 0.8500 Silver 0.3935 oz. ASW **Subject:** Hanukka **Obv:** Value **Rev:** Corfu lamp **Edge:** Plain

Date	Mintage	F	VF	XF	Unc	BU
JE5741-1980(o)	23,753	—	—	—	8.00	9.00

KM# 110.2 SHEQEL
14.4000 g., 0.8500 Silver 0.3935 oz. ASW **Subject:** Hanukka **Rev:** Corfu lamp **Edge:** Reeded

Date	Mintage	F	VF	XF	Unc	BU
JE5741-1980(o) Proof	15,428	Value: 12.00				

KM# 111 SHEQEL
5.0000 g., Copper-Nickel, 22.54 mm. **Obv:** Value **Rev:** Chalice **Edge:** Reeded and plain segments

Date	Mintage	F	VF	XF	Unc	BU
JE5741 (1981)	154,540,000	—	—	0.30	0.50	—
Note: 99,000,000 minted at (p); 39,970,000 minted at (j) and 15,570,000 minted at (b).						
JE5742 (1982)(p)	15,850,000	—	—	0.30	0.50	—
JE5743 (1983)(j)	26,360,000	—	—	0.30	0.50	—
JE5744 (1984)	32,205,000	—	—	0.30	0.50	—
Note: 26,360,200 minted at (o); 2,205,000 minted at (j).						
JE5745 (1985)(j)	500,000	—	—	—	1.00	2.00

KM# 116.1 SHEQEL
14.4000 g., 0.8500 Silver 0.3935 oz. ASW **Subject:** Hanukka **Obv:** Value at left of menorah flanked by sprigs **Rev:** Polish lamp **Edge:** Plain

Date	Mintage	F	VF	XF	Unc	BU
JE5742 -1981(p)	16,115	—	—	—	11.00	—

KM# 116.2 SHEQEL
14.4000 g., 0.8500 Silver 0.3935 oz. ASW **Subject:** Hanukka **Rev:** Polish lamp **Edge:** Reeded

Date	Mintage	F	VF	XF	Unc	BU
JE5742 -1981(f) Proof	11,186	Value: 14.00				

KM# 122   SHEQEL
14.4000 g., 0.8500 Silver 0.3935 oz. ASW   **Series:** Holyland
Sites **Obv:** Value **Rev:** Qumran caves

Date	Mintage	F	VF	XF	Unc	BU
JE5743-1982(d)	9,000			Value: 25.00		
Proof						

KM# 123   SHEQEL
14.4000 g., 0.8500 Silver 0.3935 oz. ASW   **Subject:** Hanukka
Obv: Value below menorah flanked by sprigs **Rev:** Yemen lamp

Date	Mintage	F	VF	XF	Unc	BU
JE5743-1982(p)	14,475	—	—	—	20.00	—

KM# 127   SHEQEL
14.4000 g., 0.8500 Silver 0.3935 oz. ASW   **Subject:** 35th
Anniversary - State of Israel **Obv:** Large value **Rev:** Sprig
wrapped around sword within star design

Date	Mintage	F	VF	XF	Unc	BU
JE5743-1983(f)	14,782	—	—	—	12.00	—

KM# 128   SHEQEL
14.4000 g., 0.8500 Silver 0.3935 oz. ASW   **Series:** Holyland
Sites **Obv:** Value **Rev:** Herodion Ruins

Date	Mintage	F	VF	XF	Unc	BU
JE5744-1983(d)	10,372			Value: 30.00		
Proof						

KM# 129   SHEQEL
14.4000 g., 0.8500 Silver 0.3935 oz. ASW   **Subject:** Hanukkah
Obv: Value **Rev:** Prague lamp

Date	Mintage	F	VF	XF	Unc	BU
JE5744-1983(p)	12,777	—	—	—	12.00	—

KM# 144   SHEQEL
14.4000 g., 0.8500 Silver 0.3935 oz. ASW   **Subject:** Hanukka
Obv: Vertical lined value **Rev:** Theresianstadt lamp

Date	Mintage	F	VF	XF	Unc	BU
JE5745-1984(p)	11,004	—	—	—	17.00	—

KM# 141   SHEQEL
14.4000 g., 0.8500 Silver 0.3935 oz. ASW   **Series:** Holyland
Sites **Obv:** Value **Rev:** Kidron Valley

Date	Mintage	F	VF	XF	Unc	BU
JE5745-1984(f)	6,798			Value: 30.00		
Proof						

KM# 135   SHEQEL
14.4000 g., 0.8500 Silver 0.3935 oz. ASW   **Subject:** 36th
Anniversary - State of Israel **Obv:** Value below menorah flanked
by sprigs **Rev:** Kinsmen

Date	Mintage	F	VF	XF	Unc	BU
JE5744-1984(p)	9,476	—	—	—	15.00	—

KM# 148   SHEQEL
14.4000 g., 0.8500 Silver 0.3935 oz. ASW   **Subject:** 37th
Anniversary of Independence **Obv:** Value **Rev:** Scientific
Achievement

Date	Mintage	F	VF	XF	Unc	BU
JE5745-1985(p)	8,520	—	—	—	15.00	—

KM# 155   SHEQEL
14.4000 g., 0.8500 Silver 0.3935 oz. ASW   **Obv:** Value
Rev: Ancient ship

Date	Mintage	F	VF	XF	Unc	BU
JE5745-1985(f)	12,951	—	—	—	20.00	—
Prooflike						

KM# 153   SHEQEL
14.4000 g., 0.8500 Silver 0.3935 oz. ASW   **Series:** Holyland
Sites **Obv:** Value **Rev:** Capernaum

Date	Mintage	F	VF	XF	Unc	BU
JE5746-1985(f)	6,010			Value: 28.00		
Proof						

KM# 112   2 SHEQALIM
28.8000 g., 0.8250 Silver 0.7639 oz. ASW   **Subject:** 33rd
Anniversary of independence **Obv:** Large styilized value
Rev: Stylized design within book **Edge:** Lettered

Date	Mintage	F	VF	XF	Unc	BU
JE5741-1981(o)	16,316	—	—	—	15.00	—
JE5741-1981(o)	11,317			Value: 28.00		
Proof						

KM# 117   2 SHEQALIM
28.8000 g., 0.8500 Silver 0.7870 oz. ASW   **Subject:** 34th
Anniversary of Independence **Obv:** Menorah flanked by sprigs
above text **Rev:** Head facing **Edge:** Lettered

Date	Mintage	F	VF	XF	Unc	BU
JE5742-1982(p)	13,272	—	—	—	20.00	—
JE5742-1982(f)	9,506			Value: 25.00		
Proof						

KM# 124   2 SHEQALIM
28.8000 g., 0.8500 Silver 0.7870 oz. ASW   **Subject:** Hanukka
Obv: Menorah flanked by sprigs above text and dates
Rev: Yemen lamp

Date	Mintage	F	VF	XF	Unc	BU
JE5743-1982(f)	8,996			Value: 25.00		
Proof						

KM# 130   2 SHEQALIM
28.8000 g., 0.8500 Silver 0.7870 oz. ASW **Subject:** 35th Anniversary of Independence **Rev:** Sprig wrapped around sword within star design

Date	Mintage	F	VF	XF	Unc	BU
JE5743-1983(f)	9,999				Value: 25.00	
Proof						

KM# 131   2 SHEQALIM
28.8000 g., 0.8500 Silver 0.7870 oz. ASW **Subject:** Hanukka **Obv:** Value above menorah flanked by sprigs **Rev:** Prague lamp

Date	Mintage	F	VF	XF	Unc	BU
JE5744-1983(b)	10,894				Value: 25.00	
Proof						

KM# 145   2 SHEQALIM
28.8000 g., 0.8500 Silver 0.7870 oz. ASW **Subject:** Hanukka **Obv:** Value to right of menorah flanked by sprigs **Rev:** Theresianstadt lamp

Date	Mintage	F	VF	XF	Unc	BU
JE5745-1984(b)	10,011				Value: 30.00	
Proof						

KM# 136   2 SHEQALIM
28.8000 g., 0.8500 Silver 0.7870 oz. ASW **Subject:** 36th Anniversary of Independence **Obv:** Menorah flanked by sprigs **Rev:** Kinsmen

Date	Mintage	F	VF	XF	Unc	BU
JE5744-1984(f)	8,551				Value: 25.00	
Proof						

KM# 149   2 SHEQALIM
28.8000 g., 0.8500 Silver 0.7870 oz. ASW **Subject:** 37th Anniversary of Independence **Obv:** Menorah flanked by sprigs above text within circular designs **Rev:** Scientific achievement

Date	Mintage	F	VF	XF	Unc	BU
JE5745-1985(f)	8,330				Value: 25.00	
Proof						

KM# 118   5 SHEQALIM
6.2000 g., Aluminum-Bronze, 24 mm. **Obv:** Cornucopia **Rev:** Value flanked by stars

Date	Mintage	F	VF	XF	Unc	BU
JE5742 (1982)	30,000,000	—	0.50	0.75	—	
Note: 18,000,000 minted at (so); 12,000,000 minted at (p).						
JE5743 (1983)(j)	994,000	—	—	1.00	2.00	
JE5744 (1984)	17,389,000	—	—	0.50	0.75	
Note: 9,000,000 minted at (so); 8,389,400 minted at (j).						
JE5745 (1985)(j)	250,005	—	—	1.00	2.50	

KM# 125   5 SHEQALIM
8.6300 g., 0.9000 Gold 0.2497 oz. AGW **Series:** Holyland Sites **Rev:** Qumran Caves

Date	Mintage	F	VF	XF	Unc	BU
JE5743-1982(d)	4,927				Value: 275	
Proof						

KM# 132   5 SHEQALIM
8.6300 g., 0.9000 Gold 0.2497 oz. AGW **Series:** Holyland Sites **Obv:** Value **Rev:** Herodion Ruins

Date	Mintage	F	VF	XF	Unc	BU
JE5744-1983(d)	4,346				Value: 275	
Proof						

KM# 142   5 SHEQALIM
8.6300 g., 0.9000 Gold 0.2497 oz. AGW **Series:** Holyland Sites **Obv:** Value **Rev:** Kidron Valley

Date	Mintage	F	VF	XF	Unc	BU
JE5745-1984(b)	2,601				Value: 300	
Proof						

KM# 154   5 SHEQALIM
8.6300 g., 0.9000 Gold 0.2497 oz. AGW **Series:** Holyland Sites **Obv:** Value **Rev:** Capernaum

Date	Mintage	F	VF	XF	Unc	BU
JE5746-1985(b)	2,633				Value: 275	
Proof						

KM# 113   10 SHEQALIM
17.2800 g., 0.9000 Gold 0.5000 oz. AGW **Subject:** 33rd Anniversary of Independence **Obv:** Large stylized value **Rev:** Stylized design within book

Date	Mintage	F	VF	XF	Unc	BU
JE5741-1981(o)	5,634				Value: 500	
Proof						

KM# 120   10 SHEQALIM
17.2800 g., 0.9000 Gold 0.5000 oz. AGW **Subject:** 34th Anniversary of Independence **Obv:** Menorah flanked by sprigs above text **Rev:** Head facing

Date	Mintage	F	VF	XF	Unc	BU
JE5742-1982(o)	4,875				Value: 500	
Proof						

KM# 119   10 SHEQALIM
8.0000 g., Copper-Nickel, 26 mm. **Obv:** Ancient Galley **Rev:** Value flanked by stars

Date	Mintage	F	VF	XF	Unc	BU
JE5742 (1982)	36,084,123	—	—	0.75	1.25	—
Note: 18,000,000 minted by (f) and 18,084,123 by (j).						
JE5743 (1983)(j)	17,850,750	—	—	0.75	1.25	
JE5744 (1984)(j)	31,950,200	—	—	0.75	1.25	
JE5745 (1985)	25,864,436	—	—	0.50	0.75	
Note: 15,864,436 struck by (j) and 10,000,000 by (f).						

KM# 133   10 SHEQALIM
17.2800 g., 0.9000 Gold 0.5000 oz. AGW **Subject:** 35th Anniversary of Independence **Obv:** Menorah flanked by sprigs within stylized value **Rev:** Sprig wrapped around sword within star design

Date	Mintage	F	VF	XF	Unc	BU
JE5743-1983(b)	3,814				Value: 525	
Proof						

KM# 134   10 SHEQALIM
8.0000 g., Copper-Nickel, 26 mm. **Subject:** Hanukka **Obv:** Ancient Galley **Rev:** Value flanked by stars

Date	Mintage	F	VF	XF	Unc	BU
JE5744 (1984)(j)	2,000,000	—	—	1.00	1.50	

KM# 137   10 SHEQALIM
Copper-Nickel, 26 mm. **Obv:** Head of Theodore Herzl left **Rev:** Value flanked by stars

Date	Mintage	F	VF	XF	Unc	BU
JE5744 (1984)(b)	2,002,500	—	—	1.00	1.50	

KM# 138   10 SHEQALIM
17.2800 g., 0.9000 Gold 0.5000 oz. AGW **Subject:** 36th Anniversary of Independence **Obv:** Menorah flanked by sprigs **Rev:** Kinsmen

Date	Mintage	F	VF	XF	Unc	BU
JE5744-1984(o)	3,798				Value: 500	
Proof						

KM# 150   10 SHEQALIM
17.2800 g., 0.9000 Gold 0.5000 oz. AGW **Subject:** 37th Anniversary of Independence **Obv:** Menorah, text and value within circular designs **Rev:** Scientific achievement

Date	Mintage	F	VF	XF	Unc	BU
JE5745-1985(o) Proof	3,240	Value: 500				

KM# 114.1   25 SHEQEL
26.0000 g., 0.9000 Silver 0.7523 oz. ASW **Subject:** 100th Anniversary - Birth of Zeev Jabotinsky **Obv:** State arms above value **Rev:** Head 3/4 left

Date	Mintage	F	VF	XF	Unc	BU
JE5741-1980(o)	14,469	—	—	—	12.00	—

KM# 114.2   25 SHEQEL
26.0000 g., 0.9000 Silver 0.7523 oz. ASW **Subject:** 100th Anniversary - Birth of Zeev Jabotinsky **Obv:** State arms above value **Rev:** Head left **Edge:** Reeded

Date	Mintage	F	VF	XF	Unc	BU
JE5741-1980(o) Proof	12,236	Value: 25.00				

KM# 139   50 SHEQALIM
9.0000 g., Aluminum-Bronze, 28 mm. **Obv:** Ancient coin **Rev:** Value flanked by stars

Date	Mintage	F	VF	XF	Unc	BU
JE5744 (1984)(j)	13,993,658	—	—	0.50	1.00	—
JE5745 (1985)(j)	1,000,100	—	—	1.00	2.00	—

KM# 147   50 SHEQALIM
9.0000 g., Aluminum-Bronze, 28 mm. **Obv:** Head of David Ben-Gurion left **Rev:** Value flanked by stars

Date	Mintage	F	VF	XF	Unc	BU
JE5745 (1985)	1,000,000	—	—	1.00	2.00	—

KM# 143   100 SHEQALIM
10.8200 g., Copper-Nickel, 29 mm. **Obv:** Menorah **Rev:** Value

Date	Mintage	F	VF	XF	Unc	BU
JE5744 (1984)(j)	15,028,433	—	—	0.75	1.50	—

Date	Mintage	F	VF	XF	Unc	BU
JE5744 (1984)(c)	15,000,000	—	—	0.75	1.50	—
JE5745 (1985)	19,637,806	—	—	0.75	1.50	—

KM# 146   100 SHEQALIM
10.8000 g., Copper-Nickel, 29 mm. **Subject:** Hanukka **Obv:** Menorah **Rev:** Value

Date	Mintage	F	VF	XF	Unc	BU
JE5745 (1985)(j)	2,000,000	—	—	1.00	2.00	—

KM# 151   100 SHEQALIM
10.8000 g., Copper-Nickel, 29 mm. **Obv:** Head of Ze'ev Jabotinsky 1/4 left **Rev:** Value

Date	Mintage	F	VF	XF	Unc	BU
JE5745 (1985)(p)	2,000,000	—	—	1.00	2.00	—

KM# 115   500 SHEQEL
17.2800 g., 0.9000 Gold 0.5000 oz. AGW **Subject:** 100th Anniversary - Birth of Zeèv Jabotinsky **Obv:** Menorah flanked by sprigs above value

Date	Mintage	F	VF	XF	Unc	BU
JE5741-1980(o) Proof	7,471	Value: 500				

REFORM COINAGE
100 Agorot = 1 New Sheqel
1,000 Sheqalim = 1 New Sheqel

September 4, 1985

KM# 156   AGORA
2.0400 g., Aluminum-Bronze, 17 mm. **Obv:** Ancient ship **Rev:** Value within lined square

Date	Mintage	F	VF	XF	Unc	BU
JE5745 (1985)	58,144,000	—	—	—	0.50	—
Note: 40,000,000 struck by (p) and 18,144,000 by (f).						
JE5746 (1986)	95,272,000	—	—	—	0.50	—
Note: 50,112,000 struck by (p); 30,856,000 by (f) and 14,304,000 by (j).						
JE5747 (1987)(j)	1,080,000	—	—	—	0.50	—
JE5748 (1988)(j)	15,768,000	—	—	—	0.50	—
JE5749 (1989)(j)	10,801,000	—	—	—	0.50	—
JE5750 (1990)(j)	4,968,000	—	—	—	0.50	—
JE5751 (1991)(j)	12,000	—	—	—	2.00	—
Note: In sets only, probably 5,254 melted.						

KM# 171   AGORA
2.0000 g., Aluminum-Bronze **Subject:** Hanukka **Obv:** Ancient ship **Rev:** Value within lined square

Date	Mintage	F	VF	XF	Unc	BU
JE5747 (1987)(p)	1,504,000	—	—	0.15	0.75	—
JE5748 (1988)(j)	504,000	—	—	0.20	0.75	—
JE5749 (1989)(j)	504,000	—	—	0.20	0.75	—

Date	Mintage	F	VF	XF	Unc	BU
JE5750 (1990)(j)	2,160,000	—	—	0.15	0.75	—
JE5751 (1991)(j)	432,000	—	—	0.20	0.75	—

KM# 193   AGORA
Aluminum-Bronze **Subject:** 40th Anniversary of Independence **Obv:** Ancient ship **Rev:** Value within lined square

Date	Mintage	F	VF	XF	Unc	BU
JE5748 (1988)(j)	504,000	—	—	0.25	1.00	—

KM# 157   5 AGOROT
2.9500 g., Aluminum-Bronze, 19.45 mm. **Obv:** Ancient coin **Rev:** Value within lined square **Edge:** Plain

Date	Mintage	F	VF	XF	Unc	BU
JE5745 (1985)(p)	25,000,000	—	—	0.10	0.20	—
JE5745 (1985)(f)	9,504,000	—	—	0.10	0.20	—
JE5746 (1986)(f)	6,912,050	—	—	0.10	0.20	—
JE5746 (1986)(f)	5,472,000	—	—	0.10	0.20	—
JE5747 (1987)(j)	14,257,298	—	—	0.10	0.20	—
JE5748 (1988)(j)	9,360,000	—	—	0.10	0.20	—
JE5749 (1989)(j)	4,896,000	—	—	0.10	0.20	—
JE5750 (1990)(j)	576,000	—	—	0.25	0.75	—
JE5751 (1991)(j)	4,464,000	—	—	0.10	0.20	—
JE5752 (1992)(j)	7,664,000	—	—	0.10	0.20	—
JE5752 (1992)(so)	18,432,000	—	—	0.10	0.20	—
Note: A coin-alignment error exists. Value $150.						
JE5754 (1994)(a)	5,952,000	—	—	0.10	0.15	—
JE5754 (1994)(h)	6,144,000	—	—	0.10	0.15	—
JE5755 (1995)(o)	6,144,000	—	—	0.10	0.15	—
JE5756 (1996)(sg)	6,144,000	—	—	0.10	0.15	—
JE5757 (1997)(so)	6,144,000	—	—	0.10	0.15	—
JE5758 (1998)(j)	12,288,000	—	—	0.10	0.15	—
Note: A coin-alignment error exists. Value $150.						
JE5759 (1999)(j)	6,144,000	—	—	0.10	0.15	—
JE5760 (2000)(j)	12,288,000	—	—	0.10	0.15	—
Note: A coin-alignment error exists. Value $150.						

KM# 172   5 AGOROT
3.0000 g., Aluminum-Bronze, 14.5 mm. **Subject:** Hanukka **Obv:** Ancient coin **Rev:** Value within lined square **Note:** JE5754-576 coins contain the Star of David mint mark; the JE5747-5753 coins do not.

Date	Mintage	F	VF	XF	Unc	BU
JE5747 (1987)(p)	1,004,000	—	—	0.10	0.30	—
JE5748 (1988)(j)	536,000	—	—	0.20	0.50	—
JE5749 (1989)(j)	504,000	—	—	0.20	0.50	—
JE5750 (1990)(j)	2,016,000	—	—	0.10	0.30	—
JE5751 (1991)(j)	1,488,000	—	—	0.10	0.30	—
JE5752 (1992)(j)	960,000	—	—	0.10	0.30	—
JE5753 (1993)(j)	960,000	—	—	0.10	0.30	—
JE5754 (1994)(u)	12,000	—	—	—	2.00	—
Note: In sets only						
JE5755 (1995)(u)	10,000	—	—	—	2.00	—
Note: In sets only						
JE5756 (1996)(u)	7,500	—	—	—	2.00	—
Note: In sets only						
JE5757 (1997)(u)	7,500	—	—	—	2.00	—
Note: In sets only						
JE5758 (1998)(u)	10,000	—	—	—	2.00	—
Note: In sets only						
JE5759 (1999)(u)	6,000	—	—	—	2.50	—
Note: In sets only						
JE5760 (2000)(u)	5,000	—	—	—	2.50	—
Note: In sets only						

KM# 194   5 AGOROT
3.0000 g., Aluminum-Bronze, 19.5 mm. **Subject:** 40th Anniversary of Independence **Obv:** Ancient coin **Rev:** Value within lined square

Date	Mintage	F	VF	XF	Unc	BU
JE5748 (1988)(j)	504,000	—	—	0.25	0.75	—

KM# 158 10 AGOROT
4.0000 g., Aluminum-Bronze, 22 mm. **Obv:** Menorah
Rev: Value within lined square **Edge:** Plain

Date	Mintage	F	VF	XF	Unc	BU
JE5745 (1985)(f)	45,000,000	—	—	0.10	0.20	—
JE5746 (1986)(j)	20,934,048	—	—	0.10	0.20	—
JE5746 (1986)(b)	71,820,000	—	—	0.10	0.20	—
JE5747 (1987)(j)	19,351,382	—	—	0.10	0.20	—
JE5748 (1988)(j)	8,640,298	—	—	0.10	0.20	—
JE5749 (1989)(j)	420,000	—	—	0.25	0.75	—
JE5750 (1990)(j)	2,376,000	—	—	0.10	0.20	—
JE5751 (1991)(j)	11,905,000	—	—	0.10	0.20	—

Note: Exist with 6mm or 7mm long date; thick or thin letters; and 7mm or 7.5mm value 10

Date	Mintage	F	VF	XF	Unc	BU
JE5751 (1991)(so)	30,240,000	—	—	0.10	0.20	—
JE5751 (1991)(f)	17,280,000	—	—	0.10	0.20	—
JE5752 (1992)(j)	1,728,000	—	—	0.10	0.20	—
JE5753 (1993)(so)	25,920,000	—	—	0.10	0.20	—
JE5754 (1994)(u)	30,096,000	—	—	0.10	0.20	—
JE5754 (1994)(f)	21,600,000	—	—	0.10	0.20	—
JE5755 (1995)(h)	17,280,000	—	—	0.10	0.20	—
JE5756 (1996)(so)	43,200,000	—	—	0.10	0.20	—
JE5757 (1997)(h)	21,600,000	—	—	0.10	0.20	—

Note: The Hebrew letter "heh" in the date (first letter) is open.

Date	Mintage	F	VF	XF	Unc	BU
JE5757 (1997)(u)	21,600,000	—	—	0.10	0.20	—

Note: The Hebrew letter "heh" in the date (first letter) is closed.

Date	Mintage	F	VF	XF	Unc	BU
JE5758 (1998)(so)	60,480,000	—	—	0.10	0.20	—

Note: A coin-alignment error exists. Value $150.

Date	Mintage	F	VF	XF	Unc	BU
JE5759 (1999)(a)	21,600,000	—	—	0.10	0.20	—
JE5759 (1999)(sl)	4,601,000	—	—	0.10	0.20	—
JE5759 (1999)(w)	2,000	—	—	0.10	0.20	—
JE5760 (2000)(so)	82,944,000	—	—	0.10	0.20	—

KM# 173 10 AGOROT
4.0700 g., Aluminum-Bronze, 22 mm. **Subject:** Hanukka
Obv: Menorah **Rev:** Value within lined square **Note:** JE5754-5769 have the Star of David mint mark, JE5747-5753 coins do not.

Date	Mintage	F	VF	XF	Unc	BU
JE5747 (1987)(p)	1,004,000	—	—	0.10	0.40	—
JE5748 (1988)(j)	834,000	—	—	0.10	0.40	—
JE5749 (1989)(j)	798,000	—	—	0.10	0.40	—
JE5750 (1990)(j)	2,052,000	—	—	0.10	0.40	—
JE5751 (1991)(j)	1,488,000	—	—	0.10	0.40	—
JE5752 (1992)(j)	1,404,000	—	—	0.10	0.40	—
JE5753 (1993)(j)	1,404,000	—	—	0.10	0.40	—
JE5754 (1994)(u)	12,000	—	—	*	2.00	—

Note: In sets only

Date	Mintage	F	VF	XF	Unc	BU
JE5755 (1995)(u)	10,000	—	—		2.00	—

Note: In sets only

Date	Mintage	F	VF	XF	Unc	BU
JE5756 (1996)(u)	7,500	—	—		2.00	—

Note: In sets only

Date	Mintage	F	VF	XF	Unc	BU
JE5757 (1997)(u)	7,500	—	—		2.00	—

Note: In sets only

Date	Mintage	F	VF	XF	Unc	BU
JE5758 (1998)(u)	10,000	—	—		2.00	—

Note: In sets only

Date	Mintage	F	VF	XF	Unc	BU
JE5759 (1999)(u)	6,000	—	—		2.50	—

Note: In sets only

Date	Mintage	F	VF	XF	Unc	BU
JE5760 (2000)(u)	5,000	—	—		3.00	—

Note: In sets only

KM# 195 10 AGOROT
4.0000 g., Aluminum-Bronze **Subject:** 40th Anniversary of Independence **Obv:** Menorah **Rev:** Value within lined square

Date	Mintage	F	VF	XF	Unc	BU
JE5748 (1988)(j)	504,000	—	—	0.25	0.75	—

KM# 161 SHEQEL
14.4000 g., 0.8500 Silver 0.3935 oz. ASW **Subject:** Hanukka
Obv: Value **Rev:** Ashkenaz lamp

Date	Mintage	F	VF	XF	Unc	BU
JE5745(1985)(p)	9,460	—	—	—	15.00	—

KM# 159 1/2 NEW SHEQEL
6.5200 g., Aluminum-Bronze, 25.95 mm. **Obv:** Value **Rev:** Lyre
Edge: Plain

Date	Mintage	F	VF	XF	Unc	BU
JE5745 (1985)(f)	4,032,000	—	—	0.35	0.75	—
JE5745 (1985)(j)	1,296,000	—	—	0.35	0.75	—
JE5745 (1985)(p)	15,000,000	—	—	0.35	0.75	—

Note: Exist with thick E and trimmed thin E, but which mint(s) produced which coin is not known

Date	Mintage	F	VF	XF	Unc	BU
JE5746 (1986)(j)	4,392,000	—	—	0.35	0.75	—
JE5747 (1987)(j)	144,000	—	—	1.00	2.00	—
JE5748 (1988)(j)	20,000	—	1.00	3.00	5.00	—

Note: In sets only

Date	Mintage	F	VF	XF	Unc	BU
JE5749 (1989)(j)	756,000	—	—	0.40	1.00	—
JE5750 (1990)(j)	648,000	—	—	0.40	1.00	—
JE5751 (1991)(j)	288,000	—	—	0.75	1.50	—
JE5752 (1992)(f)	2,688,000	—	—	0.35	0.75	—
JE5752 (1992)(j)	828,000	—	—	0.35	0.75	—
JE5752 (1992)(so)	10,752,000	—	—	0.35	0.75	—
JE5753 (1993)(c)	2,496,000	—	—	0.35	0.75	—
JE5753 (1993)(j)	2,688,000	—	—	0.35	0.75	—
JE5755 (1995)(a)	5,376,000	—	—	0.35	0.75	—
JE5755 (1995)(so)	5,376,000	—	—	0.35	0.75	—
JE5757 (1997)(so)	5,376,000	—	—	0.35	0.75	—
JE5758 (1998)(u)	5,376,000	—	—	0.35	0.75	—
JE5759 (1999)(so)	8,064,000	—	—	0.35	0.75	—

Note: A coin-alignment error exists. Value $200.

Date	Mintage	F	VF	XF	Unc	BU
JE5760 (2000)(so)	2,880,000	—	—			—

Note: Reported in the 2000 Annual Review, a correction in the 2002 Annual review, stated that it was in error.

KM# 167 1/2 NEW SHEQEL
Aluminum-Bronze, 26 mm. **Obv:** Value **Rev:** Bust of Edmond de Rothschild facing within names of settlements funded

Date	Mintage	F	VF	XF	Unc	BU
JE5746 (1986)(u)	2,000,000	—	—	1.00	3.00	—

KM# 168 1/2 NEW SHEQEL
7.2000 g., 0.8500 Silver 0.1968 oz. ASW **Series:** Holyland Sites
Obv: Value **Rev:** Akko

Date	Mintage	F	VF	XF	Unc	BU
JE5747-1986(u)	6,224	—	—	—	10.00	—

KM# 180 1/2 NEW SHEQEL
7.2000 g., 0.8500 Silver 0.1968 oz. ASW **Series:** Holyland Sites
Rev: Jericho

Date	Mintage	F	VF	XF	Unc	BU
JE5748-1987(p)	7,590	—	—	—	12.50	—

KM# 174 1/2 NEW SHEQEL
6.5000 g., Aluminum-Bronze, 26 mm. **Subject:** Hanukka
Obv: Value **Rev:** Lyre **Note:** Coins dated JE5754-5769 have the Star of David mint mark; the coins dated JE5747-5753 do not.

Date	Mintage	F	VF	XF	Unc	BU
JE5747 (1987)(p)	1,004,000	—	—	0.35	0.85	—
JE5748 (1988)(j)	532,000	—	—	0.40	1.00	—
JE5749 (1989)(j)	504,000	—	—	0.40	1.00	—
JE5750 (1990)(j)	2,016,000	—	—	0.35	0.85	—
JE5751 (1991)(j)	960,000	—	—	0.35	0.85	—
JE5752 (1992)(j)	288,000	—	—	0.75	1.50	—
JE5753 (1993)(j)	304,000	—	—	0.75	1.50	—
JE5754 (1994)(u)	12,000	—	—		2.00	—

Note: In sets only

Date	Mintage	F	VF	XF	Unc	BU
JE5755 (1995)(u)	10,000	—	—		2.00	—

Note: In sets only

Date	Mintage	F	VF	XF	Unc	BU
JE5756 (1996)(u)	7,500	—	—		2.00	—

Note: In sets only

Date	Mintage	F	VF	XF	Unc	BU
JE5757 (1997)(u)	7,500	—	—		2.00	—

Note: In sets only

Date	Mintage	F	VF	XF	Unc	BU
JE5758 (1998)(u)	10,000	—	—		2.00	—

Note: In sets only

Date	Mintage	F	VF	XF	Unc	BU
JE5759 (1999)(u)	6,000	—	—		2.50	—

Note: In sets only

Date	Mintage	F	VF	XF	Unc	BU
JE5760 (2000)(u)	5,000	—	—		3.00	—

Note: In sets only

KM# 188 1/2 NEW SHEQEL
7.2000 g., 0.8500 Silver 0.1968 oz. ASW **Series:** Holyland Sites
Obv: Value **Rev:** Caesarea

Date	Mintage	F	VF	XF	Unc	BU
JE5749-1988(p)	5,865	—	—	—	15.00	—

KM# 196 1/2 NEW SHEQEL
Aluminum-Bronze, 26 mm. **Subject:** 40th Anniversary of Independence **Obv:** Value **Rev:** Lyre

Date	Mintage	F	VF	XF	Unc	BU
JE5748 (1988)(j)	500,000	—	—	0.40	1.00	—

KM# 202 1/2 NEW SHEQEL
7.2000 g., 0.8500 Silver 0.1968 oz. ASW **Subject:** Holyland Sites **Obv:** Value **Rev:** Jaffa Harbor

Date	Mintage	F	VF	XF	Unc	BU
JE5750-1989(f)	4,940	—	—	—	18.00	—

KM# 209   1/2 NEW SHEQEL
7.2000 g., 0.8500 Silver 0.1968 oz. ASW   **Subject:** Holyland Sites **Obv:** Value **Rev:** Sea of Galilee sites map

Date	Mintage	F	VF	XF	Unc	BU
JE5751-1990(f)	4,346	—	—	—	20.00	—

KM# 303   1/2 NEW SHEQEL
Copper-Aluminum-Nickel, 26 mm. **Series:** Hanukka **Obv:** Value **Rev:** Theresienstadt lamp **Note:** Struck for sets only.

Date	Mintage	F	VF	XF	Unc	BU
JE5754 (1994)(u)	12,000	—	—	—	8.00	—

KM# 304   1/2 NEW SHEQEL
Copper-Aluminum-Nickel, 26 mm. **Series:** Hanukka **Obv:** Value **Rev:** Early American lamp **Note:** Struck for sets only.

Date	Mintage	F	VF	XF	Unc	BU
JE5755 (1995)(u)	10,000	—	—	—	8.00	—

KM# 368   1/2 NEW SHEQEL
14.5000 g., Copper-Aluminum-Nickel, 26 mm. **Subject:** Environment **Obv:** Value **Rev:** Flower **Edge:** Plain **Note:** Struck for sets only. Piefort only type.

Date	Mintage	F	VF	XF	Unc	BU
JE5754 (1994)(u)	8,000	—	—	—	10.00	—

KM# 392   1/2 NEW SHEQEL
Copper-Aluminum-Nickel, 26 mm. **Subject:** Medicine Anniversary **Note:** Struck for sets only. Piefort only type.

Date	Mintage	F	VF	XF	Unc	BU
JE5755 (1995)(u)	10,000	—	—	—	10.00	—

KM# 305   1/2 NEW SHEQEL
6.5000 g., Copper-Aluminum-Nickel, 26 mm. **Series:** Hanukka **Obv:** Value **Rev:** 14th century French lamp **Note:** Struck for sets only.

Date	Mintage	F	VF	XF	Unc	BU
JE5756 (1996)(u)	7,500	—	—	—	10.00	—

KM# 318   1/2 NEW SHEQEL
6.5000 g., Copper-Aluminum-Nickel, 26 mm. **Series:** Hanukka **Obv:** Value **Rev:** Russian lamp **Note:** Struck for sets only.

Date	Mintage	F	VF	XF	Unc	BU
JE5757 (1997)(u)	7,500	—	—	—	8.00	—

KM# 393   1/2 NEW SHEQEL
Copper-Aluminum-Nickel, 26 mm. **Subject:** Jerusalem 3000 **Note:** Struck for sets only. Piefort only type.

Date	Mintage	F	VF	XF	Unc	BU
JE5756 (1996)(h)	8,000	—	—	—	10.00	—

KM# 394   1/2 NEW SHEQEL
Copper-Aluminum-Nickel, 26 mm. **Subject:** First Zionist Congress Centennial **Note:** Struck for sets only. Piefort only type.

Date	Mintage	F	VF	XF	Unc	BU
JE5757 (1997)(h)	6,000	—	—	—	12.00	—

KM# 314   1/2 NEW SHEQEL
6.5000 g., Copper-Aluminum-Nickel, 26 mm. **Series:** Hanukka **Obv:** Value **Rev:** English lamp **Note:** Struck for sets only.

Date	Mintage	F	VF	XF	Unc	BU
JE5758 (1998)(u)	10,000	—	—	—	8.00	—

KM# 331   1/2 NEW SHEQEL
6.5000 g., Copper-Aluminum-Nickel, 26 mm. **Series:** Hanukka **Obv:** Value **Rev:** Menorah **Note:** Struck for sets only.

Date	Mintage	F	VF	XF	Unc	BU
JE5759 (1999)(u)	6,000	—	—	—	8.00	—

KM# 395   1/2 NEW SHEQEL
Copper-Aluminum-Nickel, 26 mm. **Subject:** 50th Anniversary - State of Israel **Note:** Struck for sets only. Piefort only type.

Date	Mintage	F	VF	XF	Unc	BU
JE5758 (1998)(h)	8,000	—	—	—	10.00	—

KM# 332   1/2 NEW SHEQEL
6.5000 g., Copper-Aluminum-Nickel, 26 mm. **Obv:** Value **Rev:** Jerusalem Hanukka lamp **Note:** Struck for sets only.

Date	Mintage	F	VF	XF	Unc	BU
JE5760 (2000)(u)	7,000	—	—	—	8.00	—

KM# 324   1/2 NEW SHEQEL
Bronze, 26 mm. **Subject:** High Tech in Israel **Obv:** Value **Rev:** Stylized mosaic bouquet **Note:** Struck for sets only. Piefort only type.

Date	Mintage	F	VF	XF	Unc	BU
JE5759 (1999)(h)	6,000	—	—	—	12.00	—

KM# 363   1/2 NEW SHEQEL
14.3200 g., Copper-Nickel-Aluminum, 25.85 mm. **Subject:** "Love Thy Neighbor" **Obv:** Value **Rev:** Arch **Edge:** Plain **Note:** Struck for sets only. Piefort only type.

Date	Mintage	F	VF	XF	Unc	BU
JE5760 (2000)(h)	4,000	—	—	—	12.00	—

KM# 160   NEW SHEQEL
4.0000 g., Copper-Nickel, 18 mm. **Obv:** Value **Rev:** Lily, state emblem and ancient Hebrew inscription

Date	Mintage	F	VF	XF	Unc	BU
JE5745 (1985)(b)	29,088,000	—	—	0.65	1.50	—
JE5746 (1986)(f)	8,000,000	—	—	0.65	1.50	—
JE5746 (1986)(j)	12,960,055	—	—	0.65	1.50	—
JE5747 (1987)(j)	216,000	—	—	1.00	3.00	—
JE5748 (1988)(j)	6,372,000	—	—	0.65	1.50	—
JE5748 (1988)(u)	14,004,000	—	—	0.65	1.50	—
JE5749 (1989)(j)	8,706,000	—	—	0.65	1.50	—
JE5750 (1990)(j)	756,000	—	—	0.75	2.00	—
JE5751 (1991)(j)	1,152,000	—	—	0.65	1.50	—
JE5752 (1992)(j)	8,640,000	—	—	0.65	1.50	—
JE5752 (1992)(j)	1,512,000	—	—	0.65	1.50	—
JE5752 (1992)(o)	17,280,000	—	—	0.65	1.50	—
JE5753 (1993)(f)	8,640,000	—	—	0.65	1.50	—

KM# 160a   NEW SHEQEL
3.4500 g., Nickel-Clad Steel, 17.97 mm. **Obv:** Value **Rev:** Lily, state emblem and ancient Hebrew inscription **Edge:** Plain

Date	Mintage	F	VF	XF	Unc	BU
JE5754 (1994)(b)	8,496,000	—	—	—	1.00	—
JE5754 (1994)(u)	12,960,000	—	—	—	1.00	—
Note: Coin alignment error exists. Value: $150.						
JE5755 (1995)(u)	25,920,000	—	—	—	1.00	—
JE5756 (1996)(u)	8,640,000	—	—	—	1.00	—
JE5757 (1997)(u)	30,240,000	—	—	—	1.00	—
JE5758 (1998)(sa)	4,295,500	—	—	—	1.00	—
JE5758 (1998)(o)		—	—	—	1.00	—
JE5759 (1999)(u)	17,280,000	—	—	—	1.00	—
JE5760 (2000)(o)	20,738,000	—	—	—	1.00	—

KM# 163   NEW SHEQEL
4.0500 g., Copper-Nickel, 18 mm. **Subject:** Hanukka **Obv:** Value **Rev:** Lily **Note:** Coins dated JE5754-5769 have the Star of David mint mark; the JE5746-5753 coins do not.

Date	Mintage	F	VF	XF	Unc	BU
JE5746 (1986)(b)	1,056,000	—	—	0.65	1.50	—
JE5747 (1987)(p)	1,004,000	—	—	0.65	1.50	—
JE5748 (1988)(j)	534,000	—	—	0.75	2.00	—
JE5749 (1989)(j)	504,000	—	—	0.75	2.00	—
JE5750 (1990)(j)	2,052,000	—	—	0.65	1.50	—
JE5751 (1991)(f)	1,080,000	—	—	0.65	1.50	—
JE5751 (1991)(j)	24,000	—	—	0.65	1.50	—
JE5752 (1992)(j)	1,044,000	—	—	0.65	1.50	—
JE5753 (1993)(j)	922,000	—	—	0.65	1.50	—
JE5754 (1994)(u)	12,000	—	—	—	2.50	—
Note: In sets only						
JE5755 (1995)(u)	10,000	—	—	—	2.50	—
JE5756 (1996)(u)	7,500	—	—	—	2.50	—
Note: In sets only						
JE5757 (1997)(u)	7,500	—	—	—	2.50	—
Note: In sets only						
JE5758 (1998)(u)	10,000	—	—	—	2.50	—
Note: In sets only						
JE5759 (1999)(u)	6,000	—	—	—	3.00	—
Note: In sets only						
JE5760 (2000)(u)	5,000	—	—	—	3.50	—
Note: In sets only						

KM# 164   NEW SHEQEL
14.4000 g., 0.8500 Silver 0.3935 oz. ASW   **Subject:** 38th Anniversary of Independence **Obv:** Value, half rainbow and menorah flanked by sprigs **Rev:** Artistic designs

Date	Mintage	F	VF	XF	Unc	BU
JE5746-1986(p)	8,010	—	—	—	12.50	—

KM# 169   NEW SHEQEL
14.4000 g., 0.8500 Silver 0.3935 oz. ASW   **Series:** Holyland Sites **Obv:** Value **Rev:** Akko

Date	Mintage	F	VF	XF	Unc	BU
JE5747-1986(f) Proof	6,117	Value: 20.00				

KM# 175   NEW SHEQEL
14.4000 g., 0.8500 Silver 0.3935 oz. ASW   **Subject:** Hanukka **Obv:** Value **Rev:** Algerian lamp

Date	Mintage	F	VF	XF	Unc	BU
JE5747-1986(f)	8,227	—	—	—	20.00	—

KM# 177   NEW SHEQEL
14.4000 g., 0.8500 Silver 0.3935 oz. ASW   **Subject:** 20th Anniversary - United Jerusalem **Obv:** Menorah flanked by sprigs within rectangle **Rev:** Circular city of Jerusalem to right of numeral two

Date	Mintage	F	VF	XF	Unc	BU
JE5747-1987(p)	8,107	—	—	—	15.00	—

KM# 181   NEW SHEQEL
14.4000 g., 0.8500 Silver 0.3935 oz. ASW   **Series:** Holyland Sites **Obv:** Value **Rev:** Jericho

Date	Mintage	F	VF	XF	Unc	BU
JE5748-1987(f) Proof	8,196	Value: 20.00				

KM# 183   NEW SHEQEL
14.4000 g., 0.8500 Silver 0.3935 oz. ASW   **Subject:** Hanukkah **Obv:** Value, text and menorah flanked by sprigs within design **Rev:** English lamp

Date	Mintage	F	VF	XF	Unc	BU
JE5748-1987(f)	7,810	—	—	—	20.00	—

KM# 185 NEW SHEQEL

14.4000 g., 0.8500 Silver 0.3935 oz. ASW **Subject:** 40th Anniversary of Indeperidence **Obv:** Large stylized value **Rev:** Stylized figures of government within large numeral 40

Date	Mintage	F	VF	XF	Unc	BU
JE5748-1988(p)	8,990	—	—	—	12.50	—

KM# 189 NEW SHEQEL

14.4000 g., 0.8500 Silver 0.3935 oz. ASW **Series:** Holyland Sites **Obv:** Value **Rev:** Caesarea

Date	Mintage	F	VF	XF	Unc	BU
JE5749-1988(f) Proof	6,560	Value: 30.00				

KM# 191 NEW SHEQEL

14.4000 g., 0.8500 Silver 0.3935 oz. ASW **Subject:** Hanukka **Obv:** Value and text within design **Rev:** Tunisian lamp

Date	Mintage	F	VF	XF	Unc	BU
JE5749-1988(u)	6,688	—	—	—	20.00	—

KM# 197 NEW SHEQEL

4.0000 g., Copper-Nickel, 18 mm. **Subject:** 40th Anniversary of Independence **Obv:** Value **Rev:** English lamp

Date	Mintage	F	VF	XF	Unc	BU
JE5748 (1988)(j)	504,000	—	—	—	1.75	—

KM# 198 NEW SHEQEL

4.0000 g., Copper-Nickel, 18 mm. **Obv:** Value **Rev:** Bust of Maimonides facing

Date	Mintage	F	VF	XF	Unc	BU
JE5748 (1988)(d)	1,000,000	—	—	—	1.75	—

KM# 199 NEW SHEQEL

14.4000 g., 0.8500 Silver 0.3935 oz. ASW **Subject:** 41st Anniversary of Independence **Obv:** Value covers left side of lined area **Rev:** Roe deer standing to right in wooded area

Date	Mintage	F	VF	XF	Unc	BU
JE5749-1989(f)	6,249	—	—	—	20.00	—

KM# 203 NEW SHEQEL

14.4000 g., 0.8500 Silver 0.3935 oz. ASW **Subject:** Holyland Sites **Obv:** Value **Rev:** Jaffa Harbor

Date	Mintage	F	VF	XF	Unc	BU
JE5750-1989(f) Proof	4,844	Value: 32.00				

KM# 205 NEW SHEQEL

14.4000 g., 0.8500 Silver 0.3935 oz. ASW **Subject:** Hanukka **Obv:** Value **Rev:** Persian lamp

Date	Mintage	F	VF	XF	Unc	BU
JE5750-1989(m)	6,171	—	—	—	25.00	—

KM# 210 NEW SHEQEL

14.4000 g., 0.8500 Silver 0.3935 oz. ASW **Subject:** Holyland Sites **Obv:** Value **Rev:** Sea of Galilee sites map

Date	Mintage	F	VF	XF	Unc	BU
JE5751-1990(f) Proof	4,735	Value: 35.00				

KM# 212 NEW SHEQEL

14.4000 g., 0.8500 Silver 0.3935 oz. ASW **Subject:** 42nd Anniversary of Independence **Obv:** Linear value **Rev:** Archaeology

Date	Mintage	F	VF	XF	Unc	BU
JE5750-1990(f)	5,509	—	—	—	22.00	—

KM# 215 NEW SHEQEL

14.4000 g., 0.8500 Silver 0.3935 oz. ASW **Subject:** Hanukkah **Obv:** Value, text and menorah flanked by sprigs **Rev:** Cochin lamp

Date	Mintage	F	VF	XF	Unc	BU
JE5751-1990(f)	5,259	—	—	—	25.00	—

KM# 220 NEW SHEQEL

14.4000 g., 0.9250 Silver 0.4282 oz. ASW **Subject:** Wildlife **Obv:** Cedar trees and value **Rev:** Dove and tree trunk

Date	Mintage	F	VF	XF	Unc	BU
JE5752-1991(f)	4,125	—	—	—	25.00	—

KM# 218 NEW SHEQEL

14.4000 g., 0.9250 Silver 0.4282 oz. ASW **Subject:** 43rd Anniversary of Independence **Obv:** Value within diagonal lines **Rev:** Plane above stylized standing figures

Date	Mintage	F	VF	XF	Unc	BU
JE5751-1991(f)	5,508	—	—	—	18.00	—

KM# 223 NEW SHEQEL

14.4000 g., 0.9250 Silver 0.4282 oz. ASW **Series:** Judaic **Obv:** Value within diagonal lines to right of cup **Rev:** Kiddush cup flanked by dates within circular design

Date	Mintage	F	VF	XF	Unc	BU
JE5752-1991(f)	4,876	—	—	—	20.00	—

KM# 342 NEW SHEQEL

3.4600 g., 0.9000 Gold 0.1001 oz. AGW **Subject:** Wildlife **Obv:** Cedar trees and value **Rev:** Dove and tree trunk

Date	Mintage	F	VF	XF	Unc	BU
JE5752-1991(o) Proof	2,515	Value: 200				

KM# 225 NEW SHEQEL

14.4000 g., 0.9250 Silver 0.4282 oz. ASW **Subject:** 44th Anniversary of Independence **Obv:** Value **Rev:** Balance scale above arch within square

Date	Mintage	F	VF	XF	Unc	BU
JE5752-1992(p)	4,047	—	—	—	35.00	—

KM# 231 NEW SHEQEL

14.4000 g., 0.9250 Silver 0.4282 oz. ASW **Series:** Wildlife **Obv:** Value at upper right of lilies **Rev:** Roe and lily

Date	Mintage	F	VF	XF	Unc	BU
JE5753-1992(f)	4,105	—	—	—	25.00	—

KM# 234 NEW SHEQEL

14.4000 g., 0.9250 Silver 0.4282 oz. ASW **Subject:** B'nai B'rith - 150th Anniversary. **Obv:** Value and menorah within stylized design **Rev:** Text within stylized design

Date	Mintage	F	VF	XF	Unc	BU
JE5752-1992	4,034	—	—	—	25.00	—

KM# 238 NEW SHEQEL
14.4000 g., 0.9250 Silver 0.4282 oz. ASW **Series:** Judaic
Obv: Value within diagonal lines to right of candles on box
Rev: Shabbat candles

Date	Mintage	F	VF	XF	Unc	BU
JE5753-1992(u)	5,564	—	—	—	25.00	—

KM# 343 NEW SHEQEL
3.4600 g., 0.9000 Gold 0.1001 oz. AGW **Series:** Wildlife
Rev: Roe and lily

Date	Mintage	F	VF	XF	Unc	BU
JE5753-1992(p)	2,000	Value: 200				
Proof						

KM# 240 NEW SHEQEL
14.4000 g., 0.9250 Silver 0.4282 oz. ASW **Subject:** 45th
Anniversary of Independence **Obv:** Value, text, dates and
menorah flanked by sprigs **Rev:** Tourism attractions

Date	Mintage	F	VF	XF	Unc	BU
JE5753-1993(u)	6,985	—	—	—	25.00	—

KM# 243 NEW SHEQEL
14.4000 g., 0.9250 Silver 0.4282 oz. ASW **Series:** Wildlife
Obv: Value at upper right of apple blossom **Rev:** Buck and young
Hart deer standing in grass

Date	Mintage	F	VF	XF	Unc	BU
JE5754-1993(f)	3,761	—	—	—	25.00	—

KM# 244 NEW SHEQEL
3.4600 g., 0.9000 Gold 0.1001 oz. AGW **Series:** Wildlife
Obv: Value at upper right of apple blossom **Rev:** Buck and young
Hart standing in grass

Date	Mintage	F	VF	XF	Unc	BU
JE5754-1993(u)	1,679	Value: 200				
Proof						

KM# 250 NEW SHEQEL
14.4000 g., 0.9250 Silver 0.4282 oz. ASW **Series:** Judaic
Obv: Torah crown at left of value within lined 1/4 square
Rev: Havdalah spicebox

Date	Mintage	F	VF	XF	Unc	BU
JE5754-1993(u)	3,288	—	—	—	20.00	—

KM# 247 NEW SHEQEL
14.4000 g., 0.9250 Silver 0.4282 oz. ASW **Obv:** Value and
menorah within beaded diagonal line **Rev:** Medal with star within
beaded diagonal lines to left of flames **Note:** Revolt and Heroism.

Date	Mintage	F	VF	XF	Unc	BU
JE5753-1993(u)	4,642	—	—	—	20.00	—

KM# 252 NEW SHEQEL
14.4000 g., 0.9250 Silver 0.4282 oz. ASW **Subject:** Environment
Obv: Slanted value **Rev:** Globe within flower design

Date	Mintage	F	VF	XF	Unc	BU
JE5754-1994(f)	3,490	—	—	—	25.00	—

KM# 256 NEW SHEQEL
14.4000 g., 0.9250 Silver 0.4282 oz. ASW **Series:** Biblical
Rev: Abraham's willingness to sacrifice Isaac

Date	Mintage	F	VF	XF	Unc	BU
JE5755-1994(f)	3,468	—	—	—	30.00	—
Prooflike						

KM# 259 NEW SHEQEL
14.4000 g., 0.9250 Silver 0.4282 oz. ASW **Subject:** Wildlife
Obv: Palm tree to right of value and text **Rev:** Leopard

Date	Mintage	F	VF	XF	Unc	BU
JE5755-1994(u)	3,286	—	—	—	32.00	—

KM# 260 NEW SHEQEL
3.4600 g., 0.9000 Gold 0.1001 oz. AGW **Subject:** Wildlife
Obv: Palm tree to right of value and text **Rev:** Leopard

Date	Mintage	F	VF	XF	Unc	BU
JE5755-1994(o)	1,355	Value: 240				
Proof						

KM# 263 NEW SHEQEL
14.4000 g., 0.9250 Silver 0.4282 oz. ASW **Subject:** Anniversary
- Medicine **Obv:** Snake on a menorrah **Rev:** Value, text and
menorah flanked by sprigs

Date	Mintage	F	VF	XF	Unc	BU
JE5755-1995(f)	3,468	—	—	—	25.00	—

KM# 267 NEW SHEQEL
14.4000 g., 0.9250 Silver 0.4282 oz. ASW **Subject:** 50th
Anniversary - Defeat of Nazi Germany **Obv:** Value above text
Rev: V-shape design with state emblems within

Date	Mintage	F	VF	XF	Unc	BU
JE5755-1995(h)	3,450	—	—	—	32.50	—
Prooflike						

KM# 271 NEW SHEQEL
14.4000 g., 0.9250 Silver 0.4282 oz. ASW **Series:** F.A.O.
Obv: Value within wheat sprigs and diagonal lines **Rev:** FAO logo

Date	Mintage	F	VF	XF	Unc	BU
JE5755-1995(v)	3,564	—	—	—	—	35.00
Prooflike						

KM# 274 NEW SHEQEL
14.4000 g., 0.9250 Silver 0.4282 oz. ASW **Subject:** Wildlife
Obv: Value and cluster of grapes **Rev:** Fox

Date	Mintage	F	VF	XF	Unc	BU
JE5756-1995(v)	2,438	—	—	—	32.00	—

KM# 275 NEW SHEQEL
3.4600 g., 0.9000 Gold 0.1001 oz. AGW **Subject:** Wildlife
Obv: Grapes **Rev:** Fox

Date	Mintage	F	VF	XF	Unc	BU
JE5756-1995(o)	837	Value: 375				
Proof						

KM# 278 NEW SHEQEL
14.4000 g., 0.9250 Silver 0.4282 oz. ASW **Subject:** Peace
Treaty with Jordan **Obv:** Text divides value and menorah flanked
by sprigs **Rev:** Sprig divides text

Date	Mintage	F	VF	XF	Unc	BU
JE5755-1995(bp)	3,301	—	—	—	—	28.00
Prooflike						

KM# 281 NEW SHEQEL
14.4000 g., 0.9250 Silver 0.4282 oz. ASW **Subject:** Biblical Arts
- Solomon's Judgment **Obv:** Value above text **Rev:** Medieval
linear design

Date	Mintage	F	VF	XF	Unc	BU
JE5755-1995(f)	2,826	—	—	—	30.00	—
Prooflike						

KM# 287 NEW SHEQEL
14.4000 g., 0.9250 Silver 0.4282 oz. ASW **Subject:** Port of
Caesarea **Obv:** Anchor to lower left of value and text **Rev:** Ancient
ship

Date	Mintage	F	VF	XF	Unc	BU
JE5755-1995(f)	2,633	—	—	—	28.00	—

KM# 284 NEW SHEQEL
14.4000 g., 0.9250 Silver 0.4282 oz. ASW **Subject:** Jerusalem
3000 **Obv:** Value flanked by menorah and design above text
Rev: Inscription at center

Date	Mintage	F	VF	XF	Unc	BU
JE5756-1996(f)	4,497	—	—	—	35.00	—
Prooflike						

KM# 290 NEW SHEQEL
14.4000 g., 0.9250 Silver 0.4282 oz. ASW **Subject:** Wildlife
Obv: Fig leaves and value **Rev:** Nightingale

Date	Mintage	F	VF	XF	Unc	BU
JE5757-1996(v)	2,451	—	—	—	—	32.00
Prooflike						

KM# 291 NEW SHEQEL
3.4600 g., 0.9000 Gold 0.1001 oz. AGW **Subject:** Wildlife
Rev: Nightingale

Date	Mintage	F	VF	XF	Unc	BU
JE5757-1996(v)	912	Value: 350				
Proof						

KM# 294 NEW SHEQEL
14.4000 g., 0.9250 Silver 0.4282 oz. ASW **Subject:** Biblical Arts
Obv: Value above design and text **Rev:** Miriam and the women

Date	Mintage	F	VF	XF	Unc	BU
JE5757-1996(u)	2,236	—	—	—	—	40.00
Prooflike						

KM# 297 NEW SHEQEL
14.4000 g., 0.9250 Silver 0.4282 oz. ASW **Obv:** Menorah above
value and text **Rev:** Head left

Date	Mintage	F	VF	XF	Unc	BU
JE5757-1996(u)	5,296	—	—	—	—	35.00

KM# 300 NEW SHEQEL
14.4000 g., 0.9250 Silver 0.4282 oz. ASW **Subject:** First Zionist
Congress Centennial **Obv:** Value flanked by menorah, star
design and text **Rev:** Half-figure left leaning on bridge

Date	Mintage	F	VF	XF	Unc	BU
JE5757-1997(u)	4,028	—	—	—	—	30.00
Prooflike						

KM# 306 NEW SHEQEL
14.4000 g., 0.9250 Silver 0.4282 oz. ASW **Subject:** Wildlife
Obv: Pomegranates, value and text **Rev:** Lion right

Date	Mintage	F	VF	XF	Unc	BU
JE5758-1997(u)	2,135	—	—	—	30.00	—
Prooflike						

KM# 307 NEW SHEQEL
3.4600 g., 0.9000 Gold 0.1001 oz. AGW **Subject:** Wildlife
Obv: Pomegranates and value **Rev:** Lion **Edge:** Reeded

Date	Mintage	F	VF	XF	Unc	BU
JE5758-1997(u)	770	Value: 400				
Proof						

KM# 310 NEW SHEQEL
14.4300 g., 0.9250 Silver 0.4291 oz. ASW **Subject:** Anniversary
Obv: Value and menorah above text **Rev:** Flag within stars

Date	Mintage	F	VF	XF	Unc	BU
JE5758-1998(u)	9,819	—	—	—	—	25.00
Prooflike						

KM# 316 NEW SHEQEL
14.4300 g., 0.9250 Silver 0.4291 oz. ASW **Subject:** Biblical -
Noah's Ark **Obv:** Dove, rainbow and value **Rev:** Stylized figure
releasing dove

Date	Mintage	F	VF	XF	Unc	BU
JE5758-1998(u)	2,198	—	—	—	—	30.00
Prooflike						

KM# 320 NEW SHEQEL
14.4300 g., 0.9250 Silver 0.4291 oz. ASW **Subject:** Wildlife
Obv: Fir trees and value **Rev:** Stork

Date	Mintage	F	VF	XF	Unc	BU
JE5759-1998(u)	2,147	—	—	—	—	30.00
Prooflike						

KM# 321 NEW SHEQEL
3.4600 g., 0.9000 Gold 0.1001 oz. AGW **Subject:** Wildlife
Obv: Fir trees and value **Rev:** Stork

Date	Mintage	F	VF	XF	Unc	BU
JE5759-1998(u)	553	Value: 400				
Proof						

KM# 325 NEW SHEQEL
14.4000 g., 0.9250 Silver 0.4282 oz. ASW, 30 mm.
Subject: High-Tech in Israel **Obv:** Value and mosaic **Rev:** O1
Computer code as bouquet

Date	Mintage	F	VF	XF	Unc	BU
JE5759-1999(u)	1,713	—	—	—	—	25.00
Prooflike						

KM# 328 NEW SHEQEL
14.4000 g., 0.9250 Silver 0.4282 oz. ASW **Subject:** The
Millennium Coin **Obv:** Value and olive branch **Rev:** Year 2000
motif incorporating dove with olive branch

Date	Mintage	F	VF	XF	Unc	BU
JE5759-1999(u)	4,629	—	—	—	—	25.00
Prooflike						

KM# 333 NEW SHEQEL
14.4000 g., 0.9250 Silver 0.4282 oz. ASW **Subject:** Biblical
Obv: Value, text and menorah to right of stars **Rev:** Abraham
looking at the stars

Date	Mintage	F	VF	XF	Unc	BU
JE5759-1999(o)	2,146	—	—	—	—	35.00
Prooflike						

KM# 336   NEW SHEQEL
14.4000 g., 0.9250 Silver 0.4282 oz. ASW, 30 mm.
Subject: Anniversary - Independence Day **Obv:** Value within dome design **Rev:** Arch above text **Rev. Insc.:** Love Thy Neighbor, As Thyself **Edge:** Plain

Date	Mintage	F	VF	XF	Unc	BU
JE5760-2000(u) Prooflike	2,516	—	—	—	—	25.00

KM# 339   NEW SHEQEL
14.4000 g., 0.9250 Silver 0.4282 oz. ASW **Subject:** Biblical - Joseph and His Brothers **Obv:** Value and text **Rev:** Joseph standing before sheaves of wheat into his brothers **Edge:** Plain

Date	Mintage	F	VF	XF	Unc	BU
JE5760-2000(u) Prooflike	2,249	—	—	—	—	25.00

KM# 347   NEW SHEQEL
14.4000 g., 0.9250 Silver 0.4282 oz. ASW, 30 mm.
Subject: Wildlife **Obv:** Acacia tree and value **Rev:** Ibex **Edge:** Plain

Date	Mintage	F	VF	XF	Unc	BU
JE5761-2000(u) Prooflike	2,000	—	—	—	—	25.00

KM# 348   NEW SHEQEL
3.4600 g., 0.9000 Gold 0.1001 oz. AGW, 18 mm.
Subject: Wildlife **Obv:** Acacia tree **Rev:** Ibex **Edge:** Reeded

Date	Mintage	F	VF	XF	Unc	BU
JE5761-2000(u) Proof	700	Value: 375				

KM# 162   2 SHEQALIM
28.8000 g., 0.8500 Silver 0.7870 oz. ASW **Subject:** Hanukka **Obv:** Value, partial feather and menorah flanked by sprigs **Rev:** Ashkenaz lamp

Date	Mintage	F	VF	XF	Unc	BU
JE5746-1985(b) Proof	9,225	Value: 25.00				

KM# 165   2 NEW SHEQALIM
28.8000 g., 0.8500 Silver 0.7870 oz. ASW **Subject:** 38th Anniversary of Independence **Obv:** Value, partial rainbow and menorah **Rev:** Artistic designs

Date	Mintage	F	VF	XF	Unc	BU
JE5746-1986(p) Proof	7,344	Value: 25.00				

KM# 176   2 NEW SHEQALIM
28.8000 g., 0.8500 Silver 0.7870 oz. ASW **Subject:** Hanukka **Obv:** Value and text **Rev:** Algerian lamp

Date	Mintage	F	VF	XF	Unc	BU
JE5747-1986(f) Proof	8,343	Value: 30.00				

KM# 178   2 NEW SHEQALIM
28.8000 g., 0.8500 Silver 0.7870 oz. ASW **Subject:** 20th Anniversary - United Jerusalem **Obv:** Stylized value **Rev:** Circular city within numeral value

Date	Mintage	F	VF	XF	Unc	BU
JE5747-1987(u) Proof	7,788	Value: 22.00				

KM# 184   2 NEW SHEQALIM
28.8000 g., 0.8500 Silver 0.7870 oz. ASW **Subject:** Hanukka **Obv:** Value above text **Rev:** English lamp

Date	Mintage	F	VF	XF	Unc	BU
JE5748-1987(d) Proof	8,039	Value: 30.00				

KM# 192   2 NEW SHEQALIM
28.8000 g., 0.8500 Silver 0.7870 oz. ASW **Subject:** Hanukka **Obv:** Value above text **Rev:** Tunisian lamp

Date	Mintage	F	VF	XF	Unc	BU
JE5749-1988(u) Proof	7,110	Value: 30.00				

KM# 186   2 NEW SHEQALIM
28.8000 g., 0.8500 Silver 0.7870 oz. ASW **Subject:** 40th Anniversary of Independence **Obv:** Menorah flanked by sprigs to to upper left of stylized value **Rev:** Stylized figures of government within large numeral 40

Date	Mintage	F	VF	XF	Unc	BU
JE5748-1988(p) Proof	9,100	Value: 22.50				

KM# 200   2 NEW SHEQALIM
28.8000 g., 0.8500 Silver 0.7870 oz. ASW **Subject:** 41st Anniversary of Independence **Obv:** Value to left within horizontal lines **Rev:** Roe deer facing right among trees

Date	Mintage	F	VF	XF	Unc	BU
JE5749-1989(f) Proof	7,062	Value: 30.00				

KM# 206   2 NEW SHEQALIM
28.8000 g., 0.8500 Silver 0.7870 oz. ASW **Subject:** Hanukka **Obv:** Value at upper left above text **Rev:** Persian lamp

Date	Mintage	F	VF	XF	Unc	BU
JE5750-1989(m) Proof	6,282	Value: 40.00				

KM# 213   2 NEW SHEQALIM
28.8000 g., 0.8500 Silver 0.7870 oz. ASW **Subject:** 42nd Anniversary of Independence **Obv:** Linear value to right of menorah flanked by sprigs **Rev:** Archaeology

Date	Mintage	F	VF	XF	Unc	BU
JE5750-1990(f) Proof	5,457	Value: 40.00				

KM# 216 2 NEW SHEQALIM
28.8000 g., 0.8500 Silver 0.7870 oz. ASW **Subject:** Hanukka
Obv: Value at lower left **Rev:** Cochin lamp

Date	Mintage	F	VF	XF	Unc	BU
JE5751-1990(f)	5,383	Value: 45.00				
Proof						

KM# 219 2 NEW SHEQALIM
28.8000 g., 0.9250 Silver 0.8565 oz. ASW **Subject:** 43rd
Anniversary of Independence **Obv:** Value to left within shaded
diagonal lines **Rev:** Plane above stylized standing figures

Date	Mintage	F	VF	XF	Unc	BU
JE5751-1991(u)	6,695	Value: 35.00				
Proof						

KM# 221 2 NEW SHEQALIM
28.8000 g., 0.9250 Silver 0.8565 oz. ASW **Subject:** Wildlife
Obv: Trees and value **Rev:** Stylized dove and tree trunk

Date	Mintage	F	VF	XF	Unc	BU
JE5752-1991(f)	5,005	Value: 40.00				
Proof						

KM# 224 2 NEW SHEQALIM
28.8000 g., 0.9250 Silver 0.8565 oz. ASW **Series:** Judaic
Obv: Value and cup **Rev:** Kiddush cup

Date	Mintage	F	VF	XF	Unc	BU
JE5752-1991(f)	6,575	Value: 30.00				
Proof						

KM# 226 2 NEW SHEQALIM
28.8000 g., 0.9250 Silver 0.8565 oz. ASW **Subject:** 44th
Anniversary of Independence **Obv:** Value **Rev:** Scales above
arched doorway

Date	Mintage	F	VF	XF	Unc	BU
JE5752-1992(p)	4,486	Value: 50.00				
Proof						

KM# 228 2 NEW SHEQALIM
28.8000 g., 0.9250 Silver 0.8565 oz. ASW **Subject:** IX Paralympic
Games **Obv:** Value to right of menorah flanked by sprigs
Rev: Shaded star in center of horizontal lines to right and upper left

Date	Mintage	F	VF	XF	Unc	BU
JE5752-1992(f)	3,718	Value: 45.00				
Proof						

KM# 235 2 NEW SHEQALIM
28.8000 g., 0.9250 Silver 0.8565 oz. ASW **Obv:** Stylized design
with value at center **Rev:** Stylized design with inscription

Date	Mintage	F	VF	XF	Unc	BU
JE5752-1992(f)	4,622	Value: 35.00				
Proof						

KM# 232 2 NEW SHEQALIM
28.8000 g., 0.9250 Silver 0.8565 oz. ASW **Series:** Wildlife
Obv: Value at upper right of lillies **Rev:** Roe deer facing left

Date	Mintage	F	VF	XF	Unc	BU
JE5753-1992(p)	4,724	Value: 45.00				
Proof						

KM# 239 2 NEW SHEQALIM
28.8000 g., 0.9250 Silver 0.8565 oz. ASW **Series:** Judaic
Obv: Value at center right within diagonal lines, lit candles on
box at lower left **Rev:** Shabbat candles

Date	Mintage	F	VF	XF	Unc	BU
JE5753-1992(p)	4,975	Value: 35.00				
Proof						

KM# 241 2 NEW SHEQALIM
28.8000 g., 0.9250 Silver 0.8565 oz. ASW **Subject:** 45th
Anniversary of Independence **Obv:** Menorah flanked by sprigs
above value and date **Rev:** Tourism objects

Date	Mintage	F	VF	XF	Unc	BU
JE5753-1993(u)	4,570	Value: 40.00				
Proof						

KM# 248 2 NEW SHEQALIM
28.8000 g., 0.9250 Silver 0.8565 oz. ASW **Subject:** Revolt and
Heroism **Obv:** Diagonal dotted lines with value to upper left
Rev: Medal with diagonal dotted lines and star to left of flame

Date	Mintage	F	VF	XF	Unc	BU
JE5753-1993(u)	4,994	Value: 38.00				
Proof						

KM# 245 2 NEW SHEQALIM
28.8000 g., 0.9250 Silver 0.8565 oz. ASW **Series:** Wildlife
Obv: Apple tree sprig to lower left of value **Rev:** Buck and young
hart deer facing left

Date	Mintage	F	VF	XF	Unc	BU
JE5754-1993(f)	5,382	Value: 40.00				
Proof						

KM# 251   2 NEW SHEQALIM

28.8000 g., 0.9250 Silver 0.8565 oz. ASW **Series:** Judaic
Obv: Torah crown to left of value **Rev:** Havdalah spicebox

Date	Mintage	F	VF	XF	Unc	BU
JE5754-1993(f)	4,750	Value: 40.00				
Proof						

KM# 253   2 NEW SHEQALIM

28.8000 g., 0.9250 Silver 0.8565 oz. ASW
Subject: Environment **Rev:** World globe and flower

Date	Mintage	F	VF	XF	Unc	BU
JE5754-1994(f)	4,272	—	—	—	40.00	—
Proof						

KM# 257   2 NEW SHEQALIM

28.8000 g., 0.9250 Silver 0.8565 oz. ASW **Series:** Biblical
Subject: Abraham's willingness to sacrifice Isaac **Obv:** Value
above text to right of menorah flanked by sprigs **Rev:** Stylized
figures below angel

Date	Mintage	F	VF	XF	Unc	BU
JE5755-1994(u)	4,439	Value: 55.00				
Proof						

KM# 261   2 NEW SHEQALIM

28.8000 g., 0.9250 Silver 0.8565 oz. ASW **Subject:** Wildlife
Obv: Palm tree **Rev:** Leopard

Date	Mintage	F	VF	XF	Unc	BU
JE5755-1994(u)	4,283	Value: 45.00				
Proof						

KM# 264   2 NEW SHEQALIM

28.8000 g., 0.9250 Silver 0.8565 oz. ASW **Subject:** Anniversary
- Medicine **Obv:** Snake on a menorah **Rev:** Value, text and
menorah flanked by sprigs

Date	Mintage	F	VF	XF	Unc	BU
JE5755-1995(f)	3,698	Value: 50.00				
Proof						

KM# 268   2 NEW SHEQALIM

28.8000 g., 0.9250 Silver 0.8565 oz. ASW **Subject:** 50th
Anniversary - Defeat of Nazi Germany **Obv:** Value above text to
right of menorah flanked by sprigs **Rev:** Shaded v-shape with
state emblems within

Date	Mintage	F	VF	XF	Unc	BU
JE5755-1995(h)	5,808	Value: 45.00				
Proof						

KM# 272   2 NEW SHEQALIM

28.8000 g., 0.9250 Silver 0.8565 oz. ASW **Series:** F.A.O.
Obv: Barley stalks and value **Rev:** FAO logo and dates

Date	Mintage	F	VF	XF	Unc	BU
JE5755-1995(v)	3,945	Value: 65.00				
Proof						

KM# 279   2 NEW SHEQALIM

28.8000 g., 0.9250 Silver 0.8565 oz. ASW **Subject:** Peace
Treaty with Jordan **Obv:** Text divides value and state arms
Rev: Sprig divides text

Date	Mintage	F	VF	XF	Unc	BU
JE5755-1995(o)	3,536	Value: 45.00				
Proof						

KM# 282   2 NEW SHEQALIM

28.8000 g., 0.9250 Silver 0.8565 oz. ASW **Series:** Biblical
Subject: Solomon's Judgment **Obv:** Value above text
Rev: Medieval linear design

Date	Mintage	F	VF	XF	Unc	BU
JE5755-1995(f)	2,993	Value: 60.00				
Proof						

KM# 288   2 NEW SHEQALIM

28.8000 g., 0.9250 Silver 0.8565 oz. ASW **Subject:** Port of
Caesarea **Rev:** Ancient ship

Date	Mintage	F	VF	XF	Unc	BU
JE5755-1995(f)	2,560	Value: 45.00				

KM# 276   2 NEW SHEQALIM

28.8000 g., 0.9250 Silver 0.8565 oz. ASW **Series:** Wildlife
Obv: Value and grape cluster **Rev:** Fox

Date	Mintage	F	VF	XF	Unc	BU
JE5756-1995(v)	3,436	Value: 50.00				
Proof						

KM# 301   2 NEW SHEQALIM

28.8000 g., 0.9250 Silver 0.8565 oz. ASW **Subject:** Anniversary
- First Zionist Congress Centennial **Obv:** Value **Rev:** Half length
figure leaning on rail facing left

Date	Mintage	F	VF	XF	Unc	BU
JE5757-1997(u)	4,281	Value: 38.00				
Proof						

KM# 298   2 NEW SHEQALIM

28.8000 g., 0.9250 Silver 0.8565 oz. ASW **Obv:** National arms
and denomination **Rev:** Head of Yitzhak Rabin left

Date	Mintage	F	VF	XF	Unc	BU
JE5756-1996(u)	5,293	Value: 60.00				
Proof						

KM# 292   2 NEW SHEQALIM

28.8000 g., 0.9250 Silver 0.8565 oz. ASW **Subject:** Wildlife
Obv: Value **Rev:** Nightingale

Date	Mintage	F	VF	XF	Unc	BU
JE5757-1996(v)	2,500	Value: 40.00				
Proof						

KM# 295   2 NEW SHEQALIM

28.8000 g., 0.9250 Silver 0.8565 oz. ASW **Subject:** Biblical
Obv: Value above text, state arms and star design at left
Rev: Miriam and the women

Date	Mintage	F	VF	XF	Unc	BU
JE5757-1996(u)	2,568	Value: 75.00				
Proof						

KM# 308 2 NEW SHEQALIM
28.8000 g., 0.9250 Silver 0.8565 oz. ASW **Subject:** Wildlife
Obv: Lion walking right **Rev:** Pomegranates at upper left of value

Date	Mintage	F	VF	XF	Unc	BU
JE5758-1997(u)	2,277	Value: 55.00				
Proof						

KM# 317 2 NEW SHEQALIM
28.8000 g., 0.9250 Silver 0.8565 oz. ASW **Subject:** Biblical - Noah's Ark **Obv:** Dove, rainbow and value **Rev:** Noah releasing dove

Date	Mintage	F	VF	XF	Unc	BU
JE5758-1998(u)	2,164	Value: 60.00				
Proof						

KM# 322 2 NEW SHEQALIM
28.8000 g., 0.9250 Silver 0.8565 oz. ASW **Subject:** Wildlife
Obv: Fir tree and value **Rev:** Stork

Date	Mintage	F	VF	XF	Unc	BU
JE5759-1998(u)	2,500	Value: 45.00				
Proof						

KM# 311 2 NEW SHEQALIM
28.8000 g., 0.9250 Silver 0.8565 oz. ASW **Subject:** 50th Anniversary of Independence **Obv:** Value to right of menorah flanked by sprigs above text **Rev:** Flag within stars

Date	Mintage	F	VF	XF	Unc	BU
JE5758-1998(u)	8,279	Value: 40.00				
Proof						

KM# 326 2 NEW SHEQALIM
28.8000 g., 0.9250 Silver 0.8565 oz. ASW, 38.7 mm.
Subject: Anniversary - High Tech in Israel **Obv:** Value and 01 computer code **Rev:** 10 computer code as bouquet

Date	Mintage	F	VF	XF	Unc	BU
JE5759-1999(u)	1,850	Value: 40.00				
Proof						

KM# 329 2 NEW SHEQALIM
28.8000 g., 0.9250 Silver 0.8565 oz. ASW **Obv:** Value and olive branch **Rev:** Year 2000 motif incorporating dove with olive branch **Edge:** The Millennium

Date	Mintage	F	VF	XF	Unc	BU
JE5759-1999(u)	4,092	Value: 40.00				
Proof						

KM# 334 2 NEW SHEQALIM
28.8000 g., 0.9250 Silver 0.8565 oz. ASW **Series:** Biblical
Obv: Menorah, value and date among stars above text
Rev: Abraham looking at stars

Date	Mintage	F	VF	XF	Unc	BU
JE5759-1999(o)	5,843	Value: 55.00				
Proof						

KM# 337 2 NEW SHEQALIM
28.8000 g., 0.9250 Silver 0.8565 oz. ASW, 38.7 mm.
Subject: Anniversary - Independence Day **Obv:** Value **Rev:** Arch above inscription **Rev. Insc.:** Love Thy Neighbor, As Thyself
Edge: Plain

Date	Mintage	F	VF	XF	Unc	BU
JE5760-2000(u)	2,258	Value: 45.00				
Proof						

KM# 340 2 NEW SHEQALIM
28.8000 g., 0.9250 Silver 0.8565 oz. ASW, 38.7 mm.
Subject: Biblical - Joseph and His Brothers **Obv:** Denomination **Rev:** Joseph standing before sheaves of wheat into brothers
Edge: Reeded

Date	Mintage	F	VF	XF	Unc	BU
JE5760-2000(u)	2,100	Value: 50.00				
Proof						

KM# 170 5 NEW SHEQALIM
8.6300 g., 0.9000 Gold 0.2497 oz. AGW **Series:** Holyland Sites
Rev: Akko

Date	Mintage	F	VF	XF	Unc	BU
JE5747-1986(b)	2,800	Value: 285				
Proof						

KM# 182 5 NEW SHEQALIM
8.6300 g., 0.9000 Gold 0.2497 oz. AGW **Series:** Holyland Sites
Obv: Value **Rev:** Jericho to left of menorah and palm trees

Date	Mintage	F	VF	XF	Unc	BU
JE5748-1987(o)	4,000	Value: 285				
Proof						

KM# 190 5 NEW SHEQALIM
8.6300 g., 0.9000 Gold 0.2497 oz. AGW **Series:** Holyland Sites
Obv: Value **Rev:** Caesarea

Date	Mintage	F	VF	XF	Unc	BU
JE5749-1988(o)	3,454	Value: 285				
Proof						

KM# 204 5 NEW SHEQALIM
8.6300 g., 0.9000 Gold 0.2497 oz. AGW **Series:** Holyland Sites
Obv: Value **Rev:** Jaffa Harbor

Date	Mintage	F	VF	XF	Unc	BU
JE5750-1989(o)	2,402	Value: 285				
Proof						

KM# 207 5 NEW SHEQALIM
8.1800 g., Copper-Nickel, 24 mm. **Obv:** Value **Rev:** Ancient column capitol **Edge:** Plain

Date	Mintage	F	VF	XF	Unc	BU
JE5750 (1990)(f)	15,000,000	—	—	—	3.75	—
JE5751 (1991)(j)	324,000	—	—	3.00	5.00	—
JE5752 (1992)(j)	413,000	—	—	3.00	5.00	—
JE5754 (1994)(v)	2,016,000	—	—	—	3.75	—
JE5755 (1995)(v)	2,160,000	—	—	—	3.75	—
JE5757 (1997)(u)	2,160,000	—	—	—	3.75	—
JE5757 (1997)(v)	2,160,000	—	—	—	3.75	—
JE5758 (1998)(h)	2,160,000	—	—	—	3.75	—
JE5759 (1999)(h)	2,160,000	—	—	—	3.75	—
JE5759 (1999)(u)	2,160,000	—	—	—	3.75	—
JE5760 (2000)(v)	4,464,000	—	—	—	3.75	—

KM# 208 5 NEW SHEQALIM
8.2000 g., Copper-Nickel, 24 mm. **Obv:** Value **Rev:** Bust of Levi Eshlol facing

Date	Mintage	F	VF	XF	Unc	BU
JE5750 (1990)(f)	1,500,000	—	—	2.50	6.00	—

KM# 211 5 NEW SHEQALIM
8.6300 g., 0.9000 Gold 0.2497 oz. AGW **Series:** Holyland Sites
Obv: Value **Rev:** Sea of Galilee map

Date	Mintage	F	VF	XF	Unc	BU
JE5751-1990(o)	1,935	Value: 350				
Proof						

KM# 217 5 NEW SHEQALIM
8.1800 g., Copper-Nickel, 24 mm. **Obv:** Value, small menorah and inscription Hanukka **Rev:** Ancient column capitol **Note:** Coins dated JE5754-5769 have the Star of David mint mark; the JE5751-5753 coins do not.

Date	Mintage	F	VF	XF	Unc	BU
JE5751 (1991)(j)	500,000	—	—	2.00	4.00	—
JE5752 (1992)(j)	486,000	—	—	2.00	4.00	—
JE5753 (1993)(j)	500,000	—	—	2.00	4.00	—
JE5754 (1994)(u)	12,000	—	—	—	4.00	—
Note: In sets only						
JE5755 (1995)(u)	10,000	—	—	—	4.00	—
Note: In sets only						
JE5756 (1996)(u)	7,500	—	—	—	4.00	—
Note: In sets only						
JE5757 (1997)(u)	7,500	—	—	—	4.00	—
Note: In sets only						
JE5758 (1998)(u)	10,000	—	—	—	4.00	—
Note: In sets only						
JE5759 (1999)(u)	6,000	—	—	—	5.00	—
Note: In sets only						

Date	Mintage	F	VF	XF	Unc	BU
JE5760 (2000)(u)	5,000	—	—	—	5.00	
Note: In sets only						
JE5761 (2001)(u)	4,000	—	—	—	7.00	
Note: In sets only						

KM# 222 5 NEW SHEQALIM
8.6300 g., 0.9000 Gold 0.2497 oz. AGW **Subject:** Wildlife
Obv: Cedar trees and value **Rev:** Dove and tree trunk within legend

Date	Mintage	F	VF	XF	Unc	BU
JE5752-1991(o)	2,000	Value: 300				
Proof						

KM# 229 5 NEW SHEQALIM
8.6300 g., 0.9000 Gold 0.2497 oz. AGW **Subject:** IX Paralympic Games **Obv:** Value at center with half horizontal lines at right **Rev:** Shaded star within horizontal lines

Date	Mintage	F	VF	XF	Unc	BU
JE5752-1992(u)	1,629	Value: 400				
Proof						

KM# 236 5 NEW SHEQALIM
8.6300 g., 0.9000 Gold 0.2497 oz. AGW **Subject:** B'nai B'rith **Obv:** Stylized design with value at upper left **Rev:** Stylized design with inscription

Date	Mintage	F	VF	XF	Unc	BU
JE5753-1992(u)	2,305	Value: 325				
Proof						

KM# 233 5 NEW SHEQALIM
8.6300 g., 0.9000 Gold 0.2497 oz. AGW **Series:** Wildlife **Obv:** Value at upper right of lily **Rev:** Roe deer facing left

Date	Mintage	F	VF	XF	Unc	BU
JE5753-1992(p)	2,150	Value: 285				
Proof						

KM# 237 5 NEW SHEQALIM
8.2000 g., Copper-Nickel **Obv:** Value **Rev:** Bust of Chiam Weizmann facing

Date	Mintage	F	VF	XF	Unc	BU
JE5753 (1993)(j)	1,500,000	—	—	—	5.00	

KM# 246 5 NEW SHEQALIM
8.6300 g., 0.9000 Gold 0.2497 oz. AGW **Series:** Wildlife **Obv:** Value at upper right of apple tree sprig **Rev:** Buck and young hart

Date	Mintage	F	VF	XF	Unc	BU
JE5754-1993(u)	1,782	Value: 285				
Proof						

KM# 254 5 NEW SHEQALIM
8.6300 g., 0.9000 Gold 0.2497 oz. AGW **Series:** Independence Day **Subject:** Environment **Obv:** Value **Rev:** World globe within flower

Date	Mintage	F	VF	XF	Unc	BU
JE5754-1994(sa)	1,407	Value: 300				
Proof						

KM# 262 5 NEW SHEQALIM
8.6300 g., 0.9000 Gold 0.2497 oz. AGW **Subject:** Wildlife **Obv:** Palm tree and value **Rev:** Leopard

Date	Mintage	F	VF	XF	Unc	BU
JE5755-1994(o)	1,355	Value: 300				
Proof						

KM# 265 5 NEW SHEQALIM
8.6300 g., 0.9000 Gold 0.2497 oz. AGW **Series:** Independence Day **Subject:** Anniversary - Medicine **Obv:** Snake on a menorah **Rev:** Value

Date	Mintage	F	VF	XF	Unc	BU
JE5755-1995(o)	1,147	Value: 350				
Proof						

KM# 277 5 NEW SHEQALIM
8.6300 g., 0.9000 Gold 0.2497 oz. AGW **Subject:** Wildlife **Obv:** Value and grape cluster **Rev:** Fox

Date	Mintage	F	VF	XF	Unc	BU
JE5756-1995(u)	877	Value: 375				
Proof						

KM# 293 5 NEW SHEQALIM
8.6300 g., 0.9000 Gold 0.2497 oz. AGW **Subject:** Wildlife **Obv:** Fig leaves and value **Rev:** Nightingale

Date	Mintage	F	VF	XF	Unc	BU
JE5757-1996(v)	805	Value: 425				
Proof						

KM# 309 5 NEW SHEQALIM
8.6300 g., 0.9000 Gold 0.2497 oz. AGW **Subject:** Wildlife **Obv:** Pomegranates and value **Rev:** Lion walking right

Date	Mintage	F	VF	XF	Unc	BU
JE5758-1997(u)	742	Value: 375				
Proof						

KM# 323 5 NEW SHEQALIM
8.6300 g., 0.9000 Gold 0.2497 oz. AGW **Subject:** Wildlife **Obv:** Fir trees and value **Rev:** Stork

Date	Mintage	F	VF	XF	Unc	BU
JE5759-1998(u)	615	Value: 400				
Proof						

KM# 350 5 NEW SHEQALIM
8.6300 g., 0.9000 Gold 0.2497 oz. AGW, 22 mm. **Subject:** Wildlife **Obv:** Acacia tree **Rev:** Ibex **Edge:** Reeded

Date	Mintage	F	VF	XF	Unc	BU
JE5761-2000(u)	600	Value: 425				
Proof						

KM# 166 10 NEW SHEQALIM
17.2800 g., 0.9000 Gold 0.5000 oz. AGW **Subject:** 38th Anniversary of Independence **Obv:** Value **Rev:** Stylized designs

Date	Mintage	F	VF	XF	Unc	BU
JE5746-1986(d)	2,485	Value: 500				
Proof						

KM# 179 10 NEW SHEQALIM
17.2800 g., 0.9000 Gold 0.5000 oz. AGW **Subject:** 39th Anniversary of Independence, 20th Anniversary of United Jerusalem

Date	Mintage	F	VF	XF	Unc	BU
JE5747-1987(p)	3,200	Value: 500				
Proof						

KM# 187 10 NEW SHEQALIM
17.2800 g., 0.9000 Gold 0.5000 oz. AGW **Subject:** 40th Anniversary of Independence **Obv:** Menorah within stylized value **Rev:** Stylized figures of government within large numeral 40

Date	Mintage	F	VF	XF	Unc	BU
JE5748-1988(m)	4,575	Value: 500				
Proof						

KM# 201 10 NEW SHEQALIM
17.2800 g., 0.9000 Gold 0.5000 oz. AGW **Subject:** 41st Anniversary of Independence **Rev:** Gazelle in forest, legend at left

Date	Mintage	F	VF	XF	Unc	BU
JE5749-1989(o)	2,743	Value: 500				
Proof						

KM# 214 10 NEW SHEQALIM
17.2800 g., 0.9000 Gold 0.5000 oz. AGW **Subject:** 42nd Anniversary of Independence **Obv:** Menorah to left of large linear value **Rev:** Archaeology

Date	Mintage	F	VF	XF	Unc	BU
JE5750-1990(p)	1,815	Value: 625				
Proof						

KM# 230 10 NEW SHEQALIM
17.2800 g., 0.9000 Gold 0.5000 oz. AGW **Subject:** 43rd Anniversary of Independence **Obv:** Value within shaded diagonal lines **Rev:** Plane above stylized standing figures

Date	Mintage	F	VF	XF	Unc	BU
JE5751-1991	2,236	Value: 500				
Proof						

KM# 227 10 NEW SHEQALIM
17.2800 g., 0.9000 Gold 0.5000 oz. AGW **Subject:** 44th Anniversary of Independence **Obv:** Value **Rev:** Scales above arched doorway **Note:** Edge varieties exist.

Date	Mintage	F	VF	XF	Unc	BU
JE5752-1992(p)	1,750	Value: 675				
Proof						

Note: Narrow spaced edge reeding

| JE5752-1992(u) | 375 | Value: 2,000 | | | | |
| Proof | | | | | | |

Note: Wide spaced edge reeding

KM# 242 10 NEW SHEQALIM
17.2800 g., 0.9000 Gold 0.5000 oz. AGW **Series:** Independence Day **Subject:** Tourism **Obv:** Value **Rev:** Tourism objects

Date	Mintage	F	VF	XF	Unc	BU
JE5753-1993(u)	1,944	Value: 500				
Proof						

KM# 249 10 NEW SHEQALIM
17.2800 g., 0.9000 Gold 0.5000 oz. AGW **Subject:** Revolt and Heroism **Obv:** Value within beaded diagonal lines **Rev:** Medal with star within beaded diagonal lines to left of flame

Date	Mintage	F	VF	XF	Unc	BU
JE5753-1993(u)	1,583	Value: 500				
Proof						

KM# 255 10 NEW SHEQALIM
17.2800 g., 0.9000 Gold 0.5000 oz. AGW **Series:** Independence Day **Subject:** Environment **Obv:** Slanted value **Rev:** World globe within flower

Date	Mintage	F	VF	XF	Unc	BU
JE5754-1994(sa)	1,482	Value: 550				
Proof						

KM# 258 10 NEW SHEQALIM
17.2800 g., 0.9000 Gold 0.5000 oz. AGW **Subject:** Biblical **Rev:** Abraham's willingness to sacrifice Isaac

Date	Mintage	F	VF	XF	Unc	BU
JE5755-1994(o)	1,209	Value: 650				
Proof						

KM# 266 10 NEW SHEQALIM
17.2800 g., 0.9000 Gold 0.5000 oz. AGW **Series:** Independence Day **Subject:** Anniversary - Medicine **Obv:** Value **Rev:** Snake on a menorah

Date	Mintage	F	VF	XF	Unc	BU
JE5755-1995(o)	1,230	Value: 600				
Proof						

KM# 269 10 NEW SHEQALIM
16.9600 g., 0.9170 Gold 0.5000 oz. AGW **Subject:** 50th Anniversary - Defeat of Nazi Germany **Obv:** Value above text to right of menorah flanked by sprigs **Rev:** Flag and emblems within v-shaped design

Date	Mintage	F	VF	XF	Unc	BU
JE5755-1995(h)	1,742	Value: 600				
Proof						

KM# 270 10 NEW SHEQALIM
7.0000 g., Bi-Metallic Aureate bonded Bronze center in Nickel bonded Steel ring, 22.95 mm. **Obv:** Value, vertical lines and text within circle **Rev:** Palm tree and baskets within half beaded circle **Edge:** Reeded

Date	Mintage	F	VF	XF	Unc	BU
JE5755 (1995)(u)	28,224,000	—	—	—	5.00	—

KM# 273 10 NEW SHEQALIM
Bi-Metallic Aureate bonded Bronze center in Nickel bonded Steel ring, 22.5 mm. **Obv:** Value, text and vertical lines within circle **Rev:** Bust of Golda Meir facing at right within vertical lines and circle

Date	Mintage	F	VF	XF	Unc	BU
JE5755 (1995)(u)	1,584,000	—	—	—	10.00	—

KM# 280 10 NEW SHEQALIM
16.9600 g., 0.9170 Gold 0.5000 oz. AGW, 30 mm. **Subject:** Peace Treaty with Jordan **Edge:** Reeded

Date	Mintage	F	VF	XF	Unc	BU
JE5755-1995(o)	1,451	Value: 550				

KM# 289 10 NEW SHEQALIM
16.9600 g., 0.9170 Gold 0.5000 oz. AGW, 30 mm. **Obv:** Anchor to lower left of value and text **Rev:** Port of Caesarea, ancient ship **Edge:** Reeded

Date	Mintage	F	VF	XF	Unc	BU
JE5755-1995(o)	625	Value: 650				
Proof						

KM# 283 10 NEW SHEQALIM
17.2800 g., 0.9000 Gold 0.5000 oz. AGW, 30 mm. **Subject:** Biblical - Solomon's Judgment **Obv:** Value above text **Rev:** Medieval linear design **Edge:** Reeded

Date	Mintage	F	VF	XF	Unc	BU
JE5756-1995(o)	961	Value: 650				
Proof						

KM# 315 10 NEW SHEQALIM
7.0000 g., Bi-Metallic Aureate bonded Bronze center in Nickel bonded Steel ring, 22.5 mm. **Subject:** Hanukka **Obv:** Value, text and menorah within circle and vertical lines **Rev:** Palm tree and baskets within half beaded circle

Date	Mintage	F	VF	XF	Unc	BU
JE5756 (1996)(u)	7,500	—	—	—	7.00	—

Note: In sets only

| JE5757 (1997)(u) | 7,500 | — | — | — | 7.00 | — |

Note: In sets only

| JE5758 (1998)(u) | 10,000 | — | — | — | 7.00 | — |

Note: In sets only

| JE5759 (1999)(u) | 6,000 | — | — | — | 8.00 | — |

Note: In sets only

| JE5760 (2000)(u) | 5,000 | — | — | — | 9.00 | — |

Note: In sets only

KM# 285 10 NEW SHEQALIM
16.9600 g., 0.9170 Gold 0.5000 oz. AGW **Subject:** Anniversary - Jerusalem's Third Millennium **Obv:** State arms left of large value **Rev:** Inscription at center

Date	Mintage	F	VF	XF	Unc	BU
JE5756-1996(sa)	1,642	Value: 650				
Proof						

KM# 296 10 NEW SHEQALIM
17.2800 g., 0.9000 Gold 0.5000 oz. AGW **Subject:** Biblical **Obv:** Value above text, state arms and star design at left **Rev:** Miriam and the women

Date	Mintage	F	VF	XF	Unc	BU
JE5757-1996(u)	855	Value: 725				
Proof						

KM# 302 10 NEW SHEQALIM
16.9600 g., 0.9170 Gold 0.5000 oz. AGW, 30 mm. **Subject:** Anniversary - First Zionist Congress Centennial **Obv:** Denomination **Rev:** Portrait of Herzl **Edge:** Reeded

Date	Mintage	F	VF	XF	Unc	BU
JE5757-1997(u)	1,326	Value: 550				
Proof						

KM# 312 10 NEW SHEQALIM
15.5500 g., 0.9990 Gold 0.4994 oz. AGW, 30 mm. **Subject:** 50th Anniversary of Independence **Obv:** Value **Rev:** Flag **Edge:** Reeded

Date	Mintage	F	VF	XF	Unc	BU
JE5758-1998(u)	2,406	Value: 520				
Proof						

KM# 319 10 NEW SHEQALIM
17.2800 g., 0.9000 Gold 0.5000 oz. AGW, 30 mm. **Subject:** Biblical - Noah's Ark **Obv:** Rainbow, dove and value **Rev:** Noah releasing dove from ark **Edge:** Reeded

Date	Mintage	F	VF	XF	Unc	BU
JE5758-1998(u)	744	Value: 750				
Proof						

KM# 327 10 NEW SHEQALIM
16.9600 g., 0.9170 Gold 0.5000 oz. AGW, 30 mm.
Subject: Anniversary - High-Tech in Israel **Obv:** Value and 01 computer code **Rev:** 01 computer code as bouquet

Date	Mintage	F	VF	XF	Unc	BU
JE5759-1999(u) Proof	751	Value: 750				

KM# 330 10 NEW SHEQALIM
16.9600 g., 0.9170 Gold 0.5000 oz. AGW **Subject:** The Millennium Coin **Obv:** Value and olive branch **Rev:** Year 2000 motif incorporating dove with olive branch

Date	Mintage	F	VF	XF	Unc	BU
JE5759-1999(u) Proof	1,859	Value: 600				

KM# 335 10 NEW SHEQALIM
17.2800 g., 0.9000 Gold 0.5000 oz. AGW, 30 mm.
Series: Biblical **Obv:** Arms above denomination **Rev:** Abraham gazing at the stars **Edge:** Reeded

Date	Mintage	F	VF	XF	Unc	BU
JE5759-1999(u) Proof	687	Value: 700				

KM# 338 10 NEW SHEQALIM
16.9600 g., 0.9170 Gold 0.5000 oz. AGW **Subject:** Anniversary - Independence Day **Obv:** Value **Rev:** Arch above inscription **Rev. Insc.:** Love Thy Neighbor, As Thyself **Edge:** Reeded

Date	Mintage	F	VF	XF	Unc	BU
JE5760-2000(u) Proof	794	Value: 725				

KM# 341 10 NEW SHEQALIM
16.9600 g., 0.9170 Gold 0.5000 oz. AGW **Series:** Biblical **Obv:** Value **Rev:** Joseph standing before sheaves of wheat into his brothers **Edge:** Reeded

Date	Mintage	F	VF	XF	Unc	BU
JE5760-2000(u) Proof	700	Value: 700				

KM# 299 20 NEW SHEQALIM
31.1035 g., 0.9990 Gold 0.9990 oz. AGW **Obv:** Menorah flanked by sprigs above text, value and date **Rev:** Yitzhak Rabin facing left

Date	Mintage	F	VF	XF	Unc	BU
JE5757-1996(va) Proof	1,949	Value: 1,000				

KM# 313 20 NEW SHEQALIM
31.1035 g., 0.9990 Gold 0.9990 oz. AGW **Subject:** 50th Anniversary of Independence **Obv:** Value **Rev:** Flag

Date	Mintage	F	VF	XF	Unc	BU
JE5758-1998(u) Proof	2,345	Value: 1,000				

KM# 286 30 NEW SHEQALIM
155.5175 g., 0.9990 Silver 4.9948 oz. ASW, 65 mm. **Subject:** Anniversary - Jerusalem's Third Millennium **Obv:** State arms left of value **Rev:** Inscription at center **Note:** Illustration reduced.

Date	Mintage	F	VF	XF	Unc	BU
JE5756-1996(f) Proof	2,929	Value: 185				

PATTERNS

KM#	Date	Mintage	Identification	Mkt Val
Pn1	1960	2	Agora. 8 fat and wide grains. Large 9.50mm 1 and date.	7,500
Pn2	1960	4	Agora. 8 thin and narrow grains. Small 9.00mm 1 and large date.	7,500
Pn3	1960	1	Agora. 8 thin and narrow grains. Large 9.50mm 1 and date.	—
Pn4	1960	1	Agora. Aluminum. 8 fate and wide grains. Small 9 mm 1. Struck as coin turn.	6,000
Pn5	JE5722-1962	3	Lira. Copper-Nickel. As KM#38 but mis-spelling of Hanukka in Hebrew. Letter "Nun" instead of "Kof"	2,500

PIEFORTS

KM#	Date	Mintage	Identification	Mkt Val
P1	JE5741 (1981)	30,217	New Agora. Copper-Nickel. 4.2000 g. 15 mm. KM#106.	2.00
P2	JE5741 (1981)	30,217	5 New Agorot. Copper-Nickel. 6.3000 g. 18.5 mm. KM#107.	2.00
P3	JE5741 (1981)	30,217	10 New Agorot. Bronze. 4.6000 g. 16 mm. KM#108.	2.50
P4	JE5741 (1981)	30,217	1/2 Sheqel. Copper-Nickel. 6.8000 g. 20 mm. KM#109.	2.50
P5	JE5741 (1981)	30,217	Sheqel. Copper-Nickel. KM111.	3.50

Note: P1-5 were struck at the Bern Mint

KM#	Date	Mintage	Identification	Mkt Val
P6	JE5742 (1982)	18,735	New Agora. Copper-Nickel. 4.2000 g. 15 mm. KM#106	2.00
P7	JE5742 (1982)	19,735	5 New Agorot. Copper-Nickel. 6.3000 g. 18.5 mm. KM#107.	2.00
P8	JE5742 (1982)	18,735	10 New Agorot. Bronze. 4.6000 g. 16 mm. KM#108.	2.50
P9	JE5742 (1982)	21,735	1/2 Sheqel. Copper-Nickel. 6.8000 g. 20 mm. KM#109.	2.50
P10	JE5742 (1982)	19,735	Sheqel. Copper-Nickel. 11.1000 g. 23 mm. KM#111.	3.00
P11	JE5742 (1982)	20,735	5 Sheqalim. Aluminum-Bronze. 12.2000 g. 24 mm. KM#118.	3.50
P12	JE5743 (1983)	17,177	New Agora. Copper-Nickel. 4.2000 g. 15 mm. Plain edge. KM#106.	1.00
P13	JE5743 (1983)	17,177	5 New Agorot. Copper-Nickel. 6.3000 g. 18.5 mm. Plain edge. KM#107.	1.50
P14	JE5743 (1983)	17,177	10 New Agorot. Bronze. 4.6000 g. 16 mm. KM#108.	1.50
P15	JE5743 (1983)	17,177	1/2 Sheqel. Copper-Nickel. 6.8000 g. 20 mm. KM#109.	2.00
P16	JE5743 (1983)	17,177	Sheqel. Copper-Nickel. 11.1000 g. 23 mm. KM#111.	2.00
P17	JE5743 (1983)	17,177	5 Sheqalim. Aluminum-Bronze. 13.0000 g. 24 mm. KM#118.	2.50
P18	JE5743 (1983)	17,177	10 Sheqalim. Copper-Nickel. 16.5000 g. 26 mm. KM#119.	3.00
P19	JE5744 (1984)	15,572	Agora. Copper-Nickel. 4.2000 g. 15 mm. Plain edge. KM#107.	1.00
P20	JE5744 (1984)	15,572	5 New Agorot. Copper-Nickel. 6.3000 g. 18.5 mm. Plain edge. KM#107.	1.50
P21	JE5744 (1984)	15,572	10 New Agorot. Bronze. 4.6000 g. 16 mm. KM#108.	1.50
P22	JE5744 (1984)	15,572	1/2 Sheqel. Copper-Nickel. 6.8000 g. 20 mm. KM#109.	2.00
P23	JE5744 (1984)	15,572	Sheqel. Copper-Nickel. 11.1000 g. 23 mm. KM#111.	2.00
P24	JE5744 (1984)	15,572	5 Sheqalim. Aluminum-Bronze. 13.0000 g. 24 mm. KM#118.	2.50
P25	JE5744 (1984)	15,572	10 Sheqalim. Copper-Nickel. 16.5000 g. 26 mm. KM#119.	3.00

Note: P6-25 were struck at the Rome Mint

KM#	Date	Mintage	Identification	Mkt Val
P26	JE5745 (1985)	14,768	Sheqel. Copper-Nickel. 11.1000 g. 23 mm. KM#111.	2.00
P27	JE5745 (1985)	14,768	5 Sheqalim. Aluminum-Bronze. 13.0000 g. 24 mm. KM#118.	2.00
P28	JE5745 (1985)	14,768	10 Sheqalim. Copper-Nickel. 16.5000 g. 26 mm. KM#119.	2.50
P29	JE5745 (1985)	14,768	50 Sheqalim. Aluminum-Bronze. 19.5000 g. 28 mm. KM#139.	3.00
P30	JE5745 (1985)	14,768	100 Sheqalim. Copper-Nickel. 23.3000 g. 29 mm. KM#143.	3.50

Note: P26-30 were struck at the Bern Mint

KM#	Date	Mintage	Identification	Mkt Val
P31	JE5746 (1986)	12,665	Agora. Aluminum-Bronze. 4.4000 g. 17 mm. KM#156.	2.00
P32	JE5746 (1986)	12,665	5 Agorot. Aluminum-Bronze. 6.6000 g. 19.5 mm. KM#157.	3.00
P33	JE5746 (1986)	12,665	10 Agorot. Aluminum-Bronze. 8.8000 g. 22 mm. KM#158.	4.00
P34	JE5746 (1986)	12,665	1/2 New Sheqel. Aluminum-Bronze. 14.5000 g. 26 mm. KM#159.	5.00
P35	JE5746 (1986)	12,665	New Sheqel. 18.0000 Copper-Nickel. 8.5000 g. KM#160.	6.00

Note: P31-35 were struck at the Paris Mint

KM#	Date	Mintage	Identification	Mkt Val
P36	JE5747 (1987)	11,529	Agora. Aluminum-Bronze center. 4.4000 g.17 mm. KM#156.	2.00
P37	JE5747 (1987)	11,529	5 Agorot. Aluminum-Bronze. 6.6000 g. 19.5 mm. KM#157.	3.00
P38	JE5747 (1987)	11,529	10 Agorot. Aluminum-Bronze. 8.8000 g. 22 mm. KM#158.	4.00
P39	JE5747 (1987)	11,529	1/2 New Sheqel. Aluminum-Bronze. 14.5000 g. 26 mm. KM#159.	5.00
P40	JE5747 (1987)	11,529	New Sheqel. Copper-Nickel. 8.5000 g. 18 mm. KM#160.	6.00
PA41	JE5748 (1988)	12,027	Agora. Nickel. 4.8000 g. 17 mm. KM#193.	2.50
P41	JE5748 (1988)	12,027	5 Agorot. Nickel. 7.2500 g. 19.5 mm. KM#194.	3.50
P42	JE5748 (1988)	12,027	10 Agorot. Nickel. 9.6500 g. 22 mm. KM#195.	4.50
P43	JE5748 (1988)	12,027	1/2 New Sheqel. Nickel. 16.0000 g. 26 mm. KM#196.	5.50
P44	JE5748 (1988)	12,027	New Sheqel. Nickel. 8.5000 g. 18 mm. KM#197.	6.00

Note: P36-44 were struck at the Stuttgart Mint

KM#	Date	Mintage	Identification	Mkt Val
P45	JE5749 (1989)	9,622	Agora. Aluminum-Bronze. 4.4000 g. 17 mm. KM#156.	2.00
P46	JE5749 (1989)	9,622	5 Agorot. Aluminum-Bronze. 6.6000 g. 19.5 mm. KM#157.	3.00
P47	JE5749 (1989)	9,622	10 Agorot. Aluminum-Bronze. 8.8000 g. 22 mm. KM#158.	4.00
P48	JE5749 (1989)	9,622	1/2 New Sheqel. Aluminum-Bronze. 14.5000 g. 26 mm. KM#159.	5.00
P49	JE5749 (1989)	9,622	New Sheqel. Copper-Nickel. 8.5000 g. 18 mm. KM#160.	6.00
P50	JE5750 (1990)	7,038	Agora. Aluminum-Bronze. 4.4000 g. 17 mm. KM#156.	2.00
P51	JE5750 (1990)	7,038	5 Agorot. Bronze. 6.6000 g. 19.5 mm. KM#157.	3.00
P52	JE5750 (1990)	—	10 Agorot. Aluminum-Bronze. 14.5000 g. 26 mm. KM#158.	4.00
P53	JE5750 (1990)	—	1/2 New Sheqel. Bronze. KM159.	5.00
P54	JE5750 (1990)	7,038	New Sheqel. Copper-Nickel. 8.5000 g. 18 mm. KM#160.	5.00
P55	JE5750 (1990)	7,038	5 New Sheqalim. Copper-Nickel. 14.5000 g. 24 mm. KM#207.	6.00

Note: P45-55 were struck at the Stuttgart mint.

KM#	Date	Mintage	Identification	Mkt Val
P56	JE5751 (1991)	6,617	Agora. Aluminum-Bronze. 4.4000 g. 17 mm. KM#156.	2.00
P57	JE5751 (1991)	6,617	5 Agorot. Aluminum-Bronze. 6.6000 g. 19.5 mm. KM#157.	3.00
P58	JE5751 (1991)	6,617	10 Agorot. Aluminum-Bronze. 8.8000 g. 22 mm. KM#158.	4.00
P59	JE5751 (1991)	6,617	1/2 New Sheqel. Aluminum-Bronze. 14.5000 g. 26 mm. KM#159.	5.00
P60	JE5751 (1991)	6,617	New Sheqel. Copper-Nickel. 8.5000 g. 18 mm. KM#160.	6.00
P61	JE5751 (1991)	6,617	5 New Sheqalim. Copper-Nickel. 14.5000 g. 24 mm. KM207.	6.00
P62	JE5752 (1992)	6,617	Agora. Aluminum-Bronze. 4.4000 g. 17 mm. KM#156.	2.00
P63	JE5752 (1992)	6,339	5 Agorot. Aluminum-Bronze. 6.6000 g. 19.5 mm. KM#157.	3.00
P64	JE5752 (1992)	6,339	10 Agorot. Aluminum-Bronze. 8.8000 g. 22 mm. KM#158.	4.00
P65	JE5752 (1992)	6,339	1/2 New Sheqel. Aluminum-Bronze. 14.5000 g. 26 mm. KM159.	5.00
P66	JE5752 (1992)	6,339	New Sheqel. Copper-Nickel. 8.5000 g. 18 mm. KM#160.	6.00
P67	JE5752 (1992)	6,339	5 New Sheqalim. Copper-Nickel. 14.5000 g. 24 mm. KM207.	6.00
P68	JE5753 (1993)	7,993	Agora. Aluminum-Bronze. 4.4000 g. 17 mm. KM#156.	2.00
P69	JE5753 (1993)	7,993	5 Agorot. Aluminum-Bronze center. 6.6000 g.19.5 mm. KM#157.	3.00
P70	JE5753 (1993)	7,993	10 Agorot. Aluminum-Bronze. 8.8000 g. 22 mm. KM#158.	4.00
P71	JE5753 (1993)	7,993	1/2 New Sheqel. Aluminum-Bronze. 14.5000 g. 26 mm. KM#159.	5.00

KM#	Date	Mintage	Identification	Mkt Val
P72	JE5753 (1993)	7,993	New Sheqel. Copper-Nickel. 8.5000 g. 18 mm. KM#160.	6.00
P73	JE5753 (1993)	7,993	5 New Sheqalim. Copper-Nickel. 14.5000 g. 24 mm. KM#207.	6.00
P74	JE5754 (1994)	8,000	Agora. Aluminum-Bronze. 4.4000 g. 17 mm. KM#156.	3.00
P75	JE5754 (1994)	8,000	5 Agorot. Aluminum-Bronze. 6.6000 g. 19.5 mm. KM#157.	4.00
P76	JE5754 (1994)	8,000	10 Agorot. Aluminum-Bronze. 8.8000 g. 22 mm. KM#158.	5.00
P77	JE5754 (1994)	8,000	1/2 New Sheqel. Aluminum-Bronze. 14.5000 g. 26 mm. KM#159.	6.00
P78	JE5754 (1994)	8,000	1/2 New Sheqel. Copper-Aluminum-Nickel. 14.5000 g. 26 mm. Value. Flower. Plain edge. KM#368.	10.00
P79	JE5754 (1994)	8,000	New Sheqel. Copper-Nickel. 8.5000 g. 18 mm. KM#160.	7.00
P80	JE5754 (1994)	8,000	5 New Sheqalim. Copper-Nickel. 14.5000 g. 24 mm. KM#207.	9.00
P81	JE5755 (1995)	10,000	Agora. Aluminum-Bronze. 4.4000 g. 17 mm. KM#156.	2.00
P82	JE5755 (1995)	10,000	5 Agorot. Aluminum-Bronze. 6.6000 g. 19.35 mm. KM#157.	3.00
P83	JE5755 (1995)	10,000	10 Agorot. Aluminum-Bronze. 8.8000 g. 22 mm. KM#158.	4.00
P84	JE5755 (1995)	10,000	1/2 New Sheqel. Aluminum-Bronze. 14.5000 g. 26 mm. KM#159.	5.00
P85	JE5755 (1995)	10,000	1/2 New Sheqel. Copper-Aluminum-Nickel. 14.5000 g. 26 mm. Value. Medical symbols. Plain edge. KM#392.	10.00
P86	JE5755 (1995)	10,000	New Sheqel. Copper-Nickel. 8.5000 g. 18 mm. KM#160.	6.00
P87	JE5755 (1995)	10,000	5 New Sheqalim. Copper-Nickel. 14.5000 g. 24 mm. KM207.	8.00
P88	JE5755 (1995)	10,000	10 New Sheqalim. Bi-Metallic. 11.0000 g. 23 mm. KM#270.	12.00

Note: P56-88 were struck at the Utrecht mint

KM#	Date	Mintage	Identification	Mkt Val
P89	JE5756 (1996)	8,000	Agora. Aluminum-Bronze. 4.4000 g. 17 mm. KM#156.	2.00
P90	JE5756 (1996)	8,000	5 Agorot. Aluminum-Bronze. 6.6000 g. 19.5 mm. KM#157	3.00
P92	JE5756 (1996)	8,000	1/2 New Sheqel. Aluminum-Bronze. 14.5000 g. 26 mm. KM#159.	5.00
P93	JE5756 (1996)	8,000	1/2 New Sheqel. Copper-Aluminum-Nickel. 14.5000 g. 26 mm. Value. Hebrew inscription. Plain edge. KM#393.	10.00
P91	JE5756 (1996)	8,000	10 Agorot. Aluminum-Bronze. 8.8000 g. 22 mm. KM#158.	4.00
P94	JE5756 (1996)	8,000	New Sheqel. Copper-Nickel. 8.5000 g. 18 mm. KM#160.	6.00
P95	JE5756 (1996)	8,000	5 New Sheqalim. Copper-Nickel. 14.5000 g. 24 mm. KM#217.	8.00
P96	JE5756 (1996)	8,000	10 New Sheqalim. Bi-Metallic. 11.0000 g. 23 mm. KM#270.	12.00
P97	JE5757 (1997)	6,000	Agora. Aluminum-Bronze. 4.4000 g. 17 mm. KM#156.	2.00
P98	JE5757 (1997)	6,000	5 Agorot. Aluminum-Bronze. 6.6000 g. 19.5 mm. KM#157.	3.00
P99	JE5757 (1997)	6,000	10 Agorot. Aluminum-Bronze. 8.8000 g. 22 mm. KM#158.	4.00
P100	JE5757 (1997)	6,000	1/2 New Sheqel. Aluminum-Bronze. 11.5000 g. 26 mm. KM#159.	5.00
P101	JE5757- (1997)	6,000	1/2 New Sheqel. Copper-Aluminum-Nickel. 14.5000 g. 26 mm. KM#394.	12.00
P102	JE5757 (1997)	6,000	New Sheqel. Aluminum-Bronze. 8.5000 g. 18 mm. KM#160.	6.00
P103	JE5757 (1997)	6,000	5 New Sheqalim. Copper-Nickel. 14.5000 g. 24 mm. KM#207.	8.00
P104	JE5757 (1997)	6,000	10 New Sheqalim. Bi-Metallic. 11.0000 g. 23 mm. KM#270.	12.00
P110	JE5758 (1998)	8,000	New Sheqel. Copper-Nickel. 8.5000 g. 18 mm. KM#160.	6.00
P105	JE5758 (1998)	8,000	Agora. Aluminum-Bronze. 4.4000 g. 17 mm. KM#156.	2.00
P106	JE5758 (1998)	8,000	5 Agorot. Aluminum-Bronze. 6.6000 g. 19.5 mm. KM#157.	3.00
P107	JE5758 (1998)	8,000	10 Agorot. Aluminum-Bronze. 8.8000 g. 22 mm. KM#158.	4.00
P108	JE5758 (1998)	8,000	1/2 New Sheqel. Aluminum-Bronze. 14.5000 g. 26 mm. KM#159.	5.00
P109	JE5758 (1998)	8,000	1/2 New Sheqel. Copper-Aluminum-Nickel. 14.3300 g. 26.3 mm. Value. Flag and stars. Plain edge. KM#395.	10.00
P111	JE5758 (1998)	8,000	5 New Sheqalim. Copper-Nickel. 14.5000 g. 24 mm. KM#207.	8.00
P112	JE5758 (1998)	8,000	10 New Sheqalim. Bi-Metallic. 11.0000 g. 23 mm. KM#270.	12.00
P116	JE5759 (1999)	6,000	1/2 New Sheqel. Aluminum-Bronze. 14.5000 g. 26 mm. KM#159.	5.00
P113	JE5759 (1999)	6,000	Agora. Aluminum-Bronze. 4.4000 g. 17 mm. KM#156.	2.00
P114	JE5759 (1999)	6,000	5 Agorot. Aluminum-Bronze. 6.6000 g. 19.5 mm. KM#157.	3.00
P115	JE5759 (1999)	6,000	10 Agorot. Aluminum-Bronze. 8.8000 g. 22 mm. KM#158.	4.00
P117	JE5759 (1999)	6,000	1/2 New Sheqel. Copper-Aluminum-Nickel. 14.5000 g. 26 mm. High Tech KM#324.	12.00
P118	JE5759 (1999)	6,000	New Sheqel. Copper-Nickel. 8.5000 g. 18 mm. KM#160a	6.00
P119	JE5759 (1999)	6,000	5 New Sheqalim. Copper-Nickel. 14.5000 g. 24 mm. KM#207.	8.00
P120	JE5759 (1999)	6,000	10 New Sheqalim. Bi-Metallic. 11.0000 g. 23 mm. KM#270.	12.00
P121	JE5760 (2000)	4,000	Agora. Aluminum-Bronze. 4.2300 g. 16.9 mm. Plain edge. KM#156.	2.00
P122	JE5760 (2000)	4,000	5 Agorot. Aluminum-Bronze. 6.3100 g. 19.4 mm. Plain edge. KM#157.	3.00
P123	JE5760 (2000)	4,000	10 Agorot. Aluminum-Bronze. 8.6000 g. 21.9 mm. Plain edge. KM#158.	4.00
P124	JE5760 (2000)	4,000	1/2 New Sheqel. Aluminum-Bronze. 14.1000 g. 26 mm. Plain edge. KM#159.	5.00
P125	JE5760 (2000)	4,000	1/2 New Sheqel. Aluminum-Bronze. 14.3200 g. 25.85 mm. Plain edge. KM#363.	12.00
P126	JE5760 (2000)	4,000	New Sheqel. Copper-Nickel. 8.3000 g. 18 mm. Plain edge. KM#160.	6.00
P127	JE5760 (2000)	4,000	5 New Sheqalim. Copper-Nickel. 14.3300 g. 23.9 mm. Plain edge. KM#207.	8.00
P128	JE5760 (2000)	4,000	10 New Sheqalim. Bi-Metallic. 11.0500 g. 22.9 mm. Reeded edge. KM#270.	12.00

MINT SETS

KM#	Date	Mintage	Identification	Issue Price	Mkt Val
MSA1	JE5709 (1949) (10)	300	KM#8 (closed link), 9-12 (with pearl), 13.1 (with pearl), 14, 15 (without pearl), 15a, 16 in "muffin tin" (small dark yellow lettering on case, Hebrew letter on the far left is below KM#8 and thick Menora between KM#13.1 and 14)	—	150
MSB1	JE5709 (1949) (10)	—	KM#8 (closed link), 9-12 (with pearl), 13.1 (with pearl), 14, 15 (without pearl), 15a, 16 in "muffin tin" (small pale yellow lettering on case, Hebrew letter on the far left below KM#8 and thin Menora between KM#13.1 and 14)	—	150
MS1	JE5709 (1949) (10)	300	KM#8 (closed link), 9-12 (with pearl), 13.1 (with pearl), 14, 15 (without pearl), 15a, 16 in "muffin tin" (two piece plastic case with clear swivel top and light blue bottom - large yellow lettering on case; Hebrew letter on the far left extends to the left of KM#8)	—	150
MS2	JE5709-5722 (1949-1962) (17)	4,000	KM#9-12, 13.1, 13.2a, 15, 15a, 16, 17, 19, 20, 24.1, 25-27, (various dates) (issued 1962)	18.50	75.00
MSA3	JE5709-5723 (1949-1963) (18)	20,000	KM#9-12, 13.1, 13.2a, 15, 15a, 16, 17, 19, 20, 24.1, 25-27, 36.1, 37 (various dates) - many circulated and cleaned (case inscribed Israel Government Coins and Medals Corporation) (issued 1964)	—	60.00
MS3	JE5723 (1949-1963) (18)	20,000	KM#9-12, 13.1, 13.2a, 15, 15a, 16, 17, 19, 20, 24.1, 25-27, 36.1, 37 (various dates) - many circulated and cleaned (case inscribed Israel Government Coins and Medals, Corporation) (issued 1964)	22.50	50.00
MS4	JE5722-5723 (1962-1963) (6)	200	KM24.1, 25-27, 36.1, 37 (KM#27 dated JE5722; others dated JE5723) (plain white card with coins individually covered by plastic), market value is for close to perfect sets	2.60	150
MSA5	JE5722-5723 (1962-1963) (6)	1,800	KM#24.1 (coin alignment; inverted reverse), 25-27, 36.1, 37 (pale blue and white card with map)	2.60	200
MSB5	JE5723 (1963) (6)	1,800	KM#24.1 (medal alignment), 25-27, 36.1, 37 (KM#27 dated JE5722) (plain white card entirely covered by plastic), market value is for close to perfect sets	2.60	200
MSC5	JE5723 (1963) (6)	1,800	KM#24.1 (medal alignment), 25-27, 36.1, 37 (all coins dated JE5723) (plain white card entirely covered by plastic), market value is for close to perfect sets	2.60	125
MS5	JE5722-5723 (1962-1963) (6)	1,800	KM#24.1, (coin alignment; inverted reverse), 25-27, 36.1, 37 (KM#27 dated JE5722; other dated JE5723) (plain white card entirely covered by plastic), market value is for close to perfect sets	2.60	200
MS6	JE5723 (1963) (6)	10,455	KM#24.1 (coin alignment; inverted reverse), 25-27, 36.1, 37 (pale blue and white card with map)	2.60	25.00
MS7	JE5723 (1963) (6)	10,455	KM#24.1,(medal alignment), 25-27, 36.1, 37 (pale blue and white card with map)	2.60	12.00
MS8	JE5725 (1965) (6)	153,424	KM24.1, 25-27, 36.1, 37 (gray and white card)	3.50	3.00
MS9	JE5726 (1966) (6)	114,714	KM24.1, 25-27, 36.1, 37 (orange and white card)	3.50	3.00
MS10	JE5727 (1967) (6)	128,124	KM24.1, 25-27, 36.1, 37 (turquoise card)	3.50	3.00
MS11	JE5728 (1968) (6)	184,552	KM24.1, 25-27, 36.1, 47.1 (blue card)	3.50	3.00
MS12	JE5729 (1969) (6)	158,052	KM24.1, 25-27, 36.1, 47.1 (reddish-brown card)	3.50	3.00
MSA13	JE5730 (1970) (6)	60,045	KM#24.1, 25-27, 36.1, 47.1 (red wallet with German insert cards)	—	4.00
MS13	JE5730 (1970) (6)	60,045	KM24.1, 25-27, 36.1, 47.1 (in red wallet with English insert cards)	3.75	3.25
MS13a	JE5730 (1970) (6)	64,800	KM24.1, 25-27, 36.1, 47.1 (blue card)	3.75	3.25
MS14	JE5731 (1971) (6)	32,543	KM24.1, 25-27, 36.1, 47.1 (blue wallet)	3.00	3.50
MS14a	JE5731 (1971) (6)	125,921	KM24.2, 25a, 26a, 27a, 36.2, 47.2 (pink plastic case)	3.50	3.00
MS15	JE5732 (1972) (6)	21,486	KM24.1, 25-27, 36.1, 47.1 (violet wallet)	3.00	3.50
MS15a	JE5732 (1972) (6)	68,513	KM24.2, 25a, 26a, 27a, 36.2, 47.2 (violet plastic case)	3.50	3.00
MS16	JE5733 (1973) (6)	98,107	KM63-68 (blue plastic case)	3.50	3.25
MSA22	JE5739 (1979) (7)	58,433	KM#24.1, 25b, 26b, 27, 36.1, 47.1, 90 (dark blue wallet with gold lettering with Hebrew insert cards)	—	3.00
MSB22	JE5739 (1979) (7)	58,433	KM#24.1, 25b, 26b, 27, 36.1, 47.1, 90 (dark blue wallet with gold lettering with Hebrew insert cards)	—	15.00
MS23	JE5739 (1979) (7)	31,590	KM#24.2, 25c, 26c, 27b, 36.2, 47.2, 90a (brown plastic case)	—	4.00
MSA53	JE5757 (1997) (7)	7,500	KM#163, 172-174, 217, 315, 318 (blue and gold laminated card)	—	35.00
MSB53	JE5757 (1997) (5)	5,000	KM#157-159, 160a, 207 (plastic case)	—	35.00
MSA54	JE5758 (1998) (7)	10,000	KM#163, 172-174, 217, 314, 315 (plastic case)	—	38.00
MS54a	JE5758 (1998) (5)	5,000	KM#157-159, 160a, 207 (plastic case)	—	14.00
MSA55	1999 (7)	6,000	KM#163, 172-174, 217, 315, 331 (plastic case)	—	35.00
MSB55	1999 (5)	6,000	KM#157-159, 160a, 207 (plastic case)	—	35.00
MSA57	JE5760 (2000) (7)	700	KM#163, 172-174, 217, 315, 332 (plasic case)	—	35.00

MINT SETS NON-STANDARD METALS

KM#	Date	Mintage	Identification	Issue Price	Mkt Val
MS17	JE5734 (1974) (6)	92,868	KM24.2, 25c, 26c, 27b, 36.2, 47.2 (violet plastic case)	3.50	3.00
MS18	JE 5735 (1975) (6)	61,686	KM24.2, 25c, 26c, 27b, 36.2, 47.2 (brown plastic case)	3.50	3.00
MS19	JE5736 (1976) (6)	64,654	KM24.2, 25c, 26c, 27b, 36.2, 47.2 (olive green plastic case)	3.50	3.00
MS20	JE5737 (1977) (6)	37,208	KM24.2, 25c, 26c, 27b, 36.2, 47.2 (reddish-brown plastic case)	3.50	3.50
MS21	JE5738 (1978) (6)	57,072	KM24.2, 25c, 26c, 27b, 36.2, 47.2 (brownish plastic case)	3.50	3.50
MS22	JE5739 (1979) (7)	58,433	KM24.1, 25b, 26b, 27, 36.1, 47.1, 90 (dark blue wallet with gold lettering and English insert cards)	—	3.00
MS24	JE5740 (1980) (7)	27,000	KM#24.1, 26b, 47.1, 106-109 (turquoise plastic case)	—	7.00
MS26	JE5740 (1980) (7)	31,348	KM96-102 (blue plastic case)	13.00	8.50
MS27	JE5742 (1982) (7)	19,660	KM106-109, 111, 118, 119 (olive green plastic case)	3.50	8.00
MS28	JE5743 (1983) (5)	17,478	KM108, 109, 111, 118, 119 (reddish-brown plasic case)	3.50	4.50
MS29	JE5744 (1984) (9)	13,403	KM#108, 109, 111, 118, 119, 134, 137, 139, 143 (orange-brown plastic case)	4.50	13.00
MS30	JE5745 (1985) (8)	15,224	KM#111, 118, 119, 139, 143, 146, 147, 151 (purple plastic case)	4.50	9.00
MS31	JE5745 (1985) (5)	7,760	KM#156-160 (gray plastic case)	10.00	20.00

KM#	Date	Mintage	Identification	Issue Price	Mkt Val
MS32	JE5746-47 (1986-87) (11)	14,305	KM#156-160, 163, 167 (JE5746), 163, 171-174 (JE5747) (silver and blue plastic case)	9.00	11.00
MS33	JE5747 (1987) (5)	14,000	KM163, 171-174 (plastic case)	—	15.00
MS34	JE5747-5748 (1987-1988) (10)	11,094	KM#156-160 (JE5747), 163, 171-174 (JE5748) (reddish-brown and gold plastic case)	10.00	12.00
MS35	JE5748 (1988) (5)	28,800	KM#163, 171-174 (reddish-brown and gold plastic case)	6.50	8.50
MS36	JE5748 (1988) (6)	15,795	KM156-160, 198 (green plasic case)	7.50	16.00
MS37	JE5748 (1988) (5)	16,649	KM#193-197 (blue plastic case)	6.50	14.00
MS38	JE5749 (1989) (5)	16,649	KM#163, 171-174 (blue plastic case)	6.50	14.00
MS39	JE5749 (1989) (10)	9,716	KM#156-160, 163, 171-174 (light green plastic case)	7.00	10.00
MS40	JE5750 (1990) (5)	7,562	KM#163, 171-174 (red plastic case)	5.00	14.00
MS41	JE5750 (1990) (6)	5,598	KM#156-160, 207 (dark green plastic case)	8.00	11.00
MS42	JE5751 (1991) (6)	7,929	KM#163, 171-174, 217 (red plastic case)	8.00	12.00
MS43	JE5750-5751 (1990-1991) (7)	6,746	KM#208 (JE5750), 156-160, 207 (JE5751) (green plastic case)	10.00	18.00
MS44	JE5752 (1992) (5)	6,886	KM#163, 172-174, 217 (dark blue plastic case)	8.00	11.00
MS45	JE5744-5753 (1984-1993) (7)	8,000	KM#137, 147, 151, 167, 198, 208, 237 (various dates) (blue folder)	15.00	18.00
MS46	JE5752 (1992) (5)	5,998	KM#157-160, 207 (pink plastic case)	8.00	16.00
MS47	JE5753 (1993) (5)	8,000	KM#163, 172-174, 217 (green folder)	9.50	12.00
MS48	JE5754 (1994) (6)	11,956	KM#163, 172-174, 217, 303 (folder)	16.00	11.00
MS49	JE5753-5754 (1993-1994) (7)	8,000	KM#158-160 (5753), 157, 158, 160a, 207 (JE5754) (folder)	—	15.00
MS50	JE5755 (1995) (6)	10,000	KM#163, 172-174, 217, 304 (folder)	17.00	25.00
MS51	JE5755 (1995) (6)	5,000	KM#157-159, 160a, 207, 270 (folder)	—	25.00
MS52	JE5756 (1996) (7)	7,500	KM#163, 172-174, 217, 305, 315 (folder)	—	35.00
MS53	JE5757 (1997) (7)	7,500	KM#163, 172-174, 217, 315, 318 (folder)	—	33.00
MS54	JE5758 (1998) (7)	10,000	KM#163, 172-174, 217, 314, 315 (folder)	—	36.00
MS55	JE5759 (1999) (7)	6,000	KM#163, 172-174, 217, 315, 331 (folder)	—	35.00
MS56	JE5760 (2000) (4)	3,000	KM#157, 158, 160A, 207 and medal (plastic case) Contains 2001 ANA issue	—	18.00
MS57	JE5760 (2000) (7)	7,000	KM#163, 172-174, 217, 315, 332 (folder)	—	33.00

OFFICIALLY ASSEMBLED HISTORICAL SETS

KM#	Date	Mintage	Identification	Issue Price	Mkt Val
HS1	1927-55 (7)	18,000	The Coin and the Moon Set, KM1, 10, 12-15, 17, plus medal	15.00	15.00
HS2	1948-1985 (9)	26,000	KM#11, 13, 14, 27, 36, 47, 107, 108, 109 plus a medal. Historical Coin Set	15.00	15.00

PIEFORT PROOF SETS (PPS)

KM#	Date	Mintage	Identification	Issue Price	Mkt Val
PPS1	JE5741 (1981) (b) (5)	30,217	KM#P1-P5.	10.00	12.00
PPS2	JE5742 (1982) (r) (6)	18,735	KM#P6-P11.	10.00	10.00
PPS3	JE5743 (1983) (d) (7)	17,177	KM#P12-P18.	10.00	12.00
PPS4	JE5744 (1984) (f) (7)	15,572	KM#P19-P25.	10.00	10.00
PPS5	JE5745 (1985) (b) (5)	14,768	KM#P26-P30	10.00	12.00
PPS6	JE5746 (1986) (p) (5)	12,665	KM#P31-P35.	12.00	18.00
PPS7	JE5747 (1987) (f) (5)	11,529	KM#P36-P40.	15.00	18.00
PPS8	JE5748 (1988) (f) (5)	12,027	KM#PA41, P41-P44.	15.00	25.00
PPS9	JE5749 (1989) (f) (5)	9,622	KM#P45-P49.	15.00	25.00
PPS10	JE5750 (1990) (f) (6)	10,000	KM#P50-P55.	15.00	25.00
PPS11	JE5751 (1991) (u) (6)	8,000	KM#P56-P61.	15.00	25.00
PPS12	JE5752 (1992) (u) (6)	8,000	KM#P68-P73.	15.00	25.00
PPS13	JE5753 (1993) (u) (6)	8,000	KM#P68-P73.	15.00	25.00
PPS14	JE5754 (1994) (u) (7)	8,000	KM#P74-P80.	—	45.00
PPS15	JE5755 (1995) (u) (8)	8,000	KM#P81-P88.	33.00	45.00
PPS16	JE5756 (1996) (b) & (u) (8)	8,000	KM#P89-P96.	—	45.00
PPS17	JE5757 (1997) (h) & (u) (8)	6,000	KM#P97-P104.	—	48.00
PPS18	JE5758 (1998) (h) & (u) (8)	8,000	KM#P105-P112.	—	45.00
PPS19	JE5759 (1999) (h) & (u) (8)	6,000	KM#P113-P120.	—	48.00
PPS20	JE5760 (2000) (8)	4,000	KM#P121-P128.	—	48.00

PROOF SETS

KM#	Date	Mintage	Identification	Issue Price	Mkt Val
PS1	1927 (14)	34	KM1-7 two each, original case	—	7,500
PS2	1927 (7)	4	KM1-7 original case	—	5,000

SPECIAL SELECT SETS

KM#	Date	Mintage	Identification	Issue Price	Mkt Val
SS1	1949	—	—	—	—

ITALIAN SOMALILAND

Italian Somaliland, a former Italian Colony in East Africa, extended south from Ras Asir to Kenya. Area: 178,218 sq. miles (461,585 sq. km). Capital: Mogadisho. In 1885, Italy obtained commercial concessions in the area of the sultan of Zanzibar, and in 1905 purchased the coast from Warshek to Brava. The Italians then extended their occupation inward. Cession of the Jubaland Province by Britain in 1924, and seizure of the sultanates of Obbia and Mejertein in 1925-27 brought direct Italian administration over the whole territory. Italian dominance continued until WW II. British troops occupied Italian Somaliland in 1941. Britain administered the colony until 1950 when it became a UN trust territory administered by Italy. On July 1, 1960, Italian Somaliland united with British Somaliland to form the Independent Somali Democratic Republic.

TITLE

الصومال الايطاليانية

Al-Somal Al-Italiyaniya(t)

MONETARY SYSTEM
100 Bese = 1 Rupia

COLONY
STANDARD COINAGE

KM# 1   BESA
Bronze **Ruler:** Vittorio Emanuele III **Obv:** Uniformed bust left **Rev:** Value and date within circle

Date	Mintage	F	VF	XF	Unc	BU
1909R	2,000,000	15.00	30.00	70.00	300	—
1910R	500,000	15.00	30.00	90.00	350	—
1913R	200,000	22.50	45.00	160	720	—
1921R	500,000	18.50	35.00	100	400	—

KM# 2   2 BESE
Bronze **Ruler:** Vittorio Emanuele III **Obv:** Uniformed bust left **Rev:** Value and date within circle

Date	Mintage	F	VF	XF	Unc	BU
1909R	500,000	18.50	37.50	145	570	—
1910R	250,000	18.50	37.50	160	600	—
1913R	300,000	22.50	45.00	225	900	—

Date	Mintage	F	VF	XF	Unc	BU
1921R	600,000	18.50	37.50	140	550	—
1923R	1,500,000	18.50	35.00	140	550	—
1924R	Inc. above	18.50	30.00	110	450	—

KM# 3   4 BESE
Bronze **Ruler:** Vittorio Emanuele III **Obv:** Uniformed bust left **Rev:** Value and date within circle

Date	Mintage	F	VF	XF	Unc	BU
1909R	250,000	27.50	55.00	180	900	—
1910R	250,000	27.50	55.00	200	1,000	—
1913R	50,000	50.00	125	520	1,550	—
1921R	200,000	30.00	60.00	200	1,020	—
1923R	1,000,000	30.00	60.00	200	1,020	—
1924R	Inc. above	30.00	75.00	230	1,130	—

KM# 4   1/4 RUPIA
2.9160 g., 0.9170 Silver 0.0860 oz. ASW **Ruler:** Vittorio Emanuele III **Obv:** Head right **Rev:** Crown above value and date flanked by sprigs

Date	Mintage	F	VF	XF	Unc	BU
1910R	400,000	20.00	40.00	150	400	—
1913R	100,000	50.00	100	300	600	—

KM# 5   1/2 RUPIA
5.8319 g., 0.9170 Silver 0.1719 oz. ASW **Ruler:** Vittorio Emanuele III **Obv:** Head right **Rev:** Crown above value and date flanked by sprigs

Date	Mintage	F	VF	XF	Unc	BU
1910R	400,000	30.00	65.00	250	650	—
1912R	100,000	35.00	70.00	225	600	—
1913R	100,000	35.00	70.00	200	550	—
1915R	50,000	55.00	120	420	1,050	—
1919R	200,000	30.00	60.00	180	450	—

KM# 6   RUPIA
11.6638 g., 0.9170 Silver 0.3439 oz. ASW **Ruler:** Vittorio Emanuele III **Obv:** Head right **Rev:** Crown above value and date flanked by sprigs

Date	Mintage	F	VF	XF	Unc	BU
1910R	300,000	40.00	90.00	275	550	—
1912R	600,000	40.00	85.00	250	500	—
1913R	300,000	40.00	75.00	225	450	—
1914R	300,000	40.00	75.00	225	450	—
1915R	250,000	40.00	75.00	225	450	—
1919R	400,000	40.00	75.00	225	450	—
1920R	1,300,000	900	1,500	3,400	7,600	—
1921R	940,000	1,850	3,750	6,000	12,550	—

REFORM COINAGE

100 Centesimi = 1 Lira

KM# 7   5 LIRE
6.0000 g., 0.8350 Silver 0.1611 oz. ASW **Ruler:** Vittorio Emanuele III **Obv:** Crowned bust right **Rev:** Crowned shield flanked by sprigs divides value with date below

Date	Mintage	F	VF	XF	Unc	BU
1925R	400,000	125	300	500	1,000	1,500

KM# 8 10 LIRE

12.0000 g., 0.8350 Silver 0.3221 oz. ASW **Ruler:** Vittorio Emanuele III **Obv:** Crowned bust right **Rev:** Crowned shield flanked by sprigs divides value with date below

Date	Mintage	F	VF	XF	Unc	BU
1925R	100,000	200	500	700	1,200	2,000

PROVAS

KM#	Date	Mintage	Identification	Mkt Val
Pr1	1909R	—	Besa. Bronze.	—
Pr2	1909R	—	2 Bese. Bronze.	—
Pr3	1909R	—	4 Bese. Bronze.	—
Pr4	1909R	—	4 Bese. Silver.	—
Pr5	1910R	—	4 Bese. Nickel.	—
Pr6	1910R	—	1/4 Rupia. Silver. Head right. Crown above value and date flanked by sprigs.	1,500
Pr7	1910R	—	1/2 Rupia. Silver. Head right. Crown above value, sprigs flank.	2,500
Pr8	1910R	—	Rupia. Silver. Head right. Crown above value and date flanked by sprigs.	4,000
Pr9	1915R	—	1/2 Rupia. Silver. 1 ANNO/DI GUERRA flanks crown.	—
Pr10	1915R	—	Rupia. Silver. 1 ANNO/DI GUERRA flanks crown.	—
Pr11	1925R	—	5 Lire. Silver. PROVA.	800
Pr12	1925R	—	5 Lire. Silver. PROVA DI STAMPA.	700
Pr13	1925R	—	10 Lire. Silver. PROVA.	1,000
Pr14	1925R	—	10 Lire. Silver. PROVA DI STAMPA.	850

TRIAL STRIKES

KM#	Date	Mintage	Identification	Mkt Val
TS2	1909	—	2 Bese. Lead.	—
TS1	1909	—	Besa. Pewter.	375
TS3	1910	—	4 Bese. Pewter.	750

ITALY

The Italian Republic, a 700-mile-long peninsula extending into the heart of the Mediterranean Sea, has an area of 116,304 sq. mi. (301,230 sq. km.) and a population of 60 million. Capital: Rome. The economy centers around agriculture, manufacturing, forestry and fishing. Machinery, textiles, clothing and motor vehicles are exported.

From the fall of Rome until modern times, 'Italy' was little more than a geographical expression. Although nominally included in the Empire of Charlemagne and the Holy Roman Empire, it was in reality divided into a number of independent states and kingdoms presided over by wealthy families, soldiers of fortune or hereditary rulers. The 19th century unification movement fostered by Mazzini, Garibaldi and Cavour attained fruition in 1860-70 with the creation of the Kingdom of Italy and the installation of Victor Emmanuel, king of Sardinia, as king of Italy. Benito Mussolini came to power during the post-World War I period of economic and political unrest, and installed a Fascist dictatorship with a figurehead king as titular Head of State. Mussolini entered Italy into the German-Japanese anti-comitern pact (Tri-Partite Pact) and withdrew from the League of Nations. The war did not go well for Italy and Germany was forced to assist Italy in its failed invasion of Greece. The Allied invasion of Sicily on July 10, 1943 and bombings of Rome brought the Fascist council to a no vote of confidence on July 23, 1943. Mussolini was arrested but soon escaped and set up a government in Salo. Rome fell to the Allied forces in June, 1944 and the country was allowed the status of cobelligerent against Germany. The Germans held northern Italy for another year. Mussolini was eventually captured and executed by partisans.

Following the defeat of the Axis powers, the Italian monarchy was dissolved by plebiscite, and the Italian Republic proclaimed.

RULERS

Vittorio Emanuele III, 1900-1946
Umberto II, 1946
Republic, 1946-

MONETARY SYSTEM

100 Centesimi = 1 Lira

KINGDOM

DECIMAL COINAGE

KM# 35 CENTESIMO

Bronze **Ruler:** Vittorio Emanuele III **Obv:** Head left **Rev:** Value and date within wreath with star above

Date	Mintage	F	VF	XF	Unc	BU
1902R	26,000	380	700	1,500	2,800	—
1903R	5,655,000	1.00	3.00	6.00	30.00	—
1904/0R	14,626,000	2.00	3.00	7.50	22.00	—
1904R	Inc. above	1.00	3.00	6.00	30.00	—
1905/0R	8,531,000	6.00	12.00	30.00	80.00	—
1905R	Inc. above	1.00	3.00	6.00	30.00	—
1908R	3,859,000	1.00	3.00	6.00	30.00	—

KM# 40 CENTESIMO

Bronze **Ruler:** Vittorio Emanuele III **Obv:** Bust left **Rev:** Female standing on prow

Date	Mintage	F	VF	XF	Unc	BU
1908R	57,000	300	650	1,100	1,800	—
1909R	3,539,000	2.00	3.00	7.00	20.00	—
1910R	3,599,000	2.00	3.00	7.00	20.00	—
1911R	700,000	18.00	40.00	75.00	120	—
1912R	3,995,000	2.00	3.00	8.00	25.00	—
1913R	3,200,000	2.00	3.00	7.00	20.00	—
1914R	11,585,000	2.00	3.00	7.00	20.00	—
1915R	9,757,000	2.00	3.00	7.00	20.00	—
1916R	9,845,000	2.00	3.00	7.00	20.00	—
1917R	2,400,000	2.00	3.00	7.00	20.00	—
1918R	2,710,000	10.00	20.00	50.00	100	—

KM# 38 2 CENTESIMI

Bronze **Ruler:** Vittorio Emanuele III **Obv:** Head left **Rev:** Value and date within wreath

Date	Mintage	F	VF	XF	Unc	BU
1903R	5,000,000	2.00	4.00	15.00	30.00	—
1905R	1,260,000	10.00	25.00	50.00	100	—
1906R	3,145,000	2.00	8.00	20.00	50.00	—
1907R	230,000	80.00	160	380	800	—
1908R	1,518,000	3.00	10.00	25.00	60.00	—

KM# 41 2 CENTESIMI

Bronze **Ruler:** Vittorio Emanuele III **Obv:** Bust left **Rev:** Female standing on prow

Date	Mintage	F	VF	XF	Unc	BU
1908R	298,000	25.00	60.00	120	300	—
1909R	2,419,000	1.00	3.00	7.00	30.00	—
1910R	590,000	15.00	45.00	100	200	—
1911R	2,777,000	1.00	3.00	7.00	30.00	—
1912R	840,000	12.00	30.00	60.00	120	—
1914R	1,648,000	2.00	5.00	15.00	40.00	—
1915R	4,860,000	1.00	3.00	5.00	25.00	—
1916R	1,540,000	2.00	4.00	10.00	35.00	—
1917R	3,638,000	1.00	3.00	7.00	30.00	—

KM# 42 5 CENTESIMI

Bronze, 25.5 mm. **Ruler:** Vittorio Emanuele III **Obv:** Bust left **Rev:** Female standing on prow

Date	Mintage	F	VF	XF	Unc	BU
1908R	824,000	25.00	40.00	90.00	190	—
1909R	1,734,000	3.00	10.00	40.00	100	—
1912R	743,000	4.00	15.00	60.00	150	—
1913R Dot after D	1,964,000	5.00	25.00	50.00	100	—
1913R Without dot after D	Inc. above	80.00	300	750	1,000	—
1915R	1,038,000	10.00	30.00	75.00	120	—
1918R	4,242,000	2.00	7.00	20.00	60.00	—

KM# 59 5 CENTESIMI

3.2600 g., Bronze, 19.8 mm. **Ruler:** Vittorio Emanuele III **Obv:** Head left **Rev:** Wheat ear divides value

Date	Mintage	F	VF	XF	Unc	BU
1919R	13,208,000	3.00	8.00	25.00	100	—
1920R	33,372,000	0.10	0.60	3.00	15.00	—
1921R	80,111,000	0.10	0.60	3.00	15.00	—
1922R	42,914,000	0.10	0.60	3.00	15.00	—
1923R	29,614,000	0.10	0.60	3.00	15.00	—
1924R	20,352,000	0.10	0.60	3.00	15.00	—
1925R	40,460,000	0.10	0.60	3.00	15.00	—
1926R	21,158,000	0.10	0.60	3.00	15.00	—
1927R	15,800,000	0.10	0.60	3.00	15.00	—
1928R	16,090,000	0.10	0.60	3.00	15.00	—
1929R	29,000,000	0.10	0.60	3.00	15.00	—
1930R	22,694,000	0.10	0.60	3.00	15.00	—
1931R	20,000,000	0.10	0.60	3.00	15.00	—
1932R	11,456,000	0.10	0.60	3.00	15.00	—
1933R	20,720,000	0.10	0.60	3.00	15.00	—
1934R	16,000,000	0.10	0.60	3.00	15.00	—
1935R	11,000,000	0.10	0.60	3.00	15.00	—
1936R	9,462,000	0.30	2.00	10.00	25.00	—
1937R	972,000	20.00	45.00	80.00	180	—

KM# 73 5 CENTESIMI

3.2000 g., Bronze **Ruler:** Vittorio Emanuele III **Obv:** Head right **Rev:** Eagle with wings spread

Date	Mintage	F	VF	XF	Unc	BU
1936R Yr. XIV	4,998,000	4.00	10.00	20.00	40.00	—
1937R Yr. XV	7,207,000	1.00	2.00	6.00	15.00	—
1938R Yr. XVI	24,000,000	0.10	0.50	2.50	5.00	—
1939R Yr. XVII	22,000,000	0.10	0.50	2.50	5.00	—

KM# 73a 5 CENTESIMI

3.0000 g., Aluminum-Bronze **Ruler:** Vittorio Emanuele III **Obv:** Head right **Rev:** Eagle with wings spread

Date	Mintage	F	VF	XF	Unc	BU
1939R Yr. XVII	10,000,000	0.20	0.50	2.00	6.00	—
1940R Yr. XVIII	16,340,000	0.20	0.50	2.00	6.00	—
1941R Yr. XIX	25,200,000	0.20	0.50	2.00	6.00	—
1942R Yr. XX	13,922,000	0.20	0.50	2.00	6.00	—
1943R Yr. XXI	372,000	3.00	6.00	15.00	30.00	—

KM# 43 10 CENTESIMI

Bronze **Ruler:** Vittorio Emanuele III **Obv:** Bust left **Rev:** Female standing on prow

Date	Mintage	F	VF	XF	Unc	BU
1908R Unique	—	—	—	—	—	—

KM# 51   10 CENTESIMI
9.9700 g., Bronze, 30.13 mm. **Ruler:** Vittorio Emanuele III
Subject: 50th Anniversary of the Kingdom **Obv:** Head left
Rev: Two classical figures standing **Edge:** Plain

Date	Mintage	F	VF	XF	Unc	BU
1911R	2,000,000	3.00	10.00	45.00	95.00	—

KM# 60   10 CENTESIMI
5.3400 g., Bronze, 23 mm. **Ruler:** Vittorio Emanuele III
Obv: Head left **Rev:** Honey Bee

Date	Mintage	F	VF	XF	Unc	BU
1919R	986,000	20.00	50.00	250	500	—
1920R	37,995,000	0.10	0.75	4.00	15.00	—
1921R	66,510,000	0.10	0.75	4.00	15.00	—
1922R	45,217,000	0.10	0.75	4.00	15.00	—
1923R	31,529,000	0.10	0.75	4.00	15.00	—
1924R	35,312,000	0.10	0.75	4.00	15.00	—
1925R	22,370,000	0.10	0.75	4.00	15.00	—
1926R	25,190,000	0.10	0.75	4.00	15.00	—
1927R	22,673,000	0.10	0.75	4.00	15.00	—
1928R	15,680,000	0.20	5.00	20.00	60.00	—
1929R	15,593,000	0.30	0.75	4.00	15.00	—
1930R	17,115,000	0.30	0.75	4.00	15.00	—
1931R	10,750,000	0.30	0.75	4.00	15.00	—
1932R	5,678,000	1.00	5.00	45.00	90.00	—
1933R	10,250,000	0.30	0.75	4.00	15.00	—
1934R	18,300,000	0.30	0.75	4.00	15.00	—
1935R	10,500,000	0.30	0.75	4.00	15.00	—
1936R	8,770,000	1.00	2.50	8.00	40.00	—
1937R	5,500,000	1.00	2.50	8.00	40.00	—

KM# 74   10 CENTESIMI
Bronze **Ruler:** Vittorio Emanuele III **Obv:** Head left **Rev:** Savoy
arms on fasces with wheat ear and oak leaf flanking

Date	Mintage	F	VF	XF	Unc	BU
1936R Yr. XIV	8,195,000	2.50	5.00	15.00	45.00	—
1937R Yr. XV	7,212,000	1.00	2.00	5.00	20.00	—
1938R Yr. XVI	18,750,000	0.30	1.00	2.00	7.00	—
1939R Yr. XVII	24,750,000	0.50	1.00	2.00	7.00	—

KM# 74a   10 CENTESIMI
4.8000 g., Aluminum-Bronze, 23 mm. **Ruler:** Vittorio
Emanuele III **Obv:** Head right **Rev:** Savoy arms on fasces with
wheat ear and oak leaf flanking

Date	Mintage	F	VF	XF	Unc	BU
1939R Yr. XVII	26,105,000	0.10	0.50	1.00	4.50	—
1940R Yr. XVIII	23,355,000	0.10	0.50	1.00	4.50	—
1941R Yr. XIX	27,050,000	0.10	0.50	1.00	4.50	—
1942R Yr. XX	18,100,000	0.10	0.50	1.00	4.50	—
1943R Yr. XXI	25,400,000	0.10	0.50	1.00	4.50	—

KM# 44   20 CENTESIMI
Nickel, 21.5 mm. **Ruler:** Vittorio Emanuele III **Obv:** Head left
admiring wheat ear **Rev:** Victory in flight with Savoy arms below

Date	Mintage	F	VF	XF	Unc	BU
1908R	14,315,000	0.50	2.00	6.00	40.00	—
1909R	19,280,000	0.50	2.00	6.00	40.00	—
1910R	21,887,000	0.50	2.00	6.00	40.00	—
1911R	13,671,000	0.50	2.00	6.00	40.00	—
1912R	21,040,000	0.50	2.00	6.00	40.00	—
1913R	20,729,000	0.50	2.00	6.00	40.00	—
1914R	14,308,000	0.50	2.00	6.00	40.00	—

Date	Mintage	F	VF	XF	Unc	BU
1919R	3,475,000	3.00	7.00	40.00	120	—
1920R	27,284,000	0.50	2.00	6.00	40.00	—
1921R	50,372,000	0.50	2.00	6.00	40.00	—
1922R	17,134,000	0.50	2.00	6.00	40.00	—
1926R	500	—	—	—	550	—
1927R	100	—	—	—	650	—
1928R	50	—	—	—	750	—
1929R	50	—	—	—	750	—
1930R	50	—	—	—	750	—
1931R	50	—	—	—	750	—
1932R	50	—	—	—	750	—
1933R	50	—	—	—	750	—
1934R	50	—	—	—	750	—
1935R	50	—	—	—	750	—

KM# 58   20 CENTESIMI
Copper-Nickel, 21.5 mm. **Ruler:** Vittorio Emanuele III
Obv: Crowned Savoy shield flanked by oak and laurel sprigs
Rev: Value and date within hexagon box **Edge:** Plain and reeded
Note: Overstruck on KM#28.

Date	Mintage	F	VF	XF	Unc	BU
1918R	43,097,000	0.50	2.00	10.00	60.00	—
1919R	33,432,000	0.50	2.00	10.00	60.00	—
1920R	923,000	5.00	15.00	60.00	150	—

KM# 75   20 CENTESIMI
Nickel, 21.5 mm. **Ruler:** Vittorio Emanuele III **Obv:** Head left
Rev: Savoy shield within head right

Date	Mintage	F	VF	XF	Unc	BU
1936R Yr. XIV	117,000	40.00	80.00	210	450	—
1937R Yr. XV	50	—	—	—	1,500	—
1938R Yr. XVII	20	—	—	—	2,000	—

KM# 75a   20 CENTESIMI
Stainless Steel, 22.5 mm. **Ruler:** Vittorio Emanuele III
Obv: Head left **Rev:** Savoy shield within head right **Edge:** Plain
Note: Magnetic.

Date	Mintage	F	VF	XF	Unc	BU
1939R Yr. XVII	10,462,000	0.20	1.00	10.00	45.00	—
1940R Yr. XVIII	35,350,000	0.20	1.00	10.00	45.00	—
1942R Yr. XX	48,500,000	0.20	1.00	10.00	55.00	—

KM# 75b   20 CENTESIMI
4.0400 g., Stainless Steel, 21.8 mm. **Ruler:** Vittorio Emanuele III
Obv: Head left **Rev:** Savoy shield within head right **Edge:** Reeded
Note: Magnetic.

Date	Mintage	F	VF	XF	Unc	BU
1939R Yr. XVII	10,462,000	0.50	3.00	10.00	20.00	—
1939R Yr. XVIII	Inc. above	0.10	0.40	1.00	2.00	—
1940R Yr. XVIII	Inc. above	0.10	0.40	1.00	2.00	—
1941R Yr. XIX	97,300,000	0.10	0.40	1.00	2.00	—
1942R Yr. XX	Inc. above	0.10	0.40	1.00	2.00	—
1943R Yr. XXI	18,453,000	0.10	0.40	1.00	2.00	—

KM# 75c   20 CENTESIMI
Stainless Steel, 22.5 mm. **Ruler:** Vittorio Emanuele III
Obv: Head left **Rev:** Savoy shield within head right **Edge:** Plain
Note: Non-magnetic.

Date	Mintage	F	VF	XF	Unc	BU
1939R Yr. XVII	Inc. above	2.00	6.00	18.00	50.00	—

KM# 75d   20 CENTESIMI
4.0300 g., Stainless Steel, 21.8 mm. **Ruler:** Vittorio Emanuele III
Obv: Head left **Rev:** Savoy shield within head right **Edge:** Reeded
Note: Non-magnetic.

Date	Mintage	F	VF	XF	Unc	BU
1939R Yr. XVII	Inc. above	0.50	1.00	2.00	3.00	—
1939R Yr. XVIII	25,300,000	0.50	1.00	2.00	3.00	—
1940R Yr. XVIII	Inc. above	0.10	0.20	2.00	3.00	—

KM# 36   25 CENTESIMI
Nickel **Ruler:** Vittorio Emanuele III **Obv:** Crowned eagle with
Savoy shield on chest **Rev:** Value above sprigs

Date	Mintage	F	VF	XF	Unc	BU
1902R	7,773,000	35.00	100	200	600	—
1903R	5,895,000	35.00	100	200	600	—

KM# 61.1   50 CENTESIMI
6.1000 g., Nickel, 24 mm. **Ruler:** Vittorio Emanuele III **Obv:** Head
left **Rev:** Four lions pulling cart with seated Aequitas **Edge:** Plain

Date	Mintage	F	VF	XF	Unc	BU
1919R	3,700,000	7.00	15.00	80.00	180	—
1920R	29,450,000	1.00	2.00	6.00	30.00	—
1921R	16,849,000	1.00	3.00	12.00	40.00	—
1924R	599,000	200	400	700	2,000	—
1925R	24,884,000	1.00	3.00	12.00	40.00	—
1926R	500	—	—	—	550	—
1927R	100	—	—	—	750	—
1928R	50	—	—	—	950	—

KM# 61.2   50 CENTESIMI
6.0000 g., Nickel, 24 mm. **Ruler:** Vittorio Emanuele III **Obv:** Head
left **Rev:** Four lions pulling cart with seated Aequitas **Edge:** Reeded

Date	Mintage	F	VF	XF	Unc	BU
1919R	Inc. above	20.00	50.00	350	1,000	—
1920R	Inc. above	2.00	14.00	180	400	—
1921R	Inc. above	2.00	14.00	200	1,500	—
1924R	Inc. above	60.00	120	400	1,000	—
1925R	Inc. above	2.00	14.00	120	1,000	—
1929R	50	—	—	—	800	—
1930R	50	—	—	—	800	—
1931R	50	—	—	—	800	—
1932R	50	—	—	—	800	—
1933R	50	—	—	—	800	—
1934R	50	—	—	—	800	—
1935R	50	—	—	—	800	—

KM# 76   50 CENTESIMI
Nickel, 24 mm. **Ruler:** Vittorio Emanuele III **Obv:** Head right
Rev: Eagle standing right on fasces

Date	Mintage	F	VF	XF	Unc	BU
1936R Yr. XIV	118,000	30.00	90.00	180	350	—
1937R Yr. XV	50	—	—	—	1,200	—
1938R Yr. XVII	20	—	—	—	2,200	—

KM# 76a   50 CENTESIMI
6.1300 g., Stainless Steel, 24 mm. **Ruler:** Vittorio Emanuele III
Obv: Head right **Rev:** Eagle standing right on fasces
Edge: Reeded **Note:** Non-magnetic.

Date	Mintage	F	VF	XF	Unc	BU
1939R Yr. XVII	9,373,000	0.10	0.50	2.00	12.00	—
1939R Yr. XVIII	10,005,000	0.10	0.50	2.00	12.00	—
1940R Yr. XVIII	19,005,000	0.10	0.50	1.00	5.00	—

KM# 76b   50 CENTESIMI
6.0000 g., Stainless Steel, 24 mm. **Ruler:** Vittorio Emanuele III
Obv: Head right **Rev:** Eagle standing right on fasces
Edge: Reeded **Note:** Magnetic.

Date	Mintage	F	VF	XF	Unc	BU
1939R Yr. XVII	9,373,000	0.10	0.50	4.00	10.00	—
1939R Yr. XVIII	Inc. above	0.10	0.50	4.00	10.00	—
1940R Yr. XVIII	19,005,000	0.10	0.40	4.00	10.00	—
1941R Yr. XIX	58,100,000	0.10	0.20	1.00	3.00	—

Date	Mintage	F	VF	XF	Unc	BU
1942R Yr. XX	26,450,000	0.10	0.20	1.00	3.00	—
1943R Yr. XXI	3,681,000	40.00	80.00	150	280	—

KM# 32 LIRA
5.0000 g., 0.8350 Silver 0.1342 oz. ASW **Ruler:** Vittorio Emanuele III **Obv:** Head right **Rev:** Crowned eagle with savoy shield

Date	Mintage	F	VF	XF	Unc	BU
1901R	2,590,000	10.00	20.00	90.00	400	—
1902R	4,084,000	8.00	16.00	75.00	280	—
1905R	700,000	150	300	1,000	2,500	—
1906R	4,665,000	8.00	16.00	75.00	300	—
1907R	8,472,000	8.00	16.00	60.00	250	—

KM# 45 LIRA
5.0000 g., 0.8350 Silver 0.1342 oz. ASW **Ruler:** Vittorio Emanuele III **Obv:** Bust right **Rev:** Quadriga with standing female figure

Date	Mintage	F	VF	XF	Unc	BU
1908R	2,212,000	30.00	75.00	325	700	—
1909R	3,475,000	15.00	50.00	280	600	—
1910R	5,525,000	10.00	25.00	75.00	250	—
1912R	5,865,000	5.00	15.00	40.00	180	—
1913R	16,177,000	5.00	10.00	30.00	90.00	—

KM# 57 LIRA
5.0000 g., 0.8350 Silver 0.1342 oz. ASW **Ruler:** Vittorio Emanuele III **Obv:** Bust right **Rev:** Quadriga with standing female figure

Date	Mintage	F	VF	XF	Unc	BU
1915R	5,229,000	5.00	30.00	60.00	120	—
1916R	1,835,000	15.00	60.00	175	450	—
1917R	9,744,000	4.00	15.00	30.00	90.00	—

KM# 62 LIRA
Nickel, 27 mm. **Ruler:** Vittorio Emanuele III **Obv:** Female seated left **Rev:** Crowned Savoy shield and value within wreath

Date	Mintage	F	VF	XF	Unc	BU
1922R	82,267,000	0.60	2.00	15.00	70.00	—
1923R	20,175,000	1.00	5.00	45.00	130	—
1924R Closed 2	29,288,000	1.00	5.00	40.00	120	—
1926R	500	—	—	—	500	—
1927R	100	—	—	—	600	—
1928R	19,996,000	4.00	10.00	70.00	180	—
1929R	50	—	—	—	1,000	—
1930R	50	—	—	—	1,000	—
1931R	50	—	—	—	1,000	—
1932R	50	—	—	—	1,000	—
1933R	50	—	—	—	1,000	—
1934R	50	—	—	—	1,000	—
1935R	50	—	—	—	1,000	—

KM# 77 LIRA
Nickel, 27 mm. **Ruler:** Vittorio Emanuele III **Obv:** Head left **Rev:** Eagle with wings open

Date	Mintage	F	VF	XF	Unc	BU
1936R Yr. XIV	119,000	30.00	110	220	450	—
1937R Yr. XV	50	—	—	—	1,150	—
1938R XVII	20	—	—	—	1,650	—

KM# 77a LIRA
8.1000 g., Stainless Steel, 27 mm. **Ruler:** Vittorio Emanuele III **Obv:** Head left **Rev:** Eagle with wings open **Edge:** Reeded **Note:** Non-magnetic.

Date	Mintage	F	VF	XF	Unc	BU
1939R Yr. XVII	10,034,000	0.20	0.60	2.00	8.00	—
1939R Yr. XVIII	15,977,000	0.20	0.60	2.00	8.00	—
1940R Yr. XVIII	25,997,000	0.20	0.50	2.00	4.00	—

KM# 77b LIRA
7.9000 g., Stainless Steel, 27 mm. **Ruler:** Vittorio Emanuele III **Obv:** Head left **Rev:** Eagle with wings open **Edge:** Reeded **Note:** Magnetic.

Date	Mintage	F	VF	XF	Unc	BU
1939R Yr. XVII	Inc. above	0.40	1.50	4.00	12.00	—
1939R Yr. XVIII	Inc. above	0.20	0.50	2.00	4.00	—
1940R Yr. XVIII	Inc. above	0.20	0.50	2.00	4.00	—
1941R Yr. XIX	8,550,000	0.20	0.50	2.00	4.00	—
1942R Yr. XX	5,700,000	0.20	1.00	4.00	10.00	—
1943R Yr. XXI	11,500,000	15.00	40.00	90.00	120	—

KM# 33 2 LIRE
10.0000 g., 0.8350 Silver 0.2684 oz. ASW **Ruler:** Vittorio Emanuele III **Obv:** Head right **Rev:** Crowned eagle with Savoy shield on chest

Date	Mintage	F	VF	XF	Unc	BU
1901R	72,000	600	1,300	3,900	7,500	—
1902R	549,000	100	350	1,100	2,200	—
1903R	54,000	1,800	3,000	7,500	16,000	—
1904R	157,000	500	1,100	2,800	6,000	—
1905R	1,643,000	100	180	400	1,100	—
1906R	970,000	110	200	500	1,200	—
1907R	1,245,000	90.00	180	480	1,100	—

KM# 46 2 LIRE
10.0000 g., 0.8350 Silver 0.2684 oz. ASW **Ruler:** Vittorio Emanuele III **Obv:** Bust right **Rev:** Quadriga with standing female

Date	Mintage	F	VF	XF	Unc	BU
1908R	2,283,000	30.00	70.00	200	550	—
1910R	719,000	100	210	600	1,700	—
1911R	535,000	200	800	1,200	2,800	—
1912R	2,166,000	30.00	70.00	200	850	—

KM# 52 2 LIRE
10.0000 g., 0.8350 Silver 0.2684 oz. ASW, 27 mm. **Ruler:** Vittorio Emanuele III **Subject:** 50th Anniversary of the Kingdom **Obv:** Head left **Rev:** Two classical figures standing

Date	Mintage	F	VF	XF	Unc	BU
1911R	1,000,000	50.00	80.00	175	400	—

KM# 55 2 LIRE
10.0000 g., 0.8350 Silver 0.2684 oz. ASW **Ruler:** Vittorio Emanuele III **Obv:** Bust right **Rev:** Quadriga with standing female

Date	Mintage	F	VF	XF	Unc	BU
1914R	10,390,000	10.00	20.00	35.00	90.00	—
1915R	7,948,000	10.00	20.00	50.00	100	—
1916R	10,923,000	10.00	20.00	35.00	90.00	—
1917R	6,123,000	30.00	60.00	120	190	—

KM# 63 2 LIRE
Nickel **Ruler:** Vittorio Emanuele III **Obv:** Bust right **Rev:** Axe head within fasces with value at left

Date	Mintage	F	VF	XF	Unc	BU
1923R	32,260,000	1.00	5.00	30.00	100	—
1924R	45,051,000	1.00	5.00	30.00	100	—
1925R	14,628,000	5.00	25.00	100	190	—
1926R	5,101,000	22.00	90.00	400	1,800	—
1927R	1,632,000	100	250	1,000	2,500	—
1928R	50	—	—	—	1,100	—
1929R	50	—	—	—	1,100	—
1930R	50	—	—	—	1,100	—
1931R	50	—	—	—	1,100	—
1932R	50	—	—	—	1,100	—
1933R	50	—	—	—	1,100	—
1934R	50	—	—	—	1,100	—
1935R	50	—	—	—	1,100	—

KM# 78 2 LIRE
Nickel **Ruler:** Vittorio Emanuele III **Obv:** Head right **Rev:** Eagle with open wings standing on fasces within wreath **Edge:** Plain

Date	Mintage	F	VF	XF	Unc	BU
1936R Yr. XIV	120,000	70.00	120	240	600	—
1937R Yr. XV	50	—	—	—	1,000	—
1939R Yr. XVII	20	—	—	—	2,500	—

KM# 78a 2 LIRE
Stainless Steel, 29 mm. **Ruler:** Vittorio Emanuele III **Obv:** Head right **Rev:** Eagle with open wings standing on fasces within wreath **Edge:** Reeded **Note:** Non-magnetic.

Date	Mintage	F	VF	XF	Unc	BU
1939R Yr. XVII	2,900,000	0.60	2.00	5.00	25.00	—
1939R Yr. XVIII	4,873,000	0.40	1.00	3.00	8.00	—
1940R Yr. XVIII	5,742,000	0.40	1.00	3.00	8.00	—

KM# 78b 2 LIRE
Stainless Steel, 29 mm. **Ruler:** Vittorio Emanuele III **Obv:** Head right **Rev:** Eagle with open wings standing on fasces within wreath **Edge:** Reeded **Note:** Magnetic.

Date	Mintage	F	VF	XF	Unc	BU
1939R Yr. XVII	Inc. above	1.00	2.00	4.00	15.00	—
1939R Yr. XVIII	Inc. above	1.00	2.00	4.00	15.00	—
1940R Yr. XVIII	Inc. above	0.40	0.90	2.00	4.00	—
1941R Yr. XIX	1,865,000	0.50	1.50	3.00	8.00	—
1942R Yr. XX	2,450,000	100	200	400	800	—
1943R Yr. XXI	600,000	70.00	160	300	580	—

KM# 34　5 LIRE
25.0000 g., 0.9000 Silver 0.7234 oz. ASW　**Ruler:** Vittorio
Emanuele III **Obv:** Head right **Rev:** Crowned eagle with Savoy
shield on chest

Date	Mintage	F	VF	XF	Unc	BU
1901R	114	10,000	20,000	40,000	60,000	—

KM# 53　5 LIRE
25.0000 g., 0.9000 Silver 0.7234 oz. ASW, 37 mm.
Ruler: Vittorio Emanuele III **Subject:** 50th Anniversary of the
Kingdom **Obv:** Head left **Rev:** Two classical figures standing

Date	Mintage	F	VF	XF	Unc	BU
1911R	60,000	1,100	1,500	2,200	3,800	—

KM# 56　5 LIRE
25.0000 g., 0.9000 Silver 0.7234 oz. ASW　**Ruler:** Vittorio
Emanuele III **Obv:** Head right **Rev:** Quadriga with standing female

Date	Mintage	F	VF	XF	Unc	BU
1914R	273,000	5,000	8,000	10,000	15,000	—

KM# 67.1　5 LIRE
5.0000 g., 0.8350 Silver 0.1342 oz. ASW, 23 mm.
Ruler: Vittorio Emanuele III **Obv:** Head left **Rev:** Eagle with open
wings standing on fascis **Edge:** *FERT*

Date	Mintage	F	VF	XF	Unc	BU
1926R	5,405,000	5.00	15.00	50.00	120	—
1927R	92,887,000	2.00	5.00	12.00	40.00	—
1928R	9,908,000	4.00	15.00	50.00	120	—
1929R	33,803,000	2.00	5.00	10.00	35.00	—
1930R	19,525,000	2.00	5.00	10.00	30.00	—
1931R	50	—	—	—	1,000	—
1932R	50	—	—	—	1,000	—
1933R	50	—	—	—	1,000	—
1934R	50	—	—	—	1,000	—
1935R	50	—	—	—	1,000	—

KM# 67.2　5 LIRE
5.0000 g., 0.8350 Silver 0.1342 oz. ASW, 23 mm.
Ruler: Vittorio Emanuele III **Obv:** Head left **Rev:** Eagle with
wings open standing on fascis **Edge:** ** FERT **

Date	Mintage	F	VF	XF	Unc	BU
1927R	Inc. above	2.00	5.00	12.00	30.00	—
1928R	Inc. above	8.00	20.00	80.00	150	—
1929R	Inc. above	2.00	5.00	10.00	30.00	—

KM# 79　5 LIRE
5.0000 g., 0.8350 Silver 0.1342 oz. ASW　**Ruler:** Vittorio
Emanuele III **Obv:** Head left **Rev:** Mother seated with three children

Date	Mintage	F	VF	XF	Unc	BU
1936R Yr. XIV	1,016,000	30.00	60.00	80.00	150	—
1937R Yr. XV	100,000	60.00	90.00	130	220	—
1938R Yr. XVIII	20	—	—	—	1,700	—
1939R Yr. XVIII	20	—	—	—	1,700	—
1940R Yr. XIX	20	—	—	—	1,700	—
1941R Yr. XX	20	—	—	—	1,700	—

KM# 47　10 LIRE
3.2258 g., 0.9000 Gold 0.0933 oz. AGW, 18 mm.
Ruler: Vittorio Emanuele III

Date	Mintage	F	VF	XF	Unc	BU
1910R Rare	—	—	—	—	—	—

Note: All but one piece melted

1912R	6,796	3,000	4,000	7,000	10,000	—
1926R	40	—	—	10,000	18,000	—
1927R	30	—	—	14,000	20,000	—

KM# 68.1　10 LIRE
10.0000 g., 0.8350 Silver 0.2684 oz. ASW　**Ruler:** Vittorio
Emanuele III **Obv:** Head left **Rev:** Biga with female **Edge:** *FERT*

Date	Mintage	F	VF	XF	Unc	BU
1926R	1,748,000	140	280	400	800	—
1927R	44,801,000	10.00	30.00	100	200	—
1928R	6,652,000	50.00	80.00	180	350	—
1929R	6,800,000	100	200	900	1,500	—
1930R	3,668,000	140	280	400	800	—
1931R	50	—	—	—	1,500	—
1932R	50	—	—	—	1,500	—
1933R	50	—	—	—	1,500	—
1934R	50	—	—	—	1,500	—

KM# 68.2　10 LIRE
10.0000 g., 0.8350 Silver 0.2684 oz. ASW　**Ruler:** Vittorio
Emanuele III **Obv:** Head left **Rev:** Biga with female **Edge:** **FERT**

Date	Mintage	F	VF	XF	Unc	BU
1927R	Inc. above	10.00	30.00	90.00	180	—
1928R	Inc. above	150	400	900	1,500	—
1929R	Inc. above	50.00	100	200	550	—

KM# 80　10 LIRE
10.0000 g., 0.8350 Silver 0.2684 oz. ASW　**Ruler:** Vittorio
Emanuele III **Obv:** Head right **Rev:** Female standing on prow

Date	Mintage	F	VF	XF	Unc	BU
1936R Yr. XIV	619,000	40.00	50.00	110	220	—
1937R Yr. XV	50	—	—	—	1,800	—
1938R Yr. XVII	20	—	—	—	3,000	—
1939R Yr. XVIII	20	—	—	—	3,000	—
1940R Yr. XIX	20	—	—	—	3,000	—
1941R Yr. XX	20	—	—	—	3,000	—

KM# 37.1　20 LIRE
6.4516 g., 0.9000 Gold 0.1867 oz. AGW　**Ruler:** Vittorio
Emanuele III **Obv:** Head left **Rev:** Crowned eagle with Savoy
shield on chest

Date	Mintage	F	VF	XF	Unc	BU
1902R	181	8,000	15,000	25,000	37,500	—
1903R	1,800	1,200	2,000	2,500	4,200	—
1905R	8,715	1,000	1,400	1,800	3,000	—
1908R Rare	—	—	—	—	—	—

KM# 37.2　20 LIRE
6.4516 g., 0.9000 Gold 0.1867 oz. AGW　**Ruler:** Vittorio
Emanuele III **Obv:** Head left **Rev:** Crowned eagle with Savoy
shield on chest **Note:** A small anchor below the neck indicates
that the gold in the coin is from Eritrea.

Date	Mintage	F	VF	XF	Unc	BU
1902R	115	8,000	15,000	28,000	52,000	—

KM# 48　20 LIRE
6.4516 g., 0.9000 Gold 0.1867 oz. AGW　**Ruler:** Vittorio
Emanuele III **Obv:** Uniformed bust left **Rev:** Female standing on
prow

Date	Mintage	F	VF	XF	Unc	BU
1910R	Est. 33,000	—	—	—	70,000	—

Note: Six pieces currently known to exist

1912R	59,000	800	1,200	1,600	2,300	—
1926R	40	—	—	10,500	17,500	—
1927R	30	—	—	12,000	20,000	—

KM# 64　20 LIRE
6.4516 g., 0.9000 Gold 0.1867 oz. AGW, 21 mm.
Ruler: Vittorio Emanuele III **Subject:** 1st Anniversary of Fascist
Government **Obv:** Head left **Rev:** Axe head within fasces with
value at left

Date	Mintage	F	VF	XF	Unc	BU
1923R	20,000	700	1,000	1,500	2,300	2,500

KM# 69　20 LIRE
15.0000 g., 0.8000 Silver 0.3858 oz. ASW　**Ruler:** Vittorio
Emanuele III **Obv:** Head right **Rev:** Standing male with fasces
approaching seated Italia

Date	Mintage	F	VF	XF	Unc	BU
1927R Yr. V	100	—	8,000	18,000	85,000	—
1927R Yr. VI	3,518,000	100	250	400	900	—
1928R Yr. VI	2,487,000	120	280	500	1,000	—
1929R Yr. VII	50	—	—	—	4,000	—
1930R Yr. VIII	50	—	—	—	4,000	—
1931R Yr. IX	50	—	—	—	4,000	—
1932R Yr. X	50	—	—	—	4,000	—
1933R Yr. XI	50	—	—	—	4,000	—
1934R Yr. XII	50	—	—	—	4,000	—

KM# 70　20 LIRE
20.0000 g., 0.6000 Silver 0.3858 oz. ASW, 35 mm.
Ruler: Vittorio Emanuele III **Subject:** 10th Anniversary - End of
World War I **Obv:** Helmeted head left **Rev:** Fasces, lion's head
and axe head **Note:** Similar 20 and 100 Lire pieces were struck
in gold. Silver and silvered brass items are modern fantasies.

Date	Mintage	F	VF	XF	Unc	BU
1928R Yr. VI	3,536,250	150	300	650	1,250	—

KM# 81   20 LIRE
20.0000 g., 0.8000 Silver 0.5144 oz. ASW **Ruler:** Vittorio Emanuele III **Obv:** Head left **Rev:** Quadriga and seated female

Date	Mintage	F	VF	XF	Unc	BU
1936R Yr. XIV	10,000	—	—	3,000	5,000	—
1937R Yr. XV	50	—	—	—	7,500	—
1938R Yr. XVII	20	—	—	—	10,000	—
1939R Yr. XVIII	20	—	—	—	10,000	—
1940R Yr. XIX	20	—	—	—	10,000	—
1941R Yr. XX	20	—	—	—	10,000	—

KM# 49   50 LIRE
16.1290 g., 0.9000 Gold 0.4667 oz. AGW **Ruler:** Vittorio Emanuele III **Obv:** Bust left **Rev:** Female with plow

Date	Mintage	F	VF	XF	Unc	BU
1910R Rare	2,096	—	—	—	—	—
1912R	11,000	1,200	1,600	2,200	3,500	5,000
1926R	40	—	—	—	28,000	—
1927R	30	—	—	—	30,000	—

KM# 54   50 LIRE
16.1290 g., 0.9000 Gold 0.4667 oz. AGW, 28 mm. **Ruler:** Vittorio Emanuele III **Subject:** 50th Anniversary of the Kingdom **Obv:** Head left **Rev:** Standing classical couple

Date	Mintage	F	VF	XF	Unc	BU
ND(1911)R	20,000	800	1,200	1,800	2,400	3,000

KM# 71   50 LIRE
4.3995 g., 0.9000 Gold 0.1273 oz. AGW **Ruler:** Vittorio Emanuele III **Obv:** Head left **Rev:** Man striding right

Date	Mintage	F	VF	XF	Unc	BU
1931R Yr. IX	19,750	300	400	500	620	—
1931R Yr. X	12,630	400	500	650	850	—
1932R Yr. X	12,000	300	400	550	700	—
1933R Yr. XI	6,463	800	1,000	1,300	2,000	—

KM# 82   50 LIRE
4.3995 g., 0.9000 Gold 0.1273 oz. AGW **Ruler:** Vittorio Emanuele III **Obv:** Head left **Rev:** Eagle with wings spread above Savoy shield

Date	Mintage	F	VF	XF	Unc	BU
1936R Yr. XIV	790	3,000	6,000	8,000	11,000	16,000

KM# 39   100 LIRE
32.2580 g., 0.9000 Gold 0.9334 oz. AGW **Ruler:** Vittorio Emanuele III **Obv:** Head left **Rev:** Crowned eagle with Savoy shield on chest

Date	Mintage	F	VF	XF	Unc	BU
1903R	966	6,000	8,000	16,000	22,500	—
1905R	1,012	5,000	7,500	13,000	17,500	—

KM# 50   100 LIRE
32.2580 g., 0.9000 Gold 0.9334 oz. AGW **Ruler:** Vittorio Emanuele III **Obv:** Bust left **Rev:** Female with plow

Date	Mintage	F	VF	XF	Unc	BU
1910R Rare	2,013	—	—	—	—	—
1912R	4,946	3,500	5,000	6,000	9,000	—
1926R	40	—	13,500	19,500	38,500	—
1927R	30	—	15,750	25,000	42,500	—

KM# 65   100 LIRE
32.2580 g., 0.9000 Gold 0.9334 oz. AGW, 32 mm. **Ruler:** Vittorio Emanuele III **Subject:** 1st Anniversary of Fascist Government **Obv:** Head left **Rev:** Axe within fasces with value at left

Date	Mintage	F	VF	XF	Unc	BU
1923R Matte finish	20,000	1,300	2,000	2,800	5,400	—
1923R Bright finish, rare	—	—	—	—	—	—

KM# 66   100 LIRE
32.2580 g., 0.9000 Gold 0.9334 oz. AGW, 35 mm. **Ruler:** Vittorio Emanuele III **Subject:** 25th year of reign, 10th Anniversary - World War I Entry **Obv:** Head left above oak sprigs **Rev:** Heroic male figure kneeling on large rock holding flag and small Victory

Date	Mintage	F	VF	XF	Unc	BU
1925R Matte finish	5,000	3,000	4,200	6,000	8,900	12,000
1925R Bright finish, rare	—	—	—	—	—	—

KM# 72   100 LIRE
8.7990 g., 0.9000 Gold 0.2546 oz. AGW **Ruler:** Vittorio Emanuele III **Obv:** Head left **Rev:** Female on prow

Date	Mintage	F	VF	XF	Unc	BU
1931R Yr. IX	34,000	350	500	900	1,100	—
1931R Yr. X	Inc. above	700	900	1,200	2,000	—
1932R Yr. X	9,081	600	700	1,100	1,500	—
1933R Yr. XI	6,464	600	800	1,200	1,600	—

KM# 83   100 LIRE
8.7990 g., 0.9000 Gold 0.2546 oz. AGW, 25 mm. **Ruler:** Vittorio Emanuele III **Obv:** Head right **Rev:** Male figure striding left

Date	Mintage	F	VF	XF	Unc	BU
1936R Yr. XIV	812	4,500	6,000	8,000	13,000	18,500

KM# 84   100 LIRE
5.1900 g., 0.9000 Gold 0.1502 oz. AGW, 20 mm. **Ruler:** Vittorio Emanuele III **Obv:** Head right **Rev:** Male figure striding left

Date	Mintage	F	VF	XF	Unc	BU
1937R Yr. XVI	249	—	16,000	25,000	35,000	45,000
1940R Yr. XVIII, rare	2	—	—	—	—	—

REPUBLIC
DECIMAL COINAGE

KM# 87   LIRA
Aluminum **Obv:** Wheat sprigs within head left **Rev:** Orange sprig

Date	Mintage	F	VF	XF	Unc	BU
1946R	104,000	60.00	110	200	400	—
1947R	12,000	200	700	1,300	1,800	—
1948R	9,000,000	0.50	4.00	7.00	30.00	—
1949R	13,200,000	0.50	4.00	7.00	30.00	—
1950R	1,942,000	1.00	3.00	10.00	40.00	—

KM# 91   LIRA
0.6200 g., Aluminum, 17 mm. **Obv:** Balance scales **Rev:** Cornucopia, value and date **Note:** The 1968-1969 and 1982-2001 dates were issued in sets only.

Date	Mintage	F	VF	XF	Unc	BU
1951R	3,680,000	0.10	0.50	3.00	10.00	—
1952R	2,720,000	4.00	8.00	20.00	40.00	—
1953R	2,800,000	0.10	0.50	3.00	10.00	—
1954R	41,040,000	0.10	0.25	0.50	2.00	—
1955R	32,640,000	0.10	0.25	0.50	2.00	—
1956R	1,840,000	4.00	8.00	15.00	30.00	—
1957R	7,440,000	0.10	0.25	0.50	2.00	—
1958R	5,280,000	0.10	0.25	0.50	2.00	—
1959R	1,680,000	0.10	0.25	0.50	2.00	—
1968R	100,000	—	—	—	25.00	—
1969R	310,000	—	—	—	4.00	—
1970R	1,011,000	—	—	—	2.00	—
1980R	1,500,000	—	—	—	4.00	—
1981R	500,000	—	—	—	4.00	—
1982R	85,000	—	—	—	4.00	—
1983R	76,000	—	—	—	25.00	—

Date	Mintage	F	VF	XF	Unc	BU
1984R	77,000	—	—	—	20.00	—
1985R	73,000	—	—	—	10.00	—
1985R Proof	20,000	Value: 10.00				
1986R	13,200	—	—	—	8.00	—
1986R Proof	17,500	Value: 12.00				
1987R	177,000	—	—	—	20.00	—
1987R Proof	—	Value: 25.00				
1988R	51,000	—	—	—	30.00	—
1988R Proof	9,000	Value: 25.00				
1989R	51,200	—	—	—	20.00	—
1989R Proof	9,260	Value: 20.00				
1990R	52,300	—	—	—	20.00	—
1990R Proof	9,600	Value: 20.00				
1991R	56,000	—	—	—	8.00	—
1991R Proof	11,000	Value: 20.00				
1992R	52,000	—	—	—	20.00	—
1992R Proof	9,500	Value: 20.00				
1993R	50,200	—	—	—	20.00	—
1993R Proof	8,500	Value: 20.00				
1994R	44,500	—	—	—	30.00	—
1994R Proof	8,500	Value: 30.00				
1995R	44,600	—	—	—	30.00	—
1995R Proof	7,960	Value: 30.00				
1996R	45,000	—	—	—	20.00	—
1996R Proof	8,000	Value: 20.00				
1997R	43,600	—	—	—	30.00	—
1997R Proof	8,440	Value: 35.00				
1998R	55,200	—	—	—	10.00	—
1998R Proof	9,000	Value: 15.00				
1999R	51,800	—	—	—	10.00	—
1999R Proof	8,000	Value: 15.00				
2000R	61,400	—	—	—	20.00	—
2000R Proof	9,000	Value: 30.00				

KM# 204 LIRA
14.6000 g., 0.8350 Silver 0.3919 oz. ASW Series: History of the Lira Subject: Lira of 1901, KM#32 Obv: Head right within circle Rev: Crowned eagle with shield on chest within beaded circle Edge: Reeded and plain

Date	Mintage	F	VF	XF	Unc	BU
1999R	—	—	—	—	55.00	60.00
1999R Proof	—	Value: 75.00				

KM# 205 LIRA
14.6000 g., 0.8350 Silver 0.3919 oz. ASW Series: History of the Lira Subject: Lira of 1915, KM#57 Obv: Head right within circle Rev: Quadriga with standing female within circle

Date	Mintage	F	VF	XF	Unc	BU
1999R	—	—	—	—	55.00	60.00
1999R Proof	—	Value: 75.00				

KM# 206 LIRA
14.6000 g., 0.8350 Silver 0.3919 oz. ASW, 34 mm. Series: History of the Lira Subject: Lira of 1922, KM#62 Obv: Seated allegorical figure within circle Rev: Crowned shield and value within wreath flanked by small circles Edge: Reeded and plain sections

Date	Mintage	F	VF	XF	Unc	BU
2000R	—	—	—	—	55.00	60.00
2000R Proof	—	Value: 75.00				

KM# 207 LIRA
14.6000 g., 0.8350 Silver 0.3919 oz. ASW, 34 mm. Series: History of the Lire Subject: Lira of 1936, KM#77 Obv: Head left within circle Rev: Eagle in front of fasces within circle flanked by sprigs Edge: Reeded and plain sections

Date	Mintage	F	VF	XF	Unc	BU
2000R	—	—	—	—	55.00	60.00
2000R Proof	—	Value: 75.00				

KM# 88 2 LIRE
1.7400 g., Aluminum Obv: Ploughman Rev: Wheat ear divides value

Date	Mintage	F	VF	XF	Unc	BU
1946R	123,000	60.00	110	210	400	—
1947R	12,000	200	700	1,300	1,800	—
1948R	7,200,000	0.50	2.00	10.00	30.00	—
1949R	1,350,000	10.00	35.00	85.00	190	—
1950R	2,640,000	0.60	2.50	10.00	35.00	—

KM# 94 2 LIRE
0.8000 g., Aluminum Obv: Honey bee Rev: Olive branch and value Note: The 1968-1969 and 1982-2001 dates were issued in sets only.

Date	Mintage	F	VF	XF	Unc	BU
1953R	4,125,000	0.20	0.50	2.00	5.00	—
1954R	22,500,000	0.20	0.50	2.00	5.00	—
1955R	2,750,000	0.20	0.50	2.00	5.00	—
1956R	1,500,000	2.00	4.00	8.00	20.00	—
1957R	6,313,000	0.20	0.50	2.00	5.00	—
1958R	125,000	25.00	100	240	400	—
1959R	2,000,000	0.20	0.50	2.00	5.00	—
1968R	100,000	—	—	—	20.00	—
1969R	310,000	—	—	—	3.00	—
1970R	1,140,000	—	—	—	2.50	—
1980R	857,000	—	—	—	2.00	—
1981R	162,000	—	—	—	2.00	—
1982R	119,000	—	—	—	2.00	—
1983R	76,000	6.00	15.00	20.00	40.00	—
1984R	77,000	—	—	8.00	15.00	—
1985R	91,220	—	—	—	10.00	—
1985R Proof	20,000	Value: 12.00				
1986R	73,200	—	—	—	10.00	—
1986R Proof	17,500	Value: 15.00				
1987R	57,500	—	—	—	18.00	—
1987R Proof	10,000	Value: 30.00				
1988R	51,050	—	—	—	25.00	—
1988R Proof	9,000	Value: 30.00				
1989R	51,200	—	—	—	25.00	—
1989R Proof	9,260	Value: 18.00				
1990R	53,300	—	—	—	25.00	—
1990R Proof	9,600	Value: 20.00				
1991R	54,000	—	—	—	25.00	—
1991R Proof	11,000	Value: 25.00				
1992R	52,000	—	—	—	8.00	—
1992R Proof	9,500	Value: 20.00				
1993R	50,200	—	—	—	25.00	—
1993R Proof	8,500	Value: 20.00				
1994R	44,500	—	—	—	25.00	—
1994R Proof	8,500	Value: 25.00				
1995R	44,588	—	—	—	40.00	—
1995R Proof	7,960	Value: 45.00				
1996R	45,000	—	—	—	20.00	—
1996R Proof	8,000	Value: 22.00				
1997R	43,600	—	—	—	40.00	—
1997R Proof	8,660	Value: 40.00				
1998R	55,200	—	—	—	10.00	—
1998R Proof	9,000	Value: 15.00				
1999R	51,800	—	—	—	15.00	—
1999R Proof	8,500	Value: 18.00				

Date	Mintage	F	VF	XF	Unc	BU
2000R	61,500	—	—	—	18.00	—
2000R Proof	9,000	Value: 20.00				

KM# 89 5 LIRE
Aluminum Obv: Female head holding torch facing right Rev: Grape cluster

Date	Mintage	F	VF	XF	Unc	BU
1946R	81,000	200	800	1,400	2,000	—
1947R	17,000	300	950	1,500	2,400	—
1948R	25,125,000	0.50	3.00	10.00	50.00	—
1949R	71,100,000	0.30	3.00	5.00	25.00	—
1950R	114,790,000	0.30	3.00	10.00	35.00	—

KM# 92 5 LIRE
1.0350 g., Aluminum, 20.12 mm. Obv: Rudder Rev: Dolphin and value Edge: Plain

Date	Mintage	F	VF	XF	Unc	BU
1951R	40,260,000	0.10	0.25	1.00	6.00	—
1952R	57,400,000	0.10	0.25	1.00	6.00	—
1953R	196,200,000	0.10	0.25	0.50	3.00	—
1954R	436,400,000	0.10	0.25	0.50	3.00	—
1955R	159,000,000	0.10	0.25	0.50	2.00	—
1956R	400,000	30.00	100	400	1,200	—
1966R	1,200,000	0.25	0.50	2.00	6.00	—
1967R	10,600,000	0.10	0.25	0.50	1.00	—
1968R	7,500,000	—	—	0.10	0.75	—
1969R	7,910,000	—	—	0.10	0.75	—
1969R Inverted 1 (die break at base of 1)	969,000	3.00	6.00	18.00	65.00	—
1970R	4,200,000	—	—	0.10	0.75	—
1971R	8,600,000	—	—	0.10	0.75	—
1972R	16,400,000	—	—	0.10	0.50	—
1973R	28,800,000	—	—	0.10	0.50	—
1974R	6,600,000	—	—	0.10	0.50	—
1975R	7,000,000	—	—	0.10	0.50	—
1976R	8,800,000	—	—	0.10	0.50	—
1977R	6,700,000	—	—	0.10	0.50	—
1978R	3,600,000	—	—	0.10	0.50	—
1979R	5,000,000	—	—	0.10	0.50	—
1980R	5,000,000	—	—	0.10	0.50	—
1981R	5,000,000	—	—	0.10	0.50	—
1982R	8,700,000	—	—	0.10	0.50	—
1983R	5,000,000	—	—	0.10	1.00	—
1984R	2,100,000	—	—	0.10	1.00	—
1985R	3,000,000	—	—	0.10	1.00	—
1985R Proof	20,000	Value: 10.00				
1986R	5,000,000	—	—	0.10	0.50	—
1986R Proof	17,500	Value: 10.00				
1987R	7,000,000	—	—	0.10	0.50	—
1987R Proof	10,000	Value: 10.00				
1988R	5,000,000	—	—	0.10	0.50	—
1988R Proof	9,000	Value: 10.00				
1989R	2,500,000	—	—	0.10	0.50	—

Note: Coin rotation

Date	Mintage	F	VF	XF	Unc	BU
1989R	—	1.00	4.00	7.00	18.00	—

Note: Medal rotation

Date	Mintage	F	VF	XF	Unc	BU
1989R Proof	9,260	Value: 10.00				
1990R	2,500,000	—	—	0.10	0.50	—
1990R Proof	9,400	Value: 10.00				
1991R	2,000,000	—	—	0.10	0.50	—
1991R Proof	11,000	Value: 10.00				
1992R	1,000,000	—	—	0.10	0.50	—
1992R Proof	8,500	Value: 10.00				
1993R	1,000,000	—	—	0.10	0.50	—
1993R Proof	9,500	Value: 14.00				
1994R	1,000,000	—	—	0.10	0.50	—
1994R Proof	8,500	Value: 14.00				
1995R	3,000,000	—	—	0.10	0.50	—
1995R Proof	7,960	Value: 15.00				
1996R	2,500,000	—	—	0.10	0.50	—
1996R Proof	8,000	Value: 15.00				
1997R	1,000,000	—	—	0.10	0.50	—
1997R Proof	8,660	Value: 15.00				
1998R	1,500,000	—	—	0.10	0.50	—
1998R Proof	9,000	Value: 10.00				
1999R	51,800	—	—	—	25.00	—
1999R Proof	8,500	Value: 15.00				
2000R	61,400	—	—	—	20.00	—
2000R Proof	10,000	Value: 20.00				

KM# 90   10 LIRE
Aluminum, 29 mm. **Obv:** Pegasus **Rev:** Olive branch divides value

Date	Mintage	F	VF	XF	Unc	BU
1946R	101,000	100	400	700	1,000	—
1947R	12,000	500	600	3,000	5,000	—
1948R	14,400,000	1.00	10.00	40.00	100	—
1949R	49,500,000	0.50	1.00	5.00	30.00	—
1950R	53,311,000	0.50	1.00	5.00	30.00	—

KM# 93   10 LIRE
1.6000 g., Aluminum, 23.25 mm. **Obv:** Plow **Rev:** Value within wheat ears **Edge:** Plain

Date	Mintage	F	VF	XF	Unc	BU
1951R	96,600,000	0.10	0.50	3.00	30.00	—
1952R	105,150,000	0.10	0.50	3.00	30.00	—
1953R	151,500,000	0.10	0.50	3.00	30.00	—
1954R	95,250,000	0.50	1.00	5.00	40.00	—
1955R	274,950,000	0.10	0.15	2.00	5.00	—
1956R	76,650,000	0.10	1.00	5.00	20.00	—
1965R	1,050,000	1.50	12.00	15.00	40.00	—
1966R	16,500,000	0.10	0.25	1.00	3.00	—
1967R	29,450,000	0.10	0.25	1.00	3.00	—
1968R	32,200,000	—	—	0.10	0.75	—
1969R	23,710,000	—	—	0.10	0.75	—
1970R	14,100,000	—	—	0.10	0.75	—
1971R	23,550,000	—	—	0.10	0.75	—
1972R	61,300,000	—	—	0.10	0.50	—
1973R	145,800,000	—	—	0.10	0.50	—
1974R	85,000,000	—	—	0.10	0.50	—
1975R	76,800,000	—	—	0.10	0.50	—
1976R	82,000,000	—	—	0.10	0.50	—
1977R	80,750,000	—	—	0.10	0.50	—
1978R	43,800,000	—	—	0.10	0.50	—
1979R	98,000,000	—	—	0.10	0.50	—
1980R	89,000,000	—	—	0.10	0.50	—
1981R	91,750,000	—	—	0.10	0.50	—
1982R	44,500,000	—	—	0.10	0.50	—
1983R	15,110,000	—	—	0.50	1.00	—
1984R	11,122,000	—	—	0.50	1.00	—
1985R	15,000,000	—	—	0.10	0.50	—
1985R Proof	20,000	Value: 10.00				
1986R	16,000,000	—	—	0.10	0.50	—
1986R Proof	17,500	Value: 8.00				
1987R	13,000,000	—	—	0.10	0.50	—
1987R Proof	10,000	Value: 8.00				
1988R	13,000,000	—	—	0.10	0.50	—
1988R Proof	9,000	Value: 10.00				
1989R	16,000,000	—	—	0.10	0.50	—
1989R Proof	9,260	Value: 10.00				
1990R	14,000,000	—	—	0.10	1.00	—
1990R Proof	9,400	Value: 10.00				
1991R	5,000,000	—	—	0.10	1.00	—
1991R Proof	11,000	Value: 10.00				
1992R	1,000,000	—	—	0.10	1.00	—
1992R Proof	9,500	Value: 10.00				
1993R	1,000,000	—	—	0.10	1.00	—
1993R Proof	8,500	Value: 10.00				
1994R	1,000,000	—	—	0.10	1.00	—
1994R Proof	8,500	Value: 10.00				
1995R	2,500,000	—	—	0.10	1.00	—
1995R Proof	7,960	Value: 15.00				
1996R	3,500,000	—	—	0.10	1.00	—
1996R Proof	8,000	Value: 15.00				
1997R	2,000,000	—	—	0.10	1.00	—
1997R Proof	8,440	Value: 15.00				
1998R	1,500,000	—	—	0.10	1.00	—
1998R Proof	9,000	Value: 10.00				
1999R	1,500,000	—	—	0.10	1.00	—
1999R Proof	8,500	Value: 10.00				
2000R	61,400	—	—	—	20.00	—
2000R Proof		Value: 18.00				

KM# 97.1   20 LIRE
3.6000 g., Aluminum-Bronze, 21.25 mm. **Obv:** Wheat sprigs within head left **Rev:** Oak leaves divide value and date

Date	Mintage	F	VF	XF	Unc	BU
1957R Serifed 7	Est. 60,075,000	0.20	0.40	2.00	10.00	—
1957R Plain 7	Inc. above	0.20	0.40	2.00	10.00	—
1958R	80,550,000	0.10	0.40	3.00	12.00	—
1959R	4,005,000	0.50	2.00	10.00	60.00	—

KM# 97.2   20 LIRE
3.6000 g., Aluminum-Bronze, 19.63 mm. **Obv:** Wheat sprigs within head left **Rev:** Oak leaves divide value and date **Edge:** Plain

Date	Mintage	F	VF	XF	Unc	BU
1968R	100,000	3.00	6.00	25.00	60.00	—
1969R	16,735,000	0.10	0.15	0.25	1.00	—
1970R	31,500,000	0.10	0.15	0.25	0.65	—
1971R	12,375,000	0.10	0.15	0.25	0.65	—
1972R	34,400,000	0.10	0.15	0.25	0.65	—
1973R	20,000,000	0.10	0.15	0.25	0.65	—
1974R	17,000,000	0.10	0.15	0.20	0.65	—
1975R	25,000,000	0.10	0.15	0.20	0.65	—
1976R	17,325,000	0.10	0.15	0.20	0.65	—
1977R	10,000,000	0.10	0.15	0.20	0.65	—
1978R	13,521,000	0.10	0.15	0.20	0.65	—
1979R	40,465,000	0.10	0.15	0.20	0.50	—
1980R	61,795,000	0.10	0.15	0.20	0.50	—
1981R	81,510,000	0.10	0.15	0.20	0.50	—
1982R	34,500,000	0.10	0.15	0.20	0.50	—
1983R	15,110,000	0.10	0.15	0.20	0.50	—
1984R	5,122,000	0.10	0.15	1.00	3.00	—
1985R	15,000,000	0.10	0.15	0.20	0.50	—
1985R Proof	20,000	Value: 10.00				
1986R	13,000,000	0.10	0.15	0.20	0.50	—
1986R Proof	17,500	Value: 10.00				
1987R	2,766,000	0.10	0.15	1.00	3.00	—
1987R Proof	10,000	Value: 10.00				
1988R	13,000,000	0.10	0.15	0.20	0.50	—
1988R Proof	9,000	Value: 15.00				
1989R	16,000,000	0.10	0.15	0.20	0.50	—
1989R Proof	9,260	Value: 10.00				
1990R	15,500,000	0.10	0.15	0.20	0.50	—
1990R Proof	9,400	Value: 10.00				
1991R	13,000,000	0.10	0.15	0.20	0.50	—
1991R Proof	11,000	Value: 10.00				
1992R	2,500,000	0.10	0.15	1.00	3.00	—
1992R Proof	9,500	Value: 10.00				
1993R	1,000,000	0.10	0.15	0.50	1.00	—
1993R Proof	8,500	Value: 10.00				
1994R	1,000,000	0.10	0.15	0.20	0.50	—
1994R Proof	8,500	Value: 10.00				
1995R	1,000,000	0.10	0.15	0.50	1.00	—
1995R Proof	7,950	Value: 15.00				
1996R	1,000,000	0.10	0.15	0.50	1.00	—
1996R Proof	8,000	Value: 10.00				
1997R	1,000,000	0.10	0.15	0.50	1.00	—
1997R Proof	8,440	Value: 20.00				
1998R	1,000,000	0.10	0.15	0.50	1.00	—
1998R Proof	9,000	Value: 10.00				
1999R	500,000	0.10	0.15	1.00	3.00	—
1999R Proof	8,500	Value: 10.00				
2000R	61,400	—	—	—	20.00	—
2000R Proof	8,960	Value: 15.00				

KM# 95.1   50 LIRE
6.2500 g., Stainless Steel, 24.8 mm. **Obv:** Head right **Rev:** Vulcan standing at anvil facing left divides date and value

Date	Mintage	F	VF	XF	Unc	BU
1954R	17,600,000	1.00	5.00	25.00	100	—
1955R	70,500,000	0.50	1.50	10.00	40.00	—
1956R	69,400,000	0.50	1.50	10.00	40.00	—
1957R	8,925,000	2.00	8.00	30.00	120	—
1958R	825,000	5.00	20.00	40.00	100	—
1959R	8,800,000	4.00	7.00	12.00	40.00	—
1960R	2,025,000	5.00	10.00	40.00	100	—
1961R	11,100,000	0.50	1.50	10.00	40.00	—
1962R	17,700,000	0.50	1.50	5.00	30.00	—
1963R	31,600,000	0.20	0.75	2.50	20.00	—
1964R	37,900,000	0.20	0.75	2.50	18.00	—
1965R	25,300,000	0.20	0.50	1.50	12.00	—
1966R	27,400,000	0.20	0.40	0.80	8.00	—
1967R	28,000,000	0.20	0.40	0.80	6.00	—
1968R	17,800,000	0.20	0.30	0.50	1.50	—
1969R	23,010,000	0.20	0.30	0.50	1.50	—
1970R	21,411,000	0.10	0.20	0.50	1.50	—
1971R	33,410,000	0.10	0.20	0.50	1.50	—
1972R	39,000,000	0.10	0.20	0.50	1.50	—
1973R	48,700,000	0.10	0.20	0.50	1.50	—
1974R	63,000,000	0.10	0.20	0.35	1.00	—
1975R	87,000,000	0.10	0.15	0.25	0.75	—
1976R	180,600,000	0.10	0.15	0.25	0.75	—
1977R	293,800,000	0.10	0.15	0.25	0.75	—
1978R	416,808,000	0.10	0.15	0.25	0.75	—

Date	Mintage	F	VF	XF	Unc	BU
1979R	321,086,000	0.10	0.15	0.25	0.75	—
1980R	94,819,000	0.10	0.15	0.25	0.75	—
1981R	139,080,000	0.10	0.15	0.25	0.75	—
1982R	54,500,000	0.10	0.15	0.25	0.75	—
1983R	20,000,000	0.10	0.15	0.25	0.75	—
1984R	10,000,000	0.10	0.15	0.25	0.75	—
1985R	10,000,000	0.10	0.15	0.25	0.75	—
1985R Proof	20,000	Value: 10.00				
1986R	15,000,000	—	—	—	0.75	—
1986R Proof	17,500	Value: 10.00				
1987R	14,682,000	0.10	0.15	0.25	0.75	—
1987R Proof	10,000	Value: 10.00				
1988R	20,000,000	0.10	0.15	0.25	0.75	—
1988R Proof	9,000	Value: 20.00				
1989R	26,500,000	0.10	0.15	0.25	0.75	—
1989R Proof	9,200	Value: 12.00				

KM# 95.2   50 LIRE
2.7300 g., Stainless Steel, 17 mm. **Obv:** Head right **Rev:** Vulcan standing at anvil facing left divides date and value **Edge:** Plain **Note:** Reduced size.

Date	Mintage	F	VF	XF	Unc	BU
1990R	45,500,000	—	0.10	0.20	0.50	—
1990R Proof	—	Value: 10.00				
1991R	60,000,000	—	0.10	0.20	0.50	—
1991R Proof	11,000	Value: 10.00				
1992R	90,000,000	—	0.10	0.20	0.50	—
1992R Proof	9,500	Value: 10.00				
1993R	160,000,000	—	0.10	0.20	0.50	—
1993R Proof	8,500	Value: 10.00				
1994R	95,255,000	—	0.10	0.20	0.50	—
1994R Proof	8,500	Value: 10.00				
1995R	82,000,000	—	0.10	0.20	0.50	—
1995R Proof	7,960	Value: 12.00				

KM# 183   50 LIRE
Copper-Nickel, 19 mm. **Obv:** Turreted head left **Rev:** Large value within wreath of produce

Date	Mintage	F	VF	XF	Unc	BU
1996R	110,000,000	—	0.10	0.20	0.50	—
1996R Proof	8,000	Value: 15.00				
1997R	10,000,000	—	0.10	0.20	1.00	—
1997R Proof	8,440	Value: 20.00				
1998R	10,000,000	—	0.10	0.20	1.00	—
1998R Proof	9,000	Value: 15.00				
1999R	55,000,000	—	0.10	0.20	1.00	—
1999R Proof	8,500	Value: 18.00				
2000R	61,400	—	—	—	12.00	—
2000R Proof	8,960	Value: 18.00				

KM# 96.1   100 LIRE
8.0000 g., Stainless Steel, 27.8 mm. **Obv:** Laureate head left **Rev:** Standing figure holding olive tree

Date	Mintage	F	VF	XF	Unc	BU
1955R	8,600,000	1.00	4.00	50.00	185	—
1956R	99,800,000	0.25	1.00	4.00	50.00	—
1957R	90,600,000	0.25	1.50	4.00	50.00	—
1958R	25,640,000	0.25	1.50	10.00	120	—
1959R	19,500,000	0.25	1.50	10.00	120	—
1960R	20,700,000	0.25	1.50	10.00	100	—
1961R	11,860,000	0.25	1.50	10.00	100	—
1962R	21,700,000	0.20	0.50	3.00	40.00	—
1963R	33,100,000	0.20	0.50	2.00	30.00	—
1964R	31,300,000	0.20	0.50	1.50	20.00	—
1965R	37,000,000	0.20	0.50	1.50	20.00	—
1966R	52,500,000	0.15	0.25	1.00	15.00	—
1967R	23,700,000	0.15	0.25	1.00	15.00	—
1968R	34,200,000	0.15	0.25	0.50	2.00	—
1969R	27,710,000	0.15	0.25	0.50	2.00	—
1970R	25,011,000	0.15	0.25	0.50	2.00	—
1971R	24,700,000	0.15	0.25	0.50	2.00	—
1972R	31,170,000	0.15	0.25	0.50	3.00	—
1973R	30,780,000	0.15	0.25	0.50	3.00	—
1974R	61,000,000	0.15	0.25	0.35	0.85	—
1975R	106,650,000	0.15	0.25	0.35	0.85	—

Date	Mintage	F	VF	XF	Unc	BU
1976R	160,020,000	0.15	0.25	0.35	0.85	—
1977R	253,980,000	0.15	0.25	0.35	0.85	—
1978R	343,626,000	0.15	0.25	0.35	0.85	—
1979R	351,583,600	0.15	0.25	0.35	0.85	—
1980R	69,938,500	0.15	0.25	0.35	0.85	—
1981R	122,381,700	0.15	0.25	0.35	0.85	—
1982R	39,500,000	0.15	0.25	0.35	0.85	—
1983R	25,000,000	0.15	0.25	1.00	3.00	—
1984R	10,000,000	0.15	0.25	1.00	3.00	—
1985R	10,000,000	0.15	0.25	1.00	3.00	—
1985R Proof	20,000	Value: 10.00				
1986R	18,000,000	0.15	0.25	0.50	1.00	—
1986R Proof	17,500	Value: 10.00				
1987R	25,000,000	0.15	0.25	0.50	1.00	—
1987R Proof	10,000	Value: 15.00				
1988R	23,000,000	0.15	0.25	0.85	1.00	—
1988R Proof	9,000	Value: 20.00				
1989R	34,000,000	0.15	0.25	0.85	1.00	—
1989R Proof	9,260	Value: 20.00				

KM# 96.2   100 LIRE

Stainless Steel **Obv:** Laureate head left **Rev:** Standing figure holding olive tree **Note:** Reduced size. Prev. KM#96a.

Date	Mintage	F	VF	XF	Unc	BU
1990R Proof	9,600	Value: 15.00				
1990R	60,000,000	—	—	—	1.00	—
1991R	100,000,000	—	—	—	1.00	—
1991R Proof	11,000	Value: 18.00				
1992R	166,000,000	—	—	—	1.00	—
1992R Proof	9,500	Value: 18.00				

KM# 102   100 LIRE

8.0000 g., Stainless Steel, 27.8 mm. **Subject:** 100th Anniversary - Birth of Guglielmo Marconi, Physicist **Obv:** Head facing **Rev:** Early radio-wave receiver flanked by date and value

Date	Mintage	F	VF	XF	Unc	BU
ND(1974)R	50,000,000	0.15	0.25	0.35	1.50	—

KM# 106   100 LIRE

8.0000 g., Stainless Steel, 27.8 mm. , Young head left **Series:** F.A.O. **Rev:** Cow nursing calf, value and date

Date	Mintage	F	VF	XF	Unc	BU
1979R	78,340,000	0.15	0.25	0.50	2.00	—

KM# 108   100 LIRE

8.0000 g., Stainless Steel, 27.8 mm. **Subject:** Centennial of Livorno Naval Academy **Obv:** Anchor and ship's wheel **Rev:** Building divides dates with flag and value below

Date	Mintage	F	VF	XF	Unc	BU
ND(1981)R	39,500,000	0.15	0.25	0.35	1.50	—

KM# 127   100 LIRE

8.0000 g., 0.8350 Silver 0.2148 oz. ASW, 27.8 mm.
Subject: 900th Anniversary - University of Bologna
Obv: Medieval student in thought **Rev:** Towered building

Date	Mintage	F	VF	XF	Unc	BU
1988R	68,000	—	—	—	18.00	—
1988R Proof	13,000	Value: 28.00				

KM# 159   100 LIRE

Copper-Nickel, 22 mm. **Obv:** Turreted head left **Rev:** Large value within circle flanked by sprigs

Date	Mintage	F	VF	XF	Unc	BU
1993R	211,501,200	0.15	0.25	0.35	0.75	—
1993R Proof	8,500	Value: 15.00				
1994R	180,000,000	0.15	0.25	0.35	0.75	—
1994R Proof	8,500	Value: 15.00				
1996R	210,000,000	0.15	0.25	0.35	0.75	—
1996R Proof	8,000	Value: 20.00				
1997R	70,000,000	0.15	0.25	0.35	0.75	—
1997R Proof	8,440	Value: 35.00				
1998R	120,000,000	0.15	0.25	0.35	0.75	—
1998R Proof	9,000	Value: 15.00				
1999R	120,000,000	0.15	0.25	0.35	0.75	—
1999R Proof	8,500	Value: 15.00				
2000R	61,400	0.15	0.25	0.35	15.00	—
2000R Proof	10,000	Value: 20.00				

KM# 171   100 LIRE

5.0000 g., 835.0000 Silver 134.22 oz. ASW **Subject:** 100th Anniversary - Bank of Italy **Rev:** Printing press **Note:** Both uncirculated and proof versions were issued in sets only.

Date	Mintage	F	VF	XF	Unc	BU
ND(1993)R	52,000	—	—	—	20.00	—
ND(1993)R Proof	10,000	Value: 35.00				

KM# 180   100 LIRE

4.5300 g., Copper-Nickel, 22 mm. **Series:** F.A.O. **Obv:** Turreted head left **Rev:** Logo and value within globe design

Date	Mintage	F	VF	XF	Unc	BU
ND(1995)R	100,000,000	0.15	0.25	0.35	0.75	—
ND(1995)R Proof	7,960	Value: 25.00				

KM# 105   200 LIRE

5.0000 g., Aluminum-Bronze, 24 mm. **Obv:** Head right **Rev:** Value within gear

Date	Mintage	F	VF	XF	Unc	BU
1977R	15,900,000	0.20	0.25	0.35	1.25	—
1978R	461,034,000	0.20	0.25	0.35	1.25	—
1979R	437,325,000	0.20	0.25	0.35	1.25	—
1980R	105,690,000	0.20	0.25	0.45	2.00	—
1981R	72,500,000	0.20	0.25	0.45	2.00	—
1982R	9,500,000	0.20	0.25	1.00	4.00	—
1983R	20,000,000	0.20	0.25	0.75	3.00	—
1984R	10,000,000	0.20	0.25	0.75	3.00	—
1985R	15,000,000	0.20	0.25	0.75	3.00	—
1985R Proof	20,000	Value: 10.00				
1986R	15,000,000	0.20	0.25	0.75	3.00	—
1986R Proof	17,500	Value: 10.00				
1987R	26,180,000	0.20	0.25	0.35	1.25	—
1987R Proof	10,000	Value: 10.00				
1988R	37,000,000	0.20	0.25	0.35	1.25	—

Date	Mintage	F	VF	XF	Unc	BU
1988R Proof	9,000	Value: 25.00				
1991R	70,000,000	0.20	0.25	0.35	1.25	—
1991R Proof	11,000	Value: 20.00				
1995R	170,000,000	0.20	0.25	0.35	1.25	—
1995R Proof	7,960	Value: 40.00				
1998R	120,000,000	0.20	0.25	0.35	1.25	—
1998R Proof	9,000	Value: 15.00				
2000R	61,400	—	—	—	15.00	—
2000R Proof	8,960	Value: 20.00				

KM# 107   200 LIRE

5.0000 g., Aluminum-Bronze, 24 mm. **Series:** F.A.O. **Subject:** International Women's Year **Obv:** Bust facing **Rev:** Seated woman with knee bent and child standing at her back facing right

Date	Mintage	F	VF	XF	Unc	BU
1980R	48,500,000	0.20	0.25	0.35	2.00	3.00

KM# 109   200 LIRE

5.0000 g., Aluminum-Bronze, 24 mm. **Subject:** World Food Day **Obv:** Villa Lubin façade **Rev:** Female advancing left holding cornucopia

Date	Mintage	F	VF	XF	Unc	BU
1981R	45,207,600	0.20	0.25	0.35	2.00	3.00

KM# 128   200 LIRE

5.0000 g., 0.8350 Silver 0.1342 oz. ASW **Subject:** 900th Anniversary - University of Bologna **Obv:** Medieval student in thought **Rev:** Courtyard view within oval rope wreath

Date	Mintage	F	VF	XF	Unc	BU
1988R	68,000	—	—	—	20.00	—
1988R Proof	13,000	Value: 30.00				

KM# 130   200 LIRE

5.0000 g., Bronzital, 24 mm. **Subject:** Taranto Naval Yards **Obv:** Head right **Rev:** Ships and dates

Date	Mintage	F	VF	XF	Unc	BU
ND(1989)R	48,000,000	—	—	—	2.00	3.00
ND(1989)R Proof	9,260	Value: 10.00				

KM# 133   200 LIRE

5.0000 g., 0.8350 Silver 0.1342 oz. ASW **Subject:** Soccer **Obv:** Head left **Rev:** Ball superimposed on world globe within assorted shields bordering

Date	Mintage	F	VF	XF	Unc	BU
1989R	86,000	—	—	—	15.00	—
1989R Proof	28,000	Value: 18.50				

KM# 138   200 LIRE

5.0000 g., 0.8350 Silver 0.1342 oz. ASW **Subject:** Christopher Columbus **Obv:** Bust 3/4 right within globe design **Rev:** Shield divides date and value above dolphin

Date	Mintage	F	VF	XF	Unc	BU
1989R	75,000	—	—	—	15.00	—
1989R Proof	25,000	Value: 22.50				

KM# 135 200 LIRE
5.0000 g., Bronzital, 24 mm. **Obv:** Head right **Rev:** State Council building divides dates and value

Date	Mintage	F	VF	XF	Unc	BU
ND(1990)R	64,500,000	—	—	—	2.00	3.00
ND(1990)R Proof	9,600	Value: 10.00				

KM# 142 200 LIRE
9.0000 g., 0.8350 Silver 0.2416 oz. ASW **Subject:** Italian Flora and Fauna **Obv:** Female head left with flora and fauna in hair **Rev:** Wolf divides date and value

Date	Mintage	F	VF	XF	Unc	BU
1991R	57,000	—	—	—	20.00	—
1991R Proof	10,000	Value: 27.50				

KM# 151 200 LIRE
5.0000 g., Aluminum-Bronze, 24 mm. **Subject:** Genoa Stamp Exposition **Obv:** Head right **Rev:** Stylized sailing ship

Date	Mintage	F	VF	XF	Unc	BU
1992R	110,000,000	—	—	—	2.50	3.50
1992R Proof	9,500	Value: 12.00				

KM# 155 200 LIRE
5.0000 g., Aluminum-Bronze, 24 mm. **Subject:** 70th Anniversary of Military Aviation **Obv:** Head right **Rev:** Quartered arms within circle

Date	Mintage	F	VF	XF	Unc	BU
1993R	170,000,000	—	—	—	2.50	3.50
1993R Proof	8,500	Value: 10.00				

KM# 172 200 LIRE
5.0000 g., 0.8350 Silver 0.1342 oz. ASW **Subject:** 100th Anniversary - Bank of Italy **Obv:** Female head left with headdress **Rev:** Hammered minting scene **Note:** Both uncirculated and proof versions were issued in sets only.

Date	Mintage	F	VF	XF	Unc	BU
ND(1993)R	52,000	—	—	—	25.00	—
ND(1993)R Proof	10,000	Value: 40.00				

KM# 164 200 LIRE
5.0000 g., Aluminum-Bronze, 24 mm. **Subject:** 180th Anniversary - Carabinieri **Obv:** Head right **Rev:** Flaming bomb above banner and value

Date	Mintage	F	VF	XF	Unc	BU
ND(1994)R	200,000,000	—	—	—	2.00	3.00
ND(1994)R Proof	8,500	Value: 12.00				

KM# 184 200 LIRE
5.0000 g., Brass, 24 mm. **Subject:** Centennial - Customs Service Academy **Obv:** Old and new buildings **Rev:** Shield above value, hat and sword

Date	Mintage	F	VF	XF	Unc	BU
ND(1996)R	200,000,000	—	—	—	1.50	2.00
ND(1996)R Proof	8,000	Value: 12.00				

KM# 186 200 LIRE
5.0000 g., Brass, 24 mm. **Subject:** Centennial - Italian Naval League **Obv:** Head right **Rev:** Naval League seal divides dates and value **Edge:** Reeded

Date	Mintage	F	VF	XF	Unc	BU
ND(1997)R	40,000,000	—	—	—	1.25	1.75
ND(1997)R Proof	8,440	Value: 15.00				

KM# 218 200 LIRE
5.0000 g., Aluminum-Bronze, 24 mm. **Subject:** The Carabinieri, Protectors of Art Heritage **Rev:** Flaming bomb and David statue **Edge:** Reeded

Date	Mintage	F	VF	XF	Unc	BU
ND(1999)R	105,000,000	—	—	—	1.50	2.00
ND(1999)R Proof	8,500	Value: 10.00				

KM# 98 500 LIRE
11.0000 g., 0.8350 Silver 0.2953 oz. ASW, 29.3 mm. **Obv:** Columbus' ships **Rev:** Bust left within wreath **Edge:** Dates in raised lettering

Date	Mintage	F	VF	XF	Unc	BU
1958R	24,240,000	—	2.00	4.50	10.00	—
1958R Proof	Inc. above	Value: 36.00				
1959R	19,360,000	—	2.00	4.50	10.00	—
1959R Proof	Inc. above	Value: 36.00				
1960R	24,080,000	—	2.00	4.50	9.00	—
1960R Proof	Inc. above	Value: 36.00				
1961R	6,560,000	—	5.00	10.00	20.00	—
1961R Proof	Inc. above	Value: 50.00				
1964R	4,880,000	—	2.00	7.50	18.00	—
1964R Proof	Inc. above	Value: 30.00				
1965R	3,120,000	—	2.00	8.00	20.00	—
1965R Proof	Inc. above	Value: 30.00				
1966R	13,120,000	—	2.00	4.50	10.00	—
Note: Varieties exist						
1966R Proof	Inc. above	Value: 25.00				
1967R	2,480,000	—	2.00	4.50	10.00	—
1967R Proof	Inc. above	Value: 25.00				
1968R	100,000	—	—	—	70.00	—
1968R Proof	Inc. above	Value: 100				
1969R	310,000	—	—	—	40.00	—
1969R Proof	Inc. above	Value: 30.00				
1970R	1,140,000	—	—	—	20.00	—
1970R Proof	Inc. above	Value: 25.00				

Date	Mintage	F	VF	XF	Unc	BU
1980R	257,270	—	—	—	15.00	—
1980R Proof	Inc. above	Value: 25.00				
1981R	162,794	—	—	—	16.50	—
1981R Proof	Inc. above	Value: 30.00				
1982R	115,000	—	—	—	16.50	—
1982R Proof	Inc. above	Value: 30.00				
1983R	76,000	—	—	—	100	—
1984R	77,000	—	—	—	80.00	—
1985R	74,600	—	—	—	30.00	—
1985R Proof	15,000	Value: 40.00				
1986R	73,200	—	—	—	30.00	—
1986R Proof	Inc. above	Value: 40.00				
1987R	57,500	—	—	—	50.00	—
1987R Proof	10,000	Value: 65.00				
1988R	51,050	—	—	—	100	—
1988R Proof	10,000	Value: 90.00				
1989R	51,200	—	—	—	50.00	—
1989R Proof	10,000	Value: 75.00				
1990R	52,300	—	—	—	40.00	—
1990R Proof	10,000	Value: 50.00				
1991R	54,000	—	—	—	40.00	—
1991R Proof	11,000	Value: 60.00				
1992R	52,000	—	—	—	35.00	—
1992R Proof	9,500	Value: 60.00				
1993R	50,200	—	—	—	35.00	—
1993R Proof	8,500	Value: 60.00				
1994R	44,500	—	—	—	80.00	—
1994R Proof	8,500	Value: 95.00				
1995R	44,558	—	—	—	100	—
1995R Proof	7,960	Value: 150				
1996R	45,000	—	—	—	40.00	—
1996R Proof	8,000	Value: 90.00				
1997R	43,600	—	—	—	90.00	—
1997R Proof	8,440	Value: 150				
1998R	55,100	—	—	—	30.00	—
1998R Proof	9,000	Value: 60.00				
1999R	51,800	—	—	—	50.00	—
1999R Proof	8,500	Value: 70.00				
2000R	61,400	—	—	—	95.00	—
2000R Proof	8,960	Value: 55.00				

KM# 99 500 LIRE
11.0000 g., 0.8350 Silver 0.2953 oz. ASW, 29.3 mm. **Subject:** Italian Unification Centennial **Obv:** Female seated left **Rev:** Quadriga

Date	Mintage	F	VF	XF	Unc	BU
ND(1961)R	27,120,000	—	BV	4.50	7.00	—
ND(1961)R Prooflike	Inc. above	—	—	—	20.00	—

KM# 100 500 LIRE
11.0000 g., 0.8350 Silver 0.2953 oz. ASW, 29.3 mm. **Subject:** 700th Anniversary - Birth of Dante Alighieri, Poet **Obv:** Head left **Rev:** Radiant sun above flame, value and date

Date	Mintage	F	VF	XF	Unc	BU
1965R	4,272,000	—	BV	5.00	12.00	—
1965R Proof	Inc. above	Value: 15.00				

KM# 103 500 LIRE
11.0000 g., 0.8350 Silver 0.2953 oz. ASW, 29.3 mm. **Subject:** 100th Anniversary - Birth of Guglielmo Marconi, Physicist **Obv:** Bust left **Rev:** Map of Italy with radio tower loops

Date	Mintage	F	VF	XF	Unc	BU
ND(1974)R	689,752	—	—	—	8.00	—
ND(1974)R Proof	Inc. above	Value: 15.00				

KM# 104   500 LIRE
11.0000 g., 0.8350 Silver 0.2953 oz. ASW, 29.3 mm.
Subject: 500th Anniversary - Birth of Michelangelo Buonarroti
Obv: Bust left **Rev:** Seated statue divides dates with value below

Date	Mintage	F	VF	XF	Unc	BU
1975R	269,000	—	—	—	10.00	—
1975R Proof	Inc. above	Value: 20.00				

KM# 110   500 LIRE
11.0000 g., 0.8350 Silver 0.2953 oz. ASW, 29.3 mm.
Subject: 2000th Anniversary - Death of Virgil **Obv:** Head left
Rev: Tree divides cow, horse and dates with value below

Date	Mintage	F	VF	XF	Unc	BU
1981R (1982)	341,000	—	—	—	14.00	—
1981R (1982) Proof	Inc. above	Value: 17.00				

KM# 111   500 LIRE
6.8000 g., Bi-Metallic Bronzital center in Acmonital ring, 25.8 mm.
Obv: Head left within circle **Rev:** Plaza within circle flanked by sprigs

Date	Mintage	F	VF	XF	Unc	BU
1982R	162,000	—	0.40	0.60	2.00	—
Note: Obverse portrait varieties exist						
1983R	137,974,000	—	0.40	0.60	2.00	—
1984R	162,000,000	—	0.40	0.60	2.00	—
1985R	162,000,000	—	0.40	0.60	2.00	—
1985R Proof	20,000	Value: 10.00				
1986R	165,000,000	—	0.40	0.60	2.00	—
1986R Proof	17,500	Value: 10.00				
1987R	200,000,000	—	0.40	0.60	2.00	—
1987R Proof	10,000	Value: 10.00				
1988R	142,000,000	—	0.40	0.60	2.00	—
1988R Proof	9,000	Value: 25.00				
1989R	155,000,000	—	0.40	0.60	2.00	—
1989R Proof	9,250	Value: 10.00				
1990R	130,000,000	—	0.40	0.60	2.00	—
1990R Proof	9,400	Value: 12.00				
1991R	140,000,000	—	0.40	0.60	2.00	—
1991R Proof	11,400	Value: 18.00				
1992R	150,000,000	—	0.40	0.60	2.00	—
Note: Obverse portrait varieties exist						
1992R Proof	9,500	Value: 18.00				
1995R	110,000,000	—	—	0.60	2.00	—
1995R Proof	7,960	Value: 35.00				
2000R	61,400	—	—	—	15.00	—
2000R Proof	10,000	Value: 30.00				

KM# 112   500 LIRE
11.0000 g., 0.8350 Silver 0.2953 oz. ASW, 29.3 mm.
Subject: 100th Anniversary - Death of Giuseppe Garibaldi
Obv: Bust right **Rev:** Island map divides value and date

Date	Mintage	F	VF	XF	Unc	BU
1982R (1983)	193,000	—	—	—	22.00	—
1982R (1983) Proof	Inc. above	Value: 30.00				

KM# 113   500 LIRE
11.0000 g., 0.8350 Silver 0.2953 oz. ASW, 29.3 mm.
Obv: Bust of G. Galiei facing **Rev:** Dog within crowned wreath dividing dates with value below

Date	Mintage	F	VF	XF	Unc	BU
ND(1983)R	198,000	—	—	—	22.00	—
ND(1983)R Proof	Inc. above	Value: 30.00				

KM# 114   500 LIRE
11.0000 g., 0.8350 Silver 0.2953 oz. ASW, 29.3 mm. **Subject:** Los Angeles Olympics **Obv:** Head right between dove at left and torch at right **Rev:** Three figures holding up Olympic flame

Date	Mintage	F	VF	XF	Unc	BU
1984R	193,000	—	—	—	22.00	—
1984R Proof	Value: 25.00					

KM# 115   500 LIRE
11.0000 g., 0.8350 Silver 0.2953 oz. ASW, 29.3 mm.
Subject: First Italian President of Common Market **Obv:** Head left with map, stars and globe within scalp **Rev:** Flags above stylized ancient stadium

Date	Mintage	F	VF	XF	Unc	BU
1985R	103,000	—	—	—	35.00	—
1985R Proof	29,000	Value: 50.00				

KM# 116   500 LIRE
11.0000 g., 0.8350 Silver 0.2953 oz. ASW, 29.3 mm.
Obv: Town's architectural montage **Rev:** Hilltop castle above two hemispheres

Date	Mintage	F	VF	XF	Unc	BU
1985R	126,000	—	—	—	25.00	—
1985R Proof	Inc. above	Value: 38.00				

KM# 117   500 LIRE
11.0000 g., 0.8350 Silver 0.2953 oz. ASW, 29.3 mm.
Subject: European Year of Music **Obv:** Muse of music left
Rev: Pipe organ frontal view

Date	Mintage	F	VF	XF	Unc	BU
1985R	96,000	—	—	—	25.00	—
1985R Proof	Inc. above	Value: 30.00				

KM# 118   500 LIRE
11.0000 g., 0.8350 Silver 0.2953 oz. ASW, 29.3 mm.
Subject: Etruscan Culture **Obv:** Standing warrior **Rev:** Two winged horses left

Date	Mintage	F	VF	XF	Unc	BU
1985R	104,000	—	—	—	15.00	—
1985R Proof	Inc. above	Value: 30.00				

KM# 123   500 LIRE
11.0000 g., 0.8350 Silver 0.2953 oz. ASW, 29.3 mm.
Subject: 200th Anniversary - Birth of Alessandro Manzoni
Obv: Bust 3/4 facing **Rev:** Headdress

Date	Mintage	F	VF	XF	Unc	BU
1985R	91,218	—	—	—	40.00	—
1985R Proof	20,000	Value: 65.00				

KM# 119   500 LIRE
11.0000 g., 0.8350 Silver 0.2953 oz. ASW, 29.3 mm.
Subject: Soccer Championship - Mexico **Obv:** Map of Italy and soccer ball **Rev:** Aztec Calendar within soccer ball

Date	Mintage	F	VF	XF	Unc	BU
1986R	91,000	—	—	—	20.00	—
1986R Proof	21,000	Value: 38.00				

KM# 120   500 LIRE
11.0000 g., 0.8350 Silver 0.2953 oz. ASW, 29.3 mm.
Subject: Year of Peace **Obv:** Head right **Rev:** Ancient tree

Date	Mintage	F	VF	XF	Unc	BU
1986R	90,000	—	—	—	20.00	—
1986R Proof	19,000	Value: 28.00				

KM# 124   500 LIRE
11.0000 g., 0.8350 Silver 0.2953 oz. ASW, 29.3 mm.
Subject: 600th Anniversary - Birth of Donatello **Obv:** Head with headdress 1/4 left **Rev:** Standing male statue to left of value and date

Date	Mintage	F	VF	XF	Unc	BU
1986R	73,000	—	—	—	40.00	—
1986R Proof	17,500	Value: 65.00				

KM# 121   500 LIRE
11.0000 g., 0.8350 Silver 0.2953 oz. ASW, 29.3 mm.
Subject: Year of the Family **Obv:** Head left **Rev:** Family scene

Date	Mintage	F	VF	XF	Unc	BU
1987R	85,000	—	—	—	20.00	—
1987R Proof	20,000	Value: 30.00				

KM# 122   500 LIRE
11.0000 g., 0.8350 Silver 0.2953 oz. ASW, 29.3 mm.
Subject: World Athletic Championships **Obv:** Stylized runner left
Rev: Ancient and modern sprinter, Coliseum in background

Date	Mintage	F	VF	XF	Unc	BU
1987R	80,000	—	—	—	20.00	—
1987R Proof	20,000	Value: 30.00				

KM# 132   500 LIRE
10.9600 g., 0.8350 Silver 0.2942 oz. ASW, 29.01 mm.
Subject: 150th Anniversary Death of Giacomo Leopardi, poet
Obv: Bust 3/4 left **Obv. Leg.:** REPUBBLICA - ITALIANA
Rev: Female standing 3/4 left at center **Rev. Leg.:** ERA IL MAGGIO
- ODOROSO **Edge:** Lettered **Edge:** GIACOMO LEOPARDI 1837-
1987

Date	Mintage	F	VF	XF	Unc	BU
1987R	58,000	—	—	—	100	—
1987R Proof	10,000	Value: 120				

KM# 125   500 LIRE
11.0000 g., 0.8350 Silver 0.2953 oz. ASW, 29.3 mm.
Subject: Summer Olympics - Seoul **Obv:** Face left with dove and
torch **Rev:** Two artistic figures within wreath above rings

Date	Mintage	F	VF	XF	Unc	BU
1988R	70,000	—	—	—	25.00	—
1988R Proof	13,000	Value: 35.00				

KM# 126   500 LIRE
11.0000 g., 0.8350 Silver 0.2953 oz. ASW, 29.3 mm. **Subject:**
40th Anniversary of Constitution **Obv:** Turreted head left **Rev:**
Oak and laurel sprig within partial text with dates and value below

Date	Mintage	F	VF	XF	Unc	BU
ND(1988)R	67,000	—	—	—	22.00	—
ND(1988)R Proof	13,000	Value: 40.00				

KM# 129   500 LIRE
11.0000 g., 0.8350 Silver 0.2953 oz. ASW, 29.3 mm.
Subject: 900th Anniversary - University of Bologna
Obv: Medieval student in thought **Rev:** Emblem

Date	Mintage	F	VF	XF	Unc	BU
1988R	68,000	—	—	—	35.00	—
1988R Proof	13,000	Value: 60.00				

KM# 144   500 LIRE
11.0000 g., 0.8350 Silver 0.2953 oz. ASW, 29.3 mm.
Subject: 100th Anniversary - Death of Giovanni Bosco **Obv:** Bust
facing **Rev:** Mother, father and seated child

Date	Mintage	F	VF	XF	Unc	BU
1988R	51,000	—	—	—	220	—
1988R Proof	9,000	Value: 250				

KM# 131   500 LIRE
11.0000 g., 0.8350 Silver 0.2953 oz. ASW, 29.3 mm.
Subject: Fight Against Cancer **Obv:** Female doctor and DNA
Rev: Heartbeat, microscope and hand

Date	Mintage	F	VF	XF	Unc	BU
1989R	46,000	—	—	—	60.00	—
1989R Proof	7,598	Value: 90.00				

KM# 134   500 LIRE
11.0000 g., 0.8350 Silver 0.2953 oz. ASW, 29.3 mm.
Subject: Soccer **Obv:** Head left with world cup trophy within hair
Rev: Map of Italy within world globe

Date	Mintage	F	VF	XF	Unc	BU
1989R	88,000	—	—	—	40.00	—
1989R Proof	28,000	Value: 50.00				

KM# 139   500 LIRE
11.0000 g., 0.8350 Silver 0.2953 oz. ASW, 29.3 mm.
Subject: Christopher Columbus **Obv:** Bust 1/4 right within globe
design **Rev:** Ships in dock

Date	Mintage	F	VF	XF	Unc	BU
1989R	75,000	—	—	—	30.00	—
1989R Proof	25,000	Value: 45.00				

KM# 145   500 LIRE
11.0000 g., 0.8350 Silver 0.2953 oz. ASW, 29.3 mm.
Subject: 350th Anniversary - Death of Tommaso Campanella
Obv: Bust 3/4 right **Rev:** Half sun face at left, half dome at right,
text below

Date	Mintage	F	VF	XF	Unc	BU
1989R	51,000	—	—	—	85.00	—
1989R Proof	9,260	Value: 100				

KM# 136   500 LIRE
11.0000 g., 0.8350 Silver 0.2953 oz. ASW, 29.3 mm.
Subject: Soccer **Obv:** Head left with world cup trophy within hair
Rev: Dove within globe and soccer ball

Date	Mintage	F	VF	XF	Unc	BU
1990R	67,500	—	—	—	25.00	—
1990R Proof	24,500	Value: 30.00				

KM# 137   500 LIRE
11.0000 g., 0.8350 Silver 0.2953 oz. ASW, 29.3 mm.
Subject: Italian Presidency of the E.E.C. Council **Obv:** Head left
Rev: Logo

Date	Mintage	F	VF	XF	Unc	BU
1990R	54,000	—	—	—	20.00	—
1990R Proof	10,000	Value: 30.00				

KM# 140   500 LIRE
11.0000 g., 0.8350 Silver 0.2953 oz. ASW, 29.3 mm.
Subject: Columbus - Discovery of America **Obv:** Head left and
new world map **Rev:** Stylized ship within an instrument

Date	Mintage	F	VF	XF	Unc	BU
1990R	75,000	—	—	—	25.00	—
1990R Proof	25,000	Value: 40.00				

KM# 146   500 LIRE
11.0000 g., 0.8350 Silver 0.2953 oz. ASW, 29.3 mm.
Subject: 500th Anniversary - Birth of Tizian **Obv:** Head left
Rev: Buildings

Date	Mintage	F	VF	XF	Unc	BU
1990R	52,300	—	—	—	60.00	—
1990R Proof	9,450	Value: 90.00				

KM# 143   500 LIRE
15.0000 g., 0.8350 Silver 0.4027 oz. ASW **Subject:** Italian Flora and Fauna **Obv:** Head facing within assorted animals and flowers **Rev:** Man within center of dead and living tree

Date	Mintage	F	VF	XF	Unc	BU
1991R	50,000	—	—	—	40.00	—
1991R Proof	9,500	Value: 45.00				

KM# 147   500 LIRE
15.0000 g., 0.8350 Silver 0.4027 oz. ASW **Subject:** 2100th Anniversary of Ponte Milvio **Obv:** Head right with bridge and shield within hair **Rev:** Stone arch bridge

Date	Mintage	F	VF	XF	Unc	BU
1991R	59,000	—	—	—	25.00	—
1991R Proof	14,000	Value: 40.00				

KM# 141   500 LIRE
11.0000 g., 0.8350 Silver 0.2953 oz. ASW **Subject:** 250th Anniversary - Death of Antonio Vivaldi **Obv:** Violinist right, building in background **Rev:** Music score and mountain scene

Date	Mintage	F	VF	XF	Unc	BU
ND(1991)R	55,000	—	—	—	100	—
ND(1991)R Proof	11,000	Value: 120				

KM# 148   500 LIRE
11.0000 g., 0.8350 Silver 0.2953 oz. ASW **Subject:** Discovery of America **Obv:** Radiant head facing **Rev:** Mapped scroll divides compass and date

Date	Mintage	F	VF	XF	Unc	BU
1991R	75,000	—	—	—	25.00	—
1991R Proof	25,000	Value: 40.00				

KM# 149   500 LIRE
15.0000 g., 0.8350 Silver 0.4027 oz. ASW **Subject:** 500th Anniversary - Death of Lorenzo de' Medici **Obv:** Bust left **Rev:** Florence tower, books, dates and value

Date	Mintage	F	VF	XF	Unc	BU
ND(1992)R	50,000	—	—	—	30.00	—
ND(1992)R Proof	11,000	Value: 50.00				

KM# 150   500 LIRE
11.0000 g., 0.8350 Silver 0.2953 oz. ASW **Subject:** Christopher Columbus **Obv:** Bust 3/4 facing **Rev:** Landing scene

Date	Mintage	F	VF	XF	Unc	BU
1992R	67,000	—	—	—	25.00	—
1992R Proof	18,000	Value: 40.00				

KM# 152   500 LIRE
15.0000 g., 0.8350 Silver 0.4027 oz. ASW **Subject:** 200th Anniversary - Birth of Gioacchino Rossini **Obv:** Bust facing **Rev:** Signature on music staff sheet

Date	Mintage	F	VF	XF	Unc	BU
1992R	45,000	—	—	—	40.00	—
1992R Proof	9,000	Value: 60.00				

KM# 153   500 LIRE
15.0000 g., 0.8350 Silver 0.4027 oz. ASW **Subject:** Olympics **Obv:** Laureate head facing and half of oval track **Rev:** Buildings and 3/4 oval track

Date	Mintage	F	VF	XF	Unc	BU
1992R	48,040	—	—	—	25.00	—
1992R Proof	12,000	Value: 45.00				

KM# 154   500 LIRE
15.0000 g., 0.8350 Silver 0.4027 oz. ASW **Subject:** Flora and Fauna **Obv:** Head left with bird and flora within hair **Rev:** Square enclosing dolphin, flamingo and other animals

Date	Mintage	F	VF	XF	Unc	BU
1992R	43,000	—	—	—	35.00	—
1992R Proof	8,500	Value: 60.00				

KM# 161   500 LIRE
11.0000 g., 0.8350 Silver 0.2953 oz. ASW **Subject:** 500th Anniversary - Death of Piero Della Francesca

Date	Mintage	F	VF	XF	Unc	BU
1992R	52,000	—	—	—	70.00	—
1992R Proof	9,500	Value: 110				

KM# 156   500 LIRE
15.0000 g., 0.8350 Silver 0.4027 oz. ASW **Subject:** 2000th Anniversary - Death of Horace **Obv:** Column divides date and value **Rev:** Bust left

Date	Mintage	F	VF	XF	Unc	BU
1993R	50,000	—	—	—	35.00	—
1993R Proof	10,000	Value: 45.00				

KM# 157   500 LIRE
15.0000 g., 0.8350 Silver 0.4027 oz. ASW **Subject:** Wildlife protection **Obv:** Head facing flanked by flowers **Rev:** Storks and swordfish divide date and value

Date	Mintage	F	VF	XF	Unc	BU
1993R	36,000	—	—	—	40.00	—
1993R Proof	10,000	Value: 50.00				

KM# 158   500 LIRE
15.0000 g., 0.8350 Silver 0.4027 oz. ASW **Subject:** 650th Anniversary - University of Pisa **Obv:** Seated figure right with open book **Rev:** Leaning Tower of Pisa to right of building

Date	Mintage	F	VF	XF	Unc	BU
1993R	41,000	—	—	—	35.00	—
1993R Proof	9,080	Value: 50.00				

KM# 160   500 LIRE
6.8000 g., Bi-Metallic Bronzital center in Acmonital ring, 25.8 mm. **Subject:** Centennial - Bank of Italy **Obv:** Head left within circle **Rev:** Monogram within design divides dates within circle **Note:** Large and small designer's name, G ROSSI, exist.

Date	Mintage	F	VF	XF	Unc	BU
ND(1993)R	Est. 90,000,000	—	—	—	2.50	—
ND(1993)R Proof	8,500	Value: 10.00				

KM# 163   500 LIRE
11.0000 g., 0.8350 Silver 0.2953 oz. ASW **Subject:** 200th Anniversary - Death of Carolo Goldoni

Date	Mintage	F	VF	XF	Unc	BU
1993R	50,000	—	—	—	70.00	—
1993R Proof	8,500	Value: 120				

KM# 173   500 LIRE
11.0000 g., 0.8350 Silver 0.2953 oz. ASW **Subject:** Centennial
- Bank of Italy **Obv:** Head left **Rev:** Statues and building **Note:**
Both uncirculated and proof versions were offered in sets only.

Date	Mintage	F	VF	XF	Unc	BU
ND(1993)R	52,000	—	—	—	40.00	—
ND(1993)R Proof	10,000	Value: 75.00				

KM# 167   500 LIRE
6.8000 g., Bi-Metallic Bronzital center in Acmonital ring, 25.8 mm.
Subject: 500th Anniversary - Publication of Mathematical Work by
Luca Pacioli **Obv:** Head left within circle **Rev:** Bust facing within circle

Date	Mintage	F	VF	XF	Unc	BU
ND(1994)R	50,000,000	—	—	—	2.00	—
ND(1994)R Proof	8,500	Value: 15.00				

KM# 181   500 LIRE
6.8000 g., Bi-Metallic Bronzital center in Acmonital ring, 25.8 mm.
Subject: Istituto Nazionale di Statistica **Obv:** Head left within
circle **Rev:** Institute building within circle

Date	Mintage	F	VF	XF	Unc	BU
ND(1996)R	96,755,000	—	—	—	2.00	—
ND(1996)R Proof	8,000	Value: 15.00				

KM# 187   500 LIRE
6.8000 g., Bi-Metallic Bronzital center in Acmonital ring, 25.8 mm.
Subject: 50th Anniversary - National Police Code **Obv:** Head left
within circle **Rev:** Mythological figure above crowned shield within
wreath and circle

Date	Mintage	F	VF	XF	Unc	BU
ND(1997)R	40,000,000	—	—	—	2.00	—
ND(1997)R Proof	8,440	Value: 25.00				

KM# 193   500 LIRE
6.8000 g., Bi-Metallic Bronzital center in Acmonital ring, 25.8 mm.
Series: F.A.O. **Subject:** 20 years - IFAD **Obv:** Allegorical portrait
Rev: Hand and grains

Date	Mintage	F	VF	XF	Unc	BU
ND(1998)R	100,000,000	—	—	—	2.00	—
ND(1998)R Proof	9,000	Value: 15.00				

KM# 203   500 LIRE
6.8200 g., Bi-Metallic Bronzital center in Acmonital ring, 25.9 mm.
Subject: European Parliamentary Elections **Obv:** Allegorical
portrait **Rev:** Ballot box **Edge:** Reeded and plain sections

Date	Mintage	F	VF	XF	Unc	BU
ND(1999)R	50,000,000	—	—	—	2.00	—
ND(1999)R Proof	8,500	Value: 15.00				

KM# 101   1000 LIRE
14.6000 g., 0.8350 Silver 0.3919 oz. ASW **Subject:** Centennial
of Rome as Italian capital **Obv:** Concordia veiled bust right
Rev: Flower-like symbol above value

Date	Mintage	F	VF	XF	Unc	BU
ND(1970)R	3,011,000	—	—	10.00	15.00	—
ND(1970)R Proof	—	Value: 35.00				

KM# 165   1000 LIRE
14.6000 g., 0.8350 Silver 0.3919 oz. ASW **Subject:** 900th
Anniversary - St. Mark's Basilica **Obv:** Church façade
Rev: Figures within boat

Date	Mintage	F	VF	XF	Unc	BU
1994R	41,000	—	—	—	35.00	—
1994R Proof	8,600	Value: 45.00				

KM# 168   1000 LIRE
14.6000 g., 0.8350 Silver 0.3919 oz. ASW **Subject:** Flora and
Fauna Protection **Obv:** Female bust facing with tree as left side
of hair **Rev:** Bird, tree and dolphin divides date and value

Date	Mintage	F	VF	XF	Unc	BU
1994R	40,000	—	—	—	35.00 *	40.00
1994R Proof	7,700	Value: 50.00				

KM# 169   1000 LIRE
14.6000 g., 0.8350 Silver 0.3919 oz. ASW **Obv:** Tintoretto in
oval **Rev:** Collage of his paintings

Date	Mintage	F	VF	XF	Unc	BU
1994R	45,000	—	—	—	110	—
1994R Proof	8,500	Value: 130				

KM# 185   1000 LIRE
14.6000 g., 0.8350 Silver 0.3919 oz. ASW **Subject:** Pietro
Mascagni **Obv:** Bust right **Rev:** Theater interior view

Date	Mintage	F	VF	XF	Unc	BU
1995R	45,000	—	—	—	200	—
1995R Proof	7,960	Value: 230				

KM# 182   1000 LIRE
14.6000 g., 0.8350 Silver 0.3919 oz. ASW **Subject:** Olympics
- Atlanta **Obv:** Female head right with laurel wreath and olympic
rings as hair style **Rev:** Torch runner, Statue of Liberty silhouette,
stadium track and value

Date	Mintage	F	VF	XF	Unc	BU
1996R	38,000	—	—	—	35.00	—
1996R Proof	7,435	Value: 45.00				

KM# 199   1000 LIRE
14.6000 g., 0.8350 Silver 0.3919 oz. ASW **Subject:** Montale
Commemorative **Note:** Both uncirculated and proof versions
were offered in sets only.

Date	Mintage	F	VF	XF	Unc	BU
1996R	45,000	—	—	—	80.00	—
1996R Proof	8,000	Value: 160				

KM# 200   1000 LIRE
14.6000 g., 0.8350 Silver 0.3919 oz. ASW **Subject:** Donizetti
Commemorative **Note:** Both uncirculated and proof versions
were offered in sets only.

Date	Mintage	F	VF	XF	Unc	BU
1997R	44,000	—	—	—	160	—
1997R Proof	8,440	Value: 300				

KM# 194   1000 LIRE
Bi-Metallic Copper-Nickel center in Aluminum-Bronze ring,
27 mm. **Subject:** European Union **Obv:** Head left within circle
Rev: Corrected map with United Germany within globe design

Date	Mintage	F	VF	XF	Unc	BU
1997R	80,000,000	—	—	—	3.00	—
1997R Proof	8,440	Value: 25.00				
1998R	180,000,000	—	—	—	3.00	—
1998R Proof	9,000	Value: 25.00				
1999R	51,800	—	—	—	15.00	—
1999R Proof	8,500	Value: 25.00				
2000R	61,400	—	—	—	20.00	—
2000R Proof	8,960	Value: 25.00				

KM# 190   1000 LIRE
Bi-Metallic Copper-Nickel center in Aluminum-Bronze ring,
27 mm. **Subject:** European Union **Obv:** Allegorical portrait
Rev: Pernazza

Date	Mintage	F	VF	XF	Unc	BU
1997R	100,000,000	—	—	—	3.50	—

KM# 201   1000 LIRE
14.6000 g., 0.8350 Silver 0.3919 oz. ASW **Obv:** Bernini bust
and St. Peter's Colonnade in background **Rev:** Architectural
renderings and sunburst **Note:** Both uncirculated and proof
versions were offered in sets only.

Date	Mintage	F	VF	XF	Unc	BU
1998R	55,200	—	—	—	50.00	—
1998R Proof	9,000	Value: 90.00				

KM# 221   1000 LIRE
14.6000 g., 0.8350 Silver 0.3919 oz. ASW, 31.4 mm.
Subject: Vittorio Alfieri **Obv:** Bust looking right **Rev:** Rope over
book **Edge:** Raised ornamentation

Date	Mintage	F	VF	XF	Unc	BU
1999R	51,800	—	—	—	80.00	—
1999R Proof	8,500	Value: 120				

KM# 235   1000 LIRE
14.6000 g., 0.8350 Silver 0.3919 oz. ASW, 31.4 mm.
Obv: Giordano Bruno **Rev:** Three sun faces

Date	Mintage	F	VF	XF	Unc	BU
2000R	8,960	—	—	—	80.00	—
2000R Proof	51,400	Value: 130				

KM# 195   2000 LIRE
16.0000 g., 0.8350 Silver 0.4295 oz. ASW **Subject:** Christian
Millennium **Obv:** Leaves and birds sprouting from globe top
Rev: Jesus above value

Date	Mintage	F	VF	XF	Unc	BU
1998R	36,300	—	—	—	55.00	—
1998R Proof	7,880	Value: 65.00				

KM# 196   2000 LIRE
16.0000 g., 0.8350 Silver 0.4295 oz. ASW **Obv:** Stars and birds
circling world globe **Rev:** Creative brain unraveling DNA above
value

Date	Mintage	F	VF	XF	Unc	BU
1998R	36,300	—	—	—	55.00	—
1998R Proof	7,880	Value: 65.00				

KM# 202   2000 LIRE
16.0000 g., 0.8350 Silver 0.4295 oz. ASW **Subject:** National
Museum in Rome **Obv:** Head left on ancient coin **Rev:** Seated
gladiator

Date	Mintage	F	VF	XF	Unc	BU
1999R	35,500	—	—	—	30.00	—
1999R Proof	6,700	Value: 60.00				

KM# 170   5000 LIRE
18.0000 g., 0.8350 Silver 0.4832 oz. ASW **Subject:** University
of Pisa **Obv:** Wings surround head facing **Rev:** Building and
design at center of circle with small towers between points

Date	Mintage	F	VF	XF	Unc	BU
1993R	42,000	—	—	—	36.00	—
1993R Proof	8,500	Value: 65.00				

KM# 175   5000 LIRE
18.0000 g., 0.8350 Silver 0.4832 oz. ASW **Subject:** 600th
Anniversary - Birth of Pisanello **Obv:** Bust left wearing floppy hat
Rev: Equestrian right

Date	Mintage	F	VF	XF	Unc	BU
1995R	38,000	—	—	—	40.00	—
1995R Proof	7,800	Value: 60.00				

KM# 178   5000 LIRE
18.0000 g., 0.8350 Silver 0.4832 oz. ASW **Subject:** Italian
Presidency of the European Union **Obv:** Female head left
Rev: Letter E, flags, stars and assorted designs

Date	Mintage	F	VF	XF	Unc	BU
1996R	38,000	—	—	—	65.00	—
1996R Proof	7,996	Value: 80.00				

KM# 189   5000 LIRE
18.0000 g., 0.8350 Silver 0.4832 oz. ASW **Subject:** Giovanni
Antonio Canal **Obv:** Bust right and Venice city view **Rev:** Harbor
full of sailboats

Date	Mintage	F	VF	XF	Unc	BU
ND(1997)R	36,000	—	—	—	35.00	—
ND(1997)R Proof	7,550	Value: 55.00				

KM# 197   5000 LIRE
18.0000 g., 0.8350 Silver 0.4832 oz. ASW **Subject:** 1999
Obv: Birds sprouting from globe **Rev:** Saint Francis selling cloth
to merchant

Date	Mintage	F	VF	XF	Unc	BU
1999R	37,600	—	—	—	30.00	—
1999R Proof	8,170	Value: 50.00				

KM# 198   5000 LIRE
18.0000 g., 0.8350 Silver 0.4832 oz. ASW **Subject:** 1999
Obv: Three birds and nine stars encircle world **Rev:** Satellite dish
and wheels

Date	Mintage	F	VF	XF	Unc	BU
1999R	37,600	—	—	—	30.00	—
1999R Proof	8,170	Value: 50.00				

KM# 166   10000 LIRE
22.0000 g., 0.8350 Silver 0.5906 oz. ASW **Subject:** World Cup
Soccer **Obv:** Head right with stars in hair **Rev:** Olive branch, value
and banner within globe

Date	Mintage	F	VF	XF	Unc	BU
1994R	43,000	—	—	—	60.00	—
1994R Proof	9,000	Value: 120				

KM# 174 10000 LIRE
22.0000 g., 0.8350 Silver 0.5906 oz. ASW **Subject:** 40th
Anniversary - Conference of Messina **Obv:** Europa on bull right
Rev: Letter E and numeral 5 within globe design and star border

Date	Mintage	F	VF	XF	Unc	BU
1995R	42,000	—	—	—	70.00	—
1995R Proof	8,050	Value: 90.00				

KM# 179 10000 LIRE
22.0000 g., 0.8350 Silver 0.5906 oz. ASW **Subject:** 50th
Anniversary of the Republic **Obv:** Bust right with star in
background **Rev:** Man leading horse right

Date	Mintage	F	VF	XF	Unc	BU
1996R	38,000	—	—	—	80.00	—
1996R Proof	7,900	Value: 100				

KM# 188 10000 LIRE
22.0000 g., 0.8350 Silver 0.5906 oz. ASW **Subject:** 200th
Anniversary - Italian Flag **Obv:** Allegorical portrait **Rev:** Woman
wearing flag like a cape

Date	Mintage	F	VF	XF	Unc	BU
ND(1997)R	36,000	—	—	—	45.00	—
ND(1997)R Proof	7,695	Value: 70.00				

KM# 192 10000 LIRE
22.0000 g., 0.8350 Silver 0.5906 oz. ASW **Subject:** Soccer
Obv: Head left **Rev:** Stylized soccer design

Date	Mintage	F	VF	XF	Unc	BU
1998R	34,000	—	—	—	45.00	—
1998R Proof	7,000	Value: 70.00				

KM# 208 10000 LIRE
22.0000 g., 0.8350 Silver 0.5906 oz. ASW, 34 mm. **Obv:** Birds
and grass sprouting **Rev:** Standing figure flanked by tall weeds
Edge: Reeded and plain sections

Date	Mintage	F	VF	XF	Unc	BU
2000R	33,700	—	—	—	35.00	—
2000R Proof	7,000	Value: 70.00				

KM# 209 10000 LIRE
22.0000 g., 0.8350 Silver 0.5906 oz. ASW, 34 mm. **Obv:** Doves
and stars around world globe **Rev:** Da Vinci's wing and airplane
design **Edge:** Reeded and plain sections

Date	Mintage	F	VF	XF	Unc	BU
2000R	—	—	—	—	35.00	—
2000R Proof	—	Value: 70.00				

KM# 176 50000 LIRE
7.5000 g., 0.9000 Gold 0.2170 oz. AGW **Subject:** Bank of Italy
Obv: Bust left **Rev:** Building and value

Date	Mintage	F	VF	XF	Unc	BU
ND(1994)R Proof	22,560	Value: 350				

KM# 223 50000 LIRE
7.5000 g., 0.9000 Gold 0.2170 oz. AGW, 20 mm. **Subject:** 800th
Anniversary - Birth of Saint Anthony of Padova **Obv:** Corner view
of Basilica **Rev:** Interior view - Chapel, date and value

Date	Mintage	F	VF	XF	Unc	BU
1995R Proof	9,221	Value: 350				

KM# 225 50000 LIRE
7.5000 g., 0.9000 Gold 0.2170 oz. AGW, 20 mm. **Subject:** 800th
Anniversary - Battistero in Parma **Obv:** Battistero **Rev:**
Decorations from the Battistero, date and value

Date	Mintage	F	VF	XF	Unc	BU
1996R Proof	7,010	Value: 600				

KM# 191 50000 LIRE
7.5000 g., 0.9000 Gold 0.2170 oz. AGW **Subject:** 1600th
Anniversary - Death of St. Ambrose **Obv:** St. Ambrose Church
in Milan **Rev:** Investiture of St. Ambrose

Date	Mintage	F	VF	XF	Unc	BU
ND(1997)R Proof	5,750	Value: 300				

KM# 228 50000 LIRE
7.5000 g., 0.9000 Gold 0.2170 oz. AGW, 20 mm. **Subject:** 850th
Anniversary - Church of San Giovanni of the Hermits in Palermo
Obv: Church of San Giovanni **Rev:** Curved arches

Date	Mintage	F	VF	XF	Unc	BU
1998R Proof	4,900	Value: 450				

KM# 230 50000 LIRE
7.5000 g., 0.9000 Gold 0.2170 oz. AGW, 20 mm. **Subject:** 900th
Anniversary - Foundation of the Cathedral in Modena **Obv:** Front
of Cathedral **Rev:** Arch with lion, date and denomination

Date	Mintage	F	VF	XF	Unc	BU
1999R Proof	5,500	Value: 350				

KM# 232 50000 LIRE
7.5000 g., 0.9000 Gold 0.2170 oz. AGW, 20 mm. **Subject:** 500th
Anniversary - Birth of Benvenuto Cellini **Obv:** Bust of Cellini
Rev: Figure, date and denomination

Date	Mintage	F	VF	XF	Unc	BU
2000R Proof	4,375	Value: 450				

KM# 177 100000 LIRE
15.0000 g., 0.9000 Gold 0.4340 oz. AGW **Subject:** Centennial
of the Bank of Italy **Obv:** Bust facing **Rev:** Value and building
Note: 1996 strikes do not exist.

Date	Mintage	F	VF	XF	Unc	BU
ND(1994)R Proof	21,196	Value: 500				

KM# 222 100000 LIRE
15.0000 g., 0.9000 Gold 0.4340 oz. AGW, 25 mm. **Subject:** 700th
Anniversary - Basilica of Santa Croce in Florence **Obv:** Front of
Basilica of Santa Croce **Rev:** Interior view, date and denomination

Date	Mintage	F	VF	XF	Unc	BU
1995R Proof	8,584	Value: 550				

KM# 224 100000 LIRE
15.0000 g., 0.9000 Gold 0.4340 oz. AGW, 25 mm.
Subject: 600th Anniversary - Foundation of Certosa Di Pavia
Obv: Exterior angled view **Rev:** Interior view

Date	Mintage	F	VF	XF	Unc	BU
1996R Proof	5,550	Value: 800				

KM# 226 100000 LIRE
15.0000 g., 0.9000 Gold 0.4340 oz. AGW, 25 mm. **Subject:**
800th Anniversary - Dedication of the Basilica Superiore of San
Nicola di Bari **Obv:** Exterior view of the Basilica **Rev:** Interior view

Date	Mintage	F	VF	XF	Unc	BU
1997R Proof	5,400	Value: 600				

KM# 227 100000 LIRE
15.0000 g., 0.9000 Gold 0.4340 oz. AGW, 25 mm. **Subject:**
650th Anniversary - Completion of the Tower - Palace of Siena
Obv: Tower **Rev:** Anniversary dates and denomination

Date	Mintage	F	VF	XF	Unc	BU
1998R Proof	4,800	Value: 600				

KM# 229 100000 LIRE
15.0000 g., 0.9000 Gold 0.4340 oz. AGW, 25 mm.
Subject: Repair of the Basilica of St. Francis of Assisi **Obv:** Front
of Basilica **Rev:** Round seal, date and denomination

Date	Mintage	F	VF	XF	Unc	BU
1999R Proof	5,047	Value: 750				

KM# 231 100000 LIRE
15.0000 g., 0.9000 Gold 0.4340 oz. AGW, 20 mm.
Subject: 700th Anniversary - First Jubilee of 1300 **Obv:** The
Quadrangle **Rev:** Detail of the fresco of Giotto

Date	Mintage	F	VF	XF	Unc	BU
2000R Proof	—	Value: 750				

TRIAL STRIKES

KM#	Date	Mintage	Identification	Mkt Val
TS1	1927R	—	20 Lire. Inscription. PROVA SENZA RITOCCO. Seated and standing figures above with KM69.	1,200
TS2	1927R	—	20 Lire. Faceless head right. PROVA TECNICA - R. SENZA RITOCCO. KM69.	1,500
TS3	1940	—	5 Lire. Silver. Helmeted bust left. Uniface.	1,500
TS4	1940	—	5 Lire. Silver. Crowned savoy shield with fases and axe within circle. Uniface. Illustration reduced.	1,500

PATTERNS
Including off metal strikes

KM#	Date	Mintage	Identification	Mkt Val
Pn2	1903R	—	10 Centesimi. Bronze.	—
Pn3	1903R	—	2 Lire. Silver Plated Bronze.	—
Pn4	1903	—	5 Lire. Silver.	1,000
PnA5	1903 (M)	—	20 Lire. Gold.	3,500
Pn5	1903R	—	20 Lire. Gilt Silver.	—
PnA6	1903 (M)	—	100 Lire. Gold.	8,500
Pn6	1903R	—	100 Lire. Gilt Bronze.	225
PnB7	1904	—	50 Lire. Brass. Head of Vittorio left. Eagle with spread wings facing, head left, crown above..	—
PnA7	1904	5	Centesimo. Bronze. KM37.	—
Pn7	1905R	—	20 Centesimi. Bronze.	—
Pn8	1905R	—	20 Centesimi. Nickel.	—
Pn9	1906R	—	20 Lire. Gilt Bronze.	225
Pn10	1907	—	20 Centesimi. Nickel.	—
Pn11	1907	—	100 Lire.	—
PnA12	1908	—	100 Lire. Silver.	5,000
Pn12	1908	—	100 Lire. Bronze.	250
Pn13	1915R	—	10 Centesimi. Nickel. Obv: Helmeted head right. Rev: Grain ear.	—
Pn14	1915R	—	10 Centesimi. Nickel. Obv: Diademed and jeweled head right. Rev: Grain ear.	—
Pn15	1915R	—	10 Centesimi. Nickel. Obv: Diademed and jeweled head right. Rev: Grain ear.	—
Pn16	1915	—	10 Centesimi. Nickel.	—

KM#	Date	Mintage	Identification	Mkt Val
Pn17	1918	—	5 Centesimi. Ferro-nickel.	250
PnA28	1918	—	25 Centesimi. Iron. Obv: Turreted and grain-wreathed head of Italia right. Rev: Denomination above ornament, PROVA S.J. below.	
Pn18	1918	—	5 Centesimi. Ferro-nickel.	250
Pn19	1918	—	5 Centesimi. Ferro-nickel.	250
Pn20	1918	—	5 Centesimi. Ferro-nickel.	250
Pn21	1918	—	5 Centesimi. Ferro-nickel.	250
Pn22	1918	—	10 Centesimi. Ferro-nickel.	—
Pn23	1918	—	20 Centesimi. Nickel.	—
Pn24	1918	—	20 Centesimi. Nickel.	—
Pn25	1918	—	20 Centesimi. Nickel.	—
Pn26	1918	—	20 Centesimi. Nickel.	—
Pn27	1918	—	20 Centesimi. Ferro-nickel.	—
Pn28	1918	—	25 Centesimi. Bronze.	—
Pn30	1918	—	50 Centesimi. Nickel.	—
Pn29	1918	—	50 Centesimi. Nickel.	—
Pn31	1919R	—	5 Centesimi. 17 mm. Ferro-nickel.	—
Pn32	1919	—	5 Centesimi. Bronze.	—
Pn33	ND(1919)	—	10 Centesimi. Bronze.	—
Pn34	1920R	—	Lira. Nickel.	—
Pn35	1920R	—	Lira. Nickel.	—
Pn36	1920R	—	Lira. Nickel.	—
PnA37	1922	—	2 Lire. Nickel.	—
PnA38	1922R	—	2 Lire. Nickel.	—
Pn38	1922R	—	2 Lire. Nickel.	—
Pn37	1922	—	2 Lire. Nickel.	—
Pn39	1926R	—	5 Lire. Silver.	—
Pn40	ND(1927)	—	20 Lire. Silver.	—
Pn41	ND(1927)	—	20 Lire. Silver.	—
Pn42	1950	—	50 Lire. Stainless Steel.	—
Pn43	1950	—	100 Lire. Silver. 20 mm.	—
Pn44	1950	—	100 Lire. Nickel-Silver.	—
Pn45	1950	—	100 Lire. Nickel.	—
Pn46	1951R	—	Lira. Aluminum.	—
Pn47	1951R	—	2 Lire. Aluminum.	—
Pn48	1951R	—	10 Lire. Aluminum.	—
Pn49	1955R	—	20 Lire. Aluminum-Bronze.	—
Pn50	1955R	—	20 Lire. Aluminum-Bronze.	—
Pn51	1956R	—	20 Lire. Aluminum-Bronze. Bottom of neck rounded.	—
Pn52	1956R	1,200	20 Lire. Aluminum-Bronze. Bottom of neck at angle.	—
Pn53	1957R	—	500 Lire. Silver.	—
Pn59	1957R	—	Florino. Gilt Bronze.	—
Pn61	1957R	—	2 Florini. Gilt Bronze.	—
Pn62	1957R	—	2 Florini. Gilt Bronze.	—
Pn60	1957R	—	Florino. Gilt Bronze.	—
Pn54	1957R	—	500 Lire. Silver.	—
Pn55	1957R	—	500 Lire. Silver.	—
Pn56	1957R	—	500 Lire. Silver.	—
Pn57	1957R	—	500 Lire. Silver.	—
Pn58	1957R	—	500 Lire. Silver.	—
Pn63	1970	—	1000 Lire. Silver.	—
Pn65	ND (1970)	—	10000 Lire. Gilt Bronze.	—
Pn64	1970	—	1000 Lire. Silver.	—

PROVAS

PROVA in field; Standard metals unless otherwise noted

KM#	Date	Mintage	Identification	Mkt Val
Pr1	1903	—	20 Lire. Head right. Standing figures facing.	4,000
Pr2	1903	—	100 Lire. Head right. Standing figures facing.	14,000
Pr3	1906 (M)	—	20 Lire. Head left. Honey bee.	11,500
Pr4	1906 (M)	—	100 Lire. Gold. Head right. Lions pulling man in chariot.	17,250
PrA4	1906	—	20 Lire. Bronze.	—
Pr5	1907R	—	20 Lire. KM48.	6,000
PrA6	1907 (M)	—	20 Lire. KM48.	6,000
Pr6	1907 (M)	—	50 Lire. Bust left. Seated figure left.	8,500
Pr7	1907R	—	100 Lire. KM50.	14,000
Pr8	1908R	—	2 Centesimi. Bronze. KM41, PROVA.	700
Pr9	1908R	—	5 Centesimi. KM42, PROVA.	700
Pr10	1908R	—	10 Centesimi. Bronze. KM43, PROVA.	4,500
Pr11	1908 (M)	—	100 Lire. Head right. Female striding left divides value and date.	17,250
PrA12	1910R	—	100 Lire. KM50, PROVA.	14,000
Pr12	1911R	—	2 Lire. KM52, PROVA.	1,600
Pr13	1911R	—	5 Lire. KM53, PROVA.	3,250
Pr14	1911R	—	50 Lire. KM54, PROVA horizontally.	5,200
PrA15	1912	—	10 Lire. KM47, PROVA.	3,450
Pr15	1912	—	20 Lire. KM48, PROVA.	4,025
Pr16	1913R	—	5 Lire. KM56.	5,000
Pr17	1914	—	2 Lire. KM55, PROVA.	5,000
Pr18	1914R	—	5 Lire. KM56.	6,000
Pr19	1914R	—	5 Lire. Copper. KM56.	—
Pr20	1914R	—	5 Lire. Copper. KM56.	—
Pr21	1914R	—	5 Lire. Silver. PROVA DI STAMPA. KM56.	10,000
Pr22	1914R	—	5 Lire. PROVA. KM56.	8,000
Pr23	1919R	—	50 Centesimi. KM61.1, PROVA.	5,000
Pr24	1919R	—	50 Centesimi. PROVA DI STAMPA. KM61.1.	8,000
Pr25	1919R	—	5 Centesimi. KM59.	—
Pr26	1919R	—	10 Centesimi. KM60, PROVA DI STAMPA.	5,000
Pr27	1921R	—	Lira. Seated figure left. Value and crowned shield within wreath. KM62, PROVA.	900

KM#	Date	Mintage	Identification	Mkt Val
Pr28	1923R	—	2 Lire. KM63, PROVA.	500
Pr29	1923R	—	2 Lire. PROVA DI STAMPA KM63.	500
Pr30	1923R P. (for Prova)	—	2 Lire. KM63.	500
Pr31	1923R	—	20 Lire. KM64, PROVA.	4,500
Pr32	1923R	—	100 Lire. KM65, PROVA.	11,500
Pr33	1923R P. (for Prova)	—	100 Lire. KM65.	12,500
Pr34	1925R	—	100 Lire. KM66, PROVA.	20,000
Pr35	1925R	—	50 Centesimi. PROVA TECNICO. KM61.	—
Pr36	1926R	—	5 Lire. Silver. KM67, PROVA.	500
Pr37	1926R	—	5 Lire. Head left. Eagle with wings open standing on fascis. PROVA DI STAMPA. KM67.	900
Pr38	1926R	—	5 Lire. LA PROVA TECNICA. KM67.	350
Pr39	1926R	—	10 Lire. PROVA at top. KM68.	500
Pr40	1926R	—	10 Lire. PROVA beneath horses. KM68.	500
Pr41	1926R	—	10 Lire. PROVA DI STAMPA. KM68.	500
Pr42	1926R	—	10 Lire. LA PROVA TECNICA. KM68.	500
Pr43	1927R	—	5 Lire. PROVA DI STAMPA above eagle. KM67.	800
Pr44	1927R Vp	—	5 Lire. PROVA DI STAMPA at right side of eagle. KM67.	700
PrA45	1927R	—	10 Lire. PROVA beneath horses. KM68.	600
PrB45	1927R Vp	—	10 Lire. PROVA DI STAMPA above. KM68.	400
Pr45	1927R Vo	—	20 Lire. KM69, Unc., circular PROVA.	13,000
Pr46	1927R Vp	—	20 Lire. PROVA DI STAMPA. KM69.	1,700
Pr49	1928R Vlo	—	20 Lire. PROVA. KM70.	1,200
Pr50	1928R Vlo	—	20 Lire. PROVA DI STAMPA. KM70.	1,450
Pr51	1928R	—	20 Lire. LA PROVA. KM70.	1,200
Pr52	1928R Vo	—	20 Lire. KM70, horizontal PROVA.	1,200
Pr53	1928R	—	20 Lire. Gold. KM70.	—
Pr54	1928R	—	20 Lire. PROVA behind head. KM69.	1,200
Pr55	1931R	—	50 Lire. KM71.	3,000
Pr56	1931R	—	100 Lire. KM72, PROVA.	3,000
Pr57	1936R	—	5 Centesimi. KM73, PROVA.	—
Pr58	1936R	—	10 Centesimi. KM74, PROVA.	300
Pr59	1936R	—	20 Centesimi. KM75, PROVA.	300
Pr60	1936R	—	50 Centesimi. KM76, PROVA.	300
Pr61	1936R	—	Lira. KM77, PROVA.	350
Pr62	1936R	—	2 Lire. Plain edge. KM78, PROVA.	350
Pr63	1936R	—	5 Lire. KM79, PROVA.	800
Pr64	1936R	—	10 Lire. KM80, PROVA.	700
Pr65	1936R	—	20 Lire. KM81, PROVA.	2,400
Pr66	1936R	—	50 Lire. KM82, PROVA.	8,600
Pr67	1936R	—	100 Lire. KM83, PROVA.	12,000
Pr68	1939R	—	5 Centesimi. KM73a, PROVA.	—
Pr69	1939R	—	10 Centesimi. KM74a, PROVA.	—
Pr70	1939R	—	20 Centesimi. Nickel-Steel. KM75a, PROVA.	600
Pr71	1939R	—	50 Centesimi. Nickel-Steel. KM76a, PROVA.	700
Pr72	1939R	—	Lira. Nickel-Steel. KM77a, PROVA.	700
Pr73	1939R	—	2 Lire. Nickel-Steel. KM78a, PROVA.	800
Pr74	1946R	—	Lira. KM87, P, Unc.	5,000
Pr75	1946R	—	2 Lire. KM88, P, Unc.	5,000
Pr76	1946R	—	5 Lire. KM89, P, Unc.	7,000
Pr77	1946R	—	10 Lire. KM90, P, Unc.	8,000
Pr78	1951R	—	Lira. KM91, PROVA, Unc.	1,500
Pr79	1951R	—	5 Lire. KM92, PROVA, Unc.	2,000
Pr80	1951R	—	10 Lire. KM93, PROVA, Unc.	2,000
Pr81	1953R	—	2 Lire. KM94, PROVA, Unc.	1,500
PrA82	1956R	—	20 Lire. P for PROVA, KM97.1, Proof.	1,200
Pr82	1956R	—	20 Lire. P for PROVA, KM97.1, Unc.	1,500
PrA83	1957R	—	500 Lire. KM98, Proof.	5,500
Pr83	1957R	1,004	500 Lire. KM98, Unc., PROVA.	12,000
PrA84	1965R	—	500 Lire. KM100, Proof.	3,000
Pr84	1965R	570	500 Lire. KM100, PROVA, Unc.	5,000
PrA85	1968R	—	20 Lire. KM97.2, Proof.	—
Pr85	1968R	999	20 Lire. KM97.2, Unc., P.	1,000
PrA86	1970R	—	1000 Lire. KM101, Proof.	750
Pr86	1970R	2,500	1000 Lire. KM101, PROVA, Unc.	1,200
PrA87	1954R	—	100 Lire. KM96, PROVA.	500
Pr87	1974R	—	100 Lire. KM96, Unc.	150
PrA88	1974R	—	100 Lire. Silver. KM102, PROVA, Unc.	300
Pr88	1974R	—	100 Lire. KM102, Proof.	300
PrA89	1974R	—	100 Lire. Copper Nickel. KM102, PROVA.	350
Pr89	1974R	—	100 Lire. Copper Nickel. KM102, Unc.	150
Pr90	1974R	—	100 Lire. Silver. KM102.	400
PrA91	1974R	—	500 Lire. KM103, PROVA, Unc.	800
Pr91	1974R	730	500 Lire. KM103, Proof.	450
PrA92	1977R	—	100 Lire. KM105, Proof.	550
Pr92	1977R	417	200 Lire. KM105, PROVA, Unc.	1,000

MINT SETS

KM#	Date	Mintage	Identification	Issue Price	Mkt Val
MS1	1968 (8)	100,000	KM91-96, 97.2, 98	6.50	180
MS2	1969 (8)	310,000	KM91-96, 97.2, 98	6.50	15.00
MS3	1970 (9)	1,011,000	KM91-96, 97.2, 98, 101	—	25.00
MS4	1980 (10)	257,272	KM91-96, 97.2, 98, 105, 107	—	18.00
MS5	1981 (11)	162,794	KM91-96, 97.2, 98, 105, 108-109	—	15.00
MS7	1982 (10)	120,000	KM91-96, 97.2, 98, 105, 111	—	24.00
MS9	1983 (10)	76,000	KM91-96, 97.2, 98, 105, 111	175	180
MS11	1984 (10)	77,000	KM91-96, 97.2, 98, 105, 111	—	70.00
MS13	1985 (10)	5,000	KM91-96, 97.2, 105, 111, 123	—	35.00
MS14	1985 (11)	75,000	KM91-96, 97.2, 98, 105, 111, 123	—	70.00
MS17	1986 (11)	73,000	KM91-96, 97.2, 98, 105, 111, 124	—	90.00
MS18	1987 (11)	58,000	KM91-96, 97.2, 98, 105, 111, 132	—	130
MS19	1988 (11)	51,000	KM91-96, 97.2, 98, 105, 111, 144	46.00	300
MS21	1988 (3)	68,000	KM127-129	—	85.00
MS22	1989 (11)	51,000	KM91-96, 97.2, 98, 111, 130, 145	—	120
MS23	1989 (2)	88,000	KM133-134	—	50.00
MS24	1989 (2)	75,000	KM138-139	—	70.00
MS25	1990 (11)	52,800	KM91-94, 95a-96a, 97.2, 98, 111, 135, 146	—	80.00
MS26	1991 (11)	64,000	KM91-94, 95a-96a, 97.2, 98, 105, 111, 141	50.00	120
MS27	1991 (2)	50,000	KM142-143	—	70.00
MS28	1992 (11)	52,000	KM91-94, 95a-96a, 97.2, 98, 111, 151, 161	50.00	90.00
MS29	1993 (11)	50,000	KM91-94, 95a, 97.2, 98, 155, 159, 160, 163	—	90.00
MS31	ND (1993) (3)	52,100	KM171-173	31.00	90.00
MS30	1994 (11)	44,500	KM91-94, 95a, 97.2, 98, 159, 164, 167, 169	—	170
MS32	1995 (11)	44,600	KM91-94, 95a, 97.2, 98, 105, 111, 180, 185	—	400
MS33	1996 (11)	45,000	KM91-94, 97.2, 98, 159, 181, 183-184, 199	—	100
MS34	1997 (10)	43,500	KM91-94, 97.2, 98, 159, 183, 186-187, 196, 200	—	220
MS35	1998 (12)	55,200	KM91-94, 97.2, 98, 105, 159, 183, 193-194, 201	—	75.00
MS36	1998 (2)	34,000	KM195-196	—	130
MS37	1999 (12)	51,800	KM#91-94, 97.2, 98, 105, 111, 159, 183, 194, 221	—	100
MS38	2000 (12)	50,000	KM#91-94, 97.2, 98, 105, 111, 159, 183, 194, 235	—	100

PROOF SETS

KM#	Date	Mintage	Identification	Issue Price	Mkt Val
PS1	1985 (10)	5,000	KM91-96, 97.2, 105, 111, 123	—	65.00
PS2	1985 (11)	15,000	KM91-96, 97.2, 98, 105, 111, 123	—	100
PS3	1986 (10)	17,500	KM91-96, 97.2, 105, 111, 124	—	100
PS4	1986 (11)	18,000	KM91-96, 97.2, 98, 105, 111, 124	—	130
PS5	1987 (11)	10,000	KM91-96, 97.2, 98, 105, 111, 132	—	140
PS6	1988 (11)	9,000	KM91-96, 97.2, 98, 105, 111, 144	100	300
PS7	1988 (3)	12,700	KM127-129	—	135
PS8	1989 (11)	9,260	KM91-96, 97.2, 98, 111, 130, 145	—	140
PS9	1990 (11)	9,400	KM91-94, 95a-96a, 97.2, 98, 111, 135, 146	—	120
PS10	1989 (2)	25,000	KM133-134	—	60.00
PS11	1989 (2)	25,000	KM138-139	—	65.00
PS12	1991 (11)	11,000	KM91-94, 95a-96a, 97.2, 98, 105, 111, 141	100	160
PS13	1992 (11)	9,500	KM91-94, 95a-96a, 97.2, 98, 111, 151, 161	90.00	160
PS14	1993 (11)	8,500	KM91-94, 95a, 97.2, 98, 155, 159, 160, 163	—	190
PS15	ND (1993) (3)	10,500	KM171-173	60.00	150
PS16	1994 (11)	8,500	KM#91-94, 95a, 97.2, 98, 159, 164, 167, 169	—	220
PS17	1995 (11)	7,960	KM#91-94, 95a, 97.2, 98, 105, 111, 180, 185	—	450
PS18	1996 (11)	8,000	KM#91-94, 97.2, 98, 159, 181, 183, 184, 199	—	220
PS19	1997 (12)	8,450	KM#91-94, 97.2, 98, 159, 183, 186, 187, 196, 200	—	430
PS20	1998 (2)	7,000	KM195-196	—	150
PS21	1998 (12)	7,000	KM#91-94, 97.2, 98, 105, 159, 183, 193, 194, 201	—	130
PS22	1999 (2)	8,700	KM197-198	—	80.00
PS23	1999 (12)	8,500	KM#91-94, 97.2, 98, 105, 111, 159, 183, 194, 221	—	180
PS24	2000 (12)	7,000	KM#91-94, 97.2, 98, 105, 111, 159, 183, 194, 235	—	240

IVORY COAST

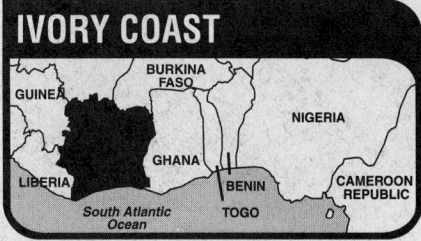

The Republic of the Ivory Coast, (Cote d'Ivoire), a former French Overseas territory located on the south side of the African bulge between Liberia and Ghana, has an area of 124,504 sq. mi. (322,463 sq. km.) and a population of 11.8 million: Capital: Yamoussoukro. The predominantly agricultural economy is one of Africa's most prosperous. Coffee, tropical woods, cocoa, and bananas are exported.

French and Portuguese navigators visited the Ivory Coast in the 15th century. French traders set up establishments in the 19th century, and gradually extended their influence along the coast and inland. The area was organized as a territory in 1893, and from 1904 to 1958 was a constituent unit of the Federation of French West Africa - as a Colony under the Third Republic and an Overseas Territory under the Fourth. In 1958 Ivory Coast became an autonomous republic within the French Community. Independence was attained on Aug. 7, 1960.

REPUBLIC
DECIMAL COINAGE

KM# 1   10 FRANCS
25.0000 g., 0.9250 Silver 0.7435 oz. ASW **Obv:** Head right **Rev:** Elephant and value within wreath **Note:** Varieties exist in 2.9mm and 3.5mm planchets.

Date	Mintage	F	VF	XF	Unc	BU
1966 Proof	—	Value: 60.00				

KM# 2   10 FRANCS
3.2000 g., 0.9000 Gold 0.0926 oz. AGW

Date	Mintage	F	VF	XF	Unc	BU
1966 Proof	2,000	Value: 95.00				

KM# 3   25 FRANCS
8.0000 g., 0.9000 Gold 0.2315 oz. AGW **Obv:** Head right **Rev:** Elephant and value within wreath

Date	Mintage	F	VF	XF	Unc	BU
1966 Proof	2,000	Value: 235				

KM# 4   50 FRANCS
16.0000 g., 0.9000 Gold 0.4630 oz. AGW **Obv:** Head right **Rev:** Elephant and value within wreath

Date	Mintage	F	VF	XF	Unc	BU
1966 Proof	2,000	Value: 460				

KM# 5   100 FRANCS
32.0000 g., 0.9000 Gold 0.9259 oz. AGW **Obv:** Head right **Rev:** Elephant within wreath

Date	Mintage	F	VF	XF	Unc	BU
1966 Proof	2,000	Value: 920				

ESSAIS
Standard metals unless otherwise noted

KM#	Date	Mintage Identification	Mkt Val
E1	1966	— 100 Francs. Silver. KM5.	85.00

PIEFORTS WITH ESSAI

KM#	Date	Mintage Identification	Mkt Val
PE1	1966	— 100 Francs. Silver. KM5.	250

PROOF SETS

KM#	Date	Mintage Identification	Issue Price	Mkt Val
PS1	1966 (4)	2,000 KM#2-5	—	1,700

JAMAICA

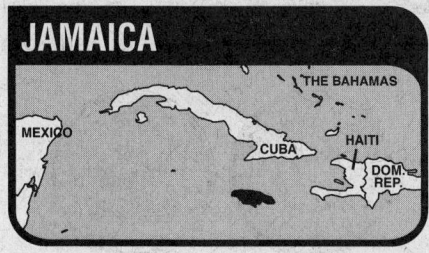

Jamaica is situated in the Caribbean Sea 90 miles south of Cuba, has an area of 4,244 sq. mi. (10,990 sq. km.) and a population of 2.1 million. Capital: Kingston. The economy is founded chiefly on mining, tourism and agriculture. Aluminum, bauxite, sugar, rum and molasses are exported.

Jamaica was discovered by Columbus on May 3, 1494, and settled by Spain in 1509. The island was captured in 1655 by a British naval force under the command of Admiral William Penn, sent by Oliver Cromwell and ceded to Britain by the Treaty of Madrid, 1670. For more than 150 years, the Jamaican economy of sugar, slaves and piracy was one of the most prosperous in the new world. Dissension between the property-oriented island legislature and the home government prompted parliament to establish a crown colony government for Jamaica in 1866. From 1958 to 1961 Jamaica was a member of the West Indies Federation, withdrawing when Jamaican voters rejected the association. The colony attained independence on Aug. 6, 1962. Jamaica is a member of the Commonwealth of Nations. Elizabeth II is the Head of State, as Queen of Jamaica.

In 1758, the Jamaican Assembly authorized stamping a certain amount of Spanish milled coinage. Token coinage by merchants aided the island's monetary supply in the early 19th century. Sterling coinage was introduced in Jamaica in 1825, with the additional silver three halfpence under William IV and Victoria. Certain issues of three pence of William IV and Victoria were intended for colonial use, including Jamaica, as were the last dates of three pence for George VI.

There was an extensive token and work tally coinage for Jamaica in the late 19th and early 20th centuries.

A decimal standard currency system was adopted on Sept. 8, 1969.

RULER
British, until 1962

MINT MARKS
C - Royal Canadian Mint, Ottawa
H - Heaton
FM - Franklin Mint, U.S.A.**
(fm) - Franklin Mint, U.S.A.*
no mint mark - Royal Mint, London
  *NOTE: During 1970 the Franklin Mint produced matte and proof coins (1 cent-1 dollar) using dies similar to/or Royal Mint without the FM mint mark.
  NOTE: From 1975-1985 the Franklin Mint produced coinage in up to 3 different qualities. Qualities of issue are designated in ( ) after each date and are defined as follows:
  (M) MATTE - Normal circulation strike or a dull finish produced by sandblasting special uncirculated (polish finish) or proof quality dies.
  (U) SPECIAL UNCIRCULATED - Polished or proof-like in appearance without any frosted features.
  (P) PROOF - The highest quality obtainable having mirror-like fields and frosted features.

MONETARY SYSTEM
4 Farthings = 1 Penny
12 Pence = 1 Shilling
8 Reales = 6 Shillings, 8 Pence
            (Commencing 1969)
100 Cents = 1 Dollar

COMMONWEALTH
REGULAR COINAGE

KM# 18   FARTHING
Copper-Nickel **Ruler:** Edward VII **Obv:** Crowned bust right within beaded circle **Rev:** Arms with horizontal shading within beaded circle

Date	Mintage	F	VF	XF	Unc	BU
1902	144,000	5.00	10.00	20.00	45.00	55.00
1903	144,000	5.00	10.00	20.00	45.00	55.00

KM# 21   FARTHING
Copper-Nickel **Ruler:** Edward VII **Obv:** Crowned bust right within beaded circle **Rev:** Arms with vertical shading within beaded circle

Date	Mintage	F	VF	XF	Unc	BU
1904	192,000	2.00	5.00	12.00	35.00	42.50
1904 Proof	—	Value: 250				
1905	192,000	2.00	5.00	12.00	35.00	42.50
1906	528,000	2.00	3.00	9.00	28.00	35.00
1907	192,000	2.00	5.00	12.00	35.00	42.50
1909	144,000	2.00	6.00	20.00	45.00	50.00
1910	48,000	5.00	15.00	30.00	50.00	65.00

KM# 24   FARTHING
Copper-Nickel **Ruler:** George V **Obv:** Crowned bust left within beaded circle **Rev:** Arms within beaded circle

Date	Mintage	F	VF	XF	Unc	BU
1914	192,000	2.00	5.00	12.00	35.00	42.50
1916H	480,000	0.75	2.00	6.00	20.00	27.50
1916H Proof	—	Value: 250				
1918C	208,000	1.00	2.00	8.00	25.00	30.00
1918C Proof	—	Value: 225				
1919C	401,000	0.75	2.00	6.00	20.00	27.50
1926	240,000	1.00	2.00	8.00	25.00	30.00
1928	480,000	0.75	2.00	6.00	20.00	25.00
1928 Proof	—	Value: 225				
1932	480,000	0.75	2.00	6.00	20.00	27.50
1932 Proof	—	—				
1934	480,000	0.75	2.00	6.00	20.00	27.50
1934 Proof	—	—				

KM# 27   FARTHING
Nickel-Brass **Ruler:** George VI **Obv:** Crowned head left **Rev:** Arms divide date

Date	Mintage	F	VF	XF	Unc	BU
1937	480,000	0.50	1.50	5.00	15.00	20.00
1937 Proof	—	Value: 175				

KM# 30   FARTHING
Nickel-Brass **Ruler:** George VI **Obv:** Crowned head left **Rev:** Arms divide date

Date	Mintage	F	VF	XF	Unc	BU
1938	480,000	0.50	1.50	5.00	15.00	20.00
1938 Proof	—	—				
1942	480,000	0.50	1.50	5.00	15.00	20.00
1945	480,000	0.50	1.50	5.00	15.00	20.00
1945 Proof	—	Value: 120				
1947	192,000	1.00	3.00	7.50	20.00	27.50
1947 Proof	—	Value: 120				

KM# 33   FARTHING
Nickel-Brass **Ruler:** George VI **Obv:** Crowned head left **Obv. Leg.:** Without AND EMPEROR OF INDIA in legend **Rev:** Arms divide date

Date	Mintage	F	VF	XF	Unc	BU
1950	288,000	0.10	0.25	0.80	3.25	15.00
1950 Proof	—	Value: 175				
1952	288,000	0.10	0.25	0.80	3.50	17.50
1952 Proof	—	Value: 175				

KM# 19 1/2 PENNY
Copper-Nickel **Ruler:** Edward VII **Obv:** Crowned bust right within beaded circle **Rev:** Arms with horizontal shading within beaded circle

Date	Mintage	F	VF	XF	Unc	BU
1902	48,000	5.00	10.00	20.00	50.00	65.00
1903	48,000	5.00	10.00	20.00	60.00	75.00

KM# 22 1/2 PENNY
Copper-Nickel, 25.3 mm. **Ruler:** Edward VII **Obv:** Crowned bust right within beaded circle **Rev:** Arms with vertical shading within beaded circle

Date	Mintage	F	VF	XF	Unc	BU
1904	48,000	1.50	5.00	25.00	70.00	85.00
1905	48,000	1.50	5.00	25.00	70.00	85.00
1906	432,000	1.00	3.00	7.50	25.00	32.50
1907	504,000	1.00	3.00	7.50	25.00	32.50
1909	144,000	3.00	5.00	10.00	40.00	45.00
1910	144,000	0.75	2.00	10.00	40.00	45.00

KM# 25 1/2 PENNY
Copper-Nickel **Ruler:** George V **Obv:** Crowned bust left within beaded circle **Rev:** Arms within beaded circle

Date	Mintage	F	VF	XF	Unc	BU
1914	96,000	3.00	6.00	25.00	75.00	95.00
1916H	192,000	0.35	1.50	6.00	20.00	27.50
1918C	251,000	0.35	1.50	6.00	20.00	27.50
1918C Proof	—	Value: 200				
1919C	312,000	0.35	1.50	7.50	20.00	27.50
1920	480,000	0.35	1.50	7.50	20.00	27.50
1926	240,000	0.35	1.50	7.50	30.00	35.00
1928	120,000	0.35	3.00	10.00	35.00	40.00
1928 Proof	—	Value: 200				

KM# 28 1/2 PENNY
Nickel-Brass **Ruler:** George VI **Obv:** Crowned head left **Rev:** Arms divide date

Date	Mintage	F	VF	XF	Unc	BU
1937	960,000	0.50	1.00	3.50	12.00	15.00
1937 Proof	—	Value: 175				

KM# 31 1/2 PENNY
Nickel-Brass **Ruler:** George VI **Obv:** Crowned head left **Rev:** Arms divide date

Date	Mintage	F	VF	XF	Unc	BU
1938	960,000	0.25	0.75	3.50	12.00	15.00
1938 Proof	—	Value: 175				
1940	960,000	0.25	0.75	3.50	12.00	15.00
1940 Proof	—	Value: 175				
1942	960,000	0.25	0.75	3.50	12.00	15.00
1945	960,000	0.25	0.75	3.50	12.00	15.00

Date	Mintage	F	VF	XF	Unc	BU
1945 Proof	—	Value: 175				
1947	960,000	0.25	0.75	3.50	12.00	15.00
1947 Proof	—	Value: 200				

KM# 34 1/2 PENNY
4.3800 g., Nickel-Brass **Ruler:** George VI **Obv:** Crowned head left **Rev:** Arms divide date

Date	Mintage	F	VF	XF	Unc	BU
1950	1,440,000	0.10	0.20	0.30	3.25	5.00
1950 Proof	—	Value: 175				
1952	1,200,000	0.10	0.20	0.30	3.25	5.00
1952 Proof	—	Value: 175				

KM# 36 1/2 PENNY
4.3400 g., Nickel-Brass **Ruler:** Elizabeth II **Obv:** Crowned bust right **Rev:** Arms divide date

Date	Mintage	F	VF	XF	Unc	BU
1955	1,440,000	0.10	0.15	0.40	2.00	3.00
1955 Proof	—	Value: 150				
1957	600,000	1.00	2.00	4.00	6.00	9.00
1957 Proof	—	Value: 250				
1958	960,000	0.10	0.20	0.50	2.00	3.00
1958 Proof	—	Value: 150				
1959	960,000	0.10	0.20	0.50	2.00	3.00
1959 Proof	—	—	—	—	—	—
1961	480,000	0.20	0.40	1.00	4.00	5.00
1961 Proof	—	—	—	—	—	—
1962	960,000	0.10	0.15	0.30	1.75	2.50
1962 Proof	—	Value: 150				
1963	960,000	0.10	0.15	0.30	1.75	2.50
1963 Proof	—	Value: 150				

KM# 38 1/2 PENNY
4.5000 g., Nickel-Brass **Ruler:** Elizabeth II **Obv:** Crowned bust right **Rev:** Arms with supporters

Date	Mintage	F	VF	XF	Unc	BU
1964	1,440,000	0.10	0.15	0.20	0.80	1.00
1965	1,200,000	0.10	0.15	0.20	0.80	1.00
1966	1,680,000	0.10	0.15	0.20	0.80	1.00

KM# 41 1/2 PENNY
Copper-Nickel-Zinc **Ruler:** Elizabeth II **Subject:** Jamaican Coinage Centennial **Obv:** Crowned bust right **Rev:** Arms with supporters

Date	Mintage	F	VF	XF	Unc	BU
1969	30,000	0.10	0.15	0.25	0.75	1.00
1969 Proof	5,000	Value: 2.50				

KM# 20 PENNY
Copper-Nickel **Ruler:** Edward VII **Obv:** Crowned bust right within beaded circle **Rev:** Arms with horizontal shading within beaded circle

Date	Mintage	F	VF	XF	Unc	BU
1902	60,000	2.25	6.00	25.00	70.00	90.00
1903	60,000	2.25	6.00	25.00	70.00	90.00

KM# 23 PENNY
8.1000 g., Copper-Nickel **Ruler:** Edward VII **Obv:** Crowned bust right within beaded circle **Rev:** Arms with vertical shading within beaded circle

Date	Mintage	F	VF	XF	Unc	BU
1904	24,000	10.00	20.00	50.00	125	150
1904 Proof	—	Value: 250				
1905	48,000	2.00	6.50	35.00	70.00	90.00
1906	156,000	1.25	2.50	12.00	45.00	60.00
1907	108,000	1.25	2.50	12.00	45.00	60.00
1909	144,000	1.25	2.50	12.00	45.00	60.00
1910	144,000	1.25	2.50	12.00	45.00	60.00

KM# 26 PENNY
Copper-Nickel **Ruler:** George V **Obv:** Crowned bust left within beaded circle **Rev:** Arms within beaded circle

Date	Mintage	F	VF	XF	Unc	BU
1914	24,000	10.00	20.00	65.00	175	200
1916H	24,000	10.00	20.00	60.00	175	200
1918C	187,000	2.00	5.00	15.00	60.00	75.00
1918C Proof	—	Value: 200				
1919C	251,000	1.25	4.75	12.00	50.00	65.00
1920	360,000	0.75	2.50	9.50	32.50	40.00
1926	240,000	0.75	2.50	9.50	35.00	40.00
1928	360,000	0.75	2.50	9.50	35.00	40.00
1928 Proof	—	Value: 200				

KM# 29 PENNY
Nickel-Brass **Ruler:** George VI **Obv:** Crowned head left **Rev:** Arms divide date

Date	Mintage	F	VF	XF	Unc	BU
1937	1,200,000	1.00	1.75	3.25	12.00	15.00
1937 Proof	—	Value: 200				

KM# 32 PENNY

Nickel-Brass **Ruler:** George VI **Obv:** Crowned head left
Rev: Arms divide date

Date	Mintage	F	VF	XF	Unc	BU
1938	1,200,000	0.35	0.65	3.25	12.00	15.00
1938 Proof	—	Value: 200				
1940	1,200,000	0.35	0.65	3.25	12.00	15.00
1940 Proof	—	Value: 200				
1942	1,200,000	0.35	0.65	3.25	12.00	15.00
1942 Proof	—	Value: 200				
1945	1,200,000	0.35	0.65	3.25	12.00	15.00
1945 Proof	—	Value: 200				
1947	480,000	3.00	7.50	10.00	25.00	32.50
1947 Proof	—	Value: 200				

KM# 35 PENNY

Nickel-Brass **Ruler:** George VI **Obv:** Crowned head left
Obv. Leg.: Without AND EMPEROR OF INDIA in legend **Rev:** Arms
divide date

Date	Mintage	F	VF	XF	Unc	BU
1950	600,000	0.20	0.35	2.00	10.00	14.00
1950 Proof	—	Value: 200				
1952	725,000	0.20	0.35	2.00	10.00	14.00
1952 Proof	—	Value: 200				

KM# 37 PENNY

7.4800 g., Nickel-Brass **Ruler:** Elizabeth II **Obv:** Crowned bust
right **Rev:** Arms divide date

Date	Mintage	F	VF	XF	Unc	BU
1953	1,200,000	0.10	0.20	0.50	1.50	2.00
1953 Proof	—	Value: 115				
1955	960,000	0.10	0.25	1.00	4.00	5.00
1955 Proof	—	Value: 115				
1957	600,000	0.10	0.25	1.00	4.00	5.00
1957 Proof	—	—	—	—	—	—
1958	1,080,000	0.10	0.20	0.30	3.00	4.50
1958 Proof	—	Value: 100				
1959	1,368,000	0.10	0.20	0.30	2.50	3.00
1959 Proof	—	—	—	—	—	—
1960	1,368,000	0.10	0.20	0.30	2.50	3.00
1960 Proof	—	—	—	—	—	—
1961	1,368,000	0.10	0.20	0.30	2.50	3.00
1961 Proof	—	—	—	—	—	—
1962	1,920,000	0.10	0.20	0.30	2.50	3.00
1962 Proof	—	Value: 100				
1963	720,000	2.00	4.00	10.00	50.00	65.00
1963 Proof	—	Value: 100				

KM# 39 PENNY

7.4700 g., Nickel-Brass **Ruler:** Elizabeth II **Obv:** Crowned bust
right **Rev:** Arms with supporters

Date	Mintage	F	VF	XF	Unc	BU
1964	480,000	0.10	0.15	0.50	1.00	1.50
1965	1,200,000	0.10	0.15	0.20	0.35	1.00
1966	1,200,000	0.10	0.15	0.20	0.35	1.00
1967	2,760,000	0.10	0.15	0.20	0.35	1.00

KM# 42 PENNY

Copper-Nickel-Zinc **Ruler:** Elizabeth II **Subject:** Jamaican
Coinage Centennial **Obv:** Crowned bust right **Rev:** Arms with
supporters

Date	Mintage	F	VF	XF	Unc	BU
1969	30,000	0.10	0.15	0.30	0.75	1.25
1969 Proof	5,000	Value: 2.50				

KM# 40 5 SHILLING

Copper-Nickel **Ruler:** Elizabeth II **Subject:** VIII Commonwealth
Games **Obv:** Arms with supporters **Rev:** Crown divides date
above inscription within chain link wreath

Date	Mintage	F	VF	XF	Unc	BU
1966	190,000	—	2.00	3.00	5.00	6.50
1966 Proof	20,000	Value: 7.00				

DECIMAL COINAGE

The Franklin Mint and Royal Mint have both been strik-
ing the 1 Cent through 1 Dollar coinage. The 1970 issues
were all struck with dies similar to/or Royal Mint without the
FM mint mark. The Royal Mint issues have the name JA-
MAICA extending beyond the native headdress feathers.
Those struck after 1970 by the Franklin Mint have the name
JAMAICA within the headdress feathers.

KM# 45 CENT

Bronze **Ruler:** Elizabeth II **Obv:** Arms with supporters
Rev: Ackee fruit above value

Date	Mintage	F	VF	XF	Unc	BU
1969	30,200,000	—	—	0.10	0.25	0.50
1969 Proof	19,000	Value: 0.50				
1970 (RM) Small date	10,000,000	—	—	0.10	0.25	0.50
1970(fm) (M); Large date	5,000	—	—	0.10	0.25	0.50
1970(fm) (P)	12,000	Value: 0.50				
1971 (RM)	5,625,000	—	—	0.10	0.25	0.50

KM# 51 CENT

Bronze **Ruler:** Elizabeth II **Obv:** Arms with supporters
Rev: Ackee fruit above value

Date	Mintage	F	VF	XF	Unc	BU
1971FM (M)	4,834	—	—	0.10	0.25	0.50
1971FM (P)	14,000	Value: 0.50				

Date	Mintage	F	VF	XF	Unc	BU
1972FM (M)	7,982	—	—	0.10	0.25	0.50
1972FM (P)	17,000	Value: 0.50				
1973FM (M)	29,000	—	—	0.10	0.25	0.50
1973FM (P)	28,000	Value: 0.50				
1974FM (M)	28,000	—	—	0.10	0.25	0.50
1974FM (P)	22,000	Value: 0.50				
1975FM (M)	36,000	—	—	0.10	0.25	0.50
1975FM (U)	4,683	—	—	—	0.25	0.50
1975FM (P)	16,000	Value: 0.50				

KM# 52 CENT

4.2000 g., Bronze **Ruler:** Elizabeth II **Series:** F.A.O. **Obv:** Arms
with supporters **Rev:** Ackee fruit above value

Date	Mintage	F	VF	XF	Unc	BU
1971	20,000	—	—	0.50	1.00	1.50
1972	5,000,000	—	—	0.10	0.30	1.00
1973	5,500,000	—	—	0.10	0.30	1.00
1974	3,000,000	—	—	0.10	0.30	1.00

KM# 64 CENT

1.2000 g., Aluminum, 20.05 mm. **Ruler:** Elizabeth II
Series: F.A.O. **Obv:** National arms **Obv. Leg.:** JAMAICA
Rev: Ackee fruit above value **Edge:** Plain

Date	Mintage	F	VF	XF	Unc	BU
1975	15,000,000	—	—	0.10	0.20	0.50
1976	16,000,000	—	—	0.10	0.20	0.50
1977	—	—	—	0.10	0.20	0.50
1978	8,400,000	—	—	0.10	0.20	0.50
1980	10,000,000	—	—	0.10	0.20	0.50
1981	8,000,000	—	—	0.10	0.20	0.50
1982	10,000,000	—	—	0.10	0.20	0.50
1983	1,342,000	—	—	—	0.15	0.50
1984	8,704,000	—	—	—	0.15	0.50
1985	5,112,000	—	—	—	0.15	0.50
1985 Proof	—	Value: 0.50				
1986	17,534,000	—	—	—	0.15	0.50
1987	9,968,000	—	—	—	0.15	0.50
1987 Proof	—	Value: 0.50				
1988 Proof	—	Value: 0.50				
1989 Proof	—	Value: 0.50				
1990	—	—	—	—	0.15	0.50
1990 Proof	—	Value: 0.50				
1991	—	—	—	—	0.15	0.50
1991 Proof	—	Value: 0.50				
1992 Proof	—	Value: 0.50				
1993 Proof	—	Value: 0.50				
1995 Proof	—	Value: 0.50				
1996	—	—	—	—	0.15	0.50
2000	—	—	—	—	—	—
2000 Proof	—	Value: 1.00				

KM# 68 CENT

1.2000 g., Aluminum, 21.05 mm. **Ruler:** Elizabeth II **Obv:** Arms
with supporters **Rev:** Ackee fruit above value

Date	Mintage	F	VF	XF	Unc	BU
1976FM (M)	28,000	—	—	—	0.15	0.50
1976FM (U)	1,802	—	—	—	0.25	0.50
1976FM (P)	24,000	Value: 0.50				
1977FM (M)	28,000	—	—	—	0.15	0.30
1977FM (U)	597	—	—	—	1.50	2.00
1977FM (P)	10,000	Value: 0.50				
1978FM (M)	28,000	—	—	—	0.15	0.30
1978FM (U)	1,282	—	—	—	0.40	0.75
1978FM (P)	6,058	Value: 0.60				
1979FM (M)	28,000	—	—	—	0.15	0.50
1979FM (U)	2,608	—	—	—	0.40	0.75
1979FM (P)	4,049	Value: 0.60				
1980FM (M)	28,000	—	—	—	0.15	0.50
1980FM (U)	3,668	—	—	—	0.35	0.70
1980FM (P)	2,688	Value: 0.75				
1981FM (U)	482	—	—	—	1.50	2.00
1981FM (P)	1,577	Value: 0.75				
1982FM (U)	—	—	—	—	0.35	0.70
1982FM (P)	—	Value: 0.75				

Date	Mintage	F	VF	XF	Unc	BU
1984FM (U)	—	—	—	—	0.35	0.70
1984FM (P)	—	Value: 0.75				

KM# 136   CENT
1.2000 g., Aluminum, 21.05 mm. **Ruler:** Elizabeth II **Note:** Mule. Two obverses of KM#64.

Date	Mintage	F	VF	XF	Unc	BU
1982FM	—	—	—	220	250	275

KM# 137   CENT
1.2000 g., Aluminum, 21.05 mm. **Ruler:** Elizabeth II **Note:** Mule. Two reverses of KM#64.

Date	Mintage	F	VF	XF	Unc	BU
1982FM	—	—	—	250	300	325

KM# 101   CENT
1.2000 g., Aluminum, 21.05 mm. **Ruler:** Elizabeth II **Subject:** 21st Anniversary of Independence **Obv:** Arms with supporters **Rev:** Ackee plant (blighia sapida)

Date	Mintage	F	VF	XF	Unc	BU
ND(1983)M (U)	—	—	—	—	0.35	0.75
ND(1983)FM (P)	—	Value: 0.75				

KM# 46   5 CENTS
2.8000 g., Copper-Nickel, 19.4 mm. **Ruler:** Elizabeth II **Obv:** Arms with supporters **Rev:** American crocodile above value

Date	Mintage	F	VF	XF	Unc	BU
1969	12,008,000	—	—	0.10	0.50	1.00
1969 Proof	30,000	Value: 0.65				
1970(fm) (M)	5,000	—	—	0.10	0.50	1.00
1970(fm) (P)	12,000	Value: 0.65				
1972	6,000,000	—	—	0.10	0.50	0.75
1975	6,010,000	—	—	0.10	0.50	0.75
1977	2,400,000	—	—	0.10	0.50	0.75
1978	2,000,000	—	—	0.10	0.50	0.75
1980	2,272,000	—	—	0.10	0.50	0.75
1981	2,001,000	—	—	0.10	0.50	0.75
1982	2,000,000	—	—	0.10	0.50	0.75
1983	992,000	—	—	0.75	1.00	1.50
1984	3,508,000	—	—	0.10	0.50	0.75
1985	4,760,000	—	—	0.10	0.50	0.75
1985 Proof	—	Value: 0.65				
1986	14,504,000	—	—	0.10	0.50	0.75
1987	13,166,000	—	—	0.10	0.50	0.75
1987 Proof	—	Value: 0.65				
1988	9,780,000	—	—	0.10	0.50	0.75
1988 Proof	—	Value: 0.65				
1989	—	—	—	0.10	0.50	0.75
1989 Proof	—	Value: 0.65				

KM# 46a   5 CENTS
2.8000 g., Nickel Plated Steel, 19.4 mm. **Ruler:** Elizabeth II **Obv:** Arms with supporters **Rev:** American crocodile above value

Date	Mintage	F	VF	XF	Unc	BU
1990	—	—	—	0.10	0.50	0.75
1990 Proof	—	Value: 0.65				
1991	—	—	—	0.10	0.50	0.75
1991 Proof	—	Value: 0.65				
1992	—	—	—	0.10	0.50	0.75
1992 Proof	—	Value: 0.65				
1993	—	—	—	0.10	0.50	0.75
1993 Proof	—	Value: 0.65				

KM# 53   5 CENTS
2.8000 g., Copper-Nickel, 19.4 mm. **Ruler:** Elizabeth II **Obv:** Arms with supporters **Rev:** American crocodile above value

Date	Mintage	F	VF	XF	Unc	BU
1971FM (M)	4,834	—	—	0.10	0.75	1.00
1971FM (P)	14,000	Value: 0.50				
1972FM (M)	7,982	—	—	0.10	0.75	1.00
1972FM (P)	17,000	Value: 0.50				
1973FM (M)	17,000	—	—	0.10	0.75	1.00
1973FM (P)	28,000	Value: 0.50				
1974FM (M)	16,000	—	—	0.10	0.75	1.00
1974FM (P)	22,000	Value: 0.50				
1975FM (M)	6,240	—	—	0.10	0.75	1.00
1975FM (U)	4,683	—	—	—	0.75	1.00
1975FM (P)	16,000	Value: 0.50				
1976FM (M)	5,560	—	—	0.10	0.75	1.00
1976FM (U)	1,802	—	—	—	0.75	1.00
1976FM (P)	24,000	Value: 0.50				
1977FM (M)	5,560	—	—	0.10	0.75	1.00
1977FM (U)	597	—	—	—	1.50	2.00
1977FM (P)	10,000	Value: 0.50				
1978FM (M)	5,560	—	—	0.10	0.75	1.00
1978FM (U)	1,282	—	—	—	0.85	1.50
1978FM (P)	6,058	Value: 0.85				
1979FM (M)	5,560	—	—	0.10	0.75	1.50

Date	Mintage	F	VF	XF	Unc	BU
1979FM (U)	2,608	—	—	—	0.80	1.60
1979FM (P)	4,049	Value: 0.85				
1980FM (M)	5,560	—	—	0.10	0.75	1.50
1980FM (U)	3,668	—	—	—	0.80	1.60
1980FM (P)	2,688	Value: 1.00				
1981FM (U)	482	—	—	—	1.50	2.00
1981FM (P)	1,577	Value: 1.00				
1982FM (U)	—	—	—	—	0.80	1.60
1982FM (P)	—	Value: 1.00				
1984FM (U)	—	—	—	—	0.80	1.60
1984FM (P)	—	Value: 1.00				

KM# 102   5 CENTS
2.8000 g., Copper-Nickel, 19.4 mm. **Ruler:** Elizabeth II **Subject:** 21st Anniversary of Independence **Obv:** Arms with supporters **Rev:** American crocodile above value

Date	Mintage	F	VF	XF	Unc	BU
ND(1983)FM (U)	—	—	—	—	1.25	1.75
ND(1983)FM (P)	—	Value: 1.75				

KM# 47   10 CENTS
5.7500 g., Copper-Nickel, 23.6 mm. **Ruler:** Elizabeth II **Obv:** Arms with supporters **Rev:** Butterfly within leafy sprigs above value

Date	Mintage	F	VF	XF	Unc	BU
1969	19,508,000	—	—	0.10	0.50	0.75
1969 Proof	30,000	Value: 0.75				
1970(fm) (M)	5,000	—	—	0.10	0.50	0.75
1970(fm) (P)	12,000	Value: 0.75				
1972	6,000,000	—	—	0.10	0.50	0.75
1975	10,010,000	—	—	0.10	0.40	0.65
1977	8,000,000	—	—	0.10	0.40	0.65
1981	8,000,000	—	—	0.10	0.30	0.60
1982	8,000,000	—	—	0.10	0.30	0.60
1983	2,000,000	—	—	0.10	0.30	0.60
1984	5,000,000	—	—	0.10	0.30	0.60
1985	8,310,000	—	—	0.10	0.30	0.60
1985 Proof	—	Value: 0.75				
1986	21,677,000	—	—	0.10	0.30	0.60
1987	29,089,000	—	—	0.10	0.30	0.60
1987 Proof	—	Value: 0.75				
1988	15,660,000	—	—	0.10	0.30	0.60
1988 Proof	—	Value: 0.75				
1989	—	—	—	0.10	0.30	0.60
1989 Proof	—	Value: 0.75				

KM# 47a   10 CENTS
5.7500 g., Nickel Plated Steel, 23.6 mm. **Ruler:** Elizabeth II **Obv:** Arms with supporters **Rev:** Butterfly within leafy sprigs above value

Date	Mintage	F	VF	XF	Unc	BU
1990	—	—	—	0.10	0.30	0.60
1990 Proof	—	Value: 0.75				

KM# 54   10 CENTS
5.7500 g., Copper-Nickel, 23.6 mm. **Ruler:** Elizabeth II **Obv:** Arms with supporters **Rev:** Butterfly within leafy sprigs above value

Date	Mintage	F	VF	XF	Unc	BU
1971FM (M)	4,834	—	—	0.10	0.35	0.70
1971FM (P)	14,000	Value: 0.75				
1972FM (M)	7,982	—	—	0.10	0.35	0.70
1972FM (P)	17,000	Value: 0.75				
1973FM (M)	15,000	—	—	0.10	0.35	0.70
1973FM (P)	28,000	Value: 0.75				
1974FM (M)	14,000	—	—	0.10	0.35	0.70
1974FM (P)	22,000	Value: 0.75				
1975FM (M)	3,120	—	—	0.10	0.35	0.75
1975FM (U)	4,683	—	—	—	0.35	0.75
1975FM (P)	16,000	Value: 0.75				
1976FM (M)	2,780	—	—	0.10	0.35	0.75
1976FM (U)	1,802	—	—	—	0.35	0.75
1976FM (P)	24,000	Value: 0.75				
1977FM (M)	2,780	—	—	0.10	0.50	0.80
1977FM (U)	597	—	—	—	1.50	2.50
1977FM (P)	10,000	Value: 0.75				
1978FM (M)	2,780	—	—	0.10	0.50	0.80
1978FM (U)	4,062	—	—	—	0.60	0.85
1978FM (P)	6,058	Value: 1.00				
1979FM (M)	2,780	—	—	0.10	0.50	0.80
1979FM (U)	2,608	—	—	—	0.60	0.85
1979FM (P)	4,049	Value: 1.00				
1980FM (M)	2,780	—	—	0.10	0.50	0.80
1980FM (U)	3,668	—	—	—	0.50	0.80
1980FM (P)	2,688	Value: 1.50				

KM# 103   10 CENTS
5.7500 g., Copper-Nickel, 23.6 mm. **Ruler:** Elizabeth II **Subject:** 21st Anniversary of Independence **Obv:** Arms with supporters **Rev:** Butterfly within leafy sprigs above value

Date	Mintage	F	VF	XF	Unc	BU
ND(1983)FM (U)	—	—	—	—	0.50	0.80
ND(1983)FM (P)	—	Value: 1.50				

KM# 146.1   10 CENTS
5.6800 g., Nickel Plated Steel. **Ruler:** Elizabeth II **Subject:** Paul Bogle **Obv:** Arms with supporters **Rev:** Bust facing

Date	Mintage	F	VF	XF	Unc	BU
1991	—	—	—	—	0.50	0.80
1991 Proof	—	Value: 1.50				
1992	—	—	—	—	0.50	0.80
1992 Proof	—	Value: 1.50				
1993	—	—	—	—	0.50	0.80
1993 Proof	—	Value: 1.50				
1994	—	—	—	—	0.50	0.80
1994 Proof	—	Value: 1.50				

KM# 146.2   10 CENTS
2.4500 g., Copper Plated Steel, 17 mm. **Ruler:** Elizabeth II **Series:** National Heroes **Subject:** Paul Bogle **Obv:** National arms **Obv. Leg.:** JAMAICA **Rev:** Bust facing **Edge:** Plain **Note:** Reduced size.

Date	Mintage	F	VF	XF	Unc	BU
1995	—	—	—	—	0.25	0.50
1995 Proof	—	Value: 2.00				
1996	—	—	—	—	0.25	0.50
2000	—	—	—	—	0.25	0.50
2000 Proof	—	Value: 2.00				

KM# 48   20 CENTS
11.3000 g., Copper-Nickel, 28.5 mm. **Ruler:** Elizabeth II **Obv:** Arms with supporters **Rev:** Mahoe trees above value

Date	Mintage	F	VF	XF	Unc	BU
1969	3,758,000	—	—	0.25	0.75	1.00
1969 Proof	30,000	Value: 1.00				
1970(fm) (M)	5,000	—	—	0.25	0.75	1.00
1970(fm) (P)	12,000	Value: 1.00				
1975	10,000	—	—	0.80	2.50	3.00
1982	1,000,000	—	—	0.25	0.65	1.00
1984	2,000,000	—	—	0.25	0.65	1.00
1986	2,530,000	—	—	0.25	0.65	1.00
1987	5,545,000	—	—	0.25	0.65	1.00
1987 Proof	—	Value: 1.00				
1988	5,016,000	—	—	0.25	0.65	1.00
1988 Proof	—	Value: 1.00				
1989	—	—	—	0.25	0.65	1.00
1989 Proof	—	Value: 1.00				
1990 Proof	—	Value: 1.00				

KM# 55 20 CENTS
11.3000 g., Copper-Nickel, 28.5 mm. **Ruler:** Elizabeth II
Obv: Arms with supporters **Rev:** Mahoe trees above value

Date	Mintage	F	VF	XF	Unc	BU
1971FM (M)	4,834	—	—	0.25	0.50	1.00
1971FM (P)	14,000	Value: 1.00				
1972FM (M)	7,982	—	—	0.25	0.50	1.00
1972FM (P)	17,000	Value: 1.00				
1973FM (M)	13,000	—	—	0.25	0.50	1.00
1973FM (P)	28,000	Value: 1.00				
1974FM (M)	12,000	—	—	0.25	0.50	1.00
1974FM (P)	22,000	Value: 1.00				
1975FM (M)	1,560	—	—	0.25	0.50	1.00
1975FM (U)	4,683	—	—	—	0.50	1.00
1975FM (P)	16,000	Value: 1.00				
1976FM (M)	1,390	—	—	0.25	0.50	1.00
1976FM (U)	1,802	—	—	—	0.50	1.00
1976FM (P)	24,000	Value: 1.00				

KM# 69 20 CENTS
11.3000 g., Copper-Nickel, 28.5 mm. **Ruler:** Elizabeth II
Series: F.A.O. **Obv:** Arms with supporters **Rev:** Mahoe trees above value

Date	Mintage	F	VF	XF	Unc	BU
1976	3,000,000	—	—	0.20	1.00	1.50
1981	—	—	—	0.20	1.00	1.50
1982	—	—	—	0.20	1.00	1.50
	Note: Mintage included with KM#48					
1984	—	—	—	0.20	1.00	1.50
1987	—	—	—	0.20	1.00	1.50

KM# 73 20 CENTS
11.3000 g., Copper-Nickel, 28.5 mm. **Ruler:** Elizabeth II
Obv: Arms with supporters **Rev:** Mahoe trees above value

Date	Mintage	F	VF	XF	Unc	BU
1977FM (M)	1,390	—	—	0.25	0.75	1.25
1977FM (U)	597	—	—	—	2.00	2.50
1977FM (P)	10,000	Value: 1.00				
1978FM (M)	1,390	—	—	0.25	0.75	1.25
1978FM (U)	1,282	—	—	—	0.75	1.25
1978FM (P)	6,058	Value: 1.50				
1979FM (M)	1,390	—	—	0.25	0.75	1.25
1979FM (U)	2,608	—	—	—	0.75	1.25
1979FM (P)	4,049	Value: 1.50				
1980FM (M)	1,390	—	—	0.25	0.60	1.00
1980FM (U)	3,668	—	—	—	0.60	1.00
1980FM (P)	2,688	Value: 2.00				
1981FM (U)	482	—	—	—	2.00	2.50
1981FM (P)	1,577	Value: 2.00				
1982FM (U)	—	—	—	—	0.60	1.00
1982FM (P)	—	Value: 2.00				
1984FM (U)	—	—	—	—	0.60	1.00
1984FM (P)	—	Value: 2.00				

KM# 90 20 CENTS
11.3000 g., Copper-Nickel, 28.5 mm. **Ruler:** Elizabeth II
Subject: World Food Day **Obv:** Arms with supporters **Rev:** Figs within leaves above value

Date	Mintage	F	VF	XF	Unc	BU
1981FM (M)	—	—	—	—	1.50	2.00

KM# 120 20 CENTS
11.3000 g., Copper-Nickel, 28.5 mm. **Ruler:** Elizabeth II
Obv: Arms with supporters **Rev:** Figs within leaves above value

Date	Mintage	F	VF	XF	Unc	BU
1981	—	—	—	—	0.60	1.00
1984	2,000,000	—	—	—	0.60	1.00
1985	2,988,000	—	—	—	0.60	1.00
1985 Proof	—	Value: 2.00				
1986	2,530,000	—	—	—	0.60	1.00
1988	—	—	—	—	0.60	1.00

KM# 104 20 CENTS
11.3000 g., Copper-Nickel, 28.5 mm. **Ruler:** Elizabeth II
Subject: 21st Anniversary of Independence **Obv:** Arms with supporters **Rev:** Mahoe trees above value

Date	Mintage	F	VF	XF	Unc	BU
ND(1983)FM (U)	—	—	—	—	0.60	1.00
ND(1983)FM (P)	—	Value: 2.00				

KM# 49 25 CENTS
14.5500 g., Copper-Nickel, 32.3 mm. **Ruler:** Elizabeth II **Obv:** Arms with supporters **Rev:** Streamer-tailed hummingbird above value

Date	Mintage	F	VF	XF	Unc	BU
1969	758,000	—	—	0.60	1.50	2.50
1969 Proof	30,000	Value: 3.00				
1970(fm) (M)	5,000	—	—	0.60	1.50	2.50
1970(fm) (P)	12,000	Value: 3.00				
1973	160,000	—	—	0.60	1.50	2.50
1975	3,110,000	—	—	0.60	1.50	2.50
1982	1,000,000	—	—	0.60	1.50	2.50
1984	2,002,000	—	—	0.60	1.50	2.50
1985	1,999,000	—	—	0.60	1.50	2.50
1985 Proof	—	Value: 3.00				
1986	2,635,000	—	—	0.60	1.50	2.50
1987	6,006,000	—	—	0.60	1.50	2.50
1987 Proof	—	Value: 3.00				
1988	3,034,000	—	—	0.60	1.50	2.50
1988 Proof	—	Value: 3.00				
1989	—	—	—	0.60	1.50	2.50
1989 Proof	—	Value: 3.00				
1990 Proof	—	Value: 3.00				

KM# 56 25 CENTS
14.5500 g., Copper-Nickel, 32.3 mm. **Ruler:** Elizabeth II
Obv: Arms with supporters **Rev:** Streamer-tailed hummingbird above value

Date	Mintage	F	VF	XF	Unc	BU
1971FM (M)	4,834	—	—	0.75	1.50	2.50
1971FM (P)	14,000	Value: 3.00				
1972FM (M)	8,382	—	—	0.75	1.50	2.50
1972FM (P)	17,000	Value: 3.00				
1973FM (M)	13,000	—	—	0.75	1.50	2.50
1973FM (P)	28,000	Value: 3.00				
1974FM (M)	12,000	—	—	0.75	1.50	2.50
1974FM (P)	22,000	Value: 3.00				
1975FM (M)	1,503	—	—	0.75	1.50	2.50
1975FM (U)	4,683	—	—	—	1.50	2.50
1975FM (P)	16,000	Value: 3.00				
1976FM (M)	1,112	—	—	0.75	1.50	2.50
1976FM (U)	1,802	—	—	—	1.50	2.50
1976FM (P)	24,000	Value: 3.00				
1977FM (M)	1,112	—	—	0.75	1.50	2.50
1977FM (U)	597	—	—	—	3.00	4.50
1977FM (P)	10,000	Value: 3.00				
1978FM (M)	1,112	—	—	0.75	1.50	2.50
1978FM (U)	1,282	—	—	0.75	1.50	2.50
1978FM (P)	6,058	Value: 3.00				
1979FM (M)	1,112	—	—	0.75	1.50	2.50
1979FM (U)	2,608	—	—	0.75	1.50	2.50
1979FM (P)	4,049	Value: 3.00				
1980FM (M)	1,112	—	—	0.75	1.50	2.50
1980FM (U)	3,668	—	—	0.75	1.50	2.50
1980FM (P)	2,688	Value: 3.50				
1981FM (U)	482	—	—	—	3.00	4.50
1981FM (P)	1,577	Value: 3.50				
1982FM (U)	—	—	—	0.75	1.50	2.50
1982FM (P)	—	Value: 3.50				
1984FM (U)	—	—	—	0.75	1.50	2.50
1984FM (P)	—	Value: 3.50				

KM# 105 25 CENTS
14.5500 g., Copper-Nickel, 32.3 mm. **Ruler:** Elizabeth II
Subject: 21st Anniversary of Independence **Obv:** Arms with supporters **Rev:** Streamer-tailed hummingbird above value

Date	Mintage	F	VF	XF	Unc	BU
ND(1983)FM (U)	—	—	—	—	1.50	3.00
ND(1983)FM (P)	—	Value: 3.00				

KM# 154 25 CENTS
14.5500 g., Copper-Nickel, 32.3 mm. **Ruler:** Elizabeth II
Subject: 25th Anniversary - Bank of Jamaica **Obv:** Arms with supporters **Rev:** Streamer-tailed hummingbird above value

Date	Mintage	F	VF	XF	Unc	BU
1985	—	—	—	0.75	3.50	6.00

KM# 147   25 CENTS
6.0000 g., Nickel Plated Steel **Ruler:** Elizabeth II **Subject:** Marcus Garvey **Obv:** Arms with supporters **Rev:** Head 1/4 right

Date	Mintage	F	VF	XF	Unc	BU
1991	—	—	—	—	1.00	1.50
1991 Proof	—	Value: 3.00				
1992	—	—	—	—	1.00	1.50
1992 Proof	—	Value: 3.00				
1993	—	—	—	—	1.00	1.50
1993 Proof	—	Value: 3.00				
1994	—	—	—	—	1.00	1.50

KM# 167   25 CENTS
3.6100 g., Copper Plated Steel, 20 mm. **Ruler:** Elizabeth II **Series:** National Heroes **Subject:** Marcus Garvey **Obv:** National arms **Obv. Leg.:** JAMAICA **Rev:** Head 1/4 right **Edge:** Plain

Date	Mintage	F	VF	XF	Unc	BU
1995	—	—	—	—	0.50	0.75
1995 Proof	—	Value: 3.00				
1996	—	—	—	—	0.50	0.75
2000	—	—	—	—	0.50	0.75
2000 Proof	—	Value: 3.00				

KM# 65   50 CENTS
12.4500 g., Copper-Nickel, 30 mm. **Ruler:** Elizabeth II **Subject:** Marcus Garvey **Obv:** Arms with supporters **Rev:** Head 1/4 right

Date	Mintage	F	VF	XF	Unc	BU
1975	12,010,000	—	0.15	0.50	1.50	2.00
1984	2,000,000	—	0.15	0.50	1.50	2.00
1985	2,119,000	—	0.15	0.50	1.50	2.00
1985 Proof	—	Value: 3.00				
1986	3,404,000	—	0.15	0.50	1.50	2.00
1987	5,545,000	—	0.15	0.50	1.50	2.00
1988	10,505,000	—	0.15	0.50	1.50	2.00
1988 Proof	—	Value: 3.00				
1989	—	—	0.15	0.50	1.50	2.00
1989 Proof	—	Value: 3.00				
1990 Proof	—	Value: 3.00				

KM# 70   50 CENTS
12.4500 g., Copper-Nickel, 30 mm. **Ruler:** Elizabeth II **Subject:** Marcus Garvey **Obv:** Arms with supporters **Rev:** Head 1/4 right

Date	Mintage	F	VF	XF	Unc	BU
1976FM (M)	1,112	—	—	0.25	1.50	2.00
1976FM (U)	1,802	—	—	—	1.50	2.00
1976FM (P)	24,000	Value: 1.50				
1977FM (M)	556	—	—	0.50	3.50	5.00
1977FM (U)	597	—	—	—	3.50	5.00
1977FM (P)	10,000	Value: 1.50				
1978FM (M)	556	—	—	0.50	3.50	5.00
1978FM (U)	1,838	—	—	—	2.00	3.00
1978FM (P)	6,058	Value: 2.50				
1979FM (M)	556	—	—	0.50	3.50	5.00
1979FM (U)	1,282	—	—	—	2.50	3.50
1979FM (P)	4,049	Value: 3.00				
1980FM (M)	556	—	—	0.50	3.50	5.00
1980FM (U)	3,668	—	—	—	2.00	3.00
1980FM (P)	2,688	Value: 3.00				

Date	Mintage	F	VF	XF	Unc	BU
1981FM (U)	482	—	—	—	3.50	5.00
1981FM (P)	1,577	Value: 3.00				
1982FM (U)	—	—	—	—	2.00	3.00
1982FM (P)	—	Value: 3.00				
1984FM (U)	—	—	—	—	2.00	3.00
1984FM (P)	—	Value: 3.00				

KM# 106   50 CENTS
12.4500 g., Copper-Nickel, 30 mm. **Ruler:** Elizabeth II **Subject:** 21st Anniversary of Independence - Marcus Garvey **Obv:** Arms with supporters **Rev:** Head 1/4 right

Date	Mintage	F	VF	XF	Unc	BU
ND(1983)FM (U)	—	—	—	—	2.00	3.00
ND(1983)FM (P)	—	Value: 4.00				

KM# 132   50 CENTS
12.4500 g., Copper-Nickel, 30 mm. **Ruler:** Elizabeth II **Subject:** 100th Anniversary - Birth of Marcus Garvey **Obv:** Arms with supporters **Rev:** Head 1/4 right

Date	Mintage	F	VF	XF	Unc	BU
1987 Proof	500	Value: 3.50				

KM# 50   DOLLAR
Copper-Nickel **Ruler:** Elizabeth II **Obv:** Arms with supporters **Rev:** Bust right

Date	Mintage	F	VF	XF	Unc	BU
1969	47,000	—	—	1.00	3.00	4.00
1969 Proof	30,000	Value: 4.50				
1970(fm) (M)	5,000	—	—	0.30	3.50	5.00
1970(fm) (P)	14,000	Value: 5.00				

KM# 57   DOLLAR
Copper-Nickel **Ruler:** Elizabeth II **Obv:** Arms with supporters **Rev:** Bust right

Date	Mintage	F	VF	XF	Unc	BU
1971FM	5,024	—	—	0.30	3.00	4.00
1971FM (P)	15,000	Value: 4.00				
1972FM (M)	7,982	—	—	0.30	2.00	3.00
1972FM (P)	17,000	Value: 3.00				
1973FM	10,000	—	—	0.30	2.00	3.00
1973FM (P)	28,000	Value: 3.00				
1974FM (M)	8,961	—	—	0.30	2.00	3.00
1974FM (P)	22,000	Value: 3.00				
1975FM (M)	5,312	—	—	0.30	2.50	3.50
1975FM (P)	4,683	—	—	—	2.50	3.50
1975FM (P)	16,000	Value: 3.00				
1976FM (M)	284	—	—	—	17.50	20.00
1976FM (U)	1,802	—	—	—	4.00	5.00
1976FM (P)	24,000	Value: 2.50				
1977FM (M)	287	—	—	—	17.50	20.00
1977FM (U)	597	—	—	—	8.00	10.00
1977FM (P)	10,000	Value: 4.00				
1978FM (U)	1,566	—	—	—	4.00	5.00
1978FM (P)	6,058	Value: 5.00				
1979FM (M)	284	—	—	—	17.50	20.00
1979FM (U)	2,608	—	—	—	4.00	5.00
1979FM (P)	4,049	Value: 5.00				

KM# 84.1   DOLLAR
Copper-Nickel **Ruler:** Elizabeth II **Obv:** Arms with supporters **Rev:** Bust right

Date	Mintage	F	VF	XF	Unc	BU
1980FM (M)	284	—	—	20.00	22.50	
1980FM (U)	3,668	—	—	—	5.00	6.00
1980FM (P)	2,688	Value: 15.00				
1981FM (U)	482	—	—	—	10.00	12.50
1981FM (P)	1,577	Value: 17.50				
1982FM (U)	—	—	—	—	7.00	10.00
1982FM (P)	—	Value: 17.50				

KM# 91   DOLLAR
Copper-Nickel **Ruler:** Elizabeth II **Subject:** World Food Day **Obv:** Arms with supporters **Rev:** World globe above produce

Date	Mintage	F	VF	XF	Unc	BU
ND(1981)FM (U)	—	—	—	—	7.50	8.50

KM# 96   DOLLAR
Copper-Nickel **Ruler:** Elizabeth II **Subject:** World Championship of Football **Obv:** Arms with supporters **Rev:** Goalie catching attempted score

Date	Mintage	F	VF	XF	Unc	BU
1982	—	—	—	—	4.50	5.50

KM# 107   DOLLAR
Copper-Nickel **Ruler:** Elizabeth II **Subject:** 21st Anniversary of Independence **Obv:** Arms with supporters **Rev:** Bust right

Date	Mintage	F	VF	XF	Unc	BU
ND(1983)FM (P)	609	Value: 20.00				
ND(1983)FM (U)	3,710	—	—	—	7.50	8.50

KM# 134   DOLLAR
Copper-Nickel **Ruler:** Elizabeth II **Subject:** 21st Anniversary of Independence **Obv:** Arms with supporters **Rev:** Number 21 divides heads facing above dates and braided rope

Date	Mintage	F	VF	XF	Unc	BU
ND(1983)FM (P)	—	Value: 14.00				

KM# 113   DOLLAR
Copper-Nickel **Ruler:** Elizabeth II **Subject:** 100th Anniversary - Birth of Bustamante **Obv:** Arms with supporters **Rev:** Bust 1/4 left

Date	Mintage	F	VF	XF	Unc	BU
1984FM (U)	—	—	—	—	3.00	4.00
1984FM (P)	268	Value: 25.00				

KM# 84.2 DOLLAR
Copper-Nickel **Ruler:** Elizabeth II **Obv:** Arms with supporters
Rev: Bust right **Edge:** Reeded

Date	Mintage	F	VF	XF	Unc	BU
1985	—	—	—	—	3.00	4.00
1985 Proof	—	Value: 7.50				
1987 Proof	—	Value: 7.50				
1988 Proof	—	Value: 7.50				
1989 Proof	—	Value: 7.50				
1990	—	—	—	—	3.00	4.00

KM# 145 DOLLAR
9.0000 g., Nickel-Brass, 23.8 mm. **Ruler:** Elizabeth II
Subject: Sir Alexander Bustamante **Obv:** Arms with supporters
Rev: Bust facing **Edge:** BANK OF JAMAICA

Date	Mintage	F	VF	XF	Unc	BU
1990	—	—	—	—	2.25	3.00
1990 Proof	—	Value: 5.00				
1991	—	—	—	—	2.25	3.00
1991 Proof	—	Value: 5.00				
1992	—	—	—	—	2.25	3.00
1992 Proof	—	Value: 10.00				
1993	—	—	—	—	2.25	3.00
1993 Proof	—	Value: 5.00				

KM# 145a DOLLAR
Brass Plated Steel, 23.8 mm. **Ruler:** Elizabeth II **Subject:** Sir
Alexander Bustamante **Obv:** Arms with supporters **Rev:** Bust
facing **Edge:** Reeded

Date	Mintage	F	VF	XF	Unc	BU
1993	—	—	—	—	2.25	3.00
1993 Proof	500	Value: 15.00				
1994	—	—	—	—	2.25	3.00

KM# 164 DOLLAR
2.9100 g., Nickel Clad Steel, 18.5 mm. **Ruler:** Elizabeth II
Series: National Heroes **Subject:** Sir Alexander Bustamante **Obv:**
National arms **Obv. Leg.:** JAMAICA **Rev:** Bust facing **Edge:** Plain

Date	Mintage	F	VF	XF	Unc	BU
1994	—	—	—	0.40	1.00	1.50
1995	—	—	—	0.40	1.00	1.50
1995 Proof	—	Value: 4.00				
1996	—	—	—	0.40	1.00	1.50
1999	—	—	—	0.40	1.00	1.50
2000	—	—	—	0.40	1.00	1.50
2000 Proof	—	Value: 4.00				

KM# 58 5 DOLLARS
42.1500 g., 0.9250 Silver 1.2535 oz. ASW **Ruler:** Elizabeth II
Obv: Arms with supporters **Rev:** Bust facing **Note:** His widow
did not like this design, and the following year it was replaced by
a left profile.

Date	Mintage	F	VF	XF	Unc	BU
1971FM	4,072	—	—	—	25.00	28.00
1971FM (P)	13,000	Value: 27.50				

KM# 59 5 DOLLARS
41.4800 g., 0.9250 Silver 1.2335 oz. ASW **Ruler:** Elizabeth II
Obv: Arms with supporters **Rev:** Head left

Date	Mintage	F	VF	XF	Unc	BU
1972FM	3,232	—	—	—	25.00	28.00
1972FM (P)	21,000	Value: 27.50				
1973FM	6,484	—	—	—	25.00	28.00
1973FM (P)	36,000	Value: 27.50				

KM# 62 5 DOLLARS
Copper-Nickel **Ruler:** Elizabeth II **Obv:** Arms with supporters
Rev: Head left

Date	Mintage	F	VF	XF	Unc	BU
1974FM (M)	8,661	—	—	—	6.00	7.50
1975FM (M)	65	—	—	—	—	—
1975FM (U)	4,683	—	—	—	7.00	8.50
1976FM (M)	56	—	—	—	—	—
1976FM (U)	1,802	—	—	—	8.00	10.00
1977FM (M)	56	—	—	—	—	—
1977FM (U)	597	—	—	—	12.00	14.00
1978FM (U)	1,338	—	—	—	7.00	9.00
1979FM (M)	56	—	—	—	—	—
1979FM (U)	2,608	—	—	—	6.00	8.00

KM# 62a 5 DOLLARS
37.6000 g., 0.5000 Silver 0.6044 oz. ASW **Ruler:** Elizabeth II
Obv: Arms with supporters **Rev:** Head left

Date	Mintage	F	VF	XF	Unc	BU
1974FM (P)	22,000	Value: 12.00				
1975FM (P)	16,000	Value: 14.00				
1976FM (P)	23,000	Value: 12.00				
1977FM (P)	10,000	Value: 14.00				
1978FM (P)	6,058	Value: 16.00				
1979FM (P)	4,049	Value: 18.00				

KM# 85.1a 5 DOLLARS
18.5600 g., 0.5000 Silver 0.2983 oz. ASW **Ruler:** Elizabeth II
Obv: Arms with supporters **Rev:** Head left

Date	Mintage	F	VF	XF	Unc	BU
1980FM (P)	2,688	Value: 15.00				
1981FM (P)	1,577	Value: 17.00				
1982FM (P)	1,040	Value: 17.00				
1984FM (P)	268	Value: 40.00				

KM# 85.1 5 DOLLARS
Copper-Nickel **Ruler:** Elizabeth II **Obv:** Arms with supporters
Rev: Head left **Note:** Similar to KM#62, but smaller size.

Date	Mintage	F	VF	XF	Unc	BU
1980FM (M)	56	—	—	—	—	—
1980FM (U)	3,668	—	—	—	15.00	17.00
1981FM (U)	482	—	—	—	20.00	22.50
1982FM (U)	—	—	—	—	10.00	12.00
1984FM (U)	—	—	—	—	10.00	12.00

KM# 108 5 DOLLARS
Copper-Nickel **Ruler:** Elizabeth II **Subject:** 21st Anniversary of
Independence **Obv:** Arms with supporters **Rev:** Head left

Date	Mintage	F	VF	XF	Unc	BU
1983FM (U)	—	—	—	—	8.00	10.00

KM# 108a 5 DOLLARS
18.5600 g., 0.5000 Silver 0.2983 oz. ASW **Ruler:** Elizabeth II
Obv: Arms with supporters **Rev:** Head left

Date	Mintage	F	VF	XF	Unc	BU
1983FM (P)	—	Value: 20.00				

KM# 85.2 5 DOLLARS
18.5600 g., 0.5000 Silver 0.2983 oz. ASW **Ruler:** Elizabeth II
Obv: Arms with supporters **Rev:** Head left

Date	Mintage	F	VF	XF	Unc	BU
1985	—	—	—	—	30.00	—
1985 Proof	—	Value: 30.00				
1987 Proof	—	Value: 30.00				
1988 Proof	—	Value: 30.00				
1989 Proof	—	Value: 30.00				
1990 Proof	500	Value: 30.00				
1991 Proof	—	Value: 30.00				
1992 Proof	—	Value: 30.00				
1993 Proof	—	Value: 30.00				

KM# 157 5 DOLLARS
Nickel Plated Steel **Ruler:** Elizabeth II **Subject:** Centennial - Birth
of Norman Manley **Obv:** Arms with supporters **Rev:** Head left

Date	Mintage	F	VF	XF	Unc	BU
1993	—	—	—	—	3.50	5.00

KM# 157a 5 DOLLARS
18.5000 g., 0.5000 Silver 0.2974 oz. ASW **Ruler:** Elizabeth II
Subject: Centennial - Birth of Norman Manley **Obv:** Arms with
supporters **Rev:** Head left

Date	Mintage	F	VF	XF	Unc	BU
1993 Proof	Est. 2,000	Value: 35.00				

KM# 163 5 DOLLARS
Steel, 21.5 mm. **Ruler:** Elizabeth II **Series:** National Heroes
Subject: Norman Manley **Obv:** National arms
Obv. Leg.: JAMAICA **Rev:** Head left

Date	Mintage	F	VF	XF	Unc	BU
1994	—	—	—	—	2.50	3.50
1995	—	—	—	—	2.50	3.50
1995 Proof	—	Value: 5.00				
1996	—	—	—	—	2.50	3.50

Date	Mintage	F	VF	XF	Unc	BU
2000	—	—	—	—	2.50	3.50
2000 Proof	—	Value: 5.00				

KM# 60   10 DOLLARS
49.2000 g., 0.9250 Silver 1.4631 oz. ASW **Ruler:** Elizabeth II
Subject: 10th Anniversary of Independence **Obv:** Arms with
supporters **Rev:** Conjoined heads facing each other above map

Date	Mintage	F	VF	XF	Unc	BU
ND(1972)	42,000	—	—	—	30.00	32.50
ND(1972) Proof	33,000	Value: 35.00				

KM# 63   10 DOLLARS
Copper-Nickel, 45 mm. **Ruler:** Elizabeth II **Subject:** Sir Henry
Morgan **Obv:** Arms with supporters **Rev:** Bust 1/4 left

Date	Mintage	F	VF	XF	Unc	BU
1974FM (M)	15,000	—	—	—	7.50	·8.50

KM# 63a   10 DOLLARS
42.8000 g., 0.9250 Silver 1.2728 oz. ASW, 45 mm.
Ruler: Elizabeth II **Subject:** Sir Henry Morgan **Obv:** Arms with
supporters **Rev:** Bust 1/4 left

Date	Mintage	F	VF	XF	Unc	BU
1974FM (P)	42,000	Value: 27.50				

KM# 66   10 DOLLARS
Copper-Nickel, 45 mm. **Ruler:** Elizabeth II **Subject:** Christopher
Columbus **Obv:** Arms with supporters **Rev:** Bust looking left at
right, ship at left

Date	Mintage	F	VF	XF	Unc	BU
1975FM (M)	30	—	—	—	—	—
1975FM (U)	5,758	—	—	—	12.00	13.00

KM# 66a   10 DOLLARS
42.8000 g., 0.9250 Silver 1.2728 oz. ASW, 45 mm.
Ruler: Elizabeth II **Subject:** Christopher Columbus **Obv:** Arms
with supporters **Rev:** Bust looking left at right, ship at left

Date	Mintage	F	VF	XF	Unc	BU
1975FM (P)	29,000	Value: 27.50				

KM# 71   10 DOLLARS
Copper-Nickel, 45 mm. **Ruler:** Elizabeth II **Subject:** Admiral
Horatio Nelson **Obv:** Arms with supporters **Rev:** Uniformed bust
1/4 left, map and ship at far left

Date	Mintage	F	VF	XF	Unc	BU
1976FM (M)	27	—	—	—	—	—
1976FM (U)	2,302	—	—	—	15.00	17.50

KM# 71a   10 DOLLARS
42.8000 g., 0.9250 Silver 1.2728 oz. ASW, 45 mm. **Ruler:**
Elizabeth II **Subject:** Admiral Horation Nelson **Obv:** Arms with
supporters **Rev:** Uniformed bust 1/4 left with ship and map at far left

Date	Mintage	F	VF	XF	Unc	BU
1976FM (P)	31,000	Value: 27.50				

KM# 74   10 DOLLARS
Copper-Nickel, 45 mm. **Ruler:** Elizabeth II **Subject:** Admiral
George Rodney **Obv:** Arms with supporters **Rev:** Bust right
looking at ship at right

Date	Mintage	F	VF	XF	Unc	BU
1977FM (M)	27	—	—	—	—	—
1977FM (U)	847	—	—	—	30.00	35.00

KM# 74a   10 DOLLARS
42.8000 g., 0.9250 Silver 1.2728 oz. ASW, 45 mm.
Ruler: Elizabeth II **Subject:** Admiral George Rodney **Obv:** Arms
with supporters **Rev:** Bust right looking at ship at right

Date	Mintage	F	VF	XF	Unc	BU
1977FM (P)	14,000	Value: 30.00				

KM# 75   10 DOLLARS
Copper-Nickel, 45 mm. **Ruler:** Elizabeth II **Subject:** Jamaican
Unity **Obv:** Arms with supporters **Rev:** Heads of many different
ethnic people forming a circle

Date	Mintage	F	VF	XF	Unc	BU
1978FM (U)	1,559	—	—	—	20.00	22.50

KM# 75a   10 DOLLARS
42.8000 g., 0.9250 Silver 1.2728 oz. ASW, 45 mm.
Ruler: Elizabeth II **Obv:** Arms with supporters **Rev:** Heads of
many different ethnic people forming a circle **Edge:** Reeded
Edge: Jamaican Unity

Date	Mintage	F	VF	XF	Unc	BU
1978FM (P)	12,000	Value: 30.00				

KM# 79   10 DOLLARS
Copper-Nickel, 45 mm. **Ruler:** Elizabeth II **Obv:** Arms with
supporters **Rev:** Butterflies and flowers above date

Date	Mintage	F	VF	XF	Unc	BU
1979FM (M)	27	—	—	—	—	—
1979FM (U)	2,608	—	—	—	35.00	45.00

KM# 79a   10 DOLLARS
42.8000 g., 0.9250 Silver 1.2728 oz. ASW, 45 mm.
Ruler: Elizabeth II **Obv:** Arms with supporters **Rev:** Butterflies
and flowers above date

Date	Mintage	F	VF	XF	Unc	BU
1979FM (P)	8,308	Value: 35.00				

KM# 80   10 DOLLARS
22.4500 g., 0.9250 Silver 0.6676 oz. ASW **Ruler:** Elizabeth II
Subject: International Year of the Child **Obv:** Arms with
supporters **Rev:** Map back of child playing cricket

Date	Mintage	F	VF	XF	Unc	BU
1979 Proof	20,000	Value: 17.00				

KM# 87   10 DOLLARS
30.2800 g., 0.5000 Silver 0.4867 oz. ASW **Ruler:** Elizabeth II
Subject: 10th Anniversary of Caribbean Development Bank
Obv: Arms with supporters **Rev:** Legend around globe, coins below

Date	Mintage	F	VF	XF	Unc	BU
ND(1980)FM (P)	2,327	Value: 30.00				

KM# 86   10 DOLLARS
Copper-Nickel **Ruler:** Elizabeth II **Obv:** Arms with supporters
Rev: Streamer-tailed Hummingbirds

Date	Mintage	F	VF	XF	Unc	BU
1980FM (M)	27	—	—	—	—	—
1980FM (U)	5,668	—	—	—	30.00	40.00

KM# 86a 10 DOLLARS
22.4500 g., 0.9250 Silver 0.6676 oz. ASW **Ruler:** Elizabeth II
Obv: Arms with supporters **Rev:** Streamer-tailed Hummingbirds

Date	Mintage	F	VF	XF	Unc	BU
1980FM (P)	5,394	Value: 40.00				

KM# 92 10 DOLLARS
28.2800 g., 0.9250 Silver 0.8410 oz. ASW **Ruler:** Elizabeth II
Subject: Wedding of Prince Charles and Lady Diana **Obv:** Arms
with supporters **Rev:** Conjoined busts right

Date	Mintage	F	VF	XF	Unc	BU
1981 Proof	40,000	Value: 20.00				

KM# 93 10 DOLLARS
Copper-Nickel **Ruler:** Elizabeth II **Obv:** Arms with supporters
Rev: American Crocodile above date

Date	Mintage	F	VF	XF	Unc	BU
1981FM (U)	804	—	—	—	30.00	35.00

KM# 93a 10 DOLLARS
22.4500 g., 0.9250 Silver 0.6676 oz. ASW **Ruler:** Elizabeth II
Obv: Arms with supporters **Rev:** American Crocodile above date

Date	Mintage	F	VF	XF	Unc	BU
1981FM (P)	3,216	Value: 40.00				

KM# 97 10 DOLLARS
Copper-Nickel **Ruler:** Elizabeth II **Obv:** Arms with supporters
Rev: Small Indian Mongoose

Date	Mintage	F	VF	XF	Unc	BU
1982FM (U)	—	—	—	—	30.00	35.00

KM# 97a 10 DOLLARS
22.4500 g., 0.9250 Silver 0.6676 oz. ASW **Ruler:** Elizabeth II
Obv: Arms with supporters **Rev:** Small Indian Mongoose

Date	Mintage	F	VF	XF	Unc	BU
1982FM (P)	1,852	Value: 40.00				

KM# 98 10 DOLLARS
22.4500 g., 0.9250 Silver 0.6676 oz. ASW **Ruler:** Elizabeth II
Subject: Soccer - World Championships **Obv:** Arms with
supporters **Rev:** Standing player with ball divides circle

Date	Mintage	F	VF	XF	Unc	BU
1982 Proof	9,775	Value: 16.50				

KM# 109 10 DOLLARS
Copper-Nickel **Ruler:** Elizabeth II **Subject:** 21st Anniversary of
Independence **Obv:** Arms with supporters **Rev:** Numeral 21
divides heads facing above dates and braided rope

Date	Mintage	F	VF	XF	Unc	BU
ND(1983)FM (U)	1,320	—	—	—	15.00	17.50

KM# 109a 10 DOLLARS
22.4500 g., 0.9250 Silver 0.6676 oz. ASW **Ruler:** Elizabeth II
Subject: 21st Anniversary of Independence **Obv:** Arms with
supporters **Rev:** Numeral 21 divides heads facing above dates
and braided rope

Date	Mintage	F	VF	XF	Unc	BU
ND(1983)FM (P)	1,187	Value: 30.00				

KM# 111 10 DOLLARS
22.4500 g., 0.9250 Silver 0.6676 oz. ASW **Ruler:** Elizabeth II
Subject: Royal visit **Obv:** Arms with supporters **Rev:** Conjoined
busts left

Date	Mintage	F	VF	XF	Unc	BU
1983	—	Value: 25.00				

KM# 114 10 DOLLARS
Copper-Nickel **Ruler:** Elizabeth II **Obv:** Arms with supporters
Rev: Blue Marlin breaking water

Date	Mintage	F	VF	XF	Unc	BU
1984FM (U)	—	—	—	—	30.00	35.00

KM# 114a 10 DOLLARS
22.4500 g., 0.9250 Silver 0.6676 oz. ASW **Ruler:** Elizabeth II
Obv: Arms with supporters **Rev:** Blue Marlin breaking water

Date	Mintage	F	VF	XF	Unc	BU
1984FM (P)	335	Value: 75.00				

KM# 115 10 DOLLARS
22.4500 g., 0.9250 Silver 0.6676 oz. ASW **Ruler:** Elizabeth II
Subject: Decade for Women **Obv:** Arms with supporters
Rev: Woman with basket on head, map behind

Date	Mintage	F	VF	XF	Unc	BU
1984 Proof	1,100	Value: 28.00				
1985 Proof	610	Value: 38.00				

KM# 125 10 DOLLARS
22.4500 g., 0.9250 Silver 0.6676 oz. ASW **Ruler:** Elizabeth II
Subject: Summer Olympics **Obv:** Arms with supporters
Rev: Sprinter

Date	Mintage	F	VF	XF	Unc	BU
1984 Proof	10,000	Value: 20.00				

KM# 123 10 DOLLARS
22.4500 g., 0.9250 Silver 0.6676 oz. ASW **Ruler:** Elizabeth II
Subject: Year of Youth **Obv:** Arms with supporters **Rev:** Collage
of many youth's heads

Date	Mintage	F	VF	XF	Unc	BU
1985 Proof	1,000	Value: 30.00				

KM# 121 10 DOLLARS
22.4500 g., 0.9250 Silver 0.6676 oz. ASW **Ruler:** Elizabeth II
Subject: XIII Commonwealth Games - Edinburgh **Obv:** Arms
with supporters **Rev:** Relay runners

Date	Mintage	F	VF	XF	Unc	BU
1986	50,000	—	—	—	16.50	18.00

KM# 121a 10 DOLLARS
28.2800 g., 0.9250 Silver 0.8410 oz. ASW **Ruler:** Elizabeth II
Obv: Arms with supporters **Rev:** Relay runners

Date	Mintage	F	VF	XF	Unc	BU
1986 Proof	20,000	Value: 22.50				

KM# 128   10 DOLLARS
22.4500 g., 0.9250 Silver 0.6676 oz. ASW **Ruler:** Elizabeth II
Subject: 100th Anniversary - Birth of Marcus Garvey **Obv:** Arms
with supporters **Rev:** Bust 1/4 right

Date	Mintage	F	VF	XF	Unc	BU
1987 Proof	1,000			Value: 35.00		

KM# 133   10 DOLLARS
22.4500 g., 0.9250 Silver 0.6676 oz. ASW **Ruler:** Elizabeth II
Subject: 25th Anniversary of Independence **Obv:** Crowned bust
right **Rev:** Arms with supporters

Date	Mintage	F	VF	XF	Unc	BU
1987 Proof	Est. 500			Value: 40.00		

KM# 138   10 DOLLARS
Copper-Nickel **Ruler:** Elizabeth II **Subject:** Year of the Worker
Obv: Arms with supporters **Rev:** Two figures standing on board
with shovel and pitch-fork above heads

Date	Mintage	F	VF	XF	Unc	BU
1988	—	—	—	—	7.00	8.00

KM# 138a   10 DOLLARS
22.4500 g., 0.9250 Silver 0.6676 oz. ASW **Ruler:** Elizabeth II
Subject: Year of the Worker **Obv:** Arms with supporters
Rev: Two standing figures on board with pitch fork and shovel
raised above heads

Date	Mintage	F	VF	XF	Unc	BU
1988 Proof	Est. 1,000			Value: 40.00		

KM# 140   10 DOLLARS
Copper-Nickel **Ruler:** Elizabeth II **Subject:** Columbus'
Discovery of the New World **Obv:** Arms with supporters
Rev: Several ships at sea

Date	Mintage	F	VF	XF	Unc	BU
1989	—	—	—	—	7.00	8.00

KM# 140a   10 DOLLARS
22.4500 g., 0.9250 Silver 0.6676 oz. ASW **Ruler:** Elizabeth II
Subject: Columbus' Discovery of the New World **Obv:** Arms with
supporters **Rev:** Several ships at sea

Date	Mintage	F	VF	XF	Unc	BU
1989 Proof	Est. 5,500			Value: 35.00		

KM# 144   10 DOLLARS
Copper-Nickel **Ruler:** Elizabeth II **Subject:** Columbus' Arrival
in New World **Obv:** Arms with supporters **Rev:** Bust 1/4 right and
ship at far right

Date	Mintage	F	VF	XF	Unc	BU
1990	—	—	—	—	7.00	8.00

KM# 144a   10 DOLLARS
22.4500 g., 0.9250 Silver 0.6676 oz. ASW **Ruler:** Elizabeth II
Subject: Columbus' Arrival in New World **Obv:** Arms with
supporters **Rev:** Bust 1/4 right and ship at far right

Date	Mintage	F	VF	XF	Unc	BU
1990 Proof	Est. 11,000			Value: 32.50		

KM# 148   10 DOLLARS
Copper-Nickel **Ruler:** Elizabeth II **Subject:** Arrival in the New
World **Obv:** Arms with supporters **Rev:** Columbus' ship - Pinta

Date	Mintage	F	VF	XF	Unc	BU
1991	—	—	—	—	7.00	8.00

KM# 148a   10 DOLLARS
22.4500 g., 0.9250 Silver 0.6676 oz. ASW **Ruler:** Elizabeth II
Subject: Arrival in the New World **Obv:** Arms with supporters
Rev: Columbus' ship - Pinta

Date	Mintage	F	VF	XF	Unc	BU
1991 Proof	Est. 5,500			Value: 35.00		

KM# 152   10 DOLLARS
22.4500 g., 0.9250 Silver 0.6676 oz. ASW **Ruler:** Elizabeth II
Subject: 500th Anniversary of Columbus' Arrival **Obv:** Arms with
supporters **Rev:** Ship

Date	Mintage	F	VF	XF	Unc	BU
1992 Proof	5,500			Value: 35.00		

KM# 155   10 DOLLARS
22.4500 g., 0.9250 Silver 0.6676 oz. ASW **Ruler:** Elizabeth II
Subject: 40th Anniversary - Coronation of Queen Elizabeth II
Obv: Arms with supporters **Rev:** Crowned bust facing holding
scepters

Date	Mintage	F	VF	XF	Unc	BU
1993 Proof	Est. 5,500			Value: 35.00		

KM# 161   10 DOLLARS
28.2800 g., 0.9250 Silver 0.8410 oz. ASW **Ruler:** Elizabeth II
Subject: Royal Visit **Obv:** Arms with supporters **Rev:** Standing
sailor beating drum on map of Jamaica to left of ship with cameo
above

Date	Mintage	F	VF	XF	Unc	BU
1994 Proof	—			Value: 35.00		

KM# 168   10 DOLLARS
20.0000 g., 0.5000 Silver 0.3215 oz. ASW **Ruler:** Elizabeth II
Subject: Ernest Hemingway 1899-1961 **Obv:** Arms with
supporters **Rev:** Bust at left looking right, ship at sea at right

Date	Mintage	F	VF	XF	Unc	BU
1994	Est. 10,000	—	—	—	20.00	22.50

KM# 187   10 DOLLARS
28.3000 g., 0.9250 Silver 0.8416 oz. ASW, 38.6 mm.
Ruler: Elizabeth II **Obv:** Arms with supporters **Rev:** Two Black-
billed parrots **Edge:** Reeded

Date	Mintage	F	VF	XF	Unc	BU
1995 Proof	1,000			Value: 80.00		

KM# 176   10 DOLLARS
28.2800 g., 0.9250 Silver 0.8410 oz. ASW **Ruler:** Elizabeth II
Subject: Olympic Games - 1996 **Obv:** Arms with supporters
Rev: Relay runner left

Date	Mintage	F	VF	XF	Unc	BU
1996 Proof	Est. 10,000			Value: 30.00		

KM# 181   10 DOLLARS
5.9400 g., Stainless Steel **Ruler:** Elizabeth II **Series:** National
Heroes **Subject:** George William Gordon **Obv:** National arms
Obv. Leg.: JAMAICA **Rev:** Bust facing **Edge:** Plain
Note: Diameter varies: 24-24.6.

Date	Mintage	F	VF	XF	Unc	BU
1999	—	—	—	—	3.00	4.00
2000	—	—	—	—	3.00	4.00
2000 Proof	—	Value: 9.00				

KM# 61   20 DOLLARS
15.7484 g., 0.5000 Gold 0.2532 oz. AGW **Ruler:** Elizabeth II
Subject: 10th Anniversary of Independence **Obv:** Arms with
supporters and dates within rope wreath **Rev:** Map of Jamaica
above ships

Date	Mintage	F	VF	XF	Unc	BU
ND(1972)	30,000	—	—	—	—	250
ND(1972) Proof	20,000	Value: 265				

KM# 182   20 DOLLARS
 Center Weight: 7.8000 g. **Center:** Bi-Metallic Copper-Nickel
center in Brass ring, 23 mm. **Ruler:** Elizabeth II **Series:** National
Heroes **Subject:** Marcus Garvey **Obv:** Value above national
arms within circle **Obv. Leg.:** JAMAICA **Rev:** Head 1/4 right within
circle **Edge:** Alternate reeding and plain

Date	Mintage	F	VF	XF	Unc	BU
2000	—	—	—	—	3.00	4.00
2000 Proof	—	Value: 15.00				

KM# 76   25 DOLLARS
136.0800 g., 0.9250 Silver 4.0468 oz. ASW **Ruler:** Elizabeth II
Subject: 25th Anniversary of Coronation **Obv:** Arms with
supporters **Rev:** Queen left on throne with crown, sceptre and orb

Date	Mintage	F	VF	XF	Unc	BU
ND(1978)	11,000	—	—	—	100	110
ND(1978) Proof	22,000	Value: 100				

KM# 81   25 DOLLARS
136.0800 g., 0.9250 Silver 4.0468 oz. ASW **Ruler:** Elizabeth II
Subject: 10th Anniversary - Investiture of Prince Charles
Obv: Arms with supporters **Rev:** Crowned half figure left in regal
dress

Date	Mintage	F	VF	XF	Unc	BU
ND(1979)	16,000	—	—	—	90.00	100
ND(1979) Proof	25,000	Value: 110				

KM# 88   25 DOLLARS
136.0800 g., 0.5000 Silver 2.1874 oz. ASW **Ruler:** Elizabeth II
Subject: 1980 Olympics **Obv:** Arms with supporters **Rev:** Circle
of heads of previous Gold Medal winners

Date	Mintage	F	VF	XF	Unc	BU
1980	—	—	—	—	55.00	65.00
1980 Proof	6,969	Value: 125				

KM# 94   25 DOLLARS
136.0800 g., 0.9250 Silver 4.0468 oz. ASW **Ruler:** Elizabeth II
Subject: Wedding of Prince Charles and Lady Diana **Obv:**
Crowned bust right **Rev:** Conjoined busts of royal couple

Date	Mintage	F	VF	XF	Unc	BU
1981(T) Proof	6,450	Value: 135				

KM# 99   25 DOLLARS
136.0800 g., 0.9250 Silver 4.0468 oz. ASW **Ruler:** Elizabeth II
Subject: World Championship Soccer Games **Obv:** Arms with
supporters **Rev:** Player kicking ball to right **Note:** Illustration reduced.

Date	Mintage	F	VF	XF	Unc	BU
1982 Proof	30,000	Value: 120				

KM# 112   25 DOLLARS
136.0800 g., 0.9250 Silver 4.0468 oz. ASW **Ruler:** Elizabeth II
Subject: Royal Visit **Obv:** Arms with supporters **Rev:** Conjoined
busts left

Date	Mintage	F	VF	XF	Unc	BU
1983 Proof	—	Value: 115				

KM# 116   25 DOLLARS
136.0800 g., 0.9250 Silver 4.0468 oz. ASW **Ruler:** Elizabeth II
Subject: Summer Olympics **Obv:** Arms with supporters
Rev: Sprinter

Date	Mintage	F	VF	XF	Unc	BU
1984 Proof	3,300	Value: 120				

KM# 126   25 DOLLARS
23.4400 g., 0.9250 Silver 0.6971 oz. ASW **Ruler:** Elizabeth II
Subject: Decade For Women **Obv:** Arms with supporters
Rev: Map and female with basket of fruit on head facing
Note: Mule. Denomination error for KM#115.

Date	Mintage	F	VF	XF	Unc	BU
1984 Proof	—				Value: 160	

KM# 119   25 DOLLARS
136.0800 g., 0.9250 Silver 4.0468 oz. ASW **Ruler:** Elizabeth II
Subject: Humpback Whale Protection **Obv:** Arms with
supporters **Rev:** Value and map divides humpback whales

Date	Mintage	F	VF	XF	Unc	BU
1985 Proof	2,600				Value: 135	

KM# 127   25 DOLLARS
23.5000 g., 0.9250 Silver 0.6988 oz. ASW **Ruler:** Elizabeth II
Subject: World Championship Soccer - Mexico **Obv:** Arms with
supporters **Rev:** Date within globe above two soccer players

Date	Mintage	F	VF	XF	Unc	BU
1986	—				40.00	50.00

KM# 130   25 DOLLARS
37.7800 g., 0.9250 Silver 1.1235 oz. ASW **Ruler:** Elizabeth II
Subject: 25th Anniversary of Independence **Obv:** Crowned bust
right **Rev:** Arms with supporters

Date	Mintage	F	VF	XF	Unc	BU
1987 Proof	1,900				Value: 32.50	

KM# 141   25 DOLLARS
23.3300 g., 0.9250 Silver 0.6938 oz. ASW **Ruler:** Elizabeth II
Subject: Olympics **Obv:** Arms with supporters **Rev:** Relay runners

Date	Mintage	F	VF	XF	Unc	BU
1988 Proof	Est. 15,000				Value: 20.00	

KM# 142   25 DOLLARS
23.3300 g., 0.9250 Silver 0.6938 oz. ASW **Ruler:** Elizabeth II
Subject: World Championship Soccer **Obv:** Arms with
supporters **Rev:** Soccer player

Date	Mintage	F	VF	XF	Unc	BU
1990 Proof	—				Value: 25.00	

KM# 150   25 DOLLARS
23.3300 g., 0.9250 Silver 0.6938 oz. ASW **Ruler:** Elizabeth II
Subject: Columbus' Jamaican Landfall of 1494 **Obv:** Arms with
supporters **Rev:** Bust of Columbus at left, Queen Isabella at right,
ship between, Island of Jamaica below

Date	Mintage	F	VF	XF	Unc	BU
1991 Matte	650	—	—	—	60.00	65.00
1991 Proof	Est. 25,000				Value: 25.00	

KM# 151   25 DOLLARS
23.3300 g., 0.9250 Silver 0.6938 oz. ASW **Ruler:** Elizabeth II
Subject: Discovery of America - Landfall **Obv:** Arms with
supporters **Rev:** Bust 1/4 right, ship within globe to right

Date	Mintage	F	VF	XF	Unc	BU
1992 Matte	550	—	—	—	60.00	65.00
1992 Proof	Est. 25,000				Value: 30.00	

KM# 159   25 DOLLARS
23.3300 g., 0.9250 Silver 0.6938 oz. ASW **Ruler:** Elizabeth II
Subject: Summer Olympic Games **Obv:** Arms with supporters
Rev: Bicyclists

Date	Mintage	F	VF	XF	Unc	BU
1992 Proof	15,000				Value: 35.00	

KM# 160   25 DOLLARS
23.3300 g., 0.9250 Silver 0.6938 oz. ASW **Ruler:** Elizabeth II
Subject: Summer Olympic Games **Obv:** Arms with supporters
Rev: Boxers

Date	Mintage	F	VF	XF	Unc	BU
1992 Proof	15,000				Value: 35.00	

KM# 165   25 DOLLARS
28.2000 g., 0.9250 Silver 0.8386 oz. ASW, 38.57 mm.
Ruler: Elizabeth II **Subject:** XV World Cup Soccer - USA
Obv: National arms **Rev:** Soccer player chasing ball, large ball
outline in background **Edge:** Reeded

Date	Mintage	F	VF	XF	Unc	BU
1994 Proof	Est. 10,000				Value: 50.00	

KM# 169   25 DOLLARS
31.4700 g., 0.9250 Silver 0.9359 oz. ASW **Ruler:** Elizabeth II
Subject: Queen Elizabeth's Wedding Anniversary and Queen
Mother's Birthday **Obv:** Arms with supporters **Rev:** Queen
Mother's wedding portrait

Date	Mintage	F	VF	XF	Unc	BU
1994 Proof	Est. 20,000				Value: 32.00	

KM# 166   25 DOLLARS
28.2000 g., 0.9250 Silver 0.8386 oz. ASW   **Ruler:** Elizabeth II
Subject: 25th Anniversary - Caribbean Development Bank
Obv: Arms with supporters **Rev:** Map within grid on globe

Date	Mintage	F	VF	XF	Unc	BU
1995	Est. 2,000	—	—	—	45.00	50.00

KM# 170   25 DOLLARS
28.2800 g., 0.9250 Silver 0.8410 oz. ASW   **Ruler:** Elizabeth II
Obv: Arms with supporters **Rev:** Tycho Brahe at right, world globe
at left

Date	Mintage	F	VF	XF	Unc	BU
1995 Proof	Est. 10,000			Value: 35.00		

KM# 173   25 DOLLARS
28.2800 g., 0.9250 Silver 0.8410 oz. ASW   **Ruler:** Elizabeth II
Subject: U.N. 50th Anniversary **Obv:** Arms with supporters
Rev: Embracing children above logo and numeral 50

Date	Mintage	F	VF	XF	Unc	BU
ND(1995) Proof	Est. 105,000			Value: 30.00		

KM# 174   25 DOLLARS
28.2800 g., 0.9250 Silver 0.8410 oz. ASW   **Ruler:** Elizabeth II
Subject: Endangered Wildlife **Obv:** Arms with supporters
Rev: Black-billed Amazon Parrots

Date	Mintage	F	VF	XF	Unc	BU
1995 Proof	Est. 10,000		Value: 45.00			

KM# 177   25 DOLLARS
28.2800 g., 0.9250 Silver 0.8410 oz. ASW   **Ruler:** Elizabeth II
Subject: World Cup Soccer **Obv:** Arms with supporters
Rev: Soccer player

Date	Mintage	F	VF	XF	Unc	BU
1998 Proof	Est. 10,000			Value: 40.00		

KM# 183   25 DOLLARS
28.2800 g., 0.9250 Silver 0.8410 oz. ASW, 38.6 mm.
Ruler: Elizabeth II **Series:** Olympics **Obv:** Arms with supporters
Rev: Two women hurdlers **Edge:** Reeded

Date	Mintage	F	VF	XF	Unc	BU
2000 Proof	5,500	—	—	—	50.00	55.00

KM# 171   50 DOLLARS
28.2800 g., 0.9250 Silver 0.8410 oz. ASW   **Ruler:** Elizabeth II
Subject: 50th Anniversary The Hon Robert Nesta Marley
Obv: Arms with supporters **Rev:** Head left

Date	Mintage	F	VF	XF	Unc	BU
1995 Proof	30,000			Value: 40.00		

KM# 175   50 DOLLARS
7.7760 g., 0.5833 Gold 0.1458 oz. AGW   **Ruler:** Elizabeth II
Obv: Arms with supporters **Rev:** Queen Mother's wedding portrait

Date	Mintage	F	VF	XF	Unc	BU
1995 Proof	Est. 5,000			Value: 145		

KM# 179   50 DOLLARS
28.2800 g., 0.9250 Silver 0.8410 oz. ASW   **Ruler:** Elizabeth II
Subject: 50th Anniversary - University of the West Indies **Obv:** Arms
with supporters **Rev:** University arms with pelican standing at top

Date	Mintage	F	VF	XF	Unc	BU
1998 Proof	20,000			Value: 40.00		

KM# 67   100 DOLLARS
7.8300 g., 0.9000 Gold 0.2266 oz. AGW   **Ruler:** Elizabeth
II **Subject:** Christopher Columbus **Obv:** Arms with supporters
Rev: Bust with hat 3/4 left

Date	Mintage	F	VF	XF	Unc	BU
1975FM (M)	100	—	—	—	—	225
1975FM (U)	10,000	—	—	—	—	220
1975FM (P)	21,000			Value: 225		

KM# 72   100 DOLLARS
7.8300 g., 0.9000 Gold 0.2266 oz. AGW   **Ruler:** Elizabeth II
Subject: Admiral Horatio Nelson **Obv:** Arms with supporters
Rev: Uniformed bust looking left, ship and map at left

Date	Mintage	F	VF	XF	Unc	BU
1976FM (M)	100	—	—	—	—	220
1976FM (P)	8,952			Value: 225		

KM# 77   100 DOLLARS
11.3400 g., 0.9000 Gold 0.3281 oz. AGW   **Ruler:** Elizabeth II
Subject: 25th Anniversary of Coronation of Elizabeth II **Obv:** Arms
with supporters **Rev:** Queen on throne with crown, sceptre and orb

Date	Mintage	F	VF	XF	Unc	BU
ND(1978)	—	—	—	—	—	320
ND(1978) Proof	5,835			Value: 325		

KM# 82   100 DOLLARS
11.3400 g., 0.9000 Gold 0.3281 oz. AGW   **Ruler:** Elizabeth II
Subject: 10th Anniversary - Investiture of Prince Charles
Obv: Arms with supporters **Rev:** Crowned half figure left in regal
dress

Date	Mintage	F	VF	XF	Unc	BU
ND(1979) Proof	2,891			Value: 325		

KM# 110   100 DOLLARS
7.1300 g., 0.9000 Gold 0.2063 oz. AGW **Ruler:** Elizabeth II
Subject: 21st Anniversary of Independence **Obv:** Arms with
supporters **Rev:** Number 21 divides heads facing above dates
and braided rope

Date	Mintage	F	VF	XF	Unc	BU
ND(1983)FM (P)	638	Value: 220				

KM# 117   100 DOLLARS
7.1300 g., 0.9000 Gold 0.2063 oz. AGW **Ruler:** Elizabeth II
Subject: 100th Anniversary - Birth of Bustamante **Obv:** Arms
with supporters **Rev:** Bust 1/4 left

Date	Mintage	F	VF	XF	Unc	BU
1984FM (P)	531	Value: 220				

KM# 122   100 DOLLARS
136.0800 g., 0.9250 Silver 4.0468 oz. ASW **Ruler:** Elizabeth II
Subject: World Championship Soccer - Mexico **Obv:** Arms with
supporters **Rev:** Date within globe above two soccer players

Date	Mintage	F	VF	XF	Unc	BU
1986 Proof	20,000	Value: 85.00				

KM# 129   100 DOLLARS
11.3400 g., 0.9000 Gold 0.3281 oz. AGW **Ruler:** Elizabeth II
Subject: 100th Anniversary - Birth of Marcus Garvey **Obv:** Arms
with supporters **Rev:** Portrait of Garvey facing

Date	Mintage	F	VF	XF	Unc	BU
1987 Proof	500	Value: 320				

KM# 139   100 DOLLARS
136.0800 g., 0.9250 Silver 4.0468 oz. ASW **Ruler:** Elizabeth II
Obv: Arms with supporters **Rev:** Streamer-tailed Hummingbird
Note: Illustration reduced.

Date	Mintage	F	VF	XF	Unc	BU
1987 Proof	—	Value: 150				

KM# 135   100 DOLLARS
136.0800 g., 0.9250 Silver 4.0468 oz. ASW **Ruler:** Elizabeth II
Subject: Summer Olympics - Relay Race **Obv:** Arms with
supporters **Rev:** Handoff of baton during relay race

Date	Mintage	F	VF	XF	Unc	BU
1988 Proof	15,000	Value: 95.00				

KM# 143   100 DOLLARS
136.0800 g., 0.9250 Silver 4.0468 oz. ASW **Ruler:** Elizabeth II
Subject: World Championship Soccer **Obv:** Arms with
supporters **Rev:** Soccer player

Date	Mintage	F	VF	XF	Unc	BU
1990 Proof	—	Value: 175				

KM# 149   100 DOLLARS
137.8000 g., 0.9250 Silver 4.0979 oz. ASW **Ruler:** Elizabeth II
Subject: Olympics - Boxing **Obv:** Arms with supporters
Rev: Boxers

Date	Mintage	F	VF	XF	Unc	BU
1992 Proof	10,000	Value: 100				

KM# 158   100 DOLLARS
11.3400 g., 0.9000 Gold 0.3281 oz. AGW **Ruler:** Elizabeth II
Subject: Centennial - Birth of Norman Manley **Obv:** Arms with
supporters **Rev:** Head left

Date	Mintage	F	VF	XF	Unc	BU
1993 Proof	500	Value: 320				

KM# 172   100 DOLLARS
15.9800 g., 0.9990 Gold 0.5132 oz. AGW **Ruler:** Elizabeth II
Subject: Robert Marley **Obv:** Arms with supporters **Rev:** Head left

Date	Mintage	F	VF	XF	Unc	BU
1995 Proof	2,000	Value: 500				

KM# 178   100 DOLLARS
15.9800 g., 0.9990 Gold 0.5132 oz. AGW **Ruler:** Elizabeth II
Subject: World Cup Soccer **Obv:** Arms with supporters
Rev: Soccer player

Date	Mintage	F	VF	XF	Unc	BU
1998 Proof	Est. 500	Value: 500				

KM# 180   100 DOLLARS
15.9700 g., 0.9167 Gold 0.4707 oz. AGW **Ruler:** Elizabeth II
Subject: 50th Anniversary - University of the West Indies
Obv: Arms with supporters **Rev:** University arms

Date	Mintage	F	VF	XF	Unc	BU
1998 Proof	1,000	Value: 450				

KM# 188   100 DOLLARS
16.0000 g., Gold, 28.3 mm. **Obv:** National arms
Obv. Leg.: JAMAICA **Rev:** Small family of four at center, rays
above, water below **Rev. Leg.:** ONE PEOPLE INTO THE
MILLENIUM / 1999 - 2000 **Edge:** Reeded

Date	Mintage	F	VF	XF	Unc	BU
2000 Proof	—	Value: 700				

KM# 78   250 DOLLARS
43.2200 g., 0.9000 Gold 1.2505 oz. AGW **Ruler:** Elizabeth II
Subject: 25th Anniversary of Coronation **Obv:** Arms with supporters
Rev: Queen seated on throne with crown, sceptre and orb

Date	Mintage	F	VF	XF	Unc	BU
ND(1978) Proof	3,005	Value: 1,250				

KM# 83   250 DOLLARS
43.2200 g., 0.9000 Gold 1.2505 oz. AGW **Ruler:** Elizabeth II
Subject: 10th Anniversary - Investiture of Prince Charles **Obv:**
Arms with supporters **Rev:** Crowned half figure left in regal dress

Date	Mintage	F	VF	XF	Unc	BU
ND(1979) Proof	1,650	Value: 1,250				

KM# 89   250 DOLLARS
11.3400 g., 0.9000 Gold 0.3281 oz. AGW **Ruler:** Elizabeth II
Subject: 1980 Olympics **Obv:** Arms with supporters **Rev:** Heads
around outer circle of previous Gold Medal winners

Date	Mintage	F	VF	XF	Unc	BU
1980 Proof	902	Value: 325				

KM# 95   250 DOLLARS
11.3400 g., 0.9000 Gold 0.3281 oz. AGW **Ruler:** Elizabeth II
Subject: Wedding of Prince Charles and Lady Diana
Obv: Crowned bust right

Date	Mintage	F	VF	XF	Unc	BU
1981 Proof	1,491	Value: 325				

KM# 100 250 DOLLARS
11.3400 g., 0.9000 Gold 0.3281 oz. AGW **Ruler:** Elizabeth II
Subject: World Championship of Football **Obv:** Arms with
supporters **Rev:** Goalie catching attempted score

Date	Mintage	F	VF	XF	Unc	BU
1982 Proof	694	Value: 325				

KM# 124 250 DOLLARS
11.3200 g., 0.9000 Gold 0.3275 oz. AGW **Ruler:** Elizabeth II
Subject: Royal Visit **Obv:** Arms with supporters **Rev:** Conjoined
heads of royal couple left

Date	Mintage	F	VF	XF	Unc	BU
1983 Proof	5,000	Value: 320				

KM# 118 250 DOLLARS
11.3400 g., 0.9000 Gold 0.3281 oz. AGW **Ruler:** Elizabeth II
Subject: Decade for Women **Obv:** Arms with supporters
Rev: Woman with basket on head facing, map in background

Date	Mintage	F	VF	XF	Unc	BU
1984 Proof	559	Value: 330				

KM# 131 250 DOLLARS
16.0000 g., 0.9000 Gold 0.4630 oz. AGW **Ruler:** Elizabeth II
Subject: 25th Anniversary of Independence **Obv:** Crowned bust
right **Rev:** Arms with supporters

Date	Mintage	F	VF	XF	Unc	BU
1987 Proof	250	Value: 460				

KM# 156 250 DOLLARS
11.3400 g., 0.9000 Gold 0.3281 oz. AGW **Ruler:** Elizabeth II
Subject: 40th Anniversary - Coronation of Queen Elizabeth
Obv: Crowned bust right **Rev:** Arms with supporters

Date	Mintage	F	VF	XF	Unc	BU
1993 Proof	Est. 500	Value: 450				

KM# 153 500 DOLLARS
11.3400 g., 0.9000 Gold 0.3281 oz. AGW **Ruler:** Elizabeth II
Subject: Columbus Quincentennial **Obv:** Arms with supporters
Rev: "500" on ship's sail

Date	Mintage	F	VF	XF	Unc	BU
1992 Proof	500	Value: 450				

KM# 162 500 DOLLARS
47.5400 g., 0.9170 Gold 1.4015 oz. AGW **Ruler:** Elizabeth II
Subject: Royal Visit **Obv:** Arms with supporters **Rev:** Drummer
on island map with yacht at right

Date	Mintage	F	VF	XF	Unc	BU
1994 Proof	100	Value: 1,350				

PIEFORTS

KM#	Date	Mintage	Identification	Mkt Val
P1	1979	—	10 Dollars. Silver. KM#80	65.00
P2	1983	32	250 Dollars. 0.9000 Gold. Design like 10 Dollars, KM#80	1,250

MINT SETS

KM#	Date	Mintage	Identification	Issue Price	Mkt Val
MS1	1969 (2)	30,000	KM#41-42	0.90	2.00
MS2	1969 (6)	30,000	KM#45-50	—	6.50
MS3	1970 (6)	5,000	KM#45-50	16.00	6.50
MS4	1971 (7)	4,072	KM#51, 53-58	19.50	17.50
MS5	1971 (6)	4,834	KM#51, 53-57	—	10.00
MS6	1972 (7)	2,982	KM#51, 53-57, 59	19.75	25.00
MS7	1972 (6)	4,000	KM#51, 53-57	10.00	10.00
MS8	1973 (7)	6,404	KM#51, 53-57, 59	19.75	20.00
MS9	1973 (6)	3,000	KM#51, 53-57	9.95	10.00
MS10	1974 (8)	8,361	KM#51, 53-57, 59, 63	25.00	20.00
MS11	1975 (8)	4,683	KM#51, 53-57, 62, 66	27.50	20.00
MS12	1976 (9)	1,802	KM#53-57, 62, 68, 70, 71	27.50	27.50
MS13	1977 (9)	597	KM#53-54, 56-57, 62, 68, 70, 73, 74	27.50	45.00
MS14	1978 (9)	1,282	KM#53-54, 56-57, 62, 68, 70, 73, 75	27.50	40.00
MS15	1979 (9)	2,608	KM#53-54, 56-57, 62, 68, 70, 73, 79	27.50	40.00
MS16	1980 (9)	3,668	KM#53-54, 56, 68, 70, 73, 84.1-86	30.00	30.00
MS17	1981 (9)	482	KM#53-54, 56, 68, 70, 73, 84.1, 85.1, 93	31.00	45.00
MS18	1982 (9)	—	KM#53-54, 56, 68, 70, 73, 84.1-85.1, 97	31.00	40.00
MS19	1983 (9)	1,210	KM#101-109	37.00	40.00
MS20	1984 (9)	—	KM#53-54, 56, 68, 70, 73, 85.1, 113-114	37.00	35.00
MS21	2000 (7)	—	KM#64, 146.2, 163, 164, 167, 181-182	25.00	27.50

PROOF SETS

KM#	Date	Mintage	Identification	Issue Price	Mkt Val
PS1	1918C (3)	—	KM#24-26	—	600
PS2	1928 (3)	20	KM#24-26	—	600
PS3	1937 (3)	—	KM#27-29	—	550
PS4	1969 (6)	8,530	KM#45-50	15.00	10.00
PS5	1969 (2)	5,000	KM#41-42	2.70	7.00
PS6	1970 (6)	11,540	KM#45-50	15.00	10.00
PS7	1971 (7)	12,739	KM#51, 53-58	26.50	17.50
PS8	1971 (6)	1,048	KM#51, 53-57	15.00	10.00
PS9	1972 (7)	16,967	KM#51, 53-57, 59	27.50	16.00
PS10	1973 (7)	28,405	KM#51, 53-57, 59	27.50	15.00
PS11	1974 (8)	22,026	KM#51, 53-57, 62a-63a	50.00	30.00
PS12	1975 (8)	15,638	KM#51, 53-57, 62a, 66a	55.00	40.00
PS13	1976 (9)	22,900	KM#53-57, 62a, 68, 70, 71a	55.00	40.00
PS14	1976 (7)	1,503	KM#53-57, 68, 70	22.50	17.00
PS15	1977	10,054	KM#53-54, 56-57, 62a, 68, 70, 73, 74a	55.00	35.00
PS16	1978 (9)	6,058	KM#53-54, 56-57, 62a, 68, 70, 73, 75a	59.00	45.00
PS17	1979 (9)	4,049	KM#53-54, 56-57, 62a, 68, 70, 73, 79a	59.00	50.00
PS18	1980 (9)	2,688	KM#53-54, 56, 68, 70, 73, 84.1, 85.1a, 86a	90.00	60.00
PS19	1981 (9)	1,577	KM#53-54, 56, 68, 70, 73, 84.1, 85.1a, 93a	92.00	80.00
PS20	1982 (9)	—	KM#53-54, 56, 68, 70, 73, 84.1, 85.1a, 97a	92.00	75.00
PS21	1983 (9)	1,210	KM#101-107, 108a-109a	—	85.00
PS22	1984 (9)	—	KM#53-54, 56, 68, 70, 73, 85.1a, 113, 114a	92.00	75.00
PS23	1985 (9)	—	KM#46-47, 49, 64-65, 84.2-85.2, 120, 123	—	75.00
PS24	1987 (9)	500	KM#46-49, 64, 84.2, 85.2, 132, 133	90.00	75.00
PS25	1988 (9)	500	KM#46-49, 64-65, 84.2, 85.2, 138a	115	80.00
PS26	1989 (9)	500	KM#46-49, 64-65, 84.2, 85.2, 140a	120	80.00
PS27	1990 (9)	500	KM#46a-47a, 48-49, 64-65, 85.2, 144, 145	125	100
PS28	1991 (7)	500	KM#46a, 64, 85.2, 145, 146-148	—	100
PS29	1992 (7)	500	KM#46a, 64, 85.2, 145-147, 152	139	140
PS30	1993 (7)	500	KM#46a, 64, 85.2, 145a, 146-147, 155	—	140
PSA31	1995 (10)	—	KM#64, 146.2, 163, 164, 167 and 187	—	—
PS31	2000 (8)	500	KM#64, 146.2, 163, 164, 167, 181-183	99.00	100

JAPAN

Japan, a constitutional monarchy situated off the east coast of Asia, has an area of 145,809 sq. mi. (377,835 sq. km.) and a population of 123.2 million. Capital: Tokyo. Japan, one of the major industrial nations of the world, exports machinery, motor vehicles, electronics and chemicals.

Japan, founded (so legend holds) in 660 B.C. by a direct descendant of the Sun Goddess, was first brought into contact with the west by a storm-blown Portuguese ship in 1542. European traders and missionaries proceeded to enlarge the contact until the Shogunate, sensing a military threat in the foreign presence, expelled all foreigners and restricted relations with the outside world in the 17th century. After Commodore Perry's U.S. flotilla visited in 1854, Japan rapidly industrialized, abolished the Shogunate and established a parliamentary form of government, and by the end of the 19th century achieved the status of a modern economic and military power. A series of wars with China and Russia, and participation with the allies in World War I, enlarged Japan territorially but brought its interests into conflict with the Far Eastern interests of the United States, Britain and the Netherlands, causing it to align with the Axis Powers for the pursuit of World War II. After its defeat in World War II, General Douglas MacArthur forced Japan to renounce military aggression as a political instrument, and he instituted constitutional democratic self-government. Japan quickly gained a position as an economic world power.

Japanese coinage of concern to this catalog includes those issued for the Ryukyu Islands (also called Liuchu), a chain of islands extending southwest from Japan toward Taiwan (Formosa), before the Japanese government converted the islands into a prefecture under the name Okinawa. Many of the provinces of Japan issued their own definitive coinage under the Shogunate.

RULERS

Emperors

Mutsuhito (Meiji), 1867-1912

明治 or 治明

Years 1-45

Yoshihito (Taisho), 1912-1926

大正 or 正大

Years 1-15

Hirohito (Showa), 1926-1989

昭和 or 和昭

Years 1-64

Akihito (Heisei), 1989-

平成

Years 1-

NOTE: The personal name of the emperor is followed by the name that he chose for his regnal era.

MONETARY SYSTEM
Commencing 1870
10 Rin = 1 Sen
100 Sen = 1 Yen

MONETARY UNITS

Rin 厘

Sen 錢

Yen 円 or 圓 or 圓

DATING

Year

2

x10

3

Reading right to left,
3x10+2 = 32 year

Meiji

Dai Nippon
Great Japan

EMPIRE

DECIMAL COINAGE

Y# 41 5 RIN
2.1000 g., Bronze, 12.8 mm. **Ruler:** Yoshihito (Taisho)
Obv: Large paulownia crest in center flanked by cherry blossoms
Rev: Value within circle of flowered wreath

Date	Mintage	F	VF	XF	Unc	BU
Yr.5(1916)	8,000,000	0.50	1.50	2.75	10.00	22.00
Yr.6(1917)	5,287,584	0.50	1.50	2.75	10.00	26.00
Yr.7(1918)	11,661,877	0.25	0.75	2.00	7.50	18.50
Yr.8(1919)	17,130,539	0.25	0.75	2.00	7.50	11.50

Y# 20 SEN
7.1300 g., Bronze, 27.8 mm. **Ruler:** Mutsuhito (Meiji)
Obv: Sunburst within beaded circle with legend separated by dots around border **Rev:** Value within center of rice wreath

Date	Mintage	F	VF	XF	Unc	BU
Yr.34(1901)	5,555,155	2.00	4.50	16.00	65.00	175
Yr.35(1902)	4,444,845	5.00	10.00	25.00	145	200
Yr.39(1906)	—	—	—	—	—	—

Note: None struck for circulation

| Yr.42(1909) | | | | | | |

Note: None struck for circulation

Y# 35 SEN
7.1300 g., Bronze, 27.8 mm. **Ruler:** Yoshihito (Taisho)
Obv: Sunburst within beaded circle with legend separated by dots around border **Rev:** Value within center of rice wreath

Date	Mintage	F	VF	XF	Unc	BU
Yr.2(1913)	15,000,000	1.50	2.25	4.00	32.00	100
Yr.3(1914)	10,000,000	1.50	2.25	4.00	32.00	75.00
Yr.4(1915)	13,000,000	1.50	2.25	4.00	32.00	75.00

Y# 42 SEN
3.7500 g., Bronze, 23 mm. **Ruler:** Yoshihito (Taisho)
Obv: Paulownia crest flanked by cherry blossoms **Rev:** Value within circle of flowered wreath

Date	Mintage	F	VF	XF	Unc	BU
Yr.5(1916)	19,193,946	0.45	0.75	1.25	30.00	100
Yr.6(1917)	27,183,078	0.25	0.45	0.75	25.00	75.00
Yr.7(1918)	121,794,756	0.25	0.45	0.75	9.50	22.00
Yr.8(1919)	209,959,359	0.15	0.25	0.50	4.50	14.50
Yr.9(1920)	118,829,256	0.15	0.25	0.50	4.50	14.50
Yr.10(1921)	252,440,000	0.15	0.25	0.50	4.50	14.50
Yr.11(1922)	253,210,000	0.15	0.25	0.50	4.50	14.50
Yr.12(1923)	155,500,000	0.15	0.25	0.50	5.50	20.00
Yr.13(1924)	106,250,000	0.15	0.25	0.50	4.50	14.50

Y# 47 SEN
3.7500 g., Bronze, 23 mm. **Ruler:** Hirohito (Showa)
Obv: Paulownia crest flanked by cherry blossoms with authority on top and date below **Rev:** Value within circle of flowered wreath

Date	Mintage	F	VF	XF	Unc	BU
Yr.2(1927)	26,500,000	1.25	2.00	2.75	32.00	75.00
Yr.4(1929)	3,000,000	2.75	5.50	12.50	45.00	100
Yr.5(1930)	5,000,000	2.00	3.50	6.00	70.00	250
Yr.6(1931)	25,001,222	0.25	0.45	1.25	12.50	35.00
Yr.7(1932)	35,066,715	0.25	0.45	1.25	9.00	29.00
Yr.8(1933)	38,936,907	0.15	0.25	0.50	2.50	12.50
Yr.9(1934)	100,004,950	0.15	0.25	0.50	2.50	12.50
Yr.10(1935)	200,009,912	0.15	0.25	0.50	1.50	6.50
Yr.11(1936)	109,170,428	0.15	0.25	0.50	1.50	6.50
Yr.12(1937)	133,196,568	0.15	0.25	0.50	1.50	6.50
Yr.13(1938)	87,649,338	0.15	0.25	0.50	1.50	6.50

Y# 55 SEN
3.7500 g., Bronze, 23 mm. **Ruler:** Hirohito (Showa) **Obv:** Bird within clouds flanked by cherry blossoms **Rev:** Value in center of sacred mirror within wave-like wreath

Date	Mintage	F	VF	XF	Unc	BU
Yr.13(1938)	113,600,000	0.15	0.25	0.50	1.50	3.50

Y# 56 SEN
0.9000 g., Aluminum, 17.6 mm. **Ruler:** Hirohito (Showa)
Obv: Bird within clouds flanked by cherry blossoms **Rev:** Value in center of sacred mirror within wave-like wreath

Date	Mintage	F	VF	XF	Unc	BU
Yr.13(1938)	45,502,266	—	0.50	1.50	8.50	17.00
Yr.14(1939) Type A	444,602,146		1.25	2.25	12.00	24.00
Yr.14(1939) Type B	Inc. above	—	0.25	0.45	1.50	2.00
Yr.15(1940)	601,110,015		0.25	0.45	1.50	2.00

Y# 59 SEN
0.6500 g., Aluminum, 16 mm. **Ruler:** Hirohito (Showa)
Obv: Value in center with authority above and date below
Rev: Chrysanthemum above Mount Fuji with value below

Date	Mintage	F	VF	XF	Unc	BU
Yr.16(1941)	1,016,620,734	—	0.15	0.25	0.50	1.00

Date	Mintage	F	VF	XF	Unc	BU
Yr.17(1942)	119,709,832	—	0.15	0.25	0.75	1.00
Yr.18(1943)	1,163,949,434	—	0.15	0.25	0.50	1.00

Y# 59a SEN
0.5500 g., Aluminum, 16 mm. **Ruler:** Hirohito (Showa)
Obv: Value in center with authority above and date below **Rev:** Chrysanthemum above Mt. Fuji with value below **Note:** Thinner

Date	Mintage	F	VF	XF	Unc	BU
Yr.18(1943)	627,160,000	—	0.15	0.50	1.00	1.50

Y# 62 SEN
1.3000 g., Tin-Zinc, 15 mm. **Ruler:** Hirohito (Showa)
Obv: Chrysanthemum flanked by sprigs with value above and below **Rev:** Authority inscribed vertically in center with date below

Date	Mintage	F	VF	XF	Unc	BU
Yr.19(1944)	1,629,580,000	—	0.15	0.25	0.50	1.00
Yr.20(1945)	Inc. above		0.25	0.50	0.75	1.50

KM# 110 SEN
0.8000 g., Reddish Brown Baked Clay, 15 mm. **Ruler:** Hirohito (Showa) **Obv:** Stylized cherry blossom surrounded by three characters "Dai Nippon" **Rev:** Mountain with character "one" at upper left

Date	Mintage	F	VF	XF	Unc	BU
ND(1945)	—	13.00	18.00	22.50	30.00	40.00

Note: Circulated unofficially for a few days before the end of WWII in Central Japan; varieties of color exist

Y# 21 5 SEN
4.6700 g., Copper-Nickel **Ruler:** Mutsuhito (Meiji)
Obv: Sunburst within circle, 3 legends separated by dots around border **Rev:** Value within rice wreath

Date	Mintage	F	VF	XF	Unc	BU
Yr.34(1901)	7,124,824	6.00	12.00	18.50	125	225
Yr.35(1902)	2,448,544	9.00	18.50	30.00	285	350
Yr.36(1903)	372,000	120	200	300	2,500	3,000
Yr.37(1904)	1,628,000	15.00	27.50	60.00	400	900
Yr.38(1905)	6,000,000	4.00	8.00	13.50	115	225
Yr.39(1906)						

Note: None struck for circulation; Spink-Taisei Hong Kong sale 9-91 BU realized $10,000

Y# 43 5 SEN
4.2800 g., Copper-Nickel, 20.6 mm. **Ruler:** Yoshihito (Taisho)
Obv: Flower-like form of sacred mirror around hole in center flanked by dots **Rev:** Chrysanthemum flanked by value with hole in center and paulownia foliage on bottom 1/2

Date	Mintage	F	VF	XF	Unc	BU
Yr.6(1917)	6,781,830	6.00	12.00	18.50	50.00	95.00
Yr.7(1918)	9,131,211	4.00	8.00	15.00	35.00	75.00
Yr.8(1919)	44,980,633	2.50	4.50	9.00	20.00	35.00
Yr.9(1920)	21,906,326	2.50	4.50	9.00	20.00	35.00

Y# 44 5 SEN
2.6300 g., Copper-Nickel, 19.1 mm. **Ruler:** Yoshihito (Taisho)
Obv: Flower-like form of sacred mirror around hole in center flanked by dots **Rev:** Chrysanthemum flanked by value with hole in center and paulownia foliage on bottom 1/2

Date	Mintage	F	VF	XF	Unc	BU
Yr.9(1920)	100,455,537	0.35	0.65	1.50	15.00	65.00
Yr.10(1921)	133,020,000	0.25	0.45	1.20	5.00	13.50
Yr.11(1922)	163,980,000	0.25	0.45	1.20	5.00	13.50
Yr.12(1923)	80,000,000	0.25	0.45	1.20	5.00	13.50

Y# 48   5 SEN

2.6300 g., Copper-Nickel, 19.1 mm.   **Ruler:** Hirohito (Showa)
Obv: Flower-like form of sacred mirror around hole in center flanked by dots **Rev:** Chrysanthemum flanked by value with hole in center and paulownia foliage on bottom 1/2

Date	Mintage	F	VF	XF	Unc	BU
Yr.7(1932)	8,000,394	0.25	0.45	1.50	7.00	40.00

Y# 53   5 SEN

2.8000 g., Nickel, 19 mm.   **Ruler:** Hirohito (Showa) **Obv:** Rings around center hole flanked by cherry blossoms with authority above and date below **Rev:** Bird with wings spread below hole in center with rays of sun on upper 1/2 of border with chrysanthemum flanked by value

Date	Mintage	F	VF	XF	Unc	BU
Yr.8(1933)	16,150,806	0.45	1.25	2.25	5.50	15.00
Yr.9(1934)	33,851,607	0.45	0.75	1.50	4.50	13.00
Yr.10(1935)	13,680,677	0.75	1.50	2.75	7.50	15.00
Yr.11(1936)	36,321,796	0.45	0.75	1.50	4.50	1.00
Yr.12(1937)	44,402,201	0.45	0.75	1.50	5.50	15.00
Yr.13(1938) 4	10,000,000	—	—	—	—	—
known						

　　Note: Almost entire mintage remelted

Y# 57   5 SEN

Aluminum-Bronze   **Ruler:** Hirohito (Showa) **Obv:** Hole in center flanked by 1/2 cherry blossoms with authority above and date below **Rev:** Hole in center divides quarters, upper and lower quarter in relief, value at either side

Date	Mintage	F	VF	XF	Unc	BU
Yr.13(1938)	40,001,977	0.45	0.75	1.25	4.00	10.00
Yr.14(1939)	97,903,873	0.45	0.75	1.25	4.00	10.00
Yr.15(1940)	34,501,716	0.45	0.75	1.25	5.00	11.00

Y# 60   5 SEN

1.2000 g., Aluminum, 19 mm.   **Ruler:** Hirohito (Showa)
Obv: Bird with wings spread with authority on top and date below
Rev: Chrysanthemum within clouds with value above and below
Note: Variety I

Date	Mintage	F	VF	XF	Unc	BU
Yr.15(1940)	410,020,460	—	0.25	0.75	3.00	6.00
Yr.16(1941)	Inc. above	—	0.25	0.50	2.25	4.50

Y# 60a   5 SEN

1.0000 g., Aluminum, 19 mm.   **Ruler:** Hirohito (Showa)
Obv: Bird with wings spread with authority on top and date below
Rev: Chrysanthemum among clouds with value above and below
Note: Variety 2

Date	Mintage	F	VF	XF	Unc	BU
Yr.16(1941)	478,023,877	1.25	2.75	6.00	37.50	55.00
Yr.17(1942)	Inc. above	—	0.25	0.65	1.50	2.00

Y# 60b   5 SEN

0.8000 g., Aluminum, 19 mm.   **Ruler:** Hirohito (Showa)
Obv: Bird with wings spread with authority on top and date below
Rev: Chrysanthemum within clouds with value above and below
Note: Variety 3

Date	Mintage	F	VF	XF	Unc	BU
Yr.18(1943)	276,493,742	—	0.25	0.75	2.00	4.00

Y# 63   5 SEN

1.9500 g., Tin-Zinc, 17 mm.   **Ruler:** Hirohito (Showa) **Obv:** Hole in center flanked by dots with authority on top and date below **Rev:** Chrysanthemum on top flanked by value above hole in center with paulownia crest within cloud-like swirls below

Date	Mintage	F	VF	XF	Unc	BU
Yr.19(1944)	70,000,000	—	0.25	0.75	2.50	3.00

Y# 65   5 SEN

2.0000 g., Tin-Zinc, 17 mm.   **Ruler:** Hirohito (Showa) **Obv:** Large value in center flanked by paulownia crests with authority above and date below **Rev:** Bird with wings spread flanked by value with chrysanthemum above

Date	Mintage	F	VF	XF	Unc	BU
Yr.20(1945)	180,000,000	—	0.45	1.00	3.50	6.00
Yr.21(1946)	Inc. above	—	0.45	1.00	3.50	4.50

KM# 111   5 SEN

1.3000 g., Reddish Brown Baked Clay, 18 mm.   **Ruler:** Hirohito (Showa) **Obv:** Heart shapes around symbol in center with authority on top and value below **Rev:** Chrysanthemum above text

Date	Mintage	F	VF	XF	Unc	BU
Yr.20(1945)	—	250	350	450	650	750

　　Note: Not issued for circulation; varieties of color exist

Y# 23   10 SEN

2.6957 g., 0.8000 Silver 0.0693 oz. ASW   **Ruler:** Mutsuhito (Meiji) **Obv:** Dragon within beaded circle, 3 legends separated by dots around border **Rev:** Value within center of flowered wreath, chrysanthemum above

Date	Mintage	F	VF	XF	Unc	BU
Yr.34(1901)	797,561	95.00	135	185	800	1,700
Yr.35(1902)	1,204,439	75.00	120	150	775	2,000
Yr.37(1904)	11,106,638	3.50	5.50	7.50	35.00	100
Yr.38(1905)	34,182,194	3.50	5.50	7.50	35.00	100
Yr.39(1906)	4,710,168	3.50	5.50	7.50	35.00	100

Y# 29   10 SEN

2.2500 g., 0.7200 Silver 0.0521 oz. ASW   **Ruler:** Mutsuhito (Meiji) **Obv:** Sunburst within cherry blossom circle with 3 legends separated by dots around border **Rev:** Value within center of flowered wreath with chrysanthemum above

Date	Mintage	F	VF	XF	Unc	BU
Yr.40(1907)	12,000,000	2.00	3.75	7.50	65.00	350
Yr.41(1908)	12,273,239	2.00	3.75	7.50	60.00	250
Yr.42(1909)	20,279,846	1.00	2.50	3.75	27.50	90.00
Yr.43(1910)	20,339,816	1.00	2.50	3.75	25.00	85.00
Yr.44(1911)	38,729,680	1.00	2.50	3.75	27.50	85.00
Yr.45(1912)	10,755,009	1.00	2.50	3.75	30.00	100

Y# 36.1   10 SEN

2.2500 g., 0.7200 Silver 0.0521 oz. ASW   **Ruler:** Yoshihito (Taisho) **Obv:** Sunburst within cherry blossom circle with 3 legends separated by dots around border **Rev:** Value within flowered wreath with chrysanthemum on top

Date	Mintage	F	VF	XF	Unc	BU
Yr.1(1912)	10,344,307	2.00	3.75	7.50	60.00	200

Y# 36.2   10 SEN

2.2500 g., 0.7200 Silver 0.0521 oz. ASW   **Ruler:** Yoshihito (Taisho) **Obv:** Sunburst within cherry blossom circle with 3 legends separated by dots around border **Rev:** Value within flowered wreath with chrysanthemum on top

Date	Mintage	F	VF	XF	Unc	BU
Yr.2(1913)	13,321,466	1.00	2.00	3.75	12.00	35.00
Yr.3(1914)	10,325,327	1.00	2.00	3.75	12.00	35.00
Yr.4(1915)	16,836,225	1.00	2.00	3.75	12.00	35.00
Yr.5(1916)	10,324,179	1.00	2.00	3.00	12.00	35.00
Yr.6(1917)	35,170,906	0.85	1.50	2.25	10.00	22.00

Y# 45   10 SEN

3.7500 g., Copper-Nickel, 22 mm.   **Ruler:** Yoshihito (Taisho) **Obv:** Flower-like form of sacred mirror around hole in center flanked by dots with authority on top and date below **Rev:** Chrysanthemum flanked by value above hole in center with paulownia foliage on bottom 1/2

Date	Mintage	F	VF	XF	Unc	BU
Yr.9(1920)	4,894,420	0.45	0.75	2.50	25.00	75.00
Yr.10(1921)	61,870,000	0.25	0.50	1.25	5.00	13.00
Yr.11(1922)	159,770,000	0.25	0.50	1.25	5.00	13.00
Yr.12(1923)	190,010,000	0.25	0.50	1.25	4.50	13.00
Yr.14(1925)	54,475,000	0.25	0.50	1.25	5.00	13.00
Yr.15(1926)	58,675,000	0.25	0.50	1.25	5.00	13.00

Y# 49   10 SEN

3.7500 g., Copper-Nickel   **Ruler:** Hirohito (Showa) **Obv:** Flower-like form of sacred mirror around hole in center flanked by dots with authority on top and date below **Rev:** Chrysanthemum flanked by value above hole in center with paulownia foliage on bottom 1/2

Date	Mintage	F	VF	XF	Unc	BU
Yr.2(1927)	36,050,000	0.25	0.45	1.25	5.00	17.00
Yr.3(1928)	41,450,000	0.25	0.45	1.25	5.00	13.00
Yr.4(1929)	10,050,000	0.45	0.75	1.50	25.00	150
Yr.6(1931)	1,850,087	0.60	1.25	2.00	9.00	30.00
Yr.7(1932)	23,151,177	0.25	0.45	1.25	5.00	15.00

Y# 54   10 SEN

4.0200 g., Nickel   **Ruler:** Hirohito (Showa) **Obv:** Center hole within 1/3 vertical portion recessed flanked by wave-like pattern with cherry blossoms **Rev:** Hole in center flanked by value and denomination, karakusa sprays are vertical in rectangular display, chrysanthemum on top, paulownia on bottom

Date	Mintage	F	VF	XF	Unc	BU
Yr.8(1933)	14,570,714	0.45	0.75	1.50	5.50	20.00
Yr.9(1934)	37,351,832	0.25	0.50	1.25	4.75	11.00
Yr.10(1935)	35,586,755	0.30	0.75	1.50	5.25	11.00
Yr.11(1936)	77,948,804	0.25	0.50	1.25	4.75	11.00
Yr.12(1937)	40,001,969	0.30	0.75	1.50	5.50	15.00

Y# 58   10 SEN

4.0000 g., Aluminum-Bronze   **Ruler:** Hirohito (Showa)
Obv: Double petal cherry blossom around center hole flanked by paulownia crest with authority on top and date below
Rev: Chrysanthemum flanked by value with sun rays on upper 1/2 above hole in center with rolling waves below

Date	Mintage	F	VF	XF	Unc	BU
Yr.13(1938)	46,999,990	0.35	0.65	1.25	4.75	11.00
Yr.14(1939)	121,500,000	0.25	0.45	1.00	4.50	11.00
Yr.15(1940)	165,000,000	0.65	1.25	2.25	12.00	26.00

Y# 61   10 SEN
1.5000 g., Aluminum, 22 mm. **Ruler:** Hirohito (Showa)
Obv: Double petal cherry blossom flanked by dots with authority on top and date below **Rev:** Chrysanthemum flanked by dots with value above and paulownia foliage below

Date	Mintage	F	VF	XF	Unc	BU
Yr.15(1940)	575,600,000	—	0.20	0.35	1.50	3.00
Yr.16(1941)	Inc. above	—	0.20	0.35	1.50	3.00

Y# 61a   10 SEN
1.2000 g., Aluminum, 22 mm. **Ruler:** Hirohito (Showa)
Obv: Double petal cherry blossom flanked by dots with authority on top and date below **Rev:** Chrysanthemum flanked by dots with value above and paulownia foliage below

Date	Mintage	F	VF	XF	Unc	BU
Yr.16(1941)	944,900,000	0.10	0.35	0.50	2.00	4.00
Yr.17(1942)	Inc. above	—	0.20	0.35	1.50	2.00
Yr.18(1943)	Inc. above	0.75	2.25	3.75	30.00	60.00

Y# 61b   10 SEN
1.0000 g., Aluminum, 22 mm. **Ruler:** Hirohito (Showa)
Obv: Double petal cherry blossom flanked by dots with authority on top and date below **Rev:** Chrysanthemum flanked by dots with value above and paulownia foliage below

Date	Mintage	F	VF	XF	Unc	BU
Yr.18(1943)	756,000,000	—	0.20	0.35	1.25	2.50

Y# 64   10 SEN
2.4000 g., Tin-Zinc, 19 mm. **Ruler:** Hirohito (Showa) **Obv:** Hole in center flanked by dots, authority on top, date on bottom **Rev:** Chrysanthemum on top flanked by value with paulownia crest within cloud-like swirls below

Date	Mintage	F	VF	XF	Unc	BU
Yr.19(1944)	450,000,000	—	0.20	0.35	1.25	1.75

KM# 112   10 SEN
2.0000 g., Reddish Brown Baked Clay, 21.9 mm. **Ruler:** Hirohito (Showa) **Obv:** Paulownia crest flanked by cherry blossoms with authority on top and date below **Rev:** Chrysanthemum in center with value above and below flanked by sprigs

Date	Mintage	F	VF	XF	Unc	BU
Yr.20(1945)	—	300	500	750	1,000	1,350

Note: Not issued for circulation; varieties of color exist

Y# 68   10 SEN
1.0000 g., Aluminum **Ruler:** Hirohito (Showa) **Obv:** Large numeral 10 overlaps double petal cherry blossom in center, authority on top, date on bottom **Rev:** Two rice stalks drooping downward, value and denomination at lower left, chrysanthemum at top

Date	Mintage	F	VF	XF	Unc	BU
Yr.20(1945)	237,590,000	—	0.20	0.35	1.00	1.50
Yr.21(1946)	Inc. above	—	0.20	0.35	1.00	1.50

Y# 24   20 SEN
5.3900 g., 0.8000 Silver 0.1386 oz. ASW, 23 mm.
Ruler: Mutsuhito (Meiji) **Obv:** Dragon within beaded circle
Rev: Chrysanthemum divides wreath, value within

Date	Mintage	F	VF	XF	Unc	BU
Yr.34(1901)	500,000	120	175	275	2,250	3,000
Yr.37(1904)	5,250,000	4.00	8.00	15.00	70.00	150
Yr.38(1905)	8,444,930	4.00	8.00	15.00	60.00	150

Y# 30   20 SEN
4.0500 g., 0.8000 Silver 0.1042 oz. ASW **Ruler:** Mutsuhito (Meiji) **Obv:** Sunburst within cherry blossom circle with 3 legends separated by dots around border **Rev:** Value and denomination within flowered wreath, chrysanthemum on top

Date	Mintage	F	VF	XF	Unc	BU
Yr.39(1906)	6,555,070	5.00	10.00	18.50	200	500
Yr.40(1907)	20,000,000	2.00	4.00	12.00	75.00	150
Yr.41(1908)	15,000,000	2.00	4.00	12.00	75.00	150
Yr.42(1909)	8,824,702	2.00	4.00	12.00	75.00	150
Yr.43(1910)	21,175,298	2.00	4.00	12.00	75.00	150
Yr.44(1911)	500,000	45.00	90.00	200	1,150	2,800

Y# 25   50 SEN
13.4800 g., 0.8000 Silver 0.3467 oz. ASW **Ruler:** Mutsuhito (Meiji) **Obv:** Dragon within beaded circle with 3 legends separated by dots around border **Rev:** Value within wreath, chrysanthemum above

Date	Mintage	F	VF	XF	Unc	BU
Yr.34(1901)	1,790,000	18.50	35.00	60.00	375	1,200
Yr.35(1902)	1,023,280	37.50	65.00	120	625	1,800
Yr.36(1903)	1,503,068	22.50	37.50	70.00	425	1,300
Yr.37(1904)	5,373,652	6.00	10.00	18.50	125	350
Yr.38(1905) Type I	9,566,100	6.00	10.00	18.50	125	350

Note: Bottom left stem cut with paint on top

Date	Mintage	F	VF	XF	Unc	BU
Yr.38 (1905) Type II	Inc. above	10.00	16.00	25.00	200	500

Note: Bottom left stem cut with paint on bottom

Y# 31   50 SEN
10.1000 g., 0.8000 Silver 0.2598 oz. ASW **Ruler:** Mutsuhito (Meiji) **Obv:** Sunburst within cherry blossom circle with 3 legends separated by dots around border **Rev:** Value and denomination within flowered wreath, chrysanthemum on top

Date	Mintage	F	VF	XF	Unc	BU
Yr.39(1906)	12,478,264	4.00	7.50	20.00	225	600
Yr.40(1907)	24,062,952	3.75	6.50	13.50	75.00	225
Yr.41(1908)	25,470,371	3.75	6.50	13.50	75.00	225
Yr.42(1909)	21,998,600	3.75	6.50	13.50	75.00	225
Yr.43(1910)	15,323,276	3.75	6.50	13.50	75.00	225
Yr.44(1911)	9,900,437	3.75	6.50	13.50	75.00	225
Yr.45(1912)	3,677,704	6.50	12.50	17.50	100	300

Y# 37.1   50 SEN
10.1300 g., 0.8000 Silver 0.2605 oz. ASW **Ruler:** Yoshihito (Taisho) **Obv:** Sunburst within cherry blossom circle, 3 legends separated by dots around border **Rev:** Value and denomination within flowered wreath, chrysanthemum on top

Date	Mintage	F	VF	XF	Unc	BU
Yr.1(1912)	1,928,649	12.50	20.00	40.00	160	450

Y# 37.2   50 SEN
10.1300 g., 0.8000 Silver 0.2605 oz. ASW **Ruler:** Yoshihito (Taisho) **Obv:** Sunburst within cherry blossom circle, 3 legends separated by dots around border **Rev:** Value and denomination within flowered wreath, chrysanthemum on top

Date	Mintage	F	VF	XF	Unc	BU
Yr.2(1913)	5,910,063	4.50	9.00	20.00	60.00	250
Yr.3(1914)	1,872,331	20.00	35.00	55.00	200	600
Yr.4(1915)	2,011,253	17.50	30.00	50.00	160	450
Yr.5(1916)	8,736,768	4.00	7.50	15.00	35.00	125
Yr.6(1917)	9,963,232	4.00	7.50	15.00	35.00	125

Y# 46   50 SEN
4.9500 g., 0.7200 Silver 0.1146 oz. ASW, 23.8 mm.
Ruler: Yoshihito (Taisho) **Obv:** Sunburst in center flanked by cherry blossoms, authority on top, date on bottom, all within sacred mirror **Rev:** Vertical value and denomination flanked by phoenix, paulownia crest flanked by karakusa sprigs, chrysanthemum on top

Date	Mintage	F	VF	XF	Unc	BU
Yr.11(1922)	76,320,000	BV	2.00	4.00	25.00	75.00
Yr.12(1923)	185,180,000	BV	1.75	2.50	18.00	25.00
Yr.13(1924)	78,520,000	BV	1.75	2.50	18.00	25.00
Yr.14(1925)	47,808,000	BV	1.75	2.50	20.00	45.00
Yr.15(1926)	32,572,000	BV	1.75	2.50	22.00	50.00

Y# 50   50 SEN
4.9500 g., 0.7200 Silver 0.1146 oz. ASW **Ruler:** Hirohito (Showa) **Obv:** Sunburst in center flanked by cherry blossoms, authority on top, date on bottom, all within sacred mirror **Rev:** Vertical value and denomination flanked by phoenix, paulownia crest flanked by karakusa sprigs, chrysanthemum on top

Date	Mintage	F	VF	XF	Unc	BU
Yr.3(1928)	38,592,000	F	BV	2.00	10.00	30.00
Yr.4(1929)	12,568,000	BV	2.00	5.00	30.00	100
Yr.5(1930)	10,200,000	BV	2.25	5.50	20.00	65.00
Yr.6(1931)	27,677,501	—	BV	2.00	9.00	18.00
Yr.7(1932)	24,132,795	—	BV	2.00	9.00	18.00
Yr.8(1933)	10,001,973	BV	2.25	7.00	22.00	65.00
Yr.9(1934)	20,003,995	—	BV	2.00	9.00	18.00
Yr.10(1935)	11,738,334	—	BV	2.00	9.00	22.00
Yr.11(1936)	44,272,796	—	BV	2.00	7.00	15.00
Yr.12(1937)	48,000,533	—	BV	2.00	7.00	15.00
Yr.13(1938)	3,600,717	50.00	75.00	125	250	350

Y# 67   50 SEN
4.5000 g., Brass **Ruler:** Hirohito (Showa) **Obv:** Stalks of wheat and rice flanked by fish, crossed pick and hoe within stalks, authority on top, date on bottom **Rev:** Phoenix among clouds, chrysanthemum on top, value and denomination on bottom
Note: Varieties exist.

Date	Mintage	F	VF	XF	Unc	BU
Yr.21(1946)	268,161,000	0.25	0.50	1.00	2.50	3.50
Yr.22(1947)	Inc. above	—	600	900	1,700	2,250

Note: Not released to circulation

Y# 69 50 SEN

2.8000 g., Brass **Ruler:** Hirohito (Showa) **Obv:** Numeral 50 within center circle flanked by dots, authority on top, date on bottom **Rev:** Value and denomination at left of 1/2 cherry blossom wreath, chrysanthemum on top

Date	Mintage	F	VF	XF	Unc	BU
Yr.22(1947)	849,234,445	0.10	0.20	0.40	0.90	1.25
Yr.23(1948)	Inc. above	0.10	0.20	0.40	0.90	1.25

Y# A25.3 YEN

26.9600 g., 0.9000 Silver 0.7801 oz. ASW, 38.1 mm.
Ruler: Mutsuhito (Meiji) **Obv:** Dragon within beaded circle, legends above, written value below **Rev:** Value within wreath, chrysanthemum above **Note:** Reduced size.

Date	Mintage	F	VF	XF	Unc	BU
Yr.34(1901)	1,256,252	25.00	50.00	95.00	225	250
Yr.35(1902)	668,782	40.00	85.00	150	300	400
Yr.36(1903)	5,131,096	22.00	40.00	70.00	140	200
Yr.37(1904)	6,970,843	22.00	40.00	70.00	200	200
Yr.38(1905)	5,031,503	22.00	40.00	70.00	200	200
Yr.39(1906)	3,471,297	25.00	50.00	95.00	450	550
Yr.41(1908)	334,705	85.00	175	300	1,000	1,000
Yr.45(1912)	5,000,000	20.00	40.00	60.00	175	175

Y# 38 YEN

26.9600 g., 0.9000 Silver 0.7801 oz. ASW **Ruler:** Yoshihito (Taisho) **Obv:** Dragon within beaded circle, 3 legends separated by dots around border **Rev:** Value and denomination within flowered wreath, chrysanthemum on top

Date	Mintage	F	VF	XF	Unc	BU
Yr.3(1914)	11,500,000	18.00	35.00	55.00	150	225

Y# 32 5 YEN

4.1666 g., 0.9000 Gold 0.1206 oz. AGW **Ruler:** Mutsuhito (Meiji) **Obv:** Sunburst superimposed on sacred mirror, legends around border, value separated by paulownia crests **Rev:** Value within wreath, chrysanthemum above

Date	Mintage	F	VF	XF	Unc	BU
Yr.36(1903)	21,956	800	950	1,250	2,250	2,750
Yr.44(1911)	59,880	750	900	1,200	2,150	2,500
Yr.45(1912)	59,880	600	750	1,000	1,750	2,000

Y# 39 5 YEN

4.1666 g., 0.9000 Gold 0.1206 oz. AGW **Ruler:** Yoshihito (Taisho) **Obv:** Sunburst within mirror, 3 legends around border, value on bottom **Rev:** Value and denomination within flowered wreath, chrysanthemum on top

Date	Mintage	F	VF	XF	Unc	BU
Yr.2(1913)	89,820	700	900	1,150	1,850	2,250
Yr.13(1924)	76,037	600	750	950	1,650	2,000

Y# 51 5 YEN

4.1666 g., 0.9000 Gold 0.1206 oz. AGW **Ruler:** Hirohito (Showa)

Date	Mintage	F	VF	XF	Unc	BU
Yr.5(1930)	852,563	20,000	35,000	50,000	65,000	75,000

Y# 33 10 YEN

8.3333 g., 0.9000 Gold 0.2411 oz. AGW **Ruler:** Mutsuhito (Meiji) **Obv:** Sunburst superimposed on sacred mirror, legends around border, value separated by paulownia crests **Rev:** Value within wreath, chrysanthemum above

Date	Mintage	VG	F	VF	XF	BU
Yr.34(1901)	1,654,682	—	400	550	750	1,250
Yr.35(1902)	3,023,940	—	400	550	750	1,350
Yr.36(1903)	2,902,184	—	400	550	750	1,350
Yr.37(1904)	724,548	—	750	1,500	2,000	4,000
Yr.40(1907)	157,684	—	450	700	1,250	2,350
Yr.41(1908)	1,160,674	—	400	550	750	1,250
Yr.42(1909)	2,165,660	—	350	550	750	1,200
Yr.43(1910)	8,982	—	7,500	10,000	15,000	25,000

Y# 34 20 YEN

16.6666 g., 0.9000 Gold 0.4822 oz. AGW **Ruler:** Mutsuhito (Meiji) **Obv:** Sunburst superimposed on sacred mirror, legends around border, authority above, date below **Rev:** Value within wreath, chrysanthemum above

Date	Mintage	VG	F	VF	XF	BU
Yr.36(1903) Rare	—	—	—	—	—	—
Yr.37(1904)	2,759,470	—	550	1,250	1,750	2,400
Yr.38(1905)	1,045,904	—	550	1,250	1,750	2,400
Yr.39(1906)	1,331,332	—	550	1,250	1,750	2,400
Yr.40(1907)	817,362	—	1,000	2,000	2,500	4,500
Yr.41(1908)	458,082	—	1,250	2,500	3,500	5,500
Yr.42(1909)	557,882	—	1,500	3,000	4,000	6,500
Yr.43(1910)	2,163,644	—	500	1,000	1,600	2,200
Yr.44(1911)	1,470,054	—	500	1,000	1,600	2,200
Yr.45(1912)	1,272,450	—	525	1,100	1,700	2,300

Y# 40.1 20 YEN

16.6666 g., 0.9000 Gold 0.4822 oz. AGW **Ruler:** Yoshihito (Taisho) **Obv:** Japanese character "first" used in date **Rev:** Value and denomination within wreath, chrysanthemum on top

Date	Mintage	VG	F	VF	XF	BU
Yr.1(1912)	177,644	—	700	1,400	2,200	3,000

Y# 40.2 20 YEN

16.6666 g., 0.9000 Gold 0.4822 oz. AGW **Ruler:** Yoshihito (Taisho) **Obv:** Sunburst within mirror, 3 legends separated by cherry blossoms, date on bottom **Rev:** Value and denomination within wreath, chrysanthemum on top

Date	Mintage	VG	F	VF	XF	BU
Yr.2(1913)	869,248	—	500	1,000	1,700	2,300
Yr.3(1914)	1,042,890	—	500	1,000	1,700	2,300
Yr.4(1915)	1,509,962	—	500	1,000	1,700	2,300
Yr.5(1916)	2,376,641	—	460	900	1,600	2,200
Yr.6(1917)	6,208,885	—	460	850	1,550	2,150

Date	Mintage	VG	F	VF	XF	BU
Yr.7(1918)	3,118,647	—	460	900	1,600	2,200
Yr.8(1919)	1,531,217	—	460	900	1,600	2,200
Yr.9(1920)	370,366	—	550	1,150	1,800	2,650

Y# 52 20 YEN

16.6666 g., 0.9000 Gold 0.4822 oz. AGW **Ruler:** Hirohito (Showa) **Obv:** Sunburst within mirror, legends separated by cherry blossoms around border **Rev:** Value and denomination within wreath, chrysanthemum on top

Date	Mintage	VG	F	VF	XF	BU
Yr.5(1930)	11,055,500	—	15,000	25,000	35,000	45,000
Yr.6(1931)	7,526,476	—	17,500	27,500	37,500	47,500
Yr.7(1932) Rare						

REFORM COINAGE

Y# 70 YEN

3.2000 g., Brass, 19.5 mm. **Ruler:** Hirohito (Showa) **Obv:** Numeral 1 within circle, flanked by dots, authority on top, date on bottom **Rev:** Value and denomination above 3/4 orange blossom wreath

Date	Mintage	F	VF	XF	Unc	BU
Yr.23(1948)	451,170,000	—	0.25	0.50	2.00	—
Yr.24(1949)	Inc. above	—	0.15	0.35	1.25	—
Yr.25(1950)	Inc. above	—	0.15	0.35	1.25	—

Y# 74 YEN

1.0000 g., Aluminum, 20 mm. **Ruler:** Hirohito (Showa) **Obv:** Sprouting branch in center, authority on top, value and denomination on bottom **Rev:** Numeral 1 within 2 inner circles, date on bottom

Date	Mintage	VG	F	VF	XF	BU
Yr.30(1955)	381,700,000	—	—	—	—	15.00
Yr.31(1956)	500,900,000	—	—	—	—	7.50
Yr.32(1957)	492,000,000	—	—	—	—	7.50
Yr.33(1958)	374,900,000	—	—	—	—	7.50
Yr.34(1959)	208,600,000	—	—	—	—	9.00
Yr.35(1960)	300,000,000	—	—	—	—	5.00
Yr.36(1961)	432,400,000	—	—	—	—	3.00
Yr.37(1962)	572,000,000	—	—	—	—	2.00
Yr.38(1963)	788,700,000	—	—	—	—	2.00
Yr.39(1964)	1,665,100,000	—	—	—	—	1.50
Yr.40(1965)	1,743,256,000	—	—	—	—	1.50
Yr.41(1966)	807,344,000	—	—	—	—	1.50
Yr.42(1967)	220,600,000	—	—	—	—	1.50
Yr.44(1969)	184,700,000	—	—	—	—	1.50
Yr.45(1970)	556,400,000	—	—	—	—	1.00
Yr.46(1971)	904,950,000	—	—	—	—	1.00
Yr.47(1972)	1,274,950,000	—	—	—	—	0.75
Yr.48(1973)	1,470,000,000	—	—	—	—	0.75
Yr.49(1974)	1,750,000,000	—	—	—	—	0.75
Yr.50(1975)	1,656,150,000	—	—	—	—	0.75
Yr.51(1976)	928,800,000	—	—	—	—	0.75
Yr.52(1977)	895,000,000	—	—	—	—	0.50
Yr.53(1978)	864,000,000	—	—	—	—	0.50
Yr.54(1979)	1,015,000,000	—	—	—	—	0.50
Yr.55(1980)	1,145,000,000	—	—	—	—	0.50
Yr.56(1981)	1,206,000,000	—	—	—	—	0.50
Yr.57(1982)	1,017,000,000	—	—	—	—	0.50
Yr.58(1983)	1,086,000,000	—	—	—	—	0.50
Yr.59(1984)	981,850,000	—	—	—	—	0.50
Yr.60(1985)	837,150,000	—	—	—	—	0.50
Yr.61(1986)	417,960,000	—	—	—	—	0.25
Yr.62(1987)	958,520,000	—	—	—	—	0.25
Yr.62(1987) Proof	230,000	Value: 1.50				
Yr.63(1988)	1,268,842,000	—	—	—	—	0.25
Yr.63(1988) Proof	200,000	Value: 1.50				
Yr.64(1989)	116,100,000	—	—	—	—	0.25

Y# 95.1 YEN

1.0000 g., Aluminum, 20 mm. **Ruler:** Akihito (Heisei) **Obv:**
Sprouting branch in center, authority on top, value and denomination
on bottom **Rev:** Numeral 1 within two circles, date on bottom

Date	Mintage	VG	F	VF	XF	BU
Yr.1(1989)	2,366,770,000	—	—	—	—	0.15
Yr.1(1989) Proof	200,000	Value: 1.50				

Y# 95.2 YEN

1.0000 g., Aluminum, 20 mm. **Ruler:** Akihito (Heisei)
Obv: Sprouting branch divides authority and value **Rev:** Value
within circles above date **Edge:** Plain

Date	Mintage	F	VF	XF	Unc	BU
Yr.2(1990)	2,768,753,000	—	—	—	—	0.15
Yr.2(1990) Proof	200,000	Value: 1.50				
Yr.3(1991)	2,300,900,000	—	—	—	—	0.15
Yr.3(1991) Proof	220,000	Value: 1.50				
Yr.4(1992)	1,298,880,000	—	—	—	—	0.15
Yr.4(1992) Proof	250,000	Value: 1.50				
Yr.5(1993)	1,260,990,000	—	—	—	—	0.15
Yr.5(1993) Proof	250,000	Value: 1.50				
Yr.6(1994)	1,040,540,000	—	—	—	—	0.15
Yr.6(1994) Proof	227,000	Value: 1.50				
Yr.7(1995)	1,041,674,000	—	—	—	—	0.15
Yr.7(1995) Proof	200,000	Value: 1.50				
Yr.8(1996)	942,024,000	—	—	—	—	0.15
Yr.8(1996) Proof	189,000	Value: 1.50				
Yr.9(1997)	782,874,000	—	—	—	—	0.15
Yr.9(1997) Proof	212,000	Value: 1.50				
Yr.10(1998)	452,412,000	—	—	—	—	0.15
Yr.10(1998) Proof	200,000	Value: 1.50				
Yr.11(1999)	66,850,000	—	—	—	—	0.15
Yr.11(1999) Proof	280,000	Value: 1.50				
Yr.12(2000)	11,800,000	—	—	—	—	0.50
Yr.12(2000) Proof	226,000	Value: 5.00				

Y# 71 5 YEN

4.0000 g., Brass **Ruler:** Hirohito (Showa) **Obv:** Pigeon within
circle with authority on top, date below **Rev:** Building within circle
flanked by value and denomination, all within wreath

Date	Mintage	VG	F	VF	XF	BU
Yr.23(1948)	74,520,000	—	—	0.50	0.75	12.50
Yr.24(1949)	179,692,000	—	—	0.15	0.40	8.00

Y# 72 5 YEN

3.7500 g., Brass, 22 mm. **Ruler:** Hirohito (Showa) **Obv:** Hole
in center flanked by seed leaf, authority on top and date below
Rev: Gear design around center hole with horizontal lines below,
large bending stalk of rice above **Note:** Old script.

Date	Mintage	VG	F	VF	XF	BU
Yr.24(1949)	111,896,000	—	—	0.15	0.25	9.00
Yr.25(1950)	181,824,000	—	—	0.15	0.25	6.50
Yr.26(1951)	197,980,000	—	—	0.15	0.25	6.50
Yr.27(1952)	55,000,000	—	—	0.30	0.60	100
Yr.28(1953)	45,000,000	—	—	0.30	0.60	6.50
Yr.32(1957)	10,000,000	—	—	4.00	8.00	40.00
Yr.33(1958)	50,000,000	—	—	0.25	0.50	3.50

Y# 72a 5 YEN

3.7500 g., Brass, 22 mm. **Ruler:** Hirohito (Showa) **Obv:** Hole
in center flanked by seed leaf with authority on top and date
below **Rev:** Gear design around center hole with horizontal lines
below, large bending stalk of rice above **Note:** New script.

Date	Mintage	VG	F	VF	XF	BU
Yr.34(1959)	33,000,000	—	—	0.25	0.50	5.00
Yr.35(1960)	34,800,000	—	—	0.20	0.40	5.00

Date	Mintage	VG	F	VF	XF	BU
Yr.36(1961)	61,000,000	—	—	0.15	0.35	4.00
Yr.37(1962)	126,700,000	—	—	0.10	0.30	3.00
Yr.38(1963)	171,800,000	—	—	0.10	0.30	2.50
Yr.39(1964)	379,700,000	—	—	0.10	0.30	2.50
Yr.40(1965)	384,200,000	—	—	0.10	0.30	2.00
Yr.41(1966)	163,100,000	—	—	0.10	0.30	2.00
Yr.42(1967)	26,000,000	—	—	0.25	0.50	2.50
Yr.43(1968)	114,000,000	—	—	—	0.10	1.50
Yr.44(1969)	240,000,000	—	—	—	0.10	1.50
Yr.45(1970)	340,000,000	—	—	—	0.10	1.50
Yr.46(1971)	362,050,000	—	—	—	0.10	1.50
Yr.47(1972)	562,950,000	—	—	—	0.10	0.75
Yr.48(1973)	745,000,000	—	—	—	0.10	0.75
Yr.49(1974)	950,000,000	—	—	—	0.10	0.75
Yr.50(1975)	970,000,000	—	—	—	0.10	0.75
Yr.51(1976)	200,000,000	—	—	—	0.10	0.75
Yr.52(1977)	340,000,000	—	—	—	0.10	0.75
Yr.53(1978)	318,000,000	—	—	—	0.10	0.75
Yr.54(1979)	317,000,000	—	—	—	0.10	0.75
Yr.55(1980)	385,000,000	—	—	—	0.10	0.75
Yr.56(1981)	95,000,000	—	—	—	0.10	1.50
Yr.57(1982)	455,000,000	—	—	—	0.10	0.75
Yr.58(1983)	410,000,000	—	—	—	0.10	0.75
Yr.59(1984)	202,850,000	—	—	—	0.10	0.75
Yr.60(1985)	153,150,000	—	—	—	0.10	1.00
Yr.61(1986)	113,960,000	—	—	—	0.10	1.50
Yr.62(1987)	631,545,000	—	—	—	0.10	0.25
Yr.62(1987) Proof	230,000	Value: 1.75				
Yr.63(1988)	368,920,000	—	—	—	—	0.25
Yr.63(1988) Proof	200,000	Value: 1.75				
Yr.64(1989)	67,332,000	—	—	—	—	0.50

Y# 96.1 5 YEN

3.7500 g., Brass, 22 mm. **Ruler:** Akihito (Heisei) **Obv:** Hole in
center flanked by a seed leaf with authority on top and date below
Rev: Gear around center hole with bending rice stalk above value

Date	Mintage	VG	F	VF	XF	BU
Yr.1(1989)	960,460,000	—	—	—	—	0.35
Yr.1(1989) Proof	200,000	Value: 1.75				

Y# 96.2 5 YEN

3.7500 g., Brass, 22 mm. **Ruler:** Akihito (Heisei) **Obv:** Hole in
center flanked by a seed leaf with authority on top and date below
Rev: Gear design around center hole with bending rice stalk
above value in horizontal lines below

Date	Mintage	F	VF	XF	Unc	BU
Yr.2(1990)	520,753,000	—	—	—	—	0.35
Yr.2(1990) Proof	200,000	Value: 1.75				
Yr.3(1991)	516,900,000	—	—	—	—	0.35
Yr.3(1991) Proof	220,000	Value: 1.75				
Yr.4(1992)	300,880,000	—	—	—	—	0.35
Yr.4(1992) Proof	250,000	Value: 1.75				
Yr.5(1993)	412,990,000	—	—	—	—	0.35
Yr.5(1993) Proof	250,000	Value: 1.75				
Yr.6(1994)	197,540,000	—	—	—	—	0.35
Yr.6(1994) Proof	227,000	Value: 1.75				
Yr.7(1995)	351,674,000	—	—	—	—	0.35
Yr.7(1995) Proof	200,000	Value: 1.75				
Yr.8(1996)	207,024,000	—	—	—	—	0.35
Yr.8(1996) Proof	189,000	Value: 1.75				
Yr.9(1997)	238,874,000	—	—	—	—	0.35
Yr.9(1997) Proof	212,000	Value: 1.75				
Yr.10(1998)	172,412,000	—	—	—	—	0.35
Yr.10(1998) Proof	200,000	Value: 1.75				
Yr.11(1999)	59,850,000	—	—	—	—	0.35
Yr.11(1999) Proof	280,000	Value: 1.75				
Yr.12(2000)	8,804,000	—	—	—	—	2.50
Yr.12(2000) Proof	226,000	Value: 5.00				

Y# 73 10 YEN

4.5000 g., Bronze, 23.5 mm. **Ruler:** Hirohito (Showa)
Obv: Temple in center with authority on top and value below
Rev: Value and denomination within wreath **Edge:** Reeded

Date	Mintage	VG	F	VF	XF	BU
Yr.26(1951)	101,068,000	—	—	0.20	0.35	150
Yr.27(1952)	486,632,000	—	—	0.20	0.35	40.00

Date	Mintage	VG	F	VF	XF	BU
Yr.28(1953)	466,300,000	—	—	0.20	0.35	40.00
Yr.29(1954)	520,900,000	—	—	0.20	0.35	50.00
Yr.30(1955)	123,100,000	—	—	0.20	0.35	50.00
Yr.32(1957)	50,000,000	—	—	0.25	0.65	100
Yr.33(1958)	25,000,000	—	—	0.40	1.00	115

Y# 73a 10 YEN

4.5000 g., Bronze, 23.5 mm. **Ruler:** Hirohito (Showa)
Obv: Temple in center with authority on top and value below
Rev: Value and denomination within wreath **Edge:** Plain

Date	Mintage	VG	F	VF	XF	BU
Yr.34(1959)	62,400,000	—	—	—	0.20	60.00
Yr.35(1960)	225,900,000	—	—	—	0.20	45.00
Yr.36(1961)	229,900,000	—	—	—	0.20	40.00
Yr.37(1962)	284,200,000	—	—	—	0.20	5.00
Yr.38(1963)	411,300,000	—	—	—	0.20	5.00
Yr.39(1964)	479,200,000	—	—	—	0.20	3.50
Yr.40(1965)	387,600,000	—	—	—	0.20	2.50
Yr.41(1966)	395,900,000	—	—	—	0.20	2.50
Yr.42(1967)	158,900,000	—	—	—	0.20	10.00
Yr.43(1968)	363,600,000	—	—	—	0.20	2.50
Yr.44(1969)	414,800,000	—	—	—	0.20	1.50
Yr.45(1970)	382,700,000	—	—	—	0.20	2.50
Yr.46(1971)	610,000,000	—	—	—	0.20	2.00
Yr.47(1972)	634,950,000	—	—	—	0.20	1.50
Yr.48(1973)	1,345,000,000	—	—	—	0.20	1.00
Yr.49(1974)	1,780,000,000	—	—	—	0.20	1.00
Yr.50(1975)	1,280,260,000	—	—	—	0.20	1.00
Yr.51(1976)	1,369,740,000	—	—	—	0.20	1.00
Yr.52(1977)	1,467,000,000	—	—	—	0.20	1.00
Yr.53(1978)	1,435,000,000	—	—	—	0.20	1.00
Yr.54(1979)	1,207,000,000	—	—	—	0.20	1.00
Yr.55(1980)	1,127,000,000	—	—	—	0.20	0.75
Yr.56(1981)	1,369,000,000	—	—	—	0.20	0.75
Yr.57(1982)	890,000,000	—	—	—	0.20	0.75
Yr.58(1983)	870,000,000	—	—	—	0.20	0.75
Yr.59(1984)	533,850,000	—	—	—	0.20	0.75
Yr.60(1985)	335,150,000	—	—	—	0.20	0.75
Yr.61(1986)	68,960,000	—	—	—	0.25	1.50
Yr.62(1987)	165,545,000	—	—	—	0.20	0.50
Yr.62(1987) Proof	230,000	Value: 1.75				
Yr.63(1988)	617,912,000	—	—	—	0.20	0.50
Yr.63(1988) Proof	200,000	Value: 1.75				
Yr.64(1989)	74,692,000	—	—	—	0.25	0.75

Y# 97.1 10 YEN

4.5000 g., Bronze, 23.5 mm. **Ruler:** Akihito (Heisei)
Obv: Temple divides authority and value **Rev:** Japanese
character "first" in date

Date	Mintage	VG	F	VF	XF	BU
Yr.1(1989)	666,108,000	—	—	—	—	0.45
Yr.1(1989) Proof	200,000	Value: 1.75				

Y# 97.2 10 YEN

4.5000 g., Bronze, 23.5 mm. **Ruler:** Akihito (Heisei) **Obv:**
Temple divides authority and value **Rev:** Value within wreath

Date	Mintage	F	VF	XF	Unc	BU
Yr.2(1990)	754,753,000	—	—	—	—	0.45
Yr.2(1990) Proof	200,000	Value: 1.75				
Yr.3(1991)	631,900,000	—	—	—	—	0.45
Yr.3(1991) Proof	220,000	Value: 1.75				
Yr.4(1992)	537,880,000	—	—	—	—	0.45
Yr.4(1992) Proof	250,000	Value: 1.75				
Yr.5(1993)	248,990,000	—	—	—	—	0.45
Yr.5(1993) Proof	250,000	Value: 1.75				
Yr.6(1994)	190,540,000	—	—	—	—	0.45
Yr.6(1994) Proof	227,000	Value: 1.75				
Yr.7(1995)	248,674,000	—	—	—	—	0.45
Yr.7(1995) Proof	200,000	Value: 1.75				
Yr.8(1996)	546,024,000	—	—	—	—	0.45
Yr.8(1996) Proof	189,000	Value: 1.75				

Date	Mintage	F	VF	XF	Unc	BU
Yr.9(1997)	490,874,000	—	—	—	—	0.45
Yr.9(1997) Proof	212,000	Value: 1.75				
Yr.10(1998)	410,412,000	—	—	—	—	0.45
Yr.10(1998) Proof	200,000	Value: 1.75				
Yr.11(1999)	358,850,000	—	—	—	—	0.45
Yr.11(1999) Proof	280,000	Value: 1.75				
Yr.12(2000)	314,800,000	—	—	—	—	0.45
Yr.12(2000) Proof	226,000	Value: 1.75				

Y# 75 50 YEN
5.5000 g., Nickel, 24 mm. **Ruler:** Hirohito (Showa)
Obv: Chrysanthemum blossom, authority on top, value at bottom
Rev: Numeral 50 within center design, regnal era on top, date on bottom

Date	Mintage	VG	F	VF	XF	BU
Yr.30(1955)	63,700,000	—	—	0.75	1.50	15.00
Yr.31(1956)	91,300,000	—	—	0.75	1.00	15.00
Yr.32(1957)	39,000,000	—	—	0.75	1.50	15.00
Yr.33(1958)	18,000,000	—	—	1.00	2.50	25.00

Y# 76 50 YEN
5.0000 g., Nickel, 25 mm. **Ruler:** Hirohito (Showa) **Rev:** Value above hole in center

Date	Mintage	VG	F	VF	XF	BU
Yr.34(1959)	23,900,000	—	—	1.00	2.50	12.50
Yr.35(1960)	6,000,000	—	—	12.50	22.50	50.00
Yr.36(1961)	16,000,000	—	—	2.00	4.00	15.00
Yr.37(1962)	50,300,000	—	—	0.75	1.25	5.00
Yr.38(1963)	55,000,000	—	—	0.75	1.25	5.00
Yr.39(1964)	69,200,000	—	—	0.75	1.25	5.00
Yr.40(1965)	189,300,000	—	—	0.75	1.00	2.00
Yr.41(1966)	171,500,000	—	—	0.75	1.25	2.50

Y# 81 50 YEN
4.0000 g., Copper-Nickel, 21 mm. **Ruler:** Hirohito (Showa)
Obv: Center hole flanked by chrysanthemums, authority on top and value below **Rev:** Numeral 50 above center hole with date below

Date	Mintage	VG	F	VF	XF	BU
Yr.42(1967)	238,400,000	—	—	—	0.75	7.50
Yr.43(1968)	200,000,000	—	—	—	0.75	5.00
Yr.44(1969)	210,000,000	—	—	—	0.75	5.00
Yr.45(1970)	269,800,000	—	—	—	0.75	5.00
Yr.46(1971)	80,950,000	—	—	—	0.75	5.00
Yr.47(1972)	138,980,000	—	—	—	0.75	4.00
Yr.48(1973)	200,970,000	—	—	—	0.75	4.00
Yr.49(1974)	470,000,000	—	—	—	0.75	2.00
Yr.50(1975)	238,120,000	—	—	—	0.75	1.50
Yr.51(1976)	241,880,000	—	—	—	0.75	1.50
Yr.52(1977)	176,000,000	—	—	—	0.75	4.00
Yr.53(1978)	234,000,000	—	—	—	0.75	1.50
Yr.54(1979)	110,000,000	—	—	—	0.75	2.00
Yr.55(1980)	51,000,000	—	—	—	0.75	2.00
Yr.56(1981)	179,000,000	—	—	—	0.75	1.00
Yr.57(1982)	30,000,000	—	—	—	0.75	2.00
Yr.58(1983)	30,000,000	—	—	—	0.75	2.00
Yr.59(1984)	29,850,000	—	—	—	0.75	2.50
Yr.60(1985)	10,150,000	—	—	—	0.75	4.00
Yr.61(1986)	9,960,000	—	—	—	0.75	2.50
Yr.62(1987)	545,000	—	—	40.00	60.00	85.00
Yr.62(1987) Proof	230,000	Value: 100				
Yr.63(1988)	108,912,000	—	—	—	—	1.50
Yr.63(1988) Proof	200,000	Value: 2.00				

Y# 101.1 50 YEN
4.0000 g., Copper-Nickel, 21 mm. **Ruler:** Akihito (Heisei)
Obv: Center hole flanked by chrysanthemums, authority at top and value below **Rev:** Numeral 50 above center hole with date below

Date	Mintage	VG	F	VF	XF	BU
Yr.1(1989)	244,800,000	—	—	—	—	1.00
Yr.1(1989) Proof	200,000	Value: 2.00				

Y# 101.2 50 YEN
4.0000 g., Copper-Nickel, 21 mm. **Ruler:** Akihito (Heisei)
Obv: Center hole flanked by chrysanthemums, authority at top and value below **Rev:** Value above hole in center

Date	Mintage	F	VF	XF	Unc	BU
Yr.2(1990)	274,753,000	—	—	—	—	1.00
Yr.2(1990) Proof	200,000	Value: 2.00				
Yr.3(1991)	208,900,000	—	—	—	—	1.00
Yr.3(1991) Proof	220,000	Value: 2.00				
Yr.4(1992)	48,880,000	—	—	—	—	1.00
Yr.4(1992) Proof	250,000	Value: 2.00				
Yr.5(1993)	50,990,000	—	—	—	—	1.00
Yr.5(1993) Proof	250,000	Value: 2.00				
Yr.6(1994)	65,540,000	—	—	—	—	1.00
Yr.6(1994) Proof	227,000	Value: 2.00				
Yr.7(1995)	111,674,000	—	—	—	—	1.00
Yr.7(1995) Proof	200,000	Value: 2.00				
Yr.8(1996)	82,024,000	—	—	—	—	1.00
Yr.8(1996) Proof	189,000	Value: 2.00				
Yr.9(1997)	149,876,000	—	—	—	—	1.00
Yr.9(1997) Proof	212,000	Value: 2.00				
Yr.10(1998)	100,412,000	—	—	—	—	1.00
Yr.10(1998) Proof	200,000	Value: 2.00				
Yr.11(1999)	58,850,000	—	—	—	—	1.00
Yr.11(1999) Proof	280,000	Value: 2.00				
Yr.12(2000)	6,800,000	—	—	—	—	7.50
Yr.12(2000) Proof	226,000	Value: 8.00				

Y# 77 100 YEN
4.8000 g., 0.6000 Silver 0.0926 oz. ASW, 22.5 mm.
Ruler: Hirohito (Showa) **Obv:** Phoenix

Date	Mintage	VG	F	VF	XF	Unc	BU
Yr.32(1957)	30,000,000	—	1.50	2.50	7.00	9.00	
Yr.33(1958)	70,000,000	—	1.50	2.50	5.00	6.00	

Y# 78 100 YEN
4.8000 g., 0.6000 Silver 0.0926 oz. ASW, 22.5 mm.
Ruler: Hirohito (Showa) **Obv:** Sheaf of rice in center with authority on top and value below **Rev:** Numeral 100 within circle flanked by 1/4 lined wreath with era on top and year below

Date	Mintage	VG	F	VF	XF	BU
Yr.34(1959)	110,000,000	—	—	1.50	2.50	7.00
Yr.35(1960)	50,000,000	—	—	1.50	2.50	9.00
Yr.36(1961)	15,000,000	—	—	1.50	2.50	9.00
Yr.38(1963)	45,000,000	—	—	1.50	2.50	9.00
Yr.39(1964)	10,000,000	—	—	1.75	3.50	9.00
Yr.40(1965)	62,500,000	—	—	1.50	2.50	4.00
Yr.41(1966)	97,500,000	—	—	1.50	2.50	4.00

Y# 79 100 YEN
4.8000 g., 0.6000 Silver 0.0926 oz. ASW, 22.5 mm.
Ruler: Hirohito (Showa) **Subject:** 1964 Olympic Games
Obv: Olympic circles on base of flaming torch flanked by authority above and value below **Rev:** Numeral 100 within center circle

Date	Mintage	VG	F	VF	XF	BU
Yr.39/1964	80,000,000	—	—	1.50	2.50	4.00

Y# 82 100 YEN
4.2000 g., Copper-Nickel, 22.5 mm. **Ruler:** Hirohito (Showa)
Obv: Cherry blossoms **Rev:** Large numeral 100 in center

Date	Mintage	VG	F	VF	XF	BU
Yr.42(1967)	432,200,000	—	—	—	1.50	7.50
	Note: Varieties exist					
Yr.43(1968)	471,000,000	—	—	—	1.50	5.00
Yr.44(1969)	323,700,000	—	—	—	1.50	7.50
Yr.45(1970)	237,100,000	—	—	—	1.50	5.00
Yr.46(1971)	481,050,000	—	—	—	1.50	2.50
Yr.47(1972)	468,950,000	—	—	—	1.50	2.00
Yr.48(1973)	680,000,000	—	—	—	1.50	2.00
Yr.49(1974)	660,000,000	—	—	—	1.50	2.00
Yr.50(1975)	437,160,000	—	—	—	1.50	2.00
Yr.51(1976)	322,840,000	—	—	—	1.50	2.00
Yr.52(1977)	440,000,000	—	—	—	1.50	2.00
Yr.53(1978)	292,000,000	—	—	—	1.50	2.00
Yr.54(1979)	382,000,000	—	—	—	1.50	2.00
Yr.55(1980)	588,000,000	—	—	—	1.50	2.00
Yr.56(1981)	348,000,000	—	—	—	1.50	2.00
Yr.57(1982)	110,000,000	—	—	—	1.50	3.00
Yr.58(1983)	50,000,000	—	—	—	1.50	5.00
Yr.59(1984)	41,850,000	—	—	—	1.50	5.00
Yr.60(1985)	58,150,000	—	—	—	1.50	5.00
Yr.61(1986)	99,960,000	—	—	—	1.50	2.00
Yr.62(1987)	193,545,000	—	—	—	1.50	2.00
Yr.62(1987) Proof	230,000	Value: 5.00				
Yr.63(1988)	362,912,000	—	—	—	1.50	2.00
Yr.63(1988) Proof	200,000	Value: 5.00				

Y# 83 100 YEN
9.0000 g., Copper-Nickel, 28 mm. **Ruler:** Hirohito (Showa)
Subject: Osaka Expo '70 **Obv:** Mt. Fuji **Rev:** Circles within world globe with value above

Date	Mintage	VG	F	VF	XF	BU
Yr.45(1970)	40,000,000	—	—	2.50	3.50	6.00

Y# 84 100 YEN
12.0000 g., Copper-Nickel, 30 mm. **Ruler:** Hirohito (Showa)
Subject: 1972 Winter Olympic Games - Sapporo **Obv:** Olympic torch with flame flanked by authority and city name **Rev:** Large numeral 100 above olympic circles flanked by flower designs

Date	Mintage	VG	F	VF	XF	BU
Yr.47/1972	30,000,000	—	—	3.00	4.50	7.50

Y# 85 100 YEN
9.8000 g., Copper-Nickel, 22.5 mm. **Ruler:** Hirohito (Showa)
Subject: Okinawa Expo '75 **Obv:** Gate of Shurei **Rev:** Value in center flanked by dolphins with legend above and below

Date	Mintage	VG	F	VF	XF	BU
Yr.50(1975)	120,000,000	—	—	1.75	2.50	3.50

Y# 86 100 YEN
12.0000 g., Copper-Nickel, 30 mm. **Ruler:** Hirohito (Showa)
Subject: 50th Anniversary of Reign **Obv:** Imperial Palace and Niju Bridge **Rev:** Chrysanthemum in center flanked by phoenix with inscription above and below

Date	Mintage	VG	F	VF	XF	BU
Yr.51(1976)	70,000,000	—	—	2.50	3.50	6.00

Y# 98.1 100 YEN
4.8000 g., Copper-Nickel, 22.5 mm. **Ruler:** Akihito (Heisei)
Obv: Cherry blossoms **Rev:** Japanese character "first" in date

Date	Mintage	VG	F	VF	XF	BU
Yr.1(1989)	368,800,000	—	—	—	—	2.00
Yr.1(1989) Proof	200,000	Value: 5.00				

Y# 98.2 100 YEN
4.8000 g., Copper-Nickel, 22.6 mm. **Ruler:** Akihito (Heisei) **Obv:** Cherry blossoms **Rev:** Large numeral 100, date in western numerals

Date	Mintage	F	VF	XF	Unc	BU
Yr.2(1990)	444,753,000	—	—	—	—	2.00
Yr.2(1990) Proof	200,000	Value: 5.00				
Yr.3(1991)	374,900,000	—	—	—	—	2.00
Yr.3(1991) Proof	220,000	Value: 5.00				
Yr.4(1992)	211,050,000	—	—	—	—	2.00
Yr.4(1992) Proof	250,000	Value: 5.00				
Yr.5(1993)	81,990,000	—	—	—	—	2.00
Yr.5(1993) Proof	250,000	Value: 5.00				
Yr.6(1994)	81,540,000	—	—	—	—	2.00
Yr.6(1994) Proof	227,000	Value: 5.00				
Yr.7(1995)	92,674,000	—	—	—	—	2.00
Yr.7(1995) Proof	200,000	Value: 5.00				
Yr.8(1996)	237,024,000	—	—	—	—	2.00
Yr.8(1996) Proof	189,000	Value: 5.00				
Yr.9(1997)	271,876,000	—	—	—	—	2.00
Yr.9(1997) Proof	212,000	Value: 5.00				
Yr.10(1998)	252,412,000	—	—	—	—	2.00
Yr.10(1998) Proof	200,000	Value: 5.00				
Yr.11(1999)	178,850,000	—	—	—	—	2.00
Yr.11(1999) Proof	280,000	Value: 5.00				
Yr.12(2000)	171,800,000	—	—	—	—	2.00
Yr.12(2000) Proof	226,000	Value: 5.00				

Y# 87 500 YEN
7.2000 g., Copper-Nickel, 26.5 mm. **Ruler:** Hirohito (Showa)
Obv: Pawlownia flower **Rev:** Numeral 500 in center flanked by cherry blossoms **Edge:** NIPPON 500

Date	Mintage	VG	F	VF	XF	BU
Yr.57(1982)	300,000,000	—	—	—	7.00	9.00
Yr.58(1983)	240,000,000	—	—	—	7.00	9.00
Yr.59(1984)	342,850,000	—	—	—	7.00	9.00
Yr.60(1985)	97,150,000	—	—	—	7.00	9.00
Yr.61(1986)	49,960,000	—	—	—	7.00	9.00

Date	Mintage	VG	F	VF	XF	BU
Yr.62(1987)	2,545,000	—	—	7.00	9.00	15.00
Yr.62(1987) Proof	230,000	Value: 25.00				
Yr.63(1988)	148,018,000	—	—	—	7.00	9.00
Yr.63(1988) Proof	200,000	Value: 15.00				
Yr.64(1989)	16,042,000	—	—	—	7.00	12.00

Y# 88 500 YEN
13.0000 g., Copper-Nickel, 30 mm. **Ruler:** Hirohito (Showa)
Subject: 1985 Tsukuba Expo **Obv:** Mt. Tsukuba above cherry blossoms **Rev:** Circles within triangular design above value flanked by cherry blossom **Edge:** TSUKUBA EXPO '85

Date	Mintage	VG	F	VF	XF	BU
Yr.60(1985)	70,000,000	—	—	—	7.50	10.00

Y# 89 500 YEN
13.0000 g., Copper-Nickel, 30 mm. **Ruler:** Hirohito (Showa)
Subject: 100th Anniversary - Governmental Cabinet System **Obv:** Prime Minister's official residence **Rev:** Large numeral 500 within center square **Edge:** NAIKAKU 100 NEN

Date	Mintage	VG	F	VF	XF	BU
Yr.60(1985)	70,000,000	—	—	—	7.50	10.00

Y# 90 500 YEN
13.0000 g., Copper-Nickel, 30 mm. **Ruler:** Hirohito (Showa)
Subject: 60 Years of Reign of Hirohito **Obv:** Large chrysanthemum with legends around border **Rev:** Shishinden Palace

Date	Mintage	VG	F	VF	XF	BU
Yr.61(1986)	50,000,000	—	—	—	8.00	12.00
Yr.62 (1987)	—	—	—	—	8.00	12.00

Y# 93 500 YEN
13.0000 g., Copper-Nickel, 30 mm. **Ruler:** Hirohito (Showa)
Subject: Opening of Seikan Tunnel **Obv:** Seikan tunnel flanked by sea gulls **Rev:** Map within ribbon above value

Date	Mintage	VG	F	VF	XF	BU
Yr.63(1988)	20,000,000	—	—	—	8.50	12.50

Y# 94 500 YEN
13.0000 g., Copper-Nickel, 30 mm. **Ruler:** Hirohito (Showa)
Subject: Opening of Seto Bridge **Obv:** Seto Bridge **Rev:** Map within ribbon above value

Date	Mintage	VG	F	VF	XF	BU
Yr.63(1988)	20,000,000	—	—	—	8.50	12.50

Y# 99.1 500 YEN
7.2000 g., Copper-Nickel, 26.5 mm. **Ruler:** Akihito (Heisei)
Obv: Pawlownia flower **Rev:** Value flanked by cherry blossoms, Japanese character "first" in date

Date	Mintage	VG	F	VF	XF	BU
Yr.1(1989)	192,652,000	—	—	—	7.00	9.00
Yr.1(1989) Proof	200,000	Value: 15.00				

Y# 99.2 500 YEN
7.2000 g., Copper-Nickel, 26.5 mm. **Ruler:** Akihito (Heisei)
Obv: Pawlownia flower **Rev:** Value flanked by cherry blossoms, date in western numerals

Date	Mintage	VG	F	VF	XF	BU
Yr.2(1990)	159,753,000	—	—	—	7.00	9.00
Yr.2(1990) Proof	200,000	Value: 15.00				
Yr.3(1991)	169,900,000	—	—	—	7.00	9.00
Yr.3(1991) Proof	220,000	Value: 15.00				
Yr.4(1992)	87,880,000	—	—	—	7.00	9.00
Yr.4(1992) Proof	250,000	Value: 15.00				
Yr.5(1993)	131,990,000	—	—	—	7.00	9.00
Yr.5(1993) Proof	250,000	Value: 15.00				
Yr.6(1994)	105,545,000	—	—	—	7.00	9.00
Yr.6(1994) Proof	227,000	Value: 15.00				
Yr.7(1995)	182,669,000	—	—	—	—	9.00
Yr.7(1995) Proof	200,000	Value: 15.00				
Yr.8(1996)	99,024,000	—	—	—	—	9.00
Yr.8(1996) Proof	189,000	Value: 15.00				
Yr.9(1997)	172,878,000	—	—	—	—	9.00
Yr.9(1997) Proof	212,000	Value: 15.00				
Yr.10(1998)	214,408,000	—	—	—	—	9.00
Yr.10(1998) Proof	200,000	Value: 15.00				
Yr.11(1999)	164,840,000	—	—	—	—	9.00
Yr.11(1999) Proof	280,000	Value: 15.00				

Y# 102 500 YEN
13.0000 g., Copper-Nickel, 30 mm. **Ruler:** Akihito (Heisei)
Subject: Enthronement of Emperor Akihito **Obv:** Carriage **Rev:** Chrysanthemum crest among leaves above value

Date	Mintage	VG	F	VF	XF	BU
Yr.2(1990)	30,000,000	—	—	—	—	13.50

Y# 106 500 YEN
13.0000 g., Copper-Nickel, 30 mm. **Ruler:** Akihito (Heisei)
Subject: 20th Anniversary - Reversion of Okinawa **Obv:** Building **Rev:** Value and denomination flanked by upright dragons

Date	Mintage	VG	F	VF	XF	BU
Yr.4(1992)	19,953,000	—	—	—	—	14.50
Yr.4(1992) Proof	47,000	Value: 27.50				

Y# 107   500 YEN
7.2000 g., Copper-Nickel, 26.5 mm. **Ruler:** Akihito (Heisei)
Subject: Royal wedding of Crown Prince **Obv:** Chrysanthemum
flanked by cherry blossom sprigs with legend around border
Rev: Pair of flying herons

Date	Mintage	VG	F	VF	XF	BU
Yr.5(1993)	29,800,000	—	—	—	—	16.00
Yr.5(1993) Proof	200,000	Value: 22.50				

Y# 110   500 YEN
7.2000 g., Copper-Nickel, 26.5 mm. **Ruler:** Akihito (Heisei)
Subject: Opening of Kansai International Airport **Obv:** Flying jet
Rev: Design within ribbon

Date	Mintage	VG	F	VF	XF	BU
Yr.6(1994)	19,900,000	—	—	—	—	14.50
Yr.6(1994) Proof	100,000	Value: 42.50				

Y# 111   500 YEN
7.2000 g., Copper-Nickel, 26.5 mm. **Ruler:** Akihito (Heisei)
Subject: 12th Asian Games **Obv:** Stylized runners **Rev:** Artistic
design above value

Date	Mintage	VG	F	VF	XF	BU
Yr.6(1994)	9,900,000	—	—	—	—	13.50
Yr.6(1994) Proof	100,000	Value: 32.50				

Y# 112   500 YEN
7.2000 g., Copper-Nickel, 26.5 mm. **Ruler:** Akihito (Heisei)
Subject: 12th Asian Games **Obv:** Stylized swimmers
Rev: Artistic design above value

Date	Mintage	VG	F	VF	XF	BU
Yr.6(1994)	9,900,000	—	—	—	—	13.50
Yr.6(1994) Proof	100,000	Value: 32.50				

Y# 113   500 YEN
7.2000 g., Copper-Nickel, 26.5 mm. **Ruler:** Akihito (Heisei)
Subject: 12th Asian Games **Obv:** Stylized jumper **Rev:** Artistic
design above value

Date	Mintage	VG	F	VF	XF	BU
Yr.6(1994)	9,900,000	—	—	—	—	13.50
Yr.6(1994) Proof	100,000	Value: 32.50				

Y# 114   500 YEN
7.2000 g., Copper-Nickel, 26.5 mm. **Ruler:** Akihito (Heisei)
Series: 1998 Nagano Winter Olympics **Obv:** Snowboarder
Rev: Bird, value and dates

Date	Mintage	VG	F	VF	XF	BU
Yr.9(1997)	19,867,000	—	—	—	—	14.50
Yr.9(1997) Proof	133,000	Value: 35.00				

Y# 117   500 YEN
7.2000 g., Copper-Nickel, 26.5 mm. **Ruler:** Akihito (Heisei)
Series: 1998 Nagano Winter Olympics **Obv:** Bobsledding
Rev: Bird, value and dates

Date	Mintage	VG	F	VF	XF	BU
Yr.9(1997)	19,867,000	—	—	—	—	14.50
Yr.9(1997) Proof	133,000	Value: 35.00				

Y# 118   500 YEN
7.2000 g., Copper-Nickel, 26.5 mm. **Ruler:** Akihito (Heisei)
Series: 1998 Nagano Winter Olympics **Obv:** Acrobat skier
Rev: Bird, value and dates

Date	Mintage	VG	F	VF	XF	BU
Yr.10(1998)	19,867,000	—	—	—	—	14.50
Yr.10(1998) Proof	133,000	Value: 35.00				

Y# 123   500 YEN
7.2000 g., Copper-Nickel, 26.5 mm. **Ruler:** Akihito (Heisei)
Subject: 10th Anniversary of Enthronement **Obv:** Mt. Fuji and
chrysanthemums **Rev:** Chrysanthemum within wreath

Date	Mintage	VG	F	VF	XF	BU
Yr.11(1999)	14,900,000	—	—	—	—	11.50
Yr.11(1999) Proof	100,000	Value: 32.00				

Y# 125   500 YEN
7.0000 g., Nickel-Brass, 26.5 mm. **Ruler:** Akihito (Heisei)
Obv: Pawlownia flower and highlighted legends **Rev:** Value with
latent zeros **Edge:** Slanted reeding

Date	Mintage	F	VF	XF	Unc	BU
Yr.12(2000)	595,743,000	—	—	—	—	9.00
Yr.12(2000) Proof	226,000	Value: 15.00				

Y# 80   1000 YEN
20.0000 g., 0.9250 Silver 0.5948 oz. ASW, 35 mm.
Ruler: Hirohito (Showa) **Series:** 1964 Olympic Games **Obv:** Mt.
Fuji within sprigs of cherry blossoms **Rev:** Value and olympic
circles flanked by cherry blossoms **Note:** Dav. #276

Date	Mintage	VG	F	VF	XF	BU
Yr.39(1964)	15,000,000	—	—	—	20.00	35.00

Y# 100   5000 YEN
15.0000 g., 0.9250 Silver 0.4461 oz. ASW, 30 mm.
Ruler: Akihito (Heisei) **Subject:** Osaka Exposition **Obv:** Head
with flowers in hair left **Rev:** Flower design above garden value

Date	Mintage	VG	F	VF	XF	Unc	BU
Yr.2 (1990)	10,000,000	—	—	—	—	—	65.00

Y# 103   5000 YEN
15.0000 g., 0.9250 Silver 0.4461 oz. ASW, 30 mm. **Subject:** Centennial of Parliament
Obv: Parliament building **Rev:** Winged figures flank central figure

Date	Mintage	VG	F	VF	XF	BU
Yr.2(1990)	5,000,000	—	—	—	—	65.00

Y# 104   5000 YEN
15.0000 g., 0.9250 Silver 0.4461 oz. ASW, 30 mm. **Ruler:** Akihito
(Heisei) **Subject:** Centennial of Judicial System **Obv:** Court room
scene **Rev:** Value within center circle and flowered wreath

Date	Mintage	VG	F	VF	XF	BU
Yr.2(1990)	5,000,000	—	—	—	—	65.00

Y# 108   5000 YEN
15.0000 g., 1.0000 Silver 0.4822 oz. ASW, 30 mm.
Ruler: Akihito (Heisei) **Subject:** Royal Wedding of Crown Prince
Obv: Chrysanthemum flanked by sprigs **Rev:** Pair of flying herons

Date	Mintage	VG	F	VF	XF	BU
Yr.5(1993)	4,800,000	—	—	—	—	70.00
Yr.5(1993) Proof	200,000	Value: 100				

Y# 115   5000 YEN
15.0000 g., 0.9250 Silver 0.4461 oz. ASW, 30 mm.
Ruler: Akihito (Heisei) **Series:** 1998 Nagano Winter Olympics
Obv: Hockey player **Rev:** Value, dates, and Serow

Date	Mintage	VG	F	VF	XF	BU
Yr.9(1997)	4,867,000	—	—	—	—	70.00
Yr.9(1997) Proof	133,000	Value: 120				

Y# 119   5000 YEN
15.0000 g., 0.9250 Silver 0.4461 oz. ASW, 30 mm.
Ruler: Akihito (Heisei) **Series:** 1998 Nagano Winter Olympics
Obv: Biathlon **Rev:** Value, dates, and antelope

Date	Mintage	VG	F	VF	XF	BU
Yr.9(1997)	4,867,000	—	—	—	—	70.00
Yr.9(1997) Proof	133,000	Value: 120				

Y# 120   5000 YEN
15.0000 g., 0.9250 Silver 0.4461 oz. ASW, 30 mm.
Ruler: Akihito (Heisei) **Series:** 1998 Nagano Winter Olympics
Obv: Paralympic skier **Rev:** Value, dates, and antelope

Date	Mintage	VG	F	VF	XF	BU
Yr.10(1998)	4,867,000	—	—	—	—	70.00
Yr.10(1998) Proof	133,000	Value: 120				

Y# 91   10000 YEN
20.0000 g., 0.9990 Silver 0.6423 oz. ASW, 35 mm.
Ruler: Hirohito (Showa) **Subject:** 60 Years - Reign of Hirohito
Obv: Large chrysanthemum with legends around border
Rev: Flying birds above center circle with hills and lines below

Date	Mintage	VG	F	VF	XF	BU
Yr.61(1986)	10,000,000	—	—	—	—	150
Yr.62 (1987)	—	—	—	—	—	150

Y# 116   10000 YEN
15.6000 g., 1.0000 Gold 0.5015 oz. AGW, 26 mm. **Ruler:** Akihito
(Heisei) **Series:** 1998 Nagano Winter Olympics **Obv:** Ski jumper
Rev: Value, dates, and gentian plant

Date	Mintage	F	VF	XF	Unc	BU
Yr.9(1997) Proof	55,000	Value: 675				

Y# 121   10000 YEN
15.6000 g., 1.0000 Gold 0.5015 oz. AGW, 26 mm. **Ruler:** Akihito
(Heisei) **Series:** 1998 Nagano Winter Olympics **Obv:** Figure
skater **Rev:** Value, dates, and gentian plant

Date	Mintage	F	VF	XF	Unc	BU
Yr.9(1997) Proof	55,000	Value: 675				

Y# 122   10000 YEN
15.6000 g., 1.0000 Gold 0.5015 oz. AGW, 26 mm. **Ruler:** Akihito
(Heisei) **Series:** 1998 Nagano Winter Olympics **Obv:** Speed
skater **Rev:** Value, dates, and gentian plant

Date	Mintage	F	VF	XF	Unc	BU
Yr.10(1998) Proof	55,000	Value: 675				

Y# 124   10000 YEN
20.0000 g., 1.0000 Gold 0.6430 oz. AGW **Ruler:** Akihito (Heisei)
Subject: 10th Anniversary of Enthronement **Obv:**
Chrysanthemum within wreath **Rev:** Stylized Green Phoenix

Date	Mintage	F	VF	XF	Unc	BU
Yr.11(1999) Proof	200,000	Value: 1,200				

Y# 109   50000 YEN
18.0000 g., 1.0000 Gold 0.5787 oz. AGW, 27 mm. **Ruler:** Akihito
(Heisei) **Subject:** Royal wedding of Crown Prince
Obv: Chrysanthemum flanked by cherry blossom sprigs
Rev: Pair of herons

Date	Mintage	VG	F	VF	XF	BU
Yr.5(1993)	1,900,000	—	—	—	—	650
Yr.5(1993) Proof	100,000	Value: 850				

Y# 92   100000 YEN
20.0000 g., 1.0000 Gold 0.6430 oz. AGW, 30 mm.
Ruler: Hirohito (Showa) **Subject:** 60 Years - Reign of Hirohito
Obv: Large chrysanthemum with legends around border
Rev: Pair of birds within artistic design

Date	Mintage	VG	F	VF	XF	BU
Yr.61(1986)	10,000,000	—	—	—	—	1,250
Yr.62(1987)	876,000	—	—	—	—	1,250
Yr.62(1987) Proof	124,000	Value: 1,350				

Y# 105   100000 YEN
30.0000 g., 1.0000 Gold 0.9645 oz. AGW, 33 mm. **Ruler:** Akihito
(Heisei) **Subject:** Enthronement of Emperor Akihito **Obv:**
Chrysanthemum within wreath **Rev:** Stylized Green Phoenix

Date	Mintage	VG	F	VF	XF	BU
Yr.3(1990)	1,900,000	—	—	—	—	1,250
Yr.3(1990) Proof	100,000	Value: 1,350				

PLATINUM BULLION COINAGE

KM# 20   10 MOMME
Platinum APW   **Ruler:** Hirohito (Showa)

Date	Mintage	VG	F	VF	XF	BU
1937	1,500	—	—	—	—	2,000

LEPROSARIUM COINAGE

KM# L11   SEN
Brass   **Issuer:** Oshima-Seisho En **Obv:** Denomination with
mulitple stamps **Rev:** "Ken" symbol = inspection

Date	Mintage	F	VF	XF	Unc	BU
ND(1912-25) Rare	—	—	—	—	—	—

KM# L20   SEN
Japanned (Lacquered) Brass   **Issuer:** Tama-Zensei En
Note: Uniface. Oval with central hole, denomination, rays at
border.

Date	Mintage	F	VF	XF	Unc	BU
ND(1926-28) Rare	—	—	—	—	—	—

KM# L1   SEN
Japanned (Lacquered) Brass   **Issuer:** Nagashima-Aisei En
Note: Uniface. Badge of Aisei En above denomination.

Date	Mintage	F	VF	XF	Unc	BU
ND(1931-48) Rare	—	—	—	—	—	—

KM# L2   SEN
Japanned Aluminum   **Issuer:** Nagashima-Aisei En

Date	Mintage	F	VF	XF	Unc	BU
ND(1931-48)	—	—	—	450	750	—

KM# L12   2 SEN
Brass   **Issuer:** Oshima-Seisho En

Date	Mintage	F	VF	XF	Unc	BU
ND(1912-25) Rare	—	—	—	—	—	—

KM# L13 5 SEN
Brass **Issuer:** Oshima-Seisho En

Date	Mintage	F	VF	XF	Unc	BU
ND(1912-25) Rare	—	—	—	—	—	—

KM# L21 5 SEN
Japanned (Lacquered) Brass **Issuer:** Tama-Zensei En **Note:** Round with central hole, perpendicular rays fill border from flower.

Date	Mintage	F	VF	XF	Unc	BU
ND(1926-28) Rare	—	—	—	—	—	—

KM# L3 5 SEN
Japanned (Lacquered) Brass **Issuer:** Nagashima-Aisei En

Date	Mintage	F	VF	XF	Unc	BU
ND(1931-48) Rare	—	—	—	—	—	—

KM# L3a 5 SEN
Japanned Aluminum **Issuer:** Nagashima-Aisei En

Date	Mintage	F	VF	XF	Unc	BU
ND(1931-48)	—	—	750	1,250	—	—

KM# L14 10 SEN
Brass **Issuer:** Oshima-Seisho En

Date	Mintage	F	VF	XF	Unc	BU
ND(1912-25) Rare	—	—	—	—	—	—

KM# L22 10 SEN
Japanned (Lacquered) Brass **Issuer:** Tama-Zensei En **Note:** Similar to 5 Sen, L21.

Date	Mintage	F	VF	XF	Unc	BU
ND(1926-28) Rare	—	—	—	—	—	—

KM# L4 10 SEN
Japanned (Lacquered) Brass **Issuer:** Nagashima-Aisei En

Date	Mintage	F	VF	XF	Unc	BU
ND(1931-48) Rare	—	—	—	—	—	—

KM# L4a 10 SEN
Japanned Aluminum **Issuer:** Nagashima-Aisei En

Date	Mintage	F	VF	XF	Unc	BU
ND(1931-48)	—	—	750	1,250	—	—

KM# L15 20 SEN
Brass **Issuer:** Oshima-Seisho En

Date	Mintage	F	VF	XF	Unc	BU
ND(1912-25) Rare	—	—	—	—	—	—

KM# L16 50 SEN
Brass **Issuer:** Oshima-Seisho En

Date	Mintage	F	VF	XF	Unc	BU
ND(1912-25) Rare	—	—	—	—	—	—

KM# L23 50 SEN
Japanned (Lacquered) Brass **Issuer:** Tama-Zensei En
Note: Rectangular with center hole. Sunset with ornate border.

Date	Mintage	F	VF	XF	Unc	BU
ND(1926-28) Rare	—	—	—	—	—	—

KM# L5 50 SEN
Japanned (Lacquered) Brass **Issuer:** Nagashima-Aisei En

Date	Mintage	F	VF	XF	Unc	BU
ND(1931-48)	—	—	900	1,500	—	—

KM# L6 YEN
Brass **Issuer:** Nagashima-Aisei En **Rev:** Stylized badge of Ansei En

Date	Mintage	F	VF	XF	Unc	BU
ND(1931-48)	—	—	1,500	2,500	—	—

OCCUPATION COINAGE

The following issues were struck at the Osaka Mint for use in the Netherlands East Indies. The only inscription found on them is Dai Nippon: Great Japan. The war situation had worsened to the point that shipping the coins became virtually impossible. Consequently, none of these coins were issued in the East Indies and almost the entire issue was lost or were remelted at the mint. Y numbers are for the Netherlands Indies and dates are from the Japanese Shinto dynastic calendar.

Y# A66 SEN
Aluminum **Obv:** Puppet's head **Note:** Prev. NEI Y#22.

Date	Mintage	F	VF	XF	Unc	BU
NE2603 (1943)	233,190,000	250	300	350	400	500
NE2604 (1944)	66,810,000	175	200	250	350	450

Y# B66 5 SEN
Aluminum **Rev:** Stick puppet **Note:** Prev. NEI Y#23.

Date	Mintage	F	VF	XF	Unc	BU
NE2603 (1943)	—	6,000	7,500	10,000	—	—

Y# 66 10 SEN
Tin Alloy **Rev:** Stick puppet **Note:** Prev. NEI Y#24.

Date	Mintage	F	VF	XF	Unc	BU
NE2603 (1943)	69,490,000	125	150	175	225	350
NE2604 (1944)	110,510,000	90.00	100	150	225	350

PATTERNS
Including off metal strikes

KM#	Date	Mintage	Identification	Mkt Val
Pn32	Yr.34 (1901)	—	Yen. Silver.	—
Pn31	Yr.34 (1901)	—	Yen. Copper.	3,250
Pn33	Yr.39 (1906)	—	5 Rin. Copper.	3,250
Pn34	Yr.41(1908)	—	Sen. Copper.	3,250
Pn35	Yr.42 (1909)	—	5 Rin. Copper.	3,250
Pn37	Yr.44 (1911)	—	Sen. Copper.	3,250
Pn36	Yr.42 (1911)	—	Sen. Copper.	—
Pn38	Yr.5 (1915)	—	Sen. Copper.	3,250
Pn39	Yr.5 (1916)	—	5 Rin. Copper.	3,250
Pn40	Yr.5 (1916)	—	5 Rin. Copper.	3,250
Pn41	Yr.5 (1916)	—	Sen. Copper.	3,250
Pn44	Yr.5 (1916)	—	5 Sen. Copper-Nickel.	3,250
Pn42	Yr.5 (1916)	—	Sen.	—
Pn43	Yr.5 (1916)	—	Sen.	—
Pn48	Yr.7 (1918)	—	50 Sen.	—
Pn45	Yr.7 (1918)	—	10 Sen. Silver.	8,250
Pn46	Yr.7 (1918)	—	20 Sen. Silver.	10,000
Pn47	Yr.7 (1918)	—	50 Sen. Silver.	11,000
Pn49	Yr.8 (1919)	—	10 Sen. Silver.	7,500
Pn50	Yr.8 (1919)	—	20 Sen. Silver.	8,500
Pn51	Yr.8 (1919)	—	20 Sen. Silver.	12,500
Pn52	Yr.9 (1920)	—	25 Sen. Silver.	—
Pn53	Yr.9 (1920)	—	50 Sen. Silver.	—
Pn54	Yr.10 (1921)	—	20 Sen. Silver. Yr.10	4,000
Pn55	Yr.12 (1923)	—	50 Sen. Tin.	850
Pn56	Yr.15 (1926)	—	50 Sen. Tin.	1,650
Pn57	Yr.2 (1927)	—	50 Sen. Brass.	625
Pn58	Yr.2 (1927)	—	50 Sen. Silver.	3,000
Pn59	Yr.2 (1927)	—	50 Sen. Brass.	575
Pn60	Yr.2 (1927)	—	50 Sen. Silver.	3,000
Pn61	Yr.3 (1928)	—	50 Sen. Tin. Y#50.	400
Pn62	Yr.8 (1933)	—	5 Sen. Nickel. Y#54.	—
Pn63	Yr.8 (1933)	—	10 Sen. Nickel. Y#53.	—
Pn64	Yr.12 (1937)	—	5 Sen. Brass.	—
Pn65	Yr.12 (1937)	—	10 Sen. Brass.	—
Pn66	Yr.13 (1938)	—	Sen. Aluminum.	—
Pn67	Yr.13 (1938)	—	5 Sen.	—
Pn68	Yr.13 (1938)	—	10 Sen.	—
Pn69	ND(1938)	—	50 Sen. White Metal. Y#50	2,500
Pn70	ND(1943)	—	Sen. Tin Alloy. Occupation issue Y#22	—
Pn71	ND(1943)	—	Sen. Red Fiber. Occupation issue Y#22	—
Pn72	Yr.2603 (1943)	—	5 Sen. Tin Alloy. Y#23.	—
PnA73	Yr.2603 (1943)	—	10 Sen. Silver. Yr. 2603; Y#24	—
Pn73	Yr.20 (1945)	—	Sen. Brass. Y#62.	—
PnA74	ND(1945)	—	Sen. Red-Brown Porcelain.	150
Pn74	Yr.20 (1945)	—	Sen. White Porcelain. Numerous designs exist.	150
Pn75	Yr.20 (1945)	—	Sen. Red-Brown Porcelain. Numerous designs exist.	150
Pn76	Yr.20 (1945)	—	5 Sen. White Porcelain. Numerous designs exist.	150
Pn77	Yr.20 (1945)	—	5 Sen. Red-Brown Porcelain. Numerous designs exist.	150
Pn78	Yr.20 (1945)	—	10 Sen. White Porcelain. Numerous designs exist.	150
Pn79	Yr.20 (1945)	—	10 Sen. Red-Brown Porcelain. Numerous designs exist.	150
Pn80	Yr.21 (1946)	—	10 Sen. Brass. Small size; Y#68.	—
Pn81	Yr.25 (1950)	—	Yen. Brass. Y#70.	—
Pn82	Yr.25 (1950)	—	10 Yen. Aluminum. Y#73.	—
Pn83	Yr.25 (1950)	—	10 Yen. Copper-Nickel.	1,000
Pn85	Yr.26 (1951)	—	10 Yen. Copper-Nickel.	1,150
Pn84	Yr.26 (1951)	—	5 Yen. Aluminum. Y#72.	—
Pn86	Yr.33 (1958)	—	5 Yen. Brass.	—

MINT SETS

KM#	Date	Mintage	Identification	Issue Price	Mkt Val
MS1	1969 (5)	6,162	Y#72a, 73a, 74, 81, 82	1.25	800
MS2	1970 (6)	26,000	Y#72a, 73a, 74, 81-83	2.00	80.00
MS3	1971 (5)	14,653	Y#72a, 73a, 74, 81, 82	1.60	120
MS4	1972 (6)	30,000	Y#72a, 73a, 74, 81, 82, 84	2.90	60.00
MS5	1975 (5)	720,000	Y#72a, 73a, 74, 81, 82	2.30	6.00
MS6	1976 (5)	580,000	Y#72a, 73a, 74, 81, 82	2.80	6.00
MS7	1977 (5)	520,000	Y#72a, 73a, 74, 81, 82	3.00	6.00
MS8	1978 (5)	488,000	Y#72a, 73a, 74, 81, 82	3.50	7.00
MS9	1979 (5)	400,000	Y#72a, 73a, 74, 81, 82	3.80	7.00
MS10	1980 (5)	520,000	Y#72a, 73a, 74, 81, 82	3.20	6.50
MS11	1981 (5)	568,000	Y#72a, 73a, 74, 81, 82	4.00	6.50
MS12	1982 (6)	632,000	Y#72a, 73a, 74, 81, 82, 87	6.80	10.00
MS13	1983 (6)	502,000	Y#72a, 73a, 74, 81, 82, 87	6.80	15.00
MS14	1984 (6)	520,000	Y#72a, 73a, 74, 81, 82, 87	7.40	18.00
MS15	1985 (7)	720,000	Y#72a, 73a, 74, 81, 82, 87, 88 Tsukuba Expo box	8.50	20.00
MS16	1985 (7)	100,000	Y#72a, 73a, 74, 81, 82, 87, 88 Tsukuba Expo box, sold on the grounds of the Expo	8.50	130
MS17	1985 (7)	746,000	Y#72a, 73a, 74, 81, 82, 87, 89	10.50	20.00
MS18	1986 (7)	642,000	Y#72a, 73a, 74, 81, 82, 87, 90	15.00	25.00
MS19	1986 (6)	519,000	Y#72a, 73a, 74, 81, 82, 87	9.20	12.00
MSA20	1986-1987 (2)	3,296	Y#92 (1986), Y#92 (1987) 60 years of Reign - Hirohito	1,868	6,000
MS20	1987 (6)	496,463	Y#72a, 73a, 74, 81, 82, 87	12.00	175

KM#	Date	Mintage	Identification	Issue Price	Mkt Val
MS21	1987 (6)	48,537	Y#72a, 73a, 74, 81, 82, 87 Cherry blossom box	12.00	200
MSB20	1987 (3)	13,832	Y#90-92 60 years of Reign - Hirohito	1,040	2,000
MS22	1988 (6)	605,021	Y#72a, 73a, 74, 81, 82, 87	12.40	13.00
MS23	1988 (6)	41,979	Y#72a, 73a, 74, 81, 82, 87 Cherry blossom box	12.40	30.00
MS24	1988 (2)	400,000	Y#93-94	15.20	20.00
MS25	1989 (6)	647,000	Y#95.1-99.1, 101.1	12.80	30.00
MS26	1990 (6)	600,000	Y#95.2-99.2, 101.2	12.00	13.00
MSA26	1990 (2)	100,000	Y#103, 104 Centenaries of Parliament and the Judicial System	94.00	175
MSA27	1991 (2)	100,000	Y#102, 105 Enthronement of Emperor Akihito (coins dated 1990)	850	1,300
MS27	1991 (6)	600,000	Y#95.2-99.2, 101.2	13.00	13.00
MS28	1991 (6)	10,000	Y#95.2-99.2, 101.2 Hiroshima cherry blossom box	13.60	60.00
MS29	1991 (6)	50,000	Y#95.2-99.2, 101.2 Osaka cherry blossom box	13.60	24.00
MS30	1991 (6)	40,000	Y#95.2-99.2, 101.2 "120th Anniversary of the Mint" box	13.60	20.00
MS34	1992 (6)	30,000	Y#95.2-99.2, 101.2 Toyama Expo box	13.60	30.00
MS31	1992 (7)	700,000	Y#95.2-99.2, 101.2, 106	18.40	26.20
MS32	1992 (6)	20,000	Y#95.2-99.2, 101.2 Hiroshima cherry blossom box	13.60	30.00
MS33	1992 (6)	50,000	Y#95.2-99.2, 101.2 Osaka cherry blossom box	13.60	25.00
MS35	1993 (7)	800,000	Y#95.2-99.2, 101.2, 107	22.50	23.00
MS36	1993 (6)	70,000	Y#95.2-99.2, 101.2 Osaka cherry blossom box	17.10	30.00
MS37	1993 (6)	30,000	Y#95.2-99.2, 101.2 Hiroshima cherry blossom box	17.10	30.00
MS38	1993 (6)	10,000	Y#95.2-99.2, 101.2 Tokyo Coin Expo box	17.10	45.00
MS39	1993 (6)	30,000	Y#95.2-99.2, 101.2 Nagano-Shinano Expo box	17.10	27.50
MS40	1993 (6)	100,000	Y#95.2-99.2, 101.2 "Respect for the Aged" box	19.80	20.00
MS41	1994 (6)	80,000	Y#95.2-99.2, 101.2 Osaka cherry blossom box	19.00	32.50
MS42	1994 (6)	20,000	Y#95.2-99.2, 101.2 Hiroshima cherry blossom box	19.00	30.00
MS43	1994 (6)	10,000	Y#95.2-99.2, 101.2 "5th International Tokyo Coin Convention" box	19.00	32.50
MS44	1994 (6)	10,000	Y#95.2-99.2, 101.2 "Transfer of the Heian Capital" box	19.00	125
MS45	1994 (6)	30,000	Y#95.2-99.2, 101.2 "Mie Festival Exposition" box	19.00	30.00
MS46	1994 (6)	570,000	Y#95.2-99.2, 101.2 Mint box	18.00	18.00
MS47	1994 (6)	100,000	Y#95.2-99.2, 101.2 "Respect for the Aged" box	22.00	20.00
MS48	1994 (6)	10,000	Y#95.2-99.2, 101.2 "Tokyo Branch Mint Coin Fair" box	19.00	30.00
MSA49	1994 (1)	20,000	Y#99.2 Mint visit souvenir folder	9.00	15.00
MS49	1995 (6)	80,000	Y#95.2-99.2, 101.2 Osaka cherry blossom box	19.00	30.00
MS50	1995 (6)	10,000	Y#95.2-99.2, 101.2 Hiroshima cherry blossom box	19.00	32.50
MS51	1995 (6)	10,000	Y#95.2-99.2, 101.2 6th Tokyo International Coin Convention	19.00	32.50
MS52	1995 (6)	10,000	Y#95.2-99.2, 101.2 "Romantopia '95" box	19.00	35.00
MS53	1995 (6)	10,000	Y#95.2-99.2, 101.2 "Coin and Banknote Fair" box	19.00	32.50
MS54	1995 (6)	12,000	Y#95.2-99.2, 101.2 50th Anniversary Hiroshima Branch Mint	19.00	32.50
MS55	1995 (6)	355,000	Y#95.2-99.2, 101.2 Mint production scenes box	18.00	18.00
MS56	1995 (6)	200,000	Y#95.2-99.2, 101.2 "Respect for the Aged" box	22.00	20.00
MS57	1995 (6)	390,000	Y#95.2-99.2, 101.2 Horyuji Temple folder	19.00	19.00
MS58	1995 (6)	192,500	Y#95.2-99.2, 101.2 Himeji Castle folder	19.00	20.00
MS59	1995 (6)	191,500	Y#95.2-99.2, 101.2 Ancient Kyoto folder	19.00	20.00
MS60	1995 (6)	177,500	Y#95.2-99.2, 101.2 Yakushima folder	19.00	20.00
MS61	1995 (6)	174,500	Y#95.2-99.2, 101.2 Shirakami Mountains folder	19.00	20.00
MS62	1995 (6)	10,000	Y#95.2-99.2, 101.2 "Tokyo Mint Fair" box	18.00	30.00
MS63	1995 (1)	20,000	Y#99.2 Mint visit souvenir folder	8.50	12.00
MS64	1995 (6)	20,000	Y#95.2-99.2, 101.2 Birthday folder	20.00	30.00
MS65	1996 (6)	80,000	Y#95.2-99.2, 101.2 Osaka cherry blossom box	17.00	35.00
MS66	1996 (6)	10,000	Y#95.2-99.2, 101.2 Hiroshima cherry blossom box	17.00	35.00
MS67	1996 (1)	10,000	Y#99.2 Mint visit souvenir folder	8.00	12.00
MS68	1996 (6)	10,000	Y#95.2-99.2, 101.2 Birthday folder	19.00	35.00
MS69	1996 (6)	10,000	Y#95.2-99.2, 101.2 "7th Tokyo International Coin Convention" box	17.00	32.50
MS70	1996 (6)	20,000	Y#95.2-99.2, 101.2 "Saga World Ceramics Expo" box	17.00	30.00
MS71	1996 (6)	8,000	Y#95.2-99.2, 101.2 "Okayama Coin, Banknote, and Stamp Exhibition" box	17.00	35.00
MS72	1996 (6)	290,000	Y#95.2-99.2, 101.2 Shirakawa district folder	18.00	23.00
MS73	1996 (6)	200,000	Y#95.2-99.2, 101.2 "Respect for the Aged" box	20.00	28.00
MS74	1996 (6)	100,000	Y#95.2-99.2, 101.2 "125th Anniversary Birth of the Yen" folder	27.00	70.00
MS75	1996 (6)	321,000	Y#95.2-99.2, 101.2 Aerial view of old and new mint box	16.00	28.00
MS76	1996 (6)	6,000	Y#95.2-99.2, 101.2 Tokyo Branch Mint fair box	17.00	32.50
MS77	1997 (1)	10,000	Y#101.2 Mint visit souvenir folder	8.00	12.00
MS78	1997 (6)	12,000	Y#95.2-99.2, 101.2 Anniversary folder	17.00	32.50
MS79	1997 (6)	80,000	Y#95.2-99.2, 101.2 Osaka cherry blossom box	16.00	32.50
MS80	1997 (6)	10,000	Y#95.2-99.2, 101.2 Hiroshima cherry blossom box	16.00	35.00
MS81	1997 (6)	10,000	Y#95.2-99.2, 101.2 "8th Tokyo International Coin Convention" box	16.00	30.00
MS82	1997 (6)	10,000	Y#95.2-99.2, 101.2 Tottori '97 Expo box	16.00	35.00
MS83	1997 (6)	10,000	Y#95.2-99.2, 101.2 Yamagata Coin, Note, and Stamp Exhibition box	16.00	35.00
MS84	1997 (6)	331,000	Y#95.2-99.2, 101.2 Mint Bureau box	14.00	20.00
MS85	1997 (6)	250,000	Y#95.2-99.2, 101.2 "Respect for the Aged" box	15.50	22.00
MS86	1997 (6)	8,000	Y#95.2-99.2, 101.2 Tokyo Mint Fair box	15.00	30.00
MS87	1997 (6)	195,000	Y#95.2-99.2, 101.2 Hiroshima Peace Dome folder	15.50	24.00
MS88	1997 (6)	205,000	Y#95.2-99.2, 101.2 Itsukushima Shrine folder	15.50	24.00
MS89	1998 (1)	10,000	Y#99.2 Mint visit souvenir folder	7.00	12.00
MS90	1998 (6)	10,000	Y#95.2-99.2, 101.2 Anniversary folder	16.00	35.00
MS91	1998 (6)	81,000	Y#95.2-99.2, 101.2 Osaka cherry blossom box	14.50	32.50
MS92	1998 (6)	10,000	Y#95.2-99.2, 101.2 Hiroshima cherry blossom box	14.50	32.50
MS93	1998 (6)	13,000	Y#95.2-99.2, 101.2 "9th Tokyo International Coin Convention" box	14.50	30.00
MS94	1998 (6)	257,000	Y#95.2-99.2, 101.2 "Respect for the Aged" box	17.00	25.00
MS95	1998 (6)	10,000	Y#95.2-99.2, 101.2 "World Cup - Japan vs. Argentina" box	17.00	45.00
MS96	1998 (6)	10,000	Y#95.2-99.2, 101.2 "World Cup - Japan vs. Croatia" box	17.00	45.00
MS97	1998 (6)	10,000	Y#95.2-99.2, 101.2 "World Cup - Japan vs. Jamaica" box	17.00	45.00
MS98	1998 (6)	336,000	Y#95.2-99.2, 101.2 Mint Bureau box	17.50	24.00
MS99	1998 (6)	6,000	Y#95.2-99.2, 101.2 Tokyo Mint Fair box	18.05	30.00
MS100	1999 (6)	20,000	Y#95.2-99.2, 101.2 Anniversary folder	19.95	35.00
MS101	1999 (1)	20,000	Y#99.2 Mint visit souvenir folder	8.55	12.00
MS102	1999 (6)	6,000	Y#95.2-99.2, 101.2 Kumamoto mint box	1,805	45.00
MS103	1999 (6)	80,000	Y#95.2-99.2, 101.2 Osaka cherry blossom box	18.05	32.50
MS104	1999 (6)	10,000	Y#95.2-99.2, 101.2 Hiroshima cherry blossom box	18.05	35.00
MS105	1999 (6)	10,000	Y#95.2-99.2, 101.2 10th Tokyo International Coin Convention box	18.05	30.00
MS106	1999 (6)	6,000	Y#95.2-99.2, 101.2 Akita exhibit box	18.55	35.00
MS107	1999 (6)	6,000	Y#95.2-99.2, 101.2 Tokyo mint box	18.55	35.00
MS108	1999 (6)	200,000	Y#95.2-99.2, 101.2 Nara Monasteries folder	18.55	32.50
MS109	1999 (6)	250,000	Y#95.2-99.2, 101.2 "Respect for the Aged" box	18.55	32.50
MS110	1999 (6)	300,000	Y#95.2-99.2, 101.2 Mint Bureau box	18.55	35.00
MS111	2000 (5)	5,000	Y#95.2-98.2, 101.2 Mint exhibition in Nagoya box	11.00	55.00
MS112	2000 (6)	65,000	Y#95.2-99.2, 101.2 Osaka cherry blossom box	11.00	50.00
MS113	2000 (6)	10,000	Y#95.2-98.2, 101.2, 125 Hiroshima cherry blossom box	11.00	45.00
MS114	2000 (5)	10,000	Y#95.2-98.2, 101.2, 125 400th Anniversary Japanese-Dutch relation at Nagsaki box	11.00	50.00
MS115	2000 (5)	10,000	Y#95.2-98.2, 101.2, 125 11th Tokyo International Coin Convention box	11.00	50.00
MS116	2000 (6)	7,000	Y#95.2-98.2, 101.2, 125 Otaru Coin and Stamp Show box	11.00	35.00
MS117	2000 (6)	4,000	Y#95.2-98.2, 101.2, 125 Tokyo Mint Fair box	11.00	45.00
MS118	2000 (5)	5,600	Y#95.2-99.2, 101.2 "Japan Coin Set" box	17.00	35.00
MS119	2000 (2)	4,000	Y#96.2, 125 "Japan Coins" short set	8.50	30.00
MS120	2000 (5)	222,300	Y#95.2-99.2, 101.2 Nikko World Cultural Sites	17.00	35.00
MS121	2000 (5)	340,200	Y#95.2-99.2, 101.2 Mint Bureau box	15.00	30.00
MS122	2000 (6)	4,500	Y#95.2-98.2, 101.2, 125 Anniversary box	18.00	50.00
MS123	2000 (12)	155,400	Y#95.2-98.2, 101.2, 125 Millennium Respect for the Aged box	19.00	30.00
MS124	2000 (12)	8,000	Y#95.2-98.2, 101.2, 125 Branch mint in Kanazawa box	16.00	35.00

PROOF SETS

KM#	Date	Mintage	Identification	Issue Price	Mkt Val
PS1	1987 (6)	230,000	Y#72a, 73a, 74, 81, 82, 87	37.40	150
PS2	1988 (6)	200,000	Y#72a, 73a, 74, 81, 82, 87	46.50	45.00
PS3	1989 (6)	200,000	Y#95.1-99.1, 101.1	47.90	45.00
PS4	1990 (6)	200,000	Y#95.2-99.2, 101.2	47.90	55.00
PS5	1991 (6)	220,000	Y#95.2-99.2, 101.2	58.75	55.00
PS6	1992 (6)	250,000	Y#95.2-99.2, 101.2	55.65	50.00
PS7	1993 (6)	250,000	Y#95.2-99.2, 101.2	72.00	50.00
PS8	1993 (3)	100,000	Y#107-109 Crown Prince's Wedding	630	900
PS9	1993 (2)	100,000	Y#107-108 Crown Prince's Wedding	100	115
PS10	1994 (6)	227,000	Y#95.2-99.2, 101.2	72.00	50.00
PS11	1994 (3)	100,000	Y#111-113 12th Asian Games	68.00	90.00
PS12	1994 (1)	100,000	Y#110 Kansai Airport	27.00	40.00
PS13	1995 (6)	200,000	Y#95.2-99.2, 101.2	72.00	55.00
PS14	1996 (6)	189,000	Y#95.2-99.2, 101.2	103	65.00
PS15	1997 (3)	33,000	Y#114-116 Nagano Olympics	413	810
PS16	1997 (3)	100,000	Y#114-115 Nagano Olympics	99.00	160
PS17	1997 (3)	33,000	Y#117, 119, 121 Nagano Olympics	406	810
PS18	1997 (2)	100,000	Y#117, 119 Nagano Olympics	97.00	160
PS19	1997 (6)	1,000	Y#95.2-99.2, 101.2 "Japan Expo Tottori '97"	59.00	1,300
PS20	1997 (6)	186,000	Y#95.2-99.2, 101.2	56.00	65.00
PS21	1997 (6)	25,000	Y#95.2-99.2, 101.2 Tokyo Bay Aqualine Opening	56.00	110
PS22	1998 (3)	33,000	Y#118, 120, 122 Nagano Olympics	375	800
PS23	1998 (2)	100,000	Y#118, 120 Nagano Olympics	90.00	100
PS24	1998 (6)	30,000	Y#95.2-99.2, 101.2 Akashi Strait Bridge Opening	59.00	85.00
PS25	1998 (6)	170,000	Y#95.2-99.2, 101.2 Mint Bureau box	62.50	60.00
PS26	1999 (6)	80,000	Y#95.2-99.2, 101.2 Old Type Coin series (20 yen medallet)	69.85	100
PS27	1999 (6)	50,000	Y#95.2-99.2, 101.2 Coastal Highway	69.85	100
PS28	1999 (6)	150,000	Y#95.2-99.2, 101.2 Bureau box	69.85	85.00
PS29	1999 (2)	100,000	Y#123, 124 10th Anniversary of Enthronement	370	400
PS30	2000 (6)	100,000	Y#95.2-98.2, 101.2, 125 Old Type Coin Series (1 yen crown medallet)	62.50	80.00
PS31	2000 (6)	126,000	Y#95.2-98.2, 101.2, 125 Mint Bureau Box	62,350	80.00

JERSEY

UNITED KINGDOM
NETHERLANDS
English Channel
BELGIUM
LUXEMBOURG
FRANCE
SWITZERLAND

The Bailiwick of Jersey, a British Crown dependency located in the English Channel 12 miles (19 km.) west of Normandy, France, has an area of 45 sq. mi. (117 sq. km.) and a population of 74,000. Capital: St. Helier. The economy is based on agriculture and cattle breeding – the importation of cattle is prohibited to protect the purity of the island's world-famous strain of milch cows.

Jersey was occupied by Neanderthal man by 100,000 B.C., and by Iberians of 2000 B.C. who left their chamber tombs in the island's granite cliffs. Roman legions almost certainly visited the island although they left no evidence of settlement. The country folk of Jersey still speak an archaic form of Norman-French, lingering evidence of the Norman annexation of the island in 933 A.D. Jersey was annexed to England in 1206, 140 years after the Norman Conquest. The dependency is administered by its own laws and customs; laws enacted by the British Parliament do not apply to Jersey unless it is specifically mentioned. During World War II, German troops occupied the island from July 1, 1940 until May 9, 1945.

Coins of pre-Roman Gaul and of Rome have been found in abundance on Jersey.

RULER
British

MINT MARK
H - Heaton, Birmingham

MONETARY SYSTEM
Commencing 1877
12 Pence = 1 Shilling
5 Shillings = 1 Crown
20 Shillings = 1 Pound
100 New Pence = 1 Pound

BRITISH DEPENDENCY
STANDARD COINAGE

KM# 9 1/24 SHILLING
Bronze **Obv:** Crowned bust right **Rev:** Pointed shield divides date

Date	Mintage	F	VF	XF	Unc	BU
1909	120,000	1.00	2.50	11.50	40.00	—

KM# 11 1/24 SHILLING
Bronze **Obv:** Crowned bust left **Rev:** Pointed shield divides date

Date	Mintage	F	VF	XF	Unc	BU
1911	72,000	1.00	2.50	11.50	40.00	—
1913	72,000	1.00	2.50	11.50	28.00	—
1923	72,000	1.00	2.50	11.50	28.00	—

KM# 13 1/24 SHILLING
Bronze **Obv:** Crowned bust left **Rev:** Shield divides date

Date	Mintage	F	VF	XF	Unc	BU
1923	72,000	0.75	3.00	5.50	22.50	—
1923 Proof	—	Value: 550				
1926	120,000	0.75	2.50	4.50	20.00	—
1926 Proof	—	Value: 550				

KM# 15 1/24 SHILLING
Bronze **Obv:** Crowned bust left **Rev:** Shield divides date

Date	Mintage	F	VF	XF	Unc	BU
1931	72,000	0.50	1.00	3.00	15.00	—
1931 Proof	—	Value: 165				
1933	72,000	0.50	1.00	3.00	15.00	—
1933 Proof	—	Value: 165				
1935	72,000	0.50	1.00	3.00	15.00	—
1935 Proof	—	Value: 165				

KM# 17 1/24 SHILLING
Bronze **Obv:** Crowned head left **Rev:** Shield divides date

Date	Mintage	F	VF	XF	Unc	BU
1937	72,000	0.50	1.00	3.00	15.00	—
1937 Proof	—	Value: 125				
1946	72,000	0.50	1.00	3.00	15.00	—
1946 Proof	—	Value: 125				
1947	72,000	0.50	1.00	3.00	15.00	—
1947 Proof	—	Value: 125				

KM# 10 1/12 SHILLING
Bronze **Obv:** Crowned bust right **Rev:** Pointed shield divides date

Date	Mintage	F	VF	XF	Unc	BU
1909	180,000	0.75	3.50	12.50	60.00	—

KM# 12 1/12 SHILLING
9.4500 g., Bronze **Obv:** Crowned bust left **Rev:** Pointed shield divides date

Date	Mintage	F	VF	XF	Unc	BU
1911	204,000	0.50	1.50	5.00	35.00	—
1913	204,000	0.50	1.50	5.00	35.00	—
1923	204,000	0.50	1.50	5.00	35.00	—

KM# 14 1/12 SHILLING
Bronze **Obv:** Crowned bust left **Rev:** Shield divides date

Date	Mintage	F	VF	XF	Unc	BU
1923	301,000	0.75	2.50	8.00	30.00	—
1926	83,000	0.75	2.50	10.00	40.00	—

KM# 16 1/12 SHILLING
9.5000 g., Bronze **Obv:** Crowned bust left **Rev:** Shield divides date

Date	Mintage	F	VF	XF	Unc	BU
1931	204,000	0.50	1.25	3.00	20.00	—
1931 Proof	—	Value: 125				
1933	204,000	0.50	1.25	3.00	20.00	—
1933 Proof	—	Value: 125				
1935	204,000	0.50	1.25	3.00	20.00	—
1935 Proof	—	Value: 125				

KM# 18 1/12 SHILLING
Bronze **Obv:** Crowned head left **Rev:** Shield divides date

Date	Mintage	F	VF	XF	Unc	BU
1937	204,000	0.50	1.00	2.50	10.00	—
1937 Proof	—	Value: 125				
1946	204,000	0.50	1.00	2.50	10.00	—
1946 Proof	—	Value: 125				
1947	444,000	0.25	0.50	1.50	7.50	—
1947 Proof	—	Value: 125				

KM# 19 1/12 SHILLING
9.5900 g., Bronze, 21.1 mm. **Subject:** Liberation Commemorative **Obv:** Crowned head left **Rev:** Shield above written value

Date	Mintage	F	VF	XF	Unc	BU
1945	1,000,000	0.25	0.50	1.00	5.00	—
1945 Proof	—	Value: 100				

Note: Struck between 1949-52

KM# 20 1/12 SHILLING
9.4000 g., Bronze **Ruler:** Elizabeth II **Obv:** Crowned head right **Rev:** Shield above written value

Date	Mintage	F	VF	XF	Unc	BU
(1954)	720,000	0.25	0.50	1.00	3.50	—
(1954) Proof	—	Value: 100				

KM# 21 1/12 SHILLING
Bronze **Ruler:** Elizabeth II **Obv:** Crowned head right **Rev:** Shield above written value

Date	Mintage	F	VF	XF	Unc	BU
1957	720,000	0.25	0.45	0.75	2.00	—
1957 Proof	2,100	Value: 7.50				

Date	Mintage	F	VF	XF	Unc	BU
1964	1,200,000	0.25	0.45	0.75	1.50	—
1964 Proof	20,000	Value: 2.00				

KM# 24   1/12 SHILLING
Bronze **Ruler:** Elizabeth II **Obv:** Crowned head right **Rev:** Shield above dates and written value

Date	Mintage	F	VF	XF	Unc	BU
ND(1960) Proof	—	Value: 65.00				

KM# 23   1/12 SHILLING
Bronze **Ruler:** Elizabeth II **Subject:** 300th Anniversary - Accession of King Charles II **Obv:** Crowned head right **Rev:** Shield above dates and written value

Date	Mintage	F	VF	XF	Unc	BU
ND (1960)	1,200,000	0.25	0.45	0.75	1.50	—
ND (1960) Proof	4,200	Value: 4.00				

KM# 26   1/12 SHILLING
Bronze **Ruler:** Elizabeth II **Subject:** Norman Conquest **Obv:** Crowned head right **Rev:** Shield divides date

Date	Mintage	F	VF	XF	Unc	BU
ND (1966)	1,200,000	0.25	0.45	0.75	1.50	—
ND (1966) Proof	30,000	Value: 2.00				

KM# 22   1/4 SHILLING (3 Pence)
Nickel-Brass **Ruler:** Elizabeth II **Obv:** Crowned head right

Date	Mintage	F	VF	XF	Unc	BU
1957	2,000,000	0.10	0.15	0.50	3.00	—
1957 Proof	6,300	Value: 7.50				
1960 Proof	4,200	Value: 8.50				

KM# 25   1/4 SHILLING (3 Pence)
Nickel-Brass **Ruler:** Elizabeth II **Obv:** Crowned head right **Rev:** Shield divides date

Date	Mintage	F	VF	XF	Unc	BU
1964	1,200,000	0.10	0.15	0.20	0.75	—
1964 Proof	20,000	Value: 2.00				

KM# 27   1/4 SHILLING (3 Pence)
Nickel-Brass **Ruler:** Elizabeth II **Subject:** Norman Conquest **Obv:** Crowned head right **Rev:** Shield divides dates

Date	Mintage	F	VF	XF	Unc	BU
ND (1966)	1,200,000	0.10	0.15	0.35	1.25	—
ND (1966) Proof	30,000	Value: 2.00				

KM# 28   5 SHILLING
Copper-Nickel **Ruler:** Elizabeth II **Subject:** Norman Conquest **Obv:** Crowned head right **Rev:** Shield divides dates

Date	Mintage	F	VF	XF	Unc	BU
ND (1966)	300,000	—	1.50	2.50	4.00	—
ND (1966) Proof	30,000	Value: 7.00				

DECIMAL COINAGE
100 New Pence = 1 Pound

Many of the following coins are also struck in silver, gold, and platinum for collectors

KM# 29   1/2 NEW PENNY
Bronze, 17.14 mm. **Ruler:** Elizabeth II **Obv:** Young bust right **Rev:** Shield above written value and date

Date	Mintage	F	VF	XF	Unc	BU
1971	3,000,000	—	—	0.10	0.20	—
1980	200,000	—	—	0.10	0.20	—
1980 Proof	10,000	Value: 1.35				

KM# 45   1/2 PENNY
Bronze, 17.14 mm. **Ruler:** Elizabeth II **Obv:** Young bust right **Rev:** Shield divides date

Date	Mintage	F	VF	XF	Unc	BU
1981	50,000	—	—	—	0.15	—
1981 Proof	15,000	Value: 0.90				

KM# 30   NEW PENNY
3.5500 g., Bronze, 20.32 mm. **Ruler:** Elizabeth II **Obv:** Young bust right **Rev:** Shield above written value

Date	Mintage	F	VF	XF	Unc	BU
1971	4,500,000	—	—	0.10	0.20	—
1980	3,000,000	—	—	0.10	0.20	—
1980 Proof	10,000	Value: 1.80				

KM# 46   PENNY
3.5500 g., Bronze, 20.32 mm. **Ruler:** Elizabeth II **Obv:** Young bust right **Rev:** Shield divides date

Date	Mintage	F	VF	XF	Unc	BU
1981	50,000	—	—	0.10	0.20	—
1981 Proof	15,000	Value: 1.10				

KM# 54   PENNY
3.6400 g., Bronze, 20.23 mm. **Ruler:** Elizabeth II **Obv:** Young bust right **Rev:** Le Hocq Watchtower, St. Clement **Edge:** Plain

Date	Mintage	F	VF	XF	Unc	BU
1983	500,000	—	—	0.10	0.25	—
1984	1,000,000	—	—	0.10	0.25	—
1985	1,000,000	—	—	0.10	0.25	—
1986	2,000,000	—	—	0.10	0.25	—
1987	1,500,000	—	—	0.10	0.25	—
1988	1,000,000	—	—	0.10	0.25	—
1989	1,500,000	—	—	0.10	0.25	—
1990	2,000,000	—	—	0.10	0.25	—
1992					0.50	—

Note: In sets only

KM# 54a   PENNY
4.2000 g., 0.9250 Silver 0.1249 oz. ASW, 20.32 mm. **Ruler:** Elizabeth II **Obv:** Young bust right **Rev:** Le Hocq Watchtower, St. Clement

Date	Mintage	F	VF	XF	Unc	BU
1983 Proof	5,000	Value: 7.00				

KM# 54b   PENNY
Copper Plated Steel, 20.32 mm. **Ruler:** Elizabeth II **Obv:** Young bust right **Rev:** Le Hocq Watchtower, St. Clement

Date	Mintage	F	VF	XF	Unc	BU
1994	2,000,000	—	—	0.10	0.50	—
1997	320,000	—	—	0.10	0.50	—

KM# 103   PENNY
3.5500 g., Copper Plated Steel, 20.27 mm. **Ruler:** Elizabeth II **Obv:** Crowned head right **Rev:** Le Hoeq Watchtower, St. Clement **Edge:** Plain

Date	Mintage	F	VF	XF	Unc	BU
1998	9,300,000	—	—	0.10	0.50	—

KM# 31   2 NEW PENCE
7.1000 g., Bronze, 25.91 mm. **Ruler:** Elizabeth II **Obv:** Young bust right **Rev:** Shield above written value

Date	Mintage	F	VF	XF	Unc	BU
1971	2,225,000	—	—	0.15	0.30	—
1975	750,000	—	—	0.15	0.40	—
1980	2,000,000	—	—	0.15	0.30	—
1980 Proof	10,000	Value: 2.25				

KM# 47   2 PENCE
7.1000 g., Bronze, 25.91 mm. **Ruler:** Elizabeth II **Obv:** Young bust right **Rev:** Shield divides date

Date	Mintage	F	VF	XF	Unc	BU
1981	50,000	—	—	0.15	0.25	—
1981 Proof	15,000	Value: 1.35				

KM# 55 2 PENCE
7.1000 g., Bronze, 25.91 mm. **Ruler:** Elizabeth II **Obv:** Young bust right **Rev:** L'Hermitage, St. Helier

Date	Mintage	F	VF	XF	Unc	BU
1983	800,000	—	—	0.15	0.25	—
1984	750,000	—	—	0.15	0.25	—
1985	250,000	—	—	0.15	0.25	—
1986	1,000,000	—	—	0.15	0.25	—
1987	2,000,000	—	—	0.15	0.25	—
1988	750,000	—	—	0.15	0.25	—
1989	1,000,000	—	—	0.15	0.25	—
1990	2,600,000	—	—	0.15	0.25	—

KM# 55a 2 PENCE
8.4000 g., 0.9250 Silver 0.2498 oz. ASW, 25.91 mm. **Ruler:** Elizabeth II **Obv:** Young bust right **Rev:** L'Hermitage, St. Helier

Date	Mintage	F	VF	XF	Unc	BU
1983 Proof	5,000	Value: 10.00				

KM# 55b 2 PENCE
Copper Plated Steel, 25.91 mm. **Ruler:** Elizabeth II **Obv:** Young bust right **Rev:** L'Hermitage, St. Helier **Note:** Released into circulation in 1998.

Date	Mintage	F	VF	XF	Unc	BU
1992	—	—	—	0.15	0.50	—
1997 In sets only	—	—	—	0.15	0.50	—

KM# 104 2 PENCE
7.1000 g., Copper Plated Steel, 25.91 mm. **Ruler:** Elizabeth II **Obv:** Head with tiara right **Rev:** L'Hermitage, St. Helier **Edge:** Plain

Date	Mintage	F	VF	XF	Unc	BU
1998	50,000	—	—	0.15	0.50	—

KM# 32 5 NEW PENCE
5.6500 g., Copper-Nickel, 23.59 mm. **Ruler:** Elizabeth II **Obv:** Young bust right **Rev:** Shield above written value

Date	Mintage	F	VF	XF	Unc	BU
1968	3,600,000	—	0.15	0.25	1.00	—
1980	800,000	—	0.15	0.25	1.00	—
1980 Proof	10,000	Value: 2.75				

KM# 48 5 PENCE
5.6500 g., Copper-Nickel, 23.59 mm. **Ruler:** Elizabeth II **Obv:** Young bust right **Rev:** Shield divides date

Date	Mintage	F	VF	XF	Unc	BU
1981	50,000	—	0.15	0.25	1.00	—
1981 Proof	15,000	Value: 1.80				

KM# 56.1 5 PENCE
5.6500 g., Copper-Nickel, 23.59 mm. **Ruler:** Elizabeth II **Obv:** Young bust right **Rev:** Seymour Tower, Grouville, L'Avathison

Date	Mintage	F	VF	XF	Unc	BU
1983	400,000	—	0.10	0.20	1.00	—
1984	300,000	—	0.10	0.20	1.00	—
1985	600,000	—	0.10	0.20	1.00	—
1986	200,000	—	0.10	0.20	1.00	—
1987	—	—	—	—	0.50	—
Note: In sets only						
1988	400,000	—	0.10	0.20	1.00	—

KM# 56.1a 5 PENCE
6.6000 g., 0.9250 Silver 0.1963 oz. ASW, 23.59 mm. **Ruler:** Elizabeth II **Obv:** Young bust right **Rev:** Seymour Tower, Grouville, L'Avathison

Date	Mintage	F	VF	XF	Unc	BU
1983 Proof	5,000	Value: 10.00				

KM# 56.2 5 PENCE
Copper-Nickel, 18 mm. **Ruler:** Elizabeth II **Obv:** Young bust right **Rev:** Seymour Tower, Grouville, L'Avathison **Note:** Reduced size.

Date	Mintage	F	VF	XF	Unc	BU
1990	4,000,000	—	—	0.15	0.35	—
1991	2,000,000	—	—	0.15	0.35	—
1992	1,000,000	—	—	0.15	0.50	—
1993	2,000,000	—	—	0.15	0.50	—
1997	5,500	—	—	—	1.00	—
Note: In sets only						

KM# 105 5 PENCE
3.2900 g., Copper-Nickel, 18 mm. **Ruler:** Elizabeth II **Obv:** Head with tiara right **Rev:** Seymour Tower, Grouville, L'Avathigon **Edge:** Reeded

Date	Mintage	F	VF	XF	Unc	BU
1998	50,000	—	—	0.15	0.50	—

KM# 33 10 NEW PENCE
11.3000 g., Copper-Nickel, 28.5 mm. **Ruler:** Elizabeth II **Obv:** Young bust right **Rev:** Shield above written value

Date	Mintage	F	VF	XF	Unc	BU
1968	1,500,000	—	0.20	0.35	1.00	—
1975	1,022,000	—	0.20	0.30	0.90	—
1980	1,000,000	—	0.20	0.30	0.75	—
1980 Proof	10,000	Value: 5.50				

KM# 49 10 PENCE
11.3000 g., Copper-Nickel, 28.5 mm. **Ruler:** Elizabeth II **Obv:** Young bust right **Rev:** Shield divides date

Date	Mintage	F	VF	XF	Unc	BU
1981	50,000	—	—	0.30	1.00	—
1981 Proof	15,000	Value: 2.25				

KM# 57.1 10 PENCE
11.3000 g., Copper-Nickel, 28.5 mm. **Ruler:** Elizabeth II **Obv:** Young bust right **Rev:** La Houque Bie, Faldouet, St. Martin

Date	Mintage	F	VF	XF	Unc	BU
1983	30,000	—	—	0.30	1.00	—
1984	100,000	—	—	0.30	1.00	—
1985	100,000	—	—	0.30	1.00	—
1986	400,000	—	—	0.30	0.75	—
1987	800,000	—	—	0.30	0.75	—
1988	650,000	—	—	0.30	0.75	—
1989	700,000	—	—	0.30	0.75	—
1990	850,000	—	—	0.30	0.75	—

KM# 57.1a 10 PENCE
13.2000 g., 0.9250 Silver 0.3925 oz. ASW, 28.5 mm. **Ruler:** Elizabeth II **Obv:** Young bust right **Rev:** La Houque Bie, Faldouet, St. Martin

Date	Mintage	F	VF	XF	Unc	BU
1983 Proof	5,000	Value: 15.00				

KM# 57.2 10 PENCE
Copper-Nickel, 24.5 mm. **Ruler:** Elizabeth II **Obv:** Young bust right **Rev:** La Houque Bie, Faldouet, St. Martin **Note:** Reduced size.

Date	Mintage	F	VF	XF	Unc	BU
1992	7,000,000	—	—	0.30	0.50	—
1997	5,500	—	—	—	1.00	—
Note: In sets only						
1998	—	—	—	—	1.00	—

KM# 53 20 PENCE
5.0000 g., Copper-Nickel, 21.4 mm. **Ruler:** Elizabeth II **Subject:** 100th Anniversary of Lighthouse at Corbiere **Obv:** Young bust right **Rev:** Date below lighthouse

Date	Mintage	F	VF	XF	Unc	BU
1982	200,000	—	—	0.50	1.50	—

KM# 53a 20 PENCE
5.8300 g., 0.9250 Silver 0.1734 oz. ASW, 21.4 mm. **Ruler:** Elizabeth II **Subject:** 100th Anniversary of Lighthouse at Corbiere **Obv:** Young bust right **Rev:** Date below lighthouse

Date	Mintage	F	VF	XF	Unc	BU
1982 Proof	1,500	Value: 15.00				

KM# 66 20 PENCE
5.0000 g., Copper-Nickel, 21.4 mm. **Ruler:** Elizabeth II **Subject:** 100th Anniversary of Lighthouse at Corbiere **Obv:** Young bust right **Rev:** Written value below lighthouse

Date	Mintage	F	VF	XF	Unc	BU
1983	400,000	—	—	0.50	1.00	—
1984	250,000	—	—	0.50	1.00	—
1986	100,000	—	—	0.50	1.00	—
1987	100,000	—	—	0.50	1.00	—
1989	100,000	—	—	0.50	1.00	—
1990	150,000	—	—	0.50	1.00	—
1992	—	—	—	—	2.00	—
Note: In sets only						
1994	200,000	—	—	0.50	1.00	—
1996	250,000	—	—	0.50	1.00	—
1997	600,000	—	—	0.50	1.00	—
1998	—	—	—	0.50	1.00	—

KM# 66a 20 PENCE
5.8300 g., 0.9250 Silver 0.1734 oz. ASW, 21.4 mm. **Ruler:** Elizabeth II **Subject:** 100th Anniversary of Lighthouse at Corbiere **Obv:** Young bust right **Rev:** Written value below lighthouse

Date	Mintage	F	VF	XF	Unc	BU
1983 Proof	5,000	Value: 15.00				

KM# 107 20 PENCE
Copper-Nickel, 21.4 mm. **Ruler:** Elizabeth II **Obv:** Head with tiara right

Date	Mintage	F	VF	XF	Unc	BU
1998	90,000	—	—	0.50	1.00	—

KM# 44   25 PENCE
Copper-Nickel **Ruler:** Elizabeth II **Subject:** Queen's Silver Jubilee **Obv:** Young bust right **Rev:** Mont Orgueil Castle and Gorey Harbour

Date	Mintage	F	VF	XF	Unc	BU
ND(1977)	262,000	—	0.75	1.25	3.75	—

KM# 44a   25 PENCE
28.2800 g., 0.9250 Silver 0.8410 oz. ASW **Ruler:** Elizabeth II **Subject:** Queen's Silver Jubilee **Obv:** Young bust right **Rev:** Mont Orgueil and sailboats

Date	Mintage	F	VF	XF	Unc	BU
ND(1977) Proof	25,000	Value: 16.50				

KM# 34   50 PENCE
13.5000 g., Copper-Nickel, 30 mm. **Ruler:** Elizabeth II **Obv:** Young bust right **Rev:** Shield above written value

Date	Mintage	F	VF	XF	Unc	BU
1969	480,000	—	—	0.90	1.50	—
1980	100,000	—	—	0.90	1.50	—
1980 Proof	10,000	Value: 9.00				

KM# 35   50 PENCE
5.4200 g., 0.9250 Silver 0.1612 oz. ASW **Ruler:** Elizabeth II **Subject:** 25th Wedding Anniversary **Obv:** Young bust right **Rev:** Mace divides map

Date	Mintage	F	VF	XF	Unc	BU
1972	24,000	—	—	3.50	5.50	—
1972 Proof	1,500	Value: 7.50				

KM# 50   50 PENCE
13.5000 g., Copper-Nickel, 30 mm. **Ruler:** Elizabeth II **Obv:** Young bust right **Rev:** Shield divides date

Date	Mintage	F	VF	XF	Unc	BU
1981	50,000	—	—	1.00	1.75	—
1981 Proof	15,000	Value: 3.00				

KM# 58.1   50 PENCE
13.5000 g., Copper-Nickel, 30 mm. **Ruler:** Elizabeth II **Obv:** Young bust right **Rev:** Grosnez Castle

Date	Mintage	F	VF	XF	Unc	BU
1983	50,000	—	—	1.00	1.75	—
1984	50,000	—	—	1.00	1.75	—
1986	30,000	—	—	1.00	1.75	—
1987	150,000	—	—	1.00	1.75	—
1988	130,000	—	—	1.00	1.75	—
1989	180,000	—	—	1.00	1.75	—
1990	370,000	—	—	1.00	1.75	—
1992		—	—	—	2.50	—

Note: In sets only

1994	200,000	—	—	1.00	1.75	—
1997	5,500	—	—	—	2.50	—

Note: In sets only

KM# 58.1a   50 PENCE
15.5000 g., 0.9250 Silver 0.4609 oz. ASW, 30 mm. **Ruler:** Elizabeth II **Obv:** Young bust right **Rev:** Grosnez Castle

Date	Mintage	F	VF	XF	Unc	BU
1983 Proof	5,000	Value: 18.00				

KM# 58.2   50 PENCE
Copper-Nickel, 27.3 mm. **Ruler:** Elizabeth II **Obv:** Young bust right **Rev:** Grosnez Castle **Note:** Small size.

Date	Mintage	F	VF	XF	Unc	BU
1997	1,500,000	—	—	—	2.50	—

KM# 63   50 PENCE
13.5000 g., Copper-Nickel, 30 mm. **Ruler:** Elizabeth II **Subject:** 40th Anniversary - Liberation of 1945 **Obv:** Crowned bust right **Rev:** Crossed flags divides dates above chain links with value below

Date	Mintage	F	VF	XF	Unc	BU
1985	65,000	—	—	1.25	2.00	—

KM# 108   50 PENCE
Copper-Nickel, 27.3 mm. **Ruler:** Elizabeth II **Obv:** Crowned bust right **Rev:** Gothic gate arch **Edge:** Plain

Date	Mintage	F	VF	XF	Unc	BU
1998	25,000	—	—	1.00	2.50	—

KM# 36   POUND
10.8400 g., 0.9250 Silver 0.3224 oz. ASW **Ruler:** Elizabeth II **Subject:** 25th Wedding Anniversary **Obv:** Young bust right **Rev:** Lillies

Date	Mintage	F	VF	XF	Unc	BU
1972	24,000	—	—	—	7.00	—
1972 Proof	1,500	Value: 12.00				

KM# 51   POUND
9.0000 g., Copper-Nickel **Ruler:** Elizabeth II **Subject:** Bicentennial - Battle of Jersey **Obv:** Young bust right **Rev:** Badge of the Royal Jersey Militia

Date	Mintage	F	VF	XF	Unc	BU
ND(1981)	200,000	—	—	2.00	3.25	—
ND(1981) Proof	15,000	Value: 8.00				

KM# 51a   POUND
10.4500 g., 0.9250 Silver 0.3108 oz. ASW **Ruler:** Elizabeth II **Subject:** Bicentennial - Battle of Jersey **Obv:** Young bust right **Rev:** Crowned shaded pointed shield within X design divides dates

Date	Mintage	F	VF	XF	Unc	BU
ND(1981) Proof	10,000	Value: 12.50				

KM# 51b   POUND
17.5500 g., 0.9170 Gold 0.5174 oz. AGW **Ruler:** Elizabeth II **Subject:** Bicentennial - Battle of Jersey **Obv:** Young bust right **Rev:** Crowned shaded pointed shield within X design divides dates

Date	Mintage	F	VF	XF	Unc	BU
ND(1981) Proof	5,000	Value: 500				

KM# 59   POUND
9.5000 g., Nickel-Brass, 22.5 mm. **Ruler:** Elizabeth II **Obv:** Young bust right **Rev:** Shield above written value **Edge:** CAESAREA INSULA

Date	Mintage	F	VF	XF	Unc	BU
1983	100,000	—	—	2.00	3.25	—

KM# 59a   POUND
11.6800 g., 0.9250 Silver 0.3473 oz. ASW, 22.5 mm. **Ruler:** Elizabeth II **Obv:** Young bust right **Rev:** Shield above written value

Date	Mintage	F	VF	XF	Unc	BU
1983 Proof	2,500	Value: 20.00				

KM# 59b   POUND
19.6500 g., 0.9170 Gold 0.5793 oz. AGW, 22.5 mm. **Ruler:** Elizabeth II **Obv:** Young bust right **Rev:** Shield above written value

Date	Mintage	F	VF	XF	Unc	BU
1983 Proof	250	Value: 575				

Note: 497 pieces were remelted

KM# 60   POUND
9.5000 g., Nickel-Brass, 22.5 mm. **Ruler:** Elizabeth II **Obv:** Young bust right **Rev:** Shield above written value **Edge:** CAESAREA INSULA

Date	Mintage	F	VF	XF	Unc	BU
1984	20,000	—	—	2.00	3.25	—

KM# 60a   POUND
11.6800 g., 0.9250 Silver 0.3473 oz. ASW, 22.5 mm. **Ruler:** Elizabeth II **Obv:** Young bust right **Rev:** Shield above written value

Date	Mintage	F	VF	XF	Unc	BU
1984 Proof	2,500	Value: 18.50				

KM# 60b   POUND
19.6500 g., 0.9170 Gold 0.5793 oz. AGW, 22.5 mm. **Ruler:** Elizabeth II **Obv:** Young bust right **Rev:** Shield above written value

Date	Mintage	F	VF	XF	Unc	BU
1984 Proof	250	Value: 575				

KM# 61   POUND
9.5000 g., Nickel-Brass, 22.5 mm. **Ruler:** Elizabeth II **Obv:** Young bust right **Rev:** Shield above written value **Edge:** CAESAREA INSULA

Date	Mintage	F	VF	XF	Unc	BU
1984	20,000	—	—	2.00	3.25	—

KM# 61a   POUND
11.6800 g., 0.9250 Silver 0.3473 oz. ASW, 22.5 mm. **Ruler:** Elizabeth II **Obv:** Young bust right **Rev:** Shield above written value

Date	Mintage	F	VF	XF	Unc	BU
1984 Proof	2,500	Value: 20.00				

KM# 61b   POUND
19.6500 g., 0.9170 Gold 0.5793 oz. AGW, 22.5 mm. **Ruler:** Elizabeth II **Obv:** Young bust right **Rev:** Shield above written value

Date	Mintage	F	VF	XF	Unc	BU
1984 Proof	250	Value: 575				

KM# 62   POUND
9.5000 g., Nickel-Brass, 22.5 mm. **Ruler:** Elizabeth II **Obv:** Young bust right **Rev:** Shield above written value **Edge:** CAESAREA INSULA

Date	Mintage	F	VF	XF	Unc	BU
1985	25,000	—	—	2.00	3.25	—

KM# 62a   POUND
11.6800 g., 0.9250 Silver 0.3473 oz. ASW, 22.5 mm. **Ruler:** Elizabeth II **Obv:** Young bust right **Rev:** Shield above written value

Date	Mintage	F	VF	XF	Unc	BU
1985 Proof	2,500	Value: 18.50				

KM# 62b   POUND
19.6500 g., 0.9170 Gold 0.5793 oz. AGW, 22.5 mm. **Ruler:** Elizabeth II **Obv:** Young bust right **Rev:** Shield above written value

Date	Mintage	F	VF	XF	Unc	BU
1985 Proof	124	Value: 600				

KM# 65   POUND
9.5000 g., Nickel-Brass, 22.5 mm. **Ruler:** Elizabeth II
Obv: Young bust right **Rev:** Shield above written value
Edge: CAESAREA INSULA

Date	Mintage	F	VF	XF	Unc	BU
1985	10,000	—	—	2.00	3.50	—

KM# 65a   POUND
11.6800 g., 0.9250 Silver 0.3473 oz. ASW, 22.5 mm. **Ruler:**
Elizabeth II **Obv:** Young bust right **Rev:** Shield above written value

Date	Mintage	F	VF	XF	Unc	BU
1985 Proof	2,500	Value: 20.00				

KM# 65b   POUND
19.6500 g., 0.9170 Gold 0.5793 oz. AGW, 22.5 mm. **Ruler:**
Elizabeth II **Obv:** Young bust right **Rev:** Shield above written value

Date	Mintage	F	VF	XF	Unc	BU
1985 Proof	108	Value: 600				

KM# 68   POUND
9.5000 g., Nickel-Brass, 22.5 mm. **Ruler:** Elizabeth II
Obv: Young bust right **Rev:** Shield above written value
Edge: CAESAREA INSULA

Date	Mintage	F	VF	XF	Unc	BU
1986	10,000	—	—	2.00	3.25	—

KM# 68a   POUND
11.6800 g., 0.9250 Silver 0.3473 oz. ASW, 22.5 mm. **Ruler:**
Elizabeth II **Obv:** Young bust right **Rev:** Shield above written value

Date	Mintage	F	VF	XF	Unc	BU
1986 Proof	2,500	Value: 20.00				

KM# 68b   POUND
19.6500 g., 0.9170 Gold 0.5793 oz. AGW, 22.5 mm. **Ruler:**
Elizabeth II **Obv:** Young bust right **Rev:** Shield above written value

Date	Mintage	F	VF	XF	Unc	BU
1986 Proof	250	Value: 575				

KM# 69   POUND
9.5000 g., Nickel-Brass, 22.5 mm. **Ruler:** Elizabeth II
Obv: Young bust right **Rev:** Shield above written value
Edge: CAESAREA INSULA

Date	Mintage	F	VF	XF	Unc	BU
1986	10,000	—	—	2.00	3.25	—

KM# 69a   POUND
11.6800 g., 0.9250 Silver 0.3473 oz. ASW, 22.5 mm. **Ruler:**
Elizabeth II **Obv:** Young bust right **Rev:** Shield above written value

Date	Mintage	F	VF	XF	Unc	BU
1986 Proof	2,500	Value: 20.00				

KM# 69b   POUND
19.6500 g., 0.9170 Gold 0.5793 oz. AGW, 22.5 mm. **Ruler:**
Elizabeth II **Obv:** Young bust right **Rev:** Shield above written value

Date	Mintage	F	VF	XF	Unc	BU
1986 Proof	250	Value: 575				

KM# 71   POUND
9.5000 g., Nickel-Brass, 22.5 mm. **Ruler:** Elizabeth II
Obv: Young bust right **Rev:** Shield above written value
Edge: CAESAREA INSULA

Date	Mintage	F	VF	XF	Unc	BU
1987	10,000	—	—	2.00	3.50	—

KM# 71a   POUND
11.6800 g., 0.9250 Silver 0.3473 oz. ASW, 22.5 mm.
Ruler: Elizabeth II **Obv:** Young bust right **Rev:** Shield above
written value

Date	Mintage	F	VF	XF	Unc	BU
1987 Proof	2,500	Value: 18.50				

KM# 71b   POUND
19.6500 g., 0.9170 Gold 0.5793 oz. AGW, 22.5 mm. **Ruler:**
Elizabeth II **Obv:** Young bust right **Rev:** Shield above written value

Date	Mintage	F	VF	XF	Unc	BU
1987 Proof	250	Value: 575				

KM# 72   POUND
9.5000 g., Nickel-Brass, 22.5 mm. **Ruler:** Elizabeth II
Obv: Young bust right **Rev:** Shield above written value
Edge: CAESAREA INSULA

Date	Mintage	F	VF	XF	Unc	BU
1987	10,000	—	—	2.00	3.25	—

KM# 72a   POUND
11.6800 g., 0.9250 Silver 0.3473 oz. ASW, 22.5 mm. **Ruler:**
Elizabeth II **Obv:** Young bust right **Rev:** Shield above written value

Date	Mintage	F	VF	XF	Unc	BU
1987 Proof	2,500	Value: 18.50				

KM# 72b   POUND
19.6500 g., 0.9170 Gold 0.5793 oz. AGW, 22.5 mm. **Ruler:**
Elizabeth II **Obv:** Young bust right **Rev:** Shield above written value

Date	Mintage	F	VF	XF	Unc	BU
1987 Proof	250	Value: 575				

KM# 73   POUND
9.5000 g., Nickel-Brass, 22.5 mm. **Ruler:** Elizabeth II
Obv: Young bust right **Rev:** Shield above written value
Edge: CAESAREA INSULA

Date	Mintage	F	VF	XF	Unc	BU
1988	10,000	—	—	2.00	4.00	—

KM# 73a   POUND
11.6800 g., 0.9250 Silver 0.3473 oz. ASW, 22.5 mm. **Ruler:**
Elizabeth II **Obv:** Young bust right **Rev:** Shield above written value

Date	Mintage	F	VF	XF	Unc	BU
1988 Proof	2,500	Value: 18.50				

KM# 73b   POUND
19.6500 g., 0.9170 Gold 0.5793 oz. AGW, 22.5 mm. **Ruler:**
Elizabeth II **Obv:** Young bust right **Rev:** Shield above written value

Date	Mintage	F	VF	XF	Unc	BU
1988 Proof	250	Value: 575				

KM# 74   POUND
9.5000 g., Nickel-Brass, 22.5 mm. **Ruler:** Elizabeth II **Obv:**
Young bust right **Rev:** Shield above written value **Edge:**
CAESAREA INSULA

Date	Mintage	F	VF	XF	Unc	BU
1988	10,000	—	—	2.00	3.25	—

KM# 74a   POUND
11.6800 g., 0.9250 Silver 0.3473 oz. ASW, 22.5 mm. **Ruler:**
Elizabeth II **Obv:** Young bust right **Rev:** Shield above written value

Date	Mintage	F	VF	XF	Unc	BU
1988 Proof	2,500	Value: 18.50				

KM# 74b   POUND
19.6500 g., 0.9170 Gold 0.5793 oz. AGW, 22.5 mm. **Ruler:**
Elizabeth II **Obv:** Young bust right **Rev:** Shield above written value

Date	Mintage	F	VF	XF	Unc	BU
1988 Proof	250	Value: 575				

KM# 75   POUND
9.5000 g., Nickel-Brass, 22.5 mm. **Ruler:** Elizabeth II
Obv: Young bust right **Rev:** Shield above written value
Edge: CAESAREA INSULA

Date	Mintage	F	VF	XF	Unc	BU
1989	25,000	—	—	2.00	3.25	—

KM# 75a   POUND
11.6800 g., 0.9250 Silver 0.3473 oz. ASW, 22.5 mm.
Ruler: Elizabeth II **Obv:** Young bust right **Rev:** Shield above written
value

Date	Mintage	F	VF	XF	Unc	BU
1989 Proof	2,500	Value: 18.50				

KM# 75b   POUND
19.6500 g., 0.9170 Gold 0.5793 oz. AGW, 22.5 mm.
Ruler: Elizabeth II **Obv:** Young bust right **Rev:** Shield above written
value

Date	Mintage	F	VF	XF	Unc	BU
1989 Proof	250	Value: 575				

KM# 84   POUND
9.5000 g., Nickel-Brass, 22.5 mm. **Ruler:** Elizabeth II **Obv:** Young
bust right **Rev:** Schooner, The Tickler **Edge:** CAESAREA INSULA

Date	Mintage	F	VF	XF	Unc	BU
1991	15,000	—	—	—	3.25	—

KM# 84a   POUND
11.6800 g., 0.9250 Silver 0.3473 oz. ASW, 22.5 mm.
Ruler: Elizabeth II **Obv:** Young bust right **Rev:** Schooner, The
Tickler

Date	Mintage	F	VF	XF	Unc	BU
1991 Proof	3,000	Value: 20.00				

KM# 84b   POUND
19.6500 g., 0.9170 Gold 0.5793 oz. AGW, 22.5 mm.
Ruler: Elizabeth II **Obv:** Young bust right **Rev:** Schooner, The
Tickler

Date	Mintage	F	VF	XF	Unc	BU
1991 Proof	250	Value: 575				

KM# 85   POUND
9.5000 g., Nickel-Brass, 22.5 mm. **Ruler:** Elizabeth II
Obv: Young bust right **Rev:** Sailing ship, Percy Douglas
Edge: CAESAREA INSULA

Date	Mintage	F	VF	XF	Unc	BU
1991	20,000	—	—	—	3.25	—

KM# 85a   POUND
11.6800 g., 0.9250 Silver 0.3473 oz. ASW, 22.5 mm.
Ruler: Elizabeth II **Obv:** Young bust right **Rev:** Sailing ship,
Percy Douglas

Date	Mintage	F	VF	XF	Unc	BU
1991 Proof	3,000	Value: 20.00				

KM# 85b   POUND
19.6500 g., 0.9170 Gold 0.5793 oz. AGW, 22.5 mm.
Ruler: Elizabeth II **Obv:** Young bust right **Rev:** Sailing ship,
Percy Douglas

Date	Mintage	F	VF	XF	Unc	BU
1991 Proof	250	Value: 575				

KM# 86   POUND
9.5000 g., Nickel-Brass, 22.5 mm. **Ruler:** Elizabeth II
Obv: Young bust right **Rev:** Brig, Hebe

Date	Mintage	F	VF	XF	Unc	BU
1992	2,000	—	—	—	3.25	—

KM# 86a   POUND
11.6800 g., 0.9250 Silver 0.3473 oz. ASW, 22.5 mm.
Ruler: Elizabeth II **Obv:** Young bust right **Rev:** Sailing ship, Hebe

Date	Mintage	F	VF	XF	Unc	BU
1992 Proof	Est. 3,000	Value: 20.00				

KM# 86b   POUND
19.6500 g., 0.9170 Gold 0.5793 oz. AGW, 22.5 mm.
Ruler: Elizabeth II **Obv:** Young bust right **Rev:** Sailing ship, Hebe

Date	Mintage	F	VF	XF	Unc	BU
1992 Proof	250	Value: 575				

KM# 87   POUND
9.5000 g., Nickel-Brass, 22.5 mm.   **Ruler:** Elizabeth II
Obv: Young bust right **Rev:** Bailiwick seal

Date	Mintage	F	VF	XF	Unc	BU
1992	20,000	—	—	—	3.50	—

KM# 87a   POUND
11.6800 g., 0.9250 Silver 0.3473 oz. ASW, 22.5 mm.   **Ruler:**
Elizabeth II **Obv:** Young bust right **Rev:** Ornamented shield

Date	Mintage	F	VF	XF	Unc	BU
1992 Proof	3,000	Value: 20.00				

KM# 87b   POUND
19.6500 g., 0.9170 Gold 0.5793 oz. AGW, 22.5 mm.   **Ruler:**
Elizabeth II **Obv:** Young bust right **Rev:** Ornamented shield

Date	Mintage	F	VF	XF	Unc	BU
1992 Proof	250	Value: 575				

KM# 88   POUND
9.5000 g., Nickel-Brass, 22.5 mm.   **Ruler:** Elizabeth II
Obv: Young bust right **Rev:** Barque, Gemini

Date	Mintage	F	VF	XF	Unc	BU
1993	—	—	—	—	3.25	—

KM# 88a   POUND
11.6800 g., 0.9250 Silver 0.3473 oz. ASW, 22.5 mm.   **Ruler:**
Elizabeth II **Obv:** Young bust right **Rev:** Sailing ship, Gemini

Date	Mintage	F	VF	XF	Unc	BU
1993 Proof	3,000	Value: 20.00				

KM# 88b   POUND
19.6500 g., 0.9170 Gold 0.5793 oz. AGW, 22.5 mm.   **Ruler:**
Elizabeth II **Obv:** Young bust right **Rev:** Sailing ship, Gemini

Date	Mintage	F	VF	XF	Unc	BU
1993 Proof	250	Value: 575				

KM# 90   POUND
9.5000 g., Nickel-Brass, 22.5 mm.   **Ruler:** Elizabeth II
Obv: Young bust right **Rev:** Brigantine, Century

Date	Mintage	F	VF	XF	Unc	BU
1993	—	—	—	—	3.25	—

KM# 90a   POUND
11.6800 g., 0.9250 Silver 0.3473 oz. ASW, 22.5 mm.
Ruler: Elizabeth II **Obv:** Young bust right **Rev:** Brigantine,
Century

Date	Mintage	F	VF	XF	Unc	BU
1993 Proof	Est. 3,000	Value: 20.00				

KM# 90b   POUND
19.6500 g., 0.9170 Gold 0.5793 oz. AGW, 22.5 mm.
Ruler: Elizabeth II **Obv:** Young bust right **Rev:** Sailing ship,
Century

Date	Mintage	F	VF	XF	Unc	BU
1993 Proof	250	Value: 575				

KM# 91   POUND
9.5000 g., Nickel-Brass, 22.5 mm.   **Ruler:** Elizabeth II
Obv: Young bust right **Rev:** Topsail Schooner, Resolute

Date	Mintage	F	VF	XF	Unc	BU
1994	60,000	—	—	—	3.25	—
1997	101,000	—	—	—	3.25	—

KM# 91a   POUND
11.6800 g., 0.9250 Silver 0.3473 oz. ASW, 22.5 mm.
Ruler: Elizabeth II **Obv:** Young bust right **Rev:** Schooner,
Resolute

Date	Mintage	F	VF	XF	Unc	BU
1994 Proof	3,000	Value: 20.00				

KM# 91b   POUND
19.6500 g., 0.9170 Gold 0.5793 oz. AGW, 22.5 mm.   **Ruler:**
Elizabeth II **Obv:** Young bust right **Rev:** Schooner, Resolute

Date	Mintage	F	VF	XF	Unc	BU
1994 Proof	250	Value: 575				

KM# 101   POUND
9.5000 g., Nickel-Brass, 22.5 mm.   **Ruler:** Elizabeth II
Obv: Head with tiara right **Rev:** Schooner, Resolute
Edge: CAESAREA INSULA

Date	Mintage	F	VF	XF	Unc	BU
1998	174,000	—	—	—	3.25	—

KM# 110   SOVEREIGN
7.9800 g., 0.9167 Gold 0.2352 oz. AGW, 22.5 mm.
Ruler: Elizabeth II **Subject:** William I - Duke of Normandy
Obv: Crowned bust right **Rev:** William seated on throne

Date	Mintage	F	VF	XF	Unc	BU
2000	Est. 2,000	—	—	—	235	—
2000 Proof	Est. 2,000	Value: 275				

KM# 37   2 POUNDS
21.6800 g., 0.9250 Silver 0.6447 oz. ASW   **Ruler:** Elizabeth II
Subject: 25th Wedding Anniversary **Obv:** Crowned bust right
Rev: Sailing ship "Alexandria"

Date	Mintage	F	VF	XF	Unc	BU
1972	24,000	—	—	—	13.00	—
1972 Proof	1,500	Value: 25.00				

KM# 52   2 POUNDS
Copper-Nickel, 38.5 mm.   **Ruler:** Elizabeth II **Subject:** Wedding
of Prince Charles and Lady Diana **Obv:** Crowned bust right
Rev: Conjoined busts right

Date	Mintage	F	VF	XF	Unc	BU
ND(1981)	150,000	—	—	—	6.00	—

KM# 52a   2 POUNDS
28.2800 g., 0.9250 Silver 0.8410 oz. ASW, 38.5 mm.
Ruler: Elizabeth II **Subject:** Wedding of Prince Charles and Lady
Diana **Obv:** Crowned bust right **Rev:** Conjoined busts right

Date	Mintage	F	VF	XF	Unc	BU
ND(1981) Proof	35,000	Value: 17.50				

KM# 52b   2 POUNDS
15.9800 g., 0.9170 Gold 0.4711 oz. AGW, 38.5 mm.
Ruler: Elizabeth II **Subject:** Wedding of Prince Charles and Lady
Diana **Obv:** Crowned bust right **Rev:** Conjoined busts right

Date	Mintage	F	VF	XF	Unc	BU
ND(1981) Proof	1,500	Value: 475				

KM# 64   2 POUNDS
Copper-Nickel, 38.5 mm.   **Ruler:** Elizabeth II **Subject:** 40th
Anniversary of Liberation of 1945 **Obv:** Crowned bust right
Rev: H.M.S. Beagle, destroyer **Edge:** OUR DEAR CHANNEL
ISLANDS WILL ALSO BE FREED TODAY

Date	Mintage	F	VF	XF	Unc	BU
1985	20,000	—	—	—	6.00	—

KM# 64a   2 POUNDS
28.2800 g., 0.9250 Silver 0.8410 oz. ASW, 38.5 mm.
Ruler: Elizabeth II **Subject:** 40th Anniversary of Liberation of
1945 **Obv:** Crowned bust right **Rev:** H.M.S. Beagle, destroyer

Date	Mintage	F	VF	XF	Unc	BU
1985 Proof	2,500	Value: 35.00				

KM# 64b   2 POUNDS
47.5400 g., 0.9170 Gold 1.4015 oz. AGW, 38.5 mm.
Ruler: Elizabeth II **Subject:** 40th Anniversary of Liberation of
1945 **Obv:** Crowned bust right **Rev:** H.M.S. Beagle, destroyer

Date	Mintage	F	VF	XF	Unc	BU
1985 Proof	40	Value: 2,000				

KM# 67.1   2 POUNDS
Copper-Nickel, 38.5 mm.   **Ruler:** Elizabeth II **Subject:** XIII
Commonwealth Games - Edinburgh **Obv:** Crowned bust right
Rev: Two sprinters **Edge:** XIII COMMONWEALTH GAMES

Date	Mintage	F	VF	XF	Unc	BU
1986	50,000	—	—	—	6.00	—

KM# 67.1a   2 POUNDS
28.2800 g., 0.5000 Silver 0.4546 oz. ASW, 38.5 mm.
Ruler: Elizabeth II **Subject:** XIII Commonwealth Games -
Edinburgh **Obv:** Crowned bust right **Rev:** Two sprinters

Date	Mintage	F	VF	XF	Unc	BU
1986	20,000	—	—	—	20.00	—

KM# 67.1b   2 POUNDS
28.2800 g., 0.9250 Silver 0.8410 oz. ASW, 38.5 mm.
Ruler: Elizabeth II **Subject:** XIII Commonwealth Games -
Edinburgh **Obv:** Crowned bust right **Rev:** Two sprinters

Date	Mintage	F	VF	XF	Unc	BU
1986 Proof	20,000	Value: 40.00				

KM# 67.2   2 POUNDS
Copper-Nickel, 38.5 mm.   **Ruler:** Elizabeth II **Subject:** XIII
Commonwealth Games - Edinburgh **Obv:** Crowned bust right
Rev: Two sprinters **Note:** Without edge inscription.

Date	Mintage	F	VF	XF	Unc	BU
1986	5,000	—	—	—	7.50	—

KM# 70   2 POUNDS
Copper-Nickel, 38.5 mm.   **Ruler:** Elizabeth II **Subject:** World
Wildlife Fund **Obv:** Crowned bust right **Rev:** Pigeons

Date	Mintage	F	VF	XF	Unc	BU
1987	23,000	—	—	—	10.00	12.50

KM# 70a 2 POUNDS
28.2800 g., 0.9250 Silver 0.8410 oz. ASW, 38.5 mm.
Ruler: Elizabeth II **Subject:** World Wildlife Fund **Obv:** Crowned
bust right **Rev:** Pigeons

Date	Mintage	F	VF	XF	Unc	BU
1987 Proof	25,000				Value: 25.00	

KM# 76 2 POUNDS
Copper-Nickel, 38.5 mm. **Ruler:** Elizabeth II **Subject:** Royal
Visit **Obv:** Crowned bust right **Rev:** Royal Mace divides map

Date	Mintage	F	VF	XF	Unc	BU
1989	10,000	—	—	—	6.00	—

KM# 76a 2 POUNDS
28.3000 g., 0.9250 Silver 0.8416 oz. ASW, 38.5 mm.
Ruler: Elizabeth II **Subject:** Royal Visit **Obv:** Crowned bust right
Rev: Royal Mace divides map

Date	Mintage	F	VF	XF	Unc	BU
1989 Proof	3,000				Value: 30.00	

KM# 77 2 POUNDS
28.3000 g., 0.9250 Silver 0.8416 oz. ASW, 38.5 mm.
Ruler: Elizabeth II **Subject:** 50th Anniversary - The Battle of
Britain **Obv:** Crowned bust right **Rev:** Spitfire divides map

Date	Mintage	F	VF	XF	Unc	BU
ND(1990) Proof	Est. 10,000				Value: 37.50	

KM# 83 2 POUNDS
Copper-Nickel, 38.5 mm. **Ruler:** Elizabeth II **Subject:** 90th
Birthday of Queen Mother **Obv:** Crowned bust right
Rev: Crowned double "E" monogram

Date	Mintage	F	VF	XF	Unc	BU
ND(1990)	10,000	—	—	—	7.00	—

KM# 83a 2 POUNDS
28.3500 g., 0.9250 Silver 0.8431 oz. ASW, 38.5 mm.
Ruler: Elizabeth II **Subject:** 90th Birthday of Queen Mother
Obv: Crowned bust right **Rev:** Crowned double "E" monogram

Date	Mintage	F	VF	XF	Unc	BU
ND(1990) Proof	3,000				Value: 55.00	

KM# 83b 2 POUNDS
15.9800 g., 0.9170 Gold 0.4711 oz. AGW **Ruler:** Elizabeth II
Subject: 90th Birthday of Queen Mother **Obv:** Crowned bust right
Rev: Crowned double "E" monogram

Date	Mintage	F	VF	XF	Unc	BU
ND(1990) Proof	90				Value: 750	

KM# 89 2 POUNDS
Copper-Nickel, 38.5 mm. **Ruler:** Elizabeth II **Subject:** 40th
Anniversary - Coronation of Queen Elizabeth II **Obv:** Crowned
bust right **Rev:** Crown, royal mace and shield

Date	Mintage	F	VF	XF	Unc	BU
ND(1993)	12,000	—	—	—	6.00	—

KM# 89a 2 POUNDS
28.2800 g., 0.9250 Silver 0.8410 oz. ASW, 38.5 mm.
Ruler: Elizabeth II **Subject:** 40th Anniversary - Coronation of
Queen Elizabeth II **Obv:** Crowned bust right **Rev:** Crown, royal
mace and shield

Date	Mintage	F	VF	XF	Unc	BU
ND(1993) Proof	Est. 10,000				Value: 55.00	

KM# 89b 2 POUNDS
15.9800 g., 0.9167 Gold 0.4710 oz. AGW **Ruler:** Elizabeth II
Subject: 40th Anniversary - Coronation of Queen Elizabeth II
Obv: Crowned bust right **Rev:** Crown, royal mace and shield

Date	Mintage	F	VF	XF	Unc	BU
ND(1993) Proof	Est. 500				Value: 525	

KM# 92 2 POUNDS
Copper-Nickel, 38.5 mm. **Ruler:** Elizabeth II **Subject:** 50th
Anniversary of Liberation **Obv:** Crowned bust right **Rev:** Bird with
sprig within letter V above dates within ribbon

Date	Mintage	F	VF	XF	Unc	BU
1995	42,000	—	—	—	7.50	9.00

Note: Also released in special wallet with 1 Pound commemorative banknote (6,000). Market value: $20.00

KM# 92a 2 POUNDS
28.2800 g., 0.9250 Silver 0.8410 oz. ASW, 38.5 mm.
Ruler: Elizabeth II **Subject:** 50th Anniversary of Liberation
Obv: Crowned bust right **Rev:** Bird with sprig within letter V above
dates within ribbon

Date	Mintage	F	VF	XF	Unc	BU
1995 Proof	7,000				Value: 55.00	

KM# 97 2 POUNDS
Copper-Nickel, 38.5 mm. **Ruler:** Elizabeth II **Subject:** Queen
Elizabeth's 70th Birthday **Obv:** Crowned bust right **Rev:** Lillies

Date	Mintage	F	VF	XF	Unc	BU
1996	Est. 20,000	—	—	—	8.00	—

KM# 97a 2 POUNDS
28.3800 g., 0.9250 Silver 0.8440 oz. ASW, 38.5 mm.
Ruler: Elizabeth II **Subject:** Queen Elizabeth's 70th Birthday
Obv: Crowned bust right **Rev:** Lillies

Date	Mintage	F	VF	XF	Unc	BU
1996	Est. 8,000	—	—	—	45.00	—

KM# 99 2 POUNDS
12.0000 g., Bi-Metallic Copper-Nickel center in Nickel-Brass ring,
28.35 mm. **Ruler:** Elizabeth II **Obv:** Crowned bust right
Rev: Value within center circle of assorted shields

Date	Mintage	F	VF	XF	Unc	BU
1997 In sets only	5,500	—	—	—	9.00	—

KM# 99a 2 POUNDS
Bi-Metallic Silver center in Gold-plated Silver ring, 28.35 mm.
Ruler: Elizabeth II **Obv:** Crowned bust right **Rev:** Value within
center circle of assorted shields

Date	Mintage	F	VF	XF	Unc	BU
1997 Proof	500				Value: 65.00	

KM# 102 2 POUNDS
12.0000 g., Bi-Metallic Copper-Nickel center in Nickel-Brass ring,
28.35 mm. **Ruler:** Elizabeth II **Obv:** Head with tiara right
Rev: Latent image value within circle of assorted shields
Edge: CAESAREA INSULA

Date	Mintage	F	VF	XF	Unc	BU
1998	800,000	—	—	—	8.50	—

KM# 38 2 POUNDS 50 PENCE
27.1000 g., 0.9250 Silver 0.8059 oz. ASW **Ruler:** Elizabeth II
Subject: 25th Wedding Anniversary **Obv:** Young bust right
Rev: European Lobster

Date	Mintage	F	VF	XF	Unc	BU
1972	24,000	—	—	—	16.00	18.00
1972 Proof	1,500				Value: 30.00	

KM# 39 5 POUNDS
2.6200 g., 0.9170 Gold 0.0772 oz. AGW **Ruler:** Elizabeth II
Subject: 25th Wedding Anniversary **Obv:** Young bust right
Rev: Garden shrew

Date	Mintage	F	VF	XF	Unc	BU
1972	8,500	—	—	—	—	85.00
1972 Proof	1,500				Value: 95.00	

KM# 78 5 POUNDS
155.5600 g., 0.9990 Silver 4.9962 oz. ASW, 65 mm.
Ruler: Elizabeth II **Subject:** 50th Anniversary - The Battle of
Britain **Obv:** Crowned bust right **Rev:** Spitfire divides map
Note: Illustration reduced.

Date	Mintage	F	VF	XF	Unc	BU
ND(1990) Proof	—				Value: 165	

KM# 100 5 POUNDS
Copper-Nickel **Ruler:** Elizabeth II **Subject:** Queen's Golden
Wedding Anniversary **Obv:** Crowned bust right **Rev:** Conjoined
busts of royal couple and coat of arms

Date	Mintage	F	VF	XF	Unc	BU
1997	6,000	—	—	—	15.00	—

KM# 100a 5 POUNDS
28.2800 g., 0.9250 Silver 0.8410 oz. ASW **Ruler:** Elizabeth II **Subject:** Queen's Golden Wedding Anniversary **Obv:** Crowned bust right **Rev:** Conjoined busts of royal couple and gold-plated coat of arms

Date	Mintage	F	VF	XF	Unc	BU
1997 Proof	Est. 30,000	Value: 65.00				

KM# 109 5 POUNDS
28.2800 g., 0.9250 Silver 0.8410 oz. ASW **Ruler:** Elizabeth II **Subject:** Millennium **Obv:** Head with tiara right **Rev:** Gold-plated island map on globe

Date	Mintage	F	VF	XF	Unc	BU
2000 Proof	32,000	Value: 47.50				

KM# 40 10 POUNDS
4.6400 g., 0.9170 Gold 0.1368 oz. AGW **Ruler:** Elizabeth II **Subject:** 25th Wedding Anniversary **Obv:** Young bust right **Rev:** Gold torque, excavated 1899 in St. Helier, Jersey.

Date	Mintage	F	VF	XF	Unc	BU
1972	8,500	—	—	—	—	145
1972 Proof	1,500	Value: 150				

KM# 79 10 POUNDS
3.1300 g., 0.9990 Gold 0.1005 oz. AGW **Ruler:** Elizabeth II **Subject:** 50th Anniversary - The Battle of Britain **Obv:** Crowned bust right **Rev:** Crowned air force badge divides dates

Date	Mintage	F	VF	XF	Unc	BU
ND Proof	Est. 500	Value: 125				

KM# 93 10 POUNDS
3.1300 g., 0.9990 Gold 0.1005 oz. AGW **Ruler:** Elizabeth II **Subject:** 50th Anniversary of Liberation **Obv:** Crowned bust right **Rev:** Red Cross bringing supplies to Jersey immediately following liberation

Date	Mintage	F	VF	XF	Unc	BU
1995	500	—	—	—	—	110

Note: Proof sets only

KM# 41 20 POUNDS
9.2600 g., 0.9170 Gold 0.2730 oz. AGW **Ruler:** Elizabeth II **Subject:** 25th Wedding Anniversary **Obv:** Young bust right **Rev:** Ormer shell

Date	Mintage	F	VF	XF	Unc	BU
1972	8,500	—	—	—	—	270
1972 Proof	1,500	Value: 280				

KM# 42 25 POUNDS
11.9000 g., 0.9170 Gold 0.3508 oz. AGW **Ruler:** Elizabeth II **Subject:** 25th Wedding Anniversary **Obv:** Young bust right **Rev:** Arms of Queen Elizabeth I

Date	Mintage	F	VF	XF	Unc	BU
1972	8,500	—	—	—	—	345
1972 Proof	1,500	Value: 350				

KM# 80 25 POUNDS
7.8100 g., 0.9990 Gold 0.2508 oz. AGW **Ruler:** Elizabeth II **Subject:** 50th Anniversary - The Battle of Britain **Obv:** Crowned bust right **Rev:** Spitfire

Date	Mintage	F	VF	XF	Unc	BU
1990 Proof	Est. 500	Value: 250				

KM# 94 25 POUNDS
7.8100 g., 0.9990 Gold 0.2508 oz. AGW **Ruler:** Elizabeth II **Subject:** 50th Anniversary of Liberation **Obv:** Crowned bust right **Rev:** Family encircled around flags with written value below

Date	Mintage	F	VF	XF	Unc	BU
1995 Proof sets only	500	—	—	—	—	245

KM# 43 50 POUNDS
22.6300 g., 0.9170 Gold 0.6672 oz. AGW **Ruler:** Elizabeth II **Subject:** 25th Wedding Anniversary **Obv:** Young bust right **Rev:** Shield above written value

Date	Mintage	F	VF	XF	Unc	BU
1972	8,500	—	—	—	—	650
1972 Proof	1,500	Value: 700				

KM# 81 50 POUNDS
15.6100 g., 0.9990 Gold 0.5014 oz. AGW **Ruler:** Elizabeth II **Subject:** 50th Anniversary - Battle of Britain **Obv:** Crowned bust right **Rev:** Crowned air force badge divides dates

Date	Mintage	F	VF	XF	Unc	BU
ND Proof	Est. 500	Value: 485				

KM# 95 50 POUNDS
15.6100 g., 0.9990 Gold 0.5014 oz. AGW **Ruler:** Elizabeth II **Subject:** 50th Anniversary of Liberation **Obv:** Crowned bust right **Rev:** Letter V divides dates above figures facing each other with flags

Date	Mintage	F	VF	XF	Unc	BU
1995 Proof	500	Value: 480				

KM# 82 100 POUNDS
31.2100 g., 0.9990 Gold 1.0024 oz. AGW **Ruler:** Elizabeth II **Subject:** 50th Anniversary - The Battle of Britain **Obv:** Crowned bust right **Rev:** Spitfire

Date	Mintage	F	VF	XF	Unc	BU
ND Proof	Est. 500	Value: 950				

KM# 96 100 POUNDS
31.2100 g., 0.9990 Gold 1.0024 oz. AGW **Ruler:** Elizabeth II **Subject:** 50th Anniversary of Liberation **Obv:** Crowned bust right **Rev:** Small shield within map with bird above within diagonal lines into map

Date	Mintage	F	VF	XF	Unc	BU
1995 Proof	500	—	—	—	—	950

PIEFORTS

KM#	Date	Mintage	Identification	Mkt Val
P1	1982	1,500	20 Pence. Silver. Date. KM53a.	25.00
P2	1995	—	2 Pounds. 0.9250 Silver. KM92a.	75.00

MINT SETS

KM#	Date	Mintage	Identification	Issue Price	Mkt Val
MS1	1972 (9)	8,500	KM35-43	348	715
MS2	1972 (4)	15,000	KM35-38	24.00	40.00
MS3	1983 (7)	25,000	KM54-59, 66	—	6.00
MS4	1987 (7)	—	KM54-55, 56.1-58.1, 66, 71	—	6.50
MSA5	1991-1994 (8)	—	Mixed dates KM#84-91	—	25.00
MS5	1992 (7)	6,000	KM54,55b, 56.2- 57.2, 58.1, 66, 86	22.50	22.50
MS6	1997 (8)	5,500	KM#54b 55b, 56.2-58.2, 66, 91, 99	—	28.00

PROOF SETS

KM#	Date	Mintage	Identification	Issue Price	Mkt Val
PS1	1957 (4)	1,050	KM21-22 two each	—	30.00
PS2.1	1960 (4)	2,100	KM22- 23 two each	—	25.00
PS2.2	1960 (4)	I.A.	KM22, 24 two each	—	150
PS3	1964 (4)	10,000	KM21, 25 two each	—	8.00
PS4	1966 (4)	15,000	KM26-27 two each	—	8.00
PS5	1966 (2)	15,000	KM28 two pieces	—	8.00
PS6	1972 (9)	1,500	KM35-43	648	975
PS7	1980 (6)	10,000	KM29-34	—	20.00
PS8	1981 (7)	15,000	KM45-51	31.00	20.00
PS9	1983 (7)	5,000	KM54a-55a, 56.1a-57.1a, 58a-59a, 66a	—	80.00
PS10	1990 (4)	500	KM79-82	1,595	1,750
PS11	1995 (4)	500	KM93-96	1,600	1,600

JORDAN

The Hashemite Kingdom of Jordan, a constitutional monarchy in southwest Asia, has an area of 37,738 sq. mi. (91,880 sq. km.) and a population of 3.5 million. Capital: Amman. Agriculture and tourism comprise Jordan's economic base. Chief exports are phosphates, tomatoe sand oranges.

Jordan is the Edom and Moab of the time of Moses. It became part of the Roman province of Arabia in 106 A.D., was conquered by the Arabs in 633-36, and was part of the Ottoman Empire from the 16th century until World War I. At that time, the regions presently known as Jordan and Israel were mandated to Great Britain by the League of Nations as Transjordan and Palestine. In 1922 Transjordan was established as the semi-autonomous Emirate of Transjordan, ruled by the Hashemite Prince Abdullah but still nominally a part of the British mandate. The mandate over Transjordan was terminated in 1946, the country becoming the independent Hashemite Kingdom of Transjordan. The kingdom was renamed the Hashemite Kingdom of Jordan in 1950.

Several 1964 and 1965 issues were limited to respective quantities of 3,000 and 5,000 examples struck to make up sets for sale to collectors.

TITLE

المملكة الاردنية الهاشمية

el-Mamlaka(t)el-Urduniya(t)el-Hashemiya(t)

RULERS
Abdullah Ibn Al-Hussein, 1946-1951
Talal Ibn Abdullah, 1951-1952
Hussein Ibn Talal, 1952-1999
Abdullah Ibn Al-Hussein, 1999-

MONETARY SYSTEM
100 Fils = 1 Dirham
1000 Fils = 10 Dirhams = 1 Dinar
                          Commencing 1992
100 Piastres = 1 Dinar

KINGDOM
DECIMAL COINAGE

KM# 1   FIL
3.0000 g., Bronze, 18 mm. **Ruler:** Abdullah Ibn Al-Hussein **Obv:** Value and date within crowned circle within sprigs **Rev:** Value within circle above date **Edge:** Plain

Date	Mintage	F	VF	XF	Unc	BU
AH1368//1949	350,000	—	1.00	1.50	3.50	—
AH1368//1949 Proof	25	Value: 250				

Note: "FIL" is an error for "FILS," the correct Arabic singular

KM# 2   FILS
3.0000 g., Bronze, 18 mm. **Ruler:** Abdullah Ibn Al-Hussein **Obv:** Value and date within crowned circle within sprigs **Rev:** Value within circle above date **Edge:** Plain

Date	Mintage	F	VF	XF	Unc	BU
AH1368//1949	Inc. above	—	0.50	0.90	2.25	—
AH1368//1949 Proof	25	Value: 250				

KM# 8   FILS
3.0000 g., Bronze, 18 mm. **Ruler:** Hussein Ibn Talal **Obv:** Value and date within crowned circle within sprigs **Rev:** Value within circle above date **Edge:** Plain

Date	Mintage	F	VF	XF	Unc	BU
AH1374//1955	200,000	—	0.35	0.50	1.00	—
AH1374//1955 Proof		Value: 100				
AH1379//1960	150,000	—	0.50	1.00	2.00	—
AH1379//1960 Proof		Value: 100				
AH1382//1963	200,000	—	0.25	0.50	1.00	—
AH1382//1963 Proof		Value: 100				

Date	Mintage	F	VF	XF	Unc	BU
AH1383//1964	3,000	—	1.50	3.00	5.00	—
Note: In sets only						
AH1385//1965	5,000	—	1.00	2.00	3.00	—
Note: In sets only						
AH1385//1965 Proof	10,000	Value: 3.00				

KM# 14   FILS
3.0000 g., Bronze, 18 mm. **Ruler:** Hussein Ibn Talal **Obv:** Head right **Rev:** Value and date within circle flanked by sprigs **Edge:** Plain

Date	Mintage	F	VF	XF	Unc	BU
AH1387-1968	60,000	—	0.35	0.75	1.25	—

KM# 35   FILS
3.0000 g., Bronze, 18 mm. **Ruler:** Hussein Ibn Talal **Obv:** Head right **Rev:** Value and date within circle flanked by sprigs **Edge:** Plain

Date	Mintage	F	VF	XF	Unc	BU
AH1398-1978 Proof	20,000	Value: 2.00				
AH1404-1984	100,000	—	0.25	0.50	1.00	—
AH1406-1985	—	—	—	1.50	2.00	—
Note: In sets only						
AH1406-1985 Proof	5,000	Value: 2.00				

KM# 3   5 FILS (1/2 Qirsh)
4.5000 g., Bronze, 21 mm. **Ruler:** Abdullah Ibn Al-Hussein **Obv:** Value and date within crowned circle within sprigs **Rev:** Value within circle above date **Edge:** Plain

Date	Mintage	F	VF	XF	Unc	BU
AH1368//1949	3,300,000	—	0.40	0.75	1.50	—
AH1368//1949 Proof	25	Value: 250				

KM# 9   5 FILS (1/2 Qirsh)
4.5000 g., Bronze, 21 mm. **Ruler:** Hussein Ibn Talal **Obv:** Value and date within crowned circle within sprigs **Rev:** Value within circle above date **Edge:** Plain

Date	Mintage	F	VF	XF	Unc	BU
AH1374-1955	3,500,000	—	0.35	0.50	0.75	—
AH1374-1955 Proof		Value: 100				
AH1379-1960	540,000	—	0.50	0.70	1.25	—
AH1379-1960 Proof		Value: 100				
AH1382-1962	250,000	—	0.45	0.70	1.25	—
AH1382-1962 Proof		Value: 100				
AH1383-1964	3,000	—	—	2.75	3.50	—
Note: In sets only						
AH1384-1964	2,500,000	—	0.30	0.50	1.00	—
AH1385-1965	5,000	—	1.25	2.50	3.00	—
Note: In sets only						
AH1385-1965 Proof	10,000	Value: 5.00				
AH1387-1967	2,000,000	—	0.10	0.20	0.40	—

KM# 15   5 FILS (1/2 Qirsh)
4.5000 g., Bronze, 21 mm. **Ruler:** Hussein Ibn Talal **Obv:** Head right **Rev:** Value and date within circle flanked by sprigs **Edge:** Plain

Date	Mintage	F	VF	XF	Unc	BU
AH1387//1968	800,000	—	0.20	0.50	0.75	—
AH1390//1970	1,400,000	—	0.10	0.25	0.50	—
AH1392//1972	400,000	—	0.10	0.25	0.65	—
AH1394//1974	2,000,000	—	0.10	0.20	0.40	—
AH1395//1975	9,000,000	—	0.10	0.15	0.30	—

KM# 36   5 FILS (1/2 Qirsh)
4.5000 g., Bronze, 21 mm. **Ruler:** Hussein Ibn Talal **Obv:** Head right **Rev:** Value and date within circle flanked by sprigs **Edge:** Plain

Date	Mintage	F	VF	XF	Unc	BU
AH1398-1978	60,200,000	—	0.10	0.15	0.30	—
AH1398-1978 Proof	20,000	Value: 2.25				
AH1406-1985	—	—	—	1.50	2.00	—
Note: In sets only						
AH1406-1985 Proof	5,000	Value: 2.50				

KM# 60   1/2 QIRSH (1/2 Piastre)
Copper Plated Steel **Ruler:** Hussein Ibn Talal **Obv:** Bust left **Rev:** Value at left within lines with date above and written value at lower right **Edge:** Plain

Date	Mintage	F	VF	XF	Unc	BU
AH1416-1996	—	—	—	0.35	0.65	1.00
AH1416-1996 Proof	—	Value: 5.00				

KM# 4   10 FILS (Qirsh, Piastre)
5.9000 g., Bronze, 25 mm. **Ruler:** Abdullah Ibn Al-Hussein **Obv:** Value and date within crowned circle within sprigs **Rev:** Value within circle above date and star **Edge:** Plain

Date	Mintage	F	VF	XF	Unc	BU
AH1368//1949	2,700,000	—	0.75	1.25	2.00	—
AH1368//1949 Proof	25	Value: 250				

KM# 10   10 FILS (Qirsh, Piastre)
5.9000 g., Bronze, 25 mm. **Ruler:** Hussein Ibn Talal **Obv:** Value and date within crowned circle within sprigs **Rev:** Value within circle above date and star **Edge:** Plain

Date	Mintage	F	VF	XF	Unc	BU
AH1374//1955	1,500,000	—	0.60	1.00	4.00	—
AH1374//1955 Proof	—	Value: 100				
AH1379//1960	60,000	—	1.25	2.00	3.50	—
AH1379//1960 Proof		Value: 100				
AH1382//1962	2,300,000	—	0.30	0.50	1.00	—
AH1382//1962 Proof		Value: 100				
AH1383//1964	1,253,000	—	0.30	0.50	1.00	—
AH1385//1965	1,003,000	—	0.20	0.40	1.00	—
AH1385//1965 Proof	10,000	Value: 5.00				
AH1387//1967	1,000,000	—	0.20	0.35	1.00	—

KM# 16   10 FILS (Qirsh, Piastre)
5.9000 g., Bronze, 25 mm. **Ruler:** Hussein Ibn Talal **Obv:** Head right **Rev:** Value and date within circle flanked by sprigs

Date	Mintage	F	VF	XF	Unc	BU
AH1387-1968	500,000	—	0.20	0.50	0.90	—
AH1390-1970	1,000,000	—	0.20	0.35	0.60	—
AH1392-1972	600,000	—	0.20	0.40	0.75	—
AH1394-1974	1,000,000	—	0.20	0.40	0.65	—
AH1395-1975	5,000,000	—	0.20	0.35	0.50	—

KM# 37   10 FILS (Qirsh, Piastre)
5.9000 g., Bronze, 25 mm. **Ruler:** Hussein Ibn Talal **Obv:** Head right **Rev:** Value and date within circle flanked by sprigs **Edge:** Plain

Date	Mintage	F	VF	XF	Unc	BU
AH1398-1978	30,000,000	—	0.10	0.15	0.40	—
AH1398-1978 Proof	20,000	Value: 3.50				
AH1404-1984	10,000,000	—	0.10	0.15	0.40	—
AH1406-1985	—	—	—	1.25	1.75	—
Note: In sets only						
AH1406-1985 Proof	5,000	Value: 5.00				
AH1409-1989	8,000,000	—	0.25	2.00	2.50	—

KM# 56   QIRSH (Piastre)
5.5000 g., Bronze Plated Steel, 25 mm. **Ruler:** Hussein Ibn Talal **Obv:** Head left **Rev:** Value to left within lines below date with written value at lower right **Edge:** Plain

Date	Mintage	F	VF	XF	Unc	BU
AH1414-1994	—	—	—	0.50	1.25	1.50
AH1416-1996	—	—	—	0.50	1.25	1.50
AH1416-1996 Proof	—	Value: 5.00				

KM# 78.1   QIRSH (Piastre)
5.4700 g., Copper Plated Steel, 25 mm. **Ruler:** Abdullah Ibn Al-Hussein **Obv:** King Abdullah II **Rev:** Christian date left, Islamic date right **Edge:** Plain

Date	Mintage	F	VF	XF	Unc	BU
AH1421-2000	—	—	—	—	1.00	1.50

KM# 78.2   QIRSH (Piastre)
5.4700 g., Copper-Plated-Steel, 24.9 mm. **Ruler:** Abdullah Ibn Al-Hussein **Obv:** King Abdullah II **Rev:** Islamic date left, Christian date right **Edge:** Plain

Date	Mintage	F	VF	XF	Unc	BU
AH1421-2000	—	—	—	—	7.50	10.00

Note: Gregorian and Hijra dates are flipped.

KM# 5   20 FILS
Copper-Nickel **Ruler:** Abdullah Ibn Al-Hussein **Obv:** Value and date within crowned circle within sprigs **Rev:** Value within circle above date and star **Edge:** Milled

Date	Mintage	F	VF	XF	Unc	BU
AH1368//1949	1,570,000	—	0.50	1.00	1.75	—
AH1368//1949 Proof	25	Value: 275				

KM# 13   20 FILS
Copper-Nickel, 19.8 mm. **Ruler:** Hussein Ibn Talal **Obv:** Value and date within crowned circle within sprigs **Rev:** Value within circle above date and star **Edge:** Milled

Date	Mintage	F	VF	XF	Unc	BU
AH1383//1964	3,000	—	—	3.00	5.00	—
Note: In sets only						
AH1385//1965	5,000	—	—	3.00	5.00	—
Note: In sets only						
AH1385//1965 Proof	10,000	Value: 5.00				

KM# 17   25 FILS (1/4 Dirham)
4.7500 g., Copper-Nickel, 22 mm. **Ruler:** Hussein Ibn Talal **Obv:** Head right **Rev:** Value and date within circle flanked by sprigs **Edge:** Milled

Date	Mintage	F	VF	XF	Unc	BU
AH1387-1968	200,000	—	0.50	0.75	1.75	—
AH1390-1970	240,000	—	0.30	0.50	1.50	—
AH1394-1974	800,000	—	0.30	0.50	1.50	—
AH1395-1975	2,000,000	—	0.30	0.50	1.50	—
AH1397-1977	1,600,000	—	0.30	0.50	1.50	—

KM# 38   25 FILS (1/4 Dirham)
4.7500 g., Copper-Nickel, 22 mm. **Ruler:** Hussein Ibn Talal **Obv:** Head right **Rev:** Value and date within circle flanked by sprigs **Edge:** Milled

Date	Mintage	F	VF	XF	Unc	BU
AH1398-1978 Proof	20,000	Value: 4.00				
AH1401-1981	2,000,000	—	0.20	0.30	0.75	—
AH1404-1984	4,000,000	—	0.20	0.30	0.75	—
AH1406-1985	—	—	—	2.50	3.00	—
Note: In sets only						
AH1406-1985 Proof	5,000	Value: 5.00				
AH1411-1991	5,000,000	—	0.20	0.30	0.75	—

KM# 53   2-1/2 PIASTRES
Stainless Steel **Ruler:** Hussein Ibn Talal **Obv:** Bust left **Rev:** Value at left within lines below date with written value to lower right **Edge:** Milled

Date	Mintage	F	VF	XF	Unc	BU
AH1412-1992	—	—	—	0.75	1.50	1.75
AH1416-1996	—	—	—	0.75	1.50	1.75
AH1416-1996 Proof	—	Value: 5.00				

KM# 6   50 FILS (1/2 Dirham)
7.5000 g., Copper-Nickel, 26 mm. **Ruler:** Abdullah Ibn Al-Hussein **Obv:** Value and date within crowned circle within sprigs **Rev:** Value within circle above date and star **Edge:** Milled

Date	Mintage	F	VF	XF	Unc	BU
AH1368//1949	2,500,000	—	0.75	2.00	3.50	—
AH1368//1949 Proof	25	Value: 275				

KM# 11   50 FILS (1/2 Dirham)
7.5000 g., Copper-Nickel, 26 mm. **Ruler:** Hussein Ibn Talal **Obv:** Value and date within crowned circle within sprigs **Rev:** Value within circle above date and star **Edge:** Milled

Date	Mintage	F	VF	XF	Unc	BU
AH1374//1955	2,500,000	—	0.75	1.50	4.00	—
AH1374//1955 Proof	—	Value: 100				
AH1382//1962	750,000	—	0.85	1.00	1.50	—
AH1382//1962 Proof	—	Value: 100				
AH1383//1964	1,003,000	—	0.40	0.60	1.00	—
AH1385//1965	1,505,000	—	0.40	0.60	1.00	—
AH1385//1965 Proof	10,000	Value: 4.50				

KM# 18   50 FILS (1/2 Dirham)
7.5000 g., Copper-Nickel, 26 mm. **Ruler:** Hussein Ibn Talal **Obv:** Head right **Rev:** Value and date within circle flanked by sprigs **Edge:** Milled

Date	Mintage	F	VF	XF	Unc	BU
AH1387-1968	400,000	—	0.75	1.00	2.75	—
AH1390-1970	1,000,000	—	0.40	0.60	1.25	—
AH1394-1974	1,000,000	—	0.40	0.60	1.25	—
AH1395-1975	2,000,000	—	0.40	0.60	1.25	—
AH1397-1977	6,000,000	—	0.40	0.60	1.25	—

KM# 39   50 FILS (1/2 Dirham)
7.5000 g., Copper-Nickel, 26 mm. **Ruler:** Hussein Ibn Talal **Edge:** Milled

Date	Mintage	F	VF	XF	Unc	BU
AH1398-1978	6,168,000	—	0.25	0.50	1.25	—
AH1398-1978 Proof	20,000	Value: 5.00				
AH1401-1981	5,000,000	—	0.25	0.50	1.25	—
AH1404-1984	10,000,000	—	0.25	0.50	1.25	—
AH1406-1985	—	—	—	2.75	3.25	—
Note: In sets only						
AH1406-1985 Proof	5,000	Value: 5.50				
AH1409-1989	6,000,000	—	0.25	0.50	1.25	—
AH1411-1991	10,000,000	—	0.25	0.50	1.25	—

KM# 54   5 PIASTRES
Nickel Plated Steel **Ruler:** Hussein Ibn Talal **Obv:** Bust left **Rev:** Value at left within lines below date with written value at lower right **Edge:** Milled

Date	Mintage	F	VF	XF	Unc	BU
AH1412-1992	—	—	—	1.00	2.00	2.50
AH1414-1993	—	—	—	1.00	2.00	2.50
AH1416-1996	—	—	—	1.00	2.00	2.50
AH1416-1996 Proof	—	Value: 5.00				
AH1418-1998	—	—	—	1.00	2.00	2.50

KM# 73   5 PIASTRES
5.0000 g., Nickel-Clad Steel, 25.8 mm. **Ruler:** Abdullah Ibn Al-Hussein **Obv:** Bust right **Rev:** Value to left within lines below date with written value at lower right **Edge:** Milled

Date	Mintage	F	VF	XF	Unc	BU
AH1421-2000	—	—	—	—	1.50	2.00

KM# 7 100 FILS (Dirham)
12.0000 g., Copper-Nickel, 30 mm. **Ruler:** Abdullah Ibn Al-Hussein **Obv:** Value and date within crowned circle within sprigs **Rev:** Value within circle above date and star **Edge:** Milled

Date	Mintage	F	VF	XF	Unc	BU
AH1368//1949	2,000,000	—	2.00	3.00	5.00	—
AH1368//1949 Proof	25	Value: 275				

KM# 12 100 FILS (Dirham)
12.0000 g., Copper-Nickel, 30 mm. **Ruler:** Hussein Ibn Talal **Obv:** Value and date within crowned circle within sprigs **Rev:** Value within circle above date and star **Edge:** Milled

Date	Mintage	F	VF	XF	Unc	BU
AH1374//1955	500,000	—	2.00	2.50	4.00	—
AH1374//1955 Proof	—	Value: 100				
AH1382//1962	600,000	—	1.00	1.50	3.00	—
AH1382//1962 Proof	—	Value: 100				
AH1383//1964 In sets only	3,000	—	1.50	3.00	5.00	—
AH1385//1965	405,000	—	1.00	1.25	2.25	—
AH1385//1965 Proof	10,000	Value: 5.00				

KM# 19 100 FILS (Dirham)
12.0000 g., Copper-Nickel, 30 mm. **Ruler:** Hussein Ibn Talal **Obv:** Head right **Rev:** Value and date within circle flanked by sprigs **Edge:** Milled

Date	Mintage	F	VF	XF	Unc	BU
AH1387-1968	175,000	—	1.00	1.50	2.50	—
AH1395-1975	2,500,000	—	0.40	1.00	2.00	—
AH1397-1977	2,000,000	—	0.40	1.00	2.00	—

KM# 40 100 FILS (Dirham)
12.0000 g., Copper-Nickel, 30 mm. **Ruler:** Hussein Ibn Talal **Obv:** Head right **Rev:** Value and date within circle flanked by sprigs **Edge:** Milled

Date	Mintage	F	VF	XF	Unc	BU
AH1398-1978	3,000,000	—	0.40	1.00	2.00	—
AH1398-1978 Proof	20,000	Value: 5.00				
AH1401-1981	4,000,000	—	0.40	1.00	2.00	—
AH1404-1984	5,000,000	—	0.40	1.00	1.50	—
AH1406-1985	—	—	—	2.50	3.50	—
Note: In sets only						
AH1406-1985 Proof	5,000	Value: 5.00				
AH1409-1989	4,000,000	—	0.40	1.00	1.50	—
AH1411-1991	6,000,000	—	0.40	1.00	1.50	—

KM# 55 10 PIASTRES
Nickel Plated Steel **Ruler:** Hussein Ibn Talal **Obv:** Bust left **Rev:** Value at left within lines below date with written value at lower right **Edge:** Milled

Date	Mintage	F	VF	XF	Unc	BU
AH1412-1992	—	—	—	1.25	2.25	2.75
AH1414-1993	—	—	—	1.25	2.25	2.75
AH1416-1996	—	—	—	1.25	2.25	2.75
AH1416-1996 Proof	—	Value: 5.00				

KM# 74 10 PIASTRES
8.0000 g., Nickel Clad Steel, 27.9 mm. **Ruler:** Abdullah Ibn Al-Hussein **Obv:** Bust right **Rev:** Value at left within lines below date with written value at lower right **Edge:** Milled

Date	Mintage	F	VF	XF	Unc	BU
AH1421-2000	—	—	—	—	4.00	5.00

KM# 20 1/4 DINAR
17.0000 g., Copper-Nickel, 34 mm. **Ruler:** Hussein Ibn Talal **Series:** F.A.O. **Obv:** Head right **Rev:** Date below olive tree within circled wreath with F.A.O. logo below **Edge:** Milled

Date	Mintage	F	VF	XF	Unc	BU
AH1389-1969	60,000	—	2.00	3.00	4.50	—

KM# 28 1/4 DINAR
17.0000 g., Copper-Nickel, 34 mm. **Ruler:** Hussein Ibn Talal **Obv:** Head right **Rev:** Date below olive tree within circled wreath **Edge:** Milled

Date	Mintage	F	VF	XF	Unc	BU
AH1390-1970	500,000	—	1.00	1.50	3.00	—
AH1394-1974	400,000	—	1.00	1.50	3.00	—
AH1395-1975	100,000	—	1.00	1.50	3.00	—

KM# 29 1/4 DINAR
19.0400 g., 0.9250 Silver 0.5662 oz. ASW, 34 mm. **Ruler:** Hussein Ibn Talal **Subject:** 10th Anniversary - Central Bank of Jordan **Obv:** Head right **Rev:** Olive tree within circled wreath with value and dates around wreath **Edge:** Milled

Date	Mintage	F	VF	XF	Unc	BU
AH1394-1974 Proof	550	Value: 200				

KM# 29a 1/4 DINAR
33.1900 g., 0.9170 Gold 0.9785 oz. AGW, 34 mm. **Ruler:** Hussein Ibn Talal **Subject:** 10th Anniversary - Central Bank of Jordan **Obv:** Head right **Rev:** Tree within circlular wreath with dates and value around wreath **Edge:** Milled

Date	Mintage	F	VF	XF	Unc	BU
AH1394-1974 Proof	100	Value: 1,350				

KM# 30 1/4 DINAR
17.0000 g., Copper-Nickel, 34 mm. **Ruler:** Hussein Ibn Talal **Subject:** 25th Anniversary of Reign **Obv:** Head facing 1/4 right within small circle flanked by sprigs, all within design with crown on top and date below **Rev:** Castle above dates **Edge:** Milled

Date	Mintage	F	VF	XF	Unc	BU
AH1397-1977	200,000	—	1.00	2.00	4.50	—

KM# 41 1/4 DINAR
17.0000 g., Copper-Nickel, 34 mm. **Ruler:** Hussein Ibn Talal **Obv:** Head right **Rev:** Date below olive tree within circled wreath

Date	Mintage	F	VF	XF	Unc	BU
AH1398-1978	200,000	—	1.00	2.00	4.00	—
AH1398-1978 Proof	20,000	Value: 5.50				
AH1401-1981	800,000	—	0.75	1.50	3.00	—
AH1406-1985	—	—	—	3.00	4.00	—
Note: In sets only						
AH1406-1985 Proof	5,000	Value: 6.50				

KM# 61 1/4 DINAR
7.4000 g., Nickel-Brass **Ruler:** Hussein Ibn Talal **Obv:** Bust left
Rev: Value in circle within artistic design **Edge:** Plain

Date	Mintage	F	VF	XF	Unc	BU
AH1416-1996	—	—	—	—	3.00	4.00
AH1416-1996 Proof	—	Value: 7.50				
AH1417-1997	—	—	—	—	3.00	4.00

KM# 21 1/2 DINAR
20.0000 g., 0.9990 Silver 0.6423 oz. ASW, 35 mm.
Ruler: Hussein Ibn Talal **Rev:** Al Harraneh Palace above value
Edge: Milled

Date	Mintage	F	VF	XF	Unc	BU
AH1389//1969 Proof	6,100	Value: 30.00				

KM# 42 1/2 DINAR
Copper-Nickel **Ruler:** Hussein Ibn Talal **Subject:** 1400th
Anniversary of Hijra (Mohammed's Pilgrimage) **Obv:** Bust facing
1/4 right **Rev:** Capitol building and sun within circle at right, sprig
to left within larger circle **Edge:** Plain

Date	Mintage	F	VF	XF	Unc	BU
AH1400-1980	2,006,000	—	1.50	2.50	5.00	—

KM# 58 1/2 DINAR
9.6800 g., Brass **Ruler:** Hussein Ibn Talal **Obv:** Bust left
Rev: Value in circle within artistic design **Edge:** Plain

Date	Mintage	F	VF	XF	Unc	BU
AH1416-1996	—	—	—	—	4.00	5.00
AH1416-1996 Proof	—	Value: 8.50				

KM# 63 1/2 DINAR
Bi-Metallic Copper-Nickel center in Aluminum-Bronze ring
Ruler: Hussein Ibn Talal **Obv:** Bust left within circle **Rev:** Value
in center of circled wreath **Edge:** Plain

Date	Mintage	F	VF	XF	Unc	BU
AH1417-1997	—	—	—	—	8.00	10.00

KM# 79 1/2 DINAR
9.6700 g., Bi-Metallic Copper-Nickel center in Brass ring, 29 mm.
Ruler: Abdullah Ibn Al-Hussein **Obv:** Bust right within circle
Rev: Value in center of circled wreath **Edge:** Plain

Date	Mintage	F	VF	XF	Unc	BU
AH1421-2000	—	—	—	—	4.00	5.00

KM# 22 3/4 DINAR
30.0000 g., 0.9990 Silver 0.9635 oz. ASW, 45 mm.
Ruler: Hussein Ibn Talal **Obv:** Similar to 1/2 Dinar, KM#21
Rev: Shrine of the Nativity, Bethlehem **Edge:** Milled

Date	Mintage	F	VF	XF	Unc	BU
AH1389//1969 Proof	5,800	Value: 50.00				

KM# 23 DINAR
40.0000 g., 0.9990 Silver 1.2847 oz. ASW, 55 mm.
Ruler: Hussein Ibn Talal **Obv:** Similar to 1/2 Dinar, KM#21
Rev: Temple Hill, Jerusalem **Edge:** Milled

Date	Mintage	F	VF	XF	Unc	BU
AH1389//1969 Proof	6,800	Value: 70.00				

KM# 47 DINAR
14.0000 g., Nickel-Bronze, 29 mm. **Ruler:** Hussein Ibn Talal
Subject: King Hussein's 50th Birthday **Obv:** Head right within
beaded circle **Rev:** Crowned sun within 3/4 wreath flanked by
dates **Edge:** Milled

Date	Mintage	F	VF	XF	Unc	BU
AH1406-1985	—	—	—	—	7.50	—
AH1406-1985 Proof	5,000	Value: 10.00				

KM# 51.1 DINAR
15.0000 g., 0.9250 Silver 0.4461 oz. ASW, 30 mm.
Ruler: Hussein Ibn Talal **Subject:** 40th Year of Reign
Obv: Uniformed bust facing **Rev:** Tughra **Edge:** Plain

Date	Mintage	F	VF	XF	Unc	BU
AH1413-1992 Proof	4,900	Value: 30.00				

KM# 51.2 DINAR
15.0000 g., 0.9250 Silver 0.4461 oz. ASW, 30 mm.
Ruler: Hussein Ibn Talal **Subject:** King's 40th Anniversary of
Reign **Obv:** Multicolor uniformed bust facing **Rev:** Tughra
Edge: Plain

Date	Mintage	F	VF	XF	Unc	BU
AH1413-1992 Proof	100	Value: 150				

KM# 52 DINAR
8.5000 g., 0.9170 Gold 0.2506 oz. AGW, 21 mm.
Ruler: Hussein Ibn Talal **Subject:** 40th Year of Reign
Obv: Uniformed bust facing **Rev:** Tughra **Edge:** Milled

Date	Mintage	F	VF	XF	Unc	BU
AH1413-1992 Proof	3,000	Value: 245				

KM# 62 DINAR
Brass **Ruler:** Hussein Ibn Talal **Subject:** 50th Anniversary -
F.A.O. **Obv:** Bust left **Rev:** F.A.O. logo within artistic design
Edge: Plain

Date	Mintage	F	VF	XF	Unc	BU
AH1415-1995	—	—	—	—	10.00	12.00

KM# 59 DINAR
Brass **Ruler:** Hussein Ibn Talal **Obv:** Bust left **Rev:** Value within
center of artistic design **Edge:** Plain

Date	Mintage	F	VF	XF	Unc	BU
AH1416-1996	—	—	—	—	8.00	10.00
AH1416-1996 Proof	—	Value: 12.00				
AH1417-1997	—	—	—	—	7.00	9.00

KM# 68 DINAR
31.1035 g., 0.9990 Silver 0.9990 oz. ASW, 40 mm.
Ruler: Hussein Ibn Talal **Subject:** 50 Years - Jordanian Independence **Obv:** Bust left **Rev:** Bust with headdress left with inscription at upper left **Edge:** Milled

Date	Mintage	F	VF	XF	Unc	BU
ND(1996) Proof	Est. 2,000				Value: 75.00	

KM# 64 DINAR
Brass **Ruler:** Hussein Ibn Talal **Obv:** Bust left **Rev:** Value within ornamented circle **Edge:** Milled

Date	Mintage	F	VF	XF	Unc	BU
AH1419-1998	—	—	—	—	5.50	6.50

KM# 65 DINAR
Brass **Ruler:** Hussein Ibn Talal **Subject:** Human Rights **Obv:** Bust left **Rev:** Commemorative legend with value within ornamented circle **Edge:** Milled

Date	Mintage	F	VF	XF	Unc	BU
AH1419-1998	—	—	—	—	7.00	8.00

KM# 24 2 DINARS
5.5200 g., 0.9000 Gold 0.1597 oz. AGW, 21 mm.
Ruler: Hussein Ibn Talal **Subject:** Forum in Jerash **Edge:** Milled

Date	Mintage	F	VF	XF	Unc	BU
AH1389//1969 Proof	2,425		Value: 180			

KM# 31 2-1/2 DINARS
28.2800 g., 0.9250 Silver 0.8410 oz. ASW, 38.61 mm.
Ruler: Hussein Ibn Talal **Subject:** Conservation **Obv:** Head right **Rev:** Rhim Gazelle **Edge:** Milled

Date	Mintage	F	VF	XF	Unc	BU
AH1397-1977	6,265	—	—	—	25.00	—
AH1397-1977 Proof	5,011		Value: 35.00			

KM# 32 3 DINARS
35.0000 g., 0.9250 Silver 1.0408 oz. ASW, 42 mm.
Ruler: Hussein Ibn Talal **Subject:** Conservation **Obv:** Head right **Rev:** Palestine sunbird and flower **Edge:** Milled

Date	Mintage	F	VF	XF	Unc	BU
AH1397-1977	6,263	—	—	—	30.00	—
AH1397-1977 Proof	4,897		Value: 35.00			

KM# 43 3 DINARS
23.3300 g., 0.9250 Silver 0.6938 oz. ASW, 38.61 mm.
Ruler: Hussein Ibn Talal **Subject:** International Year of the Child **Obv:** Bust left **Rev:** Palace of culture in Amman and two children within circle **Edge:** Milled

Date	Mintage	F	VF	XF	Unc	BU
AH1401 (1981) Proof	21,000		Value: 20.00			

KM# 25 5 DINARS
13.8200 g., 0.9000 Gold 0.3999 oz. AGW, 31 mm.
Ruler: Hussein Ibn Talal **Obv:** Bust left **Rev:** Treasury in Petra **Edge:** Milled

Date	Mintage	F	VF	XF	Unc	BU
AH1389//1969 Proof	1,950		Value: 385			

KM# 57 5 DINARS
Copper-Nickel, 38.61 mm. **Ruler:** Hussein Ibn Talal **Subject:** UN 50 Years **Obv:** Bust left **Rev:** Black iris **Edge:** Milled

Date	Mintage	F	VF	XF	Unc	BU
ND(1995)	—	—	—	—	10.00	—

KM# 57a 5 DINARS
28.2800 g., 0.9250 Silver 0.8410 oz. ASW, 38.61 mm.
Ruler: Hussein Ibn Talal **Subject:** UN 50 Years **Obv:** Bust left **Rev:** Black iris **Edge:** Milled

Date	Mintage	F	VF	XF	Unc	BU
ND(1995) Proof	100,000		Value: 50.00			

KM# 66 5 DINARS
28.2800 g., 0.9250 Silver 0.8410 oz. ASW, 38.61 mm.
Ruler: Hussein Ibn Talal **Subject:** UNICEF: For the Children of the World **Obv:** Conjoined busts of King Hussein and Queen Noor right **Rev:** Boy, girl and UNICEF logo **Edge:** Milled

Date	Mintage	F	VF	XF	Unc	BU
AH1419-1999 Proof	25,000		Value: 50.00			

KM# 71 5 DINARS
28.5000 g., Brass, 40 mm. **Ruler:** Abdullah Ibn Al-Hussein **Subject:** Millennium and Baptism of Jesus **Obv:** Bust facing **Rev:** Baptism scene **Edge:** Milled

Date	Mintage	F	VF	XF	Unc	BU
AH1420//2000 Prooflike	10,000	—	—	—	20.00	—

KM# 26 10 DINARS
27.6400 g., 0.9000 Gold 0.7997 oz. AGW, 40 mm.
Ruler: Hussein Ibn Talal **Subject:** Visit of Pope Paul VI **Obv:** Bust left **Rev:** Pope and church within circle above value

Date	Mintage	F	VF	XF	Unc	BU
AH1389//1969 Proof	1,870		Value: 825			

KM# 44 10 DINARS
30.0000 g., 0.9250 Silver 0.8921 oz. ASW, 40 mm.
Ruler: Hussein Ibn Talal **Subject:** 15th century Hijrah calendar **Obv:** Bust 1/4 right **Rev:** Capitol building and sun within circle with sprig at left within larger circle **Edge:** Milled

Date	Mintage	F	VF	XF	Unc	BU
AH1400-1980 Proof	17,000		Value: 37.50			

KM# 48   10 DINARS
15.2000 g., 0.9250 Silver 0.4520 oz. ASW, 29 mm.
Ruler: Hussein Ibn Talal **Subject:** King's 50th Birthday
Obv: Head right within beaded circle **Rev:** Crowned sun within
3/4 wreath above value **Edge:** Milled

Date	Mintage	F	VF	XF	Unc	BU
AH1406-1985	—				Value: 30.00	
Proof						

KM# 80   10 DINARS
31.1000 g., 0.9990 Silver 0.9988 oz. ASW, 40 mm. **Ruler:**
Abdullah Ibn Al-Hussein **Subject:** Abdullah II's Accession to Throne
Obv: Abdullah II **Rev:** Crowned and mantled arms **Edge:** Milled

Date	Mintage	F	VF	XF	Unc	BU
AH1420-1999	2,000				Value: 45.00	
Proof						

KM# 72   10 DINARS
31.0000 g., 0.9990 Silver 0.9956 oz. ASW, 40 mm.
Ruler: Abdullah Ibn Al-Hussein **Subject:** Millennium and
Baptism of Jesus **Obv:** Bust facing **Rev:** Baptism scene
Edge: Milled **Note:** Issued in 1999.

Date	Mintage	F	VF	XF	Unc	BU
AH1420 (2000)	5,000	—	—	—	45.00	—
Matte with Patina						
AH1420 (2000)	Inc. above	Value: 55.00				
Proof						

KM# 27   25 DINARS
69.1100 g., 0.9000 Gold 1.9997 oz. AGW, 48 mm.
Ruler: Hussein Ibn Talal **Obv:** Head right with crowned mantled
arms above **Rev:** Dome of the Rock, Jerusalem, above value
Edge: Milled

Date	Mintage	F	VF	XF	Unc	BU
AH1389//1969	1,000				Value: 2,250	
Proof						

KM# 33   25 DINARS
15.0000 g., 0.9170 Gold 0.4422 oz. AGW, 29.01 mm.
Ruler: Hussein Ibn Talal **Subject:** 25th Anniversary of Reign
Obv: Bust right **Rev:** Crowned mantled arms above dates
Edge: Milled

Date	Mintage	F	VF	XF	Unc	BU
AH1397-1977	4,724				Value: 450	
FM Proof						

KM# 45   40 DINARS
14.3100 g., 0.9170 Gold 0.4219 oz. AGW, 27 mm.
Ruler: Hussein Ibn Talal **Subject:** 15th century Hijrah calendar
Obv: Bust facing 1/4 right **Rev:** Sun rays, cloud, domed building
and box within flower design and circle **Edge:** Milled

Date	Mintage	F	VF	XF	Unc	BU
AH1400-1980	9,500				Value: 425	
Proof						

KM# 50   50 DINARS
15.9800 g., 0.9170 Gold 0.4711 oz. AGW, 28.40 mm.
Ruler: Hussein Ibn Talal **Subject:** Five-Year Plan **Obv:** Head
right with crowned mantled arms above **Rev:** Fruit flanked by
sprigs within circled gear with writing within chain wreath
Edge: Milled

Date	Mintage	F	VF	XF	Unc	BU
AH1396-1976	250	—	—	—	500	525
AH1396-1976	Inc. above	Value: 600				
Proof						

KM# 34   50 DINARS
33.4370 g., 0.9000 Gold 0.9675 oz. AGW, 34 mm.
Ruler: Hussein Ibn Talal **Subject:** Conservation **Obv:** Head right
Rev: Bird facing left **Edge:** Milled

Date	Mintage	F	VF	XF	Unc	BU
AH1397-1977	829	—	—	—	925	950
AH1397-1977	287				Value: 1,200	
Proof						

KM# 49   50 DINARS
17.0000 g., 0.9170 Gold 0.5012 oz. AGW, 29 mm.
Ruler: Hussein Ibn Talal **Subject:** King Hussein's 50th Birthday
Obv: Head right within beaded circle **Rev:** Crown above rising
sun within wreath **Edge:** Milled

Date	Mintage	F	VF	XF	Unc	BU
AH1406-1985	2,029				Value: 500	
Proof						

KM# 69   50 DINARS
16.9600 g., 0.9166 Gold 0.4998 oz. AGW, 30 mm.
Ruler: Hussein Ibn Talal **Subject:** 50 Years - Jordanian
Independence **Obv:** Bust facing **Rev:** Portrait of King Abdullah

Date	Mintage	F	VF	XF	Unc	BU
ND(1996) Proof	Est. 1,000				Value: 500	

KM# 67   50 DINARS
6.2200 g., 0.9990 Gold 0.1998 oz. AGW, 22 mm.
Ruler: Hussein Ibn Talal **Subject:** UNICEF: For the Children of
the World **Obv:** Hussein Ibn Talal and Noor Al-Hussein **Rev:** Boy,
girl and UNICEF logo

Date	Mintage	F	VF	XF	Unc	BU
AH1419-1999	10,000				Value: 200	
Proof						

KM# 81   50 DINARS
16.9600 g., 0.9166 Gold 0.4998 oz. AGW, 30 mm.
Ruler: Abdullah Ibn Al-Hussein **Subject:** Abdullah II's Accession
to the Throne **Obv:** Abdullah II **Rev:** Crowned and mantled arms
Edge: Milled

Date	Mintage	F	VF	XF	Unc	BU
AH1420-1999	1,750				Value: 520	
Proof						

KM# 82   50 DINARS
16.9600 g., 0.9166 Gold 0.4998 oz. AGW, 30 mm.
Ruler: Abdullah Ibn Al-Hussein **Subject:** Millennium and
Baptism of Jesus **Obv:** Abdullah II **Rev:** River baptism scene
Edge: Milled

Date	Mintage	F	VF	XF	Unc	BU
AH1420-2000	3,500				Value: 500	
Proof						

KM# 46 60 DINARS
17.1700 g., 0.9170 Gold 0.5062 oz. AGW, 27 mm.
Ruler: Hussein Ibn Talal **Subject:** International Year of the Child
Obv: Head right **Rev:** Palace of Culture in Amman and two children within circle **Edge:** Milled

Date	Mintage	F	VF	XF	Unc	BU
AH1401-1981 Proof	20,000	Value: 500				

PATTERNS
Including off metal strikes

KM#	Date	Mintage	Identification	Mkt Val
Pn1	AH1387	50	Fils. Gold. 5.6600 g. KM14.	250
Pn2	AH1387	50	5 Fils. Gold. 11.4000 g. KM15.	350
Pn3	AH1387	50	10 Fils. Gold. 18.8000 g. KM16.	400
Pn4	AH1387	50	25 Fils. Gold. 8.8100 g. KM17.	300
Pn5	AH1387	50	50 Fils. Gold. 13.7500 g. KM18.	1,000
Pn6	AH1387	50	Dirham. Gold. 22.8000 g. KM19.	1,200
Pn7	AH1395	170	Fils. Gold. 5.6600 g. As KM14.	300
Pn8	AH1395	170	5 Fils. Gold. 11.4000 g. As KM15.	500
Pn9	AH1395	170	10 Fils. Gold. 18.8000 g. As KM16.	550
Pn10	AH1395	170	25 Fils. Gold. 8.8100 g. As KM17.	350
Pn11	AH1395	170	50 Fils. Gold. 13.7500 g. As KM18.	550
Pn12	AH1395	170	Dirham. Gold. 22.8000 g. As KM19.	750
Pn13	AH1395	110	1/4 Dinar. Gold. 31.4500 g. As KM28.	950
Pn14	AH1412-1992	3	2-1/2 Piastres. Nickel-Plated Steel. as KM-53, denomination not frosted.	750
Pn15	AH1412-1992	3	5 Piastres. Nickel-Plated Steel. as KM-54, denomination not frosted	1,000
Pn16	AH1412-1992	3	10 Piastres. Nickel Plated Steel. as KM-55, denomination not frosted.	2,500
Pn17	AH1415-1995(1996)	1	1/4 Dinar. Nickel-Brass. Similar to KM-61, never released in circulation with the "1995" date.	—
Pn18	AH1415-1995(1996)	1	1/2 Dinar. Brass. Similar to KM-58, never released in circulation with the "1995" date.	—
Pn19	AH1415-1995(1996)	3	Dinar. Brass. as KM-62, lighter metal	450
Pn20	AH1417-1997	2	1/2 Dinar. Bi-Metallic. as KM-63, metal lighter in color	250

PIEFORTS

KM#	Date	Mintage	Identification	Mkt Val
P1	1981	2,050	3 Dinars. Silver. 46.6600 g. KM43.	150
P2	1981	61	60 Dinars. Gold. 34.3400 g. KM46.	1,200
P3	1985	700	50 Dinars. Gold. 34.3400 g. KM49.	1,000
		Note: Majority melted down; about 100 pcs. remain today		
P4	AH1413-1992	500	Dinar. 0.9167 Gold. 17.0000 g. 28.4 mm. Broad piefort of KM-52	500
P5	ND(1996)	400	50 Dinars. 0.9166 Gold. 33.9200 g. 40 mm. Milled edge. Similar to KM#69, with 40mm diameter.	1,000

MINT SETS

KM#	Date	Mintage	Identification	Issue Price	Mkt Val
MS1	1985 (8)	—	KM35-41, 47	10.75	15.00
MS2	1949-1964 (6)	—	KM5 (1949), 8 (1963), 9 (1962), Pn10-11 (1964), Pn12 (1962), mixed dates	—	10.00
MS3	1996 (8)	—	KM#53-56, 58-61	—	15.00
MS4	2000-2004 (5)	—	KM#73-74, 78.1, 79, 83	—	20.00

PROOF SETS

KM#	Date	Mintage	Identification	Issue Price	Mkt Val
PS1	1949 (6)	25	KM2-7	—	1,500
PS2	1965 (6)	10,000	KM8-13	14.40	2,000
PS3	1969 (7)	—	KM21-27	396	3,700
PS4	1969 (6)	—	KM21-26	—	1,500
PS5	1969 (4)	—	KM24-27	—	3,600
PS6	1969 (3)	5,800	KM21-23	36.00	150
PS6A	1974 (2)	100	KM#29-29a	—	1,500
PS7	1977 (3)	1,000	KM31-32, 34	780	1,300
PS8	1977 (2)	9,000	KM31-32	60.00	65.00
PS9	1978 (7)	20,000	KM35-41	27.00	25.00
PS10	1980 (2)	—	KM44-45	365	525
PS11	1985 (8)	5,000	KM35-41, 47	31.00	50.00
PS13	1996 (8)	—	KM#53-56, 58-61	30.00	45.00
PS12	1996 (3)	50	KM#68, 69 & P5	—	1,000
PS14	2006 (2)	250	KM#84-85	—	2,350

SPECIMEN SETS (SS)

KM#	Date	Mintage	Identification	Issue Price	Mkt Val
SS1	1964 (6)	3,000	KM8-13	—	14.00
SS2	1965 (6)	5,000	KM8-13	—	12.00
SS3	1968 (6)	50	KM14-19	—	300
SS4	1968 (6)	50	KMPn1-6	—	4,250
SS5	1975 (7)	110	KMPn7-13	—	2,250

KATANGA

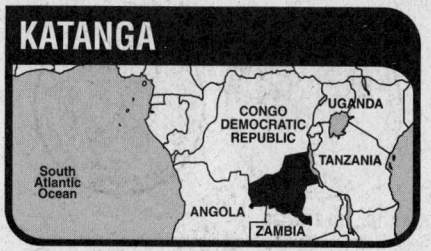

Katanga, the southern province of the former Belgian Congo, had an area of 191,873 sq. mi. (496,951 sq. km.) and was noted for its mineral wealth.

MONETARY SYSTEM
100 Centimes = 1 Franc

PROVINCE
DECIMAL COINAGE

KM# 1 FRANC
4.7000 g., Bronze **Obv:** Bananas (musax paradisiaca-Musaceae) within circle **Rev:** Cross, value and date within circle

Date	Mintage	F	VF	XF	Unc	BU
1961	—		1.25	2.00	4.00	

KM# 2 5 FRANCS
6.5400 g., Bronze, 26.3 mm. **Obv:** Bananas (musax paradisiaca-Musaceae) within circle **Rev:** Cross, value and date within circle

Date	Mintage	F	VF	XF	Unc	BU
1961	—		2.50	4.00	8.00	

KM# 2a 5 FRANCS
13.3300 g., 0.9000 Gold 0.3857 oz. AGW **Obv:** Bananas within circle **Rev:** Cross, value and date within circle

Date	Mintage	F	VF	XF	Unc	BU
1961	20,000	—			450	500

KAZAKHSTAN

The Republic of Kazakhstan (formerly Kazakhstan S.S.R.) is bordered to the west by the Caspian Sea and Russia, to the north by Russia, in the east by the Peoples Republic of China and in the south by Uzbekistan and Kirghizia. It has an area of 1,049,155 sq. mi. (2,717,300 sq. km.) and a population of 16.7 million. Capital: Astana. Rich in mineral resources including coal, tungsten, copper, lead, zinc and manganese with huge oil and natural gas reserves. Agriculture is very important, (it previously represented 20 percent of the total arable acreage of the combined U.S.S.R.) Non-ferrous metallurgy, heavy engineering and chemical industries are leaders in its economy.

The Kazakhs are a branch of the Turkic peoples which led the nomadic life of herdsmen until WW I. In the 13th century they came under Genghis Khan's eldest son Jujiand. Later they became a part of the Golden Horde, a western Mongol empire. Around the beginning of the 16th century they were divided into 3 confederacies, known as *zhuz* or hordes, in the steppes of Turkestan. At the end of the 17th century an incursion by the Kalmucks, a remnant of the Oirat Mongol confederacy, resulted in heavy losses on both sides which facilitated Russian penetration. Resistance to Russian settlements varied throughout the 1800's, but by 1900 over 100 million acres were declared Czarist state property and used for a planned peasant colonization. After a revolution in 1905 Kazakh deputies were elected. In 1916 the tsarist government ordered mobilization of all males, between 19 and 43, for auxiliary service. The Kazakhs rose in defiance which led

the governor general of Turkestan to send troops against the rebels. Shortly after the Russian revolution, Kazakh Nationalists asked for full autonomy. The Communist *coup d'etat* of Nov. 1917 led to civil war. In 1919-20 the Red army defeated the "White" Russian forces and occupied Kazakhstan and fought against the Nationalist government formed on Nov. 17, 1917 by Ali Khan Bukey Khan. The Kazakh Autonomous Soviet Socialist Republic was proclaimed on Aug. 26, 1920 within the R.S.F.S.R. Russian and Ukrainian colonization continued while 2 purges in 1927 and 1935 quelled any Kazakh feelings of priority in the matters of their country. On Dec. 5, 1936 Kazakhstan qualified for full status as an S.S.R. and held its first congress in 1937. Independence was declared on Dec. 16, 1991 and Kazakhstan joined the C.I.S.

MONETARY SYSTEM
100 Tyin = 1 Tenge

REPUBLIC
DECIMAL COINAGE

KM# 1 2 TYIN
1.9000 g., Yellow Brass, 17.2 mm. **Obv:** National emblem **Rev:** Star design divides date with value within

Date	Mintage	F	VF	XF	Unc	BU
1993	—				0.45	0.75

KM# 1a 2 TYIN
2.2000 g., Copper Clad Brass, 17.2 mm. **Obv:** National emblem **Rev:** Star design divides date with value within **Edge:** Plain

Date	Mintage	F	VF	XF	Unc	BU
1993	—				0.45	0.75

KM# 2 5 TYIN
1.9000 g., Yellow Brass, 17.2 mm. **Obv:** National emblem **Rev:** Star design divides date with value within

Date	Mintage	F	VF	XF	Unc	BU
1993	—				0.60	1.00

KM# 2a 5 TYIN
2.2400 g., Copper Clad Brass, 17.2 mm. **Obv:** National emblem **Rev:** Star design divides date with value within **Edge:** Plain

Date	Mintage	F	VF	XF	Unc	BU
1993	—				0.60	1.00

KM# 3 10 TYIN
3.3000 g., Yellow Brass, 19.95 mm. **Obv:** National emblem **Rev:** Star design divides date with value within **Edge:** Plain

Date	Mintage	F	VF	XF	Unc	BU
1993	—				0.80	1.50

KM# 3a 10 TYIN
3.1000 g., Copper Clad Brass, 19.6 mm. **Obv:** National emblem **Rev:** Star design divides date with value within

Date	Mintage	F	VF	XF	Unc	BU
1993	—				0.80	1.50

KM# 4 20 TYIN
4.5200 g., Brass Plated Zinc, 22 mm. **Obv:** National emblem
Rev: Star design divides date with value within

Date	Mintage	F	VF	XF	Unc	BU
1993	—	—	—	—	1.25	2.00

KM# 5 50 TYIN
6.8000 g., Brass Plated Zinc, 25.1 mm. **Obv:** National emblem
Rev: Star design divides date with value within

Date	Mintage	F	VF	XF	Unc	BU
1993	—	—	—	—	1.50	2.50

KM# 6 TENGE
Copper-Nickel, 17.3 mm. **Obv:** Mythical animal **Rev:** Star design
with value and date within

Date	Mintage	F	VF	XF	Unc	BU
1992	—	—	—	—	1.00	1.75
1993	—	—	—	—	0.50	0.85

KM# 23 TENGE
1.6000 g., Brass, 14.60 mm. **Obv:** National emblem **Rev:** Value
flanked by designs **Edge:** Plain

Date	Mintage	F	VF	XF	Unc	BU
1997	—	—	—	—	0.50	0.85
2000	—	—	—	—	0.50	0.85

KM# 8 3 TENGE
Copper-Nickel **Obv:** Mythical animal within circle **Rev:** Star
design with value and date within

Date	Mintage	F	VF	XF	Unc	BU
1993	—	—	—	—	0.75	1.25

KM# 9 5 TENGE
Copper-Nickel **Obv:** Mythical animal within circle **Rev:** Star
design with date and value within

Date	Mintage	F	VF	XF	Unc	BU
1993	—	—	—	—	1.25	2.00

KM# 24 5 TENGE
Brass **Obv:** National emblem **Rev:** Value flanked by designs

Date	Mintage	F	VF	XF	Unc	BU
1997	—	—	—	—	0.50	0.85
2000	—	—	—	—	0.50	0.85

KM# 10 10 TENGE
Copper-Nickel **Obv:** National emblem above value
Rev: Stylized double headed eagle within circle above date

Date	Mintage	F	VF	XF	Unc	BU
1993	—	—	—	—	2.00	3.50

KM# 25 10 TENGE
Brass **Obv:** National emblem **Rev:** Value above design

Date	Mintage	F	VF	XF	Unc	BU
1997	—	—	—	—	0.75	1.25
2000	—	—	—	—	0.75	1.25

KM# 11 20 TENGE
Copper-Nickel **Obv:** National emblem above value
Rev: Turbaned head 1/4 right within circle

Date	Mintage	F	VF	XF	Unc	BU
1993	—	—	—	—	3.50	5.50

KM# 12 20 TENGE
Copper-Nickel **Subject:** 50th Anniversary - United Nations
Obv: National emblem above value **Rev:** UN logo and
anniversary dates within circle

Date	Mintage	F	VF	XF	Unc	BU
1995	—	—	—	—	3.50	5.50

KM# 18 20 TENGE
Copper-Nickel **Subject:** 150th Anniversary - Jambyl
Obv: National emblem above value **Rev:** Man with stringed
instrument

Date	Mintage	F	VF	XF	Unc	BU
1996	—	—	—	—	3.50	5.50

KM# 19 20 TENGE
Copper-Nickel **Subject:** 5th Anniversary - Independence
Obv: National emblem above value **Rev:** Monument and
buildings

Date	Mintage	F	VF	XF	Unc	BU
1996	—	—	—	—	3.50	5.50

KM# 20 20 TENGE
Copper-Nickel **Subject:** Centennial - Birth of Muchtar Auezov
Obv: National emblem above value **Rev:** Head facing divides dates

Date	Mintage	F	VF	XF	Unc	BU
ND(1997)	—	—	—	—	3.50	5.50

KM# 26 20 TENGE
2.8600 g., Copper-Nickel, 18.3 mm. **Obv:** National emblem
Rev: Value above design **Edge:** Segmented reeding
Edge: * CTO TEHГE * Y 3 TEHГE

Date	Mintage	F	VF	XF	Unc	BU
1997	—	—	—	—	1.00	1.75
2000	—	—	—	—	1.00	1.75

KM# 21 20 TENGE
Copper-Nickel **Subject:** Year of Peace and Harmony
Obv: National emblem above value **Rev:** Stylized dove

Date	Mintage	F	VF	XF	Unc	BU
1997	—	—	—	—	3.50	5.50

KM# 22 20 TENGE
Copper-Nickel **Subject:** New Capital - Astana **Obv:** National
emblem above value **Rev:** Flower-like design

Date	Mintage	F	VF	XF	Unc	BU
1998	—	—	—	—	3.50	5.50

KM# 28 20 TENGE
Copper-Nickel **Subject:** 100th Birthday - K.I. Satbaev
Obv: National emblem above value **Rev:** Head facing

Date	Mintage	F	VF	XF	Unc	BU
1999	—	—	—	—	3.85	6.50

KM# 27 50 TENGE
Copper-Nickel **Obv:** National emblem **Rev:** Value above design

Date	Mintage	F	VF	XF	Unc	BU
1997	—	—	—	—	2.00	3.50
2000	—	—	—	—	2.00	3.50

KM# 30 50 TENGE
Copper-Nickel **Subject:** Millennium **Obv:** National emblem
above value **Rev:** Rising sun above three blocks

Date	Mintage	F	VF	XF	Unc	BU
1999	—	—	—	—	3.50	5.50

KM# 31 50 TENGE
10.7000 g., Copper-Nickel, 31 mm. **Subject:** Victorious
conclusion of World War II **Obv:** National emblem above value
Rev: Soldiers celebrating **Edge:** Reeded and plain sections

Date	Mintage	F	VF	XF	Unc	BU
ND(2000)	—	—	—	—	4.00	6.50

KM# 48 50 TENGE
11.0600 g., Copper-Nickel, 31 mm. **Subject:** 1500th Anniversary
of Akhmet Yasaui Kesenesi Mosque **Obv:** National emblem above
value **Rev:** Mosque **Edge:** Reeded and plain sections

Date	Mintage	F	VF	XF	Unc	BU
2000	—	—	—	—	3.00	5.00

KM# 33 50 TENGE
11.5000 g., Copper-Nickel **Obv:** National emblem above value
Rev: Bust 1/4 left **Edge:** Reeded and plain sections

Date	Mintage	F	VF	XF	Unc	BU
2000	—	—	—	—	4.00	6.50

KM# 13 100 TENGE
24.0000 g., 0.9250 Silver 0.7137 oz. ASW **Subject:** 150th
Anniversary - Birth of Abaj Kunabaev **Obv:** Mother and child
within circle **Rev:** Head left flanked by dates above small assorted
figures **Edge:** Lettered

Date	Mintage	F	VF	XF	Unc	BU
1995 Proof	6,000	Value: 35.00				

KM# 14 100 TENGE
24.0000 g., 0.9250 Silver 0.7137 oz. ASW **Subject:** 150th
Anniversary - Birth of Abaj Kunabaev **Obv:** Bust left **Rev:** Falconer

Date	Mintage	F	VF	XF	Unc	BU
1995 Proof	6,000	Value: 37.50				

KM# 15 100 TENGE
24.0000 g., 0.9250 Silver 0.7137 oz. ASW **Subject:** 150th
Anniversary - Birth of Abaj Kunabaev **Obv:** Bust left **Rev:** Couple
on swings

Date	Mintage	F	VF	XF	Unc	BU
1995 Proof	6,000	Value: 35.00				

KM# 16 100 TENGE
24.0000 g., 0.9250 Silver 0.7137 oz. ASW **Subject:** 150th
Anniversary - Birth of Abaj Kunabaev **Obv:** Bust left **Rev:** Town view

Date	Mintage	F	VF	XF	Unc	BU
1995 Proof	6,000	Value: 35.00				

KM# 17 100 TENGE
24.0000 g., 0.9250 Silver 0.7137 oz. ASW **Subject:** 150th
Anniversary - Birth of Abaj Kunabaev **Obv:** Bust left **Rev:** Elderly man

Date	Mintage	F	VF	XF	Unc	BU
1995 Proof	6,000	Value: 35.00				

KM# 32 100 TENGE
24.0000 g., 0.9250 Silver 0.7137 oz. ASW, 37 mm.
Subject: Millennium **Obv:** National emblem within design
Rev: Ancient and modern technologies **Edge:** Plain

Date	Mintage	F	VF	XF	Unc	BU
1999 Proof	2,000	Value: 45.00				

KM# 34 100 TENGE
24.0000 g., 0.9250 Silver 0.7137 oz. ASW, 37 mm.
Subject: 1500th Anniversary of Turkestan **Obv:** Value
Rev: Domed building **Edge:** Plain

Date	Mintage	F	VF	XF	Unc	BU
2000 Proof	3,000	Value: 45.00				

KM# 35 500 TENGE
24.0000 g., 0.9250 Silver 0.7137 oz. ASW, 37 mm.
Subject: Snow Leopard **Obv:** Value **Rev:** Prowling leopard
Edge: Plain

Date	Mintage	F	VF	XF	Unc	BU
2000 Proof	3,000	Value: 50.00				

KM# 36 500 TENGE
24.0000 g., 0.9250 Silver 0.7137 oz. ASW, 36.9 mm.
Subject: Petroglyphs of Kazakhstan **Obv:** Value within designs
Rev: "Sun God" petroglyph **Edge:** Plain

Date	Mintage	F	VF	XF	Unc	BU
2000 Proof	3,000	Value: 45.00				

KM# 29 1000 TENGE
3.1200 g., 0.9999 Gold 0.1003 oz. AGW **Subject:** Silk Road
Obv: Value in ornamental frame **Rev:** Caravan of camels around
lined cross within circle

Date	Mintage	F	VF	XF	Unc	BU
1995	—	—	—	—	110	120

KM# 45 2500 TENGE
7.7800 g., 0.9999 Gold 0.2501 oz. AGW, 20 mm. **Subject:** The Silk Road **Obv:** Value in ornamental frame **Rev:** Caravan of camels around lined cross within circle **Edge:** Reeded

Date	Mintage	F	VF	XF	Unc	BU
1995	—	—	—	—	—	275

KM# 46 5000 TENGE
15.5500 g., 0.9999 Gold 0.4999 oz. AGW, 25 mm. **Subject:** The Silk Road **Obv:** Value in ornamental frame **Rev:** Caravan of camels around lined cross within circle **Edge:** Reeded

Date	Mintage	F	VF	XF	Unc	BU
1995	—	—	—	—	—	500

KM# 47 10000 TENGE
31.1000 g., 0.9999 Gold 0.9997 oz. AGW, 32 mm. **Subject:** The Silk Road **Obv:** Value in ornamental frame **Rev:** Caravan of camels around lined cross within circle **Edge:** Reeded

Date	Mintage	F	VF	XF	Unc	BU
1995	—	—	—	—	—	1,000

PROBAS

KM#	Date	Mintage	Identification	Mkt Val
Pr1	1992	—	Tenge. Copper-Nickel. 17.3mm.	—
Pr2	1992	—	50 Tenge. Copper Nickel.	—
Pr3	1992	—	50 Tenge. Copper.	—
Pr4	1992	—	50 Tenge. Brass.	—
Pr5	1992	—	50 Tenge. Aluminum.	—

KEELING COCOS

The Territory of Cocos (Keeling) Islands, an Australian territory, comprises a group of 27 coral islands located (see arrow on map of Australia) in the Indian Ocean 1,300 miles northwest of Australia. Only Direction and Home Islands are regularly inhabited. The group has an area of 5.4 sq. mi. and a population of about 569. Calcium, phosphate and coconut products are exported.

The islands were discovered by Capt. William Keeling of the British East India Co. in 1609. Alexander Hare, an English adventurer, established a settlement on one of the southern islands in 1823, but it lasted less than a year. A permanent settlement was established on Direction Island in 1827 by Hare and Capt. John Clunies Ross, a Scot, for the purpose of storing East Indian spices for reshipment to Europe during periods of shortage. When the experiment in spice futures did not develop satisfactorily, Hare left the islands (1829 or 1830), leaving Ross as sole owner. The coral group became a British protectorate in 1856; was attached to the colony of Ceylon in 1878; and was placed under the administration of the Straits Settlements in 1882. In 1903 the group was annexed to the Straits Settlements and incorporated into the colony of Singapore until November of 1955, when it was placed under the administration of Australia.

RULER
British.

MONETARY SYSTEM
100 Cents = 1 Rupee

AUSTRALIAN TERRITORY

TOKEN COINAGE
Plastic Ivory

Tn1-Tn7 were all issued with individual serial numbers.

KM# Tn1 5 CENTS

Date	Mintage	VG	F	VF	XF	Unc
1913	5,000	60.00	100	200	325	425

KM# Tn2 10 CENTS

Date	Mintage	VG	F	VF	XF	Unc
1913	5,000	45.00	75.00	150	275	375

KM# Tn3 25 CENTS

Date	Mintage	VG	F	VF	XF	Unc
1913	5,000	20.00	30.00	50.00	90.00	185

KM# Tn4 50 CENTS

Date	Mintage	VG	F	VF	XF	Unc
1913	2,000	75.00	125	275	475	575

KM# Tn5 RUPEE

Date	Mintage	VG	F	VF	XF	Unc
1913	2,000	25.00	40.00	75.00	125	200

KM# Tn6 2 RUPEES

Date	Mintage	VG	F	VF	XF	Unc
1913	1,000	35.00	50.00	90.00	140	225

KM# Tn7 5 RUPEES

Date	Mintage	VG	F	VF	XF	Unc
1913	1,000	35.00	50.00	100	165	250

TOKEN COINAGE
Modern Plastic

KM# Tn8 CENT
Note: Aqua-color plastic.

Date	Mintage	F	VF	XF	Unc	BU
1968	—	—	—	—	90.00	—

KM# Tn9 5 CENTS
Note: Aqua-color plastic.

Date	Mintage	F	VF	XF	Unc	BU
1968	—	—	—	—	90.00	—

KM# Tn10 10 CENTS
Note: Aqua-color plastic.

Date	Mintage	F	VF	XF	Unc	BU
1968	—	—	—	—	100	—

KM# Tn11 25 CENTS
Note: Aqua-color plastic.

Date	Mintage	F	VF	XF	Unc	BU
1968	—	—	—	—	120	—

KM# Tn12 50 CENTS
Note: Aqua-color plastic.

Date	Mintage	F	VF	XF	Unc	BU
1968	—	—	—	—	135	—

KM# Tn13 RUPEE
Note: Red-color plastic.

Date	Mintage	F	VF	XF	Unc	BU
1968	—	—	—	—	140	—

KM# Tn14 2 RUPEES
Note: Red-color plastic.

Date	Mintage	F	VF	XF	Unc	BU
1968	—	—	—	—	150	—

KM# Tn15 5 RUPEES
Note: Red-color plastic.

Date	Mintage	F	VF	XF	Unc	BU
1968	—	—	—	—	175	—

KM# Tn16 10 RUPEES
Note: Red-color plastic.

Date	Mintage	F	VF	XF	Unc	BU
1968	—	—	—	—	210	—

KM# Tn17 25 RUPEES
Note: Red-color plastic.

Date	Mintage	F	VF	XF	Unc	BU
1968	—	—	—	—	245	—

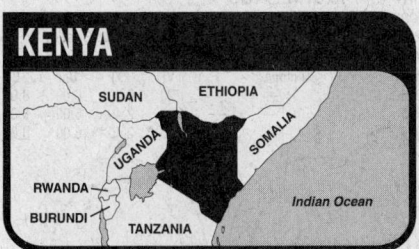

KENYA

The Republic of Kenya, located on the east coast of Central Africa, has an area of 224,961 sq. mi. (582,650 sq. km.) and a population of 20.1 million. Capital: Nairobi. The predominantly agricultural country exports coffee, tea and petroleum products.

The Arabs came to the coast of Kenya in the 8th century and established posts to conduct an ivory and slave trade. The Portuguese followed in the 16th century. After a lengthy and bitter struggle with the sultans of Zanzibar who controlled much of the southeastern coast of Africa, the Portuguese were driven away (late 17th century) and for many years Kenya was simply a port of call on the route to India. German and British interests in the 19th century produced agreements defining their respective spheres of influence. The British sphere was administrated by the Imperial East Africa Co. until 1895, when the British government purchased the company's rights in the East Africa Protectorate which, in 1920, was designated as Kenya Colony and protectorate - the latter being a 10-mile-wide coastal strip together with

Mombasa, Lamuand other small islands nominally retained by the Sultan of Zanzibar. Kenya achieved self-government in June of 1963 as a consequence of the 1952-60 Mau Mau terrorist campaign to secure land reforms and political rights for Africans. Independence was attained on Dec. 12, 1963. Kenya became a republic in 1964. It is a member of the Commonwealth of Nations. The president is Chief of State and Head of Government.

RULER
British, until 1964

MONETARY SYSTEM
100 Cents = 1 Shilling

REPUBLIC

STANDARD COINAGE

KM# 1 5 CENTS
Nickel-Brass **Obv:** Arms with supporters above value **Rev:** Bust left

Date	Mintage	F	VF	XF	Unc	BU
1966	28,000,000	—	0.25	0.50	1.00	2.00
1966 Proof	27	Value: 80.00				
1967	9,600,000	—	0.25	0.50	1.00	2.00
1968	12,000,000	—	0.25	0.50	1.00	2.00

KM# 10 5 CENTS
Nickel-Brass **Obv:** Arms with supporters divide date above value **Rev:** Bust left

Date	Mintage	F	VF	XF	Unc	BU
1969	800,000	—	0.50	1.00	2.25	4.00
1969 Proof	15	Value: 110				
1970	10,000,000	—	0.15	0.25	1.00	1.50
1971	29,680,000	—	0.15	0.25	1.00	1.50
1973 Proof	500	Value: 25.00				
1974	5,599,000	—	0.15	0.25	1.00	1.50
1975	28,000,000	—	0.15	0.25	1.00	1.50
1978	23,168,000	—	0.15	0.25	1.00	1.50

KM# 17 5 CENTS
5.6000 g., Nickel-Brass, 25.5 mm. **Obv:** Arms with supporters divide date above value **Rev:** Bust right

Date	Mintage	F	VF	XF	Unc	BU
1978	—	—	—	—	1.00	1.50
1978 Proof	—	Value: 10.00				
1980	—	—	0.15	0.25	1.00	1.50
1984	—	—	0.15	0.25	1.00	1.50
1986	—	—	0.15	0.25	1.00	1.50
1987	—	—	0.15	0.25	1.00	1.50
1989	—	—	0.15	0.25	0.75	1.25
1990	—	—	0.15	0.25	0.75	1.25
1991	—	—	0.15	0.25	0.75	1.25

KM# 2 10 CENTS
Nickel-Brass, 30.8 mm. **Obv:** Arms with supporters divide date above value **Rev:** Bust left

Date	Mintage	F	VF	XF	Unc	BU
1966	26,000,000	0.20	0.65	1.25	2.50	3.50
1966 Proof	27	Value: 80.00				
1967	7,300,000	0.20	0.65	1.25	2.50	3.50
1968	12,000,000	0.20	0.65	1.25	2.50	3.50

KM# 11 10 CENTS
5.6000 g., Nickel-Brass, 30.8 mm. **Obv:** Arms with supporters divide date above value **Rev:** Bust left

Date	Mintage	F	VF	XF	Unc	BU
1969	3,900,000	—	0.15	0.25	1.00	1.50
1969 Proof	15	Value: 110				
1970	7,200,000	—	0.15	0.25	1.00	1.50
1971	32,400,000	—	0.15	0.25	0.75	1.25
1973	3,000,000	—	0.15	0.25	1.00	1.50
1973 Proof	500	Value: 25.00				
1974	3,000,000	—	0.15	0.25	1.00	1.50
1975	3,000,000	—	0.15	0.25	1.00	1.50
1977	45,600,000	—	0.15	0.25	0.75	1.25
1978	22,600,000	—	0.15	0.25	0.75	1.25

KM# 18 10 CENTS
Nickel-Brass, 30.8 mm. **Obv:** Arms with supporters divide date above value **Rev:** Bust right

Date	Mintage	F	VF	XF	Unc	BU
1978	—	—	—	—	1.50	—
1978 Proof	—	Value: 15.00				
1980	—	—	0.15	0.25	1.50	—
1984	—	—	0.15	0.25	2.00	—
1986	—	—	0.15	0.25	2.00	—
1987	—	—	0.15	0.25	2.00	—
1989	—	—	0.15	0.25	1.50	—
1990	—	—	0.15	0.25	1.50	—
1991	—	—	0.15	0.25	1.25	—

KM# 18a 10 CENTS
9.3000 g., Brass Plated Steel, 30.8 mm. **Obv:** Arms with supporters divide date above value **Rev:** Bust right

Date	Mintage	F	VF	XF	Unc	BU
1994	—	—	0.20	0.30	1.00	1.50

KM# 31 10 CENTS
2.1700 g., Brass Plated Steel **Obv:** Value above national arms **Rev:** Bust of President Daniel Toroitich Arap Moi right

Date	Mintage	F	VF	XF	Unc	BU
1995	—	—	0.10	0.20	0.45	0.60

KM# 3 25 CENTS
Copper-Nickel **Obv:** Arms with supporters divide date above value **Rev:** Bust left

Date	Mintage	F	VF	XF	Unc	BU
1966	4,000,000	0.30	1.00	2.00	3.50	5.00
1966 Proof	27	Value: 100				
1967	4,000,000	0.30	1.00	2.00	3.50	5.00

KM# 12 25 CENTS
Copper-Nickel **Obv:** Arms with supporters divide date above value **Rev:** Bust left

Date	Mintage	F	VF	XF	Unc	BU
1969	200,000	0.50	1.00	2.50	10.00	15.00
1969 Proof	15	Value: 125				
1973 Proof	500	Value: 35.00				

KM# 4   50 CENTS
3.8200 g., Copper-Nickel, 21 mm. **Obv:** Arms with supporters divide date above value **Rev:** Bust left

Date	Mintage	F	VF	XF	Unc	BU
1966	4,000,000	0.20	0.40	1.00	4.50	—
1966 Proof	27	Value: 100				
1967	5,120,000	0.20	0.40	0.85	4.00	—
1968	6,000,000	0.20	0.40	0.85	3.50	—

KM# 13   50 CENTS
Copper-Nickel, 21 mm. **Obv:** Arms with supporters divide date above value **Rev:** Bust left

Date	Mintage	F	VF	XF	Unc	BU
1969	400,000	0.40	0.80	1.50	3.00	5.00
1969 Proof	15	Value: 125				
1971	9,600,000	—	0.20	0.40	1.00	1.50
1973	3,360,000	0.20	0.40	0.80	1.75	2.50
1973 Proof	500	Value: 25.00				
1974	12,640,000	—	0.20	0.40	1.00	1.50
1975	8,000,000	—	0.20	0.40	1.00	1.50
1977	16,000,000	—	0.20	0.40	1.00	1.50
1978	20,480,000	—	0.20	0.40	1.00	1.50

KM# 19   50 CENTS
Copper-Nickel, 21 mm. **Obv:** National arms above value **Rev:** Bust of President Daniel Toroitich Arap Moi right

Date	Mintage	F	VF	XF	Unc	BU
1978	—	—	0.20	0.40	1.00	1.35
1978 Proof	—	Value: 20.00				
1980	—	—	0.15	0.30	0.75	1.00
1989	—	—	0.15	0.30	0.75	1.00

KM# 19a   50 CENTS
Nickel-Plated Steel, 21 mm. **Obv:** National arms above value **Rev:** Bust of President Daniel Toroitich Arap Moi right

Date	Mintage	F	VF	XF	Unc	BU
1994	—	—	0.20	0.40	1.00	1.50

KM# 28   50 CENTS
3.1000 g., Brass Plated Steel, 17.9 mm. **Obv:** Value above national arms **Rev:** Bust of President Daniel Toroitich Arap Moi right

Date	Mintage	F	VF	XF	Unc	BU
1995	—	—	0.10	0.20	0.50	0.70
1997	—	—	0.10	0.20	0.50	0.70

KM# 5   SHILLING
Copper-Nickel, 27.8 mm. **Obv:** Arms with supporters divide date above value **Rev:** Bust left

Date	Mintage	F	VF	XF	Unc	BU
1966	20,000,000	0.25	0.50	1.00	3.00	5.00
1966 Proof	27	Value: 100				
1967	4,000,000	0.25	0.50	1.00	2.75	4.50
1968	8,000,000	0.20	0.40	0.80	2.25	4.00

KM# 14   SHILLING
7.9000 g., Copper-Nickel, 27.8 mm. **Obv:** Arms with supporters divide date above value **Rev:** Bust left

Date	Mintage	F	VF	XF	Unc	BU
1969	4,000,000	0.15	0.30	0.75	2.25	4.00
1969 Proof	15	Value: 125				
1971	24,000,000	0.10	0.30	0.65	2.00	3.50
1973	2,480,000	0.20	0.40	0.80	2.75	4.50
1973 Proof	500	Value: 30.00				
1974	13,520,000	0.10	0.30	0.65	2.00	3.50
1975	40,856,000	0.10	0.30	0.65	2.00	3.50
1978	20,000,000	0.10	0.30	0.65	2.00	3.50

KM# 20   SHILLING
Copper-Nickel, 27.8 mm. **Obv:** National arms above value **Rev:** Bust of President Daniel Toroitich Arap Moi 2right

Date	Mintage	F	VF	XF	Unc	BU
1978	—	0.15	0.30	0.60	1.50	2.00
1978 Proof	—	Value: 30.00				
1980	—	0.15	0.30	0.60	1.50	2.00
1989	—	0.15	0.30	0.60	1.50	2.00

KM# 20a   SHILLING
8.0000 g., Nickel-Plated Steel, 27.8 mm. **Obv:** National arms above value **Rev:** Bust of President Daniel Toroitich Arap Moi right

Date	Mintage	F	VF	XF	Unc	BU
1994	—	0.15	0.35	0.70	1.75	2.50

KM# 29   SHILLING
4.3500 g., Brass Plated Steel, 22 mm. **Obv:** Value above national arms **Rev:** Bust of President Daniel Toroitich Arap Moi right

Date	Mintage	F	VF	XF	Unc	BU
1995	—	0.10	0.20	0.40	0.75	1.00
1997	—	0.10	0.20	0.40	0.75	1.00
1998	—	0.10	0.20	0.40	0.75	1.00

KM# 6   2 SHILLINGS
Copper-Nickel **Obv:** Arms with supporters divide date above value **Rev:** Bust left **Note:** Similar to KM#2.

Date	Mintage	F	VF	XF	Unc	BU
1966	3,000,000	1.00	2.00	3.00	7.00	12.00
1966 Proof	27	Value: 120				
1968	1,100,000	1.00	2.75	4.50	10.00	15.00

KM# 15   2 SHILLINGS
Copper-Nickel **Obv:** Arms with supporters divide date above value **Rev:** Bust left **Note:** Similar to KM#11.

Date	Mintage	F	VF	XF	Unc	BU
1969	100,000	2.00	4.00	8.00	17.50	—
1969 Proof	15	Value: 150				
1971	1,920,000	0.60	1.25	3.50	12.50	—
1973 Proof	500	Value: 35.00				

KM# 16   5 SHILLINGS
Brass **Subject:** 10th Anniversary of Independence **Obv:** National arms **Rev:** Bust of President Mzee Jomo Kenyatta left

Date	Mintage	F	VF	XF	Unc	BU
1973	100,000	3.00	8.00	15.00	22.50	30.00
1973 Proof	1,500	Value: 45.00				

KM# 23   5 SHILLINGS
Copper-Nickel, 30 mm. **Obv:** National arms **Rev:** Bust of President Daniel Toroitich Arap Moi right **Edge:** Plain

Date	Mintage	F	VF	XF	Unc	BU
1985	—	0.25	0.60	1.20	3.00	5.00

KM# 23a   5 SHILLINGS
Nickel-Plated Steel **Obv:** National arms **Rev:** Bust of President Daniel Toroitich Arap Moi right **Edge:** Plain

Date	Mintage	F	VF	XF	Unc	BU
1994	—	0.50	1.00	2.25	6.00	—

KM# 30   5 SHILLINGS
3.4000 g., Bi-Metallic Brass center in Copper-Nickel ring, 20 mm. **Obv:** Value above national arms **Rev:** Bust of President Naniel Toroitich Arap Moi right

Date	Mintage	F	VF	XF	Unc	BU
1995	—	—	0.90	1.80	4.50	6.00
1997	—	—	0.90	1.80	4.50	6.00

KM# 27   10 SHILLINGS
5.0000 g., Bi-Metallic Copper-Nickel center in Brass ring, 22.9 mm. **Obv:** Value above national arms **Rev:** Bust of President Daniel Toroitich Arap Moi right

Date	Mintage	F	VF	XF	Unc	BU
1994	—	—	1.20	2.40	6.00	8.00
1995	—	—	1.20	2.40	6.00	8.00
1997	—	—	1.20	2.40	6.00	8.00

KM# 32   20 SHILLINGS
Ring: Copper-Nickel **Center:** Brass, 25.5 mm. **Obv:** Value above national arms **Rev:** Bust of President Daniel Toroitich Arap Moi right

Date	Mintage	F	VF	XF	Unc	BU
1998	—	—	1.50	3.00	7.50	10.00

KM# 7   100 SHILLINGS
7.6000 g., 0.9170 Gold 0.2241 oz. AGW **Subject:** 75th Anniversary - Birth of President Jomo Kenyatta **Obv:** Fly whisk above value and date **Rev:** Bust left

Date	Mintage	F	VF	XF	Unc	BU
1966	—	—	—	—	—	225
1966 Proof	7,500	Value: 235				

KM# 21   200 SHILLINGS
28.2800 g., 0.9250 Silver 0.8410 oz. ASW **Obv:** President Moi **Rev:** Arms with supporters above value

Date	Mintage	F	VF	XF	Unc	BU
ND (1979) Proof	Est. 9,500	Value: 100				

KM# 8   250 SHILLINGS
19.0000 g., 0.9170 Gold 0.5601 oz. AGW **Subject:** 75th Anniversary - Birth of President Jomo Kenyatta **Obv:** Rooster with axe above value and date **Rev:** Bust left

Date	Mintage	F	VF	XF	Unc	BU
1966	—	—	—	—	—	540
1966 Proof	1,000	Value: 550				

KM# 9   500 SHILLINGS
38.0000 g., 0.9170 Gold 1.1203 oz. AGW **Subject:** 75th Anniversary - Birth of President Jomo Kenyatta **Obv:** Mountain above value and date **Rev:** Bust left

Date	Mintage	F	VF	XF	Unc	BU
1966	—	—	—	—	—	1,100
1966 Proof	500	Value: 1,150				

KM# 24   500 SHILLINGS
28.2800 g., 0.9250 Silver 0.8410 oz. ASW **Subject:** 10th Anniversary of Moi as President **Obv:** Bust right **Rev:** Arms with supporters above value

Date	Mintage	F	VF	XF	Unc	BU
ND(1988) Proof	—	Value: 350				

KM# 25   500 SHILLINGS
28.3300 g., 0.9250 Silver 0.8425 oz. ASW **Subject:** 25th Anniversary of Independence **Obv:** Bust right **Rev:** Arms with supporters above value

Date	Mintage	F	VF	XF	Unc	BU
ND(1988) Proof	—	Value: 375				

KM# 26   1000 SHILLINGS
28.2800 g., 0.9250 Silver 0.8410 oz. ASW **Subject:** Silver Jubilee of Central Bank **Obv:** Bust right **Rev:** Arms with supporters above value

Date	Mintage	F	VF	XF	Unc	BU
1991 Proof	—	Value: 500				

KM# 22   3000 SHILLING
40.0000 g., 0.9170 Gold 1.1792 oz. AGW **Obv:** President Moi **Rev:** Arms with supporters above value

Date	Mintage	F	VF	XF	Unc	BU
ND (1979) Proof	2,000	Value: 1,150				

MINT SETS

KM#	Date	Mintage	Identification	Issue Price	Mkt Val
MS1	1966 (3)	—	KM7-9	—	1,350

PROOF SETS

KM#	Date	Mintage	Identification	Issue Price	Mkt Val
PS1	1966 (6)	27	KM1-6	—	575
PS2	1966 (3)	500	KM7-9	153	1,450
PS3	1969 (6)	15	KM10-15	—	750
PS4	1973 (7)	500	KM10-16	—	220
PS5	1978 (5)	9,500	KM#17-21	—	175

KIAU CHAU

Kiau Chau (Kiao Chau, Kiaochow, Kiautscho, now Jiaozhou), a former German trading enclave, including the port of Tsingtao (Qingdao), was located on the Shantung (Shandong) Peninsula of eastern China. Following the murder of two missionaries in Shantung in 1897, Germany occupied Kiaochow Bay, and during subsequent negotiations with the Chinese government obtained a 99-year lease on 177 sq. mi. of land. The enclave was established as a free port in 1899, and a customs house set up to collect tariffs on goods moving to and from the Chinese interior. The Japanese took siege to the port on Aug. 27, 1914, as their first action in World War I to deprive German sea marauders of their east Asian supply and refitting base. Aided by the British forces, the siege ended Nov. 7. Japan retained possession until 1922, when it was restored to China by the Washington Conference on China and naval armaments. It fell again to Japan in 1938, but not before the Chinese had destroyed its manufacturing facilities. It is presently a part of the Peoples Republic of China. The major city is Tsingtao (Qingdao) and is noted for its beer.

RULERS
Wilhelm II, 1897-1914
Japan, 1914-1922, 1938-1945

MONETARY SYSTEM
100 Cents = 1 Dollar

GERMAN OCCUPATION
STANDARD COINAGE

Y# 1   5 CENTS
Copper-Nickel **Ruler:** Wilhelm II **Obv:** German Imperial Eagle **Obv. Leg.:** DEUTSCH.KIAUTSHAU GEBIET **Rev:** Inscription within beaded circle **Rev. Insc.:** Kuang-hsü Yüan-pao

Date	Mintage	F	VF	XF	Unc	BU
1909	610,000	50.00	75.00	115	185	—
1909 Proof	—	Value: 450				

Y# 2   10 CENTS
Copper-Nickel **Ruler:** Wilhelm II **Obv:** German Imperial Eagle **Obv. Leg.:** DEUTSCH.KIAUTSHAU GEBIET **Rev:** Inscription within beaded circle **Rev. Insc.:** Kuang-hsü Yüan-pao

Date	Mintage	F	VF	XF	Unc	BU
1909	670,000	30.00	50.00	90.00	165	—
1909 Proof	—	Value: 500				

KIRIBATI

The Republic of Kiribati (formerly the Gilbert Islands), consists of 30 coral atolls and islands spread over more than one million sq. mi. (2,590,000 sq. km.) of the southwest Pacific Ocean, has an area of 332 sq. mi. (717 sq. km.) and a population of 64,200. Capital: Bairiki, on Tarawa. In addition to the Gilbert Islands proper, Kiribati includes Ocean Island, the Central and Southern Line Islands, and the Phoenix Islands, though possession of Canton and Enderbury of the Phoenix Islands is disputed with the United States. Most families engage in subsistence fishing. Copra and phosphates are exported, mostly to Australia and New Zealand.

The Gilbert Islands and the group formerly called the Ellice Islands (now Tuvalu) comprised a single British crown colony, the Gilbert and Ellice Islands.

Spanish mutineers first sighted the islands in 1537, succeeding visits were made by the English navigators John Byron (1764), James Cook (1777), and Thomas Gilbert and John Marshall (1788). An American, Edward Fanning, arrived in 1798. Britain declared a protectorate over the Gilbert and Ellice Islands, and in 1915 began the formation of a colony which was completed when the Phoenix Islands were added to the group in 1937. The Central and Southern Line Islands were administratively attached to the Gilbert and Ellice Islands colony in 1972, and remained attached to the Gilberts when Tuvalu was created in 1975. The colony became self-governing in 1971. Kiribati attained independence on July 12, 1979.

RULER
British, until 1979

MONETARY SYSTEM
100 Cents = 1 Dollar

REPUBLIC
DECIMAL COINAGE

KM# 1   CENT
2.6000 g., Bronze, 17.5 mm. **Subject:** Christmas Island Frigate Bird **Obv:** National arms **Rev:** Frigate bird on branch

Date	Mintage	F	VF	XF	Unc	BU
1979	90,000	—	—	0.15	0.50	1.00
1979 Proof	10,000	Value: 1.00				
1992	—	—	—	0.15	0.50	1.00

KM# 1a   CENT
2.6000 g., Bronze-Plated Steel, 17.5 mm. **Obv:** National arms **Rev:** Frigate bird on branch

Date	Mintage	F	VF	XF	Unc	BU
1992	—	—	—	—	0.50	1.00

KM# 2   2 CENTS
5.2000 g., Bronze, 21.6 mm. **Subject:** B'abal plant **Obv:** National arms **Rev:** B'abal plant below value

Date	Mintage	F	VF	XF	Unc	BU
1979	25,000	—	—	0.15	0.35	0.60
1979 Proof	10,000	Value: 1.25				
1992	—	—	—	0.15	0.35	0.60

KM# 3   5 CENTS
2.7300 g., Copper-Nickel, 19.3 mm. **Obv:** National arms **Rev:** Stump-tailed Gecko below value **Edge:** Reeded

Date	Mintage	F	VF	XF	Unc	BU
1979	20,000	—	0.15	0.30	1.50	2.50
1979 Proof	10,000	Value: 2.75				

KM# 3a   5 CENTS
Copper-Nickel-Plated Steel, 19.3 mm. **Obv:** National arms **Rev:** Stump-tailed Gecko below value

Date	Mintage	F	VF	XF	Unc	BU
1992	—	—	—	—	1.50	2.00

KM# 4   10 CENTS
5.7000 g., Copper-Nickel, 23.6 mm. **Subject:** Bread fruit **Obv:** National arms **Rev:** Bread fruit above value

Date	Mintage	F	VF	XF	Unc	BU
1979	20,000	—	0.15	0.25	1.25	1.50
1979 Proof	10,000	Value: 3.00				

KM# 5   20 CENTS
11.1500 g., Copper-Nickel, 28.45 mm. **Subject:** Dolphins **Obv:** National arms **Rev:** Dolphins above value

Date	Mintage	F	VF	XF	Unc	BU
1979	20,000	—	0.60	1.50	6.00	8.00
1979 Proof	10,000	Value: 9.00				

KM# 6   50 CENTS
15.4000 g., Copper-Nickel, 31.65 mm. **Subject:** Panda nut **Obv:** National arms **Rev:** Panda nut above value

Date	Mintage	F	VF	XF	Unc	BU
1979	20,000	—	0.50	1.00	3.00	4.50
1979 Proof	10,000	Value: 6.50				

KM# 7   DOLLAR
11.7000 g., Copper-Nickel, 30 mm. **Subject:** Outrigger sailboat **Obv:** National arms **Rev:** Outrigger sailboat above written value

Date	Mintage	F	VF	XF	Unc	BU
1979	20,000	—	0.85	1.25	4.00	5.00
1979 Proof	10,000	Value: 8.00				

KM# 41   DOLLAR
12.4000 g., Copper-Nickel, 25.8 x 38 mm. **Obv:** National arms **Rev:** Solar System **Edge:** Plain

Date	Mintage	F	VF	XF	Unc	BU
ND (1997) Proof	—	Value: 10.00				

KM# 14   2 DOLLARS
Nickel-Brass **Subject:** 10th Anniversary of Independence **Obv:** National arms above message within ribbon **Rev:** Meeting house with shell at lower left

Date	Mintage	F	VF	XF	Unc	BU
1989	—	—	—	—	5.00	6.50

KM# 21   2 DOLLARS
10.0000 g., 0.5000 Silver 0.1607 oz. ASW **Subject:** Titanic sinking **Obv:** National arms

Date	Mintage	F	VF	XF	Unc	BU
1998 Proof	—	Value: 15.00				

KM# 8   5 DOLLARS
28.1600 g., 0.5000 Silver 0.4527 oz. ASW **Subject:** Independence **Obv:** National arms **Rev:** Seated man with arms outstretched with written value below

Date	Mintage	F	VF	XF	Unc	BU
1979	1,545	—	—	—	—	22.50

KM# 8a   5 DOLLARS
28.1600 g., 0.9250 Silver 0.8374 oz. ASW **Subject:** Independence **Obv:** National arms **Rev:** Seated man with arms outstretched above written value

Date	Mintage	F	VF	XF	Unc	BU
1979 Proof	3,326	Value: 25.00				

KM# 10   5 DOLLARS
Copper-Nickel, 38.5 mm. **Subject:** 2nd Anniversary of Independence and Wedding of Prince Charles and Lady Diana **Obv:** National arms **Rev:** Wedding crown above value

Date	Mintage	F	VF	XF	Unc	BU
1981	50,000	—	—	—	7.50	9.00

KM# 10a   5 DOLLARS
28.6000 g., 0.9250 Silver 0.8505 oz. ASW, 38.5 mm. **Subject:** 2nd Anniversary of Independence and Wedding of Prince Charles and Lady Diana **Obv:** National arms **Rev:** Wedding crown above value

Date	Mintage	F	VF	XF	Unc	BU
1981 Proof	25,000	Value: 22.50				

KM# 12   5 DOLLARS
Copper-Nickel, 38.5 mm. **Subject:** Royal visit **Obv:** National arms **Rev:** Young bust right

Date	Mintage	F	VF	XF	Unc	BU
1982	—	—	—	—	5.00	6.50

KM# 12a   5 DOLLARS
Silver, 38.5 mm. **Subject:** Royal visit **Obv:** National arms **Rev:** Young bust right

Date	Mintage	F	VF	XF	Unc	BU
1982 Proof	—	Value: 35.00				

KM# 19 5 DOLLARS

31.4700 g., 0.9250 Silver 0.9359 oz. ASW **Obv:** National arms
Rev: Standing figure and ship

Date	Mintage	F	VF	XF	Unc	BU
1996 Proof	Est. 15,000				Value: 50.00	

KM# 20 5 DOLLARS

31.4700 g., 0.9250 Silver 0.9359 oz. ASW **Subject:** OLYMPIC GAMES 2000 **Obv:** National arms **Obv. Leg.:** KIRIBATI
Rev: Two high divers

Date	Mintage	F	VF	XF	Unc	BU
1996 Proof	40,000				Value: 40.00	

KM# 22 5 DOLLARS

15.5518 g., 0.9250 Silver 0.4625 oz. ASW **Subject:** Guerra & Paz **Obv:** National arms within wave-like designs **Rev:** Dove within wave-like designs **Note:** Half of two-part coin, combined with Western Samoa KM#115, issued in sets only. Value is determined by combining the two parts.

Date	Mintage	F	VF	XF	Unc	BU
ND(1997) Proof	Est. 10,000				Value: 35.00	

KM# 23 5 DOLLARS

15.5518 g., 0.9250 Silver 0.4625 oz. ASW **Subject:** Powerful empires **Obv:** National arms within wave-like designs
Rev: Helmets and hats within wave-like designs **Note:** Half of two-part coin, combined with Western Samoa KM#116, issued in sets only. Value is determined by combining the two parts.

Date	Mintage	F	VF	XF	Unc	BU
ND(1997) Proof	Est. 10,000				Value: 35.00	

KM# 24 5 DOLLARS

15.5518 g., 0.9250 Silver 0.4625 oz. ASW **Subject:** Tempora Mutantur **Obv:** National arms within wave-like designs **Rev:** Solar system within wave-like designs **Note:** Half of two-part coin, combined with Samoa KM#117, issued in sets only. Value is determined by combining the two parts.

Date	Mintage	F	VF	XF	Unc	BU
ND(1997) Proof	Est. 10,000				Value: 35.00	

KM# 24a 5 DOLLARS

Copper-Nickel **Subject:** Tempora Mutantur **Obv:** National arms within wave-like designs **Rev:** Solar system within wave-like designs. **Note:** Half of two-pary coin, combined with Samoa KM#117a. issued in pairs only. Value is determined by combining the two parts.

Date	Mintage	F	VF	XF	Unc	BU
ND(1997)	—	—	—	—	10.00	—

KM# 25 5 DOLLARS

15.5518 g., 0.9250 Silver 0.4625 oz. ASW **Subject:** People, monuments, column and compass within wave-like designs **Obv:** National arms within wave-like designs **Note:** Half of two-part coin, combined with Western Samoa KM#118, issued in sets only. Value is determined by combining the two parts.

Date	Mintage	F	VF	XF	Unc	BU
ND(1997) Proof	Est. 10,000				Value: 37.50	

KM# 31 5 DOLLARS

31.4000 g., 0.9250 Silver 0.9338 oz. ASW, 38.5 mm.
Subject: British Queen Mother **Obv:** National arms **Rev:** Windsor Castle within beaded circle **Edge:** Reeded

Date	Mintage	F	VF	XF	Unc	BU
1997 Proof	—				Value: 40.00	

KM# 42 5 DOLLARS

15.8600 g., 0.9250 Silver 0.4716 oz. ASW, 25.8 mm.
Obv: National arms **Rev:** "POWERFUL EMPIRES" Charlemagne, Spanish ship, Soviet soldier with flag **Edge:** Plain

Date	Mintage	F	VF	XF	Unc	BU
ND (1998) Proof	—				Value: 35.00	

KM# 30 5 DOLLARS

31.6000 g., 0.9250 Silver 0.9397 oz. ASW, 38.5 mm.
Subject: Whaling Ship Potomac 1842 **Obv:** National arms
Rev: Ship above sailors killing whale **Edge:** Reeded

Date	Mintage	F	VF	XF	Unc	BU
1998 Proof	—				Value: 50.00	

KM# 45 5 DOLLARS

31.3800 g., 0.9250 Silver 0.9332 oz. ASW, 38.6 mm.
Obv: Shield **Rev:** Ship LaCoquille **Edge:** Reeded

Date	Mintage	F	VF	XF	Unc	BU
1999 Proof	—				Value: 40.00	

KM# 37 5 DOLLARS

21.6400 g., Copper-Nickel, 40 mm. **Obv:** National arms
Rev: "Harmony" earth, moon and sun **Edge:** Reeded

Date	Mintage	F	VF	XF	Unc	BU
2000FM Proof	—				Value: 15.00	

KM# 28 5 DOLLARS

31.3000 g., 0.9990 Silver 1.0053 oz. ASW, 38.6 mm.
Subject: 10th Anniversary of Emperor Akihito's Reign
Obv: National arms within circle **Rev:** Conjoined busts left
Edge: Reeded

Date	Mintage	F	VF	XF	Unc	BU
2000 Proof	2,000				Value: 75.00	

KM# 13 10 DOLLARS

28.2800 g., 0.9250 Silver 0.8410 oz. ASW **Subject:** 5th Anniversary of Independence **Obv:** Value above national arms
Rev: Geographical map

Date	Mintage	F	VF	XF	Unc	BU
ND(1984)	—	—	—	—	65.00	75.00
ND(1984) Proof	2,500				Value: 45.00	

KM# 13a 10 DOLLARS

47.5200 g., 0.9170 Gold 1.4009 oz. AGW **Subject:** 5th Anniversary of Independence **Obv:** Value above national arms
Rev: Geographical map

Date	Mintage	F	VF	XF	Unc	BU
ND(1984) Proof	50				Value: 1,350	

KM# 27 10 DOLLARS

1.2441 g., 0.9990 Gold 0.0400 oz. AGW **Subject:** Titanic
Obv: National arms **Rev:** Sinking ships and lifeboats

Date	Mintage	F	VF	XF	Unc	BU
1998 Proof	—				Value: 50.00	

KM# 43 10 DOLLARS

1.2100 g., 0.9990 Gold 0.0389 oz. AGW, 13.91 mm.
Obv: National arms **Obv. Leg.:** KIRIBATI **Rev:** Manger scene, birth of Jesus Christ in Bethlehem **Rev. Leg.:** * CHRISTMAS ISLAND * KIRITIMATI * KIRIBATI **Edge:** Reeded

Date	Mintage	F	VF	XF	Unc	BU
1998 Proof	—				Value: 55.00	

KM# 44   10 DOLLARS
Gold, 13.90 mm.   **Obv:** National arms **Obv. Leg.:** KIRIBATI
Rev: Shark-tooth sword across native cloak **Edge:** Reeded

Date	Mintage	F	VF	XF	Unc	BU
2000 Proof	—	Value: 55.00				

KM# 38   10 DOLLARS
22.2200 g., 0.5000 Silver 0.3572 oz. ASW, 40 mm.
Obv: National arms **Rev:** "Hope" earth, sun and stars
Edge: Reeded

Date	Mintage	F	VF	XF	Unc	BU
2000FM Proof	—	Value: 40.00				

KM# 17   20 DOLLARS
31.4700 g., 0.9250 Silver 0.9359 oz. ASW   **Subject:** Barcelona
Olympics - Sailing **Obv:** National arms above message within
ribbon **Rev:** Radiant sun, sailboaters and seagull flying above

Date	Mintage	F	VF	XF	Unc	BU
1992 Proof	40,000	Value: 27.50				

KM# 18   20 DOLLARS
31.4700 g., 0.9250 Silver 0.9359 oz. ASW **Subject:** Endangered
Wildlife **Obv:** National arms above message within ribbon
Rev: Frigate birds

Date	Mintage	F	VF	XF	Unc	BU
1992 Proof	—	Value: 45.00				

KM# 15   20 DOLLARS
31.4700 g., 0.9250 Silver 0.9359 oz. ASW   **Subject:** Soccer -
World Cup '94 **Obv:** National arms **Rev:** Soccer players

Date	Mintage	F	VF	XF	Unc	BU
1993 Proof	Est. 10,000	Value: 32.50				

KM# 16   20 DOLLARS
31.4700 g., 0.9250 Silver 0.9359 oz. ASW **Subject:** First Space
Walk **Obv:** National arms

Date	Mintage	F	VF	XF	Unc	BU
1993 Proof	Est. 15,000	Value: 30.00				

KM# 33   20 DOLLARS
3.1103 g., 0.9250 Gold 0.0999 oz. AGW, 18 mm.
Subject: Christmas Island Holy Year 2000 **Obv:** National arms
above name and date **Rev:** Angel in flight **Edge:** Reeded

Date	Mintage	F	VF	XF	Unc	BU
1999 Proof	—	Value: 100				

KM# 39   20 DOLLARS
21.2200 g., 0.9990 Silver 0.6815 oz. ASW, 39.9 mm.
Obv: National arms **Rev:** "Faith" hands below earth
Edge: Reeded

Date	Mintage	F	VF	XF	Unc	BU
2000FM Proof	—	Value: 95.00				

KM# 26   50 DOLLARS
3.8875 g., 0.9990 Gold 0.1249 oz. AGW   **Subject:** Tempora
Mutantur **Obv:** National arms **Rev:** Solar system **Note:** Similar
to KM#24. Half of two-part coin, combined with Western Samoa
KM#119, issued in sets only. Value is determined by combining
the two parts.

Date	Mintage	F	VF	XF	Unc	BU
ND(1997) Proof	Est. 2,500	Value: 185				

KM# 34   50 DOLLARS
7.7759 g., 0.9990 Gold 0.2497 oz. AGW, 22 mm. **Subject:**
Christmas Island Holy Year 2000 **Obv:** National arms above name
and date **Rev:** The three "Wise Men" on camels **Edge:** Reeded

Date	Mintage	F	VF	XF	Unc	BU
1999 Proof	—	Value: 250				

KM# 35   100 DOLLARS
15.5518 g., 0.9990 Gold 0.4995 oz. AGW, 30 mm.
Subject: Christmas Island Holy Year 2000 **Obv:** National arms
above name and date **Rev:** Mother and child **Edge:** Reeded

Date	Mintage	F	VF	XF	Unc	BU
1999 Proof	—	Value: 475				

KM# 9   150 DOLLARS
15.9800 g., 0.9170 Gold 0.4711 oz. AGW   **Subject:** Independence
- Maneaba - a traditional meeting house **Obv:** National arms
Rev: Maneaba - a traditional meeting house

Date	Mintage	F	VF	XF	Unc	BU
1979	422	—	—	—	—	475
1979 Proof	386	Value: 500				

KM# 11   150 DOLLARS
15.9800 g., 0.9170 Gold 0.4711 oz. AGW   **Subject:** 2nd
Anniversary of Independence, and wedding of Prince Charles
and Lady Diana **Obv:** National arms

Date	Mintage	F	VF	XF	Unc	BU
1981	750	—	—	—	—	475
1981 Proof	1,500	Value: 500				

KM# 29   200 DOLLARS
31.3000 g., 0.9990 Gold 1.0053 oz. AGW, 35 mm.
Subject: 10th Anniversary of Emperor Akihito's Reign
Obv: National arms **Rev:** Conjoined busts left **Edge:** Reeded

Date	Mintage	F	VF	XF	Unc	BU
2000 Proof	500	Value: 950				

KM# 32   200 DOLLARS
16.5800 g., 0.9990 Gold 0.5325 oz. AGW, 37.8x26.2 mm.
Subject: People and Monuments **Obv:** National arms within wave-
like designs **Rev:** Eiffel Tower **Edge:** Plain **Note:** Irregular shape

Date	Mintage	F	VF	XF	Unc	BU
1999-2000 Proof	—	Value: 520				

KM# 36   500 DOLLARS
85.4700 g., 0.9990 Gold 2.7451 oz. AGW, 42.5 mm.
Obv: National arms **Rev:** Doves, children, sword point and treaty
Edge: Plain **Note:** Jagged coin half matching with Samoa
KM-136

Date	Mintage	F	VF	XF	Unc	BU
2000 Proof	99	Value: 2,750				

COMBINED PROOF SETS (CPS)

KM#	Date	Mintage	Identification	Issue Price	Mkt Val
CPS1	1997 (8)	10,000	Kiribati KM#22-25, West Samoa KM#115-118	—	240

PROOF SETS

KM#	Date	Mintage	Identification	Issue Price	Mkt Val
PS1	1979 (7)	10,000	KM1-7	34.00	55.00
PS2	1981 (2)	—	KM10a, 11	—	360
PS3	1999 (3)	—	KM#33-35	—	645
PS4	2000 (3)	—	KM#37, 38, 39	—	150

KOREA

Korea, 'Land of the Morning Calm', occupies a mountainous
peninsula in northeast Asia bounded by Manchuria, the Yellow
Sea and the Sea of Japan.

According to legend, the first Korean dynasty, that of the
House of Tangun, ruled from 2333 B.C. to 1122 B.C. It was followed by the dynasty of Kija, a Chinese scholar, which continued
until 193 B.C. and brought a high civilization to Korea. The first
recorded period in the history of Korea, the period of the Three
Kingdoms, lasted from 57 B.C. to 935 A.D. and achieved the first
political unification of the peninsula. The Kingdom of Koryo, from
which Korea derived its name, was founded in 935 and continued
until 1392, when it was superseded by the Yi Dynasty of King Yi.
Sung Kye was to last until the Japanese annexation in 1910.

At the end of the 16th century Korea was invaded and occupied for 7 years by Japan, and from 1627 until the late 19th century
it was a semi-independent tributary of China. Japan replaced
China as the predominant foreign influence at the end of the Sino-
Japanese War (1894-95), only to find her position threatened by
Russian influence from 1896 to 1904. The Russian threat was
eliminated by the Russo-Japanese War (1904-05) and in 1905
Japan established a direct protectorate over Korea. On Aug.
22,1910, the last Korean ruler signed the treaty that annexed
Korea to Japan as a government generalcy in the Japanese
Empire. Japanese suzerainty was maintained until the end of
World War II.

From 1633 to 1891 the monetary system of Korea employed
cast coins with a square center hole. Fifty-two agencies were
authorized to procure these coins from a lesser number of coin
foundries. They exist in thousands of varieties. Seed, or mother
coins, were used to make the impressions in the molds in which
the regular cash coins were cast. Czarist-Russian Korea exper-
imented with Korean coins when Alexiev of Russia, Korea's
Financial Advisor, founded the First Asian Branch of the Russo-
Korean Bank on March 1, 1898, and authorized the issuing of a
set of new Korean coins with a crowned Russian-style quasi-
eagle. British-Japanese opposition and the Russo-Japanese War
operated to end the Russian coinage experiment in 1904.

RULERS
Yi Hyong (Kojong), 1864-1897
as Emperor Kuang Mu, 1897-1907
                    Japanese Puppet
Yung Hi (Sunjong), 1907-1910

DATING

Kuang Mu

10 + 1 = 11

Nien "Year"

Ta Han "Great Korea"

Chyun III "Chon One"

JAPANESE PROTECTORATE

MILLED COINAGE

Coinage Reform of 1902

KM# 1124 1/2 CHON

3.5600 g., Bronze, 22 mm. **Ruler:** Kuang Mu **Obv:** Imperial eagle left within beaded circle **Rev:** Value within wreath below flower

Date	Mintage	F	VF	XF	Unc	BU
10 (1906)	24,000,000	5.00	15.00	50.00	150	—

KM# 1145 1/2 CHON

2.1000 g., Bronze **Ruler:** Kuang Mu

Date	Mintage	F	VF	XF	Unc	BU
11 (1907)	Rare Est. 800,000	—	—	—	—	—

KM# 1136 1/2 CHON

2.1000 g., Bronze, 19 mm. **Ruler:** Yung Hi (Sunjong) **Obv:** Imperial eagle facing left within beaded circle **Rev:** Value within wreath below flower

Date	Mintage	F	VF	XF	Unc	BU
1 (1907)	Inc. above	175	300	600	1,000	—

Note: Mintage for year 1 is included in the mintage for Year 11 of KM#1124

2 (1908)	21,000,000	10.00	30.00	65.00	250	—
3 (1909)	8,200,000	10.00	30.00	65.00	250	—
4 (1910)	5,070,000	100	300	700	1,000	—

KM# 1125 CHON

7.1300 g., Bronze, 28 mm. **Ruler:** Kuang Mu **Obv:** Imperial eagle facing left within beaded circle **Rev:** Value within wreath below flower

Date	Mintage	F	VF	XF	Unc	BU
9 (1905)	11,800,000	12.50	25.00	50.00	200	—
10 (1906)	Inc. above	10.00	20.00	50.00	200	—

KM# 1132 CHON

4.2000 g., Bronze, 23.5 mm. **Ruler:** Kuang Mu **Obv:** Imperial eagle facing left within beaded circle **Rev:** Value within wreath below flower

Date	Mintage	F	VF	XF	Unc	BU
11 (1907)	11,200,000	6.00	12.00	30.00	150	—

KM# 1137 CHON

4.2000 g., Bronze, 24 mm. **Ruler:** Yung Hi (Sunjong) **Obv:** Imperial eagle facing left within beaded circle **Rev:** Value within wreath below flower

Date	Mintage	F	VF	XF	Unc	BU
1 (1907)	Inc. above	8.00	20.00	50.00	180	—
2 (1908)	6,800,000	6.00	15.00	35.00	140	—
3 (1909)	9,200,000	6.00	15.00	30.00	140	—
4 (1910)	3,500,000	8.00	18.00	45.00	180	—

KM# 1126 5 CHON

4.5000 g., Copper-Nickel, 21 mm. **Ruler:** Kuang Mu **Obv:** Imperial eagle facing left within beaded circle **Rev:** Value within wreath below flower

Date	Mintage	F	VF	XF	Unc	BU
9 (1905)	20,000,000	12.50	30.00	60.00	150	—
9 (1905) Proof	—	Value: 1,500				
11 (1907)	160,000,000	15.00	35.00	75.00	200	—

KM# 1138 5 CHON

4.5000 g., Copper-Nickel, 21 mm. **Ruler:** Yung Hi (Sunjong)

Date	Mintage	F	VF	XF	Unc	BU
3 (1909)	—	1,200	2,300	4,000	5,000	—

KM# 1127 10 CHON

2.7000 g., 0.8000 Silver 0.0694 oz. ASW, 18 mm. **Ruler:** Kuang Mu **Obv:** Dragon within beaded circle **Rev:** Value within wreath below flower **Note:** 1.5 millimeters thick

Date	Mintage	F	VF	XF	Unc	BU
10 (1906)	2,000,000	24.00	45.00	80.00	200	—

KM# 1133 10 CHON

2.0250 g., 0.8000 Silver 0.0521 oz. ASW, 18 mm. **Ruler:** Kuang Mu **Obv:** Dragon within beaded circle **Rev:** Value within wreath below flower **Note:** 1.0 millimeters thick

Date	Mintage	F	VF	XF	Unc	BU
11 (1907)	2,400,000	28.00	50.00	125	300	—

KM# 1139 10 CHON

2.2500 g., 0.8000 Silver 0.0579 oz. ASW **Ruler:** Yung Hi (Sunjong) **Obv:** Dragon within beaded circle **Rev:** Value within wreath below flower

Date	Mintage	F	VF	XF	Unc	BU
2 (1908)	6,300,000	20.00	40.00	65.00	200	—
3 (1909) Rare	—	—	—	—	—	—
4 (1910)	9,500,000	20.00	35.00	60.00	150	—

KM# 1128 20 CHON

5.3900 g., 0.8000 Silver 0.1386 oz. ASW, 22 mm. **Ruler:** Kuang Mu **Obv:** Dragon within beaded circle **Rev:** Value within wreath below flower

Date	Mintage	F	VF	XF	Unc	BU
9 (1905)	1,000,000	50.00	100	200	400	—
9 (1905) Proof	—	Value: 2,250				

Date	Mintage	F	VF	XF	Unc	BU
10 (1906)	2,500,000	45.00	65.00	175	350	—
10 (1906) Proof	—	Value: 1,275				

KM# 1134 20 CHON

4.0500 g., 0.8000 Silver 0.1042 oz. ASW, 20 mm. **Ruler:** Kuang Mu **Obv:** Dragon within beaded circle **Rev:** Value within wreath below flower

Date	Mintage	F	VF	XF	Unc	BU
11 (1907)	1,500,000	30.00	60.00	125	300	—

KM# 1140 20 CHON

4.0500 g., 0.8000 Silver 0.1042 oz. ASW, 20 mm. **Ruler:** Yung Hi (Sunjong) **Obv:** Dragon within beaded circle **Rev:** Value within wreath below flower

Date	Mintage	F	VF	XF	Unc	BU
2 (1908)	3,000,000	27.00	50.00	100	250	—
3 (1909)	2,000,000	27.00	50.00	100	250	—
4 (1910)	2,000,000	27.00	50.00	100	250	—

KM# 1129 1/2 WON

13.4800 g., 0.8000 Silver 0.3467 oz. ASW, 31 mm. **Ruler:** Kuang Mu **Obv:** Dragon within beaded circle **Rev:** Value within wreath below flower

Date	Mintage	F	VF	XF	Unc	BU
9 (1905)	600,000	100	200	300	600	—
9 (1905) Proof	—	Value: 1,850				
10 (1906)	1,200,000	100	200	300	600	—

KM# 1135 1/2 WON

10.1300 g., 0.8000 Silver 0.2605 oz. ASW, 26.5 mm. **Ruler:** Kuang Mu **Obv:** Dragon within beaded circle **Rev:** Value within wreath below flower

Date	Mintage	F	VF	XF	Unc	BU
11 (1907)	1,000,000	100	200	350	800	—

KM# 1141 1/2 WON

10.1300 g., 0.8000 Silver 0.2605 oz. ASW, 26 mm. **Ruler:** Yung Hi (Sunjong) **Obv:** Dragon within beaded circle **Rev:** Value within wreath below flower

Date	Mintage	F	VF	XF	Unc	BU
2 (1908)	1,400,000	100	200	350	700	—

KM# 1142   5 WON
4.1666 g., 0.9000 Gold 0.1206 oz. AGW
Ruler: Yung Hi (Sunjong) **Obv:** Dragon within beaded circle
Rev: Value within wreath below flower

Date	Mintage	F	VF	XF	Unc	BU
2 (1908)	10,000	14,000	30,000	45,000	65,000	—

Note: Heritage Piedmont sale 6-2000 Gem BU realized $86,250

Date	Mintage	F	VF	XF	Unc	BU
3 (1909) 2 known						

KM# 1130   10 WON
8.3333 g., 0.9000 Gold 0.2411 oz. AGW   **Ruler:** Kuang Mu **Obv:**
Dragon within beaded circle **Rev:** Value within wreath below flower

Date	Mintage	F	VF	XF	Unc	BU
10 (1906)	5,012	—	13,000	20,000	35,000	—

KM# A1130   10 WON
8.3333 g., 0.9000 Gold 0.2411 oz. AGW   **Ruler:** Yung Hi
(Sunjong) **Obv:** Dragon within beaded circle **Rev:** Value within
wreath below flower

Date	Mintage	F	VF	XF	Unc	BU
3 (1909) 2 known						

KM# 1131   20 WON
16.6666 g., 0.9000 Gold 0.4822 oz. AGW   **Ruler:** Kuang Mu
Obv: Dragon within beaded circle **Rev:** Value within wreath
below flower

Date	Mintage	F	VF	XF	Unc	BU
10 (1906)	2,506	—	25,000	40,000	70,000	—

KM# 1144   20 WON
16.6666 g., 0.9000 Gold 0.4822 oz. AGW   **Ruler:** Yung Hi
(Sunjong) **Obv:** Dragon within beaded circle **Rev:** Value within
wreath

Date	Mintage	F	VF	XF	Unc	BU
2 (1908) Rare						
3 (1909) 2 known						

Note: Reported mintages for Year 2 (1908) of 40,000 and
Year 3 (1909) of 25,000 exist, but few are known today

KINGDOM
MILLED COINAGE
Coinage Reform of 1902

KM# 1116   5 FUN
17.2000 g., Copper   **Ruler:** Kuang Mu **Obv:** Encircled dragons
within circle **Rev:** Value within wreath below flower

Date	Mintage	F	VF	XF	Unc	BU
6 (1902)	—	10.00	25.00	50.00	150	—

KM# 1117   1/4 YANG
Copper-Nickel   **Ruler:** Kuang Mu **Obv:** Dragon within beaded
circle **Rev:** Value within wreath below flower

Date	Mintage	F	VF	XF	Unc	BU
5 (1901)	—	200	350	600	1,350	—

RUSSIAN DOMINATION
MILLED COINAGE
Coinage Reform of 1902

KM# 1121   CHON
6.8000 g., Bronze   **Ruler:** Kuang Mu **Obv:** Crowned imperial
eagle within beaded circle **Rev:** Value within wreath below flower

Date	Mintage	F	VF	XF	Unc	BU
6 (1902)	3,001,000	2,000	4,000	7,000	12,000	—

KM# 1122   5 CHON
4.3000 g., Copper-Nickel   **Ruler:** Kuang Mu **Obv:** Crowned
imperial eagle within beaded circle **Rev:** Value within wreath
below flower

Date	Mintage	F	VF	XF	Unc	BU
6 (1902)	2,800,000	1,500	2,850	5,000	9,000	—

KM# 1123   1/2 WON
13.5000 g., 0.8000 Silver 0.3472 oz. ASW   **Ruler:** Kuang Mu
Obv: Crowned imperial eagle within beaded circle **Rev:** Value
within wreath below flower

Date	Mintage	F	VF	XF	Unc	BU
5 (1901)	1,831,000	3,000	7,500	14,000	20,000	—

Note: Ponterio & Assoc. Witte Museum sale 8-89 choice
BU realized $12,500; Heritage Piedmont sale 6-2000
choice BU realized $18,400

PATTERNS
Including off metal strikes

KM#	Date	Mintage	Identification	Mkt Val
Pn33	5	—	5 Won. Copper.	—
Pn34	5	—	10 Won. Copper.	—
Pn35	6	—	20 Won. Copper.	—
Pn36	6	—	20 Won. Copper.	—
Pn37	7	—	5 Won. Copper.	—
Pn38	7	—	5 Won. Copper.	—

KOREA-NORTH

The Democratic Peoples Republic of Korea, situated in
northeastern Asia on the northern half of the Korean peninsula
between the Peoples Republic of China and the Republic of
Korea, has an area of 46,540 sq. mi. (120,540 sq. km.) and a population of 20 million. Capital: Pyongyang. The economy is based
on heavy industry and agriculture. Metals, minerals and farm produce are exported.

Japan replaced China as the predominant foreign influence
in Korea in 1895 and annexed the peninsular country in 1910.
Defeat in World War II brought an end to Japanese rule. U.S.
troops entered Korea from the south and Soviet forces entered
from the north. The Cairo conference (1943) had established that
Korea should be *free and independent*. The Potsdam conference
(1945) set the 38th parallel as the line dividing the occupation
forces of the United States and Russia. When Russia refused to
permit a U.N. commission designated to supervise reunification
elections to enter North Korea, an election was held in South

Korea which established the Republic of Korea on Aug. 15,1948.
North Korea held an unsupervised election on Aug. 25, 1948, and
on Sept. 9, 1948, proclaimed the establishment of the Democratic
Peoples Republic of Korea.

NOTE: For earlier coinage see Korea.

MONETARY SYSTEM
100 Chon = 1 Won

MINT:
Pyongyang

CIRCULATION RESTRICTIONS
W/o star: KM#1-4 - General circulation
1 star: KM#5-8 - Issued to visitors from Communist countries.
2 stars: KM#9-12 - Issued to visitors from hard currency countries.

PEOPLES REPUBLIC
DECIMAL COINAGE

KM# 1   CHON
0.6400 g., Aluminum, 16 mm.   **Obv:** National arms **Rev:** Value

Date	Mintage	F	VF	XF	Unc	BU
1959	—	0.15	0.25	0.50	1.00	—
1970	—	0.20	0.35	0.75	1.50	—

KM# 5   CHON
0.6200 g., Aluminum, 16 mm.   **Obv:** National arms within circle
Rev: Value flanked by stars

Date	Mintage	F	VF	XF	Unc	BU
1959	—			0.50	1.00	—

KM# 9   CHON
Aluminum, 16 mm.   **Obv:** National arms within circle **Rev:** Star
to left of value

Date	Mintage	F	VF	XF	Unc	BU
1959	—			0.50	1.00	—

KM# 2   5 CHON
0.8100 g., Aluminum, 18 mm.   **Obv:** National arms within circle
Rev: Value

Date	Mintage	F	VF	XF	Unc	BU
1959	—	0.50	0.75	1.00	2.00	—
1974	—	0.25	0.50	1.00	2.00	—

KM# 6   5 CHON
Aluminum, 18 mm.   **Obv:** National arms within circle **Rev:** Value
flanked by stars

Date	Mintage	F	VF	XF	Unc	BU
1974	—			1.00	2.00	—

KM# 10   5 CHON
Aluminum, 18 mm.   **Obv:** National arms within circle **Rev:** Star
to left of value

Date	Mintage	F	VF	XF	Unc	BU
1974	—			1.00	2.00	—

KM# 3 10 CHON
0.9500 g., Aluminum, 20 mm. **Obv:** National arms within circle
Rev: Value

Date	Mintage	F	VF	XF	Unc	BU
1959	—	0.50	0.75	1.00	2.00	—

KM# 7 10 CHON
Aluminum, 20 mm. **Obv:** National arms within circle **Rev:** Value flanked by stars

Date	Mintage	F	VF	XF	Unc	BU
1959	—			1.00	2.00	—

KM# 11 10 CHON
Aluminum, 20 mm. **Obv:** National arms within circle **Rev:** Star to left of value

Date	Mintage	F	VF	XF	Unc	BU
1959	—			1.00	2.00	—

KM# 4 50 CHON
2.0100 g., Aluminum, 25 mm. **Obv:** National arms within circle above value **Rev:** Leaping equestrian within radiant sun

Date	Mintage	F	VF	XF	Unc	BU
1978	—	0.75	1.00	1.75	3.00	—

KM# 8 50 CHON
Aluminum, 25 mm. **Obv:** National arms within circle above value **Rev:** Leaping equestrian divides stars within radiant sun

Date	Mintage	F	VF	XF	Unc	BU
1978	—			1.75	3.00	—

KM# 12 50 CHON
Aluminum, 25 mm. **Obv:** National arms within circle above value **Rev:** Star to left of leaping equestrian within radiant sun

Date	Mintage	F	VF	XF	Unc	BU
1978	—			1.75	3.00	—

KM# 13 WON
Copper-Nickel **Obv:** National arms above date **Rev:** Kim Il Sung's birthplace among radiant sun

Date	Mintage	F	VF	XF	Unc	BU
1987	—				4.00	—
1987 Proof	—	Value: 5.00				

KM# 18 WON
2.3200 g., Aluminum, 27 mm. **Obv:** National arms above date **Rev:** Palace

Date	Mintage	F	VF	XF	Unc	BU
1987	—				3.50	—

KM# 14 WON
Copper-Nickel **Obv:** National arms above value divides date **Rev:** Kim Il Sung's Arch of Triumph within beaded circle

Date	Mintage	F	VF	XF	Unc	BU
1987	—				4.00	—
1987 Proof	—	Value: 5.00				

KM# 15 WON
Copper-Nickel **Obv:** National arms above value **Rev:** Kim Il Sung's Tower of Juche within beaded circle

Date	Mintage	F	VF	XF	Unc	BU
1987	—				4.00	—
1987 Proof	—	Value: 5.00				

KM# 179 WON
6.7000 g., Aluminum, 40 mm. **Subject:** Birds of Korea - Dryocopus Javensis **Obv:** National arms **Rev:** White-bellied woodpecker **Edge:** Plain

Date	Mintage	F	VF	XF	Unc	BU
1999 Proof	—	Value: 16.00				

KM# 180 WON
6.7000 g., Aluminum, 40 mm. **Subject:** Birds of Korea - Lyrurus Tetrix **Obv:** National arms **Rev:** Black grouse **Edge:** Plain

Date	Mintage	F	VF	XF	Unc	BU
1999 Proof	—	Value: 16.00				

KM# 181 WON
6.7000 g., Aluminum, 40 mm. **Subject:** Birds of Korea - Syrrhaptes Paradoxus **Obv:** National arms **Rev:** Pallas's sandgrouse at water's edge **Edge:** Plain

Date	Mintage	F	VF	XF	Unc	BU
1999 Proof	—	Value: 16.00				

KM# 182 WON
6.7000 g., Aluminum, 40 mm. **Subject:** Birds of Korea - Pitta Brachyura **Obv:** National arms **Rev:** Fairy pitta trilling on branch left **Edge:** Plain

Date	Mintage	F	VF	XF	Unc	BU
1999 Proof	—	Value: 16.00				

KM# 127 WON
Copper-Nickel, 35 mm. **Subject:** Blue Dragon **Obv:** National arms **Rev:** Dragon above mountains **Edge:** Reeded

Date	Mintage	F	VF	XF	Unc	BU
2000	—				9.00	15.00

KM# 126 WON
Copper-Nickel, 32 mm. **Obv:** National arms **Rev:** "Hyonmu"
Edge: Reeded

Date	Mintage	F	VF	XF	Unc	BU
2000	—	—	—	—	8.00	12.00

KM# 126a WON
3.9400 g., Aluminum, 32 mm. **Obv:** National arms
Rev: "Hyonmu" **Edge:** Plain

Date	Mintage	F	VF	XF	Unc	BU
2000 Proof	—	Value: 16.00				

KM# 127a WON
5.2000 g., Aluminum, 35 mm. **Obv:** National arms **Rev:** Blue
Dragon **Edge:** Plain

Date	Mintage	F	VF	XF	Unc	BU
2000 Proof	—	Value: 16.00				

KM# 128 WON
22.0000 g., Copper-Nickel, 35 mm. **Subject:** Tiger **Obv:** Tiger
in mountains **Rev:** Tiger head **Edge:** Plain

Date	Mintage	F	VF	XF	Unc	BU
ND(1998) Proof	5,000	—	—	—	15.00	

KM# 155 WON
16.2000 g., Brass, 35 mm. **Subject:** Seafaring Ships
Obv: National arms **Rev:** German school ship, Prinzess Eitel
Friedrich with furled sails **Edge:** Plain

Date	Mintage	F	VF	XF	Unc	BU
ND(2000) Proof	—	Value: 10.00				

KM# 155a WON
17.0000 g., Copper-Nickel, 35 mm. **Subject:** School Ships
Obv: National arms **Rev:** German school ship, Prinzess Eitel
Friedrich with furled sails **Edge:** Plain

Date	Mintage	F	VF	XF	Unc	BU
ND(2000) Proof	200	Value: 100				

KM# 156 WON
16.8600 g., Copper-Nickel, 35 mm. **Subject:** Seafaring Ships
Obv: National arms **Rev:** German school ship, Grossherzogin
Elisabeth under full sail right **Edge:** Plain

Date	Mintage	F	VF	XF	Unc	BU
ND(2000) Proof	—	Value: 10.00				

KM# 162 WON
6.7000 g., Aluminum, 40 mm. **Subject:** 3,000 Years of Korean
History **Obv:** National arms **Rev:** Radiant map and landmarks
Edge: Plain

Date	Mintage	F	VF	XF	Unc	BU
2000 Proof	—	Value: 9.00				

KM# 162a WON
26.7500 g., Brass, 40.2 mm. **Subject:** 3,000 Years of Korean
History 3,000 Years of Korean History **Obv:** National arms
Rev: Radiant Korean map and landmarks **Edge:** Plain

Date	Mintage	F	VF	XF	Unc	BU
2000 Proof	—	Value: 17.50				

KM# 198 WON
17.0000 g., Copper-Nickel, 35 mm. **Subject:** School Ships
Obv: National arms **Rev:** SS Grossherzog Friedrich August
Edge: Plain

Date	Mintage	F	VF	XF	Unc	BU
ND(2000) Proof	200	Value: 100				

KM# 263 WON
14.3100 g., Brass, 34.2 mm. **Obv:** National arms **Rev:** Flying
squirrel **Edge:** Segmented reeding

Date	Mintage	F	VF	XF	Unc	BU
ND(2000) Proof	—	Value: 25.00				

KM# 273 WON
28.2000 g., Brass, 40.1 mm. **Obv:** National arms **Rev:** Kim Jong
Il greeting diplomat, half length figures, Korean legend **Edge:** Plain

Date	Mintage	F	VF	XF	Unc	BU
2000 Proof	—	Value: 22.00				

KM# 274 WON
28.2000 g., Brass, 40.1 mm. **Obv:** National arms **Rev:** Kim Jong
Il greeting diplomat, full length figures **Edge:** Plain

Date	Mintage	F	VF	XF	Unc	BU
2000 Proof	—	Value: 22.00				

KM# 275 WON
28.2000 g., Brass, 40.1 mm. **Obv:** National arms **Rev:** Kim Jong
Il greeting diplomat, half length figures, Cyrillic legend **Edge:** Plain

Date	Mintage	F	VF	XF	Unc	BU
2000 Proof	—	Value: 22.00				

KM# 277   WON
28.2000 g., Brass, 40.1 mm. **Obv:** National arms **Rev:** Treaty signing scene **Edge:** Plain

Date	Mintage	F	VF	XF	Unc	BU
2000 Proof	—	Value: 22.00				

KM# 22   5 WON
Copper-Nickel **Obv:** Value divides date below national arms **Rev:** Kim Il Sung's Arch of Triumph

Date	Mintage	F	VF	XF	Unc	BU
1987	—	—	—	—	7.00	8.00
1987 Proof	—	Value: 10.00				

KM# 23   5 WON
Copper-Nickel **Obv:** Radiant national arms above date and value **Rev:** Kim Il Sung's Tower of Juche

Date	Mintage	F	VF	XF	Unc	BU
1987	—	—	—	—	7.00	8.00
1987 Proof	—	Value: 10.00				

KM# 25   5 WON
Copper-Nickel **Obv:** National arms above date and value **Rev:** Kim Il Sung's birthplace

Date	Mintage	F	VF	XF	Unc	BU
1987	—	—	—	—	7.00	8.00
1987 Proof	—	Value: 10.00				

KM# 19   5 WON
Copper-Nickel **Subject:** World Festival of Youth and Students **Obv:** National arms with D.P.R. of Korea written below, value at lower left **Rev:** Flower-like design

Date	Mintage	F	VF	XF	Unc	BU
1989	—	—	—	—	7.00	8.00
1989 Proof	—	Value: 10.00				

KM# 92   5 WON
12.0000 g., 0.9990 Silver 0.3854 oz. ASW **Subject:** 50th Anniversary of Liberation **Obv:** National arms above oat sprigs and date **Rev:** Teapot in bowl

Date	Mintage	F	VF	XF	Unc	BU
1995 In proof sets only	300	Value: 50.00				

KM# 129   5 WON
13.0000 g., Copper Nickel **Subject:** 10th Singapore International Coin Show **Obv:** National arms above sprigs and date **Rev:** Multicolor logo within globe **Edge:** Plain

Date	Mintage	F	VF	XF	Unc	BU
1996	1,000	—	—	—	20.00	—

KM# 130   5 WON
27.0000 g., 0.9990 Silver 0.8672 oz. ASW, 35 mm. **Subject:** Kaesong - Sinuiju Railroad **Obv:** National arms **Rev:** Multicolor train **Edge:** Plain

Date	Mintage	F	VF	XF	Unc	BU
1996	2,000	—	—	—	40.00	—

KM# 131   5 WON
27.0000 g., 0.9990 Silver 0.8672 oz. ASW, 35 mm. **Subject:** 1st Beijing International Coin Show **Obv:** National arms **Rev:** Multicolor panda holding logo **Edge:** Plain

Date	Mintage	F	VF	XF	Unc	BU
1996	6,000	—	—	—	35.00	—

KM# 100   5 WON
26.9400 g., 0.9990 Silver 0.8652 oz. ASW **Subject:** Olympics **Obv:** National arms **Rev:** Two speed skaters

Date	Mintage	F	VF	XF	Unc	BU
1997 Proof	3,000	Value: 25.00				

KM# 132   5 WON
27.0000 g., 0.9990 Silver 0.8672 oz. ASW, 35 mm. **Subject:** 11th Singapore International Coin Show **Obv:** National arms **Rev:** Multicolor panda holding logo **Edge:** Plain

Date	Mintage	F	VF	XF	Unc	BU
1997	1,000	—	—	—	35.00	—

KM# 133   5 WON
27.0000 g., 0.9990 Silver 0.8672 oz. ASW, 35 mm. **Subject:** World Cup Soccer **Obv:** National arms **Rev:** Soccer players **Edge:** Plain

Date	Mintage	F	VF	XF	Unc	BU
1997	3,000	—	—	—	30.00	—

KM# 161   5 WON
26.8400 g., 0.9990 Silver 0.8620 oz. ASW, 40 mm. **Subject:** Korean War **Obv:** National arms **Rev:** Multicolor flags and flowers in front of monument **Edge:** Reeded

Date	Mintage	F	VF	XF	Unc	BU
1998 Proof	—	Value: 25.00				

KM# 454   5 WON
26.8700 g., 0.9990 Silver 0.8630 oz. ASW, 40.08 mm. **Subject:** Korean Folk IV **Obv:** National arms **Rev:** Girl on swing **Edge:** Plain

Date	Mintage	F	VF	XF	Unc	BU
JU87-1998 Proof	—	Value: 45.00				

KM# 424   5 WON
27.0000 g., 0.9990 Silver 0.8672 oz. ASW, 40 mm. **Obv:** National arms **Rev:** Rocket and satellite above Eastern Asia **Edge:** Plain

Date	Mintage	F	VF	XF	Unc	BU
1999 Proof	—	Value: 40.00				

KM# 123   5 WON
20.0000 g., 0.9990 Silver 0.6423 oz. ASW, 34.3 mm.
Subject: History of Seafaring **Obv:** National arms **Rev:** Sailing
Junk **Edge:** Reeded and plain sections

Date	Mintage	F	VF	XF	Unc	BU
1999 Proof	5,000	Value: 35.00				

KM# 172   5 WON
20.0000 g., 0.9990 Silver 0.6423 oz. ASW, 40 mm.
Subject: Endangered Wildlife **Obv:** National arms **Rev:** Siberian
flying squirrel **Edge:** Reeded and plain sections

Date	Mintage	F	VF	XF	Unc	BU
2000 Proof	5,000	Value: 35.00				

KM# 173   5 WON
27.0000 g., 0.9990 Silver 0.8672 oz. ASW, 40 mm.
Subject: King Tongmyong **Obv:** Mythical bird **Rev:** Crowned bust
facing **Edge:** Reeded and plain sections

Date	Mintage	F	VF	XF	Unc	BU
2000 Proof	3,000	Value: 30.00				

KM# 174   5 WON
27.0000 g., 0.9990 Silver 0.8672 oz. ASW, 40 mm.
Subject: Olympics **Obv:** National arms **Rev:** Female archer
drawing back her bow **Edge:** Plain

Date	Mintage	F	VF	XF	Unc	BU
2000 Proof	3,000	Value: 30.00				

KM# 175   5 WON
27.0000 g., 0.9990 Silver 0.8672 oz. ASW, 40 mm.
Subject: Olympics **Obv:** National arms **Rev:** Handball player
Edge: Reeded and plain sections

Date	Mintage	F	VF	XF	Unc	BU
2000 Proof	3,000	Value: 30.00				

KM# 176   5 WON
27.0000 g., 0.9990 Silver 0.8672 oz. ASW, 40 mm. **Subject:**
Olympics **Obv:** National arms **Rev:** Two wrestlers **Edge:** Plain

Date	Mintage	F	VF	XF	Unc	BU
2000 Proof	3,000	Value: 30.00				

KM# 177   5 WON
27.0000 g., 0.9990 Silver 0.8672 oz. ASW, 40 mm.
Subject: Mt. Kumgang **Obv:** Mythical bird **Rev:** Buddha statue
facing **Edge:** Reeded and plain sections

Date	Mintage	F	VF	XF	Unc	BU
2000 Proof	3,000	Value: 30.00				

KM# 199   5 WON
15.0000 g., 0.9990 Silver 0.4818 oz. ASW, 35 mm.
Subject: School Ships **Obv:** National arms **Rev:** SS
Grossherzogin Elisabeth **Edge:** Plain

Date	Mintage	F	VF	XF	Unc	BU
ND(2000) Proof	500	Value: 75.00				

KM# 200   5 WON
15.0000 g., 0.9990 Silver 0.4818 oz. ASW, 35 mm.
Subject: School Ships **Obv:** National arms **Rev:** SS Prinzess
Eitel Friedrich **Edge:** Plain

Date	Mintage	F	VF	XF	Unc	BU
ND(2000) Proof	500	Value: 75.00				

KM# 201   5 WON
15.0000 g., 0.9990 Silver 0.4818 oz. ASW, 35 mm.
Subject: School Ships **Obv:** National arms **Rev:** SS Grossherzog
Friedrich August **Edge:** Plain

Date	Mintage	F	VF	XF	Unc	BU
ND(2000) Proof	500	Value: 75.00				

KM# 213   5 WON
15.0000 g., 0.9990 Silver 0.4818 oz. ASW, 35 mm.
Subject: First Nobel Prize Winners Series - Sully Prudhomme
Obv: National arms **Rev:** Writer's portrait **Edge:** Plain

Date	Mintage	F	VF	XF	Unc	BU
ND(2000) Proof	2,000	Value: 100				

KM# 214   5 WON
15.0000 g., 0.9990 Silver 0.4818 oz. ASW, 35 mm.
Subject: First Nobel Prize Winners Series - Wilhelm C. Roentgen
Obv: National arms **Rev:** Portrait and lab scene **Edge:** Plain

Date	Mintage	F	VF	XF	Unc	BU
ND(2000) Proof	2,000	Value: 100				

KM# 215   5 WON
15.0000 g., 0.9990 Silver 0.4818 oz. ASW, 35 mm.
Subject: First Nobel Prize Winners Series - Emil A. von Behring
Obv: National arms **Rev:** Two man lab scene **Edge:** Plain

Date	Mintage	F	VF	XF	Unc	BU
ND(2000) Proof	2,000	Value: 100				

KM# 216   5 WON
15.0000 g., 0.9990 Silver 0.4818 oz. ASW, 35 mm.
Subject: First Nobel Prize Winners Series - Henri Dunant
Obv: National arms **Rev:** Portrait and war wounded scene
Edge: Plain

Date	Mintage	F	VF	XF	Unc	BU
ND(2000) Proof	2,000	Value: 100				

KM# 217   5 WON
15.0000 g., 0.9990 Silver 0.4818 oz. ASW, 35 mm.
Subject: First Nobel Prize Winners Series - Jacobus Van't Hoff
Obv: National arms **Rev:** Two chemists in lab scene **Edge:** Plain

Date	Mintage	F	VF	XF	Unc	BU
ND(2000) Proof	2,000	Value: 100				

KM# 218   5 WON
15.0000 g., 0.9990 Silver 0.4818 oz. ASW, 35 mm.
Subject: First Nobel Prize Winners Series - Frederic Passy
Obv: National arms **Rev:** Portrait and allegorical scene
Edge: Plain

Date	Mintage	F	VF	XF	Unc	BU
ND(2000) Proof	2,000	Value: 100				

KM# 268   5 WON
14.9600 g., 0.9990 Silver 0.4805 oz. ASW, 35 mm.
Obv: National arms **Rev:** Mountbatten SR-N4 hovercraft
Edge: Plain

Date	Mintage	F	VF	XF	Unc	BU
2000 Proof	—	Value: 30.00				

KM# 283 5 WON
15.0000 g., 0.9990 Silver 0.4818 oz. ASW, 35 mm.
Subject: Arirang **Obv:** National arms **Rev:** Flying female flute player **Edge:** Segmented reeding

Date	Mintage	F	VF	XF	Unc	BU
ND Proof	—	Value: 30.00				

KM# 284 5 WON
15.0000 g., 0.9990 Silver 0.4818 oz. ASW, 35 mm.
Subject: Arirang **Obv:** National arms **Rev:** Dancers holding globe over arena **Edge:** Segmented reeding

Date	Mintage	F	VF	XF	Unc	BU
ND Proof	—	Value: 30.00				

KM# 285 5 WON
15.0000 g., 0.9990 Silver 0.4818 oz. ASW, 35 mm.
Subject: Arirang **Obv:** National arms **Rev:** Uniformed heads right and outline of dove **Edge:** Segmented reeding

Date	Mintage	F	VF	XF	Unc	BU
ND Proof	—	Value: 30.00				

KM# 286 5 WON
15.0000 g., 0.9990 Silver 0.4818 oz. ASW, 35 mm. **Subject:** Arirang **Obv:** National arms **Rev:** Monument **Edge:** Segmented reeding

Date	Mintage	F	VF	XF	Unc	BU
ND Proof	—	Value: 30.00				

KM# 287 5 WON
15.0000 g., 0.9990 Silver 0.4818 oz. ASW, 35 mm.
Subject: Arirang **Obv:** National arms **Rev:** Dancer in radiant sunlight **Edge:** Segmented reeding

Date	Mintage	F	VF	XF	Unc	BU
ND Proof	—	Value: 30.00				

KM# 288 5 WON
15.0000 g., 0.9990 Silver 0.4818 oz. ASW, 35 mm.
Subject: Arirang **Obv:** National arms **Rev:** Folk dancers **Edge:** Segmented reeding

Date	Mintage	F	VF	XF	Unc	BU
ND Proof	—	Value: 30.00				

KM# 289 5 WON
15.0000 g., 0.9990 Silver 0.4818 oz. ASW, 35 mm. **Subject:** Arirang **Obv:** National arms **Rev:** Arena **Edge:** Segmented reeding

Date	Mintage	F	VF	XF	Unc	BU
ND Proof	—	Value: 30.00				

KM# 65 10 WON
Copper-Nickel **Subject:** 80th Birthday - Kim Il Sung
Obv: National arms **Rev:** Kim Il Sung birthplace

Date	Mintage	F	VF	XF	Unc	BU
1992	—	—	—	—	7.50	9.00

KM# 66 10 WON
Copper-Nickel **Subject:** 50th Birthday - Kim Il Jong
Obv: National arms **Rev:** Bust facing

Date	Mintage	F	VF	XF	Unc	BU
1992	—	—	—	—	7.50	9.00

KM# 73 10 WON
Copper-Nickel **Subject:** 80th Birthday - Kim Il Sung
Obv: National arms **Rev:** Bust facing

Date	Mintage	F	VF	XF	Unc	BU
1992	—	—	—	—	7.50	9.00

KM# 269 10 WON
31.0000 g., 0.9990 Silver 0.9956 oz. ASW, 40 mm.
Obv: National arms **Rev:** Olympic horse jumping **Edge:** Plain

Date	Mintage	F	VF	XF	Unc	BU
1995 Proof	—	Value: 35.00				

KM# 270 10 WON
31.0000 g., 0.9990 Silver 0.9956 oz. ASW, 40 mm.
Obv: National arms **Rev:** Olympic runners **Edge:** Plain

Date	Mintage	F	VF	XF	Unc	BU
1995 Proof	—	Value: 35.00				

KM# 87.1 10 WON
Copper-Nickel, 30 mm. **Subject:** International Sport and Culture Festival **Obv:** National arms **Rev:** Multicolor cartoon cat **Edge:** Plain

Date	Mintage	F	VF	XF	Unc	BU
1995	—	—	—	—	15.00	17.50

KM# 87.2 10 WON
12.9000 g., Copper-Nickel, 30 mm. **Subject:** International Sport and Culture Festival **Obv:** National arms **Rev:** Multicolor cartoon cat **Edge:** Plain

Date	Mintage	F	VF	XF	Unc	BU
1995	—	—	—	—	10.00	14.00

KM# 93 10 WON
28.0000 g., Silver **Subject:** 50th Anniversary of Liberation **Obv:** National arms above sprigs and date **Rev:** Taedong gatehouse

Date	Mintage	F	VF	XF	Unc	BU
1995 In proof sets only	300	Value: 60.00				

KM# 134.1 10 WON
12.9000 g., Copper Nickel, 30 mm. **Subject:** International Sport and Culture Festival **Obv:** National arms **Rev:** Festival logo **Edge:** Plain

Date	Mintage	F	VF	XF	Unc	BU
1995	—	—	—	—	10.00	12.00

KM# 134.2   10 WON
12.9000 g., Copper Nickel, 30 mm. **Subject:** International Sport and Culture Festival **Obv:** National arms **Rev:** Festival logo with pink flame **Edge:** Plain

Date	Mintage	F	VF	XF	Unc	BU
1995	—	—	—	—	10.00	12.00

KM# 230   10 WON
31.0000 g., 0.9990 Silver 0.9956 oz. ASW, 40.1 mm.
Subject: Brontosaurus **Obv:** National arms **Rev:** Two dinosaurs above value **Edge:** Plain

Date	Mintage	F	VF	XF	Unc	BU
1995 Proof	—	Value: 35.00				

KM# 105   10 WON
31.1035 g., 0.9990 Silver 0.9990 oz. ASW **Subject:** Fauna of Asia - Ducks **Obv:** National arms **Rev:** Multicolored pair of falcated ducks

Date	Mintage	F	VF	XF	Unc	BU
1996 Proof	1,000	Value: 45.00				

KM# 115   10 WON
30.9600 g., 0.9990 Silver 0.9944 oz. ASW **Subject:** Fauna of Asia **Obv:** National arms **Rev:** Multicolored parrot

Date	Mintage	F	VF	XF	Unc	BU
1996 Proof	1,000	Value: 50.00				

KM# 135   10 WON
31.1035 g., 0.9990 Silver 0.9990 oz. ASW, 40 mm.
Subject: Korean Workers' Party **Obv:** National arms **Rev:** Flag and radiant setting sun **Edge:** Plain

Date	Mintage	F	VF	XF	Unc	BU
1996	1,000	—	—	—	40.00	—

KM# 271   10 WON
31.0000 g., 0.9990 Silver 0.9956 oz. ASW, 40.2 mm. **Obv:** National arms **Rev:** Two green Olympic gymnasts **Edge:** Plain

Date	Mintage	F	VF	XF	Unc	BU
1996 Proof	—	Value: 40.00				

KM# 98   10 WON
31.0000 g., 0.9990 Silver 0.9956 oz. ASW **Subject:** Return of Hong Kong to China **Obv:** National arms **Rev:** Temple of Heaven above Hong Kong city view

Date	Mintage	F	VF	XF	Unc	BU
1997 Proof	2,000	Value: 65.00				

KM# 222   10 WON
30.8000 g., 0.9990 Silver 0.9892 oz. ASW, 40.2 mm.
Subject: Fauna of Asia **Obv:** National arms **Rev:** Two multicolor water birds **Edge:** Reeded

Date	Mintage	F	VF	XF	Unc	BU
1997 Proof	—	Value: 50.00				

KM# 99   10 WON
31.0000 g., 0.9990 Silver 0.9956 oz. ASW **Subject:** Ginseng **Obv:** National arms **Rev:** Multicolored ginseng plant including root, leaves and berries

Date	Mintage	F	VF	XF	Unc	BU
1997 Proof	2,000	Value: 45.00				

KM# 101   10 WON
30.8800 g., 0.9990 Silver 0.9918 oz. ASW **Subject:** Shanghai Coin Show **Obv:** National arms **Rev:** Two multicolored pandas eating bamboo

Date	Mintage	F	VF	XF	Unc	BU
1997 Proof	20,000	Value: 45.00				

KM# 120   10 WON
30.9600 g., 0.9990 Silver 0.9944 oz. ASW, 38.6 mm.
Subject: Korean War **Obv:** National arms **Rev:** Multicolored flags before monument **Edge:** Reeded and plain sections

Date	Mintage	F	VF	XF	Unc	BU
1997 Proof	20,000	Value: 35.00				

KM# 121   10 WON
30.9600 g., 0.9990 Silver 0.9944 oz. ASW, 40.3 mm.
Subject: Korean War **Obv:** National arms **Rev:** Soldier watching bridge bombardment **Edge:** Reeded and plain sections

Date	Mintage	F	VF	XF	Unc	BU
1997 Proof	20,000	Value: 40.00				

KM# 124   10 WON
30.9500 g., 0.9990 Silver 0.9940 oz. ASW, 40.3 mm.
Subject: World of Adventure **Obv:** National arms **Rev:** Multicolor sailing scene **Edge:** Segmented reeding

Date	Mintage	F	VF	XF	Unc	BU
1997 Proof	—	Value: 55.00				

KM# 136   10 WON
31.1035 g., 0.9990 Silver 0.9990 oz. ASW, 40 mm. **Subject:** Chou En Lai Centennial of Birth **Obv:** National arms above value and date **Rev:** Head facing above dates flanked by sprigs **Edge:** Plain

Date	Mintage	F	VF	XF	Unc	BU
1997	8,000	—	—	—	50.00	

KM# 137   10 WON
31.1035 g., 0.9990 Silver 0.9990 oz. ASW, 40 mm. **Subject:** Chinese National Flower **Obv:** National arms **Rev:** Multicolor flower **Edge:** Plain

Date	Mintage	F	VF	XF	Unc	BU
1997	5,000	—	—	—	55.00	

KM# 138.1   10 WON
31.1035 g., 0.9990 Silver 0.9990 oz. ASW, 40 mm. **Subject:** Giant Panda **Obv:** National arms **Rev:** Multicolor seated panda **Edge:** Plain **Note:** Previous KM#138.

Date	Mintage	F	VF	XF	Unc	BU
1997	10,000	—	—	—	50.00	—

KM# 349   10 WON
31.0000 g., 0.9990 Silver 0.9956 oz. ASW, 40.2 mm. **Obv:** National arms **Rev:** Multicolor parrot **Edge:** Plain

Date	Mintage	F	VF	XF	Unc	BU
1997 Proof	—	Value: 40.00				

KM# 164   10 WON
31.0000 g., 0.9990 Silver 0.9956 oz. ASW, 40 mm. **Subject:** 50th Anniversary - People's Republic **Obv:** National arms **Rev:** Flag, dates and value below mountains **Edge:** Reeded and plain sections

Date	Mintage	F	VF	XF	Unc	BU
1998 Proof	1,000	Value: 30.00				

KM# 102   10 WON
30.8800 g., 0.9990 Silver 0.9918 oz. ASW **Subject:** Year of the Tiger **Obv:** Tiger on mountain ledge **Rev:** Tiger head

Date	Mintage	F	VF	XF	Unc	BU
ND(1998) Proof	2,000	Value: 40.00				

KM# 110   10 WON
30.8800 g., 0.9990 Silver 0.9918 oz. ASW, 40 mm. **Subject:** Korean Folk IV **Obv:** National arms **Rev:** Girl on swing **Edge:** Segmented reeding **Note:** Large date.

Date	Mintage	F	VF	XF	Unc	BU
JU87-1998 Proof	2,000	Value: 40.00				

KM# 111.1   10 WON
30.8800 g., 0.9990 Silver 0.9918 oz. ASW, 40 mm. **Subject:** Korean Folk I **Obv:** National arms **Rev:** Two children flying a kite **Edge:** Segmented reeding **Note:** Large date.

Date	Mintage	F	VF	XF	Unc	BU
JU87-1998 Proof	2,000	Value: 40.00				

KM# 111.2   10 WON
30.8800 g., 0.9990 Silver 0.9918 oz. ASW, 40 mm. **Subject:** Korean Folk I **Obv:** National arms **Rev:** Two children flying a kite **Edge:** Plain **Note:** Small date.

Date	Mintage	F	VF	XF	Unc	BU
JU87-1998 Proof	—	Value: 60.00				

KM# 112.1   10 WON
30.8800 g., 0.9990 Silver 0.9918 oz. ASW, 40 mm. **Subject:** Korean Folk II **Obv:** National arms **Rev:** Two girls see-sawing **Edge:** Segmented reeding **Note:** Large date.

Date	Mintage	F	VF	XF	Unc	BU
JU87-1998 Proof	2,000	Value: 40.00				

KM# 112.2   10 WON
30.8800 g., 0.9990 Silver 0.9918 oz. ASW, 40 mm. **Subject:** Korean Folk II **Obv:** National arms **Rev:** Two girls see-sawing **Edge:** Plain **Note:** Small date.

Date	Mintage	F	VF	XF	Unc	BU
JU87-1998 Proof	—	Value: 60.00				

KM# 113.1   10 WON
30.8800 g., 0.9990 Silver 0.9918 oz. ASW, 40 mm. **Subject:** Korean Folk III **Obv:** National arms **Rev:** Wrestling **Edge:** Segmented reeding **Note:** Large date.

Date	Mintage	F	VF	XF	Unc	BU
JU87-1998 Proof	2,000	Value: 40.00				

KM# 113.2   10 WON
30.8800 g., 0.9990 Silver 0.9918 oz. ASW, 40 mm. **Subject:** Korean Folk III **Obv:** National arms **Rev:** Wrestling **Edge:** Plain **Note:** Small date

Date	Mintage	F	VF	XF	Unc	BU
JU87-1998 Proof	—	—	—	—	—	60.00

KM# 114.1   10 WON
30.8800 g., 0.9990 Silver 0.9918 oz. ASW, 40 mm. **Subject:** Korean Folk V **Obv:** National arms **Rev:** Three girls jumping rope **Edge:** Segmented reeding **Note:** Large date.

Date	Mintage	F	VF	XF	Unc	BU
JU87-1998 Proof	2,000	Value: 40.00				

KM# 114.2   10 WON
30.8800 g., 0.9990 Silver 0.9918 oz. ASW, 40 mm. **Subject:** Korean Folk V **Obv:** National arms **Rev:** Three girls jumping rope **Edge:** Plain **Note:** Small date

Date	Mintage	F	VF	XF	Unc	BU
JU87-1998 Proof	—	Value: 60.00				

KM# 138.2   10 WON
31.1035 g., 0.9990 Silver 0.9990 oz. ASW, 40 mm. **Subject:** Giant Panda **Obv:** National arms **Rev:** Multicolor seated Panda **Edge:** Plain

Date	Mintage	F	VF	XF	Unc	BU
1998 Proof	—	Value: 45.00				

KM# 163   10 WON
31.0000 g., 0.9990 Silver 0.9956 oz. ASW, 40 mm. **Subject:** Intrepid Symbol: Tiger **Obv:** National arms **Rev:** Snarling tiger right **Edge:** Reeded and plain sections

Date	Mintage	F	VF	XF	Unc	BU
1998 Proof	2,000	Value: 35.00				

KM# 272   10 WON
31.0000 g., 0.9990 Silver 0.9956 oz. ASW, 40 mm. **Obv:** National arms **Rev:** Olympic gymnast on high bar **Edge:** Plain

Date	Mintage	F	VF	XF	Unc	BU
1998 Proof	—	Value: 35.00				

KM# 103   10 WON
30.9600 g., 0.9990 Silver 0.9944 oz. ASW **Subject:** Year of the Rabbit **Obv:** National arms **Rev:** Multicolored rabbit with hearts with legend above

Date	Mintage	F	VF	XF	Unc	BU
1999 Proof	5,000	Value: 40.00				

KM# 107   10 WON
30.9600 g., 0.9990 Silver 0.9944 oz. ASW **Subject:** Year of the Rabbit **Obv:** National arms **Rev:** Multicolored rabbits with hearts without legend above

Date	Mintage	F	VF	XF	Unc	BU
1999 Proof	5,000	Value: 40.00				

KM# 108 10 WON
30.9600 g., 0.9990 Silver 0.9944 oz. ASW **Subject:** Blue dragon **Obv:** National arms **Rev:** Flying dragon above mountains

Date	Mintage	F	VF	XF	Unc	BU
1999 Proof	5,000			Value: 45.00		

KM# 109.1 10 WON
30.9600 g., 0.9990 Silver 0.9944 oz. ASW **Subject:** Birds of Korea **Obv:** National arms **Rev:** White-bellied woodpecker on tree limb **Edge:** Segmented reeding **Note:** Prev. KM#109

Date	Mintage	F	VF	XF	Unc	BU
1999 Proof	3,000			Value: 45.00		

KM# 109.2 10 WON
30.9600 g., 0.9990 Silver 0.9944 oz. ASW **Subject:** Birds of Korea **Obv:** National arms **Rev:** White-bellied woodpecker on tree limb **Edge:** Plain

Date	Mintage	F	VF	XF	Unc	BU
1999 Proof	Inc. above			Value: 45.00		

KM# 166 10 WON
31.0000 g., 0.9990 Silver 0.9956 oz. ASW **Subject:** Birds of Korea **Obv:** National arms **Rev:** Fairy pitta on branch **Edge:** Reeded and plain sections

Date	Mintage	F	VF	XF	Unc	BU
1999 Proof	2,000			Value: 40.00		

KM# 167 10 WON
31.0000 g., 0.9990 Silver 0.9956 oz. ASW, 40 mm.
Subject: Olympic Games **Obv:** National arms **Rev:** Man jumping hurdles above kangaroo and value **Edge:** Reeded and plain sections

Date	Mintage	F	VF	XF	Unc	BU
1999 Proof	3,000			Value: 35.00		

KM# 168 10 WON
31.0000 g., 0.9990 Silver 0.9956 oz. ASW, 40 mm.
Subject: Olympic Games **Obv:** National arms **Rev:** Diver **Edge:** Reeded and plain sections

Date	Mintage	F	VF	XF	Unc	BU
1999 Proof	3,000			Value: 35.00		

KM# 169 10 WON
31.0000 g., 0.9990 Silver 0.9956 oz. ASW, 40 mm. **Subject:** 7th World Track and Field Championships **Obv:** National arms **Rev:** Marathon winner Jong Song Ok **Edge:** Reeded and plain sections

Date	Mintage	F	VF	XF	Unc	BU
1999 Proof	1,000			Value: 35.00		

KM# 170 10 WON
31.0000 g., 0.9990 Silver 0.9956 oz. ASW, 40 mm.
Subject: First North Korean Space Satellite **Obv:** National arms **Rev:** Rocket **Edge:** Reeded and plain sections

Date	Mintage	F	VF	XF	Unc	BU
1999 Proof	5,000			Value: 35.00		

KM# 171 10 WON
31.0000 g., 0.9990 Silver 0.9956 oz. ASW, 40 mm. **Subject:** Kim Il Sung and Zhou Enlai **Obv:** National arms **Rev:** Kim Il Sung and Zhou Enlai shaking hands **Edge:** Reeded and plain sections

Date	Mintage	F	VF	XF	Unc	BU
1999 Proof	5,000			Value: 35.00		

KM# 223 10 WON
30.8000 g., 0.9990 Silver 0.9892 oz. ASW, 40.2 mm.
Subject: Birds of Korea **Obv:** National arms **Rev:** Lyrurus Tetrix, bird on ground **Edge:** Reeded

Date	Mintage	F	VF	XF	Unc	BU
1999	—	—	—	—	—	37.50

KM# 224 10 WON
30.8000 g., 0.9990 Silver 0.9892 oz. ASW, 40.2 mm.
Subject: Birds of Korea **Obv:** National arms **Rev:** Syrrhaptes Paradoxus, bird on shore **Edge:** Reeded

Date	Mintage	F	VF	XF	Unc	BU
1999 Proof	—			Value: 40.00		

KM# 125 10 WON
30.9500 g., 0.9990 Silver 0.9940 oz. ASW, 40.3 mm.
Subject: One Korea: 3,000 Years of History **Obv:** National arms **Rev:** Radiant map and landmarks **Edge:** Segmented reeding

Date	Mintage	F	VF	XF	Unc	BU
2000 Proof	—			Value: 45.00		

KM# 178 10 WON
31.0000 g., 0.9990 Silver 0.9956 oz. ASW, 40 mm.
Subject: King Tangun **Obv:** National arms **Rev:** Bust facing **Edge:** Reeded and plain sections

Date	Mintage	F	VF	XF	Unc	BU
2000 Proof	5,000			Value: 37.50		

KM# 228 10 WON
31.0400 g., 0.9990 Silver 0.9969 oz. ASW, 40.3 mm.
Subject: Hyonmu **Obv:** National arms and small legend **Rev:** Mythical creature **Edge:** Plain

Date	Mintage	F	VF	XF	Unc	BU
2000 Proof	—			Value: 40.00		

KM# 229 10 WON
31.0400 g., 0.9990 Silver 0.9969 oz. ASW, 40.3 mm.
Subject: Hyonmu **Obv:** National arms with large legend **Rev:** Mythical creature **Edge:** Plain

Date	Mintage	F	VF	XF	Unc	BU
2000 Proof	—			Value: 40.00		

KM# 276 10 WON
31.0000 g., 0.9990 Silver 0.9956 oz. ASW, 40.1 mm.
Obv: National arms **Rev:** Kim greeting diplomat with Korean legend **Edge:** Plain **Note:** Similar to KM#273.

Date	Mintage	F	VF	XF	Unc	BU
2000 Proof	—	Value: 37.50				

KM# 278 10 WON
31.0000 g., 0.9990 Silver 0.9956 oz. ASW, 40.1 mm.
Obv: National arms **Rev:** Treaty signing scene **Edge:** Plain
Note: Similar to KM#277.

Date	Mintage	F	VF	XF	Unc	BU
2000 Proof	—	Value: 37.50				

KM# 279 10 WON
31.0000 g., 0.9990 Silver 0.9956 oz. ASW, 40.1 mm.
Obv: National arms **Rev:** Kim Jong II greeting diplomat, half length figures, Cyrillic legend **Edge:** Plain **Note:** Similar to KM#275.

Date	Mintage	F	VF	XF	Unc	BU
2000 Proof	—	Value: 37.50				

KM# 280 10 WON
31.0000 g., 0.9990 Silver 0.9956 oz. ASW, 40.1 mm. **Obv:** National arms **Rev:** Kim greeting diplomat, full length view **Edge:** Plain

Date	Mintage	F	VF	XF	Unc	BU
2000 Proof	—	Value: 37.00				

KM# 281 10 WON
31.0000 g., 0.9990 Silver 0.9956 oz. ASW, 40.1 mm.
Obv: National arms **Rev:** Old couple embracing above dates and value **Edge:** Plain

Date	Mintage	F	VF	XF	Unc	BU
2000 Proof	—	Value: 37.50				

KM# 282 10 WON
31.0000 g., 0.9990 Silver 0.9956 oz. ASW, 40.1 mm.
Obv: National arms **Rev:** Two tigers **Edge:** Plain

Date	Mintage	F	VF	XF	Unc	BU
2000 Proof	—	Value: 40.00				

KM# 348 10 WON
31.0000 g., 0.9990 Silver 0.9956 oz. ASW, 40.2 mm.
Obv: National arms **Rev:** Olympic handball player **Edge:** Plain

Date	Mintage	F	VF	XF	Unc	BU
2000 Proof	—	Value: 35.00				

KM# 350 10 WON
31.0000 g., 0.9990 Silver 0.9956 oz. ASW, 40.2 mm. **Obv:** National arms **Rev:** Radiant Korean map and landmarks **Edge:** Plain

Date	Mintage	F	VF	XF	Unc	BU
2000 Proof	—	Value: 35.00				

KM# 20 20 WON
14.8000 g., 0.9990 Silver 0.4753 oz. ASW **Subject:** World Festival of Youth and Students **Obv:** National arms above D.P.R. of Korea, value, and date below **Rev:** Dove within circle of flower design

Date	Mintage	F	VF	XF	Unc	BU
1989 Proof	—	Value: 25.00				

KM# 97.1 20 WON
31.1035 g., 0.9990 Silver 0.9990 oz. ASW **Subject:** Kim II Sung's death **Obv:** National arms above value **Rev:** Bust facing **Edge:** Plain **Note:** Prev. KM#97.

Date	Mintage	F	VF	XF	Unc	BU
ND(1994) Proof	5,000	Value: 85.00				

KM# 97.2 20 WON
31.1035 g., 0.9990 Silver 0.9990 oz. ASW **Subject:** Kim II Sung's Death **Obv:** National arms **Rev:** Bust facing **Edge:** Reeded

Date	Mintage	F	VF	XF	Unc	BU
ND(1994) Proof	—	Value: 50.00				

KM# 74 20 WON
Copper-Nickel **Subject:** 1998 World Cup Soccer **Obv:** National arms **Rev:** Soccer player in front of arch

Date	Mintage	F	VF	XF	Unc	BU
1995 Proof	10,000	Value: 30.00				

KM# 94 20 WON
50.0000 g., 0.9990 Silver 1.6059 oz. ASW, 50 mm.
Subject: 50th Anniversary of Liberation **Obv:** National arms **Rev:** Fairy of Mount Kumgang

Date	Mintage	F	VF	XF	Unc	BU
1995	300	Value: 125				

Note: In proof sets only

KM# 139 20 WON
31.1035 g., 0.9990 Silver 0.9990 oz. ASW, 40 mm.
Subject: 50th Anniversary - Korean Workers' Party
Obv: National arms **Rev:** Monument **Edge:** Plain

Date	Mintage	F	VF	XF	Unc	BU
1995	—				40.00	

KM# 140 20 WON
22.0000 g., Copper Nickel, 40 mm. **Subject:** 25th Basel International Coin Show **Obv:** National arms above phone fax and telex numbers **Rev:** Multicolor island and seascape **Edge:** Plain

Date	Mintage	F	VF	XF	Unc	BU
1996	1,000				18.00	

KM# 26   30 WON
17.0200 g., 0.9990 Silver 0.5466 oz. ASW   **Subject:** Friendship
Art Festival **Obv:** National arms **Rev:** Head 3/4 left with hand
holding microphone

Date	Mintage	F	VF	XF	Unc	BU
1989 Proof	—	Value: 40.00				

KM# 52   50 WON
17.0200 g., 0.9990 Silver 0.5466 oz. ASW   **Subject:** 80th Birthday
of Kim Il Sung **Obv:** National arms **Rev:** Kim Il Sung birthplace

Date	Mintage	F	VF	XF	Unc	BU
1992 Proof	1,000	Value: 40.00				

KM# 54   50 WON
17.0200 g., 0.9990 Silver 0.5466 oz. ASW   **Subject:** 80th
Birthday of Kim Il Sung **Obv:** National arms **Rev:** Bust facing

Date	Mintage	F	VF	XF	Unc	BU
1992 Proof	1,000	Value: 45.00				

KM# 56   50 WON
17.0200 g., 0.9990 Silver 0.5466 oz. ASW   **Subject:** 50th
Birthday of Kim Jong Il **Obv:** National arms **Rev:** Bust facing

Date	Mintage	F	VF	XF	Unc	BU
1992 Proof	5,000	Value: 50.00				

KM# 88   50 WON
Copper-Nickel   **Subject:** Sportsfest **Obv:** National arms
Rev: Wrestlers

Date	Mintage	F	VF	XF	Unc	BU
1995	—	—	—	—	22.50	25.00

KM# 141   50 WON
12.9000 g., Copper Nickel, 30 mm.   **Subject:** International
Friendship Exhibition **Obv:** National arms **Rev:** Building **Edge:** Plain

Date	Mintage	F	VF	XF	Unc	BU
1995	—	—	—	—	10.00	12.00

KM# 142   50 WON
12.9000 g., Copper Nickel, 30 mm.   **Subject:** May Day Stadium
Obv: National arms **Rev:** Stadium **Edge:** Plain

Date	Mintage	F	VF	XF	Unc	BU
1995	—	—	—	—	10.00	12.00

KM# 28   100 WON
3.3100 g., 0.9990 Gold 0.1005 oz. AGW   **Subject:** 40th
Anniversary of People's Republic **Obv:** National arms
Rev: Leaping equestrian

Date	Mintage	F	VF	XF	Unc	BU
1988 Proof	—	Value: 110				

KM# 70   100 WON
7.0000 g., 0.9990 Silver 0.2248 oz. ASW   **Obv:** National arms
Rev: Two multicolored Adelie penguins

Date	Mintage	F	VF	XF	Unc	BU
1995 Proof	—	Value: 45.00				

KM# 71   100 WON
7.0000 g., 0.9990 Silver 0.2248 oz. ASW   **Subject:** 1996
Olympics **Obv:** National arms **Rev:** Sprinter

Date	Mintage	F	VF	XF	Unc	BU
1995 Proof	30,000	Value: 30.00				

KM# 72   100 WON
7.0000 g., 0.9990 Silver 0.2248 oz. ASW   **Subject:** 1998 World
Cup Soccer **Obv:** National arms **Rev:** Eiffel tower and soccer player

Date	Mintage	F	VF	XF	Unc	BU
1995 Proof	30,000	Value: 30.00				

KM# 104   100 WON
7.0000 g., 0.9990 Silver 0.2248 oz. ASW   **Subject:** Aix Galericulata
Obv: National arms **Rev:** Multicolor pair of mandarin ducks

Date	Mintage	F	VF	XF	Unc	BU
1995 Proof	Est. 30,000	Value: 40.00				

KM# 122   100 WON
7.0000 g., 0.9990 Silver 0.2248 oz. ASW, 30 mm.
Subject: Robinson Crusoe **Obv:** National arms **Rev:** Multicolor
row boat scene **Edge:** Plain

Date	Mintage	F	VF	XF	Unc	BU
1996 Proof	—	Value: 40.00				

KM# 422   100 WON
7.0000 g., 0.9990 Silver 0.2248 oz. ASW, 30 mm.   **Subject:** Return
of Hong Kong **Obv:** State emblem **Rev:** Houseboat **Edge:** Plain

Date	Mintage	F	VF	XF	Unc	BU
1996 Proof	—	Value: 25.00				

KM# 449   100 WON
7.0000 g., 0.9990 Silver 0.2248 oz. ASW, 30.04 mm.
Obv: National arms **Rev:** Olympic flame above kangeroo left on
outlined map of Australia - multicolors **Rev. Leg.:** XXVII JEUX
OLYPIQUES SYDNEY 2000 **Edge:** Plain

Date	Mintage	F	VF	XF	Unc	BU
1997 Proof	—	Value: 25.00				

KM# 450   100 WON
7.0000 g., 0.9990 Silver 0.2248 oz. ASW, 30.04 mm.
Obv: National arms **Rev:** Olympic flame at center, kangeroo at
left on large outlined map of Australia **Rev. Leg.:** OLIMPIADA
SYDNEY 2000 **Edge:** Plain

Date	Mintage	F	VF	XF	Unc	BU
1997 Proof	—	Value: 25.00				

KM# 451   100 WON
7.0000 g., 0.9990 Silver 0.2248 oz. ASW, 30.04 mm.
Obv: National arms **Rev:** Sydney Opera House at center right, bridge in background, multicolored **Rev. Leg.:** OLYMPIC GAMES SYDNEY 2000 **Edge:** Plain

Date	Mintage	F	VF	XF	Unc	BU
1997 Proof	—	Value: 25.00				

KM# 49   200 WON
14.9700 g., 0.9990 Silver 0.4808 oz. ASW   **Subject:** Olympics
Obv: Silver content statement divided by national arms
Rev: Equestrian

Date	Mintage	F	VF	XF	Unc	BU
1991 Proof	25,000	Value: 25.00				

KM# 50   200 WON
14.9700 g., 0.9990 Silver 0.4808 oz. ASW   **Subject:** Olympics
Obv: Silver content statement below national arms **Rev:** Equestrian

Date	Mintage	F	VF	XF	Unc	BU
1991 Proof	Inc. above	Value: 22.50				

KM# 64   200 WON
15.0000 g., 0.9990 Silver 0.4818 oz. ASW   **Subject:** Summer Olympic Games - Barcelona 1992 **Obv:** National arms **Rev:** Sprinter

Date	Mintage	F	VF	XF	Unc	BU
1992 Proof	25,000	Value: 20.00				

KM# 95.1   200 WON
8.0000 g., 0.9990 Gold 0.2569 oz. AGW   **Subject:** 50th Anniversary of Liberation **Obv:** National arms **Rev:** Turtle ship
Note: Prev. KM#95.

Date	Mintage	F	VF	XF	Unc	BU
1995 In proof sets only	300	Value: 420				

KM# 95.2   200 WON
8.0000 g., 0.9990 Gold 0.2569 oz. AGW, 25 mm.   **Subject:** 50th Anniversary of Liberation **Obv:** National arms with fineness closer to arms **Rev:** Turtle ship

Date	Mintage	F	VF	XF	Unc	BU
1995 Proof	—	Value: 420				

KM# 29   250 WON
7.7800 g., 0.9990 Gold 0.2499 oz. AGW   **Subject:** 40th Anniversary of People's Republic **Obv:** National arms
Rev: Leaping equestrian

Date	Mintage	F	VF	XF	Unc	BU
1988 Proof	—	Value: 250				

KM# 21   250 WON
7.7700 g., 0.9990 Gold 0.2496 oz. AGW **Subject:** World Festival of Youth and Students **Obv:** National arms above D.P.R. of Korea, value and date **Rev:** Flower design

Date	Mintage	F	VF	XF	Unc	BU
1989 Proof	—	Value: 285				

KM# 423   250 WON
15.0000 g., 0.9990 Silver 0.4818 oz. ASW, 35.1 mm.
Subject: Retrun of Hong Kong **Obv:** National arms
Rev: Multicolor Junk and city view **Edge:** Plain

Date	Mintage	F	VF	XF	Unc	BU
1996 Proof	—	Value: 35.00				

KM# 116   250 WON
20.0000 g., 0.9990 Silver 0.6423 oz. ASW   **Subject:** Millennium
Obv: National arms above value **Rev:** Dragon

Date	Mintage	F	VF	XF	Unc	BU
1998//2000 Proof	—	Value: 40.00				

KM# 225   250 WON
14.9600 g., 0.9990 Silver 0.4805 oz. ASW, 34.9 mm.
Subject: Beethoven **Obv:** National arms **Rev:** Bust 3/4 left writing
Edge: Plain

Date	Mintage	F	VF	XF	Unc	BU
1999 Proof	—	Value: 35.00				

KM# 96   400 WON
16.0000 g., Gold   **Subject:** 50th Anniversary of Liberation
Obv: National arms **Rev:** Lake on Mount Baektu

Date	Mintage	F	VF	XF	Unc	BU
1995 In proof sets only	100	Value: 700				

KM# 39   500 WON
27.0000 g., 0.9990 Silver 0.8672 oz. ASW   **Subject:** World Championship Soccer - Mexico '96 **Obv:** National arms
Rev: Soccer player

Date	Mintage	F	VF	XF	Unc	BU
1987 Proof	—	Value: 35.00				

KM# 16 500 WON
27.0000 g., 0.9990 Silver 0.8672 oz. ASW **Series:** Winter Olympics **Subject:** Hockey **Obv:** National arms **Rev:** Hockey sticks and puck

Date	Mintage	F	VF	XF	Unc	BU
1988 Proof	20,000	Value: 20.00				

KM# 17 500 WON
27.0000 g., 0.9990 Silver 0.8672 oz. ASW **Subject:** 30th Anniversary of Gorch Fock **Obv:** National arms **Rev:** Ship at sea **Edge:** Plain

Date	Mintage	F	VF	XF	Unc	BU
1988 Proof	—	Value: 35.00				

KM# 24 500 WON
27.0000 g., 0.9990 Silver 0.8672 oz. ASW **Subject:** World Championship Soccer **Obv:** National arms above date and D.P.R. of Korea **Rev:** Soccer player

Date	Mintage	F	VF	XF	Unc	BU
1988 Proof	—	Value: 25.00				

KM# 30 500 WON
15.5700 g., 0.9990 Gold 0.5001 oz. AGW **Subject:** 40th Anniversary of People's Republic **Obv:** National arms **Rev:** Leaping equestrian

Date	Mintage	F	VF	XF	Unc	BU
1988 Proof	—	Value: 500				

KM# 36 500 WON
27.0000 g., 0.9990 Silver 0.8672 oz. ASW **Series:** F.A.O. **Subject:** Food for all **Obv:** National arms

Date	Mintage	F	VF	XF	Unc	BU
1988 Proof	Est. 2,000	Value: 50.00				

KM# 27 500 WON
27.0000 g., 0.9990 Silver 0.8672 oz. ASW **Subject:** Amerigo Vespucci **Obv:** National arms **Rev:** Head left at right, map of 'Americas' at left

Date	Mintage	F	VF	XF	Unc	BU
1989 Proof	—	Value: 40.00				

KM# 32.1 500 WON
31.8200 g., 0.9990 Silver 1.0220 oz. ASW, 40 mm. **Obv:** Number 1 in date without serifs **Rev:** Fairy of Mount Kumgang playing a flute **Edge:** Plain

Date	Mintage	F	VF	XF	Unc	BU
1989 Proof	—	Value: 50.00				

KM# 32 500 WON
31.8200 g., 0.9990 Silver 1.0220 oz. ASW, 40 mm. **Obv:** National arms above date and sprigs **Rev:** Fairy of Mount Kumgang playing a flute **Edge:** Segmented reeding **Note:** Sectional reeding as follows - IIIIII II IIIIII II IIIII.

Date	Mintage	F	VF	XF	Unc	BU
1989 Proof number 1 in date without bottom serif	—	Value: 50.00				
1989 Proof	2,000	Value: 55.00				

KM# 33 500 WON
27.0000 g., 0.9990 Silver 0.8672 oz. ASW **Series:** Calgary Winter Olympics **Obv:** National arms **Rev:** Figure skater

Date	Mintage	F	VF	XF	Unc	BU
1989 Proof	—	Value: 35.00				

KM# 34 500 WON
27.0000 g., 0.9990 Silver 0.8672 oz. ASW **Series:** Barcelona Summer Olympics **Obv:** National arms **Rev:** Discus thrower

Date	Mintage	F	VF	XF	Unc	BU
1989 Proof	—	Value: 35.00				

KM# 37 500 WON
27.0000 g., 0.9990 Silver 0.8672 oz. ASW **Subject:** World Championship Soccer **Obv:** National arms **Rev:** Player kicking ball

Date	Mintage	F	VF	XF	Unc	BU
1989 Proof	15,000	Value: 50.00				

KM# 38 500 WON
27.0000 g., 0.9990 Silver 0.8672 oz. ASW **Subject:** World Championship Soccer **Obv:** National arms **Rev:** Goalie

Date	Mintage	F	VF	XF	Unc	BU
1989 Proof	—	Value: 25.00				

KM# 40 500 WON
31.8200 g., 0.9990 Silver 1.0220 oz. ASW **Subject:** Olympic table tennis **Obv:** National arms **Rev:** Table tennis player

Date	Mintage	F	VF	XF	Unc	BU
1990 Proof	15,000	Value: 25.00				

KM# 41 500 WON
31.8200 g., 0.9990 Silver 1.0220 oz. ASW **Subject:** Endangered Wildlife **Obv:** National arms **Rev:** Red-crowned crane

Date	Mintage	F	VF	XF	Unc	BU
1990 Proof	—	Value: 45.00				

KM# 44 500 WON
31.1000 g., 0.9990 Silver 0.9988 oz. ASW **Subject:** World Championship Table Tennis **Obv:** National arms **Rev:** Two male players on doubles team

Date	Mintage	F	VF	XF	Unc	BU
1991 Proof	5,000	Value: 32.50				

KM# 45 500 WON

31.1000 g., 0.9990 Silver 0.9988 oz. ASW **Subject:** World Championship Table Tennis **Obv:** National arms **Rev:** Male player

Date	Mintage	F	VF	XF	Unc	BU
1991 Proof	5,000	Value: 32.50				

KM# 46 500 WON

31.1000 g., 0.9990 Silver 0.9988 oz. ASW **Subject:** 41st World Table Tennis Championships **Obv:** National arms **Rev:** Table tennis player

Date	Mintage	F	VF	XF	Unc	BU
1991 Proof	5,000	Value: 32.50				

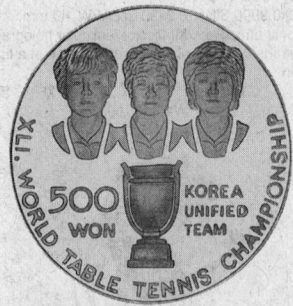

KM# 47 500 WON

31.1000 g., 0.9990 Silver 0.9988 oz. ASW **Subject:** 41st World Table Tennis Championships **Obv:** National arms **Rev:** Three busts facing above trophy

Date	Mintage	F	VF	XF	Unc	BU
1991 Proof	10,000	Value: 25.00				

KM# 48 500 WON

27.0000 g., 0.9990 Silver 0.8672 oz. ASW **Subject:** First Armoured Ship **Obv:** National arms **Rev:** First armoured ship above value

Date	Mintage	F	VF	XF	Unc	BU
1991 Proof	Est. 10,000	Value: 50.00				

KM# 63 500 WON

27.0000 g., 0.9990 Silver 0.8672 oz. ASW **Series:** Olympics **Obv:** National arms **Rev:** Women's volleyball

Date	Mintage	F	VF	XF	Unc	BU
1991 Proof	15,000	Value: 35.00				

KM# 59 500 WON

27.0000 g., 0.9990 Silver 0.8672 oz. ASW **Subject:** Environmental Protection **Obv:** National arms **Rev:** Flowers

Date	Mintage	F	VF	XF	Unc	BU
1992 Proof	1,000	Value: 55.00				

KM# 144 500 WON

27.0000 g., 0.9990 Silver 0.8672 oz. ASW, 35 mm. **Subject:** 1994 World Cup Soccer **Obv:** National arms **Rev:** Three soccer players **Edge:** Plain

Date	Mintage	F	VF	XF	Unc	BU
1992	—	—	—	—	35.00	

KM# 62.1 500 WON

31.1035 g., 0.9990 Silver 0.9990 oz. ASW, 40.3 mm. **Series:** Prehistoric Animals **Obv:** National arms **Rev:** Brontosaurus **Edge:** Reeded **Note:** Prev. KM#62.

Date	Mintage	F	VF	XF	Unc	BU
1993						
1993 Proof	—	Value: 40.00				

KM# 60 500 WON

27.0000 g., 0.9990 Silver 0.8672 oz. ASW **Series:** 1994 Olympics **Obv:** National arms **Rev:** Speed skating

Date	Mintage	F	VF	XF	Unc	BU
1993 Proof	1,000	Value: 30.00				

KM# 61 500 WON

27.0000 g., 0.9990 Silver 0.8672 oz. ASW **Series:** 1994 Olympics **Obv:** National arms **Rev:** Two-man bobsled

Date	Mintage	F	VF	XF	Unc	BU
1993 Proof	1,000	Value: 40.00				

KM# 145 500 WON

31.1035 g., 0.9990 Silver 0.9990 oz. ASW, 40 mm. **Subject:** 1994 World Cup Soccer **Obv:** National arms **Rev:** Two players and trophy cup **Edge:** Plain

Date	Mintage	F	VF	XF	Unc	BU
1994	—	—	—	—	40.00	—

KM# 62.2 500 WON

31.1035 g., 0.9990 Silver 0.9990 oz. ASW, 40.3 mm. **Series:** Prehistoric Animals **Obv:** National arms **Rev:** More vegetation by dinosaur's foot **Edge:** Reeded

Date	Mintage	F	VF	XF	Unc	BU
1995 Proof	3,000	Value: 55.00				

KM# 67 500 WON

31.1035 g., 0.9990 Silver 0.9990 oz. ASW **Series:** 1996 Atlanta Olympics **Obv:** National arms **Rev:** Relay racers

Date	Mintage	F	VF	XF	Unc	BU
1995 Proof	3,000	Value: 40.00				

KM# 68   500 WON
31.1035 g., 0.9990 Silver 0.9990 oz. ASW, 40 mm.   **Series:** 1996 Atlanta Olympics **Obv:** National arms **Rev:** Equestrian **Edge:** Plain

Date	Mintage	F	VF	XF	Unc	BU
1995 Proof	3,000				Value: 40.00	

KM# 77   500 WON
31.1035 g., 0.9990 Silver 0.9990 oz. ASW **Subject:** Fauna of Asia **Obv:** National arms **Rev:** Multicolor parrot

Date	Mintage	F	VF	XF	Unc	BU
1995 Proof	20,000				Value: 45.00	

KM# 143   500 WON
31.1035 g., 0.9990 Silver 0.9990 oz. ASW, 40 mm.   **Subject:** International Sport and Culture Festival **Obv:** National arms **Rev:** Head facing **Edge:** Plain

Date	Mintage	F	VF	XF	Unc	BU
1995	—	—	—	—	40.00	—

KM# 69   500 WON
31.1035 g., 0.9990 Silver 0.9990 oz. ASW **Subject:** Fauna of Asia **Obv:** National arms above date and sprigs **Rev:** Multicolor tiger

Date	Mintage	F	VF	XF	Unc	BU
1995 Proof	20,000				Value: 45.00	

KM# 78   500 WON
31.1035 g., 0.9990 Silver 0.9990 oz. ASW **Subject:** Fauna of Asia **Obv:** National arms **Rev:** Multicolor eagle

Date	Mintage	F	VF	XF	Unc	BU
1995 Proof	20,000				Value: 45.00	

KM# 146   500 WON
17.0000 g., 0.9990 Silver 0.5460 oz. ASW **Series:** F.A.O. **Subject:** F.A.O. 50 Years **Obv:** National arms **Rev:** F.A.O. logo above dates and value within chain-like sprigs **Edge:** Plain

Date	Mintage	F	VF	XF	Unc	BU
1995 Proof	—				Value: 35.00	

KM# 421   500 WON
31.1035 g., 0.9990 Silver 0.9990 oz. ASW, 40 mm. **Obv:** National arms **Rev:** Multicolor lenticular hologram panda and tiger heads only one of which can be seen at a time **Edge:** Plain

Date	Mintage	F	VF	XF	Unc	BU
1996 Proof	—				Value: 35.00	

KM# 75   500 WON
31.1035 g., 0.9990 Silver 0.9990 oz. ASW **Subject:** 1998 World Cup Soccer **Obv:** National arms **Rev:** Soccer player in front of arch

Date	Mintage	F	VF	XF	Unc	BU
1995 Proof	10,000				Value: 45.00	

KM# 79   500 WON
31.1035 g., 0.9990 Silver 0.9990 oz. ASW **Subject:** Fauna of Asia **Obv:** National arms **Rev:** Multicolor Eurasian eagle owl

Date	Mintage	F	VF	XF	Unc	BU
1995 Proof	20,000				Value: 50.00	

KM# 89   500 WON
31.1035 g., 0.9990 Silver multi-color 0.9990 oz. ASW **Series:** Olympics **Obv:** National arms **Rev:** Two eurythmic gymnasts

Date	Mintage	F	VF	XF	Unc	BU
1996	1,000	—	—	—	65.00	—

KM# 76   500 WON
31.1035 g., 0.9990 Silver 0.9990 oz. ASW **Subject:** Fauna of Asia **Obv:** National arms **Rev:** Multicolor panda

Date	Mintage	F	VF	XF	Unc	BU
1995 Proof	20,000				Value: 45.00	

KM# 80   500 WON
31.1035 g., 0.9990 Silver 0.9990 oz. ASW **Subject:** Fauna of Asia **Obv:** National arms **Rev:** Two multicolor falcated ducks **Note:** Enameled.

Date	Mintage	F	VF	XF	Unc	BU
1995 Proof	20,000				Value: 40.00	

KM# 90   500 WON
31.1035 g., 0.9990 Silver 0.9990 oz. ASW **Series:** Olympics **Obv:** National arms **Rev:** Soccer

Date	Mintage	F	VF	XF	Unc	BU
1996	30,000	—	—	—	45.00	—

KM# 91   500 WON
31.1035 g., 0.9990 Silver 0.9990 oz. ASW **Subject:** Fauna of Asia **Obv:** National arms **Rev:** Multicolor holographic panda

Date	Mintage	F	VF	XF	Unc	BU
1996 Proof	5,000	Value: 60.00				

KM# 106   500 WON
31.5200 g., 0.9990 Silver 1.0123 oz. ASW **Subject:** Fauna of Asia **Obv:** National arms **Rev:** Multicolor hologram of tiger

Date	Mintage	F	VF	XF	Unc	BU
1996 Proof	—	Value: 60.00				

KM# 117   500 WON
31.1035 g., 0.9990 Silver 0.9990 oz. ASW **Subject:** Fauna of Asia **Obv:** National arms **Rev:** Multicolor pearl gourami

Date	Mintage	F	VF	XF	Unc	BU
1996 Proof	—	Value: 45.00				

KM# 118   500 WON
31.1035 g., 0.9990 Silver 0.9990 oz. ASW **Subject:** Fauna of Asia **Obv:** National arms **Rev:** Multicolor clown loach

Date	Mintage	F	VF	XF	Unc	BU
1996 Proof	—	Value: 45.00				

KM# 119   500 WON
31.1035 g., 0.9990 Silver 0.9990 oz. ASW **Subject:** Fauna of Asia **Obv:** National arms **Rev:** Multicolor long-tailed angelfish

Date	Mintage	F	VF	XF	Unc	BU
1996 Proof	—	Value: 45.00				

KM# 154   500 WON
27.0000 g., 0.9990 Silver 0.8672 oz. ASW, 35.2 mm. **Subject:** First Asian Gymnastic Championship **Obv:** National arms **Rev:** Multicolor panda holding logo **Edge:** Coarse and finely reeded sections

Date	Mintage	F	VF	XF	Unc	BU
1996 Proof	—	Value: 60.00				

KM# 147   700 WON
31.1035 g., 0.9990 Gold 0.9990 oz. AGW, 35 mm. **Subject:** Korean Workers' Party **Obv:** National arms **Rev:** Flag and radiant setting sun **Edge:** Plain

Date	Mintage	F	VF	XF	Unc	BU
1996	100				—	1,000

KM# 165   700 WON
31.1000 g., 0.9990 Gold 0.9988 oz. AGW, 35 mm. **Subject:** 50th Anniversary of People's Republic **Obv:** National arms **Rev:** Flag **Edge:** Plain

Date	Mintage	F	VF	XF	Unc	BU
1998 Proof	500	Value: 975				

KM# 31   1000 WON
31.1300 g., 0.9990 Gold 0.9998 oz. AGW **Subject:** 40th Anniversary of People's Republic **Obv:** National arms **Rev:** Leaping equestrian

Date	Mintage	F	VF	XF	Unc	BU
1988 Proof	—	Value: 965				

KM# 148   1000 WON
15.5500 g., 0.9990 Gold 0.4994 oz. AGW, 27 mm. **Subject:** Death of Kim-II Sung **Obv:** National arms **Rev:** Bust facing **Edge:** Plain

Date	Mintage	F	VF	XF	Unc	BU
ND(1994)	—				—	485

KM# 149   1000 WON
31.1035 g., 0.9990 Gold 0.9990 oz. AGW, 35 mm. **Subject:** 50th Anniversary - Korean Workers' Party **Obv:** National arms **Rev:** Monument **Edge:** Plain

Date	Mintage	F	VF	XF	Unc	BU
1995	—				—	975

KM# 58   1500 WON
8.0000 g., 0.9990 Gold 0.2569 oz. AGW **Series:** Olympics **Obv:** National arms **Rev:** Gymnast

Date	Mintage	F	VF	XF	Unc	BU
1990 Proof	Est. 3,000	Value: 260				

KM# 42   1500 WON
15.5500 g., 0.9990 Gold 0.4994 oz. AGW **Subject:** Inter-parliamentary Conference **Obv:** National arms **Rev:** Buildings

Date	Mintage	F	VF	XF	Unc	BU
1991 Proof	1,000	Value: 475				

KM# 43   1500 WON
15.5500 g., 0.9990 Gold 0.4994 oz. AGW **Subject:** Inter-parliamentary Conference **Obv:** National arms **Rev:** Building

Date	Mintage	F	VF	XF	Unc	BU
1991 Proof	800	Value: 475				

KM# 51 1500 WON
8.0000 g., 0.9990 Gold 0.2569 oz. AGW **Subject:** Soccer
Obv: National arms **Rev:** Soccer player in mid-kick

Date	Mintage	F	VF	XF	Unc	BU
1991 Proof	1,000	Value: 260				

KM# 150 1500 WON
8.0000 g., 0.9990 Gold 0.2569 oz. AGW, 22 mm. **Series:**
Olympics **Obv:** National arms **Rev:** Cyclists racing **Edge:** Plain

Date	Mintage	F	VF	XF	Unc	BU
1993	—	—	—	—	—	300

KM# 53 2000 WON
31.1000 g., 0.9988 oz. AGW **Subject:** 80th Birthday
of Kim Il Sung **Obv:** National arms **Rev:** Kim Il Sung birthplace

Date	Mintage	F	VF	XF	Unc	BU
ND(1992) Proof	500	Value: 980				

KM# 55 2000 WON
31.1000 g., 0.9990 Gold 0.9988 oz. AGW **Subject:** 80th
Birthday of Kim Il Sung **Obv:** National arms **Rev:** Bust facing

Date	Mintage	F	VF	XF	Unc	BU
1992 Proof	500	Value: 980				

KM# 57 2000 WON
31.1000 g., 0.9990 Gold 0.9988 oz. AGW **Subject:** 50th
Birthday of Kim Jong Il **Rev:** Bust facing

Date	Mintage	F	VF	XF	Unc	BU
1992 Proof	500	Value: 980				

KM# 151 2000 WON
31.1035 g., 0.9990 Gold 0.9990 oz. AGW, 40 mm. **Subject:** Death
of Kim Il Sung **Obv:** National arms **Rev:** Bust facing **Edge:** Plain

Date	Mintage	F	VF	XF	Unc	BU
ND(1994)	—	—	—	—	—	960

KM# 35 2500 WON
15.5500 g., 0.9990 Gold 0.4994 oz. AGW **Subject:** 30th
Anniversary of Gorch Fock **Obv:** National arms **Rev:** Sailing ship

Date	Mintage	F	VF	XF	Unc	BU
1988 Proof	Est. 500	Value: 500				

KM# 81 2500 WON
155.5175 g., 0.9990 Silver 4.9948 oz. ASW, 65 mm.
Obv: National arms **Rev:** Multicolor panda

Date	Mintage	F	VF	XF	Unc	BU
1995 Proof	2,500	Value: 150				

KM# 82 2500 WON
155.5175 g., 0.9990 Silver 4.9948 oz. ASW **Obv:** National arms
Rev: Multicolor tiger

Date	Mintage	F	VF	XF	Unc	BU
1995 Proof	2,500	Value: 160				

KM# 83 2500 WON
155.5175 g., 0.9990 Silver 4.9948 oz. ASW **Obv:** National arms
Rev: Multicolor parrot

Date	Mintage	F	VF	XF	Unc	BU
1995 Proof	2,500	Value: 155				

KM# 85 2500 WON
155.5175 g., 0.9990 Silver 4.9948 oz. ASW **Obv:** National arms
Rev: Multicolor eurasian eagle owl

Date	Mintage	F	VF	XF	Unc	BU
1995 Proof	2,500	Value: 160				

KM# 86 2500 WON
155.5175 g., 0.9990 Silver 4.9948 oz. ASW **Obv:** National arms
Rev: Two multicolor falcated ducks

Date	Mintage	F	VF	XF	Unc	BU
1995 Proof	2,500	Value: 160				

KM# 84 2500 WON
155.5175 g., 0.9990 Silver 4.9948 oz. ASW **Obv:** National arms
Rev: Multicolor eagle

Date	Mintage	F	VF	XF	Unc	BU
1995 Proof	2,500	Value: 155				

PROOF SETS

KM#	Date	Mintage Identification	Issue Price	Mkt Val
PS1	1995 (5)	300 KM92-96	—	1,350

KOREA-SOUTH

The Republic of Korea, situated in northeastern Asia on the
southern half of the Korean peninsula between North Korea and
the Korean Strait, has an area of 38,025 sq. mi. (98,480 sq. km.)
and a population of 42.5 million. Capital: Seoul. The economy is
based on agriculture and light and medium industry. Some of the
world's largest oil tankers are built here. Automobiles, plywood,
electronics, and textile products are exported.

Japan replaced China as the predominant foreign influence
in Korea in 1895 and annexed the peninsular country in 1910.
Defeat in World War II brought an end to Japanese rule. U.S.
troops entered Korea from the south and Soviet forces entered
from the north. The Cairo conference (1943) had established that
Korea should be *free and independent*. The Potsdam conference
(1945) set the 38th parallel as the line dividing the occupation
forces of the United States and Russia. When Russia refused to
permit a U.N. commission designated to supervise reunification
elections to enter North Korea, an election was held in South
Korea on May 10, 1948. By its determination, the Republic of
Korea was inaugurated on Aug. 15,1948.

NOTE: For earlier coinage see Korea.

MONETARY SYSTEM
100 Chon = 1 Hwan

REPUBLIC
DECIMAL COINAGE

KM# 1 10 HWAN
2.4600 g., Bronze, 19.1 mm. **Obv:** Value **Rev:** Rose of Sharon

Date	Mintage	F	VF	XF	Unc	BU
KE4292(1959)	100,000,000	2.00	5.00	20.00	50.00	90.00
Note: Issued 10-20-59						
KE4294(1961)	100,000,000	0.50	1.00	2.00	5.00	8.00

KM# 2 50 HWAN
3.6900 g., Nickel-Brass, 22.86 mm. **Obv:** Value **Rev:** Iron-clad
turtle boat

Date	Mintage	F	VF	XF	Unc	BU
	24,640,000	0.60	1.00	3.00	7.00	12.00
KE4294(1961)	20,000,000	0.60	1.00	3.00	5.00	10.00

KM# 3 100 HWAN
6.7400 g., Copper-Nickel, 26 mm. **Obv:** Value flanked by
phoenix **Rev:** Bust left

Date	Mintage	F	VF	XF	Unc	BU
KE4292(1959)	—	2.00	4.00	8.00	25.00	45.00

Issued 10-30-59. Quantities of KM#1-3 dated 4292 in
uncirculated condition were countermarked "SAMPLE" in
Korean for distribution to government and banking agencies. See bank samples section at end of listing. KM#3
was withdrawn from circulation June 10, 1962, and melted; KM#1 and KM#2 continued to circulate as 1 Won and
5 Won coins for 13 years, respectively, until demonetized
and withdrawn from circulation March 22, 1975.

REFORM COINAGE
10 Hwan = 1 Won

KM# 4 WON
1.7000 g., Brass, 17.2 mm. **Obv:** Rose of Sharon
Rev: Inscription, value and date

Date	Mintage	F	VF	XF	Unc	BU
1966	7,000,000	0.25	1.00	2.00	9.00	20.00
Issued 8-16-66						
1967	48,500,000	0.10	0.50	1.00	2.00	5.00

KM# 4a WON
0.7290 g., Aluminum, 17.2 mm. **Obv:** Rose of Sharon
Rev: Inscription, value and date

Date	Mintage	F	VF	XF	Unc	BU
1968	66,500,000	—	0.25	1.00	2.00	3.50
Issued 8-26-68						
1969	85,000,000	—	0.10	0.50	1.00	3.00
1970	45,000,000	—	0.10	0.50	1.00	3.00
1974	12,000,000	—	0.25	1.00	3.00	6.00
1975	10,000,000	—	0.10	0.75	1.50	4.00
1976	20,000,000	—	—	0.20	1.00	1.75
1977	30,000,000	—	—	0.20	1.00	1.75
1978	30,000,000	—	—	0.10	0.20	0.30
1979	30,000,000	—	—	0.10	0.20	0.30
1980	20,000,000	—	—	0.10	0.20	0.30
1981	20,000,000	—	—	0.10	0.20	0.30
1982	30,000,000	—	—	0.10	2.00	0.30
1982 Proof	2,000	—	—	0.10	0.20	0.30

KM# 31 WON
0.7290 g., Aluminum, 17.2 mm. **Obv:** Rose of Sharon
Rev: Value and date

Date	Mintage	F	VF	XF	Unc	BU
1983	40,000,000	—	—	—	0.15	0.25
Issued 1-15-83						
1984	20,000,000	—	—	—	0.15	0.25
1985	10,000,000	—	—	—	0.15	0.25
1987	10,000,000	—	—	—	0.15	0.25
1988	6,500,000	—	—	—	0.15	0.25
1989	10,000,000	—	—	—	0.15	0.25
1990	6,000,000	—	—	—	0.15	0.25
1991	5,000,000	—	—	15.00	0.25	0.50
1995	15,000	—	—	—	0.15	0.25
1996	15,000	—	—	—	0.15	0.25
1997	15,000	—	—	—	0.15	0.25

Date	Mintage	F	VF	XF	Unc	BU
1998	15,000	—	—	—	0.15	0.25
1999	15,000	—	—	—	0.15	0.25
2000	30,000	—	—	—	0.15	0.25

KM# 5   5 WON
2.9500 g., Bronze, 20.4 mm. **Obv:** Iron-clad turtle boat
Rev: Value, inscription and date

Date	Mintage	F	VF	XF	Unc	BU
1966	4,500,000	0.15	0.25	1.50	50.00	100
	Note: Issued 8-16-66					
1967	18,000,000	0.15	0.25	1.00	60.00	120
1968	20,000,000	0.15	0.25	1.00	30.00	60.00
1969	25,000,000	—	0.10	0.25	10.00	20.00
1970	50,000,000	—	0.10	0.25	12.00	25.00

KM# 5a   5 WON
2.9500 g., Brass, 20 mm. **Obv:** Iron-clad turtle boat **Rev:** Value, inscription and date

Date	Mintage	F	VF	XF	Unc	BU
1970	Inc. above	—	—	0.10	1.00	3.00
	Note: Issued 7-16-70					
1971	64,038,000	—	—	—	0.25	0.50
1972	60,084,000	—	—	—	0.25	0.50
1977	1,000,000	—	—	0.10	0.65	0.50
1978	1,000,000	—	—	0.10	0.65	1.00
1979	1,000,000	—	—	0.10	0.65	1.00
1980	200,000	—	0.25	0.50	2.25	3.00
1981	200,000	—	0.25	0.50	1.50	2.00
1982	200,000	—	0.25	0.50	1.50	2.00
1982 Proof	2,000	—	—	—	—	—

KM# 32   5 WON
2.9500 g., Brass, 20.4 mm. **Obv:** Iron-clad turtle boat **Rev:** Value and date

Date	Mintage	F	VF	XF	Unc	BU
1983	6,000,000	—	—	0.10	0.20	0.30
	Note: Issued 1-15-83					
1987	1,000,000	—	—	0.10	0.30	0.60
1988	500,000	—	—	0.50	1.00	2.00
1989	600,000	—	—	0.20	0.50	0.70
1990	600,000	—	—	0.20	0.50	0.70
1991	500,000	—	—	0.10	0.20	0.30
1995	15,000	—	—	0.10	0.20	0.30
1996	15,000	—	—	0.10	0.20	0.30
1997	15,000	—	—	0.10	0.20	0.30
1999	10,000	—	—	0.10	0.20	0.30
2000	30,000	—	—	0.10	0.20	0.30

KM# 6   10 WON
4.0600 g., Bronze, 22.86 mm. **Obv:** Pagoda at Pul Guk Temple
Rev: Value, inscription and date

Date	Mintage	F	VF	XF	Unc	BU
1966	10,600,000	0.15	0.25	1.50	75.00	175
	Note: Issued 8-16-66					
1967	22,500,000	0.15	0.25	1.50	90.00	200
1968	35,000,000	0.15	0.25	1.50	35.00	75.00
1969	46,500,000	0.15	0.25	1.50	100	250
1970	157,000,000	0.15	0.25	1.50	150	350

KM# 6a   10 WON
4.0600 g., Brass, 22.86 mm. **Obv:** Pagoda at Pul Guk Temple
Rev: Value, inscription and date

Date	Mintage	F	VF	XF	Unc	BU
1970	Inc. above	—	0.35	1.25	40.00	120
	Note: Issued 7-16-70					
1971	220,000,000	—	—	0.50	2.00	3.00
1972	270,000,000	—	—	0.50	2.00	3.00
1973	30,000,000	—	0.10	0.35	15.00	30.00
1974	15,000,000	—	0.10	1.00	7.00	15.00
1975	20,000,000	—	0.10	0.50	45.00	150
1977	1,000,000	—	0.10	0.35	3.50	8.00
1978	80,000,000	—	0.10	0.15	1.25	2.00
1979	200,000,000	—	—	0.10	0.55	1.00
1980	150,000,000	—	—	0.10	0.55	1.00
1981	100,000	—	0.25	0.75	4.00	10.00

Date	Mintage	F	VF	XF	Unc	BU
1982	20,000,000	—	—	0.10	0.60	1.10
1982 Proof	2,000	—	—	—	—	—

KM# 33.1   10 WON
4.0600 g., Brass, 22.86 mm. **Obv:** Pagoda at Pul Guk Temple
Rev: Value below date

Date	Mintage	F	VF	XF	Unc	BU
1983	25,000,000	—	—	0.10	0.35	0.50
	Note: Issued 1-15-83					
1985	35,000,000	—	—	0.10	0.35	0.50
1986	195,000,000	—	—	0.10	0.35	0.50
1987	155,000,000	—	—	0.10	0.35	0.50
1988	189,000,000	—	—	0.10	0.35	0.50
1989	310,000,000	—	—	0.10	0.35	0.50
1990	395,000,000	—	—	0.10	0.35	0.50
1991	300,000,000	—	—	0.10	0.35	0.50
1992	150,000,000	—	—	0.50	1.00	2.00
1993	110,000,000	—	—	0.75	1.50	3.00
1994	300,000,000	—	—	0.10	0.35	0.50
1995	380,000,000	—	—	0.10	0.35	0.50
1996	290,000,000	—	—	0.10	0.35	0.50
1997	177,000,000	—	—	0.10	0.35	0.50
1999	377,000,000	—	—	0.10	0.35	0.50
2000	335,000,000	—	—	0.10	0.35	0.50

KM# 33.2   10 WON
4.0600 g., Brass **Obv:** Pagoda at Pul Guk Temple **Rev:** Thicker value below date

Date	Mintage	F	VF	XF	Unc	BU
1991	—	—	—	0.10	0.35	0.50
1997	—	—	—	0.10	0.35	0.50
1998	—	—	—	0.10	0.35	0.50
1999	—	—	—	0.10	0.35	0.50
2000	—	—	—	0.10	0.35	0.50

KM# 7   50 WON
2.8000 g., 0.9990 Silver 0.0899 oz. ASW, 16 mm. **Obv:** Arms within floral spray **Rev:** Half figure holding flag facing left

Date	Mintage	F	VF	XF	Unc	BU
KE4303-1970 Proof	4,350	Value: 100				
KE4304-1971 Rare	—	—	—	—	—	—

KM# 20   50 WON
4.0000 g., Copper-Nickel **Series:** F.A.O. **Obv:** Text within sagging oat sprig **Rev:** Value below date

Date	Mintage	F	VF	XF	Unc	BU
1972	6,000,000	0.20	0.40	1.00	50.00	100
	Note: Issued 12-1-72					
1973	40,000,000	—	0.15	0.25	20.00	50.00
1974	25,000,000	—	0.15	0.25	1.50	3.00
1977	1,000,000	—	0.15	0.25	5.00	10.00
1978	15,000,000	—	0.15	0.25	3.00	5.00
1979	20,000,000	—	0.10	0.20	3.00	5.00
1980	10,000,000	—	0.10	0.20	5.00	10.00
1981	25,000,000	—	0.10	0.20	2.00	3.00
1982	40,000,000	—	0.10	0.20	2.00	3.00
1982 Proof	2,000	—	—	—	—	—

KM# 34   50 WON
4.1600 g., Copper-Nickel, 21.16 mm. **Series:** F.A.O. **Obv:** Text below sagging oat sprig **Rev:** Value and date **Note:** Die varieties exist.

Date	Mintage	F	VF	XF	Unc	BU
1983	50,000,000	—	—	0.10	1.00	2.50
	Note: Issued 1-15-83					
1984	40,000,000	—	—	0.10	1.00	2.50
1985	4,000,000	—	—	0.10	2.00	4.00
1987	32,000,000	—	—	0.10	1.00	2.50
1988	53,000,000	—	—	0.10	1.00	2.50
1989	70,000,000	—	—	0.10	1.00	2.50
1990	85,000,000	—	—	0.10	2.00	4.00
1991	80,000,000	—	—	0.10	1.00	3.00
1992	50,000,000	—	—	0.10	4.00	8.00
1993	5,000,000	—	—	0.10	25.00	45.00
1994	102,000,000	—	—	0.10	1.00	3.00
1995	98,000,000	—	—	0.10	1.00	3.00
1996	52,000,000	—	—	0.10	1.00	3.00
1997	129,000,000	—	—	0.10	1.00	3.00
1998	28,000,000	—	—	0.10	3.00	5.00
1999	15,000,000	—	—	0.10	1.00	3.00
2000	86,000,000	—	—	0.10	0.50	1.00

KM# 8   100 WON
5.6000 g., 0.9990 Silver 0.1799 oz. ASW, 21 mm. **Obv:** Arms within floral spray **Rev:** Standing figure and boat

Date	Mintage	F	VF	XF	Unc	BU
KE4303-1970 Proof	4,350	Value: 400				

KM# 9   100 WON
5.4200 g., Copper-Nickel, 24 mm. **Obv:** Bust with hat facing **Rev:** Value and date within designed wreath

Date	Mintage	F	VF	XF	Unc	BU
1970	1,500,000	0.50	0.75	15.00	30.00	70.00
	Note: Issued 11-30-70					
1971	13,000,000	0.15	0.25	20.00	35.00	75.00
1972	20,000,000	—	0.20	20.00	35.00	75.00
1973	80,000,000	—	0.15	3.00	5.00	9.00
1974	50,000,000	—	0.15	20.00	50.00	120
	Note: Die varieties exist					
1975	75,000,000	—	0.15	6.00	10.00	20.00
	Note: Die varieties exist					
1977	30,000,000	—	0.15	5.00	12.00	35.00
1978	50,000,000	—	0.15	2.00	4.00	6.00
1979	130,000,000	—	0.15	1.50	2.50	4.00
1980	60,000,000	—	0.15	3.00	5.00	10.00
1981	100,000	—	0.25	2.00	4.00	6.00
1982	70,000,000	—	0.15	1.00	2.00	3.50
1982 Proof	2,000	—	—	—	—	—

KM# 21   100 WON
12.0000 g., Copper-Nickel, 30 mm. **Subject:** 30th Anniversary of Liberation **Obv:** Gate of Liberty **Rev:** Standing figures and value

Date	Mintage	F	VF	XF	Unc	BU
ND(1975)	4,998,000	0.30	0.60	0.90	2.25	—
	Note: Issued 8-15-75					
ND(1975) Proof	2,000	Value: 170				

KM# 24   100 WON
12.0000 g., Copper-Nickel, 30 mm. **Subject:** 1st Anniversary of the 5th Republic **Obv:** Yin-yang symbol within rectangle above value flanked by flames **Rev:** Cluster of flowers

Date	Mintage	F	VF	XF	Unc	BU
1981	4,980,000	0.20	0.35	0.65	2.00	—
Note: Issued 8-81						
1981 Unfrosted, Proof	18,000	Value: 25.00				
1981 Proof	2,000	Value: 165				

KM# 35.1   100 WON
5.4200 g., Copper-Nickel, 24 mm. **Obv:** Bust with hat facing **Rev:** Value and date

Date	Mintage	F	VF	XF	Unc	BU
1983	130,000,000	—	0.25	1.00	2.00	4.00
Note: Issued 1-15-83						

KM# 35.2   100 WON
5.4200 g., Copper-Nickel, 24 mm. **Obv:** Bust with hat facing **Rev:** Value and date

Date	Mintage	F	VF	XF	Unc	BU
1984	40,000,000	—	0.25	1.00	2.00	4.00
Note: Issued 1-15-83						
1985	25,000,000	—	0.25	10.00	25.00	40.00
1986	131,000,000	—	0.25	2.00	3.00	5.00
1987	170,000,000	—	0.25	1.00	2.00	4.00
1988	298,000,000	—	0.25	1.00	2.00	4.00
1989	250,000,000	—	0.25	1.00	2.00	4.00
1990	185,000,000	—	0.25	1.00	2.00	4.00
1991	400,000,000	—	0.25	1.00	2.00	4.00
1992	425,000,000	—	0.25	3.00	4.00	6.00
1993	185,000,000	—	0.25	7.00	10.00	25.00
1994	401,000,000	—	0.25	1.00	2.00	4.00
1995	228,000,000	—	0.25	1.00	2.00	4.00
1996	447,000,000	—	0.25	0.50	1.50	3.00
1997	147,000,000	—	0.25	0.50	1.50	3.00
1998	5,000,000	—	—	5.00	10.00	30.00
1999	—	—	0.25	1.00	3.00	5.00
2000	—	—	0.25	0.50	1.00	3.00

KM# 10   200 WON
11.2000 g., 0.9990 Silver 0.3597 oz. ASW, 28 mm. **Obv:** Arms within floral spray **Rev:** Celadon vase

Date	Mintage	F	VF	XF	Unc	BU
KE4303-1970 Proof	4,200	Value: 200				

KM# 11   250 WON
14.0000 g., 0.9990 Silver 0.4496 oz. ASW, 30 mm. **Obv:** Arms above flower flanked by phoenix **Rev:** Bust facing

Date	Mintage	F	VF	XF	Unc	BU
KE4303-1970 Proof	4,100	Value: 400				

KM# 12   500 WON
28.0000 g., 0.9990 Silver 0.8993 oz. ASW, 40 mm. **Obv:** Arms within floral spray **Rev:** Half length female figure holding tea cup within circle

Date	Mintage	F	VF	XF	Unc	BU
KE4303-1970 Proof	4,700	Value: 300				

KM# 22   500 WON
17.0000 g., Copper-Nickel, 32 mm. **Subject:** 42nd World Shooting Championships **Obv:** Symbol above value **Rev:** Marksman with text to right and below

Date	Mintage	F	VF	XF	Unc	BU
1978	980,000	0.35	0.75	1.50	4.50	—
1978 Unfrosted, proof	18,000	Value: 27.50				
1978 Proof	2,000	Value: 200				

KM# 27   500 WON
7.7000 g., Copper-Nickel, 26.5 mm. **Obv:** Manchurian crane **Rev:** Value and date

Date	Mintage	F	VF	XF	Unc	BU
1982	15,000,000	—	—	1.00	3.75	8.00
Note: Issued 6-12-82						
1982 Proof	2,000	—	—	—	—	—
1983	64,000,000	—	—	1.00	2.50	5.00
1984	70,000,000	—	—	1.00	2.50	5.00
1987	1,000,000	—	—	2.00	5.00	12.00
1988	27,000,000	—	—	1.00	2.50	5.00
1989	25,000,000	—	—	1.00	2.50	5.00
1990	60,000,000	—	—	1.00	2.50	5.00
1991	90,000,000	—	—	1.00	2.50	5.00
1992	105,000,000	—	—	1.00	2.50	5.00
1993	32,000,000	—	—	1.00	2.50	5.00
1994	50,600,000	—	—	1.00	2.50	5.00
1995	87,000,000	—	—	1.00	2.50	5.00
1996	122,000,000	—	—	1.00	2.50	5.00
1997	62,000,000	—	—	1.00	2.50	5.00
1999	22,000,000	—	—	1.00	2.50	5.00
2000	128,000,000	—	—	1.00	2.50	5.00

KM# 13   1000 WON
56.0000 g., 0.9990 Silver 1.7986 oz. ASW **Subject:** U.N. Forces in South Korea **Obv:** Arms within floral spray **Rev:** Korean and UN flags with four uniformed heads left within circle

Date	Mintage	F	VF	XF	Unc	BU
KE4303-1970 Proof	4,050	Value: 600				

KM# 14.1   1000 WON
3.8700 g., 0.9000 Gold 0.1120 oz. AGW, 16 mm. **Obv:** Arms within floral spray **Rev:** Great South Gate in Seoul **Mint:** Valcambi

Date	Mintage	F	VF	XF	Unc	BU
KE4303-1970 Proof	1,500	Value: 350				

KM# 14.2   1000 WON
3.8700 g., 0.9000 Gold 0.1120 oz. AGW, 16 mm. **Obv:** Arms within floral spray **Rev:** Great South Gate in Seoul **Mint:** Paris

Date	Mintage	F	VF	XF	Unc	BU
KE4303-1970(a) Proof	100	Value: 1,250				

KM# 25   1000 WON
17.0000 g., Nickel, 33 mm. **Subject:** 1st Anniversary of the 5th Republic **Obv:** Yin-yang symbol within rectangle above value flanked by flames **Rev:** Imaginary bird called Bong-hwang who represents a King

Date	Mintage	F	VF	XF	Unc	BU
1981	1,880,000	1.00	1.25	1.50	6.00	—
Note: Released in 8-81						
1981 Unfrosted, proof	18,000	Value: 27.50				
1981 Proof	2,000	Value: 250				

KM# 28   1000 WON
17.0000 g., Copper-Nickel, 33 mm. **Series:** 1988 Olympics **Obv:** Dancers **Rev:** Flower design and value within sprigs

Date	Mintage	F	VF	XF	Unc	BU
1982	1,980,000	—	—	1.25	4.00	—

Date	Mintage	F	VF	XF	Unc	BU
1982 Proof	10,000		Value: 35.00			
1982 Unfrosted, proof	10,000		Value: 20.00			

KM# 36 1000 WON

17.0000 g., Copper-Nickel, 33 mm. **Series:** 1988 Olympics **Obv:** Drummer within lined design **Rev:** Flower design and value within sprigs

Date	Mintage	F	VF	XF	Unc	BU
1983	330,000	—	—	1.25	4.00	—
1983 Proof	101,000		Value: 20.00			
1983 Unfrosted, Proof	56,000		Value: 15.00			

KM# 39 1000 WON

17.0000 g., Copper-Nickel, 33 mm. **Subject:** 200 Years of Catholic Church in Korea **Obv:** Cross above value **Rev:** Myung Dong Cathedral

Date	Mintage	F	VF	XF	Unc	BU
1984	572,000	—	—	1.50	5.00	—

KM# 41 1000 WON

17.0000 g., Copper-Nickel, 33 mm. **Subject:** 10th Asian Games **Obv:** Artistic design above flowers **Rev:** Lion dance

Date	Mintage	F	VF	XF	Unc	BU
1986	930,000	—	—	1.25	4.00	—
1986 Proof	70,000		Value: 10.00			

KM# 46 1000 WON

12.0000 g., Copper-Nickel, 30 mm. **Series:** 1988 Olympics **Obv:** Arms above floral spray **Rev:** Basketball players

Date	Mintage	F	VF	XF	Unc	BU
1986	560,000	—	—	—	4.00	—
1986 Proof	140,000		Value: 18.00			

KM# 47 1000 WON

Copper-Nickel, 30 mm. **Series:** 1988 Olympics **Obv:** Arms above floral spray **Rev:** Tennis player

Date	Mintage	F	VF	XF	Unc	BU
1987	560,000	—	—	—	4.00	—
1987 Proof	140,000		Value: 10.00			

KM# 48 1000 WON

12.0000 g., Copper-Nickel, 30 mm. **Series:** 1988 Olympics **Obv:** Arms above floral spray **Rev:** Handball players

Date	Mintage	F	VF	XF	Unc	BU
1987	560,000	—	—	—	4.00	—
1987 Proof	140,000		Value: 10.00			

KM# 49 1000 WON

Copper-Nickel, 30 mm. **Series:** 1988 Olympics **Obv:** Arms above floral spray **Rev:** Table tennis

Date	Mintage	F	VF	XF	Unc	BU
1988	560,000	—	—	—	4.00	—
1988 Proof	140,000		Value: 10.00			

KM# 78 1000 WON

12.5600 g., Copper-Nickel, 30 mm. **Subject:** Taejon International Exposition **Obv:** Circular symbols within circle **Rev:** Mascot of the Expo, Kumdori

Date	Mintage	F	VF	XF	Unc	BU
1993	590,000	—	—	—	5.00	—

Note: Metal content is copper 94% and nickel 6% giving this coin a golden brass color

KM# 87 1000 WON

Copper-Nickel **Subject:** 50th Anniversary of U.N.

Date	Mintage	F	VF	XF	Unc	BU
1995	1,000	—	—	—	10.00	—

KM# 50 2000 WON

17.0000 g., Copper-Nickel, 33 mm. **Series:** 1988 Olympics **Obv:** Arms above floral spray **Rev:** Boxing

Date	Mintage	F	VF	XF	Unc	BU
1986	560,000	—	—	—	6.50	—
1986 Proof	140,000		Value: 22.00			

KM# 51 2000 WON

17.0000 g., Nickel, 33 mm. **Series:** 1988 Olympics **Obv:** Arms above floral spray **Rev:** Tae Kwon Do

Date	Mintage	F	VF	XF	Unc	BU
1987	560,000	—	—	—	5.50	—
1987 Proof	140,000		Value: 15.00			

KM# 52 2000 WON

17.0000 g., Nickel, 33 mm. **Series:** 1988 Olympics **Subject:** Wrestling **Obv:** Arms above floral spray **Rev:** Wrestlers

Date	Mintage	F	VF	XF	Unc	BU
1987	560,000	—	—	—	5.50	—
1987 Proof	140,000		Value: 25.00			

KM# 53 2000 WON

17.0000 g., Nickel, 33 mm. **Series:** 1988 Olympics **Subject:** Weight lifting **Obv:** Arms above floral spray **Rev:** Weight lifter

Date	Mintage	F	VF	XF	Unc	BU
1988	560,000	—	—	—	5.50	—
1988 Proof	140,000		Value: 15.00			

KM# 88 2000 WON

10.7000 g., Bi-Metallic Copper-Aluminum-Nickel center in Copper-Nickel ring, 28 mm. **Subject:** New Millennium **Obv:** Astronomical observation instrument **Rev:** Stylized design **Edge:** Reeded **Mint:** KOMSCO **Note:** Korea Minting and Security Printing Corp.

Date	Mintage	F	VF	XF	Unc	BU
2000		—	—	—	9.00	10.00

KM# 15.1 2500 WON

9.6800 g., 0.9000 Gold 0.2801 oz. AGW, 26 mm. **Obv:** Arms within floral spray **Rev:** Crowned head and temple within circle **Mint:** Valcambi

Date	Mintage	F	VF	XF	Unc	BU
KE4303-1970 Proof	1,750		Value: 500			

KM# 15.2   2500 WON
9.6800 g., 0.9000 Gold 0.2801 oz. AGW **Obv:** Arms within floral
spray **Rev:** Crowned head and temple within circle **Mint:** Paris

Date	Mintage	F	VF	XF	Unc	BU
KE4303-1970(a) Proof	100	Value: 1,500				

KM# 16.1   5000 WON
19.3600 g., 0.9000 Gold 0.5602 oz. AGW, 32 mm. **Obv:** Arms
within floral spray **Rev:** Iron-clad turtle boats **Mint:** Valcambi

Date	Mintage	F	VF	XF	Unc	BU
KE4303-1970 Proof	670	Value: 1,850				

KM# 16.2   5000 WON
19.3600 g., 0.9000 Gold 0.5602 oz. AGW **Obv:** Arms within
floral spray **Rev:** Iron-clad turtle boats **Mint:** Paris

Date	Mintage	F	VF	XF	Unc	BU
KE4303-1970(a) Proof	70	Value: 2,500				

KM# 23   5000 WON
23.0000 g., 0.9000 Silver 0.6655 oz. ASW, 35 mm.
Subject: 42nd World Shooting Championships **Obv:** Artistic
design above value **Rev:** Shilla hunter motif

Date	Mintage	F	VF	XF	Unc	BU
1978	80,000	—	—	—	30.00	—
1978 Unfrosted, Proof	20,000	Value: 75.00				

KM# 54   5000 WON
16.8100 g., 0.9250 Silver 0.4999 oz. ASW, 32 mm. **Series:** 1988
Olympics **Obv:** Arms above floral spray **Rev:** Tiger mascot

Date	Mintage	F	VF	XF	Unc	BU
1986	117,500	—	—	BV	12.50	20.00
1986 Proof	227,500	Value: 22.50				

KM# 55   5000 WON
16.8100 g., 0.9250 Silver 0.4999 oz. ASW, 32 mm. **Series:** 1988
Olympics **Obv:** Arms above floral spray **Rev:** Tug of war

Date	Mintage	F	VF	XF	Unc	BU
1986	117,500	—	—	BV	13.50	22.50
1986 Proof	227,500	Value: 25.00				

KM# 60   5000 WON
16.8100 g., 0.9250 Silver 0.4999 oz. ASW, 32 mm. **Series:** 1988
Olympics **Obv:** Arms above floral spray **Rev:** Stadium

Date	Mintage	F	VF	XF	Unc	BU
1987	117,500	—	—	BV	12.50	20.00
1987 Proof	227,500	Value: 25.00				

KM# 61   5000 WON
16.8100 g., 0.9250 Silver 0.4999 oz. ASW, 32 mm. **Series:** 1988
Olympics **Obv:** Arms above floral spray **Rev:** Chegi - Kicking

Date	Mintage	F	VF	XF	Unc	BU
1987	117,500	—	—	BV	13.50	22.50
1987 Proof	227,500	Value: 25.00				

KM# 66   5000 WON
16.8100 g., 0.9250 Silver 0.4999 oz. ASW, 32 mm. **Series:** 1988
Olympics **Obv:** Arms above floral spray **Rev:** Tae Kwon Do

Date	Mintage	F	VF	XF	Unc	BU
1987	117,500	—	—	BV	12.50	20.00
1987 Proof	227,500	Value: 25.00				

KM# 67   5000 WON
16.8100 g., 0.9250 Silver 0.4999 oz. ASW, 32 mm. **Series:** 1988
Olympics **Obv:** Arms above floral spray **Rev:** Girls on swing

Date	Mintage	F	VF	XF	Unc	BU
1987	117,500	—	—	BV	13.50	22.50
1987 Proof	227,500	Value: 25.00				

KM# 70   5000 WON
16.8100 g., 0.9250 Silver 0.4999 oz. ASW, 32 mm. **Series:** 1988
Olympics **Obv:** Arms above floral spray **Rev:** Wrestling

Date	Mintage	F	VF	XF	Unc	BU
1988	117,500	—	—	BV	12.50	20.00
1988 Proof	227,500	Value: 25.00				

KM# 71   5000 WON
16.8100 g., 0.9250 Silver 0.4999 oz. ASW, 32 mm. **Series:** 1988
Olympics **Obv:** Arms above floral spray **Rev:** Boys spinning top

Date	Mintage	F	VF	XF	Unc	BU
1988	117,500	—	—	BV	12.50	20.00
1988 Proof	227,500	Value: 25.00				

KM# 79   5000 WON
16.8100 g., 0.9250 Silver 0.4999 oz. ASW, 32 mm.
Subject: Taejon International Exposition **Obv:** Circular designs
within dotted circle **Rev:** Seated figure spinning yarn

Date	Mintage	F	VF	XF	Unc	BU
1993	120,000	—	—	—	18.50	—

KM# 80   5000 WON
16.8100 g., 0.9250 Silver 0.4999 oz. ASW, 32 mm.
Subject: Taejon International Exposition **Obv:** Arms above floral
spray **Rev:** Folk musicians

Date	Mintage	F	VF	XF	Unc	BU
1993	120,000	—	—	—	18.50	—

KM# 85   5000 WON
16.0000 g., Nickel, 32 mm. **Subject:** 50th Anniversary -
Liberation from Japan **Obv:** Kim-Gu

Date	Mintage	F	VF	XF	Unc	BU
1995	25,000	—	—	—	15.00	—

KM# 96   5000 WON
22.0000 g., Bronze Enamel inlay, 38 mm. **Obv:** Head Office of
the Bank of Korea old and new buildings **Rev:** 50th Anniversary
of the Bank of Korea

Date	Mintage	F	VF	XF	Unc	BU
2000	—	—	—	—	—	—

KM# 17.1   10000 WON
38.7200 g., 0.9000 Gold 1.1203 oz. AGW **Obv:** Arms above
floral spray flanked by phoenix **Rev:** Bust facing **Mint:** Valcambi

Date	Mintage	F	VF	XF	Unc	BU
KE4303-1970 Proof	435	Value: 5,000				

KM# 17.2   10000 WON
38.7200 g., 0.9000 Gold 1.1203 oz. AGW **Obv:** Arms above
floral spray flanked by phoenix **Rev:** Bust facing **Mint:** Paris

Date	Mintage	F	VF	XF	Unc	BU
KE4303-1970(a) Proof	55	Value: 6,000				

KM# 29   10000 WON
15.0000 g., 0.9000 Silver 0.4340 oz. ASW, 30 mm. **Series:** 1988 Olympics **Obv:** Great South Gate, Seoul **Rev:** Stylized flower above value within wreath

Date	Mintage	F	VF	XF	Unc	BU
1982	280,000	—	—	12.00	13.50	15.00
1982 Unfrosted, proof	10,000	Value: 45.00				
1982 Proof	10,000	Value: 65.00				

KM# 37   10000 WON
15.0000 g., 0.9000 Silver 0.4340 oz. ASW, 30 mm. **Series:** 1988 Olympics **Obv:** Pavilion of Kyongbok Palace **Rev:** Stylized flower above value within wreath

Date	Mintage	F	VF	XF	Unc	BU
1983	137,000	—	—	12.00	13.50	15.00
1983 Unfrosted, Proof	56,000	Value: 25.00				
1983 Proof	101,000	Value: 35.00				

KM# 40   10000 WON
22.3000 g., 0.5000 Silver 0.3585 oz. ASW, 36 mm. **Subject:** 200 Years of Catholic Church in Korea **Obv:** Cross within sectioned circle above value **Rev:** Standing haloed figures facing

Date	Mintage	F	VF	XF	Unc	BU
1984	152,000	—	—	15.00	20.00	22.50

KM# 42   10000 WON
23.0000 g., 0.9000 Silver 0.6655 oz. ASW, 35 mm. **Subject:** 10th Asian Games **Obv:** Arms above floral spray **Rev:** Badminton

Date	Mintage	F	VF	XF	Unc	BU
1986	130,000	—	—	BV	13.50	15.00
1986 Proof	70,000	Value: 24.00				

KM# 43   10000 WON
23.0000 g., 0.9000 Silver 0.6655 oz. ASW, 35 mm. **Subject:** 10th Asian Games **Obv:** Arms above floral spray **Rev:** Soccer players

Date	Mintage	F	VF	XF	Unc	BU
1986	130,000	—	—	BV	13.50	15.00
1986 Proof	70,000	Value: 24.00				

KM# 56   10000 WON
33.6200 g., 0.9250 Silver 0.9998 oz. ASW, 40 mm. **Series:** 1988 Olympics **Obv:** Arms above floral spray **Rev:** Marathon runner

Date	Mintage	F	VF	XF	Unc	BU
1986	117,500	—	—	BV	20.00	25.00
1986 Proof	227,500	Value: 30.00				

KM# 57   10000 WON
33.6200 g., 0.9250 Silver 0.9998 oz. ASW, 40 mm. **Series:** 1988 Olympics **Subject:** Diving **Obv:** Arms above floral spray **Rev:** High diver

Date	Mintage	F	VF	XF	Unc	BU
1987	117,500	—	—	BV	20.00	25.00
1987 Proof	227,500	Value: 30.00				

KM# 62   10000 WON
33.6200 g., 0.9250 Silver 0.9998 oz. ASW, 40 mm. **Series:** 1988 Olympics **Subject:** Archery **Obv:** Arms above floral spray **Rev:** Archer

Date	Mintage	F	VF	XF	Unc	BU
1987	117,500	—	—	BV	20.00	25.00
1987 Proof	227,500	Value: 30.00				

Date	Mintage	F	VF	XF	Unc	BU
1988	Inc. above	—	—	—	200	
1988 Proof	Inc. above	Value: 90.00				

Note: 1988 is an error date

KM# 63   10000 WON
33.6200 g., 0.9250 Silver 0.9998 oz. ASW, 40 mm. **Series:** 1988 Olympics **Subject:** Volleyball **Obv:** Arms above floral spray **Rev:** Volleyball game

Date	Mintage	F	VF	XF	Unc	BU
1987	117,500	—	—	BV	20.00	25.00
1987 Proof	227,500	Value: 30.00				

KM# 74   10000 WON
33.6200 g., 0.9250 Silver 0.9998 oz. ASW, 40 mm. **Series:** 1988 Olympics **Subject:** Gymnastics **Obv:** Arms above floral spray **Rev:** Gymnast

Date	Mintage	F	VF	XF	Unc	BU
1988	15,000	—	—	BV	22.50	30.00
1988 Proof	110,000	Value: 40.00				

KM# 75   10000 WON
33.6200 g., 0.9250 Silver 0.9998 oz. ASW, 40 mm. **Series:** 1988 Olympics **Subject:** Equestrian events **Obv:** Arms above floral spray **Rev:** Equestrian jumping

Date	Mintage	F	VF	XF	Unc	BU
1988	15,000	—	—	BV	22.50	30.00
1988 Proof	110,000	Value: 40.00				

KM# 76   10000 WON
33.6200 g., 0.9250 Silver 0.9998 oz. ASW, 40 mm. **Series:** 1988 Olympics **Subject:** Cycling **Obv:** Arms above floral spray **Rev:** Cyclists

Date	Mintage	F	VF	XF	Unc	BU
1988	15,000	—	—	BV	22.50	30.00
1988 Proof	110,000	Value: 40.00				

KM# 77   10000 WON
33.6200 g., 0.9250 Silver 0.9998 oz. ASW, 40 mm. **Series:** 1988 Olympics **Obv:** Arms above floral spray **Rev:** Soccer players

Date	Mintage	F	VF	XF	Unc	BU
1988	15,000	—	—	BV	22.50	30.00
1988 Proof	110,000	Value: 40.00				

KM# 81   10000 WON
33.6200 g., 0.9250 Silver 0.9998 oz. ASW, 40 mm. **Subject:** Taejon International Exposition **Obv:** Stylized yin-yang within dotted circle **Rev:** Porcelain celadon

Date	Mintage	F	VF	XF	Unc	BU
1993	100,000	—	—	—	30.00	—

KM# 86   10000 WON
23.0000 g., 0.9000 Silver 0.6655 oz. ASW, 35 mm. **Subject:** 50th Anniversary of Liberation from Japan **Obv:** Ahn Jong-Kun

Date	Mintage	F	VF	XF	Unc	BU
1995	40,000	—	—	—	35.00	—

KM# 84   10000 WON
22.5000 g., 0.9250 Silver 0.6691 oz. ASW **Subject:** 50th Anniversary - Republic of Korea **Obv:** National yin-yang symbol within small circle above flowers **Rev:** Numeral 50 with doves on the 0 **Note:** With multicolor enamel and with gold-plated center insert.

Date	Mintage	F	VF	XF	Unc	BU
ND(1998)	100,000	—	—	—	35.00	—

KM# 18.1   20000 WON
77.4000 g., 0.9000 Gold 2.2395 oz. AGW, 55 mm. **Obv:** Arms within floral spray **Rev:** Gold crown - Silla Dynasty **Mint:** Valcambi

Date	Mintage	F	VF	XF	Unc	BU
KE4303-1970 Proof	382	Value: 8,750				

KM# 18.2   20000 WON
77.4000 g., 0.9000 Gold 2.2395 oz. AGW **Obv:** Arms within floral spray **Rev:** Gold Crown - Silla Dynasty **Mint:** Paris

Date	Mintage	F	VF	XF	Unc	BU
KE4303-1970(a) Proof	52	Value: 10,000				

KM# 26   20000 WON
22.5300 g., 0.9000 Silver 0.6519 oz. ASW, 35 mm. **Subject:** 1st Anniversary of the 5th Republic **Obv:** Arms above floral sprays **Rev:** Faint national yin-yang symbol above assorted uniformed busts left **Note:** Man, woman, laborer, soldier, student all symbolize the Korean will for unity.

Date	Mintage	F	VF	XF	Unc	BU
1981	80,000	—	—	25.00	30.00	—
Note: Issued 8-81						
1981 Unfrosted, proof	18,000	Value: 35.00				
1981 Proof	2,000	Value: 300				

KM# 30   20000 WON
23.0000 g., 0.9000 Silver 0.6655 oz. ASW, 35 mm. **Series:** 1988 Olympics **Obv:** Stylized torch and flame within globe **Rev:** Stylized flower above value within wreath

Date	Mintage	F	VF	XF	Unc	BU
1982	180,000	—	—	25.00	30.00	—
1982 Unfrosted, proof	10,000	Value: 50.00				
1982 Proof	10,000	Value: 70.00				

KM# 38   20000 WON
23.0000 g., 0.9000 Silver 0.6655 oz. ASW, 35 mm. **Series:** 1988 Olympics **Subject:** Wrestling **Obv:** Wrestlers **Rev:** Stylized flower above value within wreath

Date	Mintage	F	VF	XF	Unc	BU
1983	123,000	—	—	25.00	30.00	—
1983 Unfrosted, proof	56,000	Value: 40.00				
1983 Proof	101,000	Value: 45.00				

KM# 44   20000 WON
28.0000 g., 0.9000 Silver 0.8102 oz. ASW, 38 mm. **Subject:** 10th Asian Games **Obv:** Artistic design above flowers **Rev:** Runner

Date	Mintage	F	VF	XF	Unc	BU
1986	130,000	—	—	25.00	30.00	—
1986 Proof	70,000	Value: 45.00				

KM# 45   20000 WON
28.0000 g., 0.9000 Silver 0.8102 oz. ASW, 38 mm. **Subject:** 10th Asian Games **Obv:** Artistic design above flowers **Rev:** Pul Guk Temple - Kyong Ju City

Date	Mintage	F	VF	XF	Unc	BU
1986	130,000	—	—	25.00	30.00	—
1986 Proof	70,000	Value: 40.00				

KM# 19.1   25000 WON
96.8000 g., 0.9000 Gold 2.8009 oz. AGW, 60 mm. **Subject:** King Sejong The Great **Obv:** Arms within floral spray **Rev:** Seated figure facing reading from a book within circle **Mint:** Valcambi

Date	Mintage	F	VF	XF	Unc	BU
KE4303-1970 Proof	325	Value: 14,000				

KM# 19.2 25000 WON
96.8000 g., 0.9000 Gold 2.8009 oz. AGW, 60 mm.
Subject: 10th Asian Games **Obv:** Arms within floral spray
Rev: Seated figure facing reading from a book **Mint:** Paris

Date	Mintage	F	VF	XF	Unc	BU
KE4303-1970(a)	25	Value: 17,000				
Proof						

KM# 58 25000 WON
16.8100 g., 0.9250 Gold 0.4999 oz. AGW, 27 mm. **Series:** 1988
Olympics **Obv:** Arms above floral spray **Rev:** Folk dancing

Date	Mintage	F	VF	XF	Unc	BU
1986	42,500	—	—	—	—	470
1986 Proof	117,500	Value: 475				

KM# 64 25000 WON
16.8100 g., 0.9250 Gold 0.4999 oz. AGW, 27 mm. **Series:** 1988
Olympics **Obv:** Arms above floral spray **Rev:** Fan dancing

Date	Mintage	F	VF	XF	Unc	BU
1987	42,500	—	—	—	—	470
1987 Proof	117,500	Value: 475				

KM# 68 25000 WON
16.8100 g., 0.9250 Gold 0.4999 oz. AGW, 27 mm. **Series:** 1988
Olympics **Obv:** Arms above floral spray **Rev:** Kite flying

Date	Mintage	F	VF	XF	Unc	BU
1987	47,500	—	—	—	—	470
1987 Proof	47,500	Value: 475				
1988	—	—	—	—	—	470
1988 Proof	—	Value: 475				

KM# 72 25000 WON
16.8100 g., 0.9250 Gold 0.4999 oz. AGW, 27 mm. **Series:** 1988
Olympics **Obv:** Arms above floral spray **Rev:** Korean Seesaw

Date	Mintage	F	VF	XF	Unc	BU
1988	42,500	—	—	—	—	470
1988 Proof	117,500	Value: 475				

KM# 82 25000 WON
16.8100 g., 0.9250 Gold 0.4999 oz. AGW **Subject:** Taejon
International Exposition **Obv:** Stylized yin-yang within multiple
circles **Rev:** Celestial globe

Date	Mintage	F	VF	XF	Unc	BU
1993	40,000	—	—	—	—	470

KM# 59 50000 WON
33.6200 g., 0.9250 Gold 0.9998 oz. AGW, 33 mm. **Series:** 1988
Olympics **Obv:** Arms above floral spray **Rev:** Turtle boat

Date	Mintage	F	VF	XF	Unc	BU
1986 Proof	30,000	Value: 950				

KM# 65 50000 WON
33.6200 g., 0.9250 Gold 0.9998 oz. AGW, 33 mm. **Series:** 1988
Olympics **Obv:** Arms above floral spray **Rev:** Great South Gate

Date	Mintage	F	VF	XF	Unc	BU
1987 Proof	30,000	Value: 950				

KM# 69 50000 WON
33.6200 g., 0.9250 Gold 0.9998 oz. AGW, 33 mm. **Series:** 1988
Olympics **Obv:** Arms above floral spray **Rev:** Stylized horse and
rider

Date	Mintage	F	VF	XF	Unc	BU
1987 Proof	30,000	Value: 950				

KM# 73 50000 WON
33.6200 g., 0.9250 Gold 0.9998 oz. AGW, 33 mm. **Series:** 1988
Olympics **Obv:** Arms above floral spray **Rev:** Pul Guk Temple

Date	Mintage	F	VF	XF	Unc	BU
1988 Proof	30,000	Value: 950				

KM# 83 50000 WON
33.6200 g., 0.9250 Gold 0.9998 oz. AGW **Subject:** Taejon
International Exposition **Obv:** Arms above floral spray
Rev: Tower of Great Light

Date	Mintage	F	VF	XF	Unc	BU
1993	10,000	—	—	—	—	950

BANK SAMPLES
Korean

NOTE: Bank samples countermarked in Korean Sample
have been prepared for government and banking agencies.

KM#	Date	Mintage	Identification	Issue Price	Mkt Val
S1	KE4292	—	10 Hwan. Bronze. KM1.	—	65.00
S2	KE4292	—	50 Hwan. Nickel-Brass. KM2.	—	75.00
S3	KE4292	—	100 Hwan. Copper-Nickel. KM3.	—	90.00
S4	1967	—	Won. Brass. KM4.	—	—
S5	1975	—	100 Won. Copper-Nickel. KM21.	—	—
S6	1978	—	500 Won. Copper-Nickel. KM22.	—	—
S7	1978	—	5000 Won. Silver. KM23.	—	—
S8	1984	—	20000 Won. Silver. KM26.	—	—
S9	1984	—	50000 Won. Silver. KM40.	—	—

MINT SETS

KM#	Date	Mintage	Identification	Issue Price	Mkt Val
MS1	Mixed dates (6)	75,000	KM6a(1980), 32, 34, 35.1 (1983), 27, 31 (1984) Issued as a presentation set for the World Bank Conference in Seoul, October 1985.	—	60.00
MS2	1983 (6)	—	KM27, 31-32, 33.1, 34, 35.1	—	60.00
MS3	1986 (5)	130,000	KM41-45	113	100
MSA4	1988	—	KM#46-53 Olympics	—	40.00

KM#	Date	Mintage	Identification	Issue Price	Mkt Val
MS4	1991 (6)	—	KM27, 31-32, 33.1, 34, 35.2	—	12.00
MS5	1993 (6)	10,000	KM78-83	1,180	1,200
MS6	1993 (5)	30,000	KM78-82	443	450
MS7	1993 (4)	50,000	KM78-81	97.00	100

PROOF SETS

KM#	Date	Mintage	Identification	Issue Price	Mkt Val
PS1	1970 (12)	—	KM7-8, 10-13, 14.1-19.1	752	31,500
PS2	1970 (11)	—	KM7-8, 10-13, 14.2-18.2	—	22,350
PS3	1970 (6)	—	KM7-8, 10-13	53.50	1,100
PS4	1970 (6)	300	KM14.1-19.1	698	32,000
PS5	1970 (6)	25	KM14.2-19.2	—	38,250
PS6	1982 (6)	2,000	KM4a-6a, 9, 20, 27, (presentation set) Original, intact sets are worth substantially more than their individual components.	—	835
PS7	1986 (6)	350,000	KM#41, 50, 54-56, 58	275	465
PS8	1986 (5)	70,000	KM41-45	170	145
PSA9	1986 (6)	160,000	KM#46, 50, 54-56, 58	275	475
PS9	1986 (2)	—	KM46, 50	—	40.00
PS10	2001 (6)	2,002	KM#90-95	—	1,650

KUWAIT

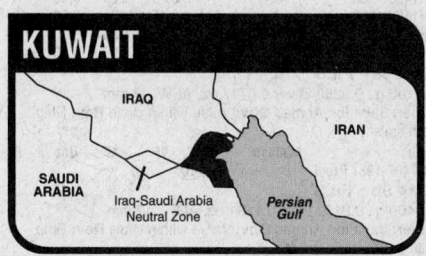

The State of Kuwait, a constitutional monarchy located on the
Arabian Peninsula at the northwestern corner of the Persian Gulf,
has an area of 6,880 sq. mi. (17,820 sq. km.) and a population of
1.7 million. Capital: Kuwait. Petroleum, the basis of the economy,
provides 95 percent of the exports.

The modern history of Kuwait began with the founding of the
city of Kuwait, 1740, by tribesmen who wandered northward from
the region of the Qatar Peninsula of eastern Arabia. Fearing that
the Turks would take over the sheikhdom, Sheikh Mubarak
entered into an agreement with Great Britain, 1899, placing
Kuwait under the protection of Britain and empowering Britain to
conduct its foreign affairs. Britain terminated the protectorate on
June19, 1961, giving Kuwait its independence (by a simple
exchange of notes) but agreeing to furnish military aid on request.

Kuwait was invaded and occupied by an army from neighboring Iraq Aug. 2, 1990. Soon thereafter Iraq declared that the
country would become a province of Iraq. An international coalition of military forces primarily based in Saudi Arabia led by the
United States under terms set by the United Nations, attacked
Iraqi military installations to liberate Kuwait. This occurred Jan.
17, 1991. Kuwait City was liberated Feb.27, and a cease-fire was
declared Feb. 28. New paper currency was introduced March 24,
1991 to replace earlier notes.

TITLE

al-Kuwait

RULER
British Protectorate, until 1961

LOCAL
Al Sabah Dynasty
Mubarak Ibn Sabah, 1896-1915
Jabir Ibn Mubarak, 1915-1917
Salim Ibn Mubarak, 1917-1921
Ahmad Ibn Jabir, 1921-1950
Abdullah Ibn Salim, 1950-1965
Sabah Ibn Salim, 1965-1977
Jabir Ibn Ahmad, 1977-

MONETARY SYSTEM
1000 Fils = 1 Dinar

SOVEREIGN EMIRATE
MODERN COINAGE

KM# 2 FILS
2.0000 g., Nickel-Brass, 17 mm. **Ruler:** Abdullah Ibn Salim
Obv: Value within circle **Rev:** Ship with sails

Date	Mintage	F	VF	XF	Unc	BU
AH1380-1961	2,000,000	—	0.50	1.00	1.50	—
AH1380-1961 Proof	60	Value: 30.00				

KM# 9   FILS
2.0000 g., Nickel-Brass, 17 mm.   **Ruler:** Jabir Ibn Ahmad
Obv: Value within circle **Rev:** Ship with sails

Date	Mintage	F	VF	XF	Unc	BU
AH1382-1962	500,000	—	0.10	0.15	0.35	—
AH1382-1962 Proof	60	Value: 30.00				
AH1384-1964	600,000	—	0.25	0.75	1.50	—
AH1385-1966	500,000	—	0.25	0.75	1.50	—
AH1386-1967	1,875,000	—	0.25	0.75	1.50	—
AH1389-1970	375,000	—	0.35	1.00	2.50	—
AH1390-1971	500,000	—	0.25	0.75	1.50	—
AH1391-1971	500,000	—	0.25	0.75	1.50	—
AH1392-1972	500,000	—	0.25	0.75	1.50	—
AH1393-1973	375,000	—	0.35	1.00	2.50	—
AH1395-1975	500,000	—	0.25	0.75	1.50	—
AH1396-1976	2,500,000	—	0.15	0.25	0.50	—
AH1397-1977	2,500,000	—	0.15	0.25	0.50	—
AH1399-1979	1,500,000	—	0.15	0.25	0.50	—
AH1400-1980	—	—	0.15	0.25	0.50	—
AH1403-1983	—	—	0.15	0.25	0.50	—
AH1407-1987	—	—	0.15	0.25	0.50	—
AH1408-1988	500,000	—	0.15	0.25	0.50	—

KM# 9a   FILS
2.4100 g., 0.9250 Silver 0.0717 oz. ASW, 17 mm.
Ruler: Jabir Ibn Ahmad **Obv:** Value within circle **Rev:** Ship with sails

Date	Mintage	F	VF	XF	Unc	BU
AH1407-1987 Proof	—	Value: 100				

KM# 9b   FILS
4.0400 g., 0.9170 Gold 0.1191 oz. AGW, 17 mm.
Ruler: Jabir Ibn Ahmad **Obv:** Value within circle **Rev:** Ship with sails

Date	Mintage	F	VF	XF	Unc	BU
AH1407-1987 Proof	—	Value: 135				

KM# 3   5 FILS
2.5000 g., Nickel-Brass, 19.5 mm.   **Ruler:** Abdullah Ibn Salim
Obv: Value within circle **Rev:** Ship with sails

Date	Mintage	F	VF	XF	Unc	BU
AH1380-1961 (1961)	2,400,000	—	0.60	1.25	2.00	—
AH1380-1961 (1961) Proof	60	Value: 35.00				

KM# 10   5 FILS
2.5000 g., Nickel-Brass, 19.5 mm.   **Ruler:** Jabir Ibn Ahmad
Obv: Value within circle **Rev:** Dhow, dates below

Date	Mintage	F	VF	XF	Unc	BU
AH1382-1962	1,800,000	—	0.10	0.20	0.45	—
AH1382-1962 Proof	60	Value: 35.00				
AH1382-1962 Proof	60	Value: 35.00				
AH1384-1964	600,000	—	0.30	0.75	2.00	—
AH1386-1967	1,600,000	—	0.20	0.35	1.00	—
AH1388-1968	800,000	—	0.30	0.75	2.25	—
AH1389-1969	—	—	0.30	0.75	2.25	—
AH1389-1970	600,000	—	0.30	0.75	2.25	—
AH1390-1971	600,000	—	0.30	0.75	2.25	—
AH1391-1971	600,000	—	0.30	0.75	2.25	—
AH1392-1972	800,000	—	0.25	0.65	1.75	—
AH1393-1973	800,000	—	0.25	0.65	1.75	—
AH1394-1974	1,200,000	—	0.10	0.20	1.00	—
AH1395-1975	5,020,000	—	0.10	0.20	0.50	—
AH1396-1976	180,000	—	0.35	1.00	3.00	—
AH1397-1977	4,000,000	—	0.10	0.20	0.40	—
AH1399-1979	6,700,000	—	0.10	0.20	0.40	—
AH1400-1980	—	—	0.10	0.20	0.40	—
AH1401-1981	7,000,000	—	0.10	0.20	0.40	—
AH1403-1983	—	—	0.10	0.20	0.40	—
AH1405-1985	—	—	0.10	0.20	0.40	—
AH1407-1987	—	—	0.10	0.20	0.40	—
AH1408-1988	3,000,000	—	0.10	0.20	0.40	—
AH1410-1990	—	—	0.10	0.20	0.40	—
AH1414-1993	—	—	0.10	0.20	0.40	—
AH1415 1994	—	—	0.10	0.20	0.40	—

Note: Varieties exist

Date	Mintage	F	VF	XF	Unc	BU
AH1415-1995	—	—	0.10	0.20	0.40	—
AH1417-1997	—	—	0.10	0.20	0.40	—

KM# 10a   5 FILS
3.0100 g., 0.9250 Silver 0.0895 oz. ASW, 19.5 mm.
Ruler: Jabir Ibn Ahmad **Obv:** Value within circle **Rev:** Ship with sails

Date	Mintage	F	VF	XF	Unc	BU
Proof	—	Value: 100				
AH1407 Proof	—	Value: 100				

KM# 10b   5 FILS
5.0500 g., 0.9170 Gold 0.1489 oz. AGW, 19.5 mm.
Ruler: Jabir Ibn Ahmad **Obv:** Value within circle **Rev:** Ship with sails

Date	Mintage	F	VF	XF	Unc	BU
AH1407-1987 Proof	—	Value: 160				

KM# 4   10 FILS
3.7500 g., Nickel-Brass, 21 mm.   **Ruler:** Abdullah Ibn Salim
Obv: Value within circle **Rev:** Ship with sails

Date	Mintage	F	VF	XF	Unc	BU
AH1380-1961	2,600,000	—	0.65	1.25	2.00	—
AH1380-1961 Proof	60	Value: 40.00				

KM# 11   10 FILS
3.7500 g., Nickel-Brass, 21 mm.   **Ruler:** Jabir Ibn Ahmad
Obv: Value within circle **Rev:** Dhow, dates below

Date	Mintage	F	VF	XF	Unc	BU
AH1382-1962	1,360,000	—	0.15	0.25	0.65	—
AH1382-1962 Proof	60	Value: 40.00				
AH1384-1964	800,000	—	0.35	0.85	2.50	—
AH1386-1967	1,360,000	—	0.30	0.75	1.75	—
AH1388-1968	672,000	—	0.35	0.85	2.50	—
AH1389-1969	480,000	—	0.50	1.00	2.75	—
AH1389-1970	640,000	—	0.35	0.85	2.50	—
AH1390-1971	480,000	—	0.50	1.00	2.75	—
AH1391-1971	800,000	—	0.35	0.85	2.50	—
AH1392-1972	1,120,000	—	0.15	0.40	2.00	—
AH1393-1973	1,440,000	—	0.15	0.40	2.00	—
AH1394-1974	1,280,000	—	0.15	0.40	2.00	—
AH1395-1975	5,280,000	—	0.15	0.25	0.75	—
AH1396-1976	2,400,000	—	0.15	0.25	0.75	—
AH1397-1977	—	—	0.15	0.25	0.75	—
AH1399-1979	6,160,000	—	0.15	0.25	0.75	—
AH1400-1980	—	—	0.15	0.25	0.75	—
AH1401-1981	8,320,000	—	0.15	0.25	0.75	—
AH1403-1983	—	—	0.15	0.25	0.75	—
AH1405-1985	—	—	0.15	0.25	0.75	—
AH1407-1987	—	—	0.15	0.25	0.75	—
AH1408-1988	5,000,000	—	0.15	0.25	0.75	—
AH1410-1990	—	—	0.15	0.25	0.75	—

Note: Varieties exist

Date	Mintage	F	VF	XF	Unc	BU
AH1415-1995	—	—	0.15	0.25	0.75	—
AH1417-1997	—	—	0.15	0.25	0.75	—
AH1418-1998	—	—	0.15	0.25	0.75	—

KM# 11a   10 FILS
4.3500 g., 0.9250 Silver 0.1294 oz. ASW, 21 mm.   **Ruler:** Jabir Ibn Ahmad **Obv:** Value within circle **Rev:** Ship with sails

Date	Mintage	F	VF	XF	Unc	BU
AH1407-1987 Proof	—	Value: 110				

KM# 11b   10 FILS
7.6300 g., 0.9170 Gold 0.2249 oz. AGW, 21 mm.   **Ruler:** Jabir Ibn Ahmad **Obv:** Value within circle **Rev:** Ship with sails

Date	Mintage	F	VF	XF	Unc	BU
AH1407-1987 Proof	—	Value: 250				

KM# 5   20 FILS
3.0000 g., Copper-Nickel, 20 mm.   **Ruler:** Abdullah Ibn Salim
Obv: Value within circle **Rev:** Ship with sails

Date	Mintage	F	VF	XF	Unc	BU
AH1380-1961	2,000,000	—	0.75	1.50	2.50	—
AH1380-1961 Proof	60	Value: 45.00				

KM# 12   20 FILS
3.0000 g., Copper-Nickel, 20 mm.   **Ruler:** Jabir Ibn Ahmad
Obv: Value within circle **Rev:** Dhow, dates below **Note:** Varieties exist

Date	Mintage	F	VF	XF	Unc	BU
AH1382-1962	1,200,000	—	0.25	0.35	0.75	—
AH1382-1962 Proof	60	Value: 45.00				
AH1384-1964	480,000	—	0.50	1.00	3.00	—
AH1386-1967	1,280,000	—	0.35	0.85	2.00	—
AH1388-1968	672,000	—	0.35	0.85	2.50	—
AH1389-1969	800,000	—	0.35	0.85	2.50	—
AH1389-1970	480,000	—	0.50	1.00	3.00	—
AH1390-1971	480,000	—	0.50	1.00	3.00	—
AH1391-1971	960,000	—	0.35	0.85	2.00	—
AH1392-1972	1,440,000	—	0.20	0.45	2.00	—
AH1393-1973	1,280,000	—	0.20	0.45	2.00	—
AH1394-1974	1,600,000	—	0.20	0.45	1.50	—
AH1395-1975	2,400,000	—	0.20	0.30	1.25	—
AH1396-1976	3,200,000	—	0.20	0.30	1.25	—
AH1397-1977	3,400,000	—	0.20	0.30	1.25	—
AH1399-1979	5,520,000	—	0.20	0.30	1.25	—
AH1400-1980	—	—	0.20	0.30	1.00	—
AH1401-1981	8,960,000	—	0.20	0.30	1.00	—
AH1403-1983	—	—	0.20	0.30	1.00	—
AH1405-1985	—	—	0.20	0.30	1.00	—
AH1407-1987	—	—	0.20	0.30	1.00	—
AH1408-1988	5,000,000	—	0.20	0.30	1.00	—
AH1410-1990	—	—	0.20	0.30	1.00	—
AH1415-1995	—	—	0.20	0.30	1.00	—
AH1417-1997	—	—	0.20	0.45	2.00	—

KM# 12a   20 FILS
3.3700 g., 0.9250 Silver 0.1002 oz. ASW, 20 mm.   **Ruler:** Jabir Ibn Ahmad **Obv:** Value within circle **Rev:** Dhow, dates below

Date	Mintage	F	VF	XF	Unc	BU
AH1407-1987 Proof	—	Value: 110				

KM# 12b   20 FILS
5.6700 g., 0.9170 Gold 0.1672 oz. AGW, 20 mm.   **Ruler:** Jabir Ibn Ahmad **Obv:** Value within circle **Rev:** Dhow, dates below

Date	Mintage	F	VF	XF	Unc	BU
AH1407-1987 Proof	—	Value: 180				

KM# 6   50 FILS
4.5000 g., Copper-Nickel, 23 mm.   **Ruler:** Sabah Ibn Salim
Obv: Value within circle **Rev:** Ship with sails

Date	Mintage	F	VF	XF	Unc	BU
AH1380-1961	1,720,000	—	0.85	1.75	2.75	—
AH1380-1961 Proof	60	Value: 60.00				

KM# 13   50 FILS
4.5000 g., Copper-Nickel, 23 mm.   **Ruler:** Jabir Ibn Ahmad
Obv: Value within circle **Rev:** Dhow, dates below

Date	Mintage	F	VF	XF	Unc	BU
AH1382-1962	900,000	—	0.50	0.75	1.25	—
AH1382-1962 Proof	60	Value: 60.00				
AH1384-1964	300,000	—	0.75	1.50	4.00	—
AH1386-1966	800,000	—	0.40	0.85	2.50	—
AH1386-1967	—	—	0.50	0.75	1.50	—
AH1388-1968	200,000	—	1.00	2.00	6.00	—
AH1389-1969	500,000	—	0.50	1.00	3.00	—
AH1390-1970	300,000	—	0.75	1.50	4.00	—
AH1391-1971	500,000	—	0.50	1.00	3.00	—
AH1392-1972	900,000	—	0.50	0.85	2.50	—
AH1393-1973	800,000	—	0.50	0.85	2.50	—
AH1394-1974	1,000,000	—	0.35	0.50	2.00	—
AH1395-1975	1,950,000	—	0.35	0.50	2.00	—
AH1396-1976	2,250,000	—	0.25	0.35	2.00	—
AH1397-1977	6,000,000	—	0.25	0.35	1.35	—
AH1399-1979	6,050,000	—	0.25	0.35	1.35	—
AH1400-1980	—	—	0.25	0.35	1.35	—
AH1401-1981	3,000,000	—	0.25	0.35	1.35	—
AH1403-1983	—	—	0.25	0.35	1.35	—
AH1405-1985	—	—	0.25	0.35	1.35	—
AH1407-1987	2,000,000	—	0.25	0.35	1.35	—
AH1408-1988	3,000,000	—	0.25	0.35	1.35	—

Date	Mintage	F	VF	XF	Unc	BU
AH1410-1990	—	—	0.25	0.35	1.35	
AH1414-1993	—	—	0.25	0.35	1.35	
AH1415-1995	—	—	0.20	0.35	1.35	
AH1417-1997	—	—	0.25	0.35	1.35	
AH1420-2000	—	—	0.25	0.35	1.25	

KM# 13a 50 FILS
5.0700 g., 0.9250 Silver 0.1508 oz. ASW, 23 mm. **Ruler:** Jabir Ibn Ahmad **Obv:** Value within circle **Rev:** Ship with sails

Date	Mintage	F	VF	XF	Unc	BU
AH1407-1987 Proof			Value: 120			

KM# 13b 50 FILS
8.5200 g., 0.9170 Gold 0.2512 oz. AGW, 23 mm. **Ruler:** Jabir Ibn Ahmad **Obv:** Value within circle **Rev:** Ship with sails

Date	Mintage	F	VF	XF	Unc	BU
AH1407-1987 Proof	—	Value: 275				

KM# 7 100 FILS
6.5000 g., Copper-Nickel, 26 mm. **Ruler:** Abdullah Ibn Salim **Obv:** Value within circle **Rev:** Ship with sails

Date	Mintage	F	VF	XF	Unc	BU
AH1380-1961	1,260,000	—	1.00	2.00	3.25	—
AH1380-1961 Proof	60	Value: 90.00				

KM# 14 100 FILS
6.5000 g., Copper-Nickel, 26 mm. **Ruler:** Jabir Ibn Ahmad **Obv:** Value within circle **Rev:** Dhow, dates below

Date	Mintage	F	VF	XF	Unc	BU
AH1382-1962	640,000	—	0.50	0.65	1.50	—
AH1382-1962 Proof	60	Value: 90.00				
AH1384-1964	160,000	—	1.75	3.00	6.00	—
AH1386-1967	640,000	—	1.00	1.50	3.00	—
AH1388-1968	160,000	—	1.75	3.00	6.00	—
AH1389-1969	320,000	—	1.00	2.00	4.00	—
AH1391-1971	240,000	—	1.25	2.00	4.00	—
AH1392-1972	400,000	—	1.00	1.50	3.00	—
AH1393-1973	480,000	—	1.00	1.50	3.00	—
AH1394-1974	480,000	—	1.00	1.50	3.00	—
AH1395-1975	3,040,000	—	0.50	0.75	1.75	—
AH1396-1976	—	—	0.50	0.75	1.75	—
AH1397-1977	1,600,000	—	0.50	0.75	1.75	—
AH1399-1979	3,040,000	—	0.50	0.75	1.75	—
AH1400-1980	—	—	0.50	0.75	1.75	—
AH1401-1981	2,960,000	—	0.50	0.75	1.75	—
AH1403-1983	—	—	0.50	0.75	1.75	—
AH1405-1985	—	—	0.50	0.75	1.75	—
AH1407-1987	2,000,000	—	0.50	0.75	1.75	—
AH1408-1988	2,000,000	—	0.50	0.75	1.75	—
AH1410-1990	—	—	0.50	0.75	1.75	—
AH1415-1995	—	—	0.50	0.75	1.75	—
Note: Varieties exist						
AH1418-1998	—	—	0.50	0.75	1.75	—
AH1420-1999	—	—	0.50	0.75	1.50	—

KM# 14a 100 FILS
7.3400 g., 0.9250 Silver 0.2183 oz. ASW, 26 mm. **Ruler:** Jabir Ibn Ahmad **Obv:** Value within circle **Rev:** Ship with sails

Date	Mintage	F	VF	XF	Unc	BU
AH1407 Proof	—	Value: 130				
AH1407-1987 Proof	—	Value: 130				

KM# 14b 100 FILS
12.3300 g., 0.9170 Gold 0.3635 oz. AGW, 26 mm. **Ruler:** Jabir Ibn Ahmad **Obv:** Value within circle **Rev:** Ship with sails

Date	Mintage	F	VF	XF	Unc	BU
AH1407-1987 Proof	—	Value: 400				

KM# 15 2 DINARS
28.2800 g., 0.5000 Silver 0.4546 oz. ASW **Ruler:** Sabah Ibn Salim **Subject:** 15th Anniversary of Independence **Obv:** Conjoined busts with traditional gutra headdresses on facing 3/4 left **Rev:** Castle, tower and ships

Date	Mintage	F	VF	XF	Unc	BU
ND(1976)	70,000	—	—	—	42.50	50.00

KM# 15a 2 DINARS
28.2800 g., 0.9250 Silver 0.8410 oz. ASW **Ruler:** Sabah Ibn Salim **Subject:** 15th Anniversary of Independence **Obv:** Castle, tower and ships **Rev:** Conjoined busts with traditional gutra headdresses on facing 3/4 left

Date	Mintage	F	VF	XF	Unc	BU
ND(1976) Proof	53,000	Value: 65.00				

KM# 24 2 DINARS
28.2800 g., 0.9250 Silver 0.8410 oz. ASW **Ruler:** Jabir Ibn Ahmad **Subject:** 50th Anniversary - United Nations **Obv:** Sailing ship within circle above dove with open wings within radiant circle **Rev:** United in peace written above designs, number 50, dates and emblem

Date	Mintage	F	VF	XF	Unc	BU
ND(1995) Proof Est. 110,000	Value: 35.00					

KM# 8 5 DINARS
13.5720 g., 0.9170 Gold 0.4001 oz. AGW **Ruler:** Abdullah Ibn Salim **Obv:** Value in Arabic in center circle **Rev:** Dhow sailing left

Date	Mintage	F	VF	XF	Unc	BU
AH1380-1961 Rare Est. 1,000						

KM# 18 5 DINARS
28.2800 g., 0.9250 Silver 0.8410 oz. ASW **Ruler:** Jabir Ibn Ahmad **Subject:** 20th Anniversary of Independence **Obv:** Building, crescent and captains wheel within circle **Rev:** Dates, building, towers and satellite dish within chained circle

Date	Mintage	F	VF	XF	Unc	BU
ND(1981) Proof	10,000	Value: 55.00				

KM# 20 5 DINARS
33.6250 g., 0.9250 Silver 0.9999 oz. ASW **Ruler:** Jabir Ibn Ahmad **Subject:** 25th Anniversary of Kuwait Currency **Obv:** Arabic value, buildings, port scene and refinery **Rev:** English legend, falcon, dhow, building and map on globe

Date	Mintage	F	VF	XF	Unc	BU
ND (1986) Proof	—	Value: 75.00				

KM# 21 50 DINARS
16.9660 g., 0.9170 Gold 0.5002 oz. AGW **Ruler:** Jabir Ibn Ahmad **Subject:** 25th Anniversary of Kuwait Independence **Obv:** Arabic legend, arched design, falcon, tent, dhow and pearl in a shell **Rev:** Radiant sun, mosque and assembly building with English and Arabic legend

Date	Mintage	F	VF	XF	Unc	BU
AH1406-1986 Proof	—	Value: 520				

KM# 17 100 DINARS
15.9800 g., 0.9170 Gold 0.4711 oz. AGW **Ruler:** Jabir Ibn Ahmad **Subject:** 15th Century of the Hijira **Obv:** Building, crescent and captain's wheel within circle **Rev:** Dates, building, towers and satellite dish within chained circle

Date	Mintage	F	VF	XF	Unc	BU
AH1401-1981 Proof	10,000	Value: 485				

KM# 16 5 DINARS
28.2800 g., 0.9250 Silver 0.8410 oz. ASW **Ruler:** Jabir Ibn Ahmad **Subject:** 15th Century of the Hijira **Obv:** Capital building within circle **Rev:** Courtyard within circle

Date	Mintage	F	VF	XF	Unc	BU
AH1401-1981 Proof	10,000	Value: 55.00				

KM# 19 100 DINARS

15.9800 g., 0.9170 Gold 0.4711 oz. AGW **Ruler:** Jabir Ibn Ahmad **Subject:** 20th Anniversary of Independence **Obv:** Capital building within circle **Rev:** Courtyard within circle

Date	Mintage	F	VF	XF	Unc	BU
AH1401-1981 Proof	10,000 Value: 485					

MINT SETS

KM#	Date	Mintage	Identification	Issue Price	Mkt Val
MS1	1973 (6)	—	KM9-14	1.75	30.00

PROOF SETS

KM#	Date	Mintage	Identification	Issue Price	Mkt Val
PS1	1961 (6)	60	KM2-7	—	300
PS2	1962 (6)	60	KM9-14	—	300
PS3	1987 (6)	—	KM9a-14a	—	675
PS4	1987 (6)	—	KM9b-14b	—	1,400

KYRGYZSTAN

The Republic of Kyrgyzstan, (formerly Kirghiz S.S.R., a Union Republic of the U.S.S.R.), is an independent state since Aug. 31, 1991, a member of the United Nations and of the C.I.S. It was the last state of the Union Republics to declare its sovereignty. Capital: Bishkek (formerly Frunze).

Originally part of the autonomous Turkestan S.S.R. founded on May 1, 1918, the Kyrgyz ethnic area was established on October 14, 1924, as the Kara-Kirghiz Autonomous Region within the R.S.F.S.R. Then on May 25, 1925, the name Kara (black) was dropped. It became an A.S.S.R. on Feb. 1, 1926, and a Union Republic of the U.S.S.R. in 1936. On Dec. 12, 1990, the name was then changed to the Republic of Kyrgyzstan.

MONETARY SYSTEM
100 Tiyin = 1 Som

REPUBLIC
STANDARD COINAGE

KM# 1 10 SOM

28.2800 g., 0.9250 Silver 0.8410 oz. ASW **Subject:** Millennium of Manas **Obv:** Arms within circle above date flanked by sprigs **Rev:** Armored equestrian above mountains, value and flying bird

Date	Mintage	F	VF	XF	Unc	BU
1995 Proof	Est. 20,000 Value: 60.00					

KM# 2 100 SOM

6.2200 g., 0.9990 Gold 0.1998 oz. AGW **Subject:** Millennium of Manas **Obv:** Arms within circle above date flanked by sprigs **Rev:** Armored equestrian above mountains, value and flying bird

Date	Mintage	F	VF	XF	Unc	BU
1995 Proof	Est. 5,000 Value: 225					

LAO

The Lao Peoples Democratic Republic, located on the Indo-Chinese Peninsula between the Socialist Republic of Vietnam and the Kingdom of Thailand, has an area of 91,428 sq. mi. (236,800 km.) and a population of 3.6 million. Capital: Vientiane. Agriculture employs 95 percent of the people. Tin, lumber and coffee are exported.

The first United Kingdom of Lan Xang (Million Elephants) was established in the mid-14th century by King Fa Ngum who ruled an area including present Laos, northeastern Thailand, and the southern part of China's Yunnan province from his capital at Luang Prabang. Thailand and Vietnam obtained control over much of the present Lao territory in the 18th century and remained dominant until France established a protectorate over the area in 1893 and incorporated it into the Union of Indo-China. The Independence of Laos was proclaimed in March of 1945, during the last days of the Japanese occupation of World War II. France reoccupied Laos in 1946, and established it as a constitutional monarchy within the French Union in 1949. In 1953 war erupted between the government and the Pathet Lao, a Communist movement supported by the Vietnamese Communist forces. Peace was declared in 1954 with Laos becoming fully independent in 1955 and the Pathet Lao being permitted to occupy two northern provinces. Civil war broke out again in 1960 with the United States supporting the government of the Kingdom of Laos and the North Vietnamese helping the Communist Pathet Lao, and continued, with intervals of truce and political compromise, until the formation of the Lao Peoples Democratic Republic on Dec. 2, 1975.

NOTE: For earlier coinage, see French Indo-China.

RULERS
Sisavang Vong, 1904-1959
Savang Vatthana, 1959-1975

MONETARY SYSTEM
100 Cents = 1 Piastre
                              Commencing 1955
100 Att = 1 Kip

MINT MARKS
(a) - Paris, privy marks only
Key - Havana
None - Berlin
    NOTE: Private bullion issues previously listed here are now listed in *Unusual World Coins*, 4th Edition, Krause Publications, Inc., 2005.

KINGDOM
STANDARD COINAGE

KM# 4 10 CENTS

1.3200 g., Aluminum, 23 mm. **Ruler:** Sisavang Vong **Obv:** Center hole in head right **Rev:** Center hole in flower design above date

Date	Mintage	F	VF	XF	Unc	BU
1952(a)	2,000,000	—	0.25	0.60	1.25	2.50

KM# 5 20 CENTS

2.2300 g., Aluminum, 27 mm. **Ruler:** Sisavang Vong **Obv:** Center hole within conjoined elephants above date **Rev:** Center hole within flower design above date

Date	Mintage	F	VF	XF	Unc	BU
1952(a)	3,000,000	—	0.35	0.75	2.00	5.00

KM# 6 50 CENTS

3.8400 g., Aluminum, 31 mm. **Ruler:** Sisavang Vong **Obv:** Center hole within pedestal holding book divides radiant sun and date **Rev:** Center hole within flower design above date

Date	Mintage	F	VF	XF	Unc	BU
1952(a)	1,400,000	—	0.75	1.25	2.50	5.00

KM# 7 1000 KIP

10.0000 g., 0.9250 Silver 0.2974 oz. ASW **Ruler:** Savang Vatthana **Subject:** King Savang Vatthana Coronation **Obv:** Head right within circle **Rev:** Radiant sun above statue dividing elephant heads with lamps flanking, all within circle

Date	Mintage	F	VF	XF	Unc	BU
1971	—			—	25.00	30.00
1971 Proof	20,000 Value: 35.00					

KM# 8 2500 KIP

20.0000 g., 0.9250 Silver 0.5948 oz. ASW **Ruler:** Savang Vatthana **Subject:** King Savang Vatthana Coronation **Obv:** Head right within circle **Rev:** Radiant sun above statue dividing elephant heads with lamps flanking, all within circle

Date	Mintage	F	VF	XF	Unc	BU
1971	—			35.00	40.00	
1971 Proof	20,000 Value: 45.00					

KM# 9 4000 KIP

4.0000 g., 0.9000 Gold 0.1157 oz. AGW **Ruler:** Savang Vatthana **Subject:** King Savang Vatthana Coronation **Obv:** Head right within circle **Rev:** Radiant sun above statue dividing elephant heads with lamps flanking, all within circle

Date	Mintage	F	VF	XF	Unc	BU
1971 Proof	10,000 Value: 130					

KM# 10 5000 KIP
40.0000 g., 0.9250 Silver 1.1895 oz. ASW Ruler: Savang
Vatthana Subject: King Savang Vatthana Coronation Obv: Head
right within circle Rev: Radiant sun above statue dividing elephant
heads with lamps flanking, circle surrounds all

Date	Mintage	F	VF	XF	Unc	BU
1971	—	—	—	—	100	110
1971 Proof	20,000	Value: 125				

KM# 16.1 5000 KIP
11.7000 g., 0.9250 Silver 0.3479 oz. ASW Ruler: Savang Vatthana
Subject: Laotian maiden Obv: Head right above conjoined elephant
heads flanked by lamps Rev: Head right above value
Note: Hologram between denomination and "•" on reverse.

Date	Mintage	F	VF	XF	Unc	BU
1975	400	—	—	—	125	—
1975 Proof	775	Value: 130				

KM# 16.2 5000 KIP
11.7000 g., 0.9250 Silver 0.3479 oz. ASW Ruler: Savang
Vatthana Subject: Laotian maiden Obv: Head right above
conjoined elephant heads flanked by lamps Rev: Head right
above value Note: Hologram between "•" and "LAOS" on reverse.

Date	Mintage	F	VF	XF	Unc	BU
ND(1975)	—	—	—	—	100	110

KM# 17 5000 KIP
11.7000 g., 0.9250 Silver 0.3479 oz. ASW Ruler: Savang
Vatthana Subject: Wat Phra Kio Museum, Vientlane Obv: Head
right above conjoined elephant heads flanked by lamps
Rev: Museum

Date	Mintage	F	VF	XF	Unc	BU
1975	400	—	—	—	125	—
1975 Proof	775	Value: 130				

KM# 11 8000 KIP
8.0000 g., 0.9000 Gold 0.2315 oz. AGW Ruler: Savang
Vatthana Subject: King Savang Vatthana Coronation Obv: Head
right within circle Rev: Radiant statue divides elephant heads
with lamps flanking, all within circle

Date	Mintage	F	VF	XF	Unc	BU
1971 Proof	10,000	Value: 225				

KM# 12 10000 KIP
80.0000 g., 0.9250 Silver 2.3791 oz. ASW Ruler: Savang
Vatthana Subject: King Savang Vatthana Coronation Obv: Head
right within circle Rev: Radiant sun above statue dividing elephant
heads with lamps flanking, circle surrounds all

Date	Mintage	F	VF	XF	Unc	BU
1971	—	—	—	—	150	165
1971 Proof	Est. 20,000	Value: 250				

KM# 18 10000 KIP
23.5000 g., 0.9250 Silver 0.6988 oz. ASW Ruler: Savang
Vatthana Subject: Wat Xieng - Thong Temple Obv: Head right
above elephant statue and lamps Rev: Temple

Date	Mintage	F	VF	XF	Unc	BU
1975	300	—	—	—	180	—
1975 Proof	650	Value: 195				

KM# 13 20000 KIP
20.0000 g., 0.9000 Gold 0.5787 oz. AGW Ruler: Savang
Vatthana Subject: King Savang Vatthana Coronation Obv: Head
right Rev: Elephant statue flanked by lamps

Date	Mintage	F	VF	XF	Unc	BU
1971 Proof	Est. 10,000	Value: 580				

KM# 14 40000 KIP
40.0000 g., 0.9000 Gold 1.1574 oz. AGW Ruler: Savang
Vatthana Subject: King Savang Vatthana Coronation
Rev: Elephant statue flanked by lamps

Date	Mintage	F	VF	XF	Unc	BU
1971 Proof	Est. 10,000	Value: 1,150				

KM# 19 50000 KIP
3.6000 g., 0.9000 Gold 0.1042 oz. AGW Ruler: Savang Vatthana
Obv: Bust of King Savang Vatthana Rev: That Luang Temple

Date	Mintage	F	VF	XF	Unc	BU
1975	100	—	—	—	200	—
1975 Proof	175	Value: 260				

KM# 20 50000 KIP
3.6000 g., 0.9000 Gold 0.1042 oz. AGW Ruler: Savang·
Vatthana Obv: Bust of King Savana Vatthana Rev: Bust of
Laotion maiden 3/4 right

Date	Mintage	F	VF	XF	Unc	BU
1975	100	—	—	—	200.	—
1975 Proof	175	Value: 260				

KM# 15 80000 KIP
80.0000 g., 0.9000 Gold 2.3148 oz. AGW Ruler: Savang
Vatthana Subject: King Savang Vatthana Coronation
Obv: Similar to 20000 Kip, KM#13, head right

Date	Mintage	F	VF	XF	Unc	BU
1971 Proof	—	Value: 2,250				

KM# 21 100000 KIP
7.3200 g., 0.9000 Gold 0.2118 oz. AGW Ruler: Savang Vatthana
Obv: Bust of King Savang Vatthana Rev: Statue of Buddha

Date	Mintage	F	VF	XF	Unc	BU
1975	100	—	—	—	375	—
1975 Proof	100	Value: 450				

PEOPLES DEMOCRATIC REPUBLIC

STANDARD COINAGE
100 Att = 1 Kip

KM# 22 10 ATT
1.2000 g., Aluminum, 21 mm. Obv: National arms Rev: Half length
figure facing holding wheat stalks divides sprigs with value above

Date	Mintage	F	VF	XF	Unc	BU
1980	—	—	0.20	0.40	0.85	—

KM# 23 20 ATT
1.5500 g., Aluminum, 23 mm. Obv: National arms Rev: Value
flanked by designs above ox, man and plow

Date	Mintage	F	VF	XF	Unc	BU
1980	—	—	0.20	0.40	0.85	—

KM# 24 50 ATT
2.5000 g., Aluminum, 26 mm. Obv: National arms Rev: Value
above fish and date flanked by palm trees

Date	Mintage	F	VF	XF	Unc	BU
1980	—	—	0.45	0.90	2.00	3.00

KM# 37 KIP
Copper-Nickel Subject: 10th Anniversary of People's
Democratic Republic Obv: National arms Rev: Value flanked by
designs above date

Date	Mintage	F	VF	XF	Unc	BU
1985	—	—	0.50	1.00	2.50	—

KM# 38   5 KIP
Copper-Nickel   **Subject:** 10th Anniversary of People's
Democratic Republic **Obv:** National arms **Rev:** Value flanked by
designs above date

Date	Mintage	F	VF	XF	Unc	BU
1985	—	—	0.75	1.50	4.00	—

KM# 39   10 KIP
Copper-Nickel   **Subject:** 10th Anniversary of People's
Democratic Republic **Obv:** National arms **Rev:** Value flanked by
designs above date

Date	Mintage	F	VF	XF	Unc	BU
1985	—	—	1.25	2.50	6.50	—

KM# 31   10 KIP
Copper-Nickel, 32.5 mm.   **Obv:** National arms **Rev:** 5-masted
clipper

Date	Mintage	F	VF	XF	Unc	BU
1988	30,000	—	—	—	9.00	—

KM# 31a   10 KIP
Nickel Bonded Steel, 32.5 mm.   **Obv:** National arms
Rev: 5-masted clipper

Date	Mintage	F	VF	XF	Unc	BU
1988	—	—	—	—	8.50	—

KM# 66   10 KIP
Copper   **Obv:** National arms **Rev:** 5-masted clipper

Date	Mintage	F	VF	XF	Unc	BU
1988	—	—	—	—	8.50	10.00
1988 Proof	100	Value: 75.00				

KM# 30   10 KIP
Copper-Nickel   **Subject:** World Soccer Championships - Italy
1990 **Obv:** National arms **Rev:** Soccer players

Date	Mintage	F	VF	XF	Unc	BU
1989	2,000	—	—	—	10.00	—

KM# 46   10 KIP
Nickel-Plated Steel   **Series:** Olympics **Obv:** National arms
Rev: Bicyclist

Date	Mintage	F	VF	XF	Unc	BU
1991	5,000	—	—	—	18.50	—

KM# 51   10 KIP
Copper-Nickel   **Series:** Endangered Wildlife **Obv:** National arms
Rev: Tiger and cubs

Date	Mintage	F	VF	XF	Unc	BU
1991	—	—	—	—	12.00	14.00

KM# 54   10 KIP
Copper   **Series:** Endangered Wildlife **Obv:** National arms
Rev: Tiger and cubs

Date	Mintage	F	VF	XF	Unc	BU
1991	—	—	—	—	12.00	15.00

KM# 50   10 KIP
Copper-Nickel   **Series:** Prehistoric Animals **Obv:** National arms
Rev: Tyranosaurus Rex

Date	Mintage	F	VF	XF	Unc	BU
1993	—	—	—	—	25.00	—

KM# 52   10 KIP
Copper-Nickel   **Series:** Prehistoric Animals **Obv:** National arms
Rev: Lufengosaurus

Date	Mintage	F	VF	XF	Unc	BU
1994	—	—	—	—	25.00	—

KM# 61   10 KIP
Copper-Nickel   **Subject:** 1996 World Food Summit **Obv:** National
arms **Rev:** Farmer plowing with ox

Date	Mintage	F	VF	XF	Unc	BU
1996	—	—	—	—	10.00	14.00

KM# 70   10 KIP
Copper-Nickel   **Series:** XXVII Olympiad **Subject:** Sydney 2000
Obv: National arms **Rev:** Sailboats, Neptune

Date	Mintage	F	VF	XF	Unc	BU
1999	10,000	—	—	—	7.00	—

KM# 40   20 KIP
Copper-Nickel   **Subject:** 10th Anniversary of People's
Democratic Republic **Obv:** National arms within circle and wreath
Rev: Value flanked by designs above date

Date	Mintage	F	VF	XF	Unc	BU
1985	—	—	1.50	2.50	7.00	—

KM# 25 50 KIP
38.2000 g., 0.9000 Silver 1.1053 oz. ASW **Subject:** 10th
Anniversary of People's Democratic Republic **Obv:** National arms
Rev: Value flanked by designs below towered building

Date	Mintage	F	VF	XF	Unc	BU
1985 Proof	2,000	Value: 42.50				

KM# 26 50 KIP
38.2000 g., 0.9000 Silver 1.1053 oz. ASW **Subject:** 10th
Anniversary of People's Democratic Republic **Obv:** National arms
Rev: Value flanked by designs below towered building

Date	Mintage	F	VF	XF	Unc	BU
1985 Proof	2,000	Value: 42.50				

KM# 27 50 KIP
38.2000 g., 0.9000 Silver 1.1053 oz. ASW **Subject:** 10th
Anniversary of People's Democratic Republic **Obv:** National arms
Rev: Value flanked by designs below building

Date	Mintage	F	VF	XF	Unc	BU
1985 Proof	2,000	Value: 42.50				

KM# 28 50 KIP
38.2000 g., 0.9000 Silver 1.1053 oz. ASW **Subject:** 10th
Anniversary of People's Democratic Republic **Obv:** National arms
Rev: Value flanked by designs below valley of jars

Date	Mintage	F	VF	XF	Unc	BU
1985 Proof	2,000	Value: 42.50				

KM# 41 50 KIP
Copper-Nickel **Subject:** 10th Anniversary of People's
Democratic Republic **Obv:** National arms within circle and wreath
Rev: Value flanked by designs above date

Date	Mintage	F	VF	XF	Unc	BU
1985	—	—	2.00	3.50	8.50	—

KM# 29 50 KIP
16.0000 g., 0.9990 Silver 0.5139 oz. ASW **Obv:** National arms
Rev: 5-masted sailship "Prussia"

Date	Mintage	F	VF	XF	Unc	BU
1988 Proof	2,000	Value: 30.00				

KM# 32 50 KIP
12.0000 g., 0.9990 Silver 0.3854 oz. ASW **Subject:** European
Soccer Championship - Germany **Obv:** National arms
Rev: Soccer players

Date	Mintage	F	VF	XF	Unc	BU
1988	5,000	—	—	25.00	—	

KM# 33 50 KIP
16.0000 g., 0.9990 Silver 0.5139 oz. ASW **Subject:** World
Soccer Championship - Mexico 86 **Obv:** National arms
Rev: Soccer players

Date	Mintage	F	VF	XF	Unc	BU
ND(1988) Proof	5,000	Value: 26.50				

KM# 34 50 KIP
16.0000 g., 0.9990 Silver 0.5139 oz. ASW **Subject:** World
Soccer Championship - Italy 1990 **Obv:** National arms
Rev: Soccer players

Date	Mintage	F	VF	XF	Unc	BU
1989 Proof	5,000	Value: 26,50				

KM# 35.1 50 KIP
16.0000 g., 0.9990 Silver 0.5139 oz. ASW **Series:** Winter
Olympics **Subject:** Ice dancing **Obv:** National arms **Rev:** Ice
dancers within design **Note:** Lightly frosted.

Date	Mintage	F	VF	XF	Unc	BU
1989 Proof	—	Value: 27.50				

KM# 35.2 50 KIP
16.0000 g., 0.9990 Silver 0.5139 oz. ASW **Series:** Winter
Olympics **Subject:** Ice dancing **Obv:** National arms **Rev:** Ice
dancers within design **Note:** Extensive frosting.

Date	Mintage	F	VF	XF	Unc	BU
1989 Proof	—	Value: 80.00				

KM# 36.1 50 KIP
16.0000 g., 0.9990 Silver 0.5139 oz. ASW **Series:** Summer
Olympics **Subject:** Water polo **Obv:** National arms **Rev:** Water
polo players within frosted water

Date	Mintage	F	VF	XF	Unc	BU
1989 Proof	5,000	Value: 50.00				

KM# 36.2   50 KIP
16.0000 g., 0.9990 Silver 0.5139 oz. ASW   **Series:** Summer
Olympics **Subject:** Water polo **Obv:** National arms **Rev:** Water
polo players within unfrosted water

Date	Mintage	F	VF	XF	Unc	BU
1989 Proof	—				Value: 27.50	

KM# 44   50 KIP
12.0000 g., 0.9990 Silver 0.3854 oz. ASW   **Subject:** World Cup
Soccer **Obv:** National arms **Rev:** Soccer Ball

Date	Mintage	F	VF	XF	Unc	BU
1991	—	—	—	—	25.00	—

KM# 45   50 KIP
20.0000 g., 0.9990 Silver 0.6423 oz. ASW   **Subject:** Wildlife
Obv: National arms **Rev:** Tiger and cubs

Date	Mintage	F	VF	XF	Unc	BU
1991	100	—	—	—	175	—
1991 Proof	—				Value: 45.00	

KM# 47   50 KIP
20.0000 g., 0.9990 Silver 0.6423 oz. ASW   **Subject:** Soccer
Obv: National arms **Rev:** Goalie

Date	Mintage	F	VF	XF	Unc	BU
1991 Proof	—				Value: 32.50	

KM# 48   50 KIP
20.0000 g., 0.9990 Silver 0.6423 oz. ASW   **Subject:** Protection
of Nature **Obv:** National arms **Rev:** Elephant

Date	Mintage	F	VF	XF	Unc	BU
1993 Proof	—				Value: 50.00	

KM# 49   50 KIP
15.9400 g., 0.9990 Silver 0.5119 oz. ASW   **Series:** Prehistoric
Animals **Obv:** National arms **Rev:** Sauroctonus

Date	Mintage	F	VF	XF	Unc	BU
1993 Proof	—				Value: 35.00	

KM# 53   50 KIP
16.0000 g., 0.9990 Silver 0.5139 oz. ASW   **Series:** Prehistoric
Animals **Obv:** National arms **Rev:** Elasmosaurus and tylosaurus
in combat

Date	Mintage	F	VF	XF	Unc	BU
1994 Proof	—				Value: 55.00	

KM# 82   50 KIP
16.0000 g., 0.9990 Silver 0.5139 oz. ASW, 37.9 mm.
Subject: Prehistoric Animals **Obv:** National arms
Rev: Elasmosaurus fighting a Tylosaurus **Edge:** Plain

Date	Mintage	F	VF	XF	Unc	BU
1994 Proof	—				Value: 55.00	

KM# 84   50 KIP
16.1000 g., 0.9990 Silver 0.5171 oz. ASW, 37.9 mm.
Obv: National arms **Rev:** Megalosaurus

Date	Mintage	F	VF	XF	Unc	BU
1994 Proof	—				Value: 40.00	

KM# 56   50 KIP
20.0000 g., 0.9990 Silver 0.6423 oz. ASW   **Series:** Olympics
Obv: National arms **Rev:** Javelin throwers

Date	Mintage	F	VF	XF	Unc	BU
1995 Proof	Est. 15,000				Value: 25.00	

KM# 57   50 KIP
20.0000 g., 0.9990 Silver 0.6423 oz. ASW   **Subject:** World Cup
Soccer **Obv:** National arms **Rev:** Player and cathedral

Date	Mintage	F	VF	XF	Unc	BU
1996	100	—	—	—	90.00	—
1996 Proof	10,000				Value: 30.00	

KM# 97   50 KIP
Silver, 37 mm.   **Subject:** World Food Summit - 1996 in Rome
Obv: National arms **Rev:** Farmer plowing with ox **Edge:** Reeded

Date	Mintage	F	VF	XF	Unc	BU
1996	—	—	—	—	—	40.00

KM# 63   50 KIP
20.0000 g., 0.9990 Silver 0.6423 oz. ASW   **Series:** XXVII
Olympiad **Obv:** National arms **Rev:** Multicolor torch and athletes
Note: Multicolor design.

Date	Mintage	F	VF	XF	Unc	BU
1996 Proof	—				Value: 42.50	

KM# 58 50 KIP
20.0000 g., 0.9990 Silver 0.6423 oz. ASW **Subject:** World Cup Soccer **Obv:** National arms **Rev:** Stadium within map of France **Note:** Multicolor design.

Date	Mintage	F	VF	XF	Unc	BU
1996 Proof	10,000	Value: 40.00				

KM# 62 50 KIP
20.0000 g., 0.9990 Silver 0.6423 oz. ASW **Series:** XXVII Olympiad **Obv:** National arms **Rev:** Archer - Diana, goddess of the hunt

Date	Mintage	F	VF	XF	Unc	BU
1996 Proof	—	Value: 40.00				

KM# 64 50 KIP
15.0000 g., 0.9990 Silver 0.4818 oz. ASW **Subject:** World of Adventure - Leif Ericson **Obv:** National arms **Rev:** Viking longship

Date	Mintage	F	VF	XF	Unc	BU
1996 Proof	—	Value: 45.00				

KM# 79 50 KIP
15.0000 g., 0.9990 Silver 0.4818 oz. ASW, 35 mm.
Series: World Cup Soccer **Obv:** National arms **Rev:** Soccer player with ball and map background **Edge:** Plain

Date	Mintage	F	VF	XF	Unc	BU
1996 Proof	—	Value: 27.50				

KM# 42 100 KIP
3.1500 g., 0.9990 Gold 0.1012 oz. AGW **Obv:** National arms and legend above value **Rev:** 5-masted sailship "Prussia"

Date	Mintage	F	VF	XF	Unc	BU
1988	500	—	—	—	155	200

KM# 43 100 KIP
3.1500 g., 0.9990 Gold 0.1012 oz. AGW **Subject:** 10th Anniversary of People's Democratic Republic **Obv:** National arms **Rev:** Radiant sun and temple

Date	Mintage	F	VF	XF	Unc	BU
1990	—	—	—	—	160	210

KM# 69 500 KIP
20.0000 g., 0.9250 Silver 0.5948 oz. ASW **Subject:** Kouprey **Obv:** National arms **Rev:** Wild bull

Date	Mintage	F	VF	XF	Unc	BU
1998 Proof	10,000	Value: 50.00				

KM# 165 1000 KIP
31.6700 g., 0.9990 Silver 1.0172 oz. ASW **Series:** Endangered Wildlife **Obv:** National arms **Rev:** Gibbon

Date	Mintage	F	VF	XF	Unc	BU
1996 Proof	—	Value: 60.00				

KM# 67 1000 KIP
31.4700 g., 0.9250 Silver 0.9359 oz. ASW **Series:** Endangered Wildlife **Obv:** National arms **Rev:** Two long-horned saola

Date	Mintage	F	VF	XF	Unc	BU
1997 Proof	15,000	Value: 45.00				

KM# 59 1200 KIP
Nickel Bonded Steel **Subject:** Food for All **Obv:** National arms **Rev:** Three people harvesting rice below logo and dates

Date	Mintage	F	VF	XF	Unc	BU
ND(1995)	—	—	—	—	8.00	

KM# 68 2000 KIP
1.2441 g., 0.9990 Gold 0.0400 oz. AGW **Subject:** That Luang **Obv:** National arms **Rev:** Temple

Date	Mintage	F	VF	XF	Unc	BU
1998 Proof	—	Value: 60.00				

KM# 72 3000 KIP
20.0000 g., 0.9250 Silver 0.5948 oz. ASW, 38.6 mm.
Subject: Retrospection Rabbit **Obv:** National arms **Rev:** Multicolor rabbit looking back **Edge:** Reeded

Date	Mintage	F	VF	XF	Unc	BU
1999 Proof	—	Value: 40.00				

KM# 91 3000 KIP
20.0000 g., 0.9250 Silver 0.5948 oz. ASW, 38.7 mm.
Subject: Year of the Rabbit **Obv:** National arms **Rev:** Rabbit leaping to right over latent image date **Edge:** Reeded

Date	Mintage	F	VF	XF	Unc	BU
1999 Proof	—	Value: 40.00				

KM# 73 3000 KIP
20.0000 g., 0.9250 Silver 0.5948 oz. ASW **Subject:** Anticipation Rabbit **Obv:** National arms **Rev:** Partially gold-plated rabbit with radiant sun background

Date	Mintage	F	VF	XF	Unc	BU
1999 Proof	—	Value: 50.00				

KM# 60 5000 KIP
7.7600 g., 0.5833 Gold 0.1455 oz. AGW **Series:** Olympics **Obv:** National arms **Rev:** Two boxers

Date	Mintage	F	VF	XF	Unc	BU
1996	Est. 3,000	—	—	—	150	165

KM# 80   5000 KIP
15.0000 g., 0.9990 Silver 0.4818 oz. ASW, 35 mm. **Series:**
Olympics **Obv:** National arms **Rev:** Archer with statue in
background **Edge:** Plain

Date	Mintage	F	VF	XF	Unc	BU
1998 Proof	—	Value: 30.00				

KM# 81   5000 KIP
15.0000 g., 0.9990 Silver 0.4818 oz. ASW, 35 mm. **Obv:**
National arms **Rev:** Multicolor torch and athletes **Edge:** Plain

Date	Mintage	F	VF	XF	Unc	BU
1998 Proof	—	Value: 50.00				

KM# 92   5000 KIP
15.0000 g., 0.9990 Silver 0.4818 oz. ASW, 35.1 mm.
Obv: National arms **Rev:** St. Thomas Aquinas **Edge:** Plain

Date	Mintage	F	VF	XF	Unc	BU
1999 Proof	—	Value: 45.00				

KM# 71   5000 KIP
20.0500 g., 0.9990 Silver 0.6440 oz. ASW **Series:** XXVII
Olympiad **Subject:** Sydney 2000 **Obv:** National arms
Rev: Sailboats, Neptune

Date	Mintage	F	VF	XF	Unc	BU
1999 Proof	5,000	Value: 35.00				

KM# 74   5000 KIP
20.0000 g., 0.9250 Silver 0.5948 oz. ASW, 39 mm. **Subject:**
Silver Dragon Fish **Obv:** National arms **Rev:** Fish **Edge:** Reeded

Date	Mintage	F	VF	XF	Unc	BU
2000-2001 Proof	10,000	Value: 40.00				

Note: Latent image date

KM# 75   5000 KIP
20.0000 g., 0.9250 Silver 0.5948 oz. ASW, 39 mm.
Subject: Red Dragon Fish **Obv:** National arms **Rev:** Red colored
fish **Edge:** Reeded

Date	Mintage	F	VF	XF	Unc	BU
2000-2001 Proof	10,000	Value: 40.00				

Note: Latent image date

KM# 93   5000 KIP
15.1400 g., 0.9990 Silver 0.4863 oz. ASW, 35.1 mm.
Subject: Third Millennium **Obv:** National arms **Rev:** World map
with date 2000/1999 **Edge:** Plain

Date	Mintage	F	VF	XF	Unc	BU
ND(2000) Proof	—	Value: 45.00				

KM# 76   5000 KIP
20.0000 g., 0.9250 Silver 0.5948 oz. ASW, 39 mm.
Subject: Golden Dragon Fish **Obv:** National arms **Rev:** Jumping
fish below gold cameo **Edge:** Reeded

Date	Mintage	F	VF	XF	Unc	BU
2000-2001 Proof	Est. 4,000	Value: 50.00				

Note: Latent image date

KM# 77   10000 KIP
1.2441 g., 0.9999 Gold 0.0400 oz. AGW, 14 mm.
Subject: Golden Dragon Fish **Obv:** National arms **Rev:** Jumping
fish **Edge:** Reeded **Note:** Date as a latent image.

Date	Mintage	F	VF	XF	Unc	BU
2000-2001	—	—	—	—	50.00	—

KM# 83   50000 KIP
7.7750 g., 0.9990 Gold 0.2497 oz. AGW, 32.2 mm.
Obv: National arms **Rev:** Red Dragon Fish **Edge:** Reeded

Date	Mintage	F	VF	XF	Unc	BU
2000-2001 Proof	3,000	Value: 250				

KM# 78   100000 KIP
15.5518 g., 0.9999 Gold 0.4999 oz. AGW, 27 mm.
Subject: Golden Dragon Fish **Obv:** National arms **Rev:**
Multicolored holographic jumping fish **Edge:** Reeded

Date	Mintage	F	VF	XF	Unc	BU
2000-2001 Proof	3,000	Value: 485				

Note: Latent image date

PIEFORTS

KM#	Date	Mintage	Identification		Mkt Val
P1	1988	—	50 Kip. Silver.		—

PIEFORTS WITH ESSAI
Standard metals unless otherwise noted

Double Thickness

KM#	Date	Mintage	Identification	Mkt Val
PE1	1952(a)	104	10 Cents.	80.00
PE2	1952(a)	104	20 Cents.	80.00
PE3	1952(a)	104	50 Cents.	100

ESSAIS
Standard metals unless otherwise noted

KM#	Date	Mintage	Identification	Mkt Val
E1	1952(a)	1,200	10 Cents.	20.00
E2	1952(a)	1,200	20 Cents.	22.50
E3	1952(a)	1,200	50 Cents.	25.00

MINT SETS

KM#	Date	Mintage	Identification	Issue Price	Mkt Val
MS1	1971 (4)	—	KM7, 8, 10, 12	—	300
MS2	1975 (6)	100	KM16-21	—	1,300
MS3	1975 (3)	300	KM16-18	—	420

PROOF SETS

KM#	Date	Mintage	Identification	Issue Price	Mkt Val
PS1	1971 (5)	10,000	KM9, 11, 13-15	467	3,000
PS2	1971 (4)	20,000	KM7, 8, 10, 12	163	450
PS3	1975 (6)	—	KM16-21	—	1,450
PS4	1975 (3)	650	KM16-18	—	450
PS5	1975 (3)	—	KM19-21	349	960
PS6	1985 (4)	2,000	KM25-28	—	180
PS7	2000-2001 (3)	3,500	KM#74-76	138	200
PS8	2000-2001 (3)	500	KM#74-76	214	300
PS9	2000-2001 (2)	800	KM#78, 83	—	700

LATVIA

The Republic of Latvia, the central Baltic state in east Europe,
has an area of 24,749 sq. mi. (43,601 sq. km.) and a population
of 2.6 million. Capital: Riga. Livestock raising and manufacturing
are the chief industries. Butter, bacon, fertilizers and telephone
equipment are exported.

The Latvians, of Aryan descent primarily from the German
Order of Livonian Knights, were nomadic tribesmen who settled
along the Baltic prior to the 13th century. Ideally situated as a trade
route and lacking a central government, conquered in 1561 by
Poland and Sweden. Following the third partition of Poland by
Austria, Prussia and Russia in 1795, Latvia came under Russian
domination and did not experience autonomy until the Russian
Revolution of 1917 provided an opportunity for freedom. The
Latvian Republic was established on Nov. 18, 1918. The republic
was occupied by Soviet troops and annexed to the Soviet Union
in 1940. Following the German occupation of 1941-44, it was
retaken by Russia and reestablished as a member republic of the
Soviet Union. Western countries, including the United States, did
not recognize Latvia's incorporation into the Soviet Union.

The coinage issued during the early 20th Century Republic
is now obsolete.

Latvia declared their independence from the U.S.S.R. on
August 22, 1991.

MONETARY SYSTEM
100 Santimu = 1 Lats

FIRST REPUBLIC
1918-1939
STANDARD COINAGE
100 Santimu = 1 Lats

KM# 1   SANTIMS
1.6500 g., Bronze, 17 mm. **Obv:** National arms above ribbon
Rev: Value and date **Edge:** Plain **Note:** Struck at Huguenin
Freres, Le Locle, Switzerland.

Date	Mintage	F	VF	XF	Unc	BU
1922	5,000,000	3.00	4.00	6.00	12.00	—
1923	10	—	—	—	1,700	—
1924	4,990,000	3.00	4.00	7.00	12.00	—
1926	5,000,000	3.00	4.00	7.00	12.00	—
1928	5,000,000	3.00	4.00	7.00	12.00	—

Note: Mint name below ribbon

1928	Inc. above	6.00	12.00	25.00	45.00	—

Note: Without mint name below ribbon

1932	5,000,000	3.00	4.00	6.00	12.00	—
1932 Proof	—	—	—	—	—	—
1935	5,000,000	3.00	4.00	6.00	12.00	—

KM# 10   SANTIMS
1.8000 g., Bronze, 17 mm. **Obv:** National arms above sprigs
Rev: Value divides sprigs above date **Edge:** Plain

Date	Mintage	F	VF	XF	Unc	BU
1937	2,700,000	3.00	4.00	7.00	14.00	—
1938	1,900,000	4.00	5.00	9.00	18.00	—
1939	3,400,000	2.00	3.00	4.00	6.00	—

Note: Most were never placed into circulation

KM# 2   2 SANTIMI
2.0000 g., Bronze, 19.5 mm. **Obv:** National arms above ribbon
Rev: Value and date **Edge:** Plain

Date	Mintage	F	VF	XF	Unc	BU
1922	10,000,000	3.00	4.00	8.00	19.00	—

Note: Mint name below ribbon

1922	Inc. above	5.00	10.00	20.00	40.00	—

Note: Without mint name below ribbon

1923	2	—	—	—	2,000	3,000
1926	5,000,000	3.00	4.00	8.00	16.00	—
1928	5,000,000	3.00	4.00	8.00	16.00	—
1932	5,000,000	3.00	4.00	8.00	16.00	—
1932 Proof	—	—	—	—	—	—

KM# 11.1   2 SANTIMI
2.0000 g., Bronze, 19 mm. **Obv:** National arms above sprigs
Rev: Value flanked by sprigs above date **Edge:** Plain

Date	Mintage	F	VF	XF	Unc	BU
1937	45,000	18.00	30.00	45.00	90.00	—

KM# 11.2   2 SANTIMI
2.0000 g., Bronze, 19.5 mm. **Obv:** National arms above sprigs
Rev: Value flanked by sprigs above date **Edge:** Plain

Date	Mintage	F	VF	XF	Unc	BU
1939	5,000,000	4.00	5.00	7.00	15.00	—

Note: Most were never placed in circulation

KM# 3 5 SANTIMI
3.0000 g., Bronze, 22 mm. **Obv:** National arms above ribbon
Rev: Value and date

Date	Mintage	F	VF	XF	Unc	BU
1922	15,000,000	3.00	4.00	7.00	14.00	—
Note: Mint name below ribbon						
1922	Inc. above	5.00	8.00	17.00	35.00	—
Note: Without name below ribbon						
1923	2	—	—	—	2,250	3,250

KM# 4 10 SANTIMU
3.0000 g., Nickel, 19 mm. **Obv:** National arms above ribbon
divides date **Rev:** Value above oat sprig **Edge:** Plain **Note:** Struck
at Huguenin.

Date	Mintage	F	VF	XF	Unc	BU
1922	15,000,000	2.00	3.00	6.00	12.00	—

KM# 5 20 SANTIMU
6.0000 g., Nickel, 21 mm. **Obv:** National arms above ribbon
divides date **Rev:** Value above oat sprig **Edge:** Plain **Note:** Struck
at Huguenin.

Date	Mintage	F	VF	XF	Unc	BU
1922	15,000,000	3.00	4.00	7.00	14.00	—

KM# 6 50 SANTIMU
6.5000 g., Nickel, 25 mm. **Obv:** National arms above ribbon
divides date **Rev:** Value to right of standing figure **Edge:** Plain
Note: Struck at Huguenin.

Date	Mintage	F	VF	XF	Unc	BU
1922	9,000,000	4.00	7.00	9.00	18.00	—

KM# 7 LATS
5.0000 g., 0.8350 Silver 0.1342 oz. ASW, 23 mm. **Obv:** Arms
with supporters **Rev:** Value and date within wreath **Edge:** Milled

Date	Mintage	F	VF	XF	Unc	BU
1923	—	—	—	1,100	—	—
1924	10,000,000	5.00	10.00	20.00	400	—

KM# 8 2 LATI
10.0000 g., 0.8350 Silver 0.2684 oz. ASW, 27 mm. **Obv:** Arms
with supporters **Rev:** Value and date within wreath **Edge:** Milled

Date	Mintage	F	VF	XF	Unc	BU
1925	6,386,000	6.00	10.00	20.00	45.00	—
1926	1,114,000	6.00	10.00	20.00	50.00	—

KM# 9 5 LATI
25.0000 g., 0.8350 Silver 0.6711 oz. ASW, 37 mm.
Obv: Crowned head right **Rev:** Arms with supporters above value
Edge: Plain with   DIEVS *** SVETI *** LATVOJU ***

Date	Mintage	F	VF	XF	Unc	BU
1929	1,000,000	20.00	25.00	35.00	70.00	—
1929 Proof	—	—	—	—	—	—
1931	2,000,000	20.00	25.00	35.00	60.00	—
1931 Proof	—	—	—	—	—	—
1932	600,000	25.00	30.00	40.00	75.00	—
1932 Proof	—	Value: 3,500				

MODERN REPUBLIC
1991-present
STANDARD COINAGE
100 Santimu = 1 Lats

KM# 15 SANTIMS
1.6000 g., Copper-Clad Steel, 15.65 mm. **Obv:** National arms
Rev: Value flanked by diamonds below lined arch **Edge:** Plain

Date	Mintage	F	VF	XF	Unc	BU
1992	—	—	—	0.15	0.45	1.00
1997	—	—	—	0.10	0.30	1.00

KM# 21 2 SANTIMI
1.9300 g., Bronze-Plated Steel, 16.97 mm. **Obv:** National arms
Rev: Lined arch above value flanked by diamonds **Edge:** Plain

Date	Mintage	F	VF	XF	Unc	BU
1992	—	—	0.10	0.50	1.00	2.00
2000	—	—	—	0.15	0.45	0.60

KM# 16 5 SANTIMI
2.5000 g., Brass, 18.5 mm. **Obv:** National arms
Obv. Leg.: LATVIJAS REPUBLIKA **Rev:** Lined arch above value
flanked by diamonds **Edge:** Plain

Date	Mintage	F	VF	XF	Unc	BU
1992	—	—	0.15	0.45	1.50	2.50

KM# 17 10 SANTIMU
3.2500 g., Brass, 19.9 mm. **Obv:** National arms **Rev:** Lined arch
above value flanked by diamonds

Date	Mintage	F	VF	XF	Unc	BU
1992	—	—	0.50	1.00	2.00	3.00

KM# 22 20 SANTIMU
4.0000 g., Brass, 21.46 mm. **Obv:** National arms **Rev:** Lined
arch above value flanked by diamonds **Edge:** Plain

Date	Mintage	F	VF	XF	Unc	BU
1992	—	—	—	1.00	2.00	4.00

KM# 13 50 SANTIMU
3.5000 g., Copper-Nickel, 18.73 mm. **Obv:** National arms
Rev: Triple sprig above value **Edge:** Reeded

Date	Mintage	F	VF	XF	Unc	BU
1992	—	—	—	2.00	4.00	5.00

KM# 12 LATS
4.8000 g., Copper-Nickel, 21.75 mm. **Obv:** Arms with supporters
Rev: Fish above value

Date	Mintage	F	VF	XF	Unc	BU
1992	—	—	—	—	4.00	7.00

KM# 23 LATS
28.2800 g., 0.9250 Silver 0.8410 oz. ASW **Series:** UN 50th
Anniversary **Obv:** National arms **Rev:** Many people holding hands

Date	Mintage	F	VF	XF	Unc	BU
1995 Proof	100,000	Value: 42.50				

KM# 39 LATS
15.2000 g., 0.9250 Silver 0.4520 oz. ASW **Subject:** Millennium
Obv: Date divides holes within circle **Rev:** Vertical holes within
circle, date on bottom **Note:** Button design.

Date	Mintage	F	VF	XF	Unc	BU
1999-2000 Proof	35,000	Value: 55.00				

KM# 44 LATS
20.0000 g., 0.9250 Silver 0.5948 oz. ASW, 34 mm.
Series: Olympics **Obv:** National arms **Rev:** Two cyclists
Edge: Lettered

Date	Mintage	F	VF	XF	Unc	BU
1999 Proof	—	Value: 35.00				

KM# 45 LATS
31.4700 g., 0.9250 Silver 0.9359 oz. ASW, 38.6 mm.
Subject: European mink **Obv:** National arms **Rev:** Mink on rock
Edge: Lettered

Date	Mintage	F	VF	XF	Unc	BU
1999 Proof	—	Value: 65.00				

KM# 46 LATS
31.4700 g., 0.9250 Silver 0.9359 oz. ASW, 38.6 mm.
Subject: Hanseatic City of Ventspils **Obv:** City arms above value
Rev: Building and ship **Edge:** "LATVIJAS REPUBLIKA
LATVIJAS BANKA"

Date	Mintage	F	VF	XF	Unc	BU
2000 Proof	—	Value: 50.00				

KM# 47 LATS
31.4700 g., 0.9250 Silver 0.9359 oz. ASW, 38.6 mm.
Subject: Earth - Roots **Obv:** Stylized "Roots" pattern
Rev: Landscape and value **Edge:** Plain

Date	Mintage	F	VF	XF	Unc	BU
2000 Proof	6,000	Value: 50.00				

KM# 48 LATS
31.4700 g., 0.9250 Silver 0.9359 oz. ASW, 38.6 mm.
Subject: UNICEF **Obv:** National arms **Obv. Leg.:** LATVIJAS
REPUBLIXA above value **Rev:** Child art and logo
Edge: "LATVIJAS BANKA" twice

Date	Mintage	F	VF	XF	Unc	BU
2000 Proof	6,000	Value: 50.00				

KM# 14 2 LATI
6.0000 g., Copper-Nickel, 24.35 mm. **Obv:** Arms with supporters
Rev: Cow grazing above value

Date	Mintage	F	VF	XF	Unc	BU
1992	—	—	—	—	8.00	9.00

KM# 18 2 LATI
Copper-Nickel **Subject:** 75th Anniversary - Declaration of
Independence **Obv:** Arms with supporters **Rev:** Artistic lined art
above value and dates

Date	Mintage	F	VF	XF	Unc	BU
ND(1993)	4,000,000	—	—	—	10.00	12.00
ND(1993) Proof	200,000	Value: 15.00				

KM# 38 2 LATI
Ring: Copper-Nickel **Center:** Brass **Obv:** Arms with supporters
within circle **Rev:** Cow above value within circle

Date	Mintage	F	VF	XF	Unc	BU
1999	—	—	—	—	10.00	12.00

KM# 19 10 LATU
25.1750 g., 0.9250 Silver 0.7487 oz. ASW **Subject:** 75th
Anniversary - Declaration of Independence **Obv:** Arms with
supporters **Rev:** Artistic lines and design above value and dates

Date	Mintage	F	VF	XF	Unc	BU
ND(1993) Proof	30,000	Value: 35.00				

KM# 24 10 LATU
31.4700 g., 0.9250 Silver 0.9359 oz. ASW **Series:** Olympics
Obv: Arms with supporters **Rev:** Man paddling canoe

Date	Mintage	F	VF	XF	Unc	BU
1994 Proof	30,000	Value: 50.00				

KM# 25 10 LATU
31.4700 g., 0.9250 Silver 0.9359 oz. ASW **Subject:** Julia Maria
Obv: National arms **Rev:** 3-masted schooner

Date	Mintage	F	VF	XF	Unc	BU
1995 Proof	20,000	Value: 50.00				

KM# 27 10 LATU
31.4700 g., 0.9250 Silver 0.9359 oz. ASW **Subject:** 800th
Anniversary - Riga **Obv:** Coat of arms from 1368 **Rev:** The Great
Gould's coat of arms from 1354

Date	Mintage	F	VF	XF	Unc	BU
1995 (1996) Proof	—	—	—	—	—	—
1995 (1996) Proof	—	Value: 50.00				

KM# 26 10 LATU
31.4700 g., 0.9250 Silver 0.9359 oz. ASW **Subject:** Riga 800
Obv: Standing figure in long robe with turban on head within
warped circle **Rev:** First city seal within circle

Date	Mintage	F	VF	XF	Unc	BU
1995 (1996) Proof Est. 8,000	Value: 50.00					

KM# 33 10 LATU
31.4700 g., 0.9250 Silver 0.9359 oz. ASW **Series:** Endangered
Wildlife **Obv:** Arms with supporters **Rev:** Grieze bird
Edge: Lettered **Edge:** LATVIJAS BANKA \ (2x)

Date	Mintage	F	VF	XF	Unc	BU
1996 Proof	15,000	Value: 55.00				

KM# 34 10 LATU
31.4700 g., 0.9250 Silver 0.9359 oz. ASW **Subject:** Riga - XVI
Century **Obv:** Old coin design above value **Rev:** Old city view

Date	Mintage	F	VF	XF	Unc	BU
1996 Proof	—	Value: 50.00				

KM# 36 10 LATU
31.3500 g., 0.9990 Silver 1.0069 oz. ASW **Subject:** 800th
Anniversary of Riga **Obv:** Old coin design with St. Christopher within
warped circle **Rev:** Old coin design with city arms within partial circle
Edge: Lettered **Edge:** LATVIJAS REPUBLIKA LATVIJAS BANKA

Date	Mintage	F	VF	XF	Unc	BU
1996 Proof	—	Value: 50.00				

KM# 28 10 LATU
31.3200 g., 0.9250 Silver 0.9314 oz. ASW **Obv:** Arms with
supporters **Rev:** 12th-century ship above its sunken remains
Edge: Lettered **Edge:** LATIJAS BANKAS

Date	Mintage	F	VF	XF	Unc	BU
1997 Proof	15,000	Value: 50.00				

KM# 42 10 LATU
1.2442 g., 0.9990 Gold 0.0400 oz. AGW, 13.92 mm. **Obv:** Arms
with supporters **Rev:** Sailing ship "Julia Maria" **Edge:** Reeded

Date	Mintage	F	VF	XF	Unc	BU
1997 Proof	—	Value: 55.00				

KM# 35 10 LATU
31.4700 g., 0.9250 Silver 0.9359 oz. ASW **Subject:** Riga - XVII
Century **Obv:** Old coin design of arms with supporters **Rev:** Aerial
view of walled city

Date	Mintage	F	VF	XF	Unc	BU
1997 Proof	—	Value: 50.00				

KM# 29 10 LATU
1.2441 g., 0.9999 Gold 0.0400 oz. AGW **Subject:** 800th
Anniversary - Riga **Obv:** City arms on old coin design **Rev:** City
arms and ship on old coin design

Date	Mintage	F	VF	XF	Unc	BU
1998 Proof	—	Value: 55.00				

KM# 30 10 LATU
31.4700 g., 0.9250 Silver 0.9359 oz. ASW **Subject:** 800th
Anniversary - Riga **Obv:** National song festival procession
Rev: Crowned Riga city arms

Date	Mintage	F	VF	XF	Unc	BU
1998 Proof	Est. 8,000	Value: 50.00				

KM# 31 10 LATU
31.4700 g., 0.9250 Silver 0.9359 oz. ASW **Subject:** 800th
Anniversary - Riga **Obv:** Liberty Monument **Rev:** City arms with
supporters

Date	Mintage	F	VF	XF	Unc	BU
1998 Proof	Est. 8,000	Value: 55.00				

KM# 32 10 LATU
31.4700 g., 0.9250 Silver 0.9359 oz. ASW **Obv:** National arms
Rev: 1925 Icebreaker "Krisjanis Valdemars"

Date	Mintage	F	VF	XF	Unc	BU
1998 Proof	10,000	Value: 50.00				

KM# 43 10 LATU
3.1100 g., 0.5830 Gold 0.0583 oz. AGW, 18.5 mm.
Series: Olympics **Obv:** Arms with supporters **Rev:** Javelin
thrower **Edge:** Reeded

Date	Mintage	F	VF	XF	Unc	BU
1999 Proof	—	Value: 65.00				

KM# 41 20 LATU
7.7760 g., 0.5830 Gold 0.1457 oz. AGW, 25 mm. **Obv:** Arms with
supporters **Rev:** Sailing ship "Gekronte Ehlendt" **Edge:** Reeded

Date	Mintage	F	VF	XF	Unc	BU
1997 Proof	—	Value: 150				

KM# 37 20 LATU
31.4100 g., 0.9210 Silver 0.9300 oz. ASW **Obv:** City arms
Rev: Melngalvgu **Edge:** Lettered **Edge:** LATVIJAS REPUBLIKA
LATVIJAS BANKA

Date	Mintage	F	VF	XF	Unc	BU
1997 Proof	—	Value: 50.00				

KM# 20 100 LATU
13.3380 g., 0.5833 Gold 0.2501 oz. AGW **Subject:** 75th
Anniversary - Declaration of Independence **Obv:** National arms
Obv. Leg.: LATVIJAS - REPUBLIKA **Rev:** Artistic lined design
above value and dates

Date	Mintage	F	VF	XF	Unc	BU
ND(1993) Proof	5,000	Value: 350				

KM# 40 100 LATU
16.2000 g., 0.9990 Gold 0.5203 oz. AGW, 24 mm.
Subject: Development **Obv:** Arms with supporters **Rev:** Partial
circle within value **Edge:** Reeded and plain sections

Date	Mintage	F	VF	XF	Unc	BU
1998 Proof	—	Value: 525				

PATTERNS
Including off metal strikes

KM#	Date	Mintage Identification	Mkt Val
Pn1	1922	— 10 Santimu. Silver. KM4.	225
Pn2	1922	— 10 Santimu. Aluminum-Bronze. KM4.	300
Pn3	1924	— 2 Lati. Silver.	300
Pn4	1938	— 2 Santimi. Bronze. KM11.2	600

MINT SETS

KM#	Date	Mintage Identification	Issue Price	Mkt Val
MS1	1992 (8)	— KM12-17, 21-22	—	25.00

PROOF SETS

KM#	Date	Mintage Identification	Issue Price	Mkt Val
PS1	ND (1993) (3)	1,800 KM18-20	—	325

LEBANON

The Republic of Lebanon, situated on the eastern shore of the Mediterranean Sea between Syria and Israel, has an area of 4,015 sq. mi. (10,400 sq. km.) and a population of 3.5 million. Capital: Beirut. The economy is based on agriculture, trade and tourism. Fruit, other foodstuffs and textiles are exported.

Almost at the beginning of recorded history, Lebanon appeared as the well-wooded hinterland of the Phoenicians who exploited its famous forests of cedar. The mountains were a Christian refuge and a Crusader stronghold. Lebanon, the history of which is essentially the same as that of Syria, came under control of the Ottoman Turks early in the 16th century. Following the collapse of the Ottoman Empire after World War I, Lebanon, along with Syria, became a French mandate. The French drew a border around the predominantly Christian Lebanon *Sanjak* or administrative subdivision and on Sept. 1, 1920 proclaimed the area the State of Grand Lebanon (*Etat du Grand Liban*) a republic under French control. France announced the independence of Lebanon on Nov. 26, 1941, but the last British and French troops didn't leave until the end of August 1946.

TITLE

al-Jomhuriya(t) al-Lubnaniya(t)

MINT MARKS
(a) - Paris, privy marks only
(u) - Utrecht, privy marks only

MONETARY SYSTEM
100 Piastres = 1 Livre (Pound)

FRENCH PROTECTORATE

STANDARD COINAGE

KM# 9   1/2 PIASTRE
4.0000 g., Copper-Nickel, 21 mm. **Obv:** Value within sprigs above date **Rev:** Value within roped wreath flanked by oat sprigs above date

Date	Mintage	F	VF	XF	Unc	BU
1934(a)	200,000	2.00	5.00	12.50	40.00	—
1936(a)	1,200,000	1.25	3.00	7.50	25.00	—

KM# 9a   1/2 PIASTRE
Zinc **Obv:** Value within sprigs above date **Rev:** Value within roped wreath flanked by oat sprigs above date

Date	Mintage	F	VF	XF	Unc	BU
1941(a)	1,000,000	0.50	1.00	4.00	10.00	—

KM# 3   PIASTRE
5.0000 g., Copper-Nickel **Obv:** Hole in center of wreath **Rev:** Hole in center flanked by lion heads with value and dates below

Date	Mintage	F	VF	XF	Unc	BU
1925(a)	1,500,000	0.50	2.00	7.50	25.00	—
1931(a)	300,000	1.00	4.00	12.50	45.00	—
1933(a)	500,000	1.00	4.00	10.00	45.00	—
1936(a)	2,200,000	0.50	1.00	6.50	20.00	—

KM# 3a   PIASTRE
Zinc **Obv:** Hole in center of wreath **Rev:** Hole in center flanked by lion heads with value and date below

Date	Mintage	F	VF	XF	Unc	BU
1940(a)	2,000,000	0.75	1.50	4.00	12.00	—

KM# 1   2 PIASTRES
2.0000 g., Aluminum-Bronze **Obv:** Cedar tree within circle above date **Rev:** Value flanked by stars

Date	Mintage	F	VF	XF	Unc	BU
1924(a)	1,800,000	1.25	3.00	12.50	50.00	—

KM# 4   2 PIASTRES
2.0000 g., Aluminum-Bronze **Obv:** Cedar tree **Rev:** Ancient ship

Date	Mintage	F	VF	XF	Unc	BU
1925(a)	1,000,000	3.00	8.00	20.00	80.00	—

KM# 10   2-1/2 PIASTRES
Aluminum-Bronze **Obv:** Hole in center of wreath **Rev:** Hole in center of flowered wreath

Date	Mintage	F	VF	XF	Unc	BU
1940(a)	1,000,000	1.00	2.00	3.50	12.00	—

KM# 2   5 PIASTRES
Aluminum-Bronze **Obv:** Cedar tree within circle **Rev:** Value flanked by stars

Date	Mintage	F	VF	XF	Unc	BU
1924(a)	1,000,000	1.25	3.00	10.00	45.00	—

KM# 5.1   5 PIASTRES
Aluminum-Bronze **Obv:** Cedar tree **Rev:** Ancient ship above value and dates

Date	Mintage	F	VF	XF	Unc	BU
1925(a)	1,500,000	1.00	2.00	8.00	30.00	—

KM# 5.2   5 PIASTRES
4.1000 g., Aluminum-Bronze **Obv:** Cedar tree **Rev:** Privy marks to left and right of "5 Piastres"

Date	Mintage	F	VF	XF	Unc	BU
1925(a)	Inc. above	1.00	2.00	7.50	30.00	—
1931(a)	400,000	1.50	4.00	12.50	40.00	—
1933(a)	500,000	1.50	4.00	12.50	40.00	—
1936(a)	900,000	1.00	2.00	7.50	25.00	—
1940(a)	1,000,000	0.75	1.50	5.00	15.00	—

KM# 6   10 PIASTRES
2.0000 g., 0.6800 Silver 0.0437 oz. ASW **Obv:** Cedar tree on rectangular box **Rev:** Crossed cornucopia above value

Date	Mintage	F	VF	XF	Unc	BU
1929	880,000	3.00	7.00	25.00	70.00	—

KM# 7   25 PIASTRES
5.0000 g., 0.6800 Silver 0.1093 oz. ASW **Obv:** Cedar tree on rectangular box **Rev:** Crossed cornucopia above value

Date	Mintage	F	VF	XF	Unc	BU
1929	600,000	3.00	7.00	25.00	75.00	—
1933(a)	200,000	4.50	15.00	40.00	125	—
1936(a)	400,000	3.50	10.00	27.50	85.00	—

KM# 8   50 PIASTRES
10.0000 g., 0.6800 Silver 0.2186 oz. ASW **Obv:** Cedar tree on rectangular box **Rev:** Crossed cornucopia with value above and below

Date	Mintage	F	VF	XF	Unc	BU
1929	500,000	5.00	10.00	40.00	125	—
1933(a)	100,000	7.00	20.00	65.00	190	—
1936(a)	100,000	7.00	17.50	50.00	140	—

WORLD WAR II COINAGE

KM# 11   1/2 PIASTRE
2.1700 g., Brass **Obv:** Hole in center flanked by english value **Rev:** Hole in center flanked by value **Note:** Three varieties known. Usually crudely struck, off-center, etc. Perfectly struck, centered uncirculated specimens command a considerable premium. Finely struck coins appear with medal rotation while crude examples have coin rotation. Size of letters also vary.

Date	Mintage	F	VF	XF	Unc	BU
ND(1941)	—	1.00	2.50	5.00	12.00	—

KM# 12   PIASTRE
Brass **Obv:** English value **Rev:** Value **Note:** Two varieties known. Usually struck, off-center, etc. Perfectly struck, centered unc. specimens command a considerable premium.

Date	Mintage	F	VF	XF	Unc	BU
ND(1941)	—	1.00	3.00	7.50	18.00	—

KM# 12a   PIASTRE
Aluminum **Obv:** English value **Rev:** Value

Date	Mintage	F	VF	XF	Unc	BU
ND(1941)	—	—	—	—	—	—

KM# 13   2-1/2 PIASTRES
Aluminum **Obv:** English value **Rev:** Value **Note:** Seven varieties known. Usually crudely struck, off-center, etc. Perfectly struck, centered unc. specimens command a considerable premium.

Date	Mintage	F	VF	XF	Unc	BU
ND(1941)	—	1.50	3.50	8.00	22.00	—

KM# 13a 2-1/2 PIASTRES
Aluminum-Bronze **Obv:** English value **Rev:** Value

Date	Mintage	F	VF	XF	Unc	BU
ND(1941)	—	—	650	850	—	—

KM# A14 5 PIASTRES
Aluminum **Obv:** English value **Rev:** Value **Note:** Did not enter circulation in significant numbers.

Date	Mintage	F	VF	XF	Unc	BU
ND(1941)	—	—	—	2,000	3,000	—

REPUBLIC

STANDARD COINAGE

KM# 19 PIASTRE
2.0400 g., Aluminum-Bronze, 18 mm.

Date	Mintage	F	VF	XF	Unc	BU
1955(a)	4,000,000	—	0.25	0.75	2.00	3.00

KM# 20 2-1/2 PIASTRES
2.7000 g., Aluminum-Bronze, 20 mm. **Obv:** Hole in center of wreath flanked by value above **Rev:** Hole in center of wreath

Date	Mintage	F	VF	XF	Unc	BU
1955(a)	5,000,000	—	0.20	0.50	1.00	1.50

KM# 14 5 PIASTRES
Aluminum **Obv:** Cedar tree divides date **Rev:** Value below boat

Date	Mintage	F	VF	XF	Unc	BU
1952(a)	3,600,000	0.75	1.50	3.00	6.00	10.00

KM# 18 5 PIASTRES
Aluminum **Obv:** Cedar tree **Rev:** Wreath with value above and below

Date	Mintage	F	VF	XF	Unc	BU
1954	4,440,000	0.25	0.50	1.00	2.50	5.00

KM# 21 5 PIASTRES
2.8500 g., Aluminum-Bronze **Obv:** Cedar tree **Rev:** Lion head and value

Date	Mintage	F	VF	XF	Unc	BU
1955(a)	3,000,000	0.20	0.50	1.00	2.00	3.50
1961(a)	—	0.20	0.40	0.75	1.50	3.00

KM# 25.1 5 PIASTRES
Nickel-Brass, 18 mm. **Obv:** Cedar tree above date **Rev:** Value within wreath

Date	Mintage	F	VF	XF	Unc	BU
1968	2,000,000	—	0.10	0.15	0.20	0.45
1969	4,000,000	—	0.10	0.15	0.20	0.45
1970	—	—	0.10	0.15	0.25	0.50

KM# 25.2 5 PIASTRES
Nickel-Brass, 18 mm. **Obv:** Cedar tree above dates **Rev:** Value within wreath

Date	Mintage	F	VF	XF	Unc	BU
1972(a)	12,000,000	—	—	0.10	0.15	0.35
1975(a)	—	—	—	0.10	0.15	0.35
1980	—	—	—	0.10	0.15	0.35

KM# 15 10 PIASTRES
1.2700 g., Aluminum, 21.8 mm. **Obv:** Cedar tree above dates **Rev:** Lion head flanked by value

Date	Mintage	F	VF	XF	Unc	BU
1952(a)	3,600,000	0.75	1.50	5.00	15.00	25.00

KM# 22 10 PIASTRES
Aluminum-Bronze, 21.8 mm. **Obv:** Boat with sail above date **Rev:** Cedar tree above value

Date	Mintage	F	VF	XF	Unc	BU
1955	2,175,000	0.50	1.00	3.50	12.50	18.50

KM# 23 10 PIASTRES
Aluminum-Bronze, 21.8 mm. **Obv:** Boat with sail above date with value at upper left **Rev:** Cedar tree above date

Date	Mintage	F	VF	XF	Unc	BU
1955(a)	6,000,000	0.20	0.40	1.00	2.00	4.00

KM# 24 10 PIASTRES
Copper-Nickel, 21.8 mm. **Obv:** Boat with sail above date with value at upper left **Rev:** Cedar tree above date

Date	Mintage	F	VF	XF	Unc	BU
1961	7,000,000	—	0.15	0.35	1.00	2.00
1961 Proof	—					

KM# 26 10 PIASTRES
Nickel-Brass, 21.8 mm. **Obv:** Cedar tree above dates **Rev:** Value within wreath

Date	Mintage	F	VF	XF	Unc	BU
1968(a)	2,000,000	—	0.10	0.15	0.25	0.50
1969(a)	5,000,000	—	—	0.10	0.20	0.45
1970(a)	8,000,000	—	—	0.10	0.20	0.45
1972(a)	12,000,000	—	—	0.10	0.20	0.45
1975(a)	—	—	—	0.10	0.20	0.45

KM# 16.1 25 PIASTRES
Aluminum-Bronze, 23.3 mm. **Obv:** Cedar tree **Rev:** Value within rectangular box divides wreath and dates

Date	Mintage	F	VF	XF	Unc	BU
1952(u)	7,200,000	0.10	0.40	0.60	1.00	2.00

KM# 16.2 25 PIASTRES
Aluminum-Bronze, 23.3 mm. **Obv:** Cedar tree **Rev:** Value within rectangular box divides wreath and dates **Note:** Different style of inscription and larger date.

Date	Mintage	F	VF	XF	Unc	BU
1961(u)	5,000,000	0.10	0.40	0.50	0.75	1.50

KM# 27.1 25 PIASTRES
Nickel-Brass, 23.3 mm. **Obv:** Cedar tree above dates **Rev:** Value within wreath

Date	Mintage	F	VF	XF	Unc	BU
1968	1,500,000	0.10	0.15	0.25	0.50	1.00
1969	2,500,000	0.10	0.15	0.20	0.40	0.85
1970	—	0.10	0.15	0.20	0.40	0.85
1972	8,000,000	0.10	0.15	0.20	0.30	0.65
1975	—	0.10	0.15	0.20	0.30	0.65

KM# 27.2 25 PIASTRES
Nickel-Brass, 23.3 mm. **Obv:** Cedar tree above dates **Rev:** Value within wreath

Date	Mintage	F	VF	XF	Unc	BU
1980	—	0.10	0.15	0.20	0.30	0.65

KM# 17 50 PIASTRES
4.9710 g., 0.6000 Silver 0.0959 oz. ASW **Obv:** Cedar tree above dates **Rev:** Value within wreath

Date	Mintage	F	VF	XF	Unc	BU
1952(u)	7,200,000	—	BV	2.50	4.50	7.00

KM# 28.1 50 PIASTRES
Nickel **Obv:** Cedar tree above dates **Rev:** Value within wreath

Date	Mintage	F	VF	XF	Unc	BU
1968	2,000,000	0.20	0.40	0.60	1.00	2.00
1969	3,488,000	0.10	0.25	0.40	0.75	1.50
1970	2,000,000	0.10	0.25	0.40	0.50	1.00
1971	2,000,000	0.10	0.25	0.40	0.50	1.00
1975	—	0.10	0.25	0.40	0.50	1.00
1978	22,400,000	0.10'	0.25	0.40	0.50	1.00

KM# 28.2 50 PIASTRES
Nickel **Obv:** Cedar tree above dates **Rev:** Value within wreath

Date	Mintage	F	VF	XF	Unc	BU
1980	—	0.10	0.25	0.40	0.50	1.00

KM# 29 LIVRE
Nickel **Series:** F.A.O. **Obv:** Cedar tree above dates **Rev:** Cluster of fruit above value

Date	Mintage	F	VF	XF	Unc	BU
1968	300,000	0.35	0.75	1.50	3.50	6.00

KM# 30 LIVRE
7.2000 g., Nickel, 27.3 mm. **Obv:** Cedar tree above dates
Rev: Value within wreath **Note:** Varieties exist.

Date	Mintage	F	VF	XF	Unc	BU
1975	—	0.20	0.40	0.60	1.00	2.00
1975 Proof						
1977	8,000,000	0.20	0.40	0.60	1.00	2.00
1980	12,000,000	0.20	0.40	0.60	1.00	2.00
1981	—	0.20	0.40	0.60	1.00	2.00

KM# 32 LIVRE
Copper-Nickel **Series:** 1980 Winter Olympics **Subject:** Lake Placid

Date	Mintage	F	VF	XF	Unc	BU
1980 Proof	40,000	Value: 20.00				

KM# 30a LIVRE
Nickel Clad Steel, 27.3 mm. **Obv:** Cedar tree above dates
Rev: Value within wreath **Note:** Varieties exist.

Date	Mintage	F	VF	XF	Unc	BU
1986	—	0.20	0.40	0.60	1.00	2.00

KM# 31 5 LIVRES
Nickel **Series:** F.A.O. **Obv:** Cedar tree above dates **Rev:** Cluster of fruit below radiant sun and value

Date	Mintage	F	VF	XF	Unc	BU
1978	1,000,000	—	—	—	3.00	5.00

KM# 33 10 LIVRES
19.0000 g., 0.5000 Silver 0.3054 oz. ASW **Series:** 1980 Winter Olympics **Subject:** Lake Placid **Obv:** Olympic rings on top of design **Rev:** Styilized flame

Date	Mintage	F	VF	XF	Unc	BU
1980 Proof	20,000	Value: 65.00				

KM# 35 10 LIVRES
Copper-Nickel **Series:** World Food Day **Obv:** Cédar tree above dates **Rev:** Man, oxen, radiant sun and value

Date	Mintage	F	VF	XF	Unc	BU
1981	15,000	—	—	—	8.50	11.50

KM# 37 50 LIVRES
2.2900 g., Stainless Steel, 18.35 mm. **Obv:** Arabic legend above large value on cedar tree within circle **Rev:** Large value "50" within circle **Rev. Leg.:** BANQUE DU LIBAN **Edge:** Plain

Date	Mintage	F	VF	XF	Unc	BU
1996	—	—	—	0.50	1.20	1.80

KM# 38 100 LIVRES
4.0000 g., Brass **Obv:** Arabic legend above large value on cedar tree **Rev:** Two banners above large value "100" **Rev. Leg.:** BANQUE DU LIBAN **Edge:** Plain

Date	Mintage	F	VF	XF	Unc	BU
1995	—	—	—	0.65	1.50	2.00
1995 Proof	—	Value: 4.00				
1996	—	—	—	0.65	1.50	2.00
2000	—	—	—	0.65	1.50	2.00

KM# 36 250 LIVRES
5.3000 g., Aluminum-Nickel-Bronze, 23.45 mm. **Obv:** Arabic legend above large value on cedar tree **Rev:** Large value "250", eliptical border design **Rev. Leg.:** BANQUE DU LIBAN **Rev. Insc.:** Small "BANQUE DU LIBAN" repeated in center **Edge:** Reeded

Date	Mintage	F	VF	XF	Unc	BU
1995	—	—	—	0.75	1.85	2.50
1995 Proof	—	Value: 5.00				
1996	—	—	—	0.75	1.85	2.50
2000	—	—	—	0.75	1.85	2.50

KM# 34 400 LIVRES
8.0000 g., 0.9000 Gold 0.2315 oz. AGW **Series:** 1980 Winter Olympics **Subject:** Lake Placid **Obv:** Olympic rings on top of design **Rev:** Stylized flame

Date	Mintage	F	VF	XF	Unc	BU
1980 Proof	1,000	Value: 600				

KM# 39 500 LIVRES
6.0600 g., Nickel Clad Steel, 24.47 mm. **Obv:** Arabic legend above large value on cedar tree **Rev:** Large value "500", thick segmented circular border **Rev. Leg.:** BANQUE DU LIBAN **Edge:** Plain

Date	Mintage	F	VF	XF	Unc	BU
1995	—	—	—	0.90	2.25	3.00
1995 Proof	—	Value: 6.00				
1996	—	—	—	0.90	2.25	3.00
2000	—	—	—	0.90	2.25	3.00

ESSAIS
Standard metals unless otherwise noted

KM#	Date	Mintage	Identification	Mkt Val
E1	1924(a)	—	5 Piastres. Aluminum-Bronze. KM2.	100
E2	1925(a)	—	Piastre. Copper-Nickel. KM3.	80.00
E3	1925(a)	—	2 Piastres. Aluminum-Bronze. KM1.	110
E4	1925(a)	—	5 Piastres. Aluminum-Bronze. KM5.1.	90.00
E5	1929(a)	—	Piastre. Copper-Nickel. KM3.	90.00
E6	1929	—	10 Piastres. Silver. KM6.	120
E7	1929	—	25 Piastres. Silver. KM7.	125
E8	1929	—	50 Piastres. Silver. KM8.	125
E9	1934 A	—	1/2 Piastre. Copper-Nickel. Value within sprigs above date. Value within roped circle flanked by sprigs above date. KM9.	100
E10	1940(a)	—	2-1/2 Piastres. Aluminum-Bronze. KM10.	50.00
E11	1972	—	5 Piastres. Nickel-Brass. KM25.	15.00
E12	1972(a)	—	10 Piastres. Nickel-Brass. KM26.	15.00
E13	1980	—	25 Piastres. Nickel-Brass. KM27.	15.00
E14	1980	—	50 Piastres. Nickel. KM28.	17.50
E15	1980	—	Livre. Nickel. KM30.	20.00
E16	1981	—	10 Livres. Copper-Nickel. KM35.	40.00

PIEFORTS

KM#	Date	Mintage	Identification	Mkt Val
P1	1980	3,000	Livre. Copper-Nickel. KM32.	45.00
P2	1980	3,000	10 Livres. Silver. KM33.	120
P3	1980	750	400 Livres. Gold. KM34.	1,400

PROOF SETS

KM#	Date	Mintage	Identification	Issue Price	Mkt Val
PS1	1995 (3)	—	KM#36, 38, 39	—	15.00

LESOTHO

The Kingdom of Lesotho, a constitutional monarchy located within the east-central part of the Republic of South Africa, has an area of 11,720 sq. mi. (30,350 sq. km.) and a population of 1.5 million. Capital: Maseru. The economy is based on subsistence agriculture and livestock raising. Wool, mohair, and cattle are exported.

Lesotho (formerly Basutoland) was sparsely populated until the end of the 16th century. Between the 16th and 19th centuries an influx of refugees from tribal wars led to the development of a distinct Basotho group. During the reign of tribal chief Mashoeshoe I (1823-70), a series of wars with the Orange Free State resulted in the loss of large areas of territory to South Africa. Mashoeshoe appealed to the British for help, and Basutoland was constituted a native state under British protection. In 1871 it was annexed to Cape Colony, but was restored to direct control by the Crown in 1884. From 1884 to 1959 legislative and executive authority was vested in a British High Commissioner. The constitution of 1959 recognized the expressed wish of the people for independence, which was attained on Oct.4, 1966.

Lesotho is a member of the Commonwealth of Nations. The king is Head of State.

RULERS
Moshoeshoe II, 1966-1990
Letsie III, 1990-1995
Moshoeshoe II, 1995-

MONETARY SYSTEM
100 Licente/Lisente = 1 Maloti/Loti

KINGDOM
STANDARD COINAGE
100 Licente/Lisente = 1 Maloti/Loti

KM# 16 SENTE
1.5000 g., Nickel-Brass, 16.5 mm. **Ruler:** Moshoeshoe II **Obv:** Uniformed bust 1/4 left **Rev:** Basotho hat and value

Date	Mintage	F	VF	XF	Unc	BU
1979	4,500,000	—	—	0.15	0.40	0.60
1979 Proof	10,000	Value: 0.65				
1980	—	—	—	0.15	0.40	0.60
1980 Proof	10,000	Value: 0.65				
1981 Proof	2,500	Value: 0.65				
1983	—	—	—	0.15	0.40	0.60
1985	—	—	—	0.15	0.40	0.60
1989	—	—	—	0.15	0.40	0.60

KM# 54 SENTE
Brass, 16.5 mm. **Ruler:** Letsie III **Obv:** Arms with supporters **Rev:** Basotho hat and value

Date	Mintage	F	VF	XF	Unc	BU
1992	—	—	—	0.15	0.75	1.00

KM# 54a SENTE
1.3900 g., Brass Plated Steel, 16.5 mm. **Ruler:** Letsie III **Obv:** Arms with supporters **Rev:** Traditional house and value

Date	Mintage	F	VF	XF	Unc	BU
1992						

KM# 17   2 LISENTE
2.5000 g., Nickel-Brass, 19.5 mm. **Ruler:** Moshoeshoe II
Obv: Uniformed bust 1/4 left **Rev:** Steer and value

Date	Mintage	F	VF	XF	Unc	BU
1979	3,000,000	—	—	0.20	0.50	0.75
1979 Proof	10,000	Value: 1.00				
1980	—	—	—	0.20	0.50	0.75
1980 Proof	10,000	Value: 1.00				
1981 Proof	2,500	Value: 2.00				
1985	—	—	—	0.20	0.50	0.75
1989	—	—	—	0.20	0.50	0.75

KM# 55   2 LISENTE
Brass, 19.5 mm. **Ruler:** Letsie III **Obv:** Arms with supporters
Rev: Bull and value

Date	Mintage	F	VF	XF	Unc	BU
1992	—	—	—	0.20	0.75	1.00

KM# 55a   2 LISENTE
2.2500 g., Brass Plated Steel, 19.5 mm. **Ruler:** Letsie III
Obv: Arms with supporters **Rev:** Bull and value **Edge:** Plain

Date	Mintage	F	VF	XF	Unc	BU
1992	—	—	—	0.20	0.75	1.00

KM# 1   5 LICENTE (Lisente)
2.8900 g., 0.9000 Silver 0.0836 oz. ASW **Ruler:** Moshoeshoe II
Subject: Independence attained **Obv:** Native bust right
Rev: Arms with supporters above value flanked by stars

Date	Mintage	F	VF	XF	Unc	BU
1966 Proof	5,000	Value: 6.00				

KM# 18   5 LICENTE (Lisente)
4.0000 g., Nickel-Brass, 23.25 mm. **Ruler:** Moshoeshoe II
Obv: Uniformed bust 1/4 left **Rev:** Single pine tree among hills,
grass and value

Date	Mintage	F	VF	XF	Unc	BU
1979	2,700,000	—	—	0.25	0.60	0.85
1979 Proof	10,000	Value: 1.25				
1980	—	—	—	0.25	0.60	0.85
1980 Proof	10,000	Value: 1.25				
1981	—	—	—	0.25	0.60	0.85
1981 Proof	2,500	Value: 2.50				
1989	—	—	—	0.25	0.60	0.85

KM# 56   5 LICENTE (Lisente)
Brass, 23.25 mm. **Ruler:** Letsie III **Obv:** Arms with supporters
Rev: Single pine tree among grass, hills and value

Date	Mintage	F	VF	XF	Unc	BU
1994	—	—	—	0.25	0.60	0.85

KM# 62   5 LICENTE (Lisente)
1.6400 g., Brass Plated Steel, 15 mm. **Ruler:** Letsie III
Obv: Arms with supporters **Rev:** Single pine tree among grass,
hills and value

Date	Mintage	F	VF	XF	Unc	BU
1998	—	—	—	0.25	0.60	0.85

KM# 2   10 LICENTE (Lisente)
5.6800 g., 0.9000 Silver 0.1643 oz. ASW **Ruler:** Moshoeshoe II
Subject: Independence Attained **Obv:** Native bust right
Rev: Arms with supporters above value flanked by stars

Date	Mintage	F	VF	XF	Unc	BU
1966 Proof	5,000	Value: 6.00				

KM# 19   10 LICENTE (Lisente)
2.0000 g., Copper-Nickel, 18.35 mm. **Ruler:** Moshoeshoe II
Obv: Uniformed bust 1/4 left **Rev:** Angora goat

Date	Mintage	F	VF	XF	Unc	BU
1979	2,000,000	—	—	0.15	0.30	1.00	1.50
1979 Proof	10,000	Value: 1.75				
1980	—	—	—	0.15	0.30	1.00	1.50
1980 Proof	10,000	Value: 1.75				
1981 Proof	2,500	Value: 3.00				
1983	—	—	—	0.15	0.30	1.00	1.50
1989	—	—	—	0.15	0.30	1.00	1.50

KM# 61   10 LICENTE (Lisente)
2.0000 g., Copper-Nickel, 18.35 mm. **Ruler:** Letsie III
Obv: Arms with supporters **Rev:** Angora goat

Date	Mintage	F	VF	XF	Unc	BU
1992	—	—	—	—	1.00	1.50

KM# 63   10 LICENTE (Lisente)
1.9600 g., Brass Plated Steel, 16 mm. **Ruler:** Moshoeshoe II
Obv: Arms with supporters **Rev:** Angora goat

Date	Mintage	F	VF	XF	Unc	BU
1998	—	—	—	—	1.00	1.50

KM# 3.1   20 LICENTE
11.2800 g., 0.9000 Silver 0.3264 oz. ASW **Ruler:** Moshoeshoe II
Subject: Independence Attained **Obv:** Native bust right **Rev:** Small
900/1000 at right of date

Date	Mintage	F	VF	XF	Unc	BU
1966 Proof	5,000	Value: 15.00				

KM# 3.2   20 LICENTE
11.2800 g., 0.9000 Silver 0.3264 oz. ASW **Ruler:** Moshoeshoe II
Subject: Independence Attained **Obv:** Native bust right **Rev:** Large
900/1000 at right of date

Date	Mintage	F	VF	XF	Unc	BU
1966 Proof	—	Value: 15.00				

KM# 64   20 LICENTE
2.6700 g., Brass Plated Steel, 18 mm. **Ruler:** Moshoeshoe II
Obv: Arms with supporters **Rev:** Flora

Date	Mintage	F	VF	XF	Unc	BU
1998	—	—	—	—	0.75	1.00

KM# 20   25 LISENTE
3.5000 g., Copper-Nickel, 21.7 mm. **Ruler:** Moshoeshoe II
Obv: Uniformed bust 1/4 left **Rev:** Woman in native costume
weaving baskets

Date	Mintage	F	VF	XF	Unc	BU
1979	1,200,000	—	0.10	0.20	1.00	1.25
1979 Proof	10,000	Value: 2.00				
1980	—	—	0.10	0.20	1.00	1.25
1980 Proof	10,000	Value: 2.00				
1981 Proof	2,500	Value: 3.50				
1985	—	—	0.10	0.20	1.00	1.25
1989	—	—	0.10	0.20	1.00	1.25

KM# 4.1   50 LICENTE (Lisente)
28.1000 g., 0.9000 Silver 0.8131 oz. ASW, 35 mm.
Ruler: Moshoeshoe II **Subject:** Independence Attained
Obv: Native bust right **Rev:** 900/1000 to right of date

Date	Mintage	F	VF	XF	Unc	BU
1966	17,500	—	—	—	16.00	18.00
1966 Proof	Inc. above	Value: 25.00				

KM# 4.2   50 LICENTE (Lisente)
28.1000 g., 0.9000 Silver 0.8131 oz. ASW **Ruler:** Moshoeshoe II
Subject: Independence Attained **Obv:** Native bust right **Rev:** Large
900/1000 to right of date

Date	Mintage	F	VF	XF	Unc	BU
1966	—	—	—	—	16.00	18.00
1966 Proof	5,000	Value: 25.00				

KM# 4.3   50 LICENTE (Lisente)
28.1000 g., 0.9000 Silver 0.8131 oz. ASW **Ruler:** Moshoeshoe II
Subject: Independence Attained **Obv:** Native bust right **Rev:** Mint
mark and fineness below date

Date	Mintage	F	VF	XF	Unc	BU
1966	—	—	—	—	16.00	18.00
1966 Proof	—	Value: 25.00				

KM# 21   50 LICENTE (Lisente)
5.5000 g., Copper-Nickel, 25.5 mm. **Ruler:** Moshoeshoe II
Obv: Uniformed bust 1/4 left **Rev:** Equestrian and value

Date	Mintage	F	VF	XF	Unc	BU
1979	480,000	—	0.35	0.50	1.25	1.50
1979 Proof	10,000	Value: 2.50				
1980	—	—	0.35	0.50	1.25	1.50
1980 Proof	10,000	Value: 2.50				
1981 Proof	2,500	Value: 4.00				
1983	—	—	0.35	0.50	1.25	1.50
1989	—	—	0.35	0.50	1.25	1.50

KM# 65   50 LICENTE (Lisente)
3.4000 g., Brass Plated Steel, 20 mm. **Ruler:** Moshoeshoe II

Date	Mintage	F	VF	XF	Unc	BU
1998	—	—	—	—	1.00	1.25

KM# 5   LOTI
3.9940 g., 0.9170 Gold 0.1177 oz. AGW **Ruler:** Moshoeshoe II
Subject: Independence Attained **Obv:** Native bust right
Rev: Arms with supporters above value flanked by stars

Date	Mintage	F	VF	XF	Unc	BU
1966 Proof	3,500	Value: 125				

KM# 8   LOTI
3.9940 g., 0.9170 Gold 0.1177 oz. AGW **Ruler:** Moshoeshoe II
Series: F.A.O. **Obv:** Native bust right **Rev:** Equestrian

Date	Mintage	F	VF	XF	Unc	BU
1969 Proof	3,000	Value: 125				

KM# 22   LOTI
11.3000 g., Copper-Nickel, 28.5 mm. **Ruler:** Moshoeshoe II
Obv: Uniformed bust 1/4 left **Rev:** Value at left of arms with
supporters

Date	Mintage	F	VF	XF	Unc	BU
1979	1,275,000	—	0.65	1.25	3.00	3.50
1979 Proof	10,000	Value: 5.00				
1980	—	—	0.75	1.50	4.00	4.50
1980 Proof	10,000	Value: 5.00				
1981 Proof	2,500	Value: 7.00				
1989	—	—	0.75	1.50	4.00	4.50

KM# 46   LOTI
11.3100 g., 0.9250 Silver 0.3363 oz. ASW **Ruler:** Moshoeshoe II
Subject: Silver Jubilee of King Moshoeshoe II **Obv:** Uniformed bust
1/4 left **Rev:** Crown above arms with supporters flanked by dates

Date	Mintage	F	VF	XF	Unc	BU
1985 Proof	2,500	Value: 17.50				

KM# 46a   LOTI
18.9800 g., 0.9170 Gold 0.5595 oz. AGW **Ruler:** Moshoeshoe II
Subject: Silver Jubilee of King Moshoeshoe II **Obv:** Uniformed bust
1/4 left **Rev:** Crown above arms with supporters flanked by dates

Date	Mintage	F	VF	XF	Unc	BU
1985 Proof	500	Value: 550				

KM# 60   LOTI
Copper-Nickel **Ruler:** Letsie III **Series:** 50th Anniversary - UN

Date	Mintage	F	VF	XF	Unc	BU
1995	—	—	—	—	8.00	9.00

KM# 66   LOTI
3.8800 g., Nickel-Plated Steel, 21 mm. **Ruler:** Letsie III **Obv:**
Native seated right **Rev:** Value at left of arms with supporters

Date	Mintage	F	VF	XF	Unc	BU
1998	—	—	—	—	1.50	2.00

KM# 6   2 MALOTI
7.9880 g., 0.9170 Gold 0.2355 oz. AGW **Ruler:** Moshoeshoe II
Obv: Native bust right **Rev:** Arms with supporters above value
flanked by stars

Date	Mintage	F	VF	XF	Unc	BU
1966 Proof	—	Value: 225				

KM# 9   2 MALOTI
7.9880 g., 0.9170 Gold 0.2355 oz. AGW **Ruler:** Moshoeshoe II
Series: F.A.O. **Obv:** Native bust right **Rev:** Figure on horseback left

Date	Mintage	F	VF	XF	Unc	BU
1969 Proof	3,000	Value: 235				

KM# 58   2 MALOTI
4.4900 g., Nickel-Clad Steel, 22 mm. **Ruler:** Moshoeshoe II
Obv: Arms with supporters **Rev:** Maize plants

Date	Mintage	F	VF	XF	Unc	BU
1996	—	—	—	—	2.50	3.00
1998	—	—	—	—	2.00	2.50

KM# 7   4 MALOTI
15.9760 g., 0.9170 Gold 0.4710 oz. AGW **Ruler:** Moshoeshoe II
Obv: Native bust right **Rev:** Arms with supporters above value
flanked by stars

Date	Mintage	F	VF	XF	Unc	BU
1966 Proof	3,500	Value: 465				

KM# 10   4 MALOTI
15.9760 g., 0.9170 Gold 0.4710 oz. AGW **Ruler:** Moshoeshoe II
Series: F.A.O. **Obv:** Native bust right **Rev:** Figure on horseback left

Date	Mintage	F	VF	XF	Unc	BU
1969 Proof	3,000	Value: 465				

KM# 67   5 MALOTI
5.4600 g., Bi-Metallic Copper-Nickel center in Brass ring,
24 mm. **Ruler:** Moshoeshoe II **Obv:** National arms **Rev:** UN
logo **Note:** 50th Anniversary of UN

Date	Mintage Mintage	F	VF	XF	Unc
1995	—	—	—	—	12.50	15.00

KM# 59   5 MALOTI
6.3700 g., Nickel-Clad Steel, 25 mm. **Ruler:** Moshoeshoe II
Obv: Arms with supporters **Rev:** Wheat sprigs and value

Date	Mintage	F	VF	XF	Unc	BU
1996	—	—	—	—	5.50	6.00
1998	—	—	—	—	4.50	5.00

KM# 11   10 MALOTI
39.9400 g., 0.9170 Gold 1.1775 oz. AGW **Ruler:** Moshoeshoe II
Series: F.A.O. **Obv:** Arms with supporters **Rev:** Farmer leading
two oxen

Date	Mintage	F	VF	XF	Unc	BU
1969 Proof	3,000	Value: 1,200				

KM# 13   10 MALOTI
25.0800 g., 0.9250 Silver 0.7458 oz. ASW **Ruler:** Moshoeshoe II
Subject: 10th Anniversary of Independence **Obv:** Uniformed bust
1/4 left divides dates **Rev:** Kneeling oriental woman with pottery
within circle

Date	Mintage	F	VF	XF	Unc	BU
1976	2,300	—	—	—	20.00	25.00
1976 Proof	2,100	Value: 30.00				

KM# 23   10 MALOTI
28.2800 g., 0.9250 Silver 0.8410 oz. ASW **Ruler:** Moshoeshoe II
Subject: Monument of King Moshoeshoe I **Obv:** Uniformed bust
1/4 left **Rev:** Native seated right

Date	Mintage	F	VF	XF	Unc	BU
1979	10,000	—	—	—	15.00	17.50
1979 Proof	5,000	Value: 20.00				

KM# 23a   10 MALOTI
12.0000 g., 0.5000 Silver 0.1929 oz. ASW **Ruler:** Moshoeshoe II
Subject: Monument of King Moshoeshoe I **Obv:** Uniformed bust
1/4 left **Rev:** Native seated right

Date	Mintage	F	VF	XF	Unc	BU
1980	10,000	—	—	—	10.00	12.00
1980 Proof	5,000	Value: 15.00				

KM# 24   10 MALOTI
28.2800 g., 0.9250 Silver 0.8410 oz. ASW   **Ruler:** Moshoeshoe II
Series: International Year of the Child **Obv:** Arms with supporters
Rev: Busts of 3 children facing, logo below **Note:** Similar to 15
Maloti, KM#25.

Date	Mintage	F	VF	XF	Unc	BU
1979 (1981)	—	—	—	—	12.00	13.50
1979 (1981) Proof	37,000	Value: 15.00				

KM# 32   10 MALOTI
23.3300 g., 0.9250 Silver 0.6938 oz. ASW   **Ruler:** Moshoeshoe II
Subject: World Soccer Championship **Obv:** Arms with supporters
Rev: Goalie in front of net

Date	Mintage	F	VF	XF	Unc	BU
1982 Proof	3,582	Value: 27.50				

KM# 34   10 MALOTI
23.3300 g., 0.9250 Silver 0.6938 oz. ASW   **Ruler:** Moshoeshoe II
Subject: World Soccer Championship **Obv:** Arms with supporters
Rev: Soccer players

Date	Mintage	F	VF	XF	Unc	BU
1982 Proof	3,000	Value: 27.50				

KM# 40   10 MALOTI
31.1000 g., 0.5000 Silver 0.4999 oz. ASW   **Ruler:** Moshoeshoe II
Subject: George Washington **Obv:** Arms with supporters **Rev:**
Bust left

Date	Mintage	F	VF	XF	Unc	BU
1982 Proof	7,355	Value: 20.00				

KM# 41   10 MALOTI
31.1000 g., 0.5000 Silver 0.4999 oz. ASW   **Ruler:** Moshoeshoe II
Subject: George Washington **Obv:** Arms with supporters
Rev: Washington on bended knee

Date	Mintage	F	VF	XF	Unc	BU
1982 Proof	4,200	Value: 24.00				

KM# 42   10 MALOTI
31.1000 g., 0.5000 Silver 0.4999 oz. ASW   **Ruler:** Moshoeshoe II
Subject: George Washington **Obv:** Arms with supporters
Rev: Washington crossing the Delaware

Date	Mintage	F	VF	XF	Unc	BU
1982 Proof	Est. 15,000	Value: 17.50				

KM# 49   10 MALOTI
23.3300 g., 0.9250 Silver 0.6938 oz. ASW   **Ruler:** Moshoeshoe II
Subject: Decade for Women **Obv:** Uniformed bust 1/4 left
Rev: Half-figure of woman with basket on head left

Date	Mintage	F	VF	XF	Unc	BU
1985 Proof	1,000	Value: 45.00				

KM# 50   10 MALOTI
28.2800 g., 0.9250 Silver 0.8410 oz. ASW   **Ruler:** Moshoeshoe II
Subject: Papal visit **Obv:** Arms with supporters **Rev:** Bust left

Date	Mintage	F	VF	XF	Unc	BU
1988 Proof	Est. 15,000	Value: 45.00				

KM# 25   15 MALOTI
33.4000 g., 0.9250 Silver 0.9933 oz. ASW   **Ruler:** Moshoeshoe II
Series: International Year of the Child **Obv:** Arms with supporters
Rev: Busts of 3 children facing, logo below

Date	Mintage	F	VF	XF	Unc	BU
1979	18,000	—	—	—	20.00	22.00
1979 Proof	7,500	Value: 25.00				

KM# 53   15 MALOTI
12.0000 g., 0.5000 Silver 0.1929 oz. ASW   **Ruler:** Moshoeshoe II
Subject: 15th Anniversary of Independence **Obv:** Uniformed bust
1/4 left **Rev:** Eagle with ribbon in talons

Date	Mintage	F	VF	XF	Unc	BU
1981 Proof	2,500	Value: 40.00				

KM# 12   20 MALOTI
79.8810 g., 0.9170 Gold 2.3550 oz. AGW   **Ruler:** Moshoeshoe II
Series: F.A.O. **Obv:** Arms with supporters **Rev:** Grazing ewe
and lamb

Date	Mintage	F	VF	XF	Unc	BU
1969 Proof	3,000	Value: 2,350				

KM# 35   25 MALOTI
16.8200 g., 0.9250 Silver 0.5002 oz. ASW   **Ruler:** Moshoeshoe II
Obv: Arms with supporters **Rev:** Bust left

Date	Mintage	F	VF	XF	Unc	BU
1981 Proof	5,000	Value: 35.00				

KM# 44   25 MALOTI
28.2800 g., 0.9250 Silver 0.8410 oz. ASW   **Ruler:** Moshoeshoe II
Series: International Year of Disabled Persons **Obv:** Arms with
supporters **Rev:** Inscription and disabled emblem divides map within
circled grid

Date	Mintage	F	VF	XF	Unc	BU
1983	—	—	—	—	32.50	37.50
1983 Proof	—	Value: 55.00				

KM# 30   30 MALOTI
0.9250 Silver   **Ruler:** Moshoeshoe II **Subject:** Wedding of Prince
Charles and Lady Diana

Date	Mintage	F	VF	XF	Unc	BU
1981 Proof	10,000	Value: 47.50				

KM# 14   50 MALOTI

4.5000 g., 0.9000 Gold 0.1302 oz. AGW **Ruler:** Moshoeshoe II
Subject: 10th Anniversary of Independence **Obv:** Arms with supporters within circle **Rev:** Young bust right divides dates

Date	Mintage	F	VF	XF	Unc	BU
ND(1976)	700	—	—	—	155	165
ND(1976) Proof	1,910	Value: 140				

KM# 27   50 MALOTI

33.6200 g., 0.9250 Silver 0.9998 oz. ASW **Ruler:** Moshoeshoe II
Subject: 110th Anniversary - Death of King Moshoeshoe I
Obv: Arms with supporters **Rev:** Hat within diamond at center, corn ear at left, alligator at right

Date	Mintage	F	VF	XF	Unc	BU
1980	2,500	—	—	—	30.00	35.00
1980 Proof	1,400	Value: 65.00				

KM# 38   50 MALOTI

33.6200 g., 0.9250 Silver 0.9998 oz. ASW **Ruler:** Moshoeshoe II
Subject: 15th Anniversary of Commonwealth Membership
Obv: Arms with supporters **Rev:** Crowned bust right

Date	Mintage	F	VF	XF	Unc	BU
1981 Proof	5,000	Value: 60.00				

KM# 15   100 MALOTI

9.0000 g., 0.9000 Gold 0.2604 oz. AGW **Ruler:** Moshoeshoe II
Subject: 10th Anniversary of Independence **Obv:** Uniformed bust 1/4 left divides dates **Rev:** Equestrian and value within circle

Date	Mintage	F	VF	XF	Unc	BU
ND(1976)	450	—	—	—	285	300
ND(1976) Proof	1,410	Value: 260				

KM# 45   200 MALOTI

15.9800 g., 0.9000 Gold 0.4624 oz. AGW **Ruler:** Moshoeshoe II
Series: International Year of Disabled Persons **Obv:** Arms with supporters **Rev:** Disabled persons design within circle

Date	Mintage	F	VF	XF	Unc	BU
1983	500	—	—	—	425	435
1983 Proof	500	Value: 450				

KM# 26   250 MALOTI

33.9300 g., 0.9170 Gold 1.0003 oz. AGW **Ruler:** Moshoeshoe II
Series: International Year of the Child **Obv:** Native bust right
Rev: Busts of 3 children facing with logo below

Date	Mintage	F	VF	XF	Unc	BU
1979	2,500	—	—	—	950	975
1979 Proof	2,000	Value: 1,000				

KM# 28   250 MALOTI

31.1000 g., 0.9170 Gold 0.9169 oz. AGW **Ruler:** Moshoeshoe II
Subject: 110th Anniversary - Death of King Moshoeshoe I
Obv: Native bust right **Rev:** Hat within diamond at center, corn ear at left, alligator at right

Date	Mintage	F	VF	XF	Unc	BU
1980	1,500	—	—	—	875	900
1980 Proof	3,000	Value: 925				

KM# 36a   250 MALOTI

15.7500 g., 0.9950 Platinum 0.5038 oz. APW
Ruler: Moshoeshoe II **Subject:** Duke of Edinburgh Youth Awards **Obv:** Arms with supporters **Rev:** Bust left

Date	Mintage	F	VF	XF	Unc	BU
1981 Proof	200	Value: 950				

KM# 33   250 MALOTI

7.1300 g., 0.9000 Gold 0.2063 oz. AGW **Ruler:** Moshoeshoe II
Subject: Soccer Games **Obv:** Arms with supporters **Rev:** Goalie

Date	Mintage	F	VF	XF	Unc	BU
1982 Proof	551	Value: 250				

KM# 51   250 MALOTI

15.9800 g., 0.9170 Gold 0.4711 oz. AGW **Ruler:** Moshoeshoe II
Subject: Papal Visit **Obv:** Bust left **Rev:** Arms with supporters

Date	Mintage	F	VF	XF	Unc	BU
1988 Proof	Est. 750	Value: 500				

KM# 29   500 MALOTI

33.9300 g., 0.9170 Gold 1.0003 oz. AGW **Ruler:** Moshoeshoe II
Subject: 110th Anniversary - Death of King Moshoeshoe I
Obv: Native bust right **Rev:** Hat within diamond at center, corn ear at left, alligator at right

Date	Mintage	F	VF	XF	Unc	BU
1980	1,500	—	—	—	950	975
1980 Proof	3,000	Value: 1,000				

KM# 39   500 MALOTI

33.9300 g., 0.9170 Gold 1.0003 oz. AGW **Ruler:** Moshoeshoe II
Subject: 15th Anniversary of Commonwealth Membership
Obv: Arms with supporters **Rev:** Crowned bust right

Date	Mintage	F	VF	XF	Unc	BU
1981 Proof	500	Value: 1,000				

KM# 31   250 MALOTI

15.9000 g., 0.9170 Gold 0.4687 oz. AGW **Ruler:** Moshoeshoe II
Subject: Wedding of Prince Charles and Lady Diana
Rev: Conjoined busts left

Date	Mintage	F	VF	XF	Unc	BU
1981	1,000	—	—	—	450	475
1981 Proof	1,500	Value: 500				

KM# 31a   250 MALOTI

15.7500 g., 0.9950 Platinum 0.5038 oz. APW
Ruler: Moshoeshoe II **Subject:** Wedding of Prince Charles and Lady Diana **Obv:** Arms with supporters **Rev:** Conjoined busts left

Date	Mintage	F	VF	XF	Unc	BU
1981 Proof	200	Value: 950				

KM# 36   250 MALOTI

16.9600 g., 0.9170 Gold 0.5000 oz. AGW **Ruler:** Moshoeshoe II
Subject: Duke of Edinburgh Youth Awards **Obv:** Arms with supporters **Rev:** Bust left

Date	Mintage	F	VF	XF	Unc	BU
1981 Proof	1,500	Value: 475				

KM# 39a 500 MALOTI
31.5000 g., 0.9950 Platinum 1.0076 oz. APW
Ruler: Moshoeshoe II **Subject:** 15th Anniversary of
Commonwealth Membership **Obv:** Arms with supporters
Rev: Crowned bust right

Date	Mintage	F	VF	XF	Unc	BU
1981 Proof	200	Value: 1,850				

KM# 57 500 MALOTI
33.9300 g., 0.9166 Gold 0.9999 oz. AGW **Ruler:** Moshoeshoe II
Subject: Royal Wedding of Prince Charles and Lady Diana **Obv:**
Arms with supporters **Rev:** Conjoined busts left

Date	Mintage	F	VF	XF	Unc	BU
ND(1981) Proof, rare	—	—	—	—	—	—

KM# 57a 500 MALOTI
33.4800 g., 0.9995 Platinum 1.0758 oz. APW **Ruler:**
Moshoeshoe II **Subject:** Royal Wedding **Obv:** Arms with
supporters **Rev:** Conjoined bust left

Date	Mintage	F	VF	XF	Unc	BU
ND(1981) Proof, rare	—	—	—	—	—	—

PATTERNS
Including off metal strikes

KM#	Date	Mintage	Identification	Mkt Val
Pn1	1966	2	5 Licente. 0.9000 Silver.	—
Pn2	1966	2	10 Licente. 0.9000 Silver.	—
Pn3	1966	2	20 Licente. 0.9000 Silver.	—
Pn4	1966	2	50 Licente. 0.9000 Silver.	—
Pn6	1966	7	2 Maloti. 0.9160 Gold.	600
Pn7	1966	7	4 Maloti. 0.9160 Gold.	800
Pn8	1966	7	10 Maloti. 0.9160 Gold. Head right. Arms with supporters above value and date.	1,100
Pn9	1966	7	20 Maloti. 0.9160 Gold.	1,400
Pn10	1979	5	15 Maloti. Copper-Nickel. KM25. Medallic alignment.	110
Pn10.2a	1979	—	15 Maloti. 0.9250 Silver. 33.5100 g.	—
Pn11	1979	15	15 Maloti. Copper-Nickel. KM25. Coin alignment.	80.00
Pn12	1979	15	250 Maloti. Brass. KM26.	75.00
Pn13	1979	5	250 Maloti. Copper-Nickel. KM26. Medallic alignment.	110
Pn14	1979	10	250 Maloti. Silver. 20.1500 g. KM26.	115
Pn15	1980	10	50 Maloti. Copper-Nickel. KM27. Medallic alignment.	125
Pn16	1980	10	50 Maloti. Copper-Nickel. Coin alignment.	125
Pn17	1980	10	250 Maloti. Brass. KM28. Coin alignment.	110
Pn18	1980	10	250 Maloti. Copper-Nickel. KM28. Medallic alignment.	100
Pn19	1980	10	500 Maloti. Brass. KM29. Coin alignment.	110
Pn20	1980	10	500 Maloti. Copper-Nickel. KM29. Medallic alignment.	110

PIEFORTS

KM#	Date	Mintage	Identification	Mkt Val
P1	1979	50	10 Maloti. Silver. KM24.	135
P2	1981	—	250 Maloti. Gold. KM31.	550
P3	1983	—	25 Maloti. Silver. KM4.	90.00
P4	1983	100	200 Maloti. Gold. KM45.	800

MINT SETS

KM#	Date	Mintage	Identification	Issue Price	Mkt Val
MS1	1976 (3)	450	KM13-15	194	315
MS2	1989 (7)	—	KM16-22	—	11.50

PROOF SETS

KM#	Date	Mintage	Identification	Issue Price	Mkt Val
PS1	1966 (7)	1,500	KM1-7	301	525
PS2	1966 (4)	7	KMPn6-9	—	3,400
PS3	1966 (4)	2	KMPn1-4	—	—
PS4	1966 (4)	3,500	KM1, 2, 3.1, 4.1	28.00	40.00
PSA5	1966 (4)	—	KM1, 2, 3.2, 4.2	28.00	40.00
PS5	1966 (3)	2,000	KM5-7	301	430
PS6	1969 (5)	3,000	KM8-12	450	3,100
PS7	1976 (3)	1,410	KM13-15	285	300
PS8	1976 (2)	—	KM14-15	270	270
PS9	1976 (2)	—	KM13-14	—	135
PS10	1979 (7)	10,000	KM16-22	34.00	15.00
PS11	1980 (8)	10,000	KM16-22, 23a	51.00	25.00
PS12	1981 (8)	2,500	KM16-22, 53	55.00	45.00

LIBERIA

The Republic of Liberia, located on the southern side of the West African bulge between Sierra Leone and Ivory Coast, has an area of 38,250 sq. mi. (111,370 sq. km) and a population of 2.2 million. Capital: Monrovia. The major industries are agriculture, mining and lumbering. Iron ore, diamonds, rubber, coffee and coca are exported.

The Liberian coast was explored and charted by Portuguese navigator Pedro de Cintra in 1461. For the three centuries following Portuguese traders visited the area regularly to trade for gold, slaves and pepper. The modern country of Liberia, Africa's first republic, was settled in1822 by the American Colonization Society as a homeland for American freed slaves, with the U.S. government furnishing funds and assisting in negotiations for procurement of land from the native chiefs. The various settlements united in 1839 to form the Commonwealth of Liberia, and in 1847 established the country as a republic with a constitution modeled after that of the United States.

U.S. money was declared legal tender in Liberia in 1943, replacing British West African currency.

Most of the Liberian pattern series, particularly of the 1888-90 period, are acknowledged to have been "unofficial" privately sponsored issues, but many collectors of Liberian coins nonetheless, avidly collect them. The "K" number designations on these pieces refer to a listing of Liberian patterns compiled and published by Ernst Kraus.

MINT MARKS
B - Bern, Switzerland
H - Heaton, Birmingham
(l) – London
(d) – Denver, U.S.A.
(s) - San Francisco, U.S.
FM - Franklin Mint, U.S.A.*
PM - Pobjoy Mint
   *NOTE: From 1975-1985 the Franklin Mint produced coinage in up to 3 different qualities. Qualities of issue are designated in ( ) after each date and are defined as follows:
   (M) MATTE - Normal circulation strike or a dull finish produced by sandblasting special uncirculated (polish finish) or proof quality dies.
   (U) SPECIAL UNCIRCULATED - Polished or prooflike in appearance without any frosted features.
   (P) PROOF - The highest quality obtainable having mirror-like fields and frosted features.

MONETARY SYSTEM
100 Cents = 1 Dollar

REPUBLIC
STANDARD COINAGE
100 Cents = 1 Dollar

KM# 10 1/2 CENT
2.4200 g., Brass, 18 mm. **Obv:** Elephant striding left, star below **Rev:** Palm tree (Elaeis guineensis-Palmae) within circle flanked by stars

Date	Mintage	F	VF	XF	Unc	BU
1937	1,000,000	0.10	0.25	0.40	1.00	2.50

KM# 10a 1/2 CENT
Copper-Nickel **Obv:** Head laureate left with star below **Rev:** Palm tree within circle flanked by stars

Date	Mintage	F	VF	XF	Unc	BU
1941	250,000	0.15	0.35	0.55	1.50	2.50

KM# 5 CENT
Bronze **Obv:** Head laureate left above star **Obv. Leg.:**
REPUBLIC OF LIBERIA **Rev:** Palm tree divides ship and radiant sun within circle, 2 stars, date and value around border

Date	Mintage	F	VF	XF	Unc	BU
1906H	180,000	4.50	10.00	35.00	75.00	—
1906H Proof	—	Value: 130				

KM# 11 CENT
5.1900 g., Brass, 25.45 mm. **Obv:** Elephant within circle above star **Rev:** Palm tree within circle above date

Date	Mintage	F	VF	XF	Unc	BU
1937	1,000,000	0.20	0.50	1.50	6.00	12.00

KM# 11a CENT
Copper-Nickel **Obv:** Elephant within circle above star **Rev:** Palm tree within circle above date

Date	Mintage	F	VF	XF	Unc	BU
1941	250,000	1.00	7.00	18.00	40.00	—

KM# 13 CENT
2.6000 g., Bronze, 18 mm. **Obv:** Elephant within circle above star **Rev:** Ship and bird to right of palm tree within 3/4 circle above date

Date	Mintage	F	VF	XF	Unc	BU
1960	500,000	—	—	0.10	0.75	2.00
1961	7,000,000	—	—	0.10	0.75	2.00
1968(l)	3,000,000	—	—	0.10	0.75	2.00
1968(s) Proof	14,000	Value: 1.25				
1969 Proof	5,056	Value: 1.25				
1970 Proof	3,464	Value: 1.25				
1971 Proof	3,032	Value: 1.25				
1972(d)	10,000,000	—	—	0.10	0.75	2.00
1972(s) Proof	4,866	Value: 1.25				
1973 Proof	11,000	Value: 1.25				
1974 Proof	9,362	Value: 1.25				
1975	5,000,000	—	—	0.10	0.75	2.00
1975 Proof	4,056	Value: 1.25				
1976 Proof	2,131	Value: 1.25				
1977	2,500,000	—	—	0.10	0.75	2.00
1977 Proof	920	Value: 1.25				
1978FM Proof	7,311	Value: 1.25				
1983FM	2,500,000	—	—	0.10	0.75	2.00
1984	2,500,000	—	—	0.10	0.75	2.00

KM# 13a CENT
Bronze **Obv:** Elephant left **Rev:** Palm tree, bird above ship at right **Edge:** O.A.U. July 1979

Date	Mintage	F	VF	XF	Unc	BU
1979FM Proof	1,857	Value: 1.50				

KM# 6 2 CENTS
Bronze **Obv:** Laureate head left above star **Obv. Leg.:**
REPUBLIC OF LIBERIA **Rev:** Palm tree divides ship and radiant sun within circle, 2 stars, date and value around border

Date	Mintage	F	VF	XF	Unc	BU
1906H	108,000	5.00	12.00	40.00	85.00	—
1906H Proof	—	Value: 160				

KM# 12 2 CENTS
Brass **Obv:** Elephant within circle above star **Rev:** Palm tree divides ship and sun within circle flanked by stars above date

Date	Mintage	F	VF	XF	Unc	BU
1937	1,000,000	0.15	0.35	1.00	6.00	9.00

KM# 12a 2 CENTS
Copper-Nickel **Obv:** Elephant within circle above star **Rev:** Palm tree divides sun and ship within circle flanked by stars above date

Date	Mintage	F	VF	XF	Unc	BU
1941	810,000	0.10	0.25	0.50	2.50	3.00
1978FM Proof	7,311	Value: 2.00				

KM# 12b 2 CENTS
Copper-Nickel **Obv:** Elephant within circle above star **Rev:** Palm tree divides sun and ship within circle flanked by stars above date **Edge:** O.A.U. July 1979

Date	Mintage	F	VF	XF	Unc	BU
1979FM Proof	1,857	Value: 4.00				

KM# 14 5 CENTS
4.1000 g., Copper-Nickel, 20 mm. **Obv:** Elephant within circle above star **Rev:** Ship and bird to right of palm tree within 3/4 circle above date

Date	Mintage	F	VF	XF	Unc	BU
1960	1,000,000	—	0.10	0.15	0.50	1.50
1961	3,200,000	—	0.10	0.15	0.50	1.50
1968 Proof	15,000	Value: 1.00				
1969 Proof	5,056	Value: 1.00				
1970 Proof	3,464	Value: 1.25				
1971 Proof	3,032	Value: 1.25				
1972(d)	3,000,000	—	0.10	0.15	0.40	1.50
1972(s) Proof	4,866	Value: 1.00				
1973 Proof	11,000	Value: 1.00				
1974 Proof	9,362	Value: 1.00				
1975	3,000,000	—	0.10	0.15	0.40	1.50
1975 Proof	4,056	Value: 1.00				
1976 Proof	2,131	Value: 1.00				
1977	—	—	0.10	0.15	0.50	1.50
1977 Proof	920	Value: 1.00				
1978FM Proof	7,311	Value: 1.00				
1983FM	1,000,000	—	0.10	0.15	0.40	1.50
1984	1,000,000	—	0.10	0.15	0.40	1.50

KM# 14a 5 CENTS
Copper-Nickel **Obv:** Elephant within circle above star **Rev:** Ship and bird to right of palm tree within 3/4 circle above date **Edge:** O.A.U. July 1979

Date	Mintage	F	VF	XF	Unc	BU
1979FM Proof	1,857	Value: 2.00				

KM# 474 5 CENTS
2.2500 g., Aluminum, 26.9 mm. **Obv:** National arms **Rev:** Dragon above value **Edge:** Plain

Date	Mintage	F	VF	XF	Unc	BU
2000	—	—	—	—	1.00	1.50

KM# 7 10 CENTS
2.3200 g., 0.9250 Silver 0.0690 oz. ASW **Obv:** Laureate head left above star **Obv. Leg.:** REPUBLIC OF LIBERIA **Rev:** Value and date within wreath

Date	Mintage	F	VF	XF	Unc	BU
1906H	35,000	5.00	25.00	75.00	165	—
1906H Proof	—	Value: 250				

KM# 15 10 CENTS
2.0700 g., 0.9000 Silver 0.0599 oz. ASW, 17 mm. **Obv:** Head with headdress left above star **Rev:** Value and date within wreath

Date	Mintage	F	VF	XF	Unc	BU
1960	1,000,000	BV	1.00	1.50	3.00	5.00
1961	1,200,000	BV	1.00	1.50	3.00	5.00

KM# 15a.1 10 CENTS
2.1000 g., Copper-Nickel **Obv:** Head with headdress left above star **Rev:** Value and date within wreath

Date	Mintage	F	VF	XF	Unc	BU
1966	2,000,000	—	0.15	0.25	0.50	0.75

KM# 15a.2 10 CENTS
1.8000 g., Copper-Nickel **Obv:** Head with headdress left above star **Rev:** Value and date within wreath

Date	Mintage	F	VF	XF	Unc	BU
1968 Proof	14,000	Value: 1.25				
1969 Proof	5,056	Value: 1.25				
1970(d)	2,500,000	—	0.15	0.25	0.50	0.75
1970(s) Proof	3,464	Value: 1.50				
1971 Proof	3,032	Value: 1.50				
1972 Proof	4,866	Value: 1.25				
1973 Proof	11,000	Value: 1.00				
1974 Proof	9,362	Value: 1.00				
1975	4,500	—	0.15	0.20	0.35	0.75
1975 Proof	4,056	Value: 1.00				
1976 Proof	2,131	Value: 1.00				
1977	—	—	0.15	0.25	0.75	1.25
1977 Proof	920	Value: 4.00				
1978FM Proof	7,311	Value: 1.00				
1983FM	500,000	—	0.15	0.25	0.75	1.25
1984FM	500,000	—	0.15	0.25	0.75	1.25
1987	10,000,000	—	0.15	0.25	0.75	1.25

KM# 15b 10 CENTS
1.8000 g., Copper-Nickel **Obv:** Head with headdress left above star **Rev:** Value and date within wreath **Edge:** O.A.U. July 1979

Date	Mintage	F	VF	XF	Unc	BU
1979FM Proof	1,857	Value: 2.00				

KM# 8 25 CENTS
5.8000 g., 0.9250 Silver 0.1725 oz. ASW **Obv:** Head laureate left above star **Obv. Leg.:** REPUBLIC OF LIBERIA **Rev:** Value and date within wreath

Date	Mintage	F	VF	XF	Unc	BU
1906H	34,000	10.00	40.00	125	275	—
1906H Proof	—	Value: 375				

KM# 16 25 CENTS
5.1800 g., 0.9000 Silver 0.1499 oz. ASW **Obv:** Head with headdress left above star **Rev:** Value and date within wreath

Date	Mintage	F	VF	XF	Unc	BU
1960	900,000	—	BV	2.75	5.00	7.00
1961	1,200,000	—	BV	2.75	5.00	7.00

KM# 16a.1 25 CENTS
5.2000 g., Copper-Nickel **Obv:** Head with headdress left above star **Rev:** Value and date within wreath

Date	Mintage	F	VF	XF	Unc	BU
1966	800,000	—	0.25	0.65	1.25	2.00

KM# 16a.2 25 CENTS
4.8000 g., Copper-Nickel, 23 mm. **Obv:** Head with headdress left above star **Rev:** Value and date within wreath **Note:** 1 and 1.15mm rim varieties exist.

Date	Mintage	F	VF	XF	Unc	BU
1968(d)	1,600,000	—	0.25	0.50	1.00	1.50
1968(s) Proof	14,000	Value: 1.50				

Date	Mintage	F	VF	XF	Unc	BU
1969 Proof	5,056	Value: 1.50				
1970 Proof	3,464	Value: 1.75				
1971 Proof	3,032	Value: 1.75				
1972 Proof	4,866	Value: 1.50				
1973	2,000,000	—	0.25	0.50	1.00	1.50
1973 Proof	11,000	Value: 1.25				
1974 Proof	9,362	Value: 1.25				
1975	1,600,000	—	0.25	0.50	1.00	1.50
1975 Proof	4,056	Value: 1.25				

KM# 16a.3 25 CENTS
5.2000 g., Copper-Nickel **Obv:** Head with headdress left above star **Rev:** Value and date within wreath **Rev. Leg.:** Large letters, higher inscription **Note:** Struck in 1988.

Date	Mintage	F	VF	XF	Unc	BU
1968 Restrike	2,400,000	—	0.25	0.50	1.00	1.50

KM# 30 25 CENTS
5.2000 g., Copper-Nickel **Series:** F.A.O. **Obv:** Head 1/4 right flanked by stars **Rev:** Woman with basket of leaves on head divides date and value within circle

Date	Mintage	F	VF	XF	Unc	BU
1976	800,000	—	0.25	0.75	1.75	3.00
1976 Proof	2,131	Value: 4.00				
1977 Proof	920	Value: 5.00				
1978FM Proof	7,311	Value: 2.50				

KM# 30a 25 CENTS
5.2000 g., Copper-Nickel **Obv:** Head 1/4 right flanked by stars **Rev:** Woman with leaves in basket on head divides date and value within circle **Edge:** O.A.U. July 1979

Date	Mintage	F	VF	XF	Unc	BU
1979FM Proof	1,857	Value: 3.50				

KM# 16b 25 CENTS
4.4600 g., Nickel Clad Steel, 22.9 mm. **Obv:** Head with headdress left above star **Rev:** Value and date within wreath **Edge:** Reeded

Date	Mintage	F	VF	XF	Unc	BU
2000	—	—	—	—	1.75	—

KM# 9 50 CENTS
11.6000 g., 0.9250 Silver 0.3450 oz. ASW **Obv:** Laureate head left above star **Obv. Leg.:** REPUBLIC OF LIBERIA **Rev:** Value and date within wreath

Date	Mintage	F	VF	XF	Unc	BU
1906H	24,000	15.00	35.00	120	475	—
1906H Proof	—	Value: 600				

KM# 17 50 CENTS
10.3700 g., 0.9000 Silver 0.3001 oz. ASW **Obv:** Head with headdress left above star **Rev:** Value and date within wreath

Date	Mintage	F	VF	XF	Unc	BU
1960	1,100,000	—	BV	5.00	9.00	12.50
1961	800,000	—	BV	5.00	9.00	12.50

KM# 17a.2 50 CENTS

8.9000 g., Copper-Nickel, 29 mm. **Obv:** Head with headdress left above star **Rev:** Value and date within wreath

Date	Mintage	F	VF	XF	Unc	BU
1968(I)	1,000,000	—	0.60	0.80	1.50	2.50
1968(s) Proof	14,000	Value: 1.50				
1969 Proof	5,056	Value: 1.50				
1970 Proof	3,464	Value: 2.50				
1971 Proof	3,032	Value: 2.50				
1972 Proof	4,866	Value: 1.50				
1973	1,000,000	—	0.60	0.75	1.25	2.00
1973 Proof	11,000	Value: 1.50				
1974 Proof	9,362	Value: 1.50				
1975	800,000	—	0.60	0.75	1.25	2.00
1975 Proof	4,056	Value: 1.50				

KM# 17a.1 50 CENTS

10.4000 g., Copper-Nickel **Obv:** Head with headdress left above star **Rev:** Value and date within wreath

Date	Mintage	F	VF	XF	Unc	BU
1966	200,000	—	0.75	1.00	1.50	2.50

KM# 17b.2 50 CENTS

9.0000 g., Nickel-Clad Steel, 28 mm. **Obv:** Head with headdress left above star **Rev:** Value and date within wreath **Edge:** Reeded

Date	Mintage	F	VF	XF	Unc	BU
2000	—	—	—	—	3.50	—

KM# 31 50 CENTS

8.9000 g., Copper-Nickel **Obv:** Head 1/4 right flanked by stars **Rev:** National arms

Date	Mintage	F	VF	XF	Unc	BU
1976	1,000,000	—	0.60	1.00	2.50	4.00
1976 Proof	2,131	Value: 5.50				
1977 Proof	920	Value: 6.50				
1978FM Proof	7,311	Value: 4.00				
1987	1,800,000	—	0.60	1.00	2.50	4.00

KM# 31a 50 CENTS

8.9000 g., Copper-Nickel **Obv:** Head 1/4 right flanked by stars **Rev:** National arms **Edge:** O.A.U. July 1979

Date	Mintage	F	VF	XF	Unc	BU
1979FM Proof	1,857	Value: 4.50				

KM# 18 DOLLAR

20.7400 g., 0.9000 Silver 0.6001 oz. ASW **Obv:** Head with headdress left above star **Rev:** Value and date within wreath

Date	Mintage	F	VF	XF	Unc	BU
1961	200,000	—	BV	10.00	12.50	16.50
1962	1,000,000	—	BV	9.50	11.00	14.50

KM# 18a.1 DOLLAR

20.7000 g., Copper-Nickel, 34 mm. **Obv:** Head with headdress left above star **Rev:** Value and date within wreath

Date	Mintage	F	VF	XF	Unc	BU
1966	1,000,000	—	1.00	1.50	2.25	3.50

KM# 18a.2 DOLLAR

18.0000 g., Copper-Nickel, 34 mm. **Obv:** Head with headdress left above star **Rev:** Value and date within wreath

Date	Mintage	F	VF	XF	Unc	BU
1968(I)	1,000,000	—	1.00	1.50	2.25	3.50
1968(s) Proof	14,000	Value: 2.00				
1969 Proof	5,056	Value: 2.00				
1970(d)	2,000,000	—	1.00	1.50	3.00	4.50
1970(s) Proof	3,464	Value: 6.00				
1971 Proof	3,032	Value: 4.50				
1972 Proof	4,866	Value: 4.50				
1973 Proof	11,000	Value: 3.00				
1974 Proof	9,362	Value: 3.00				
1975	400,000	—	1.25	1.75	3.00	4.50
1975 Proof	4,056	Value: 3.00				

KM# 32 DOLLAR

18.0000 g., Copper-Nickel, 34 mm. **Obv:** Head 1/4 right flanked by stars **Rev:** Liberia, map and date within circle flanked by stars

Date	Mintage	F	VF	XF	Unc	BU
1976	2,000,000	—	2.50	4.50	8.00	12.00
1976 Proof	2,131	Value: 12.00				
1977 Proof	920	Value: 13.50				
1978FM Proof	7,311	Value: 11.00				
1987	1,500,000	—	1.50	3.00	6.00	10.00

KM# 32a DOLLAR

18.0000 g., Copper-Nickel, 34 mm. **Obv:** Head with headdress 1/4 right flanked by stars **Rev:** Liberia, map and date within circle flanked by stars **Edge:** O.A.U. July 1979

Date	Mintage	F	VF	XF	Unc	BU
1979FM Proof	1,857	Value: 10.00				

KM# 98 DOLLAR

18.0000 g., Copper-Nickel **Series:** Preserve Planet Earth **Obv:** National arms **Rev:** Protoceratops

Date	Mintage	F	VF	XF	Unc	BU
1993	—	—	—	—	10.00	12.00

KM# 101 DOLLAR

18.0000 g., Copper-Nickel **Subject:** Nolan Ryan **Obv:** National arms **Rev:** Nolan Ryan waving baseball cap **Note:** Similar to 10 Dollars, KM#102.

Date	Mintage	F	VF	XF	Unc	BU
1993	—	—	—	—	8.50	—

KM# 109 DOLLAR

28.5200 g., Copper-Nickel **Series:** Preserve Planet Earth **Obv:** National arms **Rev:** Corythosaurus

Date	Mintage	F	VF	XF	Unc	BU
1993	—	—	—	—	10.00	14.00

KM# 112 DOLLAR

28.5200 g., Copper-Nickel **Series:** Preserve Planet Earth **Obv:** National arms **Rev:** Atchaeopteryx **Note:** Incorrect spelling

Date	Mintage	F	VF	XF	Unc	BU
1993	—	—	—	—	10.00	18.00

KM# 118 DOLLAR

28.5200 g., Copper-Nickel, 38.6 mm. **Series:** Preserve Planet Earth **Obv:** National arms **Rev:** Gorillas **Edge:** Reeded **Note:** Similar to 10 Dollars, KM#119.

Date	Mintage	F	VF	XF	Unc	BU
1994	—	—	—	—	10.00	14.00

KM# 121 DOLLAR

28.5200 g., Copper-Nickel **Series:** Preserve Planet Earth **Obv:** National arms **Rev:** Pygmy Hippopotami **Note:** Similar to 10 Dollars, KM#122.

Date	Mintage	F	VF	XF	Unc	BU
1994	—	—	—	—	10.00	14.00

KM# 124 DOLLAR

28.5200 g., Copper-Nickel **Series:** Preserve Planet Earth **Obv:** National arms **Rev:** Trionyx Turtle **Note:** Similar to 10 Dollars, KM#125.

Date	Mintage	F	VF	XF	Unc	BU
1994	—	—	—	—	10.00	14.00

KM# 115 DOLLAR

28.5200 g., Copper-Nickel **Series:** Preserve Planet Earth **Obv:** National arms **Rev:** Archaeopteryx **Note:** Correct spelling.

Date	Mintage	F	VF	XF	Unc	BU
1994	—	—	—	—	10.00	14.00

KM# 131 DOLLAR
28.5200 g., Copper-Nickel **Subject:** Babe Ruth Sultan of Swat
Obv: National arms **Rev:** Head 1/4 right divides date within circle

Date	Mintage	F	VF	XF	Unc	BU
1994	—	—	—	—	8.00	—

KM# 131a DOLLAR
Copper-Nickel, Gold Plated **Subject:** Babe Ruth Sultan of Swat
Obv: National arms **Rev:** Head 1/4 right divides date within circle
Note: Issued in a first day cover.

Date	Mintage	F	VF	XF	Unc	BU
1994	—	—	—	—	20.00	—

KM# 139 DOLLAR
Copper-Nickel **Subject:** Damon Hill- Fomula One Race Car
Obv: National arms **Rev:** Bust facing flanked by helmet and flag
above car and value within sprigs

Date	Mintage	F	VF	XF	Unc	BU
1994 Prooflike	—	—	—	—	7.00	—

KM# 248 DOLLAR
Copper-Nickel **Subject:** Hall of Fame - Roberto Clemente
Obv: National arms **Rev:** Head facing

Date	Mintage	F	VF	XF	Unc	BU
1994	—	—	—	—	8.00	—

KM# 249 DOLLAR
Copper-Nickel **Subject:** Hall of Fame - Reggie Jackson
Obv: National arms **Rev:** Baseball player divides circle above
date

Date	Mintage	F	VF	XF	Unc	BU
1994	—	—	—	—	8.00	—

KM# 411 DOLLAR
Copper-Nickel **Obv:** National arms **Rev:** Head left above small
gazelle and value

Date	Mintage	F	VF	XF	Unc	BU
1994	—	—	—	—	8.50	—

KM# 133 DOLLAR
Copper-Nickel **Series:** Preserve Planet Earth **Obv:** National
arms **Rev:** Leopard

Date	Mintage	F	VF	XF	Unc	BU
1995	—	—	—	—	12.00	14.00

KM# 136 DOLLAR
Copper-Nickel **Series:** Preserve Planet Earth **Obv:** National
arms **Rev:** Storks

Date	Mintage	F	VF	XF	Unc	BU
1995	—	—	—	—	9.00	14.00

KM# 140 DOLLAR
Copper-Nickel **Subject:** Sir Winston Churchill **Obv:** National arms
Rev: Uniformed bust right with planes, army tanks and ship at right

Date	Mintage	F	VF	XF	Unc	BU
1995	—	—	—	—	6.00	—

KM# 141 DOLLAR
Copper-Nickel **Subject:** President Franklin D. Roosevelt **Obv:**
National arms **Rev:** President Roosevelt riding in jeep

Date	Mintage	F	VF	XF	Unc	BU
1995	—	—	—	—	6.00	—

KM# 142 DOLLAR
Copper-Nickel **Subject:** General George Patton **Obv:** National
arms **Rev:** General Patton in front of map

Date	Mintage	F	VF	XF	Unc	BU
1995	—	—	—	—	6.00	—

KM# 143 DOLLAR
Copper-Nickel **Subject:** President Harry S. Truman
Obv: National arms **Rev:** President Truman facing

Date	Mintage	F	VF	XF	Unc	BU
1995	—	—	—	—	6.00	—

KM# 144 DOLLAR
Copper-Nickel **Subject:** President Charles de Gaulle
Obv: National arms **Rev:** President on Champs Elysees

Date	Mintage	F	VF	XF	Unc	BU
1995	—	—	—	—	6.00	—

KM# 158 DOLLAR
Copper-Nickel **Subject:** Dr. Sun Yat-sen **Obv:** National arms
Rev: Uniformed bust facing

Date	Mintage	F	VF	XF	Unc	BU
1995	—	—	—	—	6.50	—

KM# 161 DOLLAR
Copper-Nickel **Subject:** General Chiang Kai-shek **Obv:** National
arms **Rev:** General Chiang kai-shek

Date	Mintage	F	VF	XF	Unc	BU
1995	—	—	—	—	6.50	—

KM# 164 DOLLAR
Copper-Nickel **Subject:** Cairo Conference **Obv:** National arms
Rev: Chiang kai-shek, Roosevelt and Churchill

Date	Mintage	F	VF	XF	Unc	BU
1995	—	—	—	—	6.50	—

KM# 167 DOLLAR
Copper-Nickel **Subject:** 375th Anniversary - Pilgrim Fathers
Obv: National arms **Rev:** The "Mayflower"

Date	Mintage	F	VF	XF	Unc	BU
1995	—	—	—	—	6.00	—

KM# 168 DOLLAR
Copper-Nickel **Subject:** 375th Anniversary - Pilgrim Fathers
Obv: National arms **Rev:** First Thanksgiving scene

Date	Mintage	F	VF	XF	Unc	BU
1995	—	—	—	—	6.00	—

KM# 169 DOLLAR
Copper-Nickel **Subject:** 375th Anniversary - Pilgrim Fathers
Obv: National arms **Rev:** Cape Cod and Pilgrims in skiff

Date	Mintage	F	VF	XF	Unc	BU
1995	—	—	—	—	6.00	—

KM# 170 DOLLAR
Copper-Nickel **Subject:** 375th Anniversary - Pilgrim Fathers
Obv: National arms **Rev:** Pilgrim landing party

Date	Mintage	F	VF	XF	Unc	BU
1995	—	—	—	—	6.00	—

KM# 412 DOLLAR
Copper-Nickel **Subject:** Nations for Peace **Obv:** National arms
Rev: Paper dolls, UN logo

Date	Mintage	F	VF	XF	Unc	BU
1995	—	—	—	—	8.50	—

KM# 128 DOLLAR
Copper-Nickel **Subject:** Star Trek **Obv:** National arms
Rev: Conjoined busts facing **Note:** Similar to 10 Dollars, KM#129.

Date	Mintage	F	VF	XF	Unc	BU
1995	—	—	—	—	7.50	—

KM# 207 DOLLAR
Copper-Nickel **Subject:** Star Trek **Obv:** National arms
Rev: Starships NCC-1701 and NCC-1701D **Note:** Similar to 10
Dollars, KM#208.

Date	Mintage	F	VF	XF	Unc	BU
1996	—	—	—	—	8.50	—

KM# 210 DOLLAR
Copper-Nickel **Subject:** Star Trek **Obv:** National arms
Rev: Conjoined busts facing **Note:** Similar to 10 Dollars, KM#211.

Date	Mintage	F	VF	XF	Unc	BU
1996	—	—	—	—	8.50	—

KM# 213 DOLLAR
Copper-Nickel **Subject:** Star Trek **Obv:** National arms
Rev: Conjoined busts facing **Note:** Similar to 10 Dollars, KM#214.

Date	Mintage	F	VF	XF	Unc	BU
1996	—	—	—	—	8.50	—

KM# 216 DOLLAR
Copper-Nickel **Subject:** Star Trek **Obv:** National arms
Rev: Spock and Uhura **Note:** Similar to 10 Dollars, KM#217.

Date	Mintage	F	VF	XF	Unc	BU
1996	—	—	—	—	8.50	—

KM# 219 DOLLAR
Copper-Nickel **Subject:** Star Trek **Obv:** National arms
Rev: Conjoined busts 1/4 left **Note:** Similar to 10 Dollars,
KM#220.

Date	Mintage	F	VF	XF	Unc	BU
1996	—	—	—	—	8.50	—

KM# 222 DOLLAR
Copper-Nickel **Series:** Preserve Planet Earth **Obv:** National arms **Rev:** Grey Parrot **Note:** Similar to 10 Dollars, KM#223.

Date	Mintage	F	VF	XF	Unc	BU
1996	—	—	—	—	10.00	12.00

KM# 225 DOLLAR
Copper-Nickel **Series:** Preserve Planet Earth **Obv:** National arms **Rev:** Love Birds **Note:** Similar to 10 Dollars, KM#226.

Date	Mintage	F	VF	XF	Unc	BU
1996	—	—	—	—	10.00	12.00

KM# 254 DOLLAR
Copper-Nickel **Subject:** Chairman Mao Zedong **Obv:** National arms **Rev:** Standing figure facing **Note:** Similar to 10 Dollars, KM#256. Issued in first day cover.

Date	Mintage	F	VF	XF	Unc	BU
1996	20,000	—	—	—	7.50	—

KM# 260 DOLLAR
Copper-Nickel **Obv:** National arms **Rev:** Seated figures facing **Note:** Similar to 10 Dollars, KM#262. Issued in first day cover.

Date	Mintage	F	VF	XF	Unc	BU
1996	20,000	—	—	—	7.50	—

KM# 263 DOLLAR
Copper-Nickel **Subject:** Pioneers of the West **Obv:** National arms **Rev:** Bust of Buffalo Bill facing at right of scene fighting indians **Note:** Similar to 10 Dollars, KM#264.

Date	Mintage	F	VF	XF	Unc	BU
1996	—	—	—	—	7.50	—

KM# 266 DOLLAR
Copper-Nickel **Subject:** Pioneers of the West **Obv:** National arms **Rev:** Davy Crockett **Note:** Similar to 10 Dollars, KM#267.

Date	Mintage	F	VF	XF	Unc	BU
1996	—	—	—	—	7.50	—

KM# 269 DOLLAR
Copper-Nickel **Subject:** Pioneers of the West **Obv:** National arms **Rev:** Jim Bowie in front of the Alamo **Note:** Similar to 10 Dollars, KM#270.

Date	Mintage	F	VF	XF	Unc	BU
1996	—	—	—	—	7.50	—

KM# 272 DOLLAR
Copper-Nickel **Subject:** Pioneers of the West **Obv:** National arms **Rev:** Kit Carson **Note:** Similar to 10 Dollars, KM#273.

Date	Mintage	F	VF	XF	Unc	BU
1996	—	—	—	—	7.50	—

KM# 275 DOLLAR
Copper-Nickel **Subject:** Pioneers of the West **Obv:** National arms **Rev:** Wild Bill Hickok **Note:** Similar to 10 Dollars, KM#276.

Date	Mintage	F	VF	XF	Unc	BU
1996	—	—	—	—	7.50	—

KM# 278 DOLLAR
Copper-Nickel **Subject:** Pioneers of the West **Obv:** National arms **Rev:** Buffalo Bill **Note:** Similar to 10 Dollars, KM#279.

Date	Mintage	F	VF	XF	Unc	BU
1996	—	—	—	—	7.50	—

KM# 560 DOLLAR
Silver **Obv:** National arms **Rev:** Multicolor fish

Date	Mintage	F	VF	XF	Unc	BU
1996B Proof	— Value: 30.00					

KM# 569 DOLLAR
24.6100 g., Copper-Nickel, 38.6 mm. **Subject:** Marine Life Protection **Obv:** National arms **Rev:** Multicolor fish **Edge:** Reeded

Date	Mintage	F	VF	XF	Unc	BU
1996	—	—	—	—	30.00	—

KM# 570 DOLLAR
24.6100 g., Copper-Nickel, 38.6 mm. **Subject:** Marine Life Protection **Obv:** National arms **Rev:** Multicolor fish **Edge:** Reeded

Date	Mintage	F	VF	XF	Unc	BU
1997	—	—	—	—	30.00	—

KM# 426 DOLLAR
13.9400 g., Copper, 32 mm. **Subject:** AZA Species Survival Plan **Obv:** National arms **Rev:** Seated panda eating within circle **Edge:** Reeded

Date	Mintage	F	VF	XF	Unc	BU
1997	—	—	—	—	7.50	10.00

KM# 313 DOLLAR
Copper-Nickel **Subject:** Return of Hong Kong - Dragon **Obv:** National arms

Date	Mintage	F	VF	XF	Unc	BU
1997	—	—	—	—	8.50	9.50

KM# 320 DOLLAR
Copper-Nickel **Subject:** Fiftieth Anniversary of the Kon-Tiki Expedition **Obv:** National arms **Rev:** Sailing ship within circle

Date	Mintage	F	VF	XF	Unc	BU
1997	—	—	—	—	8.50	—

KM# 286 DOLLAR
Copper-Nickel **Subject:** WWII - Evacuation of Dunkirk **Obv:** National arms **Rev:** Star medal above dates to left of fighter planes and ships **Note:** Similar to 10 Dollars, KM#287.

Date	Mintage	F	VF	XF	Unc	BU
1997	—	—	—	—	8.50	—

KM# 288 DOLLAR
Copper-Nickel **Subject:** WWII - Liberation of the Philippines **Obv:** National arms **Rev:** Medal to right of soldiers in water **Note:** Similar to 10 Dollars, KM#289.

Date	Mintage	F	VF	XF	Unc	BU
1997	—	—	—	—	8.50	—

KM# 290 DOLLAR
Copper-Nickel **Subject:** WWII - Defense of Stalingrad **Obv:** National arms **Rev:** Soviet combat medal to left of war scene **Note:** Similar to 10 Dollars, KM#291.

Date	Mintage	F	VF	XF	Unc	BU
1997	—	—	—	—	8.50	—

KM# 292 DOLLAR
Copper-Nickel **Subject:** WWII - Arnhem **Obv:** National arms **Rev:** Netherlands bronze lion cross to right of parachutists, bridge and soldier **Note:** Similar to 10 Dollars, KM#293.

Date	Mintage	F	VF	XF	Unc	BU
1997	—	—	—	—	8.50	—

KM# 294 DOLLAR
Copper-Nickel **Subject:** WWII - Raid on the Dams **Obv:** National arms **Rev:** British distinguished flying medal **Note:** Similar to 10 Dollars, KM#295.

Date	Mintage	F	VF	XF	Unc	BU
1997	—	—	—	—	8.50	—

KM# 296 DOLLAR
Copper-Nickel **Subject:** WWII - West African Campaign **Obv:** National arms **Rev:** WWII Victory medal **Note:** Similar to 10 Dollars, KM#297.

Date	Mintage	F	VF	XF	Unc	BU
1997	—	—	—	—	8.50	—

KM# 298 DOLLAR
Copper-Nickel **Subject:** WWII - North African Campaign **Obv:** National arms **Rev:** British Africa star medal to right of tank in front of pyramid **Note:** Similar to 10 Dollars, KM#299.

Date	Mintage	F	VF	XF	Unc	BU
1997	—	—	—	—	8.50	—

KM# 300 DOLLAR
Copper-Nickel **Subject:** WWII - The Dieppe Raid **Obv:** National arms **Rev:** British Victoria cross to right of plane over half-track vehicle **Note:** Similar to 10 Dollars, KM#301.

Date	Mintage	F	VF	XF	Unc	BU
1997	—	—	—	—	8.50	—

KM# 302 DOLLAR
Copper-Nickel **Subject:** WWII - Iwo Jima **Obv:** National arms **Rev:** Purple Heart medal to upper left of damaged plane landing on a carrier **Note:** Similar to 10 Dollars, KM#303.

Date	Mintage	F	VF	XF	Unc	BU
1997	—	—	—	—	8.50	—

KM# 304 DOLLAR
Copper-Nickel **Subject:** WWII - Battle of Britain **Obv:** National arms **Rev:** British distinguished flying cross to left of pilots running to board planes **Note:** Similar to 10 Dollars, KM#305.

Date	Mintage	F	VF	XF	Unc	BU
1997	—	—	—	—	8.50	—

KM# 306 DOLLAR
Copper-Nickel **Subject:** WWII - Liberation of Paris **Obv:** National arms **Rev:** Croix de Guerre medal to right of soldiers in front of Arch de Triumph **Note:** Similar to 10 Dollars, KM#307.

Date	Mintage	F	VF	XF	Unc	BU
1997	—	—	—	—	8.50	—

KM# 308 DOLLAR
Copper-Nickel **Subject:** WWII - Burma Campaign **Obv:** National arms **Rev:** British Burma star medal **Note:** Similar to 10 Dollars, KM#309.

Date	Mintage	F	VF	XF	Unc	BU
1997	—	—	—	—	8.50	—

KM# 310 DOLLAR
Copper-Nickel **Subject:** Mahatma Gandhi **Obv:** National arms **Rev:** Seated figure facing left in front of Taj Mahal **Note:** Similar to 10 Dollars, KM#311.

Date	Mintage	F	VF	XF	Unc	BU
1997	—	—	—	—	8.00	—

KM# 324 DOLLAR
Copper-Nickel **Subject:** Jurassic Park - Stegosaurus **Obv:** National arms **Rev:** Stegosaurus **Note:** Similar to 10 Dollars, KM#325.

Date	Mintage	F	VF	XF	Unc	BU
1997	—	—	—	—	10.00	12.00

KM# 327 DOLLAR
Copper-Nickel **Subject:** Golden Wedding Anniversary **Obv:** National arms **Rev:** E & P initials above two shields **Note:** Similar to 10 Dollars, KM#328.

Date	Mintage	F	VF	XF	Unc	BU
1997	—	—	—	—	7.50	—

KM# 330 DOLLAR
Copper-Nickel **Subject:** Golden Wedding Anniversary **Obv:** National arms **Rev:** Royal couple with horse **Note:** Similar to 10 Dollars, KM#331.

Date	Mintage	F	VF	XF	Unc	BU
1997	—	—	—	—	7.50	9.00

KM# 333 DOLLAR
Copper-Nickel **Subject:** Golden Wedding Anniversary **Obv:** National arms **Rev:** Couple with dogs **Note:** Similar to 10 Dollars, KM#334.

Date	Mintage	F	VF	XF	Unc	BU
1997	—	—	—	—	7.50	9.00

KM# 336 DOLLAR
Copper-Nickel **Subject:** Golden Wedding Anniversary **Obv:** National arms **Rev:** Royal couple with children **Note:** Similar to 10 Dollars, KM#337.

Date	Mintage	F	VF	XF	Unc	BU
1997	—	—	—	—	7.50	—

KM# 344 DOLLAR
Copper-Nickel **Subject:** 150th Anniversary of Independence **Obv:** National arms **Rev:** The "Ashmon" **Note:** Similar to 10 Dollars, KM#345.

Date	Mintage	F	VF	XF	Unc	BU
1997	—	—	—	—	8.50	—

KM# 368 DOLLAR
Copper-Nickel **Subject:** Star Trek - The Next Generation **Obv:** National arms **Rev:** Romulan Warbird **Note:** Similar to 10 Dollars, KM#369.

Date	Mintage	F	VF	XF	Unc	BU
1997	—	—	—	—	7.50	—

KM# 371 DOLLAR
Copper-Nickel **Subject:** Star Trek - The Next Generation **Obv:** National arms **Rev:** Klingon Attack Cruiser **Note:** Similar to 10 Dollars, KM#372.

Date	Mintage	F	VF	XF	Unc	BU
1997	—	—	—	—	7.50	—

KM# 374 DOLLAR
Copper-Nickel **Subject:** Star Trek - The Next Generation **Obv:** National arms **Rev:** U.S.S. Enterprise NCC-1701-D **Note:** Similar to 10 Dollars, KM#375.

Date	Mintage	F	VF	XF	Unc	BU
1997	—	—	—	—	7.50	—

KM# 377 DOLLAR
Copper-Nickel **Subject:** Star Trek - The Next Generation **Obv:** National arms **Rev:** Klingon Bird of Prey **Note:** Similar to 10 Dollars, KM#378.

Date	Mintage	F	VF	XF	Unc	BU
1997	—	—	—	—	7.50	—

KM# 380 DOLLAR
Copper-Nickel **Subject:** Star Trek - The Next Generation **Obv:** National arms **Rev:** Borg Cube **Note:** Similar to 10 Dollars, KM#381.

Date	Mintage	F	VF	XF	Unc	BU
1997	—	—	—	—	7.50	—

KM# 383 DOLLAR
Copper-Nickel **Subject:** Star Trek - The Next Generation **Obv:** National arms **Rev:** Ferengi Marauder **Note:** Similar to 10 Dollars, KM#384.

Date	Mintage	F	VF	XF	Unc	BU
1997	—	—	—	—	7.50	—

KM# 386 DOLLAR
Copper-Nickel **Subject:** President Ronald Reagan
Obv: National arms **Rev:** Lincoln Memorial below head right
Note: Similar to 10 Dollars, KM#387.

Date	Mintage	F	VF	XF	Unc	BU
1998	—	—	—	—	8.50	—

KM# 401 DOLLAR
Copper-Nickel **Subject:** Christopher Columbus **Obv:** National
arms **Rev:** Bust 1/4 right above ship **Note:** Similar to 10 Dollars,
KM#402.

Date	Mintage	F	VF	XF	Unc	BU
1999	—	—	—	—	8.00	—

KM# 404 DOLLAR
Copper-Nickel **Subject:** Captain Cook **Obv:** National arms
Rev: Portrait, ship and map **Note:** Similar to 10 Dollars, KM#405.

Date	Mintage	F	VF	XF	Unc	BU
1999	—	—	—	—	8.00	—

KM# 407 DOLLAR
Copper-Nickel **Subject:** Return of Macao to China **Obv:** National
arms **Rev:** Dragon and phoenix **Note:** Similar to 10 Dollars, KM#408.

Date	Mintage	F	VF	XF	Unc	BU
1999	—	—	—	—	8.50	—

KM# 413 DOLLAR
Copper-Nickel **Subject:** The Wedding of Prince Edward
Obv: National arms **Rev:** Couple in carriage **Note:** Similar to 10
Dollars, KM#413.

Date	Mintage	F	VF	XF	Unc	BU
1999	—	—	—	—	8.00	—

KM# 571 DOLLAR
24.6100 g., Copper-Nickel, 38.6 mm. **Subject:** Marine Life
Protection **Obv:** National arms **Rev:** Multicolor fish **Edge:** Reeded

Date	Mintage	F	VF	XF	Unc	BU
1999	—	—	—	—	30.00	—

KM# 612 DOLLAR
5.3500 g., Copper Nickel, 24.9 mm. **Subject:** Millennium - Year
of the Dragon **Obv:** National arms within circle above date
Rev: Chinese dragon within circle **Edge:** Reeded

Date	Mintage	F	VF	XF	Unc	BU
2000	—	—	—	—	3.00	5.00

KM# 615 DOLLAR
5.3500 g., Copper-Nickel, 24.9 mm. **Obv:** National arms within
circle above date **Rev:** Dancing style dragon within circle
Edge: Reeded

Date	Mintage	F	VF	XF	Unc	BU
2000	—	—	—	—	3.00	5.00

KM# 635 DOLLAR
0.9990 Silver, 21 mm. **Obv:** National arms **Rev:** American
Quarter Horse

Date	Mintage	F	VF	XF	Unc	BU
2000 Proof	—	Value: 15.00				

KM# 696 DOLLAR
31.1000 g., 0.9990 Silver 0.9988 oz. ASW, 39 mm.
Subject: Millennium **Obv:** American style eagle **Rev:** Morgan
dollar style Liberty head **Edge:** Reeded

Date	Mintage	F	VF	XF	Unc	BU
2000 Proof	—	Value: 25.00				

KM# 442 DOLLAR
28.2800 g., Copper-Nickel, 38.6 mm. **Subject:** Greenwich
Meridian **Obv:** National arms **Rev:** World landmarks and
fireworks **Edge:** Reeded

Date	Mintage	F	VF	XF	Unc	BU
2000	—	—	—	—	10.00	12.00

KM# 47 2 DOLLARS
Copper-Nickel **Series:** F.A.O. **Subject:** World Fisheries
Conference **Obv:** National arms **Rev:** Longneck croaker fish

Date	Mintage	F	VF	XF	Unc	BU
1983	100,000	—	—	—	18.00	28.00

KM# 47a 2 DOLLARS
28.2800 g., 0.9250 Silver 0.8410 oz. ASW **Subject:** World
Fisheries Conference **Obv:** National arms **Rev:** Longneck
croaker fish

Date	Mintage	F	VF	XF	Unc	BU
1983 Proof	20,000	Value: 50.00				

KM# 47b 2 DOLLARS
47.5400 g., Gold **Series:** F.A.O. **Subject:** World Fisheries
Conference **Obv:** National arms **Rev:** Longneck croaker fish

Date	Mintage	F	VF	XF	Unc	BU
1983 Proof	600	Value: 1,250				

KM# 24 2-1/2 DOLLARS
4.1796 g., 0.9000 Gold 0.1209 oz. AGW **Subject:** Inauguration
of President Tolbert **Rev:** Capitol building

Date	Mintage	F	VF	XF	Unc	BU
1972 Proof	—	Value: 125				

KM# 644 2-1/2 DOLLARS
11.8000 g., Copper-Nickel, 29.5 mm. **Obv:** National arms
divides date **Rev:** Olympic torch runner facing right **Edge:** Plain

Date	Mintage	F	VF	XF	Unc	BU
1999 Proof	—	Value: 12.50				

KM# 62 5 DOLLARS
5.0000 g., 0.9000 Gold 0.1447 oz. AGW **Subject:** 25th
Anniversary of Inter-Continental Hotels **Obv:** Value below hotel
flanked by sprigs **Rev:** Letter I within football flanked by dates

Date	Mintage	F	VF	XF	Unc	BU
ND(1971) Proof	—	Value: 150				

KM# 25 5 DOLLARS
8.3592 g., 0.9000 Gold 0.2419 oz. AGW **Subject:** Inauguration
of President Tolbert **Rev:** Full masted ship at sea

Date	Mintage	F	VF	XF	Unc	BU
1972 Proof	—	Value: 250				

KM# 29 5 DOLLARS
34.1000 g., 0.9000 Silver 0.9867 oz. ASW **Obv:** National arms,
value written on top, date on bottom **Rev:** Standing elephant
looking 1/4 right above star

Date	Mintage	F	VF	XF	Unc	BU
1973	500	—	—	—	28.00	—
1973 Proof	28,000	Value: 20.00				
1974 Proof	20,000	Value: 20.00				
1975 Proof	9,017	Value: 20.00				
1976 Proof	3,683	Value: 22.00				
1977 Proof	1,640	Value: 25.00				
1978FM Proof	7,311	Value: 20.00				

KM# 29a 5 DOLLARS
34.1000 g., 0.9000 Silver 0.9867 oz. ASW **Obv:** National arms
Rev: Standing elephant looking 1/4 right above star **Edge:** O.A.U.
July 1979

Date	Mintage	F	VF	XF	Unc	BU
1979 Proof	1,857	Value: 25.00				

KM# 44 5 DOLLARS
Copper-Nickel **Subject:** Military Memorial **Obv:** National arms
above date **Rev:** Memorial statue and value flanked by shrubs

Date	Mintage	F	VF	XF	Unc	BU
1982	4,000,000	—	5.00	6.50	9.00	—
1985	2,000,000	—	5.00	6.50	9.00	—

KM# 73 5 DOLLARS
15.5500 g., 0.9990 Silver 0.4994 oz. ASW **Subject:** Formula
One - Gerhard Berger **Obv:** National arms divide date **Rev:** Head
1/4 right, racecar and flag

Date	Mintage	F	VF	XF	Unc	BU
1992 Proof	—	Value: 18.50				

KM# 76 5 DOLLARS
15.5500 g., 0.9990 Silver 0.4994 oz. ASW **Subject:** Formula
One - Nigel Mansell **Obv:** National arms **Rev:** Head right, racecar,
date and flag above sprigs

Date	Mintage	F	VF	XF	Unc	BU
1992 Proof	Est. 50,000		Value: 18.50			

KM# 78 5 DOLLARS
15.5500 g., 0.9990 Silver 0.4994 oz. ASW **Subject:** Formula
One - Ayrton Senna **Obv:** National arms **Rev:** Bust 1/4 left above
flag, racecar, dates and value

Date	Mintage	F	VF	XF	Unc	BU
1992 Proof	Est. 50,000		Value: 18.50			

KM# 79 5 DOLLARS
15.5500 g., 0.9990 Silver 0.4994 oz. ASW **Subject:** Formula
One - Riccardo Patrese **Obv:** National arms **Rev:** Head 1/4 left
to right of flag and racecar **Note:** Similar to 10 Dollars, KM#74.

Date	Mintage	F	VF	XF	Unc	BU
1992 Proof	Est. 50,000		Value: 18.50			

KM# 77 5 DOLLARS
15.5500 g., 0.9990 Silver 0.4994 oz. ASW **Subject:** Formula
One - Aguri Suzuki **Obv:** National arms **Rev:** Racecar below bust
at left **Note:** Similar to 10 Dollars, KM#84.

Date	Mintage	F	VF	XF	Unc	BU
1992 Proof	Est. 50,000		Value: 18.50			

KM# 80 5 DOLLARS
15.5500 g., 0.9990 Silver 0.4994 oz. ASW **Subject:** Formula
One - Michael Schumacher **Obv:** National arms **Rev:** Bust at
right, car at left **Note:** Similar to 10 Dollars, KM#86.

Date	Mintage	F	VF	XF	Unc	BU
1992 Proof	50,000		Value: 18.50			

KM# 81 5 DOLLARS
15.5500 g., 0.9990 Silver 0.4994 oz. ASW **Subject:** Formula
One - Alain Prost **Obv:** National arms **Rev:** Head 3/4 left above
flag, racecar, dates and value **Note:** Similar to 10 Dollars, KM#87.

Date	Mintage	F	VF	XF	Unc	BU
1992 Proof	50,000		Value: 18.50			

KM# 82 5 DOLLARS
15.5500 g., 0.9990 Silver 0.4994 oz. ASW **Subject:** Formula
One - Ukyo Katayama **Obv:** National arms **Rev:** Racecar below
bust at left **Note:** Similar to 10 Dollars, KM#88.

Date	Mintage	F	VF	XF	Unc	BU
1992 Proof	50,000		Value: 18.50			

KM# 67 5 DOLLARS
15.5500 g., 0.9990 Silver 0.4994 oz. ASW **Subject:** President
Bill Clinton **Obv:** National arms **Rev:** Head right divides date and
value above building **Note:** Similar to 10 Dollars, KM#68.

Date	Mintage	F	VF	XF	Unc	BU
1993 Proof	50,000		Value: 25.00			

KM# 97 5 DOLLARS
15.5500 g., 0.9990 Silver 0.4994 oz. ASW **Subject:** Chancellor
Willy Brandt **Obv:** National arms **Rev:** Horses pulling casket below
head right dividing dates **Note:** Similar to 10 Dollars, KM#72.

Date	Mintage	F	VF	XF	Unc	BU
1993 Proof			Value: 18.50			

KM# 103 5 DOLLARS
15.5500 g., 0.9990 Silver 0.4994 oz. ASW **Subject:** President
John F. Kennedy **Obv:** National arms **Rev:** President Kennedy
Note: Similar to 10 Dollars, KM#104.

Date	Mintage	F	VF	XF	Unc	BU
1993 Proof	50,000		Value: 20.00			

KM# 179 5 DOLLARS
15.5500 g., 0.9990 Silver 0.4994 oz. ASW **Subject:** Formula
One - Mika Hakkinen **Obv:** National arms **Rev:** Mike Hakkinen

Date	Mintage	F	VF	XF	Unc	BU
1995 Proof	50,000		Value: 20.00			

KM# 182 5 DOLLARS
15.5500 g., 0.9990 Silver 0.4994 oz. ASW **Subject:** Formula
One **Obv:** National arms **Rev:** Martin Brundle

Date	Mintage	F	VF	XF	Unc	BU
1995 Proof	Est. 50,000		Value: 20.00			

KM# 185 5 DOLLARS
15.5500 g., 0.9990 Silver 0.4994 oz. ASW **Subject:** Formula One
- Rubens Barrichello **Obv:** National arms **Rev:** Rubens Barrichello

Date	Mintage	F	VF	XF	Unc	BU
1995 Proof	Est. 50,000		Value: 20.00			

KM# 188 5 DOLLARS
15.5500 g., 0.9990 Silver 0.4994 oz. ASW **Subject:** Formula
One - David Coulthard **Obv:** National arms **Rev:** David Coulthard

Date	Mintage	F	VF	XF	Unc	BU
1995 Proof	Est. 50,000		Value: 20.00			

KM# 191 5 DOLLARS
15.5500 g., 0.9990 Silver 0.4994 oz. ASW **Subject:** Formula
One - Jean Alesi **Obv:** National arms **Rev:** Jean Alesi

Date	Mintage	F	VF	XF	Unc	BU
1995 Proof	Est. 50,000		Value: 20.00			

KM# 562 5 DOLLARS
15.5000 g., 0.9990 Silver 0.4978 oz. ASW **Obv:** National arms
Rev: Benz Patent motor car

Date	Mintage	F	VF	XF	Unc	BU
1995 Proof	—		Value: 24.50			

KM# 563 5 DOLLARS
15.5000 g., 0.9990 Silver 0.4978 oz. ASW, 32 mm.
Obv: National arms **Rev:** Bughatti Royale

Date	Mintage	F	VF	XF	Unc	BU
1995	—	—	—	—	25.00	

KM# 195 5 DOLLARS
15.5500 g., 0.9990 Silver 0.4994 oz. ASW **Subject:** Formula
One - Mark Blundell **Obv:** National arms **Rev:** Mark Brundell
Note: Similar to 10 Dollars, KM#199.

Date	Mintage	F	VF	XF	Unc	BU
1996 Proof	50,000		Value: 20.00			

KM# 196 5 DOLLARS
15.5500 g., 0.9990 Silver 0.4994 oz. ASW **Subject:** Formula
One - Johnny Herbert **Obv:** National arms **Rev:** Johnny Herbert
Note: Similar to 10 Dollars, KM#200.

Date	Mintage	F	VF	XF	Unc	BU
1996 Proof	50,000		Value: 20.00			

KM# 197 5 DOLLARS
15.5500 g., 0.9990 Silver 0.4994 oz. ASW **Subject:** Formula
One - Eddie Irvine **Obv:** National arms **Rev:** Eddie Irvine
Note: Similar to 10 Dollars, KM#201.

Date	Mintage	F	VF	XF	Unc	BU
1996 Proof	50,000		Value: 20.00			

KM# 198 5 DOLLARS
15.5500 g., 0.9990 Silver 0.4994 oz. ASW **Subject:** Formula
One - Heinz Frentzen **Obv:** National arms **Rev:** Heinz Frentzen
Note: Similar to 10 Dollars, KM#202.

Date	Mintage	F	VF	XF	Unc	BU
1996 Proof	50,000		Value: 20.00			

KM# 228 5 DOLLARS
15.5500 g., 0.9990 Silver 0.4994 oz. ASW **Subject:** Formula
One - Ayrton Senna **Obv:** National arms **Rev:** Ayrton Senna
Note: Similar to 10 Dollars, KM#229.

Date	Mintage	F	VF	XF	Unc	BU
1996 Proof	50,000		Value: 20.00			

KM# 255 5 DOLLARS
15.5500 g., 0.9990 Silver 0.4994 oz. ASW **Subject:** Chairman
Mao Zedong **Obv:** National arms **Rev:** Standing figure facing
above value **Note:** Similar to 10 Dollars, KM#256.

Date	Mintage	F	VF	XF	Unc	BU
Proof	20,000		Value: 20.00			
1996 Proof	20,000		Value: 20.00			

KM# 261 5 DOLLARS
15.5500 g., 0.9990 Silver 0.4994 oz. ASW **Subject:** Chairman
Mao Zedong and President Nixon **Obv:** National arms
Rev: Seated figures facing **Note:** Similar to 10 Dollars, KM#262.

Date	Mintage	F	VF	XF	Unc	BU
1996 Proof	20,000		Value: 20.00			

KM# 600 5 DOLLARS
21.3000 g., Copper-Nickel, 38.5 mm. **Obv:** National arms
Rev: Tiger at rest **Edge:** Reeded

Date	Mintage	F	VF	XF	Unc	BU
1997		—	—	—	10.00	

KM# A452 5 DOLLARS
Copper-Nickel **Subject:** Queen of Hearts **Obv:** National arms
Rev: Diana wearing a choker

Date	Mintage	F	VF	XF	Unc	BU
1997		—	—	—	15.00	

KM# 351 5 DOLLARS
Copper-Nickel **Subject:** Chinese Astrology **Obv:** Seated Liberty
Rev: Two rats and pumpkin

Date	Mintage	F	VF	XF	Unc	BU
1997	Est. 4,000	—	—	—	6.00	7.50

KM# 352 5 DOLLARS
Copper-Nickel **Subject:** Chinese Astrology **Obv:** Seated Liberty
Rev: Ox

Date	Mintage	F	VF	XF	Unc	BU
1997	Est. 4,000	—	—	—	5.00	7.00

KM# 353 5 DOLLARS
Copper-Nickel **Subject:** Chinese Astrology **Obv:** Seated Liberty
Rev: Tiger

Date	Mintage	F	VF	XF	Unc	BU
1997	Est. 4,000	—	—	—	6.00	7.00

KM# 354 5 DOLLARS
Copper-Nickel **Subject:** Chinese Astrology **Obv:** Seated Liberty
Rev: Rabbits

Date	Mintage	F	VF	XF	Unc	BU
1997	Est. 4,000	—	—	—	5.00	7.00

KM# 355   5 DOLLARS
Copper-Nickel **Subject:** Chinese Astrology **Obv:** Seated Liberty
Rev: Dragon

Date	Mintage	F	VF	XF	Unc	BU
1997	Est. 4,000	—	—	—	6.00	7.50

KM# 356   5 DOLLARS
12.9900 g., Copper-Nickel, 31.49 mm. **Subject:** Chinese
Astrology **Obv:** Seated Liberty **Rev:** Snake **Edge:** Reeded

Date	Mintage	F	VF	XF	Unc	BU
1997	Est. 4,000	—	—	—	5.00	6.00

KM# 357   5 DOLLARS
Copper-Nickel **Subject:** Chinese Astrology **Obv:** Seated Liberty
Rev: Horse

Date	Mintage	F	VF	XF	Unc	BU
1997	Est. 4,000	—	—	—	6.00	7.00

KM# 358   5 DOLLARS
Copper-Nickel **Subject:** Chinese Astrology **Obv:** Seated Liberty
Rev: Goat

Date	Mintage	F	VF	XF	Unc	BU
1997	Est. 4,000	—	—	—	5.00	6.00

KM# 359   5 DOLLARS
Copper-Nickel **Subject:** Chinese Astrology **Obv:** Seated Liberty
Rev: Monkey

Date	Mintage	F	VF	XF	Unc	BU
1997	Est. 4,000	—	—	—	5.00	6.00

KM# 360   5 DOLLARS
Copper-Nickel **Subject:** Chinese Astrology **Obv:** Seated Liberty
Rev: Rooster

Date	Mintage	F	VF	XF	Unc	BU
1997	Est. 4,000	—	—	—	5.00	7.00

KM# 361   5 DOLLARS
Copper-Nickel **Subject:** Chinese Astrology **Obv:** Seated Liberty
Rev: Wrinkled seated dog

Date	Mintage	F	VF	XF	Unc	BU
1997	Est. 4,000	—	—	—	6.00	7.50

KM# 362   5 DOLLARS
Copper-Nickel **Subject:** Chinese Astrology **Obv:** Seated Liberty
Rev: Pig

Date	Mintage	F	VF	XF	Unc	BU
1997	Est. 4,000	—	—	—	5.00	7.00

KM# 441   5 DOLLARS
20.5600 g., Copper-Nickel, 38.5 mm. **Obv:** National arms divide
date **Rev:** Polar bear **Edge:** Reeded

Date	Mintage	F	VF	XF	Unc	BU
1997	—	—	—	—	8.50	9.50

KM# 445   5 DOLLARS
25.1000 g., Copper-Nickel, 38.5 mm. **Subject:** Princess Diana
Obv: National arms divides date **Rev:** Crowned bust 3/4 left
Edge: Reeded

Date	Mintage	F	VF	XF	Unc	BU
1997 Proof	—	Value: 20.00				

KM# 446   5 DOLLARS
25.1000 g., Copper-Nickel, 38.5 mm. **Subject:** Diana Series -
Lady Spencer **Obv:** National arms **Rev:** Young girl's portrait
Edge: Reeded

Date	Mintage	F	VF	XF	Unc	BU
1997	—	—	—	—	15.00	16.50

KM# 447   5 DOLLARS
25.1000 g., Copper-Nickel **Subject:** First TV Interview
Obv: National arms **Rev:** Portrait of Diana with microphone

Date	Mintage	F	VF	XF	Unc	BU
1997	—	—	—	—	15.00	16.50

KM# 448   5 DOLLARS
Copper-Nickel **Subject:** Diana's Official Portrait **Obv:** National
arms **Rev:** Portrait

Date	Mintage	F	VF	XF	Unc	BU
1997	—	—	—	—	15.00	16.50

KM# 449   5 DOLLARS
Copper-Nickel **Subject:** Wedding Day **Obv:** National arms
Rev: Diana in wedding dress

Date	Mintage	F	VF	XF	Unc	BU
1997	—	—	—	—	15.00	16.50

KM# 450   5 DOLLARS
Copper-Nickel **Subject:** "People's Princess" - Diana
Obv: National arms **Rev:** Formal portrait

Date	Mintage	F	VF	XF	Unc	BU
1997	—	—	—	—	15.00	16.50

KM# 451   5 DOLLARS
Copper-Nickel **Subject:** England's Rose **Obv:** National arms
Rev: Diana with bouquet of roses

Date	Mintage	F	VF	XF	Unc	BU
1997	—	—	—	—	15.00	16.50

KM# 452   5 DOLLARS
Copper-Nickel **Series:** Diana Princess of Wales **Obv:** National
arms **Rev:** Head 3/4 left

Date	Mintage	F	VF	XF	Unc	BU
1997	—	—	—	—	—	—

KM# 453   5 DOLLARS
Copper-Nickel **Subject:** Elegance **Obv:** National arms
Rev: Diana wearing a high collar

Date	Mintage	F	VF	XF	Unc	BU
1997	—	—	—	—	15.00	16.50

KM# 454   5 DOLLARS
Copper-Nickel **Subject:** Birth of William **Obv:** National arms
Rev: Diana holding Prince William

Date	Mintage	F	VF	XF	Unc	BU
1997	—	—	—	—	15.00	16.50

KM# 455   5 DOLLARS
Copper-Nickel **Subject:** William's Christening **Obv:** National
arms **Rev:** Diana holding Prince William

Date	Mintage	F	VF	XF	Unc	BU
1997	—	—	—	—	15.00	16.50

KM# 456   5 DOLLARS
Copper-Nickel **Subject:** Birth of Prince Harry **Obv:** National
arms **Rev:** Diana holding Prince Harry

Date	Mintage	F	VF	XF	Unc	BU
1997	—	—	—	—	15.00	16.50

KM# 457   5 DOLLARS
Copper-Nickel **Subject:** Loving Mother **Obv:** National arms
Rev: Diana with Prince William and Prince Harry

Date	Mintage	F	VF	XF	Unc	BU
1997	—	—	—	—	15.00	16.50

KM# 458   5 DOLLARS
Copper-Nickel **Subject:** Royal Family **Obv:** National arms
Rev: Family portrait

Date	Mintage	F	VF	XF	Unc	BU
1997	—	—	—	—	15.00	16.50

KM# 459   5 DOLLARS
Copper-Nickel **Subject:** Queen Elizabeth and Lady Diana
Obv: National arms **Rev:** Conjoined crowned busts right

Date	Mintage	F	VF	XF	Unc	BU
1997	—	—	—	—	15.00	16.50

KM# 460   5 DOLLARS
Copper-Nickel **Obv:** National arms **Rev:** Queen Mother and Diana

Date	Mintage	F	VF	XF	Unc	BU
1997	—	—	—	—	15.00	16.50

KM# 461   5 DOLLARS
Copper-Nickel **Subject:** Visit to Wales **Obv:** National arms
Rev: Charles and Diana

Date	Mintage	F	VF	XF	Unc	BU
1997	—	—	—	—	15.00	16.50

KM# 462   5 DOLLARS
Copper-Nickel **Subject:** Australian Tour **Obv:** National arms
Rev: Charles and Diana dancing

Date	Mintage	F	VF	XF	Unc	BU
1997	—	—	—	—	15.00	16.50

KM# 463 5 DOLLARS
Copper-Nickel **Subject:** Tour of Japan **Obv:** National arms
Rev: Half length figures looking right

Date	Mintage	F	VF	XF	Unc	BU
1997	—	—	—	—	15.00	16.50

KM# 464 5 DOLLARS
Copper-Nickel, 38.5 mm. **Obv:** National arms **Rev:** Diana reading to child

Date	Mintage	F	VF	XF	Unc	BU
1997	—	—	—	—	15.00	16.50

KM# 465 5 DOLLARS
Copper-Nickel **Subject:** Charity **Obv:** National arms **Rev:** Diana with poor child

Date	Mintage	F	VF	XF	Unc	BU
1997	—	—	—	—	15.00	16.50

KM# 466 5 DOLLARS
Copper-Nickel **Obv:** National arms **Rev:** Diana with sick child

Date	Mintage	F	VF	XF	Unc	BU
1997	—	—	—	—	15.00	16.50

KM# 467 5 DOLLARS
Copper-Nickel **Obv:** National arms **Rev:** Diana's casket on gun carriage

Date	Mintage	F	VF	XF	Unc	BU
1997	—	—	—	—	15.00	16.50

KM# 496 5 DOLLARS
20.5600 g., Copper-Nickel, 38.5 mm. **Obv:** National arms
Rev: Giraffe **Edge:** Reeded

Date	Mintage	F	VF	XF	Unc	BU
1997	—	—	—	—	7.50	—

KM# 566 5 DOLLARS
Copper-Nickel **Obv:** National arms **Rev:** Elephant

Date	Mintage	F	VF	XF	Unc	BU
1997	—	—	—	—	7.00	—

KM# 578 5 DOLLARS
23.7000 g., Copper-Nickel, 38.5 mm. **Subject:** Year of the Ox
Obv: National arms **Rev:** Ox **Edge:** Reeded

Date	Mintage	F	VF	XF	Unc	BU
1997	—	—	—	—	7.50	—

KM# 579 5 DOLLARS
21.3000 g., Copper-Nickel, 38.4 mm. **Obv:** National arms
Rev: Elephant **Edge:** Reeded

Date	Mintage	F	VF	XF	Unc	BU
1997	—	—	—	—	8.50	—

KM# 580 5 DOLLARS
21.3000 g., Copper-Nickel, 38.4 mm. **Obv:** National arms
Rev: Lion **Edge:** Reeded

Date	Mintage	F	VF	XF	Unc	BU
1997	—	—	—	—	8.50	—

KM# 581 5 DOLLARS
21.3000 g., Copper-Nickel, 38.4 mm. **Obv:** National arms
Rev: Rhinoceros **Edge:** Reeded

Date	Mintage	F	VF	XF	Unc	BU
1997	—	—	—	—	8.50	—

KM# 582 5 DOLLARS
21.3000 g., Copper-Nickel, 38.4 mm. **Obv:** National arms
Rev: Zebra **Edge:** Reeded

Date	Mintage	F	VF	XF	Unc	BU
1997	—	—	—	—	8.50	—

KM# 583 5 DOLLARS
21.3000 g., Copper-Nickel, 38.4 mm. **Obv:** National arms
Rev: Two kangaroos **Edge:** Reeded

Date	Mintage	F	VF	XF	Unc	BU
1997	—	—	—	—	8.50	—

KM# 339 5 DOLLARS
Copper-Nickel **Subject:** Year of the Tiger **Obv:** National arms
Rev: Tiger with three cubs

Date	Mintage	F	VF	XF	Unc	BU
1998 (1997) Proof	—	Value: 15.00				

KM# 363 5 DOLLARS
Copper-Nickel **Subject:** RMS Titanic **Obv:** National arms
Rev: Cameo above sinking ship **Note:** Similar to 20 Dollars, KM#364.

Date	Mintage	F	VF	XF	Unc	BU
1998	—	—	—	—	10.00	—

KM# 593 5 DOLLARS
20.0000 g., Copper-Nickel, 38 mm. **Subject:** John F. Kennedy
Jr. **Obv:** National arms **Rev:** Two portraits, flag and the White House **Edge:** Reeded

Date	Mintage	F	VF	XF	Unc	BU
1999	—	—	—	—	10.00	—

KM# 828 5 DOLLARS
14.6800 g., Copper-Nickel, 33.09 mm. **Subject:** 1863
Gettysburg Battle **Obv:** National arms **Rev:** Crossed flags above cannon between busts of Generals George G. Meade and Robert E. lee **Edge:** Reeded

Date	Mintage	F	VF	XF	Unc	BU
1999	—	—	—	—	8.00	—

KM# 572 5 DOLLARS
24.9700 g., 0.9250 Silver 0.7426 oz. ASW, 38.6 mm.
Subject: Captain Cook **Obv:** National arms **Rev:** Seated Capt. Cook at right, his ship at left **Edge:** Reeded

Date	Mintage	F	VF	XF	Unc	BU
1999 Proof	—	Value: 35.00				

KM# 427 5 DOLLARS
11.1800 g., Copper-Nickel, 31.6 mm. **Series:** Millennium 2000
Zodiac **Obv:** National arms **Rev:** Snake **Edge:** Reeded

Date	Mintage	F	VF	XF	Unc	BU
2000	—	—	—	—	4.00	5.00

KM# 429 5 DOLLARS
11.1800 g., Copper-Nickel, 31.6 mm. **Series:** Millennium 2000
Zodiac **Obv:** National arms **Rev:** Ox **Edge:** Reeded

Date	Mintage	F	VF	XF	Unc	BU
2000	—	—	—	—	4.00	5.00

KM# 428 5 DOLLARS
11.1800 g., Copper-Nickel, 31.6 mm. **Series:** Millennium 2000
Zodiac **Obv:** National arms **Rev:** Two rats and pumpkin
Edge: Reeded

Date	Mintage	F	VF	XF	Unc	BU
2000	—	—	—	—	4.00	5.00

KM# 430 5 DOLLARS
11.1800 g., Copper-Nickel, 31.6 mm. **Series:** Millennium 2000
Zodiac **Obv:** National arms **Rev:** Tiger **Edge:** Reeded

Date	Mintage	F	VF	XF	Unc	BU
2000	—	—	—	—	4.00	5.00

KM# 431   5 DOLLARS
11.1800 g., Copper-Nickel, 31.6 mm. **Series:** Millennium 2000
Zodiac **Obv:** National arms **Rev:** Horse **Edge:** Reeded

Date	Mintage	F	VF	XF	Unc	BU
2000	—	—	—	—	4.00	5.00

KM# 432   5 DOLLARS
11.1800 g., Copper-Nickel, 31.6 mm. **Series:** Millennium 2000
Zodiac **Obv:** National arms **Rev:** Goat **Edge:** Reeded

Date	Mintage	F	VF	XF	Unc	BU
2000	—	—	—	—	4.00	5.00

KM# 433   5 DOLLARS
11.1800 g., Copper-Nickel, 31.6 mm. **Series:** Millennium 2000
Zodiac **Obv:** National arms **Rev:** Monkey **Edge:** Reeded

Date	Mintage	F	VF	XF	Unc	BU
2000	—	—	—	—	4.00	5.00

KM# 434   5 DOLLARS
11.1800 g., Copper-Nickel, 31.6 mm. **Series:** Millennium 2000
Zodiac **Obv:** National arms **Rev:** Rooster **Edge:** Reeded

Date	Mintage	F	VF	XF	Unc	BU
2000	—	—	—	—	4.00	5.00

KM# 435   5 DOLLARS
11.1800 g., Copper-Nickel, 31.6 mm. **Series:** Millennium 2000
Zodiac **Obv:** National arms **Rev:** Dog **Edge:** Reeded

Date	Mintage	F	VF	XF	Unc	BU
2000	—	—	—	—	3.50	5.00

KM# 436   5 DOLLARS
11.1800 g., Copper-Nickel, 31.6 mm. **Series:** Millennium 2000
Zodiac **Obv:** National arms **Rev:** Pig **Edge:** Reeded

Date	Mintage	F	VF	XF	Unc	BU
2000	—	—	—	—	4.00	5.00

KM# 437   5 DOLLARS
11.1800 g., Copper-Nickel, 31.6 mm. **Series:** Millennium 2000
Zodiac **Obv:** National arms **Rev:** Rabbit **Edge:** Reeded

Date	Mintage	F	VF	XF	Unc	BU
2000	—	—	—	—	4.00	5.00

KM# 438   5 DOLLARS
11.1800 g., Copper-Nickel, 31.6 mm. **Series:** Millennium 2000
Zodiac **Obv:** National arms **Rev:** Dragon **Edge:** Reeded

Date	Mintage	F	VF	XF	Unc	BU
2000	—	—	—	—	4.00	7.50

KM# 584   5 DOLLARS
8.5400 g., 0.9999 Silver 0.2745 oz. ASW, 30.1 mm.
Subject: Endangered Elephant **Obv:** National arms divide date
Rev: Elephant and calf **Edge:** Reeded

Date	Mintage	F	VF	XF	Unc	BU
2000 Proof	—	Value: 25.00				

KM# 589   5 DOLLARS
26.9200 g., Copper-Nickel, 40.3 mm. **Subject:** First Man on
Moon **Obv:** National arms **Rev:** Astronaut and American flag on
moon **Edge:** Reeded

Date	Mintage	F	VF	XF	Unc	BU
2000	—	—	—	—	17.50	—

KM# 651   5 DOLLARS
14.5600 g., Copper-Nickel, 33.1 mm. **Obv:** National arms
Rev: Japanese "Zero" flying over Pearl Harbor **Edge:** Reeded

Date	Mintage	F	VF	XF	Unc	BU
2000	—	—	—	—	8.00	10.00

KM# 652   5 DOLLARS
27.3300 g., Copper-Nickel, 40.2 mm. **Obv:** National arms
Rev: Titanic sinking **Edge:** Reeded

Date	Mintage	F	VF	XF	Unc	BU
2000	—	—	—	—	9.00	—

KM# 668   5 DOLLARS
26.1500 g., 0.9990 Silver Clad Copper-Nickel 0.8399 oz. ASW,
38.8 mm. **Subject:** Roy Rogers, King of the Cowboys
Obv: National arms **Rev:** Roy Rogers wearing hat flanked by
stars **Edge:** Plain

Date	Mintage	F	VF	XF	Unc	BU
2000 Proof	—	Value: 35.00				

KM# 695   5 DOLLARS
27.2500 g., Copper-Nickel, 40 mm. **Obv:** National arms
Rev: The Mayflower ship **Edge:** Reeded

Date	Mintage	F	VF	XF	Unc	BU
2000 Proof	—	Value: 10.00				

KM# 723   5 DOLLARS
12.0000 g., Nickel-Silver, 31.5 mm. **Subject:** Year of the Dragon
Obv: National arms **Obv. Leg.:** MILLENNIUM **Rev:** Chinese
Dragon, facing, type I **Edge:** Reeded

Date	Mintage	F	VF	XF	Unc	BU
2000	—	—	—	—	6.00	8.00

KM# 735   5 DOLLARS
14.8300 g., Copper Nickel, 32.00 mm. **Subject:** XXVII Olympic
Games - Sydney **Rev:** Javelin thrower **Edge:** Reeded

Date	Mintage	F	VF	XF	Unc	BU
2000 20,000	—	—	—	—	10.00	12.00

KM# 778   5 DOLLARS
Nickel-Silver, 31.5 mm. **Subject:** Year of the Dragon
Obv: National Arms **Obv. Leg.:** MILLENNIUM **Rev:** Chinese
Dragon, facing left, type II **Edge:** Reeded

Date	Mintage	F	VF	XF	Unc	BU
2000	—	—	—	—	6.00	8.00

KM# 779   5 DOLLARS
Nickel-Silver, 31.5 mm. **Subject:** Year of the Dragon
Obv: National Arms **Obv. Leg.:** MILLENNIUM **Rev:** Chinese
Dragon, facing right, type III **Edge:** Reeded

Date	Mintage	F	VF	XF	Unc	BU
2000	—	—	—	—	6.00	8.00

KM# 805   5 DOLLARS
27.7000 g., Copper-Nickel, 40.13 mm. **Series:** Wildlife of North
america **Obv:** National arms **Rev:** Upper half of Bald Eagle -
multicolor **Edge:** Reeded

Date	Mintage	F	VF	XF	Unc	BU
2000 Proof	—	Value: 10.00				

KM# 63   10 DOLLARS
11.7200 g., 0.9000 Gold 0.3391 oz. AGW **Subject:** 25th
Anniversary of Inter-Continental Hotels **Obv:** Value below hotel
building **Rev:** Letter I within football flanked by dates

Date	Mintage	F	VF	XF	Unc	BU
1971 Proof	—	Value: 350				

KM# 26   10 DOLLARS
16.7185 g., 0.9000 Gold 0.4837 oz. AGW **Subject:** Inauguration
of President Tolbert **Rev:** Head left

Date	Mintage	F	VF	XF	Unc	BU
1972 Proof	—	Value: 485				

KM# 53 10 DOLLARS
23.3300 g., 0.9250 Silver 0.6938 oz. ASW **Subject:** Decade For Women **Obv:** National arms **Rev:** Coat of arms and value

Date	Mintage	F	VF	XF	Unc	BU
1985 Proof	—				Value: 30.00	

KM# 54 10 DOLLARS
31.1000 g., 0.9990 Silver 0.9988 oz. ASW **Subject:** President John F. Kennedy **Obv:** National arms **Rev:** Head left

Date	Mintage	F	VF	XF	Unc	BU
1988 Proof	25,000				Value: 37.50	

KM# 55 10 DOLLARS
31.1000 g., 0.9990 Silver 0.9988 oz. ASW **Subject:** President Samuel Kanyon Doe **Obv:** National arms **Rev:** President Samuel Kanyon Doe **Note:** Similar to 250 Dollars, KM#56.

Date	Mintage	F	VF	XF	Unc	BU
1988 Proof	25,000				Value: 37.50	

KM# 57 10 DOLLARS
31.1000 g., 0.9990 Silver 0.9988 oz. ASW **Subject:** President George Bush **Obv:** National arms **Rev:** Head left **Note:** Similar to 250 Dollars, KM#58.

Date	Mintage	F	VF	XF	Unc	BU
1989 Proof	25,000				Value: 37.50	

KM# 59 10 DOLLARS
31.1000 g., 0.9990 Silver 0.9988 oz. ASW **Subject:** Emperor Hirohito **Obv:** National arms **Rev:** Head facing divides dates **Note:** Similar to 250 Dollars, KM#60.

Date	Mintage	F	VF	XF	Unc	BU
1989 Proof	25,000				Value: 35.00	

KM# 72 10 DOLLARS
31.1000 g., 0.9990 Silver 0.9988 oz. ASW **Subject:** Chancellor Willy Brandt - In Memorium **Obv:** National arms **Rev:** Head left, Chariot from Brandenburg Gate below

Date	Mintage	F	VF	XF	Unc	BU
1992 Proof	—				Value: 32.50	

KM# 74 10 DOLLARS
31.1000 g., 0.9990 Silver 0.9988 oz. ASW **Subject:** Formula One **Obv:** National arms **Rev:** Ricardo Patrese

Date	Mintage	F	VF	XF	Unc	BU
1992 Proof	25,000				Value: 40.00	

KM# 75 10 DOLLARS
31.1000 g., 0.9990 Silver 0.9988 oz. ASW **Subject:** Formula One **Obv:** National arms **Rev:** Nigel Mansell

Date	Mintage	F	VF	XF	Unc	BU
1992 Proof	25,000				Value: 40.00	

KM# 83 10 DOLLARS
31.1000 g., 0.9990 Silver 0.9988 oz. ASW **Subject:** Formula One **Obv:** National arms **Rev:** Gerhard Berger

Date	Mintage	F	VF	XF	Unc	BU
1992 Proof	25,000				Value: 40.00	

KM# 84 10 DOLLARS
31.1000 g., 0.9990 Silver 0.9988 oz. ASW **Subject:** Formula One **Obv:** National arms **Rev:** Aguri Suzuki

Date	Mintage	F	VF	XF	Unc	BU
1992 Proof	25,000				Value: 40.00	

KM# 85 10 DOLLARS
31.1000 g., 0.9990 Silver 0.9988 oz. ASW **Subject:** Formula One **Obv:** National arms **Rev:** Ayrton Senna

Date	Mintage	F	VF	XF	Unc	BU
1992 Proof	25,000				Value: 40.00	

KM# 86 10 DOLLARS
31.1000 g., 0.9990 Silver 0.9988 oz. ASW **Subject:** Formula One **Obv:** National arms **Rev:** Michael Schumacher

Date	Mintage	F	VF	XF	Unc	BU
1992 Proof	25,000				Value: 40.00	

KM# 87 10 DOLLARS
31.1000 g., 0.9990 Silver 0.9988 oz. ASW **Subject:** Formula One **Obv:** National arms **Rev:** Alain Prost

Date	Mintage	F	VF	XF	Unc	BU
1992 Proof	25,000				Value: 40.00	

KM# 88 10 DOLLARS
31.1000 g., 0.9990 Silver 0.9988 oz. ASW **Subject:** Formula One **Obv:** National arms **Rev:** Ukyo Katayama

Date	Mintage	F	VF	XF	Unc	BU
1992 Proof	25,000				Value: 40.00	

KM# 68 10 DOLLARS
31.1000 g., 0.9990 Silver 0.9988 oz. ASW **Subject:** President Bill Clinton **Obv:** National arms **Rev:** Head right

Date	Mintage	F	VF	XF	Unc	BU
1993 Proof	25,000				Value: 30.00	

KM# 99 10 DOLLARS
31.1000 g., 0.9990 Silver 0.9988 oz. ASW **Series:** Preserve Planet Earth **Obv:** National arms **Rev:** Protoceratops

Date	Mintage	F	VF	XF	Unc	BU
1993 Proof	25,000				Value: 40.00	

KM# 102 10 DOLLARS
31.1000 g., 0.9990 Silver 0.9988 oz. ASW **Subject:** Baseball Hall of Fame **Obv:** National arms **Rev:** Nolan Ryan waving baseball cap

Date	Mintage	F	VF	XF	Unc	BU
1993 Proof	—				Value: 30.00	

KM# 104 10 DOLLARS
31.1000 g., 0.9990 Silver 0.9988 oz. ASW **Subject:** President John F. Kennedy **Obv:** National arms **Rev:** Head left, funeral caisson below

Date	Mintage	F	VF	XF	Unc	BU
1993 Proof	25,000				Value: 40.00	

KM# 110 10 DOLLARS
31.1000 g., 0.9990 Silver 0.9988 oz. ASW **Series:** Preserve Planet Earth **Obv:** National arms **Rev:** Corythosaurus

Date	Mintage	F	VF	XF	Unc	BU
1993 Proof	25,000				Value: 35.00	

KM# 113 10 DOLLARS
31.1000 g., 0.9990 Silver 0.9988 oz. ASW **Series:** Preserve Planet Earth **Obv:** National arms **Rev:** Atchaeopteryx **Note:** Incorrect spelling.

Date	Mintage	F	VF	XF	Unc	BU
1993 Proof	25,000				Value: 35.00	

KM# 116   10 DOLLARS
31.1000 g., 0.9990 Silver 0.9988 oz. ASW **Series:** Preserve
Planet Earth **Obv:** National arms **Rev:** Archaeopteryx
Note: Correct spelling.

Date	Mintage	F	VF	XF	Unc	BU
1994 Proof	25,000		Value: 40.00			

KM# 561   10 DOLLARS
31.1035 g., 0.9990 Silver 0.9990 oz. ASW **Obv:** National arms
Rev: Mercedes Benz C-Class car

Date	Mintage	F	VF	XF	Unc	BU
1994 Proof	Est. 25,000		Value: 50.00			

KM# 119   10 DOLLARS
31.1000 g., 0.9990 Silver 0.9988 oz. ASW **Series:** Preserve
Planet Earth **Obv:** National arms **Rev:** Gorillas

Date	Mintage	F	VF	XF	Unc	BU
1994 Proof	25,000		Value: 40.00			

KM# 122   10 DOLLARS
31.1000 g., 0.9990 Silver 0.9988 oz. ASW **Series:** Preserve
Planet Earth **Obv:** National arms **Rev:** Pygmy Hippopotami

Date	Mintage	F	VF	XF	Unc	BU
1994 Proof	25,000		Value: 40.00			

KM# 125   10 DOLLARS
31.1000 g., 0.9990 Silver 0.9988 oz. ASW **Series:** Preserve
Planet Earth **Obv:** National arms **Rev:** Nile Soft-shelled Turtle

Date	Mintage	F	VF	XF	Unc	BU
1994 Proof	25,000		Value: 40.00			

KM# 127   10 DOLLARS
31.1000 g., 0.9990 Silver 0.9988 oz. ASW **Obv:** National arms
Rev: Head left with small gazelle below

Date	Mintage	F	VF	XF	Unc	BU
1994 Proof	25,000		Value: 30.00			

KM# 155   10 DOLLARS
31.1000 g., 0.9990 Silver 0.9988 oz. ASW **Obv:** National arms
Rev: General Rommel, bust 1/4 left

Date	Mintage	F	VF	XF	Unc	BU
1994 Proof	25,000		Value: 40.00			

KM# 156   10 DOLLARS
31.1000 g., 0.9990 Silver 0.9988 oz. ASW **Obv:** National arms
Rev: Field Marshal Montgomery facing

Date	Mintage	F	VF	XF	Unc	BU
1994 Proof	25,000		Value: 40.00			

KM# 157   10 DOLLARS
31.1000 g., 0.9990 Silver 0.9988 oz. ASW **Obv:** National arms
Rev: General Dwight D. Eisenhower half left

Date	Mintage	F	VF	XF	Unc	BU
1994 Proof	25,000		Value: 40.00			

KM# 281   10 DOLLARS
31.1000 g., 0.9990 Silver 0.9988 oz. ASW **Subject:** Baseball
Hall of Fame, Reggie Jackson **Obv:** National arms **Rev:** Baseball
player divides circle

Date	Mintage	F	VF	XF	Unc	BU
1994 Proof	—		Value: 40.00			

KM# 282   10 DOLLARS
31.1000 g., 0.9990 Silver 0.9988 oz. ASW **Subject:** Baseball
Hall of Fame **Obv:** National arms **Rev:** Roberto Clemente facing

Date	Mintage	F	VF	XF	Unc	BU
1994 Proof	—		Value: 40.00			

KM# 347   10 DOLLARS
31.1000 g., 0.9990 Silver 0.9988 oz. ASW **Subject:** The History
of the Motor Car **Obv:** National arms **Rev:** Mercedes-Benz
C-Class car

Date	Mintage	F	VF	XF	Unc	BU
1994 Proof	—		Value: 40.00			

KM# 129   10 DOLLARS
31.1000 g., 0.9990 Silver 0.9988 oz. ASW **Subject:** Star Trek
Obv: National arms **Rev:** Conjoined busts of Captain Kirk and
Captian Picard

Date	Mintage	F	VF	XF	Unc	BU
1995 Proof	—		Value: 47.50			

KM# 134   10 DOLLARS
31.1000 g., 0.9990 Silver 0.9988 oz. ASW **Series:** Preserve
Planet Earth **Obv:** National arms **Rev:** Leopard

Date	Mintage	F	VF	XF	Unc	BU
1995 Proof	25,000		Value: 40.00			

KM# 137   10 DOLLARS
31.1000 g., 0.9990 Silver 0.9988 oz. ASW **Series:** Preserve
Planet Earth **Obv:** National arms **Rev:** Storks

Date	Mintage	F	VF	XF	Unc	BU
1995 Proof	25,000		Value: 40.00			

KM# 145   10 DOLLARS
31.1000 g., 0.9990 Silver 0.9988 oz. ASW **Obv:** National arms
Rev: Winston Churchill overlooking planes, tanks and ship

Date	Mintage	F	VF	XF	Unc	BU
1995 Proof	25,000		Value: 40.00			

KM# 146   10 DOLLARS
31.1000 g., 0.9990 Silver 0.9988 oz. ASW **Obv:** National arms
Rev: President Franklin D. Roosevelt riding in jeep

Date	Mintage	F	VF	XF	Unc	BU
1995 Proof	25,000	Value: 40.00				

KM# 147   10 DOLLARS
31.1000 g., 0.9990 Silver 0.9988 oz. ASW **Obv:** National arms
Rev: General George Patton in front of map

Date	Mintage	F	VF	XF	Unc	BU
1995 Proof	25,000	Value: 40.00				

KM# 148   10 DOLLARS
31.1000 g., 0.9990 Silver 0.9988 oz. ASW **Obv:** National arms
Rev: President Harry S. Truman facing

Date	Mintage	F	VF	XF	Unc	BU
1995 Proof	25,000	Value: 40.00				

KM# 149   10 DOLLARS
31.1000 g., 0.9990 Silver 0.9988 oz. ASW **Obv:** National arms
Rev: President Charles de Gaulle on Champs Elysees

Date	Mintage	F	VF	XF	Unc	BU
1995 Proof	25,000	Value: 40.00				

KM# 159   10 DOLLARS
31.1000 g., 0.9990 Silver 0.9988 oz. ASW **Obv:** National arms
Rev: Sun Yat Sen bust facing

Date	Mintage	F	VF	XF	Unc	BU
1995 Proof	25,000	Value: 45.00				
1996 Proof	25,000	Value: 45.00				

KM# 162   10 DOLLARS
31.1000 g., 0.9990 Silver 0.9988 oz. ASW **Obv:** National arms
Rev: General Chiang Kai-shek

Date	Mintage	F	VF	XF	Unc	BU
1995 Proof	25,000	Value: 45.00				
1996 Proof	25,000	Value: 45.00				

KM# 165   10 DOLLARS
31.1000 g., 0.9990 Silver 0.9988 oz. ASW **Subject:** Cairo
Conference **Obv:** National arms **Rev:** Chiang Kai-shek -
Roosevelt - Churchill

Date	Mintage	F	VF	XF	Unc	BU
1995 Proof	25,000	Value: 45.00				

KM# 171   10 DOLLARS
31.1000 g., 0.9990 Silver 0.9988 oz. ASW **Subject:** 375th
Anniversary - Pilgrim Fathers **Obv:** National arms **Rev:** The
"Mayflower"

Date	Mintage	F	VF	XF	Unc	BU
1995 Proof	25,000	Value: 40.00				

KM# 172   10 DOLLARS
31.1000 g., 0.9990 Silver 0.9988 oz. ASW **Subject:** 375th
Anniversary - Pilgrim Fathers **Obv:** National arms **Rev:** Pilgrims
in skiff, Cape Cod map

Date	Mintage	F	VF	XF	Unc	BU
1995 Proof	25,000	Value: 40.00				

KM# 173   10 DOLLARS
31.1000 g., 0.9990 Silver 0.9988 oz. ASW **Subject:** 375th
Anniversary - Pilgrim Fathers **Obv:** National arms **Rev:** Pilgrim
landing party

Date	Mintage	F	VF	XF	Unc	BU
1995 Proof	25,000	Value: 40.00				

KM# 174   10 DOLLARS
31.1000 g., 0.9990 Silver 0.9988 oz. ASW **Subject:** 375th
Anniversary - Pilgrim Fathers **Obv:** National arms **Rev:** First
Thanksgiving scene

Date	Mintage	F	VF	XF	Unc	BU
1995 Proof	25,000	Value: 40.00				

KM# 180   10 DOLLARS
31.1000 g., 0.9990 Silver 0.9988 oz. ASW **Subject:** Formula
One **Obv:** National arms **Rev:** Mika Hakkinen

Date	Mintage	F	VF	XF	Unc	BU
1995 Proof	25,000	Value: 40.00				

KM# 183   10 DOLLARS
31.1000 g., 0.9990 Silver 0.9988 oz. ASW **Subject:** Formula
One **Obv:** National arms **Rev:** Martin Brundle

Date	Mintage	F	VF	XF	Unc	BU
1995 Proof	25,000	Value: 40.00				

KM# 186   10 DOLLARS
31.1000 g., 0.9990 Silver 0.9988 oz. ASW **Subject:** Formula
One **Obv:** National arms **Rev:** Rubens Barrichello

Date	Mintage	F	VF	XF	Unc	BU
1995 Proof	25,000	Value: 40.00				

KM# 189   10 DOLLARS
31.1000 g., 0.9990 Silver 0.9988 oz. ASW **Subject:** Formula
One **Obv:** National arms **Rev:** David Coulthard

Date	Mintage	F	VF	XF	Unc	BU
1995 Proof	25,000	Value: 40.00				

KM# 192   10 DOLLARS
31.1000 g., 0.9990 Silver 0.9988 oz. ASW **Subject:** Formula
One **Obv:** National arms **Rev:** Jean Alesi

Date	Mintage	F	VF	XF	Unc	BU
1995 Proof	25,000	Value: 40.00				

KM# 194   10 DOLLARS
31.1000 g., 0.9990 Silver 0.9988 oz. ASW **Subject:** Nations United
for Peace **Obv:** National arms divides date **Rev:** Logo, paper dolls

Date	Mintage	F	VF	XF	Unc	BU
1995 Proof	25,000	Value: 37.50				

KM# 564   10 DOLLARS
31.1000 g., 0.9990 Silver 0.9988 oz. ASW, 38.6 mm.
Rev: Bugatti Royale

Date	Mintage	F	VF	XF	Unc	BU
1995	—	—	—	—	40.00	—

KM# 132   10 DOLLARS
31.1000 g., 0.9990 Silver 0.9988 oz. ASW **Subject:** Centennial -
Babe Ruth - Sultan of Swat **Obv:** National arms **Rev:** Head with cap
1/4 right divides dates within circle **Note:** Similar to 1 Dollar, KM#131.

Date	Mintage	F	VF	XF	Unc	BU
1995	—	—	—	—	42.50	—

KM# 199   10 DOLLARS
31.1000 g., 0.9990 Silver 0.9988 oz. ASW **Subject:** Formula
One **Obv:** National arms **Rev:** Mark Blundell

Date	Mintage	F	VF	XF	Unc	BU
1996 Proof	25,000	Value: 40.00				

KM# 200   10 DOLLARS
31.1000 g., 0.9990 Silver 0.9988 oz. ASW **Subject:** Formula
One **Obv:** National arms **Rev:** Johnny Herbert

Date	Mintage	F	VF	XF	Unc	BU
1996 Proof	25,000	Value: 40.00				

KM# 201   10 DOLLARS
31.1000 g., 0.9990 Silver 0.9988 oz. ASW **Subject:** Formula
One **Obv:** National arms **Rev:** Eddie Irvine

Date	Mintage	F	VF	XF	Unc	BU
1996 Proof	25,000	Value: 40.00				

KM# 202   10 DOLLARS
31.1000 g., 0.9990 Silver 0.9988 oz. ASW **Subject:** Formula
One **Obv:** National arms **Rev:** Heinz Frentzen

Date	Mintage	F	VF	XF	Unc	BU
1996 Proof	25,000	Value: 40.00				

KM# 208   10 DOLLARS
31.1000 g., 0.9990 Silver 0.9988 oz. ASW **Subject:** Star Trek
Obv: National arms **Rev:** Starships NCC-1701 and NCC-1701D

Date	Mintage	F	VF	XF	Unc	BU
1996 Proof	25,000	Value: 45.00				

KM# 211   10 DOLLARS
31.1000 g., 0.9990 Silver 0.9988 oz. ASW **Subject:** Star Trek, Scott
and McCoy **Obv:** National arms **Rev:** Conjoined busts facing

Date	Mintage	F	VF	XF	Unc	BU
1996 Proof	25,000	Value: 45.00				

KM# 214   10 DOLLARS
31.1000 g., 0.9990 Silver 0.9988 oz. ASW **Subject:** Star Trek
Obv: National arms **Rev:** LaForge and Data

Date	Mintage	F	VF	XF	Unc	BU
1996 Proof	25,000	Value: 45.00				

KM# 217   10 DOLLARS
31.1000 g., 0.9990 Silver 0.9988 oz. ASW **Subject:** Star Trek
Obv: National arms **Rev:** Spock and Uhura

Date	Mintage	F	VF	XF	Unc	BU
1996 Proof	25,000	Value: 45.00				

KM# 220   10 DOLLARS
31.1000 g., 0.9990 Silver 0.9988 oz. ASW **Subject:** Star Trek
Obv: National arms **Rev:** Worf and Dr. Crusher

Date	Mintage	F	VF	XF	Unc	BU
1996 Proof	25,000	Value: 45.00				

KM# 223   10 DOLLARS
31.1000 g., 0.9990 Silver 0.9988 oz. ASW **Series:** Preserve
Planet Earth **Obv:** National arms **Rev:** Grey Parrot

Date	Mintage	F	VF	XF	Unc	BU
1996 Proof	25,000	Value: 40.00				

KM# 226   10 DOLLARS
31.1000 g., 0.9990 Silver 0.9988 oz. ASW **Series:** Preserve
Planet Earth **Obv:** National arms **Rev:** Love Birds

Date	Mintage	F	VF	XF	Unc	BU
1996 Proof	25,000	Value: 40.00				

KM# 229   10 DOLLARS
31.1000 g., 0.9990 Silver 0.9988 oz. ASW **Subject:** Formula
One **Obv:** National arms **Rev:** Ayrton Senna

Date	Mintage	F	VF	XF	Unc	BU
1996	25,000	Value: 40.00				

KM# 242   10 DOLLARS
31.1000 g., 0.9990 Silver 0.9988 oz. ASW **Subject:** President
Chiang Ching-kuo **Obv:** National arms **Rev:** Bust 1/4 right

Date	Mintage	F	VF	XF	Unc	BU
1996 Proof	25,000	Value: 45.00				

KM# 245   10 DOLLARS
31.1000 g., 0.9990 Silver 0.9988 oz. ASW **Obv:** National arms
Rev: President Lee Ten-hui

Date	Mintage	F	VF	XF	Unc	BU
1996 Proof	25,000	Value: 42.50				

KM# 256   10 DOLLARS
31.1000 g., 0.9990 Silver 0.9988 oz. ASW **Subject:** Chairman
Mao Zedong **Obv:** National arms divides date **Rev:** Standing
figure facing

Date	Mintage	F	VF	XF	Unc	BU
1996 Proof	25,000	Value: 42.50				

KM# 257   10 DOLLARS
31.1000 g., 0.9990 Silver 0.9988 oz. ASW **Obv:** National arms
Rev: Chairman Mao Zedong with gate of Heavenly Peace

Date	Mintage	F	VF	XF	Unc	BU
1996 Proof	25,000	Value: 42.50				

KM# 258   10 DOLLARS
31.1000 g., 0.9990 Silver 0.9988 oz. ASW **Obv:** National arms
Rev: Chairman Mao Zedong proclaiming People's Republic

Date	Mintage	F	VF	XF	Unc	BU
1996 Proof	25,000	Value: 42.50				

KM# 262   10 DOLLARS
31.1000 g., 0.9990 Silver 0.9988 oz. ASW **Subject:** Chairman
Mao Zedong and President Nixon **Obv:** National arms
Rev: Seated figures facing

Date	Mintage	F	VF	XF	Unc	BU
1996 Proof	25,000	Value: 40.00				

KM# 264   10 DOLLARS
31.1000 g., 0.9990 Silver 0.9988 oz. ASW **Series:** Pioneers of
the West **Obv:** National arms **Rev:** Daniel Boone

Date	Mintage	F	VF	XF	Unc	BU
1996 Proof	25,000	Value: 40.00				

KM# 267   10 DOLLARS
31.1000 g., 0.9990 Silver 0.9988 oz. ASW **Series:** Pioneers of
the West **Obv:** National arms **Rev:** Davy Crockett

Date	Mintage	F	VF	XF	Unc	BU
1996 Proof	25,000	Value: 40.00				

KM# 270 10 DOLLARS
31.1000 g., 0.9990 Silver 0.9988 oz. ASW **Series:** Pioneers of
the West **Obv:** National arms **Rev:** Jim Bowie in front of the Alamo

Date	Mintage	F	VF	XF	Unc	BU
1996 Proof	25,000		Value: 40.00			

KM# 273 10 DOLLARS
31.1000 g., 0.9990 Silver 0.9988 oz. ASW **Series:** Pioneers of
the West **Obv:** National arms **Rev:** Kit Carson

Date	Mintage	F	VF	XF	Unc	BU
1996 Proof	25,000		Value: 40.00			

KM# 276 10 DOLLARS
31.1000 g., 0.9990 Silver 0.9988 oz. ASW **Series:** Pioneers of
the West **Obv:** National arms **Rev:** Wild Bill Hickok

Date	Mintage	F	VF	XF	Unc	BU
1996 Proof	25,000		Value: 40.00			

KM# 279 10 DOLLARS
31.1000 g., 0.9990 Silver 0.9988 oz. ASW **Series:** Pioneers of
the West **Obv:** National arms **Rev:** Buffalo Bill

Date	Mintage	F	VF	XF	Unc	BU
1996 Proof	25,000		Value: 40.00			

KM# 284 10 DOLLARS
31.1000 g., 0.9990 Silver 0.9988 oz. ASW **Subject:** Return of
Macao to China **Obv:** National arms **Rev:** City views, old and new

Date	Mintage	F	VF	XF	Unc	BU
1996 Proof	Est. 6,000		Value: 32.50			

KM# 285 10 DOLLARS
31.1000 g., 0.9990 Silver 0.9988 oz. ASW **Subject:** Return of
Hong Kong to China **Obv:** National arms divide date above value
Rev: City views, old and new

Date	Mintage	F	VF	XF	Unc	BU
1996 Proof	Est. 6,000		Value: 32.50			

KM# 287 10 DOLLARS
31.1000 g., 0.9990 Silver 0.9988 oz. ASW **Series:** WWII
Subject: Evacuation from Dunkirk **Obv:** National arms **Rev:**
British 1939-45 Star Medal to left of fighter planes and ships

Date	Mintage	F	VF	XF	Unc	BU
1997 Proof	25,000		Value: 37.50			

KM# 289 10 DOLLARS
31.1000 g., 0.9990 Silver 0.9988 oz. ASW **Series:** WWII
Subject: Liberation of the Philippines **Obv:** National arms
Rev: American Asian-Pacific campaign medal to right of soldiers in
water

Date	Mintage	F	VF	XF	Unc	BU
1997 Proof	25,000		Value: 37.50			

KM# 291 10 DOLLARS
31.1000 g., 0.9990 Silver 0.9988 oz. ASW **Series:** WWII
Subject: Defense of Stalingrad **Obv:** National arms **Rev:** Soviet
distinguished combat medal to left of war scene

Date	Mintage	F	VF	XF	Unc	BU
1997 Proof	25,000		Value: 37.50			

KM# 293 10 DOLLARS
31.1000 g., 0.9990 Silver 0.9988 oz. ASW **Series:** WWII
Subject: Arnhem **Obv:** National arms **Rev:** Netherlands bronze
lion cross to right of parachutists, bridge and soldier

Date	Mintage	F	VF	XF	Unc	BU
1997 Proof	25,000		Value: 37.50			

KM# 295 10 DOLLARS
31.1000 g., 0.9990 Silver 0.9988 oz. ASW **Series:** WWII
Subject: Raid on the Dams **Obv:** National arms **Rev:** British
distinguished flying medal

Date	Mintage	F	VF	XF	Unc	BU
1997 Proof	25,000		Value: 37.50			

KM# 297 10 DOLLARS
31.1000 g., 0.9990 Silver 0.9988 oz. ASW **Series:** WWII
Subject: West African Campaign **Obv:** National arms **Rev:** WWII
Victory medal

Date	Mintage	F	VF	XF	Unc	BU
1997 Proof	25,000		Value: 37.50			

KM# 299 10 DOLLARS
31.1000 g., 0.9990 Silver 0.9988 oz. ASW **Series:** WWII
Subject: North African Campaign **Obv:** National arms **Rev:**
British Africa star medal to right of tank in front of pyramid

Date	Mintage	F	VF	XF	Unc	BU
1997 Proof	25,000		Value: 37.50			

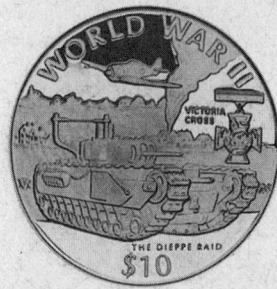

KM# 301 10 DOLLARS
31.1000 g., 0.9990 Silver 0.9988 oz. ASW **Series:** WWII
Subject: The Dieppe Raid **Obv:** National arms **Rev:** British
Victoria cross to right of plane over half-track vehicle

Date	Mintage	F	VF	XF	Unc	BU
1997 Proof	25,000		Value: 37.50			

KM# 303 10 DOLLARS
31.1000 g., 0.9990 Silver 0.9988 oz. ASW **Series:** WWII
Subject: Iwo Jima **Obv:** National arms **Rev:** Purple Heart medal
to upper left of damaged plane landing on a carrier

Date	Mintage	F	VF	XF	Unc	BU
1997 Proof	25,000		Value: 37.50			

KM# 305 10 DOLLARS
31.1000 g., 0.9990 Silver 0.9988 oz. ASW **Series:** WWII
Subject: Battle of Britain **Obv:** National arms **Rev:** British
distinguished flying cross to left of pilots running to board planes

Date	Mintage	F	VF	XF	Unc	BU
1997 Proof	25,000		Value: 37.50			

KM# 307 10 DOLLARS
31.1000 g., 0.9990 Silver 0.9988 oz. ASW **Series:** WWII
Subject: Liberation of Paris **Obv:** National arms **Rev:** Croix de
Guerre medal to right of soldiers in front of Arch de Triumph

Date	Mintage	F	VF	XF	Unc	BU
1997 Proof	25,000		Value: 37.50			

KM# 309 10 DOLLARS
31.1000 g., 0.9990 Silver 0.9988 oz. ASW **Series:** WWII
Subject: Burma Campaign **Obv:** National arms **Rev:** British
Burma star medal

Date	Mintage	F	VF	XF	Unc	BU
1997 Proof	25,000		Value: 37.50			

KM# 311 10 DOLLARS
31.1000 g., 0.9990 Silver 0.9988 oz. ASW **Subject:** Mahatma
Gandhi **Obv:** National arms **Rev:** Seated figure facing left in front
of Taj Mahal

Date	Mintage	F	VF	XF	Unc	BU
1997 Proof	25,000		Value: 40.00			

KM# 314   10 DOLLARS
31.1000 g., 0.9990 Silver 0.9988 oz. ASW **Subject:** Return of Hong Kong **Obv:** National arms **Rev:** Dragon

Date	Mintage	F	VF	XF	Unc	BU
1997 Proof	25,000	Value: 40.00				

KM# 321   10 DOLLARS
31.1000 g., 0.9990 Silver 0.9988 oz. ASW **Subject:** Fiftieth Anniversary of the Kon-Tiki Expedition **Obv:** National arms **Rev:** Mask within circle

Date	Mintage	F	VF	XF	Unc	BU
1997 Proof	25,000	Value: 40.00				

KM# 325   10 DOLLARS
31.1000 g., 0.9990 Silver 0.9988 oz. ASW **Subject:** Jurassic Park **Obv:** National arms **Rev:** Stegosaurus

Date	Mintage	F	VF	XF	Unc	BU
1997 Proof	10,000	Value: 40.00				

KM# 328   10 DOLLARS
31.1030 g., 0.9250 Gold Clad Silver 0.9249 oz. **Subject:** Golden Wedding Anniversary **Obv:** National arms **Rev:** E & P initials above 2 shields

Date	Mintage	F	VF	XF	Unc	BU
1997 Proof	10,000	Value: 50.00				

KM# 331   10 DOLLARS
31.1030 g., 0.9250 Gold Clad Silver 0.9249 oz. **Subject:** Queen Elizabeth II and Prince Philip's Golden Wedding Anniversary **Obv:** National arms **Rev:** Royal couple with horse

Date	Mintage	F	VF	XF	Unc	BU
1997 Proof	10,000	Value: 50.00				

KM# 334   10 DOLLARS
31.1030 g., 0.9250 Gold Clad Silver 0.9249 oz. **Subject:** Queen Elizabeth II and Prince Philip's Golden Wedding Anniversary **Obv:** National arms **Rev:** Royal couple with dogs

Date	Mintage	F	VF	XF	Unc	BU
1997 Proof	10,000	Value: 50.00				

KM# 337   10 DOLLARS
31.1030 g., 0.9250 Gold Clad Silver 0.9249 oz. **Subject:** Queen Elizabeth II and Prince Philip's Golden Wedding Anniversary **Obv:** National arms **Rev:** Royal couple with children

Date	Mintage	F	VF	XF	Unc	BU
1997 Proof	10,000	Value: 50.00				

KM# 345   10 DOLLARS
31.1035 g., 0.9990 Silver 0.9990 oz. ASW **Subject:** 150th Anniversary - Independence of Liberia **Obv:** National arms **Rev:** Cameo to upper left of ship above small boat

Date	Mintage	F	VF	XF	Unc	BU
1997 Proof	25,000	Value: 45.00				

KM# 346   10 DOLLARS
Copper-Nickel **Subject:** Famous Personalities of the World; Marilyn Monroe **Obv:** National arms with blank ribbons **Rev:** Head facing

Date	Mintage	F	VF	XF	Unc	BU
ND(1997) Proof	—	Value: 15.00				

KM# 348   10 DOLLARS
31.1035 g., 0.9990 Silver 0.9990 oz. ASW **Subject:** Return of Hong Kong to China **Obv:** National arms **Rev:** City view, old and new

Date	Mintage	F	VF	XF	Unc	BU
1997 Proof	Est. 8,000	Value: 32.50				

KM# 349   10 DOLLARS
31.1035 g., 0.9990 Silver 0.9990 oz. ASW **Subject:** Pending Return of Macao to China **Obv:** National arms **Rev:** City view within circle

Date	Mintage	F	VF	XF	Unc	BU
1997 Proof	Est. 8,000	Value: 32.50				

KM# 350   10 DOLLARS
31.1035 g., 0.9990 Silver 0.9990 oz. ASW **Subject:** Diana - The People's Princess **Obv:** National arms **Rev:** Princess Diana in minefield wearing protective gear

Date	Mintage	F	VF	XF	Unc	BU
1997 Proof	—	Value: 45.00				

KM# 369   10 DOLLARS
31.1035 g., 0.9990 Silver 0.9990 oz. ASW **Subject:** Star Trek - The Next Generation **Obv:** National arms **Rev:** Romulan Warbird

Date	Mintage	F	VF	XF	Unc	BU
1997 Proof	25,000	Value: 45.00				

KM# 372   10 DOLLARS
31.1035 g., 0.9990 Silver 0.9990 oz. ASW **Subject:** Star Trek - The Next Generation **Obv:** National arms **Rev:** Klingon Attack Cruiser

Date	Mintage	F	VF	XF	Unc	BU
1997 Proof	25,000	Value: 45.00				

KM# 375 10 DOLLARS
31.1035 g., 0.9990 Silver 0.9990 oz. ASW **Subject:** Star Trek - The Next Generation **Obv:** National arms **Rev:** U.S.S. Enterprise NCC-1701-D

Date	Mintage	F	VF	XF	Unc	BU
1997 Proof	25,000	Value: 45.00				

KM# 378 10 DOLLARS
31.1035 g., 0.9990 Silver 0.9990 oz. ASW **Subject:** Star Trek - The Next Generation **Obv:** National arms **Rev:** Klingon Bird of Prey

Date	Mintage	F	VF	XF	Unc	BU
1997 Proof	25,000	Value: 45.00				

KM# 381 10 DOLLARS
31.1035 g., 0.9990 Silver 0.9990 oz. ASW **Subject:** Star Trek - The Next Generation **Obv:** National arms **Rev:** Borg Cube

Date	Mintage	F	VF	XF	Unc	BU
1997 Proof	25,000	Value: 45.00				

KM# 384 10 DOLLARS
31.1035 g., 0.9990 Silver 0.9990 oz. ASW **Subject:** Star Trek - The Next Generation **Obv:** National arms **Rev:** Ferengi Marauder

Date	Mintage	F	VF	XF	Unc	BU
1997 Proof	25,000	Value: 45.00				

KM# 780 10 DOLLARS
31.9800 g., 0.9250 Silver 0.9510 oz. ASW, 38.75 mm.
Series: World's Greatest Conquerors **Obv:** National arms
Rev: Charles I **Edge:** Reeded

Date	Mintage	F	VF	XF	Unc	BU
1997FM Proof	—	Value: 50.00				

KM# 781 10 DOLLARS
31.9800 g., 0.9250 Silver 0.9510 oz. ASW, 38.75 mm.
Series: World's Greatest Conquerors **Obv:** National arms
Rev: Genghis Khan **Edge:** Reeded

Date	Mintage	F	VF	XF	Unc	BU
1997FM Proof	—	Value: 50.00				

KM# 782 10 DOLLARS
31.9800 g., 0.9250 Silver 0.9510 oz. ASW, 38.75 mm.
Series: World's Greatest Conquerors **Obv:** National arms
Rev: Tokugawa Ieyasu **Edge:** Reeded

Date	Mintage	F	VF	XF	Unc	BU
1997FM Proof	—	Value: 50.00				

KM# 783 10 DOLLARS
31.9800 g., 0.9250 Silver 0.9510 oz. ASW, 38.75 mm.
Series: World's Greatest Conquerors **Obv:** National arms
Rev: Julius Caesar **Edge:** Reeded

Date	Mintage	F	VF	XF	Unc	BU
1997FM Proof	—	Value: 50.00				

KM# 784 10 DOLLARS
31.9800 g., 0.9250 Silver 0.9510 oz. ASW, 38.75 mm.
Series: World's Greatest Conquerors **Obv:** National arms
Rev: Ramses II **Edge:** Reeded

Date	Mintage	F	VF	XF	Unc	BU
1997FM Proof	—	Value: 50.00				

KM# 785 10 DOLLARS
31.9800 g., 0.9250 Silver 0.9510 oz. ASW, 38.75 mm.
Series: World's Greatest Conquerors **Obv:** National arms
Rev: 1/2 length figure of Alexander the Great standing facing holding spear and shield **Edge:** Reeded

Date	Mintage	F	VF	XF	Unc	BU
1997FM Proof	—	Value: 50.00				

KM# 786 10 DOLLARS
31.9800 g., 0.9250 Silver 0.9510 oz. ASW, 38.75 mm.
Series: World's Greatest Conquerors **Obv:** National arms
Rev: Hannibal **Edge:** Reeded

Date	Mintage	F	VF	XF	Unc	BU
1997FM Proof	—	Value: 50.00				

KM# 787 10 DOLLARS
31.9800 g., 0.9250 Silver 0.9510 oz. ASW, 38.75 mm.
Series: World's Greatest Conquerors **Obv:** National arms
Rev: 1/2 length figure of William the Conqueror standing facing holding sword **Edge:** Reeded

Date	Mintage	F	VF	XF	Unc	BU
1997FM Proof	—	Value: 50.00				

KM# 788 10 DOLLARS
31.9800 g., 0.9250 Silver 0.9510 oz. ASW, 38.75 mm.
Series: World's Greatest Conquerors **Obv:** National arms
Rev: Constantine the Great seated facing 3/4 left **Edge:** Reeded

Date	Mintage	F	VF	XF	Unc	BU
1997FM Proof	—	Value: 50.00				

KM# 789 10 DOLLARS
31.9800 g., 0.9250 Silver 0.9510 oz. ASW, 38.75 mm.
Series: World's Greatest Conquerors **Obv:** National arms
Rev: Kyros the Great **Edge:** Reeded

Date	Mintage	F	VF	XF	Unc	BU
1997FM Proof	—	Value: 50.00				

KM# 790 10 DOLLARS
31.9800 g., 0.9250 Silver 0.9510 oz. ASW, 38.75 mm. **Series:** World's Greatest Conquerors **Obv:** National arms **Rev:** 1/2 length crowned armored bust of Attila the Hun facing 3/4 left **Edge:** Reeded

Date	Mintage	F	VF	XF	Unc	BU
1997FM Proof	—	Value: 50.00				

KM# 791 10 DOLLARS
31.9800 g., 0.9250 Silver 0.9510 oz. ASW, 38.75 mm.
Series: World's Greatest Conquerors **Obv:** National arms
Rev: 1/2 length bust of Tamerlane the Great facing 3/4 right **Edge:** Reeded

Date	Mintage	F	VF	XF	Unc	BU
1997FM Proof	—	Value: 50.00				

KM# 792 10 DOLLARS
31.9800 g., 0.9250 Silver 0.9510 oz. ASW, 38.75 mm.
Series: World's Greatest Conquerors **Obv:** National arms
Rev: Sultan Salah el-Din Yusuf bin-Ayyud **Edge:** Reeded

Date	Mintage	F	VF	XF	Unc	BU
1997FM Proof	—	Value: 50.00				

KM# 793 10 DOLLARS
31.9800 g., 0.9250 Silver 0.9510 oz. ASW, 38.75 mm.
Series: World's Greatest Conquerors **Obv:** National arms
Rev: Edward the Black Prince horseback right **Edge:** Reeded

Date	Mintage	F	VF	XF	Unc	BU
1997FM Proof	—	Value: 50.00				

KM# 794 10 DOLLARS
31.9800 g., 0.9250 Silver 0.9510 oz. ASW, 38.75 mm.
Series: World's Greatest Conquerors **Obv:** National arms
Rev: Henry V standing holding sword facing left, castle in background **Edge:** Reeded

Date	Mintage	F	VF	XF	Unc	BU
1997FM Proof	—	Value: 50.00				

KM# 795 10 DOLLARS
31.9800 g., 0.9250 Silver 0.9510 oz. ASW, 38.75 mm.
Series: World's Greatest Conquerors **Obv:** National arms
Rev: Napoleon on rearing horse left **Edge:** Reeded

Date	Mintage	F	VF	XF	Unc	BU
1997FM Proof	—	Value: 50.00				

KM# 796 10 DOLLARS
31.9800 g., 0.9250 Silver 0.9510 oz. ASW, 38.75 mm.
Series: World's Greatest Conquerors **Obv:** National arms
Rev: Duke of Marlborough **Edge:** Reeded

Date	Mintage	F	VF	XF	Unc	BU
1997FM Proof	—	Value: 50.00				

KM# 797 10 DOLLARS
31.9800 g., 0.9250 Silver 0.9510 oz. ASW, 38.75 mm.
Series: World's Greatest Conquerors **Obv:** National arms
Rev: Bust of Cortes facing 3/4 right **Edge:** Reeded

Date	Mintage	F	VF	XF	Unc	BU
1997FM Proof	—	Value: 50.00				

KM# 798 10 DOLLARS
31.9800 g., 0.9250 Silver 0.9510 oz. ASW, 38.75 mm.
Series: World's Greatest Conquerors **Obv:** National arms
Rev: Pizarro in armor standing facing holding sword, sailing ship in background **Edge:** Reeded

Date	Mintage	F	VF	XF	Unc	BU
1997FM Proof	—	Value: 50.00				

KM# 387 10 DOLLARS
31.1035 g., 0.9990 Silver 0.9990 oz. ASW **Subject:** President Ronald Reagan **Obv:** National arms **Rev:** Lincoln Memorial below head right

Date	Mintage	F	VF	XF	Unc	BU
1998 Proof	25,000	Value: 50.00				

KM# 402   10 DOLLARS
31.1035 g., 0.9990 Silver 0.9990 oz. ASW **Subject:** Christopher Columbus **Obv:** National arms **Rev:** Bust 1/4 right above ship

Date	Mintage	F	VF	XF	Unc	BU
1999 Proof	25,000	Value: 45.00				

KM# 405   10 DOLLARS
31.1035 g., 0.9990 Silver 0.9990 oz. ASW **Subject:** Captain James Cook **Obv:** National arms **Rev:** Portrait, map and ship

Date	Mintage	F	VF	XF	Unc	BU
1999 Proof	25,000	Value: 45.00				

KM# 408   10 DOLLARS
31.1035 g., 0.9990 Silver 0.9990 oz. ASW **Subject:** Return of Macao to China **Obv:** National arms **Rev:** Dragon and phoenix

Date	Mintage	F	VF	XF	Unc	BU
1999 Proof	25,000	Value: 40.00				

KM# 414   10 DOLLARS
31.1035 g., 0.9990 Silver 0.9990 oz. ASW **Subject:** The Wedding of Prince Edward and Miss Sophie Rhys-Jones **Obv:** National arms **Rev:** Couple in carriage

Date	Mintage	F	VF	XF	Unc	BU
1999 Proof	10,000	Value: 50.00				

KM# 424   10 DOLLARS
15.5517 g., 0.9990 Silver 0.4995 oz. ASW **Series:** Liberty **Subject:** John F. Kennedy and John Jr. **Obv:** National arms **Rev:** Conjoined heads left

Date	Mintage	F	VF	XF	Unc	BU
1999 Proof	—	Value: 22.50				

KM# 573   10 DOLLARS
25.1000 g., 0.9250 Silver 0.7464 oz. ASW, 38.6 mm. **Obv:** National arms **Rev:** Titanic steaming right **Edge:** Reeded

Date	Mintage	F	VF	XF	Unc	BU
1999 Proof	—	Value: 40.00				

KM# 468   10 DOLLARS
25.0000 g., 0.9250 Silver 0.7435 oz. ASW, 38.7 mm. **Obv:** National arms **Rev:** Sailing ship "Mayflower" **Edge:** Reeded

Date	Mintage	F	VF	XF	Unc	BU
1999 Proof	—	Value: 25.00				

KM# 471   10 DOLLARS
30.7500 g., 0.9990 Silver 0.9876 oz. ASW, 37.9 mm. **Subject:** Transrapid-08 Hamburg-Berlin Monorail **Obv:** National arms **Rev:** Monorail train car **Edge:** Reeded

Date	Mintage	F	VF	XF	Unc	BU
1999 Proof	—	Value: 35.00				

KM# 706   10 DOLLARS
20.1000 g., 0.9250 Silver 0.5977 oz. ASW, 34 mm. **Obv:** National arms **Rev:** Sail ship "Vijia" with captains name above **Edge:** Reeded

Date	Mintage	F	VF	XF	Unc	BU
1999 Proof	—	Value: 30.00				

KM# 594   10 DOLLARS
31.0000 g., 0.9990 Silver 0.9956 oz. ASW, 40 mm. **Subject:** John F. Kennedy Jr. **Obv:** National arms **Rev:** Two portraits, flag and the White House **Edge:** Reeded

Date	Mintage	F	VF	XF	Unc	BU
1999 Proof	—	Value: 40.00				

KM# 709   10 DOLLARS
0.5100 g., Gold, 11.1 mm.   **Subject:** American Civil War **Obv:** National arms **Rev:** Battle of Gettysburg Generals Meade and Lee **Edge:** Reeded

Date	Mintage	F	VF	XF	Unc	BU
2000 Proof	—	Value: 25.00				

KM# 821   10 DOLLARS
1.1600 g., Gold, 13.89 mm.   **Subject:** Liberian Art **Obv:** National arms **Rev:** Mask of the Dun **Edge:** Reeded

Date	Mintage	F	VF	XF	Unc	BU
2000 Proof	—	Value: 50.00				

KM# 423   10 DOLLARS
31.1035 g., 0.9990 Silver 0.9990 oz. ASW **Subject:** Millennium **Obv:** Liberty cap, crossed flags of USA and Liberia above national arms **Rev:** Morgan dollar Liberty head

Date	Mintage	F	VF	XF	Unc	BU
2000 Proof	Est. 2,000	Value: 40.00				

KM# 443   10 DOLLARS
31.1035 g., 0.9990 Silver 0.9990 oz. ASW, 38.6 mm. **Subject:** Greenwich Meridian **Obv:** National arms **Rev:** World landmarks and fireworks **Edge:** Reeded

Date	Mintage	F	VF	XF	Unc	BU
2000 Proof	25,000	Value: 47.50				

KM# 444   10 DOLLARS
25.0000 g., 0.9250 Silver 0.7435 oz. ASW, 36.8 mm. **Subject:** Millennium - Hippocrates **Obv:** National arms **Rev:** Caduceus **Edge:** Plain

Date	Mintage	F	VF	XF	Unc	BU
2000 Proof	10,000	Value: 35.00				

KM# 469   10 DOLLARS
20.5000 g., 0.9250 Silver 0.6096 oz. ASW, 38.6 mm. **Subject:** Millennium **Obv:** National arms **Rev:** Millennium Dome **Edge:** Reeded

Date	Mintage	F	VF	XF	Unc	BU
2000 Proof	2,000	Value: 32.50				

KM# 470   10 DOLLARS
20.5000 g., 0.9250 Silver 0.6096 oz. ASW **Subject:** Mutiny on the Bounty **Obv:** National arms **Rev:** Mutineers setting ship's officers adrift

Date	Mintage	F	VF	XF	Unc	BU
2000 Proof	2,000	Value: 32.50				

KM# 475   10 DOLLARS
8.4500 g., 0.9990 Silver 0.2714 oz. ASW, 30.1 mm. **Subject:** General Robert E. Lee **Obv:** National arms **Rev:** Equestrian left **Edge:** Reeded

Date	Mintage	F	VF	XF	Unc	BU
2000 Proof	—	Value: 15.00				

KM# 476   10 DOLLARS
8.4500 g., 0.9990 Silver 0.2714 oz. ASW **Obv:** National arms **Rev:** Statue of Liberty

Date	Mintage	F	VF	XF	Unc	BU
2000 Proof	—	Value: 15.00				

KM# 492 10 DOLLARS
3.3930 g., 0.9167 Gold 0.1000 oz. AGW, 16.5 mm.
Subject: US Gold Indian Design Copy **Obv:** Incuse Indian design
Rev: Incuse eagle design **Edge:** Reeded

Date	Mintage	F	VF	XF	Unc	BU
2000	—	—	—	—	125	—

KM# 499 10 DOLLARS
20.1500 g., 0.9990 Silver 0.6472 oz. ASW, 34 mm.
Obv: National arms **Rev:** Monkeys **Edge:** Reeded

Date	Mintage	F	VF	XF	Unc	BU
2000 Proof	—	Value: 30.00				

KM# 500 10 DOLLARS
8.5500 g., 0.9990 Silver 0.2746 oz. ASW, 30 mm.
Subject: American History **Obv:** National arms **Rev:** Washington
crossing the Delaware **Edge:** Reeded **Note:** The American Mint
is not an actual mint.

Date	Mintage	F	VF	XF	Unc	BU
2000 Proof	20,000	Value: 20.00				

KM# 501 10 DOLLARS
8.5500 g., 0.9990 Silver 0.2746 oz. ASW, 30 mm.
Subject: American History - Battle of Gettysburg **Obv:** National
arms **Rev:** Flags and cannon divide uniformed busts
Edge: Reeded **Note:** The American Mint is not an actual mint.

Date	Mintage	F	VF	XF	Unc	BU
2000 Proof	20,000	Value: 20.00				

KM# 502 10 DOLLARS
8.5500 g., 0.9990 Silver 0.2746 oz. ASW, 30 mm. **Subject:**
American History **Obv:** National arms **Rev:** B-17 Bomber in action
Edge: Reeded **Note:** The American Mint is not an actual mint.

Date	Mintage	F	VF	XF	Unc	BU
2000 Proof	20,000	Value: 20.00				

KM# 503 10 DOLLARS
8.5500 g., 0.9990 Silver 0.2746 oz. ASW, 30 mm.
Subject: American History - First Man on the Moon **Obv:** National
arms **Rev:** Astronaut on the moon with American flag
Edge: Reeded **Note:** The American Mint is not an actual mint.

Date	Mintage	F	VF	XF	Unc	BU
2000 Proof	20,000	Value: 20.00				

KM# 622 10 DOLLARS
21.0000 g., Copper-Nickel, 37 mm. **Subject:** Millennium
Obv: National arms **Rev:** Kneeling woman with hourglass
Edge: Reeded

Date	Mintage	F	VF	XF	Unc	BU
2000	—	—	—	—	9.00	—

KM# 645 10 DOLLARS
8.4500 g., 0.9990 Silver 0.2714 oz. ASW, 30 mm. **Obv:** National
arms **Rev:** Boeing 707 **Edge:** Reeded

Date	Mintage	F	VF	XF	Unc	BU
2000 Proof	—	Value: 20.00				

KM# 653 10 DOLLARS
14.6000 g., Copper-Nickel, 33.1 mm. **Obv:** National arms
Rev: Bust facing within U.S. flag **Edge:** Reeded

Date	Mintage	F	VF	XF	Unc	BU
2000	—	—	—	—	10.00	—

KM# 698 10 DOLLARS
29.4000 g., 0.9990 Silver 0.9442 oz. ASW, 40 mm.
Obv: National arms **Rev:** Multicolor cougar **Edge:** Reeded

Date	Mintage	F	VF	XF	Unc	BU
2000 Proof	—	Value: 35.00				

KM# 699 10 DOLLARS
21.3200 g., 0.9990 Silver 0.6847 oz. ASW, 37.4 mm.
Obv: National arms **Rev:** Three-dimensional multicolor timber
wolf in winter **Edge:** Reeded

Date	Mintage	F	VF	XF	Unc	BU
2000	—	—	—	—	30.00	—

KM# 700 10 DOLLARS
29.0600 g., 0.9990 Silver 0.9333 oz. ASW, 40 mm. **Obv:** National
arms **Rev:** Multicolor timber wolf in summer **Edge:** Reeded

Date	Mintage	F	VF	XF	Unc	BU
2000 Proof	—	Value: 35.00				

KM# 704 10 DOLLARS
Silver, 40 mm. **Subject:** Games of the XXVII Olympiad - Sydney
2000 **Obv:** National arms **Rev:** Map of Australia at upper left of
man sailing **Edge:** Reeded

Date	Mintage	F	VF	XF	Unc	BU
2000 Proof	—	Value: 45.00				

KM# 20 12 DOLLARS
6.0000 g., 0.9000 Gold 0.1736 oz. AGW **Subject:** 70th Birthday
of President Tubman **Obv:** National arms **Rev:** Bust left

Date	Mintage	F	VF	XF	Unc	BU
1965 Proof	400	Value: 185				

KM# 108 15 DOLLARS
1.0000 g., 0.9999 Gold 0.0321 oz. AGW **Series:** Preserve
Planet Earth **Obv:** National arms **Rev:** Compsognathus

Date	Mintage	F	VF	XF	Unc	BU
1993 Proof	—	Value: 35.00				

KM# 19 20 DOLLARS
18.6500 g., 0.9000 Gold 0.5396 oz. AGW **Subject:** William
Vacanarat Shadrach Tubman **Obv:** National arms **Rev:** Head 1/4
left above date flanked by stars

Date	Mintage	F	VF	XF	Unc	BU
1964B	10,000	—	—	—	525	—

KM# 19a 20 DOLLARS
0.9990 Gold **Obv:** National arms **Rev:** Head 1/4 left above date
flanked by stars

Date	Mintage	F	VF	XF	Unc	BU
1964B L Proof	100	Value: 600				

Note: Of the total issue, 10,200 were struck of .900 fine gold
and bear the "B" mint mark of the Bern Mint below the
date, while 100 were struck as proofs of .999 fine gold
and are designated by the presence of a small "L"
above the date

KM# 64 20 DOLLARS
15.8100 g., 0.9000 Gold 0.4575 oz. AGW **Subject:** 25th
Anniversary of Inter-Continental Hotels **Obv:** Value below hotel
building **Rev:** Letter I within football flanked by dates

Date	Mintage	F	VF	XF	Unc	BU
1971 Proof	—	Value: 650				

KM# 27 20 DOLLARS
33.4370 g., 0.9000 Gold 0.9675 oz. AGW **Subject:** Inauguration
of President Tolbert **Obv:** National arms **Rev:** Head left

Date	Mintage	F	VF	XF	Unc	BU
1972 Proof	—	Value: 975				

KM# 45 20 DOLLARS
28.2800 g., 0.9250 Silver 0.8410 oz. ASW **Subject:** Year of the
Scout **Obv:** National arms **Rev:** Scouts at camp, three saluting,
three seated

Date	Mintage	F	VF	XF	Unc	BU
1983	10,000	—	—	—	30.00	—
1983 Proof	10,000	Value: 48.50				

KM# 48 20 DOLLARS
28.2800 g., 0.9250 Silver 0.8410 oz. ASW **Series:** International
Year of Disabled Persons **Obv:** National arms

Date	Mintage	F	VF	XF	Unc	BU
1983	—	—	—	—	32.50	—
1983 Proof	—	Value: 50.00				

KM# 811 20 DOLLARS
1.2400 g., Gold, 13.85 mm. **Subject:** In Memory of Willy Brant
Obv: National arms **Rev:** Head of Brant right, statue at top of
Brandenburg gate below **Edge:** Reeded

Date	Mintage	F	VF	XF	Unc	BU
1992PM Proof	—	Value: 50.00				

KM# 812   20 DOLLARS
1.2400 g., 0.9999 Gold 0.0399 oz. AGW, 13.91 mm.
Series: Formula One **Obv:** National arms **Rev:** Head of Nigel
Mansell right at left, race car at lower right **Edge:** Reeded

Date	Mintage	F	VF	XF	Unc	BU
1992PM Proof	—	Value: 50.00				

KM# 813   20 DOLLARS
1.2400 g., 0.9999 Gold 0.0399 oz. AGW, 13.91 mm.
Series: Formula One **Obv:** National arms **Rev:** Head of Riccardo
Patrese **Edge:** Reeded

Date	Mintage	F	VF	XF	Unc	BU
1992PM Proof	—	Value: 50.00				

KM# 814   20 DOLLARS
1.2400 g., 0.9999 Gold 0.0399 oz. AGW, 13.91 mm.
Series: Formula One **Obv:** National arms **Rev:** Head of Gerhard
Berger **Edge:** Reeded

Date	Mintage	F	VF	XF	Unc	BU
1992PM Proof	—	Value: 50.00				

KM# 815   20 DOLLARS
1.2400 g., 0.9999 Gold 0.0399 oz. AGW, 13.91 mm.
Series: Formula One **Obv:** National arms **Rev:** Head of Ayrton
Senna **Edge:** Reeded

Date	Mintage	F	VF	XF	Unc	BU
1992PM Proof	—	Value: 50.00				

KM# 816   20 DOLLARS
1.2400 g., 0.9999 Gold 0.0399 oz. AGW, 13.89 mm.
Series: Formula One **Obv:** National arms **Rev:** Bust of Michael
Schumacher 3/4 left at right, race car at lower left **Edge:** Reeded

Date	Mintage	F	VF	XF	Unc	BU
1992PM Proof	—	Value: 59.00				

KM# 817   20 DOLLARS
1.2400 g., 0.9999 Gold 0.0399 oz. AGW, 13.91 mm.
Series: Formula One **Obv:** National arms **Rev:** Head of Alain
Prost **Edge:** Reeded

Date	Mintage	F	VF	XF	Unc	BU
1992PM Proof	—	Value: 50.00				

KM# 818   20 DOLLARS
1.2400 g., 0.9999 Gold 0.0399 oz. AGW, 13.91 mm.
Series: Formula One **Obv:** National arms **Rev:** Head of Aguri
Suzuki **Edge:** Reeded

Date	Mintage	F	VF	XF	Unc	BU
1992PM Proof	—	Value: 50.00				

KM# 819   20 DOLLARS
1.2400 g., 0.9999 Gold 0.0399 oz. AGW, 13.91 mm.
Series: Formula One **Obv:** National arms **Rev:** Head of Ukyo
Katayami **Edge:** Reeded

Date	Mintage	F	VF	XF	Unc	BU
1992PM Proof	—	Value: 50.00				

KM# 283   20 DOLLARS
1.2700 g., 0.9990 Gold 0.0408 oz. AGW **Subject:** Formula One
Obv: National arms divide date **Rev:** Damon Hill

Date	Mintage	F	VF	XF	Unc	BU
1994 Proof	25,000	Value: 65.00				

KM# 820   20 DOLLARS
1.2400 g., 0.9999 Gold 0.0399 oz. AGW, 13.84 mm.
Subject: In memory of John F. Kennedy's Visit to Berlin
Obv: National arms **Rev:** Head of JFK left, statue at top of
Brandenburg Gate below **Edge:** Reeded

Date	Mintage	F	VF	XF	Unc	BU
1995PM Proof	—	Value: 50.00				

KM# 230   20 DOLLARS
1.2700 g., 0.9990 Gold 0.0408 oz. AGW **Subject:** Formula One
Obv: National arms **Rev:** Ayrton Senna **Note:** Similar to 10
Dollars, KM#229.

Date	Mintage	F	VF	XF	Unc	BU
1996 Proof	15,000	Value: 65.00				

KM# 250   20 DOLLARS
1.2700 g., 0.9990 Gold 0.0408 oz. AGW **Subject:** Dalai Lama
Obv: National arms **Rev:** Bust with praying hands facing 1/4 left
Note: Similar to 100 Dollars, KM#252.

Date	Mintage	F	VF	XF	Unc	BU
1996 Proof	15,000	Value: 65.00				

KM# 515   20 DOLLARS
31.2200 g., 0.9990 Silver 1.0027 oz. ASW, 38.5 mm.
Subject: Princess Diana **Obv:** National arms **Rev:** Diana as a
young girl **Edge:** Reeded

Date	Mintage	F	VF	XF	Unc	BU
1997 Proof	—	Value: 40.00				

KM# 518   20 DOLLARS
31.2200 g., 0.9990 Silver 1.0027 oz. ASW, 38.5 mm.
Subject: Princess Diana **Obv:** National arms **Rev:** Diana in
wedding dress **Edge:** Reeded

Date	Mintage	F	VF	XF	Unc	BU
1997 Proof	—	Value: 40.00				

KM# 520   20 DOLLARS
31.2200 g., 0.9990 Silver 1.0027 oz. ASW, 38.5 mm.
Subject: Princess Diana "England's Rose" **Obv:** National arms
Rev: Diana with roses **Edge:** Reeded

Date	Mintage	F	VF	XF	Unc	BU
1997 Proof	—	Value: 40.00				

KM# 523   20 DOLLARS
31.2200 g., 0.9990 Silver 1.0027 oz. ASW, 38.5 mm.
Subject: Princess Diana **Obv:** National arms **Rev:** Diana with
baby William **Edge:** Reeded

Date	Mintage	F	VF	XF	Unc	BU
1997 Proof	—	Value: 40.00				

KM# 526   20 DOLLARS
31.2200 g., 0.9990 Silver 1.0027 oz. ASW, 38.5 mm.
Subject: Princess Diana **Obv:** National arms **Rev:** Diana with
two sons **Edge:** Reeded

Date	Mintage	F	VF	XF	Unc	BU
1997 Proof	—	Value: 40.00				

KM# 527   20 DOLLARS
31.2200 g., 0.9990 Silver 1.0027 oz. ASW, 38.5 mm.
Subject: Princess Diana **Obv:** National arms **Rev:** Royal family
Edge: Reeded

Date	Mintage	F	VF	XF	Unc	BU
1997 Proof	—	Value: 40.00				

KM# 528   20 DOLLARS
31.2200 g., 0.9990 Silver 1.0027 oz. ASW, 38.5 mm.
Subject: Princess Diana **Obv:** National arms **Rev:** Queen
Elizabeth II and Diana **Edge:** Reeded

Date	Mintage	F	VF	XF	Unc	BU
1997 Proof	—	Value: 37.50				

KM# 533   20 DOLLARS
31.2200 g., 0.9990 Silver 1.0027 oz. ASW, 38.5 mm.
Subject: Princess Diana **Obv:** National arms **Rev:** Diana
teaching **Edge:** Reeded

Date	Mintage	F	VF	XF	Unc	BU
1997 Proof	—	Value: 40.00				

KM# 592   20 DOLLARS
31.2200 g., 0.9990 Silver 1.0027 oz. ASW, 38.5 mm.
Subject: Princess Diana **Obv:** National arms **Rev:** Mother
Teresa and Diana **Edge:** Reeded

Date	Mintage	F	VF	XF	Unc	BU
1997 Proof	—	Value: 40.00				

KM# 498   20 DOLLARS
31.2200 g., 0.9990 Silver 1.0027 oz. ASW, 38.5 mm. **Subject:**
Year of the Ox - Type II **Obv:** National arms **Rev:** Ox within inner
circle with legend **Edge:** Reeded

Date	Mintage	F	VF	XF	Unc	BU
1997 Proof	—	Value: 40.00				

KM# 535   20 DOLLARS
31.1300 g., 0.9990 Silver 0.9998 oz. ASW, 38.6 mm.
Subject: Princess Diana - Compassion **Obv:** National arms
Rev: Diana with sick child **Edge:** Reeded

Date	Mintage	F	VF	XF	Unc	BU
1997 Proof	—	Value: 40.00				

KM# 340   20 DOLLARS
31.1035 g., 0.9990 Silver 0.9990 oz. ASW **Subject:** Year of the
Ox **Obv:** National arms **Rev:** Ox above value

Date	Mintage	F	VF	XF	Unc	BU
1997 Proof	—	Value: 30.00				

KM# 416   20 DOLLARS
31.3500 g., 0.9990 Silver 1.0069 oz. ASW **Subject:** Deng
Xiaoping **Obv:** National arms **Rev:** Bust 1/4 right above value

Date	Mintage	F	VF	XF	Unc	BU
1997 Proof	—	Value: 22.50				

KM# 417   20 DOLLARS
31.4000 g., 0.9990 Silver 1.0085 oz. ASW **Subject:** Princess
Diana In Memoriam **Obv:** National arms **Rev:** Portrait and dates

Date	Mintage	F	VF	XF	Unc	BU
1997 Proof	—	Value: 32.50				

KM# 315   20 DOLLARS
1.2400 g., 0.9990 Gold 0.0398 oz. AGW **Subject:** Return of
Hong Kong to China **Obv:** National arms **Rev:** Dragon
Note: Similar to 10 Dollars, KM#314.

Date	Mintage	F	VF	XF	Unc	BU
1997 Proof	—	Value: 65.00				

KM# 585   20 DOLLARS
31.1035 g., 0.9990 Silver 0.9990 oz. ASW, 38 mm.
Subject: Year of the Tiger **Obv:** National arms **Rev:** Tiger above
pineapple and flowers within beaded circle **Edge:** Reeded

Date	Mintage	F	VF	XF	Unc	BU
1998 Proof	—	Value: 45.00				

KM# 586   20 DOLLARS
31.1035 g., 0.9990 Silver 0.9990 oz. ASW, 38 mm. **Subject:** Year
of the Tiger **Obv:** National arms **Rev:** Roaring tiger **Edge:** Reeded

Date	Mintage	F	VF	XF	Unc	BU
1998 Proof	—	Value: 45.00				

KM# 587   20 DOLLARS
31.1035 g., 0.9990 Silver 0.9990 oz. ASW, 38 mm. **Subject:** Year
of the Tiger **Obv:** National arms **Rev:** Crouching tiger **Edge:** Reeded

Date	Mintage	F	VF	XF	Unc	BU
1998 Proof	—	Value: 45.00				

KM# 341 20 DOLLARS
31.1035 g., 0.9990 Silver 0.9990 oz. ASW **Subject:** Year of the
Tiger **Obv:** National arms **Rev:** Tiger in bamboo

Date	Mintage	F	VF	XF	Unc	BU
1998 (1997) Proof	—	Value: 40.00				

KM# 342 20 DOLLARS
24.9400 g., Silver **Subject:** Year of the Tiger **Obv:** National
arms **Rev:** Tiger lying in bamboo

Date	Mintage	F	VF	XF	Unc	BU
1998 (1997) Proof	—	Value: 40.00				

KM# 343 20 DOLLARS
24.9400 g., Silver **Subject:** Year of the Tiger **Obv:** National
arms **Rev:** Stalking tiger

Date	Mintage	F	VF	XF	Unc	BU
1998 (1997) Proof	—	Value: 40.00				

KM# 364 20 DOLLARS
31.1035 g., 0.9990 Silver 0.9990 oz. ASW **Subject:** RMS Titanic
Obv: National arms **Rev:** Cameo above sinking ship

Date	Mintage	F	VF	XF	Unc	BU
1998 Proof	25,000	Value: 50.00				

KM# 389 20 DOLLARS
31.1035 g., 0.9990 Silver 0.9990 oz. ASW **Subject:** Year of the
Rabbit **Obv:** National arms **Rev:** Rabbit running left within dotted
circle

Date	Mintage	F	VF	XF	Unc	BU
1999 Proof	8,000	Value: 40.00				

KM# 390 20 DOLLARS
31.1035 g., 0.9990 Silver 0.9990 oz. ASW **Subject:** Year of the
Rabbit **Obv:** National arms **Rev:** Rabbit sitting

Date	Mintage	F	VF	XF	Unc	BU
1999 Proof	8,000	Value: 40.00				

KM# 391 20 DOLLARS
31.1035 g., 0.9990 Silver 0.9990 oz. ASW **Subject:** Year of the
Rabbit **Obv:** National arms **Rev:** Rabbit running right

Date	Mintage	F	VF	XF	Unc	BU
1999 Proof	8,000	Value: 40.00				

KM# 418 20 DOLLARS
1.2441 g., 0.9999 Gold 0.0400 oz. AGW **Subject:** Return of
Macao to China **Obv:** National arms **Rev:** Dragon and phoenix
Note: Similar to 10 Dollars, KM#408.

Date	Mintage	F	VF	XF	Unc	BU
1999 Proof	25,000	Value: 50.00				

KM# 661 20 DOLLARS
20.6000 g., 0.9990 Silver 0.6616 oz. ASW
Obv: National arms **Rev:** R.M.S. Queen Mary **Edge:** Reeded

Date	Mintage	F	VF	XF	Unc	BU
2000 Proof	—	Value: 25.00				

KM# 574 20 DOLLARS
20.0000 g., 0.9990 Silver 0.6423 oz. ASW, 40.1 mm.
Subject: Captain Cook **Obv:** National arms **Rev:** Seated Capt.
Cook at right, his ship at left **Edge:** Reeded

Date	Mintage	F	VF	XF	Unc	BU
2000 Proof	—	Value: 30.00				

KM# 575 20 DOLLARS
31.0000 g., 0.9990 Silver 0.9956 oz. ASW, 38.7 mm.
Obv: National arms **Rev:** Hippopotamus **Edge:** Reeded

Date	Mintage	F	VF	XF	Unc	BU
2000 Proof	—	Value: 35.00				

KM# 576 20 DOLLARS
19.8500 g., 0.9990 Silver 0.6375 oz. ASW, 40.3 mm.
Subject: Olympics **Obv:** National arms **Rev:** Volleyball player
with city view behind **Edge:** Reeded

Date	Mintage	F	VF	XF	Unc	BU
2000 Proof	—	Value: 35.00				

KM# 577 20 DOLLARS
19.8500 g., 0.9990 Silver 0.6375 oz. ASW, 40.3 mm.
Subject: Olympics **Obv:** National arms **Rev:** High jumper and
Australian map **Edge:** Reeded

Date	Mintage	F	VF	XF	Unc	BU
2000 Proof	—	Value: 35.00				

KM# 736 20 DOLLARS
Silver **Subject:** XXVII Olympic Games - Sydney **Rev:** Kayaker
Edge: Reeded

Date	Mintage	F	VF	XF	Unc	BU
2000	—	—	—	27.50	—	

KM# 728 20 DOLLARS
Silver **Series:** US Presidents **Subject:** Richard Nixon

Date	Mintage	F	VF	XF	Unc	BU
2000 Proof	20,000	Value: 30.00				

KM# 472 20 DOLLARS
20.1700 g., 0.9990 Silver 0.6478 oz. ASW, 40.3 mm.
Series: American History **Obv:** National arms **Rev:** The Alamo
and defenders **Edge:** Reeded

Date	Mintage	F	VF	XF	Unc	BU
2000 Proof	—	Value: 25.00				

KM# 477 20 DOLLARS
20.0400 g., 0.9990 Silver 0.6436 oz. ASW, 40.3 mm.
Subject: Admiral David G. Farragut **Obv:** National arms
Rev: Uniformed bust 1/4 left within flag **Edge:** Reeded

Date	Mintage	F	VF	XF	Unc	BU
2000 Proof	Est. 20,000	Value: 25.00				

KM# 478 20 DOLLARS
20.0400 g., 0.9990 Silver 0.6436 oz. ASW **Subject:** Surrender
of Appomattox **Obv:** National arms **Rev:** Surrender signing scene

Date	Mintage	F	VF	XF	Unc	BU
2000 Proof	Est. 20,000	Value: 25.00				

KM# 479 20 DOLLARS
20.0400 g., 0.9990 Silver 0.6436 oz. ASW, 39.95 mm.
Subject: Abraham Lincoln **Obv:** National arms **Rev:** Bust 3/4
right **Edge:** Reeded

Date	Mintage	F	VF	XF	Unc	BU
2000 Proof	Est. 20,000	Value: 25.00				

KM# 480   20 DOLLARS
20.0400 g., 0.9990 Silver 0.6436 oz. ASW   **Subject:** Montgolfiere
Balloon **Obv:** National arms **Rev:** First hot air balloon

Date	Mintage	F	VF	XF	Unc	BU
2000 Proof	Est. 20,000	Value: 27.50				

KM# 481   20 DOLLARS
20.0400 g., 0.9990 Silver 0.6436 oz. ASW   **Subject:** Concorde
Supersonic Airliner **Obv:** National arms **Rev:** Plane in flight above
runway

Date	Mintage	F	VF	XF	Unc	BU
2000 Proof	Est. 20,000	Value: 25.00				

KM# 482   20 DOLLARS
20.0400 g., 0.9990 Silver 0.6436 oz. ASW   **Subject:** Apollo X
Obv: National arms **Rev:** Rocket launch, space capsule, large X

Date	Mintage	F	VF	XF	Unc	BU
2000 Proof	Est. 20,000	Value: 25.00				

KM# 483   20 DOLLARS
20.0400 g., 0.9990 Silver 0.6436 oz. ASW   **Subject:** Apollo VII
Obv: National arms **Rev:** Space capsule above half-length busts
of Schirra, Eisele, and Cunningham facing

Date	Mintage	F	VF	XF	Unc	BU
2000 Proof	Est. 20,000	Value: 25.00				

KM# 484   20 DOLLARS
20.0400 g., 0.9990 Silver 0.6436 oz. ASW   **Subject:** STS-1
Obv: National arms **Rev:** 3/4-length busts of Young and Crippen
facing with shuttle model

Date	Mintage	F	VF	XF	Unc	BU
2000 Proof	Est. 20,000	Value: 25.00				

KM# 485   20 DOLLARS
20.0400 g., 0.9990 Silver 0.6436 oz. ASW   **Subject:** Skylab I
Obv: National arms **Rev:** Half-length busts of Conrad, Kerwin,
and Weitz facing below Skylab

Date	Mintage	F	VF	XF	Unc	BU
2000 Proof	Est. 20,000	Value: 25.00				

KM# 486   20 DOLLARS
20.0400 g., 0.9990 Silver 0.6436 oz. ASW   **Series:** Olympics
Obv: National arms **Rev:** Hurdler

Date	Mintage	F	VF	XF	Unc	BU
2000 Proof	Est. 20,000	Value: 25.00				

KM# 487   20 DOLLARS
20.0400 g., 0.9990 Silver 0.6436 oz. ASW   **Series:** Olympics
Obv: National arms **Rev:** Equestrian

Date	Mintage	F	VF	XF	Unc	BU
2000 Proof	Est. 20,000	Value: 25.00				

KM# 488   20 DOLLARS
20.0400 g., 0.9990 Silver 0.6436 oz. ASW   **Series:** Olympics
Obv: National arms **Rev:** Two basketball players in front of flags

Date	Mintage	F	VF	XF	Unc	BU
2000 Proof	Est. 20,000	Value: 25.00				

KM# 489   20 DOLLARS
20.0400 g., 0.9990 Silver 0.6436 oz. ASW   **Series:** Olympics
Obv: National arms **Rev:** Three cyclists

Date	Mintage	F	VF	XF	Unc	BU
2000 Proof	Est. 20,000	Value: 25.00				

KM# 490   20 DOLLARS
20.0400 g., 0.9990 Silver 0.6436 oz. ASW   **Series:** Olympics
Obv: National arms **Rev:** Swimmer, cyclist, and speed walker

Date	Mintage	F	VF	XF	Unc	BU
2000 Proof	Est. 20,000	Value: 25.00				

KM# 504   20 DOLLARS
20.0000 g., 0.9990 Silver 0.6423 oz. ASW, 40.4 mm.   **Subject:**
American History **Obv:** National arms **Rev:** Treaty of Paris
signing scene **Edge:** Reeded **Note:** The American Mint is not an
actual mint.

Date	Mintage	F	VF	XF	Unc	BU
2000 Proof	20,000	Value: 40.00				

KM# 505   20 DOLLARS
20.0000 g., 0.9990 Silver 0.6423 oz. ASW, 40.4 mm.
Subject: American History - Civil War **Obv:** National arms
Rev: Bombardment of Fort Sumter scene **Edge:** Reeded
Note: The American Mint is not an actual mint.

Date	Mintage	F	VF	XF	Unc	BU
2000 Proof	20,000	Value: 40.00				

KM# 506   20 DOLLARS
20.0000 g., 0.9990 Silver 0.6423 oz. ASW, 40.4 mm.
Subject: American History **Obv:** National arms **Rev:** Bust facing
Edge: Reeded **Note:** The American Mint is not an actual mint.

Date	Mintage	F	VF	XF	Unc	BU
2000 Proof	20,000	Value: 40.00				

KM# 507   20 DOLLARS
20.0000 g., 0.9990 Silver 0.6423 oz. ASW, 40.4 mm.
Subject: American History **Obv:** National arms **Rev:** Busts of
astronauts Young and Crippen with Space Shuttle model
Edge: Reeded **Note:** The American Mint is not an actual mint.

Date	Mintage	F	VF	XF	Unc	BU
2000 Proof	20,000	Value: 40.00				

KM# 508   20 DOLLARS
31.1035 g., 0.9990 Silver 0.9990 oz. ASW, 40.7 mm.
Subject: Millennium **Obv:** Seated Liberty **Rev:** Y2K design
Edge: Reeded **Note:** The American Mint is not an actual mint.

Date	Mintage	F	VF	XF	Unc	BU
2000	2,000	—	—	—	30.00	—

KM# 509.1   20 DOLLARS
31.1035 g., 0.9990 Silver 0.9990 oz. ASW, 39 mm.
Subject: Millennium **Obv:** National arms **Rev:** Woman with
hourglass and dove **Edge:** Reeded **Note:** The American Mint is
not an actual mint.

Date	Mintage	F	VF	XF	Unc	BU
2000	—	—	—	—	30.00	—

KM# 509.2 20 DOLLARS
31.1035 g., 0.9990 Silver 0.9990 oz. ASW, 39 mm.
Subject: Millennium **Obv:** National arms **Rev:** Multicolor woman
with hourglass and dove **Edge:** Reeded **Note:** The American
Mint is not an actual mint.

Date	Mintage	F	VF	XF	Unc	BU
2000	—	—	—	30.00	—

KM# 590 20 DOLLARS
20.0000 g., 0.9990 Silver 0.6423 oz. ASW, 40 mm.
Obv: National arms **Rev:** Titanic steaming right **Edge:** Reeded

Date	Mintage	F	VF	XF	Unc	BU
2000 Proof	— Value: 30.00

KM# 591 20 DOLLARS
20.0000 g., 0.9990 Silver 0.6423 oz. ASW, 40 mm.
Subject: Apollo XVIII and Soyuz XIX **Obv:** National arms
Rev: Two space capsules about to link up **Edge:** Reeded

Date	Mintage	F	VF	XF	Unc	BU
2000 Proof	— Value: 30.00

KM# 595 20 DOLLARS
20.0000 g., 0.9990 Silver 0.6423 oz. ASW, 40 mm.
Subject: Aviation **Obv:** National arms **Rev:** Wright Brothers
airplane **Edge:** Reeded

Date	Mintage	F	VF	XF	Unc	BU
2000 Proof	20,000 Value: 35.00

KM# 596 20 DOLLARS
20.0000 g., 0.9990 Silver 0.6423 oz. ASW, 40 mm.
Subject: Aviation **Obv:** National arms **Rev:** Russian Witiaz four-
engine bi-plane **Edge:** Reeded

Date	Mintage	F	VF	XF	Unc	BU
2000 Proof	20,000 Value: 35.00

KM# 597 20 DOLLARS
20.0000 g., 0.9990 Silver 0.6423 oz. ASW, 40 mm.
Subject: Aviation **Obv:** National arms **Rev:** Curtiss R3C-2
floating bi-plane **Edge:** Reeded

Date	Mintage	F	VF	XF	Unc	BU
2000 Proof	20,000 Value: 35.00

KM# 598 20 DOLLARS
20.0000 g., 0.9990 Silver 0.6423 oz. ASW, 40 mm.
Subject: Aviation **Obv:** National arms **Rev:** Grumman F3F biplane fighter **Edge:** Reeded

Date	Mintage	F	VF	XF	Unc	BU
2000 Proof	20,000 Value: 35.00

KM# 599 20 DOLLARS
20.0000 g., 0.9990 Silver 0.6423 oz. ASW, 40 mm.
Subject: Aviation **Obv:** National arms **Rev:** Space Station
Edge: Reeded

Date	Mintage	F	VF	XF	Unc	BU
2000 Proof	20,000 Value: 35.00

KM# 609 20 DOLLARS
19.9000 g., 0.9990 Silver 0.6391 oz. ASW, 40.2 mm.
Obv: National arms **Rev:** United States Bill of Rights
Edge: Reeded

Date	Mintage	F	VF	XF	Unc	BU
2000 Proof	20,000 Value: 15.00

KM# 610 20 DOLLARS
19.9400 g., 0.9990 Silver 0.6404 oz. ASW, 40.2 mm.
Obv: National arms **Rev:** Louisiana Purchase map on flag behind
portraits of Jefferson, Lewis and Clark **Edge:** Reeded

Date	Mintage	F	VF	XF	Unc	BU
2000 Proof	— Value: 15.00

KM# 613 20 DOLLARS
31.1035 g., 0.9990 Silver 0.9990 oz. ASW, 39 mm.
Subject: "King of the Cowboys" Roy Rogers **Obv:** National arms
Obv. Leg.: ROY ROGERS, King of the Cowboys below
Rev: Bust 1/4 left **Edge:** Reeded

Date	Mintage	F	VF	XF	Unc	BU
2000 Proof	1,000 Value: 35.00

KM# 614 20 DOLLARS
31.1035 g., 0.9990 Silver 0.9990 oz. ASW, 39 mm. **Subject:**
Roy Rogers **Obv:** National arms **Obv. Leg.:** ROY ROGERS,
Happy Trails to You! below **Rev:** Bust 1/4 left **Edge:** Reeded

Date	Mintage	F	VF	XF	Unc	BU
2000 Proof	1,000 Value: 35.00

KM# 636 20 DOLLARS
31.1000 g., 0.9990 Silver 0.9988 oz. ASW, 38.6 mm.
Obv: National arms **Rev:** American Quarter Horse **Edge:** Reeded

Date	Mintage	F	VF	XF	Unc	BU
2000 Proof	— Value: 25.00

KM# 637 20 DOLLARS
20.1000 g., 0.9990 Silver 0.6456 oz. ASW, 40.2 mm.
Obv: National arms **Rev:** Berlin buildings **Edge:** Reeded

Date	Mintage	F	VF	XF	Unc	BU
2000 Proof	— Value: 30.00

KM# 638 20 DOLLARS
20.1000 g., 0.9990 Silver 0.6456 oz. ASW, 40.2 mm.
Obv: National arms **Rev:** Brussels landmarks **Edge:** Reeded

Date	Mintage	F	VF	XF	Unc	BU
2000 Proof	— Value: 30.00

KM# 639 20 DOLLARS
20.1000 g., 0.9990 Silver 0.6456 oz. ASW, 20.1 mm.
Obv: National arms **Rev:** London buildings **Edge:** Reeded

Date	Mintage	F	VF	XF	Unc	BU
2000 Proof	— Value: 30.00

KM# 640 20 DOLLARS
20.1000 g., 0.9990 Silver 0.6456 oz. ASW, 40.2 mm.
Obv: National arms **Rev:** Madrid buildings **Edge:** Reeded

Date	Mintage	F	VF	XF	Unc	BU
2000 Proof	— Value: 30.00

KM# 729 20 DOLLARS
Silver **Series:** US Presidents **Subject:** George Washington
Obv: Shield

Date	Mintage	F	VF	XF	Unc	BU
2000 Proof	20,000 Value: 30.00

KM# 641 20 DOLLARS
20.1000 g., 0.9990 Silver 0.6456 oz. ASW, 40.2 mm.
Obv: National arms **Rev:** Rome buildings **Edge:** Reeded

Date	Mintage	F	VF	XF	Unc	BU
2000 Proof	— Value: 30.00

KM# 642 20 DOLLARS
20.1000 g., 0.9990 Silver 0.6456 oz. ASW, 40.2 mm.
Obv: National arms **Rev:** Stockholm buildings **Edge:** Reeded

Date	Mintage	F	VF	XF	Unc	BU
2000 Proof	— Value: 30.00

KM# 646 20 DOLLARS
19.9100 g., 0.9990 Silver 0.6395 oz. ASW, 40 mm.
Obv: National arms **Rev:** Sailing ship **Rev. Leg.:** SOVEREIGN
OF THE SEAS **Edge:** Reeded

Date	Mintage	F	VF	XF	Unc	BU
2000 Proof	— Value: 40.00

KM# 647 20 DOLLARS
19.9100 g., 0.9990 Silver 0.6395 oz. ASW, 40 mm.
Obv: National arms **Rev:** Tall sailing ship **Rev. Leg.:** PAMIR
Edge: Reeded

Date	Mintage	F	VF	XF	Unc	BU
2000 Proof	— Value: 40.00

KM# 648 20 DOLLARS
19.9100 g., 0.9990 Silver 0.6395 oz. ASW, 40 mm.
Obv: National arms **Rev:** HMS Victory, Nelson's flag ship
Edge: Reeded

Date	Mintage	F	VF	XF	Unc	BU
2000 Proof	— Value: 40.00

KM# 649 20 DOLLARS
19.9100 g., 0.9990 Silver 0.6395 oz. ASW, 40 mm.
Obv: National arms **Rev:** LZ 127 Graf Zeppelin **Edge:** Reeded

Date	Mintage	F	VF	XF	Unc	BU
2000 Proof	— Value: 42.50

KM# 655 20 DOLLARS
20.6000 g., 0.9990 Silver 0.6616 oz. ASW, 40.3 mm.
Obv: National arms **Rev:** SS Europa **Edge:** Reeded

Date	Mintage	F	VF	XF	Unc	BU
2000 Proof	— Value: 25.00

KM# 656 20 DOLLARS
20.6000 g., 0.9990 Silver 0.6616 oz. ASW, 40.3 mm.
Obv: National arms **Rev:** "Royal William" ship **Edge:** Reeded

Date	Mintage	F	VF	XF	Unc	BU
2000 Proof	— Value: 25.00

KM# 658 20 DOLLARS
20.6000 g., 0.9990 Silver 0.6616 oz. ASW, 40.3 mm.
Obv: National arms **Rev:** The "Great Eastern" ship
Edge: Reeded

Date	Mintage	F	VF	XF	Unc	BU
2000 Proof	— Value: 25.00

KM# 660 20 DOLLARS
20.6000 g., 0.9990 Silver 0.6616 oz. ASW, 40.3 mm. **Obv:** National
arms **Rev:** Signing of the Mayflower Compact **Edge:** Reeded

Date	Mintage	F	VF	XF	Unc	BU
2000 Proof	— Value: 25.00

KM# 663 20 DOLLARS
20.2200 g., 0.9990 Silver 0.6494 oz. ASW, 40 mm. **Obv:** National
arms **Rev:** Battle of the Monitor and the Virginia **Edge:** Reeded

Date	Mintage	F	VF	XF	Unc	BU
2000 Proof	20,000 Value: 40.00

KM# 697 20 DOLLARS
31.1035 g., 0.9990 Silver 0.9990 oz. ASW, 39 mm.
Obv: National arms **Rev:** Roy Rogers **Edge:** Reeded

Date	Mintage	F	VF	XF	Unc	BU
2000 Proof	1,000 Value: 45.00

KM# 707 20 DOLLARS
20.1700 g., 0.9990 Silver 0.6478 oz. ASW, 40.3 mm.
Obv: National arms **Rev:** Boston Tea Party Scene **Edge:** Reeded

Date	Mintage	F	VF	XF	Unc	BU
2000 Proof	— Value: 35.00

KM# 710   20 DOLLARS
20.0000 g., 0.9990 Silver 0.6423 oz. ASW, 40.3 mm.
Subject: American History Series **Obv:** National arms
Rev: Columbus going ashore **Edge:** Reeded

Date	Mintage	F	VF	XF	Unc	BU
2000 Proof	20,000				Value: 25.00	

KM# 711   20 DOLLARS
20.0000 g., 0.9990 Silver 0.6423 oz. ASW, 40.3 mm.
Subject: American History Series **Obv:** National arms
Rev: Declaration of Independence signers with document in
background **Edge:** Reeded

Date	Mintage	F	VF	XF	Unc	BU
2000 Proof	20,000				Value: 25.00	

KM# 712   20 DOLLARS
20.0000 g., 0.9990 Silver 0.6423 oz. ASW, 40.3 mm.
Subject: American History Series **Obv:** National arms
Rev: Transcontinental Railroad Golden Spike ceremony scene
Edge: Reeded

Date	Mintage	F	VF	XF	Unc	BU
2000 Proof	20,000				Value: 25.00	

KM# 713   20 DOLLARS
20.0000 g., 0.9990 Silver 0.6423 oz. ASW, 40.3 mm.
Subject: American History Series **Obv:** National arms
Rev: Great Depression, Roosevelt visiting with people in a bread
line **Edge:** Reeded

Date	Mintage	F	VF	XF	Unc	BU
2000 Proof	20,000				Value: 25.00	

KM# 714   20 DOLLARS
20.0000 g., 0.9990 Silver 0.6423 oz. ASW, 40.3 mm. **Subject:**
American History Series **Obv:** National arms **Rev:** Victory over
Japan, surrender ceremony on the USS Missouri **Edge:** Reeded

Date	Mintage	F	VF	XF	Unc	BU
2000 Proof	20,000				Value: 25.00	

KM# 21   25 DOLLARS
23.3120 g., 0.9000 Gold 0.6745 oz. AGW **Subject:** 70th
Birthday of President Tubman **Obv:** Head 3/4 left above date
flanked by stars **Rev:** Trees and sun above value flanked by stars

Date	Mintage	F	VF	XF	Unc	BU
1965B	3,000	—	—	—	650	675

KM# 21a   25 DOLLARS
23.3120 g., 0.9990 Gold 0.7487 oz. AGW **Obv:** Head 3/4 left
above date flanked by stars **Rev:** Tree and sun above value
flanked by stars

Date	Mintage	F	VF	XF	Unc	BU
1965B L Proof	100				Value: 750	

KM# 23   25 DOLLARS
0.9990 Gold **Subject:** 75th Birthday of President Tubman
Obv: Birthplace of President **Rev:** Head facing above dates

Date	Mintage	F	VF	XF	Unc	BU
ND(1970)B Proof	—				Value: 725	

KM# 28   25 DOLLARS
0.9990 Gold **Subject:** Sesquicentennial - Founding of Liberia
Obv: Bust 1/4 left **Rev:** Man in canoe below tower and trees with
value above

Date	Mintage	F	VF	XF	Unc	BU
ND(1972)B Proof	3,000				Value: 725	

KM# 323   25 DOLLARS
77.7587 g., 0.9990 Silver 2.4974 oz. ASW **Subject:** 25th
Anniversary - Standard Catalog of World Coins **Obv:** National
arms **Rev:** Children, globe and world coins

Date	Mintage	F	VF	XF	Unc	BU
1997 Proof	2,500				Value: 60.00	

KM# 623   25 DOLLARS
0.7300 g., 0.9990 Gold 0.0234 oz. AGW, 11.1 mm.
Obv: National arms **Rev:** Martin Luther **Edge:** Reeded

Date	Mintage	F	VF	XF	Unc	BU
2000 Proof	—				Value: 32.00	

KM# 624   25 DOLLARS
0.7300 g., 0.9990 Gold 0.0234 oz. AGW, 11.1 mm.
Obv: National arms **Rev:** Queen Elizabeth II **Edge:** Reeded

Date	Mintage	F	VF	XF	Unc	BU
2000 Proof	—				Value: 32.00	

KM# 625   25 DOLLARS
0.7300 g., 0.9990 Gold 0.0234 oz. AGW, 11.1 mm.
Obv: National arms **Rev:** Mozart **Edge:** Reeded

Date	Mintage	F	VF	XF	Unc	BU
2000 Proof	—				Value: 32.00	

KM# 626   25 DOLLARS
0.7300 g., 0.9990 Gold 0.0234 oz. AGW, 11.1 mm.
Obv: National arms **Rev:** Christopher Columbus **Edge:** Reeded

Date	Mintage	F	VF	XF	Unc	BU
2000 Proof	—				Value: 32.00	

KM# 627   25 DOLLARS
0.7300 g., 0.9990 Gold 0.0234 oz. AGW, 11.1 mm.
Obv: National arms **Rev:** Tutankhamen **Edge:** Reeded

Date	Mintage	F	VF	XF	Unc	BU
2000 Proof	—				Value: 32.00	

KM# 628   25 DOLLARS
0.7300 g., 0.9990 Gold 0.0234 oz. AGW, 11.1 mm.
Obv: National arms **Rev:** Charlemagne **Edge:** Reeded

Date	Mintage	F	VF	XF	Unc	BU
2000 Proof	—				Value: 32.00	

KM# 629   25 DOLLARS
0.7300 g., 0.9990 Gold 0.0234 oz. AGW, 11.1 mm.
Obv: National arms **Rev:** Peter the Great **Edge:** Reeded

Date	Mintage	F	VF	XF	Unc	BU
2000 Proof	—				Value: 32.00	

KM# 630   25 DOLLARS
0.7300 g., 0.9990 Gold 0.0234 oz. AGW, 11.1 mm.
Obv: National arms **Rev:** Mikhail Gorbachev **Edge:** Reeded

Date	Mintage	F	VF	XF	Unc	BU
2000 Proof	—				Value: 32.00	

KM# 631   25 DOLLARS
0.7300 g., 0.9990 Gold 0.0234 oz. AGW, 11.1 mm.
Obv: National arms **Rev:** Julius Caesar **Edge:** Reeded

Date	Mintage	F	VF	XF	Unc	BU
2000 Proof	—				Value: 32.00	

KM# 632   25 DOLLARS
0.7300 g., 0.9990 Gold 0.0234 oz. AGW, 11.1 mm.
Obv: National arms **Rev:** George Washington **Edge:** Reeded

Date	Mintage	F	VF	XF	Unc	BU
2000 Proof	—				Value: 30.00	

KM# 633   25 DOLLARS
0.7300 g., 0.9990 Gold 0.0234 oz. AGW, 11.1 mm.
Obv: National arms **Rev:** Mahatma Gandhi **Edge:** Reeded

Date	Mintage	F	VF	XF	Unc	BU
2000 Proof	—				Value: 32.00	

KM# 634   25 DOLLARS
0.7300 g., 0.9990 Gold 0.0234 oz. AGW, 11.1 mm.
Obv: National arms **Rev:** Joan of Arc **Edge:** Reeded

Date	Mintage	F	VF	XF	Unc	BU
2000 Proof	—				Value: 32.00	

KM# 512   25 DOLLARS
0.7300 g., 0.9990 Gold 0.0234 oz. AGW, 11.1 mm.
Obv: National arms **Rev:** Bust right **Rev. Leg.:** NOFRETETE
Edge: Reeded **Note:** The American Mint is not an actual mint.

Date	Mintage	F	VF	XF	Unc	BU
2000 Proof	—				Value: 32.00	

KM# 22   30 DOLLARS
15.0000 g., 0.9000 Gold 0.4340 oz. AGW **Subject:** 70th
Birthday of President Tubman **Obv:** National arms **Rev:** Bust left

Date	Mintage	F	VF	XF	Unc	BU
1965 Proof	400				Value: 450	

KM# 69   50 DOLLARS
155.5150 g., 0.9990 Silver 4.9947 oz. ASW **Subject:** President
Bill Clinton **Obv:** National arms **Rev:** Head right divides date and
value above building **Note:** Similar to 10 Dollars, KM#68.

Date	Mintage	F	VF	XF	Unc	BU
1993 Proof	—				Value: 120	

KM# 410.1   50 DOLLARS
Copper-Nickel **Obv:** National arms **Rev:** Face on Mars with
rough texture

Date	Mintage	F	VF	XF	Unc	BU
1996	—	—	—	—	12.00	

KM# 410.2   50 DOLLARS
Copper-Nickel **Obv:** National arms **Rev:** Face on Mars with
smooth texture

Date	Mintage	F	VF	XF	Unc	BU
1996	—	—	—	—	12.00	

KM# 231   50 DOLLARS
3.1103 g., 0.9990 Gold 0.0999 oz. AGW **Subject:** Formula One
Obv: National arms **Rev:** Ayrton Senna **Note:** Similar to 10
Dollars, KM#229.

Date	Mintage	F	VF	XF	Unc	BU
1996 Proof	10,000				Value: 110	

KM# 251   50 DOLLARS
3.1103 g., 0.9990 Gold 0.0999 oz. AGW **Subject:** Dalai Lama
Obv: National arms **Rev:** Bust with praying hands 1/4 left
Note: Similar to 100 Dollars, KM#252.

Date	Mintage	F	VF	XF	Unc	BU
1996 Proof	10,000				Value: 110	

KM# 316   50 DOLLARS
3.1103 g., 0.9990 Gold 0.0999 oz. AGW **Subject:** Return of
Hong Kong to China **Obv:** National arms **Rev:** Dragon
Note: Similar to 10 Dollars, KM#314.

Date	Mintage	F	VF	XF	Unc	BU
1997 Proof	—				Value: 115	

KM# 366   50 DOLLARS
3.1103 g., 0.9990 Gold 0.0999 oz. AGW **Subject:** RMS Titanic
Obv: National arms **Rev:** Ship sinking **Note:** Similar to 20 Dollars,
KM#364.

Date	Mintage	F	VF	XF	Unc	BU
1998 Proof	Est. 2,000				Value: 115	

KM# 419   50 DOLLARS
3.1103 g., 0.9990 Gold 0.0999 oz. AGW **Subject:** Return of
Macao to China **Obv:** National arms **Rev:** Dragon and phoenix
Note: Similar to 10 Dollars, KM#408.

Date	Mintage	F	VF	XF	Unc	BU
1999 Proof	10,000				Value: 110	

KM# 33 100 DOLLARS
6.0000 g., 0.9000 Gold 0.1736 oz. AGW **Subject:** Inauguration of President Tolbert **Obv:** Bust facing **Rev:** Joined figures form a tower

Date	Mintage	F	VF	XF	Unc	BU
1976 Proof	175	Value: 225				

KM# 36 100 DOLLARS
10.9300 g., 0.9000 Gold 0.3163 oz. AGW **Subject:** 130th Anniversary of the Republic **Obv:** Bust 3/4 left **Rev:** National arms

Date	Mintage	F	VF	XF	Unc	BU
1977FM (U)	787	—	—	—	320	340
1977FM (P)	4,250	Value: 325				

KM# 37 100 DOLLARS
10.9300 g., 0.9000 Gold 0.3163 oz. AGW **Subject:** Organization of African Unity **Obv:** National arms above value flanked by stars **Rev:** Bust facing flanked by stars

Date	Mintage	F	VF	XF	Unc	BU
1979FM (P)	1,656	Value: 325				

KM# 38 100 DOLLARS
11.2000 g., 0.9000 Gold 0.3241 oz. AGW **Subject:** Organization of African Unity **Obv:** National arms **Rev:** Elephant

Date	Mintage	F	VF	XF	Unc	BU
1979FM (P)	—	Value: 320				

KM# 50 100 DOLLARS
10.9300 g., 0.9000 Gold 0.3163 oz. AGW **Subject:** 5th Anniversary of Government **Obv:** National arms **Rev:** Leopard

Date	Mintage	F	VF	XF	Unc	BU
1985FM (P)	409	Value: 450				

KM# 61 100 DOLLARS
7.1300 g., 0.9000 Gold 0.2063 oz. AGW **Series:** Decade For Women **Obv:** National arms **Rev:** Woman mashing grain

Date	Mintage	F	VF	XF	Unc	BU
1985 Proof	318	Value: 225				

KM# 70 100 DOLLARS
311.0300 g., 0.9990 Silver 9.9894 oz. ASW **Subject:** President Bill Clinton **Obv:** National arms **Rev:** Head right flanked by value and date above building

Date	Mintage	F	VF	XF	Unc	BU
1993 Proof	—	Value: 220				

KM# 100 100 DOLLARS
6.2200 g., 0.9990 Gold 0.1998 oz. AGW **Series:** Preserve Planet Earth **Obv:** National arms **Rev:** Protoceratops

Date	Mintage	F	VF	XF	Unc	BU
1993 Proof	Est. 7,500	Value: 210				

KM# 111 100 DOLLARS
6.2200 g., 0.9990 Gold 0.1998 oz. AGW **Series:** Preserve Planet Earth **Obv:** National arms **Rev:** Corythosaurus

Date	Mintage	F	VF	XF	Unc	BU
1993 Proof	7,500	Value: 210				

KM# 114 100 DOLLARS
6.2200 g., 0.9990 Gold 0.1998 oz. AGW **Series:** Preserve Planet Earth **Obv:** National arms **Rev:** Atchaeopteryx **Note:** Incorrect spelling.

Date	Mintage	F	VF	XF	Unc	BU
1993 Proof	Est. 7,500	Value: 200				

KM# 117 100 DOLLARS
6.2200 g., 0.9990 Gold 0.1998 oz. AGW **Series:** Preserve Planet Earth **Obv:** National arms **Rev:** Archaeopteryx **Note:** Correct spelling.

Date	Mintage	F	VF	XF	Unc	BU
1994 Proof	7,500	Value: 200				

KM# 120 100 DOLLARS
6.2200 g., 0.9990 Gold 0.1998 oz. AGW **Series:** Preserve Planet Earth **Obv:** National arms **Rev:** Gorillas **Note:** Similar to 10 Dollars, KM#120.

Date	Mintage	F	VF	XF	Unc	BU
1994 Proof	Est. 7,500	Value: 200				

KM# 123 100 DOLLARS
6.2200 g., 0.9990 Gold 0.1998 oz. AGW **Series:** Preserve Planet Earth **Obv:** National arms **Rev:** Pygmy Hippopotami **Note:** Similar to 10 Dollars, KM#122.

Date	Mintage	F	VF	XF	Unc	BU
1994 Proof	Est. 7,500	Value: 200				

KM# 126 100 DOLLARS
6.2200 g., 0.9990 Gold 0.1998 oz. AGW **Series:** Preserve Planet Earth **Obv:** National arms **Rev:** Trionyx Turtle **Note:** Similar to 10 Dollars, KM#125.

Date	Mintage	F	VF	XF	Unc	BU
1994 Proof	Est. 7,500	Value: 200				

KM# 130 100 DOLLARS
6.2200 g., 0.9990 Gold 0.1998 oz. AGW **Subject:** Star Trek **Obv:** National arms **Rev:** Captains Kirk and Picard **Note:** Similar to 10 Dollars, KM#129.

Date	Mintage	F	VF	XF	Unc	BU
1995 Proof	—	Value: 210				

KM# 135 100 DOLLARS
6.2200 g., 0.9990 Gold 0.1998 oz. AGW **Series:** Preserve Planet Earth **Obv:** National arms **Rev:** Leopard

Date	Mintage	F	VF	XF	Unc	BU
1995 Proof	Est. 7,500	Value: 200				

KM# 138 100 DOLLARS
6.2200 g., 0.9990 Gold 0.1998 oz. AGW **Series:** Preserve Planet Earth **Obv:** National arms **Rev:** Storks

Date	Mintage	F	VF	XF	Unc	BU
1995 Proof	Est. 7,500	Value: 200				

KM# 150 100 DOLLARS
6.2200 g., 0.9990 Gold 0.1998 oz. AGW **Subject:** Sir Winston Churchill **Obv:** National arms **Rev:** Uniformed bust right, planes, army tanks and ship

Date	Mintage	F	VF	XF	Unc	BU
1995 Proof	Est. 7,500	Value: 195				

KM# 151 100 DOLLARS
6.2200 g., 0.9990 Gold 0.1998 oz. AGW **Subject:** President Franklin D. Roosevelt **Obv:** National arms **Rev:** President Roosevelt riding in jeep

Date	Mintage	F	VF	XF	Unc	BU
1995 Proof	Est. 7,500	Value: 195				

KM# 152 100 DOLLARS
6.2200 g., 0.9990 Gold 0.1998 oz. AGW **Subject:** General George Patton **Obv:** National arms **Rev:** General Patton in front of map

Date	Mintage	F	VF	XF	Unc	BU
1995 Proof	Est. 7,500	Value: 195				

KM# 153 100 DOLLARS
6.2200 g., 0.9990 Gold 0.1998 oz. AGW **Subject:** President Harry S. Truman **Obv:** National arms **Rev:** President Truman facing

Date	Mintage	F	VF	XF	Unc	BU
1995 Proof	Est. 7,500	Value: 195				

KM# 154 100 DOLLARS
6.2200 g., 0.9990 Gold 0.1998 oz. AGW **Subject:** President Charles de Gaulle **Obv:** National arms **Rev:** President de Gaulle on Champs Elysees

Date	Mintage	F	VF	XF	Unc	BU
1995 Proof	Est. 7,500	Value: 195				

KM# 160 100 DOLLARS
6.2200 g., 0.9990 Gold 0.1998 oz. AGW **Subject:** Dr. Sun Yat-Sen **Obv:** National arms **Rev:** Uniformed bust facing

Date	Mintage	F	VF	XF	Unc	BU
1995 Proof	Est. 7,500	Value: 195				

KM# 163 100 DOLLARS
6.2200 g., 0.9990 Gold 0.1998 oz. AGW **Subject:** General Chiang Kai-shek **Obv:** National arms **Rev:** General Chiang Kai-shek

Date	Mintage	F	VF	XF	Unc	BU
1995 Proof	Est. 7,500	Value: 195				

KM# 166 100 DOLLARS
6.2200 g., 0.9990 Gold 0.1998 oz. AGW **Subject:** Cairo. Conference **Obv:** National arms **Rev:** Chiang Kai-shek, Roosevelt and Churchill

Date	Mintage	F	VF	XF	Unc	BU
1995 Proof	Est. 7,500	Value: 195				

KM# 175 100 DOLLARS
6.2200 g., 0.9990 Gold 0.1998 oz. AGW **Subject:** 375th Anniversary - Pilgrim Fathers **Obv:** National arms **Rev:** Mayflower

Date	Mintage	F	VF	XF	Unc	BU
1995 Proof	7,500	Value: 195				

KM# 176 100 DOLLARS
6.2200 g., 0.9990 Gold 0.1998 oz. AGW **Subject:** 375th Anniversary - Pilgrim Fathers **Obv:** National arms **Rev:** Cape Cod and Pilgrims in skiff

Date	Mintage	F	VF	XF	Unc	BU
1995 Proof	7,500	Value: 195				

KM# 177 100 DOLLARS
6.2200 g., 0.9990 Gold 0.1998 oz. AGW **Subject:** 375th Anniversary - Pilgrim Fathers **Obv:** National arms **Rev:** Pilgrim landing party

Date	Mintage	F	VF	XF	Unc	BU
1995 Proof	7,500	Value: 195				

KM# 178 100 DOLLARS
6.2200 g., 0.9990 Gold 0.1998 oz. AGW **Subject:** 375th Anniversary - Pilgrim Fathers **Obv:** National arms **Rev:** First Thanksgiving scene

Date	Mintage	F	VF	XF	Unc	BU
1995 Proof	7,500	Value: 195				

KM# 209 100 DOLLARS
6.2200 g., 0.9990 Gold 0.1998 oz. AGW **Subject:** Star Trek **Obv:** National arms **Rev:** Star ships NCC-1701 and NCC-1701D

Date	Mintage	F	VF	XF	Unc	BU
1996 Proof	Est. 7,500	Value: 200				

KM# 252 100 DOLLARS
6.2200 g., 0.9990 Gold 0.1998 oz. AGW **Subject:** Dalai Lama **Obv:** National arms **Rev:** Bust with praying hands facing 1/4 left

Date	Mintage	F	VF	XF	Unc	BU
1996 Proof	Est. 7,500	Value: 200				

KM# 212 100 DOLLARS
6.2200 g., 0.9990 Gold 0.1998 oz. AGW **Subject:** Star Trek **Obv:** National arms **Rev:** Scott and McCoy

Date	Mintage	F	VF	XF	Unc	BU
1996 Proof	7,500	Value: 210				

KM# 215 100 DOLLARS
6.2200 g., 0.9990 Gold 0.1998 oz. AGW **Subject:** Star Trek **Obv:** National arms **Rev:** LaForge and Data

Date	Mintage	F	VF	XF	Unc	BU
1996 Proof	25,000	Value: 200				

KM# 218 100 DOLLARS
6.2200 g., 0.9990 Gold 0.1998 oz. AGW **Subject:** Star Trek **Obv:** National arms **Rev:** Spock and Uhura **Note:** Similar to 10 Dollars, KM#217.

Date	Mintage	F	VF	XF	Unc	BU
1996 Proof	25,000	Value: 200				

KM# 221   100 DOLLARS
6.2200 g., 0.9990 Gold 0.1998 oz. AGW **Subject:** Star Trek **Obv:** National arms **Rev:** Worf and Dr. Crusher **Note:** Similar to 10 Dollars, KM#220.

Date	Mintage	F	VF	XF	Unc	BU
1996 Proof	25,000	Value: 200				

KM# 224   100 DOLLARS
6.2200 g., 0.9990 Gold 0.1998 oz. AGW **Subject:** Preserve Planet Earth **Obv:** National arms **Rev:** Grey Parrot **Note:** Similar to 10 Dollars, KM#223.

Date	Mintage	F	VF	XF	Unc	BU
1996 Proof	25,000	Value: 200				

KM# 227   100 DOLLARS
6.2200 g., 0.9990 Gold 0.1998 oz. AGW **Subject:** Preserve Planet Earth **Obv:** National arms **Rev:** Love Birds **Note:** Similar to 10 Dollars, KM#226.

Date	Mintage	F	VF	XF	Unc	BU
1996 Proof	25,000	Value: 200				

KM# 232   100 DOLLARS
6.2200 g., 0.9990 Gold 0.1998 oz. AGW **Subject:** Formula One **Obv:** National arms **Rev:** Ayrton Senna **Note:** Similar to 10 Dollars, KM#229.

Date	Mintage	F	VF	XF	Unc	BU
1996 Proof	20,000	Value: 200				

KM# 237   100 DOLLARS
6.2200 g., 0.9990 Gold 0.1998 oz. AGW **Subject:** Dr. Sun Yat-Sen

Date	Mintage	F	VF	XF	Unc	BU
1996 Proof	Est. 7,500	Value: 195				

KM# 240   100 DOLLARS
6.2200 g., 0.9990 Gold 0.1998 oz. AGW **Subject:** General Chiang Kai-shek **Obv:** National arms **Rev:** General Chiang kai-shek **Note:** Similar to 10 Dollars, KM#162.

Date	Mintage	F	VF	XF	Unc	BU
1996 Proof	Est. 7,500	Value: 195				

KM# 243   100 DOLLARS
6.2200 g., 0.9990 Gold 0.1998 oz. AGW **Subject:** President Chiang Ching-kuo **Obv:** National arms **Rev:** Bust facing **Note:** Similar to 10 Dollars, KM#242.

Date	Mintage	F	VF	XF	Unc	BU
1996 Proof	Est. 7,500	Value: 195				

KM# 246   100 DOLLARS
6.2200 g., 0.9990 Gold 0.1998 oz. AGW **Subject:** President Lee Teng-hui **Obv:** National arms **Rev:** President Lee Ten-hui **Note:** Similar to 10 Dollars, KM#245.

Date	Mintage	F	VF	XF	Unc	BU
1996 Proof	Est. 7,500	Value: 195				

KM# 253   100 DOLLARS
6.2200 g., 0.9990 Gold 0.1998 oz. AGW **Subject:** King Rama IX of Thailand **Obv:** National arms **Rev:** King seated on radiant throne

Date	Mintage	F	VF	XF	Unc	BU
1996 Proof	Est. 7,500	Value: 195				

KM# 259   100 DOLLARS
6.2200 g., 0.9990 Gold 0.1998 oz. AGW **Subject:** Mao Zedong Proclaiming People's Republic **Obv:** National arms **Rev:** Chairman Mao Zedong proclaiming People's Republic **Note:** Similar to 10 Dollars, KM#258.

Date	Mintage	F	VF	XF	Unc	BU
1996 Proof	1,996	Value: 200				

KM# 312   100 DOLLARS
6.2200 g., 0.9990 Gold 0.1998 oz. AGW **Subject:** Mahatma Gandhi **Obv:** National arms **Rev:** Seated figure looking left in front of Taj Mahal **Note:** Similar to 10 Dollars, KM#311.

Date	Mintage	F	VF	XF	Unc	BU
1997 Proof	Est. 5,000	Value: 200				

KM# 317   100 DOLLARS
6.2200 g., 0.9990 Gold 0.1998 oz. AGW **Subject:** Return of Hong Kong to China **Obv:** National arms **Rev:** Dragon **Note:** Similar to 10 Dollars, KM#314.

Date	Mintage	F	VF	XF	Unc	BU
1997 Proof	Est. 5,000	Value: 200				

KM# 322   100 DOLLARS
6.2200 g., 0.9990 Gold 0.1998 oz. AGW **Subject:** Fiftieth Anniversary of the Kon-Tiki Expedition **Obv:** National arms **Rev:** Sailing ship within circle **Note:** Similar to 1 Dollar, KM#320.

Date	Mintage	F	VF	XF	Unc	BU
1997 Proof	Est. 7,500	Value: 200				

KM# 326   100 DOLLARS
6.2200 g., 0.9990 Gold 0.1998 oz. AGW **Subject:** Jurassic Park **Obv:** National arms **Rev:** Stegosaurus **Note:** Similar to 10 Dollars, KM#325.

Date	Mintage	F	VF	XF	Unc	BU
1997 Proof	Est. 2,500	Value: 200				

KM# 329   100 DOLLARS
6.2200 g., 0.9990 Gold 0.1998 oz. AGW **Subject:** Golden Wedding Anniversary **Obv:** National arms **Rev:** E & P initials above 2 shields **Note:** Similar to 10 Dollars, KM#328.

Date	Mintage	F	VF	XF	Unc	BU
1997 Proof	Est. 3,500	Value: 200				

KM# 332   100 DOLLARS
6.2200 g., 0.9990 Gold 0.1998 oz. AGW **Subject:** Golden Wedding Anniversary **Obv:** National arms **Rev:** Royal couple with horse **Note:** Similar to 10 Dollars, KM#331.

Date	Mintage	F	VF	XF	Unc	BU
1997 Proof	Est. 3,500	Value: 200				

KM# 335   100 DOLLARS
6.2200 g., 0.9990 Gold 0.1998 oz. AGW **Subject:** Golden Wedding Anniversary **Obv:** National arms **Rev:** Royal couple with dogs **Note:** Similar to 10 Dollars, KM#334.

Date	Mintage	F	VF	XF	Unc	BU
1997 Proof	Est. 3,500	Value: 200				

KM# 338   100 DOLLARS
6.2200 g., 0.9990 Gold 0.1998 oz. AGW **Subject:** Golden Wedding Anniversary **Obv:** National arms **Rev:** Royal couple with children **Note:** Similar to 10 Dollars, KM#337.

Date	Mintage	F	VF	XF	Unc	BU
1997 Proof	Est. 3,500	Value: 200				

KM# 370   100 DOLLARS
6.2200 g., 0.9990 Gold 0.1998 oz. AGW **Subject:** Star Trek - The Next Generation **Obv:** National arms **Rev:** Romulan Warbird **Note:** Similar to 10 Dollars, KM#369.

Date	Mintage	F	VF	XF	Unc	BU
1997 Proof	Est. 7,500	Value: 200				

KM# 373   100 DOLLARS
6.2200 g., 0.9990 Gold 0.1998 oz. AGW **Subject:** Star Trek - The Next Generation **Obv:** National arms **Rev:** Klingon Attack Cruiser **Note:** Similar to 10 Dollars, KM#372.

Date	Mintage	F	VF	XF	Unc	BU
1997 Proof	Est. 7,500	Value: 200				

KM# 376   100 DOLLARS
6.2200 g., 0.9990 Gold 0.1998 oz. AGW **Subject:** Star Trek - The Next Generation **Obv:** National arms **Rev:** U.S.S. Enterprise NCC-1701-D **Note:** Similar to 10 Dollars, KM#375.

Date	Mintage	F	VF	XF	Unc	BU
1997 Proof	Est. 7,500	Value: 200				

KM# 379   100 DOLLARS
6.2200 g., 0.9990 Gold 0.1998 oz. AGW **Subject:** Star Trek - The Next Generation **Obv:** National arms **Rev:** Klingon Bird of Prey **Note:** Similar to 10 Dollars, KM#378.

Date	Mintage	F	VF	XF	Unc	BU
1997 Proof	Est. 7,500	Value: 200				

KM# 382   100 DOLLARS
6.2200 g., 0.9990 Gold 0.1998 oz. AGW **Subject:** Star Trek - The Next Generation **Obv:** National arms **Rev:** Borg Cube **Note:** Similar to 10 Dollars, KM#381.

Date	Mintage	F	VF	XF	Unc	BU
1997 Proof	Est. 7,500	Value: 200				

KM# 385   100 DOLLARS
6.2200 g., 0.9990 Gold 0.1998 oz. AGW **Subject:** Star Trek - The Next Generation **Obv:** National arms **Rev:** Ferengi Marauder **Note:** Similar to 10 Dollars, KM#384.

Date	Mintage	F	VF	XF	Unc	BU
1997 Proof	Est. 7,500	Value: 200				

KM# 473   100 DOLLARS
6.2200 g., 0.9990 Gold 0.1998 oz. AGW **Subject:** Princess Diana in Memoriam **Obv:** National arms

Date	Mintage	F	VF	XF	Unc	BU
1997 Proof	—	Value: 200				

KM# 365   100 DOLLARS
6.2200 g., 0.9990 Gold 0.1998 oz. AGW **Subject:** RMS Titanic **Obv:** National arms **Rev:** Ship sinking **Note:** Similar to 20 Dollars, KM#364.

Date	Mintage	F	VF	XF	Unc	BU
1998 Proof	Est. 5,000	Value: 210				

KM# 388   100 DOLLARS
6.2200 g., 0.9990 Gold 0.1998 oz. AGW **Subject:** President Ronald Reagan **Obv:** National arms **Rev:** Lincoln Memorial below head right **Note:** Similar to 10 Dollars, KM#387.

Date	Mintage	F	VF	XF	Unc	BU
1998 Proof	Est. 7,500	Value: 210				

KM# 392   100 DOLLARS
6.2200 g., 0.9990 Gold 0.1998 oz. AGW **Subject:** Year of the Rabbit **Obv:** National arms **Rev:** Rabbit running left **Note:** Similar to 20 Dollars, KM#389.

Date	Mintage	F	VF	XF	Unc	BU
1999 Proof	5,000	Value: 210				

KM# 393   100 DOLLARS
6.2200 g., 0.9990 Gold 0.1998 oz. AGW **Subject:** Year of the Rabbit **Obv:** National arms **Rev:** Rabbit sitting **Note:** Similar to 20 Dollars, KM#390.

Date	Mintage	F	VF	XF	Unc	BU
1999 Proof	5,000	Value: 210				

KM# 394   100 DOLLARS
6.2200 g., 0.9990 Gold 0.1998 oz. AGW **Subject:** Year of the Rabbit **Obv:** National arms **Rev:** Rabbit running right **Note:** Similar to 20 Dollars, KM#391.

Date	Mintage	F	VF	XF	Unc	BU
1999 Proof	5,000	Value: 210				

KM# 403   100 DOLLARS
6.2200 g., 0.9990 Gold 0.1998 oz. AGW **Subject:** Christopher Columbus **Obv:** National arms **Rev:** Portrait, ship **Note:** Similar to 10 Dollars, KM#402.

Date	Mintage	F	VF	XF	Unc	BU
1999 Proof	10,000	Value: 210				

KM# 406   100 DOLLARS
6.2200 g., 0.9990 Gold 0.1998 oz. AGW **Subject:** Captain James Cook **Obv:** National arms **Rev:** Portrait, ship, map **Note:** Similar to 10 Dollars, KM#405.

Date	Mintage	F	VF	XF	Unc	BU
1999 Proof	10,000	Value: 210				

KM# 409   100 DOLLARS
6.2200 g., 0.9990 Gold 0.1998 oz. AGW **Subject:** Return of Macao to China **Obv:** National arms **Rev:** Dragon and phoenix **Note:** Similar to 10 Dollars, KM#408.

Date	Mintage	F	VF	XF	Unc	BU
1999 Proof	10,000	Value: 210				

KM# 415   100 DOLLARS
6.2200 g., 0.9990 Gold 0.1998 oz. AGW **Subject:** The Wedding of Prince Edward and Miss Sophie Rhys-Jones **Obv:** National arms **Rev:** Couple in carriage **Note:** Similar to 10 Dollars, KM#414.

Date	Mintage	F	VF	XF	Unc	BU
1999 Proof	Est. 5,000	Value: 210				

KM# 106   150 DOLLARS
500.0000 g., 0.9990 Silver 16.058 oz. ASW, 85 mm. **Subject:** Preserve Planet Earth **Obv:** National arms **Rev:** Two Brachiosauros **Note:** Illustration reduced.

Date	Mintage	F	VF	XF	Unc	BU
1993 Proof	121	Value: 345				

KM# 34   200 DOLLARS
12.0000 g., 0.9000 Gold 0.3472 oz. AGW **Subject:** Inauguration of President Tolbert **Obv:** Bust facing flanked by stars **Rev:** Man holding horn within circle

Date	Mintage	F	VF	XF	Unc	BU
1976 Proof	100	Value: 350				

KM# 46   200 DOLLARS
15.9800 g., 0.9170 Gold 0.4711 oz. AGW **Subject:** Year of the Scout **Obv:** National arms **Rev:** Saluting scout divides flags above dates

Date	Mintage	F	VF	XF	Unc	BU
ND(1983)	—	—	—	—	—	450
ND(1983) Proof	—	Value: 475				

KM# 49 200 DOLLARS
15.9800 g., 0.9000 Gold 0.4624 oz. AGW **Series:** International Year of Disabled Persons **Obv:** National arms **Rev:** Standing elderly figures above disability emblem

Date	Mintage	F	VF	XF	Unc	BU
1983	500	—	—	—	—	465
1983 Proof	500	Value: 525				

KM# 395 200 DOLLARS
12.4444 g., 0.9999 Gold 0.4000 oz. AGW **Subject:** Year of the Rabbit **Obv:** National arms **Rev:** Rabbit running left **Note:** Similar to 20 Dollars, KM#389.

Date	Mintage	F	VF	XF	Unc	BU
1999 Proof	1,500	Value: 400				

KM# 396 200 DOLLARS
12.4444 g., 0.9999 Gold 0.4000 oz. AGW **Subject:** Year of the Rabbit **Obv:** National arms **Rev:** Rabbit sitting **Note:** Similar to 20 Dollars, KM#390.

Date	Mintage	F	VF	XF	Unc	BU
1999 Proof	1,500	Value: 400				

KM# 397 200 DOLLARS
12.4444 g., 0.9999 Gold 0.4000 oz. AGW **Subject:** Year of the Rabbit **Obv:** National arms **Rev:** Rabbit running right **Note:** Similar to 20 Dollars, KM#391.

Date	Mintage	F	VF	XF	Unc	BU
1999 Proof	1,500	Value: 400				

KM# 601 200 DOLLARS
500.0000 g., 0.9990 Silver 16.058 oz. ASW, 89 mm. **Obv:** National arms **Rev:** Three facing elephants **Edge:** Reeded

Date	Mintage	F	VF	XF	Unc	BU
2000 Proof	—	Value: 345				

KM# 52 250 DOLLARS
15.5000 g., 0.9990 Gold 0.4978 oz. AGW **Subject:** President John F. Kennedy **Obv:** National arms divides date **Rev:** Head left

Date	Mintage	F	VF	XF	Unc	BU
1988 Proof	5,000	Value: 500				

KM# 56 250 DOLLARS
15.5000 g., 0.9990 Gold 0.4978 oz. AGW **Subject:** President Samuel Kanyon Doe **Obv:** National arms **Rev:** Head 3/4 facing

Date	Mintage	F	VF	XF	Unc	BU
1988 Proof	Est. 5,000	Value: 500				

KM# 58 250 DOLLARS
15.5000 g., 0.9990 Gold 0.4978 oz. AGW **Subject:** President George H. W. Bush **Obv:** National arms **Rev:** Head left

Date	Mintage	F	VF	XF	Unc	BU
1989 Proof	600	Value: 515				

KM# 60 250 DOLLARS
15.5000 g., 0.9990 Gold 0.4978 oz. AGW **Subject:** Emperor Hirohito **Obv:** National arms **Rev:** Head facing divides dates

Date	Mintage	F	VF	XF	Unc	BU
1989 Proof	600	Value: 525				

KM# 89 250 DOLLARS
15.5000 g., 0.9990 Gold 0.4978 oz. AGW **Subject:** Formula One **Obv:** National arms **Rev:** Nigel Mansell **Note:** Similar to 10 Dollars, KM#75.

Date	Mintage	F	VF	XF	Unc	BU
1992 Proof	Est. 5,000	Value: 495				

KM# 90 250 DOLLARS
15.5000 g., 0.9990 Gold 0.4978 oz. AGW **Subject:** Formula One **Obv:** National arms **Rev:** Gerhard Berger **Note:** Similar to 10 Dollars, KM#83.

Date	Mintage	F	VF	XF	Unc	BU
1992 Proof	Est. 5,000	Value: 495				

KM# 91 250 DOLLARS
15.5000 g., 0.9990 Gold 0.4978 oz. AGW **Subject:** Formula One **Obv:** National arms **Rev:** Aguri Suzuki **Note:** Similar to 10 Dollars, KM#84.

Date	Mintage	F	VF	XF	Unc	BU
1992 Proof	Est. 5,000	Value: 465				

KM# 92 250 DOLLARS
15.5000 g., 0.9990 Gold 0.4978 oz. AGW **Subject:** Formula One **Obv:** National arms **Rev:** Ayrton Senna **Note:** Similar to 10 Dollars, KM#85.

Date	Mintage	F	VF	XF	Unc	BU
1992 Proof	Est. 5,000	Value: 495				

KM# 93 250 DOLLARS
15.5000 g., 0.9990 Gold 0.4978 oz. AGW **Subject:** Formula One **Obv:** National arms **Rev:** Ricardo Patrese **Note:** Similar to 10 Dollars, KM#74.

Date	Mintage	F	VF	XF	Unc	BU
1992 Proof	Est. 5,000	Value: 495				

KM# 94 250 DOLLARS
15.5000 g., 0.9990 Gold 0.4978 oz. AGW **Subject:** Formula One **Obv:** National arms **Rev:** Michael Schumacher **Note:** Similar to 10 Dollars, KM#86.

Date	Mintage	F	VF	XF	Unc	BU
1992 Proof	Est. 5,000	Value: 495				

KM# 95 250 DOLLARS
15.5000 g., 0.9990 Gold 0.4978 oz. AGW **Subject:** Formula One **Obv:** National arms **Rev:** Alain Prost **Note:** Similar to 10 Dollars, KM#87.

Date	Mintage	F	VF	XF	Unc	BU
1992 Proof	Est. 5,000	Value: 495				

KM# 96 250 DOLLARS
15.5000 g., 0.9990 Gold 0.4978 oz. AGW **Subject:** Formula One **Obv:** National arms **Rev:** Ukyo Katayama **Note:** Similar to 10 Dollars, KM#88.

Date	Mintage	F	VF	XF	Unc	BU
1992 Proof	Est. 5,000	Value: 495				

KM# 71 250 DOLLARS
15.5000 g., 0.9990 Gold 0.4978 oz. AGW **Subject:** President Bill Clinton **Obv:** National arms **Rev:** Head right **Note:** Similar to 10 Dollars, KM#68.

Date	Mintage	F	VF	XF	Unc	BU
1993 Proof	Est. 5,000	Value: 495				

KM# 105 250 DOLLARS
15.5000 g., 0.9990 Gold 0.4978 oz. AGW **Subject:** President John F. Kennedy **Obv:** National arms **Rev:** Head left, funeral caisson below **Note:** Similar to 10 Dollars, KM#104.

Date	Mintage	F	VF	XF	Unc	BU
1993 Proof	Est. 5,000	Value: 495				

KM# 181 250 DOLLARS
15.5000 g., 0.9990 Gold 0.4978 oz. AGW **Subject:** Formula One **Obv:** National arms **Rev:** Mika Hakkinen

Date	Mintage	F	VF	XF	Unc	BU
1995 Proof	Est. 5,000	Value: 495				

KM# 184 250 DOLLARS
15.5000 g., 0.9990 Gold 0.4978 oz. AGW **Subject:** Formula One **Obv:** National arms **Rev:** Martin Brundle

Date	Mintage	F	VF	XF	Unc	BU
1995 Proof	Est. 5,000	Value: 495				

KM# 187 250 DOLLARS
15.5000 g., 0.9990 Gold 0.4978 oz. AGW **Subject:** Formula One **Obv:** National arms **Rev:** Rubens Barricchello

Date	Mintage	F	VF	XF	Unc	BU
1995 Proof	Est. 5,000	Value: 495				

KM# 190 250 DOLLARS
15.5000 g., 0.9990 Gold 0.4978 oz. AGW **Subject:** Formula One **Obv:** National arms **Rev:** David Coulthard

Date	Mintage	F	VF	XF	Unc	BU
1995 Proof	Est. 5,000	Value: 495				

KM# 193 250 DOLLARS
15.5000 g., 0.9990 Gold 0.4978 oz. AGW **Subject:** Formula One **Obv:** National arms **Rev:** Jean Alesi

Date	Mintage	F	VF	XF	Unc	BU
1995 Proof	Est. 5,000	Value: 495				

KM# 565 250 DOLLARS
15.5000 g., 0.9990 Gold 0.4978 oz. AGW, 33 mm. **Obv:** National arms **Rev:** Bugatti Royale

Date	Mintage	F	VF	XF	Unc	BU
1995B	—	—	—	—	475	—

KM# 203 250 DOLLARS
15.5000 g., 0.9990 Gold 0.4978 oz. AGW **Subject:** Formula One **Obv:** National arms **Rev:** Mark Blundell

Date	Mintage	F	VF	XF	Unc	BU
1996 Proof	Est. 5,000	Value: 475				

KM# 204 250 DOLLARS
15.5000 g., 0.9990 Gold 0.4978 oz. AGW **Subject:** Formula One **Obv:** National arms **Rev:** Johnny Herbert **Note:** Similar to 10 Dollars, KM#200.

Date	Mintage	F	VF	XF	Unc	BU
1996 Proof	Est. 5,000	Value: 475				

KM# 205 250 DOLLARS
15.5000 g., 0.9990 Gold 0.4978 oz. AGW **Subject:** Formula One **Obv:** National arms **Rev:** Eddie Irvine **Note:** Similar to 10 Dollars, KM#201.

Date	Mintage	F	VF	XF	Unc	BU
1996 Proof	Est. 5,000	Value: 475				

KM# 206 250 DOLLARS
15.5000 g., 0.9990 Gold 0.4978 oz. AGW **Subject:** Formula One **Obv:** National arms **Rev:** Heinz Frentzen **Note:** Similar to 10 Dollars, KM#202.

Date	Mintage	F	VF	XF	Unc	BU
1996 Proof	Est. 5,000	Value: 475				

KM# 233 250 DOLLARS
15.5000 g., 0.9990 Gold 0.4978 oz. AGW **Subject:** Formula One **Obv:** National arms **Rev:** Ayrton Senna **Note:** Similar to 10 Dollars, KM#229.

Date	Mintage	F	VF	XF	Unc	BU
1996 Proof	Est. 5,000	Value: 475				

KM# 318 250 DOLLARS
15.5000 g., 0.9990 Gold 0.4978 oz. AGW **Subject:** Return of Hong Kong **Obv:** National arms **Rev:** Dragon **Note:** Similar to 10 Dollars, KM#314.

Date	Mintage	F	VF	XF	Unc	BU
1997 Proof	—	Value: 475				

KM# 420 250 DOLLARS
15.5000 g., 0.9990 Gold 0.4978 oz. AGW **Subject:** Return of Macao to China **Obv:** National arms **Rev:** Dragon and phoenix **Note:** Similar to 10 Dollars, KM#408.

Date	Mintage	F	VF	XF	Unc	BU
1999 Proof	Est. 5,000	Value: 475				

KM# 425 250 DOLLARS
15.5000 g., 0.9990 Gold 0.4978 oz. AGW **Subject:** Liberty **Obv:** National arms **Rev:** Conjoined heads left **Note:** Similar to 10 Dollars, KM#424.

Date	Mintage	F	VF	XF	Unc	BU
1999 Proof	375	Value: 525				

KM# 439 250 DOLLARS
15.5517 g., 0.9999 Gold 0.4999 oz. AGW, 27 mm. **Subject:** Taipai, Taiwan Rapid Transit System **Obv:** National arms above hole* and dragon **Rev:** Subway train, logo and tunnel hole* **Note:** Struck at Singapore Mint. *As first done on Albanian coins of 1988.

Date	Mintage	F	VF	XF	Unc	BU
1999 Proof	2,000	Value: 500				

KM# 107 300 DOLLARS
1000.0000 g., 0.9990 Silver 32.117 oz. ASW, 100 mm. **Series:** Preserve Planet Earth **Obv:** National arms **Rev:** Tyrannosaurus Rex attacking Triceratops **Note:** Illustration reduced.

Date	Mintage	F	VF	XF	Unc	BU
1993 Proof	151	Value: 700				

KM# 367 300 DOLLARS
1000.0000 g., 0.9990 Silver 32.117 oz. ASW. **Subject:** RMS Titanic **Obv:** National arms **Rev:** Ship sinking **Note:** Similar to 20 Dollars, KM#364.

Date	Mintage	F	VF	XF	Unc	BU
1998 Proof	Est. 500	Value: 650				

KM# 35   400 DOLLARS
24.0000 g., 0.9000 Gold 0.6944 oz. AGW Subject: Inauguration of President Tolbert Obv: Bust facing Rev: Liberia written within circle

Date	Mintage	F	VF	XF	Unc	BU
1976 Proof	25	Value: 1,250				

KM# 234   500 DOLLARS
31.1035 g., 0.9990 Gold 0.9990 oz. AGW Subject: Formula One Obv: National arms Rev: Ayrton Senna Note: Similar to 10 Dollars, KM#229.

Date	Mintage	F	VF	XF	Unc	BU
1996 Proof	Est. 2,500	Value: 975				

KM# 421   500 DOLLARS
31.1035 g., 0.9990 Gold 0.9990 oz. AGW Subject: Return of Macao to China Obv: National arms Rev: Dragon and phoenix Note: Similar to 10 Dollars, KM#408.

Date	Mintage	F	VF	XF	Unc	BU
1999 Proof	Est. 1,000	Value: 1,000				

KM# 737   500 DOLLARS
0.5850 Gold Subject: XXVII OLympic Games - Sydney Rev: Three sports figures Edge: Reeded

Date	Mintage	F	VF	XF	Unc	BU
2000	2,000					

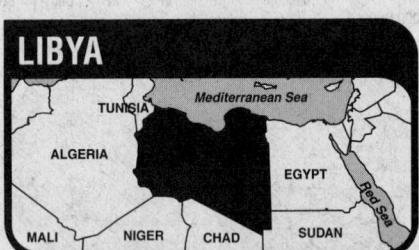

KM# 732   500 DOLLARS
373.2360 g., 0.9990 Bi-Metallic Silver with 39mm Gold inlay 11.987 oz., 89.08 mm. Subject: JFK Memorial Obv: Arms with banners above and below Obv. Leg.: REPUBLIC OF LIBERIA Rev: Conjoined heads of President John F. Kennedy and son John Jr. left Rev. Leg.: "Ask not what your country can do for you -..." Edge: Reeded Note: Illustration reduced.

Date	Mintage	F	VF	XF	Unc	BU
2000 Proof	300	Value: 2,500				

KM# 247   2500 DOLLARS
155.5175 g., 0.9990 Gold 4.9948 oz. AGW Subject: President Lee Teng-hui Obv: National arms Rev: President Lee Teng-hui Note: Similar to 10 Dollars, KM#245.

Date	Mintage	F	VF	XF	Unc	BU
1996 Proof	Est. 250	Value: 4,800				

KM# 235   2500 DOLLARS
155.5175 g., 0.9990 Gold 4.9948 oz. AGW Subject: Formula One Obv: National arms Rev: Ayrton Senna Note: Similar to 10 Dollars, KM#229.

Date	Mintage	F	VF	XF	Unc	BU
1996 Proof	Est. 250	Value: 4,800				

KM# 238   2500 DOLLARS
155.5175 g., 0.9990 Gold 4.9948 oz. AGW Subject: Dr. Sun Yat-Sen

Date	Mintage	F	VF	XF	Unc	BU
1996 Proof	Est. 250	Value: 4,800				

KM# 241   2500 DOLLARS
155.5175 g., 0.9990 Gold 4.9948 oz. AGW Subject: General Chiang Kai-shek Obv: National arms Rev: General Chiang kai-shek Note: Similar to 10 Dollars, KM#162.

Date	Mintage	F	VF	XF	Unc	BU
1996 Proof	Est. 250	Value: 4,800				

KM# 244   2500 DOLLARS
155.5175 g., 0.9990 Gold 4.9948 oz. AGW Subject: President Chiang Ching-kuo Obv: National arms Rev: Bust facing Note: Similar to 10 Dollars, KM#242.

Date	Mintage	F	VF	XF	Unc	BU
1996 Proof	Est. 250	Value: 4,800				

KM# 319   2500 DOLLARS
155.5175 g., 0.9990 Gold 4.9948 oz. AGW Subject: Return of Hong Kong Obv: National arms Rev: Dragon Note: Similar to 10 Dollars, KM#314.

Date	Mintage	F	VF	XF	Unc	BU
1997 Proof	—	Value: 4,800				

KM# 588   2500 DOLLARS
155.5175 g., 0.9990 Gold 4.9948 oz. AGW, 60 mm. Subject: Year of the Tiger Obv: National arms Rev: Tiger above pineapple and flowers within beaded circle Edge: Reeded Note: Illustration reduced.

Date	Mintage	F	VF	XF	Unc	BU
1998 Proof	—	Value: 5,000				

KM# 398   2500 DOLLARS
155.5175 g., 0.9990 Gold 4.9948 oz. AGW Subject: Year of the Rabbit Obv: National arms Rev: Rabbit running left Note: Similar to 20 Dollars, KM#389.

Date	Mintage	F	VF	XF	Unc	BU
1999 Proof	88	Value: 5,000				

KM# 399   2500 DOLLARS
155.5175 g., 0.9990 Gold 4.9948 oz. AGW Subject: Year of the Rabbit Obv: National arms Rev: Rabbit sitting Note: Similar to 20 Dollars, KM#390.

Date	Mintage	F	VF	XF	Unc	BU
1999 Proof	88	Value: 5,000				

KM# 400   2500 DOLLARS
155.5175 g., 0.9990 Gold 4.9948 oz. AGW Subject: Year of the Rabbit Obv: National arms Rev: Rabbit running right Note: Similar to 20 Dollars, KM#391.

Date	Mintage	F	VF	XF	Unc	BU
1999 Proof	88	Value: 5,000				

KM# 422   2500 DOLLARS
155.5175 g., 0.9990 Gold 4.9948 oz. AGW Subject: Return of Macao to China Obv: National arms Rev: Dragon and phoenix Note: Similar to 10 Dollars, KM#408.

Date	Mintage	F	VF	XF	Unc	BU
1999 Proof	Est. 250	Value: 5,000				

KM# 440   2500 DOLLARS
155.5175 g., 0.9999 Gold 4.9993 oz. AGW, 55 mm. Subject: Taipai, Taiwan Rapid Transit System Obv: National arms above dragon Rev: Dragon around subway train viewing sun with diamond inserts Note: Struck at Singapore Mint.

Date	Mintage	F	VF	XF	Unc	BU
ND(1999) Proof	50	Value: 5,000				

PATTERNS
Including off metal strikes

KM#	Date	Mintage Identification	Mkt Val
Pn55	1976	— 100 Dollars. Bronze. KM#33.	150
Pn56	1976	— 200 Dollars. Bronze. KM#34.	175
Pn57	1976	— 400 Dollars. Bronze. KM#35.	200

PIEFORTS

KM#	Date	Mintage Identification	Mkt Val
P1	1983	500 2 Dollars. Silver. KM#47a.	75.00
P2	1983	— 20 Dollars. Silver. KM#48.	100
P3	1983	100 200 Dollars. Gold. KM#49.	750

MINT SETS

KM#	Date	Mintage Identification	Issue Price	Mkt Val
MS1	1997 (2)	4,000 KM#351-352	50.00	60.00

PROOF SETS

KM#	Date	Mintage Identification	Issue Price	Mkt Val
PS2	1906H (5)	— KM#5-9		1,625
PS3	1968 (6)	14,396 KM#13, 14, 15a.2-18a.2	15.25	8.00
PS4	1969 (6)	5,056 KM#13, 14, 15a.2-18a.2	15.25	8.00
PS5	1970 (6)	3,464 KM#13, 14, 15a.2-18a.2	15.25	12.50
PS6	1971 (6)	3,032 KM#13, 14, 15a.2-18a.2	15.25	9.00
PS7	1972 (6)	4,866 KM#13, 14, 15a.2-18a.2	15.50	9.00
PS8	1972 (4)	— KM#24-27		1,200
PS9	1973 (7)	10,542 KM#13, 14, 15a.2-18a.2, 29	27.00	18.00
PS10	1974 (7)	9,362 KM#13, 14, 15a.2-18a.2, 29	27.00	18.00
PS11	1975 (7)	4,056 KM#13, 14, 15a.2-18a.2, 29	31.50	20.00
PS12	1976 (7)	2,131 KM#13, 14, 15a.2, 29-32	45.00	32.50
PS13	1977 (7)	920 KM#13, 14, 15a.2, 29-32	45.00	37.50
PS14	1978 (8)	7,311 KM#12a, 13, 14, 15a.2, 29-32	47.00	35.00
PS15	1979 (8)	1,857 KM#12b, 13a, 14a, 15b, 29a-32a marked O.A.U. July 1979	45.00	50.00
PS16	1997 (3)	— KM#417, 445, 473		250
PS17	1999 (2)	375 KM#424-425	345	400
PS18	2000 (2)	1,000 KM#613, 614	70.00	75.00

LIBYA

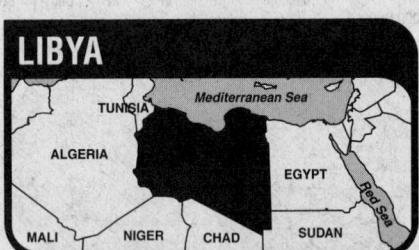

The Socialist People's Libyan Arab Jamahariya, located on the north-central coast of Africa between Tunisia and Egypt, has an area of 679,358 sq. mi. (1,759,540 sq. km.) and a population of 3.9 million. Capital: Tripoli. Crude oil, which accounts for 90 per cent of the export earnings, is the mainstay of the economy.

Libya has been subjected to foreign rule throughout most of its history, various parts of it having been ruled by the Phoenicians, Carthaginians, Vandals, Byzantines, Greeks, Romans, Egyptians, and in the following centuries the Arabs' language, culture and religion were adopted by the indigenous population. Libya was conquered by the Ottoman Turks in 1553, and remained under Turkish domination, becoming a Turkish vilayet in 1835, until it was conquered by Italy and made into a colony in 1911. The name 'Libya', the ancient Greek name for North Africa exclusive of Egypt, was given to the colony by Italy in 1934. Libya came under Allied administration after the fall of Tripoli on Jan. 23, 1943, divided into zones of British and French control. On Dec. 24, 1951, in accordance with a United Nations resolution, Libya proclaimed its independence as a constitutional monarchy, thereby becoming the first country to achieve independence through the United Nations. The monarchy was overthrown by a coup d'etat on Sept. 1, 1969, and Libya was established as a republic.

TITLES

al-Mamlaka(t) al-Libiya(t)

al-Jomhuriya(t) al-Arabiya(t) al-Libiya(t)

RULERS
Idris I, 1951-1969

MONETARY SYSTEM
10 Milliemes = 1 Piastre
100 Piastres = 1 Pound

LIBYA 1377
MONARCHY

STANDARD COINAGE
10 Milliemes = 1 Piastre; 100 Piastres = 1 Pound

KM# 1 MILLIEME
3.0000 g., Bronze, 18 mm. **Ruler:** Idris I **Obv:** Bust right
Rev: Crown divides wreath with value and date within **Note:** Date in Arabic.

Date	Mintage	F	VF	XF	Unc	BU
1952	7,750,000	—	0.15	0.25	0.75	1.50
1952 Proof	32	Value: 85.00				

KM# 6 MILLIEME
1.7500 g., Nickel-Brass, 16.03 mm. **Ruler:** Idris I **Obv:** Crowned national arms above dates **Rev:** Value within wreath

Date	Mintage	F	VF	XF	Unc	BU
AH1385-1965	11,000,000	—	0.10	0.20	0.40	0.85

KM# 2 2 MILLIEMES
6.0000 g., Bronze, 24 mm. **Ruler:** Idris I **Obv:** Bust right
Rev: Crown divides wreath with value and date within **Note:** Date in Arabic.

Date	Mintage	F	VF	XF	Unc	BU
1952	6,650,000	—	0.15	0.35	1.00	2.00
1952 Proof	32	Value: 85.00				

KM# 3 5 MILLIEMES
Bronze **Ruler:** Idris I **Obv:** Bust right **Rev:** Crown divides wreath with value and date within **Note:** Date in Arabic.

Date	Mintage	F	VF	XF	Unc	BU
1952	7,680,000	—	0.25	0.50	1.50	3.00
1952 Proof	32	Value: 85.00				

KM# 7 5 MILLIEMES
Nickel-Brass **Ruler:** Idris I **Obv:** Crowned national arms above dates **Rev:** Value within 3/4 wreath

Date	Mintage	F	VF	XF	Unc	BU
AH1385-1965	8,500,000	—	0.15	0.25	0.50	1.00

KM# 4 PIASTRE
Copper-Nickel **Ruler:** Idris I **Obv:** Bust right **Rev:** Crown divides wreath with value and date within **Note:** Date in Arabic.

Date	Mintage	F	VF	XF	Unc	BU
1952	10,200,000	—	0.35	0.60	1.25	2.50
1952 Proof	32	Value: 115				

KM# 5 2 PIASTRES
7.5300 g., Copper-Nickel, 26 mm. **Ruler:** Idris I **Obv:** Bust right **Rev:** Crown divides wreath with value and dates within **Note:** Date in Arabic.

Date	Mintage	F	VF	XF	Unc	BU
1952	6,075,000	—	0.35	0.75	1.75	3.50
1952 Proof	32	Value: 135				

KM# 8 10 MILLIEMES
Copper-Nickel **Ruler:** Idris I **Obv:** Crowned national arms above dates **Rev:** Value within wreath

Date	Mintage	F	VF	XF	Unc	BU
AH1385-1965	17,000,000	—	0.15	0.25	0.50	1.00

KM# 9 20 MILLIEMES
Copper-Nickel **Ruler:** Idris I **Obv:** Crowned national arms above dates **Rev:** Value within wreath

Date	Mintage	F	VF	XF	Unc	BU
AH1385-1965	8,750,000	—	0.20	0.50	2.00	3.50

KM# 10 50 MILLIEMES
Copper-Nickel, 26 mm. **Ruler:** Idris I **Obv:** Crowned national arms above dates **Rev:** Value within wreath

Date	Mintage	F	VF	XF	Unc	BU
AH1385-1965	8,000,000	—	0.35	0.75	3.00	5.00

KM# 11 100 MILLIEMES
Copper-Nickel **Ruler:** Idris I **Obv:** Crowned national arms above dates **Rev:** Value within wreath

Date	Mintage	F	VF	XF	Unc	BU
AH1385 (1965)	8,000,000	—	0.75	1.50	4.00	6.00

SOCIALIST PEOPLE'S REPUBLIC

STANDARD COINAGE
1000 Dirhams = 1 Dinar

KM# 12 DIRHAM
Brass Clad Steel **Obv:** Eagle flanked by dates **Rev:** Value within wreath

Date	Mintage	F	VF	XF	Unc	BU
AH1395-1975	20,000,000	—	0.25	0.50	1.50	—

KM# 18 DIRHAM
Brass Clad Steel **Obv:** Armored equestrian **Rev:** Value within wreath

Date	Mintage	F	VF	XF	Unc	BU
AH1399-1979	1,000,000	—	0.50	1.00	3.00	—

KM# 13 5 DIRHAM
Brass Clad Steel **Obv:** Eagle flanked by dates **Rev:** Value above oat sprigs within wreath

Date	Mintage	F	VF	XF	Unc	BU
AH1395-1975	23,000,000	—	0.25	0.60	2.00	—

KM# 19 5 DIRHAM
Brass Clad Steel **Obv:** Armored equestrian **Rev:** Value above oat sprigs within wreath

Date	Mintage	F	VF	XF	Unc	BU
AH1399-1979	2,000,000	—	0.75	2.00	4.00	—

KM# 14 10 DIRHAMS
Copper-Nickel Clad Steel **Obv:** Eagle flanked by dates **Rev:** Value above oat sprigs within wreath

Date	Mintage	F	VF	XF	Unc	BU
AH1395-1975	52,750,000	—	0.25	0.65	2.25	—

KM# 20 10 DIRHAMS
Copper-Nickel Clad Steel, 20 mm. **Obv:** Armored equestrian **Rev:** Value above oat sprigs within wreath

Date	Mintage	F	VF	XF	Unc	BU
AH1399-1979	4,000,000	—	0.75	2.00	4.00	—

KM# 15 20 DIRHAMS
5.6600 g., Copper-Nickel Clad Steel, 24 mm. **Obv:** Eagle flanked by dates **Rev:** Value above oat sprigs within wreath

Date	Mintage	F	VF	XF	Unc	BU
AH1395-1975	25,500,000	—	0.50	1.75	3.00	—

KM# 21 20 DIRHAMS
Copper-Nickel Clad Steel **Obv:** Armored equestrian **Rev:** Value above oat sprigs within wreath

Date	Mintage	F	VF	XF	Unc	BU
AH1399-1979	6,000,000	—	1.00	3.00	5.00	—

KM# 16 50 DIRHAMS
6.2500 g., Copper-Nickel, 25 mm. **Obv:** Eagle flanked by dates **Rev:** Value above oat sprigs within wreath

Date	Mintage	F	VF	XF	Unc	BU
AH1395-1975	25,640,000	—	1.00	2.50	6.00	—

KM# 22 50 DIRHAMS
Copper-Nickel **Obv:** Armored equestrian **Rev:** Value above oat sprigs within wreath

Date	Mintage	F	VF	XF	Unc	BU
AH1399-1979	9,120,000	—	1.50	3.50	7.00	—

KM# 17   100 DIRHAMS
Copper-Nickel **Obv:** Eagle flanked by dates **Rev. Insc.:** Value above oat sprigs within wreath

Date	Mintage	F	VF	XF	Unc	BU
AH1395-1975	15,433,000	—	1.50	3.50	8.00	—

KM# 23   100 DIRHAMS
Copper-Nickel **Obv:** Armored equestrian **Rev:** Value above oat sprigs within wreath

Date	Mintage	F	VF	XF	Unc	BU
AH1399-1979	15,000,000	—	2.00	4.50	9.00	—

KM# 24   5 DINARS
28.2800 g., 0.9250 Silver 0.8410 oz. ASW **Subject:** International Year of Disabled Persons **Obv:** Handicap symbol within center of helping hands **Rev:** Date and emblem within globe with legend above and below

Date	Mintage	F	VF	XF	Unc	BU
1981	20,000	—	—	—	65.00	—
1981 Proof	21,000	Value: 75.00				

KM# 25   70 DINARS
15.9800 g., 0.9170 Gold 0.4711 oz. AGW **Subject:** International Year of Disabled Persons **Obv:** Handicap symbol within helping hands **Rev:** Date and emblem within globe with legend above and below

Date	Mintage	F	VF	XF	Unc	BU
1981	4,000	—	—	—	475	—
1981 Proof	4,000	Value: 575				

PIEFORTS

KM#	Date	Mintage	Identification	Mkt Val
P1	1981	2,150	5 Dinars. Silver. KM24.	150
P2	1981	500	70 Dinars. Gold. KM25.	1,150

MINT SETS

KM#	Date	Mintage	Identification	Issue Price	Mkt Val
MS1	1975 (6)	—	KM12-17	—	22.50

PROOF SETS

KM#	Date	Mintage	Identification	Issue Price	Mkt Val
PS1	1952 (5)	32	KM1-5	—	450

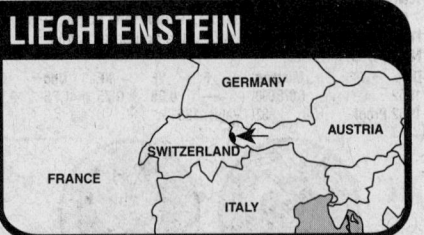

LIECHTENSTEIN

The Principality of Liechtenstein, located in central Europe on the east bank of the Rhine between Austria and Switzerland, has an area of 62 sq. mi. (160 sq. km.) and a population of 27,200. Capital: Vaduz. The economy is based on agriculture and light manufacturing. Canned goods, textiles, ceramics and precision instruments are exported.

The lordships of Schellenburg and Vaduz were merged into the principality of Liechtenstein. It was a member of the Rhine Confederation from 1806 to 1815, and of the German Confederation from 1815 to 1866 when it became independent. Liechtenstein's long and close association with Austria was terminated by World War I. In 1921 it adopted the coinage of Switzerland, and two years later entered into a customs union with the Swiss, who also operated its postal and telegraph systems and represented it in international affairs. The tiny principality abolished its army in 1868 and has avoided involvement in all European wars since that time.

RULERS
Prince John II, 1858-1929
Prince Franz I, 1929-1938
Prince Franz Josef II, 1938-1990
Prince Hans Adam II, 1990-

MINT MARKS
A - Vienna
B - Bern
M - Munich (restrikes)

MONETARY SYSTEM
100 Heller = 1 Krone

PRINCIPALITY

REFORM COINAGE
100 Heller = 1 Krone

Y# 2   KRONE
5.0000 g., 0.8350 Silver 0.1342 oz. ASW **Ruler:** Prince John II **Obv:** Head left **Obv. Leg.:** JOHANN II. FURST... **Rev:** Crowned shield within wreath divides value, date below

Date	Mintage	F	VF	XF	Unc	BU
1904	75,000	12.00	20.00	35.00	65.00	—
1910	50,000	12.00	20.00	35.00	65.00	—
1915	75,000	12.00	20.00	35.00	65.00	—

Y# 3   2 KRONEN
10.0000 g., 0.8350 Silver 0.2684 oz. ASW **Ruler:** Prince John II **Obv:** Head left **Rev:** Crowned shield within wreath flanked by value and letters

Date	Mintage	F	VF	XF	Unc	BU
1912	50,000	12.00	20.00	35.00	65.00	85.00
1915	37,500	15.00	25.00	40.00	70.00	100

Y# 4   5 KRONEN
24.0000 g., 0.9000 Silver 0.6944 oz. ASW **Ruler:** Prince John II **Obv:** Head left **Obv. Leg.:** JOHANN II. FURST... **Rev:** Crowned shield within wreath divides value above date

Date	Mintage	F	VF	XF	Unc	BU
1904	15,000	40.00	75.00	120	200	300
1910	10,000	50.00	90.00	160	245	350
1915	10,000	45.00	80.00	140	240	320

REFORM COINAGE
100 Rappen = 1 Frank

Y# 7   1/2 FRANK
2.5000 g., 0.8350 Silver 0.0671 oz. ASW **Ruler:** Prince John II **Obv:** Head left **Rev:** Crowned shield within wreath flanked by value and letters **Note:** 15,745 were melted.

Date	Mintage	F	VF	XF	Unc	BU
1924	30,000	45.00	80.00	120	225	300

Y# 8   FRANK
5.0000 g., 0.8350 Silver 0.1342 oz. ASW **Ruler:** Prince John II **Obv:** Head left **Rev:** Crowned shield within wreath flanked by value and letters **Note:** 45,355 were melted.

Date	Mintage	F	VF	XF	Unc	BU
1924	60,000	25.00	40.00	75.00	120	200

Y# 9   2 FRANKEN
10.0000 g., 0.8350 Silver 0.2684 oz. ASW **Ruler:** Prince John II **Obv:** Head left **Rev:** Crowned shield within wreath flanked by value and letters **Note:** 41,707 were melted.

Date	Mintage	F	VF	XF	Unc	BU
1924	50,000	30.00	60.00	100	185	275

Y# 10   5 FRANKEN
25.0000 g., 0.9000 Silver 0.7234 oz. ASW **Ruler:** Prince John II **Obv:** Head left **Rev:** Crowned shield within wreath flanked by value and letters **Note:** 11,260 were melted.

Date	Mintage	F	VF	XF	Unc	BU
1924	15,000	120	225	375	700	1,000

Y# 11   10 FRANKEN
3.2258 g., 0.9000 Gold 0.0933 oz. AGW **Ruler:** Prince Franz I
Obv: Bust right **Rev:** Crowned shield within wreath flanked by
value and letters

Date	Mintage	F	VF	XF	Unc	BU
1930	2,500	—	600	850	1,250	—

Y# 13   10 FRANKEN
3.2258 g., 0.9000 Gold 0.0933 oz. AGW **Ruler:** Prince Franz
Josef II **Obv:** Head left **Rev:** Crowned shield within stars

Date	Mintage	F	VF	XF	Unc	BU
1946B	10,000	—	160	220	300	—

Y# 20   10 FRANKEN
30.0000 g., 0.9000 Gold 0.8680 oz. ASW **Ruler:** Prince Franz
Josef II **Subject:** 50th Anniversary of Reign **Obv:** Head right
Rev: Crowned shield

Date	Mintage	F	VF	XF	Unc	BU
1988 Proof	35,000	Value: 45.00				

Y# 22   10 FRANKEN
30.0000 g., 0.9000 Silver 0.8680 oz. ASW **Ruler:** Prince Hans
Adam II **Subject:** Succession of Hans Adam II **Obv:** Head left
divides date **Rev:** Crowned mantled shield divides value and letters

Date	Mintage	F	VF	XF	Unc	BU
1990 Proof	35,000	Value: 40.00				

Y# 12   20 FRANKEN
6.4516 g., 0.9000 Gold 0.1867 oz. AGW **Ruler:** Prince Franz I
Obv: Bust right within circle **Rev:** Crowned shield within wreath
divides value and letters

Date	Mintage	F	VF	XF	Unc	BU
1930	2,500	—	650	950	1,400	—

Y# 14   20 FRANKEN
6.4516 g., 0.9000 Gold 0.1867 oz. AGW **Ruler:** Prince Franz
Josef II **Obv:** Head left **Rev:** Crowned shield within stars

Date	Mintage	F	VF	XF	Unc	BU
1946B	10,000	—	200	300	420	—

Y# 15   25 FRANKEN
5.6450 g., 0.9000 Gold 0.1633 oz. AGW, 22 mm. **Ruler:** Prince
Franz Josef II **Subject:** Conjoined busts left and Princess Gina
Obv: Conjoined busts left **Rev:** Crowned shield

Date	Mintage	F	VF	XF	Unc	BU
1956	17,000	—	—	2,502	350	

Y# 18   25 FRANKEN
5.6450 g., 0.9000 Gold 0.1633 oz. AGW **Ruler:** Prince Franz
Josef II **Subject:** 100th Anniversary - National Bank **Obv:** Head
right **Rev:** Crowned mantled shield

Date	Mintage	F	VF	XF	Unc	BU
1961	20,000	—	—	175	225	—

Y# 16   50 FRANKEN
11.2900 g., 0.9000 Gold 0.3267 oz. AGW, 26 mm.
Ruler: Prince Franz Josef II **Subject:** Franz Josef II and Princess
Gina **Obv:** Conjoined busts left **Rev:** Crowned shield

Date	Mintage	F	VF	XF	Unc	BU
1956	17,000	—	—	350	450	—

Y# 19   50 FRANKEN
11.2900 g., 0.9000 Gold 0.3267 oz. AGW **Ruler:** Prince Franz
Josef II **Subject:** 100th Anniversary - National Bank **Obv:** Head
right **Rev:** Crowned mantled shield

Date	Mintage	F	VF	XF	Unc	BU
1961	20,000	—	—	300	400	—

Y# 21   50 FRANKEN
10.0000 g., 0.9000 Gold 0.2893 oz. AGW **Ruler:** Prince Franz
Josef II **Subject:** 50th Anniversary of Reign **Obv:** Head right
Rev: Crowned shield divides value and letters

Date	Mintage	F	VF	XF	Unc	BU
1988 Proof	35,000	Value: 345				

Y# 23   50 FRANKEN
10.0000 g., 0.9000 Gold 0.2893 oz. AGW **Ruler:** Prince Hans
Adam II **Subject:** Succession of Hans Adam II **Obv:** Head left
divides date **Rev:** Crowned mantled shield divides value and letters

Date	Mintage	F	VF	XF	Unc	BU
1990 Proof	25,000	Value: 325				

Y# 17   100 FRANKEN
32.2580 g., 0.9000 Gold 0.9334 oz. AGW, 36 mm.
Ruler: Prince Franz Josef II **Subject:** Franz Josef II and Princess
Gina **Obv:** Conjoined busts left **Rev:** Crowned shield

Date	Mintage	F	VF	XF	Unc	BU
1952	4,000	—	1,850	2,750	3,500	—

MINT SETS

KM#	Date	Mintage	Identification	Issue Price	Mkt Val
MS1	1930 (2)	2,500	Y11-12	—	2,650
MS2	1946 (2)	10,000	Y13-14	—	725
MS3	1956 (2)	15,000	Y15-16	—	800
MS4	1961 (2)	20,000	Y18-19	—	625

PROOF SETS

KM#	Date	Mintage	Identification	Issue Price	Mkt Val
PS1	1988 (2)	35,000	Y20-21	—	400
PS2	1990 (2)	25,000	Y22-23	—	365

LITHUANIA

The Republic of Lithuania, southernmost of the Baltic states
in east Europe, has an area of 25,174 sq. mi.(65,201 sq. km.) and
a population of *3.6 million. Capital: Vilnius. The economy is
based on livestock raising and manufacturing. Hogs, cattle, hides
and electric motors are exported.

Lithuania emerged as a grand duchy in the 14th century. In
the 15th century it was a major power of central Europe, stretching
from the Baltic to the Black Sea. It was joined with Poland in 1569,
but lost Smolensk, Chernihiv, and the right bank of the river Dnepr
Ukraina in 1667, while the left bank remained under Polish –
Lithuania rule until 1793. Following the third partition of Poland by
Austria, Prussia and Russia, 1795, Lithuania came under Russian
domination and did not regain its independence until shortly
before the end of World War I when it declared itself a sovereign
republic on Feb. 16, 1918. In fall of 1920, Poland captured Vilna
(Vilnius). The republic was occupied by Soviet troops and
annexed to the U.S.S.R. in 1940. Following the German occupation of 1941-44, it was retaken by Russia and reestablished as
a member republic of the Soviet Union. Western countries, including the United States, did not recognize Lithuania's incorporation
into the Soviet Union.

Lithuania declared its independence March 11, 1990 and it
was recognized by the United States on Sept. 2, 1991, followed
by the Soviet government in Moscow on Sept. 6. They were
seated in the UN General Assembly on Sept. 17, 1991.

REPUBLIC
1918-1940

STANDARD COINAGE
100 Centas = 1 Litas

KM# 71   CENTAS
1.6000 g., Aluminum-Bronze, 16 mm. **Obv:** National arms
Rev: Value within circle divides stem of flowers **Edge:** Plain
Note: Struck at King's Norton.

Date	Mintage	F	VF	XF	Unc	BU
1925	5,000,000	7.00	15.00	25.00	50.00	—

KM# 79   CENTAS
Bronze, 16.6 mm. **Obv:** National arms **Rev:** Large value with
oat sprig at right **Edge:** Plain

Date	Mintage	F	VF	XF	Unc	BU
1936	9,995,000	5.00	10.00	20.00	40.00	—

KM# 80   2 CENTAI
2.3000 g., Bronze, 18.5 mm. **Obv:** National arms **Rev:** Large
value divides date within wreath **Edge:** Plain

Date	Mintage	F	VF	XF	Unc	BU
1936	4,951,000	7.00	15.00	25.00	50.00	—

KM# 72   5 CENTAI
Aluminum-Bronze **Obv:** National arms **Rev:** Value within circle divides stem of flowers

Date	Mintage	F	VF	XF	Unc	BU
1925	12,000,000	7.00	15.00	25.00	45.00	—

KM# 81   5 CENTAI
2.5000 g., Bronze, 20 mm. **Obv:** National arms **Rev:** Large value within wreath, date on top **Edge:** Plain

Date	Mintage	F	VF	XF	Unc	BU
1936	4,800,000	8.00	15.00	20.00	50.00	—

KM# 73   10 CENTU
3.0000 g., Aluminum-Bronze, 21 mm. **Obv:** National arms **Rev:** Value to right of sagging grain ears **Edge:** Plain

Date	Mintage	F	VF	XF	Unc	BU
1925	12,000,000	7.00	15.00	20.00	45.00	—

KM# 74   20 CENTU
4.0000 g., Aluminum-Bronze, 23 mm. **Obv:** National arms **Rev:** Value to right of sagging grain ears **Edge:** Plain

Date	Mintage	F	VF	XF	Unc	BU
1925	8,000,000	7.00	15.00	25.00	50.00	—

KM# 75   50 CENTU
5.0000 g., Aluminum-Bronze, 25 mm. **Obv:** National arms **Rev:** Value to right of sagging grain ears **Edge:** Plain

Date	Mintage	F	VF	XF	Unc	BU
1925	5,000,000	15.00	20.00	30.00	60.00	—
1925 Proof	2	Value: 1,000				

KM# 76   LITAS
2.7000 g., 0.5000 Silver 0.0434 oz. ASW, 19 mm. **Obv:** National arms **Rev:** Value above oak leaves **Edge:** Milled **Note:** Struck at Royal Mint, London.

Date	Mintage	F	VF	XF	Unc	BU
1925	5,985,000	5.00	10.00	20.00	35.00	—
1925 Proof	—	Value: 900				

Note: Struck as proof record specimens by the Royal Mint, less than 12 were issued

KM# 77   2 LITU
5.4000 g., 0.5000 Silver 0.0868 oz. ASW, 22.9 mm. **Rev:** Denomination within wreath **Edge:** Milled

Date	Mintage	F	VF	XF	Unc	BU
1925	3,000,000	5.00	10.00	20.00	40.00	—
1925 Proof	—	Value: 900				

Note: Struck as proof record specimens by the Royal Mint, less than 12 were issued

KM# 78   5 LITAI
13.5000 g., 0.5000 Silver 0.2170 oz. ASW, 29.5 mm. **Obv:** National arms **Rev:** Value within flowered wreath **Edge:** Milled

Date	Mintage	F	VF	XF	Unc	BU
1925	1,000,000	15.00	20.00	35.00	70.00	—
1925 Proof	—	Value: 900				

Note: Struck as proof record specimens by the Royal Mint, less than 12 were issued

KM# 82   5 LITAI
9.0000 g., 0.7500 Silver 0.2170 oz. ASW, 27 mm. **Obv:** National arms **Rev:** Head left **Edge:** TAUTOS GEROVE TAVO GEROVE **Note:** Designer's initials below bust.

Date	Mintage	F	VF	XF	Unc	BU
1936	2,612,000	7.00	12.00	18.00	35.00	—

KM# 83   10 LITU
18.0000 g., 0.7500 Silver 0.4340 oz. ASW, 32 mm. **Obv:** National arms **Rev:** Head left **Edge:** VIENYBEJE TAUTOS JEGA

Date	Mintage	F	VF	XF	Unc	BU
1936	720,000	15.00	20.00	30.00	50.00	80.00

KM# 84   10 LITU
18.0000 g., 0.7500 Silver 0.4340 oz. ASW, 32 mm. **Subject:** 20th Anniversary of Republic **Obv:** Columns of Gediminas above LIETUVA and dates 1918-1938 **Rev:** Head left **Edge:** VIENYBEJE TAUTOS JEGA

Date	Mintage	F	VF	XF	Unc	BU
ND(1938)	170,000	40.00	50.00	80.00	120	150

MODERN REPUBLIC
1991-present
REFORM COINAGE
100 Centas = 1 Litas

KM# 85   CENTAS
0.6200 g., Aluminum, 18.73 mm. **Obv:** National arms **Rev:** Large value to right of design

Date	Mintage	F	VF	XF	Unc	BU
1991	—	—	—	—	0.20	—

KM# 86   2 CENTAI
0.9300 g., Aluminum, 21.75 mm. **Obv:** National arms **Rev:** Large value to right of design

Date	Mintage	F	VF	XF	Unc	BU
1991	—	—	—	—	0.25	—

KM# 87   5 CENTAI
1.2400 g., Aluminum, 24.4 mm. **Obv:** National arms **Rev:** Large value to right of artistic design on pole flanked by men blowing horns

Date	Mintage	F	VF	XF	Unc	BU
1991	—	—	—	—	0.30	—

KM# 88   10 CENTU
1.2400 g., Bronze, 15.64 mm. **Obv:** National arms **Rev:** Value

Date	Mintage	F	VF	XF	Unc	BU
1991	—	—	1.00	2.00	3.00	—

KM# 106   10 CENTU
2.6700 g., Brass, 17 mm. **Obv:** National arms **Rev:** Value **Edge:** Reeded

Date	Mintage	F	VF	XF	Unc	BU
1997	—	—	—	0.10	0.30	0.40
1998	—	—	—	0.10	0.30	0.40
1999	—	—	—	0.10	0.30	0.40
2000	—	—	—	0.10	0.30	0.40
2000 Proof	5,000	Value: 1.00				

KM# 89   20 CENTU
1.8700 g., Bronze, 17.38 mm. **Obv:** National arms **Rev:** Value

Date	Mintage	F	VF	XF	Unc	BU
1991	—	1.00	2.00	3.00	6.00	—

KM# 107   20 CENTU
4.7700 g., Brass, 20.43 mm. **Obv:** National arms **Rev:** Value **Edge:** Reeded

Date	Mintage	F	VF	XF	Unc	BU
1997	—	—	—	0.30	0.50	1.00
1998	—	—	—	0.30	0.50	1.00
1999	—	—	—	0.30	0.50	1.00
2000	—	—	—	0.30	0.50	1.00
2000 Proof	5,000	Value: 1.25				

KM# 90   50 CENTU
2.7900 g., Bronze, 21.02 mm. **Obv:** National arms **Rev:** Value

Date	Mintage	F	VF	XF	Unc	BU
1991	—	2.00	3.00	5.00	10.00	—

KM# 108 50 CENTU
6.0000 g., Brass **Obv:** National arms **Rev:** Value within designed circle

Date	Mintage	F	VF	XF	Unc	BU
1997	—	—	—	0.50	1.00	1.50
1998	—	—	—	0.50	1.00	1.50
1999	—	—	—	0.50	1.00	1.50
2000	—	—	—	0.50	1.00	1.50
2000 Proof	5,000	Value: 2.00				

KM# 91 LITAS
6.2500 g., Copper-Nickel, 22.3 mm. **Obv:** National arms **Rev:** Value with lines above

Date	Mintage	F	VF	XF	Unc	BU
1991	—	3.00	5.00	7.00	15.00	—

KM# 109 LITAS
Copper-Nickel, 22.3 mm. **Subject:** 75th Anniversary - Bank of Lithuania **Obv:** National arms above value **Rev:** Bust 1/4 right

Date	Mintage	F	VF	XF	Unc	BU
1997	200,000	2.00	3.00	6.00	15.00	—

KM# 109a LITAS
7.7759 g., 0.9990 Gold 0.2497 oz. AGW, 22.3 mm. **Subject:** 75th Anniversary - Bank of Lithuania **Obv:** National arms above value **Rev:** Bust 1/4 right

Date	Mintage	F	VF	XF	Unc	BU
1997 Proof	1,500	Value: 725				

KM# 111 LITAS
6.1800 g., Copper-Nickel, 22.3 mm. **Obv:** National arms **Rev:** Value within circle above lined designs **Edge:** Reeded

Date	Mintage	F	VF	XF	Unc	BU
1998	—	—	—	1.00	1.50	2.00
1999	—	—	—	1.00	1.50	2.00
2000	—	—	—	1.00	1.50	2.00
2000 Proof	5,000	Value: 3.00				

KM# 117 LITAS
Copper-Nickel, 22.3 mm. **Subject:** The Baltic Highway **Obv:** National arms on shield within shaded circle divides date **Rev:** Six clasped hands within artistic design **Edge:** Reeded and plain sections

Date	Mintage	F	VF	XF	Unc	BU
1999	1,000,000	2.00	3.00	4.00	7.00	—

KM# 92 2 LITAI
7.5000 g., Copper-Nickel, 25 mm. **Obv:** National arms **Rev:** Value within design

Date	Mintage	F	VF	XF	Unc	BU
1991	—	3.00	6.00	9.00	18.00	—

KM# 112 2 LITAI
7.5000 g., Bi-Metallic Brass center in Copper-Nickel ring, 25 mm. **Obv:** National arms within circle **Rev:** Value within circle **Edge:** Segmented reeding

Date	Mintage	F	VF	XF	Unc	BU
1998	—	—	—	1.50	2.00	4.00
1999	—	—	—	1.50	2.00	4.00
2000	—	—	—	1.50	2.00	4.00
2000 Proof	5,000	Value: 4.00				

KM# 93 5 LITAI
Copper-Nickel **Obv:** National arms **Rev:** Value within design

Date	Mintage	F	VF	XF	Unc	BU
1991	—	4.00	7.00	12.00	20.00	—

KM# 113 5 LITAI
10.2600 g., Bi-Metallic Copper-Nickel ring in Brass center, 22.5 mm. **Obv:** National arms within circle **Rev:** Value within circle **Edge:** PENKI LITAI

Date	Mintage	F	VF	XF	Unc	BU
1998	—	—	—	4.00	7.00	10.00
1999	—	—	—	4.00	7.00	10.00
2000	—	—	—	4.00	7.00	10.00
2000 Proof	5,000	Value: 10.00				

KM# 127 5 LITAI
Outer Weight: 28.2800 g. **Outer:** 0.9250 Silver 0.8410 oz. ASW AGW , 38.61 mm. **Series:** UNICEF **Subject:** For the Children of the World **Obv:** Hill of Gediminas Castle to right of national arms on shield above value and date **Rev:** Child with pinwheel **Edge:** LIETUVOS BANKAS

Date	Mintage	F	VF	XF	Unc	BU
1998 Proof	3,000	Value: 300				

KM# 94 10 LITU
Copper-Nickel, 28.70 mm. **Subject:** 60th Anniversary - Darius and Girenas flight across the Atlantic **Obv:** National arms above value **Rev:** Conjoined pilot heads right **Edge:** SLOVE ATLANTO NUGALETOJAMS

Date	Mintage	F	VF	XF	Unc	BU
ND(1993)LMK	4,500	—	—	—	125	—

KM# 95 10 LITU
Copper-Nickel, 28.70 mm. **Subject:** Papal visit **Rev:** Bust right **Edge:** TIKEJIMAS MEILE VILTIS

Date	Mintage	F	VF	XF	Unc	BU
1993LMK	5,000	—	—	—	120	—

KM# 96 10 LITU
Copper-Nickel, 28.70 mm. **Subject:** International Song Fest **Obv:** National arms and value **Rev:** Stringed instrument below design **Edge:** SKRISKIT SKAISCIOS DAINOS

Date	Mintage	F	VF	XF	Unc	BU
1994LMK Proof	11,708	Value: 20.00				

KM# 97 10 LITU
Copper-Nickel, 28.70 mm. **Subject:** 5th World Sport Games **Obv:** National arms and value **Rev:** Runner with torch and design above divides globe **Edge:** LIETUVIAIS ESAME MES GIME

Date	Mintage	F	VF	XF	Unc	BU
1995LMK Proof	10,000	Value: 40.00				

KM# 115 10 LITU
Copper-Nickel, 28.70 mm. **Obv:** Shielded arms divide date, value below **Rev:** Vilnus building tops as seen from ground level **Edge:** VILNIUS-LIETUVOS SOSTINE

Date	Mintage	F	VF	XF	Unc	BU
1998 Proof	7,500	Value: 70.00				

KM# 116 10 LITU
Copper-Nickel, 28.70 mm. **Obv:** National arms above value **Rev:** Kaunas city arms on shield within buildings **Edge:** LAISUAS BUDAMAS, LAISVES NEISSIZADESI

Date	Mintage	F	VF	XF	Unc	BU
1999 Proof	6,028	Value: 75.00				

KM# 120 10 LITU
1.2440 g., 0.9999 Gold 0.0400 oz. AGW, 28.70 mm. **Subject:** Lithuanian gold coinage **Obv:** National arms **Rev:** Medieval minter

Date	Mintage	F	VF	XF	Unc	BU
1999 Proof	5,500	Value: 125				

KM# 98   50 LITU

23.3000 g., 0.9250 Silver 0.6929 oz. ASW, 34 mm.
Subject: 5th Anniversary - Independence **Obv:** National arms flanked by ribbon with value below **Rev:** Oak tree stump with leafed branch flanked by dates above **Edge:** TEGUL MEILE LIETUVOS DEGA MUSU SIRDYSE

Date	Mintage	F	VF	XF	Unc	BU
ND(1995)LMK	5,000	Value: 200				
Proof						

KM# 99   50 LITU

23.3000 g., 0.9250 Silver 0.6929 oz. ASW, 34 mm. **Subject:** 120th Birth Anniversary Mikalojaus K. Ciurlionis **Obv:** National arms above date at right with a pair of eagle wings at left above value **Rev:** Head 3/4 right **Edge:** PASAULIS KAIP DIDELE SIMFONIJA

Date	Mintage	F	VF	XF	Unc	BU
1995LMK Proof	6,514	Value: 75.00				

KM# 100   50 LITU

23.3000 g., 0.9250 Silver 0.6929 oz. ASW, 34 mm.
Subject: 5th Anniversary - 13 January 1991 Assault
Obv: National arms flanked by ribbon with value below
Rev: Madonna holding man **Edge:** IR KRAUJU KRIKSTYTI TAMPA VEL GYUYBE

Date	Mintage	F	VF	XF	Unc	BU
ND(1996) Proof	6,000	Value: 75.00				

KM# 103   50 LITU

23.3000 g., 0.9250 Silver 0.6929 oz. ASW, 34 mm.
Obv: National arms at upper left within patterned circle, crown at lower right above lance **Rev:** Armored bust 1/4 right **Edge:** IS PRAEITIES TAVO SUNUS TE STIPRYBE SEMIA

Date	Mintage	F	VF	XF	Unc	BU
1996LMK Proof	4,421	Value: 100				

KM# 101   50 LITU

23.3000 g., 0.9250 Silver 0.6929 oz. ASW, 34 mm.
Series: Atlanta Olympics **Obv:** National arms flanked by sprigs
Rev: Basketball players **Edge:** CITIUS. ALTIUS. FORTIUS.

Date	Mintage	F	VF	XF	Unc	BU
1996LMK Proof	6,000	Value: 60.00				

KM# 102   50 LITU

23.3000 g., 0.9250 Silver 0.6929 oz. ASW, 34 mm.
Obv: National arms at upper left within patterned circle, crown at lower right above lance **Rev:** Armored bust right **Edge:** IS PRAEITIES TAVO SUNUS TE STIPRYBE SEMIA

Date	Mintage	F	VF	XF	Unc	BU
1996LMK Proof	4,982	Value: 125				

KM# 104   50 LITU

23.3000 g., 0.9250 Silver 0.6929 oz. ASW, 34 mm.
Subject: 450th Anniversary - First Lithuanian Book **Obv:** National arms above date **Rev:** Page from book **Edge:** MARTYNAS MAZVYDAS IMKIT MANE IR SKAITYKIT

Date	Mintage	F	VF	XF	Unc	BU
1997 Proof	3,476	Value: 150				

KM# 105   50 LITU

23.3000 g., 0.9250 Silver 0.6929 oz. ASW, 34 mm.
Subject: 600th Anniversary - Karaims and Tartars settlement in Lithuania **Obv:** National arms above value **Rev:** Standing figures facing with weapons **Edge:** LIETUVA TEVYNE MUSU

Date	Mintage	F	VF	XF	Unc	BU
1997 Proof	2,635	Value: 350				

KM# 110   50 LITU

23.3000 g., 0.9250 Silver 0.6929 oz. ASW **Obv:** National arms within patterned circle above date **Rev:** Armored bust facing holding scepter

Date	Mintage	F	VF	XF	Unc	BU
1998 Proof	2,998	Value: 65.00				

KM# 114   50 LITU

23.3000 g., 0.9250 Silver 0.6929 oz. ASW **Subject:** 200th Anniversary - Birth of Adam Mickiewicz **Obv:** Feather, denomination **Rev:** Laureated profile of Adomas Mickievicius, building

Date	Mintage	F	VF	XF	Unc	BU
1998 Proof	2,860	Value: 65.00				

KM# 118   50 LITU

23.3000 g., 0.9250 Silver 0.6929 oz. ASW, 34 mm.
Subject: Grand Duke Kestutis **Obv:** National arms within patterned circle **Rev:** Armored bust facing **Edge:** IS PRAEITIES TAVO SUNVS TE STIPRYBE SEMIA **Note:** Lithuanian Mint.

Date	Mintage	F	VF	XF	Unc	BU
1999 Proof	2,500	Value: 375				

KM# 119   50 LITU

28.2800 g., 0.9250 Silver 0.8410 oz. ASW, 38.6 mm.
Subject: 100th Anniversary - Death of Vincas Kudirka
Obv: National arms within stylized bell **Rev:** Head 1/4 left
Edge: VARDAN TOS LIETUVOS VIENYBE TEZYDI
Note: Lithuanian Mint.

Date	Mintage	F	VF	XF	Unc	BU
1999 Proof	1,835	Value: 200				

KM# 123   50 LITU

28.2800 g., 0.9250 Silver 0.8410 oz. ASW, 38.1 mm.
Subject: 10th Anniversary - Baltic Way Highway **Obv:** National arms within circle divides date **Rev:** Three pairs of clasped hands **Edge:** VILNIUS RYGA TALINAS **Note:** Lithuanian Mint.

Date	Mintage	F	VF	XF	Unc	BU
1999 Proof	2,542	Value: 225				

KM# 121 50 LITU
28.2800 g., 0.9250 Silver 0.8410 oz. ASW, 38.61 mm.
Subject: 350th Anniversary - The Great Art of Artillery Book
Obv: National arms within frame **Rev:** Old rocket designs
Edge: ARS MAGNA ARTILLERIAE * MDCL

Date	Mintage	F	VF	XF	Unc	BU
2000 Proof	1,936	Value: 42.50				

KM# 125 50 LITU
23.3000 g., 0.9250 Silver 0.6929 oz. ASW, 34 mm.
Subject: Grand Duke Vytautas **Obv:** National arms on shield among other shields within patterned circle below design
Rev: Crowned armored bust holding sword facing left **Edge:** IS PRAEITIES TAVO SUNUS TESTIPRYBE SEMIA

Date	Mintage	F	VF	XF	Unc	BU
2000 Proof	2,500	Value: 300				

KM# 122 50 LITU
28.2800 g., 0.9250 Silver 0.8410 oz. ASW, 38.6 mm. **Subject:** 10th Anniversary of Independence **Obv:** National arms above value
Rev: Radiant statue of independence **Edge:** LAISVE - AMZINOJI TAUTOS VERTYBE **Note:** Struck at Lietuvos Monetu Kalykla.

Date	Mintage	F	VF	XF	Unc	BU
ND(2000) Proof	2,698	Value: 55.00				

KM# 124 50 LITU
28.2800 g., 0.9250 Silver 0.8410 oz. ASW, 38.61 mm.
Series: XXVII Summer Olympic Games **Obv:** National arms within lined diagonal design **Rev:** Man throwing discus, Olympic emblem and date **Edge:** NUGALI STIPRUS DVASIA IR KUNU

Date	Mintage	F	VF	XF	Unc	BU
2000 Proof	2,448	Value: 40.00				

KM# 128 50 LITU
28.2800 g., 0.9250 Silver 0.8410 oz. ASW, 38.61 mm.
Subject: Millennium **Obv:** National arms within lined design with stars above value **Rev:** Radiant cross within arch **Edge:** SALVE NOVUM MILLENNIUM

Date	Mintage	F	VF	XF	Unc	BU
2000 Proof	2,998	Value: 40.00				

KM# 126 100 LITU
7.7800 g., 0.9999 Gold 0.2501 oz. AGW, 22.3 mm.
Subject: Grand Duke Vytautas **Obv:** National arms above value
Rev: Crowned armored bust right holding sword **Edge:** IS PRAEITIES TAVO SUNUS TE STIPRYBE SEMIA

Date	Mintage	F	VF	XF	Unc	BU
2000 Proof	2,000	Value: 600				

PATTERNS
Including off metal strikes

KM#	Date	Mintage	Identification	Mkt Val
Pn3	1936	—	5 Litai. Silver. Plain edge. Coin struck.	2,000
Pn4	1936	—	5 Litai. Silver. Lettered edge. Coin struck.	2,000
Pn5	1936	—	5 Litai. Silver. Designer's name (J. ZIKARAS) below bust. Plain edge. KM82. Medal struck.	2,500
Pn6	1936	—	10 Litu. Silver. Plain edge. KM83.	3,500
Pn7	1938	—	2 Litai. Brass. Lettered edge.	2,800
Pn8	1938	—	2 Litai. Silver. Reeded edge.	3,000
Pn9	1938	—	2 Litai. Silver. Lettered edge.	3,000
Pn10	1938	—	2 Litai. Silver. Plain edge.	3,000
Pn11	1938	—	2 Litai. Silver. Plain edge.	3,000
Pn12	1938	—	2 Litai. Silver. Lettered edge.	3,000
Pn13	1938	—	10 Litu. Silver. Coin struck.	3,000
Pn14	1938	2	10 Litu. Gold. Lettered edge. Medal-struck presentation pieces.	—
Pn15	1994	234	50 Litu. Silver. Lettered edge.	—

TRIAL STRIKES

KM#	Date	Mintage	Identification	Mkt Val
TS1	1925	—	Centas. Aluminum-Bronze. Uniface. Obverse.	300
TS2	1925	—	Centas. Aluminum-Bronze. Uniface. Reverse.	300
TS3	1925	—	5 Centai. Aluminum-Bronze. Uniface. Obverse.	300
TS4	1925	—	5 Centai. Aluminum-Bronze. Uniface. Reverse.	300
TS5	1925	—	10 Centu. Aluminum-Bronze. Uniface. Obverse.	325
TS6	1925	—	10 Centu. Aluminum-Bronze. Uniface. Reverse.	325
TS7	1925	—	20 Centu. Aluminum-Bronze. Uniface. Obverse.	325
TS8	1925	—	20 Centu. Aluminum-Bronze. Uniface. Reverse.	325
TS9	1925	—	50 Centu. Aluminum-Bronze. Uniface. Obverse.	350
TS10	1925	—	50 Centu. Aluminum-Bronze. Uniface. Reverse.	350

MINT SETS

KM#	Date	Mintage	Identification	Issue Price	Mkt Val
MS1	1925 (5)	—	KM71-75, 2 of each	—	2,500
MS2	1991 (9)	7,000	KM85-93	7.50	45.00
MS3	2000 (6)	5,000	KM106-108, 111-113	7.50	14.00

LUXEMBOURG

The Grand Duchy of Luxembourg is located in western Europe between Belgium, Germany and France, has an area of 1,103 sq. mi. (2,586 sq. km.) and a population of 377,100. Capital: Luxembourg. The economy is based on steel.

Founded about 963, Luxembourg was a prominent country of the Holy Roman Empire; one of its sovereigns became Holy Roman Emperor as Henry VII, 1308. After being made a duchy by Emperor Charles IV, 1354, Luxembourg passed under the domination of Burgundy, Spain, Austria and France, 1443-1815, regaining autonomy under the Treaty of Vienna, 1815, as a grand duchy in union with the Netherlands, though ostensibly a member of the German Confederation. When Belgium seceded from the Kingdom of the Netherlands, 1830, Luxembourg was forced to cede its greater western section to Belgium. The tiny duchy left the German Confederation in 1867 when the Treaty of London recognized it as an independent state and guaranteed its perpetual neutrality. Luxembourg was occupied by Germany and liberated by American troops in both World Wars.

RULERS
Adolphe, 1890-1905
William IV, 1905-1912
Marie Adelaide, 1912-1919
Charlotte, 1919-1964
Jean, 1964-2000
Henri, 2000-

MINT MARKS
A - Paris
(b) - Brussels, privy marks only
H — Gunzburg
(n) – lion - Namur
(u) - Utrecht, privy marks only

PRIVY MARKS
Angel's head, two headed eagle - Brussels
Sword, Caduceus - Utrecht (1846-74 although struck at Brussels until 1909)
NOTE: Beginning in 1994 the letters "qp" for quality proof appear on Proof coins.

MONETARY SYSTEM
100 Centimes = 1 Franc

GRAND DUCHY
STANDARD COINAGE RESUMED
100 Centimes = 1 Franc

KM# 21 2-1/2 CENTIMES
Bronze **Ruler:** William III Netherlands **Obv:** Crowned ornate shield within rope wreath **Obv. Leg.:** GRAND-DUCHE DE LUXEMBOURG **Rev:** Value and date within wreath

Date	Mintage	F	VF	XF	Unc	BU
1901(u)	800,000	0.50	1.50	7.50	40.00	—
Note: BARTH on reverse						
1901(u)	Inc. above	0.50	1.50	8.50	42.00	—
Note: BAPTH on reverse						
1908(u)	400,000	0.50	1.50	9.50	45.00	—

KM# 24 5 CENTIMES
1.9500 g., Copper-Nickel, 17 mm. **Ruler:** Adolphe **Obv:** Head right **Rev:** Value within wreath

Date	Mintage	F	VF	XF	Unc	BU
1901	2,000,000	0.25	0.75	4.50	17.50	—

KM# 26 5 CENTIMES
Copper-Nickel **Ruler:** William IV **Obv:** Head right **Rev:** Value within wreath

Date	Mintage	F	VF	XF	Unc	BU
1908	1,500,000	0.35	1.00	6.50	20.00	—

KM# 27 5 CENTIMES
Zinc **Ruler:** Marie Adelaide **Obv:** Plain and beaded circle around hole in center with date below **Rev:** Value above hole in center with 1/2 wreath below

Date	Mintage	F	VF	XF	Unc	BU
1915	1,200,000	1.00	6.00	15.00	30.00	—

KM# 30 5 CENTIMES
Iron **Ruler:** Charlotte **Obv:** National arms **Rev:** Value within wreath

Date	Mintage	F	VF	XF	Unc	BU
1918	1,200,000	1.00	4.00	8.00	30.00	—
1921	600,000	10.00	20.00	40.00	80.00	—
1922	400,000	15.00	30.00	80.00	120	—

KM# 33 5 CENTIMES
Copper-Nickel **Ruler:** Charlotte **Obv:** Crowned monogram **Rev:** Value within wreath

Date	Mintage	F	VF	XF	Unc	BU
1924	3,000,000	0.20	0.40	3.00	10.00	—

KM# 40 5 CENTIMES
Bronze **Ruler:** Charlotte **Obv:** Head left **Rev:** Value

Date	Mintage	F	VF	XF	Unc	BU
1930	5,000,000	0.10	0.25	2.00	4.00	—

KM# 25 10 CENTIMES
Copper-Nickel, 20 mm. **Ruler:** Adolphe **Obv:** Head right **Rev:** Value within wreath

Date	Mintage	F	VF	XF	Unc	BU
1901	4,000,000	0.25	0.75	6.00	14.00	—

KM# 28 10 CENTIMES
Zinc **Ruler:** Marie Adelaide **Obv:** Beaded circle around hole in center with date below **Rev:** Large value above hole in center with 1/2 wreath below

Date	Mintage	F	VF	XF	Unc	BU
1915	1,400,000	1.25	4.00	8.00	20.00	—

KM# 31 10 CENTIMES
Iron **Ruler:** Charlotte **Obv:** National arms **Rev:** Value within wreath

Date	Mintage	F	VF	XF	Unc	BU
1918	1,603,000	1.50	3.50	10.00	25.00	—

Date	Mintage	F	VF	XF	Unc	BU
1921	626,000	2.00	10.00	20.00	40.00	—
1923	350,000	12.00	30.00	60.00	125	—

KM# 34 10 CENTIMES
Copper-Nickel **Ruler:** Charlotte **Obv:** Crowned monogram **Rev:** Value within wreath

Date	Mintage	F	VF	XF	Unc	BU
1924	3,500,000	0.25	0.50	2.00	8.00	—

KM# 41 10 CENTIMES
Bronze, 22 mm. **Ruler:** Charlotte **Obv:** Head left **Rev:** Value flanked by sprigs with star above

Date	Mintage	F	VF	XF	Unc	BU
1930	5,000,000	0.10	0.25	2.00	4.50	—

KM# 29 25 CENTIMES
Zinc **Ruler:** Charlotte **Obv:** Beaded circle around hole in center with date below **Rev:** Large value above hole in center with wreath below

Date	Mintage	F	VF	XF	Unc	BU
1916	800,000	1.50	6.00	12.00	25.00	—
1920	—	200	400	600	1,000	—

KM# 32 25 CENTIMES
Iron **Ruler:** Charlotte **Obv:** National arms **Rev:** Value within wreath

Date	Mintage	F	VF	XF	Unc	BU
1919	804,000	2.75	6.50	12.50	35.00	—
1920	800,000	2.75	8.00	14.00	35.00	—
1922	600,000	2.75	8.50	16.00	40.00	—

KM# 37 25 CENTIMES
Copper-Nickel **Ruler:** Charlotte **Obv:** Crowned national arms flanked by stars **Rev:** Value and date to right of sprig

Date	Mintage	F	VF	XF	Unc	BU
1927	2,500,000	0.35	0.65	5.00	25.00	—

KM# 42 25 CENTIMES
Bronze **Ruler:** Charlotte **Obv:** Crowned national arms flanked by stars **Rev:** Value and date to right of sprig

Date	Mintage	F	VF	XF	Unc	BU
1930	1,000,000	0.35	1.00	8.00	30.00	—

KM# 42a.1 25 CENTIMES
Copper-Nickel, 25 mm. **Ruler:** Charlotte **Obv:** Crowned national arms flanked by stars **Rev:** Value and date to right of sprig **Note:** Coin alignment.

Date	Mintage	F	VF	XF	Unc	BU
1938	2,000,000	0.35	1.00	3.00	10.00	—

KM# 42a.2 25 CENTIMES
Copper-Nickel, 25 mm. **Ruler:** Charlotte **Obv:** Crowned national arms flanked by stars **Rev:** Value and date to right of sprig **Note:** Medal alignment.

Date	Mintage	F	VF	XF	Unc	BU
1938	Inc. above	50.00	75.00	100	200	—

KM# 45 25 CENTIMES
Bronze, 19 mm. **Ruler:** Charlotte **Obv:** Crowned national arms flanked by diamonds **Rev:** Value and date to right of sprig

Date	Mintage	F	VF	XF	Unc	BU
1946	1,000,000	—	0.15	0.25	0.75	—
1947	1,000,000	—	0.15	0.25	0.75	—

KM# 45a.1 25 CENTIMES
Aluminum, 18.5 mm. **Ruler:** Jean **Obv:** Crowned national arms flanked by diamonds **Rev:** Value and date to right of sprig **Note:** Coin alignment.

Date	Mintage	F	VF	XF	Unc	BU
1954	7,000,000	—	—	—	0.10	0.20
1957	3,020,000	—	—	—	0.10	0.20
1960	3,020,000	—	—	—	0.10	0.20
1963	4,000,000	—	—	—	0.10	0.20
1965	2,000,000	—	—	—	0.10	0.20
1967	3,000,000	—	—	—	0.10	0.20
1968	600,000	0.10	0.25	0.50	1.00	2.00
1970	4,000,000	—	—	—	0.10	0.20
1972	4,000,000	—	—	—	0.10	0.20

KM# 45a.2 25 CENTIMES
Aluminum, 18.5 mm. **Ruler:** Jean **Obv:** Crowned national arms flanked by diamonds **Rev:** Value and date to right of sprig **Note:** Medal alignment.

Date	Mintage	F	VF	XF	Unc	BU
1954	Inc. above	10.00	20.00	30.00	40.00	—
1960	Inc. above	5.00	10.00	15.00	20.00	—
1963	Inc. above	5.00	10.00	15.00	20.00	—
1965	Inc. above	10.00	20.00	30.00	40.00	—
1967	Inc. above	10.00	20.00	30.00	40.00	—

KM# 45b 25 CENTIMES
2.9600 g., 0.9250 Silver 0.0880 oz. ASW **Ruler:** Jean **Obv:** Crowned national arms flanked by diamonds **Rev:** Value and date to right of sprig

Date	Mintage	F	VF	XF	Unc	BU
1980 Proof	3,000	Value: 12.00				

KM# 43 50 CENTIMES
Nickel **Ruler:** Charlotte **Obv:** Man working field with date below **Rev:** Value divides wheat sprays

Date	Mintage	F	VF	XF	Unc	BU
1930	2,000,000	0.25	1.00	10.00	20.00	—

KM# 35 FRANC
5.1000 g., Nickel, 22.8 mm. **Ruler:** Charlotte **Obv:** Crowned monogram **Rev:** Man working field with date below

Date	Mintage	F	VF	XF	Unc	BU
1924	1,000,000	0.25	1.50	10.00	20.00	—
1928	2,000,000	0.20	1.50	10.00	20.00	—
1935	1,000,000	0.25	2.00	14.00	30.00	—

KM# 44 FRANC
Copper-Nickel, 24 mm. **Ruler:** Charlotte **Obv:** Crowned monogram flanked by flower blossoms at top **Rev:** Woman figure divides date and value

Date	Mintage	F	VF	XF	Unc	BU
1939	5,000,000	0.25	0.75	1.50	5.00	—

KM# 46.1 FRANC
Copper-Nickel, 23 mm. **Ruler:** Charlotte **Obv:** Man working field **Rev:** Crowned monogram divides value

Date	Mintage	F	VF	XF	Unc	BU
1946	4,000,000	0.15	0.35	0.50	1.50	—
1947	2,000,000	0.20	0.40	1.00	3.00	—

KM# 46.2 FRANC
Copper-Nickel, 21 mm. **Ruler:** Charlotte **Obv:** Man working field **Rev:** Crowned monogram divides value

Date	Mintage	F	VF	XF	Unc	BU
1952	5,000,000	0.10	0.25	0.50	2.00	—
1953	2,000,000	0.10	0.25	0.50	1.50	—
1955	1,000,000	0.10	0.25	0.50	1.50	—
1957	2,000,000	—	0.10	0.25	1.00	—
1960	2,000,000	—	0.10	0.25	1.00	—
1962	2,000,000	—	0.10	0.25	1.00	—
1964	2,000,000	—	0.10	0.25	1.00	—

KM# 46.2a FRANC
4.4500 g., 0.9250 Silver 0.1323 oz. ASW, 21 mm. **Ruler:** Jean **Obv:** Man working fields **Rev:** Crowned monogram divides value

Date	Mintage	F	VF	XF	Unc	BU
1980 Proof	3,000	Value: 20.00				

KM# 55 FRANC
3.8900 g., Copper-Nickel, 21 mm. **Ruler:** Jean **Obv:** Head left **Rev:** Crown above value within wreath

Date	Mintage	F	VF	XF	Unc	BU
1965	3,000,000	—	—	0.10	0.20	0.40
1966	1,000,000	—	—	0.10	0.20	0.40
1968	3,000,000	—	—	0.10	0.20	0.40
1970	3,000,000	—	—	0.10	0.20	0.40
1972	3,000,000	—	—	0.10	0.20	0.40
1973	3,000,000	—	—	0.10	0.20	0.40
1976	3,000,000	—	—	0.10	0.20	0.40
1977	1,000,000	—	—	0.10	0.20	0.40
1978	3,000,000	—	—	0.10	0.20	0.40
1979	2,000,000	—	—	0.10	0.20	0.40
1980	4,000,000	—	—	0.10	0.20	0.40
1981	5,000,000	—	—	0.10	0.20	0.40
1982	3,000,000	—	—	0.10	0.20	0.40
1983	3,000,000	—	—	0.10	0.20	0.40
1984	3,000,000	—	—	0.10	0.20	0.40

KM# 55a FRANC
4.4700 g., 0.9250 Silver 0.1329 oz. ASW, 21 mm. **Ruler:** Jean **Obv:** Head left **Rev:** Crown above value within wreath

Date	Mintage	F	VF	XF	Unc	BU
1980 Proof	3,000	Value: 20.00				

KM# 59 FRANC
Copper-Nickel, 21 mm. **Ruler:** Jean **Obv:** Head left **Rev:** IML added

Date	Mintage	F	VF	XF	Unc	BU
1986	3,000,000	—	—	0.10	0.20	0.40
1987	3,000,000	—	—	0.10	0.20	0.40

KM# 63 FRANC
Nickel-Steel **Ruler:** Jean **Obv:** Head left **Rev:** Crown divides date above value

Date	Mintage	F	VF	XF	Unc	BU
1988	10,000,000	—	—	—	0.40	0.60
1989	3,000,000	—	—	—	0.40	0.60
1990	25,010,000	—	—	—	0.40	0.60
1991	10,010,000	—	—	—	0.40	0.60
1992 In sets only	10,000	—	—	—	0.60	1.00
1993 In sets only	10,000	—	—	—	0.60	1.00
1994 In sets only	10,000	—	—	—	0.60	1.00
1995 In sets only	10,000	—	—	—	0.60	1.00

KM# 36 2 FRANCS
Nickel **Ruler:** Charlotte **Obv:** Crowned monogram above sprig **Rev:** Man working field

Date	Mintage	F	VF	XF	Unc	BU
1924	1,000,000	1.00	4.00	20.00	40.00	—

KM# 38 5 FRANCS
8.0000 g., 0.6250 Silver 0.1607 oz. ASW, 27.8 mm. **Ruler:** Charlotte **Rev:** Wing above national arms on shield divides value

Date	Mintage	F	VF	XF	Unc	BU
1929	2,000,000	BV	3.50	12.50	25.00	—

KM# 50 5 FRANCS
Copper-Nickel **Ruler:** Charlotte **Obv:** Head left **Rev:** Value flanked by flowers below crown and ribbon

Date	Mintage	F	VF	XF	Unc	BU
1949		0.30	0.60	1.00	3.50	—

KM# 51 5 FRANCS
Copper-Nickel **Ruler:** Charlotte **Obv:** Head right **Rev:** Crowned arms divide value

Date	Mintage	F	VF	XF	Unc	BU
1962	2,000,000	0.10	0.25	0.40	1.00	—

KM# 51a 5 FRANCS
6.7400 g., 0.9250 Silver 0.2004 oz. ASW **Ruler:** Jean **Obv:** Head right **Rev:** Crowned arms divide value

Date	Mintage	F	VF	XF	Unc	BU
1980 Proof	3,000	Value: 25.00				

KM# 56 5 FRANCS
Copper-Nickel **Ruler:** Jean **Obv:** Head left **Rev:** Crown above value and date within sprigs

Date	Mintage	F	VF	XF	Unc	BU
1971	1,000,000	—	—	0.20	0.50	0.80
1976	1,000,000	—	—	0.20	0.50	0.80
1979	1,000,000	—	—	0.20	0.50	0.80
1981	1,000,000	—	—	0.20	0.50	0.80

KM# 56a 5 FRANCS
6.7800 g., 0.9250 Silver 0.2016 oz. ASW **Ruler:** Jean **Obv:** Head left **Rev:** Crown above value and date within sprigs

Date	Mintage	F	VF	XF	Unc	BU
1980 Proof	3,000	Value: 25.00				

KM# 60.1 5 FRANCS
Brass **Ruler:** Jean **Obv:** Head left **Rev:** Crown divides date above value within sprigs with IML added

Date	Mintage	F	VF	XF	Unc	BU
1986	9,000,000	—	—	0.15	0.40	0.65
1987	7,000,000	—	—	0.15	0.40	0.65
1988	2,000,000	—	—	0.15	0.40	0.65

KM# 60.2 5 FRANCS
Brass **Ruler:** Jean **Obv:** Head left **Rev:** Larger crown divides date above value within sprigs

Date	Mintage	F	VF	XF	Unc	BU
1986	—	—	—	0.15	0.40	0.65
1987	—	—	—	0.15	0.40	0.65

KM# 65 5 FRANCS
Brass **Ruler:** Jean **Obv:** Head left **Rev:** Crown divides date above value

Date	Mintage	F	VF	XF	Unc	BU
1989	2,000,000	—	—	—	0.60	1.00
1990	4,010,000	—	—	—	0.60	1.00
1991 In sets only	10,000	—	—	—	0.75	1.25
1992 In sets only	20,000	—	—	—	0.75	1.25
1993 In sets only	17,500	—	—	—	0.75	1.25
1994 In sets only	10,000	—	—	—	0.75	1.25
1995 In sets only	10,000	—	—	—	0.75	1.25

KM# 39 10 FRANCS
13.5000 g., 0.7500 Silver 0.3255 oz. ASW **Ruler:** Charlotte
Obv: Head left **Rev:** Helmeted shield **Edge:** Reeded

Date	Mintage	F	VF	XF	Unc	BU
1929	1,000,000	BV	6.00	12.00	32.50	—

KM# 57 10 FRANCS
Nickel, 27 mm. **Ruler:** Jean **Obv:** Head left **Rev:** Crown above value and date flanked by leaves

Date	Mintage	F	VF	XF	Unc	BU
1971	3,000,000	—	—	0.30	0.60	1.00
1972	3,000,000	—	—	0.30	0.60	1.00
1974	3,000,000	—	—	0.30	0.60	1.00
1976	3,000,000	—	—	0.30	0.60	1.00
1977	1,000,000	—	—	0.30	0.60	1.00
1978	1,000,000	—	—	0.30	0.60	1.00
1979	1,000,000	—	—	0.30	0.60	1.00
1980	1,000,000	—	—	0.30	0.60	1.00

KM# 57a 10 FRANCS
8.7900 g., 0.9250 Silver 0.2614 oz. ASW **Ruler:** Jean
Obv: Head left **Rev:** Crown above value and date flanked by leaves

Date	Mintage	F	VF	XF	Unc	BU
1980 Proof	3,000	Value: 30.00				

KM# 47 20 FRANCS
8.5000 g., 0.8350 Silver 0.2282 oz. ASW, 27 mm.
Ruler: Charlotte **Subject:** 600th Anniversary - John the Blind
Obv: Head left flanked by shields **Rev:** Armored Knight on horse above dates

Date	Mintage	F	VF	XF	Unc	BU
ND(1946)	100,000	BV	5.00	12.00	18.00	—
ND(1946) Proof	100	Value: 200				

KM# 58 20 FRANCS
Bronze, 25.5 mm. **Ruler:** Jean **Obv:** Head left **Rev:** Crown above value flanked by sprigs **Edge:** Dashes all around

Date	Mintage	F	VF	XF	Unc	BU
1980	3,000,000	—	—	0.60	1.00	1.50
1981	3,000,000	—	—	0.60	1.00	1.50
1982	3,000,000	—	—	0.60	1.00	1.50
1983	2,000,000	—	—	0.60	1.00	1.50

KM# 58a 20 FRANCS
10.2100 g., 0.9250 Silver 0.3036 oz. ASW, 25.5 mm.
Ruler: Jean **Obv:** Head left **Rev:** Crown above value flanked by sprigs

Date	Mintage	F	VF	XF	Unc	BU
1980 Proof	3,000	Value: 30.00				

KM# 64 20 FRANCS
6.2200 g., 0.9990 Gold 0.1998 oz. AGW **Ruler:** Jean
Subject: 150th Anniversary of the Grand Duchy **Obv:** Head left
Rev: Crowned national arms

Date	Mintage	F	VF	XF	Unc	BU
ND(1989) Proof	50,000	Value: 185				

KM# 67 20 FRANCS
Bronze, 25.5 mm. **Ruler:** Jean **Obv:** Head left **Rev:** Crown divides date above value

Date	Mintage	F	VF	XF	Unc	BU
1990	1,110,000	—	—	—	2.00	3.00
1991 In sets only	10,000	—	—	—	2.50	3.50
1992 In sets only	10,000	—	—	—	2.50	3.50
1993 In sets only	10,000	—	—	—	2.50	3.50
1994 In sets only	10,000	—	—	—	2.50	3.50
1995 In sets only	10,000	—	—	—	2.50	3.50

KM# 48 50 FRANCS
12.5000 g., 0.8350 Silver 0.3356 oz. ASW, 30 mm.
Ruler: Charlotte **Subject:** 600th Anniversary - John the Blind

Date	Mintage	F	VF	XF	Unc	BU
ND(1946)	100,000	—	10.00	15.00	35.00	—
ND(1946) Proof	100	Value: 225				

KM# 62 50 FRANCS
Nickel, 22.5 mm. **Ruler:** Jean **Obv:** Head left **Rev:** Crown divides date above value

Date	Mintage	F	VF	XF	Unc	BU
1987	3,000,000	—	—	1.50	3.50	5.00
1988	1,000,000	—	—	1.50	3.50	5.00
1989	1,200,000	—	—	1.50	3.50	5.00

KM# 66 50 FRANCS
7.0200 g., Nickel, 22.5 mm. **Ruler:** Jean **Note:** Similar to 5 Francs, KM#65.

Date	Mintage	F	VF	XF	Unc	BU
1989	2,000,000	—	—	—	3.50	5.00
1990	2,010,000	—	—	—	3.50	5.00
1991 In sets only	10,000	—	—	—	4.00	6.00
1992 In sets only	10,000	—	—	—	4.00	6.00
1993 In sets only	10,000	—	—	—	4.00	6.00
1994 In sets only	10,000	—	—	—	4.00	6.00
1995 In sets only	10,000	—	—	—	4.00	6.00

KM# 49 100 FRANCS
25.0000 g., 0.8350 Silver 0.6711 oz. ASW, 37 mm. **Ruler:** Charlotte
Subject: 600th Anniversary - John the Blind **Obv:** Head left flanked by crowned shields **Rev:** Armored Knight on horse above dates

Date	Mintage	F	VF	XF	Unc	BU
ND(1946)	98,000	—	20.00	40.00	50.00	—
ND(1946) Proof	100	Value: 250				
ND(1946) Restrike	2,000	—	—	—	100	—
Note: Without designer's name						

KM# 52 100 FRANCS
18.0000 g., 0.8350 Silver 0.4832 oz. ASW **Ruler:** Charlotte
Obv: Head right **Rev:** Crowned arms with supporters above value

Date	Mintage	F	VF	XF	Unc	BU
1963	50,000	—	—	—	10.00	15.00	—

KM# 54 100 FRANCS
18.0000 g., 0.8350 Silver 0.4832 oz. ASW **Ruler:** Charlotte
Rev: Crowned mantled arms with supporters

Date	Mintage	F	VF	XF	Unc	BU
1964	50,000	—	—	—	9.00	14.00	—

KM# 70 100 FRANCS
16.1000 g., 0.9250 Silver 0.4788 oz. ASW **Ruler:** Jean
Subject: 50th Anniversary - United Nations **Obv:** Head left
Rev: Emblem and numeral 50 to lower right of building, flags and gun

Date	Mintage	F	VF	XF	Unc	BU
ND(1995) (qp) Proof	110,000	Value: 28.50				

KM# 53.1 250 FRANCS
25.0000 g., 0.8350 Silver 0.6711 oz. ASW **Ruler:** Charlotte
Subject: Millennium of Luxembourg City **Obv:** Head right within circular inscriptions above dates **Rev:** City view above value

Date	Mintage	F	VF	XF	Unc	BU
ND(1963)	11,500	—	—	25.00	45.00	—

KM# 53.2 250 FRANCS
25.0000 g., 0.8350 Silver 0.6711 oz. ASW **Ruler:** Charlotte
Subject: Millennium of Luxembourg City **Obv:** Head right within circular inscriptions above dates **Rev:** City view above value
Note: Darkly toned by the mint.

Date	Mintage	F	VF	XF	Unc	BU
ND(1963)	8,500	—	—	40.00	60.00	—

KM# 68   250 FRANCS
18.7500 g., 0.9250 Silver 0.5576 oz. ASW **Ruler:** Jean
Subject: BE-NE-LUX Treaty **Obv:** Head left **Rev:** Houses above with flowers below dividing date and value

Date	Mintage	F	VF	XF	Unc	BU
ND(1994) (qp) Proof	30,000	Value: 30.00				

KM# 69   500 FRANCS
22.8500 g., 0.9250 Silver 0.6795 oz. ASW **Ruler:** Jean
Subject: 50th Anniversary of Liberation **Obv:** Head left **Rev:** Flag design below with inscription above within circle

Date	Mintage	F	VF	XF	Unc	BU
ND(1994)	25,000	—	—	—	35.00	—
ND(1994) (qp) Proof	25,000	Value: 42.50				

KM# 71   500 FRANCS
22.8500 g., 0.9250 Silver 0.6795 oz. ASW **Ruler:** Jean
Subject: Luxembourg - European Cultural City **Obv:** Segmented head left **Rev:** Quartered cultural pictures

Date	Mintage	F	VF	XF	Unc	BU
(19)95 (qp) Proof	10,000	Value: 45.00				

KM# 72   500 FRANCS
22.8500 g., 0.9250 Silver 0.6795 oz. ASW **Ruler:** Jean
Subject: Presidency of the European Community
Obv: Segmented portrait **Rev:** Symbolic design and dates

Date	Mintage	F	VF	XF	Unc	BU
(19)97 (qp) Proof	10,000	Value: 40.00				
(19)97 (qp) Proof	10,000	Value: 50.00				

KM# 73   500 FRANCS
22.8500 g., 0.9250 Silver 0.6795 oz. ASW **Ruler:** Jean
Subject: 1,300 years of Echternach **Obv:** Duke's segmented portrait **Rev:** City seal and anniversary dates

Date	Mintage	F	VF	XF	Unc	BU
ND(1998) (qp) Proof	10,000	Value: 40.00				

KM# 74   500 FRANCS
22.8500 g., 0.9250 Silver 0.6795 oz. ASW, 37 mm. **Ruler:** Jean
Subject: Coronation of Henry III **Obv:** Head left **Rev:** Crowned "H"

Date	Mintage	F	VF	XF	Unc	BU
2000 (qp) Proof	10,000	Value: 50.00				

ESSAIS

KM#	Date	Mintage	Identification	Mkt Val
E22	1901	20	5 Centimes. Gold. Adolph.	1,000
E23	1901	—	10 Centimes. Gold. Adolph.	1,000
E24	1908	—	10 Centimes. Gold. Wilhelm.	1,000
E25	1914	100	50 Centimes. Copper.	60.00
E26	1914	—	50 Centimes. Silver.	45.00
E27	1914	100	Franc. Copper. Bust left. Value and date within wreath.	60.00
E28	1914	—	Franc. Silver.	45.00
E29	1914	100	2 Francs. Copper.	60.00
E30	1914	—	2 Francs. Silver. Restruck after World War I.	45.00
E31	1927	—	25 Centimes. Gold.	—
E32	1929	50	5 Francs. Copper.	150
E33	1929	50	5 Francs. Bronze.	160
E34	1929	—	5 Francs. Gold.	2,000
E35	1929	50	10 Francs. Copper.	150
E36	1929	50	10 Francs. Bronze.	160
E37	1929	—	10 Francs. Silver.	1,200
E38	1929	—	10 Francs. Gold.	2,000
E39	1939	—	Franc. Gold.	1,500
E40	1945	100	25 Centimes. Copper. 25 at top.	25.00
E41	1945	100	25 Centimes. Copper. 25 at upper right.	25.00
E42	1946	100	25 Centimes. Copper.	15.00
E43	1946	500	25 Centimes. Copper.	15.00
E44	1946	500	25 Centimes. Copper.	25.00
E45	1946	500	Franc. Copper. Plain edge.	15.00
E46	1946	100	Franc. Copper. Milled edge.	20.00
E48	1946	100	Franc. Silver. Milled edge.	40.00
E49	1946	100	Franc. Silver. Small letters.	40.00
E50	1946	100	20 Francs. Copper.	100
E51	1946	50	20 Francs. Silver.	200
E52	1946	25	20 Francs. Gold.	1,200
E53	1946	100	50 Francs. Copper.	125
E54	1946	50	50 Francs. Silver.	225
E55	1946	25	50 Francs. Gold.	2,000
E56	1946	100	100 Francs. Copper.	150
E57	1946	50	100 Francs. Silver. Head left. Crowned mantled arms with supporters divides date within circle.	325
E58	1946	25	100 Francs. Gold.	3,000
E47	1946	500	Franc. Silver. Plain edge.	30.00
E59	1949	50	5 Francs. Copper.	50.00
E60	1949	50	5 Francs. Bronze-Aluminum.	50.00
E61	1962	75	5 Francs. Copper-Nickel.	30.00
E62	1962	50	5 Francs. Silver.	115
E63	1962	50	5 Francs. Gold.	1,000
E64	1963	250	20 Francs. Silver.	200
E65	1963	100	100 Francs. Bronze.	70.00
E66	1963	185	100 Francs. Silver.	60.00
E67	1963	50	100 Francs. Gold.	1,250
	1963	50	100 Francs. Gold.	1,250
E68	ND(1963)	—	250 Francs. Copper-Nickel.	50.00
E69	ND(1963)	200	250 Francs. Bronze.	50.00
E70	ND(1963)	200	250 Francs. Silver.	85.00
E71	ND(1963)	200	250 Francs. Gold.	1,450
E72	1964	200	20 Francs. Gold.	200
E73	1964	200	100 Francs. Copper-Nickel. Head left.	20.00
E74	1964	200	100 Francs. Bronze.	20.00
E75	1964	200	100 Francs. Silver.	20.00
E76	1964	200	100 Francs. Gold.	750
E77	1965	200	Franc. Copper-Nickel.	15.00
E78	1965	200	Franc. Silver.	15.00
E79	1965	200	Franc. Gold. KM55.	200
E80	1966	100	40 Francs. Gold.	400
E81	1967	100	40 Francs. Gold.	400
E82	1971	250	5 Francs. Copper-Nickel.	15.00
E83	1971	250	5 Francs. Silver.	15.00
E84	1971	250	5 Francs. Gold. KM56.	315
E85	1971	250	10 Francs. Copper-Nickel.	15.00
E86	1971	250	10 Francs. Silver.	15.00
E87	1971	250	10 Francs. Gold.	325
E88	1980	—	20 Francs. Bronze.	20.00
E89	1980	—	20 Francs. Silver.	45.00
E90	1980	500	20 Francs. Gold.	285

PATTERNS
Including off metal strikes

KM#	Date	Mintage	Identification	Mkt Val
Pn6	1901	—	2-1/2 Centimes. Copper.	125
Pn7	1901	100	2-1/2 Centimes. Silver.	165
Pn8	1901	100	5 Centimes. Copper. Without denomination.	125
Pn9	1901	100	5 Centimes. Copper-Nickel. Without denomination.	125
Pn10	1901	100	5 Centimes. Copper-Nickel. Without denomination.	—
Pn11	1901	50	5 Centimes. Silver. Without denomination.	150
Pn12	1901	20	5 Centimes. Gold. Without denomination.	1,000
Pn13	1901	100	10 Centimes. Copper. Without denomination.	90.00
Pn14	1901	100	10 Centimes. Copper-Nickel. Without denomination.	90.00
Pn15	1901	100	10 Centimes. Copper-Nickel. Plain edge. Large letters.	90.00
Pn16	1901	100	10 Centimes. Copper-Nickel. Milled edge. Large letters.	90.00
Pn17	1901	50	10 Centimes. Silver. Large letters.	150
Pn18	1901	20	10 Centimes. Gold. Without denomination.	1,000
Pn19	ND	50	Franc. Nickel. Head of William.	150
Pn20	1917	—	5 Centimes. Copper. Crossed L's.	150
Pn21	1917	—	10 Centimes. Copper.	150
Pn22	1923	100	Franc. Aluminum.	90.00
Pn23	1923	100	Franc. Bronze.	100
Pn24	1923	100	Franc. Nickel.	100
Pn25	1923	100	Franc. Silver.	135
Pn26	1923	100	2 Francs. Pewter.	125
Pn27	1923	100	2 Francs. Aluminum.	120
Pn28	1923	100	2 Francs. Bronze.	115
Pn29	1923	100	2 Francs. Nickel.	135
Pn30	1923	100	2 Francs. Silver.	150
Pn31	1924	—	Franc. Aluminum.	50.00
Pn32	1924	100	Franc. Copper.	110
Pn33	1924	100	Franc. Bronze.	110
Pn34	1924	100	Franc. Silver.	110
Pn35	1924	100	2 Francs. Copper.	100
Pn36	1924	100	2 Francs. Bronze.	110
Pn37	1930	—	5 Centimes. Copper. Crowned value.	85.00
Pn38	1930	—	5 Centimes. Copper.	75.00
Pn39	1930	—	10 Centimes. Copper.	125
Pn40	1930	—	50 Centimes. Copper-Nickel.	150
Pn41	1930	—	50 Centimes. Copper-Nickel.	160
Pn42	1939	50	Franc. Silver.	100
Pn43	1939	—	Franc. Gold.	350
Pn44	1942	—	5 Francs. Zinc.	100
Pn45	1942	—	5 Francs. Nickel.	100
Pn46	1947	100	2 Francs. Copper-Nickel.	80.00
Pn47	1947	100	5 Francs. Copper-Nickel.	85.00

PIEFORTS AND PIEFORTS WITH ESSAI

KM#	Date	Mintage	Identification	Mkt Val
PE4	1908	—	10 Centimes. Gold.	1,000
PE5	1927	100	25 Centimes. Bronze.	100
PE6	1938	100	25 Centimes. Copper-Nickel.	100

MINT SETS

KM#	Date	Mintage	Identification	Issue Price	Mkt Val
MS1	1990 (4)	10,000	KM63, 65-67	—	55.00
MS2	1991 (4)	10,000	KM63, 65-67	—	55.00
MS3	1992 (4)	10,000	KM63, 65-67	—	55.00
MS4	1993 (4)	10,000	KM63, 65-67	—	55.00
MS5	1994 (4)	10,000	KM63, 65-67	—	55.00
MS6	1995 (4)	10,000	KM63, 65-67 plus medal	—	100

PROOF SETS

KM#	Date	Mintage	Identification	Issue Price	Mkt Val
PS1	1980 (7)	3,000	KM45b, 46, 3a, 51a, 55a-58a	—	160

MACAO

The Province of Macao, a Portuguese overseas province located in the South China Sea 40 miles southwest of Hong Kong, consists of the peninsula of Macao and the islands of Taipa and Coloane. It has an area of 6.2 sq. mi.(16 sq. km.) and a population of 500,000. Capital: Macao. Macao's economy is based on light industry, commerce, tourism, fishing, and gold trading - Macao is one of the entirely free markets for gold in the world. Cement, textiles, fireworks, vegetable oils, and metal products are exported.

Established by the Portuguese in 1557, Macao is the oldest European settlement in the Far East. The Chinese, while agreeing to Portuguese settlement, did not recognize Portuguese sovereign rights and the Portuguese remained largely under control of the Chinese until 1849, when the Portuguese abolished the Chinese customhouse and declared the independence of the port. The Manchu government formally recognized the Portuguese right to *perpetual occupation* of Macao in 1887.

In 1987, Portugal and China agreed that Macao would become a Chinese Territory in 1999. In December of 1999, Macao became a special administrative zone of China.

RULER
Portuguese 1887-1999

MINT MARKS
(p) - Pobjoy Mint
(s) - Singapore Mint

Pobjoy Mint   Singapore Mint

MONETARY SYSTEM
100 Avos = 1 Pataca

PORTUGUESE COLONY

STANDARD COINAGE
100 Avos = 1 Pataca

KM# 1   5 AVOS
Bronze **Obv:** Value flanked by upper and lower dots within circle **Rev:** Shield within crowned globe flanked by stars below

Date	Mintage	F	VF	XF	Unc	BU
1952	500,000	—	3.50	15.00	30.00	50.00

KM# 1a   5 AVOS
2.6000 g., Nickel-Brass **Obv:** Value flanked by upper and lower dots within circle **Rev:** Shield within crowned globe flanked by stars below

Date	Mintage	F	VF	XF	Unc	BU
1967	5,000,000	—	0.50	1.00	2.50	—

KM# 2   10 AVOS
4.0200 g., Bronze, 20.3 mm. **Obv:** Value flanked by upper and lower dots within circle **Rev:** Shield within crowned globe flanked by stars below

Date	Mintage	F	VF	XF	Unc	BU
1952	12,500,000	—	0.30	0.80	6.00	—

KM# 2a   10 AVOS
3.9000 g., Nickel-Brass **Obv:** Value flanked by upper and lower dots within circle **Rev:** Shield within crowned globe flanked by stars below

Date	Mintage	F	VF	XF	Unc	BU
1967	5,525,000	—	0.50	1.00	2.00	—
1968	6,975,000	—	0.25	1.00	2.00	—
1975	20,000,000	—	0.10	0.50	1.50	—
1976	Inc. above	—	0.10	0.50	1.50	—

KM# 20   10 AVOS
3.3000 g., Brass, 19.1 mm. **Obv:** Portuguese shield flanked by stars below **Rev:** Value above building

Date	Mintage	F	VF	XF	Unc	BU
1982	24,580,000	—	0.10	0.50	1.50	—
1983	—	—	0.10	0.50	1.50	—
1984	—	—	0.25	0.75	2.50	—
1985	—	—	0.10	0.50	1.50	—
1988	—	—	0.10	0.50	1.50	—

KM# 20a   10 AVOS
3.2000 g., 0.9250 Silver 0.0952 oz. ASW **Obv:** Portuguese shield flanked by stars below **Rev:** Value above building

Date	Mintage	F	VF	XF	Unc	BU
1982 Proof	2,000	Value: 7.50				
1983 Proof	2,500	Value: 7.50				
1984 Proof	2,500	Value: 7.50				
1985 Proof	2,500	Value: 7.50				

KM# 20b   10 AVOS
4.0000 g., 0.9170 Gold 0.1179 oz. AGW **Obv:** Portuguese shield flanked by stars below (low star) **Rev:** Value above building

Date	Mintage	F	VF	XF	Unc	BU
1982 Proof	150	Value: 145				

KM# 20c   10 AVOS
4.5000 g., 0.9500 Platinum 0.1374 oz. APW **Obv:** Portuguese shield flanked by stars below (low star) **Rev:** Value above building

Date	Mintage	F	VF	XF	Unc	BU
1982 Proof	375	Value: 300				

KM# 70   10 AVOS
1.3800 g., Brass, 17 mm. **Obv:** MACAU written at center with date below **Rev:** Crowned design above value flanked by mint marks

Date	Mintage	F	VF	XF	Unc	BU
1993	—	—	—	—	0.75	1.25
1998	—	—	—	—	0.75	1.25

KM# 21   20 AVOS
4.7000 g., Brass, 21.1 mm. **Obv:** Portuguese shield flanked by stars below **Rev:** Value above block letter design within vertical rectangle

Date	Mintage	F	VF	XF	Unc	BU
1982	9,960,000	—	0.10	0.50	1.50	—
1983	—	—	0.10	0.50	1.50	—
1984	—	—	0.25	0.75	2.50	—
1985	—	—	0.10	0.50	1.50	—

KM# 21a   20 AVOS
4.6000 g., 0.9250 Silver 0.1368 oz. ASW, 21.1 mm. **Obv:** Portuguese shield flanked by stars below above date **Rev:** Value above block letter design within vertical rectangle

Date	Mintage	F	VF	XF	Unc	BU
1982 Proof	2,000	Value: 11.50				
1983 Proof	2,500	Value: 11.50				
1984 Proof	2,500	Value: 11.50				
1985 Proof	2,500	Value: 11.50				

KM# 21b   20 AVOS
5.5000 g., 0.9170 Gold 0.1621 oz. AGW, 21.1 mm. **Obv:** Portuguese shield flanked by stars, date below (low star) **Rev:** Value above block letter design within vertical rectangle

Date	Mintage	F	VF	XF	Unc	BU
1982 Proof	150	Value: 175				

KM# 21c   20 AVOS
6.2000 g., 0.9500 Platinum 0.1894 oz. APW, 21.1 mm. **Obv:** Portuguese shield flanked by stars, date below (low star) **Rev:** Value above block letter design within vertical rectangle

Date	Mintage	F	VF	XF	Unc	BU
1982 Proof	375	Value: 400				

KM# 71   20 AVOS
Brass, 20 mm. **Obv:** MACAU written over inner circle with date below **Rev:** Man standing above his crew on ancient ship flanked by mint marks with value above

Date	Mintage	F	VF	XF	Unc	BU
1993	—	—	—	—	1.00	1.75
1998	—	—	—	—	1.00	1.75

KM# 3   50 AVOS
Copper-Nickel, 20 mm. **Obv:** Portuguese shield within globe and cross **Rev:** Macau shield within crowned globe

Date	Mintage	F	VF	XF	Unc	BU
1952	2,560,000	—	0.75	3.50	9.00	—

KM# 7   50 AVOS
5.8000 g., Copper-Nickel, 23 mm. **Obv:** Portuguese shield within globe and cross **Rev:** Macau shield within crowned globe

Date	Mintage	F	VF	XF	Unc	BU
1972	1,600,000	—	0.50	1.50	4.00	—
1973	4,840,000	—	0.50	1.00	3.00	—

KM# 9   50 AVOS
Copper-Nickel, 23 mm. **Obv:** Value and denomination flanked by upper and lower flower buds within circle **Rev:** Macau shield within crowned globe flanked by stars and mint marks

Date	Mintage	F	VF	XF	Unc	BU
1978	3,000,000	—	0.50	1.50	4.00	—

KM# 22   50 AVOS
5.1000 g., Brass, 23 mm. **Obv:** Portuguese shield flanked by stars below above date **Rev:** Value above fallen block letters within vertical rectangle

Date	Mintage	F	VF	XF	Unc	BU
1982	16,952,000	—	0.50	1.00	3.00	—
1983	—	—	0.75	4.00	9.00	—
1984	—	—	0.75	3.50	7.00	—
1985	—	—	0.50	2.00	5.00	—

KM# 22a   50 AVOS
5.7000 g., 0.9250 Silver 0.1695 oz. ASW, 23 mm. **Obv:** Portuguese shield flanked by stars below above date **Rev:** Value above fallen block letters within vertical rectangle

Date	Mintage	F	VF	XF	Unc	BU
1982 Proof	2,000	Value: 13.50				
1983 Proof	2,500	Value: 13.50				
1984 Proof	2,500	Value: 13.50				
1985 Proof	2,500	Value: 13.50				

KM# 22b   50 AVOS
7.4000 g., 0.9170 Gold 0.2182 oz. AGW, 23 mm. **Obv:** Portuguese shield flanked by stars below (low star) **Rev:** Value above fallen block letters within vertical rectangle

Date	Mintage	F	VF	XF	Unc	BU
1982 Proof	150	Value: 220				

KM# 22c 50 AVOS
8.4000 g., 0.9500 Platinum 0.2566 oz. APW, 23 mm. **Obv:** Portuguese shield flanked by stars below above date (low star) **Rev:** Value above fallen block letters within vertical rectangle

Date	Mintage	F	VF	XF	Unc	BU
1982 Proof	375	Value: 525				

KM# 72 50 AVOS
4.5900 g., Brass, 23 mm. **Obv:** MACAU written across center of globe with date below **Rev:** Figure in ceremonial dragon costume being led by a man

Date	Mintage	F	VF	XF	Unc	BU
1993	—	—	—	—	1.50	2.50

KM# 4 PATACA
3.0000 g., 0.7200 Silver 0.0694 oz. ASW **Obv:** Portuguese shield within globe and long cross **Rev:** Macau shield within crowned globe

Date	Mintage	F	VF	XF	Unc	BU
1952	4,500,000	5.00	10.00	20.00	40.00	—

KM# 6 PATACA
10.6000 g., Nickel **Obv:** Portuguese shield within globe and long cross **Rev:** Macau shield within crowned globe

Date	Mintage	F	VF	XF	Unc	BU
1968	5,000,000	—	1.00	3.00	6.50	—
1975	6,000,000	—	0.75	2.00	5.00	—

KM# 6a PATACA
Copper-Nickel **Obv:** Portuguese shield within globe and long cross **Rev:** Macau shield within crowned globe

Date	Mintage	F	VF	XF	Unc	BU
1980	—	—	3.50	12.00	25.00	—

KM# 23.1 PATACA
9.2000 g., Copper-Nickel, 26 mm. **Obv:** Portuguese shield flanked by stars below above date (high stars) **Rev:** Artistic design flanked by upright fish

Date	Mintage	F	VF	XF	Unc	BU
1982(s)	6,427,000	—	1.00	2.00	6.00	—
1983(s)	—	—	1.50	3.50	8.00	—
1984(s)	—	—	2.00	4.50	10.00	—
1985(s)	—	—	1.50	3.50	8.00	—

KM# 23.1a PATACA
9.0000 g., 0.9250 Silver 0.2676 oz. ASW, 26 mm. **Obv:** Portuguese shield flanked by stars below above date (high stars) **Rev:** Artistic design flanked by upright fish

Date	Mintage	F	VF	XF	Unc	BU
1982(s) Proof	2,000	Value: 17.50				
1983(s) Proof	2,500	Value: 17.50				
1984(s) Proof	2,500	Value: 17.50				
1985(s) Proof	2,500	Value: 17.50				

KM# 23.1b PATACA
11.6000 g., 0.9170 Gold 0.3420 oz. AGW, 26 mm. **Obv:** Portuguese shield flanked by stars below above date (high stars) **Rev:** Artistic design flanked by upright fish

Date	Mintage	F	VF	XF	Unc	BU
1982(s) Proof	150	Value: 350				

KM# 23.1c PATACA
13.2000 g., 0.9500 Platinum 0.4032 oz. APW, 26 mm. **Obv:** Portuguese shield flanked by stars below above date (high stars) **Rev:** Artistic design flanked by upright fish

Date	Mintage	F	VF	XF	Unc	BU
1982(s) Proof	375	Value: 825				

KM# 23.2 PATACA
9.0000 g., Copper-Nickel, 26 mm. **Obv:** Portuguese shield flanked by stars below above date (low stars) **Rev:** Artistic design flanked by upright fish

Date	Mintage	F	VF	XF	Unc	BU
1982(p)	—	—	1.00	2.00	6.00	—
1983(p)	—	—	1.50	3.50	8.00	—

KM# 23.2a PATACA
5.7000 g., 0.9250 Silver 0.1695 oz. ASW, 26 mm. **Obv:** Portuguese shield flanked by stars below above date (low stars) **Rev:** Artistic design flanked by upright fish

Date	Mintage	F	VF	XF	Unc	BU
1982 Proof	—	Value: 15.00				

KM# 57 PATACA
9.1800 g., Copper-Nickel, 25.98 mm. **Obv:** MACAU written across center of globe with date below **Rev:** Lighthouse above value **Edge:** Reeded

Date	Mintage	F	VF	XF	Unc	BU
1992	—	—	—	1.20	3.00	4.00
1998	—	—	—	0.90	2.25	3.00

KM# 97 2 PATACAS
Nickel-Brass, 27.5 mm. **Obv:** MACAU written accross center of globe above date **Rev:** Church and Chinese arch **Edge:** Plain

Date	Mintage	F	VF	XF	Unc	BU
1998	—	—	—	—	3.50	5.50

KM# 5 5 PATACAS
15.0000 g., 0.7200 Silver 0.3472 oz. ASW **Obv:** Portuguese shield within globe and long cross **Rev:** Macau shield within crowned globe

Date	Mintage	F	VF	XF	Unc	BU
1952	900,000	6.00	8.00	12.00	25.00	—

KM# 5a 5 PATACAS
10.0000 g., 0.6500 Silver 0.2090 oz. ASW **Obv:** Portuguese shield within globe and long cross **Rev:** Macau shield within crowned globe

Date	Mintage	F	VF	XF	Unc	BU
1971	500,000	5.00	7.50	12.00	20.00	—

KM# 24.1 5 PATACAS
10.7000 g., Copper-Nickel, 29 mm. **Obv:** Portuguese shield flanked by stars below above date (high stars) **Rev:** Large stiylized dragon above value

Date	Mintage	F	VF	XF	Unc	BU
1982(s)	1,102,000	—	1.00	2.00	6.00	—
1983(s)	—	—	3.50	7.00	20.00	—
1984(s)	—	—	5.00	10.00	60.00	—
1985(s)	—	—	3.50	7.00	45.00	—
1988(s)	—	—	1.00	2.00	6.00	—

KM# 24.2 5 PATACAS
10.7000 g., Copper-Nickel, 29 mm. **Obv:** Portuguese shield flanked by stars below above date (low stars) **Rev:** Small stylized dragon above value

Date	Mintage	F	VF	XF	Unc	BU
1982(p)	—	—	1.00	2.00	6.00	—
1983(p)	—	—	1.00	2.00	6.00	—

KM# 24.1a 5 PATACAS
10.7000 g., 0.9250 Silver 0.3182 oz. ASW, 29 mm. **Obv:** Portuguese shield flanked by stars below above date (high stars) **Rev:** Large stiylized dragon above value

Date	Mintage	F	VF	XF	Unc	BU
1982(s) Proof	2,000	Value: 32.50				
1983(s) Proof	2,500	Value: 32.50				
1984(s) Proof	2,500	Value: 32.50				
1985(s) Proof	2,500	Value: 32.50				

KM# 24.1b 5 PATACAS
16.3000 g., 0.9170 Gold 0.4805 oz. AGW, 29 mm. **Obv:** Portuguese shield flanked by stars below above date (high stars) **Rev:** Large stiylized dragon above value

Date	Mintage	F	VF	XF	Unc	BU
1982(s) Proof	150	Value: 475				

KM# 24.1c 5 PATACAS
18.4000 g., 0.9500 Platinum 0.5620 oz. APW, 29 mm. **Obv:** Portuguese shield flanked by stars below above date (high stars) **Rev:** Large stiylized dragon above value

Date	Mintage	F	VF	XF	Unc	BU
1982(s) Proof	375	Value: 1,150				

KM# 24.2a 5 PATACAS
10.7000 g., 0.9250 Silver 0.3182 oz. ASW, 29 mm. **Obv:** Portuguese shield flanked by stars below above date (low stars) **Rev:** Small stiylized dragon above value

Date	Mintage	F	VF	XF	Unc	BU
1982(p) Proof	—	Value: 25.00				

KM# 56 5 PATACAS
10.1000 g., Copper-Nickel **Obv:** MACAU written across center of globe with date below **Rev:** Sailing ship and building scene **Edge:** Plain

Date	Mintage	F	VF	XF	Unc	BU
1992	—	—	—	—	6.50	10.00

KM# 83 10 PATACAS
Bi-Metallic Copper-Nickel center in Brass ring, 28 mm. **Obv:** MACAU written across center of globe within circle above date **Rev:** Cathedral within circle above value

Date	Mintage	F	VF	XF	Unc	BU
1997	—	—	—	—	8.50	12.50

KM# 8 20 PATACAS
18.0000 g., 0.6500 Silver 0.3761 oz. ASW **Obv:** Macau shield within globe **Rev:** Junk (ship) passing under Taipa bridge within circle

Date	Mintage	F	VF	XF	Unc	BU
1974	1,000	—	—	16.00	30.00	—

KM# 10 100 PATACAS
28.2800 g., 0.9250 Silver 0.8410 oz. ASW **Subject:** 25th Anniversary of Grand Prix **Obv:** Church facade flanked by stars **Rev:** Race car with advertising logos

Date	Mintage	F	VF	XF	Unc	BU
1978 Proof	610	Value: 150				

KM# 10a 100 PATACAS
Copper-Nickel **Subject:** 25th Anniversary of Grand Prix **Obv:** Church facade flanked by stars **Rev:** Race car with advertising logos

Date	Mintage	F	VF	XF	Unc	BU
1978	—	—	—	—	300	—

KM# 11 100 PATACAS
28.2800 g., 0.9250 Silver 0.8410 oz. ASW **Obv:** Church facade flanked by stars **Rev:** Race car without advertising **Note:** Similar to KM#10, but reissued without advertising logos on the racecar.

Date	Mintage	F	VF	XF	Unc	BU
1978 Proof	5,500	Value: 150				

KM# 14 100 PATACAS
28.2800 g., 0.9250 Silver 0.8410 oz. ASW **Subject:** Year of the Goat **Obv:** Crowned arms with supporters **Rev:** Goat

Date	Mintage	F	VF	XF	Unc	BU
1979(s) Proof	5,500	Value: 50.00				

KM# 16 100 PATACAS
28.2800 g., 0.9250 Silver 0.8410 oz. ASW **Subject:** Year of the Monkey **Obv:** Crowned arms with supporters **Rev:** Monkey swinging on a rope

Date	Mintage	F	VF	XF	Unc	BU
1980	1,000	—	—	—	65.00	—
1980 Proof	2,000	Value: 60.00				

KM# 18 100 PATACAS
28.2800 g., 0.9250 Silver 0.8410 oz. ASW **Subject:** Year of the Rooster **Obv:** Crowned arms with supporters **Rev:** Rooster

Date	Mintage	F	VF	XF	Unc	BU
1981(p)	1,000	—	—	—	60.00	—
1981(p) Proof	1,000	Value: 70.00				

KM# 25 100 PATACAS
28.2800 g., 0.9250 Silver 0.8410 oz. ASW **Subject:** Year of the Dog **Obv:** Crowned arms with supporters **Rev:** Dog

Date	Mintage	F	VF	XF	Unc	BU
1982(p)	500	—	—	—	65.00	—
1982(p) Proof	500	Value: 75.00				
1982(s)	220	—	—	—	67.50	—
1982(s) Proof	3,500	Value: 70.00				

KM# 27 100 PATACAS
28.2800 g., 0.9250 Silver 0.8410 oz. ASW **Subject:** Year of the Pig **Obv:** Crowned arms with supporters **Rev:** Pig

Date	Mintage	F	VF	XF	Unc	BU
1983(s)	2,500	—	—	—	50.00	—
1983(s) Proof	2,500	Value: 60.00				

KM# 29 100 PATACAS
28.2800 g., 0.9250 Silver 0.8410 oz. ASW **Subject:** Year of the Rat **Obv:** Crowned arms with supporters **Rev:** Rat

Date	Mintage	F	VF	XF	Unc	BU
1984(s)	2,000	—	—	—	60.00	—
1984(s) Proof	5,000	Value: 70.00				

KM# 31 100 PATACAS
28.2800 g., 0.9250 Silver 0.8410 oz. ASW **Subject:** Year of the Ox **Obv:** Crowned arms with supporters **Rev:** Ox

Date	Mintage	F	VF	XF	Unc	BU
1985(s)	10,000	—	—	—	50.00	—
1985(s) Proof	5,000	Value: 60.00				

KM# 33 100 PATACAS
28.2800 g., 0.9250 Silver 0.8410 oz. ASW **Subject:** Visit of Portugal's President Eanes **Obv:** Head left above date

Date	Mintage	F	VF	XF	Unc	BU
1985(s)	760	—	—	—	90.00	—
1985(s) Proof	2,000	Value: 65.00				

KM# 34 100 PATACAS
28.2800 g., 0.9250 Silver 0.8410 oz. ASW **Subject:** Year of the Tiger **Obv:** Crowned arms with supporters **Rev:** Tiger

Date	Mintage	F	VF	XF	Unc	BU
1986(p)	760	—	—	—	90.00	—
1986(p) Proof	3,000	Value: 60.00				

KM# 36 100 PATACAS
28.2800 g., 0.9250 Silver 0.8410 oz. ASW **Subject:** Year of the Rabbit **Obv:** Crowned arms with supporters **Rev:** Rabbit

Date	Mintage	F	VF	XF	Unc	BU
1987(p)	—	—	—	—	50.00	—
1987(p) Proof	5,000	Value: 50.00				

KM# 38 100 PATACAS
28.2800 g., 0.9250 Silver 0.8410 oz. ASW **Subject:** Year of the Dragon **Obv:** Crowned arms with supporters **Rev:** Dragon **Note:** Similar to 1,000 Patacas, KM#39.

Date	Mintage	F	VF	XF	Unc	BU
1988	—	—	—	—	50.00	—
1988 Proof	5,000	Value: 65.00				

KM# 40 100 PATACAS
28.2800 g., 0.9250 Silver 0.8410 oz. ASW **Subject:** 35th Anniversary of Grand Prix **Obv:** Sailing ship within circle **Rev:** Race car and dates within circle

Date	Mintage	F	VF	XF	Unc	BU
ND(1988) Proof	5,000	Value: 55.00				

KM# 40a 100 PATACAS
Platinum APW **Subject:** 35th Anniversary of Grand Prix **Obv:** Sailing ship within circle **Rev:** Race car within circle above dates

Date	Mintage	F	VF	XF	Unc	BU
ND(1988) Proof	10	Value: 2,850				

KM# 44 100 PATACAS
28.2800 g., 0.9250 Silver 0.8410 oz. ASW **Subject:** Year of the Snake **Obv:** Crowned arms with supporters **Rev:** Coiled snake **Note:** Similar to 1,000 Patacas, KM#45.

Date	Mintage	F	VF	XF	Unc	BU
1989(s)	2,000	—	—	—	50.00	—
1989(s) Proof	3,000	Value: 60.00				

KM# 46 100 PATACAS
28.2800 g., 0.9250 Silver 0.8410 oz. ASW **Subject:** Year of the Horse **Obv:** Crowned arms with supporters **Rev:** Horse

Date	Mintage	F	VF	XF	Unc	BU
1990(s)	1,000	—	—	—	75.00	—
1990(s) Proof	3,364	Value: 60.00				

KM# 48 100 PATACAS
28.2800 g., 0.9250 Silver 0.8410 oz. ASW **Subject:** Year of the Goat **Obv:** Crowned arms with supporters **Rev:** Goat **Note:** Similar to KM#51.

Date	Mintage	F	VF	XF	Unc	BU
1991(s)	1,000	—	—	—	50.00	—
1991(s) Proof	Est. 4,000	Value: 50.00				

KM# 52 100 PATACAS
28.2800 g., 0.9250 Silver 0.8410 oz. ASW **Subject:** Year of the Monkey **Obv:** Crowned arms with supporters **Rev:** Monkey

Date	Mintage	F	VF	XF	Unc	BU
1992(s)	1,000	—	—	—	50.00	—
1992(s) Proof	Est. 4,000	Value: 60.00				

KM# 58 100 PATACAS
28.2800 g., 0.9250 Silver 0.8410 oz. ASW **Subject:** Year of the Rooster **Obv:** Crowned arms with supporters **Rev:** Rooster

Date	Mintage	F	VF	XF	Unc	BU
1993	500	—	—	—	75.00	—
1993 Proof	Est. 4,000	Value: 50.00				

KM# 62 100 PATACAS
28.2800 g., 0.9250 Silver 0.8410 oz. ASW **Subject:** Macao Grand Prix **Obv:** Map above dates **Rev:** Checkered design divides race car and racing bike

Date	Mintage	F	VF	XF	Unc	BU
ND(1993) Proof	5,000	Value: 45.00				

KM# 66 100 PATACAS
28.2800 g., 0.9250 Silver 0.8410 oz. ASW **Subject:** Year of the Dog **Obv:** Crowned arms with supporters **Rev:** Dog

Date	Mintage	F	VF	XF	Unc	BU
1994	1,000	—	—	—	50.00	—
1994 Proof	Est. 4,000	Value: 50.00				

KM# 73 100 PATACAS
28.2800 g., 0.9250 Silver 0.8410 oz. ASW **Subject:** Year of the Pig **Obv:** Crowned arms with supporters **Rev:** Pig

Date	Mintage	F	VF	XF	Unc	BU
1995	1,000	—	—	—	60.00	—
1995 Proof	Est. 4,000	Value: 50.00				

KM# 77 100 PATACAS
28.2800 g., 0.9250 Silver 0.8410 oz. ASW **Subject:** Airpor **Obv:** Value and date within circle **Rev:** Airport scene

Date	Mintage	F	VF	XF	Unc	BU
1995 Proof	8,000	Value: 42.50				

KM# 79 100 PATACAS
28.2800 g., 0.9250 Silver 0.8410 oz. ASW **Subject:** Year of the Rat **Obv:** Crowned arms with supporters **Rev:** Rat

Date	Mintage	F	VF	XF	Unc	BU
1996	1,000	—	—	—	42.50	—
1996 Proof	Est. 4,000	Value: 50.00				

KM# 84 100 PATACAS
28.2800 g., 0.9250 Silver 0.8410 oz. ASW **Subject:** Year of the Ox **Obv:** Church facade **Rev:** Ox

Date	Mintage	F	VF	XF	Unc	BU
1997 Proof	4,000	Value: 50.00				

KM# 88 100 PATACAS
28.2800 g., 0.9250 Silver 0.8410 oz. ASW **Subject:** Year of the Tiger **Obv:** Church facade **Rev:** Tiger

Date	Mintage	F	VF	XF	Unc	BU
1998 Proof	5,000	Value: 50.00				

KM# 106 100 PATACAS
28.4000 g., 0.9250 Silver 0.8446 oz. ASW, 38.4 mm. **Subject:** 19th East Asian Insurance Conference **Obv:** Church facade **Rev:** Two hands holding world within circle **Edge:** Reeded

Date	Mintage	F	VF	XF	Unc	BU
1998 Proof	Est. 3,000	—	—	—	50.00	—

KM# 96 100 PATACAS
31.1035 g., 0.9250 Silver 0.9250 oz. ASW **Subject:** Macao returns to China **Obv:** Crowned arms with supporters **Rev:** Portuguese and Chinese ships below gold-plated cameo of the Gao Temple

Date	Mintage	F	VF	XF	Unc	BU
1999	Est. 39,000	—	—	—	65.00	—

KM# 98 100 PATACAS
28.2800 g., 0.9250 Silver 0.8410 oz. ASW, 38.6 mm. **Subject:** Year of the Dragon **Obv:** Church facade **Rev:** Dragon **Edge:** Reeded

Date	Mintage	F	VF	XF	Unc	BU
2000	1,000	—	—	—	60.00	—
2000 Proof	4,000	Value: 55.00				

KM# 49 250 PATACAS
3.9900 g., 0.9170 Gold 0.1176 oz. AGW **Subject:** Year of the Goat **Obv:** Crowned arms with supporters **Rev:** Goat **Note:** Similar to 1,000 Patacas, KM#51.

Date	Mintage	F	VF	XF	Unc	BU
1991 Proof	Est. 2,500	Value: 145				

KM# 53 250 PATACAS
3.9900 g., 0.9170 Gold 0.1176 oz. AGW **Subject:** Year of the Monkey **Obv:** Crowned arms with supporters **Rev:** Monkey **Note:** Similar to 1,000 Patacas, KM#51.

Date	Mintage	F	VF	XF	Unc	BU
1992 Proof	Est. 2,500	Value: 145				

KM# 59 250 PATACAS
3.9900 g., 0.9170 Gold 0.1176 oz. AGW **Subject:** Year of the Rooster **Obv:** Crowned arms with supporters **Rev:** Rooster **Note:** Similar to 1,000 Patacas, KM#58.

Date	Mintage	F	VF	XF	Unc	BU
1993 Proof	Est. 2,500	Value: 145				

KM# 67 250 PATACAS
3.9900 g., 0.9170 Gold 0.1176 oz. AGW **Subject:** Year of the Dog **Obv:** Church facade flanked by stars above date **Rev:** Dog **Note:** Similar to 1,000 Patacas, KM#69.

Date	Mintage	F	VF	XF	Unc	BU
1994 Proof	Est. 2,500	Value: 145				

KM# 74 250 PATACAS
3.9900 g., 0.9170 Gold 0.1176 oz. AGW **Subject:** Year of the Pig **Obv:** Church facade flanked by stars above date **Rev:** Pig

Date	Mintage	F	VF	XF	Unc	BU
1995 Proof	—	Value: 145				

KM# 80 250 PATACAS
3.9900 g., 0.9170 Gold 0.1176 oz. AGW **Subject:** Year of the Rat **Obv:** Church facade flanked by stars above date **Rev:** Rat

Date	Mintage	F	VF	XF	Unc	BU
1996 Proof	—	Value: 145				

KM# 85 250 PATACAS
3.9900 g., 0.9170 Gold 0.1176 oz. AGW **Subject:** Year of the Ox **Obv:** Church facade flanked by stars above date **Rev:** Ox **Note:** Similar to 100 Patacas, KM#84.

Date	Mintage	F	VF	XF	Unc	BU
1997 Proof	Est. 2,500	Value: 145				

KM# 89 250 PATACAS
3.9900 g., 0.9170 Gold 0.1176 oz. AGW **Subject:** Year of the Tiger **Obv:** Church facade flanked by stars above date **Rev:** Tiger **Note:** Similar to 100 Patacas, KM#88.

Date	Mintage	F	VF	XF	Unc	BU
1998 Proof	Est. 2,500	Value: 145				

KM# 93 250 PATACAS
3.9900 g., 0.9170 Gold 0.1176 oz. AGW **Subject:** Year of the Rabbit **Obv:** Church facade flanked by stars above value **Rev:** Rabbit

Date	Mintage	F	VF	XF	Unc	BU
1999 Proof	Est. 2,500	Value: 145				

KM# 99 250 PATACAS
3.9900 g., 0.9167 Gold 0.1176 oz. AGW, 19.3 mm. **Subject:** Year of the Dragon **Obv:** Church facade flanked by stars above date **Rev:** Dragon **Edge:** Reeded

Date	Mintage	F	VF	XF	Unc	BU
2000 Proof	2,500	Value: 145				

KM# 12 500 PATACAS
7.9600 g., 0.9170 Gold 0.2347 oz. AGW **Subject:** 25th Anniversary of Grand Prix **Obv:** Church facade flanked by stars above date **Rev:** Race car

Date	Mintage	F	VF	XF	Unc	BU
1978 Proof	550	Value: 300				

KM# 13 500 PATACAS
7.9600 g., 0.9170 Gold 0.2347 oz. AGW **Obv:** Church facade flanked by stars above date **Rev:** Race car without advertising

Date	Mintage	F	VF	XF	Unc	BU
1978 Proof	5,500	Value: 250				

KM# 15 500 PATACAS
7.9600 g., 0.9170 Gold 0.2347 oz. AGW **Subject:** Year of the Goat **Obv:** Crowned arms with supporters **Rev:** Goat

Date	Mintage	F	VF	XF	Unc	BU
1979 Proof	5,500	Value: 245				

KM# 41 500 PATACAS
155.5150 g., 0.9990 Silver 4.9947 oz. ASW **Subject:** 35th Anniversary of Grand Prix **Obv:** Race car within circle **Rev:** Sailing ship within circle **Note:** Similar to KM#42.

Date	Mintage	F	VF	XF	Unc	BU
1988 Proof	2,000	Value: 160				

KM# 42 500 PATACAS
7.9881 g., 0.9170 Gold 0.2355 oz. AGW **Subject:** 35th Anniversary of Grand Prix **Obv:** Sailing ship within circle **Rev:** Race car within circle

Date	Mintage	F	VF	XF	Unc	BU
ND(1988) Proof	4,500	Value: 255				

KM# 50   500 PATACAS
7.9881 g., 0.9170 Gold 0.2355 oz. AGW **Subject:** Year of the Goat **Obv:** Crowned arms with supporters **Rev:** Goat
Note: Similar to 1,000 Patacas, KM#51.

Date	Mintage	F	VF	XF	Unc	BU
1991 Proof	Est. 2,500	Value: 260				

KM# 54   500 PATACAS
7.9900 g., 0.9170 Gold 0.2356 oz. AGW **Subject:** Year of the Monkey **Obv:** Crowned arms with supporters **Rev:** Monkey
Note: Similar to 1,000 Patacas, KM#51.

Date	Mintage	F	VF	XF	Unc	BU
1992 Proof	Est. 2,500	Value: 250				

KM# 60   500 PATACAS
7.9900 g., 0.9170 Gold 0.2356 oz. AGW **Subject:** Year of the Rooster **Obv:** Church facade flanked by stars above date **Rev:** Rooster **Note:** Similar to 100 Patacas, KM#58.

Date	Mintage	F	VF	XF	Unc	BU
1993 Proof	Est. 2,500	Value: 250				

KM# 63   500 PATACAS
155.6000 g., 0.9990 Silver 4.9974 oz. ASW **Subject:** Macao Grand Prix

Date	Mintage	F	VF	XF	Unc	BU
1993 Proof	2,000	Value: 160				

KM# 64   500 PATACAS
7.9900 g., 0.9170 Gold 0.2356 oz. AGW **Subject:** Macao Grand Prix **Obv:** Map above dates **Rev:** Checkered design divides race car and racing bike

Date	Mintage	F	VF	XF	Unc	BU
ND(1993) Proof	4,500	Value: 235				

KM# 68   500 PATACAS
7.9900 g., 0.9170 Gold 0.2356 oz. AGW **Subject:** Year of the Dog **Obv:** Church facade flanked by stars above date **Rev:** Dog
Note: Similar to 1,000 Patacas, KM#69.

Date	Mintage	F	VF	XF	Unc	BU
1994 Proof	Est. 2,500	Value: 235				

KM# 75   500 PATACAS
7.9900 g., 0,9170 Gold 0.2356 oz. AGW **Subject:** Year of the Pig **Obv:** Church facade flanked by stars above date **Rev:** Pig

Date	Mintage	F	VF	XF	Unc	BU
1995 Proof	Est. 2,000	Value: 235				

KM# 81   500 PATACAS
7.9900 g., 0.9170 Gold 0.2356 oz. AGW **Subject:** Year of the Rat **Obv:** Church facade flanked by stars above date **Rev:** Rat

Date	Mintage	F	VF	XF	Unc	BU
1996 Proof	—	Value: 235				

KM# 86   500 PATACAS
7.9900 g., 0.9170 Gold 0.2356 oz. AGW **Subject:** Year of the Ox **Obv:** Church facade flanked by stars above date **Rev:** Ox
Note: Similar to 100 Patacas, KM#84.

Date	Mintage	F	VF	XF	Unc	BU
1997 Proof	2,000	Value: 250				

KM# 90   500 PATACAS
7.9900 g., 0.9170 Gold 0.2356 oz. AGW **Subject:** Year of the Tiger **Obv:** Church facade flanked by stars above date **Rev:** Tiger **Note:** Similar to 100 Patacas, KM#88.

Date	Mintage	F	VF	XF	Unc	BU
1998 Proof	2,500	Value: 250				

KM# 94   500 PATACAS
7.9900 g., 0.9170 Gold 0.2356 oz. AGW **Subject:** Year of the Rabbit **Obv:** Church facade flanked by stars above date **Rev:** Rabbit

Date	Mintage	F	VF	XF	Unc	BU
1999 Proof	Est. 2,500	Value: 250				

KM# 100   500 PATACAS
7.9900 g., 0.9167 Gold 0.2355 oz. AGW, 22.05 mm.
Subject: Year of the Dragon **Obv:** Church facade flanked by stars above date **Rev:** Dragon **Edge:** Reeded

Date	Mintage	F	VF	XF	Unc	BU
2000 Proof	2,500	Value: 260				

KM# 17   1000 PATACAS
15.9760 g., 0.9170 Gold 0.4710 oz. AGW **Subject:** Year of the Monkey **Obv:** Crowned arms with supporters **Rev:** Monkey

Date	Mintage	F	VF	XF	Unc	BU
1980 Proof	5,500	Value: 485				

KM# 19   1000 PATACAS
15.9760 g., 0.9170 Gold 0.4710 oz. AGW **Subject:** Year of the Rooster **Obv:** Crowned arms with supporters **Rev:** Rooster

Date	Mintage	F	VF	XF	Unc	BU
1981	3,500	—	—	—	—	460
1981 Proof	Inc. above	Value: 475				

KM# 26   1000 PATACAS
15.9760 g., 0.9170 Gold 0.4710 oz. AGW **Subject:** Year of the Dog **Obv:** Crowned arms with supporters **Rev:** Dog

Date	Mintage	F	VF	XF	Unc	BU
1982	256	—	—	—	—	475
1982 Proof	255	Value: 500				

KM# 28   1000 PATACAS
15.9760 g., 0.9170 Gold 0.4710 oz. AGW **Subject:** Year of the Pig **Obv:** Crowned arms with supporters **Rev:** Pig

Date	Mintage	F	VF	XF	Unc	BU
1983	400	—	—	—	—	465
1983 Proof	500	Value: 485				

KM# 30   1000 PATACAS
15.9760 g., 0.9170 Gold 0.4710 oz. AGW **Subject:** Year of the Rat **Obv:** Crowned arms with supporters **Rev:** Rat

Date	Mintage	F	VF	XF	Unc	BU
1984	2,000	—	—	—	—	450
1984 Proof	3,000	Value: 470				

KM# 32   1000 PATACAS
15.9760 g., 0.9170 Gold 0.4710 oz. AGW **Subject:** Year of the Ox **Obv:** Crowned arms with supporters **Rev:** Ox

Date	Mintage	F	VF	XF	Unc	BU
1985	10,000	—	—	—	—	450
1985 Proof	5,000	Value: 470				

KM# 35   1000 PATACAS
15.9760 g., 0.9170 Gold 0.4710 oz. AGW **Subject:** Year of the Tiger **Obv:** Crowned arms with supporters **Rev:** Tiger

Date	Mintage	F	VF	XF	Unc	BU
1986(p)	2,000	—	—	—	—	455
1986(p) Proof	3,000	Value: 480				

KM# 37   1000 PATACAS
15.9760 g., 0.9170 Gold 0.4710 oz. AGW **Subject:** Year of the Rabbit **Obv:** Crowned arms with supporters **Rev:** Rabbit

Date	Mintage	F	VF	XF	Unc	BU
1987(p)	—	—	—	—	—	450
1987(p) Proof	5,000	Value: 475				

KM# 39   1000 PATACAS
15.9760 g., 0.9170 Gold 0.4710 oz. AGW **Subject:** Year of the Dragon **Obv:** Crowned arms with supporters **Rev:** Dragon

Date	Mintage	F	VF	XF	Unc	BU
1988 Proof	5,000	Value: 475				

KM# 45   1000 PATACAS
15.9760 g., 0.9170 Gold 0.4710 oz. AGW **Subject:** Year of the Snake **Obv:** Crowned arms with supporters **Rev:** Snake

Date	Mintage	F	VF	XF	Unc	BU
1989	2,000	—	—	—	—	455
1989 Proof	3,000	Value: 480				

KM# 47   1000 PATACAS
15.9760 g., 0.9170 Gold 0.4710 oz. AGW **Subject:** Year of the Horse **Obv:** Crowned arms with supporters **Rev:** Horse

Date	Mintage	F	VF	XF	Unc	BU
1990	2,000	—	—	—	—	455
1990 Proof	3,000	Value: 480				

KM# 51   1000 PATACAS
15.9760 g., 0.9170 Gold 0.4710 oz. AGW **Obv:** Crowned arms with supporters **Rev:** Ram

Date	Mintage	F	VF	XF	Unc	BU
1991	Est. 500	—	—	—	—	465
1991 Proof	Est. 4,500	Value: 485				

KM# 55   1000 PATACAS
15.9760 g., 0.9170 Gold 0.4710 oz. AGW **Subject:** Year of the Monkey **Obv:** Crowned arms with supporters **Rev:** Monkey

Date	Mintage	F	VF	XF	Unc	BU
1992	Est. 500	—	—	—	—	460
1992 Proof	Est. 4,500	Value: 480				

KM# 61   1000 PATACAS
15.9760 g., 0.9170 Gold 0.4710 oz. AGW **Subject:** Year of the Rooster **Obv:** Church facade flanked by stars above date
Rev: Rooster

Date	Mintage	F	VF	XF	Unc	BU
1993	Est. 500	—	—	—	—	460
1993 Proof	Est. 4,500	Value: 480				

KM# 69   1000 PATACAS
15.9760 g., 0.9170 Gold 0.4710 oz. AGW **Subject:** Year of the Dog **Obv:** Church facade flanked by stars above date **Rev:** Dog

Date	Mintage	F	VF	XF	Unc	BU
1994	Est. 500	—	—	—	—	460
1994 Proof	Est. 4,500	Value: 480				

KM# 76   1000 PATACAS
15.9760 g., 0.9170 Gold 0.4710 oz. AGW **Subject:** Year of the Pig **Obv:** Church facade flanked by stars above date **Rev:** Pig

Date	Mintage	F	VF	XF	Unc	BU
1995	Est. 500	—	—	—	—	460
1995 Proof	Est. 4,500	Value: 480				

KM# 78   1000 PATACAS
15.9760 g., 0.9170 Gold 0.4710 oz. AGW **Subject:** Airport **Obv:** Stylized form **Rev:** City aerial view

Date	Mintage	F	VF	XF	Unc	BU
1995 Proof	5,000	Value: 480				

KM# 82   1000 PATACAS
15.9760 g., 0.9170 Gold 0.4710 oz. AGW **Subject:** Year of the Rat **Obv:** Church facade flanked by stars above date **Rev:** Rat

Date	Mintage	F	VF	XF	Unc	BU
1996 Proof		Value: 485				

KM# 87   1000 PATACAS
15.9760 g., 0.9170 Gold 0.4710 oz. AGW **Subject:** Year of the Ox **Obv:** Church facade flanked by stars above date **Rev:** Ox

Date	Mintage	F	VF	XF	Unc	BU
1997 Proof	5,000	Value: 485				

KM# 91 1000 PATACAS
15.9760 g., 0.9170 Gold 0.4710 oz. AGW **Subject:** Year of the Tiger **Obv:** Church facade flanked by stars above date **Rev:** Tiger

Date	Mintage	F	VF	XF	Unc	BU
1998 Proof	5,000	Value: 485				

KM# 95 1000 PATACAS
15.9760 g., 0.9170 Gold 0.4710 oz. AGW **Subject:** Year of the Rabbit **Obv:** Church facade flanked by stars above date **Rev:** Rabbit

Date	Mintage	F	VF	XF	Unc	BU
1999 Proof	4,000	Value: 485				

KM# 101 1000 PATACAS
15.9760 g., 0.9167 Gold 0.4708 oz. AGW, 28.4 mm. **Subject:** Year of the Dragon **Obv:** Church facade flanked by stars above date **Rev:** Dragon **Edge:** Reeded

Date	Mintage	F	VF	XF	Unc	BU
2000	500					460
2000 Proof	4,000	Value: 480				

KM# 43 10000 PATACAS
155.5150 g., 0.9990 Gold 4.9947 oz. AGW, 69.00 mm. **Subject:** 35th Anniversary of Grand Prix **Obv:** Chinese junk within circle **Rev:** Race car above dates within circle **Note:** Similar to 500 Patacas, KM#42.

Date	Mintage	F	VF	XF	Unc	BU
1988 Proof	500	Value: 5,000				

KM# 65 10000 PATACAS
155.5150 g., 0.9990 Gold 4.9947 oz. AGW **Subject:** Macao Grand Prix **Obv:** Map above dates **Rev:** Checkered design divides race car and racing bike **Note:** Similar to 500 Patacas, KM#64.

Date	Mintage	F	VF	XF	Unc	BU
1993 Proof	500	Value: 5,000				

SPECIAL ADMINISTRATIVE REGION (S.A.R.)

STANDARD COINAGE
100 Avos = 1 Pataca

KM# 111 10 AVOS
2.5000 g., Brass, 17 mm. **Subject:** Macao's Return to China **Obv:** City arms **Rev:** Sun Yat Sen Memorial above clasped hands with building in background

Date	Mintage	F	VF	XF	Unc	BU
1999	288,888	—	—	—	8.00	12.00

KM# 112 20 AVOS
3.2600 g., Brass, 19.5 mm. **Subject:** Macao's Return to China **Obv:** City arms **Rev:** Monetary and Foreign Exchange Authority Building

Date	Mintage	F	VF	XF	Unc	BU
1999	288,888	—	—	—	9.00	14.00

KM# 113 50 AVOS
4.5400 g., Brass, 23 mm. **Subject:** Macao's Return to China **Obv:** City arms **Rev:** Jet above bridge and ship

Date	Mintage	F	VF	XF	Unc	BU
1999	288,888	—	—	—	10.00	15.00

KM# 114 PATACA
6.0500 g., Copper-Nickel, 25.9 mm. **Subject:** Macao's Return to China **Obv:** City arms **Rev:** Cultural and recreational center building

Date	Mintage	F	VF	XF	Unc	BU
1999	288,888	—	—	—	12.00	17.00

KM# 115 2 PATACAS
5.5800 g., Copper-Nickel, 25 mm. **Subject:** Macao's Return to China **Obv:** City arms **Rev:** Cathedral and race car

Date	Mintage	F	VF	XF	Unc	BU
1999	288,888	—	—	—	15.00	20.00

KM# 116 5 PATACAS
6.6800 g., Copper-Nickel, 27 mm. **Subject:** Macao's Return to China **Obv:** City arms **Rev:** Racing dogs with Lisboa Hotel in background

Date	Mintage	F	VF	XF	Unc	BU
1999	288,888	—	—	—	18.00	22.00

KM# 117 10 PATACAS
7.2000 g., Bi-Metallic Copper-Nickel center in Brass ring, 27.8 mm. **Subject:** Macao's Return to China **Obv:** City arms **Rev:** Government House Building **Edge:** Segmented reeding

Date	Mintage	F	VF	XF	Unc	BU
1999	288,888	—	—	—	20.00	25.00

KM# 92 100 PATACAS
28.2800 g., 0.9250 Silver 0.8410 oz. ASW, 38.5 mm. **Subject:** Year of the Rabbit **Obv:** Building **Rev:** Rabbit **Edge:** Reeded

Date	Mintage	F	VF	XF	Unc	BU
1999 Proof	5,000	Value: 50.00				

KM# 127 1000 PATACAS
34.2540 g., 0.9999 Gold 1.1011 oz. AGW **Subject:** Macao returns to China **Obv:** Harbor view including Luso International Bank, Bank of China, Lisboa Hotel, two flags below **Obv. Leg.:** TERRITÓRIO DE MACAU **Rev:** Statue of Kun Iam at left of collage of historical sights, two flags below

Date	Mintage	F	VF	XF	Unc	BU
1999 Proof	1,999	Value: 2,500				

PROVAS
Standard metals

Stamped PROVA in field

KM#	Date	Mintage	Identification	Mkt Val
Pr1	1952	—	5 Avos.	20.00
Pr2	1952	—	10 Avos.	20.00
Pr3	1952	—	50 Avos.	25.00
Pr4	1952	—	Pataca.	28.00
Pr5	1952	—	5 Patacas.	32.00
Pr6	1967	—	5 Avos.	20.00
Pr7	1967	—	10 Avos.	20.00
Pr8	1968	—	10 Avos.	20.00
Pr9	1968	—	Pataca.	25.00
Pr10	1969	—	10 Avos.	10.00
Pr11	1971	—	5 Patacas.	25.00
Pr12	1972	—	50 Avos.	20.00
Pr13	1973	—	50 Avos.	20.00
Pr14	1974	—	20 Patacas.	35.00
Pr15	1975	—	Pataca.	25.00
Pr16	1988	1	10000 Patacas. 0.9990 Silver. KM#43.	—

MINT SETS

KM#	Date	Mintage	Identification	Issue Price	Mkt Val
MS1	1999 (7)	288,888	KM#111-117	23.00	95.00

PROOF SETS

KM#	Date	Mintage	Identification	Issue Price	Mkt Val
PS1	1982 (5)	2,000	KM#20a-24a	—	82.50
PS1b	1982 (5)	150	KM#20b-24b	—	1,185
PS1c	1982 (5)	375	KM#20c-24c	—	2,320
PS2	1983 (5)	2,500	KM#20a-24a	55.00	82.50
PS3	1984 (5)	2,500	KM#20a-24a	55.00	82.50
PS4	1985 (5)	2,500	KM#20a-24a	55.00	82.50
PS5	1987 (2)	—	KM#36-37	—	410
PS6	1988 (2)	—	KM#38-39	—	415
PS7	1991 (3)	2,500	KM#49-51	775	670
PS8	1992 (3)	2,500	KM#53-55	825	700
PS9	1993 (3)	2,500	KM#59-61	830	700
PS10	1994 (3)	2,500	KM#67-69	825	735
PS11	1995 (3)	2,500	KM#74-76	825	735
PS12	1997 (3)	2,500	KM#85-87	849	840
PS13	1998 (3)	2,500	KM#89-91	855	840
PS14	1999 (3)	2,500	KM#93-95	850	840
PS15	2000 (3)	2,500	KM#99-101	849	825

MACEDONIA

The Republic of Macedonia is land-locked, and is bordered in the north by Yugoslavia, to the east by Bulgaria, in the south by Greece and to the west by Albania and has an area of 9,781 sq. mi. (25,713 sq. km.) and a population at the 1991 census was 2,038,847, of which the predominating ethnic groups were Macedonians. The capital is Skopje.

The Slavs settled in Macedonia since the 6th century, who had been Christianized by Byzantium, were conquered by the non-Slav Bulgars in the 7th century and in the 9th century formed a Macedo-Bulgarian empire, the western part of which survived until Byzantine conquest in 1014. In the 14th century, it fell to Serbia, and in1355 to the Ottomans. After the Balkan Wars of 1912-13 Turkey was ousted, and Serbia received the greater part of the territory, the balance going to Bulgaria and Greece. In 1918, Yugoslav Macedonia was incorporated into Serbia as "South Serbia", becoming a republic in the S.F.R. of Yugoslavia. Claims to the historical Macedonian territory have long been a source of contention between Bulgaria and Greece.

On Nov. 20, 1991, parliament promulgated a new constitution, and declared its independence on Nov.20, 1992, but failed to secure EC and US recognition owing to Greek objections to the use of the name *Macedonia*. On Dec. 11, 1992, the UN Security Council authorized the expedition of a small peacekeeping force to prevent hostilities spreading into Macedonia.

There is a 120-member single-chamber National Assembly.

REPUBLIC

STANDARD COINAGE

KM# 1   50 DENI
4.0500 g., Brass, 21.5 mm. **Obv:** Seagull flying offshore **Rev:** Radiant value

Date	Mintage	F	VF	XF	Unc	BU
1993	11,051,000	—	0.10	0.30	0.60	1.50

KM# 2   DENAR
5.1500 g., Brass, 23.7 mm. **Obv:** Sheepdog **Obv. Leg.:** РЕПУБЛИКА МАКЕДОНИЈА **Rev:** Radiant value **Edge:** Plain

Date	Mintage	F	VF	XF	Unc	BU
1993	21,040,000	—	0.20	0.35	1.50	4.00
1997	11,200,000	—	0.20	0.35	1.50	4.00

KM# 5   DENAR
5.1500 g., Brass, 23.7 mm. **Series:** F.A.O. **Obv:** Sheep dog **Rev:** Value below F.A.O logo

Date	Mintage	F	VF	XF	Unc	BU
1995	2,314,000	—	—	—	2.00	4.00

KM# 5a   DENAR
Copper-Nickel-Zinc, 23.7 mm. **Series:** F.A.O. **Obv:** Sheep dog **Rev:** F.A.O. logo above value

Date	Mintage	F	VF	XF	Unc	BU
1995	1,001,000	—	—	—	2.50	4.50

KM# 8   DENAR
15.9800 g., 0.9167 Gold 0.4710 oz. AGW **Subject:** 5th Anniversary - UN Membership **Obv:** National emblem within circle **Rev:** Storks within circle

Date	Mintage	F	VF	XF	Unc	BU
ND(1996) Proof	1,100	Value: 485				

KM# 10   DENAR
8.0000 g., 0.9160 Gold 0.2356 oz. AGW, 23.3 mm. **Subject:** Macedonian Orthodox Church **Obv:** Half length figure of Saint facing **Rev:** Orthodox cathedral

Date	Mintage	F	VF	XF	Unc	BU
1997	5,000	—	—	—	—	245

KM# 27   DENAR
5.1000 g., Bronze, 23.8 mm. **Obv:** Byzantine copper folis coin design **Rev:** Radiant rising sun behind value **Edge:** Plain

Date	Mintage	F	VF	XF	Unc	BU
2000		—	—	—	13.00	17.00

Note: Mule of KM-9 obverse and KM-2 reverse?

KM# 9   DENAR
5.1000 g., Bronze, 23.8 mm. **Subject:** 2000 Years of Christianity **Obv:** Byzantine copper folis coin **Rev:** Ornamented cross **Edge:** Plain

Date	Mintage	F	VF	XF	Unc	BU
2000	2,000	—	—	—	12.00	15.00

KM# 9a   DENAR
7.0000 g., 0.9250 Silver 0.2082 oz. ASW, 23.8 mm. **Obv:** Byzantine copper folis coin **Rev:** Ornamented cross

Date	Mintage	F	VF	XF	Unc	BU
2000	2,000	—	—	—	—	180

KM# 9b   DENAR
8.0000 g., 0.9160 Gold 0.2356 oz. AGW, 23.8 mm. **Obv:** Byzantine copper folis coin **Rev:** Ornamented cross

Date	Mintage	F	VF	XF	Unc	BU
2000	2,000	—	—	—	200	250

KM# 3   2 DENARI
5.1500 g., Brass, 23.7 mm. **Obv:** Trout above water **Obv. Leg.:** РЕПУБЛИКА МАКЕДОНИЈА **Rev:** Radiant value **Edge:** Plain

Date	Mintage	F	VF	XF	Unc	BU
1993	8,998,000	—	0.25	0.50	1.25	3.00

KM# 6   2 DENARI
6.2500 g., Brass, 25.5 mm. **Series:** F.A.O. **Obv:** Trout above water **Rev:** Value below F.A.O logo

Date	Mintage	F	VF	XF	Unc	BU
1995	2,637,500	—	—	—	2.00	3.50

KM# 6a   2 DENARI
Copper-Nickel-Zinc, 25.5 mm. **Series:** F.A.O. **Obv:** Trout above water **Rev:** Value below F.A.O. logo

Date	Mintage	F	VF	XF	Unc	BU
1995	1,000,000	—	—	—	2.50	4.50

KM# 12   2 DENARI
7.0000 g., 0.9160 Gold 0.2061 oz. AGW, 23 mm. **Subject:** 50th Anniversary - Faculty of Economics **Obv:** Economics building **Rev:** Economics faculty logo

Date	Mintage	F	VF	XF	Unc	BU
2000	1,000	—	—	—	—	225

KM# 4   5 DENARI
7.2500 g., Brass, 27.5 mm. **Obv:** European lynx **Obv. Leg.:** РЕПУБЛИКА МАКЕДОНИЈА **Rev:** Radiant value **Edge:** Plain

Date	Mintage	F	VF	XF	Unc	BU
1993	12,330,000	—	0.35	0.75	1.75	3.50

KM# 7   5 DENARI
7.2500 g., Brass, 27.5 mm. **Series:** F.A.O. **Obv:** European lynx **Rev:** Value below F.A.O logo

Date	Mintage	F	VF	XF	Unc	BU
1995	3,123,000	—	—	—	2.00	3.50

KM# 7a   5 DENARI
Copper-Nickel-Zinc, 27.5 mm. **Series:** F.A.O. **Obv:** European lynx **Rev:** Value below F.A.O. logo

Date	Mintage	F	VF	XF	Unc	BU
1995	1,000,000	—	—	—	2.50	4.50

KM# 20   5 DENARI
7.9000 g., 0.9160 Gold 0.2326 oz. AGW, 23.8 mm. **Subject:** 60th Anniversary - First session of Parliament **Obv:** Logo of Association of Refugees from Aegean part of Macedonia **Rev:** Refugee mother with three children

Date	Mintage	F	VF	XF	Unc	BU
2000	1,500	—	—	—	200	240

KM# 11   10 DENARI
7.0000 g., 0.9160 Gold 0.2061 oz. AGW, 23 mm. **Subject:** Sts. Cyril and Methodus University **Obv:** Statue divides dates **Rev:** Macedonian Cyrillic alphabet

Date	Mintage	F	VF	XF	Unc	BU
1999	2,000	—	—	—	180	220

MINT SETS

KM#	Date	Mintage	Identification	Issue Price	Mkt Val
MS1	1993 (4)	—	KM1-4	—	7.50
MS2	1995 (3)	—	KM5a-7a	—	12.00

MADAGASCAR

ZAMBIA
ZIMBABWE
MOZAMBIQUE
SOUTH AFRICA
Indian Ocean

The Democratic Republic of Madagascar, an independent member of the French Community, located in the Indian Ocean 250 miles (402 km.) off the southeast coast of Africa, has an area of 226,656 sq. mi. (587,040 sq. km.) and a population of 10 million. Capital: Antananarivo. The economy is primarily agricultural; large bauxite deposits are being developed. Coffee, vanilla, graphite, and rice are exported.

Successive waves of immigrants from southeast Asia, Africa, Arabia and India populated Madagascar beginning about 2,000 years ago. Diago Diaz, a Portuguese navigator, sighted the island of Madagascar on Aug. 10, 1500, when his ship became separated from an India-bound fleet. Attempts at settlement by the British during the reign of Charles I and by the French during the 17th and 18th centuries were of no avail, and the island became a refuge and supply base for Indian Ocean pirates. Despite considerable influence on the island, the British accepted the imposition of a French protectorate in 1886 in return for French recognition of Britain's sphere of influence in Zanzibar. Madagascar was made a French colony in 1896 after absolute control had been established by military force. Britain occupied the island after the fall of France, 1942, to prevent its seizure by the Japanese, returning it to the Free French in 1943. On Oct. 14, 1958, following a decade of intermittent but bitter warfare, Madagascar, as the Malagasy Republic, became an autonomous state within the French Community. On June 27, 1960, it became a sovereign, independent nation, though remaining nominally within the French Community. The Malagasy Republic was renamed the Democratic Republic of Madagascar in 1975.

MONETARY SYSTEM
100 Centimes = 1 Franc

MINT MARKS
(a) - Paris, privy marks only
SA - Pretoria

FRENCH COLONY
STANDARD COINAGE

KM# 1   50 CENTIMES
Bronze   Obv: Rooster Rev: Cross of Lorraine

Date	Mintage	F	VF	XF	Unc	BU
1943SA	2,000,000	1.50	2.50	10.00	20.00	40.00

KM# 2   FRANC
Bronze   Obv: Rooster Rev: Cross of Lorraine

Date	Mintage	F	VF	XF	Unc	BU
1943SA	5,000,000	3.00	6.00	22.00	65.00	100

KM# 3   FRANC
1.3000 g., Aluminum, 23 mm.   Obv: Liberty bust left
Rev: Conjoined ox heads flanked by sprigs, value within horns

Date	Mintage	F	VF	XF	Unc	BU
1948(a)	7,400,000	0.25	0.35	0.75	2.75	3.50
1958(a)	2,600,000	0.25	0.35	0.75	2.75	3.50

KM# 4   2 FRANCS
Aluminum   Obv: Liberty bust left Rev: Conjoined ox heads flanked by sprigs, value within horns

Date	Mintage	F	VF	XF	Unc	BU
1948(a)	10,000,000	0.25	0.45	0.85	2.50	3.50

KM# 5   5 FRANCS
Aluminum   Obv: Liberty bust left Rev: Conjoined ox heads flanked by sprigs, value within horns

Date	Mintage	F	VF	XF	Unc	BU
1953(a)	30,012,000	0.25	0.55	1.00	3.00	5.00

KM# 6   10 FRANCS
Aluminum-Bronze, 20 mm.   Obv: Liberty bust left Rev: Value within horns flanked by cluster of sprigs with shaded area above value

Date	Mintage	F	VF	XF	Unc	BU
1953(a)	25,000,000	0.35	0.65	1.25	3.50	6.00

KM# 7   20 FRANCS
4.0000 g., Aluminum-Bronze   Obv: Liberty bust left Rev: Value within horns flanked by cluster of sprigs with shaded area above value

Date	Mintage	F	VF	XF	Unc	BU
1953(a)	15,000,000	0.75	1.50	3.00	6.50	9.00

TOKEN COINAGE

KM# Tn1   25 CENTIMES
Aluminum, 21 mm.   Issuer: Societe des Mines d'Or de Andavakoera.   Obv: Legend of issuer around value.
Rev: Parakeet head left.

Date	Mintage	VG	F	VF	XF	Unc
ND(1920)	—	10.00	20.00	50.00	150	340

KM# Tn2   50 CENTIMES
Aluminum, 28 mm.   Issuer: Societe des Mines d'Or de Andavakoera Note: Similar to KM#Tn1.

Date	Mintage	VG	F	VF	XF	Unc
ND(1920)	—	10.00	20.00	50.00	130	250

KM# Tn3   FRANC
Aluminum, 32 mm.   Issuer: Societe des Mines d'Or de Andavakoera Note: Similar to KM#Tn1.

Date	Mintage	VG	F	VF	XF	Unc
ND(1920)	—	9.00	18.00	35.00	100	210

MALAGASY REPUBLIC
STANDARD COINAGE

KM# 8   FRANC
2.4000 g., Stainless Steel   Obv: Poinsettia Rev: Value within horns of ox head above sprigs

Date	Mintage	F	VF	XF	Unc	BU
1965(a)	1,170,000	0.10	0.15	0.30	1.25	—
1966(a)	—	0.10	0.15	0.30	1.25	—
1970(a)	—	0.10	0.15	0.30	1.25	—
1974(a)	1,250,000	0.10	0.15	0.30	1.25	—
1975(a)	7,355,000	0.10	0.15	0.30	1.25	—
1976(a)	—	0.10	0.15	0.30	1.25	—
1977(a)	—	0.10	0.15	0.30	1.25	—
1979(a)	—	0.10	0.15	0.30	1.25	—
1980(a)	—	0.15	0.20	0.40	1.45	—
1981(a)	—	0.15	0.20	0.40	1.45	—
1982(a)	—	0.15	0.20	0.40	1.45	—
1983(a)	—	0.15	0.20	0.40	1.45	—
1986(a)	—	0.15	0.20	0.40	1.45	—
1987(a)	—	0.15	0.20	0.40	1.45	—
1988(a)	—	0.15	0.20	0.40	1.45	—
1989(a)	—	0.15	0.20	0.40	1.45	—
1991(a)	—	0.15	0.20	0.40	1.45	—
1993(a)	—	0.15	0.20	0.40	1.45	—

KM# 9   2 FRANCS
3.4000 g., Stainless Steel   Obv: Poinsettia Rev: Value within horns of ox head above sprigs

Date	Mintage	F	VF	XF	Unc	BU
1965(a)	760,000	0.15	0.25	0.50	1.50	—
1970(a)	—	0.15	0.25	0.45	1.25	—
1974(a)	1,250,000	0.15	0.25	0.45	1.25	—
1975(a)	8,250,000	0.15	0.25	0.45	1.25	—
1976(a)	—	0.15	0.25	0.45	1.25	—
1977(a)	—	0.15	0.25	0.45	1.25	—
1979(a)	—	0.15	0.25	0.45	1.25	—
1980(a)	—	0.15	0.25	0.45	1.25	—
1981(a)	—	0.15	0.25	0.45	1.25	—
1982(a)	—	0.15	0.25	0.45	1.25	—
1983(a)	—	0.15	0.25	0.45	1.25	—
1984(a)	—	0.15	0.25	0.45	1.25	—
1986(a)	—	0.15	0.25	0.45	1.25	—
1987(a)	—	0.15	0.25	0.45	1.25	—
1988(a)	—	0.15	0.25	0.45	1.25	—
1989(a)	—	0.15	0.25	0.45	1.25	—

KM# 10   5 FRANCS (Ariary)
5.0000 g., Stainless Steel   Obv: Poinsettia Rev: Value within horns of ox head above sprigs

Date	Mintage	F	VF	XF	Unc	BU
1966(a)	—	0.15	0.25	0.60	1.75	—
1967(a)	—	0.15	0.25	0.60	1.75	—
1968(a)	7,500,000	0.15	0.25	0.60	1.75	—
1970(a)	—	0.15	0.25	0.60	1.75	—
1972(a)	19,100,000	0.15	0.25	0.60	1.75	—
1976(a)	—	0.15	0.25	0.60	1.75	—
1977(a)	—	0.15	0.25	0.60	1.75	—
1979(a)	—	0.15	0.25	0.60	1.75	—
1980(a)	—	0.20	0.30	0.65	1.85	—
1981(a)	—	0.20	0.30	0.65	1.85	—
1982(a)	—	0.20	0.30	0.65	1.85	—
1983(a)	—	0.20	0.30	0.65	1.85	—
1984(a)	—	0.20	0.30	0.65	1.85	—
1986(a)	—	0.20	0.30	0.65	1.85	—
1987(a)	—	0.20	0.30	0.65	1.85	—
1988(a)	—	0.20	0.30	0.65	1.85	—
1989(a)	—	0.20	0.30	0.65	1.85	—

KM# 11   10 FRANCS (2 Ariary)
3.5000 g., Aluminum-Bronze   Series: F.A.O. Obv: Vanilla plant Rev: Value within horns of ox head flanked by sprigs and marks

Date	Mintage	F	VF	XF	Unc	BU
1970(a)	7,000,000	0.20	0.30	0.70	2.00	—
1971(a)	10,000,000	0.20	0.30	0.70	2.00	—
1972(a)	5,050,000	0.20	0.30	0.70	2.00	—
1973(a)	3,000,000	0.20	0.30	0.70	2.00	—
1974(a)	—	0.20	0.30	0.70	2.00	—
1975(a)	—	0.20	0.30	0.70	2.00	—
1976(a)	9,500,000	0.20	0.30	0.70	2.00	—
1977(a)	—	0.20	0.30	0.70	2.00	—
1978(a)	—	0.20	0.30	0.70	2.00	—
1979(a)	—	0.20	0.30	0.70	2.00	—
1980(a)	—	0.25	0.35	0.80	2.25	—

Date	Mintage	F	VF	XF	Unc	BU
1981(a)	—	0.25	0.35	0.80	2.25	—
1982(a)	—	0.25	0.35	0.80	2.25	—
1983(a)	—	0.25	0.35	0.80	2.25	—
1984(a)	—	0.25	0.35	0.80	2.25	—
1986(a)	—	0.25	0.35	0.80	2.25	—
1987(a)	3,200,000	0.25	0.35	0.80	2.25	—
1988(a)	—	0.25	0.35	0.80	2.25	—
1989(a)	—	0.25	0.35	0.80	2.25	—

Note: Struck by Royal Canadian Mint.

KM# 11a   10 FRANCS (2 Ariary)
Copper Plated Steel **Series:** F.A.O. **Obv:** Vanilla plant **Rev:** Value within horns of ox head flanked by sprigs (without other marks)

Date	Mintage	F	VF	XF	Unc	BU
1991	—	0.25	0.45	1,50	3.50	—

KM# 12   20 FRANCS (4 Ariary)
6.0000 g., Aluminum-Bronze **Series:** F.A.O. **Obv:** Cotton plant **Rev:** Value within horns of ox head above sprigs and marks

Date	Mintage	F	VF	XF	Unc	BU
1970(a)	4,000,000	0.25	0.35	0.75	2.50	—
1971(a)	2,000,000	0.25	0.35	0.75	2.50	—
1972(a)	2,000,000	0.30	0.40	0.80	2.75	—
1973(a)	3,000,000	0.30	0.40	0.80	2.75	—
1974(a)	—	0.30	0.40	0.80	2.75	—
1975(a)	—	0.30	0.40	0.80	2.75	—
1976(a)	2,700,000	0.30	0.40	0.80	2.75	—
1977(a)	—	0.30	0.40	0.80	2.75	—
1978(a)	—	0.30	0.40	0.80	2.75	—
1979(a)	—	0.30	0.40	0.80	2.75	—
1980(a)	—	0.35	0.45	0.85	3.00	—
1981(a)	—	0.35	0.45	0.85	3.00	—
1982(a)	—	0.35	0.45	0.85	3.00	—
1983(a)	—	0.35	0.45	0.85	3.00	—
1984(a)	—	0.35	0.45	0.85	3.00	—
1986(a)	—	0.35	0.45	0.85	3.00	—
1987(a)	5,200,000	0.35	0.45	0.85	3.00	—
1988(a)	—	0.35	0.45	0.85	3.00	—
1989(a)	—	0.35	0.45	0.85	3.00	—

Note: Struck by the Royal Canadian Mint

DEMOCRATIC REPUBLIC
NOTE: Reverse legends found on Malagasy Democratic Republic coinages.

A. - *Tanindrazana – Tolom – Piavotana – Fahafahana*; Fatherland – Revolution – Liberty

B. - *Tanindrazana – Fahafahana – Fahamarinana*; Fatherland – Liberty – Justice

C. - *Tanindrazana – Fahafahana – Fandrosoana*; Fatherland – Liberty - Progress

MONETARY SYSTEM
5 Francs = 1 Ariary
1 Ariary = 100 Iraimbilanja

STANDARD COINAGE

KM# 17   5 ARIARY
4.5000 g., Copper Plated Steel **Obv:** Star above value within 3/4 wreath **Rev:** Rice plant within circle **Rev. Leg.:** Motto A

Date	Mintage	F	VF	XF	Unc	BU
1992	—	0.65	1.25	2.25	4.00	—

KM# 13   10 ARIARY
Nickel **Series:** F.A.O. **Obv:** Star above value within 3/4 wreath **Rev:** Man cutting peat within circle **Rev. Leg.:** Motto A

Date	Mintage	F	VF	XF	Unc	BU
1978	8,001,000	1.50	2.75	5.00	10.00	—

KM# 13a   10 ARIARY
9.0000 g., 0.9250 Silver 0.2676 oz. ASW **Obv:** Star above value within 3/4 wreath **Rev:** Man cutting peat within circle **Rev. Leg.:** Motto A

Date	Mintage	F	VF	XF	Unc	BU
1978 Proof	3,800		Value: 20.00			

KM# 13b   10 ARIARY
Copper-Nickel **Obv:** Star above value within 3/4 wreath **Rev:** Man cutting peat within circle **Rev. Leg.:** Motto A

Date	Mintage	F	VF	XF	Unc	BU
1983	—	2.00	4.00	8.00	15.00	—

KM# 16   10 ARIARY
10.0000 g., 0.9170 Gold 0.2948 oz. AGW **Subject:** World Wildlife Fund **Obv:** Star above value within 3/4 wreath **Rev:** Ibis

Date	Mintage	F	VF	XF	Unc	BU
1988 Proof	Est. 5,000		Value: 300			

KM# 18   10 ARIARY
6.4700 g., Stainless Steel, 23.5 mm. **Obv:** Star above value within 3/4 wreath **Rev:** Man cutting peat within circle **Rev. Leg.:** Motto A

Date	Mintage	F	VF	XF	Unc	BU
1992	—	0.75	1.50	2.75	5.00	—

KM# 14   20 ARIARY
Nickel **Series:** F.A.O. **Obv:** Star above value within 3/4 wreath **Rev:** Farmer on tractor disking field **Rev. Leg.:** Motto A

Date	Mintage	F	VF	XF	Unc	BU
1978	8,001,000	2.00	4.00	8.00	16.50	—

KM# 14a   20 ARIARY
12.0000 g., 0.9250 Silver 0.3569 oz. ASW **Obv:** Star above value within 3/4 wreath **Rev:** Farmer on tractor disking field **Rev. Leg.:** Motto A

Date	Mintage	F	VF	XF	Unc	BU
1978 Proof	3,800		Value: 25.00			

KM# 14b   20 ARIARY
12.0000 g., Copper-Nickel **Obv:** Star above value within 3/4 wreath **Rev:** Man on tractor disking field **Rev. Leg.:** Motto A

Date	Mintage	F	VF	XF	Unc	BU
1983	—	2.50	4.50	9.00	17.50	—

KM# 15   20 ARIARY
19.4400 g., 0.9250 Silver 0.5781 oz. ASW **Subject:** World Wildlife Fund **Obv:** Star above value within 3/4 wreath **Rev:** Lemur

Date	Mintage	F	VF	XF	Unc	BU
1988 Proof	Est. 25,000		Value: 35.00			

KM# 19   20 ARIARY
Stainless Steel **Obv:** Star above value within 3/4 wreath **Rev:** Farmer on tractor disking field **Rev. Leg.:** Motto A

Date	Mintage	F	VF	XF	Unc	BU
1992	—	1.25	2.50	4.50	10.00	—

KM# 26   20 ARIARY
19.4400 g., 0.9250 Silver 0.5781 oz. ASW **Series:** UNICEF **Obv:** Star above value within 3/4 wreath **Rev:** Child and ring-tailed lemur in tree

Date	Mintage	F	VF	XF	Unc	BU
1996 Proof	—		Value: 32.50			

KM# 20   50 ARIARY
Stainless Steel **Obv:** Star above value within 3/4 wreath **Rev:** Avenue of Baobabs **Rev. Leg.:** Motto A

Date	Mintage	F	VF	XF	Unc	BU
1992	—	2.00	3.50	6.00	12.50	—

REPUBLIC
Madagasikara Republic
1 Ariary = 100 Iraimbilanja
STANDARD COINAGE

KM# 21 5 FRANCS (Ariary)
5.0000 g., Stainless Steel, 22 mm. **Obv:** Poinsettia **Rev:** Value within horns of ox head flanked by sprigs

Date	Mintage	F	VF	XF	Unc	BU
1996(a)	—	—	—	—	2.50	4.00

KM# 22 10 FRANCS (2 Ariary)
Copper Plated Steel, 21 mm. **Obv:** Vanilla plant **Rev:** Value within horns of ox head flanked by sprigs

Date	Mintage	F	VF	XF	Unc	BU
1996	—	—	—	—	3.00	5.00

KM# 23 5 ARIARY
4.7000 g., Copper Plated Steel, 24 mm. **Obv:** Star above value within 3/4 wreath **Rev:** Rice plant within circle **Rev. Leg.:** Motto B

Date	Mintage	F	VF	XF	Unc	BU
1994	—	—	—	—	2.50	4.00
1996	—	—	—	—	2.50	4.00

KM# 27 10 ARIARY
Stainless Steel **Issuer:** F.A.O. **Obv:** Star above value within 3/4 wreath **Rev:** Man cutting peat **Rev. Leg.:** Motto C **Edge:** Plain

Date	Mintage	F	VF	XF	Unc	BU
1999	—	—	—	—	4.50	6.50

KM# 24.1 20 ARIARY
Nickel Clad Steel, 28 mm. **Issuer:** F.A.O. **Obv:** Star above value within 3/4 wreath **Rev:** Farmer on tractor disking field **Rev. Leg.:** Motto B

Date	Mintage	F	VF	XF	Unc	BU
1994	—	—	—	—	6.50	9.00

KM# 24.2 20 ARIARY
Nickel Clad Steel, 28 mm. **Obv:** Star above value within 3/4 wreath **Rev:** Man on tractor disking field **Rev. Leg.:** Motto C

Date	Mintage	F	VF	XF	Unc	BU
1999	—	—	—	—	6.50	9.00

KM# 25.1 50 ARIARY
Stainless Steel, 30.63 mm. **Obv:** Star above value within sprays **Rev:** Avenue of Baobabs **Rev. Insc.:** Motto B **Edge:** Plain

Date	Mintage	F	VF	XF	Unc	BU
1994	—	—	—	—	8.00	12.00
1996	—	—	—	—	8.00	12.00

ESSAIS
Standard metals unless otherwise noted

KM#	Date	Mintage	Identification	Issue Price	Mkt Val
E1	1948(a)	2,000	Franc. Copper-Nickel. KM3.	—	25.00
E2	1948	2,000	2 Francs. Copper-Nickel. KM4.	—	25.00
E3	1953(a)	1,200	5 Francs. Aluminum. KM5.	—	20.00
E4	1953(a)	1,200	10 Francs. Aluminum-Bronze. KM6.	—	20.00
E5	1953(a)	1,200	20 Francs. Aluminum-Bronze. KM7.	—	20.00
E6	1965(a)	—	Franc. Stainless Steel. KM8.	—	12.00
E7	1965(a)	—	2 Francs. Stainless Steel. KM9.	—	12.00
E8	1966(a)	—	5 Francs. Stainless Steel. KM10.	—	12.00
E9	1970(a)	—	10 Francs. Aluminum-Bronze. KM11.	—	12.00
E10	1970(a)	—	20 Francs. Aluminum-Bronze. KM12.	—	12.00

PIEFORTS WITH ESSAI
Double thickness; Standard metals unless otherwise noted

KM#	Date	Mintage	Identification	Issue Price	Mkt Val
PE1	1948(a)	104	Franc. Aluminum. KM3.	—	75.00
PE2	1948(a)	104	2 Francs. Aluminum. KM4.	—	85.00
PE3	1953(a)	104	5 Francs. Aluminum. KM5.	—	90.00
PE4	1953(a)	104	10 Francs. Aluminum-Bronze. KM6.	—	65.00
PE5	1953(a)	104	20 Francs. KM7.	—	70.00

"FDC" SETS

KM#	Date	Mintage	Identification	Issue Price	Mkt Val
SS1	1970 (5)	1,500	KM8-12	2.75	11.50

PROOF SETS

KM#	Date	Mintage	Identification	Issue Price	Mkt Val
PS1	1978 (2)	3,800	KM#13a, 14a	38.00	45.00

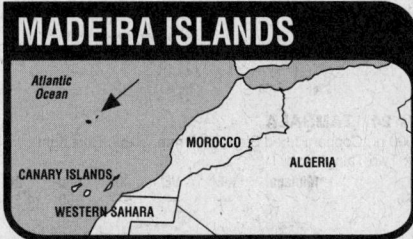

MADEIRA ISLANDS

The Madeira Islands, which belong to Portugal, are located 360 miles (492 km.) off the northwest coast of Africa. They have an area of 307 sq. mi. (795 sq. km.). The group consists of two inhabited islands named Madeira and Porto Santo and two groups of uninhabited rocks named Desertas and Selvagens. Capital: Funchal. The two staple products are wine and sugar. Bananas and pineapples are also produced for export.

Although the evidence is insufficient, it is thought that the Phoenicians visited Madeira at an early period. It is also probable that the entire archipelago was explored by Genoese adventurers; an Italian map dated 1351 shows the Madeira Islands quite clearly. The Portuguese navigator Goncalvez Zarco first sighted Porto Santo in 1418, having been driven there by a storm while he was exploring the coast of West Africa. Madeira itself was discovered in 1420. The islands were uninhabited when visited by Zarco, but soon after 1418 Madeira was quickly colonized by Prince Henry the Navigator, aided by the knights of the Order of Christ. British troops occupied the islands in 1801, and again in 1807-14.

RULER
Portuguese

PORTUGUESE COLONY
MODERN COINAGE

KM# 4 25 ESCUDOS
11.0000 g., Copper-Nickel, 28.5 mm. **Subject:** Autonomy of Madeira **Obv:** Shields above value **Rev:** Head facing

Date	Mintage	F	VF	XF	Unc	BU
1981	750,000	—	—	—	6.00	9.00

KM# 4a 25 ESCUDOS
11.0000 g., 0.9250 Silver 0.3271 oz. ASW, 28.5 mm. **Subject:** Autonomy of Madeira **Obv:** Shields above value **Rev:** Head facing

Date	Mintage	F	VF	XF	Unc	BU
1981 Proof	20,000	Value: 17.50				

KM# 5 100 ESCUDOS
Copper-Nickel, 33.8 mm. **Subject:** Autonomy of Madeira **Obv:** Shields above value **Rev:** Head facing

Date	Mintage	F	VF	XF	Unc	BU
1981	250,000	—	—	—	12.00	15.00

KM# 5a 100 ESCUDOS
16.5000 g., 0.9250 Silver 0.4907 oz. ASW, 33.8 mm. **Subject:** Autonomy of Madeira **Obv:** Shields above value **Rev:** Head facing

Date	Mintage	F	VF	XF	Unc	BU
1981 Proof	20,000	Value: 25.00				

PROVAS

KM#	Date	Mintage	Identification	Mkt Val
Pr1	1981	—	25 Escudos. Copper-Nickel. KM4.	30.00
Pr2	1981	—	100 Escudos. Copper-Nickel. KM5.	40.00

PROOF SETS

KM#	Date	Mintage	Identification	Issue Price	Mkt Val
PS1	1981 (2)	20,000	KM4a-5a	42.00	42.50

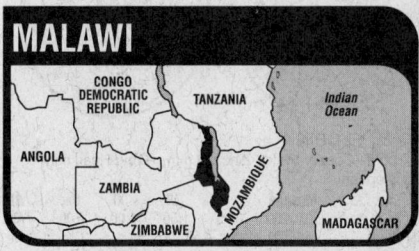

MALAWI

The Republic of Malawi (formerly Nyasaland), located in southeastern Africa to the west of Lake Malawi (Nyasa), has an area of 45,745 sq. mi. (118,480 sq. km.) and a population of 7 million. Capital: Lilongwe. The economy is predominantly agricultural. Tobacco, tea, peanuts and cotton are exported.

Although the Portuguese were the first Europeans to reach the Malawi area, the first meaningful contact was made by missionary-explorer Dr. David Livingstone. He arrived at Lake Malawi on Sept. 16, 1859, and remained to make extensive explorations in the 1860's. Subsequent clashes between settlements of Scottish missionaries and Arab slave traders, and the procurement of development rights by Cecil Rhodes, 1884, stimulated British interest and brought about the establishment of the Nyasaland protectorate in 1891. In 1953 Nyasaland reluctantly joined the Federation of Rhodesia and Nyasaland and, after prolonged protest, was granted self-government within the federation. Nyasaland became the independent nation of Malawi on July 6, 1964, and became a republic two years later. Malawi is a member of the Commonwealth of Nations. The president is the Chief of State and Head of Government.

NOTE: For earlier coinage see Rhodesia and Nyasaland.

MONETARY SYSTEM
12 Pence = 1 Shilling
2 Shillings = 1 Florin
5 Shillings = 1 Crown
20 Shillings = 1 Pound

REPUBLIC
STERLING COINAGE

KM# 6   PENNY
Bronze **Obv:** Malawi written above date and value **Rev:** Written and numeral value above designs

Date	Mintage	F	VF	XF	Unc	BU
1967	6,000,000	0.35	0.65	1.25	2.50	—
1968	3,600,000	3.00	6.00	12.00	25.00	—

KM# 1   6 PENCE
2.7900 g., Copper-Nickel-Zinc **Obv:** Head right **Rev:** Rooster

Date	Mintage	F	VF	XF	Unc	BU
1964	14,800,000	0.25	0.50	1.00	2.50	4.00
1964 Proof	10,000	Value: 1.50				
1967	6,000,000	0.50	1.00	2.50	5.00	6.50

KM# 2   SHILLING
5.3700 g., Copper-Nickel-Zinc, 23.5 mm. **Obv:** Head right **Rev:** Bundled corncobs

Date	Mintage	F	VF	XF	Unc	BU
1964	11,900,000	0.35	0.65	1.25	2.50	3.50
1964 Proof	10,000	Value: 1.50				
1968	3,000,000	0.75	1.50	3.00	5.50	7.00

KM# 3   FLORIN
11.3100 g., Copper-Nickel-Zinc, 28 mm. **Obv:** Head right **Rev:** Elephants

Date	Mintage	F	VF	XF	Unc	BU
1964	6,500,000	0.75	1.50	3.00	6.00	7.00
1964 Proof	10,000	Value: 4.50				

KM# 4   1/2 CROWN
Copper-Nickel-Zinc **Obv:** Head right **Rev:** Arms with supporters

Date	Mintage	F	VF	XF	Unc	BU
1964	6,400,000	1.00	2.00	4.00	6.00	—
1964 Proof	10,000	Value: 4.50				

KM# 5   CROWN
Nickel-Brass **Subject:** Day of the Republic - July 6, 1966 **Obv:** Head right **Rev:** Arms with supporters

Date	Mintage	F	VF	XF	Unc	BU
1966 Proof	20,000				Value: 7.50	

DECIMAL COINAGE
100 Tambala = 1 Kwacha

KM# 7.1   TAMBALA
1.7600 g., Bronze, 17 mm. **Obv:** Head right **Rev:** Rooster

Date	Mintage	F	VF	XF	Unc	BU
1971	15,000,000	0.15	0.20	0.40	0.75	1.50
1971 Proof	4,000	Value: 1.00				
1973	5,000,000	0.15	0.20	0.40	0.75	1.50
1974	12,500,000	0.15	0.20	0.40	0.75	1.50

KM# 7.2   TAMBALA
1.7800 g., Bronze, 17 mm. **Obv:** Head right with accent mark above "W" in MALAWI **Rev:** Rooster

Date	Mintage	F	VF	XF	Unc	BU
1975	10,000,000	0.15	0.20	0.40	0.75	1.50
1977	10,000,000	0.15	0.20	0.40	0.75	1.50
1979	15,000,000	0.15	0.20	0.40	0.75	1.50
1982	15,000,000	0.15	0.20	0.40	0.75	1.50

KM# 7.2a   TAMBALA
1.8000 g., Copper Plated Steel **Obv:** Head right **Rev:** Rooster divides value and date

Date	Mintage	F	VF	XF	Unc	BU
1984	201,000	0.20	0.30	0.50	0.80	1.50
1985 Proof	10,000	Value: 3.00				
1987	—	0.20	0.30	0.50	0.80	1.50
1989	—	0.20	0.30	0.50	0.80	1.50
1991	—	0.20	0.30	0.50	0.80	1.50
1994	—	0.20	0.30	0.50	0.80	1.50

KM# 24   TAMBALA
1.8000 g., Copper Plated Steel, 17.2 mm. **Obv:** Bust right **Rev:** Two Talapia fish

Date	Mintage	F	VF	XF	Unc	BU
1995	—	—	—	—	1.00	1.50

KM# 33   TAMBALA
1.6800 g., Bronze, 17.3 mm. **Obv:** Arms with supporters **Rev:** Two Talapia fish **Edge:** Plain

Date	Mintage	F	VF	XF	Unc	BU
1995	—	—	—	—	1.00	1.50

KM# 8.1   2 TAMBALA
Bronze **Obv:** Head right **Rev:** Paradise whydah bird divides date and value

Date	Mintage	F	VF	XF	Unc	BU
1971	10,000,000	0.25	0.40	0.75	1.50	2.00
1971 Proof	4,000	Value: 1.75				
1973	5,000,000	0.25	0.40	0.75	1.50	2.00
1974	5,000,000	0.25	0.40	0.75	1.50	2.00

KM# 8.2   2 TAMBALA
3.6000 g., Bronze **Obv:** Head right with accent mark above "W" in MALAWI **Rev:** Paradise whydah bird divides date and value

Date	Mintage	F	VF	XF	Unc	BU
1975	5,000,000	0.25	0.40	0.75	1.50	2.00
1977	5,000,000	0.25	0.40	0.75	1.50	2.00
1979	7,637,000	0.25	0.40	0.75	1.50	2.00
1982	15,000,000	0.25	0.40	0.75	1.50	2.00

KM# 8.2a   2 TAMBALA
3.4600 g., Copper Plated Steel **Obv:** Head right **Rev:** Paradise whydah bird divides date and value

Date	Mintage	F	VF	XF	Unc	BU
1984	150,000	0.30	0.50	0.85	2.00	—
1985 Proof	10,000	Value: 4.00				
1987	—	0.30	0.50	0.85	2.00	—
1989	—	0.30	0.50	0.85	2.00	—
1991	—	0.30	0.50	0.85	1.75	—
1994	—	0.30	0.50	0.85	1.75	—

KM# 25   2 TAMBALA
3.5000 g., Copper Plated Steel, 20.3 mm. **Obv:** Bust right **Rev:** Paradise whydah bird divides date and value

Date	Mintage	F	VF	XF	Unc	BU
1995	—	—	—	—	1.00	1.50

KM# 34   2 TAMBALA
3.5000 g., Bronze, 20.3 mm. **Obv:** Arms with supporters **Rev:** Paradise whydah bird divides date and value **Edge:** Plain

Date	Mintage	F	VF	XF	Unc	BU
1995	—	—	—	—	1.00	1.50

KM# 9.1   5 TAMBALA
2.8600 g., Copper-Nickel **Obv:** Head right **Rev:** Purple heron and value

Date	Mintage	F	VF	XF	Unc	BU
1971	7,000,000	0.25	0.45	0.85	1.75	2.00
1971 Proof	4,000	Value: 2.00				

KM# 9.2   5 TAMBALA
Copper-Nickel **Obv:** Head right with accent mark above "W" in MALAWI **Rev:** Purple heron and value

Date	Mintage	F	VF	XF	Unc	BU
1985 Proof	10,000	Value: 5.00				

KM# 9.2a   5 TAMBALA
2.8000 g., Nickel Clad Steel, 19.35 mm. **Obv:** Head right **Rev:** Purple heron and value

Date	Mintage	F	VF	XF	Unc	BU
1989	—	0.30	0.50	0.85	2.00	3.00
1994	—	0.30	0.50	0.85	2.00	3.00

KM# 26   5 TAMBALA
2.8300 g., Nickel Plated Steel, 19.35 mm. **Obv:** Bust right **Rev:** Purple heron and value

Date	Mintage	F	VF	XF	Unc	BU
1995	—	—	—	—	1.50	3.00

KM# 32.1   5 TAMBALA
Nickel Plated Steel, 19.35 mm. **Obv:** Arms with supporters **Rev:** Purple heron and value

Date	Mintage	F	VF	XF	Unc	BU
1995	—	—	—	—	2.50	3.00

KM# 10.1 10 TAMBALA
Copper-Nickel, 23.6 mm. **Obv:** Head right **Rev:** Bundled corncob divides date and value

Date	Mintage	F	VF	XF	Unc	BU
1971	4,000,000	0.30	0.50	1.00	2.25	3.00
1971 Proof	4,000	Value: 2.50				

KM# 10.2 10 TAMBALA
Copper-Nickel, 23.6 mm. **Obv:** Head right **Rev:** Bundled corncobs divide date and value

Date	Mintage	F	VF	XF	Unc	BU
1985 Proof	10,000	Value: 6.00				
1989	—	0.40	0.80	1.50	2.75	3.50

KM# 10.2a 10 TAMBALA
Nickel Clad Steel, 23.6 mm. **Obv:** Head right **Rev:** Bundled cobs of corn divide value and date

Date	Mintage	F	VF	XF	Unc	BU
1989	—	0.40	0.80	1.50	2.75	—

KM# 27 10 TAMBALA
5.6200 g., Nickel Plated Steel, 23.6 mm. **Obv:** Bust right **Rev:** Bundled corncobs divide date and value

Date	Mintage	F	VF	XF	Unc	BU
1995	—	—	—	—	2.25	3.00

KM# 11.1 20 TAMBALA
10.9700 g., Copper-Nickel, 26.5 mm. **Obv:** Head right **Rev:** Elephants

Date	Mintage	F	VF	XF	Unc	BU
1971	3,000,000	0.75	1.50	2.50	4.00	—
1971 Proof	4,000	Value: 5.00				

KM# 11.2 20 TAMBALA
Copper-Nickel, 26.5 mm. **Obv:** Head right with accent mark above "W" in MALAWI **Rev:** Elephants

Date	Mintage	F	VF	XF	Unc	BU
1985 Proof	10,000	Value: 7.00				

KM# 11.2a 20 TAMBALA
11.3300 g., Nickel Clad Steel, 26.5 mm. **Obv:** Head right **Rev:** Elephants

Date	Mintage	F	VF	XF	Unc	BU
1989	—	0.60	1.20	2.25	4.00	—
1994	—	0.60	1.20	2.25	4.00	—

KM# 29 20 TAMBALA
7.5200 g., Nickel Clad Steel, 26.5 mm. **Obv:** Bust right **Rev:** Elephants

Date	Mintage	F	VF	XF	Unc	BU
1996	—	—	—	—	3.75	4.50

KM# 19 50 TAMBALA
11.3500 g., Copper-Nickel-Zinc, 30 mm. **Obv:** Head right **Rev:** Arms with supporters **Note:** The 1989 date for this coin does not exist.

Date	Mintage	F	VF	XF	Unc	BU
1986	—	2.00	3.00	5.00	10.00	—
1994	—	2.00	3.00	5.00	10.00	—

KM# 30 50 TAMBALA
4.4000 g., Brass Plated Steel, 22 mm. **Obv:** Bust right **Rev:** Arms with supporters

Date	Mintage	F	VF	XF	Unc	BU
1996	—	—	—	—	4.50	5.00

KM# 12 KWACHA
Copper-Nickel **Subject:** Decimalization of coinage **Obv:** Head right **Rev:** Arms with supporters **Edge:** DECIMAL CURRENCY INTRODUCED FEBRUARY 15TH, 1971

Date	Mintage	F	VF	XF	Unc	BU
1971	20,000	1.00	2.00	3.50	6.00	—
1971 Proof	4,000	Value: 6.50				

KM# 20 KWACHA
8.8000 g., Nickel-Brass, 26 mm. **Obv:** Head right **Rev:** Rooster

Date	Mintage	F	VF	XF	Unc	BU
1992	—	1.00	2.00	3.00	5.50	8.00

KM# 28 KWACHA
9.0000 g., Brass Plated Steel, 26 mm. **Obv:** Bust right **Rev:** Fish eagle

Date	Mintage	F	VF	XF	Unc	BU
1996	—	—	—	—	7.00	10.00

KM# 15 5 KWACHA
28.2800 g., 0.9250 Silver 0.8410 oz. ASW **Subject:** Conservation **Obv:** Head right **Rev:** Zebras running right

Date	Mintage	F	VF	XF	Unc	BU
1978	4,048	—	—	—	25.00	—
1978 Proof	3,622	Value: 35.00				

KM# 23 5 KWACHA
Copper-Nickel **Subject:** United Nations 50th Anniversary **Obv:** Bust right **Rev:** Child reading and UN logo

Date	Mintage	F	VF	XF	Unc	BU
ND(1995)	—	—	—	—	8.50	10.00

KM# 23a 5 KWACHA
28.2800 g., 0.9250 Silver 0.8410 oz. ASW **Subject:** United Nations 50th Anniversary **Obv:** Bust right **Rev:** Child reading and UN logo

Date	Mintage	F	VF	XF	Unc	BU
ND(1995) Proof	—	Value: 32.50				

KM# 40 5 KWACHA
20.3000 g., 0.9250 Silver 0.6037 oz. ASW, 34 mm. **Obv:** Arms with supporters **Rev:** Elephant **Edge:** Reeded

Date	Mintage	F	VF	XF	Unc	BU
1997 Proof	—	Value: 27.50				

KM# 41 5 KWACHA
28.5000 g., 0.9250 Silver 0.8475 oz. ASW, 38.5 mm. **Subject:** Queen's Golden Wedding Anniversary **Obv:** Arms with supporters **Rev:** Child giving flowers to Queen above gold plated arms with supporters **Edge:** Reeded

Date	Mintage	F	VF	XF	Unc	BU
1997 Proof	—	Value: 45.00				

KM# 13 10 KWACHA
28.2800 g., 0.9250 Silver 0.8410 oz. ASW **Subject:** 10th Anniversary of Independence **Obv:** Head right **Rev:** Arms with supporters above value within chain links

Date	Mintage	F	VF	XF	Unc	BU
1974	7,556	—	—	—	17.50	20.00
1974 Proof	4,937	Value: 22.50				

KM# 14 10 KWACHA
28.2800 g., 0.9250 Silver 0.8410 oz. ASW **Subject:** 10th Anniversary of the Reserve Bank **Obv:** Head right **Rev:** Eagle with wings spread above lined design and value

Date	Mintage	F	VF	XF	Unc	BU
ND(1975)	6,870	—	—	—	17.50	20.00
ND(1975) Proof	Inc. above	Value: 22.50				

KM# 14a 10 KWACHA
0.9000 Gold Subject: 10th Anniversary of the Reserve Bank
Obv: Head right Rev: Eagle with wings spread above lined design
and value

Date	Mintage	F	VF	XF	Unc	BU
ND(1975)	—	—	—	—	1,250	—

KM# 16 10 KWACHA
35.0000 g., 0.9250 Silver 1.0408 oz. ASW Series: Conservation
Obv: Head right Rev: Sable antelope

Date	Mintage	F	VF	XF	Unc	BU
1978	4,009	—	—	—	22.00	27.50
1978 Proof	3,416	Value: 35.00				

KM# 18 10 KWACHA
28.2800 g., 0.9250 Silver 0.8410 oz. ASW Subject: 20th
Anniversary - Reserve Bank Obv: Head right Rev: Eagle with
wings spread above lined design and value

Date	Mintage	F	VF	XF	Unc	BU
ND(1985) Proof	4,000	Value: 22.50				

KM# 18a 10 KWACHA
47.5400 g., 0.9170 Gold 1.4015 oz. AGW Subject: 20th
Anniversary - Reserve Bank Obv: Head right Rev: Eagle with
wings spread above lined design and value

Date	Mintage	F	VF	XF	Unc	BU
ND(1985) Proof	50	Value: 1,650				

KM# 21 10 KWACHA
28.2800 g., 0.9250 Silver 0.8410 oz. ASW Series: Save the
Children Subject: Fishing Obv: Head right Rev: Children
carrying fish, fishermen and sailboat in background

Date	Mintage	F	VF	XF	Unc	BU
1992 Proof	20,000	Value: 35.00				

KM# 38 10 KWACHA
20.0000 g., 0.9250 Silver 0.5948 oz. ASW, 34 mm.
Subject: Olympics Obv: Arms with supporters Rev: Two runners
Edge: Reeded

Date	Mintage	F	VF	XF	Unc	BU
1999 Proof	—	Value: 35.00				

KM# 22 20 KWACHA
10.0000 g., 0.9170 Gold 0.2948 oz. AGW Series: Save the
Children Subject: Mother and children Obv: Head right
Rev: Mother and child facing left, buildings and athletic players
in background

Date	Mintage	F	VF	XF	Unc	BU
1992 Proof	Est. 3,000	Value: 325				

KM# 35 20 KWACHA
31.4000 g., 0.9250 Silver 0.9338 oz. ASW, 38.6 mm.
Series: Endangered Wildlife Subject: "The Romans" Obv: Arms
with supporters Rev: Female elephant with two calves in water
Edge: Reeded

Date	Mintage	F	VF	XF	Unc	BU
1996 Proof	—	Value: 45.00				

KM# 36 20 KWACHA
31.5500 g., 0.9250 Silver 0.9382 oz. ASW, 38.6 mm.
Subject: Queen Mother Obv: Arms with supporters Rev: Queen
Mother and two girl scouts within beaded circle Edge: Reeded

Date	Mintage	F	VF	XF	Unc	BU
1997 Proof	—	Value: 45.00				

KM# 37 20 KWACHA
31.4300 g., 0.9250 Silver 0.9347 oz. ASW, 38.5 mm.
Subject: British Queen Mother Obv: Arms with supporters
Rev: Edward VIII making his abdication speech Edge: Reeded

Date	Mintage	F	VF	XF	Unc	BU
1998 Proof	—	Value: 50.00				

KM# 31 20 KWACHA
31.5300 g., 0.9250 Silver 0.9376 oz. ASW Subject: Millennium
Obv: Head right Rev: Year 2000 flanked by seated figures below
trees all below ears of corn within vines

Date	Mintage	F	VF	XF	Unc	BU
1999 Proof	—	Value: 40.00				

KM# 17 250 KWACHA
33.4370 g., 0.9000 Gold 0.9675 oz. AGW Series: Conservation
Subject: Nyala Obv: Head right Rev: Nyala (deer)

Date	Mintage	F	VF	XF	Unc	BU
1978	566	—	—	—	—	950
1978 Proof	208	Value: 1,000				

PATTERNS
Including off metal strikes

KM#	Date	Mintage	Identification	Mkt Val
Pn1	1999	—	20 Kwacha. Silver Plated. 31.3300 g. 38.7 mm. National arms. Olympic relay runners. Reeded edge.	70.00

MINT SETS

KM#	Date	Mintage	Identification	Issue Price	Mkt Val
MS1	1971 (6)	10,000	KM7.1-11.1, 12	3.30	16.50
MS2	1978 (2)	—	KM15, 16	—	40.00

PROOF SETS

KM#	Date	Mintage	Identification	Issue Price	Mkt Val
PS1	1964 (4)	10,000	KM1-4	10.00	10.00
PS2	1971 (6)	4,000	KM7.1-11.1, 12	8.70	18.50
PS3	1978 (2)	—	KM15, 16	—	70.00
PS4	1985 (5)	10,000	KM7.2a-8.2a, 9.2-11.2	30.00	25.00

MALAY PENINSULA

KELANTAN

A state in northern Malaysia, colonized by the Javanese in
1300's. It was subject to Thailand from 1780 to 1909.

TITLE

كلنتن

Khalifa(t) Al-Mu'minin

MINT

خليفة المؤمنين

Kelantan

SULTAN
Muhammed IV, 1902-1919

SULTANATE
STANDARD COINAGE

KM# 12   PITIS
Tin, 24-29 mm.   **Ruler:** Muhammed IV **Obv:** Arabic legend
Obv. Leg.: Belanjaan Negri Kelantan Adama Mulkahu
Rev: Arabic legend **Rev. Leg.:** Duriba Fi Dhul Hijja Sanat 1321

Date	Mintage	VG	F	VF	XF	Unc
AH1321 (1903)	—	8.00	12.00	20.00	40.00	—

KM# 15   PITIS
Tin   **Ruler:** Muhammed IV **Obv:** Arabic legend
Obv. Leg.: Belanjaan Kerajaan Kelan Tan **Rev:** Arabic legend
Rev. Leg.: Duriba Fi Dhul Hijja Sanat 1321

Date	Mintage	VG	F	VF	XF	Unc
AH1321 (1903)	—	2.00	3.00	5.00	15.00	30.00

KM# 18   KEPING
Tin   **Ruler:** Muhammed IV **Obv:** Arabic legend **Obv. Leg.:** Negri
Kelantan Satu Keping **Rev:** Uninscribed, but obverse legend
shows through in negative form

Date	Mintage	VG	F	VF	XF	Unc
AH1323 (1905)	—	15.00	25.00	40.00	70.00	—

KM# 20   10 KEPINGS
Tin   **Ruler:** Muhammed IV **Obv:** Arabic legend
Obv. Leg.: Belanjaan Kerajaan Kelantin Sepuloh Keping
Rev: Border of diamonds around Arabic legend **Rev. Leg.:** Sunia
Fi Dhul Hijja Sanat 1321

Date	Mintage	VG	F	VF	XF	Unc
AH1321 (1903)	—	6.00	12.00	30.00	50.00	—

TRENGGANU

A state in eastern Malaysia on the shore of the south China
Sea. Area of dispute between Malacca and Thailand with the latter
emerging with possession. Trengganu became a British dependency in 1909.

TITLE

Khalifa(t) al-Mu'minin

MINT

ترغكانو

Trengganu

SULTANS
Zainal Abidin III, 1881-1918
Muhammed, 1918-1920
Sulaiman, 1920-1942

SULTANATE
STANDARD COINAGE

KM# 17   1/4 CENT
Tin   **Ruler:** Zainal Abidin III **Obv:** Legend within circle **Rev:** Value
within circle **Note:** Similar to 1/2 Cent, KM#16.

Date	Mintage	F	VF	XF	Unc	BU
AH1325 (1907) Rare	—	—	—	—	—	—

KM# 16   1/2 CENT
Tin, 22 mm.   **Ruler:** Zainal Abidin III **Obv:** Legend within circle
Rev: Value within circle and wreath **Note:** Recast.

Date	Mintage	VG	F	VF	XF	Unc
AH1322 (1904)	—	3.00	6.00	10.00	20.00	—

KM# 18   1/2 CENT
Tin, 22 mm.   **Ruler:** Zainal Abidin III **Obv:** Legend within circle
flanked by stars **Rev:** Value within circle and wreath
Note: Recast. Originals are rare.

Date	Mintage	VG	F	VF	XF	Unc
AH1325 (1907)	—	3.00	6.00	10.00	20.00	—

KM# 19   CENT
Tin, 29 mm.   **Ruler:** Zainal Abidin III **Obv:** Legend within beaded
circle flanked by stars **Rev:** Value within beaded circle and wreath

Date	Mintage	VG	F	VF	XF	Unc
AH1325 (1907)	—	5.00	9.00	16.00	45.00	—

KM# 20   CENT
Tin, 29 mm.   **Ruler:** Zainal Abidin III **Obv:** Legend within beaded
circle flanked by stars **Rev:** Value flanked by stars within diamond
shape within beaded circle and wreath **Note:** Although dated
AH1325 (1907), this coin was actually struck in 1920 under Sultan
Sulaiman. Authorized mintage was 1 million. Beware of thin lead
counterfeits.

Date	Mintage	VG	F	VF	XF	Unc
AH1325 (1907)	—	5.00	9.00	16.00	45.00	—

MALAYA

Malaya, a former member of the British Commonwealth located
in the southern part of the Malay peninsula, consisted of 11 states:
the un-federated Malay states of Johore, Kelantan, Kedah, Perlis
and Trengganu; the federated Malay states of Negri-Sembilan, Pahang, Perakand Selangor; former members of the Straits Settlements
Penang and Malacca. Malaya was occupied by the Japanese during
the years 1942-1945. The only local opposition to the Japanese had
come mainly from the Chinese Communists who then continued
their guerilla operations after the war, finally being defeated in 1956.
Malaya was granted full independence on Aug. 31, 1957, and
became part of Malaysia in 1963.

RULER
British

MINT MARKS
I - Calcutta Mint (1941)
I - Bombay Mint (1945)
No Mint mark - Royal Mint

MONETARY SYSTEM
100 Cents = 1 Dollar

BRITISH COLONY
STANDARD COINAGE
100 Cents = 1 Dollar

KM# 1   1/2 CENT
Bronze   **Obv:** Crowned head of King George VI left **Rev:** Value
within beaded circle **Note:** 18 mm x 18 mm.

Date	Mintage	F	VF	XF	Unc	BU
1940	6,000,000	3.00	8.00	13.00	25.00	—
1940 Proof	—	Value: 800				

KM# 2   CENT
5.8200 g., Bronze, 21 mm.   **Obv:** Crowned head of King George
VI left **Rev:** Value within beaded circle

Date	Mintage	F	VF	XF	Unc	BU
1939	20,000,000	0.25	0.60	0.80	2.50	5.00
1939 Proof	—	Value: 800				
1940	23,600,000	0.25	0.60	0.80	2.50	5.00
1940 Proof	—	Value: 800				
1941 I	33,620,000	1.00	2.50	12.00	30.00	50.00

KM# 6   CENT
4.3000 g., Bronze, 20 mm.   **Obv:** Crowned head of King George
VI left **Rev:** Value within beaded circle **Note:** Reduced size.

Date	Mintage	F	VF	XF	Unc	BU
1943	50,000,000	0.25	0.50	1.00	2.50	5.00
1943 Proof	—	Value: 500				
1945	40,033,000	0.25	0.50	1.00	2.50	5.00
1945 Proof	—	Value: 380				

KM# 3 5 CENTS
1.3600 g., 0.7500 Silver 0.0328 oz. ASW **Obv:** Crowned head of King George VI left **Rev:** Value within beaded circle

Date	Mintage	F	VF	XF	Unc	BU
1939	2,000,000	0.60	1.00	2.25	6.00	10.00
1939 Proof	—	Value: 750				
1941	4,000,000	0.50	0.80	2.00	3.00	7.00
1941 Proof	—	Value: 750				
1941 I	Inc. above	0.50	0.80	2.00	4.00	8.00

KM# 3a 5 CENTS
1.3600 g., 0.5000 Silver 0.0219 oz. ASW **Obv:** Crowned head of King George VI left **Rev:** Value within beaded circle

Date	Mintage	F	VF	XF	Unc	BU
1943	10,000,000	0.50	0.80	1.50	3.50	7.00
1943 Proof	—	Value: 750				
1945	8,800,000	0.50	0.80	1.50	3.50	7.00
1945 I	4,600,000	0.80	1.50	3.00	5.00	10.00

KM# 7 5 CENTS
1.3900 g., Copper-Nickel **Obv:** Crowned head of King George VI left **Rev:** Value within beaded circle

Date	Mintage	F	VF	XF	Unc	BU
1948	30,000,000	0.10	0.25	1.25	4.00	—
1948 Proof	—	Value: 750				
1950	40,000,000	0.10	0.25	1.25	4.00	—

KM# 4 10 CENTS
2.7100 g., 0.7500 Silver 0.0653 oz. ASW, 18 mm. **Obv:** Crowned head of King George VI left **Rev:** Value within beaded circle

Date	Mintage	F	VF	XF	Unc	BU
1939	10,000,000	1.50	2.50	3.00	5.00	9.00
1939 Proof	—	Value: 750				
1941	17,000,000	1.50	2.50	3.00	5.00	9.00
1941 Proof	—	Value: 750				
1941 I	—	—	—	3,000	4,000	

KM# 4a 10 CENTS
2.7100 g., 0.5000 Silver 0.0436 oz. ASW **Obv:** Crowned head of King George VI left **Rev:** Value within beaded circle

Date	Mintage	F	VF	XF	Unc	BU
1943	5,000,000	1.30	2.20	3.00	5.00	9.00
1943 Proof	—	Value: 750				
1945	3,152,000	1.30	2.20	5.00	10.00	20.00
1945 I	—	—	—	3,000	4,000	

KM# 8 10 CENTS
2.8500 g., Copper-Nickel, 19.5 mm. **Obv:** Crowned head of George VI left **Rev:** Value within beaded circle

Date	Mintage	F	VF	XF	Unc	BU
1948	23,885,000	0.15	0.30	1.40	6.00	—
1948 Proof	—	Value: 750				
1949	26,115,000	0.25	0.50	1.75	10.00	—
1950	65,000,000	0.15	0.30	1.25	6.00	—
1950 Proof	—	Value: 750				

KM# 5 20 CENTS
5.4300 g., 0.7500 Silver 0.1309 oz. ASW **Obv:** Crowned head of King George VI left **Rev:** Value within beaded circle

Date	Mintage	F	VF	XF	Unc	BU
1939	8,000,000	3.00	5.00	8.00	15.00	20.00
1939 Proof	—	Value: 750				

KM# 5a 20 CENTS
5.4300 g., 0.5000 Silver 0.0873 oz. ASW **Obv:** Crowned head of King George VI left **Rev:** Value within beaded circle

Date	Mintage	F	VF	XF	Unc	BU
1943	5,000,000	2.00	3.50	5.00	10.00	15.00
1943 Proof	—	Value: 750				
1945	10,000,000	3.00	9.00	15.00	25.00	35.00
1945 I	—	—	—	3,000	4,000	

KM# 9 20 CENTS
5.6900 g., Copper-Nickel, 23.4 mm. **Obv:** Crowned head of King George VI left **Rev:** Value within beaded circle

Date	Mintage	F	VF	XF	Unc	BU
1948	40,000,000	0.35	0.75	1.75	10.00	
1948 Proof	—	Value: 660				
1950	20,000,000	0.35	0.75	1.75	10.00	
1950 Proof	—	Value: 750				

MALAYA & BRITISH BORNEO

South China Sea · PHILIPPINES · MALAYSIA · BRUNEI · MALAYSIA · SINGAPORE · Indian Ocean · INDONESIA

Malaya & British Borneo, a Currency Commission named the Board of Commissioners of Currency, Malaya and British Borneo, was initiated on Jan. 1, 1952, for the purpose of providing a common currency for use in Johore, Kelantan, Kedah, Perlis, Trengganu, Negri Sembilan, Pahang, Perak, Selangor, Penang, Malacca, Singapore, North Borneo, Sarawak and Brunei.

RULER
British

MINT MARKS
KN - King's Norton, Birmingham
H - Heaton, Birmingham
No Mint mark - Royal Mint

MONETARY SYSTEM
100 Cents = 1 Dollar

BRITISH COLONY

STANDARD COINAGE
100 Cents = 1 Dollar

KM# 5 CENT
4.2700 g., Bronze **Obv:** Crowned bust of Queen Elizabeth II right **Rev:** Value within beaded circle

Date	Mintage	F	VF	XF	Unc	BU
1956	6,250,000	—	0.10	0.45	3.00	4.00
1956 Proof	—	Value: 750				
1957	12,500,000	—	0.10	0.45	3.00	4.00
1958	5,000,000	—	0.10	0.45	3.00	4.00
1958 Proof	—	Value: 750				
1961	10,000,000	—	0.10	0.45	3.00	4.00
1961 Proof	—	Value: 750				

KM# 6 CENT
1.9600 g., Bronze, 18 mm. **Obv:** Value **Rev:** Crossed encased swords

Date	Mintage	F	VF	XF	Unc	BU
1962	45,000,000			0.35	2.00	3.00
1962 Proof	Est. 25	Value: 400				

KM# 1 5 CENTS
1.4200 g., Copper-Nickel, 16 mm. **Obv:** Crowned bust of Queen Elizabeth II right **Rev:** Value within beaded circle

Date	Mintage	F	VF	XF	Unc	BU
1953	20,000,000	—	0.75	3.00	9.00	—
1953 Proof	—	Value: 750				
1957	10,000,000	—	0.75	3.00	11.00	—
1957H	10,000,000	—	0.75	3.00	11.00	—
1957H Proof	—	Value: 750				
1957KN	Inc. above	—	2.00	6.00	20.00	—
1958	10,000,000	—	1.00	3.00	9.00	—
1958 Proof	—	Value: 750				
1958H	10,000,000	—	1.25	3.00	9.00	—
1961	90,000,000	—	BV	2.00	4.00	—
1961 Proof	—	Value: 750				
1961H	5,000,000	—	2.00	10.00	30.00	—
1961KN	Inc. above	—	1.50	8.00	15.00	—

KM# 2 10 CENTS
2.9000 g., Copper-Nickel, 19.5 mm. **Obv:** Crowned bust of Queen Elizabeth II right **Rev:** Value within beaded circle

Date	Mintage	F	VF	XF	Unc	BU
1953	20,000,000	—	0.75	3.00	6.00	—
1953 Proof	—	Value: 750				
1956	10,000,000	—	0.75	3.00	6.00	—
1956 Proof	—	Value: 750				
1957H	10,000,000	—	0.75	3.00	6.00	—
1957H Proof	—	Value: 750				
1957KN	10,000,000	—	1.00	3.00	6.50	—
1958	10,000,000	—	1.00	3.00	6.50	—
1960	10,000,000	—	0.75	2.00	6.00	—
1960 Proof	—	Value: 750				
1961	60,784,000	—	0.40	1.00	4.00	—
1961 Proof	—	Value: 750				
1961H	69,220,000	—	0.40	1.00	4.00	—
1961KN	Inc. above	—	1.00	3.50	6.50	—

KM# 2a 10 CENTS
Silver, 19.5 mm. **Obv:** Crowned bust right **Rev:** Value within beaded circle **Note:** as KM#2

Date	Mintage	F	VF	XF	Unc	BU
1953 Proof	—	Value: 2,200				

KM# 3 20 CENTS
5.6800 g., Copper-Nickel, 23.51 mm. **Obv:** Crowned bust of Queen Elizabeth II right **Rev:** Value within beaded circle

Date	Mintage	F	VF	XF	Unc	BU
1954	10,000,000	—	1.25	4.00	9.00	—
1954 Proof	—	Value: 750				
1956	5,000,000	—	1.00	4.00	9.00	—
1956 Proof	—	Value: 750				
1957H	2,500,000	—	1.50	6.00	12.00	—
1957H Proof	—	Value: 700				
1957KN	2,500,000	—	1.50	6.00	12.00	—
1961	32,000,000	—	0.75	2.00	6.00	—
1961 Proof	—	Value: 750				
1961H	23,000,000	—	0.75	2.00	6.00	—

KM# 3a 20 CENTS
Silver **Obv:** Crowned bust right **Rev:** Value within beaded circle **Note:** as KM#3

Date	Mintage	F	VF	XF	Unc	BU
1954 Proof	—	Value: 9,000				

KM# 4.1 50 CENTS

9.3800 g., Copper-Nickel **Obv:** Crowned bust of Queen Elizabeth II right **Rev:** Value within beaded circle **Edge:** Security

Date	Mintage	F	VF	XF	Unc	BU
1954	8,000,000	—	2.00	6.00	16.00	—
1954 Proof	—	Value: 950				
1955H	4,000,000	—	2.00	6.50	22.00	—
1956	3,440,000	—	2.00	6.50	22.00	—
1956 Proof	—	Value: 950				
1957H	2,000,000	—	2.50	6.50	22.00	—
1957H Proof	—	Value: 950				
1957KN	2,000,000	—	3.00	8.00	25.00	—
1958H	4,000,000	—	1.50	5.00	15.00	—
1961	17,000,000	—	1.50	5.00	15.00	—
1961 Proof	—	Value: 950				
1961H	4,000,000	—	2.00	6.00	20.00	—
1961H Proof	—	Value: 950				

KM# 4.2 50 CENTS

Copper-Nickel **Obv:** Crowned bust of Queen Elizabeth II right **Rev:** Value within beaded circle **Note:** Error, without security edge.

Date	Mintage	F	VF	XF	Unc	BU
1954	Inc. above	—	200	400	800	—
1957KN	Inc. above	—	200	400	800	—
1958H	Inc. above	—	200	400	800	—
1961	Inc. above	—	200	400	800	—
1961H	Inc. above	—	200	400	800	—

MALAYSIA

The independent limited constitutional monarchy of Malaysia, which occupies the southern part of the Malay Peninsula in Southeast Asia and the northern part of the island of Borneo, has an area of 127,316 sq. mi. (329,750 sq. km.) and a population of 15.4 million. Capital: Kuala Lumpur. The economy is based on agriculture, mining and forestry. Rubber, tin, timber and palm oil are exported.

Malaysia came into being on Sept. 16, 1963, as a federation of Malaya (Johore, Kelantan, Kedah, Perlis, Trengganu, Negri Sembilan, Pahang, Perak, Selangor, Penang, Malacca), Singapore, Sabah (British North Borneo) and Sarawak. Following two serious racial riots involving Malays and Chinese, Singapore withdrew from the federation on Aug. 9, 1965. Malaysia is a member of the Commonwealth of Nations.

MINT MARK
FM - Franklin Mint, U.S.A.
***NOTE:** From 1975-1985 the Franklin Mint produced coinage in up to 3 different qualities. Qualities of issue are designated in ( ) after each date and are defined as follows:

(M) MATTE - Normal circulation strike or a dull finish produced by sandblasting special uncirculated (polish finish) or proof quality dies.

(U) SPECIAL UNCIRCULATED - Polished or prooflike in appearance without any frosted features.

(P) PROOF - The highest quality obtainable having mirror-like fields and frosted features.

MONETARY SYSTEM
100 Sen = 1 Ringgit (Dollar)

CONSTITUTIONAL MONARCHY

STANDARD COINAGE
100 Sen = 1 Ringgit (Dollar)

KM# 1 SEN

1.9500 g., Bronze **Obv:** Value **Rev:** Parliament house
Note: Varieties exist.

Date	Mintage	F	VF	XF	Unc	BU
1967	45,000,000	—	—	0.50	3.00	4.00
1967 Proof	500	Value: 15.00				

Date	Mintage	F	VF	XF	Unc	BU
1968	10,500,000	—	—	2.00	6.00	8.00
1970	2,535,000	—	—	2.00	15.00	20.00
1971	47,862,000	—	—	0.45	2.00	3.00
1973	21,400,000	—	—	0.25	1.00	1.50
1976	100	—	40.00	100	300	350
1980FM (P)	5,000	Value: 1.50				
1981FM (P)	6,628	Value: 1.50				

KM# 1a SEN

1.7200 g., Copper-Clad Steel, 17.69 mm. **Obv:** Value **Rev:** Parliament house

Date	Mintage	F	VF	XF	Unc	BU
1973	Inc. above	—	—	0.65	2.00	2.50
1976	27,406,000	—	—	0.25	1.00	1.50
1977	21,751,000	—	—	0.25	0.50	0.65
1978	30,844,000	—	—	0.25	0.50	0.65
1979	15,714,000	—	—	0.25	0.50	0.65
1980	16,152,000	—	—	0.25	0.50	0.65
1981	24,633,000	—	—	0.25	0.50	0.65
1982	37,295,000	—	—	0.25	0.50	0.65
1983	19,333,000	—	—	0.45	0.75	0.90
1984	26,267,000	—	—	0.45	0.75	0.90
1985	52,402,000	—	—	0.25	0.50	0.65
1986	48,920,000	—	—	0.25	0.50	0.65
1987	35,284,000	—	—	0.25	0.50	0.65
1988	56,749,000	—	—	0.25	0.50	0.65

KM# 49 SEN

1.8000 g., Bronze Clad Steel, 17.66 mm. **Obv:** Value divides date below flower blossom **Obv. Leg.:** BANK NEGARA MALAYSIA **Rev:** Drum **Edge:** Plain

Date	Mintage	F	VF	XF	Unc	BU
1989	28,429,000	—	—	—	0.25	0.35
1990	102,539,000	—	—	—	0.15	0.25
1991	100,314,734	—	—	—	0.15	0.25
1992	122,824,000	—	—	—	0.15	0.25
1993	153,805,875	—	—	—	0.15	0.25
1994	185,085,000	—	—	—	0.15	0.25
1995	208,611,295	—	—	—	0.15	0.25
1996	183,272,598	—	—	—	0.15	0.25
1997	172,215,681	—	—	—	0.15	0.25
1998	1,917,633,834	—	—	—	0.15	0.25
1999	265,502,565	—	—	—	0.15	0.25
2000	268,762,170	—	—	—	0.15	0.25

KM# 49a SEN

0.9250 g., Silver **Obv:** Value divides date below flower blossom **Rev:** Drum

Date	Mintage	F	VF	XF	Unc	BU
1992 Proof	—	Value: 10.00				

KM# 2 5 SEN

1.4200 g., Copper-Nickel **Obv:** Value **Rev:** Parliament house
Note: Varieties exist.

Date	Mintage	F	VF	XF	Unc	BU
1967	75,464,000	—	—	0.25	0.50	1.00
1967 Proof	500	Value: 25.00				
1968	74,536,000	—	—	0.25	0.50	1.00
1971	16,658,000	—	—	0.45	0.75	1.20
1973	102,942,000	—	—	0.25	0.50	1.00
1976	65,659,000	—	—	0.25	0.50	1.00
1977	10,609,000	—	—	0.30	0.60	1.20
1978	50,044,000	—	—	0.25	0.50	1.00
1979	38,824,000	—	—	0.25	0.50	1.00
1980	33,893,000	—	—	0.25	0.50	1.00
1980FM (P)	6,628	Value: 2.00				
1981	51,490,000	—	—	0.25	0.50	1.00
1981FM (P)	—	Value: 3.00				
1982	118,594,000	—	—	0.25	0.50	1.00
1985	15,553,000	—	—	0.25	0.50	0.65
1987	17,723,000	—	—	0.25	0.50	0.65
1988	26,788,000	—	—	0.25	0.50	0.65

KM# 50 5 SEN

1.4000 g., Copper-Nickel, 16.28 mm. **Obv:** Value divides date below flower blossom **Obv. Leg.:** BANK NEGARA MALAYSIA **Rev:** Top with string **Edge:** Reeded

Date	Mintage	F	VF	XF	Unc	BU
1989	20,484,000	—	—	—	0.20	0.30
1990	58,909,000	—	—	—	0.20	0.30
1991	46,092,000	—	—	—	0.20	0.30
1992	67,844,000	—	—	—	0.20	0.30

Date	Mintage	F	VF	XF	Unc	BU
1993	70,703,000	—	—	—	0.20	0.30
1994	83,026,000	—	—	—	0.20	0.30
1995	53,069,000	—	—	—	0.15	0.25
1996	51,812,529	—	—	—	0.15	0.25
1997	7,703,850	—	—	—	0.15	0.25
1998	1,293,910,233	—	—	—	0.15	0.25
1999	79,224,000	—	—	—	0.15	0.25
2000	61,198,528	—	—	—	0.15	0.25

KM# 50a 5 SEN

0.9250 g., Silver, 16.3 mm. **Obv:** Value divides date below flower blossom **Rev:** Top with string

Date	Mintage	F	VF	XF	Unc	BU
1992 Proof	—	Value: 10.00				

KM# 3 10 SEN

2.8200 g., Copper-Nickel, 19.3 mm. **Obv:** Value **Rev:** Parliament house **Note:** Varieties exist.

Date	Mintage	F	VF	XF	Unc	BU
1967	106,708,000	—	0.25	0.45	1.30	1.80
1967 Proof	500	Value: 35.00				
1968	128,292,000	—	0.25	0.45	1.10	1.50
1971	42,000	—	30.00	50.00	80.00	90.00
1973	214,832,000	—	0.10	0.30	1.00	1.30
1976	148,841,000	—	0.10	0.30	1.00	1.30
1977	52,720,000	—	0.10	0.30	1.00	1.30
1978	21,162,000	—	0.10	0.30	0.75	1.10
1979	50,633,000	—	0.10	0.25	0.60	1.10
1980	51,797,000	—	0.10	0.25	0.60	1.10
1980FM (P)	6,628	Value: 3.00				
1981	236,639,000	—	0.10	0.25	0.60	1.00
1981FM (P)	—	Value: 4.00				
1982	145,639,000	—	—	0.25	0.60	1.00
1983	30,832,000	—	—	0.25	0.60	1.00
1988	17,852,000	—	—	0.25	0.60	1.00

KM# 51 10 SEN

2.8200 g., Copper-Nickel, 19.43 mm. **Obv:** Value divides date below flower blossom **Obv. Leg.:** BANK NEGARA MALAYSIA **Rev:** Ceremonial table **Edge:** Reeded

Date	Mintage	F	VF	XF	Unc	BU
1989	32,392,000	—	—	—	0.25	0.40
1990	132,982,000	—	—	—	0.25	0.40
1991	133,293,000	—	—	—	0.25	0.40
1992	89,919,000	—	—	—	0.25	0.40
1993	44,224,000	—	—	—	0.25	0.40
1994	7,122,000	—	—	—	0.30	0.50
1995	82,217,000	—	—	—	0.25	0.40
1996	77,347,125	—	—	—	0.25	0.40
1997	78,955,862	—	—	—	0.25	0.40
1998	1,966,056,746	—	—	—	0.25	0.40
1999	163,080,000	—	—	—	0.25	0.40
2000	162,940,000	—	—	—	0.25	0.40

KM# 51a 10 SEN

0.9250 g., Silver, 19.3 mm. **Obv:** Value divides date below flower blossom **Rev:** Ceremonial table

Date	Mintage	F	VF	XF	Unc	BU
1992 Proof	—	Value: 10.00				

KM# 4 20 SEN

Copper-Nickel, 23.4 mm. **Obv:** Value **Rev:** Parliament house **Note:** Varieties exist.

Date	Mintage	F	VF	XF	Unc	BU
1967	49,560,000	—	0.25	1.00	3.00	5.00
1967 Proof	500	Value: 45.00				
1968	40,440,000	—	0.25	1.00	3.00	5.00
1969	15,000,000	—	0.25	1.00	3.00	5.00
1970	1,054,000	—	0.60	1.50	5.00	9.00
1971	9,958,000	—	0.25	0.50	2.00	3.50
1973	116,075,000	—	0.25	0.50	2.00	3.00
1976	47,396,000	—	0.25	0.50	2.00	3.00
1977	66,139,000	—	0.25	0.50	2.00	3.00
1978	6,847,000	—	0.25	0.50	2.00	3.00
1979	17,346,000	—	0.25	0.50	2.00	3.00
1980	32,837,000	—	0.15	0.30	2.00	3.00
1980FM (P)	6,628	Value: 4.00				

Date	Mintage	F	VF	XF	Unc	BU
1981	144,128,000	—	0.15	0.30	1.50	2.00
1981FM (P)	—	Value: 5.00				
1982	97,905,000	—	—	0.25	1.50	2.00
1983	8,105,000	—	—	0.25	1.50	2.00
1987	26,225,000	—	—	0.25	1.50	2.00
1988	67,218,000	—	—	0.25	1.50	2.00

KM# 52   20 SEN
5.6900 g., Copper-Nickel, 23.57 mm. **Obv:** Value divides date below flower blossom **Obv. Leg.:** BANK NEGARA MALAYSIA **Rev:** Basket with food and utensils **Edge:** Reeded

Date	Mintage	F	VF	XF	Unc	BU
1989	28,945,000	—	—	—	0.35	0.50
1990	56,249,000	—	—	—	0.35	0.50
1991	82,774,000	—	—	—	0.35	0.50
1992	48,975,000	—	—	—	0.35	0.50
1993	55,753,000	—	—	—	0.35	0.50
1994	2,680,000	—	—	—	0.35	0.50
1997	78,479,804	—	—	—	0.35	0.50
1998	1,161,791,361	—	—	—	0.35	0.50
2000	63,908,000	—	—	—	0.35	0.50

KM# 52a   20 SEN
0.9250 g., Silver And Enamel, 23.5 mm. **Obv:** Value divides date below flower blossom **Rev:** Basket with food and utensils

Date	Mintage	F	VF	XF	Unc	BU
1992 Proof	—	Value: 12.50				

KM# 5.1   50 SEN
Copper-Nickel, 27.8 mm. **Obv:** Value **Rev:** Parliament house

Date	Mintage	F	VF	XF	Unc	BU
1967	15,000,000	—	0.35	0.75	5.00	7.00
1967 Proof	500	Value: 55.00				
1968	12,000,000	—	0.35	0.75	5.00	7.00
1969	2,000,000	—	0.75	7.00	30.00	50.00

KM# 5.2   50 SEN
Copper-Nickel, 27.8 mm. **Obv:** Value **Rev:** Parliament house **Note:** Error, no security edge.

Date	Mintage	F	VF	XF	Unc	BU
1967	Inc. above	—	100	200	300	500
1968	Inc. above	—	100	200	300	500
1969	Inc. above	—	450	600	900	1,000

KM# 5.3   50 SEN
9.3000 g., Copper-Nickel, 27.8 mm. **Obv:** Value **Rev:** Parliament house **Edge:** MALAYSIA BANK NEGARA (repeated)

Date	Mintage	F	VF	XF	Unc	BU
1971	8,404,000	—	0.30	1.00	4.00	6.00
1973	50,135,000	—	0.25	1.00	4.00	6.00
1977	17,720,000	—	0.25	0.60	4.00	6.00
1978	11,033,000	—	0.25	0.60	4.00	6.00
1979	5,361,000	—	0.25	0.60	4.00	6.00
1980	15,911,000	—	0.25	0.50	2.00	3.50
1980FM Proof	6,628	Value: 4.50				
1981	22,969,000	—	—	0.35	2.00	3.50
1982	20,585,000	—	—	0.35	2.00	3.50
1983	11,560,000	—	—	0.35	2.00	3.50
1984	10,139,000	—	—	0.35	2.00	3.50
1985	7,115,000	—	—	0.35	2.00	3.50
1986	8,193,000	—	—	0.35	2.00	3.50
1987	7,696,000	—	—	0.35	2.00	3.00
1988	26,788,000	—	—	0.35	2.00	3.00

KM# 5.4   50 SEN
Copper-Nickel, 27.8 mm. **Obv:** Value **Rev:** Parliament house **Edge:** Plain

Date	Mintage	F	VF	XF	Unc	BU
1981FM (P)	—	Value: 12.00				

KM# 53   50 SEN
9.2800 g., Copper-Nickel, 27.78 mm. **Obv:** Value divides date below flower blossom **Obv. Leg.:** BANK NEGARA MALAYSIA **Rev:** Ceremonial kite **Edge:** Lettered **Edge:** BANK NEGARA MALAYSIA (twice)

Date	Mintage	F	VF	XF	Unc	BU
1989	6,639,057	—	—	—	0.65	0.85
1990	26,276,464	—	—	—	0.65	0.85
1991	20,720,531	—	—	—	0.65	0.85
1992	15,134,992	—	—	—	0.65	0.85
1993	7,657,991	—	—	—	0.65	0.85
1994	6,565,914	—	—	—	0.65	0.85
1995	1,650,423	—	—	—	0.65	0.85
1996	7,475,790	—	—	—	0.65	0.85
1997	16,143,327	—	—	—	0.65	0.85
1998	401,622,135	—	—	—	0.65	0.85
1999	12,085,000	—	—	—	0.65	0.85
2000	48,206,000	—	—	—	0.65	0.85

KM# 53a   50 SEN
0.9250 g., Silver, 28 mm. **Obv:** Value divides date below flower blossom **Rev:** Ceremonial kite

Date	Mintage	F	VF	XF	Unc	BU
1992 Proof	—	Value: 15.00				

KM# 7   RINGGIT
Copper-Nickel, 33.5 mm. **Subject:** 10th Anniversary - Bank Negara **Obv:** Artistic value and dollar sign within 3/4 flower wreath **Rev:** Bust with headdress left

Date	Mintage	F	VF	XF	Unc	BU
ND(1969)	1,000,000	—	1.20	2.00	6.00	8.00

KM# 7a   RINGGIT
19.9200 g., 0.9250 Silver 0.5924 oz. ASW, 33.5 mm. **Obv:** Artistic value and dollar sign within 3/4 flower wreath **Rev:** Bust with headdress left

Date	Mintage	F	VF	XF	Unc	BU
ND(1969) Proof	1,000	Value: 600				

KM# 9.1   RINGGIT
Copper-Nickel, 33.5 mm. **Obv:** Artistic value and dollar sign above date **Rev:** Parliament house within cresent **Edge:** BANK NEGARA MALAYSIA

Date	Mintage	F	VF	XF	Unc	BU
1971	2,000,000	—	0.50	0.75	2.00	—
1971 Proof	500	Value: 950				
1980	472,000	—	0.60	0.85	2.00	—
1980FM (P)	6,628	Value: 8.00				
1981	765,000	—	0.60	0.85	2.00	—
1982	202,000	—	0.60	0.85	2.00	—
1984	355,000	—	0.60	0.85	2.00	—
1985	302,000	—	0.60	0.85	2.00	—
1986	253,000	—	0.60	0.85	2.00	—

KM# 9.2   RINGGIT
Copper-Nickel, 33.5 mm. **Obv:** Artistic value and dollar sign above value **Rev:** Parliament house within cresent **Edge:** Plain

Date	Mintage	F	VF	XF	Unc	BU
1981FM (P)	—	Value: 22.00				

KM# 12   RINGGIT
Copper-Nickel, 33.5 mm. **Subject:** Kuala Lumpur Anniversary **Obv:** Artistic value and dollar sign above date **Rev:** Artistic design **Edge:** MALAYSIA BANK NEGARA **Note:** Issued in 1973.

Date	Mintage	F	VF	XF	Unc	BU
1972	500,000	—	0.60	1.00	5.00	—
1972 Proof	500	Value: 500				

KM# 13   RINGGIT
Copper-Nickel, 33.5 mm. **Subject:** 25th Anniversary - Employee Provident Fund **Obv:** Value **Rev:** Two upper circles among assorted heads

Date	Mintage	F	VF	XF	Unc	BU
1976FM (U)	500,000	—	0.60	1.00	5.00	—
1976FM (P)	7,810	Value: 28.00				

KM# 16   RINGGIT
Copper-Nickel, 33 mm. **Subject:** 3rd Malaysian 5-Year Plan **Obv:** Arms with supporters **Rev:** Head with headdress facing within circle and block-like artistic design

Date	Mintage	F	VF	XF	Unc	BU
ND(1976)	1,000,000	—	0.60	0.75	4.00	—
ND(1976)FM (P)	17,000	Value: 20.00				

KM# 22   RINGGIT
Copper-Nickel, 33.5 mm. **Subject:** 9th Southeast Asian Games **Obv:** Arms with supporters **Rev:** Kite flyer **Edge:** MALAYSIA BANK NEGARA

Date	Mintage	F	VF	XF	Unc	BU
1977	1,000,000	—	0.60	0.75	4.00	—
1977FM (P)	11,000	Value: 30.00				

KM# 25 RINGGIT
Copper-Nickel, 33.5 mm. **Subject:** 20th Anniversary of Independence **Obv:** Head facing **Rev:** Arms with supporters

Date	Mintage	F	VF	XF	Unc	BU
ND(1977)	500,000	—	0.75	1.00	5.00	
ND(1977)FM (P)	3,100	Value: 50.00				

KM# 26 RINGGIT
Copper-Nickel, 33.5 mm. **Subject:** 100th Anniversary of Natural Rubber Production **Obv:** Value and dollar sign above dates **Rev:** Artistic design with a pair of hands **Edge:** MALAYSIA BANK NEGARA

Date	Mintage	F	VF	XF	Unc	BU
ND(1977)	500,000	—	0.60	0.75	4.00	

KM# 27 RINGGIT
Copper-Nickel, 33.5 mm. **Subject:** 20th Anniversary of Bank Negara **Obv:** Value **Rev:** Building above dates

Date	Mintage	F	VF	XF	Unc	BU
ND(1979)	300,000	—	0.60	0.75	4.00	

KM# 27a RINGGIT
17.0000 g., 0.9250 Silver 0.5055 oz. ASW, 33.5 mm. **Obv:** Value **Rev:** Building above dates

Date	Mintage	F	VF	XF	Unc	BU
ND(1979) Proof	8,000	Value: 40.00				
ND(1979)FM (P)	6,628	Value: 35.00				

KM# 28 RINGGIT
Copper-Nickel, 33.5 mm. **Subject:** 15th Century of Hejira **Obv:** Value, date **Rev:** Design within spider web **Edge:** MALAYSIA BANK NEGARA

Date	Mintage	F	VF	XF	Unc	BU
AH1401(1981)	500,000	—	0.60	0.75	4.00	

KM# 29 RINGGIT
Copper-Nickel, 33.5 mm. **Subject:** 4th Malaysian Plan **Obv:** Arms with supporters **Rev:** Bust with headdress facing 1/4 right **Edge:** MALAYSIA BANK NEGARA **Note:** Tun Hussein Onn

Date	Mintage	F	VF	XF	Unc	BU
ND(1981)	1,000,000	—	0.50	0.65	4.00	
ND(1981) Proof	10,000	Value: 20.00				

KM# 32 RINGGIT
Copper-Nickel, 33.5 mm. **Subject:** 25th Anniversary of Independence **Obv:** Star design and bust with headdress with left arm raised facing right **Rev:** Arms with supporters

Date	Mintage	F	VF	XF	Unc	BU
ND(1982)	1,500,000	—	0.50	0.65	4.00	
ND(1982) Proof	15,000	Value: 20.00				

KM# 36 RINGGIT
Copper-Nickel, 33.5 mm. **Subject:** 5th Malaysian 5-Year Plan **Obv:** Arms with supporters with value and dollar sign below **Rev:** Tractor tire, plants, scale and sun within circle

Date	Mintage	F	VF	XF	Unc	BU
ND(1986)	1,000,000	—	0.50	0.65	4.00	
ND(1986) Proof	8,000	Value: 12.00				

KM# 39 RINGGIT
Copper-Nickel **Subject:** 35th Annual PATA Conference **Obv:** Value **Rev:** Standing turtle

Date	Mintage	F	VF	XF	Unc	BU
ND(1986)	500,000	—	0.50	1.50	5.00	15.00

KM# 39a RINGGIT
16.8500 g., 0.5000 Silver 0.2709 oz. ASW **Obv:** Value **Rev:** Standing turtle

Date	Mintage	F	VF	XF	Unc	BU
ND(1986) Proof	11,000	Value: 25.00				

KM# 43 RINGGIT
Copper-Zinc, 24 mm. **Subject:** 30th Anniversary of Independence **Obv:** Arms with supporters above value and dollar sign **Rev:** Numeral 30 divides dates below with flying doves and sun above

Date	Mintage	F	VF	XF	Unc	BU
ND(1987)	1,000,000	—	—	0.60	3.50	
ND(1987) Proof	20,000	Value: 16.00				

KM# 54 RINGGIT
Aluminum-Bronze, 24 mm. **Obv:** Value and dollar sign divide date with flower blossom above **Rev:** Native dagger and scabbard within designs **Note:** Varying degrees of filled die variations exist.

Date	Mintage	F	VF	XF	Unc	BU
1989	20,410,000	—	—	—	1.75	2.25
1990	80,102,000	—	—	—	1.75	2.25
1991	169,001,000	—	—	—	1.75	2.00
1992	139,042,000	—	—	—	1.75	2.00
1993	178,894,000	—	—	—	1.75	2.00

KM# 54a RINGGIT
0.9250 Silver, 24 mm. **Obv:** Value and dollar sign divide date below flower blossom **Rev:** Native dagger and scabbard within designs

Date	Mintage	F	VF	XF	Unc	BU
1992 Proof	—	Value: 15.00				

KM# 64 RINGGIT
9.3500 g., Aluminum-Bronze, 24 mm. **Obv:** Value divides date below flower blossom **Rev:** Native dagger and scabbard within designs

Date	Mintage	F	VF	XF	Unc	BU
1993	Inc. above	—	—	—	2.00	2.25
1994	36,899,000	—	—	—	1.75	2.00
1995	132,173,000	—	—	—	1.75	2.00
1996	59,460,000	—	—	—	1.75	2.00
1997	41,842,514	—	—	—	1.75	2.00
	Note: Full mintage withdrawn					
1998	607,756,026	—	—	—	1.25	1.50
	Note: Full mintage withdrawn					

KM# 65 RINGGIT
8.1500 g., Bi-Metallic Copper-Nickel center in Nickel-Brass ring, 26.5 mm. **Subject:** Thomas-Uber Cup **Obv:** City view within circle **Rev:** Two-handled cup on radiant background **Edge:** Reeded

Date	Mintage	F	VF	XF	Unc	BU
2000	2,000,000	—	—	—	4.00	5.00

KM# 10   5 RINGGIT
Copper-Nickel **Obv:** Prime Minister Abdul Rahman Putra al-Haj **Rev:** Government building in Kuala Lumpur

Date	Mintage	F	VF	XF	Unc	BU
1971	2,000,000	—	2.50	3.00	5.00	—
1971 Proof	500	Value: 900				

KM# 40   5 RINGGIT
29.0300 g., 0.5000 Silver 0.4666 oz. ASW **Subject:** PATA Conference **Obv:** Value **Rev:** Standing turtle

Date	Mintage	F	VF	XF	Unc	BU
ND(1986) Proof	11,000	Value: 50.00				

KM# 47   5 RINGGIT
Copper Plated Zinc **Subject:** 15th Southeast Asian Games **Obv:** Star design within small circle above value **Rev:** Soccer players below date and design

Date	Mintage	F	VF	XF	Unc	BU
1989	500,000	—	—	—	8.00	11.00
1989 Proof	50,000	Value: 16.00				

KM# 55   5 RINGGIT
Copper Plated Zinc **Subject:** Commonwealth Heads of State Meeting **Obv:** Underlined Malaysia flanked by dots in center, arms with supporters above and value below **Rev:** City and towers with emblem at upper right

Date	Mintage	F	VF	XF	Unc	BU
1989	150,000	—	—	—	6.00	8.00
1989 Proof	8,000	Value: 18.00				

KM# 59   5 RINGGIT
Copper Plated Zinc **Subject:** 100th Anniversary of Kuala Lumpur **Obv:** Artistic design within circle among horizontal lines with value below **Rev:** House and tower

Date	Mintage	F	VF	XF	Unc	BU
ND(1990)	100,000	—	—	—	6.00	8.00

KM# 61   5 RINGGIT
Copper-Zinc-Tin **Series:** World Wildlife Fund **Obv:** Value and dollar sign flanked by flowers with WWF below design **Rev:** Stylized stork above dates

Date	Mintage	F	VF	XF	Unc	BU
ND(1992)	—	—	—	—	6.00	8.00
ND(1992) Proof	3,000	Value: 15.00				

KM# 44   10 RINGGIT
10.8200 g., 0.5000 Silver 0.1739 oz. ASW **Subject:** 30th Anniversary of Independence **Obv:** Dollar sign and value below arms with supporters **Rev:** Numeral 30 divides date below city view

Date	Mintage	F	VF	XF	Unc	BU
ND(1987)	50,000	—	—	—	10.00	12.00
ND(1987) Proof	10,000	Value: 20.00				

KM# 57   10 RINGGIT
13.6000 g., 0.9250 Silver 0.4044 oz. ASW **Subject:** Proclamation of Melaka as a Historical City **Obv:** Arms with supporters **Rev:** Oxen pulling covered cart

Date	Mintage	F	VF	XF	Unc	BU
1989 Proof	20,000	Value: 27.00				

KM# 19   15 RINGGIT
28.2800 g., 0.9250 Silver 0.8410 oz. ASW **Series:** Conservation **Obv:** Arms with supporters **Rev:** Malaysian Gaur

Date	Mintage	F	VF	XF	Unc	BU
1976	40,000	—	—	—	25.00	32.00
1976 Proof	8,113	Value: 75.00				

KM# 48   15 RINGGIT
16.7300 g., 0.9250 Silver 0.4975 oz. ASW **Subject:** 15th Southeast Asian Games **Obv:** Sun within small circle within horizontal lines above value within 3/4 circle **Rev:** Sport players below emblem and date

Date	Mintage	F	VF	XF	Unc	BU
1989 Prooflike	50,000	—	—	—	13.50	16.00
1989 Proof	20,000	Value: 25.00				

KM# 68   15 RINGGIT
17.0000 g., Copper-Nickel, 34 mm. **Subject:** First Malaysian Grand Prix **Obv:** Value **Rev:** Track route above island maps **Edge:** Reeded

Date	Mintage	F	VF	XF	Unc	BU
1999 Proof	8,000	Value: 42.50				

KM# 14   25 RINGGIT
35.0000 g., 0.9250 Silver 1.0408 oz. ASW **Subject:** 25th Anniversary - Employee Provident Fund **Obv:** Value **Rev:** Two inner circles at top divide map of Malasia within globe

Date	Mintage	F	VF	XF	Unc	BU
1976FM (U)	100,000	—	—	—	20.00	25.00
1976FM (P)	7,796	Value: 65.00				

KM# 20   25 RINGGIT
35.0000 g., 0.9250 Silver 1.0408 oz. ASW **Series:** Conservation **Obv:** Arms with supporters **Rev:** Rhinoceros Hornbill flanked by sprigs

Date	Mintage	F	VF	XF	Unc	BU
1976	40,000	—	—	—	38.00	42.00
1976 Proof	8,008	Value: 120				

KM# 23   25 RINGGIT
35.0000 g., 0.9250 Silver 1.0408 oz. ASW **Subject:** 9th Southeast Asian Games **Obv:** Arms with supporters **Rev:** Olympic circles at upper right of mapped globe

Date	Mintage	F	VF	XF	Unc	BU
1977FM (U)	100,000	—	—	—	20.00	25.00
1977FM (P)	5,877	Value: 68.00				

KM# 33   25 RINGGIT
35.0000 g., 0.9250 Silver 1.0408 oz. ASW **Subject:** 25th
Anniversary of Independence **Obv:** Star design and bust with
headdress with arm holding dagger facing right **Rev:** Arms with
supporters

Date	Mintage	F	VF	XF	Unc	BU
ND(1982)	150,000	—	—	—	20.00	22.50
ND(1982) Proof	7,000	Value: 35.00				

KM# 35   25 RINGGIT
35.0000 g., 0.5000 Silver 0.5626 oz. ASW **Subject:** 25th
Anniversary of the National Bank **Obv:** Bust with headdress 1/4 left
Rev: Animal figure within circle and sprigs with date and value below

Date	Mintage	F	VF	XF	Unc	BU
ND(1984)	98,000	—	—	—	20.00	22.50
ND(1984) Proof	10,000	Value: 45.00				

KM# 41   25 RINGGIT
23.3300 g., 0.9250 Silver 0.6938 oz. ASW **Subject:** Women's
Decade **Obv:** Date to right of stylized design **Rev:** Animal figure
within small circle at lower left within world globe

Date	Mintage	F	VF	XF	Unc	BU
ND(1985) Proof	2,000	Value: 70.00				

KM# 37   25 RINGGIT
35.0000 g., 0.5000 Silver 0.5626 oz. ASW **Subject:** 5th
Malaysian 5-Year Plan **Obv:** Arms with supporters **Rev:** City
scene from harbor

Date	Mintage	F	VF	XF	Unc	BU
ND(1986)	80,000	—	—	—	17.50	20.00
ND(1986) Proof	5,000	Value: 32.50				

KM# 56   25 RINGGIT
21.9000 g., 0.9250 Silver 0.6513 oz. ASW **Subject:**
Commonwealth Heads of State Meeting **Obv:** Arms with
supporters above lined Malaysia in center with value below
Rev: Flag within 1/2 of world globe

Date	Mintage	F	VF	XF	Unc	BU
1989	30,000	—	—	—	17.50	20.00
1989 Proof	8,000	Value: 32.50				

KM# 60   25 RINGGIT
21.9000 g., 0.9250 Silver 0.6513 oz. ASW **Subject:** 100th
Anniversary of Kuala Lumpur **Obv:** Design within circle among
horizontal lines with value below **Rev:** Castle and tower

Date	Mintage	F	VF	XF	Unc	BU
ND(1990)	25,000	—	—	—	17.50	20.00
ND(1990) Proof	25,000	Value: 32.50				

KM# 62   25 RINGGIT
21.7700 g., 0.9250 Silver 0.6474 oz. ASW **Series:** World Wildlife
Fund **Subject:** 100th Anniversary of Kuala Lumpur **Obv:** Panda
above value and dollar sign **Rev:** Stylized fish

Date	Mintage	F	VF	XF	Unc	BU
ND(1992) Proof	50,000	Value: 32.50				

KM# 69   25 RINGGIT
21.7700 g., 0.9250 Silver 0.6474 oz. ASW, 36.25 mm.
Subject: First Malaysian Grand Prix **Obv:** Value **Rev:** Trophy
Edge: Reeded

Date	Mintage	F	VF	XF	Unc	BU
1999 Proof	3,000	Value: 60.00				

KM# 46   30 RINGGIT
22.0000 g., 0.9250 Silver 0.6542 oz. ASW **Subject:** 30th
Anniversary of the National Bank **Obv:** Value within circle
Rev: City view with sun and crescent

Date	Mintage	F	VF	XF	Unc	BU
1989	47,000	—	—	—	15.00	17.50
1989 Proof	10,000	Value: 30.00				

KM# 11   100 RINGGIT
18.6600 g., 0.9170 Gold 0.5501 oz. AGW **Subject:** Prime
Minister Abdul Rahman Putra Al-haj **Obv:** Bust 3/4 facing
Rev: Multi-storied building left of full sun

Date	Mintage	F	VF	XF	Unc	BU
1971	100,000	—	—	—	600	650
1971 Proof	500	Value: 1,800				

KM# 18   200 RINGGIT
7.3000 g., 0.9000 Gold 0.2112 oz. AGW **Subject:** 3rd Malaysian
5-Year Plan

Date	Mintage	F	VF	XF	Unc	BU
1976FM (U)	50,000	—	—	—	210	225
1976FM (P)	887	Value: 300				

KM# 24   200 RINGGIT
7.2200 g., 0.9000 Gold 0.2089 oz. AGW **Subject:** 9th Southeast
Asian Games **Obv:** Arms with supporters **Rev:** Man on horse right

Date	Mintage	F	VF	XF	Unc	BU
1977FM (U)	12,000	—	—	—	210	225
1977FM (P)	417	Value: 500				

KM# 15   250 RINGGIT
10.1100 g., 0.9000 Gold 0.2925 oz. AGW **Subject:** 25th Anniversary - Employee Provident Fund **Obv:** Value **Rev:** Inscription within circle and design

Date	Mintage	F	VF	XF	Unc	BU
1976FM (U)	30,000	—	—	—	280	380
1976FM (P)	7,706	Value: 450				

KM# 42   250 RINGGIT
8.1000 g., 0.9000 Gold 0.2344 oz. AGW **Series:** Womens' Decade **Obv:** Date below design **Rev:** World globe

Date	Mintage	F	VF	XF	Unc	BU
1985 Proof	1,500	Value: 400				

KM# 45   250 RINGGIT
7.4300 g., 0.9000 Gold 0.2150 oz. AGW **Subject:** 30th Anniversary of Independence **Obv:** Arms with supporters above value **Rev:** Numeral 30 divides dates below crossed encased swords, sun and building

Date	Mintage	F	VF	XF	Unc	BU
1987	5,000	—	—	—	210	225
1987 Proof	1,000	Value: 350				

KM# 58   250 RINGGIT
7.1300 g., 0.9000 Gold 0.2063 oz. AGW **Subject:** 15th Southeast Asian Games **Obv:** Value below full sun on lined background **Rev:** Games logo and stylized swimmer

Date	Mintage	F	VF	XF	Unc	BU
1989 Proof	2,500	Value: 310				

KM# 63   250 RINGGIT
8.6000 g., 0.9000 Gold 0.2488 oz. AGW **Series:** World Wildlife Fund **Obv:** Panda above World Wildlife Fund **Rev:** Clouded Leopard

Date	Mintage	F	VF	XF	Unc	BU
1992 Proof	3,000	Value: 310				

KM# 21   500 RINGGIT
33.4370 g., 0.9000 Gold 0.9675 oz. AGW **Series:** Conservation **Obv:** Arms with supporters **Rev:** Malayan Tapir

Date	Mintage	F	VF	XF	Unc	BU
1976	2,894	—	—	—	1,100	1,200
1976 Proof	508	Value: 2,200				

KM# 31   500 RINGGIT
10.2600 g., 0.9000 Gold 0.2969 oz. AGW **Subject:** 4th Malaysian 5-Year Plan **Obv:** Arms with supporters **Rev:** Bust 3/4 facing

Date	Mintage	F	VF	XF	Unc	BU
ND(1981)FM (U)	20,000	—	—	—	285	420
ND(1981)FM (P)	1,000	Value: 500				

KM# 34   500 RINGGIT
10.2600 g., 0.9000 Gold 0.2969 oz. AGW **Subject:** 25th Anniversary of Independence **Obv:** Arms with supporters **Rev:** Bust upholding dagger facing right **Note:** Similar to 1 Ringgit, KM#32.

Date	Mintage	F	VF	XF	Unc	BU
1982	20,000	—	—	—	320	400
1982 Proof	1,000	Value: 500				

KM# 38   500 RINGGIT
10.2600 g., 0.9000 Gold 0.2969 oz. AGW **Subject:** 5th Malaysian 5-Year Plan **Obv:** Arms with supporters **Rev:** Sun, moon and gear-like designs within circle

Date	Mintage	F	VF	XF	Unc	BU
ND(1986)	10,000	—	—	—	320	400
ND(1986) Proof	1,000	Value: 500				

KM# 70   500 RINGGIT
25.0000 g., 0.9990 Gold 0.8029 oz. AGW, 35.25 mm. **Subject:** Millennium **Obv:** Arms with supporters above value **Rev:** Flags within globe **Edge:** Reeded

Date	Mintage	F	VF	XF	Unc	BU
1999	—	—	—	—	1,100	1,200
1999 Proof	10,000	Value: 1,100				

BULLION COINAGE

KM# 121   50 RINGGIT
7.7750 g., 0.9999 Gold 0.2499 oz. AGW **Obv:** Mouse deer running right **Obv. Leg.:** BANK NEGARA MALAYSIA **Rev:** Flower

Date	Mintage	F	VF	XF	Unc	BU
2000	—	—	—	—	—	BV+30%

KM# 122   100 RINGGIT
15.5510 g., 0.9999 Gold 0.4999 oz. AGW **Obv:** Mousedeer running right **Obv. Leg.:** BANK NEGARA MALAYSIA **Rev:** Flower

Date	Mintage	F	VF	XF	Unc	BU
2000	—	—	—	—	—	BV+20%

KM# 123   200 RINGGIT
31.1030 g., 0.9999 Gold 0.9998 oz. AGW **Obv:** Mousedeer running right **Obv. Leg.:** BANK NEGARA MALAYSIA **Rev:** Flower

Date	Mintage	F	VF	XF	Unc	BU
2000	—	—	—	—	—	BV+10%

PATTERNS
Including off metal strikes

KM#	Date	Mintage Identification	Mkt Val
Pn1	SH2602 (1942)	— 20 Cents. Aluminum. Cluster of leaves within beaded circle. Value above 1/2 flower wreath. Japanese occupation.	2,500
Pn2	SH2602 (1942)	— 20 Cents. Aluminum. Japanese occupation.	2,500
Pn3	1966	— Sen. Bronze. Cattle Egret.	—
Pn4	1966	— Sen. Bronze. Single hibiscus flowers flank denomination. Parliament House.	—
Pn5	1966	— 5 Sen. Copper Nickel. Malayan Tapir.	—
Pn6	1966	— 5 Sen. Copper-Nickel. Single hibiscus flowers flank denomination. Parliament House.	—
Pn7	1966	— 10 Sen. Copper-Nickel. Pangolin.	—
Pn8	1966	— 10 Sen. Copper-Nickel. Proboscis Monkey.	—
Pn9	1966	— 10 Sen. Copper-Nickel. Single hibiscus flowers flank denomination. Parliament House.	—

KM#	Date	Mintage Identification	Mkt Val
Pn10	1966	— 20 Sen. Copper Nickel. Kijang with tall grass in background.	—
Pn11	1966	— 20 Sen. Copper Nickel. Kijang with mountains in background.	—
Pn12	1966	— 20 Sen. Copper-Nickel. Kijang on mound.	—
Pn13	1966	— 20 Sen. Copper-Nickel. Single hibiscus flowers flank denomination. Parliament House.	—

MINT SETS

KM#	Date	Mintage Identification	Issue Price	Mkt Val
MS1	1967 (5)	10,000 KM#1-5.1	—	40.00
MS2	1973 (5)	2,000 KM#1-4, 5.3	—	12.00
MS3	1980 (5)	2,000 KM#1a, 2-4, 5.3	—	12.00
MS4	1989 (6)	2,000 KM#49-54	—	12.00
MS5	1990 (6)	2,000 KM#49-54	—	12.00

PROOF SETS

KM#	Date	Mintage Identification	Issue Price	Mkt Val
PS1	1967 (5)	500 KM#1-5.1	—	400
PS2	1976 (3)	508 KM#19-21	808	2,200
PS3	1976 (2)	7,500 KM#19-20	—	300
PS4	1976 (3)	2,641 KM#16-18	—	400
PS5	1976 (3)	1,000 KM#13-15	—	500
PS6	1977 (3)	975 KM#22-24	164	650
PS7	1976-80 (8)	5,000 KM#1-4, 5.3, 9.1, 17, 23, 27a. Mixed date set. Minted by Franklin Mint and sold almost exclusively to employees of Bank Negara.	132	160
PS8	1981 (6)	— KM#1-4, 5.4, 9.2 Minted and distributed by Franklin Mint.	—	100
PS9	1981 (3)	3,000 KM#29-31	—	600
PS10	1982 (3)	4,000 KM#32-34	—	600
PS12	1986 (2)	11,000 KM#39a, 40	—	80.00
PS11	1986 (3)	2,000 KM#36-38	—	500
PS13	1987 (3)	1,000 KM#43-45	—	300
PS14	1989 (3)	2,500 KM#47, 48, 58	—	350
PS15	1989 (2)	20,000 KM#47-48	—	50.00
PS16	1989 (2)	15,000 KM#55-56	—	50.00
PS17	1992 (6)	5,000 KM#49a-54a Minted by Bank of Negara Malaysia Mint Department and sold only to bank employees.	—	80.00
PS18	1992 (3)	3,000 KM#61-63	—	300

MALDIVE ISLANDS

The Republic of Maldives, an archipelago of 2,000 coral islets in the northern Indian Ocean 417 miles (671 km.) west of Ceylon, has an area of 116 sq. mi. (298 sq. km.) and a population of 189,000. Capital: Male. Fishing employs 95 % of the male work force. Dried fish, copra and coir yarn are exported.

The Maldive Islands were visited by Arab traders and converted to Islam in 1153. After being harassed in the 16th and 17th centuries by Mopla pirates of the Malabar coast and Portuguese raiders, the Maldivians voluntarily placed themselves under the suzerainty of Ceylon. In 1887 the islands became an internally self-governing British protectorate and a nominal dependency of Ceylon. Traditionally a sultanate, the Maldives became a republic in 1953 but restored the sultanate in 1954. The Sultanate of the Maldive Islands attained complete internal and external autonomy on July 26, 1965, and on Nov. 11, 1968, again became a republic. The Maldives is a member of the Commonwealth of Nations.

RULERS
Muhammad Imad al-Din V, AH1318-1322/1900-1904AD
Muhammad Shams al-Din III, AH1322-1353/1904-1935AD
Hasan Nur al-Din II, AH1353-1364/1935-1945AD
Abdul-Majid Didi, AH1364-1371/1945-1953AD
First Republic, AH1371-1372/1953-1954AD
Muhammad Farid Didi, AH1372-1388/1954-1968AD
Second Republic, AH1388 to date/1968AD to date*

MINT NAME

محلي

Mahle (Male)

MONETARY SYSTEM
100 Lari = 1 Rupee (Rufiyaa)

SULTANATE
STANDARD COINAGE

KM# 38 LARIN
Copper Or Brass **Ruler:** Muhammad Imad al-Din V AH 1318-22 / 1900-04 AD **Note:** Weight varies: 0.80-1.10 grams.

Date	Mintage	F	VF	XF	Unc	BU
AH1319 (1901)	—	1.00	1.50	2.00	4.00	—

KM# 41 LARIN
0.9000 g., Bronze, 13 mm. **Ruler:** Muhammad Shams al-Din III AH 1322-53 / 1904-35 AD **Obv:** Legend **Rev:** Legend **Note:** Struck at Birmingham, England. Rare mint proof strikes in silver and gold exist.

Date	Mintage	F	VF	XF	Unc	BU
AH1331 (1913)	—	1.00	1.25	1.75	3.00	—

KM# 39 2 LARIAT
Copper-Brass, 13 mm. **Ruler:** Muhammad Imad al-Din V AH 1318-22 / 1900-04 AD **Obv:** Legend **Rev:** Legend **Note:** 1.4-2.2 grams. Previously listed date AH1311 is merely poor die cutting of AH1319. Many die varieties exist.

Date	Mintage	F	VF	XF	Unc	BU
AH1319 (1901)	—	1.50	3.50	5.00	7.50	—

KM# 40.1 4 LARIAT
Copper-Brass **Ruler:** Muhammad Imad al-Din V AH 1318-22 / 1900-04 AD **Obv:** Legend **Rev:** Legend **Edge:** Plain or reeded **Note:** 2.5-4.5 grams. Many die varieties exist; size varies 17 - 18mm.

Date	Mintage	F	VF	XF	Unc	BU
AH1320 (1902)	—	1.50	2.50	4.50	8.00	—

KM# 40.2 4 LARIAT
Copper-Brass **Ruler:** Muhammad Imad al-Din V AH 1318-22 / 1900-04 AD **Obv:** Legend **Rev:** Legend with Arabic "Sana(t)" below date **Note:** Silver strikes are most likely presentation pieces; size varies 16.8-18mm.

Date	Mintage	F	VF	XF	Unc	BU
AH1320 (1902)	—	3.50	8.00	12.00	16.00	—

KM# 42 4 LARIAT
3.3000 g., Bronze, 19 mm. **Ruler:** Muhammad Shams al-Din III AH 1322-53 / 1904-35 AD **Obv:** Legend **Rev:** Legend **Note:** Struck at Birmingham, England. Rare mint proof strikes in silver and gold exist.

Date	Mintage	F	VF	XF	Unc	BU
AH1331 (1913)	—	1.00	1.50	2.75	6.00	—

2ND SULTANATE
STANDARD COINAGE

KM# 43 LAARI
1.5000 g., Bronze, 15 mm. **Ruler:** Muhammad Farid Didi AH 1372-88 / 1954-68 AD **Obv:** National emblem divides dates above **Rev:** Value **Note:** Similar to Laari, KM#49.

Date	Mintage	F	VF	XF	Unc	BU
AH1379-1960	300,000	—	0.15	0.25	0.50	—
AH1379-1960 Proof	1,270	Value: 3.00				

KM# 44 2 LAARI
3.1500 g., Bronze, 18.2 mm. **Ruler:** Muhammad Farid Didi AH 1372-88 / 1954-68 AD **Obv:** National emblem divides dates above **Rev:** Value

Date	Mintage	F	VF	XF	Unc	BU
AH1379-1960	600,000	—	0.20	0.35	0.75	—
AH1379-1960 Proof	1,270	Value: 3.50				

KM# 45 5 LAARI
2.6000 g., Nickel-Brass, 20.4 mm. **Ruler:** Muhammad Farid Didi AH 1372-88 / 1954-68 AD **Obv:** National emblem divides dates above **Rev:** Value

Date	Mintage	F	VF	XF	Unc	BU
AH1379-1960	300,000	—	0.25	0.40	0.75	—
AH1379-1960 Proof	1,270	Value: 4.00				

KM# 45a 5 LAARI
Bronze **Ruler:** Muhammad Farid Didi AH 1372-88 / 1954-68 AD **Obv:** National emblem divides dates above **Rev:** Value

Date	Mintage	F	VF	XF	Unc	BU
AH1379-1960	—	0.25	0.40	0.75	—	—

KM# 46 10 LAARI
5.2000 g., Nickel-Brass, 23 mm. **Ruler:** Muhammad Farid Didi AH 1372-88 / 1954-68 AD **Obv:** National emblem divides dates above **Rev:** Value

Date	Mintage	F	VF	XF	Unc	BU
AH1379-1960	600,000	—	0.50	0.75	1.50	—
AH1379-1960 Proof	1,270	Value: 5.00				

KM# 47.1 25 LAARI
4.1000 g., Nickel-Brass, 20.4 mm. **Ruler:** Muhammad Farid Didi AH 1372-88 / 1954-68 AD **Obv:** National emblem divides dates above **Rev:** Value **Edge:** Security

Date	Mintage	F	VF	XF	Unc	BU
AH1379-1960	300,000	—	0.60	1.00	1.50	—
AH1379-1960 Proof	1,270	Value: 6.00				

KM# 47.2 25 LAARI
4.1000 g., Nickel-Brass, 20.4 mm. **Ruler:** Muhammad Farid Didi AH 1372-88 / 1954-68 AD **Obv:** National emblem divides dates above **Rev:** Value **Edge:** Reeded

Date	Mintage	F	VF	XF	Unc	BU
AH1379-1960	—	—	2.00	3.50	6.00	—

KM# 48.1 50 LAARI
5.6000 g., Nickel-Brass, 23.5 mm. **Ruler:** Muhammad Farid Didi AH 1372-88 / 1954-68 AD **Obv:** National emblem divides dates above **Rev:** Value **Edge:** Security

Date	Mintage	F	VF	XF	Unc	BU
AH1379-1960	300,000	—	1.00	1.75	2.50	—
AH1379-1960 Proof	1,270	Value: 8.00				

KM# 48.2 50 LAARI
Nickel-Brass, 23.5 mm. **Ruler:** Muhammad Farid Didi AH 1372-88 / 1954-68 AD **Obv:** National emblem divides dates above **Rev:** Value **Edge:** Reeded

Date	Mintage	F	VF	XF	Unc	BU
AH1379-1960	—	—	3.00	5.00	8.00	—

2ND REPUBLIC
STANDARD COINAGE

KM# 45b 5 LAARI
Nickel-Brass, 20.4 mm. **Obv:** National emblem divides dates above **Note:** Similar to 5 Laari, KM#45.

Date	Mintage	F	VF	XF	Unc	BU
AH1389-1970	300,000	—	0.20	0.30	0.40	—
AH1389-1970 Proof	—	Value: 3.50				
AH1399-1979	—	—	—	0.10	0.20	—
AH1399-1979 Proof	—	Value: 2.50				

STANDARD COINAGE
100 Laari = 1 Rufiyaa

KM# 49 LAARI
0.4500 g., Aluminum, 15 mm. **Obv:** National emblem divides dates above **Rev:** Value **Edge:** Plain

Date	Mintage	F	VF	XF	Unc	BU
AH1389-1970	500,000	—	0.10	0.20	0.40	—
AH1399-1979	—	—	0.10	0.20	0.40	—
AH1399-1979 Proof	100,000	Value: 1.25				

KM# 68 LAARI
0.4700 g., Aluminum, 18.2 mm. **Obv:** Value **Rev:** Palm tree within circle **Edge:** Plain

Date	Mintage	F	VF	XF	Unc	BU
AH1404-1984	—	—	—	0.10	0.15	0.20
AH1404-1984 Proof	2,500	Value: 2.50				

KM# 50 2 LAARI
Aluminum, 18.2 mm.

Date	Mintage	F	VF	XF	Unc	BU
AH1389-1970	500,000	—	0.15	0.25	0.50	—
AH1389-1970 Proof	—	—	—	—	—	—
AH1399-1979	—	—	0.15	0.25	0.50	—
AH1399-1979 Proof	100,000	Value: 1.25				

KM# 69 5 LAARI
1.0000 g., Aluminum, 20.4 mm. **Obv:** Value **Rev:** Two Bonito fish swimming upward left

Date	Mintage	F	VF	XF	Unc	BU
AH1404-1984	—	—	—	0.10	0.35	1.00
AH1404-1984 Proof	2,500	Value: 3.00				
AH1411-1990	—	—	—	0.10	0.35	1.00

KM# 46a 10 LAARI
Aluminum, 23 mm. **Obv:** National emblem divides dates above **Note:** Similar to 10 Laari, KM#46.

Date	Mintage	F	VF	XF	Unc	BU
AH1399-1979	—	—	—	0.10	0.25	—
AH1399-1979 Proof	—	Value: 2.50				

KM# 70 10 LAARI
1.9500 g., Aluminum, 23.14 mm. **Obv:** Value **Rev:** Maldivian sailing ship - Odi

Date	Mintage	F	VF	XF	Unc	BU
AH1404-1984	—	—	—	0.10	0.20	0.30
AH1404-1984 Proof	2,500	Value: 3.50				

KM# 47.3 25 LAARI
Nickel-Brass, 20.4 mm. **Obv:** National emblem divides dates above **Rev:** Palm tree **Note:** Similar to 25 Laari, KM#47.2.

Date	Mintage	F	VF	XF	Unc	BU
AH1399-1979	—	—	—	0.10	0.25	—
AH1399-1979 Proof	100,000	Value: 3.50				

KM# 71   25 LAARI
4.1500 g., Nickel-Brass, 20.4 mm. **Obv:** Value **Rev:** Mosque
and minaret at Male

Date	Mintage	F	VF	XF	Unc	BU
AH1404-1984	—	—	—	0.15	0.45	—
AH1404-1984 Proof	—	Value: 4.00				
AH1411-1990	—	—	—	0.15	0.45	—
AH1416-1996	—	—	—	0.15	0.45	—

KM# 48.3   50 LAARI
Nickel-Brass, 23.5 mm. **Obv:** National emblem divides dates
above **Rev:** Palm tree **Note:** Similar to 50 Laari, KM#48.2.

Date	Mintage	F	VF	XF	Unc	BU
AH1399-1979	—	—	0.10	0.20	0.40	—
AH1399-1979 Proof	100,000	Value: 6.50				

KM# 72   50 LAARI
5.6500 g., Nickel-Brass, 23.6 mm. **Obv:** Value **Rev:** Loggerhead
sea turtle

Date	Mintage	F	VF	XF	Unc	BU
AH1404-1984	—	—	0.15	0.35	1.50	2.50
AH1404-1984 Proof	—	Value: 6.00				
AH1411-1990	—	—	0.15	0.35	1.50	2.50
AH1415-1995	—	—	0.15	0.35	1.50	2.50

KM# 73   RUFIYAA
Copper-Nickel Clad Steel, 25.9 mm. **Obv:** Value **Rev:** National
emblem divides dates above

Date	Mintage	F	VF	XF	Unc	BU
AH1402-1982	—	—	0.20	0.50	2.00	—

KM# 73a   RUFIYAA
6.3800 g., Copper-Nickel, 25.9 mm. **Obv:** Value **Rev:** National
emblem divides dates above

Date	Mintage	F	VF	XF	Unc	BU
AH1404-1984	—	—	0.20	0.50	2.00	—
AH1404-1984 Proof	—	Value: 9.00				
AH1411-1990	—	—	0.20	0.50	2.00	—
AH1416-1996	—	—	0.20	0.50	2.00	—

KM# 88   2 RUFIYAA
11.7000 g., Brass, 25.47 mm. **Obv:** Value **Rev:** Pacific triton sea
shell **Edge:** Reeded and lettered **Edge:** REPUBLIC OF MALDIVES

Date	Mintage	F	VF	XF	Unc	BU
AH1415-1995	—	—	—	2.25	5.50	7.50

KM# 55   5 RUFIYAA
Copper-Nickel **Series:** F.A.O. **Obv:** National emblem divides
dates above **Rev:** Value below Bonito fish

Date	Mintage	F	VF	XF	Unc	BU
AH1397-1977	15,000	—	—	3.50	—	9.00

KM# 57   5 RUFIYAA
Copper-Nickel, 36 mm. **Series:** F.A.O. **Obv:** National emblem
divides dates above **Rev:** Spiny lobster divides circle

Date	Mintage	F	VF	XF	Unc	BU
AH1398-1978 (1978)	7,000	—	—	4.00	7.50	10.00

KM# 57a   5 RUFIYAA
19.1500 g., 0.9250 Silver 0.5695 oz. ASW **Series:** F.A.O.
Obv: National emblem divides dates above **Rev:** Spiny lobster
divides circle

Date	Mintage	F	VF	XF	Unc	BU
AH1398-1978 Proof	1,887	Value: 27.50				

KM# 57b   5 RUFIYAA
18.9500 g., 0.9170 Gold 0.5587 oz. AGW **Series:** F.A.O.
Obv: National emblem divides dates above **Rev:** Spiny lobster
divides circle

Date	Mintage	F	VF	XF	Unc	BU
AH1398-1978 Proof	200	Value: 650				

KM# 100   5 RUFIYAA
26.0000 g., Copper-Nickel, 38.75 mm. **Subject:** International
Year of the Reef **Obv:** National emblem divides dates above **Rev:**
Multicolor fish scene **Edge:** Reeded

Date	Mintage	F	VF	XF	Unc	BU
AH1419-1998 Proof	—	Value: 27.50				

KM# 59   10 RUFIYAA
Copper-Nickel **Series:** F.A.O. **Obv:** National emblem divides
dates above **Rev:** Woman weaving

Date	Mintage	F	VF	XF	Unc	BU
AH1399-1979	—	—	—	4.50	10.00	12.00

KM# 59a   10 RUFIYAA
25.0000 g., 0.9250 Silver 0.7435 oz. ASW **Series:** F.A.O. **Obv:**
National emblem divides dates above **Rev:** Woman weaving

Date	Mintage	F	VF	XF	Unc	BU
AH1399-1979 Proof	3,000	Value: 17.50				

KM# 62   10 RUFIYAA
Copper-Nickel **Series:** F.A.O. **Obv:** National emblem divides
dates above **Rev:** Girl making embroidery

Date	Mintage	F	VF	XF	Unc	BU
AH1400-1980	—	—	—	4.00	8.00	10.00

KM# 56   20 RUFIYAA
28.2800 g., 0.5000 Silver 0.4546 oz. ASW, 38.61 mm.
Series: F.A.O. **Obv:** National emblem divides dates above
Rev: Value flanked by fish

Date	Mintage	F	VF	XF	Unc	BU
AH1397-1977	15,000	—	—	—	12.50	15.00

KM# 61   20 RUFIYAA
28.2800 g., 0.9250 Silver 0.8410 oz. ASW, 38.61 mm.
Series: International Year of the Child **Obv:** National emblem
divides dates above **Rev:** Three children playing

Date	Mintage	F	VF	XF	Unc	BU
AH1399-1979 Proof	12,000	Value: 18.00				

KM# 65   20 RUFIYAA
Copper-Nickel, 38.61 mm. **Subject:** World Fisheries Conference
Obv: National emblem divides dates above **Rev:** Two tuna fish

Date	Mintage	F	VF	XF	Unc	BU
AH1404-1984	100,000	—	—	—	16.00	20.00

KM# 65a   20 RUFIYAA
28.2800 g., 0.9250 Silver 0.8410 oz. ASW, 38.61 mm.
Subject: World Fisheries Conference **Obv:** National emblem
divides dates above **Rev:** Two tuna fish

Date	Mintage	F	VF	XF	Unc	BU
AH1404-1984 Proof	20,000	Value: 45.00				

KM# 74   20 RUFIYAA
19.4400 g., 0.9250 Silver 0.5781 oz. ASW **Series:** Decade for
Women **Obv:** National emblem divides dates above **Rev:** Woman
sewing lace on pillow

Date	Mintage	F	VF	XF	Unc	BU
AH1405-1985 Proof	500	Value: 40.00				

KM# 97 20 RUFIYAA

31.2200 g., 0.9990 Silver 1.0027 oz. ASW, 30.3 mm.
Subject: Millennium **Obv:** National emblem **Rev:** Multicolor design **Edge:** Reeded

Date	Mintage	F	VF	XF	Unc	BU
AH1421-2000 Proof	—	Value: 50.00				

KM# 58 25 RUFIYAA

28.0500 g., 0.5000 Silver 0.4509 oz. ASW **Series:** F.A.O.
Obv: National emblem divides dates **Rev:** Sailing ship

Date	Mintage	F	VF	XF	Unc	BU
AH1398-1978	7,140	—	—	—	22.50	—

KM# 58a 25 RUFIYAA

28.2800 g., 0.9250 Silver 0.8410 oz. ASW **Series:** F.A.O.
Obv: National emblem divides dates above **Rev:** Sailing ship

Date	Mintage	F	VF	XF	Unc	BU
AH1398-1978 Proof	2,000	Value: 35.00				

KM# 58b 25 RUFIYAA

28.2500 g., 0.9170 Gold 0.8328 oz. AGW **Series:** F.A.O.
Obv: National emblem divides dates above **Rev:** Sailing ship

Date	Mintage	F	VF	XF	Unc	BU
AH1398-1978 Proof	200	Value: 850				

KM# 95 25 RUFIYAA

Copper-Nickel **Series:** 50th Anniversary - UN **Obv:** National emblem divides dates above **Rev:** UN building and logo

Date	Mintage	F	VF	XF	Unc	BU
AH1416-1996	—	—	—	—	9.50	12.50

KM# 89 50 RUFIYAA

1.2442 g., 0.9999 Gold 0.0400 oz. AGW **Obv:** National emblem divides dates above **Rev:** Skylab space station

Date	Mintage	F	VF	XF	Unc	BU
AH1415-1995	Est. 25,000	—	—	—	60.00	65.00

KM# 90 50 RUFIYAA

10.0000 g., 0.5000 Silver 0.1607 oz. ASW **Series:** 1996 Olympics
Obv: National emblem divides dates **Rev:** Sailboat and map

Date	Mintage	F	VF	XF	Unc	BU
AH1416-1996	Est. 10,000	—	—	—	20.00	22.50

KM# 99 50 RUFIYAA

31.3000 g., 0.9250 Silver 0.9308 oz. ASW, 38.5 mm.
Subject: Year of the Reef **Obv:** National emblem divides dates above **Rev:** Multicolor underwater scene **Edge:** Reeded

Date	Mintage	F	VF	XF	Unc	BU
AH1419-1998 Proof	—	Value: 50.00				

KM# 60 100 RUFIYAA

28.2800 g., 0.8000 Silver 0.7273 oz. ASW **Series:** F.A.O.
Obv: National emblem divides dates above **Rev:** Woman making mats

Date	Mintage	F	VF	XF	Unc	BU
AH1399-1979	6,000	—	—	—	18.00	20.00

KM# 60a 100 RUFIYAA

28.2800 g., 0.9250 Silver 0.8410 oz. ASW **Series:** F.A.O.
Obv: National emblem divides dates above **Rev:** Woman making mats

Date	Mintage	F	VF	XF	Unc	BU
AH1399-1979 Proof	8,000	Value: 22.50				

KM# 63 100 RUFIYAA

28.2800 g., 0.8000 Silver 0.7273 oz. ASW **Series:** F.A.O.
Obv: National emblem divides dates above **Rev:** Crown of coconut and palm

Date	Mintage	F	VF	XF	Unc	BU
AH1400-1980	6,501	—	—	—	25.00	28.00

KM# 63a 100 RUFIYAA

28.2800 g., 0.9250 Silver 0.8410 oz. ASW **Series:** F.A.O.
Obv: National emblem divides dates above **Rev:** Crown of coconut and palm

Date	Mintage	F	VF	XF	Unc	BU
AH1400-1980 Proof	3,003	Value: 45.00				

KM# 64 100 RUFIYAA

28.2800 g., 0.9250 Silver 0.8410 oz. ASW **Series:** World Food Day **Obv:** National emblem divides dates above **Rev:** Heads of 2 women working in a field

Date	Mintage	F	VF	XF	Unc	BU
AH1401-1981	10,000	—	—	—	27.50	32.50
AH1401-1981 Proof	5,000	Value: 45.00				

KM# 66 100 RUFIYAA

28.2800 g., 0.9250 Silver 0.8410 oz. ASW, 38.61 mm.
Series: International Year of Disabled Persons **Obv:** National emblem divides dates above **Rev:** Stylized yin and yang symbol

Date	Mintage	F	VF	XF	Unc	BU
AH1404-1984	—	—	—	—	25.00	28.00
AH1404-1984 Proof	—	Value: 40.00				

KM# 75 100 RUFIYAA

15.9800 g., 0.9170 Gold 0.4711 oz. AGW **Subject:** Opening of Grand Mosque and Islamic Centre **Obv:** National emblem divides dates above

Date	Mintage	F	VF	XF	Unc	BU
AH1405-1985 Proof	100	Value: 600				

KM# 67 100 RUFIYAA

15.9800 g., 0.9170 Gold 0.4711 oz. AGW **Obv:** National emblem divides dates above **Rev:** Disabled figures within lower circle under 1/2 world globe

Date	Mintage	F	VF	XF	Unc	BU
AH1404-1984	500	—	—	—	700	750
AH1404-1984 Proof	500	Value: 800				

KM# 78 100 RUFIYAA

28.2800 g., 0.9250 Silver 0.8410 oz. ASW **Subject:** Opening of Grand Mosque and Islamic Centre **Obv:** National emblem divides dates above **Rev:** Building and tower

Date	Mintage	F	VF	XF	Unc	BU
AH1405-1985 Proof	500	Value: 70.00				

KM# 76   100 RUFIYAA
28.2800 g., 0.9250 Silver 0.8410 oz. ASW
Subject: Commonwealth finance ministers meeting
Obv: National emblem divides dates above **Rev:** Grand Mosque

Date	Mintage	F	VF	XF	Unc	BU
ND(AH406) Proof	300	Value: 75.00				

KM# 87   100 RUFIYAA
10.0000 g., 0.5000 Silver 0.1607 oz. ASW **Obv:** National
emblem divides dates above **Rev:** Sailing ship "Cutty Sark"

Date	Mintage	F	VF	XF	Unc	BU
AH1414-1993 Proof	Est. 25,000	Value: 16.50				

KM# 98   100 RUFIYAA
20.0000 g., 0.8350 Silver 0.5369 oz. ASW, 34 mm. **Series:**
Olympics **Obv:** National emblem divides dates above **Rev:**
Swimmer within circle **Edge:** Reeded

Date	Mintage	F	VF	XF	Unc	BU
AH1418-1998 Proof	30,000	—	—	—	35.00	38.00

KM# 82   250 RUFIYAA
31.4700 g., 0.9250 Silver 0.9359 oz. ASW, 38.61 mm.
Series: World Football Championship **Obv:** National emblem
divides dates above **Rev:** Soccer ball trailing an inscribed ribbon

Date	Mintage	F	VF	XF	Unc	BU
AH1410-1990 Proof	—	Value: 22.50				

KM# 80   250 RUFIYAA
31.4700 g., 0.9250 Silver 0.9359 oz. ASW **Series:** 1992
Olympics **Subject:** Swimming **Obv:** National emblem divides
dates above **Rev:** Swimmer and diver

Date	Mintage	F	VF	XF	Unc	BU
AH1410-1990 Proof	—	Value: 20.00				

KM# 81   250 RUFIYAA
31.4700 g., 0.9250 Silver 0.9359 oz. ASW, 38.61 mm.
Obv: National emblem divides dates above **Rev:** Maldivian
Schooner - Dhivehi-Odi

Date	Mintage	F	VF	XF	Unc	BU
AH1410-1990 Proof	15,000	Value: 28.00				

KM# 83   250 RUFIYAA
31.4700 g., 0.9250 Silver 0.9359 oz. ASW, 38.61 mm.
Subject: World Cup '94 soccer **Obv:** National emblem divides
dates above **Rev:** Two soccer players

Date	Mintage	F	VF	XF	Unc	BU
AH1413-1993 Proof	25,000	Value: 36.50				

KM# 84   250 RUFIYAA
31.4700 g., 0.9250 Silver 0.9359 oz. ASW, 38.61 mm. **Obv:**
National emblem divides dates above **Rev:** Skylab space station

Date	Mintage	F	VF	XF	Unc	BU
AH1413-1993 Proof	1,440	Value: 32.50				

KM# 85   250 RUFIYAA
31.4700 g., 0.9250 Silver 0.9359 oz. ASW, 38.61 mm.
Series: 1996 Olympics **Subject:** Sailing **Obv:** National emblem
divides dates above **Rev:** Sailboat divides map

Date	Mintage	F	VF	XF	Unc	BU
AH1414-1993 Proof	25,000	Value: 25.00				

KM# 86   250 RUFIYAA
31.4700 g., 0.9250 Silver 0.9359 oz. ASW, 38.61 mm.
Series: Endangered Wildlife **Obv:** National emblem divides
dates above **Rev:** Turtle

Date	Mintage	F	VF	XF	Unc	BU
AH1414-1994 Proof	14,500	Value: 50.00				

KM# 96   250 RUFIYAA
31.2400 g., 0.9250 Silver 0.9290 oz. ASW, 38.61 mm.
Subject: Ibn Battuta **Obv:** National emblem divides dates above
Rev: Bust of Ibn Battuta, dhow and map

Date	Mintage	F	VF	XF	Unc	BU
AH1416-1995 Proof	—	Value: 37.50				

KM# 101   250 RUFIYAA
28.5000 g., 0.9250 Silver 0.8475 oz. ASW, 38.6 mm.
Subject: U N 50 Years **Obv:** National emblem divides dates
above **Rev:** U N building and logo **Edge:** Reeded

Date	Mintage	F	VF	XF	Unc	BU
AH1416-1996 Proof	—	Value: 100				

KM# 91   500 RUFIYAA
28.2800 g., 0.9250 Silver 0.8410 oz. ASW, 38.61 mm.
Subject: 25 Years of Independence

Date	Mintage	F	VF	XF	Unc	BU
AH1410-1990 Proof	1,000	Value: 60.00				

KM# 92   500 RUFIYAA
28.2800 g., 0.9250 Silver 0.8410 oz. ASW, 38.61 mm.
Subject: 25 Years of Republic

Date	Mintage	F	VF	XF	Unc	BU
AH1413-1993 Proof	500	Value: 65.00				

KM# 93   1000 RUFIYAA
15.9800 g., 0.9170 Gold 0.4711 oz. AGW, 28.4 mm.
Subject: 25 Years of Independence

Date	Mintage	F	VF	XF	Unc	BU
AH1410-1990 Proof	1,000	Value: 525				

KM# 94   1000 RUFIYAA
15.9800 g., 0.9170 Gold 0.4711 oz. AGW, 28.4 mm.
Subject: 25 Years of Republic

Date	Mintage	F	VF	XF	Unc	BU
AH1413-1993 Proof	500	Value: 575				

PATTERNS
Including off metal strikes

KM#	Date	Mintage	Identification	Mkt Val
Pn1	AH1319	—	Larin. Silver. KM38.	—
Pn2	AH1319	—	2 Lariat. Silver. KM39.	—
Pn3	AH1320	—	4 Lariat. Silver. KM40.2.	—

PIEFORTS

KM#	Date	Mintage	Identification	Mkt Val
P1	1979	100	20 Rufiyaa. Silver. National emblem - crescent moon, star and palm tree flanked by 2 flags. 3 children playing. KM61.	80.00
P2	1984	100	100 Rufiyaa. Silver. National emblem - crescent moon, star and palm tree flanked by 2 flags. Stylized Yin-Yang symbol. KM66.	100
P3	1984	100	100 Rufiyaa. Gold. National emblem - crescent moon, star and palm tree flanked by 2 flags. Disabled persons under an umbrella. KM67.	800

MINT SETS

KM#	Date	Mintage Identification	Issue Price	Mkt Val
MS1	1984 (6)	— KM68-73	8.75	12.50

PROOF SETS

KM#	Date	Mintage	Identification	Issue Price	Mkt Val
PS1	1960 (6)	1,270	KM43-48	—	30.00
PS2	1979 (6)	—	KM45a, 46a, 47.2, 48.2, 49-50	30.00	18.00
PS3	1979 (2)	3,000	KM59a, 60a	—	42.50
PS4	1984 (6)	2,500	KM68-72, 73a	30.00	28.00

MALI

The Republic of Mali, a landlocked country in the interior of West Africa southwest of Algeria, has an area of 482,077 sq. mi. (1,240,000 sq. km.) and a population of 8.1 million. Capital: Bamako. Livestock, fish, cotton and peanuts are exported.

Malians are descendants of the ancient Malinke Kingdom of Mali that controlled the middle Niger from the 11th to the 17th centuries. The French penetrated the Sudan (now Mali) about 1880, and established their rule in 1898 after subduing fierce native resistance. In 1904 the area became the colony of Upper Senegal-Niger (changed to French Sudan in 1920), and became part of the French Union in 1946. In 1958 French Sudan became the Sudanese Republic with complete internal autonomy. Senegal joined with the Sudanese Republic in 1959 to form the Mali Federation which, in 1960, became a fully independent member of the French Community. Upon Senegal's subsequent withdrawal from the Federation, the Sudanese, on Sept. 22, 1960, proclaimed their nation the fully independent Republic of Mali and severed all ties with France.

MINT MARK
(a) - Paris, privy marks only

REPUBLIC

STANDARD COINAGE

KM# 2   5 FRANCS
1.0000 g., Aluminum, 20 mm. **Obv:** Hippo facing **Rev:** Value above crossed leaves

Date	Mintage	F	VF	XF	Unc	BU
1961	—	0.15	0.25	0.50	2.00	6.00

KM# 1   10 FRANCS
25.0000 g., 0.9000 Silver 0.7234 oz. ASW
Subject: Independence **Obv:** Arms of Mali **Rev:** Bust facing

Date	Mintage	F	VF	XF	Unc	BU
ND(1960) Proof	10,000	Value: 35.00				

KM# 3   10 FRANCS
1.5500 g., Aluminum, 23.5 mm. **Obv:** Horse head left **Rev:** Value within leaf wreath

Date	Mintage	F	VF	XF	Unc	BU
1961	—	0.50	1.00	2.00	5.00	7.00

KM# 5   10 FRANCS
3.2000 g., 0.9000 Gold 0.0926 oz. AGW **Subject:** President Modibo Keita **Obv:** Arms of Mali **Rev:** Bust facing **Note:** Similar to 25 Francs, KM#6.

Date	Mintage	F	VF	XF	Unc	BU
1967 Proof	—	Value: 100				

KM# 11   10 FRANCS
1.5500 g., Aluminum, 23.5 mm. **Obv:** Value flanked by triangles with date below **Rev:** Rice plants

Date	Mintage	F	VF	XF	Unc	BU
1976(a)	10,000,000	1.25	2.50	4.50	12.50	15.00

KM# 13   10 FRANCS
3.2000 g., 0.9000 Gold 0.0926 oz. AGW, 23.5 mm.
Subject: Anniversary of Independence **Obv:** Designs within circle **Rev:** Bust with hat, facing **Note:** Similar to 50 Francs, KM#15.

Date	Mintage	F	VF	XF	Unc	BU
ND Proof	—					

Note: Reported not confirmed

KM# 4   25 FRANCS
2.5000 g., Aluminum, 27 mm. **Obv:** Lion's head facing **Rev:** Value within leaf wreath

Date	Mintage	F	VF	XF	Unc	BU
1961	—	0.35	0.65	1.75	4.50	10.00

KM# 6   25 FRANCS
8.0000 g., 0.9000 Gold 0.2315 oz. AGW **Subject:** President Modibo Keita **Obv:** Arms of Mali **Rev:** Bust with hat, facing

Date	Mintage	F	VF	XF	Unc	BU
1967 Proof	—	Value: 230				

KM# 12   25 FRANCS
2.5000 g., Aluminum, 27 mm. **Obv:** Value flanked by triangles with date below **Rev:** Rice plants

Date	Mintage	F	VF	XF	Unc	BU
1976(a)	10,000,000	2.50	4.00	8.00	18.00	22.00

KM# 14   25 FRANCS
8.0000 g., 0.9000 Gold 0.2315 oz. AGW **Subject:** Anniversary of Independence **Obv:** Arms of Mali **Rev:** Bust with hat, facing

Date	Mintage	F	VF	XF	Unc	BU
ND Proof	—	Value: 325				

KM# 7   50 FRANCS
16.0000 g., 0.9000 Gold 0.4630 oz. AGW **Subject:** President Modibo Keita **Obv:** Arms of Mali **Rev:** Bust with hat, facing

Date	Mintage	F	VF	XF	Unc	BU
1967 Proof	—	Value: 450				

KM# 9   50 FRANCS
4.0000 g., Nickel-Brass, 23.5 mm. **Series:** F.A.O. **Obv:** Value flanked by triangles with date below **Rev:** Millet plant

Date	Mintage	F	VF	XF	Unc	BU
1975(a)	10,000,000	0.25	0.50	1.50	3.75	5.50
1977(a)	10,000,000	0.25	0.50	1.50	3.75	5.50

KM# 15   50 FRANCS
16.0000 g., 0.9000 Gold 0.4630 oz. AGW **Subject:** Anniversary of Independence **Obv:** Arms of Mali **Rev:** Bust with hat, facing

Date	Mintage	F	VF	XF	Unc	BU
ND Proof	—	Value: 575				

KM# 8   100 FRANCS
32.0000 g., 0.9000 Gold 0.9259 oz. AGW **Subject:** President Modibo Keita **Obv:** Arms of Mali **Rev:** Bust with hat, facing

Date	Mintage	F	VF	XF	Unc	BU
1967 Proof	—	Value: 900				

KM# 10   100 FRANCS
8.0000 g., Nickel-Brass, 27.8 mm. **Series:** F.A.O. **Obv:** Value flanked by triangles with date below **Rev:** 3 Ears of corn

Date	Mintage	F	VF	XF	Unc	BU
1975(a)	23,000,000	0.65	1.25	2.50	5.00	9.00

KM# 16   100 FRANCS
32.0000 g., 0.9000 Gold 0.9259 oz. AGW **Subject:** Anniversary of Independence **Obv:** Arms of Mali **Rev:** Bust with hat, facing

Date	Mintage	F	VF	XF	Unc	BU
ND Proof	—	Value: 950				

ESSAIS

Standard metals unless otherwise noted

Some essais have surnames stamped (from die) on them. Purpose is unknown.

KM#	Date	Mintage	Identification	Mkt Val
E1	1975	—	50 Francs. Nickel-Brass. KM9.	17.50
E2	1975	—	100 Francs. Nickel-Brass. KM10.	20.00
E3	1976	—	10 Francs. Aluminum. KM11.	17.50
E4	1976	—	25 Francs. Aluminum. KM12.	20.00

PIEFORTS WITH ESSAIS

Standard metals unless otherwise noted

KM#	Date	Mintage	Identification	Mkt Val
PE1	1960	10	10 Francs. Silver. KM1.	250

PROOF SETS

KM#	Date	Mintage	Identification	Issue Price	Mkt Val
PS1	1967 (4)	—	KM5-8	—	1,225

MALTA

The Republic of Malta, an independent parliamentary democracy, is situated in the Mediterranean Sea between Sicily and North Africa. With the islands of Gozo and Comino, Malta has an area of 124 sq. mi. (320 sq. km.) and a population of 386,000. Capital: Valletta. Malta has no proven mineral resources, an agriculture insufficient to its needs, and a small, but expanding, manufacturing facility. Clothing, textile yarns and fabrics, and knitted wear are exported.

For more than 3,500 years Malta was ruled, in succession by Phoenicians, Carthaginians, Romans, Arabs, Normans, the Knights of Malta, France and Britain. Napoleon seized Malta by treachery in 1798. The French were ousted by a Maltese insurrection assisted by Britain, and in 1814 Malta, of its own free will, became a part of the British Empire. Malta obtained full independence in Sept., 1964; electing to remain within the Commonwealth with the British monarch as the nominal head of state.

Malta became a republic on Dec. 13, 1974, but remained a member of the Commonwealth of Nations. The president is Chief of State. The prime minister is the Head of Government.

RULER
British, until 1964

MONETARY SYSTEM
10 Mils = 1 Cent
100 Cents = 1 Pound

REPUBLIC

DECIMAL COINAGE

10 Mils = 1 Cent; 100 Cents = 1 Pound

KM# 5   2 MILS
0.9500 g., Aluminum, 20.3 mm. **Obv:** Maltese cross **Rev:** Value within 3/4 wreath

Date	Mintage	F	VF	XF	Unc	BU
1972	30,000	—	1.00	2.00	3.00	—
1972 Proof	13,000	Value: 5.00				
1976 (M)	5,000	—	—	—	2.00	—
1976 (P)	26,000	Value: 5.00				
1977 (U)	5,252	—	—	—	1.00	—
1977 (P)	6,884	Value: 5.00				
1978 (U)	5,252	—	—	—	1.00	—
1978 (P)	3,244	Value: 5.00				
1979 (U)	537	—	—	—	3.00	—
1979 (P)	6,577	Value: 5.00				
1980 (U)	385	—	—	—	3.00	—
1980 (P)	3,451	Value: 5.00				
1981 (U)	444	—	—	—	3.00	—
1981 (P)	1,453	Value: 5.00				

KM# 54   2 MILS
0.9500 g., Aluminum, 20.3 mm. **Subject:** 10th Anniversary of Decimalization **Obv:** Maltese cross **Rev:** Value within 3/4 wreath

Date	Mintage	F	VF	XF	Unc	BU
1982FM (U)	850	—	—	—	15.00	—
1982FM (P)	1,793	Value: 15.00				

KM# 6   3 MILS
1.4500 g., Aluminum, 23.25 mm. **Obv:** Bee and honeycomb **Rev:** Value within 3/4 wreath

Date	Mintage	F	VF	XF	Unc	BU
1972	—	—	1.00	2.00	3.00	—
1972 Proof	8,000	Value: 5.00				
1976FM (M)	5,000	—	—	—	3.00	—
1976FM (P)	26,000	Value: 5.00				
1977FM (U)	5,252	—	—	—	3.00	—
1977FM (P)	6,884	Value: 5.00				
1978FM (U)	5,252	—	—	—	3.00	—
1978FM (P)	3,244	Value: 5.00				
1979FM (U)	537	—	—	—	5.00	—
1979FM (P)	6,577	Value: 5.00				
1980FM (U)	385	—	—	—	5.00	—
1980FM (P)	3,451	Value: 5.00				
1981FM (U)	449	—	—	—	5.00	—
1981FM (P)	1,453	Value: 5.00				

KM# 55   3 MILS
1.4500 g., Aluminum, 23.25 mm. **Subject:** 10th Anniversary of Decimalization **Obv:** Bee and honeycomb **Rev:** Value

Date	Mintage	F	VF	XF	Unc	BU
1982FM (U)	850	—	—	—	4.00	—
1982FM (P)	1,793	Value: 2.00				

KM# 7   5 MILS
2.1000 g., Aluminum, 26 mm. **Obv:** Earthen lampstand **Rev:** Value within 3/4 wreath

Date	Mintage	F	VF	XF	Unc	BU
1972	4,320,000	—	1.00	2.00	3.00	—
1972 Proof	13,000	Value: 5.00				
1976FM (M)	5,000	—	—	—	3.00	—
1976FM (P)	26,000	Value: 5.00				
1977FM (U)	5,252	—	—	—	3.00	—
1977FM (P)	6,884	Value: 5.00				
1978FM (U)	5,252	—	—	—	3.00	—
1978FM (P)	3,244	Value: 5.00				
1979FM (U)	537	—	—	—	7.00	—
1979FM (P)	6,577	Value: 5.00				
1980FM (U)	385	—	—	—	7.00	—
1980FM (P)	3,451	Value: 5.00				
1981FM (U)	449	—	—	—	7.00	—
1981FM (P)	1,453	Value: 5.00				

KM# 56   5 MILS
2.1000 g., Aluminum, 26 mm. **Subject:** 10th Anniversary of Decimalization **Obv:** Earthen lampstand **Rev:** Value

Date	Mintage	F	VF	XF	Unc	BU
1982FM (U)	850	—	—	—	15.00	—
1982FM (P)	1,793	Value: 15.00				

KM# 8   CENT
7.1500 g., Bronze, 25.9 mm. **Obv:** The George Cross **Rev:** Value within 3/4 wreath

Date	Mintage	F	VF	XF	Unc	BU
1972	5,650,000	—	0.25	0.50	1.00	—
1972 Proof	13,000	Value: 5.00				
1975	1,500,000	—	0.25	0.50	1.00	—
1976FM (M)	5,000	—	—	—	5.00	—
1976FM (P)	26,000	Value: 5.00				
1977	2,793,000	—	0.25	0.50	1.00	—
1977FM (U)	5,252	—	—	—	5.00	—
1977FM (P)	6,884	Value: 5.00				
1978FM (U)	5,252	—	—	—	5.00	—
1978FM (P)	3,244	Value: 5.00				
1979FM (U)	537	—	—	—	9.00	—
1979FM (P)	6,577	Value: 5.00				
1980FM (U)	385	—	—	—	9.00	—
1980FM (P)	3,451	Value: 5.00				
1981FM (U)	449	—	—	—	9.00	—
1981FM (P)	1,453	Value: 15.00				
1982	—	—	5.00	5.00	10.00	—

KM# 57   CENT
7.1500 g., Bronze, 25.9 mm. **Subject:** 10th Anniversary of Decimalization **Obv:** The George cross **Rev:** Value

Date	Mintage	F	VF	XF	Unc	BU
1982FM (U)	850	—	—	—	15.00	—
1982FM (P)	1,793	Value: 15.00				

KM# 9   2 CENTS
2.2500 g., Copper-Zinc, 17.75 mm. **Subject:** Penthesilea, Queen of the Amazons **Obv:** Helmeted bust right **Rev:** Value within 3/4 wreath

Date	Mintage	F	VF	XF	Unc	BU
1972	5,640,000	—	0.10	0.50	1.00	—
1972 Proof	13,000	Value: 5.00				
1976	1,000,000	—	1.50	2.00	2.50	—
1976FM (M)	2,500	—	—	—	4.50	—
1976FM (P)	26,000	Value: 5.00				
1977	6,105,000	—	1.50	2.00	2.50	—
1977FM (U)	2,752	—	—	—	4.50	—
1977FM (P)	6,884	Value: 5.00				
1978FM (U)	2,752	—	—	—	4.50	—
1978FM (P)	3,244	Value: 5.00				
1979FM (U)	537	—	—	—	12.00	—
1979FM (P)	6,577	Value: 5.00				
1980FM (U)	385	—	—	—	12.00	—
1980FM (P)	3,451	Value: 5.00				
1981FM (U)	449	—	—	—	12.00	—
1981FM (P)	1,453	Value: 5.00				
1982	—	—	0.10	0.15	0.30	—

KM# 58   2 CENTS
2.2500 g., Copper-Zinc, 17.75 mm. **Subject:** 10th Anniversary of Decimalization **Obv:** Helmeted bust right **Rev:** Value

Date	Mintage	F	VF	XF	Unc	BU
1982FM (U)	850	—	—	—	10.00	—
1982FM (P)	1,793	Value: 15.00				

KM# 10 5 CENTS
5.6500 g., Copper-Nickel, 23.6 mm. **Obv:** Ritual altar in the Temple of Hagar Qim **Rev:** Value within 3/4 wreath

Date	Mintage	F	VF	XF	Unc	BU
1972	4,180,000	—	3.00	4.00	5.00	—
1972 Proof	13,000	Value: 7.00				
1976	1,009,000	—	1.00	2.00	3.00	—
1976FM (M)	2,500	—	—	—	5.00	—
1976FM (P)	26,000	Value: 2.00				
1977	—	—	1.00	2.00	3.00	—
1977FM (U)	2,752	—	—	—	5.00	—
1977FM (P)	6,884	Value: 3.00				
1978FM (U)	2,752	—	—	—	5.00	—
1978FM (P)	3,244	Value: 3.00				
1979FM (U)	537	—	—	—	15.00	—
1979FM (P)	6,577	Value: 3.00				
1980FM (U)	385	—	—	—	15.00	—
1980FM (P)	3,451	Value: 3.00				
1981FM (U)	449	—	—	—	15.00	—
1981FM (P)	1,453	Value: 3.00				

KM# 59 5 CENTS
5.6500 g., Copper-Nickel, 23.6 mm. **Subject:** 10th Anniversary of Decimalization **Obv:** Floral altar in the Temple of Hagar Qim **Rev:** Value

Date	Mintage	F	VF	XF	Unc	BU
1982FM (U)	850	—	—	—	15.00	—
1982FM (P)	1,793	Value: 3.00				

KM# 11 10 CENTS
11.3000 g., Copper-Nickel, 28.5 mm. **Obv:** Barge of the grand master **Rev:** Value within 3/4 wreath

Date	Mintage	F	VF	XF	Unc	BU
1972	10,680,000	—	4.00	6.00	8.00	—
1972 Proof	13,000	Value: 2.25				
1976FM (M)	1,000	—	—	—	8.00	—
1976FM (P)	26,000	Value: 2.50				
1977FM (U)	1,252	—	—	—	8.00	—
1977FM (P)	6,884	Value: 3.50				
1978FM (U)	1,252	—	—	—	8.00	—
1978FM (P)	3,244	Value: 3.50				
1979FM (U)	537	—	—	—	20.00	—
1979FM (P)	6,577	Value: 3.50				
1980FM (U)	385	—	—	—	20.00	—
1980FM (P)	3,451	Value: 3.50				
1981FM (U)	449	—	—	—	20.00	—
1981FM (P)	1,453	Value: 3.50				

KM# 60 10 CENTS
11.3000 g., Copper-Nickel, 28.5 mm. **Subject:** 10th Anniversary of Decimalization **Obv:** Barge of the grand master **Rev:** Value

Date	Mintage	F	VF	XF	Unc	BU
1982FM (U)	850	—	—	—	25.00	—
1982FM (P)	1,793	Value: 30.00				

KM# 29 25 CENTS
10.5500 g., Brass, 30 mm. **Subject:** 1st Anniversary - Republic of Malta **Obv:** Republic emblem within circle **Rev:** Value within 3/4 wreath

Date	Mintage	F	VF	XF	Unc	BU
1975	4,750,000	—	8.00	9.00	10.00	—
1975 Matte proof	—	—	—	—	200	—

KM# 29a 25 CENTS
Bronze, 30 mm. **Obv:** Republic emblem within circle **Rev:** Value within 3/4 wreath

Date	Mintage	F	VF	XF	Unc	BU
1975 Proof	6,000	Value: 25.00				

KM# 29b 25 CENTS
Copper-Nickel, 30 mm. **Obv:** Republic emblem within circle **Rev:** Value within 3/4 wreath

Date	Mintage	F	VF	XF	Unc	BU
1976FM (M)	300	—	—	—	40.00	—
1976FM (P)	26,000	Value: 3.00				
1977FM (U)	552	—	—	—	20.00	—
1977FM (P)	6,884	Value: 4.50				
1978FM (U)	552	—	—	—	20.00	—
1978FM (P)	3,244	Value: 4.50				
1979FM (U)	537	—	—	—	20.00	—
1979FM (P)	6,577	Value: 4.50				
1980FM (U)	385	—	—	—	20.00	—
1980FM (P)	3,451	Value: 4.50				
1981FM (U)	449	—	—	—	20.00	—
1981FM (P)	1,453	Value: 4.50				

KM# 61 25 CENTS
Copper-Nickel, 30 mm. **Subject:** 10th Anniversary of Decimalization **Obv:** Republic emblem within circle **Rev:** Value

Date	Mintage	F	VF	XF	Unc	BU
1982FM (U)	850	—	—	—	35.00	—
1982FM (P)	1,793	Value: 40.00				

KM# 12 50 CENTS
13.6000 g., Copper-Nickel, 32.95 mm. **Obv:** Great Siege Monument **Rev:** Value within 3/4 wreath

Date	Mintage	F	VF	XF	Unc	BU
1972	5,500,000	—	9.00	12.00	15.00	—
1972 Proof	13,000	Value: 4.50				
1976FM (M)	150	—	—	—	90.00	—
1976FM (P)	26,000	Value: 5.00				
1977FM (U)	402	—	—	—	25.00	—
1977FM (P)	6,884	Value: 6.00				
1978FM (U)	402	—	—	—	25.00	—
1978FM (P)	3,244	Value: 6.00				
1979FM (U)	537	—	—	—	25.00	—
1979FM (P)	6,577	Value: 6.00				
1980FM (U)	385	—	—	—	25.00	—
1980FM (P)	3,451	Value: 6.00				
1981FM (U)	449	—	—	—	25.00	—
1981FM (P)	1,453	Value: 6.00				

KM# 62 50 CENTS
13.6000 g., Copper-Nickel, 32.95 mm. **Subject:** 10th Anniversary of Decimalization **Obv:** Great Siege Monument **Rev:** Value

Date	Mintage	F	VF	XF	Unc	BU
1982FM (U)	850	—	—	40.00	—	—
1982FM (P)	1,793	Value: 40.00				

KM# 13 POUND
10.0000 g., 0.9870 Silver 0.3173 oz. ASW **Obv:** Crowned arms with supporters **Rev:** Bust left

Date	Mintage	F	VF	XF	Unc	BU
1972	55,000	—	—	16.00	17.00	18.00

Note: Appears to be proof, but officially issued as "BU"

KM# 19 POUND
10.0000 g., 0.9870 Silver 0.3173 oz. ASW **Obv:** Crowned arms with supporters **Rev:** Bust left

Date	Mintage	F	VF	XF	Unc	BU
1973	30,000	—	—	16.00	17.00	18.00

KM# 45 POUND
5.6600 g., 0.9250 Silver 0.1683 oz. ASW **Obv:** Republic emblem within circle **Rev:** Dog

Date	Mintage	F	VF	XF	Unc	BU
1977	66,000	—	—	30.00	35.00	45.00
1977 Proof	2,500	Value: 75.00				

KM# 51 POUND
5.6600 g., 0.9250 Silver 0.1683 oz. ASW **Subject:** Departure of foreign forces **Obv:** Republic emblem within circle **Rev:** Flames within helping hands divide date and value

Date	Mintage	F	VF	XF	Unc	BU
1979FM (U)	49,526	—	—	25.00	30.00	—
1979FM (P)	7,871	Value: 55.00				

KM# 14   2 POUNDS
20.0000 g., 0.9870 Silver 0.6346 oz. ASW **Obv:** Crowned arms with supporters **Rev:** Fort San Angelo

Date	Mintage	F	VF	XF	Unc	BU
1972	53,000	—	—	25.00	30.00	35.00

Note: Appears to be proof, but officially issued as "BU"

KM# 20   2 POUNDS
20.0000 g., 0.9870 Silver 0.6346 oz. ASW **Rev:** Tal-Imdina Gate

Date	Mintage	F	VF	XF	Unc	BU
1973	30,000	—	—	30.00	35.00	40.00

KM# 24   2 POUNDS
10.0000 g., 0.9870 Silver 0.3173 oz. ASW **Obv:** Crowned arms with supporters **Rev:** Bust 1/4 left

Date	Mintage	F	VF	XF	Unc	BU
1974	25,000	—	—	16.00	18.00	20.00

KM# 30   2 POUNDS
10.0000 g., 0.9870 Silver 0.3173 oz. ASW **Obv:** Crowned arms with supporters **Rev:** Bust left

Date	Mintage	F	VF	XF	Unc	BU
1975	2,000	—	—	65.00	70.00	75.00

KM# 31   2 POUNDS
10.0000 g., 0.9870 Silver 0.3173 oz. ASW **Obv:** Republic emblem within circle **Rev:** Bust left

Date	Mintage	F	VF	XF	Unc	BU
1975	18,000	—	—	16.00	18.00	20.00

KM# 40   2 POUNDS
10.0000 g., 0.9870 Silver 0.3173 oz. ASW **Obv:** Republic emblem within circle **Rev:** Bust 1/4 right

Date	Mintage	F	VF	XF	Unc	BU
1976	11,000	—	—	20.00	23.00	25.00

KM# 46   2 POUNDS
11.3100 g., 0.9250 Silver 0.3363 oz. ASW **Obv:** Republic emblem within circle **Rev:** Bust left

Date	Mintage	F	VF	XF	Unc	BU
1977	15,000	—	—	—	35.00	40.00
1977 Proof	3,692	Value: 80.00				

KM# 52   2 POUNDS
11.3100 g., 0.9250 Silver 0.3363 oz. ASW **Series:** World Food Day **Obv:** Republic emblem within circle **Rev:** Men fishing in boat below small emblem

Date	Mintage	F	VF	XF	Unc	BU
1981	1,500	—	—	—	20.00	22.00
1981 Proof	12,000	Value: 85.00				

KM# 25   4 POUNDS
20.0000 g., 0.9870 Silver 0.6346 oz. ASW **Obv:** Crowned arms with supporters **Rev:** Cottonera Gate

Date	Mintage	F	VF	XF	Unc	BU
1974	24,000	—	—	30.00	35.00	40.00

KM# 32   4 POUNDS
20.0000 g., 0.9870 Silver 0.6346 oz. ASW **Obv:** Crowned arms with supporters **Rev:** St. Agatha's tower at Gammieh

Date	Mintage	F	VF	XF	Unc	BU
1975	2,000	—	—	140	145	150

KM# 33   4 POUNDS
20.0000 g., 0.9870 Silver 0.6346 oz. ASW **Obv:** Republic emblem within circle **Rev:** St. Agatha's Tower at Gammieh

Date	Mintage	F	VF	XF	Unc	BU
1975	18,000	—	—	30.00	35.00	40.00

KM# 41   4 POUNDS
20.0000 g., 0.9870 Silver 0.6346 oz. ASW **Obv:** Republic emblem **Rev:** Fort Manoel Gate

Date	Mintage	F	VF	XF	Unc	BU
1976	10,000	—	—	40.00	40.00	45.00

KM# 15   5 POUNDS
3.0000 g., 0.9160 Gold 0.0883 oz. AGW **Obv:** Crowned arms with supporters **Rev:** Hand holding torch within map of Malta

Date	Mintage	F	VF	XF	Unc	BU
1972	18,000	—	—	—	—	115

Note: Appears to be proof, but officially issued as "BU"

KM# 47   5 POUNDS
28.2800 g., 0.9250 Silver 0.8410 oz. ASW **Obv:** Republic emblem **Rev:** Windmill divides date and value

Date	Mintage	F	VF	XF	Unc	BU
1977	15,000	—	—	—	—	100
1977 Proof	3,938	Value: 175				

KM# 53   5 POUNDS
28.2800 g., 0.9250 Silver 0.8410 oz. ASW **Subject:** International Youth Conference - UNICEF **Obv:** Republic emblem **Rev:** Kids playing game on numeral board flanked by UNICEF emblems

Date	Mintage	F	VF	XF	Unc	BU
1981 Proof	11,000	Value: 140				

KM# 16 10 POUNDS
6.0000 g., 0.9170 Gold 0.1769 oz. AGW **Obv:** Crowned arms with supporters **Rev:** Kenur, a Maltese stone charcoal stove

Date	Mintage	F	VF	XF	Unc	BU
1972	16,000	—	—	—	—	220

Note: Appears to be proof, but officially issued as "BU"

KM# 21 10 POUNDS
3.0000 g., 0.9170 Gold 0.0884 oz. AGW **Obv:** Crowned arms with supporters **Rev:** Watchtower

Date	Mintage	F	VF	XF	Unc	BU
1973	9,078	—	—	—	—	115

KM# 26 10 POUNDS
3.0000 g., 0.9170 Gold 0.0884 oz. AGW **Obv:** Crowned arms with supporters **Rev:** Zerafa flower flanked by date and value

Date	Mintage	F	VF	XF	Unc	BU
1974	9,124	—	—	—	—	110

KM# 34 10 POUNDS
3.0000 g., 0.9170 Gold 0.0884 oz. AGW **Obv:** Crowned arms with supporters **Rev:** Falcon

Date	Mintage	F	VF	XF	Unc	BU
1975	2,000	—	—	—	—	125

KM# 35 10 POUNDS
3.0000 g., 0.9170 Gold 0.0884 oz. AGW **Obv:** Republic emblem within circle **Rev:** Maltese falcon

Date	Mintage	F	VF	XF	Unc	BU
1975	6,448	—	—	—	—	125

KM# 42 10 POUNDS
3.0000 g., 0.9170 Gold 0.0884 oz. AGW **Obv:** Republic emblem within circle **Rev:** Swallowtail butterfly above value

Date	Mintage	F	VF	XF	Unc	BU
1976	4,448	—	—	—	—	120

KM# 17 20 POUNDS
12.0000 g., 0.9170 Gold 0.3538 oz. AGW **Obv:** Crowned arms with supporters **Rev:** Merill bird

Date	Mintage	F	VF	XF	Unc	BU
1972	16,000	—	—	—	—	420

Note: Appears to be proof, but officially issued as "BU"

KM# 22 20 POUNDS
6.0000 g., 0.9170 Gold 0.1769 oz. AGW **Obv:** Crowned arms with supporters **Rev:** Dolphins Fountain at Floriana

Date	Mintage	F	VF	XF	Unc	BU
1973	9,075	—	—	—	—	210

KM# 27 20 POUNDS
6.0000 g., 0.9170 Gold 0.1769 oz. AGW **Obv:** Crowned arms with supporters **Rev:** Gozo boat with lateen sails

Date	Mintage	F	VF	XF	Unc	BU
1974	8,700	—	—	—	—	210

KM# 36 20 POUNDS
6.0000 g., 0.9170 Gold 0.1769 oz. AGW **Obv:** Crowned arms with supporters **Rev:** Freshwater crab

Date	Mintage	F	VF	XF	Unc	BU
1975	2,000	—	—	—	—	210

KM# 37 20 POUNDS
6.0000 g., 0.9170 Gold 0.1769 oz. AGW **Obv:** Republic emblem within circle **Rev:** Fresh water crab

Date	Mintage	F	VF	XF	Unc	BU
1975	5,698	—	—	—	—	210

KM# 43 20 POUNDS
6.0000 g., 0.9170 Gold 0.1769 oz. AGW **Obv:** Republic emblem within circle **Rev:** Storm petrel bird

Date	Mintage	F	VF	XF	Unc	BU
1976	4,098	—	—	—	225	295

KM# 48 25 POUNDS
7.9900 g., 0.9170 Gold 0.2356 oz. AGW **Subject:** First Gozo coin **Obv:** Republic emblem within circle **Rev:** Figure holding lance facing right within circle

Date	Mintage	F	VF	XF	Unc	BU
1977	4,000	—	—	—	—	295
1977 Proof	3,249	Value: 340				

KM# 18 50 POUNDS
30.0000 g., 0.9170 Gold 0.8844 oz. AGW **Obv:** Crowned arms with supporters **Rev:** Neptune divides date and value

Date	Mintage	F	VF	XF	Unc	BU
1972	16,000	—	—	—	—	1,050

Note: Appears to be proof, but officially issued as "BU"

KM# 23 50 POUNDS
15.0000 g., 0.9170 Gold 0.4422 oz. AGW **Subject:** Auberge de Castille at Valletta **Obv:** Crowned arms with supporters **Rev:** Building with small flag on top above date and value

Date	Mintage	F	VF	XF	Unc	BU
1973	9,075	—	—	—	—	525

KM# 28 50 POUNDS
15.0000 g., 0.9170 Gold 0.4422 oz. AGW **Subject:** First Maltese coin **Obv:** Crowned arms with supporters **Rev:** Design within wreath

Date	Mintage	F	VF	XF	Unc	BU
1974	8,667	—	—	—	—	525

KM# 38 50 POUNDS
15.0000 g., 0.9170 Gold 0.4422 oz. AGW **Obv:** Crowned arms with supporters **Rev:** Ornamental stone balcony

Date	Mintage	F	VF	XF	Unc	BU
1975	2,000	—	—	—	—	560

KM# 39 50 POUNDS
15.0000 g., 0.9170 Gold 0.4422 oz. AGW **Obv:** Republic emblem within circle **Rev:** Ornamental stone balcony

Date	Mintage	F	VF	XF	Unc	BU
1975	5,500	—	—	—	—	560

KM# 44 50 POUNDS
15.0000 g., 0.9170 Gold 0.4422 oz. AGW **Obv:** Republic emblem **Rev:** Ornamental door knocker

Date	Mintage	F	VF	XF	Unc	BU
1976	3,748	—	—	—	—	525

KM# 49   50 POUNDS
15.9800 g., 0.9170 Gold 0.4711 oz. AGW **Subject:** Mnara
Obv: Republic emblem within circle **Rev:** Mnara design flanked
by value above date

Date	Mintage	F	VF	XF	Unc	BU
1977	4,000	—	—	—	—	590
1977 Proof	846	Value: 680				

KM# 50   100 POUNDS
31.9600 g., 0.9170 Gold 0.9422 oz. AGW **Rev:** Father and two
children sculpture above value

Date	Mintage	F	VF	XF	Unc	BU
1977	4,000	—	—	—	—	1,180
1977 Proof	846	Value: 1,360				

REFORM COINAGE
1982 - Present
10 Mils = 1 Cent; 100 Cents = 1 Lira = (Pound)

KM# 78   CENT
Copper-Zinc, 18 mm. **Obv:** Republic emblem within circle
Rev: Common weasel

Date	Mintage	F	VF	XF	Unc	BU
1986	21,526,000	—	0.40	0.50	1.00	—
1986 Proof	10,000	Value: 75.00				

KM# 93   CENT
2.8000 g., Copper-Zinc, 18.53 mm. **Obv:** Crowned shield within
sprigs **Rev:** Common Weasel below value **Edge:** Plain

Date	Mintage	F	VF	XF	Unc	BU
1991	—	—	0.40	0.50	1.00	—
1995	—	—	0.40	0.50	1.00	—
1998	—	—	0.40	0.50	1.00	—

KM# 79   2 CENTS
Copper-Zinc **Obv:** Republic emblem within circle **Rev:** Olive branch

Date	Mintage	F	VF	XF	Unc	BU
1986	280,000	—	1.25	1.50	2.00	—
1986 Proof	10,000	Value: 6.00				

KM# 94   2 CENTS
2.2400 g., Copper-Zinc, 17.8 mm. **Obv:** Crowned shield within
sprigs **Rev:** Olive branch and value

Date	Mintage	F	VF	XF	Unc	BU
1991	—	—	0.75	1.00	1.25	—
1992	—	—	0.75	1.00	1.25	—
1993	—	—	0.75	1.00	1.25	—
1995	—	—	0.75	1.00	1.25	—
1998	—	—	0.75	1.00	1.25	—

KM# 77   5 CENTS
Copper-Nickel, 20 mm. **Obv:** Republic emblem within circle
Rev: Freshwater crab

Date	Mintage	F	VF	XF	Unc	BU
1986	150,000	—	0.75	1.00	1.25	2.00
1986 Proof	10,000	Value: 7.00				

KM# 95   5 CENTS
3.5100 g., Copper-Nickel, 20 mm. **Obv:** Crowned shield within
sprigs **Rev:** Freshwater Crab and value **Edge:** Reeded

Date	Mintage	F	VF	XF	Unc	BU
1991	—	—	0.75	1.00	1.25	2.00
1995	—	—	0.75	1.00	1.25	2.00
1998	—	—	0.75	1.00	1.25	2.00

KM# 76   10 CENTS
5.0400 g., Copper-Nickel, 22 mm. **Obv:** Republic emblem within
circle **Rev:** Dolphin fish

Date	Mintage	F	VF	XF	Unc	BU
1986	4,188,000	—	1.25	1.50	2.00	—
1986 Proof	10,000	Value: 8.00				

KM# 96   10 CENTS
5.0000 g., Copper-Nickel, 22 mm. **Obv:** Crowned shield within
sprigs **Rev:** Dolphin fish and value

Date	Mintage	F	VF	XF	Unc	BU
1991	—	—	1.25	1.50	2.00	—
1992	—	—	1.25	1.50	2.00	—
1995	—	—	1.25	1.50	2.00	—
1998	—	—	1.25	1.50	2.00	—

KM# 80   25 CENTS
Copper-Nickel, 25 mm. **Rev:** Ghirlanda flower

Date	Mintage	F	VF	XF	Unc	BU
1986	3,090,000	—	2.25	2.50	3.00	—
1986 Proof	10,000	Value: 10.00				

KM# 97   25 CENTS
6.2300 g., Copper-Nickel, 25 mm. **Obv:** Crowned shield within
sprigs **Rev:** Ghirlanda flower and value

Date	Mintage	F	VF	XF	Unc	BU
1991	—	—	2.25	2.50	3.00	—
1993	—	—	2.25	2.50	3.00	—
1995	—	—	2.25	2.50	3.00	—
1998	—	—	2.25	2.50	3.00	—

KM# 81   50 CENTS
Copper-Nickel **Obv:** Republic emblem within circle **Rev:** Tulliera
plant

Date	Mintage	F	VF	XF	Unc	BU
1986	2,086,000	—	5.00	6.00	7.00	—
1986 Proof	10,000	Value: 15.00				

KM# 98   50 CENTS
7.9500 g., Copper-Nickel, 26.9 mm. **Obv:** Crowned shield within
sprigs **Rev:** Tulliera plant and value

Date	Mintage	F	VF	XF	Unc	BU
1991	—	—	2.50	4.50	6.00	—
1992	—	—	2.50	4.50	6.00	—
1995	—	—	2.50	5.00	10.00	—
1998	—	—	2.50	5.00	10.00	—

KM# 63   LIRA
Copper-Nickel **Subject:** World Fisheries Conference **Rev:** Man
in boat with fishing traps

Date	Mintage	F	VF	XF	Unc	BU
ND(1984)	120,000	—	—	—	20.00	—

KM# 82   LIRA
Nickel, 30 mm. **Obv:** Republic emblem within circle **Rev:** Merill
bird **Edge:** BANK CENTRALITA MALTA

Date	Mintage	F	VF	XF	Unc	BU
1986	2,272,000	—	—	4.00	8.00	12.00
1986 Proof	10,000	Value: 20.00				

KM# 99   LIRA
Nickel **Obv:** Crowned shield within sprigs **Rev:** Merill bird and value

Date	Mintage	F	VF	XF	Unc	BU
1991	—	—	—	4.00	6.00	10.00
1992	—	—	—	4.00	6.00	10.00
1994	—	—	—	4.00	6.00	10.00
1995	—	—	—	4.50	6.50	12.00
2000	—	—	—	4.50	6.50	12.00

KM# 88   2 LIRI

17.0000 g., 0.9250 Silver 0.5055 oz. ASW **Subject:** 25th
Anniversary of Independence **Obv:** Crowned shield within sprigs
Rev: Bust 1/4 right flanked by dates and value

Date	Mintage	F	VF	XF	Unc	BU
1989	75,000	—	—	—	25.00	28.00
1989 Proof	7,500	Value: 70.00				

KM# 65   5 LIRI

28.2800 g., 0.9250 Silver 0.8410 oz. ASW **Series:** International
Year of Disabled Persons **Obv:** Republic emblem **Rev:** Disabled
person design, date and value within

Date	Mintage	F	VF	XF	Unc	BU
1983	—	—	—	—	45.00	70.00
1983 Proof	—	Value: 140				

KM# 64   5 LIRI

28.2800 g., 0.9250 Silver 0.8410 oz. ASW **Subject:** World
Fisheries Conference **Obv:** Republic emblem **Rev:** Man in boat
with fishing traps

Date	Mintage	F	VF	XF	Unc	BU
ND(1984) Proof	20,000	Value: 140				

KM# 67   5 LIRI

20.0000 g., 0.9250 Silver 0.5948 oz. ASW **Subject:** Maritime
history "Strangier" (1813) **Obv:** Republic emblem within circle
Rev: Sailing ship among grid lines

Date	Mintage	F	VF	XF	Unc	BU
1984 Prooflike	15,000	—	—	—	42.50	45.00

KM# 68   5 LIRI

20.0000 g., 0.9250 Silver 0.5948 oz. ASW **Subject:** Maritime
history **Obv:** Republic emblem **Rev:** "Tigre" (1839)

Date	Mintage	F	VF	XF	Unc	BU
1984 Prooflike	15,000	—	—	—	42.50	45.00

KM# 69   5 LIRI

20.0000 g., 0.9250 Silver 0.5948 oz. ASW **Subject:** Maritime
history **Obv:** Republic emblem **Rev:** "Wignacourt" (1844)

Date	Mintage	F	VF	XF	Unc	BU
1984 Prooflike	15,000	—	—	—	42.50	45.00

KM# 70   5 LIRI

20.0000 g., 0.9250 Silver 0.5948 oz. ASW **Subject:** Maritime
history **Obv:** Republic emblem **Rev:** "Providenza" (1848)

Date	Mintage	F	VF	XF	Unc	BU
1984 Prooflike	15,000	—	—	—	42.50	45.00

KM# 71   5 LIRI

28.2800 g., 0.9250 Silver 0.8410 oz. ASW **Series:** Decade for
Women **Obv:** Republic emblem **Rev:** Woman weaving on board
within circle

Date	Mintage	F	VF	XF	Unc	BU
1984 Proof	17,000	Value: 90.00				

KM# 72   5 LIRI

20.0000 g., 0.9250 Silver 0.5948 oz. ASW **Subject:** Maritime
history **Obv:** Republic emblem **Rev:** "Malta" (1862)

Date	Mintage	F	VF	XF	Unc	BU
1985 Prooflike	15,000	—	—	—	42.50	45.00

KM# 73   5 LIRI

20.0000 g., 0.9250 Silver 0.5948 oz. ASW **Subject:** Maritime
history **Obv:** Republic emblem **Rev:** "Tagliaferro" (1882)

Date	Mintage	F	VF	XF	Unc	BU
1985 Prooflike	15,000	—	—	—	42.50	45.00

KM# 74   5 LIRI

20.0000 g., 0.9250 Silver 0.5948 oz. ASW **Subject:** Maritime
history **Obv:** Republic emblem **Rev:** "L'Isle Adam" (1883)

Date	Mintage	F	VF	XF	Unc	BU
1985 Prooflike	15,000	—	—	—	42.50	45.00

KM# 75   5 LIRI

20.0000 g., 0.9250 Silver 0.5948 oz. ASW **Subject:** Maritime
history **Obv:** Republic emblem **Rev:** "Maria Dacoutros" (1902)

Date	Mintage	F	VF	XF	Unc	BU
1985 Prooflike	15,000	—	—	—	42.50	45.00

KM# 83   5 LIRI

20.0000 g., 0.9250 Silver 0.5948 oz. ASW **Subject:** Maritime
history **Obv:** Republic emblem **Rev:** "Valetta City" (1917)

Date	Mintage	F	VF	XF	Unc	BU
1986 Prooflike	15,000	—	—	—	42.50	45.00

KM# 84   5 LIRI

20.0000 g., 0.9250 Silver 0.5948 oz. ASW **Subject:** Maritime
history **Obv:** Republic emblem **Rev:** "Knight of Malta" (1929)

Date	Mintage	F	VF	XF	Unc	BU
1986 Prooflike	15,000	—	—	—	42.50	45.00

KM# 85   5 LIRI
20.0000 g., 0.9250 Silver 0.5948 oz. ASW **Subject:** Maritime
history **Obv:** Republic emblem **Rev:** "Saver" (1943)

Date	Mintage	F	VF	XF	Unc	BU
1986 Prooflike	15,000	—	—	—	42.50	45.00

KM# 86   5 LIRI
20.0000 g., 0.9250 Silver 0.5948 oz. ASW **Subject:** Maritime
history **Obv:** Republic emblem **Rev:** "Dwejra II" (1969)

Date	Mintage	F	VF	XF	Unc	BU
1986 Prooflike	15,000	—	—	—	42.50	45.00

KM# 87   5 LIRI
28.2800 g., 0.9250 Silver 0.8410 oz. ASW **Subject:** 20th
Anniversary - Central Bank of Malta **Obv:** Crowned arms with
supporters **Rev:** Bank of Malta

Date	Mintage	F	VF	XF	Unc	BU
1988	Est. 5,000	—	—	—	—	50.00
1988 Proof	Est. 2,000	Value: 120				

KM# 90   5 LIRI
28.6000 g., 0.9250 Silver 0.8505 oz. ASW **Subject:** Papal visit
Obv: Crowned shield within sprigs **Rev:** Pope's hand with staff,
city scene in background

Date	Mintage	F	VF	XF	Unc	BU
1990	5,000	—	—	—	—	70.00
1990 Proof	4,000	Value: 140				

KM# 91   5 LIRI
28.2800 g., 0.9250 Silver 0.8410 oz. ASW **Subject:** Entry of
Malta to European Economic Community **Rev:** Two flags among
the map of Malta

Date	Mintage	F	VF	XF	Unc	BU
1990		—	—	—	—	50.00
1990 Proof	4,000	Value: 100				

KM# 92   5 LIRI
28.2800 g., 0.9250 Silver 0.8410 oz. ASW **Series:** Save the
Children **Obv:** Crowned shield within wreath **Rev:** Children playing

Date	Mintage	F	VF	XF	Unc	BU
1991 Proof	20,000	Value: 100				

KM# 100   5 LIRI
28.2800 g., 0.9250 Silver 0.8410 oz. ASW **Subject:** 50th
Anniversary of George Cross Award **Obv:** Crowned shield within
wreath **Rev:** George cross award

Date	Mintage	F	VF	XF	Unc	BU
1992		—	—	—	—	70.00
1992 Proof	10,000	Value: 140				

KM# 102   5 LIRI
28.2800 g., 0.9250 Silver 0.8410 oz. ASW **Subject:** 25th
Anniversary of Central Bank **Obv:** Arms above Central Bank
building **Rev:** Bust facing

Date	Mintage	F	VF	XF	Unc	BU
ND (1993)		—	—	—	—	50.00
ND(1993) Proof	1,500	Value: 100				

KM# 106   5 LIRI
28.2800 g., 0.9250 Silver 0.8410 oz. ASW **Subject:** 400th
Anniversary - University of Malta **Obv:** University emblems above
crowned shield within sprigs flanked by dates **Rev:** Conjoined
armored busts left

Date	Mintage	F	VF	XF	Unc	BU
ND(1993) Proof	Est. 1,000	Value: 240				

KM# 107   5 LIRI
28.2800 g., 0.9250 Silver 0.8410 oz. ASW **Subject:** World Cup
Soccer **Obv:** Crowned shield within wreath **Rev:** Goalie catching ball

Date	Mintage	F	VF	XF	Unc	BU
1993 Proof	Est. 20,000	Value: 90.00				

KM# 108   5 LIRI
31.4700 g., 0.9250 Silver 0.9359 oz. ASW **Obv:** Crowned shield
within wreath **Rev:** Sailing ship "Valletta" and fortress

Date	Mintage	F	VF	XF	Unc	BU
1994 Proof	Est. 20,000	Value: 125				

KM# 109   5 LIRI
28.2800 g., 0.9250 Silver 0.8410 oz. ASW **Series:** 50th Anniversary
- United Nations **Obv:** Crowned shield within wreath **Rev:** Small UN
logo above two half figures shaking hands, all within circle

Date	Mintage	F	VF	XF	Unc	BU
1995 Proof	125,000	Value: 100				

KM# 110 5 LIRI
31.4700 g., 0.9250 Silver 0.9359 oz. ASW Series: Olympic Games Subject: Water polo Obv: Crowned shield within wreath Rev: Men playing water volley ball

Date	Mintage	F	VF	XF	Unc	BU
1996 Proof	Est. 35,000				Value: 90.00	

KM# 115 5 LIRI
28.2800 g., 0.9250 Silver 0.8410 oz. ASW, 38.6 mm. Subject: UNICEF Obv: Crowned shield within wreath Rev: Boy with dog and computer Edge: Reeded

Date	Mintage	F	VF	XF	Unc	BU
1997 Proof	25,000				Value: 100	

KM# 111 5 LIRI
28.2800 g., 0.9250 Silver 0.8410 oz. ASW Obv: Crowned shield within wreath Rev: Bank's pyramid fountain

Date	Mintage	F	VF	XF	Unc	BU
1998 Proof	1,500				Value: 100	

KM# 112 5 LIRI
28.2800 g., 0.9250 Silver 0.8410 oz. ASW Subject: 200th Anniversary - Anti-French Revolution Obv: National arms Rev: "Blockade" medal of 1798

Date	Mintage	F	VF	XF	Unc	BU
1998 Proof	1,500				Value: 100	

KM# 113 5 LIRI
28.3500 g., 0.9250 Silver 0.8431 oz. ASW, 38.4 mm. Subject: Mattia Preti Obv: Crowned shield within wreath Rev: Portrait of Preti and John the Baptist Edge: Reeded

Date	Mintage	F	VF	XF	Unc	BU
1999 Proof	5,000				Value: 150	

KM# 114 5 LIRI
15.0000 g., 0.9250 Silver 0.4461 oz. ASW Subject: Millennium Obv: Two modern gold-plated coin designs Rev: Two ancient coin designs, gold-plated, and Malta Island map Edge: Plain Note: 40 x 20mm.

Date	Mintage	F	VF	XF	Unc	BU
2000 Proof	32,000				Value: 210	

KM# 101 25 LIRI
7.9900 g., 0.9170 Gold 0.2356 oz. AGW Subject: 50th Anniversary of George Cross Award Obv: Crowned shield within wreath Rev: George cross award

Date	Mintage	F	VF	XF	Unc	BU
1992 Proof	Est. 500				Value: 700	

KM# 66 100 LIRI
15.9800 g., 0.9170 Gold 0.4711 oz. AGW Series: International Year of Disabled Persons Obv: Republic emblem within circle Rev: Puzzle head right with missing pieces on top

Date	Mintage	F	VF	XF	Unc	BU
1983	700	—	—	—	—	775
1983 Proof	600				Value: 1,100	

KM# 89 100 LIRI
17.0000 g., 0.9170 Gold 0.5012 oz. AGW Subject: 25th Anniversary of Independence Obv: Crowned shield within sprigs Rev: Bust 1/4 right flanked by dates and value

Date	Mintage	F	VF	XF	Unc	BU
1989	5,000	—	—	—	485	595
1989 Proof	2,500				Value: 700	

ECU / LIRA COINAGE
European Currency Unit

KM# 103 LIRA (2 Ecu)
Copper-Nickel Subject: Defense of Europe Obv: Crowned shield within sprigs Rev: Cluster of sailing ships within circle

Date	Mintage	F	VF	XF	Unc	BU
1993	25,000	—	—	—	—	35.00

KM# 104 5 LIRI (10 Ecu)
25.0000 g., 0.9250 Silver 0.7435 oz. ASW Subject: Defense of Europe Obv: Crowned shield within wreath Rev: Ships at sea

Date	Mintage	F	VF	XF	Unc	BU
1993 Proof	35,000				Value: 100	

KM# 105 25 LIRI (55 Ecu)
6.7200 g., 0.9000 Gold 0.1944 oz. AGW Subject: Defense of Europe

Date	Mintage	F	VF	XF	Unc	BU
1993 Proof	2,500				Value: 560	

PIEFORTS

KM#	Date	Mintage	Identification	Issue Price	Mkt Val
P1	1981	177	5 Liri. 0.9250 Silver. KM53.	—	525
P2	1983	700	5 Liri. 0.9250 Silver. KM65.	—	420
P3	1983	—	100 Pounds. 0.9170 Gold. KM66.	—	1,700
P3	1983	—	100 Pounds. 0.9170 Gold. KM66.	—	1,700
P4	1988	500	100 Pounds. 0.9250 Silver. KM87.	80.00	280

KM#	Date	Mintage	Identification	Mkt Val
P1	1981	177	5 Liri. 0.9250 Silver. KM53.	525
P2	1983	700	5 Liri. 0.9250 Silver. KM65.	420
P3	1983	—	100 Pounds. 0.9170 Gold. KM66.	1,700
P4	1988	500	100 Pounds. 0.9250 Silver. KM87.	280

PIEFORTS

KM#	Date	Mintage	Identification	Mkt Val
P1	1981	177	5 Liri. 0.9250 Silver. KM53.	525
P2	1983	700	5 Liri. 0.9250 Silver. KM65.	420
P3	1983	—	100 Pounds. 0.9170 Gold. KM66.	1,700
P4	1988	500	100 Pounds. 0.9250 Silver. KM87.	280

MINT SETS

KM#	Date	Mintage	Identification	Issue Price	Mkt Val
MS1	1972 (8)	8,000	KM5-12	—	50.00
MS2	1972 (4)	8,000	KM15-18	210	1,785
MS3	1972 (2)	—	KM13-14	8.50	55.00
MS4	1973 (3)	9,078	KM21-23	—	840
MS5	1973 (2)	—	KM19-20	—	55.00
MS6	1974 (3)	—	KM26-28	256	840
MS7	1974 (2)	—	KM24-25	19.60	60.00
MS8	1975 (5)	2,000	KM30, 32, 34, 36, 38	276	1,150
MS9	1975 (3)	—	KM34, 36, 38	256	925
MSA10	1975 (2)	—	KM31, 33	—	60.00
MS10	1975 (2)	2,000	KM30, 32	20.00	225
MS11	1975 (3)	—	KM35, 37, 39	—	840
MS12	1976 (3)	—	KM42-44	—	875
MS13	1976 (2)	—	KM40-41	—	70.00
MS14	1977 (9)	252	KM5-12, 29b	—	160
MS15	1977 (3)	4,000	KM48-50	610	2,050
MS16	1977 (3)	15,000	KM45-47	34.50	160
MS17	1978 (9)	252	KM5-12, 29b	—	160
MS18	1979 (9)	537	KM5-12, 29b	—	125
MS19	1980 (9)	385	KM5-12, 29b	11.00	125
MS20	1981 (9)	449	KM5-12, 29b	13.25	125
MS21	1982 (9)	850	KM54-62	13.25	175
MS22	1984 (4)	15,000	KM67-70	72.00	135
MS23	1985 (4)	15,000	KM72-75	72.00	135
MS24	1986 (4)	15,000	KM83-86	72.00	135
MS25	1995 (7)	—	KM#93-97, 99, 116	—	71.50

PROOF SETS

KM#	Date	Mintage	Identification	Issue Price	Mkt Val
PS1	1972 (8)	8,000	KM5-12; plastic case	—	75.00
PS2	1976 (9)	26,248	KM5-12, 29b	27.50	90.00
PS3	1977 (9)	6,884	KM5-12, 29b	31.50	105
PS4	1977 (3)	750	KM48-50	909	2,380
PS5	1977 (3)	2,500	KM45-47	72.00	280
PS6	1978 (9)	3,244	KM5-12, 29b	—	100
PS7	1979 (10)	6,577	KM5-12, 29b, 51	41.50	100
PS8	1980 (9)	3,451	KM5-12, 29b	30.00	100
PS9	1981 (9)	1,453	KM5-12, 29b	25.30	100
PS10	1982 (9)	1,793	KM54-62	32.00	275
PS11	1986 (7)	10,000	KM76-82	29.75	150

MARSHALL ISLANDS

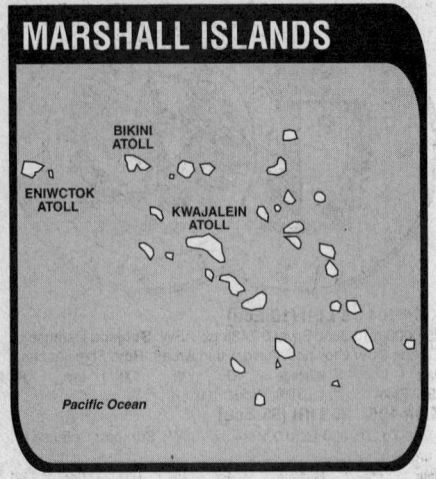

BIKINI
ATOLL

ENIWCTOK
ATOLL

KWAJALEIN
ATOLL

Pacific Ocean

The Republic of the Marshall Islands, an archipelago which is one of the four island groups that make up what is commonly known as Micronesia, consists of 33 coral atolls comprised of over 1,150 islands or islets. It is located east of the Caroline Islands and west-northwest of the Gilbert Islands halfway between Hawaii and Australia. The Ratak chain to the east and the Ralik chain to the west comprise a total land area of 70 sq. mi. (181 sq. km.) with a population of 25,000 of which about 10 % includes Americans who work at the Kwajalein Missile Range. Majuro Atoll is the government and commercial center of the Republic.

Very little is known of the history of the islands before the 16th century. It is believed that many country's vessels visited the islands while searching for new trade routes to the East. In 1788, John Marshall, a British sea captain for whom the islands were named, explored them. The Islands have undergone successive domination by the Spanish, Germans, Japanese and Americans. It was the site of some of the fiercest fighting of the entire Pacific theater during World War II. At the conclusion of the war, the United States, under the direction of the United Nations administered the affairs of the Marshall Islands.

A constitutional government was formed on May 1,1979 with Amata Kabua being elected as the head of the government. On October 1, 1986, the United States notified the United Nations that the Marshall Islands were to be recognized as a separate nation.

The USA dollar is the current monetary system. Recently, the coinage has had limited redemption policies enforced.

MINT MARKS

M - Medallic Art Co.
R - Roger Williams Mint, Rhode Island
S - Sunshine Mining Co. Mint, Idaho

REPUBLIC
NON-CIRCULATING
COLLECTOR COINAGE

The USA dollar is the current monetary system. Recently, the coinage has had limited redemption policies enforced.

KM# 1   1/2 DOLLAR
15.5510 g., 0.9990 Silver 0.4995 oz. ASW **Rev:** Pandanus Fruit

Date	Mintage	F	VF	XF	Unc	BU
1986 Proof	10,000	Value: 12.50				

KM# 2   DOLLAR
31.1030 g., 0.9990 Silver 0.9989 oz. ASW **Obv:** Similar to 1/2 Dollar, KM#1 **Rev:** Triton Shell

Date	Mintage	F	VF	XF	Unc	BU
1986 Proof	10,000	Value: 25.00				

KM# 293   DOLLAR
1.5552 g., 0.9990 Gold 0.0499 oz. AGW **Obv:** Lion **Note:** Similar to 5 Dollars, KM#295.

Date	Mintage	F	VF	XF	Unc	BU
1996	—	—	—	—	60.00	—

KM# 294   2-1/2 DOLLARS
3.1103 g., 0.9990 Gold 0.0999 oz. AGW **Obv:** Lion **Note:** Similar to 5 Dollars, KM#295.

Date	Mintage	F	VF	XF	Unc	BU
1996	—	—	—	—	120	—

KM# 6   5 DOLLARS
Copper-Nickel **Subject:** U.S. Space Shuttle - Discovery

Date	Mintage	F	VF	XF	Unc	BU
1988	756,000	—	—	—	3.50	—
1988M	431,000	—	—	—	4.50	—

KM# 13   5 DOLLARS
Copper-Nickel **Subject:** 20th Anniversary - First Men on the Moon

Date	Mintage	F	VF	XF	Unc	BU
1989	—	—	—	—	3.50	—

KM# 18   5 DOLLARS
Copper-Nickel **Subject:** To the Heroes of the Battle of Britain

Date	Mintage	F	VF	XF	Unc	BU
1990M	—	—	—	—	4.50	—

KM# 33   5 DOLLARS
Copper-Nickel **Subject:** German Unification

Date	Mintage	F	VF	XF	Unc	BU
1990M	—	—	—	—	8.00	—

KM# 38   5 DOLLARS
Copper-Nickel **Subject:** Dwight David Eisenhower **Obv:** Similar to KM#6 **Rev:** 1/2-length bust of Eisenhower saluting left

Date	Mintage	F	VF	XF	Unc	BU
1990M	—	—	—	—	5.00	—

KM# 35   5 DOLLARS
Copper-Nickel **Subject:** To the Heroes of Pearl Harbor

Date	Mintage	F	VF	XF	Unc	BU
1991M	—	—	—	—	4.00	—

KM# 37   5 DOLLARS
Copper-Nickel **Subject:** Space Shuttle Columbia

Date	Mintage	F	VF	XF	Unc	BU
1991M	—	—	—	—	5.00	—

KM# 40   5 DOLLARS
Copper-Nickel **Subject:** To the Heroes of Desert Storm

Date	Mintage	F	VF	XF	Unc	BU
1991R	—	—	—	—	6.00	—

KM# 49   5 DOLLARS
Copper-Nickel **Subject:** P-40 Warhawk of Flying Tigers

Date	Mintage	F	VF	XF	Unc	BU
1991M	—	—	—	—	4.50	—

KM# 81   5 DOLLARS
Copper-Nickel **Subject:** Reaching For New Horizons - Tipnol

Date	Mintage	F	VF	XF	Unc	BU
1992R	—	—	—	—	6.00	—

KM# 84   5 DOLLARS
Copper-Nickel **Subject:** To the Heroes of the First Air Raid on Tokyo - Doolittle **Rev:** Doolittle and the U.S.N. Hornet

Date	Mintage	F	VF	XF	Unc	BU
1992R	—	—	—	—	5.50	—

KM# 87   5 DOLLARS
Copper-Nickel **Subject:** To the Heroes of Corregidor

Date	Mintage	F	VF	XF	Unc	BU
1992R	—	—	—	—	8.00	—

KM# 90 5 DOLLARS
Copper-Nickel **Subject:** To the Heroes of Battle of Midway **Rev:** Carrier Akagi

Date	Mintage	F	VF	XF	Unc	BU
1992R	—	—	—	—	8.00	—

KM# 110 5 DOLLARS
Copper-Nickel **Subject:** Pacific Whales and Dolphins **Rev:** Humpback Whales

Date	Mintage	F	VF	XF	Unc	BU
1993R Prooflike	—	—	—	—	12.50	—

KM# 118 5 DOLLARS
Copper-Nickel **Subject:** To the Heroes of the North Atlantic **Rev:** Submarine

Date	Mintage	F	VF	XF	Unc	BU
1993R Prooflike	—	—	—	—	6.00	—

KM# 121 5 DOLLARS
Copper-Nickel **Subject:** To the Heroes of Guadalcanal **Rev:** Marine, battleship and airplanes

Date	Mintage	F	VF	XF	Unc	BU
1993R Prooflike	—	—	—	—	6.00	—

KM# 124 5 DOLLARS
Copper-Nickel **Rev:** Elvis Presley

Date	Mintage	F	VF	XF	Unc	BU
1993R Prooflike	—	—	—	—	8.00	—

KM# 126 5 DOLLARS
Copper-Nickel **Subject:** Pacific Whales and Dolphins **Rev:** Common Dolphin

Date	Mintage	F	VF	XF	Unc	BU
1993R Prooflike	—	—	—	—	12.50	—

KM# 144 5 DOLLARS
Copper-Nickel **Subject:** Christmas 1993

Date	Mintage	F	VF	XF	Unc	BU
1993	—	—	—	—	8.50	—

KM# 148 5 DOLLARS
Copper-Nickel **Subject:** Flight at Kitty Hawk

Date	Mintage	F	VF	XF	Unc	BU
1993	—	—	—	—	8.50	—

KM# 151 5 DOLLARS
Copper-Nickel **Subject:** First Men on the Moon

Date	Mintage	F	VF	XF	Unc	BU
1994	—	—	—	—	8.50	—

KM# 179 5 DOLLARS
Copper-Nickel **Subject:** To the Heroes of D-Day - Normandy Invasion

Date	Mintage	F	VF	XF	Unc	BU
1994	—	—	—	—	8.50	—

KM# 182 5 DOLLARS
Copper-Nickel **Subject:** To the Heroes of the Philippines **Rev:** MacArthur and staff

Date	Mintage	F	VF	XF	Unc	BU
1994	—	—	—	—	6.50	—

KM# 263 5 DOLLARS
Copper-Nickel **Subject:** To the Heroes of the Battle of The Bulge

Date	Mintage	F	VF	XF	Unc	BU
1994	—	—	—	—	5.50	—

KM# 187 5 DOLLARS
Copper-Nickel **Subject:** World Cup Soccer

Date	Mintage	F	VF	XF	Unc	BU
1994	—	—	—	—	5.50	—

KM# 260 5 DOLLARS
Copper-Nickel **Subject:** Christmas - Cherub

Date	Mintage	F	VF	XF	Unc	BU
1994	—	—	—	—	5.50	—

KM# 270 5 DOLLARS
Copper-Nickel **Rev:** Tornado F. MK 3 - Bomber

Date	Mintage	F	VF	XF	Unc	BU
1995	—	—	—	—	6.00	—

KM# 271 5 DOLLARS
Copper-Nickel **Subject:** Christmas **Rev:** Cherub

Date	Mintage	F	VF	XF	Unc	BU
1995	—	—	—	—	5.50	—

KM# 395 5 DOLLARS
Copper-Nickel **Obv:** State seal **Rev:** F-80 Shooting Star

Date	Mintage	F	VF	XF	Unc	BU
1995	—	—	—	—	6.50	—

KM# 185 5 DOLLARS
Copper-Nickel **Rev:** F-100 Super Sabre

Date	Mintage	F	VF	XF	Unc	BU
1995	—	—	—	—	5.50	—

KM# 186   5 DOLLARS
Copper-Nickel   **Rev:** F-16 Fighting Falcon

Date	Mintage	F	VF	XF	Unc	BU
1995	—	—	—	—	5.50	—

KM# 266   5 DOLLARS
Copper-Nickel   **Subject:** Peace - VJ Day

Date	Mintage	F	VF	XF	Unc	BU
1995	—	—	—	—	5.50	—

KM# 280   5 DOLLARS
Copper-Nickel   **Subject:** Year of the Rat

Date	Mintage	F	VF	XF	Unc	BU
1996	—	—	—	—	8.00	10.00

KM# 288   5 DOLLARS
Copper-Nickel   **Rev:** Space Shuttle Columbia

Date	Mintage	F	VF	XF	Unc	BU
1996	—	—	—	—	5.50	—

KM# 295   5 DOLLARS
7.7759 g., 0.9990 Gold 0.2497 oz. AGW   **Obv:** State seal   **Rev:** Lion

Date	Mintage	F	VF	XF	Unc	BU
1996	—	—	—	—	250	—

KM# 300   5 DOLLARS
Copper-Nickel   **Rev:** Elvis Presley

Date	Mintage	F	VF	XF	Unc	BU
1996	—	—	—	—	9.00	—

KM# 216   5 DOLLARS
Copper-Nickel   **Subject:** Peace - Victory in Europe

Date	Mintage	F	VF	XF	Unc	BU
1995	—	—	—	—	5.50	—

KM# 269   5 DOLLARS
Copper-Nickel   **Rev:** Mirage 2000C Jet Fighter

Date	Mintage	F	VF	XF	Unc	BU
1995	—	—	—	—	6.00	—

KM# 225   5 DOLLARS
Copper-Nickel   **Subject:** War in the Pacific   **Note:** Similar to 10 Dollars, KM#226.

Date	Mintage	F	VF	XF	Unc	BU
1995	—	—	—	—	9.50	—

KM# 308   5 DOLLARS
Copper-Nickel   **Subject:** Classic Cars   **Rev:** Ford Quadricycle
Note: Similar to 10 Dollars, KM#309.

Date	Mintage	F	VF	XF	Unc	BU
1996	—	—	—	—	7.50	—

KM# 303   5 DOLLARS
Copper-Nickel   **Rev:** James Dean

Date	Mintage	F	VF	XF	Unc	BU
1996	—	—	—	—	8.00	—

KM# 219   5 DOLLARS
Copper-Nickel   **Subject:** To the Heroes of the Vietnam War

Date	Mintage	F	VF	XF	Unc	BU
1995	—	—	—	—	5.50	—

KM# 222   5 DOLLARS
Copper-Nickel   **Rev:** Elvis Presley

Date	Mintage	F	VF	XF	Unc	BU
1995	—	—	—	—	9.00	—

KM# 331   5 DOLLARS
Copper-Nickel   **Subject:** Steam Locomotive   **Rev:** "Big Boy"
Note: Similar to 50 Dollar, KM#292.

Date	Mintage	F	VF	XF	Unc	BU
1996	—	—	—	—	6.00	—

KM# 311   5 DOLLARS
Copper-Nickel   **Subject:** Classic Cars   **Rev:** Model A Ford

Date	Mintage	F	VF	XF	Unc	BU
1996	—	—	—	—	7.00	—

KM# 314   5 DOLLARS
Copper-Nickel   **Subject:** Classic Cars   **Rev:** Model T Ford

Date	Mintage	F	VF	XF	Unc	BU
1996	—	—	—	—	7.00	—

KM# 253   5 DOLLARS
Copper-Nickel   **Rev:** Head of Marilyn Monroe right, 1926-1962, actress

Date	Mintage	F	VF	XF	Unc	BU
1995	—	—	—	—	7.00	—

KM# 257   5 DOLLARS
Copper-Nickel   **Series:** 50th Anniversary United Nations
Subject: Peace

Date	Mintage	F	VF	XF	Unc	BU
1995	—	—	—	—	5.50	—

KM# 297   5 DOLLARS
Copper-Nickel   **Rev:** Tiger   **Note:** Similar to 50 Dollars, KM#299.

Date	Mintage	F	VF	XF	Unc	BU
1996	—	—	—	—	17.50	—

KM# 317 5 DOLLARS
Copper-Nickel **Subject:** Classic Cars **Rev:** 1955 Thunderbird

Date	Mintage	F	VF	XF	Unc	BU
1996	—	—	—	—	10.00	—

KM# 320 5 DOLLARS
Copper-Nickel **Subject:** Classic Cars **Rev:** 1964 Mustang

Date	Mintage	F	VF	XF	Unc	BU
1996	—	—	—	—	8.50	—

KM# 353 5 DOLLARS
Copper-Nickel **Subject:** Christmas **Rev:** Two angels

Date	Mintage	F	VF	XF	Unc	BU
1996	—	—	—	—	7.50	—

KM# 403 5 DOLLARS
Copper-Nickel **Subject:** Christmas **Obv:** State seal **Rev:** Two cherubs

Date	Mintage	F	VF	XF	Unc	BU
1997	—	—	—	—	6.00	—

KM# 407 5 DOLLARS
Copper-Nickel **Subject:** Sermon on the Mount **Obv:** State seal **Rev:** Jesus preaching

Date	Mintage	F	VF	XF	Unc	BU
1997	—	—	—	—	6.00	—

KM# 323 5 DOLLARS
Copper-Nickel **Subject:** Classic Cars **Rev:** Ford Taurus

Date	Mintage	F	VF	XF	Unc	BU
1996	—	—	—	—	7.00	—

KM# 362 5 DOLLARS
Copper-Nickel **Subject:** Year of the Ox **Obv:** State seal **Rev:** Stylized Ox

Date	Mintage	F	VF	XF	Unc	BU
1997	—	—	—	—	9.00	—

KM# 364 5 DOLLARS
Copper-Nickel **Rev:** Elvis Presley

Date	Mintage	F	VF	XF	Unc	BU
1997	—	—	—	—	10.00	—

KM# 413 5 DOLLARS
Copper-Nickel **Subject:** Year of the Tiger **Obv:** State seal **Rev:** Stylized tiger

Date	Mintage	F	VF	XF	Unc	BU
1998	—	—	—	—	6.00	10.00

KM# 463 5 DOLLARS
Copper-Nickel **Subject:** History's Great Fighting Ships **Obv:** State seal **Rev:** USS Missouri

Date	Mintage	F	VF	XF	Unc	BU
1998	—	—	—	—	5.50	—

KM# 330 5 DOLLARS
Copper-Nickel **Subject:** Steam Locomotive **Rev:** Pennsylvania K4

Date	Mintage	F	VF	XF	Unc	BU
1996	—	—	—	—	6.00	—

KM# 369 5 DOLLARS
Copper-Nickel **Subject:** The Last Supper **Obv:** State seal

Date	Mintage	F	VF	XF	Unc	BU
1997	—	—	—	—	6.00	—

KM# 371 5 DOLLARS
Copper-Nickel **Subject:** To the Heroes of the Korean War **Obv:** State seal **Rev:** Soldier in poncho

Date	Mintage	F	VF	XF	Unc	BU
1997	—	—	—	—	6.00	—

KM# 464 5 DOLLARS
Copper-Nickel **Subject:** To the Heroes of the Berlin Airlift **Obv:** State seal **Rev:** C-54 landing

Date	Mintage	F	VF	XF	Unc	BU
1998	—	—	—	—	5.50	—

KM# 466 5 DOLLARS
Copper-Nickel **Subject:** Classic Cars **Obv:** State seal **Rev:** 1912 Chevy Classic Six

Date	Mintage	F	VF	XF	Unc	BU
1998	—	—	—	—	6.50	—

KM# 344 5 DOLLARS
Copper-Nickel **Rev:** Lion

Date	Mintage	F	VF	XF	Unc	BU
1996	—	—	—	—	15.00	—

KM# 345 5 DOLLARS
Copper-Nickel **Rev:** Cheetah

Date	Mintage	F	VF	XF	Unc	BU
1996	—	—	—	—	15.00	—

KM# 346 5 DOLLARS
Copper-Nickel **Rev:** Jaguar

Date	Mintage	F	VF	XF	Unc	BU
1996	—	—	—	—	15.00	—

KM# 374 5 DOLLARS
Copper-Nickel **Obv:** State seal **Rev:** Gray wolf

Date	Mintage	F	VF	XF	Unc	BU
1997	—	—	—	—	15.00	20.00

KM# 398 5 DOLLARS
Copper-Nickel **Subject:** History's Great Fighting Ships **Obv:** State seal **Rev:** USS Constitution

Date	Mintage	F	VF	XF	Unc	BU
1997	—	—	—	—	6.50	—

KM# 468 5 DOLLARS
Copper-Nickel **Subject:** Classic Cars **Obv:** State seal **Rev:** 1931 Chevy Roadster

Date	Mintage	F	VF	XF	Unc	BU
1998	—	—	—	—	6.50	—

KM# 470   5 DOLLARS
Copper-Nickel **Subject:** Classic Cars **Obv:** State seal
Rev: Cameo Carrier

Date	Mintage	F	VF	XF	Unc	BU
1998	—				6.50	

KM# 472   5 DOLLARS
Copper-Nickel **Subject:** Classic Cars **Obv:** State seal **Rev:** 1957 Chevy Bel Air

Date	Mintage	F	VF	XF	Unc	BU
1998	—	—	—	—	7.50	

KM# 474   5 DOLLARS
Copper-Nickel **Subject:** Classic Cars **Obv:** State seal **Rev:** 1957 Chevy Corvette

Date	Mintage	F	VF	XF	Unc	BU
1998	—	—	—	—	7.50	

KM# 476   5 DOLLARS
Copper-Nickel **Subject:** Classic Cars **Obv:** State seal **Rev:** 1967 Chevy Camaro

Date	Mintage	F	VF	XF	Unc	BU
1998	—	—	—	—	7.50	

KM# 478   5 DOLLARS
Copper-Nickel **Obv:** State seal **Rev:** Babe Ruth at bat

Date	Mintage	F	VF	XF	Unc	BU
1998	—	—	—	—	7.00	

KM# 481   5 DOLLARS
Copper-Nickel **Subject:** Christmas **Obv:** State seal **Rev:** Angel

Date	Mintage	F	VF	XF	Unc	BU
1998	—	—	—	—	6.00	

KM# 484   5 DOLLARS
Copper-Nickel **Rev:** Friendship 7 and Discovery blasting off

Date	Mintage	F	VF	XF	Unc	BU
1998	—	—	—	—	6.00	

KM# 486   5 DOLLARS
Copper-Nickel, 38.4 mm. **Subject:** USS United States **Obv:** National seal **Rev:** Sailing ship **Edge:** Reeded

Date	Mintage	F	VF	XF	Unc	BU
1998	—	—	—	—	10.00	

KM# 487   5 DOLLARS
Copper-Nickel, 38.4 mm. **Obv:** National seal **Rev:** USS Monitor and Merrimack battle scene **Edge:** Reeded

Date	Mintage	F	VF	XF	Unc	BU
1998	—				10.00	

KM# 488   5 DOLLARS
Copper-Nickel, 38.4 mm. **Subject:** USS Olympia **Obv:** National seal **Rev:** Battleship steaming left **Edge:** Reeded

Date	Mintage	F	VF	XF	Unc	BU
1998	—				10.00	

KM# 489   5 DOLLARS
Copper-Nickel, 38.4 mm. **Obv:** National seal **Rev:** USS Fanning and USS Nicholson **Edge:** Reeded

Date	Mintage	F	VF	XF	Unc	BU
1998	—				10.00	

KM# 490   5 DOLLARS
Copper-Nickel, 38.4 mm. **Obv:** National seal **Rev:** USS Enterprise **Edge:** Reeded

Date	Mintage	F	VF	XF	Unc	BU
1998	—				10.00	

KM# 491   5 DOLLARS
Copper-Nickel, 38.4 mm. **Obv:** National seal **Rev:** Battleship USS New Jersey **Edge:** Reeded

Date	Mintage	F	VF	XF	Unc	BU
1998	—				10.00	

KM# 492   5 DOLLARS
Copper-Nickel, 38.4 mm. **Obv:** National seal **Rev:** Heavy Cruiser USS Juneau **Edge:** Reeded

Date	Mintage	F	VF	XF	Unc	BU
1998	—				10.00	

KM# 147   10 DOLLARS
11.0000 g., 0.9990 Silver 0.3533 oz. ASW **Rev:** Greg Louganis

Date	Mintage	F	VF	XF	Unc	BU
1988 Proof	—	Value: 175				

KM# 41   10 DOLLARS
Brass **Subject:** To the Heroes of Desert Storm

Date	Mintage	F	VF	XF	Unc	BU
1991R	—	—	—	—	8.00	10.00

KM# 59   10 DOLLARS
Brass **Rev:** WWII American P-51 Mustang

Date	Mintage	F	VF	XF	Unc	BU
1991S Prooflike	Est. 50,000	—	—	—	12.50	—

KM# 60   10 DOLLARS
Brass **Rev:** WWII American B-29 Superfortress

Date	Mintage	F	VF	XF	Unc	BU
1991S Prooflike	Est. 50,000	—	—	—	12.50	—

KM# 61   10 DOLLARS
Brass **Rev:** WWII American B-25 Mitchell

Date	Mintage	F	VF	XF	Unc	BU
1991S Prooflike	Est. 50,000	—	—	—	12.50	—

KM# 62   10 DOLLARS
Brass **Rev:** WWII American PBY Catalina

Date	Mintage	F	VF	XF	Unc	BU
1991S Prooflike	Est. 50,000	—	—	—	12.50	—

KM# 63   10 DOLLARS
Brass **Rev:** WWII German BF 109 Messerschmitt

Date	Mintage	F	VF	XF	Unc	BU
1991S Prooflike	Est. 50,000	—	—	—	12.50	—

KM# 64   10 DOLLARS
Brass **Rev:** WWII British Spitfire

Date	Mintage	F	VF	XF	Unc	BU
1991S Prooflike	Est. 50,000	—	—	—	12.50	—

KM# 65   10 DOLLARS
Brass Rev: WWII Japanaese A6M Reisen

Date	Mintage	F	VF	XF	Unc	BU
1991S Prooflike	Est. 50,000	—	—	—	12.50	—

KM# 66   10 DOLLARS
Brass Rev: WWII American F6F Hellcat

Date	Mintage	F	VF	XF	Unc	BU
1991S Prooflike	Est. 50,000	—	—	—	12.50	—

KM# 67   10 DOLLARS
Brass Rev: WWII Soviet Yak 9

Date	Mintage	F	VF	XF	Unc	BU
1991S Prooflike	Est. 50,000	—	—	—	12.50	—

KM# 68   10 DOLLARS
Brass Rev: WWII American B-17 Flying Fortress

Date	Mintage	F	VF	XF	Unc	BU
1991S Prooflike	Est. 50,000	—	—	—	12.50	—

KM# 69   10 DOLLARS
Brass Rev: WWII British Hawker Hurricane

Date	Mintage	F	VF	XF	Unc	BU
1991S Prooflike	Est. 50,000	—	—	—	12.50	—

KM# 73   10 DOLLARS
Brass Subject: To the Heroes of Pearl Harbor Obv: National seal

Date	Mintage	F	VF	XF	Unc	BU
1991 Prooflike	—	—	—	—	12.50	—

KM# 70   10 DOLLARS
Brass Rev: WWII British Mosquito

Date	Mintage	F	VF	XF	Unc	BU
1991S Prooflike	Est. 50,000	—	—	—	12.50	—

KM# 71   10 DOLLARS
Brass Rev: WWII British Lancaster

Date	Mintage	F	VF	XF	Unc	BU
1991S Prooflike	Est. 50,000	—	—	—	12.50	—

KM# 96   10 DOLLARS
Brass Rev: WWII American C-47 Skytrain

Date	Mintage	F	VF	XF	Unc	BU
1991S Prooflike	Est. 50,000	—	—	—	12.50	—

KM# 98   10 DOLLARS
Brass Rev: WWII American F4U Corsair

Date	Mintage	F	VF	XF	Unc	BU
1991S Prooflike	Est. 50,000	—	—	—	12.50	—

KM# 101   10 DOLLARS
Brass Rev: WWII American P-38 Lightning

Date	Mintage	F	VF	XF	Unc	BU
1991 Prooflike	Est. 50,000	—	—	—	12.50	—

KM# 103   10 DOLLARS
Brass Rev: WWII Japanese G4M "Betty" Bomber

Date	Mintage	F	VF	XF	Unc	BU
1991S Prooflike	Est. 50,000	—	—	—	12.50	—

KM# 107   10 DOLLARS
Brass Rev: WWII Japanese KI-61 Hien "Tony"

Date	Mintage	F	VF	XF	Unc	BU
1991S Prooflike	Est. 50,000	—	—	—	12.50	—

KM# 109   10 DOLLARS
Brass Rev: WWII French D.520 Fighter

Date	Mintage	F	VF	XF	Unc	BU
1991S Prooflike	Est. 50,000	—	—	—	12.50	—

KM# 125   10 DOLLARS
Brass Rev: WWII German FW 190 Fighters

Date	Mintage	F	VF	XF	Unc	BU
1991S Prooflike	Est. 50,000	—	—	—	12.50	—

KM# 131   10 DOLLARS
Brass Rev: WWII American B-24 Liberator

Date	Mintage	F	VF	XF	Unc	BU
1991S Prooflike	Est. 50,000	—	—	—	12.50	—

KM# 140   10 DOLLARS
Brass Rev: WWII Italian S.M. 79 Sparviero

Date	Mintage	F	VF	XF	Unc	BU
1991S Prooflike	Est. 50,000	—	—	—	12.50	—

KM# 141   10 DOLLARS
Brass Rev: WWII German HE 111 Bombers

Date	Mintage	F	VF	XF	Unc	BU
1991S Prooflike	Est. 50,000	—	—	—	12.50	—

KM# 142   10 DOLLARS
Brass Rev: WWII Soviet IL-2 Shturmovik ground attack

Date	Mintage	F	VF	XF	Unc	BU
1991S Prooflike	Est. 50,000	—	—	—	12.50	—

KM# 82   10 DOLLARS
Brass Subject: Legends of Discovery Rev: Santa Maria

Date	Mintage	F	VF	XF	Unc	BU
1992R	—	—	—	—	12.50	—

KM# 85   10 DOLLARS
Brass Subject: First Air Raid on Tokyo Rev: Doolittle

Date	Mintage	F	VF	XF	Unc	BU
1992R	—	—	—	—	12.50	—

KM# 88   10 DOLLARS
Brass Subject: To the Heroes of Corregidor

Date	Mintage	F	VF	XF	Unc	BU
1992R	—	—	—	—	12.50	—

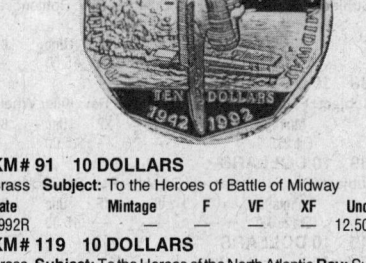

KM# 91   10 DOLLARS
Brass Subject: To the Heroes of Battle of Midway

Date	Mintage	F	VF	XF	Unc	BU
1992R	—	—	—	—	12.50	—

KM# 119   10 DOLLARS
Brass Subject: To the Heroes of the North Atlantic Rev: Submarine

Date	Mintage	F	VF	XF	Unc	BU
1993R Prooflike	—	—	—	—	14.00	—

KM# 122   10 DOLLARS
Brass Subject: To the Heroes of Guadalcanal Rev: Marine, battleship and airplanes

Date	Mintage	F	VF	XF	Unc	BU
1993R Prooflike	—	—	—	—	12.50	—

KM# 127   10 DOLLARS
Brass Subject: Pacific Whales and Dolphins Rev: Common Dolphin

Date	Mintage	F	VF	XF	Unc	BU
1993R Prooflike	—	—	—	—	15.00	—

KM# 129   10 DOLLARS
Brass Rev: Elvis Presley

Date	Mintage	F	VF	XF	Unc	BU
1993 Prooflike	—	—	—	—	16.50	—

KM# 132   10 DOLLARS
Brass Subject: Pacific Whales and Dolphins Rev: Humpback Whales

Date	Mintage	F	VF	XF	Unc	BU
1993	Est. 25,000	—	—	—	15.00	—

KM# 133   10 DOLLARS
Brass Subject: Pacific Whales and Dolphins Rev: Risso's Dolphins

Date	Mintage	F	VF	XF	Unc	BU
1993	Est. 25,000	—	—	—	15.00	—

KM# 134   10 DOLLARS
Brass **Subject:** Pacific Whales and Dolphins **Rev:** Beluga Whales

Date	Mintage	F	VF	XF	Unc	BU
1993	Est. 25,000	—	—	—	15.00	—

KM# 135   10 DOLLARS
Brass **Subject:** Pacific Whales and Dolphins **Rev:** Hector's Dolphins

Date	Mintage	F	VF	XF	Unc	BU
1993	Est. 25,000	—	—	—	15.00	—

KM# 136   10 DOLLARS
Brass **Subject:** Pacific Whales and Dolphins **Rev:** Blue Whale

Date	Mintage	F	VF	XF	Unc	BU
1993	Est. 25,000	—	—	—	15.00	—

KM# 137   10 DOLLARS
Brass **Subject:** Pacific Whales and Dolphins **Rev:** Bottlenose Dolphin

Date	Mintage	F	VF	XF	Unc	BU
1993	Est. 25,000	—	—	—	15.00	—

KM# 138   10 DOLLARS
Brass **Subject:** Pacific Whales and Dolphins **Rev:** Killer Whale

Date	Mintage	F	VF	XF	Unc	BU
1993	Est. 25,000	—	—	—	15.00	—

KM# 139   10 DOLLARS
Brass **Subject:** Pacific Whales and Dolphins **Rev:** Baiji Dolphins

Date	Mintage	F	VF	XF	Unc	BU
1993	Est. 25,000	—	—	—	15.00	—

KM# 145   10 DOLLARS
Brass **Subject:** Christmas 1993

Date	Mintage	F	VF	XF	Unc	BU
1993	Est. 25,000	—	—	—	12.50	—

KM# 149   10 DOLLARS
Brass **Subject:** Flight of the Kitty Hawk

Date	Mintage	F	VF	XF	Unc	BU
1993	—	—	—	—	12.50	—

KM# 408   10 DOLLARS
Brass **Subject:** Pacific Whales and Dolphins **Rev:** Indo-Pacific Humpbacked Dolphin

Date	Mintage	F	VF	XF	Unc	BU
1993	Est. 25,000	—	—	—	15.00	—

KM# 409   10 DOLLARS
Brass **Subject:** Pacific Whales and Dolphins **Obv:** State seal **Rev:** Long-Snouted Spinner Dolphin

Date	Mintage	F	VF	XF	Unc	BU
1993	Est. 25,000	—	—	—	15.00	—

KM# 410   10 DOLLARS
Brass **Subject:** Pacific Whales and Dolphins **Rev:** Two Sperm whales

Date	Mintage	F	VF	XF	Unc	BU
1993	Est. 25,000	—	—	—	15.00	—

KM# 411   10 DOLLARS
Brass **Subject:** Pacific Whales and Dolphins **Rev:** Minke Whale

Date	Mintage	F	VF	XF	Unc	BU
1993	Est. 25,000	—	—	—	15.00	—

KM# 152   10 DOLLARS
Brass **Subject:** First Men on the Moon

Date	Mintage	F	VF	XF	Unc	BU
1994	—	—	—	—	12.50	—

KM# 155   10 DOLLARS
Brass **Subject:** Mythological Mother Earth

Date	Mintage	F	VF	XF	Unc	BU
1994R	—	—	—	—	12.50	—

KM# 156   10 DOLLARS
Brass **Rev:** The Sun

Date	Mintage	F	VF	XF	Unc	BU
1994	—	—	—	—	14.50	—

KM# 157   10 DOLLARS
Brass **Rev:** The Moon

Date	Mintage	F	VF	XF	Unc	BU
1994	—	—	—	—	13.50	—

KM# 158   10 DOLLARS
Brass **Rev:** Pluto

Date	Mintage	F	VF	XF	Unc	BU
1994	—	—	—	—	13.50	—

KM# 159   10 DOLLARS
Brass **Rev:** Mercury

Date	Mintage	F	VF	XF	Unc	BU
1994	—	—	—	—	12.50	—

KM# 160   10 DOLLARS
Brass **Rev:** Venus

Date	Mintage	F	VF	XF	Unc	BU
1994	—	—	—	—	16.50	—

KM# 161   10 DOLLARS
Brass **Rev:** Mars

Date	Mintage	F	VF	XF	Unc	BU
1994	—	—	—	—	12.50	—

KM# 162   10 DOLLARS
Brass **Rev:** Saturn

Date	Mintage	F	VF	XF	Unc	BU
1994	—	—	—	—	13.50	—

KM# 163   10 DOLLARS
Brass **Rev:** Jupiter

Date	Mintage	F	VF	XF	Unc	BU
1994	—	—	—	—	14.50	—

KM# 164   10 DOLLARS
Brass **Rev:** Uranus

Date	Mintage	F	VF	XF	Unc	BU
1994	—	—	—	—	12.50	—

KM# 165   10 DOLLARS
Brass **Rev:** Neptune

Date	Mintage	F	VF	XF	Unc	BU
1994	—	—	—	—	14.50	—

KM# 166   10 DOLLARS
Brass **Rev:** Solar System

Date	Mintage	F	VF	XF	Unc	BU
1994	—	—	—	—	13.50	—

KM# 180   10 DOLLARS
Brass **Subject:** To the Heroes of D-Day - Normandy Invasion

Date	Mintage	F	VF	XF	Unc	BU
1994 Prooflike	—	—	—	—	12.50	—

KM# 183   10 DOLLARS
Brass **Subject:** Heroes of the Philippines **Rev:** MacArthur and staff

Date	Mintage	F	VF	XF	Unc	BU
1994 Prooflike	—	—	—	—	12.50	—

KM# 188   10 DOLLARS
Brass **Subject:** World Cup Soccer

Date	Mintage	F	VF	XF	Unc	BU
1994	—	—	—	—	12.50	—

KM# 264 10 DOLLARS
Brass **Rev:** To the Heroes of the Battle of the Bulge

Date	Mintage	F	VF	XF	Unc	BU
1994 Prooflike	—	—	—	—	12.50	

KM# 261 10 DOLLARS
Brass **Subject:** Christmas **Rev:** Cherub **Note:** Similar to 5 Dollars, KM#271.

Date	Mintage	F	VF	XF	Unc	BU
1994	—	—	—	—	12.50	—

KM# 217 10 DOLLARS
Brass **Subject:** Peace - Victory in Europe

Date	Mintage	F	VF	XF	Unc	BU
1995	—	—	—	—	12.50	—

KM# 220 10 DOLLARS
Brass **Subject:** To the Heroes of Vietnam

Date	Mintage	F	VF	XF	Unc	BU
1995 Prooflike	—	—	—	—	12.50	—

KM# 223 10 DOLLARS
Brass **Rev:** Elvis Presley

Date	Mintage	F	VF	XF	Unc	BU
1995	—	—	—	—	12.50	—

KM# 226 10 DOLLARS
Brass **Subject:** To the Heroes of the War in the Pacific

Date	Mintage	F	VF	XF	Unc	BU
1995 Prooflike	—	—	—	—	12.50	—

KM# 228 10 DOLLARS
Brass **Rev:** F-14 Tomcat

Date	Mintage	F	VF	XF	Unc	BU
1995R	Est. 25,000	—	—	—	12.50	—

KM# 229 10 DOLLARS
Brass **Rev:** F-16 Fighting Falcon

Date	Mintage	F	VF	XF	Unc	BU
1995R	Est. 25,000	—	—	—	12.50	—

KM# 230 10 DOLLARS
Brass **Rev:** Me 262A-1a Schwalbe

Date	Mintage	F	VF	XF	Unc	BU
1995R	Est. 25,000	—	—	—	12.50	—

KM# 231 10 DOLLARS
Brass **Rev:** F-104 Starfighter

Date	Mintage	F	VF	XF	Unc	BU
1995R	Est. 25,000	—	—	—	12.50	—

KM# 232 10 DOLLARS
Brass **Rev:** Mirage 2000C

Date	Mintage	F	VF	XF	Unc	BU
1995R	Est. 25,000	—	—	—	12.50	—

KM# 233 10 DOLLARS
Brass **Rev:** F-4 Phantom II

Date	Mintage	F	VF	XF	Unc	BU
1995R	Est. 25,000	—	—	—	12.50	—

KM# 234 10 DOLLARS
Brass **Rev:** Sea Harrier

Date	Mintage	F	VF	XF	Unc	BU
1995R	Est. 25,000	—	—	—	12.50	—

KM# 235 10 DOLLARS
Brass **Rev:** F-117 Nighthawk

Date	Mintage	F	VF	XF	Unc	BU
1995R	Est. 25,000	—	—	—	12.50	—

KM# 236 10 DOLLARS
Brass **Rev:** F-100 Super Sabre

Date	Mintage	F	VF	XF	Unc	BU
1995R	Est. 25,000	—	—	—	12.50	—

KM# 237 10 DOLLARS
Brass **Rev:** F-86 Sabre

Date	Mintage	F	VF	XF	Unc	BU
1995R	Est. 25,000	—	—	—	12.50	—

KM# 238 10 DOLLARS
Brass **Rev:** MIG-15

Date	Mintage	F	VF	XF	Unc	BU
1995R	Est. 25,000	—	—	—	12.50	—

KM# 239 10 DOLLARS
Brass **Rev:** G91Y

Date	Mintage	F	VF	XF	Unc	BU
1995R	Est. 25,000	—	—	—	12.50	—

KM# 240 10 DOLLARS
Brass **Rev:** SAAB 35 Draken

Date	Mintage	F	VF	XF	Unc	BU
1995R	Est. 25,000	—	—	—	12.50	—

KM# 241 10 DOLLARS
Brass **Rev:** Meteor FMK8

Date	Mintage	F	VF	XF	Unc	BU
1995R	Est. 25,000	—	—	—	12.50	—

KM# 242 10 DOLLARS
Brass **Rev:** F-105 Thunderchief

Date	Mintage	F	VF	XF	Unc	BU
1995R	Est. 25,000	—	—	—	12.50	—

KM# 243 10 DOLLARS
Brass **Rev:** Tornado FMK3

Date	Mintage	F	VF	XF	Unc	BU
1995R	Est. 25,000	—	—	—	12.50	—

KM# 254 10 DOLLARS
Brass **Rev:** Head of Marilyn Monroe right, 1926-1962, actress

Date	Mintage	F	VF	XF	Unc	BU
1995	—	—	—	—	12.50	—

KM# 258 10 DOLLARS
Brass **Series:** 50th Anniversary United Nations **Subject:** Peace

Date	Mintage	F	VF	XF	Unc	BU
1995	—	—	—	—	12.50	—

KM# 267 10 DOLLARS
Brass **Subject:** Peace - VJ Day

Date	Mintage	F	VF	XF	Unc	BU
1995	—	—	—	—	12.50	—

KM# 272 10 DOLLARS
Brass **Subject:** Christmas **Rev:** Cherub

Date	Mintage	F	VF	XF	Unc	BU
1995	—	—	—	—	12.50	—

KM# 282 10 DOLLARS
Brass **Subject:** Freedom / Liberty **Rev:** Torpedo Boat PT109

Date	Mintage	F	VF	XF	Unc	BU
1995	—	—	—	—	12.00	—

KM# 283 10 DOLLARS
Brass **Subject:** Freedom / Liberty **Rev:** President John F. Kennedy takes oath of office

Date	Mintage	F	VF	XF	Unc	BU
1995	—	—	—	—	12.50	—

KM# 284 10 DOLLARS
Brass **Subject:** Freedom / Liberty **Rev:** Peace Corps worker and native

Date	Mintage	F	VF	XF	Unc	BU
1995	—	—	—	—	12.50	—

KM# 285 10 DOLLARS
Brass **Subject:** Freedom / Liberty **Rev:** Battleships under starry sky

Date	Mintage	F	VF	XF	Unc	BU
1995	—	—	—	—	12.50	—

KM# 286 10 DOLLARS
Brass **Subject:** Freedom / Liberty **Rev:** President John F. Kennedy working at desk

Date	Mintage	F	VF	XF	Unc	BU
1995	—	—	—	—	12.50	—

KM# 287 10 DOLLARS
Brass **Subject:** Freedom / Liberty **Rev:** President John F. Kennedy's Eternal Flame

Date	Mintage	F	VF	XF	Unc	BU
1995	—	—	—	—	12.50	—

KM# 396 10 DOLLARS
Brass **Subject:** F-16 Fighting Falcon **Obv:** National seal **Rev:** Jet fighter

Date	Mintage	F	VF	XF	Unc	BU
1995	Est. 25,000	—	—	—	12.00	—

KM# 289 10 DOLLARS
Brass **Rev:** Space Shuttle Columbia

Date	Mintage	F	VF	XF	Unc	BU
1996	—	—	—	—	12.50	—

KM# 301 10 DOLLARS
Brass **Rev:** Elvis Presley

Date	Mintage	F	VF	XF	Unc	BU
1996	—	—	—	—	13.50	—

KM# 306   10 DOLLARS
Brass **Subject:** Steam Locomotive **Rev:** "Pennsylvania K4"

Date	Mintage	F	VF	XF	Unc	BU
1996	Est. 250,000	—	—	—	14.00	—

KM# 307   10 DOLLARS
Brass **Subject:** Steam Locomotive **Rev:** "Big Boy"

Date	Mintage	F	VF	XF	Unc	BU
1996	Est. 25,000	—	—	—	14.00	—

KM# 309   10 DOLLARS
Brass **Subject:** Classic Cars **Rev:** Ford Quadricycle

Date	Mintage	F	VF	XF	Unc	BU
1996 Prooflike	—	—	—	—	12.50	—

KM# 312   10 DOLLARS
Brass **Subject:** Classic Cars **Rev:** Model A Ford

Date	Mintage	F	VF	XF	Unc	BU
1996 Prooflike	—	—	—	—	12.50	—

KM# 321   10 DOLLARS
Brass **Subject:** Classic Cars **Rev:** 1964 Mustang

Date	Mintage	F	VF	XF	Unc	BU
1996 Prooflike	—	—	—	—	13.50	—

KM# 336   10 DOLLARS
Brass **Rev:** Space Shuttle - Challenger

Date	Mintage	F	VF	XF	Unc	BU
1996	—	—	—	—	12.50	—

KM# 337   10 DOLLARS
Brass **Rev:** Space Shuttle - Discovery

Date	Mintage	F	VF	XF	Unc	BU
1996	—	—	—	—	12.50	—

KM# 338   10 DOLLARS
Brass **Rev:** Space Shuttle - Atlantis

Date	Mintage	F	VF	XF	Unc	BU
1996	—	—	—	—	12.50	—

KM# 339   10 DOLLARS
Brass **Rev:** Space Shuttle - Endeavor

Date	Mintage	F	VF	XF	Unc	BU
1996	—	—	—	—	12.50	—

KM# 354   10 DOLLARS
Brass **Subject:** Christmas **Rev:** Two angels

Date	Mintage	F	VF	XF	Unc	BU
1996	—	—	—	—	12.50	—

KM# 356   10 DOLLARS
Brass **Subject:** Steam Locomotive **Rev:** "DB Class 01"

Date	Mintage	F	VF	XF	Unc	BU
1996	—	—	—	—	14.00	—

KM# 359   10 DOLLARS
Brass **Subject:** Steam Locomotive **Rev:** "RENFE Class 242"

Date	Mintage	F	VF	XF	Unc	BU
1996	—	—	—	—	14.50	—

KM# 361   10 DOLLARS
Brass **Subject:** Steam Locomotive **Rev:** "FS Group 691"

Date	Mintage	F	VF	XF	Unc	BU
1996	Est. 25,000	—	—	—	14.50	—

KM# 368   10 DOLLARS
Brass **Subject:** Steam Locomotive **Rev:** "SNCF 232. U1"

Date	Mintage	F	VF	XF	Unc	BU
1996	Est. 25,000	—	—	—	14.50	—

KM# 378   10 DOLLARS
Brass **Subject:** Steam Locomotive **Rev:** "SAR 520 Class"

Date	Mintage	F	VF	XF	Unc	BU
1996	Est. 25,000	—	—	—	14.50	—

KM# 379   10 DOLLARS
Brass **Subject:** Steam Locomotive **Rev:** "Evening Star"

Date	Mintage	F	VF	XF	Unc	BU
1996	Est. 25,000	—	—	—	14.50	—

KM# 393   10 DOLLARS
Brass **Subject:** Steam Locomotive **Rev:** QJ "Advance Forward"

Date	Mintage	F	VF	XF	Unc	BU
1996	Est. 25,000	—	—	—	14.50	—

KM# 394   10 DOLLARS
Brass **Subject:** Steam Locomotive **Obv:** State seal **Rev:** "Royal Hudson"

Date	Mintage	F	VF	XF	Unc	BU
1996	Est. 25,000	—	—	—	14.50	—

KM# 402   10 DOLLARS
Brass **Subject:** Steam Locomotive **Obv:** State seal **Rev:** C62 "Swallow"

Date	Mintage	F	VF	XF	Unc	BU
1996	Est. 25,000	—	—	—	14.50	—

KM# 304   10 DOLLARS
Brass **Rev:** James Dean **Note:** Similar to 5 Dollars, KM#303.

Date	Mintage	F	VF	XF	Unc	BU
1996	—	—	—	—	13.50	—

KM# 315   10 DOLLARS
Brass **Subject:** Classic Cars **Rev:** Model T Ford **Note:** Similar to 5 Dollars, KM#314.

Date	Mintage	F	VF	XF	Unc	BU
1996 Prooflike	—	—	—	—	12.50	—

KM# 318   10 DOLLARS
Brass **Subject:** Classic Cars **Rev:** 1955 Thunderbird **Note:** Similar to 5 Dollars, KM#317.

Date	Mintage	F	VF	XF	Unc	BU
1996 Prooflike	—	—	—	—	13.50	—

KM# 324   10 DOLLARS
Brass **Subject:** Classic Cars **Rev:** Ford Taurus **Note:** Similar to 5 Dollars, KM#323.

Date	Mintage	F	VF	XF	Unc	BU
1996 Prooflike	—	—	—	—	12.50	—

KM# 347   10 DOLLARS
Brass **Rev:** Lion **Note:** Similar to 5 Dollars, KM#344.

Date	Mintage	F	VF	XF	Unc	BU
1996	—	—	—	—	15.00	—

KM# 348   10 DOLLARS
Brass **Rev:** Cheetah **Note:** Similar to 5 Dollars, KM#345.

Date	Mintage	F	VF	XF	Unc	BU
1996	—	—	—	—	15.00	—

KM# 349   10 DOLLARS
Brass **Rev:** Jaguar **Note:** Similar to 5 Dollars, KM#346.

Date	Mintage	F	VF	XF	Unc	BU
1996	—	—	—	—	15.00	—

KM# 326   10 DOLLARS
Brass **Subject:** Steam Locomotive **Rev:** "Mallard" **Note:** Similar to 50 Dollars, KM#296.

Date	Mintage	F	VF	XF	Unc	BU
1996	Est. 25,000	—	—	—	14.00	—

KM# 298   10 DOLLARS
Brass **Rev:** Tiger **Note:** Similar to 50 Dollars, KM#299.

Date	Mintage	F	VF	XF	Unc	BU
1996	—	—	—	—	13.50	—

KM# 372   10 DOLLARS
Brass **Subject:** To the Heroes of the Korean War **Note:** Siimilar to 5 Dollars, KM#371.

Date	Mintage	F	VF	XF	Unc	BU
1997	Est. 25,000	—	—	—	12.00	—

KM# 365   10 DOLLARS
Brass **Rev:** Elvis Presley **Note:** Similar to 5 Dollars, KM#364.

Date	Mintage	F	VF	XF	Unc	BU
1997	—	—	—	—	12.50	—

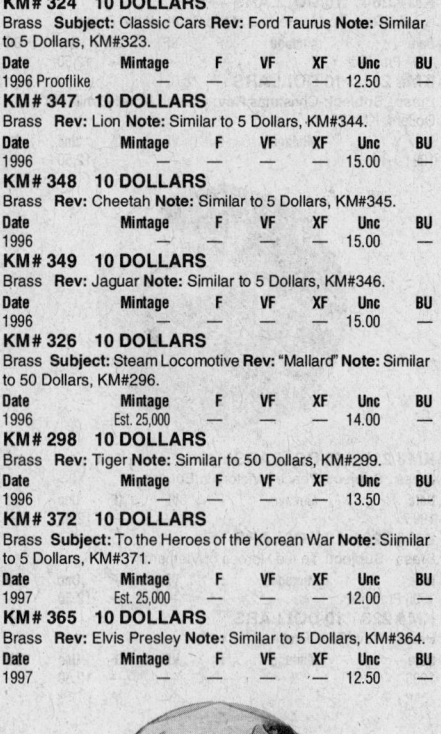

KM# 381   10 DOLLARS
Brass **Series:** Twelve Apostles **Obv:** State seal **Rev:** Andrew

Date	Mintage	F	VF	XF	Unc	BU
1997	Est. 25,000	—	—	—	12.00	—

KM# 382   10 DOLLARS
Brass **Series:** Twelve Apostles **Obv:** State seal **Rev:** Bartholomew

Date	Mintage	F	VF	XF	Unc	BU
1997	Est. 25,000	—	—	—	12.00	—

KM# 383   10 DOLLARS
Brass **Subject:** Twelve Apostles Series **Obv:** State seal **Rev:** James, Son of Zebedee

Date	Mintage	F	VF	XF	Unc	BU
1997	Est. 25,000	—	—	—	12.00	—

KM# 384   10 DOLLARS
Brass **Subject:** Twelve Apostles Series **Obv:** State seal **Rev:** James, Son of Alphaeus

Date	Mintage	F	VF	XF	Unc	BU
1997	Est. 25,000	—	—	—	12.00	—

KM# 385   10 DOLLARS
Brass **Subject:** Twelve Apostles Series **Obv:** State seal **Rev:** John

Date	Mintage	F	VF	XF	Unc	BU
1997	Est. 25,000	—	—	—	12.00	—

KM# 386   10 DOLLARS
Brass **Subject:** Twelve Apostles Series **Obv:** State seal **Rev:** Paul

Date	Mintage	F	VF	XF	Unc	BU
1997	Est. 25,000	—	—	—	12.00	—

KM# 387   10 DOLLARS
Brass **Subject:** Twelve Apostles Series **Obv:** State seal **Rev:** Matthew

Date	Mintage	F	VF	XF	Unc	BU
1997	Est. 25,000	—	—	—	12.00	—

KM# 388 10 DOLLARS
Brass **Subject:** Twelve Apostles Series **Obv:** State seal **Rev:** Peter

Date	Mintage	F	VF	XF	Unc	BU
1997	Est. 25,000	—	—	—	12.00	—

KM# 389 10 DOLLARS
Brass **Subject:** Twelve Apostles Series **Obv:** State seal **Rev:** Philip

Date	Mintage	F	VF	XF	Unc	BU
1997	Est. 25,000	—	—	—	12.00	—

KM# 390 10 DOLLARS
Brass **Subject:** Twelve Apostles Series **Obv:** State seal **Rev:** Simon

Date	Mintage	F	VF	XF	Unc	BU
1997	Est. 25,000	—	—	—	12.00	—

KM# 391 10 DOLLARS
Brass **Subject:** Twelve Apostles Series **Obv:** State seal **Rev:** Thaddaeus

Date	Mintage	F	VF	XF	Unc	BU
1997	Est. 25,000	—	—	—	12.00	—

KM# 392 10 DOLLARS
Brass **Subject:** Twelve Apostles Series **Obv:** State seal **Rev:** Thomas

Date	Mintage	F	VF	XF	Unc	BU
1997	Est. 25,000	—	—	—	12.00	—

KM# 404 10 DOLLARS
Brass **Subject:** Christmas **Obv:** State seal **Rev:** Two cherubs

Date	Mintage	F	VF	XF	Unc	BU
1997	—	—	—	—	12.00	—

KM# 406 10 DOLLARS
Brass **Obv:** National seal **Rev:** Charging bull elephant

Date	Mintage	F	VF	XF	Unc	BU
1997	—	—	—	—	13.50	—

KM# 400 10 DOLLARS
Brass **Obv:** State seal **Rev:** Deng Ziaoping

Date	Mintage	F	VF	XF	Unc	BU
1997	—	—	—	—	12.00	—

KM# 415 10 DOLLARS
Brass **Subject:** History's Great Fighting Ships **Obv:** State seal **Rev:** Viking Longship

Date	Mintage	F	VF	XF	Unc	BU
1998	Est. 25,000	—	—	—	12.00	—

KM# 417 10 DOLLARS
Brass **Subject:** History's Great Fighting Ships **Obv:** State seal **Rev:** Greek Trireme

Date	Mintage	F	VF	XF	Unc	BU
1998	Est. 25,000	—	—	—	12.00	—

KM# 419 10 DOLLARS
Brass **Subject:** History's Great Fighting Ships **Obv:** State seal **Rev:** Roman Trireme

Date	Mintage	F	VF	XF	Unc	BU
1998	Est. 25,000	—	—	—	12.00	—

KM# 421 10 DOLLARS
Brass **Subject:** History's Great Fighting Ships **Obv:** State seal **Rev:** Chinese Ming Treasure Ship

Date	Mintage	F	VF	XF	Unc	BU
1998	Est. 25,000	—	—	—	12.00	—

KM# 423 10 DOLLARS
Brass **Subject:** History's Great Fighting Ships **Obv:** State seal **Rev:** Korean Turtle Ship

Date	Mintage	F	VF	XF	Unc	BU
1998	Est. 25,000	—	—	—	12.00	—

KM# 425 10 DOLLARS
Brass **Subject:** History's Great Fighting Ships **Obv:** State seal **Rev:** Fijan War Canoe

Date	Mintage	F	VF	XF	Unc	BU
1998	Est. 25,000	—	—	—	12.00	—

KM# 427 10 DOLLARS
Brass **Subject:** History's Great Fighting Ships **Obv:** State seal **Rev:** The Bismarck

Date	Mintage	F	VF	XF	Unc	BU
1998	Est. 25,000	—	—	—	12.00	—

KM# 429 10 DOLLARS
Brass **Subject:** History's Great Fighting Ships **Obv:** State seal **Rev:** The Graf Spee

Date	Mintage	F	VF	XF	Unc	BU
1998	Est. 25,000	—	—	—	12.00	—

KM# 431 10 DOLLARS
Brass **Subject:** History's Great Fighting Ships **Obv:** State seal **Rev:** The Yamato

Date	Mintage	F	VF	XF	Unc	BU
1998	Est. 25,000	—	—	—	12.00	—

KM# 433 10 DOLLARS
Brass **Subject:** History's Great Fighting Ships **Obv:** State seal **Rev:** HMS Victory

Date	Mintage	F	VF	XF	Unc	BU
1998	Est. 25,000	—	—	—	12.00	—

KM# 435 10 DOLLARS
Brass **Subject:** History's Great Fighting Ships **Rev:** HMS Mary Rose

Date	Mintage	F	VF	XF	Unc	BU
1998	Est. 25,000	—	—	—	12.00	—

KM# 437 10 DOLLARS
Brass **Subject:** History's Great Fighting Ships **Rev:** HMS Dreadnought

Date	Mintage	F	VF	XF	Unc	BU
1998	Est. 25,000	—	—	—	12.00	—

KM# 439 10 DOLLARS
Brass **Subject:** History's Great Fighting Ships **Obv:** State Seal **Rev:** HMS Dorsetshire

Date	Mintage	F	VF	XF	Unc	BU
1998	Est. 25,000	—	—	—	12.00	—

KM# 441 10 DOLLARS
Brass **Subject:** History's Great Fighting Ships **Obv:** State Seal **Rev:** Nuestra Senora del Rosario

Date	Mintage	F	VF	XF	Unc	BU
1998	Est. 25,000	—	—	—	12.00	—

KM# 443 10 DOLLARS
Brass **Subject:** History's Great Fighting Ships **Obv:** State Seal **Rev:** Santisima Trinidad

Date	Mintage	F	VF	XF	Unc	BU
1998	Est. 25,000	—	—	—	12.00	—

KM# 445 10 DOLLARS
Brass **Subject:** History's Great Fighting Ships **Obv:** State Seal **Rev:** USS Bonhomme Richard

Date	Mintage	F	VF	XF	Unc	BU
1998	Est. 25,000	—	—	—	12.00	—

KM# 447 10 DOLLARS
Brass **Subject:** History's Great Fighting Ships **Obv:** State Seal **Rev:** USS Constellation

Date	Mintage	F	VF	XF	Unc	BU
1998	Est. 25,000	—	—	—	12.00	—

KM# 449 10 DOLLARS
Brass **Subject:** History's Great Fighting Ships **Obv:** State Seal **Rev:** USS Hartford

Date	Mintage	F	VF	XF	Unc	BU
1998	Est. 25,000	—	—	—	12.00	—

KM# 451 10 DOLLARS
Brass **Subject:** History's Great Fighting Ships **Obv:** State Seal **Rev:** USS Hornet

Date	Mintage	F	VF	XF	Unc	BU
1998	Est. 25,000	—	—	—	12.00	—

KM# 453 10 DOLLARS
Brass **Subject:** History's Great Fighting Ships **Obv:** State Seal **Rev:** USS Missouri

Date	Mintage	F	VF	XF	Unc	BU
1998	Est. 25,000	—	—	—	12.00	—

KM# 455 10 DOLLARS
Brass **Subject:** History's Great Fighting Ships **Obv:** State Seal **Rev:** USS Tautog

Date	Mintage	F	VF	XF	Unc	BU
1998	Est. 25,000	—	—	—	12.00	—

KM# 457 10 DOLLARS
Brass **Subject:** History's Great Fighting Ships **Obv:** State Seal **Rev:** Brederode

Date	Mintage	F	VF	XF	Unc	BU
1998	Est. 25,000	—	—	—	12.00	—

KM# 459 10 DOLLARS
Brass **Subject:** History's Great Fighting Ships **Obv:** State Seal **Rev:** Ville de Paris

Date	Mintage	F	VF	XF	Unc	BU
1998	Est. 25,000	—	—	—	12.00	—

KM# 461 10 DOLLARS
Brass **Subject:** History's Great Fighting Ships **Obv:** State Seal **Rev:** Galera Veneziana

Date	Mintage	F	VF	XF	Unc	BU
1998	Est. 25,000	—	—	—	12.00	—

KM# 479   10 DOLLARS
Brass **Subject:** Babe Ruth at bat **Obv:** State Seal

Date	Mintage	F	VF	XF	Unc	BU
1998	—	—	—	—	12.50	—

KM# 482   10 DOLLARS
Brass **Subject:** Christmas **Obv:** State Seal **Rev:** Angel

Date	Mintage	F	VF	XF	Unc	BU
1998	—	—	—	—	12.00	—

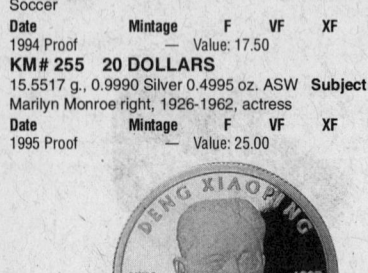

KM# 3   20 DOLLARS
3.1100 g., 0.9990 Gold 0.0999 oz. AGW **Rev:** Sun

Date	Mintage	F	VF	XF	Unc	BU
1986 Proof	Est. 5,000	Value: 100				

KM# 153   20 DOLLARS
15.5517 g., 0.9990 Silver 0.4995 oz. ASW **Subject:** First Men on the Moon

Date	Mintage	F	VF	XF	Unc	BU
1994 Proof	—	Value: 20.00				

KM# 189   20 DOLLARS
15.5517 g., 0.9990 Silver 0.4995 oz. ASW **Subject:** World Cup Soccer

Date	Mintage	F	VF	XF	Unc	BU
1994 Proof	—	Value: 17.50				

KM# 255   20 DOLLARS
15.5517 g., 0.9990 Silver 0.4995 oz. ASW **Subject:** Head of Marilyn Monroe right, 1926-1962, actress

Date	Mintage	F	VF	XF	Unc	BU
1995 Proof	—	Value: 25.00				

KM# 401   20 DOLLARS
10.3678 g., 0.9990 Silver 0.3330 oz. ASW **Subject:** Deng Xiaoping **Obv:** State seal

Date	Mintage	F	VF	XF	Unc	BU
1997 Proof	—	Value: 25.00				

KM# 20   25 DOLLARS
33.9600 g., 0.9250 Silver 1.0099 oz. ASW **Subject:** Greg Louganis **Rev:** Back dive

Date	Mintage	F	VF	XF	Unc	BU
1988	Est. 280,000	—	—	—	75.00	85.00
1988 Proof	Est. 350,000	Value: 100				

KM# 21   25 DOLLARS
33.9600 g., 0.9250 Silver 1.0099 oz. ASW **Subject:** Greg Louganis **Rev:** Twister

Date	Mintage	F	VF	XF	Unc	BU
1988	Est. 280,000	—	—	—	75.00	85.00
1988 Proof	Est. 350,000	Value: 100				

KM# 22   25 DOLLARS
33.9600 g., 0.9250 Silver 1.0099 oz. ASW **Subject:** Greg Louganis **Rev:** Jackknife

Date	Mintage	F	VF	XF	Unc	BU
1988	Est. 280,000	—	—	—	75.00	85.00
1988 Proof	Est. 350,000	Value: 100				

KM# 4   50 DOLLARS
7.7750 g., 0.9990 Gold 0.2497 oz. AGW **Rev:** Coconut

Date	Mintage	F	VF	XF	Unc	BU
1986 Proof	Est. 5,000	Value: 250				

KM# 7   50 DOLLARS
31.1000 g., 0.9990 Silver 0.9988 oz. ASW **Subject:** John Glenn in Space Orbit

Date	Mintage	F	VF	XF	Unc	BU
1989 Proof	Est. 25,000	Value: 27.50				
1989S Proof	Inc. above	Value: 23.50				

KM# 8   50 DOLLARS
31.1000 g., 0.9990 Silver 0.9988 oz. ASW **Subject:** Neil Armstrong on the Moon **Obv:** Similar to KM#12

Date	Mintage	F	VF	XF	Unc	BU
1989 Proof	Est. 25,000	Value: 27.50				
1989S Proof	Inc. above	Value: 23.50				

KM# 9   50 DOLLARS
31.1000 g., 0.9990 Silver 0.9988 oz. ASW **Subject:** American Space Station - Skylab **Obv:** Similar to KM#12

Date	Mintage	F	VF	XF	Unc	BU
1989 Proof	Est. 25,000	Value: 22.50				
1989S Proof	Inc. above	Value: 20.00				

KM# 10   50 DOLLARS
31.1000 g., 0.9990 Silver 0.9988 oz. ASW **Subject:** Apollo - Sojus Joint Mission

Date	Mintage	F	VF	XF	Unc	BU
1989 Proof	Est. 25,000	Value: 27.50				
1989S Proof	Inc. above	Value: 23.50				

KM# 11   50 DOLLARS
31.1000 g., 0.9990 Silver 0.9988 oz. ASW **Subject:** First Space Shuttle Flight

Date	Mintage	F	VF	XF	Unc	BU
1989 Proof	Est. 25,000	Value: 27.50				
1989S Proof	Inc. above	Value: 23.50				

KM# 12   50 DOLLARS
31.1000 g., 0.9990 Silver 0.9988 oz. ASW **Subject:** U.S. Space Shuttle - Discovery

Date	Mintage	F	VF	XF	Unc	BU
1989 Proof	Est. 50,000	Value: 18.50				
1989S Proof	Inc. above	Value: 16.50				

KM# 14   50 DOLLARS
31.1000 g., 0.9990 Silver 0.9988 oz. ASW **Subject:** 20th Anniversary - First Men on the Moon

Date	Mintage	F	VF	XF	Unc	BU
1989 Proof	Est. 50,000	Value: 18.50				
1989S Proof	Inc. above	Value: 16.50				

KM# 15 50 DOLLARS
31.1000 g., 0.9990 Silver 0.9988 oz. ASW **Subject:** First American Space Walk

Date	Mintage	F	VF	XF	Unc	BU
1989 Proof	Est. 25,000	Value: 27.50				
1989S Proof	Inc. above	Value: 23.50				

KM# 23 50 DOLLARS
31.1000 g., 0.9990 Silver 0.9988 oz. ASW **Subject:** First Docking In Space

Date	Mintage	F	VF	XF	Unc	BU
1989 Proof	Est. 25,000	Value: 27.50				
1989S Proof	Inc. above	Value: 23.50				

KM# 24 50 DOLLARS
31.1000 g., 0.9990 Silver 0.9988 oz. ASW **Subject:** First Man-made Satellite - 1957

Date	Mintage	F	VF	XF	Unc	BU
1989 Proof	Est. 25,000	Value: 22.50				
1989S Proof	Inc. above	Value: 20.00				

KM# 25 50 DOLLARS
31.1000 g., 0.9990 Silver 0.9988 oz. ASW **Subject:** First Man In Space - 1961

Date	Mintage	F	VF	XF	Unc	BU
1989 Proof	Est. 25,000	Value: 27.50				
1989S Proof	Inc. above	Value: 23.50				

KM# 26 50 DOLLARS
31.1000 g., 0.9990 Silver 0.9988 oz. ASW **Subject:** First Woman In Space - 1963

Date	Mintage	F	VF	XF	Unc	BU
1989 Proof	Est. 25,000	Value: 27.50				
1989S Proof	Inc. above	Value: 23.50				

KM# 27 50 DOLLARS
31.1000 g., 0.9990 Silver 0.9988 oz. ASW **Subject:** First Rendezvous In Space - 1965

Date	Mintage	F	VF	XF	Unc	BU
1989 Proof	Est. 25,000	Value: 27.50				
1989S Proof	Inc. above	Value: 23.50				

KM# 28 50 DOLLARS
31.1000 g., 0.9990 Silver 0.9988 oz. ASW **Subject:** First Space Walk - 1965

Date	Mintage	F	VF	XF	Unc	BU
1989 Proof	Est. 25,000	Value: 27.50				
1989S Proof	Inc. above	Value: 23.50				

KM# 29 50 DOLLARS
31.1000 g., 0.9990 Silver 0.9988 oz. ASW **Subject:** First Soft Landing on the Moon - 1966

Date	Mintage	F	VF	XF	Unc	BU
1989 Proof	Est. 25,000	Value: 27.50				
1989S Proof	Inc. above	Value: 23.50				

KM# 30 50 DOLLARS
31.1000 g., 0.9990 Silver 0.9988 oz. ASW **Subject:** First Probe of Venus - 1967

Date	Mintage	F	VF	XF	Unc	BU
1989 Proof	Est. 25,000	Value: 27.50				
1989S Proof	Inc. above	Value: 23.50				

KM# 31 50 DOLLARS
31.1000 g., 0.9990 Silver 0.9988 oz. ASW **Subject:** First Manned Orbit of the Moon - 1968

Date	Mintage	F	VF	XF	Unc	BU
1989 Proof	Est. 25,000	Value: 27.50				
1989S Proof	Inc. above	Value: 23.50				

KM# 32 50 DOLLARS
31.1000 g., 0.9990 Silver 0.9988 oz. ASW **Subject:** First Space Station Crew - 1971

Date	Mintage	F	VF	XF	Unc	BU
1989 Proof	Est. 25,000	Value: 27.50				
1989S Proof	Inc. above	Value: 23.50				

KM# 50 50 DOLLARS
31.1000 g., 0.9990 Silver 0.9988 oz. ASW **Subject:** First Manned Lunar Vehicle - 1971

Date	Mintage	F	VF	XF	Unc	BU
1989 Proof	Est. 25,000	Value: 27.50				
1989S Proof	Inc. above	Value: 23.50				

KM# 51 50 DOLLARS
31.1000 g., 0.9990 Silver 0.9988 oz. ASW **Subject:** First American Satellite - 1958

Date	Mintage	F	VF	XF	Unc	BU
1989 Proof	Est. 25,000	Value: 27.50				
1989S Proof	Inc. above	Value: 23.50				

KM# 52 50 DOLLARS
31.1000 g., 0.9990 Silver 0.9988 oz. ASW **Subject:** First Liquid Fuel Rocket Launch - 1926

Date	Mintage	F	VF	XF	Unc	BU
1989 Proof	Est. 25,000	Value: 27.50				
1989S Proof	Inc. above	Value: 23.50				

KM# 53 50 DOLLARS
31.1000 g., 0.9990 Silver 0.9988 oz. ASW **Subject:** First Untethered Space Walk - 1984

Date	Mintage	F	VF	XF	Unc	BU
1989 Proof	Est. 25,000	Value: 27.50				
1989S Proof	Inc. above	Value: 23.50				

KM# 54 50 DOLLARS
31.1000 g., 0.9990 Silver 0.9988 oz. ASW **Subject:** First Landing on Mars - 1976

Date	Mintage	F	VF	XF	Unc	BU
1989 Proof	Est. 25,000	Value: 27.50				
1989S Proof	Inc. above	Value: 23.50				

KM# 55 50 DOLLARS
31.1000 g., 0.9990 Silver 0.9988 oz. ASW **Subject:** First Flyby of Saturn - 1979

Date	Mintage	F	VF	XF	Unc	BU
1989 Proof	Est. 25,000	Value: 27.50				
1989S Proof	Inc. above	Value: 23.50				

KM# 56 50 DOLLARS
31.1000 g., 0.9990 Silver 0.9988 oz. ASW **Subject:** First Probe Beyond the Solar System - 1983

Date	Mintage	F	VF	XF	Unc	BU
1989 Proof	Est. 25,000	Value: 27.50				
1989S Proof	Inc. above	Value: 23.50				

KM# 57 50 DOLLARS
31.1000 g., 0.9990 Silver 0.9988 oz. ASW **Subject:** First Flyby of Jupiter - 1973

Date	Mintage	F	VF	XF	Unc	BU
1989 Proof	Est. 25,000	Value: 27.50				
1989S Proof	Inc. above	Value: 23.50				

KM# 19 50 DOLLARS
31.1000 g., 0.9990 Silver 0.9988 oz. ASW **Subject:** 50th Anniversary - Battle of Britain

Date	Mintage	F	VF	XF	Unc	BU
1990M Proof	Est. 50,000	Value: 35.00				

KM# 34 50 DOLLARS
31.1000 g., 0.9990 Silver 0.9988 oz. ASW **Subject:** German Unification

Date	Mintage	F	VF	XF	Unc	BU
1990M Proof	Est. 50,000	Value: 50.00				

KM# 39 50 DOLLARS
31.1000 g., 0.9990 Silver 0.9988 oz. ASW **Subject:** Dwight David Eisenhower

Date	Mintage	F	VF	XF	Unc	BU
1990M Proof	Est. 50,000	Value: 25.00				

KM# 36   50 DOLLARS
31.1000 g., 0.9990 Silver 0.9988 oz. ASW **Subject:** Pearl Harbor

Date	Mintage	F	VF	XF	Unc	BU
1991M Proof	Est. 50,000			Value: 27.50		

KM# 42   50 DOLLARS
31.1000 g., 0.9990 Silver 0.9988 oz. ASW **Subject:** To the Heroes of Desert Storm

Date	Mintage	F	VF	XF	Unc	BU
1991R Proof	—			Value: 24.00		

KM# 43   50 DOLLARS
31.1000 g., 0.9990 Silver 0.9988 oz. ASW **Rev:** WWII American P-51 Mustang

Date	Mintage	F	VF	XF	Unc	BU
1991 Proof	Est. 25,000			Value: 27.50		

KM# 44   50 DOLLARS
31.1000 g., 0.9990 Silver 0.9988 oz. ASW **Rev:** WWII American B-29 Superfortress

Date	Mintage	F	VF	XF	Unc	BU
1991M Proof	Est. 25,000			Value: 27.50		

KM# 45   50 DOLLARS
31.1000 g., 0.9990 Silver 0.9988 oz. ASW **Rev:** WWII German BF-109 Messerschmitt

Date	Mintage	F	VF	XF	Unc	BU
1991 Proof	Est. 25,000			Value: 27.50		

KM# 46   50 DOLLARS
31.1000 g., 0.9990 Silver 0.9988 oz. ASW **Rev:** WWII British Spitfire

Date	Mintage	F	VF	XF	Unc	BU
1991M Proof	Est. 25,000			Value: 27.50		

KM# 47   50 DOLLARS
31.1000 g., 0.9990 Silver 0.9988 oz. ASW **Rev:** WWII American PBY Catalina

Date	Mintage	F	VF	XF	Unc	BU
1991M Proof	Est. 25,000			Value: 25.00		

KM# 48   50 DOLLARS
31.1000 g., 0.9990 Silver 0.9988 oz. ASW **Rev:** WWII Japanese A6M Reisen

Date	Mintage	F	VF	XF	Unc	BU
1991M Proof	Est. 25,000			Value: 27.50		

KM# 58   50 DOLLARS
31.1000 g., 0.9990 Silver 0.9988 oz. ASW **Rev:** WWII American P-40 Warhawk

Date	Mintage	F	VF	XF	Unc	BU
1991M Proof	Est. 25,000			Value: 27.50		

KM# 72   50 DOLLARS
31.1000 g., 0.9990 Silver 0.9988 oz. ASW **Rev:** Space Shuttle Columbia - 1981

Date	Mintage	F	VF	XF	Unc	BU
1991M Proof	Est. 25,000			Value: 40.00		
1991 Proof	—			Value: 40.00		

Note: Smaller stars above moon

KM# 74   50 DOLLARS
31.1000 g., 0.9990 Silver 0.9988 oz. ASW **Rev:** WWII British Hurricane

Date	Mintage	F	VF	XF	Unc	BU
1991S Proof	Est. 24,000			Value: 25.00		

KM# 75   50 DOLLARS
31.1000 g., 0.9990 Silver 0.9988 oz. ASW **Rev:** WWII British Mosquito

Date	Mintage	F	VF	XF	Unc	BU
1991S Proof	Est. 24,000			Value: 25.00		

KM# 76   50 DOLLARS
31.1000 g., 0.9990 Silver 0.9988 oz. ASW **Rev:** WWII American B-24 Liberator

Date	Mintage	F	VF	XF	Unc	BU
1991S Proof	Est. 25,000			Value: 22.50		

KM# 77   50 DOLLARS
31.1000 g., 0.9990 Silver 0.9988 oz. ASW **Rev:** WWII American B-25 Mitchell

Date	Mintage	F	VF	XF	Unc	BU
1991S Proof	Est. 25,000			Value: 27.50		

KM# 78   50 DOLLARS
31.1000 g., 0.9990 Silver 0.9988 oz. ASW **Rev:** WWII American C-47 Skytrain

Date	Mintage	F	VF	XF	Unc	BU
1991S Proof	Est. 24,000			Value: 27.50		

KM# 79   50 DOLLARS
31.1000 g., 0.9990 Silver 0.9988 oz. ASW **Rev:** WWII American B-17 Flying Fortress

Date	Mintage	F	VF	XF	Unc	BU
1991S Proof	Est. 24,000			Value: 27.50		

KM# 80   50 DOLLARS
31.1000 g., 0.9990 Silver 0.9988 oz. ASW **Rev:** WWII American F4U Corsair

Date	Mintage	F	VF	XF	Unc	BU
1991S Proof	Est. 24,000			Value: 27.50		

KM# 93   50 DOLLARS
31.1000 g., 0.9990 Silver 0.9988 oz. ASW **Rev:** WWII American P-38 Lightning

Date	Mintage	F	VF	XF	Unc	BU
1991S Proof	Est. 25,000			Value: 27.50		

KM# 94   50 DOLLARS
31.1000 g., 0.9990 Silver 0.9988 oz. ASW **Rev:** WWII American F6F Hellcat

Date	Mintage	F	VF	XF	Unc	BU
1991S Proof	Est. 24,000			Value: 25.00		

KM# 95   50 DOLLARS
31.1000 g., 0.9990 Silver 0.9988 oz. ASW **Rev:** WWII Japanese G4M "Betty" Bomber

Date	Mintage	F	VF	XF	Unc	BU
1991S Proof	Est. 25,000			Value: 25.00		

KM# 97   50 DOLLARS
31.1000 g., 0.9990 Silver 0.9988 oz. ASW **Rev:** WWII Soviet Yak-9

Date	Mintage	F	VF	XF	Unc	BU
1991S Proof	Est. 24,000			Value: 25.00		

KM# 99   50 DOLLARS
31.1000 g., 0.9990 Silver 0.9988 oz. ASW **Rev:** WWII Japanese K1-61 Hien "Tony"

Date	Mintage	F	VF	XF	Unc	BU
1991S Proof	Est. 25,000			Value: 25.00		

KM# 100   50 DOLLARS
31.1000 g., 0.9990 Silver 0.9988 oz. ASW **Rev:** WWII French D-520 Fighter

Date	Mintage	F	VF	XF	Unc	BU
1991S Proof	Est. 25,000			Value: 25.00		

KM# 102   50 DOLLARS
31.1000 g., 0.9990 Silver 0.9988 oz. ASW **Rev:** WWII German FW 190 Fighters

Date	Mintage	F	VF	XF	Unc	BU
1991S Proof	Est. 24,000			Value: 25.00		

KM# 104 50 DOLLARS
31.1000 g., 0.9990 Silver 0.9988 oz. ASW **Rev:** WWII British Lancaster

Date	Mintage	F	VF	XF	Unc	BU
1991S Proof	Est. 25,000		Value: 25.00			

KM# 105 50 DOLLARS
31.1000 g., 0.9990 Silver 0.9988 oz. ASW **Rev:** WWII Italian S.M. 79 Sparviero Bombers

Date	Mintage	F	VF	XF	Unc	BU
1991S Proof	Est. 24,000		Value: 27.50			

KM# 106 50 DOLLARS
31.1000 g., 0.9990 Silver 0.9988 oz. ASW **Rev:** WWII German HE 111 Bombers

Date	Mintage	F	VF	XF	Unc	BU
1991S Proof	Est. 25,000		Value: 25.00			

KM# 108 50 DOLLARS
31.1000 g., 0.9990 Silver 0.9988 oz. ASW **Rev:** WWII Soviet IL-2 Shturmovik

Date	Mintage	F	VF	XF	Unc	BU
1991S Proof	Est. 24,000		Value: 22.50			

KM# 83 50 DOLLARS
31.1000 g., 0.9990 Silver 0.9988 oz. ASW **Subject:** Reaching for the Stars **Rev:** Greek ship Argo

Date	Mintage	F	VF	XF	Unc	BU
1992R Proof	—		Value: 42.50			

KM# 86 50 DOLLARS
31.1000 g., 0.9990 Silver 0.9988 oz. ASW **Subject:** To the Heroes of the Raid on Tokyo - Doolittle

Date	Mintage	F	VF	XF	Unc	BU
1992R Proof	—		Value: 45.00			

KM# 89 50 DOLLARS
31.1000 g., 0.9990 Silver 0.9988 oz. ASW **Subject:** Heroes of Corregidor

Date	Mintage	F	VF	XF	Unc	BU
1992R Proof	—		Value: 45.00			

KM# 92 50 DOLLARS
31.1000 g., 0.9990 Silver 0.9988 oz. ASW **Subject:** To the Heroes of Battle of Midway

Date	Mintage	F	VF	XF	Unc	BU
1992R Proof	—		Value: 40.00			

KM# 111 50 DOLLARS
31.1000 g., 0.9990 Silver 0.9988 oz. ASW **Subject:** Pacific Whales and Dolphins **Rev:** Humpback Whale

Date	Mintage	F	VF	XF	Unc	BU
1993R Proof	Est. 25,000		Value: 40.00			

KM# 112 50 DOLLARS
31.1000 g., 0.9990 Silver 0.9988 oz. ASW **Subject:** Pacific Whales and Dolphins **Rev:** Risso's Dolphins

Date	Mintage	F	VF	XF	Unc	BU
1993R Proof	Est. 25,000		Value: 40.00			

KM# 113 50 DOLLARS
31.1000 g., 0.9990 Silver 0.9988 oz. ASW **Subject:** Pacific Whales and Dolphins **Rev:** Beluga Whale

Date	Mintage	F	VF	XF	Unc	BU
1993R Proof	Est. 25,000		Value: 40.00			

KM# 114 50 DOLLARS
31.1000 g., 0.9990 Silver 0.9988 oz. ASW **Subject:** Pacific Whales and Dolphins **Rev:** Hector's Dolphin

Date	Mintage	F	VF	XF	Unc	BU
1993R Proof	Est. 25,000		Value: 40.00			

KM# 115 50 DOLLARS
31.1000 g., 0.9990 Silver 0.9988 oz. ASW **Subject:** Pacific Whales and Dolphins **Rev:** Blue Whales

Date	Mintage	F	VF	XF	Unc	BU
1993R Proof	Est. 25,000		Value: 40.00			

KM# 116 50 DOLLARS
31.1000 g., 0.9990 Silver 0.9988 oz. ASW **Subject:** Pacific Whales and Dolphins **Rev:** Baiji Dolphins

Date	Mintage	F	VF	XF	Unc	BU
1993R Proof	Est. 25,000		Value: 40.00			

KM# 117 50 DOLLARS
31.1000 g., 0.9990 Silver 0.9988 oz. ASW **Subject:** Pacific Whales and Dolphins **Rev:** Killer Whales

Date	Mintage	F	VF	XF	Unc	BU
1993R Proof	Est. 25,000		Value: 40.00			

KM# 120 50 DOLLARS
31.1000 g., 0.9990 Silver 0.9988 oz. ASW **Subject:** To the Heroes of the North Atlantic **Rev:** Submarine

Date	Mintage	F	VF	XF	Unc	BU
1993R Proof	—		Value: 60.00			

KM# 123 50 DOLLARS
31.1000 g., 0.9990 Silver 0.9988 oz. ASW **Subject:** To the Heroes of Guadalcanal **Rev:** Marine, battleship and airplanes

Date	Mintage	F	VF	XF	Unc	BU
1993R Proof	—		Value: 60.00			

KM# 128 50 DOLLARS
31.1000 g., 0.9990 Silver 0.9988 oz. ASW **Subject:** Pacific Whales and Dolphins **Rev:** Common Dolphins

Date	Mintage	F	VF	XF	Unc	BU
1993R Proof	—		Value: 40.00			

KM# 130 50 DOLLARS
31.1000 g., 0.9990 Silver 0.9988 oz. ASW **Rev:** Elvis Presley

Date	Mintage	F	VF	XF	Unc	BU
1993S Proof	—		Value: 37.50			

KM# 146 50 DOLLARS
31.1000 g., 0.9990 Silver 0.9988 oz. ASW **Subject:** Christmas 1993

Date	Mintage	F	VF	XF	Unc	BU
1993R Proof	—		Value: 32.50			

KM# 150 50 DOLLARS
31.1000 g., 0.9990 Silver 0.9988 oz. ASW **Subject:** Flight of the Kitty Hawk

Date	Mintage	F	VF	XF	Unc	BU
1993 Proof	—		Value: 37.50			

KM# 493 50 DOLLARS
31.1300 g., 0.9990 Silver 0.9998 oz. ASW, 38.6 mm.
Subject: Indo-Pacific Humpbacked Dolphin **Obv:** State seal **Rev:** Two dolphins and island **Edge:** Reeded **Note:** Legal tender status in question.

Date	Mintage	F	VF	XF	Unc	BU
1993 Proof	25,000		Value: 60.00			

KM# 494   50 DOLLARS
31.1300 g., 0.9990 Silver 0.9998 oz. ASW, 38.6 mm.
Subject: Minke Whale **Obv:** State seal **Rev:** Two Minke whales
and ship with coastline in background **Edge:** Reeded **Note:** Legal
tender status in question.

Date	Mintage	F	VF	XF	Unc	BU
1993 Proof	25,000	Value: 60.00				

KM# 69A   50 DOLLARS
31.1600 g., 0.9990 Silver 1.0008 oz. ASW, 39 mm. **Obv:** State
seal **Rev:** Long-Snouted Spinner Dolphins **Edge:** Reeded
Note: Legal tender status questionable

Date	Mintage	F	VF	XF	Unc	BU
1993S Proof	—	Value: 60.00				

KM# 154   50 DOLLARS
31.1000 g., 0.9990 Silver 0.9988 oz. ASW **Subject:** First Men
on the Moon

Date	Mintage	F	VF	XF	Unc	BU
1994 Proof	—	Value: 28.50				

KM# 167   50 DOLLARS
31.1000 g., 0.9990 Silver 0.9988 oz. ASW **Rev:** Mythological
Mother Earth

Date	Mintage	F	VF	XF	Unc	BU
1994 Proof	Est. 25,000	Value: 30.00				

KM# 168   50 DOLLARS
31.1000 g., 0.9990 Silver 0.9988 oz. ASW **Rev:** Sun

Date	Mintage	F	VF	XF	Unc	BU
1994 Proof	Est. 25,000	Value: 30.00				

KM# 169   50 DOLLARS
31.1000 g., 0.9990 Silver 0.9988 oz. ASW **Rev:** Moon

Date	Mintage	F	VF	XF	Unc	BU
1994 Proof	Est. 25,000	Value: 30.00				

KM# 170   50 DOLLARS
31.1000 g., 0.9990 Silver 0.9988 oz. ASW **Rev:** Pluto

Date	Mintage	F	VF	XF	Unc	BU
1994 Proof	Est. 25,000	Value: 32.50				

KM# 171   50 DOLLARS
31.1000 g., 0.9990 Silver 0.9988 oz. ASW **Rev:** Mercury

Date	Mintage	F	VF	XF	Unc	BU
1994 Proof	Est. 25,000	Value: 30.00				

KM# 172   50 DOLLARS
31.1000 g., 0.9990 Silver 0.9988 oz. ASW **Rev:** Venus

Date	Mintage	F	VF	XF	Unc	BU
1994 Proof	Est. 25,000	Value: 40.00				

KM# 173   50 DOLLARS
31.1000 g., 0.9990 Silver 0.9988 oz. ASW **Rev:** Mars

Date	Mintage	F	VF	XF	Unc	BU
1994 Proof	Est. 25,000	Value: 30.00				

KM# 174   50 DOLLARS
31.1000 g., 0.9990 Silver 0.9988 oz. ASW **Rev:** Saturn

Date	Mintage	F	VF	XF	Unc	BU
1994 Proof	Est. 25,000	Value: 30.00				

KM# 175   50 DOLLARS
31.1000 g., 0.9990 Silver 0.9988 oz. ASW **Rev:** Jupiter

Date	Mintage	F	VF	XF	Unc	BU
1994 Proof	Est. 25,000	Value: 30.00				

KM# 176   50 DOLLARS
31.1000 g., 0.9990 Silver 0.9988 oz. ASW **Rev:** Uranus

Date	Mintage	F	VF	XF	Unc	BU
1994 Proof	Est. 25,000	Value: 30.00				

KM# 177   50 DOLLARS
31.1000 g., 0.9990 Silver 0.9988 oz. ASW **Rev:** Neptune

Date	Mintage	F	VF	XF	Unc	BU
1994 Proof	Est. 25,000	Value: 32.50				

KM# 178   50 DOLLARS
31.1000 g., 0.9990 Silver 0.9988 oz. ASW **Rev:** Solar System

Date	Mintage	F	VF	XF	Unc	BU
1994 Proof	Est. 25,000	Value: 30.00				

KM# 181   50 DOLLARS
31.1000 g., 0.9990 Silver 0.9988 oz. ASW **Subject:** To the
Heroes of D-Day - Normandy Invasion

Date	Mintage	F	VF	XF	Unc	BU
1994 Proof	—	Value: 32.50				

KM# 184   50 DOLLARS
31.1000 g., 0.9990 Silver 0.9988 oz. ASW **Subject:** Heroes of
the Philippines **Rev:** MacArthur and Staff

Date	Mintage	F	VF	XF	Unc	BU
1994 Proof	—	Value: 50.00				

KM# 190   50 DOLLARS
31.1000 g., 0.9990 Silver 0.9988 oz. ASW **Subject:** World Cup
Soccer

Date	Mintage	F	VF	XF	Unc	BU
1994 Proof	—	Value: 37.50				

KM# 262   50 DOLLARS
31.1000 g., 0.9990 Silver 0.9988 oz. ASW **Subject:** Christmas
Rev: Angel

Date	Mintage	F	VF	XF	Unc	BU
1994 Proof	—	Value: 30.00				

KM# 265   50 DOLLARS
31.1000 g., 0.9990 Silver 0.9988 oz. ASW **Subject:** To the
Heroes of Battle of the Bulge

Date	Mintage	F	VF	XF	Unc	BU
1994 Proof	—	Value: 32.50				

KM# 191   50 DOLLARS
31.1000 g., 0.9990 Silver 0.9988 oz. ASW **Rev:** Jet Fighter -
F-4 Phantom II

Date	Mintage	F	VF	XF	Unc	BU
1995 Proof	25,000	Value: 28.50				

KM# 192   50 DOLLARS
31.1000 g., 0.9990 Silver 0.9988 oz. ASW **Rev:** Jet Fighter -
F-100 Super Sabre

Date	Mintage	F	VF	XF	Unc	BU
1995 Proof	25,000	Value: 27.50				

KM# 193   50 DOLLARS
31.1000 g., 0.9990 Silver 0.9988 oz. ASW **Rev:** Jet Fighter -
Mirage 2000C

Date	Mintage	F	VF	XF	Unc	BU
1995 Proof	25,000	Value: 27.50				

KM# 194   50 DOLLARS
31.1000 g., 0.9990 Silver 0.9988 oz. ASW **Rev:** Jet Fighter -
F-14 Tomcat

Date	Mintage	F	VF	XF	Unc	BU
1995 Proof	25,000	Value: 27.50				

KM# 195 50 DOLLARS
31.1000 g., 0.9990 Silver 0.9988 oz. ASW **Rev:** Jet Fighter - F-86 Sabre

Date	Mintage	F	VF	XF	Unc	BU
1995 Proof	25,000	Value: 27.50				

KM# 196 50 DOLLARS
31.1000 g., 0.9990 Silver 0.9988 oz. ASW **Rev:** Jet Fighter - MIG 15

Date	Mintage	F	VF	XF	Unc	BU
1995 Proof	25,000	Value: 27.50				

KM# 197 50 DOLLARS
31.1000 g., 0.9990 Silver 0.9988 oz. ASW **Rev:** Jet Fighter - G91R

Date	Mintage	F	VF	XF	Unc	BU
1995 Proof	25,000	Value: 30.00				

KM# 198 50 DOLLARS
31.1000 g., 0.9990 Silver 0.9988 oz. ASW **Rev:** Jet Fighter - Saab J35 Draken

Date	Mintage	F	VF	XF	Unc	BU
1995 Proof	25,000	Value: 27.50				

KM# 199 50 DOLLARS
31.1000 g., 0.9990 Silver 0.9988 oz. ASW **Rev:** Jet Fighter - Meteor F.MK8

Date	Mintage	F	VF	XF	Unc	BU
1995 Proof	25,000	Value: 27.50				

KM# 200 50 DOLLARS
31.1000 g., 0.9990 Silver 0.9988 oz. ASW **Rev:** Jet Fighter - F-105 Thunderchief

Date	Mintage	F	VF	XF	Unc	BU
1995 Proof	25,000	Value: 27.50				

KM# 201 50 DOLLARS
31.1000 g., 0.9990 Silver 0.9988 oz. ASW **Rev:** Jet Fighter - Tornado F.MK3

Date	Mintage	F	VF	XF	Unc	BU
1995 Proof	25,000	Value: 27.50				

KM# 202 50 DOLLARS
31.1000 g., 0.9990 Silver 0.9988 oz. ASW **Rev:** Jet Fighter - F-16 Fighting Falcon

Date	Mintage	F	VF	XF	Unc	BU
1995 Proof	25,000	Value: 27.50				

KM# 203 50 DOLLARS
31.1000 g., 0.9990 Silver 0.9988 oz. ASW **Rev:** Me 262A-Ia Schwable

Date	Mintage	F	VF	XF	Unc	BU
1995 Proof	25,000	Value: 27.50				

KM# 204 50 DOLLARS
31.1000 g., 0.9990 Silver 0.9988 oz. ASW **Rev:** Sea Harrier FRS. MK 1

Date	Mintage	F	VF	XF	Unc	BU
1995 Proof	25,000	Value: 27.50				

KM# 205 50 DOLLARS
31.1000 g., 0.9990 Silver 0.9988 oz. ASW **Rev:** F-117 Nighthawk

Date	Mintage	F	VF	XF	Unc	BU
1995 Proof	25,000	Value: 28.50				

KM# 206 50 DOLLARS
31.1000 g., 0.9990 Silver 0.9988 oz. ASW **Rev:** MIG - 21MF

Date	Mintage	F	VF	XF	Unc	BU
1995 Proof	25,000	Value: 28.50				

KM# 207 50 DOLLARS
31.1000 g., 0.9990 Silver 0.9988 oz. ASW **Rev:** F-104 Starfighter

Date	Mintage	F	VF	XF	Unc	BU
1995 Proof	25,000	Value: 27.50				

KM# 208 50 DOLLARS
31.1000 g., 0.9990 Silver 0.9988 oz. ASW **Rev:** Sukhoi SU-27 UB

Date	Mintage	F	VF	XF	Unc	BU
1995 Proof	25,000	Value: 28.50				

KM# 209 50 DOLLARS
31.1000 g., 0.9990 Silver 0.9988 oz. ASW **Rev:** F-80 Shooting Star

Date	Mintage	F	VF	XF	Unc	BU
1995 Proof	25,000	Value: 27.50				

KM# 210 50 DOLLARS
31.1000 g., 0.9990 Silver 0.9988 oz. ASW **Rev:** Swedish Saab JA 37 Viggen

Date	Mintage	F	VF	XF	Unc	BU
1995 Proof	25,000	Value: 27.50				

KM# 211 50 DOLLARS
31.1000 g., 0.9990 Silver 0.9988 oz. ASW **Rev:** F8U Crusader

Date	Mintage	F	VF	XF	Unc	BU
1995 Proof	25,000	Value: 27.50				

KM# 212 50 DOLLARS
31.1000 g., 0.9990 Silver 0.9988 oz. ASW **Rev:** Fiat-G91Y Jet Fighter

Date	Mintage	F	VF	XF	Unc	BU
1995 Proof	25,000	Value: 30.00				

KM# 213 50 DOLLARS
31.1000 g., 0.9990 Silver 0.9988 oz. ASW **Rev:** Mirage FIC

Date	Mintage	F	VF	XF	Unc	BU
1995 Proof	Est. 25,000	Value: 27.50				

KM# 214 50 DOLLARS
31.1000 g., 0.9990 Silver 0.9988 oz. ASW **Rev:** F-15 Eagle

Date	Mintage	F	VF	XF	Unc	BU
1995 Proof	Est. 25,000	Value: 27.50				

KM# 215 50 DOLLARS
31.1000 g., 0.9990 Silver 0.9988 oz. ASW **Obv:** State seal **Rev:** F9F-2 Panther

Date	Mintage	F	VF	XF	Unc	BU
1995 Proof	Est. 25,000	Value: 27.50				

KM# 224 50 DOLLARS
31.1000 g., 0.9990 Silver 0.9988 oz. ASW **Rev:** Elvis Presley

Date	Mintage	F	VF	XF	Unc	BU
1995 Proof	—	Value: 60.00				

KM# 256 50 DOLLARS
31.1000 g., 0.9990 Silver 0.9988 oz. ASW **Rev:** Head of Marilyn Monroe right, 1926-1962, actress

Date	Mintage	F	VF	XF	Unc	BU
1995 Proof	—	Value: 56.00				

KM# 259 50 DOLLARS
31.1000 g., 0.9990 Silver 0.9988 oz. ASW **Series:** 50th Anniversary United Nations **Subject:** Peace

Date	Mintage	F	VF	XF	Unc	BU
1995 Proof	—	Value: 45.00				

KM# 268 50 DOLLARS
31.1000 g., 0.9990 Silver 0.9988 oz. ASW **Subject:** Peace - VJ Day

Date	Mintage	F	VF	XF	Unc	BU
1995 Proof	—	Value: 45.00				

KM# 273 50 DOLLARS
31.1000 g., 0.9990 Silver 0.9988 oz. ASW **Subject:** Christmas **Rev:** Cherub

Date	Mintage	F	VF	XF	Unc	BU
1995 Proof	—	Value: 35.00				

KM# 274 50 DOLLARS
31.1000 g., 0.9990 Silver 0.9988 oz. ASW **Subject:** Freedom / Liberty **Rev:** Torpedo Boat PT-109

Date	Mintage	F	VF	XF	Unc	BU
1995 Proof	Est. 25,000	Value: 57.50				

KM# 275 50 DOLLARS
31.1000 g., 0.9990 Silver 0.9988 oz. ASW **Subject:** Freedom / Liberty **Rev:** President John F. Kennedy takes oath of office

Date	Mintage	F	VF	XF	Unc	BU
1995 Proof	Est. 25,000	Value: 57.50				

KM# 276 50 DOLLARS
31.1000 g., 0.9990 Silver 0.9988 oz. ASW **Subject:** Freedom / Liberty **Rev:** Peace Corps worker and native

Date	Mintage	F	VF	XF	Unc	BU
1995 Proof	Est. 25,000	Value: 57.50				

KM# 367 50 DOLLARS
31.1000 g., 0.9990 Silver 0.9988 oz. ASW **Obv:** State seal **Rev:** F-102A Delta Dagger

Date	Mintage	F	VF	XF	Unc	BU
1995 Proof	25,000	Value: 27.50				

KM# 397 50 DOLLARS
31.1000 g., 0.9990 Silver 0.9988 oz. ASW **Obv:** State seal **Rev:** B-52 Stratofortress

Date	Mintage	F	VF	XF	Unc	BU
1995 Proof	25,000	Value: 30.00				

KM# 277 50 DOLLARS
31.1000 g., 0.9990 Silver 0.9988 oz. ASW **Subject:** Freedom / Liberty **Rev:** Battleship and freighter

Date	Mintage	F	VF	XF	Unc	BU
1995 Proof	Est. 25,000	Value: 57.50				

KM# 278 50 DOLLARS
31.1000 g., 0.9990 Silver 0.9988 oz. ASW **Subject:** Freedom / Liberty **Rev:** President John F. Kennedy working at desk

Date	Mintage	F	VF	XF	Unc	BU
1995 Proof	Est. 25,000	Value: 57.50				

KM# 279 50 DOLLARS
31.1000 g., 0.9990 Silver 0.9988 oz. ASW **Subject:** Freedom / Liberty **Rev:** President John F. Kennedy's Eternal Flame

Date	Mintage	F	VF	XF	Unc	BU
1995 Proof	Est. 25,000	Value: 57.50				

KM# 227 50 DOLLARS
31.1000 g., 0.9990 Silver 0.9988 oz. ASW **Subject:** War in the Pacific **Note:** Similar to 10 Dollars, KM#226.

Date	Mintage	F	VF	XF	Unc	BU
1995 Proof	—	Value: 32.50				

KM# 218 50 DOLLARS
31.1000 g., 0.9990 Silver 0.9988 oz. ASW **Subject:** Victory in Europe **Note:** Similar to 5 Dollars, KM#216.

Date	Mintage	F	VF	XF	Unc	BU
1995 Proof	—	Value: 40.00				

KM# 221 50 DOLLARS
31.1000 g., 0.9990 Silver 0.9988 oz. ASW **Subject:** Vietnam Veterans **Note:** Similar to 5 Dollars, KM#219.

Date	Mintage	F	VF	XF	Unc	BU
1995 Proof	—	Value: 32.50				

KM# 281 50 DOLLARS
31.1000 g., 0.9990 Silver 0.9988 oz. ASW **Subject:** Year of the Rat **Note:** Similar to 5 Dollars, KM#280.

Date	Mintage	F	VF	XF	Unc	BU
1996 Proof	—	Value: 40.00				

KM# 305 50 DOLLARS
31.1000 g., 0.9990 Silver 0.9988 oz. ASW **Rev:** James Dean **Note:** Similar to 5 Dollars, KM#303.

Date	Mintage	F	VF	XF	Unc	BU
1996 Proof	—	Value: 50.00				

KM# 350 50 DOLLARS
31.1000 g., 0.9990 Silver 0.9988 oz. ASW **Rev:** Lion **Note:** Similar to 5 Dollars, KM#344.

Date	Mintage	F	VF	XF	Unc	BU
1996 Proof	—	Value: 42.50				

KM# 352 50 DOLLARS
31.1000 g., 0.9990 Silver 0.9988 oz. ASW **Rev:** Jaguar **Note:** Similar to 5 Dollars, KM#346.

Date	Mintage	F	VF	XF	Unc	BU
1996 Proof	—	Value: 42.50				

KM# 313 50 DOLLARS
31.1000 g., 0.9990 Silver 0.9988 oz. ASW **Subject:** Classic Cars **Rev:** Model A Ford **Note:** Similar to 10 Dollars, KM#312.

Date	Mintage	F	VF	XF	Unc	BU
1996 Proof	—	Value: 32.50				

KM# 340 50 DOLLARS
31.1000 g., 0.9990 Silver 0.9988 oz. ASW **Rev:** Space Shuttle Challenger **Note:** Similar to 10 Dollars, KM#336.

Date	Mintage	F	VF	XF	Unc	BU
1996 Proof	—	Value: 32.50				

KM# 341 50 DOLLARS
31.1000 g., 0.9990 Silver 0.9988 oz. ASW **Rev:** Space Shuttle Discovery **Note:** Similar to 10 Dollars, KM#338.

Date	Mintage	F	VF	XF	Unc	BU
1996 Proof	—	Value: 32.50				

KM# 290 50 DOLLARS
31.1000 g., 0.9990 Silver 0.9988 oz. ASW **Rev:** Space Shuttle Columbia

Date	Mintage	F	VF	XF	Unc	BU
1996 Proof	—	Value: 37.50				

KM# 291 50 DOLLARS
31.1800 g., 0.9990 Silver 1.0014 oz. ASW, 38.68 mm. **Obv:** National arms **Rev:** "Pennsylvania K4" steam locomotive **Edge:** Reeded

Date	Mintage	F	VF	XF	Unc	BU
1996 Proof	—	Value: 32.50				

KM# 292 50 DOLLARS
31.1800 g., 0.9990 Silver 1.0014 oz. ASW, 38.68 mm. **Obv:** National arms **Rev:** "Big Boy" steam locomotive **Edge:** Reeded

Date	Mintage	F	VF	XF	Unc	BU
1996 Proof	—	Value: 32.50				

KM# 296 50 DOLLARS
31.1800 g., 0.9990 Silver 1.0014 oz. ASW, 38.68 mm. **Obv:** National arms **Rev:** "Mallard" steam locomotive **Edge:** Reeded

Date	Mintage	F	VF	XF	Unc	BU
1996 Proof	—	Value: 32.50				

KM# 299 50 DOLLARS
31.1000 g., 0.9990 Silver 0.9988 oz. ASW **Rev:** Tiger

Date	Mintage	F	VF	XF	Unc	BU
1996 In set only	—	—	—	—	42.50	—

KM# 302 50 DOLLARS
31.1000 g., 0.9990 Silver 0.9988 oz. ASW **Rev:** Elvis Presley

Date	Mintage	F	VF	XF	Unc	BU
1996 Proof	—	Value: 50.00				

KM# 310 50 DOLLARS
31.1000 g., 0.9990 Silver 0.9988 oz. ASW **Subject:** Classic Cars **Rev:** Ford Quadricycle

Date	Mintage	F	VF	XF	Unc	BU
1996 Proof	—	Value: 32.50				

KM# 316 50 DOLLARS
31.1000 g., 0.9990 Silver 0.9988 oz. ASW **Subject:** Classic Cars **Rev:** Model T Ford

Date	Mintage	F	VF	XF	Unc	BU
1996 Proof	—	Value: 32.50				

KM# 319 50 DOLLARS
31.1000 g., 0.9990 Silver 0.9988 oz. ASW **Subject:** Classic Cars **Rev:** 1955 Thunderbird

Date	Mintage	F	VF	XF	Unc	BU
1996 Proof	—	Value: 50.00				

KM# 322 50 DOLLARS
31.1000 g., 0.9990 Silver 0.9988 oz. ASW **Subject:** Classic Cars **Rev:** 1964 Mustang

Date	Mintage	F	VF	XF	Unc	BU
1996 Proof	—	Value: 37.50				

KM# 325 50 DOLLARS
31.1000 g., 0.9990 Silver 0.9988 oz. ASW **Subject:** Classic
Cars **Rev:** Ford Taurus

Date	Mintage	F	VF	XF	Unc	BU
1996 Proof	—		Value: 32.50			

KM# 327 50 DOLLARS
31.1800 g., 0.9990 Silver 1.0014 oz. ASW, 38.68 mm.
Obv: National arms **Rev:** "DB Class 01" steam locomotive
Edge: Reeded

Date	Mintage	F	VF	XF	Unc	BU
1996 Proof	Est. 25,000		Value: 32.50			

KM# 328 50 DOLLARS
31.1800 g., 0.9990 Silver 1.0014 oz. ASW, 38.68 mm.
Obv: National arms **Rev:** "RENFE Class 242" steam locomotive
Edge: Reeded

Date	Mintage	F	VF	XF	Unc	BU
1996 Proof	—		Value: 32.50			

KM# 329 50 DOLLARS
31.1800 g., 0.9990 Silver 1.0014 oz. ASW, 38.68 mm.
Obv: National arms **Rev:** Steam locomotive "S Group 691"
Edge: Reeded

Date	Mintage	F	VF	XF	Unc	BU
1996 Proof	—		Value: 32.50			

KM# 342 50 DOLLARS
31.1000 g., 0.9990 Silver 0.9988 oz. ASW **Rev:** Space Shuttle
Atlantis

Date	Mintage	F	VF	XF	Unc	BU
1996 Proof	—		Value: 32.50			

KM# 343 50 DOLLARS
31.1000 g., 0.9990 Silver 0.9988 oz. ASW **Rev:** Space Shuttle
Endeavor

Date	Mintage	F	VF	XF	Unc	BU
1996 Proof	—		Value: 32.50			

KM# 351 50 DOLLARS
31.1000 g., 0.9990 Silver 0.9988 oz. ASW **Rev:** Cheetah

Date	Mintage	F	VF	XF	Unc	BU
1996 Proof	—		Value: 40.00			

KM# 355 50 DOLLARS
31.1000 g., 0.9990 Silver 0.9988 oz. ASW **Subject:** Christmas
Rev: Two angels

Date	Mintage	F	VF	XF	Unc	BU
1996 Proof	—		Value: 35.00			

KM# 357 50 DOLLARS
31.1000 g., 0.9990 Silver 0.9988 oz. ASW **Subject:** Steam
Locomotive **Rev:** "SNCF 232.U1"

Date	Mintage	F	VF	XF	Unc	BU
1996 Proof	—		Value: 40.00			

KM# 358 50 DOLLARS
31.1000 g., 0.9990 Silver 0.9988 oz. ASW **Subject:** Steam
Locomotive **Rev:** "SAR 520 Class"

Date	Mintage	F	VF	XF	Unc	BU
1996 Proof	—		Value: 40.00			

KM# 360 50 DOLLARS
31.1000 g., 0.9990 Silver 0.9988 oz. ASW **Subject:** Steam
Locomotive **Rev:** "Evening Star"

Date	Mintage	F	VF	XF	Unc	BU
1996 Proof	—		Value: 40.00			

KM# 376 50 DOLLARS
31.1000 g., 0.9990 Silver 0.9988 oz. ASW **Subject:** Steam
Locomotive **Rev:** C62 "Swallow"

Date	Mintage	F	VF	XF	Unc	BU
1996 Proof	—		Value: 40.00			

KM# 377 50 DOLLARS
31.1000 g., 0.9990 Silver 0.9988 oz. ASW **Subject:** Steam
Locomotive **Rev:** QJ "Advance Forward"

Date	Mintage	F	VF	XF	Unc	BU
1996 Proof	—		Value: 40.00			

KM# 380 50 DOLLARS
31.1000 g., 0.9990 Silver 0.9988 oz. ASW **Subject:** Steam
Locomotive **Rev:** "Royal Hudson"

Date	Mintage	F	VF	XF	Unc	BU
1996 Proof	—		Value: 40.00			

KM# 363 50 DOLLARS
31.1000 g., 0.9990 Silver 0.9988 oz. ASW **Subject:** Year of the
Ox **Obv:** State seal **Rev:** Stylized ox

Date	Mintage	F	VF	XF	Unc	BU
1997 Proof	—		Value: 57.50			

KM# 375 50 DOLLARS
31.1000 g., 0.9990 Silver 0.9988 oz. ASW **Rev:** Gray wolf

Date	Mintage	F	VF	XF	Unc	BU
1997 Proof	—		Value: 50.00			

KM# 399 50 DOLLARS
31.1000 g., 0.9990 Silver 0.9988 oz. ASW **Subject:** History's
Great Fightintg Ships **Rev:** USS Constitution; ship, dates

Date	Mintage	F	VF	XF	Unc	BU
1997 Proof	—		Value: 56.00			

KM# 405 50 DOLLARS
31.1000 g., 0.9990 Silver 0.9988 oz. ASW **Subject:** Christmas
Rev: Two cherubs

Date	Mintage	F	VF	XF	Unc	BU
1997	—	—	—	—	35.00	

KM# 366 50 DOLLARS
31.1000 g., 0.9990 Silver 0.9988 oz. ASW **Rev:** Elvis Presley
Note: Similar to 5 Dollars, KM#362.

Date	Mintage	F	VF	XF	Unc	BU
1997 Proof	—		Value: 57.50			

KM# 370 50 DOLLARS
31.1000 g., 0.9990 Silver 0.9988 oz. ASW **Subject:** The Last
Supper **Note:** Similar to 5 Dollars, KM#369.

Date	Mintage	F	VF	XF	Unc	BU
1997 Proof	—		Value: 50.00			

KM# 373 50 DOLLARS
31.1000 g., 0.9990 Silver 0.9988 oz. ASW **Subject:** To the
Heroes of the Korean War **Note:** Similar to 5 Dollars, KM#371.

Date	Mintage	F	VF	XF	Unc	BU
1997 Proof	—		Value: 40.00			

KM# 467 50 DOLLARS
31.1000 g., 0.9990 Silver 0.9988 oz. ASW **Subject:** Classic
Cars **Obv:** State seal **Rev:** 1912 Chevy Classic Six **Note:** Similar
to 5 Dollars, KM#466.

Date	Mintage	F	VF	XF	Unc	BU
1998 Proof	—		Value: 50.00			

KM# 469 50 DOLLARS
31.1000 g., 0.9990 Silver 0.9988 oz. ASW **Subject:** Classic
Cars **Obv:** State seal **Rev:** 1931 Chevy Roadster **Note:** Similar
to 5 Dollars, KM#468.

Date	Mintage	F	VF	XF	Unc	BU
1998 Proof	—		Value: 50.00			

KM# 471 50 DOLLARS
31.1000 g., 0.9990 Silver 0.9988 oz. ASW **Subject:** Classic
Cars **Obv:** State seal **Rev:** Cameo Carrier **Note:** Similar to 5
Dollars, KM#470.

Date	Mintage	F	VF	XF	Unc	BU
1998 Proof	—		Value: 50.00			

KM# 473 50 DOLLARS
31.1000 g., 0.9990 Silver 0.9988 oz. ASW **Subject:** Classic
Cars **Obv:** State seal **Rev:** 1957 Chevy Bel Air **Note:** Similar to
5 Dollars, KM#472.

Date	Mintage	F	VF	XF	Unc	BU
1998 Proof	—		Value: 50.00			

KM# 475 50 DOLLARS
31.1000 g., 0.9990 Silver 0.9988 oz. ASW **Subject:** Classic
Cars **Obv:** State seal **Rev:** 1957 Chevy Corvette **Note:** Similar
to 5 Dollars, KM#474.

Date	Mintage	F	VF	XF	Unc	BU
1998 Proof	—		Value: 50.00			

KM# 477 50 DOLLARS
31.1000 g., 0.9990 Silver 0.9988 oz. ASW **Subject:** Classic
Cars **Obv:** State seal **Rev:** 1967 Chevy Camaro **Note:** Similar to
5 Dollars, KM#476.

Date	Mintage	F	VF	XF	Unc	BU
1998 Proof	—		Value: 50.00			

KM# 414 50 DOLLARS
31.1000 g., 0.9990 Silver 0.9988 oz. ASW **Subject:** Year of the
Tiger **Rev:** Stylized tiger

Date	Mintage	F	VF	XF	Unc	BU
1998 Proof	—		Value: 50.00			

KM# 416 50 DOLLARS
31.1000 g., 0.9990 Silver 0.9988 oz. ASW **Subject:** History's
Great Fighting Ships **Rev:** Viking Longship

Date	Mintage	F	VF	XF	Unc	BU
1998 Proof	Est. 25,000		Value: 55.00			

KM# 418 50 DOLLARS
31.1000 g., 0.9990 Silver 0.9988 oz. ASW **Subject:** History's
Great Fighting Ships **Rev:** Greek Trireme

Date	Mintage	F	VF	XF	Unc	BU
1998 Proof	Est. 25,000		Value: 55.00			

KM# 420 50 DOLLARS
31.1000 g., 0.9990 Silver 0.9988 oz. ASW **Subject:** History's
Great Fighting Ships **Rev:** Roman Trireme

Date	Mintage	F	VF	XF	Unc	BU
1998 Proof	Est. 25,000		Value: 55.00			

KM# 422   50 DOLLARS
31.1000 g., 0.9990 Silver 0.9988 oz. ASW **Subject:** History's
Great Fighting Ships **Rev:** Chinese Ming Treasure Ship

Date	Mintage	F	VF	XF	Unc	BU
1998 Proof	Est. 25,000			Value: 55.00		

KM# 424   50 DOLLARS
31.1000 g., 0.9990 Silver 0.9988 oz. ASW **Subject:** History's
Great Fighting Ships **Rev:** Korean Turtle Ship

Date	Mintage	F	VF	XF	Unc	BU
1998 Proof	Est. 25,000			Value: 55.00		

KM# 426   50 DOLLARS
31.1000 g., 0.9990 Silver 0.9988 oz. ASW **Subject:** History's
Great Fighting Ships **Rev:** Fijan War Canoe

Date	Mintage	F	VF	XF	Unc	BU
1998 Proof	Est. 25,000			Value: 55.00		

KM# 428   50 DOLLARS
31.1000 g., 0.9990 Silver 0.9988 oz. ASW **Subject:** History's
Great Fighting Ships **Rev:** The Bismarck

Date	Mintage	F	VF	XF	Unc	BU
1998 Proof	Est. 25,000			Value: 55.00		

KM# 430   50 DOLLARS
31.1000 g., 0.9990 Silver 0.9988 oz. ASW **Subject:** History's
Great Fighting Ships **Rev:** The Graf Spee

Date	Mintage	F	VF	XF	Unc	BU
1998 Proof	Est. 25,000			Value: 55.00		

KM# 432   50 DOLLARS
31.1000 g., 0.9990 Silver 0.9988 oz. ASW **Subject:** History's
Great Fighting Ships **Rev:** The Yamato

Date	Mintage	F	VF	XF	Unc	BU
1998 Proof	Est. 25,000			Value: 55.00		

KM# 434   50 DOLLARS
31.1000 g., 0.9990 Silver 0.9988 oz. ASW **Subject:** History's
Great Fighting Ships **Rev:** HMS Victory

Date	Mintage	F	VF	XF	Unc	BU
1998 Proof	Est. 25,000			Value: 55.00		

KM# 436   50 DOLLARS
31.1000 g., 0.9990 Silver 0.9988 oz. ASW **Subject:** History's
Great Fighting Ships **Rev:** HMS Mary Rose

Date	Mintage	F	VF	XF	Unc	BU
1998 Proof	Est. 25,000			Value: 55.00		

KM# 438   50 DOLLARS
31.1000 g., 0.9990 Silver 0.9988 oz. ASW **Subject:** History's
Great Fighting Ships **Rev:** HMS Dreadnought

Date	Mintage	F	VF	XF	Unc	BU
1998 Proof	Est. 25,000			Value: 55.00		

KM# 440   50 DOLLARS
31.1000 g., 0.9990 Silver 0.9988 oz. ASW **Subject:** History's
Great Fighting Ships **Rev:** HMS Dorsetshire

Date	Mintage	F	VF	XF	Unc	BU
1998 Proof	Est. 25,000			Value: 55.00		

KM# 442   50 DOLLARS
31.1000 g., 0.9990 Silver 0.9988 oz. ASW **Subject:** History's
Great Fighting Ships **Obv:** State seal **Rev:** Spanish Galleon
Nuestra Senora del Rosario

Date	Mintage	F	VF	XF	Unc	BU
1998 Proof	Est. 25,000			Value: 55.00		

KM# 444   50 DOLLARS
31.1000 g., 0.9990 Silver 0.9988 oz. ASW **Subject:** History's
Great Fighting Ships **Obv:** State seal **Rev:** Spanish Galleon
Santisima Trinidad

Date	Mintage	F	VF	XF	Unc	BU
1998 Proof	Est. 25,000			Value: 55.00		

KM# 446   50 DOLLARS
31.1000 g., 0.9990 Silver 0.9988 oz. ASW **Subject:** History's
Great Fighting Ships **Obv:** State seal **Rev:** USS Bonhomme
Richard

Date	Mintage	F	VF	XF	Unc	BU
1998 Proof	Est. 25,000			Value: 55.00		

KM# 448   50 DOLLARS
31.1000 g., 0.9990 Silver 0.9988 oz. ASW **Subject:** History's
Great Fighting Ships **Obv:** State seal **Rev:** USS Constellation

Date	Mintage	F	VF	XF	Unc	BU
1998 Proof	Est. 25,000			Value: 55.00		

KM# 450   50 DOLLARS
31.1000 g., 0.9990 Silver 0.9988 oz. ASW **Subject:** History's
Great Fighting Ships **Obv:** State seal **Rev:** USS Hartford

Date	Mintage	F	VF	XF	Unc	BU
1998 Proof	Est. 25,000			Value: 55.00		

KM# 452   50 DOLLARS
31.1000 g., 0.9990 Silver 0.9988 oz. ASW **Subject:** History's
Great Fighting Ships **Obv:** State seal **Rev:** USS Hornet

Date	Mintage	F	VF	XF	Unc	BU
1998 Proof	Est. 25,000			Value: 55.00		

KM# 454   50 DOLLARS
31.1000 g., 0.9990 Silver 0.9988 oz. ASW **Subject:** History's
Great Fighting Ships **Obv:** State seal **Rev:** USS Missouri

Date	Mintage	F	VF	XF	Unc	BU
1998 Proof	Est. 25,000			Value: 55.00		

KM# 456   50 DOLLARS
31.1000 g., 0.9990 Silver 0.9988 oz. ASW **Subject:** History's
Great Fighting Ships **Obv:** State seal **Rev:** USS Tautog

Date	Mintage	F	VF	XF	Unc	BU
1998 Proof	Est. 25,000			Value: 55.00		

KM# 458   50 DOLLARS
31.1000 g., 0.9990 Silver 0.9988 oz. ASW **Subject:** History's
Great Fighting Ships **Obv:** State seal **Rev:** Dutch Ship Brederode

Date	Mintage	F	VF	XF	Unc	BU
1998 Proof	Est. 25,000			Value: 55.00		

KM# 460   50 DOLLARS
31.1000 g., 0.9990 Silver 0.9988 oz. ASW **Subject:** History's Great
Fighting Ships **Obv:** State seal **Rev:** French Ship Ville de Paris

Date	Mintage	F	VF	XF	Unc	BU
1998 Proof	Est. 25,000			Value: 55.00		

KM# 462   50 DOLLARS
31.1000 g., 0.9990 Silver 0.9988 oz. ASW **Subject:** History's Great
Fighting Ships **Obv:** State seal **Rev:** Italian Ship Galera Veneziana

Date	Mintage	F	VF	XF	Unc	BU
1998 Proof	Est. 25,000			Value: 55.00		

KM# 465   50 DOLLARS
31.1000 g., 0.9990 Silver 0.9988 oz. ASW **Subject:** To the
Heroes of the Berlin Airlift **Obv:** State seal **Rev:** C-54 Landing

Date	Mintage	F	VF	XF	Unc	BU
1998 Proof	—			Value: 55.00		

KM# 480   50 DOLLARS
31.1000 g., 0.9990 Silver 0.9988 oz. ASW **Subject:** Babe Ruth
at bat **Obv:** State seal

Date	Mintage	F	VF	XF	Unc	BU
1998 Proof	—			Value: 47.50		

KM# 483   50 DOLLARS
31.1000 g., 0.9990 Silver 0.9988 oz. ASW **Subject:** Christmas
Obv: State seal **Rev:** Angel

Date	Mintage	F	VF	XF	Unc	BU
1998 Proof	—			Value: 45.00		

KM# 485   50 DOLLARS
31.1000 g., 0.9990 Silver 0.9988 oz. ASW **Rev:** Friendship 7
and Discovery blasting off **Edge:** Reeded

Date	Mintage	F	VF	XF	Unc	BU
1998 Proof	—			Value: 56.00		

KM# 16   75 DOLLARS
155.6700 g., 0.9990 Silver 4.9997 oz. ASW, 65 mm. **Subject:** Greg
Louganis - World's Greatest Diver **Note:** Illustration reduced. An
actual mintage of 20 pieces has been reported for KM#16.

Date	Mintage	F	VF	XF	Unc	BU
1988 Proof	Est. 175,000			Value: 800		

KM# 17   100 DOLLARS
13.3300 g., 0.5830 Gold 0.2498 oz. AGW **Subject:** Greg
Louganis - World's Greatest Diver **Obv:** State seal and legend
Rev: Diver

Date	Mintage	F	VF	XF	Unc	BU
1988	Est. 280,000	—	—	—	300	320
1988 Proof	Est. 350,000			Value: 345		

KM# 5   200 DOLLARS
31.1030 g., 0.9990 Gold 0.9989 oz. AGW **Rev:** Stick chart

Date	Mintage	F	VF	XF	Unc	BU
1986 Proof	Est. 5,000	Value: 950				

MINT SETS

KM#	Date	Mintage	Identification	Issue Price	Mkt Val
MS1	1988 (3)	—	KM#20-22	—	250
MS2	1988 (4)	—	KM#17, 20-22	—	550
MS3	1992R (3)	—	KM#81-83	71.00	75.00
MS4	1992R (3)	—	KM#84-86	71.00	75.00
MS5	1992R (3)	—	KM#87-89	71.00	75.00
MS6	1992R (3)	—	KM#90-92	71.00	75.00
MS7	1992R (3)	—	KM#84, 87, 90	17.50	20.00
MS8	1992R (3)	—	KM#85, 88, 91	34.00	35.00
MS9	1992R (3)	—	KM#86, 89, 92	156	160
MS10	1995 (6)	—	KM#282-287	66.00	75.00
MS11	1998 (24)	25,000	KM#415, 417, 419, 421, 423, 425, 427, 429, 431, 433, 435, 437, 439, 441, 443, 445, 447, 449, 451, 453, 455, 457, 459, 461	288	290

PROOF SETS

KM#	Date	Mintage	Identification	Issue Price	Mkt Val
PS1	1986 (3)	5,000	KM#3-5	1,095	665
PS2	1986 (2)	10,000	KM#1-2	45.00	50.00
PS3	1988 (3)	—	KM#20-22	—	375
PS4	1988 (4)	—	KM#17, 20-22	—	700
PS5	1991 (3)	—	KM#40-42	71.00	75.00
PS6	1993 (3)	—	KM#124, 129-130	—	85.00
PS7	1994 (3)	—	KM#179-180 BU, 181	71.00	75.00
PS8	1994 (3)	—	KM#182 BU, 183 P/L, 184	71.00	75.00
PS9	1994 (3)	—	KM#260 BU, 261, 262	—	75.00
PS10	1994 (3)	—	KM#263 BU, 264, 265	—	75.00
PS11	1995 (6)	25,000	KM#274-279	—	340
PS12	1995 (3)	—	KM#216 BU, 217, 218	—	75.00
PS13	1995 (3)	—	KM#219 BU, 220, 221	—	75.00
PS14	1995 (3)	—	KM#222 BU, 223, 224	—	75.00
PS15	1995 (3)	—	KM#225 BU, 226, 227	—	75.00
PS16	1995 (3)	—	KM#253 BU, 254, 255	—	95.00
PS17	1995 (3)	—	KM#257 BU, 258, 259	—	75.00
PS18	1995 (3)	—	KM#266 BU, 267, 268	—	75.00
PS19	1996 (6)	—	KM#308, 311, 314, 317, 320, 323	33.00	40.00
PS20	1996 (6)	—	KM#309, 312, 315, 318, 321, 324	66.00	80.00
PS21	1996 (6)	—	KM#310, 313, 316, 319, 322, 325	306	325
PS22	1996 (3)	—	KM#288-290	71.00	75.00
PS23	1996 (3)	—	KM#297-299	71.00	78.00
PS24	1996 (3)	—	KM#300-302	71.00	78.00
PS25	1996 (3)	—	KM#303-305	71.00	75.00
PS26	1996 (3)	—	KM#308-310	71.00	75.00
PS27	1996 (3)	—	KM#311-313	71.00	75.00
PS28	1996 (3)	—	KM#314-316	71.00	75.00
PS29	1996 (3)	—	KM#317-319	71.00	75.00
PS30	1996 (3)	—	KM#320-322	71.00	75.00
PS31	1996 (4)	—	KM#322-325	71.00	75.00
PS32	1996 (3)	—	KM#353-355	71.00	75.00
PS33	1997 (2)	—	KM#362-363	61.00	65.00
PS34	1997 (2)	—	KM#364-366	71.00	77.50
PS35	1997 (2)	—	KM#369-370	61.00	62.50
PS36	1997 (2)	—	KM#371-373	71.00	75.00
PS37	1997 (2)	—	KM#374-375	61.00	65.00
PS38	1997 (2)	—	KM#398-399	61.00	62.50
PS39	1997 (2)	—	KM#400-401	—	37.50
PS40	1997 (3)	—	KM#403-405	71.00	75.00
PS41	1998 (24)	—	KM#416, 418, 420, 422, 424, 426, 428, 430, 432, 434, 436, 438, 440, 442, 444, 446, 448, 450, 452, 454, 456, 458, 460, 462	1,344	1,345
PS42	1998 (3)	—	KM#478-480	71.00	72.00
PS43	1998 (3)	—	KM#481-483	71.00	72.00

MARTINIQUE

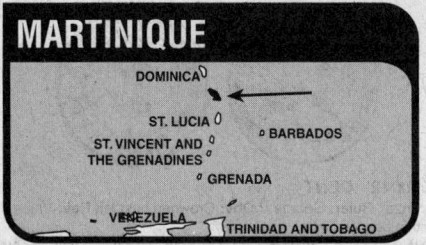

The French Overseas Department of Martinique, located in the Lesser Antilles of the West Indies between Dominica and Saint Lucia, has an area of 425 sq. mi.(1,100 sq. km.) and a population of 290,000. Capital: Fort-de-France. Agriculture and tourism are the major sources of income. Bananas, sugar, and rum are exported.

Christopher Columbus discovered Martinique, probably on June 15, 1502. France took possession on June 25, 1635, and has maintained possession since that time except for three short periods of British occupation during the Napoleonic Wars. A French department since 1946, Martinique voted a reaffirmation of that status in 1958, remaining within the new French Community. Martinique was the birthplace of Napoleon's Empress Josephine, and the site of the eruption of Mt. Pelee in 1902 that claimed 40,000 lives.

The official currency of Martinique is the French franc. The 1897-1922 coinage of the Colony of Martinique is now obsolete.

MONETARY SYSTEM
15 Sols = 1 Escalin
20 Sols = 1 Livre
66 Livres = 4 Escudos = 6400 Reis

FRENCH COLONY
DECIMAL COINAGE

KM# 40   50 CENTIMES
Copper-Nickel **Obv:** Bust left within circle with star above
Rev: Value and date within wreath

Date	Mintage	VG	F	VF	XF	Unc
1922	500,000	15.00	25.00	60.00	250	500

KM# 41   FRANC
Copper-Nickel **Obv:** Bust left within circle with star above
Rev: Value and date within wreath

Date	Mintage	VG	F	VF	XF	Unc
1922	350,000	20.00	30.00	70.00	275	600

MAURITANIA

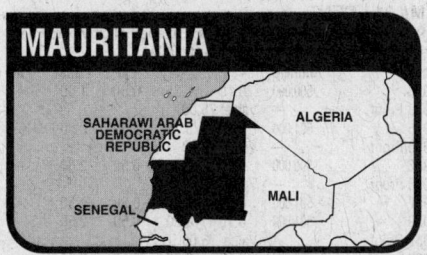

The Islamic Republic of Mauritania, located in northwest Africa bounded by Western Sahara, Mali, Algeria, Senegal and the Atlantic Ocean, has an area of 397,955 sq. mi.(1,030,700 sq. km.) and a population of 1.9 million. Capital: Nouakchott. The economy centers on herding, agriculture, fishing and mining. Iron ore, copper concentrates and fish products are exported.

The indigenous Negroid inhabitants were driven out of Mauritania by Berber invaders of the Islamic faith in the 11th century. The Berbers in turn were conquered by Arab invaders, the Beni Hassan, in the 16th century. Arab traders carried on a gainful trade in gum arabic, gold and slaves with Portuguese, Dutch, English and French traders until late in the 19th century when France took control of the area and made it a part of French West Africa, in 1920. Mauritania became a part of the French Union in 1946 and was made an autonomous republic within the new French Community in 1958, when the Islamic Republic of Mauritania was proclaimed. The republic became independent on November 28, 1960, and withdrew from the French Community in 1966.

On June 28, 1973, in a move designed to emphasize its nonalignment with France, Mauritania converted its currency from the old French-supported C.F.A. franc unit to a new unit called the Ouguiya.

MONETARY SYSTEM
5 Khoums = 1 Ouguiya

REPUBLIC
STANDARD COINAGE

KM# 1   1/5 OUGUIYA (Khoums)
Aluminum **Obv:** National emblem divides date above value
Obv. Leg.: BANQUE CENTRALE DE MAURITANIE **Rev:** Star and crescent divide sprigs within circle with legend around border

Date	Mintage	VG	F	VF	XF	Unc
AH1393//1973	1,000,000	—	0.35	0.75	1.50	3.00

KM# 2   OUGUIYA
Copper-Nickel-Aluminum **Obv:** National emblem divides date above value **Obv. Leg.:** BANQUE CENTRALE DE MAURITANIE **Rev:** Star and crescent divide sprigs below value within circle, legend around border

Date	Mintage	VG	F	VF	XF	Unc
AH1393//1973	—	—	7.00	20.00	37.50	85.00

KM# 6   OUGUIYA
3.6000 g., Copper-Nickel-Aluminum, 21 mm. **Obv:** National emblem divides date above value **Obv. Leg.:** BANQUE CENTRALE DE MAURITANIE **Rev:** Star and crescent divide sprigs with legend below value, all within circle **Edge:** Reeded

Date	Mintage	F	VF	XF	Unc	BU
AH1394//1974	—	2.50	5.50	10.00	18.50	—
AH1401//1981	—	1.50	3.00	4.50	7.50	—
AH1403//1983	—	1.00	2.00	3.50	6.50	—
AH1406//1986	—	0.75	1.50	2.50	4.50	—
AH1407//1987	—	0.50	1.00	2.00	4.00	—
AH1410//1990	—	0.50	1.00	2.00	4.00	—
AH1414//1993	—	0.50	1.00	2.00	4.00	—
AH1416//1995	—	0.50	1.00	2.00	4.00	—

KM# 3   5 OUGUIYA
5.8800 g., Copper-Nickel-Aluminum, 25 mm. **Obv:** National emblem divides date above value **Obv. Leg.:** BANQUE CENTRALE DE MAURITANIE **Rev:** Star and crescent divide sprigs below value within circle **Edge:** Plain

Date	Mintage	F	VF	XF	Unc	BU
AH1393//1973	—	2.50	5.50	10.00	15.00	—
AH1394//1974	—	2.50	5.50	10.00	17.50	—
AH1401//1981	—	2.00	4.00	6.00	12.50	—
AH1404//1984	—	1.50	2.50	4.50	10.00	—
AH1407//1987	—	0.75	1.50	2.50	5.00	—
AH1410//1990	—	0.50	1.00	2.00	4.00	—
AH1414//1993	—	0.50	1.00	2.00	4.00	—
AH1416//1995	—	0.50	1.00	2.00	4.00	—
AH1418//1997	—	0.50	1.00	2.00	4.00	—
AH1420//1999	—	0.50	1.00	2.00	4.00	—

KM# 4   10 OUGUIYA
6.0000 g., Copper-Nickel, 25 mm. **Obv:** National emblem divides date above value **Obv. Leg.:** BANQUE CENTRALE DE MAURITANIE **Rev:** Crescent and star divide sprigs below value within circle **Edge:** Reeded

Date	Mintage	F	VF	XF	Unc	BU
AH1393//1973	—	2.50	5.50	10.00	17.50	—
AH1394//1974	—	2.50	5.50	10.00	17.50	—
AH1401//1981	—	2.00	5.00	7.50	15.00	—
AH1403//1983	—	1.25	2.50	4.00	8.00	—
AH1407//1987	—	1.25	2.50	4.00	8.00	—
AH1410//1990	—	0.75	1.50	2.50	4.50	—
AH1411//1991	—	0.75	1.50	2.50	4.50	—
AH1414//1993	—	0.75	1.50	2.50	4.50	—
AH1416//1995	—	0.75	1.50	2.50	4.50	—
AH1418//1997	—	0.75	1.50	2.50	4.50	—
AH1420//1999	—	0.75	1.50	2.50	4.50	—

KM# 5   20 OUGUIYA
8.0000 g., Copper-Nickel, 28 mm. **Obv:** National emblem divides date above value **Obv. Leg.:** BANQUE CENTRALE DE MAURITANIE **Rev:** Star and crescent divide sprigs below value within circle **Edge:** Reeded

Date	Mintage	F	VF	XF	Unc	BU
AH1393//1973	—	2.00	5.00	10.00	18.00	—
AH1394//1974	—	2.00	5.00	10.00	18.00	—
AH1403//1983	—	1.25	2.50	4.00	8.00	—
AH1407//1987	—	1.25	2.50	4.00	8.00	—
AH1410//1990	—	1.25	2.50	4.00	8.00	—
AH1414//1993	—	1.25	2.50	4.00	8.00	—
AH1416//1995	—	1.25	2.50	4.00	8.00	—
AH1418//1997	—	1.25	2.50	4.00	8.00	—
AH1420//1999	—	1.25	2.50	4.00	8.00	—

KM# 7   500 OUGUIYA
26.0800 g., 0.9200 Gold 0.7714 oz. AGW **Subject:** 15th Anniversary of Independence **Obv:** Star and crescent flanked by palm trees below dates **Rev:** Value in square flanked by a camel head and fish with design above

Date	Mintage	F	VF	XF	Unc	BU
1975 (a)	1,800	—	—	—	—	750

MINT SETS

KM#	Date	Mintage	Identification	Issue Price	Mkt Val
MS1	1973 (10)	—	KM1-5, two each	20.00	275

MAURITIUS

MOZAMBIQUE · MADAGASCAR · Indian Ocean · REUNION

The Republic of Mauritius, is located in the Indian Ocean 500 miles (805 km.) east of Madagascar, has an area of 790 sq. mi. (1,860 sq. km.) and a population of 1 million. Capital: Port Louis. Sugar provides 90 percent of the export revenue.

Mauritius became independent on March 12, 1968. It is a member of the Commonwealth of Nations.

RULER
British, until 1968

MINT MARKS
H - Heaton, Birmingham
SA - Pretoria Mint

MONETARY SYSTEM
100 Cents = 1 Rupee

CROWN COLONY

STANDARD COINAGE

100 Cents = 1 Rupee

KM# 12   CENT
Bronze **Ruler:** George V **Obv:** Crowned bust left **Rev:** Value within beaded circle

Date	Mintage	F	VF	XF	Unc	BU
1911	1,000,000	1.00	6.00	22.00	40.00	100
1912	500,000	1.25	6.50	28.50	55.00	130
1917	500,000	1.00	6.00	22.00	35.00	75.00
1920	500,000	1.50	8.00	32.50	60.00	125
1921	500,000	2.00	8.00	32.50	60.00	120
1922	1,800,000	0.75	1.50	9.00	25.00	50.00
1923	200,000	3.00	17.00	45.00	75.00	175
1924	200,000	3.00	17.00	45.00	75.00	175

KM# 21   CENT
Bronze **Ruler:** George VI **Obv:** Crowned head left **Rev:** Value within beaded circle

Date	Mintage	F	VF	XF	Unc	BU
1943SA	520,000	0.50	1.25	4.00	10.00	22.00
1944SA	500,000	0.50	1.25	4.00	10.00	22.00
1945SA	500,000	0.50	1.25	4.00	10.00	22.00
1946SA	500,000	0.50	1.25	4.00	10.00	22.00
1947SA	500,000	0.50	1.25	4.00	10.00	22.00

KM# 25   CENT
Bronze **Ruler:** George VI **Obv:** Crowned head left **Rev:** Value within beaded circle

Date	Mintage	F	VF	XF	Unc	BU
1949	500,000	0.75	1.25	2.50	7.50	15.00
1949 Proof	—	Value: 100				
1952	500,000	0.75	1.25	2.50	7.50	15.00
1952 Proof	—	Value: 100				

KM# 31   CENT
1.9500 g., Bronze, 17.8 mm. **Ruler:** Elizabeth II **Obv:** Crowned head right **Rev:** Value within beaded circle

Date	Mintage	F	VF	XF	Unc	BU
1953	500,000	0.10	0.25	0.50	1.50	—
1953 Proof	—	Value: 75.00				
1955	501,000	0.10	0.25	0.50	2.50	—
1955 Proof	—	Value: 75.00				
1956	500,000	0.10	0.20	0.50	2.50	—
1956 Proof	—	Value: 75.00				
1957	501,000	0.10	0.20	0.50	2.50	—
1959	501,000	0.10	0.20	0.50	2.50	—
1959 Proof	—	Value: 75.00				
1960	500,000	0.10	0.20	0.50	2.50	—
1960 Proof	—	Value: 75.00				
1961	500,000	0.10	0.20	0.50	2.50	—
1961 Proof	—	Value: 75.00				
1962	500,000	0.10	0.20	0.50	1.50	—
1962 Proof	—	Value: 50.00				
1963	500,000	0.10	0.20	0.50	1.50	—
1963 Proof	—	Value: 50.00				
1964	1,500,000	—	0.10	0.20	0.50	—
1964 Proof	—	Value: 50.00				
1965	1,500,000	—	0.10	0.20	0.50	—
1969	500,000	—	0.10	0.15	0.30	—
1970	1,500,000	—	—	0.10	0.20	—
1971	1,000,000	—	—	0.10	0.20	—
1971 Proof	750	Value: 17.50				
1975	400,000	—	—	0.10	0.20	—
1978	—	—	—	0.10	0.20	—

KM# 13   2 CENTS
Bronze **Ruler:** George V **Obv:** Crowned bust left **Rev:** Value within beaded circle

Date	Mintage	F	VF	XF	Unc	BU
1911	500,000	2.00	12.00	25.00	40.00	85.00
1911 Proof	—	Value: 300				
1912	250,000	3.00	15.00	40.00	70.00	140
1917	250,000	1.25	14.50	22.00	50.00	80.00
1920	250,000	1.50	14.00	28.00	55.00	90.00
1921	250,000	1.50	10.00	28.00	55.00	90.00
1922	900,000	0.50	4.00	15.00	30.00	60.00
1923	400,000	1.25	5.50	28.50	55.00	95.00
1924	400,000	1.25	5.50	28.50	50.00	90.00

KM# 22   2 CENTS
3.8500 g., Bronze **Ruler:** George VI **Obv:** Crowned head left **Rev:** Value within beaded circle

Date	Mintage	F	VF	XF	Unc	BU
1943SA	290,000	0.75	2.00	4.00	10.00	22.00
1944SA	500,000	0.75	2.00	4.00	10.00	22.00
1945SA	250,000	0.75	2.00	4.00	10.00	22.00
1946SA	400,000	0.75	2.00	4.00	10.00	22.00
1947SA	250,000	0.75	2.00	4.00	10.00	22.00

KM# 26   2 CENTS
3.8500 g., Bronze, 23.2 mm. **Ruler:** George VI **Obv:** Crowned head left **Rev:** Value within beaded circle

Date	Mintage	F	VF	XF	Unc	BU
1949	250,000	0.75	1.25	2.50	6.50	12.50
1949 Proof	—	Value: 120				
1952	250,000	0.75	1.25	2.50	6.50	12.50
1952 Proof	—	Value: 120				

KM# 32   2 CENTS
3.8500 g., Bronze, 23.2 mm. **Ruler:** Elizabeth II **Obv:** Crowned head right **Rev:** Value within beaded circle

Date	Mintage	F	VF	XF	Unc	BU
1953	250,000	0.10	0.25	0.50	2.50	—
1953 Proof	—	Value: 100				
1954 Proof	—	Value: 300				
1955	501,000	0.10	0.25	0.50	2.50	—
1955 Proof	—	Value: 100				
1956	250,000	0.10	0.25	0.50	3.50	—
1956 Proof	—	Value: 100				
1957	501,000	0.10	0.25	0.50	3.50	—
1959	503,000	0.10	0.25	0.50	3.50	—
1959 Proof	—	Value: 100				
1960	250,000	0.10	0.25	0.50	3.50	—
1960 Proof	—	Value: 100				
1961	500,000	0.10	0.25	0.50	3.50	—
1961 Proof	—	Value: 100				
1962	500,000	0.10	0.25	0.50	1.50	—
1962 Proof	—	Value: 75.00				
1963	500,000	0.10	0.25	0.50	1.50	—
1963 Proof	—	Value: 75.00				
1964	1,000,000	—	0.10	0.25	0.50	—
1964 Proof	—	Value: 50.00				
1965	750,000	0.10	0.20	0.40	0.60	—
1966	500,000	0.10	0.20	0.40	0.50	—
1967	250,000	0.10	0.20	0.40	0.50	—
1969	500,000	0.10	0.20	0.40	0.50	—
1971	1,000,000	—	0.10	0.20	0.40	—
1971 Proof	750	Value: 17.50				

Date	Mintage	F	VF	XF	Unc	BU
1975	5,200,000	—	—	0.10	0.35	—
1978		—	—	0.10	0.35	—
1978 Proof	9,268	Value: 1.50				

KM# 14   5 CENTS
9.7000 g., Bronze, 28.4 mm. **Ruler:** George V **Obv:** Crowned bust left **Rev:** Value within beaded circle

Date	Mintage	F	VF	XF	Unc	BU
1917	600,000	2.00	24.50	57.50	80.00	165
1920	200,000	2.00	24.50	60.00	100	200
1921	100,000	3.00	26.50	65.00	120	250
1922	360,000	2.00	14.50	42.50	100	200
1923	400,000	3.00	16.50	45.00	120	250
1924	400,000	2.00	14.50	42.50	100	200

KM# 20   5 CENTS
9.7000 g., Bronze, 28.4 mm. **Ruler:** George VI **Obv:** Crowned head left **Rev:** Value within beaded circle

Date	Mintage	F	VF	XF	Unc	BU
1942SA	940,000	1.50	2.50	6.50	15.00	35.00
1944SA	1,000,000	1.25	1.75	4.00	10.00	22.00
1945SA	500,000	1.25	1.75	4.00	12.00	30.00

KM# 34   5 CENTS
9.7000 g., Bronze, 28.4 mm. **Ruler:** Elizabeth II **Obv:** Crowned head right **Rev:** Value within beaded circle

Date	Mintage	F	VF	XF	Unc	BU
1956	201,000	0.25	0.50	0.75	5.00	—
1956 Proof	—	Value: 100				
1957	203,000	0.25	0.50	2.00	8.00	—
1957 Proof	—	Value: 100				
1959	801,000	0.25	0.50	1.00	4.00	—
1959 Proof	—	Value: 75.00				
1960	400,000	0.25	0.50	1.00	4.00	—
1960 Proof	—	Value: 75.00				
1963	200,000	0.25	0.50	1.00	2.50	—
1963 Proof	—	Value: 70.00				
1964	600,000	0.25	0.50	1.00	2.50	—
1964 Proof	—	Value: 70.00				
1965	200,000	0.25	0.50	0.75	2.50	—
1966	200,000	0.25	0.50	0.75	1.50	—
1967	200,000	0.25	0.50	0.75	2.50	—
1969	500,000	0.10	0.15	0.25	0.50	—
1970	800,000	0.10	0.15	0.25	0.50	—
1971	500,000	0.10	0.15	0.25	0.50	—
1971 Proof	750	Value: 17.50				
1975	3,700,000	0.10	0.15	0.25	0.50	—
1978	8,000,000	—	—	0.10	0.20	—
1978 Proof	9,268	Value: 2.00				

KM# 24   10 CENTS
5.1500 g., Copper-Nickel, 23.5 mm. **Ruler:** George VI **Obv:** Crowned head left **Rev:** Value

Date	Mintage	F	VF	XF	Unc	BU
1947	500,000	1.50	4.50	18.00	45.00	—
1947 Proof	—	Value: 200				

KM# 30   10 CENTS
5.1500 g., Copper-Nickel, 23.5 mm. **Ruler:** George VI **Obv:** Crowned head left **Rev:** Value

Date	Mintage	F	VF	XF	Unc	BU
1952	250,000	0.50	1.00	3.50	9.50	17.50
1952 Proof	—	Value: 150				

KM# 33   10 CENTS
5.1500 g., Copper-Nickel, 23.5 mm. **Ruler:** Elizabeth II **Obv:** Crowned head right **Rev:** Value

Date	Mintage	F	VF	XF	Unc	BU
1954	252,000	0.20	0.35	0.75	2.50	—
1954 Proof	—	Value: 150				
1957	250,000	0.20	0.35	0.75	2.50	—
1959	253,000	0.20	0.35	0.75	2.50	—
1959 Proof	—	Value: 175				
1960	50,000	0.20	0.35	0.75	2.00	—
1960 Proof	—	Value: 175				
1963	200,000	0.15	0.30	0.60	1.50	—
1963 Proof	—	Value: 175				
1964	200,000	0.15	0.30	0.60	1.00	—
1965	200,000	0.15	0.30	0.60	1.00	—
1966	200,000	0.10	0.25	0.50	0.75	—
1969	200,000	0.10	0.25	0.50	0.75	—
1970	500,000	0.10	0.25	0.50	0.75	—
1971	300,000	0.10	0.25	0.50	0.75	—
1971 Proof	750	Value: 17.50				
1975	6,675,000	0.10	0.25	0.50	0.75	—
1978	13,000,000	0.10	0.25	0.50	0.75	—
1978 Proof	9,268	Value: 2.50				

KM# 15   1/4 RUPEE
2.9200 g., 0.9160 Silver 0.0860 oz. ASW, 19 mm. **Ruler:** George V **Obv:** Crowned bust left **Rev:** Crown above 3 emblems

Date	Mintage	F	VF	XF	Unc	BU
1934	400,000	2.50	10.00	30.00	60.00	—
1934 Proof	—	Value: 600				
1935	400,000	2.50	10.00	30.00	65.00	—
1935 Proof	—	Value: 750				
1936	400,000	2.50	10.00	30.00	60.00	—
1936 Proof	—	Value: 650				

KM# 18   1/4 RUPEE
2.9200 g., 0.9160 Silver 0.0860 oz. ASW, 19 mm. **Ruler:** George VI **Obv:** Crowned head left

Date	Mintage	F	VF	XF	Unc	BU
1938	2,000,000	3.50	15.00	40.00	85.00	—
1938 Proof	—	Value: 375				

KM# 18a   1/4 RUPEE
2.9200 g., 0.5000 Silver 0.0469 oz. ASW, 19 mm. **Ruler:** George VI **Obv:** Crowned bust left

Date	Mintage	F	VF	XF	Unc	BU
1946	2,000,000	7.50	30.00	60.00	100	—
1946 Proof	—	Value: 400				

KM# 27   1/4 RUPEE
2.9500 g., Copper-Nickel, 19 mm. **Ruler:** George VI **Obv:** Crowned head left **Rev:** Crown above 3 emblems

Date	Mintage	F	VF	XF	Unc	BU
1950	2,000,000	0.50	1.00	2.00	9.50	18.00
1950 Proof	—	Value: 175				
1951	1,000,000	0.50	1.00	2.00	9.50	18.00
1951 Proof	—	Value: 175				

KM# 36   1/4 RUPEE
2.9500 g., Copper-Nickel, 19 mm. **Ruler:** Elizabeth II **Obv:** Crowned head right **Rev:** Crown above 3 emblems

Date	Mintage	F	VF	XF	Unc	BU
1960	1,000,000	0.35	0.75	1.00	2.00	—
1960 Proof	—	Value: 100				
1964	400,000	0.25	0.50	0.75	1.50	—
1964 Proof	—	Value: 100				
1965	400,000	0.25	0.50	0.75	1.25	—
1970	400,000	0.20	0.35	0.65	1.25	—
1971	540,000	0.25	0.50	0.75	1.25	—
1971 Proof	750	Value: 17.50				
1975	8,940,000	0.15	0.30	0.60	1.00	—
1978	8,800,000	0.15	0.30	0.60	1.00	—

Note: Variety exists with lower hole in 8 filled

1978 Proof	9,268	Value: 3.50				

KM# 16   1/2 RUPEE
5.8300 g., 0.9160 Silver 0.1717 oz. ASW, 23.65 mm. **Ruler:** George V **Obv:** Crowned bust left **Rev:** Stag left **Edge:** Reeded with security

Date	Mintage	F	VF	XF	Unc	BU
1934	1,000,000	3.25	7.00	20.00	65.00	—
1934 Proof	—	Value: 450				

KM# 23   1/2 RUPEE
5.8300 g., 0.5000 Silver 0.0937 oz. ASW, 23.65 mm. **Ruler:** George VI **Obv:** Crowned head left **Rev:** Stag left

Date	Mintage	F	VF	XF	Unc	BU
1946	1,000,000	10.00	25.00	125	200	—
1946 Proof	—	Value: 700				

KM# 28   1/2 RUPEE
5.8500 g., Copper-Nickel, 23.65 mm. **Ruler:** George VI **Obv:** Crowned head left **Rev:** Stag left

Date	Mintage	F	VF	XF	Unc	BU
1950	1,000,000	0.50	1.00	1.75	12.00	—
1950 Proof	—	Value: 175				
1951	570,000	0.75	1.25	2.00	12.00	—
1951 Proof	—	Value: 225				

KM# 37.1   1/2 RUPEE
5.8500 g., Copper-Nickel, 23.65 mm. **Ruler:** Elizabeth II **Obv:** Crowned head right **Rev:** Stag left

Date	Mintage	F	VF	XF	Unc	BU
1965	200,000	0.50	1.00	2.00	9.00	—
1971	400,000	0.25	0.50	0.75	8.00	—
1971 Proof	750	Value: 22.50				
1975	4,160,000	0.25	0.50	0.75	8.00	—
1978	400,000	0.25	0.50	0.75	8.00	—
1978 Proof	9,268	Value: 6.00				

KM# 37.2 1/2 RUPEE
5.8500 g., Copper-Nickel, 23.65 mm. **Ruler:** Elizabeth II
Obv: Crowned head right **Rev:** Stag left **Edge:** Without security
feature **Note:** Error.

Date	Mintage	F	VF	XF	Unc	BU
1971	Inc. above	—	—	—	—	—

KM# 17 RUPEE
11.6600 g., 0.9160 Silver 0.3434 oz. ASW **Ruler:** George V
Obv: Crowned bust left **Rev:** National arms divide date above
value **Edge:** Reeded with security

Date	Mintage	F	VF	XF	Unc	BU
1934	1,500,000	6.00	10.00	25.00	65.00	85.00
1934 Proof	—	Value: 600				

KM# 19 RUPEE
11.6600 g., 0.9160 Silver 0.3434 oz. ASW **Ruler:** George VI
Obv: Crowned bust left **Rev:** National arms divide date above value

Date	Mintage	F	VF	XF	Unc	BU
1938	200,000	10.00	20.00	60.00	175	—
1938 Proof	—	Value: 550				

KM# 29.1 RUPEE
11.7000 g., Copper-Nickel, 29.6 mm. **Ruler:** George VI
Obv: Crowned head left **Rev:** National arms divide date above
value

Date	Mintage	F	VF	XF	Unc	BU
1950	1,500,000	0.75	1.50	3.00	16.00	—
1950 Proof	—	Value: 200				
1951	1,000,000	0.50	1.25	2.00	12.00	—
1951 Proof	—	Value: 300				

KM# 29.2 RUPEE
11.7000 g., Copper-Nickel, 29.6 mm. **Ruler:** George VI
Obv: Crowned head left **Rev:** National arms divide date above
value **Edge:** Without security feature **Note:** Error.

Date	Mintage	F	VF	XF	Unc	BU
1951	Inc. above	—	—	—	—	—

KM# 35.1 RUPEE
11.7000 g., Copper-Nickel, 29.6 mm. **Ruler:** Elizabeth II
Obv: Crowned head right **Rev:** National arms divide date
above value

Date	Mintage	F	VF	XF	Unc	BU
1956	1,000,000	0.25	0.75	1.50	7.50	—
1956 Proof	—	Value: 200				
1964	200,000	0.50	1.00	3.00	5.00	—
1971	600,000	0.25	0.60	1.00	2.00	—
1971 Proof	750	Value: 45.00				
1975	4,525,000	0.25	0.60	1.00	2.00	—
1978	2,000,000	0.25	0.60	1.00	2.00	—
1978 Proof	9,268	Value: 5.00				

KM# 35.2 RUPEE
11.7000 g., Copper-Nickel, 29.6 mm. **Ruler:** Elizabeth II
Obv: Crowned head right **Rev:** National arms divide date above
value **Edge:** Without security feature **Note:** Error.

Date	Mintage	F	VF	XF	Unc	BU
1971	Inc. above	0.25	0.75	1.25	2.50	—

COMMONWEALTH
STANDARD COINAGE
100 Cents = 1 Rupee

KM# 38 10 RUPEES
Copper-Nickel, 35 mm. **Ruler:** Elizabeth II **Subject:** Independence
Obv: Crowned head right **Rev:** Dodo bird

Date	Mintage	F	VF	XF	Unc	BU
1971	50,000	—	1.50	4.00	8.00	15.00

KM# 38a 10 RUPEES
20.0000 g., 0.9250 Silver 0.5948 oz. ASW, 35 mm.
Subject: Independence **Obv:** Crowned head right **Rev:** Dodo
bird

Date	Mintage	F	VF	XF	Unc	BU
1971 Proof	750	Value: 110				

KM# 46 10 RUPEES
Copper-Nickel **Subject:** Wedding of Prince Charles and Lady
Diana **Obv:** Young bust right **Rev:** Conjoined heads left

Date	Mintage	F	VF	XF	Unc	BU
ND(1981)	—	1.25	2.25	6.50	—	

KM# 46a 10 RUPEES
28.2800 g., 0.9250 Silver 0.8410 oz. ASW **Subject:** Wedding
of Prince Charles and Lady Diana **Obv:** Young bust right **Rev:**
Conjoined heads left

Date	Mintage	F	VF	XF	Unc	BU
ND(1981) Proof	2,090	Value: 22.50				

KM# 48 10 RUPEES
28.2800 g., 0.9250 Silver 0.8410 oz. ASW **Series:** World Food
Day **Obv:** Young bust right **Rev:** Man harvesting sugar cane

Date	Mintage	F	VF	XF	Unc	BU
1981	10,000	—	—	—	17.50	20.00
1981 Proof	5,000	Value: 27.50				

KM# 40 25 RUPEES
25.5000 g., 0.5000 Silver 0.4099 oz. ASW **Series:** Conservation
Obv: Young bust right **Rev:** Butterfly on flowers

Date	Mintage	F	VF	XF	Unc	BU
1975	—	—	—	—	25.00	28.00

KM# 40a 25 RUPEES
28.2800 g., 0.9250 Silver 0.8410 oz. ASW **Series:** Conservation
Obv: Young bust right **Rev:** Butterfly on flowers

Date	Mintage	F	VF	XF	Unc	BU
1975	12	—	—	—	100	250
1975 Proof	9,869	Value: 25.00				

KM# 43 25 RUPEES
28.4000 g., 0.5000 Silver 0.4565 oz. ASW **Subject:** Queen's Silver
Jubilee **Obv:** Young bust right **Rev:** Man harvesting sugar cane

Date	Mintage	F	VF	XF	Unc	BU
ND(1977)	—	—	—	—	9.50	11.50

KM# 43a 25 RUPEES
28.2800 g., 0.9250 Silver 0.8410 oz. ASW **Subject:** Queen's Silver
Jubilee **Obv:** Young bust right **Rev:** Man harvesting sugar cane

Date	Mintage	F	VF	XF	Unc	BU
ND(1977) Proof	47,000	Value: 14.50				

KM# 44 25 RUPEES
28.2800 g., 0.9250 Silver 0.8410 oz. ASW **Subject:** 10th
Anniversary of Independence **Obv:** Similar to 1,000 Rupees,
KM#45: bust right **Rev:** Building

Date	Mintage	F	VF	XF	Unc	BU
1978	20,000	—	—	—	16.50	18.50
1978 Proof	5,100	Value: 25.00				

KM# 49 25 RUPEES
28.2800 g., 0.9250 Silver 0.8410 oz. ASW **Series:** International
Year of Disabled Persons **Obv:** Young bust right **Rev:** Disabled
persons emblem to upper left of cluster of designs

Date	Mintage	F	VF	XF	Unc	BU
1982	11,000	—	—	—	18.50	20.00
1982 Proof	10,000	Value: 23.50				

KM# 41 50 RUPEES
32.1500 g., 0.5000 Silver 0.5168 oz. ASW **Series:** Conservation **Obv:** Young bust right **Rev:** Mauritius Kestrel

Date	Mintage	F	VF	XF	Unc	BU
1975	—	—	—	—	25.00	30.00

KM# 41a 50 RUPEES
35.0000 g., 0.9250 Silver 1.0408 oz. ASW **Series:** Conservation **Obv:** Young bust right **Rev:** Mauritius Kestrel

Date	Mintage	F	VF	XF	Unc	BU
1975	12	Value: 250				
1975 Proof	9,513	Value: 27.00				

KM# 39 200 RUPEES
15.5600 g., 0.9170 Gold 0.4587 oz. AGW **Subject:** Independence **Obv:** Crowned head right **Rev:** Couple in the forest

Date	Mintage	F	VF	XF	Unc	BU
1971	2,500	—	—	—	450	475
1971 Proof	750	Value: 500				

KM# 42 1000 RUPEES
33.4370 g., 0.9000 Gold 0.9675 oz. AGW **Series:** Conservation **Subject:** Mauritius flycatcher **Obv:** Young bust right **Rev:** Bird on nest in branch

Date	Mintage	F	VF	XF	Unc	BU
1975	1,966	—	—	—	925	950
1975 Proof	716	Value: 1,000				

KM# 45 1000 RUPEES
15.9800 g., 0.9170 Gold 0.4711 oz. AGW **Subject:** 10th Anniversary of Independence **Obv:** Bust right **Rev:** Building

Date	Mintage	F	VF	XF	Unc	BU
1978	1,000	—	—	—	450	475
1978 Proof	1,016	Value: 500				

KM# 47 1000 RUPEES
15.9800 g., 0.9170 Gold 0.4711 oz. AGW **Subject:** Wedding of Prince Charles and Lady Diana **Obv:** Young bust right **Rev:** Crowned monogram

Date	Mintage	F	VF	XF	Unc	BU
ND(1981)	28	—	—	—	600	650
ND(1981) Proof	22	Value: 950				

KM# 50 1000 RUPEES
15.9800 g., 0.9170 Gold 0.4711 oz. AGW **Series:** International Year of Disabled Persons **Obv:** Young bust right **Rev:** Disabled emblem within design

Date	Mintage	F	VF	XF	Unc	BU
1982	45	—	—	—	550	600
1982 Proof	48	Value: 925				

GOLD BULLION COINAGE

KM# 57 100 RUPEES
3.4120 g., 0.9170 Gold 0.1006 oz. AGW **Obv:** Bust 1/4 left **Rev:** Dodo bird

Date	Mintage	F	VF	XF	Unc	BU
1988	—	—	—	—	110	125

KM# 58 250 RUPEES
8.5130 g., 0.9170 Gold 0.2510 oz. AGW **Obv:** Bust 1/4 left **Rev:** Dodo bird

Date	Mintage	F	VF	XF	Unc	BU
1988	—	—	—	—	250	265

KM# 59 500 RUPEES
17.0250 g., 0.9170 Gold 0.5019 oz. AGW **Obv:** Bust 1/4 left **Rev:** Dodo bird

Date	Mintage	F	VF	XF	Unc	BU
1988	—	—	—	—	475	500

KM# 60 1000 RUPEES
34.0500 g., 0.9170 Gold 1.0038 oz. AGW **Obv:** Bust 1/4 left **Rev:** Dodo bird

Date	Mintage	F	VF	XF	Unc	BU
1988	—	—	—	—	950	1,000

REPUBLIC
STANDARD COINAGE
100 Cents = 1 Rupee

KM# 51 CENT
Copper Plated Steel **Obv:** Value within beaded circle **Rev:** Bust of Sir Seewoosagur Ramgoolam 3/4 right

Date	Mintage	F	VF	XF	Unc	BU
1987	—	—	—	—	0.20	0.40
1987 Proof	Est. 2,500	Value: 1.00				

KM# 52 5 CENTS
3.0000 g., Copper Plated Steel **Obv:** Value within beaded circle **Rev:** Bust of Sir Seewoosagur Ramgoolam 3/4 right

Date	Mintage	F	VF	XF	Unc	BU
1987	—	—	—	0.10	0.35	0.50
1987 Proof	Est. 2,500	Value: 2.00				
1990	—	—	—	0.10	0.35	0.50
1991	—	—	—	0.10	0.35	0.50
1993	—	—	—	0.10	0.35	0.50
1994	—	—	—	0.10	0.35	0.50
1995	—	—	—	0.10	0.35	0.50
1996	—	—	—	0.10	0.35	0.50
1999	—	—	—	0.10	0.35	0.50

KM# 53 20 CENTS
3.0000 g., Nickel Plated Steel **Obv:** Value within beaded circle **Rev:** Bust of Sir Seewoosagur Ramgoolam 3/4 right

Date	Mintage	F	VF	XF	Unc	BU
1987	—	—	—	0.20	0.50	0.75
1987 Proof	Est. 2,500	Value: 3.00				
1990	—	—	—	0.20	0.50	0.75
1991	—	—	—	0.20	0.50	0.75
1993	—	—	—	0.20	0.50	0.75
1994	—	—	—	0.20	0.50	0.75
1995	—	—	—	0.20	0.50	0.75
1996	—	—	—	0.20	0.50	0.75
1999	—	—	—	0.20	0.50	0.75

KM# 54 1/2 RUPEE
6.0000 g., Nickel Plated Steel **Obv:** Stag left **Rev:** Bust of Sir Seewoosagur Ramgoolam 3/4 right

Date	Mintage	F	VF	XF	Unc	BU
1987	—	—	—	0.70	1.75	2.50
1987 Proof	Est. 2,500	Value: 5.00				
1990	—	—	—	0.70	1.75	2.50
1991	—	—	—	0.70	1.75	2.50
1997	—	—	—	0.70	1.75	2.50
1999	—	—	—	0.70	1.75	2.50

KM# 55 RUPEE
Copper-Nickel **Obv:** Shield divides date above value **Rev:** Bust of Sir Seewoosagur Ramgoolam 3/4 right

Date	Mintage	F	VF	XF	Unc	BU
1987	—	—	—	0.65	1.65	2.75
1987 Proof	Est. 2,500	Value: 10.00				

Date	Mintage	F	VF	XF	Unc	BU
1990	—	—	—	0.65	1.65	2.75
1991	—	—	—	0.65	1.65	2.75
1993	—	—	—	0.65	1.65	2.75
1994	—	—	—	0.65	1.65	2.75
1997	—	—	—	0.65	1.65	2.75

KM# 56 5 RUPEES
Copper-Nickel **Obv:** Value within palm trees **Rev:** Bust of Sir Seewoosagur Ramgoolam 3/4 right

Date	Mintage	F	VF	XF	Unc	BU
1987	—	—	—	—	3.00	5.00
1987 Proof	Est. 2,500	Value: 16.00				
1991	—	—	—	—	3.00	5.00
1992	—	—	—	—	3.00	5.00

KM# 61 10 RUPEES
Copper-Nickel **Obv:** Sugar cane harvesting **Rev:** Bust of Sir Seewoosagur Ramgoolam 3/4 right

Date	Mintage	F	VF	XF	Unc	BU
1997	—	—	—	—	4.00	6.50
2000	—	—	—	—	4.00	6.50

KM# 62 10 RUPEES
28.2800 g., 0.9250 Silver 0.8410 oz. ASW **Subject:** 150th Anniversary Chamber of Commerce and Industry **Obv:** National arms above Port Louis Harbor **Rev:** Chamber of Commerce and Industry seal

Date	Mintage	F	VF	XF	Unc	BU
2000 Proof	1,000	Value: 75.00				

KM# 64 20 RUPEES
28.2800 g., 0.9250 Silver 0.8410 oz. ASW, 38 mm. **Subject:** 50th Anniversary Birth of Prince Charles Philip **Obv:** Bust of Sir Seewoosagur Ramgoolam **Rev:** Elizabeth II seated holding Prince Charles Philip **Rev. Leg.:** 1947 ELIZABETH AND PHILIP 1997

Date	Mintage	F	VF	XF	Unc	BU
1997 Proof	30,000	Value: 75.00				

KM# 63 1000 RUPEES
17.0000 g., 0.9200 Gold 0.5028 oz. AGW **Subject:** 150th Anniversary Chamber of Commerce and Industry **Obv:** National arms above Port Louis Harbor **Rev:** Chamber of Commerce and Industry seal

Date	Mintage	F	VF	XF	Unc	BU
2000 Proof	300	Value: 525				

PIEFORTS

KM#	Date	Mintage	Identification	Mkt Val
P1	ND(1822)	—	25 Sous. Copper. KM1.	375
P2	1981	—	1000 Rupees. Gold. KM47.	825
P3	1982	1,100	25 Rupees. 0.9250 Silver. KM49.	100
P4	1982	—	1000 Rupees. Gold. KM50.	1,850

MINT SETS

KM#	Date	Mintage	Identification	Issue Price	Mkt Val
MS1	1987 (6)	5,000	KM51-56	16.95	17.50
MS2	1988 (4)	—	KM57-60	1,250	1,150

PROOF SETS

KM#	Date	Mintage	Identification	Issue Price	Mkt Val
PS1	1934 (3)	20	KM15-17	—	2,100
PS2	1971 (9)	750	KM31-37, 38a, 39	200	645
PS3	1975 (2)	9,268	KM40a-41a	50.00	40.00
PS4	1978 (7)	30,000	KM31-37	22.00	20.00
PS5	1981 (2)	—	KM46a, 47	—	975
PS6	1987 (6)	2,500	KM51-56	36.95	37.50

MEXICO

The United States of Mexico, located immediately south of the United States has an area of 759,529 sq. mi. (1,967,183 sq. km.) and an estimated population of 100 million. Capital: Mexico City. The economy is based on agriculture, manufacturing and mining. Oil, cotton, silver, coffee, and shrimp are exported.

Mexico was the site of highly advanced Indian civilizations 1,500 years before conquistador Hernando Cortes conquered the wealthy Aztec empire of Montezuma, 1519-21, and founded a Spanish colony, which lasted for nearly 300 years. During the Spanish period, Mexico, then called New Spain, stretched from Guatemala to the present states of Wyoming and California, its present northern boundary having been established by the secession of Texas during 1836 and the war of 1846-48 with the United States.

Independence from Spain was declared by Father Miguel Hidalgo on Sept. 16, 1810, (Mexican Independence Day) and was achieved by General Agustin de Iturbide in 1821. Iturbide became emperor in 1822 but was deposed when a republic was established a year later. For more than fifty years following the birth of the republic, the political scene of Mexico was characterized by turmoil, which saw two emperors (including the unfortunate Maximilian), several dictators and an average of one new government every nine months passing swiftly from obscurity to oblivion. The land, social, economic and labor reforms promulgated by the Reform Constitution of Feb. 5, 1917 established the basis for sustained economic development and participative democracy that have made Mexico one of the most politically stable countries of modern Latin America.

REPUBLIC
Second
DECIMAL COINAGE
100 Centavos = 1 Peso

KM# 394 CENTAVO
Copper **Obv:** National arms **Rev:** Value below date within wreath **Note:** Reduced size. Varieties exist.

Date	Mintage	F	VF	XF	Unc	BU
1901C	220,000	15.00	22.50	35.00	65.00	—
1902C	320,000	15.00	22.50	50.00	90.00	—
1903C	536,000	7.50	12.50	20.00	50.00	—
1904/3C	148,000	35.00	50.00	75.00	125	—
1905C	110,000	100	150	300	600	—

KM# 394.1 CENTAVO
2.6100 g., Copper **Obv:** Facing eagle, snake in beak **Obv. Leg.:** REPUBLICA MEXICANA **Rev:** Value below date within wreath **Note:** Reduced size. Varieties exist.

Date	Mintage	F	VF	XF	Unc	BU
1901M	1,494,000	3.00	8.00	17.50	50.00	—
1902/899M	2,090,000	30.00	60.00	125	225	—
1902M	Inc. above	2.25	4.00	10.00	40.00	—
1903M	8,400,000	1.50	3.00	7.00	20.00	—
1904/3M	10,250,000	1.50	10.00	20.00	55.00	—
1904M	Inc. above	1.50	3.00	8.00	25.00	—
1905M	3,643,000	2.25	4.00	10.00	40.00	—

KM# 400.2 5 CENTAVOS
1.3530 g., 0.9027 Silver 0.0393 oz. ASW **Obv:** Facing eagle, snake in beak **Rev:** Value within 1/2 wreath

Date	Mintage	F	VF	XF	Unc	BU
1901Mo M	100,000	1.75	2.50	4.50	15.00	17.50
1902Mo M	144,000	1.25	2.00	3.75	12.00	15.00
1902/1Mo MoM	—	1.75	3.00	7.00	16.50	18.50
1903Mo M	500,000	1.25	2.00	3.75	12.00	15.00
1904/804Mo M	1,090,000	1.75	3.50	8.50	16.50	18.50
1904/94Mo M	Inc. above	1.75	3.75	9.00	16.50	18.50
1904Mo M	Inc. above	1.75	3.00	6.00	15.00	17.50
1905Mo M	344,000	1.75	3.00	7.00	16.50	18.50

KM# 400.3 5 CENTAVOS
1.3530 g., 0.9027 Silver 0.0393 oz. ASW **Obv:** Facing eagle, snake in beak **Rev:** Value within 1/2 wreath

Date	Mintage	F	VF	XF	Unc	BU
1901Zs Z	40,000	1.75	2.50	5.00	16.50	18.50
1902/1Zs Z	34,000	2.00	4.50	9.00	22.50	25.00
1902Zs Z	Inc. above	1.75	3.75	7.50	18.50	22.00
1903Zs Z	217,000	1.25	2.00	5.00	12.50	16.00
1904Zs Z	191,000	1.75	2.50	5.00	12.50	16.00
1904Zs M	Inc. above	1.75	2.50	6.00	16.50	18.50
1905Zs M	46,000	2.00	4.50	9.00	22.50	25.00
1905Zs M Repullica; Rare	Inc. above	—	—	—	—	—

KM# 400 5 CENTAVOS
1.3530 g., 0.9027 Silver 0.0393 oz. ASW, 14 mm. **Obv:** Facing eagle, snake in beak **Obv. Leg.:** REPUBLICA MEXICANA **Rev:** Value within 1/2 wreath **Note:** Varieties exist.

Date	Mintage	F	VF	XF	Unc	BU
1901Cn Q	148,000	1.75	2.50	4.50	15.00	18.00
1902Cn Q	262,000	1.75	3.00	6.00	16.50	20.00
Note: Narrow C, heavy serifs						
1902Cn Q	Inc. above	1.75	3.00	6.00	16.50	20.00
Note: Wide C, light serifs						
1903/1Cn Q	331,000	2.00	3.00	6.00	16.50	20.00
1903Cn Q	Inc. above	1.75	2.50	4.50	15.00	18.00
1903/1898Cn V	Inc. above	3.50	4.50	9.00	22.50	23.00
1903Cn V	Inc. above	1.75	2.50	4.50	15.00	18.00
1904Cn H	352,000	1.75	2.25	5.00	16.50	20.00
1904Cn H/C	—	1.75	2.50	5.00	16.50	20.00
1904Cn H 0/9	—	1.75	2.50	5.00	16.50	20.00

KM# 404 10 CENTAVOS
2.7070 g., 0.9030 Silver 0.0786 oz. ASW **Obv:** Facing eagle, snake in beak **Obv. Leg.:** REPUBLICA MEXICANA **Rev:** Value within 1/2 wreath **Note:** Varieties exist.

Date	Mintage	F	VF	XF	Unc	BU
1901Cn Q	235,000	1.50	2.50	5.00	18.00	20.00
1902Cn Q	186,000	1.50	2.50	5.00	20.00	22.00
1903Cn V	Inc. above	1.50	2.50	5.00	15.00	22.00
1903Cn Q	256,000	1.50	2.50	6.00	20.00	17.00
1904Cn H	307,000	1.50	2.50	5.00	15.00	17.00

KM# 404.2 10 CENTAVOS
2.7070 g., 0.9030 Silver 0.0786 oz. ASW **Obv:** Facing eagle, snake in beak **Obv. Leg.:** REPUBLICA MEXICANA **Rev:** Value within 1/2 wreath

Date	Mintage	F	VF	XF	Unc	BU
1901Mo M	80,000	2.50	3.50	7.00	22.50	25.00
1902Mo M	181,000	1.50	2.50	6.00	20.00	22.00
1903Mo M	581,000	1.50	2.50	6.00	20.00	22.00
1904Mo M	1,266,000	1.25	2.00	4.50	18.00	20.00
1904Mo MM (Error)	Inc. above	2.50	5.00	10.00	25.00	28.00
1905Mo M	266,000	2.00	3.75	7.50	20.00	22.00

KM# 404.3 10 CENTAVOS
2.7070 g., 0.9020 Silver 0.0785 oz. ASW **Obv:** Facing eagle, snake in beak **Rev:** Value within 1/2 wreath

Date	Mintage	F	VF	XF	Unc	BU
1901Zs Z	70,000	2.50	5.00	10.00	25.00	28.00
1902Zs Z	120,000	2.50	5.00	10.00	25.00	28.00
1903Zs Z	228,000	1.50	3.00	9.00	18.00	20.00
1904Zs Z	368,000	1.50	3.00	9.00	18.00	20.00
1904Zs M	Inc. above	1.50	3.00	9.00	22.00	25.00
1905Zs M	66,000	7.50	20.00	50.00	200	—

KM# 405 20 CENTAVOS
5.4150 g., 0.9030 Silver 0.1572 oz. ASW **Obv:** Facing eagle, snake in beak **Rev:** Value within 1/2 wreath

Date	Mintage	F	VF	XF	Unc	BU
1901Cn Q	185,000	5.00	10.00	30.00	120	—
1902/802Cn Q	98,000	6.00	10.00	30.00	120	—
1902Cn Q	Inc. above	4.00	9.00	30.00	120	—
1903Cn Q	93,000	4.00	9.00	30.00	120	—
1904/3Cn H	258,000	—	—	—	—	—
1904Cn H	Inc. above	5.00	10.00	30.00	120	—

KM# 405.3 20 CENTAVOS
5.4150 g., 0.9027 Silver 0.1572 oz. ASW **Obv:** Facing eagle, snake in beak **Obv. Leg.:** REPUBLICA MEXICANA **Rev:** Value within 1/2 wreath

Date	Mintage	F	VF	XF	Unc	BU
1901Zs Z	Inc. above	5.00	10.00	20.00	100	—
1901/0Zs Z	130,000	25.00	50.00	100	250	—
1902Zs Z	105,000	5.00	10.00	20.00	100	—
1903Zs Z	143,000	5.00	10.00	20.00	100	—
1904Zs Z	246,000	5.00	10.00	20.00	100	—
1904Zs M	Inc. above	5.00	10.00	50.00	300	—
1905Zs M	59,000	10.00	70.00	50.00	400	—

KM# 405.2 20 CENTAVOS
5.4150 g., 0.9030 Silver 0.1572 oz. ASW **Obv:** Facing eagle, snake in beak **Rev:** Value within 1/2 wreath **Note:** Varieties exist.

Date	Mintage	F	VF	XF	Unc	BU
1901Mo M	110,000	4.00	8.00	20.00	90.00	—
1902Mo M	120,000	4.00	8.00	20.00	90.00	—
1903Mo M	213,000	4.00	8.00	20.00	90.00	—
1904Mo M	276,000	4.00	8.00	20.00	90.00	—
1905Mo M	117,000	6.50	20.00	50.00	150	—

KM# 409 PESO
27.0730 g., 0.9030 Silver 0.7860 oz. ASW **Obv:** Facing eagle, snake in beak **Rev:** Radiant cap

Date	Mintage	F	VF	XF	Unc	BU
1901Cn JQ	1,473,000	12.00	15.00	25.00	75.00	—
1902Cn JQ	1,194,000	12.00	15.00	45.00	125	—
1903Cn JQ	1,514,000	12.00	15.00	30.00	85.00	—
1903Cn FV	Inc. above	25.00	50.00	100	225	—
1904Cn MH	1,554,000	12.00	15.00	25.00	75.00	—
1904Cn RP	Inc. above	50.00	100	150	350	—
1905Cn RP	598,000	25.00	50.00	100	250	—

KM# 410.2 PESO
1.6920 g., 0.8750 Gold 0.0476 oz. AGW **Obv:** Facing eagle, snake in beak **Obv. Leg.:** REPUBLICA MEXICANA **Rev:** Value within 1/2 wreath

Date	Mintage	F	VF	XF	Unc	BU
1901Cn Q	Inc. above	65.00	100	150	225	—
1901/0Cn Q	2,350	65.00	100	150	225	—
1902Cn Q	2,480	65.00	100	150	225	—
1902Cn/MoQ/C	Inc. above	65.00	100	150	225	—
1904Cn H	3,614	65.00	100	150	225	—
1904Cn/Mo/ H	Inc. above	65.00	100	150	250	—
1905Cn P	1,000	—	—	—	—	—

Note: Reported, not confirmed

KM# 410.5 PESO
1.6920 g., 0.8750 Gold 0.0476 oz. AGW **Obv:** Facing eagle, snake in beak **Obv. Leg.:** REPUBLICA MEXICANA **Rev:** Value within 1/2 wreath

Date	Mintage	F	VF	XF	Unc	BU
1901Mo M Small date	Inc. above	45.00	65.00	95.00	185	—
1901/801Mo M Large date	8,293	45.00	65.00	95.00	185	—
1902Mo M Large date	11,000	45.00	65.00	95.00	185	—
1902Mo M Small date	Inc. above	45.00	65.00	95.00	185	—
1903Mo M Large date	10,000	45.00	65.00	95.00	185	—
1903Mo M Small date	Inc. above	55.00	85.00	125	200	—
1904Mo M	9,845	45.00	65.00	95.00	185	—
1905Mo M	3,429	45.00	65.00	95.00	185	—

KM# 409.2 PESO
27.0730 g., 0.9027 Silver 0.7857 oz. ASW **Obv:** Facing eagle, snake in beak **Obv. Leg.:** REPUBLICA MEXICANA **Rev:** Radiant cap **Note:** Varieties exist.

Date	Mintage	F	VF	XF	Unc	BU
1901Mo AM	14,505,000	11.50	13.50	20.00	70.00	—
1902/1Mo AM	16,224,000	150	300	500	950	—
1902Mo AM	Inc. above	11.50	13.50	20.00	70.00	—
1903Mo AM	22,396,000	11.50	13.50	20.00	70.00	—
1903Mo MA (Error)	Inc. above	1,500	2,500	3,500	7,500	—
1904Mo AM	14,935,000	11.50	13.50	20.00	70.00	—
1905Mo AM	3,557,000	15.00	25.00	55.00	125	—
1908Mo AM	7,575,000	11.50	13.50	20.00	60.00	—
1908Mo GV	Inc. above	11.50	13.50	18.50	40.00	—
1909Mo GV	2,924,000	11.50	13.50	18.50	40.00	—

KM# 409.3 PESO
27.0730 g., 0.9030 Silver 0.7860 oz. ASW **Obv:** Facing eagle, snake in beak **Rev:** Radiant cap **Note:** Mint mark Zs. Varieties exist.

Date	Mintage	F	VF	XF	Unc	BU
1901Zs FZ	Inc. above	11.50	13.50	20.00	55.00	—
1901Zs AZ	5,706,000	4,000	6,500	10,000	—	—
1902Zs FZ	7,134,000	11.50	13.50	20.00	55.00	—
1903/2Zs FZ	3,080,000	12.50	15.00	50.00	125	—
1903Zs FZ	Inc. above	11.50	13.50	20.00	65.00	—
1904Zs FZ	2,423,000	12.00	15.00	25.00	85.00	—
1904Zs FM	Inc. above	12.00	15.00	25.00	75.00	—
1905Zs FM	995,000	20.00	40.00	60.00	150	—

KM# 412.6 5 PESOS
8.4600 g., 0.8750 Gold 0.2380 oz. AGW **Obv:** Facing eagle, snake in beak **Obv. Leg.:** REPUBLICA MEXICANA **Rev:** Radiant cap above scales

Date	Mintage	F	VF	XF	Unc	BU
1901Mo M	1,071	230	300	420	675	—
1902Mo M	1,478	230	300	420	675	—
1903Mo M	1,162	230	300	420	675	—
1904Mo M	1,415	230	300	420	675	—
1905Mo M	563	230	400	550	1,500	—

KM# 412.2 5 PESOS
8.4600 g., 0.8750 Gold 0.2380 oz. AGW **Obv:** Facing eagle, snake in beak **Obv. Leg.:** REPUBLICA MEXICANA **Rev:** Radiant cap above scales

Date	Mintage	F	VF	XF	Unc	BU
1903Cn Q	1,000	230	300	450	750	—

KM# 413.7 10 PESOS
16.9200 g., 0.8750 Gold 0.4760 oz. AGW **Obv:** Facing eagle, snake in beak **Obv. Leg.:** REPUBLICA MEXICANA **Rev:** Radiant cap above scales

Date	Mintage	F	VF	XF	Unc	BU
1901Mo M	562	460	520	825	1,250	—
1902Mo M	719	460	520	825	1,250	—
1903Mo M	713	460	520	825	1,250	—
1904Mo M	694	460	520	825	1,250	—
1905Mo M	401	475	600	950	1,500	—

KM# 413.2 10 PESOS
16.9200 g., 0.8750 Gold 0.4760 oz. AGW **Obv:** Facing eagle, snake in beak **Obv. Leg.:** REPUBLICA MEXICANA **Rev:** Radiant cap above scales

Date	Mintage	F	VF	XF	Unc	BU
1903Cn Q	774	475	600	1,000	1,750	—

KM# 414.2 20 PESOS
33.8400 g., 0.8750 Gold 0.9519 oz. AGW **Obv:** Facing eagle, snake in beak **Obv. Leg.:** REPUBLICA MEXICANA **Rev:** Radiant cap above scales

Date	Mintage	F	VF	XF	Unc	BU
1901Cn Q	Inc. above	BV	875	1,000	2,150	—
1901/0Cn Q	1,496	—	—	—	—	—
1902Cn Q	1,059	BV	875	1,000	2,150	—
1903Cn Q	1,121	BV	875	1,000	2,150	—
1904Cn H	4,646	BV	875	1,000	2,150	—
1905Cn P	1,738	BV	950	1,200	2,350	—

KM# 414.6 20 PESOS
33.8400 g., 0.8750 Gold 0.9519 oz. AGW **Obv:** Facing eagle, snake in beak **Obv. Leg.:** REPUBLICA MEXICANA **Rev:** Radiant cap above scales

Date	Mintage	F	VF	XF	Unc	BU
1901Mo M	29,000	—	BV	900	1,500	—
1902Mo M	38,000	—	BV	900	1,500	—
1903/2Mo M	31,000	—	BV	900	1,500	—
1903Mo M	Inc. above	—	BV	900	1,500	—
1904Mo M	52,000	—	BV	900	1,500	—
1905Mo M	9,757	—	BV	900	1,500	—

UNITED STATES
DECIMAL COINAGE
100 Centavos = 1 Peso

KM# 415 CENTAVO
3.0000 g., Bronze, 20 mm. **Obv:** National arms **Rev:** Value below date within wreath **Note:** Mint mark Mo.

Date	Mintage	F	VF	XF	Unc	BU
1905 Narrow date	6,040,000	4.00	6.50	14.00	90.00	—
1905 Wide date	—	4.00	6.50	14.00	90.00	—
1906 Narrow date	Est.	0.50	0.75	1.25	14.00	—
	67,505,000					

Note: 50,000,000 pcs. were struck at the Birmingham Mint

1906 Wide date	Inc. above	0.75	1.50	2.50	20.00	—
1910 Narrow date	8,700,000	2.00	3.00	6.50	85.00	—
1910 Wide date	—	2.00	3.00	6.50	85.00	—
1911 Narrow date	16,450,000	0.60	1.00	2.75	22.50	—
1911 Wide date	Inc. above	0.75	1.00	4.00	32.00	—
1912	12,650,000	1.00	1.35	3.25	32.00	—
1913	12,850,000	0.75	1.25	3.00	35.00	—
1914 Narrow date	17,350,000	0.75	1.00	3.00	13.50	18.00
1914 Wide date	Inc. above	0.75	1.00	3.00	13.50	18.00
1915	2,277,000	11.00	25.00	67.50	250	—
1916	500,000	45.00	80.00	170	1,200	—
1920	1,433,000	22.00	50.00	110	400	—
1921	3,470,000	5.50	15.50	47.00	275	—
1922	1,880,000	9.00	17.00	50.00	250	—
1923	4,800,000	0.75	1.25	1.75	13.50	—
1924/3	2,000,000	65.00	170	285	525	—
1924	Inc. above	4.50	11.00	22.00	235	275
1925	1,550,000	4.50	10.00	25.00	220	—
1926	5,000,000	1.00	2.00	4.00	26.00	30.00
1927/6	6,000,000	30.00	45.00	70.00	150	—
1927	Inc. above	0.75	1.25	4.50	36.00	—
1928	5,000,000	0.75	1.00	3.25	16.50	25.00
1929	4,500,000	0.75	1.00	1.75	17.00	25.00
1930	7,000,000	0.75	1.00	2.50	19.00	—
1933	10,000,000	0.25	0.35	1.75	16.50	—
1934	7,500,000	0.25	0.95	3.25	30.00	—
1935	12,400,000	0.15	0.25	0.40	11.50	—
1936	20,100,000	0.15	0.20	0.30	8.00	—
1937	20,000,000	0.15	0.25	0.35	3.25	5.00
1938	10,000,000	0.10	0.15	0.30	2.00	2.75
1939	30,000,000	0.10	0.20	0.30	1.00	1.50
1940	10,000,000	0.20	0.30	0.60	5.50	7.50
1941	15,800,000	0.15	0.25	0.35	2.00	3.00
1942	30,400,000	0.15	0.20	0.30	1.25	2.00
1943	4,310,000	0.30	0.50	5.00	8.00	10.00
1944	5,645,000	0.15	0.25	0.50	6.00	7.50
1945	26,375,000	0.10	0.15	0.25	1.00	1.25
1946	42,135,000	—	0.15	0.20	0.60	1.00
1947	13,445,000	—	0.10	0.15	0.80	1.25
1948	20,040,000	0.10	0.15	0.30	1.10	2.00
1949	6,235,000	0.10	0.15	0.30	1.25	2.00

Note: Varieties exist

KM# 416 CENTAVO
Bronze, 16 mm. **Obv:** National arms **Rev:** Value below date within wreath **Note:** Zapata issue. Struck at Mexico City Mint, mint mark Mo. Reduced size. Weight varies 1.39-1.5g.

Date	Mintage	F	VF	XF	Unc	BU
1915	179,000	18.00	30.00	50.00	75.00	—

KM# 417 CENTAVO
2.0000 g., Brass, 16 mm. **Obv:** National arms, eagle left **Rev:** Oat sprigs **Note:** Mint mark Mo.

Date	Mintage	F	VF	XF	Unc	BU
1950	12,815,000	—	0.15	0.35	1.65	2.00
1951	25,740,000	—	0.15	0.35	0.65	1.00
1952	24,610,000	—	0.10	0.25	0.40	0.75
1953	21,160,000	—	0.10	0.25	0.40	0.85
1954	25,675,000	—	0.10	0.15	0.85	1.20
1955	9,820,000	—	0.15	0.25	0.85	1.50
1956	11,285,000	—	0.15	0.25	0.80	1.25
1957	9,805,000	—	0.15	0.25	0.85	1.35
1958	12,155,000	—	0.10	0.25	0.45	0.75
1959	11,875,000	—	0.10	0.25	0.75	1.25
1960	10,360,000	—	0.10	0.10	0.40	0.65
1961	6,385,000	—	0.10	0.15	0.45	0.85
1962	4,850,000	—	0.10	0.15	0.55	0.90

Date	Mintage	F	VF	XF	Unc	BU
1963	7,775,000	—	0.10	0.15	0.25	0.45
1964	4,280,000	—	0.10	0.15	0.20	0.30
1965	2,255,000	—	0.10	0.15	0.25	0.40
1966	1,760,000	—	0.10	0.25	0.60	0.75
1967	1,290,000	—	0.10	0.15	0.40	0.60
1968	1,000,000	—	0.10	0.20	0.85	1.25
1969	1,000,000	—	0.10	0.15	0.65	0.85

KM# 418 CENTAVO
1.5000 g., Brass, 13 mm. **Obv:** National arms, eagle left **Rev:** Oat sprigs **Note:** Reduced size.

Date	Mintage	F	VF	XF	Unc	BU
1970	1,000,000	—	0.20	0.40	1.45	1.75
1972	1,000,000	—	0.20	0.45	2.50	3.25
1972/2	—	—	0.50	1.25	3.50	5.00
1973	1,000,000	—	1.65	2.75	8.50	12.00

KM# 419 2 CENTAVOS
6.0000 g., Bronze, 25 mm. **Obv:** National arms **Rev:** Value below date within wreath **Note:** Mint mark Mo.

Date	Mintage	F	VF	XF	Unc	BU
1905	50,000	150	300	500	1,200	1,350
1906 Inverted 6	9,998,000	30.00	55.00	120	375	—
1906 Wide date	Inc. above	5.00	11.00	23.00	80.00	—
1906 Narrow date	Inc. above	6.50	14.00	28.00	85.00	—

Note: 5,000,000 pieces were struck at the Birmingham Mint

1920	1,325,000	6.50	17.50	35.00	350	—
1921	4,275,000	2.50	4.75	10.00	90.00	—
1922	—	225	550	1,750	5,500	—
1924	750,000	8.50	22.50	55.00	450	—
1925	3,650,000	2.50	3.50	7.50	38.00	—
1926	4,750,000	1.00	2.25	5.50	35.00	—
1927	7,250,000	0.60	1.00	4.50	22.00	—
1928	3,250,000	0.75	1.50	4.75	30.00	—
1929	250,000	65.00	180	500	1,000	—
1935	1,250,000	4.25	9.25	22.50	200	—
1939	5,000,000	0.60	0.90	2.25	20.00	22.00
1941	3,550,000	0.45	0.60	1.25	18.00	20.00

KM# 420 2 CENTAVOS
Bronze, 20 mm. **Obv:** National arms **Rev:** Value below date within wreath **Note:** Zapata issue. Mint mark Mo. Reduced size. Weight varies 3-3.03g.

Date	Mintage	F	VF	XF	Unc	BU
1915	487,000	7.50	9.00	17.50	75.00	—

KM# 421 5 CENTAVOS
5.0000 g., Nickel, 20 mm. **Obv:** National arms **Rev:** Value and date within beaded circle **Note:** Mint mark Mo. Varieties exist.

Date	Mintage	F	VF	XF	Unc	BU
1905	1,420,000	7.00	10.00	25.00	300	375
1906/5	10,615,000	13.00	30.00	70.00	375	—
1906	Inc. above	0.75	1.35	3.25	55.00	75.00
1907	4,000,000	1.25	4.00	12.00	350	—
1909	2,052,000	3.25	10.00	48.00	360	—
1910	6,181,000	1.30	3.50	6.00	78.00	115
1911 Narrow date	4,487,000	1.00	3.00	5.00	85.00	125
1911 Wide date	Inc. above	2.50	5.00	9.00	110	160
1912 Small mint mark	420,000	90.00	100	230	725	—
1912 Large mint mark	Inc. above	70.00	95.00	175	575	—
1913	2,035,000	1.75	4.25	9.00	100	150

Note: Wide and narrow dates exist for 1913

1914	2,000,000	1.00	2.00	3.50	70.00	95.00

Note: 5,000,000 pieces appear to have been struck at the Birmingham Mint in 1914 and all of 1909-1911. The Mexican Mint report does not mention receiving the 1914 dated coins

KM# 422 5 CENTAVOS
9.0000 g., Bronze, 28 mm. **Obv:** National arms **Rev:** Value below date within wreath

Date	Mintage	F	VF	XF	Unc	BU
1914Mo	2,500,000	10.00	23.00	50.00	240	—
1915Mo	11,424,000	3.00	5.00	20.00	145	—
1916Mo	2,860,000	15.00	35.00	150	645	—
1917Mo	800,000	75.00	195	375	850	—
1918Mo	1,332,000	35.00	90.00	200	625	—
1919Mo	400,000	115	225	360	950	—
1920Mo	5,920,000	3.00	8.00	40.00	265	—
1921Mo	2,080,000	10.00	24.00	75.00	275	—
1924Mo	780,000	40.00	95.00	260	625	—
1925Mo	4,040,000	5.50	11.00	47.50	200	—
1926Mo	3,160,000	5.50	11.00	48.00	300	—
1927Mo	3,600,000	4.00	7.00	30.00	215	250
1928Mo Large date	1,740,000	11.00	18.00	65.00	250	—
1928Mo Small date	Inc. above	30.00	45.00	95.00	385	—
1929Mo	2,400,000	5.50	11.00	48.00	195	—
1930Mo	2,600,000	5.00	8.00	27.50	210	—
Note: Large oval O in date						
1930Mo	Inc. above	60.00	125	250	565	—
Note: Small square O in date						
1931Mo	—	475	750	1,450	4,000	—
1933Mo	8,000,000	1.50	2.25	3.50	27.50	35.00
1934Mo	10,000,000	1.25	1.75	2.75	25.00	40.00
1935Mo	21,980,000	0.75	1.20	2.50	22.50	30.00

KM# 423 5 CENTAVOS
4.0000 g., Copper-Nickel, 20.5 mm. **Obv:** National arms, eagle left **Rev:** Value and date within circle

Date	Mintage	F	VF	XF	Unc	BU
1936M	46,700,000	—	0.65	1.25	6.50	7.50
1937M	49,060,000	—	0.50	1.00	6.00	7.00
1938M	3,340,000	—	4.00	10.00	75.00	250
1940M	22,800,000	—	0.75	1.25	8.00	10.00
1942M	7,100,000	—	1.50	3.00	35.00	45.00

KM# 424 5 CENTAVOS
6.5000 g., Bronze, 25.5 mm. **Obv:** National arms, eagle left **Rev:** Head left

Date	Mintage	F	VF	XF	Unc	BU
1942Mo	900,000	—	25.00	75.00	375	550
1943Mo	54,660,000	—	0.50	0.75	2.50	3.50
1944Mo	53,463,000	—	0.25	0.35	0.75	1.00
1945Mo	44,262,000	—	0.25	0.35	0.75	1.25
1946Mo	49,054,000	—	0.50	1.00	2.00	3.00
1951Mo	50,758,000	—	0.75	0.90	3.00	5.00
1952Mo	17,674,000	—	1.50	2.50	9.50	11.50
1953Mo	31,568,000	—	1.25	2.00	6.00	9.00
1954Mo	58,680,000	—	0.40	1.00	2.75	4.00
1955Mo	31,114,000	—	2.00	3.00	11.00	14.00

KM# 425 5 CENTAVOS
4.0000 g., Copper-Nickel, 20.5 mm. **Obv:** National arms, eagle left **Rev:** Bust right flanked by date and value

Date	Mintage	F	VF	XF	Unc	BU
1950Mo	5,700,000	—	0.75	1.50	6.00	7.00

Note: 5,600,000 pieces struck at Connecticut melted

KM# 426 5 CENTAVOS
4.0000 g., Brass, 20.5 mm. **Obv:** National arms, eagle left **Rev:** Bust right

Date	Mintage	F	VF	XF	Unc	BU
1954Mo Dot	—	—	10.00	45.00	300	375
1954Mo Without dot	—	—	15.00	30.00	250	290
1955Mo	12,136,000	—	0.75	1.50	9.00	12.50
1956Mo	60,216,000	—	0.20	0.30	0.75	1.25
1957Mo	55,288,000	—	0.15	0.20	0.90	1.50
1958Mo	104,624,000	—	0.15	0.20	0.60	1.00
1959Mo	106,000,000	—	0.15	0.25	0.75	1.25
1960Mo	99,144,000	—	0.10	0.15	0.50	0.75
1961Mo	61,136,000	—	0.10	0.15	0.50	0.75
1962Mo	47,232,000	—	0.10	0.15	0.25	0.35
1963Mo	156,680,000	—	—	0.15	0.25	0.40
1964Mo	71,168,000	—	—	0.15	0.20	0.40
1965Mo	155,720,000	—	—	0.15	0.25	0.35
1966Mo	124,944,000	—	—	0.15	0.40	0.65
1967Mo	118,816,000	—	—	0.15	0.25	0.40
1968Mo	189,588,000	—	—	0.15	0.50	0.75
1969Mo	210,492,000	—	—	0.15	0.55	0.80

KM# 426a 5 CENTAVOS
Copper-Nickel, 20.5 mm. **Obv:** National arms, eagle left **Rev:** Bust right

Date	Mintage	F	VF	XF	Unc	BU
1960Mo	—	—	250	300	350	—
1962Mo	19	—	250	300	350	—
1965Mo	—	—	250	300	350	—

KM# 427 5 CENTAVOS
2.7500 g., Brass, 18 mm. **Obv:** National arms, eagle left **Rev:** Bust right **Note:** Due to some minor alloy variations this type is often encountered with a bronze-color toning. Reduced size.

Date	Mintage	F	VF	XF	Unc	BU
1970	163,368,000	—	0.10	0.15	0.35	0.45
1971	198,844,000	—	0.10	0.15	0.25	0.30
1972	225,000,000	—	0.10	0.15	0.25	0.30
1973 Flat top 3	595,070,000	—	0.10	0.15	0.25	0.40
1973 Round top 3	Inc. above	—	0.10	0.15	0.20	0.30
1974	401,584,000	—	0.10	0.15	0.30	0.40
1975	342,308,000	—	0.10	0.15	0.25	0.35
1976	367,524,000	—	0.10	0.15	0.40	0.60

KM# 428 10 CENTAVOS
2.5000 g., 0.8000 Silver 0.0643 oz. ASW, 18 mm. **Obv:** National arms **Rev:** Value and date within 3/4 wreath with Liberty cap above **Note:** Mint mark Mo.

Date	Mintage	F	VF	XF	Unc	BU
1905	3,920,000	—	6.00	8.00	40.00	50.00
1906	8,410,000	—	5.50	7.50	27.00	35.00
1907/6	5,950,000	—	50.00	135	275	350
1907	Inc. above	—	5.50	6.25	35.00	42.50
1909	2,620,000	—	8.50	13.00	70.00	85.00
1910/00	3,450,000	—	10.00	40.00	75.00	85.00
1910	Inc. above	—	7.00	15.00	25.00	30.00
1911 Narrow date	2,550,000	—	11.00	17.00	88.00	125
1911 Wide date	Inc. above	—	7.50	10.00	42.00	60.00
1912	1,350,000	—	10.00	18.00	130	160
1912 Low 2	Inc. above	—	10.00	18.00	115	140
1913/2	1,990,000	—	10.00	25.00	40.00	70.00
1913	Inc. above	—	7.00	10.00	33.00	40.00

Date	Mintage	F	VF	XF	Unc	BU
1914	3,110,000	—	5.50	7.00	15.00	20.00

Note: Wide and narrow dates exist for 1914

KM# 429 10 CENTAVOS
1.8125 g., 0.8000 Silver 0.0466 oz. ASW, 15 mm. **Obv:** National arms **Rev:** Value and date within 3/4 wreath with Liberty cap above **Note:** Mint mark Mo. Reduced size.

Date	Mintage	F	VF	XF	Unc	BU
1919	8,360,000	—	10.00	15.00	85.00	110

KM# 430 10 CENTAVOS
12.0000 g., Bronze, 30.5 mm. **Obv:** National arms **Rev:** Value below date within wreath **Note:** Mint mark Mo.

Date	Mintage	F	VF	XF	Unc	BU
1919	1,232,000	—	25.00	70.00	450	525
1920	6,612,000	—	15.00	50.00	400	475
1921	2,255,000	—	35.00	80.00	650	800
1935	5,970,000	—	14.00	30.00	120	175

KM# 431 10 CENTAVOS
1.6600 g., 0.7200 Silver 0.0384 oz. ASW, 15 mm. **Obv:** National arms **Rev:** Value and date within wreath with Liberty cap above **Note:** Mint mark Mo.

Date	Mintage	F	VF	XF	Unc	BU
1925/15	5,350,000	—	30.00	75.00	125	175
1925/3	Inc. above	—	20.00	40.00	125	150
1925	Inc. above	—	2.00	5.00	40.00	45.00
1926/16	2,650,000	—	30.00	75.00	125	175
1926	Inc. above	—	3.50	7.50	65.00	85.00
1927	2,810,000	—	2.25	3.00	17.50	22.50
1928	5,270,000	—	2.00	2.75	13.50	16.50
1930	2,000,000	—	3.75	5.00	18.75	25.00
1933	5,000,000	—	1.50	3.00	10.00	11.50
1934	8,000,000	—	1.75	2.50	8.00	10.00
1935	3,500,000	—	2.75	5.00	11.00	12.50

KM# 432 10 CENTAVOS
5.5000 g., Copper-Nickel, 23.5 mm. **Obv:** National arms, eagle left **Rev:** Value and date within circle **Note:** Mint mark Mo.

Date	Mintage	F	VF	XF	Unc	BU
1936	33,030,000	—	0.75	2.50	9.00	10.00
1937	3,000,000	—	8.00	45.00	215	250
1938	3,650,000	1.25	2.00	7.00	60.00	75.00
1939	6,920,000	—	1.00	3.50	27.50	30.00
1940	12,300,000	—	0.40	1.25	5.00	6.00
1942	14,380,000	—	0.60	1.50	7.00	9.00
1945	9,558,000	—	0.40	0.70	3.50	4.00
1946	46,230,000	—	0.40	0.60	2.50	3.00

KM# 433 10 CENTAVOS
5.5000 g., Bronze, 23.5 mm. **Obv:** National arms, eagle left **Rev:** Bust left **Note:** Mint mark Mo.

Date	Mintage	F	VF	XF	Unc	BU
1955	1,818,000	—	0.75	3.25	23.00	30.00
1956	5,255,000	—	0.75	3.25	23.00	28.00
1957	11,925,000	—	0.20	0.40	5.50	8.00

Date	Mintage	F	VF	XF	Unc	BU
1959	26,140,000	—	0.30	0.45	0.75	1.25
1966	5,873,000	—	0.15	0.25	0.60	1.75
1967	32,318,000	—	0.10	0.15	0.30	0.40

Sharp stem

KM# 434.1 10 CENTAVOS
1.5200 g., Copper-Nickel **Obv:** National arms, eagle left **Rev:** Upright ear of corn **Note:** Variety I- Sharp stem and wide date

Date	Mintage	F	VF	XF	Unc	BU
1974	6,000,000	—	—	0.35	0.75	1.00
1975	5,550,000	—	0.10	0.35	0.75	1.00
1976	7,680,000	—	0.10	0.20	0.30	0.40
1977	144,650,000	—	1.25	2.25	3.00	3.50
1978	271,870,000	—	—	1.00	1.50	2.25
1979	375,660,000	—	—	0.50	1.00	1.75
1980/79	21,290,000	—	—	2.45	3.75	6.00	7.00
1980	Inc. above	—	1.50	2.00	4.50	5.50

Blunt stem

KM# 434.2 10 CENTAVOS
1.5600 g., Copper-Nickel **Obv:** National arms, eagle left **Rev:** Upright ear of corn **Note:** Variety II- Blunt stem and narrow date

Date	Mintage	F	VF	XF	Unc	BU
1974	Inc. above	—	—	0.10	0.20	0.30
1977	Inc. above	—	0.15	0.50	1.25	2.25
1978	Inc. above	—	—	0.10	0.30	0.40
1979	Inc. above	—	0.15	0.35	0.85	1.50
1980	Inc. above	—	—	0.10	0.20	0.30

KM# 434.4 10 CENTAVOS
Copper-Nickel **Obv:** National arms, eagle left **Rev:** Upright ear of corn **Note:** Variety IV- Sharp stem and narrow date

Date	Mintage	F	VF	XF	Unc	BU
1974	—	—	—	—	1.50	2.50
1979	—	—	—	—	1.50	2.50

KM# 434.3 10 CENTAVOS
Copper-Nickel **Obv:** National arms, eagle left **Rev:** Upright ear of corn **Note:** Variety III- Blunt stem and wide date

Date	Mintage	F	VF	XF	Unc	BU
1980/79	—	—	—	—	5.00	6.00

KM# 435 20 CENTAVOS
5.0000 g., 0.8000 Silver 0.1286 oz. ASW, 22 mm. **Obv:** National arms **Rev:** Value and date within wreath with Liberty cap above **Note:** Mint mark Mo.

Date	Mintage	F	VF	XF	Unc	BU
1905	2,565,000	—	12.00	20.00	145	175
1906	6,860,000	—	9.00	16.50	60.00	80.00
1907 Straight 7	4,000,000	—	11.50	20.00	70.00	100
1907 Curved 7	5,435,000	—	7.50	13.50	65.00	90.00
1908	350,000	50.00	90.00	225	1,800	—
1910	1,135,000	—	11.00	16.00	80.00	95.00
1911	1,150,000	12.00	15.00	35.00	125	150
1912	625,000	20.00	40.00	70.00	335	375
1913	1,000,000	—	14.50	30.00	95.00	115
1914	1,500,000	—	10.00	21.50	62.50	75.00

KM# 436 20 CENTAVOS
3.6250 g., 0.8000 Silver 0.0932 oz. ASW, 19 mm. **Obv:** National arms **Rev:** Value and date within wreath with Liberty cap above **Note:** Mint mark Mo. Reduced size.

Date	Mintage	F	VF	XF	Unc	BU
1919	4,155,000	—	30.00	55.00	190	225

KM# 437 20 CENTAVOS
15.0000 g., Bronze, 32.5 mm. **Obv:** National arms **Rev:** Value below date within wreath **Note:** Mint mark Mo.

Date	Mintage	F	VF	XF	Unc	BU
1920	4,835,000	—	45.00	140	650	775
1935	20,000,000	—	6.00	10.00	80.00	125

KM# 438 20 CENTAVOS
3.3333 g., 0.7200 Silver 0.0772 oz. ASW, 19 mm. **Obv:** National arms **Rev:** Value and date within wreath with Liberty cap above **Note:** Mint mark Mo.

Date	Mintage	F	VF	XF	Unc	BU
1920	3,710,000	—	6.00	17.50	165	200
1921	6,160,000	—	6.00	14.00	100	145
1925	1,450,000	—	12.00	20.00	125	150
1926/5	1,465,000	—	20.00	65.00	325	375
1926	Inc. above	—	3.25	7.50	80.00	110
1927	1,405,000	—	3.50	8.00	85.00	115
1928	3,630,000	—	4.00	5.25	14.50	19.50
1930	1,000,000	—	5.00	8.00	25.00	35.00
1933	2,500,000	—	2.25	3.00	10.00	11.50
1934	2,500,000	—	2.25	4.00	11.00	12.50
1935	2,460,000	—	2.25	4.00	11.00	12.50
1937	10,000,000	—	1.75	2.25	4.00	5.00
1939	8,800,000	—	1.75	2.25	4.00	5.00
1940	3,000,000	—	1.75	2.25	3.50	5.00
1941	5,740,000	—	1.50	2.25	3.00	4.00
1942	12,460,000	—	1.50	2.25	3.25	3.75
1943	3,955,000	—	2.00	2.50	3.50	4.25

KM# 439 20 CENTAVOS
Bronze, 28.5 mm. **Obv:** National arms, eagle left **Rev:** Liberty cap divides value above Pyramid of the Sun at Teotihuacán, volcanos Ixtaccihuatl and Popocatepet in background **Edge:** Plain **Note:** Mint mark Mo.

Date	Mintage	F	VF	XF	Unc	BU
1943	46,350,000	—	1.25	3.00	18.00	25.00
1944	83,650,000	—	0.40	0.65	8.00	10.00
1945	26,801,000	—	1.25	3.50	9.50	12.00
1946	25,695,000	—	1.10	2.25	6.00	8.25
1951	11,385,000	—	3.00	8.75	90.00	110
1952	6,560,000	—	3.00	5.00	25.00	32.00
1953	26,948,000	—	0.35	0.80	8.25	12.00
1954	40,108,000	—	0.35	0.80	8.00	11.50
1955	16,950,000	—	2.75	7.00	60.00	75.00

KM# 440 20 CENTAVOS
Bronze, 28.5 mm. **Obv:** National arms, eagle left **Rev:** Liberty cap divides value above Pyramid of the Sun at Teotihuacán, volcanos Ixtaccihuatl and Popocatepet in background **Edge:** Plain **Note:** Mint mark Mo.

Date	Mintage	F	VF	XF	Unc	BU
1955 Inc. KM#439	Inc. above	—	0.75	1.75	17.00	22.00
1956	22,431,000	—	0.30	0.35	3.00	4.00
1957	13,455,000	—	0.45	1.25	9.00	12.00
1959	6,017,000	—	4.50	9.00	75.00	100
1960	39,756,000	—	0.15	0.25	0.75	1.00
1963	14,869,000	—	0.25	0.35	0.80	1.00
1964	28,654,000	—	0.25	0.40	0.90	1.25
1965	74,162,000	—	0.20	0.35	0.80	1.00
1966	43,745,000	—	0.15	0.25	0.75	1.00
1967	46,487,000	—	0.20	0.50	1.00	1.25
1968	15,477,000	—	0.30	0.55	1.35	1.65
1969	63,647,000	—	0.20	0.35	0.80	1.00

Date	Mintage	F	VF	XF	Unc	BU
1970	76,287,000	—	0.15	0.20	0.90	1.30
1971	49,892,000	—	0.30	0.50	1.25	1.50

KM# 441 20 CENTAVOS
Bronze, 28.5 mm. **Obv:** National arms, eagle left **Rev:** Liberty cap divides value above Pyramid of the Sun at Teotihuacán, volcanos Ixtaccihuatl and Popocatepet in background **Edge:** Plain

Date	Mintage	F	VF	XF	Unc	BU
1971 Inc. KM#440	Inc. above	—	0.20	0.35	1.85	2.35
1973	78,398,000	—	0.25	0.35	0.95	1.50
1974	34,200,000	—	0.20	0.35	1.25	1.75

KM# 442 20 CENTAVOS
3.0600 g., Copper-Nickel, 20 mm. **Obv:** National arms, eagle left **Rev:** Bust 3/4 facing flanked by value and date

Date	Mintage	F	VF	XF	Unc	BU
1974	112,000,000	—	0.10	0.15	0.25	0.30
1975	611,000,000	—	0.10	0.15	0.30	0.35
1976	394,000,000	—	0.10	0.15	0.35	0.45
1977	394,350,000	—	0.10	0.15	0.40	0.45
1978	527,950,000	—	0.10	0.15	0.25	0.30
1979	524,615,000	—	0.10	0.15	0.25	0.30
1979	—	—	1.25	2.00	4.00	8.00

Note: Doubled die obv. small letters

1979	—	—	1.25	2.00	4.00	8.00

Note: Doubled die obv. large letters

1980	326,500,000	—	0.15	0.20	0.30	0.40
1981 Open 8	106,205,000	—	0.30	0.50	1.00	2.00
1981 Closed 8, high date	248,500,000	—	0.30	0.50	1.00	2.00
1981 Closed 8, low date	—	—	1.00	1.50	3.50	4.25
1981/1982	—	—	40.00	75.00	175	195

Note: The 1981/1982 overdate is often mistaken as 1982/1981

1982	286,855,000	—	0.40	0.60	0.90	1.10
1983 Round top 3	100,930,000	—	0.25	0.40	1.75	2.25
1983 Flat top 3	Inc. above	—	0.25	0.50	1.25	1.75
1983 Proof	998	Value: 15.00				

KM# 491 20 CENTAVOS
3.0000 g., Bronze, 20 mm. **Subject:** Olmec Culture **Obv:** National arms, eagle left **Rev:** Mask 3/4 right with value below

Date	Mintage	F	VF	XF	Unc	BU
1983	260,000,000	—	0.20	0.25	1.25	1.75
1983 Proof	53	Value: 185				
1984	180,320,000	—	0.20	0.35	1.85	2.25

KM# 443 25 CENTAVOS
3.3330 g., 0.3000 Silver 0.0321 oz. ASW, 21.5 mm. **Obv:** National arms, eagle left **Rev:** Scale below Liberty cap **Note:** Mint mark Mo.

Date	Mintage	F	VF	XF	Unc	BU
1950	77,060,000	—	0.60	0.80	1.60	2.00
1951	41,172,000	—	0.60	0.80	1.60	2.00
1952	29,264,000	—	0.75	1.10	1.75	2.25
1953	38,144,000	—	0.65	0.85	1.60	2.00

KM# 444 25 CENTAVOS
5.5000 g., Copper-Nickel, 23 mm. **Obv:** National arms, eagle left **Rev:** Bust 3/4 facing

Date	Mintage	F	VF	XF	Unc	BU
1964	20,686,000	—	—	0.15	0.20	0.30
1966 Closed beak	180,000	—	0.65	1.00	2.25	2.50
1966 Open beak	Inc. above	—	1.75	3.50	10.00	13.50

KM# 445 50 CENTAVOS

12.5000 g., 0.8000 Silver 0.3215 oz. ASW, 30 mm.
Obv: National arms **Rev:** Value and date within 3/4 wreath with Liberty cap above **Note:** Mint mark Mo.

Date	Mintage	F	VF	XF	Unc	BU
1905	2,446,000	12.50	20.00	30.00	150	225
1906 Open 9	16,966,000	—	6.00	10.00	40.00	60.00
1906 Closed 9	Inc. above	—	5.00	9.00	35.00	50.00
1907 Straight 7	18,920,000	—	5.00	9.00	25.00	28.50
1907 Curved 7	14,841,000	—	5.25	9.00	25.00	32.00
1908	488,000	—	80.00	190	545	650
1912	3,736,000	—	11.00	14.00	45.00	60.00
1913/07	10,510,000	—	40.00	90.00	240	285
1913/2	Inc. above	—	20.00	27.50	65.00	85.00
1913	Inc. above	—	5.50	8.50	27.50	35.00
1914	7,710,000	—	6.75	13.50	32.00	45.00
1916 Narrow date	480,000	—	60.00	85.00	200	300
1916 Wide date	Inc. above	—	60.00	85.00	200	300
1917	37,112,000	—	6.00	9.50	20.00	22.50
1918	1,320,000	—	70.00	135	250	350

KM# 446 50 CENTAVOS

9.0625 g., 0.8000 Silver 0.2331 oz. ASW, 27 mm. **Obv:** National arms **Rev:** Value and date within 3/4 wreath with Liberty cap above **Note:** Mint mark Mo. Reduced size.

Date	Mintage	F	VF	XF	Unc	BU
1918/7	2,760,000	—	525	675	1,350	—
1918	Inc. above	—	17.50	55.00	300	400
1919	29,670,000	—	9.50	22.50	95.00	125

KM# 447 50 CENTAVOS

8.3333 g., 0.7200 Silver 0.1929 oz. ASW, 27 mm. **Obv:** National arms **Rev:** Value and date within 3/4 wreath with Liberty cap above **Note:** Mint mark Mo.

Date	Mintage	F	VF	XF	Unc	BU
1919	10,200,000	—	10.00	20.00	90.00	110
1920	27,166,000	—	8.00	14.00	70.00	80.00
1921	21,864,000	—	8.00	14.00	85.00	100
1925	3,280,000	—	17.50	30.00	125	160
1937	20,000,000	—	4.25	5.50	7.50	8.50
1938	100,000	—	50.00	85.00	225	300
1939	10,440,000	—	6.00	8.00	15.00	18.50
1942	800,000	—	6.00	9.00	16.00	20.00
1943	41,512,000	—	3.25	4.25	5.50	6.50
1944	55,806,000	—	3.25	4.25	5.50	6.50
1945	56,766,000	—	3.25	4.25	5.50	6.50

KM# 448 50 CENTAVOS

7.9730 g., 0.4200 Silver 0.1077 oz. ASW, 27 mm. **Obv:** National arms **Rev:** Value and date within 3/4 wreath with Liberty cap above **Note:** Mint mark Mo.

Date	Mintage	F	VF	XF	Unc	BU
1935	70,800,000	—	2.50	3.25	5.50	7.00

KM# 449 50 CENTAVOS

6.6600 g., 0.3000 Silver 0.0642 oz. ASW, 26 mm. **Obv:** National arms, eagle left **Rev:** Head with head covering right **Note:** Mint mark Mo.

Date	Mintage	F	VF	XF	Unc	BU
1950	13,570,000	—	1.50	1.85	3.00	4.50
1951	3,650,000	—	2.00	2.50	3.75	5.75

KM# 450 50 CENTAVOS

14.0000 g., Bronze, 33 mm. **Obv:** National arms, eagle left **Rev:** Head with headdress left **Note:** Mint mark Mo.

Date	Mintage	F	VF	XF	Unc	BU
1955	3,502,000	—	1.50	3.00	29.00	35.00
1956	34,643,000	—	0.75	1.50	3.75	4.50
1957	9,675,000	—	1.00	2.00	6.50	7.50
1959	4,540,000	—	0.50	0.75	2.00	2.75

KM# 451 50 CENTAVOS

6.5000 g., Copper-Nickel, 25 mm. **Obv:** National arms, eagle left **Rev:** Head with headdress left

Date	Mintage	F	VF	XF	Unc	BU
1964	43,806,000	—	0.15	0.20	0.40	0.60
1965	14,326,000	—	0.20	0.25	0.45	0.65
1966	1,726,000	—	0.20	0.40	1.30	1.75
1967	55,144,000	—	0.20	0.30	0.65	1.00
1968	80,438,000	—	0.15	0.30	0.65	0.90
1969	87,640,000	—	0.20	0.35	0.80	1.00

KM# 452 50 CENTAVOS

6.5000 g., Copper-Nickel, 25 mm. **Obv:** National arms, eagle left **Rev:** Head with headdress left **Note:** Coins dated 1975 and 1976 exist with and without dots in centers of three circles on plumage on reverse. Edge varieties exist.

Date	Mintage	F	VF	XF	Unc	BU
1970	76,236,000	—	0.15	0.20	0.80	1.00
1971	125,288,000	—	0.15	0.20	0.90	1.30
1972	16,000,000	—	1.25	2.00	3.00	4.75
1975 Dots	177,958,000	—	0.60	1.25	3.50	6.00
1975 No dots	Inc. above	—	0.15	0.20	0.75	1.00
1976 Dots	37,480,000	—	0.75	1.25	5.00	6.00
1976 No dots	Inc. above	—	0.15	0.20	0.50	0.75
1977	12,410,000	—	6.50	10.00	32.50	42.50
1978	85,400,000	—	0.15	0.25	0.50	0.75
1979 Round 2nd 9 in date	229,000,000	—	0.15	0.25	0.50	0.65
1979 Square 9's in date	Inc. above	—	0.20	0.40	1.60	2.00
1980 Narrow date, square 9	89,978,000	—	0.45	0.75	1.75	2.50
1980 Wide date, round 9	178,188,000	—	0.20	0.25	1.00	1.15
1981 Rectangular 9, narrow date	142,212,000	—	0.50	0.75	1.75	2.50
1981 Round 9, wide date	Inc. above	—	0.30	0.50	1.25	1.75
1982	45,474,000	—	0.20	0.40	1.00	1.25

Date	Mintage	F	VF	XF	Unc	BU
1983	90,318,000	—	0.50	0.75	2.00	2.50
1983 Proof	998	Value: 35.00				

KM# 492 50 CENTAVOS

Stainless Steel, 22 mm. **Subject:** Palenque Culture **Obv:** National arms, eagle left **Rev:** Head with headdress 3/4 left

Date	Mintage	F	VF	XF	Unc	BU
1983	99,540,000	—	—	0.30	1.50	2.50
1983 Proof	53	Value: 195				

KM# 453 PESO

27.0700 g., 0.9030 Silver 0.7859 oz. ASW, 39 mm. **Subject:** Caballito **Obv:** National arms **Rev:** Horse and rider facing left among sun rays **Note:** Mint mark Mo.

Date	Mintage	F	VF	XF	Unc	BU
1910	3,814,000	—	45.00	100	175	275
1911	1,227,000	—	45.00	75.00	200	300
	Note: Long lower left ray on reverse					
1911	Inc. above	—	145	250	750	950
	Note: Short lower left ray on reverse					
1912	322,000	—	100	210	365	500
1913/2	2,880,000	—	45.00	75.00	300	425
1913	Inc. above	—	45.00	70.00	175	275
	Note: 1913 coins exist with even and unevenly spaced date					
1914	120,000	—	600	1,100	3,500	—

KM# 454 PESO

18.1300 g., 0.8000 Silver 0.4663 oz. ASW, 34 mm. **Obv:** National arms **Rev:** Value and date within 3/4 wreath with Liberty cap above **Note:** Mint mark Mo.

Date	Mintage	F	VF	XF	Unc	BU
1918	3,050,000	—	35.00	125	1,350	2,400
1919	6,151,000	—	20.00	50.00	900	1,650

KM# 455 PESO

16.6600 g., 0.7200 Silver 0.3856 oz. ASW, 34 mm. **Obv:** National arms **Rev:** Value and date within 3/4 wreath with Liberty cap above **Note:** Mint mark Mo.

Date	Mintage	F	VF	XF	Unc	BU
1920/10	8,830,000	—	50.00	90.00	325	—
1920	Inc. above	—	8.00	25.00	185	300
1921	5,480,000	—	8.00	25.00	155	200
1922	33,620,000	—	BV	6.00	20.00	26.00
1923	35,280,000	—	BV	6.00	20.00	28.00
1924	33,060,000	—	BV	6.00	20.00	26.00
1925	9,160,000	—	5.00	10.00	60.00	75.00
1926	28,840,000	—	BV	6.00	20.00	25.00
1927	5,060,000	—	7.00	10.00	70.00	85.00

Date	Mintage	F	VF	XF	Unc	BU
1932 Open 9	50,770,000	—	—	BV	6.00	7.50
1932 Closed 9	Inc. above	—	—	BV	6.00	7.50
1933/2	43,920,000	—	15.00	25.00	85.00	—
1933	Inc. above	—	—	BV	6.50	8.50
1934	22,070,000	—	—	BV	8.00	10.00
1935	8,050,000	—	BV	6.00	11.50	13.50
1938	30,000,000	—	—	BV	6.00	7.50
1940	20,000,000	—	—	BV	6.50	8.00
1943	47,662,000	—	—	BV	5.75	6.50
1944	39,522,000	—	—	BV	6.00	7.00
1945	37,300,000	—	—	BV	6.00	7.00

KM# 456   PESO
14.0000 g., 0.5000 Silver 0.2250 oz. ASW, 32 mm.
Obv: National arms, eagle left **Rev:** Head with headcovering right
Note: Mint mark Mo.

Date	Mintage	F	VF	XF	Unc	BU
1947	61,460,000	—	BV	3.50	4.50	5.50
1948	22,915,000	—	3.50	4.50	5.50	6.50
1949	4,000,000	—	—	1,200	1,600	2,500

Note: Not released for circulation
1949 Proof   —   Value: 4,000

KM# 457   PESO
13.3300 g., 0.3000 Silver 0.1286 oz. ASW, 32 mm. **Obv:** National arms, eagle left **Rev:** Armored bust 3/4 left **Note:** Mint mark Mo.

Date	Mintage	F	VF	XF	Unc	BU
1950	3,287,000	—	2.50	4.00	7.00	8.50

KM# 458   PESO
16.0000 g., 0.1000 Silver 0.0514 oz. ASW, 34.5 mm.
Subject: 100th Anniversary of Constitution **Obv:** National arms, eagle left within wreath **Rev:** Head left **Edge:** INDEPENDENCIA Y LIBERTAD **Note:** Mint mark Mo.

Date	Mintage	F	VF	XF	Unc	BU
1957	500,000	—	3.50	5.00	12.50	15.00

KM# 459   PESO
16.0000 g., 0.1000 Silver 0.0514 oz. ASW, 34.5 mm. **Obv:** National arms, eagle left within wreath **Rev:** Armored bust right within wreath **Edge:** INDEPENDENCIA Y LIBERTAD **Note:** Mint mark Mo.

Date	Mintage	F	VF	XF	Unc	BU
1957	28,273,000	BV	0.75	1.00	2.50	10.00
1958	41,899,000	—	BV	0.80	1.65	9.00
1959	27,369,000	BV	1.25	2.00	5.50	8.00
1960	26,259,000	BV	0.75	1.10	3.25	4.50
1961	52,601,000	—	BV	0.90	2.25	3.00

Date	Mintage	F	VF	XF	Unc	BU
1962	61,094,000	—	BV	0.80	1.75	2.25
1963	26,394,000	—	BV	0.80	1.75	2.00
1964	15,615,000	—	BV	0.80	2.00	2.40
1965	5,004,000	—	BV	0.80	1.85	2.00
1966	30,998,000	—	BV	0.75	1.35	1.85
1967	9,308,000	—	BV	0.85	2.75	3.50

Tall date   Short date

KM# 460   PESO
9.0000 g., Copper-Nickel, 29 mm. **Obv:** National arms, eagle left **Rev:** Head left

Date	Mintage	F	VF	XF	Unc	BU
1970 Narrow date	102,715,000	—	0.25	0.35	0.65	0.80
1970 Wide date	Inc. above	—	1.25	2.50	7.50	9.00
1971	426,222,000	—	0.20	0.25	0.55	0.75
1972	120,000,000	—	0.20	0.25	0.40	0.65
1974	63,700,000	—	0.20	0.25	0.65	0.90
1975 Tall narrow date	205,979,000	—	0.25	0.45	1.00	1.35
1975 Short wide date	Inc. above	—	0.30	0.40	0.75	1.00
1976	94,489,000	—	0.15	0.20	0.50	0.75
1977 Thick date close to rim	94,364,000	—	0.25	0.45	1.00	1.25
1977 Thin date, space between sideburns and collar	Inc. above	—	1.00	2.00	6.50	13.50
1978 Closed 8	208,300,000	—	0.20	0.30	1.00	1.50
1978 Open 8	55,140,000	—	0.75	1.75	12.00	15.00
1979 Thin date	117,884,000	—	0.20	0.30	1.15	1.50
1979 Thick date	Inc. above	—	0.20	0.30	1.25	1.75
1980 Closed 8	318,800,000	—	0.25	0.35	1.00	1.25
1980 Open 8	23,865,000	—	0.75	1.50	8.00	12.00
1981 Closed 8	413,349,000	—	0.20	0.30	0.75	0.90
1981 Open 8	58,616,000	—	0.50	1.25	6.50	8.00
1982 Closed 8	235,000,000	—	0.25	0.75	2.25	2.50
1982 Open 8		—	0.75	1.50	8.00	12.00
1983 Wide date	100,000,000	—	0.30	0.45	3.00	3.50
1983 Narrow date	Inc. above	—	0.30	0.45	3.00	3.50
1983 Proof	1,051,000		Value: 38.00			

KM# 496   PESO
Stainless Steel, 24.5 mm. **Obv:** National arms, eagle left **Rev:** Armored bust right

Date	Mintage	F	VF	XF	Unc	BU
1984	722,802,000	—	0.10	0.25	0.65	1.00
1985	985,000,000	—	0.10	0.25	0.50	0.75
1986	740,000,000	—	0.10	0.25	0.50	0.75
1987	250,000,000	—	0.10	0.25	0.50	0.80
1987 Proof; 2 known		—	Value: 1,000			

KM# 461   2 PESOS
1.6666 g., 0.9000 Gold 0.0482 oz. AGW, 13 mm. **Obv:** National arms **Rev:** Date above value within wreath **Note:** Mint mark Mo.

Date	Mintage	F	VF	XF	Unc	BU
1919	1,670,000	—	BV	50.00	75.00	—
1920/10	—	BV	50.00	65.00	110	—
1920	4,282,000	—	BV	50.00	70.00	—
1944	10,000	BV	50.00	60.00	80.00	—
1945	Est. 140,000	—	—	—	BV+20%	—
1946	168,000	BV	50.00	60.00	110	—
1947	25,000	BV	50.00	60.00	80.00	—
1948 No specimens known	45,000					

Note: During 1951-1972 a total of 4,590,493 pieces were restruck, most likely dated 1945. In 1996 matte re-strikes were produced

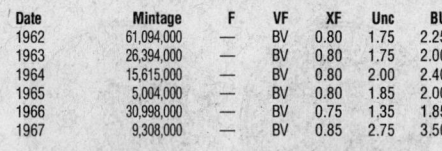

KM# 462   2 PESOS
26.6667 g., 0.9000 Silver 0.7716 oz. ASW, 39 mm. **Subject:** Centennial of Independence **Obv:** National arms, eagle left within wreath **Rev:** Winged Victory **Note:** Mint mark Mo.

Date	Mintage	F	VF	XF	Unc	BU
1921	1,278,000	—	40.00	55.00	400	650

KM# 463   2-1/2 PESOS
2.0833 g., 0.9000 Gold 0.0603 oz. AGW, 15.5 mm.
Obv: National arms **Rev:** Miguel Hidalgo y Costilla **Note:** Mint mark Mo.

Date	Mintage	F	VF	XF	Unc	BU
1918	1,704,000	—	BV	65.00	85.00	—
1919	984,000	—	BV	65.00	85.00	—
1920/10	607,000	—	BV	65.00	130	—
1920	Inc. above	—	BV	65.00	70.00	—
1944	20,000	—	BV	65.00	70.00	—
1945	Est. 180,000	—	—	—	BV+18%	—
1946	163,000	—	BV	65.00	70.00	—
1947	24,000	200	265	325	550	—
1948	63,000	—	BV	65.00	75.00	—

Note: During 1951-1972 a total of 5,025,087 pieces were restruck, most likely dated 1945. In 1996 matte re-strikes were produced

KM# 464   5 PESOS
4.1666 g., 0.9000 Gold 0.1206 oz. AGW, 19 mm. **Obv:** National arms **Rev:** Miguel Hidalgo y Costilla **Note:** Mint mark Mo.

Date	Mintage	F	VF	XF	Unc	BU
1905	18,000	120	175	245	600	—
1906	4,638,000	—	—	BV	120	—
1907/6	—	—	—	—	—	—
1907	1,088,000	—	—	BV	120	—
1910	100,000	—	—	BV	150	—
1918/7	609,000	—	—	BV	200	—
1918	Inc. above	—	—	BV	120	—
1919	506,000	—	—	BV	120	—
1920	2,385,000	—	—	BV	120	—
1955	Est. 48,000	—	—	—	BV+12%	—

Note: During 1955-1972 a total of 1,767,645 pieces were restruck, most likely dated 1955. In 1996 matte re-strikes were produced

KM# 465   5 PESOS
30.0000 g., 0.9000 Silver 0.8680 oz. ASW, 40 mm. **Obv:** National arms, eagle left **Rev:** Head with headdress left **Note:** Mint mark Mo.

Date	Mintage	F	VF	XF	Unc	BU
1947	5,110,000	—	—	BV	12.75	14.50
1948	26,740,000	—	—	BV	12.50	13.50

KM# 466   5 PESOS
27.7800 g., 0.7200 Silver 0.6430 oz. ASW, 40 mm.
Subject: Opening of Southern Railroad **Obv:** National arms, eagle left **Rev:** Radiant sun flanked by palm trees above train **Edge:** COMERCIO - AGRICULTURA - INDUSTRIA **Note:** Mint mark Mo.

Date	Mintage	F	VF	XF	Unc	BU
1950	200,000	—	22.50	40.00	50.00	55.00

Note: It is recorded that 100,000 pieces were melted to be used for the 1968 Mexican Olympic 25 Pesos

KM# 467   5 PESOS
27.7800 g., 0.7200 Silver 0.6430 oz. ASW, 40 mm. **Obv:** National arms, eagle left **Rev:** Head left within wreath **Edge:** COMERCIO - AGRICULTURA - INDUSTRIA **Note:** Mint mark Mo.

Date	Mintage	F	VF	XF	Unc	BU
1951	4,958,000	—	—	BV	10.00	12.00
1952	9,595,000	—	—	BV	9.50	11.00
1953	20,376,000	—	—	BV	9.50	11.00
1954	30,000	—	30.00	60.00	70.00	85.00

KM# 468   5 PESOS
27.7800 g., 0.7200 Silver 0.6430 oz. ASW, 40 mm. **Subject:** Bicentennial of Hidalgo's Birth **Obv:** National arms, eagle left **Rev:** Half-length figure facing to right of building and dates **Edge:** COMERCIO - AGRICULTURA - INDUSTRIA **Note:** Mint mark Mo.

Date	Mintage	F	VF	XF	Unc	BU
1953	1,000,000	—	BV	9.50	11.00	13.50

KM# 469   5 PESOS
18.0500 g., 0.7200 Silver 0.4178 oz. ASW, 36 mm.
Obv: National arms, eagle left **Rev:** Head left **Note:** Mint mark Mo.

Date	Mintage	F	VF	XF	Unc	BU
1955	4,271,000	—	BV	6.25	7.00	8.50
1956	4,596,000	—	BV	6.25	7.00	8.50
1957	3,464,000	—	BV	6.25	7.00	8.50

KM# 470   5 PESOS
18.0500 g., 0.7200 Silver 0.4178 oz. ASW, 36 mm.
Subject: 100th Anniversary of Constitution **Obv:** National arms, eagle left **Rev:** Head left **Edge:** INDEPENDENCIA Y LIBERTAD **Note:** Mint mark Mo.

Date	Mintage	F	VF	XF	Unc	BU
1957	200,000	—	6.50	7.50	13.50	15.50

KM# 471   5 PESOS
18.0500 g., 0.7200 Silver 0.4178 oz. ASW, 36 mm.
Subject: Centennial of Carranza's Birth **Obv:** National arms, eagle left **Rev:** Head left **Edge:** Plain **Note:** Mint mark Mo.

Date	Mintage	F	VF	XF	Unc	BU
1959	1,000,000	—	—	BV	7.00	9.00

Small date   Large date

KM# 472   5 PESOS
14.0000 g., Copper-Nickel, 33 mm. **Obv:** National arms, eagle left **Rev:** Armored bust right **Edge:** INDEPENDENCIA Y LIBERTAD **Note:** Small date, large date varieties.

Date	Mintage	F	VF	XF	Unc	BU
1971	28,457,000	—	0.50	0.95	2.50	3.25
1972	75,000,000	—	0.60	1.25	2.00	2.50
1973	19,405,000	—	1.25	2.00	4.50	5.50
1974	34,500,000	—	0.50	0.80	1.75	2.25
1976 Small date	26,121,000	—	0.75	1.45	3.25	4.00
1976 Large date	121,550,000	—	0.35	0.50	1.50	1.75
1977	102,000,000	—	0.35	0.50	1.50	1.75
1978	25,700,000	—	1.00	1.50	4.50	6.25

KM# 485   5 PESOS
Copper-Nickel, 27 mm. **Subject:** Quetzalcoatl **Obv:** National arms, eagle left **Rev:** Native sculpture to lower right of value and dollar sign **Edge:** LIBERTAD Y INDEPENDENCIA **Note:** Inverted and normal edge legend varieties exist for the 1980 and 1981 dates.

Date	Mintage	F	VF	XF	Unc	BU
1980	266,899,999	—	0.25	0.50	1.75	2.25
1981	30,500,000	—	0.45	0.65	2.75	3.25
1982	20,000,000	—	1.50	2.35	4.25	5.25
1982 Proof	1,051	Value: 18.00				
1983 Proof; 7 known	—	Value: 1,200				
1984	16,300,000	—	1.25	2.00	4.75	6.00
1985	76,900,000	—	2.00	3.25	4.25	5.00

KM# 502   5 PESOS
Brass, 17 mm. **Subject:** Quetzalcoatl **Obv:** National arms, eagle left **Rev:** Date and value **Note:** Circulation coinage.

Date	Mintage	F	VF	XF	Unc	BU
1985	30,000,000	—	—	0.15	0.35	0.50
1987	81,900,000	—	8.00	9.50	12.50	15.00
1988	76,600,000	—	—	0.10	0.25	0.35
1988 Proof; 2 known	—	Value: 600				

KM# 473   10 PESOS
8.3333 g., 0.9000 Gold 0.2411 oz. AGW, 22.5 mm.
Obv: National arms **Rev:** Miguel Hidalgo y Costilla **Note:** Mint mark Mo.

Date	Mintage	F	VF	XF	Unc	BU
1905	39,000	—	BV	230	275	—
1906	2,949,000	—	BV	225	245	—
1907	1,589,000	—	BV	225	245	—
1908	890,000	—	BV	225	245	—
1910	451,000	—	BV	225	245	—
1916	26,000	—	BV	235	400	—
1917	1,967,000	—	BV	225	245	—
1919	266,000	—	BV	225	260	—
1920	12,000	—	BV	450	800	—
1959	Est. 50,000	—	—	—	BV+7%	—

Note: *During 1961-1972 a total of 954,983 pieces were restruck, most likely dated 1959. In 1996 matte restrikes were produced

KM# 474   10 PESOS
28.8800 g., 0.9000 Silver 0.8356 oz. ASW, 40 mm.
Obv: National arms **Rev:** Head left **Note:** Mint mark Mo.

Date	Mintage	F	VF	XF	Unc	BU
1955	585,000	—	—	BV	12.50	14.50
1956	3,535,000	—	—	BV	12.25	13.50

KM# 475   10 PESOS
28.8800 g., 0.9000 Silver 0.8356 oz. ASW, 40 mm.
Subject: 100th Anniversary of Constitution **Obv:** National arms, eagle left **Rev:** Head left **Edge:** INDEPENDENCIA Y LIBERTAD **Note:** Mint mark Mo.

Date	Mintage	F	VF	XF	Unc	BU
1957	100,000	—	13.50	27.50	45.00	50.00

KM# 476   10 PESOS
28.8800 g., 0.9000 Silver 0.8356 oz. ASW, 40 mm.
Subject: 150th Anniversary - War of Independence
Obv: National arms, eagle left **Rev:** Conjoined busts facing flanked by dates **Note:** Mint mark Mo.

Date	Mintage	F	VF	XF	Unc	BU
1960	1,000,000	—	—	BV	12.50	15.00

KM# 477.1   10 PESOS
Copper-Nickel, 30.5 mm. **Obv:** National arms, eagle left
Rev: Miguel Hidalgo y Costilla **Note:** Thin flan - 1.6mm

Date	Mintage	F	VF	XF	Unc	BU
1974	3,900,000	—	0.50	1.00	3.00	4.00
1974 Proof	—	Value: 625				
1975	1,000,000	—	2.25	3.25	7.50	8.50
1976	74,500,000	—	0.25	0.75	1.75	2.25
1977	79,620,000	—	0.50	1.00	2.00	3.00

KM# 477.2   10 PESOS
Copper-Nickel, 30.5 mm. **Obv:** National arms, eagle left
Rev: Head left **Note:** Thick flan - 2.3mm

Date	Mintage	F	VF	XF	Unc	BU
1978	124,850,000	—	0.50	0.75	2.50	2.75
1979	57,200,000	—	0.50	0.75	2.25	2.50
1980	55,200,000	—	0.50	0.75	2.50	3.75
1981	222,768,000	—	0.40	0.60	2.25	2.65
1982	151,770,000	—	0.50	0.80	2.50	3.50
1982 Proof	1,051	Value: 40.00				
1983 Proof; 3 known	—	Value: 1,800				
1985	58,000,000	—	1.25	1.75	5.75	7.50

KM# 512   10 PESOS
3.8400 g., Stainless Steel, 19 mm. **Obv:** National arms, eagle left **Rev:** Head facing with diagonal value at left **Note:** Date varieties exist.

Date	Mintage	F	VF	XF	Unc	BU
1985	257,000,000	—	—	0.15	0.50	0.75
1986	392,000,000	—	—	0.15	0.50	1.50
1987	305,000,000	—	—	0.15	0.35	0.50
1988	500,300,000	—	—	0.15	0.25	0.35
1989	—	—	0.20	0.25	0.75	1.50
1990	—	—	—	0.25	0.75	1.25
1990 Proof; 2 known	—	Value: 550				

KM# 478   20 PESOS
16.6666 g., 0.9000 Gold 0.4822 oz. AGW, 27.5 mm.
Obv: National arms, eagle left **Rev:** Aztec Sunstone with denomination below **Edge:** Lettered **Edge:** INDEPEDENCIA Y LIBERTAD **Note:** Mint mark Mo.

Date	Mintage	F	VF	XF	Unc	BU
1917	852,000	—	—	BV	465	—
1918	2,831,000	—	—	BV	465	—

Date	Mintage	F	VF	XF	Unc	BU
1919	1,094,000	—	—	BV	465	—
1920/10	462,000	—	—	BV	465	—
1920	Inc. above	—	—	BV	500	—
1921/11	922,000	—	—	BV	465	—
1921/10	—	—	—	—	—	—
1921	Inc. above	—	—	BV	500	—
1959	Est. 13,000	—	—	—	—	—

Note: During 1960-1971 a total of 1,158,414 pieces were restruck, most likely dated 1959. In 1996 matte restrikes were produced

KM# 486   20 PESOS
Copper-Nickel, 32 mm. **Obv:** National arms, eagle left
Rev: Figure with headdress facing left within circle

Date	Mintage	F	VF	XF	Unc	BU
1980	84,900,000	—	0.50	0.85	2.25	3.00
1981	250,573,000	—	0.60	0.80	2.25	3.25
1982	236,892,000	—	1.00	1.75	2.50	3.50
1982 Proof	1,051	Value: 45.00				
1983 Proof; 3 known	—	Value: 575				
1984	55,000,000	—	1.00	1.50	2.50	4.75

KM# 508   20 PESOS
6.0000 g., Brass, 21 mm. **Obv:** National arms, eagle left
Rev: Bust facing with diagonal value at left

Date	Mintage	F	VF	XF	Unc	BU
1985 Wide date	25,000,000	—	0.10	0.20	1.00	1.25
1985 Narrow date	Inc. above	—	0.10	0.25	1.50	2.00
1986	10,000,000	—	1.00	1.75	5.00	5.50
1988	355,200,000	—	0.10	0.20	0.45	0.75
1989	—	—	0.15	0.30	1.50	2.00
1990	—	—	0.15	0.30	1.50	2.50
1990 Proof; 3 known	—	Value: 575				

Snake's tongue straight

KM# 479.1   25 PESOS
22.5000 g., 0.7200 Silver 0.5208 oz. ASW, 38 mm.
Obv: National arms, eagle left **Rev:** Olympic rings below dancing native left, numeral design in background **Note:** Type I, Rings aligned.

Date	Mintage	F	VF	XF	Unc	BU
1968	27,182,000	—	—	BV	7.50	8.50

KM# 479.2   25 PESOS
22.5000 g., 0.7200 Silver 0.5208 oz. ASW, 38 mm.
Subject: Summer Olympics - Mexico City **Obv:** National arms, eagle left **Rev:** Olympic rings below dancing native left, numeral design in background **Note:** Type II, center ring low.

Date	Mintage	F	VF	XF	Unc	BU
1968	Inc. above	—	BV	7.50	8.50	10.00

Snake's tongue curved

KM# 479.3   25 PESOS
22.5000 g., 0.7200 Silver 0.5208 oz. ASW, 38 mm.
Subject: Summer Olympics - Mexico City **Obv:** National arms, eagle left **Rev:** Olympic rings below dancing native left, numeral design in background **Note:** Snake with long curved or normal tongue. Type III, center rings low.

Date	Mintage	F	VF	XF	Unc	BU
1968	Inc. above	—	BV	7.50	9.50	11.00

KM# 480   25 PESOS
22.5000 g., 0.7200 Silver 0.5208 oz. ASW, 38 mm.
Obv: National arms, eagle left **Rev:** Bust facing

Date	Mintage	F	VF	XF	Unc	BU
1972	2,000,000	—	—	BV	7.50	8.50

KM# 497   25 PESOS
7.7760 g., 0.7200 Silver 0.1800 oz. ASW **Subject:** 1986 World Cup Soccer Games **Obv:** National arms, eagle left **Rev:** Value above soccer ball with date below

Date	Mintage	F	VF	XF	Unc	BU
1985	354,000	—	—	—	—	7.50

KM# 503   25 PESOS
8.4060 g., 0.9250 Silver 0.2500 oz. ASW **Subject:** 1986 World Cup Soccer Games **Obv:** National arms, eagle left **Rev:** Pre-Columbian hieroglyphs, ojo de buey, and soccer ball

Date	Mintage	F	VF	XF	Unc	BU
1985 Proof	277,000	Value: 12.00				

KM# 514   25 PESOS
8.4060 g., 0.9250 Silver 0.2500 oz. ASW **Subject:** 1986 World Cup Soccer Games **Obv:** National arms, eagle left **Rev:** Value above soccer ball

Date	Mintage	F	VF	XF	Unc	BU
1985 Proof	234,000	Value: 12.00				

KM# 519   25 PESOS
8.4060 g., 0.9250 Silver 0.2500 oz. ASW **Subject:** 1986 World Cup Soccer Games **Obv:** National arms, eagle left **Rev:** Soccer ball within net, date and value to left

Date	Mintage	F	VF	XF	Unc	BU
1986 Proof	—	Value: 12.00				

KM# 497a   25 PESOS
8.4060 g., 0.9250 Silver 0.2500 oz. ASW **Subject:** 1986 World Cup Soccer Games **Obv:** National arms, eagle left **Rev:** Value above soccerball with date below **Note:** Without fineness statement-reverse description

Date	Mintage	F	VF	XF	Unc	BU
1986 Proof	—	Value: 12.00				

KM# 481   50 PESOS
41.6666 g., 0.9000 Gold 1.2056 oz. AGW, 37 mm.
Subject: Centennial of Independence **Obv:** National arms **Rev:** Winged Victory **Edge:** Reeded **Note:** During 1949-1972 a total of 3,975,654 pieces were restruck, most likely dated 1947. In 1996 matte restrikes were produced. Mint mark Mo.

Date	Mintage	F	VF	XF	Unc	BU
1921	180,000	—	—	BV	1,150	1,200
1922	463,000	—	—	BV	1,150	1,200
1923	432,000	—	—	BV	1,150	1,200
1924	439,000	—	—	BV	1,150	1,200
1925	716,000	—	—	BV	1,150	1,200
1926	600,000	—	—	BV	1,150	1,200
1927	606,000	—	—	BV	1,150	1,200
1928	538,000	—	—	BV	1,150	1,200
1929	458,000	—	—	BV	1,150	1,200
1930	372,000	—	—	BV	1,150	1,200
1931	137,000	—	—	BV	1,150	1,200
1944	593,000	—	—	BV	1,150	1,200
1945	1,012,000	—	—	BV	1,150	1,200
1946	1,588,000	—	—	BV	1,150	1,200
1947	309,000	—	—	—	BV+3%	—
1947 Specimen	—	—	—	—	—	—

Note: Value, $6,500

KM# 482   50 PESOS
41.6666 g., 0.9000 Gold 1.2056 oz. AGW, 39 mm.
Obv: National arms **Rev:** Winged Victory

Date	Mintage	F	VF	XF	Unc	BU
1943	89,000	—	—	—	BV	1,150

KM# 490   50 PESOS
19.8400 g., Copper-Nickel, 35 mm. **Subject:** Coyolxauhqui **Obv:** National arms, eagle left **Rev:** Value to right of artistic designs **Edge:** Reeded **Note:** Doubled die examples of 1982 and 1983 dates exist.

Date	Mintage	F	VF	XF	Unc	BU
1982	222,890,000	—	1.00	2.50	5.00	6.00
1983	45,000,000	—	1.50	3.00	6.00	6.50
1983 Proof	1,051	Value: 40.00				
1984	73,537,000	—	1.00	1.35	3.50	4.00
1984 Proof; 4 known	—	Value: 750				

KM# 495   50 PESOS
Copper-Nickel, 23.5 mm. **Subject:** Benito Juarez **Obv:** National arms, eagle left **Rev:** Bust 1/4 left with diagonal value at left **Edge:** Reeded

Date	Mintage	F	VF	XF	Unc	BU
1984	94,216,000	—	0.65	1.25	2.70	3.00
1985	296,000,000	—	0.25	0.45	1.25	2.00
1986	50,000,000	—	6.00	10.00	12.00	14.00
1987	210,000,000	—	0.25	0.45	1.00	1.25
1988	80,200,000	—	6.25	9.00	13.50	15.50

KM# 495a   50 PESOS
Stainless Steel, 23.5 mm. **Subject:** Benito Juarez **Obv:** National arms, eagle left **Rev:** Bust 1/4 left with diagonal value at left **Edge:** Plain

Date	Mintage	F	VF	XF	Unc	BU
1988	353,300,000	—	—	0.20	1.25	1.75
1990	—	—	—	0.30	1.00	2.00
1992	—	—	—	0.25	1.00	2.75

KM# 515   50 PESOS
16.8310 g., 0.9250 Silver 0.5005 oz. ASW **Subject:** 1986 World Cup Soccer Games **Obv:** National arms, eagle left **Rev:** Value to right of soccer player

Date	Mintage	F	VF	XF	Unc	BU
1985 Proof	234,000	Value: 20.00				

KM# 498   50 PESOS
15.5520 g., 0.7200 Silver 0.3600 oz. ASW **Subject:** 1986 World Cup Soccer Games **Obv:** National arms, eagle left **Rev:** Pair of feet and soccer ball

Date	Mintage	F	VF	XF	Unc	BU
1985	347,000	—	—	—	—	6.50

KM# 498a   50 PESOS
16.8310 g., 0.9250 Silver 0.5005 oz. ASW **Subject:** 1986 World Cup Soccer Games **Obv:** National arms, eagle left **Rev:** Without fineness statement

Date	Mintage	F	VF	XF	Unc	BU
1986 Proof	10,000	Value: 20.00				

KM# 523   50 PESOS
16.8310 g., 0.9250 Silver 0.5005 oz. ASW **Subject:** 1986 World Cup Soccer Games **Obv:** National arms, eagle left **Rev:** Value to left of soccer balls

Date	Mintage	F	VF	XF	Unc	BU
1986 Proof	190,000	Value: 20.00				

KM# 532   50 PESOS
15.5500 g., 0.9990 Silver 0.4994 oz. ASW **Subject:** 50th Anniversary - Nationalization of Oil Industry **Obv:** National arms, eagle left **Rev:** Monument

Date	Mintage	F	VF	XF	Unc	BU
ND(1988)	30,000	—	—	—	20.00	22.00

KM# 504   50 PESOS
16.8310 g., 0.9250 Silver 0.5005 oz. ASW **Subject:** 1986 World Cup Soccer Games **Obv:** National arms, eagle left **Rev:** Stylized athlete as soccer forerunner

Date	Mintage	F	VF	XF	Unc	BU
1985 Proof	347,000	Value: 20.00				

| Low 7's | High 7's |

KM# 483.1   100 PESOS
27.7700 g., 0.7200 Silver 0.6428 oz. ASW, 39 mm.
Obv: National arms, eagle left **Rev:** Bust facing, sloping right shoulder, round left shoulder with no clothing folds **Edge:** Reeded

Date	Mintage	F	VF	XF	Unc	BU
1977 Low 7's	5,225,000	—	—	BV	9.50	11.50
1977 High 7's	Inc. above	—	—	BV	9.50	12.00

KM# 483.2   100 PESOS
27.7700 g., 0.7200 Silver 0.6428 oz. ASW, 39 mm.
Obv: National arms, eagle left **Rev:** Bust facing, higher right shoulder, left shoulder with clothing folds. **Note:** Mintage inc. KM#483.1

Date	Mintage	F	VF	XF	Unc	BU
1977 Date in line	—	—	—	BV	9.25	10.00
1978	9,879,000	—	—	BV	9.50	11.50
1979	784,000	—	—	BV	9.50	11.50
1979 Proof	—	Value: 650				

KM# 493   100 PESOS
Aluminum-Bronze, 26.5 mm. **Obv:** National arms, eagle left **Rev:** Head 1/4 right with diagonal value at right

Date	Mintage	F	VF	XF	Unc	BU
1984	227,809,000	—	0.45	0.60	2.50	4.00
1985	377,423,000	—	0.30	0.50	2.00	3.00
1986	43,000,000	—	1.00	2.50	4.75	7.50
1987	165,000,000	—	0.60	1.25	2.25	3.00
1988	433,100,000	—	0.30	0.50	2.00	2.75
1989	—	—	0.35	0.65	2.00	2.75
1990	—	—	0.15	0.40	1.50	2.50
1990 Proof; 1 known	—	Value: 650				
1991	—	—	0.15	0.25	1.00	2.50
1992	—	—	0.30	0.75	1.75	3.00

KM# 499   100 PESOS
31.1030 g., 0.7200 Silver 0.7200 oz. ASW **Subject:** 1986 World Cup Soccer Games **Obv:** National arms, eagle left **Rev:** Value above artistic designs and soccer ball

Date	Mintage	F	VF	XF	Unc	BU
1985	302,000	—	—	—	—	15.00

KM# 499a   100 PESOS
32.6250 g., 0.9250 Silver 0.9702 oz. ASW **Subject:** 1986 World Cup Soccer Games **Obv:** National arms, eagle left **Rev:** Without fineness statement

Date	Mintage	F	VF	XF	Unc	BU
1985 Proof	9,006	Value: 30.00				

KM# 505   100 PESOS
32.6250 g., 0.9250 Silver 0.9702 oz. ASW, 38 mm.
Subject: 1986 World Cup Soccer Games **Obv:** National arms, eagle left **Rev:** Without fineness statement

Date	Mintage	F	VF	XF	Unc	BU
1985 Proof	9,006	Value: 30.00				

KM# 521   100 PESOS
32.6250 g., 0.9250 Silver 0.9702 oz. ASW **Subject:** 1986 World Cup Soccer Games **Obv:** National arms, eagle left **Rev:** Without fineness statement

Date	Mintage	F	VF	XF	Unc	BU
1986 Proof	208,000	Value: 30.00				

KM# 524   100 PESOS
32.6250 g., 0.9250 Silver 0.9702 oz. ASW **Subject:** 1986 World Cup Soccer Games **Obv:** National arms, eagle left **Rev:** Without fineness statement

Date	Mintage	F	VF	XF	Unc	BU
1986 Proof	190,000	Value: 30.00				

KM# 537   100 PESOS
32.6250 g., 0.7200 Silver 0.7552 oz. ASW **Subject:** World Wildlife Fund **Obv:** National arms, eagle left **Rev:** Monarch butterflies

Date	Mintage	F	VF	XF	Unc	BU
1987 Proof	Est. 30,000	Value: 50.00				

KM# 533   100 PESOS
31.1030 g., 0.9990 Silver 0.9989 oz. ASW **Subject:** 50th Anniversary - Nationalization of Oil Industry **Obv:** National arms, eagle left **Rev:** Bust facing above sprigs and dates

Date	Mintage	F	VF	XF	Unc	BU
1988	10,000	—	—	—	28.00	40.00

KM# 539   100 PESOS
33.6250 g., 0.9250 Silver 0.9999 oz. ASW **Subject:** Save the Children **Obv:** National arms, eagle left **Rev:** Child flying kite, two others sitting and playing

Date	Mintage	F	VF	XF	Unc	BU
1991 Proof	30,000	Value: 45.00				

KM# 540 100 PESOS
27.0000 g., 0.9250 Silver 0.8029 oz. ASW **Subject:** Ibero - American Series **Obv:** National arms, eagle left within center of assorted arms **Rev:** Maps within circles flanked by pillars above sailboats

Date	Mintage	F	VF	XF	Unc	BU
1991 Proof	50,000	Value: 55.00				
1992 Proof	75,000	Value: 45.00				

KM# 566 100 PESOS
31.1035 g., 0.9990 Silver 0.9990 oz. ASW **Subject:** Save the Vaquita Porpoise **Obv:** National arms, eagle left **Rev:** Swimming vaquita porpoise

Date	Mintage	F	VF	XF	Unc	BU
1992 Proof	—	Value: 45.00				

KM# 509 200 PESOS
Copper-Nickel, 29.5 mm. **Subject:** 175th Anniversary of Independence **Obv:** National arms, eagle left **Rev:** Conjoined busts left

Date	Mintage	F	VF	XF	Unc	BU
1985	75,000,000	—	—	0.25	3.00	4.00

KM# 510 200 PESOS
Copper-Nickel, 29.5 mm. **Subject:** 75th Anniversary of 1910 Revolution **Obv:** National arms, eagle left **Rev:** Conjoined heads left below building

Date	Mintage	F	VF	XF	Unc	BU
1985	98,590,000	—	—	0.25	3.25	4.50

KM# 525 200 PESOS
Copper-Nickel, 29.5 mm. **Subject:** 1986 World Cup Soccer Games **Obv:** National arms, eagle left **Rev:** Soccer players **Edge:** Reeded

Date	Mintage	F	VF	XF	Unc	BU
1986	50,000,000	—	—	1.00	3.50	4.50

KM# 526 200 PESOS
62.2060 g., 0.9990 Silver 1.9979 oz. ASW **Subject:** 1986 World Cup Soccer Games **Obv:** National arms, eagle left **Rev:** Value above 3 soccer balls

Date	Mintage	F	VF	XF	Unc	BU
1986	50,000	—	—	40.00	50.00	

KM# 500.1 250 PESOS
8.6400 g., 0.9000 Gold 0.2500 oz. AGW **Subject:** 1986 World Cup Soccer Games **Obv:** National arms, eagle left **Rev:** Soccer ball within top 1/2 of design with value, date, and state below

Date	Mintage	F	VF	XF	Unc	BU
1985	100,000	—	—	—	—	260
1986	—	—	—	—	—	260

KM# 500.2 250 PESOS
8.6400 g., 0.9000 Gold 0.2500 oz. AGW **Subject:** 1986 World Cup Soccer Games **Obv:** National arms, eagle left **Rev:** Without fineness statement

Date	Mintage	F	VF	XF	Unc	BU
1985 Proof	4,506	Value: 260				
1986 Proof	—	Value: 260				

KM# 506.1 250 PESOS
8.6400 g., 0.9000 Gold 0.2500 oz. AGW **Subject:** 1986 World Cup Soccer Games **Obv:** National arms, eagle left **Rev:** Equestrian left within circle

Date	Mintage	F	VF	XF	Unc	BU
1985	88,000	—	—	—	—	255

KM# 506.2 250 PESOS
8.6400 g., 0.9000 Gold 0.2500 oz. AGW **Subject:** 1986 World Cup Soccer Games **Obv:** National arms, eagle left **Rev:** Without fineness statement

Date	Mintage	F	VF	XF	Unc	BU
1985 Proof	Est. 80,000	Value: 255				

KM# 501.1 500 PESOS
17.2800 g., 0.9000 Gold 0.5000 oz. AGW **Subject:** 1986 World Cup Soccer Games **Obv:** National arms, eagle left **Rev:** Soccer player to right within emblem

Date	Mintage	F	VF	XF	Unc	BU
1985	102,000	—	—	—	—	485
1986	—	—	—	—	—	485

KM# 501.2 500 PESOS
17.2800 g., 0.9000 Gold 0.5000 oz. AGW **Subject:** 1986 World Cup Soccer Games **Obv:** National arms, eagle left **Rev:** Without fineness statement

Date	Mintage	F	VF	XF	Unc	BU
1985 Proof	5,506	Value: 485				
1986 Proof	—	Value: 485				

KM# 507.1 500 PESOS
17.2800 g., 0.9000 Gold 0.5000 oz. AGW **Subject:** 1986 World Cup Soccer Games **Obv:** National arms, eagle left **Rev:** Soccer ball within emblem flanked by value and date

Date	Mintage	F	VF	XF	Unc	BU
1985	—	—	—	—	—	485

KM# 507.2 500 PESOS
17.2800 g., 0.9000 Gold 0.5000 oz. AGW **Subject:** 1986 World Cup Soccer Games **Obv:** National arms, eagle left **Rev:** Without fineness statement

Date	Mintage	F	VF	XF	Unc	BU
1985 Proof	—	Value: 475				

KM# 511 500 PESOS
33.4500 g., 0.9250 Silver 0.9947 oz. ASW **Subject:** 75th Anniversary of 1910 Revolution **Obv:** National arms, eagle left **Rev:** Conjoined heads left below building

Date	Mintage	F	VF	XF	Unc	BU
1985 Proof	40,000	Value: 35.00				

KM# 529 500 PESOS
Copper-Nickel, 28.5 mm. **Obv:** National arms, eagle left **Rev:** Head 1/4 right

Date	Mintage	F	VF	XF	Unc	BU
1986	20,000,000	—	—	1.00	3.25	3.50
1987	180,000,000	—	—	0.75	2.25	2.50
1988	230,000,000	—	—	0.50	2.25	2.50
1988 Proof; 2 known	—	Value: 650				
1989	—	—	—	0.75	2.25	3.00
1992	—	—	—	1.00	2.25	3.50

KM# 534 500 PESOS
17.2800 g., 0.9000 Gold 0.5000 oz. AGW **Subject:** 50th Anniversary - Nationalization of Oil Industry **Obv:** National arms, eagle left **Rev:** Monument **Note:** Similar to 5000 Pesos, KM#531.

Date	Mintage	F	VF	XF	Unc	BU
1988	—	—	—	—	—	485

KM# 513 1000 PESOS
17.2800 g., 0.9000 Gold 0.5000 oz. AGW **Subject:** 175th Anniversary of Independence **Obv:** National arms, eagle left **Rev:** Conjoined heads left below value

Date	Mintage	F	VF	XF	Unc	BU
1985 Proof	—	Value: 485				

KM# 527 1000 PESOS
31.1050 g., 0.9990 Gold 0.9990 oz. AGW **Subject:** 1986 World Cup Soccer Games **Obv:** National arms, eagle left **Rev:** Value above soccer ball and two hemispheres

Date	Mintage	F	VF	XF	Unc	BU
1986	—	—	—	—	—	950

KM# 536 1000 PESOS
15.0000 g., Aluminum-Bronze, 30.5 mm. **Obv:** National arms, eagle left **Rev:** Bust 1/4 left with diagonal value at left **Note:** Juana de Asbaje

Date	Mintage	F	VF	XF	Unc	BU
1988	229,300,000	—	0.85	2.00	4.25	5.75
1989	—	—	0.85	2.00	4.25	5.75
1990	—	—	0.85	2.00	4.00	5.50
1990 Proof; 2 known	Value: 550					
1991	—	—	1.00	2.00	3.00	7.00
1992	—	—	1.00	2.00	3.00	7.00

KM# 535 1000 PESOS
34.5590 g., 0.9999 Gold 0.9999 oz. AGW **Subject:** 50th Anniversary - Nationalization of Oil Industry **Obv:** National arms, eagle left **Rev:** Portrait of Cardenas **Note:** Similar to 5000 Pesos, KM#531.

Date	Mintage	F	VF	XF	Unc	BU
1988 Proof	—	Value: 950				

KM# 643 1000 PESOS
Aluminum-Bronze, 22 mm. **Obv:** National arms, eagle left **Rev:** Stylized boat and "ATLAN" above denomination **Note:** Unissued type due to currency reform.

Date	Mintage	F	VF	XF	Unc	BU
1991Mo	—	—	—	—	15.00	—

KM# 528 2000 PESOS
62.2000 g., 0.9990 Gold 1.9977 oz. AGW **Subject:** 1986 World Cup Soccer Games **Obv:** National arms, eagle left **Rev:** Value above soccer ball and two hemispheres

Date	Mintage	F	VF	XF	Unc	BU
1986	—	—	—	—	—	1,950

KM# 531 5000 PESOS
Copper-Nickel, 33.5 mm. **Subject:** 50th Anniversary - Nationalization of Oil Industry **Obv:** National arms, eagle left **Rev:** Monument above dates with diagonal value at left

Date	Mintage	F	VF	XF	Unc	BU
ND(1988)	50,000,000	—	—	4.75	7.75	10.00

REFORM COINAGE
1 New Peso = 1000 Old Pesos

KM# 546 5 CENTAVOS
1.5900 g., Stainless Steel, 15.58 mm. **Obv:** National arms **Rev:** Large value **Edge:** Plain

Date	Mintage	F	VF	XF	Unc	BU
1992	136,800,000	—	—	0.15	0.20	0.25
1993	234,000,000	—	—	0.15	0.20	0.25
1994	125,000,000	—	—	0.15	0.20	0.25
1995	195,000,000	—	—	0.15	0.20	0.25
1995 Proof	6,981	Value: 0.50				
1996	104,831,000	—	—	0.15	0.20	0.25
1997	153,675,000	—	—	0.15	0.20	0.25
1998	64,417,000	—	—	0.15	0.20	0.25
1999	9,949,000	—	—	0.15	0.20	0.25
2000Mo	10,871,000	—	—	0.15	0.20	0.25

KM# 547 10 CENTAVOS
2.0300 g., Stainless Steel, 17 mm. **Obv:** National arms, eagle left **Rev:** Value

Date	Mintage	F	VF	XF	Unc	BU
1992	121,250,000	—	—	0.20	0.30	0.35
1993	755,000,000	—	—	0.20	0.25	0.30
1994	557,000,000	—	—	0.20	0.25	0.30
1995	560,000,000	—	—	0.20	0.25	0.30
1995 Proof	6,981	Value: 0.50				
1996	594,216,000	—	—	0.20	0.25	0.30
1997	581,622,000	—	—	0.20	0.25	0.30
1998	602,667,000	—	—	0.20	0.25	0.30
1999	488,346,000	—	—	0.20	0.25	0.30
2000	577,546,000	—	—	0.20	0.30	0.35

KM# 548 20 CENTAVOS
Aluminum-Bronze, 19 mm. **Obv:** National arms, eagle left **Rev:** Value and date within 3/4 wreath

Date	Mintage	F	VF	XF	Unc	BU
1992	95,000,000	—	—	0.25	0.35	0.40
1993	95,000,000	—	—	0.25	0.35	0.40
1994	105,000,000	—	—	0.25	0.35	0.40
1995	180,000,000	—	—	0.25	0.35	0.40
1995 Proof	6,981	Value: 0.75				
1996	54,896,000	—	—	0.25	0.35	0.40
1997	178,807,000	—	—	0.25	0.35	0.40
1998	223,847,000	—	—	0.25	0.35	0.40
1999	233,753,000	—	—	0.25	0.35	0.40
2000	223,973,000	—	—	0.25	0.35	0.40

KM# 549 50 CENTAVOS
Aluminum-Bronze, 22 mm. **Obv:** National arms, eagle left **Rev:** Value and date within 1/2 designed wreath

Date	Mintage	F	VF	XF	Unc	BU
1992	120,150,000	—	—	0.45	0.85	1.00
1993	330,000,000	—	—	0.45	0.75	1.00
1994	100,000,000	—	—	0.45	0.75	1.00
1995	60,000,000	—	—	0.45	0.75	1.00
1995 Proof	6,981	Value: 0.90				
1996	69,956,000	—	—	0.45	0.75	1.00
1997	129,029,000	—	—	0.45	0.75	1.00
1998	223,605,000	—	—	0.45	0.75	1.00
1999	89,516,000	—	—	0.45	0.75	1.00
2000	135,112,000	—	—	0.45	0.75	1.00

KM# 550 NUEVO PESO
3.9400 g., Bi-Metallic Aluminum-Bronze center in Stainless Steel ring, 22 mm. **Obv:** National arms, eagle left **Rev:** Value

Date	Mintage	F	VF	XF	Unc	BU
1992	144,000,000	—	—	0.60	1.50	2.25
1993	329,860,000	—	—	0.60	1.50	2.25
1994	221,000,000	—	—	0.60	1.50	2.25
1995 Small date	125,000,000	—	—	0.60	1.50	2.25
1995 Large date	Inc. above	—	—	0.60	1.50	2.25
1995 Proof	6,981	Value: 2.75				

KM# 603 PESO
3.9500 g., Bi-Metallic Stainless-steel ring in Aluminum Bronze center, 21 mm. **Obv:** National arms, eagle left within circle **Rev:** Value and date within circle **Note:** Similar to KM#550 but without N.

Date	Mintage	F	VF	XF	Unc	BU
1996Mo	169,510,000	—	—	—	1.25	2.25
1997Mo	222,870,000	—	—	—	1.25	2.25
1998Mo	261,942,000	—	—	—	1.25	2.25
1999Mo	99,168,000	—	—	—	1.25	2.25
2000Mo	158,379,000	—	—	—	1.25	2.25

KM# 551 2 NUEVO PESOS
Bi-Metallic Aluminum-Bronze center in Stainless Steel ring, 23 mm. **Obv:** National arms, eagle left within circle **Rev:** Value and date within circle with assorted emblems around border

Date	Mintage	F	VF	XF	Unc	BU
1992	60,000,000	—	—	1.00	2.35	2.50
1993	77,000,000	—	—	1.00	2.35	2.50
1994	44,000,000	—	—	1.00	2.35	2.50
1995	20,000,000	—	—	1.00	2.35	2.50
1995 Proof	6,981	Value: 4.50				

KM# 604 2 PESOS
5.2100 g., Bi-Metallic Aluminum-Bronze center in Stainless Steel ring, 23 mm. **Obv:** National arms, eagle left within circle **Rev:** Value and date within center circle of assorted emblems **Note:** Similar to KM#551, but denomination without N.

Date	Mintage	F	VF	XF	Unc	BU
1996Mo	24,902,000	—	—	—	2.35	2.50
1997Mo	34,560,000	—	—	—	2.35	2.50
1998Mo	104,138,000	—	—	—	2.35	2.50
1999Mo	34,713,000	—	—	—	2.35	2.50
2000Mo	69,322,000	—	—	—	2.35	2.50

KM# 552 5 NUEVO PESOS
Bi-Metallic Aluminum-Bronze center in Stainless Steel ring, 25.5 mm. **Obv:** National arms, eagle left within circle **Rev:** Value and date within circle with bow below

Date	Mintage	F	VF	XF	Unc	BU
1992	70,000,000	—	—	2.00	4.00	4.50
1993	168,240,000	—	—	2.00	4.00	4.50
1994	58,000,000	—	—	2.00	4.00	4.50
1995 Proof	6,981	Value: 25.00				

KM# 588 5 NUEVO PESOS
27.0000 g., 0.9250 Silver 0.8029 oz. ASW **Subject:** Environmental Protection **Obv:** National arms, eagle left within center of past and present arms **Rev:** Pacific Ridley Sea Turtle

Date	Mintage	F	VF	XF	Unc	BU
1994 Proof	20,000	Value: 50.00				

KM# 629 5 PESOS
27.0000 g., 0.9250 Silver 0.8029 oz. ASW **Subject:** Jarabe Tapatio **Obv:** National arms, eagle left within center of assorted arms **Rev:** Mexican dancers

Date	Mintage	F	VF	XF	Unc	BU
1997 Proof	20,000	Value: 275				
1998 Proof	—	Value: 275				

KM# 605 5 PESOS
Bi-Metallic Aluminum-Bronze center in Stainless Steel ring, 25.5 mm. **Obv:** National arms, eagle left within circle **Rev:** Value within circle **Note:** Similar to KM#552 but denomination without N.

Date	Mintage	F	VF	XF	Unc	BU
1997Mo	39,468,000	—	—	3.00	4.00	5.00
1998Mo	103,729,000	—	—	3.00	4.00	5.00
1999Mo	59,427,000	—	—	3.00	4.00	5.00
2000Mo	20,869,000	—	—	3.00	4.00	5.00

KM# 627 5 PESOS
31.1035 g., 0.9990 Silver 0.9990 oz. ASW **Subject:** World Wildlife Fund **Obv:** National arms, eagle left **Rev:** Wolf with pup

Date	Mintage	F	VF	XF	Unc	BU
1998 Proof	Est. 15,000	Value: 75.00				

KM# 630 5 PESOS
31.1800 g., 0.9990 Silver 1.0014 oz. ASW **Subject:** Millennium Series **Obv:** National arms, eagle left within center of past and present arms **Rev:** Butterfly flanked by sprigs above hands

Date	Mintage	F	VF	XF	Unc	BU
1999-2000 Proof	75,000	Value: 45.00				

KM# 631 5 PESOS
31.1800 g., 0.9990 Silver 1.0014 oz. ASW **Subject:** Millennium Series **Obv:** National arms, eagle left within center of past and present arms **Rev:** Stylized dove as hand of peace

Date	Mintage	F	VF	XF	Unc	BU
1999-2000 Proof	75,000	Value: 40.00				

KM# 632 5 PESOS
31.1800 g., 0.9990 Silver 1.0014 oz. ASW **Subject:** Millennium Series **Obv:** National arms, eagle left within center of past and present arms **Rev:** Aztec bird design and value

Date	Mintage	F	VF	XF	Unc	BU
1999-2000 Proof	75,000	Value: 40.00				

KM# 635 5 PESOS
19.6000 g., 0.9250 Silver 0.5829 oz. ASW **Subject:** Millennium Series **Obv:** National arms, eagle left **Rev:** Naval training ship Cuauhtemoc sailing into world globe

Date	Mintage	F	VF	XF	Unc	BU
1999	—	Value: 35.00				

KM# 640 5 PESOS
31.1030 g., 0.9990 Silver 0.9989 oz. ASW, 40 mm. **Subject:** UNICEF **Obv:** National arms, eagle left **Rev:** Two children flying kite **Edge:** Reeded

Date	Mintage	F	VF	XF	Unc	BU
1999 Proof	—	Value: 45.00				

KM# 652 5 PESOS
31.1710 g., 0.9990 Silver 1.0011 oz. ASW, 40 mm. **Series:** Endangered Wildlife **Subject:** Aguila Real **Obv:** National arms, eagle left within center of past and present arms **Rev:** Golden Eagle on branch

Date	Mintage	F	VF	XF	Unc	BU
2000	50,000	—	—	—	32.50	—

KM# 655 5 PESOS
31.1710 g., 0.9990 Silver 1.0011 oz. ASW, 40 mm. **Series:** Endangered Wildlife **Subject:** Cocodrilo de Rio **Obv:** National arms, eagle left within center of past and present arms **Rev:** American Crocodile

Date	Mintage	F	VF	XF	Unc	BU
2000	50,000	—	—	—	32.50	—

KM# 656 5 PESOS
31.1710 g., 0.9990 Silver 1.0011 oz. ASW, 40 mm. **Series:** Endangered Wildlife **Subject:** Nutria de Rio **Obv:** National arms, eagle left within center of past and present arms **Rev:** Neotropical River Otter

Date	Mintage	F	VF	XF	Unc	BU
2000	50,000	—	—	—	32.50	—

KM# 657 5 PESOS
31.1710 g., 0.9990 Silver 1.0011 oz. ASW, 40 mm. **Series:** Endangered Wildlife - Berrendo **Obv:** National arms, eagle left within center of past and present arms **Rev:** Peninsular Pronghorn, giant cardon cactus in back

Date	Mintage	F	VF	XF	Unc	BU
2000	50,000	—	—	—	32.50	—

KM# 670 5 PESOS
27.0000 g., 0.9250 Silver 0.8029 oz. ASW, 40 mm. **Series:** Ibero-America **Obv:** National arms, eagle left within center of past and present arms **Rev:** Cowboy trick riding two horses **Edge:** Reeded

Date	Mintage	F	VF	XF	Unc	BU
2000 Proof	—	Value: 45.00				

KM# 553 10 NUEVO PESOS
11.1300 g., Bi-Metallic 0.925 Silver center, .1667 oz. ASW within Aluminum-Bronze ring, 27.95 mm. **Obv:** National arms **Obv. Leg.:** Estados Unidos Mexicanos **Rev:** Assorted shields within circle **Edge:** Reeded

Date	Mintage	F	VF	XF	Unc	BU
1992	20,000,000	—	—	—	7.50	8.50
1993	47,981,000	—	—	—	7.50	8.50
1994	15,000,000	—	—	—	7.50	8.50
1995	15,000,000	—	—	—	7.50	8.50
1995 Proof	6,981	Value: 15.00				

KM# 616　10 PESOS
10.3500 g., Bi-Metallic Copper-Nickel-Brass center within Brass ring, 27.95 mm.　**Obv:** National arms **Obv. Leg.:** ESTADOS UNIDOS MEXICANOS **Rev:** Aztec design

Date	Mintage	F	VF	XF	Unc	BU
1997Mo	44,837,000	—	—	—	5.00	6.50
1998Mo	203,735,000	—	—	—	5.00	6.50
1999Mo	29,842,000	—	—	—	5.00	6.50

KM# 633　10 PESOS
62.0300 g., 0.9990 Silver 1.9922 oz. ASW　**Subject:** Millennium Series **Obv:** National arms, eagle left within center of past and present arms **Rev:** Ancient and modern buildings within circle

Date	Mintage	F	VF	XF	Unc	BU
1999-2000 Proof	75,000	Value: 47.50				

KM# 636　10 PESOS
10.3500 g., Bi-Metallic Copper-Nickel center in Brass ring, 28 mm.　**Series:** Millennium **Obv:** National arms **Obv. Leg.:** ESTADOS UNIDOS MEXICANOS **Rev:** Aztec carving **Edge:** Lettered **Edge:** ANO and date repeated 3 times

Date	Mintage	F	VF	XF	Unc	BU
2000Mo	24,839,000	—	—	—	5.00	6.50

KM# 561　20 NUEVO PESOS
16.9200 g., Bi-Metallic 0.925 Silver 16.9g, (.2500 oz. ASW) center within Aluminum-Bronze ring, 31.86 mm.　**Obv:** National arms **Obv. Leg.:** ESTADOS UNIDOS MEXICANOS **Rev:** Head of Hidalgo left within wreath **Edge:** Reeded

Date	Mintage	F	VF	XF	Unc	BU
1993Mo	25,000,000	—	—	—	12.00	15.00
1994Mo	5,000,000	—	—	—	12.00	15.00
1995Mo	5,000,000	—	—	—	12.00	15.00

KM# 641　20 PESOS
6.2210 g., 0.9990 Gold 0.1998 oz. AGW, 21.9 mm.　**Subject:** UNICEF **Obv:** National arms, eagle left **Rev:** Child playing with lasso **Edge:** Reeded

Date	Mintage	F	VF	XF	Unc	BU
1999 Proof	—	Value: 275				

KM# 637　20 PESOS
Bi-Metallic Copper-Nickel center within Brass ring, 32 mm.　**Subject:** Xiuhtecuhtli **Obv:** National arms, eagle left within circle **Rev:** Aztec with torch within spiked circle

Date	Mintage	F	VF	XF	Unc	BU
2000	14,890,000	—	—	—	15.00	17.50

KM# 638　20 PESOS
Bi-Metallic Copper-Nickel center within Brass ring, 32 mm.　**Obv:** National arms, eagle left within circle **Rev:** Head 1/4 right within circle

Date	Mintage	F	VF	XF	Unc	BU
2000	14,943,000	—	—	—	15.00	17.50

KM# 571　50 NUEVO PESOS
34.1100 g., Bi-Metallic 0.925 Silver .5000 ASW center within Brass ring, 38.87 mm.　**Subject:** Nino Heroes **Obv:** National arms **Obv. Leg.:** ESTADOS UNIDOS MEXICANOS **Rev:** Six heads facing with date at upper right, all within circle and 1/2 wreath **Edge:** Reeded

Date	Mintage	F	VF	XF	Unc	BU
1993Mo	2,000,000	—	—	—	25.00	28.00
1994Mo	1,500,000	—	—	—	25.00	28.00
1995Mo	1,500,000	—	—	—	25.00	28.00

SILVER BULLION COINAGE
Libertad Series

KM# 542　1/20 ONZA (1/20 Troy Ounce of Silver)
1.5551 g., 0.9990 Silver 0.0499 oz. ASW　**Obv:** National arms, eagle left **Rev:** Winged Victory

Date	Mintage	F	VF	XF	Unc	BU
1991Mo	50,017	—	—	—	—	5.50
1992Mo	295,783	—	—	—	—	4.50
1992Mo Proof	5,000	Value: 10.00				
1993Mo	100,000	—	—	—	—	4.50
1993Mo Proof	—	Value: 10.00				
1994Mo	90,100	—	—	—	—	4.50
1994Mo Proof	10,000	Value: 10.00				
1995Mo	50,000	—	—	—	—	5.50
1995Mo Proof	2,000	Value: 12.00				

KM# 609　1/20 ONZA (1/20 Troy Ounce of Silver)
1.5551 g., 0.9990 Silver 0.0499 oz. ASW　**Obv:** National arms, eagle left **Rev:** Winged Victory

Date	Mintage	F	VF	XF	Unc	BU
1996Mo	50,000	—	—	—	—	10.00
1996Mo Proof	1,000	Value: 15.00				
1997Mo	20,000	—	—	—	—	10.00
1997Mo Proof	800	Value: 15.00				
1998Mo	6,400	—	—	—	—	10.00
1998Mo Proof	300	Value: 18.50				
1999Mo	8,401	—	—	—	—	12.00
1999Mo Proof	600	Value: 16.50				
2000Mo	63,750	—	—	—	—	12.00
2000Mo Proof	1,200	Value: 16.50				

KM# 543　1/10 ONZA (1/10 Troy Ounce of Silver)
3.1103 g., 0.9990 Silver 0.0999 oz. ASW　**Obv:** National arms, eagle left **Rev:** Winged Victory

Date	Mintage	F	VF	XF	Unc	BU
1991Mo	50,017	—	—	—	—	7.50
1992Mo	299,983	—	—	—	—	6.50
1992Mo Proof	5,000	Value: 12.00				
1993Mo	100,000	—	—	—	—	6.50
1993Mo Proof	—	Value: 12.00				
1994Mo	90,100	—	—	—	—	6.50
1994Mo Proof	10,000	Value: 12.00				
1995Mo	50,000	—	—	—	—	7.50
1995Mo Proof	2,000	Value: 13.50				

KM# 610　1/10 ONZA (1/10 Troy Ounce of Silver)
3.1103 g., 0.9990 Silver 0.0999 oz. ASW　**Obv:** National arms, eagle left **Rev:** Winged Victory

Date	Mintage	F	VF	XF	Unc	BU
1996Mo	50,000	—	—	—	—	12.00
1996Mo Proof	1,000	Value: 17.50				
1997Mo	20,000	—	—	—	—	12.00
1997Mo Proof	800	Value: 17.50				
1998Mo	6,400	—	—	—	—	12.00
1998Mo Proof	300	Value: 22.50				
1999Mo	8,400	—	—	—	—	14.00
1999Mo Proof	600	Value: 20.00				
2000Mo	33,750	—	—	—	—	14.00
2000Mo Proof	1,300	Value: 20.00				

KM# 544　1/4 ONZA (1/4 Troy Ounce of Silver)
7.7758 g., 0.9990 Silver 0.2497 oz. ASW　**Obv:** National arms, eagle left **Rev:** Winged Victory

Date	Mintage	F	VF	XF	Unc	BU
1991Mo	50,017	—	—	—	—	9.00
1992Mo	104,000	—	—	—	—	7.50
1992Mo Proof	5,000	Value: 15.00				
1993Mo	86,500	—	—	—	—	7.50
1993Mo Proof	—	Value: 15.00				
1994Mo	90,100	—	—	—	—	7.50
1994Mo Proof	15,000	Value: 15.00				
1995Mo	50,000	—	—	—	—	9.00
1995Mo Proof	2,000	Value: 16.50				

KM# 611 · 1/4 ONZA (1/4 Troy Ounce of Silver)

7.7758 g., 0.9990 Silver 0.2497 oz. ASW **Obv:** National arms, eagle left **Rev:** Winged Victory

Date	Mintage	F	VF	XF	Unc	BU
1996Mo	50,000	—	—	—	—	15.00
1996Mo Proof	1,000	Value: 20.00				
1997Mo	20,000	—	—	—	—	15.00
1997Mo Proof	800	Value: 20.00				
1998Mo	6,400	—	—	—	—	15.00
1998Mo Proof	300	Value: 32.50				
1999Mo	7,400	—	—	—	—	18.00
1999Mo Proof	600	Value: 25.00				
2000Mo	21,000	—	—	—	—	18.00
2000Mo Proof	850	Value: 25.00				

KM# 545 1/2 ONZA (1/2 Troy Ounce of Silver)

15.5517 g., 0.9990 Silver 0.4995 oz. ASW **Obv:** National arms, eagle left **Rev:** Winged Victory

Date	Mintage	F	VF	XF	Unc	BU
1991Mo	50,618	—	—	—	—	12.00
1992Mo	119,000	—	—	—	—	10.00
1992Mo Proof	5,000	Value: 17.50				
1993Mo	71,500	—	—	—	—	10.00
1993Mo Proof	—	Value: 17.50				
1994Mo	90,100	—	—	—	—	10.00
1994Mo Proof	15,000	Value: 17.50				
1995Mo	50,000	—	—	—	—	10.00
1995Mo Proof	2,000	Value: 18.50				

KM# 612 1/2 ONZA (1/2 Troy Ounce of Silver)

15.5517 g., 0.9990 Silver 0.4995 oz. ASW **Obv:** National arms, eagle left **Rev:** Winged Victory

Date	Mintage	F	VF	XF	Unc	BU
1996Mo	50,999	—	—	—	—	20.00
1996Mo Proof	1,000	Value: 30.00				
1997Mo	20,000	—	—	—	—	20.00
1997Mo Proof	800	Value: 30.00				
1998Mo	6,400	—	—	—	—	22.00
1998Mo Proof	300	Value: 45.00				
1999Mo	7,400	—	—	—	—	22.00
1999Mo Proof	600	Value: 35.00				
2000Mo	20,000	—	—	—	—	22.00
2000Mo Proof	700	Value: 35.00				

KM# 494.1 ONZA (Troy Ounce of Silver)

31.1000 g., 0.9990 Silver 0.9988 oz. ASW **Subject:** Libertad **Obv:** National arms, eagle left **Rev:** Winged Victory

Date	Mintage	F	VF	XF	Unc	BU
1982Mo	1,049,680	—	—	—	BV	27.00
1983Mo	1,001,768	—	—	—	BV	27.00
1983Mo Proof	998	Value: 225				
1984Mo	1,014,000	—	—	—	BV	27.00
1985Mo	2,017,000	—	—	—	BV	27.00
1986Mo	1,699,426	—	—	—	BV	27.00
1986Mo Proof	30,006	Value: 30.00				
1987Mo	500,000	—	—	—	BV	50.00
1987Mo	Inc. above	—	—	—	—	65.00
Doubled die						
1987Mo Proof	12,000	Value: 45.00				
1988Mo	1,500,500	—	—	—	BV	47.00
1989Mo	1,396,500	—	—	—	BV	27.00
1989Mo Proof	10,000	Value: 70.00				

KM# 494.2 ONZA (Troy Ounce of Silver)

31.1000 g., 0.9990 Silver 0.9988 oz. ASW **Obv:** National arms, eagle left **Rev:** Winged Victory **Edge:** Reeded

Date	Mintage	F	VF	XF	Unc	BU
1988Mo Proof	10,000	Value: 75.00				
1990Mo	1,200,000	—	—	—	BV	27.00
1990Mo Proof	10,000	Value: 63.00				
1991Mo	1,650,518	—	—	—	BV	30.00

KM# 494.5 ONZA (Troy Ounce of Silver)

31.1000 g., 0.9990 Silver 0.9988 oz. ASW **Subject:** Libertad **Obv:** National arms, eagle left **Rev:** Winged Victory **Edge:** Reeded edge **Note:** Mule

Date	Mintage	F	VF	XF	Unc	BU
1991Mo Proof	10,000	Value: 57.00				

KM# 494.3 ONZA (Troy Ounce of Silver)

31.1000 g., 0.9990 Silver 0.9988 oz. ASW **Subject:** Libertad **Obv:** National arms **Rev:** Winged Victory with revised design and lettering **Edge:** Reeded edge **Note:** Mule

Date	Mintage	F	VF	XF	Unc	BU
1991Mo	Inc. above	—	—	—	BV	45.00
1991Mo Proof	10,000	Value: 53.00				
1992Mo	2,458,000	—	—	—	BV	30.00
1992Mo Proof	10,000	Value: 53.00				

KM# 494.4 ONZA (Troy Ounce of Silver)

31.1000 g., 0.9990 Silver 0.9988 oz. ASW **Subject:** Libertad **Obv:** National arms, eagle left **Rev:** Winged Victory with revised design and lettering **Edge:** Reeded edge **Note:** Mule

Date	Mintage	F	VF	XF	Unc	BU
1993Mo	1,000,000	—	—	—	BV	20.00
1993Mo Proof	—	Value: 57.00				
1994Mo	400,000	—	—	—	BV	25.00
1994Mo Proof	10,000	Value: 57.00				
1995Mo	500,000	—	—	—	BV	25.00
1995Mo Proof	2,000	Value: 57.00				

KM# 613 ONZA (Troy Ounce of Silver)

33.6250 g., 0.9250 Silver 0.9999 oz. ASW **Obv:** National arms, eagle left **Rev:** Winged Victory

Date	Mintage	F	VF	XF	Unc	BU
1996Mo	280,001	—	—	—	—	27.00
1996Mo Proof	1,000	Value: 60.00				
1997Mo	119,999	—	—	—	—	27.00
1997Mo Proof	2,500	Value: 60.00				
1998Mo	67,000	—	—	—	—	42.00
1998Mo Proof	500	Value: 85.00				
1999Mo	95,000	—	—	—	—	27.00
1999Mo Proof	600	Value: 70.00				

KM# 639 ONZA (Troy Ounce of Silver)

31.1000 g., 0.9990 Silver 0.9988 oz. ASW **Subject:** Libertad **Obv:** National arms, eagle left within center of past and present arms **Rev:** Winged Victory **Edge:** Reeded

Date	Mintage	F	VF	XF	Unc	BU
2000Mo	396,400	—	—	—	—	28.00
2000Mo Proof	2,000	Value: 60.00				

KM# 614 2 ONZAS (2 Troy Ounces of Silver)

62.2070 g., 0.9990 Silver 1.9979 oz. ASW, 48 mm. **Subject:** Libertad **Obv:** National arms, eagle left within center of past and present arms **Rev:** Winged Victory **Edge:** Reeded

Date	Mintage	F	VF	XF	Unc	BU
1996Mo	50,000	—	—	—	—	35.00
1996Mo Proof	1,000	Value: 65.00				
1997Mo	15,000	—	—	—	—	35.00
1997Mo Proof	1,500	Value: 70.00				
1998Mo	7,000	—	—	—	—	45.00
1998Mo Proof	400	Value: 100				
1999Mo	5,000	—	—	—	—	60.00
1999Mo Proof	280	Value: 175				
2000Mo	12,800	—	—	—	—	60.00
2000Mo Proof	650	Value: 75.00				

KM# 615 5 ONZAS (5 Troy Ounces of Silver)

155.5175 g., 0.9990 Silver 4.9948 oz. ASW, 65 mm. **Subject:** Libertad **Obv:** National arms, eagle left within center of past and present arms **Rev:** Winged Victory **Edge:** Reeded **Note:** Illustration reduced.

Date	Mintage	F	VF	XF	Unc	BU
1996Mo	20,000	—	—	—	—	120
1996Mo Proof	1,000	Value: 200				

Date	Mintage	F	VF	XF	Unc	BU
1997Mo	10,000	—	—	—	—	120
1997Mo Proof	1,500	Value: 200				
1998Mo	3,500	—	—	—	—	220
1998Mo Proof	400	Value: 400				
1999Mo	2,800	—	—	—	—	110
1999Mo Proof	100	Value: 500				
2000Mo	5,080	—	—	—	—	110
2000Mo Proof	650	Value: 200				

GOLD BULLION COINAGE

KM# 530   1/20 ONZA (1/20 Ounce of Pure Gold)
1.7500 g., 0.9000 Gold 0.0506 oz. AGW **Obv:** Winged Victory **Rev:** Calendar stone

Date	Mintage	F	VF	XF	Unc	BU
1987Mo	—	—	—	—	—	275
1988Mo	—	—	—	—	—	

KM# 589   1/20 ONZA (1/20 Ounce of Pure Gold)
1.5551 g., 0.9990 Gold 0.0499 oz. AGW **Obv:** Winged Victory **Rev:** National arms, eagle left

Date	Mintage	F	VF	XF	Unc	BU
1991Mo	10,000	—	—	—	—	BV+30%
1992Mo	65,225	—	—	—	—	BV+30%
1993Mo	10,000	—	—	—	—	BV+30%
1994Mo	10,000	—	—	—	—	BV+30%

KM# 642   1/20 ONZA (1/20 Ounce of Pure Gold)
1.5551 g., 0.9990 Gold 0.0499 oz. AGW **Obv:** National arms, eagle left **Rev:** Native working

Date	Mintage	F	VF	XF	Unc	BU
2000Mo Proof	—	Value: 55.00				

KM# 671   1/20 ONZA (1/20 Ounce of Pure Gold)
1.5551 g., 0.9990 Gold 0.0499 oz. AGW, 16 mm. **Obv:** National arms, eagle left **Rev:** Winged Victory **Edge:** Reeded **Note:** Design similar to KM#609. Value estimates do not include the high taxes and surcharges added to the issue prices by the Mexican Government.

Date	Mintage	F	VF	XF	Unc	BU
2000Mo	5,300	—	—	—	—	BV+30%

KM# 628   1/15 ONZA (1/15 Ounce of Pure Gold)
0.9990 Gold **Obv:** Winged Victory above legend **Rev:** National arms, eagle left within circle

Date	Mintage	F	VF	XF	Unc	BU
1987Mo	—	—	—	—	—	275

KM# 541   1/10 ONZA (1/10 Ounce of Pure Gold)
3.1103 g., 0.9990 Gold 0.0999 oz. AGW **Obv:** National arms, eagle left **Rev:** Winged Victory

Date	Mintage	F	VF	XF	Unc	BU
1991Mo	10,000	—	—	—	—	BV+20%
1992Mo	50,777	—	—	—	—	BV+20%
1993Mo	10,000	—	—	—	—	BV+20%
1994Mo	10,000	—	—	—	—	BV+20%

KM# 672   1/10 ONZA (1/10 Ounce of Pure Gold)
3.1103 g., 0.9990 Gold 0.0999 oz. AGW, 20 mm. **Obv:** National arms, eagle left **Rev:** Winged Victory **Edge:** Reeded **Note:** Design similar to KM#610. Value estimates do not include the high taxes and surcharges added to the issue prices by the Mexican Government.

Date	Mintage	F	VF	XF	Unc	BU
2000Mo	3,500	—	—	—	—	BV+20%

KM# 487   1/4 ONZA (1/4 Ounce of Pure Gold)
8.6396 g., 0.9000 Gold 0.2500 oz. AGW **Obv:** National arms, eagle left **Rev:** Winged Victory **Note:** Similar to KM#488.

Date	Mintage	F	VF	XF	Unc	BU
1981Mo	313,000	—	—	—	—	BV+11%
1982Mo	—	—	—	—	—	BV+11%

KM# 590   1/4 ONZA (1/4 Ounce of Pure Gold)
7.7758 g., 0.9990 Gold 0.2497 oz. AGW **Obv:** Winged Victory above legend **Rev:** National arms, eagle left

Date	Mintage	F	VF	XF	Unc	BU
1991Mo	10,000	—	—	—	—	BV+11%
1992Mo	28,106	—	—	—	—	BV+11%
1993Mo	2,500	—	—	—	—	BV+11%
1994Mo	2,500	—	—	—	—	BV+11%

KM# 673   1/4 ONZA (1/4 Ounce of Pure Gold)
7.7758 g., 0.9990 Gold 0.2497 oz. AGW, 26.9 mm. **Obv:** National arms, eagle left **Rev:** Winged Victory **Edge:** Reeded **Note:** Design similar to KM#611. Value estimates do not include the high taxes and surcharges added to the issue prices by the Mexican Government.

Date	Mintage	F	VF	XF	Unc	BU
2000Mo	2,500	—	—	—	—	BV+12%

KM# 488   1/2 ONZA (1/2 Ounce of Pure Gold)
17.2792 g., 0.9000 Gold 0.5000 oz. AGW **Obv:** National arms, eagle left **Rev:** Winged Victory

Date	Mintage	F	VF	XF	Unc	BU
1981Mo	193,000	—	—	—	—	BV+8%
1982Mo	—	—	—	—	—	BV+8%
1989Mo Proof	704	Value: 520				

KM# 591   1/2 ONZA (1/2 Ounce of Pure Gold)
15.5517 g., 0.9990 Gold 0.4995 oz. AGW **Obv:** Winged Victory above legend **Rev:** National arms, eagle left

Date	Mintage	F	VF	XF	Unc	BU
1991Mo	10,000	—	—	—	—	BV+8%
1992Mo	25,220	—	—	—	—	BV+8%
1993Mo	2,500	—	—	—	—	BV+8%
1994Mo	2,500	—	—	—	—	BV+8%

KM# 674   1/2 ONZA (1/2 Ounce of Pure Gold)
15.5517 g., 0.9990 Gold 0.4995 oz. AGW, 32.9 mm. **Obv:** National arms, eagle left **Rev:** Winged Victory **Edge:** Reeded **Note:** Design similar to KM#612. Value estimates do not include the high taxes and surcharges added to the issue prices by the Mexican Government.

Date	Mintage	F	VF	XF	Unc	BU
2000Mo	1,500	—	—	—	—	BV+8%

KM# 489   ONZA (Ounce of Pure Gold)
34.5585 g., 0.9000 Gold 0.9999 oz. AGW **Obv:** National arms, eagle left **Rev:** Winged Victory **Note:** Similar to KM#488.

Date	Mintage	F	VF	XF	Unc	BU
1981Mo	596,000	—	—	—	—	BV+3%
1985Mo	—	—	—	—	—	BV+3%
1988Mo	—	—	—	—	—	BV+3%

KM# 592   ONZA (Ounce of Pure Gold)
31.1035 g., 0.9990 Gold 0.9990 oz. AGW **Obv:** Winged Victory above legend **Rev:** National arms, eagle left

Date	Mintage	F	VF	XF	Unc	BU
1991Mo	109,193	—	—	—	—	BV+3%
1992Mo	46,281	—	—	—	—	BV+3%
1993Mo	10,000	—	—	—	—	BV+3%
1994Mo	1,000	—	—	—	—	BV+3%

KM# 675   ONZA (Ounce of Pure Gold)
31.1035 g., 0.9990 Gold 0.9990 oz. AGW, 40 mm. **Obv:** National arms, eagle left **Rev:** Winged Victory **Edge:** Reeded **Note:** Design similar to KM#639. Value estimates do not include the high taxes and surcharges added to the issue prices by the Mexican Government.

Date	Mintage	F	VF	XF	Unc	BU
2000Mo	2,730	—	—	—	—	BV+3%

PLATINUM BULLION COINAGE

KM# 538   1/4 ONZA (1/4 Ounce)
7.7775 g., 0.9990 Platinum 0.2498 oz. APW **Obv:** National arms, eagle left **Rev:** Winged Victory

Date	Mintage	F	VF	XF	Unc	BU
1989Mo	704	Value: 450				

BULLION COINAGE
Pre-Columbian • Azteca Series

KM# 644   NUEVO PESO
7.7700 g., 0.9990 Silver 0.2496 oz. ASW, 26.8 mm. **Subject:** Eagle Warrior **Obv:** National arms, eagle left within D-shaped circle and dotted border **Rev:** Eagle warrior within D-shaped circle and dotted border **Edge:** Reeded

Date	Mintage	F	VF	XF	Unc	BU
1993Mo	1,500	—	—	—	—	15.00
1993 Proof	900	Value: 22.50				

KM# 645   2 NUEVO PESOS
15.4200 g., 0.9990 Silver 0.4952 oz. ASW, 32.9 mm. **Subject:** Eagle Warrior **Obv:** National arms, eagle left **Rev:** Eagle warrior **Edge:** Reeded

Date	Mintage	F	VF	XF	Unc	BU
1993Mo	1,500	—	—	—	—	15.00
1993 Proof	800	Value: 25.00				

KM# 646   5 NUEVO PESOS
31.0500 g., 0.9990 Silver 0.9972 oz. ASW, 40 mm. **Subject:** Eagle Warrior **Obv:** National arms, eagle left **Rev:** Eagle warrior **Edge:** Reeded

Date	Mintage	F	VF	XF	Unc	BU
1993	2,000	—	—	—	—	22.00
1993 Proof	1,000	Value: 50.00				

KM# 647   5 NUEVO PESOS
31.0000 g., 0.9990 Silver 0.9956 oz. ASW, 40 mm. **Subject:** Xochipilli **Obv:** National arms, eagle left within D-shaped circle and flower blossom border **Rev:** Seated figure sculpture within D-shaped circle and flower blossom border **Edge:** Reeded

Date	Mintage	F	VF	XF	Unc	BU
1993	2,000	—	—	—	—	25.00
1993 Proof	800	Value: 60.00				

KM# 649   5 NUEVO PESOS
31.0000 g., 0.9990 Silver 0.9956 oz. ASW, 40 mm. **Subject:** Huchucteotl **Obv:** National arms, eagle left within D-shaped circle and designed border **Rev:** Aztec sculpture within D-shaped circle and designed border **Edge:** Reeded

Date	Mintage	F	VF	XF	Unc	BU
1993	5,000	—	—	—	—	20.00
1993 Proof	800	Value: 65.00				

KM# 648   5 NUEVO PESOS
31.0000 g., 0.9990 Silver 0.9956 oz. ASW, 40 mm. **Subject:** Brasco Efigie **Obv:** National arms, eagle left within D-shaped circle and designed border **Rev:** Sculpture within D-shaped circle and designed border **Edge:** Reeded

Date	Mintage	F	VF	XF	Unc	BU
1993	2,000	—	—	—	—	25.00
1993 Proof	500	Value: 55.00				

KM# 650   10 NUEVO PESOS
155.3100 g., 0.9990 Silver 4.9881 oz. ASW, 64 mm. **Subject:** Piedra de Tizoc **Obv:** National arms, eagle left **Rev:** Warrior capturing woman **Edge:** Reeded **Note:** Illustration reduced, similar to 100 Pesos, KM# 557

Date	Mintage	F	VF	XF	Unc	BU
1992 Proof	—	Value: 150				
1993	1,000	—	—	—	—	90.00
1993 Proof	1,000	Value: 120				

KM# 554   25 PESOS
7.7758 g., 0.9990 Silver 0.2497 oz. ASW **Obv:** National arms, eagle left within D-shaped circle and designed border **Rev:** Eagle warrior right within D-shaped circle and a designed border

Date	Mintage	F	VF	XF	Unc	BU
1992	50,000	—	—	—	14.00	
1992 Proof	3,000	Value: 22.50				

KM# 555   50 PESOS
15.5517 g., 0.9990 Silver 0.4995 oz. ASW **Obv:** National arms, eagle left within D-shaped circle designed border **Rev:** Eagle warrior right within D-shaped circle and designed border

Date	Mintage	F	VF	XF	Unc	BU
1992	50,000	—	—	—	20.00	
1992 Proof	3,000	Value: 25.00				

KM# 556 100 PESOS
31.1035 g., 0.9990 Silver 0.9990 oz. ASW **Obv:** National arms, eagle left **Rev:** Eagle warrior

Date	Mintage	F	VF	XF	Unc	BU
1992	205,000	—	—	—	22.00	
1992	4,000	Value: 50.00				

KM# 562 100 PESOS
31.1035 g., 0.9990 Silver 0.9990 oz. ASW **Obv:** National arms, eagle left within D-shaped circle and designed border **Rev:** Seated figure sculpture within D-shaped circle and designed border

Date	Mintage	F	VF	XF	Unc	BU
1992 Proof	4,000	Value: 60.00				

KM# 563 100 PESOS
31.1035 g., 0.9990 Silver 0.9990 oz. ASW **Obv:** National arms, eagle left within D-shaped circle and designed border **Rev:** Brasero Efigie - The God of Rain within D-shaped circle and designed border

Date	Mintage	F	VF	XF	Unc	BU
1992 Proof	4,000	Value: 65.00				

KM# 564 100 PESOS
31.1035 g., 0.9990 Silver 0.9990 oz. ASW **Obv:** National arms, eagle left within D-shaped circle and designed border
Rev: Huehueteotl - The God of Fire within D-shaped circle and designed border

Date	Mintage	F	VF	XF	Unc	BU
1992 Proof	4,000	Value: 50.00				

KM# 558 250 PESOS
7.7758 g., 0.9990 Gold 0.2497 oz. AGW **Subject:** Native Culture **Obv:** National arms, eagle left within D-shaped circle and designed border **Rev:** Sculpture of Jaguar head within D-shaped circle and designed border

Date	Mintage	F	VF	XF	Unc	BU
1992	10,000	—	—	—	—	240
1992 Proof	2,000	Value: 285				

KM# 559 500 PESOS
15.5517 g., 0.9990 Gold 0.4995 oz. AGW **Subject:** Native Culture **Obv:** National arms, eagle left within D-shaped circle and designed border **Rev:** Sculpture of Jaguar head within D-shaped circle and designed border

Date	Mintage	F	VF	XF	Unc	BU
1992	10,000	—	—	—	—	475
1992 Proof	2,000	Value: 485				

KM# 560 1000 PESOS
31.1035 g., 0.9990 Gold 0.9990 oz. AGW **Subject:** Native Culture **Obv:** National arms, eagle left within D-shaped circle and designed border **Rev:** Sculpture of Jaguar head within D-shaped circle and designed border

Date	Mintage	F	VF	XF	Unc	BU
1992	17,850	—	—	—	—	925
1992 Proof	2,000	Value: 950				

KM# 557 10000 PESOS
155.5175 g., 0.9990 Silver 4.9948 oz. ASW, 64 mm. **Subject:** Pieora De Tizoc **Obv:** National arms, eagle left within D-shaped circle and designed border **Rev:** Native warriors within D-shaped circle and designed border **Note:** Similar to 10 Nuevo Pesos, KM#650

Date	Mintage	F	VF	XF	Unc	BU
1992	51,900	—	—	—	—	80.00
1992 Proof	3,300	Value: 160				

BULLION COINAGE
Pre-Columbian • Central Veracruz Series

KM# 567 NUEVO PESO
7.7601 g., 0.9990 Silver 0.2492 oz. ASW **Subject:** Bajo relieve de el Tajin **Obv:** National arms, eagle left within D-shaped circle and designed border **Rev:** Design within D-shaped circle and designed border

Date	Mintage	F	VF	XF	Unc	BU
1993	100,000	—	—	—	—	13.50
1993 Proof	3,300	Value: 25.00				

KM# 568 2 NUEVO PESOS
15.5516 g., 0.9990 Silver 0.4995 oz. ASW **Subject:** Bajo relieve de el Tajin **Obv:** National arms, eagle left within D-shaped circle and designed border **Rev:** Design within D-shaped circle and designed border

Date	Mintage	F	VF	XF	Unc	BU
1993	100,000	—	—	—	—	16.50
1993 Proof	3,000	Value: 25.00				

KM# 569 5 NUEVO PESOS
31.1035 g., 0.9990 Silver 0.9990 oz. ASW **Subject:** Bajo relieve de el Tajin **Obv:** National arms, eagle left within D-shaped circle and designed border **Rev:** Design within D-shaped circle and designed border

Date	Mintage	F	VF	XF	Unc	BU
1993	100,000	—	—	—	—	20.00
1993 Proof	3,000	Value: 50.00				

KM# 582 5 NUEVO PESOS
31.1035 g., 0.9990 Silver 0.9990 oz. ASW **Subject:** Palma Con Cocodrilo **Obv:** National arms, eagle left within D-shaped circle and designed border **Rev:** Aerial view of crocodile within D-shaped circle and designed border

Date	Mintage	F	VF	XF	Unc	BU
1993	4,500	—	—	—	—	20.00
1993 Proof	2,650	Value: 50.00				

KM# 583 5 NUEVO PESOS
31.1035 g., 0.9990 Silver 0.9990 oz. ASW **Subject:** Anciano Con Brasero **Obv:** National arms, eagle left within D-shaped circle and designed border **Rev:** Kneeling figure sculpture within D-shaped circle and designed border

Date	Mintage	F	VF	XF	Unc	BU
1993	2,650	—	—	—	—	25.00
1993 Proof	1,500	Value: 50.00				

KM# 584 5 NUEVO PESOS
31.1035 g., 0.9990 Silver 0.9990 oz. ASW **Subject:** Carita Sonriente **Obv:** National arms, eagle left **Rev:** Sculptured head

Date	Mintage	F	VF	XF	Unc	BU
1993	4,500	—	—	—	—	20.00
1993 Proof	3,300	Value: 50.00				

KM# 570 10 NUEVO PESOS
Center Weight: 115.5175 g. **Center:** 0.9990 Silver 3.7101 oz. ASW , 64 mm. **Subject:** Piramide Del El Tajin **Obv:** National arms, eagle left within flat shaped circle and designed border **Rev:** Pyramid within flat shaped circle and designed border **Note:** Illustration reduced.

Date	Mintage	F	VF	XF	Unc	BU
1993	50,000	—	—	—	—	80.00
1993 Proof	3,100	Value: 160				

KM# 585 25 NUEVO PESOS
7.7758 g., 0.9990 Gold 0.2497 oz. AGW **Subject:** Hacha Ceremonial **Obv:** National arms, eagle left **Rev:** Mask left **Note:** Similar to 100 New Pesos, KM#587.

Date	Mintage	F	VF	XF	Unc	BU
1993	15,500	—	—	—	—	250
1993 Proof	800	Value: 300				

KM# 586 50 NUEVO PESOS
15.5517 g., 0.9990 Gold 0.4995 oz. AGW **Subject:** Hacha Ceremonial **Obv:** National arms, eagle left **Rev:** Mask left **Note:** Similar to 100 New Pesos, KM#587.

Date	Mintage	F	VF	XF	Unc	BU
1993	15,500	—	—	—	—	485
1993 Proof	500	Value: 500				

KM# 587 100 NUEVO PESOS
31.1035 g., 0.9990 Gold 0.9990 oz. AGW **Subject:** Hacha Ceremonial **Obv:** National arms, eagle left **Rev:** Mask left

Date	Mintage	F	VF	XF	Unc	BU
1993	7,150	—	—	—	—	950
1993 Proof	500	Value: 975				

BULLION COINAGE
Pre-Columbian • Mayan Series

KM# 572   NUEVO PESO
7.7601 g., 0.9990 Silver 0.2492 oz. ASW **Subject:** Chaac Mool **Obv:** National arms, eagle left within six sided shield and designed border **Rev:** Reclining figure within six sided shield and designed border

Date	Mintage	F	VF	XF	Unc	BU
1994 Matte	30,000	—	—	—	—	13.50
1994 Proof	2,500	Value: 25.00				

KM# 573   2 NUEVO PESOS
15.5516 g., 0.9990 Silver 0.4995 oz. ASW **Subject:** Chaac Mool **Obv:** National arms, eagle left within six sided shield and designed border **Rev:** Reclining figure within six sided shield and designed border

Date	Mintage	F	VF	XF	Unc	BU
1994 Matte	30,000	—	—	—	—	16.50
1994 Proof	2,500	Value: 25.00				

KM# 574   5 NUEVO PESOS
31.1035 g., 0.9990 Silver 0.9990 oz. ASW **Subject:** Chaac Mool **Obv:** National arms, eagle left within six sided shield and designed border **Rev:** Reclining figure within six sided shield and designed border

Date	Mintage	F	VF	XF	Unc	BU
1994 Matte	50,000	—	—	—	—	20.00
1994 Proof	3,000	Value: 50.00				

KM# 575   5 NUEVO PESOS
31.1035 g., 0.9990 Silver 0.9990 oz. ASW **Subject:** Chaac Mool **Obv:** National arms, eagle left within six sided shield and designed border **Rev:** Tomb of Palenque Memorial Stone within six sided shield and designed border

Date	Mintage	F	VF	XF	Unc	BU
1994	4,500	—	—	—	—	20.00
1994 Proof	2,800	Value: 50.00				

KM# 577   5 NUEVO PESOS
31.1035 g., 0.9990 Silver 0.9990 oz. ASW **Subject:** Mascaron Del Dios Chaac **Rev:** Elaborately carved wall segment

Date	Mintage	F	VF	XF	Unc	BU
1994	4,500	—	—	—	—	20.00
1994 Proof	2,500	Value: 50.00				

KM# 578   5 NUEVO PESOS
31.1035 g., 0.9990 Silver 0.9990 oz. ASW **Subject:** Dintel 26 **Obv:** National arms, eagle left within six sided shield and designed border **Rev:** Two seated figures wall carving within six sided shield and designed border

Date	Mintage	F	VF	XF	Unc	BU
1994	4,500	—	—	—	—	20.00
1994 Proof	2,600	Value: 50.00				

KM# 676   10 NUEVO PESOS
155.5175 g., 0.9990 Silver 4.9948 oz. ASW, 65 mm. **Subject:** Piramide Del Castillo **Obv:** National arms, eagle left above metal content statement **Rev:** Pyramid above two-line inscription **Rev. Insc.:** PIRAMIDE DEL CASTILLO / CHICHEN-ITZA **Edge:** Reeded

Date	Mintage	F	VF	XF	Unc	BU
1993Mo Proof	—	Value: 325				

KM# 576   10 NUEVO PESOS
Center Weight: 115.5175 g. **Center:** 0.9990 Silver 3.7101 oz. ASW, 64 mm. **Subject:** Piramide del Castillo **Obv:** National arms, eagle left **Rev:** Pyramid **Note:** Illustration reduced.

Date	Mintage	F	VF	XF	Unc	BU
1994	20,000	—	—	—	—	85.00
1994 Proof	2,100	Value: 165				

KM# 579   25 NUEVO PESOS
7.7758 g., 0.9990 Gold 0.2497 oz. AGW **Subject:** Personaje de Jaina **Rev:** Seated figure

Date	Mintage	F	VF	XF	Unc	BU
1994	2,000	—	—	—	—	250
1994 Proof	500	Value: 300				

KM# 580   50 NUEVO PESOS
15.5517 g., 0.9990 Gold 0.4995 oz. AGW **Subject:** Personaje de Jaina **Rev:** Seated figure

Date	Mintage	F	VF	XF	Unc	BU
1994	1,000	—	—	—	—	485
1994 Proof	500	Value: 500				

KM# 581   100 NUEVO PESOS
31.1035 g., 0.9990 Gold 0.9990 oz. AGW **Subject:** Personaje de Jaina **Obv:** National arms, eagle left within six sided shield and designed border **Rev:** Seated figure within six sided shield and designed border

Date	Mintage	F	VF	XF	Unc	BU
1994	1,000	—	—	—	—	950
1994 Proof	500	Value: 975				

BULLION COINAGE
Pre-Columbian • Olmec Series

KM# 593   PESO
7.7750 g., 0.9990 Silver 0.2497 oz. ASW **Subject:** Senor De Las Limas **Obv:** National arms, eagle left within square and designed border **Rev:** Sitting figure facing within square and designed border **Note:** Similar to 5 Pesos, KM#595.

Date	Mintage	F	VF	XF	Unc	BU
1996	4,000	—	—	—	—	13.50
1996 Proof	2,200	Value: 25.00				
1998 Matte	2,400	—	—	—	—	15.00

KM# 594   2 PESOS
15.5517 g., 0.9990 Silver 0.4995 oz. ASW **Subject:** Senor De Las Limas **Obv:** National arms, eagle left within square and designed border **Rev:** Sitting figure facing within square and designed border **Note:** Similar to 5 Pesos, KM#595.

Date	Mintage	F	VF	XF	Unc	BU
1996	4,000	—	—	—	—	16.50
1996 Proof	2,200	Value: 25.00				
1998 Matte	2,400	—	—	—	—	18.00

KM# 596   5 PESOS
31.1035 g., 0.9990 Silver 0.9990 oz. ASW **Subject:** Hombre Jaguar **Obv:** National arms, eagle left within square and designed border **Rev:** Statue facing within square and designed border

Date	Mintage	F	VF	XF	Unc	BU
1996	1,500	—	—	—	—	85.00
1996 Proof	2,800	Value: 50.00				
1998 Matte	6,000	—	—	—	—	25.00
1998 Proof	4,800	Value: 50.00				

KM# 595   5 PESOS
31.1035 g., 0.9990 Silver 0.9990 oz. ASW **Subject:** Senor De Las Limas **Obv:** National arms, eagle left within square and designed border **Rev:** Seated figure facing within square and designed border

Date	Mintage	F	VF	XF	Unc	BU
1996	4,000	—	—	—	—	20.00
1996 Proof	3,000	Value: 50.00				
1998 Matte	3,400	—	—	—	—	22.00

KM# 597   5 PESOS
31.1035 g., 0.9990 Silver 0.9990 oz. ASW **Subject:** El Luchador **Obv:** National arms, eagle left **Rev:** El Luchador

Date	Mintage	F	VF	XF	Unc	BU
1996	4,500	—	—	—	—	20.00
1996 Proof	2,700	Value: 50.00				
1998 Matte	2,000	—	—	—	—	25.00

KM# 598   5 PESOS
31.1035 g., 0.9990 Silver 0.9990 oz. ASW **Subject:** Hacha Ceremonial **Obv:** National arms, eagle left within square and designed border **Rev:** Statue within square and designed border

Date	Mintage	F	VF	XF	Unc	BU
1996	4,500	—	—	—	—	20.00
1996 Proof	2,700	Value: 50.00				
1998 Matte	2,000	—	—	—	—	25.00

KM# 599   10 PESOS
Center Weight: 155.5175 g. **Center:** 0.9990 Silver 4.9948 oz. ASW, 64 mm. **Subject:** Cabeza Olmeca **Obv:** National arms, eagle left **Rev:** Native mask **Note:** Illustration reduced.

Date	Mintage	F	VF	XF	Unc	BU
1996	2,000	—	—	—	—	85.00
1996 Proof	2,750	Value: 110				
1998 Matte	2,150	—	—	—	—	85.00

KM# 600   25 PESOS
7.7758 g., 0.9990 Gold 0.2497 oz. AGW **Subject:** Sacerdote **Obv:** National arms, eagle left **Rev:** Sculpture **Note:** Similar to 100 Pesos, KM#602.

Date	Mintage	F	VF	XF	Unc	BU
1996	500	—	—	—	—	280
1996 Proof	750	Value: 300				

KM# 601   50 PESOS
15.5517 g., 0.9990 Gold 0.4995 oz. AGW **Subject:** Sacerdote **Obv:** National arms, eagle left **Rev:** Sculpture **Note:** Similar to 100 Pesos, KM#602.

Date	Mintage	F	VF	XF	Unc	BU
1996	500	—	—	—	—	485
1996 Proof	500	Value: 500				

KM# 602   100 PESOS
31.1035 g., 0.9990 Gold 0.9990 oz. AGW **Subject:** Sacerdote **Obv:** National arms, eagle left within square and designed border **Rev:** Sculpture within square and designed border

Date	Mintage	F	VF	XF	Unc	BU
1996	500	—	—	—	—	950
1996 Proof	500	Value: 975				

BULLION COINAGE
Pre-Columbian • Teotihuacan Series

KM# 617 PESO
7.7759 g., 0.9990 Silver 0.2497 oz. ASW **Subject:** Disco De La Muerte **Obv:** National arms, eagle left within oblong circle and designed border **Rev:** Sculpture within oblong circle and designed border

Date	Mintage	F	VF	XF	Unc	BU
1997	3,000	—	—	—	—	13.50
1997 Proof	1,600	Value: 25.00				
1998 Matte	2,400	—	—	—	—	15.00
1998 Proof	500	Value: 30.00				

KM# 618 2 PESOS
15.5517 g., 0.9990 Silver 0.4995 oz. ASW **Subject:** Disco De La Muerte **Obv:** National arms, eagle left within oblong circle and designed border **Rev:** Sculpture within oblong circle and designed border

Date	Mintage	F	VF	XF	Unc	BU
1997	3,000	—	—	—	—	16.50
1997 Proof	1,600	Value: 25.00				
1998	2,400	—	—	—	—	18.00
1998 Proof	500	Value: 30.00				

KM# 621 5 PESOS
31.1035 g., 0.9990 Silver 0.9990 oz. ASW **Subject:** Teotihuacan - Vasija **Obv:** National arms, eagle left within oval and designed border **Rev:** Seated woman joined to pottery vase within oval and designed border

Date	Mintage	F	VF	XF	Unc	BU
1997	4,500	—	—	—	—	20.00
1997 Proof	Est. 1,800	Value: 50.00				
1998 Matte	2,000	—	—	—	—	25.00
1998 Proof	500	Value: 60.00				

KM# 622 5 PESOS
31.1035 g., 0.9990 Silver 0.9990 oz. ASW **Subject:** Teotihuacan - Jugador de Pelota **Obv:** National arms, eagle left

Date	Mintage	F	VF	XF	Unc	BU
1997	4,500	—	—	—	—	20.00
1997 Proof	Est. 1,800	Value: 50.00				
1998 Matte	2,000	—	—	—	—	25.00
1998 Proof	500	Value: 60.00				

KM# 619 5 PESOS
31.1035 g., 0.9990 Silver 0.9990 oz. ASW **Subject:** Teotihuacan - Disco de la Muerte **Obv:** National arms, eagle left within oblong circle and designed border **Rev:** Sculpture within oblong circle and designed border

Date	Mintage	F	VF	XF	Unc	BU
1997	3,500	—	—	—	—	20.00
1997 Proof	Est. 1,800	Value: 50.00				

Date	Mintage	F	VF	XF	Unc	BU
1998	3,400	—	—	—	—	22.00
1998 Proof	500	Value: 60.00				

KM# 620 5 PESOS
31.1035 g., 0.9990 Silver 0.9990 oz. ASW **Subject:** Teotihuacan - Mascara **Obv:** National arms, eagle left within oblong circle and designed border **Rev:** Face sculpture within oblong circle and designed border

Date	Mintage	F	VF	XF	Unc	BU
1997	4,500	—	—	—	—	20.00
1997 Proof	Est. 1,800	Value: 60.00				
1998	2,000	—	—	—	—	25.00
1998 Proof	500	Value: 65.00				

KM# 623 10 PESOS
155.5175 g., 0.9990 Silver 4.9948 oz. ASW, 64 mm. **Subject:** Piramide Del Sol **Obv:** National arms, eagle left within oblong circle and designed border **Rev:** Pyramid within oblong circle and designed border **Note:** Illustration reduced.

Date	Mintage	F	VF	XF	Unc	BU
1997	1,500	—	—	—	—	85.00
1997 Proof	2,100	Value: 165				
1998 Matte	2,150	—	—	—	—	85.00

KM# 624 25 PESOS
7.7758 g., 0.9990 Gold 0.2497 oz. AGW **Subject:** Serpiente Emplumada **Obv:** National arms, eagle left **Note:** Similar to 100 Pesos, KM#626.

Date	Mintage	F	VF	XF	Unc	BU
1997	500	—	—	—	—	280
1997 Proof	200	Value: 325				

KM# 625 50 PESOS
15.5517 g., 0.9990 Gold 0.4995 oz. AGW **Subject:** Serpiente Emplumada **Obv:** National arms, eagle left **Note:** Similar to 100 Pesos, KM#626.

Date	Mintage	F	VF	XF	Unc	BU
1997	500	—	—	—	—	485
1997 Proof	200	Value: 525				

KM# 626 100 PESOS
31.1035 g., 0.9990 Gold 0.9990 oz. AGW **Subject:** Teotihuacan - Serpiente Emplumada **Obv:** National arms, eagle left

Date	Mintage	F	VF	XF	Unc	BU
1997	500	—	—	—	—	950
1997 Proof	Est. 200	Value: 1,000				

BULLION COINAGE
Pre-Columbian • Tolteca Series

KM# 661 PESO
7.7759 g., 0.9990 Silver 0.2497 oz. ASW, 27 mm. **Subject:** Jaguar **Obv:** National arms, eagle left **Rev:** Jaguar carving **Edge:** Reeded

Date	Mintage	F	VF	XF	Unc	BU
1998	6,000	—	—	—	—	13.50
1998 Proof	4,800	Value: 25.00				

KM# 662 2 PESOS
15.5517 g., 0.9990 Silver 0.4995 oz. ASW, 33 mm. **Subject:** Jaguar **Obv:** National arms, eagle left **Rev:** Jaguar carving **Edge:** Reeded

Date	Mintage	F	VF	XF	Unc	BU
1998	6,000	—	—	—	—	16.50
1998 Proof	4,800	Value: 30.00				

KM# 663 5 PESOS
31.1035 g., 0.9990 Silver 0.9990 oz. ASW, 40 mm. **Subject:** Jaguar **Obv:** National arms, eagle left within shield and designed border **Rev:** Jaguar carving within shield and designed border **Edge:** Reeded

Date	Mintage	F	VF	XF	Unc	BU
1998	6,000	—	—	—	—	20.00
1998 Proof	4,800	Value: 50.00				

KM# 664 5 PESOS
31.1035 g., 0.9990 Silver 0.9990 oz. ASW, 40 mm. **Obv:** National arms, eagle left **Rev:** Sacerdote sculpture **Edge:** Reeded

Date	Mintage	F	VF	XF	Unc	BU
1998	5,000	—	—	—	—	20.00
1998 Proof	4,800	Value: 50.00				

KM# 666 5 PESOS
31.1035 g., 0.9990 Silver 0.9990 oz. ASW, 40 mm. **Subject:** Serpiente con Craneo **Obv:** National arms, eagle left **Rev:** Large sculpture **Edge:** Reeded

Date	Mintage	F	VF	XF	Unc	BU
1998	5,000	—	—	—	—	20.00
1998 Proof	4,800	Value: 50.00				

KM# 665 5 PESOS
31.1035 g., 0.9990 Silver 0.9990 oz. ASW, 40 mm. **Subject:** Quetzalcoatl **Obv:** National arms, eagle left **Rev:** Quetzalcoatl sculpture **Edge:** Reeded

Date	Mintage	F	VF	XF	Unc	BU
1998	5,000	—	—	—	—	20.00
1998 Proof	4,800	Value: 50.00				

$10

KM# 634 10 PESOS
155.7300 g., 0.9990 Silver 5.0016 oz. ASW **Subject:** Atlantes
Obv: National arms, eagle left within shield and designed border
Rev: Three carved statues within shield and designed border

Date	Mintage	F	VF	XF	Unc	BU
1998	3,500	—	—	—	—	85.00
1998 Proof	4,200	Value: 135				

KM# 667 25 PESOS
7.7759 g., 0.9990 Gold 0.2497 oz. AGW, 23 mm. **Subject:** Aguila
Obv: National arms, eagle left **Rev:** Eagle sculpture **Edge:** Reeded

Date	Mintage	F	VF	XF	Unc	BU
1998	300	—	—	—	—	280
1998 Proof	300	Value: 325				

KM# 668 50 PESOS
15.5517 g., 0.9990 Gold 0.4995 oz. AGW, 29 mm. **Subject:** Aguila
Obv: National arms, eagle left **Rev:** Eagle sculpture **Edge:** Reeded

Date	Mintage	F	VF	XF	Unc	BU
1998	300	—	—	—	—	485
1998 Proof	300	Value: 525				

$100

KM# 669 100 PESOS
31.1035 g., 0.9990 Gold 0.9990 oz. AGW, 34.5 mm.
Subject: Aguila **Obv:** National arms, eagle left within designed
shield **Rev:** Eagle sculpture within designed shield **Edge:** Reeded

Date	Mintage	F	VF	XF	Unc	BU
1998	300	—	—	—	—	950
1998 Proof	300	Value: 975				

MEDALLIC SILVER BULLION COINAGE

KM# M49a ONZA
33.6250 g., 0.9250 Silver 0.9999 oz. ASW **Obv:** Mint mark above
coin press

Date	Mintage	F	VF	XF	Unc	BU
1949	1,000,000	—	13.00	15.00	18.00	28.00

KM# M49b.1 ONZA
33.6250 g., 0.9250 Silver 0.9999 oz. ASW **Obv:** Wide spacing
between DE MONEDA **Rev:** Mint mark below balance scale
Note: Type I

Date	Mintage	F	VF	XF	Unc	BU
1978Mo	280,000	—	—	BV	13.50	15.00

KM# M49b.2 ONZA
33.6250 g., 0.9250 Silver 0.9999 oz. ASW **Obv:** Close spacing
between DE MONEDA **Rev:** Mint mark below balance scale
Note: Type II

Date	Mintage	F	VF	XF	Unc	BU
1978Mo	Inc. above	—	—	BV	18.50	23.50

KM# M49b.3 ONZA
33.6250 g., 0.9250 Silver 0.9999 oz. ASW **Obv:** Close spacing
between DE MONEDA **Rev:** Left scale pan points to U in UNA
Note: Type III

Date	Mintage	F	VF	XF	Unc	BU
1979Mo	4,508,000	—	—	BV	17.50	22.00

KM# M49b.4 ONZA
33.6250 g., 0.9250 Silver 0.9999 oz. ASW **Obv:** Close spacing
between DE MONEDA **Rev:** Left scale pan points between U
and N of UNA **Note:** Type IV

Date	Mintage	F	VF	XF	Unc	BU
1979Mo	Inc. above	—	—	BV	17.50	22.00

KM# M49b.5 ONZA
33.6250 g., 0.9250 Silver 0.9999 oz. ASW **Obv:** Close spacing
between DE MONEDA **Rev:** Left scale pan points between U
and N of UNA **Note:** Type V

Date	Mintage	F	VF	XF	Unc	BU
1980Mo	6,104,000	—	—	BV	17.50	22.00
1980/70Mo	Inc. above	—	—	BV	17.50	25.00

MEDALLIC GOLD COINAGE

KM# M91a 10 PESOS
8.3333 g., 0.9000 Gold 0.2411 oz. AGW **Subject:** 200th
Anniversary - Birth of Hidalgo

Date	Mintage	F	VF	XF	Unc	BU
1953	—	—	—	—	BV	250

KM# M123a 10 PESOS
8.3333 g., 0.9000 Gold 0.2411 oz. AGW **Subject:** Centennial
of Constitution

Date	Mintage	F	VF	XF	Unc	BU
1957	Est. 73,000	—	—	—	BV	250

Note: Mintage includes #M122a

KM# M92a 20 PESOS
16.6666 g., 0.9000 Gold 0.4822 oz. AGW **Subject:** 200th
Anniversary - Birth of Hidalgo

Date	Mintage	F	VF	XF	Unc	BU
1953	—	—	—	—	BV	485

KM# M122a 50 PESOS
41.6666 g., 0.9000 Gold 1.2056 oz. AGW **Subject:** Centennial
of Constitution

Date	Mintage	F	VF	XF	Unc	BU
1957	—	—	—	—	BV	1,200

Note: Mintage included in total for KM#M123a

PATTERNS
Including off metal strikes

KM#	Date	Mintage	Identification	Mkt Val
Pn169	1901Cn Q	—	20 Centavos. Copper.	
Pn170	1901Cn Q	—	20 Centavos. Bronze.	425
Pn171	1904Zs FZ	—	Peso. Aluminum.	—
Pn172	1906Z	—	2 Centavos. Silver.	—
Pn173	1907Mo	—	50 Centavos. Silver. Horse and rider facing left within sun rays. National arms. Plain edge.	4,000
Pn174	1907Mo	—	50 Centavos. Silver. Incuse lettered edge, matte Proof.	3,500
Pn175	1907	—	50 Centavos. Silver. Raised lettered edge, matte Proof.	3,500
Pn176	1908Mo	—	50 Centavos. Silver. Plain edge, Proof.	3,000
Pn177	1908Mo	—	Peso. Silver. Liberty on horseback, plain edge, Proof.	—
Pn178	1909Mo	—	Peso. Silver. Plain edge, Proof.	7,000
	1909Mo	—	Peso. Silver. Plain edge, Proof.	7,000
Pn179	1909Mo	—	Peso. Silver. Incuse lettered edge, Proof.	—
Pn180	1909Mo	—	Peso. Brass. Incuse lettered edge, matte Proof.	3,250
Pn181	1909Mo	—	Peso. Brass. Raised lettered edge, matte Proof.	3,250
Pn182	1909Mo	—	Peso. Bronzed Lead. Raised lettered edge, matte Proof.	—
Pn183	1909Mo	—	Peso. Silver. Raised lettered edge, matte Proof.	—
Pn184	1910	—	2 Centavos. Bronze.	—
Pn185	1911Mo	—	Peso. Silver. Plain edge.	2,500
Pn186	1911Mo	—	Peso. Bronze. Plain edge.	2,500
Pn187	1911Mo	—	Peso. Brass. Plain edge.	2,500
Pn188	1914Mo	—	5 Centavos. Copper.	200
Pn189	1916Mo	—	20 Pesos. Copper. Arms/Aztec calendar stone.	1,150
Pn190	1936Mo	—	Centavo. Copper-Nickel.	—
Pn191	1936Mo	—	Peso. Silver. Arms/Morelos.	3,200
Pn192	1945Mo	—	50 Centavos. Nickel. Arms/Juarez.	1,250
Pn193	1947Mo	—	Peso. Silver. Arms/Morelos.	2,500
Pn194	1947Mo	—	Peso. Silver. Arms/Juarez.	2,500
Pn195	1947Mo	—	5 Pesos. Silver. Arms/Cap, balance scale, scroll.	4,250
Pn196	1947Mo	—	Onza. 0.9250 Silver. Balance scale. Coin screw press. Coin screw press/Balance scale.	1,250
Pn197	1950Mo	—	5 Pesos. Silver. Arms/Hidalgo.	1,650
Pn198	1951Mo	2	Onza. Silver. Elephant facing right. Bust with helmet left. Miner/Elephant.	4,000
Pn199	1954Mo	—	50 Centavos. Bronze. 33mm. Arms/Cuauhtémoc.	

KM#	Date	Mintage	Identification	Mkt Val
Pn200	1954Mo	—	50 Centavos. Copper-Nickel. Arms/Cuauhtémoc.	
Pn201	1955Mo	—	50 Centavos. Bronze. Arms/Cuauhtémoc.	625
Pn202	1955Mo	—	Peso. Copper-Nickel. Arms/Morelos, 32mm.	1,800
Pn203	1962Mo	—	5 Centavos. Copper-Nickel.	60.00
Pn204	1969Mo	—	Peso. Copper-Nickel. Value behind head.	2,000
Pn205	1969Mo	—	Peso. Copper-Nickel. Arms/Morelos.	1,650
Pn206	1970Mo	—	10 Centavos. Bronze. Arms/Allende.	400
Pn207	1970Mo	—	25 Centavos. Copper-Nickel. Arms/Allende.	750
Pn208	1973Mo	—	10 Pesos. Aluminum-Bronze. Arms/Hidalgo.	800
Pn209	1974Mo	—	10 Pesos. Copper-Nickel. Arms/Hidalgo.	600
Pn210	1976Mo	16	100 Pesos. 0.7200 Silver. Arms/Morelos.	—
Pn211	1978Mo	—	Onza. Silver. Coin screw press/balance scale	3,000
Pn212	1978Mo	—	Onza. 0.9250 Silver. Coin screw press / Coin belt powered press, Proof, PRUEBA	2,500
Pn213	1978Mo	—	Onza. 0.9250 Silver. Coin screw press / Coin belt powered press, Proof, PRUEBA	—
Pn214	1978Mo	—	Onza. 0.9250 Silver. Coin screw press / Native statue, Proof, PRUEBA	2,000
Pn215	1978Mo	—	Onza. 0.9250 Silver. Coin screw press / Native Statue, Proof, PRUEBA	1,750
Pn216	1979Mo	—	Onza. 0.9250 Silver.	2,000
Pn217	1979Mo	—	20 Pesos. Bronze. Arms / Mayan art	—
Pn218	1980Mo	8	20 Centavos. Copper-Nickel.	—
Pn219	1980Mo	—	Peso. Brass. Arms / Mayan art	350
Pn220	1980Mo	—	10 Pesos. 0.5000 Silver. Arms/Mayan art.	—
Pn221	1980Mo	—	10 Pesos. Bronze. Arms/Mayan art.	750
Pn222	1980Mo	—	20 Pesos. Copper-Nickel. Arms/Mayan art. Large mint mark.	300
Pn223	1980Mo	50	1/10 Onza. Silver. Arms/Radiant cap above mountain, Proof	90.00
Pn224	1981Mo	—	20 Centavos. Copper-Nickel. Small obverse design. Small arms design/Madero, Proof.	165
Pn225	1981Mo	—	20 Centavos. Copper-Nickel. Mod. portrait. Small arms design/ Modified portrait Madero, Proof.	135
Pn226	19xx	—	20 Centavos. Copper.	350
PnA227	1982	—	50 Pesos.	—
Pn227	1983Mo	—	50 Centavos. Proof.	650
Pn228	1983Mo	12	Peso. Stainless Steel. Arms/Morelos.	550
Pn229	1983	—	5 Pesos. Bronze. Arms/Mayan art.	350
Pn230	1983	—	Onza. Silver. Libertad.	1,350
Pn231	1984Mo	—	50 Pesos. Copper-Nickel. Arms/Juarez, Proof.	400
Pn232	ND	—	50 Pesos. Gold. Arms/Juarez, w/o JUAREZ.	—
Pn233	1985Mo	—	Peso. Copper.	325
Pn234	1985Mo	10	Peso. Silver. SUD design divided from date and denomination.	—
Pn235	1986Mo	33	Peso. Stainless Steel. SUD design w/date and denom., no divider	65.00
Pn236	1986	—	500 Pesos. Stainless Steel. Proof.	500
Pn237	1987	3	100 Pesos. Copper. KM#537.	—
Pn238	1987	3	100 Pesos. Copper-Nickel. KM#537.	—
Pn239	1988	3	100 Pesos. Brass.	—
Pn240	1988Mo	3	500 Pesos. Aluminum-Brass. Arms/Madero, KM#529.	500
Pn241	1988Mo	—	Onza. Silver. Plain edge. Libertad.	—
Pn242	1990Mo	—	50000 Pesos. Copper-Nickel. National arms, eagle left. Bust with hat facing. Arms/Zapato.	650
Pn244	1990	—	50000 Pesos. Silver.	800
Pn245	1990	—	100000 Pesos. Bronze. Arms/Calles.	650
Pn246	1991Mo	—	100 Pesos. Aluminum. Arms/Huitzilapan.	275
Pn247	1991	—	200 Pesos. Alum. Arms/Xochimilco.	200
Pn248	1991	—	500 Pesos. Bronze. Arms/Atenango.	400
Pn249	1991	—	1000 Pesos. Bronze. Arms/Atlan.	35.00
Pn250	1991Mo	—	2000 Pesos. Bronze. Arms/Revolution Monument.	400
Pn251	1991Mo	—	2000 Pesos. Steel. Arms/Revolution Monument.	400
Pn252	1991Mo	34	2000 Pesos. Bi-Metallic. Arms/Revolution Monument.	250
Pn253	1996Mo	—	20 Pesos. Silver center. Alum.-Bronze ring. W/o NUEVOS.	—
Pn254	1996Mo	—	50 Pesos. Silver. KM#571. W/o NUEVOS.	—
Pn255	1996Mo	—	5 Pesos. Silver. KM#627.	—

TRIAL STRIKES

KM#	Date	Mintage	Identification	Mkt Val
TS15	1980	—	8 Reales. Bronze-Plated Lead.	—
TS16	1980	—	1/10 Onza. Copper.	75.00
TS17	1980	—	1/10 Onza. Silver.	125

BANK SETS

Hard Case Sets unless otherwise noted.

KM#	Date	Mintage	Identification	Issue Price	Mkt Val
BS1	1972 (6)	—	KM#418, 427, 452, 460, 472, 480	—	30.00
BS2	1973 (5)	—	KM#418, 427 (2), 441, 472	—	20.00
BS3	1974 (7)	—	KM#427, 434.4, 441, 442, 460, 472, 477.1	—	30.00
BS4	1975 (7)	—	KM#427, 434.1, 442, 452, 460 (2), 477.1	—	20.00
BS5	1976 (9)	—	KM#427, 434.1, 442, 452 (2), 460, 472(2), 477.1	—	15.00
BS6	1977 (9)	—	KM#434.1, 434.2, 442, 452, 460 (2), 472, 477.1, 483.1	—	35.00
BS7	1977 (9)	—	KM#434.1, 434.2, 442, 452, 460 (2), 472, 477.1, 483.2 Type II for 3-ring binder	—	
BS8	1978 (9)	500	KM#434.1, 434.2, 442, 452, 460 (2), 472, 477.2, 483.2, Type I, flat pack	—	35.00
BS9	1978 (9)	—	KM#434.1, 434.2, 442, 452, 460 (2), 472, 477.2, 483.2 Type II for 3-ring binder,	—	15.00
BS10	1979 (9)	—	KM#434.1, 434.4, 442, 452 (2), 460 (2), 477.2, 483.2 Type I flat pack	11.00	25.00
BS11	1979 (8)	—	KM#434.1, 434.4, 442, 452 (2), 460, 477.2, 483.2 Type II for 3-ring binder	11.00	15.00
BS12	1980 (7)	—	KM#434.2, 442, 452 (2), 460 (2), 485, 486, 477.2	4.20	25.00
BS13	1981 (9)	—	KM#442 (2), 452 (2), 460 (2), 477.2, 485, 486	4.20	25.00
BS14	1982 (7)	—	KM#442, 452, 460, 477.2, 485, 486, 490	—	20.00
BS15	1983 (11)	—	KM#442 (2), 452 (2), 460 (2), 490, 491 (2), 492 (2)	—	20.00
BS16	1983 (11)	—	KM#442 (2), 452 (2), 460 (2), 490, 491 (2), 492 (2) 3-ring plastic page	—	12.50
BS17	1984 (8)	—	KM#485, 486, 490, 491, 493, 495 (2), 496,	—	25.00
BS22	1988 (8)	—	KM#493, 495a, 502, 508, 512, 529, 531, 536	—	20.00
BS18	1985 (12)	—	KM#477.2, 485, 493 (2), 495 (2), 496, 502, 508, 509, 510, 512	—	30.00
BS19	1985 (12)	—	KM#477.2, 485, 493 (2), 495 (2), 496, 502, 508, 509, 510, 512 3-ring plastic page	—	20.00
BS20	1986 (7)	—	KM#493, 495, 496, 508, 512, 525, 529 3-ring plastic page	—	20.00
BS21	1987 (9)	—	KM#493, 495 (2), 496, 502 (2), 512, 529 (2)	—	20.00
BS23	1989 (10)	—	KM#493 (3), 508 (3), 512, 529, 536 (2)	—	20.00
BS24	1990 (8)	—	KM#493 (2), 495a, 509 (2), 512, 536 (2)	—	20.00
BS25	1991 (4)	—	KM#493 (2), 536 (2)	—	15.00
BS26	1992 (5)	—	KM#493 (2), 495a, 529, 536	—	15.00
BS27	1992 (8)	—	KM#546-553	—	30.00
BSA28	1992-93 (9)	—	KM#546-553, 561 in heavy wooden case	—	125
BS28	1993 (7)	—	KM#546-552	—	18.00
BS29	1993 (3)	—	KM#553, 561, 571	—	35.00
BS30	1994 (7)	—	KM#546-552	—	18.00
BS31	1994 (3)	—	KM#553, 561, 571	—	35.00
BS32	1995 (9)	—	KM#546-551, 553, 561, 571	—	45.00
BS33	1996 (6)	—	KM#546-549, 603, 604	12.00	30.00
BS34	1997 (8)	—	KM#546-549, 603-605, 616	—	30.00
BS35	1998 (8)	—	KM#546-549, 603-605, 616	—	30.00
BS36	1999 (8)	—	KM#546-549, 603-605, 616	—	35.00
BS37	2000 (7)	—	KM#547-549, 603-605, 636 Set in folder	—	30.00

PROOF SETS

KM#	Date	Mintage	Identification	Issue Price	Mkt Val
PS1	1982/1983 (7)	998	KM442, 452, 460, 485, 477.2, 486, 490, 494.1	495	400
PS2	1982/1983 (8)	—	KM460, 477.2, 485, 486, 490, 491, 492, PnB169 (in white box with Mo. in gold)	—	—
PS3	1982/1983 (7)	23	KM460, 477.2, 485, 486, 490, 491, 492 (in white box with Mo in gold)	—	500
PS4	1982/1983 (7)	17	KM460, 477.2, 485, 486, 490, 491, 492 (in white box)	—	500
PS5	1982/1983 (7)	8	KM460, 477.2, 485, 486, 490, 491, 492 (in white box)	—	500
PS6	1983 (7)	3	KM460, 477.2, 485, 486, 490, 491, 492	—	—
PS7	1985/1986 (12)	—	KM497a-499a, 503-505, 514-515, 519, 521, 523-524	—	250
PS8	1985 (4)	—	KM500.2-501.2, 506.2, 507.2	—	700
PS9	1985 (3)	—	KM499a, 514, 515 (in blue box)	—	60.00
PS10	1985 (3)	—	KM503-505 (in blue box)	—	60.00
PS11	1985 (2)	—	KM511, 513	—	350
PS12	1989 (3)	704	KM488, 494.1, 538, Rainbow	730	850
PS13	1992 (5)	5,000	KM494.3, 542-545	—	87.50
PS14	1993 (5)	5,000	KM494.4, 542-545	—	87.50
PS15	1994 (5)	5,000	KM494.4, 542-545	—	85.00
PS16	1995 (7)	—	KM546-550, 552, 553, 555	45.00	48.00

MEXICO-REVOLUTIONARY

Revolution, 1910-1917

The Mexican independence movement, which is of interest and concern to collectors because of the warfare induced activity of local and state mints, began with the Sept. 16, 1810 march on the capital led by Father Miguel Hidalgo, a well-intentioned man of imagination and courage who proved to be an inept organizer and leader. Hidalgo was captured and executed within 10 months. His revolution, led by such as Morelos, Guerrero and Iturbide, continued and culminated in Mexican independence in 1821. Turbulent years followed. From 1821 to 1877 there were two emperors, several dictators and enough presidents to provide a change of government on the average of once every nine months. Porfirio Diaz, who had the longest tenure of any 19th century dictator in Latin American history, seized power in 1877 and did not relinquish it until 1911.

The final phase of Mexico's lengthy revolutionary period began in 1910 and lasted through the adoption of a liberal constitution and the election of a new congress in 1917. The 1910-1917 revolution was agrarian in character and intended to destroy the regime of Diaz and make Mexico economically and diplomatically independent. The republic experienced a state of upheaval that saw most of the leading figures of the revolution (Villa, Carranza, Obregon, Zapata, Calles) fighting each other at one time or another. Carranza eventually emerged as the most powerful figure of the early revolution. As de-facto president in 1916, he convened a constitutional convention, which produced a constitution in which the aims of the revolution were formulized. Obregon, perhaps the ablest general and wiliest politician of the lot, became Mexico's elected president in 1920, bringing the most disastrous but significant decade in Mexico's history to an end.

AGUASCALIENTES

Aguascalientes is a state in central Mexico. Its coin issues, struck by authority of Pancho Villa, represent his deepest penetration into the Mexican heartland. Lack of silver made it necessary to make all denominations in copper.

FRANCISCO PANCHO VILLA

REVOLUTIONARY COINAGE

KM# 601   CENTAVO

Copper, 17 mm. **Obv:** Liberty cap **Rev:** Value within 3/4 wreath below date **Note:** Large date weight 3.55g.

Date	Mintage	VG	F	VF	XF	Unc
1915	—	250	350	450	—	—
Note: Large date, plain edge						
1915	—	30.00	60.00	100	200	—
Note: Large date, reeded edge						
1915	—	30.00	60.00	100	130	—
Note: Small date, plain edge						
1915	—	30.00	60.00	80.00	120	—
Note: Small date, reeded edge						

KM# 602.1   2 CENTAVOS

4.2800 g., Copper **Obv:** Liberty cap **Rev:** Value within 3/4 wreath below date

Date	Mintage	VG	F	VF	XF	Unc
1915	—	40.00	100	200	350	—
Note: Round front 2, plain edge						

KM# 602.2   2 CENTAVOS

3.3500 g., Copper, 19 mm. **Obv:** Liberty cap **Rev:** Value within 1/2 wreath below date

Date	Mintage	VG	F	VF	XF	Unc
1915	—	35.00	60.00	85.00	200	•
Note: Square front 2, reeded edge						
1915 Plain edge	—	50.00	90.00	200	325	—
Note: Square front 2						

KM# 603 5 CENTAVOS
Copper, 25 mm. **Obv:** National arms **Rev:** Liberty cap and value above sprigs

Date	Mintage	VG	F	VF	XF	Unc
1915 Plain edge; Rare	—	—	—	—	—	—
1915 Reeded edge	—	10.00	20.00	30.00	50.00	—

KM# 604.1 5 CENTAVOS
7.1300 g., Copper, 25 mm. **Obv:** National arms **Rev:** Vertically shaded 5 within sprigs

Date	Mintage	VG	F	VF	XF	Unc
1915	—	100	150	225	325	—
Note: Plain edge						
1915	—	20.00	40.00	50.00	100	—
Note: Reeded edge						

KM# 604.2 5 CENTAVOS
Copper, 25 mm. **Obv:** National arms **Rev:** Horizontally shaded 5 within sprigs

Date	Mintage	VG	F	VF	XF	Unc
1915	—	30.00	50.00	80.00	150	—
Note: Plain edge						
1915	—	25.00	40.00	65.00	125	—
Note: Reeded edge						

KM# 606 20 CENTAVOS
Copper, 29 mm. **Obv:** National arms **Rev:** Value below Liberty cap within sprigs

Date	Mintage	VG	F	VF	XF	Unc
1915 Reeded edge	—	10.00	20.00	50.00	80.00	—

KM# 605 20 CENTAVOS
Copper, 29 mm. **Obv:** National arms **Rev:** Value below Liberty cap within sprigs

Date	Mintage	VG	F	VF	XF	Unc
1915 Reeded edge	—	10.00	20.00	50.00	80.00	—

KM# 600 20 CENTAVOS
Copper **Obv:** National arms **Rev:** Value below Liberty cap within sprigs **Edge:** Reeded

Date	Mintage	VG	F	VF	XF	Unc
1915	—	15.00	20.00	35.00	65.00	—

Note: Varieties exist with both plain and milled edges and many variations in the shading of the numerals

KM#	Date	Mintage	Identification	Mkt Val
P1	1915	50	Centavo. Silver. Large date. Prev. KM#601a.	650
P2	1915	—	Centavo. Silver. Small date. Prev. KM#601a.	650
P3	1915	50	2 Centavos. Silver. Prev. KM#602a.	1,200
P4	1915	50	5 Centavos. Silver. Prev. KM#604a.	3,500
P5	1915	50	20 Centavos. Silver. Plain edge. Prev. KM#605a.	3,800
P6	1915	—	20 Centavos. Silver. Prev. KM#600a.	3,000

CHIHUAHUA

Chihuahua is a northern state of Mexico bordering the U.S. It was the arena that introduced Pancho Villa to the world. Villa, an outlaw, was given a title when asked by Madero to participate in maintaining order during Madero's presidency. After Madero's death in February 1913, Villa became a persuasive leader. Chihuahua was where he made his first coins - the Parral series. The *Army of the North* pesos also came from this state. This coin helped Villa recruit soldiers because of his ability to pay in silver while others were paying in worthless paper money.

ARMY OF THE NORTH
Ejercito Del Norte
REVOLUTIONARY COINAGE

KM# 619 PESO
29.2700 g., Silver **Obv:** National arms **Rev:** Liberty cap

Date	Mintage	VG	F	VF	XF	Unc
1915	—	20.00	35.00	65.00	185	500

KM# 619a PESO
Copper **Obv:** National arms **Rev:** Liberty cap

Date	Mintage	VG	F	VF	XF	Unc
1915	—	500	1,000	1,500	2,500	—

KM# 619b PESO
Brass **Obv:** National arms **Rev:** Liberty cap **Note:** Uniface obverse

Date	Mintage	VG	F	VF	XF	Unc
1915 Rare	—	—	—	—	—	—

CONSTITUTIONALIST ARMY
Ejercito Constitucionalista
REVOLUTIONARY COINAGE

KM# 612 5 CENTAVOS
Copper **Obv:** Liberty cap **Rev:** Value above date

Date	Mintage	VG	F	VF	XF	Unc
1914	—	25.00	45.00	80.00	125	—

KM# 613 5 CENTAVOS
Copper, 25.36 mm. **Obv:** Liberty cap **Rev:** Value above date **Note:** Numerous varieties exist. Weight varies 6.3-6.93g.

Date	Mintage	VG	F	VF	XF	Unc
1914	—	1.00	2.50	4.00	10.00	—
1915	—	1.00	2.50	4.00	10.00	—

KM# 613a 5 CENTAVOS
Brass **Obv:** Liberty cap **Rev:** Value above date **Note:** Numerous varieties exist.

Date	Mintage	VG	F	VF	XF	Unc
1914	—	2.00	3.00	8.00	10.00	—
1915	—	2.00	3.00	8.00	10.00	—

KM# 613b 5 CENTAVOS
Cast Copper **Obv:** Liberty cap **Rev:** Value above date

Date	Mintage	VG	F	VF	XF	Unc
1914	—	75.00	200	300	450	—

KM# 614a 5 CENTAVOS
Copper **Obv:** National arms **Rev:** Value below date within sprigs with solid V

Date	Mintage	VG	F	VF	XF	Unc
1915 Rare	—	—	—	—	—	—

KM# 614b 5 CENTAVOS
Copper **Obv:** National arms **Rev:** Value above date **Note:** Mule.

Date	Mintage	VG	F	VF	XF	Unc
1915	—	—	350	—	—	—

KM# 614c 5 CENTAVOS
Copper **Obv:** National arms **Rev:** Liberty cap **Note:** Mule.

Date	Mintage	VG	F	VF	XF	Unc
1915 Rare	—	—	—	—	—	—

KM# 614 5 CENTAVOS
Copper **Obv:** National arms **Rev:** Value below date within sprigs with double-lined V

Date	Mintage	VG	F	VF	XF	Unc
1915 SS Unique	—	—	—	—	—	—

KM# 615 10 CENTAVOS
8.7900 g., Copper, 27.5 mm. **Obv:** Liberty cap **Rev:** Value above date

Date	Mintage	VG	F	VF	XF	Unc
1915	—	1.25	2.50	3.50	5.00	—

KM# 615a 10 CENTAVOS
8.8900 g., Brass, 27.5 mm. **Obv:** Liberty cap **Rev:** Value above date

Date	Mintage	VG	F	VF	XF	Unc
1915	—	5.00	10.00	30.00	50.00	—

Note: Many varieties exist

HIDALGO DEL PARRAL
Fuerzas Constitucionalistas
REVOLUTIONARY COINAGE

KM# 607 2 CENTAVOS
6.8500 g., Copper, 25 mm. **Obv:** Liberty cap within circle flanked by sprigs **Rev:** Value flanked by sprigs within circle

Date	Mintage	VG	F	VF	XF	Unc
1913	—	5.00	10.00	15.00	25.00	—

KM# 607a 2 CENTAVOS
Brass **Obv:** Liberty cap within circle flanked by sprigs **Rev:** Value flanked by sprigs within circle

Date	Mintage	VG	F	VF	XF	Unc
1913	—	95.00	150	200	350	—

KM# 608 50 CENTAVOS
12.6500 g., Silver **Obv:** Liberty cap **Rev:** Value flanked by sprigs below Liberty cap **Edge:** Reeded

Date	Mintage	VG	F	VF	XF	Unc
1913	—	15.00	40.00	60.00	85.00	—

KM# 609 50 CENTAVOS
12.1700 g., Silver, 30 mm. **Edge:** Plain

Date	Mintage	VG	F	VF	XF	Unc
1913	—	50.00	70.00	95.00	125	—

KM# 609a 50 CENTAVOS
Copper **Edge:** Plain

Date	Mintage	VG	F	VF	XF	Unc
1913 rare	—	200	400	525	850	—

KM# 610   PESO
Silver **Obv:** Inscription **Rev:** 1 through PESO and small circle above sprigs **Note:** Weight varies 29.18-30.9g.

Date	Mintage	VG	F	VF	XF	Unc
1913	—	1,200	2,000	3,000	6,000	14,000

KM# 611   PESO
Silver, 38 mm. **Obv:** Inscription **Rev:** Value above sprigs **Note:** Well struck counterfeits of this coin exist with the dot at the end of the word Peso even with the bottom of the O. On legitimate pieces the dot is slightly higher. Weight varies 27.3-28.85g.

Date	Mintage	VG	F	VF	XF	Unc
1913	—	35.00	40.00	120	275	475

PATTERNS
Constitutionalist Army

KM#	Date	Mintage	Identification	Mkt Val
Pn1	1913	—	Peso. Silver.	15,000
Pn2.1	1914	—	50 Centavos. Copper. 12.1800 g. 30 mm. Reeded edge.	3,500
Pn2.2	1914	—	50 Centavos. Copper. Plain edge.	3,000
			Note: Specimens exist in silver plated copper	
Pn3	1914	—	Peso. Copper.	3,500
	1914	—	Peso. Copper.	3,500
	1914	—	Peso. Copper.	3,500
Pn4	1914	—	Peso. Silver.	31,000
			Note: Silver or silver-plated copper pieces are modern fantasies.	
Pn5	1915 MS	—	5 Centavos. Copper. Prev. KM#614.	600

DURANGO

A state in north central Mexico. Another area of operation for Pancho Villa. The *Muera Huerta* peso originates in this state. The coins were made in Cuencame under the orders of Generals Cemceros and Contreras.

CUENCAME
Muera Huerta (Death to Huerta)
REVOLUTIONARY COINAGE

KM# 620   PESO
Silver **Obv:** National arms **Rev:** Liberty cap with written value flanked by stars

Date	Mintage	VG	F	VF	XF	Unc
1914	—	1,000	2,000	3,000	5,000	9,500

KM# 621   PESO
23.2000 g., Silver, 39 mm. **Obv:** National arms with continuous border **Rev:** Liberty cap with continuous border

Date	Mintage	VG	F	VF	XF	Unc
1914	—	75.00	150	300	700	1,650

KM# 621a   PESO
Copper **Obv:** National arms with continuous border **Rev:** Liberty cap with continuous border **Note:** Varieties exist.

Date	Mintage	VG	F	VF	XF	Unc
1914	—	400	600	1,000	2,000	—

KM# 621b   PESO
Brass **Obv:** National arms **Rev:** Liberty cap

Date	Mintage	VG	F	VF	XF	Unc
1914	—	—	1,000	2,000	3,500	—

KM# 622   PESO
23.4000 g., Silver, 38.5 mm. **Obv:** National arms with dot and dash border **Rev:** Liberty cap with continuous border **Note:** The so-called 20 Pesos gold Muera Huerta pieces are modern fantasies. Refer to Unusual World Coins, 4th edition, ©2005, KP Books, Inc.

Date	Mintage	VG	F	VF	XF	Unc
1914	—	60.00	100	300	500	950

ESTADO DE DURANGO
REVOLUTIONARY COINAGE

KM# 625   CENTAVO
3.2900 g., Copper, 20 mm. **Obv:** Large date in center **Rev:** Value within wreath

Date	Mintage	VG	F	VF	XF	Unc
1914	—	2.00	4.00	8.00	12.00	—

KM# 625a   CENTAVO
Brass **Obv:** Large date in center **Rev:** Value within wreath

Date	Mintage	VG	F	VF	XF	Unc
1914	—	75.00	150	300	400	—

KM# 625b   CENTAVO
Lead **Obv:** Large date in center **Rev:** Value within wreath

Date	Mintage	VG	F	VF	XF	Unc
1914	—	20.00	40.00	65.00	90.00	—

KM# 625c   CENTAVO
Copper **Obv:** Large date in center **Rev:** Value within wreath

Date	Mintage	VG	F	VF	XF	Unc
1914	—	25.00	50.00	80.00	125	—

KM# 624   CENTAVO
Cast Lead **Obv:** Date **Rev:** Value within wreath

Date	Mintage	VG	F	VF	XF	Unc
1914	—	45.00	75.00	100	200	—

KM# 626a   CENTAVO
Brass **Obv:** Date **Rev:** Value within wreath

Date	Mintage	VG	F	VF	XF	Unc
1914	—	75.00	100	200	350	—

KM# 626b   CENTAVO
Lead **Obv:** Date **Rev:** Value within wreath

Date	Mintage	VG	F	VF	XF	Unc
1914	—	20.00	40.00	70.00	125	—

Note: Varieties in size exist.

KM# 627   CENTAVO
Copper, 20 mm. **Obv:** Stars below date **Rev:** Value with retrograde N

Date	Mintage	VG	F	VF	XF	Unc
1914	—	6.00	10.00	20.00	30.00	—

KM# 627a   CENTAVO
Lead, 20 mm. **Obv:** Stars below date **Rev:** Value with retrograde N

Date	Mintage	VG	F	VF	XF	Unc
1914	—	20.00	40.00	60.00	100	—

KM# 628   CENTAVO
Aluminum **Obv:** National arms within sprigs **Rev:** Value

Date	Mintage	VG	F	VF	XF	Unc
1914	—	0.65	1.00	2.00	4.00	10.00

KM# 626   CENTAVO
Copper, 20 mm. **Obv:** Date **Rev:** Value within wreath **Note:** Weight varies 2.46-2.78g.

Date	Mintage	VG	F	VF	XF	Unc
1914	—	15.00	20.00	35.00	45.00	—

KM# 634b   5 CENTAVOS
6.8900 g., Copper-Nickel, 25.53 mm. **Obv:** National arms above sprigs **Obv. Leg.:** REPUBLICA MEXICANA **Rev:** Value **Rev. Leg.:** ESTADO DE DURANGO **Edge:** Plain

Date	Mintage	F	VF	XF	Unc	BU
1914	—	25.00	50.00	85.00	135	175

KM# 629   5 CENTAVOS
6.2000 g., Copper, 24 mm. **Obv:** Date above sprigs **Obv. Leg.:** ESTADO DE DURANGO **Rev:** Value within designed wreath

Date	Mintage	VG	F	VF	XF	Unc
1914	—	2.00	3.00	6.00	12.00	—

KM# 630   5 CENTAVOS
Copper **Obv:** Date above sprigs **Obv. Leg.:** E. DE DURANGO **Rev:** Value within designed wreath

Date	Mintage	VG	F	VF	XF	Unc
1914	—	125	275	375	600	—

KM# 631   5 CENTAVOS
5.0500 g., Copper, 23.5 mm. **Obv:** Date above sprigs
Obv. Leg.: E. DE DURANGO **Rev:** Value within designed wreath

Date	Mintage	VG	F	VF	XF	Unc
1914	—	1.25	3.00	6.00	15.00	—

KM# 631a   5 CENTAVOS
Brass **Obv:** Date above sprigs **Obv. Leg.:** E. DE DURANGO
Rev: Value within designed wreath

Date	Mintage	VG	F	VF	XF	Unc
1914	—	30.00	40.00	50.00	85.00	—

KM# 631b   5 CENTAVOS
Lead **Obv:** Date above sprigs **Obv. Leg.:** E. DE DURANGO
Rev: Value within designed wreath

Date	Mintage	VG	F	VF	XF	Unc
1914	—	45.00	70.00	100	180	—

KM# 632   5 CENTAVOS
4.6100 g., Copper, 23.5 mm. **Obv:** Date above sprigs
Obv. Leg.: E. DE DURANGO **Rev:** Roman numeral value

Date	Mintage	VG	F	VF	XF	Unc
1914	—	4.00	8.00	15.00	35.00	—

KM# 632a   5 CENTAVOS
Lead **Obv:** Date above sprigs **Obv. Leg.:** E. DE DURANGO
Rev: Roman numeral value

Date	Mintage	VG	F	VF	XF	Unc
1914	—	50.00	75.00	100	150	—

KM# 634   5 CENTAVOS
Brass **Obv:** National arms above sprigs **Obv. Leg.:** REPUBLICA
MEXICANA **Rev:** Value **Rev. Leg.:** ESTADO DE DURANGO

Date	Mintage	VG	F	VF	XF	Unc
1914	—	0.50	1.00	2.50	5.00	—

KM# 633   5 CENTAVOS
Lead **Obv:** Three stars below 1914 **Rev:** 5 CVS
Note: Counterfeits are prevalent in the market

Date	Mintage	VG	F	VF	XF	Unc
1914	—	600	2,000			—

KM# 634a   5 CENTAVOS
Copper **Obv:** National arms above sprigs
Obv. Leg.: REPUBLICA MEXICANA **Rev:** Value
Rev. Leg.: ESTADO DE DURANGO **Note:** There are numerous
varieties of these general types of the Durango 1 and 5 Centavo
pieces.

Date	Mintage	VG	F	VF	XF	Unc
1914	—	75.00	125	175	250	—

GUERRERO

Guerrero is a state on the southwestern coast of Mexico. It
was one of the areas of operation of Zapata and his forces in the
south of Mexico. The Zapata forces operated seven different
mints in this state. The date ranges were from 1914 to 1917 and
denominations from 2 Centavos to 2 Pesos. Some were cast but
most were struck and the rarest coin of the group is the Suriana
1915 2 Pesos.

EMILIANO ZAPATA
(General Salgado)
REVOLUTIONARY COINAGE

KM# 638   2 CENTAVOS
Copper, 22 mm. **Obv:** National arms **Obv. Leg.:** REPUBLICA
★ MEXICANA **Rev:** Value within wreath **Note:** Weight varies
5.4-6.03g.

Date	Mintage	VG	F	VF	XF	Unc
1915	—	75.00	125	175	250	—

KM# 635   3 CENTAVOS
Copper, 25 mm. **Obv:** National arms **Obv. Leg.:** REPUBLICA
MEXICANA **Rev:** Value within wreath **Note:** Weight varies
4.63-6.87g.

Date	Mintage	VG	F	VF	XF	Unc
1915	—	500	1,500	2,000	3,000	—

KM# 636   5 CENTAVOS
Copper, 26 mm. **Obv:** National arms **Rev:** Value within wreath

Date	Mintage	VG	F	VF	XF	Unc
1915GRO	—	800	1,200	2,000	3,000	—

KM# 637.1   10 CENTAVOS
Copper, 27-28.5 mm. **Obv:** National arms, snake head ends at
L in REPUBLICA **Obv. Leg.:** REPUBLICA MEXICANA **Rev:** Date
and value within wreath **Note:** Size varies.

Date	Mintage	VG	F	VF	XF	Unc
1915GRO	—	600	1,000	1,500	2,000	—

KM# 637.2   10 CENTAVOS
Copper, 27-28.5 mm. **Obv:** National arms, snake head ends at
C in REPUBLICA **Obv. Leg.:** REPUBLICA MEXICANA
Rev: Value within wreath **Note:** Size varies.

Date	Mintage	VG	F	VF	XF	Unc
1915GRO	—	3.00	5.00	8.00	15.00	—

KM# 637.2a   10 CENTAVOS
8.2300 g., Brass, 26 mm. **Obv:** National arms, snake head ends
at C in REPUBLICA **Obv. Leg.:** REPUBLICA MEXICANA
Rev: Value within wreath

Date	Mintage	VG	F	VF	XF	Unc
1915GRO	—	8.00	15.00	25.00	50.00	—

KM# 637.2b   10 CENTAVOS
Lead **Obv:** National arms, snake head ends at C in REPUBLICA
Obv. Leg.: REPUBLICA MEXICANA **Rev:** Value within wreath

Date	Mintage	VG	F	VF	XF	Unc
1915GRO	—	50.00	75.00	175	275	—

KM# 637.3   10 CENTAVOS
Copper **Obv:** National arms, snake head ends before A in
REPUBLICA **Obv. Leg.:** REPUBLICA MEXICANA **Rev:** Date
and value within wreath

Date	Mintage	VG	F	VF	XF	Unc
1915.GRO	—	3.00	5.00	8.00	15.00	—

KM# 637.3a   10 CENTAVOS
Brass **Obv:** National arms, snake head ends before A in
REPUBLICA **Obv. Leg.:** REPUBLICA MEXICANA **Rev:** Value
and date within wreath

Date	Mintage	VG	F	VF	XF	Unc
1915.GRO	—	12.00	20.00	50.00	100	—

KM# 639   25 CENTAVOS
Silver, 25 mm. **Obv:** Liberty cap **Obv. Leg.:** Mexicana REPUbLICA
Rev: Value above date **Note:** Weight varies 7.41-7.5g.

Date	Mintage	VG	F	VF	XF	Unc
1915	—	125	300	500	900	—

KM# 640   50 CENTAVOS
Silver, 34 mm. **Obv:** Liberty cap **Rev:** Date and value within
beaded border **Note:** Weight varies 14.5-14.8g.

Date	Mintage	VG	F	VF	XF	Unc
1915	—	1,000	2,000	3,500	5,000	—

KM# 641a   PESO (UN)
Copper **Obv:** National arms **Obv. Leg.:** REPUBLICA
MEXICANA - ★ UN PESO **Rev:** Liberty cap and rays within sprigs
Rev. Leg.: "REFORMA LIBERTAD JUSTICIA Y LEY"

Date	Mintage	Good	VG	F	VF	XF
1914GRO	—	32.00	80.00	200	500	1,500

KM# 641   PESO (UN)
Gold-Silver, 29-31 mm. **Obv:** National arms **Obv. Leg.:**
REPUBLICA MEXICANA - ★ UN PESO **Rev:** Liberty cap and
rays within sprigs **Rev. Leg.:** "REFORMA LIBERTAD JUSTICIA
Y LEY" **Rev. Insc.:** Oro:0,300 **Note:** Many die varieties exist.
Size varies. Weight varies 10.28-14.84g. Coin is 0,30g fine Gold.

Date	Mintage	VG	F	VF	XF	Unc
1914GRO	—	15.00	25.00	35.00	65.00	—

KM# 642   PESO (UN)
Gold-Silver, 30.5-31 mm.   **Obv:** National arms
Obv. Leg.: REPUBLICA MEXICANA - ★ UN PESO ★
Rev: Liberty cap and rays within sprigs **Rev. Leg.:**
"REFORMA.LIBERTAD.JUSTICIA Y LEY" **Rev. Insc.:** Oro:0,300
Note: Weight varies 12.93-14.66g. Coin is 0.300g fine Gold.

Date	Mintage	VG	F	VF	XF	Unc
1914GRO	—	50.00	75.00	100	180	—
1915GRO	—	600	1,000	1,500	1,800	—

KM# 643   2 PESOS (Dos)
Gold-Silver, 38.25-39.6 mm.   **Obv:** National arms
Obv. Leg.: REPUBLICA MEXICANA **Rev:** Radiant sun face
above high mountain peaks **Rev. Leg.:** "REFORMA LIBERTAD,
JUSTICIA Y LEY", **Rev. Insc.:** Oro:0,595 **Note:** Many varieties
exist. Coin is 0.595g fine Gold.

Date	Mintage	VG	F	VF	XF	Unc
1914GRO	—	15.00	35.00	125	200	425

KM# 643a   2 PESOS (Dos)
Copper, 38-38.5 mm.   **Obv:** National arms
Obv. Leg.: REPUBLICA MEXICANA **Rev:** Radiant sun face
above high mountain peaks **Rev. Leg.:** "REFORMA, LIBERTAD,
JUSTICIA Y LEY" **Note:** Size varies.

Date	Mintage	Good	VG	F	VF	XF
1914GRO	—	—	—	1,200	1,400	2,000

KM# 644a   2 PESOS (Dos)
Copper **Obv:** National arms **Obv. Leg.:** REPUBLICA
MEXICANA **Rev:** Radiant sun face above high and low mountain
peaks **Rev. Leg.:** "REFORMA, LIBERTAD, JUSTICIA Y LEY"

Date	Mintage	VG	F	VF	XF	Unc
1915GRO	—	400	1,000	1,200	1,800	—

KM# 644   2 PESOS (Dos)
Gold-Silver, 39-40 mm.   **Obv:** National arms **Obv. Leg.:**
REPUBLICA MEXICANA **Rev:** Radiant sun face above high and
low mountain peaks **Rev. Leg.:** "REFORMA, LIBERTAD,
JUSTICIA Y LEY" **Rev. Insc.:** Oro:0,595 **Note:** Weight varies
21.71-26.54g. Coin is 0.595g fine Gold.

Date	Mintage	VG	F	VF	XF	Unc
1915GRO	—	65.00	85.00	160	250	550

ATLIXTAC
REVOLUTIONARY COINAGE

KM# 645   10 CENTAVOS
Copper, 27.5-28 mm.   **Obv:** National arms
Obv. Leg.: REPUBLICA MEXICANA **Rev:** Value within sprigs
Note: Size varies. Weight varies 4.76-9.74g.

Date	Mintage	VG	F	VF	XF	Unc
1915	—	3.00	5.00	8.00	15.00	—

KM# 646   10 CENTAVOS
Copper, 27.55-28 mm.   **Obv:** National arms
Obv. Leg.: REPUBLICA ★ MEXICANA **Rev:** Value within sprigs
Note: Size varies. Weight varies 6.13-7.94g.

Date	Mintage	VG	F	VF	XF	Unc
1915	—	3.00	5.00	8.00	15.00	—

CACAHUATEPEC
REVOLUTIONARY COINAGE

KM# 648   5 CENTAVOS
12.1900 g., Copper, 28 mm.   **Obv:** National arms **Obv. Leg.:**
ESTADOS UNIDOS MEXICANOS **Rev:** Value within wreath

Date	Mintage	VG	F	VF	XF	Unc
1917	—	12.00	25.00	40.00	75.00	—

KM# 649   20 CENTAVOS
Silver, 21-23.8 mm.   **Obv:** National arms **Obv. Leg.:** ESTADOS
UNIDOS MEXICANOS **Rev:** Value within sprigs below liberty cap
and rays **Note:** Size varies. Weight varies 3.99-6.2g.

Date	Mintage	VG	F	VF	XF	Unc
1917	—	100	200	350	400	—

KM# 650   50 CENTAVOS
Silver, 30-30.3 mm.   **Obv:** National arms **Obv. Leg.:** ESTADOS
UNIDOS MEXICANOS **Rev:** Value and date within sprigs below
Liberty cap **Note:** Size varies. Weight varies 13.45-13.78g.

Date	Mintage	VG	F	VF	XF	Unc
1917	—	20.00	60.00	150	375	—

KM# 651   PESO (UN)
Silver, 38 mm.   **Obv:** National arms **Rev:** Liberty cap
Note: Weight varies 26.81-32.05g.

Date	Mintage	VG	F	VF	XF	Unc
1917 L.V. Go	—	2,000	4,000	6,000	9,000	—

CACALOTEPEC
REVOLUTIONARY COINAGE

KM# 652   20 CENTAVOS
Silver, 22.5 mm.   **Obv:** National arms **Obv. Leg.:** ESTADOS
UNIDOS MEXICANOS **Rev:** Date and value within sprigs below
Liberty cap and rays **Note:** Weight varies 3.89-5.73g.

Date	Mintage	VG	F	VF	XF	Unc
1917	—	1,000	1,800	3,000	5,000	—

CAMPO MORADO
REVOLUTIONARY COINAGE

KM# 653   5 CENTAVOS
4.3700 g., Copper, 23.5-24 mm.   **Obv:** National arms **Rev:** Value
within wreath **Note:** Size varies.

Date	Mintage	VG	F	VF	XF	Unc
1915 C.M.	—	9.00	15.00	22.50	35.00	—

KM# 654   10 CENTAVOS
Copper, 25.25-26 mm.   **Obv:** National arms **Rev:** Value and date
within wreath **Note:** Size varies. Weight varies. 4.48-8.77g.

Date	Mintage	VG	F	VF	XF	Unc
1915 C.M. GRO	—	6.00	10.00	20.00	30.00	—

KM# 655   20 CENTAVOS
Copper, 28 mm.   **Obv:** National arms **Rev:** Date above star and
value within wreath **Note:** Weight varies 4.48-9g.

Date	Mintage	VG	F	VF	XF	Unc
1915 C.M. GRO	—	15.00	25.00	35.00	50.00	—

KM# 657a   50 CENTAVOS
Base Silver **Obv:** National arms **Rev:** Date and value within
wreath **Note:** Regular obverse.

Date	Mintage	VG	F	VF	XF	Unc
1915 C.M. GRO	—	200	300	500	1,000	—

KM# 657   50 CENTAVOS
Copper, 30-31 mm.   **Obv:** National arms **Rev:** Date and value
within wreath **Note:** Regular obverse. Size varies. Weight varies
6.49-13.19g.

Date	Mintage	VG	F	VF	XF	Unc
1915 C.M. GRO	—	6.00	10.00	15.00	25.00	—

KM# 656 50 CENTAVOS
Copper, 29-31 mm. **Obv:** National arms **Rev:** Date and value within wreath **Note:** Size varies. Weight varies 9.81-16.77g.

Date	Mintage	VG	F	VF	XF	Unc
1915 C.M. GRO	—	12.00	20.00	30.00	60.00	—

KM# 658a PESO (UN)
Brass **Obv:** National arms **Rev:** Liberty cap

Date	Mintage	VG	F	VF	XF	Unc
1914 Co Mo Gro	—					
Unique						

KM# 659 PESO (UN)
Gold-Silver, 30-31 mm. **Obv:** National arms **Rev:** Liberty cap within sprigs **Rev. Insc.:** Oro:0,300 **Note:** Weight varies 12.26-15.81g. Coin is 0.300g fine Gold.

Date	Mintage	VG	F	VF	XF	Unc
1914 CAMPO Mo	—	15.00	30.00	45.00	60.00	—

KM# 658 PESO (UN)
Gold-Silver, 32-32.5 mm. **Obv:** National arms **Rev:** Liberty cap **Rev. Insc.:** Oro:0,300 **Note:** Weight varies 12.42-16.5g. Coin is 0.300g fine Gold.

Date	Mintage	VG	F	VF	XF	Unc
1914 Co Mo Gro	—	500	600	1,000	1,200	—

KM# 660a 2 PESOS (Dos)
Copper **Obv:** National arms **Rev:** Sun over mountains

Date	Mintage	VG	F	VF	XF	Unc
1915 Co. Mo.	—		800	1,000	1,200	—

KM# 660 2 PESOS (Dos)
Gold-Silver, 38.9-39 mm. **Obv:** National arms **Rev:** Sun over mountains **Rev. Insc.:** Oro:0,595 **Note:** Weight varies 20.6-26.02g. Coin is 0.595g fine Gold.

Date	Mintage	VG	F	VF	XF	Unc
1915 Co. Mo.	—	12.00	20.00	35.00	75.00	425

KM# 662a.1 2 PESOS (Dos)
Copper **Obv:** National arms **Rev:** Liberty cap

Date	Mintage	VG	F	VF	XF	Unc
1915 C. M. GRO	—				1,200	—

KM# 662a.2 2 PESOS (Dos)
Copper **Obv:** National arms **Rev:** Liberty cap

Date	Mintage	VG	F	VF	XF	Unc
1915 C. M. GRO	—					—
Unique						

KM# 661 2 PESOS (Dos)
29.4400 g., Gold-Silver, 39 mm. **Obv:** National arms **Rev:** Sun and mountains **Rev. Insc.:** Oro:0,595 **Note:** Coin is 0.595g fine Gold.

Date	Mintage	VG	F	VF	XF	Unc
1915 Co. Mo.	—	2,500	5,000	9,000	15,000	—

KM# 662 2 PESOS (Dos)
0.5950 g., 1.0000 Gold-Silver 0.0191 oz., 34.5-35 mm. **Obv:** National arms **Rev:** Liberty cap **Note:** Size varies. Weight varies 18.27-20.08g.

Date	Mintage	VG	F	VF	XF	Unc
1915 C. M. GRO	—	20.00	30.00	60.00	120	—

CHILPANCINGO
REVOLUTIONARY COINAGE

KM# 663 10 CENTAVOS
2.5200 g., Cast Silver, 18 mm. **Obv:** National arms **Rev:** Sun above value and sprigs

Date	Mintage	VG	F	VF	XF	Unc
1914	—	700	1,000	1,200	1,500	

Note: Many counterfeits exist.

KM# 664 20 CENTAVOS
4.9400 g., Cast Silver, 21.5 mm. **Obv:** National arms **Rev:** Sun above value and sprigs

Date	Mintage	VG	F	VF	XF	Unc
1914	—	700	1,000	1,200	1,500	

Note: Many counterfeits exist

KM# 665 2 PESOS (Dos)
22.9300 g., Gold-Silver, 39 mm. **Obv:** National arms **Rev:** Sun over mountains **Rev. Insc.:** Oro:0,595 **Note:** Coin is 0.595g fine Gold.

Date	Mintage	VG	F	VF	XF	Unc
1915 Rare	—	—	—	20,000	35,000	—

Note: Ira & Larry Goldberg - Millenia sale, 5-08 AU-55 replica. Ponterio & Associates sale, 4-09 VF realized $17,000. Spink America Gerber sale part 2, 6-96 VF realized $16,500

TAXCO
REVOLUTIONARY COINAGE

KM# 667 2 CENTAVOS
Copper, 25.25-26 mm. **Obv:** National arms **Obv. Leg.:** EDO.DE.GRO **Rev:** Value within sprigs **Note:** Size varies. Weight varies 6.81-8.55g.

Date	Mintage	VG	F	VF	XF	Unc
1915 O/T	—	25.00	40.00	60.00	90.00	—

KM# 668 5 CENTAVOS
Copper **Obv:** National arms **Obv. Leg.:** REPUBLICA ★ MEXICANA **Rev:** Value within sprigs **Note:** Weight varies 7.13-7.39g.

Date	Mintage	VG	F	VF	XF	Unc
1915	—	10.00	20.00	30.00	50.00	—

KM# 669 10 CENTAVOS
Copper, 27-28 mm. **Obv:** National arms **Obv. Leg.:** REPUBLICA ★ MEXICANA **Rev:** Date and value within sprigs **Note:** Size varies. Weight varies 7.51-8.67g.

Date	Mintage	VG	F	VF	XF	Unc
1915	—	9.00	20.00	35.00	50.00	—

KM# 670   50 CENTAVOS
5.4500 g., Copper, 27-28 mm. **Obv:** National arms with legend in large letters **Rev:** Value within sprigs **Note:** Size varies.

Date	Mintage	VG	F	VF	XF	Unc
1915	—	15.00	25.00	50.00	65.00	

KM# 671   50 CENTAVOS
Silver, 27.6-28 mm. **Obv:** National arms **Rev:** Sun above value and sprigs **Note:** Size varies. Weight varies 8.95-10.85g.

Date	Mintage	VG	F	VF	XF	Unc
1915	—	25.00	40.00	60.00	100	

KM# 672a   PESO (UN)
Brass **Obv:** National arms **Rev:** Liberty cap within sprigs

Date	Mintage	VG	F	VF	XF	Unc
1915	—	200	300	450	600	

KM# 672b   PESO (UN)
Lead **Obv:** National arms **Rev:** Liberty cap within sprigs

Date	Mintage	VG	F	VF	XF	Unc
1915	—	50.00	100	200	350	

KM# 672c   PESO (UN)
Copper **Obv:** National arms **Rev:** Liberty cap within sprigs

Date	Mintage	VG	F	VF	XF	Unc
1915	—	200	300	400	650	

KM# 673   PESO (UN)
11.6000 g., Gold-Silver, 30 mm. **Obv:** National arms **Rev:** Liberty cap within sprigs **Rev. Insc.:** Oro:0,300 **Note:** Coin is 0.300g fine Gold.

Date	Mintage	VG	F	VF	XF	Unc
1915	—	250	400	500	800	

KM# 674   PESO (UN)
Gold-Silver, 30 mm. **Obv:** National arms **Rev:** Liberty cap within sprigs **Rev. Insc.:** Oro:0,300 **Note:** Weight varies 10.51-12.79g. Coin is 0.300g fine Gold.

Date	Mintage	VG	F	VF	XF	Unc
1915	—	100	200	300	500	

KM# 672   PESO (UN)
Gold-Silver, 30-31 mm. **Obv:** National arms **Rev:** Liberty cap within sprigs **Rev. Insc.:** Oro:0,300 **Note:** Weight varies 30-31g. Coin is 0.300g fine Gold.

Date	Mintage	VG	F	VF	XF	Unc
1915	—	12.00	20.00	30.00	45.00	

PATTERNS
Including off metal strikes

KM#	Date	Mintage Identification	Mkt Val
Pn674	1914	— 2 Pesos. 1.0000 Gold-Silver.	—
Pn647	1914	— 2 Pesos. Gold-Silver. 0.3000 g. Atlixtac.	—

JALISCO

Jalisco is a state on the west coast of Mexico. The few coins made for this state show that the *Army of the North* did not restrict their operations to the northern border states. The coins were made in Guadalajara under the watchful eye of General Dieguez, commander of this segment of Villa's forces.

GUADALAJARA
REVOLUTIONARY COINAGE

KM# 675   CENTAVO
Copper **Obv:** Liberty cap **Rev:** Value

Date	Mintage	VG	F	VF	XF	Unc
1915	—	9.50	15.00	20.00	30.00	

KM# 675a   CENTAVO
Brass **Obv:** Liberty cap **Rev:** Value

Date	Mintage	VG	F	VF	XF	Unc
1915	—	—	—	300	450	

KM# A676   CENTAVO
Copper **Obv:** Liberty cap **Rev:** Retrograde value **Note:** Varieties exist.

Date	Mintage	VG	F	VF	XF	Unc
1915	—	100	300	600	1,000	

KM# 676.1   2 CENTAVOS
Copper, 20 mm. **Obv:** Liberty cap **Rev:** Value

Date	Mintage	VG	F	VF	XF	Unc
1915	—	10.00	18.00	20.00	35.00	

Note: Varieties exist.

KM# 676.2   2 CENTAVOS
Copper **Obv:** Liberty cap **Rev:** Value

Date	Mintage	VG	F	VF	XF	Unc
1915	—	200	300	500	800	

KM# 677   5 CENTAVOS
Copper, 24 mm. **Obv:** Liberty cap **Rev:** Value

Date	Mintage	VG	F	VF	XF	Unc
1915	—	6.50	12.00	15.00	25.00	

KM# 677a   5 CENTAVOS
Brass **Obv:** Liberty cap **Rev:** Value

Date	Mintage	VG	F	VF	XF	Unc
1915 rare	—	—	—	—	—	—

KM# 678   10 CENTAVOS
Copper **Obv:** Liberty cap above value and date **Rev:** Crowned shield

Date	Mintage	VG	F	VF	XF	Unc
1915	—	—	—	3,000	5,000	

KM# A678   PESO
Copper **Obv:** Liberty cap above value and date **Rev:** Crowned shield

Date	Mintage	VG	F	VF	XF	Unc
1915	—	—	—	—	17,000	—

MEXICO, ESTADO DE

Estado de Mexico is a state in central Mexico that surrounds the Federal District on three sides. The issues by the Zapata forces in this state have two distinctions – the Amecameca pieces are the crudest and the Toluca cardboard piece is the most unusual. General Tenorio authorized the crude incuse Amecameca pieces.

AMECAMECA
REVOLUTIONARY COINAGE

KM# 679   5 CENTAVOS
12.5500 g., Brass, 24.5 mm. **Obv:** Legend **Obv. Leg.:** EJERCITO CONVENCIONISTA **Rev:** Value above cent sign

Date	Mintage	VG	F	VF	XF	Unc
ND unique						

KM# 680   5 CENTAVOS
12.7700 g., Brass, 24.6 mm. **Obv:** National arms above RM **Rev:** Value above cent sign **Note:** Hand stamped.

Date	Mintage	VG	F	VF	XF	Unc
ND	—	300	400	600	800	

KM# 681a   10 CENTAVOS
Copper **Obv:** National arms above RM **Rev:** Value above cent sign **Note:** Hand stamped.

Date	Mintage	VG	F	VF	XF	Unc
ND	—	75.00	125	225	350	—

KM# 681   10 CENTAVOS
15.0000 g., Brass, 24.5-24.8 mm. **Obv:** National arms above RM **Rev:** Value above cent sign **Note:** Hand stamped. Varieties exist. Size varies.

Date	Mintage	VG	F	VF	XF	Unc
ND	—	60.00	90.00	150	200	—

KM# 682   20 CENTAVOS
Brass, 24-25 mm. **Obv:** National arms above RM **Rev:** Value above cent sign **Note:** Hand stamped. Varieties exist. Size varies. Weight varies 11.34-12.86g.

Date	Mintage	VG	F	VF	XF	Unc
ND	—	15.00	22.50	35.00	60.00	—

KM# 682a   20 CENTAVOS
Copper **Obv:** National arms above RM **Rev:** Value above cent sign **Note:** Hand stamped.

Date	Mintage	VG	F	VF	XF	Unc
ND	—	25.00	50.00	175	250	—

KM# 683   20 CENTAVOS
Copper, 19-20 mm. **Obv:** National arms above A. D. J. **Rev:** Value **Note:** Size varies. Weight varies 3.99-5.35g.

Date	Mintage	VG	F	VF	XF	Unc
ND	—	7.50	12.50	20.00	35.00	

KM# 683a   20 CENTAVOS
Brass **Obv:** National arms above A. D. J. **Rev:** Value

Date	Mintage	VG	F	VF	XF	Unc
ND	—	—	—	300	500	

KM# 684   25 CENTAVOS
Brass **Obv:** Legend **Obv. Leg.:** EJERCITO CONVENCIONISTA
Rev: Value above cent sign

Date	Mintage	VG	F	VF	XF	Unc
ND unique	—	—	—	—	—	—

KM# 685   25 CENTAVOS
Copper, 25 mm. **Obv:** National arms above sprigs **Rev:** Large numeral value **Note:** Hand stamped. Many modern counterfeits exist in all metals. Weight varies 6.32-6.99g.

Date	Mintage	VG	F	VF	XF	Unc
ND	—	15.00	20.00	30.00	40.00	

KM# 685a   25 CENTAVOS
7.9200 g., Brass, 25 mm. **Obv:** National arms above sprigs **Rev:** Large numeral value **Note:** Hand stamped.

Date	Mintage	VG	F	VF	XF	Unc
ND	—	—	—	100	300	

KM# 685b   25 CENTAVOS
Silver **Obv:** National arms above sprigs **Rev:** Large numeral value **Note:** Hand stamped.

Date	Mintage	VG	F	VF	XF	Unc
ND	—	—	—	250	400	

KM# 687   50 CENTAVOS
Copper, 23.5-29 mm. **Obv:** National arms above sprigs **Rev:** Large numeral value **Note:** Contemporary counterfeit, hand engraved. Size varies. Weight varies 8.8-10.8g.

Date	Mintage	VG	F	VF	XF	Unc
ND	—	12.00	30.00	50.00	80.00	

Note: "¢" clears top of 5

KM# 686a   50 CENTAVOS
16.0400 g., Brass, 28.5 mm. **Obv:** National arms above sprigs **Rev:** Large numeral value **Note:** Hand stamped.

Date	Mintage	VG	F	VF	XF	Unc
ND	—	100	200	300	400	

Note: Stem of "¢" above the 5

KM# 686   50 CENTAVOS
Copper, 28-28.5 mm. **Obv:** Eagle over sprays **Note:** Hand stamped. Size varies.

Date	Mintage	VG	F	VF	XF	Unc
ND	—	8.00	10.00	18.00	30.00	

TENANCINGO, TOWN
(Distrito Federal Mexico)
REVOLUTIONARY COINAGE

KM# 688.1   2 CENTAVOS
Copper **Obv:** National arms **Rev:** Value within wreath without TM below value

Date	Mintage	VG	F	VF	XF	Unc
1915	—	—	—	800	2,000	

KM# 688.2   2 CENTAVOS
Copper **Obv:** National arms **Rev:** Value within wreath with TM below value

Date	Mintage	VG	F	VF	XF	Unc
1915	—	—	400	800	2,000	

KM# 689.1   5 CENTAVOS
Copper, 19 mm. **Obv:** National arms **Rev:** Numeral value over lined C within wreath **Note:** Weight varies 2.83-2.84g.

Date	Mintage	VG	F	VF	XF	Unc
1915	—	10.00	20.00	30.00	50.00	

KM# 689.2   5 CENTAVOS
Copper, 19 mm. **Obv:** National arms **Rev:** Numeral value over lined C within wreath **Note:** Weight varies 2.83-2.84g.

Date	Mintage	VG	F	VF	XF	Unc
1915	—	100	300	500	900	

KM# 690.1   10 CENTAVOS
Copper, 25.25 mm. **Obv:** National arms **Rev:** Value over lined C within wreath below date **Note:** Weight varies 4.27-5.64g.

Date	Mintage	VG	F	VF	XF	Unc
1916	—	10.00	20.00	40.00	60.00	

KM# 690.2   10 CENTAVOS
Copper, 25.25 mm. **Obv:** National arms **Rev:** Value over lined C within wreath **Note:** Weight varies 4.27-5.64g.

Date	Mintage	VG	F	VF	XF	Unc
1916	—	100	200	400	600	

KM# 691   20 CENTAVOS
Copper, 27.5-28 mm. **Obv:** National arms **Rev:** Value and date above sprigs **Note:** Size varies. Weight varies 8.51-11.39g.

Date	Mintage	VG	F	VF	XF	Unc
1915	—	25.00	40.00	55.00	85.00	

TOLUCA, CITY
(Distrito Federal Mexico)
REVOLUTIONARY COINAGE

KM# 692.1   5 CENTAVOS
Grey Cardboard, 27-28 mm. **Obv:** Crowned shield within sprigs **Rev:** Banner accross large numeral value **Note:** Size varies. Weight varies 1.04-1.16g.

Date	Mintage	VG	F	VF	XF	Unc
1915	—	15.00	30.00	50.00	85.00	—

KM# 692.2   5 CENTAVOS
Grey Cardboard, 27-28 mm. **Obv:** Crowned shield within sprigs **Rev:** Banner accross large numeral value **Note:** Size varies. Weight varies 1.04-1.16g.

Date	Mintage	VG	F	VF	XF	Unc
1915	—	15.00	30.00	50.00	85.00	—

COUNTERMARKED COINAGE

KM# 693.1   20 CENTAVOS
Copper, 20 mm. **Countermark:** 20 within C **Obv:** National arms **Rev:** Numeral 20 within C and inner circle within sprigs **Note:** Countermark on 1 Centavo, KM#415. Varieties exist. Weight varies 2.65-2.95g.

CM Date	Host Date	Good	VG	F	VF	XF
ND(1915)	ND	—	20.00	40.00	55.00	95.00

KM# 693.2   20 CENTAVOS
Copper, 20 mm. **Countermark:** 20 within C **Obv:** National arms **Rev:** Numeral 20 within C and inner circle within 3/4 wreath **Note:** Countermark on 1 Centavo, KM#394.1. Weight varies 2.65-2.95g.

CM Date	Host Date	Good	VG	F	VF	XF
ND(1915)	1904	—	30.00	50.00	90.00	165

KM# 694 40 CENTAVOS
5.8600 g., Copper, 24.75-25 mm. **Countermark:** 40 within C
Obv: National arms **Rev:** Numeral 40 within C and inner circle within wreath **Note:** Countermark on 2 Centavos, KM#419. Varieties exist. Size varies.

CM Date	Host Date	Good	VG	F	VF	XF
ND(1915)	ND	—	25.00	40.00	60.00	100

MORELOS

Morelos is a state in south central Mexico, adjoining the federal district on the south. It was the headquarters of Emiliano Zapata. His personal quarters were at Tlatizapan in Morelos. The Morelos coins from 2 Centavos to 1 Peso were all copper except one type of 1 Peso in silver. The two operating Zapatista mints in Morelos were Atlihuayan and Tlaltizapan.

EMILIANO ZAPATA
(Zapatista)
REVOLUTIONARY COINAGE

KM# 695 2 CENTAVOS
Copper, 23 mm. **Obv:** National arms **Obv. Leg.:** E.L. DE MORELOS **Rev:** Value within wreath

Date	Mintage	VG	F	VF	XF	Unc
1915	—	1,000	1,400	1,800	2,750	

KM# 696 5 CENTAVOS
9.0000 g., Copper, 25.9 mm. **Obv:** National arms **Rev:** Value within 3/4 wreath **Rev. Leg.:** E. DE MOR. 1915

Date	Mintage	VG	F	VF	XF	Unc
1915	—	300	500	1,000	3,500	

KM# 697 10 CENTAVOS
8.6900 g., Copper, 24 mm. **Obv:** National arms **Rev:** Value within lined C and wreath

Date	Mintage	VG	F	VF	XF	Unc
1915	—	12.00	20.00	30.00	40.00	—

KM# 699 10 CENTAVOS
Copper **Obv:** National arms **Rev:** Date and value within wreath **Rev. Leg.:** E. DE MOR

Date	Mintage	VG	F	VF	XF	Unc
1915	—	1,000	2,000	3,000	5,000	

KM# 698 10 CENTAVOS
Copper, 24-24.5 mm. **Obv:** National arms **Rev:** Value within lined C and wreath with date effaced from die **Note:** Size varies. Weight varies 4.83-6.8g.

Date	Mintage	VG	F	VF	XF	Unc
ND	—	12.00	20.00	35.00	55.00	

KM# 700 10 CENTAVOS
Copper, 28 mm. **Obv:** National arms **Rev:** Date and value within wreath **Rev. Leg.:** MOR **Note:** Weight varies 5.56-8.36g.

Date	Mintage	VG	F	VF	XF	Unc
1916	—	5.00	20.00	30.00	50.00	

KM# 701 20 CENTAVOS
Copper, 23.75-24.75 mm. **Obv:** National arms **Rev:** Value within lined C and 3/4 wreath **Note:** Size varies. Weight varies 3.88-4.15g.

Date	Mintage	VG	F	VF	XF	Unc
1915	—	9.00	15.00	25.00	35.00	

KM# 702 50 CENTAVOS
Copper, 28.8 mm. **Obv:** National arms with MOR beneath eagle **Rev:** 50C monogram

Date	Mintage	VG	F	VF	XF	Unc
1915	—	300	500	900	1,450	

KM# 703a 50 CENTAVOS
Brass **Obv:** National arms above sprigs **Rev:** 50C monogram

Date	Mintage	VG	F	VF	XF	Unc
1915	—	100	200	400	600	

KM# 706 50 CENTAVOS
Copper, 28 mm. **Obv:** National arms **Rev:** Date above large numeral value **Rev. Leg.:** REFORMA LIBERTAD JUSTICIA Y LEY

Date	Mintage	VG	F	VF	XF	Unc
1915	—	350	500	850	1,200	

KM# 703 50 CENTAVOS
Copper, 28-29.5 mm. **Obv:** National arms **Rev:** Numeral value within lined C and 1/2 wreath **Note:** This coin exists with a silver and also a brass wash. Size varies. Weight varies 5.73-13.77g.

Date	Mintage	VG	F	VF	XF	Unc
1915	—	12.50	17.50	30.00	50.00	

KM# 704 50 CENTAVOS
Copper, 29-30 mm. **Obv:** National arms with Morelos written below **Rev:** Value within wreath **Note:** Size varies. Weight varies 8.56-11.47g.

Date	Mintage	VG	F	VF	XF	Unc
1916	—	12.50	20.00	30.00	50.00	—

KM# 708 PESO (UN)
Silver **Obv:** National arms **Rev:** Liberty cap within wreath

Date	Mintage	VG	F	VF	XF	Unc
1916	—	450	750	1,150	1,850	—

KM# 708a PESO (UN)
10.0000 g., Copper, 30 mm. **Obv:** National arms **Rev:** Liberty cap within wreath

Date	Mintage	VG	F	VF	XF	Unc
1916	—	500	1,000	1,200	2,300	—

PATTERNS
Including off metal strikes

KM#	Date	Mintage	Identification	Mkt Val
Pn1	1915	—	50 Centavos. Silver. 12.0000 g. 29.3 mm. KM#705.	1,500
Pn2	1915	—	50 Centavos. Copper. KM#705.	1,500
Pn3	191x	—	Peso. Silver. KM#707.	8,000
Pn4	191x	—	Peso. Copper. KM#707a.	8,000
Pn5	1916	—	Peso. Copper. KM#707b.	6,500

OAXACA

Oaxaca is one of the southern states in Mexico. The coins issued in this state represent the most prolific series of the Revolution. Most of the coins bear the portrait of Benito Juarez, have corded or plain edges and were issued by a provisional government in the state. The exceptions are the rectangular 1 and 3 Centavos pieces that begin the series.

PROVISIONAL GOVERNMENT
REVOLUTIONARY COINAGE

KM# 709 CENTAVO (UN)
Copper, 19 mm. **Obv:** Legend within beaded rectangle **Rev:** Legend within beaded rectangle **Note:** Rectangular flan.

Date	Mintage	VG	F	VF	XF	Unc
1915	—	90.00	125	400	650	—

KM# 710 CENTAVO (UN)
Copper, 18 mm. **Obv:** Bust left with date flanked by stars below **Rev:** Value within lined C and 1/2 wreath

Date	Mintage	VG	F	VF	XF	Unc
1915	—	12.00	17.50	25.00	40.00	—

KM# 710a CENTAVO (UN)
Brass **Obv:** Head left with date flanked by stars below **Rev:** Value within lined C and 1/2 wreath

Date	Mintage	VG	F	VF	XF	Unc
1915	—	50.00	100	200	350	—

KM# 711 3 CENTAVOS (Tres)
Copper, 24 mm. **Obv:** Legend within rectangle with date below, stars in corners **Rev:** Legend within rectangle with stars in corners **Rev. Leg.:** PROVISIO... **Note:** Rectangular flan.

Date	Mintage	VG	F	VF	XF	Unc
1915	—	100	200	400	600	—

KM# 712 3 CENTAVOS (Tres)
Copper **Obv:** Legend within rectangle with date below, stars in corners **Rev:** Legend within rectangle with stars in corners **Rev. Leg.:** PROVISI... **Note:** Rectangular flan.

Date	Mintage	VG	F	VF	XF	Unc
1915	—	1,000	3,000	5,000	9,000	—

KM# 713.1 3 CENTAVOS (Tres)
2.2500 g., Copper, 20 mm. **Obv:** Bust left flanked by stars below **Rev:** Value above sprigs **Note:** Without TM below value

Date	Mintage	VG	F	VF	XF	Unc
1915	—	3.00	5.00	12.00	25.00	—

KM# 713.2 3 CENTAVOS (Tres)
2.2500 g., Copper, 20 mm. **Obv:** Bust left flanked by stars below **Rev:** Value above sprigs **Edge:** Plain **Note:** Without TM below value

Date	Mintage	VG	F	VF	XF	Unc
1915	—	—	—	70.00	100	—

KM# 713.3 3 CENTAVOS (Tres)
2.2500 g., Copper, 20 mm. **Obv:** Bust left flanked by stars below **Rev:** Value above sprigs **Note:** With TM below value

Date	Mintage	VG	F	VF	XF	Unc
1915	—	100	200	400	500	—

KM# 714 3 CENTAVOS (Tres)
Copper, 20 mm. **Obv:** Bust left **Rev:** Value above sprigs **Note:** Small 3

Date	Mintage	VG	F	VF	XF	Unc
1915	—	6.00	10.00	15.00	30.00	—

KM# 715 5 CENTAVOS
Copper **Note:** JAN. 15 1915. incuse lettering

Date	Mintage	VG	F	VF	XF	Unc
1915 Rare	—	—	—	—	—	—

KM# 716 5 CENTAVOS
Copper **Obv:** Bust facing within circle **Rev:** Value above sprigs

Date	Mintage	VG	F	VF	XF	Unc
1915	—	—	—	—	8,000	—

KM# 717 5 CENTAVOS
Copper, 22 mm. **Obv:** Low relief bust left with date flanked by stars below **Rev:** Value above sprigs **Note:** Low relief with long, pointed truncation

Date	Mintage	VG	F	VF	XF	Unc
1915	—	1.50	3.00	4.50	10.00	—

KM# 718 5 CENTAVOS
Copper, 22 mm. **Obv:** Raised bust left with date flanked by stars below **Rev:** Value above sprigs **Note:** Heavy with short unfinished lapels

Date	Mintage	VG	F	VF	XF	Unc
1915	—	1.50	2.50	4.00	10.00	—

KM# 719 5 CENTAVOS
Copper, 22 mm. **Obv:** Raised bust left with date flanked by stars below **Rev:** Value above sprigs **Note:** Curved bottom

Date	Mintage	VG	F	VF	XF	Unc
1915	—	1.50	2.50	4.00	10.00	—

KM# 720 5 CENTAVOS
Copper, 22 mm. **Obv:** Bust left with date flanked by stars below **Rev:** Value above sprigs **Note:** Short truncation with closed lapels

Date	Mintage	VG	F	VF	XF	Unc
1915	—	1.50	3.00	4.50	10.00	—

KM# 721 5 CENTAVOS
Copper, 22 mm. **Obv:** Bust left with date flanked by stars below **Rev:** Value above sprigs **Note:** Short curved truncation

Date	Mintage	VG	F	VF	XF	Unc
1915	—	1.50	2.50	5.00	10.00	—

KM# 722 10 CENTAVOS
Copper **Obv:** Low relief bust left with date flanked by stars below **Rev:** Value above sprigs **Note:** Low relief with long pointed truncation

Date	Mintage	VG	F	VF	XF	Unc
1915	—	1.50	2.50	5.00	10.00	—

KM# 723 10 CENTAVOS
Copper **Obv:** Bust left with date flanked by stars below **Rev:** Value above sprigs **Note:** Obverse and reverse legend retrograde.

Date	Mintage	VG	F	VF	XF	Unc
1915 Rare	—	—	—	—	—	—

KM# 724 10 CENTAVOS
Copper, 26.5 mm. **Obv:** Raised bust left with date flanked by stars below **Rev:** Value above sprigs **Note:** Bold and unfinished truncation using 1 peso obverse die of km#740

Date	Mintage	VG	F	VF	XF	Unc
1915	—	3.00	5.00	7.00	10.00	—

KM# 725 10 CENTAVOS
Copper, 26.5 mm. **Obv:** Bust left with date flanked by stars below **Rev:** Value above sprigs **Note:** Heavy with short unfinished lapels centered high

Date	Mintage	VG	F	VF	XF	Unc
1915	—	1.50	2.50	4.00	10.00	—

KM# 726 10 CENTAVOS
Copper **Obv:** Raised bust left with date flanked by stars below **Rev:** Value above sprigs **Note:** Curved bottom

Date	Mintage	VG	F	VF	XF	Unc
1915	—	1.50	2.50	4.00	10.00	—

KM# 727.1 10 CENTAVOS
Copper **Obv:** Raised bust left with date flanked by stars below **Rev:** Value above sprigs **Note:** Short truncation with closed lapels

Date	Mintage	VG	F	VF	XF	Unc
1915	—	1.50	2.50	4.00	10.00	—

KM# 727.2 10 CENTAVOS
Copper **Obv:** Bust left with date flanked by stars below **Rev:** Value above sprigs **Note:** At present, only four pieces of this type are known. All are VF or better; T below bow with M below first leaf

Date	Mintage	VG	F	VF	XF	Unc
1915	—	—	—	400	550	—

KM# 727.3 10 CENTAVOS
Copper **Obv:** Raised bust left flanked by letters GV with date flanked by stars below **Rev:** Value above sprigs **Note:** This counterstamp appears on several different type host 10 cent coins.

Date	Mintage	VG	F	VF	XF	Unc
1915	—	100	200	300	450	—

Note: Letters GV correspond to General Garcia Vigil

KM# 730 20 CENTAVOS
Copper **Obv:** Bust left with date flanked by stars below **Rev:** Value above sprigs **Note:** 5th bust, heavy with short unfinished lapels using 20 Pesos obverse die

Date	Mintage	VG	F	VF	XF	Unc
1915	—	5.00	7.00	10.00	15.00	—

KM# 729.2   20 CENTAVOS
Copper **Counterstamp:** Liberty cap **Obv:** Bust left with date
flanked by stars below **Rev:** Value above sprigs
Note: Counterstamp: Liberty cap and rays with bold unfinished
truncation using 1 peso obverse die

Date	Mintage	VG	F	VF	XF	Unc
1915	—	100	150	300	375	—

KM# 728   20 CENTAVOS
Silver, 19 mm.   **Obv:** Low relief bust left with date flanked by
stars below **Rev:** Value above sprigs **Note:** Low relief with long
pointed truncation

Date	Mintage	VG	F	VF	XF	Unc
1915	—	800	2,000	3,000	4,000	—

KM# 728a   20 CENTAVOS
Copper, 19 mm.   **Obv:** Bust left with date flanked by stars below
Rev: Value above sprigs **Note:** Low relief with long pointed
truncation

Date	Mintage	VG	F	VF	XF	Unc
1915 Rare	—	—	—	—	—	—

KM# 729.1   20 CENTAVOS
Copper **Obv:** Raised bust left with date flanked by stars below
Rev: Value above sprigs **Note:** Unfinished truncation using 1
peso obverse die

Date	Mintage	VG	F	VF	XF	Unc
1915	—	1.50	3.00	4.50	10.00	—

KM# 731.1   20 CENTAVOS
Copper, 31 mm.   **Obv:** Raised bust left with date flanked by stars
below **Rev:** Value above sprigs **Note:** Curved bottom

Date	Mintage	VG	F	VF	XF	Unc
1915	—	1.50	2.50	5.00	10.00	—

KM# 731.2   20 CENTAVOS
Copper **Obv:** Raised bust left with date flanked by stars below
Rev: Value above sprigs **Note:** Similar to KM#731.1 but with
fourth bust.

Date	Mintage	VG	F	VF	XF	Unc
1915 Unique	—	—	—	—	—	—

KM# 732   20 CENTAVOS
Copper **Obv:** Raised bust left with date flanked by stars below
Rev: Value above sprigs

Date	Mintage	VG	F	VF	XF	Unc
1915	—	1.50	2.50	4.00	10.00	—

KM# 733   20 CENTAVOS
Copper **Obv:** Bust left with date flanked by stars below
Rev: Value above sprigs **Note:** 7th bust, short truncation with
closed lapels

Date	Mintage	VG	F	VF	XF	Unc
1915	—	1.50	3.00	4.50	10.00	—

KM# 735   50 CENTAVOS
Silver, 22 mm.   **Obv:** Raised bust left with date flanked by stars
below **Rev:** Value above sprigs **Note:** Curved bottom

Date	Mintage	VG	F	VF	XF	Unc
1915	—	8.00	15.00	30.00	50.00	—

KM# 734   50 CENTAVOS
4.0700 g., Silver, 22 mm.   **Obv:** Raised bust left with date flanked
by stars below **Rev:** Value above sprigs **Note:** Heavy with short
unfinished lapels

Date	Mintage	VG	F	VF	XF	Unc
1915	—	10.00	20.00	50.00	100	—

KM# 739   50 CENTAVOS
Billon **Obv:** Raised bust left with date flanked by stars below
Rev: Value above sprigs **Note:** Ninth bust, high nearly straight
truncation

Date	Mintage	VG	F	VF	XF	Unc
1915	—	—	—	—	4,000	—

KM# 739a   50 CENTAVOS
Copper **Obv:** Raised bust left with date flanked by stars below
Rev: Value above sprigs **Note:** Ninth bust, high nearly straight
truncation

Date	Mintage	VG	F	VF	XF	Unc
1915	—	—	—	—	—	—

KM# 736   50 CENTAVOS
Silver **Obv:** Bust left with date flanked by stars below **Rev:** Value
above sprigs **Note:** Short truncation with closed lapels

Date	Mintage	VG	F	VF	XF	Unc
1915	—	8.00	15.00	30.00	50.00	—

KM# 737   50 CENTAVOS
4.5400 g., Silver, 22 mm.   **Obv:** Bust left with date flanked by
stars below **Rev:** Value above sprigs **Note:** Short truncation with
pronounced curve

Date	Mintage	VG	F	VF	XF	Unc
1915	—	10.00	15.00	25.00	40.00	—

KM# 741   PESO (UN)
Silver **Obv:** Raised bust with date flanked by stars below
Rev: Value above sprigs **Note:** Fifth bust, heavy with short
unfinished lapels, centered high

Date	Mintage	VG	F	VF	XF	Unc
1915	—	8.00	10.00	25.00	35.00	—

KM# 740.1   PESO (UN)
Silver, 26 mm.   **Obv:** Raised bust left with date flanked by stars
below **Rev:** Written value above sprigs **Note:** Fourth bust with
heavy unfinished truncation

Date	Mintage	VG	F	VF	XF	Unc
1915	—	5.00	10.00	20.00	35.00	—

KM# 740.2   PESO (UN)
Silver, 26 mm.   **Obv:** Raised bust left with date flanked by stars
below **Rev:** Written value above sprigs **Note:** Fourth bust with
heavy unfinished truncation w/TM.

Date	Mintage	VG	F	VF	XF	Unc
1915	—	150	300	400	650	—

KM# 743   PESO (UN)
Silver **Obv:** Low relief bust left with date flanked by stars below
Rev: Value above sprigs **Note:** Seventh bust, short truncation
with closed lapels

Date	Mintage	VG	F	VF	XF	Unc
1915	—	10.00	20.00	30.00	50.00	—

KM# 743a   PESO (UN)
Silver **Obv:** Low relief bust left with date flanked by stars below
Rev: Value above sprigs **Note:** Seventh bust, short truncation
with closed lapels

Date	Mintage	VG	F	VF	XF	Unc
1915	—	35.00	75.00	150	200	—

KM# 742   PESO (UN)
Silver **Obv:** Low relief bust left with date flanked by stars below
Rev: Value above sprigs **Note:** Sixth bust; Curved bottom line

Date	Mintage	VG	F	VF	XF	Unc
1915	—	10.00	15.00	30.00	50.00	—

KM# 742a PESO (UN)
Copper Obv: Low relief bust left with date flanked by stars below
Rev: Value above sprigs Note: Sixth bust; Curved bottom line

Date	Mintage	VG	F	VF	XF	Unc
1915	—	—	—	—	500	—

KM# 744 2 PESOS (Dos)
Silver, 30 mm. Obv: Raised bust left with date flanked by stars
below Rev: Value above sprigs Note: Fourth bust, using 1 peso
obverse die

Date	Mintage	VG	F	VF	XF	Unc
1915	—	15.00	25.00	40.00	65.00	—

KM# 744a 2 PESOS (Dos)
Copper Obv: Raised bust left with date flanked by stars below Rev:
Value above sprigs Note: Fourth bust, using 1 peso obverse die

Date	Mintage	VG	F	VF	XF	Unc
1915 Rare	—	—	—	—	—	—

KM# 745 2 PESOS (Dos)
Gold-Silver, 22 mm. Obv: Low relief bust left with date flanked
by stars below Rev: Value above sprigs Note: 0.9020 Silver,
0.0100 Gold. Fifth bust, curved bottom 2 over pesos

Date	Mintage	VG	F	VF	XF	Unc
1915	—	12.00	20.00	40.00	60.00	—

KM# 745a 2 PESOS (Dos)
Copper Obv: Low relief bust left with date flanked by stars below
Rev: Value above sprigs Note: Fifth bust, curved bottom 2 over
pesos

Date	Mintage	VG	F	VF	XF	Unc
1915	—	75.00	100	150	250	—

KM# A746 2 PESOS (Dos)
Copper Obv: Raised bust left with date flanked by stars below
Rev: Balance scale below liberty cap Note: Seventh bust, short
truncation with closed lapels

Date	Mintage	VG	F	VF	XF	Unc
1915 Unique	—	—	—	—	—	—

KM# 746 2 PESOS (Dos)
Silver Obv: Raised bust left with date flanked by stars below
Rev: Balance scale below liberty cap

Date	Mintage	VG	F	VF	XF	Unc
1915	—	20.00	25.00	50.00	75.00	—

KM# A747 2 PESOS (Dos)
Silver Obv: Bust left with date flanked by stars below
Rev: Balance scale below liberty cap Note: Obverse die is free
hand engraved.

Date	Mintage	VG	F	VF	XF	Unc
1915	—	—	185	275	—	—

KM# 746a 2 PESOS (Dos)
Copper Obv: Bust left with date flanked by stars below
Rev: Balance scale below liberty cap

Date	Mintage	Good	F	VF	XF
1915	—	150	200	600	1,000

KM# 747.1 2 PESOS (Dos)
13.4400 g., Silver, 33 mm. Obv: Bust left with date flanked by
stars below Rev: Balance scale below liberty cap

Date	Mintage	VG	F	VF	XF	Unc
1915	—	15.00	20.00	50.00	90.00	—

KM# 747.2 2 PESOS (Dos)
13.4400 g., Silver, 33 mm. Obv: Bust left with date flanked by
stars below Rev: Balance scale below liberty cap

Date	Mintage	VG	F	VF	XF	Unc
1915	—	20.00	25.00	50.00	90.00	—

KM# 747.3 2 PESOS (Dos)
13.4400 g., Silver, 33 mm. Obv: Bust left with date flanked by
stars below Rev: Balance scale below liberty cap

Date	Mintage	VG	F	VF	XF	Unc
1915	—	15.00	30.00	50.00	90.00	—

KM# 748 2 PESOS (Dos)
0.9020 Silver, 22 mm. Obv: Bust left with date flanked by stars
below Rev: Value above sprigs

Date	Mintage	VG	F	VF	XF	Unc
1915	—	15.00	30.00	50.00	90.00	—

KM# 749 2 PESOS (Dos)
Silver Obv: Head left with date flanked by stars below
Rev: Value above sprigs

Date	Mintage	VG	F	VF	XF	Unc
1915 Unique	—	—	—	—	3,000	—

KM# 751 5 PESOS
16.7700 g., Silver, 30 mm. Obv: Low relief bust left with date
flanked by stars below Rev: Value above sprigs Note: Seventh
bust, short truncation with closed lapels

Date	Mintage	VG	F	VF	XF	Unc
1915	—	50.00	80.00	175	275	—

KM# 751a 5 PESOS
Copper Obv: Low relief bust left with date flanked by stars below
Rev: Value above sprigs Note: Seventh bust, short truncation
with closed lapels

Date	Mintage	VG	F	VF	XF	Unc
1915	—	125	200	300	800	—

KM# 750 5 PESOS
0.1750 Gold, 19 mm. Obv: Bust left Rev: Value above sprigs
Note: Third bust, heavy, with short unfinished lapels

Date	Mintage	VG	F	VF	XF	Unc
1915	—	150	200	300	500	800

KM# 750a 5 PESOS
Copper Obv: Bust left Rev: Value above sprigs Note: Third
bust, heavy, with short unfinished lapels

Date	Mintage	VG	F	VF	XF	Unc
1915 Unique	—	—	—	—	—	—

KM# A752 10 PESOS
0.1500 Gold Obv: Bust left with date flanked by stars below
Rev: Value above sprigs

Date	Mintage	VG	F	VF	XF	Unc
1915 Rare	—	—	—	—	—	—

KM# 752 10 PESOS
0.1750 Gold, 23 mm. Obv: Bust left with date flanked by stars
below Rev: Value above sprigs

Date	Mintage	VG	F	VF	XF	Unc
1915	—	200	300	400	600	—

KM# 752a 10 PESOS
Copper Obv: Bust left with date flanked by stars below
Rev: Value above sprigs

Date	Mintage	VG	F	VF	XF	Unc
1915	—	800	1,500	2,000	4,000	—

KM# 753 20 PESOS
0.1750 Gold Obv: Bust left with date flanked by stars below
Rev: Value above sprigs

Date	Mintage	VG	F	VF	XF	Unc
1915	—	400	500	800	1,000	1,500

KM# 754 20 PESOS
0.1750 Gold, 27 mm. Obv: Bust left with date flanked by stars
below Rev: Value above sprigs

Date	Mintage	VG	F	VF	XF	Unc
1915	—	200	400	600	900	—

KM# A753 20 PESOS
0.1500 Gold Obv: Bust left with date flanked by stars below
Rev: Value above sprigs Note: Fourth bust

Date	Mintage	VG	F	VF	XF	Unc
1915 Unique	—	—	—	—	—	—

KM# 755   60 PESOS
50.0000 g., 0.8590 Gold 1.3808 oz. AGW **Obv:** Head left within 3/4 wreath **Rev:** Balance scale below liberty cap **Edge:** Reeded

Date	Mintage	F	VF	XF	Unc	BU
1916 Rare	—	—	10,000	20,000	28,000	

KM# 755a   60 PESOS
Silver **Obv:** Head left within 3/4 wreath **Rev:** Balance scales below liberty cap **Edge:** Reeded

Date	Mintage	F	VF	XF	Unc	BU
1916	—				1,800	

KM# 755b   60 PESOS
Copper **Obv:** Head left within 3/4 wreath **Rev:** Balance scales below liberty cap **Edge:** Plain

Date	Mintage	F	VF	XF	Unc	BU
1916	—			1,000	1,800	

PUEBLA

A state of central Mexico. Puebla was a state that occasionally saw Zapata forces active within its boundaries. Also active, and an issuer of coins, was the Madero brigade who issued coins with their name two years after Madero's death. The state issue of 2, 5, 10 and 20 Centavos saw limited circulation and recent hoards have been found of some values.

CHICONCUAUTLA
Madero Brigade
REVOLUTIONARY COINAGE

KM# 756   10 CENTAVOS
6.7300 g., Copper, 27 mm. **Obv:** Date below national arms **Rev:** Letters X and C entwined

Date	Mintage	VG	F	VF	XF	Unc
1915	—	7.50	12.50	17.50	25.00	—

KM# 758   20 CENTAVOS
Copper, 28 mm. **Obv:** Date below national arms **Rev:** Value

Date	Mintage	VG	F	VF	XF	Unc
1915	—	2.50	4.00	6.50	12.00	—

KM# 757   20 CENTAVOS
Copper, 28 mm. **Obv:** Date below national arms **Rev:** Value
Note: Varieties exist.

Date	Mintage	VG	F	VF	XF	Unc
1915	—	2.50	4.00	6.50	12.00	—

TETELA DEL ORO Y OCAMPO
REVOLUTIONARY COINAGE

KM# 759   2 CENTAVOS
Copper, 16 mm. **Obv:** National arms above date **Rev:** Value

Date	Mintage	VG	F	VF	XF	Unc
1915	—	12.50	20.00	28.00	45.00	—
1915 Restrikes	—		1.00	1.50	2.00	—

KM# 760   2 CENTAVOS
Copper, 20 mm. **Obv:** National arms within beaded circle **Rev:** Value within beaded circle **Rev. Leg.:** E. DE PU.

Date	Mintage	VG	F	VF	XF	Unc
1915	—	15.00	25.00	35.00	75.00	—

KM# 761   2 CENTAVOS
Copper, 20 mm. **Obv:** National arms within beaded circle **Rev:** Value within beaded circle **Rev. Leg.:** E. DE PUE.

Date	Mintage	VG	F	VF	XF	Unc
1915	—	9.00	20.00	25.00	50.00	—

KM# 762   5 CENTAVOS
Copper, 21 mm. **Obv:** National arms within beaded circle **Rev:** Value within beaded circle

Date	Mintage	VG	F	VF	XF	Unc
1915	—	100	200	300	400	—

KM# 764   20 CENTAVOS
Copper, 24 mm. **Obv:** National arms **Rev:** Value above sprigs

Date	Mintage	VG	F	VF	XF	Unc
1915	—	50.00	100	150	225	—

KM#	Date	Mintage	Identification	Mkt Val
TS1	1915	—	10 Centavos. Copper. Uniface, KM#763.	475
TS2	1915	—	10 Centavos. Brass. Uniface, KM#763.	750
TS3	1915	—	10 Centavos. Copper. KM#761. Eagle.	1,600

SINALOA

A state along the west coast of Mexico. The cast pieces of this state have been attributed to two people - Generals Rafael Buelna and Juan Carrasco. The cap and rays 8 Reales is usually attributed to General Buelna and the rest of the series to Carrasco. Because of their crude nature it is questionable whether separate series or mints can be determined.

BUELNA / CARRASCO
CAST COINAGE
Revolutionary

KM# 766   50 CENTAVOS
Cast Silver, 29-31 mm. **Obv:** National arms **Rev:** Numeral value within wreath **Note:** Sand molded using regular 50 Centavos, KM#445. Size varies. Weight varies 12.81-14.8g.

Date	Mintage	Good	VG	F	VF	XF
ND(1905-1918)	—	200	300			

COUNTERMARKED COINAGE
Revolutionary

These are all crude sand cast coins using regular coins to prepare the mold. Prices below give a range for how much of the original coin from which the mold was prepared is visible.

KM# 765   20 CENTAVOS
Cast Silver **Obv:** National arms within beaded circle **Rev:** Value within beaded circle **Note:** Sand molded using regular 20 Centavos.

CM Date	Host Date	Good	VG	F	VF	XF
ND(ca.1915)	ND(1898-1905)	200	300			

KM# 767   50 CENTAVOS
Cast Silver **Countermark:** G.C. **Obv:** National arms with additional countermark **Rev:** Value and date within wreath with liberty cap above **Note:** Sand molded using regular 50 Centavos, KM#445.

CM Date	Host Date	Good	VG	F	VF	XF
ND	ND(1905-1918)	100	150	200	300	—

KM# 768.1   PESO
Cast Silver, 38.8-39 mm. **Note:** Sand molded using regular 8 Reales, KM#377. Size varies. Weight varies 26-33.67g.

CM Date	Host Date	Good	VG	F	VF	XF
ND(ca.1915)	ND(1824-97)	17.50	35.00	45.00	55.00	—

KM# 768.2   PESO
Cast Silver, 38.5-39 mm. **Countermark:** G.C. **Obv:** With additional countermark **Note:** Sand molded using regular 8 Reales, KM#377. Size varies. Weight varies 26-33.67g.

CM Date	Host Date	Good	VG	F	VF	XF
ND(ca.1915)	ND(1824-97)	25.00	45.00	100	150	—

KM# 770 PESO

Cast Silver, 38.5 mm. **Countermark:** G.C **Obv:** National arms with additional countermark **Rev:** Liberty cap with additional countermark **Note:** Sand molded using regular Peso, KM#409.

CM Date	Host Date	Good	VG	F	VF	XF
ND(ca.1915)	ND(1898-1909)	30.00	60.00	140	175	—

MOLDOVA

The Republic of Moldova (formerly the Moldavian S.S.R.) is bordered in the north, east and south by the Ukraine and on the west by Romania. It has an area of 13,000 sq. mi. (33,700 sq. km.) and a population of 4.4 million. The capital is Chisinau. Agricultural products are mainly cereals, grapes, tobacco, sugar beets and fruits. Food processing, clothing, building materials and agricultural machinery manufacturing dominate the industry.

The historical Romanian principality of Moldova was established in the 14th century. It fell under Turkish suzerainty in the 16th century. From 1812 to 1918 Russians occupied the eastern portion of Moldova, which they named Bessarabia. In March 1918 the Bessarabian legislature voted in favor of reunification with Romania. At the Paris Peace Conference in 1920 United States, France, U.K., and Italy a.s.o officially recognized the union. The new Soviet government did not accept the union. In 1924, due to Soviet pressure against Romania a Moldavian Autonomous Soviet Socialist Republic (A.S.S.R.) was established within the USSR on the border strip that extends east of Nistru River (today it is Transdniestria or Transdniester).

Following the Molotov-Ribbentrop Pact (1939), the Soviet - German agreement, which divided Eastern Europe, the Soviet forces, reoccupied the region in June 1940 and the Moldavian S.S.R. was proclaimed. The Transdniestra region was transferred to the new republic, while Ukrainian S.S.R. obtained possession of southern part of Bessarabia. Romanian forces liberated the region in 1941. The Soviets reconquered the territory (in 1944).

A declaration of republican sovereignty was adopted in June 1990 and in Aug. 1991 the area was renamed Moldova, an independent republic. In Dec. 1991 Moldova became a member of the C.I.S. In 1992, as a result of Russian involvement, Transdniestra seceded from Moldova. In May 1992 fighting began between Moldavian separatists (Romanians) and rebels aided by contingents of Cossacks and the Russian 14th Army. The Moldavian government made several futile requests for United Nations intervention. On July 3, 1992, Russian and Moldavian presidents agreed upon a neutral demarcation line with the withdrawal of Russian forces from Transdniestra. This status will remain until a more feasible constitution is proclaimed.

RULER
Romanian, until 1940

MONETARY SYSTEM
100 Bani = 1 Leu

REPUBLIC
DECIMAL COINAGE

KM# 1 BAN

0.6800 g., Aluminum, 14.5 mm. **Obv:** National arms **Rev:** Value divides date above monogram **Edge:** Plain

Date	Mintage	F	VF	XF	Unc	BU
1993	—	—	—	—	0.20	0.40
1995	—	—	—	—	0.20	0.40
1996	—	—	—	—	0.25	0.50
2000	—	—	—	—	0.25	0.50

KM# 2 5 BANI

0.8000 g., Aluminum, 16 mm. **Obv:** National arms **Rev:** Monogram divides sprigs below value and date **Edge:** Plain

Date	Mintage	F	VF	XF	Unc	BU
1993	—	—	—	0.15	0.35	0.50
1995	—	—	—	0.15	0.35	0.50
1996	—	—	—	0.15	0.35	0.50
1999	—	—	—	0.15	0.35	0.50
2000	—	—	—	0.15	0.35	0.50

KM# 7 10 BANI

0.8400 g., Aluminum, 16.6 mm. **Obv:** National arms **Rev:** Value, date and monogram **Edge:** Plain

Date	Mintage	F	VF	XF	Unc	BU
1995	—	—	—	—	0.40	0.60
1996	—	—	—	—	0.40	0.60
1997	—	—	—	—	0.40	0.60
1998	—	—	—	—	0.40	0.60
2000	—	—	—	—	0.40	0.60

KM# 3 25 BANI

0.9200 g., Aluminum, 17.5 mm. **Obv:** National arms **Rev:** Monogram divides sprigs below value and date **Edge:** Plain

Date	Mintage	F	VF	XF	Unc	BU
1993	—	—	—	0.20	0.50	0.75
1995	—	—	—	0.20	0.50	0.75
1999	—	—	—	0.20	0.50	0.75
2000	—	—	—	0.20	0.50	0.75

KM# 4 50 BANI

1.0700 g., Aluminum, 19 mm. **Obv:** National arms **Rev:** Monogram divides sprigs below date and value

Date	Mintage	F	VF	XF	Unc	BU
1993	—	—	—	—	0.75	1.00

KM# 10 50 BANI

3.1000 g., Brass-Clad Steel, 19 mm. **Obv:** National arms **Rev:** Value and date within grapevine **Edge:** Reeded

Date	Mintage	F	VF	XF	Unc	BU
1997	—	—	—	—	1.50	2.00

KM# 5 LEU

Nickel Clad Steel **Obv:** National arms **Rev:** Value divides date with monogram above

Date	Mintage	F	VF	XF	Unc	BU
1992	—	—	—	—	1.50	2.00

KM# 6 5 LEI

Nickel Clad Steel **Obv:** National arms **Rev:** Value flanked by monogram and date

Date	Mintage	F	VF	XF	Unc	BU
1993	—	—	—	—	3.50	4.00

KM# 11 50 LEI

16.6300 g., 0.9850 Silver 0.5266 oz. ASW, 30 mm. **Subject:** Manastirea Rudi **Obv:** National arms **Rev:** Monastary building **Edge:** Plain

Date	Mintage	F	VF	XF	Unc	BU
2000 Proof	—	Value: 35.00				

KM# 8 100 LEI

28.2800 g., 0.9250 Silver 0.8410 oz. ASW **Subject:** 5th Anniversary of Independence **Obv:** National arms **Rev:** Flying stork with grapes

Date	Mintage	F	VF	XF	Unc	BU
1996	20,000	Value: 55.00				

KM# 9 100 LEI

28.2800 g., 0.9250 Silver 0.8410 oz. ASW **Subject:** First Olympic Games Participation **Obv:** National arms **Rev:** Two men in a canoe

Date	Mintage	F	VF	XF	Unc	BU
1996	20,000	Value: 55.00				

KM# 15   100 LEI
31.1000 g., 0.9250 Silver 0.9249 oz. ASW, 37 mm.
Subject: Effigy of King Alexandru the Good **Obv:** National arms
Rev: Crowned bust facing flanked by dates and shield
Edge: Plain

Date	Mintage	F	VF	XF	Unc	BU
2000 Proof	1,000				Value: 60.00	

KM# 24   100 LEI
31.1000 g., 0.9250 Silver 0.9249 oz. ASW, 37 mm. **Subject:** Battle of Vaslui - 1475 **Obv:** National arms above value **Rev:** Battle scene, King on horse, soldiers at forefront, standard at top **Edge:** Plain

Date	Mintage	F	VF	XF	Unc	BU
2000 Proof	1,000				Value: 60.00	

KM# 28   100 LEI
31.1000 g., 0.9250 Silver 0.9249 oz. ASW, 37 mm. **Subject:** 100th Anniversary - Birth of Stefan Neaga **Obv:** Arms, date divides legend above, value below **Obv. Leg.:** REPUBLICA MOLDOVA **Rev:** Bust of Neaga facing, image of lyre at left, staff with musical notes at right **Rev. Leg.:** STEFAN NEAGA **Edge:** Plain

Date	Mintage	F	VF	XF	Unc	BU
2000 Proof	—				Value: 60.00	

MONACO

The Principality of Monaco, located on the Mediterranean coast nine miles from Nice, has an area of 0.58 sq. mi. (1.9 sq. km.) and a population of 26,000. Capital: Monaco-Ville. The economy is based on tourism and the manufacture of cosmetics, gourmet foods and highly specialized electronics. Monaco also derives its revenue from a tobacco monopoly and the sale of postage stamps for philatelic purpose. Gambling in Monte Carlo accounts for only a small fraction of the country's revenue.

Monaco derives its name from Monoikos', the Greek surname for Hercules, the mythological strong man who, according to legend, formed the Monacan headland during one of his twelve labors. Monaco has been ruled by the Grimaldi dynasty since 1297 - Prince Albert II, the present and 32nd monarch of Monaco, is still of that line - except for a period during the French Revolution until Napoleon's downfall when the Principality was annexed to France. Since 1865, Monaco has maintained a customs union with France which guarantees its privileged position as long as the royal line remains intact. Under the new constitution proclaimed on December 17, 1962, the Prince shares his power with an 18-member unicameral National Council.

RULERS
Albert I, 1889-1922
Louis II, 1922-1949
Rainier III, 1949-2005

MINT MARKS
M - Monaco
A – Paris

MINT PRIVY MARKS
(a) - Paris (privy marks only)
(p) - Thunderbolt - Poissy

MONETARY SYSTEM
10 Centimes = 1 Decime
10 Decimes = 1 Franc

PRINCIPALITY
DECIMAL COINAGE
10 Centimes = 1 Decime; 10 Decimes = 1 Franc

KM# 110   50 CENTIMES
Aluminum-Bronze **Ruler:** Louis II **Obv:** Hercules shooting bow to right **Rev:** Shield below value within circle

Date	Mintage	F	VF	XF	Unc	BU
1924 (p)	150,000	3.50	8.00	18.00	40.00	70.00

KM# 113   50 CENTIMES
Aluminum-Bronze **Ruler:** Louis II **Obv:** Hercules shooting bow to right **Rev:** Shield below value within circle

Date	Mintage	F	VF	XF	Unc	BU
1926 (p)	100,000	4.00	9.00	20.00	45.00	75.00

KM# 111   FRANC
Aluminum-Bronze **Ruler:** Louis II **Obv:** Hercules shooting bow to right **Rev:** Shield below value within circle

Date	Mintage	F	VF	XF	Unc	BU
1924 (p)	150,000	3.00	7.00	14.00	30.00	60.00

KM# 114   FRANC
Aluminum-Bronze **Ruler:** Louis II **Obv:** Hercules shooting bow to right **Rev:** Shield below value within circle

Date	Mintage	F	VF	XF	Unc	BU
1926 (p)	100,000	4.00	9.00	16.00	35.00	65.00

KM# 120   FRANC
Aluminum, 22.9 mm. **Ruler:** Louis II **Obv:** Head left **Rev:** Crowned mantled arms flanked by value below

Date	Mintage	F	VF	XF	Unc	BU
ND(1943) (a)	2,500,000	0.50	1.00	2.00	4.50	7.00

KM# 120a   FRANC
Aluminum-Bronze, 22.9 mm. **Ruler:** Louis II **Obv:** Head left **Rev:** Crowned mantled arms flanked by value below

Date	Mintage	F	VF	XF	Unc	BU
ND(1945) (a)	1,509,000	0.50	1.00	2.00	5.00	8.00

KM# 112   2 FRANCS
Aluminum-Bronze **Ruler:** Louis II **Obv:** Hercules shooting bow to right **Rev:** Shield below value within circle

Date	Mintage	F	VF	XF	Unc	BU
1924 (p)	75,000	8.00	14.00	30.00	75.00	100

KM# 115   2 FRANCS
Aluminum-Bronze **Ruler:** Louis II **Obv:** Hercules shooting bow to right **Rev:** Shield below value within circle

Date	Mintage	F	VF	XF	Unc	BU
1926 (p)	75,000	7.00	12.00	25.00	70.00	90.00

KM# 121   2 FRANCS
Aluminum **Ruler:** Louis II **Obv:** Head left **Rev:** Crowned mantled arms flanked by value below

Date	Mintage	F	VF	XF	Unc	BU
ND(1943) (a)	1,250,000	0.75	1.50	5.00	10.00	15.00

KM# 121a   2 FRANCS
Aluminum-Bronze **Ruler:** Louis II **Obv:** Head left **Rev:** Crowned mantles arms flanked by value below

Date	Mintage	F	VF	XF	Unc	BU
ND(1945) (a)	1,080,000	0.50	1.00	2.50	6.00	10.00

KM# 122   5 FRANCS
Aluminum **Ruler:** Louis II **Obv:** Head left **Rev:** Crowned mantled arms flanked by value below

Date	Mintage	F	VF	XF	Unc	BU
1945 (a)	1,000,000	1.50	3.00	7.00	15.00	20.00

KM# 123   10 FRANCS
Copper-Nickel, 26 mm. **Ruler:** Louis II **Obv:** Bust left **Rev:** Crowned mantled arms above value flanked by sprigs

Date	Mintage	F	VF	XF	Unc	BU
1946 (a)	1,000,000	1.50	3.00	6.00	12.50	20.00

KM# 130   10 FRANCS
Aluminum-Bronze **Ruler:** Rainier III **Obv:** Head left within circle **Rev:** Crowned shield flanked by value

Date	Mintage	F	VF	XF	Unc	BU
1950 (a)	500,000	0.50	1.00	2.00	4.00	6.00
1951 (a)	500,000	0.50	1.00	2.00	4.00	6.00

KM# 124   20 FRANCS (Vingt)
Copper-Nickel   **Ruler:** Louis II **Obv:** Bust left **Rev:** Crowned mantled arms above value flanked by sprigs

Date	Mintage	F	VF	XF	Unc	BU
1947 (a)	1,000,000	2.00	4.00	8.00	20.00	30.00

KM# 131   20 FRANCS (Vingt)
Aluminum-Bronze   **Ruler:** Rainier III **Obv:** Head left divides circle **Rev:** Crowned shield flanked by value

Date	Mintage	F	VF	XF	Unc	BU
1950 (a)	500,000	0.65	1.25	2.50	6.00	8.00
1951 (a)	500,000	0.65	1.25	2.50	6.00	8.00

KM# 132   50 FRANCS (Cinquante)
Aluminum-Bronze   **Ruler:** Rainier III **Obv:** Head left divides circle **Rev:** Armored equestrian divides circle above value

Date	Mintage	F	VF	XF	Unc	BU
1950 (a)	500,000	1.50	3.00	5.00	12.00	15.00

KM# 105   100 FRANCS (Cent)
32.2580 g., 0.9000 Gold 0.9334 oz. AGW   **Ruler:** Albert I **Obv:** Head left **Obv. Leg.:** ALBERT I PRINCE.... **Rev:** Crowned oval arms within wreath with ribbon above

Date	Mintage	F	VF	XF	Unc	BU
1901A	15,000	—	—	BV	900	975
1904A	10,000	—	—	BV	900	975

KM# 133   100 FRANCS (Cent)
Copper-Nickel   **Ruler:** Rainier III **Obv:** Head left divides circle **Rev:** Armored equestrian divides circle above value

Date	Mintage	F	VF	XF	Unc	BU
1950 (a)	500,000	2.00	4.00	8.00	18.00	30.00

KM# 134   100 FRANCS (Cent)
Copper-Nickel   **Ruler:** Rainier III **Obv:** Head left **Rev:** Value below crowned shield

Date	Mintage	F	VF	XF	Unc	BU
1956 (a)	500,000	1.50	2.50	5.50	15.00	25.00

REFORM COINAGE
100 Old Francs = 1 New Franc

KM# 155   CENTIME
1.6500 g., Stainless Steel   **Ruler:** Rainier III **Obv:** Crowned shield **Rev:** Sprig divides value and date

Date	Mintage	F	VF	XF	Unc	BU
1976 (a)	25,000	—	0.15	0.30	4.00	—
1977 (a)	25,000	—	0.15	0.30	4.00	—
1978 (a)	50,000	—	0.15	0.30	4.00	—
1979 (a)	50,000	—	0.15	0.30	4.00	—
1982 (a)	10,000	—	0.15	0.30	4.00	—
1995 (a)	—	—	0.15	0.30	4.00	—

KM# 156   5 CENTIMES
2.0000 g., Copper-Aluminum-Nickel   **Ruler:** Rainier III **Obv:** Head right **Rev:** Figure with hand on shield divides crown and value

Date	Mintage	F	VF	XF	Unc	BU
1976 (a)	25,000	—	0.20	0.40	4.50	—
1977 (a)	25,000	—	0.20	0.40	4.50	—
1978 (a)	75,000	—	0.20	0.40	4.50	—
1979 (a)	75,000	—	0.20	0.40	4.50	—
1982 (a)	10,000	—	0.20	0.40	4.50	—
1995 (a)	—	—	0.20	0.40	4.50	—

KM# 142   10 CENTIMES
Aluminum-Bronze   **Ruler:** Rainier III **Obv:** Head right **Rev:** Figure with hand on shield divides crown and value

Date	Mintage	F	VF	XF	Unc	BU
1962 (a)	750,000	—	0.15	0.30	1.50	—
1974 (a)	172,000	—	0.15	0.30	2.25	—
1975 (a)	172,000	—	0.15	0.30	2.25	—
1976 (a)	172,000	—	0.15	0.30	2.25	—
1977 (a)	172,000	—	0.15	0.30	2.25	—
1978 (a)	300,000	—	0.15	0.30	2.50	—
1979 (a)	300,000	—	0.15	0.30	2.50	—
1982 (a)	100,000	—	0.15	0.30	2.50	—
1995 (a)	—	—	0.15	0.30	2.50	—

KM# 143   20 CENTIMES
3.9600 g., Aluminum-Bronze, 23.5 mm.   **Ruler:** Rainier III **Obv:** Head right **Rev:** Figure with hand on shield divides crown and value

Date	Mintage	F	VF	XF	Unc	BU
1962 (a)	750,000	—	0.25	0.50	1.75	—
1974 (a)	104,000	—	0.25	0.50	2.75	—
1975 (a)	97,000	—	0.25	0.50	2.75	—
1976 (a)	103,000	—	0.25	0.50	2.75	—
1977 (a)	97,000	—	0.25	0.50	2.75	—
1978 (a)	25,000	—	0.25	0.50	2.75	—
1979 (a)	25,000	—	0.25	0.50	2.75	—
1982 (a)	100,000	—	0.25	0.50	2.75	—
1995 (a)	30,000	—	0.25	0.50	2.75	—

KM# 144   50 CENTIMES
Aluminum-Bronze   **Ruler:** Rainier III **Obv:** Head right **Rev:** Figure with hand on shield divides crown and value

Date	Mintage	F	VF	XF	Unc	BU
1962 (a)	375,000	—	1.25	2.50	4.50	12.00

KM# 145   1/2 FRANC
4.5500 g., Nickel, 20.5 mm.   **Ruler:** Rainier III **Obv:** Head right **Rev:** Crown overlapping shield, value at lower left

Date	Mintage	F	VF	XF	Unc	BU
1965 (a)	375,000	0.30	0.60	1.25	2.50	—
1968 (a)	125,000	0.30	0.60	1.25	2.50	—
1974 (a)	62,500	0.35	0.70	1.50	3.50	—
1975 (a)	62,500	0.35	0.70	1.50	3.50	—
1976 (a)	62,500	0.35	0.70	1.50	3.50	—
1977 (a)	62,500	0.35	0.70	1.50	3.50	—
1978 (a)	230,000	0.30	0.60	1.25	2.75	—
1979 (a)	230,000	0.30	0.60	1.25	2.75	—
1982 (a)	460,000	0.30	0.60	1.25	2.75	—
1989 (a)	10,000	0.30	0.60	1.25	2.75	—
1995 (a)	30,000	0.30	0.60	1.25	2.75	—

KM# 140   FRANC
Nickel   **Ruler:** Rainier III **Obv:** Head right **Rev:** Crown overlapping shield, value at lower left

Date	Mintage	F	VF	XF	Unc	BU
1960 (a)	500,000	0.35	0.70	1.50	3.25	—
1966 (a)	175,000	0.40	0.80	1.75	4.00	—
1968 (a)	250,000	0.40	0.80	1.75	4.00	—
1974 (a)	194,000	0.40	0.80	1.75	4.00	—
1975 (a)	195,000	0.40	0.80	1.75	4.00	—
1976 (a)	193,000	0.40	0.80	1.75	4.00	—
1977 (a)	188,000	0.40	0.80	1.75	4.00	—
1978 (a)	280,000	0.40	0.80	1.75	3.50	—
1979 (a)	280,000	0.40	0.80	1.75	3.50	—
1982 (a)	525,000	0.40	0.80	1.75	3.50	—
1986 (a)	50,000	0.35	0.70	1.50	3.00	—
1989 (a)	50,000	0.35	0.70	1.50	2.75	—
1995 (a)	30,000	0.35	0.70	1.50	2.75	—

KM# 157   2 FRANCS
Nickel, 26.5 mm.   **Ruler:** Rainier III **Obv:** Head right **Rev:** Monogram within crowned shield

Date	Mintage	F	VF	XF	Unc	BU
1979 (a)	162,000	0.60	0.85	1.75	4.00	—
1981 (a)	275,000	0.60	0.85	1.75	4.00	—
1982 (a)	446,000	0.60	0.85	1.75	4.00	—

KM# 166   2 FRANCS
Nickel, 26.5 mm.   **Ruler:** Rainier III **Obv:** Head left

Date	Mintage	F	VF	XF	Unc	BU
1995 (a)	—	0.60	0.85	1.75	4.00	—

KM# 141   5 FRANCS
12.0000 g., 0.8350 Silver 0.3221 oz. ASW **Ruler:** Rainier III
Obv: Head left **Rev:** Crowned arms with supporters flanked by value

Date	Mintage	F	VF	XF	Unc	BU
1960 (a)	125,000	—	—	7.50	10.00	20.00
1966 (a)	125,000	—	—	7.50	10.00	20.00

KM# 150   5 FRANCS
Nickel Clad Copper-Nickel **Ruler:** Rainier III **Obv:** Head right
Rev: Value below monogram and crown, all flanked by lined designs

Date	Mintage	F	VF	XF	Unc	BU
1971 (a)	250,000	—	1.50	2.50	4.50	10.00
1974 (a)	250,000	—	1.50	2.50	4.50	10.00
1975 (a)	14,000	—	2.50	6.00	12.50	18.00
1976 (a)	14,000	—	2.50	6.00	12.50	18.00
1977 (a)	14,500	—	2.00	5.00	10.00	16.00
1978 (a)	10,000	—	2.00	5.00	10.00	16.00
1979 (a)	10,000	—	2.00	5.00	10.00	16.00
1982 (a)	152,000	—	2.00	5.00	10.00	16.00
1989	35,000	—	2.00	5.00	10.00	16.00
1995 (a)	30,000	—	2.00	5.00	10.00	16.00

KM# 146   10 FRANCS
25.0000 g., 0.9000 Silver 0.7234 oz. ASW **Ruler:** Rainier III
Subject: 100th Anniversary - Accession of Charles III **Obv:** Head
right **Rev:** Crowned shield

Date	Mintage	F	VF	XF	Unc	BU
1966 (a)	62,500	—	—	—	25.00	45.00

KM# 151   10 FRANCS
10.2000 g., Copper-Nickel-Aluminum **Ruler:** Rainier III
Subject: 25th Anniversary of Reign **Obv:** Head left **Rev:**
Monogram within crowned arms with supporters

Date	Mintage	F	VF	XF	Unc	BU
ND(1974) (a)	25,000	—	2.50	4.50	8.00	—

KM# 154   10 FRANCS
Copper-Nickel-Aluminum **Ruler:** Rainier III **Obv:** Head left
Rev: Monogram within crowned arms with supporters

Date	Mintage	F	VF	XF	Unc	BU
1975 (a)	16,000	—	2.25	3.75	8.00	—
1976 (a)	16,000	—	2.50	4.00	9.00	—

Date	Mintage	F	VF	XF	Unc	BU
1977 (a)	18,000	—	2.25	3.25	5.50	—
1978 (a)	190,000	—	2.25	3.25	5.50	—
1979 (a)	190,000	—	2.25	3.25	5.50	—
1981 (a)	230,000	—	2.25	3.25	5.50	—
1982 (a)	230,000	—	2.25	3.25	5.50	—

KM# 160   10 FRANCS
Copper-Nickel-Aluminum **Ruler:** Rainier III **Obv:** Head of
Princess Grace left **Rev:** Single rose divides value

Date	Mintage	F	VF	XF	Unc	BU
1982 (a)	30,000	—	—	—	12.50	—

KM# 162   10 FRANCS
10.0000 g., Nickel-Aluminum-Bronze **Ruler:** Rainier III
Subject: Prince Pierre Foundation **Obv:** Bust right and single
sprig on paper to left of dates **Rev:** Small doubled wreath divides
date on top of shield flanked by symbols

Date	Mintage	F	VF	XF	Unc	BU
1989 (a)	100,000	—	—	—	6.50	—

KM# 163   10 FRANCS
Bi-Metallic Nickel center in Aluminum-Bronze ring
Ruler: Rainier III **Obv:** Value and monogram within circle
Rev: Armored knight right within circle

Date	Mintage	F	VF	XF	Unc	BU
1989 (a)	100,000	—	—	—	9.00	10.00
1991 (a)	250,000	—	—	—	14.00	15.00
1992 (a)	250,000	—	—	—	12.50	13.50
1993 (a)	250,000	—	—	—	14.00	15.00
1994 (a)	250,000	—	—	—	14.00	15.00
1995 (a)	250,000	—	—	—	9.00	10.00
1996 (a)	250,000	—	—	—	9.00	10.00
1997 (a)	250,000	—	—	—	9.00	10.00
1998 (a)	250,000	—	—	—	9.00	10.00
2000 (a)	240,000	—	—	—	9.00	10.00

KM# 165   20 FRANCS
Tri-Metallic Copper-Aluminum-Nickel center; Nickel ring;
Copper-Aluminum-Nickel outer ring, 26.8 mm. **Ruler:** Rainier III
Obv: Value and monogram within circle **Rev:** Prince's palace
within circle with crown above

Date	Mintage	F	VF	XF	Unc	BU
1992 (a)	100,000	—	—	—	15.00	16.50
1995 (a)		—	—	—	15.00	16.50
1997 (a)	120,000	—	—	—	15.00	16.50

KM# 152.1   50 FRANCS
30.0000 g., 0.9000 Silver 0.8680 oz. ASW **Ruler:** Rainier III
Subject: 25th Anniversary of Reign **Obv:** Bust right **Rev:** Crowned
monograms divide diamonds **Edge:** Commemorative inscription

Date	Mintage	F	VF	XF	Unc	BU
1974 (a)	25,000	—	—	—	42.00	65.00

KM# 152.2   50 FRANCS
30.0000 g., 0.9000 Silver 0.8680 oz. ASW **Ruler:** Rainier III
Obv: Bust right **Rev:** Crowned monograms divide diamonds
Edge: Plain

Date	Mintage	F	VF	XF	Unc	BU
1975 (a)	7,500	—	—	—	60.00	80.00
1976 (a)	6,000	—	—	—	65.00	85.00

KM# 161   100 FRANCS
15.0000 g., 0.9000 Silver 0.4340 oz. ASW **Ruler:** Rainier III
Subject: Heir Apparent Prince Albert **Obv:** Conjoined heads right
Rev: Crowned arms with supporters

Date	Mintage	F	VF	XF	Unc	BU
1982 (a)	30,000	—	—	—	75.00	80.00

KM# 164   100 FRANCS
15.0000 g., 0.9000 Silver 0.4340 oz. ASW **Ruler:** Rainier III
Subject: 40th Anniversary of Reign **Obv:** Head right
Rev: Crowned monogram above value

Date	Mintage	F	VF	XF	Unc	BU
1989 (a)	45,000	—	—	—	75.00	80.00

KM# 176   100 FRANCS
15.0000 g., 0.9500 Silver 0.4581 oz. ASW, 31 mm.
Ruler: Rainier III **Subject:** 700th Anniversary - Grimaldi Dynasty
Obv: Armored equestrian **Rev:** Robed figure drawing sword at
castle drawbridge **Edge:** Plain

Date	Mintage	F	VF	XF	Unc	BU
ND(1997)	30,000	—	—	—	55.00	85.00

KM# 175   100 FRANCS
15.0000 g., 0.9000 Silver 0.4340 oz. ASW, 31 mm. **Ruler:**
Rainier III **Subject:** 50th Anniversary of Reign - Prince Ranier III
Obv: Head right **Rev:** Crowned monogram above value **Edge:** Plain

Date	Mintage	F	VF	XF	Unc	BU
1999	20,000	—	—	—	75.00	80.00

PATTERNS
Including off metal strikes

KM#	Date	Mintage Identification	Mkt Val
Pn15	1934A	15 500 Francs. 0.9000 Gold.	3,220

ESSAIS
Standard metals unless otherwise noted

KM#	Date	Mintage	Identification	Issue Price	Mkt Val
E1	1924	—	50 Centimes. Gold. KM#110	—	2,000
E1	1924	—	50 Centimes. Gold. KM#110	—	2,000
E2	1924	12	Franc. Alum.-Bronze. KM111	—	950
E3	1924	—	Franc. Gold. KM111	—	3,000
E4	1924	12	2 Francs. Alum.-Bronze. KM112	—	1,000
E5	1924	—	2 Francs. Gold. Hercules shooting bow to right. Shield below value within circle. KM112	—	4,000
E6	ND(1943) (a)	250	Franc. 0.9000 Gold.	—	750
E7	ND(1943) (a)	1,100	Franc. Aluminum. KM120	—	28.00
E8	ND(1943) (a)	—	Franc. Alum.-Bronze. KM120	—	40.00
E9	ND(1943) (a)	250	Franc. Silver. KM120	—	150
E10	ND(1943) (a)	250	2 Francs. 0.9000 Gold.	—	800
E11	ND(1943) (a)	1,100	2 Francs. Alum. KM121	—	35.00
E12	ND(1943) (a)	1,100	2 Francs. Alum.-Bronze. KM121	—	37.00
E13	ND(1943) (a)	250	2 Francs. Silver. KM121	—	175
E14	1945 (a)	250	5 Francs. 0.9000 Gold.	—	900
E15	1945 (a)	1,100	5 Francs. Alum.. KM122	—	50.00
E16	1945 (a)	150	5 Francs. Alum.-Bronze. KM122	—	145
E17	1945 (a)	250	5 Francs. Silver. KM122	—	225
E18	1945 (a)	1,100	10 Francs. Copper-Nickel. KM123	—	40.00
E19	1945 (a)	250	10 Francs. Silver.	—	190
E20	1945 (a)	1,100	20 Francs. Copper-Nickel. KM124	—	60.00
E21	1945 (a)	250	20 Francs. Silver.	—	180
E22	1946 (a)	250	10 Francs. 0.9000 Gold.	—	950
E23	1947 (a)	250	20 Francs. 0.9000 Gold.	—	1,000
E24	1950 (a)	1,100	10 Francs.	—	25.00
E25	1950 (a)	500	10 Francs. Silver.	—	50.00
E26	1950 (a)	500	10 Francs. 0.9000 Gold. 14.5100 g.	—	500
E26	1950 (a)	500	10 Francs. 0.9000 Gold. 14.5100 g.	—	500
E27	1950 (a)	1,700	20 Francs.	—	32.00
E28	1950 (a)	—	20 Francs. Silver.	—	70.00
E29	1950 (a)	500	20 Francs. 0.9000 Gold.	—	650
E30	1950 (a)	1,700	50 Francs.	—	50.00
E31	1950 (a)	500	50 Francs. Silver.	—	90.00
E32	1950 (a)	500	50 Francs. 0.9000 Gold. 20.5200 g.	—	850
E33	1950 (a)	1,700	100 Francs.	—	50.00
E34	1950 (a)	500	100 Francs. Silver.	—	120
E35	1950 (a)	500	100 Francs. 0.9000 Gold. Head left divides circle. Armored knight on horse divides circle.	—	1,000
E36	1956 (a)	500	100 Francs. 0.9000 Gold.	—	500
E37	1956 (a)	500	100 Francs. Silver. KM134	—	150
E38	1960 (a)	—	Franc. Nickel. KM140	—	70.00
E39	1960 (a)	500	Franc. Silver.	—	70.00
E40	1960 (a)	500	Franc. 0.9200 Gold.	—	500
E41	1960 (a)	500	5 Francs. Silver.	—	100
E42	1960 (a)	500	5 Francs. 0.9200 Gold.	—	650
E43	1962 (a)	1,200	10 Centimes.	—	15.00
E44	1962 (a)	502	10 Centimes. 0.9500 Silver.	—	60.00
E45	1962 (a)	502	10 Centimes. 0.9200 Gold. Head right. Figure with hand on shield divides crown and value.	—	275
E46	1962 (a)	1,200	20 Centimes.	—	40.00
E47	1962 (a)	502	20 Centimes. 0.9500 Silver.	—	75.00
E48	1962 (a)	502	20 Centimes. 0.9200 Gold.	—	325
E49	1962 (a)	1,200	50 Centimes.	—	60.00
E50	1962 (a)	502	50 Centimes. 0.9500 Silver.	—	150
E51	1962 (a)	502	50 Centimes. 0.9200 Gold.	—	450
E52	1965 (a)	2,000	1/2 Franc. Nickel.	—	40.00
E53	1965 (a)	1,000	1/2 Franc. Silver.	—	60.00
E54	1965 (a)	1,000	1/2 Franc. 0.9200 Gold.	—	300
E55	1966 (a)	500	5 Francs. 0.9200 Gold.	—	600
E56	1966 (a)	100	10 Francs.	—	140
E57	1966 (a)	1,000	10 Francs. 0.9200 Gold.	—	850
E58	1971 (a)	1,000	5 Francs.	—	40.00
E59	1971 (a)	1,000	5 Francs. Silver.	—	100
E60	1971 (a)	500	5 Francs. 0.9200 Gold.	—	500
E61	1974 (a)	1,000	5 Francs. Silver.	—	60.00
E62	1974 (a)	1,000	5 Francs. Gold.	—	325
E63	1974 (a)	1,000	10 Francs.	—	45.00
E64	1974 (a)	1,000	10 Francs. Silver.	—	110
E65	1974 (a)	1,000	10 Francs. Gold.	—	345
E66	1974 (a)	1,000	50 Francs.	—	125
E67	1974 (a)	1,000	50 Francs. Gold.	—	1,200
E68	1976	1,600	Centime. Stainless Steel. KM155	—	30.00
E69	1976	1,600	5 Centimes. Copper-Aluminum-Nickel. KM156	—	35.00
E70	1976	1,600	10 Centimes. Aluminum-Bronze. KM142	—	35.00
E71	1979	—	2 Francs. Nickel. KM157	—	70.00
E71.2	1982	—	2 Francs. 0.9000 Silver. 8.8600 g. 26.4 mm. Prince Rainier III. Crowned shield behind monogram. Reeded edge.	—	75.00
E72	1982 (a)	4,000	10 Francs. Nickel-Aluminum-Bronze.	—	45.00
E73	1982 (a)	30,000	10 Francs. Silver.	—	20.00
E74	1982 (a)	1,000	10 Francs. Gold.	—	385
E75	1982 (a)	1,000	100 Francs. 0.9000 Silver. KM161	—	60.00
E76	1982 (a)	1,000	100 Francs. Gold. Conjoined heads right. Crowned arms with supporters.	—	400

PIEFORTS
Double thickness; Standard metals unless otherwise stated

KM#	Date	Mintage	Identification	Issue Price	Mkt Val
P18a	1974 (a)	—	10 Francs. Gold. Without Essai	—	750
P19a	1974 (a)	250	50 Francs. Gold. Without Essai	—	2,100

PIEFORTS WITH ESSAI
Double thickness; Standard metals unless otherwise noted

KM#	Date	Mintage	Identification	Issue Price	Mkt Val
PE1	ND(1943) (a)	15	Franc. 0.9000 Gold.	—	1,200
PE2	ND(1943) (a)	15	2 Francs. 0.9000 Gold.	—	1,400
PE3	1945 (a)	15	5 Francs. 0.9000 Gold.	—	1,500
PE4	1946 (a)	16	10 Francs. 0.9000 Gold. Bust left. Crowned shield and value flanked by sprigs.	—	1,100
PE5	1947 (a)	16	20 Francs. 0.9000 Gold.	—	1,350
PE6	1950 (a)	—	10 Francs. Silver.	—	85.00
PE6a	1950 (a)	325	10 Francs. 0.9000 Gold.	—	275
PE7	1950 (a)	—	20 Francs. Silver.	—	90.00
PE7a	1950 (a)	325	20 Francs. 0.9000 Gold.	—	315
PE8	1950 (a)	—	50 Francs. Silver.	—	160
PE8a	1950 (a)	325	50 Francs. 0.9000 Gold. 40.8700 g.	—	500
PE9	1950 (a)	—	100 Francs. Silver.	—	160
PE9a	1950 (a)	325	100 Francs. 0.9000 Gold.	—	500
PE10	1956 (a)	20	100 Francs. 0.9000 Gold.	—	1,200
PE11	1960 (a)	—	Franc. 0.9200 Gold.	—	645
PE12	1960 (a)	25	5 Francs. 0.9200 Gold.	—	1,200
PE13	1962 (a)	100	10 Centimes. 0.9500 Silver.	—	140
PE13a	1962 (a)	25	10 Centimes. 0.9200 Gold.	—	725
PE14	1962 (a)	100	20 Centimes. 0.9500 Silver.	—	140
PE14a	1962 (a)	25	20 Centimes. 0.9200 Gold.	—	820
PE15	1962 (a)	100	50 Centimes. 0.9500 Silver.	—	200
PE15a	1962 (a)	25	50 Centimes. 0.9200 Gold.	—	900
PE16	1966 (a)	150	5 Francs. Nickel.	—	60.00
PE16a	1971 (a)	250	5 Francs. Silver.	—	150
PE16b	1971 (a)	250	5 Francs. 0.9200 Gold.	—	625
PE17	1974 (a)	250	5 Francs. Silver.	—	150
PE17a	1974 (a)	250	5 Francs. Gold. Head right. Crowned monogram and value flanked by lined designs.	—	625
PE18	1974 (a)	250	10 Francs. Silver.	—	200
PE18a	1974 (a)	250	10 Francs. Gold.	—	500
PE19	1974 (a)	250	50 Francs. Without Essai	—	125
PE19a	1974 (a)	250	50 Francs. Gold.	—	2,500
PE20	1982 (a)	250	10 Francs. Silver.	—	180
PE20a	1982 (a)	250	10 Francs. Gold.	—	500
PE21	1982 (a)	250	100 Francs. Silver.	—	260
PE21a	1982 (a)	250	100 Francs. Gold.	—	800

SPECIMEN SETS (SS)

KM#	Date	Mintage	Identification	Issue Price	Mkt Val
SS1	1974 (7)	7	KM140, 142, 143, 145, 150, 151, 152.1. 3,000 sets not released.	45.00	500
SS2	1975 (7)	8	KM140, 142, 143, 145, 150, 152.2, 154	—	200
SS3	1976 (9)	6,000	KM140, 142, 143, 145, 150, 152.2, 154-156	—	120
SS6	1982 (11)	10,000	KM140, 142, 143, 145, 150, 154-157, 160, 161	—	150
SS7	1995 (9)	—	KM140, 142, 143, 150, 155, 156, 163, 165, 166	—	120

MONGOLIA

The State of Mongolia, (formerly the Mongolian People's Republic) a landlocked country in central Asia between Russia and the People's Republic of China, has an area of 604,250 sq. mi. (1,565,000 sq. km.) and a population of 2.26 million. Capital: Ulaan Baator. Animal herds and flocks are the chief economic asset. Wool, cattle, butter, meat and hides are exported.

Mongolia (often referred to as Outer Mongolia), one of the world's oldest countries, attained its greatest power in the 13th century when Genghis Khan and his successors conquered all of China and extended their influence westward as far as Hungary and Poland. The empire dissolved in later centuries and in 1691 was brought under suzerainty of the Manchus, who had conquered China in 1644. Afterward the Chinese republican movement led by Sun Yat-sen overthrew the Manchus and set up the Chinese Republic in 1911. Mongolia, with the support of Russia, proclaimed their independence from China and, on March 13, 1921 a Provisional People's Government was established and later, on Nov. 26, 1924 the government proclaimed the Mongolian People's Republic.

Although nominally a dependency of China, Outer Mongolia voted at a plebiscite Oct. 20, 1945 to sever all ties with China and become an independent nation. Opposition to the communist party developed in late 1989 and after demonstrations and hunger strikes, the Politburo resigned on March 12, 1990 and the new State of Mongolia was organized.

On Feb. 12, 1992 it became the first to discard communism as the national political system by adopting a new constitution.

For earlier issues see Russia - Tannu Tuva.

MONETARY SYSTEM
100 Mongo = 1 Tugrik

PEOPLE'S REPUBLIC
DECIMAL COINAGE

KM# 1   MONGO
Copper, 21 mm. **Obv:** Soembo arms, text **Rev:** Value within 1/2 wreath

Date	Mintage	F	VF	XF	Unc	BU
AH15 (1925)	—	5.00	8.00	12.00	25.00	—

KM# 9   MONGO
Aluminum-Bronze **Obv:** Soembo arms, text **Rev:** Value within 1/2 wreath

Date	Mintage	F	VF	XF	Unc	BU
AH27 (1937)	—	2.50	3.50	7.50	16.50	—

KM# 15   MONGO
Aluminum-Bronze **Obv:** National arms within circle **Rev:** Value within 1/2 wreath

Date	Mintage	F	VF	XF	Unc	BU
AH35 (1945)	—	2.00	3.00	5.50	12.50	—

KM# 21   MONGO
Aluminum **Obv:** Wreath around center hole with inscription around border **Rev:** Value above hole in center and 3/4 wreath

Date	Mintage	F	VF	XF	Unc	BU
1959	9,000,000	0.25	0.60	1.00	2.00	—

KM# 27 MONGO
0.7500 g., Aluminum, 17.5 mm. **Obv:** National arms **Rev:** Value above 1/2 wreath

Date	Mintage	F	VF	XF	Unc	BU
1970	—	0.25	0.60	0.85	1.50	—
1977	—	0.25	0.60	0.85	1.50	—
1980	—	0.25	0.60	0.85	1.50	—
1981	—	0.25	0.60	0.85	1.50	—

KM# 2 2 MONGO
Copper, 24 mm. **Obv:** Soembo arms, text **Rev:** Value within 1/2 wreath

Date	Mintage	F	VF	XF	Unc	BU
AH15 (1925)	—	3.50	6.50	12.00	25.00	—

KM# 10 2 MONGO
Aluminum-Bronze, 22 mm. **Obv:** Soembo, text **Rev:** Value within 1/2 wreath

Date	Mintage	F	VF	XF	Unc	BU
AH27 (1937)	—	2.50	3.50	6.00	14.00	—

KM# 16 2 MONGO
Aluminum-Bronze **Obv:** National arms within circle **Rev:** Value within 1/2 wreath

Date	Mintage	F	VF	XF	Unc	BU
AH35 (1945)	—	1.00	2.00	4.00	9.00	—

KM# 22 2 MONGO
Aluminum **Obv:** Wreath around center hole with inscription around border **Rev:** Value above center hole and 3/4 wreath

Date	Mintage	F	VF	XF	Unc	BU
1959	4,000,000	0.25	0.65	1.50	3.50	—

KM# 28 2 MONGO
1.0500 g., Aluminum, 20 mm. **Obv:** National arms above date **Rev:** Value within 1/2 wreath **Edge:** Plain

Date	Mintage	F	VF	XF	Unc	BU
1970	—	0.25	0.65	1.20	2.50	—
1977	—	0.25	0.65	1.20	2.50	—
1980	—	0.25	0.65	1.20	2.50	—
1981	—	0.25	0.65	1.20	2.50	—

KM# 3.1 5 MONGO
Copper, 32 mm. **Obv:** Soembo arms, text **Rev:** Value within 1/2 wreath

Date	Mintage	F	VF	XF	Unc	BU
AH15 (1925)	—	5.00	10.00	20.00	40.00	—

Note: Variety in obverse legend exists

KM# 3.2 5 MONGO
Copper, 32 mm. **Note:** Error: letter "m" looking like a horse's tail omitted in nayramdax (Vertically written word lower left of Soyombo)

Date	Mintage	F	VF	XF	Unc	BU
1925	—	—	—	—	45.00	—

KM# 11 5 MONGO
Aluminum-Bronze, 28 mm. **Obv:** Soembo arms, text **Rev:** Value within 1/2 wreath

Date	Mintage	F	VF	XF	Unc	BU
AH27 (1937)	—	2.75	3.50	6.00	14.00	—

KM# 17 5 MONGO
Aluminum-Bronze **Obv:** National arms within circle **Rev:** Value within 1/2 wreath

Date	Mintage	F	VF	XF	Unc	BU
AH35 (1945)	—	1.75	2.50	5.00	12.00	—

KM# 23 5 MONGO
Aluminum **Obv:** Wreath around hole in center with inscription around border **Rev:** Value above hole in center and 1/2 wreath

Date	Mintage	F	VF	XF	Unc	BU
1959	2,400,000	0.25	1.00	2.00	4.00	—

KM# 29 5 MONGO
1.6000 g., Aluminum, 23 mm. **Obv:** Date below national arms **Rev:** Value within 1/2 wreath

Date	Mintage	F	VF	XF	Unc	BU
1970	—	0.25	0.85	1.75	3.50	—
1977	—	0.25	0.85	1.75	3.50	—
1980	—	0.25	0.85	1.75	3.50	—
1981	—	0.25	0.85	1.75	3.50	—

KM# 4 10 MONGO
1.7996 g., 0.5000 Silver 0.0289 oz. ASW, 17 mm. **Obv:** Soembo arms, text **Rev:** Value within 1/2 wreath

Date	Mintage	VG	F	VF	XF	Unc
AH15 (1925)	1,500,000	—	3.00	5.00	10.00	22.00

KM# 12 10 MONGO
Copper-Nickel **Obv:** Soembo arms, text **Rev:** Value within 1/2 wreath

Date	Mintage	F	VF	XF	Unc	BU
AH27 (1937)	—	2.00	3.50	7.00	16.00	—

KM# 18 10 MONGO
Copper-Nickel **Obv:** National arms within circle **Rev:** Value within 1/2 wreath

Date	Mintage	F	VF	XF	Unc	BU
AH35 (1945)	—	1.50	3.00	5.00	12.00	—

KM# 24 10 MONGO
Aluminum **Obv:** National arms within circle **Rev:** Value within 3/4 wreath

Date	Mintage	F	VF	XF	Unc	BU
1959	3,000,000	0.75	1.50	3.00	6.00	—

KM# 30 10 MONGO
2.3000 g., Copper-Nickel, 18.5 mm. **Obv:** Date below national arms **Rev:** Value within 1/2 wreath

Date	Mintage	F	VF	XF	Unc	BU
1970	—	0.35	0.85	1.75	3.50	—
1977	—	0.35	0.85	1.75	3.50	—
1980	—	0.35	0.85	1.75	3.50	—
1981	—	0.35	0.85	1.75	3.50	—

KM# 5 15 MONGO
2.6994 g., 0.5000 Silver 0.0434 oz. ASW, 19 mm. **Obv:** Soembo arms, text **Rev:** Value within 1/2 wreath

Date	Mintage	VG	F	VF	XF	Unc
AH15 (1925)	417,000	—	3.50	6.00	12.00	25.00

KM# 13 15 MONGO
Copper-Nickel **Obv:** Soembo arms, text **Rev:** Value within 1/2 wreath

Date	Mintage	F	VF	XF	Unc	BU
AH27 (1937)	—	2.00	3.00	6.00	14.00	—

KM# 19   15 MONGO

Copper-Nickel **Obv:** National arms within circle **Rev:** Value within 3/4 wreath

Date	Mintage	F	VF	XF	Unc	BU
AH35 (1945)	—	1.50	2.25	4.00	9.00	

KM# 25   15 MONGO

Aluminum **Obv:** National arms within circle **Rev:** Value within 3/4 wreath

Date	Mintage	F	VF	XF	Unc	BU
1959	4,600,000	0.35	0.85	1.75	4.00	

KM# 31   15 MONGO

4.0500 g., Copper-Nickel, 22 mm. **Obv:** Date below national arms **Rev:** Value within 1/2 wreath

Date	Mintage	F	VF	XF	Unc	BU
1970	—	0.25	0.65	1.25	2.75	—
1977	—	0.25	0.65	1.25	2.75	—
1980	—	0.25	0.65	1.25	2.75	—
1981	—	0.25	0.65	1.25	2.75	—

KM# 6   20 MONGO

3.5992 g., 0.5000 Silver 0.0579 oz. ASW, 22 mm. **Obv:** Soembo arms, text **Rev:** Value within 1/2 wreath

Date	Mintage	VG	F	VF	XF	Unc
AH15 (1925)	1,625,000	—	4.00	7.50	15.00	30.00

KM# 14   20 MONGO

Copper-Nickel **Obv:** Soembo arms, text **Rev:** Value within 1/2 wreath

Date	Mintage	F	VF	XF	Unc	BU
AH27 (1937)	—	2.50	4.50	10.00	20.00	

KM# 20   20 MONGO

Copper-Nickel **Obv:** National arms within circle **Rev:** Value within 3/4 wreath

Date	Mintage	F	VF	XF	Unc	BU
AH35 (1945)	—	1.50	2.50	5.00	12.00	

KM# 26   20 MONGO

Aluminum **Obv:** National arms within circle **Rev:** Value within 3/4 wreath

Date	Mintage	F	VF	XF	Unc	BU
1959	3,600,000	0.60	1.25	2.25	4.50	

KM# 32   20 MONGO

5.9000 g., Copper-Nickel, 25 mm. **Obv:** Date below national arms **Rev:** Value within 1/2 wreath

Date	Mintage	F	VF	XF	Unc	BU
1970	—	0.40	0.80	1.50	3.50	—
1977	—	0.40	0.80	1.50	3.50	—
1980	—	0.40	0.80	1.50	3.50	—
1981	—	0.40	0.80	1.50	3.50	—

KM# 7   50 MONGO

9.9979 g., 0.9000 Silver 0.2893 oz. ASW, 27 mm. **Obv:** Soembo arms, text **Rev:** Value within 1/2 wreath

Date	Mintage	VG	F	VF	XF	Unc
AH15 (1925)	920,000	—	7.50	12.00	20.00	40.00

KM# 33   50 MONGO

8.6000 g., Copper-Nickel, 27.5 mm. **Obv:** Date below national arms **Rev:** Value within 1/2 wreath

Date	Mintage	F	VF	XF	Unc	BU
1970	—	0.50	1.00	1.75	3.75	—
1977	—	0.50	1.00	1.75	3.75	—
1980	—	0.50	1.00	1.75	3.75	—
1981	—	0.50	1.00	1.75	3.75	—

KM# 8   TUGRIK

19.9957 g., 0.9000 Silver 0.5786 oz. ASW, 34 mm. **Obv:** Soembo arms, text **Rev:** Value within 1/2 wreath

Date	Mintage	VG	F	VF	XF	Unc
AH15 (1925)	400,000	—	12.00	17.00	25.00	50.00

KM# 34   TUGRIK

14.9000 g., Aluminum-Bronze, 32 mm. **Subject:** 50th Anniversary of the Revolution **Obv:** National arms **Rev:** Man on horse left within beaded circle **Edge:** ONE TUGRIK 1921 - 1971 **Note:** Date on edge.

Date	Mintage	F	VF	XF	Unc	BU
ND(1971)	—	—	4.00	6.00	10.00	

KM# 34a   TUGRIK

Copper-Nickel, 32 mm. **Obv:** National arms **Rev:** Man on horse left within beaded circle

Date	Mintage	F	VF	XF	Unc	BU
ND(1971)	—	6.00	8.00	12.00	18.00	

KM# 34b   TUGRIK

18.4000 g., Silver, 32 mm. **Obv:** National arms **Rev:** Man on horse left within beaded circle

Date	Mintage	F	VF	XF	Unc	BU
(1971) Proof	—	Value: 50.00				

KM# 34c   TUGRIK

30.0000 g., Gold, 32 mm. **Subject:** 50th Anniversary of the Revolution **Obv:** National arms **Rev:** Man on horse left within beaded circle **Note:** Mintage: 5-10 pieces.

Date	Mintage	F	VF	XF	Unc	BU
(1971) Proof	—	Value: 2,500				

KM# 41   TUGRIK

14.9000 g., Aluminum-Bronze, 32 mm. **Subject:** 60th Anniversary of the Revolution **Obv:** National arms **Rev:** Man on horse left within beaded circle **Edge:** Lettered

Date	Mintage	F	VF	XF	Unc	BU
1981	—	—	4.00	7.50	9.00	

KM# 42   TUGRIK

14.9000 g., Aluminum-Bronze, 32 mm. **Subject:** Soviet - Mongolian Space Flight **Obv:** National arms **Rev:** Conjoined helmeted heads left with stars at upper left and date at lower right **Edge:** Smooth

Date	Mintage	F	VF	XF	Unc	BU
1981	—	—	3.00	6.00		

KM# 43   TUGRIK

14.9000 g., Aluminum-Bronze, 32 mm. **Subject:** 60th Anniversary of the State Bank **Obv:** National arms **Rev:** Value within design with date within 1/2 wreath **Edge:** Lettered

Date	Mintage	F	VF	XF	Unc	BU
1984	—	—	3.00	6.00		

Note: Edge varieties exist

KM# 44 TUGRIK
14.9000 g., Aluminum-Bronze, 32 mm. **Subject:** 60th Anniversary of the People's Republic **Obv:** National arms **Rev:** Soembo arms and value within 1/2 wreath **Edge:** Lettered

Date	Mintage	F	VF	XF	Unc	BU
1984	—	—	—	3.00	5.50	

KM# 48 TUGRIK
14.9000 g., Aluminum-Bronze, 32 mm. **Subject:** Year of Peace **Obv:** National arms **Rev:** Dove above hands and 3/4 wreath **Edge:** Lettered

Date	Mintage	F	VF	XF	Unc	BU
1986	—	—	—	3.50	7.50	

KM# 49 TUGRIK
14.9000 g., Aluminum-Bronze, 32 mm. **Subject:** 65th Anniversary of the Revolution **Obv:** National arms **Rev:** Bust left **Edge:** Lettered

Date	Mintage	F	VF	XF	Unc	BU
1986	—	—	—	3.00	5.50	

KM# 52 TUGRIK
14.9000 g., Aluminum-Bronze, 32 mm. **Subject:** 170th Anniversary - Birth of Karl Marx **Obv:** National arms **Rev:** Head facing flanked by dates

Date	Mintage	F	VF	XF	Unc	BU
ND(1988)	—	—	—	4.00	12.50	

KM# 35 10 TUGRIK
Copper-Nickel **Subject:** 50th Anniversary of State Bank **Obv:** National arms **Rev:** State bank

Date	Mintage	F	VF	XF	Unc	BU
ND(1974)	—	—	—	—	9.00	
ND(1974)	—	—	—	—	9.00	

KM# 36 25 TUGRIK
28.2800 g., 0.9250 Silver 0.8410 oz. ASW **Subject:** Conservation **Obv:** National arms **Rev:** Arfali sheep

Date	Mintage	F	VF	XF	Unc	BU
1976	5,348	—	—	—	25.00	—
1976 Proof	6,096	Value: 30.00				

KM# 39.1 25 TUGRIK
19.4400 g., 0.9250 Silver 0.5781 oz. ASW **Series:** International Year of the Child **Obv:** National arms **Rev:** Children riding camel

Date	Mintage	F	VF	XF	Unc	BU
1980 Proof	14,000	Value: 25.00				

KM# 39.2 25 TUGRIK
19.2600 g., 0.9250 Silver 0.5728 oz. ASW, 36.1 mm. **Obv:** National arms **Rev:** Children riding camel, two countermarks at 5 o'clock **Edge:** Reeded

Date	Mintage	F	VF	XF	Unc	BU
1980 Proof	—	Value: 50.00				

KM# 47 25 TUGRIK
19.4400 g., 0.9250 Silver 0.5781 oz. ASW **Series:** Decade for Women **Obv:** National arms **Rev:** Figure with hat holding child

Date	Mintage	F	VF	XF	Unc	BU
1984 Proof	1,249	Value: 37.50				

KM# 50 25 TUGRIK
28.2800 g., 0.9250 Silver 0.8410 oz. ASW **Series:** World Wildlife Fund **Obv:** National arms **Rev:** Snow leopard

Date	Mintage	F	VF	XF	Unc	BU
1987 Matte	850	—	—	—	25.00	
1987 Proof	25,000	Value: 30.00				

KM# 54 25 TUGRIK
28.2800 g., 0.9250 Silver 0.8410 oz. ASW **Series:** Save the Children Fund **Obv:** National arms **Rev:** Child playing horse head fiddle

Date	Mintage	F	VF	XF	Unc	BU
1989 Proof	20,000	Value: 28.50				

KM# 37 50 TUGRIK
35.0000 g., 0.9250 Silver 1.0408 oz. ASW **Subject:** Conservation **Obv:** National arms **Rev:** Camel running left above value flanked by bushes

Date	Mintage	F	VF	XF	Unc	BU
1976	5,328	—	—	—	25.00	—
1976 Proof	5,900	Value: 30.00				

KM# 57 50 TUGRIK
31.1000 g., 0.9990 Silver 0.9988 oz. ASW **Subject:** Discovery of America **Obv:** National arms **Rev:** Portrait of Columbus and ship within circle and legend

Date	Mintage	F	VF	XF	Unc	BU
1992 Proof	20,000	Value: 32.50				

KM# 170 50 TUGRIK
31.1000 g., 0.9990 Silver 0.9988 oz. ASW **Subject:** Year of the Monkey **Obv:** National arms **Rev:** Monkey

Date	Mintage	F	VF	XF	Unc	BU
1992	Est. 20,000	—	—	—	80.00	

KM# 53 100 TUGRIK
28.0000 g., 0.9000 Silver 0.8102 oz. ASW **Subject:** Dinosaurs **Obv:** National arms **Rev:** Nemectosaurus

Date	Mintage	F	VF	XF	Unc	BU
1989	1,000	—	—	—	80.00	—

KM# 55 100 TUGRIK
28.0000 g., 0.9000 Silver 0.8102 oz. ASW **Subject:** Secret history of the Mongols **Obv:** State emblem above denomination within English legend **Rev:** Portrait of Genghis Khan in light clothing

Date	Mintage	F	VF	XF	Unc	BU
1990	4,000	—	—	—	50.00	—

KM# 58 100 TUGRIK
1.5600 g., 0.9990 Gold 0.0501 oz. AGW **Subject:** Discovery of America - Columbus **Obv:** National arms **Rev:** Portrait of Columbus and ship within circle and legend

Date	Mintage	F	VF	XF	Unc	BU
1992 Proof	Est. 10,000	Value: 55.00				

KM# 59 200 TUGRIK
3.1100 g., 0.9990 Gold 0.0999 oz. AGW **Subject:** Discovery of America - Columbus **Obv:** National arms **Rev:** Portrait of Columbus and ship within circle and legend

Date	Mintage	F	VF	XF	Unc	BU
1992 Proof	Est. 10,000	Value: 120				

KM# 45   250 TUGRIK
7.1300 g., 0.9000 Gold 0.2063 oz. AGW **Series:** Decade for Women **Obv:** National arms **Rev:** Figure on horseback left, value

Date	Mintage	F	VF	XF	Unc	BU
1984 Proof	510	Value: 220				

KM# 72   300 TUGRIK
7.7700 g., 0.9990 Gold 0.2496 oz. AGW **Subject:** Japanese royal wedding **Obv:** National arms above value **Rev:** Royal couple facing each other

Date	Mintage	F	VF	XF	Unc	BU
1993 Proof	Est. 500	Value: 250				

KM# 38   750 TUGRIK
33.4370 g., 0.9000 Gold 0.9675 oz. AGW **Subject:** Conservation **Rev:** Przewalski horses

Date	Mintage	F	VF	XF	Unc	BU
1976	929	—	—	—	—	950
1976 Proof	374	Value: 975				

KM# 40   750 TUGRIK
18.7900 g., 0.9000 Gold 0.5437 oz. AGW **Series:** International Year of the Child **Obv:** National arms **Rev:** Children dancing

Date	Mintage	F	VF	XF	Unc	BU
1980 Proof	32,000	Value: 600				

KM# 56   1000 TUGRIK
20.7000 g., 0.9000 Gold 0.5989 oz. AGW **Subject:** Secret history of the Mongols **Obv:** State emblem above denomination within English legend **Rev:** Portrait of Genghis Khan in heavy clothing

Date	Mintage	F	VF	XF	Unc	BU
1990	Est. 4,000	—	—	—	—	625

KM# 60   1000 TUGRIK
31.1000 g., 0.9990 Gold 0.9988 oz. AGW **Subject:** Discovery of America **Obv:** National arms divide date above value **Rev:** Portrait of Columbus and ship within circle and legend

Date	Mintage	F	VF	XF	Unc	BU
1992 Proof	2,000	Value: 1,000				

KM# 171   1000 TUGRIK
Gold **Subject:** Year of the Monkey **Obv:** National arms **Rev:** Monkey

Date	Mintage	F	VF	XF	Unc	BU
1992	Est. 2,000	—	—	—	—	1,000

STATE

DECIMAL COINAGE

KM# 122   20 TUGRIK
Aluminum **Obv:** Soembo arms, text **Rev:** Value

Date	Mintage	F	VF	XF	Unc	BU
1994	—	—	—	—	1.50	1.75

KM# 84   50 TUGRIK
15.0000 g., 0.9990 Silver 0.4818 oz. ASW **Obv:** State emblem above value **Rev:** Bust with hat 1/4 left

Date	Mintage	F	VF	XF	Unc	BU
1992 Proof	Est. 1,000	Value: 30.00				

KM# 86   50 TUGRIK
31.1035 g., 0.9990 Silver 0.9990 oz. ASW **Subject:** Year of the Monkey **Obv:** State emblem above value **Rev:** Sitting monkey

Date	Mintage	F	VF	XF	Unc	BU
1992 Proof	20,000	Value: 40.00				

KM# 166   50 TUGRIK
31.1035 g., 0.9990 Silver 0.9990 oz. ASW **Subject:** Discovery of America - Columbus **Obv:** State emblem above value **Rev:** Portrait of Columbus and ship within circle and legend

Date	Mintage	F	VF	XF	Unc	BU
1992 Proof	—	Value: 42.50				

KM# 61   50 TUGRIK
31.1035 g., 0.9990 Silver 0.9990 oz. ASW **Subject:** Year of the Rooster **Obv:** State emblem above value **Rev:** Rooster

Date	Mintage	F	VF	XF	Unc	BU
1993 Proof	20,000	Value: 40.00				

KM# 69   50 TUGRIK
31.1035 g., 0.9990 Silver 0.9990 oz. ASW **Subject:** Japanese Royal Wedding **Obv:** State emblem above value **Rev:** Busts facing each other

Date	Mintage	F	VF	XF	Unc	BU
1993 Proof	1,962	Value: 47.50				

KM# 75   50 TUGRIK
31.1035 g., 0.9990 Silver 0.9990 oz. ASW **Subject:** Year of the Dog **Obv:** State emblem above value **Rev:** Two dogs

Date	Mintage	F	VF	XF	Unc	BU
1994 Proof	4,000	Value: 45.00				

KM# 123   50 TUGRIK
Aluminum **Obv:** Soembo arms, text **Rev:** Value within design

Date	Mintage	F	VF	XF	Unc	BU
1994	—	—	—	—	1.75	2.00

KM# 94   50 TUGRIK
Copper-Nickel **Subject:** Year of the Pig **Obv:** State emblem above value **Rev:** Pig

Date	Mintage	F	VF	XF	Unc	BU
1995 Proof	50,000	Value: 15.00				

KM# 104   50 TUGRIK
Copper-Nickel **Subject:** Year of the Rat **Obv:** Soembo arms within deigned circle **Rev:** Rat among flowers and plants

Date	Mintage	F	VF	XF	Unc	BU
1996 Proof	50,000	Value: 17.50				

KM# 126   50 TUGRIK
Copper-Nickel **Subject:** Year of the Ox **Obv:** National emblem **Rev:** Ox

Date	Mintage	F	VF	XF	Unc	BU
1997 Proof	25,000	Value: 17.00				

KM# 172   50 TUGRIK
Copper-Nickel **Subject:** Year of the Tiger **Obv:** National emblem **Rev:** Tiger

Date	Mintage	F	VF	XF	Unc	BU
1998	25,000	—	—	—	17.00	—

KM# 159   50 TUGRIK
20.0000 g., Copper-Nickel, 38 mm. **Subject:** Year of the Rabbit **Obv:** National emblem **Rev:** Rabbit **Edge:** Plain

Date	Mintage	F	VF	XF	Unc	BU
1999 Prooflike	25,000	—	—	—	17.00	—

KM# 87   100 TUGRIK
1.5600 g., 0.9990 Gold 0.0501 oz. AGW **Subject:** Year of the Monkey **Obv:** National emblem **Rev:** Monkey **Note:** Similar to 50 Tugrik, KM#86.

Date	Mintage	F	VF	XF	Unc	BU
1992 Proof	10,000	Value: 75.00				

KM# 167   100 TUGRIK
1.5600 g., 0.9990 Gold 0.0501 oz. AGW **Subject:** Discovery of America - Columbus **Obv:** National emblem **Rev:** Portrait of Columbus and ship within circle and legend

Date	Mintage	F	VF	XF	Unc	BU
1992 Proof	—	Value: 60.00				

KM# 62.1   100 TUGRIK
1.5600 g., 0.9990 Gold 0.0501 oz. AGW **Subject:** Year of the Rooster **Obv:** National emblem **Rev:** Rooster **Note:** Similar to 50 Tugrik, KM#61.

Date	Mintage	F	VF	XF	Unc	BU
1993 Proof	30,000	Value: 60.00				

KM# 62.2   100 TUGRIK
1.5600 g., 0.9990 Gold 0.0501 oz. AGW **Obv:** National arms above value **Rev:** Rooster left **Note:** Handstruck.

Date	Mintage	F	VF	XF	Unc	BU
1993 Proof	500	Value: 250				

Note: Strikes tend to be crude and do not have ".999" on them.

KM# 70   100 TUGRIK
1.5600 g., 0.9990 Gold 0.0501 oz. AGW **Subject:** Japanese Royal Wedding **Obv:** State emblem above value **Rev:** Busts facing each other **Note:** Similar to 50 Tugrik, KM#69.

Date	Mintage	F	VF	XF	Unc	BU
1993 Proof	Est. 3,000	Value: 75.00				

KM# 124   100 TUGRIK
Copper-Nickel **Obv:** Soembo arms, text **Rev:** Value below building

Date	Mintage	F	VF	XF	Unc	BU
1994	—	—	—	—	2.50	3.00

KM# 88   200 TUGRIK
3.1100 g., 0.9990 Gold 0.0999 oz. AGW **Subject:** Year of the
Monkey **Obv:** National emblem **Rev:** Seated monkey
Note: Similar to 50 Tugrik, KM#86.

Date	Mintage	F	VF	XF	Unc	BU
1992 Proof	—				Value: 120	

KM# 168   200 TUGRIK
3.1100 g., 0.9990 Gold 0.0999 oz. AGW **Subject:** Discovery of
America - Columbus **Obv:** State emblem above value
Rev: Portrait of Columbus and ship within circle and legend

Date	Mintage	F	VF	XF	Unc	BU
1992 Proof	—				Value: 120	

KM# 63   200 TUGRIK
3.1100 g., 0.9990 Gold 0.0999 oz. AGW **Subject:** Year of the
Rooster **Obv:** National emblem above value at left, country name
at right **Rev:** Rooster **Note:** Similar to 50 Tugrik, KM#61.

Date	Mintage	F	VF	XF	Unc	BU
1993 Proof	500				Value: 200	

KM# 71   200 TUGRIK
3.1100 g., 0.9990 Gold 0.0999 oz. AGW **Subject:** Japanese
Royal Wedding **Obv:** National arms above value **Rev:** Busts
facing each other **Note:** Similar to 50 Tugrik, KM#69.

Date	Mintage	F	VF	XF	Unc	BU
1993 Proof	100				Value: 300	

KM# 76   200 TUGRIK
3.1100 g., 0.9990 Gold 0.0999 oz. AGW **Subject:** Year of the
Dog. **Obv:** National emblem **Rev:** Dogs

Date	Mintage	F	VF	XF	Unc	BU
1994 Proof	500				Value: 175	

KM# 125   200 TUGRIK
Copper-Nickel **Obv:** Soembo arms, text **Rev:** Value below building

Date	Mintage	F	VF	XF	Unc	BU
1994	—	—	—	—	3.00	4.00

KM# 80   250 TUGRIK
31.4700 g., 0.9250 Silver 0.9359 oz. ASW **Subject:** Endangered
Wildlife **Obv:** Soembo arms within 3/4 wreath **Rev:** Wolves

Date	Mintage	F	VF	XF	Unc	BU
1993 Proof	Est. 15,000				Value: 40.00	

Note: KM#89 previously listed here has been reported as
never released

Date	Mintage	F	VF	XF	Unc	BU
1993 Proof	15,000				Value: 45.00	

Note: KM#89 previously listed here has been reported as
never released

KM# 100   250 TUGRIK
31.4700 g., 0.9250 Silver 0.9359 oz. ASW **Subject:** Endangered
Wildlife **Obv:** National emblem **Rev:** Przewalski's Horses

Date	Mintage	F	VF	XF	Unc	BU
1992 Proof	20,000				Value: 40.00	

KM# 110   250 TUGRIK
31.4700 g., 0.9359 oz. ASW **Series:** Endangered
Wildlife **Obv:** National emblem **Rev:** Saiga Antelope

Date	Mintage	F	VF	XF	Unc	BU
1993 Proof	Est. 10,000				Value: 40.00	

KM# 64   250 TUGRIK
155.5000 g., 0.9990 Silver 4.9942 oz. ASW **Subject:** Year of
the Rooster **Obv:** National emblem **Rev:** Rooster **Note:** Similar
to 50 Tugrik, KM#61.

Date	Mintage	F	VF	XF	Unc	BU
1993	300				Value: 150	

KM# 77   250 TUGRIK
155.5000 g., 0.9990 Silver 4.9942 oz. ASW, 65 mm.
Subject: Year of the Dog **Obv:** National emblem **Rev:** Two
Pekingese **Note:** Illustration reduced.

Date	Mintage	F	VF	XF	Unc	BU
1994 Proof	200				Value: 300	

KM# 112   250 TUGRIK
31.4700 g., 0.9250 Silver 0.9359 oz. ASW **Series:** Olympics
Subject: Archery **Obv:** Soembo arms within wreath **Rev:** Archer

Date	Mintage	F	VF	XF	Unc	BU
1994 Proof	—				Value: 27.50	
1995 Proof	Est. 40,000				Value: 30.00	

KM# 111   250 TUGRIK
31.4700 g., 0.9250 Silver 0.9359 oz. ASW **Series:** Olympics
Subject: Boxing **Obv:** National emblem

Date	Mintage	F	VF	XF	Unc	BU
1994 Proof	Est. 5,000				Value: 50.00	

KM# 186   250 TUGRIK
31.4000 g., 0.9250 Silver 0.9338 oz. ASW, 38.4 mm.
Subject: Sojus 39 and Saljut 6 **Obv:** National arms **Rev:** 2 space
capsules **Edge:** Reeded

Date	Mintage	F	VF	XF	Unc	BU
1994 Proof	—				Value: 55.00	

KM# 103   250 TUGRIK
31.4700 g., 0.9250 Silver 0.9359 oz. ASW **Subject:** World Cup
soccer **Obv:** National arms **Rev:** Soccer players

Date	Mintage	F	VF	XF	Unc	BU
1994 Proof	—				Value: 30.00	

KM# 73   500 TUGRIK
15.5500 g., 0.9990 Gold 0.4994 oz. AGW **Subject:** Japanese
Royal Wedding **Obv:** State emblem above value **Rev:** Busts
facing each other

Date	Mintage	F	VF	XF	Unc	BU
1993 Proof	160				Value: 550	

KM# 95   500 TUGRIK
31.1035 g., 0.9990 Silver 0.9990 oz. ASW **Subject:** Year of the
Pig **Obv:** Soembo arms within circle **Rev:** Wild pig

Date	Mintage	F	VF	XF	Unc	BU
1995 Proof	3,000				Value: 50.00	

KM# 101.1 500 TUGRIK
31.1035 g., 0.9990 Silver 0.9990 oz. ASW **Subject:** Moscow -
Beijing Railroad **Obv:** National arms **Rev:** Map without trains

Date	Mintage	F	VF	XF	Unc	BU
ND(1995) Proof	20,000	Value: 35.00				

KM# 101.2 500 TUGRIK
31.1035 g., 0.9990 Silver 0.9990 oz. ASW, 40.1 mm. **Obv:**
Soembo arms within circle **Rev:** Map with trains **Edge:** Plain

Date	Mintage	F	VF	XF	Unc	BU
ND (1995) Proof	—	Value: 45.00				

KM# 203 500 TUGRIK
31.1500 g., 0.9990 Silver 1.0005 oz. ASW, 38 mm.
Subject: The Straits Times 150th Anniversary **Obv:** National
emblem **Rev:** Rolled newspapers and logo **Edge:** Plain

Date	Mintage	F	VF	XF	Unc	BU
ND(1995) Proof	—	Value: 40.00				

KM# 105 500 TUGRIK
31.1035 g., 0.9990 Silver 0.9990 oz. ASW **Subject:** Year of the
Rat **Obv:** National emblem **Rev:** Rat **Note:** Similar to 50 Tugrik,
KM#104, but with gold plated rat.

Date	Mintage	F	VF	XF	Unc	BU
1996 Proof	500	Value: 90.00				

KM# 216 500 TUGRIK
1.1800 g., 0.9999 Gold 0.0379 oz. AGW, 13.91 mm.
Subject: 1996 Summer Olympics - Atlanta **Obv:** National
emblem at left, value below **Rev:** Archer **Edge:** Reeded

Date	Mintage	F	VF	XF	Unc	BU
1996 Proof	—	Value: 55.00				

KM# 187 500 TUGRIK
31.6000 g., 0.9250 Silver 0.9397 oz. ASW **Series:** Endangered
Wildlife **Obv:** National emblem **Rev:** Pelican

Date	Mintage	F	VF	XF	Unc	BU
1996 Proof	—	—	—	—	—	65.00

KM# 132 500 TUGRIK
25.0000 g., 0.9250 Silver 0.7435 oz. ASW **Subject:** Aquila
Rapax **Obv:** Soembo arms above value **Rev:** Aquila rapax sitting
among rocks

Date	Mintage	F	VF	XF	Unc	BU
1996 Proof	3,500	Value: 45.00				

KM# 133 500 TUGRIK
25.0000 g., 0.9250 Silver 0.7435 oz. ASW **Subject:** Equus
Ferus **Obv:** National emblem **Rev:** Horse running left

Date	Mintage	F	VF	XF	Unc	BU
1996 Proof	3,500	Value: 45.00				

KM# 134 500 TUGRIK
25.0000 g., 0.9250 Silver 0.7435 oz. ASW **Subject:** Cameleus
Ferus **Obv:** National emblem **Rev:** Camel right

Date	Mintage	F	VF	XF	Unc	BU
1996 Proof	3,500	Value: 45.00				

KM# 135 500 TUGRIK
25.0000 g., 0.9250 Silver 0.7435 oz. ASW **Subject:** Panthera
Tigris Altaica **Obv:** National emblem **Rev:** Three tigers

Date	Mintage	F	VF	XF	Unc	BU
1996 Proof	3,500	Value: 40.00				

KM# 193 500 TUGRIK
19.4400 g., 0.9250 Silver 0.5781 oz. ASW, 36 mm.
Subject: UNICEF **Obv:** National arms **Rev:** Three costumed
children **Edge:** Reeded

Date	Mintage	F	VF	XF	Unc	BU
1997 Proof	25,000	Value: 25.00				

KM# 127 500 TUGRIK
31.1035 g., 0.9990 Silver With Partial Gold Plating 0.9990 oz.
Subject: Year of the Ox **Obv:** National emblem **Rev:** Ox
Note: Similar to 50 Tugrik, KM#126.

Date	Mintage	F	VF	XF	Unc	BU
1997 Proof	3,000	Value: 50.00				

KM# 197 500 TUGRIK
Gold **Obv:** National emblem **Rev:** Sumo wrestling

Date	Mintage	F	VF	XF	Unc	BU
1998 Proof	—	Value: 50.00				

KM# 155 500 TUGRIK
15.0000 g., 0.9250 Silver 0.4461 oz. ASW **Series:** 1988
Olympics **Obv:** Soembo arms **Rev:** Skier

Date	Mintage	F	VF	XF	Unc	BU
1998	—	Value: 30.00				

KM# 156 500 TUGRIK
20.0000 g., 0.5000 Silver 0.3215 oz. ASW **Series:** 2000
Olympics **Obv:** National emblem **Rev:** 2 Wrestlers

Date	Mintage	VG	F	VF	XF	Unc
1998 Proof	—	Value: 28.00				

KM# 157 500 TUGRIK
31.4700 g., 0.9990 Silver 1.0107 oz. ASW **Subject:** Endangered
wildlife **Obv:** National emblem **Rev:** Tiger and cubs

Date	Mintage	F	VF	XF	Unc	BU
1998 Proof	—	Value: 50.00				

KM# 158 500 TUGRIK
1.2241 g., 0.9990 Gold 0.0393 oz. AGW **Subject:** Buddhist
Diety Maitreya **Obv:** National emblem **Rev:** Statue

Date	Mintage	F	VF	XF	Unc	BU
1998 Proof	—	Value: 50.00				

KM# 173 500 TUGRIK
31.1045 g., 0.9990 Silver 0.9990 oz. ASW **Subject:** Year of the
Tiger **Obv:** National emblem **Rev:** Tiger

Date	Mintage	F	VF	XF	Unc	BU
1998	25,000	—	—	—	25.00	—

KM# 173a 500 TUGRIK
31.1045 g., 0.9990 Silver 0.9990 oz. ASW **Subject:** Year of the
Tiger **Obv:** National emblem **Rev:** Tiger **Note:** Gold-plated tiger.

Date	Mintage	F	VF	XF	Unc	BU
1998	3,000	—	—	—	50.00	—

KM# 174 500 TUGRIK
1.2441 g., 0.9990 Gold 0.0400 oz. AGW **Subject:** Year of the
Tiger **Obv:** National emblem **Rev:** Tiger

Date	Mintage	F	VF	XF	Unc	BU
1998	—	—	—	—	—	50.00

KM# 178   500 TUGRIK
31.6100 g., 0.9250 Silver 0.9400 oz. ASW **Subject:** Millennium 2000 **Obv:** National emblem **Rev:** Rider and multicolor speckled hologram

Date	Mintage	F	VF	XF	Unc	BU
1998 Proof	Est. 10,000				Value: 37.50	

KM# 160   500 TUGRIK
31.1045 g., 0.9990 Silver 0.9990 oz. ASW **Subject:** Year of the Rabbit **Obv:** Soembo arms within circle **Rev:** Rabbit running left

Date	Mintage	F	VF	XF	Unc	BU
1999	3,000	—	—	—	40.00	—

KM# 196   500 TUGRIK
19.8200 g., 0.5000 Silver 0.3186 oz. ASW, 34 mm. **Obv:** National emblem **Rev:** Two Bactrian camels **Edge:** Reeded

Date	Mintage	F	VF	XF	Unc	BU
1999 Proof	—	—	—	—	45.00	—

KM# 202   500 TUGRIK
31.4400 g., 0.9250 Silver 0.9350 oz. ASW, 38.6 mm. **Subject:** Princess Diana **Obv:** National emblem **Rev:** Diana by minefield **Edge:** Plain

Date	Mintage	F	VF	XF	Unc	BU
1999 Proof	—				Value: 45.00	

KM# 160a   500 TUGRIK
31.1045 g., 0.9990 Silver 0.9990 oz. ASW **Subject:** Year of the Rabbit **Obv:** Soembo arms within circle **Rev:** Rabbit running left **Note:** Gold plated rabbit.

Date	Mintage	F	VF	XF	Unc	BU
1999	3,000	—	—	—	50.00	—

KM# 161   500 TUGRIK
1.2441 g., 0.9990 Gold 0.0400 oz. AGW **Subject:** Year of the Rabbit **Obv:** Soembo arms within circle **Rev:** Rabbit running left

Date	Mintage	F	VF	XF	Unc	BU
1999	5,000	—	—	—	—	50.00

KM# 179   500 TUGRIK
25.2700 g., 0.9250 Silver 0.7515 oz. ASW **Subject:** Sita Tara **Obv:** Soembo arms above value **Rev:** Seated figure facing

Date	Mintage	F	VF	XF	Unc	BU
1999 Proof	2,500				Value: 46.50	

KM# 180   500 TUGRIK
25.0000 g., 0.9250 Bi-Metallic Goldine center in Silver ring 0.7435 oz. **Subject:** Genius of the Millennium - Gutenberg **Obv:** National emblem **Rev:** Open Bible, dates **Note:** Goldine center is square.

Date	Mintage	F	VF	XF	Unc	BU
1999 Proof	2,500				Value: 43.50	

KM# 181   500 TUGRIK
25.0000 g., 0.9250 Bi-Metallic Goldine center in Silver ring 0.7435 oz., 38.61 mm. **Subject:** Genius of the Millennium - Da Vinci **Obv:** National emblem **Obv. Leg.:** MONGOLIA **Rev:** Male figure study **Rev. Leg.:** LEONARDO DA VINCI **Edge:** Reeded **Note:** Goldine center is triangular.

Date	Mintage	F	VF	XF	Unc	BU
1999 Proof	2,500				Value: 50.00	

KM# 181a   500 TUGRIK
25.0000 g., 0.9250 Bi-Metallic Copper center in silver ring 0.7435 oz., 38.61 mm. **Subject:** Genius of the Millennium - Da Vinci **Obv:** National emblem **Obv. Leg.:** MONGOLIA **Rev:** Male figure study **Rev. Leg.:** LEONARDO DA VINCI **Edge:** Reeded **Note:** Copper center is triangular.

Date	Mintage	F	VF	XF	Unc	BU
1999 Proof	—				Value: 50.00	

KM# 182   500 TUGRIK
25.0000 g., 0.9250 Bi-Metallic Goldine center in Silver ring 0.7435 oz. **Subject:** Genius of the Millennium - Newton **Obv:** National emblem **Rev:** Solar system diagram **Note:** Goldine center is round.

Date	Mintage	F	VF	XF	Unc	BU
1999 Proof	2,500				Value: 46.50	

KM# 183   500 TUGRIK
25.0000 g., 0.9250 Bi-Metallic Goldine center in Silver ring 0.7435 oz. **Subject:** Genius of the Millennium - von Goethe **Obv:** National emblem **Rev:** Bust facing **Note:** Goldine center is round.

Date	Mintage	F	VF	XF	Unc	BU
1999 Proof	2,500				Value: 43.50	

KM# 184   500 TUGRIK
25.0000 g., 0.9250 Bi-Metallic Goldine center in Silver ring 0.7435 oz. **Subject:** Genius of the Millennium - Edison **Obv:** National emblem **Rev:** Light bulb, telephone, record player **Note:** Goldine center is square.

Date	Mintage	F	VF	XF	Unc	BU
1999 Proof	2,500				Value: 43.50	

Note: KM#90, previously listed here, has been reported as never released.

KM# 217   500 TUGRIK
1.2100 g., Gold **Subject:** Troops of Chinggis Khan **Obv:** National emblem, value below **Rev:** Chinggis at right giving directions to charioteer at left

Date	Mintage	F	VF	XF	Unc	BU
2000 Proof	—				Value: 55.00	

KM# 65   600 TUGRIK
373.2000 g., 0.9990 Silver 11.986 oz. ASW **Subject:** Year of the Rooster **Obv:** National emblem **Rev:** Rooster **Note:** Similar to 50 Tugrik, KM#61.

Date	Mintage	F	VF	XF	Unc	BU
1993 Proof	200				Value: 500	

KM# 91   1000 TUGRIK
31.1000 g., 0.9990 Gold 0.9988 oz. AGW **Subject:** Year of the Monkey **Obv:** National emblem **Rev:** Monkey **Note:** Similar to 50 Tugrik, KM#86.

Date	Mintage	F	VF	XF	Unc	BU
1992 Proof	2,000				Value: 975	

KM# 85   1000 TUGRIK
20.0000 g., 0.9000 Gold 0.5787 oz. AGW **Obv:** National arms above value **Rev:** Ugedei Khan, Son of Genghis

Date	Mintage	F	VF	XF	Unc	BU
1992 Proof	500				Value: 625	

KM# 169   1000 TUGRIK
20.0000 g., 0.9000 Gold 0.5787 oz. AGW **Subject:** Discovery of America - Columbus **Obv:** State emblem above value **Rev:** Portrait of Columbus and ship within circle and legend

Date	Mintage	F	VF	XF	Unc	BU
1992 Proof	Est. 2,000				Value: 575	

KM# 66   1000 TUGRIK
31.1000 g., 0.9990 Gold 0.9988 oz. AGW **Subject:** Year of the Rooster **Obv:** National emblem above value at left, country name at right **Rev:** Rooster **Note:** Similar to 50 Tugrik, KM#61.

Date	Mintage	F	VF	XF	Unc	BU
1993 Proof	1,000				Value: 975	

KM# 74   1000 TUGRIK
20.0000 g., 0.9000 Gold 0.5787 oz. AGW   **Subject:** Japanese Royal Wedding **Obv:** State emblem above value **Rev:** Busts of couple facing each other

Date	Mintage	F	VF	XF	Unc	BU
1993 Proof	145	Value: 800				

KM# 78   1000 TUGRIK
31.1035 g., 0.9990 Gold 0.9990 oz. AGW   **Subject:** Year of the Dog **Obv:** National emblem **Rev:** Pekingese

Date	Mintage	F	VF	XF	Unc	BU
1994 Proof	500	Value: 950				

KM# 96   1000 TUGRIK
3.1100 g., 0.9990 Gold 0.0999 oz. AGW   **Subject:** Year of the Pig **Obv:** National emblem **Rev:** Wild boar **Note:** Similar to 500 Tugrik, KM#95.

Date	Mintage	F	VF	XF	Unc	BU
1995 Proof	500	Value: 200				

KM# 148   1000 TUGRIK
4.4100 g., 0.9000 Gold 0.1276 oz. AGW   **Subject:** Moscow - Ulaan Blaatar - Bejing Railroad **Obv:** Soembo arms within circle **Rev:** Steam locomotive

Date	Mintage	F	VF	XF	Unc	BU
1995 Proof	—	Value: 135				

KM# 106   1000 TUGRIK
3.1100 g., 0.9990 Gold 0.0999 oz. AGW   **Subject:** Year of the Rat **Obv:** National emblem **Rev:** Rat **Note:** Similar to 50 Tugrik, KM#104.

Date	Mintage	F	VF	XF	Unc	BU
1996 Proof	500	Value: 150				

KM# 115   1000 TUGRIK
156.6100 g., 0.9990 Silver 5.0299 oz. ASW, 65.5 mm.
Series: Olympics **Obv:** Soembo arms **Rev:** Ancient runners within circle **Note:** With gold inlay. Illustration reduced.

Date	Mintage	F	VF	XF	Unc	BU
1996 Matte	—	—	—	—	225	—

KM# 128   1000 TUGRIK
3.1100 g., 0.9990 Gold 0.0999 oz. AGW   **Subject:** Year of the Ox **Obv:** National emblem **Rev:** Ox **Note:** Similar to 50 Tugrik, KM#126.

Date	Mintage	F	VF	XF	Unc	BU
1997 Proof	500	Value: 120				

KM# 185   1000 TUGRIK
1.2441 g., 0.9999 Gold 0.0400 oz. AGW   **Subject:** Genius of the Millennium - Da Vinci **Obv:** National arms **Rev:** Male figure study **Note:** Similar to 500 Tugrik, KM#181.

Date	Mintage	F	VF	XF	Unc	BU
1999 Proof	25,000	Value: 50.00				

KM# 201   1000 TUGRIK
7.7200 g., Gold, 24.8 mm. **Obv:** Soembo arms **Rev:** Tiger head with diamond inset eyes **Edge:** Reeded

Date	Mintage	F	VF	XF	Unc	BU
1999 Proof	—	Value: 450				

KM# 116   1200 TUGRIK
7.7000 g., 0.9990 Silver 0.2473 oz. ASW   **Subject:** Chinggis Khan **Obv:** Soemba arms **Rev:** Bust 3/4 right, dates below **Note:** Similar to 5,000 Tugrik, KM#118.

Date	Mintage	F	VF	XF	Unc	BU
1996	Est. 10,000	—	—	—	10.00	12.00
1996 Proof	Est. 10,000	Value: 15.00				

KM# 149   1200 TUGRIK
7.7000 g., 0.9990 Silver 0.2473 oz. ASW   **Subject:** Ugedei Khan **Obv:** National emblem **Rev:** Head 3/4 facing, dates at right

Date	Mintage	F	VF	XF	Unc	BU
1997 Proof	Est. 10,000	Value: 15.00				

KM# 113   2000 TUGRIK
7.7760 g., 0.5830 Gold 0.1457 oz. AGW   **Series:** Endangered Wildlife **Obv:** Soembo arms within wreath **Rev:** Snow leopard

Date	Mintage	F	VF	XF	Unc	BU
1994 Proof	Est. 5,000	Value: 175				

KM# 114   2000 TUGRIK
7.7760 g., 0.5830 Gold 0.1457 oz. AGW   **Series:** Olympics **Obv:** Soembo arms within wreath **Rev:** Boxer

Date	Mintage	F	VF	XF	Unc	BU
1994 Proof	Est. 5,000	Value: 175				

KM# 175   2000 TUGRIK
7.7760 g., 0.5830 Gold 0.1457 oz. AGW   **Subject:** Year of the Tiger **Obv:** National emblem **Rev:** Tiger

Date	Mintage	F	VF	XF	Unc	BU
1998	—	—	—	—	—	170

KM# 97   2500 TUGRIK
155.5150 g., 0.9990 Silver 4.9947 oz. ASW, 65 mm.
Subject: Year of the Pig **Obv:** Soemba arms **Rev:** Wild pigs eating in the wild **Note:** Illustration reduced.

Date	Mintage	F	VF	XF	Unc	BU
1995 Proof	300	Value: 160				

KM# 102   2500 TUGRIK
155.5150 g., 0.9990 Silver 4.9947 oz. ASW, 65.14 mm.
Subject: Moscow - Ulaan Baatar - Beijing Railroad **Obv:** Soemba arms **Rev:** Passenger train crossing trestle left **Edge:** Plain **Note:** Illustration reduced.

Date	Mintage	F	VF	XF	Unc	BU
1995 Proof	5,000	Value: 125				

KM# 107   2500 TUGRIK
155.5150 g., 0.9990 Silver 4.9947 oz. ASW, 65 mm. **Subject:** Year of the Rat **Obv:** Soemba arms **Rev:** Gold-plated rat

Date	Mintage	F	VF	XF	Unc	BU
1996 Proof	300	Value: 250				

KM# 117 2500 TUGRIK
15.5500 g., 0.9990 Silver 0.4994 oz. ASW **Obv:** National emblem **Rev:** Chinggis Khan **Note:** Similar to 5000 Tugrik, KM#118

Date	Mintage	F	VF	XF	Unc	BU
1996	Est. 10,000	—	—	—	20.00	22.50
1996 Proof	Est. 10,000	Value: 30.00				

KM# 129 2500 TUGRIK
155.5150 g., 0.9990 Silver With Partial Gold Plating 4.9947 oz. **Subject:** Year of the Ox **Obv:** National emblem **Rev:** Man riding ox, flowered spray around upper right

Date	Mintage	F	VF	XF	Unc	BU
1997 Proof	300	Value: 200				

KM# 150 2500 TUGRIK
15.5517 g., 0.9990 Silver 0.4995 oz. ASW **Obv:** Soembo arms above value **Rev:** Bust with hat 1/4 left

Date	Mintage	F	VF	XF	Unc	BU
1997 Proof	Est. 10,000	Value: 30.00				

KM# 162 2500 TUGRIK
155.1750 g., 0.9990 Silver 4.9838 oz. ASW, 65 mm. **Subject:** Year of the Rabbit **Obv:** National emblem **Rev:** Rabbit **Edge:** Plain **Note:** Struck at B.H. Mayer's.

Date	Mintage	F	VF	XF	Unc	BU
1999 Proof	1,500	Value: 175				

KM# 163 2500 TUGRIK
7.7759 g., 0.9990 Gold 0.2497 oz. AGW, 22.5 mm. **Subject:** Year of the Rabbit **Obv:** National emblem **Rev:** Rabbit **Edge:** Plain **Note:** Struck at B.H. Mayer's.

Date	Mintage	F	VF	XF	Unc	BU
1999 Proof	1,500	Value: 265				

KM# 81 4000 TUGRIK
15.5940 g., 0.9999 Gold 0.5013 oz. AGW **Obv:** Soembo arms above value **Rev:** Horse and rider left

Date	Mintage	F	VF	XF	Unc	BU
1992 Proof	Est. 9,000	Value: 650				

KM# 67 5000 TUGRIK
155.5000 g., 0.9990 Gold 4.9942 oz. AGW **Subject:** Year of the Rooster **Obv:** National emblem above denomination at left, country name at right **Rev:** Rooster **Note:** Similar to 50 Tugrik, KM#51.

Date	Mintage	F	VF	XF	Unc	BU
1993 Proof	50	Value: 5,000				

KM# 79 5000 TUGRIK
155.5000 g., 0.9990 Gold 4.9942 oz. AGW **Subject:** Year of the Dog **Obv:** National emblem **Rev:** Dog

Date	Mintage	F	VF	XF	Unc	BU
1994 Proof	25	Value: 5,200				

KM# 118 5000 TUGRIK
3.1000 g., 0.9990 Silver 0.0996 oz. ASW **Obv:** Soembo arms above value **Rev:** Bust 3/4 facing, dates below

Date	Mintage	F	VF	XF	Unc	BU
1996	Est. 10,000	—	—	—	30.00	35.00
1996 Proof	Est. 10,000	Value: 50.00				

KM# 194 5000 TUGRIK
6.2200 g., 0.9990 Gold 0.1998 oz. AGW **Subject:** UNICEF **Obv:** National emblem and value **Rev:** Three costumed children **Edge:** Reeded

Date	Mintage	F	VF	XF	Unc	BU
1997 Proof	10,000	Value: 200				

KM# 136 5000 TUGRIK
155.5175 g., 0.9990 Silver 4.9948 oz. ASW **Subject:** Aquila Rapax **Obv:** National emblem and value **Rev:** Bird standing on rock **Note:** Similar to 500 Tugrik, KM#132.

Date	Mintage	F	VF	XF	Unc	BU
1997 Proof	750	Value: 225				

KM# 137 5000 TUGRIK
155.5175 g., 0.9990 Silver 4.9948 oz. ASW **Subject:** Eguus Fergus **Obv:** National emblem and value **Rev:** Horse running left **Note:** Similar to 500 Tugrik, KM#133.

Date	Mintage	F	VF	XF	Unc	BU
1997 Proof	750	Value: 225				

KM# 139 5000 TUGRIK
155.5175 g., 0.9990 Silver 4.9948 oz. ASW **Subject:** Panthera Tigris Altaica **Obv:** National emblem and value **Rev:** Tiger lying on rock **Note:** Similar to 500 Tugrik, KM#135.

Date	Mintage	F	VF	XF	Unc	BU
1997 Proof	750	Value: 225				

KM# 151 5000 TUGRIK
31.1035 g., 0.9990 Silver 0.9990 oz. ASW **Obv:** National emblem **Rev:** Ugedei Khan

Date	Mintage	F	VF	XF	Unc	BU
1997 Proof	Est. 10,000	Value: 50.00				

KM# 138 5000 TUGRIK
155.5175 g., 0.9990 Silver 4.9948 oz. ASW **Subject:** Camelus Ferus **Obv:** National emblem and value **Rev:** Camel right **Note:** Similar to 500 Tugrik, KM#134.

Date	Mintage	F	VF	XF	Unc	BU
1997 Proof	750	Value: 225				

KM# 82 8000 TUGRIK
31.1620 g., 0.9999 Gold 1.0017 oz. AGW **Obv:** Soembo arms above value **Rev:** Chinggis Khan standing

Date	Mintage	F	VF	XF	Unc	BU
1992 Proof	Est. 3,000	Value: 1,200				

KM# 98 10000 TUGRIK
31.1035 g., 0.9990 Gold 0.9990 oz. AGW **Subject:** Year of the Pig **Obv:** National emblem **Rev:** Wild boar **Note:** Similar to 500 Tugrik, KM#95.

Date	Mintage	F	VF	XF	Unc	BU
1995 Proof	300	Value: 975				

KM# 108 10000 TUGRIK
31.1035 g., 0.9990 Gold 0.9990 oz. AGW **Subject:** Year of the Rat **Obv:** National emblem **Rev:** Rat **Note:** Similar to 50 Tugrik, KM#104.

Date	Mintage	F	VF	XF	Unc	BU
1996 Proof	300	Value: 975				

KM# 140 10000 TUGRIK
1000.1000 g., 0.9990 Silver 32.120 oz. ASW **Subject:** Aquila Rapax **Obv:** National emblem and value **Rev:** Bird standing on rock **Note:** Similar to 500 Tugrik, KM#132.

Date	Mintage	F	VF	XF	Unc	BU
1996 Prooflike	450	—	—	—	—	600

KM# 143 10000 TUGRIK
1000.1000 g., 0.9990 Silver 32.120 oz. ASW **Subject:** Panthera Tigris Alaica **Obv:** National emblem and value **Rev:** Tiger lying on rock **Note:** Similar to 500 Tugrik, KM#135.

Date	Mintage	F	VF	XF	Unc	BU
1996 Proof	450	—	—	—	—	600

KM# 141 10000 TUGRIK
1000.1000 g., 0.9990 Silver 32.120 oz. ASW **Subject:** Equus Ferus **Obv:** National emblem and value **Rev:** Horse running left **Note:** Similar to 500 Tugrik, KM#133.

Date	Mintage	F	VF	XF	Unc	BU
1996 Prooflike	450	—	—	—	—	600

KM# 142 10000 TUGRIK
1000.1000 g., 0.9990 Silver 32.120 oz. ASW **Subject:** Camelus Ferus **Obv:** National emblem and value **Rev:** Camel right **Note:** Similar to 500 Tugrik, KM#134.

Date	Mintage	F	VF	XF	Unc	BU
1996 Prooflike	450	—	—	—	—	600

KM# 130 10000 TUGRIK
31.1035 g., 0.9990 Gold 0.9990 oz. AGW **Subject:** Year of the Ox **Obv:** National emblem **Rev:** Ox **Note:** Similar to 2,500 Tugrik, KM#129.

Date	Mintage	F	VF	XF	Unc	BU
1997 Proof	300	Value: 950				

KM# 176 10000 TUGRIK
31.1035 g., 0.9990 Gold 0.9990 oz. AGW **Subject:** Year of the Tiger **Obv:** National emblem **Rev:** Tiger

Date	Mintage	F	VF	XF	Unc	BU
1998	250	—	—	—	—	975

KM# 164 10000 TUGRIK
31.1035 g., 0.9990 Gold 0.9990 oz. AGW **Subject:** Year of the Rabbit **Obv:** National emblem **Rev:** Rabbit

Date	Mintage	F	VF	XF	Unc	BU
1999	250	—	—	—	—	975

KM# 68 12000 TUGRIK
373.2000 g., 0.9990 Gold 11.986 oz. AGW **Subject:** Year of the Rooster **Obv:** National emblem above denomination at left, country name at right **Rev:** Rooster **Note:** Similar to 50 Tugrik, KM#61.

Date	Mintage	F	VF	XF	Unc	BU
1993 Proof	25	Value: 12,000				

KM# 119 12000 TUGRIK
7.7700 g., 0.9999 Gold 0.2498 oz. AGW **Subject:** Chinggis Khan **Obv:** National emblem and value **Rev:** Bust 3/4 facing **Note:** Similar to 50,000 Tugrik, KM#121.

Date	Mintage	F	VF	XF	Unc	BU
1996 Rare	10	—	—	—	—	—
1996 Proof, rare	10	—	—	—	—	—

KM# 119a 12000 TUGRIK
7.7700 g., 0.9990 Gold 0.2496 oz. AGW **Subject:** Chinggis Khan **Obv:** National emblem and value **Rev:** Bust 3/4 facing

Date	Mintage	F	VF	XF	Unc	BU
1996	Est. 10,000	—	—	—	—	250
1996 Proof	Est. 10,000	Value: 260				

KM# 152 12000 TUGRIK
7.7750 g., 0.9990 Gold 0.2497 oz. AGW **Obv:** Soembo arms above value **Rev:** Ugedei Khan with hat, facing

Date	Mintage	F	VF	XF	Unc	BU
1997 Proof	Est. 10,000	Value: 300				

KM# 120   25000 TUGRIK
15.5500 g., 0.9999 Gold 0.4999 oz. AGW   **Subject:** Chinggis Khan **Obv:** National emblem and value **Rev:** Bust 3/4 facing **Note:** Similar to 50,000 Tugrik, KM#121.

Date	Mintage	F	VF	XF	Unc	BU
1996 Rare	10	—	—	—	—	—
1996 Proof, Rare	10	—	—	—	—	—

KM# 120a   25000 TUGRIK
15.5500 g., 0.9990 Gold 0.4994 oz. AGW   **Subject:** Chinggis Khan **Obv:** National emblem and value **Rev:** Bust 3/4 facing

Date	Mintage	F	VF	XF	Unc	BU
1996	Est. 10,000	—	—	—	—	475
1996 Proof	Est. 10,000		Value: 485			

KM# 144   25000 TUGRIK
15.5940 g., 0.9999 Gold 0.5013 oz. AGW   **Subject:** Aquila Rapaz **Obv:** National emblem and value **Rev:** Bird standing on rock **Note:** Similar to 500 Tugrik, KM#132.

Date	Mintage	F	VF	XF	Unc	BU
1996 Proof	300		Value: 485			

KM# 145   25000 TUGRIK
15.5940 g., 0.9999 Gold 0.5013 oz. AGW   **Obv:** National emblem and value **Rev:** Horse running left **Note:** Similar to 500 Tugrik, KM#133.

Date	Mintage	F	VF	XF	Unc	BU
1996 Proof	300		Value: 485			

KM# 146   25000 TUGRIK
15.5940 g., 0.9999 Gold 0.5013 oz. AGW   **Subject:** Cameleus Ferus **Obv:** National emblem and value **Rev:** Camel right **Note:** Similar to 500 Tugrik, KM#134.

Date	Mintage	F	VF	XF	Unc	BU
1996 Proof	300		Value: 485			

KM# 147   25000 TUGRIK
15.5940 g., 0.9999 Gold 0.5013 oz. AGW   **Subject:** Panthera Tigris Altaica **Obv:** National emblem and value **Rev:** Tiger lying on rock **Note:** Similar to 500 Tugrik, KM#135.

Date	Mintage	F	VF	XF	Unc	BU
1996 Proof	300		Value: 485			

KM# 153   25000 TUGRIK
15.5517 g., 0.9990 Gold 0.4995 oz. AGW   **Subject:** Ugedei Khan **Obv:** National arms **Rev:** Bust 1/4 left

Date	Mintage	F	VF	XF	Unc	BU
1997 Proof	Est. 10,000		Value: 600			

KM# 99   50000 TUGRIK
155.5150 g., 0.9990 Gold 4.9947 oz. AGW   **Subject:** Year of the Pig **Obv:** National emblem **Rev:** Pigs in field **Note:** Similar to 2500 Tugrik, KM#97

Date	Mintage	F	VF	XF	Unc	BU
1995 Proof	25		Value: 5,200			

KM# 109   50000 TUGRIK
155.5150 g., 0.9990 Gold 4.9947 oz. AGW   **Subject:** Year of the Rat **Obv:** National emblem **Rev:** Rat **Note:** Similar to 50 Tugrik, KM#104.

Date	Mintage	F	VF	XF	Unc	BU
1996 Proof	25		Value: 5,000			

KM# 121   50000 TUGRIK
31.1000 g., 0.9999 Gold 0.9997 oz. AGW   **Obv:** Soembo arms above value **Rev:** Chinggis Khan bust 3/4 facing

Date	Mintage	F	VF	XF	Unc	BU
1996 Rare	10	—	—	—	—	—
1996 Proof, rare	10	—	—	—	—	—

KM# 121a   50000 TUGRIK
31.1000 g., 0.9990 Gold 0.9988 oz. AGW   **Subject:** Chinggis Khan **Obv:** Soembo arms above value **Rev:** Bust 3/4 facing

Date	Mintage	F	VF	XF	Unc	BU
1996	Est. 10,000	—	—	—	—	975
1996 Proof	Est. 10,000		Value: 1,000			

KM# 131   50000 TUGRIK
155.5150 g., 0.9999 Gold 4.9992 oz. AGW   **Subject:** Year of the Ox **Obv:** National emblem **Rev:** Ox **Note:** Similar to 2,500 Tugrik, KM#129.

Date	Mintage	F	VF	XF	Unc	BU
1997 Proof	25		Value: 5,000			

KM# 154   50000 TUGRIK
31.1035 g., 0.9990 Gold 0.9990 oz. AGW   **Obv:** Soembo arms above value **Rev:** Ugedei Khan bust 3/4 facing

Date	Mintage	F	VF	XF	Unc	BU
1997 Proof	Est. 10,000		Value: 1,200			

KM# 177   50000 TUGRIK
155.5150 g., 0.9999 Gold 4.9992 oz. AGW   **Subject:** Year of the Tiger **Obv:** National emblem **Rev:** Tiger

Date	Mintage	F	VF	XF	Unc	BU
1998	99	—	—	—	—	5,000

KM# 165   50000 TUGRIK
155.5150 g., 0.9999 Gold 4.9992 oz. AGW   **Subject:** Year of the Rabbit **Obv:** National emblem **Rev:** Rabbit

Date	Mintage	F	VF	XF	Unc	BU
1999	99	—	—	—	—	5,000

KM# 83   250000 TUGRIK
1000.1000 g., 0.9999 Gold 32.149 oz. AGW, 85 mm. **Subject:** Chinggis Khan **Obv:** Soemba arms **Rev:** Head facing

Date	Mintage	F	VF	XF	Unc	BU
1992 Proof	Est. 300		Value: 30,000			

PIEFORTS

KM#	Date	Mintage	Identification	Mkt Val
P1	1980	92	25 Tugrik. Silver. KM39.	135
P2	1980	550	750 Tugrik. Gold. KM40.	775

MINT SETS

KM#	Date	Mintage	Identification	Issue Price	Mkt Val
MS1	1980 (8)	—	KM27-33, 41	—	25.00
MS2	1996 (3)	10,000	KM116-118	—	40.00
MS3	1996 (3)	10	KM119-121	—	—
MS4	1996 (3)	10,000	KM119a-121a	—	1,100

PROOF SETS

KM#	Date	Mintage	Identification	Issue Price	Mkt Val
PS1	1996 (3)	—	KM105, 106, 108	—	700
PS2	1996 (3)	10,000	KM116-118. The *10,000 mintage limit is per denomination including proof and BU single coins as well as coins included in sets.	—	70.00
PS3	1996 (3)	10	KM119-121	—	—
PS4	1996	10,000	KM119a-121a. The *10,000 mintage limit is per denomination including proof and BU single coins as well as coins included in sets.	—	1,700
PS5	1996 (4)	10	KM116-118, 121	—	—
PS6	1996 (4)	10,000	KM116-118, 121a. The *10,000 mintage limit is per denomination including proof and BU single coins as well as coins included in sets.	—	1,000
PS7	1996 (4)	10	KM118, 119-121	—	—
PS8	1996 (4)	10,000	KM118, 119a-121a. The *10,000 mintage limit is per denomination including proof and BU single coins as well as coins included in sets.	—	1,750
PS9	1997 (3)	10,000	KM149-151	—	100
PS10	1997 (3)	10,000	KM152-154	—	2,150

MONTENEGRO

The former independent kingdom of Montenegro, now one of the nominally autonomous federated units of Yugoslavia, was located in southeastern Europe north of Albania. As a kingdom, it had an area of 5,333 sq. mi. (13,812 sq. km.) and a population of about 250,000. Capital: Podgorica.

Montenegro became an independent state in 1355 following the break-up of the Serb empire. During the Turkish invasion of Albania and Herzegovina in the 15th century, the Montenegrins moved their capital to the remote mountain village of Cetinje where they maintained their independence through two centuries of intermittent attack, emerging as the only one of the Balkan states not subjugated by the Turks. When World War I began, Montenegro joined with Serbia and was subsequently invaded and occupied by the Austrians. Austria withdrew upon the defeat of the Central Powers, permitting the Serbians to move in and maintain the occupation. Montenegro then joined the kingdom of the Serbs, Croats and Slovenes, which later became Yugoslavia.

The coinage, issued under the autocratic rule of Prince Nicholas, is obsolete.

RULER
Nicholas I, as Prince, 1860-1910 as King, 1910-1918

MINT MARK
(a) - Paris, privy marks only

MONETARY SYSTEM
100 Para, = 1 Perper,

KINGDOM

STANDARD COINAGE

KM# 1   PARA
Bronze **Ruler:** Nicholas I **Obv:** Crowned arms **Rev:** Value

Date	Mintage	F	VF	XF	Unc	BU
1906	200,000	10.00	20.00	42.00	120	—

KM# 16   PARA
Bronze **Ruler:** Nicholas I **Obv:** Crowned arms **Rev:** Value

Date	Mintage	F	VF	XF	Unc	BU
1913	100,000	13.00	30.00	73.00	160	—
1914	200,000	7.00	18.00	40.00	120	—
1914 Proof	—		Value: 675			

KM# 2   2 PARE
Bronze **Ruler:** Nicholas I **Obv:** Crowned arms **Rev:** Value

Date	Mintage	F	VF	XF	Unc	BU
1906	600,125	5.00	12.00	24.00	55.00	—
1908	250,000	9.00	22.00	40.00	100	—

KM# 17 2 PARE
Bronze **Ruler:** Nicholas I **Obv:** Crowned arms **Rev:** Value

Date	Mintage	F	VF	XF	Unc	BU
1913	500,000	5.00	8.00	18.00	40.00	—
1914	400,000	6.00	12.00	24.00	54.00	—

KM# 3 10 PARA
Nickel **Ruler:** Nicholas I **Obv:** Crowned arms **Rev:** Value

Date	Mintage	F	VF	XF	Unc	BU
1906	750,156	2.50	6.00	14.00	28.00	—
1908	250,000	3.00	6.50	16.00	36.00	—

KM# 18 10 PARA
Nickel **Ruler:** Nicholas I

Date	Mintage	F	VF	XF	Unc	BU
1913	200,000	3.50	6.00	18.00	42.00	—
1914	800,000	2.50	5.00	14.00	28.00	—

KM# 4 20 PARA
Nickel **Ruler:** Nicholas I **Obv:** Crowned arms **Rev:** Value

Date	Mintage	F	VF	XF	Unc	BU
1906	600,156	3.00	6.00	14.00	28.00	—
1908	400,000	3.00	7.00	15.00	35.00	—

KM# 19 20 PARA
Nickel **Ruler:** Nicholas I **Obv:** Crowned arms **Rev:** Value

Date	Mintage	F	VF	XF	Unc	BU
1913	200,000	4.00	6.00	18.00	45.00	—
1914	800,000	3.00	6.00	14.00	28.00	—

KM# 5 PERPER
5.0000 g., 0.8350 Silver 0.1342 oz. ASW **Ruler:** Nicholas I **Obv:** Head right **Rev:** Crowned mantled arms within sprigs above date and value **Note:** Approximately 30 percent melted.

Date	Mintage	F	VF	XF	Unc	BU
1909	500,018	.12.00	22.00	45.00	100	—

KM# 14 PERPER
5.0000 g., 0.8350 Silver 0.1342 oz. ASW **Ruler:** Nicholas I **Obv:** Head right **Rev:** Crowned mantled arms within sprigs above value and date

Date	Mintage	F	VF	XF	Unc	BU
1912	520,008	8.00	14.00	30.00	85.00	—
1914	500,000	9.00	18.00	35.00	90.00	—

KM# 7 2 PERPERA
10.0000 g., 0.8350 Silver 0.2684 oz. ASW **Ruler:** Nicholas I **Obv:** Head right **Rev:** Crowned mantled arms within sprigs above date and value

Date	Mintage	F	VF	XF	Unc	BU
1910	300,006	15.00	35.00	72.00	185	—

KM# 20 2 PERPERA
10.0000 g., 0.8350 Silver 0.2684 oz. ASW **Ruler:** Nicholas I **Obv:** Head right **Rev:** Crowned mantled arms within sprigs above date and value

Date	Mintage	F	VF	XF	Unc	BU
1914	200,008	15.00	35.00	75.00	190	—

KM# 6 5 PERPERA
24.0000 g., 0.9000 Silver 0.6944 oz. ASW **Ruler:** Nicholas I **Obv:** Head right **Rev:** Crowned and mantled arms **Note:** Approximately 50 percent melted.

Date	Mintage	F	VF	XF	Unc	BU
1909	60,010	75.00	165	375	900	—

KM# 15 5 PERPERA
24.0000 g., 0.9000 Silver 0.6944 oz. ASW **Ruler:** Nicholas I **Obv:** Head right **Rev:** Crowned mantled arms within sprigs above date and value

Date	Mintage	F	VF	XF	Unc	BU
1912	40,002	80.00	175	350	855	—
1914	20,002	85.00	160	330	980	1,020

KM# 8 10 PERPERA
3.3875 g., 0.9000 Gold 0.0980 oz. AGW **Ruler:** Nicholas I **Obv:** Head right **Rev:** Crowned mantled arms within sprigs above date and value

Date	Mintage	F	VF	XF	Unc	BU
1910	40,000	125	220	350	700	—

KM# 9 10 PERPERA
3.3875 g., 0.9000 Gold 0.0980 oz. AGW **Ruler:** Nicholas I **Subject:** 50th Year of Reign **Obv:** Head laureate left **Rev:** Crowned mantled arms within sprigs above date and value

Date	Mintage	F	VF	XF	Unc	BU
1910	35,003	140	260	375	750	—

KM# 10 20 PERPERA
6.7751 g., 0.9000 Gold 0.1960 oz. AGW **Ruler:** Nicholas I **Obv:** Head right **Rev:** Crowned mantled arms within sprigs above date and value

Date	Mintage	F	VF	XF	Unc	BU
1910	30,000	200	300	700	1,200	1,500

KM# 11 20 PERPERA
6.7751 g., 0.9000 Gold 0.1960 oz. AGW **Ruler:** Nicholas I **Subject:** 50th Year of Reign **Obv:** Laureate head left **Rev:** Crowned mantled arms within sprigs above date and value

Date	Mintage	F	VF	XF	Unc	BU
1910	30,003	200	300	700	1,200	1,500

KM# 12 100 PERPERA
33.8753 g., 0.9000 Gold 0.9802 oz. AGW **Ruler:** Nicholas I **Obv:** Head right **Rev:** Crowned and mantled arms

Date	Mintage	F	VF	XF	Unc	BU
1910	301	—	5,500	10,000	17,500	20,000
1910 Proof	25	Value: 35,000				

KM# 13 100 PERPERA
33.8753 g., 0.9000 Gold 0.9802 oz. AGW **Ruler:** Nicholas I **Subject:** 50th Year of Reign **Obv:** Laureate head left **Rev:** Crowned mantled arms within sprigs above date and value

Date	Mintage	F	VF	XF	Unc	BU
1910	501	—	5,500	9,750	17,250	20,000
1910 Proof	Inc. above	Value: 20,000				

PATTERNS

KM#	Date	Mintage	Identification	Mkt Val
Pn1	1915	—	Para. With ESSAI. Struck at Paris.	1,210
Pn2	1915	—	2 Pare. With ESSAI. Struck at Paris.	1,210
Pn3	1915	—	10 Para. With ESSAI. Struck at Paris.	—
Pn4	1915	—	20 Para. With ESSAI. Struck at Paris.	—
Pn5	1915	—	Perper. With ESSAI. Struck at Paris.	1,550

KM#	Date	Mintage	Identification	Mkt Val
Pn6	1915	—	2 Perpera. With ESSAI. Struck at Paris.	2,000
Pn7	1915	—	5 Perpera. With ESSAI. Struck at Paris. Bears the monogram EL for Edmond Lindauer, who copied the work of S. Schwarz of the Vienna Mint, where the regular issue coinage was struck.	8,100

TRIAL STRIKES

KM#	Date	Mintage	Identification	Mkt Val
TS1	ND(1910)	—	100 Perpera. Hallmarked edge. Uniface.	6,200
TS2	ND(1910)	—	100 Perpera. TITRE ZZK ESSAI.	5,100

MONTSERRAT

Montserrat, a British crown colony located in the Lesser Antilles of the West Indies 27 miles (43 km.) southwest of Antigua, has an area of 38 sq. mi. (100 sq. km.) and a population of 18,500. Capital: Plymouth. The island - actually a range of volcanic peaks rising from the Caribbean - exports cotton, limes and vegetables.

Columbus discovered Montserrat in 1493 and named it after Monserrado, a mountain in Spain. It was colonized by the English in 1632 and, except for brief periods of French occupancy in 1667 and 1782-83, has remained a British possession from that time. Currency of the British Caribbean Territories (Eastern Group) was used until later when the East Caribbean States coinage was introduced. Until becoming a separate colony in 1956, Montserrat was a presidency of the Leeward Islands.

The early 19th century countermarks of a crowned 3, 4, 7, 9 or 18 over M as documented by Major Pridmore have been more correctly listed under St. Bartholomew.

RULER
British

MONETARY SYSTEM
100 Cents = 1 Dollar

BRITISH COLONY
MODERN COINAGE

KM# 30   4 DOLLARS
28.3000 g., Copper-Nickel, 38.5 mm.   Series: F.A.O.
Obv: National shield Rev: Value flanked by plants

Date	Mintage	F	VF	XF	Unc	BU
1970	13,000	4.00	8.00	15.00	30.00	45.00
1970 Proof	2,000	Value: 50.00				

MOROCCO

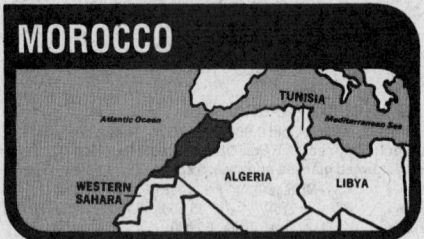

The Kingdom of Morocco, situated on the northwest corner of Africa, has an area of 275,117 sq. mi. (446,550 sq. km.) and a population of 28.5 million. Capital: Rabat. The economy is essentially agricultural. Phosphates, fresh and preserved vegetables, canned fish, and raw materials are exported.

Morocco's strategic position at the gateway to Western Europe has been the principal determinant of its violent, frequently unfortunate history. Time and again the fertile plain between the rugged Atlas Mountains and the sea has echoed the battle's trumpet as Phoenicians, Romans, Vandals, Visigoths,

Byzantine Greeks and Islamic Arabs successively conquered and occupied the land. Modern Morocco is a remnant of an early empire formed by the Arabs at the close of the 7th century, which encompassed all of northwest Africa, and most of the Iberian Peninsula. During the 17th and 18th centuries, while under the control of native dynasties, it was the headquarters of the famous Sale pirates. Morocco's strategic position involved it in the competition of 19th century European powers for political influence in Africa, and resulted in the division of Morocco into French and Spanish spheres of interest, which were established as protectorates in 1912. Morocco became independent on March 2, 1956, after France agreed to end its protectorate. Spain signed similar agreements on April 7 of the same year.

TITLES

المغربية

Al-Maghribiya(t)

المملكة المغربية

Al-Mamlaka(t) al-Maghribiya(t)

المحمدية الشريفة

Al-Mohammediya(t) esh-Sherifiya(t)

RULERS
Abd al-Aziz, AH1311-1326/1894-1908AD
Abd al-Hafiz, AH1326-1330/1908-1912AD

French Protectorate, AH1330/1912AD
Yusuf, AH1330-1346/1912-1927AD
Mohammed V, AH1346-1375/1927-1955AD

Kingdom
Mohammed V, AH1376-1381/1956-1962AD
Al-Hasan II, AH1381-1420/1962-1999AD
Mohammed VI, AH1420- /1999- AD

MINTS

(a) - Paris privy marks only

Silver Coins   Bronze Coins
Bi - England (Birmingham)

بانكلند

Ln = bi-England (London)

بباريز

Pa = bi-Bariz (Paris)

فاس

Fs = Fes (Fas, Fez)

Py - Poissy Inscribed "Paris" but with thunderbolt privy mark.

NOTE: Some of the above forms of the mint names are shown as they appear on the coins, not in regular Arabic script.
NOTES: On the silver coins the denominations are written in words and each series has its own characteristic names:
Y#9-13 (1313-1319) Denomination in 'Preferred' Dirhams.
Y#18-22 (1320-1323) Denomination in fractions of a Rial, but on the 3 larger sizes, the equivalent is given in "Urti parts", 1 Rial 20 = Urti parts.
Y#23-25 (1329) Denomination in Dirhams and in fraction of a Rial.
Y#30-33 (1331-1336) Denomination in Yusuti or "Treasury" Dirhams.
On most of the larger denominations, the denomination is given in the form of a rhymed couplet.
NOTE: Various copper and silver coins dated AH1297-1311 are believed to be patterns. Copper coins similar to Y#14-17, but without denomination on reverse, are patterns.
NOTE: 1, 2, 5 and 10 Mazunas of AH1320 Fes exist in medal alignment and coin alignment (rare). AH1321-1323 Fes strikes are medal alignment only.

KINGDOM
Filali Sharifs - Alawi Dynasty

Abd al-Aziz
AH1311-1326/1894-1908AD
MILLED COINAGE

Y# 9.2   1/2 DIRHAM
1.4558 g., 0.8350 Silver 0.0391 oz. ASW Obv: Star of David within inner circle flanked by arrow heads facing inwards Rev: Star of David within inner circle flanked by arrow heads facing inwards

Date	Mintage	F	VF	XF	Unc	BU
AH1319	572,000	15.00	40.00	120	280	—

REFORM COINAGE
AH1320 / 1902AD

Y# 14.1   MUZUNA
1.0000 g., Bronze Obv: Date within circle Rev: Value within circle

Date	Mintage	F	VF	XF	Unc	BU
AH1320Bi	3,000,000	4.50	9.00	20.00	50.00	—
AH1321Bi	900,000	8.00	20.00	50.00	130	—

Y# 14.2   MUZUNA
1.0000 g., Bronze Obv: Date within circle Rev: Value within circle Note: Varieties exist.

Date	Mintage	F	VF	XF	Unc	BU
AH1320Fs	—	80.00	200	400	—	—

Y# 15.1   2 MAZUNAS
2.0000 g., Bronze Obv: Date within circle Rev: Value within circle

Date	Mintage	F	VF	XF	Unc	BU
AH1320Bi	1,500,000	8.50	18.50	35.00	75.00	—
AH1321Bi	450,000	15.00	35.00	60.00	120	—

Y# 15.2   2 MAZUNAS
2.0000 g., Bronze Note: Normal rim design; varieties exist.

Date	Mintage	F	VF	XF	Unc	BU
AH1320Fs	—	30.00	100	250	—	—
AH1322Fs	—	100	300	600	—	—
AH1323Fs	—	50.00	150	350	—	—

Y# 15.3   2 MAZUNAS
2.0000 g., Bronze Obv: Date within circle Rev: Value within circle, rim design reversed

Date	Mintage	F	VF	XF	Unc	BU
AH1320Fs Rare						

Y# 15.4   2 MAZUNAS
2.0000 g., Bronze, 20.1 mm. Note: Normal rim design.

Date	Mintage	F	VF	XF	Unc	BU
AH1321Pa	6,500,000	2.00	6.00	12.00	30.00	—

Y# 16.1   5 MAZUNAS
5.0000 g., Bronze Obv: Date within circle Rev: Value within circle

Date	Mintage	F	VF	XF	Unc	BU
AH1320Bi	2,400,000	2.00	5.00	10.00	30.00	—
AH1321Bi	720,000	4.00	10.00	20.00	50.00	—

Y# 16.2   5 MAZUNAS
5.0000 g., Bronze Obv: Date within circle Rev: Value within circle Note: Varieties exist.

Date	Mintage	F	VF	XF	Unc	BU
AH1320Fs	—	25.00	50.00	130	—	—
AH1322Fs	—	40.00	90.00	240	—	—

Y# 16.3 5 MAZUNAS
5.0000 g., Bronze **Obv:** Date within circle **Rev:** Value within circle

Date	Mintage	F	VF	XF	Unc	BU
AH1321Pa	7,950,000	2.00	5.00	10.00	30.00	—

Y# 17.1 10 MAZUNAS
10.0000 g., Bronze

Date	Mintage	F	VF	XF	Unc	BU
AH1320Be	2,400,000	2.00	5.00	15.00	40.00	—
AH1321Be	2,600,000	2.00	5.00	15.00	40.00	—

Y# 17.2 10 MAZUNAS
10.0000 g., Bronze **Obv:** Date within circle **Rev:** Value within circle

Date	Mintage	F	VF	XF	Unc	BU
AH1320Bi	1,200,000	3.00	6.00	18.00	50.00	—
AH1321Bi	360,000	4.00	12.00	35.00	100	—

Y# 17.3 10 MAZUNAS
10.0000 g., Bronze **Obv:** Date within circle **Rev:** Value within circle **Note:** Varieties exist.

Date	Mintage	F	VF	XF	Unc	BU
AH1320Fs Small letters	—	200	350	600	1,000	—
AH1320Fs Large letters	—	20.00	60.00	150	300	—
AH1321Fs	—	18.00	50.00	150	300	—
AH1323Fs Large 10	—	75.00	150	300	600	—
AH1323Fs Small 10	—	85.00	175	475	850	—

Y# 18.1 1/20 RIAL (1/2 Dirham)
1.2500 g., 0.8350 Silver 0.0336 oz. ASW **Obv:** Inscription **Rev:** Value and date

Date	Mintage	F	VF	XF	Unc	BU
AH1320Ln	3,920,000	2.00	6.00	20.00	50.00	—
AH1321Ln	2,105,000	3.00	8.00	25.00	55.00	—

Y# 18.2 1/20 RIAL (1/2 Dirham)
1.2500 g., 0.8350 Silver 0.0336 oz. ASW

Date	Mintage	F	VF	XF	Unc	BU
AH1320Pa	2,400,000	3.00	8.00	25.00	55.00	—

Y# 19 1/10 RIAL (Dirham)
2.5000 g., 0.8350 Silver 0.0671 oz. ASW

Date	Mintage	F	VF	XF	Unc	BU
AH1320Ln	2,940,000	3.00	8.00	25.00	55.00	—
AH1321Ln	770,000	6.00	18.00	40.00	100	—

Y# 20.1 1/4 RIAL (2-1/2 Dirhams)
6.2500 g., 0.8350 Silver 0.1678 oz. ASW, 25 mm. **Obv:** Inscription within inner circle, legend around border **Rev:** Inscription and date within the Star of David, legend flanked by star points

Date	Mintage	F	VF	XF	Unc	BU
AH1320Be	1,380,000	4.00	12.50	45.00	120	—

Date	Mintage	F	VF	XF	Unc	BU
AH1321Be	4,450,000	3.00	8.00	30.00	80.00	—
AH1321Be Proof; Rare	5	—	—	—	—	—

Y# 20.2 1/4 RIAL (2-1/2 Dirhams)
6.2500 g., 0.8350 Silver 0.1678 oz. ASW, 25 mm.

Date	Mintage	F	VF	XF	Unc	BU
AH1320Ln	3,056,000	4.00	12.50	35.00	90.00	—
AH1321Ln	1,889,000	5.00	15.00	45.00	100	—

Y# 20.3 1/4 RIAL (2-1/2 Dirhams)
6.2500 g., 0.8350 Silver 0.1678 oz. ASW, 25 mm.

Date	Mintage	F	VF	XF	Unc	BU
AH1320Pa	480,000	12.00	30.00	125	300	—
AH1321Pa	160,000	40.00	80.00	250	550	—

Y# 21.1 1/2 RIAL (5 Dirhams)
12.5000 g., 0.8350 Silver 0.3356 oz. ASW, 32 mm.

Date	Mintage	F	VF	XF	Unc	BU
AH1320Be	2,510,000	10.00	25.00	80.00	180	—

Y# 21.2 1/2 RIAL (5 Dirhams)
12.5000 g., 0.8350 Silver 0.3356 oz. ASW, 32 mm.

Date	Mintage	F	VF	XF	Unc	BU
AH1320Ln	900,000	12.00	30.00	90.00	200	—
AH1321Ln	1,041,000	10.00	25.00	80.00	180	—

Y# 21.3 1/2 RIAL (5 Dirhams)
12.5000 g., 0.8350 Silver 0.3356 oz. ASW, 32 mm.

Date	Mintage	F	VF	XF	Unc	BU
AH1321Pa	1,800,000	8.00	20.00	70.00	160	—
AH1322Pa	540,000	15.00	40.00	110	240	—
AH1323Pa	1,090,000	12.00	30.00	90.00	200	—

Y# 22.1 RIAL (10 Dirhams)
25.0000 g., 0.9000 Silver 0.7234 oz. ASW, 37 mm.

Date	Mintage	F	VF	XF	Unc	BU
AH1320Ln	330,000	25.00	70.00	160	300	—

Y# 22.2 RIAL (10 Dirhams)
25.0000 g., 0.9000 Silver 0.7234 oz. ASW, 37 mm.
Obv: Inscription within circle, legend around border
Rev: Inscription and date within the Star of David, legend flanked by star points

Date	Mintage	F	VF	XF	Unc	BU
AH1321Pa	300,000	25.00	70.00	160	300	—

Abd al-Hafiz
AH1326-1330/1908-1912AD
REFORM COINAGE
AH1320 / 1902AD

Y# 23 1/4 RIAL (2-1/2 Dirhams)
6.2500 g., 0.8350 Silver 0.1678 oz. ASW **Obv:** Inscription below star within sprays **Rev:** Mint, name and date within doubled tri-lobe star

Date	Mintage	F	VF	XF	Unc	BU
AH1329Pa	3,900,000	12.00	25.00	60.00	130	—

Y# 24 1/2 RIAL (5 Dirhams)
12.5000 g., 0.8350 Silver 0.3356 oz. ASW **Obv:** Star above inscription within sprays **Rev:** Mint, name and date within doubled tri-lobe star

Date	Mintage	F	VF	XF	Unc	BU
AH1329Pa	6,200,000	10.00	22.00	55.00	120	—

Y# 25 RIAL (10 Dirhams)
25.0000 g., 0.9000 Silver 0.7234 oz. ASW **Obv:** Star above inscription within sprays **Rev:** Mint, name and date within doubled tri-lobe star

Date	Mintage	F	VF	XF	Unc	BU
AH1329Pa	10,100,000	12.00	25.00	55.00	120	—

PRIVATE TOKEN COINAGE
Enterprise Collet et Gouvernet

KM# Tn1 FRANC
Aluminum **Issuer:** Entreprise Collet et Gouvernet

Date	Mintage	F	VF	XF	Unc	BU
ND	—	20.00	50.00	100	185	—

KM# Tn2 2 FRANCS
Aluminum

Date	Mintage	F	VF	XF	Unc	BU
ND	—	25.00	55.00	120	245	—

KM# Tn3 5 FRANCS
Aluminum

Date	Mintage	F	VF	XF	Unc	BU
ND	—	35.00	60.00	145	275	—

KM# Tn4 5 FRANCS
Aluminum

Date	Mintage	F	VF	XF	Unc	BU
ND	—	35.00	60.00	145	275	—

Yusuf
AH1330-1346/1912-1927AD

REFORM COINAGE
AH1320 / 1902AD

Y# 26 MUZUNA
Bronze **Obv:** Value within star **Rev:** Mint name and date within doubled tri-lobe star

Date	Mintage	F	VF	XF	Unc	BU
AH1330Pa	1,850,000	2.00	7.00	20.00	40.00	—

Y# 27 2 MAZUNAS
Bronze **Obv:** Value within star **Rev:** Mint name and date within doubled tri-lobe star

Date	Mintage	F	VF	XF	Unc	BU
AH1330Pa	2,790,000	2.00	5.00	20.00	45.00	—

Note: Coins reportedly dated 1331Pa probably bore date AH1330

Y# 28.1 5 MAZUNAS
Bronze **Obv:** Value within star **Rev:** Mint name and date within doubled tri-lobe star

Date	Mintage	F	VF	XF	Unc	BU
AH1330Pa	2,983,000	2.00	5.00	20.00	50.00	—
AH1340Pa	2,000,000	2.00	5.00	20.00	50.00	—

Y# 28.2 5 MAZUNAS
Bronze **Obv:** Value within star **Rev:** Mint name and date within doubled tri-lobe star

Date	Mintage	F	VF	XF	Unc	BU
AH1340Py	2,010,000	2.00	5.00	20.00	50.00	—

Y# 29.1 10 MAZUNAS
Bronze **Obv:** Value within star **Rev:** Mint name and date within doubled tri-lobe star

Date	Mintage	F	VF	XF	Unc	BU
AH1330Pa	1,500,000	2.00	6.00	22.00	55.00	—
AH1340Pa	1,000,000	2.00	6.00	22.00	55.00	—

Y# 29.2 10 MAZUNAS
Bronze **Obv:** Value within star **Rev:** Mint name and date within doubled tri-lobe star, privy marks

Date	Mintage	F	VF	XF	Unc	BU
AH1340Py	1,000,000	2.00	6.00	22.00	55.00	—

Y# 30 1/10 RIAL (Dirham)
2.5000 g., 0.8350 Silver 0.0671 oz. ASW **Obv:** Inscription **Rev:** Mint name and date

Date	Mintage	F	VF	XF	Unc	BU
AH1331Pa	500,000	30.00	45.00	75.00	200	—
AH1331Pa Proof	—	Value: 800				

Y# 31 1/4 RIAL (2-1/2 Dirhams)
6.2500 g., 0.8350 Silver 0.1678 oz. ASW **Obv:** Inscription and date within the Star of David, legend flanked by star points **Rev:** Mint name and date within circle

Date	Mintage	F	VF	XF	Unc	BU
AH1331Pa	1,700,000	30.00	45.00	90.00	225	—

Y# 32 1/2 RIAL (5 Dirhams)
0.8350 Silver **Obv:** Inscription and date within the Star of David, legend flanked by star points **Rev:** Mint name and date within circle

Date	Mintage	F	VF	XF	Unc	BU
AH1331Pa	4,300,000	10.00	20.00	40.00	125	—
AH1336Pa	7,200,000	6.00	11.00	25.00	60.00	—

Y# 33 RIAL (10 Dirhams)
25.0000 g., 0.9000 Silver 0.7234 oz. ASW **Obv:** Inscription and date within the Star of David, legend flanked by star points **Rev:** Mint name and date within circle

Date	Mintage	F	VF	XF	Unc	BU
AH1331Pa	4,200,000	12.00	20.00	60.00	120	—
AH1336Pa	2,500,000	13.00	22.00	70.00	130	—

FRENCH PROTECTORATE

Yusuf
AH1330-1346/1912-1927AD

STANDARD COINAGE
100 Centimes = 1 Franc

Y# 34.1 25 CENTIMES
Copper-Nickel, 24 mm. **Obv:** Hole in center of the star of David within circle, without privy marks **Rev:** Hole in center flanked by value within circle, without privy marks

Date	Mintage	F	VF	XF	Unc	BU
ND(1921)Pa	8,000,000	1.00	3.00	8.00	30.00	—

Y# 34.2 25 CENTIMES
Copper-Nickel, 24 mm. **Obv:** Hole in center of the star of David within circle **Rev:** Hole in center flanked by value within circle

Date	Mintage	F	VF	XF	Unc	BU
ND(1924)Py	2,037,000	2.00	4.00	15.00	45.00	—

Y# 34.3 25 CENTIMES
Copper-Nickel, 24 mm. **Rev:** Thunderbolt and torch at left and right of CENTIMES

Date	Mintage	F	VF	XF	Unc	BU
ND(1924)Py	Inc. above	2.00	4.00	15.00	45.00	—

Y# 35.1 50 CENTIMES
Nickel **Obv:** Star within circle ,without privy marks **Rev:** Value within artistic designed star, without privy marks

Date	Mintage	F	VF	XF	Unc	BU
ND(1921)Pa	7,976,000	0.50	1.00	6.50	25.00	—

Y# 35.2 50 CENTIMES
Nickel **Obv:** Star within circle **Rev:** Value within artistic designed star, thunderbolt at bottom

Date	Mintage	F	VF	XF	Unc	BU
ND(1924)Py	3,000,000	1.00	2.00	8.00	30.00	—

Y# 36.1 FRANC
Nickel, 27 mm. **Obv:** Star within circle, without privy marks **Rev:** Value within artistic designed star, without privy marks

Date	Mintage	F	VF	XF	Unc	BU
ND(1921)Pa	8,325,000	0.50	1.00	6.50	25.00	—

Y# 36.2 FRANC
Nickel, 27 mm. **Obv:** Star within circle **Rev:** Value within artistic designed star, thunderbolt below 1

Date	Mintage	F	VF	XF	Unc	BU
ND(1924)Py	4,796,000	1.25	2.50	10.00	35.00	—

Mohammed V
AH1346-1381/1927-1962AD

STANDARD COINAGE
100 Centimes = 1 Franc

Y# 40 50 CENTIMES
Aluminum-Bronze **Obv:** Star **Rev:** Value flanked by dates

Date	Mintage	F	VF	XF	Unc	BU
AH1364-1945(a)	24,000,000	—	0.50	2.00	6.00	—

Y# 41 FRANC
Aluminum-Bronze **Obv:** Legend around star **Rev:** Value flanked by dates

Date	Mintage	F	VF	XF	Unc	BU
AH1364-1945(a)	24,000,000	—	0.50	2.00	6.00	—

Y# 46 FRANC
Aluminum, 19.5 mm. **Obv:** Legend around star **Rev:** Value flanked by dates

Date	Mintage	F	VF	XF	Unc	BU
AH1370-1951(a)	33,000,000	—	0.25	1.00	3.00	—

Note: Note: Y#46-51 were struck for more than 20 years without change of date, until a new currency was introduced in 1974

Y# 42 2 FRANCS
Aluminum-Bronze **Obv:** Legend around star **Rev:** Value flanked by dates

Date	Mintage	F	VF	XF	Unc	BU
AH1364-1945(a)	12,000,000	—	1.00	5.00	12.00	—

Y# 47 2 FRANCS
Aluminum, 22 mm. **Obv:** Legend around star **Rev:** Value flanked by dates

Date	Mintage	F	VF	XF	Unc	BU
AH1370-1951(a)	20,000,000	—	0.25	1.00	3.00	—

Y# 37 5 FRANCS
5.0000 g., 0.6800 Silver 0.1093 oz. ASW **Obv:** Date within small circle of doubled tri-lobe star, all within circle **Rev:** Value within doubled square within circle

Date	Mintage	F	VF	XF	Unc	BU
AH1347(a)	4,000,000	—	3.00	15.00	35.00	—
AH1352(a)	5,000,000	—	2.00	12.00	28.00	—

Y# 43 5 FRANCS
Aluminum-Bronze **Obv:** Date within small circle of doubled tri-lobe star, all within circle **Rev:** Value in doubled square within circle

Date	Mintage	F	VF	XF	Unc	BU
AH1365(a)	20,000,000	0.25	0.50	3.00	10.00	—

Y# 48 5 FRANCS
Aluminum, 25 mm. **Obv:** Date within small circle of doubled tri-lobe star, all within circle **Rev:** Value flanked by marks in doubled square within circle

Date	Mintage	F	VF	XF	Unc	BU
AH1370(a)	23,000,000	0.15	0.30	1.00	5.00	—

Y# 38 10 FRANCS
10.0000 g., 0.6800 Silver 0.2186 oz. ASW **Obv:** Date in small circle of doubled tri-lobe star, all within circle **Rev:** Date in doubled square within circle

Date	Mintage	F	VF	XF	Unc	BU
AH1347(a)	1,600,000	4.50	10.00	22.00	50.00	—
AH1352(a)	2,900,000	3.00	5.00	15.00	40.00	—

Y# 44 10 FRANCS
Copper-Nickel **Obv:** Date in small circle of doubled tri-lobe star, all within circle **Rev:** Value in doubled square within circle

Date	Mintage	F	VF	XF	Unc	BU
AH1366(a)	20,000,000	0.50	1.00	2.00	6.00	—

Y# 49 10 FRANCS
Aluminum-Bronze, 20 mm. **Obv:** Star flanked by designs, date on bottom **Rev:** Value flanked by designs

Date	Mintage	F	VF	XF	Unc	BU
AH1371(a)	40,000,000	0.15	0.50	2.00	6.00	—

Y# 39 20 FRANCS
20.0000 g., 0.6800 Silver 0.4372 oz. ASW **Obv:** Date in inner circle of doubled tri-lobe star, all within circle **Rev:** Value in doubled square within circle

Date	Mintage	F	VF	XF	Unc	BU
AH1347(a)	177,000	7.50	22.00	60.00	120	—
AH1352(a)	2,000,000	4.00	8.00	30.00	60.00	—

Y# 45 20 FRANCS
Copper-Nickel **Obv:** Date in inner circle of doubled tri-lobe star, all within circle **Rev:** Value in doubled square within circle

Date	Mintage	F	VF	XF	Unc	BU
AH1366(a)	6,000,000	0.35	0.65	2.00	6.00	—
AH1366(a) Proof	—	Value: 50.00				

Y# 50 20 FRANCS
Aluminum-Bronze, 23.8 mm. **Obv:** Star flanked by designs, date on bottom **Rev:** Value flanked by designs

Date	Mintage	F	VF	XF	Unc	BU
AH1371(a)	20,000,000	0.25	0.50	1.00	4.00	—

Y# 51 50 FRANCS
Aluminum-Bronze, 27 mm. **Obv:** Date in inner circle of doubled tri-lobe star, all within circle **Rev:** Value in doubled square within circle

Date	Mintage	F	VF	XF	Unc	BU
AH1371(a)	20,600,000	0.35	0.65	2.00	8.00	—

Y# 51a 50 FRANCS
Gold **Obv:** Date in inner circle of doubled tri-lobe star, all within circle **Rev:** Value within doubled square within circle

Date	Mintage	F	VF	XF	Unc	BU
AH1371(a) Rare	—	—	—	—	—	—

Y# A54　100 FRANCS
2.5000 g., 0.7200 Silver 0.0579 oz. ASW **Obv:** Star flanked by designs, date on bottom **Rev:** Value flanked by designs

Date	Mintage	F	VF	XF	Unc	BU
AH1370(a)	10,000,000	—	—	—	500	—

Note: Nearly all specimens were melted, only 100 known

Y# 52　100 FRANCS
4.0000 g., 0.7200 Silver 0.0926 oz. ASW **Obv:** Star within small circle in center of larger star with designs in points **Rev:** Value within beaded circle, legend around border

Date	Mintage	F	VF	XF	Unc	BU
AH1372-1953(a)	20,000,000	—	2.50	10.00	20.00	—

Y# 53　200 FRANCS
8.0000 g., 0.7200 Silver 0.1852 oz. ASW **Obv:** Star within small circle in center of larger star with designs in points **Rev:** Value and date within beaded circle

Date	Mintage	F	VF	XF	Unc	BU
AH1372-1953 (1953) (a)	10,176,000	—	3.50	12.00	25.00	—

Y# 54　500 FRANCS
22.5000 g., 0.9000 Silver 0.6510 oz. ASW **Obv:** Bust left within circle **Rev:** Crown in center of star flanked by dates and value

Date	Mintage	F	VF	XF	Unc	BU
AH1376-1956(a)	2,000,000	—	9.00	18.00	40.00	—

KINGDOM
1956-

Mohammed V
AH1346-1381/1927-1962AD

REFORM COINAGE
100 Francs = 1 Dirham

Y# 55　DIRHAM
6.0000 g., 0.6000 Silver 0.1157 oz. ASW **Obv:** Head left **Rev:** Crowned arms with supporters flanked by dates above and value below

Date	Mintage	F	VF	XF	Unc	BU
AH1380-1960(a)	33,000,000	—	1.00	3.00	8.00	—

al-Hassan II
AH1381-1420/1962-1999AD

REFORM COINAGE
100 Francs = 1 Dirham

Y# 56　DIRHAM
Nickel, 23.6 mm. **Obv:** Head left **Rev:** Crowned arms with supporters

Date	Mintage	F	VF	XF	Unc	BU
AH1384-1965(a)	30,000,000	—	0.50	0.75	2.00	—
AH1388-1968(a)	5,000,000	1.00	2.00	4.00	10.00	—
AH1389-1969(a)	17,200,000	—	0.50	0.75	2.00	—

Y# 57　5 DIRHAMS
11.7500 g., 0.7200 Silver 0.2720 oz. ASW **Obv:** Head left **Rev:** Crowned arms with supporters

Date	Mintage	F	VF	XF	Unc	BU
AH1384-1965(a)	2,000,000	—	5.00	12.00	30.00	—
AH1384-1965(a) Proof	200	Value: 60.00				

REFORM COINAGE
100 Santimat = 1 Dirham

Y# 87　1/2 DIRHAM
Copper-Nickel **Obv:** Head left **Rev:** Crowned arms with supporters

Date	Mintage	F	VF	XF	Unc	BU
AH1407-1987	—	—	—	—	1.50	—

Y# 63　DIRHAM
6.0000 g., Copper-Nickel, 24 mm. **Obv:** Head left **Rev:** Crowned arms with supporters

Date	Mintage	F	VF	XF	Unc	BU
AH1394-1974	32,850,000	—	0.30	0.50	1.00	—

Y# 63a　DIRHAM
0.9170 Gold, 24 mm. **Obv:** Head left **Rev:** Crowned arms with supporters

Date	Mintage	F	VF	XF	Unc	BU
AH1394-1974 Proof	30	Value: 685				

Y# 88　DIRHAM
Copper-Nickel **Obv:** Head left **Rev:** Crowned arms with supporters

Date	Mintage	F	VF	XF	Unc	BU
AH1407-1987	—	—	—	—	2.75	—

Y# 58　SANTIM
0.7000 g., Aluminum, 17 mm. **Obv:** Crowned arms with supporters **Rev:** Value flanked by designs

Date	Mintage	F	VF	XF	Unc	BU
AH1394-1974	10,240,000	—	—	0.50	2.00	—

Y# 58a　SANTIM
0.9170 Gold, 17 mm. **Obv:** Crowned arms with supporters **Rev:** Value flanked by designs

Date	Mintage	F	VF	XF	Unc	BU
AH1394-1974 Proof	30	Value: 425				

Y# 93　SANTIM
0.7000 g., Aluminum, 17 mm. **Obv:** Crowned arms with supporters **Rev:** Fish above value

Date	Mintage	F	VF	XF	Unc	BU
AH1407-1987	—	—	—	6.00	12.00	—

Note: Most were melted

Y# 59　5 SANTIMAT
2.0000 g., Brass, 17.5 mm. **Series:** F.A.O. **Obv:** Crowned arms with supporters **Rev:** Value at lower right of captains wheel

Date	Mintage	F	VF	XF	Unc	BU
AH1394-1974	54,820,000	—	—	0.15	1.00	—

Y# 59a　5 SANTIMAT
0.9170 Gold, 17.5 mm. **Series:** F.A.O. **Obv:** Crowned arms with supporters **Rev:** Value at lower right of captain's wheel

Date	Mintage	F	VF	XF	Unc	BU
AH1394-1974 Proof	30	Value: 485				

Y# 83　5 SANTIMAT
2.0000 g., Brass, 17.5 mm. **Series:** F.A.O. **Obv:** Crowned arms with supporters **Rev:** Value to upper left of center design **Edge:** Plain

Date	Mintage	F	VF	XF	Unc	BU
AH1407-1987	—	—	—	—	1.00	—

Y# 60　10 SANTIMAT
3.0000 g., Brass, 20 mm. **Series:** F.A.O. **Obv:** Crowned arms with supporters **Rev:** Value at lower left of designs

Date	Mintage	F	VF	XF	Unc	BU
AH1394-1974	67,950,000	—	—	0.15	1.00	—

Y# 60a　10 SANTIMAT
0.9170 Gold, 20 mm. **Series:** F.A.O. **Obv:** Crowned arms with supporters **Rev:** Value at lower left of designs

Date	Mintage	F	VF	XF	Unc	BU
AH1394-1974 Proof	30	Value: 575				

Y# 84　10 SANTIMAT
3.4000 g., Brass, 20 mm. **Series:** F.A.O. **Obv:** Crowned arms with supporters **Rev:** Single ear of corn to left of value **Edge:** Reeded

Date	Mintage	F	VF	XF	Unc	BU
AH1407-1987	—	—	—	—	1.00	—

Y# 61 20 SANTIMAT
4.0000 g., Brass, 23 mm. **Obv:** Head left **Rev:** Crowned arms with supporters

Date	Mintage	F	VF	XF	Unc	BU
AH1394-1974	59,840,000	—	0.30	0.40	1.00	—

Y# 61a 20 SANTIMAT
0.9170 Gold, 23 mm. **Obv:** Head left **Rev:** Crowned arms with supporters

Date	Mintage	F	VF	XF	Unc	BU
AH1394-1974 Proof	30	Value: 585				

Y# 85 20 SANTIMAT
4.0000 g., Brass, 23 mm. **Series:** F.A.O. **Obv:** Crowned arms with supporters **Rev:** Value to right of designs

Date	Mintage	F	VF	XF	Unc	BU
AH1407-1987	—	—	—	—	1.00	—

Y# 62 50 SANTIMAT
4.0000 g., Copper-Nickel, 21 mm. **Obv:** Head left **Rev:** Crowned arms with supporters

Date	Mintage	F	VF	XF	Unc	BU
AH1394-1974	40,380,000	—	0.20	0.40	1.00	—

Y# 62a 50 SANTIMAT
0.9170 Gold, 21 mm. **Obv:** Head left **Rev:** Crowned arms with supporters

Date	Mintage	F	VF	XF	Unc	BU
AH1394-1974 Proof	30	Value: 585				

Y# 64 5 DIRHAMS
Copper-Nickel **Series:** World Food Conference **Obv:** Head left **Rev:** Small value within center of designs

Date	Mintage	F	VF	XF	Unc	BU
AH1395-1975	500,000	—	—	4.00	12.00	15.00
AH1395-1975 Proof	500	Value: 80.00				

Y# 64a 5 DIRHAMS
12.0000 g., 0.9250 Silver 0.3569 oz. ASW **Series:** World Food Conference **Obv:** Head left **Rev:** Small value within center of designs

Date	Mintage	F	VF	XF	Unc	BU
AH1395-1975 Proof	200	Value: 150				

Y# 64b 5 DIRHAMS
23.6500 g., 0.9000 Gold 0.6843 oz. AGW **Series:** World Food Conference **Obv:** Head left **Rev:** Small value within center of designs

Date	Mintage	F	VF	XF	Unc	BU
AH1395-1975 Proof	20	Value: 1,000				

Y# 72 5 DIRHAMS
12.0000 g., Copper-Nickel, 29 mm. **Obv:** Head left **Rev:** Crowned arms with supporters

Date	Mintage	F	VF	XF	Unc	BU
AH1400-1980	10,000,000	—	1.50	4.00	10.00	12.00

Y# 82 5 DIRHAMS
6.8000 g., Bi-Metallic Aluminum-Bronze center in Stainless Steel ring, 26.2 mm. **Obv:** Head left within circle **Rev:** Crowned arms with supporters and value within circle

Date	Mintage	F	VF	XF	Unc	BU
AH1407-1987	—	—	2.00	4.50	7.50	9.00

Y# 92 10 DIRHAMS
12.0000 g., Bi-Metallic Copper-Nickel center in Brass ring, 28 mm. **Obv:** Hooded head left within circle with star below **Rev:** Crowned arms with supporters and value within circle with star above

Date	Mintage	F	VF	XF	Unc	BU
AH1415-1995	—	—	—	—	8.00	10.00

Y# 65 50 DIRHAMS
35.0000 g., 0.9250 Silver 1.0408 oz. ASW **Subject:** 20th Anniversary of Independence **Obv:** Head left **Rev:** Crowned arms with supporters

Date	Mintage	F	VF	XF	Unc	BU
AH1395-1975	6,000	—	—	—	30.00	40.00
AH1395-1975 Proof	4,400	Value: 60.00				

Y# 65a 50 DIRHAMS
60.1400 g., 0.9000 Gold 1.7401 oz. AGW **Subject:** 20th Anniversary of Independence **Obv:** Head left **Rev:** Crowned arms with supporters

Date	Mintage	F	VF	XF	Unc	BU
AH1395-1975	40	Value: 1,750				

Y# 67 50 DIRHAMS
35.0000 g., 0.9250 Silver 1.0408 oz. ASW **Series:** International Women's Year **Obv:** Head left **Rev:** Hand within circled design

Date	Mintage	F	VF	XF	Unc	BU
AH1395-1975	6,000	—	—	—	40.00	45.00
AH1395-1975 Proof	4,400	Value: 60.00				

Y# 67a 50 DIRHAMS
60.1400 g., 0.9000 Gold 1.7401 oz. AGW **Series:** International Women's Year **Obv:** Head left **Rev:** Hand within circled design

Date	Mintage	F	VF	XF	Unc	BU
AH1395-1975 Proof	20	Value: 1,750				

Y# 68 50 DIRHAMS
35.0000 g., 0.9250 Silver 1.0408 oz. ASW **Subject:** Anniversary - Green March **Obv:** Head left **Rev:** Pointed artistic design with stars on points flanked by dates **Note:** Reverse inscriptions vary slightly for each date.

Date	Mintage	F	VF	XF	Unc	BU
AH1396-1976	11,000	—	—	—	30.00	40.00
AH1396-1976 Proof	4,400	Value: 50.00				
AH1397-1977	3,500	—	—	—	50.00	60.00
AH1397-1977 Proof	200	Value: 150				
AH1398-1978	5,000	—	—	—	40.00	45.00
AH1398-1978 Proof	300	Value: 120				
AH1399-1979	3,000	—	—	—	55.00	60.00
AH1399-1979 Proof	300	Value: 150				
AH1400-1980	1,000	—	—	—	100	115
AH1400-1980 Proof	200	Value: 225				

Y# 68a 50 DIRHAMS
60.1400 g., 0.9000 Gold 1.7401 oz. AGW **Subject:** Anniversary - Green March **Obv:** Head left **Rev:** Pointed artistic design with stars on points flanked by dates **Note:** Reverse inscriptions vary slightly for each date.

Date	Mintage	F	VF	XF	Unc	BU
AH1396-1976 Proof	20	Value: 1,850				
AH1397-1977 Proof	20	Value: 1,800				
AH1398-1978 Proof	70	Value: 1,750				
AH1399-1979 Proof	70	Value: 1,750				
AH1400-1980 Proof	30	Value: 1,750				

Y# 70 50 DIRHAMS
35.0000 g., 0.9250 Silver 1.0408 oz. ASW **Series:** International Year of the Child **Obv:** Head left **Rev:** Design divides world globe flanked by dates

Date	Mintage	F	VF	XF	Unc	BU
AH1399-1979	5,000	—	—	—	40.00	45.00
AH1399-1979 Proof	500	Value: 100				

Y# 70a 50 DIRHAMS
60.1400 g., 0.9000 Gold 1.7401 oz. AGW **Series:** International Year of the Child **Obv:** Head left **Rev:** Designs divide globe flanked by dates

Date	Mintage	F	VF	XF	Unc	BU
AH1399-1979 Proof	70	Value: 1,750				

Y# 76   50 DIRHAMS
35.0000 g., 0.9250 Silver 1.0408 oz. ASW **Subject:** 50th Birthday - King Hassan **Obv:** Head left **Rev:** Crowned arms with supporters flanked by oat sprig, curvey line and dates with value below

Date	Mintage	F	VF	XF	Unc	BU
AH1399-1979	5,000	—	—	—	40.00	45.00
AH1399-1979 Proof	500	Value: 100				

Y# 76a   50 DIRHAMS
60.1400 g., 0.9000 Gold 1.7401 oz. AGW **Subject:** 50th Birthday - King Hassan **Obv:** Head left **Rev:** Crowned arms with supporters flanked by oat sprig, curvy line and dates with value below

Date	Mintage	F	VF	XF	Unc	BU
AH1399-1979 Proof	70	Value: 1,750				

Y# 75   100 DIRHAMS
25.0000 g., 0.9250 Silver 0.7435 oz. ASW **Subject:** 9th Mediterranean Games **Obv:** Head left **Rev:** Olympic circles flanked by dates

Date	Mintage	F	VF	XF	Unc	BU
AH1403-1983	5,000	—	—	—	40.00	45.00
AH1403-1983 Proof	500	Value: 80.00				

Y# 77   100 DIRHAMS
15.0000 g., 0.9250 Silver 0.4461 oz. ASW **Series:** 6th Panarab Sports Games - Olympics **Obv:** Head left **Rev:** Olympic rings above map

Date	Mintage	F	VF	XF	Unc	BU
AH1405-1985	2,300	—	—	—	50.00	55.00
AH1405-1985 Proof	300	Value: 150				

Y# 78   100 DIRHAMS
15.0000 g., 0.9250 Silver 0.4461 oz. ASW **Subject:** 10th Anniversary of Green March **Obv:** Seated figure right **Rev:** Crowned arms with supporters

Date	Mintage	F	VF	XF	Unc	BU
AH1406-1985	1,200	—	—	—	60.00	70.00
AH1406-1985 Proof	200	Value: 200				

Y# 78a   100 DIRHAMS
21.5000 g., 0.9000 Gold 0.6221 oz. AGW **Subject:** 10th Anniversary of the Green March **Obv:** Seated figure right **Rev:** Crowned arms with supporters

Date	Mintage	F	VF	XF	Unc	BU
AH1406-1985 Proof	30	Value: 700				

Y# 79   100 DIRHAMS
15.0000 g., 0.9250 Silver 0.4461 oz. ASW **Subject:** 25th Year - Reign of King Hassan **Obv:** Head left flanked by dates **Rev:** Cheering citizens

Date	Mintage	F	VF	XF	Unc	BU
AH1406-1986	—	—	—	—	40.00	45.00
AH1406-1986 Proof	—	Value: 100				

Y# 80   100 DIRHAMS
15.0000 g., 0.9250 Silver 0.4461 oz. ASW **Subject:** Visit of the Pope **Obv:** Popes shaking hands **Rev:** Crowned arms with supporters

Date	Mintage	F	VF	XF	Unc	BU
AH1406-1986	—	—	—	—	100	120
AH1406-1986 Proof	2,000	Value: 200				

Y# 86   100 DIRHAMS
15.0000 g., 0.9250 Silver 0.4461 oz. ASW **Subject:** Opening of the Rabat Mint **Obv:** Head left **Rev:** Cluster of square designs flanked by dates

Date	Mintage	F	VF	XF	Unc	BU
AH1407-1987	—	—	—	—	40.00	45.00
AH1407-1987 Proof	—	Value: 80.00				

Y# 74   150 DIRHAMS
35.0000 g., 0.9250 Silver 1.0408 oz. ASW **Subject:** 15th Hejira Calendar Century **Obv:** Crowned arms with supporters flanked by dates **Rev:** Artistic design within circle flanked by dates

Date	Mintage	F	VF	XF	Unc	BU
AH1401-1980	3,000	—	—	—	50.00	60.00
AH1401-1980 Proof	300	Value: 150				

Y# 74a   150 DIRHAMS
60.1400 g., 0.9000 Gold 1.7401 oz. AGW **Subject:** 15th Hejira Calendar Century **Obv:** Crowned arms with supporters flanked by dates **Rev:** Artistic design within circle flanked by dates

Date	Mintage	F	VF	XF	Unc	BU
AH1401-1980 Proof	30	Value: 1,850				

Y# 73   150 DIRHAMS
35.0000 g., 0.9250 Silver 1.0408 oz. ASW **Subject:** 20th Anniversary - King Hassan's Coronation **Obv:** Crowned arms with supporters flanked by dates **Rev:** Crowned arms with supporters

Date	Mintage	F	VF	XF	Unc	BU
AH1401-1981	3,000	—	—	—	50.00	60.00
AH1401-1981 Proof	300	Value: 150				

Y# 73a   150 DIRHAMS
60.1400 g., 0.9000 Gold 1.7401 oz. AGW **Subject:** 20th Anniversary - King Hassan's Coronation **Obv:** Head left **Rev:** Crowned arms with supporters flanked by dates

Date	Mintage	F	VF	XF	Unc	BU
AH1401-1981 Proof	30	Value: 1,750				

Y# 81   200 DIRHAMS
15.0000 g., 0.9250 Silver 0.4461 oz. ASW **Subject:** Moroccan - American Friendship Treaty **Obv:** Head left **Rev:** Radiant sun behind crossed flags

Date	Mintage	F	VF	XF	Unc	BU
AH1408-1987 Proof Est. 5,000		Value: 40.00				

Y# 81a   200 DIRHAMS
121.5000 g., 0.9000 Gold 3.5155 oz. AGW **Subject:** Moroccan - American Friendship Treaty **Obv:** Head left **Rev:** Radiant sun behind crossed flags

Date	Mintage	F	VF	XF	Unc	BU
AH1408-1987	30	—	—	—	4,000	—

Y# 97   200 DIRHAMS
15.0000 g., 0.9250 Silver 0.4461 oz. ASW, 31.3 mm. **Subject:** African Cup Soccer Games **Obv:** Head left **Rev:** Games logo **Edge:** Reeded

Date	Mintage	F	VF	XF	Unc	BU
AH1408-1988	—	—	—	—	40.00	50.00

Y# 91   200 DIRHAMS
15.0000 g., 0.9250 Silver 0.4461 oz. ASW **Subject:** First Francophone Games **Obv:** Head left **Rev:** Games emblem

Date	Mintage	F	VF	XF	Unc	BU
AH1409-1989	5,000	—	—	—	30.00	35.00
AH1409-1989 Proof	500	Value: 95.00				

Y# 89   200 DIRHAMS
15.0000 g., 0.9250 Silver 0.4461 oz. ASW, 31.3 mm.
Subject: 35th Anniversary of Independence **Obv:** Head left
Rev: Crowned arms with supporters **Edge:** Reeded

Date	Mintage	F	VF	XF	Unc	BU
AH1411-1990	—	—	—	—	60.00	65.00
AH1411-1990 Proof	—	Value: 120				

Y# 90   200 DIRHAMS
15.0000 g., 0.9250 Silver 0.4461 oz. ASW, 31.3 mm.   **Subject:**
King's Tunisian Visit **Obv:** Head left **Rev:** Inscription **Edge:** Reeded

Date	Mintage	F	VF	XF	Unc	BU
AH1411-1990 Proof	—	Value: 95.00				
AH1411-1990	—	—	—	—	50.00	60.00

Y# 96   200 DIRHAMS
15.0000 g., 0.9250 Silver 0.4461 oz. ASW, 31.3 mm.
Subject: 30th Anniversary of Reign **Obv:** Crowned arms with
supporters **Rev:** King on horseback amidst crowd **Edge:** Reeded

Date	Mintage	F	VF	XF	Unc	BU
AH1411-1991 Proof	—	Value: 95.00				
AH1411-1991	—	—	—	—	50.00	60.00

Y# 98   200 DIRHAMS
15.0000 g., 0.9250 Silver 0.4461 oz. ASW, 31.3 mm.
Subject: Revolution, 40th Anniversary **Obv:** Head left
Rev: Building within circle **Edge:** Reeded

Date	Mintage	F	VF	XF	Unc	BU
AH1414-1993	2,000	—	—	—	50.00	60.00
AH1414-1993 Proof	300	Value: 120				

Y# 99   200 DIRHAMS
15.0000 g., 0.9250 Silver 0.4461 oz. ASW, 31.3 mm.
Subject: 33rd Anniversary of Hassan's Inauguration **Obv:** Head
left **Rev:** Mosque within circle **Edge:** Reeded

Date	Mintage	F	VF	XF	Unc	BU
AH1414-1993	2,000	—	—	—	50.00	60.00
AH1414-1993 Proof	300	Value: 120				

Y# 100   200 DIRHAMS
15.0000 g., 0.9250 Silver 0.4461 oz. ASW, 31.3 mm.
Subject: GATT Agreement **Obv:** Head left **Rev:** Tower within
world globe **Edge:** Reeded

Date	Mintage	F	VF	XF	Unc	BU
AH1414-1994 Proof	300	Value: 120				
AH1414-1994	2,000	—	—	—	50.00	60.00

Y# 100a   200 DIRHAMS
21.5000 g., 0.9000 Gold 0.6221 oz. AGW, 31.3 mm.
Subject: GATT Agreement **Obv:** Head left **Rev:** Tower within
world globe **Edge:** Reeded

Date	Mintage	F	VF	XF	Unc	BU
AH1416-1995 Proof	—	—	—	—	—	—

Y# 101   200 DIRHAMS
15.0000 g., 0.9250 Silver 0.4461 oz. ASW, 31.3 mm.
Subject: 40th Anniversary of Independence **Obv:** Head left
Rev: Crowned arms with supporters **Edge:** Reeded

Date	Mintage	F	VF	XF	Unc	BU
AH1416-1995	—	—	—	—	60.00	65.00
AH1416-1995 Proof	—	Value: 120				

Y# 102   200 DIRHAMS
15.0000 g., 0.9250 Silver 0.4461 oz. ASW, 31.3 mm.
Subject: 50th Anniversary of United Nations **Obv:** Head left
Rev: UN logo and value within circle **Edge:** Reeded

Date	Mintage	F	VF	XF	Unc	BU
AH1416-1995	—	—	—	—	60.00	65.00
AH1416-1995 Proof	—	Value: 120				

Y# 103   200 DIRHAMS
15.0000 g., 0.9250 Silver 0.4461 oz. ASW, 31.3 mm.
Subject: Rabat 800th Anniversary **Obv:** Head left **Rev:** City view
within circle **Edge:** Reeded

Date	Mintage	F	VF	XF	Unc	BU
AH1416-1995	—	—	—	—	60.00	65.00
AH1416-1995 Proof	—	Value: 120				

Y# 104   200 DIRHAMS
15.0000 g., 0.9250 Silver 0.4461 oz. ASW, 31.3 mm.
Subject: 20th Anniversary of the Green March **Obv:** Head left
Rev: Arabic inscription **Edge:** Reeded

Date	Mintage	F	VF	XF	Unc	BU
AH1416-1995	—	—	—	—	60.00	65.00
AH1416-1995 Proof	—	Value: 120				

Y# 105   200 DIRHAMS
15.0000 g., 0.9250 Silver 0.4461 oz. ASW, 31.3 mm.
Subject: 50th Anniversary Human Rights Declaration **Obv:** Head
left **Rev:** Logo, legend and inscription **Edge:** Reeded

Date	Mintage	F	VF	XF	Unc	BU
AH1419-1998	—	—	—	—	60.00	65.00

Y# 66   250 DIRHAMS
6.4500 g., 0.9000 Gold 0.1866 oz. AGW   **Subject:** Birthday of
King Hassan **Obv:** Head left **Rev:** Crowned arms with supporters
flanked by dates

Date	Mintage	F	VF	XF	Unc	BU
AH1395-1975	5,000	—	—	—	—	190
AH1395-1975 Proof	1,270	Value: 220				
AH1396-1976	3,200	—	—	—	—	190
AH1396-1976 Proof	450	Value: 220				
AH1397-1977	3,000	—	—	—	—	190
AH1397-1977 Proof	800	Value: 220				
AH1398-1978	2,000	—	—	—	—	190
AH1398-1978 Proof	150	Value: 220				

Y# 71   500 DIRHAMS
12.9000 g., 0.9000 Gold 0.3733 oz. AGW   **Subject:** Birthday of
King Hassan **Obv:** Head left **Rev:** Crowned arms with supporters
flanked by oat sprig, curvy line and dates

Date	Mintage	F	VF	XF	Unc	BU
AH1399-1979	3,000	—	—	—	—	360
AH1399-1979 Proof	300	Value: 360				
AH1400-1980	100	—	—	—	—	420
AH1400-1980 Proof	100	Value: 500				
AH1401-1981	100	—	—	—	—	420
AH1401-1981 Proof	100	Value: 500				
AH1402-1982	100	—	—	—	—	420
AH1402-1982 Proof	100	Value: 500				
AH1403-1983	2,500	—	—	—	—	360
AH1403-1983 Proof	Inc. above	Value: 360				
AH1404-1984	100	—	—	—	—	420
AH1404-1984 Proof	100	Value: 500				
AH1405-1985	275	—	—	—	—	375
AH1405-1985 Proof	125	Value: 475				
AH1406-1986 Proof	—	Value: 450				
AH1407-1987 Proof	—	Value: 450				
AH1408-1988 Proof	—	Value: 450				
AH1409-1989 Proof	—	Value: 450				
AH1410-1990 Proof	—	Value: 450				
AH1411-1991 Proof	—	Value: 450				
AH1412-1992 Proof	—	Value: 450				
AH1413-1993 Proof	—	Value: 450				

Mohammed VI
AH1420/1999AD
REFORM COINAGE
100 Santimat = 1 Dirham

Y# 94   250 DIRHAMS
25.0000 g., 0.9250 Silver 0.7435 oz. ASW, 37 mm.
Subject: First Anniversary of Mohammed VI's Enthronement
Obv: Hooded bust left **Rev:** Crowned arms with supporters flanked by dates **Edge:** Reeded

Date	Mintage	F	VF	XF	Unc	BU
AH1421-2000	—	—	—	—	—	55.00
AH1421-2000 Proof	— Value: 90.00					

Y# 106   250 DIRHAMS
25.0000 g., 0.9250 Silver 0.7435 oz. ASW, 37 mm.
Subject: Green March 25th Anniversary **Obv:** Head 3/4 left
Rev: Map **Edge:** Reeded

Date	Mintage	F	VF	XF	Unc	BU
AH1421-2000	—	—	—	—	—	50.00

ESSAIS

KM#	Date	Mintage	Identification	Mkt Val
E1	AH1329(a) (Pa)	—	5 Dirhams. Silver. Y24.	600
E2	AH1330(a) (Pa)	—	Muzuna. Bronze. Y26.	300
E3	AH1330(a) (Pa)	—	2 Mazunas. Bronze. Y27.	300
E4	AH1330(a) (Pa)	—	5 Mazunas. Bronze. Value within star. Mint name and date within tri-lobe star. Y28.	350
E5	AH1330(a) (Pa)	—	10 Mazunas. Bronze. Y29.	375
E6	AH1331(a) (Pa)	—	5 Dirhams. Nickel.	750
E7	AH1331(a) (Pa)	—	5 Dirhams. Aluminum-Bronze.	750
E8	AH1331(a) (Pa)	—	5 Dirhams. Aluminum. Y32.	750
E9	ND (Py)	—	25 Centimes. Copper-Nickel. Without hole or ESSAI. Y34.	300
E9a	ND(a) (Py)	—	25 Centimes. Copper-Nickel. With hole. Y34.	300
E9b	ND	—	25 Centimes. Hole in center flanked by value within circle. Incuse "Essai".	—
E10	ND(a) (Py)	—	50 Centimes. Star within circle. Value within artistic designed star.	175
E10a	NDPy	—	50 Centimes. Nickel. Y35.	—
E11	ND(a) (Py)	—	Franc. Nickel. Y36.	275
E12	AH1340(a) (Py)	—	5 Mazunas. Bronze. Value within center of star. Mint name and date within doubled tri-lobe star. Y28.	450
E13	AH1340(a) (a)	—	10 Mazunas. Bronze. Y29.	500
E14	AH1346(a) (Pa)	—	10 Francs. Nickel. Head laureate right. Value in doubled square within circle.	—
E15	AH1346(a) (Pa)	—	10 Francs. Nickel. Without ESSAI.	—
E16	ND(a) (Pa)	—	5 Dirhams. Nickel. Head laureate right. Inscription within the star of David.	2,500
E17	ND(a) (Pa)	—	5 Dirhams. Nickel. Without ESSAI.	2,500
E18	ND(a) (Pa)	—	5 Dirhams. Aluminum-Bronze.	2,500
E19	ND(a) (Pa)	—	5 Dirhams. Aluminum-Bronze. Without ESSAI.	2,500
E20	AH1347(a) (Pa)	—	5 Francs. Silver. Y37.	300
E21	AH1347(a) (Pa)	—	10 Francs. Silver. Date in inner circle of doubled tri-lobe star, all within circle. Value in small circle among doubled square design, all within circle.	1,500
E22	AH1347(a) (Pa)	—	10 Francs. Silver. Without ESSAI.	450
E23	AH1347(a) (Pa)	—	10 Francs. Silver. Y38.	350

KM#	Date	Mintage	Identification	Mkt Val
E24	AH1347(a) (Pa)	—	20 Francs. Date in inner circle of doubled tri-lobe star, all within circle. Value in small circle of doubled square design, all within circle.	—
E25	AH1347(a) (Pa)	—	20 Francs. Without ESSAI.	—
E26	AH1347(a) (Pa)	—	20 Francs. Silver. Y39.	400
E28	AH1361(a) (a)	—	50 Centimes. Aluminum-Bronze. Y40.	250
E29	AH1361(a) (a)	—	Franc. Aluminum-Bronze. Y41.	250
E30	AH1361(a) (a)	—	2 Francs. Aluminum-Bronze. Y42.	250
E31	AH1365(a) (a)	—	50 Centimes. Aluminum-Bronze center. Y40.	300
E32	AH1365(a) (a)	—	Franc. Aluminum-Bronze. Y41.	200
E33	AH1365(a) (a)	—	2 Francs. Alum.-Bronze. Y42.	200
E34	AH1365(a) (a)	—	5 Francs. Alum.-Bronze. Y43.	80.00
E35	AH1366(a) (a)	1,100	10 Francs. Copper-Nickel. Y44.	80.00
E36	AH1366(a) (a)	1,100	20 Francs. Copper-Nickel. Y45.	80.00
E37	AH1370(a) (a)	1,100	Franc. Aluminum. Y46.	50.00
E38	AH1370(a) (a)	1,100	2 Francs. Alum. center. Y47.	50.00
E39	AH1370(a) (a)	1,100	5 Francs. Aluminum. Y48.	60.00
E40	AH1370(a) (a)	1,100	100 Francs. 0.7200 Silver. Y-A54.	80.00

Note: KM#E37-E40 were issued in a set with Tunisia, KM#E28-E30.

KM#	Date	Mintage	Identification	Mkt Val
E41	AH1371(a) (a)	1,100	10 Francs. Alum.-Bronze. Y49.	60.00
E42	AH1371(a) (a)	1,100	20 Francs. Alum.-Bronze. Y50.	50.00
E43	AH1371(a) (a)	1,100	50 Francs. Aluminum-Bronze. Value in doubled square design within circle. Date in small circle within doubled tri-lobe star, all within circle. Y51.	45.00

Note: KM#E41-43 also issued in 3-piece boxed sets.

KM#	Date	Mintage	Identification	Mkt Val
E44	AH1372(a) (a)	1,100	100 Francs. Silver. Y52.	75.00
E45	AH1372(a) (a)	1,100	200 Francs. Silver. Y53.	90.00
E46	AH1384	—	5 Dirhams. Silver. Y#57.	—
E47	AH1384	—	Dirham. Nickel. Y#56.	—

PATTERNS
Including off metal strikes

KM#	Date	Mintage	Identification	Mkt Val
Pn29	AH1319Fs	—	1/4 Falus. Bronze. 0.7210 g. 12.5 mm. Machine struck.	—
Pn30	AH1319Fs	—	1/2 Falus. Bronze. 1.4430 g. 13 mm.	—
Pn31	AH1319Mr	—	1/2 Falus. Cast Bronze. 1.4430 g. 14 mm.	—
Pn32	AH1319Fs	—	Falus. Bronze. 2.8860 g. 16 mm.	—
Pn33	AH1319Mr	—	Falus. Cast Bronze. 2.8860 g. 17 mm.	—
Pn34	AH1319Mr	—	2 Falus. Cast Bronze. 5.7730 g. 22 mm.	—
Pn35	AH1319Fs	—	4 Falus. Bronze. 11.5460 g. 25 mm.	—
Pn36	AH1319Mr	—	4 Falus. Cast Bronze. 11.5460 g. 27 mm.	—
Pn37	AH1320Fs	—	1/2 Falus. Bronze. 1.4430 g. 13 mm. Machine struck.	—
Pn38	AH1320Fs	—	2 Falus. Bronze. 5.7730 g. 20 mm. Machine struck.	—
Pn39	AH1320Fs	—	4 Falus. Bronze. 11.5460 g. 25 mm. Machine struck.	—
Pn40	AH1320Be	—	Muzuna. Bronze.	—
Pn41	AH1320Pa	—	Muzuna. Bronze.	—
Pn42	AH1320Be	—	2 Mazunas. Bronze.	—
Pn43	AH1320Fs	—	2 Mazunas. Bronze. Y#15.1 w/out "2".	—
Pn44	AH1320Be	—	5 Mazunas. Bronze.	—
Pn45	AH1320Fs	—	5 Mazunas. Bronze. Y#16.1 without "5".	—
Pn46	AH1320Pa	—	5 Mazunas. Bronze.	—
Pn47	AH1320Be	—	10 Mazunas. Bronze. Y#17.2.	—
Pn48	AH1320Pa	—	10 Mazunas. Bronze.	—
Pn49	AH1320Be	—	1/20 Rial. Silver.	—
Pn50	AH1320Be	—	1/10 Rial. Silver.	—
Pn51	AH1320Be	—	Rial. Silver.	—
Pn53	AH1321Be	—	1/20 Rial. Silver.	—
Pn54	AH1321Be	—	1/10 Rial. Silver.	—
Pn55	AH1321Be	—	1/2 Rial. Silver.	—
Pn56	AH1321Be	—	Rial. Silver.	—

PIEFORTS
Double thickness

KM#	Date	Mintage	Identification	Mkt Val
PA1	NDPy	—	Franc. Nickel. Y#36.2.	—
P1	AH1395	10	5 Dirhams. Gold. Y64b.	1,100
P1a	ND(1395)	—	Franc. Nickel. Y#36.2.	—
P2	AH1395	40	50 Dirhams. Silver. Y65	400
P3	AH1395	10	50 Dirhams. Gold. Y65a.	2,500
P4	AH1395	10	50 Dirhams. Gold. Y67a	2,500
P5	AH1395	10	250 Dirhams. Gold. Y66	400
P7	AH1396	10	250 Dirhams. Gold. Y66	400
P6	AH1395	10	50 Dirhams. Gold. Y68a.	2,100
P8	AH1396	10	50 Dirhams. Gold. Y68a.	2,500
P9	AH1397	15	250 Dirhams. Gold. Y66.	375
P10	AH1397	10	50 Dirhams. Gold. Y68a.	2,500
P11	AH1398	20	250 Dirhams. Gold. Y66.	350
P12	AH1399	20	50 Dirhams. Gold. Y68a.	2,000
P13	AH1399	20	50 Dirhams. Silver. Y70.	500
P14	AH1399	20	50 Dirhams. 0.9250 Silver. Y76	500
P15	AH1399	20	50 Dirhams. Gold. Y76a.	2,000
P16	AH1399	20	500 Dirhams. Gold. Y71.	800
P17	AH1400	10	50 Dirhams. Gold. Y68.	2,000
P19	AH1401	10	150 Dirhams. 0.9000 Gold. Y73a.	2,500
P18	AH1401	10	150 Dirhams. 0.9000 Gold. Y74a.	2,500

PIEFORTS WITH ESSAI

KM#	Date	Mintage	Identification	Mkt Val
PEC1	ND(a)	—	50 Centimes. Nickel. Y#35.1.	300
PED1	NDPa	—	50 Centimes. Copper-Nickel. Star within circle. Value within artistic designed star. Small module with 12 sides.	1,500
PEE1	NDPa	—	50 Centimes. Copper-Nickel. Star within circle. Value within artistic designed star. Large module with 12 sides.	1,500
PEF1	ND(AH1340)Py	—	5 Mazunas. Bronze. Y#28.2.	500
PEG1	ND(AH1340)Py	—	10 Mazunas. Bronze. Y#29.2.	600
PEB1	NDPy	—	25 Centimes. Copper-Nickel. Y#34.2; Without hole.	300
PEA1	AH1361(a)	—	50 Centimes. Alum.-Bronze. Y40.	175
PE1	AH1361(a) (a)	—	Franc. Aluminum-Bronze. Y41.	300
PE2	AH1361(a) (a)	—	2 Francs. Aluminum-Bronze. Y42.	350
PE3	AH1364(a) (a)	104	50 Centimes. Alum.-Bronze. Y40.	350
PE4	AH1364 (a)	104	Franc. Aluminum-Bronze. Y41	300
PE5	AH1364(a) (a)	104	2 Francs. Aluminum-Bronze. Y42.	375
PE6	AH1365(a) (a)	104	5 Francs. Aluminum-Bronze. Y43.	350
PE7	AH1366(a) (a)	104	10 Francs. Copper-Nickel center. Y44.	350
PE8	AH1366(a) (a)	104	20 Francs. Copper-Nickel. Y45.	350
PEA9	ND(AH1370)	—	Franc. Aluminum. Y#46.	175
PEB9	ND(AH1370)	—	2 Francs. Aluminum. Y#47.	200
PEC9	ND(AH1370)	—	5 Francs. Aluminum. Y#48.	200
PED9	ND(AH1371)	—	10 Francs. Alum.-Bronze. Y#49.	150
PEE9	ND(AH1371)	—	20 Francs. Alum.-Bronze. Y#50.	150
PEF9	ND(AH1371)	—	50 Francs. Alum.-Bronze. Y#51.	120
PEG9	ND(AH1370)	—	100 Francs. Silver. Y-A54.	150
PE9	AH1372(a) (a)	104	100 Francs. Copper-Nickel. Y52.	350
PE10	AH1372(a) (a)	104	200 Francs. Gold. Y53.	400
PE11	AH1372(a) (a)	—	200 Francs. Gold. Y53.	1,000

TRIAL STRIKES
Uniface

KM#	Date	Mintage	Identification	Mkt Val
TS1	AH1347	—	10 Francs. Silvered Bronze.	800
TS2	AH1347	—	10 Francs. Silvered Bronze. Value in doubled square design within circle. Uniface.	800
TS3	AH1347	—	20 Francs. Silvered Bronze.	600
TS4	AH1347	—	20 Francs. Silvered Bronze. Value in doubled square design within circle. Uniface.	600

MINT SETS

KM#	Date	Mintage	Identification	Issue Price	Mkt Val
MS1	AH1370-84 (8)	—	Y#46-48(AH1370), 49-51(AH1371), 56-57(AH1384)	—	80.00
MS2	1974-75 (7)	20,000	Y#58-63 (1974), Y#64 (1975)	20.00	50.00

PROOF SETS

KM#	Date	Mintage	Identification	Issue Price	Mkt Val
PS1	1974 (6)	30	Y#58a-63a	—	3,650

MOZAMBIQUE

The Republic of Mozambique, a former overseas province of Portugal, stretches for 1,430 miles (2,301 km.) along the southeast coast of Africa, has an area of 302,330 sq. mi. (801,590 sq. km.) and a population of 14.1 million, 99 % of whom are native Africans of the Bantu tribes. Capital: Maputo. Agriculture is the chief industry. Cashew nuts, cotton, sugar, copra and tea are exported.

Vasco de Gama explored all the coast of Mozambique in 1498 and found Arab trading posts already established along the coast. Portuguese settlement dates from the establishment of the trading post of Mozambique in 1505. Within five years Portugal absorbed all the former Arab sultanates along the east African coast. The area was organized as a colony in 1907 and became an overseas province in 1952. In Sept. of 1974, after more than a decade of guerrilla warfare with the forces of the Mozambique Liberation Front, Portugal agreed to the independence of Mozambique, effective June 25, 1975. The Socialist party, led by President Joaquim Chissano was in power until the 2nd of November, 1990 when they became a republic.

Mozambique became a member of the Commonwealth of Nations in November 1995. The President is Head of State; the Prime Minister is Head of Government.

RULER
Portuguese, until 1975

MONETARY SYSTEM
100 Centavos = 1 Escudo

PORTUGUESE COLONY

DECIMAL COINAGE
100 Centavos = 1 Escudo

KM# 63   10 CENTAVOS
Bronze **Obv:** Value **Rev:** Arms

Date	Mintage	F	VF	XF	Unc	BU
1936	2,000,000	2.00	10.00	35.00	50.00	—

KM# 72   10 CENTAVOS
3.9400 g., Bronze, 22.57 mm. **Obv:** Value **Rev:** Arms within crowned globe **Edge:** Plain

Date	Mintage	F	VF	XF	Unc	BU
1942	2,000,000	1.00	2.50	12.50	20.00	—

KM# 83   10 CENTAVOS
1.7000 g., Bronze, 16 mm. **Obv:** Value **Rev:** Arms within crowned globe

Date	Mintage	F	VF	XF	Unc	BU
1960	3,750,000	—	0.50	1.25	3.00	—
1961	10,300,000	—	0.25	1.00	2.50	—

KM# 64   20 CENTAVOS
Bronze **Obv:** Value **Rev:** Arms

Date	Mintage	F	VF	XF	Unc	BU
1936	2,500,000	2.00	14.50	50.00	90.00	—

KM# 71   20 CENTAVOS
Bronze **Obv:** Value **Rev:** Arms within crowned globe

Date	Mintage	F	VF	XF	Unc	BU
1941	2,000,000	1.75	14.50	50.00	90.00	—

KM# 75   20 CENTAVOS
Bronze, 20.3 mm. **Obv:** Value **Rev:** Arms within crowned globe

Date	Mintage	F	VF	XF	Unc	BU
1949	8,000,000	0.75	1.50	4.00	10.00	—
1950	12,500,000	0.75	1.50	3.00	8.50	—

KM# 85   20 CENTAVOS
2.5300 g., Bronze, 18 mm. **Obv:** Value **Rev:** Arms within crowned globe

Date	Mintage	F	VF	XF	Unc	BU
1961	12,500,000	—	0.25	1.00	2.50	—

KM# 88   20 CENTAVOS
1.8000 g., Bronze, 16 mm. **Obv:** Value **Rev:** Arms within crowned globe **Edge:** Plain **Note:** Reduced size.

Date	Mintage	F	VF	XF	Unc	BU
1973	1,798,000	1.00	2.00	3.00	7.50	—
1974	13,044,000	1.00	2.50	3.75	9.00	—

KM# 65   50 CENTAVOS
Copper-Nickel **Obv:** Value **Rev:** Arms

Date	Mintage	F	VF	XF	Unc	BU
1936	2,500,000	5.00	45.00	125	225	—

KM# 73   50 CENTAVOS
4.0000 g., Bronze **Obv:** Value **Rev:** Arms within crowned globe

Date	Mintage	F	VF	XF	Unc	BU
1945	2,500,000	1.50	3.50	25.00	50.00	80.00

KM# 76   50 CENTAVOS
Nickel-Bronze **Obv:** Value **Rev:** Arms within crowned globe

Date	Mintage	F	VF	XF	Unc	BU
1950	20,000,000	1.00	3.00	12.00	22.00	32.00
1951	16,000,000	1.00	3.00	10.00	20.00	30.00

KM# 81   50 CENTAVOS
Bronze **Obv:** Value **Rev:** Arms within crowned globe

Date	Mintage	F	VF	XF	Unc	BU
1953	5,010,000	0.50	1.50	4.00	10.00	—
1957	24,990,000	—	0.50	1.25	4.50	8.00

KM# 89   50 CENTAVOS
4.5300 g., Bronze, 22.49 mm. **Obv:** Value **Rev:** Arms within crowned globe

Date	Mintage	F	VF	XF	Unc	BU
1973	6,841,000	—	0.50	1.00	3.00	—
1974	23,810,000	—	0.50	1.00	4.00	—

KM# 66   ESCUDO
8.0000 g., Copper-Nickel **Obv:** Value **Rev:** Arms

Date	Mintage	F	VF	XF	Unc	BU
1936	2,000,000	4.00	25.00	150	240	—

KM# 74   ESCUDO
Bronze **Obv:** Value **Rev:** Arms within crowned globe

Date	Mintage	F	VF	XF	Unc	BU
1945	2,000,000	2.00	15.00	45.00	110	200

KM# 77   ESCUDO
Nickel-Bronze, 27 mm. **Obv:** Value **Rev:** Arms within crowned globe

Date	Mintage	F	VF	XF	Unc	BU
1950	10,000,000	2.00	15.00	45.00	90.00	—
1951	10,000,000	1.50	3.00	12.50	30.00	—

KM# 82   ESCUDO
8.0000 g., Bronze, 26 mm. **Obv:** Value **Rev:** Arms within crowned globe

Date	Mintage	F	VF	XF	Unc	BU
1953	2,013,000	0.75	1.50	15.00	25.00	35.00
1957	2,987,000	0.75	1.50	17.50	35.00	45.00
1962	600,000	0.50	1.25	15.00	22.50	30.00
1963	3,258,000	0.50	0.75	4.00	12.50	18.00
1965	5,000,000	—	0.25	1.50	3.50	6.00
1968	4,500,000	—	0.25	1.50	3.50	6.00
1969	1,642,000	—	0.50	1.75	4.00	7.00
1973	501,000	0.20	0.50	2.00	6.50	9.00
1974	25,281,000	—	0.25	1.50	3.00	5.00

KM# 61   2-1/2 ESCUDOS
3.5000 g., 0.6500 Silver 0.0731 oz. ASW **Obv:** Shield within globe and maltese cross **Rev:** Arms

Date	Mintage	F	VF	XF	Unc	BU
1935	1,200,000	4.50	12.50	40.00	100	—

KM# 68   2-1/2 ESCUDOS
3.5000 g., 0.6500 Silver 0.0731 oz. ASW **Obv:** Shield within globe and maltese cross **Rev:** Arms within crowned globe

Date	Mintage	F	VF	XF	Unc	BU
1938	1,000,000	3.50	10.00	35.00	65.00	—
1942	1,200,000	2.50	7.50	30.00	55.00	—
1950	4,000,000	1.50	2.50	7.50	20.00	—
1951	4,000,000	2.00	6.50	25.00	50.00	—

KM# 78   2-1/2 ESCUDOS
3.5000 g., Copper-Nickel **Obv:** Shield within globe and maltese cross **Rev:** Arms within crowned globe

Date	Mintage	F	VF	XF	Unc	BU
1952	4,000,000	0.50	8.00	50.00	80.00	125
1953	4,000,000	0.30	5.00	25.00	45.00	85.00

Date	Mintage	F	VF	XF	Unc	BU
1954	4,000,000	0.25	3.00	12.00	22.00	40.00
1955	4,000,000	0.30	1.50	13.50	42.50	80.00
1965	8,000,000	0.10	0.25	1.00	4.00	12.00
1973	1,767,000	0.25	0.65	2.50	6.50	15.00

KM# 62   5 ESCUDOS
7.0000 g., 0.6500 Silver 0.1463 oz. ASW **Obv:** Shield within globe and maltese cross **Rev:** Arms

Date	Mintage	F	VF	XF	Unc	BU
1935	1,000,000	5.50	22.50	65.00	120	—

KM# 69   5 ESCUDOS
7.0000 g., 0.6500 Silver 0.1463 oz. ASW **Obv:** Shield within globe and maltese cross **Rev:** Arms within crowned globe

Date	Mintage	F	VF	XF	Unc	BU
1938	800,000	7.50	20.00	80.00	130	—
1949	8,000,000	2.75	5.50	25.00	45.00	—

KM# 84   5 ESCUDOS
4.0000 g., 0.6500 Silver 0.0836 oz. ASW **Obv:** Shield within globe and maltese cross **Rev:** Arms within crowned globe

Date	Mintage	F	VF	XF	Unc	BU
1960	8,000,000	1.50	2.25	3.50	7.00	10.00

KM# 86   5 ESCUDOS
Copper-Nickel **Obv:** Shield within globe and maltese cross **Rev:** Arms within crowned globe

Date	Mintage	F	VF	XF	Unc	BU
1971	8,000,000	0.20	0.50	1.00	3.00	6.00
1973	3,352,000	0.20	0.50	1.75	4.50	7.00

KM# 67   10 ESCUDOS
12.5000 g., 0.8350 Silver 0.3356 oz. ASW **Obv:** Shield within globe and maltese cross **Rev:** Arms

Date	Mintage	F	VF	XF	Unc	BU
1936	497,000	10.00	20.00	67.50	130	—

KM# 70   10 ESCUDOS
12.5000 g., 0.8350 Silver 0.3356 oz. ASW **Obv:** Shield within globe and maltese cross **Rev:** Arms within crowned globe

Date	Mintage	F	VF	XF	Unc	BU
1938	530,000	20.00	35.00	75.00	165	245

KM# 79   10 ESCUDOS
5.0000 g., 0.7200 Silver 0.1157 oz. ASW **Obv:** Shield within globe and maltese cross **Rev:** Arms within crowned globe

Date	Mintage	VG	F	VF	XF	Unc
1952	1,503,000	—	2.00	4.50	15.00	35.00
1954	1,335,000	—	2.00	4.50	20.00	50.00
1955	1,162,000	—	2.00	4.50	15.00	35.00
1960	2,000,000	—	2.00	3.00	6.00	12.00

KM# 79a   10 ESCUDOS
5.0000 g., 0.6800 Silver 0.1093 oz. ASW **Obv:** Shield within globe and maltese cross **Rev:** Arms within crowned globe

Date	Mintage	F	VF	XF	Unc	BU
1966	500,000	1.75	2.75	5.50	12.50	—

KM# 79b   10 ESCUDOS
Copper-Nickel **Obv:** Shield within globe and maltese cross **Rev:** Arms within crowned globe

Date	Mintage	F	VF	XF	Unc	BU
1968	5,000,000	0.30	0.70	2.50	5.00	—
1970	4,000,000	0.30	0.70	2.50	5.00	—
1974	3,366,000	0.40	1.00	3.00	6.50	—

KM# 80   20 ESCUDOS
10.0000 g., 0.7200 Silver 0.2315 oz. ASW **Obv:** Shield within globe and maltese cross **Rev:** Arms within crowned globe

Date	Mintage	F	VF	XF	Unc	BU
1952	1,004,000	3.75	4.50	10.00	25.00	—
1955	996,000	3.75	5.00	12.50	30.00	—
1960	2,000,000	3.75	4.25	6.50	12.50	—

KM# 80a   20 ESCUDOS
10.0000 g., 0.6800 Silver 0.2186 oz. ASW **Obv:** Shield within globe and maltese cross **Rev:** Arms within crowned globe

Date	Mintage	F	VF	XF	Unc	BU
1966	250,000	3.75	5.50	9.50	18.00	—

KM# 87   20 ESCUDOS
Nickel **Obv:** Shield within globe **Rev:** Arms within circle

Date	Mintage	F	VF	XF	Unc	BU
1971	2,000,000	0.35	0.75	1.75	5.00	—
1972	1,158,000	0.50	1.00	2.50	6.00	—

REPUBLIC

DECIMAL COINAGE
100 Centimos = 1 Metica

KM# 90   CENTIMO
Aluminum **Obv:** Head right **Rev:** Value and flower sprig

Date	Mintage	F	VF	XF	Unc	BU
1975	15,050,000	—	—	60.00	120	200

KM# 91   2 CENTIMOS
Copper-Zinc **Obv:** Head right **Rev:** Value and flower sprig

Date	Mintage	F	VF	XF	Unc	BU
1975	8,242,000	—	—	70.00	125	—

KM# 92   5 CENTIMOS
Copper-Zinc **Obv:** Head right **Rev:** Value and flower sprig

Date	Mintage	F	VF	XF	Unc	BU
1975	14,898,000	—	—	60.00	110	—

KM# 93   10 CENTIMOS
Copper-Zinc **Obv:** Head right **Rev:** Value and 3 flower sprigs

Date	Mintage	F	VF	XF	Unc	BU
1975	18,000,000	—	—	50.00	90.00	—

KM# 94   20 CENTIMOS
Copper-Nickel **Obv:** Head right **Rev:** Value and flower sprig

Date	Mintage	F	VF	XF	Unc	BU
1975	8,050,000	—	—	120	200	—

KM# 95   50 CENTIMOS
Copper-Nickel **Obv:** Head right **Rev:** Value and 2 1/2 seeds

Date	Mintage	F	VF	XF	Unc	BU
1975	3,050,000	—	—	145	265	—

KM# 96 METICA
Copper-Nickel **Obv:** Head right **Rev:** Plant in vase

Date	Mintage	F	VF	XF	Unc	BU
1975	2,550,000	—	—	50.00	85.00	—

KM# 97 2-1/2 METICAIS
Copper-Nickel **Obv:** Head right **Rev:** Leafy plant

Date	Mintage	F	VF	XF	Unc	BU
1975	1,500,000	—	—	145	225	—

REFORM COINAGE
100 Centavos = 1 Metical; 1980

KM# 98 50 CENTAVOS
1.4000 g., Aluminum, 20 mm. **Obv:** Emblem **Rev:** Value above xylophone

Date	Mintage	F	VF	XF	Unc	BU
1980	5,160,000	0.15	0.30	0.60	1.25	2.00
1981	—	—	—	—	—	—
1982	—	0.15	0.30	0.60	1.25	2.00

KM# 99 METICAL
8.0000 g., Brass, 26 mm. **Obv:** Emblem **Rev:** Female student and value

Date	Mintage	F	VF	XF	Unc	BU
1980	32,000	1.50	3.00	5.00	12.00	22.00
1981	—	—	—	—	—	—
1982	—	1.50	3.00	5.00	12.00	22.00

KM# 99a METICAL
Aluminum **Obv:** Emblem **Rev:** Female student and value

Date	Mintage	F	VF	XF	Unc	BU
1986	—	0.20	0.40	0.60	1.00	—

KM# 100 2-1/2 METICAIS
Aluminum, 22.6 mm. **Obv:** Emblem **Rev:** Ship and crane in harbor **Note:** 1.80-2.00 grams.

Date	Mintage	F	VF	XF	Unc	BU
1980	1,088,000	0.25	0.50	1.00	1.75	—
1981	—	—	—	—	—	—
1982	—	0.25	0.50	1.00	1.75	—
1986	—	0.25	0.50	1.00	1.75	—

Note: Edge varieties exist

KM# 101 5 METICAIS
2.6000 g., Aluminum, 24.5 mm. **Obv:** Emblem **Rev:** Tractor and value

Date	Mintage	F	VF	XF	Unc	BU
1980	7,736,000	0.35	0.75	1.25	2.00	—
1981	—	—	—	—	—	—
1982	—	0.35	0.75	1.25	2.00	—
1986	—	0.35	0.75	1.25	2.00	—

KM# 102 10 METICAIS
9.1000 g., Copper-Nickel, 28 mm. **Obv:** Emblem **Rev:** Industrial skyline

Date	Mintage	F	VF	XF	Unc	BU
1980	152,000	0.75	1.50	2.50	6.00	—
1981	—	0.75	1.50	2.50	6.00	—

KM# 102a 10 METICAIS
Aluminum, 28 mm. **Obv:** Emblem **Rev:** Industrial skyline

Date	Mintage	F	VF	XF	Unc	BU
1986	—	0.25	0.45	1.00	2.00	—

KM# 103 20 METICAIS
12.0000 g., Copper-Nickel, 30 mm. **Obv:** Emblem **Rev:** Panzer tank

Date	Mintage	F	VF	XF	Unc	BU
1980	78,000	1.00	2.00	4.00	9.00	—
1986	—	1.00	2.00	4.00	9.00	—

KM# 103a 20 METICAIS
Aluminum, 30 mm. **Obv:** Emblem **Rev:** Panzer tank

Date	Mintage	F	VF	XF	Unc	BU
1986	—	0.40	0.80	1.50	3.00	—

KM# 106 50 METICAIS
Copper-Nickel, 35 mm. **Subject:** World Fisheries Conference **Obv:** Emblem above value and date **Rev:** Traditional fishing raft

Date	Mintage	F	VF	XF	Unc	BU
1983	130,000	2.50	5.00	8.00	14.00	—

KM# 106a 50 METICAIS
22.0000 g., 0.9250 Silver 0.6542 oz. ASW, 35 mm. **Subject:** World Fisheries Conference **Obv:** Emblem above value and date **Rev:** Traditional fishing raft

Date	Mintage	F	VF	XF	Unc	BU
1983 Proof	21,000	Value: 50.00				

KM# 106b 50 METICAIS
22.0000 g., 0.9000 Gold 0.6366 oz. AGW **Subject:** World Fisheries Conference **Obv:** Emblem above value and date **Rev:** Traditional fishing raft

Date	Mintage	F	VF	XF	Unc	BU
1983 Proof	135	Value: 1,000				

KM# 112 50 METICAIS
Aluminum **Obv:** Emblem **Rev:** Woman and soldier with provisions

Date	Mintage	F	VF	XF	Unc	BU
1986	—	0.75	1.50	2.50	5.50	7.50

KM# 107 250 METICAIS
28.2800 g., 0.9250 Silver 0.8410 oz. ASW **Subject:** 10th Anniversary of Independence **Obv:** Emblem **Rev:** Star and map divides circle, value within 1/2 circle

Date	Mintage	F	VF	XF	Unc	BU
1985 Proof	2,000	Value: 42.50				

KM# 107a 250 METICAIS
Copper-Nickel **Obv:** Emblem **Rev:** Star and map divides circle, value within 1/2 circle

Date	Mintage	F	VF	XF	Unc	BU
1985	—	—	—	—	15.00	—

KM# 104 500 METICAIS
19.4000 g., 0.8000 Silver 0.4990 oz. ASW **Subject:** 5th Anniversary of Independence **Obv:** Emblem above value **Rev:** 1/2 Figure, corn stalks and small building

Date	Mintage	F	VF	XF	Unc	BU
1980 Proof	5,000	Value: 65.00				

KM# 110 500 METICAIS
16.0000 g., 0.9990 Silver 0.5139 oz. ASW **Subject:** Defense of Nature **Obv:** Emblem and value **Rev:** Lions

Date	Mintage	F	VF	XF	Unc	BU
1989 Proof	2,500	Value: 35.00				

KM# 111 500 METICAIS
16.0000 g., 0.9990 Silver 0.5139 oz. ASW **Subject:** Defense of Nature **Obv:** Emblem and value **Rev:** Moorish Idol Fish

Date	Mintage	F	VF	XF	Unc	BU
1989 Proof	2,000	Value: 35.00				

KM# 113 500 METICAIS
16.0000 g., 0.9990 Silver 0.5139 oz. ASW **Subject:** Defense of Nature **Obv:** Emblem and value **Rev:** Giraffes

Date	Mintage	F	VF	XF	Unc	BU
1990 Proof	2,000	Value: 35.00				

KM# 109 1000 METICAIS
Copper-Nickel **Subject:** Visit of Pope John Paul II **Obv:** Emblem above value **Rev:** Bust right

Date	Mintage	F	VF	XF	Unc	BU
1988	Est. 80,000	—	—	—	8.00	10.00

KM# 109a 1000 METICAIS
28.2800 g., 0.9250 Silver 0.8410 oz. ASW **Obv:** Emblem above value and date **Rev:** Bust right

Date	Mintage	F	VF	XF	Unc	BU
1988 Proof	Est. 3,500	Value: 42.50				

KM# 108 2000 METICAIS
17.5000 g., 0.9170 Gold 0.5159 oz. AGW **Subject:** 10th Anniversary of Independence **Obv:** Emblem above value **Rev:** Star and map divides circle, value at right

Date	Mintage	F	VF	XF	Unc	BU
1985 Proof	100	Value: 675				

KM# 105 5000 METICAIS
17.2790 g., 0.9000 Gold 0.5000 oz. AGW **Subject:** 5th Anniversary of Independence **Obv:** Emblem above value **Rev:** Figure at left, corn plants in background with tractor above

Date	Mintage	F	VF	XF	Unc	BU
1980 Proof	2,000	Value: 485				

REFORM COINAGE
100 Centavos = 1 Metical; 1994

KM# 115 METICAL
Brass Clad Steel, 17 mm. **Obv:** Emblem **Rev:** Female student

Date	Mintage	F	VF	XF	Unc	BU
1994	—	—	—	—	0.50	1.00

KM# 116 5 METICAIS
Brass Clad Steel **Obv:** Emblem **Rev:** Kingfisher

Date	Mintage	F	VF	XF	Unc	BU
1994	—	—	—	—	1.50	2.50

KM# 117 10 METICAIS
Brass Clad Steel, 23 mm. **Obv:** Emblem **Rev:** Cotton plant

Date	Mintage	F	VF	XF	Unc	BU
1994	—	—	—	—	1.25	2.00

KM# 118 20 METICAIS
Brass Clad Steel, 26 mm. **Obv:** Emblem **Rev:** Pepper plant

Date	Mintage	F	VF	XF	Unc	BU
1994	—	—	—	—	1.50	2.50

KM# 119 50 METICAIS
Nickel Clad Steel **Obv:** Emblem **Rev:** Leopard's head

Date	Mintage	F	VF	XF	Unc	BU
1994	—	—	—	—	3.00	5.00

KM# 120 100 METICAIS
Nickel Clad Steel, 27 mm. **Obv:** Emblem **Rev:** Lobster

Date	Mintage	F	VF	XF	Unc	BU
1994	—	—	—	—	3.50	5.00

KM# 121 500 METICAIS
Nickel Clad Steel, 30 mm. **Obv:** Emblem **Rev:** Building

Date	Mintage	F	VF	XF	Unc	BU
1994	—	—	—	—	4.50	5.50

KM# 127 500 METICAIS
Nickel Clad Steel **Series:** 2000 Summer Olympics - Sydney

Date	Mintage	F	VF	XF	Unc	BU
1998 Proof	10,000	Value: 7.50				

KM# 122 1000 METICAIS
Nickel Clad Steel, 31.5 mm. **Obv:** Emblem **Rev:** Building

Date	Mintage	F	VF	XF	Unc	BU
1994	—	—	—	—	5.00	6.00

KM# 128 1000 METICAIS
24.6200 g., 0.9250 Silver 0.7322 oz. ASW **Series:** 2000 Summer Olympics - Sydney

Date	Mintage	F	VF	XF	Unc	BU
1998 Proof	10,000	Value: 32.50				

KM# 125 5000 METICAIS
411.4224 g., 0.9990 Silver 13.213 oz. ASW, 97 mm. **Obv:** National arms **Rev:** Rhinoceros right **Edge:** Reeded **Note:** Illustration reduced.

Date	Mintage	F	VF	XF	Unc	BU
1997 Proof	2,000	Value: 300				

KM# 124 5000 METICAIS
14.0000 g., Nickel Clad Steel, 28.5 mm. **Obv:** Emblem **Rev:** High power electric lines

Date	Mintage	F	VF	XF	Unc	BU
1998	—	—	—	—	5.00	6.00

KM# 114.1 10000 METICAIS
20.0000 g., 0.9990 Silver 0.6423 oz. ASW **Subject:** World Cup Soccer **Obv:** Emblem **Rev:** Soccer player, 999 at right

Date	Mintage	F	VF	XF	Unc	BU
1994 Proof	—	Value: 65.00				

KM# 114.2 10000 METICAIS
20.0000 g., 0.9990 Silver 0.6423 oz. ASW **Obv:** Emblem **Rev:** Soccer player without 999

Date	Mintage	F	VF	XF	Unc	BU
1994 Proof	—	Value: 65.00				

KM# 123 10000 METICAIS
21.0600 g., 0.9990 Silver 0.6764 oz. ASW **Subject:** World Cup Soccer **Obv:** Emblem **Rev:** Soccer players and net, 999 at lower left

Date	Mintage	F	VF	XF	Unc	BU
1994 Proof	—	Value: 65.00				

KM# 126 10000 METICAIS
822.8449 g., 0.9990 Silver 26.427 oz. ASW, 100 mm. **Obv:** National arms **Rev:** Elephant charging **Edge:** Reeded **Note:** Illustration reduced.

Date	Mintage	F	VF	XF	Unc	BU
1997 Proof	2,000	Value: 500				

KM# 129 10000 METICAIS
822.8449 g., 0.9990 Silver 26.427 oz. ASW **Series:** 2000 Summer Olympics - Sydney

Date	Mintage	F	VF	XF	Unc	BU
1998 Proof	2,000	Value: 425				

PATTERNS
Including off metal strikes

KM#	Date	Mintage Identification	Mkt Val
Pn1	1994	— 10000 Meticais. Copper-Nickel. KM#114.1.	—
Pn2	1994	— 10000 Meticais. Copper-Nickel. KM#123.	—

PIEFORTS

KM#	Date	Mintage Identification	Issue Price	Mkt Val
P1	1983	600 50 Meticais. 0.9250 Silver.	—	70.00

PROVAS
Standard Metals

KM#	Date	Mintage Identification	Issue Price	Mkt Val
Pr1	1935	— 2-1/2 Escudos. Silver. KM#61	—	125
Pr2	1935	— 5 Escudos. Silver. KM62.	—	145
Pr3	1936	— 10 Centavos. Bronze. KM63.	—	60.00
Pr4	1936	— 20 Centavos. Bronze. KM64.	—	60.00
Pr5	1936	— 50 Centavos. Copper-Nickel. KM65.	—	90.00
Pr6	1936	— Escudo. Copper-Nickel. KM66	—	90.00
Pr7	1936	— 10 Escudos. Silver. KM67.	—	180
Pr8	1938	— 2-1/2 Escudos. Silver. KM61.	—	100
Pr9	1938	— 5 Escudos. Silver. KM69.	—	120
Pr10	1938	— 10 Escudos. Silver. KM70.	—	130
Pr11	1941	— 10 Centavos. Bronze. KM71.	—	65.00
Pr12	1942	— 10 Centavos. Bronze. KM72.	—	40.00
Pr13	1942	— 2-1/2 Escudos. Silver. KM68.	—	75.00
Pr14	1945	— 50 Centavos. Bronze. KM73.	—	40.00
Pr15	1945	— Escudo. Bronze. KM74.	—	40.00
Pr16	1948	— 2-1/2 Escudos.	—	175
Pr17	1949	— 20 Centavos. Bronze. KM75.	—	40.00
Pr18	1949	— 5 Escudos. Silver. KM69.	—	75.00
PrA19	1950	— 20 Centavos. Bronze. KM75.	—	85.00
Pr19	1950	— 50 Centavos. Nickel-Bronze. KM76.	—	45.00
Pr20	1950	— Escudo. Nickel-Bronze. KM77.	—	45.00
Pr21	1950	— 2-1/2 Escudos. Silver. KM68.	—	80.00
Pr22	1951	— 50 Centavos. Nickel-Bronze. KM76.	—	35.00
Pr23	1951	— Escudo. Nickel-Bronze. KM77.	—	35.00
Pr24	1951	— 2-1/2 Escudos. Silver. KM68.	—	65.00
Pr25	1951	— 5 Escudos.	—	—
Pr26	1952	— 2-1/2 Escudos. Copper-Nickel. KM78.	—	65.00
Pr27	1952	— 5 Escudos.	—	—
Pr28	1952	— 10 Escudos. Silver. KM79	—	65.00
Pr29	1952	— 20 Escudos. Silver. KM80.	—	75.00
Pr30	1953	— 50 Centavos. Bronze. KM81.	—	35.00

KM#	Date	Mintage Identification	Issue Price	Mkt Val
Pr31	1953	— Escudo. Bronze. KM82.	—	35.00
Pr32	1953	— 2-1/2 Escudos. Copper-Nickel. KM78.	—	45.00
Pr34	1954	— 10 Escudos. Silver. KM79.	—	65.00
Pr35	1955	— 2-1/2 Escudos. Copper-Nickel. KM78.	—	45.00
Pr36	1955	— 10 Escudos. Silver. KM79.	—	65.00
Pr37	1955	— 20 Escudos. Silver. KM80.	—	65.00
Pr38	1957	— 50 Centavos. Bronze. KM81.	—	35.00
Pr39	1957	— Escudo. Bronze. KM82.	—	35.00
Pr40	1960	— 10 Centavos. Bronze. KM83.	—	35.00
Pr41	1960	— 5 Escudos. Silver. KM84	—	65.00
Pr42	1960	— 10 Escudos. Silver. KM79.	—	65.00
Pr43	1960	— 20 Escudos. Silver. KM80.	—	65.00
Pr44	1961	— 10 Centavos. Bronze. KM83.	—	35.00
Pr45	1961	— 20 Centavos. Bronze. KM85.	—	35.00
Pr46	1962	— Escudo. Bronze. KM82.	—	35.00
Pr47	1963	— Escudo. Bronze. KM82.	—	35.00
Pr48	1965	— Escudo. Bronze. KM82.	—	35.00
Pr49	1965	— 2-1/2 Escudos. Copper-Nickel. KM78.	—	45.00
Pr50	1966	— 10 Escudos. Silver. KM79a.	—	65.00
Pr51	1966	— 20 Escudos. Silver. KM80a.	—	75.00
Pr52	1968	— Escudo. Bronze. KM82.	—	35.00
Pr53	1968	— 10 Escudos. Copper-Nickel. KM79b.	—	45.00
Pr54	1968	— 20 Escudos.	—	45.00
Pr55	1969	— Escudo. Bronze. KM82.	—	35.00
Pr56	1969	— 20 Escudos.	—	45.00
Pr57	1970	— 10 Escudos. Copper-Nickel. KM79b.	—	45.00
Pr58	1970	— 20 Escudos.	—	45.00
Pr59	1971	— 5 Escudos. Copper-Nickel. KM86.	—	45.00
Pr60	1971	— 20 Escudos. Nickel. KM87.	—	45.00
Pr61	1972	— 20 Escudos. Nickel. KM87.	—	85.00
Pr62	1973	— 20 Centavos. Bronze. KM88.	—	65.00
Pr63	1973	— 50 Centavos. Bronze. KM89.	—	85.00
Pr64	1973	— Escudo. Bronze. KM82.	—	65.00
Pr65	1973	— 2-1/2 Escudos. Copper-Nickel. KM78.	—	85.00
Pr66	1973	— 5 Escudos. Copper-Nickel. KM86.	—	85.00
Pr68	1974	— 20 Centavos. Bronze. KM88.	—	65.00
Pr69	1974	— 50 Centavos. Bronze. KM89.	—	85.00
Pr70	1974	— Escudo. Bronze. KM82.	—	65.00

MINT SETS

KM#	Date	Mintage Identification	Issue Price	Mkt Val
MS1	1980 (6)	— KM#98-103	—	30.00

SPECIMEN SETS (SS)

KM#	Date	Mintage Identification	Issue Price	Mkt Val
SS1	1975 (8)	— KM#90-97	—	2,250

MUSCAT & OMAN

RULERS
al-Bu Sa'id Dynasty
Feisal ibn Turkee, AH1285-1332/1888-1913AD
Taimur ibn Faisal, AH1332-1351/1913-1932AD
Sa'id ibn Taimur, AH1351-1390/1932-1970AD

MONETARY SYSTEM
Until 1970

4 Baiza = 1 Anna
64 Baiza = 1 Rupee
200 Baiza = 1 Saidi (Dasin Dog)/Dhofari Rial
1970-1972
1000 (new) Baiza = 1 Saidi Rial
Commencing 1972
1000 Baiza = 1 Omani Rial
NOTE: For later coin issues, please refer to Oman.

SULTANATE
COUNTERMARKED COINAGE

C# 19.1 1/4 ANNA
Copper **Ruler:** Faisal bin Turkee **Countermark:** ST
Note: Countermark in Arabic on 1/4 Anna, KM#3.

CM Date	Host Date	Good	VG	F	VF	XF
1913	AH1315	15.00	25.00	40.00	60.00	—
1913	AH1315	15.00	25.00	40.00	60.00	—

C# 19.2 1/4 ANNA
Copper **Ruler:** Faisal bin Turkee **Countermark:** ST
Note: Countermark in Arabic on 1/4 Anna, KM#8. Countermark for Sultan Taimur or Sayyid Taimur.

CM Date	Host Date	Good	VG	F	VF	XF
1913	AH1312	15.00	25.00	45.00	70.00	—

C# 20.1 1/4 ANNA
Copper **Ruler:** Faisal bin Turkee **Countermark:** SS **Note:** Large 10mm countermark in Arabic on 1/4 Anna, KM#3.

CM Date	Host Date	Good	VG	F	VF	XF
1932	AH1312	30.00	50.00	80.00	120	—
1932	AH1315	30.00	50.00	80.00	120	—

C# 20.2 1/4 ANNA
Copper **Ruler:** Faisal bin Turkee **Countermark:** SS **Note:** Large 10mm countermark in Arabic on 1/4 Anna, KM#8.

CM Date	Host Date	Good	VG	F	VF	XF
ND(1932)	AH1312	30.00	50.00	80.00	120	—

C# 21.1 1/4 ANNA
Copper **Ruler:** Faisal bin Turkee **Countermark:** SS **Note:** Small 8mm countermark in Arabic on 1/4 Anna, KM#3.

CM Date	Host Date	Good	VG	F	VF	XF
ND(1932)	AH1312	30.00	50.00	80.00	120	—

C# 21.2 1/4 ANNA
Copper **Ruler:** Faisal bin Turkee **Countermark:** SS **Note:** Small 8mm countermark in Arabic on 1/4 Anna, KM#8. Countermark for Sultan Sa'id or Sayyid Sa'id.

CM Date	Host Date	Good	VG	F	VF	XF
ND(1932)	AH1312	30.00	50.00	80.00	120	—

REFORM COINAGE
1000 (new) Baisa = 1 Saidi Rial

KM# 25 2 BAISA (Baiza)
Copper-Nickel **Ruler:** Sa'id bin Taimur **Obv:** Arms flanked by marks **Rev:** Arabic legend and inscription

Date	Mintage	F	VF	XF	Unc	BU
AH1365	1,500,000	0.50	0.75	1.00	2.00	—
AH1365 Proof	—	Value: 4.00				

Note: Coins of AH1365 have the monetary unit spelled "Baiza", on all other coins it is spelled "Baisa". Most of the proof issues of the AH1359 and 1365 dated coins of Muscat and Oman now on the market are probably later restrikes produced by the Bombay Mint

KM# 36 2 BAISA (Baiza)
1.7500 g., Bronze, 16 mm. **Ruler:** Sa'id bin Taimur **Obv:** Arms **Rev:** Value flanked by marks

Date	Mintage	F	VF	XF	Unc	BU
AH1390	4,000,000	0.15	0.20	0.30	0.50	—
AH1390 Proof	—	Value: 2.50				

KM# 30   3 BAISA
Bronze, 20 mm. **Ruler:** Sa'id bin Taimur **Obv:** Arms **Rev:** Value flanked by marks

Date	Mintage	F	VF	XF	Unc	BU
AH1378	8,000,000	0.75	1.00	1.50	2.50	—
AH1378 Proof	—	—	—	—	—	—

Note: Struck for use in Dhofar Province

KM# 32   3 BAISA
Bronze, 18 mm. **Ruler:** Sa'id bin Taimur **Obv:** Arms **Rev:** Value flanked by marks

Date	Mintage	F	VF	XF	Unc	BU
AH1380	10,000,000	0.35	0.50	0.60	1.25	—
AH1380 Proof	Inc. above	—	—	—	—	—

Note: Struck for use in Muscat Province

KM# 26   5 BAISA (Baiza)
Copper-Nickel, 21 mm. **Ruler:** Sa'id bin Taimur **Obv:** Arms **Rev:** Arabic legend and inscription

Date	Mintage	F	VF	XF	Unc	BU
AH1365	3,849,000	1.00	1.25	1.50	2.50	—
AH1365 Proof	—	Value: 5.00				

Note: Coins of AH1365 have the monetary unit spelled "Baiza", on all other coins it is spelled "Baisa"

KM# 33   5 BAISA (Baiza)
Copper-Nickel **Ruler:** Sa'id bin Taimur **Obv:** Arms **Rev:** Sailing ship within circle

Date	Mintage	F	VF	XF	Unc	BU
AH1381	5,000,000	0.40	0.60	1.00	2.00	—
AH1381 Proof	Inc. above	—	—	—	—	—

Note: Struck for use in Muscat Province

KM# 37   5 BAISA (Baiza)
3.1000 g., Bronze, 19 mm. **Ruler:** Sa'id bin Taimur **Obv:** Arms **Rev:** Value flanked by marks

Date	Mintage	F	VF	XF	Unc	BU
AH1390	3,400,000	0.15	0.20	0.30	0.50	—
AH1390 Proof	—	Value: 2.00				

KM# 22   10 BAISA
Copper-Nickel **Ruler:** Sa'id bin Taimur **Obv:** Arms **Rev:** Inscription

Date	Mintage	F	VF	XF	Unc	BU
AH1359	572,000	2.50	3.25	4.00	6.00	—
AH1359 Proof	—	Value: 8.50				

Note: Struck for use in Dhofar Province

KM# 22a   10 BAISA
Gold **Ruler:** Sa'id bin Taimur **Obv:** Arms **Rev:** Inscription

Date	Mintage	F	VF	XF	Unc	BU
AH1359 Proof	—	Value: 1,850				

KM# 38   10 BAISA
4.7000 g., Bronze, 22.5 mm. **Ruler:** Sa'id bin Taimur **Obv:** Arms **Rev:** Value flanked by marks

Date	Mintage	F	VF	XF	Unc	BU
AH1390	4,500,000	0.15	0.20	0.35	0.75	—
AH1390 Proof	—	Value: 2.50				

KM# 23   20 BAISA (Baiza)
Copper-Nickel **Ruler:** Sa'id bin Taimur **Obv:** Arms **Rev:** Inscription

Date	Mintage	F	VF	XF	Unc	BU
AH1359	35,000	3.00	5.00	7.50	12.50	—
AH1359 Proof	—	Value: 14.50				

Note: Struck for use in Dhofar Province

KM# 23a   20 BAISA (Baiza)
Gold **Ruler:** Sa'id bin Taimur **Obv:** Arms **Rev:** Inscription

Date	Mintage	F	VF	XF	Unc	BU
AH1359 Proof	—	Value: 1,650				

KM# 27   20 BAISA (Baiza)
Copper-Nickel **Ruler:** Sa'id bin Taimur **Obv:** Arms **Rev:** Arabic legend and inscription

Date	Mintage	F	VF	XF	Unc	BU
AH1365	1,135,000	1.00	2.00	2.75	4.50	—
AH1365 Proof	—	Value: 7.00				

KM# 28   20 BAISA (Baiza)
Copper-Nickel **Ruler:** Sa'id bin Taimur **Obv:** Arms **Rev:** Inscription **Note:** Mule.

Date	Mintage	F	VF	XF	Unc	BU
AH1359/1365 Restrike	—	—	—	—	17.50	—

KM# 39   25 BAISA
2.9000 g., Copper-Nickel, 18 mm. **Ruler:** Sa'id bin Taimur **Obv:** Arms **Rev:** Value flanked by marks

Date	Mintage	F	VF	XF	Unc	BU
AH1390	2,000,000	0.20	0.30	0.45	1.00	—
AH1390 Proof	—	Value: 2.75				

KM# 39a   25 BAISA
6.0100 g., 0.9160 Gold 0.1770 oz. AGW **Ruler:** Sa'id bin Taimur **Obv:** Arms **Rev:** Value flanked by marks

Date	Mintage	F	VF	XF	Unc	BU
AH1390 Proof	350	Value: 195				

KM# 24   50 BAISA
Ruler: Obv: Rev:

Date	Mintage	F	VF	XF	Unc	BU
AH1359	65,000	2.00	6.50	8.50	12.50	—
AH1359 Proof	—	Value: 16.50				

Note: Struck for use in Dhofar Province

KM# 24a   50 BAISA
Gold **Ruler:** Sa'id bin Taimur **Obv:** Arms **Rev:** Inscription

Date	Mintage	F	VF	XF	Unc	BU
AH1359 Proof	—	Value: 1,750				

KM# 40   50 BAISA
6.4000 g., Copper-Nickel, 24 mm. **Ruler:** Sa'id bin Taimur **Obv:** Arms **Rev:** Value flanked by marks

Date	Mintage	F	VF	XF	Unc	BU
AH1390	1,600,000	0.25	0.45	0.75	1.50	—
AH1390 Proof	—	Value: 3.50				

KM# 40a   50 BAISA
12.8100 g., 0.9160 Gold 0.3772 oz. AGW **Ruler:** Sa'id bin Taimur **Obv:** Arms **Rev:** Value flanked by marks

Date	Mintage	F	VF	XF	Unc	BU
AH1390 Proof	350	Value: 425				

KM# 41   100 BAISA
Copper-Nickel **Ruler:** Sa'id bin Taimur **Obv:** Arms **Rev:** Value flanked by marks

Date	Mintage	F	VF	XF	Unc	BU
AH1390	1,000,000	0.35	0.50	0.85	1.75	—
AH1390 Proof	—	Value: 5.00				

KM# 41a   100 BAISA
22.6300 g., 0.9160 Gold 0.6664 oz. AGW **Ruler:** Sa'id bin Taimur **Obv:** Arms **Rev:** Value flanked by marks

Date	Mintage	F	VF	XF	Unc	BU
AH1390 Proof	350	Value: 725				

KM# 29   1/2 DHOFARI RIAL
14.0300 g., 0.5000 Silver 0.2255 oz. ASW **Ruler:** Sa'id bin Taimur **Obv:** Arms above sprig **Rev:** Inscription within circle and wreath

Date	Mintage	F	VF	XF	Unc	BU
AH1367	200,000	12.00	14.00	18.00	28.00	—
AH1367 Proof	—	Value: 45.00				

Note: Struck for use in Dhofar Province

KM# 29a   1/2 DHOFARI RIAL
24.0300 g., 0.9170 Gold 0.7084 oz. AGW **Ruler:** Sa'id bin Taimur **Obv:** Arms above sprig **Rev:** Inscription within circle and wreath

Date	Mintage	F	VF	XF	Unc	BU
AH1367 Proof	2	Value: 5,500				

Note: Struck for presentation purposes

KM# 34 1/2 SAIDI RIAL
14.0300 g., 0.5000 Silver 0.2255 oz. ASW **Ruler:** Sa'id bin Taimur
Obv: Arms **Rev:** Value

Date	Mintage	F	VF	XF	Unc	BU
AH1380	300,000	3.75	4.50	6.00	9.00	—
AH1380 Proof	—	Value: 75.00				
AH1381	850,000	3.75	4.50	6.00	9.00	—

KM# 34a 1/2 SAIDI RIAL
25.6000 g., 0.9160 Gold 0.7539 oz. AGW **Ruler:** Sa'id bin Taimur
Obv: Arms **Rev:** Value

Date	Mintage	F	VF	XF	Unc	BU
AH1381 Proof	150	Value: 850				
AH1382 Proof	100	Value: 900				
AH1390 Proof	350	Value: 800				

Note: Struck for presentation purposes

KM# 31 SAIDI RIAL
28.0700 g., 0.8330 Silver 0.7517 oz. ASW **Ruler:** Sa'id bin Taimur
Obv: Arms within circle, designs around border **Rev:** Value and date

Date	Mintage	F	VF	XF	Unc	BU
AH1378	1,000,000	—	12.50	16.00	20.00	—
AH1378 Proof	100	Value: 650				

KM# 31a SAIDI RIAL
28.0700 g., 0.5000 Silver 0.4512 oz. ASW **Ruler:** Sa'id bin Taimur
Obv: Arms within circle, designs around border **Rev:** Value and date

Date	Mintage	F	VF	XF	Unc	BU
AH1378	400,000	—	10.00	12.50	15.00	—

KM# 31b SAIDI RIAL
46.6500 g., 0.9160 Gold 1.3738 oz. AGW, 33.7 mm.
Ruler: Sa'id bin Taimur **Obv:** Arms within circle, designs around
border **Rev:** Value and date

Date	Mintage	F	VF	XF	Unc	BU
AH1378 Proof	100	Value: 1,550				
AH1390 Proof	350	Value: 1,400				

Note: Struck for presentation purposes

KM# 35 15 SAIDI RIALS
7.9900 g., 0.9160 Gold 0.2353 oz. AGW **Ruler:** Sa'id bin Taimur

Date	Mintage	F	VF	XF	Unc	BU
AH1381	2,000	—	—	—	245	275
AH1381 Proof	100	Value: 575				

Note: Struck for presentation purposes

MINT SETS

KM#	Date	Mintage	Identification	Issue Price	Mkt Val
MS1	AH1390 (1970) (6)	5,500	KM#36-41	—	7.50

PROOF SETS

KM#	Date	Mintage	Identification	Issue Price	Mkt Val
PS1	AH1359, 65, 57 (1940, 45, 47) (6)	—	KM#22-26, 29	—	75.00
PS2	AH1359, 65, 57 (1940, 45, 47) (6)	—	KM#22, 24-27, 29	—	70.00
PS3	AH1390 (1970) (6)	2,102	KM#36-41	11.00	16.50
PS4	AH1390 (1970) (3)	350	KM#39a-41a	—	1,150

MYANMAR

The Union of Myanmar, formerly Burma, a country of Southeast Asia fronting on the Bay of Bengal and the Andaman Sea,
has an area of 261,218 sq. mi. (678,500 sq. km.) and a population
of 38.8 million. Capital: Yangon (Rangoon) until 2005; followed
thereafter by Naypyidaw. Myanmar is an agricultural country
heavily dependent on its leading product (rice), which occupies
two-thirds of the cultivated area and accounts for 40% of the value
of exports. Mineral resources are extensive, but production is low.
Petroleum, lead, tin, silver, zinc, nickel cobalt, and precious
stones are exported.

The British East India Company, while unsuccessful in its
1612 effort to establish posts along the Bay of Bengal, was
enabled by the Anglo-Burmese Wars of 1824-86 to expand to the
whole of Burma and to secure its annexation to British India. In
1937, Burma was separated from India, becoming a separate British colony with limited self-government. Burma became an independent nation outside the British Commonwealth on Jan. 4,
1948, the constitution of 1948 providing for a parliamentary
democracy and the nationalization of certain industries. However,
political and economic problems persisted, and on March 2, 1962,
Gen. Ne Win took over the government, suspended the constitution, installed himself as chief of state, and pursued a social-
istic program with nationalization of nearly all industry and trade.
On Jan. 4, 1974, a new constitution adopted by referendum established Burma as a socialist republic under one-party rule. The
country name was changed to Myanmar in 1989.

Burmese coins are frequently known by the equivalent Indian
denominations, although their values are inscribed in Burmese
units. Upper Burma was annexed in 1885 and the Burmese coinage remained in circulation until 1889, when Indian coins became
current throughout Burma. Coins were again issued in the old Burmese denominations after independence in 1948, but decimal
issues replaced these in 1952. The Chula-Sakarat (CS) dating is
sometimes referred to as BE-Burmese Era and began in 638AD.

RULER
British, 1886-1948

MONETARY SYSTEM
                    (Until 1952)
4 Pyas = 1 Pe
2 Pe = 1 Mu
2 Mu = 1 Mat

5 Mat = 1 Kyat
    NOTE: Originally 10 light Mu = 1 Kyat,
eventually 8 heavy Mu = 1 Kyat.
                    Indian Equivalents
1 Silver Kyat = 1 Rupee = 16 Annas
1 Gold Kyat = 1 Mohur = 16 Rupees

UNION OF BURMA
STANDARD COINAGE

KM# 27 2 PYAS
Copper-Nickel **Obv:** Chinze **Rev:** Value and date flanked by
sprays

Date	Mintage	F	VF	XF	Unc	BU
1949	7,000,000	0.25	0.50	1.00	3.00	—
1949 Proof	100	Value: 100				

KM# 28 PE
Copper-Nickel **Obv:** Chinze **Rev:** Value and date flanked by sprays

Date	Mintage	F	VF	XF	Unc	BU
1949	8,000,000	0.35	0.75	1.75	4.00	—
1949 Proof	100	Value: 100				
1950	9,500,000	0.35	0.75	1.75	4.00	—
1950 Proof	—					
1951	6,500,000	0.50	1.00	2.00	5.00	—
1951 Proof	—					

KM# 29 2 PE
Copper-Nickel **Obv:** Chinze **Rev:** Value and date flanked by sprays

Date	Mintage	F	VF	XF	Unc	BU
1949	7,100,000	0.50	1.00	2.00	5.00	—
1949 Proof	100	Value: 100				
1950	8,500,000	0.50	1.00	2.00	5.00	—
1950 Proof	—					
1951	7,480,000	0.50	1.00	2.00	5.00	—
1951 Proof	—					

KM# 30 4 PE
Nickel **Obv:** Chinze **Rev:** Value and date flanked by sprays

Date	Mintage	F	VF	XF	Unc	BU
1949	6,500,000	1.25	2.50	5.00	15.00	—
1949 Proof	100	Value: 100				
1950	6,120,000	1.00	2.00	4.00	12.00	—

KM# 31 8 PE
Nickel **Obv:** Chinze **Rev:** Value and date flanked by sprays

Date	Mintage	F	VF	XF	Unc	BU
1949	3,270,000	1.50	3.00	6.00	25.00	—
1949 Proof	100	Value: 100				
1950	3,900,000	1.25	2.50	5.00	20.00	—
1950 Proof	—					

KM# 31a 8 PE
Copper-Nickel **Obv:** Chinze flanked by stars **Rev:** Value and date flanked by sprays

Date	Mintage	VG	F	VF	XF	Unc
CS1314-1952	1,642,000	—	50.00	100	150	200
CS1314-1952 Proof	—	Value: 400				

DECIMAL COINAGE
100 Pyas = 1 Kyat

KM# 32 PYA
2.2000 g., Bronze, 18 mm. **Obv:** Chinze **Rev:** Value and date flanked by sprays

Date	Mintage	VG	F	VF	XF	Unc
1952	500,000	—	0.10	0.15	0.20	0.35
1952 Proof	100	Value: 60.00				
1953	14,000,000	—	0.10	0.15	0.20	0.35
1953 Proof	—	—	—	—	—	—
1955	30,000,000	—	0.10	0.15	0.20	0.35
1955 Proof	—	—	—	—	—	—
1956 Proof	100	Value: 60.00				
1962 Proof	100	Value: 60.00				
1965	15,000,000	—	0.10	0.15	0.20	0.35
1965 Proof	—	—	—	—	—	—

KM# 38 PYA
0.6000 g., Aluminum, 17 mm. **Subject:** Aung San **Obv:** Head 1/4 right flanked by stars below **Rev:** Value and date flanked by sprays

Date	Mintage	VG	F	VF	XF	Unc
1966	8,000,000	—	0.10	0.15	0.25	0.65

KM# 33 5 PYAS
3.1700 g., Copper-Nickel **Obv:** Chinze **Rev:** Value flanked by sprays

Date	Mintage	VG	F	VF	XF	Unc
1952	20,000,000	—	0.10	0.15	0.35	0.75
1952 Proof	100	Value: 65.00				
1953	59,700,000	—	0.10	0.15	0.35	0.75
1953 Proof	—	—	—	—	—	—
1955	40,272,000	—	0.10	0.15	0.35	0.75
1955 Proof	—	—	—	—	—	—
1956	20,000,000	—	0.10	0.15	0.35	0.75
1956 Proof	100	Value: 65.00				
1961	12,000,000	—	0.10	0.15	0.35	0.75
1961 Proof	—	—	—	—	—	—
1962	10,000,000	—	0.10	0.15	0.35	0.75
1962 Proof	100	Value: 65.00				
1963	40,400,000	—	0.10	0.15	0.25	0.60
1963 Proof	—	—	—	—	—	—
1965	43,600,000	—	0.10	0.15	0.20	0.40
1965 Proof	—	—	—	—	—	—
1966	20,000,000	—	0.10	0.15	0.20	0.40
1966 Proof	—	—	—	—	—	—

KM# 39 5 PYAS
0.9000 g., Aluminum, 18.4 mm. **Subject:** Aung San **Obv:** Head 1/4 right flanked by stars below **Rev:** Value and date flanked by sprays

Date	Mintage	VG	F	VF	XF	Unc
1966	—	—	0.10	0.20	0.35	0.75

KM# 51 5 PYAS
Aluminum-Bronze **Series:** F.A.O. **Obv:** Rice plant **Rev:** Value and date within square

Date	Mintage	VG	F	VF	XF	Unc
1987	—	—	0.10	0.20	0.40	1.00

KM# 34 10 PYAS
4.4600 g., Copper-Nickel **Obv:** Chinze **Rev:** Value and date flanked by sprays

Date	Mintage	VG	F	VF	XF	Unc
1952	20,000,000	—	0.10	0.20	0.40	1.00
1952 Proof	100	Value: 70.00				
1953	37,250,000	—	0.10	0.20	0.40	1.00
1953 Proof	—	—	—	—	—	—
1955	22,750,000	—	0.10	0.20	0.40	1.00
1955 Proof	—	—	—	—	—	—
1956	35,000,000	—	0.10	0.20	0.40	1.00
1956 Proof	100	Value: 70.00				
1962	6,000,000	—	0.10	0.20	0.40	1.00
1962 Proof	100	Value: 70.00				
1963	10,750,000	—	0.10	0.20	0.40	1.00
1963 Proof	10,750,000	—	—	—	—	—
1965	32,619,999	—	0.10	0.20	0.40	1.00
1965 Proof	—	—	—	—	—	—

KM# 40 10 PYAS
1.0000 g., Aluminum **Subject:** Aung San **Obv:** Head 1/4 right flanked by stars below **Rev:** Value and date flanked by sprays

Date	Mintage	VG	F	VF	XF	Unc
1966	—	—	0.15	0.30	0.60	1.25

KM# 49 10 PYAS
3.0000 g., Brass, 20.45 mm. **Series:** F.A.O. **Obv:** Rice plant **Rev:** Value within square

Date	Mintage	VG	F	VF	XF	Unc
1983	—	—	0.15	0.30	0.60	1.00

KM# 35 25 PYAS
Copper-Nickel **Obv:** Chinze flanked by stars **Rev:** Value and date flanked by sprays

Date	Mintage	VG	F	VF	XF	Unc
1952	13,540,000	—	0.10	0.20	0.50	1.25
1952 Proof	100	Value: 75.00				
1954	18,000,000	—	0.10	0.20	0.50	1.25
1954 Proof	—	—	—	—	—	—
1955 Proof	—	Value: 75.00				
1956	14,000,000	—	0.10	0.20	0.50	1.25
1956 Proof	100	Value: 75.00				
1959	6,000,000	—	0.10	0.20	0.50	1.25
1959 Proof	—	—	—	—	—	—
1961	4,000,000	—	0.10	0.20	0.50	1.25
1961 Proof	—	—	—	—	—	—
1962	3,200,000	—	0.10	0.20	0.50	1.25
1962 Proof	100	Value: 75.00				
1963	16,000,000	—	0.10	0.15	0.30	0.75
1963 Proof	—	—	—	—	—	—

Date	Mintage	VG	F	VF	XF	Unc
1965	26,000,000	—	0.10	0.15	0.30	0.75
1965 Proof	—	—	—	—	—	—

KM# 41 25 PYAS
1.8000 g., Aluminum **Subject:** Aung San **Obv:** Head 1/4 right flanked by stars below **Rev:** Value and date flanked by sprays

Date	Mintage	VG	F	VF	XF	Unc
1966	—	—	0.15	0.30	0.60	1.25

KM# 48 25 PYAS
4.3000 g., Bronze, 22.35 mm. **Series:** F.A.O. **Obv:** Rice plant **Rev:** Value and date within square

Date	Mintage	VG	F	VF	XF	Unc
1980	—	—	0.15	0.30	0.60	1.00

KM# 50 25 PYAS
Bronze **Series:** F.A.O. **Obv:** Rice plant **Rev:** Large value

Date	Mintage	VG	F	VF	XF	Unc
1986	—	—	0.10	0.20	0.35	0.60

KM# 36 50 PYAS
7.8000 g., Copper-Nickel **Obv:** Chinze flanked by stars **Rev:** Value and date flanked by vine sprigs

Date	Mintage	VG	F	VF	XF	Unc
1952	2,500,000	—	0.20	0.50	0.75	1.75
1952 Proof	100	Value: 80.00				
1954	12,000,000	—	0.20	0.50	0.75	1.75
1954 Proof	—	—	—	—	—	—
1956	8,000,000	—	0.20	0.50	0.75	1.75
1956 Proof	100	Value: 80.00				
1961	2,000,000	—	0.15	0.40	0.75	1.75
1961 Proof	—	—	—	—	—	—
1962	600,000	—	0.25	0.75	1.25	2.25
1962 Proof	100	Value: 80.00				
1963	4,800,000	—	0.15	0.25	0.65	1.25
1963 Proof	—	—	—	—	—	—
1965	2,800,000	—	0.15	0.40	0.75	1.75
1965 Proof	—	—	—	—	—	—
1966	3,400,000	—	0.10	0.30	0.75	1.75
1966 Proof	—	—	—	—	—	—

KM# 42 50 PYAS
2.0000 g., Aluminum **Subject:** Aung San **Obv:** Head 1/4 right flanked by stars below **Rev:** Value and date flanked by sprays

Date	Mintage	VG	F	VF	XF	Unc
1966	—	—	0.15	0.40	1.00	2.25

KM# 46 50 PYAS
5.7000 g., Brass, 24.6 mm. **Series:** F.A.O. **Obv:** Rice plant
Rev: Value within square

Date	Mintage	VG	F	VF	XF	Unc
1975	—	—	0.15	0.35	0.70	1.25
1976	—	—	0.15	0.35	0.70	1.25

KM# 37 KYAT
11.6500 g., Copper-Nickel, 30.5 mm. **Obv:** Chinze flanked by stars **Rev:** Value and date flanked by sprays

Date	Mintage	VG	F	VF	XF	Unc
1952	2,500,000	—	0.35	0.75	1.50	3.00
1952 Proof	100	Value: 85.00				
1953	7,500,000	—	0.25	0.50	1.00	2.00
1953 Proof	—	—	—	—	—	—
1956	3,500,000	—	0.35	0.75	1.50	3.00
1956 Proof	100	Value: 85.00				
1962 Proof	100	Value: 85.00				
1965	1,000,000	—	0.35	0.75	1.50	3.00
1965 Proof	—	—	—	—	—	—

KM# 47 KYAT
7.2000 g., Copper-Nickel, 26.45 mm. **Series:** F.A.O. **Obv:** Rice plant **Rev:** Value within square

Date	Mintage	VG	F	VF	XF	Unc
1975	20,000,000	—	0.25	0.50	1.00	2.00

REVOLUTIONARY COINAGE
Patriotic Liberation Army

KM# 43 MU
2.0000 g., 1.0000 Gold 0.0643 oz. AGW **Obv:** Peacock
Rev: Legend within star

Date	Mintage	F	VF	XF	Unc	BU
1970-71	—	—	—	—	—	160

KM# 44 2 MU
4.0000 g., 1.0000 Gold 0.1286 oz. AGW **Obv:** Peacock
Rev: Legend within star flanked by stars at points

Date	Mintage	F	VF	XF	Unc	BU
1970-71	—	—	—	—	—	260
1970-71	—	—	—	—	—	280

KM# 45 4 MU
8.0000 g., 1.0000 Gold 0.2572 oz. AGW **Obv:** Peacock
Rev: Legend within star

Date	Mintage	F	VF	XF	Unc	BU
1970-71	—	—	—	—	—	500

UNION OF MYANMAR
DECIMAL COINAGE
100 Pyas = 1 Kyat

KM# 60 KYAT
2.9500 g., Bronze, 19.03 mm. **Obv:** Chinze flanked by stars **Rev:** Value **Edge:** Plain

Date	Mintage	F	VF	XF	Unc	BU
1999	—	—	—	—	0.25	0.40

KM# 57 10 PYAS
Brass **Obv:** Rice plant **Obv. Leg.:** Myanmar Central Bank **Rev:** Value within square **Note:** Similar to KM#49.

Date	Mintage	VG	F	VF	XF	Unc
1991	—	—	0.15	0.30	0.60	1.00

KM# 58 25 PYAS
5.0000 g., Copper Plated Steel **Obv:** Rice plant
Obv. Leg.: Myanmar Central Bank **Rev:** Large value

Date	Mintage	VG	F	VF	XF	Unc
1991	—	—	0.15	0.30	0.60	1.00

KM# 59 50 PYAS
Brass, 24.6 mm. **Obv:** Rice plant **Obv. Leg.:** Myanmar Central Bank **Rev:** Value within square **Edge:** Reeded

Date	Mintage	VG	F	VF	XF	Unc
1991	—	—	0.15	0.35	0.70	1.25

KM# 61 5 KYATS
2.7300 g., Brass, 20 mm. **Obv:** Chinze flanked by stars
Rev: Value **Edge:** Plain

Date	Mintage	F	VF	XF	Unc	BU
1999	—	—	—	—	0.50	0.75

KM# 62 10 KYATS
4.4500 g., Brass **Obv:** Chinze flanked by stars **Rev:** Value

Date	Mintage	F	VF	XF	Unc	BU
1999	—	—	—	—	0.75	1.00

KM# 63 50 KYATS
5.0600 g., Copper-Nickel, 23.85 mm. **Obv:** Chinze flanked by stars **Rev:** Value **Edge:** Reeded

Date	Mintage	F	VF	XF	Unc	BU
1999	—	—	—	—	1.75	2.00

KM# 64 100 KYATS
7.5200 g., Copper-Nickel, 26.8 mm. **Obv:** Chinze flanked by stars **Rev:** Value **Edge:** Reeded

Date	Mintage	F	VF	XF	Unc	BU
1999	—	—	—	—	3.00	3.50

KM# A51 300 KYAT
1.2441 g., 0.9990 Gold 0.0400 oz. AGW **Subject:** Year of the Tiger **Obv:** Lotus flower **Rev:** Tiger

Date	Mintage	F	VF	XF	Unc	BU
1998	—	—	—	—	45.00	50.00

KM# 52 500 KYAT
20.0000 g., 0.9250 Silver 0.5948 oz. ASW **Subject:** Year of the Tiger **Obv:** Lotus flower **Rev:** Stalking tiger

Date	Mintage	F	VF	XF	Unc	BU
1998 Proof	Est. 15,000	Value: 50.00				

KM# 53 500 KYAT
20.0000 g., 0.9250 Silver 0.5948 oz. ASW **Subject:** Year of the Tiger **Obv:** Lotus flower **Rev:** Tiger drinking

Date	Mintage	F	VF	XF	Unc	BU
1998 Proof	Est. 15,000	Value: 50.00				

KM# 54   500 KYAT
20.0000 g., 0.9250 Silver 0.5948 oz. ASW **Subject:** Year of the
Tiger **Obv:** Lotus flower **Rev:** Tiger

Date	Mintage	F	VF	XF	Unc	BU
1998 Proof	1,014,999	Value: 50.00				

KM# 55   2000 KYAT
7.7759 g., 0.9999 Gold 0.2500 oz. AGW **Subject:** Year of the
Tiger **Obv:** Lotus flower **Rev:** Stalking tiger

Date	Mintage	F	VF	XF	Unc	BU
1998 Proof	1,998	Value: 275				

KM# 56   5000 KYAT
15.5518 g., 0.9999 Gold 0.4999 oz. AGW **Subject:** Year of the
Tiger **Obv:** Lotus flower **Rev:** Tiger

Date	Mintage	F	VF	XF	Unc	BU
1998 Proof	5,798	Value: 500				

PROOF SETS

KM#	Date	Mintage	Identification	Issue Price	Mkt Val
PS1	1949 (5)	100	KM#27-31	—	500
PS2	1952 (6)	100	KM#32-37	—	435
PS3	1956 (6)	100	KM#32-37	—	435
PS4	1962 (6)	100	KM#32-37	—	435
PS5	1998 (3)	3,998	KM#52-54	—	145
PS6	1998 (2)	1,998	KM#55-56	—	745

NAGORNO-KARABAKH

Nagorno-Karabakh, an ethnically Armenian enclave inside
Azerbaijan (pop., 1991 est.: 193,000), SW region. It occupies an
area of 1,700 sq mi (4,400 square km) on the NE flank of the Karabakh Mountain Range, with the capital city of Stepanakert.

Russia annexed the area from Persia in 1813, and in 1923
it was established as an autonomous province of the Azerbaijan
S.S.R. In 1988 the region's ethnic Armenian majority demonstrated against Azerbaijani rule, and in 1991, after the breakup of
the U.S.S.R. brought independence to Armenia and Azerbaijan,
war broke out between the two ethnic groups. On January 8, 1992
the leaders of Nagorno-Karabakh declared independence as the
Republic of Mountainous Karabakh (RMK). Since 1994, following
a cease-fire, ethnic Armenians have held Karabakh, though officially it remains part of Azerbaijan. Karabakh remains sovereign,
but the political and military condition is volatile and tensions frequently flare into skirmishes.

Its marvelous nature and geographic situation, have all facilitated Karabakh to be a center of science, poetry and, especially,
of the musical culture of Azerbaijan.

REPUBLIC
STANDARD COINAGE

KM# 13   25000 DRAMS
31.2200 g., 0.9990 Silver 1.0027 oz. ASW, 38.9 mm.
Obv: National arms **Rev:** Maps **Edge:** Plain

Date	Mintage	F	VF	XF	Unc	BU
1998 Proof	—	Value: 60.00				

KM# 14   25000 DRAMS
31.2200 g., 0.9990 Silver 1.0027 oz. ASW, 38.9 mm.
Obv: National arms **Rev:** "1700" in cross design with inscription
301AD **Edge:** Plain

Date	Mintage	F	VF	XF	Unc	BU
1998 Proof	—	Value: 60.00				

KM# 15   25000 DRAMS
31.2200 g., 0.9990 Silver 1.0027 oz. ASW, 38.9 mm.
Subject: 1700th Anniversary of Christianity in Armenia
Obv: National arms **Rev:** Standing Saint and church **Edge:** Plain

Date	Mintage	F	VF	XF	Unc	BU
1998 Proof	—	Value: 60.00				

KM# 16   25000 DRAMS
31.2200 g., 0.9990 Silver 1.0027 oz. ASW, 38.9 mm.
Obv: National arms **Rev:** Head left **Edge:** Plain

Date	Mintage	F	VF	XF	Unc	BU
1998 Proof	—	Value: 60.00				

KM# 16a   25000 DRAMS
31.2200 g., 0.9990 Gold Plated Silver 1.0027 oz. ASW AGW,
38.9 mm. **Obv:** National arms **Rev:** Head left **Edge:** Plain

Date	Mintage	F	VF	XF	Unc	BU
1998 Proof	—	Value: 70.00				

KM# 17   25000 DRAMS
31.2200 g., 0.9990 Silver 1.0027 oz. ASW, 38.9 mm.
Obv: National arms **Rev:** Head right with laurels **Edge:** Plain

Date	Mintage	F	VF	XF	Unc	BU
1998 Proof	—	Value: 60.00				

KM# 18   25000 DRAMS
31.2200 g., 0.9990 Silver 1.0027 oz. ASW, 38.9 mm. **Obv:** National
arms **Rev:** Standing figure reading book right **Edge:** Plain

Date	Mintage	F	VF	XF	Unc	BU
1998 Proof	—	Value: 60.00				

KM# 1   25000 DRAMS
31.2000 g., 0.9990 Silver 1.0021 oz. ASW, 39 mm.
Obv: National arms **Rev:** Head left above two fists **Edge:** Reeded
Note: Struck at Lialoosin Inc., Los Angeles, CA.

Date	Mintage	F	VF	XF	Unc	BU
1998 Proof	—	Value: 60.00				

KM# 1a   25000 DRAMS
Gold Plated Silver **Obv:** National arms **Rev:** Head left above
two fists

Date	Mintage	F	VF	XF	Unc	BU
1998 Proof	—	Value: 65.00				

KM# 5   25000 DRAMS
30.8000 g., 0.9990 Silver 0.9892 oz. ASW **Obv:** National arms
Rev: Two stone faced monuments **Edge:** Plain **Note:** Struck at
Lialoosin Inc., Los Angeles, CA.

Date	Mintage	F	VF	XF	Unc	BU
1998(2000) Proof	—	Value: 75.00				

KM# 5a 25000 DRAMS
Gold Plated Silver, 38.8 mm. **Obv:** National arms **Rev:** Two stone faced monuments

Date	Mintage	F	VF	XF	Unc	BU
1998(2000) Proof	—	Value: 85.00				

KM# 2 50000 DRAM
155.5175 g., 0.9990 Silver 4.9948 oz. ASW, 63.8 mm. **Obv:** National arms **Rev:** Head left above two fists **Edge:** 5 T.O. .999 A6 **Note:** Struck at Lialoosin Inc., Los Angeles, CA.

Date	Mintage	F	VF	XF	Unc	BU
1998 Proof	—	Value: 300				

KM# 2a 50000 DRAM
Gold Plated Silver **Obv:** National arms **Rev:** Head left above two fists

Date	Mintage	F	VF	XF	Unc	BU
1998 Proof	—	Value: 325				

KM# 3 50000 DRAM
7.8000 g., 0.9000 Gold 0.2257 oz. AGW, 22 mm. **Obv:** National arms **Rev:** Head left above two fists **Edge:** Plain **Note:** Struck at Lialoosin Inc., Los Angeles, CA.

Date	Mintage	F	VF	XF	Unc	BU
1998 Proof	—	Value: 400				

KM# 4 50000 DRAM
155.5175 g., 0.9990 Silver 4.9948 oz. ASW, 63.8 mm. **Obv:** National arms **Rev:** Two monumental portraits **Edge:** 5 T.O. .999 AG **Note:** Struck at Lialoosin Inc., Los Angeles, CA.

Date	Mintage	F	VF	XF	Unc	BU
1998 Proof	—	Value: 300				

KM# 4a 50000 DRAM
Gold Plated Silver **Obv:** National arms **Rev:** Two monumental portraits

Date	Mintage	F	VF	XF	Unc	BU
1998 Proof	—	Value: 325				

NAMIBIA

The Republic of Namibia, once the German colonial territory of German Southwest Africa, and later Southwest Africa, is situated on the Atlantic coast of southern Africa, bounded on the north by Angola, on the east by Botswana, and on the south by South Africa. It has an area of 318,261 sq. mi. (824,290 sq. km.) and a population of *1.4 million. Capital: Windhoek. Diamonds, copper, lead, zinc, and cattle are exported.

South Africa undertook the administration of Southwest Africa under the terms of a League of Nations mandate on Dec. 17, 1920. When the League of Nations was dissolved in 1946, its supervisory authority for Southwest Africa was inherited by the United Nations. In 1946 the UN denied South Africa's request to annex Southwest Africa. South Africa responded by refusing to place the territory under a UN trusteeship. In 1950 the International Court of Justice ruled that South Africa could not unilaterally modify the international status of Southwest Africa. A 1966 UN resolution declaring the mandate terminated was rejected by South Africa, and the status of the area remained in dispute. In June 1968 the UN General Assembly voted to rename the territory Namibia. In 1971 the International Court of Justice ruled that South Africa's presence in Namibia was illegal. In Dec. 1973 the UN appointed a UN Commissioner and a multi-racial Advisory Council was appointed. An interim government was formed in 1977 and independence was to be declared by Dec. 31, 1978. This resolution was rejected by major UN powers. In April 1978 South Africa accepted a plan for UN-supervised elections, which led to a political abstention by the Southwest Africa People's Organization (SWAPO) party leading to dissolving of the Minister's Council and National Assembly in Jan. 1983. A Multi-Party Conference (MPC) was formed in May 1984, which held talks with SWAPO. The MPC petitioned South Africa for self-government and on June 17, 1985 the Transitional Government of National Unity was installed. Negotiations were held in 1988 between Angola, Cuba, and South Africa reaching a peaceful settlement on Aug. 5, 1988. By April 1989 Cuban troops were to withdraw from Angola and South African troops from Namibia. The Transitional Government resigned on Feb. 28, 1988 for the upcoming elections of the constituent assembly in Nov. 1989. Independence was finally achieved on March 12, 1990 within the Commonwealth of Nations. The President is the Head of State; the Prime Minister is Head of Government.

MONETARY SYSTEM
100 Cents = 1 Namibia Dollar
1 Namibia Dollar = 1 South African Rand

REPUBLIC
1990 - present
DECIMAL COINAGE

KM# 1 5 CENTS
2.2000 g., Nickel Plated Steel, 16.9 mm. **Obv:** National arms **Rev:** Value left, aloe plant within 3/4 sun design

Date	Mintage	F	VF	XF	Unc	BU
1993	—	—	—	0.20	0.50	0.75

KM# 16 5 CENTS
3.1000 g., Stainless Steel, 20.03 mm. **Series:** F.A.O **Obv:** Arms with supporters **Rev:** Fish below value **Edge:** Plain

Date	Mintage	F	VF	XF	Unc	BU
1999	—	—	—	—	1.00	1.50
2000	—	—	—	—	1.00	1.50

KM# 2 10 CENTS
3.3900 g., Nickel Plated Steel, 21.5 mm. **Obv:** National arms **Rev:** Camelthorn tree right, partial sun design left, value below

Date	Mintage	F	VF	XF	Unc	BU
1993	—	—	—	0.35	1.00	1.25
1996	—	—	—	0.35	1.00	1.25
1998	—	—	—	0.35	1.00	1.25

KM# 3 50 CENTS
4.4300 g., Nickel Plated Steel, 24 mm. **Obv:** National arms **Rev:** Quiver tree right, partial sun design upper left, value below

Date	Mintage	F	VF	XF	Unc	BU
1993	—	—	—	0.75	1.75	2.00
1996	—	—	—	0.75	1.75	2.00

KM# 4 DOLLAR
4.9600 g., Brass, 22.3 mm. **Obv:** National arms **Rev:** Value divides Bateleur eagle at right, partial sun design at left

Date	Mintage	F	VF	XF	Unc	BU
1993	—	—	—	1.25	3.50	6.00
1996	—	—	—	1.25	3.50	6.00
Note: Edge varieties exist for 1996						
1998	—	—	—	1.25	3.50	6.00

KM# 6 DOLLAR
Copper-Nickel **Subject:** 5th Year of Independence **Obv:** Arms with supporters within beaded border **Rev:** Hills within beaded border

Date	Mintage	F	VF	XF	Unc	BU
1995	50,000	—	—	—	10.00	—

KM# 7 DOLLAR
Copper-Nickel **Subject:** Miss Universe **Obv:** Arms with supporters within beaded border **Rev:** Multicolor gemsbok within beaded border

Date	Mintage	F	VF	XF	Unc	BU
1995	50,000	—	—	—	14.00	—

KM# 12 DOLLAR
Copper-Nickel **Subject:** Marine Life Protection **Obv:** Arms with supporters **Rev:** Multicolor whale and calf

Date	Mintage	F	VF	XF	Unc	BU
1998 Proof	7,500	Value: 25.00				

KM# 5 5 DOLLARS
6.2200 g., Brass, 24.9 mm. **Obv:** National arms **Rev:** Partial sun design at top, value at center, African fish eagle below

Date	Mintage	F	VF	XF	Unc	BU
1993	—	—	—	4.00	7.50	10.00

KM# 18 5 DOLLARS
1.2700 g., 0.9999 Gold 0.0408 oz. AGW, 13.9 mm. **Subject:** 10 Years of Independence **Obv:** Arms with supporters **Rev:** Two lions within circle **Edge:** Reeded

Date	Mintage	F	VF	XF	Unc	BU
2000 Proof	8,000	Value: 40.00				

KM# 8 10 DOLLARS
25.0000 g., 0.9250 Silver 0.7435 oz. ASW **Subject:** 5th Year of Independence **Obv:** Arms with supporters **Rev:** Multicolor desert view

Date	Mintage	F	VF	XF	Unc	BU
1995 Proof	10,000	Value: 32.50				

KM# 9   10 DOLLARS
Copper-Nickel **Subject:** U.N. 50th Anniversary **Obv:** Arms with supporters **Rev:** Farm scene

Date	Mintage	F	VF	XF	Unc	BU
1995	—	—	—	—	12.50	14.50

KM# 9a   10 DOLLARS
28.2800 g., 0.9250 Silver 0.8410 oz. ASW **Subject:** U.N. 50th Anniversary **Obv:** Arms with supporters **Rev:** Farm scene

Date	Mintage	F	VF	XF	Unc	BU
1995 Proof	—	Value: 50.00				

KM# 10   10 DOLLARS
25.0000 g., 0.9250 Silver 0.7435 oz. ASW **Subject:** Miss Universe **Obv:** Arms with supporters **Rev:** Multicolor leopard

Date	Mintage	F	VF	XF	Unc	BU
1995 Proof	10,000	Value: 35.00				

KM# 11   10 DOLLARS
25.0000 g., 0.9250 Silver 0.7435 oz. ASW **Series:** Olympic Games 1996 **Obv:** Arms with supporters **Rev:** Runner and cheetah

Date	Mintage	F	VF	XF	Unc	BU
1996 Proof	—	Value: 35.00				

KM# 13   10 DOLLARS
25.0000 g., 0.9250 Silver 0.7435 oz. ASW **Subject:** Marine Life Protection **Obv:** Arms with supporters **Rev:** Multicolor whale and calf **Note:** Similar to 1 Dollar, KM#12.

Date	Mintage	F	VF	XF	Unc	BU
1998 Proof	—	Value: 60.00				

KM# 19   10 DOLLARS
25.0000 g., 0.9000 Silver 0.7234 oz. ASW, 37.3 mm. **Subject:** 10 Years of Independence **Obv:** Arms with supporters **Rev:** Two multicolor lions **Edge:** Reeded

Date	Mintage	F	VF	XF	Unc	BU
2000 Proof	3,000	Value: 40.00				

KM# 14   20 DOLLARS
155.5175 g., 0.9990 Silver 4.9948 oz. ASW **Obv:** Arms with supporters **Rev:** Multicolor whale and calf **Note:** Similar to 1 Dollar, KM#12.

Date	Mintage	F	VF	XF	Unc	BU
1998 Proof	—	Value: 350				

KM# 17   100 DOLLARS
31.1035 g., 0.9999 Gold 0.9999 oz. AGW **Series:** Olympic Games 1996 **Obv:** Arms with supporters **Rev:** Runner and cheetah **Note:** Similar to 10-Dollar, KM#11.

Date	Mintage	F	VF	XF	Unc	BU
1996 Proof	400	Value: 975				

KM# 15   100 DOLLARS
31.1035 g., 0.9999 Gold 0.9999 oz. AGW **Subject:** Marine Life Protection **Obv:** Arms with supporters **Rev:** Multicolor whale and calf **Note:** Similar to 1 Dollar, KM#12.

Date	Mintage	F	VF	XF	Unc	BU
1998 Proof	125	Value: 1,100				

ESSAIS

KM#	Date	Mintage	Identification		Mkt Val
E1	1996	30	10 Dollars. Copper-Nickel. Multi-color, KM#11.		200
E2	1996	30	100 Dollars. Copper-Nickel. Multi-color, KM#17.		220

MINT SETS

KM#	Date	Mintage	Identification	Issue Price	Mkt Val
MS1	1993 (5)	—	KM#1-5		

NAURU

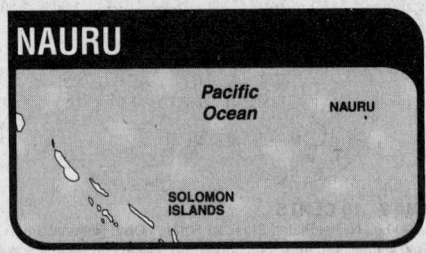

Pacific Ocean · NAURU · SOLOMON ISLANDS

The Republic of Nauru, formerly Pleasant Island, is an island republic in the western Pacific Ocean west of the Gilbert Islands. It has an area of 8-1/2 sq. mi. and a population of 7,254. It is known for its phosphate deposits.

The island was discovered in 1798. It was annexed by Germany in 1888 and made a part of the Marshall Island protectorate. In 1914 the island was occupied by Australia and placed under mandate in 1919. During World War II it was seized by the Japanese in August, 1942. It became a joint Australian, British and New Zealand trust territory in 1947 and remained as such until it became an independent republic in 1968. Nauru has a unique relationship with the Commonwealth of Nations.

RULER
British, until 1968

MONETARY SYSTEM
100 Cents = 1 (Australian) Dollar

REPUBLIC

DECIMAL COINAGE

KM# 12   DOLLAR
Copper-Nickel, 38.6 mm. **Obv:** National arms **Obv. Leg.:** BANK OF NAURU **Rev:** Queen Elizabeth and Winston Churchill standing facing while inspecting bomb damage to palace in 1940 **Rev. Leg.:** QUEEN ELIZABETH THE QUEEN MOTHER **Edge:** Reeded

Date	Mintage	F	VF	XF	Unc	BU
1996 Proof	—	Value: 12.00				

KM# 16   2 DOLLARS
Silver **Obv:** National arms **Obv. Leg.:** BANK OF NAURU **Rev:** Castle Mey in Scotland

Date	Mintage	F	VF	XF	Unc	BU
1998 Proof	—	Value: 40.00				

KM# 1   10 DOLLARS
38.7000 g., 0.9250 Silver 1.1509 oz. ASW **Subject:** Silver Jubilee of Independence **Obv:** National arms **Rev:** Value and ingot

Date	Mintage	F	VF	XF	Unc	BU
1993 Proof	1,000	Value: 85.00				

KM# 2   10 DOLLARS
31.4700 g., 0.9250 Silver 0.9359 oz. ASW **Subject:** Noah's Ark **Obv:** National arms **Rev:** Man, woman and animals in ark

Date	Mintage	F	VF	XF	Unc	BU
1993 Proof	Est. 15,000	Value: 65.00				

KM# 5   10 DOLLARS
31.4700 g., 0.9250 Silver 0.9359 oz. ASW **Series:** Endangered Wildlife **Obv:** National arms **Rev:** Songbirds

Date	Mintage	F	VF	XF	Unc	BU
1993 Proof	Est. 10,000	Value: 55.00				

KM# 3   10 DOLLARS
31.4700 g., 0.9250 Silver 0.9359 oz. ASW **Subject:** World Cup Soccer **Obv:** National arms **Rev:** Soccer player and soccer ball

Date	Mintage	F	VF	XF	Unc	BU
1994 Proof	30,000	Value: 45.00				

KM# 6   10 DOLLARS
31.4700 g., 0.9250 Silver 0.9359 oz. ASW **Subject:** Queen Mother Visits Bombed Palace **Obv:** National arms **Rev:** Figures standing in front of bombed building

Date	Mintage	F	VF	XF	Unc	BU
1994 Proof	Est. 30,000	Value: 45.00				

KM# 7   10 DOLLARS
31.4700 g., 0.9250 Silver 0.9359 oz. ASW **Subject:** John Fearn **Obv:** National arms **Rev:** Ship

Date	Mintage	F	VF	XF	Unc	BU
1994 Proof	Est. 15,000	Value: 50.00				

KM# 8   10 DOLLARS
31.4700 g., 0.9250 Silver 0.9359 oz. ASW **Obv:** National arms **Rev:** Bust with telescope facing right

Date	Mintage	F	VF	XF	Unc	BU
1994 Proof	Est. 10,000	Value: 52.50				

KM# 9   10 DOLLARS
31.4700 g., 0.9250 Silver 0.9359 oz. ASW **Series:** Olympics **Obv:** National arms **Rev:** Weight lifter

Date	Mintage	F	VF	XF	Unc	BU
1995 Proof	Est. 30,000	Value: 45.00				

KM# 4   50 DOLLARS
8.0500 g., 0.9000 Gold 0.2329 oz. AGW **Series:** 1996 Olympics **Obv:** National arms **Rev:** Javelin throwing

Date	Mintage	F	VF	XF	Unc	BU
1994 Proof	3,000	Value: 235				

KM# 10   50 DOLLARS
7.7760 g., 0.5833 Gold 0.1458 oz. AGW **Obv:** National arms **Rev:** Crowned emblem above steamship

Date	Mintage	F	VF	XF	Unc	BU
1994 Proof	Est. 3,000	Value: 165				

KM# 11   50 DOLLARS
7.7760 g., 0.5833 Gold 0.1458 oz. AGW **Subject:** Endangered Wildlife **Obv:** National arms **Rev:** Sea otter

Date	Mintage	F	VF	XF	Unc	BU
1995 Proof	Est. 2,000	Value: 175				

KM# 17   50 DOLLARS
7.7800 g., 0.5830 Gold 0.1458 oz. AGW **Obv:** National arms **Obv. Leg.:** BANK OF NAURU **Rev:** Queen Elizabeth and Winston Churchill standing facing while inspecting bomb damage to palace in 1940 **Rev. Leg.:** QUEEN ELIZABETH THE QUEEN MOTHER

Date	Mintage	F	VF	XF	Unc	BU
1998 Proof	—	Value: 185				

The Kingdom of Nepal, the world's only surviving Hindu kingdom, is a landlocked country occupying the southern slopes of the Himalayas. It has an area of 56,136 sq. mi. (140,800 sq. km.) and a population of 18 million. Capital: Kathmandu. Nepal has deposits of coal, copper, iron and cobalt, but they are largely unexploited. Agriculture is the principal economic activity. Rice, timber and jute are exported, with tourism being the other major foreign exchange earner.

Apart from a brief Muslim invasion in the 14th century, Nepal was able to avoid the mainstream of Northern Indian politics, due to its impregnable position in the mountains. It is therefore a unique survivor of the medieval Hindu and Buddhist culture of Northern India, which was largely destroyed by the successive waves of Muslim invasions.

Apart from agriculture, Nepal owed its prosperity to its position on one of the easiest trade routes between the great monasteries of central Tibet, and India. Nepal made full use of this, and a trading community was set up in Lhasa during the 16th century, and Nepalese coins became the accepted currency medium in Tibet.

A popular revolution in 1950 toppled the Rana family and reconstituted power in the throne. In 1959 King Mahendra declared Nepal a constitutional monarchy, and in 1962 a new constitution set up a system of *panchayat* (village council) democracy. In 1990, following political unrest, the king's powers were reduced. The country then adopted a system of parliamentary democracy.

On June 2, 2001 tragedy struck the royal family when Crown Prince Dipendra used an assault rifle to kill his father, mother and other members of the royal family as the result of a dispute over his current lady friend. He died 48 hours later, as King, from self inflicted gunshot wounds. Gyanendra began his second reign as King (his first was a short time as a toddler, 1950-51).

DATING
Saka Era (SE)

Up until 1888AD all coins of the Gorkha Dynasty were dated in the Saka era (SE). To convert from Saka to AD take Saka date and add 78 to arrive at the AD date. Coins dated with this era have SE before the date in the following listing.

Bikram Samvat Era (VS)

From 1888AD most copper coins were dated in the Bikram Samvat (VS) era. To convert take VS date - 57 = AD date. Coins with this era have VS before the year in the listing. With the exception of a few gold coins struck in 1890 & 1892, silver and gold coins only changed to the VS era in 1911AD, but now this era is used for all coins struck in Nepal.

RULERS

SHAH DYNASTY

पृथ्वी वीर विक्रम

Prithvi Bir Bikram
SE1803-1833/1881-1911AD, VS1938-1968/

लदमी दिव्येश्वरी

Queen of Prithvi Bir Bikram: Lakshmi Divyeswari

त्रिभुवनवीर विक्रम

Tribhuvana Bir Bikram
VS1968-2007, 2007-2011/1911-1950, 1951-1955AD (first reign)
VS2058- / 2001- AD (second reign)

ज्ञानेन्दवीर विक्रम

Gyanendra Bir Bikram
VS2007/1950-1951AD

महेन्द्रवीर विक्रम

Mahendra Bir Bikram
VS2012-2028/1955-1971AD

रन्न राज लदमी

Queen of Mahendra Bir Bikram: Ratna Rajya Lakshmi

बीरेन्द्र वीर विक्रम

Birendra Bir Bikram
VS2028-2058 /1971-2001AD

ऐश्वर्य राज्य लद्मी दृवी

Queen of Birendra Bir Bikram: Aishvarya Rajya Lakshmi
VS2028-2058 /1971-2001AD

MONETARY SYSTEM
Many of the mohars circulated in Tibet as well as in Nepal, and on a number of occasions coins were struck from bullion supplied by the Tibetan authorities. The smaller denominations never circulated in Tibet, but some of the mohars were cut for use as small change in Tibet.

In these listings only major changes in design have been noted. There are numerous minor varieties of ornamentation or spelling. With a few exceptions, most all coins were struck at Kathmandu.

COPPER

Initially the copper paisa was not fixed in value relative to the silver coins, and generally fluctuated in value from 1/32 mohar in 1865AD to around 1/50 mohar after 1880AD, and was fixed at that value in 1903AD.
4 Dam = 1 Paisa
2 Paisa = 1 Dyak, Adhani

COPPER and SILVER
Decimal Series
100 Paisa = 1 Rupee

Although the value of the copper paisa was fixed at 100 paisa to the rupee in 1903, it was not until 1932 that silver coins were struck in the decimal system.

GOLD COINAGE

Nepalese gold coinage, until recently, did not carry any denominations and was traded for silver, etc. at the local bullion exchange rate. The three basic weight standards used in the following listing are distinguished for convenience, although all were known as Asarphi (gold coin) locally as follows:

GOLD MOHAR
5.60 g multiples and fractions

TOLA
12.48 g multiples and fractions

GOLD RUPEE or ASHRPHI/ASARFI
11.66 g multiples and fractions
(Reduced to 10.00 g in 1966)

NOTE: In some instances the gold and silver issues were struck from the same dies.

NUMERALS
Nepal has used more variations of numerals on their coins than any other nation. The most common are illustrated in the numeral chart in the introduction. The chart below illustrates some variations encompassing the last four centuries.

1	2	3	4	5	6	7	8	9	0
१	२	३	४	५	६	७	८	९	०

NUMERICS

Half	आधा
One	एक
Two	इड
Four	चार

Five	पाच
Ten	दसा
Twenty	विसा
Twenty-five	पचीसा
Fifty	पचासा
Hundred	सय

DENOMINATIONS

Paisa	पैसा
Dam	दाम
Mohar	मोरु
Rupee	रुपैयाँ
Ashrapi	असार्फो
Asarphi (Asarfi)	अभ्रफी

DIE VARIETIES

Although the same dies were usually used both for silver and gold minor denominations, the gold Mohar is easily recognized being less ornate. The following illustrations are of a silver Mohar, KM#602 and a gold Mohar KM#615 issued by Surendra Bikram Saha Deva in the period SE1769-1803/1847-1881AD. Note the similar reverse legend. The obverse usually will start with the character for the word Shri either in single or multiples, the latter as Shri Shri Shri or Shri 3.

OBVERSE

SILVER SE1791	GOLD SE1793

LEGEND

श्री श्रीश्री सुरेन्द्र बिकम साहदेव

Shri Shri Shri Surendra Bikrama Saha Deva (date).

REVERSE

SILVER	GOLD

LEGEND
(in center)

श्री ३ भवानी

Shri 3 Bhavani
(around outer circle)

श्री श्री श्री गोरपनाथ

Shri Shri Shri Gorakhanatha

KINGDOM
Shah Dynasty

Prithvi Bir Bikram
VS1938-1968 / 1881-1911AD

COPPER COINAGE

KM# 620.1 DAM
Copper

Date	Mintage	F	VF	XF	Unc	BU
SE(18)18 (1896)	—	7.50	12.00	15.00	20.00	—

Note: Reverse inscription SARKAR

Date	Mintage	F	VF	XF	Unc	BU
SE(18)19 (1897)	—	7.50	12.00	15.00	20.00	—

Note: Reverse inscription SURKAR (error)

KM# 620.2 DAM
Copper Rev. Insc.: "Sarkar"

Date	Mintage	F	VF	XF	Unc	BU
VS(19)64 (1907)	—	7.50	12.00	15.00	20.00	—

KM# 621 DAM
Copper

Date	Mintage	F	VF	XF	Unc	BU
VS(19)68 (1911)	—	4.50	7.50	10.00	17.50	—
VS(19)68 (1911) Proof	—	Value: 60.00				

KM# 622 1/2 PAISA
Copper, 19 mm.

Date	Mintage	F	VF	XF	Unc	BU
VS(19)64 (1907)	—	4.50	7.50	10.00	17.50	—
VS(19)68 (1911)	—	4.50	7.50	10.00	17.50	—
VS(19)68 (1911) Proof	—	Value: 60.00				

KM# 623 PAISA
Copper Obv: Trident Rev: Legend in four lines

Date	Mintage	Good	VG	F	VF	XF
SE1810 (1888)	—	30.00	50.00	75.00	100	—

KM# 625 PAISA
Copper Obv: Two footprints above khukris

Date	Mintage	Good	VG	F	VF	XF
VS1945 (1888)	—	3.00	5.00	8.50	13.50	—
VS1948 (1891)	—	9.00	15.00	22.50	35.00	—

KM# 624 PAISA
Copper Obv: Crossed khukris, circular legend, border of flowers
Note: Two reverse die varieties

Date	Mintage	Good	VG	F	VF	XF
VS1945 (1888)	—	30.00	50.00	75.00	100	—
Note: Without obverse footprints						
VS1945 (1888)	—	30.00	50.00	75.00	100	—

KM# 626 PAISA
Copper Obv: Border of XXX's Rev: Border of XXX's

Date	Mintage	Good	VG	F	VF	XF
VS1948 (1891)	—	1.00	1.50	3.00	5.00	—
VS1948 (1891) Inverted date	—	2.00	3.00	5.00	8.00	—
VS1949 (1892)	—	2.00	3.00	5.00	8.00	—

KM# 627 PAISA
Copper Obv: Border of crescents Rev: Border of crescents

Date	Mintage	Good	VG	F	VF	XF
VS1949 (1892)	—	1.00	1.50	3.00	5.00	—
VS1950 (1893)	—	1.00	1.50	3.00	5.00	—
VS1951 (1894)	—	1.25	1.75	3.50	6.00	—

KM# 628 PAISA
Copper Obv: Legend within sprays Rev: Legend within sprays
Note: Varieties in sprays exist. Coin and medal alignment varieties exist. Also struck between VS1343-1357/1943-57AD.

Date	Mintage	Good	VG	F	VF	XF
VS1949 (1892)	—	1.00	1.50	3.00	5.00	—
VS1950 (1893)	—	1.00	1.50	3.00	5.00	—
VS1951 (1894)	—	1.00	1.50	3.00	5.00	—
VS1952 (1895)	—	1.00	1.50	3.00	5.00	—
VS1953 (1896)	—	1.00	1.50	3.00	5.00	—
VS1954 (1897)	—	1.00	1.50	3.00	5.00	—
VS1955 (1898)	—	1.00	1.50	3.00	5.00	—
VS1956 (1899)	—	1.00	1.50	3.00	5.00	—
VS1957 (1900)	—	1.00	1.50	3.00	5.00	—
VS1959 (1902)	—	1.00	1.50	3.00	5.00	—
VS1960 (1903)	—	1.00	1.50	3.00	5.00	—
VS1961 (1904)	—	1.00	1.50	3.00	5.00	—
VS1962 (1905)	—	1.00	1.50	3.00	5.00	—
VS(19)62 (1905)	—	—	—	—	—	—
VS1963 (1906)	—	1.00	1.50	3.00	5.00	—

Date	Mintage	Good	VG	F	VF	XF
VS1964 (1907)	—	1.00	1.50	3.00	5.00	—
VS(19)64 (1907)	—					—

KM# 629 PAISA
Copper **Obv:** Legend within squares **Rev:** Legend within squares

Date	Mintage	Good	VG	F	VF	XF
VS1959 (1902)	—	1.00	1.50	2.50	4.00	—
VS1962 (1905)	—	1.00	1.50	2.50	4.00	—
VS1963 (1906)	—	1.00	1.50	2.50	4.00	—
VS1964 (1907)	—	1.00	1.50	2.50	4.00	—
VS1965 (1908)	—	1.00	1.50	2.50	4.00	—
VS1966 (1909)	—	1.00	1.50	2.50	4.00	—
VS1967 (1910)	—	1.00	1.50	2.50	4.00	—
VS1968 (1911)	—	1.00	1.50	2.50	4.00	—

KM# 630 PAISA
Copper-Iron Alloy **Obv:** Legend within square **Rev:** Legend within circle **Note:** Magnetic and non-magnetic alloy.

Date	Mintage	Good	VG	F	VF	XF
VS1959 (1902)	—	7.50	12.50	20.00	33.50	—

KM# 631 PAISA
Copper, 23 mm. **Note:** Also Tribhuvaua Bir Bikram struck a Paisa VS1968, see KM#685.1.

Date	Mintage	F	VF	XF	Unc	BU
VS1964 (1907)	—	5.50	9.00	15.00	22.50	—
VS1968 (1911)	—	8.50	13.50	20.00	30.00	—
VS1968 (1911) Proof	—	Value: 90.00				

KM# 632 2 PAISA (Dak)
Copper **Obv:** Circular legends **Rev:** Circular legends **Note:** Varieties exist with dot or with cross below khukris.

Date	Mintage	Good	VG	F	VF	XF
VS1948 (1891)	—	2.00	3.00	5.00	8.00	—
VS1949 (1892)	—	2.50	3.50	5.00	8.00	—
VS1950 (1893)	—	2.50	3.50	5.00	8.00	—

KM# 633 2 PAISA (Dak)
Copper-Iron Alloy **Obv:** Legend within square **Rev:** Legend within circle **Note:** Magnetic and non-magnetic alloy. Similar to KM#630.

Date	Mintage	Good	VG	F	VF	XF
VS1959 (1902)	—	12.50	17.50	25.00	50.00	—

KM# 634 2 PAISA (Dak)
Copper, 26.5 mm.

Date	Mintage	F	VF	XF	Unc	BU
VS1964 (1907)	—	8.50	13.50	20.00	30.00	—
VS1968 (1911)	—	9.00	15.00	22.50	35.00	—
VS1968 (1911) Proof	—	Value: 110				

SILVER COINAGE

KM# 635 DAM
0.0400 g., Silver **Note:** Uniface. Five characters around sword.

Date	Mintage	VG	F	VF	XF	Unc
ND(1881-1911)	—	—	8.00	10.00	15.00	25.00

KM# 636 DAM
0.0400 g., Silver **Note:** Four characters around sword.

Date	Mintage	VG	F	VF	XF	Unc
ND(1881-1911)	—	—	15.00	25.00	30.00	40.00

KM# 637 1/32 MOHAR
0.1800 g., Silver, 11 mm. **Obv:** Sun and moon

Date	Mintage	VG	F	VF	XF	Unc
ND(1881-1911)	—	5.00	8.50	12.50	16.50	—

KM# 638 1/32 MOHAR
0.1800 g., Silver, 11 mm. **Obv:** Without sun and moon

Date	Mintage	VG	F	VF	XF	Unc
ND(1881-1911)	—	5.00	8.50	12.50	16.50	—

KM# 639 1/16 MOHAR
0.3500 g., Silver, 13 mm. **Note:** Varieties exist.

Date	Mintage	VG	F	VF	XF	Unc
ND(1881-1911)	—	—	6.00	10.00	13.50	20.00

KM# 640 1/8 MOHAR
0.7000 g., Silver **Note:** Varieties exist.

Date	Mintage	VG	F	VF	XF	Unc
ND(1881-1911)	—	—	7.50	12.50	18.50	27.50

KM# 641 1/4 MOHAR
1.4000 g., Silver **Rev:** Two moons **Note:** Handstruck

Date	Mintage	VG	F	VF	XF	Unc
SE1804 (1882)	—	15.00	17.50	25.00	35.00	—
SE1806 (1884)	—	20.00	25.00	35.00	45.00	—
SE1808 (1886)	—	15.00	17.50	25.00	35.00	—
SE1811 (1889)	—	20.00	25.00	35.00	45.00	—

KM# 642 1/4 MOHAR
1.4000 g., Silver **Rev:** Moon and spiral sun **Note:** Machine struck

Date	Mintage	VG	F	VF	XF	Unc
SE1816 (1894)	—	1.75	3.00	5.00	7.00	—
SE1817 (1895)	—	1.75	3.00	5.00	7.00	—

KM# 643 1/4 MOHAR
1.4000 g., Silver **Rev:** Moon and dot for sun **Note:** Machine struck. Also struck between SE1804-1817.

Date	Mintage	VG	F	VF	XF	Unc
SE1827 (1905)	—	1.75	3.00	5.00	7.00	—

KM# 644 1/4 MOHAR
1.4000 g., Silver, 15.5 mm. **Note:** Machine struck.

Date	Mintage	VG	F	VF	XF	Unc
SE1833 (1911)	—	1.75	3.00	5.00	7.00	—
SE1833 (1911) Proof	—	Value: 25.00				

KM# 647 1/2 MOHAR
2.7700 g., Silver, 21 mm. **Edge:** Plain **Note:** Machine struck. Varieties exist. Also struck between SE1803-1817.

Date	Mintage	F	VF	XF	Unc	BU
SE1824 (1902)	—	20.00	25.00	30.00	35.00	—

KM# 648 1/2 MOHAR
2.7700 g., Silver, 21 mm. **Note:** Machine struck.

Date	Mintage	F	VF	XF	Unc	BU
SE1826 (1904)	—	3.00	5.00	7.00	10.00	—
SE1827 (1905)	—	3.00	5.00	7.00	10.00	—
SE1829 (1907)	—	3.50	5.50	8.50	11.50	—

KM# 649 1/2 MOHAR
2.7700 g., Silver, 19 mm. **Edge:** Milled **Note:** Machine struck.

Date	Mintage	F	VF	XF	Unc	BU
SE1832 (1910)	—	20.00	25.00	30.00	35.00	—
SE1833 (1911)	—	2.25	3.50	5.00	7.00	—
SE1833 (1911) Proof	—	Value: 35.00				

KM# 651.1 MOHAR
5.6000 g., Silver, 26 mm. **Edge:** Plain **Note:** Machine struck. Also struck between SE1807-1822.

Date	Mintage	F	VF	XF	Unc	BU
SE1823 (1901)	—	4.50	6.50	8.00	10.00	—
SE1824 (1902)	—	4.50	6.50	8.00	10.00	—
SE1825 (1903)	—	4.50	6.50	8.00	10.00	—
SE1826 (1904)	—	4.50	6.50	8.00	10.00	—
SE1827 (1905)	—	4.50	6.50	8.00	10.00	—

KM# 652 MOHAR
5.6000 g., Silver, 26 mm. **Rev:** Gold die, in error

Date	Mintage	F	VF	XF	Unc	BU
SE1825 (1903)	—	10.00	15.00	25.00	32.50	—

KM# 651.2 MOHAR
5.6000 g., Silver, 26 mm. **Edge:** Milled **Note:** Machine struck.

Date	Mintage	F	VF	XF	Unc	BU
SE1826 (1904)	—	4.50	6.50	8.00	10.00	—
SE1827 (1905)	—	4.50	6.50	8.00	10.00	—
SE1828 (1906)	—	4.50	6.50	8.00	10.00	—
SE1829 (1907)	—	4.50	6.50	8.00	10.00	—
SE1830 (1908)	—	4.50	6.50	8.00	10.00	—
SE1831 (1909)	—	4.50	6.50	8.00	10.00	—
SE1832 (1910)	—	4.50	6.50	8.00	10.00	—
SE1833 (1911)	—	—	25.00	35.00	50.00	—

Note: The date SE1833 was only issued in presentation sets

KM# A653 2 MOHARS
11.2000 g., Silver, 27 mm. **Note:** Hand struck using gold dies.

Date	Mintage	F	VF	XF	Unc	BU
SE1803 (1881)	—	40.00	60.00	80.00	100	—

KM# 653 2 MOHARS
11.2000 g., Silver, 27 mm. **Note:** Machine struck.

Date	Mintage	F	VF	XF	Unc	BU
SE1804 (1882)	—	40.00	60.00	80.00	100	—

Note: Milled edge

| SE1811 (1889) | — | 40.00 | 60.00 | 80.00 | 100 | — |

Note: Plain edge

| SE1817 (1895) | — | 8.00 | 12.50 | 17.50 | 25.00 | — |

Note: Plain edge

KM# 654 2 MOHARS
11.2000 g., Silver, 29 mm. **Edge:** Plain **Note:** Machine struck using gold dies.

Date	Mintage	F	VF	XF	Unc	BU
SE1821 (1899)	—	10.00	15.00	25.00	45.00	—

KM# 655 2 MOHARS
11.2000 g., Silver, 27 mm. **Edge:** Milled **Note:** Machine struck.

Date	Mintage	F	VF	XF	Unc	BU
SE1829 (1907)	—	15.00	27.50	40.00	60.00	—
SE1831 (1909)	—	6.50	9.00	12.50	20.00	—

KM# 656 2 MOHARS
Silver, 29 mm. **Note:** Machine struck.

Date	Mintage	F	VF	XF	Unc	BU
SE1832 (1910)	—	7.00	9.00	11.50	18.50	—

Date	Mintage	F	VF	XF	Unc	BU
SE1833 (1911)		6.50	8.00	10.00	16.50	—
SE1833 (1911) Proof		Value: 75.00				

KM# 657 4 MOHARS
22.4000 g., Silver **Edge:** Plain

Date	Mintage	F	VF	XF	Unc	BU
SE1817 (1895)	—	60.00	100	140	200	—

KM# 658 4 MOHARS
22.4000 g., Silver, 29 mm. **Edge:** Milled

Date	Mintage	F	VF	XF	Unc	BU
SE1833 (1911)	—	60.00	100	140	200	—
SE1833 (1911) Proof	—	Value: 450				

GOLD COINAGE

KM# 659 DAM
0.0400 g., Gold **Note:** Uniface. Five characters around sword. Similar to 1/64 Mohar, KM#664.

Date	Mintage	VG	F	VF	XF	Unc
ND(1881-1911)	—	10.00	14.00	20.00	27.50	

KM# 660 DAM
0.0400 g., Gold **Note:** Uniface. Four characters around sword. Similar to 1/64 Mohar, KM#663.

Date	Mintage	VG	F	VF	XF	Unc
ND(1881-1911)	—	10.00	14.00	20.00	27.50	

Actual Size   **2 x Actual Size**

KM# 661 DAM
0.0400 g., Gold **Note:** Uniface. Circle around characters.

Date	Mintage	VG	F	VF	XF	Unc
ND(1881-1911)	—	10.00	14.00	20.00	27.50	

Actual Size   **2 x Actual Size**

KM# 662 DAM
0.0400 g., Gold **Note:** Uniface. Two characters below sword. Varieties exist.

Date	Mintage	VG	F	VF	XF	Unc
ND(1881-1911)	—	10.00	14.00	20.00	27.50	

Actual Size   **2 x Actual Size**

KM# 663 1/64 MOHAR
0.0900 g., Gold **Note:** Uniface. Four characters around sword.

Date	Mintage	VG	F	VF	XF	Unc
ND(1881-1911)	—	12.50	17.50	22.50	30.00	

Actual Size   **2 x Actual Size**

KM# 664 1/64 MOHAR
0.0900 g., Gold **Note:** Uniface. Five characters around sword.

Date	Mintage	VG	F	VF	XF	Unc
ND(1881-1911)	—	12.50	17.50	22.50	30.00	

KM# 665 1/32 MOHAR
0.1800 g., Gold **Note:** Uniface. Five characters around sword.

Date	Mintage	VG	F	VF	XF	Unc
ND(1881-1911)	—	20.00	40.00	75.00	100	

KM# 666 1/32 MOHAR
0.1800 g., Gold **Note:** Uniface. Four characters around sword.

Date	Mintage	VG	F	VF	XF	Unc
ND(1881-1911)	—	15.00	30.00	75.00	100	

KM# 667 1/16 MOHAR
0.3500 g., Gold

Date	Mintage	VG	F	VF	XF	Unc
ND(1881-1911)	—	15.00	40.00	75.00	100	

KM# 668 1/16 MOHAR
0.3500 g., Gold

Date	Mintage	F	VF	XF	Unc	BU
SE(18)33 (1911)	—	15.00	30.00	75.00	100	
SE(18)33 (1911) Proof						

KM# 669.1 1/8 MOHAR
0.7000 g., Gold **Obv:** Six characters

Date	Mintage	F	VF	XF	Unc	BU
ND (1881)	—	22.50	40.00	75.00	100	—

KM# 669.2 1/8 MOHAR
0.7000 g., Gold **Obv:** Five characters **Note:** Varieties exist.

Date	Mintage	F	VF	XF	Unc	BU
ND (1881)	—	22.50	40.00	75.00	100	—

KM# 670 1/8 MOHAR
0.7000 g., Gold

Date	Mintage	F	VF	XF	Unc	BU
SE(18)33 (1911)	—	22.50	40.00	75.00	100	—

KM# 671.1 1/4 MOHAR
1.4000 g., Gold

Date	Mintage	F	VF	XF	Unc	BU
SE1808 (1886)	—	45.00	60.00	80.00	100	—
SE1811 (1889)	—	45.00	60.00	80.00	100	—
SE1817 (1895)	—	40.00	50.00	60.00	80.00	—
SE1823 (1901)	—	45.00	60.00	80.00	100	—
SE1829 (1907)	—	40.00	50.00	60.00	80.00	—

KM# 671.2 1/4 MOHAR
1.4000 g., Gold

Date	Mintage	F	VF	XF	Unc	BU
SE1833 (1911) Proof	—	—	—	—	—	—
SE1833 (1911)	—	40.00	50.00	60.00	80.00	—

KM# 672.1 1/2 MOHAR
2.8000 g., Gold

Date	Mintage	F	VF	XF	Unc	BU
SE1805 (1883)	—	70.00	80.00	90.00	110	—

KM# 672.2 1/2 MOHAR
2.8000 g., Gold

Date	Mintage	F	VF	XF	Unc	BU
SE1817 (1895)	—	70.00	80.00	90.00	110	—

KM# 672.3 1/2 MOHAR
2.8000 g., Gold

Date	Mintage	F	VF	XF	Unc	BU
SE1823 (1901)	—	75.00	85.00	100	125	—

KM# 672.4 1/2 MOHAR
2.8000 g., Gold

Date	Mintage	F	VF	XF	Unc	BU
SE1829 (1907)	—	70.00	80.00	90.00	110	—

KM# 672.5 1/2 MOHAR
2.8000 g., Gold

Date	Mintage	F	VF	XF	Unc	BU
SE1833 (1911) Proof	—	—	—	—	—	—
SE1833 (1911)	—	70.00	80.00	90.00	110	—

KM# 673.1 MOHAR
5.6000 g., Gold

Date	Mintage	F	VF	XF	Unc	BU
SE1804 (1882)	—	140	150	165	200	350
SE1805 (1883)	—	140	150	165	200	350
SE1809 (1887)	—	140	150	165	200	350
SE1817 (1895)	—	140	150	165	200	350

Date	Mintage	F	VF	XF	Unc	BU
SE1820 (1898)	—	140	150	165	200	350
SE1823 (1901)	—	140	150	165	200	350
SE1825 (1903)	—	140	150	165	200	350
SE1826 (1904)	—	140	150	165	200	350
SE1827 (1905)	—	140	150	165	200	350

KM# 673.3 MOHAR
5.6000 g., Gold

Date	Mintage	F	VF	XF	Unc	BU
VS1949 (1892)	—	125	135	150	185	—

KM# 673.2 MOHAR
5.6000 g., Gold Edge: Milled

Date	Mintage	F	VF	XF	Unc	BU
SE1828 (1906)	—	140	150	165	200	350
SE1829 (1907)	—	140	150	165	200	350
SE1831 (1909)	—	140	150	165	200	350
SE1833 (1911) Proof	—	—	—	—	—	—
SE1833 (1911)	—	140	150	165	200	350

KM# 674.1 TOLA
12.4800 g., Gold Note: Oblique edge milling.

Date	Mintage	F	VF	XF	Unc	BU
SE1803 (1881)	—	265	275	295	345	—
SE1805 (1883)	—	265	275	295	345	—
SE1810 (1888)	—	265	275	295	345	—
SE1811 (1889)	—	265	275	295	345	—

KM# 674.2 TOLA
12.4800 g., Gold Note: Vertical edge milling.

Date	Mintage	F	VF	XF	Unc	BU
SE1803 (1881)	—	265	275	295	345	—
SE1804 (1882)	—	265	275	295	345	—

KM# 674.3 TOLA
12.4800 g., Gold Edge: Plain

Date	Mintage	F	VF	XF	Unc	BU
SE1807 (1885)	—	300	310	320	345	—
SE1817 (1895)	—	300	310	320	345	—
SE1820 (1898)	—	300	310	320	345	—
SE1823 (1901)	—	300	310	320	345	—
SE1824 (1902)	—	300	310	320	345	—
SE1825 (1903)	—	300	310	320	345	—
SE1826 (1904)	—	300	310	320	345	—

KM# 675.2 TOLA
12.4800 g., Gold Edge: Plain

Date	Mintage	F	VF	XF	Unc	BU
VS1947 (1890)	—	265	275	295	335	—

KM# 675.3 TOLA
12.4800 g., Gold Note: Oblique edge milling.

Date	Mintage	F	VF	XF	Unc	BU
VS1949 (1892)	—	265	275	295	335	—

KM# 675.1 TOLA
12.4800 g., Gold Edge: Vertical milling

Date	Mintage	F	VF	XF	Unc	BU
SE1828 (1906)	—	300	310	320	345	—
SE1829 (1907)	—	300	310	320	345	—
SE1831 (1909)	—	300	310	320	345	—
SE1832 (1910)	—	300	310	320	345	—
SE1833 (1911) Proof	—	—	—	—	—	—
SE1833 (1911)	—	300	310	320	345	—

KM# 676 DUITOLA ASARPHI
23.3200 g., Gold

Date	Mintage	F	VF	XF	Unc	BU
SE1811 (1889)	—	625	725	825	1,000	—

KM# 677 DUITOLA ASARPHI
23.3200 g., Gold Rev: Die of 4 Mohars, KM#657

Date	Mintage	F	VF	XF	Unc	BU
SE1817 (1895)	—	625	725	825	1,000	—

KM# 678 DUITOLA ASARPHI
23.3200 g., Gold Edge: Plain

Date	Mintage	F	VF	XF	Unc	BU
SE1825 (1902)	—	625	725	850	1,000	—

KM# 679 DUITOLA ASARPHI
23.3200 g., Gold Edge: Milled

Date	Mintage	F	VF	XF	Unc	BU
SE1829 (1907)	—	600	650	700	800	—

KM# 680 DUITOLA ASARPHI
23.3200 g., Gold Edge: Milled

Date	Mintage	F	VF	XF	Unc	BU
SE1833 (1911) Proof	—	—	—	—	—	—
SE1833 (1911)	—	600	650	700	800	—

Tribhuvana Bir Bikram
VS1968-2007 / 1911-1950AD

COPPER COINAGE

KM# 684 1/2 PAISA
Copper Note: Struck only for presentation sets.

Date	Mintage	F	VF	XF	Unc	BU
VS1978 (1921)	—	—	—	50.00	75.00	—
VS1985 (1928)	—	—	—	50.00	75.00	—

KM# 685.1 PAISA
Copper Note: Machine struck. Also Prithvi Bir Bikram struck a Paisa VS1968, see KM#631.

Date	Mintage	Good	VG	F	VF	XF
VS1968 (1911)	—	10.00	20.00	50.00	75.00	—

KM# 685.2 PAISA
Copper **Note:** Hand struck. Many varieties exist.

Date	Mintage	Good	VG	F	VF	XF
VS1969 (1912)	—	1.00	1.50	2.25	3.50	—
VS1970 (1913)	—	1.00	1.50	2.25	3.50	—
VS1971 (1914)	—	1.00	1.50	2.25	3.50	—
VS1972 (1915)	—	1.00	1.50	2.25	3.50	—
VS1973 (1916)	—	1.00	1.50	2.25	3.50	—
VS1974 (1917)	—	1.00	1.50	2.25	3.50	—
VS1975 (1918)	—	1.00	1.50	2.25	3.50	—
VS1976 (1919)	—	1.00	1.50	2.25	3.50	—
VS1977 (1920)	—	1.00	1.50	2.25	3.50	—

KM# 687.4 PAISA
3.7500 g., Brass **Obv:** Fine style crossed khukris

Date	Mintage	VG	F	VF	XF	Unc
VS1975 (1918)	—	0.50	1.25	1.75	3.00	6.00
VS1976 (1919)	—	0.50	1.25	1.75	3.00	6.00

KM# 686.1 PAISA
5.2000 g., Copper, 23.5 mm. **Rev:** Without "Nepal" below

Date	Mintage	F	VF	XF	Unc	BU
VS1975 (1918)	—	—	—	37.50	50.00	—

KM# 686.2 PAISA
3.7000 g., Copper, 21.5 mm. **Rev:** Without "Nepal" below

Date	Mintage	Good	VG	F	VF	XF
VS1975 (1918)	—	—	—	60.00	90.00	—

Note: The above issues are believed to be patterns

KM# 687.1 PAISA
Copper, 21.5 mm. **Obv:** Outlined Khukris **Note:** Machine struck. Fine style. Weight varies: 3.50-3.80 g.

Date	Mintage	F	VF	XF	Unc	BU
VS1977 (1920)	—	1.25	1.75	3.00	6.00	—
VS1977 (1920)	—	1.25	1.75	3.00	6.00	—
Note: Inverted date						
VS1978	—	1.25	1.75	3.00	6.00	—

KM# 687.3 PAISA
3.7500 g., Copper, 21 mm. **Obv:** Outlined Khukris left over right and right over left **Note:** Crude, hand struck. Varieties of the Khukris exist

Date	Mintage	Good	VG	F	VF	XF
VS1978 (1921)	—	2.00	3.00	4.50	7.50	—
VS1979 (1922)	—	2.00	3.00	4.50	7.50	—
VS1980 (1923)	—	4.00	5.00	7.50	12.50	—
VS1981 (1924)	—	4.00	5.00	7.50	12.50	—
VS1982 (1925)	—	4.00	5.00	7.50	12.50	—
VS1983 (1926)	—	4.00	5.00	7.50	12.50	—

KM# 687.2 PAISA
Copper, 22 mm. **Obv:** Outlined Khukris always right over left **Note:** Machine struck. Weight varies: 2.6-3.1 grams. Prev. KM#688.

Date	Mintage	F	VF	XF	Unc	BU
VS1978 (1921)	—	1.25	1.75	3.00	6.00	—
VS1979 (1922)	—	1.25	1.75	3.00	6.00	—

Date	Mintage	F	VF	XF	Unc	BU
VS1980 (1923)	—	1.50	3.00	5.00	10.00	—
VS1981 (1924)	—	1.50	3.00	5.00	10.00	—
VS1982 (1925)	—	1.25	1.75	3.00	6.00	—
VS1984 (1927)	—	1.25	1.75	3.00	6.00	—
VS1985 (1928)	—	1.25	1.75	3.00	6.00	—
VS1986 (1929)	—	1.25	1.75	3.00	6.00	—
VS1987 (1930)	—	1.25	1.75	3.00	6.00	—

KM# 689.4 2 PAISA
Brass **Obv:** Fine style crossed khukris

Date	Mintage	VG	F	VF	XF	Unc
VS1976 (1919)	—	1.00	2.00	3.00	5.00	—

KM# 689.1 2 PAISA
Copper, 26 mm. **Obv:** Outlined Khukris **Note:** Machine struck. Varieties of the Khukris exist. Weight varies: 6.9-7.5 grams.

Date	Mintage	VG	F	VF	XF	Unc
VS1976 (1919)	—	1.00	2.00	3.00	5.00	—
VS1977 (1920)	—	1.00	2.00	3.00	5.00	—
VS1977 (1920)	—	3.50	5.00	8.50	13.50	—
Inverted date						

KM# 689.3 2 PAISA
5.0000 g., Copper **Obv:** Outlined Khukris always right over left **Note:** Machine struck. Weight varies: 5.00-5.700 grams.

Date	Mintage	VG	F	VF	XF	Unc
VS1978 (1921)	—	1.00	2.00	3.00	4.50	—
VS1979 (1922)	—	1.00	2.00	3.00	4.50	—
VS1980 (1923)	—	1.00	2.00	3.00	4.50	—
VS1981 (1924)	—	1.00	2.00	3.00	4.50	—
VS1982 (1925)	—	1.00	2.00	3.00	4.50	—
VS1983 (1926)	—	1.00	2.00	3.00	4.50	—
VS1984 (1927)	—	1.00	2.00	3.00	4.50	—
VS1991 (1934)	—	1.50	2.50	4.00	6.00	—

KM# 689.2 2 PAISA
Copper **Obv:** Outlined Khukris left over right and right over left **Note:** Crude struck. Varieties of the Khukris exist. Weight varies: 4.6-5.5 grams.

Date	Mintage	Good	VG	F	VF	XF
VS1978 (1921)	—	1.00	2.00	3.50	6.50	—
VS1979 (1922)	—	1.00	2.00	3.50	6.50	—
VS1980 (1923)	—	1.00	2.00	3.50	6.50	—
VS1981 (1924)	—	1.00	2.00	3.50	6.50	—
VS1982 (1925)	—	1.00	2.00	3.50	6.50	—
VS1983 (1926)	—	1.00	2.00	3.50	6.50	—
VS1984 (1927)	—	1.00	2.00	3.50	6.50	—
VS1985 (1928)	—	1.00	2.00	3.50	6.50	—
VS1986 (1929)	—	1.50	2.50	4.00	7.50	—
VS1987 (1930)	—	1.50	2.50	4.00	7.50	—
VS1988 (1931)	—	2.00	3.00	5.00	9.00	—

KM# 690.1 5 PAISA
Copper, 29.5 mm. **Obv:** Outlined Khukris **Note:** Weight varies: 18.1-18.8 g.

Date	Mintage	F	VF	XF	Unc	BU
VS1976 (1919)	—	6.00	10.00	14.00	20.00	—
Note: Fine style						

Date	Mintage	F	VF	XF	Unc	BU
VS1977 (1920)	—	1.25	2.25	3.50	6.00	—
VS1977 (1920)	—	3.00	5.00	8.50	12.50	—
Inverted date						

KM# 690.2 5 PAISA
Copper **Obv:** Outlined Khukris, left over right and right over left **Note:** Crude hand struck. Weight varies: 11.0-13.2 g. Size varies: 29.0-32.5mm.

Date	Mintage	F	VF	XF	Unc	BU
VS1978 (1921)	—	1.75	3.00	5.00	8.00	—
VS1979 (1922)	—	1.75	3.00	5.00	8.00	—
VS1980 (1923)	—	1.75	3.00	5.00	8.00	—
VS1981 (1924)	—	1.75	3.00	5.00	8.00	—
VS1982 (1925)	—	1.75	3.00	5.00	8.00	—
VS1983 (1926)	—	1.75	3.00	5.00	8.00	—
VS1984 (1927)	—	1.75	3.00	5.00	8.00	—
VS1985 (1928)	—	1.75	3.00	5.00	8.00	—
VS1986 (1929)	—	1.75	3.00	5.00	8.00	—
VS1987 (1930)	—	1.75	3.00	5.00	8.00	—
VS1988 (1931)	—	6.00	10.00	14.00	20.00	—
VS1989 (1932)	—	1.75	3.00	5.00	8.00	—

KM# 690.3 5 PAISA
14.0000 g., Copper **Obv:** Outlined Khukris always right over left **Note:** Machine struck. Weight varies: 13.5-14.0 g. Varieties exist. Size varies: 29.0-30.0mm.

Date	Mintage	F	VF	XF	Unc	BU
VS1978 (1921)	—	1.25	2.25	3.50	5.00	—
VS1979 (1922)	—	1.25	2.25	3.50	5.00	—
VS1979 (1922)	—	1.25	2.25	3.50	5.00	—
Backwards date						
VS1980 (1923)	—	1.25	2.25	3.50	5.00	—
VS1981 (1924)	—	1.25	2.25	3.50	5.00	—
VS1982 (1925)	—	1.25	2.25	3.50	5.00	—
VS1983 (1926)	—	1.25	2.25	3.50	5.00	—
VS1984 (1927)	—	1.25	2.25	3.50	5.00	—
VS1991 (1934)	—	15.00	20.00	25.00	30.00	—

SILVER COINAGE

KM# 691 DAM
0.0400 g., Silver **Note:** Uniface.

Date	Mintage	F	VF	XF	Unc	BU
ND (1911)	—	15.00	25.00	30.00	50.00	—

KM# 692 1/4 MOHAR
1.4000 g., Silver, 16 mm.

Date	Mintage	VG	F	VF	XF	Unc
VS1969 (1912)	—	1.75	3.00	5.00	7.00	—
VS1970 (1913)	—	1.75	3.00	5.00	7.00	—

KM# 693 1/2 MOHAR
2.8000 g., Silver

Date	Mintage	F	VF	XF	Unc	BU
VS1968 (1911)	—	2.25	3.50	5.00	7.00	—
VS1970 (1913)	—	2.25	3.50	5.00	7.00	—
VS1971 (1914)	—	2.25	3.50	5.00	7.00	—

KM# 681 1/2 MOHAR

2.7700 g., Silver **Note:** In the name of "Queen Lakshmi Divyeswari" - Regent for Tribhuvana Bir Bikram.

Date	Mintage	F	VF	XF	Unc	BU
VS1971 (1914)	—	4.00	6.00	9.00	11.50	—

KM# 694 MOHAR

5.6000 g., Silver

Date	Mintage	F	VF	XF	Unc	BU
VS1968 (1911)	—	4.50	6.50	8.00	10.00	—
VS1969 (1912)	—	4.50	6.50	8.00	10.00	—
VS1971 (1914)	—	4.50	6.50	8.00	10.00	—

KM# 682 MOHAR

5.6000 g., Silver **Note:** In the name of "Queen Lakshmi Divyeswari" - Regent for Tribhuvana Bir Bikram.

Date	Mintage	F	VF	XF	Unc	BU
VS1971 (1914)	—	4.50	6.50	9.00	11.50	—

KM# 695 2 MOHARS

11.2000 g., Silver, 29 mm. **Note:** Varieties exist for this type.

Date	Mintage	F	VF	XF	Unc	BU
VS1968 (1911)	—	BV	7.50	10.00	16.50	—
VS1969 (1912)	—	BV	7.50	10.00	16.50	—
VS1970 (1913)	—	BV	7.50	10.00	16.50	—
VS1971 (1914)	—	BV	7.50	10.00	16.50	—
VS1972 (1915)	—	BV	7.50	10.00	16.50	—
VS1973 (1916)	—	BV	7.50	10.00	16.50	—
VS1974 (1917)	—	BV	7.50	10.00	16.50	—
VS1975 (1918)	—	BV	7.50	10.00	16.50	—
VS1976 (1919)	—	BV	7.50	10.00	16.50	—
VS1977 (1920)	—	BV	7.50	10.00	16.50	—
VS1978 (1921)	—	BV	7.50	10.00	16.50	—
VS1979 (1922)	—	BV	7.50	10.00	16.50	—
VS1980 (1923)	—	BV	7.50	10.00	16.50	—
VS1982 (1925)	—	BV	7.50	10.00	16.50	—
VS1983 (1926)	—	BV	7.50	10.00	16.50	—
VS1984 (1927)	—	BV	7.50	10.00	16.50	—
VS1985 (1928)	—	BV	7.50	10.00	16.50	—
VS1986 (1929)	—	BV	7.50	10.00	16.50	—
VS1987 (1930)	—	BV	7.50	10.00	16.50	—
VS1988 (1931)	—	BV	7.50	10.00	16.50	—
VS1989 (1932)	—	BV	7.50	10.00	16.50	—

KM# 696 4 MOHARS

22.4000 g., Silver

Date	Mintage	F	VF	XF	Unc	BU
VS1971 (1914)	—	40.00	75.00	125	175	—

GOLD COINAGE

KM# 697 DAM

0.0400 g., Gold **Note:** Uniface.

Date	Mintage	F	VF	XF	Unc	BU
ND (1911)	—	28.00	40.00	75.00	100	—

KM# 697a DAM

0.0400 g., Gold **Note:** Uniface, machine struck.

Date	Mintage	F	VF	XF	Unc	BU
ND (1911)	—	28.00	40.00	70.00	100	—

KM# 698 1/32 MOHAR

0.1800 g., Gold **Note:** Uniface.

Date	Mintage	F	VF	XF	Unc	BU
ND (1911)	—	38.00	60.00	90.00	125	—

KM# 699 1/16 MOHAR

0.3500 g., Gold

Date	Mintage	F	VF	XF	Unc	BU
VS(19)77 (1920)	—	50.00	90.00	120	150	—

KM# 700 1/8 MOHAR

0.7000 g., Gold

Date	Mintage	F	VF	XF	Unc	BU
VS(19)76 (1919)	—	75.00	120	150	200	—

KM# 701 1/2 MOHAR

2.8000 g., Gold

Date	Mintage	F	VF	XF	Unc	BU
VS1969 (1912)	—					—

KM# 717 1/2 MOHAR

2.8000 g., Gold

Date	Mintage	F	VF	XF	Unc	BU
VS1995 (1938)	—					—

KM# 702 MOHAR

5.6000 g., Gold

Date	Mintage	F	VF	XF	Unc	BU
VS1969 (1912)	—	135	140	150	200	300
VS1975 (1918)	—	135	140	150	200	300
VS1978 (1921)	—	135	140	150	200	300
VS1979 (1922)	—	135	140	150	200	300
VS1981 (1924)	—	135	140	150	200	300
VS1983 (1926)	—	135	140	150	200	300
VS1985 (1928)	—	135	140	150	200	300
VS1986 (1929)	—	135	140	150	200	300
VS1987 (1930)	—	135	140	150	200	300
VS1989 (1932)	—	135	140	150	200	300
VS1990 (1933)	—	135	140	150	200	300
VS1991 (1934)	—	135	140	150	200	300
VS1998 (1941)	—	135	140	150	200	300
VS1999 (1942)	—	135	140	150	200	300
VS2000 (1943)	—	135	140	150	200	300
VS2003 (1946)	—	135	140	150	200	300
VS2005 (1948)	—	135	140	150	200	300

KM# 683 MOHAR

5.6000 g., Gold **Note:** In the name of "Queen Lakshmi Divyeswari" - Regent for Tribhuvana Bir Bikram.

Date	Mintage	F	VF	XF	Unc	BU
VS1971 (1914)	—	135	140	150	185	—

KM# 722 MOHAR

5.6000 g., Gold

Date	Mintage	F	VF	XF	Unc	BU
VS1993 (1936)	376,000	—				—
VS1994 (1937)	283,000	—				—

KM# 703.1 ASHRAPHI (Tola)

Gold **Rev:** Moon and sun in center **Rev. Leg.:** SRI 3 BHAVANI

Date	Mintage	F	VF	XF	Unc	BU
VS1969 (1912)	—	285	300	310	335	—
VS1974 (1917)	—	285	300	310	335	—
VS1975 (1918)	—	285	300	310	335	—
VS1976 (1919)	—	285	300	310	335	—
VS1977 (1920)	—	285	300	310	335	—
VS1978 (1921)	—	285	300	310	335	—
VS1979 (1922)	—	285	300	310	335	—
VS1980 (1923)	—	285	300	310	335	—
VS1981 (1924)	—	285	300	310	335	—
VS1982 (1925)	—	285	300	310	335	—

Date	Mintage	F	VF	XF	Unc	BU
VS1983 (1926)	—	285	300	310	335	—
VS1984 (1927)	—	285	300	310	335	—
VS1985 (1928)	—	285	300	310	335	—
VS1986 (1929)	—	285	300	310	335	—
VS1987 (1930)	—	285	300	310	335	—
VS1988 (1931)	—	285	300	310	335	—
VS1989 (1932)	—	285	300	310	335	—
VS1990 (1933)	—	285	300	310	335	—
VS1991 (1934)	—	285	300	310	335	—
VS1998 (1941)	—	285	300	310	335	—
VS1999 (1942)	—	285	300	310	335	—
VS2000 (1943)	—	285	300	310	335	—
VS2003 (1946)	—	285	300	310	335	—

KM# 703.3 ASHRAPHI (Tola)

Gold **Rev:** 3 dots each side in center **Rev. Leg.:** SRI BHAVANI

Date	Mintage	F	VF	XF	Unc	BU
VS2033 (1976)	—	265	270	285	315	—

KM# 703.2 ASHRAPHI (Tola)

Gold

Date	Mintage	F	VF	XF	Unc	BU
VS2005 (1948)	—	285	300	310	335	—

KM# 727 ASHRAPHI (Tola)

Gold **Obv:** Trident between moon and sun above crossed Khukris in center

Date	Mintage	F	VF	XF	Unc	BU
VS1992 (1935)	—	300	310	320	350	400

KM# 728 DUITOLA ASARPHI

Gold **Note:** Similar to 1 Tola, KM#703.

Date	Mintage	F	VF	XF	Unc	BU
VS2005 (1948)	—	550	575	600	700	—

DECIMAL COINAGE

100 Paisa = 1 Rupee

KM# 704 1/4 PAISA

Copper, 14 mm. **Obv:** Footprints above crossed daggers within circle **Rev:** Crescent moon and star flank center dagger **Note:** Struck only for presentation sets.

Date	Mintage	F	VF	XF	Unc	BU
VS2000 (1943)	—	—	—	—	40.00	—
VS2004 (1947)	—	—	—	—	40.00	—

KM# 705 1/2 PAISA

Copper, 16 mm. **Obv:** Footprints above crossed daggers within circle **Rev:** Crescent moon and star flank dagger at center **Note:** Struck only for presentation sets.

Date	Mintage	F	VF	XF	Unc	BU
VS2004 (1947)	—	—	—	—	40.00	—

KM# 706.1 PAISA

Copper, 23 mm. **Obv:** Footprints above crossed daggers within circle **Rev:** Right wreath with sharp end **Note:** Prev. KM#706.

Date	Mintage	F	VF	XF	Unc	BU
VS1990 (1933)	—	0.75	1.50	3.00	5.00	—
VS1991 (1934)	—	0.75	1.50	3.00	5.00	—
VS1992 (1935)	—	0.75	1.50	3.00	5.00	—

KM# 706.2 PAISA

Copper, 23 mm. **Obv:** Footprints above crossed daggers within circle **Rev:** Right wreath with round end

Date	Mintage	VG	F	VF	XF	Unc
VS1993	—	—	0.75	1.50	3.00	5.00
VS1994	456,000	—	0.75	1.50	3.00	5.00
VS1995	—	—	0.75	1.50	3.00	5.00
VS1996	—	—	0.75	1.50	3.00	5.00

KM# 707 PAISA
Copper, 20 mm.

Date	Mintage	F	VF	XF	Unc	BU
VS2005 (1948)	—	0.75	1.25	1.75	2.50	—

KM# 707a PAISA
Brass, 20 mm. **Obv:** Footprints above crossed daggers within circle **Rev:** Crescent moon and star flank dagger at center

Date	Mintage	F	VF	XF	Unc	BU
VS2003 (1946)	—	0.30	0.50	0.75	1.00	—
VS2004 (1947)	—	3.00	5.00	7.00	10.00	—
VS2005 (1948)	—	0.30	0.50	0.75	1.00	—
VS2001 (1948)	—	0.30	0.50	0.75	1.00	—
VS2006 (1949)	—	0.60	1.00	1.25	1.75	—

KM# 709.1 2 PAISA
Copper, 27 mm. **Obv:** Footprints above crossed daggers within circle **Rev:** Crescent moon and star flank dagger ant center
Note: 2mm wide rim.

Date	Mintage	F	VF	XF	Unc	BU
VS1992 (1935)	—	1.00	2.00	3.00	5.00	—
VS1993 (1936)	473,000	1.00	2.00	3.00	5.00	—
VS1994 (1937)	1,133,000	1.00	2.00	3.00	5.00	—
VS1995 (1938)	—	1.00	2.00	3.00	5.00	—
VS1996 (1939)	—	1.00	2.00	3.00	5.00	—
VS1997 (1940)	—	1.00	2.00	3.00	5.00	—

KM# 709.2 2 PAISA
Copper, 25 mm. **Obv:** Footprints above crossed daggers within circle **Rev:** Crescent moon and star flank dagger at center
Note: Rim is 1mm wide or less.

Date	Mintage	F	VF	XF	Unc	BU
VS1992 (1935)	—	0.60	1.00	1.75	3.00	—
VS1993 (1936)	—	0.60	1.00	1.75	3.00	—
VS1994 (1937)	—	0.50	0.75	1.50	2.50	—
VS1995 (1938)	—	2.00	3.50	5.00	7.50	—
VS1996 (1939)	—	0.30	0.50	1.00	1.50	—
VS1997 (1940)	—	0.50	0.75	1.50	2.50	—
VS1998 (1941)	—	0.50	0.75	1.50	2.50	—
VS1999 (1942)	—	0.50	0.75	1.50	2.50	—

KM# 708 2 PAISA
Copper, 27 mm. **Obv:** Footprints above crossed daggers within circle **Rev:** Crescent moon and star flank trident at center

Date	Mintage	VG	F	VF	XF	Unc
VS1992 (1935)	—	3.00	5.00	8.50	13.50	—

KM# 710 2 PAISA
Copper, 23 mm. **Obv:** Footprints above crossed daggers within circle **Rev:** Crescent moon and star flank dagger at center

Date	Mintage	F	VF	XF	Unc	BU
VS1999 (1942)	—	0.30	0.50	1.00	2.00	—
VS2000 (1943)	—	0.30	0.50	1.00	2.00	—
VS2003 (1946)	—	0.30	0.50	1.00	2.00	—
VS2005 (1948)	—	3.00	5.00	7.00	10.00	—

KM# 710a 2 PAISA
Brass   **Obv:** Footprints above crossed daggers within circle **Rev:** Crescent moon and star flank dagger at center

Date	Mintage	F	VF	XF	Unc	BU
VS1999 (1942)	—	0.30	0.50	1.00	2.00	—
VS2000 (1943)	—	0.30	0.50	1.00	2.00	—
VS2001 (1944)	—	0.30	0.50	1.00	2.00	—
VS2005 (1948)	—	1.75	3.00	5.00	7.50	—
VS2008 (1951)	—	0.30	0.50	1.00	2.00	—
VS2009 (1952)	—	0.30	0.50	1.00	2.00	—
VS2010 (1953)	—	0.30	0.50	1.00	2.00	—

KM# 711 5 PAISA
Copper, 30 mm. **Obv:** Footprints above crossed daggers within circle **Rev:** Crescent moon and star flank trident at center

Date	Mintage	F	VF	XF	Unc	BU
VS1992 (1935)	—	1.50	3.00	4.50	6.50	—
VS1993 (1936)	878,000	1.50	3.00	4.50	6.50	—
VS1994 (1937)	403,000	1.50	3.00	4.50	6.50	—
VS1995 (1938)	—	1.00	2.00	3.00	6.50	—
VS1996 (1939)	—	1.50	3.00	4.50	6.50	—
VS1997 (1940)	—	1.50	3.00	4.50	6.50	—
VS1998 (1941)	—					

KM# 712 5 PAISA
Copper-Nickel-Zinc   **Obv:** Lamp within center circle
Rev: Crescent moon and star flank trident above inscription

Date	Mintage	F	VF	XF	Unc	BU
VS2000 (1943)	—	0.65	1.00	1.50	2.50	—
VS2009 (1952)	—	1.75	3.00	5.00	8.50	—
VS2010 (1953)	—	1.25	2.00	3.00	5.00	—

KM# 712a 5 PAISA
Copper-Nickel   **Obv:** Lamp within center circle
Rev. Insc.: Crescent moon and star flank trident above inscription

Date	Mintage	F	VF	XF	Unc	BU
VS2010 (1953)	—	0.65	1.00	1.50	2.50	—
Restrike						

KM# 714 20 PAISA
2.2161 g., 0.3330 Silver 0.0237 oz. ASW **Obv:** Trident
Rev: Dagger flanked by garlands from above

Date	Mintage	F	VF	XF	Unc	BU
VS1989 (1932)	—	2.25	4.00	5.00	6.50	
VS1991 (1934)	—	1.75	3.50	4.50	6.00	
VS1992 (1935)	—	1.75	3.50	4.50	6.00	
VS1993 (1936)	—	1.75	3.50	4.50	6.00	
VS1994 (1937)	—	3.75	6.50	10.00	15.00	
VS1995 (1938)	—	1.75	3.50	4.50	6.00	
VS1996 (1939)	—	1.75	3.50	4.50	6.00	
VS1997 (1940)	—	1.75	3.50	4.50	6.00	
VS1998 (1941)	—	1.75	3.50	4.50	6.00	
VS1999 (1942)	—	1.75	3.50	4.50	6.00	
VS2000 (1943)	—	1.75	3.50	4.50	6.00	
VS2001 (1944)	—	1.75	3.50	4.50	6.00	
VS2003 (1946)	—	1.75	3.50	4.50	6.00	
VS2004 (1947)	—	1.75	3.50	4.50	6.00	

KM# 715 20 PAISA
2.2161 g., 0.3330 Silver 0.0237 oz. ASW

Date	Mintage	F	VF	XF	Unc	BU
VS1989 (1932)	—	2.25	4.00	6.00	8.50	

Note: The date VS1989 is given in different style characters.
Refer to 50 Paisa KM#719 and 1 Rupee, KM#724 for style

KM# 716 20 PAISA
2.2161 g., 0.3330 Silver 0.0237 oz. ASW

Date	Mintage	F	VF	XF	Unc	BU
VS2006 (1949)	—	0.75	1.00	1.25	1.75	
VS2007 (1950)	—					
VS2009 (1952)	—	0.75	1.00	1.50	2.50	
VS2010 (1953)	—	0.75	1.00	1.50	2.50	

KM# 718 50 PAISA
5.5403 g., 0.8000 Silver 0.1425 oz. ASW **Obv:** Trident within small center circle **Rev:** Dagger flanked by garlands from above

Date	Mintage	F	VF	XF	Unc	BU
VS1989 (1932)	—	5.50	6.50	8.00	10.00	—
VS1991 (1934)	—	2.75	4.50	7.00	10.00	—
VS1992 (1935)	—	2.75	4.50	7.00	10.00	—
VS1993 (1936)	—	2.75	4.50	7.00	10.00	—
VS1994 (1937)	—	2.75	4.50	7.00	10.00	—
VS1995 (1938)	—	2.75	4.50	7.00	10.00	—
VS1996 (1939)	—	2.75	4.50	7.00	10.00	—
VS1997 (1940)	—	2.75	4.50	7.00	10.00	—
VS1998 (1941)	—	2.75	4.50	7.00	10.00	—
VS1999 (1942)	—	2.75	4.50	7.00	10.00	—
VS2000 (1943)	—	2.75	4.50	7.00	10.00	—
VS2001 (1944)	—	2.75	4.50	7.00	10.00	—
VS2003 (1946)	—	2.75	4.50	7.00	10.00	—
VS2004 (1947)	—	2.75	4.50	7.00	10.00	—
VS2005 (1948)	—	2.75	4.50	7.00	10.00	—

KM# 719 50 PAISA
5.5403 g., 0.8000 Silver 0.1425 oz. ASW **Obv:** Trident within small center circle **Rev:** Dagger flanked by garlands from above

Date	Mintage	F	VF	XF	Unc	BU
VS1989 (1932)	—	2.50	4.50	7.00	9.00	—

Note: The date is given in different style characters

KM# 720 50 PAISA
5.5403 g., 0.3330 Silver 0.0593 oz. ASW **Obv:** Four dots around trident **Rev:** Dagger flanked by garlands from above

Date	Mintage	F	VF	XF	Unc	BU
VS2005 (1948)	—	45.00	65.00	90.00	125	—

KM# 721 50 PAISA
5.5403 g., 0.3330 Silver 0.0593 oz. ASW **Obv:** Without dots around trident **Rev:** Dagger flanked by garlands from above

Date	Mintage	F	VF	XF	Unc	BU
VS2006 (1949)	—	1.50	2.00	2.75	4.50	—
VS2007 (1950)	—	1.50	2.00	2.75	4.50	—
VS2009/7 (1952)	—	1.50	2.25	3.00	5.00	—
VS2009 (1952)	—	1.50	2.00	2.75	4.50	—
VS2010 (1953)	—	1.50	2.00	2.75	4.50	—

KM# 713 1/16 RUPEE
Silver **Obv:** Inscription **Rev:** Inscription

Date	Mintage	F	VF	XF	Unc	BU
VS(19)96 (1939)	—	12.50	20.00	32.50	50.00	—

KM# 723 RUPEE

11.0806 g., 0.8000 Silver 0.2850 oz. ASW **Obv:** Trident within small center circle **Rev:** Dagger flanked by garlands from above

Date	Mintage	F	VF	XF	Unc	BU
VS1989 (1932)	—	4.50	6.00	8.00	20.00	—
VS1991 (1934)	—	4.50	6.00	8.00	16.50	—
VS1992 (1935)	—	4.50	6.00	8.00	16.50	—
VS1993 (1936)	1,717,000	4.50	6.00	8.00	16.50	—
VS1994 (1937)	2,097,000	4.50	6.00	8.00	16.50	—
VS1995 (1938)	—	4.50	6.00	8.00	16.50	—
VS1996 (1939)	—	4.50	6.00	8.00	16.50	—
VS1997 (1940)	—	4.50	6.00	8.00	16.50	—
VS1998 (1941)	—	4.50	6.00	8.00	16.50	—
VS1999 (1942)	—	4.50	6.00	8.00	16.50	—
VS2000 (1943)	—	4.50	6.00	8.00	16.50	—
VS2001 (1944)	—	4.50	6.00	8.00	16.50	—
VS2003 (1946)	—	4.50	6.00	8.00	16.50	—
VS2005 (1948)	—	4.50	6.00	8.00	16.50	—

KM# 724 RUPEE

11.0806 g., 0.8000 Silver 0.2850 oz. ASW **Obv:** Trident within small center circle **Rev:** Dagger flanked by garlands from above

Date	Mintage	F	VF	XF	Unc	BU
VS1989 (1932)	—	7.50	10.00	12.50	15.00	—

Note: The date is given in different style characters

KM# 725 RUPEE

11.0806 g., 0.3330 Silver 0.1186 oz. ASW **Obv:** Four dots around trident **Rev:** Dagger flanked by garlands from above

Date	Mintage	F	VF	XF	Unc	BU
VS2005 (1948)	—	5.00	7.50	10.00	13.50	—

KM# 726 RUPEE

11.0806 g., 0.3330 Silver 0.1186 oz. ASW **Obv:** Without dots around trident **Rev:** Dagger flanked by garlands from above

Date	Mintage	F	VF	XF	Unc	BU
VS2006 (1949)	—	2.50	3.50	5.00	7.50	—
VS2007 (1950)	—	2.50	3.50	5.00	7.50	—
VS2008 (1951)	—	2.50	3.50	5.00	7.50	—
VS2009 (1951)	—	2.50	3.50	5.00	7.50	—
VS2010 (1952)	—	2.50	3.50	5.00	7.50	—

ASARFI GOLD COINAGE
(Asarphi)

Fractional designations are approximate for this series. Actual Gold Weight (AGW) is used to identify each type.

KM# 741 1/2 ASARPHI

5.8000 g., Gold **Obv:** Head of Tribhuvan Bir Bikram right on 5-pointed star **Note:** Portrait type.

Date	Mintage	F	VF	XF	Unc	BU
VS2010 (1953)	—		145	165	185	—

Note: KM#741 is normally found as a restrike ca. 1968

ANONYMOUS COINAGE

KM# 733 PAISA

Brass, 18 mm. **Obv:** Sun rising above three hills within grain sprigs **Rev:** Dagger in front of hills within circle

Date	Mintage	F	VF	XF	Unc	BU
VS2010 (1953)	—	8.00	15.00	20.00	25.00	—
VS2011 (1954)	—	17.50	25.00	35.00	40.00	—
VS2012 (1955) Restrike	—	—	1.00	1.50	2.00	—

KM# 734 PAISA

Brass, 17.5 mm.

Date	Mintage	F	VF	XF	Unc	BU
VS2012 (1955)	—	1.25	2.00	2.50	3.50	—

KM# 735 2 PAISA

Brass, 21 mm. **Obv:** Sun rising above three hills within grain sprigs **Rev:** Dagger in front of hills within circle

Date	Mintage	F	VF	XF	Unc	BU
VS2010 (1953)	—	12.50	20.00	37.50	60.00	—
VS2011 (1954)	—	30.00	40.00	50.00	75.00	—
VS2011 (1954) Restrike	—	—	—	1.50	2.50	—

KM# 749 2 PAISA

Brass, 19.5 mm. **Obv:** Sun rising above three hills within grain sprigs **Rev:** Dagger in front of hills within circle

Date	Mintage	F	VF	XF	Unc	BU
VS2012 (1955)	—	0.30	0.50	0.75	1.50	—
VS2013 (1956)	—	0.30	0.50	0.75	1.50	—
VS2014 (1957)	—	0.30	0.50	0.75	1.50	—

KM# 754 4 PAISA

Brass **Obv:** Legend around center circle **Rev:** Date below center circle

Date	Mintage	F	VF	XF	Unc	BU
VS2012 (1955)	—	1.00	1.75	3.00	5.00	—

KM# 736 5 PAISA

3.8900 g., Bronze **Obv:** Sun rising above three hills within grain sprigs **Rev:** Hand divides date within decorative outline

Date	Mintage	F	VF	XF	Unc	BU
VS2010 (1953)	—	2.75	4.50	7.00	10.00	—
VS2011 (1954)	—	0.65	1.00	2.75	5.00	—
VS2012 (1955)	—	0.30	0.50	0.75	1.25	—
VS2013 (1956)	—	0.30	0.50	0.75	1.25	—
VS2014 (1957)	—	0.30	0.50	0.75	1.25	—

KM# 736a 5 PAISA

4.0400 g., Copper-Nickel **Obv:** Sun rising above three hills within grain sprigs **Rev:** Hand divides date within decorative outline

Date	Mintage	F	VF	XF	Unc	BU
VS2014 (1957)	—					—

KM# 737 10 PAISA

Bronze **Obv:** Sun rising above three hills within grain sprigs **Rev:** Dagger in front of three hills within circle

Date	Mintage	F	VF	XF	Unc	BU
VS2010 (1953)	—	2.75	4.50	7.00	10.00	—
VS2011 (1954)	—	0.15	0.25	0.50	1.00	—
VS2011 (1954) Restrike	—	—	—	0.15	0.25	—
VS2012 (1955)	—	0.15	0.25	0.50	1.00	—

KM# 738 20 PAISA

Copper-Nickel, 18 mm. **Obv:** Sun rising above three hills within grain sprigs **Rev:** Dagger in front of three hills within circle

Date	Mintage	F	VF	XF	Unc	BU
VS2010 (1953)	—	12.50	20.00	30.00	40.00	—
VS2010 (1953) Restrike	—	—	—	2.50	3.00	—
VS2011 (1954)	—	32.50	40.00	50.00	60.00	—

KM# 739 25 PAISA

Copper-Nickel, 19 mm. **Obv:** Sun rising above three hills within grain sprigs **Rev:** Dagger in front of three hills within circle

Date	Mintage	F	VF	XF	Unc	BU
VS2010 (1953)	—	2.00	3.50	4.50	6.00	—
VS2011 (1954)	—	2.00	3.50	4.50	6.00	—
VS2012 (1955)	—	1.25	2.00	2.50	3.50	—
VS2014 (1957)	—	1.25	2.00	2.50	3.50	—

KM# 768 1/5 ASARPHI

2.3300 g., Gold

Date	Mintage	F	VF	XF	Unc	BU
VS2010 (1953)	—	—	65.00	75.00	100	—

Note: Coins dated VS2010 are normally found as restrikes ca. 1968

VS2012 (1955).						

KM# 774 1/4 ASARPHI

2.9000 g., Gold

Date	Mintage	F	VF	XF	Unc	BU
VS2010 (1953)	—	—	75.00	85.00	95.00	125

Note: Coins dated VS2010 are normally found as restrikes ca. 1968

VS2012 (1955)						

Gyanendra Bir Bikram
VS2007 / 1950-51AD (first reign)

DECIMAL COINAGE
100 Paisa = 1 Rupee

KM# 729 50 PAISA

5.5403 g., 0.3330 Silver 0.0593 oz. ASW **Obv:** Trident within small center circle **Rev:** Dagger flanked by garlands from above

Date	Mintage	F	VF	XF	Unc	BU
VS2007 (1950)	26	—	175	275	350	—

KM# 731 MOHAR

Gold

Date	Mintage	F	VF	XF	Unc	BU
VS2007 (1950) Rare						

KM# 730   RUPEE
11.0806 g., 0.3330 Silver 0.1186 oz. ASW **Obv:** Trident within small center circle **Rev:** Dagger flanked by garlands from above

Date	Mintage	F	VF	XF	Unc	BU
VS2007 (1950)	—	4.50	6.50	9.00	15.00	—

KM# 732   TOLA
Gold

Date	Mintage	F	VF	XF	Unc	BU
VS2007 (1950) Rare	—	—	—	—	—	—

Trivhuvan Bir Bikram
VS2007-2011 / 1951-1955AD (second reign)

DECIMAL COINAGE
100 Paisa = 1 Rupee

KM# 740   50 PAISA
Copper-Nickel, 25 mm. **Obv:** Head of Tribhuvan Bir Bikram right on 5-pointed star **Rev:** Sun rising back of hills, grain sprigs flank

Date	Mintage	F	VF	XF	Unc	BU
VS2010 (1953)	—	0.50	1.00	2.00	4.00	—
VS2011 (1954)	—	0.35	0.75	1.50	3.00	—

KM# 742   RUPEE
Copper-Nickel **Obv:** Head of Tribhuvan Bir Bikram right on 5-pointed star **Note:** Equal denticles at rim.

Date	Mintage	F	VF	XF	Unc	BU
VS2010 (1953)	—	0.75	1.25	2.25	4.50	—
VS2011 (1954)	—	0.75	1.25	2.25	4.50	—

KM# 743   RUPEE
Copper-Nickel **Obv:** Head of Tribhuvan Bir Bikram right on 5-pointed star **Rev:** Sun rising back of hills, grain sprigs flank **Note:** Unequal denticles at rim.

Date	Mintage	F	VF	XF	Unc	BU
VS2011 (1954)	—	0.75	1.25	2.25	4.50	—

ASARFI GOLD COINAGE
(Asarphi)

Fractional designations are approximate for this series. Actual Gold Weight (AGW) is used to identify each type.

KM# 744   ASARPHI
11.6600 g., Gold **Obv:** Head of Tribhuvan Bir Bikram right on 5-pointed star

Date	Mintage	F	VF	XF	Unc	BU
VS2010 (1953)	—	—	300	325	350	—

Note: KM#744 normally found as a restrike ca. 1968

Mahendra Bir Bikram
VS2012-2028 / 1955-1971AD

DECIMAL COINAGE
100 Paisa = 1 Rupee

KM# 745.1   PAISA
Brass, 18 mm. **Subject:** Mahendra Coronation **Obv:** Crown **Rev:** Numeral at center, sprigs at sides **Note:** Prev. KM#745.

Date	Mintage	F	VF	XF	Unc	BU
VS2013 (1956) Narrow rim	—	0.30	0.50	0.75	1.00	—

KM# 746   PAISA
Brass, 16 mm. **Obv:** Crescent and star flank trident at center **Rev:** Numerals with shading

Date	Mintage	F	VF	XF	Unc	BU
VS2014 (1957)	—	0.10	0.15	0.25	0.40	—
VS2015 (1958)	—	0.10	0.15	0.25	0.40	—
VS2018 (1961)	—	0.10	0.15	0.25	0.40	—
VS2019 (1962)	—	0.10	0.15	0.25	0.40	—
VS2020 (1963)	—	0.10	0.15	0.25	0.40	—

KM# 745.2   PAISA
Brass **Subject:** Mahendra coronation

Date	Mintage	F	VF	XF	Unc	BU
VS2013 (1958) Wide rim	—	0.30	0.50	0.75	1.00	—

KM# 747   PAISA
1.4500 g., Brass, 16.5 mm. **Obv:** Crescent moon and star flank trident at center **Rev:** Numerals without shading

Date	Mintage	F	VF	XF	Unc	BU
VS2021 (1964)	—	0.10	0.15	0.20	0.30	—
VS2022 (1965)	—	0.10	0.15	0.25	0.40	—

KM# 748   PAISA
0.6100 g., Aluminum, 16.6 mm. **Obv:** Flower above hills **Rev:** National flower

Date	Mintage	F	VF	XF	Unc	BU
VS2023 (1966)	—	—	0.10	0.15	0.25	—
VS2025 (1968)	—	—	0.10	0.15	0.25	—
VS2026 (1969)	—	—	0.10	0.15	0.25	—
VS2027 (1970) Proof	2,187	Value: 1.25				
VS2028 (1971)	—	—	0.10	0.15	0.25	—
VS2028 (1971) Proof	2,380	Value: 1.25				

KM# 750.1   2 PAISA
Brass, 20.5 mm. **Subject:** Mahendra Coronation **Obv:** Crown **Rev:** Numeral at center **Note:** Narrow rim.

Date	Mintage	F	VF	XF	Unc	BU
VS2013 (1956)	—	0.30	0.50	0.75	1.00	—

KM# 750.2   2 PAISA
Brass **Subject:** Mahendra coronation **Obv:** Crown **Rev:** Numeral at center **Note:** Wide rim.

Date	Mintage	F	VF	XF	Unc	BU
VS2013 (1956)	—	0.30	0.50	0.75	1.00	—

KM# 751   2 PAISA
2.1600 g., Brass, 19.1 mm. **Obv:** Crescent moon and sun flank trident **Rev:** Numerals with shading

Date	Mintage	F	VF	XF	Unc	BU
VS2014 (1957)	—	0.10	0.15	0.25	0.40	—
VS2015 (1958)	—	0.10	0.15	0.25	0.40	—
VS2016 (1959)	—	0.10	0.15	0.25	0.40	—
VS2018 (1961)	—	0.10	0.15	0.25	0.40	—
VS2019 (1962)	—	0.10	0.15	0.25	0.40	—
VS2020 (1963)	—	0.10	0.15	0.25	0.40	—

KM# 752   2 PAISA
Brass **Obv:** Crescent moon and sun flank trident at center **Rev:** Numerals without shading

Date	Mintage	F	VF	XF	Unc	BU
VS2021 (1964)	—	0.10	0.15	0.20	0.35	—
VS2022 (1965)	—	0.10	0.15	0.25	0.50	—
VS2023 (1966)	—	0.10	0.15	0.25	0.50	—

KM# 753   2 PAISA
0.9100 g., Aluminum, 18.6 mm. **Obv:** Trident with sun and moon flanking above hills **Rev:** Himalayan Monal pheasant

Date	Mintage	F	VF	XF	Unc	BU
VS2023 (1966)	—	—	0.10	0.15	0.75	—
VS2024 (1967)	—	—	0.10	0.15	0.75	—
VS2025 (1968)	—	—	0.10	0.15	0.75	—
VS2026 (1969)	—	—	0.10	0.15	0.75	—
VS2027 (1970)	—	—	0.10	0.15	0.75	—
VS2027 (1970) Proof	2,187	Value: 1.50				
VS2028 (1971)	—	—	0.10	0.15	0.75	—
VS2028 (1971) Proof	2,380	Value: 1.50				

KM# 756.1   5 PAISA
Bronze, 22 mm. **Subject:** Mahendra Coronation **Obv:** Crown **Rev:** Numeral within floral outline **Note:** Wide rim with accent mark.

Date	Mintage	F	VF	XF	Unc	BU
VS2013 (1955)	—	10.00	20.00	30.00	40.00	—

KM# 756.2   5 PAISA
Bronze, 22 mm. **Subject:** Mahendra coronation **Obv:** Crown **Rev:** Numeral within floral outline **Note:** Narrow rim.

Date	Mintage	F	VF	XF	Unc	BU
VS2013 (1955) Restrike	—	0.35	0.60	1.00	1.50	—

KM# 756.3   5 PAISA
Bronze, 22 mm. **Subject:** Mahendra coronation **Obv:** Crown **Rev:** Numeral within floral outline **Note:** Without accent mark.

Date	Mintage	F	VF	XF	Unc	BU
VS2013 (1955)	—	1.00	2.00	3.00	5.00	—

KM# 757 5 PAISA
3.8500 g., Bronze, 22.5 mm. **Obv:** Trident at center
Rev: Numerals with shading

Date	Mintage	F	VF	XF	Unc	BU
VS2014 (1957)	—	0.10	0.20	0.30	0.75	—
VS2015 (1958)	—	0.10	0.20	0.30	0.75	—
VS2016 (1959)	—	0.10	0.30	0.50	1.00	—
VS2017 (1960)	—	0.10	0.20	0.30	0.75	—
VS2018 (1961)	—	0.10	0.20	0.30	0.75	—
VS2019 (1962)	—	0.10	0.20	0.30	0.75	—
VS2020 (1963)	—	0.10	0.20	0.30	0.75	—

KM# 758 5 PAISA
Aluminum-Bronze, 22.5 mm. **Obv:** Crescent moon and sun flank
trident at center **Rev:** Numerals without shading

Date	Mintage	F	VF	XF	Unc	BU
VS2021 (1964)	—	0.50	1.00	1.50	2.50	—

KM# 758a 5 PAISA
3.0800 g., Bronze, 21 mm. **Obv:** Crescent moon and sun flank
trident at center **Rev:** Numeral within shaded floral outline

Date	Mintage	F	VF	XF	Unc	BU
VS2021 (1964)	—	0.10	0.15	0.25	0.50	—
VS2022 (1965)	—	0.10	0.15	0.30	0.60	—
VS2023 (1966)	—	0.10	0.15	0.30	0.60	—

KM# 759 5 PAISA
Aluminum, 21 mm. **Obv:** Trident with sun and moon flanking
above hills **Rev:** Ox left

Date	Mintage	F	VF	XF	Unc	BU
VS2023 (1966)	—	—	0.15	0.25	1.00	—
VS2024 (1967)	—	—	0.10	0.20	1.00	—
VS2025 (1968)	—	—	0.10	0.20	1.00	—
VS2026 (1969)	—	—	0.10	0.20	1.00	—
VS2027 (1970)	—	—	0.10	0.20	1.00	—
VS2027 (1970) Proof	2,187	Value: 1.75				
VS2028 (1971)	—	—	0.10	0.20	1.00	—
VS2028 (1971) Proof	2,038	Value: 1.75				

KM# 761 10 PAISA
Bronze, 24.5 mm. **Subject:** Mahendra Coronation **Obv:** Crown
Rev: Shaded numeral

Date	Mintage	F	VF	XF	Unc	BU
VS2013 (1956)	—	0.25	0.50	0.75	1.50	—

KM# 762 10 PAISA
6.3000 g., Bronze, 25 mm. **Obv:** Crescent moon and sun flank
trident **Rev:** Numerals with shading

Date	Mintage	F	VF	XF	Unc	BU
VS2014 (1957)	—	2.75	4.50	7.00	10.00	—
VS2015 (1958)	—	0.15	0.25	0.50	0.75	—
VS2016 (1959)	—	3.00	5.00	7.00	10.00	—
VS2018 (1961)	—	0.15	0.25	0.50	0.75	—
VS2019 (1962)	—	0.15	0.25	0.50	0.75	—
VS2020 (1963)	—	0.15	0.25	0.50	0.75	—

KM# 763 10 PAISA
Aluminum-Bronze **Obv:** Crescent moon and sun flank trident at
center **Rev:** Numerals without shading

Date	Mintage	F	VF	XF	Unc	BU
VS2021 (1964)	—	0.75	1.25	2.00	3.00	—

KM# 764 10 PAISA
4.9300 g., Bronze, 25 mm. **Note:** Modified design.

Date	Mintage	F	VF	XF	Unc	BU
VS2021 (1964)	—	0.10	0.15	0.25	0.50	—
VS2022 (1965)	—	0.10	0.15	0.25	0.50	—
VS2023 (1966)	—	0.10	0.15	0.25	0.50	—

KM# 765 10 PAISA
Brass **Obv:** Trident with sun and moon flanking above hills
Rev: Ox left

Date	Mintage	F	VF	XF	Unc	BU
VS2023 (1966)	—	—	0.15	0.25	1.00	—
VS2024 (1967)	—	—	0.15	0.25	1.00	—
VS2025 (1968)	—	—	15.00	17.50	20.00	—
VS2026 (1969)	—	—	0.10	0.20	1.00	—
VS2027 (1970)	—	—	0.10	0.20	1.00	—
VS2027 (1970) Proof	2,187	Value: 2.00				
VS2028 (1971)	—	—	0.10	0.20	1.00	—
VS2028 (1971) Proof	2,380	Value: 2.00				

Note: Birendra Bir Bikram also struck a 10 Paisa VS2028,
see KM#806

KM# 766 10 PAISA
4.0600 g., Brass, 21 mm. **Series:** F.A.O. **Obv:** Grain sprig at
center **Rev:** Ox left

Date	Mintage	F	VF	XF	Unc	BU
VS2028 (1971)	1,500,000	—	0.10	0.20	1.00	—

KM# 770 25 PAISA
Copper-Nickel **Subject:** Mahendra Coronation

Date	Mintage	F	VF	XF	Unc	BU
VS2013 (1956)	—	0.30	0.50	0.70	1.00	—

KM# 771 25 PAISA
Copper-Nickel, 19 mm. **Obv:** Four characters in line above
trident **Rev:** Small character at bottom (outer circle)

Date	Mintage	F	VF	XF	Unc	BU
VS2015 (1958)	—	1.50	2.50	4.00	6.00	—
VS2018 (1961)	—	0.25	0.40	0.60	0.80	—

Date	Mintage	F	VF	XF	Unc	BU
VS2020 (1963)	—	0.25	0.40	0.60	0.80	—
VS2021 (1964)	—	0.30	0.50	0.75	1.00	—
VS2022 (1965)	—	2.00	3.50	6.00	9.00	—

KM# 771a 25 PAISA
2.9900 g., 840.0000 Silver 80.746 oz. ASW **Obv:** Trident within
small center circle **Rev:** Dagger flanked by garlands from above

Date	Mintage	F	VF	XF	Unc	BU
VS2017/6/5 (1960)	—	—	—	—	100	—

KM# 772 25 PAISA
3.0500 g., Copper-Nickel, 19 mm. **Obv:** Trident within small
center circle **Rev:** Large different character at bottom

Date	Mintage	F	VF	XF	Unc	BU
VS2021 (1964)	—	0.30	0.50	0.70	1.00	—
VS2022 (1965)	—	0.30	0.50	0.70	1.00	—
VS2023 (1966)	—	0.30	0.50	0.70	1.00	—

KM# 773 25 PAISA
Copper-Nickel **Obv:** Five characters in line above trident
Rev: Dagger flanked by garlands from above

Date	Mintage	F	VF	XF	Unc	BU
VS2024 (1967)	—	—	0.35	0.50	0.75	—
VS2025 (1968)	—	—	15.00	20.00	25.00	—
VS2026 (1969)	—	—	0.35	0.50	0.75	—
VS2027 (1970)	—	—	0.35	0.50	0.75	—
VS2027 (1970) Proof	2,187	Value: 2.50				
VS2028 (1971)	—	—	0.35	0.50	0.75	—
VS2028 (1971) Proof	2,380	Value: 2.50				
VS2030 (1973)	—	—	0.35	0.50	0.75	—

KM# 777 50 PAISA
Copper-Nickel, 25 mm. **Obv:** Trident within small center circle
Rev: Small character at bottom

Date	Mintage	F	VF	XF	Unc	BU
VS2011 (1954)	—	0.50	1.00	1.50	3.00	—
VS2012 (1955)	—	0.25	0.50	0.75	1.00	—
VS2013 (1956)	—	0.25	0.50	1.00	2.00	—
VS2014 (1957)	—	0.25	0.50	1.00	2.00	—
VS2015 (1958)	—	0.25	0.50	1.00	2.00	—
VS2016 (1959)	—	0.25	0.50	1.00	2.00	—
VS2017 (1960)	—	0.25	0.30	0.75	1.25	—
VS2018 (1961)	—	0.25	0.50	1.00	2.00	—
VS2020 (1963)	—	0.25	0.30	0.75	1.50	—

KM# 795 50 PAISA
Copper-Nickel **Obv:** Trident within small center circle
Rev: Dagger flanked by garlands from above **Note:** In the name
of "Queen Ratna Rajya Lakshmi".

Date	Mintage	F	VF	XF	Unc	BU
VS2012 (1955)	—	3,000	100	125	150	—

KM# 776   50 PAISA
Copper-Nickel   **Subject:** Mahendra Coronation **Obv:** Crown
Rev: Dagger flanked by garlands from above

Date	Mintage	F	VF	XF	Unc	BU
VS2013 (1956)	—	0.35	0.75	1.00	1.50	—

KM# 778   50 PAISA
Copper-Nickel, 25 mm.   **Obv:** Trident within small center circle
Rev: Large different character at bottom

Date	Mintage	F	VF	XF	Unc	BU
VS2021 (1964)	—	0.25	0.35	0.50	0.75	—
VS2022 (1965)	—	0.25	0.50	0.75	1.50	—
VS2023 (1966)	—	0.25	0.50	0.75	1.00	—

KM# 779   50 PAISA
Copper-Nickel   **Obv:** Four characters in line above trident
Rev: Dagger flanked by garlands from above **Note:** Reduced
size, 23.5mm.

Date	Mintage	F	VF	XF	Unc	BU
VS2023 (1966)	—	0.25	0.50	0.75	1.50	—

KM# 780   50 PAISA
Copper-Nickel   **Obv:** Five characters in line above trident
Rev: Dagger flanked by garlands from above

Date	Mintage	F	VF	XF	Unc	BU
VS2025 (1968)	—	—	0.30	0.50	1.00	—
VS2026 (1969)	—	—	0.30	0.50	0.85	—
VS2027 (1970) Proof	2,187	Value: 3.00				
VS2028 (1971) Proof	2,380	Value: 3.00				
VS2030 (1973)	—	—	0.30	0.50	0.85	—

KM# 784   RUPEE
Copper-Nickel, 30 mm.

Date	Mintage	F	VF	XF	Unc	BU
VS2011 (1954)	—	1.25	2.25	3.50	5.00	—
VS2012 (1955)	—	1.00	1.75	2.50	4.00	—

KM# 797   RUPEE
Copper-Nickel   **Obv:** Trident within center circle **Rev:** Dagger
flanked by garlands from above **Note:** In the name of "Queen
Ratna Rajya Lakshmi".

Date	Mintage	F	VF	XF	Unc	BU
VS2012 (1955)	2,000	—	100	150	175	—

KM# 785   RUPEE
Copper-Nickel, 28.5 mm.   **Obv:** Trident within center circle
Rev: Small character at bottom **Note:** Reduced size.

Date	Mintage	F	VF	XF	Unc	BU
VS2012 (1955)	—	0.50	0.85	1.25	1.75	—
VS2013 (1956)	—	0.50	0.85	1.25	1.75	—
VS2014 (1957)	—	0.50	0.85	1.25	1.75	—
VS2015 (1958)	—	0.50	0.85	1.25	1.75	—
VS2016 (1959)	—	0.50	0.85	1.25	1.75	—
VS2018 (1961)	—	0.50	0.85	1.25	1.75	—
VS2020 (1963)	—	0.50	0.85	1.25	1.75	—

KM# 790   RUPEE
Copper-Nickel   **Subject:** Mahendra Coronation **Obv:** Crown
Rev: Dagger flanked by garlands from above

Date	Mintage	F	VF	XF	Unc	BU
VS2013 (1956)	—	1.25	1.75	2.50	—	

KM# 786   RUPEE
Copper-Nickel, 28.5 mm.   **Obv:** Trident within center circle
Rev: Large character at bottom

Date	Mintage	F	VF	XF	Unc	BU
VS2021 (1964)	—	0.50	0.75	1.00	1.50	—
VS2022 (1965)	—	0.50	1.00	1.50	2.50	—
VS2023 (1966)	—	4.50	7.50	10.00	15.00	—

KM# 787   RUPEE
Copper-Nickel, 27 mm.   **Obv:** Four characters in line above
trident **Rev:** Dagger flanked by garlands from above
Note: Reduced size.

Date	Mintage	F	VF	XF	Unc	BU
VS2023 (1966)	—	0.75	1.00	1.35	2.00	—

KM# 788   RUPEE
Copper-Nickel   **Obv:** Five characters in line above trident **Rev:**
Dagger flanked by garlands from above

Date	Mintage	F	VF	XF	Unc	BU
VS2025 (1968)	—	—	1.00	1.50	2.00	—
VS2026 (1969)	—	—	1.00	1.40	2.00	—

Date	Mintage	F	VF	XF	Unc	BU
VS2027 (1970) Proof	2,187	Value: 4.50				
VS2028 (1971) Proof	2,380	Value: 4.50				

KM# 794   10 RUPEE
15.6000 g., 0.6000 Silver 0.3009 oz. ASW   **Series:** F.A.O.
Obv: Bust of Mahendra Bir Bikram left **Rev:** Trident and 1/2
cogwheel above grain sprig

Date	Mintage	F	VF	XF	Unc	BU
VS2025 (1968)	1,000,000	—	5.00	7.00	10.00	—

ASARFI GOLD COINAGE
(Asarphi)

Fractional designations are approximate for this series.
Actual Gold Weight (AGW) is used to identify each type.

KM# 767   1/6 ASARPHI
1.9000 g., Gold   **Subject:** Mahendra Coronation

Date	Mintage	F	VF	XF	Unc	BU
VS2013 (1956)	—	—	50.00	70.00	110	—

KM# 775   1/4 ASARPHI
2.5000 g., Gold   **Obv:** Trident within small circle at center
Rev: Dagger flanked by garlands from above **Note:** Reduced
weight.

Date	Mintage	F	VF	XF	Unc	BU
VS2026 (1969)	—	—	—	85.00	120	—

KM# 782   1/2 ASARPHI
5.8000 g., Gold   **Obv:** Trident within small circle at center
Rev: Dagger flanked by garlands from above

Date	Mintage	F	VF	XF	Unc	BU
VS2012 (1955)	—	—	150	170	200	—
VS2019 (1962)	—	—	150	170	200	—

KM# 796   1/2 ASARPHI
Gold   **Note:** In the name of "Queen Ratna Rajya Lakshmi".

Date	Mintage	F	VF	XF	Unc	BU
VS2012 (1955)	—	—	—	—	—	—

KM# 781   1/2 ASARPHI
5.8000 g., Gold   **Subject:** Mahendra Coronation

Date	Mintage	F	VF	XF	Unc	BU
VS2013 (1956)	—	—	150	170	200	—

KM# 783   1/2 ASARPHI
5.0000 g., Gold   **Subject:** Birendra Marriage

Date	Mintage	F	VF	XF	Unc	BU
VS2026 (1969)	—	—	—	160	190	—

KM# 789   ASARPHI
Gold   **Obv:** Trident within small center circle **Rev:** Dagger flanked
by garlands from above

Date	Mintage	F	VF	XF	Unc	BU
VS2012 (1955)	—	—	300	345	375	—
VS2019 (1962)	—	—	300	345	375	—

KM# 798   ASARPHI
11.6600 g., Gold   **Note:** In the name of "Queen Ratna Rajya
Lakshmi".

Date	Mintage	F	VF	XF	Unc	BU
VS2012 (1955)	—	—	300	345	375	—
VS2018 (1960)	—	—	300	345	375	—

KM# 791 ASARPHI

Gold **Subject:** Mahendra Coronation

Date	Mintage	F	VF	XF	Unc	BU
VS2013 (1956)	—	—	300	345	375	—

KM# 792 ASARPHI

10.0000 g., Gold **Obv:** Trident within small center circle
Rev: Dagger flanked by garlands from above

Date	Mintage	F	VF	XF	Unc	BU
VS2026 (1969)	—	—	300	335	365	—

KM# 793 2 ASARFI

Gold

Date	Mintage	F	VF	XF	Unc	BU
VS2012 (1955)	—	—	600	650	750	—

Birendra Bir Bikram
VS2028-2058 / 1971-2001 AD

DECIMAL COINAGE
100 Paisa = 1 Rupee

KM# 799 PAISA

Aluminum **Obv:** Trident with sun and moon flanking above hills
Rev: National flower

Date	Mintage	F	VF	XF	Unc	BU
VS2028 (1971)	10,000	—	0.20	0.30	0.40	—
VS2029 (1972)	3,036,000	—	0.10	0.15	0.25	—
VS2029 (1972) Proof	3,943	Value: 0.60				
VS2030 (1973)	1,279,000	—	0.10	0.15	0.25	—
VS2030 (1973) Proof	8,891	Value: 0.40				
VS2031 (1974)	430,000	—	0.10	0.15	0.25	—
VS2031 (1974) Proof	11,000	Value: 0.40				
VS2032 (1975)	324,000	—	0.10	0.15	0.25	—
VS2033 (1976)	217,000	—	—	0.10	0.25	—
VS2034 (1977)	1,040,000	—	0.10	0.15	0.25	—
VS2035 (1978)	394,000	—	0.10	0.15	0.25	—
VS2036 (1979)	—	—	0.10	0.15	0.25	—

KM# 800 PAISA

Aluminum **Subject:** Birendra Coronation **Obv:** Crown

Date	Mintage	F	VF	XF	Unc	BU
VS2031 (1974)	75,000	—	0.10	0.15	0.25	—

KM# 800a PAISA

Copper-Nickel **Subject:** Birendra Coronation **Obv:** Crown
Rev: Dagger flanked by garlands from above

Date	Mintage	F	VF	XF	Unc	BU
VS2031 (1974) Proof	1,000	Value: 2.50				

KM# 1012 PAISA

Aluminum **Obv:** Crown **Rev:** Value

Date	Mintage	F	VF	XF	Unc	BU
VS2039 (1982)	—	—	4.00	6.00	8.00	—
VS2040 (1983)	42,000	—	—	—	—	—

KM# 801 2 PAISA

Aluminum, 20 mm. **Obv:** Flower above hills with sun and moon
flanking **Rev:** Himalayan Monal pheasant

Date	Mintage	F	VF	XF	Unc	BU
VS2028 (1971)	8,319	—	0.20	0.30	0.75	—
VS2029 (1972)	5,206,000	—	0.10	0.15	0.75	—
VS2029 (1972) Proof	3,943	Value: 1.00				

Date	Mintage	F	VF	XF	Unc	BU
VS2030 (1973)	2,563,000	—	0.10	0.15	0.75	—
VS2030 (1973) Proof	8,891	Value: 0.75				
VS2031 (1974) Proof	11,000	Value: 0.75				
VS2033 (1976)	72,000	—	0.10	0.15	0.75	—
VS2035 (1978)	26,000	—	0.10	0.15	0.75	—

KM# 802 5 PAISA

1.1400 g., Aluminum, 20.5 mm. **Obv:** Trident with sun and moon
flanking above hills **Rev:** Ox left

Date	Mintage	F	VF	XF	Unc	BU
VS2028 (1971)	3,700,000	—	0.10	0.20	0.75	—
VS2029 (1972)	23,578,000	—	0.10	0.20	0.75	—
VS2029 (1972) Proof	3,943	Value: 1.00				
VS2030 (1973)	12,320,000	—	0.10	0.20	0.75	—
VS2030 (1973) Proof	8,891	Value: 1.00				
VS2031 (1974)	15,730,000	—	0.10	0.20	0.75	—
VS2031 (1974) Proof	11,000	Value: 1.00				
VS2032 (1975)	19,747,000	—	0.10	0.20	0.75	—
VS2033 (1976)	29,619,000	—	0.10	0.20	0.75	—
VS2034 (1977)	27,222,000	—	0.10	0.20	0.75	—
VS2035 (1978)	27,613,000	—	0.10	0.20	0.75	—
VS2036 (1979)	—	—	0.10	0.20	0.75	—
VS2037 (1980)	13,235,000	—	0.10	0.20	0.75	—
VS2038 (1981)	15,137,000	—	0.10	0.20	0.75	—
VS2039 (1982)	8,971,000	—	0.10	0.20	0.75	—

KM# 803 5 PAISA

1.2300 g., Aluminum, 21.0 mm. **Series:** F.A.O. **Obv:** Value

Date	Mintage	F	VF	XF	Unc	BU
VS2031 (1974)	4,584,000	—	0.10	0.15	0.25	—

KM# 804 5 PAISA

Aluminum **Subject:** Birendra Coronation **Obv:** Crown
Rev: Dagger flanked by garlands from above

Date	Mintage	F	VF	XF	Unc	BU
VS2031 (1974)	2,869,000	—	0.10	0.25	0.50	—

KM# 804a 5 PAISA

Copper-Nickel **Subject:** Birendra Coronation **Obv:** Crown
Rev: Dagger flanked by garlands from above

Date	Mintage	F	VF	XF	Unc	BU
VS2031 (1974) Proof	1,000	Value: 3.00				

KM# 1013 5 PAISA

0.8500 g., Aluminum, 18 mm. **Obv:** Crown **Rev:** Value

Date	Mintage	F	VF	XF	Unc	BU
VS2039 (1982)	8,971,000	—	7.00	10.00	15.00	—
VS2040 (1983)	6,430,000	—	—	0.10	0.25	—
VS2041 (1984)	9,634,000	—	—	0.10	0.25	—
VS2042 (1985)	58,000	—	—	0.10	0.25	—
VS2043 (1986)	2,937,000	—	—	0.10	0.25	—
VS2044 (1987)	3,126,000	—	—	0.10	0.25	—
VS2045 (1988)	1,030,000	—	—	0.10	0.25	—
VS2046 (1989)	—	—	—	0.10	0.25	—
VS2047 (1990)	—	—	—	0.10	0.25	—

KM# 806 10 PAISA

Brass **Obv:** Trident with sun and moon flanking above hills
Rev: Ox left

Date	Mintage	F	VF	XF	Unc	BU
VS2028 (1971)	5,035	—	—	—	1.50	—
In sets only						

Note: Mahendra Bir Bikram also struck a 10 Paisa VS2028,
see KM#765.

KM# 807 10 PAISA

4.1400 g., Brass, 21 mm. **Obv:** Trident with sun and moon
flanking above hills **Rev:** Value with grain sprigs at sides of coin

Date	Mintage	F	VF	XF	Unc	BU
VS2029 (1972)	3,297,000	—	0.15	0.25	0.40	—
VS2029 (1972) Proof	3,943	Value: 1.00				
VS2030 (1973)	5,670,000	—	0.15	0.25	0.40	—
VS2030 (1973) Proof	8,891	Value: 0.70				
VS2031 (1974) Proof	11,000	Value: 0.70				

KM# 808 10 PAISA

Aluminum **Subject:** Birendra Coronation **Obv:** Crown
Rev: Dagger flanked by garlands from above

Date	Mintage	F	VF	XF	Unc	BU
VS2031 (1974)	192,000	—	0.10	0.20	0.35	—

KM# 808a 10 PAISA

Copper-Nickel **Subject:** Birendra Coronation **Obv:** Crown
Rev: Dagger flanked by garlands from above

Date	Mintage	F	VF	XF	Unc	BU
VS2031 (1974) Proof	1,000	Value: 3.50				

KM# 809 10 PAISA

Brass **Series:** F.A.O. International Women's Year **Obv:** Busts
left **Rev:** Value within grain sprigs

Date	Mintage	F	VF	XF	Unc	BU
VS2032 (1975)	2,500,000	—	0.10	0.15	0.25	—

KM# 810 10 PAISA

Brass **Subject:** Agricultural Developement **Obv:** Crown
Rev: Value

Date	Mintage	F	VF	XF	Unc	BU
VS2033 (1976)	10,000,000	—	0.10	0.15	0.25	—

KM# 811 10 PAISA

Aluminum **Series:** International Year of the Child **Obv:** Trident
within small circle at center **Rev:** Symbol at center, rising sun
above

Date	Mintage	F	VF	XF	Unc	BU
VS2036 (1979)	213,000	—	0.10	0.15	0.25	—

KM# 812   10 PAISA
Aluminum **Subject:** Education for Village Women **Obv:** Trident within small circle at center **Rev:** Open book

Date	Mintage	F	VF	XF	Unc	BU
VS2036 (1979)	Inc. above	—	0.10	0.15	0.50	—

KM# 1014.1   10 PAISA
1.3000 g., Aluminum, 21.5 mm. **Obv:** Crown **Rev:** Large ears of grain

Date	Mintage	F	VF	XF	Unc	BU
VS2039 (1982)	796	—	7.00	10.00	15.00	—
VS2040 (1983)	—	—	—	0.10	0.30	—
VS2041 (1984)	7,834,000	—	—	0.10	0.30	—
VS2042 (1985)	99,000	—	—	0.10	0.30	—

KM# 1014.2   10 PAISA
1.3000 g., Aluminum, 21.5 mm. **Obv:** Crown **Rev:** Small ears of grain

Date	Mintage	F	VF	XF	Unc	BU
VS2041 (1984)	—	—	—	0.10	0.30	—
VS2042 (1985)	Inc. above	—	—	0.10	0.30	—
VS2043 (1986)	10,000	—	—	0.10	0.30	—
VS2044 (1987)	30,172,000	—	—	0.10	0.30	—
VS2045 (1988)	4,140,000	—	—	0.10	0.30	—
VS2046 (1989)	—	—	—	0.10	0.30	—
VS2047 (1990)	—	—	—	0.10	0.30	—
VS2048 (1991)	—	—	—	0.10	0.30	—
VS2049 (1992)	—	—	—	0.10	0.30	—
VS2050 (1993)	—	—	—	0.10	0.20	—

KM# 1014.3   10 PAISA
0.7200 g., Aluminum, 17 mm. **Obv:** Crown **Rev:** Value, grain ears flank **Edge:** Plain **Note:** Reduced size.

Date	Mintage	F	VF	XF	Unc	BU
VS2051 (1994)	—	—	—	0.10	0.30	—
VS2052 (1995)	—	—	—	0.10	0.30	—
VS2053 (1996)	—	—	—	0.10	0.30	—
VS2054 (1997)	—	—	—	0.10	0.30	—
VS2055 (1998)	—	—	—	0.10	0.30	—
VS2056 (1999)	—	—	—	0.10	0.30	—
VS2057 (2000)	—	—	—	0.10	0.30	—

KM# 813   20 PAISA
Brass **Series:** F.A.O. **Obv:** Trident within small circle at center

Date	Mintage	F	VF	XF	Unc	BU
VS2035 (1978)	234,000	—	0.35	0.75	1.00	—

KM# 814   20 PAISA
Brass **Series:** International Year of the Child **Obv:** Trident within small center circle **Rev:** Emblem below rising sun

Date	Mintage	F	VF	XF	Unc	BU
VS2036 (1979)	30,000	—	0.35	0.75	1.00	—

KM# 815   25 PAISA
3.0000 g., Copper-Nickel **Obv:** Trident within small center circle **Rev:** Dagger flanked by garlands from above **Note:** Varieties exist.

Date	Mintage	F	VF	XF	Unc	BU
VS2028 (1971)	5,691	—	0.40	0.60	0.80	—
VS2029 (1972) Proof	3,943	Value: 1.25				
VS2030 (1973)	8,676,000	—	0.30	0.40	0.50	—
VS2030 (1973) Proof	8,891	Value: 0.80				
VS2031 (1974)	1,172,000	—	0.35	0.50	0.75	—
VS2031 (1974) Proof	11,900	Value: 0.80				
VS2032 (1975)	4,584,000	—	0.30	0.40	0.50	—
VS2033 (1976)	1,837,000	—	0.30	0.40	0.50	—
VS2034 (1977)	3,808,000	—	0.30	0.40	0.50	—
VS2035 (1978)	5,964,000	—	0.30	0.40	0.50	—
VS2036 (1979)	—	—	0.30	0.40	0.50	—
VS2037 (1980)	2,047,000	—	0.30	0.40	0.50	—
VS2038 (1981)	1,580,000	—	0.30	0.40	0.50	—
VS2039 (1982)	7,185,000	—	0.30	0.40	0.50	—

KM# 816.1   25 PAISA
2.9300 g., Copper-Nickel, 18.8 mm. **Subject:** Birendra Coronation **Obv:** Crown **Rev:** Dagger flanked by garlands from above

Date	Mintage	F	VF	XF	Unc	BU
VS2031 (1974)	431,000	—	0.35	0.50	0.75	—

KM# 816.2   25 PAISA
Copper-Nickel **Subject:** Birendra Coronation **Obv:** Crown **Rev:** Dagger flanked by garlands from above **Edge:** Reeded

Date	Mintage	F	VF	XF	Unc	BU
VS2031 (1974) Proof	1,000	Value: 4.00				

KM# 817   25 PAISA
Brass **Series:** World Food Day **Obv:** Trident within small center circle **Rev:** Corn ear at left, logo at right

Date	Mintage	F	VF	XF	Unc	BU
VS2038 (1981)	2,000,000	—	—	0.10	0.30	—

KM# 818   25 PAISA
Brass **Series:** International Year of Disabled Persons **Obv:** Trident within small center circle **Rev:** Emblem at center

Date	Mintage	F	VF	XF	Unc	BU
VS2038 (1981)	Inc. above	—	0.10	0.25	0.50	—

KM# 1015.1   25 PAISA
1.8000 g., Aluminum, 24.5 mm. **Obv:** Crown **Rev:** Value flanked by grain ears

Date	Mintage	F	VF	XF	Unc	BU
VS2039 (1982)	—	—	4.00	6.00	8.00	—
VS2040 (1983)	7,603,000	—	0.10	0.25	0.50	—
VS2041 (1984)	15,534,000	—	0.10	0.25	0.50	—
VS2042 (1985)	12,586,000	—	0.10	0.25	0.50	—
VS2043 (1986)	54,000	—	0.10	0.25	0.50	—
VS2044 (1987)	13,633,000	—	0.10	0.25	0.50	—
VS2045 (1988)	13,046,000	—	0.10	0.25	0.50	—
VS2046 (1989)	—	—	0.10	0.25	0.50	—
VS2047 (1990)	—	—	0.10	0.25	0.50	—
VS2048 (1991)	—	—	0.10	0.25	0.50	—

Date	Mintage	F	VF	XF	Unc	BU
VS2049 (1992)	—	—	0.10	0.25	0.50	—
VS2050 (1993)	—	—	0.10	0.25	0.50	—

KM# 1015.2   25 PAISA
1.5000 g., Aluminum, 20 mm. **Obv:** Crown **Rev:** Value flanked by grain ears **Edge:** Plain **Note:** Reduced size.

Date	Mintage	F	VF	XF	Unc	BU
VS2051 (1994)	—	—	0.10	0.25	0.50	—
VS2052 (1995)	—	—	0.10	0.25	0.50	—
VS2053 (1996)	—	—	0.10	0.25	0.50	—
VS2054 (1997)	—	—	0.10	0.25	0.50	—
VS2055 (1998)	—	—	0.10	0.25	0.50	—
VS2056 (1999)	—	—	0.10	0.25	0.50	—
VS2057 (2000)	—	—	0.10	0.25	0.50	—

KM# 821   50 PAISA
5.0000 g., Copper-Nickel, 23.5 mm. **Obv:** Trident within small center circle **Rev:** Dagger flanked by garlands from above

Date	Mintage	F	VF	XF	Unc	BU
VS2028 (1971)	5,343	—	0.35	0.50	1.00	—
VS2029 (1972)	347,000	—	0.35	0.50	0.90	—
VS2029 (1972) Proof	3,943	Value: 1.50				
VS2030 (1973)	998,000	—	0.35	0.50	0.90	—
VS2030 (1973) Proof	8,891	Value: 1.00				
VS2031 (1974)	16,000	—	0.35	0.50	1.00	—
VS2031 (1974) Proof	11,900	Value: 1.00				
VS2032 (1975)	227,000	—	0.35	0.50	0.90	—

Note: Dot in moon on reverse

Date	Mintage	F	VF	XF	Unc	BU
VS2033 (1976)	3,446,000	—	0.35	0.50	0.75	—
VS2034 (1977)	6,016,000	—	0.35	0.50	0.75	—
VS2035 (1978)	2,355,000	—	0.35	0.50	0.75	—
VS2036 (1979)	—	—	0.35	0.50	0.75	—
VS2037 (1980)	4,861,000	—	0.35	0.50	0.75	—
VS2038 (1981)	929,000	—	0.35	0.50	0.75	—
VS2039 (1982)	2,954,000	—	0.35	0.50	0.75	—

KM# 821a   50 PAISA
5.0900 g., Copper-Nickel, 20 mm. **Obv:** Trident within small center circle **Rev:** Dagger flanked by garlands from above

Date	Mintage	F	VF	XF	Unc	BU
VS2039 (1971)	Inc. above	—	0.10	0.25	0.50	—
VS2040 (1983)	72,000	—	0.10	0.25	0.50	—
VS2041 (1984)	5,917,000	—	0.10	0.25	0.50	—

KM# 822.1   50 PAISA
Copper-Nickel **Subject:** Birendra Coronation **Obv:** Crown **Rev:** Dagger flanked by garlands from above **Note:** 1mm thick.

Date	Mintage	F	VF	XF	Unc	BU
VS2031 (1974)	136,000	—	0.50	0.75	1.25	—

KM# 822.2   50 PAISA
Copper-Nickel **Subject:** Birendra Coronation **Edge:** Reeded **Note:** 1.5mm thick.

Date	Mintage	F	VF	XF	Unc	BU
VS2031 (1974) Proof	1,000	Value: 5.00				

KM# 846   50 PAISA
4.9000 g., Copper-Nickel, 23.56 mm. **Obv:** Trident within small center circle **Rev:** Dagger flanked by garlands from above **Note:** In the name of Queen Aishvarya Rajya Lakshmi

Date	Mintage	F	VF	XF	Unc	BU
VS2031 (1974)	—	—	—	—	1.00	—

KM# 823   50 PAISA
Copper-Nickel   Series: World Food Day   Obv: Trident within small center circle   Rev: Corn ear at left, logo at right

Date	Mintage	F	VF	XF	Unc	BU
VS2038 (1981)	2,000,000	—	0.10	0.30	0.60	—

KM# 824   50 PAISA
Copper-Nickel   Series: International Year of Disabled Persons   Obv: Trident within small center circle   Rev: Emblem at center

Date	Mintage	F	VF	XF	Unc	BU
VS2038 (1981)	Inc. above	—	0.50	0.75	1.25	—

KM# 1016   50 PAISA
3.0000 g., Copper-Nickel, 20 mm.   Subject: Family Planning   Obv: Logo above inscription   Rev: Value

Date	Mintage	F	VF	XF	Unc	BU
VS2041 (1984)	—	—	0.10	0.25	0.50	—

KM# 1018   50 PAISA
Stainless Steel, 23.5 mm.   Obv: Small trident in center   Rev: Dagger flanked by garlands from above

Date	Mintage	F	VF	XF	Unc	BU
VS2044 (1987)	6,341,000	—	0.10	0.25	0.50	—
VS2045 (1988)	7,350,000	—	0.10	0.25	0.50	—

Note: Varieties with small and large Nepalese "5" exist

| VS2046 (1989) | — | — | 0.10 | 0.25 | 0.50 | — |

KM# 1072   50 PAISA
1.4100 g., Aluminum, 22.5 mm.   Obv: Royal crown   Rev: Crown   Edge: Plain   Note: Coins dated VS2051 exist in two minor varieties being struck at Kathmandu (round edge) and Singapore (sharp edge).

Date	Mintage	F	VF	XF	Unc	BU
VS2051 (1994)	—	—	0.10	0.20	0.40	—
VS2052 (1995)	—	—	0.10	0.20	0.40	—
VS2053 (1996)	—	—	0.10	0.20	0.40	—
VS2054 (1997)	—	—	0.10	0.20	0.40	—
VS2055 (1998)	—	—	0.10	0.20	0.40	—
VS2056 (1999)	—	—	0.10	0.20	0.40	—
VS2057 (2000)	—	—	0.10	0.20	0.40	—

KM# 828.1   RUPEE
10.2000 g., Copper-Nickel   Obv: Trident within small center circle   Rev: Dagger flanked by garlands from above

Date	Mintage	F	VF	XF	Unc	BU
VS2028 (1971)	5,030	—	0.50	1.00	2.00	—
VS2029 (1972)	22,000	—	0.50	1.00	1.50	—
VS2029 (1972) Proof	3,943	Value: 2.50				
VS2030 (1973)	5,667	—	0.50	1.00	2.00	—
VS2030 (1973) Proof	8,891	Value: 2.00				
VS2031 (1974) Proof	11,000	Value: 1.50				

KM# 829.1   RUPEE
Copper-Nickel   Subject: Birendra Coronation   Obv: Crown at center of ornamental frame   Rev: Dagger flanked by garlands from above   Note: 2 millimeters thick.

Date	Mintage	F	VF	XF	Unc	BU
VS2031 (1973)	—	—	0.75	1.25	1.75	—

KM# 829.2   RUPEE
Copper-Nickel   Subject: Birendra Coronation   Obv: Crown at center of ornamental frame   Rev: Dagger flanked by garlands from above   Edge: Reeded   Note: 2.5 millimeters thick.

Date	Mintage	F	VF	XF	Unc	BU
VS2031 (1973) Proof	1,000	Value: 6.00				

KM# 848   RUPEE
Copper-Nickel   Obv: Trident within small circle at center   Rev: Dagger flanked by garlands from above   Note: In the name of Queen Aishvarya Rajya Lakshmi.

Date	Mintage	F	VF	XF	Unc	BU
VS2031 (1974)	—	—	—	—	150	—

KM# 831   RUPEE
Copper-Nickel   Series: F.A.O. International Women's Year   Obv: Busts left   Rev: Value above logo, grain ears flank

Date	Mintage	F	VF	XF	Unc	BU
VS2032 (1975)	1,500,000	—	0.25	0.50	1.25	—

KM# 828a   RUPEE
7.5000 g., Copper-Nickel, 27.5 mm.   Note: Reduced weight. Coins dated VS2036 were struck at the Canberra Mint and have a very shiny surface. High quality examples of VS2034 were struck at Canberra Mint while dull surfaced examples were probably struck at Kathmandu Mint.

Date	Mintage	F	VF	XF	Unc	BU
VS2033 (1976)	58,000	—	0.50	1.00	1.50	—
VS2034 (1977)	30,000,000	—	0.25	0.50	1.00	—
VS2035 (1978)	—	—	0.25	0.50	1.00	—
VS2036 (1979)	30,000,000	—	0.25	0.50	1.00	—

KM# 828.2   RUPEE
Copper-Nickel   Note: Reduced size: 23mm. Like 821a.

Date	Mintage	F	VF	XF	Unc	BU
VS2039 (1982)	—	—	0.25	0.50		

KM# 1019   RUPEE
Copper-Nickel   Subject: Family Planning   Obv: Logo at center within design   Rev: Value

Date	Mintage	F	VF	XF	Unc	BU
VS2041 (1984)	21,000	—	—	—	0.75	—

KM# 1061   RUPEE
6.7500 g., Stainless Steel   Obv: Small trident in center   Rev: Dagger flanked by garlands from above

Date	Mintage	F	VF	XF	Unc	BU
VS2045 (1988) Prooflike	—	—	0.25	0.50	1.00	—
VS2048 (1991) Prooflike	—	—	0.25	0.50	1.00	—
Note: Varieties exist						
VS2049 (1992) Prooflike	—	—	0.25	0.50	1.25	—

KM# 1073   RUPEE
3.5000 g., Brass Plated Steel, 22 mm.   Obv: Small trident at center   Rev: Large legends   Edge: Plain   Note: Sharp and round edge varieties.

Date	Mintage	F	VF	XF	Unc	BU
VS2051 (1994)	—	—	0.25	0.50	1.00	—
VS2052 (1995)	—	—	0.25	0.50	1.00	—

KM# 1152   RUPEE
28.1600 g., 0.9990 Copper-Nickel 0.9044 oz., 38.5 mm.   Subject: UN 50th Anniversary   Obv: Traditional design   Rev: UN 50 logo   Edge: Reeded

Date	Mintage	F	VF	XF	Unc	BU
VS2052 (1995)	—	—	—	—	—	8.00

KM# 1073a   RUPEE
4.0800 g., Brass, 20 mm.   Obv: Traditional design   Rev: Small legends

Date	Mintage	F	VF	XF	Unc	BU
VS2052 (1995)	—	—	—	—	1.00	—
VS2053 (1996)	—	—	—	—	1.00	—

Date	Mintage	F	VF	XF	Unc	BU
VS2054 (1997)	—	—	—	—	1.00	—
VS2055 (1998)	—	—	—	—	1.00	—
VS2056 (1999)	—	—	—	—	1.00	—
VS2057 (2000)	—	—	—	—	1.00	—

KM# 1092 RUPEE
Brass Plated Steel, 22 mm. **Series:** U.N. 50th Anniversary **Obv:** Traditional design **Rev:** UN logo and dates

Date	Mintage	F	VF	XF	Unc	BU
VS2052 (1995)	—	—	—	—	1.75	—

KM# 1115 RUPEE
Brass, 20 mm. **Subject:** Visit Nepal '98 **Obv:** Traditional design **Rev:** Moon and sun flanking mountaintop

Date	Mintage	F	VF	XF	Unc	BU
VS2054 (1997)	—	—	—	—	1.00	—

KM# 1139 RUPEE
Brass, 20 mm. **Subject:** Gorkhapatra Centenary **Obv:** Traditional design **Rev:** Inscription within wreath of ten people reading newspapers **Rev. Insc.:** "Gorkhapata 1958-VS2057"

Date	Mintage	F	VF	XF	Unc	BU
VS2057 (2000)	—	—	—	—	1.00	—

KM# 832 2 RUPEES
Copper-Nickel **Series:** World Food Day **Obv:** Trident within circle at center **Rev:** Corn ear at left, logo at right

Date	Mintage	F	VF	XF	Unc	BU
VS2038 (1981)	1,000,000	—	0.50	0.75	1.50	—

KM# 1025 2 RUPEES
Copper-Nickel **Series:** F.A.O. **Obv:** Traditional design **Note:** Size of obverse square varies. With or without dot in reverse sun.

Date	Mintage	F	VF	XF	Unc	BU
VS2039 (1982)	366,000	—	0.50	0.75	1.50	—

KM# 1020 2 RUPEES
Copper-Nickel **Subject:** Family Planning **Obv:** Emblem within decorative outlines **Rev:** Value

Date	Mintage	F	VF	XF	Unc	BU
VS2041 (1984)	11,000	—	0.50	0.75	1.50	—

KM# 1074.1 2 RUPEES
4.9600 g., Brass Plated Steel, 24.4 mm. **Obv:** Small trident at center **Rev:** Building above value **Edge:** Plain **Note:** Sharp and round edge varieties exist.

Date	Mintage	F	VF	XF	Unc	BU
VS2051 (1994)	—	—	0.35	0.60	1.25	—
VS2052 (1995)	—	—	0.35	0.60	1.25	—

KM# 1074.2 2 RUPEES
Brass, 25 mm.

Date	Mintage	F	VF	XF	Unc	BU
VS2053 (1996)	—	—	0.35	0.60	1.25	—
VS2055 (1998)	—	—	0.35	0.60	1.25	—
VS2056 (1999)	—	—	0.35	0.60	1.25	—
VS2057 (2000)	—	—	0.35	0.60	1.25	—

KM# 1116 2 RUPEES
Brass, 25 mm. **Subject:** Visit Nepal '98 **Obv:** Traditional design **Rev:** Moon and sun flanking mountaintop

Date	Mintage	F	VF	XF	Unc	BU
VS2053 (1996)	—	—	—	—	1.25	—
VS2054 (1997)	—	—	—	—	1.25	—

KM# 833 5 RUPEE
Copper-Nickel **Subject:** Rural Women's Advancement **Obv:** Trident within small circle at center

Date	Mintage	F	VF	XF	Unc	BU
VS2037 (1980)	50,000	—	0.75	1.50	3.00	—

KM# 834 5 RUPEE
Copper-Nickel, 28.7-30.0 mm. **Subject:** National Bank Silver Jubilee **Obv:** Trident within small circle at center **Rev:** Small figurine of native god at center **Note:** Size varies.

Date	Mintage	F	VF	XF	Unc	BU
VS2038 (1981)	64,000	—	0.75	1.50	3.00	—

KM# 1009 5 RUPEE
Copper-Nickel **Obv:** Traditional design **Rev:** Dagger flanked by garlands from above **Note:** Circulation coinage

Date	Mintage	F	VF	XF	Unc	BU
VS2039 (1982)	Inc. above	—	0.50	1.00	2.00	—
VS2040 (1983)	478,000	—	0.30	0.50	1.00	—

KM# 1017 5 RUPEE
Copper-Nickel **Subject:** Family Planning **Obv:** Value **Rev:** Logo above inscription

Date	Mintage	F	VF	XF	Unc	BU
VS2041 (1984)	458,000	—	0.50	1.00	2.00	—

KM# 1023 5 RUPEE
Copper-Nickel **Subject:** Year of Youth **Obv:** Value **Rev:** Emblem below hills

Date	Mintage	F	VF	XF	Unc	BU
VS2042 (1985)	1,124,000	—	—	—	2.50	—

KM# 1047 5 RUPEE
Copper-Nickel **Subject:** Social Services **Obv:** Value **Rev:** Ox left within small center circle

Date	Mintage	F	VF	XF	Unc	BU
VS2042 (1985)	Inc. above	—	—	—	3.50	—

KM# 1028 5 RUPEE
Copper-Nickel **Series:** World Food Day **Obv:** Traditional design **Rev:** Fish left below logo

Date	Mintage	F	VF	XF	Unc	BU
VS2043 (1986)	99,000	—	—	—	3.50	—

KM# 1042 5 RUPEE
Copper-Nickel **Subject:** 15th World Buddhist Conference **Obv:** Value **Rev:** Figure at center of globe within ornamented circle **Note:** Two different obverse dies exist.

Date	Mintage	F	VF	XF	Unc	BU
VS2043//1986	135,000	—	—	—	3.50	—

KM# 1030 5 RUPEE
Copper-Nickel **Subject:** 10th Year of National Social Security Administration **Obv:** Traditional design **Rev:** Emblem at center

Date	Mintage	F	VF	XF	Unc	BU
VS2044 (1987)	104,000	—	—	—	3.50	—
VS2045 (1988)	—	—	—	—	3.50	—

KM# 1043 5 RUPEE
Copper **Subject:** 3rd SAARC Summit **Obv:** Traditional design **Rev:** Summit emblem

Date	Mintage	F	VF	XF	Unc	BU
VS2044 (1987)	2,000	—	—	—	6.50	—

KM# 1053 5 RUPEE
Copper-Nickel **Series:** World Food Day **Obv:** Traditional design **Rev:** Emblem above symbols

Date	Mintage	F	VF	XF	Unc	BU
VS2047 (1990)	—	—	—	—	4.00	—

KM# 1063 5 RUPEE
Copper-Nickel **Subject:** New Constitution **Obv:** Traditional design **Rev:** Flags above open book

Date	Mintage	F	VF	XF	Unc	BU
VS2047 (1990)	—	—	—	—	3.25	—

KM# 1062 5 RUPEE
Copper-Nickel **Subject:** Parliament Session **Obv:** Traditional design **Rev:** Outlined drawings symbolizing figures of parliament

Date	Mintage	F	VF	XF	Unc	BU
VS2048 (1991)	—	—	—	—	3.00	—

KM# 1075.1 5 RUPEE
6.5200 g., Brass Plated Steel, 27 mm. **Obv:** Traditional design **Rev:** Temple **Edge:** Plain

Date	Mintage	F	VF	XF	Unc	BU
VS2051 (1994)	—	—	—	—	1.50	—

KM# 1075.2 5 RUPEE
Brass, 25 mm. **Edge:** Reeded

Date	Mintage	F	VF	XF	Unc	BU
VS2053 (1996)	—	—	—	—	1.50	—

KM# 1117 5 RUPEE
Copper, 25 mm. **Subject:** Visit Nepal '98 **Obv:** Traditional design **Rev:** Sun and moon flanking mountaintop **Edge:** Reeded

Date	Mintage	F	VF	XF	Unc	BU
VS2054 (1997)	—	—	—	—	1.50	—

KM# 835 10 RUPEE
8.0000 g., 0.2500 Silver 0.0643 oz. ASW **Series:** F.A.O. **Obv:** Value and dates **Rev:** Family scene

Date	Mintage	F	VF	XF	Unc	BU
VS2031 (1974)	39,000	—	—	4.00	6.00	—

KM# 1004 10 RUPEE
Copper-Nickel, 40 mm. **Subject:** 30th Anniversary - Ascent of Mt. Everest **Obv:** Traditional design **Rev:** Mount Everest

Date	Mintage	F	VF	XF	Unc	BU
VS2040 (1983)	2,000	—	—	—	12.50	—

KM# 1076 10 RUPEE
8.0000 g., Brass Plated Steel, 29 mm. **Obv:** Traditional design **Rev:** Closed book

Date	Mintage	F	VF	XF	Unc	BU
VS2051 (1994)	—	—	—	—	2.50	—

KM# 1083 10 RUPEE
Copper-Nickel **Subject:** 75th Anniversary - International Labor Organization **Obv:** Traditional design **Rev:** Logo above legend

Date	Mintage	F	VF	XF	Unc	BU
VS2051 (1994)	—	—	—	—	4.50	—

KM# 1089 10 RUPEE
Copper-Nickel **Subject:** 50th Anniversary - F.A.O. Logo **Obv:** Traditional design **Rev:** Logo with grain ears flanking

Date	Mintage	F	VF	XF	Unc	BU
VS2052 (1995)	—	—	—	—	4.00	—

KM# 1118 10 RUPEE
Copper-Nickel, 25 mm. **Subject:** Visit Nepal '98 **Obv:** Traditional design **Rev:** Moon and sun flanking mountaintop **Edge:** Reeded

Date	Mintage	F	VF	XF	Unc	BU
VS2054 (1997)	—	—	—	—	3.00	—

KM# 836 20 RUPEE
14.8500 g., 0.5000 Silver 0.2387 oz. ASW **Series:** F.A.O. International Women's Year **Obv:** Busts left **Rev:** Value within grain sprigs

Date	Mintage	F	VF	XF	Unc	BU
VS2032 (1975)	50,000	—	—	4.50	7.50	—

KM# 837 20 RUPEE
14.8500 g., 0.2500 Silver 0.1194 oz. ASW **Series:** International Year of the Child **Obv:** Trident within small circle at center **Rev:** Emblem below rising sun

Date	Mintage	F	VF	XF	Unc	BU
VS2036 (1979)	—	—	—	4.00	6.00	—

KM# 837a 20 RUPEE
15.0000 g., 0.9250 Silver 0.4461 oz. ASW **Obv:** Trident within small circle at center **Rev:** Emblem below rising sun

Date	Mintage	F	VF	XF	Unc	BU
VS2036 (1979)	1,000	Value: 27.50				
Proof						

KM# 1048.1 25 RUPEE
12.0000 g., 0.2500 Silver 0.0964 oz. ASW **Subject:** 25th Anniversary of Panchayat **Obv:** Thin 25 **Rev:** Small rosette **Note:** Varieties exist with hollow or solid hand-like symbol below on obverse.

Date	Mintage	F	VF	XF	Unc	BU
VS2042 (1985)	9,962,000	—	—	—	10.00	—

KM# 1048.2 25 RUPEE
12.0000 g., 0.2500 Silver 0.0964 oz. ASW **Subject:** 25th Anniversary of Panchayat **Obv:** Thick 25 **Rev:** Large rosette **Note:** Varieties exist with hollow or solid hand-like symbol below on obverse.

Date	Mintage	F	VF	XF	Unc	BU
VS2042 (1985)	Inc. above	—	—	—	10.00	—

KM# 839 25 RUPEE
25.6000 g., 0.5000 Silver 0.4115 oz. ASW **Series:** Conservation **Obv:** Bust of Birendra Bir Bikram right **Rev:** Himalayan Monal Pheasant

Date	Mintage	F	VF	XF	Unc	BU
VS2031 (1974)	11,000	—	—	8.50	20.00	—

KM# 839a 25 RUPEE
28.2800 g., 0.9250 Silver 0.8410 oz. ASW **Obv:** Bust of Birendra Bir Bikram right **Rev:** Himalayan Monal Pheasant

Date	Mintage	F	VF	XF	Unc	BU
VS2031 (1974) Proof	11,000	Value: 24.00				

KM# 842 50 RUPEE
25.0000 g., 0.5000 Silver 0.4019 oz. ASW **Subject:** Education for Village Women **Obv:** Traditional design **Rev:** Open book

Date	Mintage	F	VF	XF	Unc	BU
VS2036 (1979)	15,000	—	—	—	12.50	—

KM# 842a 50 RUPEE
25.0000 g., 0.9250 Silver 0.7435 oz. ASW **Obv:** Traditional design **Rev:** Open book

Date	Mintage	F	VF	XF	Unc	BU
VS2036 (1979) Proof	1,000	Value: 40.00				

KM# 838 25 RUPEE
25.6000 g., 0.5000 Silver 0.4115 oz. ASW **Subject:** Birendra Coronation **Obv:** Crown **Rev:** Dagger flanked by garlands from above **Edge:** Reeded **Note:** 2mm thick.

Date	Mintage	F	VF	XF	Unc	BU
VS2031 (1974)	75,000	—	—	7.00	10.00	—

KM# 838a 25 RUPEE
28.2800 g., 0.9250 Silver 0.8410 oz. ASW **Obv:** Crown **Rev:** Dagger flanked by garlands from above **Edge:** Reeded **Note:** 3mm thick.

Date	Mintage	F	VF	XF	Unc	BU
VS2031 (1974) Proof	2,000	Value: 22.50				

KM# 1135 25 RUPEE
8.5000 g., Copper Nickel, 29 mm. **Subject:** Silver Jubilee of King's Accession **Obv:** Traditional design **Rev:** Crown on radiant emblem **Edge:** Plain

Date	Mintage	F	VF	XF	Unc	BU
VS2053 (1996)	—	—	—	—	3.50	—

KM# 1126 25 RUPEE
Copper-Nickel **Subject:** Silver Jubilee **Obv:** Traditional design **Rev:** Stylized face design

Date	Mintage	F	VF	XF	Unc	BU
VS2055 (1998)	—	—	—	—	4.50	—

KM# 843 50 RUPEE
14.9000 g., 0.5000 Silver 0.2395 oz. ASW **Series:** International Year of Disabled Persons **Obv:** Traditional design **Rev:** Emblem within grain ears

Date	Mintage	F	VF	XF	Unc	BU
VS2038 (1981)	16,000	—	—	—	8.50	—

KM# A851 50 RUPEE
15.0000 g., 0.4000 Silver 0.1929 oz. ASW **Series:** International Year of the Child **Note:** Similar to 100 Rupee, KM#851.

Date	Mintage	F	VF	XF	Unc	BU
VS2038 (1981)	—	—	—	—	—	—

KM# 1051 25 RUPEE
12.0000 g., 0.2500 Silver 0.0964 oz. ASW **Obv:** Crown **Rev:** Value

Date	Mintage	F	VF	XF	Unc	BU
VS2041 (1984)	—	—	—	—	15.00	—

KM# 841 50 RUPEE
31.8000 g., 0.5000 Silver 0.5112 oz. ASW **Series:** Conservation **Obv:** Bust right **Rev:** Red panda

Date	Mintage	F	VF	XF	Unc	BU
VS2031 (1974)	11,000	—	—	10.00	22.00	—

KM# 841a 50 RUPEE
35.0000 g., 0.9250 Silver 1.0408 oz. ASW **Obv:** Bust right **Rev:** Red panda

Date	Mintage	F	VF	XF	Unc	BU
VS2031 (1974) Proof	10,000	Value: 25.00				

KM# 1046 50 RUPEE
15.0000 g., 0.5000 Silver 0.2411 oz. ASW **Subject:** 50th Anniversary of Kathmandu Mint **Obv:** Trident within small center circle **Rev:** Mint press

Date	Mintage	F	VF	XF	Unc	BU
VS2039 (1982)	8,765	—	—	13.50	17.50	—

KM# 1119 50 RUPEE
Bronze **Obv:** Traditional square in circle design **Rev:** Buddha's portrait and Ashoka pillar **Note:** Lord Buddha; Similar to 1500 Rupee, KM#1120.

Date	Mintage	F	VF	XF	Unc	BU
VS2055 (1998)	30,000	—	—	—	10.00	—

KM# 1136 50 RUPEE
Brass, 37.5 mm. **Subject:** 50th Anniversary - Radio Nepal
Obv: Traditional design **Rev:** Stylized design **Edge:** Plain

Date	Mintage	F	VF	XF	Unc	BU
VS2056 (1999)	—			—	10.00	—

KM# 1137 50 RUPEE
Brass, 37.5 mm. **Subject:** St. Xavier's Golden Jubilee
Obv: Traditional design **Rev:** Coat of arms **Edge:** Plain

Date	Mintage	F	VF	XF	Unc	BU
VS2057 (2000)	—			—	10.00	—

KM# 1127 50 RUPEE
Brass, 38.7 mm. **Subject:** Buddha **Obv:** Traditional square
design **Rev:** Buddha and four figures **Edge:** Reeded

Date	Mintage	F	VF	XF	Unc	BU
VS2057 (2000)	30,000			—	10.00	—

KM# 1165 100 RUPEE
25.0000 g., 0.5000 Silver 0.4019 oz. ASW, 36 mm. **Obv:** Crown in
square design **Rev:** Garland draped above sword **Edge:** Reeded

Date	Mintage	F	VF	XF	Unc	BU
VS2031 (1974)	1,000	Value: 50.00				
Proof						

KM# 850.2 100 RUPEE
25.4900 g., 0.9250 Silver 0.7580 oz. ASW **Series:** World Food
Day **Obv:** Traditional design **Rev:** Figure working in field **Note:**
Obverse and reverse are different.

Date	Mintage	F	VF	XF	Unc	BU
VS2038 (1981)	—	Value: 80.00				

KM# 851 100 RUPEE
19.4400 g., 0.5000 Silver 0.3125 oz. ASW **Series:** International
Year of the Child **Obv:** Crowned bust right **Rev:** Children filling
water jug

Date	Mintage	F	VF	XF	Unc	BU
VS2031(1974)	9,270	Value: 17.50				
Proof						

Note: Struck in 1981

KM# 850.1 100 RUPEE
25.4900 g., 0.5000 Silver 0.4097 oz. ASW **Series:** World Food
Day **Obv:** Traditional design **Rev:** Figure working in field

Date	Mintage	F	VF	XF	Unc	BU
VS2038 (1981)	18,000	—	—	—	22.50	—

KM# 1005 100 RUPEE
31.1000 g., 0.9250 Silver 0.9249 oz. ASW, 38.6 mm.
Subject: 30th Anniversary Ascent of Mt. Everest **Obv:** Trident
within small circle at center **Rev:** Mount Everest

Date	Mintage	F	VF	XF	Unc	BU
VS2040 (1983)	1,500	Value: 50.00				
Proof						

KM# 1024 100 RUPEE
15.0000 g., 0.5000 Silver 0.2411 oz. ASW **Subject:** Year of
Youth **Obv:** Value **Rev:** Emblem below hills

Date	Mintage	F	VF	XF	Unc	BU
VS2042 (1985)	8,199	—	—	—	12.00	—

KM# 1114 100 RUPEE
12.0400 g., 0.6000 Silver 0.2322 oz. ASW **Series:** 50th
Anniversary - F.A.O. **Obv:** Traditional design **Rev:** Logo at center,
grain ears flank

Date	Mintage	F	VF	XF	Unc	BU
VS2052 (1995)	—			—	15.00	—

KM# 1102 100 RUPEE
Copper-Nickel **Series:** Nepal Wildlife **Rev:** Multicolor tiger

Date	Mintage	F	VF	XF	Unc	BU
VS2054 (1998)	25,000			—	40.00	—

KM# 1103 100 RUPEE
Copper-Nickel **Series:** Nepal Wildlife **Obv:** Traditional design
Rev: Multicolor Great Indian rhino

Date	Mintage	F	VF	XF	Unc	BU
VS2054-1998	25,000			—	40.00	—

KM# 1141 100 RUPEE
12.5000 g., 0.5000 Silver 0.2009 oz. ASW **Series:** International
Year of Older Persons **Obv:** Traditional design **Rev:** Emblem and
inscription

Date	Mintage	F	VF	XF	Unc	BU
VS2056 (1999)	—			—	10.00	—

KM# 1031 200 RUPEE
15.0000 g., 0.6000 Silver 0.2893 oz. ASW **Subject:** 10th
Anniversary of National Social Security Administration
Obv: Traditional design **Rev:** Emblem at center within small circle

Date	Mintage	F	VF	XF	Unc	BU
VS2044 (1987)	4,145	—	—	—	25.00	—

KM# 1007   250 RUPEE
28.2800 g., 0.9250 Silver 0.8410 oz. ASW   Subject: 10th
Anniversary of Reign Obv: Conjoined busts left Rev: Value

Date	Mintage	F	VF	XF	Unc	BU
VS2038 (1981)	10,000	Value: 95.00				
Proof						

KM# 1010   250 RUPEE
28.2800 g., 0.9250 Silver 0.8410 oz. ASW   Subject: Year of the
Scout Obv: Traditional design Rev: Boy and girl scouts planting
seedling

Date	Mintage	F	VF	XF	Unc	BU
VS2039 (1982)	10,000	—	—	—	45.00	50.00
VS2039 (1982)	Inc. above	Value: 55.00				
Proof						

KM# 1026   250 RUPEE
19.4400 g., 0.9250 Silver 0.5781 oz. ASW   Series: Wildlife
Preservation Obv: Traditional design Rev: Musk deer

Date	Mintage	F	VF	XF	Unc	BU
VS2043 (1986)	20,000	Value: 30.00				
Proof						

KM# 1049   250 RUPEE
19.4400 g., 0.9250 Silver 0.5781 oz. ASW   Subject: Silver
Jubilee of Nepal Red Cross Society Obv: Traditional design
Rev: Emblem at center

Date	Mintage	F	VF	XF	Unc	BU
VS2045 (1988)	6,360	—	—	—	23.50	28.50

KM# 1052   250 RUPEE
19.4400 g., 0.9250 Silver 0.5781 oz. ASW   Subject: 25th
Anniversary of Nepalese Power Company Obv: Traditional
design Rev: Rising sun back of hills

Date	Mintage	F	VF	XF	Unc	BU
VS2046 (1989)	—	—	—	—	23.50	28.50

KM# 1055   250 RUPEE
19.4400 g., 0.9250 Silver 0.5781 oz. ASW   Series: Save the
Children Obv: Traditional design Rev: Children dancing

Date	Mintage	F	VF	XF	Unc	BU
VS2047 (1990)	20,000	Value: 22.50				
Proof						

KM# 1134.1   250 RUPEE
18.1000 g., 0.9250 Silver 0.5383 oz. ASW, 36 mm.
Subject: Silver Jubilee - Nepal Disabled Association Note: Large
figures, large inscriptions.

Date	Mintage	F	VF	XF	Unc	BU
VS2052(1995)	—	Value: 27.50				

KM# 1134.2   250 RUPEE
17.7000 g., 0.5000 Silver 0.2845 oz. ASW, 36 mm.
Subject: Nepal Disabled Association Obv: Traditional square
design Rev: Human figures Logo and value Edge: Reeded
Note: Small figures, small inscriptions

Date	Mintage	F	VF	XF	Unc	BU
VS2052(1995)	—	—	—	—	25.00	—

KM# 1134.3   250 RUPEE
17.7000 g., 0.5000 Silver 0.2845 oz. ASW, 36 mm. Subject: Nepal
Disabled Association Obv: Traditional square design with small
inscriptions Rev: Human figures logo and value Edge: Reeded

Date	Mintage	F	VF	XF	Unc	BU
VS2052(1995)	—	—	—	—	25.00	—

KM# 1029   300 RUPEE
25.2900 g., 0.5000 Silver 0.4065 oz. ASW   Subject: First Scout
Jamboree in Nepal Obv: Traditional design Rev: Emblems within
temple outline, hills in background

Date	Mintage	F	VF	XF	Unc	BU
VS2043 (1986)	6,967	—	—	—	27.50	32.50

KM# 1044   300 RUPEE
25.0000 g., 0.9250 Silver 0.7435 oz. ASW   Subject: 3rd SAARC
Summit Obv: Traditional design Rev: Summit emblem

Date	Mintage	F	VF	XF	Unc	BU
VS2044 (1987)	5,000	—	—	—	22.50	27.50

KM# 1057   300 RUPEE
18.0500 g., 0.9250 Silver 0.5368 oz. ASW   Obv: Traditional
design Rev: Rastriya Banijya Bank logo

Date	Mintage	F	VF	XF	Unc	BU
VS2047 (1990)	—	—	—	—	22.50	27.50

KM# 1064   300 RUPEE
18.3150 g., 0.9250 Silver 0.5447 oz. ASW   Subject: New
Constitution Obv: Traditional design Rev: Flags above open book

Date	Mintage	F	VF	XF	Unc	BU
VS2047 (1990)	—	—	—	—	22.50	27.50

KM# 1065   300 RUPEE
18.3150 g., 0.9250 Silver 0.5447 oz. ASW   Subject: Parliament
Session Obv: Traditional design Rev: Outlined figures
symbolizing members of parliament

Date	Mintage	F	VF	XF	Unc	BU
VS2048 (1991)	—	—	—	—	22.50	27.50

KM# 1068   300 RUPEE
17.8100 g., 0.9250 Silver 0.5296 oz. ASW   Obv: Traditional
design Rev: Figure between hands holding grains, hills in
background

Date	Mintage	F	VF	XF	Unc	BU
VS2049 (1992)	—	—	—	—	22.50	27.50

KM# 1094 300 RUPEE
18.1300 g., 0.9250 Silver 0.5392 oz. ASW **Subject:** Rastriya Beema Sansthan Silver Jubilee **Obv:** Traditional design **Rev:** Eyes below design

Date	Mintage	F	VF	XF	Unc	BU
VS2049 (1992)	—	—	—	—	22.50	27.50

KM# 1142 300 RUPEE
18.0000 g., 0.9250 Silver 0.5353 oz. ASW **Subject:** 75th Anniversary of I.L.O.

Date	Mintage	F	VF	XF	Unc	BU
VS2051 (1994)	—	—	—	—	22.50	27.50

KM# 1032 350 RUPEE
23.3000 g., 0.5000 Silver 0.3745 oz. ASW **Subject:** Crown Prince, Sacred Thread Ceremony **Obv:** Traditional design

Date	Mintage	F	VF	XF	Unc	BU
VS2044 (1987)	5,217	—	—	—	30.00	35.00

KM# 1035 500 RUPEE
35.0000 g., 0.5000 Silver 0.5626 oz. ASW **Subject:** 50th Anniversary of National Bank **Obv:** Traditional design **Rev:** Figure at center of designed globe

Date	Mintage	F	VF	XF	Unc	BU
VS2044 (1987)	19,000	—	—	—	45.00	50.00

KM# 1166 500 RUPEE
31.1000 g., 0.9990 Silver 0.9988 oz. ASW, 38.7 mm. **Obv:** Traditional design **Rev:** Ceremonial vase

Date	Mintage	F	VF	XF	Unc	BU
VS2046(1989)	5,000	—	—	—	45.00	50.00

KM# 1058 500 RUPEE
31.4700 g., 0.9250 Silver 0.9359 oz. ASW **Subject:** 1992 Olympic games - Barcelona **Obv:** Traditional design **Rev:** Boxers

Date	Mintage	F	VF	XF	Unc	BU
VS2049 (1992) Proof	Est. 40,000	Value: 18.50				

KM# 1069 500 RUPEE
31.4700 g., 0.9250 Silver 0.9359 oz. ASW **Subject:** XV World Soccor Championship - USA **Rev:** Soccer goal being scored

Date	Mintage	F	VF	XF	Unc	BU
VS2049 (1992) Proof	20,000	Value: 28.50				

KM# 1071 500 RUPEE
31.8300 g., 0.9250 Silver 0.9466 oz. ASW **Series:** 1992 Olympics - Ski Jumping **Obv:** Traditional design **Rev:** Ski jumper

Date	Mintage	F	VF	XF	Unc	BU
VS2049 (1992) Proof	Est. 40,000	Value: 17.50				

KM# 1090 500 RUPEE
31.4700 g., 0.9250 Silver 0.9359 oz. ASW **Series:** Endangered Wildlife **Obv:** Traditional design **Rev:** Red Panda

Date	Mintage	F	VF	XF	Unc	BU
VS2049 (1992) Proof	Est. 15,000	Value: 30.00				

KM# 1070 500 RUPEE
31.4700 g., 0.9250 Silver 0.9359 oz. ASW **Series:** Endangered Wildlife **Obv:** Traditional design **Rev:** Himalayan Black Bear

Date	Mintage	F	VF	XF	Unc	BU
VS2050 (1993) Proof	10,000	Value: 45.00				

KM# 1066 500 RUPEE
31.7500 g., 0.9250 Silver 0.9442 oz. ASW **Series:** 1994 Olympics **Obv:** Traditional design **Rev:** Cross-country skiing

Date	Mintage	F	VF	XF	Unc	BU
VS2050 (1993) Proof	40,000	Value: 22.50				

KM# 1084 500 RUPEE
28.2800 g., 0.9250 Silver 0.8410 oz. ASW, 38.6 mm. **Subject:** 40th Anniversary - Conquest of Mt. Everest **Obv:** King's name above Napelese calendar date surrounded by religious and cultural emblems **Rev:** Route taken by Sir Edmund Hillary and Sherpa Norgay Tensing's ascent in 1953 to the summit of the highest mountain in the world

Date	Mintage	F	VF	XF	Unc	BU
VS2050 (1993) Proof	Est. 10,000	Value: 32.50				

KM# 1091 500 RUPEE
31.4700 g., 0.9250 Silver 0.9359 oz. ASW **Series:** Endangered Wildlife **Rev:** Tiger

Date	Mintage	F	VF	XF	Unc	BU
VS2050 (1993) Proof	Est. 15,000	Value: 40.00				

KM# 1133 500 RUPEE
35.2000 g., 0.9000 Silver 1.0185 oz. ASW **Subject:** International Monetary Fund **Obv:** Traditional design **Rev:** Conjoined globes within rectangle above banner

Date	Mintage	F	VF	XF	Unc	BU
VS2051 (1994)	—	—	—	—	45.00	50.00

KM# 1192 500 RUPEE
35.0000 g., 825.0000 Silver 928.31 oz. ASW **Subject:** 50th Anniversary World Bank **Obv:** Traditional design **Rev:** World Bank globe logo

Date	Mintage	F	VF	XF	Unc	BU
VS2051	—	—	—	—	30.00	—

KM# 1077 500 RUPEE
31.1035 g., 0.9250 Silver 0.9250 oz. ASW **Obv:** Traditional design **Rev:** Buddha

Date	Mintage	F	VF	XF	Unc	BU
VS2052 (1995) Proof	15,000	Value: 37.50				

KM# 1125   500 RUPEE
31.3500 g., 0.9990 Silver 1.0069 oz. ASW **Obv:** Traditional
design **Rev:** Gold-plated lotus flowers

Date	Mintage	F	VF	XF	Unc	BU
VS2052 (1995) Proof	Est. 7,000	Value: 45.00				

KM# 1138   500 RUPEE
19.4400 g., 0.9250 Silver 0.5781 oz. ASW, 36 mm.
Series: UNICEF **Obv:** Traditional design **Rev:** Standing girl
serving seated boy **Edge:** Reeded

Date	Mintage	F	VF	XF	Unc	BU
1997 Proof	25,000	Value: 25.00				

KM# 1143   500 RUPEE
25.2000 g., 0.9250 Silver 0.7494 oz. ASW **Subject:** 50th
Anniversary of Universal Declaration of Human Rights
Obv: Traditional design **Rev:** Logo above inscription

Date	Mintage	F	VF	XF	Unc	BU
VS2055 (1998)	—	—	—	—	22.50	27.50

KM# 1041   600 RUPEE
31.1030 g., 0.9990 Silver 0.9989 oz. ASW **Subject:** 60th
Birthday - Queen Mother **Obv:** Traditional design **Rev:** Bust left

Date	Mintage	F	VF	XF	Unc	BU
VS2045 (1988) Proof	5,000	Value: 60.00				

KM# 844   1000 RUPEE
33.4370 g., 0.9000 Gold 0.9675 oz. AGW **Series:** Conservation
Obv: Crowned bust right **Rev:** Great Indian Rhinoceros
Note: Very small quantity restruck in 1979.

Date	Mintage	F	VF	XF	Unc	BU
VS2031 (1974)	2,176	—	—	—	925	
VS2031 (1974) Proof	671	Value: 975				

KM# 1000   1000 RUPEE
33.4370 g., 0.9000 Gold 0.9675 oz. AGW **Subject:** Rural
Women's Advancement

Date	Mintage	F	VF	XF	Unc	BU
VS2038 (1981) Proof	500	Value: 975				

KM# 1036   1000 RUPEE
155.5150 g., 0.9990 Silver 4.9947 oz. ASW, 65 mm.
Obv: Traditional design **Rev:** Snow Leopard **Note:** Illustration
reduced.

Date	Mintage	F	VF	XF	Unc	BU
VS2045 (1988) Proof	5,000	Value: 150				

KM# 1169   1000 RUPEE
40.0000 g., 0.5000 Silver 0.6430 oz. ASW, 40 mm.
Obv: Traditional square calendar with trident in circle at center
Rev: Living Goddess Kumari **Edge:** Reeded

Date	Mintage	F	VF	XF	Unc	BU
VS2057(2000)	—	—	—	—	50.00	55.00

KM# 1095   1500 RUPEE
31.1035 g., 0.9250 Silver 0.9250 oz. ASW **Subject:** Buddha's
Birth **Obv:** Traditional square in circle design **Rev:** Figure
standing in center, cameo at right, small figure at left

Date	Mintage	F	VF	XF	Unc	BU
VS2054 (1997) Proof	15,000	Value: 35.00				

KM# 1120   1500 RUPEE
20.0000 g., 0.9250 Silver 0.5948 oz. ASW **Subject:** Lord
Buddha **Obv:** Traditional square in circle design **Rev:** Portrait of
Buddha, Ashoka pillar, portrait halo glows under ultraviolet light

Date	Mintage	F	VF	XF	Unc	BU
VS2055 (1998) Proof	15,000	Value: 50.00				

KM# 1168   1500 RUPEE
0.9990 Silver, 38 mm. **Obv:** Traditional square design
Rev: Tiger in tall grass **Edge:** Reeded

Date	Mintage	F	VF	XF	Unc	BU
VS2054-1998	—	—	—	—	50.00	60.00

KM# 1128   1500 RUPEE
20.0000 g., 0.9250 Silver 0.5948 oz. ASW, 38.7 mm.
Subject: Buddha **Obv:** Traditional square design **Rev:** Buddha
with golden aura **Edge:** Reeded

Date	Mintage	F	VF	XF	Unc	BU
VS2057 (2000)	—	—	—	—	50.00	60.00

KM# 1100   2000 RUPEE
31.2400 g., 0.9990 Silver 1.0033 oz. ASW, 40 mm.
Subject: Silver Jubilee of King's Accession **Obv:** Traditional
design **Rev:** Multicolor crown

Date	Mintage	F	VF	XF	Unc	BU
VS2053 (1996) Proof	Est. 5,000	Value: 40.00				

KM# 1121 2000 RUPEE
20.0000 g., 0.9250 Silver 0.5948 oz. ASW **Obv:** Traditional square in circle design **Rev:** Buddha's portrait with gold insert halo, Ashoka pillar at right **Note:** Lord Buddha; Similar to 1500 Rupee, KM#1120.

Date	Mintage	F	VF	XF	Unc	BU
VS2055 (1998) Proof	5,000	Value: 75.00				

KM# 1104 2000 RUPEE
31.1700 g., 0.9990 Silver 1.0011 oz. ASW **Series:** Nepal Wildlife **Obv:** Traditional design **Rev:** Multicolored leopard

Date	Mintage	F	VF	XF	Unc	BU
VS2054-1998 Proof	8,000	Value: 45.00				

KM# 1105 2000 RUPEE
31.1700 g., 0.9990 Silver 1.0011 oz. ASW **Series:** Nepal Wildlife **Obv:** Traditional design **Rev:** Multicolor elephants

Date	Mintage	F	VF	XF	Unc	BU
VS2054-1998 Proof	8,000	Value: 45.00				

KM# 1085 2500 RUPEE
155.5100 g., 0.9990 Silver 4.9946 oz. ASW **Subject:** Conquest of Mt. Everest **Obv:** Traditional design **Rev:** Busts facing in front of Mount Everest **Note:** Illustration reduced.

Date	Mintage	F	VF	XF	Unc	BU
VS2050 (1993)	Est. 3,000	Value: 145				

KM# 1078 2500 RUPEE
155.5100 g., 0.9990 Silver 4.9946 oz. ASW **Obv:** Traditional design **Rev:** Buddha **Note:** Similar to 500 Rupee, KM#1077.

Date	Mintage	F	VF	XF	Unc	BU
VS2052 (1995) Proof	3,000	Value: 200				

KM# 1101 5000 RUPEE
155.5000 g., 0.9990 Silver 4.9942 oz. ASW, 65 mm. **Subject:** Silver Jubilee of King's Accession **Obv:** Traditional design **Rev:** Multicolor crown

Date	Mintage	F	VF	XF	Unc	BU
VS2053 (1996) Proof	Est. 2,500	Value: 200				

KM# 1106 5000 RUPEE
155.5518 g., 0.9990 Silver 4.9959 oz. ASW **Series:** Nepal Wildlife **Rev:** Multicolor elephants **Note:** Similar to 2000 Rupee, KM#1105.

Date	Mintage	F	VF	XF	Unc	BU
VS2054 (1997) Proof	500	Value: 250				

ASARFI GOLD COINAGE
(Asarphi)

Fractional designations are approximate for this series. Actual Gold Weight (AGW) is used to identify each type.

KM# 1167 1/3 ASARFI
11.6500 g., 0.9000 Gold 0.3371 oz. AGW, 28.5 mm. **Obv:** Traditional design **Rev:** Ceremonial Vase **Note:** The Prince's Coming of Age

Date	Mintage	F	VF	XF	Unc	BU
VS2046(1989)	1,000	—	—	—	350	—

KM# 1050a 0.3G ASARPHI
0.2500 g., 0.9990 Gold 0.0080 oz. AGW

Date	Mintage	F	VF	XF	Unc	BU
VS2051 (1994)	—	—	—	—	40.00	—
VS2052 (1995)	—	—	—	—	40.00	—
VS2053 (1996)	—	—	—	—	35.00	—
VS2054 (1997)	—	—	—	—	35.00	—
VS2055 (1998)	—	—	—	—	35.00	—
VS2056 (1999)	—	—	—	—	35.00	—
VS2057 (2000)	—	—	—	—	35.00	—

KM# 1129 0.3G ASARPHI
0.3000 g., 0.9999 Gold 0.0096 oz. AGW, 7 mm. **Subject:** Buddha **Obv:** Traditional square design **Rev:** Buddha with halo **Edge:** Reeded

Date	Mintage	F	VF	XF	Unc	BU
VS2057 (2000)	25,000	—	—	—	12.00	—

KM# 825 5.0G ASARPHI
5.0000 g., 0.9990 Gold 0.1606 oz. AGW

Date	Mintage	F	VF	XF	Unc	BU
VS2028 (1971)	4	—	—	—	—	—
VS2030 (1973)	—	—	—	—	165	—
VS2031 (1974)	—	—	—	—	165	—
VS2036 (1979)	36	—	—	—	165	—
VS2037 (1980)	45	—	—	—	165	—

Note: Reports indicate a mintage of 44 pieces struck in .960 gold in 1980

VS2038 (1981)	—	—	—	—	165	—

KM# 822a 5.0G ASARPHI
5.0000 g., 0.9990 Gold 0.1606 oz. AGW **Subject:** Birendra Coronation **Obv:** Crown at center **Rev:** Dagger flanked by garlands from above

Date	Mintage	F	VF	XF	Unc	BU
VS2031 (1974)	500	—	—	—	160	—

KM# 1021 5.0G ASARPHI
5.0000 g., 0.9000 Gold 0.1447 oz. AGW **Obv:** Traditional design **Rev:** Dagger flanked by garlands from above

Date	Mintage	F	VF	XF	Unc	BU
VS2039 (1982)	23	—	—	—	175	—

KM# 1021a 5.0G ASARPHI
0.5000 g., 0.9990 Gold 0.0161 oz. AGW **Obv:** Traditional design **Rev:** Dagger flanked by garlands from above

Date	Mintage	F	VF	XF	Unc	BU
VS2042 (1985)	—	—	—	—	125	—
VS2043 (1986)	—	—	—	—	125	—
VS2044 (1987)	—	—	—	—	125	—
VS2045 (1988)	—	—	—	—	120	—
VS2046 (1989)	—	—	—	—	120	—
VS2048 (1991)	—	—	—	—	120	—
VS2049 (1992)	—	—	—	—	120	—
VS2050 (1993)	—	—	—	—	115	—
VS2051 (1994)	—	—	—	—	115	—
VS2052 (1995)	—	—	—	—	115	—
VS2053 (1996)	—	—	—	—	115	—
VS2054 (1997)	—	—	—	—	115	—
VS2056 (1999)	—	—	—	—	115	—

KM# 1060 5.0G ASARPHI
5.0000 g., 0.9990 Gold 0.1606 oz. AGW **Subject:** The New Constitution **Obv:** Traditional design **Rev:** Flags above open book **Note:** Similar to 10 Asarphi, KM#1054.

Date	Mintage	F	VF	XF	Unc	BU
VS2047 (1990)	—	—	—	—	175	—

KM# 1144 5.0G ASARPHI
5.0000 g., 0.9990 Gold 0.1606 oz. AGW **Subject:** New Parliament Session

Date	Mintage	F	VF	XF	Unc	BU
VS2048 (1991)	—	—	—	—	175	—

KM# 827 10.0G ASARPHI
10.0000 g., 0.9990 Gold 0.3212 oz. AGW **Obv:** Traditional design **Rev:** Dagger flanked by garlands from above

Date	Mintage	F	VF	XF	Unc	BU
VS2028 (1971)	Est. 4	—	—	—	—	—
VS2030 (1973)	50	—	—	—	350	—
VS2031 (1974)	—	—	—	—	350	—
VS2033 (1976)	—	—	—	—	350	—
VS2035 (1978)	—	—	—	—	350	—
VS2036 (1979)	52	—	—	—	350	—
VS2037 (1980)	30	—	—	—	350	—

Note: Reports indicate a mintage of 44 pieces struck in .960 gold in 1980

VS2038 (1981)	—	—	—	—	350	—

KM# 829a 10.0G ASARPHI
10.0000 g., 0.9990 Gold 0.3212 oz. AGW **Subject:** Birendra Coronation **Obv:** Crown **Rev:** Dagger flanked by garlands from above

Date	Mintage	F	VF	XF	Unc	BU
VS2031 (1974) Proof	Est. 500	Value: 350				

KM# 829b 10.0G ASARPHI
10.0000 g., 0.5000 White Gold 0.1607 oz. AGW

Date	Mintage	F	VF	XF	Unc	BU
VS2031 (1974) Proof	Est. 250	Value: 350				

Note: Sometimes referred to as 1000 Rupees

KM# 852 10.0G ASARPHI
11.6600 g., 0.9000 Gold 0.3374 oz. AGW **Series:** International Year of the Child **Obv:** Crowned bust right **Rev:** Child reading, emblems flank

Date	Mintage	F	VF	XF	Unc	BU
VS2038 (1974) Proof	4,055	Value: 350				

Note: Struck in 1981

KM# 1022 10.0G ASARPHI
10.0000 g., 0.9000 Gold 0.2893 oz. AGW **Obv:** Traditional design **Rev:** Dagger flanked by garlands from above

Date	Mintage	F	VF	XF	Unc	BU
VS2039 (1982)	25	—	—	—	300	—

KM# 1006 10.0G ASARPHI
10.0000 g., 0.5000 Gold 0.1607 oz. AGW **Subject:** 30th Anniversary Ascent of Mt. Everest **Obv:** Trident within small circle at center **Rev:** Mount Everest

Date	Mintage	F	VF	XF	Unc	BU
VS2040 (1983) Proof	350	Value: 225				

KM# 1022a 10.0G ASARPHI
10.0000 g., 0.9990 Gold 0.3212 oz. AGW

Date	Mintage	F	VF	XF	Unc	BU
VS2042 (1985)	—	—	—	—	375	—
VS2046 (1989)	—	—	—	—	360	—
VS2048 (1991)	—	—	—	—	360	—
VS2049 (1992)	—	—	—	—	360	—
VS2050 (1993)	—	—	—	—	350	—
VS2052 (1995)	—	—	—	—	350	—
VS2054 (1997)	—	—	—	—	350	—
VS2056 (1999)	—	—	—	—	350	—

KM# 1034 10.0G ASARPHI
10.0000 g., Gold **Subject:** Crown Prince, Sacred Thread Ceremony **Obv:** Traditional design

Date	Mintage	F	VF	XF	Unc	BU
VS2044 (1987)	1,962	—	—	—	350	—

KM# 1054 10.0G ASARPHI
10.0000 g., 0.9990 Gold 0.3212 oz. AGW **Subject:** The New Constitution **Obv:** Traditional design **Rev:** Flags above open book

Date	Mintage	F	VF	XF	Unc	BU
VS2047 (1990)	—	—	—	—	325	—

KM# 1145 10.0G ASARPHI
10.0000 g., 0.9990 Gold 0.3212 oz. AGW **Subject:** 50th Anniversary International Monetary Fund

Date	Mintage	F	VF	XF	Unc	BU
VS2051 (1994)	—	—	—	—	325	—

KM# 1146 10.0G ASARPHI
10.0000 g., 0.9990 Gold 0.3212 oz. AGW **Subject:** 50th Anniversary World Bank

Date	Mintage	F	VF	XF	Unc	BU
VS2051 (1994)	—	—	—	—	325	—

KM# 1147 10.0G ASARPHI
10.0000 g., 0.9990 Gold 0.3212 oz. AGW **Subject:** Queen Aishwariya Golden Anniversary

Date	Mintage	F	VF	XF	Unc	BU
VS2056 (1999)	—	—	—	—	325	—

KM# 1122 1/25-OZ. ASARFI
1.2441 g., 0.9999 Gold 0.0400 oz. AGW **Obv:** Traditional square in circle design **Rev:** Buddha's portrait and Ashoka pillar **Note:** Lord Buddha; Similar to Asarfi KM#1124.

Date	Mintage	F	VF	XF	Unc	BU
VS2055 (1998) Proof	30,000	Value: 45.00				

KM# 1130 1/25-OZ. ASARFI
1.2441 g., 0.9999 Gold 0.0400 oz. AGW, 18 mm.
Subject: Buddha **Obv:** Traditional square design **Rev:** Buddha with halo **Edge:** Reeded

Date	Mintage	F	VF	XF	Unc	BU
VS2057 (2000)	30,000	—	—	—	45.00	—

KM# 1033 1/20-OZ. ASARFI
5.8300 g., 0.9600 Gold 0.1799 oz. **Subject:** Crown Prince, Sacred Thread Ceremony **Obv:** Traditional design

Date	Mintage	F	VF	XF	Unc	BU
VS2044 (1987)	2,774	—	—	—	190	—

KM# 1079 1/20-OZ. ASARFI
1.5532 g., 0.9990 Gold 0.0499 oz. AGW **Obv:** Traditional design **Rev:** Buddha **Note:** Similar to 1-oz. Asarfi, KM#1082.

Date	Mintage	F	VF	XF	Unc	BU
VS2052 (1995)	15,000	—	—	—	50.00	—

KM# 1096 1/20-OZ. ASARFI
1.5532 g., 0.9990 Gold 0.0499 oz. AGW **Subject:** Buddha's Birth **Obv:** Traditional design **Rev:** Standing figure at center, cameo at right, small figure at left **Note:** Similar to 1500 Rupee, KM#1095.

Date	Mintage	F	VF	XF	Unc	BU
VS2054 (1997)	15,000	—	—	—	55.00	—

KM# 1107 1/20-OZ. ASARFI
1.5552 g., 0.9990 Gold 0.0499 oz. AGW **Series:** Nepal Wildlife **Obv:** Traditional design **Rev:** Multicolor leopard **Note:** Similar to 2000 Rupees, KM#1104.

Date	Mintage	F	VF	XF	Unc	BU
VS2054 (1998) Proof	15,000	Value: 75.00				

KM# 1108 1/20-OZ. ASARFI
1.5552 g., 0.9990 Gold 0.0499 oz. AGW **Series:** Nepal Wildlife **Obv:** Traditional design **Rev:** Multicolor tiger **Note:** Similar to 100 Rupees, KM#1102.

Date	Mintage	F	VF	XF	Unc	BU
VS2054 (1998) Proof	15,000	Value: 75.00				

KM# 1050 1/10-OZ. ASARFI
2.5000 g., 0.9000 Gold 0.0723 oz. AGW

Date	Mintage	F	VF	XF	Unc	BU
VS2039 (1982)	11	—	—	—	150	—

KM# 1037 1/10-OZ. ASARFI
3.1100 g., 0.9990 Gold 0.0999 oz. AGW **Obv:** Traditional design **Rev:** Snow leopard **Note:** Similar to 1-oz. Asarphi, KM#1040.

Date	Mintage	F	VF	XF	Unc	BU
VS2045 (1988)	Est. 10,000	—	—	—	110	—
VS2045 (1988) Proof	2,000	Value: 120				

KM# 1080 1/10-OZ. ASARFI
3.1100 g., 0.9990 Gold 0.0999 oz. AGW **Obv:** Traditional design **Rev:** Buddha **Note:** Similar to 1-oz. Asarphi, KM#1082.

Date	Mintage	F	VF	XF	Unc	BU
VS2052 (1995)	15,000	—	—	—	110	—

KM# 1097 1/10-OZ. ASARFI
3.1100 g., 0.9990 Gold 0.0999 oz. AGW **Subject:** Buddha's Birth **Obv:** Traditional design **Rev:** Standing figure at center, cameo at right, small figure at left **Note:** Similar to 1500 Rupee, KM#1095.

Date	Mintage	F	VF	XF	Unc	BU
VS2054 (1997)	15,000	—	—	—	110	—

KM# 1109 1/10-OZ. ASARFI
3.1104 g., 0.9990 Gold 0.0999 oz. AGW **Series:** Nepal Wildlife **Obv:** Traditional design **Rev:** Multicolor leopard **Note:** Similar to 2000 Rupees, KM#1104.

Date	Mintage	F	VF	XF	Unc	BU
VS2054 (1998) Proof	10,000	Value: 110				

KM# 1123 1/10-OZ. ASARFI
3.1104 g., 0.9999 Gold 0.1000 oz. AGW **Obv:** Traditional square in circle design **Rev:** Buddha's portrait and Ashoka pillar **Note:** Lord Buddha; Similar to Asarfi KM#1124.

Date	Mintage	F	VF	XF	Unc	BU
VS2055 (1998) Proof	15,000	Value: 110				

KM# 1131 1/10-OZ. ASARFI
3.1100 g., 0.9990 Gold 0.0999 oz. AGW, 18 mm.
Subject: Buddha **Obv:** Traditional square design **Rev:** Buddha with halo **Edge:** Reeded

Date	Mintage	F	VF	XF	Unc	BU
VS2057 (2000)	30,000	—	—	—	110	—

KM# 819 1/4-OZ. ASARFI
2.5000 g., 0.9990 Gold 0.0803 oz. AGW **Obv:** Traditional design **Rev:** Dagger flanked by garlands from above

Date	Mintage	F	VF	XF	Unc	BU
VS2028 (1971)	4	—	—	—	—	—
VS2030 (1973)	—	—	—	—	115	—
VS2031 (1974)	—	—	—	—	115	—
VS2036 (1979)	—	—	—	—	115	—
VS2037 (1980)	48	—	—	—	115	—

KM# 816a 1/4-OZ. ASARFI
7.7700 g., 0.9990 Gold 0.2496 oz. AGW **Subject:** Birendra Coronation **Obv:** Crown **Rev:** Dagger flanked by garlands from above

Date	Mintage	F	VF	XF	Unc	BU
VS2031 (1974)	500	—	—	—	250	—

KM# 1038 1/4-OZ. ASARFI
7.7700 g., 0.9990 Gold 0.2496 oz. AGW **Obv:** Traditional design **Rev:** Snow leopard **Note:** Similar to 1-oz. Asarphi, KM#1040, Bullion Series.

Date	Mintage	F	VF	XF	Unc	BU
VS2045 (1988)	8,000	—	—	—	250	—
VS2045 (1988)	2,000	Value: 260				

KM# 1059 1/4-OZ. ASARFI
7.7700 g., 0.9990 Gold 0.2496 oz. AGW **Obv:** Traditional design **Rev:** Flags above open book **Note:** Similar to 1-oz. Asarphi, KM#1054.

Date	Mintage	F	VF	XF	Unc	BU
VS2047 (1990)	—	—	—	—	250	—

KM# 1056 1/4-OZ. ASARFI
11.6600 g., 0.9000 Gold 0.3374 oz. AGW **Series:** Save the Children **Obv:** Traditional design **Rev:** Older and younger children

Date	Mintage	F	VF	XF	Unc	BU
VS2047 (1990) Proof	3,000	Value: 340				

KM# 1093 1/4-OZ. ASARFI
7.7760 g., 0.9990 Gold 0.2497 oz. AGW **Series:** Olympics **Obv:** Traditional design **Rev:** Runner and temple

Date	Mintage	F	VF	XF	Unc	BU
VS2052 (1995)	Est. 3,000	—	—	—	250	—

KM# 1081 1/4-OZ. ASARFI
7.7759 g., 0.9990 Gold 0.2497 oz. AGW **Obv:** Traditional design **Rev:** Buddha **Note:** Similar to 1-oz. Asarphi, KM#1082.

Date	Mintage	F	VF	XF	Unc	BU
VS2052 (1995)	15,000	—	—	—	250	—

KM# 1098 1/4-OZ. ASARFI
7.7759 g., 0.9990 Gold 0.2497 oz. AGW **Subject:** Buddha's Birth **Obv:** Traditional design **Rev:** Standing figure at center, cameo at right, small figure at left **Note:** Similar to 1500 Rupees, KM#1095.

Date	Mintage	F	VF	XF	Unc	BU
VS2054 (1997)	15,000	—	—	—	250	—

KM# 1110 1/4-OZ. ASARFI
7.7759 g., 0.9990 Gold 0.2497 oz. AGW **Series:** Nepal Wildlife **Obv:** Traditional design **Rev:** Multicolor elephants **Note:** Similar to 2000 Rupees, KM#1105.

Date	Mintage	F	VF	XF	Unc	BU
VS2054 (1998) Proof	2,000	Value: 250				

KM# 1111 1/4-OZ. ASARFI
7.7759 g., 0.9990 Gold 0.2497 oz. AGW **Series:** Nepal Wildlife **Obv:** Traditional design **Rev:** Multicolor tiger **Note:** Similar to 100 Rupees, KM#1102.

Date	Mintage	F	VF	XF	Unc	BU
VS2054 (1998) Proof	2,000	Value: 250				

KM# 1112 1/4-OZ. ASARFI
7.7759 g., 0.9990 Gold 0.2497 oz. AGW **Series:** Nepal Wildlife **Obv:** Traditional design **Rev:** Multicolor rhinoceros **Note:** Similar to 100 Rupees, KM#1103.

Date	Mintage	F	VF	XF	Unc	BU
VS2054 (1998) Proof	2,000	Value: 250				

KM# 1113 1/4-OZ. ASARFI
7.7759 g., 0.9990 Gold 0.2497 oz. AGW **Series:** Nepal Wildlife **Obv:** Traditional design **Rev:** Multicolor leopard **Note:** Similar to 100 Rupees, KM#1104.

Date	Mintage	F	VF	XF	Unc	BU
VS2054 (1998) Proof	2,000	Value: 250				

KM# 1008 1/2-OZ. ASARFI
15.9800 g., 0.9000 Gold 0.4624 oz. AGW **Subject:** 10th Anniversary of Reign **Rev:** Dagger flanked by garlands from above

Date	Mintage	F	VF	XF	Unc	BU
VS2038 (1981)	27	—	—	—	500	—
VS2038 (1981) Proof	5,092	Value: 475				

KM# 1011 1/2-OZ. ASARFI
15.9800 g., 0.9170 Gold 0.4711 oz. AGW **Series:** Year of the Scout **Obv:** Traditional design **Rev:** Girl scout filling water jug

Date	Mintage	F	VF	XF	Unc	BU
VS2039 (1982)	2,000	—	—	—	475	—

KM# 1045 1/2-OZ. ASARFI
15.0000 g., 0.9000 Gold 0.4340 oz. AGW **Subject:** 3rd SAARC Summit **Obv:** Traditional design **Rev:** Summit emblem **Note:** Similar to 300 Rupees, KM#1044.

Date	Mintage	F	VF	XF	Unc	BU
VS2044 (1987)	1,000	—	—	—	440	—

KM# 1039 1/2-OZ. ASARFI
15.5500 g., 0.9990 Gold 0.4994 oz. AGW **Obv:** Traditional design **Rev:** Snow leopard **Note:** Similar to 1-oz. Asarphi, KM#1040.

Date	Mintage	F	VF	XF	Unc	BU
VS2045 (1988)	Est. 8,000	—	—	—	500	—
VS2045 (1988) Proof	2,000	Value: 525				

KM# 1124 1/2-OZ. ASARFI
15.5518 g., 0.9999 Gold 0.4999 oz. AGW **Obv:** Traditional square in circle design **Rev:** Lord Buddha, Ashoka pillar

Date	Mintage	F	VF	XF	Unc	BU
VS2055 (1998) Proof	2,500	Value: 500				

KM# 1132 1/2-OZ. ASARFI
15.5518 g., 0.9999 Gold 0.4999 oz. AGW, 27 mm.
Subject: Buddha **Obv:** Traditional square design **Rev:** Buddha with halo **Edge:** Reeded

Date	Mintage	F	VF	XF	Unc	BU
VS2057 (2000) Proof	2,500	Value: 500				

KM# 1027 1-OZ. ASARFI
31.1000 g., 0.9990 Gold 0.9988 oz. AGW **Series:** Wildlife Protection **Obv:** Traditional design **Rev:** Ganges River Dolphins

Date	Mintage	F	VF	XF	Unc	BU
VS2043 (1986)	5,000	Value: 1,000				

KM# 1040 1-OZ. ASARFI
31.1000 g., 0.9999 Gold 0.9997 oz. AGW **Obv:** Traditional design **Rev:** Snow leopard

Date	Mintage	F	VF	XF	Unc	BU
VS2045 (1988)	Est. 10,000	—	—	—	1,000	—
VS2045 (1988) Proof	2,000	Value: 1,100				

KM# 1082 1-OZ. ASARFI
31.1035 g., 0.9990 Gold 0.9999 oz. AGW **Obv:** Traditional design **Rev:** Buddha

Date	Mintage	F	VF	XF	Unc	BU
VS2052 (1995) Proof	2,500	Value: 1,000				

KM# 1099 1-OZ. ASARFI
31.1035 g., 0.9990 Gold 0.9999 oz. AGW **Subject:** Buddha's Birth **Obv:** Traditional square in circle design **Rev:** Standing figure at center, cameo at right, small figure at left

Date	Mintage	F	VF	XF	Unc	BU
VS2054 (1997) Proof	2,500	Value: 1,000				

KM# 1086 1-1/2 OZ. ASARFI
44.6400 g., 0.9167 Gold 1.3156 oz. AGW **Subject:** Conquest of Mt. Everest **Obv:** Traditional design **Rev:** Mount Everest

Date	Mintage	F	VF	XF	Unc	BU
VS2050 (1993) Proof	Est. 100	Value: 1,400				

PATTERNS
Including off metal strikes

KM#	Date	Mintage	Identification	Mkt Val
Pn1	SE1810	—	Paisa.	—
Pn3	VS1975	—	5 Paisa. Copper. KM#690.1	—

PIEFORTS

KM#	Date	Mintage	Identification	Mkt Val
P1	VS2038	88	100 Rupee. Silver. KM#851.	100
P2	VS2039	48	Asarphi.	1,250

MINT SETS

KM#	Date	Mintage	Identification	Issue Price	Mkt Val
MS1	1932 (3)	—	—		—
MS2	1949 (3)	—	KM#716, 718, 723 (restrikes)		8.00
MS3	1953 (8)	—	KM#733, 735-740, 742		160
MSA4	1953 (7)	—	KM#745.1, 750.1, 756.3, 761, 770, 776, 790 Coronation		10.00
MS4	1955 (3)	—	KM#712 (2000); 733; 749 (2012)	0.85	5.00
MS5	1956 (7)	—	KM#745.1, 750.1, 756.2, 761, 770, 776, 790		50.00
MS6	1956 (7)	—	KM#745.1, 750.1, 756.3, 761, 770, 776, 790 (restrikes)		13.50
MS7	1957 (4)	—	KM#740 (2011), 742, 738 (2010), 769 (2011)	2.05	12.00
MS8	1957 (6)	—	KM#709.1 (1996), 755 (2014), 760 (2011); 2 pieces each	0.85	7.00
MS9	1964 (7)	—	KM#747, 752, 758, 763, 772, 778, 785		10.00
MS10	1964 (7)	—	KM#747, 752, 758a, 764, 772, 778, 785		50.00
MS11	1965 (7)	—	KM#747, 752 (2022), 758, 763, 772, 778, 786 (2021)	2.75	10.00
MS12	1966 (7)	—	KM#748, 753, 759, 765, 772, 779, 787		7.00
MS13	1967 (7)	—	KM#748, 753, 759, 765, 772, 779, 787		5.00
MS14	1971 (7)	—	KM#799, 801, 802, 806, 815, 821, 828		5.00
MS15	1974 (7)	—	KM#800, 804, 808, 816.1, 822.1, 829.1, 838		12.50
MS16	1974 (2)	—	KM#829.1, 841	32.50	30.00
MS17	1975 (5)	—	KM#808, 816.1, 822.1, 829.1, 838		13.00
MS18	1975 (3)	—	KM#809, 831, 836		9.00
MSA19	1996, 1995, 2011 (3)	—	KM#709.2 (1996); 711 (1995); 737 (2011)		7.00
MS19	1997 (3)	—	KM#1096-1098		285

PROOF SETS

KM#	Date	Mintage	Identification	Issue Price	Mkt Val
PS1	1911 (9)	—	KM621, 622, 631, 634, 644, 649, 651.2, 656, 658, Copper, Silver		—
PS2	1911 (6)	—	KM668, 671.2, 672.5, 673.2, 675.1, 680, Gold		—
PS3	1970 (7)	2,187	KM#748, 753, 759, 765, 773, 780, 788	10.00	15.00
PS4	1971 (7)	2,380	KM#748, 753, 759, 765, 773, 780, 788	10.00	15.00
PS5	1972 (7)	3,943	KM#799, 801, 802, 807, 815, 821, 828	10.00	8.50
PS6	1973 (7)	8,891	KM#799, 801, 802, 807, 815, 821, 828	10.00	6.00
PS7	1974 (7)	10,543	KM#799, 801, 802, 807, 815, 821, 828	10.00	5.50
PS8	1974 (2)	30,000	KM#839a, 841a	50.00	42.00

KM#	Date	Mintage	Identification	Issue Price	Mkt Val
PS9	1981 (7)	1,000	KM#800a, 804a, 808a, 816.2, 822.2, 829.2, 838a (dated 1974)Coins dated 2031 (1974) but this set was issued in 1981 to celebrate the 7th Anniversary of the Coronation.	62.00	50.00
PS10	1988 (4)	2,000	KM#1037-1040	—	1,800
PS11	1995-97 (2)	—	KM#1077, 1099	—	940

NETHERLANDS

The Kingdom of the Netherlands, a country of western Europe fronting on the North Sea and bordered by Belgium and Germany, has an area of 15,770 sq. mi. (41,500 sq. km.) and a population of 16.1 million. Capital: Amsterdam, but the seat of government is at The Hague. The economy is based on dairy farming and a variety of industrial activities. Chemicals, yarns and fabrics, and meat products are exported.

After being a part of Charlemagne's empire in the 8th and 9th centuries, the Netherlands came under control of Burgundy and the Austrian Hapsburgs, and finally was subjected to Spanish dominion in the 16th century. Led by William of Orange, the Dutch revolted against Spain in 1568. The seven northern provinces formed the Union of Utrecht and declared their independence in 1581, becoming the Republic of the United Netherlands. In the following century, the *Golden Age* of Dutch history, the Netherlands became a great sea and colonial power, a patron of the arts and a refuge for the persecuted. The United Dutch Republic ended in 1795 when the French formed the Batavian Republic. Napoleon made his brother Louis, the King of Holland in 1806, however he abdicated in 1810 when Napoleon annexed Holland. The French were expelled in 1813, and all the provinces of Holland and Belgium were merged into the Kingdom of the United Netherlands under William I, in 1814. The Belgians withdrew in 1830 to form their own kingdom, the last substantial change in the configuration of European Netherlands. German forces invaded in 1940 as the royal family fled to England where a government-in-exile was formed.

WORLD WAR II COINAGE

U.S. mints in the name of the government in exile and its remaining Curacao and Suriname Colonies during the years 1941-45 minted coinage of the Netherlands. Homeland Types - KM #152, 153, 163, 164, 161.1 and 161.2 -. The Curacao and Suriname strikes, distinguished by the presence of a palm tree in combination with a mint mark (P-Philadelphia; D-Denver; S-San Francisco) flanking the date, are incorporated under those titles in this volume. Pieces of this period struck in the name of the homeland bear an acorn and mint mark and are incorporated in the following tabulation.

NOTE: Excepting the World War II issues struck at U.S. mints, all of the modern coins were struck at the Utrecht Mint and bear the caduceus mint mark of that facility. They also bear the mintmasters' marks.

RULERS
KINGDOM OF THE NETHERLANDS
Wilhelmina I, 1890-1948
Juliana, 1948-1980
Beatrix, 1980—

MINT MARKS
D - Denver, 1943-1945
P - Philadelphia, 1941-1945
S - San Francisco, 1944-1945

MINT PRIVY MARKS
Utrecht

Date	Privy Mark
1806-present	Caduceus

MINTMASTERS' PRIVY MARKS
U. S. Mints

Date	Privy Mark
1941-45	Palm tree

Utrecht Mint

Date	Privy Mark
1888-1909	Halberd
1909	Halberd and star
1909-1933	Seahorse
1933-42	Grapes
1943-1945	No privy mark
1945-69	Fish
1969-79	Cock
1980	Cock and star (temporal)
1980-88	Anvil with hammer
1989-99	Bow and arrow
2000-	Bow, arrow and star

NOTE: A star adjoining the privy mark indicates that the piece was struck at the beginning of the term of office of a successor. (The star was used only if the successor had not chosen his own mark yet.)

NOTE: Since October, 1999, the Dutch Mint has taken the title of Royal Dutch Mint.

MONETARY SYSTEM
Until January 29, 2002
100 Cents = 1 Gulden

KINGDOM
DECIMAL COINAGE

KM# 109 1/2 CENT
1.2500 g., Bronze, 14 mm. Ruler: Wilhelmina I Obv: Crowned rampant lion left within beaded circle, date below
Obv. Leg.: KONINGRIJK DER NEDERLANDEN Rev: Value within wreath Edge: Reeded

Date	Mintage	F	VF	XF	Unc	BU
1901	6,000,000	1.00	5.00	10.00	30.00	60.00

KM# 133 1/2 CENT
1.2500 g., Bronze, 14 mm. Ruler: Wilhelmina I Obv: Crowned arms with 17 small shields within beaded circle
Obv. Leg.: KONINGRIJK DER NEDERLANDEN Rev: Value within wreath Edge: Reeded

Date	Mintage	F	VF	XF	Unc	BU
1903	10,000,000	1.00	2.00	3.00	10.00	20.00
1906	10,000,000	1.00	2.00	3.00	10.00	20.00

KM# 138 1/2 CENT
1.2500 g., Bronze, 14 mm. Ruler: Wilhelmina I Obv: Crowned arms with 15 large shields within beaded circle, date and legend Rev: Value within wreath Edge: Reeded

Date	Mintage	F	VF	XF	Unc	BU
1909	5,000,000	1.00	2.00	3.00	10.00	17.50
1911	5,000,000	1.00	2.00	3.00	10.00	20.00
1912	5,000,000	1.00	2.00	3.00	10.00	20.00
1914	5,000,000	1.00	2.00	3.00	10.00	20.00
1915	2,500,000	5.00	10.00	15.00	25.00	60.00
1916	4,000,000	2.00	4.00	7.00	15.00	30.00
1917	5,000,000	1.00	2.00	4.00	10.00	15.00
1921	1,500,000	5.00	10.00	15.00	25.00	50.00
1922/1	—	200	500	1,000	1,400	1,850
1922	2,500,000	5.00	10.00	15.00	25.00	45.00
1928	4,000,000	1.00	2.00	3.00	8.00	15.00
1930	6,000,000	1.00	1.50	2.50	6.00	10.00
1934	5,000,000	0.75	1.75	2.50	5.00	8.00
1936	5,000,000	0.75	1.75	2.50	5.00	8.00
1937	1,600,000	1.00	2.50	4.00	8.00	12.50
1938	8,400,000	0.75	1.50	2.00	3.00	5.00
1940	6,000,000	0.75	1.50	2.00	3.00	5.00

KM# 130 CENT
2.5000 g., Bronze, 19 mm. Ruler: Wilhelmina I Obv: Crowned arms with 15 large shields within beaded circle
Obv. Leg.: KONINKRIJK DER NEDERLANDEN Rev: Value within wreath Edge: Reeded

Date	Mintage	F	VF	XF	Unc	BU
1901	10,000,000	1.00	2.50	5.00	20.00	50.00

KM# 131 CENT
2.5000 g., Bronze, 19 mm. Ruler: Wilhelmina I Obv: Crowned arms with 10 large shields within beaded circle Obv. Leg.: KONINGRIJK DER NEDERLANDEN Rev: Value within wreath Edge: Reeded

Date	Mintage	F	VF	XF	Unc	BU
1901	10,000,000	1.00	2.50	5.00	20.00	50.00

KM# 132.1 CENT
2.5000 g., Bronze, 19 mm. Ruler: Wilhelmina I Obv: Crowned arms with 15 medium shields within beaded circle
Obv. Leg.: KONINGRIJK DER NEDERLANDEN Rev: Value within wreath Edge: Reeded

Date	Mintage	F	VF	XF	Unc	BU
1902	10,000,000	1.00	2.00	3.00	15.00	30.00
1904	15,000,000	1.00	2.00	3.00	15.00	30.00
1905	10,000,000	1.00	2.00	3.00	15.00	30.00
1906	9,000,000	1.00	2.00	3.00	15.00	30.00
1907	6,000,000	6.00	12.00	30.00	60.00	120

KM# 132.2 CENT
2.5000 g., Bronze, 19 mm. Ruler: Wilhelmina I Obv: 15 medium shields in field Obv. Leg.: KONINGRIJK DER NEDERLANDEN Rev: Value within wreath Edge: Plain

Date	Mintage	F	VF	XF	Unc	BU
1906 Proof	—	Value: 875				

KM# 152 CENT
2.5000 g., Bronze, 19 mm. Ruler: Wilhelmina I Obv: Crowned arms with 17 small shields within beaded circle Rev: Value within wreath

Date	Mintage	F	VF	XF	Unc	BU
1913	5,000,000	2.50	6.00	12.00	28.00	60.00
1914	9,000,000	1.00	2.00	3.00	15.00	40.00
1915	10,800,000	1.00	2.00	3.00	12.00	20.00
1916 Proof	—	Value: 200				
1916	21,700,000	0.75	1.00	2.00	10.00	20.00
1917	20,000,000	0.75	1.00	2.00	10.00	15.00
1918	10,000,000	1.00	2.00	4.00	12.00	20.00
1919	6,000,000	2.75	5.00	10.00	20.00	30.00
1920	11,400,000	0.75	1.50	2.00	10.00	15.00
1921	12,600,000	0.75	1.50	2.00	10.00	15.00
1922	20,000,000	0.75	1.50	2.00	10.00	15.00
1924	1,400,000	15.00	30.00	55.00	110	160
1925	18,600,000	0.75	1.50	2.00	10.00	15.00
1926	10,000,000	0.75	1.50	2.00	10.00	15.00
1927	10,000,000	0.75	1.50	2.00	10.00	15.00
1928	10,000,000	0.75	1.50	2.00	10.00	15.00
1929	20,000,000	0.75	1.50	2.00	8.00	12.00
1930	10,000,000	0.75	1.50	2.00	8.00	12.00
1931	3,400,000	3.50	7.50	12.50	35.00	50.00
1937	10,000,000	0.50	1.00	1.50	5.00	8.00
1938	16,600,000	0.50	1.00	1.50	5.00	8.00
1939	22,000,000	0.50	1.00	1.50	5.00	7.00
1940	24,600,000	0.50	1.00	1.50	5.00	7.00
1941	66,600,000	0.25	0.60	1.00	2.50	4.00

Note: For similar coins dated 1942P see Curacao; 1943P, 1957-1960 see Suriname

KM# 170 CENT
2.0000 g., Zinc, 17 mm. Ruler: Wilhelmina I Obv: Circled cross with banner below Rev: Value, waves, date and sprig Edge: Reeded

Date	Mintage	F	VF	XF	Unc	BU
1941	31,800,000	1.00	2.00	4.00	15.00	25.00
1942	241,000,000	0.25	0.50	1.00	3.00	8.00
1943	71,000,000	0.50	1.00	2.00	5.00	15.00
1944	29,600,000	2.00	4.00	4.00	15.00	25.00

KM# 175 CENT
2.0000 g., Bronze, 14 mm. Ruler: Wilhelmina I Obv: Head left Rev: Value divides date Edge: Plain

Date	Mintage	F	VF	XF	Unc	BU
1948 Proof	—	Value: 80.00				
1948	175,000,000	0.05	0.10	0.50	3.50	9.00

KM# 180 CENT
2.0000 g., Bronze, 14 mm. **Ruler:** Juliana **Obv:** Head right **Rev:** Value divides date

Date	Mintage	F	VF	XF	Unc	BU
1950	46,400,000	0.10	0.20	2.00	6.00	15.00
1950 Proof	—	Value: 50.00				
1951	45,800,000	0.10	0.20	2.00	6.00	15.00
1951 Proof	—	Value: 50.00				
1952	68,000,000	0.10	0.20	2.00	6.00	15.00
1952 Proof	—	Value: 50.00				
1953	54,000,000	0.10	0.20	2.00	6.00	15.00
1953 Proof	—	Value: 50.00				
1954 Proof	—	Value: 50.00				
1954	54,000,000	0.10	0.20	2.00	6.00	15.00
1955	52,000,000	0.10	0.20	2.00	6.00	15.00
1955 Proof	—	Value: 50.00				
1956	34,800,000	0.10	0.20	2.00	6.00	10.00
1956 Proof	—	Value: 50.00				
1957	48,000,000	0.10	0.20	0.25	6.00	10.00
1957 Proof	—	Value: 50.00				
1958	34,000,000	0.10	0.20	0.25	6.00	10.00
1958 Proof	—	Value: 50.00				
1959	36,000,000	0.10	0.20	1.00	6.00	10.00
1959 Proof	—	Value: 50.00				
1960	40,000,000	0.10	0.20	1.00	2.00	6.00
1960 Proof	—	Value: 50.00				
1961	52,000,000	0.10	0.20	1.00	1.50	3.00
1961 Proof	—	Value: 50.00				
1962	57,000,000	0.10	0.20	1.00	1.50	3.00
1962 Proof	—	Value: 50.00				
1963 Proof	—	Value: 50.00				
1963	70,000,000	0.10	0.20	1.00	1.50	3.00
1964	73,000,000	0.10	0.20	1.00	1.50	3.00
1964 Proof	—	Value: 50.00				
1965	91,000,000	0.10	0.20	1.00	1.50	3.00
1965 Proof	—	Value: 50.00				
1966 large date	104,000,000	0.10	0.20	1.00	1.50	3.00
1966 Proof, large date	—	Value: 50.00				
1966 small date	Inc. above	0.10	0.20	1.00	1.50	3.00
1966 Proof, small date	—	Value: 50.00				
1967	140,000,000	0.10	0.20	1.00	1.50	3.00
1967 Proof	—	Value: 50.00				
1968	28,000,000	0.10	0.20	1.00	1.50	3.00
1968 Proof	—	Value: 50.00				
1969 fish privy mark	50,000,000	0.10	0.20	0.30	0.75	1.25
1969 Proof, fish privy mark	—	Value: 50.00				
1969 cock privy mark	50,000,000	0.10	0.20	0.30	0.75	1.25
1969 Proof, cock privy mark	—	Value: 50.00				
1970	100,000,000	0.10	0.20	0.30	0.75	1.25
1970 Proof	—	Value: 50.00				
1971	70,000,000	—	—	—	0.75	1.25
1972	40,000,000	—	—	—	0.75	1.25
1973	34,000,000	—	—	—	0.75	1.25
1974	46,000,000	—	—	—	0.75	1.25
1975	25,000,000	—	—	—	0.75	1.25
1976	15,000,000	—	—	—	0.75	1.25
1977	15,000,000	—	—	—	0.75	1.25
1978	15,000,000	‣	—	—	0.75	1.25
1979	15,000,000	—	—	—	0.75	1.25
1980 cock and star privy mark	15,300,000	—	—	0.10	0.20	0.50

KM# 134 2-1/2 CENT
4.0000 g., Bronze, 23.5 mm. **Ruler:** Wilhelmina I **Obv:** Crowned arms with 15 large shields within beaded circle **Obv. Leg.:** KONINGRIJK DER NEDERLANDEN **Rev:** Value within wreath **Edge:** Reeded

Date	Mintage	F	VF	XF	Unc	BU
1903	4,000,000	2.00	3.50	6.50	20.00	50.00
1904	4,000,000	2.00	3.50	6.50	20.00	50.00
1905	4,000,000	2.00	3.50	6.50	20.00	50.00
1906	8,000,000	2.00	3.50	6.50	20.00	40.00

KM# 150 2-1/2 CENT
4.0000 g., Bronze, 23 mm. **Ruler:** Wilhelmina I **Obv:** Crowned arms with 15 large shields within beaded circle **Obv. Leg.:** KONINGRIJK. **Rev:** Value within wreath

Date	Mintage	F	VF	XF	Unc	BU
1912	2,000,000	4.00	8.00	16.50	50.00	100
1913	4,000,000	2.50	4.50	8.00	15.00	50.00
1914	2,000,000	4.00	8.00	16.50	50.00	100
1915	3,000,000	3.00	6.00	12.00	25.00	55.00
1916	8,000,000	2.00	3.50	6.00	15.00	50.00
1918	4,000,000	2.50	4.00	8.00	22.50	50.00
1919	2,000,000	6.00	12.00	25.00	50.00	100
1929	8,000,000	2.00	3.50	6.00	10.00	25.00
1941	19,800,000	1.25	2.00	3.00	6.00	9.00

KM# 171 2-1/2 CENT
2.0000 g., Zinc, 20 mm. **Ruler:** Wilhelmina I **Obv:** Two swans on roof **Rev:** Value with four waves

Date	Mintage	F	VF	XF	Unc	BU
1941	27,600,000	1.00	3.00	5.00	15.00	40.00
1942	Est. 200,000	750	3,500	5,500	8,500	12,000

Note: Almost entire issue melted, about 30 pieces known

KM# 137 5 CENTS
4.5000 g., Copper-Nickel, 12 mm. **Ruler:** Wilhelmina I **Obv:** Crown flanked by sprigs **Rev:** Value within wreath

Date	Mintage	F	VF	XF	Unc	BU
1907	6,000,000	3.00	6.00	10.00	20.00	35.00
1908	5,430,000	4.00	8.00	12.50	22.50	40.00
1909	2,570,000	20.00	30.00	40.00	80.00	150

KM# 153 5 CENTS
4.5000 g., Copper-Nickel, 21.3 mm. **Ruler:** Wilhelmina I **Obv:** Orange branch within circle **Rev:** Value within shells and beaded circle

Date	Mintage	F	VF	XF	Unc	BU
1913	6,000,000	1.50	3.00	5.00	15.00	30.00
1914	7,400,000	1.50	3.00	5.00	15.00	30.00
1923	10,000,000	1.50	3.00	5.00	15.00	30.00
1929	8,000,000	1.50	3.00	5.00	15.00	30.00
1932	2,000,000	5.50	12.00	20.00	35.00	65.00
1933	1,400,000	20.00	30.00	50.00	70.00	140
1934	2,600,000	4.00	6.00	10.00	20.00	40.00
1936	2,600,000	4.00	6.00	10.00	20.00	40.00
1938	4,200,000	2.00	3.50	4.50	10.00	20.00
1939	4,600,000	2.00	3.50	4.50	10.00	20.00
1940	7,200,000	2.00	3.00	4.00	9.00	15.00

Note: For a similar coin dated 1943, see Curacao

KM# 172 5 CENTS
2.6000 g., Zinc, 18 mm. **Ruler:** Wilhelmina I **Obv:** Two crossed horse heads and sun within square **Rev:** Value within circle flanked by nine waves and sprig

Date	Mintage	F	VF	XF	Unc	BU
1941	32,200,000	1.00	2.50	6.00	18.00	35.00
1942	11,800,000	2.00	3.50	9.00	22.00	40.00
1943	7,000,000	5.00	8.00	16.50	42.50	75.00

KM# 176 5 CENTS
2.5000 g., Bronze, 21 mm. **Ruler:** Wilhelmina I **Obv:** Head left **Rev:** Value divides date and orange branch

Date	Mintage	F	VF	XF	Unc	BU
1948 Proof	—	Value: 100				
1948	23,600,000	—	0.10	0.75	7.00	17.50

KM# 181 5 CENTS
3.5000 g., Bronze, 21 mm. **Ruler:** Juliana **Obv:** Head right **Rev:** Value divides date and orange branch

Date	Mintage	F	VF	XF	Unc	BU
1950 Proof	—	Value: 70.00				
1950	20,000,000	—	0.10	0.25	7.50	25.00
1951 Proof	—	Value: 70.00				
1951	16,200,000	—	0.10	0.25	7.50	25.00
1952	14,400,000	—	0.10	0.25	7.50	30.00
1952 Proof	—	Value: 70.00				
1953 Proof	—	Value: 70.00				
1953	12,000,000	—	0.10	0.25	7.50	30.00
1954	14,000,000	—	0.10	0.25	7.50	30.00
1954 Proof	—	Value: 70.00				
1955	11,400,000	—	0.10	0.25	7.50	30.00
1955 Proof	—	Value: 70.00				
1956	7,400,000	—	0.15	0.35	8.50	30.00
1956 Proof	—	Value: 70.00				
1957	16,000,000	—	0.10	0.25	6.50	30.00
1957 Proof	—	Value: 70.00				
1958 Proof	—	Value: 70.00				
1958	9,000,000	—	0.10	0.25	8.50	30.00
1960	11,000,000	—	0.10	0.25	3.50	20.00
1960 Proof	—	Value: 40.00				
1961	12,000,000	—	0.10	0.25	3.50	20.00
1961 Proof	—	Value: 40.00				
1962 Proof	—	Value: 40.00				
1962	15,000,000	—	0.10	0.25	2.00	20.00
1963 Proof	—	Value: 40.00				
1963	18,000,000	—	0.10	0.25	2.00	20.00
1964 Proof	—	Value: 40.00				
1964	21,000,000	—	0.10	0.25	2.00	20.00
1965 Proof	—	Value: 40.00				
1965	28,000,000	—	0.10	0.25	1.50	20.00
1966 Proof	—	Value: 40.00				
1966	22,000,000	—	0.10	0.25	2.00	20.00
1967 leaves far from rim	32,000,000	—	—	0.20	1.50	15.00
1967 Proof, leaves far from rim	—	Value: 50.00				
1967 leaves touching rim	Inc. above	—	0.15	0.50	1.50	15.00
1967 Proof, leaves touching rim	—	Value: 40.00				
1969 fish privy mark	5,000,000	—	0.15	0.50	3.50	20.00
1969 Proof, fish privy mark	—	Value: 40.00				
1969 cock privy mark	11,000,000	—	—	0.10	1.00	20.00
1969 Proof, cock privy mark	—	Value: 40.00				
1970	22,000,000	—	—	0.10	0.75	10.00
1970 Proof	—	Value: 40.00				
1970 date close to rim	Inc. above	—	—	0.10	0.75	5.00
1970 Proof, date close to rim	—	Value: 40.00				
1971	25,000,000	—	—	0.10	0.50	5.00
1972	25,000,000	—	—	0.10	0.50	5.00
1973	22,000,000	—	—	0.10	0.50	5.00
1974	20,000,000	—	—	—	0.50	5.00
1975	46,000,000	—	—	—	0.25	1.50
1976	50,000,000	—	—	—	0.25	1.50
1977	50,000,000	—	—	—	0.25	1.50
1978	60,000,000	—	—	—	0.25	1.50
1979	80,000,000	—	—	—	0.25	1.50
1980 cock and star privy mark	252,500,000	—	—	—	0.10	0.35

KM# 202   5 CENTS

3.5000 g., Bronze, 21 mm.   **Ruler:** Beatrix **Obv:** Head left with vertical inscription **Rev:** Value within vertical lines **Edge:** Plain

Date	Mintage	F	VF	XF	Unc	BU
1982 Proof	10,000	Value: 10.00				
1982	47,100,000	—	—	—	0.10	0.40
1983 Proof	15,000	Value: 7.50				
1983	60,200,000	—	—	—	0.10	0.40
1984 Proof	20,000	Value: 4.00				
1984	70,700,000	—	—	—	0.10	0.40
1985 Proof	17,000	Value: 4.00				
1985	36,100,000	—	—	—	0.10	0.40
1986 Proof	20,000	Value: 4.00				
1986	7,700,000	—	—	—	0.50	1.50
1987 Proof	18,000	Value: 4.00				
1987	33,299,999	—	—	—	—	0.40
1988 Proof	20,000	Value: 4.00				
1988	22,600,000	—	—	—	—	0.40
1989 Proof	15,000	Value: 4.00				
1989	27,100,000	—	—	—	—	0.40
1990 Proof	15,000	Value: 4.00				
1990	39,300,000	—	—	—	—	0.40
1991 Proof	14,000	Value: 4.00				
1991	73,100,000	—	—	—	—	0.40
1992 Proof	13,000	Value: 4.00				
1992	52,700,000	—	—	—	—	0.40
1993 Proof	12,000	Value: 4.00				
1993	40,000,000	—	—	—	—	0.40
1994 Proof	13,000	Value: 4.00				
1994	14,000,000	—	—	—	—	1.50
1995 Proof	12,000	Value: 4.00				
1995	6,000,000	—	—	—	0.75	3.00
1996 Proof	14,000	Value: 4.00				
1996	40,000,000	—	—	—	—	0.40
1997 Proof	12,000	Value: 4.00				
1997	36,000,000	—	—	—	—	0.40
1998 Proof	12,000	Value: 4.00				
1998	65,099,999	—	—	—	—	0.40
1999 Proof	15,000	Value: 4.00				
1999	16,480,000	—	—	—	—	0.40
2000 Proof	15,000	Value: 4.00				
2000	30,076,000	—	—	—	—	0.40

KM# 119   10 CENTS

1.4000 g., 0.6400 Silver 0.0288 oz. ASW, 15 mm.
Ruler: Wilhelmina I **Obv:** Small crowned head left divides legend
Obv. Leg.: WILHELMINA... **Rev:** Value and date within wreath
Edge: Reeded

Date	Mintage	F	VF	XF	Unc	BU
1901	2,000,000	10.00	25.00	70.00	150	300

KM# 135   10 CENTS

1.4000 g., 0.6400 Silver 0.0288 oz. ASW, 15 mm.
Ruler: Wilhelmina I **Obv:** Head left **Rev:** Value in wreath

Date	Mintage	F	VF	XF	Unc	BU
1903	6,000,000	4.00	12.00	30.00	50.00	85.00

KM# 136   10 CENTS

1.4000 g., 0.6400 Silver 0.0288 oz. ASW, 15 mm.
Ruler: Wilhelmina I **Obv:** Small head left with continous legend
Rev: Value in wreath

Date	Mintage	F	VF	XF	Unc	BU
1904	3,000,000	6.00	16.50	30.00	70.00	150
1905	2,000,000	8.00	25.00	50.00	100	250
1906	4,000,000	4.00	14.50	25.00	55.00	110

KM# 145   10 CENTS

1.4000 g., 0.6400 Silver 0.0288 oz. ASW, 15 mm.
Ruler: Wilhelmina I **Obv:** Small head left with continuous legend
Rev: Value within wreath **Edge:** Reeded

Date	Mintage	F	VF	XF	Unc	BU
1910	2,250,000	10.00	25.00	45.00	100	200
1911	4,000,000	4.00	9.00	22.00	45.00	100
1912	4,000,000	4.00	9.00	22.00	45.00	85.00
1913	5,000,000	3.00	7.00	15.00	40.00	75.00
1914	9,000,000	1.50	4.00	10.00	25.00	45.00
1915	5,000,000	1.75	5.00	12.00	30.00	65.00
1916	5,000,000	1.75	5.00	12.00	30.00	65.00
1917	10,000,000	1.50	3.50	8.00	16.00	30.00
1918	20,000,000	1.00	2.50	5.00	13.50	30.00
1919	10,000,000	1.50	3.50	8.00	16.00	30.00
1921	5,000,000	2.00	6.00	10.00	22.00	70.00
1925	5,000,000	2.00	6.00	10.00	22.00	70.00

KM# 163   10 CENTS

1.4000 g., 0.6400 Silver 0.0288 oz. ASW, 15 mm.
Ruler: Wilhelmina I **Obv:** Small head left with continuous legend
Rev: Value within wreath **Edge:** Reeded

Date	Mintage	F	VF	XF	Unc	BU
1926	2,700,000	2.50	6.00	15.00	55.00	150
1927	2,300,000	2.50	6.00	15.00	60.00	150
1928	10,000,000	0.75	2.00	5.00	16.00	40.00
1930	5,000,000	1.00	3.50	7.50	22.00	40.00
1934	2,000,000	2.50	6.00	15.00	60.00	120
1935	8,000,000	0.75	1.50	3.50	10.00	20.00
1936	15,000,000	0.50	0.75	2.00	5.00	10.00
1937	18,600,000	0.50	0.75	2.00	3.50	5.00
1938	21,400,000	0.50	0.75	2.00	3.50	5.00
1939	20,000,000	0.50	0.75	2.00	3.50	5.00
1941	43,000,000	0.50	0.50	1.50	2.25	3.00
1943 Acorn privy mark	—	0.75	1.00	2.00	10.00	20.00
1944	120,000,000	0.50	0.75	1.25	2.00	3.00
1944	25,400,000	1,200	3,000	6,000	11,000	15,000

Note: Almost entire issue melted

Date	Mintage	F	VF	XF	Unc	BU
1944	64,040,000	1.00	2.00	4.50	15.00	30.00
1945	90,560,000	120	300	550	1,000	1,500

Note: For similar coins dated 1941P-1943P with palm tree privy mark, see Curacao and Suriname

KM# 173   10 CENTS

3.3000 g., Zinc, 22 mm.   **Ruler:** Wilhelmina I **Obv:** Three tulips flanked by dots within circle **Rev:** Value flanked by sprigs
Edge: Reeded

Date	Mintage	F	VF	XF	Unc	BU
1941	29,800,000	0.75	1.50	3.50	10.00	30.00
1942	95,600,000	0.25	0.50	2.00	5.00	20.00
1943	29,000,000	0.75	1.50	3.50	10.00	30.00

KM# 177   10 CENTS

1.5000 g., Nickel, 15 mm.   **Ruler:** Wilhelmina I **Obv:** Head left
Rev: Crowned value divides date **Edge:** Reeded

Date	Mintage	F	VF	XF	Unc	BU
1948 Proof	—	Value: 100				
1948	69,200,000	—	0.10	0.50	3.00	10.00

KM# 182   10 CENTS

1.5000 g., Nickel, 15 mm.   **Ruler:** Juliana **Obv:** Head right
Rev: Crowned value divides date **Edge:** Reeded

Date	Mintage	F	VF	XF	Unc	BU
1950 Proof	—	Value: 80.00				
1950	56,600,000	—	0.10	0.35	0.75	3.50
1951 Proof	—	Value: 60.00				
1951	54,200,000	—	0.10	0.35	0.75	5.00

Date	Mintage	F	VF	XF	Unc	BU
1954	8,200,000	—	0.20	0.50	1.00	10.00
1954 Proof	—	Value: 60.00				
1955	18,200,000	—	0.10	0.35	0.75	10.00
1955 Proof	—	Value: 60.00				
1956	12,000,000	—	0.10	0.35	0.75	10.00
1956 Proof	—	Value: 60.00				
1957	18,600,000	—	0.10	0.35	0.75	10.00
1957 Proof	—	Value: 60.00				
1958 Proof	—	Value: 60.00				
1958	34,000,000	—	0.10	0.35	0.75	10.00
1959 Proof	—	Value: 50.00				
1959	44,000,000	—	0.10	0.35	0.75	10.00
1960	12,000,000	—	0.10	0.35	0.75	10.00
1960 Proof	—	Value: 50.00				
1961 Proof	—	Value: 50.00				
1961	25,000,000	—	—	0.10	0.25	5.00
1962 Proof	—	Value: 50.00				
1962	30,000,000	—	—	0.10	0.25	5.00
1963 Proof	—	Value: 60.00				
1963	35,000,000	—	—	0.10	0.25	5.00
1964 Proof	—	Value: 60.00				
1964	41,000,000	—	—	0.10	0.25	5.00
1965 Proof	—	Value: 60.00				
1965	59,000,000	—	—	0.10	0.25	5.00
1966 Proof	—	Value: 50.00				
1966	44,000,000	—	—	—	0.10	5.00
1967 Proof	—	Value: 50.00				
1967	39,000,000	—	—	—	0.10	2.00
1968 Proof	—	Value: 40.00				
1968	42,000,000	—	—	—	0.10	2.00
1969 fish privy mark	29,100,000	—	—	—	0.10	2.00
1969 Proof, fish privy mark	—	Value: 40.00				
1969 cock privy mark	24,000,000	—	—	—	0.10	2.00
1969 Proof, cock privy mark	—	Value: 40.00				
1970 Proof	—	Value: 40.00				
1970	50,000,000	—	—	—	0.10	1.00
1971	55,000,000	—	—	—	0.10	1.00
1972	60,000,000	—	—	—	0.10	1.00
1973	90,000,000	—	—	—	0.10	1.00
1974	75,000,000	—	—	—	0.20	1.50
1975	110,000,000	—	—	—	0.10	0.50
1976	85,000,000	—	—	—	0.10	0.50
1977	100,000,000	—	—	—	0.10	0.50
1978	110,000,000	—	—	—	0.10	0.50
1979	120,000,000	—	—	—	0.10	0.50
1980 cock and star privy mark	195,300,000	—	—	—	0.10	0.50

KM# 203   10 CENTS

1.5000 g., Nickel, 15 mm.   **Ruler:** Beatrix **Obv:** Head left with vertical inscription **Rev:** Value and vertical lines **Edge:** Reeded

Date	Mintage	F	VF	XF	Unc	BU
1982 Proof	10,000	Value: 10.00				
1982	10,300,000	—	—	—	0.10	0.50
1983 Proof	15,000	Value: 8.00				
1983	38,200,000	—	—	—	—	0.50
1984 Proof	20,000	Value: 4.00				
1984	42,200,000	—	—	—	0.10	0.50
1985 Proof	17,000	Value: 4.00				
1985	29,100,000	—	—	—	0.10	0.50
1986 Proof	20,000	Value: 4.00				
1986	23,100,000	—	—	—	0.10	0.50
1987 Proof	18,000	Value: 4.00				
1987	21,700,000	—	—	—	0.10	0.50
1988 Proof	20,000	Value: 6.00				
1988	2,200,000	—	—	—	0.25	2.00
1989 Proof	15,000	Value: 5.00				
1989	5,300,000	—	—	—	—	1.50
1990 Proof	15,000	Value: 4.00				
1990	13,300,000	—	—	—	—	0.50
1991 Proof	14,000	Value: 4.00				
1991	41,100,000	—	—	—	—	0.50
1992 Proof	13,000	Value: 4.00				
1992	41,300,000	—	—	—	—	0.50
1993 Proof	12,000	Value: 4.00				
1993	30,100,000	—	—	—	—	0.50
1994 Proof	13,000	Value: 4.00				
1994	25,685,000	—	—	—	—	0.50
1995 Proof	12,000	Value: 4.00				
1995	35,100,000	—	*	—	—	0.50
1996 Proof	14,000	Value: 4.00				
1996	34,900,000	—	—	—	—	0.50
1997 Proof	12,000	Value: 4.00				
1997	20,100,000	—	—	—	—	0.50
1998 Proof	12,000	Value: 4.00				
1998	24,540,000	—	—	—	—	0.50
1999 Proof	15,000	Value: 4.00				
1999	50,040,000	—	—	—	—	1.50
2000 Proof	15,000	Value: 4.00				
2000	75,476,000	—	—	—	—	0.50

KM# 120.1 25 CENTS
3.5750 g., 0.6400 Silver 0.0736 oz. ASW, 19 mm.
Ruler: Wilhelmina I **Obv:** Bust with wide truncation **Rev:** Value within wreath **Edge:** Reeded

Date	Mintage	F	VF	XF	Unc	BU
1901	1,600,000	40.00	100	275	700	1,100

KM# 120.2 25 CENTS
3.5750 g., 0.6400 Silver 0.0736 oz. ASW, 19 mm.
Ruler: Wilhelmina I **Obv:** Head left **Rev:** Value within wreath **Edge:** Reeded

Date	Mintage	F	VF	XF	Unc	BU
1901	Inc. above	8.00	22.00	45.00	150	225
1901 Proof	3	Value: 1,500				
1902	1,200,000	8.00	25.00	50.00	120	225
1903	1,200,000	8.00	25.00	50.00	120	200
1904	1,600,000	7.00	20.00	40.00	100	200
1905	1,200,000	8.00	25.00	50.00	120	180
1906	2,000,000	6.00	18.00	35.00	85.00	140

KM# 146 25 CENTS
3.5750 g., 0.6400 Silver 0.0736 oz. ASW, 19 mm.
Ruler: Wilhelmina I **Obv:** Bust left, legend **Rev:** Value within wreath **Edge:** Reeded

Date	Mintage	F	VF	XF	Unc	BU
1910	880,000	18.00	35.00	75.00	200	400
1910 Proof	—	Value: 600				
1911	1,600,000	8.00	20.00	40.00	150	300
1912	1,600,000	8.00	20.00	40.00	150	300
1913	1,200,000	20.00	40.00	75.00	180	275
1914	5,600,000	3.50	8.00	20.00	75.00	100
1915	2,000,000	4.50	12.00	25.00	100	200
1916	2,000,000	4.50	12.00	25.00	100	200
1917	4,000,000	3.50	8.00	20.00	50.00	100
1918	6,000,000	3.50	6.00	12.00	32.00	50.00
1919	4,000,000	3.50	8.00	20.00	50.00	85.00
1925	2,000,000	4.50	12.00	20.00	100	150

KM# 164 25 CENTS
3.5750 g., 0.6400 Silver 0.0736 oz. ASW, 19 mm.
Ruler: Wilhelmina I **Obv:** Small head left **Rev:** Value within wreath **Edge:** Reeded

Date	Mintage	F	VF	XF	Unc	BU
1926	2,000,000	6.00	12.00	30.00	120	200
1928	8,000,000	BV	1.75	5.00	18.00	110
1939	4,000,000	BV	1.25	2.00	5.00	8.00
1940	9,000,000	BV	1.25	2.00	5.00	8.00
1941	40,000,000	—	BV	1.50	2.50	4.50
1943 acorn privy mark	—	BV	1.50	3.50	12.50	20.00
1944 acorn privy mark	40,000,000	—	BV	1.50	2.50	5.50
1945 acorn privy mark	92,000,000	40.00	110	200	300	500

Note: For similar coins dated 1941P and 1943P with palm tree privy mark, see Curacao

KM# 174 25 CENTS
5.0000 g., Zinc, 26 mm. **Ruler:** Wilhelmina I **Obv:** Sailing boat **Rev:** Value flanked by sprigs

Date	Mintage	F	VF	XF	Unc	BU
1941	34,600,000	0.75	1.50	3.50	12.00	25.00
1942	27,800,000	0.75	1.50	3.50	12.00	25.00
1943	13,600,000	2.50	6.00	12.00	35.00	60.00

KM# 178 25 CENTS
3.0000 g., Nickel, 19 mm. **Ruler:** Wilhelmina I **Obv:** Head left **Rev:** Crowned value divides date **Edge:** Reeded

Date	Mintage	F	VF	XF	Unc	BU
1948 Proof	—	Value: 150				
1948	27,400,000	—	0.10	0.50	4.00	12.00

KM# 183 25 CENTS
3.0000 g., Nickel, 19 mm. **Ruler:** Juliana **Obv:** Head right **Rev:** Crowned value divides date **Edge:** Reeded

Date	Mintage	F	VF	XF	Unc	BU
1950	43,000,000	—	0.20	0.30	1.50	6.50
1950 Proof	—	Value: 75.00				
1951	33,200,000	—	0.20	0.30	1.50	10.00
1951 Proof	—	Value: 65.00				
1954	6,400,000	—	0.50	1.50	2.00	10.00
1954 Proof	—	Value: 65.00				
1955	10,000,000	—	0.20	0.30	1.50	10.00
1955 Proof	—	Value: 65.00				
1956	8,000,000	—	0.20	0.30	1.50	10.00
1956 Proof	—	Value: 65.00				
1957	8,000,000	—	0.20	0.30	1.50	10.00
1957 Proof	—	Value: 65.00				
1958	15,000,000	—	0.20	0.30	1.50	10.00
1958 Proof	—	Value: 65.00				
1960	9,000,000	—	0.20	0.30	1.50	10.00
1960 Proof	—	Value: 60.00				
1961	6,000,000	—	0.40	1.25	1.50	10.00
1961 Proof	—	Value: 50.00				
1962	12,000,000	—	0.20	0.30	1.00	10.00
1962 Proof	—	Value: 50.00				
1963	18,000,000	—	0.20	0.30	1.00	10.00
1963 Proof	—	Value: 50.00				
1964	25,000,000	—	0.20	0.30	1.00	10.00
1964 Proof	—	Value: 50.00				
1965	18,000,000	—	0.20	0.30	1.00	5.00
1965 Proof	—	Value: 50.00				
1966	25,000,000	—	—	0.20	0.75	5.00
1966 Proof	—	Value: 60.00				
1967	18,000,000	—	—	0.20	0.75	5.00
1967 Proof	—	Value: 60.00				
1968	26,000,000	—	—	0.20	0.75	5.00
1968 Proof	—	Value: 60.00				
1969 fish privy mark	14,000,000	—	—	0.20	0.30	5.00
1969 Proof, fish privy mark	—	Value: 60.00				
1969 cock privy mark	21,000,000	—	—	0.20	0.75	5.00
1969 Proof, cock privy mark	—	Value: 60.00				
1970	39,000,000	—	—	0.20	0.30	2.00
1970 Proof	—	Value: 60.00				
1971	40,000,000	—	—	0.20	0.30	2.00
1972	50,000,000	—	—	0.20	0.30	1.00
1973	45,000,000	—	—	0.20	0.30	1.00
1974	10,000,000	—	—	0.20	0.50	1.50
1975	25,000,000	—	—	0.20	0.30	1.00
1976	64,000,000	—	—	0.20	0.30	1.00
1977	55,000,000	—	—	0.20	0.30	1.00
1978	35,000,000	—	—	0.20	0.30	1.00
1979	45,000,000	—	—	0.20	0.30	1.00
1980 cock and star privy mark	159,300,000	—	—	—	0.20	0.50

KM# 183a 25 CENTS
0.7800 g., Aluminum **Ruler:** Juliana **Obv:** Head right **Rev:** Crowned value divides date **Note:** Thought by many sources to be a pattern.

Date	Mintage	F	VF	XF	Unc	BU
1980 Proof	15	Value: 500				

KM# 204 25 CENTS
3.0000 g., Nickel, 19 mm. **Ruler:** Beatrix **Obv:** Head left with vertical inscription **Obv. Insc.:** Beatrix/Konincin Der/Nederlanden **Rev:** Value within vertical and horizontal lines **Edge:** Reeded

Date	Mintage	F	VF	XF	Unc	BU
1982	18,300,000	—	—	—	0.20	0.60
1982 Proof	10,000	Value: 15.00				
1983	18,200,000	—	—	—	0.20	0.60
1983 Proof	15,000	Value: 12.00				
1984	19,200,000	—	—	—	0.20	0.60
1984 Proof	20,000	Value: 6.00				
1985	29,100,000	—	—	—	0.20	0.60
1985 Proof	17,000	Value: 6.00				
1986	20,300,000	—	—	—	0.20	0.60
1986 Proof	20,000	Value: 6.00				
1987	30,100,000	—	—	—	0.20	0.60
1987 Proof	18,000	Value: 6.00				
1988	17,400,000	—	—	—	0.20	0.60
1988 Proof	20,000	Value: 6.00				
1989	30,500,000	—	—	—	0.20	0.60
1989 Proof	15,000	Value: 6.00				
1990	23,100,000	—	—	—	0.20	0.60
1990 Proof	15,000	Value: 6.00				
1991	25,100,000	—	—	—	0.20	0.60
1991 Proof	14,000	Value: 6.00				
1992	41,600,000	—	—	—	0.20	0.60
1992 Proof	13,000	Value: 6.00				
1993	15,100,000	—	—	—	0.25	1.00
1993 Proof	12,000	Value: 6.00				
1994	1,700,000	—	—	—	1.00	5.00
1994 Proof	13,000	Value: 10.00				
1995	30,300,000	—	—	—	0.20	0.60
1995 Proof	12,000	Value: 8.00				
1996	24,900,000	—	—	—	0.20	0.60
1996 Proof	14,000	Value: 6.00				
1997	29,900,000	—	—	—	0.20	0.60
1997 Proof	12,000	Value: 6.00				
1998	69,660,000	—	—	—	0.20	0.60
1998 Proof	12,000	Value: 6.00				
1999	10,720,074	—	—	—	0.20	0.80
1999 Proof	15,000	Value: 6.00				
2000	31,176,000	—	—	—	0.20	0.60
2000 Proof	15,000	Value: 6.00				

KM# 121.2 1/2 GULDEN
5.0000 g., 0.9450 Silver 0.1519 oz. ASW, 22 mm.
Ruler: Wilhelmina I **Obv:** Head left **Rev:** Crowned Arms without 50 C. below shield **Edge:** Reeded

Date	Mintage	F	VF	XF	Unc	BU
1904	1,000,000	25.00	60.00	150	275	400
1905	4,000,000	7.00	15.00	35.00	90.00	150
1906	1,000,000	30.00	70.00	200	300	500
1907	3,300,000	7.00	15.00	35.00	90.00	150
1907 Proof	—	Value: 400				
1908	4,000,000	7.00	15.00	35.00	90.00	150
1909	3,000,000	7.00	15.00	35.00	90.00	150

KM# 147 1/2 GULDEN
5.0000 g., 0.9450 Silver 0.1519 oz. ASW, 22 mm.
Ruler: Wilhelmina I **Obv:** Head left **Rev:** Crowned Arms **Edge:** Reeded

Date	Mintage	F	VF	XF	Unc	BU
1910	4,000,000	7.00	16.50	50.00	100	200
1912	4,000,000	7.00	16.50	50.00	100	200
1913	8,000,000	6.00	10.00	30.00	65.00	125
1919	8,000,000	6.00	10.00	30.00	65.00	125

KM# 160 1/2 GULDEN
5.0000 g., 0.7200 Silver 0.1157 oz. ASW, 22 mm.
Ruler: Wilhelmina I **Obv:** Head left **Rev:** Crowned Arms **Edge:** Reeded

Date	Mintage	F	VF	XF	Unc	BU
1921	5,000,000	BV	2.75	5.00	22.00	40.00
1921 Proof	—	Value: 250				
1922	11,240,000	BV	2.50	3.50	15.00	22.00
1928	5,000,000	BV	2.75	5.00	22.00	30.00
1929	9,500,000	—	BV	3.00	12.00	18.00
Note: Pearls contact the edge						
1929	Inc. above	BV	5.00	25.00	50.00	100
Note: Pearls from the edge						
1930	18,500,000	—	BV	2.75	9.00	15.00

KM# 122.1 GULDEN

10.0000 g., 0.9450 Silver 0.3038 oz. ASW, 28 mm.
Ruler: Wilhelmina I **Obv:** Crowned head left
Obv. Leg.: WILHELMINA... **Rev:** Crowned arms divide value
Rev. Leg.: DER NEDERLANDEN... **Edge:** GOD * ZIJ * MET *
ONS *

Date	Mintage	F	VF	XF	Unc	BU
1901	2,000,000	25.00	65.00	150	300	400
1901 Proof	—	Value: 950				

KM# 122.2 GULDEN

10.0000 g., 0.9450 Silver 0.3038 oz. ASW **Ruler:** Wilhelmina I
Obv: Head left **Rev:** Crowned arms without 100 C. below shield
Edge: GOD*ZY*MET*ONS*

Date	Mintage	F	VF	XF	Unc	BU
1904	2,000,000	12.00	35.00	75.00	175	350
1905	1,000,000	25.00	65.00	150	300	800
1905 Proof	—	Value: 1,500				
1906	500,000	150	300	900	1,250	2,000
1906 Proof	—	Value: 4,000				
1907	5,100,000	8.00	20.00	45.00	100	150
1908	4,700,000	8.00	20.00	45.00	100	150
1908 Proof	—	Value: 750				
1909	2,000,000	20.00	35.00	90.00	175	300

KM# 148 GULDEN

10.0000 g., 0.9450 Silver 0.3038 oz. ASW, 28 mm.
Ruler: Wilhelmina I **Obv:** Head left **Obv. Leg.:** Crowned arms
Edge: GOD * ZIJ * MET * ONS *

Date	Mintage	F	VF	XF	Unc	BU
1910	1,000,000	50.00	200	500	800	1,500
1910 Proof	—	Value: 2,000				
1911	2,000,000	20.00	45.00	150	300	600
1912	3,000,000	10.00	35.00	75.00	200	300
1913	8,000,000	7.00	20.00	65.00	100	150
1914	15,785,000	6.00	15.00	32.50	75.00	130
1915	14,215,000	6.00	16.50	35.00	75.00	130
1916	5,000,000	16.00	50.00	85.00	175	225
1917	2,300,000	20.00	65.00	100	200	250

KM# 161.1 GULDEN

10.0000 g., 0.7200 Silver 0.2315 oz. ASW, 28 mm.
Ruler: Wilhelmina I **Obv:** Head left **Obv. Leg.:** Ends below
truncation **Rev:** Crowned arms **Edge:** GOD * ZIJ * MET * ONS *

Date	Mintage	F	VF	XF	Unc	BU
1922	9,550,000	BV	3.75	15.00	40.00	75.00
1922 Proof	—	Value: 450				
1923	8,050,000	BV	3.75	20.00	40.00	75.00
1924	8,000,000	BV	4.50	20.00	40.00	75.00
1928	6,150,000	BV	3.75	15.00	50.00	100
1929	32,350,000	—	BV	4.00	10.00	18.00
1930	13,500,000	—	BV	5.00	12.00	35.00
1931	38,100,000	—	BV	4.00	10.00	15.00
1938	5,000,000	BV	4.25	7.00	18.00	25.00
1939	14,200,000	—	BV	3.75	7.00	15.00

Date	Mintage	F	VF	XF	Unc	BU
1940	21,300,000	—	BV	3.75	7.00	15.00
1940 Proof	—	Value: 200				
1944 acorn privy mark	105,125,000	80.00	250	450	600	800

KM# 161.2 GULDEN

10.0000 g., 0.7200 Silver 0.2315 oz. ASW, 28 mm.
Ruler: Wilhelmina I **Obv:** Head left **Obv. Leg.:** Ends at right of
truncation **Rev:** Crowned arms **Edge:** GOD * ZIJ * MET * ONS
* **Note:** For similar coins dated 1943D with palm tree privy mark,
see Netherlands East Indies

Date	Mintage	F	VF	XF	Unc	BU
1944 acorn privy mark	Inc. above	7.50	20.00	35.00	55.00	100
1945 acorn privy mark	25,375,000	225	600	1,200	1,750	2,500

Note: Only a small number placed into circulation

KM# 184 GULDEN

6.5000 g., 0.7200 Silver 0.1505 oz. ASW, 25 mm. **Ruler:** Juliana
Obv: Head right **Rev:** Crowned arms divide date **Edge:** GOD *
ZIJ * MET * ONS *

Date	Mintage	F	VF	XF	Unc	BU
1954	6,600,000	—	—	BV	4.00	6.00
1954 Proof	—	Value: 120				
1955	37,500,000	—	—	BV	3.00	5.00
1955 Proof	—	Value: 120				
1956	38,900,000	—	—	BV	3.00	5.00
1956 Proof	—	Value: 120				
1957	27,000,000	—	—	BV	3.00	5.00
1957 Proof	—	Value: 120				
1958	30,000,000	—	—	BV	4.50	15.00
1958 Proof	—	Value: 120				
1963	5,000,000	—	—	BV	4.50	7.50
1963 Proof	—	Value: 120				
1964	9,000,000	—	—	BV	3.00	5.00
1964 Proof	—	Value: 120				
1965	21,000,000	—	—	BV	3.00	4.00
1965 Proof	—	Value: 120				
1966	5,000,000	—	—	BV	3.00	5.00
1966 Proof	—	Value: 120				
1967	7,000,000	—	—	BV	4.50	6.00
1967 Proof	—	Value: 120				

KM# 184a GULDEN

6.0000 g., Nickel, 25 mm. **Ruler:** Juliana **Obv:** Head right
Rev: Crowned arms divide date

Date	Mintage	F	VF	XF	Unc	BU
1967	31,000,000	—	—	0.75	2.00	5.00
1967 Proof	—	Value: 100				
1968	61,000,000	—	—	0.75	2.00	5.00
1969 fish	27,500,000	—	—	—	2.50	6.00
1969 Proof, fish	—	Value: 100				
1969 cock	15,500,000	—	—	—	2.50	6.00
1969 Proof, cock	—	Value: 100				
1970	18,000,000	—	—	0.75	2.00	10.00
1970 Proof	—	Value: 100				
1971	50,000,000	—	—	—	0.75	2.00
1972	60,000,000	—	—	—	0.75	2.00
1973	27,000,000	—	—	—	0.75	3.00
1975	9,000,000	—	—	—	2.00	5.00
1976	32,000,000	—	—	—	0.75	2.00
1977	38,000,000	—	—	—	0.75	2.00
1978	30,000,000	—	—	—	0.75	2.00
1979	25,000,000	—	—	—	0.75	2.00
1980 cock and star privy mark	118,300,000	—	—	—	0.65	1.00

KM# 200 GULDEN

6.0000 g., Nickel, 25 mm. **Ruler:** Beatrix **Subject:** Investiture
of New Queen **Obv:** Conjoined heads left **Rev:** Crowned arms
divide date **Edge:** GOD * ZIJ * MET * ONS *

Date	Mintage	F	VF	XF	Unc	BU
1980	30,500,000	—	—	—	0.65	1.00

KM# 200b GULDEN

Gold, 25 mm. **Ruler:** Beatrix **Subject:** Investiture of New Queen
Obv: Conjoined heads left **Rev:** Crowned arms divide date
Note: G added (for gold).

Date	Mintage	F	VF	XF	Unc	BU
1980 Rare	7	—	—	—	—	—

KM# 200a GULDEN

6.5000 g., Silver, 25 mm. **Ruler:** Beatrix **Subject:** Investiture of
New Queen **Obv:** Conjoined heads left **Rev:** Crowned arms divide
date **Edge:** GOD * ZIJ * MET * ONS * **Note:** Z added (for silver).

Date	Mintage	F	VF	XF	Unc	BU
1980	157	—	—	—	—	1,000

KM# 205 GULDEN

6.0000 g., Nickel, 25 mm. **Ruler:** Beatrix **Obv:** Head left with
vertical inscription **Rev:** Value within vertical and horizontal lines
Edge: GOD * ZIJ * MET * ONS *

Date	Mintage	F	VF	XF	Unc	BU
1982	31,300,000	—	—	—	—	1.25
1982 Proof	10,000	Value: 20.00				
1983	5,200,000	—	—	—	—	1.50
1983 Proof	15,000	Value: 15.00				
1984	4,200,000	—	—	—	—	1.50
1984 Proof	20,000	Value: 7.50				
1985	3,100,000	—	—	—	—	2.50
1985 Proof	17,000	Value: 7.50				
1986	12,100,000	—	—	—	—	1.75
1986 Proof	15,000	Value: 7.50				
1987	20,100,000	—	—	—	—	1.75
1987 Proof	20,000	Value: 7.50				
1988	13,600,000	—	—	—	—	1.75
1988 Proof	20,000	Value: 7.50				
1989	1,100,000	—	—	—	—	3.50
1989 Proof	15,000	Value: 7.50				
1990	1,100,000	—	—	—	—	3.50
1990 Proof	15,000	Value: 7.50				
1991	500,000	—	—	—	—	4.00
1991 Proof	14,000	Value: 7.50				
1992	10,100,000	—	—	—	—	1.50
1992 Proof	13,000	Value: 7.50				
1993	15,100,000	—	—	—	—	1.50
1993 Proof	12,000	Value: 7.50				
1994	16,600,000	—	—	—	—	1.50
1994 Proof	13,000	Value: 7.50				
1995	12,600,000	—	—	—	—	1.50
1995 Proof	12,000	Value: 7.50				
1996	6,660,000	—	—	—	—	1.50
1996 Proof	14,000	Value: 7.50				
1997	12,800,000	—	—	—	—	1.50
1997 Proof	12,000	Value: 7.50				
1998	15,100,000	—	—	—	—	1.75
1998 Proof	12,000	Value: 7.50				
1999	8,900,000	—	—	—	—	1.25
1999 Proof	15,000	Value: 7.50				
2000	37,680,000	—	—	—	—	1.25
2000 Proof	15,000	Value: 7.50				

KM# 230 GULDEN

11.0000 g., 0.7500 Gold 0.2652 oz. AGW **Ruler:** Beatrix
Rev: Small tulip, "750" added **Edge:** GOD ZIJ MET ONS
Note: Similar to KM#205.

Date	Mintage	F	VF	XF	Unc	BU
1999 Proof	1,000	Value: 1,500				

Note: Approximately 480 of the mintage were melted down

KM# 165 2-1/2 GULDEN
25.0000 g., 0.7200 Silver 0.5787 oz. ASW, 38 mm.
Ruler: Wilhelmina I **Obv:** Head left **Rev:** Crowned arms divide value **Edge:** GOD * ZIJ * MET * ONS *

Date	Mintage	F	VF	XF	Unc	BU
1929	4,400,000	BV	10.00	25.00	75.00	100
1930	11,600,000	BV	9.00	12.00	20.00	30.00
1931	4,400,000	BV	9.00	12.00	20.00	30.00
1932	6,320,000	BV	9.00	12.00	20.00	30.00
1932 Deep hair lines	Inc. above	70.00	125	250	350	600
1933	3,560,000	BV	9.50	15.00	25.00	50.00
1933 Deep hair lines	Inc. above	70.00	125	250	350	500
1937	4,000,000	—	BV	10.00	20.00	30.00
1938	2,000,000	BV	10.00	18.00	30.00	45.00
1938 Deep hair lines	Inc. above	45.00	100	235	325	450
1939	3,760,000	—	BV	10.00	20.00	30.00
1940	4,640,000	12.00	20.00	30.00	50.00	100

Note: For similar coins dated 1943D with palm tree privy mark, see Netherlands East Indies

KM# 185 2-1/2 GULDEN
15.0000 g., 0.7200 Silver 0.3472 oz. ASW, 33 mm.
Ruler: Juliana **Obv:** Head right **Rev:** Crowned arms divide value **Edge:** GOD * ZIJ * MET * ONS *

Date	Mintage	F	VF	XF	Unc	BU
1959	7,200,000	—	—	BV	5.50	10.00
1959 Proof	—	Value: 250				
1960	12,800,000	—	—	BV	5.50	10.00
1960 Proof	—	Value: 250				
1961	10,000,000	—	—	BV	5.50	10.00
1961 Proof	—	Value: 250				
1962	5,000,000	—	—	BV	5.50	10.00
1962 Proof	—	Value: 250				
1963	4,000,000	—	BV	5.50	9.00	14.00
1963 Proof	—	Value: 250				
1964	2,800,000	—	BV	6.00	10.00	15.00
1964 Proof	—	Value: 250				
1966	5,000,000	—	—	BV	5.50	9.00
1966 Proof	—	Value: 250				

KM# 191 2-1/2 GULDEN
10.0000 g., Nickel, 29 mm. **Ruler:** Juliana **Obv:** Head right **Rev:** Crowned arms divide value **Edge:** GOD * ZIJ * MET * ONS *

Date	Mintage	F	VF	XF	Unc	BU
1969	1,200,000	—	—	1.00	3.00	10.00

Note: Fish privy mark

| 1969 Proof | — | Value: 200 | | | | |

Note: Fish privy mark with front hair lock

| 1969 Proof, 2 known | — | Value: 3,500 | | | | |

Note: Fish privy mark without front hair lock

| 1969 | 15,600,000 | — | — | — | 3.00 | 5.00 |

Note: Cock privy mark

| 1969 Proof | — | Value: 200 | | | | |

Note: Cock privy mark

1970	22,000,000	—	—	—	5.00	20.00
1970 Proof	—	Value: 150				
1971	8,000,000	—	—	—	2.50	4.00
1972	20,000,000	—	—	—	2.50	4.00
1978	5,000,000	—	—	—	3.00	6.00

Date	Mintage	F	VF	XF	Unc	BU
1980	37,300,000	—	—	—	2.50	4.00

Note: Cock and star privy mark

KM# 197 2-1/2 GULDEN
10.0000 g., Nickel, 29 mm. **Ruler:** Juliana **Subject:** 400th Anniversary - The Union of Utrecht **Obv:** Head right **Rev:** Text, value and date **Edge:** GOD * ZIJ * MET * ONS *

Date	Mintage	F	VF	XF	Unc	BU
1979	25,000,000	—	—	—	1.00	2.00

KM# 201 2-1/2 GULDEN
10.0000 g., Nickel, 29 mm. **Ruler:** Beatrix **Subject:** Investiture of New Queen **Obv:** Conjoined heads left **Rev:** Crowned arms divide date **Edge:** GOD * ZIJ * MET * ONS *

Date	Mintage	F	VF	XF	Unc	BU
1980	30,500,000	—	—	—	1.00	2.00

KM# 201b 2-1/2 GULDEN
Gold **Ruler:** Beatrix **Subject:** Investiture of New Queen **Obv:** Conjoined heads left **Rev:** Crowned arms divide date **Edge:** GOD * ZIJ * MET * ONS * **Note:** G added (for gold).

Date	Mintage	F	VF	XF	Unc	BU
1980 Rare	7	—	—	—	—	—

KM# 201a 2-1/2 GULDEN
Silver **Ruler:** Beatrix **Subject:** Investiture of New Queen **Obv:** Conjoined heads left **Rev:** Crowned arms divide date **Edge:** GOD * ZIJ * MET * ONS * **Note:** Z added (for silver).

Date	Mintage	F	VF	XF	Unc	BU
1980	157	—	—	—	—	1,800

KM# 206 2-1/2 GULDEN
10.0000 g., Nickel, 29 mm. **Ruler:** Beatrix **Obv:** Head left with vertical inscription **Rev:** Value within horizontal, vertical and diagonal lines **Edge:** GOD * ZIJ * MET * ONS *

Date	Mintage	F	VF	XF	Unc	BU
1982	14,300,000	—	—	—	—	2.00
1982 Proof	10,000	Value: 35.00				
1983	3,800,000	—	—	—	—	2.50
1983 Proof	15,000	Value: 27.50				
1984	5,200,000	—	—	—	—	2.50
1984 Proof	20,000	—	—	—	—	—
1985	3,100,000	—	—	—	—	4.50
1985 Proof	17,000	Value: 16.00				
1986	5,800,000	—	—	—	—	4.50
1986 Proof	20,000	Value: 16.00				
1987	2,500,000	—	—	—	—	8.50
1987 Proof	18,000	Value: 16.00				
1988	6,200,000	—	—	—	—	4.50
1988 Proof	20,000	Value: 16.00				
1989	4,099,999	—	—	—	—	4.00
1989 Proof	15,000	Value: 16.00				
1990	1,100,000	—	—	—	—	3.00
1990 Proof	15,000	Value: 16.00				
1991	500,000	—	—	—	—	10.00
1991 Proof	14,000	Value: 16.00				
1992	500,000	—	—	—	—	10.00
1992 Proof	13,000	Value: 16.00				
1993	500,000	—	—	—	—	10.00
1993 Proof	12,000	Value: 16.00				
1994	500,000	—	—	—	—	10.00
1994 Proof	13,000	Value: 16.00				
1995	240,000	—	—	—	—	12.00
1995 Proof	12,000	Value: 16.00				
1996	240,000	—	—	—	—	12.00
1996 Proof	14,000	Value: 16.00				
1997	300,000	—	—	—	—	12.00

Date	Mintage	F	VF	XF	Unc	BU
1997 Proof	12,000	Value: 16.00				
1998	300,000	—	—	—	—	12.00
1998 Proof	12,000	Value: 16.00				
1999	400,000	—	—	—	—	12.00
1999 Proof	15,000	Value: 16.00				
2000	500,000	—	—	—	—	12.00
2000 Proof	15,000	Value: 16.00				

KM# 151 5 GULDEN
3.3600 g., 0.9000 Gold 0.0972 oz. AGW, 18 mm.
Ruler: Wilhelmina I **Obv:** Bust right **Rev:** Crowned arms divide value **Edge:** Reeded **Note:** Counterfeits are prevalent.

Date	Mintage	F	VF	XF	Unc	BU
1912	1,000,000	90.00	100	120	200	250
1912 Matte Proof	120	Value: 1,200				

KM# 210 5 GULDEN
9.2500 g., Bronze Clad Nickel, 23.5 mm. **Ruler:** Beatrix **Obv:** Head left with vertical inscription **Rev:** Value within horizontal, vertical and diagonal lines **Edge:** GOD * ZIJ * MET * ONS *

Date	Mintage	F	VF	XF	Unc	BU
1987 Proof	2	—	—	—	—	—
1988	73,700,000	—	—	—	—	8.00
1988 Proof	20,000	Value: 12.50				
1989	69,100,000	—	—	—	—	8.00
1989 Proof	15,000	Value: 12.50				
1990	47,300,000	—	—	—	—	8.00
1990 Proof	15,000	Value: 15.00				
1991	17,100,000	—	—	—	—	8.00
1991 Proof	14,000	Value: 15.00				
1992	500,000	—	—	—	—	8.00
1992 Proof	13,000	Value: 15.00				
1993	5,500,000	—	—	—	—	5.00
1993 Proof	12,000	Value: 15.00				
1994	488,000	—	—	—	—	12.00
1994 Proof	13,000	Value: 17.50				
1995	488,000	—	—	—	—	12.00
1995 Proof	12,000	Value: 17.50				
1996	240,000	—	—	—	—	12.00
1996 Proof	14,000	Value: 17.50				
1997	278,000	—	—	—	—	12.00
1997 Proof	12,000	Value: 17.50				
1998	204,000	—	—	—	—	12.00
1998 Proof	12,000	Value: 16.00				
1999	280,000	—	—	—	—	12.00
1999 Proof	15,000	Value: 16.00				
2000	385,000	—	—	—	—	10.00
2000 Proof	15,000	Value: 16.00				

KM# 231 5 GULDEN
9.2500 g., Brass Plated Nickel, 23.5 mm. **Ruler:** Beatrix **Subject:** Soccer **Obv:** Head left **Rev:** Value within soccerball **Edge:** Reeded **Edge:** GOD * ZIJ * MET * ONS * **Note:** A joint issue proof set exists containing the Netherlands KM#231, Belgium KM#213-214 plus a medal.

Date	Mintage	F	VF	XF	Unc	BU
2000 Proof	Est. 1,000	Value: 175				

Note: Small mintmarks

| 2000 | 2,500,000 | — | — | — | 4.00 | 8.50 |
| 2000 Proof | 19,000 | Value: 12.50 | | | | |

Note: Large mintmarks

KM# 149 10 GULDEN
6.7290 g., 0.9000 Gold 0.1947 oz. AGW, 22.5 mm.
Ruler: Wilhelmina I **Obv:** Head right **Rev:** Crowned arms divide value **Edge:** Reeded

Date	Mintage	F	VF	XF	Unc	BU
1911	774,544	—	—	—	BV	225
1911 Proof	8	Value: 1,750				
1912	3,000,000	—	—	—	BV	200
1912 Proof	20	Value: 1,500				
1913	1,133,476	—	—	—	BV	200
1917	4,000,000	—	—	—	BV	200

KM# 162 10 GULDEN
6.7290 g., 0.9000 Gold 0.1947 oz. AGW, 22.5 mm.
Ruler: Wilhelmina I **Obv:** Head right **Rev:** Crowned arms divide value **Edge:** Reeded

Date	Mintage	F	VF	XF	Unc	BU
1925	2,000,000	—	—	—	BV	200
1925 Proof	12	Value: 2,000				
1926	2,500,000	—	—	—	BV	200
1926 Proof	—	Value: 1,300				
1927	1,000,000	—	—	—	BV	200
1932	4,323,954	—	—	—	BV	200
1933	2,462,101	—	—	—	BV	200

KM# 195 10 GULDEN
25.0000 g., 0.7200 Silver 0.5787 oz. ASW, 38 mm.
Ruler: Juliana **Subject:** 25th Anniversary of Liberation
Obv: Head right within beaded border **Rev:** Head left within beaded border **Edge:** GOD * ZIJ * MET * ONS *

Date	Mintage	F	VF	XF	Unc	BU
ND(1970)	5,980,000	—	—	—	9.50	
ND(1970) Prooflike	20,000	—	—	—	—	40.00
ND(1970) Proof	40	Value: 1,000				

KM# 196 10 GULDEN
25.0000 g., 0.7200 Silver 0.5787 oz. ASW, 38 mm.
Ruler: Juliana **Subject:** 25th Anniversary of Reign **Obv:** Head right within beaded border **Rev:** Crowned arms divide date within beaded border **Edge:** GOD * ZIJ * MET * ONS *

Date	Mintage	F	VF	XF	Unc	BU
1973	4,505,000	—	—	—	9.50	12.50
1973 Proof	105,570	Value: 17.50				

KM# 216 10 GULDEN
15.0000 g., 0.7200 Silver 0.3472 oz. ASW, 33 mm. **Ruler:** Beatrix
Subject: BE-NE-LUX Treaty **Obv:** Head left. **Rev:** Three Parliament buildings on top, 3 designs in circles within vertical lines, all flanked by dates and value **Edge:** GOD * ZIJ * MET * ONS *

Date	Mintage	F	VF	XF	Unc	BU
1994 Proof	66,500	Value: 20.00				

Note: 25,000 pieces issued in sets only

Date	Mintage	F	VF	XF	Unc	BU
1994	2,000,000	—	—	—	8.00	10.00

Note: 100,000 pieces melted

KM# 220 10 GULDEN
15.0000 g., 0.8000 Silver 0.3858 oz. ASW, 33 mm.
Ruler: Beatrix **Subject:** 300th Anniversary - Death of Hugo de Groot **Obv:** Head left **Rev:** Value and date above supine head facing upward **Edge:** GOD * ZIJ * MET * ONS *

Date	Mintage	F	VF	XF	Unc	BU
1995	1,500,000	—	—	—	8.00	10.00

Note: 110,000 pieces melted

Date	Mintage	F	VF	XF	Unc	BU
1995 Proof	37,500	Value: 20.00				

KM# 223 10 GULDEN
15.0000 g., 0.8000 Silver 0.3858 oz. ASW, 33 mm.
Ruler: Beatrix **Subject:** Artist Jan Steen - Lute Player **Obv:** Head left **Rev:** Jan Steen as lute player **Edge:** GOD * ZIJ * MET * ONS *

Date	Mintage	F	VF	XF	Unc	BU
1996	1,500,000	—	—	—	8.00	10.00

Note: 395,000 pieces melted

Date	Mintage	F	VF	XF	Unc	BU
1996 Proof	25,000	Value: 22.50				

KM# 224 10 GULDEN
15.0000 g., 0.8000 Silver 0.3858 oz. ASW, 33 mm.
Ruler: Beatrix **Subject:** Marshall Plan **Obv:** Head left **Rev:** Marshall head 3/4 left divides value **Edge:** GOD * ZIJ * MET * ONS *

Date	Mintage	F	VF	XF	Unc	BU
1997	1,010,000	—	—	—	8.00	12.00

Note: 55,000 pieces melted

Date	Mintage	F	VF	XF	Unc	BU
1997 Proof	27,000	Value: 20.00				

KM# 228 10 GULDEN
15.0000 g., 0.8000 Silver 0.3858 oz. ASW, 33 mm.
Ruler: Beatrix **Subject:** Millennium **Obv:** Head above 12 concentric rings within beaded border **Rev:** Head above 12 concentric rings within beaded border **Edge:** GOD ZIJ MET ONS

Date	Mintage	F	VF	XF	Unc	BU
1999	1,250,000	—	—	—	8.00	10.00
1999 Proof	50,000	Value: 20.00				

KM# 207 50 GULDEN
25.0000 g., 0.9250 Silver 0.7435 oz. ASW, 38 mm.
Ruler: Beatrix **Subject:** Dutch-American Friendship **Obv:** Head left **Rev:** Value within lion and eagle **Edge:** GOD * ZIJ * MET * ONS *

Date	Mintage	F	VF	XF	Unc	BU
ND (1982)	189,986	—	—	—	35.00	45.00
ND(1982) Proof	49,998	Value: 55.00				
2000 Proof	—	Value: 55.00				

KM# 207a 50 GULDEN
Gold **Ruler:** Beatrix **Subject:** Dutch-American Friendship **Obv:** Head left **Rev:** Value within lion and eagle **Edge:** GOT ZIJ MET ONS

Date	Mintage	F	VF	XF	Unc	BU
ND(1982) Rare	2					

KM# 208 50 GULDEN
25.0000 g., 0.9250 Silver 0.7435 oz. ASW, 38 mm. **Ruler:** Beatrix
Subject: 400th Anniversary - Death of William of Orange **Obv:** Head left **Rev:** Signature of William **Edge:** GOD * ZIJ * MET * ONS *

Date	Mintage	F	VF	XF	Unc	BU
1984	1,000,000	—	—	—	15.00	20.00

Note: 145,000 pieces melted down

Date	Mintage	F	VF	XF	Unc	BU
1984 Prooflike	106,378	—	—	—	15.00	30.00
1984 Proof	56,200	Value: 30.00				

KM# 209 50 GULDEN
25.0000 g., 0.9250 Silver 0.7435 oz. ASW **Ruler:** Beatrix
Subject: Golden Wedding Anniversary - Queen Mother and Prince Bernhard **Obv:** Outlined profile left, triangular points at right **Rev:** Value within conjoined outlined heads right, 1/2 star border with letters within points **Edge:** GOD * ZIJ * MET * ONS *

Date	Mintage	F	VF	XF	Unc	BU
1987	1,500,000	—	—	—	15.00	20.00

Note: 535,000 pieces melted down

Date	Mintage	F	VF	XF	Unc	BU
1987 Prooflike	80,400	—	—	—	—	20.00
1987 Proof	52,872	Value: 25.00				

KM# 212   50 GULDEN
25.0000 g., 0.9250 Silver 0.7435 oz. ASW, 38 mm.
Ruler: Beatrix **Subject:** 300th Anniversary of William and Mary **Obv:** Patterned head left **Rev:** Conjoined heads right **Edge:** GOD * ZIJ * MET * ONS *

Date	Mintage	F	VF	XF	Unc	BU
1988	900,000	—	—	—	15.00	20.00

Note: 235,000 pieces melted

Date	Mintage	F	VF	XF	Unc	BU
1988 Prooflike	52,500	—	—	—	—	20.00
1988 Proof	35,500	Value: 25.00				

KM# 212a   50 GULDEN
Gold **Ruler:** Beatrix **Subject:** 300th Anniversary of William and Mary **Obv:** Patterned head left **Rev:** Conjoined heads right **Edge:** GOD ZIJ MET ONS

Date	Mintage	F	VF	XF	Unc	BU
1988 Rare	4					

KM# 214   50 GULDEN
25.0000 g., 0.9250 Silver 0.7435 oz. ASW, 38 mm.
Ruler: Beatrix **Subject:** 100 Years of Queens **Rev:** Heads of Queens Emma, Wilhelmina, Juliana, and Beatrix like rocks **Edge:** GOD * ZIJ * MET * ONS *

Date	Mintage	F	VF	XF	Unc	BU
1990	800,000	—	—	—	15.00	20.00

Note: 210,000 pieces melted

Date	Mintage	F	VF	XF	Unc	BU
1990 Prooflike	50,400	—	—	—	—	20.00
1990 Proof	34,500	Value: 25.00				

KM# 215   50 GULDEN
25.0000 g., 0.9250 Silver 0.7435 oz. ASW, 38 mm. **Ruler:** Beatrix **Subject:** Silver Wedding Anniversary **Obv:** Half face left **Rev:** Half face left **Edge:** GOD * ZIJ * MET * ONS *

Date	Mintage	F	VF	XF	Unc	BU
1991	600,000	—	—	—	18.00	20.00

Note: 60,000 pieces melted

Date	Mintage	F	VF	XF	Unc	BU
1991 Prooflike	45,800	—	—	—	—	30.00
1991 Proof	34,700	Value: 25.00				

KM# 217   50 GULDEN
25.0000 g., 0.9250 Silver 0.7435 oz. ASW, 38 mm.
Ruler: Beatrix **Subject:** Maastricht Treaty **Obv:** Head left with title within ribbon **Rev:** Value, date and name within rippled banner with stars **Edge:** GOD * ZIJ * MET * ONS *

Date	Mintage	F	VF	XF	Unc	BU
1994	550,000	—	—	—	15.00	20.00

Note: 170,000 pieces melted

Date	Mintage	F	VF	XF	Unc	BU
1994 Prooflike	28,000	—	—	—	—	20.00
1994 Proof	24,500	Value: 25.00				

KM# 219   50 GULDEN
25.0000 g., 0.9250 Silver 0.7435 oz. ASW, 38 mm. **Ruler:** Beatrix **Subject:** 50th Anniversary of Liberation **Obv:** Head 1/4 left **Rev:** Large numeral value and legend **Edge:** GOD * ZIJ * MET * ONS *

Date	Mintage	F	VF	XF	Unc	BU
ND(1995)	650,000	—	—	—	15.00	20.90

Note: 220,000 pieces melted

Date	Mintage	F	VF	XF	Unc	BU
ND(1995) Prooflike	27,500	—	—	—	—	20.00
ND(1995) Proof	26,000	Value: 25.00				

KM# 227   50 GULDEN
25.0000 g., 0.9250 Silver 0.7435 oz. ASW, 38 mm.
Ruler: Beatrix **Subject:** 350th Anniversary - Treaty of Munster **Obv:** Head 1/4 left within circle **Rev:** Head 1/4 right within circle **Edge:** GOD*ZIJ*MET*ONS*

Date	Mintage	F	VF	XF	Unc	BU
1998	450,000	—	—	—	15.00	20.00

Note: 180,000 pieces melted

Date	Mintage	F	VF	XF	Unc	BU
1998 Prooflike	20,000	—	—	—	—	25.00
1998 Proof	20,000	Value: 35.00				

EURO COINAGE
European Union Issues

KM# 234   EURO CENT
2.3000 g., Copper Plated Steel, 16.2 mm. **Ruler:** Beatrix **Obv:** Head left among stars **Rev:** Value and globe **Edge:** Plain

Date	Mintage	F	VF	XF	Unc	BU
1999	47,800,000	—	—	—	0.50	0.75
1999 Proof	16,500					

Date	Mintage	F	VF	XF	Unc	BU
2000	276,800,000	—	—	—	0.35	0.50
2000 Proof	16,500					

KM# 235   2 EURO CENT
3.0000 g., Copper Plated Steel, 18.7 mm. **Ruler:** Beatrix **Obv:** Head left among stars **Rev:** Value and globe **Edge:** Grooved

Date	Mintage	F	VF	XF	Unc	BU
1999	109,000,000	—	—	—	0.50	0.75
1999 Proof	16,500	—	—	—	—	—
2000	122,000,000	—	—	—	0.50	0.75
2000 Proof	16,500	—	—	—	—	—

KM# 236   5 EURO CENT
3.9000 g., Copper Plated Steel, 21.25 mm. **Ruler:** Beatrix **Obv:** Head left among stars **Rev:** Value and globe **Edge:** Plain

Date	Mintage	F	VF	XF	Unc	BU
1999	213,000,000	—	—	—	0.50	0.75
1999 Proof	16,500	—	—	—	—	—
2000	184,200,000	—	—	—	0.50	0.75
2000 Proof	16,500	—	—	—	—	—

KM# 237   10 EURO CENT
4.1000 g., Brass, 19.7 mm. **Ruler:** Beatrix **Obv:** Head left among stars **Rev:** Value and map

Date	Mintage	F	VF	XF	Unc	BU
1999	149,700,000	—	—	—	0.75	1.00
1999 Proof	16,500	—	—	—	—	—
2000	156,700,000	—	—	—	0.75	1.00
2000 Proof	16,500	—	—	—	—	—

KM# 238   20 EURO CENT
5.7000 g., Brass, 22.2 mm. **Ruler:** Beatrix **Obv:** Head left among stars **Rev:** Value and map **Edge:** Notched

Date	Mintage	F	VF	XF	Unc	BU
1999	86,500,000	—	—	—	1.00	1.25
1999 Proof	16,500	—	—	—	—	—
2000	67,500,000	—	—	—	1.00	1.25
2000 Proof	16,500	—	—	—	—	—

KM# 239   50 EURO CENT
7.8000 g., Brass, 24.2 mm. **Ruler:** Beatrix **Obv:** Head left among stars **Rev:** Value and map **Edge:** Notched

Date	Mintage	F	VF	XF	Unc	BU
1999	99,600,000	—	—	—	1.25	1.50
1999 Proof	16,500	—	—	—	—	—
2000	87,000,000	—	—	—	1.25	1.50
2000 Proof	16,500	—	—	—	—	—

KM# 240 EURO

7.5000 g., Bi-Metallic Copper-Nickel center in Brass ring, 23.2 mm. **Ruler:** Beatrix **Obv:** Half head left within 1/2 circle and star border, name within vertical lines **Rev:** Value and map within circle **Edge:** Plain and reeded sections

Date	Mintage	F	VF	XF	Unc	BU
1999	63,500,000	—	—	—	2.50	3.00
1999 Proof	16,500	—	—	—	—	—
2000	62,800,000	—	—	—	2.50	3.00
2000 Proof	16,500	—	—	—	—	—

KM# 241 2 EURO

8.5000 g., Bi-Metallic Brass center in Copper-Nickel ring, 25.7 mm. **Ruler:** Beatrix **Obv:** Profile left within 1/2 circle and star border, name within vertical lines **Rev:** Value and map within circle **Edge:** Reeded Edge: "GOD*ZIJ*MET*ONS*"

Date	Mintage	F	VF	XF	Unc	BU
1999	9,900,000	—	—	—	6.00	8.00
1999 Proof	16,500	—	—	—	—	—
2000	24,400,000	—	—	—	5.00	6.00
2000 Proof	16,500	—	—	—	—	—

TRADE COINAGE

KM# 83.1 DUCAT

3.4940 g., 0.9830 Gold 0.1104 oz. AGW, 21 mm. **Obv:** Standing knight divides date **Rev:** Inscription within ornamented square **Edge:** Slant-reeded

Date	Mintage	F	VF	XF	Unc	BU
1901	29,284	400	1,000	1,500	2,400	2,900
1903/1	91,000	400	1,000	1,850	2,400	2,900
1903	Inc. above	250	700	1,000	1,700	2,500
1905	87,995	175	450	700	1,000	1,500
1906	29,379	400	1,000	1,500	2,400	2,900
1908	91,006	175	450	700	1,000	1,500
1909	106,021	400	1,000	1,500	2,400	3,000
	Note: Halberd with star privy mark					
1909	30,182	400	1,000	2,000	3,000	4,000
	Note: Sea horse privy mark					
1910	421,447	125	375	525	900	1,100
1910 Proof	—	Value: 1,700				
1912	147,860	125	375	525	900	1,100
1912 Proof	—	Value: 1,200				
1913	205,464	125	375	525	900	1,100
1914	246,560	125	375	525	900	1,100
1916	116,997	125	375	525	900	1,100
1916 Proof	—	Value: 2,000				
1917	216,892	—	BV	110	125	155
1920	293,389	—	BV	110	125	155
1920 Proof	—	Value: 800				
1921	409,001	—	BV	110	120	135
1922	49,837	120	350	500	900	1,200
1923	106,674	BV	110	250	400	600
1924	84,206	BV	110	250	400	600
1925	573,071	—	BV	110	120	135
1925 Proof	Inc. above	Value: 600				
1926	191,311	—	BV	110	125	155
1927	654,424	—	—	—	BV	110
1928	571,801	—	—	—	BV	110
1932	88,268	200	500	900	1,700	2,500
1937	116,660	BV	110	115	120	145

KM# 190.1 DUCAT

3.4940 g., 0.9830 Gold 0.1104 oz. AGW, 21 mm. **Ruler:** Beatrix **Obv:** Knight with right leg bent divides date **Rev:** Inscription within decorated square

Date	Mintage	F	VF	XF	Unc	BU
1960	3,605	BV	120	300	400	450
1972 Prooflike	29,205	—	—	—	—	115
1974 Prooflike	86,558	—	—	—	—	115
1974	Est. 2,000	—	—	300	600	700
	Note: Medal struck					
1975 Prooflike	204,788	—	—	—	—	110
1976 Prooflike	37,844	—	—	115	150	200
	Note: Of 37,844 pieces struck, 32,000 were melted					
1978 Prooflike	29,305	—	—	—	115	125
1985 Prooflike	103,863	—	—	—	—	110

KM# 190.2 DUCAT

3.4940 g., 0.9830 Gold 0.1104 oz. AGW **Ruler:** Beatrix **Obv:** Knight divides date with larger letters in legend **Rev:** Inscription within decorated square

Date	Mintage	F	VF	XF	Unc	BU
1986 Prooflike	95,091	—	—	—	—	115
1989 Proof	24,478	Value: 115				
1990 Proof	17,500	Value: 115				
1991 Proof	11,500	Value: 115				
1992 Proof	14,400	Value: 115				
1993 Proof	11,100	Value: 120				
1994 Proof	11,500	Value: 120				
1995 Proof	11,000	Value: 120				
1996 Proof	12,000	Value: 120				
1997 Proof	11,500	Value: 120				
1998 Proof	8,500	Value: 125				
1999 Proof	7,550	Value: 125				
2000 Proof	8,000	Value: 125				

KM# 211 2 DUCAT

6.9880 g., 0.9830 Gold 0.2208 oz. AGW, 26 mm. **Ruler:** Beatrix **Obv:** Knight divides date within beaded circle **Rev:** Inscription within decorated square

Date	Mintage	F	VF	XF	Unc	BU
1988 Prooflike	23,759	—	—	—	—	215
1989 Proof	17,862	Value: 215				
1991 Proof	10,000	Value: 220				
1992 Proof	11,800	Value: 220				
1996 Proof	10,500	Value: 220				
1999 Proof	6,250	Value: 225				
2000 Proof	7,000	Value: 220				

SILVER BULLION COINAGE

KM# 213 SILVER DUCAT

28.2500 g., 0.8730 Silver 0.7929 oz. ASW, 40 mm. **Ruler:** Beatrix **Obv:** Crowned arms divide date **Rev:** Knight standing with the arms of Utrecht

Date	Mintage	F	VF	XF	Unc	BU
1989 Proof	35,797	Value: 20.00				

Date	Mintage	F	VF	XF	Unc	BU
1992 Proof	17,200	Value: 30.00				
1993 Proof	12,500	Value: 35.00				

KM# 218 SILVER DUCAT

28.2500 g., 0.8730 Silver 0.7929 oz. ASW, 40 mm. **Ruler:** Beatrix **Subject:** Seven Provinces - Groningen **Obv:** Crowned arms divide date **Rev:** Knight standing with arms of Groningen

Date	Mintage	F	VF	XF	Unc	BU
1994 Proof	11,000	Value: 50.00				

KM# 221 SILVER DUCAT

28.2500 g., 0.8730 Silver 0.7929 oz. ASW, 40 mm. **Ruler:** Beatrix **Subject:** Seven Provinces - Zeeland **Obv:** Crowned arms of the Netherlands **Rev:** Knight standing with arms of Zeeland

Date	Mintage	F	VF	XF	Unc	BU
1995 Proof	11,000	Value: 30.00				

KM# 222 SILVER DUCAT

28.2500 g., 0.8730 Silver 0.7929 oz. ASW, 40 mm. **Ruler:** Beatrix **Subject:** Seven Provinces - Holland **Obv:** Crowned arms divide date **Rev:** Knight standing with arms of Holland

Date	Mintage	F	VF	XF	Unc	BU
1996 Proof	12,500	Value: 30.00				

KM# 225 SILVER DUCAT

28.2500 g., 0.8730 Silver 0.7929 oz. ASW, 40 mm. **Ruler:** Beatrix **Subject:** Seven Provinces - Gelderland **Obv:** Crowned arms of the Netherlands **Rev:** Knight standing with arms of Gelderland

Date	Mintage	F	VF	XF	Unc	BU
1997 Proof	11,500	Value: 30.00				

KM# 226 SILVER DUCAT

28.2500 g., 0.8730 Silver 0.7929 oz. ASW, 40 mm. **Ruler:** Beatrix **Subject:** Seven Provinces - Friesland **Obv:** Crowned arms of the Netherlands **Rev:** Knight standing with shield of Friesland

Date	Mintage	F	VF	XF	Unc	BU
1998 Proof	11,100	Value: 30.00				

KM# 229 SILVER DUCAT

28.2500 g., 0.8730 Silver 0.7929 oz. ASW, 40 mm. **Ruler:** Beatrix **Subject:** Seven Provinces - Utrecht **Obv:** Crowned arms divide date **Rev:** Knight standing with arms of Utrecht

Date	Mintage	F	VF	XF	Unc	BU
1999 Proof	9,500	Value: 30.00				

KM# 232 SILVER DUCAT

28.2500 g., 0.8730 Silver 0.7929 oz. ASW, 40 mm. **Ruler:** Beatrix
Subject: Seven Provinces - Overijssel **Obv:** Crowned shield divides
date **Rev:** Knight with crowned shield **Edge:** Reeded

Date	Mintage	F	VF	XF	Unc	BU
2000 Proof	10,100	Value: 30.00				

PATTERNS

Including off metal strikes

KM#	Date	Mintage	Identification	Mkt Val
Pn96	1902	—	Cent. Gold. KM132.	—
Pn97	1903	—	1/2 Cent. Gold. KM133.	—
Pn98	1903	—	2-1/2 Cent. Gold. KM134.	—
Pn99	1903	—	10 Cents. Gold. KM135.	—
Pn100	1903	—	25 Cents. Gold. KM120.2	—
PnA101	190x	—	5 Cents. Small 5. Reverse small 5.	—
Pn101	190x	—	5 Cents. Bronze. Large 5. Reverse large 5.	—
Pn101a	190x	—	5 Cents. Silver.	—
PNA102	190x	—	5 Cents. Bronze. 27 mm.	—
Pn102	190x	—	5 Cents. Bronze. 29 mm.	—
Pn103	190x	—	10 Cents. Nickel.	—
Pn104	1904	—	Cent. Bronze-Nickel Plug.	—
Pn105	1904	—	5 Cents. Bronze.	—
Pn106	1904	—	5 Cents. Bronze. Holed.	—
Pn107	1904	—	5 Cents. Nickel.	—
Pn108	1904	—	5 Cents. Nickel. Holed.	—
Pn109	1904	—	5 Cents.	—
PnA110	1904	—	1/2 Gulden. Gold. KM121.2	—
Pn110	1905	—	5 Cents. Silver. Plain edge.	1,100
PnA111	1906	—	5 Cents. Bronze.	—
Pn111	1906	—	5 Cents. Nickel.	—
Pn112	1906	—	5 Cents. Nickel.	—
Pn113	1906	—	5 Cents. Nickel.	—
Pn114	1906	—	5 Cents. Silver.	—
Pn115	1906	—	10 Cents. Nickel.	—
PnA117	1906	—	10 Cents.	—
Pn117	1907	—	5 Cents. Bronze. Crown.	—
Pn118	1907	—	5 Cents. Nickel. Small crown.	—
Pn119	1908	—	Gulden. Bronze. KM122.	—
Pn120	1910	—	10 Cents. Gold. KM145.	—
PnA121	1911	—	Gulden. Bronze.	1,100
PnB121	1912	—	5 Cents. Nickel. "Proof".	—
Pn121	1913	—	2-1/2 Gulden. Silver. KM148.	—
Pn122	1928	—	Gulden. Silver. 28 mm.	350
PnA123	1928	—	Gulden. Gold. 28 mm.	700
Pn123	1928	—	Gulden. Silver. 19 mm.	250
PnA124	1928	—	Gulden. Gold. 19 mm.	550
Pn124	1929	—	Gulden. Silver.	—
PnA125	1929	—	2-1/2 Gulden. Bronze.	1,250
Pn125	1929	—	2-1/2 Gulden. Silver.	550
PnA126	1929	—	2-1/2 Gulden. Gold.	1,300
Pn126	1934	—	10 Cents. Bronze. KM163.	—
PnA127	1935	—	5 Cents. Gold.	4,000
Pn127	1941	—	Cent. Zinc. KM170 with center hole.	550
Pn128	1941	—	2-1/2 Cent. Zinc. KM171 with center hole.	550
Pn129	1941	—	10 Cents. Zinc.	180
PnA130	1969	—	Cent. Nickel.	—
Pn130	1969	—	5 Cents. Nickel. Plain edge.	—
Pn131	1969	—	5 Cents. Nickel.	—
Pn132	1969	—	5 Cents. Aluminum. 1.5000 g.	—
Pn133	1969	—	5 Cents. Aluminum. 1.2200 g.	—
PnA134	1969	—	5 Cents. Nickel-Brass.	—
PnB134	1969	—	25 Cents. Brass.	—
PnC134	1970	—	Cent. Aluminum.	—
Pn134	1973	—	10 Cents. Silver.	—
Pn134A	1975	—	25 Cents. Aluminum. KM#1830.	—
Pn135	1979	—	10 Gulden. Nickel.	—
Pn136	1980	15	25 Cents. Aluminum. KM183a.	500
Pn138	1980	—	Gulden. Gold. KM200b.	—
Pn139	1980	—	Gulden. Silver. KM200a.	700
Pn140	1980	—	2-1/2 Gulden. Gold. KM201b.	—
Pn141	1980	—	2-1/2 Gulden. Silver. KM201a.	800
Pn142	1982	—	5 Cents. Bronze. 17 mm.	—
Pn143	1982	—	5 Cents. Tombac.	—
Pn144	1982	—	5 Cents. Brass.	—
Pn145	1982	—	5 Cents. Copper Clad Steel.	—
Pn146	1982	—	Gulden. Nickel.	—
Pn147	1982	—	50 Cents. Gold. KM207.	—
Pn148	1984	—	5 Cents. Tombac.	200
Pn149	1984	—	10 Cents. Bronze.	200
Pn150	1985	—	5 Cents. Nickel. Plain edge.	200
PnA151	1985	—	25 Cents. Aluminum. KM204	300
Pn151	1986	—	25 Cents. Brass. KM204.	300

KM#	Date	Mintage	Identification	Mkt Val
Pn152	1986	—	25 Cents. Aluminum. KM204.	300
Pn152A	1986	—	Gulden. Copper Nickel. KM#206.	300
Pn152B	1986	—	2-1/2 Gulden. Copper Nickel. KM#206	400
Pn153	1986	—	Ducat. Tombac. KM190.2.	500
Pn154	1987	—	5 Cents. Nickel. KM202.	—
Pn155	1988	—	5 Cents. Nickel Clad Steel.	—
Pn156	1988	—	5 Cents. Copper Clad Steel.	—
Pn157	1988	—	5 Cents. Brass Clad Steel.	—
PnA158	1988	—	50 Gulden. Tombac.	750
PnB158	1988	—	50 Gulden. Silver.	850
Pn158	1988	—	50 Gulden. Gold. KM212.	—
Pn159	1990	—	5 Cents. Aluminum.	—
Pn160	1991	—	5 Cents. Nickel. KM202.	—
Pn161	1991	—	50 Gulden. Silver. 1/4 Circle. Queen Beatrix and Prince Claus	—
Pn163	1999	—	Euro Cent. Nickel.	100
Pn164	2000	—	2 Euro Cent. Copper Nickel. KM#241	250

PIEFORTS

KM#	Date	Mintage	Identification	Mkt Val
P19	1905	—	1/2 Gulden. Silver. KM121.2	4,000
		Note: Triple weight		
P20	1905	—	Gulden. Silver. KM122.2	5,000
		Note: Triple weight		
P21	1910	—	25 Cents. Bronze. KM146.	—
P22	1948	—	Cent. Silver. KM175.	—
P23	1948	—	5 Cents. Silver. KM176.	—
P24	1948	—	10 Cents. Silver. KM177.	—
P25	1948	—	25 Cents. Silver. KM178.	—
PA26	1956	—	Gulden. Silver. similar to KM#184	—
P26	1958	—	Gulden. Silver. KM184.	—

MINT SETS

KM#	Date	Mintage	Identification	Issue Price	Mkt Val
MS1	1999 (8)	65,000	KM#234-241 Charity set, Clinic Clowns	15.00	10.00
MS99	1999 (6)	3,500	KM#202-206, 210 King Willem III	17.50	35.00
MS100	1999 (6)	74	KM#202-206, 210 VOC ship "De Akerendam" with original golden ducat dated 1724 Utrecht KM#7	1,250	1,300
MS101	1999 (6)	1,000	KM#202-206, 210 P.W.S.	75.00	—
MS102	2000 (6)	3,500	KM#202-206, 210 Queen Wilhelmina	17.50	30.00
MS103	2000 (6)	105,000	KM#202-206, 210 Introduction Euro-coins, no medal	15.00	16.00
MS104	2000 (6)	4,000	KM#202-206, 210 400 year Nederland-Japan	17.50	22.50
MS105	2000 (6)	18,300	KM#202-206, 210 Baby set plus bear medal	15.50	35.00
MS106	2000 (6)	1,000	KM#202-206, 210 United Seven Provinces Gelderland	40.00	40.00
MS107	2000 (6)	1,000	KM#202-206, 210 United Seven Provinces Overijsel	40.00	40.00
MS108	2000 (6)	1,000	KM#202-206, 210 Bouers Met Visie	45.00	45.00
MS118	1999 (8)	65,000	KM#234-241 Charity set, clinicclowns	15.00	17.00
MS119	2000 (8)	13,850	KM#234-241 RABO bank	—	35.00
MS120	2000 (8)	68,000	KM#234-241 Charity set, naturmonuments	15.00	17.00
MS2	2000 (6)	50,000	KM#202-206, 210	12.00	10.00
MS3	2000 (8)	68,000	KM#234-241 Charity set, Nature Monuments	15.00	10.00
MS3A	2000 (8)	13,850	KM#234-241 RABO Bank	—	40.00

PROOF SETS

KM#	Date	Mintage	Identification	Issue Price	Mkt Val
PSA1	1928-29 (3)	—	PN122-123, 125	—	1,150
PSB1	1928-29 (3)	—	PnA123-A124, A126	—	2,250
PS1	1948 (4)	50	KM175-178 with PROEF	—	4,000
PS2	1948 (4)	—	KM175-178	—	400
PS3	1949	—	KM180-183, head left, rare.	—	—
PS4	1950 (4)	—	KM180-183 with PROEF	—	4,000
PS5	1950 (4)	—	KM180-183	—	325
PS6	1951 (4)	—	KM180-183	—	275
PS7	1952 (2)	—	KM180-181	—	275
PS8	1953 (2)	—	KM180-181	—	275
PS9	1954 (5)	—	KM180-184	—	300
PS10	1955 (5)	—	KM180-184	—	250
PS11	1956 (5)	—	KM180-184	—	250
PS12	1957 (5)	—	KM18-184	—	250
PS13	1958 (5)	—	KM180-184	—	250
PS14	1959 (3)	—	KM180, 182, 185	—	600
PS15	1960 (3)	—	KM180-183, 185	—	450
PS16	1961 (5)	—	KM180-183, 185	—	600
PS17	1962 (5)	40	KM180-183, 185	—	600
PS18	1963 (6)	40	KM180-185	—	600
PS19	1964 (6)	40	KM180-185	—	600
PS20	1965 (6)	—	KM180-184	—	600
PS21	1966 (6)	—	KM180-185	—	600
PS22	1967 (5)	—	KM180-183, 184a	—	400
PS23	1968 (3)	—	KM180, 182-184	—	400
PS24	1969 (6)	—	KM180-183, 184a, 191. Cock.	—	400
PS25	1969 (6)	—	KM180-183, 184a, 191. Fish.	—	400
PS26	1970 (6)	—	KM180-183, 184a, 191	—	400
PS27	1982 (5)	10,000	KM202-206	35.00	50.00
PS28	1983 (5)	15,000	KM202-206	35.00	20.00
PS29	1984 (5)	20,406	KM202-206	35.00	15.00

KM#	Date	Mintage	Identification	Issue Price	Mkt Val
PS30	1985 (5)	17,100	KM202-206	35.00	15.00
PS31	1986 (5)	19,500	KM202-206	35.00	15.00
PS32	1987 (5)	18,100	KM202-206, Utrecht medal	35.00	15.00
PS33	1988 (6)	19,550	KM202-206, 210, Groningen medal	38.00	15.00
PS34	1989 (6)	15,300	KM202-206,210, Flevoland medal	50.00	15.00
PS35	1989 (3)	6,400	KM190.2, 211, 213	260	275
PS36	1990 (6)	15,100	KM202-206, 210, N. Brabant medal. Set also includes 1974 25 Cents.	50.00	45.00
PS37	1991 (6)	14,240	KM202-206, 210,Drenthe medal	50.00	40.00
PS38	1992 (6)	12,600	KM202-206, 210, Zeeland medal	53.50	40.00
PS39	1992 (3)	6,300	KM190.2, 211, 213	270	235
PS40	1993 (6)	12,000	KM202-206, 210, Limburg medal	53.50	40.00
PS41	1994 (6)	12,500	KM202-206, 210, Friesland medal	59.50	40.00
PS42	1994 (3)	25,000	BE NE LUX, Belgium KM195, Netherlands KM216, Luxemburg KM68	65.00	55.00
PS43	1995 (6)	11,500	KM202-206, 210, Zuid-Holland medal	59.50	40.00
PS44	1996 (6)	13,500	KM202-206, 210 Booklet, 5 cents, Stuiver	60.00	65.00
PS45	1996 (2)	6,500	KM190.2, 211	248	225
PS46	1997 (6)	12,000	KM202-206, 210 Booklet, 10 Cents	60.00	70.00
PS47	1998 (7)	12,000	KM202-206, 210 Booklet, 25 Cents	60.00	50.00
PS48	1999 (6)	15,000	KM202-206, 210, Booklet, 1 Guilder	50.00	40.00
PS49	1999 (3)	2,500	KM190.2, 211, 229	—	280
PS50	1999 (2)	1,800	KM190.2, 211	—	240
PS51	2000 (6)	15,000	KM#202-206, 210 Booklet 2-1/2 Guilder	50.00	40.00
PS52	2000 (2)	500	KM190.2, 211 Golden ducats	—	230
PS53	2000 (3)	1,000	KM#190.2, 211,232 Golden Ducats and Silver Ducat	—	270
PS60	2000 (7)	15,000	KM#202-207, 210 Booklet 2 1/2 guilder	50.00	60.00
PS61	2000 (2)	500	KM#190.2, 211 Golden ducats	—	230
PS62	2000 (3)	1,000	KM#190.2, 211, 232 Golden ducats + silver ducat	—	270

PROOF-LIKE SETS (PL)

KM#	Date	Mintage	Identification	Issue Price	Mkt Val
PL1	1999 (8)	16,500	KM#234-241	50.00	40.00
PL2	2000 (8)	16,500	KM#234-241	50.00	40.00
PL10	1999 (8)	16,500	KM#234-241	50.00	—
PL11	2000 (8)	16,500	KM#234-241	50.00	—

SELECT SETS (FLEUR DE COIN)

KM#	Date	Mintage	Identification	Issue Price	Mkt Val
SS2	1971 (6)	1,000	KM180-183, 184a, 191	—	750
SS3	1972 (1)	2,000	KM191	—	35.00
SS4	1972 (5)	2,000	KM180-183, 184a	—	250
SS5	1973 (5)	10,000	KM180-183, 184a	—	50.00
SS6	1974 (3)	10,000	KM180-182	6.50	30.00
SS7	1975 (5)	12,000	KM180-183, 184a Set also includes 1974 25 cents.	6.50	50.00
SS8	1976 (5)	15,000	KM180-183, 184a	6.50	60.00
SS9	1977 (5)	17,000	KM180-183, 184a	6.50	50.00
SS10	1978 (6)	21,500	KM180-183, 184a, 191	6.50	30.00
SS11	1979 (6)	50,000	KM180-183, 184a, 191	6.50	10.00
SS12	1980 (6)	249,732	KM180-183, 184a, 191	6.50	4.00
SS13	1980 (6)	504,000	KM200-201	12.00	4.00
SS14	1980 (2)	157	KM200-201	—	2,500
SS15	1980 (2)	7	KM200b-201b. Gold.	—	—
SS16	1982 (5)	242,701	KM202-206	12.00	4.00
SS17	1983	156,165	KM202-206	12.00	4.00
SS18	1984 (5)	131,748	KM202-206	12.00	4.00
SS19	1985 (5)	113,079	KM202-206	12.00	8.00
SS20	1986 (5)	112,190	KM202-206	12.00	8.00
SS21	1987 (5)	120,850	KM202-206, Utrecht medal	15.00	8.00
SS22	1988 (6)	132,957	KM202-206, 210, Groningen medal	15.00	5.00
SS23	1988 (6)	5,000	KM202-206, 210, ERU medal	—	100
SS24	1989 (6)	103,607	KM202-206, 210, Flevoland medal	15.00	5.00
SS25	1990 (6)	102,750	KM202-206, 210, N-Brabant medal	15.00	6.00
SS26	1991 (6)	100,000	KM202-206, 210, Drenthe medal	15.00	6.00
SS27	1991 (6)	4,000	KM202-206, 210, RABO Bank medal	—	40.00
SS28	1992 (6)	94,000	KM202-206, 210, Zeeland medal	15.00	6.00
SS29	1992 (6)	3,000	KM202-206, 210, numismatic year medal	17.50	25.00
SS30	1993 (6)	87,000	KM202-206, 210, Limburg medal	15.00	6.00
SS31	1993 (6)	2,900	KM202-206, 210, V.O.C. medal	17.50	37.50
SS32	1994 (6)	85,000	KM202-206, 210, Friesland medal	15.00	6.00
SS33	1994 (6)	3,000	KM202-206, 210, millennium of mint	17.50	25.00

KM#	Date	Mintage	Identification	Issue Price	Mkt Val
SS34	1995 (6)	81,000	KM202-206, 210, Zuid-Holland medal	15.00	6.00
SS35	1995 (6)	2,500	KM202-206, 210, Royal mint medal	17.50	30.00
SS36	1995 (6)	1,500	KM202-206, 210, Ehrbecker mint medal	—	25.00
SS37	1995 (6)	1,500	KM202-206, 210, Province of Utrecht medal	14.50	600
SS38	1995 (6)	800	KM202-206, 210, DeCampen medal, Lion Daalder from shipwreck	200	175
SS39	1996 (6)	1,500	KM202-206, 210, Utrecht: Town of the Mint medal	17.50	6.00
SS40	1996 (6)	80,000	KM202-206, 210, Overyssel medal	15.00	6.00
SS41	1996 (6)	3,000	KM202-206, 210, French Occupation (1795-1813) medal	17.50	20.00
SS42	1996 (6)	2,100	KM202-206, 210, Baby set	17.50	30.00
SS43	1996 (6)	350	KM202-206, 210, DeCampen medal, 1/2 Lion Daalder from shipwreck	240	200
SS44	1996 (6)	1,300	KM202-206, 210, Westpark I medal	—	20.00
SS45	1996 (6)	1,000	KM202-206, 210, Province of Utrecht II medal	—	850
SS46	1997 (6)	85,000	KM202-206, 210, Gelderland medal	15.00	6.00
SS47	1997 (6)	3,500	KM202-206, 210, King Willem I medal	17.50	22.00
SS48	1997 (6)	—	KM202-206, 210, Baby set	17.50	32.50
SS49	1997 (6)	1,430	KM202-206, 210, Ice skating/11 cities medal	45.00	25.00
SS50	1997 (6)	700	KM202-206, 210, Westpark II medal	—	40.00
SS51	1997 (6)	1,000	KM202-206, 210, Den Besterd I medal	—	40.00
SS52	1997 (6)	500	KM202-206, 210, Den Besterd II medal	—	100
SS53	1997 (6)	1,000	KM202-206, 210, Czar Peter medal	—	80.00
SS54	1997 (6)	500	KM202-206, 210, 't Vliegent heart medal, Ducaton from shipwreck	240	225
SS55	1997 (6)	1,150	KM202-206, 210, Royal Navy medal	—	250
SS56	1997 (6)	700	KM202-206, 210, BFBN medal	—	130
SS57	1997 (6)	1,500	KM202-206, 210, Maasdonk medal	50.00	18.00
SS58	1997 (6)	1,000	KM202-206, 210, BNN medal	75.00	75.00
SS59	1997 (6)	1,000	KM202-206, 210, Overyssel medal	—	900
SS60	1997 (6)	1,000	KM202-206, 210, van Rembrandt U Rijn I medal	45.00	30.00
SS61	1997 (6)	1,000	KM202-206, 210, van Gogh I medal	45.00	30.00
SS62	1997 (6)	1,000	KM202-206, 210, Stuurman medal	75.00	50.00
SS63	1998 (7)	83,500	KM202-206, 210, N. Holland medal	15.00	6.00
SS64	1998 (6)	3,500	KM202-206, 210, King Willem II medal	17.50	20.00
SS65	1998 (6)	100	KM202-206, 210, 't Vliegent heart medal, Ducaton from shipwreck	1,000	600
SS66	1998 (6)	8,400	KM202-206, 210, Baby set	17.50	22.50
SS67	1998 (6)	1,000	KM202-206, 210, van Rijn II medal	40.00	40.00
SS68	1998 (6)	1,000	KM202-206, 210, van Gogh II medal	40.00	40.00
SS69	1998 (6)	1,000	KM202-206, 210, Frans Hals medal	50.00	35.00
SS70	1998 (6)	1,000	KM202-206, 210, Statenjacht medal	—	30.00
SS71	1998 (6)	1,000	KM202-206,210, Theo Peters medal	—	40.00
SS72	1998 (6)	1,000	KM202-206,210, Vermeer medal	—	40.00
SS73	1998 (6)	1,000	KM202-206, 210, Knippenberg medal	—	40.00
SS74	1998 (6)	2,500	KM202-206, 210, Holland medal	40.00	6.00
SS75	1998 (6)	2,500	KM202-206, 210, Zeeland medal	40.00	6.00
SS76	1999 (6)	3,500	KM202-206, 210, King Willem III medal	17.50	20.00
SS77	1999 (6)	1,000	KM202-206, 210, Statenjacht medal	30.00	20.00
SS78	1999 (6)	2,500	KM202-206, 210, Friesland medal	40.00	6.00
SS79	1999 (6)	2,500	KM202-206, 210, West Friesland medal	40.00	6.00
SS80	1999 (6)	—	KM202-206, 210, Baby set	15.50	17.50
SS80A	1999 (6)	1,000	KM202-206, 210 P.W.S.	75.00	50.00
SS81	1999 (7)	74	KM#202-206, 210, VOC ship "De Akerendam" with original golden ducat dated 1724 Utrecht (KM#7)	1,250	1,200
SS83	2000 (6)	3,500	KM202-206, 210, Queen Wilhelmina medal	17.50	20.00
SS84	2000 (6)	105,000	KM#202-206, 210 Introduction of Euro coins	15.00	6.00
SS85	2000 (6)	4,000	KM#202-206, 210 400-year Nederland - Janpan	17.50	10.00
SS86	2000 (6)	18,300	KM#202-206, 210 Baby set plus bear medal	15.50	20.00
SS87	2000 (6)	1,000	KM#202-206, 210 United Seven Provinces Gelderland medal	40.00	30.00
SS88	2000 (6)	1,000	KM#202-206, 210 United Seven Provinces Overijsel Medal	40.00	30.00
SS89	2000 (6)	1,000	KM#202-206, 210 Bouwers Met Visie	45.00	100

NETHERLANDS ANTILLES

The Netherlands Antilles, comprises two groups of islands in the West Indies: Aruba (until 1986), Bonaire and Curacao and their dependencies near the Venezuelan coast and St. Eustatius, Saba, and the southern part of St. Martin (St. Maarten) southeast of Puerto Rico. The island group has an area of 371 sq. mi. (960 sq. km.) and a population of 225,000. Capital: Willemstad. Chief industries are the refining of crude oil and tourism. Petroleum products and phosphates are exported.

On Dec. 15, 1954, the Netherlands Antilles were given complete domestic autonomy and granted equality within the Kingdom with Surinam and the Netherlands. On Jan. I, 1986, Aruba achieved status aparte as the fourth part of the Dutch realm that was a step towards total independence.

RULERS
Juliana, 1948-1980
Beatrix, 1980-

MINT MARKS
Y – York Mint

Utrecht Mint
(privy marks only)

Date	Privy Mark
1945-1969	Fish
1969	Fish with star
1970-1979	Cock
1980	Cock with star
1982-1988	Anvil with hammer
1988-1999	Bow and arrow
2000	Bow and arrow with star
2001	Wine tendril with grapes
2002	Wine tendril with grapes and star
2003	Sails of a clipper

FM - Franklin Mint, U.S.A.
NOTE: See Kingdom of the Netherlands for more details.
NOTE: From 1975-1985 the Franklin Mint produced coinage in up to 3 different qualities. Qualities of issue are designated in ( ) after each date and are defined as follows:

(M) MATTE - Normal circulation strike or a dull finish produced by sandblasting special uncirculated (polish finish) or proof quality dies.

(U) SPECIAL UNCIRCULATED - Polished or prooflike in appearance without any frosted features.

(P) PROOF - The highest quality obtainable having mirror-like fields and frosted features.

MONETARY SYSTEM
100 Cents = 1 Gulden

DUTCH ADMINISTRATION

DECIMAL COINAGE

KM# 1 CENT
2.5000 g., Bronze, 19 mm. **Ruler:** Juliana **Obv:** Rampant lion left **Rev:** Value within wreath **Edge:** Reeded

Date	Mintage	F	VF	XF	Unc	BU
1952	1,000,000	1.50	2.50	5.00	12.50	14.00
1952 Proof	100	Value: 40.00				
1954	1,000,000	1.50	2.50	5.00	12.50	14.00
1954 Proof	200	Value: 45.00				
1957	1,000,000	0.50	1.00	2.50	6.00	14.00
1957 Proof	250	Value: 35.00				
1959	1,000,000	0.50	1.00	2.50	6.00	10.00
1959 Proof	250	Value: 30.00				
1960 Proof	300	Value: 30.00				
1961	1,000,000	0.35	0.60	1.25	2.50	4.50
1961 Proof	—	Value: 25.00				
1963	1,000,000	0.35	0.60	1.25	2.50	4.50
1963 Proof	—	Value: 20.00				

Date	Mintage	F	VF	XF	Unc	BU
1964 Proof	—	Value: 20.00				
1965	1,200,000	0.35	0.60	1.25	2.50	4.00
1965 Proof	—	Value: 20.00				
1967	850,000	0.35	0.60	1.25	2.50	4.50
1967 Proof	—	Value: 20.00				
1968 fish	900,000	0.35	0.60	1.25	2.50	4.50
1968 star and fish	700,000	0.75	1.00	2.00	4.00	9.00
Note: Struck in 1969						
1970	200,000	0.75	1.00	2.00	4.00	9.00
1970 Proof	—	Value: 25.00				

KM# 8 CENT
2.5000 g., Bronze, 19 mm. **Ruler:** Juliana **Obv:** Crowned shield above date and ribbon **Rev:** Value flanked by stars **Edge:** Plain

Date	Mintage	F	VF	XF	Unc	BU
1970	1,200,000	0.10	0.40	0.75	1.50	2.50
1970 Proof	—	Value: 17.50				
1971	3,000,000	0.10	0.40	0.75	1.50	2.50
1971 Proof	—	Value: 17.50				
1972	1,000,000	0.10	0.40	0.75	1.50	2.50
1973	3,000,000	0.10	0.20	0.40	0.80	2.00
1973 Proof	—	Value: 17.50				
1974	3,000,000	0.10	0.20	0.40	0.80	2.00
1974 Proof	—	Value: 17.50				
1975	2,000,000	0.10	0.20	0.40	0.80	2.00
1975 Proof	—	Value: 17.50				
1976	3,000,000	—	0.20	0.40	0.80	2.00
1977	4,000,000	—	0.20	0.40	0.80	2.00
1978	2,000,000	—	0.20	0.40	0.80	2.00
Note: 1969 date is now listed in the Patterns section						

KM# 8a CENT
0.8000 g., Aluminum, 19 mm. **Ruler:** Juliana **Obv:** Crowned shield above date and ribbon **Rev:** Value flanked by stars **Edge:** Plain

Date	Mintage	F	VF	XF	Unc	BU
1979	7,512,000	—	0.10	0.25	0.50	0.75
1979 Proof	—	Value: 7.50				
1980	2,518,000	—	0.10	0.25	0.50	1.25
1981	2,423,000	—	0.10	0.25	0.50	0.75
1982	2,410,000	—	0.10	0.25	0.50	0.75
1983	2,925,000	—	0.10	0.25	0.50	0.75
1984	3,626,000	—	0.10	0.25	0.50	0.75
1985	3,024,000	—	0.10	0.25	0.50	0.75

KM# 32 CENT
0.7000 g., Aluminum, 14 mm. **Ruler:** Beatrix **Obv:** Orange blossom within circle **Rev:** Value within circle of geometric designed border **Edge:** Reeded

Date	Mintage	F	VF	XF	Unc	BU
1989(u)	1,365,000	—	—	0.10	0.20	0.50
1990(u)	2,711,000	—	—	0.10	0.20	0.50
1991(u)	4,016,000	—	—	0.10	0.20	0.50
1992(u)	3,049,000	—	—	0.10	0.20	0.50
1993(u)	3,997,000	—	—	0.10	0.20	0.50
1994(u)	1,997,000	—	—	0.10	0.20	0.50
1995(u)	997,000	—	—	0.10	0.20	0.50
1996(u)	3,595,000	—	—	0.10	0.20	0.50
1997(u)	4,107,000	—	—	0.10	0.20	0.50
1998(u)	5,757,000	—	—	0.10	0.20	0.50
1999(u)	15,876,000	—	—	0.10	0.20	0.50
2000(u)	6,607,500	—	—	0.10	0.20	0.50

KM# 5 2-1/2 CENTS
4.0000 g., Bronze, 23.5 mm. **Ruler:** Juliana **Obv:** Rampant lion left **Rev:** Value within orange wreath **Edge:** Reeded

Date	Mintage	F	VF	XF	Unc	BU
1956	400,000	0.50	1.25	2.50	5.00	8.00
1956 Proof	500	Value: 25.00				
1959	1,000,000	0.50	1.00	2.00	4.00	5.00
1959 Proof	250	Value: 25.00				
1965 fish	500,000	0.50	1.00	2.00	4.00	6.00

Date	Mintage	F	VF	XF	Unc	BU
1965 Proof	—	Value: 25.00				
1965 fish and star	150,000	1.00	2.00	4.00	7.50	17.50

Note: Struck in 1969

KM# 9   2-1/2 CENTS

4.0000 g., Bronze, 23.5 mm. **Ruler:** Juliana **Obv:** Crowned shield above date and ribbon **Rev:** Value flanked by stars **Edge:** Plain

Date	Mintage	F	VF	XF	Unc	BU
1970	500,000	0.40	0.75	1.50	3.00	2.75
1970 Proof	—	Value: 20.00				
1971	3,000,000	0.10	0.25	0.50	1.00	1.50
1971 Proof	—	Value: 20.00				
1973	1,000,000	0.10	0.15	0.35	0.75	1.00
1973 Proof	—	Value: 20.00				
1974	1,000,000	0.10	0.15	0.35	0.75	1.00
1974 Proof	—	Value: 20.00				
1975	1,000,000	0.10	0.15	0.35	0.75	1.00
1976	1,000,000	0.10	0.15	0.35	0.75	1.00
1977	1,000,000	0.10	0.15	0.35	0.75	1.00
1978	1,500,000	0.10	0.15	0.35	0.75	1.00

Note: 1969 date is now found in the Patterns section

KM# 9a   2-1/2 CENTS

1.2000 g., Aluminum, 23.5 mm. **Ruler:** Juliana **Obv:** Crowned shield above date and ribbon **Rev:** Value flanked by stars **Edge:** Plain

Date	Mintage	F	VF	XF	Unc	BU
1979	2,012,000	—	0.10	0.25	0.50	0.75
1979 Proof	—	Value: 10.00				
1980	2,018,000	—	0.10	0.25	0.50	0.75
1981	1,023,000	—	0.10	0.25	0.50	0.75
1982	1,010,000	—	0.10	0.25	0.50	0.75
1983	1,025,000	—	0.10	0.25	0.50	0.75
1984	1,026,000	—	0.10	0.25	0.50	0.75
1985	1,024,000	—	0.10	0.25	0.50	0.75

KM# 6   5 CENTS

4.5000 g., Copper-Nickel, 21.3 mm. **Ruler:** Juliana **Obv:** Orange blossom within circle **Rev:** Value within circle, pearls and shells around border **Edge:** Plain

Date	Mintage	F	VF	XF	Unc	BU
1957	500,000	0.35	0.75	1.50	3.00	6.00
1957 Proof	250	Value: 40.00				
1962	250,000	1.25	2.50	5.00	10.00	12.00
1962 Proof	200	Value: 30.00				
1963	400,000	0.35	0.75	1.50	3.00	6.00
1963 Proof	—	Value: 30.00				
1965	500,000	0.35	0.75	1.50	3.00	6.00
1965 Proof	—	Value: 30.00				
1967	600,000	0.35	0.75	1.50	3.00	6.00
1967 Proof	—	Value: 30.00				
1970	450,000	0.35	0.75	1.50	3.00	6.00
1970 Proof	—	Value: 30.00				

Note: KM#A13, previously listed here, is now under Patterns

KM# 13   5 CENTS

4.5000 g., Copper-Nickel, 21.3 mm. **Ruler:** Juliana **Obv:** Crowned shield **Rev:** Value flanked by stars **Edge:** Plain

Date	Mintage	F	VF	XF	Unc	BU
1971	2,000,000	0.10	0.15	0.30	0.60	0.95
1971 Proof	—	Value: 22.50				
1974	500,000	0.30	0.60	1.25	2.50	2.75
1974 Proof	—	Value: 22.50				
1975	2,000,000	0.10	0.15	0.30	0.60	0.95
1975 Proof	—	Value: 22.50				
1976	1,500,000	0.10	0.15	0.30	0.60	0.95
1977	1,000,000	0.10	0.15	0.30	0.60	0.95
1978	1,500,000	0.10	0.15	0.30	0.60	0.95
1979	1,512,000	0.10	0.15	0.30	0.60	0.95
1980	1,518,000	—	0.15	0.30	0.60	0.95
1981	1,022,999	—	0.15	0.30	0.60	0.95
1982	1,010,000	—	0.15	0.30	0.60	0.95
1983	1,024,999	—	0.15	0.30	0.60	0.95
1984	1,526,000	—	0.15	0.30	0.60	0.95
1985	1,524,000	—	0.15	0.30	0.60	0.95

KM# 33   5 CENTS

1.1600 g., Aluminum, 16 mm. **Ruler:** Beatrix **Obv:** Orange blossom within circle **Rev:** Value within circle, geometric designed border **Edge:** Reeded

Date	Mintage	F	VF	XF	Unc	BU
1989	915,000	—	—	0.25	0.60	0.75
1990	1,811,000	—	—	0.25	0.60	0.75
1991	2,513,000	—	—	0.25	0.60	0.75
1992	1,599,000	—	—	0.25	0.60	0.75
1993	2,497,000	—	—	0.25	0.60	0.75
1994	1,497,000	—	—	0.25	0.60	0.75
1995	997,000	—	—	0.25	0.60	0.75
1996	796,000	—	—	0.25	0.60	0.75
1997	2,207,000	—	—	0.25	0.60	0.75
1998	2,507,000	—	—	0.25	0.60	0.75
1999	2,501,000	—	—	0.25	0.60	0.75
2000	1,007,500	—	—	0.25	0.60	0.75

KM# 3   1/10 GULDEN

1.4000 g., 0.6400 Silver 0.0288 oz. ASW, 15 mm. **Ruler:** Juliana **Obv:** Head right **Rev:** Value **Edge:** Reeded

Date	Mintage	F	VF	XF	Unc	BU
1954	200,000	1.50	3.00	8.00	15.00	30.00
1954 Proof	200	Value: 40.00				
1956	250,000	1.00	2.00	4.00	8.00	12.00
1956 Proof	500	Value: 40.00				
1957	250,000	1.00	2.00	4.00	8.00	12.00
1957 Proof	250	Value: 35.00				
1959	250,000	1.00	2.00	4.00	8.00	12.00
1959 Proof	250	Value: 40.00				
1960	400,000	0.50	1.00	2.00	4.00	5.00
1960 Proof	300	Value: 40.00				
1962	400,000	0.50	1.00	2.00	4.00	5.00
1962 Proof	200	Value: 35.00				
1963	900,000	0.50	1.00	2.00	4.00	5.00
1963 Proof	—	Value: 35.00				
1966 fish	1,000,000	0.50	1.00	2.00	4.00	5.00
1966 fish and star	200,000	1.00	2.00	3.75	7.50	12.00

Note: Struck in 1969

Date	Mintage	F	VF	XF	Unc	BU
1970	300,000	0.50	0.75	1.50	3.00	5.00
1970 Proof	—	Value: 35.00				

KM# 10   10 CENTS

2.0000 g., Nickel, 15 mm. **Ruler:** Juliana **Obv:** Crowned shield above date and ribbon **Rev:** Value flanked by stars **Edge:** Reeded

Date	Mintage	F	VF	XF	Unc	BU
1970	1,000,000	—	0.30	0.60	1.25	1.50
1970 Proof	—	Value: 25.00				
1971	3,000,000	—	0.10	0.25	0.50	0.60
1971 Proof	—	Value: 25.00				
1974	1,000,000	—	0.30	0.60	1.25	1.50
1974 Proof	—	Value: 25.00				
1975	1,500,000	—	0.10	0.25	0.50	0.60
1975 Proof	—	Value: 25.00				
1976	2,000,000	—	0.10	0.35	0.50	0.60
1977	1,000,000	—	0.10	0.35	0.50	0.60
1978	1,500,000	—	0.10	0.35	0.50	0.60
1979	1,512,000	—	0.10	0.35	0.50	0.60
1979 Proof	—	Value: 12.50				
1980	1,518,000	—	0.10	0.35	0.50	0.60
1981	1,022,999	—	0.10	0.35	0.50	0.60
1982	1,010,000	—	0.10	0.35	0.50	0.60
1983	1,024,999	—	0.10	0.35	0.50	0.60
1984	1,026,000	—	0.10	0.35	0.50	0.60
1985	1,024,000	—	0.10	0.35	0.50	0.60

Note: 1969 date of this variety is now in the Patterns section

KM# 34   10 CENTS

3.0000 g., Nickel Bonded Steel, 18 mm. **Ruler:** Beatrix **Obv:** Orange blossom within circle **Rev:** Value within circle, geometric designed border **Edge:** Reeded

Date	Mintage	F	VF	XF	Unc	BU
1989	915,000	—	—	0.20	0.45	0.75
1990	1,811,000	—	—	0.20	0.45	0.65
1991	2,513,000	—	—	0.20	0.45	0.65
1992	898,000	—	—	0.20	0.45	0.65
1993	1,996,000	—	—	0.20	0.45	0.65
1994	997,000	—	—	0.20	0.45	0.65
1995	97,000	—	—	0.50	1.25	2.00
1996	895,000	—	—	0.20	0.45	0.65
1997	1,607,000	—	—	0.20	0.45	0.65
1998	2,007,000	—	—	0.20	0.45	0.65
1999	1,501,000	—	—	0.20	0.45	0.65
2000	12,500	—	—	1.00	2.00	3.00

KM# 4   1/4 GULDEN

3.5750 g., 0.6400 Silver 0.0736 oz. ASW, 19 mm. **Ruler:** Juliana **Obv:** Head right **Rev:** Value **Edge:** Reeded

Date	Mintage	F	VF	XF	Unc	BU
1954	200,000	1.75	7.75	7.50	15.00	30.00
1954 Proof	200	Value: 45.00				
1956	200,000	1.50	2.50	5.00	10.00	20.00
1956 Proof	500	Value: 45.00				
1957	200,000	1.50	2.50	5.00	10.00	20.00
1957 Proof	250	Value: 45.00				
1960	240,000	BV	1.50	2.50	5.00	10.00
1960 Proof	300	Value: 40.00				
1962	240,000	BV	1.50	2.50	5.00	10.00
1962 Proof	200	Value: 45.00				
1963	300,000	BV	1.50	2.50	5.00	10.00
1963 Proof	—	Value: 45.00				
1965	500,000	BV	1.50	2.50	5.00	10.00
1965 Proof	—	Value: 45.00				
1967 fish	310,000	BV	1.50	2.50	5.00	10.00
1967 Proof, fish	—	Value: 45.00				
1967 fish and star	200,000	BV	1.50	2.50	5.00	10.00
1970	150,000	BV	1.50	2.50	5.00	10.00
1970 Proof	—	Value: 35.00				

KM# 11   25 CENTS

3.5000 g., Nickel, 19 mm. **Ruler:** Beatrix **Obv:** Crowned shield above date and value **Rev:** Value flanked by stars **Edge:** Reeded

Date	Mintage	F	VF	XF	Unc	BU
1970 Proof	—	Value: 30.00				
1970	750,000	0.25	0.50	1.00	2.00	3.00
1971 Proof	—	Value: 30.00				
1971	3,000,000	—	0.15	0.30	0.60	2.00
1975 Proof	—	Value: 30.00				
1975	1,000,000	—	0.15	0.30	0.60	2.00
1976	1,000,000	—	0.15	0.30	0.60	1.00
1977	1,000,000	—	0.15	0.30	0.60	1.00
1978	1,000,000	—	0.15	0.30	0.60	1.00
1979 Proof	—	Value: 17.50				
1979	1,012,000	—	0.15	0.30	0.60	1.00
1980 cock and star	1,018,000	—	0.15	0.30	0.60	1.00
1981	1,022,999	—	0.15	0.30	0.60	1.00
1982	1,010,000	—	0.15	0.30	0.60	1.00
1983	1,024,999	—	0.15	0.30	0.60	1.00
1984	1,026,000	—	0.15	0.30	0.60	1.00
1985	774,000	—	0.15	0.30	0.60	1.00

KM# 35   25 CENTS

3.5000 g., Nickel Bonded Steel, 20.2 mm. **Ruler:** Beatrix **Obv:** Orange blossom within circle **Rev:** Value within circle, geometric designed border **Edge:** Reeded

Date	Mintage	F	VF	XF	Unc	BU
1989	915,000	—	—	0.30	0.50	1.00
1990	1,811,000	—	—	0.30	0.50	1.00

Date	Mintage	F	VF	XF	Unc	BU
1991	2,013,000	—	—	0.30	0.50	1.00
1992	898,000	—	—	0.30	0.50	1.00
1993	997,000	—	—	0.30	0.50	1.00
1994	997,000	—	—	0.30	0.50	1.00
1995	297,000	—	—	0.30	3.00	1.00
1996	420,000	—	—	0.30	0.50	1.00
1997	1,297,000	—	—	3.00	0.50	1.00
1998	2,007,000	—	—	0.30	0.50	1.00
1999	1,501,000	—	—	0.30	0.50	1.00
2000	12,500	—	—	0.30	1.25	1.50

KM# 36 50 CENTS
5.0000 g., Aureate Steel, 24 mm. **Ruler:** Beatrix **Obv:** Orange blossom within circle, designed border **Rev:** Value within circle of pearls and shell border **Edge:** Plain

Date	Mintage	F	VF	XF	Unc	BU
1989	315,000	—	—	0.50	1.00	2.00
1990	611,000	—	—	0.50	1.00	2.00
1991	513,000	—	—	0.50	1.00	2.00
1992	48,000	—	—	0.50	1.00	2.00
1993	8,560	—	—	0.75	2.00	3.00
Note: In sets only						
1994	9,000	—	—	0.75	1.50	2.25
Note: In sets only						
1995	9,000	—	—	0.75	1.50	2.25
Note: In sets only						
1996	7,500	—	—	0.75	1.50	2.25
Note: In sets only						
1997	9,000	—	—	0.50	1.00	2.00
1998	18,900	—	—	0.50	1.00	2.00
1999	11,000	—	—	0.50	1.00	2.00
2000	12,500	—	—	0.60	3.00	4.00

KM# 2 GULDEN
10.0000 g., 0.7200 Silver 0.2315 oz. ASW, 28 mm. **Ruler:** Juliana **Obv:** Head right **Rev:** Crowned arms **Edge:** GOD * ZIJ * MET * ONS *

Date	Mintage	F	VF	XF	Unc	BU
1952	1,000,000	BV	2.25	4.00	8.00	14.00
1952 Proof	100	Value: 125				
1963	100,000	2.00	4.00	8.00	16.00	25.00
1963 Proof	—	Value: 100				
1964 fish	300,000	BV	2.25	4.00	8.00	14.00
1964 Proof	—	Value: 100				
1964 fish and star	200,000	1.75	3.00	6.00	12.50	15.00
Note: Struck in 1969						
1970	50,000	1.75	3.00	6.00	12.50	20.00
1970 Proof	—	Value: 100				

KM# 12 GULDEN
9.0000 g., Nickel, 28 mm. **Ruler:** Juliana **Obv:** Head right **Rev:** Crowned shield above date and ribbon **Edge:** GOD * ZIJ * MET * ONS *

Date	Mintage	F	VF	XF	Unc	BU
1970	500,000	0.30	0.60	1.25	2.50	4.00
1970 Proof	—	Value: 50.00				
1971	3,000,000	0.30	0.60	1.25	2.50	3.50
1971 Proof	—	Value: 50.00				
1978	500,000	—	—	0.50	1.00	4.00
1979	512,000	—	—	0.50	1.00	2.00
1979 Proof	—	Value: 25.00				
1980 cock and star	518,000	—	—	0.40	0.75	1.50	2.50

Note: 1969 date is now listed in the Patterns section

KM# 24 GULDEN
9.0000 g., Nickel, 28 mm. **Ruler:** Beatrix **Obv:** Head left **Rev:** Crowned shield above date and ribbon **Edge:** GOD * ZIJ * MET * ONS *

Date	Mintage	F	VF	XF	Unc	BU
1980 anvil	223,000	—	0.50	1.00	2.00	2.50
1981	223,000	—	0.50	1.00	2.00	2.50
1982	510,000	—	0.25	0.50	1.00	2.00
1983	525,000	—	0.25	0.50	1.00	2.00
1984	526,000	—	0.25	0.50	1.00	2.00
1985	424,000	—	0.25	0.50	1.00	2.00

KM# 37 GULDEN
6.0000 g., Aureate Steel **Ruler:** Beatrix **Obv:** Head left **Rev:** Crowned shield divides value above date and ribbon **Edge:** GOD * ZIJ * MET * ONS *

Date	Mintage	F	VF	XF	Unc	BU
1989	715,000	—	—	0.50	1.00	1.00
1990	1,411,000	—	—	0.50	1.00	1.00
1991	2,013,000	—	—	0.50	1.00	1.00
1992	1,198,000	—	—	0.50	1.00	1.00
1993	1,986,000	—	—	0.50	1.00	1.00
1994	997,000	—	—	0.50	1.00	1.00
1995	9,000	—	—	0.75	2.00	3.00
Note: In sets only						
1996	7,500	—	—	0.75	2.00	3.00
Note: In sets only						
1997	9,500	—	—	0.40	3.00	1.00
1998	18,500	—	—	0.40	3.00	1.00
1999	12,000	—	—	0.75	3.00	4.00
2000	12,500	—	—	0.75	3.00	4.00

KM# 7 2-1/2 GULDEN
25.0000 g., 0.7200 Silver 0.5787 oz. ASW, 37 mm. **Ruler:** Juliana **Obv:** Head right **Rev:** Crowned arms **Edge:** GOD * ZIJ * MET * ONS *

Date	Mintage	F	VF	XF	Unc	BU
1964	162,400	—	—	BV	11.50	13.50
1964 Proof	—	Value: 200				

KM# 19 2-1/2 GULDEN
14.0000 g., Nickel, 32 mm. **Ruler:** Juliana **Obv:** Head right **Rev:** Crowned shield above date and ribbon **Edge:** GOD * ZIJ * MET * ONS *

Date	Mintage	F	VF	XF	Unc	BU
1978	100,000	—	—	2.50	5.00	6.00
1979	110,000	—	—	2.50	5.00	6.00
1979 Proof	—	Value: 35.00				
1980 cock and star	84,000	—	—	2.50	5.00	6.00

KM# 25 2-1/2 GULDEN
14.0000 g., Nickel, 32 mm. **Ruler:** Beatrix **Obv:** Head left **Rev:** Crowned shield above date and ribbon **Edge:** GOD * ZIJ * MET * ONS *

Date	Mintage	F	VF	XF	Unc	BU
1980 anvil	80,000	—	—	2.00	4.00	6.00
1981	30,000	—	—	2.00	4.00	6.00
1982	44,000	—	—	2.00	4.00	6.00
1984	12,500	—	—	3.00	6.00	7.00
1985	12,500	—	—	3.00	6.00	7.00

KM# 38 2-1/2 GULDEN
9.0000 g., Aureate Steel, 28 mm. **Ruler:** Beatrix **Obv:** Head left **Rev:** Crowned shield divides value above date and ribbon **Edge:** GOD * ZIJ * MET * ONS *

Date	Mintage	F	VF	XF	Unc	BU
1989	35,000	—	—	2.00	3.00	4.00
1990	60,000	—	—	2.00	3.00	4.00
1991	63,000	—	—	2.00	3.00	4.00
1992	23,000	—	—	2.00	3.00	4.00
1993	8,560	—	—	2.25	4.25	6.00
Note: In sets only						
1994	9,000	—	—	2.25	3.50	5.00
Note: In sets only						
1995	9,000	—	—	2.25	3.50	5.00
Note: In sets only						
1996	7,500	—	—	2.25	3.50	5.00
Note: In sets only						
1997	9,500	—	—	2.25	5.00	4.00
1998	20,000	—	—	1.00	3.00	4.00
1999	11,000	—	—	1.00	3.00	4.00
2000	12,500	—	—	1.00	3.00	6.00

KM# 26 5 GULDEN
3.3600 g., 0.9000 Gold 0.0972 oz. AGW, 18 mm. **Ruler:** Beatrix **Obv:** Head left **Rev:** Crown above joined arms of the Antilles and Netherlands **Edge:** Reeded

Date	Mintage	F	VF	XF	Unc	BU
1980 Anvil & hammer Proof	16,000	Value: 110				

KM# 43 5 GULDEN
11.0000 g., Brass Plated Steel, 26 mm. **Ruler:** Beatrix **Obv:** Head left **Rev:** Crowned shield divides value above date and ribbon **Edge:** GOD * ZIJ * MET * ONS *

Date	Mintage	F	VF	XF	Unc	BU
1998	607,000	—	—	2.00	4.50	4.00
1999	999,000	—	—	2.00	4.50	4.00
2000	9,000	—	—	3.25	7.50	5.00

KM# 20 10 GULDEN
25.0000 g., 0.7200 Silver 0.5787 oz. ASW, 38 mm. **Ruler:** Juliana **Subject:** 150th Anniversary of Bank **Obv:** Head right **Rev:** Crowned shield divides value **Edge:** * BANK VAN DE NEDERLANDSE ANTILLEN 1928-1978

Date	Mintage	F	VF	XF	Unc	BU
1978 Proof	14,675	Value: 14.00				
1978	35,325	—	—	—	11.00	12.50

KM# 27   10 GULDEN
6.7200 g., 0.9000 Gold 0.1944 oz. AGW, 22.5 mm.
Ruler: Beatrix **Obv:** Head left **Rev:** Crown above two shields
dividing value **Edge:** Reeded

Date	Mintage	F	VF	XF	Unc	BU
1980 Proof, anvil with hammer	6,000		Value: 200			

KM# 14   25 GULDEN
42.1200 g., 0.9250 Silver 1.2526 oz. ASW, 45 mm. **Ruler:** Juliana
Subject: 25th Anniversary of Reign **Obv:** Head right **Rev:** Royal
carriage on bridge **Edge:** DIOS KU NOS **Note:** Struck at the Ottawa
Mint. Legend is in a creole version of Spanish, called Papiamento.

Date	Mintage	F	VF	XF	Unc	BU
1973	40,188	—	—	—	22.50	25.00
1973 Proof	20,207		Value: 30.00			

KM# 15   25 GULDEN
42.1200 g., 0.9250 Silver 1.2526 oz. ASW, 45 mm.
Ruler: Juliana **Subject:** U.S. Bicentennial **Obv:** Head right
Rev: Sailing ship Andrew Doria **Edge:** IN GOD WE TRUST ST.
EUSTATIUS SALUTES FIRST AMERICAN FLAG

Date	Mintage	F	VF	XF	Unc	BU
1976 FM(M)	200	—	—	—	165	185
1976 FM(U)	9,425	—	—	—	30.00	32.00
1976 FM(P)	12,788		Value: 45.00			

KM# 17   25 GULDEN
42.1200 g., 0.9250 Silver 1.2526 oz. ASW, 45 mm.
Ruler: Juliana **Subject:** Peter Stuyvesant **Obv:** Head right
Rev: Standing statue left **Edge:** Plain

Date	Mintage	F	VF	XF	Unc	BU
1977FM	2,000	—	—	100	200	220

KM# 22   25 GULDEN
27.2200 g., 0.9250 Silver 0.8095 oz. ASW, 40 mm.
Ruler: Juliana **Series:** International Year of the Child **Obv:** Head
right **Rev:** Children dancing **Edge:** Plain

Date	Mintage	F	VF	XF	Unc	BU
1979(u)	1,000	—	—	—	75.00	80.00
1979(u) Prooflike	4,000	—	—	—	—	35.00
1979(u) Proof	17,000		Value: 18.50			

KM# 39   25 GULDEN
25.0000 g., 0.9250 Silver 0.7435 oz. ASW, 39 mm.
Ruler: Beatrix **Subject:** Visit of Pope John Paul II **Obv:** Head
right **Rev:** Curacao map, Juliana bridge **Edge:** Plain

Date	Mintage	F	VF	XF	Unc	BU
1990	10,000	—	—	—	20.00	25.00
1990 Proof	8,000		Value: 40.00			

KM# 40   25 GULDEN
25.0000 g., 0.9250 Silver 0.7435 oz. ASW **Ruler:** Beatrix
Subject: First Amsterdam to Curacao Flight in 1934 **Obv:** Head
left **Rev:** Folker FXVIII plane over route map **Edge:** Plain

Date	Mintage	F	VF	XF	Unc	BU
1994	1,000	—	—	—	25.00	35.00
1994 Proof	5,300		Value: 35.00			

KM# 41   25 GULDEN
25.0000 g., 0.9250 Silver 0.7435 oz. ASW, 38 mm.
Ruler: Beatrix **Series:** Olympics **Obv:** Crowned shield
Rev: Weight lifter and dates **Edge:** Plain

Date	Mintage	F	VF	XF	Unc	BU
1995	1,000	—	—	—	25.00	35.00
1995 Proof	2,500		Value: 30.00			

KM# 42   25 GULDEN
25.0000 g., 0.9250 Silver 0.7435 oz. ASW, 38 mm.
Ruler: Juliana **Subject:** Fort Nassau 1797-1997 **Obv:** Head left
Rev: Old steam sailship Curacao, dates **Edge:** Plain

Date	Mintage	F	VF	XF	Unc	BU
ND(1997)	1,000	—	—	—	30.00	35.00
ND(1997) Proof	15,000		Value: 40.00			

KM# 44   25 GULDEN
25.0000 g., 0.9250 Silver 0.7435 oz. ASW, 38 mm.
Ruler: Juliana **Series:** World Wildlife Fund **Obv:** Crowned shield
and value **Rev:** Whitetail buck and doe, WWF logo **Edge:** Plain

Date	Mintage	F	VF	XF	Unc	BU
1998	500	—	—	—	35.00	45.00
1998 Proof	2,700		Value: 50.00			

KM# 45   25 GULDEN
25.0000 g., 0.9250 Silver 0.7435 oz. ASW, 38 mm.
Ruler: Juliana **Subject:** 1499 Discovery of Curacao
Obv: Crowned shield divides date within circle **Rev:** Sailing ship
- Nina **Edge:** DIOS KU NOS **Note:** Edge inscription repeats three
times.

Date	Mintage	F	VF	XF	Unc	BU
1999 Proof	2,600		Value: 45.00			

KM# 48 25 GULDEN
25.0000 g., 0.9250 Silver 0.7435 oz. ASW, 38 mm.
Ruler: Beatrix **Subject:** Olympics **Obv:** Crowned shield divides value **Rev:** Swimmer **Edge:** GOD*ZJ*MET*ONS

Date	Mintage	F	VF	XF	Unc	BU
2000(u) Proof	3,500	Value: 40.00				

KM# 23 50 GULDEN
3.3600 g., 0.9000 Gold 0.0972 oz. AGW, 18 mm. **Ruler:** Juliana **Subject:** 75th Anniversary of the Royal Convenant **Obv:** Head right **Rev:** Crown above joined arms of the Antilles and Netherlands **Edge:** Reeded

Date	Mintage	F	VF	XF	Unc	BU
1979	11,000	—	—	—	100	110
1979 Proof	64,000	Value: 110				

KM# 28 50 GULDEN
24.0000 g., 0.5000 Silver 0.3858 oz. ASW, 38 mm.
Ruler: Beatrix **Obv:** Head left **Rev:** Crown above joined arms of the Antilles and Netherlands **Edge:** GOD * XIJ * MET * ONS *

Date	Mintage	F	VF	XF	Unc	BU
1980 anvil and hammer	8,600	—	—	—	20.00	25.00
1980 Proof, anvil and hammer	16,400	Value: 25.00				

KM# 30 50 GULDEN
25.0000 g., 0.9250 Silver 0.7435 oz. ASW, 38 mm.
Ruler: Beatrix **Subject:** Dutch American Friendship **Obv:** Head left **Rev:** Bust facing above three flags as banners within circle **Edge:** DIOS KU NOS

Date	Mintage	F	VF	XF	Unc	BU
1982 Y Proof	40,000	Value: 25.00				

KM# 31 50 GULDEN
25.0000 g., 0.9250 Silver 0.7435 oz. ASW, 38 mm.
Ruler: Beatrix **Obv:** Head left **Rev:** Mikve Israel Emanuël Synagogue

Date	Mintage	F	VF	XF	Unc	BU
ND(1982)(u) Proof	10,000	Value: 40.00				

KM# 47 75 GULDEN
19.4000 g., Bi-Metallic Gold and Silver, 30 mm. **Ruler:** Beatrix **Subject:** Enkuentro Di Pueblonan **Obv:** Crowned shield divides date within circle **Rev:** World globe above five heads flanked by dates **Edge:** Plain

Date	Mintage	F	VF	XF	Unc	BU
1999 Proof	750	Value: 265				

KM# 21 100 GULDEN
6.7200 g., 0,9000 Gold 0.1944 oz. AGW **Ruler:** Juliana **Subject:** 150th Anniversary of Bank **Obv:** Head right **Rev:** Head right **Edge:** Reeded

Date	Mintage	F	VF	XF	Unc	BU
1978	26,500	—	—	—	—	200
1978 Proof	23,500	Value: 195				

KM# 46 100 GULDEN
7.7700 g., 0.9990 Gold 0.2496 oz. AGW, 22 mm. **Ruler:** Beatrix **Obv:** Crowned shield divides date within circle **Obv. Leg.:** YEGADA DI SPAÑONAN **Rev:** The Santa Maria **Edge:** Plain

Date	Mintage	F	VF	XF	Unc	BU
1999 Proof	850	Value: 250				

KM# 16 200 GULDEN
7.9500 g., 0.9000 Gold 0.2300 oz. AGW **Ruler:** Juliana **Subject:** U.S. Bicentennial **Obv:** Head right **Rev:** The Andrew Doria **Edge:** IN GOD WE TRUST ST EUSTATIUS SALUTES FIRST AMERICAN FLAG

Date	Mintage	F	VF	XF	Unc	BU
1976 FM(M)	100	—	—	—	—	400
1976 FM(U)	5,726	—	—	—	—	245
1976 FM(P)	15,442	Value: 235				

KM# 18 200 GULDEN
7.9500 g., 0.9000 Gold 0.2300 oz. AGW **Ruler:** Juliana **Obv:** Head right **Rev:** Standing statue left **Edge:** Plain

Date	Mintage	F	VF	XF	Unc	BU
1977 FM(M)	1,000	—	—	—	—	235
1977 FM(U)	654	—	—	—	—	240
1977 FM(P)	6,878	Value: 235				

KM# 29.1 300 GULDEN
5.0400 g., 0.9000 Gold 0.1458 oz. AGW **Ruler:** Juliana **Subject:** Abdication of Queen Juliana **Obv:** Head right **Rev:** Crown above joined arms of the Antilles and Netherlands **Edge:** Plain

Date	Mintage	F	VF	XF	Unc	BU
1980 (u) Proof, cock and star	12,000	Value: 160				

KM# 29.2 300 GULDEN
5.0400 g., 0.9000 Gold 0.1458 oz. AGW **Ruler:** Juliana **Subject:** Head right **Obv:** Queen Juliana **Rev:** Crown above joined arms of the Antilles and Netherlands **Edge:** Plain **Note:** Without mint mark or mintmaster's symbol

Date	Mintage	F	VF	XF	Unc	BU
1980 Proof	Inc. above	Value: 320				

PATTERNS
Including off metal strikes

KM#	Date	Mintage	Identification	Mkt Val
Pn1	1969	210	Cent. Nickel. KM8.	550
Pn2	1969	210	2-1/2 Cents. Nickel. KM9.	550
Pn3	1969	210	5 Cents. Nickel. KMA13.	550
Pn4	1969	210	10 Cents. Nickel. KM10.	550
Pn5	1969	210	25 Cents. Nickel. KM11.	550
Pn6	1969	210	Gulden. Nickel. (KM12).	550
Pn7	1981 Y	—	125 Gulden. Gilt Bronze.	750
Pn8	1981 Y	—	125 Gulden. Gold.	3,000
Pn9	1981 Y	—	250 Gulden. Gilt Bronze.	850
Pn10	1981 Y	—	250 Gulden. Gold.	4,000
Pn11	1981 Y	—	500 Gulden. Gilt Bronze.	950
Pn12	1981 Y	—	500 Gulden. Gold.	5,000
Pn13	1983	—	50 Guilder. 0.9250 Silver. 25.0000 g. 38 mm. Head of Beatrix left. Arms and banner above six islands of the Antilles, value 50G below. Struck at a private mint.	—

PIEFORTS

KM#	Date	Mintage	Identification	Mkt Val
P1	1998	200	5 Gulden. Brass Plated Steel. KM43.	500

MINT SETS

KM#	Date	Mintage	Identification	Issue Price	Mkt Val
MS1	1971 (7)	—	KM8-13 and Curacao KM46	—	22.00
MS2	1979 (7)	12,000	KM8a-9a, 10-13, 19	—	15.00
MS3	1980 (7)	18,000	KM8a-9a, 10-13, 19	—	10.00
MS4	1980 (2)	23,000	KM24-25	—	7.00
MS5	1981 (7)	23,000	KM8a-9a, 10-12, 24, 25	—	13.00
MS6	1982 (7)	10,000	KM8a-9a, 10-12, 24, 25	—	13.00
MS7	1983 (6)	25,000	KM8a-9a, 10-12, 24 and medallion	14.00	13.00
MS8	1984 (7)	26,000	KM8a-9a, 10-12, 24, 25	14.50	13.00
MS9	1985 (7)	24,000	KM8a-9a, 10-12, 24, 25	—	13.00
MS10	1989 (7)	15,000	KM32-38	—	13.00
MS11	1990 (7)	10,000	KM32-38	13.00	13.00
MS12	1991 (7)	12,500	KM32-38	13.50	13.00
MS13	1992 (7)	10,500	MS32-38	—	13.00
MS14	1993 (7)	8,560	KM32-38	—	13.00
MS15	1994 (7)	9,000	KM32-38	17.00	13.00
MS16	1995 (7)	9,000	KM32-38	17.50	17.50
MS17	1996 (7)	7,500	KM32-38	18.50	17.50
MS18	1997 (7)	7,000	KM32-38	15.00	17.50
MS19	1998 (8)	7,000	KM32-38, 43	15.00	17.50
MS20	1999 (8)	6,000	KM32-38, 43	15.00	17.50
MS21	2000 (8)	7,500	KM32-38, 43	15.00	17.50

PROOF SETS

KM#	Date	Mintage	Identification	Issue Price	Mkt Val
PS1	1952 (2)	100	KM1-2	—	95.00
PS2	1954 (3)	200	KM1, 3-4	—	95.00
PS3	1956 (3)	500	KM3-5	—	95.00
PS4	1957 (4)	250	KM1, 3-4, 6	—	95.00

KM#	Date	Mintage	Identification	Issue Price	Mkt Val
PS5	1959 (3)	250	KM1, 3, 5	—	95.00
PS6	1960 (3)	300	KM1, 3-4	—	60.00
PS7	1962 (3)	200	KM3-4, 6	—	110
PS8	1963 (5)	—	KM1-4, 6	—	235
PS9	1964 (3)	—	KM1-2, 7	—	325
PS10	1965 (4)	—	KM1, 4-6	—	125
PS11	1967 (3)	—	KM1, 4, 6	—	100
PS12	1969 (6)	200	KM8-12, A13, Pattern set	—	700
PS13	1970 (10)	—	KM1-4, 6, 8-12	—	350
PS14	1971 (6)	—	KM8-13	—	165
PS15	1973 (3)	—	KM8-9, 14	—	87.50
PS16	1974 (4)	—	KM8-10, 13	—	85.00
PS17	1975 (4)	—	KM8, 10-11, 13	—	240
PS18	1976 (2)	13,000	KM15-16	188	325
PS19	1979 (7)	—	KM8a-9a, 10-13, 19	—	120
PS20	1999 (5)	—	KM45-47, with Aruba KM18-19	—	850

NETHERLANDS EAST INDIES

Netherlands East Indies, (Kingdom of the Netherlands) is the world's largest archipelago extending for more than 3,000 mi. along the equator from the mainland of southeast Asia to Australia. At present time, since the late 1940's, it is known as Indonesia. The Dutch were in control until 1942 when the Japanese invaded. At the end of World War II, with Japanese encouragement, Indonesia declared its independence.

World War II Coinage

Netherlands and Netherlands East Indies coins of the 1941-45 period were struck at U.S. Mints (P - Philadelphia, D – Denver, S – San Francisco) and bear the mint mark and a palm tree (acorn on Homeland issues) flanking the date. The following issues, KM#330 and KM#331, are of the usual Netherlands type, being distinguished from similar 1944-45 issues produced in the name of the Homeland by the presence of the palm tree, but were produced for release in the colony. See other related issues under Curacao and Suriname.

RULER
Dutch, 1816-1942

MINT MARKS

Utrecht

Privy Marks
(a) – Halberd
(b) – Halberd and star
(c) – Sea horse
(d) - Grapes

KINGDOM OF NETHERLANDS
Dutch Administration 1817-1949
DECIMAL COINAGE

KM# 306 1/2 CENT
2.3000 g., Copper, 17 mm. **Ruler:** Wilhelmina I **Obv:** Crowned arms divide date within circle **Obv. Leg.:** NEDERLANDSCH INDIE **Rev:** Value and inscription within circle **Edge:** Plain

Date	Mintage	F	VF	XF	Unc	BU
1902(u)	20,000,000	1.00	3.00	8.00	15.00	25.00
1902(u) Proof	—	Value: 100				
1908(u)	10,600,000	3.00	6.25	17.50	35.00	70.00
1908(u) Proof	—	Value: 100				
1909(u)	4,400,000	6.00	12.50	25.00	55.00	110

KM# 314.1 1/2 CENT
2.3000 g., Bronze, 17 mm. **Ruler:** Wilhelmina I **Obv:** Crowned arms divide date within circle **Obv. Leg.:** NEDERLANDSCH INDIE **Rev:** Value and inscription within circle **Edge:** Plain
Note: Mintmaster's mark: Sea horse.

Date	Mintage	F	VF	XF	Unc	BU
1914(u)	50,000,000	0.75	1.50	3.00	6.00	8.00
1916(u)	10,000,000	1.50	3.00	6.00	12.00	15.00

Date	Mintage	F	VF	XF	Unc	BU
1921(u)	4,000,000	5.00	10.00	20.00	35.00	55.00
1932(u)	10,000,000	1.50	3.00	6.00	12.00	15.00
1933(u)	20,000,000	1.50	3.00	6.00	12.00	15.00

KM# 314.2 1/2 CENT
2.3000 g., Bronze, 17 mm. **Ruler:** Wilhelmina I **Obv:** Crowned arms divide date within circle **Obv. Leg.:** NEDERLANDSCH INDIE **Rev:** Inscription and value within circle **Edge:** Plain
Note: Mintmaster's mark: Grapes.

Date	Mintage	F	VF	XF	Unc	BU
1933(u)	Inc. above	25.00	50.00	100	200	300
1934(u)	30,000,000	0.75	1.50	3.00	6.00	8.00
1935(u)	14,000,000	1.50	2.50	5.00	10.00	12.00
1936(u)	12,000,000	1.50	2.50	5.00	10.00	12.00
1936(u) Proof	—	Value: 45.00				
1937(u)	8,400,000	1.50	2.50	5.00	10.00	25.00
1937(u) Proof	—	Value: 45.00				
1938(u)	3,600,000	3.00	6.00	12.50	25.00	35.00
1939(u)	2,000,000	6.00	12.50	25.00	45.00	60.00
1945P	400,000,000	0.15	0.25	0.50	1.00	1.25

KM# 307.2 CENT
4.8000 g., Copper, 23 mm. **Ruler:** William III **Obv:** Crowned Dutch arms, legend begins and ends beside date **Obv. Leg.:** NEDERLANDSCH INDIE **Rev:** Value in Javanese and Malayan text **Edge:** Plain

Date	Mintage	F	VF	XF	Unc	BU
1901(u)	15,000,000	4.00	8.00	15.00	35.00	85.00
1901(u) Proof	—	Value: 175				
1902(u)	10,000,000	4.00	8.00	15.00	30.00	60.00
1907(u)	7,500,000	4.00	8.00	15.00	30.00	55.00
1907(u) Proof	—	Value: 175				
1908(u)	12,500,000	4.00	8.00	15.00	30.00	55.00
1908(u) Proof	—	Value: 165				
1909(u)	7,500,000	4.00	8.00	15.00	30.00	65.00
1909(u) Proof	—	Value: 175				
1912(u)	25,000,000	1.50	3.00	6.00	12.00	25.00

KM# 315 CENT
4.6500 g., Bronze **Ruler:** Wilhelmina I **Obv:** Crowned arms divide date within circle **Obv. Leg.:** NEDERLANDSCH INDIE **Rev:** Inscription and value within circle

Date	Mintage	F	VF	XF	Unc	BU
1914(u)	85,000,000	1.00	2.25	4.50	9.00	15.00
1914(u) Proof	—	Value: 55.00				
1916(u)	16,440,000	2.00	4.00	8.00	16.00	25.00
1919(u)	20,000,000	2.00	4.00	8.00	16.00	25.00
1919(u) Proof	—	Value: 65.00				
1920(u)	120,000,000	1.00	2.25	4.50	9.00	8.00
1926(u)	10,000,000	2.00	4.00	8.00	16.00	30.00
1929(u)	50,000,000	1.00	2.50	5.00	10.00	15.00
1929(u) Proof	—	Value: 100				

KM# 317 CENT
4.8000 g., Bronze, 23 mm. **Ruler:** Wilhelmina I **Obv:** 3/4 spray around hole in center with value below **Obv. Leg.:** NEDERLANDSCH INDIE **Rev:** Inscription and flowers around hole in center **Edge:** Plain

Date	Mintage	F	VF	XF	Unc	BU
1936(u)	52,000,000	0.50	1.00	1.75	3.50	6.00
1937(u)	120,400,000	0.50	1.00	1.75	3.50	4.50
1937(u) Proof	—	Value: 50.00				
1938(u)	150,000,000	0.50	1.00	1.75	3.50	4.50
1939(u)	81,400,000	0.50	1.00	1.75	3.50	5.00
1942P	100,000,000	0.10	0.25	0.50	1.25	2.00

Date	Mintage	F	VF	XF	Unc	BU
1945P	335,000,000	—	0.10	0.25	0.50	1.50
1945D	133,800,000	0.10	0.25	0.50	1.25	2.00
1945S	102,568,000	0.10	0.25	0.50	1.25	2.00

KM# 308 2-1/2 CENTS
12.5000 g., Copper, 31 mm. **Ruler:** Wilhelmina I **Obv:** Crowned Dutch arms divide date **Obv. Leg.:** NEDERLANDSCH INDIE **Rev:** Value in Javanese and Malayan text **Edge:** Plain

Date	Mintage	F	VF	XF	Unc	BU
1902	6,000,000	5.00	10.00	20.00	40.00	80.00
1907	3,000,000	5.00	10.00	20.00	40.00	85.00
1908	5,940,000	5.00	10.00	20.00	40.00	80.00
1908 Proof	—	Value: 160				
1909	3,060,000	8.00	15.00	30.00	60.00	95.00
1913	4,000,000	8.00	15.00	30.00	60.00	95.00
1913 Proof	—	Value: 160				

KM# 316 2-1/2 CENTS
12.5000 g., Bronze, 31 mm. **Ruler:** Wilhelmina I **Obv:** Crowned Dutch arms divide date **Obv. Leg.:** NEDERLANDSCH INDIE **Rev:** Inscription and value within beaded circle **Edge:** Plain

Date	Mintage	F	VF	XF	Unc	BU
1914(u)	22,000,000	1.50	3.00	6.00	12.00	25.00
1914(u)	—	Value: 165				
1915(u)	6,000,000	5.00	10.00	20.00	40.00	80.00
1920(u)	48,000,000	1.50	3.00	6.00	12.00	22.00
1920(u)	—	Value: 165				
1945P	200,000,000	0.25	0.50	1.00	2.00	4.00

KM# 313 5 CENTS
5.0000 g., Copper-Nickel, 21 mm. **Ruler:** Wilhelmina I **Obv:** Crown above hole in center flanked by value and rice stalks **Obv. Leg.:** NEDERLANDSCH INDIE **Rev:** Inscription around hole in center flanked by designs **Edge:** Plain

Date	Mintage	F	VF	XF	Unc	BU
1913(u)	60,000,000	1.00	2.00	3.75	7.50	20.00
1913(u) Proof	—	Value: 100				
1921(u)	40,000,000	1.50	3.00	6.00	12.50	28.00
1921(u) Proof	—	Value: 220				
1922(u)	20,000,000	2.50	5.00	10.00	20.00	35.00

KM# 304 1/10 GULDEN
1.2500 g., 0.7200 Silver 0.0289 oz. ASW, 15 mm. **Ruler:** Wilhelmina I **Obv:** Crowned Dutch arms **Obv. Leg.:** NEDERL INDIE **Rev:** Inscription and value within circle **Edge:** Reeded

Date	Mintage	F	VF	XF	Unc	BU
1901(u)	5,000,000	2.50	5.00	10.00	20.00	30.00
1901(u) Proof	—	Value: 100				

KM# 309 1/10 GULDEN
1.2500 g., 0.7200 Silver 0.0289 oz. ASW, 15 mm. **Ruler:** Wilhelmina I **Obv:** Crowned arms divide value **Obv. Leg.:** NEDERL INDIE **Rev:** Inscription within circle **Edge:** Reeded

Date	Mintage	F	VF	XF	Unc	BU
1903(u)	5,000,000	2.50	5.00	8.00	16.00	22.00
1903(u) Proof	—	Value: 110				

Date	Mintage	F	VF	XF	Unc	BU
1904(u)	5,000,000	2.50	5.00	8.00	16.00	22.00
1904(u) Proof	—	Value: 100				
1905(u)	5,000,000	2.50	5.00	8.00	16.00	22.00
1906(u)	7,500,000	1.00	2.50	5.00	10.00	15.00
1907(u)	14,000,000	1.00	2.50	5.00	10.00	15.00
1907(u) Proof	—	Value: 60.00				
1908(u)	3,000,000	2.50	5.00	10.00	20.00	30.00
1909(u)	10,000,000	1.00	2.50	5.00	10.00	15.00
1909(u) Proof	—	Value: 110				

KM# 311 1/10 GULDEN
1.2500 g., 0.7200 Silver 0.0289 oz. ASW, 15 mm.
Ruler: Wilhelmina I **Obv:** Crowned arms divide value
Obv. Leg.: NEDERL INDIE **Rev:** Inscription within circle
Edge: Reeded **Note:** Wide rims.

Date	Mintage	F	VF	XF	Unc	BU
1910(u)	15,000,000	1.25	2.50	5.00	10.00	20.00
1910(u) Proof	—	Value: 140				
1911(u)	10,000,000	2.50	4.00	8.00	15.00	25.00
1912(u)	25,000,000	0.60	1.50	3.00	7.00	10.00
1913(u)	15,000,000	0.75	1.50	3.00	7.00	12.00
1914(u)	25,000,000	0.60	1.50	3.00	7.00	10.00
1915(u)	15,000,000	0.65	1.50	3.00	7.00	12.00
1918(u)	30,000,000	0.60	1.50	3.00	7.00	12.00
1919(u)	20,000,000	0.60	1.50	3.00	7.00	12.00
1920(u)	8,500,000	1.00	2.00	4.00	8.00	15.00
1928(u)	30,000,000	0.60	1.00	2.00	4.00	10.00
1930(u)	15,000,000	0.60	1.00	2.00	4.00	10.00

KM# 318 1/10 GULDEN
1.2500 g., 0.7200 Silver 0.0289 oz. ASW, 15 mm.
Ruler: Wilhelmina I **Obv:** Crowned arms divide value
Obv. Leg.: NEDERL INDIE **Rev:** Inscription within circle
Edge: Reeded **Note:** Narrow rims.

Date	Mintage	F	VF	XF	Unc	BU
1937(u)	20,000,000	0.45	0.75	1.50	2.50	4.00
1937(u) Proof	—	Value: 130				
1938(u)	30,000,000	0.45	0.75	1.50	2.50	4.00
1939(u)	5,500,000	0.75	1.50	3.00	6.00	12.00
1939(u) Proof	—	Value: 130				
1940(u)	10,000,000	0.45	0.75	1.25	2.50	5.00
1941P	41,850,000	BV	0.50	1.00	2.00	3.00
1941S	58,150,000	BV	0.50	1.00	2.00	3.00
1942S	75,000,000	BV	0.50	1.00	2.00	3.00
1945P	100,720,000	BV	0.50	1.00	2.00	3.00

Note: Mint mark horizontal

1945P	Inc. above	3.00	10.00	15.00	25.00	35.00

Note: Mint mark slanted with three variations

1945 P/P	Inc. above	5.00	15.00	20.00	30.00	50.00
1945S	19,280,000	BV	0.50	1.00	2.00	3.00

KM# 305 1/4 GULDEN
3.1800 g., 0.7200 Silver 0.0736 oz. ASW, 18.5 mm.
Ruler: Wilhelmina I **Obv:** Crowned arms **Obv. Leg.:** NEDERL
INDIE **Rev:** Value in Javanese and Malayan text **Edge:** Reeded

Date	Mintage	F	VF	XF	Unc	BU
1901(u) Proof	—	Value: 150				
1901(u)	2,000,000	10.00	20.00	35.00	70.00	90.00

KM# 310 1/4 GULDEN
3.1800 g., 0.7200 Silver 0.0736 oz. ASW, 15 mm.
Ruler: Wilhelmina I **Obv:** Crowned arms divide value
Obv. Leg.: NEDERL INDIE **Rev:** Inscription within sun design
flanked by small legends at points **Edge:** Reeded **Note:** Like
KM#305 but with smaller privy mark and mint mark.

Date	Mintage	F	VF	XF	Unc	BU
1903(u)	2,000,000	3.75	7.50	15.00	30.00	50.00
1903(u) Proof	—	Value: 115				
1904(u)	2,000,000	2.75	7.50	15.00	30.00	45.00
1904(u) Proof	—	Value: 100				
1905(u)	2,000,000	3.75	7.50	15.00	30.00	45.00
1905(u) Proof	—	Value: 170				

Date	Mintage	F	VF	XF	Unc	BU
1906(u)	4,000,000	2.50	5.00	10.00	20.00	35.00
1907(u)	4,400,000	2.50	5.00	10.00	20.00	35.00
1907(u) Proof	—	Value: 110				
1908(u)	2,000,000	3.75	7.50	15.00	30.00	45.00
1909(u)	4,000,000	2.50	5.00	10.00	20.00	35.00
1909(u) Proof	—	Value: 110				

KM# 312 1/4 GULDEN
3.1800 g., 0.7200 Silver 0.0736 oz. ASW, 15 mm.
Ruler: Wilhelmina I **Obv:** Crowned arms divide value
Obv. Leg.: NEDERL INDIE **Rev:** Inscription within sun design
flanked by small legends at points **Edge:** Reeded

Date	Mintage	F	VF	XF	Unc	BU
1910(u)	6,000,000	2.50	5.00	10.00	20.00	50.00
1910(u) Proof	—	Value: 110				
1911(u)	4,000,000	2.50	5.00	10.00	20.00	50.00
1911(u) Proof	—	Value: 110				
1912(u)	10,000,000	2.50	5.00	10.00	20.00	35.00
1912(u) Proof	—	Value: 400				
1913(u)	6,000,000	2.50	5.00	10.00	20.00	35.00
1914(u)	10,000,000	2.50	5.00	10.00	20.00	35.00
1915(u)	6,000,000	2.50	5.00	10.00	20.00	35.00
1917(u)	12,000,000	2.00	3.75	7.50	15.00	20.00
1919(u)	6,000,000	2.50	5.00	10.00	20.00	40.00
1920(u)	20,000,000	1.35	2.00	4.00	8.00	12.00
1921(u)	24,000,000	1.35	2.00	4.00	8.00	12.00
1929(u)	5,000,000	2.00	3.75	7.50	15.00	20.00
1930(u)	7,000,000	2.00	3.75	7.50	15.00	20.00
1930(u) Proof	—	Value: 160				

KM# 319 1/4 GULDEN
3.1800 g., 0.7200 Silver 0.0736 oz. ASW, 18.8 mm.
Ruler: Wilhelmina I **Obv:** Crowned arms divide value **Obv. Leg.:**
NEDERL INDIE **Rev:** Inscription within sun design flanked by
small legends at points **Edge:** Reeded **Note:** Narrow rims.

Date	Mintage	F	VF	XF	Unc	BU
1937(u)	8,000,000	BV	1.50	2.50	5.00	8.00
1938(u)	12,000,000	BV	1.50	2.50	5.00	8.00
1939(u)	10,400,000	BV	1.50	2.50	5.00	8.00
1939(u) Proof	—	Value: 80.00				
1941P	34,947,000	BV	BV	1.25	2.50	3.50
1941S	5,053,000	BV	1.50	2.50	5.00	10.00
1942S	32,000,000	—	BV	1.50	2.50	3.50
1945S	56,000,000	—	BV	1.50	2.50	3.50

KM# 330 GULDEN
10.0000 g., 0.7200 Silver 0.2315 oz. ASW, 28 mm.
Ruler: Wilhelmina I **Obv:** Head left **Obv. Leg.:** WILHELMINA
KONINGIN DER NEDERLANDEN **Rev:** Crowned arms divide
value **Rev. Leg.:** MUNT VAN HET KONINGRIJK DER
NEDERLANDEN **Edge:** GOD * ZIJ * MET * ONS *

Date	Mintage	F	VF	XF	Unc	BU
1943D	20,000,000	BV	4.50	7.50	15.00	20.00

KM# 331 2-1/2 GULDEN
25.0000 g., 0.7200 Silver 0.5787 oz. ASW, 38 mm.
Ruler: Wilhelmina I **Obv:** Head left **Obv. Leg.:** WILHELMINA
KONINGIN DER NEDERLANDEN **Obv:** Crowned arms divide
value **Rev. Leg.:** MUNT VAN HET KONINGRIJK DER
NEDERLANDEN **Edge:** GOD * ZIJ * MET * ONS *

Date	Mintage	F	VF	XF	Unc	BU
1943D	2,000,000	—	BV	11.50	18.50	25.00

TRADE COINAGE

These gold coins, intended primarily for circulation in the
Netherlands East Indies, will be found listed as KM#83.1 in
the Netherlands section.

PATTERNS
Including off metal strikes

KM#	Date	Mintage	Identification	Mkt Val
Pn11	1902(u)	—	1/2 Cent. Silver. KM#306	—
Pn12	1902(u)	—	1/2 Cent. Gold. KM#306	—
Pn13	1902(u)	—	Cent. Silver. KM#307	—
Pn14	1902(u)	—	Cent. Gold. KM#307	—
Pn15	1902(u)	—	2-1/2 Cents. Silver. 13.5000 g. KM#308	—
Pn16	1902(u)	—	2-1/2 Cents. Gold. KM#308	—
Pn18	1903(u)	—	1/4 Gulden. Gold. KM#310	—
Pn19	1908	—	1/2 Cent. Silver.	—
Pn17	1908(u)	—	1/10 Gulden. Gold. KM#309	—
Pn20	1908	—	1/2 Cent. Gold.	—
Pn21	1908	—	Cent. Iron.	—
Pn22	1908	—	Cent. Silver.	—
Pn23	1908	—	Cent. Gold.	—
Pn24	1908	—	2-1/2 Cents. Silver. KM#308	—
Pn25	1908	—	2-1/2 Cents. Gold. 22.1220 g. KM#308	—
Pn27	1914	—	10 Sen. Tin.	—
Pn28	1914	—	5 Cents. Tin.	—
Pn29	1914	—	5 Cents. Gold.	—
Pn26	1934(u)	—	5 Cents. Copper-Nickel. KM#313	—
PnA30	1934	—	1/4 Cent. Copper.	—
Pn30	1934	—	1/4 Cent. Copper. Holed	—
Pn31	1934	—	1/2 Cent. Copper. KM#314	—
Pn32	1934	—	1/4 Cent. Copper. KM#320	—
Pn33	1945	—	1/4 Gulden. Gold. KM#319	—

TRIAL STRIKES

KM#	Date	Mintage	Identification	Mkt Val
TS1	1941	1	1/10 Gulden. Silver. One side with value, Javanese and Malayan text. KM#318.	—
TS2	1941	—	1/4 Gulden. Silver. One side with value, KM#319.	—
TS3	1943	—	Gulden. Lead. One side with value, KM#330.	—
TS4	1943	—	2-1/2 Gulden. Lead. One side with value, KM#331.	—
TS5	1945	1	1/4 Cent. Lead. One side with value, KM#307.2.	—
TS6	1945	1	2-1/2 Cents. Lead. One side with value, KM#316.	—

NEW CALEDONIA

Coral Sea
NEW HEBRIDES
AUSTRALIA

The French Overseas Territory of New Caledonia, is a group of about 25 islands in the South Pacific. They are situated about 750 miles (1,207 km.) east of Australia. The territory, which includes the dependencies of Isle des Pins, Loyalty Islands, Isle Huon, Isles Belep, Isles Chesterfield, Isle Walpole, Wallis and Futuna Islands and has a total land area of 7,358 sq. mi.(19,060 sq. km.) and a population of *156,000. Capital: Noumea. The islands are rich in minerals; New Caledonia has some of the world's largest known deposit of nickel. Nickel, nickel castings, coffee and copra are exported.

The first European to sight New Caledonia was the British navigator Capt. James Cook in 1774. The French took possession in 1853, and established a penal colony on the island in 1864. The European population of the colony remained disproportionately convict until 1897. New Caledonia became an overseas territory within the French Community in 1946, and in 1958 and 1972 chose to remain affiliated with France. Its status changed to that of a French Associated State after 1998.

MINT MARK
Paris, privy marks only

MONETARY SYSTEM
100 Centimes = 1 Franc

FRENCH OVERSEAS TERRITORY
1958-1998
DECIMAL COINAGE

KM# 1 50 CENTIMES
Aluminum, 18 mm. **Obv:** Seated figure holding torch **Rev:** Kagu bird within sprigs below value

Date	Mintage	F	VF	XF	Unc	BU
1949(a)	1,000,000	—	0.50	1.00	3.50	7.50

KM# 2 FRANC
1.3000 g., Aluminum, 23 mm. **Obv:** Seated figure holding torch **Rev:** Kagu bird within sprigs below value

Date	Mintage	F	VF	XF	Unc	BU
1949(a)	4,000,000	—	0.25	0.75	2.00	5.00

KM# 8 FRANC
1.3000 g., Aluminum, 23 mm. **Obv:** Seated figure holding torch **Rev:** Kagu bird within sprigs below value

Date	Mintage	F	VF	XF	Unc	BU
1971(a)	1,000,000	—	0.25	0.75	1.75	4.50

KM# 10 FRANC
1.3000 g., Aluminum, 23 mm. **Obv:** Seated figure holding torch, legend added **Obv. Leg.:** I. E. O. M. **Rev:** Kagu bird within sprigs below value

Date	Mintage	F	VF	XF	Unc	BU
1972(a)	600,000	—	0.25	0.75	1.75	4.00
1973(a)	1,000,000	—	0.10	0.25	1.00	2.00
1977(a)	1,500,000	—	0.10	0.25	1.00	2.00
1981(a)	1,000,000	—	0.10	0.20	0.75	1.50
1982(a)	1,000,000	—	0.10	0.20	0.75	1.50
1983(a)	2,000,000	—	0.10	0.20	0.75	1.50
1984(a)	—	—	0.10	0.20	0.75	1.50
1985(a)	2,000,000	—	0.10	0.20	0.75	1.50
1988(a)	2,000,000	—	0.10	0.20	0.75	1.50
1989(a)	1,000,000	—	0.10	0.20	0.75	1.50
1990(a)	1,500,000	—	0.10	0.20	0.75	1.50
1991(a)	1,600,000	—	0.10	0.20	0.75	1.50
1994(a)	2,000,000	—	0.10	0.20	0.70	1.25
1996(a)	1,900,000	—	0.10	0.20	0.70	1.25
1997(a)	1,200,000	—	0.10	0.20	0.70	1.25
1998(a)	400,000	—	0.10	0.25	0.75	1.50
1999(a)	1,200,000	—	0.10	0.20	0.70	1.25
2000(a)	1,300,000	—	—	0.15	0.50	1.00

KM# 3 2 FRANCS
2.2600 g., Aluminum, 27 mm. **Obv:** Seated figure holding torch **Rev:** Kagu bird within sprigs below value

Date	Mintage	F	VF	XF	Unc	BU
1949(a)	3,000,000	—	0.35	1.00	2.50	5.50

KM# 9 2 FRANCS
2.2000 g., Aluminum, 27 mm. **Obv:** Seated figure holding torch **Rev:** Kagu bird within sprigs below value

Date	Mintage	F	VF	XF	Unc	BU
1971(a)	1,000,000	—	0.35	1.25	2.25	3.50

KM# 14 2 FRANCS
2.2000 g., Aluminum, 27 mm. **Obv:** Seated figure holding torch, legend added **Obv. Leg.:** I. E. O. M. **Rev:** Kagu bird and value within sprigs

Date	Mintage	F	VF	XF	Unc	BU
1973(a)	400,000	—	0.20	0.75	2.00	3.00
1977(a)	1,500,000	—	0.20	0.50	1.50	2.50
1982(a)	1,000,000	—	0.20	0.35	1.00	2.25
1983(a)	2,000,000	—	0.20	0.35	0.75	2.00
1987(a)	2,000,000	—	0.20	0.35	0.75	2.00
1989(a)	1,200,000	—	0.20	0.35	0.75	2.00
1990(a)	1,500,000	—	0.20	0.35	0.75	2.00
1991(a)	1,500,000	—	0.20	0.35	0.75	2.00
1995(a)	400,000	—	0.20	0.35	0.75	2.00
1996(a)	900,000	—	0.20	0.35	0.75	2.00
1997(a)	400,000	—	0.20	0.35	0.75	2.00
1998(a)	400,000	—	0.20	0.35	0.85	2.25
1999(a)	800,000	—	0.20	0.35	0.85	2.25
2000(a)	700,000	—	—	0.25	0.75	2.00

KM# 4 5 FRANCS
3.7500 g., Aluminum, 31 mm. **Obv:** Seated figure holding torch **Rev:** Kagu bird and value within sprigs

Date	Mintage	F	VF	XF	Unc	BU
1952(a)	4,000,000	—	0.50	1.50	3.50	6.00

KM# 16 5 FRANCS
3.7500 g., Aluminum, 31 mm. **Obv:** Seated figure holding torch, legend added **Obv. Leg.:** I. E. O. M. **Rev:** Kagu bird and value within sprigs

Date	Mintage	F	VF	XF	Unc	BU
1983(a)	500,000	—	0.45	0.75	2.50	4.50
1986(a)	1,000,000	—	0.45	0.75	2.50	3.50
1989(a)	500,000	—	0.45	0.75	2.50	3.50
1990(a)	500,000	—	0.45	0.75	2.25	3.50
1991(a)	480,000	—	0.45	0.75	2.25	3.50
1992(a)	480,000	—	0.45	0.75	2.00	3.00
1994(a)	1,200,000	—	0.45	0.75	2.00	3.00
1997(a)	240,000	—	0.35	0.65	1.75	3.00
1998(a)	120,000	—	0.35	0.65	1.75	3.00
1999(a)	480,000	—	0.35	0.50	1.50	3.00
2000(a)	400,000	—	0.35	0.50	1.50	3.00

KM# 5 10 FRANCS
6.0000 g., Nickel, 24 mm. **Obv:** Liberty head left **Rev:** Sailboat above value

Date	Mintage	F	VF	XF	Unc	BU
1967(a)	400,000	—	1.00	2.00	4.00	7.00
1970(a)	1,000,000	—	0.50	1.00	2.50	5.00

KM# 11 10 FRANCS
6.0000 g., Nickel, 24 mm. **Obv:** Liberty head left **Obv. Leg.:** I. E. O. M. **Rev:** Sailboat above value

Date	Mintage	F	VF	XF	Unc	BU
1972(a)	600,000	—	0.70	1.50	2.00	5.25
1973(a)	400,000	—	0.70	1.00	2.00	4.25
1977(a)	1,000,000	—	0.70	1.00	1.50	4.00
1983(a)	800,000	—	0.60	0.85	1.50	4.00
1986(a)	1,000,000	—	0.60	0.85	1.50	4.00
1989(a)	500,000	—	0.60	0.85	1.50	4.00
1990(a)	500,000	—	0.60	0.85	1.25	3.75
1991(a)	500,000	—	0.50	0.75	1.25	3.75
1992(a)	500,000	—	0.50	0.75	1.25	3.75
1995(a)	200,000	—	0.50	0.75	1.25	3.50
1996(a)	300,000	—	0.50	0.75	1.25	3.50
1997(a)	300,000	—	0.50	0.75	1.25	3.50
1998(a)	300,000	—	0.50	0.75	1.25	3.50
1999(a)	500,000	—	0.50	0.75	1.25	3.50
2000(a)	350,000	—	—	0.65	1.25	2.75

KM# 6 20 FRANCS
10.0000 g., Nickel, 28.5 mm. **Rev:** Three zebu heads left

Date	Mintage	F	VF	XF	Unc	BU
1967(a)	300,000	—	1.25	2.50	5.00	8.50
1970(a)	1,200,000	—	0.60	1.00	3.00	5.50

KM# 12 20 FRANCS
10.0000 g., Nickel, 28.5 mm. **Obv:** Liberty head left
Obv. Leg.: I. O. E. M. **Rev:** Three ox heads above value

Date	Mintage	F	VF	XF	Unc	BU
1972(a)	700,000	—	0.85	2.00	3.00	5.00
1977(a)	350,000	—	0.85	2.50	4.00	6.50
1983(a)	600,000	—	0.75	1.75	3.00	5.00
1986(a)	800,000	—	0.75	1.50	2.00	4.50
1990(a)	500,000	—	0.75	1.50	2.00	4.50
1991(a)	500,000	—	0.75	1.50	2.00	4.50
1992(a)	500,000	—	0.75	1.50	2.00	4.50
1996(a)	150,000	—	0.75	1.50	2.00	4.50
1997(a)	—	—	0.75	1.00	1.75	3.25
1999(a)	300,000	—	0.75	15.00	2.00	4.50
2000(a)	250,000	—	0.75	1.50	200	4.50

KM# 7 50 FRANCS
15.0000 g., Nickel, 33 mm. **Obv:** Liberty head left **Rev:** Small
hut within pines and palm, value at bottom

Date	Mintage	F	VF	XF	Unc	BU
1967(a)	700,000	—	1.50	3.00	6.50	10.00

KM# 13 50 FRANCS
15.0000 g., Nickel, 33 mm. **Obv:** Liberty head left **Obv. Leg.:** I.
E. O. M. **Rev:** Hut above value in center of palm and pine trees

Date	Mintage	F	VF	XF	Unc	BU
1972(a)	300,000	—	1.25	2.00	5.00	7.00
1983(a)	300,000	—	1.25	2.00	4.50	6.50
1987(a)	300,000	—	1.00	2.00	4.50	6.50
1991(a)	450,000	—	1.00	1.85	3.00	4.25
1992(a)	450,000	—	1.00	1.85	3.00	4.25
1996(a)	—	—	1.00	1.75	3.00	4.25
1997(a)	150,000	—	1.00	1.75	3.00	4.25
2000(a)	1,000,000	—	1.00	1.75	3.00	4.25

KM# 15 100 FRANCS
10.0000 g., Nickel-Bronze, 30 mm. **Obv:** Liberty head left
Rev: Hut above value in center of palm and pine trees

Date	Mintage	F	VF	XF	Unc	BU
1976(a)	2,000,000	—	1.50	2.50	6.00	9.00
1984(a)	600,000	—	1.50	2.50	6.00	8.50
1987(a)	800,000	—	1.50	2.50	5.50	7.00
1988(a)	—	—	1.50	2.50	5.50	7.00
1991(a)	500,000	—	1.35	2.25	4.00	6.00
1992(a)	500,000	—	1.35	2.25	4.00	6.00
1994(a)	250,000	—	1.35	2.25	4.00	6.00
1995(a)	—	—	—	2.00	3.50	5.50
1996(a)	250,000	—	1.35	2.25	4.00	6.00
1997(a)	190,000	—	1.35	2.00	3.50	5.50
1998(a)	310,000	—	1.25	2.00	3.50	5.50

Date	Mintage	F	VF	XF	Unc	BU
1999(a)	400,000	—	1.25	2.00	3.50	5.50
2000(a)	300,000	—	1.25	2.00	3.50	5.50

ESSAIS

KM#	Date	Mintage	Identification	Issue Price	Mkt Val
E1	1948(a)	1,100	50 Centimes. Nickel-Bronze. Sitting figure holding sprig. Bird with wings open. Incuse design, flat rim.	—	20.00
E1a	1948(a)	—	50 Centimes. Aluminum. Incuse design, flat rim.	—	45.00
E2	1948(a)	1,100	50 Centimes. Nickel-Bronze. Incuse design, raised rim.	—	25.00
E2a	1948(a)	—	50 Centimes. Aluminum. Incuse design, raised rim.	—	40.00
E3	1948(a)	1,100	Franc. Nickel-Bronze. Incuse design, flat rim.	—	25.00
E3a	1948(a)	—	Franc. Aluminum. Incuse design, flat rim.	—	50.00
E4	1948(a)	1,100	Franc. Nickel-Bronze. Incuse design, raised rim.	—	30.00
E4a	1948(a)	—	Franc. Aluminum. Incuse design, raised rim.	—	45.00
E5	1948(a)	1,100	2 Francs. Nickel-Bronze. Incuse design, flat rim.	—	30.00
E5a	1948(a)	—	2 Francs. Aluminum. Incuse design, flat rim.	—	55.00
E6	1948(a)	1,100	2 Francs. Nickel-Bronze. Incuse design, raised rim.	—	20.00
E6a	1948(a)	—	2 Francs. Aluminum. Incuse design, raised rim.	—	50.00
E7	1949(a)	2,000	50 Centimes. Copper Nickel. KM1.	—	17.50
E8	1949(a)	2,000	Franc. Copper Nickel. KM2.	—	20.00
E9	1949(a)	2,000	2 Francs. Copper Nickel. KM3.	—	22.50
E10	1952(a)	1,200	5 Francs. Aluminum. KM4.	—	25.00
E11	1967(a)	1,700	10 Francs. Nickel. KM5.	—	15.00
E12	1967(a)	1,700	20 Francs. Nickel. KM6.	—	15.00
E13	1967(a)	1,700	50 Francs. Nickel. KM7.	—	15.00
E14	1976(a)	1,900	100 Francs. Nickel-Bronze. KM15.	—	27.50

PIEFORTS

An unknown quantity of gold pieforts were melted in 1983.

KM#	Date	Mintage	Identification	Issue Price	Mkt Val
P1	1967(a)	500	10 Francs. Nickel. KM5.	—	25.00
P1a	1967(a)	50	10 Francs. 0.9500 Silver. KM5.	—	150
P1b	1967(a)	20	10 Francs. 0.9200 Gold. KM5.	—	950
P2	1967(a)	500	20 Francs. Nickel. KM6.	—	30.00
P2a	1967(a)	50	20 Francs. 0.9500 Silver. KM6.	—	175
P2b	1967(a)	20	20 Francs. 0.9200 Gold. KM6.	—	1,250
P3	1967(a)	500	50 Francs. Nickel. KM7.	—	35.00
P3a	1967(a)	50	50 Francs. 0.9500 Silver. KM7.	—	200
P3b	1967(a)	20	50 Francs. 0.9200 Gold. KM7.	—	1,750
P4	1979(a)	150	Franc. Aluminum center. Similar to KM10.	—	10.00
P4a	1979(a)	250	Franc. 0.9250 Silver. Similar to KM10.	—	25.00
P4b	1979(a)	94	Franc. 0.9200 Gold. Similar to KM10.	—	550
P5	1979(a)	150	2 Francs. Aluminum. Similar to KM14.	—	15.00
P5a	1979(a)	250	2 Francs. 0.9250 Silver. Similar to KM14.	—	50.00
P5b	1979(a)	96	2 Francs. 0.9200 Gold. Similar to KM14.	—	925
P6	1979(a)	150	5 Francs. Aluminum. Similar to KM4.	—	25.00
P6a	1979(a)	250	5 Francs. 0.9250 Silver. Similar to KM4.	—	75.00
P6b	1979(a)	94	5 Francs. 0.9200 Gold. Similar to KM4.	—	1,700
P7	1979(a)	150	10 Francs. Nickel. Similar to KM11.	—	40.00
P7a	1979(a)	250	10 Francs. 0.9250 Silver. Similar to KM11.	—	100
P7b	1979(a)	93	10 Francs. 0.9200 Gold. Similar to KM11.	—	850
P8	1979(a)	150	20 Francs. Nickel center. Similar to KM12.	—	40.00
P8a	1979(a)	250	20 Francs. 0.9250 Silver. Similar to KM12.	—	100
P8b	1979(a)	95	20 Francs. 0.9200 Gold. Liberty head left. Three ox heads, value at lower left. Similar to KM12.	—	1,200
P9	1979(a)	150	50 Francs. Nickel. Similar to KM13.	—	50.00
P9a	1979(a)	250	50 Francs. 0.9250 Silver. Similar to KM13.	—	100
P9b	1979(a)	96	50 Francs. 0.9200 Gold. Similar to KM13.	—	2,000
P10	1979(a)	150	100 Francs. Nickel-Bronze. Similar to KM15.	—	85.00
P10a	1979(a)	350	100 Francs. 0.9250 Silver. Similar to KM15.	—	125
P10b	1979(a)	96	100 Francs. 0.9200 Gold. Similar to KM15.	—	1,500

PIEFORTS WITH ESSAI
Double thickness

KM#	Date	Mintage	Identification	Issue Price	Mkt Val
PE1	1949(a)	104	50 Centimes. Aluminum. KM1.	—	60.00
PE2	1949(a)	104	Franc. Aluminum. KM2.	—	70.00

KM#	Date	Mintage	Identification	Issue Price	Mkt Val
PE3	1949(a)	104	2 Francs. Aluminum. KM3.	—	80.00
PE4	1952(a)	104	5 Francs. Aluminum. KM4.	—	90.00

SPECIMEN SETS (SS)

KM#	Date	Mintage	Identification	Issue Price	Mkt Val
SS1	1967 (3)	2,200	KM5-7. This set issued with New Hebrides and French Polynesia 1967 set.	10.00	20.00

NEW GUINEA

Spanish navigator Jorge de Menezes, who landed on the northwest shore in 1527, discovered New Guinea, the world's largest island after Greenland. European interests, attracted by exaggerated estimates of the resources of the area, resulted in the island being claimed in part by Spain, the Netherlands, Great Britain and Germany.

RULER
British, 1910-1952

MONETARY SYSTEM
12 Pence = 1 Shilling
20 Shillings = 1 Pound

AUSTRALIAN TERRITORY
STANDARD COINAGE

12 Pence = 1 Shilling; 20 Shillings = 1 Pound

KM# 1a 1/2 PENNY
Nickel **Obv:** Hole in center flanked by scepters with crown above and value below **Rev:** Hole in center flanked by designs

Date	Mintage	F	VF	XF	Unc	BU
1929 Proof	—				Value: 800	

KM# 1 1/2 PENNY
Copper-Nickel **Obv:** Hole in center flanked by scepters with crown above and value below **Rev:** Hole in center flanked by designs
Note: Entire mintage returned to Melbourne Mint which later sold 400 pcs. in sets with KM#2. The balance of mintage was destroyed.

Date	Mintage	F	VF	XF	Unc	BU
1929	25,000	—	—	275	495	650
1929 Proof	—				Value: 450	

KM# 2 PENNY
Copper-Nickel **Obv:** Hole in center flanked by scepters with crown above and value below **Rev:** Hole in center flanked by designs
Note: Entire mintage returned to Melbourne Mint which later sold 400 pcs. in sets with KM#1. The balance of mintage was destroyed.

Date	Mintage	F	VF	XF	Unc	BU
1929 Proof	—				Value: 800	
1929	63,000	—	—	275	495	650

KM# 2a PENNY
Nickel **Obv:** Hole in center flanked by scepters with crown above and value below **Rev:** Hole in center flanked by designs

Date	Mintage	F	VF	XF	Unc	BU
1929 Proof	—				Value: 800	

KM# 6 PENNY
Bronze **Obv:** Hole in center flanked by swimming birds with crown above and monogram below **Rev:** Artistic design around hole in center

Date	Mintage	F	VF	XF	Unc	BU
1936	360,000	1.20	1.50	2.50	5.00	10.00
1936 Proof	—				Value: 300	

KM# 7   PENNY
Bronze **Obv:** Hole in center flanked by swimming birds with crown above and monogram below **Rev:** Artistic design around hole in center

Date	Mintage	F	VF	XF	Unc	BU
1938	360,000	2.50	5.00	9.50	15.00	20.00
1944	240,000	1.50	3.00	6.00	10.00	15.00

KM# 3   3 PENCE
Copper-Nickel **Obv:** Hole in center divides date with crown above and monogram below **Rev:** Square-star design around hole in center

Date	Mintage	F	VF	XF	Unc	BU
1935	1,200,000	2.50	5.00	10.00	20.00	30.00
1935 Proof	— Value: 250					

KM# 10   3 PENCE
Copper-Nickel **Obv:** Hole in center divides date with crown above and monogram below **Rev:** Square-star design around hole in center

Date	Mintage	F	VF	XF	Unc	BU
1944	500,000	2.00	4.00	8.50	20.00	30.00

KM# 4   6 PENCE
Copper-Nickel **Obv:** Hole in center divides date with crown above and monogram below **Rev:** Star design around hole in center

Date	Mintage	F	VF	XF	Unc	BU
1935	2,000,000	2.00	4.00	8.00	22.50	32.50
1935 Proof	— Value: 250					

KM# 9   6 PENCE
Copper-Nickel **Obv:** Hole in center divides date with crown above and monogram below **Rev:** Star design around hole in center

Date	Mintage	F	VF	XF	Unc	BU
1943	130,000	3.50	6.00	15.00	40.00	55.00

KM# 5   SHILLING
5.3800 g., 0.9250 Silver 0.1600 oz. ASW, 23.5 mm. **Obv:** Hole in center flanked by crossed scepters with crown above and star below **Rev:** Hole in center flanked by artistic designs

Date	Mintage	F	VF	XF	Unc	BU
1935	2,100,000	BV	2.75	3.75	6.50	8.00
1936	1,360,000	BV	2.75	3.75	6.50	8.00

KM# 8   SHILLING
5.3800 g., 0.9250 Silver 0.1600 oz. ASW, 23.5 mm. **Obv:** Hole in center flanked by crossed scepters with crown above and star below **Rev:** Hole in center flanked by artistic designs

Date	Mintage	F	VF	XF	Unc	BU
1938	3,400,000	BV	2.75	3.75	6.50	8.00
1945	2,000,000	BV	2.75	3.75	6.50	8.00

PROOF SETS

KM#	Date	Mintage	Identification	Issue Price	Mkt Val
PS1	1929 (2)	—	KM#1, 2	—	1,400
PS2	1929 (2)	20	KM#1a, 2a	—	1,600

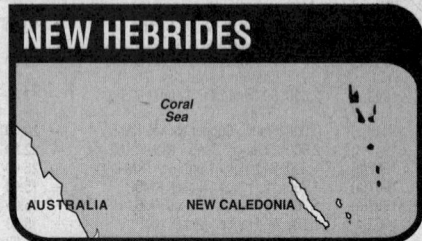

NEW HEBRIDES

Coral Sea

AUSTRALIA   NEW CALEDONIA

The New Hebrides were discovered by Portuguese navigator Pedro de Quiros in 1606, visited by French explorer Bougainville in 1768, and named by British navigator Capt. James Cook in 1774. Ships of all nations converged on the islands to trade for sandalwood, prompting France and Britain to relinquish their individual claims and declare the islands a neutral zone in 1878. The New Hebrides were placed under the control of a mixed Anglo-French commission of naval officers during the native uprisings of 1887, until achieving independence as Vanuatu, within the Commonwealth of nations on September 30, 1980.

MINT MARK
(a) - Paris, privy marks only

MONETARY SYSTEM
100 Centimes = 1 Franc

FRENCH/BRITISH CONDOMINIUM
(Jointly Governed Territory)

STANDARD COINAGE

KM# 4.1   FRANC
Nickel-Brass **Obv:** Liberty head left, date below
Obv. Leg.: REPVBLIQVE FRANCAISE **Rev:** Frigate bird above value

Date	Mintage	F	VF	XF	Unc	BU
1970(a)	435,000	—	0.25	0.50	0.85	1.75

KM# 4.2   FRANC
Nickel-Brass **Obv:** I.E.O.M. below head **Obv. Leg.:** REPVBLIQVE FRANCAISE **Rev:** Frigate bird above value

Date	Mintage	F	VF	XF	Unc	BU
1975(a)	350,000	—	0.20	0.40	0.75	—
1978(a)	200,000	—	0.20	0.40	0.75	—
1979(a)	350,000	—	0.20	0.40	0.75	—
1982(a)		—	0.20	0.40	0.75	—

KM# 5.1   2 FRANCS
3.0000 g., Nickel-Brass **Obv:** Liberty head left, date below
Obv. Leg.: REPVBLIQVE FRANCAISE **Rev:** Frigate bird above value

Date	Mintage	F	VF	XF	Unc	BU
1970(a)	264,000	—	0.50	0.75	1.50	2.50

KM# 5.2   2 FRANCS
Nickel-Brass **Obv:** Liberty head left, I.E.O.M. and date below head **Obv. Leg.:** REPVBLIQVE FRANCAISE **Rev:** Frigate bird above value

Date	Mintage	F	VF	XF	Unc	BU
1973(a)	200,000	—	0.20	0.50	1.00	—
1975(a)	300,000	—	0.20	0.50	1.00	—
1978(a)	150,000	—	0.20	0.50	1.00	—
1979(a)	250,000	—	0.20	0.50	1.00	—

KM# 6.1   5 FRANCS
Nickel-Brass **Obv:** Liberty head left, date below
Obv. Leg.: REPVBLIQVE FRANCAISE **Rev:** Frigate bird above value

Date	Mintage	F	VF	XF	Unc	BU
1970(a)	375,000	—	0.50	0.75	1.65	2.75

KM# 6.2   5 FRANCS
Nickel-Brass **Obv:** Liberty head left, I.E.O.M. and date below head **Obv. Leg.:** REPVBLIQVE FRANCAISE **Rev:** Frigate bird above value

Date	Mintage	F	VF	XF	Unc	BU
1975(a)	350,000	—	0.30	0.75	1.25	—
1979(a)	250,000	—	0.30	0.75	1.25	—

KM# 2.1   10 FRANCS
Nickel **Obv:** Liberty head left, date below **Obv. Leg.:** REPVBLIQVE FRANCAISE **Rev:** Mask left flanked by designs with value below

Date	Mintage	F	VF	XF	Unc	BU
1967(a)	200,000	—	0.30	1.00	1.85	3.00
1970(a)	400,000	—	0.30	1.00	1.85	3.00

KM# 2.2   10 FRANCS
6.0000 g., Nickel **Obv:** Liberty head left, I.E.O.M. and date below head **Obv. Leg.:** REPVBLIQVE FRANCAISE **Rev:** Mask left flanked by designs with value below

Date	Mintage	F	VF	XF	Unc	BU
1973(a)	200,000	—	0.30	1.15	1.85	2.75
1975(a)	300,000	—	0.30	1.15	1.85	2.75

Date	Mintage	F	VF	XF	Unc	BU
1977(a)	200,000	—	0.30	1.15	1.85	2.75
1979(a)	400,000	—	0.30	1.15	1.85	2.75

KM# 3.1   20 FRANCS
Nickel **Obv:** Liberty head left, date below
Obv. Leg.: REPVBLEQVE FRANCAISE **Rev:** Mask left flanked by designs with value below

Date	Mintage	F	VF	XF	Unc	BU
1967(a)	250,000	—	0.60	1.25	2.25	4.00
1970(a)	300,000	—	0.60	1.25	2.25	4.00

KM# 3.2   20 FRANCS
Nickel **Obv:** Liberty head left, I.E.O.M. and date below head
Obv. Leg.: REPVBLIQVE FRANCAISE **Rev:** Mask left flanked by designs, value at bottom

Date	Mintage	F	VF	XF	Unc	BU
1973(a)	300,000	—	0.60	1.25	2.25	3.25
1975(a)	150,000	—	0.60	1.25	2.25	3.25
1977(a)	150,000	—	0.60	1.25	2.25	3.25
1979(a)	300,000	—	0.60	1.25	2.25	3.25

KM# 7   50 FRANCS
Nickel **Obv:** Liberty head left, I.E.O.M. and date below head
Obv. Leg.: REPVBLIQVE FRANCAISE **Rev:** Scepter above value

Date	Mintage	F	VF	XF	Unc	BU
1972(a)	200,000	—	1.00	2.00	3.00	5.00

KM# 1   100 FRANCS
25.0000 g., 0.8350 Silver 0.6711 oz. ASW **Obv:** Liberty head left, date below **Obv. Leg.:** REPVBLIQVE FRANCAISE
Rev: Scepter above value

Date	Mintage	F	VF	XF	Unc	BU
1966(a)	200,000	—	—	—	15.00	25.00

ESSAIS

KM#	Date	Mintage	Identification	Issue Price	Mkt Val
E1	1966(a)	3,000	100 Francs. Liberty head left, date below. Sword hilt above value.	—	80.00
E2	1967(a)	1,700	10 Francs.	—	20.00
E3	1967(a)	1,700	20 Francs.	—	20.00
E4	1970(a)	1,250	Franc.	—	20.00
E5	1970(a)	1,700	2 Francs.	—	20.00
E6	1970(a)	1,250	5 Francs.	—	20.00
E7	1972(a)	1,300	50 Francs.	—	22.00

PATTERNS
Including off metal strikes

KM#	Date	Mintage	Identification	Mkt Val
Pn1	1979	60	500 Francs. Copper-Nickel-Aluminum.	350
Pn2	1979	60	500 Francs. 0.9990 Silver.	500
Pn3	1979	3	500 Francs. 0.9990 Gold. 62.2000 g.	6,000
Pn4	1979	1	500 Francs. 0.9990 Platinum. 62.2000 g.	9,000

PIEFORTS WITH ESSAI
Double thickness

KM#	Date	Mintage	Identification	Issue Price	Mkt Val
PE1	1966(a)	500	100 Francs.	—	150
PE2	1966(a)	50	100 Francs. 0.9200 Gold.	—	4,750
PE3	1967(a)	500	10 Francs. Liberty head left, date below. Mask left, flanked by designs, value on bottom.	—	15.00
PE4	1967(a)	50	10 Francs. 0.9500 Silver.	—	75.00
PE5	1967(a)	20	10 Francs. 0.9200 Gold.	—	650
PE6	1967(a)	500	20 Francs.	—	15.00
PE7	1967(a)	50	20 Francs. 0.9500 Silver.	—	125
PE8	1967(a)	20	20 Francs. 0.9200 Gold.	—	1,000
PE10	1974(a)	500	100 Francs. 0.9250 Silver.	—	100
PE11	1974(a)	119	100 Francs. 0.9200 Gold.	—	4,000
PE12	1979(a)	150	Franc.	—	10.00
PE13	1979	250	Franc. 0.9250 Silver.	—	20.00
PE14	1979(a)	123	Franc. 0.9200 Gold.	—	400
PE15	1979(a)	150	2 Francs.	—	12.50
PE16	1979(a)	250	2 Francs. 0.9250 Silver.	—	20.00
PE17	1979(a)	115	2 Francs. 0.9200 Gold.	—	450
PE18	1979(a)	150	5 Francs.	—	15.00
PE19	1979(a)	250	5 Francs. 0.9250 Silver.	—	20.00
PE20	1979(a)	116	5 Francs. 0.9200 Gold.	—	800
PE21	1979(a)	150	10 Francs.	—	17.50
PE22	1979(a)	250	10 Francs. 0.9250 Silver.	—	20.00
PE23	1979(a)	116	10 Francs. 0.9200 Gold.	—	550
PE24	1979(a)	150	20 Francs.	—	20.00
PE25	1979(a)	250	20 Francs. 0.9250 Silver.	—	20.00
PE26	1979(a)	115	20 Francs. 0.9200 Gold.	—	1,000
PE27	1979(a)	150	50 Francs.	—	25.00
PE28	1979(a)	250	50 Francs. 0.9250 Silver.	—	100
PE29	1979(a)	116	50 Francs. 0.9200 Gold.	—	1,600

"FDC" SETS

This fleur-de-coin set was issued with New Caledonia and French Polynesia 1967 sets.

KM#	Date	Mintage	Identification	Issue Price	Mkt Val
SS1	1966-67 (3)	2,200	KM#1, 2.1, 3.1	10.00	20.00

NEW ZEALAND

New Zealand, a parliamentary state located in the Southwest Pacific 1,250 miles (2,011 km.) east of Australia, has an area of 103,883 sq. mi. (268,680 sq. km.) and a population of *3.4 million. Capital: Wellington. Wool, meat, dairy products and some manufactured items are exported.

The first European to sight New Zealand was the Dutch navigator Abel Tasman in 1642. The islands were explored by British navigator Capt. James Cook who surveyed it in 1769 and annexed the land to Great Britain. The British government disavowed the annexation and for the next 70 years the only white settlers to arrive were adventurers attracted by the prospects of lumbering, sealing and whaling. Great Britain annexed the land in 1840 by treaty with the native chiefs and made it a dependency of New South Wales. The colony was granted self-government in1852, a ministerial form of government in 1856, and full dominion status on Sept. 26, 1907. Full internal and external autonomy, which New Zealand had in effect possessed for many years, was formally extended in 1947.New Zealand is a member of the Commonwealth of Nations. Elizabeth II is Head of State as Queen of New Zealand.

Prior to 1933 British coins were the official legal tender but Australian coins were accepted in small transactions. Currency fluctuations caused a distinctive New Zealand coinage to be introduced in 1933. The 1935 Waitangi crown and proof set were originally intended to mark the introduction but delays caused their date to be changed to 1935. The 1940 half crown marked the centennial of British rule, the 1949 and 1953 crowns commemorated Royal visits and the 1953 proof set marked the coronation of Queen Elizabeth.

Decimal Currency was introduced in 1967 with special sets commemorating the last issued of pound sterling (1965) and the first of the decimal issues. Since then dollars and set of coins have been issued nearly every year.

RULER
British

MINTS
(l) – British Royal Mint (Llantrisant)
(c) – Royal Australian Mint (Canberra)
(o) – Royal Canadian Mint
(n) – Norwegian Mint
(p) – South African Mint (Pretoria)

MONETARY SYSTEM
4 Farthings = 1 Penny
12 Pence = 1 Shilling
20 Shillings = 1 Pound

STATE
1907 - present
POUND STERLING COINAGE

KM# 12   1/2 PENNY
5.8000 g., Bronze, 25.4 mm. **Ruler:** George VI **Obv:** Head left
Rev: Hei Tiki

Date	Mintage	F	VF	XF	Unc	BU
1940	3,432,000	0.20	0.50	8.00	20.00	40.00
1940 Proof; 5 known	—	Value: 1,000				
1941	960,000	0.10	0.25	8.00	50.00	70.00
1941 Proof	—	Value: 275				
1942	1,920,000	1.00	2.50	30.00	100	230
1944	2,035,000	0.10	0.25	7.00	15.00	35.00
1945	1,516,000	0.10	0.25	7.00	15.00	35.00
1945 Proof	—	Value: 210				
1946	3,120,000	0.10	0.25	7.00	12.50	28.00
1946 Proof	—	Value: 210				
1947	2,726,400	0.10	0.25	5.00	12.50	22.00
1947 Proof	—	Value: 180				

KM# 20   1/2 PENNY
Bronze, 25.4 mm. **Ruler:** George VI **Obv:** Head left **Rev:** Hei Tiki

Date	Mintage	F	VF	XF	Unc	BU
1949	1,766,400	0.10	0.25	5.00	12.50	22.00
1949 Proof	—	Value: 180				
1950	1,425,600	0.10	0.25	6.00	15.00	35.00
1950 Proof	—	Value: 210				
1951	2,342,400	0.10	0.25	4.00	8.00	12.00
1951 Proof	—	Value: 180				
1952	2,400,000	0.10	0.20	3.00	5.00	8.00
1952 Proof	—	Value: 180				

KM# 23.1   1/2 PENNY
Bronze, 25.4 mm. **Ruler:** Elizabeth II **Obv:** Laureate bust right without shoulder strap **Rev:** Hei Tiki

Date	Mintage	F	VF	XF	Unc	BU
1953	720,000	0.20	0.50	5.00	12.50	20.00
1953 Proof	7,000	Value: 5.00				
1953 Matte proof	—	Value: 110				
1954	240,000	3.00	6.00	40.00	85.00	125
1954 Proof	—	Value: 170				
1955	240,000	3.00	6.00	40.00	85.00	125
1955	—	Value: 170				

KM# 23.2   1/2 PENNY
5.6000 g., Bronze, 25.4 mm. **Ruler:** Elizabeth II **Obv:** Laureate bust right with shoulder strap **Rev:** Hei Tiki

Date	Mintage	F	VF	XF	Unc	BU
1956	1,200,000	0.10	0.25	4.00	10.00	18.00
1956 Proof	—	Value: 150				

Date	Mintage	F	VF	XF	Unc	BU
1957	1,440,000	0.10	0.25	4.00	10.00	18.00
1957 Proof	—	Value: 150				
1958	1,920,000	0.10	0.25	4.00	10.00	18.00
1958 Proof	—	Value: 150				
1959	1,920,000	0.10	0.20	3.00	8.00	17.00
1959 Proof	—	Value: 150				
1960	2,400,000	0.10	0.20	2.00	4.00	8.00
1960 Proof	—	Value: 150				
1961	2,880,000	0.10	0.15	4.00	7.00	10.00
1961 Proof	—	Value: 150				
1962	2,880,000	0.10	0.15	4.00	7.00	10.00
1962 Proof	—	Value: 150				
1963	1,680,000	0.10	0.15	0.30	1.00	2.00
1963 Proof	—	Value: 150				
1964	2,885,000	0.10	0.15	0.20	0.75	2.50
1964 Proof	—	Value: 100				
1965 Prooflike	25,000	—	—	—	—	1.00
1965	5,200,000	0.10	0.15	0.20	0.50	2.50
1965 Proof	10	—	—	—	—	—

KM# 13 PENNY
9.5600 g., Bronze, 31 mm. **Ruler:** George VI **Obv:** Head left
Rev: Tui bird sitting on branch

Date	Mintage	F	VF	XF	Unc	BU
1940	5,424,000	0.20	0.50	8.00	25.00	45.00
1940 Proof	—	Value: 1,200				
	Note: 5 known					
1941	1,200,000	0.20	0.50	30.00	100	175
1942	3,120,000	1.00	5.00	35.00	110	195
1942 Proof	—	Value: 350				
1943	8,400,000	0.20	0.40	8.00	25.00	45.00
1943 Proof	—	Value: 300				
1944	3,696,000	0.20	0.40	8.00	25.00	45.00
1944 Proof	—	Value: 300				
1945	4,764,000	0.20	0.40	8.00	25.00	45.00
1945 Proof	—	Value: 300				
1946	6,720,000	0.20	0.40	6.00	15.00	25.00
1946 Proof	—	Value: 300				
1947	5,880,000	0.20	0.40	5.00	12.50	22.00
1947 Proof	—	Value: 300				

KM# 13a PENNY
Bronze, 31 mm. **Ruler:** George VI **Obv:** Head left **Rev:** Tui bird sitting on branch **Note:** Burnished

Date	Mintage	F	VF	XF	Unc	BU
1945	—	—	—	100	180	250

Note: Struck in error by the Royal Mint on Great Britain blanks

KM# 21 PENNY
Bronze, 31 mm. **Ruler:** George VI **Obv:** Head left **Rev:** Tui bird sitting on branch

Date	Mintage	F	VF	XF	Unc	BU
1949	2,016,000	0.20	0.40	5.00	12.50	25.00
1949 Proof	—	Value: 300				
1950	5,784,000	0.20	0.40	5.00	12.50	20.00
1950 Proof	—	Value: 210				
1951	6,888,000	0.20	0.40	5.00	10.00	20.00
1951 Proof	—	Value: 210				
1952	10,800,000	0.20	0.40	5.00	10.00	20.00
1952 Proof	—	Value: 190				

KM# 24.1 PENNY
9.4000 g., Bronze, 31 mm. **Ruler:** Elizabeth II **Obv:** Laureate bust right without shoulder strap **Rev:** Tui bird sitting on branch

Date	Mintage	F	VF	XF	Unc	BU
1953	2,400,000	0.20	0.40	5.00	10.00	20.00
1953 Proof	7,000	Value: 10.00				
1953 Matte proof	—	Value: 110				
1954	1,080,000	1.00	3.00	25.00	50.00	120
1954 Proof	—	Value: 210				
1955	3,720,000	0.20	0.30	3.00	10.00	20.00
1955 Proof	—	Value: 190				
1956	Inc. below	25.00	45.00	350	700	1,100

KM# 24.2 PENNY
9.5000 g., Bronze, 31 mm. **Ruler:** Elizabeth II **Obv:** Laureate bust right with shoulder strap **Rev:** Tui bird sitting on branch

Date	Mintage	F	VF	XF	Unc	BU
1956	3,600,000	0.20	0.30	3.00	8.00	16.00
1956 Proof	—	Value: 190				
1957	2,400,000	0.20	0.30	3.00	8.00	16.00
1957 Proof	—	Value: 150				
1958	10,800,000	0.20	0.30	3.00	8.00	16.00
1958 Proof	—	Value: 190				
1959	8,400,000	0.20	0.30	3.00	8.00	16.00
1959 Proof	—	Value: 190				
1960	7,200,000	0.20	0.30	2.00	4.00	6.50
1960 Proof	—	Value: 170				
1961	7,200,000	0.20	0.30	1.00	2.00	4.00
1961 Proof	—	Value: 170				
1962	6,000,000	—	0.20	1.00	2.00	4.00
1962 Proof	—	Value: 170				
1963	2,400,000	—	0.20	0.50	1.00	2.50
1963 Proof	—	Value: 170				
1964	18,000,000	—	0.20	0.25	0.50	1.00
1964 Proof	—	Value: 170				
1965	200,000	—	—	—	5.00	6.00
1965 Prooflike	25,000	—	—	—	—	5.00
1965 Proof	10	—	—	—	—	—

KM# 1 3 PENCE
0.5000 Silver, 16.3 mm. **Ruler:** George V **Subject:** Crossed Patu **Obv:** Crowned bust left **Rev:** Crossed patu flanked by value and date

Date	Mintage	F	VF	XF	Unc	BU
1933	6,000,000	1.00	3.00	10.00	20.00	40.00
1933 Proof	Est. 20	Value: 600				
1934	6,000,000	1.00	3.00	10.00	20.00	40.00
1934 Proof	Est. 20	Value: 1,700				
1935	40,000	100	220	500	900	1,250
1935 Proof	364	Value: 1,400				
1936	2,760,000	1.00	3.00	12.00	22.50	50.00
1936 Proof	—	Value: 600				

KM# 7 3 PENCE
1.4000 g., 0.5000 Silver 0.0225 oz. ASW, 16.3 mm. **Ruler:** George VI **Subject:** Crossed Patu **Obv:** Head left **Rev:** Crossed patu flanked by value and date

Date	Mintage	F	VF	XF	Unc	BU
1937	2,880,000	1.00	3.00	10.00	20.00	45.00
1937 Proof	Est. 200	Value: 400				
1939	3,000,000	1.00	3.00	10.00	20.00	45.00
1939 Proof	—	Value: 550				
1940	2,000,000	1.00	3.00	12.00	25.00	50.00
1940 Proof	—	Value: 550				

Date	Mintage	F	VF	XF	Unc	BU
1941	1,760,000	2.00	20.00	70.00	200	400
1941 Proof	—	Value: 500				
1942	3,120,000	1.00	3.00	10.00	20.00	40.00
1942 With 1 dot	Est. 250,000	4.00	60.00	200	400	600
1943	4,400,000	1.00	2.00	6.00	15.00	35.00
1944	2,840,000	1.00	2.50	6.00	15.00	35.00
1944 Proof	—	Value: 500				
1945	2,520,000	1.00	2.00	6.00	15.00	27.50
1945 Proof	—	Value: 500				
1946	6,080,000	1.00	2.00	6.00	15.00	25.00
1946 Proof	—	Value: 450				

KM# 7a 3 PENCE
Copper-Nickel, 16.3 mm. **Ruler:** George VI **Obv:** Head left **Rev:** Crossed patu flanked by value and date

Date	Mintage	F	VF	XF	Unc	BU
1947	6,400,000	0.10	1.00	6.00	15.00	30.00
1947 Proof	Est. 20	Value: 400				

KM# 15 3 PENCE
1.4000 g., Copper-Nickel, 16.3 mm. **Ruler:** George VI **Obv:** Head left **Rev:** Crossed patu flanked by value and date

Date	Mintage	F	VF	XF	Unc	BU
1948	4,000,000	0.10	1.00	6.00	15.00	30.00
1948 Proof	—	Value: 250				
1950	800,000	1.00	7.50	50.00	100	200
1950 Proof	—	Value: 300				
1951	3,600,000	0.10	0.75	3.00	6.00	12.00
1951 Proof	—	Value: 225				
1952	8,000,000	0.10	0.75	3.00	6.00	10.00
1952 Proof	—	Value: 225				

KM# 25.1 3 PENCE
1.4000 g., Copper-Nickel, 16.3 mm. **Ruler:** Elizabeth II **Obv:** Laureate bust right without shoulder strap **Rev:** Crossed patu flanked by value and date

Date	Mintage	F	VF	XF	Unc	BU
1953	4,000,000	0.10	0.75	3.00	6.00	12.00
1953 Proof	7,000	Value: 7.00				
1953 Matte proof	—	Value: 130				
1954	4,000,000	0.10	2.00	3.00	6.00	10.00
1954 Proof	—	Value: 225				
1955	4,000,000	0.10	0.75	3.00	6.00	10.00
1955 Proof	—	Value: 225				
1956 Proof	—	Value: 300				
1956	Inc. below	2.50	6.00	125	220	400

KM# 25.2 3 PENCE
1.4000 g., Copper-Nickel, 16.3 mm. **Ruler:** Elizabeth II **Obv:** Laureate bust right with shoulder strap **Rev:** Crossed patu flanked by value and date

Date	Mintage	F	VF	XF	Unc	BU
1956	4,800,000	0.10	0.15	1.00	4.00	8.00
1956 Proof	—	Value: 225				
1957	8,000,000	0.10	0.15	0.50	2.00	4.00
1957 Proof	—	Value: 225				
1958	4,800,000	0.10	0.15	1.00	4.00	8.00
1958 Proof	—	Value: 225				
1959	4,000,000	0.10	0.15	1.00	4.00	8.00
1959 Proof	—	Value: 225				
1960	4,000,000	0.10	0.15	0.50	1.00	2.00
1960 Proof	—	Value: 225				
1961	4,800,000	0.10	0.15	0.50	2.00	4.00
1961 Proof	—	Value: 225				
1962	6,000,000	0.10	0.15	0.20	0.75	1.25
1962 Proof	—	Value: 225				
1963	6,000,000	0.10	0.15	0.20	0.75	1.25
1963 Proof	—	Value: 225				
1964	6,400,000	0.10	0.15	0.20	0.40	0.75
1964 Proof	—	Value: 175				
1965	4,200,000	—	0.10	0.20	0.40	0.75
1965 Prooflike	25,000	—	—	—	—	1.00
1965 Proof	10	—	—	—	—	—

KM# 2 6 PENCE
2.8300 g., 0.5000 Silver 0.0455 oz. ASW, 19.3 mm.
Ruler: George V **Obv:** Crowned bust left **Rev:** Huia bird sitting on branch

Date	Mintage	F	VF	XF	Unc	BU
1933	3,000,000	1.00	8.00	25.00	60.00	100
1933 Proof	20	Value: 750				
1934 Proof	20	Value: 1,750				
1934	3,600,000	1.00	8.00	25.00	60.00	100
1935 Proof	364	Value: 500				
1935	560,000	2.00	15.00	75.00	175	325
1936	1,480,000	1.00	12.00	35.00	70.00	125
1936 Proof	—					

KM# 8 6 PENCE
2.8300 g., 0.5000 Silver 0.0455 oz. ASW, 19.3 mm.
Ruler: George VI **Obv:** Head left **Rev:** Huia bird sitting on branch

Date	Mintage	F	VF	XF	Unc	BU
1937	1,280,000	1.00	8.00	30.00	65.00	125
1937 Proof	Est. 200	Value: 350				
1939	700,000	1.50	12.00	35.00	70.00	150
1939 Proof	—	Value: 350				
1940	800,000	1.50	8.00	35.00	70.00	150
1940 Proof	—	Value: 350				
1941	440,000	2.00	35.00	120	250	475
1941 Proof	—	Value: 550				
1942	360,000	2.00	35.00	120	250	475
1943	1,800,000	1.00	7.00	20.00	45.00	100
1944	1,160,000	1.50	7.00	20.00	45.00	100
1944 Proof	—	Value: 300				
1945	940,000	1.50	7.00	20.00	45.00	100
1945 Proof	—	Value: 300				
1946	—	Value: 300				
1946	2,120,000	1.00	8.00	20.00	45.00	60.00

KM# 8a 6 PENCE
Copper-Nickel, 19.3 mm. **Ruler:** George VI **Obv:** Head left **Rev:** Huia bird sitting on branch

Date	Mintage	F	VF	XF	Unc	BU
1947	3,200,000	0.20	5.00	20.00	40.00	80.00
1947 Proof	Est. 20	Value: 300				

KM# 16 6 PENCE
Copper-Nickel, 19.3 mm. **Ruler:** George VI **Obv:** Head left **Rev:** Huia bird sitting on branch

Date	Mintage	F	VF	XF	Unc	BU
1948	2,000,000	0.20	5.00	20.00	45.00	85.00
1948 Proof	—	Value: 275				
1950	800,000	2.00	15.00	60.00	125	220
1950 Proof	—	Value: 275				
1951	1,800,000	0.20	1.00	2.50	4.00	6.00
1951 Proof	—	Value: 275				
1952	3,200,000	0.20	6.00	15.00	30.00	50.00
1952 Proof	—	Value: 225				

KM# 26.1 6 PENCE
Copper-Nickel, 19.3 mm. **Ruler:** Elizabeth II **Obv:** Laureate bust right without shoulder strap **Rev:** Huia bird sitting on branch

Date	Mintage	F	VF	XF	Unc	BU
1953	1,200,000	0.20	3.00	8.00	15.00	22.50
1953 Proof	7,000	Value: 7.00				

Date	Mintage	F	VF	XF	Unc	BU
1953 Matte proof	—	—	—	—	125	
1954	1,200,000	0.20	3.00	8.00	20.00	35.00
1954 Proof	—	Value: 175				
1955	1,600,000	0.20	3.00	8.00	20.00	35.00
1955 Proof	—	Value: 200				
1957	Inc. below	5.00	17.50	150	400	650
1957 Proof	—	Value: 600				

KM# 26.2 6 PENCE
2.8000 g., Copper-Nickel, 19.3 mm. **Ruler:** Elizabeth II **Obv:** Laureate bust right with shoulder strap **Rev:** Huia bird sitting on branch

Date	Mintage	F	VF	XF	Unc	BU
1956	2,000,000	0.20	2.00	5.00	10.00	22.50
1956 Proof	—	Value: 200				
1957	2,400,000	0.10	0.20	3.00	5.00	10.00
1957 Proof	—	Value: 200				
1958	3,000,000	0.10	0.20	3.00	5.00	10.00
1958 Proof	—	Value: 200				
1959	2,000,000	0.10	0.15	1.00	5.00	10.00
1959 Proof	—	Value: 200				
1960	1,600,000	0.10	0.15	1.00	2.00	4.00
1960 Proof	—	Value: 200				
1961	800,000	0.10	0.15	1.00	2.00	4.00
1961 Proof	—	Value: 200				
1962	1,200,000	0.10	0.15	1.00	2.00	6.00
1962 Proof	—	Value: 200				
1963	800,000	0.10	0.15	0.75	2.00	4.00
1963 Proof	—	Value: 200				
1964	3,800,000	—	0.10	0.15	0.50	6.00
1964 Proof	—	Value: 175				
1965	8,600,000	—	0.10	0.50	1.00	
1965 Broken wing	Inc. above	3.50	7.00	12.00	30.00	40.00
1965 Prooflike	25,000	—	—	—	—	1.00
1965 Proof	10	—	—	—	—	

KM# 3 SHILLING
5.6500 g., 0.5000 Silver 0.0908 oz. ASW, 23.62 mm.
Ruler: George V **Obv:** Crowned bust left **Rev:** Crouched Maori warrior left

Date	Mintage	F	VF	XF	Unc	BU
1933	2,000,000	1.50	10.00	25.00	110	225
1933 Proof	Est. 20	Value: 1,500				
1934	3,400,000	1.50	10.00	25.00	110	225
1934 Proof	Est. 20	Value: 2,500				
1935	1,680,000	2.00	20.00	60.00	200	400
1935 Proof	364	Value: 500				

KM# 9 SHILLING
5.6500 g., 0.5000 Silver 0.0908 oz. ASW, 23.62 mm.
Ruler: George VI **Obv:** Head left **Rev:** Crouched Maori warrior left

Date	Mintage	F	VF	XF	Unc	BU
1937	890,000	2.00	10.00	25.00	70.00	125
1937 Proof	Est. 200	Value: 550				
1940	500,000	2.50	12.00	30.00	90.00	200
1940 Proof	—	Value: 550				
1941	360,000	4.00	40.00	125	250	500
1941 Proof	—	Value: 550				
1942	240,000	4.00	40.00	125	250	500
1942 Broken back	Est. 80,000	8.00	95.00	350	650	—
1943	900,000	2.00	10.00	25.00	50.00	100
1944	480,000	2.50	12.00	30.00	60.00	150
1944 Proof	—	Value: 550				
1945	1,030,000	2.00	9.00	20.00	40.00	75.00
1945 Proof	—	Value: 550				
1946	1,060,000	2.00	9.00	20.00	37.50	72.00
1946 Proof	—	Value: 550				

KM# 9a SHILLING
5.5000 g., Copper-Nickel, 23.62 mm. **Ruler:** George VI **Obv:** Head left **Rev:** Crouched Maori warrior left

Date	Mintage	F	VF	XF	Unc	BU
1947	2,800,000	1.00	8.00	35.00	80.00	230
1947 Proof	Est. 20	Value: 350				

KM# 17 SHILLING
Copper-Nickel, 23.62 mm. **Ruler:** George VI **Obv:** Head left **Rev:** Crouched Maori warrior left

Date	Mintage	F	VF	XF	Unc	BU
1948	1,000,000	1.00	8.00	35.00	80.00	180
1948 Proof	—	Value: 350				
1950	600,000	1.00	8.00	35.00	80.00	200
1950 Proof	—	Value: 350				
1951	1,200,000	1.00	8.00	35.00	70.00	150
1951 Proof	—	Value: 350				
1952	600,000	2.00	10.00	35.00	80.00	160
1952 Proof	—	Value: 350				

KM# 27.1 SHILLING
Copper-Nickel, 23.62 mm. **Ruler:** Elizabeth II **Obv:** Laureate bust right without shoulder strap **Rev:** Crouched Maori warrior left

Date	Mintage	F	VF	XF	Unc	BU
1953	200,000	1.50	5.00	12.00	25.00	45.00
1953 Proof	14,000	Value: 8.00				
1953 Matte proof	—	Value: 125				
1954 Proof	—	—	—	—	—	—
1955	200,000	2.00	15.00	60.00	120	220
1955 Proof	—	Value: 350				

KM# 27.2 SHILLING
5.6400 g., Copper-Nickel, 23.62 mm. **Ruler:** Elizabeth II **Obv:** Laureate bust right with shoulder strap **Rev:** Crouched Maori warrior left

Date	Mintage	F	VF	XF	Unc	BU
1956	800,000	0.20	1.00	8.00	15.00	27.50
1956 Proof	—	Value: 350				
1957	800,000	0.20	1.00	8.00	15.00	27.50
1957 Proof	—	Value: 350				
1958	1,000,000	0.20	1.00	8.00	15.00	25.00
1958 Proof	—	Value: 350				
1958 Broken back	—	8.00	20.00	40.00	120	220
1959	600,000	0.20	1.00	5.00	12.50	25.50
1959 Proof	—	Value: 350				
1960	600,000	0.20	1.00	5.00	12.50	22.50
1960 Proof	—	Value: 350				
1961	400,000	0.20	0.50	5.00	12.00	20.00
1961 Proof	—	Value: 350				
1962	1,000,000	0.20	0.30	1.00	2.50	5.00
1962 Proof	—	Value: 350				
1962 No Horizon	—	10.00	20.00	30.00	70.00	110
1963	600,000	0.15	0.25	0.75	2.50	7.50
1963 Proof	—	Value: 350				
1964	3,400,000	0.10	0.15	0.30	1.00	2.00
1964 Proof	—	Value: 350				
1965	3,500,000	0.10	0.15	0.30	1.00	2.00
1965 Prooflike	25,000	—	—	—	—	1.25
1965 Proof	10	—	—	—	—	—

KM# 4 FLORIN
11.3100 g., 0.5000 Silver 0.1818 oz. ASW, 28.58 mm.
Ruler: George V **Obv:** Crowned bust left **Rev:** Kiwi bird

Date	Mintage	F	VF	XF	Unc	BU
1933	2,100,000	2.50	17.50	35.00	110	250
1933 Proof	Est. 20	Value: 600				

Date	Mintage	F	VF	XF	Unc	BU
1934	2,850,000	2.50	17.50	35.00	110	225
1934 Proof	Est. 20	Value: 2,000				
1935	755,000	2.50	30.00	60.00	190	500
1935 Proof	364	Value: 700				
1936	150,000	6.00	80.00	400	1,500	4,000
1936 Proof	—	Value: 1,250				

KM# 10.1   FLORIN
11.3100 g., 0.5000 Silver 0.1818 oz. ASW, 28.58 mm.
Ruler: George VI **Obv:** Head left **Rev:** Kiwi bird with rounded back

Date	Mintage	F	VF	XF	Unc	BU
1937	1,190,000	2.50	17.50	40.00	110	170
1937 Proof	Est. 200	Value: 600				
1940	500,000	3.00	35.00	150	500	1,000
1940 Proof	—	Value: 800				
1941	820,000	2.50	15.00	30.00	70.00	150
1941 Proof	—	Value: 600				
1942	150,000	2.50	20.00	40.00	100	190
1943	1,400,000	2.50	15.00	30.00	70.00	170
1944	140,000	6.00	35.00	120	220	500
1944 Proof	—	Value: 800				
1945	515,000	3.00	15.00	35.00	70.00	180
1945 Proof	—	Value: 650				
1946	1,200,000	2.50	12.00	30.00	60.00	125
1946 Proof	—	Value: 650				

KM# 10.2   FLORIN
11.3100 g., 0.5000 Silver 0.1818 oz. ASW, 28.58 mm.
Ruler: George VI **Obv:** Head left **Rev:** Flat back on Kiwi

Date	Mintage	F	VF	XF	Unc	BU
1946	Est. 300,000	4.00	40.00	200	500	800

KM# 10.2a   FLORIN
Copper-Nickel, 28.58 mm. **Ruler:** George VI **Obv:** Head left **Rev:** Kiwi bird

Date	Mintage	F	VF	XF	Unc	BU
1947	2,500,000	1.00	10.00	30.00	70.00	175
1947 Proof	Est. 20	Value: 450				

KM# 18   FLORIN
Copper-Nickel, 28.58 mm. **Ruler:** George VI **Obv:** Head left **Rev:** Kiwi bird

Date	Mintage	F	VF	XF	Unc	BU
1948	1,750,000	1.00	10.00	30.00	70.00	175
1948 Proof	—	Value: 400				
1949	3,500,000	1.00	10.00	30.00	70.00	175
1949 Proof	—	Value: 400				
1950	3,500,000	0.75	4.00	8.00	20.00	35.00
1950 Proof	—	Value: 400				
1951	2,000,000	0.75	4.00	8.00	20.00	35.00
1951 Proof	—	Value: 400				

KM# 28.1   FLORIN
Copper-Nickel, 28.58 mm. **Ruler:** Elizabeth II **Obv:** Laureate bust right without shoulder strap **Rev:** Kiwi bird

Date	Mintage	F	VF	XF	Unc	BU
1953	250,000	2.00	4.00	12.00	25.00	45.00
1953 Proof	7,000	Value: 12.50				
1953 Matte proof	—	Value: 180				
1954	—					

KM# 28.2   FLORIN
Copper-Nickel, 28.58 mm. **Ruler:** Elizabeth II **Obv:** Laureate bust right with shoulder strap **Rev:** Kiwi bird

Date	Mintage	F	VF	XF	Unc	BU
1961	1,500,000	0.75	1.50	4.00	10.00	20.00
1961 Proof	—	Value: 375				
1962	1,500,000	0.75	1.50	3.50	8.00	15.00
1962 Proof	—	Value: 375				
1963	100,000	2.00	3.50	6.00	10.00	20.00
1963 Proof	—	Value: 375				
1964	7,000,000	0.20	0.50	1.00	3.00	6.00
1964 Proof	—	Value: 375				
1965	9,450,000	0.20	0.50	0.75	1.00	1.50
1965 Prooflike	25,000	—	—	—	—	2.50
1965 Proof	10	—	—	—	—	—

KM# 5   1/2 CROWN
14.1400 g., 0.5000 Silver 0.2273 oz. ASW, 32 mm.
Ruler: George V **Obv:** Crowned bust left **Rev:** Crowned shield within ornamental design

Date	Mintage	F	VF	XF	Unc	BU
1933	2,000,000	3.50	20.00	45.00	200	300
1933 Proof	Est. 20	Value: 650				
1934	2,720,000	3.50	20.00	45.00	200	350
1934 Proof	Est. 20	Value: 2,250				
1935	612,000	5.00	40.00	110	350	650
1935 Proof	364	Value: 700				

KM# 11   1/2 CROWN
14.1400 g., 0.5000 Silver 0.2273 oz. ASW, 32 mm.
Ruler: George VI **Obv:** Head left **Rev:** Crowned shield within ornamental design

Date	Mintage	F	VF	XF	Unc	BU
1937	672,000	4.00	22.50	60.00	200	300
1937 Proof	200	Value: 700				
1941	776,000	4.00	22.50	40.00	100	220
1941 Proof	—	Value: 700				
1942	240,000	4.00	25.00	50.00	120	250
1943	1,120,000	3.50	15.00	37.50	80.00	180
1944	180,000	6.00	45.00	180	375	750
1944 Proof	—	Value: 700				

Date	Mintage	F	VF	XF	Unc	BU
1945	420,000	4.00	15.00	45.00	120	225
1945 Proof	—	Value: 700				
1946	960,000	3.50	15.00	45.00	115	175
1946 Proof	—	Value: 700				

KM# 14   1/2 CROWN
14.1400 g., 0.5000 Silver 0.2273 oz. ASW, 32 mm.
Ruler: George VI **Subject:** New Zealand Centennial **Obv:** Head left **Rev:** Radiant sun above city, standing figure in foreground

Date	Mintage	F	VF	XF	Unc	BU
1940	100,800	10.00	13.00	20.00	35.00	60.00
1940 Proof	—	Value: 5,000				

KM# 11a   1/2 CROWN
Copper-Nickel, 32 mm. **Ruler:** George VI **Obv:** Head left **Rev:** Crowned shield within ornamental design

Date	Mintage	F	VF	XF	Unc	BU
1947	1,600,000	1.25	5.00	30.00	120	200
1947 Proof	Est. 20	Value: 550				

KM# 19   1/2 CROWN
Copper-Nickel, 32 mm. **Ruler:** George VI **Obv:** Head left **Rev:** Crowned shield within ornamental design

Date	Mintage	F	VF	XF	Unc	BU
1948	1,400,000	1.25	5.00	30.00	120	200
1948 Proof	—	Value: 500				
1949	2,800,000	1.25	5.00	30.00	120	200
1949 Proof	—	Value: 500				
1950	3,600,000	1.25	2.50	15.00	25.00	45.00
	Note: K. G. close to dots					
1950 Proof	—	Value: 500				
1950	Inc. above	2.00	8.00	25.00	60.00	100
	Note: K. G. close to rim					
1950 Proof	—	Value: 500				
1951	1,200,000	1.25	2.50	12.00	25.00	40.00
1951 Proof	—	Value: 500				

KM# 29.1   1/2 CROWN
Copper-Nickel, 32 mm. **Ruler:** Elizabeth II **Obv:** Laureate bust right without shoulder strap **Rev:** Crowned shield within ornamental design

Date	Mintage	F	VF	XF	Unc	BU
1953	120,000	3.50	6.00	20.00	25.00	55.00
1953 Proof	7,000	Value: 20.00				
1953 Matte proof	—	Value: 245				

KM# 29.2 1/2 CROWN
Copper-Nickel, 32 mm. **Ruler:** Elizabeth II **Obv:** Laureate bust right with shoulder strap **Rev:** Crowned shield within ornamental design

Date	Mintage	F	VF	XF	Unc	BU
1961	80,000	4.00	8.00	15.00	30.00	60.00
1961 Proof	—	Value: 450				
1962	600,000	1.25	2.00	3.00	4.00	8.00
1962 Proof	—	Value: 450				
1963	400,000	1.25	2.50	3.50	6.00	8.00
1963 Proof	—	Value: 450				
1965	200,000	1.25	2.50	3.50	4.00	5.00
1965 Prooflike	25,000	—	—	—	—	5.00
1965 Proof	10	—	—	—	—	—

KM# 6 CROWN
28.2800 g., 0.5000 Silver 0.4546 oz. ASW, 38.8 mm.
Ruler: George V **Subject:** Treaty of Waitangi in 1840.
Obv: Crowned bust left **Rev:** Crown above standing figures shaking hands **Note:** 364 Proofs issued in sets, 104 issued loose.

Date	Mintage	F	VF	XF	Unc	BU
1935	660	1,200	2,000	3,000	4,250	5,000
1935 Proof	468	Value: 5,500				

KM# 22 CROWN
28.2800 g., 0.5000 Silver 0.4546 oz. ASW, 38.8 mm.
Ruler: George VI **Subject:** Proposed Royal Visit **Obv:** Head left
Rev: Silver fern leaf flanked by stars

Date	Mintage	F	VF	XF	Unc	BU
1949	200,000	BV	12.00	16.00	25.00	40.00
1949 Proof	Est. 3	Value: 12,000				

KM# 30 CROWN
Copper-Nickel, 38.8 mm. **Ruler:** Elizabeth II **Subject:** Queen Elizabeth II Coronation **Obv:** Laureate bust right **Rev:** Crowned monogram flanked by stars above design

Date	Mintage	F	VF	XF	Unc	BU
1953	250,000	—	5.00	6.50	10.00	12.50
1953 Proof	7,000	Value: 80.00				
1953 Matte proof	—	Value: 345				
	Note: Mintage: 4-10.					

DECIMAL COINAGE
100 Cents = 1 Dollar

- (c) Royal Australian Mint, Canberra
- (l) Royal Mint, Llantrisant
- (o) Royal Canadian Mint, Ottawa
- (m) B.H. Mayer, Germany
- (n) Norwegian Mint, Kongsberg
- (p) South African Mint, Pretoria
- (v) Valcambi SA, Switzerland
- (w) Perth Mint, Western Australia

KM# 31.1 CENT
2.0500 g., Bronze, 17.5 mm. **Ruler:** Elizabeth II **Obv:** Young bust right **Rev:** Value within silver fern leaf **Note:** Rounded, high relief portrait.

Date	Mintage	F	VF	XF	Unc	BU
1967(l)	120,000,000	—	—	0.10	0.15	0.25
1967(l) Prooflike	50,000	—	—	—	—	0.80
1967 Proof	10	—	—	—	—	—
1968	35,000	—	—	—	2.00	—
	Note: In sets only					
1968 Prooflike	40,000	—	—	—	—	2.00
1969	50,000	—	—	—	2.00	—
	Note: In sets only					
1969 Prooflike	50,000	—	—	—	—	2.00
1970(c)	10,060,000	—	—	0.10	0.50	1.00
1970 Prooflike	20,010	—	—	—	—	1.00
1971(c)	10,000,000	—	—	0.10	6.00	8.00
	Note: Serifs on date numerals					
1971(l)	15,000	—	—	0.10	3.00	5.00
	Note: Without serifs					
1971(l) Proof	5,000	Value: 12.50				
1972(c)	10,055,000	—	0.20	1.00	5.00	7.00
1972(c) Proof	8,045	Value: 5.00				
1973(c)	15,055,000	—	—	0.10	5.00	7.00
1973(c) Proof	8,000	Value: 5.00				
1974(c)	35,035,000	—	—	0.10	0.50	1.00
1974(c) Proof	8,000	Value: 4.00				
1975(l)	60,015,000	—	—	0.10	0.50	1.00
1975(l) Proof	10,000	Value: 4.00				
1976(l)	20,016,000	—	—	0.10	0.50	1.00
1976(l) Proof	11,000	Value: 4.00				
1977 In sets only	20,000	—	—	—	4.00	6.00
1977 Proof	12,000	Value: 6.00				
1978(o)	15,023,000	—	—	0.10	0.50	1.00
1978(o) Proof	15,000	Value: 2.00				
1979(o)	35,025,000	—	—	0.10	0.50	1.00
1979(o) Proof	16,000	Value: 2.00				
1980(o)	40,000,000	—	—	0.10	0.50	1.00
	Note: Oval O in date					
1980(l)	27,000	—	—	—	0.50	1.00
	Note: Round 0 in date. In sets only.					
1980(l) Proof	17,000	Value: 2.00				
1981(o)	10,000,000	—	—	0.10	0.50	1.00
	Note: Oval hole in 8					
1981(l)	25,000	—	—	—	0.50	1.00
	Note: Round hole in 8. In sets only.					
1981(l) Proof	18,000	Value: 2.00				
	Note: Round hole in 8					
1982(o)	10,000,000	—	—	0.10	0.50	1.00
	Note: Blunt-tipped 2					
1982(l)	25,000	—	—	—	0.50	1.00

Date	Mintage	F	VF	XF	Unc	BU
	Note: Round-tipped 2					
1982(l) Proof	18,000	Value: 2.00				
	Note: Round-tipped 2					
1983(o)	—	—	—	0.10	0.50	1.00
	Note: Round-top 3					
1983(l)	25,000	—	—	0.10	0.50	1.00
	Note: Flat-top 3. In sets only.					
1983(l) Proof	18,000	Value: 2.00				
	Note: Flat-top 3					
1984(l)	25,000	—	—	0.10	0.50	1.00
	Note: In sets only.					
1984(l) Proof	15,000	Value: 2.00				
1985(c)	20,000	—	—	0.10	0.50	1.00
	Note: In sets only.					
1985(c) Proof	12,000	Value: 2.00				

KM# 31.2 CENT
2.0500 g., Bronze, 17.5 mm. **Obv:** Crowned bust right **Rev:** Value within silver fern leaf **Note:** Die recut, low relief portrait.

Date	Mintage	F	VF	XF	Unc	BU
1984(o)	30,000,000	—	—	0.10	0.50	1.00
1985(o)	40,000,000	—	—	0.10	0.50	1.00

KM# 58 CENT
2.0500 g., Bronze, 17.5 mm. **Ruler:** Elizabeth II **Obv:** Crowned head right **Rev:** Value within silver fern leaf **Edge:** Plain

Date	Mintage	F	VF	XF	Unc	BU
1986(o)	25,000,000	—	—	0.10	0.50	1.00
1986(l)	18,000	—	—	—	1.00	—
	Note: In sets only.					
1986(l) Proof	10,000	Value: 1.00				
1987(o)	27,500,000	—	—	0.10	0.50	1.00
1987(l)	18,000	—	—	—	1.00	—
	Note: In sets only.					
1987(l) Proof	10,000	Value: 1.00				
1988(l)	15,000	—	—	—	5.00	7.50
	Note: In sets only					
1988(l) Proof	9,000	Value: 2.00				
	Note: 1988 cent was struck for sets only					

KM# 33 2 CENTS
4.1500 g., Bronze, 21.1 mm. **Ruler:** Elizabeth II **Obv:** Young bust right **Rev:** Value within kowhai leaves **Note:** Mule with Bahamas KM#3.

Date	Mintage	F	VF	XF	Unc	BU
ND(1967)	Est. 50,000	—	8.00	15.00	22.50	30.00

KM# 32.1 2 CENTS
4.1500 g., Bronze, 21.1 mm. **Ruler:** Elizabeth II **Obv:** Young bust right **Rev:** Value within kowhai leaves **Note:** Rounded, high relief portrait.

Date	Mintage	F	VF	XF	Unc	BU
1967(l)	75,000,000	—	—	0.10	0.15	0.25
1967(l) Prooflike	50,000	—	—	—	—	0.75
1967(l) Proof	10	—	—	—	—	—
1968	35,000	—	—	—	2.00	3.00
	Note: In sets only					
1968 Prooflike	40,000	—	—	—	—	1.25
1969(c)	20,510,000	—	—	0.15	0.25	0.50
1969 Prooflike	50,000	—	—	—	—	1.25
1970(c)	30,000	—	—	—	2.00	3.00
	Note: In sets only					
1970 Prooflike	20,010	—	—	—	—	1.25
1971(c)	15,050,000	—	0.10	1.00	5.00	6.00
	Note: Serifs on date numerals					
1971(l)	15,000	—	—	2.00	4.00	5.00
	Note: Without serifs					
1971(l) Proof	5,000	Value: 12.50				
1972(c)	17,525,000	—	0.10	1.00	5.00	6.00
1972(c) Proof	8,045	Value: 5.00				
1973(c)	38,565,000	—	—	0.10	5.00	6.00
1973(c) Proof	8,000	Value: 5.25				
1974(c)	50,015,000	—	0.10	0.50	1.00	2.00
1974(c) Proof	8,000	Value: 3.00				
1975(l)	20,015,000	—	—	0.10	1.00	1.50
1975(l) Proof	10,000	Value: 3.00				

Date	Mintage	F	VF	XF	Unc	BU
1976(I)	15,016,000	—	—	0.10	1.00	1.50
1976(I) Proof	11,000	Value: 3.00				
1977(I)	20,000,000	—	—	0.10	1.00	1.50
1977(I) Proof	12,000	Value: 3.00				
1978(o)	23,000	—	—	—	5.00	6.00
Note: In sets only						
1978(o) Proof	15,000	Value: 3.00				
1979(o)	25,000	—	—	—	5.00	6.00
Note: In sets only						
1979(o) Proof	16,000	Value: 3.00				
1980(o)	10,000,000	—	—	0.10	1.00	1.25
Note: Oval 0 in date						
1980(I)	27,000	—	—	—	1.00	1.25
Note: Round 0 in date. In sets only.						
1980(I) Proof	17,000	Value: 3.00				
1981(o)	25,000,000	—	—	0.10	1.00	1.25
Note: Oval hole in 8						
1981(I)	25,000	—	—	—	1.00	1.25
Note: Round hole in 8. In sets only.						
1981(I) Proof	18,000	Value: 3.00				
1982(o)	50,000,000	—	—	0.10	1.00	1.25
Note: Blunt open 2						
1982(I)	25,000	—	—	—	1.00	1.25
Note: Pointed tight 2. In sets only.						
1982(I) Proof	18,000	Value: 3.00				
1983(o)	15,000,000	—	—	0.10	1.00	1.25
Note: Round-topped 3						
1983(I)	25,000	—	—	—	1.00	1.25
Note: Flat-topped 3. In sets only.						
1983(I) Proof	18,000	Value: 3.00				
1984(I)	25,000	—	—	—	1.00	1.25
Note: Smooth shoulder folds. In sets only.						
1984(I) Proof	15,000	Value: 2.00				
1985(c)	20,000	—	—	—	2.00	2.50
Note: In sets only.						
1985(c) Proof	12,000	Value: 2.00				

KM# 32.2 2 CENTS
Bronze, 21.1 mm. Obv: Crowned bust right Rev: Value within kowhai leaves Note: Die recut, low relief portrait.

Date	Mintage	F	VF	XF	Unc	BU
1984(o)	10,000,000	—	—	0.10	1.00	1.50
1985(o)	22,500,000	—	—	0.10	1.00	1.50

KM# 59 2 CENTS
4.1500 g., Bronze, 21.1 mm. Ruler: Elizabeth II Obv: Crowned head right Rev: Kowhai

Date	Mintage	F	VF	XF	Unc	BU
1986(I)	18,000	—	—	—	8.00	9.50
Note: In sets only						
1986(I) Proof	10,000	Value: 8.00				
1987(o)	36,250,000	—	—	—	1.00	1.25
1987(I)	18,000	—	—	—	2.00	2.50
Note: In sets only.						
1987(I) Proof	10,000	Value: 2.00				
1988(I)	15,000	—	—	—	5.00	7.50
Note: In sets only						
1988(I) Proof	9,000	Value: 1.25				

KM# 34.1 5 CENTS
2.8300 g., Copper-Nickel, 19.43 mm. Ruler: Elizabeth II Subject: Tuatara Obv: Young bust right Rev: Value below tuatara Note: Rounded, high relief portrait. Many recalled and melted in 2006.

Date	Mintage	F	VF	XF	Unc	BU
1967(I)	26,000,000	—	—	0.10	0.20	0.50
1967(I)	Inc. above	3.00	5.00	15.00	30.00	50.00
Note: Without sea line at right of Tuatara						
1967(I)	Inc. above	3.00	5.00	15.00	30.00	50.00
Note: No tail triangle under chin						
1967(I) Prooflike	50,000	—	—	—	—	1.00
1967(I) Proof	10	—	—	—	—	—
1968	35,000	—	—	—	1.00	2.00
Note: In sets only						
1968 Prooflike	40,000	—	—	—	—	2.00
1969(c)	10,260,000	—	—	0.10	0.50	1.00
1969 Prooflike	50,000	—	—	—	—	2.00
1970(c)	11,202,000	—	—	0.10	0.50	1.00
1970 Prooflike	20,010	—	—	—	—	2.00
1971(c)	11,152,000	—	0.10	0.50	5.00	10.00
Note: Serifs on date numerals						
1971(I)	15,000	—	—	0.50	3.00	6.00
Note: Without serifs						
1971(I) Proof	5,000	Value: 5.00				
1972(c)	20,015,000	—	—	—	1.00	2.00
1972(c) Proof	8,000	Value: 5.00				
1973(c)	4,038,999	—	—	0.10	1.00	2.00
Note: 2nd hardest date to find, after 2004						
1973(c) Proof	8,000	Value: 4.50				
1974(c)	18,015,000	—	—	0.10	1.50	3.00
1974(c) Proof	8,000	Value: 4.00				
1975(c)	32,015,000	—	—	0.10	0.50	1.00
1975(c) Proof	10,000	Value: 4.50				
1976	16,000	—	—	—	5.00	6.00

Date	Mintage	F	VF	XF	Unc	BU
Note: In sets only						
1976 Proof	11,000	Value: 2.00				
1977	20,000	—	—	—	5.00	6.00
Note: In sets only						
1977 Proof	12,000	Value: 3.00				
1978(o)	20,023,000	—	—	0.10	0.40	1.00
1978(o) Proof	15,000	Value: 3.00				
1979(o)	25,000	—	—	—	4.00	6.00
Note: In sets only						
1979(o) Proof	16,000	Value: 3.00				
1980(o)	12,000,000	—	—	0.10	0.50	1.00
Note: Oval O in date						
1980(I)	27,000	—	—	—	0.50	1.00
Note: Round O in date. In sets only.						
1980(I) Proof	17,000	Value: 2.00				
1981(o)	20,000,000	—	—	0.10	0.50	1.00
Note: Oval hole in 8						
1981(I)	25,000	—	—	—	0.50	0.50
Note: Round hole in 8. In sets only.						
1981(I) Proof	18,000	Value: 2.00				
1982(o)	50,000,000	—	—	0.10	0.50	1.00
Note: Blunt 2						
1982(I)	25,000	—	—	0.50	1.00	2.00
Note: Pointed 2. In sets only.						
1982(I) Proof	18,000	Value: 3.00				
1983(I)	25,000	—	—	—	3.00	4.00
Note: In sets only						
1983(I) Proof	18,000	Value: 3.00				
1984(I)	25,000	—	—	—	3.00	4.00
Note: In sets only						
1984(I) Proof	15,000	Value: 3.00				
1985(c)	20,000	—	—	0.50	1.00	2.00
Note: In sets only.						
1985(c) Proof	12,000	Value: 2.00				

KM# 64 5 CENTS
Copper-Nickel Ruler: Elizabeth II Obv: Young bust right Rev: Small ship Note: Mule with Canada KM#77.

Date	Mintage	F	VF	XF	Unc	BU
1981(o)	Rare;	—	—	—	—	—
Serif on 1						

KM# 34.2 5 CENTS
2.8300 g., Copper-Nickel, 19.43 mm. Subject: Tuatara Obv: Crowned bust right Rev: James Berry Note: Die recut, low relief.

Date	Mintage	F	VF	XF	Unc	BU
1985(o)	14,000,000	—	—	0.10	0.50	1.00

KM# 60 5 CENTS
2.8300 g., Copper-Nickel, 19.43 mm. Ruler: Elizabeth II Obv: Crowned head right Rev: Value below tuatara Note: Many recalled and melted in 2006.

Date	Mintage	F	VF	XF	Unc	BU
1986(o)	18,000,000	—	—	0.10	0.50	1.00
1986(I)	18,000	—	—	—	1.00	2.00
Note: In sets only.						
1986(I) Proof	10,000	Value: 3.00				
1987(o)	40,000,000	—	—	0.10	0.50	1.00
1987(I)	18,000	—	—	—	2.00	3.00
Note: In sets only.						
1987(I) Proof	10,000	Value: 3.00				
1988(o)	16,000,000	—	—	0.10	0.50	1.00
Note: Round-topped numerals						
1988(I)	15,000	—	—	—	2.00	2.50
Note: Flat-topped numerals. In sets only.						
1988(I) Proof	9,000	Value: 3.00				
1989(o)	36,000,000	—	—	0.10	0.50	1.00
1989(c)	15,000	—	—	—	1.00	1.50
Note: In sets only.						
1989(c) Proof	8,500	Value: 3.00				
1990(c)	18,000	—	—	—	3.00	4.00
Note: In sets only						
1990(c) Proof	10,000	Value: 3.00				
1991(c)	20,000	—	—	—	3.00	4.00
Note: In sets only						
1991(c) Proof	9,000	Value: 4.00				
1992(I)	15,000	—	—	—	3.00	4.00
Note: In sets only						
1992(I) Proof	9,000	Value: 4.00				
1993(I)	15,000	—	—	—	3.00	4.00
Note: In sets only						
1993(I) Proof	10,000	Value: 4.00				
1994(I)	20,026,000	—	—	0.10	0.50	1.00
1994(I) Proof	10,000	Value: 3.00				
1995(I)	40,010,000	—	—	0.10	0.50	1.00
1995(I) Proof	4,000	Value: 3.00				
1996(n)	19,008,000	—	—	0.10	0.50	1.00
1996(I) Proof	4,000	Value: 3.00				
1997(n)	14,000,000	—	—	0.10	0.50	1.00
1997(I) Proof	2,500	Value: 5.00				
1998(p)	8,000,000	—	—	0.10	0.50	1.00
1998(I) Proof	2,000	Value: 3.00				

KM# 72 5 CENTS
2.8300 g., Copper-Nickel, 19.43 mm. Ruler: Elizabeth II Subject: 1990 Anniversary Celebrations Obv: Crowned head right Rev: Stylized kotuku bird

Date	Mintage	F	VF	XF	Unc	BU
1990	10,000	—	—	—	6.00	8.00
Note: In sets only.						

KM# 72a 5 CENTS
3.2700 g., 0.9250 Silver 0.0972 oz. ASW, 19.43 mm. Ruler: Elizabeth II Obv: Crowned head right Rev: Stylized kotuku bird

Date	Mintage	F	VF	XF	Unc	BU
1990 Proof	7,000	Value: 15.00				

KM# 116 5 CENTS
2.8300 g., Copper-Nickel, 19.43 mm. Ruler: Elizabeth II Obv: Head with tiara right Rev: Value below tuatara Edge: Reeded Note: Many recalled and melted in 2006.

Date	Mintage	F	VF	XF	Unc	BU
1999(p)	25,040,000	—	—	0.10	0.50	1.00
1999(p) Wart on nose		—	—	—	6.00	8.00
Note: Die crack error						
1999(I)	3,199	—	—	—	5.00	6.00
Note: In sets only.						
1999(I) Proof	1,800	Value: 3.00				
2000(o)	26,000,000	—	—	0.10	0.50	1.00
2000(c)	3,000	—	—	—	12.00	15.00
Note: In sets only.						
2000(c) Proof	1,500	Value: 15.00				

KM# 35 10 CENTS
5.6500 g., Copper-Nickel, 23.62 mm. Ruler: Elizabeth II Obv: Young bust right Rev: Value above Maori mask, koruru Note: Many recalled and melted in 2006.

Date	Mintage	F	VF	XF	Unc	BU
1967(I)	17,000,000	—	—	0.10	0.25	0.50
1967(I) Prooflike	50,000	—	—	—	—	1.00
1967(I) Proof	10	—	—	—	—	—
1968	35,000	—	—	1.00	2.00	3.00
Note: In sets only						
1968 Prooflike	40,000	—	—	—	—	2.00
1969	3,050,000	—	—	0.15	0.50	1.00
1969 Proof	50,000	Value: 2.00				

KM# 41.1 10 CENTS
5.6500 g., Copper-Nickel, 23.62 mm. Ruler: Elizabeth II Obv: Young bust right Rev: Value above Maori mask, koruru Note: Rounded, high relief portrait. Many recalled and melted in 2006.

Date	Mintage	F	VF	XF	Unc	BU
1970	2,046,000	—	—	0.15	0.50	1.00
1970 Prooflike	20,010	—	—	—	—	1.50
1971(c)	2,800,000	—	0.10	5.00	30.00	40.00
Note: Serifs on date numerals						
1971(I)	15,000	—	—	1.00	2.00	3.00
Note: Without serifs						
1971(I) Proof	5,000	Value: 5.00				
1972(c)	2,039,000	—	—	0.15	1.00	2.00
1972(c) Proof	8,000	Value: 5.00				
1973(c)	3,525,000	—	—	0.10	1.00	2.00
1973(c) Proof	8,000	Value: 3.00				
1974(c)	4,619,000	—	—	0.10	1.00	2.00
1974(c) Proof	8,000	Value: 3.00				
1975(I)	7,015,000	—	—	0.10	1.00	2.00

Date	Mintage	F	VF	XF	Unc	BU
1975(I) Proof	10,000	Value: 3.00				
1976(I)	5,016,000	—	—	0.10	1.00	2.00
1976(I) Proof	11,000	Value: 3.00				
1977(I)	5,000,000	—	—	0.10	1.00	2.00
1977(o) Proof	12,000	Value: 3.00				
1978(o)	16,023,000	—	—	0.10	1.00	2.00
1978(o) Proof	15,000	Value: 3.00				
1979(o)	6,000,000	—	—	0.10	0.50	1.00
1979(o) Proof	16,000	Value: 3.00				
1980(o)	28,000,000	—	—	0.10	0.50	1.00
Note: Oval O in date						
1980(I)	27,000	—	—	—	1.00	
Note: Round O in date. In sets only.						
1980(I) Proof	17,000	Value: 3.00				
1981(I)	5,000,000	—	—	0.10	0.50	1.00
Note: Oval holes in 8						
1981(I)	25,000	—	—	0.10	0.50	1.00
Note: Round holes in 8. In sets only.						
1981(I) Proof	18,000	Value: 3.00				
1982(o)	18,000,000	—	—	0.10	0.50	1.00
Note: Blunt open 2						
1982(I)	25,000	—	—	—	1.00	2.00
Note: Point-tipped 2. In sets only.						
1982(I) Proof	18,000	Value: 3.00				
1983(I)	25,000	—	—	—	3.00	4.00
Note: In sets only						
1983(I) Proof	18,000	Value: 3.00				
1984(I)	25,000	—	—	—	3.00	4.00
Note: In sets only						
1984(I) Proof	15,000	Value: 4.00				
1985(c)	20,000	—	—	—	3.00	4.00
Note: In sets only.						
1985(c) Proof	12,000	Value: 4.00				

KM# 41.2 10 CENTS
5.6500 g., Copper-Nickel, 23.62 mm. **Obv:** Crowned bust right **Note:** Recut due, low relief.

Date	Mintage	F	VF	XF	Unc	BU
1985(o)	8,000,000	—	—	0.50	3.00	4.00
Note: Wiry hair, bushy eyebrow						

KM# 61 10 CENTS
5.6500 g., Copper-Nickel, 23.62 mm. **Ruler:** Elizabeth II **Obv:** Crowned head right **Rev:** Value above Maori mask, koruru **Note:** Many recalled and melted in 2006.

Date	Mintage	F	VF	XF	Unc	BU
1986(I)	18,000	—	—	—	3.00	4.00
Note: In sets only						
1986(I) Proof	10,000	Value: 4.00				
1987(o)	21,000,000	—	—	0.10	0.50	1.00
1987(I)	18,000	—	—	—	1.00	2.00
Note: In sets only.						
1987(I) Proof	10,000	Value: 3.00				
1988(c)	26,702,000	—	—	0.10	0.50	1.00
1988(I)	15,000	—	—	—	1.00	2.00
Note: In sets only.						
1988(I) Proof	9,000	Value: 3.00				
1989(o)	9,000,000	—	—	—	0.50	1.00
1989(c)	14,600	—	—	—	2.50	3.50
Note: In sets only.						
1989(c) Proof	8,500	Value: 3.00				
1990(c)	18,000	—	—	—	2.00	3.00
Note: In sets only						
1990(c) Proof	10,000	Value: 3.00				
1991(c)	20,000	—	—	—	2.00	3.00
Note: In sets only						
1991(c) Proof	15,000	Value: 3.00				
1992	15,000	—	—	—	2.00	3.00
Note: In sets only.						
1992 Proof	9,000	Value: 3.00				
1993	15,000	—	—	—	2.00	3.00
Note: In sets only.						
1993 Proof	10,000	Value: 3.00				
1994	7,000	—	—	—	2.00	3.00
Note: In sets only.						
1994 Proof	4,600	Value: 3.00				
1995	6,000	—	—	—	1.00	2.00
Note: In sets only.						
1995 Proof	3,560	Value: 3.00				
1996(n)	12,960,000	—	—	—	0.50	1.00
1996(n) Proof	2,569	Value: 3.00				
1997(n)	8,000,000	—	—	—	0.50	1.00
1997(I) Proof	2,132	Value: 3.00				
1998	4,000	—	—	—	8.00	10.00
Note: In sets only						
1998(I) Proof	2,000	Value: 3.00				

KM# 73 10 CENTS
5.6500 g., Copper-Nickel, 23.62 mm. **Ruler:** Elizabeth II **Subject:** 1990 Anniversary Celebrations **Obv:** Crowned head right **Rev:** Value above sailboats within rainbow design

Date	Mintage	F	VF	XF	Unc	BU
1990	10,000	—	—	—	7.00	9.00

KM# 73a 10 CENTS
6.5300 g., 0.9250 Silver 0.1942 oz. ASW, 23.62 mm. **Ruler:** Elizabeth II **Subject:** 1990 Anniversary Celebrations **Obv:** Crowned head right **Rev:** Value above sailboats within rainbow design

Date	Mintage	F	VF	XF	Unc	BU
1990 Proof	7,000	Value: 10.00				

KM# 117 10 CENTS
5.6600 g., Copper-Nickel, 23.62 mm. **Ruler:** Elizabeth II **Obv:** Head with tiara right **Rev:** Value above koruru **Note:** Many recalled and melted in 2006.

Date	Mintage	F	VF	XF	Unc	BU
1999(I)	3,199	—	—	—	10.00	12.00
Note: In sets only.						
1999(I) Proof	1,800	Value: 10.00				
2000(o)	11,000,000	—	—	0.10	0.30	0.50
2000(I)	4,500	—	—	—	12.00	15.00
Note: In sets only.						
2000(I) Proof	1,500	Value: 15.00				

KM# 36.1 20 CENTS
11.3100 g., Copper-Nickel, 28.58 mm. **Ruler:** Elizabeth II **Obv:** Young bust right **Rev:** Value below Kiwi bird with sprigs above **Note:** Rounded, high relief portrait. Prev. KM#36. Many recalled and melted in 2006.

Date	Mintage	F	VF	XF	Unc	BU
1967(I)	13,000,000	—	—	0.20	0.50	1.00
1967(I) Prooflike	50,000	—	—	—	—	1.00
1967(I) Proof	10	—	—	—	—	—
1968	35,000	—	—	—	2.00	3.00
Note: In sets only						
1968 Prooflike	40,000	—	—	—	—	2.00
1969	2,500,000	—	—	0.20	1.00	1.50
1969 Prooflike	50,000	—	—	—	—	2.00
1970	30,000	—	—	—	2.00	3.00
Note: In sets only						
1970 Prooflike	20,010	—	—	—	—	3.00
1971(c)	1,600,000	—	1.00	5.00	30.00	40.00
Note: Serifs on date numerals						
1971(I)	15,000	—	—	1.00	2.50	4.00
Note: Without serifs						
1971(I) Proof	5,000	Value: 10.00				
1972(c)	1,531,000	—	—	0.20	2.00	—
1972(c) Proof	8,000	Value: 12.50				
1973(c)	3,043,000	—	—	0.20	2.00	—
1973(c) Proof	8,000	Value: 7.00				
1974(c)	4,527,000	—	—	0.20	2.00	—
1974(c) Proof	8,000	Value: 8.00				
1975(I)	5,015,000	—	—	0.20	2.00	—
Note: About 15-20 examples are known struck on a Hong Kong $2 planchet						
1975(I) Proof	12,000	Value: 6.50				
1976(I)	7,516,000	—	—	0.20	2.00	—
1976(I) Proof	11,000	Value: 6.00				
1977(I)	7,500,000	—	—	0.20	2.00	—
1977(I) Proof	12,000	Value: 6.50				
1978(I)	2,523,000	—	—	0.20	2.00	—
1978(o) Proof	15,000	Value: 5.00				
1979(o)	8,025,000	—	—	0.20	2.00	—
1979(o) Proof	16,000	Value: 5.00				
1980(o)	9,000,000	—	—	0.15	2.00	—
Note: Oval O in date						
1980(I)	27,000	—	—	0.15	1.00	—

Date	Mintage	F	VF	XF	Unc	BU
Note: Round O in date. In sets only.						
1980(I) Proof	17,000	Value: 5.00				
1981(o)	7,500,000	—	—	0.15	1.00	—
Note: Oval holes in 8						
1981(I)	25,000	—	—	—	2.00	—
Note: Round holes in 8. In sets only.						
1981(I) Proof	18,000	Value: 4.00				
1982(o)	17,500,000	—	—	0.15	2.00	—
Note: Blunt 2						
1982(I)	25,000	—	—	—	1.00	—
Note: Pointed 2. In sets only.						
1982(I) Proof	18,000	Value: 5.00				
1983(o)	2,500,000	—	—	0.15	3.00	—
Note: Round topped 3						
1983(I)	25,000	—	—	—	1.00	—
Note: Flat topped 3. In sets only.						
1983(I) Proof	18,000	Value: 4.00				
1984(I)	25,000	—	—	—	1.00	—
Note: In sets only.						
1984(I) Proof	18,000	Value: 4.00				
1985(c)	20,000	—	—	—	1.00	—
Note: Round tip 5. In sets only.						
1985(c) Proof	18,000	Value: 4.00				

KM# 36.2 20 CENTS
11.3100 g., Copper-Nickel, 28.58 mm. **Obv:** Crowned bust right **Note:** Die recut, low relief. Many recalled and melted in 2006.

Date	Mintage	F	VF	XF	Unc	BU
1984(o)	1,500,000	—	—	0.15	2.00	—
1985(o)	6,000,000	—	—	0.15	2.00	—

KM# 62 20 CENTS
11.3100 g., Copper-Nickel, 28.58 mm. **Ruler:** Elizabeth II **Obv:** Crowned head right **Rev:** Kiwi

Date	Mintage	F	VF	XF	Unc	BU
1986(o)	12,500,000	—	—	0.15	1.00	—
1986(I)	18,000	—	—	—	2.00	—
Note: In sets only.						
1986(I) Proof	10,000	Value: 4.00				
1987(o)	14,000,000	—	—	0.15	1.00	—
1987(I)	18,000	—	—	—	2.00	—
Note: In sets only.						
1987(I) Proof	10,000	Value: 4.00				
1988(c)	12,500,000	—	—	0.15	1.00	—
1988(I)	15,000	—	—	—	2.00	—
Note: In sets only.						
1988(I) Proof	9,000	Value: 4.00				
1989(o)	5,000,000	—	—	0.15	1.00	—
1989(c) Proof	8,500	Value: 4.00				
1989(c)	15,000	—	—	—	2.00	—
Note: In sets only.						

KM# 74 20 CENTS
11.3100 g., Copper-Nickel, 28.58 mm. **Ruler:** Elizabeth II **Subject:** 1990 Anniversary Celebrations **Obv:** Crowned head right **Rev:** Ship, H.M.S. Tory

Date	Mintage	F	VF	XF	Unc	BU
1990(c)	10,000	—	—	—	10.00	—
Note: In sets only.						

KM# 74a 20 CENTS
13.0700 g., 0.9250 Silver 0.3887 oz. ASW, 28.58 mm. **Ruler:** Elizabeth II **Subject:** 1990 Anniversary Celebrations **Obv:** Crowned head right **Rev:** Ship, H.M.S. Tory

Date	Mintage	F	VF	XF	Unc	BU
1990(c) Proof	7,000	Value: 12.00				

KM# 81 20 CENTS
11.3100 g., Copper-Nickel, 28.58 mm. **Ruler:** Elizabeth II **Obv:** Crowned head right **Rev:** Value below Pukaki **Note:** Many recalled and melted in 2006.

Date	Mintage	F	VF	XF	Unc	BU
1990(I)	5,000,000	—	—	0.20	1.00	—
1990(c)	18,000	—	—	—	2.00	—
Note: In sets only.						
1990(c) Proof	10,000	Value: 4.00				
1991(c)	20,000	—	—	—	3.00	—
Note: In sets only						
1991(c) Proof	15,000	Value: 4.00				

Date	Mintage	F	VF	XF	Unc	BU
1992(I)	15,000	—	—	—	4.00	—
Note: In sets only						
1992(I) Proof	9,000	Value: 4.00				
1993(I)	15,000	—	—	—	4.00	—
Note: In sets only						
1993(I) Proof	10,000	Value: 4.00				
1994(I)	7,000	—	—	—	4.00	—
Note: In sets only						
1994(I) Proof	4,600	Value: 5.00				
1995(I)	6,000	—	—	—	4.00	—
Note: In sets only						
1995(I) Proof	3,560	Value: 10.00				
1996(I)	5,150	—	—	—	5.00	—
Note: In sets only						
1996(I) Proof	2,569	Value: 5.00				
1997(I)	4,150	—	—	—	5.00	—
Note: In sets only						
1997(I) Proof	2,132	Value: 10.00				
1998(I)	4,000	—	—	—	5.00	—
Note: In sets only						
1998(I) Proof	2,000	Value: 10.00				

KM# 81a   20 CENTS
13.0700 g., 0.9250 Silver Piefort issue comemorating the Maori language 0.3887 oz. ASW, 28.58 mm. **Ruler:** Elizabeth II **Obv:** Crowned head right **Rev:** Value below Pukaki

Date	Mintage	F	VF	XF	Unc	BU
1995(I) Proof	Est. 2,500	Value: 15.00				

KM# 118   20 CENTS
11.3100 g., Copper-Nickel, 28.58 mm. **Ruler:** Elizabeth II **Obv:** Head with tiara right **Rev:** Value below Pukaki **Note:** Many recalled and melted in 2006.

Date	Mintage	F	VF	XF	Unc	BU
1999(I)	3,199	—	—	—	—	5.00
Note: In sets only						
1999(I) Proof	1,800	Value: 10.00				
2000(I)	3,000	—	—	—	—	5.00
Note: In sets only						
2000(I) Proof	1,500	Value: 10.00				

KM# 37.1   50 CENTS
13.6100 g., Copper-Nickel, 31.75 mm. **Ruler:** Elizabeth II **Obv:** Young bust right **Rev:** Ship, H.M.S. Endeavour **Note:** Rounded, high relief portrait. Many recalled and melted in 2006.

Date	Mintage	F	VF	XF	Unc	BU
1967(I)	10,000,000	—	—	0.30	1.00	—
1967(I)	Est. 750,000	—	5.00	20.00	100	—
Note: Dot above 1						
1967(I) Prooflike	50,000	—	—	—	—	2.00
1967(I)	10	—	—	—	—	—
1968	35,000	—	—	—	2.00	—
Note: In sets only						
1968 Prooflike	40,000	—	—	—	—	3.00
1970	30,000	—	—	—	2.00	—
Note: In sets only						
1970 Prooflike	20,010	—	—	—	—	3.00
1971(c)	1,123,000	0.15	1.00	5.00	40.00	—
Note: Serifs on date numerals						
1971(I)	15,000	—	—	0.50	5.00	—
Note: Without serifs						
1971(I) Proof	5,000	Value: 40.00				
1972(c)	1,423,000	—	—	0.50	5.00	—
1972(c) Proof	8,045	Value: 15.00				
1973(c)	2,523,000	—	—	0.50	5.00	—
1973(c) Proof	8,000	Value: 10.00				
1974(c)	1,215,000	—	—	0.50	5.00	—
1974(c) Proof	8,000	Value: 10.00				
1975(I)	3,815,000	—	—	0.50	4.00	—
1975(I) Proof	10,000	Value: 7.50				
1976(I)	2,016,000	—	—	0.50	3.00	—
1976(I) Proof	11,000	Value: 7.50				
1977(I)	2,000,000	—	—	0.50	3.00	—
1977(I) Proof	12,000	Value: 7.50				
1978(o)	2,023,000	—	—	0.50	3.00	—

Date	Mintage	F	VF	XF	Unc	BU
1978(o) Proof	15,000	Value: 6.00				
1979(o)	2,425,000	—	—	0.50	3.00	—
1979(o) Proof	16,000	Value: 6.00				
1980(o)	8,000,000	—	0.30	0.50	3.00	—
Note: Thin 8 in date						
1980(I)	27,000	—	—	0.50	2.00	—
Note: Thick 8 in date. In sets only.						
1980(I) Proof	17,000	Value: 6.00				
1981(o)	4,000,000	—	0.30	0.50	3.00	—
Note: Blunt end on 9, oval holes in 8						
1981(I)	25,000	—	—	0.50	2.00	—
Note: Pointed end on 9, round holes in 8. In sets only.						
1981(I) Proof	18,000	Value: 6.00				
1982(o)	6,000,000	—	—	0.50	3.00	—
Note: Blunt end on 2						
1982(I)	25,000	—	—	0.50	3.00	—
Note: Pointed end on 2. In sets only.						
1982(I) Proof	18,000	Value: 6.00				
1983(I)	25,000	—	—	—	3.00	—
Note: In sets only						
1983(I) Proof	18,000	Value: 6.00				
1984(I)	25,000	—	—	—	3.00	—
Note: In sets only.						
1984(I) Proof	15,000	Value: 5.00				
1985(c)	20,000	—	—	0.50	3.00	—
Note: In sets only.						
1985(c) Proof	12,000	Value: 5.00				

KM# 39   50 CENTS
13.6100 g., Copper-Nickel, 31.75 mm. **Ruler:** Elizabeth II **Subject:** 200th Anniversary - Captain Cook's Voyage **Obv:** Young bust right **Rev:** Ship, H.M.S. Endeavour **Edge:** Cook Bi-Centenary 1769-1969 **Note:** Similar to KM#37.

Date	Mintage	F	VF	XF	Unc	BU
1969	50,000	—	—	1.00	3.00	—
1969 Prooflike	50,000	—	—	—	—	3.00

KM# 37.2   50 CENTS
13.6100 g., Copper-Nickel, 31.75 mm. **Obv:** Crowned bust right **Rev:** Value in upper left **Note:** Recut die, low relief. Many recalled and melted in 2006.

Date	Mintage	F	VF	XF	Unc	BU
1984(o)	2,000,000	—	—	—	3.00	—
1985(o)	2,000,000	—	—	0.50	4.00	—

KM# 95   50 CENTS
Nickel **Ruler:** Elizabeth II **Obv:** Young bust right **Rev:** Voyageur, date and value below **Note:** Mule with Canada Dollar, KM#120..

Date	Mintage	F	VF	XF	Unc	BU
1985 6 known	—	—	1,200	1,900	—	—

KM# 63   50 CENTS
13.6100 g., Copper-Nickel, 31.75 mm. **Ruler:** Elizabeth II **Obv:** Crowned head right **Rev:** Ship, H.M.S. Endeavour **Note:** Many recalled and melted in 2006.

Date	Mintage	F	VF	XF	Unc	BU
1986(o)	5,200,000	—	—	0.50	2.00	—
1986(I)	8,000	—	—	1.00	2.00	—
Note: In sets only.						
1986(I) Proof	10,000	Value: 5.00				
1987(o)	3,600,000	—	—	0.50	2.00	—
1987(I)	18,000	—	—	1.00	2.00	—
Note: In sets only.						
1987(I) Proof	10,000	Value: 5.00				
1988(c)	8,800,000	—	—	0.50	2.00	—
Note: Two die varieties known						
1988(I)	15,000	—	—	—	2.00	—
Note: In sets only						
1988(I) Proof	9,000	Value: 5.00				
1989(c)	15,000	—	—	—	3.00	—
Note: In sets only						
1989(c) Proof	8,500	Value: 5.00				
1990(c)	18,000	—	—	—	5.00	—
Note: In sets only						
1990(c) Proof	10,000	Value: 5.00				
1991(c)	20,000	—	—	—	3.00	—

Date	Mintage	F	VF	XF	Unc	BU
Note: In sets only						
1991(c) Proof	15,000	Value: 5.00				
1992(I)	15,000	—	—	—	4.00	—
Note: In sets only						
1992(I) Proof	9,000	Value: 5.00				
1993(I)	15,000	—	—	—	4.00	—
Note: In sets only						
1993(I) Proof	10,000	Value: 5.00				
1995(I)	10,000	—	—	—	4.00	—
Note: In sets only						
1995(I) Proof	4,000	Value: 5.00				
1996(I)	5,150	—	—	—	4.00	—
1996(I) Proof	2,569	Value: 5.00				
1997(I)	4,150	—	—	—	5.00	—
1997(I) Proof	2,132	Value: 5.00				
1998(I)	4,000	—	—	—	4.00	—
1998(I) Proof	2,000	Value: 5.00				

KM# 75   50 CENTS
13.6100 g., Copper-Nickel, 31.75 mm. **Ruler:** Elizabeth II **Subject:** 1990 Anniversary Celebrations **Obv:** Crowned head right **Rev:** Child with shovel sitting beside tree, value slanted at right

Date	Mintage	F	VF	XF	Unc	BU
1990(c)	10,000	—	—	—	8.00	—
Note: In sets only.						

KM# 75a   50 CENTS
15.7400 g., 0.9250 Silver 0.4681 oz. ASW, 31.75 mm. **Ruler:** Elizabeth II **Subject:** 1990 Anniversary Celebrations **Obv:** Crowned head right **Rev:** Child with shovel sitting beside tree with slanted value at right

Date	Mintage	F	VF	XF	Unc	BU
1990(c) Proof	7,000	Value: 20.00				
Note: In sets only.						

KM# 90   50 CENTS
Bi-Metallic Aluminum-Bronze center in Copper-Nickel ring, 32 mm. **Ruler:** Elizabeth II **Subject:** H.M.S. Endeavour **Obv:** Crowned head right within circle **Rev:** Sailing ship within circle

Date	Mintage	F	VF	XF	Unc	BU
1994	52,500	—	—	—	15.00	—

KM# 90a   50 CENTS
Ring: 0.9250 Silver **Center:** Aluminum-Bronze, 32 mm. **Ruler:** Elizabeth II **Subject:** H.M.S. Endeavour **Obv:** Crowned head right within circle **Rev:** Sailing ship within circle

Date	Mintage	F	VF	XF	Unc	BU
1994 Proof	10,000	Value: 25.00				

KM# 90b   50 CENTS
Ring: 0.3750 Gold **Center:** 0.9160 Gold, 32 mm. **Ruler:** Elizabeth II **Subject:** H.M.S. Endeavour **Obv:** Crowned head right within circle **Rev:** Sailing ship within circle

Date	Mintage	F	VF	XF	Unc	BU
1994 Proof	500	Value: 400				

KM# 119 50 CENTS
13.6100 g., Copper-Nickel, 31.75 mm. **Ruler:** Elizabeth II
Obv: Head with tiara right **Rev:** Ship, H.M.S. Endeavour
Note: Many recalled and melted in 2006.

Date	Mintage	F	VF	XF	Unc	BU
1999	3,199	—	—	—	4.00	—
Note: In sets only						
1999 Proof	1,800	Value: 5.00				
2000	3,000	—	—	—	4.00	—
Note: In sets only						
2000 Proof	1,500	Value: 5.00				

KM# 38.1 DOLLAR
Copper-Nickel, 38.8 mm. **Ruler:** Elizabeth II
Subject: Decimalization Commemorative **Obv:** Young bust right
Rev: Crowned shield within silver fern leaves **Edge:** DECIMAL
CURRENCY INTRODUCED JULY 10 1967

Date	Mintage	F	VF	XF	Unc	BU
1967(I)	250,000	—	—	0.75	1.00	—
1967 Prooflike	50,000	—	—	—	—	2.00
1967 Proof	10	—	—	—	—	—

KM# 38.2 DOLLAR
Copper-Nickel, 38.8 mm. **Ruler:** Elizabeth II **Obv:** Young bust
right **Rev:** Crowned shield within silver fern leaves **Edge:** Reeded
Note: Regular issue.

Date	Mintage	F	VF	XF	Unc	BU
1971(I)	45,000	—	—	2.00	3.00	—
1971 Proof	5,000	Value: 25.00				
1972(c)	42,000	—	—	2.00	3.00	—
1972(c) Proof	8,045	Value: 10.00				
1972(c) RAM case; Proof	3,000	Value: 30.00				
1973(c)	37,000	—	—	2.00	3.00	—
1973 Proof	16,000	Value: 5.00				
1975(I)	30,000	—	—	2.00	3.00	—
1975 Proof	20,000	Value: 5.00				
1976(I)	36,000	—	—	2.00	4.00	—
1976 Proof	22,000	Value: 5.00				

KM# 40.1 DOLLAR
Copper-Nickel, 38.8 mm. **Ruler:** Elizabeth II **Subject:** 200th
Anniversary - Captain Cook's Voyage **Obv:** Young bust right
Rev: Map flanked by bust at left and ship at right
Edge: COMMEMORATING COOK BI-CENTENERY 1769-1969

Date	Mintage	F	VF	XF	Unc	BU
1969(c)	450,000	—	—	1.00	2.00	—
1969 Prooflike	50,000	—	—	—	—	3.00

KM# 40.2 DOLLAR
Copper-Nickel, 38.8 mm. **Ruler:** Elizabeth II **Obv:** Young bust
right **Rev:** Map flanked by bust at left and ship at right **Edge:** No
hyphen in edge inscription

Date	Mintage	F	VF	XF	Unc	BU
1969(c)	Inc. above	—	—	—	4.00	—

KM# 40.3 DOLLAR
Copper Nickel, 38.8 mm. **Ruler:** Elizabeth II **Obv:** Young bust
right **Rev:** Map flanked by bust at left and ship at right **Edge:** No
I in BI-CENTENARY

Date	Mintage	F	VF	XF	Unc	BU
1969(c)	Inc. above					

KM# 42 DOLLAR
Copper-Nickel, 38.8 mm. **Ruler:** Elizabeth II **Subject:** Royal
Visit **Obv:** Young bust right **Rev:** Mount Cook, known as Aorangi

Date	Mintage	F	VF	XF	Unc	BU
1970(c)	315,000	—	—	0.75	1.00	—
1970 Prooflike	20,000	—	—	—	—	2.00

KM# 43 DOLLAR
Copper-Nickel, 38.8 mm. **Ruler:** Elizabeth II **Subject:** Cook
Islands **Obv:** Young bust right **Rev:** Sailing ship to left of bust 1/4 left

Date	Mintage	F	VF	XF	Unc	BU
1970	25,070	—	—	4.00	9.00	—
1970 Proof	5,030	Value: 30.00				

KM# 44 DOLLAR
Copper-Nickel, 38.8 mm. **Ruler:** Elizabeth II
Subject: Commonwealth Games **Obv:** Young bust right
Rev: Square emblem flanked by athletes

Date	Mintage	F	VF	XF	Unc	BU
1974	515,000	—	—	1.00	1.75	—

KM# 44a DOLLAR
27.2160 g., 0.9250 Silver 0.8094 oz. ASW, 38.8 mm.
Ruler: Elizabeth II **Subject:** Commonwealth Games **Obv:** Young
bust right **Rev:** Square emblem flanked by athletes

Date	Mintage	F	VF	XF	Unc	BU
1974 Proof	18,000	Value: 16.00				

KM# 45 DOLLAR
Copper-Nickel, 38.8 mm. **Ruler:** Elizabeth II **Subject:** New
Zealand Day **Obv:** Young bust right **Rev:** Great Egret

Date	Mintage	F	VF	XF	Unc	BU
1974(c)	50,000	—	—	3.00	5.00	12.00
1974 Proof	5,000	Value: 40.00				

KM# 46 DOLLAR
Copper-Nickel, 38.8 mm. **Ruler:** Elizabeth II **Subject:** Waitangi
Day and Queen's Silver Jubilee **Obv:** Young bust right
Rev: Treaty House **Edge:** Reeded

Date	Mintage	F	VF	XF	Unc	BU
1977	90,000	—	—	2.00	3.00	—

KM# 46a DOLLAR
27.2160 g., 0.9250 Silver 0.8094 oz. ASW, 38.8 mm.
Ruler: Elizabeth II **Subject:** Waitangi Day and Queen's 25th
Anniversary **Obv:** Young bust right **Rev:** Treaty House
Edge: Reeded

Date	Mintage	F	VF	XF	Unc	BU
1977 Proof	27,000	Value: 12.50				

KM# 47 DOLLAR
Copper-Nickel, 38.8 mm. **Ruler:** Elizabeth II **Subject:** 25th Anniversary of Coronation and Opening of Parliament Building **Obv:** Young bust right **Rev:** Parliament Building

Date	Mintage	F	VF	XF	Unc	BU
1978(I)	123,000	—	—	1.00	2.00	—

KM# 47a DOLLAR
27.2160 g., 0.9250 Silver 0.8094 oz. ASW, 38.8 mm.
Ruler: Elizabeth II **Subject:** 25th Anniversary of Coronation and Opening of Parliament Building **Obv:** Young bust right **Rev:** Parliament Building

Date	Mintage	F	VF	XF	Unc	BU
1978(o) Proof	33,000		Value: 12.50			

KM# 50 DOLLAR
Copper-Nickel, 38.8 mm. **Ruler:** Elizabeth II **Subject:** Royal Visit **Obv:** New head right **Rev:** English Oak **Edge:** Reeded

Date	Mintage	F	VF	XF	Unc	BU
1981(I)	100,000	—	—	1.00	2.00	—

KM# 50a DOLLAR
27.2160 g., 0.9250 Silver 0.8094 oz. ASW, 38.8 mm.
Ruler: Elizabeth II **Subject:** Royal Visit **Obv:** New head right **Rev:** English Oak **Edge:** Reeded

Date	Mintage	F	VF	XF	Unc	BU
1981(I) Proof	38,000		Value: 12.50			

KM# 53 DOLLAR
Copper-Nickel, 38.8 mm. **Ruler:** Elizabeth II **Subject:** 50 Years of New Zealand Coinage **Obv:** Young bust right **Rev:** Crowned arms with supporters above various coins **Edge:** Reeded

Date	Mintage	F	VF	XF	Unc	BU
1983(I)	65,000	—	—	1.00	4.00	—

KM# 53a DOLLAR
27.2160 g., 0.9250 Silver 0.8094 oz. ASW, 38.8 mm.
Ruler: Elizabeth II **Subject:** 50 Years of New Zealand Coinage **Obv:** Young bust right **Rev:** Crowned arms with supporters above various coins **Edge:** Reeded

Date	Mintage	F	VF	XF	Unc	BU
1983(I) Proof	35,000		Value: 12.50			

KM# 48 DOLLAR
Copper-Nickel, 38.8 mm. **Ruler:** Elizabeth II **Obv:** New head right **Rev:** Crowned shield within silver fern **Edge:** Reeded

Date	Mintage	F	VF	XF	Unc	BU
1979(o)	25,000	—	—	1.00	2.00	—
1979(o) Proof	85,000	—	—	—	4.00	—

KM# 48a DOLLAR
27.2160 g., 0.9250 Silver 0.8094 oz. ASW, 38.8 mm.
Ruler: Elizabeth II **Obv:** New head right **Rev:** Crowned shield within silver fern **Edge:** Reeded

Date	Mintage	F	VF	XF	Unc	BU
1979(o) Proof	35,000		Value: 12.50			

KM# 51 DOLLAR
Copper-Nickel, 38.8 mm. **Ruler:** Elizabeth II **Obv:** New head right **Rev:** Takahe bird **Edge:** Reeded

Date	Mintage	F	VF	XF	Unc	BU
1982(I)	65,000	—	—	1.00	8.00	12.00

KM# 51a DOLLAR
27.2160 g., 0.9250 Silver 0.8094 oz. ASW, 38.8 mm.
Ruler: Elizabeth II **Obv:** New head right **Rev:** Takahe bird **Edge:** Reeded

Date	Mintage	F	VF	XF	Unc	BU
1982(I) Proof	35,000		Value: 17.50			

KM# 54 DOLLAR
Copper-Nickel, 38.8 mm. **Ruler:** Elizabeth II **Subject:** Chatham Island **Obv:** Young bust right **Rev:** Black Robin on branch **Edge:** Reeded

Date	Mintage	F	VF	XF	Unc	BU
1984(I)	65,000	—	—	1.00	2.50	12.50

KM# 54a DOLLAR
27.2160 g., 0.9250 Silver 0.8094 oz. ASW, 38.8 mm.
Ruler: Elizabeth II **Subject:** Chatham Island **Obv:** Young bust right **Rev:** Black Robin on branch **Edge:** Reeded

Date	Mintage	F	VF	XF	Unc	BU
1984(I) Proof	30,000		Value: 17.50			

KM# 49 DOLLAR
Copper-Nickel, 38.8 mm. **Ruler:** Elizabeth II **Obv:** New head right **Rev:** Fantail bird sitting on branch **Edge:** Reeded

Date	Mintage	F	VF	XF	Unc	BU
1980(I)	115,000	—	—	1.00	3.00	7.50

KM# 49a DOLLAR
27.2160 g., 0.9250 Silver 0.8094 oz. ASW, 38.8 mm.
Ruler: Elizabeth II **Obv:** New head right **Rev:** Fantail bird sitting on branch **Edge:** Reeded

Date	Mintage	F	VF	XF	Unc	BU
1980(I) Proof	44,000		Value: 20.00			

KM# 52 DOLLAR
Copper-Nickel, 38.8 mm. **Ruler:** Elizabeth II **Subject:** Royal Visit **Obv:** Young bust right **Rev:** Conjoined busts of Prince Charles and Lady Diana right **Edge:** Reeded

Date	Mintage	F	VF	XF	Unc	BU
1983(I)	40,000	—	—	1.00	4.00	—

KM# 52a DOLLAR
27.2160 g., 0.9250 Silver 0.8094 oz. ASW, 38.8 mm.
Ruler: Elizabeth II **Subject:** Royal Visit **Obv:** Young bust right **Rev:** Conjoined busts of Prince Charles and Lady Diana right **Edge:** Reeded

Date	Mintage	F	VF	XF	Unc	BU
1983(I) Proof	17,000		Value: 12.50			

KM# 55 DOLLAR
Copper-Nickel, 38.8 mm. **Ruler:** Elizabeth II **Subject:** Black Stilt **Obv:** Young bust right **Edge:** Reeded

Date	Mintage	F	VF	XF	Unc	BU
1985(c)	60,000	—	—	1.00	4.00	9.00

KM# 55a DOLLAR
27.2160 g., 0.9250 Silver 0.8094 oz. ASW, 38.8 mm.
Ruler: Elizabeth II **Subject:** Black Stilt **Obv:** Young bust right **Rev:** Black stilt and chicks **Edge:** Reeded

Date	Mintage	F	VF	XF	Unc	BU
1985(c) Proof	25,000		Value: 17.50			

KM# 56 DOLLAR
Copper-Nickel, 38.8 mm. **Ruler:** Elizabeth II **Subject:** Royal Visit **Obv:** Crowned head right **Rev:** Crowned E within wreath of houhere, clematis, Mt. Cook lilly, rata, pohutukawa, kowhai, kaka beak, manuka and fern fronds **Edge:** Reeded

Date	Mintage	F	VF	XF	Unc	BU
1986(I)	40,000	—	—	1.00	3.00	—

KM# 56a DOLLAR
27.2160 g., 0.9250 Silver 0.8094 oz. ASW, 38.8 mm.
Ruler: Elizabeth II **Subject:** Royal Visit **Obv:** Crowned head right **Rev:** Crowned E within wreath of houhere, clematis, Mt. Cook lilly, rata, pohutukawa, kowhai, kaka beak, manuka and fern fronds **Edge:** Reeded

Date	Mintage	F	VF	XF	Unc	BU
1986(I) Proof	12,500	Value: 12.50				

KM# 57 DOLLAR
Copper-Nickel, 38.8 mm. **Ruler:** Elizabeth II **Obv:** Crowned head right **Rev:** Kakapo bird **Edge:** Reeded

Date	Mintage	F	VF	XF	Unc	BU
1986(c)	53,000	—	—	1.00	5.00	10.00

KM# 57a DOLLAR
27.2160 g., 0.9250 Silver 0.8094 oz. ASW, 38.8 mm.
Ruler: Elizabeth II **Obv:** Crowned head right **Rev:** Kakapo bird **Edge:** Reeded

Date	Mintage	F	VF	XF	Unc	BU
1986(I) Proof	20,500	Value: 24.00				

KM# 65 DOLLAR
Copper-Nickel, 38.8 mm. **Ruler:** Elizabeth II **Subject:** National Parks Centennial **Obv:** Crowned head right **Rev:** Mountains within circular design **Edge:** Reeded

Date	Mintage	F	VF	XF	Unc	BU
1987(I)	53,000	—	—	1.00	3.00	—

KM# 65a DOLLAR
27.2160 g., 0.9250 Silver 0.8094 oz. ASW, 38.8 mm.
Ruler: Elizabeth II **Subject:** National Parks Centennial **Obv:** Crowned head right **Rev:** Mountains within circular design **Edge:** Reeded

Date	Mintage	F	VF	XF	Unc	BU
1987(I) Proof	20,500	Value: 12.50				

KM# 66 DOLLAR
Copper-Nickel, 38.8 mm. **Ruler:** Edward VIII **Obv:** Crowned head right **Rev:** Yellow-eyed Penguin

Date	Mintage	F	VF	XF	Unc	BU
1988(I)	45,000	—	—	2.00	10.00	22.00

KM# 66a DOLLAR
27.2160 g., 0.9250 Silver 0.8094 oz. ASW, 38.8 mm.
Ruler: Elizabeth II **Obv:** Crowned head right **Rev:** Yellow-eyed Penguin

Date	Mintage	F	VF	XF	Unc	BU
1988 Proof	18,500	Value: 25.00				

KM# 67 DOLLAR
Copper-Nickel, 38.8 mm. **Ruler:** Elizabeth II **Subject:** XIV Commonwealth Games **Obv:** Crowned head right **Rev:** Runner

Date	Mintage	F	VF	XF	Unc	BU
1989(c)	35,000	—	—	1.00	2.00	—

KM# 67a DOLLAR
27.2160 g., 0.9250 Silver 0.8094 oz. ASW, 38.8 mm.
Ruler: Elizabeth II **Subject:** XIV Commonwealth Games **Obv:** Crowned head right **Rev:** Runner

Date	Mintage	F	VF	XF	Unc	BU
1989 Proof	8,600	Value: 12.50				

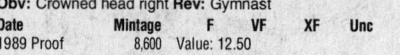

KM# 68 DOLLAR
Copper-Nickel, 38.8 mm. **Ruler:** Elizabeth II **Subject:** XIV Commonwealth Games **Obv:** Crowned head right **Rev:** Gymnast

Date	Mintage	F	VF	XF	Unc	BU
1989	35,000	—	—	1.00	2.00	—

KM# 68a DOLLAR
27.2160 g., 0.9250 Silver 0.8094 oz. ASW, 38.8 mm.
Ruler: Elizabeth II **Subject:** XIV Commonwealth Games **Obv:** Crowned head right **Rev:** Gymnast

Date	Mintage	F	VF	XF	Unc	BU
1989 Proof	8,600	Value: 12.50				

KM# 69 DOLLAR
Copper-Nickel, 38.8 mm. **Ruler:** Elizabeth II **Subject:** XIV Commonwealth Games **Obv:** Crowned head right **Rev:** Swimmer

Date	Mintage	F	VF	XF	Unc	BU
1989	35,000	—	—	1.00	2.00	—

KM# 69a DOLLAR
27.2160 g., 0.9250 Silver 0.8094 oz. ASW, 38.8 mm.
Ruler: Elizabeth II **Subject:** XIV Commonwealth Games **Obv:** Crowned head right **Rev:** Swimmer

Date	Mintage	F	VF	XF	Unc	BU
1989 Proof	8,600	Value: 12.50				

KM# 70 DOLLAR
Copper-Nickel, 38.8 mm. **Ruler:** Elizabeth II **Subject:** XIV Commonwealth Games **Obv:** Crowned head right **Rev:** Weight lifter

Date	Mintage	F	VF	XF	Unc	BU
1989	35,000	—	—	1.00	2.00	—

KM# 70a DOLLAR
27.2160 g., 0.9250 Silver 0.8094 oz. ASW, 38.8 mm.
Ruler: Elizabeth II **Subject:** XIV Commonwealth Games **Obv:** Crowned head right **Rev:** Weight lifter

Date	Mintage	F	VF	XF	Unc	BU
1989 Proof	8,600	Value: 12.50				

KM# 78 DOLLAR
8.0000 g., Aluminum-Bronze, 23 mm. **Ruler:** Elizabeth II **Obv:** Crowned head right **Rev:** Kiwi Bird **Note:** Regular circulation issue.

Date	Mintage	F	VF	XF	Unc	BU
1990(I)	40,000,000	—	—	1.00	3.00	5.00
1990(c)	10,000	—	—	—	4.00	5.00
Note: In sets only.						
1991(I)	10,000,000	—	—	1.00	3.00	5.00
1991(c)	20,000	—	—	—	3.00	5.00
Note: In sets only.						
1991(c) Proof	15,000	Value: 20.00				
1992(I)	15,000	—	—	—	15.00	—
Note: In sets only						
1992(I) Proof	9,000	Value: 20.00				
1993(I)	15,000	—	—	—	10.00	—
Note: In sets only						
1993(I) Proof	10,000	Value: 20.00				
1994(I)	16,000	—	—	—	20.00	—
Note: In sets only						
1994(I) Proof	4,600	Value: 25.00				
1995(I)	6,000	—	—	—	20.00	—
Note: In sets only						
1995(I) Proof	3,560	Value: 25.00				
1996(I)	5,150	—	—	—	20.00	—
Note: In sets only						
1996(I) Proof	4,000	Value: 25.00				
1997(I)	4,150	—	—	—	20.00	—
Note: In sets only						
1997(I) Proof	2,132	Value: 25.00				
1998(I)	4,000	—	—	—	20.00	—
Note: In sets only						
1998(I) Proof	2,000	Value: 25.00				

KM# 76 DOLLAR
Copper-Nickel, 38.8 mm. **Ruler:** Elizabeth II **Subject:** 1990 Anniversary Celebrations - Treaty of Waitangi **Obv:** Crowned head right **Rev:** Treaty signing scene

Date	Mintage	F	VF	XF	Unc	BU
1990	—	—	—	1.00	3.00	—

KM# 76a DOLLAR
27.2160 g., 0.9250 Silver 0.8094 oz. ASW, 38.8 mm. **Ruler:** Elizabeth II **Subject:** 1990 Anniversary Celebrations - Treaty of Waitangi **Obv:** Crowned head right **Rev:** Treaty signing scene

Date	Mintage	F	VF	XF	Unc	BU
1990 Proof	20,000	Value: 16.00				

KM# 78a DOLLAR
8.0000 g., 0.9250 Silver 0.2379 oz. ASW, 23 mm. **Ruler:** Elizabeth II **Obv:** Crowned head right **Rev:** Kiwi Bird

Date	Mintage	F	VF	XF	Unc	BU
1990 Proof	10,000	Value: 30.00				

KM# 120 DOLLAR
8.0000 g., Aluminum-Bronze **Ruler:** Elizabeth II **Obv:** Head with tiara right **Rev:** Kiwi bird within sprigs

Date	Mintage	F	VF	XF	Unc	BU
1999	3,199	—	—	—	—	20.00
Note: In sets only						
1999 Proof	1,800	Value: 20.00				
2000(o)	5,000,000	—	—	—	1.00	3.00
2000 Proof	1,500	Value: 5.00				

KM# 79 2 DOLLARS
10.0000 g., Aluminum-Bronze, 26.5 mm. **Ruler:** Elizabeth II **Obv:** Crowned head right **Rev:** Kotuku, white heron

Date	Mintage	F	VF	XF	Unc	BU
1990(c)	18,000	—	—	—	3.00	5.00
1990(I)	30,000,000	—	—	2.00	3.00	5.00
1991(I)	10,000,000	—	—	2.00	3.00	5.00
1991(c)	20,000	—	—	—	3.00	5.00
1991(c) Proof	15,000	Value: 6.00				
1992(I)	15,000	—	—	—	6.00	—
Note: In sets only						
1992(I) Proof	9,000	Value: 6.00				
1994(I)	7,000	—	—	—	6.00	—
Note: In sets only						
1994(I) Proof	4,600	Value: 6.00				
1995(I)	6,000	—	—	—	6.00	—
Note: In sets only						
1995(I) Proof	3,560	Value: 20.00				
1996(I)	5,150	—	—	—	20.00	—
Note: In sets only						
1996(I) Proof	2,569	Value: 20.00				
1997(I)	4,150	—	—	—	—	—
Note: In sets only.						
1997(I) Proof	2,132	—	—	—	—	—
1997(p)	1,000,000	—	—	—	3.00	5.00
Note: Entire mintage recalled, but many left in circulation						
1998(p)	6,000,000	—	—	—	3.00	5.00
1998(p) Proof	2,000	Value: 6.00				

KM# 79a 2 DOLLARS
10.0000 g., 0.9250 Silver 0.2974 oz. ASW, 26.5 mm. **Ruler:** Elizabeth II **Obv:** Crowned head right **Rev:** Kotuku, white heron

Date	Mintage	F	VF	XF	Unc	BU
1990 Proof	10,000	Value: 25.00				

KM# 87 2 DOLLARS
Aluminum-Bronze **Ruler:** Elizabeth II **Obv:** Crowned head right **Rev:** Sacred Kingfisher

Date	Mintage	F	VF	XF	Unc	BU
1993	40,000	—	—	—	7.50	12.00

KM# 87a 2 DOLLARS
10.0000 g., 0.9250 Silver 0.2974 oz. ASW **Ruler:** Elizabeth II **Obv:** Crowned head right **Rev:** Sacred Kingfisher

Date	Mintage	F	VF	XF	Unc	BU
1993 Proof	10,000	Value: 20.00				

KM# 121 2 DOLLARS
10.0000 g., Aluminum-Bronze, 26.5 mm. **Ruler:** Elizabeth II **Obv:** Head with tiara right **Rev:** Great Egret above value

Date	Mintage	F	VF	XF	Unc	BU
1999(p)	5,050,000	—	—	—	3.00	5.00
1999(I) Proof	2,000	Value: 25.00				
2000	3,000	—	—	—	2.50	5.00
Note: In sets only						
2000(I) Proof	1,500	Value: 25.00				

KM# 71 5 DOLLARS
Aluminum-Bronze **Ruler:** Elizabeth II **Obv:** Crowned head right **Rev:** ANZAC Memorial

Date	Mintage	F	VF	XF	Unc	BU
1990 Proof	60,000	Value: 17.50				
Note: Set only, issued with Australian 1990 $5 as pair						

KM# 80 5 DOLLARS
Copper-Nickel **Ruler:** Elizabeth II **Subject:** Rugby World Cup **Obv:** Crowned head right **Rev:** Champion cup flanked by rugby players

Date	Mintage	F	VF	XF	Unc	BU
1991	120,000	—	—	—	4.50	6.00

KM# 80a 5 DOLLARS
27.2200 g., 0.9250 Silver 0.8095 oz. ASW **Ruler:** Elizabeth II **Subject:** Rugby World Cup **Obv:** Crowned head right **Rev:** Champion cup flanked by rugby players

Date	Mintage	F	VF	XF	Unc	BU
1991 Proof	30,000	Value: 16.00				

KM# 82 5 DOLLARS
Copper-Nickel **Ruler:** Elizabeth II **Subject:** 25th Anniversary of Decimal Currency **Obv:** Crowned head right **Rev:** Silver fern leaf above various coins

Date	Mintage	F	VF	XF	Unc	BU
1992	34,000	—	—	—	5.00	6.00

KM# 82a 5 DOLLARS
27.2200 g., 0.9250 Silver 0.8095 oz. ASW **Ruler:** Elizabeth II **Subject:** 25th Anniversary of Decimal Currency **Obv:** Crowned head right **Rev:** Silver fern leaf above various coins

Date	Mintage	F	VF	XF	Unc	BU
1992 Proof	17,000	Value: 16.00				

KM# 83 5 DOLLARS
Copper-Nickel **Ruler:** Elizabeth II **Series:** The Discoverers **Subject:** Mythological Maori Hero - Kupe **Obv:** Crowned head right **Rev:** Bust right

Date	Mintage	F	VF	XF	Unc	BU
1992	40,000	—	—	—	5.00	—

KM# 84 5 DOLLARS
Copper-Nickel **Ruler:** Elizabeth II **Series:** The Discoverers **Subject:** Abel Tasman **Obv:** Crowned head right

Date	Mintage	F	VF	XF	Unc	BU
1992	40,000	—	—	—	5.00	—

KM# 85 5 DOLLARS
Copper-Nickel **Ruler:** Elizabeth II **Series:** The Discoverers **Subject:** Captain James Cook **Obv:** Crowned head right **Rev:** Bust 1/4 right

Date	Mintage	F	VF	XF	Unc	BU
1992	40,000	—	—	—	5.00	—

KM# 86 5 DOLLARS
Copper-Nickel **Ruler:** Elizabeth II **Series:** The Discoverers
Subject: Christopher Columbus **Obv:** Crowned head right
Rev: Bust 1/4 right

Date	Mintage	F	VF	XF	Unc	BU
1992	40,000	—	—	—	5.00	—

KM# 88 5 DOLLARS
Copper-Nickel **Ruler:** Elizabeth II **Subject:** 40th Anniversary of
Coronation **Obv:** Crowned head right **Rev:** Coronation emblem
within squares, all within artistic designed circle

Date	Mintage	F	VF	XF	Unc	BU
1993	15,000	—	—	—	5.00	7.00

KM# 88a 5 DOLLARS
27.2200 g., 0.9250 Silver 0.8095 oz. ASW **Ruler:** Elizabeth II
Subject: 40th Anniversary of Coronation **Obv:** Crowned head
right **Rev:** Coronation emblem within squares, all within artistic
designed circle

Date	Mintage	F	VF	XF	Unc	BU
1993 Proof	15,000	Value: 20.00				

KM# 88b 5 DOLLARS
47.5250 g., 0.9170 Gold 1.4011 oz. AGW **Ruler:** Elizabeth II
Subject: 40th Anniversary of Coronation **Obv:** Crowned head
right **Rev:** Coronation emblem within squares, all within artistic
designed circle

Date	Mintage	F	VF	XF	Unc	BU
1993 Proof	210	Value: 1,450				

KM# 89 5 DOLLARS
31.4700 g., 0.9250 Silver 0.9359 oz. ASW **Ruler:** Elizabeth II
Subject: Endangered Wildlife **Obv:** Crowned head right
Rev: Hooker Sea Lions

Date	Mintage	F	VF	XF	Unc	BU
1993 Proof	20,000	Value: 30.00				

KM# 91 5 DOLLARS
28.2800 g., 0.9250 Silver 0.8410 oz. ASW **Ruler:** Elizabeth II
Obv: Crowned head right **Rev:** Queen mother and infant
Elizabeth within beaded circle

Date	Mintage	F	VF	XF	Unc	BU
1994 Proof	34,600	Value: 30.00				

KM# 96 5 DOLLARS
31.4700 g., 0.9250 Silver 0.9359 oz. ASW **Ruler:** Elizabeth II
Series: Winter Olympics - 1994 **Obv:** Crowned head right
Rev: Downhill skier

Date	Mintage	F	VF	XF	Unc	BU
1994 Proof	33,300	Value: 30.00				

KM# 92 5 DOLLARS
31.4700 g., 0.9250 Silver 0.9359 oz. ASW **Ruler:** Elizabeth II
Subject: Antarctica **Obv:** Crowned head right **Rev:** James Clark
Ross

Date	Mintage	F	VF	XF	Unc	BU
1995 Proof	13,000	Value: 30.00				

KM# 93 5 DOLLARS
Copper-Nickel **Ruler:** Elizabeth II **Obv:** Crowned head right
Rev: Tui bird sitting on branch

Date	Mintage	F	VF	XF	Unc	BU
1995	11,000	—	—	—	12.50	15.00

KM# 93a 5 DOLLARS
28.2800 g., 0.9250 Silver 0.8410 oz. ASW **Ruler:** Elizabeth II
Obv: Crowned head right **Rev:** Tui bird sitting on branch

Date	Mintage	F	VF	XF	Unc	BU
1995 Proof	7,000	Value: 25.00				

KM# 97 5 DOLLARS
Copper-Nickel, 38.61 mm. **Ruler:** Elizabeth II **Obv:** Crowned
head right **Rev:** Kaka (Bush Parrot)

Date	Mintage	F	VF	XF	Unc	BU
1996	11,000	—	—	—	12.00	25.00

KM# 97a 5 DOLLARS
28.2800 g., 0.9250 Silver 0.8410 oz. ASW **Ruler:** Elizabeth II
Obv: Crowned head right **Rev:** Kaka (Bush parrot)

Date	Mintage	F	VF	XF	Unc	BU
1996 Proof	7,000	Value: 30.00				

KM# 99 5 DOLLARS
Copper-Nickel, 38.61 mm. **Ruler:** Elizabeth II **Subject:** Auckland
City of Sails **Obv:** Crowned head right **Rev:** Bridge and boats

Date	Mintage	F	VF	XF	Unc	BU
1996(I)	6,000	—	—	—	8.00	10.00

KM# 99a 5 DOLLARS
28.2800 g., 0.9250 Silver 0.8410 oz. ASW **Ruler:** Elizabeth II
Subject: Auckland - City of Sails **Obv:** Crowned head right
Rev: Bridge and boats

Date	Mintage	F	VF	XF	Unc	BU
1996 Proof	3,000	Value: 40.00				

KM# 101 5 DOLLARS
28.4500 g., 0.9250 Silver 0.8461 oz. ASW **Ruler:** Elizabeth II
Obv: Crowned head right **Rev:** Crowned belt wreath flanked by
flowers

Date	Mintage	F	VF	XF	Unc	BU
1996(I)	3,000	—	—	—	50.00	—

Note: In sets only with $20 commemorative banknote

KM# 102 5 DOLLARS
25.2200 g., 0.9250 Silver 0.7500 oz. ASW **Ruler:** Elizabeth II
Subject: De Heemskerck **Obv:** Crowned head right **Rev:** Sailship
on globe with map

Date	Mintage	F	VF	XF	Unc	BU
1996(o) Proof	18,000	Value: 45.00				

KM# 103 5 DOLLARS
Copper-Nickel, 38.61 mm. **Ruler:** Elizabeth II **Subject:** WWF
Conserving Nature **Obv:** Crowned head right **Rev:** Saddleback bird

Date	Mintage	F	VF	XF	Unc	BU
1997(I)	8,000	—	—	—	9.00	12.00

KM# 103a 5 DOLLARS
28.2800 g., 0.9250 Silver 0.8410 oz. ASW **Ruler:** Elizabeth II
Subject: WWF Conserving Nature **Obv:** Crowned head right
Rev: Saddleback bird

Date	Mintage	F	VF	XF	Unc	BU
1997 Proof	19,000	Value: 35.00				

KM# 105 5 DOLLARS
Copper-Nickel **Ruler:** Elizabeth II **Subject:** Queen's Golden
Wedding Anniversary **Obv:** Crowned head right **Rev:** Coronation
scene

Date	Mintage	F	VF	XF	Unc	BU
1997	9,000	—	—	—	20.00	—

KM# 105a 5 DOLLARS
28.2800 g., 0.9250 Silver 0.8410 oz. ASW **Ruler:** Elizabeth II
Subject: Queen's Golden Wedding Anniversary **Obv:** Crowned
head right **Rev:** Coronation scene

Date	Mintage	F	VF	XF	Unc	BU
1997 Proof	32,500	Value: 25.00				

KM# 106 5 DOLLARS
Ruler: Elizabeth II **Subject:** City of Christchurch **Obv:** Crowned
head right **Rev:** Value above church

Date	Mintage	F	VF	XF	Unc	BU
1997	5,000	—	—	—	10.00	15.00

KM# 106a 5 DOLLARS
28.2800 g., 0.9250 Silver 0.8410 oz. ASW **Ruler:** Elizabeth II
Subject: City of Christchurch **Obv:** Crowned head right
Rev: Value above church

Date	Mintage	F	VF	XF	Unc	BU
1997	3,000	Value: 40.00				

KM# 107 5 DOLLARS
Copper-Nickel **Ruler:** Elizabeth II **Obv:** Crowned head right
Rev: Royal Albatross

Date	Mintage	F	VF	XF	Unc	BU
1998	6,500	—	—	—	10.00	18.00

KM# 107a 5 DOLLARS
29.2000 g., 0.9250 Silver 0.8684 oz. ASW **Ruler:** Elizabeth II
Obv: Crowned head right **Rev:** Royal Albatross

Date	Mintage	F	VF	XF	Unc	BU
1998 Proof	2,500	Value: 65.00				

KM# 109 5 DOLLARS
Copper-Nickel **Ruler:** Elizabeth II **Subject:** Pride in New
Zealand **Obv:** Crowned head right **Rev:** Four stars

Date	Mintage	F	VF	XF	Unc	BU
1998(v) in sets only	2,000	—	—	—	10.00	—

KM# 109a 5 DOLLARS
6.0000 g., 0.9990 Silver 0.1927 oz. ASW **Ruler:** Elizabeth II
Subject: Pride in New Zealand **Obv:** Crowned head right
Rev: Four stars

Date	Mintage	F	VF	XF	Unc	BU
1998(v) in sets only	1,200	—	—	—	15.00	—

KM# 110 5 DOLLARS
Copper-Nickel **Ruler:** Elizabeth II **Subject:** Pride in New
Zealand **Obv:** Crowned head right **Rev:** Fleece

Date	Mintage	F	VF	XF	Unc	BU
1998(v) in sets only	2,000	—	—	—	10.00	—

KM# 110a 5 DOLLARS
6.0000 g., 0.9990 Silver 0.1927 oz. ASW **Ruler:** Elizabeth II
Subject: Pride in New Zealand **Obv:** Crowned head right
Rev: Fleece

Date	Mintage	F	VF	XF	Unc	BU
1998(v) in sets only	1,200	—	—	—	15.00	—

KM# 111 5 DOLLARS
Copper-Nickel **Ruler:** Elizabeth II **Subject:** Pride in New
Zealand **Obv:** Crowned head right **Rev:** Wheat sheaf

Date	Mintage	F	VF	XF	Unc	BU
1998(v) in sets only	2,000	—	—	—	10.00	—

KM# 111a 5 DOLLARS
6.0000 g., 0.9990 Silver 0.1927 oz. ASW **Ruler:** Elizabeth II
Subject: Pride in New Zealand **Obv:** Crowned head right **Rev:**
Wheat sheaf

Date	Mintage	F	VF	XF	Unc	BU
1998(v) in sets only	1,200	—	—	—	15.00	—

KM# 112 5 DOLLARS
Copper-Nickel **Ruler:** Elizabeth II **Subject:** Pride in New
Zealand **Obv:** Crowned head right **Rev:** Crossed hammers

Date	Mintage	F	VF	XF	Unc	BU
1998(v) in sets only	2,000	—	—	—	10.00	—

KM# 112a 5 DOLLARS
6.0000 g., 0.9990 Silver 0.1927 oz. ASW **Ruler:** Elizabeth II
Subject: Pride in New Zealand **Obv:** Crowned head right
Rev: Crossed hammers

Date	Mintage	F	VF	XF	Unc	BU
1998(v) in sets only	1,200	—	—	—	15.00	—

KM# 113 5 DOLLARS
Copper-Nickel **Ruler:** Elizabeth II **Subject:** Dunedin
Obv: Crowned head right **Rev:** Larnach Castle

Date	Mintage	F	VF	XF	Unc	BU
1998(v)	4,000	—	—	—	10.00	—

KM# 113a 5 DOLLARS
28.2800 g., 0.9250 Silver 0.8410 oz. ASW **Ruler:** Elizabeth II
Subject: Dunedin **Obv:** Crowned head right **Rev:** Larnach Castle

Date	Mintage	F	VF	XF	Unc	BU
1998 Proof	2,500	Value: 30.00				

KM# 115 5 DOLLARS
Copper-Nickel **Ruler:** Elizabeth II **Obv:** Head with tiara right
Rev: Morepork on branch

Date	Mintage	F	VF	XF	Unc	BU
1999	7,500	—	—	—	15.00	27.00

KM# 115a 5 DOLLARS
28.2800 g., 0.9990 Silver 0.9083 oz. ASW **Ruler:** Elizabeth II
Obv: Head with tiara right **Rev:** Morepork

Date	Mintage	F	VF	XF	Unc	BU
1999 Proof	7,000	Value: 45.00				

KM# 123 5 DOLLARS
31.0500 g., 0.9250 Silver 0.9234 oz. ASW, 38.7 mm.
Ruler: Elizabeth II **Subject:** Wellington Harbour Capital
Obv: Head with tiara right **Rev:** City view with ship **Edge:** Reeded

Date	Mintage	F	VF	XF	Unc	BU
1999(v) Proof	2,500	Value: 30.00				

KM# 125 5 DOLLARS
32.2000 g., Copper-Nickel, 38.6 mm. **Ruler:** Elizabeth II
Obv: Head with tiara right **Rev:** Perching cormorant bird
Edge: Reeded

Date	Mintage	F	VF	XF	Unc	BU
2000(v) Frosted finish	5,500	—	—	—	12.00	17.50

KM# 127 5 DOLLARS
32.2000 g., Copper-Nickel, 38.6 mm. **Ruler:** Elizabeth II
Obv: Queen's portrait from dies of Solomon Islands KM67-68
Rev: Pied Cormorant for dies of New Zealand KM125
Edge: Reeded **Note:** Mule.

Date	Mintage	F	VF	XF	Unc	BU
2000(v)	Est. 50	—	—	—	—	1,000

Note: This coin is included in a New Zealand mint set dated 2000

KM# 125a 5 DOLLARS
31.1300 g., 0.9990 Silver 0.9998 oz. ASW **Ruler:** Elizabeth II
Obv: Head with tiara right **Rev:** Perching cormorant
Note: Heavier than the official weight of 28.28 grams.

Date	Mintage	F	VF	XF	Unc	BU
2000(v) Proof	5,000	Value: 35.00				

KM# 94   10 DOLLARS
Aluminum-Bronze **Ruler:** Elizabeth II **Obv:** Crowned head right
Rev: Gold Prospector

Date	Mintage	F	VF	XF	Unc	BU
1995(I)	7,000	—	—	—	—	15.00

KM# 94a   10 DOLLARS
0.9990 Gold **Ruler:** Elizabeth II **Obv:** Crowned head right
Rev: Gold Prospector

Date	Mintage	F	VF	XF	Unc	BU
1995(I) Proof	600	Value: 435				

KM# 98   10 DOLLARS
Aluminum-Bronze **Ruler:** Elizabeth II **Subject:** Sinking of General
Grant **Obv:** Crowned head right **Rev:** Sinking ship above value

Date	Mintage	F	VF	XF	Unc	BU
1996(I) Prooflike	6,000	—	—	—	—	15.00

KM# 98a   10 DOLLARS
0.9990 Gold **Ruler:** Elizabeth II **Subject:** Sinking of The General
Grant **Obv:** Crowned head right **Rev:** Sinking ship above value

Date	Mintage	F	VF	XF	Unc	BU
1996(I) Proof	650	Value: 450				

KM# 104   10 DOLLARS
Aluminum-Bronze **Ruler:** Elizabeth II **Subject:** Gabriel's Gully
Obv: Crowned head right **Rev:** Prospector climbing hill with
shovel in hand

Date	Mintage	F	VF	XF	Unc	BU
1997(I)	3,000	—	—	—	—	17.50

KM# 104a   10 DOLLARS
0.9990 Gold **Ruler:** Elizabeth II **Subject:** Gabriel's Gully
Obv: Crowned head right **Rev:** Prospector climbing hill with shovel
in hand

Date	Mintage	F	VF	XF	Unc	BU
1997(I) Proof	650	Value: 435				

KM# 114   10 DOLLARS
Copper-Zinc **Ruler:** Elizabeth II **Subject:** Century of Motoring
Obv: Crowned head right **Rev:** Karl Benz driving his automobile

Date	Mintage	F	VF	XF	Unc	BU
1998(v)	2,000	—	—	—	—	15.00

KM# 114a   10 DOLLARS
Copper-Nickel, Gold Plated **Ruler:** Elizabeth II **Subject:** Century
of Motoring **Obv:** Crowned head right **Rev:** Karl Benz driving his
automobile

Date	Mintage	F	VF	XF	Unc	BU
1998(v) Proof	1,500	Value: 45.00				

KM# 124   10 DOLLARS
15.4500 g., 0.9990 Silver 0.4962 oz. ASW, 29.9 mm.
Ruler: Elizabeth II **Obv:** Crowned head right **Rev:** Kiwi bird below
silver fern leaf **Edge:** Reeded

Date	Mintage	F	VF	XF	Unc	BU
1998	1,500	—	—	—	110	120

KM# 122   10 DOLLARS
28.3700 g., 0.9250 Silver 0.8437 oz. ASW **Ruler:** Elizabeth II
Subject: New Zealand - First to the Future **Obv:** Head with tiara
right **Rev:** Gold-plated map of New Zealand, gold printed radiant
sun **Edge:** Reeded

Date	Mintage	F	VF	XF	Unc	BU
2000(1999) Proof	33,000	Value: 40.00				

KM# 100   20 DOLLARS
31.1030 g., 0.9250 Silver 0.9249 oz. ASW **Ruler:** Elizabeth II
Subject: Salute to Bravery **Obv:** Crowned head right **Rev:** Cameo
at left, Captain Charles Upham, Victoria Cross and Bar at right

Date	Mintage	F	VF	XF	Unc	BU
1995 Proof	3,500	Value: 40.00				

KM# 108   20 DOLLARS
28.2800 g., 0.9250 Silver 0.8410 oz. ASW **Ruler:** Elizabeth II
Subject: Queen's Golden Wedding Anniversary **Obv:** Crowned
head right **Rev:** Coronation scene **Note:** Similar to 5 Dollars,
KM#105.

Date	Mintage	F	VF	XF	Unc	BU
1997 Proof	32,500	Value: 40.00				

KM# 77   150 DOLLARS
16.9500 g., 0.9170 Gold 0.4997 oz. AGW **Ruler:** Elizabeth II
Obv: Crowned head right **Rev:** Kiwi

Date	Mintage	F	VF	XF	Unc	BU
1990 Proof	10,000	Value: 485				

KM# 126   150 DOLLARS
15.6000 g., 0.9950 Platinum 0.4990 oz. APW, 30 mm.
Ruler: Elizabeth II **Obv:** Crowned head right **Rev:** Two Kiwi and
fern **Edge:** Reeded

Date	Mintage	F	VF	XF	Unc	BU
1998 Proof	350	Value: 620				

PATTERNS
Including off metal strikes

KM#	Date	Mintage	Identification	Mkt Val
Pn2	1933	—	3 Pence. Silver.	20,000
Pn3	1933	—	Shilling. Silver.	50,000
Pn4	1935	—	Crown. Silver.	75,000

PIEFORTS

KM#	Date	Mintage	Identification	Mkt Val
P1	1992	5,000	Dollar. 0.9250 Silver. KM78.	100

MINT SETS

KM#	Date	Mintage	Identification	Issue Price	Mkt Val
MSA1	1965 (7)	75,000	KM23.2-29.2, green label, flat pack	2.50	5.00
MS1	1965 (7)	100,000	KM23.2-29.2, pink label, flat pack	2.00	3.00
MS2	1967 (7)	250,000	KM31-32, 34-37, 38.1	4.50	2.00
MS4	1968 (6)	35,000	KM31-32, 34-37	2.15	3.00
MS5	1969 (7)	50,000	KM31-32, 34-36, 39-40	3.25	3.00
MS7	1970 (7)	30,000	KM31-32, 34, 36-37, 41-42	3.50	5.00
MS10	1971 (7)	15,000	KM31-32, 36-37, 38.2, 41	3.50	5.00
MS12	1972 (7)	15,000	KM31-32, 34, 36-37, 38.2, 41	3.50	4.00

KM#	Date	Mintage	Identification	Issue Price	Mkt Val
MS14	1973 (7)	15,000	KM31-32, 34, 36-37, 38.2, 41	3.50	5.00
MS17	1974 (7)	15,000	KM31-32, 34, 36-37, 41, 44	4.35	6.00
MS20	1975 (7)	15,000	KM31-32, 34, 36-37, 38.2, 41	4.50	4.00
MS22	1976 (7)	16,000	KM31-32, 34, 36-37, 38.2, 41	4.75	5.00
MS23	1977 (7)	20,000	KM31-32, 34, 36-37, 41, 46	4.75	5.00
MS24	1978 (7)	23,000	KM31-32, 34, 36-37, 41, 47	5.25	5.00
MS25	1979 (7)	25,000	KM31-32, 34, 36-37, 41, 48	5.50	5.00
MS26	1980 (7)	27,000	KM31-32, 34, 36-37, 41, 49	5.75	6.00
MS27	1981 (7)	25,000	KM31-32, 34, 36-37, 41, 50	5.75	5.00
MS28	1982 (7)	25,000	KM31-32, 34, 36-37, 41, 51	6.00	6.00
MS29	1983 (7)	25,000	KM31-32, 34, 36-37, 41, 53	6.25	5.00
MS30	1984 (7)	25,000	KM31-32, 34, 36-37, 41, 54	4.75	6.00
MS31	1985 (7)	20,000	KM31-32, 34, 36-37, 41, 55	4.00	6.00
MS32	1986 (7)	18,000	KM57-63	5.00	6.00
MS33	1987 (7)	18,000	KM58-63, 65	7.50	6.00
MS34	1988 (7)	15,000	KM58-63, 66	8.00	10.00
MS36	1990 (6)	18,000	KM60-61, 63, 78-79, 81	13.00	12.50
MS35	1989 (5)	14,600	KM60-63, 67	14.60	8.00
MS37	1990 (5)	10,000	KM72-76	11.00	25.00
MS38	1991 (7)	20,000	KM60-61, 63, 78-81	16.00	12.00
MS39	1992 (7)	15,000	KM60-61, 63, 78-79, 81-82	15.00	25.00
MS40	1992 (4)	40,000	KM83-86	—	20.00
MS41	1993 (6)	15,000	KM60-61, 63, 78, 81, 87	—	12.00
MS42	1994 (6)	7,000	KM60-61, 78-79,81,90	20.00	25.00
MS43	1995 (7)	6,000	KM60-61, 63, 78-79, 81, 93	17.00	25.00
MS44	1996 (7)	5,150	KM60-61, 63, 78-79, 81, 97	17.00	25.00
MS45	1997 (7)	4,150	KM60-63, 78-79, 81, 103	—	40.00
MS46	1998 (7)	4,000	KM60-61, 63, 78-79, 81, 107	15.00	25.00
MS47	1998 (4)	2,000	KM109-112	—	50.00
MS48	1999 (7)	3,199	KM115-121	20.00	30.00
MS49	2000 (7)	3,000	KM116-121, 127	18.00	50.00

PROOF SETS

KM#	Date	Mintage	Identification	Issue Price	Mkt Val
PS1	1933 (5)	20	KM1-5	—	2,850
PS2	1934 (5)	20	KM1-5	—	9,000
PS3	1935 (6)	364	KM1-6	—	8,000
PS4	1937 (5)	200	KM7-11	—	2,700
PS5	1947 (5)	20	KM7a-11a	—	2,150
PSA6	1950 (7)	—	KM15-21	—	2,100
PS6	1953 (8)	7,000	KM23-30	—	50.00
PS7	1953 (8)	—	KM23-30, Matte Proof	—	1,350
PS8	1954 (4)	—	KM23.1-26.1	—	750
PS9	1954 (6)	—	KM23.1-28.1	—	1,350
PS10	1965 (7)	10	KM23.2-29.2	—	—
PS11	1967 (7)	10	KM31-32,34-38, V.I.P. Set	—	—
PSA12	1970 (7)	10	KM#31.1-32.1, 34.1, 36.1-37.1, 41.1-42, official card, red plush case, V.I.P. set	—	—
PS12	1971 (7)	5,000	KM31-32, 34, 36-37, 38.2, 41	15.00	70.00
PS13	1972 (7)	8,000	KM31-32, 34, 36-37, 38.2, 41	16.00	10.00
PS14	1973 (7)	8,000	KM31-32, 34, 36-37, 38.2, 41	16.00	7.00
PS15	1974 (7)	8,000	KM31-32, 34, 36-37, 41, 44a	14.00	15.00
PS16	1975 (7)	10,000	KM31-32, 34, 36-37, 38.2, 41	18.50	7.00
PS17	1976 (7)	11,000	KM31-32, 34, 36-37, 38.2, 41	19.00	7.00
PS18	1977 (7)	12,000	KM31-32, 34, 36-37, 41, 46a	19.50	12.50
PS19	1977 (7)	10	KM31-32, 34, 36-37, 41, 46a, Official card	—	—
PS20	1978 (7)	15,000	KM31-32, 34, 36-37, 41, 47a	23.50	12.50
PS21	1979 (7)	16,000	KM31-32, 34, 36-37, 41, 48a	25.50	12.50
PS22	1980 (7)	17,000	KM31-32, 34, 36-37, 41, 49a	42.00	12.50
PS23	1981 (7)	18,000	KM31-32, 34, 36-37, 41, 50a	37.00	12.50
PS24	1982 (7)	18,000	KM31-32, 34, 36-37, 41, 51a	33.00	12.50
PS25	1983 (7)	18,000	KM31-32, 34, 36-37, 41, 53a	40.00	12.50
PS26	1984 (7)	15,000	KM31-32, 34, 36-37, 41, 54a	28.00	12.50
PS27	1985 (7)	11,500	KM31-32, 34, 36-37, 41, 55a	27.00	12.50
PS28	1986 (7)	10,000	KM57a, 58-63	30.00	15.00
PS29	1987 (7)	10,000	KM58-63, 65a	38.00	15.00
PS30	1988 (7)	9,000	KM58-63, 66a	43.00	25.00
PS31	1989 (7)	8,500	KM60-63, 67a	44.50	20.00
PS32	1989 (4)	8,600	KM67a-70a	132	50.00
PS33	1990 (6)	10,000	KM60-61, 63, 78a-79a, 81	52.00	60.00
PS34	1990 (5)	7,000	KM72a-76a	110	80.00
PS35	1991 (7)	15,000	KM60-61, 63, 78-79, 80a, 81	61.00	30.00
PS36	1992 (7)	9,000	KM60-61, 63, 78-79, 81, 82a	58.00	25.00
PS37	1993 (6)	10,000	KM60-61, 63, 78, 81, 87a	75.00	25.00
PS38	1994 (6)	4,600	KM60-61, 78-79, 81, 90a	45.00	50.00
PS39	1995 (7)	3,560	KM60-61, 63, 78-79, 81, 93a	45.00	80.00
PS39A	1996 (5)	2,560	KM#60-61, 78-79, 81, 90	—	110
PS40	1997 (7)	2,132	KM60-63, 78-79, 81, 103a	—	130
PS41	1998 (7)	2,000	KM60-61, 63, 78-79, 81, 107a	55.00	180
PS42	1998 (4)	1,200	KM109a-112a	—	75.00
PS43	1999 (7)	1,800	KM115a, 116-121	59.00	180
PS44	2000 (7)	1,500	KM116-121, 128a	40.00	375

PROOF-LIKE SETS (PL)

KM#	Date	Mintage	Identification	Issue Price	Mkt Val
PLS1	1965 (7)	25,000	KM23.2-29.2 flat pack, blue label	—	7.00
PLS2	1965 (7)	400	KM23.2-29.2 red plush case	—	—
PLS3	1967 (7)	49,500	KM31-32, 34-38 flat pack, blue label	5.00	3.00
PLS4	1967	500	KM31-32, 34-38 blue plush case	—	110
PLS6	1968 (6)	40,000	KM31-32, 34-37 flat pack, blue label	5.00	2.50
PLS7	1968 (6)	I.A.	KM31-32, 34-37 blue plush case	—	7.50
PLS8	1969 (7)	50,000	KM31-32, 34-36, 39-40 flat pack, blue label	5.00	4.00

KM#	Date	Mintage	Identification	Issue Price	Mkt Val
PLS9	1969 (7)		I.A. KM31-32, 34-36, 39-40 blue plush case	—	10.00
PLS101970 (7)		20,000	KM31-32, 34, 36-37, 41-42, flat pack, blue label	5.00	7.00
PLS111970 (7)			I.A. KM31-32, 34, 36-37, 41-42, blue plush case	—	12.50

NICARAGUA

The Republic of Nicaragua, situated in Central America between Honduras and Costa Rica, has an area of 50,193 sq. mi. (129,494 sq. km.) and a population of *3.7 million. Capital: Managua. Agriculture, mining (gold and silver) and hardwood logging are the principal industries. Cotton, meat, coffee and sugar are exported.

Columbus sighted the coast of Nicaragua on Sept. 12,1502 during the course of his last voyage of discovery. It was first visited in 1522 by conquistadors from Panama, under the command of Gil Gonzalez. Francisco Hernandez de Cordoba established the first settlements in 1524 at Granada and Leon. Nicaragua was incorporated, for administrative purpose, in the Captaincy General of Guatemala, which included every Central American state but Panama. On September 15, 1821 the Captaincy General of Guatemala declared itself and all the Central American provinces independent of Spain. The next year Nicaragua united with the Mexican Empire of Augustin de Iturbide, only to join in 1823 the federation of the Central American Republic. Within Nicaragua rival cities or juntas such as Leon, Granada and El Viejo vied for power, wealth and influence, often attacking each other at will. To further prove their legitimacy as well as provide an acceptable circulating coinage in those turbulent times (1821-1825), provisional mints functioned intermittently at Granada, Leon and El Viejo. The early coinage reflected traditional but crude Spanish colonial cob-style designs. Nicaragua's first governor was Pedro Arias Davila, appointed on June 1, 1827. When the federation was dissolved, Nicaragua declared itself an independent republic on April 30, 1838.

Dissension between the Liberals and Conservatives of the contending cities kept Nicaragua in turmoil, which made it possible for William Walker to make himself President in 1855. The two major political parties finally united to drive him out and in 1857 he was expelled. A relative peace followed, but by1912, Nicaragua had requested the U.S. Marines to restore order, which began a U.S. involvement that lasted until the Good Neighbor Policy was adopted in 1933. Anastasio Somoza Garcia assumed the Presidency in 1936. This family dynasty dominated Nicaragua until its overthrow in 1979. Formal elections in 1990 renewed a democratic government in power.

MINT MARKS
H - Heaton, Birmingham
HF - Huguenin Freres, Le Locle, Switzerland
Mo - Mexico City
    -Philadelphia, Pa.
    -Sherritt Mint, Canada
    -Waterbury, Ct.

MONETARY SYSTEM
100 Centavos = 1 Peso

REPUBLIC
DECIMAL COINAGE

KM# 10   1/2 CENTAVO
Bronze   Obv: National emblem Rev: Value within sprigs

Date	Mintage	F	VF	XF	Unc	BU
1912H	900,000	1.00	2.50	15.00	40.00	—
1912H Proof	—	Value: 275				
1915H	320,000	1.50	4.00	30.00	100	—
1916H	720,000	1.50	4.00	30.00	100	—
1917	720,000	1.50	4.00	20.00	65.00	—
1922	400,000	2.00	5.00	20.00	80.00	—
1924	400,000	1.00	3.00	12.00	70.00	—
1934	500,000	1.00	3.00	10.00	45.00	—
1936	600,000	0.50	0.75	5.00	35.00	—
1937	1,000,000	0.40	0.60	4.00	20.00	—

KM# 11   CENTAVO
Bronze   Obv: National emblem Rev: Value within sprigs

Date	Mintage	F	VF	XF	Unc	BU
1912H	450,000	1.00	3.00	10.00	45.00	—
1912H Proof	—	Value: 275				
1914H	300,000	5.00	10.00	30.00	85.00	—
1915H	500,000	5.00	10.00	35.00	100	—
1916H	450,000	5.00	10.00	35.00	100	—
1917	450,000	3.00	7.00	28.00	75.00	—
1919	750,000	2.00	6.00	18.00	50.00	—
1920	700,000	1.00	4.50	14.50	45.00	—
1922	500,000	1.00	4.50	14.50	45.00	—
1924	300,000	2.00	6.00	22.00	65.00	—
1927	250,000	3.50	8.50	28.00	75.00	—
1928	500,000	2.00	6.00	18.00	45.00	—
1929	500,000	1.00	3.50	13.50	35.00	—
1930	250,000	3.00	8.00	25.00	70.00	—
1934	500,000	1.50	4.00	12.00	35.00	—
1935	500,000	1.00	4.00	12.00	35.00	—
1936	500,000	1.00	3.00	8.00	25.00	—
1937	1,000,000	0.75	2.00	7.00	30.00	—
1938	2,000,000	0.75	1.50	5.00	15.00	—
1940	2,000,000	0.75	1.50	5.00	15.00	—

KM# 20   CENTAVO
Brass   Obv: National emblem Rev: Value within sprigs

Date	Mintage	F	VF	XF	Unc	BU
1943	1,000,000	0.50	1.50	4.50	18.00	—

KM# 12   5 CENTAVOS
5.0000 g., Copper-Nickel   Obv: National emblem Rev: Value within sprigs

Date	Mintage	F	VF	XF	Unc	BU
1912H	460,000	4.00	10.00	25.00	75.00	—
1912H Proof	—	Value: 300				
1914H	300,000	4.00	10.00	30.00	85.00	—
1915H	160,000	8.00	20.00	50.00	225	—
1919	100,000	4.00	10.00	30.00	110	—
1920	150,000	4.00	10.00	30.00	100	—
1927	100,000	4.00	10.00	30.00	100	—
1928	100,000	4.00	10.00	30.00	100	—
1929	100,000	5.00	12.00	35.00	120	—
1930	100,000	4.00	10.00	30.00	100	—
1934	200,000	3.00	10.00	25.00	90.00	—
1935	200,000	2.00	5.00	20.00	85.00	—
1936	300,000	1.50	3.00	15.00	65.00	—
1937	300,000	1.50	3.00	10.00	40.00	—
1938	800,000	1.00	2.00	8.00	30.00	—
1940	800,000	1.00	2.00	6.00	20.00	—

KM# 21   5 CENTAVOS
Brass   Obv: Bust facing within circle Rev: Radiant sun and hills within circle Edge: Plain

Date	Mintage	F	VF	XF	Unc	BU
1943	2,000,000	0.75	2.50	10.00	60.00	—

KM# 24.1   5 CENTAVOS
3.0000 g., Copper-Nickel   Obv: Bust facing within circle Rev: Radiant sun and hills within circle Edge: B. N. N Note: Reduced size. Medal rotation.

Date	Mintage	F	VF	XF	Unc	BU
1946	4,000,000	0.10	0.25	2.50	18.00	—
1946 Proof	—	Value: 200				

Date	Mintage	F	VF	XF	Unc	BU
1950	—	0.10	0.25	2.50	18.00	—
1952	4,000,000	0.10	0.25	3.50	25.00	—
1952 Proof	—	Value: 250				
1954	4,000,000	0.10	0.15	0.25	5.00	—
1954 Proof	—	Value: 250				
1956	5,000,000	0.10	0.15	0.50	5.00	—
1956 Proof	—	Value: 250				

KM# 24.2   5 CENTAVOS
Copper-Nickel   Obv: Bust facing within circle Rev: Radiant sun and hills within circle Edge: B. C. N. Note: Medal rotation.

Date	Mintage	F	VF	XF	Unc	BU
1962	3,000,000	—	0.10	0.15	2.00	—
1962 Proof	—	Value: 200				
1964	4,000,000	—	0.10	0.15	2.00	—
1965	10,000,000	—	0.10	0.15	2.00	—

KM# 24.2a   5 CENTAVOS
3.0000 g., Nickel Clad Steel   Obv: Bust facing within circle Rev: Radiant sun and hills within circle Note: Medal rotation.

Date	Mintage	F	VF	XF	Unc	BU
1972	10,020,000	—	—	0.10	0.50	—

KM# 24.3   5 CENTAVOS
3.0000 g., Copper-Nickel   Obv: Bust facing within circle Rev: Radiant sun and hills within circle Edge: Reeded Note: Coin rotation.

Date	Mintage	F	VF	XF	Unc	BU
1972 Proof	20,000	Value: 2.50				

KM# 27   5 CENTAVOS
Aluminum, 21.5 mm.   Obv: National emblem within circle Rev: Value within circle Note: Medal rotation.

Date	Mintage	F	VF	XF	Unc	BU
1974	18,000,000	—	—	0.10	0.50	—

KM# 28   5 CENTAVOS
1.4600 g., Aluminum, 21.5 mm.   Series: F.A.O. Obv: National emblem within circle Rev: Value within circle Note: Medal rotation.

Date	Mintage	F	VF	XF	Unc	BU
1974	2,000,000	—	—	0.40	2.00	—

KM# 49   5 CENTAVOS
1.0400 g., Aluminum, 16.8 mm.   Obv: Head with hat facing Rev: Value Note: Coin rotation.

Date	Mintage	F	VF	XF	Unc	BU
1981	5,000,000	—	—	0.40	1.50	—

KM# 55   5 CENTAVOS
0.7500 g., Aluminum, 15 mm.   Obv: Hat above date and sprigs Rev: Value Note: Medal rotation.

Date	Mintage	F	VF	XF	Unc	BU
1987	38,000,000	—	—	0.40	1.00	—

KM# 80   5 CENTAVOS
2.1100 g., Chromium Plated Steel, 14.97 mm. **Obv:** National emblem **Rev:** Bird flying over map **Edge:** Plain **Note:** Coin rotation.

Date	Mintage	F	VF	XF	Unc	BU
1994	20,000,000	—	—	—	0.50	0.75

KM# 13   10 CENTAVOS
2.5000 g., 0.8000 Silver 0.0643 oz. ASW **Obv:** Bust facing within circle **Rev:** Radiant sun and hills within circle **Note:** All dates struck with medal rotation except 1935, which appears only in coin rotation.

Date	Mintage	F	VF	XF	Unc	BU
1912H	230,000	2.50	7.00	25.00	100	—
1912H Proof	—	Value: 300				
1914H	220,000	3.00	10.00	35.00	115	—
1914H Proof	—	Value: 375				
1927	500,000	2.00	4.00	20.00	85.00	—
1928	1,000,000	1.25	3.00	15.00	65.00	—
1930	150,000	1.50	4.00	30.00	95.00	—
1935	250,000	1.25	3.00	12.50	45.00	—
1936	250,000	1.25	3.00	10.00	30.00	—

KM# 17.1   10 CENTAVOS
4.0000 g., Copper-Nickel **Obv:** Bust facing within circle **Rev:** Radiant sun and hills within circle **Edge:** B.N.N **Note:** Medal rotation.

Date	Mintage	F	VF	XF	Unc	BU
1939	2,500,000	1.25	3.00	10.00	30.00	—
1939 Proof	—	Value: 250				
1946	2,000,000	1.25	3.00	10.00	30.00	—
1946 Proof	—	Value: 200				
1950	2,000,000	0.25	0.50	3.00	20.00	—
1950 Proof	—	Value: 200				
1952	1,500,000	0.25	0.50	3.00	25.00	—
1952 Proof	—	Value: 200				
1954	3,000,000	0.10	0.25	1.50	10.00	—
1954 Proof	—	Value: 200				
1956	5,000,000	0.10	0.20	1.00	6.00	—
1956 Proof	—	Value: 200				

KM# 17.2   10 CENTAVOS
3.9100 g., Copper-Nickel **Obv:** Bust facing within circle **Rev:** Radiant sun and hills within circle **Edge:** B.C.N **Note:** Medal rotation.

Date	Mintage	F	VF	XF	Unc	BU
1962	4,000,000	—	0.10	0.15	5.00	—
1962 Proof	—	Value: 225				
1964	4,000,000	—	0.10	0.15	5.00	—
1965	12,000,000	—	0.10	0.15	1.00	—

KM# 17.2a   10 CENTAVOS
Nickel Clad Steel **Obv:** Bust facing within circle **Rev:** Radiant sun and hills within circle **Note:** Medal rotation. Previous KM#17.3a.

Date	Mintage	F	VF	XF	Unc	BU
1972	10,020,000	—	0.10	0.15	0.30	—

KM# 22   10 CENTAVOS
Brass **Obv:** Bust facing within circle **Rev:** Radiant sun and hills within circle **Edge:** Reeded **Note:** Coin rotation.

Date	Mintage	F	VF	XF	Unc	BU
1943	2,000,000	0.50	1.00	5.00	50.00	—

KM# 17.3   10 CENTAVOS
Copper-Nickel, 17 mm. **Issuer:** Banco Central De Nicaragua **Obv:** Bust facing within circle - Francisco Hernandez de Cordoba **Obv. Leg.:** Republica de Nicaragua **Rev:** Radiant sun and hills within circle, Seal of the Central America Federation **Rev. Leg.:** In God We Trust (En Dios Confiamos) **Edge:** Reeded **Note:** Coin rotation.

Date	Mintage	F	VF	XF	Unc	BU
1972 Proof	20,000	Value: 2.50				

Note: In sets only

KM# 30   10 CENTAVOS
Aluminum **Obv:** Map within circle **Rev:** Value within circle

Date	Mintage	F	VF	XF	Unc	BU
1974	18,000,000	—	—	0.10	0.20	—

KM# 29   10 CENTAVOS
Aluminum **Series:** F.A.O. **Obv:** Map within circle **Rev:** Value within circle **Note:** Medal rotation.

Date	Mintage	F	VF	XF	Unc	BU
1974	2,000,000	—	—	0.10	1.00	—

KM# 31   10 CENTAVOS
Copper-Nickel

Date	Mintage	F	VF	XF	Unc	BU
1978	20,000,000	—	—	0.40	2.00	—

KM# 50   10 CENTAVOS
Aluminum **Obv:** Head with hat facing **Rev:** Value **Note:** Coin rotation.

Date	Mintage	F	VF	XF	Unc	BU
1981	10,000,000	—	—	0.15	1.00	—

KM# 56   10 CENTAVOS
0.9000 g., Aluminum, 17 mm. **Obv:** Hat above date and sprigs **Rev:** Value **Note:** Medal rotation.

Date	Mintage	F	VF	XF	Unc	BU
1987	16,000,000	—	—	0.15	0.40	—

KM# 81   10 CENTAVOS
Chromium Plated Steel **Obv:** National emblem **Rev:** Bird flying above map **Note:** Coin rotation.

Date	Mintage	F	VF	XF	Unc	BU
1994	6,439,000	—	—	—	0.75	1.00

KM# 14   25 CENTAVOS
6.2500 g., 0.8000 Silver 0.1607 oz. ASW **Obv:** Bust facing within circle **Rev:** Radiant sun and hills within circle **Note:** Medal rotation.

Date	Mintage	F	VF	XF	Unc	BU
1912H	320,000	3.00	10.00	35.00	90.00	—
1912H Proof	—	Value: 350				
1914H	100,000	5.00	15.00	50.00	170	—
1928	200,000	3.00	10.00	30.00	90.00	—
1929	20,000	8.00	35.00	90.00	275	—
1930	20,000	8.00	35.00	90.00	250	—
1936	100,000	2.75	8.00	20.00	65.00	—

KM# 18.1   25 CENTAVOS
5.0000 g., Copper-Nickel, 23 mm. **Obv:** Bust facing within circle **Rev:** Radiant sun and hills within circle **Edge:** B N N (repeated)

Date	Mintage	F	VF	XF	Unc	BU
1939	1,000,000	2.00	6.00	15.00	50.00	—
1939 Proof	—	Value: 300				
1946	1,000,000	1.50	4.00	12.00	40.00	—
1946 Proof	—	Value: 280				
1950	1,000,000	0.25	0.50	1.50	20.00	—
1950 Proof	—	Value: 300				
1952	1,000,000	0.25	0.50	1.50	15.00	—
1952 Proof	—	Value: 280				
1954	2,000,000	0.10	0.20	0.50	6.00	—
1954 Proof	—	Value: 280				
1956	3,000,000	0.10	0.20	0.50	5.00	—
1956 Proof	—	Value: 280				

KM# 23   25 CENTAVOS
Brass, 26.8 mm. **Obv:** Bust facing within circle **Rev:** Radiant sun and hills within circle **Edge:** Reeded **Note:** Coin rotation.

Date	Mintage	F	VF	XF	Unc	BU
1943	1,000,000	0.50	1.50	8.50	50.00	—

KM# 18.2   25 CENTAVOS
5.1000 g., Copper-Nickel, 23 mm. **Obv:** Bust facing within circle **Rev:** Radiant sun and hills within circle **Edge:** B. C. N. **Note:** Medal rotation.

Date	Mintage	F	VF	XF	Unc	BU
1964	3,000,000	0.10	0.20	0.40	4.00	—
1965	4,400,000	0.10	0.20	0.30	4.00	—

KM# 18.3   25 CENTAVOS
Copper-Nickel **Obv:** Bust facing within circle **Rev:** Radiant sun and hills within circle **Edge:** Reeded

Date	Mintage	F	VF	XF	Unc	BU
1972 Proof	20,000	Value: 2.50				
	Note: Coin rotation					
1972	4,000,000	—	0.10	0.15	2.00	—
1974	6,000,000	—	0.10	0.15	2.00	—
	Note: Medal rotation					

KM# 51   25 CENTAVOS
3.4000 g., Nickel Clad Steel **Obv:** Head with hat facing **Rev:** Value **Note:** Coin rotation.

Date	Mintage	F	VF	XF	Unc	BU
1981	10,000,000	—	—	0.25	1.50	—
1985	8,000,000	5.00	10.00	20.00	35.00	—

KM# 57   25 CENTAVOS
1.3500 g., Aluminum, 19 mm. **Obv:** Hat above date and sprigs **Rev:** Value **Note:** Medal rotation.

Date	Mintage	F	VF	XF	Unc	BU
1987	—	—	—	0.25	2.00	—

KM# 82   25 CENTAVOS
Chromium Plated Steel   **Obv:** National emblem **Rev:** Bird flying above map **Note:** Coin rotation.

Date	Mintage	F	VF	XF	Unc	BU
1994	2,500,000	—	—	—	1.00	1.50

KM# 15   50 CENTAVOS
12.5000 g., 0.8000 Silver 0.3215 oz. ASW   **Obv:** Bust facing within circle **Rev:** Radiant sun and hills within circle **Note:** Medal rotation.

Date	Mintage	F	VF	XF	Unc	BU
1912H	260,000	5.50	15.00	75.00	200	—
1912H Proof	—	Value: 500				
1929	20,000	6.50	20.00	90.00	275	—

KM# 19.1   50 CENTAVOS
7.9200 g., Copper-Nickel   **Obv:** Bust facing within circle **Rev:** Radiant sun and hills within circle **Edge:** B. N. N **Note:** Medal rotation.

Date	Mintage	F	VF	XF	Unc	BU
1939	1,000,000	3.00	8.00	20.00	65.00	—
1939 Proof	—	Value: 300				
1946	500,000	2.00	5.00	12.50	50.00	—
1946 Proof	—	Value: 300				
1950	500,000	1.00	2.00	10.00	50.00	—
1950 Proof	—	Value: 300				
1952	1,000,000	0.75	1.50	5.00	30.00	—
1952 Proof	—	Value: 300				
1954	2,000,000	0.50	1.00	4.00	15.00	—
1954 Proof	—	Value: 300				
1956	2,000,000	0.50	1.00	4.00	15.00	—
1956 Proof	—	Value: 300				

KM# 19.2   50 CENTAVOS
Copper-Nickel   **Obv:** Bust facing within circle **Rev:** Radiant sun and hills within circle **Edge:** B. C. N

Date	Mintage	F	VF	XF	Unc	BU
1965	600,000	0.50	1.25	4.50	15.00	—
1965 Proof	—	Value: 150				

KM# 19.3   50 CENTAVOS
Copper-Nickel   **Obv:** Bust facing within circle **Rev:** Radiant sun and hills within circle **Edge:** Reeded

Date	Mintage	F	VF	XF	Unc	BU
1972	—	—	—	—	—	—
1972 Proof	20,000	Value: 2.50				
Note: Coin rotation						
1974	2,000,000	0.10	0.25	0.50	3.50	—
Note: Medal rotation						

KM# 42   50 CENTAVOS
7.0000 g., Copper-Nickel   **Obv:** Head with hat facing **Rev:** Value **Note:** Coin rotation.

Date	Mintage	F	VF	XF	Unc	BU
1980Mo	15,000,000	0.10	0.25	0.50	1.75	—

KM# 42a   50 CENTAVOS
6.1600 g., Nickel Clad Steel, 25.9 mm.   **Obv:** Head with hat facing **Rev:** Value **Note:** Coin rotation.

Date	Mintage	F	VF	XF	Unc	BU
1983	10,000,000	—	—	0.40	2.50	—
1985	10,000,000	3.50	7.50	15.00	23.00	—

KM# 58   50 CENTAVOS
4.8500 g., Aluminum-Bronze, 22 mm.   **Obv:** Hat above date and sprigs **Rev:** Value **Note:** Medal rotation.

Date	Mintage	F	VF	XF	Unc	BU
1987	12,000,000	—	—	0.40	2.50	—

KM# 83   50 CENTAVOS
4.6800 g., Chromium Plated Steel, 22 mm.   **Obv:** National emblem **Rev:** Bird flying above map **Note:** Coin rotation.

Date	Mintage	F	VF	XF	Unc	BU
1994	12,000,000	—	—	—	1.25	1.75

KM# 88   50 CENTAVOS
4.8000 g., Nickel Clad Steel, 22 mm.   **Obv:** National emblem **Rev:** Value above sprigs within circle, date flanked by stars

Date	Mintage	F	VF	XF	Unc	BU
1997	24,000,000	—	—	—	1.25	1.75

KM# 16   CORDOBA
25.0000 g., 0.9000 Silver 0.7234 oz. ASW   **Obv:** Bust facing within circle **Rev:** Radiant sun and hills within circle **Note:** Medal rotation.

Date	Mintage	F	VF	XF	Unc	BU
1912H	35,000	30.00	75.00	285	1,950	—
1912H Proof	—	Value: 2,850				

KM# 26   CORDOBA
9.4500 g., Copper-Nickel, 28.9 mm.   **Obv:** Bust facing within circle **Rev:** Radiant sun and hills within circle **Edge:** Reeded

Date	Mintage	F	VF	XF	Unc	BU
1972	20,000,000	0.10	0.20	2.00	4.00	—
Note: Medal rotation						
1972 Proof	40,000	Value: 10.00				
Note: Coin rotation						

KM# 43   CORDOBA
8.8400 g., Copper-Nickel   **Obv:** Head with hat facing **Rev:** Value **Note:** Coin rotation.

Date	Mintage	F	VF	XF	Unc	BU
1980Mo	10,000,000	0.10	0.20	0.50	2.00	—
1983Mo	10,000,000	0.10	0.20	0.50	2.00	—

KM# 43a   CORDOBA
Nickel Clad Steel   **Obv:** Head with hat facing **Rev:** Value **Note:** Coin rotation.

Date	Mintage	F	VF	XF	Unc	BU
1984	10,000,000	—	0.10	0.50	2.00	—
1985	10,000,000	1.00	2.00	7.00	35.00	—

KM# 59   CORDOBA
6.1500 g., Aluminum-Bronze, 24 mm.   **Obv:** Hat above date and sprigs **Rev:** Value **Note:** Medal rotation.

Date	Mintage	F	VF	XF	Unc	BU
1987	23,000,000	—	0.75	1.00	3.75	—

KM# 77   CORDOBA
27.0000 g., 0.9250 Silver 0.8029 oz. ASW   **Subject:** Ibero - American Series **Obv:** National emblem within assorted arms around border **Rev:** Map behind standing figures shaking hands within circle

Date	Mintage	F	VF	XF	Unc	BU
1991 Proof	10,000	Value: 65.00				

KM# 84   CORDOBA
13.8200 g., 0.9250 Silver 0.4110 oz. ASW   **Subject:** National Ruben Dario Theater **Obv:** Dancing native and map **Rev:** Theatrical masks on theatre

Date	Mintage	F	VF	XF	Unc	BU
1994 Proof	2,000	Value: 42.50				

KM# 85   CORDOBA
14.1700 g., 0.9250 Silver 0.4214 oz. ASW   **Subject:** 100th Anniversary - City of Boaco **Obv:** National emblem **Rev:** Building

Date	Mintage	F	VF	XF	Unc	BU
1995 Proof	1,000	Value: 45.00				

KM# 87   CORDOBA
13.9600 g., 0.8250 Silver 0.3703 oz. ASW   **Subject:** 50th Anniversary - F.A.O **Obv:** National emblem **Rev:** F.A.O. logo within circle

Date	Mintage	F	VF	XF	Unc	BU
1995 Proof	2,200	Value: 37.50				

KM# 89   CORDOBA
6.2500 g., Nickel Clad Steel, 25 mm. **Obv:** National emblem
Rev: Value above sprigs within circle

Date	Mintage	F	VF	XF	Unc	BU
1997	39,000,000	—	—	—	2.50	3.00
2000	35,000,000	—	—	—	2.50	3.00

KM# 44   5 CORDOBAS
Copper-Nickel, 27 mm. **Obv:** Value **Rev:** Head with hat facing
Note: Medal rotation.

Date	Mintage	F	VF	XF	Unc	BU
1980	10,000,000	0.15	0.25	1.00	3.00	—

KM# 44a   5 CORDOBAS
Nickel Clad Steel **Obv:** Value **Rev:** Head with hat facing
Note: Medal rotation.

Date	Mintage	F	VF	XF	Unc	BU
1984	8,000,000	—	0.25	1.00	3.50	—

KM# 60   5 CORDOBAS
7.5000 g., Aluminum-Bronze, 25.9 mm. **Obv:** Hat above date
and sprigs **Rev:** Value

Date	Mintage	F	VF	XF	Unc	BU
1987	23,000,000	—	1.00	2.50	4.00	—

KM# 86   5 CORDOBAS
27.0000 g., 0.9250 Silver 0.8029 oz. ASW **Subject:** Wildlife
Protection **Obv:** National emblem

Date	Mintage	F	VF	XF	Unc	BU
1994 Proof	20,000	Value: 45.00				

KM# 96   5 CORDOBAS
27.0000 g., 0.9250 Silver 0.8029 oz. ASW, 40 mm.
Subject: Ibero-America **Obv:** National emblem within assorted
arms border **Rev:** Two folk dancers **Edge:** Reeded

Date	Mintage	F	VF	XF	Unc	BU
1997 Proof	—	Value: 65.00				

KM# 90   5 CORDOBAS
7.8000 g., Nickel Clad Steel, 27.8 mm. **Obv:** National emblem
Rev: Value above sprigs within circle **Note:** Coin rotation.

Date	Mintage	F	VF	XF	Unc	BU
1997	11,000,000	—	—	—	4.00	5.00
2000	25,000,000	—	—	—	4.00	5.00

KM# 76   10 CORDOBAS
25.7000 g., 0.9990 Silver 0.8254 oz. ASW **Subject:** Soccer
Obv: National emblem within circle **Rev:** Soccer champions with
arms raised

Date	Mintage	F	VF	XF	Unc	BU
1991 Proof	10,000	Value: 65.00				

KM# 78   10 CORDOBAS
19.9500 g., 0.9990 Silver 0.6407 oz.,ASW **Subject:** Spanish
Royal Visit **Obv:** National emblem within circle **Rev:** Heads 1/4
left on map

Date	Mintage	F	VF	XF	Unc	BU
1991 Proof	5,000	Value: 55.00				

KM# 95   10 CORDOBAS
27.2000 g., 0.9250 Silver 0.8089 oz. ASW, 40 mm. **Subject:** Ibero-
America Series **Obv:** National emblem within circle of assorted arms
Rev: Man on horse with two milk cans **Edge:** Reeded

Date	Mintage	F	VF	XF	Unc	BU
1999 Proof	—	Value: 75.00				

KM# 32   20 CORDOBAS
5.0300 g., 0.9250 Silver 0.1496 oz. ASW **Subject:** Earthquake
Relief Issue **Obv:** National emblem **Rev:** Bird at center of cog
wheel design, plant sprigs in sections

Date	Mintage	F	VF	XF	Unc	BU
1975 Proof	1,750	Value: 20.00				

Note: Medal rotation

1975	2,491	—	—	—	14.50	—

KM# 25   50 CORDOBAS
35.6000 g., 0.9000 Gold 1.0301 oz. AGW **Subject:** 100th
Anniversary - Birth of Ruben Dario **Obv:** National emblem within
circle **Rev:** Bust 3/4 facing within circle

Date	Mintage	F	VF	XF	Unc	BU
1967HF Prooflike	16,000	—	—	—	—	975

Note: 500 pieces were issued in blue boxes with certificates;
Boxed examples command a premium

KM# 33   50 CORDOBAS
12.5700 g., 0.9250 Silver 0.3738 oz. ASW **Subject:** U.S.
Bicentennial **Obv:** National emblem **Rev:** Liberty bell divides
dates **Note:** Mintages are included with KM#34.

Date	Mintage	F	VF	XF	Unc	BU
1975	—	—	—	—	21.50	—
1975 Proof	—	Value: 30.00				

Note: Medal rotation

KM# 34   50 CORDOBAS
12.5700 g., 0.9250 Silver 0.3738 oz. ASW **Subject:** Earthquake
Relief Issue **Obv:** National emblem **Rev:** "The Bud" painting by
Annigoni

Date	Mintage	F	VF	XF	Unc	BU
1975	4,482	—	—	—	18.00	—
1975 Proof	3,500	Value: 27.50				

KM# 61   50 CORDOBAS
16.6000 g., 0.8250 Silver 0.4403 oz. ASW **Series:** Winter
Olympics **Obv:** National emblem within circle **Rev:** Skier

Date	Mintage	F	VF	XF	Unc	BU
1988 Proof	10,000	Value: 22.50				

KM# 62   50 CORDOBAS
16.6000 g., 0.8250 Silver 0.4403 oz. ASW **Series:** Olympics
Obv: National emblem within circle **Rev:** Sailboat

Date	Mintage	F	VF	XF	Unc	BU
1988 Proof	10,000	Value: 22.50				

KM# 91   50 CORDOBAS
27.0000 g., 0.9250 Silver 0.8029 oz. ASW, 40 mm.
Subject: Central Bank 40th Anniversary **Obv:** National emblem
within circle and wreath **Rev:** Bust 1/4 left **Edge:** Reeded

Date	Mintage	F	VF	XF	Unc	BU
2000 Proof	1,000	Value: 75.00				

KM# 35   100 CORDOBAS
25.1400 g., 0.9250 Silver 0.7476 oz. ASW **Subject:** U.S.
Bicentennial **Obv:** National emblem **Rev:** Betsy Ross sewing flag
on left, astronaut placing flag on moon on right **Note:** Mintages
included with KM#36.

Date	Mintage	F	VF	XF	Unc	BU
1975	—	—	—	—	35.00	—
1975 Proof	—	Value: 45.00				

Note: Medal rotation

KM# 36   100 CORDOBAS
25.1400 g., 0.9250 Silver 0.7476 oz. ASW **Subject:** Earthquake
Relief Issue **Obv:** National emblem **Rev:** World globe in front of
assorted flags

Date	Mintage	F	VF	XF	Unc	BU
1975	4,682	—	—	—	35.00	—
1975 Proof	3,500	Value: 45.00				

Note: Medal rotation

KM# 37   200 CORDOBAS
2.1000 g., 0.9000 Gold 0.0608 oz. AGW **Subject:** Pieta by
Michelangelo **Obv:** National emblem **Rev:** Sitting figure holding
lying figure on lap within circle

Date	Mintage	F	VF	XF	Unc	BU
1975 Proof	1,650	Value: 90.00				
1975	1,200	—	—	—	65.00	80.00

KM# 79   250 CORDOBAS
171.0700 g., 0.9990 Silver 5.4943 oz. ASW **Subject:** Spanish
Royal Visit **Obv:** National emblem within circle **Rev:** Heads 1/4
left on map

Date	Mintage	F	VF	XF	Unc	BU
1992 Proof	—	Value: 145				

KM# 38   500 CORDOBAS
5.4000 g., 0.9000 Gold 0.1562 oz. AGW **Subject:** Colonial Church,
La Merced **Obv:** National emblem **Rev:** Colonial church within circle

Date	Mintage	F	VF	XF	Unc	BU
1975 Proof	100	Value: 650				
1975	200	—	—	—	—	350

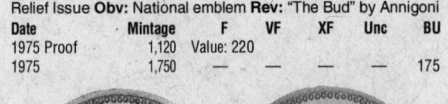

KM# 39   500 CORDOBAS
5.4000 g., 0.9000 Gold 0.1562 oz. AGW **Subject:** Earthquake
Relief Issue **Obv:** National emblem **Rev:** "The Bud" by Annigoni

Date	Mintage	F	VF	XF	Unc	BU
1975 Proof	1,120	Value: 220				
1975	1,750	—	—	—	—	175

KM# 45   500 CORDOBAS
14.0000 g., 0.9250 Silver 0.4163 oz. ASW **Obv:** Map **Rev:** Head
with hat facing **Note:** Medal rotation.

Date	Mintage	F	VF	XF	Unc	BU
1980Mo Proof	7,000	Value: 35.00				

KM# 46   500 CORDOBAS
14.0000 g., 0.9250 Silver 0.4163 oz. ASW **Obv:** Map **Rev:** Bust
right **Note:** Medal rotation.

Date	Mintage	F	VF	XF	Unc	BU
1980Mo Proof	7,000	Value: 35.00				

KM# 47   500 CORDOBAS
14.0000 g., 0.9250 Silver 0.4163 oz. ASW **Obv:** National emblem
Rev: Bust of Rigoberto Lopez Perez 1/4 left **Note:** Medal rotation.

Date	Mintage	F	VF	XF	Unc	BU
1980Mo Proof	7,000	Value: 35.00				

KM# 69   500 CORDOBAS
14.0000 g., 0.9990 Silver 0.4496 oz. ASW **Subject:** 50th
Anniversary - A. C. Sandino **Obv:** National emblem
Rev: Birthplace of Augusto Cesar Sandino

Date	Mintage	F	VF	XF	Unc	BU
ND(1984) Proof	1,000	Value: 45.00				

KM# 70   500 CORDOBAS
14.0000 g., 0.9990 Silver 0.4496 oz. ASW **Subject:** 50th
Anniversary - Sandono's Death **Obv:** National emblem
Rev: Facing busts of Generals Sandino, Estrada and Umanzor

Date	Mintage	F	VF	XF	Unc	BU
ND(1984) Proof	1,000	Value: 45.00				

KM# 73   500 CORDOBAS
14.0000 g., 0.9990 Silver 0.4496 oz. ASW **Subject:** 50th
Anniversary - The Murder of General Augusto Cesar Sandino
Obv: National emblem **Rev:** Bust with hat facing

Date	Mintage	F	VF	XF	Unc	BU
ND(1984) Proof	1,000	Value: 45.00				

KM# 63 500 CORDOBAS
Aluminum **Obv:** Hat above date and sprigs **Rev:** Value

Date	Mintage	F	VF	XF	Unc	BU
1987	—	—	—	2.50	6.50	—

KM# 40 1000 CORDOBAS
9.5000 g., 0.9000 Gold 0.2749 oz. AGW **Subject:** U.S. Bicentennial
Obv: National emblem **Rev:** Liberty bell divides dates

Date	Mintage	F	VF	XF	Unc	BU
1975 Proof	2,270	Value: 300				
1975	3,380	—	—	—	—	285

KM# 48 1000 CORDOBAS
20.0000 g., 0.9000 Gold 0.5787 oz. AGW **Subject:** 1st
Anniversary of Revolution **Obv:** Three 1/2 figures with guns
raised **Rev:** Busts of Sandino and Fonseca

Date	Mintage	F	VF	XF	Unc	BU
1980Mo Proof	6,000	Value: 575				

KM# 52 1000 CORDOBAS
20.0000 g., 0.9170 Gold 0.5896 oz. AGW **Subject:** 50th
Anniversary - The Murder of General Augusto Cesar Sandino
Obv: National emblem **Rev:** Bust with hat facing

Date	Mintage	F	VF	XF	Unc	BU
1984 Proof	1,000	Value: 620				

KM# 53 1000 CORDOBAS
20.0000 g., 0.9170 Gold 0.5896 oz. AGW **Obv:** National emblem
Rev: Birthplace of Augusto Cesar Sandino

Date	Mintage	F	VF	XF	Unc	BU
1984 Proof	1,000	Value: 620				

KM# 54 1000 CORDOBAS
20.0000 g., 0.9170 Gold 0.5896 oz. AGW **Obv:** National emblem
Rev: Facing busts of Generals Sandino, Estrada and Umanzor

Date	Mintage	F	VF	XF	Unc	BU
1984 Proof	1,000	Value: 620				

KM# 41 2000 CORDOBAS
19.2000 g., 0.9000 Gold 0.5555 oz. AGW **Subject:** U.S.
Bicentennial **Obv:** National emblem **Rev:** Betsy Ross sewing flag
on left, astronaut placing flag on moon on right

Date	Mintage	F	VF	XF	Unc	BU
1975 Proof	100	Value: 850				
1975	320	—	—	—	—	650

KM# 65 2000 CORDOBAS
16.6000 g., 0.8250 Silver 0.4403 oz. ASW **Subject:** Soccer
Obv: National emblem within circle **Rev:** Soccer player

Date	Mintage	F	VF	XF	Unc	BU
1988 Proof	5,000	Value: 40.00				

KM# 64 10000 CORDOBAS
20.0000 g., 0.9990 Silver 0.6423 oz. ASW **Subject:** Discovery of
Nicaragua by Columbus **Obv:** National emblem **Rev:** Sailing ship
and small boat

Date	Mintage	F	VF	XF	Unc	BU
1989 Proof	Est. 10,000	Value: 45.00				

KM# 66 10000 CORDOBAS
26.4000 g., 0.9990 Silver 0.8479 oz. ASW **Obv:** National emblem
within circle **Rev:** Two soccer players

Date	Mintage	F	VF	XF	Unc	BU
1990 Proof	5,000	Value: 45.00				

KM# 67 10000 CORDOBAS
26.0000 g., 0.9990 Silver 0.8350 oz. ASW **Subject:** Discovery of
America **Obv:** National emblem within circle **Rev:** Sailing ship

Date	Mintage	F	VF	XF	Unc	BU
1990 Proof	10,000	Value: 47.50				

KM# 68 10000 CORDOBAS
26.0000 g., 0.9990 Silver 0.8350 oz. ASW **Series:** 1992 Summer
Olympics **Obv:** National emblem within circle **Rev:** Bicyclist

Date	Mintage	F	VF	XF	Unc	BU
1990 Proof	10,000	Value: 40.00				

KM# 71 10000 CORDOBAS
26.0000 g., 0.9990 Silver 0.8350 oz. ASW **Subject:** Wildlife
Protection **Obv:** National emblem within circle **Rev:** Ocelot

Date	Mintage	F	VF	XF	Unc	BU
1990 Proof	5,000	Value: 50.00				

KM# 72.1 10000 CORDOBAS
20.4000 g., 0.9990 Silver 0.6552 oz. ASW **Series:** 1992
Summer Olympics **Obv:** National emblem within circle
Rev: Horse jumping

Date	Mintage	F	VF	XF	Unc	BU
1990 Proof	10,000	Value: 60.00				

KM# 72.2 10000 CORDOBAS
20.0000 g., 0.9990 Silver 0.6423 oz. ASW **Series:** 1992
Summer Olympics **Obv:** National emblem within circle
Rev: Horse jumping, 999 added at 4 o'clock

Date	Mintage	F	VF	XF	Unc	BU
1990 Proof	Inc. above	Value: 42.50				

KM# 74 10000 CORDOBAS
25.9000 g., 0.9990 Silver 0.8318 oz. ASW **Series:** 1992
Summer Olympics **Obv:** National emblem within circle
Rev: Tennis player proclaiming victory

Date	Mintage	F	VF	XF	Unc	BU
1990 Proof	10,000	Value: 50.00				

KM# 75 10000 CORDOBAS
20.0000 g., 0.9990 Silver 0.6423 oz. ASW **Series:** 1992 Winter Olympics **Obv:** National emblem within circle **Rev:** Figure skater

Date	Mintage	F	VF	XF	Unc	BU
1990 Proof	10,000				Value: 47.50	

REVOLUTIONARY TOKEN COINAGE

KM# Tn1 10 PESOS
18.0000 g., Lead **Issuer:** General Augusto Cesar Sandino, 1925-1934

Date	Mintage	VG	F	VF	XF	Unc
ND(1927)	—	400	700	1,200	2,500	—

PATTERNS
Including off metal strikes.

KM#	Date	Mintage	Identification	Mkt Val
Pn10	1912H	2	1/2 Centavo. Silver. KM10; 2 known.	
Pn11	1912H	1	1/2 Centavo. Gold. KM10; unique.	
Pn12	1912H	2	Centavo. Silver. KM11; 2 known.	4,000
Pn13	1912H	1	Centavo. Gold. KM#11.	
Pn14	1912H	2	5 Centavos. Silver. KM12.	
Pn15	1912H	1	5 Centavos. Gold. KM12.	
Pn16	1912H	1	10 Centavos. Gold. KM13.	
Pn17	1912H	1	25 Centavos. Gold. KM14.	
Pn18	1912H	1	50 Centavos. Gold. KM#15.	
Pn19	1912H	1	Cordoba. Gold. KM16.	
Pn20	1975	—	20 Cordobas. Silver. KM32 with 4.65 gram Plata Fino, LEY 925 below date.	
Pn21	1975	—	50 Cordobas. Silver. KM34 with 11.63 gram. Plata Fino, LEY 925 below date.	
Pn22	1975	—	100 Cordobas. Silver. KM36 with 23.25 gram. Plata Fino, LEY 925 below date.	

TRIAL STRIKES

KM#	Date	Mintage	Identification	Mkt Val
TS1	ND(1912)	—	10 Centavos. Aluminum. Obverse.	350
TS2	ND(1912)	—	10 Centavos. Aluminum. Bust facing within circle. Radiant sun and hills within circle. Reverse.	350
TS3	ND(1912)	—	25 Centavos. Aluminum. Obverse.	360
TS4	ND(1912)	—	25 Centavos. Aluminum. Reverse.	360
TS5	ND(1912)	—	50 Centavos. Aluminum. Bust facing within circle. Radiant sun and hills within circle. Obverse.	375
TS6	ND(1912)	—	50 Centavos. Aluminum.	375
TS7	ND(1912)	—	Cordoba. 18.0000 Aluminum. Obverse.	—
TS8	ND(1912)	—	Cordoba. 18.0000 Aluminum. Reverse.	—
TS9	1965	—	5 Centavos. Nickel. Raised "Trial" left of bust on obverse, above rays on reverse. KM24.2.	—
TS10	1965	—	10 Centavos. Nickel. Raised "Trial" left of bust on obverse, above rays on reverse. KM17.2.	—

MINT SETS

KM#	Date	Mintage	Identification	Issue Price	Mkt Val
MS1	1975 (5)	—	KM37-41	—	1,150
MS2	1975 (5)	2,250	KM32-36	—	110

PROOF SETS

KM#	Date	Mintage	Identification	Issue Price	Mkt Val
PS1	1912 (7)	10	KM10-16	—	4,500
PS2	1912 (3)	2	Pn10, Pn12, Pn14	—	4,500
PS3	1912 (7)	1	Pn11, Pn13, Pn15-19	—	—
PS4	1972 (5)	20,000	KM17.3-19.3, 24.3, 26	8.00	15.00
PS5	1975 (7)	—	KM32, 33, 35, 37, 38, 40, 41	—	1,900
PS6	1975 (5)	2,000	KM32-36	—	160
PS7	1975 (3)	—	KM32, 33, 35	115	90.00
PS8	1975 (3)	—	KM34, 36, 39	—	295
PS9	1975 (2)	—	KM37, 39	—	300

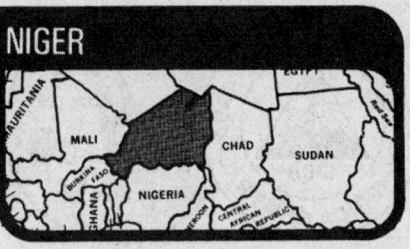

NIGER

The Republic of Niger, located in West Africa's Sahara region 1,000 miles (1,609 km.) from the Mediterranean shore, has an area of 489,191 sq. mi. (1,267,000 sq. km.) and a population of *7.4 million. Capital: Niamey. The economy is based on subsistence agriculture and raising livestock. Peanuts, peanut oil, and livestock are exported.

Although four-fifths of Niger is arid desert, it was, some 6,000 years ago inhabited and an important economic crossroads. Its modern history began in the 19th century with the beginning of contacts with British and German explorers searching for the mouth of the Niger River. Niger was incorporated into French West Africa in 1896, but it was 1922 before all native resistance was quelled and Niger became a French colony. In 1958 the voters approved the new French Constitution and elected to become an autonomous republic within the French Community. On Aug. 3, 1960, Niger withdrew from the Community and proclaimed its independence.

REPUBLIC
DECIMAL COINAGE

KM# 1 10 FRANCS
4.2000 g., 0.9000 Gold 0.1215 oz. AGW **Subject:** Independence Commemorataive **Obv:** President Diori Hamani left **Rev:** Flagged arms

Date	Mintage	F	VF	XF	Unc	BU
ND(1960) Proof	1,000				Value: 120	

KM# 7 10 FRANCS
3.2000 g., 0.9000 Gold 0.0926 oz. AGW **Obv:** Ostriches **Rev:** Flagged arms

Date	Mintage	F	VF	XF	Unc	BU
1968 Proof	1,000				Value: 125	

KM# 8.1 10 FRANCS
20.0000 g., 0.9000 Silver 0.5787 oz. ASW **Obv:** Lion **Rev:** Flagged arms **Note:** Sharp details, raised rim.

Date	Mintage	F	VF	XF	Unc	BU
1968 Proof	1,000				Value: 65.00	

KM# 8.2 10 FRANCS
24.5400 g., 0.9000 Silver 0.7101 oz. ASW **Obv:** Exists with and without accent marks above first "E" in REPUBLIQUE **Rev:** Flagged arms **Note:** Dull details, machined-down rim

Date	Mintage	F	VF	XF	Unc	BU
1968 Proof	—	—	—	—	50.00	—

KM# 2 25 FRANCS
8.0000 g., 0.9000 Gold 0.2315 oz. AGW **Subject:** Independence Commemorative **Obv:** President Diori Hamani left **Rev:** Flagged arms

Date	Mintage	F	VF	XF	Unc	BU
ND(1960) Proof	1,000				Value: 245	

KM# 9 25 FRANCS
8.0000 g., 0.9000 Gold 0.2315 oz. AGW **Obv:** Barbary sheep **Rev:** Flagged arms

Date	Mintage	F	VF	XF	Unc	BU
1968 Proof	1,000				Value: 245	

KM# 3 50 FRANCS
16.0000 g., 0.9000 Gold 0.4630 oz. AGW **Subject:** Independence Commemorative **Obv:** President Diori Hamani left **Rev:** Flagged arms

Date	Mintage	F	VF	XF	Unc	BU
ND(1960) Proof	1,000				Value: 475	

KM# 10 50 FRANCS
16.0000 g., 0.9000 Gold 0.4630 oz. AGW **Subject:** Independence Commemorative **Obv:** Lion **Rev:** Flagged arms

Date	Mintage	F	VF	XF	Unc	BU
1968 Proof	1,000				Value: 475	

KM# 4 100 FRANCS
32.0000 g., 0.9000 Gold 0.9259 oz. AGW **Subject:** Independence Commemorative **Obv:** President Diori Hamani left **Rev:** Flagged arms

Date	Mintage	F	VF	XF	Unc	BU
ND(1960) Proof	1,000				Value: 925	

KM# 11 100 FRANCS
32.0000 g., 0.9000 Gold 0.9259 oz. AGW **Subject:** Independence Commemorative **Obv:** President Diori Hamani left **Rev:** Flagged arms

Date	Mintage	F	VF	XF	Unc	BU
1968 Proof	1,000	Value: 925				

KM# 5 500 FRANCS
10.0000 g., 0.9000 Silver 0.2893 oz. ASW **Subject:** Independence Commemorative **Obv:** President Diori Hamani left **Rev:** Flagged arms

Date	Mintage	F	VF	XF	Unc	BU
ND(1960) Proof	—	Value: 35.00				

KM# 6 1000 FRANCS
20.0000 g., 0.9000 Silver 0.5787 oz. ASW **Subject:** Independence Commemorative **Obv:** President Diori Hamani left **Rev:** Flagged arms

Date	Mintage	F	VF	XF	Unc	BU
ND(1960) Proof	—	Value: 55.00				

ESSAIS

KM#	Date	Mintage	Identification	Issue Price	Mkt Val
E1	1960	—	10 Francs. Silver. 39.4000 g. Lion facing. Arms. Thick planchet.	—	125
E2	1960	—	25 Francs.	—	200
E3	1960	—	50 Francs.	—	325
E4	1960	—	100 Francs.	—	500
E5	ND(1960)	1,000	500 Francs. Silver. KM5.	—	40.00
E6	ND(1960)	1,000	1000 Francs. Silver. KM6.	—	60.00
E7	1968	—	10 Francs. Gold. 31.7800 g. KM8.	—	1,750
E8	1968	—	10 Francs. Silver.	—	35.00
E9	1968	—	25 Francs. Silver.	—	40.00
E10	1968	—	50 Francs. Silver.	—	45.00
E11	1968	—	100 Francs. Silver.	—	50.00

PATTERNS
Including off metal strikes

KM#	Date	Mintage	Identification	Mkt Val
Pn1	1968	—	10 Francs. Copper. 18.8200 g. Reeded edge. KM8.1.	225

PROOF SETS

KM#	Date	Mintage	Identification	Issue Price	Mkt Val
PS1	1960 (4)	1,000	KM1-4	—	1,600
PS2	1968 (4)	—	KM7, 9-11	—	1,650

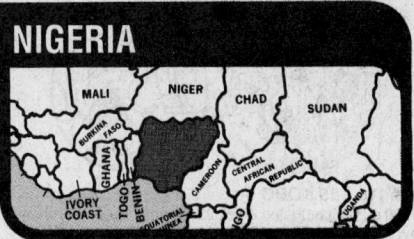

NIGERIA

Nigeria, situated on the Atlantic coast of West Africa has an area of 356,669 sq. mi. (923,770 sq. km.).

Following the Napoleonic Wars, the British expanded their trade with the interior of Nigeria. The Berlin Conference of 1885 recognized British claims to a sphere of influence in that area, and in the following year the Royal Niger Company was chartered. Direct British control of the territory was initiated in 1900, and in 1914 the amalgamation of Northern and Southern Nigeria into the Colony and Protectorate of Nigeria was effected. In 1960, following a number of territorial and constitutional changes, Nigeria was granted independence within the British Commonwealth as a federation of the Northern, Western and Eastern regions. Nigeria altered its political relationship with Great Britain on Oct. 1, 1963, by proclaiming itself a republic. It did, however, elect to remain a member of the Commonwealth of Nations.

On May 30, 1967, the Eastern Region of the republic an area occupied principally by the proud and resourceful Ibo tribe – seceded from Nigeria and proclaimed itself the independent Republic of Biafra with Odumegwu Ojukwu as Chief of State. Civil war erupted and raged for 31 months. Casualties, including civilian, were about two million, the majority succumbing to malnutrition and disease. Biafra surrendered to the federal government on January 15, 1970.

For earlier coinage refer to British West Africa.

Arms Mottos
Short: Unity and faith
Long: Unity and Faith, Peace and Progress

BRITISH PROTECTORATE OF NIGERIA
POUND STERLING COINAGE

KM# 1 1/2 PENNY
Bronze **Ruler:** Elizabeth II **Obv:** Crown above center hole flanked by curved sprig **Rev:** Star design around center hole

Date	Mintage	F	VF	XF	Unc	BU
1959	52,800,000	—	0.15	0.25	1.00	—
1959 Proof	6,031	Value: 2.50				

KM# 2 PENNY
7.5000 g., Bronze, 28 mm. **Ruler:** Elizabeth II **Obv:** Crown above center hole flanked by curved sprig **Rev:** Star design around center hole

Date	Mintage	F	VF	XF	Unc	BU
1959	93,368,000	—	0.15	0.25	2.00	—
1959 Proof	6,031	Value: 2.50				

KM# 3 3 PENCE
Nickel-Brass **Ruler:** Elizabeth II **Obv:** Crowned head right **Rev:** Cotton plant

Date	Mintage	F	VF	XF	Unc	BU
1959	52,000,000	—	0.20	0.40	2.00	—
1959 Proof	6,031	Value: 3.50				

KM# 4 6 PENCE
2.5000 g., Copper-Nickel, 17.8 mm. **Ruler:** Elizabeth II **Obv:** Crowned head right **Rev:** Cocoa beans

Date	Mintage	F	VF	XF	Unc	BU
1959	35,000,000	—	0.40	0.80	2.50	—
1959 Proof	6,031	Value: 5.00				

KM# 5 SHILLING
5.0000 g., Copper-Nickel, 22.8 mm. **Ruler:** Elizabeth II **Obv:** Crowned head right **Rev:** Palm divides date

Date	Mintage	F	VF	XF	Unc	BU
1959	18,000,000	—	0.65	1.45	3.50	—
1959 Proof	6,031	Value: 6.50				
1961	48,584,000	—	0.65	1.45	3.50	—
1962	39,416,000	—	0.65	1.45	3.50	—

KM# 6 2 SHILLING
Copper-Nickel, 27 mm. **Ruler:** Elizabeth II **Obv:** Crowned head right **Rev:** Flowers **Edge:** Security

Date	Mintage	F	VF	XF	Unc	BU
1959	15,000,000	—	1.25	2.50	6.00	—
1959 Proof	6,031	Value: 9.00				

FEDERAL REPUBLIC
DECIMAL COINAGE
100 Kobo = 1 Naira

KM# 7 1/2 KOBO
3.5300 g., Bronze **Ruler:** Elizabeth II **Obv:** Arms with supporters **Rev:** Value flanked by flowers

Date	Mintage	F	VF	XF	Unc	BU
1973	166,618,000	—	0.45	1.00	3.50	—
1973 Proof	10,000	Value: 3.50				

KM# 8.1 KOBO
Bronze **Ruler:** Elizabeth II **Obv:** Arms with supporters and short motto **Rev:** Value flanked by oil derricks

Date	Mintage	F	VF	XF	Unc	BU
1973 Proof	10,000	Value: 3.50				
1973	586,944,000	—	0.25	0.50	2.00	—
1974	14,500,000	—	0.25	0.50	3.00	—

KM# 8.2 KOBO
Bronze **Ruler:** Elizabeth II **Obv:** Arms with supporters and long motto **Rev:** Value flanked by oil derricks

Date	Mintage	F	VF	XF	Unc	BU
1987	—	—	0.50	1.50	6.00	—
1988	—	—	0.50	1.50	6.00	—

KM# 8.2a KOBO
2.5700 g., Copper Plated Steel, 17 mm. **Ruler:** Elizabeth II
Obv: Arms with supporters and long motto **Rev:** Value flanked by oil derricks

Date	Mintage	F	VF	XF	Unc	BU
1991	—	—	—	—	0.25	0.45

KM# 9.1 5 KOBO
Copper-Nickel **Ruler:** Elizabeth II **Obv:** Arms with supporters and short motto **Rev:** Cocoa beans

Date	Mintage	F	VF	XF	Unc	BU
1973 Proof	10,000	Value: 4.00				
1973	96,920,000	—	0.35	0.75	2.75	—
1974	—	—	0.45	0.85	3.00	—
1976	9,800,000	—	0.45	0.85	3.00	—
1986	—	—	0.45	0.85	3.00	—

KM# 9.2 5 KOBO
Copper-Nickel **Ruler:** Elizabeth II **Obv:** Arms with supporters and long motto **Rev:** Cocoa beans

Date	Mintage	F	VF	XF	Unc	BU
1987	—	—	1.00	2.50	7.00	—
1988	—	—	1.00	2.50	7.00	—
1989	—	—	1.00	2.50	7.00	—

KM# 10.1 10 KOBO
Copper-Nickel, 22.8 mm. **Ruler:** Elizabeth II **Obv:** Arms with supporters and short motto **Rev:** Value at left of oil palms

Date	Mintage	F	VF	XF	Unc	BU
1973 Proof	10,000	Value: 5.00				
1973	340,870,000	—	0.50	1.00	3.50	—
1974	—	—	0.60	1.20	3.75	—
1976	7,000,000	—	0.60	1.20	3.75	—

KM# 10.2 10 KOBO
4.0000 g., Copper-Nickel, 22.8 mm. **Ruler:** Elizabeth II **Obv:** Arms with supporters and long motto **Rev:** Value to left of oil palms

Date	Mintage	F	VF	XF	Unc	BU
1987	—	—	1.25	3.50	9.00	—
1988	—	—	1.25	3.50	9.00	—
1989	—	—	1.25	3.50	9.00	—
1990	—	—	1.25	3.50	9.00	—

KM# 12 10 KOBO
3.4800 g., Copper Plated Steel, 19.9 mm. **Ruler:** Elizabeth II **Obv:** Arms with supporters and long motto **Rev:** Value to left of oil palms

Date	Mintage	F	VF	XF	Unc	BU
1991	—	—	—	—	0.45	0.75

KM# 11 25 KOBO
Copper-Nickel **Ruler:** Elizabeth II **Obv:** Arms with supporters and short motto **Rev:** Groundnuts **Edge:** Security

Date	Mintage	F	VF	XF	Unc	BU
1973	4,616,000	—	1.00	2.50	7.50	—
1973 Proof	10,000	Value: 8.50				
1975	—	—	1.00	2.50	7.50	—

KM# 11a 25 KOBO
4.4900 g., Copper Plated Steel, 22.45 mm. **Ruler:** Elizabeth II **Obv:** Arms with supporters and long motto **Rev:** Groundnuts **Edge:** Reeded

Date	Mintage	F	VF	XF	Unc	BU
1991	—	—	—	—	0.65	1.00

KM# 13.1 50 KOBO
5.5300 g., Nickel Plated Steel, 24.72 mm. **Ruler:** Elizabeth II **Obv:** Arms with supporters with long motto **Rev:** Corn and value

Date	Mintage	F	VF	XF	Unc	BU
1991	—	—	—	—	1.25	1.50

KM# 13.2 50 KOBO
5.5300 g., Nickel Clad Steel, 24.72 mm. **Obv:** Arms with supporters with long motto **Rev:** Corn with value

Date	Mintage	F	VF	XF	Unc	BU
1993	—	—	—	—	1.25	1.50

KM# 14 NAIRA
12.1500 g., Nickel Plated Steel, 27.5 mm. **Ruler:** Elizabeth II **Obv:** Arms with supporters and long motto **Rev:** Head 1/4 right

Date	Mintage	F	VF	XF	Unc	BU
1991	—	—	—	—	1.75	2.00
1993	—	—	—	—	1.75	2.00

KM# 15 100 NAIRA
28.2800 g., 0.9250 Silver 0.8410 oz. ASW **Ruler:** Elizabeth II **Subject:** 100 Years - Banking in Nigeria **Obv:** Arms with supporters **Rev:** Bank building **Edge:** Reeded

Date	Mintage	F	VF	XF	Unc	BU
1994 Proof	5,000	Value: 650				

Note: Issue price at Bank in Lagos approximately $1,400

KM# 16 1000 NAIRA
47.5400 g., 0.9166 Gold 1.4009 oz. AGW **Ruler:** Elizabeth II **Subject:** 100 Years - Banking in Nigeria **Obv:** Arms with supporters **Rev:** Bank building **Edge:** Reeded

Date	Mintage	F	VF	XF	Unc	BU
1994 Proof	100	Value: 2,250				

PATTERNS
Including off metal strikes

KM#	Date	Mintage Identification	Mkt Val
Pn1	1962	— Shilling. Bronze. KM5.	200
Pn2	1973	— 10 Kobo. Bronze. KM10.	175

TRIAL STRIKES

KM#	Date	Mintage Identification	Mkt Val
TS1	1962	— Shilling. Copper-Nickel. "TRIAL" in field on obverse and reverse.	120

PROOF SETS

KM#	Date	Mintage Identification	Issue Price	Mkt Val
PS1	1959 (6)	1,031 KM1-5, 6.1, red case, originals	—	45.00
PS2	1959 (6)	5,000 KM1-5, 6.1, blue case, restrikes	—	30.00
PS3	1973 (5)	102,000 KM7, 8.1-10.1,11	14.70	25.00

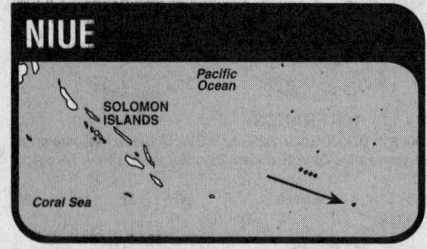

NIUE

Niue, or Savage Island, a dependent state of New Zealand is located in the Pacific Ocean east of Tonga and southeast of Samoa. The size is 100 sq. mi. (260 sq. km.) with a population of *2,000. Chief village and port is Alofi. Bananas and copra are exported.

Discovered by Captain Cook in 1774, it was originally part of the Cook Islands administration but has been separate since 1922.

MINT MARK
PM - Pobjoy Mint

NEW ZEALAND DEPENDENT STATE
DECIMAL COINAGE

KM# 85 DOLLAR
10.0200 g., 0.5000 Silver 0.1611 oz. ASW **Ruler:** Elizabeth II **Obv:** Crowned arms within sprigs **Rev:** Sailing ship, value and emblem

Date	Mintage	F	VF	XF	Unc	BU
1996 Proof	—	Value: 7.50				

KM# 113 DOLLAR
10.0200 g., 0.5000 Silver 0.1611 oz. ASW **Ruler:** Elizabeth II **Series:** Endangered Wildlife **Obv:** Crowned arms within sprigs **Rev:** Jaguar on tree limb

Date	Mintage	F	VF	XF	Unc	BU
1996 Proof	—	Value: 15.00				

KM# 122 DOLLAR
10.0000 g., 0.5000 Silver 0.1607 oz. ASW, 30 mm. **Ruler:** Elizabeth II **Series:** Protect Our World **Obv:** Crowned arms within sprigs **Rev:** Oak tree **Edge:** Reeded

Date	Mintage	F	VF	XF	Unc	BU
1996 Proof	—	Value: 8.00				

KM# 87 DOLLAR

Copper-Nickel **Ruler:** Elizabeth II **Obv:** Crowned arms within sprigs **Rev:** Bust facing **Rev. Leg.:** . . . The People's Princess

Date	Mintage	F	VF	XF	Unc	BU
1997	—	—	—	—	3.00	4.50

KM# 88 DOLLAR

Copper-Nickel **Ruler:** Elizabeth II **Obv:** Crowned arms within sprigs **Rev:** Bust facing **Rev. Leg.:** . . . Princess of Wales **Note:** Similar to 10 Dollars, KM#91.

Date	Mintage	F	VF	XF	Unc	BU
1997	—	—	—	—	3.00	4.50

KM# 89 DOLLAR

Copper-Nickel **Ruler:** Elizabeth II **Obv:** Crowned arms within sprigs **Rev:** Head left above sprigs **Rev. Leg.:** . . . Princess of Wales **Note:** Similar to 10 Dollars, KM#92.

Date	Mintage	F	VF	XF	Unc	BU
1997	—	—	—	—	3.00	4.50

KM# 102 DOLLAR

Copper-Nickel **Ruler:** Elizabeth II **Obv:** Crowned head right **Rev:** Bust facing **Rev. Leg.:** . . . In Memoriam **Note:** Similar to 10 Dollars, KM#104.

Date	Mintage	F	VF	XF	Unc	BU
1998	—	—	—	—	3.00	4.50

KM# 103 DOLLAR

Copper-Nickel **Ruler:** Elizabeth II **Obv:** Crowned head right **Rev:** Bust facing **Rev. Leg.:** . . . Princess of Wales **Note:** Similar to 10 Dollars, KM#105.

Date	Mintage	F	VF	XF	Unc	BU
1998	—	—	—	—	3.00	4.50

KM# 115 DOLLAR

Copper-Nickel **Ruler:** Elizabeth II **Subject:** 50th Anniversary of Peanuts **Obv:** Crowned head right **Rev:** Snoopy and Woodstock **Note:** Similar to 10 Dollars, KM#116.

Date	Mintage	F	VF	XF	Unc	BU
2000	Est. 100,000	—	—	—	12.00	14.00

KM# 174 DOLLAR

21.0000 g., Copper-Nickel, 38.6 mm. **Ruler:** Elizabeth II **Subject:** Marine Life Protection **Obv:** Crowned head right **Rev:** Multicolor fish scene **Edge:** Reeded

Date	Mintage	F	VF	XF	Unc	BU
2000	—	—	—	—	14.00	25.00

KM# 1 5 DOLLARS

Copper-Nickel **Ruler:** Elizabeth II **Series:** Olympics **Subject:** Tennis **Obv:** Crowned arms within sprigs **Rev:** Boris Becker

Date	Mintage	F	VF	XF	Unc	BU
1987	80,000	—	—	—	6.00	8.00

KM# 5 5 DOLLARS

Copper-Nickel **Ruler:** Elizabeth II **Subject:** 24th Olympiad Tennis Games, Seoul 1988 **Obv:** Crowned arms within sprigs **Rev:** Steffi Graf

Date	Mintage	F	VF	XF	Unc	BU
1987	50,000	—	—	—	6.00	8.00

KM# 11 5 DOLLARS

Copper-Nickel **Ruler:** Elizabeth II **Subject:** 24th Olympic Games, Seoul 1988 **Obv:** Crowned arms within sprigs **Rev:** 3/4 Tennis player with cup

Date	Mintage	F	VF	XF	Unc	BU
1988	80,000	—	—	—	6.00	8.00

KM# 12 5 DOLLARS

Copper-Nickel **Ruler:** Elizabeth II **Series:** Olympics **Subject:** Soccer **Obv:** Crowned arms within sprigs **Rev:** Soccer player left of cameo

Date	Mintage	F	VF	XF	Unc	BU
1988	50,000	—	—	—	4.00	6.00

KM# 15 5 DOLLARS

Copper-Nickel **Ruler:** Elizabeth II **Subject:** 24th Olympic Games, Seoul 1988 **Obv:** Crowned arms within sprigs **Rev:** Cameos of Navratilova, Graf and Evert, tennis champions

Date	Mintage	F	VF	XF	Unc	BU
1988	80,000	—	—	—	6.00	8.00

KM# 17 5 DOLLARS

Copper-Nickel, 38.8 mm. **Ruler:** Elizabeth II **Obv:** Crowned arms within sprigs **Rev:** Head of John F. Kennedy left

Date	Mintage	F	VF	XF	Unc	BU
1988	80,000	—	—	—	3.50	5.00

KM# 22 5 DOLLARS

Copper-Nickel **Ruler:** Elizabeth II **Obv:** Crowned arms within sprigs **Rev:** Head of General Douglas MacArthur 3/4 left

Date	Mintage	F	VF	XF	Unc	BU
1989	—	—	—	—	5.00	7.00

KM# 24 5 DOLLARS

Copper-Nickel **Ruler:** Elizabeth II **Obv:** Crowned arms within sprigs **Rev:** Tennis player

Date	Mintage	F	VF	XF	Unc	BU
1989	Est. 50,000	—	—	—	4.00	6.00

KM# 67 5 DOLLARS

Copper-Nickel **Ruler:** Elizabeth II **Subject:** 24th Olympic Games, Seoul 1988 **Obv:** Crowned arms within sprigs **Rev:** Steffi Graf

Date	Mintage	F	VF	XF	Unc	BU
1989	—	—	—	—	4.00	6.00

KM# 29   5 DOLLARS
Copper-Nickel, 38.8 mm.   **Ruler:** Elizabeth II **Obv:** Crowned arms within sprigs **Rev:** Bust of General Eisenhower facing within flags

Date	Mintage	F	VF	XF	Unc	BU
1990	—	—	—	—	5.00	7.00

KM# 31   5 DOLLARS
Copper-Nickel, 38.8 mm.   **Ruler:** Elizabeth II **Obv:** Crowned arms within sprigs **Rev:** General George S. Patton

Date	Mintage	F	VF	XF	Unc	BU
1990	—	—	—	—	5.00	7.00

KM# 33   5 DOLLARS
Copper-Nickel, 38.8 mm.   **Ruler:** Elizabeth II **Obv:** Crowned arms within sprigs **Rev:** Admiral William Halsey

Date	Mintage	F	VF	XF	Unc	BU
1990	—	—	—	—	5.00	7.00

KM# 35   5 DOLLARS
Copper-Nickel, 38.8 mm.   **Ruler:** Elizabeth II **Obv:** Crowned arms within sprigs **Rev:** Bust of President Franklin D. Roosevelt facing

Date	Mintage	F	VF	XF	Unc	BU
1990	—	—	—	—	5.00	7.00

KM# 37   5 DOLLARS
Copper-Nickel, 38.8 mm.   **Ruler:** Elizabeth II **Obv:** Crowned arms within sprigs **Rev:** Sir Winston Churchill

Date	Mintage	F	VF	XF	Unc	BU
1990	—	—	—	—	5.00	7.00

KM# 143   5 DOLLARS
28.3400 g., Copper-Nickel, 38.6 mm.   **Ruler:** Elizabeth II **Subject:** XIV Football World Championship Italy '90 **Obv:** Crowned arms within sprigs **Rev:** Head right at lower left of map and soccer player **Edge:** Reeded

Date	Mintage	F	VF	XF	Unc	BU
1990	60,000	—	—	—	4.00	6.00

KM# 144   5 DOLLARS
28.1500 g., Copper-Nickel, 38.5 mm.   **Ruler:** Elizabeth II **Subject:** Basketball Centennial **Obv:** Crowned arms within sprigs **Rev:** Two female basketball players **Edge:** Reeded

Date	Mintage	F	VF	XF	Unc	BU
1991	28,000	—	—	—	4.00	6.00

KM# 58   5 DOLLARS
9.9300 g., 0.5000 Silver 0.1596 oz. ASW   **Ruler:** Elizabeth II **Series:** World Cup Soccer **Obv:** Crowned arms within sprigs **Rev:** Soccer player and Statue of Liberty

Date	Mintage	F	VF	XF	Unc	BU
1991 Proof	150,000			Value: 9.00		

KM# 55   5 DOLLARS
10.0000 g., 0.5000 Silver 0.1607 oz. ASW   **Ruler:** Elizabeth II **Obv:** Crowned arms within sprigs **Rev:** Ship, HMS Bounty

Date	Mintage	F	VF	XF	Unc	BU
1992 Proof	Est. 150,000			Value: 9.00		

KM# 60   5 DOLLARS
10.0000 g., 0.5000 Silver 0.1607 oz. ASW   **Ruler:** Elizabeth II **Series:** Endangered Wildlife **Obv:** Crowned arms within sprigs **Rev:** Jaguar

Date	Mintage	F	VF	XF	Unc	BU
1992 Proof	Est. 25,000			Value: 17.50		

KM# 61   5 DOLLARS
10.0000 g., 0.5000 Silver 0.1607 oz. ASW   **Ruler:** Elizabeth II **Series:** Olympics 1996 **Obv:** Crowned arms within sprigs **Rev:** Sprinter

Date	Mintage	F	VF	XF	Unc	BU
1992 Proof	100,000			Value: 8.00		

KM# 68   5 DOLLARS
9.8500 g., 0.5000 Silver 0.1583 oz. ASW   **Ruler:** Elizabeth II **Subject:** First Moon Landing **Obv:** Crowned arms within sprigs **Rev:** Man on moon

Date	Mintage	F	VF	XF	Unc	BU
1992 Proof	—			Value: 8.00		

KM# 76   5 DOLLARS
10.0000 g., 0.9250 Silver 0.2974 oz. ASW   **Ruler:** Elizabeth II **Obv:** Crowned arms within sprigs **Rev:** Kennedy, Brandenburg Gate

Date	Mintage	F	VF	XF	Unc	BU
1992 Proof	Est. 50,000			Value: 10.00		

KM# 80   5 DOLLARS
9.9500 g., 0.5000 Silver 0.1599 oz. ASW   **Ruler:** Elizabeth II **Series:** Endangered Wildlife **Obv:** Crowned arms within sprigs **Rev:** Dolphins

Date	Mintage	F	VF	XF	Unc	BU
1992 Proof	—			Value: 17.50		

KM# 62 5 DOLLARS
9.9500 g., 0.5000 Silver 0.1599 oz. ASW **Ruler:** Elizabeth II
Series: Protect Our World **Obv:** Crowned arms within sprigs
Rev: Oak tree

Date	Mintage	F	VF	XF	Unc	BU
1993 Proof	—	Value: 12.50				

KM# 114 5 DOLLARS
31.3200 g., 0.9250 Silver 0.9314 oz. ASW, 38.51 mm.
Ruler: Elizabeth II **Subject:** Cook's Pacific Voyages
Obv: National arms **Rev:** Head of Captain Cook in oval frame at left, sailing ship H.M.S. Resolution at right **Edge:** Reeded

Date	Mintage	F	VF	XF	Unc	BU
1996 Proof	—	Value: 40.00				

KM# 175 5 DOLLARS
31.8400 g., 0.9250 Silver 0.9469 oz. ASW, 38.6 mm.
Ruler: Elizabeth II **Subject:** Victorian Age **Obv:** Crowned head right
Rev: Queen Victoria and Prince Albert wedding portrait
Edge: Reeded

Date	Mintage	F	VF	XF	Unc	BU
1996 Proof	—	Value: 25.00				

KM# 173 5 DOLLARS
31.2200 g., 0.9250 Silver 0.9284 oz. ASW, 38.6 mm.
Ruler: Elizabeth II **Subject:** Queen Mother **Obv:** Crowned arms within sprigs **Rev:** Queen Mother viewing London bomb damage
Edge: Reeded

Date	Mintage	F	VF	XF	Unc	BU
1997 Proof	—	Value: 20.00				

KM# 145 5 DOLLARS
31.0000 g., 0.9250 Silver 0.9326 oz. ASW, 38.4 mm. **Ruler:**
Elizabeth II **Subject:** Queen Mother **Obv:** Crowned head right
Rev: Silver Wedding scene within circle **Edge:** Reeded

Date	Mintage	F	VF	XF	Unc	BU
1998 Proof	—	Value: 20.00				

KM# 171 5 DOLLARS
31.2500 g., 0.9250 Silver 0.9293 oz. ASW, 35.5 mm.
Ruler: Elizabeth II **Subject:** Pygoplites Diacantus **Obv:** Crowned head right **Rev:** Three gold-plated fish **Edge:** Plain

Date	Mintage	F	VF	XF	Unc	BU
1999 Proof	—	Value: 75.00				

KM# 120 5 DOLLARS
31.4200 g., 0.9250 Silver 0.9344 oz. ASW **Ruler:** Elizabeth II
Subject: Pterois Radiata **Obv:** Crowned head right **Rev:** Gold colored Clearfin lion fish **Edge:** Plain

Date	Mintage	F	VF	XF	Unc	BU
1999 Proof	—	Value: 75.00				

KM# 121 5 DOLLARS
31.4200 g., 0.9250 Silver 0.9344 oz. ASW **Ruler:** Elizabeth II
Subject: Fourcipiger Longirostris **Obv:** Crowned head right
Rev: Gold colored big long nosed Butterfly fish **Edge:** Plain

Date	Mintage	F	VF	XF	Unc	BU
1999 Proof	—	Value: 75.00				

KM# 172 5 DOLLARS
28.4000 g., 0.9250 Silver with gilt outer ring 0.8446 oz. ASW,
38.5 mm. **Ruler:** Elizabeth II **Subject:** Queen Mother
Obv: Crowned head right **Rev:** Queen Mother's engagement
portrait **Edge:** Reeded

Date	Mintage	F	VF	XF	Unc	BU
2000 Proof	—	Value: 18.00				

KM# 46 10 DOLLARS
10.0000 g., 0.9250 Silver 0.2974 oz. ASW **Ruler:** Elizabeth II
Series: Summer Olympics **Obv:** Crowned arms within sprigs
Rev: Runners

Date	Mintage	F	VF	XF	Unc	BU
1991 Proof	150,000	Value: 12.50				

KM# 56 10 DOLLARS
10.0000 g., 0.9250 Silver 0.2974 oz. ASW **Ruler:** Elizabeth II
Series: Summer Olympics **Obv:** Crowned arms within sprigs
Rev: Discus Thrower

Date	Mintage	F	VF	XF	Unc	BU
1991 Proof	50,000	Value: 11.50				

KM# 59 10 DOLLARS
31.5300 g., 0.9999 Silver 1.0136 oz. ASW **Ruler:** Elizabeth II
Series: World Cup Soccer **Obv:** Crowned arms within sprigs
Rev: Handshake above value with hands holding crowned arms
below

Date	Mintage	F	VF	XF	Unc	BU
1991 Proof	20,000	Value: 18.50				

KM# 69 10 DOLLARS
31.4300 g., 0.9999 Silver 1.0104 oz. ASW **Ruler:** Elizabeth II
Subject: Cook's Pacific Voyages **Obv:** Crowned arms within
sprigs **Rev:** Cameo left of sailing ship

Date	Mintage	F	VF	XF	Unc	BU
1992 Proof	—	Value: 25.00				

KM# 70   10 DOLLARS
31.4300 g., 0.9999 Silver 1.0104 oz. ASW   **Ruler:** Elizabeth II
Subject: Moon Landing **Obv:** Crowned arms within sprigs
Rev: Luna 9

Date	Mintage	F	VF	XF	Unc	BU
1992 Proof	Est. 15,000	Value: 20.00				

KM# 74   10 DOLLARS
31.4700 g., 0.9250 Silver 0.9359 oz. ASW   **Ruler:** Elizabeth II
Series: Endangered Wildlife **Obv:** Crowned arms within sprigs
Rev: Whales

Date	Mintage	F	VF	XF	Unc	BU
1992 Proof	25,000	Value: 22.50				

KM# 78   10 DOLLARS
31.4700 g., 0.9250 Silver 0.9359 oz. ASW   **Ruler:** Elizabeth II
Subject: The Resolution **Obv:** Crowned arms within sprigs
Rev: Three-masted ship

Date	Mintage	F	VF	XF	Unc	BU
1992 Proof	Est. 15,000	Value: 20.00				

KM# 86   10 DOLLARS
31.0400 g., 0.9250 Silver 0.9231 oz. ASW   **Ruler:** Elizabeth II
Obv: Crowned arms within sprigs **Rev:** Head 1/4 left and rocket
launch

Date	Mintage	F	VF	XF	Unc	BU
1992 Proof	—	Value: 22.00				

KM# 81   10 DOLLARS
1.2440 g., 0.9990 Gold 0.0400 oz. AGW   **Ruler:** Elizabeth II
Subject: Liberty Gold Bullion **Obv:** Crowned head right
Rev: Statue of Liberty

Date	Mintage	F	VF	XF	Unc	BU
1997	—	—	—		45.00	

KM# 90   10 DOLLARS
28.2800 g., 0.9250 Silver 0.8410 oz. ASW   **Ruler:** Elizabeth II
Obv: Crowned arms within sprigs **Rev:** Bust facing
Rev. Leg.: . . . The People's Princess

Date	Mintage	F	VF	XF	Unc	BU
1997 Proof	Est. 10,000	Value: 16.00				

KM# 91   10 DOLLARS
28.2800 g., 0.9250 Silver 0.8410 oz. ASW   **Ruler:** Elizabeth II
Obv: Crowned arms within sprigs **Rev:** Bust facing
Rev. Leg.: . . . Princess of Wales

Date	Mintage	F	VF	XF	Unc	BU
1997 Proof	Est. 10,000	Value: 16.00				

KM# 92   10 DOLLARS
28.2800 g., 0.9250 Silver 0.8410 oz. ASW   **Ruler:** Elizabeth II
Obv: Crowned arms within sprigs **Rev:** Head left above sprigs
Rev. Leg.: . . . Princess of Wales

Date	Mintage	F	VF	XF	Unc	BU
1997 Proof	Est. 10,000	Value: 16.00				

KM# 104   10 DOLLARS
28.2800 g., 0.9250 Silver 0.8410 oz. ASW   **Ruler:** Elizabeth II
Obv: Crowned head right **Rev:** Bust facing **Rev. Leg.:** . . . In
Memoriam

Date	Mintage	F	VF	XF	Unc	BU
1998 Proof	Est. 10,000	Value: 16.00				

KM# 105   10 DOLLARS
28.2800 g., 0.9250 Silver 0.8410 oz. ASW   **Ruler:** Elizabeth II
Obv: Crowned head right **Rev:** Bust facing
Rev. Leg.: . . . Princess of Wales

Date	Mintage	F	VF	XF	Unc	BU
1998 Proof	Est. 10,000	Value: 16.00				

KM# 116   10 DOLLARS
28.2800 g., 0.9250 Silver 0.8410 oz. ASW   **Ruler:** Elizabeth II
Subject: 50th Anniversary of Peanuts **Obv:** Crowned head right
Rev: Snoopy and Woodstock

Date	Mintage	F	VF	XF	Unc	BU
2000 Proof	Est. 10,000	Value: 22.00				

KM# 182   10 DOLLARS
1.2400 g., Gold, 13.89 mm.   **Ruler:** Elizabeth II **Obv:** National
arms **Rev:** 2 Black and Gold Angelfish **Edge:** Reeded

Date	Mintage	F	VF	XF	Unc	BU
2000 Proof	—	Value: 55.00				

KM# 57   20 DOLLARS
31.4700 g., 0.9250 Silver 0.9359 oz. ASW   **Ruler:** Elizabeth II
Subject: 40th Anniversary of Coronation **Obv:** Crowned head
right **Rev:** Crowned monogram within 3/4 wreath with value and
dates below

Date	Mintage	F	VF	XF	Unc	BU
1993 Proof	Est. 10,000	Value: 20.00				

KM# 63   20 DOLLARS
31.4700 g., 0.9250 Silver 0.9359 oz. ASW   **Ruler:** Elizabeth II
Series: Protect Our World **Obv:** Crowned arms within sprigs
Rev: Hand holding seedling

Date	Mintage	F	VF	XF	Unc	BU
1993 Proof	Est. 10,000	Value: 20.00				

KM# 64 20 DOLLARS
31.4700 g., 0.9250 Silver 0.9359 oz. ASW **Ruler:** Elizabeth II
Obv: Crowned arms within sprigs **Rev:** Bust right and Statue of
Liberty

Date	Mintage	F	VF	XF	Unc	BU
1993 Proof	—				Value: 20.00	

KM# 93 20 DOLLARS
1.2440 g., 0.9990 Gold 0.0400 oz. AGW **Ruler:** Elizabeth II
Obv: Crowned arms within sprigs **Rev:** Bust facing
Rev. Leg.: ...The People's Princess

Date	Mintage	F	VF	XF	Unc	BU
1997 Proof	Est. 10,000				Value: 45.00	

KM# 94 20 DOLLARS
1.2440 g., 0.9990 Gold 0.0400 oz. AGW **Ruler:** Elizabeth II
Obv: Crowned arms within sprigs **Rev:** Bust facing
Rev. Leg.: ...Princess of Wales

Date	Mintage	F	VF	XF	Unc	BU
1997 Proof	Est. 10,000				Value: 45.00	

KM# 95 20 DOLLARS
1.2440 g., 0.9990 Gold 0.0400 oz. AGW **Ruler:** Elizabeth II
Obv: Crowned arms within sprigs **Rev:** Head left above sprigs
Rev. Leg.: ...Princess of Wales

Date	Mintage	F	VF	XF	Unc	BU
1997 Proof	Est. 10,000				Value: 45.00	

KM# 106 20 DOLLARS
1.2440 g., 0.9990 Gold 0.0400 oz. AGW **Ruler:** Elizabeth II
Obv: Crowned head right **Rev:** Bust facing **Rev. Leg.:** ...In
Memoriam

Date	Mintage	F	VF	XF	Unc	BU
1998 Proof	Est. 10,000				Value: 45.00	

KM# 107 20 DOLLARS
1.2440 g., 0.9990 Gold 0.0400 oz. AGW **Ruler:** Elizabeth II
Obv: Crowned head right **Rev:** Bust facing **Rev. Leg.:** ...Princess
of Wales

Date	Mintage	F	VF	XF	Unc	BU
1998 Proof	Est. 10,000				Value: 45.00	

KM# 117 20 DOLLARS
1.2400 g., 0.9990 Gold 0.0398 oz. AGW **Ruler:** Elizabeth II
Subject: 50th Anniversary of Peanuts **Obv:** Crowned head right
Rev: Snoopy and Woodstock

Date	Mintage	F	VF	XF	Unc	BU
2000 Proof	Est. 10,000				Value: 45.00	

KM# 79 25 DOLLARS
1.2441 g., 0.9990 Gold 0.0400 oz. AGW **Ruler:** Elizabeth II
Subject: Death of John F. Kennedy **Obv:** National arms
Rev: Half length figure of JFK left **Edge:** Reeded

Date	Mintage	F	VF	XF	Unc	BU
1994 Proof	Est. 25,000				Value: 50.00	

KM# 178 25 DOLLARS
1.2300 g., 0.9999 Gold 0.0395 oz. AGW, 13.93 mm.
Ruler: Elizabeth II **Obv:** National arms **Rev:** Sailing ship "H.M.S.
Bounty" **Edge:** Reeded

Date	Mintage	F	VF	XF	Unc	BU
1996 Proof	—				Value: 55.00	

KM# 179 25 DOLLARS
1.2200 g., 0.9999 Gold 0.0392 oz. AGW, 13.86 mm.
Ruler: Elizabeth II **Subject:** Protect our World **Obv:** National arms
Rev: Tree **Edge:** Reeded

Date	Mintage	F	VF	XF	Unc	BU
1996 Proof	—				Value: 55.00	

KM# 82 25 DOLLARS
3.1000 g., 0.9990 Gold 0.0996 oz. AGW **Ruler:** Elizabeth II
Series: Liberty Gold Bullion **Obv:** Crowned head right
Rev: Statue of Liberty

Date	Mintage	F	VF	XF	Unc	BU
1997	—	—	—	—	—	110

KM# 96 25 DOLLARS
3.1000 g., 0.9990 Gold 0.0996 oz. AGW **Ruler:** Elizabeth II
Obv: Crowned arms within sprigs **Rev:** Bust facing
Rev. Leg.: ...The People's Princess

Date	Mintage	F	VF	XF	Unc	BU
1997 Proof	Est. 7,500				Value: 110	

KM# 97 25 DOLLARS
3.1000 g., 0.9990 Gold 0.0996 oz. AGW **Ruler:** Elizabeth II
Obv: Crowned arms within sprigs **Rev:** Bust facing
Rev. Leg.: ...Princess of Wales

Date	Mintage	F	VF	XF	Unc	BU
1997 Proof	Est. 7,500				Value: 110	

KM# 98 25 DOLLARS
3.1000 g., 0.9990 Gold 0.0996 oz. AGW **Ruler:** Elizabeth II
Obv: Crowned arms within sprigs **Rev:** Head left above sprigs
Rev. Leg.: . . . Princess of Wales

Date	Mintage	F	VF	XF	Unc	BU
1997 Proof	Est. 7,500				Value: 110	

KM# 181 25 DOLLARS
1.2400 g., Gold, 13.89 mm. **Ruler:** Elizabeth II
Subject: Entering the New Century - For a Better World
Obv: National arms **Rev:** 2 hands holding a plant **Edge:** Reeded

Date	Mintage	F	VF	XF	Unc	BU
1999 Proof	—				Value: 55.00	

KM# 2 50 DOLLARS
27.1000 g., 0.6250 Silver 0.5445 oz. ASW **Ruler:** Elizabeth II
Series: Olympics **Subject:** Tennis **Obv:** Crowned arms within
sprigs **Rev:** Boris Becker

Date	Mintage	F	VF	XF	Unc	BU
1987 Proof	20,000				Value: 22.50	

KM# 6 50 DOLLARS
27.1000 g., 0.6250 Silver 0.5445 oz. ASW **Ruler:** Elizabeth II
Subject: 24th Olympiad Tennis Games, Seoul 1988
Obv: Crowned arms within sprigs **Rev:** Steffi Graf

Date	Mintage	F	VF	XF	Unc	BU
1987 Proof	20,000				Value: 22.50	

KM# 13 50 DOLLARS
27.1000 g., 0.6250 Silver 0.5445 oz. ASW **Ruler:** Elizabeth II
Subject: 24th Olympic Games, Seoul 1988 **Obv:** Crowned arms
within sprigs **Rev:** Steffi Graf **Note:** Similar to 5 Dollars, KM#11.

Date	Mintage	F	VF	XF	Unc	BU
1988 Proof	Est. 20,000				Value: 28.00	

KM# 14 50 DOLLARS
27.1000 g., 0.6250 Silver 0.5445 oz. ASW **Ruler:** Elizabeth II
Series: Olympics **Subject:** Soccer **Obv:** Crowned arms within
sprigs **Rev:** Soccer player to left of cameo

Date	Mintage	F	VF	XF	Unc	BU
1988 Proof	Est. 20,000				Value: 16.50	

KM# 16 50 DOLLARS
27.1000 g., 0.6250 Silver 0.5445 oz. ASW **Ruler:** Elizabeth II
Subject: 24th Olympic Games, Seoul 1988 **Obv:** Crowned arms
within sprigs **Rev:** Cameos of Navratilova, Graf and Evert, tennis
champions

Date	Mintage	F	VF	XF	Unc	BU
1988 Proof	Est. 20,000				Value: 28.00	

KM# 18 50 DOLLARS
28.2800 g., 0.9250 Silver 0.8410 oz. ASW **Ruler:** Elizabeth II
Obv: Crowned arms within sprigs **Rev:** Head left

Date	Mintage	F	VF	XF	Unc	BU
1988 Proof	20,000				Value: 18.00	

KM# 43 50 DOLLARS
28.2800 g., 0.9250 Silver 0.8410 oz. ASW **Ruler:** Elizabeth II
Subject: Soccer **Obv:** Crowned arms within sprigs **Rev:** Soccer
players divide circle

Date	Mintage	F	VF	XF	Unc	BU
1988 Proof					Value: 20.00	

KM# 23 50 DOLLARS
31.1030 g., 0.9990 Silver 0.9989 oz. ASW **Ruler:** Elizabeth II
Obv: Crowned arms within sprigs **Rev:** General Douglas MacArthur

Date	Mintage	F	VF	XF	Unc	BU
1989 Proof	Est. 50,000				Value: 20.00	

KM# 25 50 DOLLARS
28.2800 g., 0.9250 Silver 0.8410 oz. ASW **Ruler:** Elizabeth II
Series: Davis Cup Tennis **Obv:** Crowned arms within sprigs
Rev: Conjoined busts of tennis players

Date	Mintage	F	VF	XF	Unc	BU
1989 Proof	Est. 20,000				Value: 22.50	

KM# 27 50 DOLLARS
28.2800 g., 0.9250 Silver 0.8410 oz. ASW **Ruler:** Elizabeth II
Series: 1992 Olympics **Subject:** Rowing **Obv:** Crowned arms
within sprigs **Rev:** Men rowing boats within circle

Date	Mintage	F	VF	XF	Unc	BU
1989 Proof	Est. 30,000				Value: 20.00	

KM# 44   50 DOLLARS
28.2800 g., 0.9250 Silver 0.8410 oz. ASW   **Ruler:** Elizabeth II
Subject: 24th Olympic Games, Seoul 1988 **Obv:** Crowned arms within sprigs **Rev:** Steffi Graf

Date	Mintage	F	VF	XF	Unc	BU
1989 Proof	20,000	Value: 20.00				

KM# 30   50 DOLLARS
31.1030 g., 0.9990 Silver 0.9989 oz. ASW   **Ruler:** Elizabeth II
Obv: Crowned arms within sprigs **Rev:** General Eisenhower within flags

Date	Mintage	F	VF	XF	Unc	BU
1990 Proof	Est. 50,000	Value: 18.50				

KM# 32   50 DOLLARS
31.1030 g., 0.9990 Silver 0.9989 oz. ASW   **Ruler:** Elizabeth II
Obv: Crowned arms within sprigs **Rev:** General George S. Patton

Date	Mintage	F	VF	XF	Unc	BU
1990 Proof	Est. 50,000	Value: 18.50				

KM# 34   50 DOLLARS
31.1030 g., 0.9990 Silver 0.9989 oz. ASW   **Ruler:** Elizabeth II
Obv: Crowned arms within sprigs **Rev:** Admiral William Halsey

Date	Mintage	F	VF	XF	Unc	BU
1990 Proof	Est. 50,000	Value: 18.50				

KM# 36   50 DOLLARS
31.1030 g., 0.9990 Silver 0.9989 oz. ASW   **Ruler:** Elizabeth II
Obv: Crowned arms within sprigs **Rev:** President Franklin D. Roosevelt

Date	Mintage	F	VF	XF	Unc	BU
1990 Proof	Est. 50,000	Value: 18.50				

KM# 38   50 DOLLARS
31.1030 g., 0.9990 Silver 0.9989 oz. ASW   **Ruler:** Elizabeth II
Obv: Crowned arms within sprigs **Rev:** Sir Winston Churchill

Date	Mintage	F	VF	XF	Unc	BU
1990 Proof	Est. 50,000	Value: 18.50				

KM# 47   50 DOLLARS
38.2000 g., 0.9250 Silver 1.1360 oz. ASW   **Ruler:** Elizabeth II
Subject: Soccer **Obv:** Crowned arms within sprigs **Rev:** Player kicking soccer ball

Date	Mintage	F	VF	XF	Unc	BU
1990 Proof	20,000	Value: 22.50				

KM# 75   50 DOLLARS
28.5600 g., 0.9250 Silver 0.8493 oz. ASW   **Ruler:** Elizabeth II
Subject: Soccer **Obv:** Crowned arms within sprigs **Rev:** Soccer players

Date	Mintage	F	VF	XF	Unc	BU
1990 Proof	20,000	Value: 18.00				

KM# 71   50 DOLLARS
7.7000 g., 0.5830 Gold 0.1443 oz. AGW   **Ruler:** Elizabeth II
Series: Olympics **Obv:** Crowned arms within sprigs **Rev:** Discus thrower

Date	Mintage	F	VF	XF	Unc	BU
1992 Proof	6,000	Value: 165				

KM# 65   50 DOLLARS
155.5175 g., 0.9990 Silver 4.9948 oz. ASW   **Ruler:** Elizabeth II
Obv: Crowned arms within sprigs **Rev:** Head left with apollo rocket

Date	Mintage	F	VF	XF	Unc	BU
1993 Proof	—	Value: 100				

KM# 66   50 DOLLARS
7.7760 g., 0.5830 Gold 0.1457 oz. AGW   **Ruler:** Elizabeth II
Obv: Crowned arms within sprigs **Rev:** Bust left and rocket launch

Date	Mintage	F	VF	XF	Unc	BU
1993 Proof	—	Value: 165				

KM# 72   50 DOLLARS
156.1700 g., 0.9990 Silver 5.0158 oz. ASW, 65 mm.
Ruler: Elizabeth II **Series:** World Cup Soccer **Obv:** Crowned arms within sprigs **Rev:** Statue of Liberty, stars and various buildings within soccer ball design **Note:** Illustration reduced.

Date	Mintage	F	VF	XF	Unc	BU
1994 Proof	Est. 3,000	Value: 135				

KM# 83   50 DOLLARS
6.2200 g., 0.9990 Gold 0.1998 oz. AGW   **Ruler:** Elizabeth II
Series: Liberty Gold Bullion **Obv:** Crowned head right
Rev: Statue of Liberty

Date	Mintage	F	VF	XF	Unc	BU
1997	—	—	—	—	—	200

KM# 108   50 DOLLARS
3.1100 g., 0.9999 Gold 0.1000 oz. AGW   **Ruler:** Elizabeth II
Obv: Crowned head right **Rev:** Bust facing **Rev. Leg.:** ...In Memoriam

Date	Mintage	F	VF	XF	Unc	BU
1998 Proof	Est. 7,500	Value: 110				

KM# 109   50 DOLLARS
3.1100 g., 0.9999 Gold 0.1000 oz. AGW   **Ruler:** Elizabeth II
Obv: Crowned head right **Rev:** Bust facing **Rev. Leg.:** ...Princess of Wales

Date	Mintage	F	VF	XF	Unc	BU
1998 Proof	Est. 7,500	Value: 100				

KM# 118   50 DOLLARS
3.1103 g., 0.9990 Gold 0.0999 oz. AGW   **Ruler:** Elizabeth II
Subject: 50th Anniversary of Peanuts **Obv:** Crowned head right
Rev: Snoopy and Woodstock

Date	Mintage	F	VF	XF	Unc	BU
2000 Proof	Est. 7,500	Value: 100				

KM# 7 100 DOLLARS
155.5175 g., 0.9990 Silver 4.9948 oz. ASW **Ruler:** Elizabeth II
Subject: 24th Olympiad Tennis Games, Seoul 1988
Obv: Crowned arms within sprigs **Rev:** Steffi Graf

Date	Mintage	F	VF	XF	Unc	BU
1987	Est. 5,000		Value: 85.00			

KM# 3 100 DOLLARS
155.5175 g., 0.9990 Silver 4.9948 oz. ASW, 65 mm.
Ruler: Elizabeth II **Series:** Olympics **Subject:** Tennis
Obv: Crowned arms within sprigs **Rev:** Boris Becker
Note: Illustration reduced.

Date	Mintage	F	VF	XF	Unc	BU
1987 Proof	Est. 5,000		Value: 85.00			

KM# 77 100 DOLLARS
Silver **Ruler:** Elizabeth II **Obv:** Crowned arms within sprigs
Rev: Steffi Graf with cup **Note:** Similar to $5 KM#11.

Date	Mintage	F	VF	XF	Unc	BU
1988	—	—	—		90.00	—

KM# 19 100 DOLLARS
155.5175 g., 0.9990 Silver 4.9948 oz. ASW **Ruler:** Elizabeth II
Obv: Crowned arms within sprigs **Rev:** Head left

Date	Mintage	F	VF	XF	Unc	BU
1988 Proof	3,000		Value: 85.00			

KM# 21 100 DOLLARS
155.5175 g., 0.9990 Silver 4.9948 oz. ASW **Ruler:** Elizabeth II
Subject: Soccer **Obv:** Crowned arms within sprigs **Rev:** Soccer
player

Date	Mintage	F	VF	XF	Unc	BU
1988 Proof	3,000		Value: 90.00			

KM# 40 100 DOLLARS
155.5175 g., 0.9990 Silver 4.9948 oz. ASW **Ruler:** Elizabeth II
Subject: 24th Olympic Games, Seoul 1988 **Obv:** Crowned arms
within sprigs **Rev:** Cameos of Navratilova, Graf and Evert, tennis
champions

Date	Mintage	F	VF	XF	Unc	BU
1988 Proof	Est. 3,000		Value: 95.00			

KM# 28 100 DOLLARS
155.5175 g., 0.9990 Silver 4.9948 oz. ASW, 65 mm.
Ruler: Elizabeth II **Subject:** 24th Olympic Games, Seoul 1988
Obv: Crowned arms within sprigs **Rev:** Steffi Graf
Note: Illustration reduced.

Date	Mintage	F	VF	XF	Unc	BU
1989 Proof	3,000		Value: 95.00			

KM# 73 100 DOLLARS
154.8500 g., 0.9990 Silver 4.9734 oz. ASW, 65 mm.
Ruler: Elizabeth II **Subject:** Soccer **Obv:** Crowned arms within
sprigs **Rev:** 1990 World Champion Italian soccer team
Note: Illustration reduced.

Date	Mintage	F	VF	XF	Unc	BU
1990 Proof	Est. 3,000		Value: 100			

KM# 84 100 DOLLARS
15.5517 g., 0.9990 Gold 0.4995 oz. AGW **Ruler:** Elizabeth II
Series: Liberty Gold Bullion **Obv:** Crowned head right **Rev:**
Statue of Liberty

Date	Mintage	F	VF	XF	Unc	BU
1997 Proof	—		Value: 520			

KM# 99 100 DOLLARS
6.2200 g., 0.9990 Gold 0.1998 oz. AGW **Ruler:** Elizabeth II
Obv: Crowned arms within sprigs **Rev:** Bust facing **Rev. Leg.:**
...The People's Princess

Date	Mintage	F	VF	XF	Unc	BU
1997 Proof	Est. 5,000		Value: 210			

KM# 100 100 DOLLARS
6.2200 g., 0.9990 Gold 0.1998 oz. AGW **Ruler:** Elizabeth II
Obv: Crowned arms within sprigs **Rev:** Bust facing **Rev. Leg.:**
...Princess of Wales

Date	Mintage	F	VF	XF	Unc	BU
1997 Proof	Est. 5,000		Value: 210			

KM# 101 100 DOLLARS
6.2200 g., 0.9990 Gold 0.1998 oz. AGW **Ruler:** Elizabeth II
Obv: Crowned arms within sprigs **Rev:** Head left above sprigs
Rev. Leg.: ...Princess of Wales

Date	Mintage	F	VF	XF	Unc	BU
1997 Proof	Est. 5,000		Value: 210			

KM# 110 100 DOLLARS
6.2200 g., 0.9990 Gold 0.1998 oz. AGW **Ruler:** Elizabeth II
Obv: Crowned head right **Rev:** Bust facing **Rev. Leg.:** ...In
Memoriam

Date	Mintage	F	VF	XF	Unc	BU
1998 Proof	Est. 5,000		Value: 210			

KM# 111 100 DOLLARS
6.2200 g., 0.9990 Gold 0.1998 oz. AGW **Ruler:** Elizabeth II
Obv: Crowned head right **Rev:** Bust facing **Rev. Leg.:** ...Princess
of Wales

Date	Mintage	F	VF	XF	Unc	BU
1998 Proof	Est. 5,000		Value: 210			

KM# 119 100 DOLLARS
6.2200 g., 0.9990 Gold 0.1998 oz. AGW **Ruler:** Elizabeth II
Subject: 50th Anniversary of Peanuts **Obv:** Crowned head right
Rev: Snoopy and Woodstock

Date	Mintage	F	VF	XF	Unc	BU
2000 Proof	Est. 5,000		Value: 210			

KM# 4 200 DOLLARS
311.0350 g., 0.9990 Silver 9.9896 oz. ASW **Ruler:** Elizabeth II
Series: Olympics **Subject:** Tennis **Obv:** Crowned arms within
sprigs **Rev:** Tennis player

Date	Mintage	F	VF	XF	Unc	BU
1987 Proof	Est. 3,000		Value: 200			

KM# 8 200 DOLLARS
311.0350 g., 0.9990 Silver 9.9896 oz. ASW **Ruler:** Elizabeth II
Subject: 24th Olympiad Tennis Games, Seoul 1988
Obv: Crowned arms within sprigs **Rev:** Tennis player

Date	Mintage	F	VF	XF	Unc	BU
1987 Proof	Est. 3,000		Value: 200			

KM# 42 200 DOLLARS
6.9117 g., 0.9000 Gold 0.2000 oz. AGW **Ruler:** Elizabeth II
Obv: Crowned arms within sprigs **Rev:** General Douglas MacArthur
1/4 left

Date	Mintage	F	VF	XF	Unc	BU
1989 Proof	Est. 2,500		Value: 220			

KM# 50 200 DOLLARS
6.9117 g., 0.9000 Gold 0.2000 oz. AGW **Ruler:** Elizabeth II
Obv: Crowned arms within sprigs **Rev:** General George S. Patton

Date	Mintage	F	VF	XF	Unc	BU
1989 Proof	—		Value: 220			

KM# 45 200 DOLLARS
6.9117 g., 0.9000 Gold 0.2000 oz. AGW **Ruler:** Elizabeth II
Obv: Crowned arms within sprigs **Rev:** General Dwight David
Eisenhower in front of flags

Date	Mintage	F	VF	XF	Unc	BU
1990 Proof	2,500		Value: 220			

KM# 51 200 DOLLARS
6.9117 g., 0.9000 Gold 0.2000 oz. AGW **Ruler:** Elizabeth II
Obv: Crowned arms within sprigs **Rev:** Admiral William Halsey

Date	Mintage	F	VF	XF	Unc	BU
1990 Proof	—		Value: 220			

KM# 52 200 DOLLARS
6.9117 g., 0.9000 Gold 0.2000 oz. AGW **Ruler:** Elizabeth II **Obv:** Crowned arms within sprigs **Rev:** President Franklin D. Roosevelt

Date	Mintage	F	VF	XF	Unc	BU
1990 Proof	—			Value: 220		

KM# 53 200 DOLLARS
6.9117 g., 0.9000 Gold 0.2000 oz. AGW **Ruler:** Elizabeth II **Obv:** Crowned arms within sprigs **Rev:** Sir Winston Churchill

Date	Mintage	F	VF	XF	Unc	BU
1990 Proof	—			Value: 220		

KM# 9 250 DOLLARS
8.4830 g., 0.9170 Gold 0.2501 oz. AGW **Ruler:** Elizabeth II **Series:** Olympics **Subject:** Tennis **Obv:** Crowned arms within sprigs **Rev:** Boris Becker

Date	Mintage	F	VF	XF	Unc	BU
1987 Proof	1,000			Value: 265		

KM# 10 250 DOLLARS
8.4830 g., 0.9170 Gold 0.2501 oz. AGW **Ruler:** Elizabeth II **Subject:** 24th Olympiad Tennis Games, Seoul 1988 **Obv:** Crowned arms within sprigs **Rev:** Steffi Graf

Date	Mintage	F	VF	XF	Unc	BU
1987 Proof	1,000			Value: 265		

KM# 20 250 DOLLARS
10.0000 g., 0.9170 Gold 0.2948 oz. AGW **Ruler:** Elizabeth II **Obv:** Crowned arms within sprigs **Rev:** John F. Kennedy left

Date	Mintage	F	VF	XF	Unc	BU
1988 Proof	5,000			Value: 320		

KM# 39 250 DOLLARS
10.0000 g., 0.9170 Gold 0.2948 oz. AGW **Ruler:** Elizabeth II **Subject:** Soccer **Obv:** Crowned arms within sprigs **Rev:** Soccer player to left of cameo

Date	Mintage	F	VF	XF	Unc	BU
1988 Proof	Est. 5,000			Value: 320		

KM# 41 250 DOLLARS
10.0000 g., 0.9170 Gold 0.2948 oz. AGW **Ruler:** Elizabeth II **Subject:** 24th Olympic Games, Seoul 1988 **Obv:** Crowned arms within sprigs **Rev:** Cameos of Navratilova, Graf and Evert, tennis champions

Date	Mintage	F	VF	XF	Unc	BU
1988 Proof	Est. 5,000			Value: 320		

KM# 48 250 DOLLARS
10.0000 g., 0.9170 Gold 0.2948 oz. AGW **Ruler:** Elizabeth II **Subject:** 24th Olympic Games, Seoul 1988 **Obv:** Crowned arms within sprigs **Rev:** Steffi Graf with cup

Date	Mintage	F	VF	XF	Unc	BU
1988 Proof	5,000			Value: 320		

KM# 26 250 DOLLARS
10.0000 g., 0.9170 Gold 0.2948 oz. AGW **Ruler:** Elizabeth II **Series:** Davis Cup Tennis **Obv:** Crowned arms within sprigs **Rev:** Davis cup

Date	Mintage	F	VF	XF	Unc	BU
1989 Proof	500			Value: 325		

KM# 49 250 DOLLARS
10.0000 g., 0.9170 Gold 0.2948 oz. AGW **Ruler:** Elizabeth II **Subject:** 24th Olympic Games, Seoul 1988 **Obv:** Crowned arms within sprigs **Rev:** Steffi Graf

Date	Mintage	F	VF	XF	Unc	BU
1989 Proof	3,000			Value: 325		

KM# 54 250 DOLLARS
10.0000 g., 0.9170 Gold 0.2948 oz. AGW **Ruler:** Elizabeth II **Subject:** Soccer - Italian **Obv:** Crowned arms within sprigs

Date	Mintage	F	VF	XF	Unc	BU
1990 Proof	Est. 2,500			Value: 325		

KM# A113 250 DOLLARS
15.5500 g., 0.9999 Gold 0.4999 oz. AGW **Ruler:** Elizabeth II **Obv:** Crowned head right **Rev:** Bust facing **Rev. Leg.:** ... Princess of Wales

Date	Mintage	F	VF	XF	Unc	BU
1998 Proof	3,000			Value: 545		

KM# 112 250 DOLLARS
15.5500 g., 0.9999 Gold 0.4999 oz. AGW **Ruler:** Elizabeth II **Obv:** Crowned head right **Rev:** Bust facing **Rev. Leg.:** ...In Memoriam

Date	Mintage	F	VF	XF	Unc	BU
1998 Proof	Est. 3,000			Value: 545		

PATTERNS
Including off metal strikes

KM#	Date	Mintage	Identification	Mkt Val
Pn1	1990	2	5 Dollars. Silver. Silver Proof, KM33.	—
Pn2	1990	2	5 Dollars. Silver. Silver Proof, KM35.	—
Pn3	1990	2	5 Dollars. Silver. Silver Proof, KM37.	—

NORWAY

The Kingdom of Norway (*Norge, Noreg*), a constitutional monarchy located in northwestern Europe, has an area of 150,000sq. mi. (324,220 sq. km.), including the island territories of Spitzbergen (Svalbard) and Jan Mayen, and a population of *4.2 million. Capital: Oslo (Christiania). The diversified economic base of Norway includes shipping, fishing, forestry, agriculture, and manufacturing. Nonferrous metals, paper and paperboard, paper pulp, iron, steel and oil are exported.

A united Norwegian kingdom was established in the 9th century, the era of the indomitable Norse Vikings who ranged far and wide, visiting the coasts of northwestern Europe, the Mediterranean, Greenland and North America. In the 13th century the Norse kingdom was united briefly with Sweden, then passed through inheritance in 1380 to the rule of Denmark which was maintained until 1814. In 1814 Norway fell again under the rule of Sweden. The union lasted until 1905 when the Norwegian Parliament arranged a peaceful separation and invited a Danish prince (King Haakon VII) to ascend the throne of an independent Kingdom of Norway.

RULERS
Swedish, 1814-1905
Haakon VII, 1905-1957
Olav V, 1957-1991
Harald V, 1991-

MINT MARK
(h) - Crossed hammers – Kongsberg

MINT OFFICIALS' INITIALS

Letter	Date	Name
AB, B	1961-1980	Arne Jon Bakken
AB*	1980	Ole R. Kolberg
I, IT	1880-1918	Ivar Trondsen, engraver
IAR	-	Angrid Austlid Rise, engraver
K	1981	Ole R. Kolberg
OH	1959	Oivind Hansen, engraver

MONETARY SYSTEM
100 Ore = 1 Krone (30 Skilling)

KINGDOM
DECIMAL COINAGE

KM# 352 ORE
2.0000 g., Bronze **Obv:** Crowned arms divide monograms **Rev:** Value within wreath, crossed hammers divide date below **Note:** Varieties exist.

Date	Mintage	VG	F	VF	XF	BU
1902	4,500,000	—	2.00	5.00	15.00	45.00

KM# 361 ORE
2.0000 g., Bronze **Ruler:** Haakon VII **Obv:** Crowned shield divides monogram **Rev:** Value within sprigs

Date	Mintage	VG	F	VF	XF	BU
1906	3,000,000	—	2.00	3.00	10.00	27.50
1907	2,550,000	—	2.00	3.00	12.00	30.00

KM# 367 ORE
2.0000 g., Bronze **Ruler:** Haakon VII **Obv:** Crowned monogram within circle **Rev:** Value

Date	Mintage	VG	F	VF	XF	BU
1908	1,450,000	—	10.00	20.00	45.00	165
1910	2,480,000	—	1.00	2.50	12.00	40.00
1911	3,270,000	—	1.00	2.50	15.00	75.00
1912	2,850,000	—	3.00	10.00	40.00	240
1913	2,840,000	—	1.00	2.50	7.50	35.00
1914	5,020,000	—	1.00	2.50	10.00	40.00
1915	1,540,000	—	10.00	25.00	75.00	325
1921	3,805,000	—	25.00	45.00	105	275
1922	Inc. above	—	0.50	2.00	15.00	55.00
1923	770,000	—	6.00	17.50	35.00	175
1925	3,000,000	—	0.50	1.50	15.00	60.00
1926	2,200,000	—	0.50	1.50	15.00	60.00
1927	800,000	—	4.00	10.00	30.00	165
1928	3,000,000	—	0.25	0.75	4.50	25.00
1929	4,990,000	—	0.25	0.75	4.50	20.00
1930 large date	2,009,999	—	0.50	1.00	6.00	27.50
1930 small date	Inc. above	—	0.50	1.00	6.00	27.50
1931	2,000,000	—	0.50	1.00	6.00	25.00
1932	2,500,000	—	0.50	1.00	6.00	25.00
1933	2,000,000	—	0.50	1.00	6.00	20.00
1934	2,000,000	—	0.50	1.00	6.00	25.00
1935	5,495,000	—	0.25	0.75	2.50	12.50
1936	6,855,000	—	0.25	0.75	2.50	12.50
1937	6,020,000	—	0.20	0.50	1.50	10.00
1938	4,920,000	—	0.20	0.50	1.50	10.00
1939	2,500,000	—	0.20	0.50	1.50	12.50
1940	5,010,000	—	0.20	0.50	1.50	10.00
1941	12,260,000	—	0.10	0.25	1.50	5.00
1946	2,200,000	—	0.10	0.25	1.50	12.00
1947	4,870,000	—	0.10	0.25	0.90	6.00
1948	9,405,000	—	0.10	0.25	0.90	5.00
1949	2,785,000	—	0.10	0.25	0.90	8.00
1950	5,730,000	—	0.10	0.25	0.90	5.00
1951	16,670,000	—	0.10	0.25	0.90	5.00
1952	Inc. above	—	0.10	0.25	0.90	4.00

KM# 367a ORE
1.7400 g., Iron **Ruler:** Haakon VII **Obv:** Crowned monogram **Rev:** Value

Date	Mintage	VG	F	VF	XF	BU
1918	6,000,000	—	5.00	10.00	20.00	65.00
1919	12,930,000	—	1.50	3.50	12.00	30.00
1920	4,445,000	—	6.00	12.50	35.00	165
1921	2,270,000	—	30.00	40.00	75.00	210

KM# 387 ORE
1.7400 g., Iron **Ruler:** Haakon VII **Subject:** World War II German Occupation **Obv:** Shield **Rev:** Value

Date	Mintage	VG	F	VF	XF	BU
1941	13,410,000	—	0.15	0.50	1.75	12.50
1942	37,710,000	—	0.15	0.50	1.75	6.00
1943	33,030,000	—	0.15	0.50	1.75	6.00
1944	8,820,000	—	0.25	0.75	2.25	6.50
1945	1,740,000	—	4.00	8.00	15.00	35.00

KM# 398 ORE
2.0000 g., Bronze, 11 mm. **Ruler:** Haakon VII **Obv:** Crowned monogram divides date **Rev:** Value

Date	Mintage	VG	F	VF	XF	BU
1952	—	—	—	0.10	1.00	6.50

Note: Mintage included with KM#367

Date	Mintage	VG	F	VF	XF	BU
1953	7,440,000	—	—	0.10	0.75	4.50
1954	7,650,000	—	—	0.10	0.75	4.50
1955	8,635,000	—	—	0.10	0.75	4.50
1956	11,705,000	—	—	0.10	0.75	4.50
1957	15,750,000	—	—	0.10	0.50	3.25

KM# 403 ORE
2.0000 g., Bronze, 11 mm. **Ruler:** Olav V **Obv:** Crowned monogram **Rev:** Squirrel and value **Note:** Varieties exist.

Date	Mintage	VG	F	VF	XF	BU
1958	2,820,000	—	0.25	0.50	2.25	8.00
1959	9,120,000	—	0.10	0.20	0.85	7.00
1960	7,890,000	—	—	0.10	0.30	3.00
1961	5,670,600	—	—	0.10	0.30	3.00
1962	12,180,000	—	—	0.10	0.25	2.00
1963	8,010,000	—	—	0.10	0.30	2.50
1964	11,020,000	—	—	—	0.10	0.75
1965	8,081,000	—	—	—	0.15	2.00
1966	12,431,000	—	—	—	0.15	1.25
1967	13,026,000	—	—	—	0.10	0.75
1968	125,500	—	0.50	1.00	2.25	8.50
1969	6,290,500	—	—	—	0.10	0.50
1970	6,607,500	—	—	—	0.10	0.50
1971	18,966,000	—	—	—	0.10	0.45
1972	21,102,984	—	—	—	0.10	0.45

KM# 353 2 ORE
4.0000 g., Bronze, 21 mm. **Obv:** Crowned arms divide monograms **Rev:** Value within wreath, crossed hammers divide date below

Date	Mintage	VG	F	VF	XF	BU
1902	1,005,000	—	1.50	4.00	15.00	150

KM# 362 2 ORE
4.0000 g., Bronze, 21 mm. **Ruler:** Haakon VII **Obv:** Crowned shield **Rev:** Value within sprigs

Date	Mintage	VG	F	VF	XF	BU
1906	500,000	—	5.00	15.00	50.00	325
1907	980,000	—	3.00	5.00	25.00	145

KM# 371 2 ORE
4.0000 g., Bronze, 21 mm. **Ruler:** Haakon VII **Obv:** Crowned momogram within circle **Rev:** Value

Date	Mintage	VG	F	VF	XF	BU
1909	520,000	—	6.00	20.00	60.00	250
1910	500,000	—	6.00	20.00	100	500
1911	195,000	—	6.00	17.50	70.00	375
1912	805,000	—	6.00	17.50	70.00	425
1913	2,010,000	—	0.75	2.00	12.00	125
1914	2,990,000	—	0.75	2.00	12.00	125
1915	Inc. above	—	5.00	20.00	95.00	500
1921	2,028,000	—	0.50	1.00	17.00	90.00
1922	2,288,000	—	0.50	1.00	17.00	75.00
1923	745,000	—	1.00	2.00	30.00	145
1928	2,250,000	—	0.50	1.00	12.50	70.00
1929	750,000	—	1.00	2.00	20.00	120
1931	1,570,000	—	0.50	1.00	15.00	75.00
1932	630,000	—	3.50	7.50	45.00	210
1933	750,000	—	0.50	1.50	10.00	75.00
1934	500,000	—	0.50	1.50	10.00	75.00
1935	2,223,000	—	0.25	1.00	7.50	45.00
1936	4,533,000	—	0.25	1.00	7.50	45.00
1937	3,790,000	—	0.20	0.50	2.75	20.00
1938	3,765,000	—	0.20	0.50	2.75	20.00
1939	4,420,000	—	0.20	0.50	2.75	20.00
1940	2,655,000	—	0.20	0.50	2.75	20.00
1946	1,575,000	—	0.50	3.50	20.00
1947	4,679,000	—	0.10	0.25	1.25	10.00
1948	1,002,999	—	1.00	3.00	5.00	12.50
1949	1,455,000	—	0.10	0.25	1.00	9.00
1950	5,790,000	—	0.10	0.25	1.00	6.00
1951	10,540,000	—	0.10	0.25	1.00	5.00
1952	Inc. above	—	0.10	0.25	1.00	5.00

KM# 371a 2 ORE
3.4800 g., Iron, 21 mm. **Ruler:** Haakon VII **Obv:** Crowned monogram **Rev:** Value

Date	Mintage	VG	F	VF	XF	BU
1917	720,000	—	80.00	145	250	500
1918	1,280,000	—	35.00	50.00	110	250
1919	3,365,000	—	10.00	15.00	55.00	285
1920	2,635,000	—	10.00	15.00	55.00	300

KM# 394 2 ORE
3.4700 g., Iron, 21 mm. **Ruler:** Haakon VII **Obv:** Shield **Rev:** Value **Note:** World War II German occupation issue.

Date	Mintage	VG	F	VF	XF	BU
1943	6,575,000	—	0.50	0.75	1.75	9.00
1944	9,805,000	—	0.50	0.75	1.75	9.00
1945	2,520,000	—	1.50	3.00	6.00	20.00

KM# 399 2 ORE
4.0000 g., Bronze, 21 mm. **Ruler:** Haakon VII **Obv:** Crowned monogram divides date **Rev:** Value

Date	Mintage	VG	F	VF	XF	BU
1952	Inc. above	—	—	0.10	0.85	8.50
1953	6,705,000	—	—	0.10	0.85	7.00
1954	2,805,000	—	—	0.10	0.85	10.00
1955	3,600,000	—	—	0.10	0.85	10.00

Date	Mintage	VG	F	VF	XF	BU
1956	6,780,000	—	—	0.10	0.85	7.00
1957	6,090,000	—	—	0.10	0.85	7.00

KM# 404 2 ORE
4.0000 g., Bronze, 21 mm. **Ruler:** Olav V **Obv:** Crowned monogram **Rev:** Moor hen and value, small lettering

Date	Mintage	VG	F	VF	XF	BU
1958	2,700,000	—	0.20	0.50	1.75	10.00

KM# 410 2 ORE
4.0000 g., Bronze, 21 mm. **Ruler:** Olav V **Obv:** Crowned monogram **Rev:** Moor hen and value, large lettering

Date	Mintage	VG	F	VF	XF	BU
1959	4,125,000	—	0.10	0.20	1.25	8.00
1960	3,735,000	—	—	0.10	0.85	16.50
1961	4,477,000	—	—	0.10	0.35	2.00
1962	6,205,000	—	—	0.10	0.35	2.00
1963	4,840,000	—	—	0.10	0.35	2.00
1964	7,250,000	—	—	0.10	0.20	1.50
1965	6,241,000	—	—	0.10	0.30	3.00
1966	10,485,000	—	—	—	0.15	2.50
1967	11,993,000	—	—	—	0.15	1.50
1968	3,467	—	—	—	—	1,000

Note: In mint sets only

Date	Mintage	VG	F	VF	XF	BU
1969	315,600	—	0.50	1.00	1.75	6.00
1970	6,794,000	—	—	—	0.10	1.25
1971	15,462,000	—	—	—	0.10	1.00
1972	15,897,984	—	—	—	0.10	1.00

KM# 349 5 ORE
8.0000 g., Bronze, 27 mm. **Obv:** Crowned arms divide monograms **Rev:** Value within wreath, crossed hammers divide date below

Date	Mintage	VG	F	VF	XF	BU
1902	705,000	—	2.50	6.00	55.00	400

KM# 364 5 ORE
8.0000 g., Bronze, 27 mm. **Ruler:** Haakon VII **Obv:** Crowned shield divides monogram **Rev:** Value within sprigs

Date	Mintage	VG	F	VF	XF	BU
1907	200,000	—	3.50	12.50	70.00	285

KM# 368 5 ORE
8.0000 g., Bronze, 27 mm. **Ruler:** Haakon VII **Obv:** Crowned monogram within circle **Rev:** Numeral and written value

Date	Mintage	VG	F	VF	XF	BU
1908	600,000	—	25.00	45.00	130	600
1911	480,000	—	2.00	15.00	65.00	340
1912	520,000	—	6.00	25.00	135	825
1913	1,000,000	—	1.25	5.00	30.00	200

Date	Mintage	VG	F	VF	XF	BU
1914	1,000,000	—	1.25	5.00	30.00	200
1915	Inc. above	—	10.00	35.00	145	900
1916	300,000	—	6.00	15.00	60.00	450
1921	683,000	—	1.50	7.50	60.00	280
1922	2,296,000	—	1.25	5.00	30.00	150
1923	456,000	—	2.50	10.00	60.00	260
1928	848,000	—	0.60	3.00	25.00	110
1929	452,000	—	3.00	10.00	60.00	300
1930	1,292,000	—	0.60	2.50	30.00	150
1931	808,000	—	0.60	2.50	30.00	120
1932	500,000	—	3.00	15.00	45.00	225
1933	300,000	—	3.00	12.00	65.00	350
1935	496,000	—	1.50	5.00	25.00	160
1936	760,000	—	1.00	2.50	20.00	115
1937	1,552,000	—	0.50	1.50	12.00	50.00
1938	1,332,000	—	0.50	1.50	12.00	50.00
1939	1,370,000	—	0.50	1.50	9.00	50.00
1940	2,554,000	—	0.30	1.00	7.00	32.50
1941	3,576,000	—	0.30	1.00	6.00	32.50
1951	8,128,000	—	0.25	0.50	2.25	10.00
1952	Inc. above	—	1.50	3.50	9.00	50.00

KM# 368a 5 ORE
6.6900 g., Iron, 27 mm. **Ruler:** Haakon VII **Obv:** Crowned monogram within circle **Rev:** Numeral and written value

Date	Mintage	VG	F	VF	XF	BU
1917	1,700,000	—	25.00	40.00	70.00	125
1918/7	432,000	—	135	225	—	850
1918	Inc. above	—	135	250	425	950
1919	3,464,000	—	12.00	30.00	70.00	250
1920	1,629,000	—	25.00	55.00	120	550

KM# 388 5 ORE
6.9400 g., Iron, 27 mm. **Ruler:** Haakon VII **Note:** World War II German occupation issue.

Date	Mintage	VG	F	VF	XF	BU
1941	6,608,000	—	0.50	1.50	5.50	40.00
1942	10,312,000	—	0.50	1.50	5.00	20.00
1943	6,184,000	—	0.75	2.00	7.00	32.50
1944	4,256,000	—	1.25	3.00	9.00	32.50
1945	408,000	—	145	165	270	600

KM# 400 5 ORE
8.0000 g., Bronze, 27 mm. **Ruler:** Haakon VII **Obv:** Crowned monogram divides date **Rev:** Value

Date	Mintage	VG	F	VF	XF	BU
1952	—	—	0.10	0.50	2.50	35.00
	Note: Mintage included with KM#368					
1953	6,216,000	—	0.10	0.35	2.25	20.00
1954	4,536,000	—	0.10	0.35	2.25	20.00
1955	6,570,000	—	0.10	0.35	2.25	20.00
1956	2,959,000	—	0.10	0.35	2.25	30.00
1957	5,624,000	—	0.10	0.35	2.25	12.50

KM# 405 5 ORE
8.0000 g., Bronze, 27 mm. **Ruler:** Olav V **Obv:** Head left **Rev:** Moose

Date	Mintage	VG	F	VF	XF	BU
1958	2,205,000	—	1.00	2.00	6.00	60.00
1959	3,208,000	—	0.10	0.50	2.25	25.00
1960	5,519,000	—	0.10	0.20	1.25	17.00
1961	4,554,000	—	0.10	0.20	1.25	15.00
1962	7,764,000	—	0.10	0.15	0.75	9.00
1963	3,204,000	—	0.10	0.15	0.75	9.00
1964	6,108,000	—	—	0.10	0.50	3.00
1965	6,841,000	—	—	0.10	0.50	7.00
1966	8,415,000	—	—	0.10	0.50	3.00
1967	9,071,000	—	—	0.10	0.45	3.00

Date	Mintage	VG	F	VF	XF	BU
1968	4,286,000	—	—	0.10	0.85	8.00
1969	4,328,000	—	—	0.10	0.35	1.25
1970	7,350,600	—	—	0.10	0.35	1.25
1971	13,450,100	—	—	0.10	0.35	1.25
1972	19,001,784	—	—	—	0.15	1.00
1973	9,584,175	—	—	—	0.15	1.00

KM# 415 5 ORE
3.0000 g., Bronze, 19 mm. **Ruler:** Olav V **Obv:** Arms **Rev:** Value **Note:** Varieties exist.

Date	Mintage	VG	F	VF	XF	BU
1973	52,886,175	—	—	—	0.10	0.45
1974	37,150,223	—	—	—	0.10	0.45
1975	32,478,744	—	—	—	0.10	0.45
1976	24,232,824	—	—	—	0.10	0.25
1977	29,646,000	—	—	—	0.10	0.25
1978	13,838,000	—	—	—	0.10	0.25
1979	25,255,000	—	—	—	0.10	0.25
1980	12,315,000	—	—	—	0.10	0.25
1980 Without star	27,515,000	—	—	—	0.10	0.25
1981	24,529,000	—	—	—	0.10	0.25
1982	21,900,650	—	—	—	0.10	0.25

KM# 350 10 ORE
1.5000 g., 0.4000 Silver 0.0193 oz. ASW, 15 mm. **Obv:** Crowned monogram **Obv. Leg.:** BRODERFOLKENES VEL **Rev:** Crowned arms divide date

Date	Mintage	VG	F	VF	XF	BU
1901	2,021,100	—	10.00	22.00	30.00	50.00
1903	1,500,700	—	10.00	20.00	35.00	55.00

KM# 372 10 ORE
1.4500 g., 0.4000 Silver 0.0186 oz. ASW, 15 mm. **Ruler:** Haakon VII **Obv:** Crowned monogram **Rev:** Value

Date	Mintage	VG	F	VF	XF	BU
1909	2,000,000	—	6.50	13.00	30.00	100
1911	1,650,000	—	9.00	22.00	60.00	200
1912	2,350,000	—	6.00	12.00	30.00	85.00
1913	2,000,000	—	6.00	11.00	28.00	70.00
1914	1,180,000	—	11.00	25.00	50.00	150
1915	2,820,000	—	3.00	5.00	13.00	100
1916	1,500,000	—	10.00	17.00	45.00	130
1917	5,950,000	—	1.50	3.00	5.00	20.00
1918	Inc. above	—	3.00	5.00	13.00	50.00
1918/7	1,650,000	—	15.00	35.00	75.00	—
1919	Inc. above	—	1.50	3.00	5.00	20.00
1919/7	7,800,000	—	15.00	35.00	75.00	—

KM# 378 10 ORE
1.5000 g., Copper-Nickel, 15 mm. **Ruler:** Haakon VII **Obv:** Crowned monogram **Rev:** Value flanked by designs

Date	Mintage	VG	F	VF	XF	BU
1920	2,535,000	—	10.00	20.00	30.00	60.00
1921	6,465,000	—	7.00	15.00	25.00	55.00
1922	3,965,000	—	7.00	15.00	20.00	55.00
1923	7,135,000	—	15.00	25.00	30.00	55.00

KM# 383 10 ORE
1.5000 g., Copper-Nickel, 15 mm. **Ruler:** Haakon VII **Obv:** Crown above center hole **Rev:** Value above center hole

Date	Mintage	VG	F	VF	XF	BU
1924	12,079,100	—	0.30	0.75	9.00	40.00
1925	7,050,700	—	0.30	0.75	9.00	60.00
1926	11,764,200	—	0.30	0.75	9.00	40.00
1927	526,000	5.00	10.00	20.00	120	625
1937	5,000,000	—	0.30	0.75	5.00	40.00
1938	3,412,600	—	0.30	0.75	5.00	35.00

Date	Mintage	VG	F	VF	XF	BU
1939	1,538,400	—	1.00	2.50	9.50	65.00
1940	4,800,000	—	0.30	0.75	1.75	17.50
1941	10,150,000	—	0.30	0.75	1.75	10.00
1945	1,718,000	—	0.10	0.25	1.75	15.00
1946	3,723,200	—	0.10	0.25	1.75	9.00
1947	7,256,700	—	0.10	0.25	1.75	6.50
1948	3,104,500	—	0.10	0.25	2.00	7.00
1949	11,545,500	—	0.10	0.25	1.75	7.00
1951	5,150,000	—	0.10	0.25	1.75	7.00

KM# 389 10 ORE
1.2500 g., Zinc, 15 mm. **Ruler:** Haakon VII **Obv:** Shield flanked by designs **Rev:** Value flanked by designs **Note:** World War II German occupation issue.

Date	Mintage	F	VF	XF	Unc	BU
1941	15,309,900	0.75	2.00	6.00	—	32.50
1942	50,387,600	0.35	1.00	3.50	—	12.50
1943	13,377,700	0.75	2.00	5.50	—	35.00
1944	3,549,400	7.50	12.50	30.00	—	135
1945	5,645,500	4.00	8.00	18.00	—	50.00

KM# 391 10 ORE
1.1500 g., Nickel-Brass, 15 mm. **Ruler:** Haakon VII **Obv:** Crown above center hole **Rev:** Value above center hole **Note:** World War II government in exile issue.

Date	Mintage	VG	F	VF	XF	BU
1942	6,000,000	—	—	—	150	250
	Note: All except 9,667 were melted					

KM# 396 10 ORE
1.5000 g., Copper-Nickel, 15 mm. **Ruler:** Haakon VII **Obv:** Crowned monogram divides date **Rev:** Value flanked by designs

Date	Mintage	VG	F	VF	XF	BU
1951	17,400,000	—	0.10	0.30	2.50	60.00
1952	Inc. above	—	0.10	0.20	1.50	20.00
1953	7,700,000	—	0.10	0.20	1.50	20.00
1954	10,105,000	—	0.10	0.20	1.50	20.00
1955	9,829,500	—	0.10	0.20	1.50	50.00
1956	10,066,000	—	0.10	0.20	1.50	20.00
1957	22,900,000	—	0.10	0.20	1.50	12.00

KM# 406 10 ORE
1.5000 g., Copper-Nickel, 15 mm. **Ruler:** Olav V **Obv:** Crowned monogram **Rev:** Honey bee and value, small lettering

Date	Mintage	VG	F	VF	XF	BU
1958	1,425,000	—	0.50	1.50	3.00	30.00

KM# 411 10 ORE
1.5000 g., Copper-Nickel, 15 mm. **Ruler:** Olav V **Obv:** Crowned monogram **Rev:** Honey bee and value, large lettering

Date	Mintage	VG	F	VF	XF	BU
1959	2,500,000	—	—	0.75	3.00	20.00
1960	12,490,200	—	—	0.10	0.60	7.00
1961	10,385,000	—	—	0.10	0.60	20.00
1962	16,210,000	—	—	0.10	0.60	5.00
1963	17,560,000	—	—	0.10	0.60	5.00
1964	9,781,000	—	—	0.10	0.35	1.35
1965	10,561,000	—	—	0.10	0.60	14.00
1966	16,610,000	—	—	0.10	0.50	3.00
1967	18,243,000	—	—	0.10	0.35	5.00
1968	24,998,300	—	—	0.10	0.35	7.00
1969	27,157,200	—	—	0.10	0.25	2.25
1970	639,300	—	0.50	1.00	2.25	5.00
1971	8,903,800	—	—	0.10	0.25	1.35
1972	24,834,484	—	—	—	0.25	1.00
1973	22,300,925	—	—	—	0.25	1.00

KM# 416 10 ORE
1.2500 g., Copper-Nickel, 15 mm. **Ruler:** Olav V **Obv:** Crowned monogram divides date **Rev:** Value **Note:** Varieties exist in monogram.

Date	Mintage	VG	F	VF	XF	BU
1974	30,995,223	—	—	—	0.10	0.60
1975	21,845,496	—	—	—	0.10	0.60
1976	42,403,074	—	—	—	0.10	0.40
1977	43,304,000	—	—	—	0.10	0.40
1978	37,395,000	—	—	—	0.10	0.40
1979	25,808,000	—	—	—	0.10	0.40
1980	28,620,000	—	—	—	0.10	0.40
1980 Without star	14,050,000	—	—	—	0.10	0.40
1981	43,083,400	—	—	—	0.10	0.40
1982	40,974,256	—	—	—	0.10	0.40
1983	45,637,300	—	—	—	0.10	0.40
1984	100,066,000	—	—	—	0.10	0.35
1985	103,108,000	—	—	—	0.10	0.35
1986	146,392,000	—	—	—	0.10	0.35
1987	166,040,000	—	—	—	0.10	0.35
1988	94,677,000	—	—	—	0.10	0.35
1989	97,273,500	—	—	—	0.10	0.35
1990	150,290,000	—	—	—	0.10	0.35
1991	79,597,000	—	—	—	0.10	0.35

KM# 360 25 ORE
2.4200 g., 0.6000 Silver 0.0467 oz. ASW **Obv:** Crowned arms within wreath **Obv. Leg.:** BRODERFOLKENES VEL **Rev:** Value within wreath, crossed hammers divide date below

Date	Mintage	VG	F	VF	XF	BU
1901	606,900	9.00	21.00	40.00	60.00	130
1902	611,700	9.00	21.00	40.00	60.00	130
1904	600,000	9.00	21.00	40.00	60.00	130

KM# 373 25 ORE
2.4200 g., 0.6000 Silver 0.0467 oz. ASW **Ruler:** Haakon VII **Obv:** Arms flanked by designs **Rev:** Crowned cross with monogram

Date	Mintage	VG	F	VF	XF	BU
1909	600,000	8.00	16.00	30.00	55.00	110
1911	400,000	15.00	30.00	45.00	80.00	200
1912	200,000	50.00	100	150	270	650
1913	400,000	12.00	20.00	35.00	70.00	165
1914	399,600	12.00	18.00	50.00	100	200
1915	1,032,300	4.50	10.00	15.00	40.00	110
1916	368,000	17.00	35.00	50.00	80.00	225
1917	400,000	15.00	30.00	45.00	70.00	200
1918/6	800,000	6.00	12.00	20.00	40.00	65.00
1918	inc. above	5.00	12.00	20.00	40.00	110
1919	1,600,000	3.50	6.00	12.00	25.00	90.00

KM# 381 25 ORE
4.4000 g., Copper-Nickel, 17 mm. **Ruler:** Haakon VII **Obv:** Crowned monogram **Rev:** Arms flanked by designs

Date	Mintage	VG	F	VF	XF	BU
1921	4,800,000	4.00	10.00	15.00	20.00	40.00
1922	14,200,000	4.00	10.00	15.00	20.00	40.00
1923	5,200,000	8.00	16.50	25.00	35.00	60.00

KM# 382 25 ORE
2.4000 g., Copper-Nickel, 17 mm. **Ruler:** Haakon VII **Obv:** Crowned monogram, hole in center **Rev:** Arms flanked by designs, hole in center

Date	Mintage	VG	F	VF	XF	BU
1921	—	1.50	3.00	5.00	75.00	625
1922	—	1.50	3.00	4.00	45.00	375

Date	Mintage	VG	F	VF	XF	BU
1923	—	1.00	1.50	3.00	25.00	190

Note: Respective mintages included with KM#381

KM# 384 25 ORE
2.4000 g., Copper-Nickel, 17 mm. **Ruler:** Haakon VII **Obv:** Crowned cross with monogram, hole in center **Rev:** Center hole flanked by designs, crown above

Date	Mintage	VG	F	VF	XF	BU
1924	4,000,000	—	0.50	2.00	7.00	65.00
1927	6,200,000	—	0.50	1.50	7.00	65.00
1929	800,000	—	1.50	6.00	42.00	275
1939	1,220,000	—	0.25	0.75	3.50	70.00
1940	1,160,000	—	0.25	0.75	3.50	50.00
1946	1,850,000	—	0.20	0.50	1.75	20.00
1947	2,592,000	—	0.20	0.50	1.75	15.00
1949	2,602,000	—	0.20	0.50	1.75	15.00
1950	2,800,000	—	0.20	0.50	1.75	15.00

KM# 392 25 ORE
2.4000 g., Nickel-Brass, 17 mm. **Ruler:** Haakon VII **Obv:** Crowned monograms form cross, hole at center **Rev:** Crown on top divides date, hole in center flanked by designs, value on bottom **Note:** World War II government in exile issue.

Date	Mintage	VG	F	VF	XF	BU
1942	2,400,000	—	—	—	150	275

Note: All but 10,300 were melted

KM# 395 25 ORE
2.0000 g., Zinc, 17 mm. **Ruler:** Haakon VII **Obv:** Shield flanked by designs **Rev:** Value flanked by designs **Note:** World War II German occupation.

Date	Mintage	VG	F	VF	XF	BU
1943	14,104,800	—	1.00	1.50	4.00	25.00
1944	3,030,500	2.00	4.00	7.50	20.00	50.00
1945	3,010,000	3.00	6.00	10.00	22.00	60.00

KM# 401 25 ORE
2.4000 g., Copper-Nickel, 17 mm. **Ruler:** Haakon VII **Obv:** Crowned monogram divides date **Rev:** Value flanked by designs **Note:** Mint marks exist with mint mark on square or without square.

Date	Mintage	VG	F	VF	XF	BU
1952	4,060,000	—	0.10	0.25	1.20	30.00
1953	3,320,000	—	0.10	0.25	1.20	35.00
1954	3,140,000	—	0.10	0.25	1.20	30.00
1955	2,000,000	—	0.10	0.25	1.20	75.00
1956	3,980,000	—	0.10	0.25	1.20	30.00
1957	7,660,000	—	0.10	0.25	1.20	20.00

KM# 407 25 ORE
2.4000 g., Copper-Nickel, 17 mm. **Ruler:** Olav V **Obv:** Head left **Rev:** Bird above value

Date	Mintage	VG	F	VF	XF	BU
1958	1,316,000	—	0.50	1.00	3.00	40.00
1959	1,184,000	—	0.50	1.00	3.00	35.00
1960	3,964,200	—	—	0.10	1.25	20.00
1961	4,656,000	—	—	0.10	1.00	7.50
1962	6,304,000	—	—	0.10	1.00	7.50
1963	3,640,000	—	—	0.10	1.00	7.50
1964	4,953,000	—	—	0.10	0.50	2.75
1965	2,798,000	—	—	0.10	0.65	30.00
1966	6,075,000	—	—	0.10	0.65	3.00
1967	6,641,000	—	—	0.10	0.65	3.00
1968	4,963,400	—	—	0.10	0.50	5.00
1969	12,426,500	—	—	0.10	0.15	2.00
1970	1,545,400	—	—	0.15	0.75	6.50

Date	Mintage	VG	F	VF	XF	BU
1971	5,247,200	—	—	—	0.10	1.25
1972	7,928,584	—	—	—	0.10	1.25
1973	8,516,175	—	—	—	0.10	1.25

KM# 417 25 ORE
2.0000 g., Copper-Nickel, 17 mm. **Ruler:** Olav V **Obv:** Crowned monograms in cross formation **Rev:** Value

Date	Mintage	VG	F	VF	XF	BU
1974	8,048,223	—	—	—	0.10	0.65
1975	15,594,696	—	—	—	0.10	0.65
1976	24,721,074	—	—	—	0.10	0.50
1977	20,150,000	—	—	—	0.10	0.50
1978	11,259,000	—	—	—	0.10	0.50
1979	16,666,000	—	—	—	0.10	0.50
1980	6,289,000	—	—	—	0.10	0.50
1980 Without star	8,176,000	—	—	—	0.10	0.50
1981	17,971,000	—	—	—	0.10	0.50
1982	16,862,650	—	—	—	0.10	0.50

KM# 356 50 ORE
5.0000 g., 0.6000 Silver 0.0964 oz. ASW **Obv:** Head left **Obv. Leg.:** OSCAR II NORGES... **Rev:** Crowned shield within wreath, crossed hammers divide date below

Date	Mintage	VG	F	VF	XF	BU
1901	404,000	7.00	14.00	35.00	70.00	200
1902	301,200	7.00	14.00	35.00	70.00	200
1904	100,500	35.00	70.00	165	260	550

KM# 374 50 ORE
5.0000 g., 0.6000 Silver 0.0964 oz. ASW **Ruler:** Haakon VII **Obv:** Head right **Rev:** Crowned shield flanked by designs

Date	Mintage	VG	F	VF	XF	BU
1909	200,000	14.00	27.00	35.00	65.00	175
1911	200,000	14.00	40.00	60.00	90.00	250
1912	200,000	30.00	60.00	90.00	150	325
1913	200,000	14.00	40.00	60.00	90.00	250
1914	800,000	3.50	8.00	15.00	25.00	120
1915	300,000	12.00	23.00	40.00	60.00	150
1916	700,000	4.50	9.00	19.00	45.00	150
1918	3,090,000	2.50	5.00	8.00	12.00	100
1919	1,219,000	3.00	6.00	9.00	18.00	60.00

KM# 379 50 ORE
4.8000 g., Copper-Nickel, 22 mm. **Ruler:** Haakon VII **Obv:** Crowned monograms form cross **Rev:** Crowned shield flanked by designs

Date	Mintage	VG	F	VF	XF	BU
1920	1,236,000	15.00	25.00	35.00	60.00	125
1921	7,345,000	4.00	8.00	12.00	25.00	50.00
1922	3,000,000	4.00	8.00	12.00	25.00	50.00
1923	4,540,000	25.00	60.00	85.00	115	185

KM# 380 50 ORE
4.8000 g., Copper-Nickel, 22 mm. **Ruler:** Haakon VII **Obv:** Crowned monograms form cross with hole in center **Rev:** Crowned shield flanked by designs, hole in center **Note:** Respective mintages are included with KM#379.

Date	Mintage	VG	F	VF	XF	BU
1920	—	—	30.00	90.00	300	—
1921	—	—	3.00	15.00	135	700

Date	Mintage	VG	F	VF	XF	BU
1922	—	—	2.50	10.00	85.00	500
1923	—	—	2.50	6.00	70.00	350

KM# 386   50 ORE
4.8000 g., Copper-Nickel, 22 mm.   **Ruler:** Haakon VII
Obv: Crowned monograms form cross with hole in center
Rev: Center hole flanked by designs, crown above, value below

Date	Mintage	VG	F	VF	XF	BU
1926	2,000,000	—	0.35	1.50	17.50	95.00
1927	2,502,100	—	0.35	1.50	12.00	75.00
1928/7	1,458,200	—	0.50	2.50	20.00	110
1928	Inc. above	—	0.35	1.50	20.00	110
1929	600,000	—	1.50	6.00	70.00	600
1939	900,000	—	0.25	0.60	5.00	165
1940	2,193,000	—	0.20	0.50	3.50	40.00
1941	2,373,000	—	0.20	0.50	3.50	25.00
1945	1,354,000	—	0.20	0.50	2.50	32.50
1946	1,532,500	—	0.20	0.50	3.50	20.00
1947	2,465,300	—	0.20	0.50	3.50	12.50
1948	5,911,400	—	0.20	0.40	1.75	12.50
1949	1,029,600	—	0.25	1.00	5.00	25.00

KM# 390   50 ORE
Zinc, 22 mm.   **Ruler:** Haakon VII **Obv:** Shield flanked by designs
Rev: Value flanked by designs **Note:** World War II German
occupation issue.

Date	Mintage	VG	F	VF	XF	BU
1941	7,760,800	—	1.25	3.00	15.00	80.00
1942	7,605,550	—	1.00	2.50	7.00	50.00
1943	3,348,500	7.00	15.00	25.00	60.00	200
1944	1,542,400	5.00	10.00	15.00	35.00	65.00
1945	226,000	90.00	180	285	425	675

KM# 393   50 ORE
4.8000 g., Nickel-Brass, 22 mm.   **Ruler:** Haakon VII
Obv: Crowned monograms form cross with hole in center
Rev: Center hole flanked by designs, crown above, value below
Note: World War II government in exile issue.

Date	Mintage	VG	F	VF	XF	BU
1942	1,600,000	—	—	—	150	300

Note: All but 9,238 were melted

KM# 402   50 ORE
4.8000 g., Copper-Nickel, 22 mm.   **Ruler:** Haakon VII
Obv: Crowned monogram **Rev:** Crowned shield divides date

Date	Mintage	VG	F	VF	XF	BU
1953	2,370,000	—	0.20	0.60	1.75	35.00
1954	230,000	1.25	5.00	15.00	85.00	600
1955	1,930,000	—	0.10	0.40	2.25	75.00
1956	1,630,000	—	0.10	0.40	2.25	65.00
1957	1,800,000	—	0.10	0.40	2.25	32.50

KM# 408   50 ORE
4.8000 g., Copper-Nickel, 22 mm.   **Ruler:** Olav V **Obv:** Head left
Rev: Dog right divides date and value

Date	Mintage	VG	F	VF	XF	BU
1958	1,560,000	—	0.25	0.75	3.00	90.00
1959	340,000	—	1.00	2.00	12.00	90.00
1960	1,584,000	—	—	0.10	1.75	20.00
1961	2,424,600	—	—	0.10	0.85	12.50
1962	3,064,000	—	—	0.10	0.85	12.50
1963	2,168,000	—	—	0.10	0.85	12.50
1964	2,692,000	—	—	0.10	0.60	8.00
1965	1,248,000	—	0.25	0.75	3.00	55.00
1966	4,262,000	—	—	0.10	0.50	8.00
1967	4,001,000	—	—	0.10	0.50	6.50
1968	5,430,800	—	—	0.10	0.50	12.50
1969	7,591,000	—	—	0.10	0.50	3.00
1970	481,000	—	0.25	0.75	2.25	6.50
1971	2,489,300	—	—	0.10	0.50	3.00
1972	4,452,784	—	—	0.10	0.50	3.00
1973	3,317,175	—	—	0.10	0.50	3.00

KM# 418   50 ORE
4.8000 g., Copper-Nickel, 22 mm.   **Ruler:** Olav V **Obv:** Crowned
shield divides date **Rev:** Value **Note:** Varieties in shield exist.

Date	Mintage	VG	F	VF	XF	BU
1974	8,494,223	—	—	0.10	0.15	0.75
1975	10,123,496	—	—	0.10	0.15	0.75
1976	15,177,324	—	—	0.10	0.15	0.65
1977	19,411,750	—	—	0.10	0.15	0.50
1978	15,305,000	—	—	0.10	0.15	0.50
1979	10,152,000	—	—	0.10	0.15	0.50
1980 Without star	7,066,000	—	—	0.10	0.15	0.50
1980	7,082,000	—	—	0.10	0.15	0.50
1981	3,402,000	—	—	0.10	0.15	0.50
1982	11,156,650	—	—	0.10	0.15	0.40
1983	15,762,300	—	—	0.10	0.15	0.40
1984	8,615,000	—	—	0.10	0.15	0.40
1985	4,444,000	—	—	0.10	0.15	0.40
1986	4,178,000	—	—	0.10	0.15	0.40
1987	5,167,000	—	—	0.10	0.15	0.40
1988	9,610,000	—	—	0.10	0.15	0.35
1989	5,785,000	—	—	0.10	0.15	0.35
1990	1,729,000	—	—	0.10	0.15	0.50
1991	2,924,008	—	—	0.10	0.15	0.35
1992	6,802,027	—	—	0.10	0.15	0.35
1992 Proof	20,000	Value: 10.00				
1993	8,056,000	—	—	0.10	0.15	0.35
1994	7,173,000	—	—	0.10	0.15	0.35
1994 Proof	12,000	Value: 10.00				
1995	6,835,000	—	—	—	—	0.35
1995 Proof	—	Value: 10.00				
1996	4,500,000	—	—	—	—	0.40
1996 Proof	—	Value: 10.00				

KM# 460   50 ORE
3.6000 g., Bronze, 18.49 mm.   **Ruler:** Harald V **Obv:** Crown
Rev: Stylized animal and value **Edge:** Plain

Date	Mintage	VG	F	VF	XF	BU
1996	81,956,200	—	—	—	—	0.50
1997	24,089,873	—	—	—	—	0.40
1997 Proof	—	Value: 10.00				
1998	30,913,000	—	—	—	—	0.40
1998 Proof	—	Value: 10.00				
1999	25,314,273	—	—	—	—	0.40
1999 Proof	—	Value: 10.00				
2000	18,979,552	—	—	—	—	0.40
2000 Proof	—	Value: 10.00				

KM# 357   KRONE
7.5000 g., 0.8000 Silver 0.1929 oz. ASW   **Obv:** Head left
Obv. Leg.: OSCAR II NORGES... **Rev:** Crowned arms within
wreath, crossed hammers divide date below **Note:** Without 30 SK

Date	Mintage	VG	F	VF	XF	BU
1901	151,800	17.00	30.00	70.00	200	550
1904	100,100	35.00	70.00	150	230	650

KM# 369   KRONE
7.5000 g., 0.8000 Silver 0.1929 oz. ASW   **Ruler:** Haakon VII
Obv: Head right **Rev:** Order of St. Olaf

Date	Mintage	VG	F	VF	XF	BU
1908	180,000	26.00	50.00	80.00	120	280
	Note: Crossed hammers on shield					
1908	170,000	21.00	40.00	60.00	100	215
	Note: Crossed hammers without shield					
1910	100,000	50.00	—	150	250	600
1912	200,000	30.00	45.00	100	160	325
1913	230,000	22.00	40.00	90.00	125	285
1914	602,000	11.00	19.00	35.00	50.00	125
1915	498,000	12.00	22.00	40.00	90.00	125
1916	400,000	12.00	25.00	40.00	100	280
1917	600,000	11.00	19.00	30.00	55.00	95.00

KM# 385   KRONE
7.0000 g., Copper-Nickel, 25 mm.   **Ruler:** Haakon VII
Obv: Crowned monograms form cross with hole in center
Rev: Crowned order chain with hole in center

Date	Mintage	VG	F	VF	XF	BU
1925	8,686,000	—	0.30	3.00	25.00	140
1926	1,984,000	—	0.50	4.00	35.00	240
1927	1,000,000	—	1.00	5.00	65.00	550
1936	700,000	—	1.25	5.50	65.00	500
1937	1,000,000	—	1.00	4.00	45.00	350
1938	926,000	—	0.60	2.50	20.00	150
1939	2,253,000	—	0.60	1.50	10.00	95.00
1940	3,890,000	—	0.30	1.00	6.00	75.00
1946	5,499,000	—	0.25	0.50	3.00	20.00
1947	802,000	—	1.00	2.00	12.00	65.00
1949	7,846,000	—	0.20	0.50	3.00	15.00
1950	9,942,000	—	0.20	0.50	3.00	15.00
1951	4,761,000	—	0.20	0.50	3.00	15.00

KM# 397.1   KRONE
7.0000 g., Copper-Nickel, 25 mm.   **Ruler:** Haakon VII
Obv: Crowned monogram **Rev:** Crowned shield divides date
Note: Thin border dentilations

Date	Mintage	F	VF	XF	Unc	BU
1951	3,819,000	0.20	0.50	2.50	32.50	40.00

KM# 397.2   KRONE
7.0000 g., Copper-Nickel, 25 mm.   **Ruler:** Haakon VII
Obv: Crowned monogram **Rev:** Crowned shield divides date
Note: Thick border dentilations.

Date	Mintage	VG	F	VF	XF	BU
1953	1,465,000	—	0.20	0.50	2.50	70.00
1954	3,045,000	—	0.20	0.50	2.50	70.00
1955	1,970,000	—	0.20	0.50	2.50	100
1956	4,300,000	—	0.20	0.50	2.50	60.00
1957	7,630,000	—	0.20	0.50	2.50	40.00

KM# 409 KRONE
7.0000 g., Copper-Nickel, 25 mm. **Ruler:** Olav V **Obv:** Head left **Rev:** Horse

Date	Mintage	VG	F	VF	XF	BU
1958	540,000	—	3.00	10.00	50.00	325
1959	4,450,000	—	—	0.20	2.50	35.00
1960	1,790,200	—	—	0.20	2.50	30.00
1961	3,933,600	—	—	0.20	0.85	15.00
1962	6,015,000	—	—	0.20	0.85	15.00
1963	4,677,000	—	—	0.20	0.85	15.00
1964	3,469,000	—	—	0.20	0.60	7.50
1965	3,222,000	—	—	0.20	1.20	70.00
1966	3,084,000	—	—	0.20	0.85	30.00
1967	6,680,000	—	—	0.20	0.85	15.00
1968	6,149,200	—	—	0.20	0.85	70.00
1969	5,185,500	—	—	0.20	0.40	7.00
1970	8,637,900	—	—	0.20	0.50	17.00
1971	10,257,800	—	—	0.20	0.40	7.00
1972	13,179,394	—	—	0.20	0.40	4.75
1973	9,140,175	—	—	0.20	0.40	4.75

KM# 419 KRONE
7.0000 g., Copper-Nickel, 25 mm. **Ruler:** Olav V **Obv:** Head left **Rev:** Value and date below crown **Note:** Varieties with and without star mint mark exist.

Date	Mintage	VG	F	VF	XF	BU
1974	16,537,223	—	—	0.20	0.35	1.25
1975	26,043,966	—	—	0.20	0.35	1.25
1976	35,926,574	—	—	0.20	0.35	0.85
1977	26,263,500	—	—	0.20	0.35	0.85
1978	23,360,000	—	—	0.20	0.35	0.85
1979	15,896,500	—	—	0.20	0.35	0.85
1980	5,918,000	—	—	0.20	0.35	2.50
1981	16,308,150	—	—	0.20	0.35	0.75
1982	29,187,000	—	—	0.20	0.35	0.75
1983	24,293,300	—	—	0.20	0.35	0.75
1984	3,677,000	—	—	0.20	0.35	1.50
1985	10,985,000	—	—	0.20	0.35	0.75
1986	5,612,500	—	—	0.20	0.35	0.75
1987	11,015,500	—	—	0.20	0.35	0.75
1988	14,880,000	—	—	0.20	0.35	0.75
1989	5,605,000	—	—	0.20	0.35	0.65
1990	8,804,000	—	—	0.20	0.35	0.65
1990 Proof	15,110	Value: 85.00				
1991	21,064,500	—	—	0.20	0.35	0.65

KM# 436 KRONE
7.0000 g., Copper-Nickel, 25 mm. **Ruler:** Harald V **Obv:** Head right **Rev:** Value and date below crown

Date	Mintage	VG	F	VF	XF	BU
1992	7,425,500	—	—	0.20	0.35	0.65
1992 Proof	20,000	Value: 10.00				
1993	12,295,000	—	—	0.20	0.35	0.65
1994	25,951,000	—	—	0.20	0.35	0.65
1994 Proof	12,000	Value: 10.00				
1995	12,883,000	—	—	0.20	0.35	0.65
1995 Proof	—	Value: 10.00				
1996	20,844,000	—	—	0.20	0.35	0.65
1996 Proof	—	Value: 10.00				

KM# 462 KRONE
4.3000 g., Copper-Nickel, 21 mm. **Ruler:** Harald V **Obv:** Crowned monograms form cross within circle with center hole **Rev:** Bird on vine above center hole date and value below

Date	Mintage	VG	F	VF	XF	BU
1997	141,099,873	—	—	—	—	0.65
1997 Proof	—	Value: 10.00				
1998	139,493,000	—	—	—	—	0.65
1998 Proof	—	Value: 10.00				
1999	74,454,273	—	—	—	—	0.65
1999 Proof	—	Value: 10.00				
2000	42,689,277	—	—	—	—	0.65
2000 Proof	—	Value: 10.00				

KM# 359 2 KRONER
15.0000 g., 0.8000 Silver 0.3858 oz. ASW, 31 mm. **Obv:** Head left **Obv. Leg.:** OSCAR II NORGES... **Rev:** Crowned arms within wreath, crossed hammers divide date below **Note:** Restrikes are made by the Royal Mint, Norway, in gold, silver and bronze.

Date	Mintage	VG	F	VF	XF	BU
1902	153,100	50.00	85.00	125	225	500
1904	75,600	50.00	100	150	250	525

KM# 363 2 KRONER
15.0000 g., 0.8000 Silver 0.3858 oz. ASW, 31 mm. **Ruler:** Haakon VII **Subject:** Norway Independence **Obv:** Crowned mantled shield **Rev:** Inscription and date within tree, wreath of grasped hands surround

Date	Mintage	VG	F	VF	XF	BU
1906	100,000	23.00	40.00	70.00	115	225

KM# 365 2 KRONER
15.0000 g., 0.8000 Silver 0.3858 oz. ASW, 31 mm. **Ruler:** Haakon VII **Obv:** Crowned mantled shield **Rev:** Inscription and date within tree, wreath of grasped hands surround

Date	Mintage	VG	F	VF	XF	BU
1907	54,600	30.00	65.00	110	175	325

KM# 366 2 KRONER
15.0000 g., 0.8000 Silver 0.3858 oz. ASW, 31 mm. **Ruler:** Haakon VII **Subject:** Border watch **Obv:** Crowned and mantled arms **Rev:** Inscription and date within tree, wreath of grasped hands surround

Date	Mintage	VG	F	VF	XF	BU
1907	27,500	125	225	375	600	950

KM# 370 2 KRONER
15.0000 g., 0.8000 Silver 0.3858 oz. ASW, 31 mm. **Ruler:** Haakon VII **Obv:** Head right **Rev:** Crowned shield within designed circle, various emblems around border

Date	Mintage	VG	F	VF	XF	BU
1908	200,000	—	50.00	85.00	125	250
1910	150,000	—	80.00	125	175	425
1912	150,000	—	65.00	100	150	400
1913	270,000	—	45.00	65.00	90.00	175
1914	255,000	—	45.00	70.00	95.00	215
1915	225,000	—	40.00	65.00	95.00	215
1916	250,000	—	60.00	85.00	125	265
1917	377,500	—	30.00	40.00	60.00	165

KM# 377 2 KRONER
15.0000 g., 0.8000 Silver 0.3858 oz. ASW, 31 mm. **Ruler:** Haakon VII **Subject:** Constitution centennial **Obv:** Crowned shield **Rev:** Standing figure facing right

Date	Mintage	VG	F	VF	XF	BU
1914	225,600	10.00	20.00	40.00	70.00	165

KM# 412 5 KRONER
11.5000 g., Copper-Nickel, 29.5 mm. **Ruler:** Olav V **Obv:** Head left **Rev:** Crowned shield divides value

Date	Mintage	VG	F	VF	XF	BU
1963	7,074,000	—	—	1.00	3.50	30.00
1964	7,346,000	—	—	1.00	2.25	15.00
1965	2,233,000	—	—	1.00	3.00	90.00
1966	2,502,000	—	—	1.00	3.00	65.00
1967	583,000	—	1.00	1.75	6.50	60.00
1968	1,813,400	—	—	1.00	2.25	45.00
1969	2,403,700	—	—	1.00	2.25	12.00
1970	202,300	—	1.50	2.50	6.50	22.50
1971	177,900	—	1.50	2.50	7.00	27.50
1972	2,208,704	—	—	—	1.25	3.50
1973	2,778,055	—	—	—	1.25	7.50

KM# 420 5 KRONER
11.5000 g., Copper-Nickel, 29.5 mm. **Ruler:** Olav V **Obv:** Head left **Rev:** Crowned shield divides date **Note:** Varieties exist with large and small shields.

Date	Mintage	VG	F	VF	XF	BU
1974	1,983,423	—	—	—	1.00	7.50
1975	2,946,442	—	—	—	1.00	4.50
1976	9,055,574	—	—	—	1.00	2.25
1977	4,629,600	—	—	—	1.00	1.50
1978	5,853,000	—	—	—	1.00	1.50
1979	6,818,000	—	—	—	1.00	1.50
1980	1,578,400	—	—	—	1.00	2.50
1981	1,104,800	—	—	—	1.00	2.25
1982	3,919,890	—	—	—	1.00	1.50
1983	2,932,260	—	—	—	1.00	1.50
1984	1,233,000	—	—	—	1.00	2.25
1985	1,399,600	—	—	—	1.00	1.50
1987	900,200	—	—	—	1.00	2.50
1988	865,200	—	—	—	1.00	2.50

KM# 421 5 KRONER
11.5000 g., Copper-Nickel, 29.5 mm. **Ruler:** Olav V **Subject:** 100th Anniversary of Krone System **Obv:** Crowned shield divides value **Rev:** Balance scale and miner

Date	Mintage	VG	F	VF	XF	BU
ND(1975)	1,191,813	—	—	1.00	1.50	3.50

KM# 422 5 KRONER
11.5000 g., Copper-Nickel, 29.5 mm. **Ruler:** Olav V **Subject:** 150th Anniversary - Immigration to America **Obv:** Value below arms **Rev:** Sailing ship, The "Restaurasjonen"(Restoration)

Date	Mintage	VG	F	VF	XF	BU
ND(1975)	1,222,827	—	—	1.00	1.50	3.50

KM# 423 5 KRONER
11.5000 g., Copper-Nickel, 29.5 mm. **Ruler:** Olav V **Subject:** 350th Anniversary of Norwegian Army **Obv:** Value below arms **Rev:** Sword divides crowned monograms

Date	Mintage	VG	F	VF	XF	BU
ND(1978)	2,989,768	—	—	1.00	1.50	3.00

KM# 428 5 KRONER
11.5000 g., Copper-Nickel, 29.5 mm. **Ruler:** Olav V **Subject:** 300th Anniversary of the Mint **Obv:** Crossed mining tools below crown, circle surrounds **Rev:** Conjoined heads left and right within circle

Date	Mintage	VG	F	VF	XF	BU
1986	2,345,500	—	—	1.00	1.50	3.00
1986 Prooflike	5,000	—	—	—	—	—

KM# 430 5 KRONER
11.5000 g., Copper-Nickel, 29.5 mm. **Ruler:** Olav V **Subject:** 175th Anniversary of the National Bank **Obv:** Arms **Rev:** Stein above date and inscription

Date	Mintage	VG	F	VF	XF	BU
1991	512,000	—	—	—	—	7.00

KM# 437 5 KRONER
11.5000 g., Copper-Nickel, 29.5 mm. **Ruler:** Harald V **Obv:** Crowned shield divides date

Date	Mintage	VG	F	VF	XF	BU
1992	549,600	—	—	—	—	2.25
Note: 100,000 are in mint sets						
1992 Proof	20,000	Value: 10.00				
1993	509,600	—	—	—	—	2.50
1994	2,111,800	—	—	—	—	2.00
1994 Proof	12,000	Value: 10.00				

KM# 456 5 KRONER
11.5000 g., Copper-Nickel, 29.5 mm. **Ruler:** Harald V **Obv:** Head right **Rev:** Old coin design divides value above legend and date **Note:** 1,000 years of Norwegian coinage

Date	Mintage	VG	F	VF	XF	BU
1995	500,000	—	—	—	—	3.50
1995 Proof	12,000	Value: 22.50				

KM# 458 5 KRONER
11.5000 g., Copper-Nickel, 29.5 mm. **Ruler:** Harald V **Subject:** 50th Anniversary - United Nations **Obv:** Head right **Rev:** Standing figure with arms outstretched, children holding hands by tree

Date	Mintage	VG	F	VF	XF	BU
ND(1995)	500,000	—	—	—	—	3.50

KM# 459 5 KRONER
11.5000 g., Copper-Nickel, 29.5 mm. **Ruler:** Harald V **Subject:** Centennial - Nansen's Return From the Arctic **Obv:** Head right **Rev:** Sailing ship facing

Date	Mintage	VG	F	VF	XF	BU
1996	1,381,909	—	—	—	—	3.00
1996 Proof	12,000	Value: 22.50				

KM# 461 5 KRONER
11.5000 g., Copper-Nickel, 29.5 mm. **Ruler:** Harald V **Subject:** 350th Anniversary - Norwegian Postal Service **Obv:** Arms **Rev:** Horse and rider left

Date	Mintage	VG	F	VF	XF	BU
ND(1997)	1,742,073	—	—	—	—	3.00
ND(1997) Proof	12,000	Value: 10.00				

KM# 463 5 KRONER
7.8500 g., Copper-Nickel, 26 mm. **Ruler:** Harald V **Subject:** Order of St. Olaf **Obv:** Hole at center of order chain **Rev:** Center hole divides sprigs, value above and date below

Date	Mintage	VG	F	VF	XF	BU
1998	47,701,000	—	—	—	—	1.50
1998 Proof	10,000	Value: 12.50				
1999	21,754,273	—	—	—	—	1.50
1999 Proof	10,000	Value: 12.50				
2000	9,691,387	—	—	—	—	1.50
2000 Proof	10,000	Value: 12.50				

KM# 358 10 KRONER
4.4803 g., 0.9000 Gold 0.1296 oz. AGW **Obv:** Head right **Obv. Leg.:** OSCAR II NORGES... **Rev:** Crowned arms within wreath

Date	Mintage	VG	F	VF	XF	Unc
1902	24,100	BV	125	200	375	600

KM# 375 10 KRONER
4.4803 g., 0.9000 Gold 0.1296 oz. AGW **Ruler:** Haakon VII
Obv: Crowned head right **Rev:** King Olaf Haraldson, the Saint

Date	Mintage	F	VF	XF	Unc	BU
1910	52,600	BV	175	275	450	—

KM# 413 10 KRONER
20.0000 g., 0.9000 Silver 0.5787 oz. ASW, 35 mm.
Ruler: Haakon VII **Subject:** Constitution sesquicentennial
Obv: Crowned shield **Rev:** Eidsval Mansion **Edge:** ENIGE OG
TRO TIL DOVRE FALLER **Note:** Edge lettering varieties exist.

Date	Mintage	VG	F	VF	XF	BU
ND(1964)	1,408,000	—	—	—	9.00	11.50

KM# 427 10 KRONER
9.0000 g., Copper-Zinc-Nickel **Ruler:** Olav V **Obv:** Head left
within circle **Rev:** Value within small circle at center of order chain

Date	Mintage	VG	F	VF	XF	BU
1983	20,193,060	—	—	—	2.00	5.50
1984	11,073,500	—	—	—	1.75	3.25
1985	22,457,550	—	—	—	1.75	3.00
1986	29,060,950	—	—	—	1.75	3.00
1987	8,809,750	—	—	—	1.75	3.25
1988	2,630,500	—	—	—	1.75	3.25
1989	3,259,000	—	—	—	1.75	3.25
1990	3,004,000	—	—	—	1.75	3.25
1991	20,287,150	—	—	—	1.75	2.75

KM# 457 10 KRONER
6.8000 g., Copper-Zinc-Nickel, 24 mm. **Ruler:** Harald V
Obv: Head right **Rev:** Stylized church rooftop, value and date

Date	Mintage	VG	F	VF	XF	BU
1995	60,740,000	—	—	—	—	3.50
1995 Proof	—	Value: 10.00				
1996	36,372,000	—	—	—	—	3.50
1996 Proof	—	Value: 10.00				
1997	1,229,873	—	—	—	—	3.50
1997 Proof	—	Value: 10.00				
1998	1,058,000	—	—	—	—	3.50
1998 Proof	—	Value: 10.00				
1999	1,059,273	—	—	—	—	3.50
1999 Proof	—	Value: 10.00				
2000	1,096,727	—	—	—	—	3.50
2000 Proof	—	Value: 10.00				

KM# 355 20 KRONER
8.9600 g., 0.9000 Gold 0.2593 oz. AGW **Obv:** Head right **Obv.**
Leg.: OSCAR II NORGES... **Rev:** Crowned arms within wreath

Date	Mintage	VG	F	VF	XF	Unc
1902	50,400	—	—	BV	265	350

KM# 376 20 KRONER
8.9600 g., 0.9000 Gold 0.2593 oz. AGW **Ruler:** Haakon VII
Obv: Crowned head right **Rev:** King Olaf II, the Saint

Date	Mintage	F	VF	XF	Unc	BU
1910	250,000	—	BV	300	450	—

KM# 453 20 KRONER
9.9000 g., Copper-Zinc-Nickel, 27.5 mm. **Ruler:** Harald V
Obv: Head right **Rev:** Value above 1/2 ancient boat

Date	Mintage	VG	F	VF	XF	BU
1994	18,598,000	—	—	—	—	6.50
1994 Proof	12,000	Value: 25.00				
1995	21,760,000	—	—	—	—	6.50
1995 Proof	—	Value: 25.00				
1996	1,519,500	—	—	—	—	6.50
1996 Proof	—	Value: 25.00				
1997	1,049,873	—	—	—	—	6.50
1997 Proof	—	Value: 25.00				
1998	5,007,000	—	—	—	—	6.50
1998 Proof	—	Value: 25.00				
1999	6,171,000	—	—	—	—	6.50
1999 Proof	—	Value: 25.00				
2000	11,113,370	—	—	—	—	6.50
2000 Proof	10,000	Value: 25.00				

KM# 464 20 KRONER
9.9000 g., Copper-Zinc-Nickel **Ruler:** Harald V **Subject:** 700th
Anniversary - Akershus Fortress **Obv:** Seal of King Hadon V
Rev: Fortress

Date	Mintage	F	VF	XF	Unc	BU
1999	5,121,986	—	—	—	7.50	—

KM# 465 20 KRONER
9.9000 g., Nickel-Bronze **Ruler:** Harald V **Subject:** Vinland
Obv: Head right **Rev:** Viking ship hull reflected

Date	Mintage	F	VF	XF	Unc	BU
1999	1,048,700	—	—	—	7.50	—
1999 Proof	2,500	Value: 30.00				
	Note: In sets only					

KM# 468 20 KRONER
9.9000 g., Nickel-Brass **Ruler:** Harald V **Subject:** Millennium
Obv: Head right **Rev:** Unknown road into the future

Date	Mintage	F	VF	XF	Unc	BU
2000	1,032,307	—	—	—	12.50	—

KM# 414 25 KRONER
29.0000 g., 0.8750 Silver 0.8158 oz. ASW, 39 mm.
Ruler: Olav V **Subject:** 25th Anniversary of Liberation
Obv: Head right **Rev:** Crowned monogram **Edge:** Repeated
pattern of circles and rectangles

Date	Mintage	VG	F	VF	XF	BU
1970	1,203,700	—	—	—	—	13.50

KM# 424 50 KRONER
27.0000 g., 0.9250 Silver 0.8029 oz. ASW **Ruler:** Olav V
Subject: 75th Birthday of King Olav V **Obv:** Head left **Rev:** Single
flowered stem divides signature and dates

Date	Mintage	VG	F	VF	XF	BU
ND(1978)	800,000	—	—	—	—	15.00

KM# 431 50 KRONER
16.8100 g., 0.9250 Silver 0.4999 oz. ASW **Ruler:** Olav V
Subject: 1994 Olympics **Obv:** Head left **Rev:** Skiers within circle

Date	Mintage	VG	F	VF	XF	BU
1991	80,016	—	—	—	—	37.50

KM# 432 50 KRONER
16.8100 g., 0.9250 Silver 0.4999 oz. ASW **Ruler:** Olav V
Subject: 1994 Olympics **Obv:** Head left **Rev:** Child skiing

Date	Mintage	VG	F	VF	XF	BU
1991	120,000	—	—	—	—	37.50

KM# 438   50 KRONER
16.8100 g., 0.9250 Silver 0.4999 oz. ASW **Ruler:** Harald V
Subject: 1994 Olympics **Obv:** Head right **Rev:** Grandfather and child within circle

Date	Mintage	VG	F	VF	XF	BU
1992	74,000	—	—	—	—	37.50

KM# 439   50 KRONER
16.8100 g., 0.9250 Silver 0.4999 oz. ASW **Ruler:** Harald V
Subject: 1994 Olympics **Obv:** Head right **Rev:** 2 children on sled

Date	Mintage	VG	F	VF	XF	BU
1992	88,000	—	—	—	—	37.50

KM# 447   50 KRONER
16.8100 g., 0.9250 Silver 0.4999 oz. ASW **Ruler:** Harald V
Subject: 1994 Olympics **Obv:** Head right **Rev:** Cross-country skiers

Date	Mintage	VG	F	VF	XF	BU
1993	65,000	—	—	—	—	37.50

KM# 448   50 KRONER
16.8100 g., 0.9250 Silver 0.4999 oz. ASW **Ruler:** Harald V
Subject: 1994 Olympics **Obv:** Head right **Rev:** Children ice skating within circle

Date	Mintage	VG	F	VF	XF	BU
1993	77,000	—	—	—	—	37.50

KM# 454   50 KRONER
16.8100 g., 0.9250 Silver 0.4999 oz. ASW **Ruler:** Harald V
Subject: 50th Anniversary - United Nations **Obv:** Head right
Rev: Standing figure facing, children holding hands under tree

Date	Mintage	VG	F	VF	XF	BU
ND(1995) Proof	200,000			Value: 42.50		

KM# 455   50 KRONER
16.8100 g., 0.9250 Silver 0.4999 oz. ASW **Ruler:** Harald V
Subject: 50th Anniversary - End of World War II **Obv:** Arms
Rev: Stylized dove above dates

Date	Mintage	VG	F	VF	XF	BU
ND(1995) Proof	50,000			Value: 45.00		

KM# 426   100 KRONER
24.7300 g., 0.9250 Silver 0.7354 oz. ASW **Ruler:** Olav V
Subject: 25th Anniversary of King Olav's Reign **Obv:** Head left
Rev: Tilted shield under artistic designed shield

Date	Mintage	VG	F	VF	XF	BU
1982	800,000	—	—	—	—	25.00

KM# 433   100 KRONER
33.6200 g., 0.9250 Silver 0.9998 oz. ASW **Ruler:** Olav V
Subject: 1994 Olympics **Obv:** Head left **Rev:** Cross-country skier within circle

Date	Mintage	VG	F	VF	XF	BU
1991	88,000	—	—	—	—	60.00

KM# 434   100 KRONER
33.6200 g., 0.9250 Silver 0.9998 oz. ASW **Ruler:** Olav V
Subject: 1994 Olympics **Obv:** Head left **Rev:** 2 speed skaters

Date	Mintage	VG	F	VF	XF	BU
1991	116,000	—	—	—	—	60.00

KM# 440   100 KRONER
33.6200 g., 0.9250 Silver 0.9998 oz. ASW **Ruler:** Harald V
Subject: 1994 Olympics **Obv:** Head right **Rev:** Ski jumper within circle

Date	Mintage	VG	F	VF	XF	BU
1992	85,000	—	—	—	—	60.00

KM# 441   100 KRONER
33.6200 g., 0.9250 Silver 0.9998 oz. ASW **Ruler:** Harald V
Subject: 1994 Olympics **Obv:** Head right **Rev:** Hockey players

Date	Mintage	VG	F	VF	XF	BU
1992	81,000	—	—	—	—	60.00

KM# 443   100 KRONER
33.6200 g., 0.9250 Silver 0.9998 oz. ASW **Ruler:** Harald V
Subject: World Cycling Championships **Obv:** Arms **Rev:** Cyclist

Date	Mintage	VG	F	VF	XF	BU
1993	9,288	—	—	—	—	70.00

KM# 444   100 KRONER
33.6200 g., 0.9250 Silver 0.9998 oz. ASW **Ruler:** Harald V
Subject: World Cycling Championships **Obv:** Arms **Rev:** 7 cyclists

Date	Mintage	VG	F	VF	XF	BU
1993	9,288	—	—	—	—	70.00

KM# 449   100 KRONER
33.6200 g., 0.9250 Silver 0.9998 oz. ASW **Ruler:** Harald V
Subject: 1984 Olympics **Obv:** Head right **Rev:** Female figure skater within circle

Date	Mintage	VG	F	VF	XF	BU
1993	96,000	—	—	—	—	60.00

KM# 450   100 KRONER
33.6200 g., 0.9250 Silver 0.9998 oz. ASW **Ruler:** Harald V
Subject: 1984 Olympics **Obv:** Head right **Rev:** Alpine skier

Date	Mintage	VG	F	VF	XF	BU
1993	85,000	—	—	—	—	60.00

KM# 466   100 KRONER
33.8000 g., 0.9250 Silver 1.0052 oz. ASW **Ruler:** Harald V
Subject: Year 2000 **Obv:** National arms **Rev:** Cut tree trunk exposing rings

Date	Mintage	F	VF	XF	Unc	BU
1999 Proof	50,000	Value: 70.00				

KM# 429   175 KRONER
26.5000 g., 0.9250 Silver 0.7881 oz. ASW **Ruler:** Olav V
Subject: 175th Anniversary of Constitution **Obv:** Crowned arms within order chain **Rev:** Building

Date	Mintage	VG	F	VF	XF	BU
ND(1989)	85,000	—	—	—	—	75.00
ND(1989) Proof	15,000	Value: 225				

KM# 425   200 KRONER
26.8000 g., 0.6250 Silver 0.5385 oz. ASW **Ruler:** Olav V
Subject: 35th Anniversary of Liberation **Obv:** Arms **Rev:** Akershus Castle

Date	Mintage	VG	F	VF	XF	BU
1980	298,399	—	—	—	—	45.00

KM# 435   1500 KRONER
17.0000 g., 0.9170 Gold 0.5012 oz. AGW **Ruler:** Olav V
Subject: 1994 Olympics **Obv:** Head left **Rev:** Ancient Norwegian skier

Date	Mintage	VG	F	VF	XF	BU
1991 Proof	30,000	Value: 500				

KM# 442   1500 KRONER
17.0000 g., 0.9170 Gold 0.5012 oz. AGW **Ruler:** Harald V
Subject: 1994 Olympics **Obv:** Head right **Rev:** Birkebeiners

Date	Mintage	VG	F	VF	XF	BU
1992 Proof	30,000	Value: 500				

KM# 445   1500 KRONER
17.0000 g., 0.9170 Gold 0.5012 oz. AGW **Ruler:** Harald V
Subject: World Cycling Championships **Obv:** Arms **Rev:** Two 19th century cyclists

Date	Mintage	VG	F	VF	XF	BU
1993 Proof	6,390	Value: 500				

KM# 446   1500 KRONER
17.0000 g., 0.9170 Gold 0.5012 oz. AGW **Ruler:** Harald V
Subject: Edvard Grieg **Obv:** Crowned shield **Rev:** Figure playing piano

Date	Mintage	VG	F	VF	XF	BU
1993 Proof	5,139	Value: 550				

KM# 451   1500 KRONER
17.0000 g., 0.9170 Gold 0.5012 oz. AGW **Ruler:** Harald V
Subject: 1994 Olympics **Obv:** Head right **Rev:** Telemark skier

Date	Mintage	VG	F	VF	XF	BU
1993 Proof	30,000	Value: 500				

KM# 452   1500 KRONER
17.0000 g., 0.9170 Gold 0.5012 oz. AGW **Ruler:** Harald V
Subject: Roald Amundsen **Obv:** Head right **Rev:** Bust left with skis on shoulder

Date	Mintage	VG	F	VF	XF	BU
1993 Proof	22,000	Value: 500				

KM# 467   1500 KRONER
16.9600 g., 0.9170 Gold 0.5000 oz. AGW **Ruler:** Olav V
Subject: Year 2000 **Obv:** Head right **Rev:** Tree and roots

Date	Mintage	VG	F	VF	XF	BU
2000 Proof	7,500	Value: 500				

PATTERNS
Including off metal strikes

KM#	Date	Mintage Identification	Mkt Val
Pn40	1958	6 Ore.	—

MINT SETS

KM#	Date	Mintage	Identification	Issue Price	Mkt Val
MS1	1960 (7)	200	KM403, 405, 407-411	—	—
MS2	1961 (7)	475	KM403, 405, 407-411	—	—
MS3	1962 (7)	570	KM403, 405, 407-411	—	—
MS4	1963 (8)	430	KM403, 405, 407-412	—	—
MS6	1964 (8)	1,200	KM403, 405, 407-412	—	—
MS7	1965 (8)	1,800	KM403, 405, 407-412. Plastic.	—	400
MS8	1966 (8)	1,400	KM403, 405, 407-412. Plastic.	—	300
MS9	1967 (8)	2,490	KM403, 405, 407-412. Soft plastic.	—	250
MS11	1968 (8)	1,167	KM403, 405, 407-412. Soft plastic.	—	1,275
MS12	1968 (8)	2,300	KM403, 405, 407-412. Sandhill.	—	1,400
MS13	1969 (8)	3,140	KM403, 405, 407-412	—	55.00
MS14	1969 (8)	7,450	KM403, 405, 407-412. Sandhill.	—	125
MS15	1970 (8)	2,005	KM403, 405, 407-412. Soft plastic.	—	100
MS16	1970 (8)	7,311	KM403, 405, 407-412. Sandhill.	—	225
MS17	1971 (8)	2,010	KM403, 405, 407-412. Soft plastic.	—	100
MS18	1971 (8)	4,055	KM403, 405, 407-412. Sandhill.	—	265
MS19	1972 (8)	6,549	KM403, 405, 407-412. Soft plastic.	—	30.00
MS20	1972 (8)	6,435	KM403, 405, 407-412. Sandhill.	—	125
MS21	1973 (7)	7,085	KM405, 407-409, 411-412, 415. Soft plastic.	—	30.00
MS22	1973 (7)	13,090	KM405, 407-409, 411-412, 415. Sandhill.	6.00	100
MS23	1974 (6)	10,275	KM415-420. Soft plastic.	3.00	30.00
MS24	1974 (6)	29,695	KM415-420. Sandhill.	—	45.00
MS25	1975 (8)	30,207	KM415-422. Sandhill.	5.00	75.00
MS26	1975 (7)	5,287	KM415-421. Soft plastic.	5.00	25.00
MS27	1976 (6)	5,000	KM415-420. Soft plastic.	3.00	23.00
MS28	1976 (6)	25,000	KM415-420. Sandhill.	3.00	60.00
MS29	1977 (6)	5,000	KM415-420. Soft plastic.	3.40	25.00
MS30	1977 (6)	25,000	KM415-420. Sandhill.	3.40	60.00
MS31	1978 (6)	5,000	KM415-420. Soft plastic.	3.40	25.00

KM#	Date	Mintage	Identification	Issue Price	Mkt Val
MS32	1978 (6)	30,000	KM415-420. Sandhill.	3.40	60.00
MS33	1979 (6)	8,000	KM415-420. Soft plastic.	3.40	9.00
MS34	1979 (6)	50,000	KM415-420. Sandhill.	3.40	27.00
MS35	1980 (6)	10,000	KM415-420. Soft plastic.	3.40	20.00
MS36	1980 (6)	70,000	KM415-420. Sandhill.	3.40	35.00
MS37	1981 (6)	100,000	KM415-420. Hard plastic.	4.25	19.00
MS38	1982 (6)	102,650	KM415-420	4.50	26.00
MS39	1983 (4)	102,300	KM416, 418-420	5.00	17.00
MS40	1984 (5)	101,000	KM416, 418-420, 427	5.00	21.00
MS41	1985 (5)	110,000	KM416, 418-420, 427	5.00	21.00
MS42	1986 (5)	100,000	KM416, 418-419, 427-428	7.00	30.00
MS43	1987 (5)	85,000	KM416, 418-420, 427	7.00	30.00
MS44	1988 (5)	102,000	KM416, 418, 419, 420, 427	7.00	22.00
MS45	1989 (5)	101,000	KM416, 418-419, 427	8.00	23.00
MS46	1990 (4)	103,000	KM416, 418-419, 427, plus mint medal	8.00	23.00
MS47	1991/1992 (5)	100,000	KM416, 418, 427, 436-437	—	11.00
MS48	1991/1993 (5)	100,000	KM416, 418, 427, 436-437	—	20.00
MS49	1994 (5)	100,000	KM418, 427, 436-437, 453	—	18.00
MS50	1995 (5)	100,000	KM418, 436, 453, 456, 457	—	20.00
MS51	1996 (5)	90,000	KM418, 436, 453, 457, 459	—	25.00
MS52	1997 (5)	90,000	KM453, 457, 460, 461, 462	—	25.00
MS53	1998 (5)	90,000	KM453, 457, 460, 462, 463	—	25.00
MS54	1999 (5)	—	KM453, 457, 460, 462, 463	—	50.00
MS55	1999 (5)	50,000	KM457, 460 462-464. Souvenir folder.	13.00	15.00
MS56	1999 (5)	35,000	KM457, 460, 462-464. Baby coin set.	14.30	30.00
MS57	1999 (5)	—	KM457, 460, 462-464 plus medal.	26.00	26.00
MS58	2000 (5)	—	KM453, 457, 460, 462, 463. Hard case.	—	45.00

PROOF SETS

KM#	Date	Mintage	Identification	Issue Price	Mkt Val
PS1	1992 (3)	20,000	KM418, 436-437	—	45.00
PS2	1993 (3)	12,000	KM443-445	—	650
PS3	1994 (4)	15,000	KM418, 436-437, 453	—	60.00
PS4	1995 (5)	14,459	KM418, 436, 453, 456, 457	—	80.00
PS5	1996 (5)	11,551	KM418, 436, 453, 457, 459	—	80.00
PS6	1997 (5)	15,000	KM453, 457, 460, 461, 462. Norwegian Heritage Set.	—	65.00
PS7	1997 (5)	12,000	KM453, 457, 460, 461, 462	—	70.00
PS8	1998 (5)	14,097	KM453, 457, 460, 462, 463. Norwegian Heritage Set.	—	65.00
PS9	1998 (5)	12,000	KM453, 457, 460, 462, 463	—	70.00
PS10	1999 (5)	15,000	KM453, 457, 460, 462, 463	60.00	80.00
PS11	1999 (5)	2,500	KM457, 460, 462-463, 465. Heritage Set.	—	150
PS12	2000 (5)	10,000	KM453, 457, 460, 462, 463	—	65.00

OMAN

The Sultanate of Oman (formerly Muscat and Oman), an independent monarchy located in the southeastern part of the Arabian Peninsula, has an area of 82,030 sq. mi. (212,460 sq. km.) and a population of *1.3 million. Capital: Muscat. The economy is based on agriculture, herding and petroleum. Petroleum products, dates, fish and hides are exported.

The Portuguese who captured Muscat, the capital and chief port, in 1508, made the first European contact with Muscat and Oman. They occupied the city, utilizing it as a naval base and factory and holding it against land and sea attacks by Arabs and Persians until finally ejected by local Arabs in 1650. It was next occupied by the Persians who maintained control until 1741, when it was taken by Ahmed ibn Sa'id of the present ruling family. Muscat and Oman was the most powerful state in Arabia during the first half of the 19th century, until weakened by the persistent attack of interior nomadic tribes. British influence, initiated by the signing of a treaty of friendship with the Sultanate in 1798, remains a dominant fact of the civil and military phases of the government, although Britain recognizes the Sultanate as a sovereign state.

Sultan Sa'id bin Taimur was overthrown by his son, Qabus bin Sa'id, on July 23, 1970. The new sultan changed the nation's name to Sultanate of Oman.

TITLES

Muscat

Oman .

SULTANATE
DECIMAL COINAGE

1000 (new) Baisa = 1 Saidi Rial

KM# 42 1/2 SAIDI RIAL
25.6000 g., 0.9170 Gold 0.7547 oz. AGW **Ruler:** Qabus bin Sa'id AH1390-/1970AD- **Obv:** National arms within circle **Rev:** Value and date

Date	Mintage	F	VF	XF	Unc	BU
AH1391 (1971) Proof	100	Value: 850				

Note: Struck for presentation purposes

KM# 44 SAIDI RIAL
46.6500 g., 0.9170 Gold 1.3753 oz. AGW **Ruler:** Qabus bin Sa'id AH1390-/1970AD- **Obv:** National arms within circle with star and moon border **Rev:** Value and date

Date	Mintage	F	VF	XF	Unc	BU
AH1391 (1971) Proof	100	Value: 1,500				
AH1394 (1974) Proof	250	Value: 1,400				

Note: Struck for presentation purposes

KM# 43 15 SAIDI RIALS
5.8100 g., 0.9170 Gold 0.1713 oz. AGW **Ruler:** Qabus bin Sa'id AH1390-/1970AD- **Obv:** National arms **Rev:** Value

Date	Mintage	F	VF	XF	Unc	BU
AH1391 (1971) Proof	112	Value: 650				

Note: Struck for presentation purposes

KM# 53 15 SAIDI RIALS
7.9800 g., 0.9170 Gold 0.2353 oz. AGW **Ruler:** Qabus bin Sa'id AH1390-/1970AD- **Obv:** National arms **Rev:** Value and date

Date	Mintage	F	VF	XF	Unc	BU
AH1391 (1971) Proof	224	Value: 550				

Note: Struck for presentation purposes

REFORM COINAGE

1000 Baisa = 1 Omani Rial

KM# 50 5 BAISA
3.1000 g., Bronze, 19 mm. **Ruler:** Qabus bin Sa'id AH1390-/1970AD- **Obv:** National arms **Rev:** Value and date

Date	Mintage	F	VF	XF	Unc	BU
AH1395 (1975)	6,000,000	—	0.10	0.30	0.75	1.00
AH1400 (1979)	3,000,000	—	0.10	0.30	0.75	1.00
AH1406 (1985)	2,000,000	—	0.10	0.30	0.75	1.00
AH1410 (1989)	5,000,000	—	0.10	0.30	0.75	1.00

KM# 76 5 BAISA
Bronze **Ruler:** Qabus bin Sa'id AH1390-/1970AD- **Subject:** 20th National Day - Sultan Qaboos **Obv:** National emblem **Rev:** Sports Complex

Date	Mintage	F	VF	XF	Unc	BU
AH1411 (1990) Proof	3,200	Value: 5.00				

KM# 150 5 BAISA
2.6500 g., Bronze Clad Steel, 18.98 mm. **Ruler:** Qabus bin Sa'id AH1390-/1970AD- **Obv:** National arms **Rev:** Value and dates **Edge:** Plain

Date	Mintage	F	VF	XF	Unc	BU
AH1420-1999	—			0.20	0.50	0.75

KM# 51 10 BAISA
4.7000 g., Bronze, 22.5 mm. **Ruler:** Qabus bin Sa'id AH1390-/1970AD- **Series:** F.A.O. **Obv:** Date palms **Rev:** Value and date

Date	Mintage	F	VF	XF	Unc	BU
AH1395 (1975)	1,000,000	—	0.15	0.30	0.65	—

KM# 52 10 BAISA
4.7000 g., Bronze, 22.5 mm. **Ruler:** Qabus bin Sa'id AH1390-/1970AD- **Series:** F.A.O. **Obv:** National arms **Rev:** Value and date

Date	Mintage	F	VF	XF	Unc	BU
AH1395 (1975)	6,000,000	—	0.15	0.40	1.00	1.35
AH1400 (1979)	5,250,000	—	0.15	0.40	1.00	1.35
AH1406 (1985)	3,000,000	—	0.15	0.40	1.00	1.35
AH1410 (1989)	6,000,000	—	0.15	0.40	1.00	1.35
AH1418 (1997)		—	0.15	0.40	1.00	1.35

KM# 77 10 BAISA
Bronze Clad Steel **Ruler:** Qabus bin Sa'id AH1390-/1970AD- **Subject:** 20th National Day - Central Bank of Oman **Obv:** National emblem **Rev:** Central Bank building

Date	Mintage	F	VF	XF	Unc	BU
AH1411 (1990) Proof	3,200	Value: 5.00				

KM# 94 10 BAISA
Bronze Clad Steel, 22.5 mm. **Ruler:** Qabus bin Sa'id AH1390-/1970AD- **Series:** F.A.O. **Subject:** 50 Years **Obv:** National arms **Rev:** FAO symbol and dates

Date	Mintage	F	VF	XF	Unc	BU
ND	—				1.25	—
ND(1995)	224	—	—	—	1.25	—

KM# 151 10 BAISA
4.0400 g., Bronze Clad Steel, 22.48 mm. **Ruler:** Qabus bin Sa'id AH1390-/1970AD- **Obv:** National arms **Rev:** Value and both dates **Edge:** Plain

Date	Mintage	F	VF	XF	Unc	BU
AH1420-1999	—	—	—	0.30	0.75	1.00

KM# 75 15 BAISA
20.0000 g., 0.9250 Silver 0.5948 oz. ASW **Ruler:** Qabus bin Sa'id AH1390-/1970AD- **Subject:** 15th Anniversary - Reign of Sultan **Obv:** Head 1/4 left within 3/4 wreath and circular design **Rev:** Crowned Arms over country map within circle

Date	Mintage	F	VF	XF	Unc	BU
AH1406 (1985) Proof	2,000	Value: 160				

KM# 45 25 BAISA
5.9600 g., 0.9170 Gold 0.1757 oz. AGW, 18 mm. **Ruler:** Qabus bin Sa'id AH1390-/1970AD- **Obv:** National arms **Rev:** Value and date

Date	Mintage	F	VF	XF	Unc	BU
AH1392 (1972)	100	—	—	—	225	—
AH1392 (1972) Proof	50	Value: 250				
AH1394 (1974) Proof	250	Value: 200				
AH1395 (1975) Proof	250	Value: 200				

Note: Struck for presentation purposes

KM# 45a 25 BAISA
3.0300 g., Copper-Nickel, 18 mm. **Ruler:** Qabus bin Sa'id AH1390-/1970AD- **Obv:** National arms **Rev:** Value and date

Date	Mintage	F	VF	XF	Unc	BU
AH1395 (1975)	4,500,000	—	0.20	0.50	1.20	1.60
AH1400 (1979)	5,250,000	—	0.20	0.50	1.20	1.60
AH1406 (1985)	4,000,000	—	0.20	0.50	1.20	1.60
AH1410 (1989)	7,000,000	—	0.20	0.50	1.20	1.60
AH1418 (1997)	—	—	0.20	0.50	1.20	1.60

KM# 78 25 BAISA
Copper-Nickel **Ruler:** Qabus bin Sa'id AH1390-/1970AD- **Subject:** 20th National Day - Royal Hospital **Obv:** National emblem **Rev:** Royal Hospital building

Date	Mintage	F	VF	XF	Unc	BU
AH1411 (1990) Proof	3,200	Value: 7.00				

KM# 152 25 BAISA
3.0300 g., Copper-Nickel, 17.95 mm. **Ruler:** Qabus bin Sa'id AH1390-/1970AD- **Obv:** National arms **Rev:** Value and both dates **Edge:** Plain

Date	Mintage	F	VF	XF	Unc	BU
AH1420-1999	—	—	0.15	0.35	0.90	1.25

KM# 46 50 BAISA
12.8900 g., 0.9170 Gold 0.3800 oz. AGW **Ruler:** Qabus bin Sa'id AH1390-/1970AD- **Obv:** National arms **Rev:** Value and date

Date	Mintage	F	VF	XF	Unc	BU
AH1392 (1972)	200	—	—	—	450	—
AH1392 (1972) Proof	50	Value: 500				
AH1394 (1974) Proof	250	Value: 450				
AH1395 (1975) Proof	250	Value: 450				

Note: Struck for presentation purposes

KM# 46a 50 BAISA
6.4000 g., Copper-Nickel, 24 mm. **Ruler:** Qabus bin Sa'id AH1390-/1970AD- **Obv:** National arms **Rev:** Value and date

Date	Mintage	F	VF	XF	Unc	BU
AH1395 (1975)	2,500,000	—	0.30	0.70	1.80	2.40
AH1400 (1979)	2,750,000	—	0.30	0.70	1.80	2.40
AH1406 (1985)	4,000,000	—	0.30	0.70	1.80	2.40
AH1410 (1989)	4,000,000	—	0.30	0.70	1.80	2.40
AH1418 (1997)	—	—	0.30	0.70	1.80	2.40

KM# 79 50 BAISA
Copper-Nickel **Ruler:** Qabus bin Sa'id AH1390-/1970AD- **Subject:** 20th National Day - Irrigation Canal **Obv:** National emblem **Rev:** Canal and palm trees

Date	Mintage	F	VF	XF	Unc	BU
AH1411 (1990) Proof	3,200	Value: 8.00				

KM# 95 50 BAISA
6.4000 g., Copper-Nickel, 24 mm. **Ruler:** Qabus bin Sa'id AH1390-/1970AD- **Subject:** U.N. - 50 Years **Obv:** National arms **Rev:** UN symbol and anniversary dates

Date	Mintage	F	VF	XF	Unc	BU
ND (1995)	—	—	—	—	3.00	—

KM# 153 50 BAISA
6.4000 g., Copper-Nickel, 24 mm. **Ruler:** Qabus bin Sa'id AH1390-/1970AD- **Obv:** National arms **Rev:** Value with both dates **Edge:** Reeded

Date	Mintage	F	VF	XF	Unc	BU
AH1420-1999	—	—	0.25	0.60	1.50	2.00

KM# 47 100 BAISA
22.7400 g., 0.9170 Gold 0.6704 oz. AGW **Ruler:** Qabus bin Sa'id AH1390-/1970AD- **Obv:** National arms **Rev:** Value and date

Date	Mintage	F	VF	XF	Unc	BU
AH1392 (1972)	200	—	—	—	745	—
AH1392 (1972) Proof	50	Value: 800				
AH1394 (1974) Proof	250	Value: 750				
AH1395 (1975) Proof	250	Value: 750				

Note: Struck for presentation purposes

KM# 68 100 BAISA
4.2000 g., Copper-Nickel, 21.5 mm. **Ruler:** Qabus bin Sa'id AH1390-/1970AD- **Obv:** National arms **Rev:** Arms and date

Date	Mintage	VG	F	VF	XF	Unc
AH1404-1983	4,000,000	—	—	0.40	0.80	2.25

KM# 80 100 BAISA
Copper-Nickel **Ruler:** Qabus bin Sa'id AH1390-/1970AD- **Subject:** 20th National Day - Sultan Qaboos University **Obv:** National emblem **Rev:** University building

Date	Mintage	F	VF	XF	Unc	BU
AH1411 (1990) Proof	3,200	Value: 10.00				

KM# 82 100 BAISA
Bi-Metallic Aluminumn-Bronze center in Copper-Nickel ring, 25 mm. **Ruler:** Qabus bin Sa'id AH1390-/1970AD- **Subject:** 100 Years of Coinage **Obv:** Arms within circle **Rev:** Fortress within circle

Date	Mintage	F	VF	XF	Unc	BU
AH1411-1991	—	—	—	—	5.00	7.00
AH1411-1991 Proof	1,000	Value: 20.00				

KM# 57 1/4 OMANI RIAL
12.8900 g., 0.9170 Gold 0.3800 oz. AGW **Ruler:** Qabus bin Sa'id AH1390-/1970AD- **Subject:** Fort al Hazam **Obv:** National arms **Rev:** Fort

Date	Mintage	F	VF	XF	Unc	BU
AH1397 (1976) Proof	1,000	Value: 425				
AH1408 (1987) Proof	250	Value: 500				

KM# 66 1/4 OMANI RIAL
6.5000 g., Aluminum-Bronze, 26 mm. **Ruler:** Qabus bin Sa'id AH1390-/1970AD- **Obv:** National arms and dates **Rev:** Value

Date	Mintage	VG	F	VF	XF	Unc
AH1400-1980	4,000,000	—	—	0.75	1.00	2.00

KM# 48 1/2 OMANI RIAL
25.6000 g., 0.9170 Gold 0.7547 oz. AGW **Ruler:** Qabus bin Sa'id AH1390-/1970AD- **Obv:** National arms **Rev:** Value and date

Date	Mintage	F	VF	XF	Unc	BU
AH1392 (1972) Proof	124	Value: 850				
AH1394 (1974)	250	—	—	—	825	—
AH1395 (1975)	250	—	—	—	825	—

Note: Struck for presentation purposes

KM# 58 1/2 OMANI RIAL
19.6700 g., 0.9170 Gold 0.5799 oz. AGW **Ruler:** Qabus bin Sa'id AH1390-/1970AD- **Subject:** Fort Mirbat **Obv:** National arms **Rev:** Fort

Date	Mintage	F	VF	XF	Unc	BU
AH1397 (1976) Proof	1,000	Value: 650				
AH1408 (1987) Proof	250	Value: 700				

KM# 64 1/2 OMANI RIAL
Copper-Nickel **Ruler:** Qabus bin Sa'id AH1390-/1970AD- **Series:** F.A.O. **Obv:** National arms flanked by dates **Rev:** Fruit above value

Date	Mintage	VG	F	VF	XF	Unc
AH1398-1978	15,000	—	—	2.75	3.50	5.00

KM# 69 1/2 OMANI RIAL
19.6700 g., 0.9170 Gold 0.5799 oz. AGW **Ruler:** Qabus bin Sa'id AH1390-/1970AD- **Subject:** 10th National Day **Obv:** Crowned arms **Rev:** Value

Date	Mintage	VG	F	VF	XF	Unc
AH1400-1979 Proof	600	Value: 650				

Note: Struck for presentation purposes

KM# 67 1/2 OMANI RIAL
10.0000 g., Aluminum-Bronze, 30 mm. **Ruler:** Qabus bin Sa'id AH1390-/1970AD- **Obv:** National arms and dates **Rev:** Value

Date	Mintage	VG	F	VF	XF	Unc
AH1400-1980	2,000,000	—	—	2.75	3.50	5.00

KM# 87 1/2 OMANI RIAL
10.0000 g., 0.9170 Gold 0.2948 oz. AGW **Ruler:** Qabus bin Sa'id AH1390-/1970AD- **Subject:** Youth Year **Obv:** National arms, date and value **Rev:** Youth with banner within sprigs

Date	Mintage	VG	F	VF	XF	Unc
AH1403-1982 Proof	1,000	Value: 325				

KM# 85 1/2 OMANI RIAL
28.2800 g., 0.9250 Silver 0.8410 oz. ASW **Ruler:** Qabus bin Sa'id AH1390-/1970AD- **Subject:** Year of Agriculture **Obv:** National arms within circle **Rev:** Dates within small circle, farm fields on top 1/2

Date	Mintage	VG	F	VF	XF	Unc
AH1409-1988 Proof	300	Value: 135				

KM# 86 1/2 OMANI RIAL
28.2800 g., 0.9250 Silver 0.8410 oz. ASW **Ruler:** Qabus bin Sa'id AH1390-/1970AD- **Subject:** Year of Industry **Obv:** National arms **Rev:** Gears with map at center

Date	Mintage	F	VF	XF	Unc	BU
AH1411 (1990) Proof	810	Value: 110				

KM# 91 1/2 OMANI RIAL
15.0000 g., 0.9250 Silver 0.4461 oz. ASW **Ruler:** Qabus bin Sa'id AH1390-/1970AD- **Subject:** Youth Year **Obv:** National arms within circle flanked by stars **Rev:** Radiant design

Date	Mintage	F	VF	XF	Unc	BU
AH1413 (1992) Proof	600	Value: 85.00				

KM# 134 1/2 OMANI RIAL
15.0000 g., 0.9250 Silver 0.4461 oz. ASW **Ruler:** Qabus bin Sa'id AH1390-/1970AD- **Subject:** Youth Year **Obv:** Crowned arms **Rev:** Radiant design

Date	Mintage	F	VF	XF	Unc	BU
AH1413 (1992) Proof; Rare	310	—	—	—	—	—

KM# 92 1/2 OMANI RIAL
28.2800 g., 0.9250 Silver 0.8410 oz. ASW **Ruler:** Qabus bin Sa'id AH1390-/1970AD- **Subject:** Heritage Year **Obv:** National arms within circle **Rev:** Radiant design

Date	Mintage	F	VF	XF	Unc	BU
AH1414 (1993) Proof	840	Value: 100				

KM# 111 1/2 OMANI RIAL
28.2800 g., 0.9250 Silver 0.8410 oz. ASW **Ruler:** Qabus bin Sa'id AH1390-/1970AD- **Subject:** 250th Anniversary - Al Bu Sa'id Dynasty **Obv:** Bust facing flanked by dates **Rev:** National arms within artistic designed border

Date	Mintage	VG	F	VF	XF	Unc
1994 (AH1414) Proof	500	Value: 110				

KM# 54 OMANI RIAL
46.6500 g., 0.9170 Gold 1.3753 oz. AGW **Ruler:** Qabus bin Sa'id AH1390-/1970AD- **Obv:** National arms **Rev:** Value and date **Note:** Similar to KM#44.

Date	Mintage	F	VF	XF	Unc	BU
AH1392 (1972) Proof	124	Value: 1,550				
AH1394 (1974) Proof	250	Value: 1,500				
AH1395 (1975) Proof	250	Value: 1,500				

Note: Struck for presentation purposes

KM# 59 OMANI RIAL
25.6000 g., 0.9170 Gold 0.7547 oz. AGW **Ruler:** Qabus bin Sa'id AH1390-/1970AD- **Subject:** Fort Buraimi **Obv:** National arms and value **Rev:** Fort

Date	Mintage	F	VF	XF	Unc	BU
AH1397 (1976) Proof	1,000	Value: 825				
AH1408 (1987) Proof	250	Value: 850				

KM# 65 OMANI RIAL
15.0000 g., 0.5000 Silver 0.2411 oz. ASW **Ruler:** Qabus bin Sa'id AH1390-/1970AD- **Series:** F.A.O. **Obv:** National arms flanked by dates **Rev:** Fish above value

Date	Mintage	VG	F	VF	XF	Unc
AH1398-1978	15,000	—	—	—	8.50	14.50

KM# 70 OMANI RIAL
25.6000 g., 0.9170 Gold 0.7547 oz. AGW **Ruler:** Qabus bin Sa'id AH1390-/1970AD- **Subject:** 10th National Day

Date	Mintage	F	VF	XF	Unc	BU
AH1400 (1979) Proof	300	Value: 825				

Note: Struck for presentation purposes

KM# 84a OMANI RIAL

20.0000 g., 0.9170 Gold 0.5896 oz. AGW, 30 mm.
Ruler: Qabus bin Sa'id AH1390-/1970AD- **Subject:** Youth Year
Obv: National arms above value **Rev:** Youth with banner

Date	Mintage	F	VF	XF	Unc	BU
AH1403 (1982) Proof	900	Value: 650				

KM# 84 OMANI RIAL

14.8400 g., 0.9250 Silver 0.4413 oz. ASW **Ruler:** Qabus bin
Sa'id AH1390-/1970AD- **Subject:** Youth Year **Obv:** National
arms above value **Rev:** Youth with banner

Date	Mintage	VG	F	VF	XF	Unc
AH1403-1982 Proof	1,200	Value: 75.00				

KM# 112 OMANI RIAL

20.0000 g., 0.9170 Gold 0.5896 oz. AGW **Ruler:** Qabus bin Sa'id
AH1390-/1970AD- **Subject:** Youth Year **Obv:** National arms
Rev: Radiant design **Note:** Similar to 1/2 Omani Rial, KM#91.

Date	Mintage	F	VF	XF	Unc	BU
AH1413 (1992) Proof	900	Value: 650				

KM# 135 OMANI RIAL

20.0000 g., 0.9170 Gold 0.5896 oz. AGW **Ruler:** Qabus bin Sa'id
AH1390-/1970AD- **Subject:** Youth Year **Obv:** Crowned arms
Rev: Radiant design **Note:** Similar to 1/2 Omani Rial, KM#91.

Date	Mintage	F	VF	XF	Unc	BU
AH1413 (1992) Proof; Rare	110	—	—	—	—	—

KM# 93 OMANI RIAL

39.9400 g., 0.9167 Gold 1.1771 oz. AGW **Ruler:** Qabus bin Sa'id
AH1390-/1970AD- **Subject:** Heritage Year **Obv:** National arms
Rev: Radiant design **Note:** Similar to 1/2 Omani Rial, KM#92.

Date	Mintage	F	VF	XF	Unc	BU
AH1414 (1993) Proof	1,000	Value: 1,250				

KM# 146 OMANI RIAL

39.9400 g., 0.9167 Gold 1.1771 oz. AGW **Ruler:** Qabus bin
Sa'id AH1390-/1970AD- **Subject:** 250th Anniversary - Al Bu Sa'id
Dynasty **Obv:** Portrait **Rev:** National arms and value
Note: Similar to 1/2 Omani Rial, KM#111.

Date	Mintage	F	VF	XF	Unc	BU
AH1414 (1994) Proof	500	Value: 1,300				

KM# 96 OMANI RIAL

10.0000 g., 0.9250 Silver 0.2974 oz. ASW, 30 mm.
Ruler: Qabus bin Sa'id AH1390-/1970AD- **Subject:** F.A.O. - 50
Years **Obv:** National arms within circle **Rev:** FAO symbol and
anniversary dates

Date	Mintage	F	VF	XF	Unc	BU
ND (1995) Proof	—	Value: 30.00				

KM# 114 OMANI RIAL

28.2800 g., 0.9250 Silver 0.8410 oz. ASW **Ruler:** Qabus bin
Sa'id AH1390-/1970AD- **Obv:** National arms within circle
Rev: Al-Hazm castle

Date	Mintage	VG	F	VF	XF	Unc
AH1416-1995 Proof	—	Value: 37.50				

KM# 115 OMANI RIAL

28.2800 g., 0.9250 Silver 0.8410 oz. ASW **Ruler:** Qabus bin
Sa'id AH1390-/1970AD- **Obv:** National arms **Rev:** Al-Jalali fort

Date	Mintage	VG	F	VF	XF	Unc
AH1416-1995 Proof	—	Value: 37.50				

KM# 116 OMANI RIAL

28.2800 g., 0.9250 Silver 0.8410 oz. ASW **Ruler:** Qabus bin
Sa'id AH1390-/1970AD- **Obv:** National arms **Rev:** Al-Mirani fort

Date	Mintage	VG	F	VF	XF	Unc
AH1416-1995 Proof	—	Value: 37.50				

KM# 117 OMANI RIAL

28.2800 g., 0.9250 Silver 0.8410 oz. ASW **Ruler:** Qabus bin
Sa'id AH1390-/1970AD- **Obv:** National arms **Rev:** Al-Rustaq fort

Date	Mintage	VG	F	VF	XF	Unc
AH1416-1995 Proof	—	Value: 37.50				

KM# 118 OMANI RIAL

28.2800 g., 0.9250 Silver 0.8410 oz. ASW **Ruler:** Qabus bin
Sa'id AH1390-/1970AD- **Obv:** National arms **Rev:** Al-Wafi castle

Date	Mintage	VG	F	VF	XF	Unc
AH1416-1995 Proof	—	Value: 37.50				

KM# 119 OMANI RIAL

28.2800 g., 0.9250 Silver 0.8410 oz. ASW **Ruler:** Qabus bin Sa'id
AH1390-/1970AD- **Obv:** National arms **Rev:** Bait Al-Falaj fort

Date	Mintage	VG	F	VF	XF	Unc
AH1416-1995 Proof	—	Value: 37.50				

KM# 120 OMANI RIAL

28.2800 g., 0.9250 Silver 0.8410 oz. ASW **Ruler:** Qabus bin
Sa'id AH1390-/1970AD- **Obv:** National arms **Rev:** Bait Al-
Na'Aman castle

Date	Mintage	VG	F	VF	XF	Unc
AH1416-1995 Proof	—	Value: 37.50				

KM# 121 OMANI RIAL

28.2800 g., 0.9250 Silver 0.8410 oz. ASW **Ruler:** Qabus bin
Sa'id AH1390-/1970AD- **Obv:** National arms **Rev:** Bahla fort

Date	Mintage	VG	F	VF	XF	Unc
AH1416-1995 Proof	—	Value: 37.50				

KM# 122 OMANI RIAL

28.2800 g., 0.9250 Silver 0.8410 oz. ASW **Ruler:** Qabus bin
Sa'id AH1390-/1970AD- **Obv:** National arms **Rev:** Barka fort

Date	Mintage	VG	F	VF	XF	Unc
AH1416-1995 Proof	—	Value: 37.50				

KM# 123   OMANI RIAL
28.2800 g., 0.9250 Silver 0.8410 oz. ASW **Ruler:** Qabus bin Sa'id AH1390-/1970AD- **Obv:** National arms **Rev:** Barkat-Al-Mauz castle

Date	Mintage	VG	F	VF	XF	Unc
AH1416-1995 Proof	—	Value: 37.50				

KM# 124   OMANI RIAL
28.2800 g., 0.9250 Silver 0.8410 oz. ASW **Ruler:** Qabus bin Sa'id AH1390-/1970AD- **Obv:** National arms **Rev:** Buraimi fort

Date	Mintage	VG	F	VF	XF	Unc
AH1416-1995 Proof	—	Value: 37.50				

KM# 125   OMANI RIAL
28.2800 g., 0.9250 Silver 0.8410 oz. ASW **Ruler:** Qabus bin Sa'id AH1390-/1970AD- **Obv:** National arms **Rev:** Ja'Alan Bani Bu Hassan castle

Date	Mintage	VG	F	VF	XF	Unc
AH1416-1995 Proof	—	Value: 37.50				

KM# 126   OMANI RIAL
28.2800 g., 0.9250 Silver 0.8410 oz. ASW **Ruler:** Qabus bin Sa'id AH1390-/1970AD- **Obv:** National arms **Rev:** Jabrin castle

Date	Mintage	VG	F	VF	XF	Unc
AH1416-1995 Proof	—	Value: 37.50				

KM# 127   OMANI RIAL
28.2800 g., 0.9250 Silver 0.8410 oz. ASW **Ruler:** Qabus bin Sa'id AH1390-/1970AD- **Obv:** National arms **Rev:** Khasab fort

Date	Mintage	VG	F	VF	XF	Unc
AH1416-1995 Proof	—	Value: 37.50				

KM# 128   OMANI RIAL
28.2800 g., 0.9250 Silver 0.8410 oz. ASW **Ruler:** Qabus bin Sa'id AH1390-/1970AD- **Obv:** National arms **Rev:** Matrah fort

Date	Mintage	VG	F	VF	XF	Unc
AH1416-1995 Proof	—	Value: 37.50				

KM# 129   OMANI RIAL
28.2800 g., 0.9250 Silver 0.8410 oz. ASW **Ruler:** Qabus bin Sa'id AH1390-/1970AD- **Obv:** National arms **Rev:** Mirbat castle

Date	Mintage	VG	F	VF	XF	Unc
AH1416-1995 Proof	—	Value: 37.50				

KM# 130   OMANI RIAL
28.2800 g., 0.9250 Silver 0.8410 oz. ASW **Ruler:** Qabus bin Sa'id AH1390-/1970AD- **Obv:** National arms **Rev:** Nakhl fort

Date	Mintage	VG	F	VF	XF	Unc
AH1416-1995 Proof	—	Value: 37.50				

KM# 131   OMANI RIAL
28.2800 g., 0.9250 Silver 0.8410 oz. ASW **Ruler:** Qabus bin Sa'id AH1390-/1970AD- **Obv:** National arms **Rev:** Nizwa fort

Date	Mintage	VG	F	VF	XF	Unc
AH1416-1995 Proof	—	Value: 37.50				

KM# 132   OMANI RIAL
28.2800 g., 0.9250 Silver 0.8410 oz. ASW **Ruler:** Qabus bin Sa'id AH1390-/1970AD- **Obv:** National arms **Rev:** Sohar fort

Date	Mintage	VG	F	VF	XF	Unc
AH1416-1995 Proof	—	Value: 37.50				

KM# 133   OMANI RIAL
28.2800 g., 0.9250 Silver 0.8410 oz. ASW **Ruler:** Qabus bin Sa'id AH1390-/1970AD- **Obv:** National arms **Rev:** Sur castle

Date	Mintage	VG	F	VF	XF	Unc
AH1416-1995 Proof	—	Value: 37.50				

KM# 140   OMANI RIAL
13.9000 g., 0.9250 Silver 0.4134 oz. ASW **Ruler:** Qabus bin Sa'id AH1390-/1970AD- **Subject:** 25th National Day Anniversary - Burj Al Nahda **Obv:** National arms **Rev:** Burj Al Nahda

Date	Mintage	F	VF	XF	Unc	BU
1995 Proof	—	Value: 65.00				

KM# 140a   OMANI RIAL
22.8000 g., 0.9160 Gold 0.6714 oz. AGW **Ruler:** Qabus bin Sa'id AH1390-/1970AD- **Subject:** 25th National Day Anniversary - Burj Al Nahda **Obv:** National arms **Rev:** Burj Al Nahda

Date	Mintage	F	VF	XF	Unc	BU
1995 Proof	—	Value: 750				

KM# 145   OMANI RIAL
28.2800 g., 0.9250 Silver 0.8410 oz. ASW, 30 mm. **Ruler:** Qabus bin Sa'id AH1390-/1970AD- **Subject:** U.N. - 50 Years **Obv:** National arms **Rev:** UN symbol and anniversary dates

Date	Mintage	F	VF	XF	Unc	BU
ND(1995) Proof	25,000	Value: 40.00				

KM# 101   OMANI RIAL
31.4700 g., 0.9250 Silver 0.9359 oz. ASW **Ruler:** Qabus bin Sa'id AH1390-/1970AD- **Subject:** 26th National Day Anniversary - Sultanah **Obv:** National arms

Date	Mintage	F	VF	XF	Unc	BU
1996 Proof	—	Value: 45.00				

KM# 102   OMANI RIAL
37.8000 g., 0.9160 Gold 1.1132 oz. AGW **Ruler:** Qabus bin Sa'id AH1390-/1970AD- **Subject:** 26th National Day Anniversary - Sultanah **Obv:** National arms **Rev:** Sailing ship - Sultanah within circle

Date	Mintage	F	VF	XF	Unc	BU
1996 Proof	—	Value: 1,200				

KM# 103   OMANI RIAL
28.2800 g., 0.9250 Silver 0.8410 oz. ASW **Ruler:** Qabus bin Sa'id AH1390-/1970AD- **Subject:** 26th National Day Anniversary - Al Battil **Obv:** National arms **Rev:** Sailing ship - Al Battil

Date	Mintage	F	VF	XF	Unc	BU
1996 Proof	—	Value: 35.00				

KM# 104   OMANI RIAL
28.2800 g., 0.9250 Silver 0.8410 oz. ASW **Ruler:** Qabus bin Sa'id AH1390-/1970AD- **Subject:** 26th National Day Anniversary - Al Badan **Obv:** National arms **Rev:** Sailing ship - Al Badan within circle

Date	Mintage	F	VF	XF	Unc	BU
1996 Proof	—	Value: 35.00				

KM# 105   OMANI RIAL
28.2800 g., 0.9250 Silver 0.8410 oz. ASW **Ruler:** Qabus bin Sa'id AH1390-/1970AD- **Subject:** 26th National Day Anniversary - Al Baghlah **Obv:** National arms **Rev:** Sailing ship - Al Baghlah

Date	Mintage	F	VF	XF	Unc	BU
1996 Proof	—	Value: 35.00				

KM# 106   OMANI RIAL
28.2800 g., 0.9250 Silver 0.8410 oz. ASW **Ruler:** Qabus bin Sa'id AH1390-/1970AD- **Subject:** 26th National Day Anniversary - Al Boum **Obv:** National arms **Rev:** Sailing ship - Al Boum within circle

Date	Mintage	F	VF	XF	Unc	BU
1996 Proof	—	Value: 35.00				

KM# 107   OMANI RIAL
28.2800 g., 0.9250 Silver 0.8410 oz. ASW **Ruler:** Qabus bin Sa'id AH1390-/1970AD- **Subject:** 26th National Day Anniversary - Al Jalbout **Obv:** National arms **Rev:** Sailing ship - Al Jalbout

Date	Mintage	F	VF	XF	Unc	BU
1996 Proof	—	Value: 35.00				

KM# 108   OMANI RIAL
28.2800 g., 0.9250 Silver 0.8410 oz. ASW **Ruler:** Qabus bin Sa'id AH1390-/1970AD- **Subject:** 26th National Day Anniversary - Al Sanbuq **Obv:** National arms **Rev:** Sailing ship - Al Sanbuq

Date	Mintage	F	VF	XF	Unc	BU
1996 Proof	—	Value: 35.00				

KM# 109   OMANI RIAL
28.2800 g., 0.9250 Silver 0.8410 oz. ASW **Ruler:** Qabus bin Sa'id AH1390-/1970AD- **Subject:** 26th National Day Anniversary - Al Ghanjah **Obv:** National arms **Rev:** Sailing ship - Al Ghanjah within circle

Date	Mintage	F	VF	XF	Unc	BU
1996 Proof	—	Value: 35.00				

KM# 110   OMANI RIAL
28.2800 g., 0.9250 Silver 0.8410 oz. ASW **Ruler:** Qabus bin Sa'id AH1390-/1970AD- **Subject:** 26th National Day Anniversary - Al Lateen **Obv:** National arms **Rev:** Sailing ship - Al Lateen

Date	Mintage	F	VF	XF	Unc	BU
1996 Proof	—	Value: 35.00				

KM# 136   OMANI RIAL
28.2800 g., 0.9250 Silver 0.8410 oz. ASW, 38.6 mm. **Ruler:** Qabus bin Sa'id AH1390-/1970AD- **Subject:** 27th National Day Anniversary - Al Nahdha **Rev:** Al Nahdha Tower, coconut tree and Frankincense tree from the Dhofar Region

Date	Mintage	F	VF	XF	Unc	BU
AH1418-1997 Proof	—	Value: 45.00				

KM# 136a   OMANI RIAL
37.8000 g., 0.9167 Gold 1.1140 oz. AGW, 38.6 mm. **Ruler:** Qabus bin Sa'id AH1390-/1970AD- **Subject:** 27th National Day Anniversary - Al Nahdha **Rev:** Al Nahdha Tower, coconut tree and Frankincense tree from the Dhofar Region

Date	Mintage	F	VF	XF	Unc	BU
AH1418-1997 Proof	—	Value: 1,250				

KM# 138   OMANI RIAL
28.2800 g., 0.9250 Silver 0.8410 oz. ASW **Ruler:** Qabus bin Sa'id AH1390-/1970AD- **Series:** World Wildlife Fund **Obv:** National arms and value within circle **Rev:** Leopard

Date	Mintage	F	VF	XF	Unc	BU
1997 Proof	15,000	Value: 40.00				

KM# 113   OMANI RIAL
28.2800 g., 0.9250 Silver 0.8410 oz. ASW, 38.6 mm. **Ruler:** Qabus bin Sa'id AH1390-/1970AD- **Series:** World Wildlife Fund **Obv:** National arms **Rev:** Mountain gazelle

Date	Mintage	F	VF	XF	Unc	BU
1997 Proof	15,000	Value: 40.00				

KM# 139   OMANI RIAL
28.2800 g., 0.9250 Silver 0.8410 oz. ASW, 38.6 mm. **Ruler:** Qabus bin Sa'id AH1390-/1970AD- **Subject:** 28th National Day Anniversary - Private Sector Year **Obv:** National arms within circle **Rev:** Radiant design

Date	Mintage	F	VF	XF	Unc	BU
AH1418 (1997) Proof	—	Value: 45.00				

KM# 139a   OMANI RIAL
37.8000 g., 0.9167 Gold 1.1140 oz. AGW, 38.6 mm. **Ruler:** Qabus bin Sa'id AH1390-/1970AD- **Subject:** 28th National Day Anniversary - Private Sector Year **Obv:** National arms **Rev:** Radiant design

Date	Mintage	F	VF	XF	Unc	BU
AH1418 (1997)	—	—	—	—	—	1,250

KM# 149   OMANI RIAL
28.2800 g., 0.9250 Silver 0.8410 oz. ASW, 38.61 mm. **Ruler:** Qabus bin Sa'id AH1390-/1970AD- **Subject:** 29th National Day Anniversary - 1420/1999 **Obv:** National arms **Rev:** Palm tree (Khalas) and camels caravan

Date	Mintage	F	VF	XF	Unc	BU
ND(1999)	—	—	—	—	100	—

KM# 149a OMANI RIAL
37.8000 g., 0.9167 Gold 1.1140 oz. AGW, 38.61 mm.
Ruler: Qabus bin Sa'id AH1390-/1970AD- **Subject:** 29th
National Day Anniversary - 1420/1999 **Obv:** National arms
Rev: Palm tree (Khalas) and camels caravan

Date	Mintage	F	VF	XF	Unc	BU
ND(1999)	—	—	—	—	—	1,250

KM# 147a OMANI RIAL
37.8000 g., 0.9160 Gold 1.1132 oz. AGW, 38.61 mm.
Ruler: Qabus bin Sa'id AH1390-/1970AD- **Subject:** 30th
National Day **Obv:** National arms **Rev:** Factory and symbols of
commerce, value in center circle **Edge:** Reeded

Date	Mintage	F	VF	XF	Unc	BU
2000	—	—	—	—	—	1,250

KM# 147 OMANI RIAL
27.8700 g., 0.9250 Silver 0.8288 oz. ASW, 38.61 mm.
Ruler: Qabus bin Sa'id AH1390-/1970AD- **Subject:** 30th
National Day **Obv:** National arms **Rev:** Factory and symbols of
commerce, value in center circle **Edge:** Reeded

Date	Mintage	F	VF	XF	Unc	BU
2000 Proof	300	—	—	—	100	—

KM# 148 OMANI RIAL
27.8700 g., 0.9250 Silver 0.8288 oz. ASW, 38.6 mm. **Ruler:**
Qabus bin Sa'id AH1390-/1970AD- **Subject:** Central Bank's 25th
Anniversary **Obv:** National arms **Rev:** Central Bank of Oman

Date	Mintage	F	VF	XF	Unc	BU
ND(2000) Proof	500	—	—	—	100	—

KM# 81 2 OMANI RIALS
20.0000 g., 0.9250 Silver 0.5948 oz. ASW **Ruler:** Qabus bin
Sa'id AH1390-/1970AD- **Subject:** 20th National Day - Sultan
Sa'id **Obv:** Crowned arms **Rev:** Head 1/4 left within circle

Date	Mintage	VG	F	VF	XF	Unc
AH1411-1990 Proof	3,200	Value: 50.00				

KM# 60 2-1/2 OMANI RIALS
28.2800 g., 0.9250 Silver 0.8410 oz. ASW **Ruler:** Qabus bin
Sa'id AH1390-/1970AD- **Subject:** Conservation **Obv:** National
arms **Rev:** Caracal

Date	Mintage	F	VF	XF	Unc	BU
AH1397 (1976)	4,539	—	—	—	25.00	—
AH1397 (1976) Proof	4,407	Value: 32.00				

KM# 71 2-1/2 OMANI RIALS
28.2800 g., 0.9250 Silver 0.8410 oz. ASW **Ruler:** Qabus bin
Sa'id AH1390-/1970AD- **Obv:** Crowned arms **Rev:** Verreaux's
eagle in flight

Date	Mintage	VG	F	VF	XF	Unc
AH1407-1986	—	—	—	—	—	—
Proof; Rare						

Note: Struck for presentation purposes

KM# 73 2-1/2 OMANI RIALS
28.2800 g., 0.9250 Silver 0.8410 oz. ASW **Ruler:** Qabus bin
Sa'id AH1390-/1970AD- **Series:** World Wildlife Fund
Obv: National arms **Rev:** Verreaux's eagle in flight

Date	Mintage	VG	F	VF	XF	Unc
AH1407-1987 Proof	25,000	Value: 30.00				

KM# 83 2-1/2 OMANI RIALS
28.2800 g., 0.9250 Silver 0.8410 oz. ASW **Ruler:** Qabus bin
Sa'id AH1390-/1970AD- **Series:** Save the Children
Obv: Crowned arms **Rev:** Three children playing

Date	Mintage	F	VF	XF	Unc
AH1411-1991 Proof	Est. 20,000	Value: 37.50			

KM# 97 2-1/2 OMANI RIALS
28.2800 g., 0.9250 Silver 0.8410 oz. ASW **Ruler:** Qabus bin
Sa'id AH1390-/1970AD- **Obv:** Crowned arms **Rev:** Three
children playing

Date	Mintage	VG	F	VF	XF	Unc
AH1411-1991	—	—	—	—	—	—
Proof; Rare						

Note: Struck for presentation purposes

KM# 61 5 OMANI RIALS
35.0000 g., 0.9250 Silver 1.0408 oz. ASW **Ruler:** Qabus bin
Sa'id AH1390-/1970AD- **Subject:** Conservation **Obv:** National
arms **Rev:** Arabian White Oryx

Date	Mintage	F	VF	XF	Unc	BU
AH1397 (1976)	4,359	—	—	—	25.00	—
AH1397 (1976) Proof	4,401	Value: 30.00				

KM# 62 5 OMANI RIALS
45.6500 g., 0.9170 Gold 1.3458 oz. AGW **Ruler:** Qabus bin
Sa'id AH1390-/1970AD- **Subject:** 7th Anniversary - Reign of
Sultan Qabus bin Sa'id **Obv:** National arms **Rev:** Bust 3/4 left

Date	Mintage	F	VF	XF	BU
AH1397 (1976) Proof	1,000	Value: 1,500			
AH1408 (1987) Proof	250	Value: 1,600			

KM# 89 5 OMANI RIALS
20.0000 g., 0.9170 Gold 0.5896 oz. AGW **Ruler:** Qabus bin
Sa'id AH1390-/1970AD- **Subject:** Agricultural Year
Obv: National arms **Rev:** Farm fields above dates within center
circle **Note:** Similar to 1/2 Omani Rial, KM#85.

Date	Mintage	F	VF	XF	Unc	BU
AH1409 (1988) Proof	200	Value: 650				

KM# 90 5 OMANI RIALS
20.0000 g., 0.9170 Gold 0.5896 oz. AGW **Ruler:** Qabus bin
Sa'id AH1390-/1970AD- **Subject:** Industry Year **Obv:** National
arms **Rev:** Gears **Note:** Similar to 1/2 Omani Rial, KM#86.

Date	Mintage	F	VF	XF	Unc	BU
AH1411-1991	410	Value: 625				
(1990) Proof						

KM# 141 5 OMANI RIALS
18.8000 g., 0.9250 Silver 0.5591 oz. ASW **Ruler:** Qabus bin
Sa'id AH1390-/1970AD- **Subject:** 25th National Day Anniversary
- Burj Al Sahwa **Obv:** National arms and value within circle
Rev: Monument

Date	Mintage	F	VF	XF	Unc	BU
1995 Proof	—	Value: 75.00				

KM# 141a 5 OMANI RIALS
31.0000 g., 0.9160 Gold 0.9129 oz. AGW **Ruler:** Qabus bin
Sa'id AH1390-/1970AD- **Obv:** National arms and value within
circle **Rev:** Monument

Date	Mintage	F	VF	XF	Unc	BU
1995 Proof	—	Value: 1,000				

KM# 142 10 OMANI RIALS
23.2000 g., 0.9250 Silver 0.6899 oz. ASW **Ruler:** Qabus bin
Sa'id AH1390-/1970AD- **Subject:** 25th National Day Anniversary
- Central Bank **Obv:** National arms and value **Rev:** Central Bank
of Oman

Date	Mintage	F	VF	XF	Unc	BU
1995 Proof	—	Value: 85.00				

KM# 142a 10 OMANI RIALS
36.4000 g., 0.9160 Gold 1.0719 oz. AGW **Ruler:** Qabus bin
Sa'id AH1390-/1970AD- **Subject:** 25th National Day Anniversary
- Central Bank **Obv:** National arms and value **Rev:** Central Bank
of Oman

Date	Mintage	F	VF	XF	Unc	BU
1995 Proof	—	Value: 1,150				

KM# 49 15 OMANI RIALS
7.9900 g., 0.9170 Gold 0.2356 oz. AGW **Ruler:** Qabus bin Sa'id
AH1390-/1970AD- **Obv:** National arms **Rev:** Value

Date	Mintage	F	VF	XF	Unc	BU
AH1392 (1972) Proof	124	Value: 375				
AH1394 (1974)	300	—	—	—	285	—

Note: Struck for presentation purposes

KM# 55 15 OMANI RIALS
7.9900 g., 0.9170 Gold 0.2356 oz. AGW **Ruler:** Qabus bin Sa'id AH1390-/1970AD- **Subject:** 10th National Day **Obv:** Crowned arms **Rev:** Value

Date	Mintage	F	VF	XF	Unc	BU
AH1400 (1979) Proof	1,000	Value: 400				

Note: Struck for presentation purposes

KM# 56 15 OMANI RIALS
20.0000 g., 0.9170 Gold 0.5896 oz. AGW **Ruler:** Qabus bin Sa'id AH1390-/1970AD- **Subject:** 15th Anniversary - Reign of Sultan **Obv:** Head 1/4 left within 3/4 wreath and designed border **Rev:** Crowned arms over country map within circle

Date	Mintage	F	VF	XF	Unc	BU
AH1406 (1985) Proof	2,000	Value: 650				

KM# 56a 15 OMANI RIALS
31.0100 g., 0.9170 Gold 0.9142 oz. AGW **Ruler:** Qabus bin Sa'id AH1390-/1970AD- **Subject:** 15th Anniversary - Reign of Sultan **Obv:** Head 1/4 left within 3/4 wreath and designed border **Rev:** Crowned arms over country map within circle

Date	Mintage	F	VF	XF	Unc	BU
AH1406 (1985) Proof	200	Value: 1,000				

KM# 98 20 OMANI RIALS
20.0000 g., 0.9170 Gold 0.5896 oz. AGW **Ruler:** Qabus bin Sa'id AH1390-/1970AD- **Subject:** 20th National Day - Sultan Sa'id **Obv:** National arms **Rev:** Bust 1/4 left within circle and designs around border **Note:** Similar to 2 Omani Rials, KM#81.

Date	Mintage	F	VF	XF	Unc	BU
AH1411 (1990) Proof	1,200	Value: 650				

KM# 137.1 20 OMANI RIALS
48.6500 g., 0.9167 Gold 1.4338 oz. AGW **Ruler:** Qabus bin Sa'id AH1390-/1970AD- **Subject:** 20th Anniversary of Sultan's Reign **Obv:** Crowned arms within designed circle, legend above and below **Rev:** Value within designed circle with dates below flanked by leaves

Date	Mintage	F	VF	XF	Unc	BU
AH1411 (1990)	500	—	—	—	—	1,600

KM# 137.2 20 OMANI RIALS
65.3700 g., 0.9170 Gold 1.9272 oz. AGW **Ruler:** Qabus bin Sa'id AH1390-/1970AD- **Subject:** 20th Anniversary of Sultan's Reign **Obv:** Crowned arms within designed circle with legend above and below **Rev:** Value within designed circle above dates flanked by leaves **Note:** Prev. KM#137.

Date	Mintage	VG	F	VF	XF	Unc
AH1411-1990 Proof	—	Value: 2,200				

KM# 143 20 OMANI RIALS
27.4000 g., 0.9250 Silver 0.8148 oz. ASW **Ruler:** Qabus bin Sa'id AH1390-/1970AD- **Subject:** 25th National Day Anniversary **Obv:** National arms and value **Rev:** Radiant value within circle

Date	Mintage	F	VF	XF	Unc	BU
1995 Proof	—	Value: 95.00				

KM# 143a 20 OMANI RIALS
41.2000 g., 0.9160 Gold 1.2133 oz. AGW **Ruler:** Qabus bin Sa'id AH1390-/1970AD- **Subject:** 25th National Day Anniversary **Obv:** National arms and value **Rev:** Radiant value within circle

Date	Mintage	F	VF	XF	Unc	BU
1995 Proof	—	Value: 1,350				

KM# 74 25 OMANI RIALS
10.0000 g., 0.9170 Gold 0.2948 oz. AGW **Ruler:** Qabus bin Sa'id AH1390-/1970AD- **Series:** World Wildlife Fund **Obv:** National arms within circle **Rev:** Masked Booby

Date	Mintage	VG	F	VF	XF	Unc
AH1407-1987 Proof	5,000	Value: 325				

KM# 99 25 OMANI RIALS
10.0000 g., 0.9170 Gold 0.2948 oz. AGW **Ruler:** Qabus bin Sa'id AH1390-/1970AD- **Series:** World Wildlife Fund **Obv:** Crown above arms with legends above and below **Rev:** Masked booby

Date	Mintage	F	VF	XF	Unc	BU
AH1407-1987 Proof; Rare	—	—	—	—	—	—

Note: Struck for presentation purposes

KM# 88 25 OMANI RIALS
10.0000 g., 0.9170 Gold 0.2948 oz. AGW **Ruler:** Qabus bin Sa'id AH1390-/1970AD- **Series:** Save the Children **Obv:** National arms within circle **Rev:** School Master with pupils

Date	Mintage	VG	F	VF	XF	Unc
AH1411-1991 Proof	Est. 3,000	Value: 300				

KM# 100 25 OMANI RIALS
10.0000 g., 0.9170 Gold 0.2948 oz. AGW **Ruler:** Qabus bin Sa'id AH1390-/1970AD- **Series:** Save the Children **Obv:** Crown above arms with legends above and below **Rev:** School Master with pupils

Date	Mintage	F	VF	XF	Unc	BU
AH1411-1991 Proof; Rare	—	—	—	—	—	—

Note: Struck for presentation purposes

KM# 144 25 OMANI RIALS
31.7000 g., 0.9250 Silver 0.9427 oz. ASW **Ruler:** Qabus bin Sa'id AH1390-/1970AD- **Subject:** 25th National Day Anniversary - Sultan Qaboos bin Said **Obv:** National arms and value **Rev:** Multicolor bust facing

Date	Mintage	F	VF	XF	Unc	BU
1995 Proof	—	Value: 100				

KM# 144a 25 OMANI RIALS
50.2000 g., 0.9160 Gold 1.4783 oz. AGW **Ruler:** Qabus bin Sa'id AH1390-/1970AD- **Subject:** 25th National Day Anniversary - Sultan Qaboos bin Said **Obv:** National arms and value **Rev:** Multicolor bust facing

Date	Mintage	F	VF	XF	Unc	BU
1995 Proof	—	Value: 1,600				

KM# 63 75 OMANI RIALS
33.4370 g., 0.9000 Gold 0.9675 oz. AGW **Ruler:** Qabus bin Sa'id AH1390-/1970AD- **Subject:** Conservation **Obv:** National arms above date **Rev:** Arabian Tahr

Date	Mintage	F	VF	XF	Unc	BU
AH1397 (1976)	825	—	—	—	—	1,000
AH1397 (1976) Proof	325	Value: 1,150				

PROOF SETS

KM#	Date	Mintage	Identification	Issue Price	Mkt Val
PS1	AH1394 (3)	250	KM#45-47	—	1,400
PS2	AH1395 (3)	250	KM#45-47	—	1,400
PS3	AH1397 (3)	—	KM#60, 61, 63	780	1,200
PS4	AH1397 (2)	—	KM#60, 61	60.00	65.00
PS5	AH1411 (6)	3,200	KM#76-81	84.50	95.00
PSA6	1996 (2)	—	KM#101-102	640	1,250
PS6	AH1416 (20)	—	KM#114-133	—	750
PS7	1996 (4)	—	KM#103-106	125	140
PS8	1996 (4)	—	KM#107-110	125	140
PS9	1996 (8)	—	KM#103-110	247	280

PAKISTAN

The Islamic Republic of Pakistan, located on the Indian subcontinent between India and Afghanistan, has an area of 310,404 sq. mi. (803,940 sq. km.) and a population of 130 million. Capital: Islamabad. Pakistan is mainly an agricultural land although the industrial base is expanding rapidly. Yarn, textiles, cotton, rice, medical instruments, sports equipment and leather are exported.

Afghan and Turkish intrusions into northern India between the 11th and 18th centuries resulted in large numbers of Indians being converted to Islam. The idea of a separate Moslem state independent of Hindu India developed in the 1930's and was agreed to by Britain in 1946. The Islamic majority areas of India, consisting of the separate geographic entities known as East and West Pakistan, achieved self-government as Pakistan, with dominion status in the British Commonwealth, when the British withdrew from India on Aug. 14, 1947. Pakistan became a republic in 1956. When a basic constitutional crisis initiated by the election of Dec. 1, 1970 - the first direct general election in Pakistani history - could not be resolved by the leaders of East and West Pakistan, the East Pakistanis seceded from the Islamic Republic of Pakistan (March 26, 1971) and formed the independent People's Republic of Bangladesh. After many years of vacillation between civilian and military regimes, the people of Pakistan held a free national election in November, 1988 and installed the first of a series of democratic governments under a parliamentary system.

TITLE

پاکستان

Pakistan

MONETARY SYSTEM
100 Paisa = 1 Rupee

ISLAMIC REPUBLIC
STANDARD COINAGE

3 Pies = 1 Pice; 4 Pice = 1 Anna; 16 Annas = 1 Rupee

KM# 11 PIE
1.2500 g., Bronze, 15.87 mm. **Obv:** Crescent and star above tughra **Rev:** Value and date flanked by stars within wreath **Edge:** Plain

Date	Mintage	F	VF	XF	Unc	BU
1951	2,950,000	0.25	0.50	1.00	2.50	—
1951 Proof	—	Value: 4.00				

Date	Mintage	F	VF	XF	Unc	BU
1953	110,000	3.00	5.00	7.00	10.00	—
1953 Proof	—	Value: 5.00				
1955	211,000	0.25	0.75	1.50	3.00	—
1955 Proof	—	Value: 15.00				
1956	3,390,000	0.25	0.50	1.00	2.50	—
1957		0.25	0.50	1.00	2.50	—

KM# 1 PICE
1.5500 g., Bronze, 21.3 mm. **Obv:** Legend around center hole **Rev:** Crescent and star divides value around the top, center hole divides date **Note:** Varieties exist.

Date	Mintage	F	VF	XF	Unc	BU
1948	101,070,000	0.20	0.40	0.75	1.50	—
1948 Proof	—	Value: 2.00				
1949	25,740,000	0.20	0.40	0.75	1.50	—
1949 Proof	—	Value: 2.00				
1951	14,050,000	0.20	0.45	0.85	1.75	—
1952	41,680,000	0.20	0.40	0.75	1.50	—

KM# 12 PICE
2.3000 g., Nickel-Brass, 20.59 mm. **Obv:** Crescent and star above tughra **Rev:** Value flanked by oat sprigs **Edge:** Plain

Date	Mintage	F	VF	XF	Unc	BU
1953	47,540,000	0.15	0.30	0.50	1.00	—
1953 Proof	—	Value: 1.50				
1955	31,280,000	0.15	0.30	0.50	1.00	—
1956	9,710,000	0.50	0.70	1.00	1.50	—
1957	57,790,000	0.15	0.30	0.50	1.00	—
1958	52,470,000	0.15	0.30	0.50	1.00	—
1959	41,620,000	0.15	0.30	0.50	1.00	—

KM# 2 1/2 ANNA
2.9000 g., Copper-Nickel, 19.8 mm. **Obv:** Tughra and date flanked by stars within sprigs, circle surrounds **Rev:** Crescent, stars and value above sprigs within circle

Date	Mintage	F	VF	XF	Unc	BU
1948	73,920,000	0.15	0.30	0.50	1.00	—
1948 Proof	—	Value: 1.50				
1949 Dot after date	16,940,000	0.50	0.75	1.00	1.50	—
1951	75,360,000	0.15	0.30	0.50	1.00	—

KM# 13 1/2 ANNA
2.5000 g., Nickel-Brass, 19.8 mm. **Obv:** Crescent and star above tughra **Rev:** Date divides wreath, value in center

Date	Mintage	F	VF	XF	Unc	BU
1953	8,350,000	0.20	0.35	0.60	1.15	—
1953 Proof	—	Value: 1.50				
1955	17,310,000	0.15	0.30	0.50	1.00	—
1958	38,250,000	0.15	0.30	0.50	1.00	—

KM# 3 ANNA
3.7500 g., Copper-Nickel, 21.0 mm. **Obv:** Tughra and date flanked by stars above sprigs within circle **Rev:** Crescent and star above sprigs within circle

Date	Mintage	F	VF	XF	Unc	BU
1948	73,460,000	0.15	0.30	0.50	1.00	—
1948 Proof	—	Value: 1.50				

Date	Mintage	F	VF	XF	Unc	BU
1949	11,140,000	0.20	0.35	0.60	1.15	—
1949 Dot after date		0.50	0.75	1.00	1.50	—

Note: Mintage included with KM#8.

Date	Mintage	F	VF	XF	Unc	BU
1951	40,800,000	0.15	0.30	0.50	1.00	—
1952	15,430,000	0.20	0.35	0.60	1.15	—

KM# 8 ANNA
3.7500 g., Copper-Nickel, 21.0 mm. **Obv:** Tughra and date flanked by stars above sprigs within circle **Rev:** Crescent, stars and value above sprigs within circle

Date	Mintage	F	VF	XF	Unc	BU
1950	94,830,000	3.00	4.50	6.50	10.00	—
1950 Proof	—	Value: 15.00				

KM# 14 ANNA
2.9000 g., Copper-Nickel, 19.5 mm. **Obv:** Crescent and star above tughra **Rev:** Date divides wreath, value in center

Date	Mintage	F	VF	XF	Unc	BU
1953	9,350,000	0.15	0.30	0.50	1.00	—
1953 Proof	—	Value: 1.50				
1954	35,360,000	0.15	0.30	0.50	1.00	—
1955	6,230,000	0.20	0.35	0.60	1.15	—
1956	4,580,000	0.20	0.35	0.60	1.15	—
1957	12,500,000	0.15	0.30	0.50	1.00	—
1958	44,320,000	0.15	0.30	0.50	1.00	—

KM# 4 2 ANNAS
5.8000 g., Copper-Nickel, 25.4 mm. **Obv:** Tughra and date flanked by stars above sprigs within circle **Rev:** Crescent, stars and value above sprigs within circle

Date	Mintage	F	VF	XF	Unc	BU
1948	55,930,000	0.15	0.30	0.50	1.00	—
1948 Proof	—	Value: 1.50				
1949	19,720,000	0.20	0.35	0.60	1.15	—
1949 Dot after date		0.50	0.75	1.00	1.50	—

Note: Mintage included with KM#9.

Date	Mintage	F	VF	XF	Unc	BU
1951	33,130,000	0.15	0.30	0.50	1.00	—

KM# 9 2 ANNAS
5.8000 g., Copper-Nickel, 25.4 mm. **Obv:** Tughra and date flanked by stars above sprigs within circle **Rev:** Crescent, stars and value above sprigs within circle

Date	Mintage	F	VF	XF	Unc	BU
1950	21,190,000	3.50	5.00	7.50	12.50	—
1950 Proof	—	Value: 20.00				

KM# 15 2 ANNAS
5.8000 g., Copper-Nickel, 25.4 mm. **Obv:** Crescent and star above tughra **Rev:** Date divides wreath, value in center

Date	Mintage	F	VF	XF	Unc	BU
1953	7,910,000	0.15	0.30	0.50	1.00	—
1953 Proof	—	Value: 1.50				

Date	Mintage	F	VF	XF	Unc	BU
1954	5,740,000	0.15	0.30	0.50	1.00	—
1955	6,230,000	0.15	0.30	0.50	1.00	—
1956	1,370,000	0.20	0.35	0.60	1.15	—
1957	2,570,000	0.20	0.35	0.60	1.15	—
1958	6,200,000	0.15	0.30	0.50	1.00	—
1959	8,010,000	0.15	0.30	0.50	1.00	—

KM# 5 1/4 RUPEE
2.7500 g., Nickel, 19 mm. **Obv:** Tughra and date flanked by stars above sprigs **Rev:** Crescent, stars and value above sprigs **Edge:** Reeded

Date	Mintage	F	VF	XF	Unc	BU
1948	52,680,000	0.20	0.30	0.50	1.00	—
1948 Proof	—	Value: 2.25				
1949	46,000,000	0.20	0.30	0.50	1.00	—
1951	19,120,000	0.20	0.35	0.60	1.15	—

KM# 10 1/4 RUPEE
2.7500 g., Nickel, 19 mm. **Obv:** Tughra and date flanked by stars above sprigs **Rev:** Crescent, stars and value above sprigs **Edge:** Reeded

Date	Mintage	F	VF	XF	Unc	BU
1950	19,400,000	5.00	7.50	12.00	20.00	—
1950 Proof	—	Value: 25.00				

KM# 6 1/2 RUPEE
6.0000 g., Nickel, 24 mm. **Obv:** Tughra and date flanked by stars above sprigs **Rev:** Crescent, stars and value above sprigs **Edge:** Reeded

Date	Mintage	F	VF	XF	Unc	BU
1948	33,260,000	0.40	0.60	0.75	1.50	—
1948 Proof	—	Value: 2.00				
1949	20,300,000	0.40	0.60	0.75	1.50	—
1951	11,430,000	0.40	0.65	0.90	1.75	—

KM# 7 RUPEE
11.5000 g., Nickel, 28 mm. **Obv:** Tughra and date flanked by stars above sprigs **Rev:** Crescent, stars and value above sprigs **Edge:** Reeded **Note:** Varieties exist.

Date	Mintage	F	VF	XF	Unc	BU
1948	46,200,000	0.75	1.25	2.00	3.75	—
1948 Proof	—	Value: 5.00				
1949	37,100,000	0.75	1.25	2.00	3.75	—

DECIMAL COINAGE

100 Paisa = 1 Rupee

KM# 16 PICE
1.4000 g., Bronze, 16 mm. **Obv:** Crescent and star above tughra **Rev:** Date and value flanked by oat sprigs

Date	Mintage	F	VF	XF	Unc	BU
1961	74,910,000	0.15	0.30	0.50	1.00	—

KM# 17 PAISA
1.4000 g., Bronze, 16 mm. **Obv:** Crescent and star above tughra **Rev:** Value and date flanked by oat sprigs

Date	Mintage	F	VF	XF	Unc	BU
1961	134,650,000	0.15	0.25	0.40	0.80	—
1961 Proof	—	Value: 1.50				
1962	149,380,000	0.15	0.25	0.40	0.80	—
1963	127,810,000	0.15	0.25	0.40	0.80	—

KM# 24 PAISA
1.5000 g., Bronze, 17 mm. **Obv:** Crescent and star above tughra **Rev:** Value flanked by oat sprigs

Date	Mintage	F	VF	XF	Unc	BU
1964	39,890,000	0.20	0.35	0.50	1.00	—
1964 Proof	—	Value: 1.50				
1965	69,660,000	0.20	0.35	0.50	1.00	—

KM# 24a PAISA
1.5000 g., Nickel-Brass, 17 mm. **Obv:** Crescent and star above tughra **Rev:** Value flanked by oat sprigs

Date	Mintage	F	VF	XF	Unc	BU
1965	32,950,000	0.20	0.35	0.50	1.00	—
1966	179,370,000	0.15	0.25	0.40	0.80	—

KM# 29 PAISA
0.6000 g., Aluminum, 17 mm. **Obv:** Crescent and star above tughra **Rev:** Value flanked by oat sprigs

Date	Mintage	F	VF	XF	Unc	BU
1967	170,070,000	—	0.20	0.40	0.75	—
1968	—	—	0.20	0.40	0.75	—
1969	—	—	0.20	0.40	0.75	—
1970	204,606,000	—	0.20	0.40	0.75	—
1971	191,880,000	—	0.20	0.40	0.75	—
1972	108,510,000	—	0.20	0.40	0.75	—
1973	Inc. above	—	0.20	0.40	0.75	—

KM# 33 PAISA
0.7500 g., Aluminum, 17 mm. **Series:** F.A.O. **Obv:** Crescent within monument with star at upper left **Rev:** Value flanked by abstract cotton plant **Edge:** Plain

Date	Mintage	F	VF	XF	Unc	BU
1974	14,230,000	—	0.20	0.40	0.75	—
1975	43,000,000	—	0.20	0.40	0.75	—
1976	49,180,000	—	0.20	0.40	0.75	—
1977	62,750,000	—	0.20	0.40	0.75	—
1978	20,380,000	—	0.20	0.40	0.75	—
1978/7	—	—	4.00	6.00	8.00	—
1979	5,630,000	—	2.00	3.00	4.00	—

KM# 25 2 PAISA
2.2500 g., Bronze, 18.0 mm. **Obv:** Crescent and star above tughra **Rev:** Value within sprigs

Date	Mintage	F	VF	XF	Unc	BU
1964	67,660,000	0.15	0.35	0.50	1.00	—
1964 Proof	—	Value: 1.50				
1965	27,880,000	0.15	0.35	0.50	1.00	—
1966	50,590,000	0.15	0.35	0.50	1.00	—

KM# 28 2 PAISA
0.7500 g., Aluminum, 18 mm. **Obv:** Crescent and star above tughra **Rev:** Value within sprigs

Date	Mintage	F	VF	XF	Unc	BU
1966	11,940,000	—	0.35	0.50	1.00	—
1967	73,970,000	—	0.35	0.50	1.00	—
1968	—	—	0.35	0.50	1.00	—

KM# 25a 2 PAISA
0.7500 g., Aluminum, 18.0 mm. **Obv:** Crescent and star above tughra **Rev:** Value within sprigs

Date	Mintage	F	VF	XF	Unc	BU
1968	—	—	0.35	0.50	1.00	—
1969	—	—	0.35	0.50	1.00	—
1970	24,401,000	—	0.35	0.50	1.00	—
1971	10,140,000	—	0.35	0.50	1.00	—
1972	4,040,000	—	0.65	1.00	2.00	—

KM# 34 2 PAISA
1.0000 g., Aluminum, 19.0 mm. **Series:** F.A.O. **Obv:** Crescent within monument with star at upper left **Rev:** Value flanked by rice plant

Date	Mintage	F	VF	XF	Unc	BU
1974	3,600,000	—	0.35	0.50	1.00	—
1975	4,020,000	—	0.35	0.50	1.00	—
1976	5,750,000	—	0.50	0.75	1.50	—

KM# 18 5 PICE
2.7500 g., Nickel-Brass, 24.0 mm. **Obv:** Crescent and star above tughra **Rev:** Sailboat with value on sails

Date	Mintage	F	VF	XF	Unc	BU
1961	40,050,000	0.20	0.35	0.75	1.50	—

KM# 19 5 PAISA
2.7500 g., Nickel-Brass, 21.0 mm. **Obv:** Crescent and star above tughra **Rev:** Sailboat with value on sails

Date	Mintage	F	VF	XF	Unc	BU
1961	40,790,000	0.20	0.35	0.75	1.50	—
1961 Proof	—	Value: 1.50				
1962	48,200,000	0.20	0.35	0.75	1.50	—
1963	45,020,000	0.20	0.35	0.75	1.50	—

KM# 26 5 PAISA
2.7500 g., Nickel-Brass, 21.0 mm. **Obv:** Crescent and star above tughra **Rev:** Sailboat with value on the sails

Date	Mintage	F	VF	XF	Unc	BU
1964	82,730,000	0.20	0.35	0.50	1.00	—
1965	72,570,000	0.20	0.35	0.50	1.00	—
1966	32,900,000	0.20	0.35	0.50	1.00	—
1967	24,470,000	0.20	0.35	0.50	1.00	—

Date	Mintage	F	VF	XF	Unc	BU
1968	—	0.20	0.35	0.50	1.00	—
1969	5,690,000	0.20	0.35	0.50	1.00	—
1970	24,655,000	0.20	0.35	0.50	1.00	—
1971	23,860,000	0.20	0.35	0.50	1.00	—
1972	40,345,000	0.20	0.35	0.50	1.00	—
1973	Inc. above	0.20	0.35	0.50	1.00	—
1974	7,695,000	0.65	1.00	2.00	3.00	—

KM# 35 5 PAISA
1.0000 g., Aluminum, 21.0 mm. **Series:** F.A.O. **Obv:** Crescent within monument with star at upper left **Rev:** Value within sugar cane

Date	Mintage	F	VF	XF	Unc	BU
1974	23,395,000	—	0.35	0.50	1.00	—
1975	50,030,000	—	0.35	0.50	1.00	—
1976	58,255,000	—	0.35	0.50	1.00	—
1977	32,840,000	—	0.35	0.50	1.00	—
1978	61,940,000	—	0.35	0.50	1.00	—
1979	65,485,000	—	0.35	0.50	1.00	—
1980	55,940,000	—	0.35	0.50	1.00	—
1981	18,290,000	—	0.35	0.50	1.00	—

KM# 52 5 PAISA
1.0000 g., Aluminum, 19.12 mm. **Obv:** Crescent, star and date above sprigs **Rev:** Value within sugar cane flanked by stars **Edge:** Plain

Date	Mintage	F	VF	XF	Unc	BU
1981	16,730,000	—	0.35	0.50	1.00	—
1982	51,210,000	—	0.35	0.50	1.00	—
1983	42,915,000	—	0.35	0.50	1.00	—
1984	45,105,000	—	0.35	0.50	1.00	—
1985	46,555,000	—	0.35	0.50	1.00	—
1986	20,065,000	—	0.35	0.50	1.00	—
1987	37,710,000	—	0.35	0.50	1.00	—
1988	40,150,000	—	0.35	0.50	1.00	—
1989	—	—	0.35	0.50	1.00	—
1990	—	—	0.35	0.50	1.00	—
1991	—	—	0.35	0.50	1.00	—
1992	—	—	0.35	0.50	1.00	—

KM# 20 10 PICE
4.7500 g., Copper-Nickel, 23.0 mm. **Obv:** Crescent and star above tughra **Rev:** Date divides wreath, value in center

Date	Mintage	F	VF	XF	Unc	BU
1961	22,230,000	0.20	0.35	0.75	1.50	—

KM# 21 10 PAISA
4.7500 g., Copper-Nickel, 23.0 mm. **Obv:** Crescent and star above tughra **Rev:** Date divides wreath, value in center

Date	Mintage	F	VF	XF	Unc	BU
1961	31,090,000	0.20	0.35	0.75	1.50	—
1961 Proof	—	Value: 2.00				
1962	29,440,000	0.20	0.35	0.75	1.50	—
1963	19,760,000	0.20	0.35	0.75	1.50	—

KM# 27   10 PAISA
4.7500 g., Copper-Nickel, 23.0 mm. **Obv:** Crescent and star above tughra **Rev:** Value within wreath

Date	Mintage	F	VF	XF	Unc	BU
1964	52,580,000	0.20	0.35	0.50	1.00	—
1965	51,540,000	0.20	0.35	0.50	1.00	—
1966	—	0.20	0.35	0.50	1.00	—
1967	16,430,000	0.20	0.35	0.50	1.00	—
1968		0.20	0.35	0.50	1.00	—

KM# 31   10 PAISA
4.0000 g., Copper-Nickel, 22.0 mm. **Obv:** Crescent and star above tughra **Rev:** Value within wreath **Note:** Reduced size.

Date	Mintage	F	VF	XF	Unc	BU
1969	—	0.20	0.35	0.50	1.00	—
1970	30,250,000	0.20	0.35	0.50	1.00	—
1971	26,270,000	0.20	0.35	0.50	1.00	—
1972	24,845,000	0.20	0.35	0.50	1.00	—
1973	Inc. above	0.20	0.35	0.50	1.00	—
1974	4,780,000	0.20	0.35	0.50	1.00	—

KM# 36   10 PAISA
1.2500 g., Aluminum, 22.0 mm. **Series:** F.A.O. **Obv:** Crescent within monument with star at upper left **Rev:** Value within wheat ears

Date	Mintage	F	VF	XF	Unc	BU
1974	18,640,000	—	0.35	0.50	1.00	—
1975	28,875,000	—	0.35	0.50	1.00	—
1976	43,755,000	—	0.35	0.50	1.00	—
1977	29,045,000	—	0.35	0.50	1.00	—
1978	55,185,000	—	0.35	0.50	1.00	—
1979	56,100,000	—	0.35	0.50	1.00	—
1980	40,985,000	—	0.35	0.50	1.00	—
1981	15,500,000	—	0.35	0.50	1.00	—

KM# 53   10 PAISA
1.1900 g., Aluminum, 22 mm. **Obv:** Crescent, star and date above sprigs **Rev:** Value within square **Edge:** Plain

Date	Mintage	F	VF	XF	Unc	BU
1981	7,995,000	—	0.35	0.50	1.00	—
1982	39,770,000	—	0.35	0.50	1.00	—
1983	44,705,000	—	0.35	0.50	1.00	—
1984	35,255,000	—	0.35	0.50	1.00	—
1985	41,545,000	—	0.35	0.50	1.00	—
1986	43,280,000	—	0.35	0.50	1.00	—
1987	39,090,000	—	0.35	0.50	1.00	—
1988	42,510,000	—	0.35	0.50	1.00	—
1989	—	—	0.35	0.50	1.00	—
1990	—	—	0.35	0.50	1.00	—
1991	—	—	0.35	0.50	1.00	—
1992	—	—	0.35	0.50	1.00	—
1993	—	—	0.35	0.50	1.00	—

KM# 22   25 PAISA
2.9000 g., Nickel, 19 mm. **Obv:** Crescent and star above tughra **Rev:** Value flanked by flower sprigs **Edge:** Reeded

Date	Mintage	F	VF	XF	Unc	BU
1963	16,900,000	0.20	0.35	0.50	1.00	—
1964	7,990,000	0.20	0.35	0.50	1.00	—

Date	Mintage	F	VF	XF	Unc	BU
1965	9,290,000	0.20	0.35	0.50	1.00	—
1966	6,650,000	0.20	0.35	0.50	1.00	—
1967	3,740,000	0.20	0.35	0.50	1.00	—

KM# 30   25 PAISA
4.0000 g., Copper-Nickel, 20 mm. **Obv:** Crescent and star above tughra **Rev:** Value below flowers **Edge:** Reeded

Date	Mintage	F	VF	XF	Unc	BU
1967	5,500,000	0.20	0.35	0.50	1.00	—
	Note: Mintage unconfirmed					
1968	5,500,000		0.35	0.50	1.00	
	Note: Mintage unconfirmed					
1969	—	0.20	0.35	0.50	1.00	
1970	30,392,000	0.20	0.35	0.50	1.00	
1971	12,664,000	0.20	0.35	0.50	1.00	
1972	10,824,000	0.20	0.35	0.50	1.00	
1973	—	0.20	0.35	0.50	1.00	
1974	9,756,000	0.20	0.35	0.50	1.00	

KM# 37   25 PAISA
4.0000 g., Copper-Nickel, 20 mm. **Obv:** Crescent within monument with star at upper left **Rev:** Value within flowers **Edge:** Reeded

Date	Mintage	F	VF	XF	Unc	BU
1975	14,264,000	0.20	0.35	0.50	1.00	—
1976	20,440,000	0.20	0.35	0.50	1.00	—
1977	22,092,000	0.20	0.35	0.50	1.00	—
1978	33,544,000	0.20	0.35	0.50	1.00	—
1979	29,648,000	0.20	0.35	0.50	1.00	—
1980	49,556,000	0.20	0.35	0.50	1.00	—
1981	33,952,000	0.20	0.35	0.50	1.00	—

KM# 58   25 PAISA
2.5000 g., Copper-Nickel, 18 mm. **Obv:** Crescent, star and date above sprigs **Rev:** Value within artistic designed wreath **Edge:** Reeded **Note:** Varieties in date and crescent size exist.

Date	Mintage	F	VF	XF	Unc	BU
1981	5,648,000	0.20	0.35	0.50	1.00	—
1982	28,940,000	0.20	0.35	0.50	1.00	—
1983	40,844,000	0.20	0.35	0.50	1.00	—
1984	50,988,000	0.20	0.35	0.50	1.00	—
1985	53,748,000	0.20	0.35	0.50	1.00	—
1986	75,764,000	0.20	0.35	0.50	1.00	—
1987	53,560,000	0.20	0.35	0.50	1.00	—
1988	58,900,000	0.20	0.35	0.50	1.00	—
1989	—	0.20	0.35	0.50	1.00	—
1990	—	0.20	0.35	0.50	1.00	—
1991	—	0.20	0.35	0.50	1.00	—
1992	—	0.20	0.35	0.50	1.00	—
1993	—	0.20	0.35	0.50	1.00	—
1994	—	0.20	0.35	0.50	1.00	—
1995	—	0.20	0.35	0.50	1.00	—
1996	—	0.20	0.35	0.50	1.00	—

KM# 23   50 PAISA
5.8000 g., Nickel, 24 mm. **Obv:** Crescent and star above tughra **Rev:** Value flanked by flowers **Edge:** Reeded

Date	Mintage	F	VF	XF	Unc	BU
1963	8,110,000	0.20	0.35	0.50	1.00	—
1964	4,580,000	0.20	0.35	0.50	1.00	—
1965	8,980,000	0.20	0.35	0.50	1.00	—
1966	2,860,000	0.20	0.35	0.50	1.00	—
1968	—	0.20	0.35	0.50	1.00	—
1969	—	0.20	0.35	0.50	1.00	—

KM# 32   50 PAISA
5.0000 g., Copper-Nickel, 22 mm. **Obv:** Crescent and star above tughra **Rev:** Value below flowers **Edge:** Reeded

Date	Mintage	F	VF	XF	Unc	BU
1969	9,240,000	0.20	0.35	0.50	1.00	—
1970	Inc. above	0.20	0.35	0.50	1.00	—
1971	4,670,000	0.20	0.35	0.50	1.00	—
1972	4,900,000	0.20	0.35	0.50	1.00	—
1974	1,128,000	0.50	0.75	1.00	2.00	—

KM# 38   50 PAISA
5.0000 g., Copper-Nickel, 23 mm. **Obv:** Crescent within monument with star at upper left **Rev:** Value within circle and designed wreath **Edge:** Reeded **Note:** Varieties in date size exist.

Date	Mintage	F	VF	XF	Unc	BU
1975	9,180,000	0.20	0.35	0.50	1.00	—
1976	—	0.20	0.35	0.50	1.00	—
1977	5,548,000	0.20	0.35	0.50	1.00	—
1978	18,252,000	0.20	0.35	0.50	1.00	—
1979	14,596,000	0.20	0.35	0.50	1.00	—
1980	22,332,000	0.20	0.35	0.50	1.00	—
1981	13,552,000	0.20	0.35	0.50	1.00	—

KM# 39   50 PAISA
5.8300 g., Copper-Nickel, 24 mm. **Subject:** 100th Anniversary - Birth of Mohammad Ali Jinnah **Obv:** Value within circle and designed wreath **Rev:** Bust facing flanked by dates **Edge:** Reeded

Date	Mintage	F	VF	XF	Unc	BU
1976	5,600,000	0.35	0.50	1.00	1.50	2.00

KM# 54   50 PAISA
4.0000 g., Copper-Nickel, 21 mm. **Obv:** Crescent, star and date above sprigs **Rev:** Value within circle and leaf wreath **Edge:** Reeded

Date	Mintage	F	VF	XF	Unc	BU
1981	4,612,000	0.20	0.35	0.50	1.00	—
1982	15,844,000	0.20	0.35	0.50	1.00	—
1983	9,608,000	0.20	0.35	0.50	1.00	—
1984	17,520,000	0.20	0.35	0.50	1.00	—
1985	20,144,000	0.20	0.35	0.50	1.00	—
1986	14,116,000	0.20	0.35	0.50	1.00	—
1987	23,044,000	0.20	0.35	0.50	1.00	—
1988	37,140,000	0.20	0.35	0.50	1.00	—
1989	—	0.20	0.35	0.50	1.00	—
1990	—	0.20	0.35	0.50	1.00	—
1991	—	0.20	0.35	0.50	1.00	—
1992	—	0.20	0.35	0.50	1.00	—
1993	—	0.20	0.35	0.50	1.00	—
1994	—	0.20	0.35	0.50	1.00	—
1995	—	0.20	0.35	0.50	1.00	—
1996	—	0.20	0.35	0.50	1.00	—

KM# 51 50 PAISA
5.0000 g., Copper-Nickel, 23 mm. **Subject:** 1,400th Hejira Anniversary **Obv:** Crescent and star above design **Rev:** Value within wreath **Edge:** Reeded

Date	Mintage	F	VF	XF	Unc	BU
AH1401 (1981)	—	0.50	0.75	1.00	2.00	2.50

KM# 45 RUPEE
7.5000 g., Copper-Nickel, 27.5 mm. **Subject:** Islamic Summit Conference **Obv:** Islamic summit minar flanked by designs **Rev:** Design within inner circle **Edge:** Reeded

Date	Mintage	F	VF	XF	Unc	BU
1977	5,074,000	0.50	0.75	1.00	2.00	2.50

KM# 46 RUPEE
7.5000 g., Copper-Nickel, 27.5 mm. **Subject:** 100th Anniversary - Birth of Allama Mohammad Iqbal **Obv:** Value and date above sprigs **Rev:** Head leaning on arm facing 1/4 left **Edge:** Reeded

Date	Mintage	F	VF	XF	Unc	BU
1977	5,000,000	0.50	0.75	1.00	2.00	2.50

KM# 57.1 RUPEE
6.5000 g., Copper-Nickel, 26.5 mm. **Obv:** Crescent, star and date above sprigs **Rev:** Value within sprigs **Edge:** Reeded

Date	Mintage	F	VF	XF	Unc	BU
1979	—	0.30	0.40	0.55	1.15	—
1980	14,522,000	0.30	0.40	0.55	1.15	—
1981	12,038,000	0.30	0.40	0.55	1.15	—

KM# 57.2 RUPEE
6.0000 g., Copper-Nickel, 25 mm. **Obv:** Crescent, star and date above sprigs **Rev:** Value within sprigs **Edge:** Reeded

Date	Mintage	F	VF	XF	Unc	BU
1981	4,084,000	0.25	0.40	0.60	1.20	—
1982	27,878,000	0.20	0.35	0.50	1.00	—
1983	18,746,000	0.20	0.35	0.50	1.00	—
1984	14,562,000	0.20	0.35	0.50	1.00	—
1985	4,934,000	0.25	0.40	0.60	1.20	—
1986	11,840,000	0.20	0.35	0.50	1.00	—
1987	50,416,000	0.20	0.35	0.50	1.00	—
1988	10,644,000	0.20	0.35	0.50	1.00	—
1990	—	0.20	0.35	0.50	1.00	—
1991	—	0.20	0.35	0.50	1.00	—

KM# 55 RUPEE
6.5000 g., Copper-Nickel, 26.5 mm. **Subject:** 1,400th Hejira Anniversary **Obv:** Crescent and star above design **Rev:** Value within wreath **Edge:** Reeded

Date	Mintage	F	VF	XF	Unc	BU
AH1401 (1981)	45,000	0.50	0.75	1.25	2.50	3.00

KM# 56 RUPEE
6.0000 g., Copper-Nickel, 25 mm. **Series:** World Food Day **Obv:** Crescent, star and date above sprigs **Rev:** F.A.O. logo within circle **Edge:** Reeded

Date	Mintage	F	VF	XF	Unc	BU
1981	45,000	0.35	0.75	1.50	3.00	3.50

KM# 62 RUPEE
4.0000 g., Bronze, 20 mm. **Obv:** Head left **Rev:** Mosque above value **Edge:** Reeded

Date	Mintage	F	VF	XF	Unc	BU
1998	—	0.20	0.25	0.35	0.65	0.75
1999	—	0.20	0.25	0.35	0.65	0.75
2000	—	0.20	0.25	0.35	0.65	0.75

KM# 63 2 RUPEES
4.0000 g., Nickel-Brass, 22.5 mm. **Obv:** Crescent, star and date above sprigs **Rev:** Mosque **Edge:** Reeded

Date	Mintage	F	VF	XF	Unc	BU
1998	—	0.20	0.30	0.45	0.85	1.00
1999	—	0.25	0.45	0.75	1.25	1.50

KM# 64 2 RUPEES
5.0000 g., Nickel-Brass, 22.5 mm. **Obv:** Crescent, star and date above sprigs **Rev:** Value below mosque and clouds **Edge:** Reeded

Date	Mintage	F	VF	XF	Unc	BU
1999	—	0.20	0.30	0.45	0.85	1.00
2000	—	0.20	0.30	0.45	0.85	1.00

KM# 59 5 RUPEES
20.0000 g., Copper, 35 mm. **Subject:** United Nations 50th Year **Obv:** Crescent and star above grain sprigs **Rev:** 50, UN logo **Edge:** Reeded **Note:** Four die varieties are reported to exist.

Date	Mintage	F	VF	XF	Unc	BU
1995	500,000	—	—	—	5.50	6.00

KM# 61 10 RUPEES
10.0000 g., Copper-Nickel, 26 mm. **Subject:** 25th Anniversary - Pakistan's Senate **Obv:** Crescent, star and date above sprigs **Rev:** Shield within sprigs above banner and dates to left of numeral 25 **Edge:** Reeded

Date	Mintage	F	VF	XF	Unc	BU
1998	100,000	—	—	4.00	6.50	7.50

KM# 60 50 RUPEES
20.0000 g., Copper-Nickel, 35 mm. **Subject:** 50th Anniversary - National Independence **Obv:** Star and crescent **Rev:** Flag and dates **Edge:** Reeded

Date	Mintage	F	VF	XF	Unc	BU
1997	500,000	—	—	4.50	7.50	8.00

KM# 40 100 RUPEES
28.2800 g., 0.9250 Silver 0.8410 oz. ASW, 38.6 mm. **Series:** Conservation **Obv:** Crescent within monument with star at upper left **Rev:** Tropogan pheasant

Date	Mintage	F	VF	XF	Unc	BU
1976	5,120	—	—	—	40.00	50.00
1976 Proof	5,837	Value: 60.00				

KM# 41 100 RUPEES
20.4400 g., 0.9250 Silver 0.6078 oz. ASW, 36 mm. **Subject:** 100th Anniversary - Birth of Mohammad Ali Jinnah **Obv:** Crescent and star **Rev:** Bust facing flanked by dates

Date	Mintage	F	VF	XF	Unc	BU
ND(1976)	1,300	—	—	—	35.00	40.00
ND(1976) Proof	2,800	Value: 45.00				

KM# 47   100 RUPEES
20.4400 g., 0.9250 Silver 0.6078 oz. ASW, 36 mm.
Subject: Islamic Summit Conference **Obv:** Islamic building
Rev: Islamic summit minar

Date	Mintage	F	VF	XF	Unc	BU
1977	1,500	—	—	—	35.00	40.00
1977 Proof	2,500	Value: 45.00				

KM# 48   100 RUPEES
20.4400 g., 0.9250 Silver 0.6078 oz. ASW, 36 mm.
Subject: 100th Anniversary - Birth of Allama Mohammad Iqbal
Obv: Value and date above sprigs **Rev:** Head leaning on hand
divides dates

Date	Mintage	F	VF	XF	Unc	BU
1977	3,000	—	—	—	35.00	40.00
1977 Proof	300	Value: 50.00				

KM# 42   150 RUPEES
35.0000 g., 0.9250 Silver 1.0408 oz. ASW, 42 mm.
Series: Conservation **Obv:** Crescent within monument with star
at upper left **Rev:** Gavial crocodile and value

Date	Mintage	F	VF	XF	Unc	BU
1976	5,119	—	—	—	40.00	50.00
1976 Proof	5,637	Value: 60.00				

KM# 43   500 RUPEES
4.5000 g., 0.9170 Gold 0.1327 oz. AGW, 19 mm. **Subject:** 100th
Anniversary - Birth of Mohammad Ali Jinnah **Obv:** Crescent and
star **Rev:** Bust facing flanked by dates

Date	Mintage	F	VF	XF	Unc	BU
ND(1976)	500	—	—	—	160	185
ND(1976) Proof	500	Value: 210				

KM# 49   500 RUPEES
3.6400 g., 0.9170 Gold 0.1073 oz. AGW, 19 mm. **Subject:** 100th
Anniversary - Birth of Allama Mohammad Iqbal **Obv:** Value and
date above sprigs **Rev:** Head leaning on hand flanked by dates

Date	Mintage	F	VF	XF	Unc	BU
1977	500	—	—	—	150	175
1977 Proof	200	Value: 215				

KM# 50   1000 RUPEES
9.0000 g., 0.9170 Gold 0.2653 oz. AGW, 25 mm.
Subject: Islamic Summit Conference **Obv:** Islamic summit minar
Rev: Design within center circle

Date	Mintage	F	VF	XF	Unc	BU
1977	400	—	—	—	300	400
1977 Proof	400	Value: 500				

KM# 44   3000 RUPEES
33.4370 g., 0.9000 Gold 0.9675 oz. AGW, 39 mm.
Obv: Crescent within monument with star at upper left **Rev:** Astor
Markhor and value

Date	Mintage	F	VF	XF	Unc	BU
1976	902	—	—	—	—	1,000
1976 Proof	273	Value: 1,150				

PATTERNS
Including off-metal strikes

KM#	Date	Mintage	Identification	Mkt Val
Pn1	1947	—	Rupee. Nickel Alloy. Toughra within circle. GOVERNMENT OF PAKISTAN. Crescent and star, dates flanking.	—
Pn2	1947	—	Rupee. Nickel Alloy. Toughra within circle, dates below. GOVERNMENT OF PAKISTAN. Crescent with star.	—
Pn3	1947	—	Rupee. Nickel Alloy. Crescent and star, denomination and wreath below. Toughra, date at right, wreath below. GOVERNMENT OF PAKISTAN.	—
Pn4	ND(1995)	—	Rupee. Copper Alloys. Crescent and star, wheat ears below. UN logo, large 50.	—

MINT SETS

KM#	Date	Mintage	Identification	Issue Price	Mkt Val
MS1	1948 (7)	—	KM1-7	—	10.00
MS2	1948, 1951, 1953 (8)	—	KM5-7 (1948), 11 (1951), 12-15 (1953). Restrikes have been issued.	4.00	12.50
MS3	1948, 1961 (6)	—	KM5-7 (1948), 17, 19, 21 (1961). Restrikes have been issued.	2.00	6.50
MS4	1948, 1964 (7)	—	KM7 (1948), 22-27 (1964). Restrikes have been issued.	2.00	6.50
MS5	1948, 1975 (7)	—	KM7 (1948), 33-38 (1975). Restrikes have been issued.	—	5.00
MS6	1951, 1953 (5)	—	KM11 (1951), 12-15 (1953). Restrikes have been issued.	—	8.00
MS7	1961 (3)	—	KM17, 19, 21	—	3.50
MS8	1976 (2)	—	KM41, 43	63.00	225
MS9	1976 (2)	—	KM40, 42	—	68.00
MS10	1977 (2)	—	KM47, 50	—	445

PROOF SETS

KM#	Date	Mintage	Identification	Issue Price	Mkt Val
PS1	1948 (7)	5,000	KM1-7	4.00	15.50
PS3	1950 (3)	—	KM8-10	—	60.00
PS4	1953 (5)	—	KM11-15	2.00	11.50
PS5	1961 (3)	—	KM17, 19, 21	1.00	5.00
PS6	1976 (2)	—	KM41, 43	90.50	250
PS7	1976 (2)	—	KM40, 42	—	120
PS8	1977 (2)	—	KM47, 50	—	550
PS9	1977 (2)	—	KM#45	—	40.00

PALAU

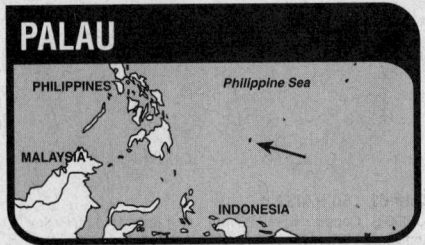

The Republic of Palau, a group of about 100 islands and
islets, is generally considered a part of the Caroline Islands. It is
located about 1,000 miles southeast of Manila and about the
same distance southwest of Saipan and has an area of 179 sq.
mi. and a population of 12,116. Capital: Koror.

The islands were administered as part of the Caroline Islands
under the Spanish regime until they were sold to Germany in
1899. Seized by Japan in 1914, it was mandated to them in 1919
and Koror was made the administrative headquarters of all the
Japanese mandated islands in 1921. During World War II the
islands were taken by the Allies, in 1944, with the heaviest fighting
taking place on Peleliu. They became part of the U.S. Trust Territory of the Pacific Islands in 1947. In 1980 they became internally
self-governing and independent. Control over foreign policy,
except defense, was approved in 1986. Palau became an independent nation in 1995.

REPUBLIC
MILLED COINAGE

KM# 1   DOLLAR
Copper-Nickel   **Subject:** Year of Marine Life Protection
Obv: Sailboat, mermaid and value within beaded circle
Rev: Multicolor design within beaded circle

Date	Mintage	F	VF	XF	Unc	BU
1992 Proof	Est. 50,000	Value: 30.00				

KM# 3   DOLLAR
Copper-Nickel   **Series:** Marine Life Protection **Obv:** Mermaid
sitting upright **Rev:** Multicolor ocean scene

Date	Mintage	F	VF	XF	Unc	BU
1993 Proof	50,000	Value: 30.00				

KM# 5 DOLLAR

Copper-Nickel **Series:** Marine Life Protection **Obv:** Ship, mermaid and value **Rev:** Multicolor ocean scene

Date	Mintage	F	VF	XF	Unc	BU
1994 Proof	50,000	Value: 30.00				

KM# 8 DOLLAR

Copper-Nickel **Subject:** Independence **Obv:** Neptune and mermaid **Rev:** Multicolor ocean scene

Date	Mintage	F	VF	XF	Unc	BU
1994 Proof	50,000	Value: 32.50				

KM# 11 DOLLAR

Copper-Nickel **Subject:** Marine Life Protection **Obv:** Mermaid with harp **Rev:** Multicolor sea horse and lion fish

Date	Mintage	F	VF	XF	Unc	BU
1995 Proof	30,000	Value: 37.50				

KM# 14 DOLLAR

Copper-Nickel **Subject:** United Nations 50th Anniversary **Obv:** Mermaid above seahorses, value below **Rev:** Multicolor ocean scene with emblem on bottom

Date	Mintage	F	VF	XF	Unc	BU
1995 Proof	30,000	Value: 25.00				

KM# 25 DOLLAR

Copper-Nickel **Series:** Marine Life Protection **Obv:** Two mermaids **Rev:** Multicolor high-relief dolphin

Date	Mintage	F	VF	XF	Unc	BU
1998 Proof	13,000	Value: 37.50				

KM# 26 DOLLAR

1.2441 g., 0.9999 Gold 0.0400 oz. AGW, 13.94 mm. **Series:** Marine Life Protection **Obv:** Two mermaids **Rev:** Jumping dolphin

Date	Mintage	F	VF	XF	Unc	BU
1998 Proof	10,000	Value: 45.00				

KM# 30 DOLLAR

Copper-Nickel **Series:** Marine Life Protection **Obv:** Mermaid with cockatoo **Rev:** Multicolor high-relief turtle

Date	Mintage	F	VF	XF	Unc	BU
1998 Proof	—	Value: 37.50				

KM# 31 DOLLAR

1.2441 g., 0.9999 Gold 0.0400 oz. AGW, 13.94 mm. **Series:** Marine Life Protection **Obv:** Mermaid holding cockatoo **Rev:** Sea turtle

Date	Mintage	F	VF	XF	Unc	BU
1998 Proof	—	Value: 45.00				

KM# 35 DOLLAR

Copper-Nickel **Series:** Marine Life Protection **Obv:** Mermaid and dolphin **Rev:** Multicolor high-relief manta ray

Date	Mintage	F	VF	XF	Unc	BU
1999 Proof	—	Value: 37.50				

KM# 82 DOLLAR

1.2441 g., 0.9999 Gold 0.0400 oz. AGW, 13.94 mm. **Obv:** Seated Mermaid and sailboat **Rev:** Multicolor shark **Edge:** Reeded

Date	Mintage	F	VF	XF	Unc	BU
1999 Proof	—	Value: 45.00				

KM# 36 DOLLAR

1.2441 g., 0.9999 Gold 0.0400 oz. AGW, 13.94 mm. **Series:** Marine Life Protection **Obv:** Mermaid and dolphin **Rev:** Manta ray

Date	Mintage	F	VF	XF	Unc	BU
1999 Proof	—	Value: 45.00				

KM# 40 DOLLAR

Copper-Nickel **Series:** Marine Life Protection **Obv:** Mermaid and sailboat **Rev:** Multicolor shark

Date	Mintage	F	VF	XF	Unc	BU
1999 Proof	—	Value: 37.50				

KM# 43 DOLLAR

26.6500 g., Copper-Nickel **Series:** Marine Life Protection **Obv:** Mermaid and ship **Rev:** Multicolor fish and coral

Date	Mintage	F	VF	XF	Unc	BU
2000 Proof	—	Value: 35.00				

KM# 58 DOLLAR

26.8000 g., Copper-Nickel, 37.2 mm. **Obv:** Diving Mermaid **Rev:** Multicolor jumping swordfish **Edge:** Reeded

Date	Mintage	F	VF	XF	Unc	BU
2000 Proof	—	Value: 37.50				

KM# 59 DOLLAR

26.8000 g., Copper-Nickel, 37.2 mm. **Obv:** Seated Mermaid **Rev:** Multicolor fish and wreck **Edge:** Reeded

Date	Mintage	F	VF	XF	Unc	BU
2000 Proof	—	Value: 35.00				

KM# 83   DOLLAR
1.2441 g., 0.9999 Gold 0.0400 oz. AGW, 13.94 mm. **Obv:** Diving
Mermaid **Rev:** Multicolor jumping Swordfish **Edge:** Reeded

Date	Mintage	F	VF	XF	Unc	BU
2000 Proof	—				Value: 45.00	

KM# 84   DOLLAR
1.2441 g., 0.9999 Gold 0.0400 oz. AGW, 13.94 mm. **Obv:**
Seated Mermaid **Rev:** Multicolor fish and wreck **Edge:** Reeded

Date	Mintage	F	VF	XF	Unc	BU
2000 Proof	—				Value: 45.00	

KM# 85   DOLLAR
1.2441 g., 0.9999 Gold 0.0400 oz. AGW, 13.94 mm. **Obv:** Seated
Mermaid and ship **Rev:** Multicolor fish and coral **Edge:** Reeded

Date	Mintage	F	VF	XF	Unc	BU
2000 Proof	—				Value: 45.00	

KM# 2   5 DOLLARS
25.0000 g., 0.9000 Silver 0.7234 oz. ASW **Series:** Marine Life
Protection **Obv:** Neptune and spear **Rev:** Multicolor ocean scene

Date	Mintage	F	VF	XF	Unc	BU
1992 Proof	Est. 6,000				Value: 75.00	

KM# 4   5 DOLLARS
25.0000 g., 0.9000 Silver 0.7234 oz. ASW **Series:** Marine Life
Protection **Obv:** Neptune in shell, horses, dolphin and value
Rev: Multicolor ocean scene

Date	Mintage	F	VF	XF	Unc	BU
1993 Proof	6,000				Value: 75.00	

KM# 6   5 DOLLARS
25.0000 g., 0.9000 Silver 0.7234 oz. ASW **Series:** Marine Life
Protection **Obv:** Neptune and seascape **Rev:** Multicolor ocean
scene

Date	Mintage	F	VF	XF	Unc	BU
1994 Proof	10,000				Value: 70.00	

KM# 9   5 DOLLARS
25.0000 g., 0.9000 Silver 0.7234 oz. ASW **Series:** Independence
Obv: Mermaid and Neptune **Rev:** Nautilus and seascape

Date	Mintage	F	VF	XF	Unc	BU
1994 Proof	—				Value: 78.00	

KM# 12   5 DOLLARS
25.0000 g., 0.9000 Silver 0.7234 oz. ASW **Series:** Marine Life
Protection **Rev:** Sea horse and lion fish

Date	Mintage	F	VF	XF	Unc	BU
1995 Proof	7,500				Value: 75.00	

KM# 15   5 DOLLARS
25.0000 g., 0.9000 Silver 0.7234 oz. ASW **Subject:** United
Nations 50th Anniversary **Obv:** Mermaid above seahorses
Rev: Multicolor ocean scene

Date	Mintage	F	VF	XF	Unc	BU
1995 Proof	5,500				Value: 60.00	

KM# 46   5 DOLLARS
24.6400 g., 0.9000 Silver 0.7129 oz. ASW **Series:** Marine Life
Protection **Obv:** Mermaid and sailboat **Rev:** Multicolor shark

Date	Mintage	F	VF	XF	Unc	BU
1998 Proof	—				Value: 75.00	
1999 Proof	—				Value: 75.00	

KM# 27   5 DOLLARS
25.0000 g., 0.9000 Silver 0.7234 oz. ASW **Series:** Marine Life
Protection **Obv:** Two mermaids **Rev:** Multicolor high-relief
dolphin **Note:** Similar to Dollar, KM#25.

Date	Mintage	F	VF	XF	Unc	BU
1998 Proof	5,000				Value: 78.00	

KM# 32   5 DOLLARS
25.0000 g., 0.9000 Silver 0.7234 oz. ASW **Series:** Marine Life
Protection **Obv:** Mermaid holding cockatoo **Rev:** Multicolor high-
relief turtle **Note:** Similar to Dollar, KM#30.

Date	Mintage	F	VF	XF	Unc	BU
1998 Proof	—				Value: 75.00	

KM# 44   5 DOLLARS
24.6400 g., 0.9000 Silver 0.7129 oz. ASW **Series:** Marine Life
Protection **Obv:** Neptune and ship **Rev:** Multicolor dolphin
jumping **Edge:** Reeded

Date	Mintage	F	VF	XF	Unc	BU
1998 Proof	5,000				Value: 78.00	

KM# 45   5 DOLLARS
24.6400 g., 0.9000 Silver 0.7129 oz. ASW **Series:** Marine Life
Protection **Obv:** Neptune and two dolphins **Rev:** Multicolor sea
turtle

Date	Mintage	F	VF	XF	Unc	BU
1998 Proof	3,000				Value: 75.00	

KM# 37   5 DOLLARS
25.0000 g., 0.9000 Silver 0.7234 oz. ASW, 37 mm. **Subject:**
Marine Life Protection **Obv:** Mermaid and dolphin **Rev:** Multicolor
high relief manta ray **Edge:** Reeded

Date	Mintage	F	VF	XF	Unc	BU
1999 Proof	—				Value: 70.00	

KM# 47   5 DOLLARS
24.6400 g., 0.9000 Silver 0.7129 oz. ASW **Series:** Marine Life
Protection **Obv:** Mermaid in profile, sailboat **Rev:** Multicolor
manta ray

Date	Mintage	F	VF	XF	Unc	BU
1999 Proof	—				Value: 75.00	

KM# 16   5 DOLLARS
25.0000 g., 0.9250 Silver 0.7435 oz. ASW **Series:** International
Coins **Subject:** Spanish 5 Peseta - 1896-1899 **Obv:** Crowned
Spanish arms **Rev:** Young head left

Date	Mintage	F	VF	XF	Unc	BU
1999 Proof	—				Value: 27.50	

KM# 17 5 DOLLARS
25.0000 g., 0.9250 Silver 0.7435 oz. ASW **Series:** International Coins **Subject:** Prussian 5 Mark - 1891-1908 **Obv:** Crowned arms **Rev:** Head right

Date	Mintage	F	VF	XF	Unc	BU
1999 Proof	—				Value: 27.50	

KM# 18 5 DOLLARS
25.0000 g., 0.9250 Silver 0.7435 oz. ASW **Series:** International Coins **Subject:** German East Africa **Obv:** Elephant above value **Rev:** Uniformed bust of Paul Emil von Lettow-Vorbeck facing, colonial arms at lower right

Date	Mintage	F	VF	XF	Unc	BU
1999 Proof	—				Value: 35.00	

KM# 19 5 DOLLARS
25.0000 g., 0.9250 Silver 0.7435 oz. ASW **Series:** International Coins **Subject:** German Cameroon **Obv:** Kaiser Wilhelm I facing right **Rev:** Germania and colonial arms

Date	Mintage	F	VF	XF	Unc	BU
1999 Proof	—				Value: 30.00	

KM# 20 5 DOLLARS
25.0000 g., 0.9250 Silver 0.7435 oz. ASW **Series:** International Coins **Subject:** Kiau Chau **Obv:** Ships in harbor **Rev:** Emblem based on 1909 coinage

Date	Mintage	F	VF	XF	Unc	BU
1999 Proof	—				Value: 30.00	

KM# 21 5 DOLLARS
25.0000 g., 0.9250 Silver 0.7435 oz. ASW **Series:** International Coins **Subject:** German New Guinea **Obv:** Large ship **Rev:** Colonial arms

Date	Mintage	F	VF	XF	Unc	BU
1999 Proof	—				Value: 30.00	

KM# 22 5 DOLLARS
25.0000 g., 0.9250 Silver 0.7435 oz. ASW **Series:** International Coins **Subject:** German Samoa **Obv:** Armored bust left of Kaiser Wilhelm II facing left **Rev:** Colonial arms

Date	Mintage	F	VF	XF	Unc	BU
1999 Proof	—				Value: 30.00	

KM# 23 5 DOLLARS
25.0000 g., 0.9250 Silver 0.7435 oz. ASW **Series:** International Coins **Subject:** German South West Africa **Obv:** Whilhelm II portrait from Prussian 5 Mark coin of 1913-1914 **Rev:** Colonial arms and trooper on camel

Date	Mintage	F	VF	XF	Unc	BU
1999 Proof	—				Value: 32.50	

KM# 24 5 DOLLARS
25.0000 g., 0.9250 Silver 0.7435 oz. ASW **Series:** International Coins **Subject:** German Togo **Obv:** Seated Germania **Rev:** Colonial arms

Date	Mintage	F	VF	XF	Unc	BU
1999 Proof	—				Value: 27.50	

KM# 48 5 DOLLARS
24.6400 g., 0.9000 Silver 0.7129 oz. ASW **Series:** Marine Life Protection **Obv:** Neptune seated **Rev:** Multicolor fish and coral

Date	Mintage	F	VF	XF	Unc	BU
2000 Proof	—				Value: 65.00	

KM# 73 5 DOLLARS
25.0000 g., 0.9000 Silver 0.7234 oz. ASW, 37.2 mm. **Subject:** Marine Life Protection **Obv:** Neptune seated **Rev:** Multicolor jumping swordfish **Edge:** Reeded

Date	Mintage	F	VF	XF	Unc	BU
2000 Proof	—				Value: 75.00	

KM# 74 5 DOLLARS
25.0000 g., 0.9000 Silver 0.7234 oz. ASW, 37.2 mm. **Subject:** Marine Life Protection **Obv:** Neptune behind ancient ship **Rev:** Multicolor fish and wreck **Edge:** Reeded

Date	Mintage	F	VF	XF	Unc	BU
2000 Proof	—				Value: 75.00	

KM# 51 5 DOLLARS
24.9400 g., 0.9000 Silver 0.7216 oz. ASW, 38.6 mm. **Subject:** Our World - Our Future **Obv:** Half-length dancer with leis **Rev:** Multicolor world map **Edge:** Reeded

Date	Mintage	F	VF	XF	Unc	BU
2000 Proof	—				Value: 45.00	

KM# 112   10 DOLLARS
1.4900 g., 0.9990 Gold 0.0479 oz. AGW, 11 x 19 mm.
Obv: Value, date and inscription **Rev:** Mermaid **Edge:** Plain

Date	Mintage	F	VF	XF	Unc	BU
1995 Proof	—	Value: 55.00				

KM# 7   20 DOLLARS
155.5175 g., 0.9990 Silver 4.9948 oz. ASW, 63.9 mm.
Subject: Marine - Life Protection **Rev:** Multicolor ocean scene
Note: Illustration reduced.

Date	Mintage	F	VF	XF	Unc	BU
1994 Proof	3,000	Value: 95.00				

KM# 42   20 DOLLARS
155.5175 g., 0.9990 Silver 4.9948 oz. ASW, 63.9 mm.
Subject: Independence - October 1994 **Obv:** Mermaid and
Neptune **Rev:** Multicolor seascape **Note:** Illustration reduced.

Date	Mintage	F	VF	XF	Unc	BU
ND(1994) Proof	—	Value: 95.00				

KM# 13   20 DOLLARS
155.5175 g., 0.9990 Silver 4.9948 oz. ASW **Series:** Marine Life
Protection **Obv:** Seated mermaid with harp **Rev:** Seahorse and
lion fish **Note:** Similar to Dollar, KM#11.

Date	Mintage	F	VF	XF	Unc	BU
1995 Proof	3,000	Value: 95.00				

KM# 41   20 DOLLARS
15.6500 g., 0.9990 Silver 0.5026 oz. ASW, 64.5 mm.
Series: 50th Anniversary - United Nations Member
Obv: Mermaid driving quadriga **Rev:** Multicolor seascape, globe
of earth below **Note:** Illustration reduced.

Date	Mintage	F	VF	XF	Unc	BU
1995 Proof	—	Value: 95.00				

KM# 28   20 DOLLARS
155.5175 g., 0.9990 Silver 4.9948 oz. ASW **Series:** Marine Life
Protection **Obv:** Two mermaids **Rev:** Multicolor high-relief
dolphin **Note:** Similar to Dollar, KM#25.

Date	Mintage	F	VF	XF	Unc	BU
1998 Proof	700	Value: 100				

KM# 33   20 DOLLARS
155.5175 g., 0.9990 Silver 4.9948 oz. ASW **Series:** Marine Life
Protection **Obv:** Mermaid with cockatoo **Rev:** Multicolor high-
relief turtle **Note:** Similar to Dollar, KM#30.

Date	Mintage	F	VF	XF	Unc	BU
1998 Proof	500	Value: 110				

KM# 38   20 DOLLARS
155.5175 g., 0.9990 Silver 4.9948 oz. ASW **Series:** Marine Life
Protection **Obv:** Mermaid with dolphin **Rev:** Multicolor high-relief
manta ray **Note:** Similar to Dollar, KM#35.

Date	Mintage	F	VF	XF	Unc	BU
1999 Proof	500	Value: 110				

KM# 49   20 DOLLARS
153.9400 g., 0.9990 Silver 4.9441 oz. ASW **Series:** Marine Life
Protection **Obv:** Seated mermaid and sailboat **Rev:** Multicolor
shark **Edge:** Reeded

Date	Mintage	F	VF	XF	Unc	BU
1999 Proof	500	Value: 110				

KM# 55   20 DOLLARS
154.8400 g., 0.9990 Silver 4.9730 oz. ASW, 64.5 mm.
Subject: Marine Life Protection **Obv:** Diving mermaid
Rev: Multicolor jumping swordfish scene **Edge:** Reeded

Date	Mintage	F	VF	XF	Unc	BU
2000 Proof	500	Value: 110				

KM# 50   20 DOLLARS
153.9400 g., 0.9990 Silver 4.9441 oz. ASW **Subject:** Marine -
Life Protection **Obv:** Mermaid and ship **Rev:** Multicolor fish and
coral **Note:** Illustration reduced.

Date	Mintage	F	VF	XF	Unc	BU
2000 Proof	500	Value: 110				

KM# 54   20 DOLLARS
154.8400 g., 0.9990 Silver 4.9730 oz. ASW, 64.5 mm.
Subject: Marine Life Protection **Obv:** Seated mermaid
Rev: Multicolor sunken ship and fish scene **Edge:** Reeded
Note: Illustration reduced.

Date	Mintage	F	VF	XF	Unc	BU
2000 Proof	500	Value: 110				

KM# 10   200 DOLLARS
31.1035 g., 0.9990 Gold 0.9990 oz. AGW **Subject:** Independence
Obv: Mermaid and Neptune **Rev:** Nautilus and seascape

Date	Mintage	F	VF	XF	Unc	BU
1994 Proof	—	Value: 975				

KM# 29   200 DOLLARS
31.1035 g., 0.9990 Gold 0.9990 oz. AGW **Subject:** Marine - Life
Protection **Obv:** Two mermaids **Rev:** Multicolor high-relief
dolphin **Note:** Similar to Dollar, KM#25.

Date	Mintage	F	VF	XF	Unc	BU
1998 Proof	200	Value: 975				

KM# 34   200 DOLLARS
31.1035 g., 0.9990 Gold 0.9990 oz. AGW **Subject:** Marine - Life
Protection **Obv:** Mermaid with cockatoo **Rev:** Multicolor high-
relief turtle **Note:** Similar to Dollar, KM#30.

Date	Mintage	F	VF	XF	Unc	BU
1998 Proof	—	Value: 975				

KM# 39   200 DOLLARS
31.1035 g., 0.9990 Gold 0.9990 oz. AGW **Subject:** Marine - Life
Protection **Obv:** Mermaid with dolphin **Rev:** Multicolor high-relief
manta ray **Note:** Similar to Dollar, KM#35.

Date	Mintage	F	VF	XF	Unc	BU
1999 Proof	—	Value: 975				

ESSAIS
Standard metals unless otherwise noted

KM#	Date	Mintage	Identification	Issue Price	Mkt Val
E1	1992	—	Dollar. 0.9990 Gold. 25.9600 g. Seated mermaid and sailboat. Multicolor sea life. KM1.	—	1,500
E2	1992	—	5 Dollars. 0.9990 Gold. 25.9700 g. Seated Neptune and ship. Multicolor sea life. Reeded edge. KM2.	—	1,500
E3	1995	30	Dollar. Silver. KM41.	—	125
E4	1995	30	5 Dollars. Copper-Nickel. KM41.	—	100
E5	1995	30	200 Dollars. Copper-Nickel. KM41.	—	120
E6	1995	30	200 Dollars. Silver. KM41.	—	185
E7	1998	20	Dollar. Silver. KM25.	—	145
E8	1998	20	5 Dollars. Copper-Nickel. KM25.	—	145
E9	1998	20	200 Dollars. Silver. KM25.	—	145
E10	1999	—	200 Dollars. Copper-Nickel. Shark, m/c.	—	300
E11	2000	—	200 Dollars. Copper-Nickel. 3 fish, m/c.	—	300

PROOF SETS

KM#	Date	Mintage	Identification	Issue Price	Mkt Val
PS1	1992	—	KME1, E2	—	3,000
PS2	1995 (4)	20	KME3, E4, E5, E6	—	600
PS3	1998 (3)	20	KME7, E8, E9	—	450

PALESTINE

Palestine, which corresponds to Canaan of the Bible, was settled by the Philistines about the 12th century B.C. and shortly thereafter was settled by the Jews who established the kingdoms of
Israel and Judah. Because of its position as part of the land bridge
connecting Asia and Africa, Palestine was invaded and conquered
by nearly all of the historic empires of ancient Europe and Asia. In
the 16th century it became a part of the Ottoman Empire. After falling to the British in World War I, it, together with Transjordan, was
mandated to Great Britain by the League of Nations, 1922.

For more than half a century prior to the termination of the
British mandate over Palestine, 1948, Zionist leaders had sought
to create a Jewish homeland for Jews who were dispersed
throughout the world. For almost as long, Jews fleeing persecution had immigrated to Palestine. The Nazi persecutions of the
1930s and 1940s increased the Jewish movement to Palestine and
generated international support for the creation of a Jewish
state, first promulgated by the Balfour Declaration of 1917, which
asserted British support for the endeavor. The state of Israel was
proclaimed as the Jewish state in the territory that was Palestine.
The remainder of that territory was occupied by Jordanian and
Egyptian armies. Israel demonetized the coins of Palestine on
Sept. 15, 1948, the Jordan government declared Palestine currency no longer legal tender on June 30, 1951, and Egypt
declared it no longer legal tender in Gaza on June 9, 1951.

TITLES

فلسطين

Filastin

פלשתינה (א"י).

Paleshtina (E.I.)

MONETARY SYSTEM
1000 Mils = 1 Pound
1000 Mils = 1 Pound

BRITISH ADMINISTRATION
MIL COINAGE

KM# 1   MIL
3.2000 g., Bronze, 21 mm. **Obv:** Inscription PALESTINE, in English, Hebrew and Arabic **Rev:** Value, plant **Edge:** Plain

Date	Mintage	F	VF	XF	Unc	BU
1927	10,000,000	0.75	2.00	4.00	12.00	15.00
1927 Proof	66	Value: 650				
1935	704,000	2.00	3.00	5.00	25.00	50.00
1937	1,200,000	1.50	4.00	25.00	150	250
1939	3,700,000	1.50	3.00	10.00	30.00	50.00
1939 Proof	—	Value: 400				
1940	396,000	10.00	25.00	75.00	200	—
1941	1,920,000	1.50	3.50	9.00	20.00	30.00
1942	4,480,000	1.00	2.00	4.00	25.00	40.00
1943	2,800,000	1.00	2.00	5.00	35.00	45.00
1944	1,400,000	1.00	3.00	6.00	18.00	25.00
1946	1,632,000	2.00	4.00	8.00	35.00	50.00
1946 Proof	—	Value: 500				
1947	2,880,000	—	—	—	—	10,000

Note: Only 5 known; The entire issue was to be melted down

KM# 2   2 MILS
7.8000 g., Bronze, 28 mm. **Obv:** Inscription PALESTINE, in English, Hebrew and Arabic **Rev:** Value, plant **Edge:** Plain

Date	Mintage	F	VF	XF	Unc	BU
1927	5,000,000	2.00	3.00	5.00	20.00	30.00
1927 Proof	66	Value: 700				
1941	1,600,000	1.50	3.00	6.00	45.00	—
1941 Proof	—	Value: 400				
1942	2,400,000	1.00	2.50	7.50	25.00	40.00
1945	960,000	2.00	5.00	20.00	150	—
1946	960,000	6.00	15.00	50.00	175	—
1947	480,000					

Note: The entire issue was melted down, but at least one is reported to be in the British Museum's collection

KM# 3   5 MILS
2.9000 g., Copper-Nickel, 20 mm. **Obv:** Wreath around center hole, with enscription PALESTINE in English, Hebrew and Arabic **Rev:** Value above center hole **Edge:** Plain

Date	Mintage	F	VF	XF	Unc	BU
1927	10,000,000	1.00	2.00	5.00	25.00	35.00
1927 Proof	66	Value: 550				
1934	500,000	6.50	12.50	50.00	175	—
1935	2,700,000	1.00	2.00	7.00	40.00	60.00
1939	2,000,000	1.00	2.00	5.00	30.00	45.00
1939 Proof	—	Value: 425				
1941	400,000	10.00	15.00	30.00	125	175
1941 Proof	—	Value: 375				
1946	1,000,000	2.00	4.00	8.00	30.00	45.00
1946 Proof	—	Value: 450				
1947	1,000,000	—	—	—	—	25,000

Note: Almost the entire issue was melted down, with only 3 remaining pieces known to exist

KM# 3a   5 MILS
Bronze, 20 mm. **Obv:** Wreath around center hole, with inscription PALESTINE in English, Hebrew and Arabic **Rev:** Value above center hole **Edge:** Plain

Date	Mintage	F	VF	XF	Unc	BU
1942	2,700,000	—	4.00	10.00	50.00	60.00
1944	1,000,000	2.00	5.00	10.00	50.00	60.00

KM# 4   10 MILS
6.5000 g., Copper-Nickel, 27 mm. **Obv:** Date above and below center hole, with inscription PALESTINE in English, Hebrew and Arabic **Rev:** Wreath around center hole with value above and below **Edge:** Plain

Date	Mintage	F	VF	XF	Unc	BU
1927	5,000,000	2.00	6.50	10.00	45.00	60.00
1927 Proof	66	Value: 575				
1933	500,000	4.00	8.00	75.00	400	—
1933 Proof	—	Value: 350				
1934	500,000	5.00	12.00	60.00	300	—
1934 Proof	—	Value: 375				
1935	1,150,000	3.00	10.00	40.00	250	—
1935 Proof	—	Value: 425				
1937	750,000	3.50	10.00	20.00	175	—
1937 Proof	—	Value: 425				
1939	1,000,000	2.00	6.00	17.00	100	—
1939 Proof	—	Value: 350				
1940	1,500,000	1.50	6.00	18.00	100	—
1940 Proof	—	Value: 100				
1941	400,000	8.00	20.00	50.00	125	200
1941 Proof	—	Value: 350				
1942	600,000	5.00	12.00	25.00	175	—
1946	1,000,000	5.00	18.00	25.00	75.00	—
1946 Proof	—	Value: 300				
1947	1,000,000					

Note: The entire issue was melted down but at least one coin is reported to be in the British Museum's collection

KM# 4a   10 MILS
6.5000 g., Bronze, 27 mm. **Obv:** Date above and below center hole, with inscription PALESTINE in English, Hebrew and Arabic **Rev:** Wreath around center hole with value above and below **Edge:** Plain

Date	Mintage	F	VF	XF	Unc	BU
1942	1,000,000	5.00	8.00	15.00	125	—
1943	1,000,000	8.50	15.00	40.00	180	—

KM# 5   20 MILS
11.3000 g., Copper-Nickel, 30.5 mm. **Obv:** Wreath around center hole with dates below, with inscription PALESTINE in English, Hebrew and Arabic **Rev:** Value above and below center hole **Edge:** Plain

Date	Mintage	F	VF	XF	Unc	BU
1927	1,500,000	10.00	15.00	50.00	120	—
1927 Proof	66	Value: 800				
1933	250,000	20.00	40.00	80.00	400	—
1934	125,000	50.00	80.00	180	750	—
1934 Proof	—	—	—	—	—	—
1935	575,000	15.00	22.00	50.00	300	—
1940	200,000	20.00	40.00	90.00	400	—
1940 Proof	—	Value: 500				
1941	100,000	75.00	110	200	1,000	—
1941 Proof	—	Value: 1,200				

KM# 5a   20 MILS
11.3000 g., Bronze, 30.5 mm. **Obv:** Wreath around center hole with dates below, with inscription PALESTINE in English, Hebrew and Arabic **Rev:** Value above and below center hole **Edge:** Plain

Date	Mintage	F	VF	XF	Unc	BU
1942	1,100,000	15.00	25.00	70.00	250	—
1944	1,000,000	25.00	60.00	200	600	—

KM# 6   50 MILS
5.8319 g., 0.7200 Silver 0.1350 oz. ASW, 23.5 mm. **Obv:** Plant flanked by dates within circle, with inscription PALESTINE in English, Hebrew and Arabic **Rev:** Written and numeric value **Edge:** Reeded

Date	Mintage	F	VF	XF	Unc	BU
1927	8,000,000	8.00	12.00	35.00	80.00	100
1927 Proof	66	Value: 775				
1931	500,000	30.00	60.00	175	500	—
1933	1,000,000	20.00	25.00	50.00	125	—
1934	398,861	30.00	60.00	75.00	180	—
1935	5,600,000	5.00	8.00	12.00	40.00	50.00
1939	3,000,000	6.00	8.00	15.00	40.00	50.00
1939 Proof	—	Value: 275				
1940	2,000,000	8.00	18.00	30.00	75.00	—
1940 Proof	—	Value: 150				
1942	5,000,000	8.00	8.00	15.00	40.00	50.00

KM# 7   100 MILS
11.6638 g., 0.7200 Silver 0.2700 oz. ASW, 29 mm. **Obv:** Plant flanked by dates, with inscription PALESTINE in English, Hebrew and Arabic **Rev:** Value within circle **Edge:** Reeded

Date	Mintage	F	VF	XF	Unc	BU
1927	2,000,000	12.00	25.00	50.00	120	—
1927 Proof	66	Value: 850				
1931	250,000	90.00	150	250	1,000	1,500
1931 Proof	—	Value: 1,400				
1933	500,000	30.00	60.00	150	375	—
1934	200,000	100	150	225	550	—
1935	2,850,000	12.00	15.00	28.00	110	—
1939	1,500,000	10.00	15.00	30.00	135	—
1939 Proof	—	Value: 250				
1940	1,000,000	18.00	30.00	50.00	150	—
1942	2,500,000	15.00	25.00	35.00	120	—

MINT SETS

KM#	Date	Mintage Identification	Issue Price	Mkt Val
MS1	1927 (14)	— KM1-7, two each	—	1,750

PROOF SETS

KM#	Date	Mintage Identification	Issue Price	Mkt Val
PS1	1927 (14)	34 KM1-7, two each, original case	—	8,500
PS2	1927 (7)	4 KM1-7, original case	—	5,000

PANAMA

The Republic of Panama, a Central American Country situated between Costa Rica and Colombia, has an area of 29,762 sq. mi. (78,200 sq. km.) and a population of *2.4 million. Capital: Panama City. The Panama Canal is the country's biggest asset; servicing world related transit trade and international commerce. Bananas, refined petroleum, sugar and shrimp are exported.

Discovered in 1501 by the Spanish conquistador Rodrigo Galvan de Bastidas, the land of Panama was soon explored and after a few attempts at settlement was successfully colonized by the Spanish. It was in Panama in 1513 that Vasco Nunez de Balboa became the first European to see the Pacific Ocean. The first Pacific-coast settlement, founded in 1519 on the site of a village the natives called Panama, was named *Nuestra Senora de la Asuncion de Panama* (Our Lady of the Assumption of Panama). The settlement soon became a city and eventually, albeit briefly, an Audiencia (judicial tribunal).

In 1578 the city of Panama, being a primary transshipment center for treasure and supplies to and from Spain's South Pacific-coast colonies, was chosen for a new mint, and minting had begun there by 1580. By late 1582 or 1583 production was halted, possibly due to the fact that there were no nearby silver mines to sustain it. In it's brief operation, the Panama Mint must not have made many coins, as the corpus of surviving specimens known today from this colonial mint is less than 40.

The city of Panama, known today as the Old City of Panama, was sacked and burned in 1671 by the famous Henry Morgan in one of the greatest pirate victories against the Spanish Main.

Panama declared its independence in 1821 and joined the Confederation of Greater Colombia. In 1903, after Colombia rejected a treaty enabling the United States to build a canal across the Isthmus, Panama with the support of the United States proclaimed its independence from Colombia and became a sovereign republic.

The 1904 2-1/2 centesimos known as the 'Panama Pill' or 'Panama Pearl' is one of the world's smaller silver coins and a favorite with collectors.

MINT MARKS

FM - Franklin Mint, U.S.A.*
CHI in circle - Valcambi Mint, Balerna, Switzerland
RCM – Royal Canadian Mint

*NOTE: From 1975-1985 the Franklin Mint produced coinage in up to 3 different qualities. Qualities of issue are designated in ( ) after each date and are defined as follows:

(M) MATTE - Normal circulation strike or a dull finish produced by sandblasting special uncirculated (polish finish) or proof quality dies.

(U) SPECIAL UNCIRCULATED - Polished or proof-like in appearance without any frosted features.

(P) PROOF - The highest quality obtainable having mirror-like fields and frosted features.

MONETARY SYSTEM

100 Centesimos = 1 Balboa

REPUBLIC
DECIMAL COINAGE

KM# 6   1/2 CENTESIMO
Copper-Nickel, 16 mm. **Obv:** Bust of Balboa left **Rev:** Written value **Note:** Previously listed re-engraved overdates were struck from very common doubled dies. The plain date in unc. is scarcer.

Date	Mintage	F	VF	XF	Unc	BU
1907	1,000,000	1.00	2.00	3.00	12.00	15.00
1907 Proof	—	Value: 200				

KM# 14   CENTESIMO
Bronze, 19.05 mm. **Subject:** Uracca **Obv:** Written value above sprigs **Rev:** Bust with headcovering left

Date	Mintage	F	VF	XF	Unc	BU
1935	200,000	4.50	6.50	15.00	35.00	80.00
1937	200,000	3.50	5.50	12.50	25.00	60.00

KM# 17   CENTESIMO
Bronze, 19.05 mm. **Subject:** 50th Anniversary of the Republic **Obv:** Written value above sprigs **Rev:** Bust of Uracca with headcovering left

Date	Mintage	F	VF	XF	Unc	BU
1953	1,500,000	0.10	0.50	1.00	4.00	7.00

KM# 22   CENTESIMO
3.1000 g., Bronze, 19.05 mm. **Obv:** Written value above sprigs with stars above **Obv. Leg.:** Bust with headcovering left **Note:** Varieties exist.

Date	Mintage	F	VF	XF	Unc	BU
1961	2,500,000	—	0.25	0.50	2.50	5.00
1962	2,000,000	—	0.25	0.50	2.00	5.00
1962 Proof	Est. 50	Value: 200				
1966	3,000,000	—	0.25	0.50	2.00	3.00
1966 Proof	13,000	Value: 1.00				
1967	7,600,000	—	0.25	0.50	2.00	3.00
1967 Proof	20,000	Value: 1.00				
1968	25,000,000	—	0.25	0.50	2.00	3.00

Date	Mintage	F	VF	XF	Unc	BU
1968 Proof	23,000	Value: 3.00				
1969 Proof	14,000	Value: 3.00				
1970 Proof	9,528	Value: 3.00				
1971 Proof	11,000	Value: 3.00				
1972 Proof	13,000	Value: 3.00				
1973 Proof	17,000	Value: 3.00				
1974	Est. 10,000,000	—	0.10	0.30	2.00	3.00

Note: The 1974 circulation coins were stuck at West Point, NY.

Date	Mintage	F	VF	XF	Unc	BU
1974 Proof	Est. 18,000	Value: 3.00				

Note: The 1974 proof coins were struck at San Francisco

Date	Mintage	F	VF	XF	Unc	BU
1975	10,000,000	—	0.15	0.35	2.00	3.00
1977	10,000,000	—	0.15	0.35	2.00	3.00
1978	10,000,000	—	0.15	0.35	2.00	3.00
1979	10,000,000	—	0.15	0.35	2.00	3.00
1980	20,500,000	—	0.15	0.35	2.00	3.00
1982	20,000,000	—	0.25	0.50	2.00	5.00
1983	5,000,000	—	0.25	0.50	2.00	5.00
1983FM (P)	—	Value: 3.00				
1984FM (P)	—	Value: 3.00				
1985FM (P)	—	Value: 3.00				

Note: Unauthorized striking

Date	Mintage	F	VF	XF	Unc	BU
1986	20,000,000	—	0.25	0.50	2.00	4.00
1987	20,000,000	—	0.25	0.50	2.00	4.00

KM# 33.1   CENTESIMO
2.5000 g., Copper Coated Zinc, 19.05 mm. **Obv:** National arms **Rev:** Covered head 1/4 left **Note:** Medal rotation.

Date	Mintage	F	VF	XF	Unc	BU
1975 (RCM)	500,000	—	0.10	0.20	1.00	3.00
1975 (M)	125,000	—	0.10	0.25	1.00	3.00
1975 (U)	1,410	—	—	3.00	5.00	
1975FM (P)	41,000	Value: 3.00				
1976 (RCM)	50,000	—	0.15	0.50	1.50	3.00
1976 (M)	63,000	—	0.15	0.50	1.50	3.00
1976 (U)	12,000	Value: 3.00				
1977	63,000	—	0.15	0.50	1.50	3.00
1977 (U)	9,548	Value: 3.00				
1979 (U)	20,000	—	0.50	1.00	2.00	3.00
1979 (P)	5,949	Value: 3.00				
1980 (U)	40,000	—	0.25	0.50	1.50	3.00
1981 (P)	1,973	Value: 3.00				
1982 (U)	5,000	—	0.75	1.50	3.50	5.00
1982FM (P)	1,480	Value: 3.00				

KM# 33.2   CENTESIMO
2.5000 g., Copper Coated Zinc, 19.05 mm. **Obv:** National arms **Rev:** Covered head of Urraca 1/4 left **Edge:** 1830 BOLIVAR 1980

Date	Mintage	F	VF	XF	Unc	BU
1980FM (P)	2,629	Value: 3.00				

KM# 45   CENTESIMO
2.5000 g., Copper Coated Zinc, 19.05 mm. **Subject:** 75th Anniversary of Independence **Obv:** National coat of arms **Rev:** Covered head 1/4 left **Note:** Medal rotation.

Date	Mintage	F	VF	XF	Unc	BU
1978FM (U)	50,000	—	0.10	0.25	1.00	3.00
1978FM (P)	11,000	Value: 3.00				

KM# 22a   CENTESIMO
2.5000 g., Copper Coated Zinc, 19.05 mm. **Obv:** Value above sprigs with stars above **Rev:** Covered head left

Date	Mintage	F	VF	XF	Unc	BU
1983	45,000,000	—	0.25	1.00	2.00	4.00

KM# 124   CENTESIMO
2.5000 g., Copper Plated Zinc, 19.05 mm. **Obv:** Written value **Rev:** Covered head 1/4 left **Edge:** Plain

Date	Mintage	F	VF	XF	Unc	BU
1991	—	—	—	—	1.00	2.00
1993	30,000,000	—	—	—	1.00	2.00

KM# 125   CENTESIMO
2.4400 g., Copper Plated Zinc, 18.96 mm. **Obv:** Written value **Obv. Leg.:** REPUBLICA DE PANAMA **Rev:** Native Urraca bust left **Edge:** Plain

Date	Mintage	F	VF	XF	Unc	BU
1996RCM	180,000,000	—	—	0.15	0.45	0.60

KM# 132   CENTESIMO
1.6400 g., Aluminum, 22.8 mm. **Series:** F.A.O. **Subject:** XXI Century F.A.O. Food Security **Obv:** National coat of arms **Rev:** Ship in canal **Edge:** Plain **Note:** Medal rotation.

Date	Mintage	F	VF	XF	Unc	BU
2000	—	—	—	—	5.00	10.00

KM# 15   1-1/4 CENTESIMOS
3.1000 g., Bronze **Obv:** Written value **Rev:** Uniformed bust left

Date	Mintage	F	VF	XF	Unc	BU
1940	1,600,000	0.45	1.25	2.50	10.00	15.00

KM# 1   2-1/2 CENTESIMOS
1.2500 g., 0.9000 Silver 0.0362 oz. ASW **Obv:** Uniformed bust left **Rev:** National arms **Note:** This coin is popularly referred to as the "Panama Pill."

Date	Mintage	F	VF	XF	Unc	BU
1904	400,000	9.00	15.00	20.00	27.50	40.00

KM# 7.1   2-1/2 CENTESIMOS
Copper-Nickel **Obv:** National coat of arms **Rev:** Value above stars **Rev. Leg.:** DOS Y MEDIOS

Date	Mintage	F	VF	XF	Unc	BU
1907	800,000	1.25	4.00	18.00	50.00	80.00

KM# 7.2   2-1/2 CENTESIMOS
Copper-Nickel **Obv:** National coat of arms **Rev:** Value above stars **Rev. Leg.:** DOS Y MEDIO

Date	Mintage	F	VF	XF	Unc	BU
1916	800,000	2.50	6.00	35.00	100	150
1918 7 Known	—	—	1,800	3,000	—	—

Note: Unauthorized issue, 1 million pieces were struck and nearly all were melted in June 1918.

KM# 8   2-1/2 CENTESIMOS
3.2700 g., Copper-Nickel **Obv:** Uniformed bust left **Rev:** Written value

Date	Mintage	F	VF	XF	Unc	BU
1929	1,000,000	1.00	3.00	35.00	120	200
1929 Proof	—					

KM# 16 2-1/2 CENTESIMOS
Copper-Nickel **Obv:** Uniformed bust left **Rev:** Written value

Date	Mintage	F	VF	XF	Unc	BU
1940	1,200,000	1.00	1.25	2.50	15.00	25.00

KM# 32 2-1/2 CENTESIMOS
1.6500 g., Copper-Nickel Clad Copper, 15 mm. **Series:** F.A.O. **Obv:** National coat of arms **Rev:** Hand holding leafy plant flanked by stars below

Date	Mintage	F	VF	XF	Unc	BU
1973	2,000,000	—	0.10	0.15	0.25	0.50
1975	1,000,000	—	0.25	0.50	1.00	2.00

KM# 34.1 2-1/2 CENTESIMOS
Copper-Nickel Clad Copper, 10 mm. **Subject:** Victoriano Lorenzo **Obv:** National coat of arms **Rev:** Head facing **Note:** Medal rotation.

Date	Mintage	F	VF	XF	Unc	BU
1975 (RCM)	40,000	—	1.00	2.00	3.00	6.00
1975 (M)	50,000	—	1.00	2.00	3.00	6.00
1975 (U)	1,410	—	1.50	3.00	4.00	6.00
1975FM (P)	41,000	Value: 5.00				
1976 (RCM)	20,000	—	1.00	2.00	3.50	6.00
1976 (M)	25,000	—	1.00	2.00	3.50	6.00
1976FM (P)	24,000	Value: 5.00				
1977 (U)	25,000	—	1.00	2.00	3.50	8.00
1977FM (P)	9,548	Value: 5.00				
1979 (U)	12,000	—	1.00	2.00	3.50	8.00
1979FM (P)	5,949	Value: 5.00				
1980 (U)	40,000	—	0.75	1.00	3.50	8.00
1981FM (P)	1,973	Value: 5.00				
1982FM (U)	2,000	—	2.50	3.50	8.50	10.00
1982FM (P)	1,480	Value: 9.00				

KM# 34.2 2-1/2 CENTESIMOS
Copper-Nickel Clad Copper, 10 mm. **Edge:** 1830 BOLIVAR 1980

Date	Mintage	F	VF	XF	Unc	BU
1980FM (P)	2,629	Value: 8.00				

KM# 46 2-1/2 CENTESIMOS
Copper-Nickel Clad Copper, 10 mm. **Subject:** 75th Anniversary of Independence **Obv:** National coat of arms **Rev:** Head facing **Note:** Medal rotation.

Date	Mintage	F	VF	XF	Unc	BU
1978FM (U)	40,000	—	2.00	2.50	3.50	8.00
1978FM (P)	11,000	Value: 5.00				

KM# 85 2-1/2 CENTESIMOS
Copper-Nickel Clad Copper, 10 mm. **Subject:** Victoriano Lorenzo **Obv:** National coat of arms **Rev:** Head facing

Date	Mintage	F	VF	XF	Unc	BU
1983FM (P)	—	Value: 10.00				
1984FM (P)	—	Value: 18.00				
1985FM (P)	—	Value: 15.00				
Note: Unauthorized striking						

KM# 2 5 CENTESIMOS
2.5000 g., 0.9000 Silver 0.0723 oz. ASW **Obv:** Uniformed bust left **Rev:** National coat of arms

Date	Mintage	F	VF	XF	Unc	BU
1904	1,500,000	4.00	6.00	12.00	35.00	75.00
1904 Proof	12	Value: 1,750				
1916	100,000	90.00	135	195	300	425

KM# 9 5 CENTESIMOS
5.0000 g., Copper-Nickel, 21.2 mm. **Obv:** National coat of arms **Rev:** Numeric value

Date	Mintage	F	VF	XF	Unc	BU
1929	500,000	2.50	6.00	15.00	75.00	100
1932	332,000	3.00	7.00	20.00	100	120

KM# 23.1 5 CENTESIMOS
5.0000 g., Copper-Nickel, 21.2 mm. **Obv:** National coat of arms **Rev:** Numeric value

Date	Mintage	F	VF	XF	Unc	BU
1961	1,000,000	—	0.50	1.00	2.50	5.00

KM# 23.2 5 CENTESIMOS
5.0000 g., Copper-Nickel, 21.2 mm. **Obv:** National coat of arms **Rev:** Numeric value **Note:** The 1962 & 1966 Royal Mint strikes are normally sharper in detail. The stars on the reverse above the eagle are flat while previous dates are raised. Varieties exist.

Date	Mintage	F	VF	XF	Unc	BU
1962	2,600,000	—	0.25	0.50	2.00	5.00
1962 Proof	Est. 25	Value: 350				
1966	4,900,000	—	0.15	0.35	2.00	5.00
1966 Proof	13,000	Value: 2.00				
1967	2,600,000	—	0.25	0.50	2.25	5.00
1967 Proof	20,000	Value: 1.00				
1968	6,000,000	—	0.10	0.20	2.00	5.00
1968 Proof	23,000	Value: 2.00				
1969 Proof	14,000	Value: 2.00				
1970	5,000,000	—	0.10	0.20	2.00	5.00
1970 Proof	9,528	Value: 2.00				
1971 Proof	11,000	Value: 2.00				
1972 Proof	13,000	Value: 2.00				
1973	5,000,000	—	0.10	0.20	2.00	5.00
1973 Proof	17,000	Value: 2.00				
1974 Proof	19,000	Value: 2.00				
1975	5,000,000	—	0.10	0.35	2.50	6.00
1982	8,000,000	—	0.10	0.35	2.50	6.00
1983	7,500,000	—	0.10	0.35	2.50	6.00
1993	6,000,000	—	0.10	0.25	2.00	5.00
1993 Proof	—	Value: 250				
Note: The 1993 proof strike was not authorized by the Panamanian government						

KM# 35.1 5 CENTESIMOS
5.0000 g., Copper-Nickel Clad Copper, 21.2 mm. **Subject:** Carlos J. Finlay **Obv:** National coat of arms **Rev:** Head 1/4 left **Note:** Medal rotation.

Date	Mintage	F	VF	XF	Unc	BU
1975 (RCM)	80,000	—	0.15	0.40	1.00	5.00
1975FM (M)	15,000	—	0.25	0.60	2.00	7.00
1975FM (U)	1,410	—	—	—	2.50	10.00
1975FM (P)	41,000	Value: 2.00				
1976 (RCM)	20,000	—	0.25	0.75	2.00	6.00
1976FM (M)	13,000	—	0.25	0.75	2.00	6.00
1976FM (P)	12,000	Value: 5.00				
1977FM (U)	13,000	—	0.25	0.75	2.00	6.00
1977FM (P)	9,548	Value: 5.00				
1979FM (U)	12,000	—	0.25	0.75	2.00	6.00
1979FM (P)	5,949	Value: 5.00				
1980FM (U)	43,000	—	0.25	0.50	1.50	6.00
1981FM (P)	1,973	Value: 8.00				
1982FM (U)	3,000	—	15.00	20.00	30.00	35.00
1982FM (P)	1,480	Value: 8.00				

KM# 35.2 5 CENTESIMOS
5.0000 g., Copper-Nickel Clad Copper, 21.2 mm. **Obv:** National coat of arms **Rev:** Head 1/4 left **Edge:** 1830 BOLIVAR 1980 **Note:** Medal rotation.

Date	Mintage	F	VF	XF	Unc	BU
1980FM (P)	2,629	Value: 5.00				

KM# 47 5 CENTESIMOS
5.0000 g., Copper-Nickel Clad Copper, 21.2 mm. **Subject:** 75th Anniversary of Independence **Obv:** National coat of arms **Rev:** Head 1/4 left **Note:** Medal rotation.

Date	Mintage	F	VF	XF	Unc	BU
1978FM (U)	30,000	—	0.25	0.50	1.00	5.00
1978FM (P)	11,000	Value: 2.00				

KM# 86 5 CENTESIMOS
5.0000 g., Copper-Nickel Clad Copper, 21.2 mm. **Obv:** National coat of arms **Rev:** Numeric value

Date	Mintage	F	VF	XF	Unc	BU
1983FM (P)	—	Value: 5.00				
1984FM (P)	—	Value: 5.00				
1985FM (P)	—	Value: 7.00				
Note: Unauthorized striking						

KM# 126 5 CENTESIMOS
5.0400 g., Copper-Nickel, 21.2 mm. **Obv:** National coat of arms **Rev. Leg.:** Numeric value **Edge:** Plain

Date	Mintage	F	VF	XF	Unc	BU
1996	4,000,000	—	—	—	0.40	1.00

KM# 3 10 CENTESIMOS
5.0000 g., 0.9000 Silver 0.1447 oz. ASW **Obv:** Armored bust left **Rev:** National coat of arms

Date	Mintage	F	VF	XF	Unc	BU
1904	1,100,000	5.00	12.00	35.00	100	150
1904 Proof	12	Value: 1,750				

KM# 36.1 10 CENTESIMOS
2.2500 g., Copper-Nickel Clad Copper, 17.9 mm. **Subject:** Manuel E. Amador **Obv:** National coat of arms **Rev:** Head 1/4 right **Note:** Medal rotation.

Date	Mintage	F	VF	XF	Unc	BU
1975 (RCM)	50,000	—	0.25	0.50	1.00	5.00
1975FM (M)	13,000	—	0.25	0.50	1.50	6.00
1975FM (U)	1,410	—	—	—	2.50	8.00
1975FM (P)	41,000	Value: 2.00				
1976 (RCM)	20,000	—	0.25	1.00	1.50	5.00
1976FM (M)	6,250	—	1.00	1.50	3.00	8.00
1976FM (P)	12,000	Value: 5.00				
1977FM (U)	6,250	—	1.00	1.50	5.00	10.00
1977FM (P)	9,548	Value: 5.00				
1979FM (U)	10,000	—	0.75	1.25	3.50	10.00
1979FM (P)	5,949	Value: 5.00				
1980FM (U)	40,000	—	0.50	1.00	3.00	6.00
1981FM (P)	1,973	Value: 6.00				
1982FM (U)	2,500	—	1.00	2.00	5.00	12.00
1982FM (P)	1,480	Value: 6.00				

KM# 36.2 10 CENTESIMOS
Copper-Nickel Clad Copper, 17.9 mm. **Obv:** National coat of arms **Rev:** Head 1/4 right **Edge:** 1830 BOLIVAR 1980
Note: Medal rotation.

Date	Mintage	F	VF	XF	Unc	BU
1980 FM (P)	2,629	Value: 12.00				

KM# 48 10 CENTESIMOS
2.2500 g., Copper-Nickel Clad Copper, 17.9 mm. **Subject:** 75th Anniversary of Independence **Obv:** National coat of arms **Rev:** Bust 1/4 right **Note:** Medal rotation.

Date	Mintage	F	VF	XF	Unc	BU
1978 FM (U)	20,000	—	0.25	0.50	1.50	4.00
1978 FM (P)	11,000	Value: 3.00				

KM# 10.1 1/10 BALBOA
2.5000 g., 0.9000 Silver 0.0723 oz. ASW, 17.9 mm. **Obv:** National coat of arms **Rev:** Armored bust left **Note:** High relief.

Date	Mintage	F	VF	XF	Unc	BU
1930	500,000	2.00	4.00	8.00	35.00	60.00
1930 Matte proof	20	—	—	—	1,000	—
1931	200,000	5.00	8.00	25.00	100	125
1932	150,000	6.00	10.00	25.00	100	150
1933	100,000	12.00	30.00	75.00	200	400
1934	75,000	15.00	35.00	75.00	250	400
1947	1,000,000	BV	4.00	7.00	25.00	40.00

KM# 18 1/10 BALBOA
2.5000 g., 0.9000 Silver 0.0723 oz. ASW, 17.9 mm. **Subject:** 50th Anniversary of the Republic **Obv:** National coat of arms **Rev:** Armored bust left

Date	Mintage	F	VF	XF	Unc	BU
1953	3,300,000	—	BV	1.50	6.00	10.00

KM# 24 1/10 BALBOA
2.5000 g., 0.9000 Silver 0.0723 oz. ASW, 17.9 mm. **Obv:** National coat of arms **Rev:** Armored bust left

Date	Mintage	F	VF	XF	Unc	BU
1961	2,500,000	—	BV	1.50	3.50	8.00

KM# 10.2 1/10 BALBOA
2.5000 g., 0.9000 Silver 0.0723 oz. ASW, 17.9 mm. **Obv:** National coat of arms **Rev:** Armored bust left **Note:** Low relief.

Date	Mintage	F	VF	XF	Unc	BU
1962	5,000,000	—	BV	1.25	3.00	8.00
1962 Proof	Est. 25	Value: 500				

KM# 10a 1/10 BALBOA
2.2500 g., Copper-Nickel Clad Copper, 17.9 mm. **Obv:** National coat of arms **Rev:** Armored bust left

Date	Mintage	F	VF	XF	Unc	BU
1966 Type 1	6,955,000	—	0.75	1.00	3.00	3.50

Note: The Type I is similar to the 1962 strike on a thick flan (London) with diamonds on both sides of DE

Date	Mintage	F	VF	XF	Unc	BU
1966 Type 2	1,000,000	—	1.25	3.50	10.00	12.00

Note: The Type II strike similar to the 1947 strikes on a thin flan (U.S.) with elongated diamonds on both sides of DE

Date	Mintage	F	VF	XF	Unc	BU
1966 Proof	13,000	Value: 3.00				

Note: Thick and thin planchets

Date	Mintage	F	VF	XF	Unc	BU
1967 Proof	20,000	Value: 3.00				
1968	5,000,000	—	0.20	0.30	2.50	3.00
1968 Proof	23,000	Value: 2.00				
1969 Proof	14,000	Value: 2.00				
1970	7,500,000	—	0.15	0.25	2.00	2.50
1970 Proof	9,528	Value: 2.00				
1971 Proof	11,000	Value: 2.00				
1972 Proof	13,000	Value: 2.00				
1973	10,000,000	—	0.15	0.20	2.00	3.00
1973 Proof	17,000	Value: 2.00				
1974 Proof	18,000	Value: 2.00				
1975	500,000	—	0.25	0.50	2.50	3.50
1980	5,000,000	—	0.20	0.50	2.25	3.00
1982	7,740,000	—	0.25	0.50	2.00	2.50
1983 (RCM)	7,750,000	—	0.15	0.25	1.75	2.50
1986 (RCM)	1,000,000	—	0.15	0.25	1.50	2.50
1993	7,000,000	—	0.15	0.25	1.00	2.00
1993 Proof	—	Value: 300				

Note: Unauthorized striking

KM# 87 1/10 BALBOA
2.2500 g., Copper-Nickel Clad Copper, 17.9 mm. **Obv:** National coat of arms **Rev:** Armored bust left **Note:** Medal rotation.

Date	Mintage	F	VF	XF	Unc	BU
1983FM (P)	—	Value: 8.00				
1984FM (P)	—	Value: 8.00				
1985FM (P)	—	Value: 10.00				

Note: Unauthorized striking

KM# 127 1/10 BALBOA
2.2800 g., Copper-Nickel Clad Copper, 17.9 mm. **Obv:** National coat of arms **Obv. Leg.:** REPUBLICA DE PANAMA **Rev:** Armored bust of Balboa left **Edge:** Reeded

Date	Mintage	F	VF	XF	Unc	BU
1996RCM	21,000,000	—	—	0.25	0.60	1.00

KM# 4 25 CENTESIMOS
12.5000 g., 0.9000 Silver 0.3617 oz. ASW **Obv:** Armored bust left **Rev:** National coat of arms

Date	Mintage	F	VF	XF	Unc	BU
1904	16,000,000	7.00	20.00	30.00	120	150
1904 Proof	12	Value: 3,000				

KM# 37.1 25 CENTESIMOS
5.6500 g., Copper-Nickel Clad Copper, 24.25 mm. **Obv:** National coat of arms **Rev:** Head 1/4 left **Note:** Medal rotation.

Date	Mintage	F	VF	XF	Unc	BU
1975 (RCM)	40,000	—	0.35	0.50	1.00	5.00
1975FM (M)	5,000	—	1.00	2.00	4.00	8.00
1975FM (U)	1,410	—	—	—	4.00	8.00
1975FM (P)	41,000	Value: 3.00				
1976 (RCM)	12,000	—	0.45	0.60	1.50	5.00
1976FM (M)	2,500	—	0.75	1.50	3.50	8.00
1976FM (P)	12,000	Value: 5.00				
1977FM (U)	2,500	—	0.75	1.50	3.50	8.50
1977FM (P)	9,548	Value: 5.00				
1979FM (U)	4,000	—	1.00	2.00	5.00	9.00
1979FM (P)	5,949	Value: 5.00				
1980FM (U)	4,000	—	1.00	2.00	4.00	10.00
1981FM (P)	1,973	Value: 5.00				
1982FM (U)	2,000	—	1.50	—	5.00	10.00
1982FM (P)	1,480	Value: 5.00				

KM# 37.2 25 CENTESIMOS
5.6500 g., Copper-Nickel Clad Copper, 24.25 mm. **Edge:** 1830 BOLIVAR 1980

Date	Mintage	F	VF	XF	Unc	BU
1980 FM (P)	2,629	Value: 10.00				

KM# 49 25 CENTESIMOS
5.6500 g., Copper-Nickel Clad Copper, 24.25 mm. **Subject:** 75th Anniversary of Independence **Obv:** National coat of arms **Rev:** Head 1/4 left **Note:** Medal rotation.

Date	Mintage	F	VF	XF	Unc	BU
1978 FM (U)	8,000	—	0.75	1.25	2.50	10.00
1978 FM (P)	11,000	Value: 5.00				

KM# 11.1 1/4 BALBOA
6.2500 g., 0.9000 Silver 0.1808 oz. ASW, 24.25 mm. **Obv:** National coat of arms **Rev:** Armored bust left

Date	Mintage	F	VF	XF	Unc	BU
1930	400,000	BV	5.00	25.00	50.00	85.00
1930 Matte proof	20	—	—	—	2,000	—
1931	48,000	18.00	70.00	350	1,100	2,000
1932	126,000	6.00	9.00	75.00	200	300
1933	120,000	5.00	8.00	40.00	275	400
1934	90,000	5.00	9.00	45.00	200	400
1947	700,000	BV	4.00	6.00	35.00	70.00

KM# 19 1/4 BALBOA
6.2500 g., 0.9000 Silver 0.1808 oz. ASW, 24.25 mm. **Obv:** National coat of arms **Rev:** Armored bust left

Date	Mintage	F	VF	XF	Unc	BU
1953	1,200,000	BV	4.00	7.00	15.00	30.00
1953 Proof	Est. 5	Value: 1,350				

KM# 25 1/4 BALBOA
6.2500 g., 0.9000 Silver 0.1808 oz. ASW, 24.25 mm. **Obv:** National coat of arms **Rev:** Armored bust left

Date	Mintage	F	VF	XF	Unc	BU
1961	2,000,000	BV	2.50	3.00	7.00	9.00

KM# 11.2 1/4 BALBOA
6.2500 g., 0.9000 Silver 0.1808 oz. ASW, 24.25 mm. **Obv:** National coat of arms **Rev:** Armored bust left **Note:** Low relief.

Date	Mintage	F	VF	XF	Unc	BU
1962	4,000,000	—	BV	3.00	6.00	9.00
1962 Proof	25	Value: 500				

KM# 11 1/4 BALBOA
5.6500 g., Copper-Nickel Clad Copper, 24.25 mm. **Obv:** National coat of arms **Rev:** Armored bust left **Note:** Varieties exist.

Date	Mintage	F	VF	XF	Unc	BU
1966	7,400,000	—	0.35	0.50	1.50	4.00
1966 Proof	13,000	Value: 5.00				
1967 Proof	20,000	Value: 5.00				
1968	1,200,000	—	0.35	0.60	2.00	5.00
1968 Proof	23,000	Value: 5.00				
1969 Proof	14,000	Value: 5.00				
1970	2,000,000	—	0.35	0.60	1.25	4.00
1970 Proof	9,528	Value: 5.00				
1971 Proof	11,000	Value: 5.00				
1972 Proof	13,000	Value: 5.00				
1973	800,000	—	0.40	1.00	2.00	5.00
1973 Proof	17,000	Value: 5.00				
1974 Proof	18,000	Value: 5.00				
1975	1,500,000	—	0.35	0.50	3.00	7.00
1979	2,000,000	—	0.25	0.50	2.00	3.00
1980	2,000,000	—	0.25	0.50	2.00	3.00
1982	3,000,000	—	0.25	0.50	1.50	2.50
1983 (RCM)	6,000,000	—	0.25	0.50	1.00	2.00
1986 (RCM)	3,000,000	—	0.25	0.50	1.50	2.50
1993	4,000,000	—	0.25	0.50	1.00	2.00
1993 Proof	—	Value: 350				

Note: The 1993 Proof strikes were not authorized by the Panamanian government

KM# 88 1/4 BALBOA
5.6500 g., Copper-Nickel Clad Copper, 24.25 mm. **Obv:** National coat of arms **Rev:** Armored bust left **Note:** Medal rotation

Date	Mintage	F	VF	XF	Unc	BU
1983FM (P)	—	Value: 10.00				
1984FM (P)	—	Value: 10.00				
1985FM (P)	—	Value: 12.00				

Note: Unauthorized striking

KM# 128 1/4 BALBOA
5.6500 g., Copper-Nickel Clad Copper, 24.25 mm. **Obv:** National coat of arms **Obv. Leg.:** REPUBLICA DE PANAMA **Rev:** Armored bust of Balboa left **Edge:** Reeded

Date	Mintage	F	VF	XF	Unc	BU
1996RCM	7,200,000	—	—	0.60	1.00	1.50

KM# 5 50 CENTESIMOS
25.0000 g., 0.9000 Silver 0.7234 oz. ASW **Obv:** Armored bust left **Rev:** National coat of arms

Date	Mintage	F	VF	XF	Unc	BU
1904	1,800,000	32.00	60.00	120	200	300
1904 Proof	12	Value: 6,000				
1905	1,000,000	35.00	80.00	150	350	750

Note: 1,000,000 of both 1904 and 1905 dates were melted in 1931 for the metal to issue 1 Balboa coin at San Francisco Mint

KM# 38.1 50 CENTESIMOS
11.3000 g., Copper-Nickel Clad Copper, 30.6 mm. **Subject:** Fernando de Lesseps **Obv:** National coat of arms **Rev:** Head 1/4 right **Note:** Medal rotation.

Date	Mintage	F	VF	XF	Unc	BU
1975 (RCM)	20,000	—	1.00	1.50	2.50	6.00
1975FM (M)	2,000	—	1.50	3.00	5.00	10.00
1975FM (U)	1,410	—	—	—	7.00	12.00
1975FM (P)	41,000	Value: 8.00				
1976 (RCM)	12,000	—	1.25	2.00	5.00	8.00
1976FM (M)	1,250	—	3.00	6.00	13.00	16.00
1976FM (P)	12,000	Value: 9.00				
1977FM (U)	1,250	—	3.00	6.00	13.00	18.00
1977FM (P)	9,548	Value: 10.00				
1979FM (U)	2,000	—	4.00	6.00	13.00	18.00
1979FM (P)	5,949	Value: 10.00				
1980FM (U)	2,000	—	4.00	6.00	13.00	18.00
1981FM (P)	1,973	Value: 12.00				
1982FM (U)	1,000	—	8.00	12.00	20.00	28.00
1982FM (P)	1,480	Value: 12.00				

Note: (Error) Without edge lettering

KM# 38.2 50 CENTESIMOS
11.3000 g., Copper-Nickel Clad Copper, 30.6 mm. **Obv:** National coat of arms **Rev:** Head 1/4 right **Edge:** 1830 BOLIVAR 1980 **Note:** Medal rotation.

Date	Mintage	F	VF	XF	Unc	BU
1980 FM (P)	2,629	Value: 12.00				
1980 Proof	Inc. above	Value: 135				

Note: (error) without edge lettering

KM# 50 50 CENTESIMOS
11.3000 g., Copper-Nickel Clad Copper, 30.6 mm. **Subject:** 75th Anniversary of Independence **Obv:** National coat of arms **Rev:** Bust 1/4 right **Note:** Medal rotation.

Date	Mintage	F	VF	XF	Unc	BU
1978FM (U)	8,000	—	1.50	3.00	5.00	10.00
1978FM (P)	11,000	Value: 8.00				

KM# 12.1 1/2 BALBOA
12.5000 g., 0.9000 Silver 0.3617 oz. ASW, 30.6 mm. **Obv:** National coat of arms **Rev:** Armored bust left **Note:** High relief.

Date	Mintage	F	VF	XF	Unc	BU
1930	300,000	5.50	10.00	40.00	100	125
1930 Matte proof	20	Value: 2,200				
1932	63,000	9.00	18.00	120	400	750
1933	120,000	7.00	12.00	50.00	300	500
1934	90,000	7.00	10.00	35.00	275	400
1947	450,000	5.00	7.50	12.00	45.00	95.00

KM# 20 1/2 BALBOA
12.5000 g., 0.9000 Silver 0.3617 oz. ASW, 30.6 mm. **Obv:** National coat of arms **Rev:** Armored bust left

Date	Mintage	F	VF	XF	Unc	BU
1953	600,000	—	BV	5.00	15.00	25.00
1953 Proof	Est. 5	Value: 1,850				

KM# 26 1/2 BALBOA
12.5000 g., 0.9000 Silver 0.3617 oz. ASW, 30.6 mm. **Obv:** National coat of arms **Rev:** Armored bust left

Date	Mintage	F	VF	XF	Unc	BU
1961	350,000	BV	5.00	6.50	10.00	18.00

KM# 12.2 1/2 BALBOA
12.5000 g., 0.9000 Silver 0.3617 oz. ASW, 30.6 mm. **Obv:** National coat of arms **Rev:** Armored bust left **Note:** Low relief.

Date	Mintage	F	VF	XF	Unc	BU
1962	700,000	—	BV	6.00	9.00	12.00
1962 Proof	25	Value: 750				

KM# 12a.1 1/2 BALBOA
12.5000 g., 0.4000 Silver Clad 0.1607 oz. ASW, 30.6 mm. **Obv:** National coat of arms **Rev:** Normal helmet **Note:** Varieties exist.

Date	Mintage	F	VF	XF	Unc	BU
1966 (RCM)	1,000,000	—	BV	3.50	5.00	7.00
1966 (RCM) Proof	13,000	Value: 7.00				
1967	300,000	—	BV	3.50	9.00	15.00
1967 Proof	20,000	Value: 6.00				
1968	1,000,000	—	BV	3.50	5.00	7.00
1968 Proof	23,000	Value: 6.00				
1969 Proof	14,000	Value: 6.00				
1970	610,000	—	BV	3.50	6.00	8.00
1970 Proof	9,528	Value: 7.00				
1971 Proof	11,000	Value: 7.00				
1972 Proof	13,000	Value: 7.00				
1993 Proof	—	Value: 450				

Note: The 1993 Proof strike was not authorized by the Panamanian government

KM# 12a.2   1/2 BALBOA
12.5000 g., 0.4000 Silver Clad 0.1607 oz. ASW, 30.6 mm.
Obv: National coat of arms **Rev:** Error: Type II helmet rim incomplete.

Date	Mintage	F	VF	XF	Unc	BU
1966	Inc. above	BV	3.50	7.50	15.00	25.00

KM# 12b   1/2 BALBOA
11.3000 g., Copper-Nickel Clad Copper, 30.6 mm. **Obv:** National coat of arms **Rev:** Armored bust left **Note:** Varieties exist.

Date	Mintage	F	VF	XF	Unc	BU
1973	1,000,000	—	1.00	1.50	3.00	6.00
1973 Proof	17,000	Value: 5.00				
1974 Proof	18,000	Value: 5.00				
1975	1,200,000	—	0.75	1.50	3.00	6.00
1979	1,000,000	—	—	1.00	3.00	6.00
1980	400,000	—	—	1.75	3.50	8.00
1982	400,000	—	—	1.75	3.50	8.00
1983 (RCM)	1,850,000	—	—	1.00	3.00	8.00
1986 (RCM)	200,000	—	2.00	3.00	7.50	10.00
1993	600,000	—	0.75	1.25	3.00	—

KM# 89   1/2 BALBOA
11.3000 g., Copper-Nickel Clad Copper, 30.6 mm. **Obv:** National coat of arms **Rev:** Armored bust left **Note:** Medal rotation.

Date	Mintage	F	VF	XF	Unc	BU
1983FM (P)	—	Value: 10.00				
1984FM (P)	—	Value: 10.00				
1985FM (P)	—	Value: 18.00				

Note: Unauthorized striking

KM# 129   1/2 BALBOA
11.3000 g., Copper-Nickel Clad Copper, 30.54 mm.
Obv: National coat of arms **Obv. Leg.:** REPUBLICA DE PANAMA **Rev:** Armored bust of Balboa left **Edge:** Reeded

Date	Mintage	F	VF	XF	Unc	BU
1996RCM	200,000	—	1.00	2.50	6.00	8.00

KM# 13   BALBOA
26.7300 g., 0.9000 Silver 0.7734 oz. ASW, 38.1 mm.
Subject: Vasco Nunez de Balboa **Obv:** Standing figure with arm on shield **Rev:** Armored bust left

Date	Mintage	F	VF	XF	Unc	BU
1931	200,000	BV	16.00	20.00	75.00	100
1931 Proof	20	Value: 3,000				
1934	225,000	BV	16.00	20.00	60.00	90.00
1947	500,000	BV	10.00	16.00	20.00	25.00

KM# 21   BALBOA
26.7300 g., 0.9000 Silver 0.7734 oz. ASW, 38.1 mm.
Subject: 50th Anniversary of the Republic **Obv:** Standing figure with hand on shield **Rev:** Armored bust left

Date	Mintage	F	VF	XF	Unc	BU
1953	50,000	BV	16.00	20.00	35.00	50.00

KM# 27   BALBOA
26.7300 g., 0.9000 Silver 0.7734 oz. ASW, 38.1 mm.
Obv: National coat of arms **Rev:** Armored bust left **Note:** More than 200,000 of 1966 dates were melted down in 1971 for silver for the 20 Balboas. Varieties exist.

Date	Mintage	F	VF	XF	Unc	BU
1966 (RCM)	300,000	—	—	BV	16.00	18.00
1966 (RCM) Proof	13,000	Value: 22.00				
1967 Proof	20,000	Value: 20.00				
1968 Proof	23,000	Value: 20.00				
1969 Proof	14,000	Value: 20.00				
1970 Proof	13,000	Value: 22.00				
1971 Proof	18,000	Value: 22.00				
1972 Proof	10,081	Value: 24.00				
1973 Proof	30,000	Value: 20.00				
1974 Proof	30,000	Value: 20.00				

KM# 39.1   BALBOA
Copper-Nickel Clad Copper, 38.1 mm. **Obv:** National coat of arms **Rev:** Armored head 1/4 left

Date	Mintage	F	VF	XF	Unc	BU
1975FM (M)	4,035	—	—	—	15.00	25.00
1975FM (U)	1,410	—	—	—	35.00	50.00
1976FM (M)	625	—	—	—	80.00	100
1977FM (U)	625	—	—	—	80.00	100
1979FM (U)	1,000	—	—	—	80.00	100
1980FM (U)	1,000	—	—	—	80.00	100
1982FM (U)	500	—	—	—	100	150

KM# 39.1a   BALBOA
26.7300 g., 0.9250 Silver 0.7949 oz. ASW, 38.1 mm. **Obv:** National coat of arms **Rev:** Armored head 1/4 left **Note:** Medal rotation.

Date	Mintage	F	VF	XF	Unc	BU
1975FM (P)	45,000	Value: 18.00				
1976FM (P)	14,000	Value: 20.00				
1977FM (P)	11,000	Value: 30.00				
1979FM (P)	7,160	Value: 30.00				

KM# 39.1b   BALBOA
20.7400 g., 0.5000 Silver 0.3334 oz. ASW, 38.1 mm.
Obv: National coat of arms **Rev:** Armored head 1/4 left

Date	Mintage	F	VF	XF	Unc	BU
1981FM (P)	2,633	Value: 30.00				
1982FM (P)	1,837	Value: 30.00				

KM# 39.2   BALBOA
Copper-Nickel Clad Copper, 38.1 mm. **Obv:** Erroneous silver content (LEY .925) below arms **Rev:** Armored head 1/4 left

Date	Mintage	F	VF	XF	Unc	BU
1975 (RCM)	10,000	—	—	—	8.00	15.00
1976 (RCM)	12,000	—	—	—	8.00	15.00

KM# 39.4   BALBOA
Copper-Nickel Clad Copper, 38.1 mm. **Obv:** Erroneous silver content (LEY .500) below arms **Rev:** Armored head 1/4 left

Date	Mintage	F	VF	XF	Unc	BU
1982FM (U)	11	—	—	—	500	—

KM# 51   BALBOA
Copper-Nickel Clad Copper, 38.1 mm. **Subject:** 75th Anniversary of Independence **Obv:** National coat of arms **Rev:** Armored head 1/4 left **Note:** Medal rotation.

Date	Mintage	F	VF	XF	Unc	BU
1978FM (U)	4,000	—	—	—	25.00	—

KM# 51a   BALBOA
0.9250 Silver, 38.1 mm. **Obv:** National coat of arms **Rev:** Armored head 1/4 left

Date	Mintage	F	VF	XF	Unc	BU
1978FM (P)	13,000	Value: 30.00				

KM# 39.3   BALBOA
20.7400 g., 0.5000 Silver 0.3334 oz. ASW, 38.1 mm.
Obv: National coat of arms **Rev:** Armored head 1/4 left **Edge:** 1830 BALBOA 1980

Date	Mintage	F	VF	XF	Unc	BU
1980FM (P)	2,629	Value: 30.00				

KM# 76   BALBOA
22.4000 g., Copper Nickel, 37.8 mm. **Subject:** Death of General Omar Torrijos **Obv:** National coat of arms **Rev:** Uniformed bust right

Date	Mintage	F	VF	XF	Unc	BU
1982	200,000	—	—	1.50	9.00	15.00
1982 Proof	50	Value: 250				

Note: Frosted obverse

Date	Mintage	F	VF	XF	Unc	BU
1982 Proof	200	Value: 200				

Note: Frosted obverse and reverse

Date	Mintage	F	VF	XF	Unc	BU
1983	200,000	—	—	2.00	10.00	18.00
1984	200,000	—	—	2.00	10.00	18.00

KM# 90   BALBOA
20.7400 g., 0.5000 Silver 0.3334 oz. ASW, 38.1 mm.
Obv: National coat of arms **Rev:** Armored bust left

Date	Mintage	F	VF	XF	Unc	BU
1983FM (P)	1,602	Value: 40.00				
1984FM (P)	1,044	Value: 50.00				
1985FM (P)	954	Value: 75.00				

KM# 28   5 BALBOAS
35.7000 g., 0.9250 Silver 1.0617 oz. ASW, 39 mm.
Subject: 11th Central American and Caribbean Games
Obv: National coat of arms **Rev:** Discus thrower **Note:** Medal rotation.

Date	Mintage	F	VF	XF	Unc	BU
1970FM	1,647,000	—	BV	15.00	22.50	30.00
1970FM (U)	603,000	—	—	BV	22.50	27.50
1970FM (P)	59,000	Value: 32.00				

KM# 30   5 BALBOAS
35.0000 g., 0.9000 Silver 1.0127 oz. ASW, 38.8 mm.
Subject: F.A.O. **Obv:** National coat of arms **Rev:** Hand holding leafy plant

Date	Mintage	F	VF	XF	Unc	BU
1972	70,000	—	BV	14.00	20.00	25.00
1972 Proof	10,000	Value: 32.00				

KM# 40.1a   5 BALBOAS
35.1200 g., 0.9250 Silver 1.0444 oz. ASW, 39 mm.
Obv: National coat of arms **Rev:** Head facing

Date	Mintage	F	VF	XF	Unc	BU
1975FM (P)	41,000	Value: 25.00				
1976FM (P)	12,000	Value: 27.50				
1977FM (P)	9,548	Value: 30.00				
1979FM (P)	5,949	Value: 35.00				

KM# 40.1b   5 BALBOAS
23.3300 g., 0.5000 Silver 0.3750 oz. ASW, 39 mm. **Obv:** National coat of arms **Rev:** Head facing **Note:** Medal rotation.

Date	Mintage	F	VF	XF	Unc	BU
1981FM (P)	1,973	Value: 45.00				
1982FM (P)	1,480	Value: 50.00				

KM# 40.1   5 BALBOAS
Copper-Nickel Clad Copper, 39 mm. **Subject:** Belisario Porras
Obv: National coat of arms **Rev:** Head facing **Note:** Medal rotation.

Date	Mintage	F	VF	XF	Unc	BU
1975FM (M)	5,125	—	—	—	18.00	25.00
1975FM (U)	1,410	—	—	—	25.00	40.00
1976FM (M)	125	—	—	—	175	200
1977FM (M)	125	—	—	—	175	200
1979FM (U)	1,000	—	—	—	30.00	50.00
1980FM (U)	1,000	—	—	—	30.00	50.00
1982FM (U)	1,200	—	—	—	25.00	50.00

KM# 40.2   5 BALBOAS
Copper-Nickel Clad Copper, 38.8 mm. **Obv:** Erroneous silver content (LEY .925) below arms **Rev:** Head facing

Date	Mintage	F	VF	XF	Unc	BU
1975	4,000	—	—	—	20.00	—
1976	5,000	—	—	—	20.00	—

KM# 40.3   5 BALBOAS
23.3300 g., 0.5000 Silver 0.3750 oz. ASW, 39 mm. **Obv:** National coat of arms **Rev:** Head facing **Edge:** 1830 BALBOA 1980

Date	Mintage	F	VF	XF	Unc	BU
1980FM (P)	2,629	Value: 30.00				

KM# 40.4   5 BALBOAS

KM# 40.4   5 BALBOAS
23.3300 g., 0.5000 Silver 0.3750 oz. ASW, 39 mm. **Obv:** Erroneous silver content (LEY .925) below arms **Rev:** Head facing

Date	Mintage	F	VF	XF	Unc	BU
1982FM (P)	—	Value: 75.00				

KM# 40.5   5 BALBOAS
Copper-Nickel Clad Copper, 39 mm. **Obv:** Erroneous silver content (LEY .500) below arms **Rev:** Head facing

Date	Mintage	F	VF	XF	Unc	BU
1982FM (U)	200	—	—	—	275	325

KM# 52   5 BALBOAS
Copper-Nickel Clad Copper **Subject:** 75th Anniversary of Independence **Obv:** National coat of arms **Rev:** Bust facing

Date	Mintage	F	VF	XF	Unc	BU
1978FM (U)	2,000	—	—	—	25.00	35.00

KM# 52a   5 BALBOAS
35.1200 g., 0.9250 Silver 1.0444 oz. ASW **Obv:** National coat of arms **Rev:** Bust facing

Date	Mintage	F	VF	XF	Unc	BU
1978FM (P)	11,000	Value: 35.00				

KM# 58   5 BALBOAS
35.1200 g., 0.9250 Silver 1.0444 oz. ASW **Subject:** Panama Canal Treaty Implementation **Obv:** National coat of arms **Rev:** Flag

Date	Mintage	F	VF	XF	Unc	BU
1979FM (P)	6,854	Value: 35.00				

KM# 63   5 BALBOAS
24.1100 g., 0.5000 Silver 0.3876 oz. ASW **Subject:** Champions of Boxing **Obv:** National coat of arms **Rev:** Boxer and flag

Date	Mintage	F	VF	XF	Unc	BU
1980 Proof	1,261	Value: 50.00				

KM# 77   5 BALBOAS
24.1600 g., 0.9250 Silver 0.7185 oz. ASW **Subject:** Champions of Soccer **Obv:** National coat of arms **Rev:** Soccer ball and world globe

Date	Mintage	F	VF	XF	Unc	BU
1982 Proof	9,446	Value: 45.00				

KM# 91   5 BALBOAS
23.3300 g., 0.5000 Silver 0.3750 oz. ASW **Obv:** National coat of arms **Rev:** Armored bust left

Date	Mintage	F	VF	XF	Unc	BU
1983FM (P)	1,776	Value: 75.00				
1984FM (P)	889	Value: 85.00				

KM# 104   5 BALBOAS
23.3300 g., 0.5000 Silver 0.3750 oz. ASW **Subject:** Discovery of the Pacific Ocean

Date	Mintage	F	VF	XF	Unc	BU
1985FM (P)	765	Value: 250				

KM# 53   10 BALBOAS
42.4800 g., 0.9250 Silver 1.2633 oz. ASW, 45.6 mm.
Subject: Panama Canal Treaty Ratification **Obv:** National coat of arms **Rev:** Map within circle

Date	Mintage	F	VF	XF	Unc	BU
1978FM (P)	12,000	Value: 35.00				
1978FM (P) FDC	Inc. above	Value: 50.00				

KM# 53a   10 BALBOAS
Nickel, 45.6 mm. **Obv:** National coat of arms **Rev:** Map within circle

Date	Mintage	F	VF	XF	Unc	BU
1978	300,000	—	—	12.00	15.00	20.00

KM# 59   10 BALBOAS
42.4800 g., 0.9250 Silver 1.2633 oz. ASW **Subject:** Panama Canal Treaty Implementation **Obv:** National coat of arms **Rev:** Ship and flag

Date	Mintage	F	VF	XF	Unc	BU
1979FM (P)	7,229	Value: 40.00				

KM# 64   10 BALBOAS
26.5000 g., 0.5000 Silver 0.4260 oz. ASW **Subject:** Balseria Game **Obv:** National coat of arms **Rev:** Dancing figure

Date	Mintage	F	VF	XF	Unc	BU
1980 Proof	1,267				Value: 75.00	

KM# 78   10 BALBOAS
26.5000 g., 0.5000 Silver 0.4260 oz. ASW **Subject:** Champions of Soccer **Obv:** National coat of arms **Rev:** Soccer players

Date	Mintage	F	VF	XF	Unc	BU
1982 Proof	9,076				Value: 50.00	

KM# 79   10 BALBOAS
26.5000 g., 0.5000 Silver 0.4260 oz. ASW **Subject:** International Year of the Child **Obv:** National coat of arms **Rev:** Three dancing figures, 2 emblems on the bottom

Date	Mintage	F	VF	XF	Unc	BU
1982 Proof	8,460				Value: 45.00	

KM# 130   10 BALBOAS
31.0000 g., 0.9250 Silver 0.9219 oz. ASW **Subject:** Panama Canal Transfer **Obv:** Bust left **Rev:** Ship in canal under Panamanian flag

Date	Mintage	F	VF	XF	Unc	BU
1999 Proof	4,500				Value: 45.00	

KM# 29   20 BALBOAS
129.5900 g., 0.9250 Silver 3.8538 oz. ASW, 61 mm.
Subject: 150th Anniversary of Central American Independence
Obv: National coat of arms **Rev:** Head right **Note:** Illustration reduced.

Date	Mintage	F	VF	XF	Unc	BU
1971FM (M)	69,000	—	BV	55.00	85.00	95.00
1971FM (U)	—	—	BV	55.00	90.00	110
1971FM (P)	40,000				Value: 95.00	

KM# 31   20 BALBOAS
129.5900 g., 0.9250 Silver 3.8538 oz. ASW, 61 mm.
Subject: Simon Bolivar **Obv:** National coat of arms **Rev:** Head right

Date	Mintage	F	VF	XF	Unc	BU
1972FM (M)	37,000	—	BV	55.00	80.00	90.00
1972FM (P)	48,000				Value: 80.00	
1973FM (M)	94,000	—	BV	55.00	80.00	90.00
1973FM (P)	74,000				Value: 80.00	
1974FM (M)	99,000	—	BV	55.00	80.00	90.00
1974FM (P)	161,000				Value: 80.00	
1975FM (M)	2,500	—	BV	55.00	85.00	95.00
1975FM (U)	—	—	BV	55.00	100	125
1975FM (P)	62,000				Value: 80.00	
1976FM (M)	22,000				Value: 90.00	
1976FM (M)	2,500	85.00	90.00	100	125	250

Note: A substantial portion of the 1976 mintage was melted.

KM# 44   20 BALBOAS
129.5900 g., 0.9250 Silver 3.8538 oz. ASW, 61 mm.
Subject: Vasco Nunez de Balboa **Obv:** National coat of arms **Rev:** 3/4-length standing armored figure facing left, raised right arm holding sword, left arm a flag **Note:** Illustration reduced.

Date	Mintage	F	VF	XF	Unc	BU
1977FM (U)	2,879	BV	80.00	90.00	110	125
1977FM (P)	24,000				Value: 100	

Date	Mintage	F	VF	XF	Unc	BU
1979FM (U)	2,500	BV	80.00	90.00	110	125
1979FM (P)	13,000				Value: 100	

KM# 54   20 BALBOAS
129.5900 g., 0.9250 Silver 3.8538 oz. ASW, 61 mm. **Subject:** 75th Anniversary of Independence **Obv:** National coat of arms **Rev:** 3/4-length Balboa standing facing left, upraised right arm holding sword, left arm a flag **Note:** Illustration reduced.

Date	Mintage	F	VF	XF	Unc	BU
1978FM (U)	2,500	BV	80.00	90.00	110	125
1978FM (P)	23,000				Value: 95.00	

KM# 65   20 BALBOAS
119.8800 g., 0.5000 Silver 1.9270 oz. ASW, 61 mm.
Subject: Sesquicentenarium - Death of Simon Bolivar
Obv: National coat of arms **Rev:** Armored figure on horse
Note: Illustration reduced.

Date	Mintage	F	VF	XF	Unc	BU
1980FM (U)	1,000	—	—	—	135	150
1980FM (P)	3,714				Value: 135	

KM# 71   20 BALBOAS
118.5700 g., 0.5000 Silver 1.9060 oz. ASW, 61 mm.
Subject: Simon Bolivar, El Libertador **Obv:** National coat of arms **Rev:** Armored figure on rearing horse in center of assorted flags **Note:** Illustration reduced.

Date	Mintage	F	VF	XF	Unc	BU
1981FM (U)	500	—	—	—	200	225
1981FM (P)	3,528				Value: 150	

KM# 72 20 BALBOAS
2.1400 g., 0.5000 Gold 0.0344 oz. AGW **Obv:** National coat of arms **Rev:** Figure of Eight Butterfly

Date	Mintage	F	VF	XF	Unc	BU
1981FM (U)	205	—	—	—	225	250
1981FM (P)	4,445	Value: 100				
1981FM (P) FDC	Inc. above	Value: 120				

KM# 81 20 BALBOAS
2.1400 g., 0.5000 Gold 0.0344 oz. AGW **Obv:** National coat of arms **Rev:** Hummingbird

Date	Mintage	F	VF	XF	Unc	BU
1982FM (U)	140	—	—	—	—	300
1982FM (P)	3,445	Value: 100				
1982FM (P) FDC	Inc. above	Value: 120				

KM# 80 20 BALBOAS
119.8800 g., 0.5000 Silver 1.9270 oz. ASW, 61 mm.
Subject: Balboa - Discoverer of the Pacific **Obv:** National coat of arms **Rev:** Standing armored figures **Note:** Illustration reduced.

Date	Mintage	F	VF	XF	Unc	BU
1982FM (P)	2,352	Value: 180				

KM# 92 20 BALBOAS
2.1400 g., 0.5000 Gold 0.0344 oz. AGW **Obv:** National coat of arms **Rev:** Banded Butterfly fish

Date	Mintage	F	VF	XF	Unc	BU
1983FM (U)	—	—	—	—	—	250
1983FM (P)	1,671	Value: 100				
1983FM (P) FDC	Inc. above	Value: 150				

KM# 93 20 BALBOAS
118.5700 g., 0.5000 Silver 1.9060 oz. ASW, 61 mm.
Subject: 200th Anniversary - Birth of Bolivar **Obv:** National coat of arms **Rev:** 1/2-Length bust left holding scroll

Date	Mintage	F	VF	XF	Unc	BU
1983FM (U)	500	—	—	—	200	—
1983FM (P)	3,186	Value: 80.00				

KM# 97 20 BALBOAS
2.1400 g., 0.5000 Gold 0.0344 oz. AGW **Obv:** National coat of arms **Rev:** Puma

Date	Mintage	F	VF	XF	Unc	BU
1984FM (U)	100	—	—	—	—	750
1984FM (P)	357	Value: 400				
1984FM (P) FDC		Value: 500				

KM# 98 20 BALBOAS
119.8800 g., 0.5000 Silver 1.9270 oz. ASW, 61 mm.
Obv: National coat of arms **Rev:** Balboa and Indian guide
Note: Illustration reduced.

Date	Mintage	F	VF	XF	Unc	BU
1984FM (P)	1,760	Value: 200				

KM# 102 20 BALBOAS
2.1400 g., 0.5000 Gold 0.0344 oz. AGW **Obv:** National coat of arms **Rev:** Harpy Eagle

Date	Mintage	F	VF	XF	Unc	BU
1985FM (P)	817	Value: 250				
1985FM (P) FDC	Inc. above	Value: 275				

KM# 105 20 BALBOAS
119.8800 g., 0.5000 Silver 1.9270 oz. ASW, 61 mm.
Subject: Discovery of the Pacific Ocean **Obv:** National coat of arms **Rev:** Armored head and eagle facing left

Date	Mintage	F	VF	XF	Unc	BU
1985FM (P)	1,402	Value: 200				

KM# 73 50 BALBOAS
5.3700 g., 0.5000 Gold 0.0863 oz. AGW **Subject:** Christmas 1981 **Obv:** National coat of arms **Rev:** Stylized dove flanked by flowers

Date	Mintage	F	VF	XF	Unc	BU
1981FM (U)	154	—	—	—	—	250
1981FM (P)	1,940	Value: 95.00				
1981FM (P) FDC	Inc. above	Value: 110				

KM# 82 50 BALBOAS
5.3700 g., 0.5000 Gold 0.0863 oz. AGW **Subject:** Christmas 1982 **Obv:** National coat of arms **Rev:** Star of Bethlehem flanked by flowers

Date	Mintage	F	VF	XF	Unc	BU
1982FM (U)	60	—	—	—	—	450
1982FM (P)	1,361	Value: 100				
1982FM (P) FDC	Inc. above	Value: 110				

KM# 94 50 BALBOAS
5.3700 g., 0.5000 Gold 0.0863 oz. AGW **Subject:** Christmas 1983 **Obv:** National coat of arms **Rev:** Poinsettia

Date	Mintage	F	VF	XF	Unc	BU
1983FM (U)	—	—	—	—	—	225
1983FM (P)	1,283	Value: 120				
1983FM (P) FDC	Inc. above	Value: 130				

KM# 99 50 BALBOAS
5.3700 g., 0.5000 Gold 0.0863 oz. AGW **Subject:** Peace at Christmas **Obv:** National coat of arms **Rev:** Lion and lamb

Date	Mintage	F	VF	XF	Unc	BU
1984FM (P)	—	Value: 600				
1984FM (P) FDC	—	Value: 750				

KM# 55 75 BALBOAS
10.6000 g., 0.5000 Gold 0.1704 oz. AGW **Subject:** 75th Anniversary of Independence **Obv:** National coat of arms **Rev:** Flag flanked by dates, flowers and stars

Date	Mintage	F	VF	XF	Unc	BU
ND1978FM (U)	410	—	—	—	—	200
ND1978FM (P)	9,161	Value: 170				
1978FM (P) FDC	Inc. above	Value: 180				

KM# 41 100 BALBOAS
8.1600 g., 0.9000 Gold 0.2361 oz. AGW **Subject:** 500th Anniversary - Birth of Balboa **Obv:** National coat of arms **Rev:** Armored head 1/4 left

Date	Mintage	F	VF	XF	Unc	BU
1975FM (U)	44,000	—	—	—	—	230
1975FM (P)	75,000	Value: 235				
1975FM (P) FDC	Inc. above	Value: 245				
1976FM (M)	50	—	—	—	—	600
1976FM (U)	3,013	—	—	—	—	275
1976FM (P)	11,000	Value: 235				
1976FM (P) FDC	Inc. above	Value: 245				
1977FM (M)	50	—	—	—	—	600
1977FM (U)	324	—	—	—	—	300
1977FM (P)	5,092	Value: 235				
1977FM (P) FDC	Inc. above	Value: 245				

KM# 56   100 BALBOAS

8.1600 g., 0.9000 Gold 0.2361 oz. AGW **Subject:** Peace and Progress **Obv:** National coat of arms **Rev:** Dove orchid within circle

Date	Mintage	F	VF	XF	Unc	BU
1978FM (M)	50	—	—	—	—	500
1978FM (U)	300	—	—	—	—	325
1978FM (P)	6,086	Value: 235				
1978FM (P) FDC	Inc. above	Value: 245				

KM# 60   100 BALBOAS

8.1600 g., 0.9000 Gold 0.2361 oz. AGW **Subject:** Pre-Columbian Art - Golden Turtle **Obv:** National coat of arms **Rev:** Stylized turtle

Date	Mintage	F	VF	XF	Unc	BU
1979FM (M)	50	—	—	—	—	400
1979FM (U)	240	—	—	—	—	350
1979FM (P)	4,829	Value: 235				
1979FM (P) FDC	Inc. above	Value: 245				

KM# 66   100 BALBOAS

8.1600 g., 0.9000 Gold 0.2361 oz. AGW **Subject:** Pre-Columbian Art - Golden Condor **Obv:** National coat of arms **Rev:** Stylized condor within circle

Date	Mintage	F	VF	XF	Unc	BU
1980FM (U)	209	—	—	—	—	425
1980FM (P)	2,411	Value: 235				
1980FM (P) FDC	Inc. above	Value: 250				

KM# 67   100 BALBOAS

7.1300 g., 0.5000 Gold 0.1146 oz. AGW **Subject:** Panama Canal Centennial **Obv:** National coat of arms **Rev:** Bust 1/4 left

Date	Mintage	F	VF	XF	Unc	BU
ND (1980)FM (U)	77	—	—	—	—	750
ND (1980)FM (P)	2,468	Value: 135				
ND(1980)FM (P) FDC	Inc. above	Value: 150				

KM# 74   100 BALBOAS

7.1300 g., 0.5000 Gold 0.1146 oz. AGW **Subject:** Pre-Columbian Art **Obv:** National coat of arms **Rev:** Cocle Peoples' Ceremonial Mask

Date	Mintage	F	VF	XF	Unc	BU
1981FM (U)	174	—	—	—	—	475
1981FM (P)	1,841	Value: 180				
1981FM (P) FDC	Inc. above	Value: 195				

KM# 83   100 BALBOAS

7.1300 g., 0.5000 Gold 0.1146 oz. AGW **Subject:** Pre-Columbian Art **Obv:** National coat of arms **Rev:** Native design within quartered circle

Date	Mintage	F	VF	XF	Unc	BU
1982FM (U)	26	—	—	—	—	850
1982FM (P)	578	Value: 225				
1882FM (P) FDC	Inc. above	Value: 300				

KM# 95   100 BALBOAS

7.1300 g., 0.5000 Gold 0.1146 oz. AGW **Subject:** Pre-Columbian Art **Obv:** National coat of arms **Rev:** Cocle style birds

Date	Mintage	F	VF	XF	Unc	BU
1983FM (U)		—	—	—	—	350
1983FM (P)	1,308	Value: 180				
1983FM (P) FDC	Inc. above	Value: 200				

KM# 100   100 BALBOAS

7.1300 g., 0.5000 Gold 0.1146 oz. AGW **Subject:** Pre-Columbian Art **Obv:** National coat of arms **Rev:** Native art

Date	Mintage	F	VF	XF	Unc	BU
1984FM (U)	—	—	—	—	—	400
1984FM (P)	—	Value: 180				
1984FM (P) FDC	—	Value: 200				

KM# 131   100 BALBOAS

8.3000 g., 0.9000 Gold 0.2402 oz. AGW **Subject:** Panama Canal Transfer **Obv:** Bust left **Rev:** Ship in canal under Panamanian flag

Date	Mintage	F	VF	XF	Unc	BU
1999 Proof	1,000	Value: 300				

KM# 43   150 BALBOAS

9.3000 g., 0.9990 Platinum 0.2987 oz. APW **Subject:** 150th Anniversary - Pan Congress **Obv:** National coat of arms **Rev:** Bust left divides dates

Date	Mintage	F	VF	XF	Unc	BU
ND (1976)FM (M)	30	—	—	—	—	950
ND (1976)FM (U)	510	—	—	—	—	610
ND (1976)FM (P)	13,000	Value: 620				
ND(1976)FM (P) FDC	Inc. above	Value: 625				

KM# 68   150 BALBOAS

7.6700 g., 0.5000 Gold 0.1233 oz. AGW **Subject:** Sesqui-centenarium - Death of Simon Bolivar **Obv:** National coat of arms **Rev:** Armored bust 1/4 left

Date	Mintage	F	VF	XF	Unc	BU
ND (1980)FM (U)	169	—	—	—	—	550
ND (1980)FM (P)	1,837	Value: 225				
ND(1980)FM (P) FDC	Inc. above	Value: 250				

KM# 61   200 BALBOAS

9.5000 g., 0.9800 Platinum 0.2993 oz. APW **Subject:** Panama Canal Treaty Implementation **Obv:** National coat of arms **Rev:** Flag above map

Date	Mintage	F	VF	XF	Unc	BU
1979FM (P)	2,178	Value: 620				
1979FM (P) FDC	Inc. above	Value: 625				

KM# 69   200 BALBOAS

9.9300 g., 0.9800 Platinum 0.3129 oz. APW **Subject:** Champions of Boxing **Obv:** National coat of arms **Rev:** Boxer and flag

Date	Mintage	F	VF	XF	Unc	BU
1980 Proof	219	Value: 650				

KM# 42   500 BALBOAS

41.7000 g., 0.9000 Gold 1.2066 oz. AGW **Subject:** 500th Anniversary - Birth of Balboa **Obv:** National coat of arms **Rev:** Kneeling armored figure, sword in left hand, flag in right

Date	Mintage	F	VF	XF	Unc	BU
1975FM (M)	10	—	—	—	—	3,000
1975FM (U)	1,496	—	—	—	—	1,150
1975FM (P)	9,824	Value: 1,175				
1975FM (P) FDC	Inc. above	Value: 1,175				
1976FM (M)	10	—	—	—	—	3,000
1976FM (U)	160	—	—	—	—	1,150
1976FM (P)	2,669	Value: 1,175				
1976FM (P) FDC	Inc. above	Value: 1,175				
1977FM (M)	10	—	—	—	—	2,500
1977FM (U)	59	—	—	—	—	1,500
1977FM (P)	1,980	Value: 1,175				
1977FM (P) FDC	Inc. above	Value: 1,175				

KM# 57   500 BALBOAS

41.7000 g., 0.9000 Gold 1.2066 oz. AGW **Subject:** 30th Anniversary - Organization of American States **Obv:** Coat of arms and value **Rev:** Map of North America and South America in inner circle

Date	Mintage	F	VF	XF	Unc	BU
ND(1978)FM (M)	10	—	—	—	—	2,250
ND(1978)FM (U)	106	—	—	—	—	1,250
ND(1978)FM (P)	2,009	Value: 1,175				
ND(1978)FM (P) FDC	Inc. above	Value: 1,175				

KM# 62   500 BALBOAS
41.7000 g., 0.9000 Gold 1.2066 oz. AGW **Obv:** National coat
of arms **Rev:** Jaguar

Date	Mintage	F	VF	XF	Unc	BU
1979FM (U)	130	—	—	—	—	1,250
1979FM (P)	1,657	Value: 1,175				
1979FM (P) FDC	Inc. above	Value: 1,175				

KM# 70   500 BALBOAS
37.1800 g., 0.5000 Gold 0.5977 oz. AGW **Obv:** National coat
of arms **Rev:** Great egrets

Date	Mintage	F	VF	XF	Unc	BU
1980FM (U)	54	—	—	—	—	1,650
1980FM (P)	612	Value: 700				
1980FM (P) FDC	Inc. above	Value: 800				

KM# 75   500 BALBOAS
37.1800 g., 0.5000 Gold 0.5977 oz. AGW **Obv:** National coat
of arms **Rev:** Sailfish

Date	Mintage	F	VF	XF	Unc	BU
1981FM (U)	41	—	—	—	—	2,000
1981FM (P)	487	Value: 750				
1981FM (P) FDC	Inc. above	Value: 800				

KM# 84   500 BALBOAS
37.1800 g., 0.5000 Gold 0.5977 oz. AGW **Subject:** Death of
General Omar Torrijos **Obv:** National coat of arms
Rev: Uniformed bust right

Date	Mintage	F	VF	XF	Unc	BU
1982FM (U)	97	—	—	—	—	1,400

Date	Mintage	F	VF	XF	Unc	BU
1982FM (P)	398	Value: 800				
1982FM (P) FDC	Inc. above	Value: 950				

KM# 96   500 BALBOAS
37.1800 g., 0.5000 Gold 0.5977 oz. AGW **Obv:** National coat
of arms **Rev:** Owl Butterfly

Date	Mintage	F	VF	XF	Unc	BU
1983FM (U)	73	—	—	—	—	1,250
1983FM (P)	469	Value: 750				
1983FM (P) FDC	Inc. above	Value: 900				

KM# 101   500 BALBOAS
37.1200 g., 0.5000 Gold 0.5967 oz. AGW **Subject:** Golden
Eagle **Obv:** National coat of arms **Rev:** National eagle holding a
ribbon, stars above

Date	Mintage	F	VF	XF	Unc	BU
1984FM (U)	10	—	—	—	—	5,000
1984FM (P)	156	Value: 1,750				
1984FM (P) FDC	Inc. above	Value: 1,800				

KM# 103   500 BALBOAS
37.1800 g., 0.5000 Gold 0.5977 oz. AGW **Subject:** National
Eagle **Obv:** National coat of arms **Rev:** National eagle holding
an ribbon, stars above

Date	Mintage	F	VF	XF	Unc	BU
1985FM (P)	184	Value: 1,600				
1985FM (P) FDC	Inc. above	Value: 1,650				

PATTERNS
Including off metal strikes.

KM#	Date	Mintage	Identification	Mkt Val
Pn1	1904	—	2-1/2 Centesimos. Silver.	1,500
Pn2	1907	—	Half Cent.	3,500
PnA3	1907	—	1/2 Centesimo. Bronze. KM6.	—
Pn3	1907	—	2-1/2 Centesimos. Silver.	—
PnB4	1953	—	Centesimo. Silver. 17a	—
PnC4	1953	—	Centesimo. 0.9000 Gold. 17b	—
PnD4	1953	—	1/10 Balboa. Silver.	—
PnE4	1953	—	1/10 Balboa. 0.9000 Gold. 18a	—
PnF4	1953	—	1/4 Balboa. Silver.	—
PnG4	1953	—	1/4 Balboa. 0.9000 Gold. 19a	—
PnH4	1953	—	1/2 Balboa. Silver.	—
Pnl4	1953	—	1/2 Balboa. 0.9000 Gold. 20a	—
PnA4	1953	—	Centesimo. Copper. KM17	—
Pn4	1986	—	Balboa. Copper-Nickel. Type I.	4,000
Pn5	1986	—	Balboa. Copper Nickel. Type II.	4,000

KM#	Date	Mintage	Identification	Mkt Val
Pn6	1987	—	1/10 Balboa. Copper-Nickel Clad Copper. Similar to KM10a.	1,000
Pn7	1987	—	1/4 Balboa. Copper-Nickel Clad Copper. Similar to KM11a.	1,500
Pn8	1987	—	1/2 Balboa. Copper-Nickel Clad Copper. Similar to KM12.	2,000
Pn9	1988	—	1/10 Balboa. Copper-Nickel. KM24.	—
Pn10	1988	—	1/4 Balboa. Copper-Nickel. KM25.	1,500
Pn11	1988	—	1/2 Balboa. Copper-Nickel. KM26.	2,000

PIEFORTS

KM#	Date	Mintage	Identification	Mkt Val
P1	1982	—	Centesimo. 0.4000 Gold. The 1982 series of 1-50 Centesimos were struck as pieforts in .400 Gold outside the normal minting facility without consent from the National Bank of Panama.	550
P2	1982	—	5 Centesimos. 0.4000 Gold.	650
P3	1982	—	1/10 Balboa. 0.4000 Gold.	750
P4	1982	20	1/4 Balboa. 0.4000 Gold.	950
P5	1982	—	50 Centesimos. 0.4000 Gold.	1,000

TRIAL STRIKES

KM#	Date	Mintage	Identification	Mkt Val
TS1	1982	—	Centesimo. 0.4000 Gold. The 1982 series of 1-50 Centesimos were struck as uniface trial strikes in .400 Gold outside the normal minting facility without consent from the National Bank or authorization from the Government of Panama. Reverse piefort.	250
TS2	1982	—	Centesimo. 0.4000 Gold. Obverse piefort.	250
TS3	1982	—	5 Centesimos. 0.4000 Gold. Reverse piefort	300
TS4	1982	—	5 Centesimos. 0.4000 Gold. Obverse piefort	300
TS5	1982	—	1/10 Balboa. 0.4000 Gold. Reverse piefort	375
TS6	1982	—	1/10 Balboa. 0.4000 Gold. Obverse piefort	375
TS7	1982	—	1/4 Balboa. 0.4000 Gold. Reverse piefort	500
TS8	1982	—	1/4 Balboa. 0.4000 Gold. Obverse piefort	500
TS9	1982	—	50 Centesimos. 0.4000 Gold. Reverse piefort	500
TS10	1982	—	50 Centesimos. 0.4000 Gold. Obverse piefort	500
TS11	ND(1983) FM	—	1/4 Balboa. Copper-Nickel Clad Copper. Obverse, KM#88.	700
TS12	ND(1983) FM	—	1/2 Balboa. Copper-Nickel Clad Copper. Obverse, KM#89.	1,400

MINT SETS

KM#	Date	Mintage Identification	Issue Price	Mkt Val
MS1	1975 (8)	1,410 KM33.1-40.1	25.00	90.00

PROOF SETS

KM#	Date	Mintage Identification	Issue Price	Mkt Val
PS1	1904 (4)	12 KM2-5	—	12,500
PS2	1930 (3)	20 KM10.1-12.1	—	5,200
PS3	1962 (5)	25 KM10.2-12.2, 22, 23.2	—	2,850
PS4	1966 (6)	12,701 KM10a-11a, 12a.1, 22, 23.2, 27	15.25	30.00
PS5	1967 (6)	19,983 KM10a-11a, 12a.1, 22, 23.2, 27	15.25	27.00
PS6	1968 (6)	23,210 KM10a-11a, 12a.1, 22, 23.2, 27	15.25	28.00
PS7	1969 (6)	14,000 KM10a-11a, 12a.1, 22, 23.2, 27	15.25	28.00
PS8	1970 (6)	9,528 KM10a-11a, 12a.1, 22, 23.2, 27	15.25	32.00
PS9	1971 (6)	10,696 KM10a-11a, 12a.1, 22, 23.2, 27	15.25	30.00
PS10	1972 (6)	13,322 KM10a-11a, 12a.1, 22, 23.2, 27	15.25	30.00
PS11	1973 (6)	16,946 KM10a-11a, 12b, 22, 23.2, 27	17.50	24.00
PS12	1974 (6)	17,521 KM10a-11a, 12b, 22, 23.2, 27	17.50	24.00
PS13	1975 (9)	37,041 KM31, 33.1-38.1, 39.1a-40.1a	130	115
PS14	1975 (8)	4,057 KM33.1-38.1, 39.1a-40.1a	50.00	70.00
PS15	1976 (9)	10,610 KM31, 33.1-38.1, 39.1a-40.1a	102	120
PS16	1976 (8)	1,792 KM33.1-38.1, 39.1a-40.1a	50.00	70.00
PS17	1976 (2)	11,479 KM31, 34.1	51.00	75.00
PS18	1977 (9)	8,093 KM33.1-38.1, 39.1a-40.1a, 44	100	135
PS19	1977 (8)	1,455 KM33.1-38.1, 39.1a-40.1a	50.00	100
PS20	1978 (9)	9,667 KM45-50, 51a, 52a, 54	110	140
PS21	1978 (8)	1,122 KM45-50, 51a, 52a	—	100
PS22	1979 (9)	4,974 KM33.1-38.1, 39.1a-40.1a, 44	132	160
PS23	1979 (8)	975 KM33.1-38.1, 39.1a-40.1a	60.00	100
PS24	1979 (2)	1,775 KM58-59	125	80.00
PS25	1980 (9)	1,686 KM33.2-38.2, 39.3-40.3, 65	287	250
PS26	1980 (8)	943 KM33.2-38.2, 39.3-40.3	87.00	170
PS27	1981 (9)	1,279 KM33.1-38.1, 39.1b-40.1b, 71	212	240
PS28	1981 (8)	694 KM33.1-38.1, 39.1b-40.1b	87.00	100
PS29	1982 (9)	746 KM33.1-38.1, 39.1b-40.1b, 80	212	300

KM#	Date	Mintage	Identification	Issue Price	Mkt Val
PS30	1982 (9)	—	Error set; KM33.1-38.1, 39.1b, 40.4, 80	212	275
PS31	1982 (8)	734	KM33.1-38.1, 39.1b, 40.1b	87.00	150
PS32	1982 (8)	—	Error set; KM33.1-38.1, 39.1b, 40.4	—	135
PS33	1983 (9)	—	KM22, 85-91, 93	87.00	180
PS34	1983 (8)	—	KM22, 85-91	—	125
PS35	1984 (9)	—	KM22, 85-91, 98	—	345
PS36	1984 (8)	—	KM22, 85-91	72.00	150
PS37	1985 (8)	765	KM22, 85-90, 104	72.00	300
PS39	1993 (4)	—	KM10a-11a, 12a.1, 23.2	—	1,350

PALO SECO

Palo Seco Leper Colony was established in Balboa, Canal Zone in 1907. It is known today as Palo Seco Hospital. The original issue of tokens totaled $1,800.00 of which $1,492.75 was destroyed on November 28, 1955. The issue was backed by United States Currency and was replaced by United States circulation coinage.

COLONY
LEPROSARIUM TOKEN COINAGE

KM# Tn1   CENT
Brass, 19 mm. **Obv:** Square center hole **Rev:** Square center hole divides values

Date	Mintage	VG	F	VF	XF	Unc
ND(1919)	—	75.00	150	250	—	—

KM# Tn2   5 CENTS
Brass, 21 mm. **Obv:** Square center hole divides legend **Rev:** Square center hole divides values

Date	Mintage	VG	F	VF	XF	Unc
ND(1919)	—	100	175	300	—	—

KM# Tn3   10 CENTS
Aluminum, 18 mm. **Obv:** Center hole divides legend **Rev:** Center hole divides values

Date	Mintage	VG	F	VF	XF	Unc
ND(1919)	—	125	200	400	—	—

KM# Tn4   25 CENTS
Aluminum, 24 mm. **Obv:** Center hole divides legend **Rev:** Center hole divides values

Date	Mintage	VG	F	VF	XF	Unc
ND(1919)	—	150	250	500	—	—

KM# Tn5   50 CENTS
Aluminum, 30.5 mm. **Obv:** Center hole divides legend **Rev:** Center hole divides values

Date	Mintage	VG	F	VF	XF	Unc
ND(1919)	—	400	600	1,000	—	—

KM# Tn6   DOLLAR
Aluminum, 38 mm. **Obv:** Center hole divides legend **Rev:** Center hole divides values

Date	Mintage	VG	F	VF	XF	Unc
ND(1919)	—	600	900	1,500	—	—

PAPUA NEW GUINEA

Papua New Guinea occupies the eastern half of the island of New Guinea. It lies north of Australia near the equator and borders on West Irian. The country, which includes nearby Bismark archipelago, Buka and Bougainville, has an area of 178,260 sq. mi. (461,690 sq. km.) and a population of 3.7 million that is divided into more than 1,000 separate tribes speaking more than 700 mutually unintelligible languages. Capital: Port Moresby. The economy is agricultural, and exports copra, rubber, cocoa, coffee, tea, gold and copper

In 1884 Germany annexed the area known as German New Guinea (also Neu Guinea or Kaiser Wilhelmsland) comprising the northern section of eastern New Guinea, and granted its administration and development to the Neu-Guinea Compagnie. Administration reverted to Germany in 1889 following the failure of the company to exercise adequate administration. While a German protectorate, German New Guinea had an area of 92,159 sq. mi. (238,692 sq. km.) and a population of about 250,000. Capital: Herbertshohe, 1 of 4 capitals of German New Guinea. The seat of government was transferred to Rabaul in 1910. Copra was the chief crop.

Australian troops occupied German New Guinea in Aug. 1914, shortly after Great Britain declared war on Germany. It was mandated to Australia by the League of Nations in 1920, known as the Territory of New Guinea. The territory was invaded and most of it was occupied by Japan in 1942. Following the Japanese surrender, it came under U.N. trusteeship, Dec. 13, 1946, with Australia as the administering power.

The Papua and New Guinea act, 1949, provided for the government of Papua and New Guinea as one administrative unit. On Dec. 1, 1973, Papua New Guinea became self-governing with Australia retaining responsibility for defense and foreign affairs. Full independence was achieved on Sept. 16, 1975. Papua New Guinea is a member of the Commonwealth of Nations. Elizabeth II is Head of State.

MINT MARK
FM - Franklin Mint, U.S.A.
   NOTE: From 1975-1985 the Franklin Mint produced coinage in up to 3 different qualities. Qualities of issue are designated in ( ) after each date and are defined as follows:
   (M) MATTE - Normal circulation strike or a dull finish produced by sandblasting special uncirculated (polish finish) or proof quality dies.
   (U) SPECIAL UNCIRCULATED - Polished or prooflike in appearance without any frosted features.
   (P) PROOF - The highest quality obtainable having mirror-like fields and frosted features.
MONETARY SYSTEM
100 Toea = 1 Kina

CONSTITUTIONAL MONARCHY
Commonwealth of Nations
STANDARD COINAGE

100 Toea = 1 Kina

KM# 1   TOEA
2.0000 g., Bronze, 17.65 mm. **Obv:** National emblem **Rev:** Butterfly and value **Edge:** Plain

Date	Mintage	F	VF	XF	Unc	BU
1975	14,400,000	—	—	0.15	0.35	1.00
1975FM (M)	83,000	—	—	—	0.45	1.00

Date	Mintage	F	VF	XF	Unc	BU
1975FM (U)	4,134	—	—	—	1.00	1.50
1975FM (P)	67,000	Value: 1.00				
1976	25,175,000	—	—	—	0.35	1.00
1976FM (M)	84,000	—	—	—	0.35	1.00
1976FM (U)	976	—	—	—	1.00	1.50
1976FM (P)	16,000	Value: 1.00				
1977FM (M)	84,000	—	—	—	0.35	1.00
1977FM (U)	603	—	—	—	1.50	2.50
1977FM (P)	7,721	Value: 1.25				
1978	—	—	—	—	0.35	1.00
1978FM (M)	83,000	—	—	—	0.35	1.00
1978FM (U)	777	—	—	—	1.00	1.50
1978FM (P)	5,540	Value: 1.50				
1979FM (M)	84,000	—	—	—	0.35	1.00
1979FM (U)	1,366	—	—	—	1.00	1.50
1979FM (P)	2,728	Value: 1.50				
1980FM (U)	1,160	—	—	—	1.00	1.50
1980FM (P)	2,125	Value: 1.50				
1981	—	—	—	—	1.00	1.50
1981FM (P)	10,000	Value: 1.25				
1981FM (M)	—	—	—	—	0.35	1.00
1982FM (M)	—	—	—	—	1.00	1.50
1982FM (P)	—	Value: 2.25				
1983	—	—	—	—	0.45	1.25
1983FM (U)	360	—	—	—	1.00	1.50
1983FM (P)	—	Value: 2.25				
1984	—	—	—	—	0.45	1.25
1984FM (P)	—	Value: 2.25				
1987	—	—	—	—	0.45	1.25
1990	—	—	—	—	0.45	1.25
1995	—	—	—	—	0.45	1.25
1996	—	—	—	—	0.45	1.25

KM# 2   2 TOEA
4.0000 g., Bronze, 21.72 mm. **Obv:** National emblem **Rev:** Lion fish **Edge:** Plain

Date	Mintage	F	VF	XF	Unc	BU
1975	11,400,000	—	—	0.10	0.60	1.00
1975FM (M)	42,000	—	—	—	0.65	1.00
1975FM (U)	4,134	—	—	—	1.00	1.50
1975FM (P)	67,000	Value: 1.50				
1976	15,175,000	—	—	0.10	0.50	1.00
1976FM (M)	42,000	—	—	—	0.50	1.00
1976FM (U)	976	—	—	—	1.00	1.50
1976FM (P)	16,000	Value: 1.50				
1977FM (M)	42,000	—	—	—	0.50	1.00
1977FM (U)	603	—	—	—	1.50	2.50
1977FM (P)	7,721	Value: 1.75				
1978	—	—	—	—	0.50	1.00
1978FM (M)	42,000	—	—	—	0.50	1.00
1978FM (U)	777	—	—	—	1.00	1.50
1978FM (P)	5,540	Value: 1.75				
1979FM (M)	42,000	—	—	—	0.50	1.00
1979FM (U)	1,366	—	—	—	1.00	1.50
1979FM (P)	2,728	Value: 1.75				
1980FM (U)	1,160	—	—	—	1.00	1.50
1980FM (P)	2,125	Value: 1.75				
1981	—	—	—	—	0.50	1.25
1981FM (P)	10,000	Value: 1.50				
1982FM (M)	—	—	—	—	1.00	1.50
1982FM (P)	—	Value: 2.50				
1983	—	—	—	—	0.50	1.25
1983FM (U)	360	—	—	—	1.50	2.50
1983FM (P)	—	Value: 2.50				
1984	—	—	—	—	0.50	1.25
1984 Proof	—	Value: 2.50				
1987	—	—	—	—	0.50	1.25
1990	—	—	—	—	0.50	1.25
1995	—	—	—	—	0.50	1.25
1996	—	—	—	—	0.50	1.25

KM# 3   5 TOEA
3.0000 g., Copper-Nickel, 19.53 mm. **Obv:** National emblem **Rev:** Plateless turtle

Date	Mintage	F	VF	XF	Unc	BU
1975	11,000,000	—	0.15	0.25	0.75	2.00
1975FM (M)	17,000	—	—	—	0.75	2.00
1975FM (U)	4,134	—	—	—	1.25	3.00
1975FM (P)	67,000	Value: 2.00				
1976	24,000,000	—	0.15	0.25	0.75	2.00
1976FM (M)	17,000	—	—	—	0.75	3.00
1976FM (U)	976	—	—	—	1.25	3.00
1976FM (P)	16,000	Value: 2.00				
1977FM (M)	17,000	—	—	—	0.75	2.00
1977FM (U)	603	—	—	—	1.75	3.00

Date	Mintage	F	VF	XF	Unc	BU
1977FM (P)	7,721	Value: 2.25				
1978	2,000	—	—	—	2.50	3.00
1978FM (M)	17,000	—	—	—	0.75	2.00
1978FM (U)	777	—	—	—	1.25	3.00
1978FM (P)	5,540	Value: 2.25				
1979	—	—	—	—	0.75	2.00
1979FM (M)	17,000	—	—	—	0.75	2.00
1979FM (U)	1,366	—	—	—	1.25	2.00
1979FM (P)	2,728	Value: 2.25				
1980FM (U)	1,160	—	—	—	1.25	2.00
1980FM (P)	2,125	Value: 2.25				
1981FM (P)	10,000	Value: 2.00				
1982	—	—	—	—	0.75	2.00
1982FM (M)	—	—	—	—	1.25	2.00
1982FM (P)	—	Value: 3.00				
1983FM (U)	360	—	—	—	2.25	5.00
1983FM (P)	—	Value: 3.00				
1984	—	—	—	—	0.75	2.00
1984FM (P)	—	Value: 3.00				
1987	—	—	—	—	0.75	2.00
1990	—	—	—	—	0.75	2.00
1995	—	—	—	—	0.75	2.00
1996	—	—	—	—	0.75	2.00
1998	—	—	—	—	0.75	2.00
1999	—	—	—	—	0.75	2.00

Date	Mintage	F	VF	XF	Unc	BU
1980FM (P)	2,125	Value: 3.00				
1981	—	—	0.25	0.50	1.25	1.50
1981FM (P)	10,000	Value: 2.50				
1982FM (M)	—	—	—	—	2.00	2.25
1982FM (P)	—	Value: 4.00				
1983FM (U)	360	—	—	—	3.00	3.50
1983FM (P)	—	Value: 4.00				
1984	—	—	0.25	0.50	1.25	1.50
1984FM (P)	—	Value: 4.00				
1987	—	—	0.25	0.50	1.25	1.50
1990	—	—	0.25	0.50	1.25	1.50
1995	—	—	0.25	0.50	1.25	1.50
1998	—	—	0.25	0.50	1.25	1.50
1999	—	—	0.25	0.50	1.25	1.50

Date	Mintage	F	VF	XF	Unc	BU
1978FM (P)	5,540	Value: 5.00				
1979FM (M)	829	—	—	—	8.50	9.50
1979FM (U)	1,366	—	—	—	3.50	6.50
1979FM (P)	2,728	Value: 6.00				
1980FM (U)	1,160	—	—	—	3.50	6.50
1980FM (U)	2,125	Value: 5.00				
1981FM (P)	10,000	Value: 5.00				
1982FM (M)	—	—	—	—	3.50	6.50
1982FM (P)	—	Value: 7.50				
1983FM (U)	360	—	—	—	14.50	15.50
1983FM (P)	—	Value: 7.00				
1984FM (P)	—	Value: 7.00				
1995	—	—	—	—	3.50	6.00
1996	—	—	—	—	3.50	6.00
1998	—	—	—	—	3.50	6.00
1999	—	—	—	—	3.50	6.00

KM# 4 10 TOEA

5.6700 g., Copper-Nickel, 23.72 mm. **Obv:** National emblem
Rev: Cuscus and value **Edge:** Reeded

Date	Mintage	F	VF	XF	Unc	BU
1975	8,600,000	—	0.20	0.35	0.65	1.50
1975FM (M)	8,300	—	—	—	1.00	1.75
1975FM (U)	4,134	—	—	—	1.50	2.00
1975FM (P)	67,000	Value: 2.00				
1976	—	—	0.20	0.35	0.65	1.50
1976FM (M)	8,300	—	—	—	1.00	1.75
1976FM (U)	976	—	—	—	1.50	2.00
1976FM (P)	16,000	Value: 2.00				
1977FM (M)	8,300	—	—	—	1.00	1.75
1977FM (U)	603	—	—	—	2.25	2.75
1977FM (P)	7,721	Value: 2.50				
1978FM (M)	8,300	—	—	—	1.00	1.75
1978FM (U)	777	—	—	—	1.50	2.00
1978FM (P)	5,540	Value: 2.75				
1979FM (M)	8,300	—	—	—	1.00	1.75
1979FM (U)	1,366	—	—	—	1.50	2.00
1979FM (P)	2,728	Value: 2.75				
1980FM (U)	1,160	—	—	—	1.50	2.00
1980FM (P)	2,125	Value: 2.75				
1981FM (P)	10,000	Value: 2.75				
1982FM (M)	—	—	—	—	1.50	2.00
1982FM (P)	—	Value: 3.50				
1983FM (U)	360	—	—	—	2.50	3.00
1983FM (P)	—	Value: 3.50				
1984FM (P)	—	Value: 3.50				
1995	—	—	—	0.60	1.50	2.00
1996	—	—	—	0.60	1.50	2.00
1999	—	—	—	0.60	1.50	2.00

KM# 15 50 TOEA

Copper-Nickel **Subject:** South Pacific Festival of Arts
Obv: National emblem **Rev:** Design divides circles

Date	Mintage	F	VF	XF	Unc	BU
1980	—	—	0.75	1.25	2.50	—
1980FM (U)	1,160	—	—	—	10.00	—
1980FM (P)	2,125	Value: 6.50				

KM# 31 50 TOEA

Copper-Nickel **Subject:** 9th South Pacific Games **Obv:** National emblem **Rev:** Games emblem

Date	Mintage	F	VF	XF	Unc	BU
1991	25,000	—	—	—	4.00	—

KM# 7 5 KINA

Copper-Nickel, 40 mm. **Obv:** National emblem **Rev:** New Guinea eagle

Date	Mintage	F	VF	XF	Unc	BU
1975FM (M)	166	—	—	—	32.00	—
1975FM (U)	4,134	—	—	—	6.50	—
1976FM (M)	166	—	—	—	32.00	—
1976FM (U)	976	—	—	—	8.50	—
1977FM (M)	166	—	—	—	32.00	—
1977FM (U)	603	—	—	—	18.00	—
1978FM (M)	166	—	—	—	32.00	—
1978FM (U)	777	—	—	—	10.00	—
1979FM (M)	166	—	—	—	32.00	—
1979FM (U)	1,366	—	—	—	7.50	—
1980FM (U)	1,160	—	—	—	7.50	—

KM# 7a 5 KINA

27.6000 g., 0.5000 Silver 0.4437 oz. ASW, 40 mm.
Obv: National emblem **Rev:** New Guinea eagle

Date	Mintage	F	VF	XF	Unc	BU
1975FM (P)	67,000	Value: 8.50				
1976FM (P)	16,000	Value: 8.50				
1977FM (P)	7,721	Value: 8.00				
1978FM (P)	5,540	Value: 8.00				
1979FM (P)	2,728	Value: 8.50				
1980FM (P)	2,125	Value: 9.00				

KM# 5 20 TOEA

11.3000 g., Copper-Nickel, 28.65 mm. **Obv:** National emblem
Rev: Bennett's Cassowary and value

Date	Mintage	F	VF	XF	Unc	BU
1975	15,500,000	—	0.30	0.65	1.25	1.75
1975FM (M)	4,150	—	—	—	1.50	2.00
1975FM (U)	4,134	—	—	—	1.50	2.00
1975FM (P)	67,000	Value: 2.50				
1976FM (M)	4,150	—	—	—	1.50	2.00
1976FM (U)	976	—	—	—	1.75	2.25
1976FM (P)	16,000	Value: 2.50				
1977FM (M)	4,150	—	—	—	1.75	2.25
1977FM (U)	603	—	—	—	2.25	2.75
1977FM (P)	7,721	Value: 3.00				
1978	2,500,000	—	0.35	0.70	1.25	1.75
1978FM (M)	4,150	—	—	—	1.50	2.00
1978FM (U)	777	—	—	—	1.75	2.25
1978FM (P)	5,540	Value: 3.00				
1979FM (M)	4,150	—	—	—	1.50	2.00
1979FM (U)	1,366	—	—	—	1.75	2.25
1979FM (P)	2,728	Value: 3.00				
1980FM (U)	1,160	—	—	—	1.75	2.25

KM# 41 50 TOEA

13.6300 g., Copper-Nickel, 30 mm. **Subject:** Silver Jubilee of Bank
Obv: National emblem **Rev:** Symbolic design **Edge:** Reeded

Date	Mintage	F	VF	XF	Unc	BU
1998	—	—	—	—	4.50	—

KM# 6 KINA

Copper-Nickel, 33 mm. **Obv:** Symbolic design around center hole **Rev:** Crocodiles flank center hole

Date	Mintage	F	VF	XF	Unc	BU
1975	2,000,000	—	1.35	2.00	3.50	7.50
1975FM (U)	4,134	—	—	—	3.50	7.50
1975FM (M)	829	—	—	—	8.50	9.50
1975FM (P)	67,000	Value: 5.00				
1976FM (U)	829	—	—	—	8.50	9.50
1976FM (U)	976	—	—	—	3.50	7.50
1976FM (P)	16,000	Value: 5.00				
1977FM (M)	829	—	—	—	8.50	9.50
1977FM (U)	603	—	—	—	12.50	13.50
1977FM (P)	7,721	Value: 6.00				
1978FM (M)	829	—	—	—	8.50	9.50
1978FM (U)	777	—	—	—	3.50	6.00

KM# 18 5 KINA

28.2800 g., 0.5000 Silver 0.4546 oz. ASW **Series:** International Year of the Child **Obv:** National emblem **Rev:** Kneeling figure holding fish

Date	Mintage	F	VF	XF	Unc	BU
1981	8,775	—	—	—	10.00	12.00

KM# 20 5 KINA
Copper-Nickel, 40 mm. **Subject:** Defense of the Kokoda Trail **Obv:** National emblem **Rev:** Standing figures

Date	Mintage	F	VF	XF	Unc	BU
1982FM (M)	—	—	—	—	3.50	—

KM# 20a 5 KINA
28.2800 g., 0.9250 Silver 0.8410 oz. ASW, 40 mm. **Subject:** Defense of the Kokoda Trail **Obv:** National emblem **Rev:** Standing figures

Date	Mintage	F	VF	XF	Unc	BU
1982FM (P)	1,795	Value: 17.50				

KM# 23 5 KINA
Copper-Nickel, 40 mm. **Subject:** 10th Anniversary - Bank of Papua New Guinea **Obv:** National emblem **Rev:** Bank divides symbolic design above and value below

Date	Mintage	F	VF	XF	Unc	BU
1983FM (U)	360	—	—	—	7.50	—

KM# 23a 5 KINA
28.2800 g., 0.9250 Silver 0.8410 oz. ASW, 40 mm. **Subject:** 10th Anniversary - Bank of Papua New Guinea **Obv:** National emblem **Rev:** Bank divides symbolic design above and value below

Date	Mintage	F	VF	XF	Unc	BU
1983FM (P)	673	Value: 20.00				

KM# 25 5 KINA
28.2800 g., 0.9250 Silver 0.8410 oz. ASW, 40 mm. **Subject:** New Parliament Building **Obv:** National emblem **Rev:** Building **Note:** Prev. KM#25a.

Date	Mintage	F	VF	XF	Unc	BU
1984FM (P) Proof	—	Value: 18.50				

KM# 28 5 KINA
28.2800 g., 0.9250 Silver 0.8410 oz. ASW **Series:** Decade for Women **Obv:** National emblem **Rev:** Half-figure picking berries off branch

Date	Mintage	F	VF	XF	Unc	BU
1984FM Proof	1,050	Value: 17.50				

KM# 34 5 KINA
23.3300 g., 0.9250 Silver 0.6938 oz. ASW **Obv:** National emblem **Rev:** Queen Alexandra butterfly (o. alexandrae)

Date	Mintage	F	VF	XF	Unc	BU
1992FM	500	—	—	—	50.00	—
1992FM (P)	—	Value: 80.00				

KM# 37 5 KINA
27.7800 g., 0.9000 Silver 0.8038 oz. ASW **Subject:** Centennial of First Coinage **Obv:** National emblem within sprigs **Rev:** Raggiana Bird of Paradise

Date	Mintage	F	VF	XF	Unc	BU
ND(1994) Proof	7,500	Value: 35.00				

KM# 39 5 KINA
31.4700 g., 0.9250 Silver 0.9359 oz. ASW **Series:** Endangered Wildlife **Obv:** National emblem **Rev:** Two Ribbon Sweetlips fish

Date	Mintage	F	VF	XF	Unc	BU
1997 Proof	10,000	Value: 30.00				

KM# 43 5 KINA
31.5000 g., 0.9250 Silver 0.9368 oz. ASW, 38.6 mm. **Obv:** National emblem **Rev:** Sailing ship **Edge:** Reeded

Date	Mintage	F	VF	XF	Unc	BU
1997 Proof	—	Value: 20.00				

KM# 44 5 KINA
31.4300 g., 0.9250 Silver 0.9347 oz. ASW, 38.6 mm. **Subject:** Green Tree Python **Obv:** National emblem **Rev:** Snake in tree **Edge:** Reeded

Date	Mintage	F	VF	XF	Unc	BU
1997	—					
1998 Proof	—	Value: 50.00				

KM# 47 5 KINA
31.3500 g., 0.9250 Silver 0.9323 oz. ASW, 38.6 mm. **Subject:** British Queen Mother **Obv:** National emblem **Rev:** Cameo above Sandringham Palace **Edge:** Reeded

Date	Mintage	F	VF	XF	Unc	BU
1997 Proof	—	Value: 20.00				

KM# 40 5 KINA
20.0000 g., 0.9000 Silver 0.5787 oz. ASW **Series:** Olympic Games 2000 **Obv:** National emblem **Rev:** Sailboarder

Date	Mintage	F	VF	XF	Unc	BU
1997 Proof	—	Value: 14.50				

KM# 45 5 KINA
31.8500 g., 0.9250 Silver 0.9472 oz. ASW, 38.6 mm. **Subject:** Queen Mother **Obv:** National emblem **Rev:** Investiture of Prince Charles **Edge:** Reeded

Date	Mintage	F	VF	XF	Unc	BU
1998 Proof	—	Value: 20.00				

KM# 48 5 KINA
31.5300 g., 0.9250 Silver 0.9376 oz. ASW, 38.6 mm. **Subject:** Princess Diana **Obv:** National emblem **Rev:** Diana and Bishop Tutu **Edge:** Reeded

Date	Mintage	F	VF	XF	Unc	BU
1998 Proof	—	Value: 25.00				

KM# 8 10 KINA
Copper-Nickel, 45 mm. **Obv:** National emblem **Rev:** Raggiana Bird of Paradise

Date	Mintage	F	VF	XF	Unc	BU
1975FM (M)	82	—	—	—	60.00	—
1975FM (U)	4,134	—	—	—	10.00	—
1976FM (M)	82	—	—	—	60.00	—
1976FM (U)	976	—	—	—	12.00	—
1978FM (M)	168	—	—	—	50.00	—
1978FM (U)	777	—	—	—	15.00	—
1979FM (M)	82	—	—	—	60.00	—
1979FM (U)	1,366	—	—	—	10.00	—

Date	Mintage	F	VF	XF	Unc	BU
1980FM (U)	776	—	—	—	12.50	—
1983FM (U)	360	—	—	—	15.00	—

KM# 8a 10 KINA
41.6000 g., 0.9250 Silver 1.2371 oz. ASW, 45 mm.
Obv: National emblem **Rev:** Raggiana Bird of Paradise

Date	Mintage	F	VF	XF	Unc	BU
1975FM (P)	79,000	Value: 25.00				
1976FM (P)	21,000	Value: 25.00				
1978FM (P)	7,352	Value: 25.00				
1979FM (P)	4,147	Value: 25.00				
1980FM (P)	2,752	Value: 28.00				
1983FM (P)	1,025	Value: 28.00				

KM# 8a.1 10 KINA
40.6000 g., 0.9250 Silver 1.2074 oz. ASW, 42 mm.
Subject: Reduced size **Obv:** National emblem **Rev:** Raggiana Bird of Paradise **Edge:** Reeded

Date	Mintage	F	VF	XF	Unc	BU
1983FM Proof	1,025	Value: 32.50				

KM# 11 10 KINA
Copper-Nickel, 45 mm. **Subject:** Silver Jubilee of Queen Elizabeth II **Obv:** National emblem **Rev:** Young bust right

Date	Mintage	F	VF	XF	Unc	BU
1977FM (M)	82	—	—	—	50.00	—
1977FM (U)	603	—	—	—	15.00	—

KM# 11a 10 KINA
40.0000 g., 0.9250 Silver 1.1895 oz. ASW, 45 mm.
Subject: Silver Jubilee of Queen Elizabeth II **Obv:** National emblem **Rev:** Young bust right

Date	Mintage	F	VF	XF	Unc	BU
1977FM (P)	14,000	Value: 25.00				

KM# 21 10 KINA
Copper-Nickel, 45 mm. **Subject:** Royal visit **Obv:** National emblem **Rev:** Conjoined heads right

Date	Mintage	F	VF	XF	Unc	BU
1982FM (M)	—	—	—	—	6.50	—

KM# 21a 10 KINA
40.5000 g., 0.9250 Silver 1.2044 oz. ASW, 45 mm.
Subject: Royal visit **Obv:** National emblem **Rev:** Conjoined heads right

Date	Mintage	F	VF	XF	Unc	BU
1982FM (P)	1,185	Value: 27.50				

KM# 26 10 KINA
35.6000 g., 0.9250 Silver 1.0587 oz. ASW **Subject:** Papal visit **Obv:** National emblem **Rev:** Pope with arms outstretched with national arms above **Note:** Prev. KM#26a.

Date	Mintage	F	VF	XF	Unc	BU
1984FM (P)	597	Value: 30.00				

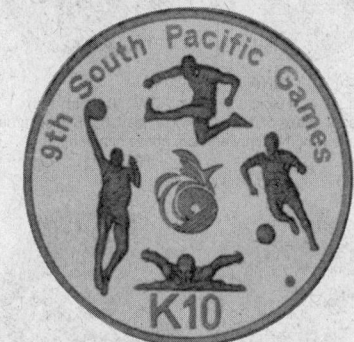

KM# 30 10 KINA
42.1200 g., 0.9250 Silver 1.2526 oz. ASW **Subject:** 9th South Pacific Games **Obv:** National emblem **Rev:** Assorted olympic athletes around emblem

Date	Mintage	F	VF	XF	Unc	BU
1991 Proof	1,971	Value: 30.00				

KM# 33 10 KINA
1.5710 g., 0.9990 Gold 0.0505 oz. AGW **Obv:** National emblem **Rev:** Butterfly

Date	Mintage	F	VF	XF	Unc	BU
1992 Proof	—	Value: 60.00				

KM# 33a 10 KINA
1.5710 g., 0.9950 Platinum 0.0503 oz. APW **Obv:** National emblem **Rev:** Butterfly

Date	Mintage	F	VF	XF	Unc	BU
1992 Proof	—	Value: 100				

KM# 46 10 KINA
155.5000 g., 0.9990 Silver 4.9942 oz. ASW, 64.9 mm.
Subject: Queen Mother **Obv:** National emblem **Rev:** Queen Mary with the Duchess of York **Edge:** Reeded **Note:** Illustration reduced.

Date	Mintage	F	VF	XF	Unc	BU
1998 Proof	3,000	Value: 110				

KM# 36 25 KINA
136.0000 g., 0.9250 Silver And Enamel 4.0444 oz., 63 mm.
Obv: National emblem within wreath **Rev:** Raggiana Bird of Paradise **Note:** Illustration reduced.

Date	Mintage	F	VF	XF	Unc	BU
ND(1994) Proof	1,000	Value: 145				

KM# 42 50 KINA
6.2200 g., 0.9000 Gold 0.1800 oz. AGW, 21.9 mm. **Obv:** Crowned head right **Rev:** Golden butterfly and value **Edge:** Reeded

Date	Mintage	F	VF	XF	Unc	BU
1993 Proof	—	Value: 185				

KM# 38 50 KINA
7.9700 g., 0.9000 Gold 0.2306 oz. AGW **Subject:** Centennial of First Coinage **Obv:** National emblem within wreath **Rev:** Bird of Paradise **Note:** Similar to 5 Kina, KM#37.

Date	Mintage	F	VF	XF	Unc	BU
1994 Proof-like	100	—	—	—	—	235
1994 Proof	1,500	Value: 240				

KM# 9 100 KINA
9.5700 g., 0.9000 Gold 0.2769 oz. AGW **Subject:** Independence **Obv:** Head 3/4 left **Rev:** Bird of paradise

Date	Mintage	F	VF	XF	Unc	BU
1975FM (M)	100	—	—	—	—	—
1975FM (U)	8,081	—	—	—	—	—
1975FM (P)	18,000	Value: 280				

KM# 10 100 KINA
9.5700 g., 0.9000 Gold 0.2769 oz. AGW **Subject:** 1st Anniversary of Independence **Obv:** Symbolic design around center hole **Rev:** National emblem above circular designs around center hole

Date	Mintage	F	VF	XF	Unc	BU
1976FM (M)	100	—	—	—	—	—
1976FM (U)	250	—	—	—	—	—
1976FM (P)	8,020	Value: 280				

KM# 12 100 KINA
9.5700 g., 0.9000 Gold 0.2769 oz. AGW **Obv:** National emblem **Rev:** Papuan hornbill

Date	Mintage	F	VF	XF	Unc	BU
1977FM (M)	100	—	—	—	—	—
1977FM (U)	362	—	—	—	—	—
1977FM (P)	3,460	Value: 280				

KM# 13 100 KINA
9.5700 g., 0.9000 Gold 0.2769 oz. AGW **Obv:** National emblem **Rev:** Bird-wing butterfly

Date	Mintage	F	VF	XF	Unc	BU
1978FM (U)	400	—	—	—	—	—
1978FM (P)	4,751	Value: 280				

KM# 14 100 KINA
9.5700 g., 0.9000 Gold 0.2769 oz. AGW **Obv:** National emblem **Rev:** Four Faces of the Nation

Date	Mintage	F	VF	XF	Unc	BU
1979FM (M)	102	—	—	—	—	—
1979FM (U)	286	—	—	—	—	—
1979FM (P)	3,492	Value: 280				

KM# 16 100 KINA
7.8300 g., 0.5000 Gold 0.1259 oz. AGW **Subject:** South Pacific Festival of Arts **Obv:** National emblem **Rev:** Design divides circle

Date	Mintage	F	VF	XF	Unc	BU
1980 Proof	7,500	Value: 130				

KM# 17 100 KINA
9.5700 g., 0.9000 Gold 0.2769 oz. AGW **Subject:** 5th Anniversary of Independence **Obv:** National emblem **Rev:** Map and flag

Date	Mintage	F	VF	XF	Unc	BU
1980FM (M)	30	—	—	—	—	345
1980FM (P)	1,118	Value: 280				

KM# 19 100 KINA
9.5700 g., 0.9000 Gold 0.2769 oz. AGW **Obv:** Head 1/4 left **Rev:** Bird of paradise and stars

Date	Mintage	F	VF	XF	Unc	BU
1981FM (P)	685	Value: 280				

KM# 22 100 KINA
9.5700 g., 0.9000 Gold 0.2769 oz. AGW **Subject:** Royal Visit **Obv:** National emblem **Rev:** Conjoined heads right

Date	Mintage	F	VF	XF	Unc	BU
1982FM (P)	484	Value: 280				

KM# 24 100 KINA
9.5700 g., 0.9000 Gold 0.2769 oz. AGW **Subject:** 10th Anniversary - Bank of Papua New Guinea **Obv:** Symbol around center hole **Rev:** National emblem above center hole

Date	Mintage	F	VF	XF	Unc	BU
1983FM (P)	378	Value: 280				

KM# 27 100 KINA
9.5700 g., 0.9000 Gold 0.2769 oz. AGW **Subject:** 100th Anniversary - Founding of British and German Protectorates **Obv:** National emblem **Rev:** Value above flags

Date	Mintage	F	VF	XF	Unc	BU
1984FM (P)	274	Value: 280				

KM# 29 100 KINA
9.5700 g., 0.9000 Gold 0.2769 oz. AGW **Obv:** National emblem **Rev:** Queen Alexandra Butterfly

Date	Mintage	F	VF	XF	Unc	BU
1990	500	—	—	—	—	290
1990 Proof	Est. 5,000	Value: 280				
1992 Proof	Est. 5,000	Value: 280				

KM# 29a 100 KINA
9.5700 g., 0.9950 Platinum 0.3061 oz. APW **Obv:** National emblem **Rev:** Queen Alexandra butterfly

Date	Mintage	F	VF	XF	Unc	BU
1992	500	—	—	—	—	535
1992 Proof	Est. 5,000	Value: 520				

KM# 35 100 KINA
9.5700 g., 0.9000 Gold 0.2769 oz. AGW **Subject:** 9th South Pacific Games **Obv:** National emblem **Rev:** Artistic design

Date	Mintage	F	VF	XF	Unc	BU
1991 Proof	5,000	Value: 280				

PIEFORTS

KM#	Date	Mintage	Identification	Mkt Val
P1	1982	39	5 Kina. Silver. KM18.	100

MINT SETS

KM#	Date	Mintage	Identification	Issue Price	Mkt Val
MS1	1975FM (8)	4,134	KM1-8	30.00	22.50
MS2	1976FM (8)	976	KM1-8	30.00	35.00
MS3	1977FM (8)	603	KM1-7, 11	30.00	55.00
MS4	1978FM (8)	777	KM#1-8	30.00	35.00
MS5	1979FM (8)	1,366	KM1-8	31.00	30.00
MS6	1980FM (9)	—	KM1-8, 15	35.00	30.00
MS7	1982FM (8)	—	KM1-6, 20, 21	36.00	30.00
MS8	1983FM (8)	360	KM1-6, 8, 23	36.00	30.00

PROOF SETS

KM#	Date	Mintage	Identification	Issue Price	Mkt Val
PS1	1975FM (8)	42,340	KM1-6, 7a, 8a	60.00	27.50
PS2	1976FM (8)	16,323	KM1-6, 7a, 8a	60.00	27.50
PS3	1977FM (8)	7,721	KM1-6, 7a, 11a	60.00	35.00
PS4	1978FM (8)	5,540	KM1-6, 7a, 8a	70.00	40.00
PS5	1979FM (8)	2,728	KM1-6, 7a, 8a	72.00	45.00
PS6	1980FM (9)	—	KM1-6, 7a, 8a, 15	130	60.00
PS7	1981FM (6)	10,000	KM1-6	29.00	10.00
PS8	1982FM (8)	—	KM1-6, 20a, 21a	92.00	90.00
PS9	1983FM (8)	—	KM1-6, 8a.1, 23a	132	100
PS10	1984FM (8)	—	KM1-6, 25, 26	133	100
PS11	1992 (4)	250	KM29a, 33, 33a, 34	—	800

PARAGUAY

The Republic of Paraguay, a landlocked country in the heart of South America surrounded by Argentina, Bolivia and Brazil, has an area of 157,048 sq. mi. (406,750 sq. km.) and a population of *4.5 million, 95 percent of whom are of mixed Spanish and Indian descent. Capital: Asuncion. The country is predominantly agrarian, with no important mineral deposits or oil reserves. Meat, timber, hides, oilseeds, tobacco and cotton account for 70 percent of Paraguay's export revenue.

Paraguay was first visited by a ship-wrecked Spaniard named Alejo Garcia, in 1524. The interior was explored by Sebastian Cabot in 1527 and 1528, when he sailed up the Parana and Paraguay rivers. Asuncion, which would become the center of a Spanish colonial province embracing much of southern South America, was established by the Spanish explorer Juan de Salazar on Aug. 15,1537. For 150 years the history of Paraguay was largely the history of the agricultural colonies established by the Jesuits in the south and east to Christianize the Indians. In 1811, following the outbreak of the South American wars of independence, Paraguayan patriots over-threw the local Spanish authorities and proclaimed their country's independence.

During the Triple Alliance War (1864-1870) in which Paraguay faced Argentina, Brazil and Uruguay, Asuncion's ladies gathered in an Assembly on Feb. 24, 1867 and decided to give up their jewelry in order to help the national defense. The President of the Republic, Francisco Solano Lopez accepted the offering and ordered one twentieth of it be used to mint the first Paraguayan gold coins according to the Decree of the 11th of Sept.,1867.

Two dies were made, one by Bouvet, and another by an American, Leonard Charles, while only the die made by Bouvet was eventually used.

MINT MARK
HF – LeLocle (Swiss)

REPUBLIC
DECIMAL COINAGE

KM# 6 5 CENTAVOS
Copper-Nickel **Obv:** Seated lion with liberty cap on pole, date below **Obv. Leg.:** REPUBLICA DEL PARAGUAY **Rev:** Value within wreath

Date	Mintage	F	VF	XF	Unc	BU
1903	600,000	2.00	8.00	25.00	75.00	—

KM# 9 5 CENTAVOS
Copper-Nickel **Obv:** Radiant star within wreath **Rev:** Value within flower chain

Date	Mintage	F	VF	XF	Unc	BU
1908	400,000	2.50	8.00	30.00	75.00	—

KM# 7 10 CENTAVOS
Copper-Nickel **Obv:** Seated lion with liberty cap on pole, date below **Obv. Leg.:** REPUBLICA DEL PARAGUAY **Rev:** Value within wreath

Date	Mintage	F	VF	XF	Unc	BU
1903	1,200,000	1.50	4.00	15.00	35.00	—

KM# 10 10 CENTAVOS
Copper-Nickel **Obv:** Radiant star within wreath **Rev:** Value within flower chain

Date	Mintage	F	VF	XF	Unc	BU
1908	800,000	2.50	6.50	25.00	75.00	—

KM# 8 20 CENTAVOS
Copper-Nickel **Obv:** Seated lion with liberty cap on pole, date below **Obv. Leg.:** REPUBLICA DEL PARAGUAY **Rev:** Value within wreath

Date	Mintage	F	VF	XF	Unc	BU
1903	750,000	1.50	4.00	20.00	65.00	—

KM# 11 20 CENTAVOS
Copper-Nickel **Obv:** Radiant star within wreath **Rev:** Value

Date	Mintage	F	VF	XF	Unc	BU
1908	1,000,000	2.50	7.00	35.00	80.00	—

KM# 12 50 CENTAVOS
2.0000 g., Copper-Nickel **Obv:** Radiant star within wreath **Rev:** Value

Date	Mintage	F	VF	XF	Unc	BU
1925	4,000,000	0.50	1.50	5.00	15.00	—

KM# 15 50 CENTAVOS
0.9000 g., Aluminum, 17.5 mm. **Obv:** Radiant star within wreath **Rev:** Value

Date	Mintage	F	VF	XF	Unc	BU
1938	400,000	0.50	1.00	3.50	10.00	—

KM# 13 PESO
2.9300 g., Copper-Nickel, 19 mm. **Obv:** Radiant star within wreath **Rev:** Value

Date	Mintage	F	VF	XF	Unc	BU
1925	3,500,000	0.50	1.00	5.00	10.00	—

KM# 16 PESO
Aluminum **Obv:** Radiant star within wreath **Rev:** Value

Date	Mintage	F	VF	XF	Unc	BU
1938	—	0.50	1.50	3.00	8.00	—

KM# 14 2 PESOS
4.0000 g., Copper-Nickel, 22 mm. **Obv:** Radiant star within wreath **Rev:** Value

Date	Mintage	F	VF	XF	Unc	BU
1925	2,500,000	0.50	1.00	6.00	12.00	—

KM# 17 2 PESOS
1.7600 g., Aluminum, 22.5 mm. **Obv:** Radiant star within wreath **Rev:** Value

Date	Mintage	F	VF	XF	Unc	BU
1938	—	0.50	1.50	3.00	10.00	—

KM# 18 5 PESOS
Copper-Nickel **Obv:** Radiant star within wreath **Rev:** Value

Date	Mintage	F	VF	XF	Unc	BU
1939	4,000,000	1.00	3.50	10.00	20.00	—

KM# 19 10 PESOS
Copper-Nickel **Obv:** Radiant star within wreath **Rev:** Value

Date	Mintage	F	VF	XF	Unc	BU
1939	4,000,000	1.00	2.00	7.00	18.00	—

REFORM COINAGE
100 Centimos = 1 Guarani

KM# 20 CENTIMO
2.0000 g., Aluminum-Bronze, 17.5 mm. **Obv:** Flower within circle **Rev:** Value within wreath

Date	Mintage	F	VF	XF	Unc	BU
1944	3,500,000	0.10	0.50	1.00	5.00	—
1948	2,000,000	0.10	0.50	1.00	4.00	—
1950	1,096,000	0.10	0.25	0.75	3.00	—

KM# 21 5 CENTIMOS
Aluminum-Bronze **Obv:** Passion flower within circle **Rev:** Value within wreath

Date	Mintage	F	VF	XF	Unc	BU
1944	2,195,000	0.10	0.50	1.00	4.00	—
1947HF	13,111,000	0.10	0.20	0.50	2.00	—

KM# 22 10 CENTIMOS
Aluminum-Bronze **Obv:** Orchid within circle **Rev:** Value within wreath

Date	Mintage	F	VF	XF	Unc	BU
1944	975,000	0.25	0.75	3.00	6.00	—
1947	6,656,000	0.10	0.25	1.00	3.00	—
1947HF	—	0.20	0.50	2.00	5.00	—

KM# 25 10 CENTIMOS
Aluminum-Bronze **Obv:** Seated lion with liberty cap on pole within circle **Rev:** Value within wreath

Date	Mintage	F	VF	XF	Unc	BU
1953	5,000,000	0.10	0.15	0.50	1.00	—
1953 Proof; 1 known	—	Value: 375				

Note: Medal die rotation

KM# 26 15 CENTIMOS
Aluminum-Bronze **Obv:** Seated lion with liberty cap on pole within circle **Rev:** Value within wreath

Date	Mintage	F	VF	XF	Unc	BU
1953	5,000,000	0.10	0.20	0.35	1.00	—
1953 Proof; 1 known	—	Value: 375				

Note: Medal die rotation

KM# 23 25 CENTIMOS
Aluminum-Bronze **Obv:** Orchid within circle **Rev:** Value within wreath

Date	Mintage	F	VF	XF	Unc	BU
1944	700,000	0.25	1.00	3.00	12.00	—
1948HF	600,000	0.25	0.75	2.50	9.00	—
1951HF	1,000,000	0.25	0.75	1.50	5.00	—

KM# 27 25 CENTIMOS
Aluminum-Bronze **Obv:** Seated lion with liberty cap on pole within circle **Rev:** Value within wreath

Date	Mintage	F	VF	XF	Unc	BU
1953	2,000,000	0.10	0.15	0.30	1.00	2.00
1953 Proof; 1 known	—	Value: 450				

Note: Medal die rotation

KM# 24 50 CENTIMOS
Aluminum-Bronze **Obv:** Seated lion with liberty cap on pole within circle **Rev:** Value within wreath

Date	Mintage	F	VF	XF	Unc	BU
1944	2,485,000	0.25	1.00	2.00	7.00	—
1951	2,893,000	0.25	0.50	1.25	3.00	4.00

KM# 28 50 CENTIMOS
Aluminum-Bronze **Obv:** Seated lion with liberty cap on pole within circle **Rev:** Value within wreath

Date	Mintage	F	VF	XF	Unc	BU
1953	2,000,000	0.10	0.15	0.30	1.00	2.50
1953 Proof; 1 known	—	Value: 450				
Note: Medal die rotation						

KM# 151 GUARANI
2.9000 g., Stainless Steel **Obv:** Soldier 3/4 facing **Rev:** Tobacco plant and value

Date	Mintage	F	VF	XF	Unc	BU
1975	10,000,000	—	—	0.15	0.50	0.75
1975 Proof	1,000	Value: 6.00				
1976	12,000,000	—	—	0.10	0.40	0.65
1976 Proof	1,000	Value: 8.00				

KM# 151a GUARANI
6.9900 g., Gold, 18 mm.

Date	Mintage	F	VF	XF	Unc	BU
1976 Proof	—	—	—	—	—	—

KM# 165a GUARANI
6.9900 g., Gold, 18 mm.

Date	Mintage	F	VF	XF	Unc	BU
1978 Proof	—	—	—	—	—	—
1980 Proof	—	—	—	—	—	—

KM# 165 GUARANI
2.6000 g., Stainless Steel **Series:** F.A.O. **Obv:** Standing 3/4 figure facing **Rev:** Plant and value **Note:** Varieties exist.

Date	Mintage	F	VF	XF	Unc	BU
1978	15,000,000	—	—	0.15	0.50	0.75
1978 Proof	—	Value: 6.00				
1980	13,000,000	—	—	0.15	0.50	0.75
1980 Proof	1,000	Value: 6.00				
1984	15,000,000	—	—	0.10	0.30	0.50
1986	15,000,000	—	—	0.10	0.30	0.50
1988	15,000,000	—	—	0.10	0.30	0.50

KM# 192 GUARANI
1.5000 g., Brass Plated Steel, 15.03 mm. **Series:** F.A.O. **Edge:** Reeded

Date	Mintage	F	VF	XF	Unc	BU
1993	5,000,000	—	—	0.15	0.50	0.75

KM# 193 GUARANI
27.0000 g., 0.9250 Silver 0.8029 oz. ASW **Subject:** Encuentro De Dos Mundos **Obv:** National arms within circle of assorted arms **Rev:** Dancer and artistic design within circle

Date	Mintage	F	VF	XF	Unc	BU
1997 Proof	—	Value: 60.00				

KM# 196 GUARANI
27.1000 g., 0.9250 Silver 0.8059 oz. ASW, 40 mm. **Subject:** Ibero-America Series **Obv:** National arms within circle of assorted arms **Rev:** Cowboy on horse **Edge:** Reeded

Date	Mintage	F	VF	XF	Unc	BU
2000 Proof	—	Value: 65.00				

KM# 152 5 GUARANIES
3.8000 g., Stainless Steel, 20 mm. **Obv:** Half-length figure with jug looking right **Rev:** Cotton plant and value

Date	Mintage	F	VF	XF	Unc	BU
1975	7,500,000	—	—	0.15	0.50	0.75
1975 Proof	1,000	Value: 6.00				

KM# 166b 5 GUARANIES
Gold, 20 mm.

Date	Mintage	F	VF	XF	Unc	BU
1978 Proof	10	—	—	—	—	—
1980 Proof	1,000	—	—	—	—	—

KM# 166 5 GUARANIES
3.8000 g., Stainless Steel, 20 mm. **Series:** F.A.O. **Obv:** Half-length figure with jug looking right **Rev:** Cotton plant and value **Note:** Varieties exist.

Date	Mintage	F	VF	XF	Unc	BU
1978	10,000,000	—	—	0.15	0.60	0.85
1978 Proof	—	Value: 6.00				
1980	12,000,000	—	—	0.15	0.60	0.85
1980 Proof	1,000	Value: 6.00				
1984	15,000,000	—	—	0.10	0.40	0.60
1986	15,000,000	—	—	0.10	0.40	0.60

KM# 166a 5 GUARANIES
1.9500 g., Nickel-Bronze, 16.97 mm. **Series:** F.A.O. **Obv:** Half-length figure with jug looking right **Rev:** Cotton plant and value **Edge:** Reeded

Date	Mintage	F	VF	XF	Unc	BU
1992	15,000,000	—	—	0.10	0.30	0.50

KM# 153 10 GUARANIES
4.5000 g., Stainless Steel, 22 mm. **Obv:** Bust 1/4 left **Rev:** Cow head left and value

Date	Mintage	F	VF	XF	Unc	BU
1975	10,000,000	—	0.10	0.20	0.75	1.00
1975 Proof	1,000	Value: 8.00				
1976	10,000,000	—	0.10	0.20	0.75	1.00
1976 Proof	1,000	Value: 10.00				

KM# 153a 10 GUARANIES
Gold, 22 mm.

Date	Mintage	F	VF	XF	Unc	BU
1976 Proof	—	—	—	—	—	—

KM# 167a 10 GUARANIES
Gold, 22 mm.

Date	Mintage	F	VF	XF	Unc	BU
1978 Proof	10	—	—	—	—	—
1980 Proof	—	—	—	—	—	—

KM# 167 10 GUARANIES
4.5000 g., Stainless Steel, 22 mm. **Series:** F.A.O. **Obv:** Bust 1/4 left **Rev:** Cow head left and value **Note:** Varieties exist.

Date	Mintage	F	VF	XF	Unc	BU
1978	15,000,000	—	0.10	0.20	0.75	1.00
1978 Proof	—	Value: 8.00				
1980	15,000,000	—	0.10	0.20	0.75	1.00
1980 Proof	1,000	Value: 8.00				
1984	20,000,000	—	0.10	0.15	0.50	0.75
1986	35,000,000	—	0.10	0.15	0.50	0.75
1988	40,000,000	—	0.10	0.15	0.50	0.75

KM# 178 10 GUARANIES
2.6900 g., Nickel-Bronze, 19.34 mm. **Series:** F.A.O. **Obv:** Bust 1/4 left **Rev:** Cow head left and value **Edge:** Reeded

Date	Mintage	F	VF	XF	Unc	BU
1990	40,000,000	—	—	0.10	0.40	0.60

KM# 178a 10 GUARANIES
Brass Plated Steel **Series:** F.A.O. **Obv:** Bust of Garay 1/4 left **Rev:** Cow's head left at left of value **Note:** Magnetic.

Date	Mintage	F	VF	XF	Unc	BU
1996	20,000,000	—	—	0.10	0.40	0.60

KM# 154 50 GUARANIES
7.4000 g., Stainless Steel, 26 mm. **Obv:** Uniformed bust facing **Rev:** Value above dam on the Acaray River

Date	Mintage	F	VF	XF	Unc	BU
1975	9,500,000	0.20	0.40	0.60	1.25	1.50
1975 Proof	1,000	Value: 10.00				

KM# 169a 50 GUARANIES
Gold, 25 mm.

Date	Mintage	F	VF	XF	Unc	BU
1980 Proof	10	—	—	—	—	—

KM# 169 50 GUARANIES
7.4000 g., Stainless Steel, 26.1 mm. **Obv:** Bust of General Estigarribia facing **Obv. Leg.:** REPUBLICA DEL PARAGUAY **Rev:** Acaray River Dam **Note:** Examples of each date differ slightly.

Date	Mintage	F	VF	XF	Unc	BU
1980	10,700,000	0.20	0.40	0.60	1.25	1.50
1980 Proof	1,000	Value: 10.00				
1986	15,000,000	0.20	0.40	0.60	1.25	1.50
1988	25,000,000	0.20	0.30	0.50	1.00	1.25

KM# 191 50 GUARANIES
3.7700 g., Copper-Zinc-Nickel, 21.69 mm. **Obv:** Bust of Major General J.F. Estigarribia facing **Obv. Leg.:** REPUBLICA DEL PARAGUAY **Rev:** Acary River Dam **Rev. Leg.:** REPRESA ACARAY **Edge:** Reeded

Date	Mintage	F	VF	XF	Unc	BU
1992	35,000,000	—	—	—	0.75	1.00

KM# 191a 50 GUARANIES
Brass Plated Steel **Obv:** Uniformed bust facing **Rev:** Value above river dam **Note:** Magnetic

Date	Mintage	F	VF	XF	Unc	BU
1995	25,000,000	—	—	—	0.75	1.00
1998	22,000,000	—	—	—	0.75	1.00

KM# 177 100 GUARANIES
10.4500 g., Copper-Zinc-Nickel **Obv:** Bust of General Jose E. Dias facing **Obv. Leg.:** REPUBLICA DEL PARAGUAY **Rev:** Ruins of Humaita **Rev. Insc.:** RUINAS DE HUMAITA 1865/70

Date	Mintage	F	VF	XF	Unc	BU
1990	35,000,000	—	—	—	2.25	2.75

KM# 177a 100 GUARANIES
5.4500 g., Brass Plated Steel **Obv:** Bust of General Jose E. Dias facing **Obv. Leg.:** REPUBLICA DEL PARAGUAY **Rev:** Ruins of Humaita **Rev. Insc.:** RUINAS DE HUMAITA 1865/70 **Note:** Reduced weight and thickness.

Date	Mintage	F	VF	XF	Unc	BU
1993	35,000,000	—	—	—	1.50	2.00
1995	10,000,000	—	—	—	1.50	2.00
1996	30,000,000	—	—	—	1.50	2.00

KM# 31 150 GUARANIES
25.0000 g., 0.9990 Silver 0.8029 oz. ASW **Obv:** National arms **Rev:** Uniformed bust of General A. Stroessner facing

Date	Mintage	F	VF	XF	Unc	BU
1972 Proof	Est. 10,000	Value: 60.00				

KM# 32 150 GUARANIES
25.0000 g., 0.9990 Silver 0.8029 oz. ASW **Subject:** Munich Olympics **Obv:** National arms **Rev:** Runner flanked by design and Olympic rings

Date	Mintage	F	VF	XF	Unc	BU
1972 Proof	Est. 10,000	Value: 70.00				

KM# 33 150 GUARANIES
25.0000 g., 0.9990 Silver 0.8029 oz. ASW **Subject:** Munich Olympics **Obv:** National arms **Rev:** Broad jumper

Date	Mintage	F	VF	XF	Unc	BU
1972 Proof	Est. 10,000	Value: 70.00				

KM# 34 150 GUARANIES
25.0000 g., 0.9990 Silver 0.8029 oz. ASW **Subject:** Munich Olympics **Obv:** National arms **Rev:** Soccer player

Date	Mintage	F	VF	XF	Unc	BU
1972 Proof	Est. 10,000	Value: 70.00				

KM# 35 150 GUARANIES
25.0000 g., 0.9990 Silver 0.8029 oz. ASW **Subject:** Munich Olympics **Obv:** National arms **Rev:** Hurdler

Date	Mintage	F	VF	XF	Unc	BU
1972 Proof	Est. 10,000	Value: 70.00				

KM# 36 150 GUARANIES
25.0000 g., 0.9990 Silver 0.8029 oz. ASW **Subject:** Munich Olympics **Obv:** National arms **Rev:** High jumper

Date	Mintage	F	VF	XF	Unc	BU
1972 Proof	Est. 10,000	Value: 70.00				

KM# 37 150 GUARANIES
25.0000 g., 0.9990 Silver 0.8029 oz. ASW **Subject:** Munich Olympics **Obv:** National arms **Rev:** Boxer

Date	Mintage	F	VF	XF	Unc	BU
1973 Proof	Est. 10,000	Value: 70.00				

KM# 59 150 GUARANIES
25.0000 g., 0.9990 Silver 0.8029 oz. ASW **Obv:** National arms **Rev:** Mariscal Jose F. Estigarribia

Date	Mintage	F	VF	XF	Unc	BU
1973 Proof	Est. 10,000	Value: 55.00				

KM# 60 150 GUARANIES
25.0000 g., 0.9990 Silver 0.8029 oz. ASW **Obv:** National arms **Rev:** Mariscal Francisco Solano Lopez

Date	Mintage	F	VF	XF	Unc	BU
1973 Proof	Est. 10,000	Value: 55.00				

KM# 61   150 GUARANIES
25.0000 g., 0.9990 Silver 0.8029 oz. ASW   **Obv:** National arms
Rev: General Jose E. Diaz

Date	Mintage	F	VF	XF	Unc	BU
1973 Proof	Est. 10,000			Value: 52.50		

KM# 62   150 GUARANIES
25.0000 g., 0.9990 Silver 0.8029 oz. ASW   **Obv:** National arms
Rev: General Bernardino Cabaliero

Date	Mintage	F	VF	XF	Unc	BU
1973 Proof	Est. 10,000			Value: 52.50		

KM# 63   150 GUARANIES
25.0000 g., 0.9990 Silver 0.8029 oz. ASW   **Obv:** National arms
Rev: Teotihucana Culture sculpture

Date	Mintage	F	VF	XF	Unc	BU
1973 Proof	Est. 10,000			Value: 52.50		

KM# 64   150 GUARANIES
25.0000 g., 0.9990 Silver 0.8029 oz. ASW   **Obv:** National arms
Rev: Huasteca Culture sculpture

Date	Mintage	F	VF	XF	Unc	BU
1973 Proof	Est. 10,000			Value: 52.50		

KM# 65   150 GUARANIES
25.0000 g., 0.9990 Silver 0.8029 oz. ASW   **Obv:** National arms
Rev: Mixteca Culture animal sculpture

Date	Mintage	F	VF	XF	Unc	BU
1973 Proof	Est. 10,000			Value: 52.50		

KM# 66   150 GUARANIES
25.0000 g., 0.9990 Silver 0.8029 oz. ASW   **Obv:** National arms
Rev: Veracruz Ceramica Vase

Date	Mintage	F	VF	XF	Unc	BU
1973 Proof	Est. 10,000			Value: 52.50		

KM# 67   150 GUARANIES
25.0000 g., 0.9990 Silver 0.8029 oz. ASW   **Obv:** National arms
Rev: Veracruz Culture sculpture facing

Date	Mintage	F	VF	XF	Unc	BU
1973 Proof	Est. 10,000			Value: 52.50		

KM# 68   150 GUARANIES
25.0000 g., 0.9990 Silver 0.8029 oz. ASW   **Obv:** National arms
Rev: Albrecht Durer facing

Date	Mintage	F	VF	XF	Unc	BU
1973 Proof	Est. 10,000			Value: 65.00		

KM# 69   150 GUARANIES
25.0000 g., 0.9990 Silver 0.8029 oz. ASW   **Obv:** National arms
Rev: Johann Wolfgang Goethe

Date	Mintage	F	VF	XF	Unc	BU
1973 Proof	Est. 10,000			Value: 65.00		

KM# 107   150 GUARANIES
25.0000 g., 0.9990 Silver 0.8029 oz. ASW   **Obv:** National arms
Rev: Head of President Abraham Lincoln left

Date	Mintage	F	VF	XF	Unc	BU
1974 Proof	Est. 10,000			Value: 75.00		

KM# 108   150 GUARANIES
25.0000 g., 0.9990 Silver 0.8029 oz. ASW   **Obv:** National arms
Rev: Ludwig van Beethoven

Date	Mintage	F	VF	XF	Unc	BU
1974 Proof	Est. 10,000			Value: 75.00		

KM# 109   150 GUARANIES
25.0000 g., 0.9990 Silver 0.8029 oz. ASW   **Obv:** National arms
Rev: Head of Otto von Bismarck right

Date	Mintage	F	VF	XF	Unc	BU
1974 Proof	Est. 10,000			Value: 75.00		

KM# 110   150 GUARANIES
25.0000 g., 0.9990 Silver 0.8029 oz. ASW   **Obv:** National arms
Rev: Head of Albert Einstein left

Date	Mintage	F	VF	XF	Unc	BU
1974 Proof	Est. 10,000			Value: 85.00		

KM# 111   150 GUARANIES
25.0000 g., 0.9990 Silver 0.8029 oz. ASW   **Obv:** National arms
Rev: Head of Giuseppe Garibaldi facing

Date	Mintage	F	VF	XF	Unc	BU
1974 Proof	Est. 10,000			Value: 65.00		

KM# 112   150 GUARANIES
25.0000 g., 0.9990 Silver 0.8029 oz. ASW **Obv:** National arms
Rev: Head of Alessandro Manzoni facing

Date	Mintage	F	VF	XF	Unc	BU
1974 Proof	Est. 10,000	Value: 57.50				

KM# 113   150 GUARANIES
25.0000 g., 0.9990 Silver 0.8029 oz. ASW **Obv:** National arms
Rev: William Tell and son facing

Date	Mintage	F	VF	XF	Unc	BU
1974 Proof	Est. 10,000	Value: 57.50				

KM# 114   150 GUARANIES
25.0000 g., 0.9990 Silver 0.8029 oz. ASW **Obv:** National arms
Rev: Head of John F. Kennedy left

Date	Mintage	F	VF	XF	Unc	BU
1974 Proof	Est. 10,000	Value: 55.00				

KM# 115   150 GUARANIES
25.0000 g., 0.9990 Silver 0.8029 oz. ASW **Obv:** National arms
Rev: Head of Konrad Adenauer left

Date	Mintage	F	VF	XF	Unc	BU
1974 Proof	Est. 10,000	Value: 65.00				

KM# 116   150 GUARANIES
25.0000 g., 0.9990 Silver 0.8029 oz. ASW **Obv:** National arms
Rev: Head of Winston Churchill left

Date	Mintage	F	VF	XF	Unc	BU
1974 Proof	Est. 10,000	Value: 55.00				

KM# 117   150 GUARANIES
25.0000 g., 0.9990 Silver 0.8029 oz. ASW **Obv:** National arms
Rev: Head of Pope John XXIII left

Date	Mintage	F	VF	XF	Unc	BU
1974 Proof	Est. 10,000	Value: 65.00				

KM# 118   150 GUARANIES
25.0000 g., 0.9990 Silver 0.8029 oz. ASW **Obv:** National arms
Rev: Head of Pope Paul VI left

Date	Mintage	F	VF	XF	Unc	BU
1974 Proof	Est. 10,000	Value: 65.00				

KM# 155   150 GUARANIES
25.0000 g., 0.9990 Silver 0.8029 oz. ASW **Obv:** National arms
Rev: Parliament building

Date	Mintage	F	VF	XF	Unc	BU
1975 Proof	Est. 10,000	Value: 55.00				

KM# 156   150 GUARANIES
25.0000 g., 0.9990 Silver 0.8029 oz. ASW **Subject:** Apollo 11
Mission **Obv:** National arms **Rev:** Eagle landing on moon with earth at left

Date	Mintage	F	VF	XF	Unc	BU
1975 Proof	Est. 10,000	Value: 65.00				

KM# 157   150 GUARANIES
25.0000 g., 0.9990 Silver 0.8029 oz. ASW **Subject:** Apollo 15
Mission **Obv:** National arms **Rev:** Apollo mission design within circle

Date	Mintage	F	VF	XF	Unc	BU
1975 Proof	Est. 10,000	Value: 65.00				

KM# 158   150 GUARANIES
25.0000 g., 0.9990 Silver 0.8029 oz. ASW **Obv:** National arms
Rev: Friendship Bridge

Date	Mintage	F	VF	XF	Unc	BU
1975 Proof	Est. 10,000	Value: 57.50				

KM# 159   150 GUARANIES
25.0000 g., 0.9990 Silver 0.8029 oz. ASW **Obv:** National arms
Rev: Holy Trinity Church

Date	Mintage	F	VF	XF	Unc	BU
1975 Proof	Est. 10,000	Value: 57.50				

KM# 160   150 GUARANIES
25.0000 g., 0.9990 Silver 0.8029 oz. ASW **Obv:** National arms
Rev: Ruins of Humaita

Date	Mintage	F	VF	XF	Unc	BU
1975 Proof	Est. 10,000	Value: 57.50				

KM# 29   300 GUARANIES
26.6000 g., 0.7200 Silver 0.6157 oz. ASW **Subject:** 4th Term of President Stroessner **Obv:** Seated lion with liberty cap on pole within circle **Rev:** Head left

Date	Mintage	F	VF	XF	Unc	BU
1968	250,000	—	—	12.50	15.00	18.00

KM# 194   500 GUARANIES
Brass Plated Steel **Obv:** Head of General Bernardino Caballero facing **Rev:** Bank of Paraguay within circle

Date	Mintage	F	VF	XF	Unc	BU
1997	20,000,000	—	—	—	2.50	3.00

KM# 195   500 GUARANIES
7.8200 g., Brass Plated Steel **Obv:** Head of General Bernardino Caballero facing **Obv. Leg.:** REPUBLICA DEL PARAGUAY **Rev:** Bank above value within circle **Rev. Leg.:** BANCO CENTRAL DEL PARAGUAY

Date	Mintage	F	VF	XF	Unc	BU
1997	—	—	—	—	35.00	50.00
1998	15,000,000	—	—	—	2.50	3.00

KM# 38   1500 GUARANIES
10.7000 g., 0.9000 Gold 0.3096 oz. AGW **Obv:** National arms **Rev:** Uniformed bust of General A. Stroessner facing

Date	Mintage	F	VF	XF	Unc	BU
1972 Proof	Est. 1,500	Value: 345				

KM# 39   1500 GUARANIES
10.7000 g., 0.9000 Gold 0.3096 oz. AGW **Subject:** Munich Olympics **Obv:** National arms **Rev:** Runner

Date	Mintage	F	VF	XF	Unc	BU
1972 Proof	Est. 1,500	Value: 750				

KM# 40   1500 GUARANIES
10.7000 g., 0.9000 Gold 0.3096 oz. AGW **Subject:** Munich Olympics **Obv:** National arms **Rev:** Broad jumper

Date	Mintage	F	VF	XF	Unc	BU
1972 Proof	Est. 1,500	Value: 750				

KM# 41   1500 GUARANIES
10.7000 g., 0.9000 Gold 0.3096 oz. AGW **Subject:** Munich Olympics **Obv:** National arms **Rev:** Soccer

Date	Mintage	F	VF	XF	Unc	BU
1972 Proof	Est. 1,500	Value: 750				

KM# 42   1500 GUARANIES
10.7000 g., 0.9000 Gold 0.3096 oz. AGW **Subject:** Munich Olympics **Obv:** National arms **Rev:** Hurdler

Date	Mintage	F	VF	XF	Unc	BU
1972 Proof	Est. 1,500	Value: 750				

KM# 43   1500 GUARANIES
10.7000 g., 0.9000 Gold 0.3096 oz. AGW **Subject:** Munich Olympics **Obv:** National arms **Rev:** High Jumper

Date	Mintage	F	VF	XF	Unc	BU
1973 Proof	1,500	Value: 750				

KM# 44   1500 GUARANIES
10.7000 g., 0.9000 Gold 0.3096 oz. AGW **Subject:** Munich Olympics **Obv:** National arms **Rev:** Boxer

Date	Mintage	F	VF	XF	Unc	BU
1973 Proof	Est. 1,500	Value: 750				

KM# 70   1500 GUARANIES
10.7000 g., 0.9000 Gold 0.3096 oz. AGW **Obv:** National arms **Rev:** Mariscal Jose F. Estigarriba

Date	Mintage	F	VF	XF	Unc	BU
1973 Proof	Est. 1,500	Value: 400				

KM# 71   1500 GUARANIES
10.7000 g., 0.9000 Gold 0.3096 oz. AGW **Obv:** National arms **Rev:** Head of Mariscal Francisco Solano Lopez facing

Date	Mintage	F	VF	XF	Unc	BU
1973 Proof	Est. 1,500	Value: 400				

KM# 72   1500 GUARANIES
10.7000 g., 0.9000 Gold 0.3096 oz. AGW **Obv:** National arms **Rev:** Bust of General Jose E. Diaz facing

Date	Mintage	F	VF	XF	Unc	BU
1973 Proof	Est. 1,500	Value: 400				

KM# 73   1500 GUARANIES
10.7000 g., 0.9000 Gold 0.3096 oz. AGW **Obv:** National arms **Rev:** Head of General Bernardino Caballero facing

Date	Mintage	F	VF	XF	Unc	BU
1973 Proof	Est. 1,500	Value: 400				

KM# 74   1500 GUARANIES
10.7000 g., 0.9000 Gold 0.3096 oz. AGW **Obv:** National arms **Rev:** Teotihucana Culture sculpture facing

Date	Mintage	F	VF	XF	Unc	BU
1973 Proof	Est. 1,500	Value: 400				

KM# 75   1500 GUARANIES
10.7000 g., 0.9000 Gold 0.3096 oz. AGW **Obv:** National arms **Rev:** Huasteca Culture sculpture

Date	Mintage	F	VF	XF	Unc	BU
1973 Proof	Est. 1,500	Value: 400				

KM# 76   1500 GUARANIES
10.7000 g., 0.9000 Gold 0.3096 oz. AGW **Obv:** National arms **Rev:** Mixteca Culture sculpture

Date	Mintage	F	VF	XF	Unc	BU
1973 Proof	Est. 1,500	Value: 400				

KM# 77   1500 GUARANIES
10.7000 g., 0.9000 Gold 0.3096 oz. AGW **Obv:** National arms **Rev:** Veracruz Ceramica vase

Date	Mintage	F	VF	XF	Unc	BU
1973 Proof	Est. 1,500	Value: 400				

KM# 78   1500 GUARANIES
10.7000 g., 0.9000 Gold 0.3096 oz. AGW **Obv:** National arms **Rev:** Veracruz Culture sculpture

Date	Mintage	F	VF	XF	Unc	BU
1973 Proof	Est. 1,500	Value: 400				

KM# 79   1500 GUARANIES
10.7000 g., 0.9000 Gold 0.3096 oz. AGW **Obv:** National arms **Rev:** Bust of Albrecht Durer facing

Date	Mintage	F	VF	XF	Unc	BU
1973 Proof	Est. 1,500	Value: 400				

KM# 80   1500 GUARANIES
10.7000 g., 0.9000 Gold 0.3096 oz. AGW **Obv:** National arms **Rev:** Bust of Johann Wolfgang Goethe facing

Date	Mintage	F	VF	XF	Unc	BU
1973 Proof	Est. 1,500	Value: 400				

KM# 119   1500 GUARANIES
10.7000 g., 0.9000 Gold 0.3096 oz. AGW **Obv:** National arms **Rev:** Bust of President Abraham Lincoln left

Date	Mintage	F	VF	XF	Unc	BU
1974 Proof	Est. 1,500	Value: 400				

KM# 120   1500 GUARANIES
10.7000 g., 0.9000 Gold 0.3096 oz. AGW **Obv:** National arms **Rev:** Bust of Ludwig van Beethoven left

Date	Mintage	F	VF	XF	Unc	BU
1974 Proof	Est. 1,500	Value: 750				

KM# 121   1500 GUARANIES
10.7000 g., 0.9000 Gold 0.3096 oz. AGW **Obv:** National arms **Rev:** Head of Otto von Bismarck right

Date	Mintage	F	VF	XF	Unc	BU
1974 Proof	Est. 1,500	Value: 400				

KM# 122   1500 GUARANIES
10.7000 g., 0.9000 Gold 0.3096 oz. AGW **Obv:** National arms **Rev:** Head of Albert Einstein left

Date	Mintage	F	VF	XF	Unc	BU
1974 Proof	Est. 1,500	Value: 400				

KM# 123   1500 GUARANIES
10.7000 g., 0.9000 Gold 0.3096 oz. AGW **Obv:** National arms **Rev:** Giuseppe Garibaldi facing

Date	Mintage	F	VF	XF	Unc	BU
1974 Proof	Est. 1,500	Value: 400				

KM# 124   1500 GUARANIES
10.7000 g., 0.9000 Gold 0.3096 oz. AGW **Obv:** National arms **Rev:** Alessandro Manzoni facing

Date	Mintage	F	VF	XF	Unc	BU
1974 Proof	Est. 1,500	Value: 400				

KM# 125   1500 GUARANIES
10.7000 g., 0.9000 Gold 0.3096 oz. AGW **Obv:** National arms **Rev:** William Tell and son facing

Date	Mintage	F	VF	XF	Unc	BU
1974 Proof	Est. 1,500	Value: 400				

KM# 126   1500 GUARANIES
10.7000 g., 0.9000 Gold 0.3096 oz. AGW **Obv:** National arms
Rev: Head of John F. Kennedy left

Date	Mintage	F	VF	XF	Unc	BU
1974 Proof	Est. 1,500	Value: 400				

KM# 127   1500 GUARANIES
10.7000 g., 0.9000 Gold 0.3096 oz. AGW **Obv:** National arms
Rev: Head of Konrad Adenauer left

Date	Mintage	F	VF	XF	Unc	BU
1974 Proof	Est. 1,500	Value: 400				

KM# 128   1500 GUARANIES
10.7000 g., 0.9000 Gold 0.3096 oz. AGW **Obv:** National arms
Rev: Head of Winston Churchill left

Date	Mintage	F	VF	XF	Unc	BU
1974 Proof	Est. 1,500	Value: 400				

KM# 129   1500 GUARANIES
10.7000 g., 0.9000 Gold 0.3096 oz. AGW **Obv:** National arms
Rev: Head of Pope John XXIII left

Date	Mintage	F	VF	XF	Unc	BU
1974 Proof	Est. 1,500	Value: 400				

KM# 130   1500 GUARANIES
10.7000 g., 0.9000 Gold 0.3096 oz. AGW **Obv:** National arms
Rev: Head of Pope Paul VI left

Date	Mintage	F	VF	XF	Unc	BU
1974 Proof	Est. 1,500	Value: 400				

KM# 179   1500 GUARANIES
10.7000 g., 0.9000 Gold 0.3096 oz. AGW **Obv:** National arms
Rev: Parliament building

Date	Mintage	F	VF	XF	Unc	BU
1975 Proof	1,500	Value: 400				

KM# 180   1500 GUARANIES
10.7000 g., 0.9000 Gold 0.3096 oz. AGW **Subject:** Apollo 11
Mission **Obv:** National arms **Rev:** Eagle landing on moon with
earth at left

Date	Mintage	F	VF	XF	Unc	BU
1975 Proof	1,500	Value: 500				

KM# 181   1500 GUARANIES
10.7000 g., 0.9000 Gold 0.3096 oz. AGW **Subject:** Apollo 15
Mission **Obv:** National arms **Rev:** Apollo mission design within circle

Date	Mintage	F	VF	XF	Unc	BU
1975 Proof	1,500	Value: 500				

KM# 182   1500 GUARANIES
10.7000 g., 0.9000 Gold 0.3096 oz. AGW **Obv:** National arms
Rev: Friendship Bridge

Date	Mintage	F	VF	XF	Unc	BU
1975 Proof	1,500	Value: 400				

KM# 183   1500 GUARANIES
10.7000 g., 0.9000 Gold 0.3096 oz. AGW **Obv:** National arms
Rev: Holy Trinity Chruch

Date	Mintage	F	VF	XF	Unc	BU
1975 Proof	1,500	Value: 400				

KM# 184   1500 GUARANIES
10.7000 g., 0.9000 Gold 0.3096 oz. AGW **Obv:** National arms
Rev: Ruins of Humaita

Date	Mintage	F	VF	XF	Unc	BU
1975 Proof	Est. 1,500	Value: 400				

KM# 45   3000 GUARANIES
21.3000 g., 0.9000 Gold 0.6163 oz. AGW **Obv:** National arms
Rev: Uniformed bust of General A. Stroessner facing

Date	Mintage	F	VF	XF	Unc	BU
1972 Proof	Est. 1,500	Value: 650				

KM# 46   3000 GUARANIES
21.3000 g., 0.9000 Gold 0.6163 oz. AGW **Subject:** Munich
Olympics **Obv:** National arms **Rev:** Runner

Date	Mintage	F	VF	XF	Unc	BU
1972 Proof	Est. 1,500	Value: 1,500				

KM# 47   3000 GUARANIES
21.3000 g., 0.9000 Gold 0.6163 oz. AGW **Subject:** Munich
Olympics **Obv:** Radiant star within wreath **Rev:** Broad jumper

Date	Mintage	F	VF	XF	Unc	BU
1972 Proof	Est. 1,500	Value: 1,500				

KM# 48   3000 GUARANIES
21.3000 g., 0.9000 Gold 0.6163 oz. AGW **Subject:** Munich
Olympics **Obv:** National arms **Rev:** Soccer

Date	Mintage	F	VF	XF	Unc	BU
1972 Proof	Est. 1,500	Value: 1,500				

KM# 49   3000 GUARANIES
21.3000 g., 0.9000 Gold 0.6163 oz. AGW **Subject:** Munich
Olympics **Obv:** National arms **Rev:** Hurdler

Date	Mintage	F	VF	XF	Unc	BU
1972 Proof	Est. 1,500	Value: 1,500				

KM# 50   3000 GUARANIES
21.3000 g., 0.9000 Gold 0.6163 oz. AGW **Subject:** Munich
Olympics **Obv:** National arms **Rev:** High jumper

Date	Mintage	F	VF	XF	Unc	BU
1972 Proof	Est. 1,500	Value: 1,500				

KM# 51   3000 GUARANIES
21.3000 g., 0.9000 Gold 0.6163 oz. AGW **Subject:** Munich
Olympics **Obv:** National arms **Rev:** Boxer

Date	Mintage	F	VF	XF	Unc	BU
1973 Proof	Est. 1,500	Value: 1,500				

KM# 81   3000 GUARANIES
21.3000 g., 0.9000 Gold 0.6163 oz. AGW **Obv:** National arms
Rev: Head of Mariscal Jose F. Estigarriba facing

Date	Mintage	F	VF	XF	Unc	BU
1973 Proof	Est. 1,500	Value: 750				

KM# 82   3000 GUARANIES
21.3000 g., 0.9000 Gold 0.6163 oz. AGW **Obv:** National arms
Rev: Bust of Mariscal Francisco Solano Lopez facing

Date	Mintage	F	VF	XF	Unc	BU
1973 Proof	Est. 1,500	Value: 750				

KM# 83   3000 GUARANIES
21.3000 g., 0.9000 Gold 0.6163 oz. AGW   **Obv:** National arms
Rev: Bust of General Jose E. Diaz facing

Date	Mintage	F	VF	XF	Unc	BU
1973 Proof	Est. 1,500	Value: 750				

KM# 88   3000 GUARANIES
21.3000 g., 0.9000 Gold 0.6163 oz. AGW   **Obv:** National arms
Rev: Veracruz Ceramica vase

Date	Mintage	F	VF	XF	Unc	BU
1973 Proof	Est. 1,500	Value: 750				

KM# 132   3000 GUARANIES
21.3000 g., 0.9000 Gold 0.6163 oz. AGW   **Obv:** National arms
Rev: Bust of Ludwig van Beethoven left

Date	Mintage	F	VF	XF	Unc	BU
1974 Proof	Est. 1,500	Value: 1,350				

KM# 84   3000 GUARANIES
21.3000 g., 0.9000 Gold 0.6163 oz. AGW   **Obv:** National arms
Rev: Bust of General Bernardino Caballero facing

Date	Mintage	F	VF	XF	Unc	BU
1973 Proof	Est. 1,500	Value: 750				

KM# 89   3000 GUARANIES
21.3000 g., 0.9000 Gold 0.6163 oz. AGW   **Obv:** National arms
Rev: Veracruz Culture sculpture facing

Date	Mintage	F	VF	XF	Unc	BU
1973 Proof	Est. 1,500	Value: 750				

KM# 133   3000 GUARANIES
21.3000 g., 0.9000 Gold 0.6163 oz. AGW   **Obv:** National arms
Rev: Bust of Otto von Bismarck right

Date	Mintage	F	VF	XF	Unc	BU
1974 Proof	Est. 1,500	Value: 750				

KM# 85   3000 GUARANIES
21.3000 g., 0.9000 Gold 0.6163 oz. AGW   **Obv:** National arms
Rev: Teotihucana Culture sculpture facing

Date	Mintage	F	VF	XF	Unc	BU
1973 Proof	Est. 1,500	Value: 750				

KM# 90   3000 GUARANIES
21.3000 g., 0.9000 Gold 0.6163 oz. AGW   **Obv:** National arms
Rev: Bust of Albrecht Durer facing

Date	Mintage	F	VF	XF	Unc	BU
1973 Proof	Est. 1,500	Value: 750				

KM# 134   3000 GUARANIES
21.3000 g., 0.9000 Gold 0.6163 oz. AGW   **Obv:** National arms
Rev: Head of Albert Einstein left

Date	Mintage	F	VF	XF	Unc	BU
1974 Proof	Est. 1,500	Value: 750				

KM# 86   3000 GUARANIES
21.3000 g., 0.9000 Gold 0.6163 oz. AGW   **Obv:** National arms
Rev: Huasteca Culture sculpture

Date	Mintage	F	VF	XF	Unc	BU
1973 Proof	Est. 1,500	Value: 750				

KM# 91   3000 GUARANIES
21.3000 g., 0.9000 Gold 0.6163 oz. AGW   **Obv:** National arms
Rev: Bust of Johann Wolfgang von Goethe facing

Date	Mintage	F	VF	XF	Unc	BU
1973 Proof	Est. 1,500	Value: 750				

KM# 135   3000 GUARANIES
21.3000 g., 0.9000 Gold 0.6163 oz. AGW   **Obv:** National arms
Rev: Head of Giuseppe Garibaldi facing

Date	Mintage	F	VF	XF	Unc	BU
1974 Proof	Est. 1,500	Value: 750				

KM# 87   3000 GUARANIES
21.3000 g., 0.9000 Gold 0.6163 oz. AGW   **Obv:** National arms
Rev: Mixteca Culture sculpture

Date	Mintage	F	VF	XF	Unc	BU
1973 Proof	Est. 1,500	Value: 750				

KM# 131   3000 GUARANIES
21.3000 g., 0.9000 Gold 0.6163 oz. AGW   **Obv:** National arms
Rev: Bust of President Abraham Lincoln left

Date	Mintage	F	VF	XF	Unc	BU
1974 Proof	Est. 1,500	Value: 750				

KM# 136   3000 GUARANIES
21.3000 g., 0.9000 Gold 0.6163 oz. AGW   **Obv:** National arms
Rev: Bust of Alessandro Manzoni facing

Date	Mintage	F	VF	XF	Unc	BU
1974 Proof	Est. 1,500	Value: 750				

KM# 137   3000 GUARANIES
21.3000 g., 0.9000 Gold 0.6163 oz. AGW   **Obv:** National arms
Rev: William Tell and son facing

Date	Mintage	F	VF	XF	Unc	BU
1974 Proof	Est. 1,500	Value: 750				

KM# 138   3000 GUARANIES
21.3000 g., 0.9000 Gold 0.6163 oz. AGW   **Obv:** National arms
Rev: Head of President John F. Kennedy left

Date	Mintage	F	VF	XF	Unc	BU
1974 Proof	Est. 1,500	Value: 750				

KM# 139   3000 GUARANIES
21.3000 g., 0.9000 Gold 0.6163 oz. AGW   **Obv:** National arms
Rev: Head of Konrad Adenauer left

Date	Mintage	F	VF	XF	Unc	BU
1974 Proof	Est. 1,500	Value: 750				

KM# 140   3000 GUARANIES
21.3000 g., 0.9000 Gold 0.6163 oz. AGW   **Obv:** National arms
Rev: Head of Sir Winston Churchill left

Date	Mintage	F	VF	XF	Unc	BU
1974 Proof	Est. 1,500	Value: 750				

KM# 141   3000 GUARANIES
21.3000 g., 0.9000 Gold 0.6163 oz. AGW   **Obv:** National arms
Rev: Head of Pope John XXIII left

Date	Mintage	F	VF	XF	Unc	BU
1974 Proof	Est. 1,500	Value: 750				

KM# 142   3000 GUARANIES
21.3000 g., 0.9000 Gold 0.6163 oz. AGW   **Obv:** National arms
Rev: Head of Pope Paul VI left

Date	Mintage	F	VF	XF	Unc	BU
1974 Proof	Est. 1,500	Value: 750				

KM# 161   3000 GUARANIES
21.3000 g., 0.9000 Gold 0.6163 oz. AGW   **Obv:** National arms
Rev: Holy Trinity Chruch

Date	Mintage	F	VF	XF	Unc	BU
1975 Proof	—	Value: 700				

KM# 162   3000 GUARANIES
21.3000 g., 0.9000 Gold 0.6163 oz. AGW   **Obv:** National arms
Rev: Parliament building

Date	Mintage	F	VF	XF	Unc	BU
1975 Proof	—	Value: 700				

KM# 163   3000 GUARANIES
21.3000 g., 0.9000 Gold 0.6163 oz. AGW   **Obv:** National arms
Rev: Friendship bridge

Date	Mintage	F	VF	XF	Unc	BU
1975 Proof	—	Value: 700				

KM# 164   3000 GUARANIES
21.3000 g., 0.9000 Gold 0.6163 oz. AGW   **Obv:** National arms
Rev: Humaita ruins

Date	Mintage	F	VF	XF	Unc	BU
1975 Proof	—	Value: 700				

KM# 175   3000 GUARANIES
21.3000 g., 0.9000 Gold 0.6163 oz. AGW   **Subject:** Apollo 11
Mission **Obv:** National arms **Rev:** Eagle landing on moon with
earth at upper left

Date	Mintage	F	VF	XF	Unc	BU
1975 Proof	—	Value: 1,000				

KM# 176   3000 GUARANIES
21.3000 g., 0.9000 Gold 0.6163 oz. AGW   **Subject:** Apollo 15
Mission within circle **Obv:** National arms **Rev:** Apollo mission
design within circle

Date	Mintage	F	VF	XF	Unc	BU
1975 Proof	—	Value: 1,000				

KM# 52   4500 GUARANIES
31.9000 g., 0.9000 Gold 0.9230 oz. AGW   **Obv:** National arms
Rev: General A. Stroessner

Date	Mintage	F	VF	XF	Unc	BU
1972 Proof	Est. 1,500	Value: 975				

KM# 53   4500 GUARANIES
31.9000 g., 0.9000 Gold 0.9230 oz. AGW   **Subject:** Munich
Olympics **Obv:** National arms **Rev:** Runner

Date	Mintage	F	VF	XF	Unc	BU
1972 Proof	Est. 1,500	Value: 2,700				

KM# 54   4500 GUARANIES
31.9000 g., 0.9000 Gold 0.9230 oz. AGW   **Subject:** Munich
Olympics **Obv:** National arms **Rev:** Broad jumper

Date	Mintage	F	VF	XF	Unc	BU
1972 Proof	Est. 1,500	Value: 2,700				

KM# 55   4500 GUARANIES
31.9000 g., 0.9000 Gold 0.9230 oz. AGW   **Subject:** Munich
Olympics **Obv:** National arms **Rev:** Soccer

Date	Mintage	F	VF	XF	Unc	BU
1972 Proof	Est. 1,500	Value: 2,700				

KM# 56   4500 GUARANIES
31.9000 g., 0.9000 Gold 0.9230 oz. AGW   **Subject:** Munich
Olympics **Obv:** National arms **Rev:** Hurdler

Date	Mintage	F	VF	XF	Unc	BU
1972 Proof	Est. 1,500	Value: 2,700				

KM# 57   4500 GUARANIES
31.9000 g., 0.9000 Gold 0.9230 oz. AGW   **Subject:** Munich
Olympics **Obv:** National arms **Rev:** High jumper

Date	Mintage	F	VF	XF	Unc	BU
1972 Proof	Est. 1,500	Value: 2,700				

KM# 58   4500 GUARANIES
31.9000 g., 0.9000 Gold 0.9230 oz. AGW   **Subject:** Munich
Olympics **Obv:** National arms **Rev:** Boxer

Date	Mintage	F	VF	XF	Unc	BU
1973 Proof	Est. 1,500	Value: 2,700				

KM# 92   4500 GUARANIES
31.9000 g., 0.9000 Gold 0.9230 oz. AGW   **Obv:** National arms
Rev: Bust of Mariscal Jose F. Estigarribia facing

Date	Mintage	F	VF	XF	Unc	BU
1973 Proof	Est. 1,500	Value: 1,200				

KM# 93   4500 GUARANIES
31.9000 g., 0.9000 Gold 0.9230 oz. AGW   **Obv:** National arms
Rev: Bust of Mariscal Francisco Solano Lopez facing

Date	Mintage	F	VF	XF	Unc	BU
1973 Proof	Est. 1,500		Value: 1,200			

KM# 94   4500 GUARANIES
31.9000 g., 0.9000 Gold 0.9230 oz. AGW   **Obv:** National arms
Rev: Head of General Jose E. Diaz facing

Date	Mintage	F	VF	XF	Unc	BU
1973 Proof	Est. 1,500		Value: 1,200			

KM# 95   4500 GUARANIES
31.9000 g., 0.9000 Gold 0.9230 oz. AGW   **Obv:** National arms
Rev: Head of General Bernardino Caballero facing

Date	Mintage	F	VF	XF	Unc	BU
1973 Proof	Est. 1,500		Value: 1,200			

KM# 96   4500 GUARANIES
31.9000 g., 0.9000 Gold 0.9230 oz. AGW   **Obv:** National arms
Rev: Teotihucana Culture sculpture

Date	Mintage	F	VF	XF	Unc	BU
1973 Proof	Est. 1,500		Value: 1,200			

KM# 97   4500 GUARANIES
31.9000 g., 0.9000 Gold 0.9230 oz. AGW   **Obv:** National arms
Rev: Huasteca Culture sculpture

Date	Mintage	F	VF	XF	Unc	BU
1973 Proof	Est. 1,500		Value: 1,200			

KM# 98   4500 GUARANIES
31.9000 g., 0.9000 Gold 0.9230 oz. AGW   **Obv:** National arms
Rev: Mixteca Culture sculpture

Date	Mintage	F	VF	XF	Unc	BU
1973 Proof	Est. 1,500		Value: 1,200			

KM# 99   4500 GUARANIES
31.9000 g., 0.9000 Gold 0.9230 oz. AGW   **Obv:** National arms
Rev: Veracruz Ceramica sculpture

Date	Mintage	F	VF	XF	Unc	BU
1973 Proof	Est. 1,500		Value: 1,200			

KM# 100   4500 GUARANIES
31.9000 g., 0.9000 Gold 0.9230 oz. AGW   **Obv:** National arms
Rev: Veracruz Culture bust

Date	Mintage	F	VF	XF	Unc	BU
1973 Proof	Est. 1,500		Value: 1,200			

KM# 101   4500 GUARANIES
31.9000 g., 0.9000 Gold 0.9230 oz. AGW   **Obv:** National arms
Rev: Bust of Albrecht Durer facing

Date	Mintage	F	VF	XF	Unc	BU
1973 Proof	Est. 1,500		Value: 1,200			

KM# 102   4500 GUARANIES
31.9000 g., 0.9000 Gold 0.9230 oz. AGW   **Obv:** National arms
Rev: Johann Wolfgang Goethe facing

Date	Mintage	F	VF	XF	Unc	BU
1973 Proof	Est. 1,500		Value: 1,200			

KM# 103   4500 GUARANIES
31.9000 g., 0.9000 Gold 0.9230 oz. AGW   **Obv:** National arms
Rev: Ludwig van Beethoven left

Date	Mintage	F	VF	XF	Unc	BU
1974 Proof	Est. 1,500		Value: 2,100			

KM# 104   4500 GUARANIES
31.9000 g., 0.9000 Gold 0.9230 oz. AGW   **Obv:** National arms
Rev: Head of Otto von Biscarck right

Date	Mintage	F	VF	XF	Unc	BU
1974 Proof	Est. 1,500		Value: 1,200			

KM# 105   4500 GUARANIES
31.9000 g., 0.9000 Gold 0.9230 oz. AGW   **Obv:** National arms
Rev: Giuseppe Gàribaldi facing

Date	Mintage	F	VF	XF	Unc	BU
1974 Proof	Est. 1,500		Value: 1,200			

KM# 106   4500 GUARANIES
31.9000 g., 0.9000 Gold 0.9230 oz. AGW   **Obv:** National arms
Rev: Alessandro Manzoni facing

Date	Mintage	F	VF	XF	Unc	BU
1974 Proof	Est. 1,500		Value: 1,200			

KM# 143   4500 GUARANIES
31.9000 g., 0.9000 Gold 0.9230 oz. AGW   **Obv:** National arms
Rev: President Abraham Lincoln left

Date	Mintage	F	VF	XF	Unc	BU
1974 Proof	Est. 1,500		Value: 1,200			

KM# 144   4500 GUARANIES
31.9000 g., 0.9000 Gold 0.9230 oz. AGW   **Obv:** National arms
Rev: Albert Einstein left

Date	Mintage	F	VF	XF	Unc	BU
1974 Proof	Est. 1,500		Value: 1,200			

KM# 145   4500 GUARANIES
31.9000 g., 0.9000 Gold 0.9230 oz. AGW   **Obv:** National arms
Rev: William Tell and son facing

Date	Mintage	F	VF	XF	Unc	BU
1974 Proof	Est. 1,500		Value: 1,200			

KM# 146   4500 GUARANIES
31.9000 g., 0.9000 Gold 0.9230 oz. AGW   **Obv:** National arms
Rev: President John F. Kennedy left

Date	Mintage	F	VF	XF	Unc	BU
1974 Proof	Est. 1,500		Value: 1,200			

KM# 147   4500 GUARANIES
31.9000 g., 0.9000 Gold 0.9230 oz. AGW   **Obv:** National arms
Rev: Konrad Adenauer left

Date	Mintage	F	VF	XF	Unc	BU
1974 Proof	Est. 1,500		Value: 1,200			

KM# 148   4500 GUARANIES
31.9000 g., 0.9000 Gold 0.9230 oz. AGW   **Obv:** National arms
Rev: Sir Winston Churchill left

Date	Mintage	F	VF	XF	Unc	BU
1974 Proof	Est. 1,500		Value: 1,200			

KM# 149   4500 GUARANIES
31.9000 g., 0.9000 Gold 0.9230 oz. AGW   **Obv:** National arms
Rev: Pope JOhn XXIII left

Date	Mintage	F	VF	XF	Unc	BU
1974 Proof	Est. 1,500		Value: 1,200			

KM# 150   4500 GUARANIES
31.9000 g., 0.9000 Gold 0.9230 oz. AGW   **Obv:** National arms
Rev: Pope Paul VI left

Date	Mintage	F	VF	XF	Unc	BU
1974 Proof	Est. 1,500		Value: 1,200			

KM# 185   4500 GUARANIES
31.9000 g., 0.9000 Gold 0.9230 oz. AGW   **Obv:** National arms
Rev: Parliament building

Date	Mintage	F	VF	XF	Unc	BU
1975 Proof	Est. 1,500		Value: 1,200			

KM# 186   4500 GUARANIES
31.9000 g., 0.9000 Gold 0.9230 oz. AGW   **Subject:** Apollo 11
Mission **Obv:** National arms **Rev:** Eagle landing on moon with
earth at upper left

Date	Mintage	F	VF	XF	Unc	BU
1975 Proof	Est. 1,500		Value: 1,200			

KM# 187   4500 GUARANIES
31.9000 g., 0.9000 Gold 0.9230 oz. AGW   **Subject:** Apollo 15
Mission **Obv:** National arms **Rev:** Apollo mission designs within
circle

Date	Mintage	F	VF	XF	Unc	BU
1975 Proof	Est. 1,500		Value: 1,200			

KM# 188   4500 GUARANIES
31.9000 g., 0.9000 Gold 0.9230 oz. AGW   **Obv:** National arms
Rev: Friendship bridge

Date	Mintage	F	VF	XF	Unc	BU
1975 Proof	Est. 1,500		Value: 1,200			

KM# 189   4500 GUARANIES
31.9000 g., 0.9000 Gold 0.9230 oz. AGW   **Obv:** National arms
Rev: Holy Trinity Church

Date	Mintage	F	VF	XF	Unc	BU
1975 Proof	Est. 1,500		Value: 1,200			

KM# 190   4500 GUARANIES
31.9000 g., 0.9000 Gold 0.9230 oz. AGW   **Obv:** National arms
Rev: Ruins of Humaita

Date	Mintage	F	VF	XF	Unc	BU
1975 Proof	Est. 1,500		Value: 1,200			

KM# 30   10000 GUARANIES
46.0100 g., 0.9000 Gold 1.3313 oz. AGW   **Subject:** 4th Term of
President Stroessner **Obv:** Seated lion with liberty cap on pole
within circle **Rev:** Head of President Stroessner left **Note:** Similar
to 300 Guaranies KM#29. KM#30 struck for presentation.

Date	Mintage	F	VF	XF	Unc	BU
ND(1968) Proof	Est. 50		Value: 4,500			

KM# 171   10000 GUARANIES
28.7000 g., 0.9990 Silver 0.9218 oz. ASW   **Obv:** Bank building
Rev: Conjoined busts of Caballero and Stroessner left

Date	Mintage	F	VF	XF	Unc	BU
ND(1987) Proof	1,000		Value: 42.00			

KM# 173   10000 GUARANIES
28.7000 g., 0.9990 Silver 0.9218 oz. ASW   **Subject:** 8th Term
of President A. Stroessner **Obv:** Seated lion with Liberty cap on
pole within circle **Rev:** Bust of President A. Stroessner left

Date	Mintage	F	VF	XF	Unc	BU
ND(1988) Proof	1,000		Value: 42.00			

KM# 168   70000 GUARANIES
46.0000 g., 0.9000 Gold 1.3310 oz. AGW   **Subject:** 6th Term of
President A. Stroessner **Obv:** Seated lion with Liberty cap on
pole within circle **Rev:** Bust of President A. Stroessner left

Date	Mintage	F	VF	XF	Unc	BU
ND(1978) Proof	300		Value: 1,450			

KM# 170   100000 GUARANIES
46.0000 g., 0.9000 Gold 1.3310 oz. AGW   **Subject:** 7th Term of
President A. Stroessner **Obv:** Seated lion with Liberty cap on
pole within circle **Rev:** Bust of President A. Stroessner left

Date	Mintage	F	VF	XF	Unc	BU
ND(1983) Proof	300		Value: 1,450			

KM# 172 250000 GUARANIES
46.0000 g., 0.9170 Gold 1.3561 oz. AGW **Obv:** Bank building within circle **Rev:** Conjoined busts of Caballero and Stroessner left

Date	Mintage	F	VF	XF	Unc	BU
ND(1987) Proof	Est. 500				Value: 1,450	

Note: 250 pieces remelted

KM# 174 300000 GUARANIES
46.0000 g., 0.9170 Gold 1.3561 oz. AGW **Subject:** 8th Term of President A. Stroessner **Obv:** Seated lion with Liberty cap on pole within circle **Rev:** Bust of President A. Stroessner left

Date	Mintage	F	VF	XF	Unc	BU
ND(1988) Proof	Est. 500				Value: 1,450	

Note: 250 pieces remelted

PATTERNS
Including off metal strikes

KM#	Date	Mintage	Identification	Mkt Val
Pn40	1925	—	2 Pesos. Aluminum. Narrow flan, KM14.	100
Pn41	1925	—	2 Pesos. Aluminum. Broad flan, KM14.	125
Pn42	1939	—	5 Pesos. Brass. KM#8.	175
Pn43	1939	—	5 Pesos. Copper. KM18.	175
Pn44	1976	—	10 Guarani. Gold.	450
Pn45	1976	—	10 Guaranies. Gold.	750
Pn46	1978	—	10 Guarani. Gold.	450
Pn47	1978	—	5 Guaranies. Gold.	550
Pn48	1978	—	10 Guaranies. Gold.	750
Pn49	1980	—	10 Guarani. Gold.	450
Pn50	1980	—	5 Guaranies. Gold.	550
Pn51	1980	—	10 Guaranies. Gold.	750
Pn52	1980	—	50 Guaranies. Gold.	1,100

PROOF SETS

KM#	Date	Mintage	Identification	Issue Price	Mkt Val
PS1	1953 (4)	1	KM25-28	—	1,650
PS2	1972 (24)	150	KM31-36, 38-43, 45-50, 52-57	—	—
PS3	1973 (48)	150	KM37, 44, 51, 58-102	—	—
PS4	1974 (48)	150	KM103-150	—	—
PS5	1975 (24)	150	KM155-164, 175-176, 179-190	—	—
PS6	1975 (4)	1,000	KM151-154	—	30.00
PS7	1976 (2)	1,000	KM151, 153	—	20.00
PS8	1976 (2)	—	KM#151a, 153a	—	—
PS9	1978 (3)	—	KM#165, 166, 167	—	—
PS10	1978 (3)	—	KM#165a, 166b, 167a	—	—
PS11	1980 (4)	1,000	KM165-167, 169	—	30.00
PS12	1980 (4)	—	KM#165a, 166b, 167a, 169a	—	—
PS13	1988 (3)	—	KM#165, 167, 169	—	20.00

The Republic of Peru, located on the Pacific coast of South America, has an area of 496,225 sq. mi. (1,285,220sq. km.) and a population of *21.4 million. Capital: Lima. The diversified economy includes mining, fishing and agriculture. Fishmeal, copper, sugar, zinc and iron ore are exported.

Once part of the great Inca Empire that reached from northern Ecuador to central Chile, the conquest of Peru by Francisco Pizarro began in 1531. Desirable as the richest of the Spanish viceroyalties, it was torn by warfare between avaricious Spaniards until the arrival in 1569 of Francisco de Toledo, who initiated 2-1/2 centuries of efficient colonial rule, which made Lima the most aristocratic colonial capital and the stronghold of Spain's American possessions. Jose de San Martin of Argentina proclaimed Peru's independence on July 28, 1821; Simon Bolivar of Venezuela secured it in December, 1824 when he defeated the last Spanish army in South America. After several futile attempts to re-establish its South American Empire, Spain recognized Peru's independence in 1879.

Andres de Santa Cruz, whose mother was a high-ranking Inca, was the best of Bolivia's early presidents, and temporarily united Peru and Bolivia 1836-39, thus realizing his dream of a Peruvian/Bolivian confederation. This prompted the separate coinages of North and South Peru. Peruvian resistance and Chilean intervention finally broke up the confederation, sending Santa Cruz into exile. A succession of military strongman presidents ruled Peru until Marshall Castilla revitalized Peruvian politics in the mid-19th century and repulsed Spain's attempt to reclaim its one-time colony. Subsequent loss of southern territory to Chile in the War of the Pacific, 1879-81, and gradually increasing rejection of foreign economic domination, combined with recent serious inflation, affected the country numismatically.

As a result of the discovery of silver at Pofosi in 1545, a mint was eventually authorized in 1565 with the first coinage taking place in 1568. The mint had an uneven life span during the Spanish Colonial period from 1568-72. It was closed from 1573-76, reopened from 1577-88. It remained closed until 1659-1660 when an unauthorized coinage in both silver and gold were struck. After being closed in 1660, it remained closed until 1684 when it struck cob style coins until 1752.

MINT MARKS
AREQUIPA, AREQ = Arequipa
AYACUCHO = Ayacucho
(B) = Brussels
CUZCO (monogram), Cuzco, Co. Cuzco
L, LM, LIMAE (monogram), Lima
(monogram), LIMA = Lima
(L) = London
PASCO (monogram), Pasco, Paz, Po= Pasco
P, (P) = Philadelphia
S = San Francisco
(W) = Waterbury, CT, USA

MINT ASSAYERS' INITIALS
The letter(s) following the dates of Peruvian coins are the assayer's initials appearing on the coins. They generally appear at the 11 o'clock position on the Colonial coinage and at the 5 o'clock position along the rim on the obverse or reverse on the Republican coinage.

DATING
Peruvian 5, 10 and 20 centavos, issued from 1918-1944, bear the dates written in Spanish. The following table translates those written dates into numerals:

1918 - UN MIL NOVECIENTOS DIECIOCHO
1919 - UN MIL NOVECIENTOS DIECINUEVE
1920 - UN MIL NOVECIENTOS VEINTE
1921 - UN MIL NOVECIENTOS VEINTIUNO
1923 - UN MIL NOVECIENTOS VEINTITRES
1926 - UN MIL NOVECIENTOS VEINTISEIS
1934 - UN MIL NOVECIENTOS TREINTICUATRO
1935 - UN MIL NOVECIENTOS TREINTICINCO
1937 - UN MIL NOVECIENTOS TREINTISIETE
1939 - UN MIL NOVECIENTOS TREINTINUEVE
1940 - UN MIL NOVECIENTOS CUARENTA
1941 - UN MIL NOVECIENTOS CUARENTIUNO
U.S. Mints
1942 - MIL NOVECIENTOS CUARENTA Y DOS
Lima Mint
1942 - UN MIL NOVECIENTOS CUARENTIDOS
U.S. Mints
1943 - MIL NOVECIENTOS CUARENTA Y TRES
1944 - MIL NOVECIENTOS CUARENTA Y CUATRO
Lima Mint
1944 - MIL NOVECIENTOS CUARENTICUATRO

MONETARY SYSTEM
100 Centavos (10 Dineros) = 1 Sol
10 Soles = 1 Libra

REPUBLIC
DECIMAL COINAGE
100 Centavos (10 Dineros) = 1 Sol; 10 Soles = 1 Libra

KM# 208.1 CENTAVO
Bronze **Obv:** Radiant star design around center circle with small date below and legend above **Rev:** Value within wreath, CENTAVO straight **Note:** Thick planchet.

Date	Mintage	F	VF	XF	Unc	BU
1901	600,000	1.00	3.00	8.00	20.00	—
1904	1,000,000	8.00	15.00	30.00	60.00	—

KM# 211 CENTAVO
Bronze **Obv:** Radiant star design around center circle **Rev:** Value within wreath, CENTAVO curved **Note:** Thick planchet. Engravers initial R appears below ribbon on most or all new dies, but often became weak or filled. Most coins show at least a faint trace of an R. Date varieteis also exist.

Date	Mintage	F	VF	XF	Unc	BU
1909/999 R	Inc. above	10.00	20.00	35.00	70.00	—
1909 R	Inc. above	10.00	20.00	35.00	70.00	—
1909	252,000	10.00	20.00	35.00	70.00	—
1915	250,000	3.00	6.00	10.00	30.00	—
1916	360,000	1.00	2.00	7.00	20.00	—
1916 R	Inc. above	1.00	2.00	6.00	15.00	—
1917	830,000	1.00	2.00	6.00	15.00	—
1917 R	Inc. above	1.00	2.00	6.00	15.00	—
1918	1,060,000	1.00	2.00	5.00	14.00	—
1918 R	Inc. above	1.00	2.00	5.00	14.00	—
1920	360,000	1.00	2.50	7.00	20.00	—
1920 R	Inc. above	1.00	2.50	7.00	20.00	—
1933 R Inc. KM208.2	—	1.00	2.50	7.00	20.00	—
1934 Inc. KM#208.2	—	4.50	8.00	20.00	55.00	—
1935 R Inc. KM#208.2	—	4.00	7.00	20.00	50.00	—
1936 R Inc. KM#208.2	—	1.50	3.50	7.00	20.00	—
1937	—	—	—	—	—	—
1937 R Inc. KM#208.2	—	1.50	3.50	7.00	20.00	—
1939 R Inc. KM#208.2	—	4.50	8.00	20.00	55.00	—

KM# 208.2 CENTAVO
Bronze **Obv:** Large date and legend **Rev:** CENTAVO straight **Note:** Thick planchet. Varieties exist.

Date	Mintage	F	VF	XF	Unc	BU
1933	275,000	1.50	3.00	8.00	20.00	—
1934	1,185,000	1.00	2.00	5.00	15.00	—
1935	1,105,000	1.00	2.00	5.00	15.00	—
1936	565,000	1.50	3.00	8.00	20.00	—
1937/6	735,000	1.00	2.00	4.00	20.00	—
1937	Inc. above	0.75	1.50	2.50	15.00	—
1938	340,000	0.75	1.50	2.50	15.00	—
1939	1,225,000	1.50	3.00	5.50	20.00	—
1940	1,250,000	1.50	3.00	5.50	20.00	—
1941	2,593,000	0.40	0.75	1.50	10.00	—

KM# 208a CENTAVO
Bronze **Obv:** Large date and legend **Rev:** Straight centavo **Note:** Thin planchet.

Date	Mintage	F	VF	XF	Unc	BU
1941 Inc. KM#208.2	—	0.40	0.75	2.00	8.00	—
1942	2,865,000	0.50	1.00	2.50	10.00	—
1944	—	10.00	20.00	35.00	70.00	—

KM# 211a CENTAVO
Bronze **Obv:** Radiant star design around center circle, large date and legend **Rev:** Value within wreath, CENTAVO curved **Note:** Thin planchet. Many varieties exist.

Date	Mintage	F	VF	XF	Unc	BU
1941 Inc. KM#208.2	—	1.00	2.00	5.00	15.00	—
1942 Inc. KM#208a	—	0.50	1.00	3.00	10.00	—
1943	—	2.50	5.00	15.00	35.00	—
1944	2,490,000	0.15	0.40	1.00	4.00	—
1945	2,157,000	0.15	0.40	1.00	4.00	—
1946	3,198,000	0.15	0.40	1.00	4.00	—
1947	2,976,000	0.15	0.40	1.00	4.00	—
1948	3,195,000	0.15	0.40	1.00	4.00	—
1949	1,104,000	0.25	0.65	2.00	6.00	—

KM# 227 CENTAVO

1.0200 g., Zinc, 14.98 mm. **Obv:** Radiant star design around center circle **Rev:** Value within wreath, curved centavo **Edge:** Plain **Note:** Varieties exist.

Date	Mintage	F	VF	XF	Unc	BU
1950	3,196,000	0.35	0.25	1.25	5.00	—
1951	3,289,000	0.25	0.40	0.65	3.00	—

Note: Copper-plated examples of type dated 1951 are known

1952	3,050,000	0.25	0.40	0.65	3.00	—
1953	3,260,000	0.35	0.60	1.00	4.00	—
1954	3,215,000	0.75	1.50	2.50	10.00	—
1955	3,400,000	0.25	0.40	0.65	3.00	—
1956 Pointed 6	2,500,000	0.25	0.40	0.65	3.00	—
1956 Knobbed 6	Inc. above	0.25	0.40	0.65	3.00	—
1957	4,400,000	0.40	0.85	2.00	7.00	—
1958/7	—	0.35	0.60	1.00	4.00	—
1958/8	3,200,000	0.50	1.00	2.00	7.00	—
1958	2,600,000	0.35	0.60	1.00	4.00	—
1959/8	Inc. above	0.35	0.75	1.50	5.00	—
1959	0.25	0.40	0.65	3.00	—
1960/50	3,060,000	0.35	0.60	1.00	4.00	—
1960	0.75	1.50	3.00	8.00	—
1961/51	2,600,000	0.25	0.40	1.00	3.00	—
1961	Inc. above	0.25	0.40	1.00	3.00	—
1962/52	2,600,000	0.25	0.40	1.00	3.00	—
1962	Inc. above	0.25	0.40	1.00	3.00	—
1963/53	2,400,000	0.25	0.40	1.00	3.00	—
1963	Inc. above	0.25	0.40	1.00	3.00	—
1965	360,000	0.75	1.50	3.00	10.00	—

KM# 187 CENTAVO

Bronze **Obv:** Radiant star design around center circle **Rev:** Value within wreath **Note:** Earlier dates 1875-1878 are listed as KM#187.1a in our 19th Century book.

Date	Mintage	F	VF	XF	Unc	BU
1919(P)	4,000,000	0.50	1.00	2.50	10.00	—

KM# 212.1 2 CENTAVOS

Copper Or Bronze **Obv:** Date at bottom **Rev:** Curved "CENTAVOS" **Note:** Thick planchet. Engraver's initial C appeared below ribbon on most or all new dies, but often became weak or filled. Most coins show at least a faint trace of C. Other varieties also exist.

Date	Mintage	F	VF	XF	Unc	BU
1917 C	73,000	4.00	6.50	15.00	40.00	—
1918/17	580,000	3.50	6.00	12.00	40.00	—
1918	Inc. above	3.50	6.00	15.00	40.00	—
1918/17 C	Inc. above	4.00	10.00	20.00	50.00	—
1918 C	Inc. above	3.50	6.00	15.00	40.00	—
1920/7 C	328,000	2.00	4.00	10.00	30.00	—
1920	Inc. above	1.00	2.00	5.00	15.00	—
1920 C	Inc. above	1.00	2.00	5.00	15.00	—
1933	285,000	1.00	2.00	5.00	15.00	—
1933 C	Inc. above	1.00	2.00	5.00	15.00	—
1934	973,000	0.75	1.50	4.00	15.00	—
1934 C	Inc. above	0.75	1.50	4.00	15.00	—
1935	950,000	0.75	1.50	4.00	15.00	—
1935 C	Inc. above	0.75	1.50	4.00	15.00	—
1936	763,000	0.75	1.50	4.00	15.00	—
1936/5 C	Inc. above	1.50	2.50	8.00	20.00	—
1936 C	Inc. above	0.75	1.25	3.00	12.00	—
1937	963,000	0.75	1.50	4.00	15.00	—
1937 C	Inc. above	0.75	1.50	4.00	15.00	—
1938 C	428,000	1.00	1.75	4.00	15.00	—
1939/8 C	—	—	—	—	—	—

Note: Reported, not confirmed

1939/8	—	1.50	2.50	8.00	20.00	—
1939 C Inverted A for V in CENTAVOS	783,000	0.75	1.50	4.00	15.00	—
1940	—	1.00	2.00	4.00	15.00	—
1940 C	565,000	1.00	1.75	4.00	15.00	—
1941/0	Inc. above	1.00	2.00	4.00	15.00	—
1941/0 C	Inc. above	1.00	2.00	4.00	15.00	—
1941/22	Inc. above	1.00	2.00	4.00	15.00	—
1941	Inc. above	1.00	2.00	4.00	15.00	—
1941 C	Inc. above	2.00	5.00	12.00	20.00	—

KM# 212.2 2 CENTAVOS

5.8000 g., Copper Or Bronze, 23.93 mm. **Obv:** Radiant star design around center circle **Rev:** Value within sprays **Edge:** Plain **Note:** Thin planchet. Varieties exist.

Date	Mintage	F	VF	XF	Unc	BU
1941/32	870,000	1.00	2.00	3.50	10.00	—
1941/33 C	Inc. above	1.00	2.00	3.50	10.00	—
1941/33	Inc. above	1.00	2.00	3.50	10.00	—
1941/38	Inc. above	1.00	2.00	3.50	10.00	—
1941/38 C	Inc. above	1.00	2.00	3.50	10.00	—
1941/39 C	Inc. above	1.00	2.00	3.50	10.00	—
1941/0	Inc. above	1.00	2.00	3.50	10.00	—
1941	Inc. above	0.50	1.00	2.00	7.00	—
1942/22	4,418,000	—	0.50	1.00	5.00	—
1942/32	4,418,000	—	0.50	1.00	5.00	—
1942	Inc. above	0.25	0.50	1.00	5.00	—
1943/2	1,829,000	0.50	1.00	3.00	10.00	—
1943	Inc. above	0.50	1.00	3.00	10.00	—
1944	2,068,000	1.00	2.00	4.00	12.00	—

Date	Mintage	F	VF	XF	Unc	BU
1945	2,288,000	1.00	2.00	4.00	12.00	—
1946	2,121,000	0.25	0.50	0.75	4.00	—
1947	1,280,000	0.25	0.50	0.75	4.00	—
1948	1,518,000	0.25	0.50	0.75	5.00	—
1949/8	938,000	0.25	0.60	4.00	7.00	—
1949	Inc. above	0.50	1.00	4.00	7.00	—

KM# 228 2 CENTAVOS

Zinc **Obv:** Radiant star design around center circle **Rev:** Value within wreath

Date	Mintage	F	VF	XF	Unc	BU
1950	1,702,000	0.35	0.75	1.25	3.00	—
1951	3,289,000	0.35	0.75	1.25	3.00	—

Note: Copper-plated examples of type dated 1951 exist

1952	1,155,000	0.35	0.75	1.25	3.00	—
1953	1,150,000	0.40	0.85	1.50	4.00	—
1954	—	2.00	4.00	10.00	30.00	—
1955	1,185,000	0.35	0.75	1.25	3.00	—
1956	400,000	0.50	1.00	2.00	5.00	—
1957	520,000	1.50	3.00	6.00	25.00	—
1958	200,000	1.25	2.50	4.50	15.00	—

KM# A212 2 CENTAVOS

Copper Or Bronze **Obv:** Radiant star design around center circle **Rev:** Value within wreath **Note:** Sharper diework. Earlier date 1895 listed as KM#188.2 in 19th Century book.

Date	Mintage	F	VF	XF	Unc	BU
1919(P)	3,000,000	0.35	0.75	2.00	9.00	—

KM# 213.1 5 CENTAVOS

Copper-Nickel **Obv:** Date: UN MIL NOVECIENTOS DIECIOCHO **Rev:** Value to right of sprig

Date	Mintage	F	VF	XF	Unc	BU
1918	4,000,000	0.50	1.25	2.50	10.00	—
1919	10,000,000	0.40	1.00	2.00	7.00	—
1923	2,000,000	1.00	2.00	3.50	12.50	—
1926	4,000,000	1.50	3.00	6.00	20.00	—

KM# 213.2 5 CENTAVOS

3.0000 g., Copper-Nickel **Obv:** Head right **Rev:** Value to right of sprig

Date	Mintage	F	VF	XF	Unc	BU
1934	4,000,000	0.75	2.00	3.00	9.00	—
1934 Proof	— Value: 200					
1935	4,000,000	0.50	1.25	2.00	6.00	—
1935 Proof	—	—	—	—	—	—
1937	2,000,000	0.75	2.00	3.00	9.00	—
1937 Proof	—	—	—	—	—	—
1939	2,000,000	0.50	1.25	2.00	6.00	—
1939 Proof	—	—	—	—	—	—
1940	2,000,000	0.50	1.25	2.00	6.00	—
1940 Proof	—	—	—	—	—	—
1941	2,000,000	0.50	1.25	2.00	6.00	—
1941 Proof	—	—	—	—	—	—

KM# 213.2a.1 5 CENTAVOS

Brass **Obv:** Date: MIL NOVECIENTOS CUARENTA Y DOS **Rev:** Value to right of sprig

Date	Mintage	F	VF	XF	Unc	BU
1942	4,000,000	1.00	3.00	5.00	20.00	—
1943	4,000,000	1.00	3.00	5.00	20.00	—
1944	4,000,000	1.00	2.75	4.50	20.00	—

KM# 213.2a.2 5 CENTAVOS

Brass **Obv:** Head right with date spelled out **Rev:** Value to right of sprig

Date	Mintage	F	VF	XF	Unc	BU
1942S	4,000,000	2.50	4.50	10.00	50.00	—
1943S	4,000,000	2.50	4.50	8.00	40.00	—

KM# 213.2a.3 5 CENTAVOS

Brass **Obv:** Date: MIL NOVECIENTOS CUARENTICUATRO **Rev:** Value to right of sprig

Date	Mintage	F	VF	XF	Unc	BU
1944	1,106,000	1.50	3.50	6.00	15.00	—

KM# 223.1 5 CENTAVOS

2.0000 g., Brass **Obv:** Head right with short legend **Rev:** Value to right of sprig **Note:** Thick planchet.

Date	Mintage	F	VF	XF	Unc	BU
1945	2,768,000	0.35	0.75	1.50	4.00	—
1946/5	4,270,000	1.00	2.50	5.00	14.00	—
1946	Inc. above	0.25	0.50	1.00	3.50	—

KM# 223.3 5 CENTAVOS

Brass **Obv:** Head right with long legend with 3mm gap above head **Rev:** Value to right of sprig **Note:** Thick planchet.

Date	Mintage	F	VF	XF	Unc	BU
1947	7,683,000	0.25	0.50	1.00	3.00	—
1948	6,711,000	0.25	0.50	1.00	3.00	—
1949	—	0.25	0.50	1.00	3.00	—
1949/8	5,550,000	1.00	2.00	4.00	10.00	—

KM# 223.4 5 CENTAVOS

Brass **Obv:** Head right **Rev:** Value to right of sprig **Note:** Thick planchet.

Date	Mintage	F	VF	XF	Unc	BU
1949	Inc. above	1.00	2.00	4.00	10.00	—
1950	7,933,000	0.25	0.50	1.00	3.00	—
195.1	8,064,000	0.25	0.50	1.00	3.00	—
1951	Inc. above	1.00	2.00	4.00	35.00	—

KM# 223.2 5 CENTAVOS

2.8500 g., Brass, 17 mm. **Obv:** Head right **Rev:** Value to right of sprig **Note:** Thin planchet. Varieties exist.

Date	Mintage	F	VF	XF	Unc	BU
1951	Inc. above	0.10	0.25	0.50	6.00	—
1952	7,840,000	0.10	0.25	0.50	6.00	—
1953 AFP	6,976,000	0.10	0.25	0.50	6.00	—
1954	6,244,000	0.10	0.20	0.40	1.00	—
1955	8,064,000	0.10	0.20	0.40	2.00	—
1956	16,200,000	—	0.10	0.35	1.50	—
1957 Small date	16,000,000	—	0.10	0.25	1.00	—
1957 Large date	Inc. above	—	0.10	0.25	1.00	—
1958	4,600,000	—	0.10	0.25	1.00	—
1959	8,300,000	—	0.10	0.25	1.00	—
1960/50	9,900,000	—	0.10	0.25	1.00	—
1960 Large date	Inc. above	—	0.10	0.20	1.00	—
1960 Small date	Inc. above	—	0.10	0.20	1.00	—
1961	10,200,000	—	0.10	0.20	1.00	—
1962 Curved 9	11,064,000	—	0.10	0.20	1.00	—
1962 Straight 9	Inc. above	—	0.10	0.20	1.00	—
1963	12,012,000	—	0.10	0.20	1.00	—
1964/3	12,304,000	—	0.10	0.35	1.50	—
1964	Inc. above	—	—	0.10	1.00	—
1965 Small date	12,500,000	—	—	0.10	1.00	—
1965 Large date	Inc. above	—	0.10	0.20	1.00	—
1965 Proof	— Value: 20.00					

KM# 232 5 CENTAVOS

Brass, 17 mm. **Obv:** Head right **Rev:** Value to right of torch within chain circle

Date	Mintage	F	VF	XF	Unc	BU
1954	2,080,000	1.00	2.00	4.00	8.00	—

KM# 290 5 CENTAVOS

1.4400 g., Brass **Subject:** 400th Anniversary of Lima Mint **Obv:** National arms above value **Rev:** Pillars of Hercules within inner circle

Date	Mintage	F	VF	XF	Unc	BU
1965 Proof	— Value: 100					
1965	712,000	—	—	0.25	1.00	—

KM# 244.1 5 CENTAVOS

Brass **Obv:** National arms within circle above date **Rev:** Value to left of flower sprig

Date	Mintage	F	VF	XF	Unc	BU
1966 Proof	1,000	Value: 15.00				
1966	14,620,000	—	—	0.10	0.20	0.35

Note: PAREJA in field at lower left of arms

| 1967 | 14,088,000 | — | — | 0.10 | 0.20 | 0.35 |
| 1968 | 17,880,000 | — | — | 0/10 | 0.20 | 0.35 |

KM# 244.1a 5 CENTAVOS

Silver Plated Brass **Obv:** National arms within circle above date **Rev:** Value to left of flower sprig

Date	Mintage	F	VF	XF	Unc	BU
1967	—	—	—	—	—	—

KM# 244.1b 5 CENTAVOS

Silver **Obv:** National arms within circle above date **Rev:** Value to left of flower sprig

Date	Mintage	F	VF	XF	Unc	BU
1967	—	—	—	—	—	—

KM# 244.2 5 CENTAVOS

1.5000 g., Brass **Obv:** National arms within circle **Rev:** Value to left of flower sprig **Edge:** Plain

Date	Mintage	F	VF	XF	Unc	BU
1969	17,880,000	—	—	—	0.10	0.20
1970	—	—	—	—	0.10	0.20
1971	24,320,000	—	—	—	0.10	0.20
1972	24,342,000	—	—	—	0.10	0.20
1973	25,074,000	—	—	—	0.10	0.20

KM# 244.3 5 CENTAVOS

1.4500 g., Brass, 14.8 mm. **Obv:** National arms within circle **Rev:** Value to left of flower sprig **Edge:** Plain

Date	Mintage	F	VF	XF	Unc	BU
1973	Inc. above	—	—	—	0.10	0.20
1974	—	—	—	—	0.10	0.20
1975	—	—	—	—	0.10	0.20

KM# 206.2 1/2 DINERO
1.2500 g., 0.9000 Silver 0.0362 oz. ASW **Obv:** National arms above date **Rev:** Seated Liberty flanked by shield and column **Note:** Most coins 1900-06 show faint to strong traces of 9/8 or 90/89 in date. Non-overdates without such traces are scarce. Most coins of 1907-17 have engraver's initial R at left of shield tip on reverse. Many other varieties exist.

Date	Mintage	F	VF	XF	Unc	BU
1901/801 JF	500,000	65.00	1.25	2.50	6.00	—
1901/801/701 JF	Inc. above	0.65	1.25	2.50	6.00	—
1901/891/791	Inc. above	0.65	1.25	2.00	5.00	—
1901/891 JF	Inc. above	0.65	1.25	2.00	5.00	—
1901 JF	Inc. above	0.75	1.50	3.50	10.00	—
1902/802 JF	616,000	0.65	1.25	2.00	5.00	—
1902/892 JF	Inc. above	0.65	1.25	2.00	5.00	—
1902/92	Inc. above	0.65	1.25	2.00	5.00	—
1902 JF	Inc. above	0.75	1.50	3.50	10.00	—
1903/803 JF	1,798,000	0.65	1.50	3.00	9.00	—
1903/893 JF	Inc. above	0.65	1.50	3.00	9.00	—
1903/897 JF	Inc. above	0.60	1.00	2.50	7.00	—
1903 JF	Inc. above	0.75	1.50	3.00	10.00	—
1904/804 JF	723,000	0.65	1.25	2.00	5.00	—
1904/804 JF FFLIZ Error	Inc. above	3.00	6.00	12.00	25.00	—
1904/884 JF	Inc. above	0.65	1.25	2.00	6.00	—
1904/891 JF	Inc. above	0.65	1.25	2.00	6.00	—
1904/893 JF	Inc. above	0.65	1.25	2.00	5.00	—
1904/894 JF	Inc. above	0.65	1.25	2.00	5.00	—
1904/894 JF FFLIZ Error	Inc. above	2.00	4.50	8.00	12.00	—
1904 JF	Inc. above	0.75	1.50	3.50	10.00	—
1904 JF FFLIZ Error	Inc. above	2.00	4.50	8.00	12.00	—
1905/805 JF	1,400,000	0.75	1.50	3.50	8.00	—
1905/891 JF	Inc. above	1.00	2.00	4.50	12.00	—
1905/893 JF	Inc. above	1.00	2.00	4.50	12.00	—
1905/894	Inc. above	1.00	2.00	4.50	12.00	—
1905/895 JF	Inc. above	0.60	1.25	2.00	5.00	—
1905/3 JF	Inc. above	1.00	2.00	4.50	12.00	—
1905 JF	Inc. above	0.75	1.50	3.50	10.00	—
1906/806 JF	900,000	0.75	1.50	3.50	8.00	—
1906/886 JF	Inc. above	0.75	1.50	3.50	8.00	—
1906/895 JF	Inc. above	0.75	1.50	3.50	8.00	—
1906/896 JF	Inc. above	0.60	1.25	2.00	5.00	—
1906 JF	Inc. above	0.75	1.50	3.00	10.00	—
1907 FG	600,000	0.75	1.50	3.00	10.00	—
1908/7 FG	200,000	1.50	3.00	6.00	15.00	—
1908 FG	Inc. above	0.75	1.50	3.50	10.00	—
1909/7 FG	—	3.00	6.00	12.50	30.00	—
1909 FG	—	0.75	1.50	3.50	8.00	—
1910 FG	640,000	0.60	1.00	2.00	5.00	—
1911 FG	460,000	0.60	1.25	2.00	5.00	—
1912 FG	120,000	0.65	1.25	2.50	6.00	—
1913 FG	480,000	0.60	1.00	2.00	5.00	—
1914/3 FG	—	0.75	1.50	3.50	10.00	—
1914/03 FG	—	1.00	2.50	5.50	15.00	—
1914/04 FG	—	1.00	2.50	5.50	15.00	—
1914 FG	—	0.60	1.00	2.00	5.00	—
1916/3 FG	860,000	0.60	1.00	2.00	5.00	—
1916/3 FG FERUANA Error	—	1.00	2.00	4.50	12.00	—
1916 FG	Inc. above	BV	0.75	1.75	4.50	—
1916/5 FG PERUANA Error	Inc. above	1.00	2.00	4.50	12.00	—
1916/5 FG FERUANA Error	Inc. above	1.00	2.00	4.50	12.00	—
1916/5 Without FERUANA	Inc. above	1.00	2.00	4.50	12.00	—
1916 FG FERUANA Error	Inc. above	1.00	2.00	4.50	15.00	—
1916 Matte	—	—	—	—	—	—
1917/87 FG	140,000	0.60	1.00	2.00	5.00	—
1917 FG	Inc. above	0.60	1.00	2.00	5.00	—

KM# 214.1 10 CENTAVOS
Copper-Nickel **Obv:** Head right **Rev:** Value to right of sprig

Date	Mintage	F	VF	XF	Unc	BU
1918	3,000,000	0.40	1.00	2.00	12.00	—
1919	2,500,000	0.40	1.00	2.00	12.00	—
1920	3,080,000	0.35	0.75	1.50	10.00	—
1921	6,920,000	0.35	0.75	1.50	10.00	—
1926	3,000,000	2.50	5.00	8.50	25.00	—

KM# 214.2 10 CENTAVOS
3.8600 g., Copper-Nickel **Obv:** Head right **Rev:** Value to right of sprig

Date	Mintage	F	VF	XF	Unc	BU
1935	1,000,000	0.75	1.50	3.00	12.00	—
1935 Proof	—	Value: 150				
1937	1,000,000	0.40	1.00	2.00	7.00	—
1937 Proof	—	—	—	—	—	—
1939	2,000,000	0.35	0.75	1.25	5.00	—
1939 Proof	—	—	—	—	—	—
1940	2,000,000	0.35	0.75	1.25	5.00	—
1940 Proof	—	Value: 175				
1941	2,000,000	0.35	0.75	1.25	5.00	—
1941 Proof	—	—	—	—	—	—

KM# 214a.1 10 CENTAVOS
Brass **Obv:** Head right, date begins MIL..., spelled out w/a "Y" **Rev:** Value to right of sprig

Date	Mintage	F	VF	XF	Unc	BU
1942	2,000,000	1.50	3.00	6.00	20.00	—
1943	2,000,000	1.50	3.00	6.00	20.00	—
1944	2,000,000	1.50	3.50	7.00	25.00	—

KM# 214a.2 10 CENTAVOS
Brass **Obv:** Head right **Rev:** Value to right of sprig **Edge:** Plain

Date	Mintage	F	VF	XF	Unc	BU
1942S	2,000,000	6.00	12.00	20.00	50.00	—
1943S	2,000,000	1.50	3.00	6.00	20.00	—

KM# 214a.3 10 CENTAVOS
Brass **Obv:** Date behins MIL..., spelled out with an "I" **Rev:** Value to right of sprig

Date	Mintage	F	VF	XF	Unc	BU
1942	—	5.00	9.00	15.00	40.00	—

KM# 214a.4 10 CENTAVOS
Brass **Obv:** Date behins MIL..., spelled out with an "I" **Rev:** Value to right of sprig **Note:** Varieties exist.

Date	Mintage	F	VF	XF	Unc	BU
1944	—	3.50	7.00	12.00	35.00	—

KM# 224.1 10 CENTAVOS
Brass **Obv:** Head right with short legend **Rev:** Value to right of sprig **Note:** Thick planchet.

Date	Mintage	F	VF	XF	Unc	BU
1945	2,810,000	0.25	0.50	1.50	4.00	—
1946/5	4,863,000	0.50	1.00	2.50	8.00	—
1946	Inc. above	0.35	0.75	2.00	7.00	—

KM# 226.1 10 CENTAVOS
3.8900 g., Brass **Obv:** Long legend with 3mm gap above head **Rev:** Value to right of sprig **Note:** Thick planchet.

Date	Mintage	F	VF	XF	Unc	BU
1947	6,806,000	0.25	0.50	1.00	3.00	—
1948	5,771,000	0.25	0.50	1.25	4.00	—
1949/8	4,730,000	0.50	1.00	1.50	7.50	—

KM# 226.2 10 CENTAVOS
Brass **Obv:** Head right **Rev:** Value to right of sprig

Date	Mintage	F	VF	XF	Unc	BU
1949	Inc. above	0.25	0.50	1.00	5.00	—
1950	5,298,000	0.20	0.40	0.80	4.00	—
1950 AFP	Inc. above	0.25	0.50	1.25	8.00	—
1951	7,324,000	6.00	10.00	15.00	40.00	—
1951/0 AFP	—	0.25	0.50	1.00	4.00	—
1951 AFP	—	0.20	0.40	0.80	3.00	—

KM# 224.2 10 CENTAVOS
2.5100 g., Brass **Obv:** Head right **Rev:** Value to right of sprig **Note:** Thin planchet - 1.3mm. Date varieties exist.

Date	Mintage	F	VF	XF	Unc	BU
1951	Inc. above	0.10	0.20	0.40	2.00	—
1951 AFP	—	0.10	0.20	0.40	2.00	—
1952	6,694,000	0.10	0.20	0.40	3.00	—
1952 AFP	—	0.10	0.20	0.40	3.00	—
1953	5,668,000	0.10	0.20	0.40	2.00	—
1953 AFP	—	0.10	0.20	0.40	2.00	—
1954	7,786,000	—	0.10	0.35	1.50	—
1954 AFP	—	—	0.10	0.35	1.50	—
1955	6,690,000	—	0.10	0.35	1.50	—
1955 AFP	—	—	0.10	0.35	1.50	—
1956/5	8,410,000	0.10	0.35	0.75	3.50	—
1956	Inc. above	—	0.20	0.25	1.00	—
1956 AFP	—	—	0.20	0.40	2.00	—
1957	8,420,000	—	0.10	0.25	1.00	—
1957 AFP	—	—	0.10	0.25	1.00	—
1958	10,380,000	—	0.10	0.25	1.00	—
1958 AFP	—	—	—	—	—	—
1959	8,300,000	—	0.10	0.25	1.00	—
1959 AFP	—	—	—	—	—	—
1960	12,600,000	—	0.10	0.15	1.00	—
1961	12,700,000	—	0.10	0.15	1.00	—
1962	14,598,000	—	0.10	0.15	1.00	—
1963	16,100,000	—	0.10	0.15	1.00	—
1964	16,504,000	—	0.10	0.15	1.00	—
1965	17,808,000	—	0.10	0.15	1.00	—
1965 Proof	—	Value: 25.00				

KM# 233 10 CENTAVOS
Brass, 20 mm. **Obv:** Head right **Rev:** Value to upper right of torch, all within chain circle

Date	Mintage	F	VF	XF	Unc	BU
1954	1,818,000	1.00	2.00	4.50	10.00	—

KM# 237 10 CENTAVOS
2.1000 g., Brass **Subject:** 400th Anniversary of Lima Mint **Obv:** National arms above value **Rev:** Pillars of Hercules within inner circle

Date	Mintage	F	VF	XF	Unc	BU
1965	572,000	—	—	0.35	1.00	—
1965 Proof	—	Value: 150				

KM# 245.1 10 CENTAVOS
Brass **Obv:** National arms within circle **Rev:** Value to left of flower sprig **Edge:** Reeded **Note:** Date varieties exist.

Date	Mintage	F	VF	XF	Unc	BU
1966	14,930,000	—	—	0.10	0.75	1.25
Note: PAREJA in field at lower left of arms						
1966 Proof	1,000	Value: 15.00				
1967	19,330,000	—	—	0.10	0.75	1.25
1968	24,390,000	—	—	0.10	0.75	1.25

KM# 245.2 10 CENTAVOS
2.1700 g., Brass, 17.90 mm. **Obv:** National arms within circle **Rev:** Value to left of flower sprig **Edge:** Reeded **Note:** Date varieties exist.

Date	Mintage	F	VF	XF	Unc	BU
1967	—	—	—	0.10	0.25	0.40
1968	—	—	—	0.10	0.20	0.35
1969	24,390,000	—	—	0.10	0.25	0.40
1970	29,110,000	—	—	0.10	0.20	0.35
1971	30,590,000	—	—	0.10	0.20	0.35
1972	34,442,000	—	—	0.10	0.20	0.35
1973	33,864,000	—	—	0.10	0.20	0.35

KM# 245.1a 10 CENTAVOS
Silver Plated Brass **Obv:** National arms within circle **Rev:** Value to left of flower sprig

Date	Mintage	F	VF	XF	Unc	BU
1967	—	—	—	—	—	—

KM# 245.3 10 CENTAVOS
2.1800 g., Brass **Obv:** National arms within circle **Rev:** Value to left of flower sprig **Edge:** Plain

Date	Mintage	F	VF	XF	Unc	BU
1973	Inc. above	—	—	0.10	0.15	0.25
1974	—	—	—	0.10	0.15	0.25
1975	10,430,000	—	—	0.10	0.15	0.25

KM# 263 10 CENTAVOS
Brass **Obv:** National arms within circle **Rev:** Value

Date	Mintage	F	VF	XF	Unc	BU
1975	—	—	—	0.10	0.15	0.25

KM# 204.2 DINERO
2.5000 g., 0.9000 Silver 0.0723 oz. ASW **Obv:** National arms above date **Rev:** Seated Liberty flanked by shield and column **Note:** Varieties exist.

Date	Mintage	F	VF	XF	Unc	BU
1902/1 JF	375,000	1.20	2.00	3.50	15.00	—
1902/891 JF	Inc. above	1.20	2.00	3.50	15.00	—
1902/892 JF	Inc. above	1.20	2.00	3.50	15.00	—
1902/897 JF	Inc. above	1.20	2.00	3.50	15.00	—
1902 JF	Inc. above	1.20	2.00	4.00	18.00	—
1903/803 JF	887,000	1.20	2.00	3.50	15.00	—
1903/807 JF	Inc. above	1.20	2.00	3.50	15.00	—
1903/892 JF	Inc. above	1.20	2.00	3.50	12.00	—
1903/893 JF	Inc. above	1.20	2.00	3.50	12.00	—
1903/92 JF	Inc. above	1.20	2.00	3.50	15.00	—
1903 JF	Inc. above	1.20	2.00	3.50	15.00	—
1904 JF	380,000	1.20	2.50	4.00	15.00	—
1905/1 JF	700,000	1.20	2.50	4.00	15.00	—
1905/3 JF	Inc. above	1.20	2.50	4.00	15.00	—
1905 JF	Inc. above	1.20	2.00	3.50	15.00	—
1906 JF	826,000	1.20	2.00	3.50	15.00	—
1907 JF Rare	500,000	—	—	—	—	—
1907 FG/JF	Inc. above	1.25	2.50	4.50	15.00	—
1907 FG	Inc. above	1.20	1.75	3.00	12.00	—
1908/6 FG/JF	Inc. above	1.20	2.00	4.00	15.00	—
1908 FG/JF	200,000	1.20	2.25	4.00	15.00	—
1908 FG/GF	Inc. above	1.20	2.00	3.00	15.00	—
1908 FG	Inc. above	1.20	1.75	3.00	15.00	—
1909 FG	—	2.00	4.00	8.00	20.00	—
1909 FG/FO	—	2.00	4.00	8.00	20.00	—
1909 FG/FF	—	2.00	4.00	8.00	20.00	—
1910 FG	210,000	BV	1.25	3.00	15.00	—
1910 FG/JF	Inc. above	1.20	2.25	4.00	18.00	—
1910 FG/JG	Inc. above	1.20	2.25	4.00	18.00	—
1911 FG	200,000	1.20	1.50	3.00	15.00	—
1911 FG/JF	Inc. above	1.20	2.25	4.00	18.00	—
1911 FG/JG	—	1.20	2.25	4.00	18.00	—
1912 FG	400,000	BV	1.25	3.00	15.00	—
1912/02 FG/JG	Inc. above	1.20	2.25	4.00	18.00	—
1912 FG/JF	Inc. above	1.20	2.25	4.00	18.00	—
1912 FG/JG	Inc. above	1.20	2.25	4.00	18.00	—

Date	Mintage	F	VF	XF	Unc	BU
1913/1 FG/JF	Inc. above	1.20	2.25	4.00	18.00	—
1913/2 FG	360,000	1.20	2.25	4.00	18.00	—
1913/7 FG/G	Inc. above	1.20	2.25	4.00	18.00	—
1913 FG	Inc. above	BV	1.25	3.00	15.00	—
1913 FG/G	Inc. above	BV	1.25	2.50	12.00	—
1913 FG/JB	Inc. above	1.50	3.00	5.50	18.00	—
1916 FG Large date	430,000	1.25	2.50	4.50	15.00	—
1916 FG Small date	Inc. above	BV	1.25	2.00	6.00	—
1916 FG/JG	Inc. above	2.00	5.00	7.50	20.00	—
1916 FG/FF	Inc. above	2.00	5.00	7.50	20.00	—

KM# 215.1   20 CENTAVOS
7.0000 g., Copper-Nickel, 24 mm. **Obv:** Date spelled: UN MIL NOVECIENTOS DIECIOCHO **Rev:** Value to right of sprig

Date	Mintage	F	VF	XF	Unc	BU
1918	2,500,000	0.40	1.00	5.00	20.00	—
1919	1,250,000	1.25	2.50	5.00	20.00	—
1920	1,464,000	1.25	2.25	4.00	25.00	—
1921	8,536,000	0.85	3.00	6.00	25.00	—
1926	2,500,000	2.50	5.00	9.00	30.00	—

KM# 215.2   20 CENTAVOS
Copper-Nickel, 24 mm. **Obv:** Head right **Rev:** Value to right of sprig

Date	Mintage	F	VF	XF	Unc	BU
1940	1,000,000	0.25	0.75	1.75	5.50	—
1940 Proof	—	Value: 175				
1941	1,000,000	0.35	1.00	2.50	7.50	—
1941 Proof	—	Value: 150				

KM# 215a.1   20 CENTAVOS
Brass, 24 mm. **Obv:** Date spelling: MIL NOVECIENTOS CUARENTA Y TRES **Rev:** Value to right of sprig

Date	Mintage	F	VF	XF	Unc	BU
1942	500,000	3.00	6.00	13.50	60.00	—
1943	500,000	3.00	6.00	13.50	60.00	—
1944	500,000	4.00	7.50	16.50	65.00	—

KM# 215a.2   20 CENTAVOS
Brass, 24 mm. **Obv:** Head right **Rev:** Value to right of sprig

Date	Mintage	F	VF	XF	Unc	BU
1942S	500,000	6.00	12.00	50.00	150	—
1943S	500,000	3.00	6.00	12.50	200	—

KM# 221.1   20 CENTAVOS
Brass, 24 mm. **Obv:** Head right, divided legend **Rev:** Value to right of sprig **Note:** Thick planchet.

Date	Mintage	F	VF	XF	Unc	BU
1942	300,000	1.00	2.50	5.00	12.50	—
1943	1,900,000	0.75	1.50	2.50	7.50	—
1944	2,963,000	0.60	1.25	2.00	6.00	—

KM# 221.3   20 CENTAVOS
Brass **Obv:** Head right, continuous legend **Rev:** Value to right of sprig

Date	Mintage	F	VF	XF	Unc	BU
1945	3,043,000	0.25	—	0.75	1.50	—
1946/5	Inc. above	0.25	0.65	1.00	2.00	—
1946	Inc. above	0.25	0.50	0.75	1.50	—

KM# 221.2   20 CENTAVOS
6.8300 g., Brass, 24 mm. **Obv:** AFP on truncation, continuous legend **Rev:** Value to right of sprig

Date	Mintage	F	VF	XF	Unc	BU
1946	3,410,000	0.25	0.50	0.85	3.00	—
1947	4,307,000	0.25	0.50	0.85	3.00	—
1948	3,578,000	0.25	0.50	0.85	3.00	—
1949/8	2,709,000	0.75	1.50	2.50	6.50	—

KM# 221.2a   20 CENTAVOS
Copper **Obv:** Head right **Rev:** Value to right of sprig

Date	Mintage	F	VF	XF	Unc	BU
1947	300	—	—	—	150	—

KM# 221.4   20 CENTAVOS
Brass **Obv:** Different style legend **Rev:** Value to right of sprig

Date	Mintage	F	VF	XF	Unc	BU
1949	Inc. above	0.50	1.00	1.75	4.50	—
1950	2,427,000	1.00	1.75	3.00	8.00	—
1951	2,941,000	3.00	7.50	15.00	40.00	—

KM# 221.2b   20 CENTAVOS
3.8000 g., Brass, 23 mm. **Obv:** Head right **Rev:** Value to right of sprig **Note:** Thin planchet - 1.3mm. AFP. Date varieties exist.

Date	Mintage	F	VF	XF	Unc	BU
1951	Inc. above	0.20	0.40	0.75	2.00	—
1951 Without AFP	—	—	—	—	—	—
1952	4,410,000	0.20	0.40	0.75	2.50	—
1952 Without AFP	Inc. above	—	—	—	—	—
1953	2,615,000	0.20	0.40	1.50	8.00	—
1954	1,816,000	1.50	2.50	4.00	12.00	—
1955 Large oval 9	4,050,000	0.10	0.15	0.30	1.50	—
1955 Small oval 9	Inc. above	0.20	0.40	1.50	8.00	—
1955 Round nine	Inc. above	—	—	—	—	—
1956	3,760,000	0.10	0.15	0.30	1.50	—
1957	3,680,000	0.10	0.15	0.30	1.00	—
1958	3,100,000	0.10	0.15	0.30	1.00	—
1959	5,450,000	0.10	0.20	0.40	1.00	—
1959 Without AFP	—	—	—	—	—	—
1960/90 With AFP	—	—	—	—	—	—
1960/90 Without AFP	—	—	—	—	—	—
1960	6,750,000	—	0.10	0.20	1.00	—
1960 Without AFP	—	0.25	0.75	1.50	4.00	—
1961	6,800,000	—	0.10	0.20	1.00	—
1961 Without AFP	—	—	—	—	—	—
1962	7,357,000	—	0.10	0.20	1.00	—
1963/2	8,843,000	0.15	0.25	0.50	2.00	—
1963	Inc. above	—	0.10	0.20	1.00	—
1964	9,550,000	—	0.10	0.20	1.00	—
1965 With inverted V for A in AFP	—	—	0.10	0.20	1.00	—
1965 Without AFP	—	0.10	0.15	0.30	1.00	—
1965 Proof	—	Value: 35.00				

KM# 234   20 CENTAVOS
Brass, 24 mm. **Subject:** President Castilla **Obv:** Head right **Rev:** Value to right of torch within chain circle **Edge:** Reeded **Note:** Thin planchet - 1.3mm. AFP.

Date	Mintage	F	VF	XF	Unc	BU
1954	799,000	2.00	4.00	8.00	15.00	—

KM# 221.2c   20 CENTAVOS
Copper-Nickel **Obv:** Head right **Rev:** Value to right of sprig **Edge:** Reeded **Note:** Thin planchet - 1.3mm. AFP.

Date	Mintage	F	VF	XF	Unc	BU
1958	—	—	—	—	150	—
1963	—	8.00	15.00	25.00	—	—
1965 Proof	—	Value: 30.00				

KM# 264   20 CENTAVOS
Brass **Obv:** National arms within circle **Rev:** Value

Date	Mintage	F	VF	XF	Unc	BU
1975	—	0.10	0.20	0.50	1.00	1.50

KM# 205.2   1/5 SOL
5.0000 g., 0.9000 Silver 0.1447 oz. ASW **Obv:** National arms **Rev:** Libertad incuse **Edge:** Plain **Note:** Die varieties exist. Some coins 1911-17 have engraver's initial R left of shield on reverse.

Date	Mintage	F	VF	XF	Unc	BU
1901 JF	638,000	BV	2.50	5.50	12.00	—
1903/1 JF	702,000	2.50	4.00	7.00	17.50	—
1903/13 JF	Inc. above	BV	3.50	6.00	15.00	—
1903 JF	Inc. above	BV	3.25	5.50	12.00	—
1906 JF	660,000	BV	3.25	5.50	12.00	—
1907 JF	1,370,000	BV	2.25	4.00	10.00	—
1907 FG	Inc. above	BV	3.25	5.50	12.00	—
1908/7 FG	560,000	BV	3.50	6.00	15.00	—
1908 FG	Inc. above	BV	3.25	5.50	15.00	—
1909 FG	42,000	2.50	4.00	9.00	27.50	—
1910/00 FG	165,000	3.00	7.00	15.00	35.00	—
1910 FG	Inc. above	3.00	7.00	12.00	25.00	—
1911 FG	250,000	BV	3.25	5.50	9.00	—
1911 FG-R	Inc. above	BV	3.25	5.50	9.00	—
1912 FG	300,000	BV	2.25	4.00	8.00	—
1912 R	—	BV	2.25	4.00	8.00	—
1912/1 FG-R	—	BV	2.50	5.00	10.00	—
1912 FG-R	Inc. above	BV	3.25	5.50	15.00	—
1913 FG	223,000	BV	3.50	6.00	15.00	—
1913 FG-R	Inc. above	BV	3.50	6.00	15.00	—
1914 FG	10,000	5.00	12.00	25.00	55.00	—
1915 FG	—	25.00	40.00	75.00	125	—
1916 FG,	425,000	2.50	5.00	10.00	25.00	—
1916 FG-R	Inc. above	BV	3.25	5.00	9.00	—
1917 FG-R	20,000	8.00	17.00	35.00	75.00	—

KM# 238   25 CENTAVOS
Brass **Subject:** 400th Anniversary of Lima Mint **Obv:** National arms above value **Rev:** Pillars of Hercules within inner circle

Date	Mintage	F	VF	XF	Unc	BU
ND(1965)	1,113,000	—	0.25	0.35	0.75	—
1965 Proof	—	Value: 200				

KM# 246.1   25 CENTAVOS
Brass **Obv:** PAREJA in field at lower left of arms **Rev:** Value to left of flower sprig **Edge:** Reeded

Date	Mintage	F	VF	XF	Unc	BU
1966 PAREJA in field at lower left of arms	9,300,000	—	0.15	0.25	0.50	0.75
1966 Proof	1,000	Value: 15.00				
1967	8,150,000	—	0.15	0.25	0.50	0.75
1968	7,440,000	—	0.15	0.25	0.50	0.75

KM# 246.1a   25 CENTAVOS
Silver Plated Brass **Obv:** National arms within circle **Rev:** Value to left of flower sprig

Date	Mintage	F	VF	XF	Unc	BU
1967	Inc. above	—	—	—	—	—

KM# 246.2   25 CENTAVOS
3.2000 g., Brass, 21.03 mm. **Obv:** National arms within circle **Rev:** Value to left of flower sprig **Edge:** Reeded

Date	Mintage	F	VF	XF	Unc	BU
1968 AP	Inc. above	—	0.15	0.25	0.50	0.75
1969 AP on reverse	7,440,000	—	0.20	0.40	1.00	1.50
1969 With inverted V for A in AP	Inc. above	—	0.20	0.40	1.00	1.50
1969 Without AP	Inc. above	—	0.15	0.25	0.50	0.75
1970	6,341,000	—	0.20	0.40	1.00	1.50
1971	3,196,000	—	0.20	0.40	1.00	1.50
1972	5,523,000	—	0.20	0.40	1.00	1.50
1973	7,492,000	—	0.15	0.25	0.50	0.75

KM# 259   25 CENTAVOS
3.1000 g., Brass **Obv:** National arms within circle **Rev:** Value to left of flower sprig

Date	Mintage	F	VF	XF	Unc	BU
1973	Inc. above	—	0.10	0.15	0.25	0.40
1974	—	—	0.10	0.15	0.25	0.40
1975	—	—	0.10	0.15	0.25	0.40

KM# 203   1/2 SOL
12.5000 g., 0.9000 Silver 0.3617 oz. ASW **Obv:** National arms above date **Rev:** Seated Liberty flanked by shield and column **Note:** Mint mark: LIMA. Date varieties exist. Most coins have engraver's initials JR left of shield tip on reverse.

Date	Mintage	F	VF	XF	Unc	BU
1907 LIMA FG-JR	1,000,000	BV	6.00	10.00	20.00	—
1908/7 LIMA FG-JR	30,000	15.00	30.00	75.00	300	—
1908 LIMA FG-JR	Inc. above	12.00	25.00	65.00	175	—
1914 LIMA FG-JR	173,000	BV	6.50	15.00	35.00	—
1915 LIMA FG-JR	570,000	BV	5.50	7.50	15.00	—
1916 LIMA FG	384,000	BV	5.50	7.50	15.00	—
1916 LIMA FG-JR	—	BV	5.50	7.50	15.00	—
1917 LIMA FG-JR	178,000	BV	6.00	10.00	20.00	—

KM# 216   1/2 SOL
12.5000 g., 0.5000 Silver 0.2009 oz. ASW, 30 mm. **Obv:** National arms above date **Rev:** Seated Liberty flanked by shield and column **Note:** Date varieties exist. Engraver's initials appear on stems of obverse wreath.

Date	Mintage	F	VF	XF	Unc	BU
1922 LIMA LIBERTAD incuse, J.R. on reverse	465,000	BV	7.00	25.00	80.00	—
1922 LIMA LIBERTAD in relief	Inc. above	BV	7.00	25.00	80.00	—
1923 LIMA GM LIBER/TAD, round-top 3	2,520,000	BV	4.00	10.00	30.00	—
1923/2 LIMA Flat-top 3	Inc. above	BV	3.25	5.50	20.00	—
1923 LIMA Flat-top 3	Inc. above	BV	3.50	7.00	25.00	—
1924 LIMA GM	238,000	BV	6.50	20.00	50.00	—
1926 LIMA GM	694,000	BV	3.50	7.50	25.00	—
1927 LIMA GM	2,640,000	BV	3.25	5.50	15.00	—
1928/7 LIMA GM	3,028,000	—	—	—	—	—

Date	Mintage	F	VF	XF	Unc	BU
1928LIMA GM	Inc. above	BV	3.25	5.50	15.00	—
1929LIMA GM	3,068,000	BV	3.25	5.50	15.00	—
1935LIMA AP	2,653,000	BV	3.25	5.00	14.00	—
1935LIMA	—	—	—	—	—	—

KM# 220.1 1/2 SOL
Brass Obv: Five palm leaves point to llama on shield Rev: Value and legend

Date	Mintage	F	VF	XF	Unc	BU
1935	10,000,000	0.50	1.25	2.25	7.00	—
1935 Proof	—	Value: 200				
1941	4,000,000	0.50	1.25	2.25	7.00	—

KM# 220.2 1/2 SOL
Brass Obv: Arms within wreath Rev: Value and legend

Date	Mintage	F	VF	XF	Unc	BU
1942	4,000,000	1.50	3.00	5.00	20.00	—
1943	4,000,000	3.00	6.50	12.50	35.00	—
1944	Inc. above	1.50	3.00	5.00	20.00	—

KM# 220.4 1/2 SOL
7.3200 g., Brass Obv: Three palm leaves point to llama on shield Rev: Value and legend Note: Dates 1941-44 have thick flat-top 4 without serifs. 1945 has narrow 4 like KM#220.5.

Date	Mintage	F	VF	XF	Unc	BU
1941	2,000,000	3.00	6.50	12.50	35.00	—
1942	Inc. above	1.50	3.00	5.00	15.00	—
1942 AP	—	—	—	—	—	—
1943	2,000,000	0.50	1.00	2.00	12.00	—
1944	Inc. above	0.40	0.85	1.75	7.00	—
1944/2	4,000,000	—	—	—	—	—
1944 AP	Inc. above	—	—	—	—	—
1945	4,000,000	0.75	1.50	3.00	10.00	—

KM# 220.3 1/2 SOL
Brass Obv: National arms within wreath Rev: Value and legend Note: The coins struck in Philadelphia and San Francisco have a serif on the "4" of the date; the Lima and London coins do not.

Date	Mintage	F	VF	XF	Unc	BU
1942S	1,668,000	1.50	3.00	5.00	15.00	—
1943S	6,332,000	1.50	3.00	5.00	15.00	—

KM# 220.5 1/2 SOL
7.6000 g., Brass, 27 mm. Obv: Three palm leaves point to llama on shield Rev: Value and legend Note: 1942, 1944 AP, and all 1945-49 have narrow 4 without serif on crossbar. 1944 without AP has flat-top 4 like KM#220.4. Engraver's initials AP appear on wreath stems of some 1944-45, all 1946 and some 1947 coins. Varieties exist, including narrow and wide dates for 1956 and 1961 issues.

Date	Mintage	F	VF	XF	Unc	BU
1942 Long-top 2	Inc. above	1.50	3.00	5.00	15.00	—
1944	Inc. above	0.75	1.50	3.00	10.00	—
1944 AP	Inc. above	0.50	1.00	2.00	7.00	—
1945	Inc. above	0.75	1.50	3.00	10.00	—
1945 AP	Inc. above	0.75	1.50	3.00	10.00	—
1946/5 AP	3,744,000	2.00	3.50	6.50	17.50	—
1946 AP	Inc. above	0.40	0.75	1.25	7.00	—
1947 AP	6,066,000	0.40	0.75	1.25	7.00	—
1947	Inc. above	0.40	0.75	1.25	7.00	—
1948	3,324,000	0.40	0.75	1.25	7.00	—
1949/8	420,000	1.00	2.00	4.00	12.00	—
1949	Inc. above	1.50	3.00	6.00	18.00	—
1950	91,000	1.25	2.25	4.50	15.00	—
1951/8	930,000	0.50	1.00	2.00	7.00	—
1951	Inc. above	0.50	1.00	2.00	7.00	—
1952	935,000	0.75	1.50	3.00	10.00	—
1953	817,000	0.50	1.00	2.00	7.00	—
1954	637,000	0.75	1.50	3.00	10.00	—
1955	1,383,000	0.15	0.35	0.75	4.00	—
1956	2,309,000	0.10	0.25	0.40	1.50	—
1957	2,700,000	0.10	0.25	0.50	2.00	—
1958	2,691,000	0.10	0.25	0.40	1.50	—
1959	3,609,000	0.10	0.25	0.40	1.50	—
1960	5,600,000	0.10	0.20	0.35	0.75	—
1961 Narrow date	4,400,000	0.10	0.20	0.35	0.75	—
1961 Wide date	Inc. above	0.10	0.20	0.35	0.75	—
1962	3,540,000	0.10	0.20	0.35	1.00	—
1963	4,345,000	0.10	0.20	0.35	0.75	—
1964	5,315,000	0.10	0.20	0.35	1.50	—
1965	7,090,000	0.10	0.20	0.35	1.75	—
1965 Proof	—	Value: 75.00				

KM# 239 1/2 SOL
Brass Subject: 400th Anniversary of Lima Mint Obv: National arms above value Rev: Pillars of Hercules within inner circle

Date	Mintage	F	VF	XF	Unc	BU
ND(1965)	10,971,000	—	0.10	0.20	0.50	—
ND(1965) Proof	—	Value: 400				

KM# 247 1/2 SOL
Brass, 22.5 mm. Obv: National arms within circle Rev: Value to right of llama

Date	Mintage	F	VF	XF	Unc	BU
1966	13,720,000	—	0.10	0.20	1.00	2.50
1966 Proof	1,000	Value: 20.00				
1967	15,500,000	—	0.10	0.20	1.00	2.50
1967 PAREJA on obverse and reverse	—	—	0.10	0.20	1.00	2.50
1968	13,890,000	3.00	7.00	15.00	30.00	—
1968 JAS	—	—	0.10	0.20	1.00	2.50
1969	13,890,000	—	0.10	0.20	1.00	2.50
1970	11,901,000	—	0.10	0.20	1.00	2.50

Note: Date varieties exist

1971	7,524,000	—	0.15	0.20	1.00	2.50
1972	19,441,000	—	0.10	0.20	1.00	2.50
1973	14,951,000	—	0.10	0.20	1.00	2.50

KM# 247a 1/2 SOL
Silver Plated Brass Obv: National arms within circle Rev: Value to right of llama

Date	Mintage	F	VF	XF	Unc	BU
1967	—	—	—	—	—	—

KM# 247b 1/2 SOL
Silver Obv: National arms within circle Rev: Value to right of llama

Date	Mintage	F	VF	XF	Unc	BU
1967	—	—	—	—	—	—

KM# 260 1/2 SOL
4.1600 g., Brass, 22.5 mm. Obv: National arms within circle Rev: Value to right of llama Edge: Reeded

Date	Mintage	F	VF	XF	Unc	BU
1973	Inc. above	—	0.10	0.20	1.00	2.50
1974/1	—	—	0.10	0.20	1.00	2.50
1974	14,518,000	—	0.10	0.20	1.00	2.50
1975	14,039,000	—	0.10	0.20	1.00	2.50

KM# 265 1/2 SOL
2.1000 g., Brass, 17.97 mm. Obv: National arms within circle Rev: Value Edge: Plain Note: Without mint mark.

Date	Mintage	F	VF	XF	Unc	BU
1975	62,682,000	—	0.10	0.20	0.30	0.50
1976	388,771,000	—	0.10	0.20	0.30	0.50

KM# 268 1/2 SOL
9.3500 g., 0.9000 Gold 0.2705 oz. AGW Subject: 150th Anniversary - Battle of Ayacucho Obv: National arms Rev: Monument and value

Date	Mintage	F	VF	XF	Unc	BU
1976	10,000	—	—	—	—	275

KM# 196.26 SOL
25.0000 g., 0.9000 Silver 0.7234 oz. ASW Obv: National arms above date Rev: Libertad incuse Note: Type XII. Legends have smaller lettering. Varieties exist.

Date	Mintage	F	VF	XF	Unc	BU
1914 FG	620,000	—	BV	15.00	25.00	—
1915 FG	Inc. above	—	BV	15.00	22.00	—

KM# 196.28 SOL
25.0000 g., 0.9000 Silver 0.7234 oz. ASW Obv: National arms above date Rev: LIBERTAD in relief Note: Type III.

Date	Mintage	F	VF	XF	Unc	BU
1916 FG	Inc. above	—	BV	15.00	22.00	—

KM# 196.27 SOL
25.0000 g., 0.9000 Silver 0.7234 oz. ASW Obv: National arms above date Rev: LIBERTAD incuse

Date	Mintage	F	VF	XF	Unc	BU
1916 FG	1,927,000	—	BV	15.00	22.00	—

KM# 217.1 SOL
25.0000 g., 0.5000 Silver 0.4019 oz. ASW, 37 mm. Obv: National arms, fineness omitted Rev: LEBERTAD in relief

Date	Mintage	F	VF	XF	Unc	BU
1922 Rare	—	—	—	—	—	—
1923	3,600	15.00	30.00	70.00	275	—

KM# 217.2 SOL
25.0000 g., 0.5000 Silver 0.4019 oz. ASW, 37 mm. Obv: National arms above date Rev: LIBERTAD incuse

Date	Mintage	F	VF	XF	Unc	BU
1923	1,400	35.00	75.00	165	475	—

KM# 218.1 SOL
25.0000 g., 0.5000 Silver 0.4019 oz. ASW, 37 mm. Obv: National arms Rev: Seated Liberty flanked by shield and column Note: Small letters. The Philadelphia and Lima strikings may be distinguished by the fact that the letters in the legends are smaller on those pieces produced at Philadelphia. All bear the name of the Lima Mint.

Date	Mintage	F	VF	XF	Unc	BU
1923	Est. 2,369,000	BV	8.00	10.00	15.00	—
1924/823	3,113,000	8.00	10.00	20.00	40.00	—
1924/824	Inc. above	8.00	10.00	20.00	40.00	—

Date	Mintage	F	VF	XF	Unc	BU
1924	Inc. above	BV	8.00	10.00	15.00	—
1925	1,291,000	BV	8.00	12.00	20.00	—
1926	2,157,000	BV	8.00	10.00	15.00	—

KM# 218.2 SOL
25.0000 g., 0.5000 Silver 0.4019 oz. ASW, 37 mm. **Obv:** National arms, engraver's initials GM on stems flanking date **Rev:** Seated Liberty flanked by shield and column **Note:** Large letters.

Date	Mintage	F	VF	XF	Unc	BU
1924	96,000	8.00	10.00	20.00	65.00	—
1925	1,004,999	BV	8.00	9.00	15.00	—
1930	76,000	BV	8.00	10.00	20.00	—
1931	24,000	BV	8.00	10.00	22.00	—
1933	5,000	8.00	12.00	20.00	40.00	—
1934/3	2,855,000	BV	8.00	10.00	20.00	—
1934	Inc. above	BV	8.00	9.00	15.00	—
1935	695,000	BV	8.00	10.00	20.00	—

KM# 222 SOL
14.5300 g., Brass, 33 mm. **Obv:** National arms **Rev:** Value within circle **Note:** Date varieties exist.

Date	Mintage	F	VF	XF	Unc	BU
1943	10,000,000	0.35	1.25	3.00	8.00	—
1944	Inc. above	0.35	1.25	3.00	7.00	—
1945	—	0.50	1.50	3.50	9.00	—
1946	1,752,000	0.50	1.50	3.00	8.00	—
1947	3,302,000	0.35	1.00	2.00	6.00	—
1948	1,992,000	0.35	1.00	2.00	6.00	—
1949/8	751,000	2.00	4.00	7.00	20.00	—
1949	Inc. above	3.50	7.50	12.00	25.00	—
1950	1,249,000	7.00	10.00	15.00	25.00	—
1951	Inc. above	0.25	0.50	1.50	6.00	—
1951/0	2,093,999	0.25	0.50	1.50	6.00	—
1952	2,037,000	0.25	0.50	1.50	6.00	—
1953	1,243,000	3.00	6.00	10.00	25.00	—
1954	1,220,000	0.35	0.75	1.75	6.00	—
1955	1,323,000	0.35	0.75	1.75	6.00	—
1956	3,450,000	0.15	0.35	0.75	3.00	—
1957	3,086,000	0.15	0.35	1.00	5.00	—
1958 Wide date	3,390,000	0.15	0.35	0.75	3.00	—
1958 Narrow date	Inc. above	0.15	0.35	0.75	3.00	—
1959	4,975,000	0.15	0.35	1.00	5.00	—
1960	5,800,000	0.15	0.35	0.75	1.50	—
1961	5,200,000	0.15	0.35	0.75	2.00	—
1962	5,102,000	0.15	0.35	0.75	1.50	—
1963	5,499,000	0.15	0.35	0.75	2.00	—
1964 Wide date	5,888,000	0.15	0.35	0.75	2.00	—
1964 Narrow date	Inc. above	0.15	0.35	0.75	2.00	—
1965	5,504,000	0.15	0.35	0.75	2.00	—
1965 Proof	—	Value: 75.00				

KM# 240 SOL
Brass, 28 mm. **Subject:** 400th Anniversary of the Lima Mint **Obv:** National arms above value **Rev:** Pillars of Hercules within inner circle

Date	Mintage	F	VF	XF	Unc	BU
ND(1965)	3,103,000	—	0.35	0.75	1.50	—
ND(1965) Proof	—	Value: 500				

KM# 248 SOL
9.2000 g., Brass, 28 mm. **Obv:** National arms **Rev:** Llama

Date	Mintage	F	VF	XF	Unc	BU
1966	16,410,000	—	0.10	0.25	1.00	3.00
1966 Proof	1,000	Value: 25.00				
1967	13,920,000	—	0.10	0.25	1.00	3.00
1968	12,260,000	—	0.10	0.25	1.00	3.00
1969	12,260,000	—	0.10	0.25	1.00	3.00
1970	12,336,000	—	0.10	0.25	1.00	3.00
1971	11,927,000	—	0.10	0.25	1.00	3.00
1972	3,945,000	—	0.10	0.25	1.00	3.00
1973	12,856,000	—	0.10	0.25	1.00	3.00
1974	14,966,000	—	0.10	0.25	1.00	3.00
1975	—	—	0.10	0.25	1.00	3.00

KM# 248a SOL
Silver Plated Brass **Obv:** National arms **Rev:** Llama

Date	Mintage	F	VF	XF	Unc	BU
1967	—	—	—	—	—	—

KM# 248b SOL
Silver **Obv:** National arms **Rev:** Llama

Date	Mintage	F	VF	XF	Unc	BU
1967	—	—	—	—	—	—

KM# 266.1 SOL
3.2400 g., Brass, 21 mm. **Obv:** National arms within circle **Rev:** Value **Edge:** Plain

Date	Mintage	F	VF	XF	Unc	BU
1975	354,485,000	—	—	0.10	0.25	0.40
1976	114,660,000	—	—	0.10	0.25	0.40

KM# 269 SOL
23.4000 g., 0.9000 Gold 0.6771 oz. AGW **Subject:** 150th Anniversary - Battle of Ayacucho **Obv:** National arms within circle **Rev:** Monument divides value within circle **Note:** Mint mark in monogram.

Date	Mintage	F	VF	XF	Unc	BU
1976LIMA	10,000	—	—	—	—	650

KM# 266.2 SOL
2.0000 g., Brass **Obv:** National arms within circle **Rev:** Value **Edge:** Plain **Note:** Mint mark in monogram.

Date	Mintage	F	VF	XF	Unc	BU
1978LIMA	9,000,000	—	—	0.15	0.35	0.50
1979LIMA	4,842,000	—	—	0.15	0.35	0.50
1980LIMA	28,826,000	—	—	0.15	0.35	0.50
1981LIMA	55,785,000	—	—	0.15	0.35	0.50

KM# 235 5 SOLES
2.3404 g., 0.9000 Gold 0.0677 oz. AGW **Obv:** National arms above date **Rev:** Seated Liberty flanked by shield and column

Date	Mintage	F	VF	XF	Unc	BU
1956	4,510	—	—	BV	65.00	—
1957	2,146	—	—	BV	65.00	—
1959	1,536	—	—	BV	65.00	—
1960	8,133	—	—	BV	65.00	—
1961	1,154	—	—	BV	65.00	—
1962	1,550	—	—	BV	65.00	—
1963	3,945	—	—	BV	65.00	—
1964	2,063	—	—	BV	65.00	—
1965	14,000	—	—	BV	65.00	—
1966	4,738	—	—	BV	65.00	—
1967	3,651	—	—	BV	65.00	—
1969	127	—	—	BV	175	—

KM# 252 5 SOLES
2.3000 g., Copper-Nickel **Obv:** National arms within circle **Rev:** Value above designed Incan cup, written value around bottom half

Date	Mintage	F	VF	XF	Unc	BU
1969	10,000,000	0.20	0.40	0.60	1.50	2.00

KM# 254 5 SOLES
Copper-Nickel **Subject:** 150th Anniversary of Independence **Obv:** National arms **Rev:** Bust of Tupac Amaru right **Note:** Mint mark in monogram.

Date	Mintage	F	VF	XF	Unc	BU
1971LIMA	3,480,000	0.20	0.40	0.80	2.00	—

KM# 257 5 SOLES
7.8800 g., Copper-Nickel, 25.57 mm. **Obv:** National arms within circle **Rev:** Bust of Tupac Amaru **Edge:** Reeded **Note:** Mint mark in monogram.

Date	Mintage	F	VF	XF	Unc	BU
1972	2,068,000	—	0.10	0.35	1.00	—
1973	475,000	—	0.10	0.35	1.00	—
1974	—	—	0.10	0.35	1.50	—
1975	—	—	0.10	0.35	1.50	—

KM# 267 5 SOLES
4.4000 g., Copper-Nickel, 22 mm. **Obv:** National arms **Rev:** Bust of Tupac Amaru **Note:** Mint mark in monogram.

Date	Mintage	F	VF	XF	Unc	BU
1975	—	—	0.10	0.35	1.00	1.75
1976	17,016,000	—	0.10	0.35	1.00	1.75
1977	94,272,000	—	0.10	0.35	1.00	1.75

KM# 271 5 SOLES
4.2400 g., Brass, 22.49 mm. **Obv:** National arms within circle **Rev:** Value **Edge:** Plain **Note:** Mint mark in monogram.

Date	Mintage	F	VF	XF	Unc	BU
1978	38,015,000	—	0.10	0.20	0.60	1.00
1979	64,524,000	—	0.10	0.20	0.60	1.00
1980	76,964,000	—	0.10	0.20	0.60	1.00
1981	31,632,000	—	0.10	0.20	0.60	1.00
1982	23,252,000	—	0.10	0.20	0.60	1.00
1983	650	20.00	30.00	40.00	60.00	—

KM# 236 10 SOLES
4.6070 g., 0.9000 Gold 0.1333 oz. AGW **Obv:** National arms above date **Rev:** Seated Liberty flanked by shield and column

Date	Mintage	F	VF	XF	Unc	BU
1956	5,410	—	—	BV	130	—
1957	1,300	—	—	BV	130	—
1959	1,103	—	—	BV	130	—
1960	7,178	—	—	BV	130	—
1961	1,634	—	—	BV	130	—
1962	1,676	—	—	BV	130	—
1963	3,372	—	—	BV	130	—
1964	1,554	—	—	BV	130	—
1965	14,000	—	—	BV	130	—
1966	2,601	—	—	BV	130	—
1967	3,002	—	—	BV	130	—
1968	100	—	BV	130	220	—
1969	100	—	BV	130	220	—

KM# 253 10 SOLES
10.0000 g., Copper-Nickel **Obv:** National arms within circle **Rev:** Stylized fish below value

Date	Mintage	F	VF	XF	Unc	BU
1969	15,000,000	0.25	0.50	0.75	1.75	2.50

KM# 255 10 SOLES
Copper-Nickel **Subject:** 150th Anniversary of Independence **Obv:** National arms **Rev:** Bust of Tupac Amaru right **Note:** Mint mark in monogram.

Date	Mintage	F	VF	XF	Unc	BU
1971LIMA	2,460,000	0.25	0.50	1.00	2.50	—

KM# 258   10 SOLES

11.7000 g., Copper-Nickel, 30.94 mm. **Obv:** National arms within circle **Rev:** Bust of Tupac Amaru right **Edge:** Reeded **Note:** Mint mark in monogram.

Date	Mintage	F	VF	XF	Unc	BU
1972	2,235	—	0.10	0.40	1.25	
1973	1,765	—	0.10	0.40	1.25	
1974	—	—	0.10	0.40	1.25	
1975	—	—	0.10	0.40	1.25	

KM# 272.1   10 SOLES

Brass **Obv:** National arms, small letters: inner circle 18.1mm **Rev:** Head with hat 3/4 right **Edge:** Plain **Note:** Mint mark in monogram.

Date	Mintage	F	VF	XF	Unc	BU
1978	46,970,000	—	0.10	0.40	0.85	1.50

KM# 272.2   10 SOLES

5.6500 g., Brass, 24.48 mm. **Subject:** Tupac Amaru **Obv:** Small arms , large letters, inner circle 17.2mm **Rev:** Head with hat 3/4 right **Rev. Leg.:** TUPAC AMARU, SOLES DE ORO **Edge:** Plain **Note:** Mint mark in monogram.

Date	Mintage	F	VF	XF	Unc	BU
1978	—	—	0.10	0.40	0.85	1.50
1979	82,220,000	—	0.10	0.40	0.85	1.50
1980	99,595,000	—	0.10	0.40	0.85	1.50
1981	25,660,000	—	0.10	0.40	0.85	1.50
1982	61,035,000	—	0.10	0.40	0.85	1.50
1983	15,820,000	—	0.10	0.40	0.85	1.50

KM# 287   10 SOLES

Brass **Subject:** 150th Anniversary - Birth of Admiral Grau **Obv:** Value within circle **Rev:** Head 1/4 right **Note:** Mint mark in monogram.

Date	Mintage	F	VF	XF	Unc	BU
1984	30,000,000	—	—	0.20	0.50	0.75

KM# 229   20 SOLES

9.3614 g., 0.9000 Gold 0.2709 oz. AGW, 22 mm. **Obv:** National arms **Rev:** Seated Liberty flanked by shield and column

Date	Mintage	F	VF	XF	Unc	BU
1950	1,800	—	—	BV	270	—
1951	9,264	—	—	BV	260	275
1952	424	—	—	BV	270	—
1953	1,435	—	—	BV	270	—
1954	1,732	—	—	BV	270	—
1955	1,971	—	—	BV	270	—
1956	1,201	—	—	BV	270	—
1957	11,000	—	—	BV	260	275
1958	11,000	—	—	BV	260	275
1959	12,000	—	—	BV	260	275
1960	7,753	—	—	BV	260	275
1961	1,825	—	—	BV	270	—
1962	2,282	—	—	BV	270	—
1963	3,892	—	—	BV	270	—
1964	1,302	—	—	BV	270	—
1965	12,000	—	—	BV	260	275
1966	4,001	—	—	BV	260	275
1967	5,003	—	—	BV	260	275
1968	640	—	—	BV	270	—
1969	640	—	—	BV	270	—

KM# 241   20 SOLES

8.0000 g., 0.9000 Silver 0.2315 oz. ASW **Subject:** 400th Anniversary of Lima Mint. **Obv:** National arms above value **Rev:** Pillars of Hercules within inner circle

Date	Mintage	F	VF	XF	Unc	BU
ND(1965)	150,000	—	—	—	7.00	—

KM# 219   50 SOLES

33.4363 g., 0.9000 Gold 0.9675 oz. AGW **Obv:** Head with headdress left **Rev:** Sculpture

Date	Mintage	F	VF	XF	Unc	BU
1930	5,584	—	—	975	1,600	
1931	5,538	—	—	975	1,500	
1967	10,000	—	—	—	950	
1968	300	—	—	—	950	
1969	403	—	—	—	950	

KM# 230   50 SOLES

23.4056 g., 0.9000 Gold 0.6772 oz. AGW **Obv:** National arms **Rev:** Seated Liberty flanked by shield and column **Note:** Similar to KM#229.

Date	Mintage	F	VF	XF	Unc	BU
1950	1,927	—	—	BV	660	—
1951	5,292	—	—	BV	650	665
1952	1,201	—	—	BV	660	—
1953	1,464	—	—	BV	660	—
1954	1,839	—	—	BV	660	—
1955	1,898	—	—	BV	660	—
1956	11,000	—	—	BV	650	665
1957	11,000	—	—	BV	650	665
1958	11,000	—	—	BV	650	665
1959	5,734	—	—	BV	650	665
1960	2,139	—	—	BV	660	—
1961	1,110	—	—	BV	660	—
1962	3,319	—	—	BV	660	—
1963	3,089	—	—	BV	660	—
1964/3	2,425	—	—	BV	660	—
1964	Inc. above	—	—	BV	660	—
1965	23,000	—	—	BV	650	665
1966	3,409	—	—	BV	650	665
1967	5,805	—	—	BV	650	665
1968	443	—	—	BV	660	—
1969	443	—	—	BV	660	—
1970	553	—	—	BV	660	—

KM# 242   50 SOLES

23.4056 g., 0.9000 Gold 0.6772 oz. AGW **Subject:** 400th Anniversary of Lima Mint **Obv:** National arms above value **Rev:** Pillars of Hercules within inner circle

Date	Mintage	F	VF	XF	Unc	BU
ND(1965)	17,000	—	—	—	650	665

KM# 250   50 SOLES

23.4056 g., 0.9000 Gold 0.6772 oz. AGW **Subject:** 100th Anniversary of Peru-Spain Naval Battle **Obv:** National arms above value **Rev:** Victory standing on globe divides dates

Date	Mintage	F	VF	XF	Unc	BU
ND(1966)	6,409	—	—	—	650	665

KM# 256   50 SOLES

21.4500 g., 0.8000 Silver 0.5517 oz. ASW **Subject:** 150th Anniversary of Independence **Obv:** National arms within circle **Rev:** Bust of Tupac Amaru right **Note:** Mint mark in monogram.

Date	Mintage	F	VF	XF	Unc	BU
1971LIMA	100,000	—	—	—	12.50	15.00

KM# 273   50 SOLES

9.0000 g., Aluminum-Bronze **Obv:** National arms **Rev:** Value within circle **Note:** Mint mark in monogram.

Date	Mintage	F	VF	XF	Unc	BU
1979	1,323,000	—	0.15	0.35	1.00	—
1980	452,573,000	—	0.10	0.20	0.50	—
1981	19,923,000	—	0.10	0.20	0.50	—
1982LIMA	18,471,000	—	0.10	0.20	0.50	—
1982 Without LIMA	Inc. above	—	0.15	0.35	1.00	—
1983	8,175,000	—	0.10	0.20	0.50	—

KM# 297   50 SOLES

Brass **Subject:** 150th Anniversary - Birth of Admiral Grau **Obv:** Value within circle **Rev:** Head 1/4 right **Note:** Mint mark in monogram.

Date	Mintage	F	VF	XF	Unc	BU
1984	11,475,000	—	—	0.20	0.50	—

KM# 321   50 SOLES

Brass, 17 mm. **Subject:** Admiral Grau **Obv:** Value within circle **Rev:** Head 1/4 right **Edge:** Plain

Date	Mintage	F	VF	XF	Unc	BU
1985LIMAE	8,525,000	—	—	0.20	0.50	—

KM# 249   20 SOLES

7.9700 g., 0.9000 Silver 0.2306 oz. ASW **Subject:** 100th Anniversary of Peru-Spain Naval Battle **Obv:** National arms above value **Rev:** Victory standing on globe flanked by dates

Date	Mintage	F	VF	XF	Unc	BU
ND(1966)	4,001	—	—	—	16.50	—

KM# 231   100 SOLES

46.8071 g., 0.9000 Gold 1.3543 oz. AGW **Obv:** National arms **Rev:** Seated Liberty flanked by shield and column

Date	Mintage	F	VF	XF	Unc	BU
1950	1,176	—	—	BV	1,300	1,350
1951	8,241	—	—	BV	1,300	1,350
1952	126	—	—	2,000	3,000	3,500
1953	498	—	—	BV	1,300	1,350
1954	1,808	—	—	BV	1,300	1,350
1955	901	—	—	BV	1,300	1,350
1956	1,159	—	—	BV	1,300	1,350
1957	550	—	—	BV	1,300	1,350
1958	101	—	—	3,000	4,000	4,500
1959	4,710	—	—	BV	1,300	1,350
1960	2,207	—	—	BV	1,300	1,350
1961	6,982	—	—	BV	1,300	1,350
1962	9,678	—	—	BV	1,300	1,350
1963	7,342	—	—	BV	1,300	1,350
1964	11,000	—	—	BV	1,300	1,350
1965	23,000	—	—	BV	1,300	1,350
1966	3,409	—	—	BV	1,300	1,350
1967	6,431	—	—	BV	1,300	1,350

Date	Mintage	F	VF	XF	Unc	BU
1968	540	—	—	BV	1,300	1,350
1969	540	—	—	BV	1,300	1,350
1970	425	—	—	BV	1,300	1,350

KM# 243   100 SOLES
46.8071 g., 0.9000 Gold 1.3543 oz. AGW **Subject:** 400th Anniversary of Lima Mint **Obv:** National arms **Rev:** Pillars of Hercules within inner circle

Date	Mintage	F	VF	XF	Unc	BU
ND(1965)	27,000	—	—	—	1,300	1,350

KM# 251   100 SOLES
46.8071 g., 0.9000 Gold 1.3543 oz. AGW **Subject:** 100th Anniversary of Peru-Spain Naval Battle **Obv:** National arms **Rev:** Victory standing on globe divides dates

Date	Mintage	F	VF	XF	Unc	BU
ND(1966)	6,253	—	—	—	1,300	1,350

KM# 261   100 SOLES
22.4500 g., 0.8000 Silver 0.5774 oz. ASW **Subject:** Centennial Peru-Japan Trade Relations **Obv:** National arms **Rev:** Value to left of flower sprig within circle **Note:** Mint mark in monogram.

Date	Mintage	F	VF	XF	Unc	BU
1973LIMA	375,000	—	—	—	12.50	16.00

KM# 283   100 SOLES
11.6600 g., Copper-Nickel, 29.83 mm. **Obv:** National arms **Rev:** Value within circle **Edge:** Reeded **Note:** Without mint mark.

Date	Mintage	F	VF	XF	Unc	BU
1980	100,000,000	—	0.20	0.40	1.50	—
1980 Proof	—	Value: 8.00				
1982	—	—	0.20	0.40	1.50	—

KM# 288   100 SOLES
3.0000 g., Brass **Subject:** 150th Anniversary - Birth of Admiral Grau **Obv:** Value within circle **Rev:** Head 1/4 right **Note:** Mint mark in monogram.

Date	Mintage	F	VF	XF	Unc	BU
1984LIMA	20,000,000	—	0.15	0.35	1.00	—

KM# 262   200 SOLES
22.0000 g., 0.8000 Silver 0.5658 oz. ASW **Subject:** Aviation Heroes - Chavez and Guinones **Obv:** National arms **Rev:** Conjoined heads left within circle **Note:** No mint mark.

Date	Mintage	F	VF	XF	Unc	BU
1974	25,000	—	—	—	16.00	—
1975	90,000	—	—	—	12.00	—
1976	25,000	—	—	—	20.00	—
1977	3,000	—	—	—	30.00	—
1978	3,000	—	—	—	30.00	—

KM# 270   400 SOLES
28.1000 g., 0.9000 Silver 0.8131 oz. ASW **Subject:** 150th Anniversary - Battle of Ayacucho **Obv:** National arms **Rev:** Monument divides value within circle **Note:** Mint mark in monogram.

Date	Mintage	F	VF	XF	Unc	BU
1976LIMA	350,000	—	—	—	18.00	20.00

KM# 289   500 SOLES
5.2000 g., Brass **Subject:** 150th Anniversary - Birth of Admiral Grau **Obv:** Value within circle **Rev:** Head 1/4 right **Note:** Mint mark in monogram.

Date	Mintage	F	VF	XF	Unc	BU
1984LIMA	16,962,000	—	0.20	0.50	2.00	—

KM# 310   500 SOLES
5.1200 g., Brass **Subject:** Admiral Grau **Obv:** National arms **Rev:** Head 1/4 right without date **Note:** Mint mark in monogram.

Date	Mintage	F	VF	XF	Unc	BU
1985LIMA	13,038,000	—	0.20	0.50	2.50	—

KM# 275   1000 SOLES
15.5500 g., 0.5000 Silver 0.2500 oz. ASW **Subject:** National Congress **Obv:** National arms within circle **Rev:** Building **Edge:** Smooth with incuse stars **Note:** Mint mark in monogram.

Date	Mintage	F	VF	XF	Unc	BU
1979LIMA	200,000	—	—	—	6.00	7.50

KM# 276   5000 SOLES
31.1077 g., 0.9250 Silver 0.9251 oz. ASW **Subject:** 100th Anniversary - Battle of Iquique **Obv:** National arms **Rev:** Ship **Note:** Mint mark in monogram.

Date	Mintage	F	VF	XF	Unc	BU
1979LIMA	100,000	—	—	15.00	20.00	22.50

KM# 284   5000 SOLES
23.3700 g., 0.9250 Silver 0.6950 oz. ASW **Subject:** Champions of Soccer **Obv:** National arms **Rev:** Soccer players **Note:** Mint mark in monogram.

Date	Mintage	F	VF	XF	Unc	BU
1982LIMA Proof	8,250	Value: 26.50				

KM# 285   5000 SOLES
Silver **Subject:** Champions of Soccer **Obv:** National arms **Rev:** Soccer players in front of world globe **Note:** Mint mark in monogram.

Date	Mintage	F	VF	XF	Unc	BU
1982LIMA Proof	8,300	Value: 26.50				

KM# 286   10000 SOLES
16.8000 g., 0.9250 Silver 0.4996 oz. ASW **Subject:** Battle of La Brena and General Caceres **Obv:** National arms **Rev:** Head left **Note:** Mint mark in monogram.

Date	Mintage	F	VF	XF	Unc	BU
1982LIMA	100,000	—	—	—	12.50	14.50

KM# 277 50000 SOLES

16.8600 g., 0.9170 Gold 0.4970 oz. AGW **Subject:** Alfonso Urgarte **Obv:** National arms within circle **Rev:** Head left **Note:** Mint mark in monogram.

Date	Mintage	F	VF	XF	Unc	BU
1979LIMA	10,000	—	—	—	500	525

KM# 278 50000 SOLES

16.8600 g., 0.9170 Gold 0.4970 oz. AGW **Subject:** Elias Aguirre **Obv:** National arms within circle **Rev:** Head left **Note:** Mint mark in monogram.

Date	Mintage	F	VF	XF	Unc	BU
1979LIMA	10,000	—	—	—	500	525

KM# 279 50000 SOLES

16.8600 g., 0.9170 Gold 0.4970 oz. AGW **Subject:** F. Garcia Calderon **Obv:** National arms within circle **Rev:** Bust left **Note:** Mint mark in monogram.

Date	Mintage	F	VF	XF	Unc	BU
1979LIMA	10,000	—	—	—	500	525

KM# 280 100000 SOLES

33.9000 g., 0.9170 Gold 0.9994 oz. AGW **Subject:** Francisco Bolognese **Obv:** National arms within circle **Rev:** Bust left **Note:** Mint mark in monogram.

Date	Mintage	F	VF	XF	Unc	BU
1979LIMA	10,000	—	—	—	975	1,000

KM# 281 100000 SOLES

33.9000 g., 0.9170 Gold 0.9994 oz. AGW **Subject:** Andres A. Caceres **Obv:** National arms within circle **Rev:** Head left **Note:** Mint mark in monogram.

Date	Mintage	F	VF	XF	Unc	BU
1979LIMA	10,000	—	—	—	975	1,000

KM# 282 100000 SOLES

33.9000 g., 0.9170 Gold 0.9994 oz. AGW **Subject:** Miguel Grau **Obv:** National arms within circle **Rev:** Bust left **Note:** Mint mark in monogram.

Date	Mintage	F	VF	XF	Unc	BU
1979LIMA	10,000	—	—	—	975	1,000

REFORM COINAGE
1000 Soles de Oro = 1 Inti

KM# 291 CENTIMO

1.5000 g., Brass, 15 mm. **Subject:** General Grau **Obv:** Value within circle **Rev:** Head 1/4 right **Note:** Mint mark: LIMA (monogram)

Date	Mintage	F	VF	XF	Unc	BU
1985LIMA	4,199,999	—	—	—	0.25	0.45

KM# 292 5 CENTIMOS

2.0000 g., Brass, 17 mm. **Subject:** General Grau **Obv:** Value within circle **Rev:** Head 1/4 right **Note:** Mint mark: LIMA (monogram)

Date	Mintage	F	VF	XF	Unc	BU
1985LIMA	20,000,000	—	—	—	0.35	0.50

KM# 293 10 CENTIMOS

2.9000 g., Brass, 19 mm. **Subject:** General Grau **Obv:** Value within circle **Rev:** Head 1/4 right **Rev. Leg.:** GRAN ALMIRANTE MIGUEL GRAU **Edge:** Plain **Note:** Mint mark: LIMA (monogram)

Date	Mintage	F	VF	XF	Unc	BU
1985LIMA	143,900,000	—	—	—	0.50	0.85
1986LIMA	48,730,000	—	—	—	0.65	1.00
1987LIMA	42,370,000	—	—	—	0.65	1.00

KM# 294 20 CENTIMOS

4.0600 g., Brass, 21 mm. **Subject:** General Grau **Obv:** Value within circle **Rev:** Head 1/4 right **Rev. Leg.:** GRAN ALMIRANTE MIGUEL GRAU **Edge:** Plain **Note:** Mint mark: LIMA (monogram)

Date	Mintage	F	VF	XF	Unc	BU
1985LIMA	4,739,000	—	—	—	1.25	1.50
1986LIMA	96,699,000	—	—	—	1.00	1.25
1987LIMA	59,668,000	—	—	—	1.00	1.25

KM# 295 50 CENTIMOS

5.2000 g., Brass, 23 mm. **Subject:** General Grau **Obv:** Value within circle **Rev:** Head 1/4 right **Note:** Mint mark: LIMA (monogram)

Date	Mintage	F	VF	XF	Unc	BU
1985LIMA	43,320,000	—	—	—	1.25	1.50
1986LIMA	72,802,000	—	—	—	1.25	1.50

Date	Mintage	F	VF	XF	Unc	BU
1987LIMA	63,878,000	—	—	—	1.25	1.50
1988LIMA	80,000,000	—	—	—	1.25	1.50

KM# 301a 1/2 INTI

Copper-Nickel **Subject:** Pachacutec **Obv:** Map within design and stylized bow **Rev:** Native head left divides date

Date	Mintage	F	VF	XF	Unc	BU
1989						

KM# 301 1/2 INTI

16.8000 g., 0.9250 Silver 0.4996 oz. ASW **Subject:** Pachacutec **Obv:** Map within design and stylized bow **Rev:** Native head left divides date **Note:** Mint mark: LIMA (monogram)

Date	Mintage	F	VF	XF	Unc	BU
1989LIMA	—	—	—	—	20.00	22.50

KM# 296 INTI

7.0000 g., Copper-Nickel, 25 mm. **Subject:** Admiral Grau **Obv:** National arms **Rev:** Head 1/4 right **Rev. Leg.:** GRAN ALMIRANTE MIGUEL GRAU, value **Edge:** Reeded **Note:** Mint mark: LIMA (monogram)

Date	Mintage	F	VF	XF	Unc	BU
1985LIMA	15,760,000	—	—	—	1.75	2.00
1986LIMA	87,240,000	—	—	—	1.25	1.50
1987LIMA	120,000,000	—	—	—	1.00	1.25
1988LIMA	17,304,000	—	—	—	1.75	2.00

KM# 300 5 INTIS

8.2000 g., Copper-Nickel, 27 mm. **Subject:** Admiral Grau **Obv:** National arms **Rev:** Head 1/4 right **Rev. Leg.:** GRAN ALMIRANTE MIGUEL GRAU, value **Edge:** Reeded **Note:** Mint mark: LIMA (monogram)

Date	Mintage	F	VF	XF	Unc	BU
1985LIMA	3,972	—	—	—	—	—
1986LIMA	28,000	—	—	—	3.50	5.00
1987LIMA	20,106,000	—	—	—	2.50	3.00
1988LIMA	34,084,000	—	—	—	2.50	3.00

KM# 298 100 INTIS

11.1100 g., 0.9250 Silver 0.3304 oz. ASW **Subject:** 150th Anniversary - Birth of Marshal Caceres **Obv:** National arms above value **Rev:** Head right **Note:** Mint mark: LIMA (monogram)

Date	Mintage	F	VF	XF	Unc	BU
ND(1986)LIMA	10,000	—	—	—	17.50	20.00

KM# 299 200 INTIS

22.0400 g., 0.9250 Silver 0.6554 oz. ASW **Subject:** 150th Anniversary - Birth of Marshal Caceres **Obv:** National arms above value **Rev:** Head right **Note:** Mint mark: LIMA (monogram)

Date	Mintage	F	VF	XF	Unc	BU
ND(1986)LIMA	—	—	—	—	32.50	35.00

REFORM COINAGE
1/M Intis = 1 Nuevo Sol; 100 (New) Centimos = 1 Nuevo Sol

KM# 303.1 CENTIMO

Brass **Obv:** National arms **Rev:** Value flanked by designs **Note:** LIMA monogram is mint mark.

Date	Mintage	F	VF	XF	Unc	BU
1991 CHAVEZ	—	—	—	—	0.35	0.50
1992 CHAVEZ	—	—	—	—	0.45	0.65
1993 CHAVEZ	—	—	—	—	0.35	0.50
1994 CHAVEZ	—	—	—	—	0.35	0.50

KM# 303.2 CENTIMO

Brass **Obv:** National arms **Obv. Leg.:** No accent in Peru **Rev:** Large braille, no accent mark above E in centimo, no Chavez **Note:** LIMA monogram is mint mark.

Date	Mintage	F	VF	XF	Unc	BU
1997	—	—	—	—	0.35	—

KM# 303.3 CENTIMO

1.7300 g., Brass, 15.94 mm. **Obv:** National arms **Obv. Leg.:** Accent mark in Peru **Rev:** Large braille, accent in centimo, no Chavez **Edge:** Plain **Note:** LIMA monogram is mint mark.

Date	Mintage	F	VF	XF	Unc	BU
1999	—	—	—	—	2.50	—

KM# 304.1   5 CENTIMOS

2.2600 g., Brass **Obv:** National arms **Rev:** Value flanked by designs **Note:** LIMA monogram is mint mark.

Date	Mintage	F	VF	XF	Unc	BU
1991 CHAVEZ	—	—	—	—	0.45	0.65
1992 CHAVEZ	—	—	—	—	0.50	0.75
1993	—	—	—	—	0.45	0.65
1993 CHAVEZ	—	—	—	—	0.45	0.65
1994	—	—	—	—	0.45	0.65
1995	—	—	—	—	0.45	0.65
1996	—	—	—	—	0.45	0.65

KM# 304.2   5 CENTIMOS

2.7800 g., Brass, 17.92 mm. **Obv:** National arms **Rev:** Small braille with no accent mark above E in centimos, no Chavez **Edge:** Plain **Note:** LIMA monogram is mint mark.

Date	Mintage	F	VF	XF	Unc	BU
1997	—	—	—	—	0.35	0.50
1998	—	—	—	—	0.35	0.50

KM# 304.3   5 CENTIMOS

Brass **Obv:** National arms **Rev:** Small braille with accent mark above E in centimos **Note:** LIMA monogram is mint mark.

Date	Mintage	F	VF	XF	Unc	BU
2000	—	—	—	—	0.35	0.50

KM# 305.1   10 CENTIMOS

3.5000 g., Brass, 20.47 mm. **Obv:** National arms within octagon **Rev:** Value flanked by designs within octagon **Edge:** Plain **Note:** LIMA monogram is mint mark.

Date	Mintage	F	VF	XF	Unc	BU
1991	—	—	—	—	0.65	0.85
1992	—	—	—	—	0.75	1.00
1993	—	—	—	—	0.65	0.85
1993 CHAVEZ	—	—	—	—	0.65	0.85
1994	—	—	—	—	0.65	0.85
1995	—	—	—	—	0.65	0.85
1996	—	—	—	—	0.65	0.85

KM# 305.2   10 CENTIMOS

3.5000 g., Brass **Obv:** National arms within octagon **Rev:** Value flanked by designs within octagon **Note:** LIMA monogram mint mark.

Date	Mintage	F	VF	XF	Unc	BU
1997	—	—	—	—	0.65	0.85
1998 LIMA	—	—	—	—	0.65	0.85

KM# 305.3   10 CENTIMOS

3.5000 g., Brass, 20.47 mm. **Obv:** National arms within octagon **Rev:** Value flanked by designs within octagon **Edge:** Plain **Note:** LIMA monogram is mint mark.

Date	Mintage	F	VF	XF	Unc	BU
1999	—	—	—	—	0.65	0.85
2000	—	—	—	—	0.65	0.85

KM# 306.1   20 CENTIMOS

4.4300 g., Brass, 23 mm. **Obv:** National arms **Rev:** Value **Edge:** Plain **Note:** LIMA monogram is mint mark. Varieties exist.

Date	Mintage	F	VF	XF	Unc	BU
1991 CHAVEZ	—	—	—	—	0.85	1.20
1992 CHAVEZ	—	—	—	—	0.85	1.20
1993 CHAVEZ	—	—	—	—	0.85	1.20
1994	—	—	—	—	0.85	1.20
1996	—	—	—	—	0.85	1.20

KM# 306.2   20 CENTIMOS

4.5300 g., Brass, 23 mm. **Obv:** National arms, accent above "u" **Rev:** Small braille dots, accent above "e" **Edge:** Plain **Note:** LIMA monogram is mint mark. Prev. KM#306.3.

Date	Mintage	F	VF	XF	Unc	BU
2000 LIMA	—	—	—	—	0.85	1.20

KM# 307.1   50 CENTIMOS

5.5200 g., Copper-Nickel, 22 mm. **Obv:** National arms within octagon **Rev:** Value flanked by sprig and monogram within octagon **Edge:** Reeded **Note:** LIMA monogram is mint mark.

Date	Mintage	F	VF	XF	Unc	BU
1991	—	—	—	—	1.50	1.75
1992	—	—	—	—	1.75	2.00
1993	—	—	—	—	1.50	1.75
1994	—	—	—	—	1.50	1.75
1996	—	—	—	—	1.50	1.75

KM# 307.2   50 CENTIMOS

5.5200 g., Copper-Nickel, 22 mm. **Obv:** National arms within octagon **Rev:** Value flanked by sprig and monogram within octagon **Edge:** Reeded **Note:** LIMA monogram is mint mark.

Date	Mintage	F	VF	XF	Unc	BU
1997	—	—	—	—	1.50	1.75
1998	—	—	—	—	1.50	1.75

KM# 307.3   50 CENTIMOS

5.5200 g., Copper-Nickel, 22 mm. **Obv:** National arms within octagon **Rev:** Value flanked by sprig and monogram within octagon **Edge:** Reeded **Note:** LIMA monogram is mint mark.

Date	Mintage	F	VF	XF	Unc	BU
2000	—	—	—	—	1.50	1.75

KM# 302   NUEVO SOL

27.0000 g., 0.9250 Silver 0.8029 oz. ASW **Series:** Ibero - American **Obv:** National arms within assorted emblems around border **Rev:** Supine conjoined heads with hands holding a cornstalk and cross **Note:** LIMA monogram is mint mark.

Date	Mintage	F	VF	XF	Unc	BU
1991 Proof	60,000	Value: 50.00				

KM# 308.1   NUEVO SOL

7.3000 g., Copper-Nickel, 25.48 mm. **Obv:** National arms within octagon **Rev:** Written value flanked by sprig and monogram within octagon **Edge:** Reeded **Note:** LIMA monogram is mint mark.

Date	Mintage	F	VF	XF	Unc	BU
1991	—	—	—	—	5.00	5.50
1992	—	—	—	—	5.00	5.50
1993	—	—	—	—	5.00	5.50
1994	—	—	—	—	4.00	4.50
1995	—	—	—	—	4.00	4.50
1996	—	—	—	—	4.00	4.50

KM# 327   NUEVO SOL

27.0000 g., 0.9250 Silver 0.8029 oz. ASW, 39 mm. **Series:** Ibero-American **Obv:** National arms within assorted emblems around border **Rev:** Opposite conjoined heads with hands holding cornstalk and cross **Note:** LIMA monogram is mint mark.

Date	Mintage	F	VF	XF	Unc	BU
ND(1991) Proof	—	Value: 55.00				

KM# 308.2   NUEVO SOL

7.3000 g., Copper-Nickel, 25.48 mm. **Obv:** National arms within octagon **Rev:** Written value flanked by sprig and monogram within octagon **Edge:** Reeded **Note:** LIMA monogram is mint mark.

Date	Mintage	F	VF	XF	Unc	BU
1991	—	5.00	10.00	25.00	55.00	—

KM# 311   NUEVO SOL

33.6250 g., 0.9250 Silver 0.9999 oz. ASW **Subject:** Pre-Inca Moche Cultural Artifacts **Obv:** National arms **Rev:** Cultural artifacts within designed circle **Note:** LIMA monogram is mint mark.

Date	Mintage	F	VF	XF	Unc	BU
1994	3,300					
1994 Proof	2,000	Value: 55.00				

KM# 314   NUEVO SOL

20.0000 g., 0.9990 Silver 0.6423 oz. ASW **Series:** Environmental Protection **Obv:** National arms **Rev:** Two Young Vicunas **Note:** LIMA monogram is mint mark.

Date	Mintage	F	VF	XF	Unc	BU
1994 Proof	30,000	Value: 50.00				

KM# 317 NUEVO SOL
20.0000 g., 0.9990 Silver 0.6423 oz. ASW **Series:** Environmental Protection **Obv:** National arms **Rev:** Llama, monkey and crocodile **Note:** LIMA monogram is mint mark.

Date	Mintage	F	VF	XF	Unc	BU
1994 Proof	20,000	Value: 50.00				

KM# 312 NUEVO SOL
33.6250 g., 0.9170 Gold 0.9913 oz. AGW **Obv:** National arms **Rev:** Cultural artifacts within circle **Note:** LIMA monogram is mint mark. Similar to KM#311.

Date	Mintage	F	VF	XF	Unc	BU
1994	899	—	—	—	—	950
1994 Proof	100	Value: 975				

KM# 325 NUEVO SOL
33.6250 g., 0.9250 Silver 0.9999 oz. ASW, 37.1 mm. **Subject:** Centennial - Birth of Jose Carlos Mariategui **Obv:** National arms **Rev:** Bust half right **Edge:** Reeded **Note:** LIMA monogram is mint mark.

Date	Mintage	F	VF	XF	Unc	BU
1994 Proof	—	Value: 100				

KM# 338 NUEVO SOL
39.3000 g., 0.9250 Silver 1.1687 oz. ASW, 37.19mm mm. **Obv:** National arms **Obv. Leg.:** BANCO CENTRAL DE RESERVA DEL PERÚ **Rev:** Military bust of Grand Marshall Luis José de Orbegoso y Moncada 3/4 right **Rev. Leg.:** PROCER de la INDEPENDENCIA y PRESIDENTE de la REPUBLICA **Edge:** Reeded

Date	Mintage	F	VF	XF	Unc	BU
1995 Proof	—	Value: 60.00				

KM# 318 NUEVO SOL
33.6250 g., 0.9250 Silver 0.9999 oz. ASW **Subject:** Centennial of Victor Raul Haya de la Torre **Obv:** National arms **Rev:** Head right **Note:** LIMA monogram is mint mark.

Date	Mintage	F	VF	XF	Unc	BU
1995	883	—	—	—	100	—

KM# 319 NUEVO SOL
33.6250 g., 0.9250 Silver 0.9999 oz. ASW **Subject:** National Mineral and Petroleum Society Centennial **Obv:** National arms **Rev:** Miner, oil derrick and cart **Note:** LIMA monogram is mint mark.

Date	Mintage	F	VF	XF	Unc	BU
1996	—	—	—	—	45.00	—

KM# 336 NUEVO SOL
33.6250 g., 0.9250 Silver 0.9999 oz. ASW, 36.9 mm. **Subject:** Central Bank's 75th Anniversary **Obv:** National arms above date **Rev:** Radiant 75 design **Edge:** Reeded

Date	Mintage	F	VF	XF	Unc	BU
1997LIMAE Proof	—	Value: 50.00				

KM# 337 NUEVO SOL
33.6250 g., 0.9250 Silver 0.9999 oz. ASW, 37 mm. **Obv:** National arms above date **Rev:** Grand Marshal Ramon Castilla **Edge:** Reeded

Date	Mintage	F	VF	XF	Unc	BU
1997LIMAE Proof	—	Value: 50.00				

KM# 328 NUEVO SOL
33.5200 g., 0.9250 Silver 0.9968 oz. ASW, 37 mm. **Subject:** Centennial - Birth of Raul Porras Barrenechea **Obv:** National arms **Rev:** Bust facing **Edge:** Reeded **Note:** LIMA monogram is mint mark.

Date	Mintage	F	VF	XF	Unc	BU
1997 Proof	1,000	Value: 55.00				

KM# 323 NUEVO SOL
33.4700 g., 0.9250 Silver 0.9953 oz. ASW, 37.1 mm. **Subject:** Centennial of Chorrillos Military School **Obv:** National arms **Rev:** Monument and building divide dates **Edge:** Reeded **Note:** LIMA monogram is mint mark.

Date	Mintage	F	VF	XF	Unc	BU
1998 Proof	—	Value: 47.50				

KM# 322 NUEVO SOL
33.6250 g., 0.9250 Silver 0.9999 oz. ASW **Subject:** Centennial of Japanese Immigration **Obv:** National arms **Rev:** Radiant sun above maps **Note:** LIMA monogram is mint mark.

Date	Mintage	F	VF	XF	Unc	BU
1999 Proof	—	Value: 47.50				

KM# 308.3 NUEVO SOL
7.3000 g., Copper-Nickel, 25.48 mm. **Obv:** National arms within octagon **Rev:** Value flanked by sprig and monogram within octagon **Edge:** Reeded **Note:** LIMA monogram is mint mark.

Date	Mintage	F	VF	XF	Unc	BU
1999	—	—	—	—	4.00	4.50
2000	—	—	—	—	4.00	4.50

KM# 326 NUEVO SOL
26.9500 g., 0.9250 Silver 0.8014 oz. ASW, 40 mm. **Series:** Ibero-American **Obv:** National arms within circle of assorted arms **Rev:** Horse and rider in courtyard **Edge:** Reeded **Note:** LIMA monogram is mint mark.

Date	Mintage	F	VF	XF	Unc	BU
2000 Proof	—	Value: 60.00				

KM# 313 2 NUEVOS SOLES
5.5800 g., Bi-Metallic Brass center in Steel ring, 22.22 mm. **Obv:** National arms within circle **Rev:** Stylized bird in flight to left of value within circle **Edge:** Plain **Note:** LIMA monogram is mint mark.

Date	Mintage	F	VF	XF	Unc	BU
1994LIMA	—	—	—	—	4.50	5.00
1995LIMA	—	—	—	—	4.50	5.00

KM# 316 5 NUEVOS SOLES
6.6700 g., Bi-Metallic Brass center in Steel ring, 24.27 mm.
Obv: National arms within circle **Rev:** Stylized bird in flight to left of value within circle **Edge:** Plain **Note:** LIMA monogram is mint mark.

Date	Mintage	F	VF	XF	Unc	BU
1994LIMA	—	—	—	—	6.50	7.00
1995LIMA	—	—	—	—	6.50	7.00
2000LIMA	—	—	—	—	6.50	7.00

KM# 309 20 NUEVOS SOLES
33.6250 g., 0.9250 Silver 0.9999 oz. ASW **Subject:** Rio De Janeiro Protocal **Obv:** National arms **Rev:** Angel above map, dates at left **Note:** LIMA monogram is mint mark.

Date	Mintage	F	VF	XF	Unc	BU
1992	50,000	—	—	—	28.50	32.50

KM# 315 20 NUEVOS SOLES
33.6250 g., 0.9250 Silver 0.9999 oz. ASW **Obv:** National arms **Rev:** Head right **Note:** LIMA monogram is mint mark.

Date	Mintage	F	VF	XF	Unc	BU
1992 Proof	—	Value: 28.50				

KM# 320 50 NUEVOS SOLES
33.6250 g., 0.9250 Silver 0.9999 oz. ASW **Subject:** Peru-Japan Commercial Exchange **Obv:** National arms **Rev:** Stylized bird design **Note:** LIMA monogram is mint mark.

Date	Mintage	F	VF	XF	Unc	BU
1993	—	—	—	—	42.50	47.50

TRADE COINAGE

KM# 210 1/5 LIBRA (Pound)
1.5976 g., 0.9170 Gold 0.0471 oz. AGW **Obv:** Shield within sprigs with small radiant sun above **Rev:** Head with headband right **Note:** Struck at Lima.

Date	Mintage	F	VF	XF	Unc	BU
1906 GOZF	106,000	—	—	—	45.00	—
1907 GOZF	31,000	—	—	—	45.00	—
1907 GOZG	—	—	—	—	45.00	—
1909 GOZG	—	—	—	—	45.00	—
1910 GOZG	—	—	—	—	45.00	—
1911 GOZF	62,000	—	—	—	45.00	—
1911 GOZG	—	—	—	—	45.00	—
1912 GOZG	—	—	—	—	45.00	—
1912 POZG	—	—	—	—	45.00	—
1913 POZG	60,000	—	—	—	45.00	—
1914 POZG	25,000	—	—	—	45.00	—
1914 PBLG	Inc. above	—	—	—	—	—
	Note: Reported, not confirmed					
1915	10,000	—	—	—	45.00	—
1916	13,000	—	—	—	—	—
	Note: Reported, not confirmed					
1917	3,896	—	—	—	45.00	—
1918	16,000	—	—	—	45.00	—
1919	10,000	—	—	—	45.00	—
1920	72,000	—	—	—	45.00	—
1922	8,110	—	—	—	45.00	—
1923	27,000	—	—	—	45.00	—
1924	—	—	—	—	45.00	—
1925	20,000	—	—	—	45.00	—
1926	11,000	—	—	—	45.00	—
1927	14,000	—	—	—	45.00	—
1928	9,322	—	—	—	45.00	—
1929	8,971	—	—	—	45.00	—
1930	9,991	—	—	—	55.00	—
1953 BBR	9,821	—	—	—	50.00	—
1955 ZBR	10,000	—	—	—	50.00	—
1958 ZBR	5,098	—	—	—	45.00	—
1959 ZBR	6,308	—	—	—	45.00	—
1960 ZBR	6,083	—	—	—	45.00	—
1961 ZBR	12,000	—	—	—	45.00	—
1962 ZBR	5,431	—	—	—	45.00	—
1963 ZBR	11,000	—	—	—	45.00	—
1964 ZBR	25,000	—	—	—	45.00	—
1965 ZBR	19,000	—	—	—	45.00	—
1966 ZBR	60,000	—	—	—	45.00	—
1967 BBR	9,914	—	—	—	45.00	—
1968 BBR	—	—	—	—	45.00	—
1968 BBB	4,781	—	—	—	45.00	—
1969 BBB	15,000	—	—	—	45.00	—

KM# 209 1/2 LIBRA (Pound)
3.9940 g., 0.9170 Gold 0.1177 oz. AGW **Obv:** Shield within sprigs with radiant sun above **Rev:** Head with headband right

Date	Mintage	F	VF	XF	Unc	BU
1902 ROZF	7,800	—	BV	110	120	—
1903 ROZF	7,245	—	BV	110	120	—

Date	Mintage	F	VF	XF	Unc	BU
1904 ROZF	8,360	—	BV	110	120	—
1905 ROZF	8,010	—	BV	110	120	—
1905 GOZF	Inc. above	—	BV	110	120	—
1906 GOZF	9,176	—	BV	110	120	—
1907 GOZG	—	—	BV	110	120	—
1908 GOZG	8,180	—	BV	110	120	—
1953 BBR	9,210	—	BV	110	120	—
1955 ZBR	14,000	—	—	BV	110	—
1961 ZBR	752	—	—	BV	110	—
1962 ZBR	4,286	—	—	BV	110	—
1963 ZBR	908	—	—	BV	110	—
1964 ZBR	10,000	—	—	BV	110	—
1965 ZBR	5,490	—	—	BV	110	—
1966 ZBR	44,000	—	—	BV	110	—
1967 BBR	—	—	—	BV	110	—
1968 BBB	Inc. above	—	—	BV	110	—
1968 BBR	—	—	—	BV	110	—
1969 BBB	4,400	—	—	BV	110	—

KM# 207 LIBRA (Pound)
7.9881 g., 0.9170 Gold 0.2355 oz. AGW **Obv:** Shield within sprigs with radiant sun above **Rev:** Head with headband right

Date	Mintage	VG	F	VF	XF	Unc
1901 ROZF	81,000	—	—	—	BV	225
1902 ROZF	89,000	—	—	—	BV	225
1903 ROZF	100,000	—	—	—	BV	225
1904 ROZF	33,000	—	—	—	BV	225
1905 GOZF	—	—	—	—	BV	225
1905 ROZF	141,000	—	—	—	BV	225
1906 GOZF	201,000	—	—	—	BV	225
1907 GOZG	Inc. above	—	—	—	BV	225
1908 GOZG	36,000	—	—	—	BV	225
1909 GOZG	52,000	—	—	—	BV	225
1910 GOZG	47,000	—	—	—	BV	225
1911 GOZG	42,000	—	—	—	BV	225
1912 GOZG	54,000	—	—	—	BV	225
1912 POZG	Inc. above	—	—	—	BV	225
1913 POZG	—	—	—	—	BV	225
1914 POZG	—	—	—	—	BV	225
1914 PBLG	119,000	—	—	—	BV	225
1915 PVG	91,000	—	—	—	BV	225
1915 PMGG	Inc. above	—	—	—	BV	225
1915	Inc. above	—	—	—	BV	225
1916	582,000	—	—	—	BV	225
1917	1,928,000	—	—	—	BV	225
1918	600,000	—	—	—	BV	225
1919	Inc. above	—	—	—	BV	225
1920	152,000	—	—	—	BV	225
1921	Inc. above	—	—	—	BV	225
1922	13,000	—	—	—	BV	225
1923	15,000	—	—	—	BV	225
1924	8,113	—	—	—	BV	225
1925	9,068	—	—	—	BV	225
1926	4,596	—	—	—	BV	225
1927	8,360	—	—	—	BV	225
1928	2,184	—	—	—	BV	225
1929	3,119	—	—	—	BV	225
1930	1,050	—	—	—	BV	225
1959 ZBR	605	—	—	—	BV	250
1961 ZBR	402	—	—	—	BV	250
1962 ZBR	6,203	—	—	—	BV	225
1963 ZBR	302	—	—	—	BV	260
1964 ZBR	13,000	—	—	—	BV	225
1965 ZBR	9,917	—	—	—	BV	225
1966 ZBR	39,000	—	—	—	BV	225
1967 BBR	2,002	—	—	—	BV	225
1968 BBR	7,307	—	—	—	BV	225
1969 BBR	7,307	—	—	—	BV	225

TOKEN COINAGE

KM# Tn3 50 CENTAVOS
Silver **Subject:** National Defense **Obv:** Inca warrior Cahuide attacking with war club

Date	Mintage	F	VF	XF	Unc	BU
1932	—	8.50	12.50	18.50	30.00	—

KM# Tn1 SOL
0.9000 Silver **Note:** Medal rotation.

Date	Mintage	F	VF	XF	Unc	BU
1910	—	8.50	12.50	18.50	30.00	40.00

KM# Tn4 SOL
Silver **Subject:** National Defense **Obv:** Inca warrior Cahuide attacking with war club **Note:** Medal rotation.

Date	Mintage	F	VF	XF	Unc	BU
1932	—	7.00	12.00	17.50	30.00	—

KM# Tn2 5 SOLES
2.3404 g., 0.9000 Gold 0.0677 oz. AGW

Date	Mintage	F	VF	XF	Unc	BU
1910	—	60.00	80.00	110	150	200

KM# Tn5 5 SOLES
Silver **Subject:** National Defense **Obv:** Inca warrior Cahuide attacking with war club

Date	Mintage	F	VF	XF	Unc	BU
1932	—	12.00	17.50	28.50	45.00	—

KM# Tn6 10 SOLES
Gold Plated Silver **Subject:** National Defense **Obv:** Inca warrior Cahuide attacking with war club

Date	Mintage	F	VF	XF	Unc	BU
1932	—	15.00	20.00	38.50	55.00	—

PATTERNS
Including off metal strikes

KM#	Date	Mintage	Identification	Mkt Val
PnF26	1930	3	50 Soles. Native inscription.	—
PnG26	1932	—	50 Centavos.	—
Pn26	1932	—	Sol.	—
Pn27	1932	—	5 Soles.	—
PnA28	1932	—	10 Soles.	—
pnB28	1946	—	1/2 Sol. Copper-Nickel.	150
Pn28	1947	—	100 Soles. Gilt Bronze.	—
Pn29	1948	—	Sol. Aluminum.	—
PnA30	1949	—	Centavo. Zinc. KM#211.	75.00
PnB30	1949	—	2 Centavos. Zinc. KM#212.2.	50.00
Pn30	1952	—	1 Sol De Oro. Brass.	—
PnA31	1958	—	20 Centavos. Copper Nickel.	50.00
Pn31	1958	—	50 Soles. Silver. With PRUEBA.	900
Pn32	1964	—	50 Soles. Silver. With PRUEBA.	900
PnA33	1965	—	5 Centavos. Copper-Nickel-Zinc. KM#290.	900
Pn33	1965	—	50 Soles. Silver. With PRUEBA.	900
Pn34	1966	200	Sol. Silver. With PAREJA.	—
Pn35	1967	—	1/2 Sol. With PAREJA.	—
Pn36	1967	7	50 Soles. Silver.	—
Pn37	1988	—	Inti. Brass. KM#296.	—
Pn38	198x	—	5 Intis. Copper-Nickel-Zinc. KM#300.	—
Pn39	1988	—	10 Intis. Brass.	—

TRIAL STRIKES

KM#	Date	Mintage	Identification	Mkt Val
TS4	1935	—	Sol. Silver. KM#218.1. Alloy percentage: N. 3/25, PLT/0, NKL 10 ZNC/55 CRE.	—
TS5	1935	—	Sol. Silver. KM#218.1. Alloy percentage: N. 4/20, PLT/15, NKL 10 ZNC/55 CRE.	—

PROOF SETS

KM#	Date	Mintage	Identification	Issue Price	Mkt Val
PS2	1965 (5)	10	KM#237-240, 290	—	1,500
PS3	1965 (5)	—	KM#220.5, 221.2b, 222, 223.2, 224.2	—	300
PS4	1966 (5)	1,000	KM244.1-246.1, 247-248	—	100

SPECIMEN SETS (SS)

KM#	Date	Mintage	Identification	Issue Price	Mkt Val
SS1	1964 (5)	—	KM220.5, 221.2b, 222, 223.2, 224.2	—	200
SS2	1965 (5)	—	KM220.5, 221.2b, 222, 223.2, 224.2	—	150
SS3	1965 (5)	—	KM220.5, 221.2b, 222, 223.2, 224.2	—	150
SS4	1966 (5)	—	KM244.1-246.1, 247-248	—	150

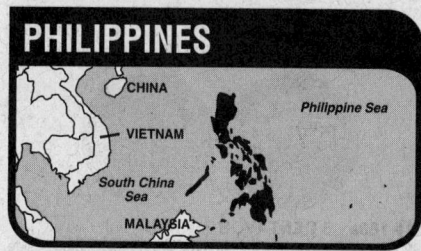

PHILIPPINES

The Republic of the Philippines, an archipelago in the western Pacific 500 miles (805 km.) from the southeast coast of Asia, has an area of 115,830 sq. mi. (300,000 sq. km.) and a population of *64.9 million. Capital: Manila. The economy of the 7,000-island group is based on agriculture, forestry and fishing. Timber, coconut products, sugar and hemp are exported.

Migration to the Philippines began about 30,000 years ago when land bridges connected the islands with Borneo and Sumatra. Ferdinand Magellan claimed the islands for Spain in 1521. The first permanent settlement was established by Miguel de Legazpi at Cebu April 1565. Manila was established in 1572. A British expedition captured Manila and occupied the Spanish colony in October 1762, but returned it to Spain by the treaty of Paris, 1763. Spain held the Philippines despite growing Filipino nationalism until 1898 when they were ceded to the United States at the end of the Spanish-American War. The Philippines became a self-governing commonwealth under the United States in 1935, and attained independence as the Republic of the Philippines on July 4, 1946.

MINT MARKS
(b) Brussels, privy marks only
BSP - Bangko Sentral Pilipinas
D - Denver, 1944-1945
(Lt) - Llantrisant
M, MA - Manila
PM - Pobjoy Mint
S - San Francisco, 1903-1947
SGV - Madrid
(Sh) - Sherritt
(US) - United States
FM - Franklin Mint, U.S.A.*
(VDM) - Vereinigte Deutsche Metall Werks; Altona, Germany
Star - Manila (Spanish) = Manila
*NOTE: From 1975-1977 the Franklin Mint produced coinage in up to 3 different qualities. Beginning in 1978 only (U) and (P) were struck. Qualities of issue are designated in ( ) after each date and are defined as follows:
(M) MATTE - Normal circulation strike or a dull finish produced by sandblasting special uncirculated (polish-finish) or proof quality dies.
(U) SPECIAL UNCIRCULATED - Polished or prooflike in appearance without any frosted features.
(P) PROOF - The highest quality obtainable having mirror-like fields and frosted features.

MONETARY SYSTEM
4 Quartos = 1 Real
8 Reales = 1 Peso

UNITED STATES ADMINISTRATION

DECIMAL COINAGE

KM# 162 1/2 CENTAVO
Bronze **Obv:** Man seated beside hammer and anvil **Rev:** Eagle above stars and striped shield

Date	Mintage	F	VF	XF	Unc	BU
1903	12,084,000	0.50	1.00	2.00	10.00	20.00
1903 Proof	2,558	Value: 65.00				
1904	5,654,000	0.50	1.25	2.00	15.00	35.00
1904 Proof	1,355	Value: 85.00				
1905 Proof	471	Value: 350				
1906 Proof	500	Value: 200				
1908 Proof	500	Value: 200				

KM# 163 CENTAVO
4.7000 g., Bronze **Obv:** Man seated beside hammer and anvil **Rev:** Eagle above stars and striped shield

Date	Mintage	F	VF	XF	Unc	BU
1903	10,790,000	0.50	1.25	2.50	20.00	40.00
1903 Proof	2,558	Value: 75.00				
1904	17,040,000	0.50	1.25	2.50	15.00	30.00
1904 Proof	1,355	Value: 85.00				
1905	10,000,000	0.50	1.50	2.00	25.00	45.00
1905 Proof	471	Value: 175				
1906 Proof	500	Value: 150				
1908 Proof	500	Value: 150				
1908S	2,187,000	2.50	4.00	11.00	60.00	90.00
1909S	1,738,000	7.00	12.00	25.00	100	150
1910S	2,700,000	2.00	5.00	10.00	55.00	80.00
1911S	4,803,000	1.00	3.00	6.50	30.00	60.00
1912S	3,000,000	3.00	7.00	12.50	80.00	125
1913S	5,000,000	2.00	4.00	7.00	40.00	75.00
1914S	5,000,000	1.00	2.50	5.00	40.00	75.00
1915S	2,500,000	20.00	30.00	95.00	600	1,300
1916S	4,330,000	6.00	12.50	25.00	120	150
1917/6S	7,070,000	35.00	65.00	150	375	550
1917S	Inc. above	3.00	4.50	7.50	30.00	90.00
1918S	11,660,000	2.00	4.00	10.00	70.00	150
1918S Large S	Inc. above	100	175	300	1,300	1,900
1919S	4,540,000	0.75	2.50	6.50	60.00	125
1920S	2,500,000	4.50	9.50	15.00	150	300
1920	3,552,000	1.00	5.00	10.00	125	250
1921	7,283,000	0.75	3.50	5.00	50.00	100
1922	3,519,000	0.50	2.50	9.00	75.00	125
1925M	9,332,000	0.50	3.00	7.50	25.00	65.00
1926M	9,000,000	0.50	2.25	5.00	20.00	60.00
1927M	9,270,000	0.35	2.00	6.00	30.00	60.00
1928M	9,150,000	0.35	2.00	4.00	35.00	75.00
1929M	5,657,000	1.00	3.00	6.00	35.00	85.00
1930M	5,577,000	0.50	2.00	4.50	30.00	65.00
1931M	5,659,000	0.50	2.50	4.50	25.00	55.00
1932M	4,000,000	0.75	2.50	6.00	40.00	65.00
1933M	8,393,000	0.25	2.00	4.00	20.00	50.00
1934M	3,179,000	0.75	2.50	10.00	60.00	90.00
1936M	17,455,000	0.25	2.00	5.00	40.00	75.00

KM# 164 5 CENTAVOS
Copper-Nickel, 21.3 mm. **Obv:** Man seated beside hammer and anvil **Rev:** Eagle above stars and striped shield

Date	Mintage	F	VF	XF	Unc	BU
1903	8,910,000	0.50	1.25	2.25	25.00	35.00
1903 Proof	2,558	Value: 85.00				
1904	1,075,000	0.75	2.00	5.00	27.00	40.00
1904 Proof	1,355	Value: 95.00				
1905 Proof	471	Value: 175				
1906 Proof	500	Value: 150				
1908 Proof	500	Value: 150				
1916S	300,000	35.00	60.00	125	600	1,100
1917S	2,300,000	2.00	5.00	10.00	125	250
1918/7S	—	3.00	9.00	18.50	150	—
1918S	2,780,000	2.00	6.00	12.50	120	200
1919S	1,220,000	2.50	10.00	15.50	150	300
1920	1,421,000	3.00	7.50	12.50	150	250
1921	2,132,000	2.00	5.00	10.00	90.00	180
1925M	1,000,000	10.00	17.50	25.00	160	250
1926M	1,200,000	5.00	6.50	17.50	125	175
1927M	1,000,000	2.00	5.00	8.50	55.00	100
1928M	1,000,000	3.00	5.00	7.50	50.00	75.00

KM# 173 5 CENTAVOS
Copper-Nickel **Obv:** Man seated beside hammer and anvil **Rev:** Eagle above stars and striped shield **Note:** Mule.

Date	Mintage	F	VF	XF	Unc	BU
1918S	—	250	600	1,750	4,000	8,000

KM# 175 5 CENTAVOS
4.7500 g., Copper-Nickel, 19 mm. **Obv:** Man seated beside hammer and anvil **Rev:** Eagle above stars and striped shield

Date	Mintage	F	VF	XF	Unc	BU
1930M	2,905,000	1.00	2.50	5.00	35.00	65.00
1931M	3,477,000	1.00	2.70	5.00	50.00	75.00
1932M	3,956,000	1.00	2.50	4.50	40.00	60.00
1934M	2,154,000	1.00	3.50	7.00	65.00	125
1935M	2,754,000	1.00	1.75	6.50	80.00	120

KM# 165 10 CENTAVOS
2.6924 g., 0.9000 Silver 0.0779 oz. ASW **Obv:** Female standing beside hammer and anvil **Rev:** Eagle above stars and striped shield

Date	Mintage	F	VF	XF	Unc	BU
1903	5,103,000	1.25	3.00	5.00	35.00	60.00
1903 Proof	2,558	Value: 85.00				
1903S	1,200,000	11.00	17.50	30.00	350	800
1904	11,000	15.00	25.00	35.00	80.00	135
1904 Proof	1,355	Value: 80.00				
1904S	5,040,000	1.50	3.50	5.00	50.00	95.00
1905 Proof	471	Value: 150				
1906 Proof	500	Value: 125				

KM# 169 10 CENTAVOS
2.0000 g., 0.7500 Silver 0.0482 oz. ASW **Obv:** Female standing beside hammer and anvil **Rev:** Eagle above stars and striped shield

Date	Mintage	F	VF	XF	Unc	BU
1907	1,501,000	1.50	4.00	6.00	40.00	95.00
1907S	4,930,000	1.25	2.00	3.00	40.00	75.00
1908 Proof	500	Value: 125				
1908S	3,364,000	1.25	2.00	4.00	35.00	75.00
1909S	312,000	15.00	27.50	75.00	400	900
1910S	—	—	—	—	—	—

Note: Unknown in any collection. Counterfeits of the 1910S are commonly encountered

1911S	1,101,000	3.00	6.50	15.00	125	300
1912S	1,010,000	2.25	6.00	14.00	125	260
1913S	1,361,000	1.50	5.00	9.00	110	200
1914S	1,180,000	2.00	5.00	15.00	175	300
1915S	450,000	6.00	24.00	35.00	300	650
1917S	5,991,000	1.00	1.50	4.00	40.00	65.00
1918S	8,420,000	1.00	1.50	3.00	25.00	40.00
1919S	1,630,000	1.25	2.00	5.00	45.00	90.00
1920	520,000	4.50	6.50	12.50	85.00	200
1921	3,863,000	1.00	1.50	2.75	25.00	40.00
1929M	1,000,000	1.25	1.50	5.00	25.00	35.00
1935M	1,280,000	1.25	1.50	2.25	20.00	30.00

KM# 166 20 CENTAVOS
5.3849 g., 0.9000 Silver 0.1558 oz. ASW **Obv:** Female standing beside hammer and anvil **Rev:** Eagle above stars and striped shield

Date	Mintage	F	VF	XF	Unc	BU
1903	5,353,000	1.75	2.50	6.00	40.00	90.00
1903 Proof	2,558	Value: 125				
1903S	150,000	10.00	20.00	60.00	750	1,100
1904	11,000	16.00	30.00	40.00	100	175
1904 Proof	1,355	Value: 125				
1904S	2,060,000	3.00	5.00	12.50	100	175
1905 Proof	471	Value: 200				
1905S	420,000	7.50	15.00	35.00	200	700
1906 Proof	500	Value: 150				

KM# 170 20 CENTAVOS
4.0000 g., 0.7500 Silver 0.0964 oz. ASW **Obv:** Female standing beside hammer and anvil **Rev:** Eagle above stars and striped shield

Date	Mintage	F	VF	XF	Unc	BU
1907	1,251,000	2.25	4.00	10.00	125	200
1907S	3,165,000	2.25	3.00	6.00	35.00	125

Date	Mintage	F	VF	XF	Unc	BU
1908 Proof	500	Value: 200				
1908S	1,535,000	2.25	4.50	12.50	60.00	125
1909S	450,000	10.00	30.00	75.00	375	950
1910S	500,000	15.00	25.00	70.00	400	950
1911S	505,000	10.00	30.00	60.00	275	850
1912S	750,000	5.00	15.00	35.00	200	350
1913S/S	949,000	9.00	20.00	50.00	250	400
1913S	Inc. above	3.00	7.50	15.00	175	300
1914S	795,000	3.50	8.00	25.00	200	450
1915S	655,000	12.50	17.50	45.00	425	950
1916S	1,435,000	6.00	10.00	20.00	125	225
1917S	3,151,000	1.75	3.00	5.00	45.00	85.00
1918S	5,560,000	1.75	2.50	5.00	35.00	75.00
1919S	850,000	1.75	5.00	10.00	100	200
1920	1,046,000	2.50	5.00	15.00	125	175
1921	1,843,000	BV	2.00	7.00	75.00	100
1929M	1,970,000	BV	2.50	5.00	25.00	50.00

KM# 174   20 CENTAVOS
4.0000 g., 0.7500 Silver 0.0964 oz. ASW **Obv:** Female standing beside hammer and anvil **Rev:** Eagle above stars and striped shield **Note:** Mule.

Date	Mintage	F	VF	XF	Unc	BU
1928M	100,000	5.00	15.00	50.00	800	1,300

KM# 167   50 CENTAVOS
13.4784 g., 0.9000 Silver 0.3900 oz. ASW **Obv:** Female standing beside hammer and anvil **Rev:** Eagle above stars and striped shield

Date	Mintage	F	VF	XF	Unc	BU
1903	3,102,000	4.00	6.50	11.00	55.00	85.00
1903 Proof	2,558	Value: 150				
1903S 2 Known	—	—	—	22,000	—	—
1904	11,000	25.00	40.00	70.00	125	225
1904 Proof	1,355	Value: 175				
1904S	2,160,000	5.00	11.00	15.00	125	200
1905 Proof	471	Value: 300				
1905S	852,000	8.00	17.50	35.00	600	2,000
1906 Proof	500	Value: 275				

KM# 171   50 CENTAVOS
10.0000 g., 0.7500 Silver 0.2411 oz. ASW **Obv:** Female standing beside hammer and anvil **Rev:** Eagle above stars and striped shield

Date	Mintage	F	VF	XF	Unc	BU
1907	1,201,000	6.00	11.00	40.00	200	450
1907S	2,112,000	4.00	8.00	35.00	125	300
1908 Proof	500	Value: 250				
1908S	1,601,000	5.00	10.00	30.00	250	2,000
1909S	528,000	6.00	15.00	70.00	300	800
1917S	674,000	10.00	15.00	25.00	150	300
1918S	2,202,000	4.00	5.00	10.00	100	150
1919S	1,200,000	4.00	5.00	14.00	125	175
1920	420,000	4.00	5.50	11.00	35.00	95.00
1921	2,317,000	BV	4.00	6.00	30.00	60.00

KM# 168   PESO
26.9568 g., 0.9000 Silver 0.7800 oz. ASW **Obv:** Female standing beside hammer and anvil **Rev:** Eagle above stars and striped shield

Date	Mintage	F	VF	XF	Unc	BU
1903	2,791,000	16.00	20.00	27.00	125	450
1903 Proof	2,558	Value: 250				
1903S	11,361,000	15.00	18.00	25.00	110	175
1904	11,000	65.00	75.00	110	265	400
1904 Proof	1,355	Value: 325				
1904S	6,600,000	15.00	18.00	25.00	160	240
1905S curved serif on 1	6,056,000	15.00	25.00	35.00	225	350
1905S straight serif on 1		30.00	45.00	75.00	500	2,000
1905 Proof	471	Value: 1,000				
1906 Proof	500	Value: 900				
1906S	201,000	1,000	1,600	2,600	16,000	30,000

Note: Counterfeits of the 1906S exist

KM# 172   PESO
20.0000 g., 0.8000 Silver 0.5144 oz. ASW **Obv:** Female standing beside hammer and anvil **Rev:** Eagle above stars and striped shield

Date	Mintage	F	VF	XF	Unc	BU
1907 Proof, 2 known	—	—	—	—	—	—
1907S	10,276,000	6.50	8.00	10.00	75.00	125
1908 Proof	500	Value: 750				
1908S	20,955,000	6.00	8.00	10.00	75.00	125
1909S	7,578,000	7.50	10.00	15.00	90.00	140
1910S	3,154,000	10.00	12.50	25.00	250	525
1911S	463,000	20.00	30.00	65.00	750	2,700
1912S	680,000	20.00	35.00	80.00	1,500	6,500

UNITED STATES ADMINISTRATION
Commonwealth
DECIMAL COINAGE

KM# 179   CENTAVO
5.3000 g., Bronze, 25 mm. **Obv:** Male seated beside hammer and anvil **Rev:** Eagle above shield

Date	Mintage	F	VF	XF	Unc	BU
1937M	15,790,000	0.25	2.00	3.00	20.00	35.00
1938M	10,000,000	0.25	1.50	3.00	15.00	25.00
1939M	6,500,000	0.25	2.00	4.00	30.00	50.00
1940M	4,000,000	0.25	1.25	2.25	15.00	25.00
1941M	5,000,000	0.25	2.00	3.50	20.00	35.00
1944S	58,000,000	—	0.25	0.50	1.50	3.00

KM# 180   5 CENTAVOS
4.8000 g., Copper-Nickel **Obv:** Male seated beside hammer and anvil **Rev:** Eagle with wings open above shield

Date	Mintage	F	VF	XF	Unc	BU
1937M	2,494,000	1.00	2.50	5.50	45.00	75.00
1938M	4,000,000	0.50	1.25	2.50	20.00	35.00
1941M	2,750,000	1.00	2.50	6.00	40.00	90.00

KM# 180a   5 CENTAVOS
4.9200 g., Copper-Nickel-Zinc, 19 mm. **Obv:** Male seated beside hammer and anvil **Rev:** Eagle with wings open above shield

Date	Mintage	F	VF	XF	Unc	BU
1944	21,198,000	—	0.50	1.00	2.00	3.00
1944S	14,040,000	—	0.25	0.30	1.25	2.50
1945S	72,796,000	—	0.25	0.30	1.00	2.50

KM# 181   10 CENTAVOS
2.0000 g., 0.7500 Silver 0.0482 oz. ASW, 16.7 mm. **Obv:** Female standing beside hammer and anvil **Rev:** Eagle with wings open above shield

Date	Mintage	F	VF	XF	Unc	BU
1937M	3,500,000	1.00	2.00	3.00	20.00	30.00
1938M	3,750,000	BV	1.00	2.00	12.50	18.00
1941M	2,500,000	BV	1.50	2.50	10.00	15.00
1944D	31,592,000	—	—	BV	2.00	3.50
1945D	137,208,000	—	—	BV	2.00	3.00

Note: 1937, 1938, and 1941 dated strikes have inverted W's for M's

KM# 182   20 CENTAVOS
4.0000 g., 0.7500 Silver 0.0964 oz. ASW, 21 mm. **Obv:** Female standing beside hammer and anvil **Rev:** Eagle with wings open above shield

Date	Mintage	F	VF	XF	Unc	BU
1937M	2,665,000	BV	1.75	3.00	20.00	35.00
1938M	3,000,000	BV	1.50	2.50	12.00	20.00
1941M	1,500,000	BV	1.50	2.50	10.00	20.00
1944D	28,596,000	—	—	BV	2.00	3.00
1944D/S	—	12.00	16.50	17.50	40.00	50.00
1945D	82,804,000	—	—	BV	2.00	3.00

KM# 176   50 CENTAVOS
10.0000 g., 0.7500 Silver 0.2411 oz. ASW, 27.5 mm. **Subject:** Establishment of the Commonwealth **Obv:** Busts facing each other **Rev:** Eagle above shield

Date	Mintage	F	VF	XF	Unc	BU
1936	20,000	—	30.00	65.00	110	150

KM# 183 50 CENTAVOS
10.0000 g., 0.7500 Silver 0.2411 oz. ASW, 27.5 mm.
Obv: Female standing beside hammer and anvil **Rev:** Eagle with wings open above shield

Date	Mintage	F	VF	XF	Unc	BU
1944S	19,187,000	—	—	BV	5.00	7.50
1945S	18,120,000	—	—	BV	5.00	7.50

KM# 177 PESO
20.0000 g., 0.9000 Silver 0.5787 oz. ASW, 35 mm.
Subject: Establishment of the Commonwealth **Obv:** Conjoined busts left **Rev:** Eagle with wings open above shield

Date	Mintage	F	VF	XF	Unc	BU
1936	10,000	—	50.00	75.00	150	250

KM# 178 PESO
20.0000 g., 0.9000 Silver 0.5787 oz. ASW, 35 mm.
Subject: Establishment of the Commonwealth **Obv:** Conjoined busts left **Rev:** Eagle with wings open above shield

Date	Mintage	F	VF	XF	Unc	BU
1936	10,000	—	50.00	75.00	150	250

REPUBLIC
DECIMAL COINAGE

KM# 186 CENTAVO
Bronze, 19 mm. **Obv:** Shield of arms **Rev:** Male seated beside hammer and anvil

Date	Mintage	F	VF	XF	Unc	BU
1958	20,000,000	—	—	0.10	0.25	0.50
1960	40,000,000	—	—	0.10	0.15	0.35
1962	30,000,000	—	—	0.10	0.15	0.35
1963	130,000,000	—	—	0.10	0.15	0.25

KM# 187 5 CENTAVOS
4.8000 g., Brass, 21 mm. **Obv:** Shield of arms **Rev:** Male seated beside hammer and anvil

Date	Mintage	F	VF	XF	Unc	BU
1958	10,000,000	—	—	0.10	0.25	0.50
1959	10,000,000	—	—	0.10	0.20	0.50
1960	40,000,000	—	—	0.10	0.15	0.40
1962	40,000,000	—	—	0.10	0.15	0.40
1963	50,000,000	—	—	0.10	0.15	0.40

Date	Mintage	F	VF	XF	Unc	BU
1964	100,000,000	—	—	—	0.10	0.40
1966	10,000,000	—	—	0.10	0.20	0.50

KM# 188 10 CENTAVOS
2.0000 g., Copper-Zinc-Nickel, 17.8 mm. **Obv:** Shield of arms **Rev:** Female standing beside hammer and anvil

Date	Mintage	F	VF	XF	Unc	BU
1958	10,000,000	—	—	0.15	0.25	0.50
1960	70,000,000	—	—	0.15	0.20	0.40
1962	50,000,000	—	—	0.15	0.20	0.40
1963	50,000,000	—	—	0.15	0.20	0.40
1964	100,000,000	—	—	0.10	0.20	0.40
1966	110,000,000	—	—	0.10	0.20	0.45

KM# 189.1 25 CENTAVOS
5.0000 g., Copper-Zinc-Nickel **Obv:** Shield of arms **Rev:** Female standing beside hammer and anvil

Date	Mintage	F	VF	XF	Unc	BU
1958	10,000,000	—	—	0.25	0.50	0.75
1960	10,000,000	—	—	0.30	0.50	0.75
1962	40,000,000	—	—	0.25	0.50	0.75
1964	49,800,000	—	—	0.20	0.35	0.75
1966	50,000,000	—	0.25	0.50	1.00	1.25

KM# 189.2 25 CENTAVOS
Copper-Zinc-Nickel **Obv:** Shield of arms **Rev:** Female standing beside hammer and anvil

Date	Mintage	F	VF	XF	Unc	BU
1966	40,000,000	—	—	0.20	0.40	1.00
1966 Matte finish	Inc. above	—	—	—	—	—

KM# 184 50 CENTAVOS
10.0000 g., 0.7500 Silver 0.2411 oz. ASW, 27.5 mm. **Obv:** Shield of arms above date and value **Rev:** Uniformed bust right

Date	Mintage	F	VF	XF	Unc	BU
1947S	200,000	—	BV	5.00	8.00	11.00

KM# 190 50 CENTAVOS
10.0000 g., Copper-Zinc-Nickel, 30.3 mm. **Obv:** Shield of arms **Rev:** Female standing beside hammer and anvil

Date	Mintage	F	VF	XF	Unc	BU
1958	5,000,000	—	0.30	0.45	1.00	1.50
1964	25,000,000	—	0.20	0.30	0.75	1.25

KM# 191 1/2 PESO
12.5000 g., 0.9000 Silver 0.3617 oz. ASW **Subject:** 100th Anniversary Birth of Dr. Jose Rizal **Obv:** Shield of arms **Rev:** Head left

Date	Mintage	F	VF	XF	Unc	BU
ND(1961)	100,000	—	—	6.00	7.00	9.00

KM# 185 PESO
20.0000 g., 0.9000 Silver 0.5787 oz. ASW, 35.5 mm. **Obv:** Shield of arms above date and value **Rev:** Uniformed bust right

Date	Mintage	F	VF	XF	Unc	BU
1947S	100,000	—	BV	12.00	18.50	20.00

KM# 192 PESO
26.0000 g., 0.9000 Silver 0.7523 oz. ASW **Subject:** 100th Anniversary Birth of Dr. Jose Rizal **Obv:** Shield of arms **Rev:** Bust 1/4 right divides dates

Date	Mintage	F	VF	XF	Unc	BU
ND(1961)	100,000	—	—	BV	9.00	11.00

KM# 193 PESO
26.0000 g., 0.9000 Silver 0.7523 oz. ASW **Subject:** 100th Anniversary Birth of Andres Bonifacio **Obv:** Shield of arms **Rev:** Head 1/4 left divides dates

Date	Mintage	F	VF	XF	Unc	BU
ND(1963)	100,000	—	—	BV	10.00	11.00

KM# 194 PESO
26.0000 g., 0.9000 Silver 0.7523 oz. ASW **Subject:** 100th Anniversary Birth of Apolinario Mabini **Obv:** Shield of arms **Rev:** Head 1/4 right divides dates

Date	Mintage	F	VF	XF	Unc	BU
ND(1964)	100,000	—	—	BV	10.00	11.00

KM# 195   PESO

26.0000 g., 0.9000 Silver 0.7523 oz. ASW **Subject:** 25th
Anniversary of Bataan Day **Obv:** Shield of arms **Rev:** Flaming
broken sword flanked by sprigs, dates and stars

Date	Mintage	F	VF	XF	Unc	BU
ND(1967)	100,000	—	—	BV	10.00	11.00

Note: KM#195 is a prooflike issue

REFORM COINAGE
100 Sentimos = 1 Piso

KM# 196   SENTIMO
Aluminum **Obv:** Shield of arms **Rev:** Head left

Date	Mintage	F	VF	XF	Unc	BU
1967	10,000,000	—	—	—	0.25	—
1968	27,940,000	—	—	—	0.10	—
1969/6	12,060,000	—	—	—	0.20	—
1970	130,000,000	—	—	—	0.10	—
1974 0	165,000,000	—	—	—	0.10	—
1974 1 Proof	10,000	Value: 3.50				

KM# 205   SENTIMO
1.2200 g., Aluminum, 19 mm. **Obv:** Head 3/4 right
Rev: Redesigned bank seal within circle **Edge:** Plain

Date	Mintage	F	VF	XF	Unc	BU
1975FM (M)	108,000	—	—	—	0.50	—
1975FM (U)	5,875	—	—	—	2.00	—
1975FM (P)	37,000	Value: 1.50				
1975(Lt)	10,000,000	—	—	—	0.10	—
1975(US)	60,190,000	—	—	—	0.10	—
1976FM (M)	10,000	—	—	—	0.75	—
1976FM (U)	1,826	—	—	1.00	2.50	—
1976FM (P)	9,901	Value: 1.50				
1976(US)	60,000,000	—	—	—	0.10	—
1977	4,808,000	—	—	—	0.25	—
1977FM (M)	10,000	—	—	—	1.00	—
1977FM (U)	354	—	—	—	4.00	—
1977FM (P)	4,822	Value: 2.00				
1978	24,813,000	—	—	—	0.10	—
1978FM (U)	10,000	—	—	—	1.00	—
1978FM (P)	4,792	Value: 2.00				

KM# 224   SENTIMO
Aluminum **Obv:** Head 3/4 right **Rev:** Redesigned bank seal
within circle **Note:** Varieties exist in date.

Date	Mintage	F	VF	XF	Unc	BU
1979BSP	—	—	—	—	0.25	—
1979FM (U)	10,000	—	—	—	1.00	—
1979FM (P)	3,645	Value: 2.00				
1980BSP	12,601,000	—	—	—	0.25	—
1980FM (U)	10,000	—	—	—	0.75	—
1980FM (P)	3,133	Value: 2.00				
1981BSP	33,391,000	—	—	—	0.20	—
1981FM (U)	—	—	—	—	1.00	—
1981FM (P)	1,795	Value: 2.00				
1982BSP	51,730,000	—	—	—	0.10	—
1982FM (P)	—	Value: 2.00				

KM# 238   SENTIMO
0.7000 g., Aluminum, 15.5 mm. **Obv:** Head left **Rev:** Sea shell
and value within circle

Date	Mintage	F	VF	XF	Unc	BU
1983	62,090,000	—	—	—	0.50	—
1983 Proof	—	Value: 2.00				
1984	320,000	—	—	—	0.75	—
1985	16,000	—	—	—	1.00	—
1986	80,000	—	—	—	1.00	—
1987	13,570,000	—	—	—	0.75	—
1988	26,861,000	—	—	—	0.75	—
1989	—	—	—	—	0.75	—
1990	—	—	—	—	—	12.00
1991	—	—	—	—	—	20.00
1992	—	—	—	—	—	20.00
1993	—	—	2.00	5.00	10.00	16.50

KM# 273   SENTIMO
2.0000 g., Copper Plated Steel **Obv:** Value and date
Rev: Central bank seal within circle and gear design, 1993 (date
Cenral Bank was established) below **Rev. Leg.:** BANGKO
SENTRAL NG PILIPINAS - 1993

Date	Mintage	F	VF	XF	Unc	BU
1995	—	—	—	—	0.15	0.20
1996	—	—	—	—	0.15	0.20
1997	—	—	—	—	0.15	0.20
1998	—	—	—	—	0.15	0.20
1999	—	—	—	—	0.15	0.20
2000	—	—	—	—	0.15	0.20

KM# 197   5 SENTIMOS
Brass, 18 mm. **Obv:** Shield above banner **Rev:** Head right

Date	Mintage	F	VF	XF	Unc	BU
1967	40,000,000	—	—	—	0.30	—
1968	50,000,000	—	—	—	0.30	—
1970	5,000,000	—	—	1.00	3.50	—
1972	71,744,000	—	—	—	0.30	—
1974	90,025,000	—	—	—	0.30	—
1974 Proof	10,000	Value: 4.00				

KM# 206   5 SENTIMOS
2.4000 g., Brass **Obv:** Head 3/4 left **Rev:** Redesigned bank seal
within circle

Date	Mintage	F	VF	XF	Unc	BU
1975FM (M)	104,000	—	—	—	0.50	—
1975FM (U)	5,875	—	—	—	2.50	—
1975FM (P)	37,000	Value: 2.00				
1975(US)	98,928,000	—	—	—	0.10	—
1975(Lt)	10,000,000	—	—	—	0.10	—
1976FM (M)	10,000	—	—	—	1.50	—
1976FM (U)	1,826	—	—	—	2.50	—
1976FM (P)	9,901	Value: 1.50				
1976(US)	98,000,000	—	—	—	0.20	—
1977	19,367,000	—	—	—	0.35	—
1977FM (M)	10,000	—	—	—	1.25	—
1977FM (U)	354	—	—	—	4.00	—
1977FM (P)	4,822	Value: 2.50				
1978	61,838,000	—	—	—	0.20	—
1978FM (U)	10,000	—	—	—	1.50	—
1978FM (P)	4,792	Value: 2.50				

KM# 225   5 SENTIMOS
2.5000 g., Brass **Obv:** Head 3/4 left **Rev:** Redesigned bank seal
within circle

Date	Mintage	F	VF	XF	Unc	BU
1979BSP	12,805,000	—	—	—	0.30	—
1979FM (U)	10,000	—	—	—	1.25	—

Date	Mintage	F	VF	XF	Unc	BU
1979FM (P)	3,645	Value: 2.50				
1980BSP	111,339,000	—	—	—	0.10	—
1980FM (U)	—	—	—	—	1.75	—
1980FM (P)	3,133	Value: 2.50				
1981BSP	—	—	—	—	0.10	—
1981FM (U)	—	—	—	—	1.25	—
1981FM (P)	1,795	Value: 3.00				
1982BSP	—	—	—	—	0.10	—
1982FM (P)	—	Value: 3.00				

KM# 239   5 SENTIMOS
1.2000 g., Aluminum, 17 mm. **Obv:** Head right **Rev:** Orchid and
value

Date	Mintage	F	VF	XF	Unc	BU
1983	100,016,000	—	—	—	0.50	—
1983 Proof	—	Value: 2.00				
1984	141,744,000	—	—	—	0.40	—
1985	50,416,000	—	—	—	0.25	—
1986	11,664,000	—	—	—	0.35	—
1987	79,008,000	—	—	—	0.10	—
1988	90,487,000	—	—	—	0.10	—
1989	—	—	—	—	0.25	—
1990	—	—	—	—	0.25	—
1991	—	—	—	—	3.75	—
1992	—	—	—	—	0.25	—

KM# 268   5 SENTIMOS
1.9000 g., Copper Plated Steel, 15.43 mm. **Obv:** Numeral value
around center hole **Rev:** Hole in center with date, bank and name
around border, 1993 (date Cenral Bank was established) below
Rev. Leg.: BANGKO CENTRAL NG PILIPINAS - 1993 **Edge:** Plain

Date	Mintage	F	VF	XF	Unc	BU
1995	—	—	—	0.10	0.25	0.30
1996	—	—	—	0.10	0.25	0.30
1997	—	—	—	0.10	0.25	0.30
1998	—	—	—	0.10	0.25	0.30
1999	—	—	—	0.10	0.25	0.30
2000	—	—	—	0.10	0.25	0.30

KM# 198   10 SENTIMOS
2.0000 g., Copper-Zinc-Nickel, 18 mm. **Obv:** Shield of arms
Rev: Bust left

Date	Mintage	F	VF	XF	Unc	BU
1967	50,000,000	—	—	—	0.35	—
1968	60,000,000	—	—	—	0.35	—
1969	40,000,000	—	—	—	0.35	—
1970	50,000,000	—	—	—	0.35	—
1971	80,000,000	—	—	—	0.35	—
1972	121,390,000	—	—	—	0.35	—
1974	60,208,000	—	—	—	0.35	—
1974 Proof	10,000	Value: 4.00				

KM# 207   10 SENTIMOS
2.0000 g., Copper-Nickel **Obv:** Head 3/4 right **Rev:** Redesigned
bank seal within circle

Date	Mintage	F	VF	XF	Unc	BU
1975FM (M)	104,000	—	—	—	0.50	—
1975FM (U)	5,875	—	—	—	2.50	—
1975FM (P)	37,000	Value: 2.50				
1975(VDM)	10,000,000	—	—	—	0.25	—
1975(US)	50,000,000	—	—	—	0.20	—
1976FM (M)	10,000	—	—	—	0.50	—
1976FM (U)	1,826	—	—	—	5.00	—
1976FM (P)	9,901	Value: 2.00				
1976(US)	50,000,000	—	—	—	0.20	—
1977	29,314,000	—	—	—	0.25	—
1977FM (M)	10,000	—	—	—	1.50	—
1977FM (U)	354	—	—	—	6.00	—
1977FM (P)	4,822	Value: 3.00				
1978	60,042,000	—	—	—	0.10	—
1978FM (U)	10,000	—	—	—	3.00	—
1978FM (P)	4,792	Value: 3.00				

KM# 226   10 SENTIMOS
Copper-Nickel, 18 mm. **Obv:** Head 3/4 right **Rev:** Redesigned bank seal within circle **Note:** Varieties with thick and thin legends exist for coins with BSP mint mark.

Date	Mintage	F	VF	XF	Unc	BU
1979BSP	6,446,000	—	—	—	0.50	—
1979FM (U)	10,000	—	—	—	2.00	—
1979FM (P)	3,645	Value: 3.00				
1980BSP	—	—	—	—	0.30	—
1980FM (U)	10,000	—	—	—	1.50	—
1980FM (P)	3,133	Value: 3.25				
1981BSP	—	—	—	—	0.30	—
1981FM (U)	—	—	—	*	2.00	—
1981FM (P)	1,795	Value: 3.50				
1982BSP	—	—	—	—	0.30	—
1982FM (P)	—	Value: 3.50				
1982FM (U)	—	Value: 23.00				

KM# 240.1   10 SENTIMOS
2.4500 g., Aluminum, 18.95 mm. **Series:** F.A.O. **Subject:** World Conference on Fisheries **Obv:** Head left **Rev:** Fish and value within circle **Edge:** Plain

Date	Mintage	F	VF	XF	Unc	BU
1983	95,640,000	—	—	—	8.00	—
1983 Proof	—	Value: 8.00				
1986	—	—	—	—	1.00	—
1987	Inc. below	—	—	—	1.00	—

KM# 240.2   10 SENTIMOS
1.5000 g., Aluminum, 19 mm. **Series:** F.A.O. **Subject:** World Conference on Fisheries **Obv:** Head left **Rev:** Fish and value within circle

Date	Mintage	F	VF	XF	Unc	BU
1983	—	—	—	—	0.50	1.50
1984	235,900,000	—	—	—	0.35	1.00
1985	90,169,000	—	—	—	0.35	1.00
1986	4,270,000	—	—	—	0.50	0.65
1987	99,520,000	—	—	—	0.50	0.75
1988	117,166,000	—	—	—	0.35	0.50
1989	—	—	—	—	0.35	0.50
1990	—	—	—	—	0.35	0.50
1991	—	—	—	—	0.35	0.50
1992	—	—	—	—	0.35	0.50
1993	—	—	—	—	0.50	7.00
1994	—	—	—	—	0.50	7.00

KM# 270.1   10 SENTIMOS
2.4600 g., Bronze Plated Steel, 16.9 mm. **Obv:** Value and date **Rev:** Central Bank seal within circle and gear design, 1993 (date Cenral Bank was established) below **Rev. Leg.:** BANGKO SENTRAL NG PILIPINAS - 1993 **Edge:** Reeded

Date	Mintage	F	VF	XF	Unc	BU
1995	—	—	—	0.10	0.30	0.40
1996	—	—	—	0.40	1.00	1.50
1997	—	—	—	0.10	0.30	0.40
1990	—	—	—	0.10	0.30	0.40
1999	—	—	—	0.10	0.30	0.40

KM# 199   25 SENTIMOS
4.0000 g., Copper-Zinc-Nickel, 21 mm. **Obv:** Shield of arms **Rev:** Head left

Date	Mintage	F	VF	XF	Unc	BU
1967	40,000,000	—	—	0.10	0.50	—
1968	10,000,000	—	—	0.10	0.50	—

Date	Mintage	F	VF	XF	Unc	BU
1969	10,000,000	—	—	0.10	0.50	—
1970	40,000,000	—	—	0.10	0.40	—
1971	60,000,000	—	—	0.10	0.40	—
1972	90,000,000	—	—	0.10	0.40	—
1974	10,000,000	—	—	0.10	0.50	—
1974 Proof	10,000	Value: 12.00				

KM# 208   25 SENTIMOS
4.0000 g., Copper-Nickel, 21 mm. **Obv:** Head 3/4 left **Rev:** Redesigned bank seal within circle

Date	Mintage	F	VF	XF	Unc	BU
1975FM (M)	104,000	—	—	—	0.75	—
1975FM (U)	5,875	—	—	—	5.00	—
1975FM (P)	37,000	Value: 3.00				
1975(US)	10,000,000	—	—	0.10	0.40	—
1975(VDM)	10,000,000	—	—	0.10	0.40	—
1976FM (M)	10,000	—	—	0.10	1.00	—
1976FM (U)	1,826	—	—	—	6.50	—
1976FM (P)	9,901	Value: 2.00				
1976(US)	10,000,000	—	—	0.10	0.25	—
1977	24,654,000	—	—	0.10	0.25	—
1977FM (M)	10,000	—	—	—	1.25	—
1977FM (U)	354	—	—	—	5.00	—
1977FM (P)	4,822	Value: 4.50				
1978	40,466,000	—	—	0.10	0.25	—
1978FM (U)	10,000	—	—	—	2.50	—
1978FM (P)	4,792	Value: 4.00				

KM# 227   25 SENTIMOS
Copper-Nickel, 21 mm. **Obv:** Head 3/4 left **Rev:** Redesigned bank seal within circle

Date	Mintage	F	VF	XF	Unc	BU
1979BSP	20,725,000	—	—	0.10	0.50	—
1979FM (U)	10,000	—	—	—	2.50	—
1979FM (P)	3,645	Value: 2.00				
1980BSP	—	—	—	0.10	0.75	—
1980FM (U)	10,000	—	—	—	1.25	—
1980FM (P)	3,133	Value: 4.50				
1981BSP	—	—	—	0.10	1.00	—
1981FM (U)	—	—	—	—	3.00	—
1981FM (P)	1,795	Value: 5.00				
1982BSP	—	—	—	0.10	0.50	—
1982FM (P)	—	Value: 5.00				
1982FM (U)	—	Value: 34.00				

KM# 241.1   25 SENTIMOS
3.9000 g., Brass, 21 mm. **Obv:** Juan Luna right **Rev:** Butterfly

Date	Mintage	F	VF	XF	Unc	BU
1983	92,944,000	—	—	0.15	1.00	2.00
1983 Proof	—	Value: 2.50				
1984	254,324,000	—	—	0.15	0.75	2.00
1985	84,922,000	—	—	0.15	0.75	1.25
1986	65,244,000	—	—	0.15	0.75	2.00
1987	1,680,000	—	—	0.50	2.00	2.75
1988	51,062,000	—	—	—	0.75	2.00
1989	—	—	—	—	0.75	1.50
1990	—	—	—	—	0.75	2.00

KM# 241.2   25 SENTIMOS
2.2400 g., Brass **Obv:** Juan Luna right **Rev:** Butterfly **Note:** Reduced size.

Date	Mintage	F	VF	XF	Unc	BU
1991	—	—	—	—	1.00	1.25
1992	—	—	—	—	1.00	1.25
1993	—	—	—	—	5.00	7.00
1994	—	—	—	—	4.00	6.50

KM# 271   25 SENTIMOS
3.8000 g., Brass, 20 mm. **Obv:** Value and date **Rev:** Central Bank seal within circle and gear design, 1993 (date Cenral Bank was established) below **Rev. Leg.:** BANGKO SENTRAL NG PILIPINAS - 1993 **Edge:** Plain

Date	Mintage	F	VF	XF	Unc	BU
1995	—	—	0.15	0.30	0.75	1.00
1996	—	—	0.15	0.30	0.75	1.00
1997	—	—	0.15	0.30	0.75	1.00
1998	—	—	0.15	0.30	0.75	1.00
1999	—	—	0.15	0.30	0.75	1.00
2000	—	—	0.15	0.30	0.75	1.00

KM# 200   50 SENTIMOS
8.0000 g., Copper-Zinc-Nickel, 27.5 mm. **Obv:** Shield of arms **Rev:** Marcelo H. del Pilar right

Date	Mintage	F	VF	XF	Unc	BU
1967	20,000,000	—	0.10	0.25	0.75	1.25
1971	10,000,000	—	0.10	0.50	1.00	2.00
1972 Knob on 2	30,000,000	—	0.10	0.75	1.50	2.50
1972 Plain 2	20,517,000	—	0.10	0.50	1.25	2.25
1974	5,004,000	—	0.40	0.60	12.00	15.00
1974 Proof	10,000	Value: 20.00				
1975	5,714,000	—	0.10	0.20	1.00	2.00

KM# 242.1   50 SENTIMOS
6.0000 g., Copper-Nickel, 25 mm. **Obv:** Head of Marcelo H. del Pilar left **Rev:** Eagle with talons out **Note:** Eagle's name: PITHECOPHAGA

Date	Mintage	F	VF	XF	Unc	BU
1983	27,644,000	—	0.10	0.50	1.25	2.00
1983 Proof	—	Value: 4.25				
1984	121,408,000	—	0.10	0.20	1.00	1.50
1985	107,048,000	—	0.10	0.20	1.00	1.50
1986	120,000,000	—	0.10	0.20	0.75	1.25
1987	1,078,000	—	0.10	1.00	1.50	2.50
1988	24,008,000	—	0.10	0.20	1.00	1.50
1989	—	—	0.10	0.20	1.00	2.50
1990	—	—	0.10	0.20	1.00	1.50

KM# 242.2   50 SENTIMOS
6.0000 g., Copper-Nickel, 25 mm. **Obv:** Head of Marcelo H. del Pilar left **Rev:** Eagle attacking **Note:** Error eagle's name: PITHECOBHAGA

Date	Mintage	F	VF	XF	Unc	BU
1983	Inc. above	—	2.00	2.50	7.50	—

KM# 242.3   50 SENTIMOS
3.0000 g., Brass **Obv:** Head of Marcelo H. Pilar left **Rev:** Eagle with talons out **Note:** Reduced size.

Date	Mintage	F	VF	XF	Unc	BU
1991	—	—	—	0.25	1.50	2.00
1992	—	—	—	0.25	1.50	2.00
1993	—	—	—	—	5.00	7.00
1994	—	—	—	—	3.50	4.00

KM# 201 PISO

26.4500 g., 0.9000 Silver 0.7653 oz. ASW **Subject:** Centennial - Birth of Aguinaldo **Obv:** Shield of arms **Rev:** Bust facing divides dates

Date	Mintage	F	VF	XF	Unc	BU
ND(1969) Prooflike	100,000	—	—	BV	10.00	11.00

KM# 202 PISO

Nickel, 38.3 mm. **Subject:** Pope Paul VI Visit **Obv:** Bust of Ferdinand Marcos left **Rev:** Bust of Pope Paul VI right

Date	Mintage	F	VF	XF	Unc	BU
1970	70,000	—	—	—	2.50	3.00

KM# 202a PISO

26.4500 g., 0.9000 Silver 0.7653 oz. ASW, 38.3 mm. **Obv:** Bust of Ferdinand Marcos left **Rev:** Bust of Pope Paul VI right

Date	Mintage	F	VF	XF	Unc	BU
1970	30,000	—	—	—	11.00	12.00

KM# 202b PISO

19.3000 g., 0.9170 Gold 0.5690 oz. AGW **Subject:** Pope Paul VI Visit **Obv:** Bust of Ferdinand Marcos left **Rev:** Bust of Pope Paul VI right

Date	Mintage	F	VF	XF	Unc	BU
1970	1,000	—	—	—	—	575

KM# 203 PISO

Copper-Zinc-Nickel, 33 mm. **Obv:** Shield of arms **Rev:** Head of Jose Rizal left

Date	Mintage	F	VF	XF	Unc	BU
1972	121,821,000	—	0.25	0.50	1.00	2.50
1974	45,631,000	—	0.25	0.50	1.00	3.00
1974 Proof	10,000	Value: 30.00				

KM# 209.1 PISO

9.5000 g., Copper-Nickel, 29 mm. **Obv:** Head of Jose Rizal 1/4 right within octogon **Rev:** Shield of arms

Date	Mintage	F	VF	XF	Unc	BU
1975FM (M)	104,000	—	—	—	2.00	—
1975FM (U)	5,877	—	—	—	5.50	—
1975FM (P)	37,000	Value: 3.00				
1975(VDM)	10,000,000	—	0.15	0.25	1.25	—
1975(US)	30,000,000	—	0.15	0.25	0.75	1.00
1976FM (M)	10,000	—	—	—	2.00	—
1976FM (U)	1,826	—	—	—	8.00	—
1976FM (P)	9,901	Value: 3.00				
1976(US)	30,000,000	—	0.15	0.25	0.75	—
1977	14,771,000	—	0.15	0.25	0.75	—
1977FM (M)	12,000	—	—	—	3.00	—
1977FM (U)	354	—	—	—	5.00	—
1977FM (P)	4,822	Value: 3.00				
1978	19,408,000	—	0.15	0.25	1.00	—
1978FM (U)	10,000	—	—	—	4.00	—
1978FM (P)	4,792	Value: 7.50				

KM# 209.2 PISO

9.5000 g., Copper-Nickel, 29 mm. **Obv:** Head of Jose Rizal 1/4 right within octogon **Rev:** Shield of arms **Rev. Insc.:** ISANG BANSA ISANG DIWA

Date	Mintage	F	VF	XF	Unc	BU
1979BSP	321,000	—	0.15	0.25	1.50	—
1979FM (U)	10,000	—	—	—	1.50	—
1979FM (P)	3,645	Value: 3.00				
1980BSP	19,693,000	—	0.15	0.25	0.75	1.00
1980FM (U)	10,000	—	—	—	4.25	—
1980FM (P)	3,133	Value: 12.50				
1981BSP	7,944,000	—	0.15	0.25	1.00	—
1981FM (U)	10,000	—	—	—	4.00	—
1981FM (P)	1,795	Value: 6.00				
1982FM (P)		Value: 7.00				
1982BSP Large date	52,110,000	—	0.15	0.25	1.00	—
1982BSP Small date	Inc. above	—	0.15	0.25	1.00	—

KM# 243.1 PISO

9.5000 g., Copper-Nickel, 28.9 mm. **Obv:** Head of Jose Rizal right **Rev:** Tamaraw bull **Edge:** Reeded **Note:** Large legends and design elements.

Date	Mintage	F	VF	XF	Unc	BU
1983	55,869,000	—	—	0.30	1.25	2.00
1983 Proof		Value: 6.50				
1984	4,997,000	—	—	1.00	2.00	3.00
1985	182,592,000	—	—	0.30	1.00	1.75
1986	19,072,000	—	—	0.30	1.25	2.25
1987	1,391,000	—	—	3.00	5.00	6.25
1988	54,636,000	—	—	0.30	1.25	2.00
1989		—	—	—	—	8.00

KM# 243.2 PISO

4.0000 g., Stainless Steel, 21.6 mm. **Obv:** Head of Jose Rizal right **Rev:** Tamaraw bull **Edge:** Plain **Note:** Reduced size.

Date	Mintage	F	VF	XF	Unc	BU
1991	—	—	—	0.50	1.25	2.25
1992	—	—	—	0.50	1.25	2.25
1993	—	—	—	—	3.50	4.00
1994	—	—	—	—	5.00	6.50

KM# 243.3 PISO

Copper-Nickel **Obv:** Head of Jose Rizal right **Rev:** Tamaraw bull **Note:** Smaller legends and design elements.

Date	Mintage	F	VF	XF	Unc	BU
1989	—	—	—	0.30	1.00	1.50
1990	—	—	—	0.30	1.00	1.25

KM# 251 PISO

Copper-Nickel, 28.5 mm. **Subject:** Philippine Cultures Decade **Obv:** Shield of arms divides date **Rev:** Three conjoined vertical busts right

Date	Mintage	F	VF	XF	Unc	BU
1989	—	—	—	—	4.50	—
1989 Matte	—	—	—	—	9.00	—

KM# 257 PISO

Copper-Nickel **Obv:** Shield of arms **Rev:** Waterfall, ship, and flower within circle

Date	Mintage	F	VF	XF	Unc	BU
ND(1991)	—	—	—	—	1.25	2.00
ND(1991) Matte	—	—	—	—	8.00	—

Note: Special striking by CB

KM# 260 PISO

Nickel Clad Steel, 21.5 mm. **Subject:** 50th Anniversary - Battle of Kagitingan **Obv:** Shield of arms **Rev:** Military head left, cross, flag and dates

Date	Mintage	F	VF	XF	Unc	BU
ND(1992)	—	—	—	—	2.50	—

KM# 269 PISO

6.0700 g., Copper-Nickel, 24 mm. **Obv:** Head of Jose Rizal right, value and date **Rev:** Bank seal within circle and gear design, 1993 (date Cenral Bank was established) below **Rev. Leg.:** BANGKO SENTRAL NG PILIPINAS - 1993 **Edge:** Reeded

Date	Mintage	F	VF	XF	Unc	BU
1995	—	—	0.20	0.40	1.00	1.50
1996	—	—	0.25	0.50	1.25	1.75
1997	—	—	0.25	0.50	1.25	1.75
1998	—	—	0.25	0.50	1.25	1.75
1999	—	—	0.25	0.50	1.25	1.75
2000	—	—	0.25	0.50	1.25	1.75

KM# 244 2 PISO

12.0000 g., Copper-Nickel, 31 mm. **Obv:** Head of Andres
Bonifacio left **Rev:** Coconut palm

Date	Mintage	F	VF	XF	Unc	BU
1983	15,640,000	—	—	0.35	2.50	3.50
1983 Proof	—	Value: 5.00				
1984	121,111,000	—	—	0.35	1.00	1.50
1985	115,211,000	—	—	0.35	1.25	1.50
1986	25,260,000	—	—	0.35	1.25	1.50
1987	2,196,000	—	—	5.00	8.00	10.00
1988	16,094,000	—	—	—	7.00	10.00
1989	—	—	—	—	1.25	1.50
1990	—	—	—	—	1.25	1.50

KM# 253 2 PISO

12.0000 g., Copper-Nickel, 31 mm. **Obv:** Design within beaded
circle **Rev:** Head of Elpidio Quirino right

Date	Mintage	F	VF	XF	Unc	BU
ND(1991)	10,000,000	—	—	—	1.25	2.00
ND(1991) Matte	—	—	—	—	10.00	—

Note: Special striking by CB

KM# 258 2 PISO

5.0100 g., Stainless Steel, 23.5 mm. **Obv:** Head of Andres
Bonifacio left **Rev:** Coconut palm

Date	Mintage	F	VF	XF	Unc	BU
1991	—	—	—	—	2.50	3.50
1992	—	—	—	—	3.00	3.50
1993	—	—	—	—	3.00	3.50
1994	—	—	—	—	2.50	3.50

KM# 261 2 PISO

Nickel Clad Steel, 23.5 mm. **Obv:** Design within beaded circle
Rev: Head of Manuel A. Roxas right

Date	Mintage	F	VF	XF	Unc	BU
ND(1992)	—	—	—	—	2.50	3.00
ND(1992) Matte	—	—	—	—	10.00	—

Note: Special striking by CB

KM# 256 2 PISO

Copper-Nickel **Obv:** Triangular design within circle **Rev:** Head
of Jose Laurel right

Date	Mintage	F	VF	XF	Unc	BU
ND(1992)	—	—	—	1.75	2.00	3.00
ND(1992) Matte	—	—	—	—	10.00	—

Note: Special striking by CB

KM# 210.1 5 PISO

Nickel, 36.5 mm. **Obv:** Shield of arms above value **Rev:** Head
of Ferdinand E. Marcos left

Date	Mintage	F	VF	XF	Unc	BU
1975FM (M)	3,850	—	—	—	12.00	—
1975FM (U)	7,875	—	—	—	6.00	—
1975FM (P)	39,000	Value: 5.00				
1975(Sh)	20,000,000	—	0.50	0.75	1.00	1.50
1976FM (M)	10,000	—	—	—	4.00	—
1976FM (U)	1,826	—	—	—	15.00	—
1976FM (P)	9,901	Value: 6.00				
1977FM (M)	10,000	—	—	—	4.00	—
1977FM (U)	354	—	—	—	10.00	—
1977FM (P)	4,822	Value: 9.00				
1978FM (U)	10,000	—	—	—	2.00	—
1978FM (P)	4,792	Value: 6.00				
1982	—	—	0.50	0.75	1.50	—

KM# 210.2 5 PISO

Nickel, 36.5 mm. **Obv:** Shield of arms **Obv. Insc.:** ISANG BANSA
ISANG DIWA below shield **Rev:** Head of Ferdinand E. Marcos left

Date	Mintage	F	VF	XF	Unc	BU
1979FM (U)	10,000	—	—	—	11.00	—
1979FM (P)	3,645	Value: 8.00				
1980FM (U)	10,000	—	—	—	2.25	—
1980FM (P)	3,133	Value: 10.00				
1981FM (U)	11,000	—	—	—	4.00	—
1981FM (P)	1,795	Value: 10.00				
1982FM (P)	—	Value: 10.00				
1982FM (U); Prooflike	—	—	—	—	10.00	—

KM# 259 5 PISO

Nickel-Brass, 25.5 mm. **Obv:** Head of Emilio Aguinaldo right
Rev: Pterocarpus Indicus Flower

Date	Mintage	F	VF	XF	Unc	BU
1991	—	—	—	—	3.00	3.50
1992	—	—	—	—	3.50	4.50
1993	—	—	—	—	9.00	18.00
1994	—	—	—	—	10.00	15.00

KM# 262 5 PISO

Nickel-Brass, 25.5 mm. **Subject:** 30th Chess Olympiad
Obv: Shield of arms **Rev:** Stylized horse head on chess board
Note: Varieties exist.

Date	Mintage	F	VF	XF	Unc	BU
1992	—	—	—	—	11.00	12.50

KM# 263 5 PISO

Nickel-Brass, 25.5 mm. **Subject:** Leyte Gulf Landings
Obv: Shield of arms **Rev:** Standing figures

Date	Mintage	F	VF	XF	Unc	BU
ND(1994)	7,800	—	—	—	8.50	10.00

KM# 272 5 PISO

7.6700 g., Nickel-Brass, 25.5 mm. **Obv:** Head of Emilio
Aguinaldo right, value and date within scalloped border
Rev: Central Bank seal within circle and gear design within
scalloped border, 1993 (date Cenral Bank was established) below
Rev. Leg.: BANGKO SENTRAL NG PILIPINAS - 1993
Edge: Plain

Date	Mintage	F	VF	XF	Unc	BU
1995	—	—	0.45	0.90	4.00	6.00
1996	—	—	0.45	0.90	2.25	3.00
1997	—	—	0.35	0.70	1.75	2.50

Note: Struck at Royal Canadian Mint, without designer initials

1997BSP	—	—	0.35	0.70	1.75	2.50

Note: With designer initials below shoulder

1998	—	—	—	—	2.50	4.00

Note: Struck at Royal Canadian Mint, without designer initials

1998	—	—	0.35	0.70	1.75	2.50

Note: With designer initials below shoulder

1999	—	—	0.35	0.70	1.75	2.50

KM# 250 10 PISO

Nickel, 36 mm. **Subject:** People Power Revolution **Obv:** Shield
of arms divides date **Rev:** Group of people

Date	Mintage	F	VF	XF	Unc	BU
1988	—	—	—	—	4.00	5.00

KM# 278 10 PISO
8.7000 g., Bi-Metallic Brass center in Copper-Nickel ring,
26.5 mm. **Obv:** Conjoined heads right within circle **Rev:** Bank
seal within circle and gear design, 1993 (date Cenral Bank was
established) below **Rev. Leg.:** BANGKO SENTRAL NG
PILIPINAS - 1993 **Edge:** Plain and reeded sections

Date	Mintage	F	VF	XF	Unc	BU
2000	—	—	0.75	1.50	3.75	5.00

KM# 204 25 PISO
26.4000 g., 0.9000 Silver 0.7639 oz. ASW **Subject:** 25th
Anniversary of Bank **Obv:** Shield of arms **Rev:** Bank in front of clouds

Date	Mintage	F	VF	XF	Unc	BU
ND(1974)	90,000	—	—	—	10.00	11.00

KM# 204a 25 PISO
26.4000 g., 0.9000 Silver 0.7639 oz. ASW **Obv:** Shield of arms
Rev: Bank in front of clouds

Date	Mintage	F	VF	XF	Unc	BU
ND(1974) Proof	10,000	Value: 18.00				

KM# 211 25 PISO
25.0000 g., 0.5000 Silver 0.4019 oz. ASW **Obv:** Head of Emilio
Aguinaldo 1/4 right **Rev:** Shield of arms

Date	Mintage	F	VF	XF	Unc	BU
1975FM (M)	10,000	—	—	—	8.00	10.00
1975FM (U)	5,875	—	—	—	15.00	16.50
1975FM (P)	37,000	Value: 12.00				

KM# 214 25 PISO
25.0000 g., 0.5000 Silver 0.4019 oz. ASW **Series:** F.A.O.
Obv: Shield of arms **Rev:** Half figure with hat holding grain

Date	Mintage	F	VF	XF	Unc	BU
1976FM (M)	22,000	—	—	—	8.00	10.00
1976FM (U)	1,826	—	—	—	20.00	22.50
1976FM (P)	9,901	Value: 12.00				

KM# 217 25 PISO
25.0000 g., 0.5000 Silver 0.4019 oz. ASW **Subject:** Banaue
Rice Terraces **Obv:** Shield of arms **Rev:** Hilly designs within circle

Date	Mintage	F	VF	XF	Unc	BU
1977FM (M)	10,000	—	—	—	13.50	15.00
1977FM (U)	354	—	—	—	30.00	35.00
1977FM (P)	4,822	Value: 15.00				

KM# 221 25 PISO
25.0000 g., 0.5000 Silver 0.4019 oz. ASW **Subject:** 100th
Anniversary - Birth of Quezon **Obv:** Shield of arms
Rev: Monument divides dates within beaded circle

Date	Mintage	F	VF	XF	Unc	BU
ND(1978)FM (U)	10,000	—	—	—	15.00	16.50
ND(1978)FM (P)	9,930	Value: 20.00				

KM# 228 25 PISO
25.0000 g., 0.5000 Silver 0.4019 oz. ASW **Subject:** UN
Conference on Trade and Development **Obv:** Conference center
buildings **Rev:** UN logo

Date	Mintage	F	VF	XF	Unc	BU
1979FM (U)	10,000	—	—	—	8.00	10.00
1979FM (P)	7,093	Value: 20.00				

KM# 230 25 PISO
25.0000 g., 0.5000 Silver 0.4019 oz. ASW **Subject:** 100th
Anniversary - Birth of Gen. Douglas MacArthur **Obv:** Uniformed
figures **Rev:** Uniformed bust with pipe facing 1/4 left

Date	Mintage	F	VF	XF	Unc	BU
ND(1980)FM (U)	9,800	—	—	—	18.00	20.00
ND(1980)FM (P)	6,318	Value: 40.00				

KM# 232 25 PISO
25.0000 g., 0.5000 Silver 0.4019 oz. ASW **Subject:** World Food
Day **Obv:** Shield of arms **Rev:** Fish, corn, grain and fruit

Date	Mintage	F	VF	XF	Unc	BU
1981FM (U)	10,000	—	—	—	10.00	11.00
1981FM (P)	3,033	Value: 25.00				

KM# 235 25 PISO
25.0000 g., 0.5000 Silver 0.4019 oz. ASW **Obv:** Shield of arms
Rev: Conjoined heads of Marcos and Reagan right

Date	Mintage	F	VF	XF	Unc	BU
1982	8,000	—	—	—	35.00	40.00
1982 Proof	250	Value: 450				

KM# 246 25 PISO
18.4100 g., 0.9250 Silver 0.5475 oz. ASW **Subject:** President
Aquino's visit in Washington **Obv:** Head of President Aquino left
Rev: Head of President Reagan right **Note:** Photo reduced.

Date	Mintage	F	VF	XF	Unc	BU
1986 Proof	Est. 1,000	Value: 350				

KM# 212 50 PISO
27.4000 g., 0.9250 Silver 0.8148 oz. ASW **Subject:** 3rd
Anniversary of the New Society **Obv:** Shield of arms **Rev:** Head
of Marcos left

Date	Mintage	F	VF	XF	Unc	BU
1975FM (M)	10,000	—	—	—	16.50	18.00
1975FM (U)	7,875	—	—	—	17.50	20.00
1975FM (P)	54,000	Value: 10.00				

KM# 215 50 PISO
27.4000 g., 0.9250 Silver 0.8148 oz. ASW **Subject:** I.M.F. Meeting
Obv: Map **Rev:** Stylized star in center of world globe emblems

Date	Mintage	F	VF	XF	Unc	BU
1976 Proof	5,477	Value: 22.00				
1976FM (M)	10,000	—	—	—	17.50	20.00
1976FM (U)	1,826	—	—	—	30.00	35.00
1976FM (P)	15,000	Value: 17.50				

KM# 218 50 PISO
27.4000 g., 0.9250 Silver 0.8148 oz. ASW **Subject:** Inauguration
of New Mint Facilities **Obv:** Shield of arms **Rev:** Two coins under
star and building within circle

Date	Mintage	F	VF	XF	Unc	BU
1977FM (M)	10,000	—	—	—	18.00	20.00
1977FM (U)	354	—	—	—	45.00	55.00
1977FM (P)	6,704	Value: 18.00				

KM# 222 50 PISO
27.4000 g., 0.9250 Silver 0.8148 oz. ASW **Subject:** 100th
Anniversary - Birth of Manuel L. Quezon **Obv:** Shield of arms
Rev: Head right, dates and shield

Date	Mintage	F	VF	XF	Unc	BU
ND(1978)FM (U)	10,000	—	—	—	18.00	20.00
ND(1978)FM (P)	9,969	Value: 22.00				

KM# 229 50 PISO
27.4000 g., 0.9250 Silver 0.8148 oz. ASW **Subject:**
International Year of the Child **Obv:** Shield of arms **Rev:** Child's
bust facing, logo at right

Date	Mintage	F	VF	XF	Unc	BU
1979FM (U)	10,000	—	—	—	16.50	18.00
1979FM (P)	27,000	Value: 16.00				
1979 Piefort Proof	—	Value: 210				

KM# 233 50 PISO
27.4000 g., 0.9250 Silver 0.8148 oz. ASW **Subject:** Pope John
Paul II Visit **Obv:** Standing figure praying **Rev:** Head 1/4 left

Date	Mintage	F	VF	XF	Unc	BU
1981FM (U)	10,000	—	—	—	33.00	35.00
1981FM (P)	3,353	Value: 50.00				

KM# 236 50 PISO
27.4000 g., 0.9250 Silver 0.8148 oz. ASW **Subject:** 40th
Anniversary of Bataan-Corregidor **Obv:** Shield of arms
Rev: Conjoined military heads left

Date	Mintage	F	VF	XF	Unc	BU
ND(1982)FM (U)	13,000	—	—	—	22.00	25.00
ND(1982)FM (P)	4,626	Value: 35.00				

KM# 245 100 PISO
25.0000 g., 0.5000 Silver 0.4019 oz. ASW **Subject:** 75th
Anniversary - University of the Philippines **Obv:** Shield of arms
Rev: Nude statue divides building above dates

Date	Mintage	F	VF	XF	Unc	BU
ND(1983)	15,000	—	—	—	17.50	20.00
ND(1983) Proof	2,000	Value: 30.00				

KM# 264 100 PISO
10.0000 g., 0.9250 Silver 0.2974 oz. ASW **Subject:** Papal Visit
1995-Pope John Paul II **Obv:** Shield of arms **Rev:** Head left

Date	Mintage	F	VF	XF	Unc	BU
ND(1994) Proof	1,000	Value: 80.00				

KM# 279 100 PISO
16.7300 g., 0.8000 Silver 0.4303 oz. ASW **Subject:** Leyte Gulf
Landing

Date	Mintage	F	VF	XF	Unc	BU
ND(1994) Proof	1,000	Value: 55.00				

KM# 254 150 PISO
16.8200 g., 0.9250 Silver 0.5002 oz. ASW **Subject:** Southeast
Asian Games **Obv:** Shield of arms **Rev:** Official logo

Date	Mintage	F	VF	XF	Unc	BU
1991 Prooflike	—	—	—	—	60.00	
1991 Proof	5,000	Value: 50.00				

KM# 248 200 PISO
25.0000 g., 0.9250 Silver 0.7435 oz. ASW **Subject:** World
Wildlife Fund **Obv:** Shield of arms **Rev:** Mindoro Buffalo

Date	Mintage	F	VF	XF	Unc	BU
1987 Proof	25,000	Value: 40.00				

KM# 252 200 PISO
25.0000 g., 0.9250 Silver 0.7435 oz. ASW **Subject:** Save the
Children Fund **Obv:** Shield of arms **Rev:** Children playing

Date	Mintage	F	VF	XF	Unc	BU
1990 Proof	Est. 20,000	Value: 60.00				

KM# 265 200 PISO
15.5600 g., 0.9990 Silver 0.4997 oz. ASW **Subject:** Papal Visit
1995 **Obv:** Shield of arms **Rev:** Bust of John Paul II left
Note: Similar to 100 Piso, KM#264.

Date	Mintage	F	VF	XF	Unc	BU
ND(1994) Proof	1,000	Value: 100				

KM# 249 500 PISO
28.0000 g., 0.9250 Silver 0.8327 oz. ASW **Subject:** People Power
Revolution **Obv:** Shield of arms divides date **Rev:** Group of people

Date	Mintage	F	VF	XF	Unc	BU
1988 Proof	Est. 7,500	Value: 50.00				

KM# 280 500 PISO
23.1000 g., 0.9250 Silver 0.6870 oz. ASW **Subject:** Leyte Gulf
Landing

Date	Mintage	F	VF	XF	Unc	BU
ND(1994) Proof	1,000	Value: 100				

KM# 276 500 PISO
28.2800 g., 0.9250 Silver 0.8410 oz. ASW **Subject:** Centennial
- Andres Bonifacio 1897-1997

Date	Mintage	F	VF	XF	Unc	BU
ND(1997) Proof	2,625	Value: 120				

KM# 274　500 PISO
28.2800 g., 0.9250 Silver 0.8410 oz. ASW **Subject:** Carlos P. Romulo Centennial **Obv:** Shield above value **Rev:** Bust left and dates

Date	Mintage	F	VF	XF	Unc	BU
ND(1998) Proof	Est. 2,100				Value: 80.00	

KM# 277　500 PISO
28.2800 g., 0.9250 Silver 0.8410 oz. ASW **Subject:** Centennial - Emilio F. Aguinaldo 1898-1998

Date	Mintage	F	VF	XF	Unc	BU
ND(1998) Proof	2,100				Value: 100	

KM# 275　500 PISO
28.2800 g., 0.9250 Silver 0.8410 oz. ASW **Subject:** 50th Anniversary - Central Bank **Obv:** Old and new bank buildings **Rev:** Old and new bank seals

Date	Mintage	F	VF	XF	Unc	BU
ND(1999) Proof	Est. 5,000				Value: 60.00	

KM# 213　1000 PISO
9.9500 g., 0.9000 Gold 0.2879 oz. AGW **Subject:** 3rd Anniversary of the New Society **Obv:** Shield **Rev:** Head left

Date	Mintage	F	VF	XF	Unc	BU
1975	23,000					275
1975 Proof	13,000				Value: 280	

KM# 281　1000 PISO
31.1000 g., 0.9990 Silver 0.9988 oz. ASW **Subject:** Leyte Gulf Landing

Date	Mintage	F	VF	XF	Unc	BU
ND(1994) Proof	1,000				Value: 125	

KM# 216　1500 PISO
20.5500 g., 0.9000 Gold 0.5946 oz. AGW **Subject:** I.M.F. Meeting **Obv:** Map **Rev:** Stylized star in center of world globe emblems

Date	Mintage	F	VF	XF	Unc	BU
1976	5,500					575
1976 Proof	6,500				Value: 575	

KM# 219　1500 PISO
20.5500 g., 0.9000 Gold 0.5946 oz. AGW **Subject:** 5th Anniversary of the New Society **Obv:** Head facing **Rev:** Redesigned bank seal within circle

Date	Mintage	F	VF	XF	Unc	BU
ND(1977)	4,000					
ND(1977) Proof	6,000				Value: 575	

KM# 223　1500 PISO
20.5500 g., 0.9000 Gold 0.5946 oz. AGW **Subject:** Inauguration of New Mint Facilities **Obv:** Flowers **Rev:** Bank, gold bars, paper money and coins

Date	Mintage	F	VF	XF	Unc	BU
1978	3,000					
1978 Proof	3,000				Value: 575	

KM# 234　1500 PISO
9.9500 g., 0.9000 Gold 0.2879 oz. AGW **Subject:** Pope John Paul II Visit **Obv:** Standing figure in prayer, crowd in background **Rev:** Bust 3/4 left

Date	Mintage	F	VF	XF	Unc	BU
1981 Proof	1,000				Value: 425	
1982 Proof						

KM# 237　1500 PISO
9.7800 g., 0.9000 Gold 0.2830 oz. AGW **Subject:** 40th Anniversary of Bataan-Corregidor **Obv:** Shield of arms **Rev:** Conjoined military heads left

Date	Mintage	F	VF	XF	Unc	BU
ND(1982)FM (U)	1,000					325
ND(1982)FM (P)	445				Value: 400	

KM# 282　2000 PISO
10.0000 g., 0.5000 Gold 0.1607 oz. AGW, 27 mm. **Subject:** Asia Pacific Economic Cooperation **Obv:** Head of Fidel Ramos 3/4 right **Rev:** World globe logo and value **Edge:** Reeded

Date	Mintage	F	VF	XF	Unc	BU
1996 Proof	3,000				Value: 225	

KM# 231　2500 PISO
14.5700 g., 0.5000 Gold 0.2342 oz. AGW **Subject:** 100th Anniversary - Birth of General Douglas MacArthur **Obv:** Military standing figures **Rev:** Uniformed bust with pipe facing 1/4 left

Date	Mintage	F	VF	XF	Unc	BU
ND(1980)FM (P)	3,073				Value: 300	

KM# 247　2500 PISO
15.0000 g., 0.5000 Gold 0.2411 oz. AGW **Subject:** President Aquino's Visit in Washington **Obv:** Bust of President Aquino left **Rev:** Bust of President Reagan right

Date	Mintage	F	VF	XF	Unc	BU
1986 Proof	Est. 250				Value: 575	

KM# 266　2500 PISO
7.9800 g., 0.9167 Gold 0.2352 oz. AGW **Subject:** Papal Visit 1995 **Obv:** Shield of arms **Rev:** Pope John Paul II left **Note:** Similar to 100 Piso, KM#264.

Date	Mintage	F	VF	XF	Unc	BU
ND(1994) Proof	—				Value: 425	

KM# 220　5000 PISO
68.7400 g., 0.9000 Gold 1.9890 oz. AGW **Subject:** 5th Anniversary of the New Society **Obv:** Design within beaded circle **Rev:** Conjoined busts of Ferdindand and Imelda Marcos right

Date	Mintage	F	VF	XF	Unc	BU
ND(1977)FM (U)	100					2,250
ND(1977)FM (P)	3,832				Value: 1,950	

KM# 267　5000 PISO
16.8100 g., 0.9250 Gold 0.4999 oz. AGW **Subject:** Papal Visit 1995 **Obv:** Shield of arms **Rev:** Bust of Pope John Paul II left **Note:** Similar to 100 Piso, KM#264.

Date	Mintage	F	VF	XF	Unc	BU
ND(1994) Proof	—				Value: 525	

KM# 283   5000 PISO
Gold **Subject:** 50th Anniversary - Central Bank in the Philippines

Date	Mintage	F	VF	XF	Unc	BU
1999 Proof	2,000	Value: 500				

KM# 255   10000 PESOS
33.5500 g., 0.9250 Gold 0.9977 oz. AGW **Subject:** People Power 1992 **Obv:** Bust of Aquino facing 3/4 right **Rev:** Map, scroll, dates and dove

Date	Mintage	F	VF	XF	Unc	BU
ND(1992) Proof	1,600	Value: 975				

PATTERNS
Including off metal strikes

KM#	Date	Mintage	Identification	Mkt Val
Pn20	1922	—	Centavo. Silver. KM#163.	—
Pn21	ND(1965-66)	—	Peso. Silver. Marcos	—
Pn22	1966	—	Centavo. Copper. Central Bank	100
Pn23	1966	—	5 Centavos. Brass.	100
Pn24	1966	—	5 Centavos. Copper.	100
Pn25	1966	—	10 Centavos. Silver.	125
Pn26	1966	—	10 Centavos. Copper.	100
Pn27	1966	—	25 Centavos. Brass.	100
PnA28	1966	—	50 Centavos. Copper. Similar to Pn28. Conjoined busts of Ferdinand and Imelda Marcos.	90.00
PnB28	1966	—	50 Centavos. Copper. As Pn28	90.00
Pn28	1966	—	50 Centavos. Silver.	200
Pn29	1966	—	Piso. Silver.	200
Pn30	1966	—	Peso. Silver. Ferd and Imelda Marcos	—
PnA31	1966	—	Piso. Copper. Similar to Pn28. As Pn38.	150
PnB31	1966	—	Piso. Brass. Similar to Pn38 wtihout eagle and lion on arms.	150
Pn31	1967	—	Sentimo. Copper.	100
Pn32	1967	—	5 Sentimos.	125
Pn33	1967	—	5 Sentimos. Copper. Similar to Pn32. Similar to Pn27.	125
PnA34	1967	—	25 Sentimos. Copper. Design similar to Pn28, legend as Pn34. Similar to Pn27.	100
PnB34	1967	—	10 Centavos. Bronze. Bust of Francisco Baltazar.	125
Pn34	1967	—	25 Sentimos. Silver.	125
PnA35	1967	—	50 Centavos. Copper. As Pn36. Small conjoined busts of Ferdinand and Imelda Marcos.	125
PnB35	1967	—	50 Sentimos. Bronze. Similar to Pn28. Bust of Juan Luna.	150
Pn35	1967	—	50 Sentimos. Copper. Large conjoined busts of Ferdinand and Imelda Marcos.	150
Pn36	1967	—	50 Sentimos. Silver. Del Pilar left. Del Pilar	125
Pn37	1967	—	50 Sentimos. Copper. Del Pilar left. Del Pilar	125
PnA38	1967	—	Peso. Copper. Similar to KM#195	150
PnB38	1967	—	Peso. Brass. Similar to KM#195	150
Pn38	1968	—	Peso. Silver. Sower walking left.	225
Pn39	1968	—	Piso. Silver. Sower walking right.	225
PnA40	1969	—	Peso. Copper. Similar to KM#195. As Pn40.	150
Pn40	1969	—	Piso. Silver. Dated 1966. Aquinaldo	225
Pn41	ND(1970)	—	Peso. Copper. Similar to KM#195. Conjoined busts of Marcos and Pope Paul VI left.	95.00
Pn42	1970	—	Peso. Copper. Similar to KM#195. Bust of Pope Paul VI 3/4 right.	95.00

PIEFORTS
All standard metals unless otherwise indicated

KM#	Date	Mintage	Identification	Mkt Val
P1	1979	—	50 Piso. Silver. KM#229.	150

TRIAL STRIKES

KM#	Date	Mintage	Identification	Mkt Val
TS8	1967	—	Peso. Brass. KM#195. Bataan Day	75.00

MINT SETS

KM#	Date	Mintage	Identification	Issue Price	Mkt Val
MS1	1936 (3)	—	KM#176-178	—	500
MS2	1947 (2)	—	KM#184-185	—	25.00
MS3	1958 (5)	—	KM#186-190	—	3.00
MS4	1970 (2)	—	KM#202-202a	—	15.00
MS5	1975 (8)	5,877	KM#205-208, 209.1, 210.1, 211-212. Enclosed in Franklin Mint folder	33.50	30.00
MS6	1975 (8)	3,850	KM#205-208, 209.1, 210.1, 211-212	—	45.00

KM#	Date	Mintage	Identification	Issue Price	Mkt Val
MS7	1976 (8)	1,826	KM#205-208, 209.1, 210.1, 214-215. Enclosed in Franklin Mint folder	—	100
MS8	1976 (8)	10,000	KM#205-208, 209.1, 210.1, 214-215	—	30.00
MS9	1977 (8)	354	KM#205-208, 209.1, 210.1, 217-218; Enclosed in Franklin Mint folder.	—	100
MSA11	1977 (8)	10,000	KM#205-208, 209.1, 210.1, 217-218	—	30.00
MS11	1978 (8)	10,000	KM#205-210, 221-222	—	30.00
MS12	1979 (8)	10,000	KM#209.2-210.2, 224-229	—	30.00
MS13	1980 (7)	9,800	KM#209.2-210.2, 224-227, 230	—	30.00
MS14	1981 (8)	10,000	KM#209.2-210.2, 224-227, 232-233	—	65.00
MS15	1982 (5)	—	KM#209.2, 224-227	—	2.50
MS16	1983 (8)	—	KM#238-239, 240.2, 241, 242.1, 243-245BRM	—	35.00
MS17	1983 (7)	—	KM#238-239, 240.1, 241, 242.1, 243-244	—	5.00
MS18	1983 (7)	—	KM#238-239, 240.2, 241.1, 242.1, 243-244	—	10.00
MS19	1985 (7)	—	KM#238-239, 240.2, 241.1, 242.1, 243-244	—	5.00
MS20	1986 (7)	—	KM#238-239, 240.2, 241.1, 243-244	—	5.00
MS21	1987 (7)	—	KM#238-239, 240.2, 241.1, 242.1, 243-244	—	5.00
MS22	1988 (7)	—	KM#238-239, 240.2, 241.1, 242.1, 243-244	—	5.00
MS23	1989 (7)	—	KM#238-239, 240.2, 241.1, 242.1, 243-244	—	5.00
MS24	1989 (7)	—	KM#238-239, 240.2, 241, 242.1, 243-244	—	5.00
MS25	1990 (7)	—	KM#238-239, 240.2, 241.1, 242.1, 243-244	—	5.00
MS26	1990 (7)	—	KM#238-239, 240.2, 241.1, 242.1, 243-244	—	5.00
MS27	1991 (8)	—	KM#238-239, 240.2, 241.2, 242.3, 243.2, 258-259	—	10.00
MS28	1992 (8)	—	KM#238-239, 240.2, 241.2, 242.3, 243.2, 258-259	—	10.00
MS29	1995 (6)	—	KM#268-273	—	12.00
MS30	1996 (6)	—	KM#268-273	—	12.00
MS31	1997 (6)	—	KM#268-273	—	20.00
MS32	1998 (5)	—	KM#268-269, 271-273	—	20.00
MS33	1999 (5)	—	KM#268-269, 271-273	—	20.00
MS34	2000 (5)	—	KM#268-269, 271, 273, 278	—	—

PROOF SETS

KM#	Date	Mintage	Identification	Issue Price	Mkt Val
PS1i	1903 (7)	I.A.	KM#162-168 (impaired)	—	500
PS1	1903 (7)	2,558	KM#162-168	—	1,000
PS2	1904 (7)	1,355	KM#162-168	—	1,250
PS2i	1904 (7)	I.A.	KM#162-168 (impaired)	—	600
PS3	1905 (7)	471	KM#162-168	—	2,750
PS3i	1905 (7)	I.A.	KM#162-168 (impaired)	—	1,500
PS4	1906 (7)	500	KM#162-168	—	2,500
PS4i	1906 (7)	I.A.	KM#162-168 (impaired)	—	1,100
PS5	1908 (7)	500	KM#162-164, 169-172	—	2,500
PS5i	1908 (7)	I.A.	KM#162-164, 169-172 (impaired)	—	1,100
PS6	1958 (5)	—	KM#186-190, Not confirmed	—	—
PS7	1974 (6)	10,000	KM#196-200, 203; Not released to the general public	—	80.00
PS8	1975 (8)	36,516	KM#205-208, 209.1-210.1, 211-212	67.00	30.00
PS9	1975 (6)	—	KM#205-208, 209.1-210.1	—	—
PS10	1976 (8)	9,901	KM#205-208, 209.1-210.1, 214-215	67.00	30.00
PS11	1977 (8)	4,822	KM#205-208, 209.1-210.1, 217-218	70.00	40.00
PS12	1978 (8)	4,792	KM#205-208, 209.1-210.1, 220-221	70.00	45.00
PS13	1978 (2)	3,911	KM#221-222	46.00	30.00
PS14	1979 (8)	3,645	KM#209.2-210.2, 224-229	68.00	40.00
PS15	1979 (2)	2,448	KM#228-229	47.50	30.00
PS16	1980 (7)	3,133	KM#209.2-210.2, 224-227, 230	65.00	65.00
PS17	1981 (8)	1,795	KM#209.2-210.2, 224-227, 232-233	—	110
PS18	1981 (2)	—	KM#232, 233	—	65.00
PS19	1982 (7)	—	KM#209.2-210.2, 224-227, 236	52.00	65.00
PS20	1983 (8)	—	KM#238-239, 240.1, 241, 242.1, 243-245	50.00	85.00
PS21	1986 (2)	—	KM#246-247	—	600
PS22	ND(1994) (3)	—	KM#264-265, 267 Papal Visit 1995	—	800
PS23	1994 (4)	—	KM#263, 279-281 50th Anniversary of Leyte Gulf Landings	—	275

CULION ISLAND

The Culion Leper Colony was established around 1903 on the island of Culion about 150 miles southeast of Manila by the Commission of Public Health. The first issue of coins valid only in the colony was produced by a private firm, Frank & Company. Later issues were struck at the Manila Mint.

MINT MARK
PM = Philippine Mint at Manila

MONETARY SYSTEM
100 Centavos = 1 Peso

CULION LEPER COLONY
Philippine Commission of Public Health
LEPROSARIUM COINAGE

KM# 1   1/2 CENTAVO
Aluminum **Obv:** Value **Rev:** Caduceus

Date	Mintage	F	VF	XF	Unc	BU
1913	17,000	—	5.00	8.00	10.00	

Note: Some authorities doubt that this coin circulated

KM# 2   CENTAVO
Aluminum

Date	Mintage	Good	VG	F	VF	XF
1913	33,000	30.00	40.00	110	150	—

Note: This coin exists with thick and thin planchets

KM# 3   CENTAVO
Copper-Nickel **Obv:** Bust 1/4 right **Rev:** Eagle above shield **Note:** Similar to KM#4 but first die, better strike.

Date	Mintage	Good	VG	F	VF	XF
1927PM	30,000	10.00	15.00	25.00	50.00	140

Note: Type I - One-button coat, legible motto, "7" in date over "T" in Centavo

KM# 4   CENTAVO
Copper-Nickel **Obv:** Bust 1/4 right **Rev:** Eagle with wings open above shield **Note:** Second die, poor strike. This coin exists with thick and thin planchets.

Date	Mintage	Good	VG	F	VF	XF
1927PM	Inc. above	12.00	18.00	25.00	70.00	150

Note: Type II - One-button coat, illegible motto, end of ribbon two widths from shield edge, "7" over "N"

KM# A5   CENTAVO
Copper Nickel

Date	Mintage	Good	VG	F	VF	XF
1927PM	Inc. above	35.00	50.00	100	200	375

Note: Type III - Two-button coat, illegible motto, end of ribbon one width from shield edge

KM# 5   CENTAVO
Copper-Nickel **Obv:** Bust of Rizal in circle **Rev:** Legend **Rev. Leg.:** PHILIPPINE HEALTH SERVICE/LEPER COIN ONE CENTAVO

Date	Mintage	Good	VG	F	VF	XF
1930 Rare	—	—	—	—	—	—

KM# 6   5 CENTAVOS
Aluminum **Obv:** Value, legend **Rev:** Caduceus

Date	Mintage	Good	VG	F	VF	XF
1913	6,600	70.00	80.00	125	250	—

KM# 7   5 CENTAVOS
Copper-Nickel **Obv:** Bust 1/4 right **Rev:** Eagle with wings open above shield

Date	Mintage	Good	VG	F	VF	XF
1927	16,000	5.00	7.50	10.00	25.00	40.00

KM# 8   10 CENTAVOS
Aluminum **Obv:** Value **Rev:** Caduceus **Note:** Similar to 1/2 Centavo, KM#1.

Date	Mintage	Good	VG	F	VF	XF
1913	6,600	8.00	30.00	50.00	100	—

KM# 9 10 CENTAVOS
Aluminum **Obv:** Value **Rev:** Caduceus **Note:** Similar to 1 Peso, KM#14.

Date	Mintage	Good	VG	F	VF	XF
1920	20,000	7.50	12.50	17.50	40.00	100

KM# 10 10 CENTAVOS
Copper-Nickel **Obv:** Bust 1/4 left within circle **Rev:** Value within circle

Date	Mintage	VG	F	VF	XF	Unc
1930	17,000	—	7.50	10.00	20.00	100

Note: One pattern in copper, has been authenticated by ANACS

KM# 11 20 CENTAVOS
Aluminum **Obv:** Value **Rev:** Caduceus **Note:** Similar to 1/2 Centavo, KM#1.

Date	Mintage	Good	VG	F	VF	XF
1913	10,000	17.50	45.00	60.00	150	—

KM# 12 20 CENTAVOS
Aluminum **Obv:** Value **Rev:** Caduceus

Date	Mintage	Good	VG	F	VF	XF
1920	10,000	5.00	10.00	20.00	45.00	—

KM# 13 20 CENTAVOS
Copper-Nickel **Obv:** Value, legend **Rev:** Caduceus

Date	Mintage	VG	F	VF	XF	Unc
1922PM	10,000	—	20.00	25.00	40.00	—

Note: This coin exists with thick and thin planchets

KM# 15 PESO
Aluminum **Obv:** Value **Rev:** Caduceus

Date	Mintage	VG	F	VF	XF	Unc
1920	4,000	16.00	20.00	30.00	60.00	—

Note: Pointed serif on "1", (narrow numerals)

1920	—	50.00	—	—	220	—

Note: Blunt serif on "1" (rounder numerals)

KM# 16 PESO
Copper-Nickel **Obv:** Value **Rev:** Caduceus **Note:** Varieties exist.

Date	Mintage	VG	F	VF	XF	Unc
1922	8,280	—	15.00	20.00	40.00	—

KM# 17 PESO
Copper-Nickel **Obv:** Value **Rev:** Caduceus with curved wings
Note: Similar to KM#16, but caduceus has curved wings.

Date	Mintage	VG	F	VF	XF	Unc
1922PM	Inc. above	—	200	275	300	—

KM# 18 PESO
Copper-Nickel **Obv:** Bust 3/4 right **Rev:** Eagle with wings open above shield

Date	Mintage	VG	F	VF	XF	Unc
1925	20,000	—	10.00	15.00	20.00	250

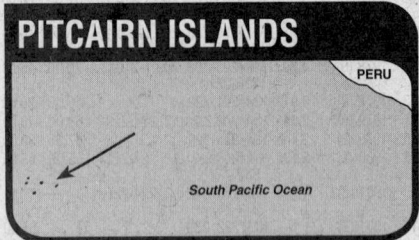

KM# 14 PESO
Aluminum **Obv:** Value **Rev:** Caduceus

Date	Mintage	VG	F	VF	XF	Unc
1913	8,600	10.00	15.00	20.00	40.00	—

Note: This coin exists with thick and thin planchets

PITCAIRN ISLANDS

South Pacific Ocean

PERU

A small volcanic island, along with the uninhabited islands of Oeno, Henderson, and Ducie, constitute the British Colony of Pitcairn Islands. The main island has an area of about 2 sq. mi. (5 sq. km.) and a population of *68. It is located 1350 miles southeast of Tahiti. The islanders subsist on fishing, garden produce and crops. The sale of postage stamps and carved curios to passing ships brings cash income.

Discovered in 1767 by a British naval officer, Pitcairn was not occupied until 1790 when Fletcher Christian and nine mutineers from the British ship, *HMS Bounty*, along with some Tahitian men and women went ashore, and survived in obscurity until discovered by American whalers in 1808.

Adamstown is the chief settlement, located on the north coast, one of the few places that island-made longboats can land. The primary religion is Seventh-day Adventist and a public school provides basic education. In 1898 the settlement was placed under the jurisdiction of the Commissioner for the Western Pacific. Since 1970 this British settlement has been governed through a locally elected council under a governor.

New Zealand currency has been used since July 10, 1967.

BRITISH COLONY
REGULAR COINAGE

KM# 3 DOLLAR
Copper-Nickel, 38.5 mm. **Subject:** Drafting of Constitution, 1838-1988 **Obv:** Crowned bust right **Rev:** Sailing ship

Date	Mintage	F	VF	XF	Unc	BU
ND(1988)	—	—	—	—	8.00	—

KM# 3a DOLLAR
28.2800 g., 0.9250 Silver 0.8410 oz. ASW, 38.5 mm.
Subject: Drafting of constitution, 1838-1988 **Obv:** Crowned bust right **Rev:** Sailing ship

Date	Mintage	F	VF	XF	Unc	BU
ND(1988) Proof	—	Value: 40.00				

KM# 4 DOLLAR
Copper-Nickel, 38.5 mm. **Subject:** HMAV Bounty, 1789-1989 **Obv:** Crowned bust right **Rev:** Sailing ship

Date	Mintage	F	VF	XF	Unc	BU
ND(1989)	50,000	—	—	—	8.00	—

KM# 4a DOLLAR
28.2800 g., 0.9250 Silver 0.8410 oz. ASW, 38.5 mm.
Subject: HMAV Bounty, 1789-1989 **Obv:** Crowned bust right **Rev:** Sailing ship

Date	Mintage	F	VF	XF	Unc	BU
ND(1989) Proof	20,000	Value: 40.00				

KM# 7 DOLLAR
Copper-Nickel, 38.5 mm. **Subject:** Establishment of Settlement, 1790-1990 **Obv:** Crowned bust right **Rev:** Ship in flames

Date	Mintage	F	VF	XF	Unc	BU
ND(1990)	—	—	—	—	8.00	—

KM# 7a DOLLAR
28.2800 g., 0.9250 Silver 0.8410 oz. ASW, 38.5 mm.
Subject: Establishment of Settlement, 1790-1990 **Obv:** Crowned bust right **Rev:** Ship in flames

Date	Mintage	F	VF	XF	Unc	BU
ND(1990) Proof	10,000	Value: 45.00				

KM# 10 DOLLAR
Copper-Nickel, 38.5 mm. **Subject:** British Queen Mother **Obv:** Crowned bust right **Rev:** Queen Mother at right, Order of the Garter at left within beaded circle **Note:** Struck at the British Royal Mint.

Date	Mintage	F	VF	XF	Unc	BU
1997	—	—	—	—	10.00	—

KM# 11 5 DOLLARS
31.5600 g., 0.9250 Silver 0.9385 oz. ASW, 38.5 mm. **Subject:** Queen Mother **Obv:** Crowned bust right **Rev:** Queen Mother and the Order of the Garter at left within beaded circle **Edge:** Reeded

Date	Mintage	F	VF	XF	Unc	BU
1997 Proof	—	Value: 50.00				

KM# 13 10 DOLLARS
Silver **Subject:** 50th Wedding Anniversary of Queen Elizabeth II and Philip **Obv:** Bust right, legend above, date below **Rev:** Queen Elizabeth II and Philip with Prince Charles in baby buggy, legend above, value below

Date	Mintage	F	VF	XF	Unc	BU
1997 Proof	—	Value: 50.00				

KM# 1 50 DOLLARS
155.6000 g., 0.9990 Silver 4.9974 oz. ASW, 65 mm. **Subject:** Drafting of Constitution, 1838-1988 **Obv:** Crowned bust right **Rev:** Sailing ship **Note:** Illustration reduced.

Date	Mintage	F	VF	XF	Unc	BU
ND(1988) Proof	10,000	Value: 165				

KM# 5 50 DOLLARS
155.6000 g., 0.9990 Silver 4.9974 oz. ASW, 65 mm. **Subject:** HMAV Bounty, 1789-1989 **Obv:** Crowned bust right **Rev:** Sailing ship **Note:** Similar to 250 Dollars, KM#6.

Date	Mintage	F	VF	XF	Unc	BU
ND(1989) Proof	10,000	Value: 135				

KM# 8 50 DOLLARS
155.6000 g., 0.9990 Silver 4.9974 oz. ASW, 65 mm. **Subject:** Establishment of Settlement, 1790-1990 **Obv:** Crowned bust right **Rev:** Ship in flames **Note:** Similar to 250 Dollars, KM#9.

Date	Mintage	F	VF	XF	Unc	BU
ND(1990) Proof	2,500	Value: 225				

KM# 2 250 DOLLARS
15.9800 g., 0.9170 Gold 0.4711 oz. AGW **Subject:** Drafting of Constitution, 1838-1988 **Obv:** Crowned bust right **Rev:** Sailing ship

Date	Mintage	F	VF	XF	Unc	BU
ND(1988) Proof	2,500	Value: 475				

KM# 6 250 DOLLARS
15.9800 g., 0.9170 Gold 0.4711 oz. AGW **Subject:** HMAV Bounty, 1789-1989 **Obv:** Crowned bust right **Rev:** Ship

Date	Mintage	F	VF	XF	Unc	BU
ND(1989) Proof	2,500	Value: 475				

KM# 9 250 DOLLARS
15.9800 g., 0.9170 Gold 0.4711 oz. AGW **Subject:** Establishment of Settlement, 1790-1990 **Obv:** Crowned bust right **Rev:** Burning of the Bounty, ship in flames within circle

Date	Mintage	F	VF	XF	Unc	BU
ND(1990) Proof	500	Value: 475				

POLAND

The Republic of Poland, located in central Europe, has an area of 120,725 sq. mi. (312,680 sq. km.) and a population of *38.2 million. Capital: Warszawa (Warsaw). The economy is essentially agricultural, but industrial activity provides the products for foreign trade. Machinery, coal, coke, iron, steel and transport equipment are exported.

Poland, which began as a Slavic duchy in the 10th century and reached its peak of power between the 14th and 16th centuries, has had a turbulent history of invasion, occupation or partition by Mongols, Turkey, Transylvania, Sweden, Austria, Prussia and Russia.

The first partition took place in 1772. Prussia took Polish Pomerania, Russia took part of the eastern provinces, and Austria occupied Galicia and its capital city Lwów. The second partition occurred in 1793 when Russia took another slice of the eastern provinces and Prussia took what remained of western Poland. The third partition, 1795, literally removed Poland from the map. Russia took what was left of the eastern provinces. Prussia seized most of central Poland, including Warsaw. Austria took what was left of the south. Napoleon restored to Poland much of the territory lost to Prussia and Austria, but after his defeat another partition returned the Duchy of Warsaw to Prussia, made Kraków into a tiny republic, and declared what remained to be the Kingdom of Poland under the czar and in permanent union with Russia.

Poland re-emerged as an independent state recognized by the Treaty of Versailles on June 28, 1919, and maintained its independence until 1939 when it was invaded by, and partitioned between, Germany and Russia. Poland's present boundaries were determined by the U.S.-British-Russian agreement of Aug. 16, 1945. The Government of National Unity was replaced when the Polish Communist-Socialist faction claimed victory at the polls in 1947 and established a Peoples Democratic Republic' of the Soviet type in 1952. On December 29, 1989 Poland was proclaimed as the Republic of Poland.

MINT MARKS
MV, MW, MW-monogram - Warsaw Mint, 1965-
FF - Stuttgart Germany 1916-1917
(w) - Warsaw 1923-39 (opened officially in 1924) arrow mintmark
CHI - Valcambi, Switzerland
Other letters appearing with date denote the Mintmaster at the time the coin was struck.

GERMAN OCCUPATION

REGENCY COINAGE
100 Fenigow = 1 Marka

Y# 4 FENIG
1.9700 g., Iron, 15 mm. **Obv:** Value **Rev:** Crowned eagle with wings open

Date	Mintage	F	VF	XF	Unc	BU
1918FF	51,484,000	0.50	1.00	3.00	10.00	30.00
1918FF Proof	—	Value: 200				

Y# 5 5 FENIGOW
2.5300 g., Iron, 18 mm. **Obv:** Value **Rev:** Crowned eagle with wings open

Date	Mintage	F	VF	XF	Unc	BU
1917FF	18,700,000	0.25	0.75	1.50	3.50	—
1917FF Proof	—	Value: 100				
1918FF	22,690,000	0.25	0.75	1.50	3.50	—
1918FF Proof	—	Value: 200				

Y# 6 10 FENIGOW
3.5600 g., Iron, 21 mm. **Obv:** Value **Rev:** Crowned eagle with wings open

Date	Mintage	F	VF	XF	Unc	BU
1917FF	33,000,000	7.50	15.00	20.00	28.00	—
Note: Obverse legend touches edge						
1917FF Proof	—	Value: 100				
1917FF	Inc. above	0.25	0.75	1.25	3.50	—
Note: Obverse legend away from edge						
1918FF	14,990,000	0.50	1.00	2.00	5.00	—
Note: Obverse legend away from edge						
1918FF Proof	—	Value: 200				
Note: Obverse legend away from edge						

Y# 6a 10 FENIGOW
3.5600 g., Zinc, 21 mm. **Obv:** Value **Rev:** Crowned eagle with wings open **Note:** Error planchet.

Date	Mintage	F	VF	XF	Unc	BU
1917FF	—	25.00	45.00	85.00	150	—

Y# 7 20 FENIGOW
3.9000 g., Iron, 23 mm. **Obv:** Value **Rev:** Crowned eagle with wings open

Date	Mintage	F	VF	XF	Unc	BU
1917FF	1,900,000	2.00	4.00	6.00	11.50	—
1918FF	19,260,000	0.75	1.25	2.50	5.50	—

Y# 7a 20 FENIGOW
Zinc **Obv:** Value **Rev:** Crowned eagle with wings open **Note:** Error planchet.

Date	Mintage	F	VF	XF	Unc	BU
1917FF	—	35.00	60.00	100	200	—

REPUBLIC

STANDARD COINAGE
100 Groszy = 1 Zloty

Y# 8 GROSZ
1.5000 g., Brass, 14.7 mm. **Obv:** Crowned eagle with wings open **Rev:** Stylized value **Note:** Some authorities consider this strike a pattern.

Date	Mintage	F	VF	XF	Unc	BU
1923	—	—	—	—	200	—

Y# 8a   GROSZ
1.5000 g., Bronze, 14.7 mm. **Obv:** Crowned eagle with wings open **Rev:** Stylized value

Date	Mintage	F	VF	XF	Unc	BU
1923	30,000,000	0.25	0.50	1.75	10.00	—
1925(w)	40,000,000	0.25	0.50	1.75	9.00	—
1927(w)	17,000,000	0.25	0.50	1.75	10.00	—
1928(w)	13,600,000	0.25	0.50	1.75	9.00	—
1930(w)	22,500,000	4.00	10.00	25.00	40.00	—
1931(w)	9,000,000	0.50	1.00	2.00	10.00	—
1932(w)	12,000,000	0.50	1.00	2.00	10.00	—
1933(w)	7,000,000	0.50	1.00	2.00	10.00	—
1934(w)	5,900,000	0.50	1.00	2.00	12.00	—
1935(w)	7,300,000	0.50	1.00	2.00	5.00	—
1936(w)	12,600,000	0.50	1.00	2.00	5.00	—
1937(w)	17,370,000	0.25	0.50	0.75	2.50	—
1938(w)	20,530,000	0.25	0.50	0.75	2.50	—
1939(w)	12,000,000	0.25	0.50	0.75	2.50	—

Y# 9   2 GROSZE
2.0000 g., Brass, 17.6 mm. **Obv:** Crowned eagle with wings open **Rev:** Stylized value

Date	Mintage	F	VF	XF	Unc	BU
1923	20,500,000	3.50	12.50	22.50	45.00	60.00

Y# 9a   2 GROSZE
2.0000 g., Bronze, 17.6 mm. **Obv:** Crowned eagle with wings open **Rev:** Stylized value

Date	Mintage	F	VF	XF	Unc	BU
1925(w)	39,000,000	0.50	2.00	4.50	10.00	—
1927(w)	15,300,000	0.50	2.00	4.50	10.00	—
1928(w)	13,400,000	0.50	2.00	4.50	10.00	—
1930(w)	20,000,000	0.50	2.00	4.50	10.00	—
1931(w)	9,500,000	1.75	2.50	5.50	12.75	—
1932(w)	6,500,000	2.00	4.00	6.00	15.00	—
1933(w)	7,000,000	2.00	4.00	6.00	15.00	—
1934(w)	9,350,000	1.75	3.00	7.50	17.50	—
1935(w)	5,800,000	0.20	0.75	2.00	5.00	—
1936(w)	5,800,000	0.20	0.75	2.00	5.00	—
1937(w)	17,360,000	0.20	0.40	0.60	2.50	—
1938(w)	20,530,000	0.20	0.40	0.60	2.50	—
1939(w)	12,000,000	0.20	0.40	0.60	2.50	—

Y# 10   5 GROSZY
3.0000 g., Brass, 20. mm. **Obv:** Crowned eagle with wings open **Rev:** Stylized value

Date	Mintage	F	VF	XF	Unc	BU
1923	32,000,000	0.50	2.00	5.00	10.00	—

Y# 10a   5 GROSZY
3.0000 g., Bronze, 20 mm. **Obv:** Crowned eagle with wings open **Rev:** Stylized value

Date	Mintage	F	VF	XF	Unc	BU
1923 Proof	350	Value: 150				
1925(w)	45,500,000	0.20	0.40	4.00	8.00	—
1928(w)	8,900,000	0.20	0.40	5.00	10.00	—
1930(w)	14,200,000	0.20	0.40	5.00	12.00	—
1931(w)	1,500,000	0.50	1.00	10.00	20.00	—
1934(w)	420,000	5.00	7.50	35.00	75.00	—
1935(w)	4,660,000	0.20	0.40	0.60	5.00	—
1936(w)	4,660,000	0.20	0.40	0.60	5.00	—
1937(w)	9,050,000	0.20	0.40	0.60	2.50	—
1938(w)	17,300,000	0.20	0.40	0.60	2.50	—
1939(w)	10,000,000	0.20	0.40	0.60	2.50	—

Y# 11   10 GROSZY
2.0000 g., Nickel, 17.6 mm. **Obv:** Crowned eagle with wings open **Rev:** Value within wreath

Date	Mintage	F	VF	XF	Unc	BU
1923	100,000,000	0.20	0.45	0.80	1.25	—

Y# 12   20 GROSZY
3.0000 g., Nickel, 20 mm. **Obv:** Crowned eagle with wings open **Rev:** Value within wreath

Date	Mintage	F	VF	XF	Unc	BU
1923	150,000,000	0.35	0.75	1.25	2.00	—
1923 Proof	10	Value: 300				

Y# 13   50 GROSZY
5.0000 g., Nickel, 23 mm. **Obv:** Crowned eagle with wings open **Rev:** Value within wreath

Date	Mintage	F	VF	XF	Unc	BU
1923	100,000,000	0.40	0.80	1.50	3.50	—
1923 Proof	10	Value: 350				

Y# 15   ZLOTY
5.0000 g., 0.7500 Silver 0.1206 oz. ASW, 23 mm. **Obv:** Crowned eagle with wings open **Rev:** Bust left **Edge:** Reeded

Date	Mintage	F	VF	XF	Unc	BU
1924 (Paris)	16,000,000	2.50	6.00	20.00	55.00	—
Note: Torch and cornucopia flank date						
1924 (Birmingham); Proof	8	Value: 600				
1925 (London)	24,000,000	2.50	5.00	12.00	30.00	—
Note: Dot after date						
1925 (London); Proof	—	Value: 4,000				

Y# 14   ZLOTY
7.0000 g., Nickel, 25 mm. **Obv:** Crowned eagle with wings open **Rev:** Value within stylized design

Date	Mintage	F	VF	XF	Unc	BU
1929(w)	32,000,000	0.75	1.50	2.50	7.00	—

Y# 16   2 ZLOTE
10.0000 g., 0.7500 Silver 0.2411 oz. ASW, 27 mm. **Obv:** Crowned eagle with wings open **Rev:** Head left **Edge:** Reeded

Date	Mintage	F	VF	XF	Unc	BU
1924 (Paris)	8,200,000	5.50	10.00	20.00	85.00	—
Note: Torch and cornucopia flank date						
1924 H (Birmingham)	1,200,000	17.50	35.00	175	450	
1924 (Birmingham); Proof	60	Value: 600				

Date	Mintage	F	VF	XF	Unc	BU
1924 (Philadelphia)	800,000	10.00	20.00	60.00	125	—
Note: Without privy marks, coin alignment						
1925 (London)	11,000,000	5.00	9.00	17.50	47.50	—
Note: Dot after date						
1925 (Philadelphia)	5,200,000	6.50	12.00	40.00	75.00	—
Note: Without privy marks						

Y# 20   2 ZLOTE
4.4000 g., 0.7500 Silver 0.1061 oz. ASW, 22 mm. **Obv:** National arms **Obv. Leg.:** RRZECZPOSPOLITA POLSKA **Rev:** Radiant head of Queen Jadwiga left **Edge:** Milled

Date	Mintage	F	VF	XF	Unc	BU
1932(w)	15,700,000	2.50	5.00	9.00	15.00	20.00
1933(w)	9,250,000	2.25	4.00	7.00	13.50	16.50
1934(w)	250,000	4.00	7.00	12.00	27.50	—

Y# 27   2 ZLOTE
4.4000 g., 0.7500 Silver 0.1061 oz. ASW, 22 mm. **Obv:** Crowned eagle with wings open **Rev:** Head of Jozef Pilsudski left **Edge:** Reeded

Date	Mintage	F	VF	XF	Unc	BU
1934(w)	10,425,000	3.00	6.00	10.00	25.00	—
1936(w)	75,000	20.00	75.00	150	300	—

Y# 30   2 ZLOTE
4.4000 g., 0.7500 Silver 0.1061 oz. ASW, 22 mm. **Subject:** 15th Anniversary of Gdynia Seaport **Obv:** Crowned eagle with wings open **Rev:** Sailing ship

Date	Mintage	F	VF	XF	Unc	BU
1936(w)	3,918,000	3.00	6.00	12.00	30.00	—

Y# 17.1   5 ZLOTYCH
25.0000 g., 0.9000 Silver 0.7234 oz. ASW, 37 mm. **Subject:** Adoption of the Constitution **Obv:** Crowned eagle with wings open **Rev:** 100 pearls in circle **Edge:** SALUS REIPUBLICAS SUPREMA LEX

Date	Mintage	F	VF	XF	Unc	BU
1925(w)	100	175	350	750	1,650	—

Y# 17.1a   5 ZLOTYCH
Gold **Obv:** Crowned eagle with wings open **Rev:** Adoption of the Constitution

Date	Mintage	F	VF	XF	Unc	BU
1925(w) Rare	2	—	—	—	—	—

Y# 17.2   5 ZLOTYCH
25.0000 g., 0.9000 Silver 0.7234 oz. ASW **Obv:** Without monogram by date **Rev:** Adoption of the Constitution

Date	Mintage	F	VF	XF	Unc	BU
1925(w)	1,000	—	—	600	1,000	—

Y# 17.2a   5 ZLOTYCH
Bronze **Obv:** Crowned imperial eagle **Rev:** Adoption of the Constitution

Date	Mintage	F	VF	XF	Unc	BU
1925(w)	100	—	—	250	350	—

Y# 17.2c   5 ZLOTYCH
Gold **Obv:** Without monogram by date **Rev:** Adoption of the Constitution

Date	Mintage	F	VF	XF	Unc	BU
1925(w) Rare	1	—	—	—	—	—

Y# 17.3 5 ZLOTYCH
25.0000 g., 0.9000 Silver 0.7234 oz. ASW **Obv:** Monogram by date **Rev:** 81 pearls in circle

Date	Mintage	F	VF	XF	Unc	BU
1925(w)	1,000	.—		600	1,000	—

Y# 17.3a 5 ZLOTYCH
43.3300 g., 0.9000 Gold 1.2537 oz. AGW **Obv:** Crowned eagle with wings open, mint mark to right of date **Rev:** Adoption of the Constitution **Edge:** SALUS REIPUBLICAE SUPREMA LEX

Date	Mintage	F	VF	XF	Unc	BU
1925(w) Rare	1	—	—	—	—	—

Y# 17.4 5 ZLOTYCH
43.3300 g., 0.9000 Gold 1.2537 oz. AGW **Obv:** Without monogram by date, with mint mark **Rev:** Adoption of the Constitution

Date	Mintage	F	VF	XF	Unc	BU
1925(w)	1,000	—	—	1,250	1,350	—

Y# 17.4a 5 ZLOTYCH
Tombac **Obv:** Crowned imperial eagle **Rev:** Adoption of the Constitution

Date	Mintage	F	VF	XF	Unc	BU
1925(w)	100	—	—	300	400	—

Y# 18 5 ZLOTYCH
18.0000 g., 0.7500 Silver 0.4340 oz. ASW, 33 mm. **Obv:** Crowned eagle with wings open **Rev:** Winged Victory right **Edge:** SALUS REIPUBLICAE SUPREMA LEX

Date	Mintage	F	VF	XF	Unc	BU
1928(w)	7,500,000	15.00	30.00	65.00	125	—
Note: Conjoined arrow and K mint mark						
1928 Error	Inc. above	40.00	75.00	100	225	—
Note: "SUPRMA" edge inscription						
1928 Without mint mark	10,000,000	13.50	25.00	65.00	125	—
Note: 4,300,000 struck in London and 5,700,000 in Belgium						
1930(w)	5,900,000	100	350	800	—	—
1931(w)	2,200,000	120	400	850	—	—
1932(w)	3,100,000	150	450	950	—	—

Y# 19.1 5 ZLOTYCH
18.0000 g., 0.7500 Silver 0.4340 oz. ASW, 33 mm. **Subject:** Centennial of 1830 Revolution **Obv:** Crowned eagle with wings open flanked by value **Rev:** Pole with flag and banner divides dates **Edge:** SALUS REIPUBLICAE SUPREMA LEX

Date	Mintage	F	VF	XF	Unc	BU
1930(w)	1,000,000	8.00	16.50	45.00	120	—

Y# 19.2 5 ZLOTYCH
18.0000 g., 0.7500 Silver 0.4340 oz. ASW **Obv:** Crowned imperial eagle **Rev:** Pole with flag and banner divides dates **Note:** High relief.

Date	Mintage	F	VF	XF	Unc	BU
1930(w)	200	75.00	175	375	800	—

Y# 21 5 ZLOTYCH
11.0000 g., 0.7500 Silver 0.2652 oz. ASW, 28 mm. **Obv:** National arms flanked by value **Obv. Leg.:** RZECZPOSPOLITA POLSKA **Rev:** Radiant head of Queen Jadwiga left **Edge:** Reeded

Date	Mintage	F	VF	XF	Unc	BU
1932 (Warsaw : tiny arrow in space between talons of eagle's left claw)	1,000,000	15.00	50.00	225	500	—
1932 (London); without mint mark	3,000,000	—	BV	6.50	18.00	28.00
1933(w)	11,000,000	—	BV	5.00	15.00	20.00
1933(w) Proof	100	—	—	—	—	—
1934(w)	250,000	BV	5.00	10.00	25.00	—

Y# 25 5 ZLOTYCH
11.0000 g., 0.7500 Silver 0.2652 oz. ASW, 28 mm. **Obv:** Rifle Corps symbol below eagle with wings open **Rev:** Head of Jozef Pilsudski left **Edge:** Reeded

Date	Mintage	F	VF	XF	Unc	BU
1934(w)	300,000	6.00	9.00	17.50	40.00	—

Y# 28 5 ZLOTYCH
11.0000 g., 0.7500 Silver 0.2652 oz. ASW, 28 mm. **Obv:** Radiant crowned eagle with wings open **Rev:** Head of Jozef Pilsudski left **Edge:** Reeded

Date	Mintage	F	VF	XF	Unc	BU
1934(w)	6,510,000	BV	5.00	9.00	22.00	30.00
1935(w)	1,800,000	BV	5.00	10.00	25.00	35.00
1936(w)	1,800,000	BV	5.00	10.00	25.00	35.00
1938(w)	289,000	5.00	7.50	15.00	30.00	—

Y# 31 5 ZLOTYCH
11.0000 g., 0.7500 Silver 0.2652 oz. ASW, 28 mm. **Subject:** 15th Anniversary of Gdynia Seaport **Obv:** Crowned eagle with wings open **Rev:** Sailing ship **Edge:** Reeded

Date	Mintage	F	VF	XF	Unc	BU
1936(w)	1,000,000	7.00	12.00	25.00	60.00	—

Y# 32 10 ZLOTYCH
3.2258 g., 0.9000 Gold 0.0933 oz. AGW, 19 mm. **Obv:** Crowned eagle with wings open **Rev:** Crowned head left **Note:** Never released into circulation; similar design to Y#33.

Date	Mintage	F	VF	XF	Unc	BU
ND(1925)(w)	50,350		BV	100	200	300

Y# 22 10 ZLOTYCH
22.0000 g., 0.7500 Silver 0.5305 oz. ASW, 34 mm. **Obv:** National arms **Obv. Leg.:** RZECZPOSPOLITA POLSKA **Rev:** Radiant head of Queen Jadwiga left **Edge:** Reeded

Date	Mintage	F	VF	XF	Unc	BU
1932(w)	3,100,000	BV	9.50	15.00	40.00	50.00
Note: Warsaw Mint : tiny arrow in space between talons of eagle's left claw						
1932	6,000,000	BV	9.50	15.00	40.00	50.00
Note: London Mint: without mint mark						
1932(w) Proof	100	—	—	—	—	—
1933(w)	2,800,000	BV	9.50	15.00	40.00	50.00
1933(w) Proof	100	—	—	—	—	—

Y# 23 10 ZLOTYCH
22.0000 g., 0.7500 Silver 0.5305 oz. ASW, 34 mm. **Subject:** Jan III Sobieski's Victory Over the Turks **Obv:** Crowned eagle with wings open **Rev:** Uniformed bust right **Edge:** Reeded

Date	Mintage	F	VF	XF	Unc	BU
ND(1933)(w)	300,000	10.00	20.00	35.00	80.00	—
ND(1933)(w) Proof	100	—	—	—	—	—

Y# 24 10 ZLOTYCH
22.0000 g., 0.7500 Silver 0.5305 oz. ASW, 34 mm. **Subject:** 70th Anniversary of 1863 Insurrection **Obv:** Crowned eagle with wings open **Rev:** Head of Romuald Traugutt 3/4 facing divides dates **Edge:** Reeded

Date	Mintage	F	VF	XF	Unc	BU
ND(1933)(w)	300,000	12.00	20.00	45.00	100	—
ND(1933)(w) Proof	100	—	—	—	—	—

Y# 26 10 ZLOTYCH
22.0000 g., 0.7500 Silver 0.5305 oz. ASW, 34 mm. **Obv:** Rifle Corps symbol below eagle with wings open **Rev:** Head of Jozef Pilsudski left **Edge:** Reeded

Date	Mintage	F	VF	XF	Unc	BU
1934(w)	300,000	10.00	20.00	40.00	85.00	—

Y# 29 10 ZLOTYCH
22.0000 g., 0.7500 Silver 0.5305 oz. ASW, 34 mm. **Obv:** Eagle with wings open with no symbols below **Rev:** Head of Jozef Pilsudski left **Edge:** Reeded

Date	Mintage	F	VF	XF	Unc	BU
1934(w)	200,000	12.00	10.00	40.00	90.00	—
1935(w)	1,670,000	BV	10.00	14.00	35.00	50.00
1936(w)	2,130,000	BV	10.00	14.00	35.00	50.00
1937(w)	908,000	BV	10.00	16.00	50.00	—
1938(w)	234,000	10.00	12.00	22.00	60.00	—
1939(w)	—	BV	10.00	16.00	50.00	—

Y# 33 20 ZLOTYCH
6.4516 g., 0.9000 Gold 0.1867 oz. AGW, 21 mm. **Obv:** Crowned eagle with wings open **Rev:** Crowned head of Boleslaw I left **Edge:** Reeded **Note:** Never released into circulation.

Date	Mintage	F	VF	XF	Unc	BU
ND(1925)(w)	27,240	—	BV	200	300	400

WWII GERMAN OCCUPATION

OCCUPATION COINAGE

Y# 34 GROSZ
1.1700 g., Zinc, 14.7 mm. **Obv:** Crowned eagle with wings open **Rev:** Stylized value

Date	Mintage	F	VF	XF	Unc	BU
1939(w)	33,909,000	0.50	1.00	1.75	3.50	—

Y# 35 5 GROSZY
1.7200 g., Zinc, 16 mm. **Obv:** Crowned eagle with wings open, hole in center **Rev:** Stylized value, hole in center

Date	Mintage	F	VF	XF	Unc	BU
1939(w)	15,324,000	0.50	1.50	2.00	5.00	—

Y# 36 10 GROSZY
2.0000 g., Zinc, 17.6 mm. **Obv:** Crowned imperial eagle **Rev:** Value

Date	Mintage	F	VF	XF	Unc	BU
1923(w)	42,175,000	0.10	0.20	0.40	2.00	—

Note: Actually struck in 1941-44

Y# 37 20 GROSZY
2.9700 g., Zinc, 20 mm. **Obv:** Crowned eagle with wings open **Rev:** Value within wreath

Date	Mintage	F	VF	XF	Unc	BU
1923(w)	40,025,000	0.15	0.25	0.50	2.00	—

Note: Actually struck in 1941-44

Y# 38 50 GROSZY
5.0000 g., Nickel Plated Iron, 23 mm. **Obv:** Crowned eagle with wings open **Rev:** Value within wreath

Date	Mintage	F	VF	XF	Unc	BU
1938(w)	32,000,000	1.00	2.00	4.00	8.50	—

Y# 38a 50 GROSZY
Iron **Obv:** Crowned eagle with wings open **Rev:** Value within wreath

Date	Mintage	F	VF	XF	Unc	BU
1938(w)	—	1.25	2.50	5.00	10.00	—

Note: Varieties exist

TOKEN COINAGE
Lodz Ghetto, 1942-1944

A major industrial city in western Poland before World War II and site of the first wartime ghetto under German occupation (May 1940). It was also the last ghetto to close during the war (August 1944). Token coinage was struck in 1942 and 1943, in the name of the Jewish Elders of Litzmannstadt. This series has seen very little circulation, but is commonly found in conditions from slightly to badly corroded. The badly corroded specimens have the appearance of zinc.

KM# Tn1 10 PFENNIG
Aluminum-Magnesium **Rev:** Value

Date	Mintage	VG	F	VF	XF	Unc
1942	Est. 100,000	60.00	125	200	—	—

Note: Most were destroyed or remelted as the design was too similar to regular German coinage

KM# Tn5 10 PFENNIG
Aluminum-Magnesium **Obv:** Star in circle **Rev:** Value

Date	Mintage	VG	F	VF	XF	Unc
1942	100,000	35.00	50.00	65.00	125	—

KM# Tn2 5 MARK
Aluminum **Obv:** Value **Rev:** Star at upper left, GETTO and date lower right

Date	Mintage	VG	F	VF	XF	Unc
1943	600,000	5.00	10.00	25.00	45.00	—

KM# Tn2a 5 MARK
Aluminum-Magnesium **Obv:** Value **Rev:** Star at upper left, GETTO and date lower right

Date	Mintage	VG	F	VF	XF	Unc
1943	Inc. above	20.00	40.00	75.00	—	—

KM# Tn3 10 MARK
Aluminum **Obv:** Value **Rev:** Star at upper left, GETTO and date lower right **Note:** Thick and thin planchets exist.

Date	Mintage	VG	F	VF	XF	Unc
1943	100,000	5.00	10.00	25.00	45.00	—

KM# Tn3a 10 MARK
Aluminum-Magnesium **Obv:** Value **Rev:** Star at upper left, GETTO and date lower right

Date	Mintage	VG	F	VF	XF	Unc
1943	Inc. above	25.00	45.00	85.00	—	—

KM# Tn4 20 MARK
Aluminum **Obv:** Value **Rev:** Star at upper left, GETTO and date lower right **Note:** Beware of numerous counterfeits.

Date	Mintage	VG	F	VF	XF	Unc
1943	—	75.00	110	150	250	—

REPUBLIC
Post War

STANDARD COINAGE

Y# 39 GROSZ
0.5000 g., Aluminum, 14.7 mm. **Obv:** Eagle with wings open **Rev:** Value at upper right of sprig **Note:** 116,000 were struck at Warsaw, the remainder at Budapest.

Date	Mintage	F	VF	XF	Unc	BU
1949	400,116,000	0.10	0.20	0.30	0.75	—

Y# 40 2 GROSZE
0.5800 g., Aluminum, 16 mm. **Obv:** Eagle with wings open **Rev:** Value at upper right of sprig **Edge:** Reeded **Note:** 106,000 were struck at Warsaw, the remainder at Budapest.

Date	Mintage	F	VF	XF	Unc	BU
1949	300,106,000	0.10	0.25	0.50	1.00	—

Y# 41 5 GROSZY
3.0000 g., Bronze, 20 mm. **Obv:** Eagle with wings open **Rev:** Value at upper right of sprig

Date	Mintage	F	VF	XF	Unc	BU
1949	300,000,000	0.10	0.25	0.50	1.00	—

Y# 41a 5 GROSZY
1.0000 g., Aluminum, 20 mm. **Obv:** Eagle with wings open **Rev:** Value at upper right of sprig

Date	Mintage	F	VF	XF	Unc	BU
1949	200,000,000	0.10	0.25	0.75	1.50	—

Y# 42 10 GROSZY
2.0000 g., Copper-Nickel, 17.6 mm. **Obv:** Eagle with wings open **Rev:** Value above sprig

Date	Mintage	F	VF	XF	Unc	BU
1949	200,000,000	0.20	0.40	0.60	1.50	—

Y# 42a 10 GROSZY
0.7000 g., Aluminum, 17.6 mm. **Obv:** Eagle with wings open
Rev: Value above sprig

Date	Mintage	F	VF	XF	Unc	BU
1949	31,047,000	0.10	0.25	0.75	2.50	—

Y# 43 20 GROSZY
2.8900 g., Copper-Nickel, 20 mm. **Obv:** Eagle with wings open
Rev: Value above sprig

Date	Mintage	F	VF	XF	Unc	BU
1949	133,383,000	0.25	0.45	0.75	2.00	—

Y# 43a 20 GROSZY
1.0000 g., Aluminum, 20 mm. **Obv:** Eagle with wings open
Rev: Value above sprig

Date	Mintage	F	VF	XF	Unc	BU
1949	197,472,000	0.10	0.25	0.75	2.50	—

Y# 44 50 GROSZY
5.0000 g., Copper-Nickel, 23 mm. **Obv:** Eagle with wings open
Rev: Value above sprig **Edge:** Reeded

Date	Mintage	F	VF	XF	Unc	BU
1949	109,000,000	0.35	0.65	1.00	2.50	—

Y# 44a 50 GROSZY
1.6000 g., Aluminum, 23 mm. **Obv:** Eagle with wings open
Rev: Value above sprig **Edge:** Reeded

Date	Mintage	F	VF	XF	Unc	BU
1949	59,393,000	0.10	0.25	1.50	5.00	—

Y# 45 ZLOTY
7.0000 g., Copper-Nickel, 25 mm. **Obv:** Eagle with wings open
Rev: Value within wreath **Edge:** Reeded

Date	Mintage	F	VF	XF	Unc	BU
1949	87,053,000	1.00	1.50	2.25	4.00	—

Y# 45a ZLOTY
2.1200 g., Aluminum, 25 mm. **Obv:** Eagle with wings open
Rev: Value within wreath **Edge:** Reeded

Date	Mintage	F	VF	XF	Unc	BU
1949	43,000,000	0.10	0.25	2.50	6.00	—

PEOPLES REPUBLIC

STANDARD COINAGE

Y# A46 5 GROSZY
0.6100 g., Aluminum, 16 mm. **Obv:** Eagle with wings open
Rev: Value to upper right of sprig

Date	Mintage	F	VF	XF	Unc	BU
1958	53,521,000	—	—	0.10	0.20	—
1959	28,564,000	—	—	0.10	0.15	—
1960	12,246,000	—	0.50	1.50	2.75	—
1961	29,502,000	—	—	0.10	0.20	—
1962	90,257,000	—	—	0.10	0.15	—
1963	20,878,000	—	—	0.10	0.15	—
1965MW	5,050,000	—	0.75	2.00	4.00	—
1967MW	10,056,000	—	0.75	2.00	4.00	—
1968MW	10,196,000	—	0.75	2.00	4.00	—
1970MW	20,095,000	—	—	0.10	0.20	—
1971MW	20,000,000	—	—	0.10	0.20	—
1972MW	10,000,000	—	—	0.10	0.20	—

Y# AA47 10 GROSZY
0.7000 g., Aluminum, 17.6 mm. **Obv:** Eagle with wings open
Rev: Value above sprig **Edge:** Plain **Note:** Varieties in date size exist.

Date	Mintage	F	VF	XF	Unc	BU
1961	73,400,000	—	0.75	2.50	4.00	—
1962	25,362,000	—	1.75	5.00	20.00	—
1963	40,434,000	—	—	0.50	1.50	—
1965MW	50,521,000	—	0.25	1.00	2.00	—
1966MW	70,749,000	—	—	0.50	1.50	—
1967MW	62,059,000	—	—	0.50	1.50	—
1968MW	62,204,000	—	—	0.50	1.50	—
1969MW	71,566,000	—	—	0.50	1.00	—
1970MW	38,844,000	—	—	0.10	0.50	—
1971MW	50,000,000	—	—	0.10	0.50	—
1972MW	60,000,000	—	—	0.10	0.50	—
1973MW	80,000,000	—	—	0.10	0.25	—
1973 Rare						
1974	50,000,000	—	—	0.10	0.15	—

Note: Struck at Kremnica Mint

Date	Mintage	F	VF	XF	Unc	BU
1975MW	50,000,000	—	—	0.10	0.15	—
1976MW	100,000,000	—	—	—	0.10	—
1977MW	100,000,000	—	—	—	0.10	—
1978MW	71,204,000	—	—	—	0.10	—
1979MW	73,191,000	—	—	—	0.10	—
1979MW Proof	5,000	Value: 1.00				
1980MW	60,623,000	—	—	—	0.10	—
1980MW Proof	5,000	Value: 1.00				
1981MW	70,000,000	—	—	—	0.10	—
1981MW Proof	5,000	Value: 1.00				
1983MW	9,600,000	—	—	—	0.10	—
1985MW	9,957,000	—	—	—	0.10	—

Y# A47 20 GROSZY
1.0000 g., Aluminum, 20 mm. **Obv:** Eagle with wings open
Rev: Value above sprig **Edge:** Plain **Note:** Date varieties exist.

Date	Mintage	F	VF	XF	Unc	BU
1957	3,940,000	—	5.00	17.00	40.00	—
1961	53,108,000	—	1.75	3.75	8.00	—
1962	19,140,000	—	2.00	5.00	12.50	—
1963	41,217,000	—	—	0.50	2.00	—
1965MW	32,022,000	—	—	0.50	2.00	—
1966MW	23,860,000	—	—	0.50	2.00	—
1967MW	29,099,000	—	—	1.00	5.00	—
1968MW	29,191,000	—	—	1.00	5.00	—
1969MW	40,227,000	—	—	0.50	1.50	—
1970MW	20,028,000	—	—	0.10	1.00	—
1971MW	20,000,000	—	—	0.10	1.00	—
1972MW	60,000,000	—	—	0.10	1.00	—
1973	50,000,000	—	—	0.10	0.50	—

Note: Struck at Kremnica Mint

Date	Mintage	F	VF	XF	Unc	BU
1973MW	65,000,000	—	—	0.10	0.50	—

Note: Struck at Kremnica Mint

Date	Mintage	F	VF	XF	Unc	BU
1975MW	50,000,000	—	—	0.10	0.50	—
1976MW Large date	100,000,000	—	—	0.10	0.50	—
1976MW Small date	Inc. above	—	—	0.10	0.50	—
1977MW	80,730,000	—	—	0.10	0.20	—
1978MW	50,730,000	—	—	0.10	0.20	—
1979MW	45,252,000	—	—	0.10	0.20	—
1979MW Proof	5,000	Value: 1.00				
1980MW	30,020,000	—	—	0.10	0.20	—
1980MW Proof	5,000	Value: 1.00				
1981MW	60,082,000	—	—	0.10	0.20	—
1981MW Proof	5,000	Value: 1.00				
1983MW	—	—	—	0.10	0.20	—
1985MW	16,227,000	—	—	0.10	0.20	—

Y# 48.1 50 GROSZY
1.6000 g., Aluminum, 23 mm. **Obv:** Eagle with wings open
Rev: Value above sprig **Edge:** Reeded

Date	Mintage	F	VF	XF	Unc	BU
1957	91,316,000	—	0.75	2.00	5.00	—
1965MW	22,090,000	—	0.25	1.50	4.00	—
1967MW	2,027,000	—	1.25	4.00	15.00	—

Date	Mintage	F	VF	XF	Unc	BU
1968MW	2,065,000	—	1.25	4.00	15.00	—
1970MW	3,273,000	—	0.15	0.30	2.00	—
1971MW	7,000,000	—	0.10	0.25	1.00	—
1972MW	10,000,000	—	0.10	0.25	0.50	—
1973MW	39,000	—	0.10	0.20	0.50	—
1974MW	33,000,000	—	0.10	0.20	0.50	—
1975	25,000,000	—	0.10	0.20	0.50	—

Note: Struck at Kremnica Mint

Date	Mintage	F	VF	XF	Unc	BU
1976	25,000,000	—	0.10	0.20	0.40	—

Note: Struck at Kremnica Mint

Date	Mintage	F	VF	XF	Unc	BU
1977MW	50,000,000	—	0.10	0.20	0.40	—
1978MW	50,020,000	—	0.10	0.20	0.40	—
1978	18,600,000	—	0.10	0.20	0.40	—

Note: Struck at Kremnica Mint

Date	Mintage	F	VF	XF	Unc	BU
1982MW	16,067,000	—	0.10	0.20	0.40	—
1982MW Proof	5,000	Value: 3.50				
1983MW	39,667,000	—	0.10	0.20	0.40	—
1984MW	44,217,000	—	0.10	0.20	0.40	—
1985MW	49,052,000	—	0.10	0.20	0.40	—

Y# 48.2 50 GROSZY
1.6000 g., Aluminum, 23 mm. **Obv:** Eagle with wings open
Rev: Value above sprig **Edge:** Reeded

Date	Mintage	F	VF	XF	Unc	BU
1986MW	45,796,000	—	0.10	0.20	0.40	—
1986MW Proof	5,000	Value: 3.50				
1987MW	21,257,000	—	0.10	0.20	0.40	—
1987MW Proof	5,000	Value: 3.50				

Y# 49.1 ZLOTY
2.1200 g., Aluminum, 25 mm. **Obv:** Eagle with wings open
Rev: Value within wreath **Edge:** Reeded

Date	Mintage	F	VF	XF	Unc	BU
1957	58,631,000	—	1.00	3.50	20.00	—
1965MW	15,015,000	—	0.50	1.00	3.00	—
1966MW	18,185,000	—	0.75	2.00	4.00	—
1967MW	1,002,000	—	2.25	6.00	15.00	—
1968MW	1,176,000	—	2.25	6.00	15.00	—
1969MW	3,024,000	—	1.25	3.00	6.00	—
1970MW	6,016,000	—	0.15	0.50	1.50	—
1971MW	6,000,000	—	0.15	0.50	1.00	—
1972MW	7,000,000	—	0.15	0.50	1.00	—
1973MW	15,000,000	—	0.10	0.50	1.00	—
1974MW	42,000,000	—	0.10	0.15	0.50	—
1975	22,000,000	—	0.10	0.15	0.50	—

Note: Struck at Kremnica Mint

Date	Mintage	F	VF	XF	Unc	BU
1975MW	33,000,000	—	0.10	0.15	0.50	—
1976	22,000,000	—	0.10	0.50	1.00	—

Note: Struck at Kremnica Mint

Date	Mintage	F	VF	XF	Unc	BU
1977MW	65,000,000	—	0.10	0.50	1.00	—
1978	16,399,999	—	0.10	0.50	1.50	—

Note: Struck at Kremnica Mint

Date	Mintage	F	VF	XF	Unc	BU
1978MW	80,000,000	—	0.10	0.50	1.00	—
1980MW	100,002,000	—	0.10	0.15	0.50	—
1980MW Proof	5,000	Value: 2.50				
1981MW	4,082,000	—	0.10	0.15	1.00	—
1981MW Proof	5,000	Value: 2.50				
1982MW	59,643,000	—	0.10	0.15	0.30	—
1982MW Proof	5,000	Value: 3.50				
1983MW	49,636,000	—	0.10	0.15	0.25	—
1984MW	61,036,000	—	0.10	0.15	0.25	—
1985MW	167,939,000	—	0.10	0.15	0.25	—

Y# 49.2 ZLOTY
2.2000 g., Aluminum, 25 mm. **Obv:** Eagle with wings open
Rev: Value within wreath **Edge:** Reeded

Date	Mintage	F	VF	XF	Unc	BU
1986MW	130,697,000	—	0.10	0.15	0.25	—
1986MW Proof	5,000	Value: 3.50				
1987MW	100,081,000	—	0.10	0.15	0.25	—
1987MW Proof	5,000	Value: 3.50				

Date	Mintage	F	VF	XF	Unc	BU
1988MW	96,400,000	—	0.10	0.15	0.25	—
1988MW Proof	5,000	Value: 3.50				

Y# 49.3 ZLOTY
0.5700 g., Aluminum, 16 mm. **Obv:** Eagle with wings open
Rev: Value within wreath **Edge:** Reeded

Date	Mintage	F	VF	XF	Unc	BU
1989MW	49,410,000	—	0.10	0.15	0.25	—
1989MW Proof	5,000	Value: 3.50				
1990MW	30,667,000	—	0.10	0.15	0.25	—
1990MW Proof	5,000	Value: 3.50				

Y# 46 2 ZLOTE
2.7000 g., Aluminum, 27 mm. **Obv:** Eagle with wings open
Rev: Value above design and fruit **Edge:** Reeded

Date	Mintage	F	VF	XF	Unc	BU
1958	83,640,000	—	0.20	1.50	6.00	—
1959	7,170,000	—	0.50	4.00	20.00	—
1960	36,131,000	—	0.20	0.50	3.00	—
1970MW	2,013,999	—	0.30	1.00	4.00	—
1971MW	3,000,000	—	0.20	1.00	4.00	—
1972MW	3,000,000	—	0.20	1.00	4.00	—
1973MW	10,000,000	—	0.15	0.50	1.50	—
1974MW	46,000,000	—	0.15	0.30	1.00	—

Y# 80.1 2 ZLOTE
3.0000 g., Brass, 21 mm. **Obv:** Eagle with wings open
Rev: Value above design **Edge:** Reeded

Date	Mintage	F	VF	XF	Unc	BU
1975	25,000,000	—	0.15	0.25	0.50	—
Note: Struck at Leningrad Mint						
1976	60,000,000	—	0.15	0.25	0.50	—
Note: Struck at Leningrad Mint						
1977	50,000,000	—	0.15	0.25	0.50	—
Note: Struck at Leningrad Mint						
1978	2,600,000	—	0.15	0.25	1.75	—
Note: Struck at Leningrad Mint						
1978MW	2,382,000	—	0.15	0.25	1.75	—
1979MW	85,752,000	—	0.15	0.25	0.50	—
1979MW Proof	5,000	Value: 2.50				
1980MW	66,610,000	—	0.15	0.25	0.50	—
1980MW Proof	5,000	Value: 2.50				
1981MW	40,306,000	—	0.15	0.25	0.50	—
1981MW Proof	5,000	Value: 2.50				
1982MW	43,318,000	—	0.15	0.25	0.50	—
1982MW Proof	5,000	Value: 3.50				
1983MW	35,244,000	—	0.15	0.25	0.50	—
1984MW	59,999,000	—	0.15	0.25	0.50	—
1985MW	100,300,000	—	0.15	0.25	0.50	—

Y# 80.2 2 ZLOTE
3.0000 g., Brass, 21 mm. **Obv:** Eagle with wings open
Rev: Value above design **Edge:** Reeded

Date	Mintage	F	VF	XF	Unc	BU
1986MW	60,718,000	—	0.15	0.25	0.50	—
1986MW Proof	5,000	Value: 3.50				
1987MW	44,673,000	—	0.15	0.25	0.50	—
1987MW Proof	5,000	Value: 3.50				
1988MW	94,651,000	—	0.15	0.25	0.50	—
1988MW Proof	5,000	Value: 3.50				

Y# 80.3 2 ZLOTE
0.7100 g., Aluminum, 18 mm. **Obv:** Eagle with wings open
Rev: Value above design **Edge:** Reeded

Date	Mintage	F	VF	XF	Unc	BU
1989MW	91,494,000	—	0.10	0.20	0.40	—
1989MW Proof	5,000	Value: 3.50				
1990MW	40,723,000	—	0.10	0.20	0.40	—
1990MW Proof	5,000	Value: 3.50				

Y# 47 5 ZLOTYCH
3.4500 g., Aluminum, 29 mm. **Obv:** Eagle with wings open
Rev: Fisherman with net **Edge:** Reeded

Date	Mintage	F	VF	XF	Unc	BU
1958	1,328,000	—	7.50	12.50	20.00	—
Note: Two date varieties exist for strikes dated 1958						
1959	56,811,000	—	0.75	2.50	7.00	—
1960	16,300,999	—	0.25	1.50	5.00	—
1971MW	16,300,999	—	7.50	12.50	20.00	—
1973MW	5,000,000	—	0.20	1.00	4.00	—
1974MW	46,000,000	—	0.20	0.50	2.50	—

Y# 81.1 5 ZLOTYCH
5.0000 g., Brass, 24 mm. **Obv:** Eagle with wings open
Rev: Value **Edge:** Reeded **Note:** Varieties in the letter size exist.

Date	Mintage	F	VF	XF	Unc	BU
1975	25,000,000	—	0.20	0.40	0.85	—
Note: Struck at Leningrad Mint						
1976	60,000,000	—	0.20	0.40	0.85	—
Note: Struck at Leningrad Mint						
1977	50,000,000	—	0.20	0.40	0.85	—
Note: Struck at Leningrad Mint						
1978MW Rare	—	—	—	—	—	—
1979MW	5,098,000	—	0.20	0.40	1.50	—
1979MW	5,000	Value: 3.50				
1980MW	10,100,000	—	0.20	0.40	0.85	—
1980MW Proof	5,000	Value: 2.50				
1981MW	4,008,000	—	0.20	0.40	1.75	—
1981MW Proof	5,000 #	Value: 2.50				
1982MW	25,379,000	—	0.20	0.40	0.85	—
1982MW Proof	5,000	Value: 3.50				
1983MW	30,531,000	—	0.20	0.40	0.85	—
1984MW	85,598,000	—	0.20	0.40	0.85	—
1985MW	20,501,000	—	0.20	0.40	0.85	—

Y# 81.2 5 ZLOTYCH
5.0000 g., Brass, 24 mm. **Obv:** Eagle with wings open
Rev: Value **Edge:** Reeded

Date	Mintage	F	VF	XF	Unc	BU
1986MW	57,108,000	—	0.20	0.40	0.85	—
1986MW Proof	5,000	Value: 3.50				
1987MW	58,843,000	—	0.20	0.40	0.85	—
1987MW Proof	5,000	Value: 3.50				
1988MW	18,668,000	—	0.20	0.40	0.85	—
1988MW Proof	5,000	Value: 3.50				

Y# 81.3 5 ZLOTYCH
0.8800 g., Aluminum, 20 mm. **Obv:** Eagle with wings open
Rev: Value **Edge:** Reeded

Date	Mintage	F	VF	XF	Unc	BU
1989MW	30,253,000	—	0.15	0.30	0.65	—
1989MW Proof	5,000	Value: 3.50				
1990MW	38,248,000	—	0.15	0.30	0.65	—
1990MW Proof	5,000	Value: 3.50				

Y# 50 10 ZLOTYCH
12.9000 g., Copper-Nickel, 31 mm. **Obv:** Eagle with wings open
Rev: Head of Tadeusz Kosciuszko left **Edge:** Reeded

Date	Mintage	F	VF	XF	Unc	BU
1959	13,107,000	—	0.60	2.00	6.50	—
1960	27,551,000	—	0.60	2.00	6.50	—
1966MW	4,157,000	—	1.00	8.00	18.00	—

Y# 50a 10 ZLOTYCH
9.5000 g., Copper-Nickel, 28 mm. **Obv:** Eagle with wings open
Rev: Head of Tadeusz Kosciuszko left **Note:** Reduced size.

Date	Mintage	F	VF	XF	Unc	BU
1969MW	5,428,000	—	0.50	1.75	5.00	—
1970MW	13,783,000	—	0.50	1.00	2.00	—
1971MW	12,000,000	—	0.50	1.00	2.00	—
1972MW	10,000,000	—	0.50	1.00	2.00	—
1973MW	3,900,000	—	0.50	2.00	8.00	—

Y# 51 10 ZLOTYCH
12.9000 g., Copper-Nickel, 31 mm. **Obv:** Eagle with wings open
Rev: Bust of Mikolaj Kopernik facing **Edge:** Reeded

Date	Mintage	F	VF	XF	Unc	BU
1959	12,559,000	—	0.75	1.25	2.50	—
1965MW	3,000,000	—	1.00	5.00	15.00	—

Y# 51a 10 ZLOTYCH
9.5000 g., Copper-Nickel, 28 mm. **Obv:** Eagle with wings open
Rev: Bust of Mikolaj Kopernik facing **Note:** Reduced size.

Date	Mintage	F	VF	XF	Unc	BU
1967MW	2,128,000	—	0.75	2.00	7.50	—
1968MW	9,389,000	—	0.75	1.25	2.50	—
1969MW	8,612,000	—	0.75	1.25	2.75	—

Y# 52   10 ZLOTYCH

12.9000 g., Copper-Nickel, 31 mm. **Subject:** 600th Anniversary of Jagiello University **Obv:** Eagle with wings open **Rev:** Stylized crowned head left **Edge:** Reeded **Note:** Legends raised.

Date	Mintage	F	VF	XF	Unc	BU
ND(1964)	2,610,000	—	0.50	1.50	3.50	—

Y# 52a   10 ZLOTYCH

12.9000 g., Copper-Nickel, 31 mm. **Subject:** 600th Anniversary of Jagiello University **Obv:** Eagle with wings open **Rev:** Stylized crowned head left **Edge:** Reeded **Note:** Legends incuse.

Date	Mintage	F	VF	XF	Unc	BU
ND(1964)	2,612,000	—	0.50	1.50	3.50	—

Y# 54   10 ZLOTYCH

12.9000 g., Copper-Nickel, 31 mm. **Subject:** 700th Anniversary of Warsaw **Obv:** Eagle with wings open **Rev:** Nike of Warsaw with sword **Edge:** Reeded

Date	Mintage	F	VF	XF	Unc	BU
1965MW	3,492,000	—	0.75	2.00	3.50	5.00

Y# 55   10 ZLOTYCH

12.9000 g., Copper-Nickel, 31 mm. **Subject:** 700th Anniversary of Warsaw **Obv:** Stylized eagle with wings open **Rev:** Sigismund Pillar **Edge:** Reeded

Date	Mintage	F	VF	XF	Unc	BU
1965MW	2,000,000	—	0.75	2.00	3.50	5.00

Y# 56   10 ZLOTYCH

9.5000 g., Copper-Nickel, 28 mm. **Subject:** 200th Anniversary of Warsaw Mint **Obv:** Stylized eagle with wings open **Rev:** Sigismund Pillar **Edge:** W DWUSETNA ROCZNICE MENNICY WARSZAWSKIEJ

Date	Mintage	F	VF	XF	Unc	BU
1966MW	102,000	—	2.50	6.50	22.50	40.00

Y# 58   10 ZLOTYCH

9.5000 g., Copper-Nickel, 28 mm. **Subject:** 20th Anniversary - Death of General Swierczewski **Obv:** Eagle with wings open **Rev:** Military head left **Edge:** Reeded

Date	Mintage	F	VF	XF	Unc	BU
1967MW	2,000,000	—	0.50	1.00	2.25	—

Y# 59   10 ZLOTYCH

9.5000 g., Copper-Nickel, 28 mm. **Subject:** Centennial - Birth of Marie Sklodowska Curie **Obv:** Eagle with wings open **Rev:** Head facing **Edge:** Reeded

Date	Mintage	F	VF	XF	Unc	BU
1967MW	2,000,000	—	0.50	1.00	2.25	—

Y# 60   10 ZLOTYCH

9.5000 g., Copper-Nickel, 28 mm. **Subject:** 25th Anniversary - Peoples Army **Obv:** Eagle with wings open standing on perch **Rev:** XXV and helmeted head right **Edge:** Reeded

Date	Mintage	F	VF	XF	Unc	BU
1968MW	2,000,000	—	0.50	1.00	2.25	—

Y# 61   10 ZLOTYCH

9.5000 g., Copper-Nickel, 28 mm. **Subject:** 25th Anniversary - Peoples Republic **Obv:** Eagle with wings open within circle **Rev:** Radiant design within circle **Edge:** Reeded

Date	Mintage	F	VF	XF	Unc	BU
1969MW	2,000,000	—	0.50	1.00	2.25	—

Y# 62   10 ZLOTYCH

9.5000 g., Copper-Nickel, 28 mm. **Subject:** 25th Anniversary - Provincial Annexations **Obv:** Eagle with wings open, shield divides value **Rev:** Assorted shields **Edge:** Reeded

Date	Mintage	F	VF	XF	Unc	BU
1970MW	2,000,000	—	0.50	1.00	2.25	—

Y# 63   10 ZLOTYCH

9.5000 g., Copper-Nickel, 28 mm. **Series:** F.A.O. **Obv:** Eagle with wings open on shield **Rev:** Atlantic turbot and ear of barley **Edge:** Reeded

Date	Mintage	F	VF	XF	Unc	BU
1971MW	2,000,000	—	0.75	1.50	3.50	5.00

Y# 64   10 ZLOTYCH

9.5000 g., Copper-Nickel, 28 mm. **Subject:** 50th Anniversary - Battle of Upper Silesia **Obv:** Eagle with wings open divides date **Rev:** Design and emblem **Edge:** Reeded

Date	Mintage	F	VF	XF	Unc	BU
1971MW	2,000,000	—	0.50	1.00	2.25	—

Y# 65   10 ZLOTYCH

9.5000 g., Copper-Nickel, 28 mm. **Subject:** 50th Anniversary - Gdynia Seaport **Obv:** Eagle with wings open **Rev:** Map and emblem **Edge:** Reeded

Date	Mintage	F	VF	XF	Unc	BU
1972MW	2,000,000	—	0.50	1.00	2.25	—

Y# 73   10 ZLOTYCH

7.7000 g., Copper-Nickel, 25 mm. **Obv:** Eagle with wings open divides date **Rev:** Head of Boleslaw Prus left **Edge:** Reeded

Date	Mintage	F	VF	XF	Unc	BU
1975MW	35,000,000	—	0.25	0.65	1.25	—
1976MW	20,000,000	—	0.25	0.65	1.25	—
1977MW	25,000,000	—	0.25	0.65	1.25	—
1978MW	4,006,999	—	0.25	0.75	2.25	—
1981MW	2,655,000	—	0.25	1.00	3.75	—
1981MW Proof	5,000	Value: 5.50				
1982MW	16,341,000	—	0.25	0.65	1.25	—
1982MW Proof	5,000	Value: 6.50				
1983MW	14,248,000	—	0.25	0.65	1.25	—
1984MW	19,064,000	—	0.25	0.65	1.25	—

Y# 74   10 ZLOTYCH

7.7000 g., Copper-Nickel, 25 mm. **Obv:** Eagle with wings open **Rev:** Head of Adam Micklewicz left **Edge:** Reeded

Date	Mintage	F	VF	XF	Unc	BU
1975MW	35,000,000	—	0.25	0.65	1.25	—
1976MW	20,000,000	—	0.25	0.65	1.25	—

Y# 152.1   10 ZLOTYCH
7.7000 g., Copper-Nickel, 25 mm.   **Obv:** Eagle with wings open
Rev: Value **Edge:** Reeded

Date	Mintage	F	VF	XF	Unc	BU
1984MW	15,756,000	—	0.20	0.50	1.00	—
1985MW	5,282,000	—	0.20	0.50	1.00	—
1986MW	31,043,000	—	0.20	0.50	1.00	—
1986MW Proof	5,000	Value: 4.00				
1987MW	69,636,000	—	0.20	0.50	1.00	—
1987MW Proof	5,000	Value: 4.00				
1988MW	102,493,000	—	0.20	0.50	1.00	—
1988MW Proof	5,000	Value: 4.00				

Y# 152.2   10 ZLOTYCH
4.2700 g., Brass, 22 mm.   **Obv:** Imperial eagle **Rev:** Value
Edge: Reeded

Date	Mintage	F	VF	XF	Unc	BU
1989MW	80,800,000	—	0.20	0.40	0.80	—
1989MW Proof	5,000	Value: 4.00				
1990MW	106,892,000	—	0.20	0.40	0.80	—
1990MW Proof	5,000	Value: 4.00				

Y# 67   20 ZLOTYCH
10.1500 g., Copper-Nickel, 29 mm.   **Obv:** Eagle with wings open
within circle **Rev:** Value within designed waterfall **Edge:** Reeded

Date	Mintage	F	VF	XF	Unc	BU
1973	25,000,000	—	0.25	1.00	2.50	—
Note: Struck at Kremnica Mint						
1974	12,000,000	—	0.25	0.75	1.50	—
Note: Struck at Kremnica Mint						
1976	20,000,000	—	0.25	0.75	1.50	—
Note: Struck at Warsaw Mint						

Y# 69   20 ZLOTYCH
10.1500 g., Copper-Nickel, 29 mm.   **Obv:** Eagle with wings open,
value below **Rev:** Bust of Marceli Nowotko 1/4 left **Edge:** Reeded

Date	Mintage	F	VF	XF	Unc	BU
1974MW	10,000,000	—	0.25	1.00	2.50	—
1975	10,000,000	—	0.25	1.00	2.00	—
Note: Struck at Kremnica Mint						
1976	20,000,000	—	0.25	0.75	1.50	—
Note: Struck at Kremnica Mint						
1976MW	30,000,000	—	0.25	0.75	1.50	—
1977MW	16,000,000	—	0.25	1.00	2.00	—
1983MW	152,000	—	0.25	5.00	12.50	—

Y# 70   20 ZLOTYCH
10.1500 g., Copper-Nickel, 29 mm.   **Subject:** 25th Anniversary
of the Comcon **Obv:** Imperial eagle above value **Rev:** Half
sunflower, half cog wheel **Edge:** Reeded

Date	Mintage	F	VF	XF	Unc	BU
1974MW	2,000,000	—	0.75	1.25	2.50	—

Y# 75   20 ZLOTYCH
10.1500 g., Copper-Nickel, 29 mm.   **Subject:** International
Women's Year **Obv:** Polish eagle above value **Rev:** Stylized head
left **Edge:** Reeded

Date	Mintage	F	VF	XF	Unc	BU
1975MW	2,000,000	—	0.75	1.25	2.50	—

Y# 95   20 ZLOTYCH
10.1500 g., Copper-Nickel, 29 mm.   **Obv:** Imperial eagle above
value **Rev:** Head of Maria Konopnicka facing **Edge:** Reeded

Date	Mintage	F	VF	XF	Unc	BU
1978MW	2,010,000	—	0.75	1.25	2.75	—

Y# 97   20 ZLOTYCH
10.1500 g., Copper-Nickel, 29 mm.   **Subject:** First Polish
Cosmonaut **Obv:** Imperial eagle above value **Rev:** Cosmonaut
head 1/4 left **Edge:** Reeded

Date	Mintage	F	VF	XF	Unc	BU
1978MW	2,009,000	—	0.75	1.25	2.75	—

Y# 99   20 ZLOTYCH
10.1500 g., Copper-Nickel, 29 mm.   **Series:** International Year
of the Child **Obv:** Imperial eagle above value **Rev:** Children
playing **Edge:** Reeded

Date	Mintage	F	VF	XF	Unc	BU
1979MW	2,007,000	—	1.00	1.50	3.00	—
1979MW Proof	5,000	Value: 12.00				

Y# 108   20 ZLOTYCH
10.1500 g., Copper-Nickel, 29 mm.   **Series:** 1980 Olympics
Obv: Imperial eagle above value **Rev:** Runner **Edge:** Reeded

Date	Mintage	F	VF	XF	Unc	BU
1980MW	2,012,000	—	1.00	1.75	5.00	—
1980MW Proof	5,000	Value: 12.00				

Y# 112   20 ZLOTYCH
10.1500 g., Copper-Nickel, 29 mm.   **Subject:** 50th Anniversary
- Training Ship Daru Pomorza **Obv:** Imperial eagle above value
Rev: Sailing ship **Edge:** Reeded

Date	Mintage	F	VF	XF	Unc	BU
1980MW	2,069,200	—	1.00	1.75	3.50	—
1980MW Proof	5,000	Value: 10.00				

Y# 153.1   20 ZLOTYCH
8.7000 g., Copper-Nickel, 26.5 mm.   **Obv:** Eagle with wings open
Rev: Value **Edge:** Reeded **Note:** Circulation coinage.

Date	Mintage	F	VF	XF	Unc	BU
1984MW	12,703,000	—	0.25	0.60	1.25	1.50
1985MW	15,514,000	—	0.25	0.60	1.25	1.50
1986MW	37,959,000	—	0.25	0.60	1.25	1.50
1986MW Proof	5,000	Value: 4.00				
1987MW	22,213,000	—	0.25	0.60	1.25	1.50
1987MW Proof	5,000	Value: 4.00				
1988MW	14,994,000	—	0.25	0.60	1.25	1.50
1988MW Proof	5,000	Value: 4.00				

Y# 153.2   20 ZLOTYCH
5.6500 g., Copper-Nickel, 24 mm.   **Obv:** Eagle with wings open
Rev: Value **Edge:** Reeded **Note:** Reduced size.

Date	Mintage	F	VF	XF	Unc	BU
1989MW	95,974,000	—	0.25	0.35	0.75	1.00
1989MW Proof	5,000	Value: 4.00				
1990MW	104,712,000	—	0.25	0.35	0.75	1.00
1990MW Proof	5,000	Value: 4.00				

Y# 66   50 ZLOTYCH
12.7500 g., 0.7500 Silver 0.3074 oz. ASW, 30 mm.   **Obv:** Eagle
with wings open **Rev:** Head of Fryderyk Chopin left

Date	Mintage	F	VF	XF	Unc	BU
1972MW Proof	49,999	Value: 20.00				
1974MW Proof	10,375	Value: 22.00				

Y# 100 50 ZLOTYCH
11.7000 g., Copper-Nickel, 30.5 mm. **Obv:** Imperial eagle above value **Rev:** Bust of Duke Mieszko I 3/4 left **Edge:** Reeded

Date	Mintage	F	VF	XF	Unc	BU
1979MW	2,640,000	—	1.00	2.00	5.00	—
1979MW Proof	5,000	Value: 15.00				

Y# 114 50 ZLOTYCH
11.7000 g., Copper-Nickel, 30.5 mm. **Obv:** Imperial eagle above value **Rev:** King Boleslaw I Chrobry **Edge:** Reeded

Date	Mintage	F	VF	XF	Unc	BU
1980MW	2,564,000	—	1.00	2.00	5.00	—
1980MW Proof	5,000	Value: 12.50				

Y# 117 50 ZLOTYCH
11.7000 g., Copper-Nickel, 30.5 mm. **Obv:** Imperial eagle above value **Rev:** Crowned bust of Duke Kazimierz I Odnowiciel facing **Edge:** Reeded

Date	Mintage	F	VF	XF	Unc	BU
1980MW	2,504,000	—	1.00	2.00	5.00	—
1980MW Proof	5,000	Value: 12.50				

Y# 122 50 ZLOTYCH
11.7000 g., Copper-Nickel, 30.5 mm. **Obv:** Imperial eagle above value **Rev:** General Broni Wladyslaw Sikorski left **Edge:** Reeded

Date	Mintage	F	VF	XF	Unc	BU
1981MW	2,505,000	—	1.00	2.00	5.00	—
1981MW Proof	5,000	Value: 12.50				

Y# 124 50 ZLOTYCH
11.7000 g., Copper-Nickel, 30.5 mm. **Obv:** Imperial eagle above value **Rev:** Crowned bust of King Boleslaw II Smialy 1/4 right **Edge:** Reeded

Date	Mintage	F	VF	XF	Unc	BU
1981MW	2,538,000	—	1.00	2.00	4.50	—
1981MW Proof	5,000	Value: 12.00				

Y# 128 50 ZLOTYCH
11.7000 g., Copper-Nickel, 30.5 mm. **Obv:** Imperial eagle above value **Rev:** Head of King Wladyslaw I Herman 3/4 left **Edge:** Reeded

Date	Mintage	F	VF	XF	Unc	BU
1981MW	2,500,000	—	1.00	2.00	4.50	—
1981MW Proof	5,000	Value: 12.00				

Y# 127 50 ZLOTYCH
11.7000 g., Copper-Nickel, 30.5 mm. **Series:** F.A.O. - World Food Day **Obv:** Imperial eagle above value **Rev:** F.A.O. logo within circle **Edge:** Reeded

Date	Mintage	F	VF	XF	Unc	BU
1981MW	2,524,000	—	1.00	2.00	4.50	—
1981MW Proof	5,000	Value: 12.00				

Y# 133 50 ZLOTYCH
11.7000 g., Copper-Nickel, 30.5 mm. **Obv:** Imperial eagle above value **Rev:** King Boleslaw III Krzywousty **Edge:** Reeded

Date	Mintage	F	VF	XF	Unc	BU
1982MW	2,616,000	—	1.00	2.00	4.50	—
1982MW Proof	5,000	Value: 12.50				

Y# 142 50 ZLOTYCH
11.7000 g., Copper-Nickel, 30.5 mm. **Subject:** 150th Anniversary of Great Theater **Obv:** Imperial eagle above value **Rev:** Theater building **Edge:** Reeded

Date	Mintage	F	VF	XF	Unc	BU
1983MW	615,000	—	1.00	4.00	8.00	—

Y# 145 50 ZLOTYCH
11.7000 g., Copper-Nickel, 30.5 mm. **Obv:** Imperial eagle above value **Rev:** King Jan III Sobieski facing **Edge:** Reeded

Date	Mintage	F	VF	XF	Unc	BU
1983MW	2,576,000	—	1.00	2.00	4.50	—

Y# 146 50 ZLOTYCH
11.7000 g., Copper-Nickel, 30.5 mm. **Obv:** Imperial eagle above value **Rev:** Bust of Ignacy Lukasiewicz right **Edge:** Reeded

Date	Mintage	F	VF	XF	Unc	BU
1983MW	612,000	—	1.00	4.00	8.00	—

Y# 57 100 ZLOTYCH
20.0000 g., 0.9000 Silver 0.5787 oz. ASW, 35 mm. **Subject:** Polish Millennium **Obv:** Eagle with wings open within assorted shields around border **Rev:** Two figures standing behind shield within circle

Date	Mintage	F	VF	XF	Unc	BU
1966MW	196,859	—	—	9.50	13.50	22.50

Y# 68 100 ZLOTYCH
16.5000 g., 0.6250 Silver 0.3315 oz. ASW, 32 mm. **Subject:** 500th Anniversary - Birth of Mikolaj Kopernik, scientist **Obv:** Eagle with wings open within circle **Rev:** Head of Mikolaj Kopernik 1/4 left

Date	Mintage	F	VF	XF	Unc	BU
1973MW Proof	51,000	Value: 20.00				
1974MW Proof	50,000	Value: 20.00				

Y# 71 100 ZLOTYCH
16.5000 g., 0.6250 Silver 0.3315 oz. ASW, 32 mm. **Subject:** 40th Anniversary - Death of Maria Sklodowska Curie **Obv:** Imperial eagle above value **Rev:** Profile of Curie left with radiation lines running from the symbol of the element at right

Date	Mintage	F	VF	XF	Unc	BU
1974MW Proof	50,000	Value: 15.50				

Y# 76 100 ZLOTYCH
16.5000 g., 0.6250 Silver 0.3315 oz. ASW, 32 mm. **Obv:** Imperial eagle above value **Rev:** Royal castle in Warsaw

Date	Mintage	F	VF	XF	Unc	BU
1975MW Proof	50,177	Value: 15.50				

Y# 77   100 ZLOTYCH
16.5000 g., 0.6250 Silver 0.3315 oz. ASW, 32 mm.   **Obv:** Imperial eagle above value **Rev:** Ignacy Jan Paderewski, composer, left

Date	Mintage	F	VF	XF	Unc	BU
1975MW Proof	60,184	Value: 12.50				

Y# 78   100 ZLOTYCH
16.5000 g., 0.6250 Silver 0.3315 oz. ASW, 32 mm.   **Obv:** Imperial eagle above value **Rev:** Bust of Helena Modrzejewska right

Date	Mintage	F	VF	XF	Unc	BU
1975MW Proof	60,158	Value: 12.50				

Y# 82   100 ZLOTYCH
16.5000 g., 0.6250 Silver 0.3315 oz. ASW, 32 mm.
Obv: Imperial eagle above value **Rev:** Tadeusz Kosciuszko right

Date	Mintage	F	VF	XF	Unc	BU
1976MW Proof	100,148	Value: 12.50				

Y# 84   100 ZLOTYCH
16.5000 g., 0.6250 Silver 0.3315 oz. ASW, 32 mm.
Obv: Imperial eagle above value **Rev:** Head of Kazimierz Pulaski left

Date	Mintage	F	VF	XF	Unc	BU
1976MW Proof	100,334	Value: 12.50				

Y# 87   100 ZLOTYCH
16.5000 g., 0.6250 Silver 0.3315 oz. ASW, 32 mm.
Series: Environment Protection **Obv:** Imperial eagle above value
Rev: Buffalo

Date	Mintage	F	VF	XF	Unc	BU
1977MW Proof	30,050	Value: 30.00				

Y# 88   100 ZLOTYCH
16.5000 g., 0.6250 Silver 0.3315 oz. ASW, 32 mm.   **Obv:** Imperial eagle above value **Rev:** Henryk Sienkiewicz, Writer, left

Date	Mintage	F	VF	XF	Unc	BU
1977MW Proof	20,000	Value: 20.00				

Y# 89   100 ZLOTYCH
16.5000 g., 0.6250 Silver 0.3315 oz. ASW, 32 mm.   **Obv:** Imperial eagle above value **Rev:** Head of Wladyslaw Reymont 1/4 right

Date	Mintage	F	VF	XF	Unc	BU
1977MW Proof	20,150	Value: 30.00				

Y# 91   100 ZLOTYCH
16.5000 g., 0.6250 Silver 0.3315 oz. ASW, 32 mm.
Obv: Imperial eagle above value **Rev:** Castle

Date	Mintage	F	VF	XF	Unc	BU
1977MW Proof	30,000	Value: 27.50				

Y# 92   100 ZLOTYCH
16.5000 g., 0.6250 Silver 0.3315 oz. ASW, 32 mm.
Obv: Imperial eagle above value **Rev:** Bust of Adam Mickiewicz facing

Date	Mintage	F	VF	XF	Unc	BU
1978MW Proof	30,000	Value: 16.50				

Y# 93   100 ZLOTYCH
16.5000 g., 0.6250 Silver 0.3315 oz. ASW, 32 mm.
Series: Environment Protection **Obv:** Imperial eagle above value
Rev: Moose heading left

Date	Mintage	F	VF	XF	Unc	BU
1978MW Proof	30,000	Value: 30.00				

Y# 94   100 ZLOTYCH
16.5000 g., 0.6250 Silver 0.3315 oz. ASW, 32 mm.
Subject: 100th Anniversary - Birth of Janusz Korczak
Obv: Imperial eagle above value **Rev:** Bust facing

Date	Mintage	F	VF	XF	Unc	BU
1978MW Proof	30,000	Value: 16.50				

Y# 96   100 ZLOTYCH
16.5000 g., 0.6250 Silver 0.3315 oz. ASW, 32 mm.
Series: Environment Protection **Obv:** Imperial eagle above value
Rev: Beaver

Date	Mintage	F	VF	XF	Unc	BU
1978MW Proof	30,000	Value: 30.00				

Y# 98   100 ZLOTYCH
16.5000 g., 0.6250 Silver 0.3315 oz. ASW, 32 mm.   **Obv:** Imperial eagle above value **Rev:** Head of Henryk Wieniawski 3/4 left

Date	Mintage	F	VF	XF	Unc	BU
1979MW Proof	30,000	Value: 16.50				

Y# 103   100 ZLOTYCH
16.5000 g., 0.6250 Silver 0.3315 oz. ASW, 32 mm.
Obv: Imperial eagle above value **Rev:** Ludwik Zamenhof left

Date	Mintage	F	VF	XF	Unc	BU
1979MW Proof	30,000	Value: 16.50				

Y# 104   100 ZLOTYCH
16.5000 g., 0.6250 Silver 0.3315 oz. ASW, 32 mm. **Series:**
Environment Protection **Obv:** Imperial eagle above value **Rev:** Lynx

Date	Mintage	F	VF	XF	Unc	BU
1979MW Proof	20,000	Value: 27.50				

Y# 105   100 ZLOTYCH
16.5000 g., 0.6250 Silver 0.3315 oz. ASW, 32 mm.
Series: Environment Protection **Obv:** Imperial eagle above value
Rev: Chamois

Date	Mintage	F	VF	XF	Unc	BU
1979MW Proof	20,000	Value: 27.50				

Y# 120   100 ZLOTYCH
16.5000 g., 0.6250 Silver 0.3315 oz. ASW, 32 mm. **Subject:**
450th Anniversary - Birth of Jan Kochanowski, Poet **Obv:** Imperial
eagle above value **Rev:** Bust of Jan Kochanowski 1/4 right

Date	Mintage	F	VF	XF	Unc	BU
1980MW Proof	10,000	Value: 45.00				

Y# 109   100 ZLOTYCH
16.5000 g., 0.6250 Silver 0.3315 oz. ASW, 32 mm. **Series:** 1980
Olympics **Obv:** Imperial eagle above value **Rev:** Olympic rings
and runner

Date	Mintage	F	VF	XF	Unc	BU
1980MW Proof	10,000	Value: 32.50				

Y# 121   100 ZLOTYCH
16.5000 g., 0.6250 Silver 0.3315 oz. ASW, 32 mm.
Series: Environment Protection **Obv:** Imperial eagle above value
Rev: Cappercaillie

Date	Mintage	F	VF	XF	Unc	BU
1980MW Proof	18,000	Value: 27.50				

Y# 123   100 ZLOTYCH
16.5000 g., 0.6250 Silver 0.3315 oz. ASW, 32 mm. **Obv:** Imperial
eagle above value **Rev:** General Broni Wladyslaw Sikorski left

Date	Mintage	F	VF	XF	Unc	BU
1981MW Proof	12,000	Value: 20.00				

Y# 126   100 ZLOTYCH
16.5000 g., 0.6250 Silver 0.3315 oz. ASW, 32 mm.
Series: Environment Protection **Obv:** Imperial eagle above value
Rev: Horse right

Date	Mintage	F	VF	XF	Unc	BU
1981MW Proof	12,000	Value: 30.00				

Y# 136   100 ZLOTYCH
14.1500 g., 0.7500 Silver 0.3412 oz. ASW, 30 mm.
Subject: Visit of Pope John Paul II **Obv:** Imperial eagle above
value **Rev:** Bust left

Date	Mintage	F	VF	XF	Unc	BU
1982CHI	8,700	—	—	—	55.00	—
1982CHI Proof	3,750	Value: 100				
1985CHI Unique	—	—	—	—	—	—
1985CHI Proof	5	—	—	—	—	—
1986CHI	80	—	—	—	450	—
1986CHI Proof	128	Value: 500				

Y# 141   100 ZLOTYCH
16.5000 g., 0.6250 Silver 0.3315 oz. ASW **Series:** Environment
Protection **Obv:** Imperial eagle above value **Rev:** Stork walking
right

Date	Mintage	F	VF	XF	Unc	BU
1982MW Proof	12,000	Value: 30.00				

Y# 147   100 ZLOTYCH
16.5000 g., 0.6250 Silver 0.3315 oz. ASW, 32 mm.
Series: Environment Protection **Obv:** Imperial eagle above value
Rev: Bear walking right

Date	Mintage	F	VF	XF	Unc	BU
1983MW Proof	8,000	Value: 40.00				

Y# 148   100 ZLOTYCH
10.8000 g., Copper-Nickel, 29.5 mm. **Obv:** Imperial eagle above
value **Rev:** Wincenty Witos 3/4 facing **Edge:** Reeded

Date	Mintage	F	VF	XF	Unc	BU
1984MW	1,530,000	—	—	—	3.00	5.00

Y# 151   100 ZLOTYCH
10.8000 g., Copper-Nickel, 29.5 mm. **Subject:** 40th Anniversary
of Peoples Republic **Obv:** Imperial eagle above value **Rev:** 40
PRL within design **Edge:** Reeded

Date	Mintage	F	VF	XF	Unc	BU
1984MW	2,595,000	—	—	—	3.00	5.00

Y# 155   100 ZLOTYCH
10.8000 g., Copper-Nickel, 29.5 mm. **Obv:** Imperial eagle above
value **Rev:** King Przemyslaw II **Edge:** Reeded

Date	Mintage	F	VF	XF	Unc	BU
1985MW	2,924,000	—	—	—	3.00	5.00

Y# 157   100 ZLOTYCH
9.6000 g., Nickel Plated Steel, 29.5 mm. **Subject:** Polish
Women's Memorial Hospital Center **Obv:** Imperial eagle above
value **Rev:** Woman breast-feeding Child **Edge:** Reeded

Date	Mintage	F	VF	XF	Unc	BU
1985MW	1,927,000	—	—	—	3.00	5.00

Y# 160   100 ZLOTYCH
10.8000 g., Copper-Nickel, 29.5 mm. **Obv:** Imperial eagle above
value **Rev:** Bust of King Wladyslaw I Lokietek 1/4 right
Edge: Reeded

Date	Mintage	F	VF	XF	Unc	BU
1986MW	2,540,000	—	—	—	3.00	5.00
1986MW Proof	5,000	Value: 12.00				

Y# 167   100 ZLOTYCH
10.8000 g., Copper-Nickel, 29.5 mm. **Obv:** Imperial eagle above
value **Rev:** King Kazimierz III half left **Edge:** Reeded

Date	Mintage	F	VF	XF	Unc	BU
1987MW	2,479,000	—	—	—	3.50	5.50
1987MW Proof	5,000	Value: 12.50				

Y# 182   100 ZLOTYCH
10.8000 g., Copper-Nickel, 29.5 mm. **Subject:** 70th Anniversary
- Wielkopolskiego Insurrection **Obv:** Imperial eagle above value
Rev: Uniformed conjoined busts left **Edge:** Reeded

Date	Mintage	F	VF	XF	Unc	BU
1988MW	2,513,000	—	—	—	3.00	5.00
1988MW Proof	5,000	Value: 12.00				

Y# 183 100 ZLOTYCH
10.8000 g., Copper-Nickel, 29.5 mm. **Obv:** Imperial eagle above value **Rev:** Queen Jadwiga 1384-1399 **Edge:** Reeded

Date	Mintage	F	VF	XF	Unc	BU
1988MW	2,469,000	—	—	—	3.00	5.00
1988MW Proof	5,000	Value: 12.00				

Y# 72 200 ZLOTYCH
14.4700 g., 0.6250 Silver 0.2908 oz. ASW, 31 mm.
Subject: 30th Anniversary - Polish Peoples Republic **Obv:** Eagle with wings open within square with value below **Rev:** XXX LAT PRL in square within shaded design **Edge:** Reeded

Date	Mintage	F	VF	XF	Unc	BU
1974MW	13,062,000	—	—	—	6.50	7.50
1974MW Proof	6,000	Value: 22.50				

Y# 79 200 ZLOTYCH
14.4700 g., 0.7500 Silver 0.3489 oz. ASW, 31 mm. **Subject:** 30th Anniversary - Victory Over Fascism **Obv:** Eagle with wings open divides date **Rev:** Conjoined military heads left **Edge:** Reeded

Date	Mintage	F	VF	XF	Unc	BU
1975MW	1,826,000	—	—	—	7.00	10.00
1975MW Proof	2,600	Value: 25.00				

Y# 86 200 ZLOTYCH
14.4700 g., 0.6250 Silver 0.2908 oz. ASW, 31 mm. **Series:** XXI Olympics **Obv:** Imperial eagle above value **Rev:** Rings and torch **Edge:** Reeded

Date	Mintage	F	VF	XF	Unc	BU
1976MW	2,072,000	—	—	—	8.50	12.00
1976MW Proof	11,000	Value: 22.50				

Y# 101 200 ZLOTYCH
17.6000 g., 0.7500 Silver 0.4244 oz. ASW, 33 mm. **Obv:** Imperial eagle above value **Rev:** Uniformed bust of Duke Mieszko I 1/4 left

Date	Mintage	F	VF	XF	Unc	BU
1979MW Proof	12,150	Value: 150				

Y# 110 200 ZLOTYCH
17.6000 g., 0.7500 Silver 0.4244 oz. ASW, 33 mm.
Series: Winter Olympics **Obv:** Imperial eagle above value **Rev:** Torch below ski jumper

Date	Mintage	F	VF	XF	Unc	BU
1980MW Proof	32,040	Value: 16.50				

Y# 110a 200 ZLOTYCH
17.6000 g., 0.7500 Silver 0.4244 oz. ASW, 33 mm.
Series: Winter Olympics **Obv:** Imperial eagle above value **Rev:** Ski jumper, no torch below

Date	Mintage	F	VF	XF	Unc	BU
1980MW Proof	28,040	Value: 14.50				

Y# 115 200 ZLOTYCH
17.6000 g., 0.7500 Silver 0.4244 oz. ASW, 33 mm.
Obv: Imperial eagle above value **Rev:** King Boleslaw I Chrobry

Date	Mintage	F	VF	XF	Unc	BU
1980MW Proof	12,000	Value: 100				

Y# 118 200 ZLOTYCH
17.6000 g., 0.7500 Silver 0.4244 oz. ASW, 33 mm.
Obv: Imperial eagle above value **Rev:** Bust of Duke Kazimierz I facing

Date	Mintage	F	VF	XF	Unc	BU
1980MW Proof	12,000	Value: 45.00				

Y# 125 200 ZLOTYCH
17.6000 g., 0.7500 Silver 0.4244 oz. ASW, 33 mm. **Obv:** Imperial eagle above value **Rev:** King Bolaslaw II Smialy 3/4 facing

Date	Mintage	F	VF	XF	Unc	BU
1981MW Proof	12,000	Value: 45.00				

Y# 129 200 ZLOTYCH
17.6000 g., 0.7500 Silver 0.4244 oz. ASW, 33 mm.
Obv: Imperial eagle above value **Rev:** Bust of King Wladyslaw I Herman left within circle

Date	Mintage	F	VF	XF	Unc	BU
1981MW Proof	12,000	Value: 45.00				

Y# 130 200 ZLOTYCH
17.6000 g., 0.7500 Silver 0.4244 oz. ASW, 33 mm.
Subject: World Soccer Championship Games in Spain
Obv: Imperial eagle above value **Rev:** Stylized soccer player, date and names within grid-lined background

Date	Mintage	F	VF	XF	Unc	BU
1982MW Proof	21,000	Value: 16.50				

Y# 132 200 ZLOTYCH
17.6000 g., 0.7500 Silver 0.4244 oz. ASW, 33 mm.
Obv: Imperial eagle above value **Rev:** King Boleslaw III Krzywousty

Date	Mintage	F	VF	XF	Unc	BU
1982MW Proof	12,000	Value: 50.00				

Y# 137 200 ZLOTYCH
28.3000 g., 0.7500 Silver 0.6824 oz. ASW, 40 mm.
Subject: Visit of Pope John Paul II **Obv:** Imperial eagle above value **Rev:** Bust left

Date	Mintage	F	VF	XF	Unc	BU
1982CHI	3,000	—	—	—	475	575
1982CHI Proof	3,650	Value: 600				
1985CHI Unique	—	—	—	—	—	—
1985CHI Proof	5	—	—	—	—	—
1986CHI	32	—	—	—	850	—
1986CHI Proof	75	Value: 900				

Y# 143   200 ZLOTYCH
17.6000 g., 0.7500 Silver 0.4244 oz. ASW, 33 mm.
Obv: Imperial eagle above value **Rev:** King Jan III Sobieski

Date	Mintage	F	VF	XF	Unc	BU
1983MW Proof	11,000	Value: 45.00				

Y# 149   200 ZLOTYCH
17.6000 g., 0.7500 Silver 0.4244 oz. ASW, 33 mm. **Series:**
Winter Olympics **Obv:** Imperial eagle above value **Rev:** Ice skater

Date	Mintage	F	VF	XF	Unc	BU
1984MW Proof	15,000	Value: 22.50				

Y# 150   200 ZLOTYCH
17.6000 g., 0.7500 Silver 0.4244 oz. ASW, 33 mm. **Series:**
Summer Olympics **Obv:** Imperial eagle above value **Rev:** Hurdler

Date	Mintage	F	VF	XF	Unc	BU
1984MW Proof	16,000	Value: 20.00				

Y# 83   500 ZLOTYCH
30.0000 g., 0.9000 Gold 0.8680 oz. AGW, 32 mm. **Obv:** Imperial
eagle above value **Rev:** Head of Tadeusz Kosciuszko right

Date	Mintage	F	VF	XF	Unc	BU
1976MW Proof	2,318	Value: 1,250				

Y# 85   500 ZLOTYCH
30.0000 g., 0.9000 Gold 0.8680 oz. AGW, 32 mm. **Obv:** Imperial
eagle above value **Rev:** Kazimierz Pulaski left

Date	Mintage	F	VF	XF	Unc	BU
1976MW Proof	2,315	Value: 1,250				

Y# 154   500 ZLOTYCH
16.5000 g., 0.6250 Silver 0.3315 oz. ASW, 32 mm.
Series: Environment Protection **Obv:** Imperial eagle above value
Rev: Swan and two chicks

Date	Mintage	F	VF	XF	Unc	BU
1984MW Proof	10,000	Value: 45.00				

Y# 156   500 ZLOTYCH
16.5000 g., 0.7500 Silver 0.3978 oz. ASW, 32 mm.
Obv: Imperial eagle above value **Rev:** King Przemyslaw II

Date	Mintage	F	VF	XF	Unc	BU
1985MW Proof	8,000	Value: 65.00				

Y# 158   500 ZLOTYCH
16.5000 g., 0.7500 Silver 0.3978 oz. ASW, 32 mm.
Subject: 40th Anniversary of United Nations **Obv:** Imperial eagle
above value **Rev:** UN logo within sprigs

Date	Mintage	F	VF	XF	Unc	BU
1985MW Proof	10,000	Value: 27.50				

Y# 159   500 ZLOTYCH
16.5000 g., 0.7500 Silver 0.3978 oz. ASW, 32 mm.
Series: Environmental Protection **Obv:** Imperial eagle above
value **Rev:** Red squirrel

Date	Mintage	F	VF	XF	Unc	BU
1985MW Proof	8,000	Value: 45.00				

Y# 161   500 ZLOTYCH
16.5000 g., 0.7500 Silver 0.3978 oz. ASW, 32 mm. **Obv:** Imperial
eagle above value **Rev:** King Wladyslaw I Lokietek half right

Date	Mintage	F	VF	XF	Unc	BU
1986MW Proof	8,000	Value: 65.00				

Y# 162   500 ZLOTYCH
16.5000 g., 0.7500 Silver 0.3978 oz. ASW, 32 mm.
Series: Environment Protection **Obv:** Eagle with wings open
divides date **Rev:** Owl with 2 chicks

Date	Mintage	F	VF	XF	Unc	BU
1986MW Proof	12,000	Value: 50.00				

Y# 225   500 ZLOTYCH
16.5000 g., 0.7500 Silver 0.3978 oz. ASW, 32 mm.
Obv: Imperial eagle above value **Rev:** Soccer ball in net

Date	Mintage	F	VF	XF	Unc	BU
1986MW Proof	16,000	Value: 30.00				

Y# 165   500 ZLOTYCH
16.5000 g., 0.7500 Silver 0.3978 oz. ASW, 32 mm. **Series:**
Olympics **Obv:** Imperial eagle above value **Rev:** Equestrian

Date	Mintage	F	VF	XF	Unc	BU
1987MW Proof	15,000	Value: 25.00				

Y# 166   500 ZLOTYCH
16.5000 g., 0.7500 Silver 0.3978 oz. ASW, 32 mm.
Subject: European Championship Soccer Games **Obv:** Imperial
eagle above value **Rev:** Soccer player

Date	Mintage	F	VF	XF	Unc	BU
1987MW Proof	12,000	Value: 27.50				

Y# 172   500 ZLOTYCH
16.5000 g., 0.7500 Silver 0.3978 oz. ASW, 32 mm.
Series: Winter Olympics **Obv:** Imperial eagle above value
Rev: Ice hockey goalie

Date	Mintage	F	VF	XF	Unc	BU
1987MW Proof	15,000	Value: 18.50				

Y# 173   500 ZLOTYCH
16.5000 g., 0.7500 Silver 0.3978 oz. ASW, 32 mm. **Obv:** Imperial eagle above value **Rev:** Bust of King Kazimierz III 3/4 facing

Date	Mintage	F	VF	XF	Unc	BU
1987MW Proof	8,000	Value: 60.00				

Y# 181   500 ZLOTYCH
16.5000 g., 0.7500 Silver 0.3978 oz. ASW, 32 mm. **Obv:** Imperial eagle above value **Rev:** Crowned bust of Queen Jadwiga facing

Date	Mintage	F	VF	XF	Unc	BU
1988MW Proof	8,000	Value: 200				

Y# 184   500 ZLOTYCH
16.5000 g., 0.7500 Silver 0.3978 oz. ASW, 32 mm. **Obv:** Imperial eagle above value **Rev:** Colosseum within split soccer ball

Date	Mintage	F	VF	XF	Unc	BU
1988MW Proof	15,000	Value: 22.50				

Y# 185   500 ZLOTYCH
10.8000 g., Copper-Nickel, 29.5 mm. **Subject:** 50th Anniversary - Beginning of WWII **Obv:** Imperial eagle above value **Rev:** Infantry soldiers advancing **Edge:** Reeded

Date	Mintage	F	VF	XF	Unc	BU
1989MW	10,135,000	—	—	—	2.50	4.00
1989MW Proof	5,000	Value: 12.00				

Y# 194   500 ZLOTYCH
10.8000 g., Copper-Nickel, 29.5 mm. **Obv:** Imperial eagle above value **Rev:** Bust of King Wladyslaw II 1/4 left **Edge:** Reeded

Date	Mintage	F	VF	XF	Unc	BU
1989MW	2,544,000	—	—	—	3.00	5.00
1989MW Proof	5,000	Value: 12.00				

Y# 138   1000 ZLOTYCH
3.4000 g., 0.9000 Gold 0.0984 oz. AGW, 18 mm. **Subject:** Visit of Pope John Paul II **Obv:** Eagle with wings open divides date **Rev:** 1/2 Figure of Pope 1/4 left

Date	Mintage	F	VF	XF	Unc	BU
1982CHI	900	—	—	—	—	450
1982CHI Proof	1,700	Value: 500				
1985CHI Unique	—	—	—	—	—	—
1985CHI Proof	2	—	—	—	—	—
1986CHI	83	—	—	—	—	700
1986CHI Proof	53	Value: 850				

Y# 144   1000 ZLOTYCH
14.5000 g., 0.6250 Silver 0.2914 oz. ASW, 31 mm. **Subject:** Visit of Pope John Paul II **Obv:** Imperial eagle above value **Rev:** Bust left

Date	Mintage	F	VF	XF	Unc	BU
1982MW	803,000	—	—	—	10.00	12.00
1983MW	1,530,000	—	—	—	9.00	10.00
1983MW Proof	10,000	Value: 27.50				

Y# 168   1000 ZLOTYCH
3.1100 g., 0.9990 Gold 0.0999 oz. AGW, 18 mm.
Subject: Papal Visit in America **Obv:** Imperial eagle above value **Rev:** Half figure of Pope 3/4 left **Note:** Similar to KM#163.

Date	Mintage	F	VF	XF	Unc	BU
1987MW Proof	201	Value: 400				

Y# 174   1000 ZLOTYCH
3.1100 g., 0.9990 Gold 0.0999 oz. AGW, 18 mm. **Subject:** 10th Anniversary of Pope John Paul II **Obv:** Imperial eagle above value **Rev:** Bust left **Note:** Similar to KM#177.

Date	Mintage	F	VF	XF	Unc	BU
1988MW Proof	1,000	Value: 225				

Y# 186   1000 ZLOTYCH
3.1100 g., 0.9990 Gold 0.0999 oz. AGW, 18 mm. **Subject:** Pope John Paul II **Obv:** Imperial eagle above value **Rev:** Bust left on patterned background

Date	Mintage	F	VF	XF	Unc	BU
1989MW In sets only	Est. 1,000	—	—	—	—	200

Y# 90   2000 ZLOTYCH
8.0000 g., 0.9000 Gold 0.2315 oz. AGW, 21 mm. **Obv:** Eagle with wings open divides date **Rev:** Head of Fryderyk Chopin left

Date	Mintage	F	VF	XF	Unc	BU
1977MW Proof	4,000	Value: 375				

Y# 102   2000 ZLOTYCH
8.0000 g., 0.9000 Gold 0.2315 oz. AGW, 21 mm. **Obv:** Eagle with wings open divides date **Rev:** Duke Mieszko I

Date	Mintage	F	VF	XF	Unc	BU
1979MW Proof	3,000	Value: 375				

Y# 106   2000 ZLOTYCH
8.0000 g., 0.9000 Gold 0.2315 oz. AGW, 21 mm. **Obv:** Eagle with wings open divides date **Rev:** Head of Mikolaj Kopernik 1/4 right

Date	Mintage	F	VF	XF	Unc	BU
1979MW Proof	5,000	Value: 350				

Y# 107   2000 ZLOTYCH
8.0000 g., 0.9000 Gold 0.2315 oz. AGW, 21 mm. **Obv:** Eagle with wings open divides date **Rev:** Profile of Maria Skiodowska Curie left, symbol at right

Date	Mintage	F	VF	XF	Unc	BU
1979MW Proof	5,000	Value: 350				

Y# 111   2000 ZLOTYCH
8.0000 g., 0.9000 Gold 0.2315 oz. AGW, 21 mm. **Series:** Winter Olympics **Obv:** Imperial eagle above value **Rev:** Ski jumper

Date	Mintage	F	VF	XF	Unc	BU
1980MW Proof	5,250	Value: 350				

Y# 116   2000 ZLOTYCH
8.0000 g., 0.9000 Gold 0.2315 oz. AGW, 24 mm. **Obv:** Imperial eagle above value **Rev:** King Boleslaw I Chrobry

Date	Mintage	F	VF	XF	Unc	BU
1980MW Proof	2,500	Value: 375				

Y# 119   2000 ZLOTYCH
8.0000 g., 0.9000 Gold 0.2315 oz. AGW, 21 mm. **Obv:** Imperial eagle above value **Rev:** Kazimierz I

Date	Mintage	F	VF	XF	Unc	BU
1980MW Proof	2,500	Value: 375				

Y# 131   2000 ZLOTYCH
8.0000 g., 0.9000 Gold 0.2315 oz. AGW, 21 mm. **Obv:** Imperial eagle above value **Rev:** Wladyslaw I Herman **Note:** Similar to 200 Zlotych, Y#129.

Date	Mintage	F	VF	XF	Unc	BU
1981MW Proof	3,113	Value: 375				

Y# 135   2000 ZLOTYCH
8.0000 g., 0.9000 Gold 0.2315 oz. AGW, 21 mm. **Obv:** Imperial eagle above value **Rev:** Boleslaw II

Date	Mintage	F	VF	XF	Unc	BU
1981MW Proof	—	Value: 375				

Y# 139   2000 ZLOTYCH
6.8000 g., 0.9000 Gold 0.1968 oz. AGW, 23 mm. **Subject:** Visit of Pope John Paul II **Obv:** Imperial eagle above value **Rev:** Half-figure of Pope 1/4 left

Date	Mintage	F	VF	XF	Unc	BU
1982CHI	500	—	—	—	—	800
1982CHI Proof	1,250	Value: 900				
1985CHI Unique	—	—	—	—	—	—
1985CHI Proof	Est. 2	—	—	—	—	—
1986CHI	Est. 54	—	—	—	—	1,250
1986CHI Proof	Est. 79	Value: 1,300				

Y# 169   2000 ZLOTYCH
7.7700 g., 0.9990 Gold 0.2496 oz. AGW, 22 mm.
Subject: Papal Visit in America **Obv:** Imperial eagle above value **Rev:** 1/2-figure of Pope with staff left **Note:** Similar to KM#163.

Date	Mintage	F	VF	XF	Unc	BU
1987MW Proof	201	Value: 600				

Y# 175   2000 ZLOTYCH
7.7700 g., 0.9990 Gold 0.2496 oz. AGW, 22 mm. **Subject:** 10th Anniversary of Pope John Paul II **Obv:** Imperial eagle above value **Rev:** Bust left **Note:** Similar to KM#177.

Date	Mintage	F	VF	XF	Unc	BU
1988 Proof	1,000	Value: 300				

Y# 187   2000 ZLOTYCH
7.7700 g., 0.9990 Gold 0.2496 oz. AGW, 22 mm. **Obv:** Imperial eagle above value **Rev:** Bust left on patterned background **Note:** Pope John Paul II.

Date	Mintage	F	VF	XF	Unc	BU
1989MW In sets only	Est. 1,000	—	—	—	—	275

Y# 170   5000 ZLOTYCH
15.5500 g., 0.9990 Gold 0.4994 oz. AGW, 27 mm.
Subject: Papal Visit in America **Obv:** Imperial eagle above value **Rev:** Half-figure of Pope with staff left **Note:** Similar to KM#163.

Date	Mintage	F	VF	XF	Unc	BU
1987MW Proof	201	Value: 750				

Y# 176   5000 ZLOTYCH
15.5500 g., 0.9990 Gold 0.4994 oz. AGW, 27 mm.
Subject: 10th Anniversary of Pope John Paul II **Obv:** Imperial
eagle above value **Rev:** Bust left **Note:** Similar to KM#177.

Date	Mintage	F	VF	XF	Unc	BU
1988MW Proof	1,000	Value: 600				

Y# 188   5000 ZLOTYCH
15.5500 g., 0.9990 Gold 0.4994 oz. AGW, 27 mm. **Obv:** Imperial
eagle above value **Rev:** Bust left on patterned background
Note: Pope John Paul II.

Date	Mintage	F	VF	XF	Unc	BU
1989MW In sets only	Est. 1,000,000	—	—	—	—	500

Y# 191   5000 ZLOTYCH
16.5000 g., 0.7500 Silver 0.3978 oz. ASW, 32 mm. **Obv:** Eagle
with wings open divides date **Rev:** Circular design in front of bust
facing 1/4 left, building in background

Date	Mintage	F	VF	XF	Unc	BU
1989MW Proof	20,000	Value: 45.00				

Y# 192   5000 ZLOTYCH
16.5000 g., 0.7500 Silver 0.3978 oz. ASW, 32 mm.
Obv: Imperial eagle above value **Rev:** Torunia Town Hall

Date	Mintage	F	VF	XF	Unc	BU
1989MW Proof	20,000	Value: 40.00				

Y# 193   5000 ZLOTYCH
16.5000 g., 0.7500 Silver 0.3978 oz. ASW, 32 mm.
Obv: Imperial eagle above value **Rev:** Henryk Sucharski

Date	Mintage	F	VF	XF	Unc	BU
1989MW Proof	25,000	Value: 35.00				

Y# 197   5000 ZLOTYCH
16.5000 g., 0.7500 Silver 0.3978 oz. ASW, 32 mm.
Obv: Imperial eagle above value **Rev:** Bust of King Wladyslaw II

Date	Mintage	F	VF	XF	Unc	BU
1989MW Proof	8,000	Value: 85.00				

Y# 198   5000 ZLOTYCH
16.5000 g., 0.7500 Silver 0.3978 oz. ASW, 32 mm.
Obv: Imperial eagle above value **Rev:** Half-length portrait of King
Wladyslaw II

Date	Mintage	F	VF	XF	Unc	BU
1989MW Proof	2,500	Value: 325				

Y# 140   10000 ZLOTYCH
34.5000 g., 0.9000 Gold 0.9982 oz. AGW, 40 mm.
Subject: Visit of Pope John Paul II **Obv:** Imperial eagle above
value **Rev:** Half-figure of Pope 1/4 left

Date	Mintage	F	VF	XF	Unc	BU
1982CHI	200	—	—	—	—	2,000
1982CHI Proof	700	Value: 2,150				
1985CHI Proof, unique	—	—	—	—	—	—
1986CHI	Est. 6	—	—	—	—	—
1986CHI Proof	Est. 13	—	—	—	—	—

Y# 399   10000 ZLOTYCH
28.3100 g., 0.9000 Silver 0.8191 oz. ASW, 40.2 mm.
Subject: Pope John Paul II **Obv:** Imperial eagle above value
Rev: Bust of Pope left **Edge:** Plain

Date	Mintage	F	VF	XF	Unc	BU
1986 Proof	9	Value: 2,000				

Y# 164   10000 ZLOTYCH
19.3000 g., 0.7500 Silver 0.4654 oz. ASW, 35 mm.
Subject: Papal Visit **Obv:** Imperial eagle above value **Rev:** 1/2
Figure of Pope 1/4 left

Date	Mintage	F	VF	XF	Unc	BU
1987MW	908,000	—	—	—	30.00	40.00
1987MW Proof	15,000	Value: 75.00				

Y# 171   10000 ZLOTYCH
31.1030 g., 0.9990 oz. AGW, 32 mm.
Subject: Papal Visit in America **Obv:** Imperial eagle above value
Rev: Half-figure of Pope left **Note:** Similar to KM#163.

Date	Mintage	F	VF	XF	Unc	BU
1987MW Proof	201	Value: 1,450				

Y# 177   10000 ZLOTYCH
31.1030 g., 0.9990 Gold 0.9989 oz. AGW, 32 mm.
Subject: 10th Anniversary of Pope John Paul II **Obv:** Imperial
eagle above value **Rev:** Bust left

Date	Mintage	F	VF	XF	Unc	BU
1988MW	1,000	—	—	—	—	1,000
1988MW Proof	1,000	Value: 1,100				

Y# 177a   10000 ZLOTYCH
31.1030 g., 0.9990 Silver 0.9989 oz. ASW, 32 mm.
Subject: 10th Anniversary of Pope John Paul II **Obv:** Imperial
eagle above value **Rev:** Bust left

Date	Mintage	F	VF	XF	Unc	BU
1988MW	5,000	—	—	—	—	—
1988MW Proof	—	Value: 375				

Y# 179   10000 ZLOTYCH
31.1030 g., 0.9990 Silver 0.9989 oz. ASW, 32 mm.
Subject: Pope John Paul - Christmas **Obv:** Imperial eagle above
value **Rev:** Bust of Pope left with right hand raised

Date	Mintage	F	VF	XF	Unc	BU
1988MW Proof	5,000	Value: 325				

Y# 189   10000 ZLOTYCH
31.1030 g., 0.9990 Gold 0.9989 oz. AGW, 32 mm.
Subject: Pope John Paul II **Obv:** Imperial eagle above value
Rev: Bust left on patterned background

Date	Mintage	F	VF	XF	Unc	BU
1989MW Proof	Est. 2,000	Value: 1,000				

Y# 189a   10000 ZLOTYCH
31.1000 g., 0.9990 Silver 0.9988 oz. ASW, 32 mm.
Obv: Imperial eagle above value **Rev:** Pope John Paul II

Date	Mintage	F	VF	XF	Unc	BU
1989MW	—	—	—	—	—	—
1989MW Proof	5,000	Value: 350				

Y# 237   10000 ZLOTYCH
31.1000 g., 0.9990 Silver 0.9988 oz. ASW, 32 mm.
Obv: Imperial eagle above value **Rev:** 3/4 Figure of Pope right

Date	Mintage	F	VF	XF	Unc	BU
1989MW Proof	—	Value: 150				

Y# 223 20000 ZLOTYCH
19.3000 g., 0.7500 Silver 0.4654 oz. ASW, 35 mm.
Obv: Imperial eagle above value **Rev:** Soccer ball, map, and globe

Date	Mintage	F	VF	XF	Unc	BU
1989 Proof	25,000	Value: 35.00				

Y# 224 20000 ZLOTYCH
19.3000 g., 0.7500 Silver 0.4654 oz. ASW, 35 mm. **Obv:** Eagle with wings open divides date **Rev:** Soccer player behind vertical lines, all within circle

Date	Mintage	F	VF	XF	Unc	BU
1989 Proof	25,000	Value: 35.00				

Y# 180 50000 ZLOTYCH
19.3000 g., 0.7500 Silver 0.4654 oz. ASW, 35 mm. **Subject:** 70 Years of Polish Independence **Obv:** Imperial eagle above value **Rev:** Head left

Date	Mintage	F	VF	XF	Unc	BU
1988	1,000,000	—	—	—	20.00	25.00
1988 Proof	20,000	Value: 65.00				

Y# 163 200000 ZLOTYCH
373.2420 g., 0.9990 Gold 11.987 oz. AGW, 70 mm.
Subject: Papal Visit in America **Obv:** Imperial eagle above value **Rev:** Half-figure with staff left **Note:** Illustration reduced.

Date	Mintage	F	VF	XF	Unc	BU
1987 Proof	101	Value: 12,500				

Y# 178 200000 ZLOTYCH
373.2420 g., 0.9990 Gold 11.987 oz. AGW, 70 mm. **Subject:** 10th Anniversary of Pope John Paul II **Obv:** Imperial eagle above value **Rev:** Bust with chin resting on thumbs left **Note:** Illustration reduced.

Date	Mintage	F	VF	XF	Unc	BU
1988MW Proof	300	Value: 12,500				

Y# 190 200000 ZLOTYCH
373.2420 g., 0.9990 Gold 11.987 oz. AGW, 70 mm. **Obv:** Imperial eagle above value **Rev:** Pope John Paul II **Note:** Similar to KM#189.

Date	Mintage	F	VF	XF	Unc	BU
1989MW Proof	Est. 200	Value: 12,500				

REPUBLIC
Democratic
STANDARD COINAGE

Y# 216 50 ZLOTYCH
6.8000 g., Copper-Nickel, 26 mm. **Obv:** Crowned eagle with wings open, date below **Rev:** Value with sprig in 0

Date	Mintage	F	VF	XF	Unc	BU
1990MW	28,707,000	—	—	—	1.25	2.00
1990MW Proof	5,000	Value: 12.00				

Y# 214 100 ZLOTYCH
7.6800 g., Copper-Nickel, 28 mm. **Obv:** Crowned eagle with wings open **Rev:** Value with sprig in first 0

Date	Mintage	F	VF	XF	Unc	BU
1990MW	37,341,000	—	—	—	2.00	3.00
1990MW Proof	5,000	Value: 15.00				

Y# 195 10000 ZLOTYCH
10.8000 g., Copper-Nickel, 29.5 mm. **Subject:** 10th Anniversary of Solidarity **Obv:** Crowned eagle with wings open divides date **Rev:** Solidarity monument with city view background **Edge:** Reeded

Date	Mintage	F	VF	XF	Unc	BU
1990MW	15,164,000	—	—	—	4.50	6.00
1990MW Proof	5,000	Value: 16.50				

Y# 217 10000 ZLOTYCH
9.4700 g., Nickel Plated Steel, 29.5 mm. **Subject:** 200th Anniversary of Polish Constitution **Obv:** Crowned eagle with wings open divides date **Rev:** Crowned eagle above inscription, crowned monogram below **Edge:** Reeded

Date	Mintage	F	VF	XF	Unc	BU
1991MW	2,605,000	—	—	—	6.00	8.00

Y# 246 10000 ZLOTYCH
10.8000 g., Copper-Nickel, 29.5 mm. **Obv:** Crowned eagle with wings open divides date **Rev:** Wladyslaw III 3/4 left **Edge:** Reeded

Date	Mintage	F	VF	XF	Unc	BU
1992MW	2,500,000	—	—	—	3.50	5.00

Y# 219 20000 ZLOTYCH
9.4500 g., 0.9990 Gold 0.3035 oz. AGW, 32.1 mm.
Subject: 10th Anniversary of Solidarity **Obv:** Crowned eagle **Rev:** Solidarity monument with city view background **Edge:** alternating plain and reeded **Note:** Similar to 10000 Zlotych, Y#195.

Date	Mintage	F	VF	XF	Unc	BU
1990 Proof	1,004	Value: 300				

Y# 215 20000 ZLOTYCH
9.4500 g., Bi-Metallic Copper-Nickel center in Brass ring, 32 mm. **Subject:** 225th Anniversary of Warsaw Mint **Obv:** Crowned eagle with wings open divides date, all within circle **Rev:** Crowned monogram divides date, all within circle

Date	Mintage	F	VF	XF	Unc	BU
1991MW	100,000	—	—	—	18.00	22.00

Y# 243 20000 ZLOTYCH
10.8000 g., Copper-Nickel, 29.5 mm. **Obv:** Imperial eagle above value **Rev:** Barn swallows **Edge:** Reeded

Date	Mintage	F	VF	XF	Unc	BU
1993MW	520,000	—	—	—	7.50	15.00

Y# 244 20000 ZLOTYCH
10.8000 g., Copper-Nickel, 29.5 mm. **Obv:** Crowned eagle with wings open divides date, all within circle **Rev:** Lancut Castle **Edge:** Reeded

Date	Mintage	F	VF	XF	Unc	BU
1993MW	500,000	—	—	—	4.50	6.00

Y# 256 20000 ZLOTYCH
10.8000 g., Copper-Nickel, 29.5 mm. **Obv:** Imperial eagle above value **Rev:** Kazimierz IV **Edge:** Reeded

Date	Mintage	F	VF	XF	Unc	BU
1993	1,500,000	—	—	—	4.50	6.00

Y# 261   20000 ZLOTYCH
10.8000 g., Copper-Nickel, 29.5 mm. **Series:** Olympics
Obv: Crowned eagle with wings open divides date **Rev:** Slalom
skier **Edge:** Reeded

Date	Mintage	F	VF	XF	Unc	BU
1993	988,000	—	—	—	7.50	10.00

Y# 265   20000 ZLOTYCH
10.8000 g., Copper-Nickel, 29.5 mm. **Subject:** 75th Anniversary -
Disabled Association **Obv:** Crowned eagle with wings open divides
date **Rev:** Shield and rose within designed circle **Edge:** Reeded

Date	Mintage	F	VF	XF	Unc	BU
1994	76,000	—	—	—	4.50	6.00

Y# 270   20000 ZLOTYCH
10.8000 g., Copper-Nickel, 29.5 mm. **Obv:** Crowned eagle with
wings open divides date **Rev:** New mint building **Edge:** Reeded

Date	Mintage	F	VF	XF	Unc	BU
1994	252,000	—	—	—	4.50	6.00

Y# 271   20000 ZLOTYCH
10.8000 g., Copper-Nickel, 29.5 mm. **Subject:** 200th Anniversary
- Kosciuszko Insurrection **Obv:** Crowned eagle with wings open
divides date **Rev:** Head left in circle within ship **Edge:** Milled

Date	Mintage	F	VF	XF	Unc	BU
1994	100,000	—	—	—	5.00	7.00

Y# 272   20000 ZLOTYCH
10.8000 g., Copper-Nickel, 29.5 mm. **Obv:** Imperial eagle above
value **Rev:** Zygmunt I, 1506-1548 **Edge:** Reeded

Date	Mintage	F	VF	XF	Unc	BU
1994	1,500,000	—	—	—	4.50	6.00

Y# 220   50000 ZLOTYCH
7.7000 g., 0.9990 Gold 0.2473 oz. AGW, 22 mm. **Subject:** 10th
Anniversary of Solidarity **Obv:** Imperial eagle above value
Rev: Solidarity monument with city view background
Note: Similar to 10000 Zlotych, Y#195.

Date	Mintage	F	VF	XF	Unc	BU
1990 Proof	1,001	Value: 400				

Y# 229   50000 ZLOTYCH
11.3000 g., Copper-Nickel, 32 mm. **Subject:** 200th Anniversary
of Order Virtuti Militari **Obv:** Crowned eagle with wings open
divides date, all within beaded circle **Rev:** Military medal and
crowned monogram

Date	Mintage	F	VF	XF	Unc	BU
1992 Proof	125,000	Value: 12.50				

Y# 196.1   100000 ZLOTYCH
31.1000 g., 0.9990 Silver 0.9988 oz. ASW, 32 mm.
Subject: 10th Anniversary of Solidarity **Obv:** Imperial eagle
above value **Rev:** Solidarity monument with city view background
Edge: Plain

Date	Mintage	F	VF	XF	Unc	BU
1990	520,000	—	—	—	22.00	25.00
1990 Proof	125,000	Value: 85.00				

Y# 196.2   100000 ZLOTYCH
31.1000 g., 0.9990 Silver 0.9988 oz. ASW, 31.9 mm. **Subject:** 10th
Anniversary of Solidarity **Obv:** Imperial eagle above value **Rev:**
Solidarity monument with city view background **Note:** Reduced size.

Date	Mintage	F	VF	XF	Unc	BU
1990 Proof	—	Value: 65.00				

Y# 199   100000 ZLOTYCH
31.1000 g., 0.9990 Silver 0.9988 oz. ASW, 35 mm.
Obv: Imperial eagle above value **Rev:** Fryderyk Chopin
Edge: Reeded

Date	Mintage	F	VF	XF	Unc	BU
1990 Proof	10,000	Value: 35.00				

Y# 200   100000 ZLOTYCH
31.1000 g., 0.9990 Silver 0.9988 oz. ASW, 39 mm. **Obv:** Imperial
eagle above value **Rev:** Uniformed figure on horse **Edge:** Milled

Date	Mintage	F	VF	XF	Unc	BU
1990 Proof	10,000	Value: 35.00				

Y# 201   100000 ZLOTYCH
31.1000 g., 0.9990 Silver 0.9988 oz. ASW, 39 mm.
Obv: Imperial eagle above value **Rev:** Uniformed bust of
Marszalek Pilsudski 1/4 left **Edge:** Reeded

Date	Mintage	F	VF	XF	Unc	BU
1990 Proof	10,000	Value: 35.00				

Y# 221   100000 ZLOTYCH
15.5500 g., 0.9990 Gold 0.4994 oz. AGW **Subject:** 10th
Anniversary of Solidarity **Obv:** Imperial eagle above value
Rev: Buildiings, symbols **Note:** Similar to 10000 Zlotych, Y#195.

Date	Mintage	F	VF	XF	Unc	BU
1990 Proof	Est. 1,000	Value: 475				

Y# 235   100000 ZLOTYCH
16.5000 g., 0.7500 Silver 0.3978 oz. ASW, 32 mm.
Series: WWII **Obv:** Crowned eagle with wings open divides date
Rev: Cavalry facing right, flanked by trees **Edge:** Reeded

Date	Mintage	F	VF	XF	Unc	BU
1991 Proof	12,000	Value: 27.50				

Y# 236   100000 ZLOTYCH
16.5000 g., 0.7500 Silver 0.3978 oz. ASW, 32 mm.
Series: WWII **Subject:** Defense of Narvik **Obv:** Imperial eagle
above value **Rev:** Polish troops **Edge:** Reeded

Date	Mintage	F	VF	XF	Unc	BU
1991 Proof	12,000	Value: 27.50				

Y# 238 100000 ZLOTYCH
16.5000 g., 0.7500 Silver 0.3978 oz. ASW, 32 mm.
Series: WWII **Obv:** Imperial eagle above value **Rev:** Polish
troops at Battle of Tobruk **Edge:** Reeded

Date	Mintage	F	VF	XF	Unc	BU
1991 Proof	12,000	Value: 27.50				

Y# 239 100000 ZLOTYCH
16.5000 g., 0.7500 Silver 0.3978 oz. ASW, 32 mm.
Series: WWII **Obv:** Imperial eagle above value **Rev:** Polish pilots
in Battle of Britain **Edge:** Reeded

Date	Mintage	F	VF	XF	Unc	BU
1991 Proof	12,000	Value: 27.50				

Y# 227 100000 ZLOTYCH
16.5000 g., 0.7500 Silver 0.3978 oz. ÀSW, 32 mm.
Subject: Unification of Upper Silesia and Poland **Obv:** Imperial
eagle above value **Rev:** Bust 3/4 left, inscription at left
Edge: Reeded

Date	Mintage	F	VF	XF	Unc	BU
1992 Proof	30,000	Value: 27.50				

Y# 268 100000 ZLOTYCH
16.5000 g., 0.9000 Silver 0.4774 oz. ASW, 32 mm.
Subject: Warsaw Uprising **Obv:** Imperial eagle above value
Rev: Soldier with gun

Date	Mintage	F	VF	XF	Unc	BU
1994 Proof	150,000	Value: 32.50				

Y# 240 200000 ZLOTYCH
19.3600 g., 0.7500 Silver 0.4668 oz. ASW, 35 mm. **Obv:** Imperial
eagle above value **Rev:** Gen. Dyw. Stefan Rowecki "Grot" facing

Date	Mintage	F	VF	XF	Unc	BU
1990 Proof	25,000	Value: 45.00				
1991 Proof	—	Value: 45.00				

Y# 202 200000 ZLOTYCH
155.5000 g., 0.9990 Silver 4.9942 oz. ASW, 65 mm.
Obv: Imperial eagle above value **Rev:** Fryderyk Chopin
Edge: Reeded **Note:** Similar to 100,000 Zlotych, Y#199.

Date	Mintage	F	VF	XF	Unc	BU
1990 Proof	10,000	Value: 175				

Y# 203 200000 ZLOTYCH
155.5000 g., 0.9990 Silver 4.9942 oz. ASW, 65 mm.
Obv: Imperial eagle above value **Rev:** Uniformed figure on horse
Edge: Reeded **Note:** Similar to 100,000 Zlotych, Y#200.

Date	Mintage	F	VF	XF	Unc	BU
1990 Proof	10,000	Value: 175				

Y# 204 200000 ZLOTYCH
155.5000 g., 0.9990 Silver 4.9942 oz. ASW, 65 mm.
Obv: Imperial eagle above value **Rev:** Bust of Marszalek
Pilsudski 1/4 left **Note:** Similar to 100,000 Zlotych, Y#201.

Date	Mintage	F	VF	XF	Unc	BU
1990 Proof	10,000	Value: 175				

Y# 205 200000 ZLOTYCH
31.1000 g., 0.9990 Gold 0.9988 oz. AGW, 32 mm. **Obv:** Imperial
eagle above value **Rev:** Fryderyk Chopin

Date	Mintage	F	VF	XF	Unc	BU
1990 Proof	13,000	Value: 975				

Y# 206 200000 ZLOTYCH
31.1000 g., 0.9990 Gold 0.9988 oz. AGW, 32 mm. **Obv:** Imperial
eagle above value **Rev:** Tadeusz Kosciuszko

Date	Mintage	F	VF	XF	Unc	BU
1990 Proof	13,000	Value: 975				

Y# 207 200000 ZLOTYCH
31.1000 g., 0.9990 Gold 0.9988 oz. AGW, 32 mm. **Obv:** Imperial
eagle above value **Rev:** Marszalek Pilsudski **Edge:** Reeded

Date	Mintage	F	VF	XF	Unc	BU
1990 Proof	10,000	Value: 975				

Y# 222 200000 ZLOTYCH
31.1000 g., 0.9990 Gold 0.9988 oz. AGW, 32 mm.
Subject: Solidarity **Obv:** Solidarity monument with city view
background **Rev:** Solidarity monument with city view background

Date	Mintage	F	VF	XF	Unc	BU
1990 Proof	Est. 1,000	Value: 1,000				

Y# 250 200000 ZLOTYCH
19.2650 g., 0.9990 Silver 0.6187 oz. ASW, 35 mm.
Obv: Imperial eagle above value **Rev:** Bust of Gen. Komorowski
facing

Date	Mintage	F	VF	XF	Unc	BU
1990 Proof	25,000	Value: 27.50				

Y# 218 200000 ZLOTYCH
38.9000 g., 0.9990 Silver 1.2494 oz. ASW, 40 mm. **Subject:** 200th
Anniversary of Polish Constitution **Obv:** Imperial eagle above value
Rev: Crowned eagle perched on sprigs above engraved stone

Date	Mintage	F	VF	XF	Unc	BU
1991 Proof	100,000	Value: 27.50				

Y# 226 200000 ZLOTYCH
31.1000 g., 0.9250 Silver 0.9249 oz. ASW, 40 mm.
Series: Albertville Olympics **Obv:** Imperial eagle above value
Rev: Slalom skier

Date	Mintage	F	VF	XF	Unc	BU
1991 Proof	20,000	Value: 28.50				

Y# 228 200000 ZLOTYCH
31.1000 g., 0.9250 Silver 0.9249 oz. ASW, 40 mm.
Series: Barcelona Olympics **Obv:** Imperial eagle above value
Rev: Weight lifter

Date	Mintage	F	VF	XF	Unc	BU
1991 Proof	20,000	Value: 42.50				

Y# 241 200000 ZLOTYCH
31.1600 g., 0.9250 Silver 0.9266 oz. ASW, 40 mm.
Series: Barcelona Olympics **Obv:** Imperial eagle above value
Rev: Two sailboats

Date	Mintage	F	VF	XF	Unc	BU
1991 Proof	20,000	Value: 37.50				

Y# 242 200000 ZLOTYCH
19.3300 g., 0.7500 Silver 0.4661 oz. ASW, 35 mm.
Subject: 70th Anniversary of Poznan Fair **Obv:** Imperial eagle
above value **Rev:** Monument and globe design, dates above and
below

Date	Mintage	F	VF	XF	Unc	BU
1991 Proof	20,000	Value: 30.00				

Y# 251 200000 ZLOTYCH
19.3300 g., 0.7500 Silver 0.4661 oz. ASW, 35 mm.
Obv: Imperial eagle above value **Rev:** Bust of Gen. Okulicki 3/4 facing

Date	Mintage	F	VF	XF	Unc	BU
1991 Proof	25,000	Value: 27.50				

Y# 252 200000 ZLOTYCH
19.3300 g., 0.7500 Silver 0.4661 oz. ASW, 35 mm. **Obv:** Imperial eagle above value **Rev:** Bust of Gen. Tokarzewski - Karaszewicz

Date	Mintage	F	VF	XF	Unc	BU
1991 Proof	25,000	Value: 27.50				

Y# 230 200000 ZLOTYCH
31.1000 g., 0.9990 Silver 0.9988 oz. ASW, 40 mm.
Subject: Discovery of America **Obv:** Imperial eagle above value **Rev:** Portrait and ship

Date	Mintage	F	VF	XF	Unc	BU
1992 Proof	20,000	Value: 40.00				

Y# 231 200000 ZLOTYCH
31.1000 g., 0.9990 Silver 0.9988 oz. ASW, 40 mm.
Subject: Seville Expo '92 **Obv:** Imperial eagle above value **Rev:** Building facade and logo

Date	Mintage	F	VF	XF	Unc	BU
1992 Proof	45,000	Value: 28.00				

Y# 232 200000 ZLOTYCH
16.5000 g., 0.7500 Silver 0.3978 oz. ASW, 32 mm.
Series: WWII **Obv:** Imperial eagle above value **Rev:** Polish protection of WWII sea convoys

Date	Mintage	F	VF	XF	Unc	BU
1992 Proof	15,000	Value: 27.50				

Y# 233 200000 ZLOTYCH
16.5000 g., 0.7500 Silver 0.3978 oz. ASW, 32 mm.
Obv: Imperial eagle above value **Rev:** Bust of Stanislaw Staszic 3/4 left within sprigs

Date	Mintage	F	VF	XF	Unc	BU
1992 Proof	20,000	Value: 27.50				

Y# 253 200000 ZLOTYCH
16.5000 g., 0.7500 Silver 0.3978 oz. ASW, 32 mm.
Obv: Imperial eagle above value **Rev:** Bust of Wladyslaw II 1/4 left

Date	Mintage	F	VF	XF	Unc	BU
1992 Proof	5,000	Value: 30.00				

Y# 254 200000 ZLOTYCH
16.5000 g., 0.7500 Silver 0.3978 oz. ASW, 32 mm. **Obv:** Imperial eagle above value **Rev:** Bust of Wladyslaw III 1/4 left

Date	Mintage	F	VF	XF	Unc	BU
1992 Proof	20,000	Value: 60.00				

Y# 255 200000 ZLOTYCH
16.5000 g., 0.7500 Silver 0.3978 oz. ASW, 32 mm.
Subject: 750th Anniversary - City of Szczecin **Obv:** Imperial eagle above value **Rev:** Crowned phoenix head within shield flanked by dates

Date	Mintage	F	VF	XF	Unc	BU
1993 Proof	20,000	Value: 27.50				

Y# 257 200000 ZLOTYCH
16.5000 g., 0.7500 Silver 0.3978 oz. ASW, 32 mm.
Obv: Imperial eagle above value **Rev:** Bust of Kazimierz IV 3/4 right

Date	Mintage	F	VF	XF	Unc	BU
1993 Proof	15,000	Value: 32.50				

Y# 258 200000 ZLOTYCH
16.5000 g., 0.7500 Silver 0.3978 oz. ASW, 32 mm. **Obv:** Crowned eagle with wings open divides date **Rev:** Kazimierz IV enthroned

Date	Mintage	F	VF	XF	Unc	BU
1993 Proof	5,000	Value: 75.00				

Y# 259 200000 ZLOTYCH
16.5000 g., 0.7500 Silver 0.3978 oz. ASW, 32 mm.
Series: WWII **Obv:** Imperial eagle above value **Rev:** Polish partisans sabotaging railways

Date	Mintage	F	VF	XF	Unc	BU
1993 Proof	10,000	Value: 55.00				

Y# 262 200000 ZLOTYCH
16.5000 g., 0.7500 Silver 0.3978 oz. ASW, 32 mm. **Series:** WWII
Obv: Imperial eagle above value **Rev:** Battle of Monte Cassino

Date	Mintage	F	VF	XF	Unc	BU
1994 Proof	15,000	Value: 37.50				

Y# 266 200000 ZLOTYCH
16.5000 g., 0.7500 Silver 0.3978 oz. ASW, 32 mm.
Subject: 75th Anniversary - Disabled Association **Obv:** Imperial eagle above value **Rev:** Shield and rose within designed circle

Date	Mintage	F	VF	XF	Unc	BU
1994 Proof	15,000	Value: 35.00				

Y# 273 200000 ZLOTYCH

16.5000 g., 0.7500 Silver 0.3978 oz. ASW, 32 mm. **Obv:** Imperial eagle above value **Rev:** Half-length figure of Zygmunt I 1/4 right

Date	Mintage	F	VF	XF	Unc	BU
1994 Proof	15,000	Value: 30.00				

Y# 274 200000 ZLOTYCH

16.5000 g., 0.7500 Silver 0.3978 oz. ASW, 32 mm.
Obv: Imperial eagle above value **Rev:** Bust of Zygmunt I facing

Date	Mintage	F	VF	XF	Unc	BU
1994 Proof	5,000	Value: 65.00				

Y# 275 200000 ZLOTYCH

16.5000 g., 0.7500 Silver 0.3978 oz. ASW, 32 mm.
Subject: 200th Anniversary - Kosciuszko Insurrection
Obv: Imperial eagle above value **Rev:** Cameo bust left within ship

Date	Mintage	F	VF	XF	Unc	BU
1994 Proof	15,000	Value: 32.50				

Y# 245 300000 ZLOTYCH

31.1600 g., 0.9250 Silver 0.9266 oz. ASW, 40 mm.
Subject: 50th Anniversary of Warsaw Ghetto Uprising
Obv: Imperial eagle above value **Rev:** Outreached arms above bricks

Date	Mintage	F	VF	XF	Unc	BU
1993 Proof	30,000	Value: 32.50				

Y# 247 300000 ZLOTYCH

31.1600 g., 0.9250 Silver 0.9266 oz. ASW, 40 mm. **Series:** 1994 Olympics **Obv:** Eagle with wings open divides date
Rev: Lillehammer

Date	Mintage	F	VF	XF	Unc	BU
1993 Proof	20,000	Value: 32.50				

Y# 248 300000 ZLOTYCH

31.1450 g., 0.9990 Silver 1.0003 oz. ASW, 40 mm.
Obv: Imperial eagle above value **Rev:** Barn swallow feeding young

Date	Mintage	F	VF	XF	Unc	BU
1993 Proof	20,000	Value: 135				

Y# 249 300000 ZLOTYCH

31.1450 g., 0.9990 Silver 1.0003 oz. ASW, 40 mm.
Obv: Imperial eagle above value **Rev:** Lancut Castle

Date	Mintage	F	VF	XF	Unc	BU
1993 Proof	20,000	Value: 45.00				

Y# 260 300000 ZLOTYCH

31.1000 g., 0.9990 Silver 0.9988 oz. ASW, 40 mm.
Obv: Imperial eagle above value **Rev:** Aerial view of Zamosc

Date	Mintage	F	VF	XF	Unc	BU
1993 Proof	20,000	Value: 32.50				

Y# 263 300000 ZLOTYCH

31.1600 g., 0.9250 Silver 0.9266 oz. ASW **Obv:** Imperial eagle above value **Rev:** St. Maksymilian Kolbe

Date	Mintage	F	VF	XF	Unc	BU
1994 Proof	15,000	Value: 40.00				

Y# 264 300000 ZLOTYCH

31.1000 g., 0.9250 Silver 0.9249 oz. ASW, 40 mm.
Subject: 70th Anniversary - Polish National Bank **Obv:** Crowned eagle with wings open divides date **Rev:** Bust facing in front of buildings

Date	Mintage	F	VF	XF	Unc	BU
1994 Proof	20,880	Value: 50.00				

Y# 269 300000 ZLOTYCH

31.1035 g., 0.9990 Silver 0.9990 oz. ASW, 40 mm.
Subject: Warsaw Uprising **Obv:** Imperial eagle above value
Rev: Fighting soldiers, dates, designs and cross

Date	Mintage	F	VF	XF	Unc	BU
1994 Proof	30,000	Value: 35.00				

Y# 208 500000 ZLOTYCH

62.2000 g., 0.9990 Gold 1.9977 oz. AGW, 39 mm. **Obv:** Imperial eagle above value **Rev:** Fryderyk Chopin **Note:** Similar to 100,000 Zlotych, Y#199.

Date	Mintage	F	VF	XF	Unc	BU
1990 Proof	16	Value: 2,150				

Y# 209 500000 ZLOTYCH

62.2000 g., 0.9990 Gold 1.9977 oz. AGW, 39 mm. **Obv:** Imperial eagle above value **Rev:** Uniformed figure on horse **Note:** Similar to 100,000 Zlotych, Y#200.

Date	Mintage	F	VF	XF	Unc	BU
1990 Proof	12	Value: 2,150				

Y# 210 500000 ZLOTYCH

62.2000 g., 0.9990 Gold 1.9977 oz. AGW, 39 mm. **Obv:** Imperial eagle above value **Rev:** Bust of Marszalek Pilsudski 1/4 left
Note: Similar to 100,000 Zlotych, Y#201.

Date	Mintage	F	VF	XF	Unc	BU
1990 Proof	16	Value: 2,150				

Y# 211 1000000 ZLOTYCH

373.2000 g., 0.9990 Gold 11.986 oz. AGW, 65 mm.
Obv: Imperial eagle above value **Rev:** Fryderyk Chopin
Note: Similar to 100,000 Zlotych, Y#199.

Date	Mintage	F	VF	XF	Unc	BU
1990	1	Value: 12,500				

Y# 212 1000000 ZLOTYCH

373.2000 g., 0.9990 Gold 11.986 oz. AGW, 65 mm.
Obv: Imperial eagle above value **Rev:** Uniformed figure on horse **Note:** Similar to 100,000 Zlotych, Y#200.

Date	Mintage	F	VF	XF	Unc	BU
1990 Proof	1	Value: 12,500				

Y# 213 1000000 ZLOTYCH

373.2000 g., 0.9990 Gold 11.986 oz. AGW, 65 mm.
Obv: Imperial eagle above value **Rev:** Bust of Marszalek Pilsudski 1/4 left **Note:** Similar to 100,000 Zlotych, Y#201.

Date	Mintage	F	VF	XF	Unc	BU
1990 Proof	1	Value: 12,500				

REFORM COINAGE

100 Old Zlotych = 1 Grosz; 10,000 Old Zlotych = 1 Zloty

As far back as 1990, production was initiated for the new 1 Grosz - 1 Zlotych coins for a forthcoming monetary reform. It wasn't announced until the Act of July 7, 1994 and was enacted on January 1, 1995.

Y# 276 GROSZ

1.6400 g., Brass, 15.5 mm. **Obv:** National arms **Obv. Leg.:** RZECZPOSPOLITA POLSKA **Rev:** Drooping oak leaf over value **Edge:** Reeded

Date	Mintage	F	VF	XF	Unc	BU
1990MW	29,140,000	—	—	—	0.10	0.20
1991MW	79,000,000	—	—	—	0.10	0.20
1992MW	362,000,000	—	—	—	0.10	0.20
1993MW	80,780,000	—	—	—	0.10	0.20
1995MW	102,280,109	—	—	—	0.10	0.20
1997MW	103,080,002	—	—	—	0.10	0.20
1998MW	255,830,003	—	—	—	0.10	0.20
1999MW	204,470,000	—	—	—	0.10	0.20
2000MW	211,410,000	—	—	—	0.10	0.20

Y# 277 2 GROSZE

2.1300 g., Brass, 17.5 mm. **Obv:** National arms **Obv. Leg.:** RZECZPOSPOLITA POLSKA **Rev:** Drooping oak leaves above value **Edge:** Plain

Date	Mintage	F	VF	XF	Unc	BU
1990MW	34,400,000	—	—	—	0.15	0.25
1991MW	97,410,000	—	—	—	0.15	0.25
1992MW	157,000,003	—	—	—	0.15	0.25
1997MV	92,400,002	—	—	—	0.15	0.25
1998MW	154,840,050	—	—	—	0.15	0.25
1999MW	187,900,000	—	—	—	0.15	0.25
2000MW	92,400,000	—	—	—	0.15	0.25

Y# 278 5 GROSZY

2.5900 g., Brass, 19.5 mm. **Obv:** National arms **Obv. Leg.:** RZECZPOSPOLITA POLSKA **Rev:** Value at upper left of oak leaves **Edge:** Segmented reeding

Date	Mintage	F	VF	XF	Unc	BU
1990MW	70,240,000	—	—	—	0.25	0.45
1991MW	171,040,000	—	—	—	0.25	0.45
1992MW	103,784,000	—	—	—	0.25	0.45
1993MW	20,280,101	—	—	—	0.25	0.45
1998MW	93,472,002	—	—	—	0.25	0.45
1999MW	99,024,000	—	—	—	0.25	0.45
2000MW	75,600,000	—	—	—	0.25	0.45

Y# 279 10 GROSZY

2.5100 g., Copper-Nickel, 16.5 mm. **Obv:** National arms **Obv. Leg.:** RZECZPOSPOLITA POLSKA **Rev:** Value within wreath

Date	Mintage	F	VF	XF	Unc	BU
1990MW	43,055,000	—	—	—	0.40	0.60
1991MW	123,164,300	—	—	—	0.40	0.60
1992MW	210,005,000	—	—	—	0.40	0.60
1993MW	80,240,008	—	—	—	0.40	0.60
1998MW	62,695,000	—	—	—	0.40	0.60
1999MW	47,040,000	—	—	—	0.40	0.60
2000MW	104,060,000	—	—	—	0.40	0.60

Y# 280 20 GROSZY

3.2200 g., Copper-Nickel, 18.5 mm. **Obv:** National arms **Obv. Leg.:** RZECZPOSPOLITA POLSKA **Rev:** Value within artistic design **Edge:** Reeded

Date	Mintage	F	VF	XF	Unc	BU
1990MW	25,100,000	—	—	—	0.65	0.85
1991MW	75,400,000	—	—	—	0.65	0.85

Date	Mintage	F	VF	XF	Unc	BU
1992MW	106,100,001	—	—	—	0.65	0.85
1996MW	29,745,000	—	—	—	0.65	0.85
1997MW	59,755,000	—	—	—	0.65	0.85
1998MW	52,500,000	—	—	—	0.65	0.85
1999MW	25,985,000	—	—	—	0.65	0.85
2000MW	52,135,000	—	—	—	0.65	0.85

Y# 281 50 GROSZY

3.9400 g., Copper-Nickel, 20.5 mm. **Obv:** National arms **Obv. Leg.:** RZECZPOSPOLITA POLSKA **Rev:** Value to right of sprig **Edge:** Reeded

Date	Mintage	F	VF	XF	Unc	BU
1990MW	29,152,000	—	—	—	1.00	1.25
1991MW	99,120,000	—	—	—	1.00	1.25
1992MW	116,000,000	—	—	—	1.00	1.25
1994MW		—	—	—	1.00	1.25
1995MW	101,600,113	—	—	—	1.00	1.25

Y# 282 ZLOTY

5.0300 g., Copper-Nickel, 23 mm. **Obv:** National arms **Obv. Leg.:** RZECZPOSPOLITA POLSKA **Rev:** Value within wreath

Date	Mintage	F	VF	XF	Unc	BU
1990MW	20,040,000	—	—	—	1.75	2.00
1991MW	60,080,000	—	—	—	1.75	2.00
1992MW	102,240,000	—	—	—	1.75	2.00
1993MW	20,904,000	—	—	—	1.75	2.00
1994MW	69,956,000	—	—	—	1.75	2.00
1995MW	99,740,122	—	—	—	1.75	2.00

Y# 283 2 ZLOTE

5.2100 g., Bi-Metallic Copper-Nickel center in Brass ring, 21.5 mm. **Obv:** National arms within circle **Obv. Leg.:** RZECZPOSPOLITA POLSKA **Rev:** Value flanked by oak leaves

Date	Mintage	F	VF	XF	Unc	BU
1994MW	79,644,000	—	—	—	4.00	4.50
1995MW	122,880,020	—	—	—	4.00	4.50

Y# 285 2 ZLOTE

10.8000 g., Copper-Nickel, 29.5 mm. **Subject:** 55th Anniversary - Katyn Forest Massacre **Obv:** Crowned eagle with wings open divides date **Rev:** Burned forest

Date	Mintage	F	VF	XF	Unc	BU
1995	300,000	—	—	—	3.50	5.50

Y# 289 2 ZLOTE

10.8000 g., Copper-Nickel, 29.5 mm. **Obv:** Crowned eagle with wings open **Rev:** Catfish

Date	Mintage	F	VF	XF	Unc	BU
1995	300,000	—	—	—	14.00	25.00

Y# 297 2 ZLOTE

10.8000 g., Copper-Nickel, 26.8 mm. **Subject:** 75th Anniversary - Battle of Warsaw **Obv:** Crowned eagle with wings open divides date **Rev:** Armored figures behind figure with cross

Date	Mintage	F	VF	XF	Unc	BU
1995	300,000	—	—	—	3.50	5.50

Y# 300 2 ZLOTE

10.8000 g., Copper-Nickel, 29.5 mm. **Series:** 1996 Olympic Games **Obv:** Crowned eagle with wings open divides date **Rev:** Centennial

Date	Mintage	F	VF	XF	Unc	BU
1995	350,000	—	—	—	3.50	5.50

Y# 303 2 ZLOTE

10.8000 g., Copper-Nickel, 29.5 mm. **Series:** 1996 Olympics - Atlanta **Obv:** Crowned eagle with wings open divides date **Rev:** Wrestling

Date	Mintage	F	VF	XF	Unc	BU
1995	300,000	—	—	—	3.50	5.50

Y# 310 2 ZLOTE

10.8000 g., Copper-Nickel, 29.5 mm. **Obv:** Crowned eagle with wings open divides date, all within circle **Rev:** Lazienki Royal Palace

Date	Mintage	F	VF	XF	Unc	BU
1995	287,000	—	—	—	3.75	6.00

Y# 306 2 ZLOTE

8.1500 g., Brass, 27 mm. **Obv:** Imperial eagle above value **Rev:** Bust of Zygmunt II

Date	Mintage	F	VF	XF	Unc	BU
1996	200,000	—	—	—	10.00	12.00

Y# 311   2 ZLOTE
Copper-Zinc-Tin, 27 mm. **Obv:** Crowned eagle with wings open
Rev: Hedgehog with young

Date	Mintage	F	VF	XF	Unc	BU
1996	300,000	—	—	—	17.50	30.00

Y# 313   2 ZLOTE
8.1500 g., Copper-Aluminum-Zinc-Tin, 27 mm. **Obv:** Crowned
eagle with wings open divides date, all within circle **Rev:** Castle
and shield

Date	Mintage	F	VF	XF	Unc	BU
1996	300,000	—	—	—	3.00	5.00

Y# 315   2 ZLOTE
8.1500 g., Copper-Aluminum-Zinc-Tin, 27 mm. **Obv:** Crowned
eagle with wings open divides date **Rev:** Heads opposite divide dates

Date	Mintage	F	VF	XF	Unc	BU
1996	300,000	—	—	—	3.00	5.00

Y# 325   2 ZLOTE
8.1500 g., Brass, 27 mm. **Obv:** Crowned eagle with wings open
divides date **Rev:** Head of Stefan Batory 1/4 right

Date	Mintage	F	VF	XF	Unc	BU
1997	315,000	—	—	—	3.50	5.50

Y# 329   2 ZLOTE
8.1500 g., Brass, 27 mm. **Subject:** Jelonek Rogacz - Lucanus
cervus. **Obv:** Crowned eagle with wings open **Rev:** Stag beetle

Date	Mintage	F	VF	XF	Unc	BU
1997	315,000	—	—	—	10.00	25.00

Y# 331   2 ZLOTE
8.1500 g., Brass, 27 mm. **Obv:** Crowned eagle with wings open
Rev: Zamek W Pieskowej Skale

Date	Mintage	F	VF	XF	Unc	BU
1997	315,000	—	—	—	3.00	5.00

Y# 333   2 ZLOTE
8.5000 g., Copper-Aluminum-Zinc-Tin, 27 mm. **Obv:** Crowned
eagle with wings open divides date **Rev:** Head with headdress
left, antelope and ostrich within globe design

Date	Mintage	F	VF	XF	Unc	BU
1997	420,000	—	—	—	5.00	7.00

Y# 335   2 ZLOTE
Brass, 26.8 mm. **Series:** Nagano Olympics **Obv:** Crowned eagle
with wings open divides date **Rev:** Snow boarder

Date	Mintage	F	VF	XF	Unc	BU
1998	400,000	—	—	—	3.00	5.00

Y# 336   2 ZLOTE
8.1500 g., Brass, 27 mm. **Obv:** Imperial eagle above value **Rev:**
Sigismund III (1587-1632)

Date	Mintage	F	VF	XF	Unc	BU
1998	400,000	—	—	—	3.00	5.00

Y# 340   2 ZLOTE
8.1500 g., Brass, 27 mm. **Obv:** Crowned eagle with wings open
Rev: Toad right

Date	Mintage	F	VF	XF	Unc	BU
1998	400,000	—	—	—	15.00	22.00

Y# 344   2 ZLOTE
8.1500 g., Brass, 27 mm. **Subject:** Discovery of Radium and
Polomium **Obv:** Crowned eagle with wings open divides date
Rev: Seated and standing figure among scientific figures of
radium and polomium

Date	Mintage	F	VF	XF	Unc	BU
1998	400,000	—	—	—	3.00	5.00

Y# 347   2 ZLOTE
Brass, 26.8 mm. **Obv:** Imperial eagle above value **Rev:** Zamek
W. Korniku - Palace

Date	Mintage	F	VF	XF	Unc	BU
1998	400,000	—	—	—	3.50	5.50

Y# 349   2 ZLOTE
8.1500 g., Brass, 27 mm. **Subject:** 80th Anniversary - Polish
Independence **Obv:** Crowned eagle with wings open divides date
Rev: 1918 on flaming map

Date	Mintage	F	VF	XF	Unc	BU
1998	400,000	—	—	—	3.00	5.00

Y# 352   2 ZLOTE
8.1500 g., Brass, 27 mm. **Subject:** 200th Birthday - Adam
Mickiewicz **Obv:** Crowned eagle with wings open divides date
Rev: Head of Adam Mickiewicz 3/4 facing **Note:** With and without
dash between value and denomination.

Date	Mintage	F	VF	XF	Unc	BU
1998	420,000	—	—	—	3.00	5.00

Y# 355   2 ZLOTE
8.1500 g., Brass, 27 mm. **Obv:** Crowned eagle with wings open
Rev: Gray wolves and cubs **Edge:** POLSKI NARODOWY BANK

Date	Mintage	F	VF	XF	Unc	BU
1999	420,000	—	—	—	14.00	25.00

Y# 356   2 ZLOTE
8.1500 g., Brass, 27 mm. **Obv:** Crowned eagle with wings open
divides date **Rev:** Bust of Juliusz Slosacki 1/4 right

Date	Mintage	F	VF	XF	Unc	BU
1999	420,000	—	—	—	3.00	5.00

Y# 357 2 ZLOTE
8.1500 g., Brass, 27 mm. **Subject:** Poland's Accession to NATO **Obv:** Crowned eagle with wings open divides date **Rev:** NATO globe, soldiers rappelling from helicopter **Edge:** NARODOWY BANK POLSKI

Date	Mintage	F	VF	XF	Unc	BU
1999	400,000	—	—	—	3.00	5.00

Y# 358 2 ZLOTE
8.1500 g., Brass, 27 mm. **Obv:** Crowned eagle with wings open divides date **Rev:** Head of Ernest Malinowski facing above slanted text

Date	Mintage	F	VF	XF	Unc	BU
1999	420,000	—	—	—	3.00	5.00

Y# 363 2 ZLOTE
8.1500 g., Brass, 27 mm. **Obv:** Crowned eagle with wings open divides date **Rev:** Laski and Erasmus **Edge:** NARODOWY BANK POLSKI

Date	Mintage	F	VF	XF	Unc	BU
1999	420,000	—	—	—	3.00	5.00

Y# 365 2 ZLOTE
8.1500 g., Brass, 27 mm. **Obv:** Imperial eagle above value **Rev:** Fryderyk Chopin with stylized piano and music score **Edge:** NARODOWY BANK POLSKI

Date	Mintage	F	VF	XF	Unc	BU
1999	420,000	—	—	—	3.00	5.00

Y# 368 2 ZLOTE
Brass, 26.8 mm. **Obv:** Crowned eagle with wings open divides date **Rev:** Wladyslaw IV 1/4 right **Edge:** NARODOWY BANK POLSKI

Date	Mintage	F	VF	XF	Unc	BU
1999	500,000	—	—	—	3.00	5.00

Y# 372 2 ZLOTE
Brass, 26.8 mm. **Obv:** Crowned eagle with wings open divides date, all within circle **Rev:** Palace behind Potlocki family arms

Date	Mintage	F	VF	XF	Unc	BU
1999	450,000	—	—	—	3.50	5.50

Y# 404 2 ZLOTE
8.1500 g., Brass, 26.7 mm. **Subject:** Workers revolt in December 1970 **Obv:** Crowned eagle **Rev:** Fist **Edge:** "NBP" repeatedly

Date	Mintage	F	VF	XF	Unc	BU
2000	750,000	—	—	—	3.00	5.00

Y# 374 2 ZLOTE
8.3100 g., Bi-Metallic Copper-Nickel center in Brass ring, 26.8 mm. **Subject:** Millennium **Obv:** Crowned eagle in center **Rev:** Latent image dates in center **Edge:** NARODOWY BANK POLSKI

Date	Mintage	F	VF	XF	Unc	BU
2000	2,000,000	—	—	—	3.00	5.00

Y# 376 2 ZLOTE
8.1500 g., Brass, 26.8 mm. **Subject:** Holy Year **Obv:** Crowned eagle with wings open divides date **Rev:** Cross with holy symbolic animals

Date	Mintage	F	VF	XF	Unc	BU
2000	1,500,000	—	—	—	5.00	7.00

Y# 377 2 ZLOTE
8.1500 g., Brass, 26.8 mm. **Subject:** 1000th Anniversary - Gniezno Convention **Obv:** Crowned eagle with wings open divides date **Rev:** Denar coin design of Boleslaw Chrobry

Date	Mintage	F	VF	XF	Unc	BU
2000	450,000	—	—	—	5.00	7.00

Y# 388 2 ZLOTE
8.1400 g., Brass, 26.8 mm. **Subject:** "Dudek-Upupa epops" **Obv:** Crowned eagle with wings open **Rev:** Long-billed Hoopoe **Edge:** NARODOWY BANK POLSKI

Date	Mintage	F	VF	XF	Unc	BU
2000	500,000	—	—	—	5.00	9.00

Y# 389 2 ZLOTE
8.1400 g., Brass, 26.8 mm. **Subject:** 1000th Anniversary - Wroclawia (Breslau) **Obv:** Polish eagle **Rev:** Jesus with city view in background

Date	Mintage	F	VF	XF	Unc	BU
2000	500,000	—	—	—	3.00	5.00

Y# 390 2 ZLOTE
8.1400 g., Brass, 26.8 mm. **Obv:** Crowned eagle with wings open divides date, all within circle **Rev:** Wilanowie Palace

Date	Mintage	F	VF	XF	Unc	BU
2000	500,000	—	—	—	3.00	5.00

Y# 394 2 ZLOTE
8.2200 g., Brass, 26.8 mm. **Subject:** Solidarity **Obv:** Crowned eagle with wings open divides date **Rev:** Solidarity logo, map, children **Edge:** NARODOWY BANK POLSKI

Date	Mintage	F	VF	XF	Unc	BU
2000	750,000	—	—	—	3.00	5.00

Y# 398 2 ZLOTE
8.2200 g., Brass, 26.8 mm. **Obv:** Crowned eagle with wings open divides date **Rev:** Bust of Jan II Kazimierz facing 1/4 left **Edge:** POLSKA NARODOWY BANK **Note:** Jan II Kazimierz - 1648-68.

Date	Mintage	F	VF	XF	Unc	BU
2000	450,000	—	—	—	3.00	5.00

Y# 284 5 ZLOTYCH
6.5400 g., Bi-Metallic Brass center in Copper-Nickel ring, 24 mm. **Obv:** National arms within circle **Obv. Leg.:** RZECZPOSPOLITA POLSKA **Rev:** Value within circle flanked by oak leaves

Date	Mintage	F	VF	XF	Unc	BU
1994MW	112,896,033	—	—	—	7.00	8.00
1996MW	52,940,003	—	—	—	7.00	8.00

Y# 287   10 ZLOTYCH
16.5500 g., 0.7500 Silver 0.3991 oz. ASW, 32 mm. **Obv:** Crowned
eagle with wings open divides date **Rev:** Capture of Berlin

Date	Mintage	F	VF	XF	Unc	BU
1995 Proof	12,000	Value: 45.00				

Y# 301   10 ZLOTYCH
16.4400 g., 0.9250 Silver 0.4889 oz. ASW **Series:** 1996 Olympics
Obv: Imperial eagle above value **Rev:** Centennial - Atlanta

Date	Mintage	F	VF	XF	Unc	BU
1995 Proof	20,000	Value: 120				

Y# 305   10 ZLOTYCH
16.5000 g., 0.9250 Silver 0.4907 oz. ASW **Subject:** Centennial
of Organized Peasant Movement **Obv:** Imperial eagle above
value **Rev:** Wincenty Witos

Date	Mintage	F	VF	XF	Unc	BU
1995 Proof	20,000	Value: 45.00				

Y# 307   10 ZLOTYCH
16.5000 g., 0.9250 Silver 0.4907 oz. ASW **Obv:** Imperial eagle
above value **Rev:** Bust of Zygmunt II August left

Date	Mintage	F	VF	XF	Unc	BU
1996 Proof	13,000	Value: 45.00				

Y# 308   10 ZLOTYCH
16.5000 g., 0.9250 Silver 0.4907 oz. ASW **Obv:** Imperial eagle
above value **Rev:** Half-length figure facing left

Date	Mintage	F	VF	XF	Unc	BU
1996 Proof	5,000	Value: 80.00				

Y# 317   10 ZLOTYCH
16.5000 g., 0.9250 Silver 0.4907 oz. ASW, 32 mm.
Obv: Imperial eagle above value **Rev:** Stanislaw Mikolajczyk

Date	Mintage	F	VF	XF	Unc	BU
1996 Proof	13,500	Value: 45.00				

Y# 318   10 ZLOTYCH
16.5000 g., 0.9250 Silver 0.4907 oz. ASW, 32 mm.
Obv: Imperial eagle above value **Rev:** Mazurka of Dabrowski

Date	Mintage	F	VF	XF	Unc	BU
1996 Proof	14,000	Value: 50.00				

Y# 324   10 ZLOTYCH
16.5000 g., 0.9250 Silver 0.4907 oz. ASW, 32 mm.
Subject: 40th Anniversary - Poznan Workers Protest
Obv: Crowned eagle with wings open **Rev:** Figures around
inscription and date

Date	Mintage	F	VF	XF	Unc	BU
1996 Proof	13,050	Value: 45.00				

Y# 321   10 ZLOTYCH
16.5000 g., 0.9250 Silver 0.4907 oz. ASW **Subject:** St. Adalbert's
Martyrdom **Obv:** Crowned eagle with wings open **Rev:** Baptism and
funeral scenes **Edge:** 997-1997 (STAR) repeated 7 times

Date	Mintage	F	VF	XF	Unc	BU
1997 Proof	25,000	Value: 45.00				

Y# 322   10 ZLOTYCH
16.5000 g., 0.9250 Silver 0.4907 oz. ASW, 32 mm. **Subject:** 46th
Eucharistic Congress **Obv:** Crowned eagle with wings open within
design **Rev:** Pope left with arms raised **Edge:** MIEDZYNAR-
ODOWY KONGRES EUCHARYSTYCZNY - WROCLAW 1997

Date	Mintage	F	VF	XF	Unc	BU
1997 Proof	Est. 50,000	Value: 40.00				

Y# 326   10 ZLOTYCH
16.5000 g., 0.9250 Silver 0.4907 oz. ASW, 32 mm.   **Obv:**
Crowned eagle with wings open **Rev:** Stefan Batory 3/4 right

Date	Mintage	F	VF	XF	Unc	BU
1997 Proof	5,250	Value: 200				

Y# 327   10 ZLOTYCH
14.1400 g., 0.9250 Silver 0.4205 oz. ASW **Obv:** Crowned eagle
with wings open **Rev:** Stefan Batory

Date	Mintage	F	VF	XF	Unc	BU
1997 Proof	15,000	Value: 185				

Y# 334   10 ZLOTYCH
14.1400 g., 0.9250 Silver 0.4205 oz. ASW **Obv:** Crowned eagle
with wings open **Rev:** Pawel Edmund Strzelecki **Edge:** 200
LECIE URODZIN

Date	Mintage	F	VF	XF	Unc	BU
1997 Proof	20,000	Value: 45.00				

Y# 337   10 ZLOTYCH
14.1400 g., 0.9250 Silver 0.4205 oz. ASW, 32 mm. **Obv:** Crowned
eagle with wings open **Rev:** Crowned bust of Zygmunt III 1/4 left

Date	Mintage	F	VF	XF	Unc	BU
1998 Proof	22,000	Value: 45.00				

Y# 338   10 ZLOTYCH
14.1400 g., 0.9250 Silver 0.4205 oz. ASW **Subject:** Sigismund
III (1587-1632) **Obv:** Crowned eagle with wings open
Rev: Seated King 1/4 left

Date	Mintage	F	VF	XF	Unc	BU
1998 Proof	7,000	Value: 40.00				

Y# 341   10 ZLOTYCH
14.1400 g., 0.9250 Silver 0.4205 oz. ASW, 32 mm. **Series:** 1998
Winter Olympics **Obv:** Crowned eagle with wings open
Rev: Snowboarder

Date	Mintage	F	VF	XF	Unc	BU
1998 Proof	30,000	Value: 18.50				

Y# 342 10 ZLOTYCH
14.1400 g., 0.9250 Silver 0.4205 oz. ASW, 32 mm.
Obv: Crowned eagle with wings open **Rev:** Brigadier General
August Emil Fieldorf

Date	Mintage	F	VF	XF	Unc	BU
1998 Proof	14,000	Value: 45.00				

Y# 345 10 ZLOTYCH
14.1400 g., 0.9250 Silver 0.4205 oz. ASW, 32 mm.
Subject: 20th Anniversary of Pontificate **Obv:** Value and eagles
in cross design **Rev:** Pope John Paul II

Date	Mintage	F	VF	XF	Unc	BU
1998 Proof	65,000	Value: 65.00				

Y# 350 10 ZLOTYCH
14.1400 g., 0.9250 Silver 0.4205 oz. ASW **Subject:** 80th
Anniversary - Polish Independence **Obv:** Crowned eagle with
wings open within stylized flames **Rev:** Anniversary dates

Date	Mintage	F	VF	XF	Unc	BU
1998 Proof	16,000	Value: 35.00				

Y# 351 10 ZLOTYCH
14.1400 g., 0.9250 Silver 0.4205 oz. ASW, 32 mm.
Subject: Universal Declaration of Human Rights **Obv:** Crowned
eagle with wings open divides date **Rev:** Human figure between
two hands **Edge:** 50 ROCZNICA UCHWALENIA (three times)

Date	Mintage	F	VF	XF	Unc	BU
1998 Proof	16,000	Value: 35.00				

Y# 359 10 ZLOTYCH
14.1400 g., 0.9250 Silver 0.4205 oz. ASW, 32 mm.
Subject: Poland's Accession to NATO **Obv:** Crowned eagle with
wings open within quartered circle **Rev:** NATO globe, soldiers
rapelling from helicopter

Date	Mintage	F	VF	XF	Unc	BU
1999 Proof	16,000	Value: 30.00				

Y# 360 10 ZLOTYCH
14.1400 g., 0.9250 Silver 0.4205 oz. ASW, 32 mm. **Obv:** Crucifix
designs and crowned eagle **Rev:** Bust of Pope left and radiant dove

Date	Mintage	F	VF	XF	Unc	BU
1999 Proof	70,000	Value: 47.50				

Y# 362 10 ZLOTYCH
14.1400 g., 0.9250 Silver 0.4205 oz. ASW **Obv:** Crowned eagle
with wings open **Rev:** Queen Jadwiga and coat of arms
Edge: 1400-2000 (five times) **Note:** Cracow University.

Date	Mintage	F	VF	XF	Unc	BU
1999 Proof	22,000	Value: 32.50				

Y# 364 10 ZLOTYCH
14.1400 g., 0.9250 Silver 0.4205 oz. ASW, 32 mm.
Obv: Crowned eagle above windowed brick wall **Rev:** Laski with
Erasmus in background **Edge:** 500 LECIE URODZIN (twice)
Note: Jan Laski 1490-1560.

Date	Mintage	F	VF	XF	Unc	BU
1999 Proof	15,000	Value: 32.50				

Y# 366 10 ZLOTYCH
14.1400 g., 0.9250 Silver 0.4205 oz. ASW, 32 mm. **Obv:** Crowned
eagle over twisted chords **Rev:** Head right with stylized design

Date	Mintage	F	VF	XF	Unc	BU
1999 Proof	27,000	Value: 32.50				

Y# 369 10 ZLOTYCH
14.1400 g., 0.9250 Silver 0.4205 oz. ASW **Obv:** Crowned eagle
with wings open **Rev:** Portrait of Wladyslaw IV, dates

Date	Mintage	F	VF	XF	Unc	BU
1999 Proof	20,000	Value: 32.50				

Y# 370 10 ZLOTYCH
14.1400 g., 0.9250 Silver 0.4205 oz. ASW **Obv:** Crowned eagle
with wings open **Rev:** Framed half-length portrait of Wladyslaw IV

Date	Mintage	F	VF	XF	Unc	BU
1999 Proof	13,000	Value: 60.00				

Y# 378 10 ZLOTYCH
14.1400 g., 0.9250 Silver 0.4205 oz. ASW, 32 mm. **Obv:** World
globe and crowned eagle **Rev:** Bust of E. Malinowski facing, train
in background **Edge:** 100-LECIE SMIERCI (twice)

Date	Mintage	F	VF	XF	Unc	BU
1999 Proof	20,000	Value: 32.50				

Y# 379 10 ZLOTYCH
14.1400 g., 0.9250 Silver 0.4205 oz. ASW, 32 mm.
Obv: Inscription and crowned eagle **Rev:** Bust of Juliusz Slowacki
1/4 right **Edge:** Plain

Date	Mintage	F	VF	XF	Unc	BU
1999 Proof	20,000	Value: 30.00				

Y# 380 10 ZLOTYCH
14.1400 g., 0.9250 Silver 0.4205 oz. ASW **Subject:** Holy Year
Obv: Crowned eagle in frame **Rev:** Cross with symbols of the
evangelists **Edge:** WIELKI JUBILEUSZ ROKU 2000

Date	Mintage	F	VF	XF	Unc	BU
2000 Proof	60,000	Value: 32.50				

Y# 381 10 ZLOTYCH
14.1400 g., 0.9250 Silver 0.4205 oz. ASW **Subject:** 1000th
Anniversary - Gniezno Convention **Obv:** Old coin designs in
oxidized center, crowned eagle within circle **Rev:** Seated figures
of Boleslaw Chrobry and Otto III in oxidized center **Edge:** Plain

Date	Mintage	F	VF	XF	Unc	BU
2000 Proof	32,000	Value: 32.50				

Y# 392 10 ZLOTYCH
14.2000 g., 0.9250 Silver 0.4223 oz. ASW **Subject:** 1000 Years
Wroclaw (Breslau) **Obv:** Crowned eagle in front of city view
Rev: City arms in arch **Edge:** Plain

Date	Mintage	F	VF	XF	Unc	BU
2000 Proof	32,000	Value: 30.00				

Y# 395 10 ZLOTYCH
14.2200 g., 0.9250 Silver 0.4229 oz. ASW, 32 mm.
Subject: Solidarity **Obv:** Crowned eagle with wings open divides
date **Rev:** Solidarity logo and two children **Edge:** Plain

Date	Mintage	F	VF	XF	Unc	BU
2000 Proof	40,000	Value: 27.50				

Y# 400 10 ZLOTYCH
14.1400 g., 0.9250 Silver 0.4205 oz. ASW, 32 mm.
Subject: Jan Kazimierz II (1648-68) **Obv:** Crowned eagle with
wings open divides date **Rev:** Half-length figure facing 1/4 left
Edge: Plain

Date	Mintage	F	VF	XF	Unc	BU
2000 Proof	14,000	Value: 30.00				

Y# 401 10 ZLOTYCH
14.1400 g., 0.9250 Silver 0.4205 oz. ASW **Subject:** Jan Kazimierz
II (1648-68) **Obv:** Crowned eagle **Rev:** Jan II Kazimierz 1/4 left

Date	Mintage	F	VF	XF	Unc	BU
2000 Proof	20,000	Value: 30.00				

Y# 403 10 ZLOTYCH
14.1400 g., 0.9250 Silver 0.4205 oz. ASW **Subject:** Rapperswil
Polish Museum **Obv:** Crowned eagle and value between two
buildings **Rev:** Eagle-topped column **Edge:** GDANSK GDYNIA
SZCZECIN ELBLAG SLUPSK

Date	Mintage	F	VF	XF	Unc	BU
2000 Proof	37,000	Value: 30.00				

Y# 405 10 ZLOTYCH
14.1400 g., 0.9250 Silver 0.4205 oz. ASW **Subject:** Grudnia 1970
Obv: Two crowned eagles **Rev:** Shadow figures on pavement

Date	Mintage	F	VF	XF	Unc	BU
2000 Proof	37,000	Value: 30.00				

   Note: Antiqued finish

Y# 286 20 ZLOTYCH
31.1100 g., 0.9250 Silver 0.9252 oz. ASW, 38.6 mm.
Subject: Katyn Forest Massacre **Obv:** Crowned eagle with wings
open divides date **Rev:** Burned forest

Date	Mintage	F	VF	XF	Unc	BU
1995 Proof	30,000	Value: 37.50				

Y# 288 20 ZLOTYCH
31.1100 g., 0.9990 Silver 0.9992 oz. ASW, 38.6 mm.
Subject: 500th Anniversary - Plock Province **Obv:** Imperial eagle
above value **Rev:** Eagle on shield divides dates, castle in
background

Date	Mintage	F	VF	XF	Unc	BU
1995 Proof	15,000	Value: 45.00				

Y# 290 20 ZLOTYCH
31.1100 g., 0.9990 Silver 0.9992 oz. ASW **Obv:** Crowned eagle
with wings open **Rev:** Catfish

Date	Mintage	F	VF	XF	Unc	BU
1995 Proof	20,000	Value: 250				

Y# 291 20 ZLOTYCH
31.1100 g., 0.9990 Silver 0.9992 oz. ASW **Subject:** 50th
Anniversary - United Nations **Obv:** Imperial eagle above value
Rev: ONZ in front of half globe with designs

Date	Mintage	F	VF	XF	Unc	BU
1995 Proof	20,000	Value: 37.50				

Y# 296 20 ZLOTYCH
31.1700 g., 0.9990 Silver 1.0011 oz. ASW **Obv:** Crowned eagle
with wings open divides date, all within circle **Rev:** Royal Palace
and swans

Date	Mintage	F	VF	XF	Unc	BU
1995 Proof	20,000	Value: 130				

Y# 298 20 ZLOTYCH
30.9200 g., 0.9250 Silver 0.9195 oz. ASW **Subject:** 75th
Anniversary - Battle of Warsaw **Obv:** Imperial eagle above value
Rev: Armored figures behind figure with cross

Date	Mintage	F	VF	XF	Unc	BU
1995 Proof	20,000	Value: 40.00				

Y# 302 20 ZLOTYCH
31.0500 g., 0.9250 Silver 0.9234 oz. ASW, 38.6 mm.
Obv: Imperial eagle above value **Rev:** Copernicus and Ecu

Date	Mintage	F	VF	XF	Unc	BU
1995 Proof	15,000	Value: 150				

Y# 304 20 ZLOTYCH
31.1000 g., 0.9250 Silver 0.9249 oz. ASW, 38.6 mm. **Series:** 1996 Olympics - Atlanta **Obv:** Imperial eagle above value **Rev:** Wrestlers

Date	Mintage	F	VF	XF	Unc	BU
1995 Proof	16,700	Value: 65.00				

Y# 309 20 ZLOTYCH
31.1000 g., 0.9250 Silver 0.9249 oz. ASW, 38.6 mm. **Subject:** 400th Anniversary - Warsaw as Capital City **Obv:** Imperial eagle above value **Rev:** Buildings, statue and cross

Date	Mintage	F	VF	XF	Unc	BU
1996 Proof	16,500	Value: 45.00				

Y# 312 20 ZLOTYCH
31.1000 g., 0.9250 Silver 0.9249 oz. ASW, 38.6 mm. **Obv:** Crowned eagle with wings open **Rev:** Hedgehog with young

Date	Mintage	F	VF	XF	Unc	BU
1996 Proof	18,000	Value: 500				

Y# 314 20 ZLOTYCH
31.1000 g., 0.9250 Silver 0.9249 oz. ASW, 38.6 mm. **Obv:** Imperial eagle within circle outlined in crosses, value below **Rev:** Bishop's arms and Lidzibark Warminski castle

Date	Mintage	F	VF	XF	Unc	BU
1996 Proof	15,000	Value: 50.00				

Y# 319 20 ZLOTYCH
31.1000 g., 0.9250 Silver 0.9249 oz. ASW **Subject:** Millennium of Gdansk (Danzig) **Obv:** Imperial eagle above value **Rev:** Arms with supporters divide dates in front of city silhouette **Edge:** MONUMENTUM MILLENNII CIVITATIS GEDANENSIS

Date	Mintage	F	VF	XF	Unc	BU
1996 Proof	20,000	Value: 100				

Y# 330 20 ZLOTYCH
28.5200 g., 0.9250 Silver 0.8481 oz. ASW, 38.6 mm. **Obv:** Crowned eagle with wings open **Rev:** Stag beetle **Rev. Leg.:** JELONEK ROGACZ - Lucanus cervus

Date	Mintage	F	VF	XF	Unc	BU
1997 Proof	15,000	Value: 345				

Y# 332 20 ZLOTYCH
28.2800 g., 0.9250 Silver 0.8410 oz. ASW, 38.6 mm. **Obv:** Crowned eagle with wings open divides date, all within circle **Rev:** Zamek W Pieskowej Skale

Date	Mintage	F	VF	XF	Unc	BU
1997 Proof	15,100	Value: 160				

Y# 343 20 ZLOTYCH
28.2800 g., 0.9250 Silver 0.8410 oz. ASW, 38.6 mm. **Obv:** Crowned eagle with wings open **Rev:** Ropucha Paskowka - Natterjack Toad

Date	Mintage	F	VF	XF	Unc	BU
1998 Proof	20,000	Value: 250				

Y# 348 20 ZLOTYCH
28.2800 g., 0.9250 Silver 0.8410 oz. ASW, 38.6 mm. **Subject:** Zamek W. Koniku **Obv:** Crowned eagle with wings open **Rev:** Palace among diamond design

Date	Mintage	F	VF	XF	Unc	BU
1998 Proof	20,000	Value: 70.00				

Y# 354 20 ZLOTYCH
28.2800 g., 0.9250 Silver 0.8410 oz. ASW, 38.6 mm. **Subject:** Discovery of Radium and Polonium **Obv:** Atom design **Rev:** Madame and Monsieur Curie and formulas

Date	Mintage	F	VF	XF	Unc	BU
1998 Proof	20,000	Value: 50.00				

Y# 373 20 ZLOTYCH
28.2800 g., 0.9250 Silver 0.8410 oz. ASW **Subject:** Radzyn Podlaski Palace **Obv:** Crowned eagle within inner circle **Rev:** Palace behind sculptured arms

Date	Mintage	F	VF	XF	Unc	BU
1999 Proof	15,000	Value: 145				

Y# 382 20 ZLOTYCH
28.2800 g., 0.9250 Silver 0.8410 oz. ASW, 38.6 mm. **Obv:** Imperial eagle above value **Rev:** Wolf family

Date	Mintage	F	VF	XF	Unc	BU
1999 Proof	21,000	Value: 275				

Y# 387 20 ZLOTYCH
28.3700 g., 0.9250 Silver 0.8437 oz. ASW **Obv:** Imperial eagle above value **Rev:** Dudek - Upupa epops - Eurasian Hoopoe

Date	Mintage	F	VF	XF	Unc	BU
2000 Proof	24,000	Value: 125				

Y# 391   20 ZLOTYCH
28.2400 g., 0.9250 Silver 0.8398 oz. ASW, 38.5 mm.
Obv: Crowned eagle **Rev:** View of Palace through front gate
Edge: Plain

Date	Mintage	F	VF	XF	Unc	BU
2000 Proof	24,000	Value: 75.00				

Y# 328   100 ZLOTYCH
8.0000 g., 0.9000 Gold 0.2315 oz. AGW, 24 mm. **Obv:** Crowned
eagle with wings open divides date **Rev:** Bust of Stefan Batory
1/4 right

Date	Mintage	F	VF	XF	Unc	BU
1997 Proof	2,000	Value: 275				

Y# 339   100 ZLOTYCH
8.0000 g., 0.9000 Gold 0.2315 oz. AGW, 21 mm. **Obv:** Crowned
eagle with wings open divides date **Rev:** Sigismund III 1/4 left

Date	Mintage	F	VF	XF	Unc	BU
1998 Proof	2,000	Value: 275				

Y# 361   100 ZLOTYCH
8.0000 g., 0.9000 Gold 0.2315 oz. AGW, 21 mm. **Obv:** Crowned
eagle in inner circle **Rev:** Pope John Paul II left

Date	Mintage	F	VF	XF	Unc	BU
1999 Proof	7,000	Value: 250				

Y# 371   100 ZLOTYCH
8.0000 g., 0.9000 Gold 0.2315 oz. AGW, 21 mm. **Obv:** Crowned
eagle with wings open divides date **Rev:** Wladyslaw IV in frame

Date	Mintage	F	VF	XF	Unc	BU
1999 Proof	2,300	Value: 275				

Y# 383   100 ZLOTYCH
8.0000 g., 0.9000 Gold 0.2315 oz. AGW **Obv:** Crowned eagle
with wings open divides date **Rev:** Bust of Zygmunt II left

Date	Mintage	F	VF	XF	Unc	BU
1999 Proof	2,000	Value: 245				

Y# 384   100 ZLOTYCH
8.0000 g., 0.9000 Gold 0.2315 oz. AGW **Subject:** 100th
Anniversary - Gniezno Convention **Obv:** Old coin designs
Rev: Seated figures of Boleslaw Chrobry and Otto III

Date	Mintage	F	VF	XF	Unc	BU
2000 Proof	2,200	Value: 245				

Y# 396   100 ZLOTYCH
8.0000 g., 0.9000 Gold 0.2315 oz. AGW **Obv:** Crowned eagle
with wings open divides date **Rev:** Queen Jadwiga facing
Edge: Plain

Date	Mintage	F	VF	XF	Unc	BU
2000 Proof	2,000	Value: 275				

Y# 402   100 ZLOTYCH
8.0000 g., 0.9000 Gold 0.2315 oz. AGW, 21 mm. **Subject:** Jan
Kazimierz II (1648-68) **Obv:** Crowned eagle with wings open
Rev: Armored bust 1/4 left with names and dates on shoulder
Edge: Plain

Date	Mintage	F	VF	XF	Unc	BU
2000 Proof	2,000	Value: 275				

Y# 299   200 ZLOTYCH
15.5000 g., 0.9000 Gold 0.4485 oz. AGW **Subject:** XII Chopin
Piano Competition **Obv:** Crowned eagle with wings open divides
date **Rev:** Bust of Chopin 1/4 right below tree **Edge:** Lettered

Date	Mintage	F	VF	XF	Unc	BU
1995 Proof	500	Value: 925				

Y# 316   200 ZLOTYCH
15.5000 g., 0.9000 Gold 0.4485 oz. AGW **Obv:** Stylized design
to right of eagle **Rev:** Henryk Sienkiewicz

Date	Mintage	F	VF	XF	Unc	BU
1996 Proof	Est. 1,000	Value: 450				

Y# 320   200 ZLOTYCH
15.5000 g., 0.9000 Gold 0.4485 oz. AGW **Subject:** Millennium
of Gdansk (Danzig) **Obv:** Crowned eagle with wings open within
shield **Rev:** City arms in old coin style

Date	Mintage	F	VF	XF	Unc	BU
1996 Proof	2,000	Value: 450				

Y# 323   200 ZLOTYCH
15.5000 g., 0.9000 Gold 0.4485 oz. AGW **Subject:** St. Adalbert's
Martyrdom **Obv:** Crowned eagle with wings open within circle
Rev: Figure standing within center design flanked by other figures

Date	Mintage	F	VF	XF	Unc	BU
1997 Proof	2,000	Value: 450				

Y# 346   200 ZLOTYCH
15.5000 g., 0.9000 Gold 0.4485 oz. AGW **Obv:** Imperial eagle
above value **Rev:** Standing Pope with arms wide open

Date	Mintage	F	VF	XF	Unc	BU
1998 Proof	5,000	Value: 450				

Y# 353   200 ZLOTYCH
15.5000 g., 0.9000 Gold 0.4485 oz. AGW **Subject:** 200th
Birthday - Adam Mickiewicz **Obv:** Small crowned eagle at lower
right, quote written above **Rev:** Portrait with silhouette

Date	Mintage	F	VF	XF	Unc	BU
1998 Proof	3,000	Value: 450				

Y# 367   200 ZLOTYCH
15.5000 g., 0.9000 Gold 0.4485 oz. AGW **Obv:** Crowned eagle
on sash, music design **Rev:** Head of Fryderyk Chopin 1/4 left
with music background

Date	Mintage	F	VF	XF	Unc	BU
1999 Proof	2,200	Value: 450				

Y# 385   200 ZLOTYCH
15.5000 g., 0.9000 Gold 0.4485 oz. AGW **Obv:** Crowned eagle
with wings open, feather at right **Rev:** Head of Juliusz Slowacki left

Date	Mintage	F	VF	XF	Unc	BU
1999 Proof	1,900	Value: 450				

Y# 386 200 ZLOTYCH
15.5000 g., 0.9000 Gold 0.4485 oz. AGW **Subject:** 1000th Anniversary - Gniezno Convention **Obv:** Old coin designs **Rev:** Seated figures of Boleslaw Chrobry and Otto III

Date	Mintage	F	VF	XF	Unc	BU
2000 Proof	1,250	Value: 450				

Y# 393 200 ZLOTYCH
15.5000 g., 0.9000 Gold 0.4485 oz. AGW, 27 mm. **Subject:** 1000 Years - Wroclzaw (Breslau) **Obv:** Crowned eagle with wings open within beaded circle **Rev:** Bust of Jesus facing, holding city arms **Edge:** Plain

Date	Mintage	F	VF	XF	Unc	BU
2000 Proof	2,000	Value: 450				

Y# 397 200 ZLOTYCH
23.3200 g., 0.9000 Gold 0.6748 oz. AGW, 32 mm. **Subject:** Solidarity **Obv:** Crowned eagle with wings open **Rev:** Multicolor Soldiarity logo, map and two children **Edge:** Plain

Date	Mintage	F	VF	XF	Unc	BU
2000 Proof	2,500	Value: 650				

Y# 375 200 ZLOTYCH
13.6000 g., Gold And Silver **Subject:** Millennium **Obv:** Crowned eagle and world globe **Rev:** Various computer, DNA and atomic symbols **Note:** .900 Gold center in .925 Silver inner ring in a .900 Gold outer ring.

Date	Mintage	F	VF	XF	Unc	BU
2000 Proof	6,000	Value: 250				

Y# 267 1000 ZLOTYCH
27.9500 g., 0.9250 Silver 0.8312 oz. ASW **Subject:** World Cup Soccer **Rev:** Soccer stadium

Date	Mintage	F	VF	XF	Unc	BU
1994MW Proof	10,000	Value: 65.00				

GOLD BULLION COINAGE

Y# 292 50 ZLOTYCH
3.1000 g., 0.9999 Gold 0.0997 oz. AGW, 18 mm. **Obv:** Crowned eagle with wings open, all within circle **Rev:** Golden eagle

Date	Mintage	F	VF	XF	Unc	BU
1995	5,000	—	—	—	BV	165
1996	2,500	—	—	—	BV	175
1997	2,000	—	—	—	BV	175
1998	1,500	—	—	—	BV	180
1999	2,000	—	—	—	BV	175
2000	2,000	—	—	—	BV	175

Y# 293 100 ZLOTYCH
7.7800 g., 0.9999 Gold 0.2501 oz. AGW, 22 mm. **Obv:** Crowned eagle with wings open, all within circle **Rev:** Golden eagle

Date	Mintage	F	VF	XF	Unc	BU
1995	3,000	—	—	—	BV	265
1996	2,500	—	—	—	BV	265
1997	2,000	—	—	—	BV	265
1998	500	—	—	—	BV	300
1999	1,000	—	—	—	BV	275
2000	500	—	—	—	BV	300

Y# 294 200 ZLOTYCH
15.5000 g., 0.9000 Gold 0.4485 oz. AGW, 27 mm. **Obv:** Crowned eagle with wings open within beaded circle **Rev:** Golden eagle

Date	Mintage	F	VF	XF	Unc	BU
1995	2,000	—	—	—	BV	625
1996	2,500	—	—	—	BV	625
1997	1,500	—	—	—	BV	650
1998	500	—	—	—	BV	700
1999	1,000	—	—	—	BV	650
2000	500	—	—	—	BV	700

Y# 295 500 ZLOTYCH
31.1035 g., 0.9999 Gold 0.9999 oz. AGW **Obv:** Crowned eagle with wings open within beaded circle **Rev:** Golden eagle

Date	Mintage	F	VF	XF	Unc	BU
1995	2,500	—	—	—	BV	1,000
1996	2,500	—	—	—	BV	1,000
1997	3,500	—	—	—	BV	975
1998	1,000	—	—	—	BV	1,250
1999	1,500	—	—	—	BV	650
2000	500	—	—	—	BV	1,500

TRIAL STRIKES

KM#	Date	Mintage	Identification	Mkt Val
TS1	1923	—	Grosz. Copper. Uniface.	75.00
TS2	1923	—	Grosz. Copper. Uniface.	75.00

PATTERNS
Including off metal strikes

KM#	Date	Mintage	Identification	Mkt Val
Pn232	1919	—	50 Groszy. Nickel. 7.5600 g. Small eagle.	—

| Pn233 | 1919 | — | 50 Groszy. Nickel. Large eagle. | — |

Pn234	1922	60	100 Marek. Copper. 8.8400 g.	550
Pn235	1922	100	100 Marek. Bronze. 8.8400 g.	200
Pn236	1922	10	100 Marek. Brass. 8.8400 g.	—
Pn237	1922	4	100 Marek. Tin. 4.5700 g.	—
Pn238	1922	50	100 Marek. Silver. 8.8000 g.	350
Pn239	1922	3	100 Marek. Gold.	—

Pn240	1923	120	50 Marek. Bronze. 5.1300 g.	200
Pn241	1923	12	50 Marek. Silver. 5.2500 g.	—
Pn242	1923	1	50 Marek. Gold.	—

| Pn243 | 1923 | 30 | Grosz. Bronze. 1.5000 g. | 300 |

| Pn244 | 1923 | 125 | 2 Grosze. Bronze. 1.5600 g. | 350 |
| Pn245 | 1923 | — | 2 Grosze. Gold. | — |

| Pn246 | 1923 | 10 | 5 Groszy. Brass. 3.0000 g. | — |
| Pn247 | 1923 | 100 | 5 Groszy. Silver. 3.2900 g. | 200 |

| Pn248 | 1923 | 3 | 5 Groszy. Brass. 3.0000 g. | 250 |

KM#	Date	Mintage	Identification	Mkt Val	KM#	Date	Mintage	Identification	Mkt Val	KM#	Date	Mintage	Identification	Mkt Val
Pn249	1923	30	20 Groszy. Brass. 4.5200 g.	125	Pn261	1924	3	2 Zlote. Silver. 10.0000 g. Larger eagle.	—	Pn283	1925	100	100 Zlotych. Bronze. 3.5000 g. Kopernik Commemorative.	200
Pn250	1923	30	50 Groszy. Brass. 4.5200 g.	—						Pn284	1925	50	100 Zlotych. Silver. 4.1500 g.	400
										Pn285	1925	1	100 Zlotych. Gold.	—
Pn251	1923	—	50 Groszy. Nickel. HUGUENIN in 0 of 50.	—	Pn262	1924	120	20 Zlotych. Bronze. 3.3500 g.	200					
					Pn263	1924	10	20 Zlotych. Silver. 5.6900 g.	500	Pn286	1926	20	2 Grosze. Nickel. 2.4700 g.	—
					Pn264	1924	10	20 Zlotych. Gold.	—	Pn287	1926	100	2 Grosze. Silver. 2.2900 g.	200
					Pn266	1924	2	50 Zlotych. Lead. 7.8000 g.	—	Pn288	1927	100	Grosz. Silver. 5.2500 g.	—
					Pn267	1924	2	50 Zlotych. Aluminum. 2.8000 g.	—	Pn289	1927	6	Grosz. Gold.	—
					Pn268	1924	1	50 Zlotych. Gold.	—	Pn290	1927	100	2 Zlote.	125
Pn265	1924	105	50 Zlotych. Copper. 10.4200 g.	200	Pn269	1925	15	5 Groszy. Brass. 3.0000 g.	—					
Pn252	1924	10	20 Groszy. Nickel. 3.0000 g.	—										
					Pn272	1925	100	10 Zlotych. Bronze. 3.3100 g.	200					
					Pn273	1925	50	10 Zlotych. Silver. 4.3700 g.	300	Pn291	1927	10	2 Zlote. Bronze. 9.8600 g. With PROBA.	
Pn253	1924	15	Zloty. Silver. 5.0000 g. ESSAI.		Pn274	1925	1	10 Zlotych. Gold.	—					
					Pn275	1925	105	20 Zlotych. Bronze. 5.3900 g.	200	Pn292	1927	100	2 Zlote. Silver. 10.0000 g. Warsau Mint, with proba	4,500
					Pn276	1925	10	20 Zlotych. Copper. 5.3900 g.	300					
					Pn277	1925	12	20 Zlotych. Silver. 4.3200 g.	450					
					Pn278	1925	5	20 Zlotych. Gold.	—					
Pn254	1924	40	Zloty. Silver. With torch.	800	Pn279	1925	35	20 Zlotych. Brass. 3.2700 g. Boleslaus I, Y#33.	—					
Pn255	1924 H	8	Zloty. Silver.	—	Pn280	1925	20	20 Zlotych. Nickel. 3.5000 g. Boleslaus I, Y#33.	—					
										Pn293	1927	81	5 Zlotych. Silver. 18.4000 g. With MM, PROBA.	500
										Pn294	1927	20	5 Zlotych. Silver. 18.4000 g. Without MM, without PROBA.	—
										Pn295	1927	100	5 Zlotych. Silver. 16.0000 g. Without MM, with PROBA.	—
Pn256	1924	40	2 Zlote. Brass. 9.6500 g.	350										
Pn257	1924	100	2 Zlote. Brass. 10.0000 g. Rotated dies.	300	Pn281	1925	2	100 Zlotych. Silver. 24.2000 g. Plain edge.	—					
										Pn296	1928	2	Zloty. Copper. 7.9000 g.	—
										Pn297	1928	2	Zloty. Tombac. 6.0000 g.	—
										Pn298	1928	25	Zloty. Nickel. 6.8400 g.	—
										Pn300	1928	35	Zloty. Nickel. 7.0000 g. Mint mark.	—
Pn258	1924	15	2 Zlote. Silver. 10.0000 g. ESSAI. Paris Mint.	—										
Pn259	1924 H	60	2 Zlote. Silver. 10.0000 g.	900						Pn299	1928	110	Zloty. Nickel. 7.0000 g.	2,500
Pn260	1924	10	2 Zlote. Silver. 10.0000 g.	—	Pn282	1925	100	100 Zlotych. Silver. 24.5300 g. Edge lettering: SALUS REIPUBLICAE SUPREMA LEX.	—	Pn301	1928	35	Zloty. Bronze. 7.0000 g.	—

KM#	Date	Mintage	Identification	Mkt Val
Pn302	1928		15 Zloty. Nickel. 7.0700 g.	—
Pn303	1928		8 Zloty. Tombac. 6.0000 g.	—
Pn304	1928		2 Zloty. Copper. 6.9800 g.	—
Pn305	1928		125 Zloty. Bronze. 6.0000 g.	400
Pn306	1928		— Zloty. Nickel. Madonna.	—
Pn307	1928		— 2 Zlotych. Aluminum. Madonna.	—
Pn308	1928		— 2 Zlotych. Copper. Madonna.	—
Pn309	1928		— 2 Zlotych. Silver. Madonna.	—
Pn310	1928		— 2 Zlotych. Gold. Madonna.	1,250
Pn311	1928		— 2 Zlotych. Platinum. Madonna.	1,500
Pn312	1928		— 5 Zlotych. Aluminum. Madonna.	—
Pn313	1928		— 5 Zlotych. Copper. Madonna.	—
Pn314	1928		— 5 Zlotych. Nickel. Madonna.	—
Pn315	1928		— 5 Zlotych. Silver. Madonna.	375
Pn316	1928		— 5 Zlotych. Gold. Madonna.	1,750
Pn317	1928		— 5 Zlotych. Platinum. Madonna.	2,250
Pn318	1928		20 5 Zlotych. Silver. 18.4000 g. Nike.	—

KM#	Date	Mintage	Identification	Mkt Val
Pn319	1928		— 5 Zlotych. Tombac. ESSAI/30.	1,250
Pn320	1928		20 5 Zlotych. Tombac. Denticals instead of dots.	900
Pn321	1929		10 Zloty. Aluminum. 2.2800 g.	—
Pn322	1929		12 Zloty. Bronze. 4.8700 g.	—
Pn323	1929		115 Zloty. Nickel. 6.8400 g. Without PROBA.	100
Pn324	1930		20 5 Zlotych. Bronze. 16.0000 g. PROBA.	250
Pn325	1930		200 5 Zlotych. Bronze. Without PROBA.	—
Pn326	1932		100 Zloty. Bronze. 2.0500 g.	125
Pn327	1932		120 Zloty. Silver. 2.0200 g.	85.00
Pn328	1932		100 2 Zlote. Bronze. 3.8700 g.	125
Pn329	1932		110 2 Zlote. Silver. 4.4000 g.	150
Pn330	1932		100 10 Zlotych. Silver. 22.0000 g.	350
Pn331	1932		10 10 Zlotych. Bronze. 19.2200 g.	—
Pn332	1932		100 10 Zlotych. Bronze. 19.7000 g.	250
PnA333	1933		— 2 Zlote. Silver. PROBA.	—
Pn333	1933		100 5 Zlotych. Bronze. 10.0700 g.	200
Pn334	1933		100 5 Zlotych. Silver. 11.0000 g.	250
Pn335	1933		100 10 Zlotych. Silver. 22.0000 g.	850

KM#	Date	Mintage	Identification	Mkt Val
Pn336	1933		100 10 Zlotych. Silver. 28.6700 g. PROBA, Y#23.	850
Pn337	1933		100 10 Zlotych. Silver. 30.0000 g. Klippe.	650
Pn338	1933		100 10 Zlotych. Silver. 28.8100 g. Klippe. Y#24.	1,000
Pn339	1934		100 5 Zlotych. Bronze. 9.4700 g. PROBA.	150
Pn340	1934		100 5 Zlotych. Silver. 11.0000 g. PROBA.	250
Pn341	1934		100 5 Zlotych. Silver. 11.0000 g. Without PROBA.	—

KM#	Date	Mintage	Identification	Mkt Val
PnA342	1934	—	10 Zlotych. Silver.	—
Pn342	1934	2	10 Zlotych. Aluminum.	500
Pn343	1934	130	10 Zlotych. Iron-Plated Nickel. 4.9700 g.	250
Pn344	1934	3	10 Zlotych. Tombac. 10.3000 g.	700

KM#	Date	Mintage	Identification	Mkt Val
Pn345	1934	100	10 Zlotych. Silver. 22.0000 g. PROBA.	900
Pn346	1934	100	10 Zlotych. Silver. 22.0000 g. Without PROBA.	—
Pn347	1934	100	10 Zlotych. Bronze. 19.4000 g. PROBA.	—
Pn348	1934	3	10 Zlotych. Silver. 15.0000 g.	1,000

KM#	Date	Mintage	Identification	Mkt Val
Pn349	1934	300	10 Zlotych. Silver. 41.1900 g. Klippe. Illustration reduced.	1,250
Pn351	1936	110	5 Zlotych.	300

KM#	Date	Mintage	Identification	Mkt Val
Pn350	1936	100	2 Zlote. Silver. 4.4000 g. With PROBA.	200
PnA351	1936	100	2 Zlote. Silver. 4.4000 g. Without PROBA.	—

KM#	Date	Mintage	Identification	Mkt Val
Pn352	1936	200	5 Zlotych. Bronze. 17.4600 g. Klippe.	600

KM#	Date	Mintage	Identification	Mkt Val
Pn353	1936	200	5 Zlotych. Silver. 19.8400 g. Klippe. Illustration reduced.	1,250
PnA356	1938	100	20 Groszy. Nickeled Iron. Without PROBA.	—
Pn354	1938	100	10 Groszy. Bronze. 4.9000 g.	200
Pn355	1938	100	20 Groszy. Nickeled Iron. 3.4900 g. With PROBA.	120
Pn356	1938	120	50 Groszy. Iron.	100
Pn357	1938	10	50 Groszy. Aluminum.	—
Pn358	1938	100	50 Groszy. Iron. 4.5000 g.	100
Pn359	1938	1	50 Groszy. Bronze. 3.4000 g.	—
Pn360	1938	3	50 Groszy. Aluminum.	—
Pn361	1938	200	50 Groszy. Iron-Plated Nickel.	75.00
Pn362	1939	200	Grosz. Zinc. 14.7000 g.	75.00
Pn363	1939	200	2 Grosze. Zinc. 1.7500 g.	75.00
Pn364	1939	200	5 Groszy. Zinc. 1.7200 g. 2/hole.	75.00
Pn365	1981M W	3,000	2000 Zlotych. Gold. 8.0000 g. Boleslaw II.	—

PIEFORTS

KM#	Date	Mintage	Identification	Mkt Val
P1	1989	—	10000 Zlotych. Gold. Y#189.	—
'P2	1989	—	10000 Zlotych. Silver. Y#237.	—

PROBAS
Standard metals unless otherwise stated

In Poland, rejected coin designs are often minted in large numbers for sale to collectors. These coins have the word PROBA on them, usually stamped incuse. The coins struck in nickel are not available to the general public. Of the 500 pieces struck, 250 pieces are distributed among the members of the Polish Numismatic Society and the other 250 pieces are distributed between various banks and museums.

KM#	Date	Mintage	Identification	Mkt Val
PrA1	1929	—	Zloty. Nickel. Crowned eagle with wings open. Value within fruit wreath.	
Pr1	1949	—	Grosz. Aluminum.	—
Pr2	1949	100	Grosz. Brass. Y#39.	65.00
Pr3	1949	500	Grosz. Nickel. Y#39.	40.00
Pr4	1949	100	2 Grosze. Brass. Y#40.	65.00
Pr5	1949	500	2 Grosze. Nickel. Y#40.	45.00
Pr6	1949	—	2 Grosze. Aluminum.	—
Pr7	1949	100	5 Groszy. Brass. Y#41.	75.00
PrA7	1949	500	5 Groszy. Nickel. Y#41.	45.00
Pr8	1949	100	5 Groszy. Brass.	—
Pr9	1949	—	5 Groszy. Aluminum. Eagle with wings open. Value at upper right of spray.	—
Pr10	1949	—	10 Groszy. Aluminum.	—
Pr11	1949	100	10 Groszy. Brass. Y#42.	65.00
Pr12	1949	500	10 Groszy. Nickel. Y#42.	45.00
Pr13	1949	100	20 Groszy. Brass. Y#43.	65.00
Pr14	1949	500	20 Groszy. Nickel. Y#43.	45.00
Pr15	1949	—	20 Groszy. Aluminum.	—
Pr16	1949	100	50 Groszy. Brass. Y#44.	65.00
Pr17	1949	20	50 Groszy. Tombac. Y#44.	—

KM#	Date	Mintage	Identification	Mkt Val
Pr18	1949	500	50 Groszy. Nickel. Y#44.	45.00
Pr19	1949	—	50 Groszy. Aluminum.	—

| Pr20 | 1949 | 100 | Zloty. Brass. Y#45. | 80.00 |
| Pr21 | 1949 | — | Zloty. Aluminum. | — |

| Pr22 | 1949 | 500 | Zloty. Nickel. Y#45. | 45.00 |

| Pr23 | 1957 | 100 | 20 Groszy. Brass. Y#A47. | 80.00 |

| Pr24 | 1957 | 100 | 50 Groszy. Brass. Y#48.1. | 80.00 |
| Pr25 | 1957 | 500 | 50 Groszy. Nickel. Y#48.1. | 45.00 |

Pr26	1957	100	Zloty. Brass. Y#49.1.	80.00
Pr27	1957	500	Zloty. Nickel. Y#49.1.	45.00
Pr28	1957	5	Zloty. Copper-Nickel-Zinc. Y#49.1 without PROBA.	—

| Pr29 | 1958 | 100 | 5 Groszy. Brass. Y#A46. | — |

| Pr30 | 1958 | 245 | 50 Groszy. Aluminum. Eagle with wings open. Value above crossed hammers. | 35.00 |
| Pr31 | 1958 | 500 | 50 Groszy. Nickel. Crossed hammers. | 35.00 |

| Pr32 | 1958 | 198 | 50 Groszy. Aluminum. Eagle with wings open. Antenna below value. | 35.00 |
| Pr33 | 1958 | 500 | 50 Groszy. Nickel. Antenna below denomination. | 35.00 |

KM#	Date	Mintage	Identification	Mkt Val
Pr34	1958	212	50 Groszy. Alum. Eagle with wings open. Value above spears of grain.	35.00
Pr35	1958	500	50 Groszy. Nickel. 50 above spears of grain.	35.00

| Pr36 | 1958 | 234 | Zloty. Aluminum. Eagle with wings open. 1 Between spears of grain. | 30.00 |
| Pr37 | 1958 | 500 | Zloty. Nickel. 1 between spears of grain. | 35.00 |

| Pr38 | 1958 | 235 | Zloty. Aluminum. Eagle with wings open. Value in spears of grain within diamond shape design. | 35.00 |
| Pr39 | 1958 | 500 | Zloty. Nickel. 1 within circle. | 35.00 |

| Pr40 | 1958 | 211 | Zloty. Aluminum. Eagle with wings open. Value among acorns and oak leaves. | 30.00 |
| Pr41 | 1958 | 500 | Zloty. Nickel. Acorns and oak leaves. | 35.00 |

Pr42	1958	210	Zloty. Aluminum. Eagle with wings open. Value between doves, low relief.	30.00
Pr43	1958	53	Zloty. Aluminum. 1 between doves, high relief.	125
Pr44	1958	500	Zloty. Nickel. 1 between birds.	35.00

| Pr45 | 1958 | 100 | 2 Zlote. Brass. Y#46. | 55.00 |

| Pr46 | 1958 | 5 | 5 Zlotych. Aluminum. Eagle with wings open. Hammer and shovel without PROBA. | — |

KM#	Date	Mintage	Identification	Mkt Val
Pr47	1958	5	5 Zlotych. Brass. Eagle with wings open. Ship and value.	—
Pr48	1958	20	5 Zlotych. Aluminum. Ship, without PROBA.	150

| Pr49 | 1958 | 500 | 5 Zlotych. Nickel. Ship. | 35.00 |
| Pr50 | 1958 | 10 | 5 Zlotych. Aluminum. Without PROBA, reverse of Pr49. | — |

| Pr51 | 1958 | 5 | 10 Zlotych. Aluminum. Eagle with wings open. Caliper and gear, without PROBA. | 100 |

Pr52	1958	10	10 Zlotych. Aluminum. Eagle with wings open. Kosciuszko with ornaments, without PROBA.	—
Pr53	1958	10	10 Zlotych. Copper-Nickel. Eagle with wings open. Kosciuszko with ornaments, without PROBA.	—
Pr54	1958	5	10 Zlotych. Aluminum. With ornaments and PROBA.	100
Pr55	1958	5	10 Zlotych. Brass. Eagle with wings open. Kosciuszko with ornaments without PROBA.	—
Pr56	1958	5	10 Zlotych. Copper-Nickel. Eagle with wings open. Kosciuszko with ornaments and PROBA.	—
Pr57	1958	10	10 Zlotych. Aluminum.	—

| Pr58 | 1958 | 5 | 10 Zlotych. Copper-Nickel. Eagle with wings open. Without ornaments and PROBA, high relief. | — |

KM#	Date	Mintage	Identification	Mkt Val
Pr59	1959	500	2 Zlote. Nickel. Y#46.	30.00
Pr60	1959	100	5 Zlotych. Brass. Y#47.	65.00
Pr61	1959	500	5 Zlotych. Nickel. Y#47.	30.00
Pr62	1959	500	5 Zlotych. Nickel. Eagle with wings open. Value within industrial collage.	30.00
Pr63	1959	500	5 Zlotych. Nickel. Eagle with wings open. Value to left of hammer and shovel.	30.00
Pr64	1959	10	10 Zlotych. Aluminum. Y#51.	—
Pr65	1959	500	10 Zlotych. Nickel. Y#51.	30.00
Pr66	1960	196	5 Zlotych. Aluminum. Ship.	—
Pr67	1960	500	5 Zlotych. Nickel. Eagle with wings open. Ship and value.	32.50
Pr68	1960	500	10 Zlotych. Nickel. Eagle with wings open. Value above caliper and gear.	30.00
Pr69	1960	500	10 Zlotych. Nickel. Eagle with wings open. Kosciuszko with ornaments and PROBA.	30.00
Pr70	1960	500	10 Zlotych. Nickel. Eagle with wings open. Kosciuszko with PROBA in front of neck.	30.00
Pr71	1960	10	100 Zlotych. Nickel. Y#57, with crosshatched field.	—
Pr72	1960	500	100 Zlotych. Nickel. Y#57, with crosshatched field.	35.00
Pr73	1960	50	100 Zlotych. 0.5000 Silver. Without PROBA, Y#57 with crosshatched field.	60.00
Pr74	1960	20	100 Zlotych. 0.7500 Silver. Y#57, with crosshatched field.	60.00
Pr75	1960	500	100 Zlotych. Nickel. Y#57.	35.00
Pr76	1960	12	100 Zlotych. 0.7500 Silver. Eagle with wings open flanked by shields. Conjoined heads right.	125
Pr77	1960	14	100 Zlotych. 0.7500 Silver.	125
Pr78	1960	4	100 Zlotych. 0.7000 Silver. High relief.	—
Pr79	1960	9	100 Zlotych. 0.7000 Silver. Flat relief.	—
Pr80	1960	20	100 Zlotych. 0.5000 Silver.	125
Pr81	1960	13	100 Zlotych. 0.7500 Silver. Eagle with wings open within circle, assorted shields around border. Conjoined heads right.	125
Pr82	1960	500	100 Zlotych. Nickel.	30.00
Pr83	1960	5	100 Zlotych. 0.7500 Silver.	150
Pr84	1960	500	100 Zlotych. Nickel.	30.00
Pr85	1960	29	100 Zlotych. 0.7000 Silver.	125
Pr86	1960	500	100 Zlotych. Nickel. Eagle with wings open within circle. Conjoined heads left within circle.	30.00
Pr87	1960	12	100 Zlotych. 0.7500 Silver.	135
Pr88	1960	500	100 Zlotych. Nickel. Eagle with wings open. Conjoined heads right.	30.00
Pr89	1960	6	100 Zlotych. 0.7500 Silver.	—
Pr90	1962	500	10 Groszy. Nickel. Y#AA47.	30.00
Pr91	1963	500	5 Groszy. Nickel. Y#A46.	30.00
Pr92	1963	500	20 Groszy. Nickel. Y#A47.	30.00
Pr93	1964	125	10 Zlotych. Copper-Nickel. Raised legend, Y#52.	50.00
Pr94	1964	500	10 Zlotych. Nickel. Y#52a.	25.00

KM#	Date	Mintage	Identification	Mkt Val
Pr95	1964	125	10 Zlotych. Copper-Nickel. Incuse legend, Y#52a.	50.00
Pr96	1964	5	10 Zlotych. Tombac. Y#52a.	90.00
Pr97	1964	500	10 Zlotych. Nickel. Y#52a.	25.00

KM#	Date	Mintage	Identification	Mkt Val
Pr98	1964	30	10 Zlotych. Copper-Nickel-Zinc. Eagle with wings open. Seated King facing, PROBA raised.	7.00
Pr99	1964	30,000	10 Zlotych. Copper-Nickel. 12.9000 g. PROBA incuse.	7.00
Pr100	1964	I.A.	10 Zlotych. Copper-Nickel. Eagle with wings open. Without PROBA.	150
Pr101	1964	500	10 Zlotych. Nickel. Eagle with wings open. PROBA raised.	20.00

KM#	Date	Mintage	Identification	Mkt Val
Pr102	1964	500	10 Zlotych. Nickel. Crowned eagle. Raised PROBA.	25.00
Pr103	1964	10	10 Zlotych. Copper-Nickel.	—

KM#	Date	Mintage	Identification	Mkt Val
Pr104	1964	10	10 Zlotych. Copper-Nickel. Shield on eagle with wings open. Standing figure holding spears of grain.	—
Pr105	1964	500	10 Zlotych. Nickel.	25.00

KM#	Date	Mintage	Identification	Mkt Val
Pr106	1964	10	10 Zlotych. Copper-Nickel.	—

KM#	Date	Mintage	Identification	Mkt Val
Pr107	1964	10	10 Zlotych. Copper-Nickel.	—

KM#	Date	Mintage	Identification	Mkt Val
Pr108	1964	20	10 Zlotych. Copper-Nickel. Eagle with wings open above inscription and date. Vertical inscription flanked by designs.	—
Pr109	1964	500	10 Zlotych. Nickel.	25.00

KM#	Date	Mintage	Identification	Mkt Val
Pr110	1964	10	10 Zlotych. Copper-Nickel. Eagle with wings open above inscription and date. Value below stylized tree.	—

KM#	Date	Mintage	Identification	Mkt Val
Pr111	1964	10	10 Zlotych. Copper-Nickel. Eagle with wings open. Value below stylized tree.	—
Pr112	1964	500	10 Zlotych. Nickel.	25.00

KM#	Date	Mintage	Identification	Mkt Val
Pr113	1964	10	10 Zlotych. Copper-Nickel. Shield on eagle with wings open. Value below stylized tree.	—

KM#	Date	Mintage	Identification	Mkt Val
Pr114	1964	20	10 Zlotych. Copper-Nickel. Eagle with wings open. Value below designs.	—
Pr115	1964	500	10 Zlotych. Nickel.	25.00

KM#	Date	Mintage	Identification	Mkt Val
Pr116	1964	20	20 Zlotych. Copper-Nickel. Shield on eagle with wings open. Standing figure holding spears of grain.	—

KM#	Date	Mintage	Identification	Mkt Val
Pr117	1964	500	20 Zlotych. Nickel.	25.00

KM#	Date	Mintage	Identification	Mkt Val
Pr118	1964	20	20 Zlotych. Copper-Nickel.	—

KM#	Date	Mintage	Identification	Mkt Val
Pr119	1964	10	20 Zlotych. Copper-Nickel. Eagle with wings open. Vertical inscription flanked by designs.	—

KM#	Date	Mintage	Identification	Mkt Val
Pr120	1964	20	20 Zlotych. Copper-Nickel. Eagle with wings open above inscription and date. Vertical inscription flanked by designs.	—
Pr121	1964	500	20 Zlotych. Nickel.	25.00

KM#	Date	Mintage	Identification	Mkt Val
Pr122	1964	20	20 Zlotych. Copper-Nickel. Eagle with wings open. Value below tree.	—
Pr123	1964	500	20 Zlotych. Nickel.	25.00

KM#	Date	Mintage	Identification	Mkt Val
Pr124	1964	20	20 Zlotych. Copper-Nickel. Shield on eagle with wings open. Value below tree.	—

KM#	Date	Mintage	Identification	Mkt Val
Pr125	1964	20	20 Zlotych. Copper-Nickel. Eagle with wings open. Value below designs.	—

KM#	Date	Mintage	Identification	Mkt Val
Pr126	1964	500	20 Zlotych. Nickel.	25.00
Pr127	1965	20	10 Zlotych. Copper-Nickel.	—
Pr128	1965	500	10 Zlotych. Nickel.	25.00

Pr129	1965	20	10 Zlotych. Copper-Nickel. Y#54.	—
Pr130	1965	500	10 Zlotych. Nickel. Y#54.	95.00

Pr131	1965	30,000	10 Zlotych. Copper-Nickel. 12.9000 g. Eagle with wings open. Mermaid holding sword and shield.	10.00
Pr132	1965	500	10 Zlotych. Nickel.	35.00

Pr133	1965	30,000	10 Zlotych. Copper-Nickel. 12.9000 g. Eagle with wings open. Mermaid holding sword and shield flanked by ship and house, value at bottom.	10.00
Pr134	1965	500	10 Zlotych. Nickel.	35.00

Pr135	1965	20	10 Zlotych. Copper-Nickel. Eagle with wings open. Value, monument and flying birds.	—
Pr136	1965	500	10 Zlotych. Nickel.	25.00

Pr137	1965	5	10 Zlotych. Aluminum. Kopernik.	—

Pr138	1966	25	10 Zlotych. Copper-Nickel. Eagle with wings open. Head left.	—
Pr139	1966	500	10 Zlotych. Nickel.	25.00

KM#	Date	Mintage	Identification	Mkt Val
Pr140	1966	500	10 Zlotych. Nickel. Eagle with with wings open. Value, monument and flying birds.	25.00
Pr141	1966	10	10 Zlotych. Copper-Nickel.	—
Pr142	1966	10	100 Zlotych. Copper-Nickel.	—
Pr143	1966	10	100 Zlotych. 0.7500 Silver.	—

Pr144	1966	500	100 Zlotych. Nickel. Y#57.	25.00
Pr145	1966	500	100 Zlotych. Nickel.	25.00

Pr146	1966	31,000	100 Zlotych. 0.9000 Silver. 20.0000 g. Eagle with wings open within circle, assorted shields around border. Conjoined half figures facing right, flanked by value.	22.50

Pr147	1966	500	100 Zlotych. Nickel. Eagle with wings open. Conjoined heads right.	25.00
Pr148	1966	30,000	100 Zlotych. 0.9000 Silver. 2 heads.	22.50
Pr149	1967	10	10 Zlotych. Copper-Nickel. Plain edge. Y#59.	—
Pr150	1967	16	10 Zlotych. Copper-Nickel. Milled edge. Y#59.	—
Pr151	1967	500	10 Zlotych. Nickel. Y#59.	25.00

KM#	Date	Mintage	Identification	Mkt Val
Pr152	1967	20	10 Zlotych. Copper-Nickel. Eagle with wings open above inscription and value. Head facing 1/4 left.	—
Pr153	1967	500	10 Zlotych. Nickel.	25.00

Pr154	1967	16	10 Zlotych. Copper-Nickel. Eagle with wings open. Head left.	—
Pr155	1967	10	10 Zlotych. Plain edge.	—
Pr156	1967	500	10 Zlotych. Nickel.	25.00

Pr157	1967	25	10 Zlotych. Copper-Nickel. Eagle with wings open. Head left.	—
Pr158	1967	500	10 Zlotych. Nickel.	15.00
Pr159	1967	40	10 Zlotych. Copper-Nickel.	—
Pr160	1967	500	10 Zlotych. Nickel.	15.00
Pr161	1967	17	10 Zlotych. Aluminum. Kopernik.	—
Pr162	1967	1	10 Zlotych. Copper-Nickel. Kopernik.	—
Pr163	1967	10	10 Zlotych. Aluminum. Kopernik.	—

Pr164	1968	20	10 Zlotych. Copper-Nickel. Eagle with wings open perched on design. 1/4 helmeted head right, XXV to left.	—
Pr165	1968	500	10 Zlotych. Nickel.	25.00

Pr166	1969	20	10 Zlotych. Copper-Nickel. Eagle with wings open within circle. Design divides date within radiant circle, PROBA at lower right.	—
Pr167	1969	500	10 Zlotych. Nickel. PROBA at lower right.	—
Pr168	1969	5	10 Zlotych. Gold. PROBA at lower right.	—
	1969	5	10 Zlotych. Gold. PROBA at lower right.	—
Pr169	1969	20	10 Zlotych. Copper-Nickel. Eagle with wings open within circle. PROBA at lower right.	—
Pr170	1969	500	10 Zlotych. Nickel. PROBA at right.	—
Pr171	1969	500	10 Zlotych. Nickel. Wthout PROBA.	25.00

KM#	Date	Mintage Identification	Mkt Val

Pr172 1969   20   10 Zlotych. Copper-Nickel. Eagle with wings open within circle, bold letters around border. 1/4 head right on mirror, bold letters around border.   —

Pr173 1969   500   10 Zlotych. Nickel.   25.00

Pr174 1969   20   10 Zlotych. Copper-Nickel. Eagle with wings open within circle. Letters and numbers within blocks.   —

Pr175 1969   500   10 Zlotych. Nickel.   25.00

Pr176 1970   20   10 Zlotych. Copper-Nickel. Eagle with wings open flanked by shields. Conjoined heads right. 25th Anniversary of Provincial Annexation   —

Pr177 1970   500   10 Zlotych. Nickel. 25th Anniversary of Provincial Annexation.   20.00

Pr178 1970   10   10 Zlotych. Copper-Nickel. Without PROBA.   —

Pr179 1970   20   10 Zlotych. Copper-Nickel. Y#62.   —
Pr180 1970   500   10 Zlotych. Nickel. Y#62.   20.00
Pr181 1970   300   10 Zlotych. Silver. Y#62.   40.00
Pr182 1970   5   10 Zlotych. Aluminum. Kopernik.   —
Pr183 1971   20   10 Zlotych. Copper-Nickel. Y#63.   —
Pr184 1971   500   10 Zlotych. Nickel. Y#63.   20.00

Pr185 1971   51,000   10 Zlotych. Copper-Nickel. Eagle with wings open. Baby nursing in front of world globe, FAO above.   12.50

Pr186 1971   500   10 Zlotych. Nickel. FAO, baby nursing.   20.00

Pr187 1971   52,000   10 Zlotych. Copper-Nickel. 9.5000 g. Eagle with wings open. Spears of grain on top of globe, F.A.O. logo between spears.   12.50

Pr188 1971   500   10 Zlotych. Nickel. FAO, wheat.   20.00

Pr189 1971   20   10 Zlotych. Copper-Nickel. Y#64.   —
Pr190 1971   500   10 Zlotych. Nickel. Y#64.   20.00

Pr191 1971   20   10 Zlotych. Copper-Nickel. Eagle with wings open within eagle with wings open, all within circle. Medal in front of inscription.   —

Pr192 1971   500   10 Zlotych. Nickel. Medal.   20.00

Pr193 1972   20   10 Zlotych. Copper-Nickel. Y#65 but date inside legend.   25.00

Pr194 1972   500   10 Zlotych. Nickel. Y#65 but date inside legend.   —

Pr195 1972   20   10 Zlotych. Copper-Nickel. Y#65.   —
Pr196 1972   500   10 Zlotych. Nickel. Y#65.   20.00
Pr197 1972   —   50 Zlotych. Copper-Nickel.   —
Pr198 1972   20   50 Zlotych. 0.7500 Silver. Y#66, Chopin.   —
Pr199 1972   500   50 Zlotych. Nickel. Y#66.   18.00
Pr200 1972   —   50 Zlotych. Bronze. Chopin, without PROBA.   —
Pr201 1972   20   50 Zlotych. 0.7500 Silver. Chopin, without PROBA.   —

Pr202 1972   15,000   50 Zlotych. 0.7500 Silver. Stylized eagle with wings open within circle. Stylized head of Chopin 3/4 right. Chopin.   20.00

Pr203 1972   500   50 Zlotych. Nickel. Chopin.   20.00

Pr204 1973   20   10 Zlotych. Copper-Nickel. Eagle with wings open above inscription and date. Design above inscription and value.   —

Pr205 1973   500   10 Zlotych. Nickel.   20.00

Pr206 1973   20   10 Zlotych. Copper-Nickel. Eagle with wings open. Design within dates.   —

Pr207 1973   500   10 Zlotych. Nickel.   20.00

Pr208 1973   10   10 Zlotych. Copper-Nickel. Kopernik.   —
Pr209 1973   500   10 Zlotych. Nickel. Kopernik.   —
Pr210 1973   20   20 Zlotych. Copper-Nickel. Plain edge. Without PROBA, Y#67.   —

Pr211 1973   20   20 Zlotych. Copper-Nickel. Eagle with wings open within circle. Value within designed waterfall. Ornamented edge.   30.00

Pr212 1973   13,000   20 Zlotych. Copper-Nickel. 10.1500 g. Milled edge. Y#67.   —
Pr213 1973   500   20 Zlotych. Nickel. Y#67.   20.00

Pr214 1973   16,000   20 Zlotych. Copper-Nickel. 10.1500 g. Tree.   —
Pr215 1973   500   20 Zlotych. Nickel. Tree.   20.00
Pr216 1973   —   100 Zlotych. Copper. Kopernik.   —
Pr217 1973   20   100 Zlotych. 0.6250 Silver. Kopernik.   —
Pr218 1973   500   100 Zlotych. Nickel. Kopernik.   20.00

KM#	Date	Mintage Identification	Mkt Val

Pr219 1973   500 100 Zlotych. Nickel. Y#68.   15.00
Pr220 1973   5,000 100 Zlotych. 0.6250 Silver. Y#68.   15.00

Pr221 1973   1,222 100 Zlotych. 0.6250 Silver. Eagle with wings open divides date. Head of Kopernik 1/4 right.   35.00
Pr222 1973   500 100 Zlotych. Nickel. Kopernik.   20.00

Pr223 1974   40 10 Zlotych. Copper-Nickel. Sienkiewicz.   —
Pr224 1974   500 10 Zlotych. Nickel. Sienkiewicz.   20.00

Pr225 1974   40 10 Zlotych. Copper-Nickel. Y#74.   —
Pr226 1974   500 10 Zlotych. Nickel. Y#74.   20.00

Pr227 1974 10,000 20 Zlotych. Copper-Nickel. Y#69.   —
Pr228 1974   500 20 Zlotych. Nickel. Y#69.   20.00

Pr229 1974   20 20 Zlotych. Copper-Nickel. 4 laborers.   —
Pr230 1974   500 20 Zlotych. Nickel. 4 laborers.   20.00
Pr231 1974   20 20 Zlotych. Copper-Nickel.

Pr232 1974   500 20 Zlotych. Nickel.   —

Pr233 1974   20 20 Zlotych. Copper-Nickel. XXX LAT PRL.   —
Pr234 1974   500 20 Zlotych. Nickel. XXX LAT PRL.   20.00

Pr235 1974   20 20 Zlotych. Copper-Nickel. Y#70.   —
Pr236 1974   500 20 Zlotych. Nickel. Y#70.   —

Pr237 1974   20 20 Zlotych. Copper-Nickel. Eagle with wings open above value. Letters within circle of 1/2 gear and 1/2 flower design.   —
Pr238 1974   500 20 Zlotych. Nickel.   20.00

Pr239 1974   500 100 Zlotych. Nickel. Eagle with wings open. Profile of Curie left, symbol at right.   17.50
Pr240 1974 10,000 100 Zlotych. 0.6250 Silver. Curie left.   12.50
Pr241 1974   500 100 Zlotych. Nickel. Y#71.   30.00
Pr242 1974   10 100 Zlotych. 0.6250 Silver. Y#71.   20.00

Pr243 1974   500 100 Zlotych. Nickel. Curie right.   15.00
Pr244 1974 10,000 100 Zlotych. 0.6250 Silver. Curie right.   12.50

Pr245 1974   500 100 Zlotych. Nickel. Royal Castle in Warsaw.   —
Pr246 1974   20 100 Zlotych. 0.6250 Silver. Royal Castle in Warsaw.   —

Pr247 1974   500 200 Zlotych. Nickel. Eagle with wings open within square. Triple x and letters within square.   20.00
Pr248 1974   20 200 Zlotych. 0.6250 Silver.   —
Pr249 1975   — 10 Zlotych. Aluminum. Boleslaw Prus.   —
Pr250 1975   40 10 Zlotych. Copper-Nickel. Boleslaw Prus.   —
Pr251 1975   500 10 Zlotych. Nickel. Boleslaw Prus.   20.00

Pr252 1975   20 20 Zlotych. Copper-Nickel. Year of the Woman.   —
Pr253 1975   500 20 Zlotych. Nickel. Year of the Woman.   20.00

Pr254 1975   20 20 Zlotych. Copper-Nickel. Eagle with wings open above value. Globe. Globe.   —
Pr255 1975   500 20 Zlotych. Nickel. Globe.   15.00
Pr256 1975   5,000 100 Zlotych. 0.6250 Silver. Y#76.   12.50

Pr257 1975   500 100 Zlotych. Nickel. Y#78.   17.50

Pr258 1975   20 100 Zlotych. 0.6250 Silver. Y#78.

KM#	Date	Mintage	Identification	Mkt Val
Pr259	1975	500	100 Zlotych. Nickel. Modrzejewska.	17.50
Pr260	1975	20	100 Zlotych. 0.6250 Silver. Modrzejewska.	—
Pr261	1975	500	100 Zlotych. Nickel. Y#77.	17.50
Pr262	1975	20	100 Zlotych. 0.6250 Silver. Y#77.	—

Pr263	1975	500	100 Zlotych. Nickel. Paderewski.	12.50
Pr264	1975	20	100 Zlotych. 0.6250 Silver. Paderewski.	—

Pr265	1975	500	200 Zlotych. Nickel. Eagle with wings open above value. Name written in front of swords.	20.00
Pr266	1975	10,000	200 Zlotych. 0.7500 Silver.	22.50

Pr267	1975	500	200 Zlotych. Nickel. Eagle with wings open. Hammer head flanked by dates with triple x on top.	20.00
Pr268	1975	10,000	200 Zlotych. 0.7500 Silver.	17.50

Pr269	1975	500	200 Zlotych. Nickel. Y#79.	20.00
Pr270	1975	2,600	200 Zlotych. 0.7500 Silver. Y#79.	—
Pr271	1976	20	20 Zlotych. Copper-Nickel. 30 Years of Budget Bill.	—
Pr272	1976	500	20 Zlotych. Nickel. 30 Years of Budget Bill.	—
Pr273	1976	20	20 Zlotych. Copper-Nickel. 30 Years of Budget Bill - PRL.	—
Pr274	1976	500	20 Zlotych. Nickel. PRL.	—

Pr275	1976	500	100 Zlotych. Nickel. Y#82.	20.00
Pr276	1976	20	100 Zlotych. 0.6250 Silver. Y#82.	—

KM#	Date	Mintage	Identification	Mkt Val
Pr277	1976	3,000	100 Zlotych. 0.6250 Silver. Kosciuszko.	35.00
Pr278	1976	500	100 Zlotych. Nickel. Kosciuszko.	20.00
Pr279	1976	20	100 Zlotych.	—

Pr280	1976	500	100 Zlotych. Nickel. Pulaski.	20.00
Pr281	1976	3,000	100 Zlotych. 0.6250 Silver. Pulaski.	35.00

Pr282	1976	20	200 Zlotych. 0.6250 Silver. Olympics.	—
Pr283	1976	—	200 Zlotych. Nickel. Olympic rings and torch.	—

Pr284	1976	500	200 Zlotych. Nickel. Y#86.	30.00
Pr285	1976	6,048	200 Zlotych. 0.7500 Silver. Y#86.	20.00

Pr286	1976	500	200 Zlotych. Nickel. Eagle with wings open divides date. Stylized head with Olympic circles left.	25.00
Pr287	1976	6,050	200 Zlotych. 0.6250 Silver.	30.00
Pr288	1976	500	500 Zlotych. Nickel. Y#83.	20.00
Pr289	1976	300	500 Zlotych. 0.9000 Gold. Y#83.	700
Pr290	1976	500	500 Zlotych. Nickel. Kosciuszko.	20.00
Pr291	1976	500	500 Zlotych. Nickel. Y#85.	20.00
Pr292	1976	300	500 Zlotych. 0.9000 Gold. Y#85.	700
Pr293	1976	500	500 Zlotych. Nickel. Pulaski facing.	20.00
Pr294	1977	100	20 Zlotych. Copper-Nickel. Y#96.	—
Pr295	1977	200	20 Zlotych. Nickel. Y#96.	—

KM#	Date	Mintage	Identification	Mkt Val
Pr296	1977	500	100 Zlotych. Nickel. Y#88.	—

Pr297	1977	3,000	100 Zlotych. 0.6250 Silver. Y#88.	42.50

Pr298	1977	500	100 Zlotych. Nickel. Sienkiewicz facing.	12.50
Pr299	1977	3,000	100 Zlotych. 0.6250 Silver. Sienkiewicz facing.	40.00
Pr300	1977	500	100 Zlotych. Nickel. Y#89.	—
Pr301	1977	3,100	100 Zlotych. 0.6250 Silver. Y#89.	25.00

Pr302	1977	500	100 Zlotych. Nickel. Reymont profile left.	—
Pr303	1977	3,100	100 Zlotych. 0.6250 Silver. Reymont profile left.	38.00

Pr304	1977	500	100 Zlotych. Nickel. Eagle with wings open divides date. Catfish.	35.00
Pr305	1977	5,100	100 Zlotych. 0.6250 Silver. Fish.	45.00

Pr306	1977	500	100 Zlotych. Nickel. Y#91.	25.00
Pr307	1977	100	100 Zlotych. 0.6250 Silver. Y#91.	—

KM#	Date	Mintage Identification	Mkt Val

Pr308 1977 500 100 Zlotych. Nickel. Distant Krakow castle. —
Pr309 1977 3,100 100 Zlotych. 0.6250 Silver. Distant Krakow castle. 42.50

Pr310 1977 500 100 Zlotych. Nickel. Bison. 35.00
Pr311 1977 5,400 100 Zlotych. 0.6250 Silver. Bison. 45.00
Pr312 1977 6 2000 Zlotych. Gold. Chopin. —
Pr313 1977 500 2000 Zlotych. Nickel. Chopin. —
Pr314 1978 100 20 Zlotych. Copper-Nickel. Y#97. —
Pr315 1978 500 20 Zlotych. Nickel. Y#97. —
Pr316 1978 100 20 Zlotych. Copper-Nickel. Y#96. —
Pr317 1978 500 20 Zlotych. Nickel. Y#96. —

Pr318 1978 100 100 Zlotych. 0.6250 Silver. Y#92. —
Pr319 1978 500 100 Zlotych. Nickel. Y#92. —
Pr320 1978 100 100 Zlotych. 0.6250 Silver. Similar to KM#PrM255 but with lock of hair at left of face. —
Pr321 1978 500 100 Zlotych. Nickel. Similar to KM#PrK255. —
Pr322 1978 500 100 Zlotych. Nickel. Mickiewicz profile. —

Pr323 1978 3,100 100 Zlotych. 0.6250 Silver. Eagle with wings open divides date. Head of Mickiewicz left. 40.00
Pr324 1978 100 100 Zlotych. 0.6250 Silver. Y#93. —
Pr325 1978 100 100 Zlotych. Nickel. Y#93. —
Pr326 1978 500 100 Zlotych. Nickel. Elk head. —

Pr327 1978 3,100 100 Zlotych. 0.6250 Silver. Eagle with wings open divides date. Moose head. 50.00
Pr328 1978 500 100 Zlotych. Nickel. Beaver on wood. —
Pr329 1978 3,100 100 Zlotych. 0.6250 Silver. Beaver on wood. 50.00

Pr330 1978 500 100 Zlotych. Nickel. Beaver on grass. 65.00
Pr331 1978 3,100 100 Zlotych. 0.6250 Silver. Beaver on grass. 50.00
Pr332 1978 100 100 Zlotych. 0.6250 Silver. Y#94. —
Pr333 1978 500 100 Zlotych. Nickel. Y#94. —

Pr334 1978 500 100 Zlotych. Nickel. Eagle with wings open divides date. Head of Korczak right. —
Pr335 1978 3,100 100 Zlotych. 0.6250 Silver. Korczak. 22.50

Pr336 1978 500 100 Zlotych. Nickel. Eagle with wings open divides date. Globe within legend. —
Pr337 1978 3,100 100 Zlotych. 0.6250 Silver. Globe in legend. 47.50
Pr338 1979 500 2 Zlotych. Nickel. —
Pr339 1979 500 5 Zlotych. Nickel. —
Pr340 1979 500 20 Zlotych. Nickel. I.Y.C., dancers. —
Pr341 1979 4,100 20 Zlotych. 0.6250 Silver. I.Y.C. 25.00

Pr342 1979 500 20 Zlotych. Nickel. I.Y.C. Health Center. —
Pr343 1979 30,000 20 Zlotych. Copper-Nickel. I.Y.C. Health Center. 6.00

Pr344 1979 100 50 Zlotych. Copper-Nickel. Eagle with wings open divides date. Mieszko I. —
Pr345 1979 500 50 Zlotych. Nickel. Mieszko I. —
Pr346 1979 100 100 Zlotych. 0.6250 Silver. Y#98. —
Pr347 1979 500 100 Zlotych. Nickel. Y#98. —
Pr348 1979 500 100 Zlotych. Nickel. Wieniawski profile. —

Pr349 1979 3,100 100 Zlotych. 0.6250 Silver. Wieniawski profile. 25.00
Pr350 1979 100 100 Zlotych. 0.6250 Silver. Y#104. —
Pr351 1979 500 100 Zlotych. Nickel. Y#104. —

Pr352 1979 500 100 Zlotych. Nickel. Eagle with wings open divides date. Lynx. 65.00
Pr353 1979 4,100 100 Zlotych. 0.6250 Silver. Lynx. 45.00
Pr354 1979 100 100 Zlotych. 0.6250 Silver. Y#105. —
Pr355 1979 500 100 Zlotych. Nickel. Y#105. —

Pr356 1979 500 100 Zlotych. Nickel. Mountain goat on rock. 75.00
Pr357 1979 4,100 100 Zlotych. 0.6250 Silver. Mountain goat on rock. 45.00
Pr358 1979 100 100 Zlotych. 0.6250 Silver. Y#103. —
Pr359 1979 500 100 Zlotych. Nickel. Y#103. —

Pr360 1979 500 100 Zlotych. Nickel. Eagle with wings open divides date. Head of Zamenhof facing. —
Pr361 1979 3,100 100 Zlotych. 0.6250 Silver. Zamenhof facing. 30.00
Pr362 1979 100 200 Zlotych. 0.7500 Silver. Y#101. —
Pr363 1979 500 200 Zlotych. Nickel. Y#101. —
Pr364 1979 500 200 Zlotych. Nickel. Mieszko. —
Pr365 1979 4,100 200 Zlotych. 0.7500 Silver. Mieszko I. 25.00
Pr366 1979 5 2000 Zlotych. 0.9000 Gold. Y#106. —
Pr367 1979 500 2000 Zlotych. Nickel. Y#106. —
Pr368 1979 6 2000 Zlotych. 0.9000 Gold. Y#107. —
Pr369 1979 500 2000 Zlotych. Nickel. Y#107. —
Pr370 1979 4 2000 Zlotych. 0.9000 Gold. Y#102. —
Pr371 1979 — 2000 Zlotych. Bronze. Y#102. —
Pr372 1979 500 2000 Zlotych. Nickel. Y#102. —
Pr373 1979 4 2000 Zlotych. 0.9000 Gold. Mieszko I, PrG266. —
Pr374 1979 — 2000 Zlotych. Bronze. PrG266. —
Pr375 1979 500 2000 Zlotych. Nickel. PrG266. —
Pr376 1980 100 20 Zlotych. 0.6250 Silver. Y#108. —
Pr377 1980 500 20 Zlotych. Nickel. Y#108. 75.00

KM#	Date	Mintage	Identification	Mkt Val

KM#	Date	Mintage	Identification	Mkt Val
PrA378	1980	100	20 Zlotych. Nickel. Eagle with wings open divides date. Stylized runner with torch, Olympic rings at right.	90.00
Pr378	1980	100	20 Zlotych. Copper-Nickel. Y#112.	—
Pr379	1980	500	20 Zlotych. Nickel. Y#112.	—
Pr380	1980	20	20 Zlotych. Copper-Nickel. Ship.	—
Pr381	1980	500	20 Zlotych. Nickel. Ship.	—

Pr382	1980	500	20 Zlotych. Nickel. 1905-Lodz.	—
Pr383	1980	10,000	20 Zlotych. Copper-Nickel. 1905-Lodz.	—
Pr384	1980	20	20 Zlotych. Copper-Nickel. 75th Anniversary of Lodz riots.	—
Pr385	1980	500	20 Zlotych. Nickel. 75th Anniversary of Lodz riots.	—
Pr386	1980	20	50 Zlotych. Copper-Nickel. Y#114.	—
Pr387	1980	500	50 Zlotych. Nickel. 11.6400 g. 30.5 mm. Reeded edge. Y#114.	65.00
Pr388	1980	20	50 Zlotych. Copper-Nickel. Boleslaw I inscription below.	—
Pr389	1980	500	50 Zlotych. Nickel. Boleslaw I, inscription below.	—
Pr390	1980	20	50 Zlotych. Copper-Nickel. Y#117.	—

Pr391	1980	500	100 Zlotych. Nickel. Eagle with wings open divides date. Ship.	—
Pr392	1980	4,000	100 Zlotych. 0.6250 Silver. Ship.	38.50
Pr393	1980	100	100 Zlotych. Copper-Nickel. Olympic flame and rings.	—

| Pr394 | 1980 | 500 | 100 Zlotych. Nickel. Eagle with wings open divides date. Stylized runner holding torch, Olympic rings at right. | 90.00 |
| Pr395 | 1980 | 4,100 | 100 Zlotych. 0.6250 Silver. Olympic flame and rings. | 35.00 |

PrA396	1980	500	100 Zlotych. Nickel. Y#109.	90.00
Pr396	1980	20	100 Zlotych. 0.6250 Silver. Y#121.	—
Pr397	1980	500	100 Zlotych. Nickel. Y#121.	—

Pr398	1980	500	100 Zlotych. Nickel. Eagle with wings open divides date. Birds.	65.00
Pr399	1980	4,018	100 Zlotych. 0.6250 Silver. Birds.	45.00
Pr400	1980	100	100 Zlotych. 0.6250 Silver. Y#120.	—
Pr401	1980	500	100 Zlotych. Nickel.	—

Pr402	1980	500	100 Zlotych. Nickel. Larger head of Kochanowski.	—
Pr403	1980	4,100	100 Zlotych. 0.6250 Silver. Larger head of Kochanowski.	20.00
Pr404	1980	100	200 Zlotych. 0.7500 Silver. Y#110.	—
Pr405	1980	500	200 Zlotych. Nickel. Y#110.	90.00
Pr406	1980	100	200 Zlotych. 0.7500 Silver. Y#110a.	—
Pr407	1980	500	200 Zlotych. Nickel. Y#110a.	90.00

Pr408	1980	500	200 Zlotych. Nickel. Eagle with wings open divides date. Olympic skier with torch mm.	100
Pr409	1980	3,620	200 Zlotych. 0.7500 Silver. Olympic skier with torch mm.	45.00
Pr410	1980	500	200 Zlotych. Nickel. Olympic skier without mm.	100
Pr411	1980	3,620	200 Zlotych. 0.7500 Silver. Olympic skier without mm.	45.00
Pr412	1980	20	200 Zlotych. 0.7500 Silver. Y#115.	—
Pr413	1980	500	200 Zlotych. Nickel. Y#115.	—
Pr414	1980	500	200 Zlotych. Nickel. Boleslaw I torso.	—
Pr415	1980	4,020	200 Zlotych. 0.7500 Silver. Boleslaw I torso.	25.00
Pr416	1980	20	200 Zlotych. 0.7500 Silver. Y#118.	—
Pr417	1980	500	200 Zlotych. Nickel. Y#118.	—
Pr418	1980	500	200 Zlotych. Nickel. Kazimierz I torso.	—
Pr419	1980	4,020	200 Zlotych. 0.7500 Silver. Kazimierz I torso.	25.00
Pr420	1980	3	2000 Zlotych. 0.9000 Gold. Y#111.	—
Pr421	1980	—	2000 Zlotych. Bronze. Y#111.	—
	1980	—	2000 Zlotych. Bronze. Y#111.	—

Pr422	1980	500	2000 Zlotych. Nickel. Y#111.	—
Pr423	1980	6	2000 Zlotych. 0.9000 Gold. Y#116.	—
Pr424	1980	500	2000 Zlotych. Nickel. Y#116.	—
Pr425	1980	6	2000 Zlotych. 0.9000 Gold. Odnowiciel.	—
Pr426	1980	500	2000 Zlotych. Nickel. Odnowiciel.	—
Pr427	1980	500	2000 Zlotych. Nickel. Olympic skier without torch mm.	—

| Pr428 | 1980 | 1,500 | 2000 Zlotych. 0.9000 Gold. Eagle with wings open divides date. Olympic skier without torch mm. | 350 |
| Pr429 | 1981 | 500 | 100 Zlotych. Nickel. Restoration of Krakow. | — |

Pr430	1981	30,000	20 Zlotych. Copper-Nickel. Restoration of Krakow.	8.50
Pr431	1981	20	50 Zlotych. Copper-Nickel. Y#122.	—
Pr432	1981	500	50 Zlotych. Nickel. Y#122.	—
Pr433	1981	20	50 Zlotych. Copper-Nickel. Y#124.	—
Pr434	1981	500	50 Zlotych. Nickel. Y#124.	—
Pr435	1981	20	50 Zlotych. Copper-Nickel. Y#128.	—
Pr436	1981	500	50 Zlotych. Nickel. Y#128.	—
Pr437	1981	20	50 Zlotych. Copper-Nickel. Y#127.	—
Pr438	1981	500	50 Zlotych. Nickel. Y#127.	—
Pr439	1981	120	100 Zlotych. 0.6250 Silver. Y#123.	—
Pr440	1981	500	100 Zlotych. Nickel. Y#123.	—

| Pr441 | 1981 | 500 | 100 Zlotych. Nickel. Sikorski. | — |
| Pr442 | 1981 | 5,020 | 100 Zlotych. 0.6250 Silver. Sikorski. | 27.50 |

Pr443	1981	500	100 Zlotych. Nickel. St. Mary's Church.	—
Pr444	1981	4,020	100 Zlotych. 0.6250 Silver. St. Mary's Church.	26.50
Pr445	1981	20	100 Zlotych. 0.6250 Silver. Y#126.	—
Pr446	1981	500	100 Zlotych. Nickel. Y#126.	—

Pr447	1981	500	100 Zlotych. Nickel.	40.00
Pr448	1981	4,020	100 Zlotych. 0.6250 Silver. Horses.	40.00
Pr449	1981	20	100 Zlotych. 0.7500 Silver. Y#125.	—
Pr450	1981	500	200 Zlotych. Nickel. Y#125.	—
Pr451	1981	500	200 Zlotych. Nickel. Boleslaw II.	—
Pr452	1981	4,020	200 Zlotych. 0.7500 Silver. Boleslaw II.	25.00
Pr453	1981	20	200 Zlotych. 0.7500 Silver. Y#129.	—
Pr454	1981	500	200 Zlotych. Nickel. Y#129.	—

KM#	Date	Mintage	Identification	Mkt Val	KM#	Date	Mintage	Identification	Mkt Val	KM#	Date	Mintage	Identification	Mkt Val

Pr455	1981	500	200 Zlotych. Nickel. Wladyslaw I Herman.	—
Pr456	1981	4,020	200 Zlotych. 0.7500 Silver.	—
Pr457	1981	—	200 Zlotych. 0.7500 Silver. Wladyslaw I.	—
Pr458	1981	4	2000 Zlotych. 0.9000 Gold. Y#126.	—
Pr459	1981	500	2000 Zlotych. Nickel. Y#126.	—
Pr460	1981	4	2000 Zlotych. 0.9000 Gold. Y#131.	—
Pr461	1981	500	2000 Zlotych. 0.9000 Gold. Y#131.	—
Pr462	1982	20	50 Zlotych. Copper-Nickel. Y#133.	—
Pr463	1982	500	50 Zlotych. Nickel. Y#133.	—
Pr464	1982	500	100 Zlotych. Nickel. Y#141.	—

| Pr465 | 1982 | 500 | 100 Zlotych. Nickel. Eagle with wings open divides date. Storks. | 65.00 |
| Pr466 | 1982 | 4,000 | 100 Zlotych. 0.6250 Silver. Storks. | 45.00 |

Pr467	1982	20	200 Zlotych. 0.7500 Silver. Y#132.	—
Pr468	1982	500	200 Zlotych. Nickel. Y#132.	—
Pr469	1982	500	200 Zlotych. Nickel.	—
Pr470	1982	3,000	200 Zlotych. 0.7500 Silver.	60.00
Pr471	1982	6,000	200 Zlotych. 0.7500 Silver. Soccer player leaning right.	30.00
Pr472	1982	6,002	200 Zlotych. 0.7500 Silver. Soccer player leaning left.	60.00

| Pr473 | 1982 | 500 | 200 Zlotych. Nickel. Soccer player leaning right. | — |
| Pr474 | 1982 | 500 | 200 Zlotych. Nickel. Without Espana 82, Y#130. | — |

| Pr475 | 1982 | 500 | 200 Zlotych. Nickel. Eagle with wings open divides date. Stylized soccer player leaning left. | — |

| Pr476 | 1982 | 500 | 500 Zlotych. Nickel. Eagle with wings open divides date. Ship. | — |
| Pr477 | 1982 | 25,000 | 500 Zlotych. 0.6250 Silver. Ship. | 25.00 |

Pr478	1982	10,000	1000 Zlotych. 0.7500 Silver. Pope John Paul II.	35.00
Pr479	1982	500	1000 Zlotych. Nickel. Y#144.	—
Pr480	1982	500	1000 Zlotych. Nickel.	—
Pr481	1983	20	50 Zlotych. Copper-Nickel. Y#142.	—
Pr482	1983	500	50 Zlotych. Nickel. Y#142.	—
Pr483	1983	20	50 Zlotych. Copper-Nickel. Y#145.	—
Pr484	1983	500	50 Zlotych. Nickel. Y#145.	—
Pr485	1983	20	50 Zlotych. Copper-Nickel. Y#146.	—
Pr486	1983	500	50 Zlotych. Nickel. Y#146.	—
Pr487	1983	500	100 Zlotych. Nickel. Y#147.	—
Pr488	1983	500	100 Zlotych. Nickel.	—

| Pr489 | 1983 | 3,000 | 100 Zlotych. 0.6250 Silver. Bears. | 60.00 |
| Pr490 | 1983 | 500 | 200 Zlotych. Nickel. Y#143. | 95.00 |

| Pr491 | 1983 | 500 | 200 Zlotych. Nickel. Eagle with wings open divides date. Horse and rider rearing above fallen indian. | — |
| Pr492 | 1983 | 4,000 | 200 Zlotych. 0.7500 Silver. Jan III Sobieski. | 60.00 |

| Pr493 | 1983 | 500 | 500 Zlotych. Nickel. Eagle with wings open divides date. Gymnast. | — |
| Pr494 | 1983 | 7,000 | 500 Zlotych. 0.7500 Silver. Gymnast. | 35.00 |

Pr495	1983	500	500 Zlotych. Nickel. Eagle with wings open divides date. Speed skater within horizontal lines.	—
Pr496	1983	6,000	500 Zlotych. 0.7500 Silver. Speed skater.	35.00
Pr497	1984	500	10 Zlotych. Nickel. Y#152.1.	—
Pr498	1984	500	20 Zlotych. Nickel. Y#153.1.	—
Pr499	1984	500	100 Zlotych. Nickel. Y#148.	—
Pr500	1984	500	100 Zlotych. Nickel. Reeded edge. Y#151.	—
Pr501	1984	500	200 Zlotych. Nickel. Y#149.	—
Pr502	1984	500	200 Zlotych. Nickel. Y#150.	—
Pr503	1984	500	500 Zlotych. Nickel. Y#154.	—

| Pr504 | 1984 | 500 | 1000 Zlotych. Nickel. Wincenty Witos. | — |
| Pr505 | 1984 | 3,000 | 1000 Zlotych. 0.6250 Silver. Wincenty Witos. | 35.00 |

| Pr506 | 1984 | 500 | 1000 Zlotych. Nickel. PRL. | — |
| Pr507 | 1984 | 2,004 | 1000 Zlotych. 0.6250 Silver. 40th Anniversary of Peoples Republic. | 35.00 |

Pr508	1984	500	1000 Zlotych. Nickel. Eagle with wings open divides date. Swan.	90.00
Pr509	1984	5,700	1000 Zlotych. 0.6250 Silver. Environment.	60.00
Pr510	1985	500	100 Zlotych. Nickel. Y#155.	—
Pr511	1985	500	100 Zlotych. Nickel. Y#157.	—

Pr512	1985	500	200 Zlotych. Nickel. Eagle with wings open divides date. Fallen soccer player within net design.	—
Pr513	1985	15,000	200 Zlotych. Copper-Nickel.	8.50
Pr514	1985	500	200 Zlotych. Nickel. Hospital Center.	—

KM#	Date	Mintage	Identification	Mkt Val
Pr515	1985	37,300	200 Zlotych. Nickel Plated Iron. Hospital Center	16.50
Pr516	1985	500	500 Zlotych. Nickel. Y#156.	—
Pr517	1985	500	500 Zlotych. Nickel. Y#158.	—
Pr518	1985	500	500 Zlotych. Nickel. Y#159.	—
Pr519	1985	500	1000 Zlotych. Nickel. Przemyslaw II.	—
Pr520	1985	2,500	1000 Zlotych. 0.7500 Silver. Przemyslaw II.	15.00
Pr521	1985	500	1000 Zlotych. Nickel. Eagle with wings open divides date. Heart design. Hospital Center.	—
Pr522	1985	2,500	1000 Zlotych. 0.7500 Silver. Hospital Center.	25.00
Pr523	1985	500	1000 Zlotych. Nickel. U.N.	—
Pr524	1985	2,500	1000 Zlotych. 0.7500 Silver. U.N.	40.00
Pr525	1985	500	1000 Zlotych. Nickel. Eagle with wings open divides date. Squirrel.	90.00
Pr526	1985	2,500	1000 Zlotych. 0.7500 Silver. Squirrel.	85.00
Pr527	1986	500	50 Groszy. Nickel. Y#48.2.	—
Pr528	1986	500	Zloty. Nickel. Y#49.2.	—
Pr529	1986	500	2 Zlote. Nickel. Y#80.2.	—
Pr530	1986	500	5 Zlotych. Nickel. Y#81.2.	—
Pr531	1986	500	100 Zlotych. Nickel. Y#160.	—

KM#	Date	Mintage	Identification	Mkt Val
Pr532	1986	500	200 Zlotych. Nickel. Y#162.	60.00
Pr533	1986	6,000	200 Zlotych. Copper-Nickel. Y#162.	45.00
Pr534	1986	500	200 Zlotych. Nickel. Wladyslaw.	—
Pr535	1986	10,000	200 Zlotych. Copper-Nickel. Wladyslaw.	15.00
Pr536	1986	500	500 Zlotych. Nickel. Y#161.	—
Pr537	1986	500	500 Zlotych. Nickel. Y#162.	—
Pr538	1986	500	500 Zlotych. Nickel. Y#166.	—
Pr539	1986	—	500 Zlotych. Nickel. Y#225.	—
Pr540	1986	500	1000 Zlotych. Nickel. Soccer.	—
Pr541	1986	9,000	1000 Zlotych. 0.7500 Silver. Eagle with wings open divides date. Soccer ball and globe.	—
Pr542	1986	500	1000 Zlotych. Nickel. Education.	—
Pr543	1986	25,400	1000 Zlotych. 0.6250 Silver. Education.	—
Pr544	1986	22,000	1000 Zlotych. 0.7500 Silver. Hospital Center.	40.00
Pr545	1986	500	1000 Zlotych. Nickel. Wladyslaw I.	—
Pr546	1986	2,500	1000 Zlotych. 0.7500 Silver. Wladyslaw I.	30.00

KM#	Date	Mintage	Identification	Mkt Val
Pr547	1986	500	1000 Zlotych. Nickel. Eagle with wings open divides date. Owl.	90.00
Pr548	1986	6,000	1000 Zlotych. 0.7500 Silver. Owl.	60.00
Pr549	1986	—	1000 Zlotych. Nickel. Eagle with wings open divides date. School design.	—
Pr550	1986	—	1000 Zlotych. 0.6250 Silver. School aid.	—
Pr551	1987	500	100 Zlotych. Nickel. Y#167.	—
Pr552	1987	500	200 Zlotych. Nickel. Eagle with wings open divides date. Europe soccer.	—
Pr553	1987	15,000	200 Zlotych. Copper-Nickel. Europe soccer.	12.00
Pr554	1987	500	200 Zlotych. Nickel. Olympics - Tennis.	—
Pr555	1987	10,000	200 Zlotych. Copper-Nickel. Olympics - Tennis.	13.50
Pr556	1987	500	500 Zlotych. Nickel. Y#165.	—
Pr557	1987	500	500 Zlotych. Nickel. Y#166.	—
Pr558	1987	500	500 Zlotych. Nickel. Y#172.	—
Pr559	1987	500	500 Zlotych. Nickel. Y#173.	—
Pr560	1987	500	1000 Zlotych. Nickel. Wratislavia.	—

KM#	Date	Mintage	Identification	Mkt Val
Pr561	1987	24,000	1000 Zlotych. 0.7500 Silver. Wratislavia.	15.00
Pr562	1987	500	1000 Zlotych. Nickel. Slaskie Museum.	—
Pr563	1987	11,500	1000 Zlotych. 0.7500 Silver. Slaskie Museum.	20.00

KM#	Date	Mintage	Identification	Mkt Val
Pr564	1987	500	1000 Zlotych. Nickel. Olympic cross country skier.	—
Pr565	1987	10,000	1000 Zlotych. 0.7500 Silver. Olympic cross country skier.	15.00

KM#	Date	Mintage	Identification	Mkt Val
Pr566	1987	500	1000 Zlotych. Nickel. Eagle with wings open divides date. Olympic archery.	—
Pr567	1987	10,000	1000 Zlotych. 0.7500 Silver. Olympic archery.	37.50

KM#	Date	Mintage	Identification	Mkt Val
Pr568	1987	500	1000 Zlotych. Nickel. Eagle with wings open divides date. Kazimierz III.	—
Pr569	1987	2,500	1000 Zlotych. 0.7500 Silver. Kazimierz III.	75.00

KM#	Date	Mintage	Identification	Mkt Val
Pr570	1987	9	1000 Zlotych. Gold. Y#168.	—

KM#	Date	Mintage	Identification	Mkt Val
Pr571	1987	9	2000 Zlotych. Gold. Y#169; Similar design to Pr570.	—
Pr572	1987	9	5000 Zlotych. Gold. Y#170; Similar design to Pr570.	—

KM#	Date	Mintage	Identification	Mkt Val
Pr573	1987	9	10000 Zlotych. Gold. Y#171; Similar design to Pr570.	—

KM#	Date	Mintage	Identification	Mkt Val
Pr574	1987	5	200000 Zlotych. Gold. Y#163; Similar design to Pr570. Photo reduced.	—

KM#	Date	Mintage	Identification	Mkt Val
Pr575	1988	500	200 Zlotych. Nickel. Eagle with wings open divides date. Soccer 1990.	—
Pr576	1988	10,000	200 Zlotych. Copper-Nickel. Soccer 1990.	12.50
Pr577	1988	7,000	500 Zlotych. Silver. Soccer 1990, Y#184.	—

KM#	Date	Mintage	Identification	Mkt Val
Pr578	1988	500	1000 Zlotych. Nickel. Queen Jadwiga.	—
Pr579	1988	2,500	1000 Zlotych. 0.7500 Silver. Queen Jadwiga.	250

KM#	Date	Mintage	Identification	Mkt Val
Pr580	1988	500	1000 Zlotych. Nickel. Eagle with wings open divides date. Soccer 1990.	—
Pr581	1988	7,000	1000 Zlotych. 0.7500 Silver. Soccer 1990.	27.50

KM#	Date	Mintage	Identification	Mkt Val
Pr582	1991	300	20000 Zlotych. 0.9990 Gold. Pope John Paul II right. Similar design to Pr583.	375

KM#	Date	Mintage	Identification	Mkt Val
Pr583	1991	—	50000 Zlotych. 0.9990 Gold. Pope John Paul II right.	500

KM#	Date	Mintage	Identification	Mkt Val
Pr584	1991	—	100000 Zlotych. 0.9990 Gold. Eagle with wings open divides date. Bust of Pope 1/4 right. Similar design to Pr583.	600
Pr585	1991	—	200000 Zlotych. 0.9990 Gold. Pope John Paul II right. Similar design to Pr583.	750

KM#	Date	Mintage	Identification	Mkt Val
Pr586	1994	—	1000 Zlotych. Copper-Nickel. Y#267.	—

BANK SETS

KM#	Date	Mintage	Identification	Issue Price	Mkt Val
BS1	1990-1994 (9)	—	Y#276-284 National Bank assembled mixed date set	—	15.30

MINT SETS

KM#	Date	Mintage	Identification	Issue Price	Mkt Val
MS1	1964 (2)	—	Y#52, 52a	—	15.00
MS2	1983 (11)	—	Y#AA47, A47, 48.1, 49.1, 69, 80.1, 81.1, 73, 142, 145, 146	—	37.50
MS3	1984 (9)	—	Y#48.1, 49.1, 80.1, 81.1, 73, 152.1, 153.1(Part 1), 148, 151 (Part 2)	—	18.50
MS4	1985 (10)	—	Y#AA47, A47, 48.1, 49.1, 73, 80.1, 81.1, 152.1, 153.1 (Part 1), 155, 157 (Part 2)	—	17.50

PROOF SETS

KM#	Date	Mintage	Identification	Issue Price	Mkt Val
PS1	1979 (6)	5,000	Y#AA47, A47, 80.1, 81.1, 99, 100	—	35.00
PS2	1980 (9)	5,000	Y#AA47, A47, 49.1, 80.1, 81.1, 108, 112, 114, 117	—	55.00
PS3	1981 (10)	5,000	Y#AA47, A47, 49.1, 80.1, 81.1, 73, 122, 124, 127, 128	—	60.00
PS4	1982 (6)	5,000	Y#48.1, 49.1, 80.1, 81.1, 73, 133	—	35.00
PS5	1986 (7)	5,000	Y#48.2, 49.2, 80.2, 81.2, 152.1, 153.1, 160	—	35.00
PS6	1987 (7)	5,000	Y#48.2, 49.2, 80.2, 81.2, 152.1, 153.1, 167	—	35.00
PS7	1988 (7)	5,000	Y#49.2, 80.2, 81.2, 152.1, 153.1, 182, 183 plus medal	—	42.50
PS8	1989 (7)	5,000	Y#49.3, 80.3, 81.3, 152.2, 153.2, 185, 194	—	42.50
PS9	1990 (8)	5,000	Y#49.3, 80.3, 81.3, 152.2, 153.2, 216, 214, 195	—	62.50

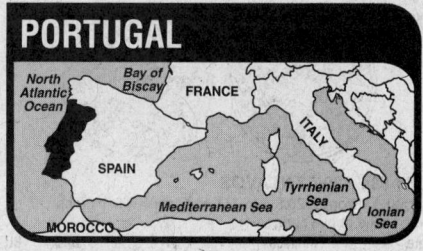

PORTUGAL

The Portuguese Republic, located in the western part of the Iberian Peninsula in southwestern Europe, has an area of 35,553 sq. mi. (92,080 sq. km.) and a population of *10.5 million. Capital: Lisbon. Portugal's economy is based on agriculture, tourism, minerals, fisheries and a rapidly expanding industrial sector. Textiles account for 33% of the exports and Portuguese wine is world famous. Portugal has become Europe's number one producer of copper and the world's largest producer of cork.

After centuries of domination by Romans, Visigoths and Moors, Portugal emerged in the 12th century as an independent kingdom financially and philosophically prepared for the great period of exploration that would soon follow. Attuned to the inspiration of Prince Henry the Navigator (1394-1460), Portugal's daring explorers of the 15th and 16th centuries roamed the world's oceans from Brazil to Japan in an unprecedented burst of energy and endeavor that culminated in 1494 with Portugal laying claim to half the transoceanic world. Unfortunately for the fortunes of the tiny kingdom, the Portuguese population was too small to colonize this vast territory. Less than a century after Portugal laid claim to half the world, English, French and Dutch trading companies had seized the lion's share of the world's colonies and commerce, and Portugal's place as an imperial power was lost forever. The monarchy was overthrown in 1910 and a republic was established.

On April 25, 1974, the government of Portugal was seized by a military junta which reached agreements providing for independence for the Portuguese overseas provinces of Portuguese Guinea (*Guinea-Bissau*), Mozambique, Cape Verde Islands, Angola, and St. Thomas and Prince Islands (*Sao Tome and Principe*).

On January 1, 1986, Portugal became the eleventh member of the European Economic Community and in the first half of 1992 held its first EEC Presidency.

RULERS
Carlos I, 1889-1908
Manuel II, 1908-1910
Republic, 1910 to date

MONETARY SYSTEM
Beginning in 1836 all coins were expressed in terms of Reis and arranged in a decimal sequence (until 1910).
Commencing 1910
100 Centavos = 1 Escudo

KINGDOM
DECIMAL COINAGE

KM# 530   5 REIS
2.8000 g., Bronze **Ruler:** Carlos I **Obv:** Head right
Obv. Leg.: CARLOS I REI... **Rev:** Value within wreath

Date	Mintage	F	VF	XF	Unc	BU
1901	1,070,000	2.50	12.50	40.00	90.00	—
1904	720,000	0.75	1.75	12.50	28.00	—
1905	1,340,000	0.75	1.50	6.00	15.00	—
1906/0	1,260	0.30	1.00	2.50	8.00	—
1906/9	Inc. above	0.25	0.75	2.00	7.00	—
1906	Inc. above	0.75	2.00	4.00	10.00	—

KM# 555   5 REIS
Bronze **Ruler:** Manuel II **Obv:** Head left **Rev:** Value within wreath

Date	Mintage	F	VF	XF	Unc	BU
1910	1,000,000	0.30	1.00	2.50	7.00	—

KM# 548   100 REIS
2.5000 g., 0.8350 Silver 0.0671 oz. ASW, 20 mm.
Ruler: Manuel II **Obv:** Bust left **Obv. Leg.:** EMANVEL II PORTVG: ET ALGARB: REX

Date	Mintage	F	VF	XF	Unc	BU
1909	6,363,000	1.50	3.50	6.50	22.00	—
1910	Inc. above	1.25	2.50	4.00	10.00	—

KM# 534   200 REIS
5.0000 g., 0.9170 Silver 0.1474 oz. ASW **Ruler:** Carlos I
Obv: Head right **Obv. Leg.:** CARLOS I... **Rev:** Value within wreath

Date	Mintage	VG	F	VF	XF	Unc
1901	205,000	30.00	100	200	400	—
1903	200,000	12.50	35.00	65.00	115	—

KM# 549   200 REIS
5.0000 g., 0.8350 Silver 0.1342 oz. ASW **Ruler:** Manuel II
Obv: Head left **Obv. Leg.:** EMANVEL II... **Rev:** Crown above value within wreath

Date	Mintage	VG	F	VF	XF	Unc
1909	7,656,000	2.25	3.50	6.50	12.00	25.00

KM# 535   500 REIS
12.5000 g., 0.9170 Silver 0.3685 oz. ASW, 30 mm.
Ruler: Carlos I **Obv:** Head right **Obv. Leg.:** CARLOS I...
Rev: Crowned arms within wreath

Date	Mintage	VG	F	VF	XF	Unc
1901	1,050,000	7.50	22.50	40.00	75.00	150
1903	680,000	6.50	9.00	15.00	30.00	60.00
1906	Inc. above	12.00	30.00	60.00	90.00	200
1906/3	240,000	15.00	35.00	70.00	100	250
1907	384,000	6.00	8.00	12.00	18.00	35.00
1908	1,840,000	5.50	7.50	11.50	16.00	25.00

KM# 547   500 REIS
12.5000 g., 0.9170 Silver 0.3685 oz. ASW, 30 mm.
Ruler: Manuel II **Obv:** Head left **Obv. Leg.:** EMANVEL II..
Rev: Crowned shield within sprigs

Date	Mintage	VG	F	VF	XF	Unc
1908	2,500,000	BV	6.00	10.00	18.00	30.00
1909	Inc. above	8.00	25.00	45.00	85.00	190
1909/8	1,513,000	8.00	25.00	45.00	85.00	195

KM# 556   500 REIS
12.5000 g., 0.9170 Silver 0.3685 oz. ASW, 30 mm.
Ruler: Manuel II **Subject:** Peninsular War Centennial **Obv:** Head left **Obv. Leg.:** EMANVEL II... **Rev:** Crowned shield

Date	Mintage	VG	F	VF	XF	Unc
1910	200,000	12.50	35.00	55.00	90.00	175

KM# 557   500 REIS
12.5000 g., 0.9170 Silver 0.3685 oz. ASW, 30 mm.
Ruler: Manuel II **Subject:** Marquis De Pombal **Obv:** Head left **Obv. Leg.:** EMANVEL II... **Rev:** Seated Victory flanked by crowned shield and bust statue

Date	Mintage	VG	F	VF	XF	Unc
1910	400,000	10.00	15.00	25.00	45.00	85.00
1910 Proof	—	Value: 600				

KM# 558   1000 REIS
25.0000 g., 0.9170 Silver 0.7370 oz. ASW, 37 mm.
Ruler: Manuel II **Subject:** Peninsular War Centennial **Obv:** Head left **Obv. Leg.:** EMANVEL II... **Rev:** Crowned shield

Date	Mintage	VG	F	VF	XF	Unc
1910	200,000	20.00	45.00	75.00	125	250
1910 Proof	—	Value: 900				

REPUBLIC
DECIMAL COINAGE

KM# 565   CENTAVO
Bronze **Obv:** Value **Rev:** Shield within designed circle

Date	Mintage	F	VF	XF	Unc	BU
1917	2,250,000	0.50	1.00	2.00	4.00	6.00
1918	22,996,000	0.50	1.00	2.00	3.00	5.00
1920	12,535,000	0.50	1.00	2.50	5.00	7.00
1921	4,492,000	10.00	30.00	40.00	70.00	—
1922 Rare	Inc. above	—	—	—	—	—

KM# 567   2 CENTAVOS
Iron **Obv:** Value **Rev:** Shield within designed circle

Date	Mintage	F	VF	XF	Unc	BU
1918	170,000	65.00	150	300	700	—

Note: Most lower grades have oxidation and will sell for less

KM# 568   2 CENTAVOS
Bronze

Date	Mintage	F	VF	XF	Unc	BU
1918	4,295,000	0.50	0.75	2.00	4.00	6.00
1920	10,109,000	0.50	1.50	2.50	5.00	7.00
1921	679,000	25.00	50.00	100	150	—

KM# 566   4 CENTAVOS
Copper-Nickel **Obv:** Value **Rev:** Liberty head left

Date	Mintage	F	VF	XF	Unc	BU
1917	4,961,000	0.35	0.65	1.50	4.00	7.00
1919	10,067,000	0.35	0.65	1.75	4.50	8.00

KM# 569 5 CENTAVOS
Bronze **Obv:** Value **Rev:** Shield within designed circle

Date	Mintage	F	VF	XF	Unc	BU
1920	114,000	35.00	70.00	120	200	—
1921	5,916,000	0.75	2.00	4.00	7.00	9.00
1922	Inc. above	125	250	500	750	—

KM# 572 5 CENTAVOS
Bronze **Obv:** Value **Rev:** Liberty head left

Date	Mintage	F	VF	XF	Unc	BU
1924	6,480,000	0.50	1.50	4.50	10.00	—
1925	7,260,000	3.50	7.50	22.00	40.00	—
1927	26,320,000	0.25	0.75	1.50	5.00	10.00

KM# 563 10 CENTAVOS
2.5000 g., 0.8350 Silver 0.0671 oz. ASW **Obv:** Liberty head left
Rev: Shield within designed circle within wreath

Date	Mintage	F	VF	XF	Unc	BU
1915	3,418,000	1.25	2.50	3.50	8.00	12.00

KM# 570 10 CENTAVOS
Copper-Nickel **Obv:** Value **Rev:** Liberty head left

Date	Mintage	F	VF	XF	Unc	BU
1920	1,120,000	3.00	6.00	12.00	20.00	—
1921	1,285,000	3.00	6.00	15.00	25.00	—

KM# 573 10 CENTAVOS
4.0000 g., Bronze **Obv:** Value **Rev:** Liberty head left

Date	Mintage	F	VF	XF	Unc	BU
1924	1,210,000	3.00	12.50	45.00	100	—
1925	9,090,000	0.75	1.50	11.00	35.00	—
1926	26,250,000	0.75	2.75	14.50	40.00	—
1930	1,730,000	55.00	125	250	550	—
1938	2,000,000	5.00	20.00	40.00	100	—
1940	3,384,000	1.50	4.00	10.00	25.00	—

KM# 583 10 CENTAVOS
2.0000 g., Bronze, 17 mm. **Obv:** Circles within cross **Rev:** Value above sprig

Date	Mintage	F	VF	XF	Unc	BU
1942	1,035,000	2.00	4.00	22.50	45.00	—
1943	18,765,000	2.00	5.00	10.00	40.00	—
1944	5,090,000	2.00	5.00	10.00	40.00	—
1945	6,090,000	2.00	4.50	10.00	35.00	—
1946	7,740,000	1.00	2.50	8.00	40.00	—
1947	9,283,000	1.00	2.00	5.00	20.00	—
1948	5,900,000	10.00	30.00	75.00	150	—
1949	15,240,000	0.25	1.00	5.00	15.00	20.00
1950	8,860,000	1.50	5.00	10.00	60.00	—
1951	5,040,000	1.50	5.00	15.00	75.00	—

Date	Mintage	F	VF	XF	Unc	BU
1952	4,960,000	2.50	12.00	35.00	125	—
1953	7,548,000	1.50	3.00	5.00	10.00	15.00
1954	2,452,000	1.50	5.00	15.00	60.00	—
1955	10,000,000	0.10	0.50	2.50	6.00	—
1956	3,336,000	0.10	0.50	2.00	5.00	7.50
1957	6,654,000	0.10	0.25	2.00	5.00	—
1958	7,320,000	0.10	0.25	2.00	5.00	—
1959	7,140,000	0.10	0.25	2.00	4.00	5.00
1960	15,055,000	0.10	0.25	2.00	2.00	—
1961	5,020,000	—	0.10	1.50	4.00	—
1962	14,980,000	—	0.10	0.50	1.00	1.50
1963	5,393,000	—	0.10	1.25	2.50	—
1964	10,257,000	—	0.10	0.75	1.50	2.00
1965	15,550,000	—	0.10	1.00	1.75	—
1966	10,200,000	—	0.10	0.50	1.00	—
1967	18,592,000	—	0.10	0.50	1.00	1.50
1968	22,515,000	—	0.10	0.50	1.00	2.00
1969	3,871,000	0.10	0.25	1.25	2.50	—

KM# 594 10 CENTAVOS
0.5000 g., Aluminum, 15 mm. **Obv:** Circles within cross
Obv. Leg.: REPVBLICA PORTVGVESA **Rev:** Value above sprig
Edge: Plain

Date	Mintage	F	VF	XF	Unc	BU
1969	—	700	1,250	1,950	3,500	—
1970 Rare						
1971	25,673,000	—	—	0.50	1.00	—
1972	10,558,000	—	—	0.50	1.00	—
1973	3,149,000	—	—	1.25	3.50	—
1974	17,043,000	—	—	0.50	1.00	—
1975	22,410,000	—	—	0.50	1.00	—
1976	19,907,000	—	—	0.50	1.00	—
1977	8,431,000	—	—	0.50	1.00	—
1978	2,205,000	—	—	0.50	1.00	—
1979	9,083,000	—	—	1.00	2.50	—

KM# 562 20 CENTAVOS
5.0000 g., 0.8350 Silver 0.1342 oz. ASW **Obv:** Liberty head left
Rev: Shield within designed circle and wreath

Date	Mintage	F	VF	XF	Unc	BU
1913	540,000	5.00	35.00	75.00	175	—
1916	706,000	3.00	30.00	40.00	100	—

KM# 571 20 CENTAVOS
Copper-Nickel **Obv:** Value and date within circle **Rev:** Liberty head left within circle

Date	Mintage	F	VF	XF	Unc	BU
1920	1,568,000	3.50	7.00	15.00	20.00	—
1921	3,030,000	4.00	8.00	14.00	22.50	—
1922	580,000	500	900	1,500	3,000	—

KM# 574 20 CENTAVOS
Bronze, 24 mm. **Obv:** Value **Rev:** Liberty head left

Date	Mintage	F	VF	XF	Unc	BU
1924	6,220,000	1.00	4.00	20.00	50.00	—
1925	10,580,000	1.00	4.00	20.00	50.00	—

KM# 584 20 CENTAVOS
3.0000 g., Bronze, 20.8 mm. **Obv:** Circles within cross
Rev: Value above sprig

Date	Mintage	F	VF	XF	Unc	BU
1942	10,170,000	1.50	3.50	25.00	60.00	—
1943	Inc. above	1.50	3.00	20.00	60.00	—
1944	7,290,000	1.50	3.00	20.00	60.00	—
1945	7,552,000	1.00	2.00	25.00	60.00	—
1948	2,750,000	2.50	12.00	35.00	135	—
1949	12,250,000	0.10	0.50	6.00	15.00	20.00
1951	3,185,000	0.50	2.00	20.00	150	—
1952	1,815,000	2.00	12.00	35.00	200	—
1953	9,426,000	—	0.75	4.00	8.00	—
1955	5,574,000	—	0.75	4.00	8.00	—
1956	6,450,000	—	0.50	2.75	6.00	7.50
1958	7,470,000	—	0.50	2.75	6.00	7.50
1959	4,780,000	—	0.50	2.75	6.00	7.50
1960	4,790,000	—	0.50	3.50	8.00	—
1961	5,180,000	—	0.50	3.50	8.00	—
1962	2,500,000	0.25	1.50	10.00	18.00	25.00
1963	7,990,000	—	0.25	2.00	3.50	4.50
1964	7,010,000	—	0.25	1.50	3.00	4.00
1965	7,365,000	—	0.25	1.00	2.50	—
1966	8,074,999	—	0.25	0.50	2.00	—
1967	9,220,000	—	0.25	0.50	2.00	—
1968	10,372,000	—	0.25	0.50	1.50	2.00
1969	8,657,000	—	0.25	1.00	3.00	—

KM# 595 20 CENTAVOS
1.7000 g., Bronze, 16 mm. **Obv:** Circles within cross **Rev:** Value above sprig

Date	Mintage	F	VF	XF	Unc	BU
1969	10,891,000	—	0.25	0.75	2.50	—
1970	16,120,000	—	0.25	1.00	3.00	—
1971	1,933,000	—	1.00	2.50	7.50	—
1972	16,354,000	—	—	0.25	1.00	—
1973	4,900,000	—	—	0.25	1.00	—
1974	26,975,000	—	—	0.25	1.00	—

KM# 561 50 CENTAVOS
12.5000 g., 0.8350 Silver 0.3356 oz. ASW **Obv:** Liberty head left **Rev:** Shield within designed circle and wreath

Date	Mintage	F	VF	XF	Unc	BU
1912	1,695,000	7.00	9.00	15.00	30.00	—
1913	4,443,000	BV	8.00	10.00	20.00	—
1914	4,992,000	7.00	9.00	15.00	30.00	—
1916	5,080,000	BV	8.00	10.00	20.00	—

KM# 575 50 CENTAVOS
Aluminum-Bronze **Obv:** Seated figure **Rev:** Shield within designed circle and wreath

Date	Mintage	F	VF	XF	Unc	BU
1924	810,000	65.00	125	250	450	—
1925	—	1,000	1,500	3,500	7,000	—
1926	4,340,000	2.00	6.00	18.00	40.00	55.00

KM# 577 50 CENTAVOS
4.4500 g., Copper-Nickel, 23 mm. **Obv:** Liberty head right
Rev: Shield within designed circle and wreath above value

Date	Mintage	F	VF	XF	Unc	BU
1927	2,330,000	2.50	12.50	30.00	125	150
1928	6,823,000	2.50	12.50	30.00	175	—
1929	9,779,000	2.50	12.50	30.00	125	150
1930	1,116,000	2.50	20.00	200	500	—
1931	7,127,000	8.00	22.00	200	500	—
1935	902,000	25.00	55.00	300	700	—
Note: For exclusive use in Azores						
1938	923,000	25.00	55.00	300	800	—
1940	2,000,000	1.00	5.00	30.00	125	—
1944	2,974,000	0.25	1.00	7.00	20.00	30.00
1945	5,700,000	0.25	1.00	5.50	15.00	25.00
1946	4,334,000	—	2.00	10.00	35.00	45.00
1947	6,998,000	0.10	1.00	9.00	20.00	30.00
1951	4,610,000	—	0.50	2.75	10.00	15.00
1952	2,421,000	0.10	1.00	4.00	20.00	40.00
1953	2,369,000	0.10	1.00	12.50	50.00	75.00
1955	3,057,000	0.10	0.50	3.00	9.00	12.00
1956	3,003,000	—	0.50	3.00	6.00	8.00
1957	3,940,000	—	0.50	3.00	6.50	9.00
1958	2,687,000	—	0.50	4.00	9.00	12.00
1959	4,027,000	—	0.50	2.00	6.00	8.00
1960	2,592,000	—	0.50	2.00	5.50	7.50
1961	3,324,000	—	0.50	2.00	4.00	7.50
1962	6,678,000	—	0.25	1.00	2.50	3.50
1963	2,346,000	—	0.25	3.00	9.00	12.00
1964	7,654,000	—	0.25	1.00	1.75	2.75
1965	3,366,000	—	0.25	1.00	2.50	3.50
1966	6,085,000	—	0.25	1.00	2.50	3.50
1967	19,391,000	—	0.25	1.00	2.50	3.50
1968	11,448,000	—	0.25	1.00	2.00	3.00

KM# 596 50 CENTAVOS
4.2500 g., Bronze, 22.5 mm. **Obv:** Circles within cross **Obv. Leg.:** REPVBLICA PORTVGVESA **Rev:** Value above spears of grain

Date	Mintage	F	VF	XF	Unc	BU
1969	3,481,000	—	—	1.00	3.50	—
1970	17,280,000	—	—	1.00	3.00	—
1971	9,139,000	—	—	1.00	3.00	—
1972	24,729,000	—	—	1.00	3.00	—
1973	35,588,000	—	—	0.75	2.50	—
1974	28,719,000	—	—	0.75	2.50	—
1975	17,793,000	—	—	0.75	2.50	—
1976	23,734,000	—	—	0.75	2.50	—
1977	16,340,000	—	—	0.75	2.50	—
1978	48,348,000	—	—	0.75	2.25	—
1979	61,652,000	—	—	0.75	2.00	—

KM# 560 ESCUDO
25.0000 g., 0.8350 Silver 0.6711 oz. ASW, 37 mm.
Subject: October 5, 1910. Birth of the Republic **Obv:** Bust holding torch facing left **Obv. Leg.:** REPUBLICA PORTUGUESA 5 de Outubro de 1910 **Rev:** Shield within designed circle and wreath

Date	Mintage	F	VF	XF	Unc	BU
1910	1,000,000	100	150	200	300	—

Note: Struck in 1914

KM# 564 ESCUDO
25.0000 g., 0.8350 Silver 0.6711 oz. ASW, 37 mm. **Obv:** Liberty head left

Date	Mintage	F	VF	XF	Unc	BU
1915	1,818,000	15.00	35.00	50.00	80.00	—
1916	1,405,000	15.00	40.00	60.00	90.00	—

KM# 576 ESCUDO
Aluminum-Bronze **Obv:** Sitting figure **Rev:** Shield within designed circle, value divides wreath

Date	Mintage	F	VF	XF	Unc	BU
1924	2,709,000	10.00	20.00	40.00	80.00	—
1926	2,346,000	85.00	175	300	700	—

KM# 578 ESCUDO
8.0000 g., Copper-Nickel, 26.5 mm.

Date	Mintage	F	VF	XF	Unc	BU
1927	1,917,000	2.00	12.00	65.00	200	—
1928	7,462,000	1.00	5.00	35.00	225	—
1929	1,617,000	1.00	15.00	75.00	300	—
1930	1,911,000	6.00	25.00	250	1,000	—
1931	2,039,000	7.50	25.00	250	900	—
1935	—	125	325	1,000	6,000	—
Note: For exclusive use in Azores						
1939	304,000	12.00	85.00	325	750	—
1940	1,259,000	1.00	25.00	50.00	150	—
1944	993,000	25.00	100	250	600	—
1945	Inc. above	0.50	1.50	22.00	75.00	—
1946	2,507,000	0.50	1.50	12.50	75.00	—
1951	2,500,000	0.50	1.00	6.00	10.00	15.00
1952	2,500,000	1.50	4.00	45.00	125	—
1957	1,656,000	0.10	0.50	4.50	10.00	20.00
1958	1,447,000	0.10	0.50	4.50	12.00	20.00
1959	1,908,000	0.10	0.50	4.50	10.00	20.00
1961	2,505,000	0.10	0.25	2.50	5.00	7.00
1962	2,757,000	0.10	0.25	2.00	5.00	7.00
1964	1,611,000	0.10	0.25	2.00	5.00	7.00
1965	1,683,000	0.10	0.25	1.50	3.00	4.00
1966	2,607,000	0.10	0.20	1.50	4.00	4.00
1968	4,099,000	0.10	0.20	1.50	3.50	5.00

KM# 597 ESCUDO
8.0000 g., Bronze, 26 mm. **Obv:** Circles within cross **Obv. Leg.:** REPVBLICA PORTVGVESA **Rev:** Value above spears of grain **Edge:** Plain

Date	Mintage	F	VF	XF	Unc	BU
1969	3,020,000	—	0.10	1.50	5.00	—
1970	6,009,000	—	0.10	1.50	4.00	—
1971	7,860,000	—	0.10	1.50	4.00	—
1972	3,815,000	—	0.10	1.50	4.50	—
1973	20,467,000	—	0.10	1.00	3.00	—
1974	11,444,000	—	0.10	1.00	3.00	—
1975	8,473,000	—	0.10	0.50	3.00	—
1976	7,353,000	—	0.10	0.50	2.00	—
1977	6,218,000	—	0.10	0.50	2.00	—
1978	7,061,000	—	0.10	0.50	2.00	—
1979	14,241,000	—	0.10	0.25	1.50	—

KM# 614 ESCUDO
3.0000 g., Nickel-Brass, 18 mm. **Obv:** Shield **Rev:** Value
Note: Prev. KM#611.

Date	Mintage	F	VF	XF	Unc	BU
1981	30,165,000	—	—	0.10	1.00	—
1982	53,018,000	—	—	0.10	1.00	—
1983	53,165,000	—	—	0.10	0.50	—
1984	59,463,000	—	—	0.10	0.50	—
1985	46,832,000	—	—	0.10	0.50	—
1986	8,029,999	—	—	0.10	4.00	—

KM# 612 ESCUDO
Nickel-Brass, 18 mm. **Subject:** World Roller Hockey Championship Games **Obv:** Shield **Rev:** Hockey player

Date	Mintage	F	VF	XF	Unc	BU
ND(1983)	1,990,000	—	0.10	0.25	0.75	—

KM# 631 ESCUDO
1.6900 g., Nickel-Brass, 16 mm. **Obv:** Design above shield **Rev:** Flower design above value **Edge:** Reeded

Date	Mintage	F	VF	XF	Unc	BU
1986	14,882,000	—	—	0.10	0.35	—
1987	21,922,000	—	—	0.10	0.35	—
1988	17,168,000	—	—	0.10	0.35	—
1989	17,194,000	—	—	0.10	0.35	—
1990	19,008,000	—	—	0.10	0.35	—
1991	21,500,000	—	—	—	0.35	—
1992	22,000,000	—	—	—	0.35	—
1993	10,505,000	—	—	—	0.35	—
1994	—	—	—	—	0.35	—
1995	—	—	—	—	0.50	—
Note: In Mint sets only						
1996	—	—	—	—	0.35	—
1996 Proof	7,000	Value: 0.50				
1997	—	—	—	—	—	—
1997 Proof	—	Value: 0.50				
1998	—	—	—	—	0.35	—
1998 Proof	—	Value: 2.00				
1999	—	—	—	—	0.35	—
2000	—	—	—	—	0.35	—

KM# 580 2-1/2 ESCUDOS
3.5000 g., 0.6500 Silver 0.0731 oz. ASW, 20.41 mm. **Obv:** Early sailing ship **Rev:** Shield on globe **Edge:** Reeded

Date	Mintage	F	VF	XF	Unc	BU
1932	2,592,000	5.00	20.00	50.00	120	—
1933	2,457,000	15.00	40.00	100	200	—
1937	1,000,000	150	350	700	1,500	—
1940	2,763,000	3.00	10.00	25.00	70.00	—
1942	3,847,000	BV	3.00	6.50	20.00	—
1943	8,302,000	BV	1.75	2.50	10.00	15.00
1944	9,134,000	BV	1.50	2.25	7.00	10.00
1945	6,316,000	BV	3.50	10.00	20.00	30.00
1946	3,208,000	BV	3.00	7.50	15.00	25.00
1947	2,610,000	BV	3.00	7.50	15.00	25.00
1948	1,814,000	10.00	20.00	40.00	110	—
1951	4,000,000	BV	1.25	2.00	5.00	7.00

KM# 590 2-1/2 ESCUDOS
3.5000 g., Copper-Nickel, 20 mm. **Obv:** Ship **Rev:** Shield flanked by stars

Date	Mintage	F	VF	XF	Unc	BU
1963	12,711,000	—	0.50	20.00	32.00	45.00
1964	17,948,000	—	0.50	20.00	32.00	45.00

Date	Mintage	F	VF	XF	Unc	BU
1965	19,512,000	—	0.25	5.00	11.00	15.00
1966	3,828,000	—	2.00	35.00	55.00	80.00
1967	5,545,000	—	0.25	7.00	18.00	—
1968	6,087,000	—	0.25	2.00	3.50	5.00
1969	9,969,000	—	0.25	1.75	3.00	4.00
1970	2,400,000	—	0.25	2.25	4.00	5.00
1971	6,791,000	—	0.25	1.50	3.00	4.00
1972	6,713,000	—	0.25	1.75	3.00	4.00
1973	9,104,000	—	0.25	1.00	2.00	3.00
1974	22,743,000	—	0.10	0.75	2.50	3.50
1975	16,623,999	—	0.10	0.50	1.50	2.00
1976	21,516,000	—	0.10	0.50	1.50	2.00
1977	45,726,000	—	0.10	0.50	1.50	2.00
1978	27,375,000	—	0.10	0.25	0.75	1.00
1979	44,804,000	—	0.10	0.25	0.75	1.00
1980	22,319,000	—	0.10	0.25	1.00	1.25
1981	25,420,000	—	0.10	0.20	1.00	1.25
1982	45,910,000	—	0.10	0.20	0.75	1.00
1983	62,946,000	—	0.10	0.20	0.75	1.00
1984	58,210,000	—	0.10	0.20	0.75	1.00
1985	60,142,000	—	0.10	0.20	0.75	1.00

KM# 605   2-1/2 ESCUDOS
3.5000 g., Copper-Nickel, 20 mm. **Subject:** 100th Anniversary - Death of Alexandre Herculano, Poet **Obv:** Shield **Rev:** Bust facing flanked by dates

Date	Mintage	F	VF	XF	Unc	BU
ND(1977)	5,990,000	—	0.20	0.75	2.00	—
ND(1977) Proof	13,000	Value: 3.50				

KM# 613   2-1/2 ESCUDOS
3.5000 g., Copper-Nickel, 20 mm. **Subject:** World Roller Hockey Championship Games **Obv:** Shield **Rev:** Hockey player

Date	Mintage	F	VF	XF	Unc	BU
ND(1983)	1,990,000	—	0.10	0.25	1.00	—

KM# 617   2-1/2 ESCUDOS
3.5000 g., Copper-Nickel, 20 mm. **Series:** F.A.O. **Obv:** Shield **Rev:** Ear of corn, FAO and date

Date	Mintage	F	VF	XF	Unc	BU
1983	995,000	—	0.10	0.35	1.25	—

KM# 581   5 ESCUDOS
7.0000 g., 0.6500 Silver 0.1463 oz. ASW, 25 mm. **Obv:** Ship **Rev:** Shield in front of circular design

Date	Mintage	F	VF	XF	Unc	BU
1932	800,000	10.00	35.00	200	600	—
1933	6,717,000	2.50	5.50	20.00	60.00	—
1934	1,012,000	4.00	15.00	50.00	120	—
1937	1,500,000	30.00	80.00	200	600	—
1940	1,500,000	4.00	15.00	50.00	120	—
1942	2,051,000	2.50	4.50	9.00	20.00	25.00
1943	1,354,000	6.00	20.00	60.00	140	—
1946	404,000	4.00	12.50	25.00	55.00	—
1947	2,420,000	BV	3.00	5.00	12.00	—
1948	2,017,999	BV	3.00	5.00	11.00	15.00
1951	966,000	BV	3.00	5.00	11.00	15.00

KM# 587   5 ESCUDOS
7.0000 g., 0.8000 Silver 0.1800 oz. ASW, 25 mm. **Subject:** 500th Anniversary - Death of Prince Henry the Navigator **Obv:** Shield **Rev:** Head with sombrero facing 1/4 left

Date	Mintage	F	VF	XF	Unc	BU
1960INCM	800,000	—	2.50	3.50	6.50	10.00
1960INCM Matte	—	—	—	—	20.00	—

Note: A small quantity of these coins were given a matte finish by the Lisbon Mint on private contract

KM# 591   5 ESCUDOS
7.0000 g., Copper-Nickel, 24.5 mm. **Obv:** Ship **Obv. Leg.:** REPUBLICA PORTUGUESA **Rev:** Shield flanked by stars

Date	Mintage	F	VF	XF	Unc	BU
1963	2,200,000	—	0.50	15.00	30.00	—
1964	4,268,000	—	0.50	12.50	25.00	35.00
1965	7,294,000	—	0.35	12.50	25.00	35.00
1966	8,119,999	—	0.35	10.00	25.00	35.00
1967	8,128,000	—	0.25	7.00	20.00	25.00
1968	5,023,000	—	0.25	3.00	5.00	10.00
1969	3,571,000	—	0.10	2.00	5.00	6.00
1970	1,200,000	—	0.10	2.50	5.50	7.00
1971	2,721,000	—	0.10	2.00	5.00	6.00
1972	1,880,000	—	0.10	2.00	6.00	—
1973	2,836,000	—	0.10	1.25	4.00	—
1974	3,984,000	—	0.10	1.00	3.50	—
1975	7,496,000	—	0.10	1.00	2.50	3.50
1976	11,379,000	—	0.10	1.00	2.50	3.50
1977	29,058,000	—	0.10	0.50	1.50	2.00
1978	672,000	2.00	5.00	10.00	—	—
1979	19,546,000	—	0.10	0.50	1.50	—
1980	46,244,000	—	0.10	0.50	1.50	2.00
1981	15,267,000	—	0.10	0.50	1.50	2.00
1982	31,318,000	—	0.10	0.50	1.50	2.00
1983	51,056,000	—	0.10	0.50	1.50	2.00
1984	46,794,000	—	0.10	0.50	1.50	2.00
1985	45,441,000	—	0.10	0.50	1.25	1.75
1986	18,753,000	—	0.10	0.50	1.50	—

KM# 606   5 ESCUDOS
7.0000 g., Copper-Nickel, 24.5 mm. **Subject:** 100th Anniversary - Death of Alexandre Herculano, Poet **Obv:** Shield **Obv. Leg.:** REPUBLICA PORTUGUESA **Rev:** Bust 1/4 right flanked by dates **Rev. Leg.:** CENTENARIO DA MORTE DE ALEXANDRE HERCULANO 1877 1977

Date	Mintage	F	VF	XF	Unc	BU
ND(1977)INCM	5,990,000	—	0.35	1.00	2.00	2.50
ND(1977)INCM Proof	10,000	Value: 4.00				

KM# 615   5 ESCUDOS
7.0000 g., Copper-Nickel, 24.5 mm. **Subject:** World Roller Hockey Championship Games **Obv:** Shield **Rev:** Hockey player

Date	Mintage	F	VF	XF	Unc	BU
ND(1983)	1,990,000	—	0.25	0.50	1.00	1.50

KM# 618   5 ESCUDOS
7.0000 g., Copper-Nickel, 24.5 mm. **Series:** F.A.O. **Obv:** Shield **Rev:** Bull

Date	Mintage	F	VF	XF	Unc	BU
ND(1983)	995,000	—	0.30	0.75	1.50	2.50

KM# 632   5 ESCUDOS
Nickel-Brass **Obv:** Design above shield **Rev:** Star design above value

Date	Mintage	F	VF	XF	Unc	BU
1986	21,426,000	—	0.10	0.25	0.50	—
1987	40,548,000	—	0.10	0.25	0.50	—
1988	19,382,000	—	0.10	0.25	0.50	—
1989	27,641,000	—	0.10	0.25	0.50	—
1990	77,977,000	—	0.10	0.25	0.50	—
1991	32,000,000	—	—	—	0.50	—
1992	16,000,000	—	—	—	0.50	—
1993	8,300,000	—	—	—	0.50	—
1994	—	—	—	—	0.50	—
1995	—	—	—	—	0.50	—
1996	—	—	—	—	0.50	—
1996 Proof	7,000	Value: 0.75				
1997	—	—	—	—	0.50	—
1997 Proof	—	Value: 0.75				
1998	—	—	—	—	0.50	—
1998 Proof	—	Value: 0.75				
1999	—	—	—	—	0.50	—
2000	—	—	—	—	0.50	—

KM# 579   10 ESCUDOS
12.5000 g., 0.8350 Silver 0.3356 oz. ASW, 30 mm. **Subject:** Battle of Ourique **Obv:** Crowned shield flanked by value **Obv. Leg.:** REPUBLICA PORTUGUESA **Rev:** Armored figure on horse holding sword **Rev. Leg.:** Comemoração da Batalha de Ourique 1139

Date	Mintage	F	VF	XF	Unc	BU
1928	200,000	15.00	25.00	50.00	75.00	—

KM# 582   10 ESCUDOS
12.5000 g., 0.8350 Silver 0.3356 oz. ASW, 30 mm. **Obv:** Ship **Rev:** Shield in front of circular design

Date	Mintage	F	VF	XF	Unc	BU
1932	3,220,000	5.50	10.00	20.00	60.00	—
1933	1,780,000	30.00	70.00	200	500	—
1934	400,000	15.00	30.00	50.00	150	—
1937	500,000	60.00	150	400	650	—
1940	1,200,000	10.00	20.00	40.00	60.00	—
1942	186,000	200	400	700	1,200	—
1948	507,000	30.00	75.00	150	220	—

KM# 586   10 ESCUDOS
12.5000 g., 0.8350 Silver 0.3356 oz. ASW, 30 mm. **Obv:** Ship **Rev:** Shield above circular design flanked by value

Date	Mintage	F	VF	XF	Unc	BU
1954	5,764,000	—	BV	5.50	8.00	10.00
1955	4,056,000	—	BV	5.50	8.00	10.00

KM# 588   10 ESCUDOS
12.5000 g., 0.8000 Silver 0.3215 oz. ASW, 30 mm.
Subject: 500th Anniversary - Death of Prince Henry the Navigator
Obv: Shield flanked by designs **Rev:** Head with sombrero facing 1/4 left

Date	Mintage	F	VF	XF	Unc	BU
1960INCM	200,000	—	9.00	20.00	30.00	35.00
1960INCM Matte	—	—	—	—	50.00	—

Note: A small quantity of these coins were given a matte finish by the Lisbon Mint on private contract

KM# 600   10 ESCUDOS
10.0000 g., Copper-Nickel Clad Nickel, 28 mm. **Obv:** Ship
Obv. Leg.: REPUBLICA PORTUGUESA **Rev:** Shield flanked by stars **Rev. Leg.:** CONFIANCA ESPERANCA FRATERNIDADE
Note: Edge lettering exists in both normal and upside down positions for all years.

Date	Mintage	F	VF	XF	Unc	BU
1971	3,876,000	—	0.25	0.75	2.00	2.50
1972	2,694,000	—	0.25	1.00	2.50	3.50
1973	5,418,000	—	0.25	0.75	2.00	2.50
1974	4,043,000	—	0.25	0.75	2.00	2.50

KM# 633   10 ESCUDOS
Nickel-Brass   **Obv:** Design above shield **Rev:** Artistic design above value

Date	Mintage	F	VF	XF	Unc	BU
1986	12,818,000	—	0.20	0.40	1.00	1.50
1987	32,814,999	—	0.20	0.40	1.00	1.50
1988	32,579,000	—	0.20	0.40	1.00	1.50
1989	12,788,000	—	0.20	0.40	1.00	1.50
1990	26,500,000	—	0.20	0.40	1.00	1.50
1991	9,500,000	—	—	—	1.00	1.75
1992	5,600,000	—	—	—	1.00	1.75
1993	20,000	—	—	—	10.00	—
Note: In Mint sets only						
1994	20,000	—	—	—	10.00	—
Note: In Mint sets only						
1995	—	—	—	—	10.00	—
Note: In Mint sets only						
1996	—	—	—	—	1.00	—
1996 Proof	7,000	Value: 2.50				
1997	—	—	—	—	—	—
1997 Proof	—	Value: 2.50				
1998	—	—	—	—	1.00	—
1998 Proof	—	Value: 3.00				
1999	—	—	—	—	—	—
2000	—	—	—	—	1.00	—

KM# 638   10 ESCUDOS
7.4000 g., Nickel-Brass   **Subject:** Rural World **Obv:** Design above shield **Rev:** Hand holding sprig flanked by stars all around

Date	Mintage	F	VF	XF	Unc	BU
1987	2,000,000	—	0.40	0.60	1.50	—

KM# 585   20 ESCUDOS
21.0000 g., 0.8000 Silver 0.5401 oz. ASW, 34 mm. **Subject:** 25th Anniversary of Financial Reform **Obv:** Shield above globe, value at left, all within circle **Rev:** Seated figure facing left reading a book

Date	Mintage	F	VF	XF	Unc	BU
1953	1,000,000	—	BV	11.50	12.50	14.50
1953 Matte	—	—	—	—	35.00	—

Note: A small quantity of these coins were given a matte finish by the Lisbon Mint on private contract

KM# 589   20 ESCUDOS
21.0000 g., 0.8000 Silver 0.5401 oz. ASW, 34 mm.
Subject: 500th Anniversary - Death of Prince Henry the Navigator
Obv: Shield flanked by designs **Rev:** Head with sombrero facing 1/4 left

Date	Mintage	F	VF	XF	Unc	BU
1960	200,000	—	12.00	20.00	30.00	40.00
1960 Matte	—	—	—	—	55.00	—

Note: A small quantity of these coins were given a matte finish by the Lisbon Mint on private contract

KM# 592   20 ESCUDOS
10.0000 g., 0.6500 Silver 0.2090 oz. ASW **Subject:** Opening of Salazar Bridge **Obv:** Shield and value within artistic design
Rev: Salazar bridge

Date	Mintage	F	VF	XF	Unc	BU
1966	2,000,000	—	BV	4.50	5.50	7.00
1966 Matte	200	—	—	—	35.00	—

Note: A small quantity of these coins were given a matte finish by the Lisbon Mint on private contract

KM# 634.1   20 ESCUDOS
6.9000 g., Copper-Nickel, 26.5 mm. **Obv:** Shield divides date with value below **Obv. Leg.:** REPUBLICA PORTUGUESA
Rev: Nautical windrose

Date	Mintage	F	VF	XF	Unc	BU
1986INCM	45,361,000	—	0.15	0.25	1.00	1.50
1987INCM	68,216,000	—	0.15	0.25	1.00	1.50
1988INCM	57,482,000	—	0.15	0.25	1.00	1.50
1989INCM	25,060,000	—	0.15	0.25	1.00	1.50
1990INCM	50,000	—	—	—	10.00	—
Note: In Mint sets only						
1991INCM	50,000	—	—	—	10.00	—
Note: In Mint sets only						
1992INCM	20,000	—	—	—	10.00	—
Note: In Mint sets only						
1993INCM	20,000	—	—	—	10.00	—
Note: In Mint sets only						
1994INCM	20,000	—	—	—	10.00	—
Note: In Mint sets only						
1995INCM	—	—	—	—	10.00	—

Date	Mintage	F	VF	XF	Unc	BU
Note: In Mint sets only						
1996INCM	—	—	—	—	10.00	—
Note: In Mint sets only						
1996INCM Proof	7,000	Value: 2.50				
1997INCM	—	—	—	—	10.00	—
Note: In Mint sets only						
1997INCM Proof	—	Value: 2.50				
1998INCM	15,000,000	—	—	—	1.00	1.50
1999INCM	20,000,000	—	—	—	1.00	1.50

KM# 634.2   20 ESCUDOS
Copper-Nickel **Obv:** Larger shield divides date with larger value below **Rev:** Nautical windrose

Date	Mintage	F	VF	XF	Unc	BU
1998	—	—	—	—	1.00	—
1998 Proof	—	Value: 4.00				
1999	—	—	—	—	1.00	—
2000	—	—	—	—	1.00	—

KM# 607   25 ESCUDOS
Copper-Nickel **Obv:** Value to right of shield **Rev:** Head laureate left

Date	Mintage	F	VF	XF	Unc	BU
1977	7,657,000	—	0.40	1.00	2.00	4.50
1978	12,277,000	—	0.40	1.50	3.00	5.00

KM# 608   25 ESCUDOS
Copper-Nickel, 26.5 mm. **Subject:** 100th Anniversary - Death of Alexandre Herculano, Poet **Obv:** Shield **Rev:** Bust flanked by dates facing 1/4 right

Date	Mintage	F	VF	XF	Unc	BU
ND(1977)	5,990,000	—	0.50	1.00	2.50	4.75
ND(1977) Proof	13,000	Value: 7.00				

KM# 609   25 ESCUDOS
Copper-Nickel **Subject:** International Year of the Child
Obv: Shield **Rev:** Two faces, one facing left, the other 3/4 right

Date	Mintage	F	VF	XF	Unc	BU
1979	990,000	—	0.50	1.00	2.50	—
1979 Prooflike	10,000	—	—	—	8.00	—

KM# 607a   25 ESCUDOS
10.8000 g., Copper-Nickel, 28.5 mm. **Obv:** Value to right of shield **Rev:** Head laureate left **Note:** Increased size; prev. KM#610.

Date	Mintage	F	VF	XF	Unc	BU
1980	750,000	—	0.40	0.80	1.50	—
1981	19,924,000	—	0.40	0.80	1.50	3.50
1982	12,158,000	—	0.40	0.80	1.50	3.50
1983	5,622,000	—	0.40	0.80	1.50	—
1984	3,453,000	—	—	1.00	3.00	—
1985	25,027,000	—	0.40	0.80	1.50	2.50
1986	—	—	0.50	1.00	4.00	—

KM# 616   25 ESCUDOS
Copper-Nickel, 28.5 mm. **Subject:** World Roller Hockey
Championship Games **Obv:** Shield **Rev:** Suited hockey player

Date	Mintage	F	VF	XF	Unc	BU
ND(1983)	1,990,000	—	0.50	1.00	2.00	2.50

KM# 619   25 ESCUDOS
Copper-Nickel, 28.5 mm. **Series:** F.A.O. **Obv:** Shield **Rev:** Fish,
F.A.O. and date

Date	Mintage	F	VF	XF	Unc	BU
1983	995,000	—	0.60	1.25	2.25	3.00

KM# 623   25 ESCUDOS
Copper-Nickel, 28.5 mm. **Subject:** 10th Anniversary of
Revolution **Obv:** Waves breaking over shield **Rev:** Stylized 25

Date	Mintage	F	VF	XF	Unc	BU
ND(1984)	1,980,000	—	0.40	1.00	1.50	2.00

KM# 624   25 ESCUDOS
Copper-Nickel, 28.5 mm. **Subject:** International Year of Disabled
Persons **Obv:** Shield **Rev:** Head 1/4 left with legend above

Date	Mintage	F	VF	XF	Unc	BU
ND(1984)	1,990,000	—	0.40	1.00	2.00	2.50

KM# 627   25 ESCUDOS
Copper-Nickel, 28.5 mm. **Subject:** 600th Anniversary - Battle
of Aljubarrota **Obv:** Shield within circle **Rev:** Seated crowned
figure flanked by shields

Date	Mintage	F	VF	XF	Unc	BU
ND(1985)	500,000	—	0.50	1.00	2.75	

KM# 627a   25 ESCUDOS
10.8300 g., 0.9250 Silver 0.3221 oz. ASW, 28.5 mm.
Obv: Shield within circle **Rev:** Seated crowned figure flanked
by shields

Date	Mintage	F	VF	XF	Unc	BU
ND(1985)	20,000	—	—	—	15.00	

Note: In Mint sets only

ND(1985)	5,000	Value: 40.00				

Note: In Proof sets only

KM# 635   25 ESCUDOS
Copper-Nickel, 28.5 mm. **Subject:** Admission to European
Common Market **Obv:** Shield **Rev:** Small square and lined design

Date	Mintage	F	VF	XF	Unc	BU
1986	4,990,000	—	0.40	1.00	2.00	—

KM# 635a   25 ESCUDOS
11.0000 g., 0.9250 Silver 0.3271 oz. ASW, 28.5 mm.
Obv: Shield **Rev:** Small square and lined design

Date	Mintage	F	VF	XF	Unc	BU
1986 Proof	5,000	Value: 200				

KM# 593   50 ESCUDOS
18.0000 g., 0.6500 Silver 0.3761 oz. ASW **Subject:** 500th
Anniversary - Birth of Pedro Alvares Cabral, Navigator,
Discoverer of Brazil **Obv:** Crowned shield **Rev:** Bust with
headdress right within circle

Date	Mintage	F	VF	XF	Unc	BU
1968	1,000,000	—	—	—	8.50	10.00
1968 Matte	400	—	—	—	32.50	

Note: A small quantity of these coins were given a matte
finish by the Lisbon Mint on private contract

KM# 598   50 ESCUDOS
18.0000 g., 0.6500 Silver 0.3761 oz. ASW **Subject:** 500th
Anniversary - Birth of Vasco daGama, Discoverer of the sea route
to India **Obv:** Shield within maltese cross **Rev:** Head with
headdress left

Date	Mintage	F	VF	XF	Unc	BU
ND(1969)	1,000,000	—	—	—	8.50	10.00
ND(1969) Matte	400	—	—	—	32.50	

Note: A small quantity of these coins were given a matte
finish by the Lisbon Mint on private contract

KM# 599   50 ESCUDOS
18.0000 g., 0.6500 Silver 0.3761 oz. ASW **Subject:** 100th
Anniversary - Birth of Marechal Carmona, President **Obv:** Shield
Rev: Uniformed bust 3/4 right

Date	Mintage	F	VF	XF	Unc	BU
ND(1969)	500,000	—	—	—	9.00	11.00
ND(1969) Matte	400	—	—	—	32.50	

Note: A small quantity of these coins were given a matte
finish by the Lisbon Mint on private contract

KM# 601   50 ESCUDOS
18.0000 g., 0.6500 Silver 0.3761 oz. ASW **Subject:** 125th
Anniversary - Bank of Portugal **Obv:** Circles within circled cross
design **Rev:** Stylized tree

Date	Mintage	F	VF	XF	Unc	BU
ND(1971)	500,000	—	—	—	10.00	12.00
ND(1971) Matte		—	—	—	32.50	

Note: A small quantity of these coins were given a matte
finish by the Lisbon Mint on private contract

KM# 602   50 ESCUDOS
18.0000 g., 0.6500 Silver 0.3761 oz. ASW, 34.5 mm.
Subject: 400th Anniversary of Heroic Epic 'Os Lusiadas'
Obv: Book appears as part of Quinas Cross, all within circle
Rev: Victory within design flanked by dates, all within circle

Date	Mintage	F	VF	XF	Unc	BU
ND(1972)	1,000,000	—	—	—	8.50	10.00
ND(1972) Matte		—	—	—	32.50	

Note: A small quantity of these coins were given a matte
finish by the Lisbon Mint on private contract

KM# 636   50 ESCUDOS
9.4100 g., Copper-Nickel, 31 mm. **Obv:** Shield divides date with
value below **Rev:** Sailboat, water and fish

Date	Mintage	F	VF	XF	Unc	BU
1986	51,110,000	—	—	—	2.25	2.75
1987	28,248,000	—	—	—	2.25	2.75
1988	41,905,000	—	—	—	2.25	2.75
1989	18,327,000	—	—	—	2.25	2.75
1990	50,000	—	—	—	15.00	—

Note: In Mint sets only

1991	2,000,000	—	—	—	3.00	—
1992	20,000	—	—	—	15.00	—

Note: In Mint sets only

1993	20,000	—	—	—	15.00	—

Note: In Mint sets only

1994	20,000	—	—	—	15.00	—

Note: In Mint sets only

1995	20,000	—	—	—	15.00	—

Note: In Mint sets only

1996		—	—	—	8.00	—

Note: In Mint sets only

1996 Proof	7,000	Value: 5.00				
1997		—	—	—	8.00	—

Note: In Mint sets only

1997 Proof		Value: 5.00				
1998	6,000,000	—	—	—	8.00	—

Note: In Mint sets only

1998 Proof		Value: 6.00				
1999		—	—	—	3.00	—
2000		—	—	—	3.00	—

KM# 603 100 ESCUDOS
18.0000 g., 0.6500 Silver 0.3761 oz. ASW **Subject:** 1974 Revolution **Obv:** Small cross design within circle with numeral and written value above **Rev:** Inscription and date flanked by vertical block designs

Date	Mintage	F	VF	XF	Unc	BU
ND(1976)	950,000	—	BV	7.50	9.00	10.00
ND(1976) Proof	10,000	Value: 15.00				

KM# 625 100 ESCUDOS
Copper-Nickel, 33.5 mm. **Subject:** International Year of Disabled Persons **Obv:** Shield **Rev:** Styilized head facing 1/4 right

Date	Mintage	F	VF	XF	Unc	BU
ND(1984)	990,000	—	0.75	1.50	2.50	3.50

KM# 628 100 ESCUDOS
Copper-Nickel, 33.5 mm. **Subject:** 50th Anniversary - Death of Fernando Pessoa - Poet **Obv:** Shield above value **Rev:** Four conjoined faces facing right and flying birds within circle

Date	Mintage	F	VF	XF	Unc	BU
1985	480,000	—	0.75	2.00	3.50	4.50

KM# 628a 100 ESCUDOS
16.5000 g., 0.9250 Silver 0.4907 oz. ASW, 33.5 mm. **Obv:** Shield above value **Rev:** Four conjoined faces facing right and flying birds within circle

Date	Mintage	F	VF	XF	Unc	BU
1985 Proof	5,000	Value: 200				

KM# 629 100 ESCUDOS
Copper-Nickel, 33.5 mm. **Subject:** 800th Anniversary - Death of King Alfonso Henriques **Obv:** Cross design within oblong circle flanked by designs, date and value **Rev:** Armored head left

Date	Mintage	F	VF	XF	Unc	BU
1985	500,000	—	0.75	2.00	4.00	—

KM# 629a 100 ESCUDOS
16.5000 g., 0.9250 Silver 0.4907 oz. ASW, 33.5 mm. **Subject:** 800th Anniversary - Death of King Alfonso Henriques **Obv:** Cross design within oblong circle flanked by designs, date and value **Rev:** Armored head left

Date	Mintage	F	VF	XF	Unc	BU
1985	20,000	—	—	—	27.00	—
1985 Proof	5,000	Value: 110				

KM# 630 100 ESCUDOS
Copper-Nickel, 33.5 mm. **Subject:** 600th Anniversary - Battle of Aljubarrota **Obv:** Shield within circle **Rev:** Standing figure facing within pillar arch

Date	Mintage	F	VF	XF	Unc	BU
ND(1985)	500,000	—	0.75	2.00	3.50	4.50

KM# 630a 100 ESCUDOS
16.5000 g., 0.9250 Silver 0.4907 oz. ASW, 33.5 mm. **Subject:** 600th Anniversary - Battle of Aljubarrota **Obv:** Shield within circle **Rev:** Standing figure facing within pillar arch

Date	Mintage	F	VF	XF	Unc	BU
ND(1985)	20,000	—	—	—	22.00	—
ND(1985) Proof	5,000	Value: 80.00				

KM# 637 100 ESCUDOS
15.0000 g., Copper-Nickel, 33.5 mm. **Subject:** World Cup Soccer - Mexico 86 **Edge:** Reeded

Date	Mintage	F	VF	XF	Unc	BU
1986INCM	500,000	—	—	2.00	3.50	4.50

KM# 637a 100 ESCUDOS
16.5000 g., 0.9250 Silver 0.4907 oz. ASW, 33.5 mm. **Subject:** World Cup Soccer - Mexico 86 **Edge:** Reeded

Date	Mintage	F	VF	XF	Unc	BU
1986	50,000	—	—	—	—	12.50
1986 Proof	20,000	Value: 27.50				

KM# 639 100 ESCUDOS
Copper Nickel, 34 mm. **Subject:** Golden Age of Portuguese Discoveries - Gil Eanes **Obv:** Shield within circle **Rev:** Ship with flag on top of sails

Date	Mintage	F	VF	XF	Unc	BU
1987	1,000,000	—	0.75	1.00	2.50	3.50

KM# 639a 100 ESCUDOS
16.5000 g., 0.9250 Silver 0.4907 oz. ASW, 34 mm. **Subject:** Goldén Age of Portuguese Discoveries - Gil Eanes **Obv:** Shield within circle **Rev:** Ship with flag on top of sails

Date	Mintage	F	VF	XF	Unc	BU
1987	50,000	—	—	—	10.00	12.50
1987 Proof	22,000	Value: 20.00				

KM# 639b 100 ESCUDOS
24.0000 g., 0.9170 Gold 0.7075 oz. AGW, 34 mm. **Subject:** Golden Age of Portuguese Discoveries - Gil Eanes **Obv:** Shield within circle **Rev:** Ship with flag on top of sails

Date	Mintage	F	VF	XF	Unc	BU
1987	5,772	—	—	—	—	675

KM# 640 100 ESCUDOS
Copper-Nickel, 34 mm. **Subject:** Golden Age of Portuguese Discoveries - Nuno Tristao **Obv:** Shield flanked by crowns within circle **Rev:** Ship

Date	Mintage	F	VF	XF	Unc	BU
1987	1,000,000	—	0.75	1.00	2.50	3.50

KM# 640a 100 ESCUDOS
16.5000 g., 0.9250 Silver 0.4907 oz. ASW, 34 mm. **Subject:** Golden Age of Portuguese Discoveries - Nuno Tristao **Obv:** Shield flanked by crowns within circle **Rev:** Ship

Date	Mintage	F	VF	XF	Unc	BU
1987	50,000	—	—	—	12.50	—
1987 Proof	20,000	Value: 20.00				

KM# 640b 100 ESCUDOS
24.0000 g., 0.9170 Gold 0.7075 oz. AGW, 34 mm. **Subject:** Golden Age of Portuguese Discoveries - Nuno Tristao **Obv:** Shield flanked by crowns within circle **Rev:** Ship

Date	Mintage	F	VF	XF	Unc	BU
1987	5,497	—	—	—	—	675

KM# 640c 100 ESCUDOS
31.1190 g., 0.9990 Palladium 0.9995 oz. **Subject:** Golden Age of Portuguese Discoveries - Nuno Tristao **Obv:** Shield flanked by crowns within circle **Rev:** Ship

Date	Mintage	F	VF	XF	Unc	BU
1987	323	—	—	—	—	500
1987 Proof	2,000	Value: 475				

KM# 641 100 ESCUDOS
Copper-Nickel, 34 mm. **Subject:** Golden Age of Portuguese Discoveries - Diogo Cao **Obv:** Shield to upper right of design with value below **Rev:** Compass within center of sailboat and map

Date	Mintage	F	VF	XF	Unc	BU
1987	1,000,000	—	0.75	1.00	2.50	3.50

KM# 641a 100 ESCUDOS
16.5000 g., 0.9250 Silver 0.4907 oz. ASW, 34 mm. **Subject:** Golden Age of Portuguese Discoveries - Diogo Cao **Obv:** Shield to upper right of center design with value below **Rev:** Compass within center of sailboat and map

Date	Mintage	F	VF	XF	Unc	BU
1987	50,000	—	—	—	12.50	—
1987 Proof	20,000	Value: 20.00				

KM# 641b 100 ESCUDOS
24.0000 g., 0.9170 Gold 0.7075 oz. AGW, 34 mm. **Subject:** Golden Age of Portuguese Discoveries - Diogo Cao **Obv:** Shield to upper right of center design with value below **Rev:** Compass within center of sailboat and map

Date	Mintage	F	VF	XF	Unc	BU
1987	5,256	—	—	—	—	675
1987 Proof	5,387	Value: 675				

KM# 644 100 ESCUDOS
Copper-Nickel, 34 mm. **Subject:** Amadeo de Souza Cardoso **Obv:** Shield and value to left of design **Rev:** Head facing flanked by dates with design at left

Date	Mintage	F	VF	XF	Unc	BU
1987	800,000	—	0.75	1.25	2.50	3.50

KM# 644a   100 ESCUDOS
21.0000 g., 0.9250 Silver 0.6245 oz. ASW, 34 mm.
Subject: Amadeo De Souza Cardoso **Obv:** Shield and value to left of design **Rev:** Head facing flanked by dates to right of design

Date	Mintage	F	VF	XF	Unc	BU
1987	30,000	—	—	—	18.50	—
1987 Proof	15,000	Value: 28.50				

KM# 642   100 ESCUDOS
Copper-Nickel, 34 mm. **Subject:** Golden Age of Portuguese Discoveries - Bartolomeu Dias **Obv:** Shield within circle **Rev:** Stylized boat and map

Date	Mintage	F	VF	XF	Unc	BU
ND(1988)	1,000,000	—	0.75	1.00	2.50	3.50

KM# 642a   100 ESCUDOS
16.5000 g., 0.9250 Silver 0.4907 oz. ASW, 34 mm.
Subject: Golden Age of Portuguese Discoveries - Bartolomeu Dias **Obv:** Shield within circle **Rev:** Stylized boat and map

Date	Mintage	F	VF	XF	Unc	BU
ND(1988)	50,000	—	—	—	10.00	12.50
ND(1988) Proof	20,000	Value: 20.00				

KM# 642b   100 ESCUDOS
24.0000 g., 0.9170 Gold 0.7075 oz. AGW, 34 mm.
Subject: Golden Age of Portuguese Discoveries - Bartolomeu Dias **Obv:** Shield within circle **Rev:** Stylized boat and map

Date	Mintage	F	VF	XF	Unc	BU
ND(1988)	5,503	—	—	—	—	675

KM# 642c   100 ESCUDOS
31.1190 g., 0.9990 Platinum 0.9995 oz. APW **Subject:** Golden Age of Portuguese Discoveries - Bartolomeu Dias **Obv:** Shield within circle **Rev:** Stylized boat and map

Date	Mintage	F	VF	XF	Unc	BU
ND(1988)	907	—	—	—	—	2,000
ND(1988) Proof	2,000	Value: 1,950				

KM# 645.2   100 ESCUDOS
Bi-Metallic Aluminumn-Bronze center in Copper-Nickel ring, 25.5 mm. **Rev:** Pedro Nunes **Edge:** Six reeded and six plain sections

Date	Mintage	F	VF	XF	Unc	BU
1989	Inc. above	—	1.00	1.50	3.00	5.00
1990	Inc. above	—	1.25	2.00	3.50	5.50
1991	Inc. above	—	1.00	1.50	3.00	5.00

KM# 646   100 ESCUDOS
Copper-Nickel, 34 mm. **Subject:** Discovery of the Canary Islands **Obv:** Shield with supporters above value **Rev:** Ship

Date	Mintage	F	VF	XF	Unc	BU
1989	2,000,000	—	—	1.00	2.50	4.00

KM# 646a   100 ESCUDOS
21.0000 g., 0.9250 Silver 0.6245 oz. ASW, 34 mm.
Subject: Discovery of the Canary Islands **Obv:** Shield with supporters above value **Rev:** Ship

Date	Mintage	F	VF	XF	Unc	BU
1989	50,000	—	—	—	12.50	—
1989 Proof	23,000	Value: 20.00				

KM# 646b   100 ESCUDOS
24.0000 g., 0.9170 Gold 0.7075 oz. AGW **Subject:** Discovery of the Canary Islands **Obv:** Shield with supporters above value **Rev:** Ship

Date	Mintage	F	VF	XF	Unc	BU
1989 Proof	2,981	Value: 700				

KM# 647   100 ESCUDOS
Copper-Nickel, 34 mm. **Subject:** Discovery of Madeira **Obv:** Cross and shield **Rev:** Ship

Date	Mintage	F	VF	XF	Unc	BU
1989	2,000,000	—	—	1.00	2.50	4.00

KM# 647a   100 ESCUDOS
21.0000 g., 0.9250 Silver 0.6245 oz. ASW, 34 mm.
Subject: Discovery of Madeira **Obv:** Cross and shield **Rev:** Ship

Date	Mintage	F	VF	XF	Unc	BU
1989	50,000	—	—	—	12.50	—
1989 Proof	20,000	Value: 20.00				

KM# 647b   100 ESCUDOS
24.0000 g., 0.9170 Gold 0.7075 oz. AGW, 34 mm.
Subject: Discovery of Madeira **Obv:** Cross and shield **Rev:** Ship

Date	Mintage	F	VF	XF	Unc	BU
1989 Proof	2,996	Value: 700				

KM# 647c   100 ESCUDOS
31.1190 g., 0.9990 Palladium 0.9995 oz. **Subject:** Discovery of Madeira **Obv:** Cross and shield **Rev:** Ship

Date	Mintage	F	VF	XF	Unc	BU
1989 Proof	2,500	Value: 475				

KM# 648   100 ESCUDOS
Copper-Nickel, 34 mm. **Subject:** Discovery of the Azores **Obv:** Shield at right within design **Rev:** Ship and stars within design

Date	Mintage	F	VF	XF	Unc	BU
ND(1989)	2,000,000	—	—	1.00	2.50	—

KM# 648a   100 ESCUDOS
21.0000 g., 0.9250 Silver 0.6245 oz. ASW, 34 mm.
Subject: Discovery of the Azores **Obv:** Shield at right within design **Rev:** Ship and stars within design

Date	Mintage	F	VF	XF	Unc	BU
ND(1989)	50,000	—	—	—	12.50	—
ND(1989) Proof	20,000	Value: 20.00				

KM# 648b   100 ESCUDOS
24.0000 g., 0.9170 Gold 0.7075 oz. AGW **Subject:** Discovery of the Avores **Obv:** Shield to right within design **Rev:** Ship and stars within design

Date	Mintage	F	VF	XF	Unc	BU
ND(1989) Proof	5,495	Value: 700				

KM# 645.1   100 ESCUDOS
8.3000 g., Bi-Metallic Aluminum-Bronze center in Copper-Nickel ring, 25.5 mm. **Obv:** Shield within globe above value within circle **Rev:** Armored 1/2 length figure holding globe facing left within circle **Edge:** Five reeded and five plain sections **Note:** Varieties exist with fine and bold letters.

Date	Mintage	F	VF	XF	Unc	BU
1989	20,000,000	—	—	1.00	2.50	3.00
1990	52,000,000	—	—	1.00	2.50	3.00
1991	45,500,000	—	—	1.00	2.50	3.00
1992	14,500,000	—	—	1.00	2.50	3.00
1993	20,000	—	—	—	—	15.00
Note: In Mint sets only						
1994	20,000	—	—	—	—	15.00
Note: In Mint sets only						
1996		—	—	—	—	15.00
Note: In Mint sets only						
1996 Proof	7,000	Value: 10.00				

Date	Mintage	F	VF	XF	Unc	BU
1997	—	—	—	—	2.50	—
1997 Proof	—	Value: 2.50				
1998	—	—	—	—	2.50	—
1998 Proof	—	Value: 10.00				
1999	—	—	—	—	2.50	—
2000	—	—	—	—	2.50	—

KM# 649   100 ESCUDOS
Copper-Nickel, 34 mm. **Subject:** Celestial Navigation **Obv:** Value in center flanked by shield and circled star designs **Rev:** Artistic designs

Date	Mintage	F	VF	XF	Unc	BU
1990	2,000,000	—	—	1.00	2.50	—

KM# 649a   100 ESCUDOS
21.0000 g., 0.9250 Silver 0.6245 oz. ASW, 34 mm.
Subject: Celestial Navigation **Obv:** Value in center flanked by shield and circled star designs **Rev:** Artistic designs

Date	Mintage	F	VF	XF	Unc	BU
1990	50,000	—	—	—	12.50	—
1990 Proof	20,000	Value: 20.00				

KM# 649b   100 ESCUDOS
24.0000 g., 0.9170 Gold 0.7075 oz. AGW, 34 mm.
Subject: Celestial Navigation **Obv:** Value in center flanked by shield and circled star designs **Rev:** Artistic designs

Date	Mintage	F	VF	XF	Unc	BU
1990 Proof	2,958	Value: 700				

KM# 649c   100 ESCUDOS
31.1190 g., 0.9990 Platinum 0.9995 oz. APW **Subject:** Celestial Navigation **Obv:** Value in center flanked by shield and circled star designs **Rev:** Artistic designs

Date	Mintage	F	VF	XF	Unc	BU
1990 Proof	2,500	Value: 1,950				

KM# 651   100 ESCUDOS
Copper-Nickel, 33 mm. **Subject:** 350th Anniversary - Restoration of Portuguese Independence **Obv:** Shield within beaded circle **Rev:** Half length figure facing left holding sword under design

Date	Mintage	F	VF	XF	Unc	BU
ND(1990)	1,000,000	—	—	1.00	2.50	4.00

KM# 651a   100 ESCUDOS
18.5000 g., 0.9250 Silver 0.5502 oz. ASW, 33 mm.
Subject: 350th Anniversary - Restoration of Portuguese **Obv:** Shield within beaded circle **Rev:** Half length figure facing left holding sword under design

Date	Mintage	F	VF	XF	Unc	BU
ND(1990)	25,000	—	—	—	20.00	—
ND(1990) Proof	10,000	Value: 40.00				

KM# 656   100 ESCUDOS
Copper-Nickel, 33 mm. **Rev:** Camilo Castelo Branco

Date	Mintage	F	VF	XF	Unc	BU
1990	1,000,000	—	—	1.00	2.50	3.50

KM# 656a   100 ESCUDOS
18.5000 g., 0.9250 Silver 0.5502 oz. ASW, 33 mm. **Rev:** Camilo Castelo Branco

Date	Mintage	F	VF	XF	Unc	BU
1990	25,000	—	—	—	18.50	—
1990 Proof	10,000	Value: 42.00				

KM# 664   100 ESCUDOS
Copper-Nickel, 33 mm.   **Subject:** Centenary of the death of Antero de Quental **Obv:** Hand above national arms and value **Obv. Leg.:** REPUBLICA PORTUGUESA AÇORES **Rev:** Portrait, signature, life dates and name **Rev. Leg.:** ANTERO DE QUENTAL 1842 1891 **Edge:** Reeded

Date	Mintage	F	VF	XF	Unc	BU
1991INCM	1,000,000	—	—	3.00	4.50	

KM# 664a   100 ESCUDOS
26.5000 g., 0.9250 Silver 0.7881 oz. ASW, 36 mm.   **Subject:** Antero DeQuental **Obv:** Hand above national arms and value **Rev:** Portrait, signature, name and life dates **Edge:** Reeded

Date	Mintage	F	VF	XF	Unc	BU
1991INCM	20,000	—	—	—	—	18.50
1991INCM Proof		—	Value: 42.00				

KM# 678   100 ESCUDOS
Bi-Metallic Aluminumn-Bronze center in Copper-Nickel ring, 25.5 mm.   **Subject:** 50th Anniversary - F.A.O. **Obv:** Shield within globe above value within circle **Rev:** F.A.O. logo within oat wreath

Date	Mintage	F	VF	XF	Unc	BU
1995	500,000	—	—	1.50	4.00	
1995 Proof	17,000	Value: 15.00					

KM# 680   100 ESCUDOS
Copper-Nickel, 33 mm.   **Subject:** 400th Anniversary - Antonio Prior de Crato **Obv:** Bird, shield, cross and designs within circle **Rev:** Bust 1/4 right within circle

Date	Mintage	F	VF	XF	Unc	BU
ND(1995)	—	—	—	1.00	2.50	4.00

KM# 680a   100 ESCUDOS
18.5000 g., 0.9250 Silver 0.5502 oz. ASW, 33 mm.   **Subject:** 400th Anniversary - Antonio Prior de Crato **Obv:** Bird, shield, cross and designs within circle **Rev:** Bust 1/4 right within circle

Date	Mintage	F	VF	XF	Unc	BU
ND(1995)	5,000	—	—	—	—	30.00
ND(1995) Proof	10,000	Value: 32.50					

KM# 693   100 ESCUDOS
Bi-Metallic Aluminumn-Bronze center in Copper-Nickel ring, 25.5 mm.   **Subject:** Lisbon World Expo '98 **Obv:** Shield and flying bird above value **Rev:** Monk Seal

Date	Mintage	F	VF	XF	Unc	BU
1997	—	—	—	1.50	5.00	9.00
1997 Proof	7,000	Value: 20.00					

KM# 722.1   100 ESCUDOS
Bi-Metallic Brass center in Copper-Nickel ring, 25 mm. **Obv:** National arms, value and country name**Obv. Leg.:** REPUBLICA PORTUGUESA **Rev:** UNICEF logo **Edge:** Reeded and plain sections

Date	Mintage	F	VF	XF	Unc	BU
1999INCM	—	—	—	—	5.00	6.50

KM# 722.2   100 ESCUDOS
Bi-Metallic Brass center in Copper-Nickel ring, 25 mm.   **Subject:** UNICEF **Obv:** Shield within globe in center circle, numeral and written value in outer circle **Obv. Leg.:** REPUBLICA PORTUGUSA **Rev:** Silhouette heads of mother and baby and partial globe in center circle flanked by sprigs **Edge:** Reeded and plain sections **Note:** Legend Obverse with error. There is an "E" missing on the word PORTUGUESA.

Date	Mintage	F	VF	XF	Unc	BU
1999INCM	—	—	—	—	6.00	7.50

KM# 655   200 ESCUDOS
9.8000 g., Bi-Metallic Copper-Nickel center in Aluminum-Bronze ring, 28 mm.   **Obv:** Shield within globe above value **Obv. Leg.:** REPUBLICA PORTUGUESA **Rev:** Armored 1/2 length bust right holding flower within circle **Rev. Leg.:** GARCIA DE ORTA **Edge:** Segmented reeding

Date	Mintage	F	VF	XF	Unc	BU
1991	33,000,000	—	—	1.25	3.00	4.00
1991 Proof		—	Value: 1.10				
1992	11,000,000	—	—	1.50	3.50	5.00
1993	20,000	—	—	—	18.00	—
	Note: In Mint sets only					
1996		—	—	—	18.00	—
	Note: In Mint sets only					
1996 Proof	7,000	Value: 20.00					
1997	5,000,000	—	—	1.50	4.00	—
1997 Proof		—	Value: 20.00				
1998	17,866,000	—	—	1.50	4.00	—
1998 Proof		—	Value: 20.00				
1999	5,998,000	—	—	1.50	4.00	—
2000		—	—	1.50	4.00	—

KM# 658   200 ESCUDOS
Copper-Nickel, 36 mm.   **Subject:** Columbus and Portugal **Obv:** Shield and value to left of design**Rev:** Head left, map, cross, dates and 1/2 star design

Date	Mintage	F	VF	XF	Unc	BU
1991	1,500,000	—	—	1.50	3.50	5.00

KM# 658a   200 ESCUDOS
26.5000 g., 0.9250 Silver 0.7881 oz. ASW, 36 mm.   **Subject:** Columbus and Portugal **Obv:** Shield and value to left of design **Rev:** Head left, map, cross, dates and 1/2 star design

Date	Mintage	F	VF	XF	Unc	BU
1991	10,000	—	—	—	16.50	
1991 Proof	15,000	Value: 30.00					

KM# 658b   200 ESCUDOS
27.2000 g., 0.9170 Gold 0.8019 oz. AGW   **Subject:** Columbus and Portugal **Obv:** Shield, value and date to left of design **Rev:** Head left, map, cross, dates and 1/2 star design

Date	Mintage	F	VF	XF	Unc	BU
1991 Proof	3,500	Value: 775					

KM# 658c   200 ESCUDOS
31.1190 g., 0.9990 Platinum 0.9995 oz. APW **Subject:** Columbus and Portugal **Obv:** Shield, value and date to left of design **Rev:** Head left, map, cross, dates and 1/2 star design

Date	Mintage	F	VF	XF	Unc	BU
1991 Proof	2,500	Value: 1,950					

KM# 658d   200 ESCUDOS
31.1190 g., 0.9990 Palladium 0.9995 oz.   **Subject:** Columbus and Portugal **Obv:** Shield, value and date to left of design **Rev:** Head left, map, cross, dates and 1/2 star design

Date	Mintage	F	VF	XF	Unc	BU
1991 Proof	2,500	Value: 475					

KM# 659   200 ESCUDOS
Copper-Nickel, 36 mm.   **Subject:** Westward Navigation **Obv:** Shield and value within design **Rev:** Stylized ship

Date	Mintage	F	VF	XF	Unc	BU
1991	1,500,000	—	—	1.50	4.50	—

KM# 659a   200 ESCUDOS
26.5000 g., 0.9250 Silver 0.7881 oz. ASW, 36 mm.   **Subject:** Westward Navigation **Obv:** Shield and value within design **Rev:** Stylized ship

Date	Mintage	F	VF	XF	Unc	BU
1991	10,000	—	—	—	15.00	16.50
1991 Proof	15,000	Value: 25.00					

KM# 659b   200 ESCUDOS
27.2000 g., 0.9170 Gold 0.8019 oz. AGW   **Subject:** Westward Navigation **Obv:** Shield and value within design **Rev:** Stylized ship

Date	Mintage	F	VF	XF	Unc	BU
1991 Proof	3,500	Value: 775					

KM# 659c   200 ESCUDOS
31.1190 g., 0.9990 Platinum 0.9995 oz. APW **Subject:** Westward Navigation **Obv:** Shield and value within design **Rev:** Stylized ship

Date	Mintage	F	VF	XF	Unc	BU
1991 Proof	2,500	Value: 1,950					

KM# 659d   200 ESCUDOS
31.1190 g., 0.9990 Palladium 0.9995 oz.   **Subject:** Westward Navigation **Obv:** Shield and value within design **Rev:** Stylized ship

Date	Mintage	F	VF	XF	Unc	BU
1991 Proof	2,500	Value: 475					

KM# 660   200 ESCUDOS
Copper-Nickel, 36 mm.   **Subject:** New World - America **Obv:** Shield within design **Rev:** Head 1/4 left and ships

Date	Mintage	F	VF	XF	Unc	BU
ND(1992)	1,300,000	—	—	1.50	4.50	—

KM# 660a   200 ESCUDOS
26.5000 g., 0.9250 Silver 0.7881 oz. ASW, 36 mm.   **Subject:** New World - America **Obv:** Shield within design **Rev:** Head 1/4 left and ships

Date	Mintage	F	VF	XF	Unc	BU
ND(1992)	10,000	—	—	—	16.50	
ND(1992) Proof	15,000	Value: 25.00					

KM# 660b   200 ESCUDOS
27.2000 g., 0.9170 Gold 0.8019 oz. AGW   **Subject:** New World - America **Obv:** Shield within design **Rev:** Head 1/4 left and ships

Date	Mintage	F	VF	XF	Unc	BU
ND(1992) Proof	6,000	Value: 775					

KM# 660c   200 ESCUDOS
31.1190 g., 0.9990 Platinum 0.9995 oz. APW **Subject:** New World - America **Obv:** Shield within design **Rev:** Head 1/4 left and ships

Date	Mintage	F	VF	XF	Unc	BU
ND(1992) Proof	2,500	Value: 1,950					

KM# 660d   200 ESCUDOS
31.1190 g., 0.9990 Palladium 0.9995 oz.   **Subject:** New World - America **Obv:** Shield within design **Rev:** Head 1/4 left and ships

Date	Mintage	F	VF	XF	Unc	BU
ND(1992) Proof	2,500	Value: 475					

KM# 661 200 ESCUDOS
Copper-Nickel, 36 mm. **Obv:** Shield and value within thin lined cross **Rev:** Standing figure and map

Date	Mintage	F	VF	XF	Unc	BU
ND(1992)	1,300,000	—	—	1.50	4.50	—

KM# 661a 200 ESCUDOS
26.5000 g., 0.9250 Silver 0.7881 oz. ASW, 36 mm. **Obv:** Shield and value within thin lined cross **Rev:** Standing figure and map

Date	Mintage	F	VF	XF	Unc	BU
ND(1992)	10,000	—	—	—	16.50	—
ND(1992) Proof	15,000	Value: 25.00				

KM# 661b 200 ESCUDOS
27.2000 g., 0.9170 Gold 0.8019 oz. AGW **Obv:** Shield and value within thin lined cross **Rev:** Standing figure and map

Date	Mintage	F	VF	XF	Unc	BU
ND(1992) Proof	3,500	Value: 775				

KM# 661c 200 ESCUDOS
31.1190 g., 0.9990 Platinum 0.9995 oz. APW **Obv:** Shield and value within thin lined cross **Rev:** Standing figure and map

Date	Mintage	F	VF	XF	Unc	BU
ND(1992) Proof	2,500	Value: 1,950				

KM# 661d 200 ESCUDOS
31.1190 g., 0.9990 Palladium 0.9995 oz. **Obv:** Shield and value within thin lined cross **Rev:** Standing figure and map

Date	Mintage	F	VF	XF	Unc	BU
ND(1992) Proof	2,500	Value: 450				

KM# 662 200 ESCUDOS
Copper-Nickel, 36 mm. **Series:** Olympics **Rev:** Stylized runner

Date	Mintage	F	VF	XF	Unc	BU
1992	1,000,000	—	—	1.50	4.50	—

KM# 662a 200 ESCUDOS
26.5000 g., 0.9250 Silver 0.7881 oz. ASW, 36 mm. **Series:** Olympics **Rev:** Stylized runner

Date	Mintage	F	VF	XF	Unc	BU
1992	20,000	—	—	—	17.50	—
1992 Proof	30,000	Value: 32.50				

KM# 663 200 ESCUDOS
21.0000 g., Copper-Nickel, 36 mm. **Subject:** Portugal's Presidency of the European Community **Obv:** Shield within wave-like design **Obv. Leg.:** REPUBLICA PORTUGUESA **Rev:** Circle of stars within wave-like design **Rev. Leg.:** PRESIDENCIA DA COMUNIDADE EUROPEIA - 1992 **Edge:** Reeded

Date	Mintage	F	VF	XF	Unc	BU
1992INCM	1,000,000	—	—	1.50	4.50	—

KM# 663a 200 ESCUDOS
26.5000 g., 0.9250 Silver 0.7881 oz. ASW, 36 mm. **Subject:** Portugal's Presidency of the European Community **Obv:** Shield within wave-like design **Rev:** Circle of stars within wave-like design

Date	Mintage	F	VF	XF	Unc	BU
1992	20,000	—	—	—	20.00	—
1992 Proof	30,000	Value: 35.00				

KM# 665 200 ESCUDOS
Copper-Nickel, 36 mm. **Subject:** Tanegashima - Site 1st Portuguese Landing in Japan **Obv:** Shield **Rev:** Ship

Date	Mintage	F	VF	XF	Unc	BU
ND(1993)	1,000,000	—	—	1.50	4.50	—

KM# 665a 200 ESCUDOS
26.5000 g., 0.9250 Silver 0.7881 oz. ASW, 36 mm. **Subject:** Tanegashima - Site 1st Portuguese Landing in Japan **Obv:** Shield **Rev:** Ship

Date	Mintage	F	VF	XF	Unc	BU
ND(1993)	30,000	—	—	—	18.50	—
ND(1993) Proof	22,000	Value: 30.00				

KM# 665b 200 ESCUDOS
27.2000 g., 0.9170 Gold 0.8019 oz. AGW **Subject:** Tanegashima - 1st Portuguese Ship to Japan **Obv:** Shield **Rev:** Ship

Date	Mintage	F	VF	XF	Unc	BU
ND(1993) Proof	7,000	Value: 775				

KM# 666 200 ESCUDOS
Copper-Nickel, 36 mm. **Subject:** Espingarda **Obv:** Inscription divides globe and shield **Rev:** Mounted cavalryman shooting rifle

Date	Mintage	F	VF	XF	Unc	BU
1993	1,000,000	—	—	1.50	4.50	—

KM# 666a 200 ESCUDOS
26.5000 g., 0.9250 Silver 0.7881 oz. ASW, 36 mm. **Subject:** Espingarda **Obv:** Inscription divides globe and shield **Rev:** Mounted cavalryman shooting rifle

Date	Mintage	F	VF	XF	Unc	BU
1993	30,000	—	—	—	18.50	—
1993 Proof	20,000	Value: 35.00				

KM# 666b 200 ESCUDOS
27.2000 g., 0.9170 Gold 0.8019 oz. AGW **Subject:** Espingarda **Obv:** Inscription divides globe and shield **Rev:** Mounted cavalryman shooting rifle

Date	Mintage	F	VF	XF	Unc	BU
1993 Proof	7,000	Value: 775				

KM# 666c 200 ESCUDOS
31.1190 g., 0.9990 Palladium 0.9995 oz. **Subject:** Espingarda **Obv:** Inscription divides globe and shield **Rev:** Mounted cavalryman shooting rifle

Date	Mintage	F	VF	XF	Unc	BU
1993 Proof	2,000	Value: 475				

KM# 667 200 ESCUDOS
Copper-Nickel, 36 mm. **Obv:** Ship at right of shield **Rev:** Armored busts and date to right of column

Date	Mintage	F	VF	XF	Unc	BU
1993	1,000,000	—	—	1.50	4.50	—

KM# 667a 200 ESCUDOS
26.5000 g., 0.9250 Silver 0.7881 oz. ASW, 36 mm. **Obv:** Ship at right of shield **Rev:** Armored busts and date to right of column

Date	Mintage	F	VF	XF	Unc	BU
1993	30,000	—	—	—	18.50	—
1993 Proof	20,000	Value: 35.00				

KM# 667b 200 ESCUDOS
27.2000 g., 0.9170 Gold 0.8019 oz. AGW **Obv:** Ship at right of shield **Rev:** Armored busts and date to right of column

Date	Mintage	F	VF	XF	Unc	BU
1993 Proof	7,000	Value: 775				

KM# 668 200 ESCUDOS
Copper-Nickel, 36 mm. **Rev:** Arte Namban

Date	Mintage	F	VF	XF	Unc	BU
1993	1,000,000	—	—	1.50	4.50	—

KM# 668a 200 ESCUDOS
26.5000 g., 0.9250 Silver 0.7881 oz. ASW, 36 mm. **Rev:** Arte Namban

Date	Mintage	F	VF	XF	Unc	BU
1993	30,000	—	—	—	18.50	—
1993 Proof	22,000	Value: 35.00				

KM# 668b 200 ESCUDOS
27.2000 g., 0.9170 Gold 0.8019 oz. AGW **Rev:** Arte Namban

Date	Mintage	F	VF	XF	Unc	BU
1993 Proof	7,000	Value: 775				

KM# 668c 200 ESCUDOS
31.1190 g., 0.9990 Platinum 0.9995 oz. APW **Rev:** Arte Namban

Date	Mintage	F	VF	XF	Unc	BU
1993 Proof	2,000	Value: 1,950				

KM# 669 200 ESCUDOS
Bi-Metallic Copper-Nickel center in Aluminum-Bronze ring, 28 mm. **Subject:** Lisbon - European Cultural Capital **Obv:** Shield within globe above value within circle **Rev:** Cultural building within circle

Date	Mintage	F	VF	XF	Unc	BU
1994	1,000,000	—	—	—	4.50	—
1994 Proof	7,000	Value: 20.00				

KM# 670 200 ESCUDOS
Copper-Nickel, 36 mm. **Obv:** Shield to left of ships **Rev:** Bust 1/4 right flanked by dates and symbol

Date	Mintage	F	VF	XF	Unc	BU
ND(1994)	750,000	—	—	—	5.50	—

KM# 670a 200 ESCUDOS
26.5000 g., 0.9250 Silver 0.7881 oz. ASW, 36 mm. **Obv:** Shield to upper left of ships **Rev:** Bust 1/4 right flanked by dates and symbol

Date	Mintage	F	VF	XF	Unc	BU
ND(1994)	20,000	—	—	—	17.50	—
ND(1994) Proof	13,000	Value: 27.50				

KM# 670b 200 ESCUDOS
27.2000 g., 0.9170 Gold 0.8019 oz. AGW **Obv:** Shield to upper left of ships **Rev:** Bust 1/4 right flanked by dates and symbol

Date	Mintage	F	VF	XF	Unc	BU
ND(1994) Proof	2,000	Value: 775				

KM# 671   200 ESCUDOS
Copper-Nickel, 36 mm.   **Subject:** Treaty of Tordesilhas
Obv: Ship flanked by map, shield, designs and value **Rev:** Left 1/2 of coin is conjoined crowned heads right, arms above, right 1/2 of coin is crown head left, arms on bottom

Date	Mintage	F	VF	XF	Unc	BU
ND(1994)	750,000	—	—	—	5.50	—

KM# 671a   200 ESCUDOS
26.5000 g., 0.9250 Silver 0.7881 oz. ASW, 36 mm.   **Subject:** Treaty of Tordesilhas **Obv:** Ship flanked by map, shield, designs and value **Rev:** Left 1/2 of coin is conjoined crowned heads right, arms above, right 1/2 of coin is crown head left, arms on bottom

Date	Mintage	F	VF	XF	Unc	BU
ND(1994)	20,000	—	—	—	17.50	—
ND(1994) Proof	13,000	Value: 27.50				

KM# 671b   200 ESCUDOS
27.2000 g., 0.9170 Gold 0.8019 oz. AGW   **Subject:** Treaty of Tordesilhas **Obv:** Ship flanked by map, shield, designs and value **Rev:** Left 1/2 of coin is conjoined crowned heads right, arms above, right 1/2 of coin is crown head left, arms on bottom

Date	Mintage	F	VF	XF	Unc	BU
ND(1994) Proof	2,000	Value: 775				

KM# 671c   200 ESCUDOS
31.1190 g., 0.9990 Palladium 0.9995 oz.   **Subject:** Treaty of Tordesilhas **Obv:** Ship flanked by map, shield, designs and value **Rev:** Left 1/2 of coin is conjoined crowned heads right, arms above, right 1/2 of coin is crown head left, arms on bottom

Date	Mintage	F	VF	XF	Unc	BU
ND(1994) Proof	1,000	Value: 475				

KM# 672   200 ESCUDOS
Copper-Nickel, 36 mm.   **Subject:** Dividing Up The World **Obv:** Shield, map, value and date **Rev:** Ship, map and divided arms

Date	Mintage	F	VF	XF	Unc	BU
1994	750,000	—	—	—	5.50	—

KM# 672a   200 ESCUDOS
26.5000 g., 0.9250 Silver 0.7881 oz. ASW, 36 mm.
Subject: Dividing up the World **Obv:** Shield, value, date and map **Rev:** Ship, map and divided arms

Date	Mintage	F	VF	XF	Unc	BU
1994	20,000	—	—	—	17.50	—
1994 Proof	12,000	Value: 27.50				

KM# 672b   200 ESCUDOS
27.2000 g., 0.9170 Gold 0.8019 oz. AGW   **Subject:** Dividing Up The World **Obv:** Shield, map, value and date **Rev:** Ship, map and divided arms

Date	Mintage	F	VF	XF	Unc	BU
1994 Proof	3,000	Value: 775				

KM# 673   200 ESCUDOS
Copper-Nickel, 36 mm.   **Obv:** Water divides shield and design **Rev:** Crowned 1/2 length figure facing

Date	Mintage	F	VF	XF	Unc	BU
ND(1994)	750,000	—	—	—	5.50	—

KM# 673a   200 ESCUDOS
26.5000 g., 0.9250 Silver 0.7881 oz. ASW, 36 mm.   **Obv:** Water divides shield and design **Rev:** Crowned 1/2 length figure facing

Date	Mintage	F	VF	XF	Unc	BU
ND(1994)	20,000	—	—	—	18.50	—
ND(1994) Proof	13,000	Value: 37.50				

KM# 673b   200 ESCUDOS
27.2000 g., 0.9170 Gold 0.8019 oz. AGW   **Obv:** Water divides shield and design **Rev:** Crowned 1/2 length figure facing

Date	Mintage	F	VF	XF	Unc	BU
ND(1994) Proof	2,000	Value: 775				

KM# 673c   200 ESCUDOS
31.1190 g., 0.9990 Platinum 0.9995 oz. APW   **Obv:** Water divides shield and design **Rev:** Crowned 1/2 length figure facing

Date	Mintage	F	VF	XF	Unc	BU
ND(1994) Proof	1,000	Value: 1,950				

KM# 679   200 ESCUDOS
Bi-Metallic Copper-Nickel center in Aluminum-Bronze ring, 28 mm.   **Subject:** 50th Anniversary - United Nations **Obv:** Shield within globe above value **Rev:** Numeral 50 and emblem in center of puzzle pieces

Date	Mintage	F	VF	XF	Unc	BU
1995	500,000	—	—	—	5.50	—
1995 Proof	17,000	Value: 20.00				

KM# 681   200 ESCUDOS
Copper-Nickel, 36 mm.   **Obv:** Shield and globe above date and value **Rev:** Armored standing figure

Date	Mintage	F	VF	XF	Unc	BU
1995	750,000	—	—	—	5.00	—

KM# 681a   200 ESCUDOS
26.5000 g., 0.9250 Silver 0.7881 oz. ASW, 36 mm.   **Obv:** Shield and globe above date and value **Rev:** Armored standing figure

Date	Mintage	F	VF	XF	Unc	BU
1995	20,000	—	—	—	18.50	—
1995 Proof	13,000	Value: 32.50				

KM# 681b   200 ESCUDOS
27.2000 g., 0.9170 Gold 0.8019 oz. AGW   **Obv:** Shield and globe above date and value **Rev:** Armored standing figure

Date	Mintage	F	VF	XF	Unc	BU
1995 Proof	4,000	Value: 775				

KM# 682   200 ESCUDOS
Copper-Nickel, 36 mm.   **Obv:** Shield, value, fruit sprig and flower sprig **Rev:** Moluca Islands and ship

Date	Mintage	F	VF	XF	Unc	BU
1995	750,000	—	—	—	5.00	—

KM# 682a   200 ESCUDOS
26.5000 g., 0.9250 Silver 0.7881 oz. ASW, 36 mm.   **Obv:** Shield, value, fruit sprig and flower sprig **Rev:** Moluca Islands and ship

Date	Mintage	F	VF	XF	Unc	BU
1995	20,000	—	—	—	18.50	—
1995 Proof	13,000	Value: 35.00				

KM# 682b   200 ESCUDOS
27.2000 g., 0.9170 Gold 0.8019 oz. AGW   **Obv:** Shield, value, fruit sprig and flower sprig **Rev:** Moluca Islands and ship

Date	Mintage	F	VF	XF	Unc	BU
1995 Proof	4,000	Value: 775				

KM# 682c   200 ESCUDOS
31.1190 g., 0.9995 Palladium 1.0000 oz.   **Obv:** Shield, value, fruit sprig and flower sprig **Rev:** Moluca Islands and ship

Date	Mintage	F	VF	XF	Unc	BU
1995	1,000	Value: 475				

KM# 683   200 ESCUDOS
Copper-Nickel, 36 mm.   **Obv:** Tree, ship and shield **Rev:** Solor and Timor Islands

Date	Mintage	F	VF	XF	Unc	BU
1995	750,000	—	—	—	5.00	—

KM# 683a   200 ESCUDOS
26.5000 g., 0.9250 Silver 0.7881 oz. ASW, 36 mm.   **Obv:** Shield, tree and ship **Rev:** Solor and Timor Islands

Date	Mintage	F	VF	XF	Unc	BU
1995	20,000	—	—	—	18.50	—
1995 Proof	13,000	Value: 35.00				

KM# 683b   200 ESCUDOS
27.2000 g., 0.9170 Gold 0.8019 oz. AGW   **Obv:** Ship, tree and shield **Rev:** Solar and Timor Islands

Date	Mintage	F	VF	XF	Unc	BU
1995 Proof	4,000	Value: 775				

KM# 684   200 ESCUDOS
Copper-Nickel, 36 mm.   **Obv:** Shield, dates, globe and value **Rev:** Map and ships

Date	Mintage	F	VF	XF	Unc	BU
1995	750,000	—	—	—	5.00	—

KM# 684a   200 ESCUDOS
26.5000 g., 0.9250 Silver 0.7881 oz. ASW, 36 mm.   **Obv:** Shield, dates, globe and value **Rev:** Map and ships

Date	Mintage	F	VF	XF	Unc	BU
1995	20,000	—	—	—	18.50	—
1995 Proof	13,000	Value: 35.00				

KM# 684b   200 ESCUDOS
27.2000 g., 0.9170 Gold 0.8019 oz. AGW   **Obv:** Shield, dates, globe and value **Rev:** Map and ships

Date	Mintage	F	VF	XF	Unc	BU
1995 Proof	4,000	Value: 775				

KM# 684c   200 ESCUDOS
31.1190 g., 0.9995 Platinum 1.0000 oz. APW   **Obv:** Shield, dates, globe and value **Rev:** Map and ships

Date	Mintage	F	VF	XF	Unc	BU
1995	1,000	Value: 1,950				

KM# 687   200 ESCUDOS
Bi-Metallic Copper-Nickel center in Brass ring, 28 mm.
Series: Olympics **Subject:** XXVI Olympic Games Atlanta
Obv: Shield, value and olympic circles **Obv. Leg.:** REPUBLICA PORTUGUESA **Rev:** High jumper **Rev. Leg.:** XXVI JOGOS OLIMPICOS 1896 Atlanta 1996 **Edge:** Segmented reeding

Date	Mintage	F	VF	XF	Unc	BU
1996INCM	1,000,000	—	—	2.25	5.00	—
1996INCM Proof	7,000	Value: 20.00				

KM# 687a   200 ESCUDOS
26.4500 g., 0.9250 Silver 0.7866 oz. ASW   **Series:** Olympics **Obv:** Shield, value and olympic circles **Rev:** High jumper

Date	Mintage	F	VF	XF	Unc	BU
1996 Proof	20,000	Value: 50.00				

KM# 689   200 ESCUDOS
Copper-Nickel, 36 mm. **Subject:** 1512 Portugal - Siam Alliance
Obv: Ship, shield, dates and value **Rev:** Portuguese and
Siamese arms

Date	Mintage	F	VF	XF	Unc	BU
1996					5.00	—

KM# 689a   200 ESCUDOS
26.5000 g., 0.9250 Silver 0.7881 oz. ASW, 36 mm.
Subject: 1512 Portugal - Siam Alliance **Obv:** Ship, shield, dates
and value **Rev:** Portuguese and Siamese arms

Date	Mintage	F	VF	XF	Unc	BU
1996	20,000	—	—	—	17.50	—
1996 Proof	11,000	Value: 32.50				

KM# 689b   200 ESCUDOS
27.0000 g., 0.9166 Gold 0.7956 oz. AGW **Subject:** 1512
Portugal - Siam Alliance **Obv:** Ship, shield, dates and value
Rev: Portuguese and Siamese arms

Date	Mintage	F	VF	XF	Unc	BU
1996 Proof	3,000	Value: 775				

KM# 690   200 ESCUDOS
Copper-Nickel, 36 mm. **Subject:** 1513 Portuguese Arrival in
China **Obv:** Shield within globe flanked by leafy sprigs **Rev:** Ship,
map and building

Date	Mintage	F	VF	XF	Unc	BU
1996				—	6.00	—

KM# 690a   200 ESCUDOS
26.5000 g., 0.9250 Silver 0.7881 oz. ASW, 36 mm.
Subject: 1513 Portuguese Arrival in China **Obv:** Shield within
globe flanked by leafy sprigs **Rev:** Ship, map and building

Date	Mintage	F	VF	XF	Unc	BU
1996	20,000	—	—	—	22.50	—
1996 Proof	10,000	Value: 40.00				

KM# 690b   200 ESCUDOS
27.2000 g., 0.9166 Gold 0.8015 oz. AGW **Subject:** 1513
Portuguese Arrival in China **Obv:** Shield within globe flanked by
leafy sprigs **Rev:** Ship, map and building

Date	Mintage	F	VF	XF	Unc	BU
1996 Proof	3,000	Value: 775				

KM# 690c   200 ESCUDOS
31.1190 g., 0.9995 Palladium 1.0000 oz. **Subject:** 1513
Portuguese Arrival in China **Obv:** Shield within globe flanked by
leafy sprigs **Rev:** Ship, map and building

Date	Mintage	F	VF	XF	Unc	BU
1996 Proof	1,000	Value: 475				

KM# 691   200 ESCUDOS
Copper-Nickel, 36 mm. **Subject:** 1557 Portuguese
Establishment in Macau **Obv:** Shield at upper left above building
Rev: Building at upper left of ship

Date	Mintage	F	VF	XF	Unc	BU
1996	—	—	—	—	5.00	—

KM# 691a   200 ESCUDOS
26.5000 g., 0.9250 Silver 0.7881 oz. ASW, 36 mm.
Subject: 1557 Portuguese Establishment in Macau **Obv:** Shield
at upper left above building **Rev:** Building at upper left of ship

Date	Mintage	F	VF	XF	Unc	BU
1996	20,000	—	—	—	17.50	—
1996 Proof	10,000	Value: 32.50				

KM# 691b   200 ESCUDOS
27.2000 g., 0.9166 Gold 0.8015 oz. AGW **Subject:** 1557
Portuguese establishment in Macau **Obv:** Shield at upper left
above building **Rev:** Building at upper left of ship

Date	Mintage	F	VF	XF	Unc	BU
1996 Proof	4,000	Value: 775				

KM# 692   200 ESCUDOS
Copper-Nickel, 36 mm. **Subject:** 1582 Portuguese Discovery
of Taiwan **Obv:** Flower sprig to left of shield **Rev:** Ship

Date	Mintage	F	VF	XF	Unc	BU
1996				—	5.00	—

KM# 692a   200 ESCUDOS
26.5000 g., 0.9250 Silver 0.7881 oz. ASW, 36 mm. **Subject:**
1582 Portuguese Discovery of Taiwan **Obv:** Flower sprig to left
of shield **Rev:** Ship

Date	Mintage	F	VF	XF	Unc	BU
1996	20,000	—	—	—	17.50	—
1996 Proof	10,000	Value: 32.50				

KM# 692b   200 ESCUDOS
27.2000 g., 0.9166 Gold 0.8015 oz. AGW **Subject:** 1582
Portuguese dscovery of Taiwan **Obv:** Flower sprig to left of shield
Rev: Ship

Date	Mintage	F	VF	XF	Unc	BU
1996 Proof	3,000	Value: 775				

KM# 692c   200 ESCUDOS
31.1190 g., 0.9995 Platinum 1.0000 oz. APW **Subject:** 1582
Portuguese Discovery of Taiwan **Obv:** Flower sprig to left of shield
Rev: Ship

Date	Mintage	F	VF	XF	Unc	BU
1996 Proof	1,000	Value: 1,950				

KM# 694   200 ESCUDOS
9.7300 g., Bi-Metallic Copper-Nickel center in Copper-Aluminum
ring, 28 mm. **Subject:** Lisbon World Expo '98 **Obv:** Shield and
value within circle **Obv. Leg.:** REPUBLICA PORTUGUESA
Rev: Dolphins **Rev. Leg.:** EXPOSICÃO MUNDIAL DE LISBOA
- EXPO'98 **Edge:** Segmented reeding

Date	Mintage	F	VF	XF	Unc	BU
1997INCM	—	—	—	—	6.00	—
1997INCM Proof	7,000	Value: 20.00				

KM# 697   200 ESCUDOS
Copper-Nickel, 36 mm. **Obv:** National arms **Rev:** S. Francisco
Xavier

Date	Mintage	F	VF	XF	Unc	BU
1997	—	—	—	—	5.00	—

KM# 697a   200 ESCUDOS
26.5000 g., 0.9250 Silver 0.7881 oz. ASW, 36 mm.
Obv: National arms **Rev:** S. Francisco Xavier

Date	Mintage	F	VF	XF	Unc	BU
1997	25,000	—	—	—	17.50	—
1997 Proof	25,000	Value: 30.00				

KM# 697b   200 ESCUDOS
27.2000 g., 0.9167 Gold 0.8016 oz. AGW **Obv:** National arms
Rev: St. Francis Xavier

Date	Mintage	F	VF	XF	Unc	BU
1997 Proof	4,000	Value: 775				

KM# 698   200 ESCUDOS
Copper-Nickel, 36 mm. **Obv:** Shield to left of designs and value
Rev: Two seated figures talking

Date	Mintage	F	VF	XF	Unc	BU
1997				—	5.00	—

KM# 698a   200 ESCUDOS
26.5000 g., 0.9250 Silver 0.7881 oz. ASW, 36 mm. **Obv:** Shield
to left of designs and value **Rev:** Two seated figures talking

Date	Mintage	F	VF	XF	Unc	BU
1997	25,000	—	—	—	17.50	—
1997 Proof	24,000	Value: 32.50				

KM# 698b   200 ESCUDOS
27.2000 g., 0.9167 Gold 0.8016 oz. AGW **Obv:** Shield to left of
designs and value **Rev:** Two seated figures talking

Date	Mintage	F	VF	XF	Unc	BU
1997 Proof	5,000	Value: 775				

KM# 699   200 ESCUDOS
Copper-Nickel, 36 mm. **Obv:** Shield and map of South America
Rev: Bto. Jose de Anchieta

Date	Mintage	F	VF	XF	Unc	BU
1997				—	5.00	—

KM# 699a   200 ESCUDOS
26.5000 g., 0.9250 Silver 0.7881 oz. ASW, 36 mm. **Obv:** Shield
and map of South America **Rev:** Bto. Jose de Anchieta

Date	Mintage	F	VF	XF	Unc	BU
1997	25,000	—	—	—	17.50	—
1997 Proof	24,000	Value: 32.50				

KM# 699b   200 ESCUDOS
27.2000 g., 0.9167 Gold 0.8016 oz. AGW **Obv:** Shield and map
of South America **Rev:** Bto. Jose de Anchieta

Date	Mintage	F	VF	XF	Unc	BU
1997 Proof	4,000	Value: 775				

KM# 699c   200 ESCUDOS
31.1190 g., 0.9995 Palladium 1.0000 oz. **Obv:** Shield and map
of South America **Rev:** Bto. Jose de Anchieta

Date	Mintage	F	VF	XF	Unc	BU
1997 Proof	1,000	Value: 475				

KM# 700   200 ESCUDOS
Copper-Nickel, 36 mm. **Obv:** National cross and shield
Rev: Irmao Bento de Gois, map of China's coast

Date	Mintage	F	VF	XF	Unc	BU
1997				—	5.00	—

KM# 700a   200 ESCUDOS
26.5000 g., 0.9250 Silver 0.7881 oz. ASW, 36 mm.
Obv: National cross and shield **Rev:** Irmao Bento de Gois, map
of China's coast

Date	Mintage	F	VF	XF	Unc	BU
1997	25,000	—	—	—	17.50	—
1997 Proof	24,000	Value: 32.50				

KM# 700b 200 ESCUDOS
27.2000 g., 0.9160 Gold 0.8010 oz. AGW **Obv:** National cross and shield **Rev:** Irmao Bento de Gois, map of China's coast

Date	Mintage	F	VF	XF	Unc	BU
1997 Proof	4,000				Value: 775	

KM# 700c 200 ESCUDOS
31.1190 g., 0.9995 Platinum 1.0000 oz. APW **Obv:** National cross and shield **Rev:** Irmao Bento de Gois, map of China's coast

Date	Mintage	F	VF	XF	Unc	BU
1997 Proof	1,000				Value: 1,950	

KM# 706 200 ESCUDOS
Bi-Metallic Copper-Nickel center in Aluminum-Bronze ring, 28 mm. **Subject:** International Year of the Oceans Expo **Obv:** Small shield within sprigs above value **Rev:** Expo 98 and fish within sprigs

Date	Mintage	F	VF	XF	Unc	BU
1998	Est. 50,000	—	—	—	4.50	—
1998 Proof	Est. 20,000		Value: 12.00			

KM# 709 200 ESCUDOS
Copper-Nickel, 36 mm. **Obv:** Three ships, shield, and value **Rev:** Portrait of Vasco Da Gama, dates

Date	Mintage	F	VF	XF	Unc	BU
1998	—	—	—	—	5.00	—

KM# 709a 200 ESCUDOS
26.5000 g., 0.9250 Silver 0.7881 oz. ASW, 36 mm. **Obv:** Three ships, shield, and value **Rev:** Bust of Vasco da Gama left, dates

Date	Mintage	F	VF	XF	Unc	BU
1998	—	—	—	—	17.50	—
1998 Proof	25,000		Value: 32.50			

KM# 709b 200 ESCUDOS
27.2000 g., 0.9167 Gold 0.8016 oz. AGW **Obv:** Three ships, shield, and value **Rev:** Bust of Vasco da Gama left, dates

Date	Mintage	F	VF	XF	Unc	BU
1998 Proof	5,000				Value: 775	

KM# 709c 200 ESCUDOS
31.1190 g., 0.9995 Platinum 1.0000 oz. APW **Obv:** Three ships, shield, and value **Rev:** Bust of Vasco da Gama, dates

Date	Mintage	F	VF	XF	Unc	BU
1998 Proof	1,000				Value: 1,950	

KM# 710 200 ESCUDOS
Copper-Nickel, 36 mm. **Subject:** Discovery of Africa **Obv:** Shield, ship, and palm tree **Rev:** Ship, map, and hunter

Date	Mintage	F	VF	XF	Unc	BU
1998	—	—	—	—	5.00	—

KM# 710a 200 ESCUDOS
26.5000 g., 0.9250 Silver 0.7881 oz. ASW, 36 mm. **Subject:** Discovery of Africa **Obv:** Shield, ship, and palm tree **Rev:** Ship, map, and hunter

Date	Mintage	F	VF	XF	Unc	BU
1998	25,000	—	—	—	17.50	—
1998 Proof	26,000		Value: 30.00			

KM# 710b 200 ESCUDOS
27.2000 g., 0.9167 Gold 0.8016 oz. AGW **Subject:** Discovery of Africa **Obv:** Shield, ship, and palm tree **Rev:** Ship, map, and hunter

Date	Mintage	F	VF	XF	Unc	BU
1998 Proof	5,000				Value: 775	

KM# 711 200 ESCUDOS
Copper-Nickel, 36 mm. **Subject:** Mozambique **Obv:** Shield above mermaid **Rev:** Two ships and island map

Date	Mintage	F	VF	XF	Unc	BU
1998	—	—	—	—	5.00	—

KM# 711a 200 ESCUDOS
26.5000 g., 0.9250 Silver 0.7881 oz. ASW, 36 mm. **Subject:** Mozambique **Obv:** Shield above mermaid **Rev:** Two ships and island map

Date	Mintage	F	VF	XF	Unc	BU
1998	25,000	—	—	—	17.50	—
1998 Proof	25,000		Value: 30.00			

KM# 711b 200 ESCUDOS
27.2000 g., 0.9167 Gold 0.8016 oz. AGW **Subject:** Mozambique **Obv:** Shield above mermaid **Rev:** Two ships and island map

Date	Mintage	F	VF	XF	Unc	BU
1998 Proof	6,000		Value: 775			

KM# 712 200 ESCUDOS
Copper-Nickel, 36 mm. **Subject:** India 1498 **Obv:** Shield and sailing ship **Rev:** Ship and coastal map of India

Date	Mintage	F	VF	XF	Unc	BU
1998	—	—	—	—	5.00	—

KM# 712a 200 ESCUDOS
26.5000 g., 0.9250 Silver 0.7881 oz. ASW, 36 mm. **Subject:** India 1498 **Obv:** Shield and sailing ship **Rev:** Ship and coastal map of India

Date	Mintage	F	VF	XF	Unc	BU
1998	25,000	—	—	—	17.50	—
1998 Proof	25,000		Value: 32.50			

KM# 712b 200 ESCUDOS
27.2000 g., 0.9167 Gold 0.8016 oz. AGW **Subject:** India 1498 **Obv:** Shield and sailing ship **Rev:** Ship and coastal map of India

Date	Mintage	F	VF	XF	Unc	BU
1998 Proof	5,000		Value: 775			

KM# 712c 200 ESCUDOS
31.1190 g., 0.9995 Palladium 1.0000 oz. **Subject:** India 1498 **Obv:** Shield and sailing ship **Rev:** Ship and coastal map of India

Date	Mintage	F	VF	XF	Unc	BU
1998 Proof	1,000		Value: 475			

KM# 716 200 ESCUDOS
Copper-Nickel, 36 mm. **Subject:** Death on the Sea **Obv:** Shield, globe and ropes **Rev:** Stylized sinking ship **Edge:** Reeded

Date	Mintage	F	VF	XF	Unc	BU
1999INCM	—	—	—	—	4.00	—

KM# 716a 200 ESCUDOS
26.5000 g., 0.9250 Silver 0.7881 oz. ASW, 36 mm. **Subject:** Death on the Sea **Obv:** Shield, globe and ropes **Rev:** Stylized sinking ship **Edge:** Reeded

Date	Mintage	F	VF	XF	Unc	BU
1999INCM	10,000	—	—	—	20.00	—
1999INCM Proof	10,000		Value: 35.00			

KM# 716b 200 ESCUDOS
27.2000 g., 0.9167 Gold 0.8016 oz. AGW, 36 mm. **Subject:** Death on the Sea **Obv:** Shield, globe and ropes **Rev:** Stylized sinking ship **Edge:** Reeded

Date	Mintage	F	VF	XF	Unc	BU
1999INCM Proof	1,000		Value: 775			

KM# 717 200 ESCUDOS
Copper-Nickel, 36 mm. **Subject:** Pedro Alvares Cabral - Brasil 1500 **Obv:** Fleet of sailing ships **Rev:** Bust right superimposed on map of South American coastline, anchor marks spot of Porto Seguro **Edge:** Reeded

Date	Mintage	F	VF	XF	Unc	BU
1999INCM	—	—	—	—	4.00	—

KM# 717a 200 ESCUDOS
26.5000 g., 0.9250 Silver 0.7881 oz. ASW, 36 mm. **Subject:** Brasil 1500 **Obv:** Fleet of sailing ships **Rev:** Head right

Date	Mintage	F	VF	XF	Unc	BU
1999INCM	1,000	—	—	—	20.00	—
1999 Proof	1,000		Value: 35.00			

KM# 717b 200 ESCUDOS
27.2000 g., 0.9167 Gold 0.8016 oz. AGW **Subject:** Brasil 1500 **Obv:** Fleet of sailing ships **Rev:** Head right

Date	Mintage	F	VF	XF	Unc	BU
1999 Proof	1,000		Value: 775			

KM# 718 200 ESCUDOS
Copper-Nickel, 36 mm. **Subject:** Brasil **Obv:** Natives, palm trees, arms at right superimposed on coastline map of Brazil **Rev:** Ship, native, and map **Edge:** Reeded

Date	Mintage	F	VF	XF	Unc	BU
1999	—	—	—	—	4.00	—

KM# 718a 200 ESCUDOS
26.5000 g., 0.9250 Silver 0.7881 oz. ASW, 36 mm. **Subject:** Brasil **Obv:** Natives, palm trees **Rev:** Ship, native, and map

Date	Mintage	F	VF	XF	Unc	BU
1999	Est. 10,000	—	—	—	20.00	—
1999 Proof	Est. 10,000		Value: 35.00			

KM# 718b 200 ESCUDOS
27.2000 g., 0.9167 Gold 0.8016 oz. AGW **Subject:** Brasil **Obv:** Natives and palm trees **Rev:** Ship, native, and map

Date	Mintage	F	VF	XF	Unc	BU
1999 Proof	1,000		Value: 775			

KM# 719 200 ESCUDOS
Copper-Nickel, 36 mm. **Subject:** Duarte Pacheco Pereira **Obv:** Arms above sailing ships, value below **Rev:** Armored half-length bust facing **Edge:** Reeded

Date	Mintage	F	VF	XF	Unc	BU
1999	—	—	—	—	4.00	—

KM# 719a 200 ESCUDOS
26.5000 g., 0.9250 Silver 0.7881 oz. ASW, 36 mm.
Subject: Duarte Pacheco Pereira **Rev:** Armored half-length bust facing

Date	Mintage	F	VF	XF	Unc	BU
1999	1,000	—	—	—	20.00	—
1999 Proof	1,000	Value: 35.00				

KM# 719b 200 ESCUDOS
27.2000 g., 0.9167 Gold 0.8016 oz. AGW **Subject:** Duarte Pacheco Pereira **Rev:** Armored half-length bust facing

Date	Mintage	F	VF	XF	Unc	BU
1999 Proof	1,000	Value: 775				

KM# 720 200 ESCUDOS
Bi-Metallic Copper-Nickel center in Brass ring, 28 mm.
Obv: Shield within globe above value **Rev:** Stylized dove on wheels and logo **Edge:** Segmented reeding

Date	Mintage	F	VF	XF	Unc	BU
1999INCM	—	—	—	—	6.50	7.50

KM# 726 200 ESCUDOS
Bi-Metallic Copper-Nickel center in Nickel-Brass ring, 28 mm.
Obv: Torch, cross design and value **Rev:** Olympic logo
Edge: Reeded and plain sections

Date	Mintage	F	VF	XF	Unc	BU
2000INCM	10,000	—	—	—	4.00	—
2000INCM Proof	5,000	Value: 7.50				

KM# 729a 200 ESCUDOS
26.5000 g., 0.9250 Silver 0.7881 oz. ASW, 36 mm.
Subject: Terra Dos Corte-Real **Obv:** Cross above shield
Rev: Ship above 1501-1502 **Edge:** Reeded

Date	Mintage	F	VF	XF	Unc	BU
2000 Proof	Est. 10,000	Value: 37.50				
2000	Est. 10,000	—	—	—	25.00	—

KM# 730a 200 ESCUDOS
26.5000 g., 0.9250 Silver 0.7881 oz. ASW **Subject:** Terra Florida **Obv:** Maltese crosses above compass **Rev:** Ship below maltese cross within map **Edge:** Reeded

Date	Mintage	F	VF	XF	Unc	BU
2000 Proof	Est. 10,000	Value: 37.50				
2000	Est. 10,000	—	—	—	25.00	—

KM# 728a 200 ESCUDOS
26.5000 g., 0.9250 Silver 0.7881 oz. ASW, 36 mm.
Subject: Terra do Lavrado **Obv:** Shield and compass **Rev:** Labrador coast and ship **Edge:** Reeded

Date	Mintage	F	VF	XF	Unc	BU
2000 Proof	Est. 10,000	Value: 37.50				
2000	Est. 10,000	—	—	—	25.00	—

KM# 728 200 ESCUDOS
21.1000 g., Copper-Nickel, 36 mm. **Subject:** Terra Do Lavrado **Obv:** Compass and shield **Rev:** Labrador coast and ship
Edge: Reeded

Date	Mintage	F	VF	XF	Unc	BU
2000INCM	—	—	—	—	4.00	—

KM# 728b 200 ESCUDOS
27.2000 g., 0.9166 Gold 0.8015 oz. AGW, 36 mm.
Subject: Terra do Lavrado **Obv:** Shield and compass
Rev: Labrador coast and ship **Edge:** Reeded

Date	Mintage	F	VF	XF	Unc	BU
2000 Proof	Est. 1,375	Value: 775				

KM# 729 200 ESCUDOS
21.1400 g., Copper-Nickel, 36 mm. **Subject:** Terra Dos Corte-Real **Obv:** Cross above shield **Rev:** Ship above 1501-1502
Edge: Reeded

Date	Mintage	F	VF	XF	Unc	BU
2000INCM	—	—	—	—	4.00	—

KM# 729b 200 ESCUDOS
27.2000 g., 0.9166 Gold 0.8015 oz. AGW **Subject:** Terra dos Corte-Real **Obv:** Cross above shield **Rev:** Ship above 1501-1502 **Edge:** Reeded

Date	Mintage	F	VF	XF	Unc	BU
2000 Proof	Est. 1,375	Value: 775				

KM# 729c 200 ESCUDOS
31.1190 g., 0.9995 Palladium 1.0000 oz. **Subject:** Terra Dos Corte-Real **Obv:** Cross above shield **Rev:** Ship above 1501-1502 **Edge:** Reeded

Date	Mintage	F	VF	XF	Unc	BU
2000 Proof	Est. 250	Value: 550				

KM# 730 200 ESCUDOS
21.1400 g., Copper-Nickel, 36 mm. **Subject:** Terra Florida
Obv: Maltese crosses above compass **Rev:** Ship below maltese cross within map **Edge:** Reeded

Date	Mintage	F	VF	XF	Unc	BU
2000INCM	—	—	—	—	4.00	—

KM# 730b 200 ESCUDOS
27.2000 g., 0.9166 Gold 0.8015 oz. AGW **Obv:** Maltese crosses above compass **Rev:** Ship below maltese cross within map
Edge: Reeded **Edge:** Terra Florida

Date	Mintage	F	VF	XF	Unc	BU
2000 Proof	Est. 1,375	Value: 775				

KM# 731 200 ESCUDOS
21.1400 g., Copper-Nickel, 36 mm. **Subject:** Fernao De Magalhaes **Obv:** Shield, ship, and value **Rev:** Bearded portrait
Edge: Reeded

Date	Mintage	F	VF	XF	Unc	BU
2000INCM	—	—	—	—	4.00	—

KM# 731a 200 ESCUDOS
26.5000 g., 0.9250 Silver 0.7881 oz. ASW **Subject:** Fernao de Magalhaes **Obv:** Shield, ship, and value **Rev:** Bearded portrait
Edge: Reeded

Date	Mintage	F	VF	XF	Unc	BU
2000	Est. 10,000	—	—	—	25.00	—
2000 Proof	Est. 10,000	Value: 37.50				

KM# 731b 200 ESCUDOS
27.2000 g., 0.9166 Gold 0.8015 oz. AGW **Subject:** Fernao de Magalhaes **Obv:** Shield, ship, and value **Rev:** Bearded portrait
Edge: Reeded

Date	Mintage	F	VF	XF	Unc	BU
2000 Proof	Est. 1,375	Value: 775				

KM# 731c 200 ESCUDOS
31.1190 g., 0.9995 Platinum 1.0000 oz. APW **Subject:** Fernao de Magalhaes **Obv:** Shield, ship, and value **Rev:** Bearded portrait
Edge: Reeded

Date	Mintage	F	VF	XF	Unc	BU
2000 Proof	Est. 250	Value: 1,950				

KM# 604 250 ESCUDOS
25.0000 g., 0.6800 Silver 0.5465 oz. ASW **Subject:** 1974 Revolution **Obv:** Value above cross design within circle
Rev: Design flanked by dates with value above

Date	Mintage	F	VF	XF	Unc	BU
ND(1976)	950,000	—	—	10.00	12.00	—
ND(1976) Proof	10,000	Value: 18.50				

KM# 626 250 ESCUDOS
Copper-Nickel, 37 mm. **Subject:** World Fisheries Conference
Obv: Shield within horizontal lines **Rev:** Cluster of fish within triangular design facing right

Date	Mintage	F	VF	XF	Unc	BU
ND(1984)	24,000	—	—	30.00	65.00	—

KM# 626a 250 ESCUDOS
23.0000 g., 0.9250 Silver 0.6840 oz. ASW, 37 mm. **Series:** World Fisheries Conference **Obv:** Shield within horizontal lines
Rev: Cluster of fish within triangular design facing right
Edge: Reeded

Date	Mintage	F	VF	XF	Unc	BU
ND(1984) Proof	8,000	Value: 150				

KM# 643 250 ESCUDOS
Copper-Nickel, 37 mm. **Subject:** Seoul Olympics **Obv:** Shield in front of lined flower-like design **Rev:** Runners

Date	Mintage	F	VF	XF	Unc	BU
1988	850,000	—	—	2.50	5.00	—

KM# 643a 250 ESCUDOS
28.0000 g., 0.9250 Silver 0.8327 oz. ASW, 37 mm.
Subject: Seoul Olympics **Obv:** Shield in front of lined flower-like design **Rev:** Runners

Date	Mintage	F	VF	XF	Unc	BU
1988	70,000	—	—	—	17.50	—
1988 Proof	30,000	Value: 27.50				

KM# 650   250 ESCUDOS
Copper-Nickel, 37 mm. **Subject:** 850th Anniversary - Founding of Portugal **Obv:** Small churches in cross formation at left of design **Rev:** Sword divides cresent flanked by dates below design within circle

Date	Mintage	F	VF	XF	Unc	BU
1989	750,000	—	—	2.50	5.00	—

KM# 650a   250 ESCUDOS
28.0000 g., 0.9250 Silver 0.8327 oz. ASW, 37 mm.
Subject: 850th Anniversary - Founding of Portugal **Obv:** Small churches in cross formation to left of design **Rev:** Sword divides cresent flanked by dates below design within circle

Date	Mintage	F	VF	XF	Unc	BU
1989	15,000	—	—	—	22.50	—
1989 Proof	30,000	Value: 40.00				

KM# 620   500 ESCUDOS
7.0000 g., 0.8350 Silver 0.1879 oz. ASW **Subject:** XVII European Art Exhibition **Obv:** Cross and globe divides date **Rev:** Stylized castle within 1/2 beaded circle

Date	Mintage	F	VF	XF	Unc	BU
1983	200,000	—	—	6.00	12.00	—
1983 Proof	8,500	Value: 30.00				

KM# 686b   500 ESCUDOS
14.0000 g., 0.9250 Silver 0.4163 oz. ASW **Subject:** 800th Anniversary - Birth of Saint Anthony **Obv:** Church to left of shield, date and value **Rev:** Seated figure holding cross and book within arch

Date	Mintage	F	VF	XF	Unc	BU
1995 Proof	10,000	Value: 45.00				

KM# 686c   500 ESCUDOS
17.5000 g., 0.9177 Gold 0.5163 oz. AGW **Subject:** 800th Anniversary - Birth of Saint Anthony **Obv:** Church to left of shield, date and value **Rev:** Seated figure holding cross and book within arch

Date	Mintage	F	VF	XF	Unc	BU
1995 Proof	5,000	Value: 525				

KM# 686   500 ESCUDOS
14.0000 g., 0.5000 Silver 0.2250 oz. ASW **Subject:** 800th Anniversary - Birth of Saint Anthony **Obv:** Castle to left of shield, date and value **Rev:** Seated figure holding cross and book within arch **Note:** Prev. KM686a

Date	Mintage	F	VF	XF	Unc	BU
1995	—	—	—	—	8.50	10.00

KM# 702   500 ESCUDOS
13.8700 g., 0.5000 Silver 0.2230 oz. ASW **Obv:** Shield **Rev:** Bank seal - Banco de Portugal

Date	Mintage	F	VF	XF	Unc	BU
ND(1996)	—	—	—	—	8.50	10.00

KM# 701   500 ESCUDOS
14.0000 g., 0.5000 Silver 0.2250 oz. ASW **Obv:** Shield superimposed on radiant sun **Rev:** Head facing

Date	Mintage	F	VF	XF	Unc	BU
ND(1997)	—	—	—	—	7.50	9.50

KM# 701a   500 ESCUDOS
14.0000 g., 0.9250 Silver 0.4163 oz. ASW **Obv:** Shield superimposed on radiant sun **Rev:** Head facing

Date	Mintage	F	VF	XF	Unc	BU
ND(1997) Proof	—	Value: 37.50				

KM# 701b   500 ESCUDOS
Silver And Gold **Obv:** Shield superimposed on radiant sun **Rev:** Head facing **Note:** 14.0000 gram, .925 Silver, .4051 ounce with 3.1000 gram .9167 gold, .0914 ounce lamination on reverse.

Date	Mintage	F	VF	XF	Unc	BU
ND(1997) Proof	15,000	Value: 125				

KM# 705   500 ESCUDOS
14.0000 g., 0.5000 Silver 0.2250 oz. ASW **Obv:** Shield, design within circle and value **Rev:** Bridge

Date	Mintage	F	VF	XF	Unc	BU
1998	—	—	—	—	7.50	9.50
1998 Proof	30,000	Value: 42.50				

KM# 705a   500 ESCUDOS
Bi-Metallic Gold center in Silver ring **Obv:** Shield, design within circle and value **Rev:** Bridge **Note:** 14.000 gram, .925 Silver, .4164 ounce with 3.1000 gram .9167 gold, .0914 ounce lamination on reverse.

Date	Mintage	F	VF	XF	Unc	BU
1998 Proof	15,000	Value: 135				

KM# 723   500 ESCUDOS
14.0000 g., 0.5000 Silver 0.2250 oz. ASW, 30 mm.
Subject: Macao's Return to China **Obv:** Partial bridge above shield and value **Rev:** Bridge above monument **Edge:** Reeded

Date	Mintage	F	VF	XF	Unc	BU
1999INCM	—	—	—	—	6.00	7.50

KM# 725   500 ESCUDOS
14.0000 g., 0.5000 Silver 0.2250 oz. ASW **Subject:** Eca de Queiroz, death centennial **Obv:** Portuguese national shield in center flanked by laurel leaves **Obv. Leg.:** REPUBLICA PORTUGUESA CENTENARIO DA MORTE DE EÇA DE QUEIROZ **Rev:** Portrait of Eça de Queiroz facing left **Rev. Leg.:** EÇA DE QUEIROZ 1900 2000 **Edge:** Reeded

Date	Mintage	F	VF	XF	Unc	BU
ND(2000)INCM	500,000	—	—	5.25	8.50	10.00
ND(2000)INCM Proof	10,000	Value: 45.00				

KM# 725a   500 ESCUDOS
14.0000 g., 0.9250 Silver 0.4163 oz. ASW **Subject:** Eca de Queiroz **Obv:** Shield flanked by sprigs above value **Rev:** Stylized portrait left **Edge:** Reeded **Note:** 14.000 gram, .925 Silver, .4164 ounce with 3.1000 gram .9167 gold, .1000 ounce lamination on reverse.

Date	Mintage	F	VF	XF	Unc	BU
ND(2000) Proof	10,000	Value: 175				

KM# 621   750 ESCUDOS
12.5000 g., 0.8350 Silver 0.3356 oz. ASW **Subject:** XVII European Art Exhibition **Obv:** Cross and globe divides date **Rev:** Crowned shield within circle

Date	Mintage	F	VF	XF	Unc	BU
1983	200,000	—	—	7.50	15.00	—
1983 Proof	8,500	Value: 35.00				

KM# 611   1000 ESCUDOS
17.0000 g., 0.9250 Silver 0.5055 oz. ASW **Subject:** 400th Anniversary - Death of Louis de Camoes **Obv:** Shield within globe above sprig **Rev:** Armored bust 1/4 right flanked by dates

Date	Mintage	F	VF	XF	Unc	BU
ND(1983)	150,000	—	—	—	18.50	—
ND(1983) Proof	10,000	Value: 42.50				

KM# 622   1000 ESCUDOS
21.0000 g., 0.8350 Silver 0.5637 oz. ASW **Subject:** XVII European Art Exhibition **Obv:** Cross and globe divides date **Rev:** Crowned shield within center circle

Date	Mintage	F	VF	XF	Unc	BU
1983	200,000	—	—	9.50	17.50	—
1983 Proof	8,500	Value: 40.00				

KM# 696a   1000 ESCUDOS
28.0000 g., 0.9250 Silver 0.8327 oz. ASW **Subject:** N. S. Da Conceicao Padroeira de Portugal **Obv:** Shield **Rev:** Madonna and child

Date	Mintage	F	VF	XF	Unc	BU
ND(1996) Proof	—	Value: 45.00				

KM# 657   1000 ESCUDOS
27.0000 g., 0.5000 Silver 0.4340 oz. ASW **Series:** Ibero - American **Obv:** Shield within globe in center of assorted emblems around border **Rev:** Ship and assorted emblems within map and circle

Date	Mintage	F	VF	XF	Unc	BU
ND(1992)INCM	326,000	—	—	—	17.50	—

KM# 657a   1000 ESCUDOS
27.0000 g., 0.9250 Silver 0.8029 oz. ASW **Series:** Ibero - American **Obv:** Shield within globe in center of assorted emblems around border **Rev:** Ship and assorted emblems within circle

Date	Mintage	F	VF	XF	Unc	BU
ND(1992) Proof	30,000	Value: 65.00				

KM# 685   1000 ESCUDOS
28.0000 g., 0.5000 Silver 0.4501 oz. ASW, 40 mm. **Subject:** 500th Anniversary - Death of John II **Obv:** Design within circle **Obv. Leg.:** REPUBLICA PORTUGUESA **Rev:** Head right and 1/2 of ship **Rev. Leg.:** D. JOÃO II : REI DE PORTUGAL : 1495-1995

Date	Mintage	F	VF	XF	Unc	BU
ND(1995)INCM	600,000	—	—	—	13.50	15.00

KM# 685a   1000 ESCUDOS
28.0000 g., 0.9250 Silver 0.8327 oz. ASW **Subject:** 500th Anniversary - Death of John II **Obv:** Design within circle **Rev:** Head right and 1/2 of ship

Date	Mintage	F	VF	XF	Unc	BU
ND(1995) Proof	15,000	Value: 40.00				

KM# 695   1000 ESCUDOS
28.0000 g., 0.5000 Silver 0.4501 oz. ASW **Subject:** 100th Anniversary - Portuguese Oceanic Expedition **Obv:** Shield and fish **Rev:** Ship below two facing busts

Date	Mintage	F	VF	XF	Unc	BU
1997	—	—	—	—	14.50	16.50

KM# 695a   1000 ESCUDOS
28.0000 g., 0.9250 Silver 0.8327 oz. ASW **Subject:** 100th Anniversary - Portuguese Oceanic Expedition **Obv:** Shield and fish **Rev:** Two busts above ship

Date	Mintage	F	VF	XF	Unc	BU
1997 Proof	Est. 15,000	Value: 40.00				

KM# 675   1000 ESCUDOS
28.0000 g., 0.5000 Silver 0.4501 oz. ASW, 40 mm. **Subject:** Treaty of Tordesilhas **Obv:** Upright design above value **Rev:** Cross on top of shield within mapped scroll

Date	Mintage	F	VF	XF	Unc	BU
ND(1994)INCM	570,000	—	—	—	14.50	16.50

KM# 675a   1000 ESCUDOS
28.0000 g., 0.9250 Silver 0.8327 oz. ASW **Subject:** Treaty of Tordesilhas **Obv:** Upright design above value **Rev:** Cross on top of shield within mapped scroll

Date	Mintage	F	VF	XF	Unc	BU
ND(1994) Proof	10,000	Value: 45.00				

KM# 688   1000 ESCUDOS
28.0000 g., 0.5000 Silver 0.4501 oz. ASW **Subject:** Restoration of the Frigate Ferdinand II and Gloria **Obv:** Shield, figure head, ship's hull **Rev:** Ship below two facing busts

Date	Mintage	F	VF	XF	Unc	BU
ND(1996)	—	—	—	—	14.50	16.50

KM# 688a   1000 ESCUDOS
28.0000 g., 0.9250 Silver 0.8327 oz. ASW **Subject:** Restoration of the Frigate Ferdinand II and Gloria **Obv:** Shield, figure head, ship's hull **Rev:** Two facing busts above ship

Date	Mintage	F	VF	XF	Unc	BU
ND(1996) Proof	15,000	Value: 45.00				

KM# 703   1000 ESCUDOS
28.0000 g., 0.5000 Silver 0.4501 oz. ASW, 40 mm. **Subject:** Credito Publico **Obv:** Shield within hexagonal design **Obv. Leg.:** REPUBLICA PORTUGUESA **Rev:** Hexagonal design **Rev. Leg.:** IGCP II CENTENÁRIO DO CRÉDITO PÚBLICO

Date	Mintage	F	VF	XF	Unc	BU
1997INCM	320,000	—	—	—	13.50	15.00

KM# 703a   1000 ESCUDOS
28.0000 g., 0.9250 Silver 0.8327 oz. ASW, 40 mm. **Subject:** Credito Publico **Obv:** Shield within hexagonal design **Obv. Leg.:** REPUBLICA PORTUGUESA **Rev:** Hexagonal design **Rev. Leg.:** IGCP II CENTENARIO DO CREDITO PUBLICO

Date	Mintage	F	VF	XF	Unc	BU
1997INCM Proof	15,000	Value: 50.00				

KM# 676   1000 ESCUDOS
28.0000 g., 0.5000 Silver 0.4501 oz. ASW **Subject:** Endangered Wildlife **Obv:** Shield within globe in center of assorted emblems **Rev:** Gray wolves within circle

Date	Mintage	F	VF	XF	Unc	BU
1994	70,000	—	—	—	125	—

KM# 676a   1000 ESCUDOS
28.0000 g., 0.9250 Silver 0.8327 oz. ASW **Subject:** Endangered Wildlife **Obv:** Shield within globe in center of assorted emblems **Rev:** Grey wolves within circle

Date	Mintage	F	VF	XF	Unc	BU
1994 Proof	30,000	Value: 150				

KM# 696   1000 ESCUDOS
28.0000 g., 0.5000 Silver 0.4501 oz. ASW, 40 mm. **Subject:** N. S. Da Conceicao Padroeira de Portugal **Obv:** Shield **Obv. Leg.:** REPUBLICA PORTUGUESA 1996 **Rev:** Madonna and child **Rev. Leg.:** N.S.DA CONCEICAO PADROEIRA DE PORTUGAL

Date	Mintage	F	VF	XF	Unc	BU
ND(1996)INCM	620,000	—	—	—	13.50	15.00

KM# 704   1000 ESCUDOS
27.0000 g., 0.5000 Silver 0.4340 oz. ASW **Obv:** Shield within circle of assorted shields **Rev:** Pauliteiros dancers

Date	Mintage	F	VF	XF	Unc	BU
1997	—	—	—	—	13.50	15.00

KM# 704a 1000 ESCUDOS

27.0000 g., 0.9250 Silver 0.8029 oz. ASW **Obv:** Shield within circle of assorted shields **Rev:** Pauliteiros dancers

Date	Mintage	F	VF	XF	Unc	BU
1997 Proof	—	Value: 45.00				

KM# 707 1000 ESCUDOS

27.0000 g., 0.5000 Silver 0.4340 oz. ASW, 40 mm. **Subject:** International Year of the Oceans Expo 98 **Obv:** Shield and logo **Rev:** Styilized expo designs

Date	Mintage	F	VF	XF	Unc	BU
1998	1,000,000	—	—	—	13.50	15.00

KM# 707a 1000 ESCUDOS

27.0000 g., 0.9250 Silver 0.8029 oz. ASW **Subject:** International Year of the Oceans Expo **Obv:** Shield and logo **Rev:** Styilized expo designs

Date	Mintage	F	VF	XF	Unc	BU
1998 Proof	Est. 20,000	Value: 45.00				

KM# 708 1000 ESCUDOS

27.0000 g., 0.5000 Silver 0.4340 oz. ASW **Subject:** 500th Anniversary - Misericordia Church **Obv:** Basket and rope design **Rev:** Crowned praying figure flanked by cherubs and other figures below

Date	Mintage	F	VF	XF	Unc	BU
ND(1998)	—	—	—	—	13.50	15.00

KM# 708a 1000 ESCUDOS

27.0000 g., 0.9250 Silver 0.8029 oz. ASW **Subject:** 500th Anniversary - Misericordia Church **Obv:** Basket and rope design **Rev:** Crowned praying figure flanked by cherubs and other figures below

Date	Mintage	F	VF	XF	Unc	BU
ND(1998) Proof	—	Value: 45.00				

KM# 713 1000 ESCUDOS

27.0000 g., 0.5000 Silver 0.4340 oz. ASW **Obv:** Two ships, crowned shield, armillary sphere **Rev:** King Dom Manuel I seated on throne with sword

Date	Mintage	F	VF	XF	Unc	BU
1998	—	—	—	—	13.50	15.00

KM# 713a 1000 ESCUDOS

27.0000 g., 0.9250 Silver 0.8029 oz. ASW **Obv:** Two ships, crowned shield, armillary sphere **Rev:** King Dom Manuel I seated on throne with sword

Date	Mintage	F	VF	XF	Unc	BU
1998 Proof	Est. 15,000	Value: 45.00				

KM# 714 1000 ESCUDOS

27.0000 g., 0.5000 Silver 0.4340 oz. ASW, 40 mm. **Subject:** 75th Anniversary - League of Combatants **Obv:** Stylized shield **Obv. Leg.:** REPUBLICA PORTUGUESA **Rev:** Sword and laurel branch **Rev. Leg.:** LIGA DOS COMBATENTES 1923 1998

Date	Mintage	F	VF	XF	Unc	BU
1998INCM	500,000	—	—	10.00	13.50	15.00

KM# 714a 1000 ESCUDOS

27.0000 g., 0.9250 Silver 0.8029 oz. ASW **Subject:** 75th Anniversary - League of Combatants **Obv:** Stylized shield **Rev:** Sword and laurel branch

Date	Mintage	F	VF	XF	Unc	BU
1998 Proof	—	Value: 45.00				

KM# 715 1000 ESCUDOS

27.0000 g., 0.5000 Silver 0.4340 oz. ASW **Subject:** 25th Anniversary - Revolution of April 25 **Obv:** Circles within cross design above value and date **Rev:** Date and mirrored anniversary number

Date	Mintage	F	VF	XF	Unc	BU
1999	—	—	—	—	13.50	15.00

KM# 715a 1000 ESCUDOS

27.0000 g., 0.9250 Silver 0.8029 oz. ASW **Subject:** 25th Anniversary - Revolution of April 25 **Obv:** Circles within cross design above value and date **Rev:** Date and mirrored anniversary number

Date	Mintage	F	VF	XF	Unc	BU
1999 Proof	Est. 15,000	Value: 45.00				

KM# 721 1000 ESCUDOS

27.2000 g., 0.5000 Silver 0.4372 oz. ASW, 39 mm. **Subject:** Millennium of Atlantic Sailing **Obv:** Shield above logo **Rev:** Stylized face looking down on ship **Edge:** Reeded

Date	Mintage	F	VF	XF	Unc	BU
1999INCM	—	—	—	—	18.50	20.00

KM# 721a 1000 ESCUDOS

27.0000 g., 0.9250 Silver 0.8029 oz. ASW **Subject:** Millennium of Atlantic Sailing **Obv:** Shield above logo **Rev:** Stylized face looking down on ship **Edge:** Reeded

Date	Mintage	F	VF	XF	Unc	BU
1999INCM Proof	15,000	Value: 45.00				

KM# 724 1000 ESCUDOS

27.0000 g., 0.5000 Silver 0.4340 oz. ASW, 40.2 mm. **Subject:** Presidency of the European Union **Obv:** Shield and cave drawings **Rev:** Stylized design **Edge:** Reeded

Date	Mintage	F	VF	XF	Unc	BU
2000	450,000	—	—	—	13.50	15.00

KM# 727 1000 ESCUDOS

27.0000 g., 0.5000 Silver 0.4340 oz. ASW, 40 mm. **Series:** Ibero-America **Obv:** Shield within center of assorted shields **Rev:** Lusitano horses and rider **Edge:** Reeded

Date	Mintage	F	VF	XF	Unc	BU
2000INCM	Est. 450,000	—	—	—	22.50	25.00

KM# 724a 1000 ESCUDOS

27.0500 g., 0.9250 Silver 0.8044 oz. ASW **Obv:** Shield and cave drawings **Rev:** Stylized design

Date	Mintage	F	VF	XF	Unc	BU
2000 Proof	10,000	Value: 75.00				

KM# 727a 1000 ESCUDOS

27.0000 g., 0.9250 Silver 0.8029 oz. ASW, 40 mm. **Series:** Ibero-America **Obv:** Shield within center of assorted shields **Rev:** Lusitano horses and rider **Edge:** Reeded

Date	Mintage	F	VF	XF	Unc	BU
2000 Proof	Est. 20,000	—	—	—	100	120

KM# 732 1000 ESCUDOS

27.0000 g., 0.5000 Silver 0.4340 oz. ASW **Subject:** D. Joso De Castro **Obv:** Shield within globe above value **Rev:** Bearded stylized bust

Date	Mintage	F	VF	XF	Unc	BU
2000	—	—	—	—	20.00	22.50

ESSAIS

KM#	Date	Mintage	Identification	Mkt Val
E1	1986	30	100 Escudos. Copper Nickel. KM637	—
E2	1998	—	100 Escudos. Silver. "ENSAIO" on obverse and reverse.	—
E3	1998	—	100 Escudos. Silver. "ENSAIO" on reverse only.	—

PATTERNS
Including off metal strikes

KM#	Date	Mintage	Identification	Mkt Val
Pn200	1903	—	2 Reis. Nickel. Plain royal arms.	—
Pn201	1903	—	20 Reis. Nickel. Royal arms with wreath.	350
Pn202	1903	—	20 Reis. Nickel. Plain edge. Without wreath.	350
Pn203	1903	—	20 Reis. Nickel. Reeded edge. Value on reeded edge.	275
Pn204	1903	—	20 Reis. Nickel. Plain edge. Value on plain edge.	275

KM#	Date	Mintage	Identification	Mkt Val
Pn205	1903	—	100 Reis. Silver. Crowned value.	1,500
Pn206	1903	—	200 Reis. Silver. Crowned value.	2,200
Pn207	ND	—	20 Centavos. Silver. Two reverses.	600
Pn208	1912	—	50 Centavos. Copper. Plain edge. Type as adopted.	750
Pn209	1912	—	50 Centavos. Silver. Reeded edge. Type as adopted.	1,000
Pn210	1912	—	Escudo. Gold. 'October 5, 1910'.	600
Pn211	1912	—	Escudo. Gold. Obverse variety.	600
Pn212	1912	—	Escudo. Gold.	600
Pn213	1919	—	4 Centavos. Copper Nickel. Plain edge. Wide border.	—
Pn214	1919	—	4 Centavos. Copper Nickel. Reeded edge. Wide border.	—
Pn215	1919	—	4 Centavos. Copper Nickel. Plain edge. Semi-wide border.	—
Pn216	1919	—	4 Centavos. Copper Nickel. Alternate edge. Narrow border.	—
Pn218	1920	—	10 Centavos. Brass. Plain edge. Larger type.	—
Pn217	1920	—	10 Centavos. Copper Nickel. Plain edge. Larger type.	1,500
Pn219	1920	—	5 Escudos. Copper. 'Abundance Through Labor'	1,000
Pn220	1920	—	5 Escudos. Copper Nickel. 'Abundance Through Labor'	1,000
Pn221	1920	—	5 Escudos. Gold. 'Abundance Through Labor'	—
Pn222	1921	—	10 Centavos. Bronze. Reeded edge. 19mm	500
Pn224	1927	—	50 Centavos. Silver. Obverse 1924 type.	500
Pn223	1927	—	50 Centavos. Silver. Reeded edge. Large type.	500
Pn225	1927	—	Escudo. Silver. Reverse 1924 type.	—
Pn226	1928	—	Escudo. Brass.	650
Pn227	1928	—	10 Escudos. Copper. 'Battle of Orique'.	750
Pn228	1929	—	10 Escudos. Brass. 'Battle of Orique'.	—
Pn229	1932	—	5 Escudos. Copper Nickel. Type adopted.	—
Pn230	1932	—	10 Escudos. Copper.	225
Pn231	1932	—	10 Escudos. Copper Nickel. Type adopted.	225
Pn232	1940	—	10 Escudos. Copper Nickel. Large type.	225
Pn233	1953	—	20 Escudos. Copper. 'National Revival'.	650
Pn235	1953	—	20 Escudos. Silver. Variety of type adopted.	1,250
Pn234	1953	—	20 Escudos. Gold. 'National Revival'.	—
Pn236	1961	—	2-1/2 Escudos. Nickel. Reeded edge.	—
Pn237	1961	—	2-1/2 Escudos. Nickel. Reeded edge.	—
Pn238	1961	—	2-1/2 Escudos. Copper Nickel.	—
Pn241	1961	—	10 Escudos. Silver.	—
Pn242	1961	—	10 Escudos. Copper Nickel. Legend in relief.	—
Pn243	ND	—	10 Centavos. Aluminum.	—
Pn246	ND	—	10 Centavos. Nickel. Reeded edge. Type adopted.	—
Pn247	ND	—	10 Centavos. Nickel. Plain edge. Type adopted.	—
Pn248	ND	—	10 Centavos. Bronze-Aluminum. Plain edge.	—
Pn239	1961	—	10 Centavos. Silver. Legend incuse.	600
Pn240	1961	—	10 Centavos. Copper Nickel.	350
Pn244	ND	—	20 Centavos. Brass.	225
Pn245	ND	—	5 Escudos. Brass. Type adopted.	225
Pn249	1966	—	Escudo. Bronze-Aluminum.	200
Pn250	1966	—	Escudo. Bronze-Aluminum. Reeded edge.	200
Pn251	1966	—	20 Centavos. Nickel. Reeded edge.	350
Pn252	1968	—	10 Centavos. Aluminum. Similar to 1942 type.	225
Pn253	1969	—	10 Centavos. Aluminum. Large type as adopted.	—
Pn254	1970	—	Escudo. Nickel. Type adopted.	100
Pn255	1970	—	20 Escudos. Nickel. Reeded edge.	200
Pn256	1970	—	20 Escudos. Nickel. Plain edge.	200
Pn257	1970	—	20 Escudos. Nickel. Reeded edge.	200
Pn258	1970	—	20 Escudos. Nickel. Plain edge.	200
Pn259	1979	—	50 Centavos. Reeded edge.	125
Pn260	1979	—	Escudo. Reeded edge.	125
Pn261	1979	—	5 Escudos. Aluminum.	150
Pn262	ND	—	250 Escudos. Copper Nickel. Decade of Women, United Nations.	—
Pn263	1989	—	100 Escudos.	1,650

PROVAS

Stamped

KM#	Date	Mintage	Identification	Mkt Val
PrA7	1942	—	10 Centavos. Bronze. KM583.	—
PrB7	1942	—	20 Centavos. Bronze. KM584.	55.00
Pr7	1943	—	5 Escudos. Silver. KM581.	35.00
Pr8	1943	—	10 Centavos. Bronze. KM583.	20.00
Pr9	1943	—	20 Centavos. Bronze. KM584.	20.00
Pr10	1960	—	5 Escudos. Silver. KM587.	15.00
Pr11	1960	—	10 Escudos. Silver. KM588.	20.00
Pr12	1960	—	20 Escudos.	30.00
PrA11	1960	—	5 Escudos. Silver. Matte. KM#587.	250
PrA13	1962	—	10 Centavos. Bronze. KM583.	—
PrB13	1962	—	20 Centavos. Bronze. KM584.	—
PrC13	1962	—	50 Centavos. Copper Nickel. KM577.	—
PrD13	1962	—	Escudo. Copper-Nickel. KM578.	—
Pr13	1964	—	Escudo. Copper-Nickel. KM578.	—
Pr14	1964	—	2-1/2 Escudos. Copper-Nickel. KM590.	—
Pr15	1966	—	20 Centavos. Bronze. KM584.	—
Pr16	1966	—	Escudo. Copper-Nickel. KM578.	—

KM#	Date	Mintage	Identification	Mkt Val
Pr17	1966	—	2-1/2 Escudos. Copper-Nickel. KM590.	17.50
Pr18	1966	—	5 Escudos. Copper-Nickel. KM591.	15.00
Pr19	1966	—	20 Escudos. Silver. Salazar Bridge. KM592.	25.00
Pr20	1966	—	20 Escudos. Gold. Salazar Bridge. KM592.	2,500
Pr21	1968	—	50 Escudos. Silver. KM593.	30.00
Pr23	1969	—	50 Escudos. Silver. KM598. 'Prova' in relef.	35.00
Pr24	1969	—	50 Escudos. Silver. KM599.	30.00
Pr22	1969	—	50 Escudos. Silver. KM598. 'Prova' incuse.	30.00
Pr25	1971	—	50 Escudos. Silver. KM601.	30.00
Pr26	1972	—	50 Escudos. Silver. KM602.	30.00
Pr27	ND(1984)	100	25 Escudos. Copper-Nickel. Shield below wave-like design. Styilized value. KM623. Revolution.	15.00
Pr28	1985	5,000	100 Escudos. Copper-Nickel. KM629, Henrique.	—

TRIAL STRIKES

KM#	Date	Mintage	Identification	Mkt Val
TS33	1910	—	1000 Reis. Nickel Alloy. KM558; ALP	400
TS34	1915	—	Escudo. Nickel Alloy. KM564; ALP.	400
TS35	1927	—	5 Centavos. Bronze. Reverse.	—
TS36	ND	—	20 Centavos. Brass. Reverse, Roman numeral.	—
TS37	ND(1927)	—	50 Centavos. Brass. Reverse.	—
TS38	ND(1927)	—	2 Escudos. Brass. Uniface, KM#591.	25.00
TS36	ND(1963)	—	20 Centavos. Brass. Reverse, Roman numeral.	—

MINT SETS

KM#	Date	Mintage	Identification	Issue Price	Mkt Val
MS1	1960 (3)	—	KM587-589	—	45.00
MS2	1982 (4)	10,000	KM612-613, 615-616	3.00	7.00
MS3	1983 (5)	50,000	KM620-622	30.00	30.00
MS4	1983 (3)	5,000	KM617-619	4.00	25.00
MS5	1984 (2)	10,000	KM624-625	3.00	25.00
MS6	1985 (2)	20,000	KM627a, 630a	20.00	37.50
MSA6	1985 (2)	—	KM627, 630	—	10.00
MS7	1986 (5)	50,000	KM631-634, 636	6.00	30.00
MS8	1987/8 (4)	40,000	KM639a-642a	78.00	70.00
MS9	1987/8 (4)	5,000	KM639b-642b	2,080	2,200
MS10	1987 (6)	5,000	KM631-634, 636, 638	10.00	30.00
MS11	1988 (5)	30,000	KM631-634, 636	10.00	20.00
MS12	1989 (6)	50,000	KM631-634, 636, 645.1	12.00	20.00
MS13	1990 (6)	50,000	KM631-634, 636, 645.1	15.00	17.50
MS14	1989/90 (4)	30,000	KM646a-649a	79.50	80.00
MSA14	1989/90 (4)	—	KM646-649	—	15.00
MS15	1991 (7)	—	KM631-634, 636, 645.1, 655	17.50	17.50
MS16	1992 (7)	—	KM631-634, 636, 645.1, 655	—	32.50
MS17	1993 (7)	—	KM631-634, 636, 645.1, 655	—	25.00
MS18	1993 (4)	30,000	KM665a-668a	79.50	75.00
MS19	1994 (7)	—	KM631-634, 636, 645.1, 669	—	32.50
MS20	1994 (4)	—	KM670a-673a	—	90.00
MS21	1995 (7)	—	KM631-634, 636, 678-679	—	20.00
MS23	1995 (2)	5,000	KM678 679	—	60.00
MS22	1995 (4)	20,000	KM681a-684a	77.50	70.00
MS24	1996 (8)	—	KM631-634, 636, 645.1, 655, 687	—	35.00
MS25	1996 (4)	10,000	KM689a, 690a, 691a, 692a	105	70.00
MS26	1997 (9)	20,000	KM631-634, 636, 645.1, 655, 693-694	32.50	30.00
MS27	1998 (8)	50,000	KM631-634, 636, 645.1, 655, 706	32.50	30.00
MS28	1998 (4)	25,000	KM709a-712a	95.00	95.00
MS29	1999 (9)	—	KM631-634, 636, 645.1, 655, 720, 722	—	30.00
MS30	1999 (4)	10,000	KM716a-719a	95.00	95.00
MS31	2000 (4)	10,000	KM#728a-731a	65.00	95.00

PROOF SETS

KM#	Date	Mintage	Identification	Issue Price	Mkt Val
PS1	1960 (3)	—	KM587-589; matte finish	—	115
PS2	1974 (2)	10,000	KM603-604	6.00	35.00
PS3	1977 (3)	10,000	KM605-606, 608	2.50	25.00
PS4	1983 (3)	8,500	KM620-622	60.00	100
PS5	1985 (2)	5,000	KM627a, 630a	40.00	150
PS6	1985 (2)	5,000	KM628, 628a	35.00	300
PS7	1987 (4)	20,000	KM639a-642a	128	150
PS8	1987/88 (4)	2,000	KM639a, 640c, 641b, 642c; Prestige	2,200	2,750
PS9	1989/90 (4)	20,000	KM646a-649a	138	150
PS10	1989/90 (4)	5,000	KM646b-649b	2,425	2,450
PS11	1989/90 (4)	2,500	KM646a, 647c, 648b, 649c; Prestige	2,650	2,800
PS12	1991/92 (4)	15,000	KM658a-661a	150	150
PS13	1991/92 (4)	3,500	KM658b-661b	2,350	2,350
PS14	1991/92 (4)	2,500	KM658c-661c; Prestige	2,400	3,000
PS15	1993 (7)	—	KM631-634, 636, 645.1, 655	—	100
PS16	1993 (4)	22,000	KM665a-668a	150	150
PS17	1993 (4)	5,000	KM665b-668b	1,980	2,500
PS18	1993 (4)	2,000	KM665a, 666c, 667b, 668c; Prestige	2,300	2,150
PS19	1994 (7)	—	KM631-634, 636, 645.1, 669	—	50.00
PS20	1994 (4)	10,000	KM670a-673a	—	150
PS21	1994 (4)	—	KM670b-673b	—	2,400
PS22	1994 (4)	1,000	KM670a, 671c, 672b, 673c; Prestige	—	2,175
PS23	1995 (7)	7,000	KM631-634, 636, 678, 679	47.50	50.00
PS24	1995 (4)	13,000	KM681a-684a	150	150

KM#	Date	Mintage	Identification	Issue Price	Mkt Val
PS25	1995 (4)	2,000	KM681b-684b	1,980	2,000
PS26	1995 (4)	1,000	KM681a, 682c, 683b, 684c	1,800	2,100
PS27	1995 (2)	10,000	KM678, 679	—	35.00
PS28	1996 (4)	7,000	KM631-634, 636, 645.1, 655, 687	—	50.00
PS29	1996 (4)	10,000	KM689a, 690a, 691a, 692a	160	150
PS30	1996 (4)	2,000	KM689b, 690b, 691b, 692b	—	2,000
PS31	1996 (4)	1,000	KM689a, 690c, 691b, 692c	—	2,100
PS32	1997 (9)	7,000	KM631-634, 636, 645.1, 655, 693-694	55.00	50.00
PS33	1997 (4)	24,000	KM697a-700a	145	150
PS34	1997 (4)	4,000	KM697b-700b	1,980	2,000
PS35	1997 (4)	1,000	KM697a, 698b, 699c, 700c	2,000	2,250
PS36	1998 (8)	20,000	KM631-634, 636, 645.1, 655, 706	52.50	50.00
PS37	1998 (4)	25,000	KM709a-712a	150	150
PS38	1998 (4)	5,000	KM709b-712b	1,980	1,980
PS39	1998 (4)	1,000	KM709c, 710a, 711b, 712c	2,000	2,250
PS40	1999 (4)	10,000	KM716a-719a	150	150
PS41	1999 (4)	1,000	KM716b-719b	1,800	1,800
PS42	2000 (4)	10,000	KM#728a-731a	125	150
PS43	2000 (4)	1,000	KM#728b-731b	1,405	1,850
PS44	2000 (4)	250	KM#728a, 729c, 730b, 731c	2,988	3,000

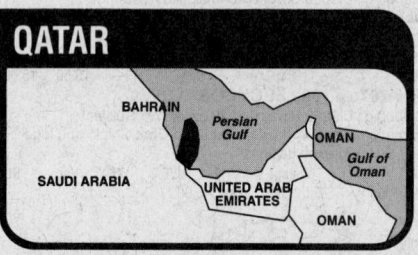

QATAR

The State of Qatar, an emirate in the Persian Gulf between Bahrain and Trucial Oman, has an area of 4,247sq. mi. (11,000 sq. km.) and a population of *469,000. Capital: Doha. Oil is the chief industry and export.

Qatar was under Turkish control from 1872 until the beginning of World War I when the Ottoman Turks evacuated the Qatar Peninsula. In 1916 Sheikh Abdullah placed Qatar under the protection of Great Britain and gave Britain responsibility for its defense and foreign relations. Qatar joined with Dubai in a Monetary Union and issued coins and paper money in 1966 and 1969. When Britain announced in 1968 that it would end treaty relationships with the Persian Gulf sheikhdoms in 1971, this union was dissolved; Qatar joined Bahrain and the seven trucial sheikhdoms (called the United Arab Emirates) in an effort to form a union of Arab Emirates. However the nine sheikhdoms were unable to agree on terms of union, and Qatar declared its independence as the State of Qatar on Sept. 3, 1971.

TITLE

دولة قطر

Daulat Qatar

RULERS

Al-Thani Dynasty
Qasim Bin Muhammad, 1876-1913
Abdullah Bin Qasim, 1913-1948
Ali Bin Abdullah, 1948-1960
Ahmad Bin Ali, 1960-1972
Khalifah bin Hamad, 1972-1995
Hamad bin Khalifah, 1995-

MONETARY SYSTEM
100 Dirhem = 1 Riyal

STATE

STANDARD COINAGE

KM# 2 DIRHAM
1.5000 g., Bronze, 15 mm. **Ruler:** Khalifah Bin Hamad
Obv: Value **Rev:** Sail boat and palm trees flanked by beads

Date	Mintage	F	VF	XF	Unc	BU
AH1393 - 1973	500,000	—	0.25	0.50	1.00	2.00

KM# 3 5 DIRHAMS
3.7500 g., Bronze, 22 mm. **Ruler:** Khalifah Bin Hamad
Obv: Value **Rev:** Sail boat and palm trees flanked by beads
Edge: Plain

Date	Mintage	F	VF	XF	Unc	BU
AH1393 - 1973	1,000,000	—	0.15	0.30	0.75	1.50
AH1398 - 1978	1,000,000	—	0.15	0.30	0.75	1.50

KM# 1 10 DIRHAMS
7.5000 g., Bronze, 27 mm. **Ruler:** Khalifah Bin Hamad
Obv: Value **Rev:** Sail boat and palm trees flanked by beads

Date	Mintage	F	VF	XF	Unc	BU
AH1392 - 1972	1,500,000	—	0.50	1.00	2.50	4.00
AH1393 - 1973	1,500,000	—	0.25	0.50	1.50	3.00

KM# 8 25 DIRHAMS
3.5000 g., Copper-Nickel, 19 mm. **Ruler:** Hamad bin Khalifah
Obv: Value **Obv. Leg.:** STATE OF QATAR **Rev:** Sail boat and
palm trees flanked by beads **Edge:** Reeded

Date	Mintage	F	VF	XF	Unc	BU
AH1419-1998	—	—	0.30	0.65	1.50	2.50
AH1421-2000	—	—	0.30	0.65	1.50	2.50

KM# 5 50 DIRHAMS
6.5000 g., Copper-Nickel, 25 mm. **Ruler:** Khalifah Bin Hamad
Obv: Value **Rev:** Sail boat and palm trees flanked by beads

Date	Mintage	F	VF	XF	Unc	BU
AH1393 - 1973	1,500,000	—	0.40	0.85	2.00	3.00
AH1398 - 1978	2,000,000	—	0.40	0.85	2.25	3.25
AH1401 - 1981	—	—	0.40	0.85	2.25	3.25
AH1407 - 1987	—	—	0.40	0.85	2.25	3.25
AH1410 - 1990	—	—	0.40	0.85	2.25	3.25
AH1414 - 1993	—	—	0.40	0.85	2.25	3.25
AH1419 - 1998	—	—	0.40	0.85	2.25	3.25

KM# 9 50 DIRHAMS
6.5000 g., Copper-Nickel, 24 mm. **Ruler:** Hamad bin Khalifah
Obv: Arms **Rev:** Value **Edge:** Reeded

Date	Mintage	F	VF	XF	Unc	BU
AH1421-2000	—	—	—	—	2.00	3.00

KM# 6 100 RIYALS
22.2000 g., 0.9250 Silver 0.6602 oz. ASW, 37 mm.
Ruler: Hamad bin Khalifah **Subject:** Central Bank **Obv:** National
arms **Rev:** Bank building **Edge:** Plain

Date	Mintage	F	VF	XF	Unc	BU
ND(1998) Proof	400	Value: 250				

KM# 10 200 RIYALS
22.2000 g., 0.9250 Silver 0.6602 oz. ASW, 37 mm. **Ruler:** Hamad
bin Khalifah **Subject:** Qatar University 25th Anniversary
Obv: National arms **Rev:** University logo, value and dates
Edge: Plain

Date	Mintage	F	VF	XF	Unc	BU
ND(1998) Proof	1,000	Value: 275				

KM# 7 500 RIYALS
17.0000 g., 0.9170 Gold 0.5012 oz. AGW, 31 mm.
Ruler: Hamad bin Khalifah **Subject:** Central Bank **Obv:** National
arms **Rev:** Bank building **Edge:** Plain

Date	Mintage	F	VF	XF	Unc	BU
ND(1998) Proof	100	Value: 700				

QATAR & DUBAI

The State of Qatar, which occupies the Qatar Peninsula jutting into the Persian Gulf from eastern Saudi Arabia, has an area of 4,247 sq. mi. (11,000 sq. km.) and a population of *469,000. Capital: Doha. The traditional occupations of pearling, fishing, and herding have been replaced in economics by petroleum-related industries. Crude oil, petroleum products, and tomatoes are exported.

Dubai is one of the seven sheikhdoms comprising the United Arab Emirates (formerly Trucial States) located along the southern shore of the Persian Gulf. It has a population of about 60,000. Capital (of the United Arab Emirates): Abu Dhabi.

Qatar, which initiated protective treaty relations with Great Britain in 1916, achieved independence on Sept. 3,1971, upon withdrawal of the British military presence from the Persian Gulf, and replaced its special treaty arrangement with Britain with a treaty of general friendship. Dubai attained independence on Dec. 1, 1971, upon termination of Britain's protective treaty with the trucial Sheikhdoms, and on Dec. 2, 1971, entered into the union of the United Arab Emirates.

Despite the fact that the Emirate of Qatar and the Sheikhdom of Dubai were merged under a monetary union, the two territories were governed independently from each other. Qatar now uses its own currency while Dubai uses the United Arab Emirates currency and coins.

TITLE

Qatar Wa Dubai

RULER
Ahmad II, 1960-1972

MONETARY SYSTEM
100 Dirhem = 1 Riyal

BRITISH PROTECTORATE
STANDARD COINAGE

KM# 1 DIRHEM
1.5000 g., Bronze, 15 mm. **Ruler:** Ahmad II **Obv:** Value
Rev: Goitered gazelle

Date	Mintage	F	VF	XF	Unc	BU
AH1386 - 1966	1,000,000	—	2.00	4.00	8.00	12.00

KM# 2 5 DIRHEMS
3.7500 g., Bronze, 22 mm. **Ruler:** Ahmad II **Obv:** Value
Rev: Goitered gazelle

Date	Mintage	F	VF	XF	Unc	BU
AH1386 - 1966	2,000,000	—	2.50	4.50	8.00	15.00
AH1389 - 1969	2,000,000	—	2.50	4.50	8.00	15.00

KM# 3 10 DIRHEMS
7.5000 g., Bronze, 27 mm. **Ruler:** Ahmad II **Obv:** Value
Rev: Goitered gazelle

Date	Mintage	F	VF	XF	Unc	BU
AH1386 - 1966	2,000,000	—	3.50	6.00	10.00	18.00
AH1391 - 1971	1,500					

Note: Official mintage figure reported for Qatar by British Royal Mint.

KM# 4 25 DIRHEMS
3.5000 g., Copper-Nickel, 20 mm. **Ruler:** Ahmad II **Obv:** Value
Rev: Goitered gazelle

Date	Mintage	F	VF	XF	Unc	BU
AH1386 - 1966	2,000,000	—	4.50	7.50	12.50	20.00
AH1389 - 1969	2,000,000	—	4.50	7.50	12.50	20.00

KM# 5 50 DIRHEMS
6.5000 g., Copper-Nickel, 25 mm. **Ruler:** Ahmad II **Obv:** Value
Rev: Goitered gazelle

Date	Mintage	F	VF	XF	Unc	BU
AH1386 - 1966	2,000,000	—	6.00	9.00	15.00	22.00

RAS AL-KHAIMAH

Ras al-Khaimah is only one of the coin issuing emirates that was not one of the original members of the United Arab Emirates. It was a part of Sharjah. It has an estimated area of 650 sq. mi. (1700 sq. km.) and a population of 30,000. Ras al Khaimah is the only member of the United Arab Emirates that has agriculture as its principal industry.

TITLE

Ras al-Khaimah(t)

RULERS
Sultan bin Salim al-Qasimi,/1921-1948
Saqr Bin Muhammad al-Qasimi,/1948—

MONETARY SYSTEM
100 Dirhams = 1 Rial

UNITED ARAB EMIRATE

NON-CIRCULATING
LEGAL TENDER COINAGE

KM# 28 50 DIRHAMS
Copper-Nickel **Ruler:** Saqr bin Muhammad al Qasimi
Obv: Value within circle **Rev:** Falcon within circle flanked by stars

Date	Mintage	F	VF	XF	Unc	BU
AH1390 - 1970	—	—	—	—	55.00	

KM# 1 RIAL
3.9500 g., 0.6400 Silver 0.0813 oz. ASW **Ruler:** Saqr bin
Muhammad al Qasimi **Obv:** Value within circle **Rev:** Crossed
flags within wreath

Date	Mintage	F	VF	XF	Unc	BU
AH1389 - 1969	—	—	—	—	12.50	—
AH1389 - 1969 Proof	1,500	Value: 25.00				

KM# 2 2 RIALS
6.4500 g., 0.8350 Silver 0.1731 oz. ASW **Ruler:** Saqr bin
Muhammad al Qasimi **Obv:** Value within circle **Rev:** Crossed
flags within wreath

Date	Mintage	F	VF	XF	Unc	BU
AH1389 - 1969	—	—	—	—	17.50	—
AH1389 - 1969 Proof	1,500	Value: 35.00				

KM# 29 2-1/2 RIALS
7.5000 g., 0.9250 Silver 0.2230 oz. ASW **Ruler:** Saqr bin
Muhammad al Qasimi **Obv:** Head with headdress 1/4 right within
circle flanked by stars **Rev:** Falcon within circle

Date	Mintage	F	VF	XF	Unc	BU
AH1390 - 1970	—	—	—	—	75.00	—

KM# 3 5 RIALS
15.0000 g., 0.8350 Silver 0.4027 oz. ASW **Ruler:** Saqr bin
Muhammad al Qasimi **Obv:** Value within circle **Rev:** Crossed
flags within wreath

Date	Mintage	F	VF	XF	Unc	BU
AH1389 - 1969	—	—	—	—	25.00	—
AH1389 - 1969 Proof	1,500	Value: 45.00				

KM# 17 7-1/2 RIYALS
22.5000 g., 0.9250 Silver 0.6691 oz. ASW **Ruler:** Saqr bin
Muhammad al Qasimi **Subject:** Centennial of Rome **Obv:** Value
within circle **Rev:** Man plowing

Date	Mintage	F	VF	XF	Unc	BU
1970 Proof	Est. 2,000	Value: 120				

KM# 32 7-1/2 RIYALS
22.5000 g., 0.9250 Silver 0.6691 oz. ASW **Ruler:** Saqr bin
Muhammad al Qasimi **Subject:** World Championship Football
Obv: Value within circle **Rev:** Jules Rimet Cup flanked by shields

Date	Mintage	F	VF	XF	Unc	BU
1970 Proof	Est. 2,000	Value: 235				

KM# 30 7-1/2 RIYALS
22.5000 g., 0.9250 Silver 0.6691 oz. ASW **Ruler:** Saqr bin
Muhammad al Qasimi **Obv:** Head with headdress 1/4 right within
circle flanked by stars **Rev:** Falcon within circle

Date	Mintage	F	VF	XF	Unc	BU
AH1390 (1970)	—	—	—	—	100	—

KM# 5 7-1/2 RIYALS
22.5000 g., 0.9250 Silver 0.6691 oz. ASW **Ruler:** Saqr bin
Muhammad al Qasimi **Obv:** Value within circle **Rev:** Head of
Giacomo Agostini left

Date	Mintage	F	VF	XF	Unc	BU
ND (1970) Proof	Est. 2,000	Value: 400				

KM# 31 10 RIYALS
30.0000 g., 0.9250 Silver 0.8921 oz. ASW **Ruler:** Saqr bin
Muhammad al Qasimi **Subject:** 1st Anniversary - Death of
Dwight Eisenhower **Obv:** Value within circle **Rev:** Head left

Date	Mintage	F	VF	XF	Unc	BU
1970	4,500	—	—	—	18.50	20.00
1970 Proof	1,400	Value: 37.50				

KM# 6 10 RIYALS
30.0000 g., 0.9250 Silver 0.8921 oz. ASW **Ruler:** Saqr bin
Muhammad al Qasimi **Subject:** World Championship Football
Obv: Value within circle **Rev:** Jules Rimet Cup in front of soccer ball

Date	Mintage	F	VF	XF	Unc	BU
1970 Proof	Est. 2,000	Value: 350				

KM# 18 10 RIYALS
30.0000 g., 0.9250 Silver 0.8921 oz. ASW **Ruler:** Saqr bin
Muhammad al Qasimi **Subject:** Centennial of Rome **Obv:** Value
within circle **Rev:** Emperor standing with charging horses

Date	Mintage	F	VF	XF	Unc	BU
1970 Proof	Est. 2,000	Value: 175				

KM# 7 10 RIYALS
30.0000 g., 0.9250 Silver 0.8921 oz. ASW **Ruler:** Saqr bin
Muhammad al Qasimi **Subject:** Felice Gimondi **Obv:** Value
within circle **Rev:** Head left

Date	Mintage	F	VF	XF	Unc	BU
ND (1970) Proof	Est. 2,000	Value: 450				

KM# 8   15 RIYALS
45.0000 g., 0.9250 Silver 1.3382 oz. ASW **Ruler:** Saqr bin
Muhammad al Qasimi **Subject:** Champions of Sport **Obv:** Value
within circle **Rev:** Cluster of heads all facing left

Date	Mintage	F	VF	XF	Unc	BU
ND(1970) Proof	Est. 2,000	Value: 625				

KM# 19   15 RIYALS
45.0000 g., 0.9250 Silver 1.3382 oz. ASW **Ruler:** Saqr bin
Muhammad al Qasimi **Subject:** Centennial of Rome **Obv:** Value
within circle **Rev:** Three heads facing right

Date	Mintage	F	VF	XF	Unc	BU
1970 Proof	Est. 2,000	Value: 220				

KM# 33   15 RIYALS
45.0000 g., 0.9250 Silver 1.3382 oz. ASW **Ruler:** Saqr bin
Muhammad al Qasimi **Subject:** World Championship Football -
Jules Rimet Cup **Obv:** Value within circle **Rev:** Jules Rimet Cup
flanked by shields

Date	Mintage	F	VF	XF	Unc	BU
1970 Proof	—	Value: 525				

KM# 21   50 RIYALS
10.3500 g., 0.9000 Gold 0.2995 oz. AGW **Ruler:** Saqr bin
Muhammad al Qasimi **Subject:** Centennial of Italian Unification
Obv: Value within circle **Rev:** Head left

Date	Mintage	F	VF	XF	Unc	BU
1970 Proof	Est. 2,000	Value: 400				

KM# 10   50 RIYALS
10.3500 g., 0.9000 Gold 0.2995 oz. AGW **Ruler:** Saqr bin
Muhammad al Qasimi **Subject:** Gigi Riva **Obv:** Value within
circle **Rev:** Head left

Date	Mintage	F	VF	XF	Unc	BU
ND (1970) Proof	Est. 2,000	Value: 425				

KM# 22   75 RIYALS
15.5300 g., 0.9000 Gold 0.4494 oz. AGW **Ruler:** Saqr bin
Muhammad al Qasimi **Subject:** Centennial of Italian Unification,
Rome as the Capital **Obv:** Value within circle **Rev:** Figure with
gun walking left

Date	Mintage	F	VF	XF	Unc	BU
1970 Proof	Est. 2,000	Value: 525				

KM# 11   75 RIYALS
15.5300 g., 0.9000 Gold 0.4494 oz. AGW **Ruler:** Saqr bin
Muhammad al Qasimi **Subject:** Gianni Rivera **Obv:** Value within
circle **Rev:** Head left

Date	Mintage	F	VF	XF	Unc	BU
ND (1970) Proof	Est. 2,000	Value: 500				

KM# 12   100 RIYALS
20.7000 g., 0.9000 Gold 0.5989 oz. AGW **Ruler:** Saqr bin
Muhammad al Qasimi **Subject:** World Chmapionship Football -
Jules Rimet Cup **Obv:** Value within circle **Rev:** Jules Rimet Cup
in front of soccer ball

Date	Mintage	F	VF	XF	Unc	BU
1970 Proof	Est. 2,000	Value: 675				

KM# 23   100 RIYALS
20.7000 g., 0.9000 Gold 0.5989 oz. AGW **Ruler:** Saqr bin
Muhammad al Qasimi **Subject:** Centennial of Italian Unification
- WWI Victory

Date	Mintage	F	VF	XF	Unc	BU
1970 Proof	Est. 2,000	Value: 625				

KM# 24   100 RIYALS
31.0500 g., 0.9000 Gold 0.8984 oz. AGW **Ruler:** Saqr bin
Muhammad al Qasimi **Subject:** Centennial of Italian Unification
Rev: Standing Italia

Date	Mintage	F	VF	XF	Unc	BU
1970 Proof	Est. 2,000	Value: 1,000				

KM# 13   150 RIYALS
31.0500 g., 0.9000 Gold 0.8984 oz. AGW **Ruler:** Saqr bin
Muhammad al Qasimi **Series:** 1972 Munich Olympics **Obv:** Value
within circle **Rev:** Figures within olympic circles and flaming torch

Date	Mintage	F	VF	XF	Unc	BU
ND (1970) Proof	3,060	Value: 1,850				

KM# 25   200 RIYALS
41.4000 g., 0.9000 Gold 1.1979 oz. AGW **Ruler:** Saqr bin
Muhammad al Qasimi **Subject:** Centennial of Italian Unification
- Romulus and Remus **Obv:** Value within circle **Rev:** Wolf within
designed circle

Date	Mintage	F	VF	XF	Unc	BU
1970 Proof	Est. 2,000	Value: 1,300				

KM# 14   200 RIYALS
41.4000 g., 0.9000 Gold 1.1979 oz. AGW **Ruler:** Saqr bin
Muhammad al Qasimi **Subject:** Champions of Sport
Note: Similar to KM#8.

Date	Mintage	F	VF	XF	Unc	BU
ND (1970) Proof	Est. 2,000	Value: 1,450				

ESSAIS

KM#	Date	Mintage	Identification	Mkt Val
E1	1969	—	Riyal. Value within circle. Crossed flags within wreath. With ASSAY.	15.00
E2	1969	—	2 Riyals. Value within circle. Crossed flags within wreath. With ASSAY.	22.50
E3	1969	—	5 Riyals. Value within circle. Crossed flags within wreath. With ASSAY.	37.50
E4	1970	—	10 Riyals. With ASSAY.	45.00

MINT SETS

KM#	Date	Mintage	Identification	Issue Price	Mkt Val
MS1	1969 (3)	—	KM#1-3	—	55.00

PROOF SETS

KM#	Date	Mintage	Identification	Issue Price	Mkt Val
PS1	1969 (3)	1,500	KM#1-3	10.80	100
PS2	(1970) (9)	—	KM#5-8, 10-14	—	6,850
PS3	1970 (8)	—	KM#17-19, 21-25	—	4,500
PS4	(1970) (5)	—	KM#10-14	—	5,000
PS5	1970 (5)	—	KM#21-25	—	4,000
PS6	(1970) (4)	—	KM#5-8	41.50	2,000
PS7	1970 (3)	—	KM#17-19	—	600
PS8	1970 (4)	—	KM#6, 10-12	—	2,000

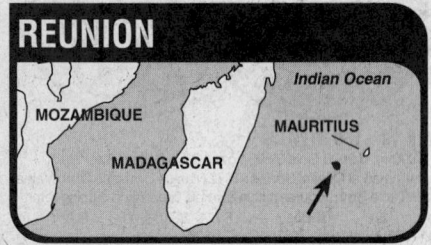

REUNION

MOZAMBIQUE

Indian Ocean

MADAGASCAR

MAURITIUS

The Department of Reunion, an overseas department of France located in the Indian Ocean 400 miles (640 km.) east of Madagascar, has an area of 969 sq. mi. (2,510 sq. km.) and a population of *566,000. Capital: Saint-Denis. The island's volcanic soil is extremely fertile. Sugar, vanilla, coffee and rum are exported.

Although first visited by Portuguese navigators in the 16th century, Reunion was uninhabited when claimed for France by Capt. Goubert in 1638. The French first colonized the Isle de Bourbon in 1662 as a layover station for ships rounding the Cape of Good Hope to India. It was renamed Reunion in 1793. The island remained in French possession except for the period of 1810-15, when the British occupied it. Reunion became an overseas department of France in 1946, and in 1958 voted to continue that status within the new French Union.

During the first half of the 19th century, Reunion was officially known as Isle de Bonaparte (1801-14) and Isle de Bourbon (1814-48). Reunion coinage of those periods is so designated.

The world debut of the Euro was here on January 1, 2002.

MINT MARK
(a) – Paris, privy marks only

MONETARY SYSTEM
100 Centimes = 1 Franc

FRENCH OVERSEAS DEPARTMENT

STANDARD COINAGE

KM# 6.1 FRANC
Aluminum, 23 mm. **Obv:** Winged liberty head left **Rev:** Sugar cane plants divide value **Edge:** Plain

Date	Mintage	F	VF	XF	Unc	BU
1948(a)	3,000,000	—	0.35	0.60	2.50	3.00
1964(a)	1,000,000	—	0.35	0.60	3.00	3.50
1968(a)	450,000	—	0.60	1.25	4.50	5.50
1969(a)	500,000	—	0.60	0.85	3.50	4.00
1971(a)	800,000	—	0.60	0.85	3.00	3.50
1973(a)	500,000	—	0.60	0.85	3.50	4.00

KM# 6.2 FRANC
Aluminum **Note:** Thinner planchet.

Date	Mintage	F	VF	XF	Unc	BU
1969(a)	Inc. above	—	0.75	1.50	5.00	6.00

KM# 7 FRANC
Aluminum **Obv:** Winged liberty head left **Rev:** Sugar cane plants divide value **Note:** Mule.

Date	Mintage	F	VF	XF	Unc	BU
1948(a)	Inc. above	—	650	1,300	2,600	—

KM# 8 2 FRANCS
Aluminum **Obv:** Winged liberty head left **Rev:** Sugar cane plants divide value

Date	Mintage	F	VF	XF	Unc	BU
1948(a)	2,000,000	—	0.35	0.85	3.50	4.00
1968(a)	100,000	—	3.00	5.00	10.00	12.50
1969(a)	150,000	—	1.75	3.50	6.50	9.00
1970(a)	300,000	—	0.85	1.75	4.00	4.50
1971(a)	300,000	—	0.85	1.75	4.00	4.50
1973(a)	500,000	—	0.85	1.75	4.00	4.50

KM# 9 5 FRANCS
Aluminum **Obv:** Winged liberty head left **Rev:** Sugar cane plants divides value

Date	Mintage	F	VF	XF	Unc	BU
1955(a)	3,000,000	—	0.60	1.00	3.00	3.50
1969(a)	100,000	—	2.50	5.00	9.00	11.50
1970(a)	200,000	—	1.75	3.50	6.50	9.00
1971(a)	100,000	—	1.75	3.50	6.50	9.00
1972(a)	300,000	—	0.85	1.75	3.50	4.00
1973(a)	250,000	—	0.85	1.75	3.50	4.00

KM# 10 10 FRANCS
Aluminum-Bronze **Obv:** Winged liberty head left **Rev:** Crowned shield divides value

Date	Mintage	F	VF	XF	Unc	BU
1955(a)	1,500,000	—	0.45	0.75	3.00	3.50
1962(a)	700,000	—	1.75	3.50	6.50	9.00
1964(a)	1,000,000	—	0.45	0.75	3.00	3.50

KM# 10a 10 FRANCS
Aluminum-Nickel-Bronze **Obv:** Winged Liberty head left **Rev:** Crowned shield divides value

Date	Mintage	F	VF	XF	Unc	BU
1964(a)	Inc. above	—	0.45	0.75	3.00	3.50
1969(a)	300,000	—	1.25	2.50	6.00	7.00
1970(a)	300,000	—	1.25	2.50	5.00	6.00
1971(a)	200,000	—	1.75	3.75	7.50	10.00
1972(a)	400,000	—	1.25	2.50	6.00	7.00
1973(a)	700,000	—	0.85	1.75	3.50	4.00

KM# 11 20 FRANCS
Aluminum-Bronze **Obv:** Winged liberty head left **Rev:** Crowned shield divides value

Date	Mintage	F	VF	XF	Unc	BU
1955(a)	1,250,000	—	0.75	1.50	4.00	4.50
1960(a)	100,000	—	3.00	6.00	12.00	15.00
1961(a)	300,000	—	2.50	4.75	8.00	10.00
1962(a)	190,000	—	2.75	5.50	9.00	12.00
1964(a)	750,000	—	0.75	1.50	3.50	4.00

KM# 11a 20 FRANCS
Aluminum-Nickel-Bronze **Obv:** Winged Liberty head left **Rev:** Crowned shield divides value

Date	Mintage	F	VF	XF	Unc	BU
1969(a)	200,000	—	2.75	5.50	9.00	12.00
1970(a)	200,000	—	2.75	5.50	9.00	12.00
1971(a)	200,000	—	2.75	5.50	9.00	12.00
1972(a)	300,000	—	2.00	3.50	6.50	8.50
1973(a)	550,000	—	0.75	1.50	3.50	4.50

KM# 12 50 FRANCS
Nickel **Obv:** Winged liberty head left **Rev:** Crowned shield divides value

Date	Mintage	F	VF	XF	Unc	BU
1962(a)	1,000,000	—	1.50	2.50	5.00	6.00
1964(a)	500,000	—	2.00	3.00	6.00	7.50
1969(a)	100,000	—	2.75	5.00	9.00	12.00
1970(a)	100,000	—	2.75	5.00	9.00	12.00
1973(a)	350,000	—	2.00	3.50	6.50	8.00

KM# 13 100 FRANCS
8.5400 g., Nickel, 26.5 mm. **Obv:** Winged liberty head left **Rev:** Crowned shield divides value

Date	Mintage	F	VF	XF	Unc	BU
1964(a)	2,000,000	—	1.00	2.00	4.00	5.00
1969(a)	200,000	—	2.25	4.50	7.50	9.50
1970(a)	150,000	—	2.25	5.00	9.00	12.00
1971(a)	200,000	—	2.75	6.00	12.50	15.00
1972(a)	300,000	—	2.00	3.50	6.00	7.50
1973(a)	550,000	—	2.25	4.50	7.50	9.50

TOKEN COINAGE

KM# Tn1 5 CENTIMES
Aluminum **Note:** Bank token. Demonetized 1941.

Date	Mintage	F	VF	XF	Unc	BU
1920	500,000	30.00	75.00	200	550	900

KM# Tn2 10 CENTIMES
Aluminum **Note:** Bank token. Demonetized 1941.

Date	Mintage	F	VF	XF	Unc	BU
1920	250,000	35.00	75.00	200	550	900

KM# Tn3 25 CENTIMES
Aluminum **Note:** Bank token. Demonetized 1941.

Date	Mintage	F	VF	XF	Unc	BU
1920	120,000	50.00	100	275	800	1,250

ESSAIS

Standard metals unless otherwise noted

KM#	Date	Mintage	Identification	Mkt Val
E3	1948(a)	2,000	Franc. Copper-Nickel. KM6.1.	50.00
E4	1948(a)	2,000	2 Francs. Copper-Nickel. KM8.	50.00
E5	1955(a)	1,200	5 Francs. Aluminum. KM9.	35.00
E6	1955(a)	2,000	10 Francs. Aluminum-Bronze. KM10.	35.00
E7	1955(a)	1,200	20 Francs. Aluminum-Bronze. KM11.	40.00
E8	1962(a)	1,200	50 Francs. Nickel. KM12.	40.00
E9	1964(a)	2,000	50 Francs. Nickel. KM12.	40.00
E10	1964(a)	2,000	100 Francs. Nickel. KM13.	50.00

PIEFORTS WITH ESSAI

Double thickness; standard metals unless otherwise noted

KM#	Date	Mintage	Identification	Mkt Val
PE3	1948(a)	104	Franc. Aluminum. KM6.1.	100
PE4	1948(a)	104	2 Francs. Aluminum. KM8.	110

"FDC" SETS

KM#	Date	Mintage	Identification	Issue Price	Mkt Val
SS1	1964 (5)	—	KM6.1, 10-13. Issued with Comoros set.	—	25.00

RHODESIA

The Republic of Rhodesia or Southern Rhodesia (now known as the Republic of Zimbabwe), located in the east-central part of southern Africa, has an area of 150,804 sq. mi. (390,580sq. km.) and a population of *10.1 million. Capital: Harare (formerly Salisbury). The economy is based on agriculture and mining. Tobacco, sugar, asbestos, copper, chrome, ore and coal are exported.

The Rhodesian area contains extensive evidence of the habitat of paleolithic man and earlier civilizations, notably the world-famous ruins of Zimbabwe, a gold-trading center that flourished about the 14th or 15th century A.D. The Portuguese of the 16th century were the first Europeans to attempt to develop south-central Africa, but it remained for Cecil Rhodes and the British South Africa Co. to open the hinterlands. Rhodes obtained a concession for mineral rights from local chiefs in 1888 and administered his African empire (named Southern Rhodesia in 1895) through the British South Africa Co. until 1923, when the British government annexed the area after the white settlers voted for existence as a separate entity, rather than for incorporation into the Union of South Africa. From Sept. of 1953 through 1963 Southern Rhodesia was joined with the British Protectorates of Northern Rhodesia and Nyasaland into a multiracial federation, known as the Federation of Rhodesia and Nyasaland. When the federation was dissolved at the end of 1963, Northern Rhodesia and Nyasaland became the independent states of Zambia and Malawi.

Britain was prepared to grant independence to Southern Rhodesia but declined to do so when the politically dominant white Rhodesians refused to give assurances of representative government. On Nov. 11, 1965, following two years of unsuccessful negotiation with the British government, Prime Minister Ian Smith issued an unilateral declaration of independence. Britain responded with economic sanctions supported by the United Nations. After further futile attempts to effect an accommodation, the Rhodesian Parliament severed all ties with Britain and on March 2, 1970, established the Republic of Rhodesia.

On March 3, 1978, Prime Minister Ian Smith and three moderate black nationalist leaders signed an agreement providing for black majority rule. The name of the country was changed to Zimbabwe Rhodesia. Following a conference in London in December 1979, the opposition government conceded and it was agreed that the British Government should resume control. A British Governor soon returned to Southern Rhodesia. One of his first acts was to affirm the nullification of the purported declaration of independence. On April 18, 1980 pursuant to an act of the British Parliament, the colony of Southern Rhodesia became independent as the Republic of Zimbabwe, which remains a member of the British Commonwealth of Nations.

RULER
British, until 1966

MONETARY SYSTEM
12 Pence = 1 Shilling = 10 Cents
10 Shillings = 1 Dollar
20 Shillings = 1 Pound

BRITISH COLONY
Self-Governing
POUND COINAGE

KM# 8   3 PENCE = 2-1/2 CENTS
Copper-Nickel **Obv:** Crowned bust of Queen Elizabeth II right **Rev:** Three spear points divides date

Date	Mintage	F	VF	XF	Unc	BU
1968	2,400,000	0.25	0.50	0.75	2.00	—
1968 Double shaft error	—	—	10.00	20.00	35.00	—
1968 Proof	10	Value: 1,200				

KM# 1   6 PENCE = 5 CENTS
Copper-Nickel, 19.5 mm. **Obv:** Crowned bust of Queen Elizabeth II right **Rev:** Flame lily

Date	Mintage	F	VF	XF	Unc	BU
1964	13,500,000	0.15	0.25	0.40	1.25	—
1964 Proof	2,060	Value: 15.00				

KM# 2   SHILLING = 10 CENTS
Copper-Nickel, 23.5 mm. **Obv:** Crowned bust of Queen Elizabeth II right **Rev:** Shield

Date	Mintage	F	VF	XF	Unc	BU
1964	15,500,000	0.15	0.25	0.65	1.50	—
1964 Proof	2,060	Value: 18.00				

KM# 3   2 SHILLINGS = 20 CENTS
Copper-Nickel **Obv:** Crowned bust of Queen Elizabeth II right **Rev:** Native headdress

Date	Mintage	F	VF	XF	Unc	BU
1964	10,500,000	0.25	0.50	1.25	3.00	—
1964 Proof	2,060	Value: 20.00				

KM# 4   2-1/2 SHILLINGS = 25 CENTS
14.0000 g., Copper-Nickel, 32.5 mm. **Obv:** Crowned bust of Queen Elizabeth II right **Rev:** Sable antelope

Date	Mintage	F	VF	XF	Unc	BU
1964	11,500,000	0.50	1.00	2.00	4.50	6.00
1964 Proof	2,060	Value: 25.00				

KM# 5   10 SHILLINGS
3.9940 g., 0.9160 Gold 0.1176 oz. AGW **Obv:** Crowned bust right **Rev:** Sable antelope

Date	Mintage	F	VF	XF	Unc	BU
1966 Proof	6,000	Value: 130				

KM# 6   POUND
7.9881 g., 0.9160 Gold 0.2352 oz. AGW **Obv:** Crowned bust right **Rev:** Lion

Date	Mintage	F	VF	XF	Unc	BU
1966 Proof	5,000	Value: 250				

KM# 7   5 POUNDS
39.9403 g., 0.9160 Gold 1.1762 oz. AGW **Obv:** Crowned bust of Queen Elizabeth II right **Rev:** Arms with supporters divides date

Date	Mintage	F	VF	XF	Unc	BU
1966 Proof	3,000	Value: 1,200				

REPUBLIC
DECIMAL COINAGE

KM# 9   1/2 CENT
Bronze, 20 mm. **Obv:** Value and date to upper left of sprig **Rev:** Arms with supporters

Date	Mintage	F	VF	XF	Unc	BU
1970	10,000,000	—	0.10	0.50	1.00	—
1970 Proof	12	Value: 1,000				
1971	2,000,000	—	0.10	0.50	1.25	—
1972	2,000,000	—	0.10	0.50	1.25	—
1972 Proof	12	Value: 1,000				
1975	10,001,000	—	0.10	0.20	0.50	—
1975 Proof	10	Value: 1,000				
1977	—	—	—	800	1,500	—

Note: Circulation mintage melted, less than 10 surviving specimens known

1977 Proof	10	Value: 1,500				

KM# 10   CENT
4.0000 g., Bronze, 22.5 mm. **Obv:** Value and date to upper left of sprig **Rev:** Arms with supporters

Date	Mintage	F	VF	XF	Unc	BU
1970	25,000,000	—	0.10	0.50	1.00	—
1970 Proof	12	Value: 900				
1971	15,000,000	—	0.10	0.50	1.00	—
1972	10,000,000	—	0.10	0.50	1.00	—
1972 Proof	12	Value: 900				
1973	5,000,000	—	0.10	0.50	1.50	—
1973 Proof	10	Value: 900				
1974	—	—	0.10	0.50	1.00	—
1975	10,000,000	—	0.10	0.50	1.00	—
1975 Proof	10	Value: 900				
1976	20,000,000	—	0.10	0.20	0.50	—
1976 Proof	10	Value: 900				
1977	10,000,000	—	0.10	0.20	0.50	—

KM# 11   2-1/2 CENTS
Copper-Nickel **Obv:** Three spear points divides date below value **Rev:** Arms with supporters

Date	Mintage	F	VF	XF	Unc	BU
1970	4,000,000	0.15	0.25	0.70	1.50	—
1970 Proof	12	Value: 950				

KM# 12   5 CENTS
3.0000 g., Copper-Nickel **Obv:** Flame lily divides date **Rev:** Arms with supporters

Date	Mintage	F	VF	XF	Unc	BU
1973	—	0.25	0.75	1.50	3.00	—
1973 Proof	10	Value: 950				

KM# 13 5 CENTS
Copper-Nickel **Obv:** Flame lily **Rev:** Arms with supporters

Date	Mintage	F	VF	XF	Unc	BU
1975	3,500,000	0.15	0.25	0.50	1.00	—
1975 Proof	10	Value: 900				
1976	8,038,000	0.15	0.25	0.50	1.00	—
1977	3,015,000	0.25	0.75	1.50	3.00	—

KM# 14 10 CENTS
Copper-Nickel **Obv:** Arms with supporters **Rev:** Shield, value and date

Date	Mintage	F	VF	XF	Unc	BU
1975	2,003,000	0.15	0.30	0.60	1.50	—
1975 Proof	10	Value: 950				

KM# 15 20 CENTS
Copper-Nickel **Obv:** Arms with supporters **Rev:** Native headdress, value and date

Date	Mintage	F	VF	XF	Unc	BU
1975	1,937,000	0.50	0.75	1.00	3.00	—
1975 Proof	10	Value: 950				
1977	—	0.50	0.75	1.50	3.50	—

KM# 16 25 CENTS
Copper-Nickel **Obv:** Arms with supporters **Rev:** Sable antelope, value and date

Date	Mintage	F	VF	XF	Unc	BU
1975	1,011,000	0.50	1.00	2.00	5.00	7.50
1975 Proof	10	Value: 950				

PROOF SETS

KM#	Date	Mintage	Identification	Issue Price	Mkt Val
PS1	1964 (8)	10	KM#1-4 Double set	—	250
PS2	1964 (4)	2,060	KM#1-4	—	50.00
PS3	1966 (3)	2,000	KM#5-7	280	1,600
PS4	1968 (2)	3	KM#8 Double set	—	2,250
PS5	1970 (6)	3	KM#9-11 Double set	—	5,000
PS6	1973 (2)	2	KM#12 Double set	—	1,500
PS7	1975 (8)	1	KM#13-16 Double set	—	7,000
PS8	1975 (6)	4	KM#9, 10, 13-16	—	5,000
PS9	1975 (4)	4	KM#13-16	—	3,500

RHODESIA & NYASALAND

The Federation of Rhodesia and Nyasaland was located in the east-central part of southern Africa. The multiracial federation has an area of about 487,000 sq. mi. (1,261,330 sq. km.) and a population of 6.8 million. Capital: Salisbury, in Southern Rhodesia.

The geographical unity of the three British possessions suggested the desirability of political and economic union as early as 1924. Despite objections by the African constituency of Northern Rhodesia and Nyasaland, who feared that African self-determination would be retarded by the dominant influence of prosperous and self-governing Southern Rhodesia. The Central African Federation was established in Sept. of 1953. As feared by the European constituency, Southern Rhodesia despite the fact that the three component countries largely retained their pre-federation political structure effectively and profitably dominated the Federation. It was dissolved at the end of 1963, largely because of the effective opposition of the Nyasaland African Congress. Northern Rhodesia and Nyasaland became the independent states of Zambia and Malawi in 1964. Southern Rhodesia unilaterally declared its independence the following year, which was not recognized by the British Government.

For earlier coinage refer to Southern Rhodesia. For later coinage refer to Malawi, Zambia, Rhodesia and Zimbabwe.

RULER
Elizabeth II, 1952-1964

MONETARY SYSTEM
12 Pence = 1 Shilling
5 Shillings = 1 Crown
20 Shillings = 1 Pound

FEDERATION
STANDARD COINAGE

KM# 1 1/2 PENNY
Bronze, 21 mm. **Ruler:** Elizabeth II **Obv:** Hole in center flanked by giraffes with crown above **Rev:** Value around hole in center flanked by sprigs

Date	Mintage	F	VF	XF	Unc	BU
1955	720,000	0.15	0.25	0.50	4.00	6.00
1955 Proof	2,010	Value: 5.00				
1956	480,000	0.20	0.50	1.00	4.00	6.00
1956 Proof	—	Value: 400				
1957	1,920,000	0.10	0.15	0.25	4.00	6.00
1957 Proof	—	Value: 400				
1958	2,400,000	0.10	0.15	0.25	4.00	6.00
1958 Proof	—	Value: 400				
1964	1,440,000	0.10	0.15	0.25	4.00	6.00

KM# 2 PENNY
6.3000 g., Bronze **Ruler:** Elizabeth II **Obv:** Hole in center and crown flanked by elephants **Rev:** Value around hole in center flanked by sprigs

Date	Mintage	F	VF	XF	Unc	BU
1955	2,040,000	0.15	0.25	0.75	4.50	7.50
1955 Proof	2,010	Value: 5.50				

Date	Mintage	F	VF	XF	Unc	BU
1956	4,800,000	0.15	0.25	0.50	4.50	7.50
1956 Proof	—	Value: 400				
1957	7,200,000	0.10	0.15	0.25	4.50	7.50
1957 Proof	—					
1958	2,880,000	0.10	0.15	0.25	4.50	7.50
1958 Proof	—	Value: 400				
1961	4,800,000	0.10	0.15	0.25	4.50	7.50
1961 Proof	—					
1962	6,000,000	0.10	0.15	0.25	4.50	7.50
1963	6,000,000	0.10	0.15	0.25	4.50	7.50
1963 Proof	—	Value: 400				

KM# 3 3 PENCE
Copper-Nickel, 16.3 mm. **Ruler:** Elizabeth II **Obv:** Bust right **Rev:** Flame lily divides date

Date	Mintage	F	VF	XF	Unc	BU
1955	1,200,000	0.20	0.50	1.00	4.00	—
1955 Proof	10	Value: 400				
1956	3,200,000	0.50	1.00	2.50	20.00	—
1956 Proof	—	Value: 600				
1957	6,000,000	0.20	0.50	0.75	3.00	—
1957 Proof	—	Value: 600				
1962	4,000,000	0.20	0.50	0.75	3.00	—
1962 Proof	—					
1963	2,000,000	0.20	0.50	0.75	3.00	—
1963 Proof	—					
1964	3,600,000	0.15	0.25	0.50	1.50	—

KM# 3a 3 PENCE
1.4100 g., 0.5000 Silver 0.0227 oz. ASW, 16.3 mm. **Ruler:** Elizabeth II **Obv:** Bust laureate right **Rev:** Flame lily divides date

Date	Mintage	F	VF	XF	Unc	BU
1955 Proof	2,000	Value: 7.50				

KM# 4 6 PENCE
Copper-Nickel **Ruler:** Elizabeth II **Obv:** Bust right **Rev:** Lion standing on rock

Date	Mintage	F	VF	XF	Unc	BU
1955	400,000	0.50	1.00	2.50	7.50	10.00
1955 Proof	10	Value: 400				
1956	800,000	0.75	2.00	7.00	40.00	—
1956 Proof	—					
1957	4,000,000	0.20	0.50	1.00	4.00	7.50
1957 Proof	—					
1962	2,800,000	0.20	0.50	1.00	4.00	8.00
1962 Proof	—					
1963	800,000	5.00	10.00	20.00	45.00	—
1963 Proof	—					

KM# 4a 6 PENCE
2.8300 g., 0.5000 Silver 0.0455 oz. ASW **Ruler:** Elizabeth II **Obv:** Bust laureate right **Rev:** Lion staning on rock

Date	Mintage	F	VF	XF	Unc	BU
1955 Proof	2,000	Value: 10.00				

KM# 5 SHILLING
Copper-Nickel **Ruler:** Elizabeth II **Obv:** Bust right **Rev:** Sable antelope

Date	Mintage	F	VF	XF	Unc	BU
1955	200,000	1.50	2.50	7.00	18.00	—
1955 Proof	10	Value: 400				
1956	1,700,000	0.75	1.50	3.50	30.00	—
1956 Proof	—					
1957	3,500,000	0.50	1.00	2.50	8.00	10.00
1957 Proof	—					

KM# 5a SHILLING
5.6600 g., 0.5000 Silver 0.0910 oz. ASW **Ruler:** Elizabeth II **Obv:** Bust laureate right **Rev:** Antelope

Date	Mintage	F	VF	XF	Unc	BU
1955 Proof	2,000	Value: 25.00				

KM# 6 2 SHILLINGS
Copper-Nickel **Ruler:** Elizabeth II **Obv:** Bust right **Rev:** Eagle with talons in fish flanked by initials

Date	Mintage	F	VF	XF	Unc	BU
1955	1,750,000	1.25	2.50	5.00	12.50	—
1955 Proof	10	Value: 400				
1956	1,850,000	1.25	2.50	4.50	12.00	—
1956 Proof	—	—	—	—	—	—
1957	1,500,000	1.25	2.50	4.50	12.00	—
1957 Proof	—	—	—	—	—	—

KM# 6a 2 SHILLINGS
11.3100 g., 0.5000 Silver 0.1818 oz. ASW **Ruler:** Elizabeth II **Obv:** Bust laureate right **Rev:** Eagle with talons in fish

Date	Mintage	F	VF	XF	Unc	BU
1955 Proof	2,000	Value: 30.00				

KM# 7 1/2 CROWN
Copper-Nickel **Ruler:** Elizabeth II **Obv:** Bust right **Rev:** Arms with supporters

Date	Mintage	F	VF	XF	Unc	BU
1955	1,600,000	1.50	3.00	6.00	15.00	—
1955 Proof	10	Value: 550				
1956	160,000	7.50	15.00	35.00	250	—
1956 Proof	—	—	—	—	—	—
1957	2,400,000	7.50	15.00	35.00	75.00	—
1957 Proof	—	—	—	—	—	—

KM# 7a 1/2 CROWN
14.1400 g., 0.5000 Silver 0.2273 oz. ASW **Ruler:** Elizabeth II **Obv:** Bust laureate right **Rev:** Arms with supporters

Date	Mintage	F	VF	XF	Unc	BU
1955 Proof	2,000	Value: 35.00				

PROOF SETS

KM#	Date	Mintage	Identification	Issue Price	Mkt Val
PS1	1955 (7)	10	KM1-7	—	2,200
PS2	1955 (7)	2,000	KM1-2, 3a-7a	—	110

ROMANIA

Romania (formerly the Socialist Republic of Romania), a country in southeast Europe, has an area of 91,699 sq. mi. (237,500 sq. km.) and a population of 23.2 million. Capital: Bucharest. Machinery, foodstuffs, raw minerals and petroleum products are exported. Heavy industry and oil have become increasingly important to the economy since 1959.

A new constitution was adopted in 1923. During this period in history, the Romanian government struggled with domestic problems, agrarian reform and economic reconstruction.

On August 23, 1944, King Mihai I proclaimed an armistice with the Allied Forces. The Romanian army drove out the Germans and Hungarians in northern Transylvania, but the country was subsequently occupied by the Soviet army. That monarchy was abolished on December 30, 1947, and Romania became a "People's Republic" based on the Soviet regime. The process of sovietization included Soviet regime. The anti-Communist combative resistance movement developed frequent purges of dissidents: mainly political but also clerical, cultural and peasants. Romanian elite disappeared into the concentration camps. The anti-Communist combative resistance movement developed in spite of the Soviet army presence until 1956. The partisans remained in the mountains until 1964. With the accession of N. Ceausescu to power, Romania began to exercise a considerable degree of independence, refusing to participate in the invasion of Czechoslovakia (August 1968). In 1965, it was proclaimed a "Socialist Republic". After 1977, an oppressed and impoverished domestic scene worsened.

On December 17, 1989, an anti-Communist revolt in Timisoara. On December 22, 1989 the Communist government was overthrown. Ceausescu and his wife were arrested and later executed. The new government established a republic, the constitutional name being Romania.

RULERS
Carol I (as Prince), 1866-81 (as King), 1881-1914
Ferdinand I, 1914-1927
Mihai I, 1927-1930
Carol II, 1930-1940
Mihai I, 1940-1947

MINT MARKS
(a) - Paris, privy marks only
(b) - Brussels, privy marks only
angel head (1872-1876),
no marks (1894-1924)
B - Bucharest (1870-1900)
B - Hamburg, Germany
C - Candescu, chief engineer of the Bucharest Mint (1870-)
FM - Franklin Mint, USA
H - Heaton, Birmingham, England
HF - Huguenin Freres & Co., Le Locle, Switzerland
J - Hamburg
KN - Kings Norton, Birmingham, England
(p) - Thunderbolt - Poissy, France
zig zag (1924)
V - Vienna, Austria
W - Watt (James Watt & Co.)
Huguenin - Le Locle, Switzerland
( ) - no marks, 1930 (10, 20 Lei),
1932 (100 Lei), Royal Mint – London

MINT OFFICIALS' INITIALS

Initials	Date	Name
BASSARAB		Costache Bassarab
IOANA BASSARAB	1941-45	Ioana Bassarab Starostescu
E.W. BECKER (wing)	1939-40	E.W. Becker
P.M. DAMMANN	1922	P.M. Dammann
C.D.	1990	C. Dumitrescu
V.G.	1990	Vasile Gabor
H.I.; H.IONESCU	1939-52	Haralamb Ionescu
I. Jalea	1935-41	Ion Jalea
LAVRILLIER	1930-32	A. Larrillier
A.M.; A. MICHAUX	1906	Alfons Michaux
A. MURNU (torch)	1940	A. Murnu
		Henry Auguste Jules Patey
A. ROMANESCU	1946	A.Rromanescu
A. SCHARFF	1894-1901	Anton Scharff
TASSET	1910-14	Ernst Paulini Tasset

MONETARY SYSTEM
100 Bani = 1 Leu

KINGDOM
STANDARD COINAGE

KM# 31 5 BANI
2.5000 g., Copper-Nickel, 19 mm. **Ruler:** Carol I **Obv:** Crown above banner and hole in center **Rev:** Hole in center flanked by designs with value above and date below

Date	Mintage	F	VF	XF	Unc	BU
1905	2,000,000	1.00	2.50	10.00	25.00	—
1905 Proof	—	Value: 42.00				
1906	48,000,000	0.50	1.50	4.00	12.00	—
1906J	24,000,000	0.50	1.50	5.00	14.00	—

KM# 32 10 BANI
4.0000 g., Copper-Nickel, 22 mm. **Ruler:** Carol I **Obv:** Crown above banner and hole in center **Rev:** Hole in center flanked by designs with value above and date below

Date	Mintage	F	VF	XF	Unc	BU
1905	10,820,000	1.00	4.00	15.00	40.00	—
1906	24,180,000	0.50	1.50	8.00	30.00	—
1906J	17,000,000	0.50	1.50	9.00	32.00	—

KM# 33 20 BANI
6.0000 g., Copper-Nickel, 25 mm. **Ruler:** Carol I **Obv:** Crown above banner and hole in center **Rev:** Hole in center flanked by designs with value above and date below

Date	Mintage	F	VF	XF	Unc	BU
1905	2,500,000	3.00	10.00	26.00	85.00	—
1906	3,000,000	2.00	5.00	22.00	75.00	—
1906J	2,500,000	2.00	4.50	20.00	80.00	—

KM# 44 25 BANI
0.8960 g., Aluminum, 19 mm. **Ruler:** Ferdinand I **Obv:** Eagle above hole in center **Rev:** Hole in center of value with crown at right **Note:** Center hole sizes vary from 4 to 4.5mm.

Date	Mintage	F	VF	XF	Unc	BU
1921	20,000,000	0.50	1.50	3.00	8.00	—

KM# 23 50 BANI
2.5000 g., 0.8350 Silver 0.0671 oz. ASW **Ruler:** Carol I **Obv:** Head left **Rev:** Value, date within wreath **Edge:** Reeded

Date	Mintage	F	VF	XF	Unc	BU
1901	194,205	10.00	30.00	75.00	250	—

KM# 41 50 BANI
2.5000 g., 0.8350 Silver 0.0671 oz. ASW, 18 mm. **Ruler:** Carol I **Obv:** Head left **Rev:** Crown above design **Edge:** Reeded

Date	Mintage	F	VF	XF	Unc	BU
1910	3,600,000	1.50	3.50	8.50	20.00	—
1910 Proof	—	Value: 180				
1911	3,000,000	2.00	4.00	15.00	40.00	—
1912	1,800,000	1.50	3.50	13.00	30.00	—
1914	1,600,000	1.25	2.00	6.00	15.00	20.00
1914 Proof	—	Value: 135				

Note: Edge varieties (round or flat) exist

KM# 45 50 BANI
1.2030 g., Aluminum, 21 mm. **Ruler:** Ferdinand I **Obv:** Eagle above hole in center **Rev:** Hole in center of value with crown at right **Note:** Center hole size varies from 4 to 4.5mm.

Date	Mintage	F	VF	XF	Unc	BU
1921	30,000,000	0.50	1.50	4.00	9.00	—

KM# 24 LEU
5.0000 g., 0.8350 Silver 0.1342 oz. ASW, 23 mm. **Ruler:** Carol I **Edge:** Reeded

Date	Mintage	F	VF	XF	Unc	BU
1901	369,614	10.00	50.00	150	350	600
1901 Proof	—	Value: 1,000				

KM# 34 LEU
5.0000 g., 0.8350 Silver 0.1342 oz. ASW, 14 mm. **Ruler:** Carol I **Subject:** 40th Anniversary - Reign of Carol I **Obv:** Bearded head left **Rev:** Head left **Edge:** Reeded **Note:** Designer's name below truncation on reverse.

Date	Mintage	F	VF	XF	Unc	BU
ND(1906)	2,500,000	5.00	13.00	28.00	80.00	—
ND(1906) Proof	—	Value: 250				

KM# 42   LEU
5.0000 g., 0.8350 Silver 0.1342 oz. ASW **Ruler:** Carol I
Obv: Bearded head left **Rev:** Standing figure walking right
Edge: Reeded

Date	Mintage	F	VF	XF	Unc	BU
1910	4,600,000	3.00	6.00	18.00	35.00	—

Note: Edge varieties (round or flat) exist

1910 Proof	—	Value: 350				
1911	2,573,000	4.00	8.00	15.00	42.00	—
1912	3,540,000	3.00	5.00	10.00	32.00	—
1914	4,282,935	2.50	3.50	8.00	30.00	40.00

Note: Edge varieties (round or flat) exist

| 1914 Proof | — | Value: 120 | | | | |

KM# 46   LEU
3.5000 g., Copper-Nickel, 21 mm. **Ruler:** Ferdinand I
Obv: Crowned arms with supporters flanked by stars **Rev:** Value
above sprig **Edge:** Reeded

Date	Mintage	F	VF	XF	Unc	BU
1924(b) Thin	100,000,000	0.50	1.50	5.00	14.00	—
1924(p) Thick	100,006,000	0.50	1.50	6.00	16.00	—

KM# 56   LEU
2.7500 g., Nickel-Brass, 18 mm. **Ruler:** Carol II **Obv:** Crown
and date above sprig **Rev:** Ear of corn divides value **Edge:** Plain
Note: Without mint mark.

Date	Mintage	F	VF	XF	Unc	BU
1938	27,900,000	0.20	0.60	1.75	5.00	—
1939	72,200,000	0.20	0.50	1.50	3.00	—
1940	Inc. above	0.20	0.50	1.00	3.00	—
1941	Inc. above	0.20	0.50	1.50	3.50	—

KM# 25   2 LEI
10.0000 g., 0.8350 Silver 0.2684 oz. ASW **Ruler:** Carol I
Obv: Head left **Obv. Insc.:** CAROL I.... **Rev:** Crowned arms with
supporters within crowned mantle, divided value **Edge:** Reeded

Date	Mintage	F	VF	XF	Unc	BU
1901	12,476	450	800	1,500	3,000	—

KM# 43   2 LEI
10.0000 g., 0.8350 Silver 0.2684 oz. ASW **Ruler:** Carol I
Obv: Bearded head left **Rev:** Standing figure walking right

Date	Mintage	F	VF	XF	Unc	BU
1910	1,800,000	5.00	8.00	18.00	45.00	—

Note: Edge varieties (round and flat) exist

1910 Proof	—	Value: 250				
1911	1,000,000	6.00	12.00	30.00	60.00	—
1912	1,500,000	5.00	7.50	15.00	45.00	—
1914	2,452,000	4.50	6.00	13.00	38.00	50.00

Note: Edge varieties (round and flat) exist

| 1914 Proof | — | Value: 140 | | | | |

KM# 47   2 LEI
7.0000 g., Copper-Nickel, 25 mm. **Ruler:** Ferdinand I
Obv: Crowned arms with supporters flanked by stars **Rev:** Value
above sprig **Edge:** Reeded

Date	Mintage	F	VF	XF	Unc	BU
1924(b)	50,000,000	1.00	1.75	5.00	15.00	—
1924(p)	50,008,000	1.00	1.75	6.00	17.00	—

KM# 58   2 LEI
3.2000 g., Zinc, 20 mm. **Ruler:** Mihai I **Obv:** Crown above date
Rev: Value within wreath

Date	Mintage	F	VF	XF	Unc	BU
1941	101,778,000	0.50	2.00	6.00	14.00	—

KM# 17.2   5 LEI
25.0000 g., 0.9000 Silver 0.7234 oz. ASW, 38 mm.
Ruler: Carol I **Edge:** Reeded

Date	Mintage	F	VF	XF	Unc	BU
1901B	82,460	75.00	150	500	1,200	—
1901B Proof	—	Value: 3,000				

KM# 35   5 LEI
25.0000 g., 0.9000 Silver 0.7234 oz. ASW, 38 mm.
Ruler: Carol I **Subject:** 40th Anniversary - Reign of Carol I
Obv: Bearded head left **Rev:** Head left **Edge:** Reeded

Date	Mintage	F	VF	XF	Unc	BU
ND(1906)	200,000	80.00	200	500	1,000	—
ND(1906) Proof	—	Value: 1,500				

KM# 48   5 LEI
3.5000 g., Nickel-Brass, 21 mm. **Ruler:** Mihai I **Obv:** Head left
Rev: Crowned shield divides value flanked by stars **Edge:** Reeded

Date	Mintage	F	VF	XF	Unc	BU
1930H	15,000,000	1.50	3.00	10.00	35.00	—
1930KN	15,000,000	1.50	4.00	12.00	40.00	—
1930(a)	30,000,000	1.00	3.00	8.00	33.00	—

KM# 61   5 LEI
4.5000 g., Zinc, 23 mm. **Ruler:** Mihai I **Obv:** Crown above date
Rev: Oat sprigs to right of value

Date	Mintage	F	VF	XF	Unc	BU
1942	140,000,000	0.50	1.25	3.00	8.00	—

KM# 49   10 LEI
5.0000 g., Nickel-Brass, 23 mm. **Ruler:** Carol II **Obv:** Head left
Rev: Crowned eagle with crowned shield on chest divides value
Edge: Reeded

Date	Mintage	F	VF	XF	Unc	BU
1930	15,000,000	1.00	3.50	12.00	70.00	—
1930 Proof	—	Value: 200				
1930(a)	30,000,000	1.00	3.00	10.00	65.00	—
1930H	7,500,000	2.50	4.50	18.00	75.00	—
1930KN	7,500,000	3.00	7.00	20.00	80.00	—
1930(a) Proof	—	Value: 200				

KM# 36   12-1/2 LEI
4.0325 g., 0.9000 Gold 0.1167 oz. AGW, 19 mm. **Ruler:** Carol I
Subject: 40th Anniversary - Reign of Carol I **Obv:** Bearded bust
left **Rev:** Crowned eagle and banner

Date	Mintage	F	VF	XF	Unc	BU
1906	32,000	150	250	500	800	—

KM# 37   20 LEI
6.4516 g., 0.9000 Gold 0.1867 oz. AGW, 20 mm. **Ruler:** Carol I
Subject: 40th Anniversary - Reign of Carol I **Obv:** Bearded head
left **Rev:** Head left **Edge:** Reeded

Date	Mintage	F	VF	XF	Unc	BU
ND(1906)(b)	15,000	BV	250	600	900	—

KM# 50   20 LEI
7.5000 g., Nickel-Brass, 27 mm. **Ruler:** Mihai I **Obv:** Young head
left **Rev:** Figures holding hands divides value **Edge:** Reeded

Date	Mintage	F	VF	XF	Unc	BU
1930 London	40,000,000	2.50	7.00	22.00	45.00	—
1930 Proof	—	Value: 200				
1930H	5,000,000	3.00	8.00	28.00	60.00	—
1930KN	5,000,000	3.50	12.00	35.00	82.00	—

KM# 51 20 LEI

7.5000 g., Nickel-Brass, 27 mm. **Ruler:** Carol II **Obv:** Head left
Rev: Crowned eagle with crowned shield on chest divides value
Edge: Reeded

Date	Mintage	F	VF	XF	Unc	BU
1930	6,750,000	2.00	5.00	18.00	35.00	—
1930 Proof	—	—	—	—	—	—
1930(a)	17,500,000	1.40	4.00	13.00	27.00	—
1930(a) Proof	—	Value: 180				
1930KN	7,750,000	3.00	8.00	30.00	63.00	—
1930KN Proof	—	Value: 200				
1930H	7,750,000	2.50	5.00	20.00	48.00	—
1930H Proof	—	Value: 220				

KM# 62 20 LEI

6.0000 g., Zinc, 26 mm. **Ruler:** Mihai I **Obv:** Crown above date
Rev: Value within wreath **Edge:** Reeded

Date	Mintage	F	VF	XF	Unc	BU
1942	44,000,000	0.75	1.50	3.00	8.50	—
1943	25,783,000	1.00	2.25	4.00	9.00	—
1944	5,034,000	1.50	3.00	5.00	13.00	—

KM# 38 25 LEI

8.0650 g., 0.9000 Gold 0.2334 oz. AGW, 30 mm. **Ruler:** Carol I
Subject: 40th Anniversary - Reign of Carol I **Obv:** Uniformed
bust left **Rev:** Crowned eagle and banner

Date	Mintage	F	VF	XF	Unc	BU
ND(1906)(b)	24,000	BV	375	650	1,000	—

KM# 39 50 LEI

16.1300 g., 0.9000 Gold 0.4667 oz. AGW, 35 mm. **Ruler:** Carol I
Subject: 40th Anniversary - Reign of Carol I **Obv:** Uniformed
bust left **Rev:** Equestrian

Date	Mintage	F	VF	XF	Unc	BU
ND(1906)(b)	28,000	BV	600	1,200	2,400	—

KM# 55 50 LEI

5.8300 g., Nickel, 24 mm. **Ruler:** Carol II **Obv:** Helmeted head
left **Rev:** Crowned shield within sprigs divides value
Edge: Reeded **Note:** 16,731 pieces melted.

Date	Mintage	F	VF	XF	Unc	BU
1937	12,000,000	1.25	2.50	8.00	25.00	—
1938	8,000,000	3.00	6.00	18.00	45.00	—

KM# 40 100 LEI

32.2600 g., 0.9000 Gold 0.9334 oz. AGW, 36 mm. **Ruler:** Carol I
Subject: 40th Anniversary - Reign of Carol I **Note:** Similar to KM#35.

Date	Mintage	F	VF	XF	Unc	BU
ND(1906)(b)	3,000	BV	1,250	2,500	4,000	—

KM# 52 100 LEI

14.0000 g., 0.5000 Silver 0.2250 oz. ASW, 31 mm.
Ruler: Carol II **Obv:** Head right **Rev:** Crowned eagle divides
wreath with value within **Edge:** Reeded

Date	Mintage	F	VF	XF	Unc	BU
1932(a)	2,000,000	10.00	20.00	60.00	250	325
1932	16,400,000	5.00	10.00	30.00	180	250
1932 Proof	—	Value: 800				

KM# 54 100 LEI

8.2000 g., Nickel, 27 mm. **Ruler:** Carol II **Obv:** Head left
Rev: Crowned shield within sprigs flanked by value
Edge: Reeded **Note:** 17,030 pieces melted.

Date	Mintage	F	VF	XF	Unc	BU
1936	20,230,000	2.00	4.00	12.00	35.00	—
1938	3,250,000	3.00	8.00	20.00	60.00	—

KM# 64 100 LEI

8.5000 g., Nickel Clad Steel, 28 mm. **Ruler:** Mihai I **Obv:** Head
right **Rev:** Crown divides wreath with date and value within
Edge: Incuse lettering **Edge:** NIHIL SINE DEO

Date	Mintage	F	VF	XF	Unc	BU
1943	40,590,000	0.25	0.50	2.00	7.00	—

Note: Portrait varieties exist

| 1944 | 21,289,000 | 0.25 | 0.50 | 3.00 | 10.00 | — |

KM# 63 200 LEI

6.0000 g., 0.8350 Silver 0.1611 oz. ASW, 24 mm. **Ruler:** Mihai I
Obv: Head right **Rev:** Crowned arms with supporters
Edge: Incuse lettering **Edge:** NIHIL SINE DEO

Date	Mintage	F	VF	XF	Unc	BU
1942	30,025,000	2.75	4.00	8.00	22.00	—

KM# 66 200 LEI

7.5000 g., Brass, 27 mm. **Ruler:** Mihai I **Obv:** Head right
Rev: Crown divides wreath with date and value within **Note:** Many
were silver-plated privately.

Date	Mintage	F	VF	XF	Unc	BU
1945	1,399,000	1.00	2.00	6.00	16.00	—

KM# 53 250 LEI

13.5000 g., 0.7500 Silver 0.3255 oz. ASW, 29 mm.
Ruler: Carol II **Obv:** Head left **Rev:** Crowned eagle with shield
on chest

Date	Mintage	F	VF	XF	Unc	BU
1935	4,500,000	22.00	60.00	180	400	700

Note: Bank reports show that between 1937-39 4,490,670
pieces were withdrawn and remelted

KM# 57 250 LEI

12.0000 g., 0.8350 Silver 0.3221 oz. ASW, 30 mm.
Ruler: Carol II **Obv:** Head right **Rev:** Crowned shield divides
wreath with date and value within **Edge:** Incuse lettering, line
interrupted by two rhombs **Edge:** MUNCA CREDINTA REGE
NATIUNE

Date	Mintage	F	VF	XF	Unc	BU
1939	10,000,000	7.00	12.00	36.00	110	—
1940	8,000,000	12.00	22.00	56.00	160	—

KM# 59.1 250 LEI

12.0000 g., 0.8350 Silver 0.3221 oz. ASW **Ruler:** Carol II
Obv: Head left **Rev:** Date divided by portcullis **Edge:** Incuse
lettering **Edge:** TOTUL PENTRU TARA **Note:** Mintage unissued
and reportedly melted.

Date	Mintage	F	VF	XF	Unc	BU
1940	—	—	—	3,500	4,000	—

KM# 59.2 250 LEI

12.0000 g., 0.8350 Silver 0.3221 oz. ASW **Ruler:** Mihai I
Obv: Head left **Rev:** Crowned shield divides date with value and
date within **Edge:** Incuse lettering **Edge:** NIHIL SINE DEO

Date	Mintage	F	VF	XF	Unc	BU
1941	2,250,000	9.00	15.00	35.00	100	—

KM# 59.3 250 LEI

12.0000 g., 0.8350 Silver 0.3221 oz. ASW **Ruler:** Mihai I
Obv: Head left **Edge:** Lettered **Edge:** NIHIL SINE DEO

Date	Mintage	F	VF	XF	Unc	BU
1941B	13,750,000	6.50	9.50	16.00	50.00	—

KM# 60   500 LEI
25.0000 g., 0.8350 Silver 0.6711 oz. ASW, 37 mm.   **Ruler:** Mihai I
Subject: Basarabia Reunion **Obv:** Young head left **Rev:** Crowned
kneeling figure presenting putna monastery to Lord **Edge:** Incuse
lettering **Edge:** PRIN STATORNICIE LA IZBANADA +

Date	Mintage	F	VF	XF	Unc	BU
1941	775,000	BV	14.50	17.50	36.00	—

KM# 65   500 LEI
12.0000 g., 0.7000 Silver 0.2701 oz. ASW, 32 mm.   **Ruler:** Mihai I
Obv: Head left **Rev:** Crowned arms with supporters within crowned
mantle divides date **Edge:** Incuse lettering **Edge:** NIHIL SINE DEO

Date	Mintage	F	VF	XF	Unc	BU
1944	9,731,000	BV	6.00	9.00	18.00	—

KM# 67   500 LEI
10.0000 g., Brass, 30 mm.   **Ruler:** Mihai I **Obv:** Head left **Rev:**
Crowned arms with supporters within crowned mantle divides
date **Edge:** Reeded **Note:** Many were silver-plated privately.

Date	Mintage	F	VF	XF	Unc	BU
1945	3,422,000	1.00	2.00	4.00	10.00	—

KM# 68   500 LEI
1.5000 g., Aluminum, 24 mm.   **Ruler:** Mihai I **Obv:** Head right
Rev: Value above sprig **Edge:** Reeded **Note:** Without designer's
name, the result of a filled die.

Date	Mintage	F	VF	XF	Unc	BU
1946	5,823,000	1.00	3.00	6.00	15.00	—

KM# 69   2000 LEI
5.1000 g., Brass, 24 mm.   **Ruler:** Mihai I **Obv:** Head right
Rev: Crowned arms with supporters **Edge:** Incuse lettering
Edge: NIHIL SINE DEO **Note:** Many were silver-plated privately.

Date	Mintage	F	VF	XF	Unc	BU
1946	24,619,000	0.50	1.00	3.00	8.00	—

KM# 76   10000 LEI
10.0000 g., Brass, 27 mm.   **Ruler:** Mihai I **Obv:** Head right
Rev: Crowned shield to left of value and sprigs **Edge:** Incuse
lettering **Edge:** NIHIL SINE DEO **Note:** Many were silver-plated
privately.

Date	Mintage	F	VF	XF	Unc	BU
1947	11,850,000	1.00	2.00	4.00	9.00	—

KM# 70   25000 LEI
12.5000 g., 0.7000 Silver 0.2813 oz. ASW, 32 mm.
Ruler: Mihai I **Obv:** Head right **Rev:** Crowned shield to left of
value and sprigs **Edge:** Incuse lettering **Edge:** NIHIL SINE DEO

Date	Mintage	F	VF	XF	Unc	BU
1946	2,372,000	BV	6.50	10.00	20.00	—

KM# 71   1.0000 LEI
25.0000 g., 0.7000 Silver 0.5626 oz. ASW, 37 mm.
Ruler: Mihai I **Obv:** Head right **Rev:** Standing figure releasing
dove with crowned shield at lower right, value at lower left
Edge: Incuse lettering **Edge:** NIHIL SINE DEO

Date	Mintage	F	VF	XF	Unc	BU
1946	2,002,000	BV	11.50	13.50	25.00	—

REFORM COINAGE
Aug. 15, 1947; 100 Bani = 1 Leu

KM# 72   50 BANI
1.7000 g., Brass, 16 mm.   **Ruler:** Mihai I **Obv:** Crown above date
Rev: Value **Edge:** Plain

Date	Mintage	F	VF	XF	Unc	BU
1947	13,266,000	1.00	2.00	4.00	11.00	—

KM# 73   LEU
2.5000 g., Brass, 18 mm.   **Ruler:** Mihai I **Obv:** Crowned shield
Rev: Value within oat sprig **Edge:** Plain

Date	Mintage	F	VF	XF	Unc	BU
1947	88,341,000	1.00	2.25	4.50	12.00	—

KM# 74   2 LEI
3.5000 g., Bronze, 21 mm.   **Ruler:** Mihai I **Obv:** Crowned shield
and date **Rev:** Value within oat sprigs **Edge:** Plain

Date	Mintage	F	VF	XF	Unc	BU
1947	40,000,000	1.00	2.50	6.00	18.00	—

KM# 75   5 LEI
1.5000 g., Aluminum, 23 mm.   **Ruler:** Mihai I **Obv:** Head right
Rev: Value to left of oat sprig

Date	Mintage	F	VF	XF	Unc	BU
1947	56,026,000	1.50	3.00	9.00	26.00	—

PEOPLE'S REPUBLIC
STANDARD COINAGE

KM# 78   LEU
1.8300 g., Copper-Nickel-Zinc, 16 mm.   **Obv:** Radiant sun and
lighthouse **Rev:** Value and date **Edge:** Plain

Date	Mintage	F	VF	XF	Unc	BU
1949	—	0.75	1.50	3.00	9.00	—
1950	—	0.75	1.50	4.00	12.00	—
1951	—	1.00	2.00	10.00	24.00	—

KM# 78a   LEU
0.6100 g., Aluminum, 16 mm.   **Obv:** Radiant sun and lighthouse
Rev: Value and date

Date	Mintage	F	VF	XF	Unc	BU
1951	—	1.00	2.00	5.00	12.00	—
1952	—	9.00	16.00	30.00	80.00	—

KM# 79   2 LEI
2.4400 g., Copper-Nickel-Zinc, 18 mm.   **Obv:** Ear of corn flanked
by oat and flower sprig **Rev:** Value and date **Edge:** Plain

Date	Mintage	F	VF	XF	Unc	BU
1950	—	1.00	2.50	5.50	12.00	—
1951	—	2.00	5.00	12.00	26.00	—

KM# 79a   2 LEI
0.8400 g., Aluminum, 18 mm.   **Obv:** Ear of corn flanked by oat
and flower sprig **Rev:** Value and date

Date	Mintage	F	VF	XF	Unc	BU
1951	—	0.75	2.00	7.00	15.00	—
1952	—	12.00	25.00	45.00	110	—

KM# 77   5 LEI
1.5000 g., Aluminum, 23 mm.   **Obv:** National emblem **Rev:** Value
within wreath **Edge:** Plain

Date	Mintage	F	VF	XF	Unc	BU
1948	—	1.50	2.50	5.00	18.00	—
1949	—	1.25	2.00	4.00	14.00	—
1950	—	1.25	2.00	3.50	11.00	—
1951	—	1.25	2.00	5.50	18.00	—

KM# 80   20 LEI
2.1200 g., Aluminum, 26 mm. **Obv:** National emblem
Rev: Blacksmith at anvil, factory in background **Edge:** Plain

Date	Mintage	F	VF	XF	Unc	BU
1951	—	3.00	7.00	20.00	50.00	—

REFORM COINAGE
Jan. 26, 1952; 20 "old" Lei + 1 "new" Lei; 100 Bani = 1 Leu

KM# 81.1   BAN
1.0000 g., Copper-Nickel-Zinc, 16 mm. **Obv:** National emblem
Rev: Value and date **Edge:** Reeded

Date	Mintage	F	VF	XF	Unc	BU
1952	—	0.20	0.50	1.00	2.00	—

KM# 81.2   BAN
1.0000 g., Copper-Nickel-Zinc **Obv:** National emblem
Rev: Value and date

Date	Mintage	F	VF	XF	Unc	BU
1953	—	1.00	2.00	8.00	18.00	—
1954	—	3.00	8.00	20.00	52.00	—

KM# 82.1   3 BANI
2.0000 g., Copper-Nickel-Zinc, 18 mm. **Obv:** National emblem
Rev: Value and date **Edge:** Reeded

Date	Mintage	F	VF	XF	Unc	BU
1952	—	1.00	2.00	4.00	10.00	—

KM# 82.2   3 BANI
2.0000 g., Copper-Nickel-Zinc **Obv:** National emblem
Rev: Value and date

Date	Mintage	F	VF	XF	Unc	BU
1953	—	0.50	1.00	3.00	10.00	—
1954	—	20.00	50.00	75.00	180	—

KM# 83.1   5 BANI
2.4000 g., Copper-Nickel-Zinc, 20 mm. **Obv:** National emblem
Rev: Value and date **Edge:** Reeded

Date	Mintage	F	VF	XF	Unc	BU
1952	—	0.50	1.00	3.00	8.00	—

KM# 83.2   5 BANI
2.4000 g., Copper-Nickel-Zinc, 20 mm. **Obv:** National emblem
Rev: Value and date

Date	Mintage	F	VF	XF	Unc	BU
1953	—	0.25	0.50	2.00	8.00	—
1954	—	0.25	0.50	1.50	6.00	—
1955	—	0.25	0.50	1.50	5.00	—

Date	Mintage	F	VF	XF	Unc	BU
1956	—	0.25	0.50	1.25	4.50	—
1957	—	0.25	0.50	1.75	5.00	—

KM# 89   5 BANI
1.7000 g., Nickel Clad Steel, 16 mm. **Obv:** National emblem,
RPR on ribbon **Rev:** Value and date **Edge:** Plain

Date	Mintage	F	VF	XF	Unc	BU
1963	—	0.20	0.50	1.00	2.00	—

KM# 84.1   10 BANI
1.8000 g., Copper-Nickel, 17 mm. **Obv:** National emblem
Rev: Value and date within wreath **Edge:** Reeded

Date	Mintage	F	VF	XF	Unc	BU
1952	—	2.00	3.00	10.00	26.00	—

KM# 84.2   10 BANI
1.8000 g., Copper-Nickel **Obv:** National emblem
Obv. Leg.: ROMANA **Rev:** Value and date within wreath

Date	Mintage	F	VF	XF	Unc	BU
1954	—	0.30	1.50	4.00	10.00	—

KM# 84.3   10 BANI
1.8000 g., Copper-Nickel **Obv:** National emblem
Obv. Leg.: ROMINA **Rev:** Value and date within wreath

Date	Mintage	F	VF	XF	Unc	BU
1955	—	0.10	0.20	0.75	4.00	—
1956	—	0.10	0.20	0.75	3.50	—

KM# 87   15 BANI
2.8700 g., Nickel Clad Steel, 19.5 mm. **Obv:** National emblem
Rev: Value within wreath **Edge:** Plain

Date	Mintage	F	VF	XF	Unc	BU
1960	—	0.10	0.40	1.00	3.00	—

KM# 85.1   25 BANI
3.6000 g., Copper-Nickel, 22 mm. **Obv:** National emblem
Rev: Value and date within wreath **Edge:** Reeded

Date	Mintage	F	VF	XF	Unc	BU
1952	—	2.00	4.00	16.00	35.00	—

KM# 85.2   25 BANI
3.6000 g., Copper-Nickel **Obv:** National emblem
Obv. Leg.: ROMANA **Rev:** Value and date within wreath

Date	Mintage	F	VF	XF	Unc	BU
1953	—	0.20	0.75	2.50	7.00	—
1954	—	0.20	0.60	2.00	6.00	—

KM# 85.3   25 BANI
3.6000 g., Copper-Nickel **Obv:** National emblem
Obv. Leg.: ROMINA **Rev:** Value and date within wreath

Date	Mintage	F	VF	XF	Unc	BU
1955	—	0.15	0.35	1.00	4.00	—

KM# 88   25 BANI
3.3800 g., Nickel Clad Steel **Obv:** National emblem **Rev:** Value
above tractor **Edge:** Plain

Date	Mintage	F	VF	XF	Unc	BU
1960	—	0.15	0.30	1.00	4.00	—

KM# 86   50 BANI
4.5500 g., Copper-Nickel, 25 mm. **Obv:** National emblem
Rev: Blacksmith at anvil, factory in background **Edge:** Reeded

Date	Mintage	F	VF	XF	Unc	BU
1955	—	0.50	1.00	3.00	14.00	—
1956	—	0.50	1.00	4.00	16.00	—

KM# 90   LEU
5.0600 g., Nickel Clad Steel, 24 mm. **Obv:** National emblem
Rev: Tractor **Edge:** Plain

Date	Mintage	F	VF	XF	Unc	BU
1963	—	0.25	0.50	1.00	3.00	—

KM# 91   3 LEI
5.8600 g., Nickel Clad Steel, 27 mm. **Obv:** National emblem
Rev: Oil refinery **Edge:** Plain

Date	Mintage	F	VF	XF	Unc	BU
1963	—	0.25	0.50	1.50	4.00	—

SOCIALIST REPUBLIC

STANDARD COINAGE

KM# 92   5 BANI
1.7000 g., Nickel Clad Steel, 16 mm. **Obv:** National emblem,
ROMANIA on ribbon **Rev:** Value and date **Edge:** Plain

Date	Mintage	F	VF	XF	Unc	BU
1966	—	0.10	0.50	1.00	2.00	—

KM# 92a   5 BANI
0.6000 g., Aluminum, 16 mm. **Obv:** National emblem,
ROMANIA on ribbon **Rev:** Value and date **Edge:** Plain

Date	Mintage	F	VF	XF	Unc	BU
1975	—	0.10	0.50	1.00	—

KM# 93   15 BANI
2.8800 g., Nickel Clad Steel, 19.5 mm. **Obv:** National emblem
Rev: Value within wreath **Edge:** Plain

Date	Mintage	F	VF	XF	Unc	BU
1966	—	—	0.50	1.00	2.00	—

KM# 93a   15 BANI
1.0000 g., Aluminum, 19.5 mm. **Obv:** National emblem
Rev: Value within wreath **Edge:** Plain

Date	Mintage	F	VF	XF	Unc	BU
1975	—	—	0.10	0.50	1.50	—

KM# 94   25 BANI
3.3800 g., Nickel Clad Steel, 22 mm. **Obv:** National emblem
Rev: Value above tractor **Edge:** Plain

Date	Mintage	F	VF	XF	Unc	BU
1966	—	—	0.20	1.00	2.50	—

KM# 94a   25 BANI
1.3000 g., Aluminum, 22 mm. **Obv:** National emblem **Rev:** Value
above tractor **Edge:** Plain

Date	Mintage	F	VF	XF	Unc	BU
1982	—	0.20	0.50	1.00	3.00	—

KM# 95   LEU
5.0600 g., Nickel Clad Steel, 24.6 mm. **Obv:** National emblem
Rev: Tractor

Date	Mintage	F	VF	XF	Unc	BU
1966	—	0.10	0.25	0.75	2.00	—

KM# 96   3 LEI
5.8600 g., Nickel Clad Steel, 27 mm. **Obv:** National emblem
Rev: Oil refinery **Edge:** Waves

Date	Mintage	F	VF	XF	Unc	BU
1966	—	0.25	0.50	1.20	4.00	—

KM# 97   5 LEI
2.8000 g., Aluminum, 29 mm. **Obv:** National emblem **Rev:** Value
within design **Edge:** Security

Date	Mintage	F	VF	XF	Unc	BU
1978	—	0.25	0.50	1.50	5.00	—

KM# 100   50 LEI
15.0000 g., 0.9250 Silver 0.4461 oz. ASW **Subject:** 2,050th
Anniversary of First Independent State **Obv:** National emblem
Rev: Fighting figures within circle

Date	Mintage	F	VF	XF	Unc	BU
1983FM Proof	7,000	Value: 400				
1983FM Proof	1,000	Value: 600				

Note: Serially numbered on edges

KM# 98   100 LEI
30.0000 g., 0.9250 Silver 0.8921 oz. ASW **Subject:** 2,050th
Anniversary of First Independent State **Obv:** National emblem
divides date **Rev:** Head with headdress left flanked by diamonds

Date	Mintage	F	VF	XF	Unc	BU
1982FM Proof	7,500	Value: 525				
1983FM Proof	7,000	Value: 650				
1983FM Proof	1,000	Value: 850				

Note: Serially numbered on edge

KM# 99   500 LEI
8.0000 g., 0.9000 Gold 0.2315 oz. AGW **Subject:** 2,050th
Anniversary of First Independent State **Obv:** National emblem
divides date **Rev:** Fighting figures within circle

Date	Mintage	F	VF	XF	Unc	BU
1982FM Proof	7,500	Value: 1,200				
1983FM Proof	7,000	Value: 1,500				
1983FM Proof	1,000	Value: 2,000				

Note: Edge numbered

KM# 101   1000 LEI
16.0000 g., 0.9000 Gold 0.4630 oz. AGW **Subject:** 2,050th
Anniversary of First Independent State **Obv:** National emblem
divides date **Rev:** Head with headdress left flanked by diamonds

Date	Mintage	F	VF	XF	Unc	BU
1983FM Proof	7,000	Value: 1,800				
1983FM Proof	1,000	Value: 3,000				

Note: Edge numbered

REPUBLIC
STANDARD COINAGE

KM# 113   LEU
2.5000 g., Copper Clad Steel, 19 mm. **Subject:** National Bank
of Romania **Obv:** Monogram above date and sprigs **Rev:** Value
above oat sprigs **Edge:** Plain

Date	Mintage	F	VF	XF	Unc	BU
1992	Est. 60,000,000	0.20	0.50	1.25	3.50	—

KM# 115   LEU
2.5200 g., Copper Clad Steel, 19 mm. **Obv:** Value flanked by
sprigs **Rev:** Shield divides date

Date	Mintage	F	VF	XF	Unc	BU
1993	Est. 61,000,000	—	0.10	0.25	1.50	—
1994	Est. 10,000,000	—	—	0.20	1.00	—
1995	2,000,000	—	—	0.10	1.00	—
1996	272,000	—	0.50	1.00	4.00	—
2000 Proof	4,500	Value: 4.50				

KM# 112   5 LEI
3.3500 g., Aluminum, 21 mm. **Subject:** Prince Mihai Viteazul
Note: Similar to 100 Lei, KM#111. Not released for circulation;
majority were melted.

Date	Mintage	F	VF	XF	Unc	BU
1991	—	—	—	—	200	—

KM# 114   5 LEI
3.3000 g., Nickel Plated Steel, 20.99 mm. **Obv:** Value flanked
by oak leaves **Rev:** Shield divides date **Edge:** Plain

Date	Mintage	F	VF	XF	Unc	BU
1992 CD VG	Est. 30,000,000	—	0.25	0.60	3.00	—
1993 CD	Est. 70,000,000	—	—	0.30	2.00	—
1994	Est. 10,000,000	—	—	0.30	1.50	—
1995	25,000,000	—	—	0.20	1.00	—
1996	—	—	—	0.20	1.00	—
2000 Proof	4,500	Value: 4.50				

KM# 108   10 LEI
4.6500 g., Nickel-Clad Steel, 23 mm. **Subject:** Revolution
Anniversary **Obv:** Flag and sprig **Rev:** Value within wreath
Edge: Security scroll **Note:** Rotated die varieties exist.

Date	Mintage	F	VF	XF	Unc	BU
1990	30,000,000	—	0.50	1.00	3.00	—
1991	31,303,000	—	0.25	0.60	2.20	—
1992	60,000,000	—	0.25	0.50	1.50	—

KM# 116   10 LEI
4.7000 g., Nickel-Clad Steel, 23 mm. **Obv:** Value within sprigs
Rev: Shield divides date **Edge:** Plain

Date	Mintage	F	VF	XF	Unc	BU
1993	Est. 6,000,000	—	0.75	1.50	3.50	—
1994	Est. 7,000,000	—	0.50	1.00	3.00	—
1995	30,000,000	—	—	0.30	1.50	—
1996	5,000	—	—	—	—	—
2000 Proof	4,500	Value: 4.50				

KM# 117.1   10 LEI
5.2000 g., Nickel Plated Steel, 23.2 mm. **Series:** F.A.O.
Subject: 50 Years - F.A.O. **Obv:** Shield flanked by sprigs and
diamonds above value **Rev:** F.A.O logo and dates **Edge:** Plain

Date	Mintage	F	VF	XF	Unc	BU
1995	200,000	—	—	3.50	8.00	—

KM# 117.2 10 LEI
Nickel Plated Steel, 23.3 mm. **Series:** F.A.O. **Subject:** 50 Years - F.A.O. **Obv:** Shield flanked by sprigs and diamonds **Rev:** F.A.O logo and dates **Note:** Obverse description: N in diamond at right for Numismatists

Date	Mintage	F	VF	XF	Unc	BU
1995	30,000	—	—	4.00	10.00	—

KM# 120 10 LEI
Nickel Plated Steel **Series:** 1996 Olympic Games - U.S.A. **Obv:** Shield above sprigs flanked by value **Rev:** Swimmer

Date	Mintage	F	VF	XF	Unc	BU
1996	10,000	—	—	7.00	16.00	—

KM# 121 10 LEI
Nickel Plated Steel **Series:** 1996 Olympic Games - U.S.A. **Obv:** Shield above sprig flanked by value **Rev:** Four Olympic scenes

Date	Mintage	F	VF	XF	Unc	BU
1996	10,000	—	—	7.00	16.00	—

KM# 122 10 LEI
Nickel Plated Steel **Series:** 1996 Olympic Games - U.S.A. **Obv:** Shield above sprig flanked by value **Rev:** Windsurfer

Date	Mintage	F	VF	XF	Unc	BU
1996	10,000	—	—	7.00	16.00	—

KM# 123 10 LEI
Nickel Plated Steel **Series:** 1996 Olympic Games - U.S.A. **Obv:** Shield above sprig flanked by value **Rev:** Sailboat with two racers

Date	Mintage	F	VF	XF	Unc	BU
1996	10,000	—	—	7.00	16.00	—

KM# 124 10 LEI
Nickel Plated Steel **Series:** 1996 Olympic Games - U.S.A. **Obv:** Shield above sprigs divide value **Rev:** Canoe with two racers

Date	Mintage	F	VF	XF	Unc	BU
1996	10,000	—	—	7.00	16.00	—

KM# 125 10 LEI
Nickel Plated Steel **Series:** 1996 Olympic Games - U.S.A. **Obv:** Shield above sprigs divide value **Rev:** Scullcraft with racers

Date	Mintage	F	VF	XF	Unc	BU
1996	10,000	—	—	7.00	16.00	—

KM# 126 10 LEI
Nickel Plated Steel **Subject:** World Food Summit - Rome **Obv:** Shield above value **Rev:** Logo above inscription

Date	Mintage	F	VF	XF	Unc	BU
1996	50,000	—	—	7.00	16.00	—

KM# 134 10 LEI
Nickel Plated Steel **Subject:** Euro Soccer **Obv:** Shield divides value **Rev:** Stylized soccer players

Date	Mintage	F	VF	XF	Unc	BU
1996	50,000	—	—	6.00	14.00	—

KM# 109 20 LEI
5.0000 g., Brass Clad Steel, 24 mm. **Obv:** Crowned bust of Prince Stefan Cel Mare facing, flanked by dots **Rev:** Value and date within half sprigs and dots **Edge:** Plain **Note:** Date varieties exist.

Date	Mintage	F	VF	XF	Unc	BU
1991	Est. 43,200,000	—	—	1.00	3.00	—
1992	Est. 48,000,000	—	—	0.80	3.00	—
1993	Est. 33,800,000	—	—	0.80	3.00	—
1994	Est. 5,000,000	—	—	1.25	3.00	—
1995	8,000,000	—	—	0.75	3.00	—
1996	500,000	—	0.75	2.00	7.00	—
2000 Proof	4,500	Value: 6.00				

KM# 110 50 LEI
5.9000 g., Brass Clad Steel, 26 mm. **Obv:** Bust left flanked by dots **Rev:** Sprig divides date and value **Edge:** Plain

Date	Mintage	F	VF	XF	Unc	BU
1991	Est. 29,600,000	—	—	1.50	3.00	—
1992	Est. 70,800,000	—	—	1.00	2.00	—
Note: 1992 date varieties exist						
1993	Est. 34,600,000	—	—	1.00	2.00	—
1994	Est. 30,000,000	—	—	1.00	2.00	—
1995	20,000,000	—	—	1.00	2.20	—
1996	4,900,000	—	—	2.00	4.00	—
2000 Proof	4,500	Value: 7.00				

KM# 111 100 LEI
8.7500 g., Nickel Plated Steel, 29 mm. **Obv:** Bust with headdress 1/4 right **Rev:** Value within sprigs **Edge:** ROMANIA

Date	Mintage	F	VF	XF	Unc	BU
1991	Est. 12,600,000	—	—	2.50	6.00	—
1992	Est. 70,500,000	—	—	1.50	3.50	—

Date	Mintage	F	VF	XF	Unc	BU
Note: Reported edge varieties for 1992 with TOTUL PENTRU TARA; without ROMANIA are presumed essais						
1993	Est. 78,000,000	—	—	1.50	3.00	—
1994	Est. 125,000,000	—	—	1.50	3.00	—
1995	30,000,000	—	—	1.50	3.50	—
1996	11,000,000	—	—	2.50	9.00	—
2000 Proof	4,500	Value: 7.50				

KM# 118 100 LEI
27.5000 g., 0.9250 Silver 0.8178 oz. ASW, 37 mm. **Series:** F.A.O. **Subject:** 50 Years - F.A.O. **Obv:** Shield flanked by sprigs and diamonds above value **Rev:** F.A.O logo and dates **Edge:** Plain

Date	Mintage	F	VF	XF	Unc	BU
1995	30,000	—	—	—	26.00	—

KM# 119 100 LEI
27.0000 g., 0.9250 Silver 0.8029 oz. ASW, 37 mm. **Subject:** Euro Soccer **Obv:** Shield **Rev:** Players **Edge:** Plain

Date	Mintage	F	VF	XF	Unc	BU
1996 Proof	12,000	Value: 30.00				

KM# 127 100 LEI
27.0000 g., 0.9250 Silver 0.8029 oz. ASW, 37 mm. **Series:** 1996 Olympic Games - U.S.A. **Obv:** Shield divides value above sprig **Rev:** Swimmer **Edge:** Plain

Date	Mintage	F	VF	XF	Unc	BU
1996 Proof	10,000	Value: 30.00				

KM# 128 100 LEI
27.0000 g., 0.9250 Silver 0.8029 oz. ASW, 37 mm. **Series:** 1996 Olympic Games - U.S.A. **Obv:** Shield divides value above sprig **Rev:** Four olympic scenes **Edge:** Plain

Date	Mintage	F	VF	XF	Unc	BU
1996 Proof	10,000	Value: 30.00				

KM# 129 100 LEI
27.0000 g., 0.9250 Silver 0.8029 oz. ASW, 37 mm. **Series:** 1996 Olympic Games - U.S.A. **Obv:** Shield divides value above sprig **Rev:** Windsurfer

Date	Mintage	F	VF	XF	Unc	BU
1996 Proof	10,000	Value: 30.00				

KM# 130   100 LEI
27.0000 g., 0.9250 Silver 0.8029 oz. ASW, 37 mm. **Series:** 1996 Olympic Games - U.S.A. **Obv:** Shield divides value above sprig **Rev:** Sailboat with three crewmen

Date	Mintage	F	VF	XF	Unc	BU
1996 Proof	10,000	Value: 30.00				

KM# 131   100 LEI
27.0000 g., 0.9250 Silver 0.8029 oz. ASW, 37 mm. **Series:** 1996 Olympic Games - U.S.A. **Obv:** Shield divides value above sprig **Rev:** Canoe with two canoeists

Date	Mintage	F	VF	XF	Unc	BU
1996 Proof	10,000	Value: 30.00				

KM# 132   100 LEI
27.0000 g., 0.9250 Silver 0.8029 oz. ASW, 37 mm. **Series:** 1996 Olympic Games - U.S.A. **Obv:** Shield divides value above sprig **Rev:** Scullcraft with rowers

Date	Mintage	F	VF	XF	Unc	BU
1996 Proof	10,000	Value: 32.00				

KM# 133   100 LEI
27.5000 g., 0.9250 Silver 0.8178 oz. ASW, 37 mm. **Subject:** World Food Summit - Rome **Edge:** Plain

Date	Mintage	F	VF	XF	Unc	BU
1996 Proof	5,000	Value: 38.00				

KM# 135   100 LEI
27.0000 g., 0.9250 Silver 0.8029 oz. ASW, 37 mm. **Subject:** 50th Anniversary - UNICEF **Obv:** Shield above value **Rev:** UNICEF logo on world globe **Edge:** Plain

Date	Mintage	F	VF	XF	Unc	BU
1996 Proof	5,000	Value: 38.00				

KM# 138   100 LEI
27.0000 g., 0.9250 Silver 0.8029 oz. ASW, 37 mm. **Subject:** 120th Anniversary of Independence **Obv:** Shield above value **Rev:** Three soldiers with flag behind cannon **Edge:** Plain

Date	Mintage	F	VF	XF	Unc	BU
1998 Proof	Est. 5,000	Value: 60.00				

KM# 139   100 LEI
27.0000 g., 0.9250 Silver 0.8029 oz. ASW, 37 mm. **Subject:** Andrei Saguna **Obv:** Shield divides value **Rev:** Bust facing 1/4 right with dates and church towers **Edge:** Plain

Date	Mintage	F	VF	XF	Unc	BU
1998 Proof	2,000	Value: 80.00				

KM# 140   100 LEI
27.0000 g., 0.9250 Silver 0.8029 oz. ASW, 37 mm. **Series:** Olympic Games - Nagano 1998 **Obv:** Value above shield to right of stylized flame and snow flakes **Rev:** Bobsled **Edge:** Plain

Date	Mintage	F	VF	XF	Unc	BU
1998 Proof	2,000	Value: 60.00				

KM# 141   100 LEI
27.0000 g., 0.9250 Silver 0.8029 oz. ASW, 37 mm. **Series:** Olympic Games - Nagano 1998 **Rev:** Figure skaters

Date	Mintage	F	VF	XF	Unc	BU
1998 Proof	2,000	Value: 60.00				

KM# 142   100 LEI
27.0000 g., 0.9250 Silver 0.8029 oz. ASW, 37 mm. **Series:** Olympic Games - Nagano 1998 **Rev:** Slalom skier

Date	Mintage	F	VF	XF	Unc	BU
1998 Proof	2,000	Value: 60.00				

KM# 143   100 LEI
27.0000 g., 0.9250 Silver 0.8029 oz. ASW, 37 mm. **Subject:** World Cup Soccer - France 1998 **Obv:** Value within goal net with shield at right **Rev:** Eiffel Tower in front of soccer ball **Edge:** Plain

Date	Mintage	F	VF	XF	Unc	BU
1998 Proof	5,000	Value: 65.00				

KM# 149   100 LEI
27.0000 g., 0.9250 Silver 0.8029 oz. ASW, 37 mm. **Subject:** Visit of Pope John Paul II - May 7-9, 1999 **Obv:** Shield on quatrefoil **Rev:** Portraits of Pope and Patriarch Theoctist **Edge:** Plain

Date	Mintage	F	VF	XF	Unc	BU
1999 Proof	2,000	Value: 400				

KM# 152   100 LEI
1.2240 g., 0.9990 Gold 0.0393 oz. AGW, 13.92 mm. **Subject:** History of Gold **Obv:** Shield within ornamental circle above value **Rev:** Gold Dacian helmet found at Poiana Cotofeneti

Date	Mintage	F	VF	XF	Unc	BU
1999 Proof	25,000	Value: 150				

KM# 148   100 LEI
27.0000 g., 0.9250 Silver 0.8029 oz. ASW, 37 mm. **Subject:** 100th Anniversary - Belgica Expedition **Obv:** Shield, birds and compas face **Rev:** The sailing ship Belgica and bust of scientist Emil Racovita **Edge:** Plain

Date	Mintage	F	VF	XF	Unc	BU
1999 Proof	20,000	Value: 35.00				

KM# 136   500 LEI
8.6400 g., 0.9000 Gold 0.2500 oz. AGW, 24 mm. **Subject:** Revolution of 1848 **Obv:** Upper and lower shield divides value **Rev:** Half length figure with head facing right flanked by dates

Date	Mintage	F	VF	XF	Unc	BU
1998 Proof	Est. 2,000	Value: 400				

KM# 145   500 LEI
3.7000 g., Aluminum, 25 mm. **Obv:** Shield within sprigs **Rev:** Value within 3/4 wreath **Edge:** Lettered **Edge:** ROMANIA (three times)

Date	Mintage	F	VF	XF	Unc	BU
1998	—	—	—	0.75	2.00	—
1999	—	—	—	0.75	2.00	—
2000	—	—	—	0.75	2.00	—
2000 Proof	4,500	Value: 6.00				

KM# 146 500 LEI
3.6000 g., Aluminum, 25 mm. **Obv:** Shield, value and date within design **Rev:** Solar eclipse **Edge:** Lettered **Edge:** ROMANIA (three times)

Date	Mintage	VG	F	VF	XF	Unc
1999	4,000,000	—	—	—	1.00	4.00

KM# 147 500 LEI
Aluminum, 25 mm. **Subject:** Solar eclipse **Obv:** Shield, eclipse and observatory **Rev:** Solar eclipse **Edge:** Lettered **Edge:** ROMANIA (3x)

Date	Mintage	VG	F	VF	XF	Unc
1999						

Note: This design never gained broad release and is considered to be a pattern by several authorities

KM# 154 500 LEI
27.0000 g., 0.9990 Silver 0.8672 oz. ASW, 37 mm.
Subject: Alexander the Good of Moldavia **Obv:** Old seal design and value **Rev:** Crowned bust 1/4 left, church at left **Edge:** Plain

Date	Mintage	F	VF	XF	Unc	BU
2000 Proof	Est. 1,000	Value: 100				

KM# 137 1000 LEI
31.1035 g., 0.9990 Gold 0.9990 oz. AGW, 35 mm.
Subject: Revolution of 1848 **Obv:** Crossed flags and shield flanked by value **Rev:** Victory flanked by dates **Edge:** Plain

Date	Mintage	F	VF	XF	Unc	BU
1998 Proof	Est. 1,000	Value: 1,100				

KM# 144 1000 LEI
31.1035 g., 0.9990 Gold 0.9990 oz. AGW, 35 mm.
Subject: 80th Anniversary - Union of Transylvania **Obv:** Shield to right of value **Rev:** Large building and the arms of Wallachia, Moldova and Transylvania **Edge:** Plain

Date	Mintage	F	VF	XF	Unc	BU
1998 Proof	2,000	Value: 975				

KM# 151 1000 LEI
31.1035 g., 0.9990 Gold 0.9990 oz. AGW, 35 mm.
Subject: Visit of Pope John Paul II - May 7-9, 1999 **Obv:** Shield **Rev:** Portraits of Pope and Patriarch Theocist **Edge:** Plain

Date	Mintage	F	VF	XF	Unc	BU
1999 Proof	1,000	Value: 1,300				

KM# 153 1000 LEI
2.0000 g., Aluminum, 22.2 mm. **Subject:** Constantin Brancoveanu **Obv:** Value above shield within lined circle **Rev:** Bust with headdress facing **Edge:** Plain with serrated sections

Date	Mintage	VG	F	VF	XF	Unc
2000				—	0.50	3.00
2000 Proof	4,500	Value: 10.00				

KM# 157 2000 LEI
31.1030 g., 0.9990 Gold 0.9989 oz. AGW, 35 mm.
Subject: 150th Anniversary - Birth of Mihai Eminesu, Poet **Obv:** Shield and quill within circle **Rev:** Bust 3/4 left **Edge:** Plain

Date	Mintage	VG	F	VF	XF	Unc
2000 Proof	1,500	Value: 1,000				

KM# 155 5000 LEI
31.1030 g., 0.9990 Gold 0.9989 oz. AGW, 35 mm.
Subject: Michael the Brave's Unification of Romania in 1600 **Obv:** Shield and old seal within circle **Rev:** Bust with headdress and church **Edge:** Plain

Date	Mintage	F	VF	XF	Unc	BU
2000 Proof	Est. 1,500	Value: 1,000				

KM# 182 5000 LEI
31.1030 g., 0.9990 Gold 0.9989 oz. AGW, 35 mm.
Subject: 2000 Years of Christianity **Rev:** Jesus Christ

Date	Mintage	F	VF	XF	Unc	BU
2000 Proof	Est. 1,000	Value: 1,000				

ESSAIS

KM#	Date	Mintage	Identification	Mkt Val
E1	1905	—	10 Bani. Copper-Nickel. KM29. With center hole.	200
E2	1910	—	50 Bani. Silver. Head left. Crown above sprigs.	350
E3	1910	—	Leu. Silver.	350
E4	1910	—	2 Lei. Silver.	350
E5	1914	—	50 Bani. Silver.	200
E6	1914	—	50 Bani. Silver. KM41	150
E7	1914	—	Leu. Silver.	250
E8	1914	—	Leu. Silver. KM42.	
E9	1914	—	2 Lei. Silver. Head left. Crowned arms with supporters within crowned mantle flanked by value.	275
E10	1914	—	2 Lei. Silver. KM43.	
E11	1924	—	2 Lei. Silver.	125

PATTERNS
Including off metal strikes

KM#	Date	Mintage	Identification	Mkt Val
Pn49	1905	—	5 Bani. White Metal. KM28.	100
Pn50	1905	—	5 Bani. Pewter. KM28.	—
Pn51	1905	—	5 Bani. Aluminum. KM28.	—
Pn52	1905	—	5 Bani. Zinc. KM28.	—
Pn53	1905	—	5 Bani. Bronze. KM28.	—
Pn54	1905	—	5 Bani. Brass. KM28.	125
Pn55	1905	—	5 Bani. Copper. KM28. With center hole.	125
Pn56	1905	—	5 Bani. Copper. KM28.	500
Pn57	1905	—	5 Bani. Gilt Copper. KM28.	—
Pn58	1905	—	5 Bani. Silver. KM31. Without center hole.	1,500
Pn59	1905	—	5 Bani. Bronze. KM31. Without center hole.	—

KM#	Date	Mintage	Identification	Mkt Val
Pn60	1905	—	5 Bani. Pewter. KM31. Without center hole.	100
Pn61	1905	—	5 Bani. Aluminum. KM31. Without center hole.	—
Pn62	1905	—	5 Bani. Zinc. KM31. Without center hole.	—
Pn63	1905	—	5 Bani. Copper-Nickel. KM31. Without center hole.	—
Pn64	1905	—	5 Bani. Gold. Without center hole.	2,000
Pn65	1905	—	5 Bani. Gold. Without center hole.	1,500
PnA66	1905	—	10 Bani. White Metal. With center hole.	—
PnB66	1905	—	10 Bani. White Metal. Without center hole.	—
Pn66	1905	—	10 Bani. Pewter. KM29. With center hole.	125
Pn67	1905	—	10 Bani. Brass. KM29. With center hole.	125
Pn68	1905	—	10 Bani. Aluminum. KM29. With center hole.	75.00
PnA69	1905	—	10 Bani. Bronze. KM29. Red. With center hole.	—
Pn69	1905	—	10 Bani. Bronze. KM29. Red. Without center hole.	100
Pn70	1905	—	10 Bani. Bronze. KM29. Green. Without center hole.	100
Pn71	1905	—	10 Bani. Zinc. KM29.	160
PnA72	1905	—	10 Bani. Gilt Bronze. KM29. With center hole.	—
Pn72	1905	—	10 Bani. Gilt Bronze. KM29. Without center hole.	100
Pn73	1905	—	10 Bani. Copper-Nickel-Zinc. With center hole.	150
Pn74	1905	—	10 Bani. Nickel. KM29. With center hole.	—
Pn75	1905	—	10 Bani. Silver. KM29. Without center hole.	400
Pn76	1905	—	10 Bani. Silver. KM29. With center hole.	400
PnA77	1905	—	10 Bani. Gilt Copper. With branches and small date. Without center hole.	—
Pn77	1905	—	10 Bani. Copper. KM29. Without center hole.	100
Pn78	1905	—	10 Bani. Gold. Without branches. KM29. Without center hole.	1,800
Pn79	1905	—	10 Bani. Gold. KM29. With center hole.	1,500
	1905	—	10 Bani. Gold. KM29. With center hole.	1,500
Pn80	1905	—	10 Bani. Pewter. KM32. Without center hole.	150
Pn81	1905	—	10 Bani. Brass. KM32. Without center hole.	150
Pn82	1905	—	10 Bani. Aluminum. KM32. Without center hole.	100
Pn83	1905	—	10 Bani. Bronze. KM32. Without center hole.	125
Pn84	1905	—	10 Bani. Gold. KM32. Without center hole.	1,250
Pn85	1905	—	20 Bani. Lead. KM30.	100
Pn86	1905	—	20 Bani. Brass. KM30.	150
Pn87	1905	—	20 Bani. Copper. KM30.	125
Pn88	1905	—	20 Bani. Aluminum. KM30.	100
Pn89	1905	—	20 Bani. White Metal. KM30.	100
Pn90	1905	—	20 Bani. Zinc. KM30.	—
Pn91	1905	—	20 Bani. Pewter. KM30.	—
Pn92	1905	—	20 Bani. Gilt Bronze. KM30.	125
PnA93	1905	—	20 Bani. Bronze. KM30.	—
Pn93	1905	—	20 Bani. Silver. KM30.	250
Pn94	1905	—	20 Bani. Gold. Without center hole.	1,750
Pn95	1905	—	20 Bani. Gold. With center hole.	1,500
Pn96	1905	—	20 Bani. Brass. KM33. Without center hole.	—
Pn97	1905	—	20 Bani. Copper. KM33. Without center hole.	200
Pn98	1905	—	20 Bani. Aluminum. KM33. Without center hole.	—
Pn99	1905	—	20 Bani. Pewter. KM33. Without center hole.	200
Pn100	1905	—	20 Bani. Silver. KM33. Without center hole.	400
Pn101	1906	—	Leu. White Metal.	125
Pn102	1906	—	Leu. Brass.	150
Pn103	1906	—	Leu. Aluminum.	100
Pn104	1906	—	Leu. Copper.	125
Pn105	1906	—	Leu. Gilt Bronze.	125
Pn106	1906	—	Leu. Copper-Nickel.	—
Pn107	1906	—	Leu. Gilt Bronze.	125
Pn108	1906	—	Leu. Silver.	250
Pn109	1906	—	Leu. Gold.	—
Pn110	1906	—	5 Lei. Silver.	4,500
Pn111	1906	—	12-1/2 Lei. Lead.	250
Pn112	1906	—	12-1/2 Lei. White Metal.	250
Pn113	1906	—	12-1/2 Lei. Brass.	250
Pn114	1906	—	12-1/2 Lei. Pewter.	—
Pn115	1906	—	12-1/2 Lei. Gilt Bronze.	250
PnA116	1906	—	12-1/2 Lei. Bronze. Plain edge.	250
Pn116	1906	—	12-1/2 Lei. Aluminum.	250
Pn117	1906	—	12-1/2 Lei. Aluminum. Gilt.	250
Pn118	1906	—	12-1/2 Lei. Copper.	350
Pn119	1906	—	12-1/2 Lei. Copper-Nickel.	—
Pn120	1906	—	12-1/2 Lei. Silver.	550
Pn121	1906	—	12-1/2 Lei. Gold.	1,400
Pn122	1906	—	12-1/2 Lei. Gold. Pale.	2,500
Pn123	1906	—	20 Lei. Copper.	450
Pn124	1906	—	20 Lei. Bronze.	300

KM#	Date	Mintage	Identification	Mkt Val
Pn125	1906	—	20 Lei. White Metal.	—
Pn126	1906	—	20 Lei. White Metal. Gilt.	—
Pn127	1906	—	20 Lei. Gold.	1,400
Pn128	1906	—	20 Lei. Gold. Pale.	2,500
Pn129	1906	—	25 Lei. Pewter.	250
Pn130	1906	—	25 Lei. Zinc.	400
Pn131	1906	—	25 Lei. Lead.	200
Pn132	1906	—	25 Lei. Copper.	175
Pn133	1906	—	25 Lei. Gilt Copper.	—
Pn134	1906	—	25 Lei. Aluminum.	175
Pn135	1906	—	25 Lei. Brass.	175
Pn136	1906	—	25 Lei. Bronze. Antique.	175
Pn137	1906	—	25 Lei. Gilt Bronze.	175
Pn138	1906	—	25 Lei. Silver.	1,000
Pn139	1906	—	25 Lei. Gold.	2,650
Pn140	1906	—	25 Lei. Gold. Pale.	4,500
Pn141	1906	—	50 Lei. Aluminum.	350
Pn142	1906	—	50 Lei. Bronze.	400
Pn143	1906	—	50 Lei. White Metal.	—
Pn144	1906	—	50 Lei. Pewter.	425
Pn145	1906	—	50 Lei. Brass.	400
Pn146	1906	—	50 Lei. Silver.	850
Pn148	1906	—	100 Lei. Copper.	650
Pn149	1906	—	100 Lei. Bronze.	650
Pn150	1906	—	100 Lei. Silver.	—
Pn151	1906	—	100 Lei. Gold.	5,500
PnA152	1910	—	10 Bani. Zinc.	—
Pn152	1910	—	10 Bani. Copper.	—
Pn153	1910	—	50 Bani. Lead.	—
Pn154	1910	—	50 Bani. Tin.	—
PnA155	1910	—	50 Bani. Pewter. Plain edge.	—
Pn155	1910	—	50 Bani. Pewter. Milled edge.	100
Pn156	1910	—	50 Bani. White Metal.	75.00
Pn157	1910	—	50 Bani. Aluminum.	60.00
Pn158	1910	—	50 Bani. Zinc.	—
Pn159	1910	—	50 Bani. Copper.	—
Pn160	1910	—	50 Bani. Copper-Nickel.	—
Pn161	1910	—	50 Bani. Brass.	75.00
PnA162	1910	—	50 Bani. Bronze. Plain edge. Thin planchet.	—
PnB162	1910	—	50 Bani. Bronze. Plain edge. Thick planchet.	—
PnC162	1910	—	50 Bani. Bronze. Milled edge. Thin planchet.	—
PnD162	1910	—	50 Bani. Bronze. Milled edge. Thick planchet.	—
Pn162	1910	—	50 Bani. Nickel.	100
Pn163	1910	—	Leu. Lead.	100
Pn164	1910	—	Leu. Aluminum.	100
Pn165	1910	—	Leu. Bronze.	100
Pn166	1910	—	Leu. Gilt Bronze.	100
Pn167	1910	—	Leu. Pewter.	125
Pn168	1910	—	Leu. Zinc.	—
PnA169	1910	—	Leu. Gilt Copper.	—
Pn169	1910	—	Leu. Copper.	—
Pn170	1910	—	Leu. Copper-Nickel.	—
Pn171	1910	—	2 Lei. Lead.	100
Pn172	1910	—	2 Lei. Tin.	150
Pn173	1910	—	2 Lei. Pewter.	150
Pn174	1910	—	2 Lei. Aluminum.	100
Pn175	1910	—	2 Lei. Brass.	100
PnA176	1910	—	2 Lei. Gilt Copper.	—
Pn176	1910	—	2 Lei. Copper.	—
Pn177	1910	—	2 Lei. Gilt Bronze.	100
PnA178	1910	—	2 Lei. Bronze.	—
Pn178	1910	—	2 Lei. Nickel.	—
PnA179	1910	—	2 Lei. Silver.	—
PnB179	1914	—	Leu. Silver.	350
PnC179	1914	—	2 Lei. Silver.	450
PnE180	1921	—	25 Bani. Copper. Without hole.	300
PnF180	1921	—	25 Bani. Bronze. With hole.	200
PnA181	1921	—	50 Bani. Bronze. Without hole.	300
PnB181	1921	—	50 Bani. Bronze. With hole.	200
PnB181	1921	—	1.25 Leu. Nickel. Without hole.	700
Pn179	1921	—	25 Bani. Aluminum. HF at left of date.	125
PnA180	1921	—	25 Bani. Bronze. HF at left of date.	200
PnB180	1921	—	25 Bani. Copper-Nickel.	185
PnC180	1921	—	25 Bani. Bronze. Without hole.	185
PnD180	1921	—	25 Bani. Nickel.	200
Pn180	1921	—	50 Bani. Nickel. With hole.	200
PnC181	1921	—	50 Bani. Bronze. With hole.	200
Pn181	1921	—	1.25 Leu. Nickel. With hole.	500
PnA182	1921	—	5 Lei. Billon. Arms, cornucopia. Hand numbered 1-15. Struck at Paris.	—
Pn182	1921	—	5 Lei. Copper-Nickel.	450
Pn183	1921	—	5 Lei. Nickel.	—
PnC201	1922	—	100 Lei. Bronze.	—
PnA195	1922	—	5 Bani. Copper.	300
Pn184	1922	—	25 Bani. Aluminum.	175
Pn185	1922	—	50 Bani. Aluminum.	175
Pn186	1922	—	Leu. Bronze.	220
Pn187	1922	—	Leu. Nickel.	250
Pn188	1922	—	Leu. Copper-Nickel.	210
Pn189	1922	—	2 Lei. Bronze.	250
Pn190	1922	—	2 Lei. Nickel.	250
Pn191	1922	—	2 Lei. Brass.	150
Pn192	1922	—	5 Lei. Bronze.	300
Pn193	1922	—	5 Lei. Copper-Nickel.	300
Pn194	1922	—	5 Lei. Nickel.	300
Pn195	1922	—	5 Lei. Brass.	300
Pn196	1922	—	5 Lei. Copper-Nickel.	300
Pn197	1922	—	20 Lei. Gold.	2,000
Pn198	1922	—	25 Lei. Gold.	2,750
Pn199	1922	—	50 Lei. Gold.	4,500
Pn200	1922	—	100 Lei. Gold.	6,000
PnB201	1923	—	2 Lei. Copper.	600
PnA201	1923	—	Leu. Nickel.	275
Pn201	1924	—	Leu. Nickel.	65.00
Pn202	1924	—	Leu. Aluminum.	45.00
Pn203	1924	—	Leu. Tin.	45.00
Pn204	1924	—	Leu. Zinc.	—
Pn205	1924	—	Leu. Copper.	—
Pn206	1924	—	Leu. Brass.	110
Pn207	1924	—	Leu. Bronze.	60.00
Pn208	1924	—	Leu. Gilt Bronze.	50.00
Pn209	1924	—	Leu. Silver. Plain edge.	125
Pn210	1924	—	Leu. Silver. Reeded edge.	125
Pn211	1924	—	2 Lei. Zinc.	75.00
Pn212	1924	—	2 Lei. Aluminum.	50.00
Pn213	1924	—	2 Lei. Tin.	—
Pn214	1924	—	2 Lei. Bronze.	240
Pn215	1924	—	2 Lei. Brass.	100
Pn216	1924	—	2 Lei. Copper.	65.00
Pn217	1924	—	2 Lei. Nickel.	75.00
PnA217	1924	—	2 Lei. Copper-Nickel.	—
Pn218	1924	—	2 Lei. Silver. Plain edge. Thick planchet.	200
PnA219	1930	—	10 Lei. Copper-Nickel. KM49.	100
Pn219	1930	—	20 Lei. Gold. Plain.	—
Pn220	1930	—	20 Lei. Gold. Ornamented.	—
Pn221	1930	—	100 Lei. Gold. Plain.	—
Pn222	1930	—	100 Lei. Gold. Ornamented.	—
Pn223	1931	—	20 Lei. Gold. Plain.	—
Pn224	1931	—	20 Lei. Gold. Ornamented.	—
Pn225	1931	—	100 Lei. Gold. Plain.	—
Pn226	1931	—	100 Lei. Gold. Ornamented.	—
Pn227	1932	—	20 Lei. Gold. Plain.	—
Pn228	1932	—	20 Lei. Gold. Ornamented.	—
Pn229	1932	—	100 Lei. Silver. Y62.	75.00
Pn230	1932	—	100 Lei. Gold. Plain.	—
Pn231	1932	—	100 Lei. Gold. Ornamented.	—
Pn232	1933	—	20 Lei. Gold. Plain.	—
Pn233	1933	—	20 Lei. Gold. Ornamented.	—
Pn234	1933	—	100 Lei. Gold. Plain.	—
Pn235	1933	—	100 Lei. Gold. Ornamented.	—
Pn236	1934	—	20 Lei. Gold. Plain.	—
Pn237	1934	—	20 Lei. Gold. Ornamented.	—
Pn238	1934	—	100 Lei. Gold. Plain.	—
Pn239	1934	—	100 Lei. Gold. Ornamented.	—
Pn240	1935	—	20 Lei. Gold. Plain.	—
Pn241	1935	—	20 Lei. Gold. Ornamented.	—
Pn242	1935	—	50 Lei. Silver.	—
Pn243	1935	—	100 Lei. Gold. Plain.	—
Pn244	1935	—	100 Lei. Gold. Ornamented.	—
Pn245	1935	—	200 Lei. Silver.	450
PnA245	1935	—	250 Lei. Nickel.	—
PnB245	1935	—	250 Lei. Brass.	—
PnA250	1936	—	100 Lei. Copper.	500
Pn246	1936	—	20 Lei. Gold. Plain.	—
Pn247	1936	—	20 Lei. Gold. Ornamented.	—
Pn248	1936	—	50 Lei. Nickel.	—
Pn249	1936	—	100 Lei. Gold. Plain.	—
Pn250	1936	—	100 Lei. Gold. Ornamented.	—
PnA251	1937	—	50 Lei. Nickel. KM55.	120
Pn251	1937	—	Leu. Copper-Nickel-Zinc.	250
Pn252	ND 1937	—	Leu. Copper-Nickel-Zinc.	—
Pn253	1937	—	2 Lei. Copper-Nickel-Zinc.	—
Pn254	1937	—	20 Lei. Gold. Plain.	—
Pn255	1937	—	20 Lei. Gold. Ornamented.	—
Pn256	1937	—	50 Lei. Copper-Nickel-Zinc.	240
Pn257	1937	—	100 Lei. Gold. Plain.	—
Pn258	1937	—	100 Lei. Gold. Ornamented.	—
Pn259	1938	—	Leu. Copper-Nickel-Zinc.	400
Pn260	1938	—	20 Lei. Gold. Plain.	—
Pn261	1938	—	20 Lei. Gold. Ornamented.	—
Pn262	1938	—	100 Lei. Gold. Plain.	—
Pn263	1938	—	100 Lei. Gold. Ornamented.	—
Pn264	1939	—	20 Lei. Gold. Plain.	—
Pn265	1939	—	20 Lei. Gold. Ornamented.	—
Pn266	1939	—	20 Lei. Gold. Arms.	—
Pn267	1939	—	20 Lei. Gold. Eagle.	—
Pn268	1939	—	100 Lei. Gold. Plain.	—
Pn269	1939	—	100 Lei. Gold. Ornamented.	—
Pn270	1939	—	100 Lei. Gold. Bust.	—
Pn271	1940	—	20 Lei. Gold. Plain.	3,300
Pn272	1940	—	20 Lei. Gold. Ornamented.	3,300
Pn273	1940	—	100 Lei. Gold. Plain.	—
Pn274	1940	—	100 Lei. Gold. Ornamented.	—
Pn275	1940	—	250 Lei. 0.7500 Silver. Iron guard emblem.	9,000
Pn276	1941	—	Leu. Zinc.	—
Pn277	1941	—	Leu. Copper-Nickel-Zinc.	—
PnA278	1944	—	20 Lei. Gilt Copper.	200
Pn278	1944	—	20 Lei. Copper-Nickel-Zinc.	750
PnA279	1944	—	500 Lei. Silver. Plain edge.	180
Pn279	1944	—	500 Lei. Silver.	300
Pn280	1945	—	100 Lei. Nickel Clad Steel.	125
PnA280	1945	—	200 Lei. Aluminum.	—
Pn281	1945	—	500 Lei. Brass. Nickel plated.	125
Pn282	1945	—	2000 Lei. Brass. Nickel plated.	—
PnC283	1946	—	25000 Lei. Silver. Without number.	5,000
PnA283	1946	—	1000 Lei. Aluminum.	—
PnB283	1946	—	500 Lei.	—
Pn283	1946	—	25000 Lei. Silver. With number	3,000
PnA284	1952	—	10 Bani. Copper-Nickel. With cogged wheel instead of wreath.	—
PnB284	1956	—	10 Bani. Aluminum.	100
PnC284	1956	—	50 Bani. Aluminum.	200
Pn284	1958	—	5 Bani. Copper-Nickel-Zinc.	150
PnD284	ND 1958	—	5 Bani. Aluminum-Bronze.	—
Pn285	1960	—	10 Bani. Nickel. 20 teeth to wheel.	200
PnA285	1960	—	10 Bani. Nickel. 12 teeth to wheel.	400
PnB285	1966	—	5 Bani. Aluminum.	—
PnC285	1966	—	15 Bani. Aluminum.	—
PnD285	1966	—	15 Bani. Brass.	—
PnE285	1966	—	15 Bani. Copper.	100
PnF285	1966	—	3 Lei. Silver.	7,500
PnG285	1966	—	5 Lei. Copper. Factory.	300
PnH285	1966	—	5 Lei. Copper.	300
PnI285	1966	—	5 Lei. Brass.	300
PnJ285	1984	—	100 Lei. Silver.	10,000
PnK285	ND (1984)	—	100 Lei. Silver.	10,000
PnL285	1987	—	2 Lei. Nickel Plated Steel.	250
Pn286	1987	—	10 Lei. Aluminum.	75.00
Pn287	1987	—	10 Lei. Aluminum.	70.00
Pn288	1987	—	10 Lei. Aluminum.	70.00
Pn289	1987	—	10 Lei. Bronze.	80.00
Pn290	1987	—	10 Lei. Nickel. Steel plated.	75.00
PnA290	1987	—	10 Lei. Nickel Plated Steel.	—
PnB290	1987	—	10 Lei. Aluminum.	—
PnC290	1987	—	10 Lei. Brass.	—
Pn291	1988	—	10 Lei. Aluminum.	75.00
Pn292	1988	—	10 Lei. Aluminum.	75.00
PnA293	1990	—	10 Lei. Aluminum.	100
PnB293	1991	—	Leu. Copper-Nickel. 3 oak leaves.	60.00
Pn293	1991	—	5 Lei. Iron. Nickel clad. Similar to 100 Lei, KM#111.	70.00
Pn294	1991	—	5 Lei. Similar to 100 Lei, KM#111.	70.00
PnA296	1991	—	20 Lei. Aluminum.	70.00
PnB296	1991	—	20 Lei. Nickel Plated Steel. Similar to 100 Lei, KM#111.	95.00
PnC296	1991	—	50 Lei. Aluminum.	60.00
PnD296	1991	—	50 Lei. Copper-Nickel.	60.00
Pn296	1991	—	50 Lei. Silver. KM110.	250
PnA297	1991	—	100 Lei. Brass. King Stephen.	300
PnB297	1991	—	100 Lei. Brass. Prince M. Viteazul.	200
PnC297	1991	—	100 Lei. Alum. Prince M. Viteazul.	150
PnD297	1991	—	100 Lei. Nickel Plated Steel. Lettered edge.	180
PnE297	1991	—	100 Lei. Nickel Plated Steel. Sinus line edge.	90.00
PnF297	1991	—	100 Lei. Nickel Plated Steel. Lettered edge.	90.00
PnG297	1991	—	100 Lei. Nickel Plated Steel. Lettered edge.	90.00
PnH297	ND (1992)	—	Leu. Nickel.	80.00
Pn297	1992	—	Leu. Silver.	100
Pn298	ND (1992)	—	Leu. Nickel.	80.00
PnA299	1992	—	Leu. Silver.	100
PnB299	1992	—	5 Lei. Brass.	70.00
PnC299	1992	—	5 Lei. Copper-Nickel.	70.00
PnD299	1992	—	5 Lei. Nickel Plated Steel.	70.00
Pn299	1992	—	5 Lei. Aluminum.	50.00
PnA300	1993	—	Leu. Copper. Like KM#113.	80.00
PnB300	1995	—	100 Lei. Aluminum. KM#118.	40.00
PnA315 C1	1996	125	100 Lei. Brass center. Copper-Nickel ring. 37 mm. Nationl arms. Gymnast on balance beam. Plain with denomination edge. Piefort version.	
PnB326	1996	125	100 Lei. Bronze.	30.00
Pn300	1996	—	10 Lei. Nickel Plated Steel. Similar to KM#117. KM#134.	35.00
Pn301	1996	—	100 Lei. Aluminum. KM#119.	45.00
Pn302	1996	—	100 Lei. Brass. KM#119.	50.00
Pn303	1996	—	100 Lei. Copper-Nickel. KM#127. Brass plated.	45.00
Pn304	1996	—	100 Lei. Aluminum. KM#127.	40.00
Pn305	1996	—	100 Lei. Copper-Nickel. KM#128. Brass plated.	45.00
Pn306	1996	—	100 Lei. Aluminum. KM#128.	40.00
Pn307	1996	—	100 Lei. Copper-Nickel. KM#129. Brass plated.	45.00
Pn351A	1996	—	100 Lei. Brass. 37 mm. National arms. Skier. Plain with denomination edge.	30.00
Pn308	1996	—	100 Lei. Aluminum. KM#129.	40.00
Pn309	1996	—	100 Lei. Copper-Nickel. KM#130. Brass plated.	45.00
Pn310	1996	—	100 Lei. Aluminum. KM#130.	40.00
Pn311	1996	—	100 Lei. Copper-Nickel. KM#131. Brass plated.	45.00
Pn312	1996	—	100 Lei. Aluminum. KM#131.	40.00
Pn313	1996	—	100 Lei. Copper-Nickel. KM#132. Brass plated.	45.00
Pn314	1996	—	100 Lei. Aluminum. KM#132.	40.00
Pn316	1996	—	100 Lei. Aluminum. KM#133.	45.00
Pn317	1996	—	100 Lei. Brass. KM#135.	50.00
Pn318	1996	—	500 Lei. Brass. KM#147. Arms without outline.	90.00
Pn319	1996	—	500 Lei. Aluminum. KM#147. Arms without outline.	90.00
Pn320	1996	—	500 Lei. Nickel. KM#147. Arms without outline.	90.00
Pn321	1996	—	500 Lei. Aluminum. KM#147. Arms without outline. Bimetal.	100
Pn322	1996	—	3000 Lei. Copper. 1 ECU. Dracula.	100

KM#	Date	Mintage	Identification	Mkt Val
Pn323	1996	—	3000 Lei. 1 ECU. Dracula. Golden brass.	100
Pn324	1996	—	3000 Lei. Silver. 1 ECU. Dracula.	150
Pn325	1996	—	3000 Lei. Alum. 1 ECU. Dracula.	120
Pn326	1998	—	100 Lei. Silver. KM#119. Eiffel Tower. Golden brass.	60.00
Pn327	1998	—	100 Lei. Alum. KM#119. Eiffel Tower.	60.00
Pn328	1998	—	100 Lei. Brass. One player.	100
Pn329	1998	—	100 Lei. One player. Bimetal.	100
Pn330	1998	—	100 Lei. Brass. Two players.	60.00
Pn331	1998	—	100 Lei. Bi-Metallic. Two players.	100
Pn332	1998	—	100 Lei. Bi-Metallic. Gaelic cock.	100
Pn350a	1998	—	100 Lei. Brass. Hockey.	35.00
Pn333	1998	—	500 Lei. Silver.	—
Pn334	1998	—	500 Lei. Golden brass.	—
Pn353A	1998	—	100 Lei. Brass. Ice dancing.	35.00
Pn335	1998	—	500 Lei. Brass. KM#136.	25.00
Pn336	1998	—	1000 Lei. Silver. Arms at 6.	200
Pn337	1998	—	1000 Lei. Brass. Arms at 6.	80.00
Pn338	1998	—	1000 Lei. Arms at 9. Golden brass.	90.00
Pn339	1998	—	500 Lei. Brass. KM#147. Arms without outline.	90.00
Pn340	1998	—	500 Lei. Nickel. KM#147. Arms without outline.	40.00
Pn341	1998	—	500 Lei. Aluminum. KM#147. Arms without outline.	30.00
Pn342	1998	—	500 Lei. Aluminum. KM#147. Arms without outline. Bimetal.	45.00
Pn343	1998	—	100 Lei. Brass.	—
Pn344	1998	—	100 Lei. Bi-Metallic. KM#138.	—
Pn345	1998	—	100 Lei. Aluminum. KM#138.	—
Pn346	1998	—	100 Lei. Brass.	—
Pn347	1998	—	100 Lei. Silver.	—
Pn348	1998	—	100 Lei. Bi-Metallic.	—
Pn349	1998	—	100 Lei. Aluminum.	—
Pn350	1998	125	100 Lei. Alum. 37 mm. National arms. Two hockey players. Plain with denomination edge.	30.00
Pn352	1998	—	100 Lei. Brass. Women single.	35.00
Pn353	1998	125	100 Lei. Aluminum. 37 mm. National arms. Two ice dancers. Plain with denomination edge.	30.00
Pn354	1998	—	100 Lei. Brass. Ice dancing. without inscription.	50.00
Pn355	1998	—	100 Lei. Brass. Bobsled, without inscription.	30.00
Pn356	1998	—	100 Lei. Brass. Slalom, without inscription.	50.00
Pn357	1998	—	1000 Lei. Brass. Large.	—
Pn358	1998	—	1000 Lei. Brass. Thin.	—
Pn359	1998	—	1000 Lei. Golden brass.	—
Pn366	1999	—	500 Lei. Aluminum. Solar Eclipse. Lettered edge. KM#147.	—
Pn360	1999	—	100 Lei. Brass. Young.	100
Pn361	1999	—	100 Lei. Brass. Old.	70.00
Pn362	1999	—	100 Lei. Brass.	—
Pn363	1999	—	100 Lei. Brass.	—
Pn364	1999	—	100 Lei. Alum. Plain edge. KM146.	100
Pn365	1999	—	100 Lei. Alum. Plain edge. KM147.	100

PIEFORTS

KM#	Date	Mintage	Identification	Mkt Val
P3	1905	—	20 Bani. Aluminum-Bronze.	200
P4	1905	—	20 Bani. Bronze.	200
P5	1906	—	12-1/2 Lei. Gold.	—
P6	1906	—	25 Lei. Gold.	—
P7	1906	—	50 Lei. Lead.	325
P8	1906	—	50 Lei. Copper.	325
P9	1906	—	50 Lei. Silver.	1,200
P10	1906	—	50 Lei. Gold.	—

TRIAL STRIKES

KM#	Date	Mintage	Identification	Mkt Val
TS1	1906	—	5 Lei. Silver.	4,500
TS2	1906	—	100 Lei. Silver.	400
TS3	1910	—	Leu. Pewter. Milled edge. Thin planchet.	—
TS4	1910	—	Leu. Pewter. Milled edge. Thick planchet.	—
TS5	1996	—	10 Lei. Nickel Plated Steel. KM#134.	100

MINT SETS

KM#	Date	Mintage	Identification	Issue Price	Mkt Val
MS1	1982FM (2)	—	KM#98-99	429	1,700
MS2	1983FM (4)	—	KM#98-101	850	4,700

PROOF SETS

KM#	Date	Mintage	Identification	Issue Price	Mkt Val
PS3	2000 (8)	—	KM109-111, 114-116, 145, 153 140th Anniversary Foundation Romanian Academy	—	45.00

RUSSIA (U.S.S.R.)

Russia, formerly the central power of the Union of Soviet Socialist Republics and now of the Commonwealth of Independent States occupies the northern part of Asia and the eastern part of Europe, has an area of 17,075,400 sq. km. and a population of *146.2 million. Capital: Moscow. Exports include iron and steel, crude oil, timber, and nonferrous metals.

The first Russian dynasty was founded in Novgorod by the Viking Rurik in 862 A.D. under Yaroslav the Wise (1019-54). The subsequent Kievan state became one of the great commercial and cultural centers of Europe before falling to the Mongols of the Batu Khan, 13th century, who were suzerains of Russia until late in the 15th century when Ivan III threw off the Mongol yoke. The Russian Empire was enlarged, solidified and Westernized during the reigns of Ivan the Terrible, Peter the Great and Catherine the Great, and by 1881 extended to the Pacific and into Central Asia. Contemporary Russian history began in March of 1917 when Tsar Nicholas II abdicated under pressure and was replaced by a provisional government composed of both radical and conservative elements. This government rapidly lost ground to the Bolshevik wing of the Socialist Democratic Labor Party which attained power following the Bolshevik Revolution which began on Nov. 7, 1917. After the Russian Civil War, the regional governments, national states and armies became federal republics of the Russian Socialist Federal Soviet Republic. These autonomous republics united to form the Union of Soviet Socialist Republics that was established as a federation under the premiership of Lenin on Dec. 30, 1922.

In the fall of 1991, events moved swiftly in the Soviet Union. Estonia, Latvia and Lithuania won their independence and were recognized by Moscow, Sept. 6. The Commonwealth of Independent States was formed Dec. 8, 1991 in Mensk by Belarus, Russia and Ukraine. It was expanded at a summit Dec. 21, 1991 to include 11 of the 12 remaining republics (excluding Georgia) of the old U.S.S.R.

EMPIRE

RULER
Nicholas II, 1894-1917

MINT MARKS
Л – Leningrad, 1991
M – Moscow, 1990
СП – St. Petersburg, 1999
СПБ – St. Petersburg, 1724-1914
СПМД – St. Petersburg, 1999

(sp) (l) – LMD (ЛМД) monogram in oval, (Leningrad), (St. Petersburg) 1977-1997

(m) – MMD (ММД) monogram in oval, Moscow, 1977-

MINT OFFICIALS' INITIALS

Leningrad Mint

Initials	Years	Mint Official
АГ	1921-22	A.F. Hartman
ПЛ	1922-27	P.V. Latishev

London Mint

Т.Р.	1924	Thomas Ross
ФР	1924	Thomas Ross

St. Petersburg Mint

ФЗ	1899-1901	Felix Zaleman
АР	1901-05	Alexander Redko
ЭБ	1906-13	Elikum Babayantz
ВС	1913-17	Victor Smirnov

NOTE: St. Petersburg Mint became Petrograd in 1914 and Leningrad in 1924. It was renamed St. Petersburg in 1991.

MONETARY SYSTEM
1/4 Kopek = Polushka ПОЛУШКА
1/2 Kopek = Denga, Denezhka ДЕНГА, ДЕНЕЖКА
Kopek = КОП_ИКА
(2, 3 & 4) Kopeks КОП_ИКИ
(5 and up) Kopeks КОП_ЕКЪ
(1924 – 5 and up) Kopeks КОПЕЕК
50 Kopeks = Poltina, Poltinnik ПОЛТИНА,…ПОЛРУБЛЪ
100 Kopeks = Rouble, Ruble РУБЛЪ
10 Roubles = Imperial ИМПЕРIАЛЪ
10 Roubles = Chervonetz ЧЕРВОНЕЦ

NOTE: Mintage figures for years after 1885 are for fiscal years and may or may not reflect actual rarity, the commemorative and 1917 silver figures being exceptions.

STANDARD COINAGE

Y# 47.1   1/4 KOPEK
0.8000 g., Copper **Ruler:** Nicholas II **Obv:** Crowned monogram above sprays **Rev:** Value, date **Edge:** Reeded

Date	Mintage	F	VF	XF	Unc	BU
1909СПБ	2,000,000	8.00	7.00	15.00	30.00	—
1910СПБ	8,000,000	5.00	10.00	20.00	40.00	—
1909-1910 Common date Proof	—	Value: 125				

Y# 47.2   POLUSHKA (1/4 Kopek)
0.8000 g., Copper **Ruler:** Nicholas II **Obv:** Crowned monogram above sprays **Rev:** Value, date

Date	Mintage	F	VF	XF	Unc	BU
1915	500,000	5.00	10.00	15.00	30.00	—
1916	1,200,000	50.00	100	170	350	—

Y# 48.1   1/2 KOPEK
1.6000 g., Copper, 16 mm. **Ruler:** Nicholas II **Obv:** Crowned monogram above sprays **Rev:** Value and date **Edge:** Reeded

Date	Mintage	F	VF	XF	Unc	BU
1908СПБ	8,000,000	5.00	7.00	12.00	25.00	—
1909СПБ	49,500,000	5.00	7.00	15.00	30.00	—
1910СПБ	24,000,000	3.00	8.00	15.00	30.00	40.00
1911СПБ	35,800,000	4.00	8.00	15.00	30.00	40.00
1912СПБ	28,000,000	3.00	8.00	15.00	30.00	40.00
1913СПБ	50,000,000	2.00	5.00	7.00	15.00	25.00
1914СПБ	14,000,000	4.00	7.00	15.00	30.00	40.00
1908-14 Common date Proof	—	Value: 200				

Y# 48.2   1/2 KOPEK
1.6000 g., Copper **Ruler:** Nicholas II **Obv:** Crowned monogram above sprays **Rev:** Value and date **Note:** Struck at Petrograd without mint mark.

Date	Mintage	F	VF	XF	Unc	BU
1915	12,000,000	4.00	8.00	15.00	30.00	40.00
1916	9,400,000	4.00	8.00	15.00	30.00	40.00

Y# 9.2   KOPEK
3.3000 g., Copper, 21.5 mm. **Ruler:** Nicholas II **Obv:** Crowned double-headed imperial eagle within circle **Rev:** Value flanked by stars within beaded circle **Edge:** Reeded

Date	Mintage	F	VF	XF	Unc	BU
1901СПБ	30,000,000	2.00	3.00	5.00	15.00	—
1902СПБ	20,000,000	3.00	10.00	20.00	35.00	—
1903СПБ	74,400,000	2.00	3.00	5.00	15.00	—
1904СПБ	30,600,000	2.00	3.00	5.00	15.00	—
1905СПБ	23,000,000	2.00	3.00	5.00	15.00	—
1906СПБ	20,000,000	2.00	3.00	5.00	15.00	—
1907СПБ	20,000,000	2.00	3.00	5.00	15.00	—
1908СПБ	40,000,000	2.00	3.00	5.00	15.00	—
1909СПБ	27,500,000	2.00	3.00	5.00	15.00	—
1910СПБ	36,500,000	2.00	3.00	5.00	15.00	—
1911СПБ	38,150,000	2.00	3.00	5.00	15.00	—
1912СПБ	31,850,000	2.00	3.00	5.00	15.00	—
1913СПБ	61,500,000	2.00	3.00	5.00	15.00	—
1914СПБ	32,500,000	2.00	3.00	5.00	15.00	—
1901-14 Common date Proof	—	Value: 150				

Y# 9.3   KOPEK
3.3000 g., Copper **Ruler:** Nicholas II **Obv:** Crowned double-headed imperial eagle within circle **Rev:** Value flanked by stars within beaded circle **Note:** Struck at Petrograd without mint mark.

Date	Mintage	F	VF	XF	Unc	BU
1915	58,000,000	2.00	3.00	6.00	15.00	—
1916	46,500,000	3.00	4.00	7.00	15.00	—
1917 Unique						

Y# 10.2   2 KOPEKS
6.6000 g., Copper **Ruler:** Nicholas II **Obv:** Crowned double-headed imperial eagle within circle **Rev:** Value flanked by stars within circle **Edge:** Reeded

Date	Mintage	F	VF	XF	Unc	BU
1901СПБ	20,000,000	4.00	6.00	10.00	18.00	—
1902СПБ	10,000,000	4.00	6.00	10.00	18.00	—

Date	Mintage	F	VF	XF	Unc	BU
1903СПБ	29,200,000	4.00	6.00	10.00	18.00	—
1904СПБ	13,300,000	4.00	6.00	10.00	18.00	—
1905СПБ	15,000,000	4.00	6.00	10.00	18.00	—
1906СПБ	6,250,000	4.00	6.00	10.00	18.00	—
1907СПБ	7,500,000	4.00	6.00	10.00	18.00	—
1908СПБ	19,000,000	4.00	6.00	10.00	18.00	—
1909СПБ	16,250,000	4.00	6.00	10.00	18.00	—
1910СПБ	12,000,000	4.00	6.00	10.00	18.00	—
1911СПБ	17,200,000	4.00	6.00	10.00	18.00	—
1912СПБ	17,050,000	4.00	6.00	10.00	18.00	—
1913СПБ	26,000,000	4.00	6.00	10.00	18.00	—
1914СПБ	20,000,000	4.00	6.00	10.00	18.00	—
1901-14 Common date proof	—	Value: 175				

Y# 10.3   2 KOPEKS
Copper **Ruler:** Nicholas II **Obv:** Crowned double-headed imperial eagle **Rev:** Value within circle **Note:** Struck at Petrograd without mint mark.

Date	Mintage	F	VF	XF	Unc	BU
1915	33,750,000	5.00	7.00	10.00	20.00	—
1916	31,500,000	7.00	8.00	12.00	24.00	—
1917 Rare	—	—	—	—	—	—

Y# 11.2   3 KOPEKS
8.0000 g., Copper, 18.23 mm. **Ruler:** Nicholas II **Obv:** Crowned double imperial eagle within circle **Rev:** Value flanked by stars within beaded circle **Edge:** Reeded

Date	Mintage	F	VF	XF	Unc	BU
1901СПБ	10,000,000	4.00	6.00	12.00	24.00	—
1902СПБ	3,333,000	5.00	10.00	17.00	35.00	—
1903СПБ	11,400,000	4.00	6.00	12.00	24.00	—
1904СПБ	6,934,000	5.00	10.00	17.00	35.00	—
1905СПБ	3,333,000	5.00	9.00	20.00	35.00	—
1906СПБ	5,667,000	5.00	9.00	20.00	35.00	—
1907СПБ	2,500,000	5.00	9.00	20.00	35.00	—
1908СПБ	12,667,000	4.00	6.00	12.00	24.00	—
1909СПБ	6,733,000	4.00	6.00	12.00	24.00	—
1910СПБ	6,667,000	4.00	6.00	12.00	24.00	—
1911СПБ	9,467,000	4.00	6.00	12.00	24.00	—
1912СПБ	8,533,000	5.00	10.00	20.00	39.00	—
1913СПБ	15,333,000	4.00	7.00	12.00	25.00	—
1914СПБ	8,167,000	4.00	7.00	12.00	25.00	—
1901-14СПБ Common date proof	—	Value: 200				

Y# 11.3   3 KOPEKS
Copper **Ruler:** Nicholas II **Obv:** Crowned double-headed imperial eagle **Rev:** Value flanked by stars within beaded circle **Note:** Struck at Petrograd without mint mark.

Date	Mintage	F	VF	XF	Unc	BU
1915	19,833,000	5.00	10.00	20.00	40.00	—
1916	25,667,000	5.00	10.00	20.00	45.00	—
1917 Rare	—	—	—	—	—	—

Y# 19a.1   5 KOPEKS
0.8998 g., 0.5000 Silver 0.0145 oz. ASW **Ruler:** Nicholas II **Obv:** Crowned double-headed imperial eagle **Rev:** Crown above date and value within wreath **Edge:** Reeded

Date	Mintage	F	VF	XF	Unc	BU
1901СПБ АР	Inc. above	4.00	7.00	12.00	25.00	50.00
1901СПБ ФЗ	5,790,000	4.00	7.00	12.00	25.00	50.00
1902СПБ АР	6,000,000	4.00	7.00	12.00	25.00	50.00
1903СПБ АР	9,000,000	4.00	7.00	12.00	25.00	50.00
1904СПБ АР Rare	9					
1905СПБ АР	10,000,000	5.00	8.00	15.00	40.00	100
1906СПБ ЭБ	4,000,000	5.00	8.00	15.00	40.00	100
1908СПБ ЭБ	400,000	5.00	8.00	15.00	40.00	100
1909СПБ ЭБ	3,100,000	5.00	8.00	15.00	40.00	100
1910СПБ ЭБ	2,500,000	5.00	8.00	15.00	40.00	100
1911СПБ ЭБ	2,700,000	5.00	8.00	15.00	40.00	100
1912СПБ ЭБ	3,000,000	5.00	8.00	15.00	40.00	100
1913СПБ ЭБ Proof	Inc. below	Value: 150				
1913СПБ ВС	1,300,000	5.00	8.00	15.00	40.00	100
1914СПБ ВС	4,200,000	5.00	8.00	15.00	40.00	100
1901-14 Common date proof	—	Value: 150				

Y# 12.2   5 KOPEKS
16.4000 g., Copper, 32.6 mm. **Ruler:** Nicholas II **Obv:** Crowned double-headed imperial eagle within circle **Rev:** Value flanked by stars within beaded circle **Edge:** Reeded

Date	Mintage	F	VF	XF	Unc	BU
1911СПБ	3,800,000	15.00	25.00	40.00	80.00	—
1912СПБ	2,700,000	20.00	30.00	50.00	100	—

Y# 19a.2   5 KOPEKS
0.8998 g., 0.5000 Silver 0.0145 oz. ASW **Ruler:** Nicholas II **Obv:** Crowned double-headed imperial eagle **Rev:** Crown above value and date within wreath **Note:** Struck at Petrograd without mint mark.

Date	Mintage	F	VF	XF	Unc	BU
1915 ВС	3,000,000	4.00	7.00	15.00	30.00	50.00

Y# 12.3   5 KOPEKS
Copper **Ruler:** Nicholas II **Obv:** Crowned double-headed imperial eagle **Rev:** Value flanked by stars within beaded circle **Note:** Struck at Petrograd without mint mark.

Date	Mintage	F	VF	XF	Unc	BU
1916	8,000,000	50.00	90.00	160	270	—
1917 Rare	—	—	—	—	—	—

Y# 20a.2   10 KOPEKS
1.7996 g., 0.5000 Silver 0.0289 oz. ASW **Ruler:** Nicholas II **Obv:** Crowned double-headed imperial eagle, ribbons on crown **Rev:** Crown above value and date within wreath **Edge:** Reeded

Date	Mintage	F	VF	XF	Unc	BU
1901СПБ АР	Inc. above	3.00	6.00	12.00	25.00	—
1901СПБ ФЗ	15,000,000	3.00	6.00	12.00	25.00	—
1902СПБ АР	17,000,000	3.00	6.00	12.00	25.00	—
1903СПБ АР	28,500,000	3.00	6.00	12.00	25.00	—
1904СПБ АР	20,000,000	3.00	6.00	12.00	25.00	—
1905СПБ АР	25,000,000	3.00	6.00	12.00	25.00	—
1906СПБ ЭБ	17,500,000	3.00	6.00	12.00	25.00	—
1907СПБ ЭБ		3.00	6.00	12.00	25.00	—
1908СПБ ЭБ	8,210,000	3.00	6.00	12.00	25.00	—
1909СПБ ЭБ	25,290,000	3.00	6.00	12.00	25.00	—
1910СПБ ЭБ	20,000,000	3.00	6.00	12.00	25.00	—
1911СПБ ЭБ	19,180,000	3.00	6.00	12.00	25.00	—
1912СПБ ЭБ	20,000,000	3.00	6.00	12.00	25.00	—
1913СПБ ЭБ Proof	Inc. below	Value: 250				
1913СПБ ВС	7,250,000	3.00	6.00	12.00	25.00	—
1914СПБ ВС	51,250,000	3.00	6.00	12.00	25.00	—
1901-14 Common date proof	—	Value: 250				

Y# 20a.3   10 KOPEKS
1.7996 g., 0.5000 Silver 0.0289 oz. ASW **Ruler:** Nicholas II **Obv:** Crowned double-headed imperial eagle, ribbons on crown **Rev:** Crown above value and date within wreath **Edge:** Reeded **Note:** Struck at Petrograd without mintmaster initials.

Date	Mintage	F	VF	XF	Unc	BU
1915 ВС	82,500,000	3.00	5.00	7.00	14.00	—
1916 ВС	121,500,000	3.00	5.00	10.00	20.00	—
1917 ВС	17,600,000	10.00	35.00	60.00	120	—

Y# 20a.1   10 KOPEKS
1.7996 g., 0.5000 Silver 0.0289 oz. ASW **Ruler:** Nicholas II **Obv:** Crowned double-headed imperial eagle, ribbons on crown **Rev:** Crown above value and date within wreath **Note:** Struck at Osaka, Japan without mintmaster initials.

Date	Mintage	F	VF	XF	Unc	BU
1916	70,001,000	2.00	3.00	10.00	20.00	—

Y# 21a.2   15 KOPEKS
2.6994 g., 0.5000 Silver 0.0434 oz. ASW **Ruler:** Nicholas II **Obv:** Crowned double-headed imperial eagle, ribbons on crown **Rev:** Crown above date and value within wreath **Edge:** Reeded

Date	Mintage	F	VF	XF	Unc	BU
1901СПБ ФЗ	6,670,000	6.00	12.00	20.00	35.00	—
1901СПБ АР	Inc. above	6.00	12.00	20.00	35.00	—
1902СПБ АР	28,667,000	6.00	12.00	20.00	35.00	—

Date	Mintage	F	VF	XF	Unc	BU
1903СПБ АР	16,667,000	6.00	12.00	20.00	35.00	—
1904СПБ АР	15,600,000	4.00	7.00	12.00	25.00	—
1905СПБ АР	24,000,000	4.00	7.00	12.00	25.00	—
1906СПБ ЭБ	23,333,000	4.00	7.00	12.00	25.00	—
1907СПБ ЭБ	30,000,000	4.00	7.00	12.00	25.00	—
1908СПБ ЭБ	29,000,000	4.00	7.00	12.00	25.00	—
1909СПБ ЭБ	21,667,000	4.00	7.00	12.00	25.00	—
1911СПБ ЭБ	6,313,000	7.00	15.00	20.00	35.00	—
1912СПБ ЭБ	13,333,000	10.00	15.00	30.00	60.00	—
1912СПБ ВС Rare	Inc. above	—	—	—	—	—
1913СПБ ЭБ Proof	Inc. below	Value: 250				
1913СПБ ВС	5,300,000	7.00	12.00	18.00	35.00	—
1914СПБ ВС	43,367,000	4.00	7.00	12.00	25.00	—
1901-14 Common date proof	—	Value: 250				

Y# 21a.3 15 KOPEKS
2.6994 g., 0.5000 Silver 0.0434 oz. ASW **Ruler:** Nicholas II
Obv: Crowned double-headed imperial eagle, ribbons on crown
Rev: Crown above value and date within wreath **Note:** Struck at Petrograd without mintmaster initials.

Date	Mintage	F	VF	XF	Unc	BU
1915 ВС	59,333,000	3.00	5.00	10.00	20.00	—
1916 ВС	96,773,000	3.00	5.00	10.00	20.00	—
1917 ВС	14,320,000	20.00	40.00	70.00	140	—

Y# 21a.1 15 KOPEKS
2.6994 g., 0.5000 Silver 0.0434 oz. ASW **Ruler:** Nicholas II
Obv: Crowned double-headed imperial eagle, ribbons on crown
Rev: Crown above value and date within wreath **Edge:** Reeded
Note: Struck at Osaka, Japan without mintmaster initials.

Date	Mintage	F	VF	XF	Unc	BU
1916	96,666,000	BV	2.00	5.00	12.00	—

Y# 22a.1 20 KOPEKS
3.5992 g., 0.5000 Silver 0.0579 oz. ASW, 22 mm.
Ruler: Nicholas II **Obv:** Crowned double-headed imperial eagle, ribbons on crown **Rev:** Crown above value and date within wreath

Date	Mintage	F	VF	XF	Unc	BU
1901СПБ ФЗ	7,750,000	4.00	6.00	12.00	24.00	—
1901СПБ АР Proof	Inc. above	Value: 300				
1902СПБ АР	10,000,000	4.00	6.00	12.00	24.00	—
1903СПБ АР	Inc. above	4.00	6.00	12.00	24.00	—
1904СПБ АР	13,000,000	4.00	6.00	12.00	24.00	—
1905СПБ АР	11,000,000	4.00	6.00	12.00	24.00	—
1906СПБ ЭБ	15,000,000	4.00	6.00	12.00	24.00	—
1907СПБ ЭБ	20,000,000	4.00	6.00	12.00	24.00	—
1908СПБ ЭБ	5,000,000	4.00	6.00	12.00	24.00	—
1909СПБ ЭБ	18,875,000	4.00	6.00	12.00	24.00	—
1910СПБ ЭБ	11,000,000	4.00	6.00	12.00	24.00	—
1911СПБ ЭБ	7,100,000	4.00	6.00	12.00	24.00	—
1912СПБ ЭБ	15,000,000	4.00	6.00	12.00	24.00	—
1912СПБ ВС Rare	Inc. above					
1913СПБ ЭБ Proof	Inc. below	Value: 250				
1913СПБ ВС	4,250,000	4.00	6.00	12.00	24.00	—
1914СПБ ВС	52,750,000	3.00	5.00	10.00	20.00	25.00
1901-14 Common date proof	—	Value: 250				

Y# 22a.2 20 KOPEKS
3.5992 g., 0.5000 Silver 0.0579 oz. ASW **Ruler:** Nicholas II
Obv: Crowned double-headed imperial eagle, ribbons on crown
Rev: Crown above value and date within wreath **Note:** Struck at Petrograd without mint mark.

Date	Mintage	F	VF	XF	Unc	BU
1915 ВС	105,500,000	2.00	4.00	8.00	15.00	20.00
1916 ВС	131,670,000	3.00	5.00	10.00	20.00	30.00
1917 ВС	3,500,000	20.00	40.00	80.00	170	—
1915-17 Common date proof	—	Value: 250				

Y# 57 25 KOPEKS
4.9990 g., 0.9000 Silver 0.1446 oz. ASW **Ruler:** Nicholas II
Obv: Head left **Rev:** Crowned double-headed imperial eagle, ribbons on crown **Note:** Struck at St. Petersburg without mint mark.

Date	Mintage	F	VF	XF	Unc	BU
1901 Proof	Est. 200	Value: 1,250				

Y# 58.2 50 KOPEKS
9.9980 g., 0.9000 Silver 0.2893 oz. ASW **Ruler:** Nicholas II
Obv: Head left **Rev:** Crowned double-headed imperial eagle, ribbons on crown **Note:** Without mint mark, moneyer's initials on edge.

Date	Mintage	F	VF	XF	Unc	BU
1901 АР	412,000	25.00	50.00	100	250	—
1901 ФЗ	Inc. above	25.00	50.00	100	250	—
1902 АР	36,000	25.00	50.00	100	300	—
1903 АР Proof	—	Value: 2,000				
1904 АР	4,010,000	100	200	400	1,200	—
1906 ЭБ	10,000	30.00	70.00	150	400	—
1907 ЭБ	200,000	25.00	50.00	100	250	—
1908 ЭБ	40,000	25.00	50.00	100	250	—
1909 ЭБ	50,000	25.00	50.00	100	250	—
1910 ЭБ	150,000	25.00	50.00	100	250	—
1911 ЭБ	800,000	20.00	40.00	80.00	200	—
1912 ЭБ	7,085,000	15.00	30.00	50.00	100	—
1913 ЭБ	6,420,000	15.00	30.00	70.00	150	—
1913 ВС	Inc. above	15.00	20.00	40.00	80.00	—
1914 ВС	1,200,000	15.00	25.00	50.00	100	—
1901-14 Common date proof	—	Value: 500				

Y# 59.3 ROUBLE
19.9960 g., 0.9000 Silver 0.5786 oz. ASW **Ruler:** Nicholas II
Obv: Head left **Rev:** Crowned double-headed imperial eagle, ribbons on crown **Note:** Without mint mark, moneyer's initials on edge.

Date	Mintage	F	VF	XF	Unc	BU
1901 ФЗ	2,608,000	30.00	60.00	120	350	700
1901 АР	Inc. above	80.00	150	350	800	4,000
1902 АР	140,000	110	140	300	700	1,200
1903 АР	56,000	120	170	400	900	—
1904 АР	12,000	150	250	600	1,200	—
1905 АР	21,000	140	200	500	1,000	—
1906 ЭБ	46,000	120	200	500	1,000	—
1907 ЭБ	400,000	80.00	140	300	700	2,000
1908 ЭБ	130,000	140	300	700	1,300	—
1909 ЭБ	51,000	100	200	400	900	—
1910 ЭБ	75,000	70.00	140	300	800	3,750
1911 ЭБ	129,000	70.00	140	300	700	2,750
1912 ЭБ	2,111,000	40.00	70.00	140	500	600
1913 ЭБ	22,000	120	250	500	1,000	—
1913 ВС	Inc. above	120	250	500	1,000	—
1914 ВС	536,000	60.00	120	350	700	2,000
1915 ВС	5,000	60.00	120	350	700	3,600
	Note: Varieties exist with plain edge, these are mint errors and rare					
1901-15 Common date proof	—	Value: 4,000				

Y# 68 ROUBLE
19.9960 g., 0.9000 Silver 0.5786 oz. ASW, 34 mm.
Ruler: Nicholas II **Subject:** Centennial - Napolean's Defeat
Obv: Crowned double-headed imperial eagle with various crowned shields **Rev:** Inscription and date within beaded circle

Date	Mintage	F	VF	XF	Unc	BU
1912 ЭБ	46,000	300	600	900	1,200	2,750
1912 ЭБ Proof	—	Value: 4,500				

Y# 69 ROUBLE
19.9960 g., 0.9000 Silver 0.5786 oz. ASW, 34 mm.
Ruler: Nicholas II **Subject:** Alexander III Memorial **Obv:** Head left **Rev:** Monument

Date	Mintage	F	VF	XF	Unc	BU
1912 ЭБ	2,100	800	1,700	3,000	5,500	9,500
1912 ЭБ Proof	—	Value: 10,000				

Y# 70 ROUBLE
19.9960 g., 0.9000 Silver 0.5786 oz. ASW, 34 mm.
Ruler: Nicholas II **Subject:** 300th Anniversary - Romanov Dynasty **Obv:** Conjoined heads facing 1/4 right **Rev:** Crowned double-headed imperial eagle **Note:** Struck at St. Petersburg without mint mark.

Date	Mintage	F	VF	XF	Unc	BU
1913 ВС	1,472,000	35.00	70.00	120	200	300

Y# 71 ROUBLE
19.9960 g., 0.9000 Silver 0.5786 oz. ASW, 34 mm.
Ruler: Nicholas II **Subject:** 200th Anniversary - Battle of Gangut
Obv: Armored bust right **Rev:** Crowned double-headed imperial eagle

Date	Mintage	F	VF	XF	Unc	BU
1914 ВС	Est. 30,000	1,500	4,000	6,500	8,500	9,500
	Note: Only 317 pieces were issued through 1917, but an unknown number of restrikes were made in the 1920's					
1914 ВС Proof	—	Value: 12,500				

Y# 62 5 ROUBLES
4.3013 g., 0.9000 Gold 0.1245 oz. AGW **Ruler:** Nicholas II
Obv: Head left **Rev:** Crowned double-headed imperial eagle, ribbons on crown **Note:** Struck at St. Petersburg without mint mark.

Date	Mintage	F	VF	XF	Unc	BU
1901 ФЗ	7,500,000	BV	280	300	330	400
1901 АР	Inc. above	BV	280	300	330	400
1902 АР	6,240,000	BV	280	300	330	400
1903 АР	5,148,000	BV	280	300	330	400
1904 АР	2,016,000	BV	280	300	330	400
1906 ЭБ	10	—	—	7,000	10,000	—
1907 ЭБ	109	—	—	4,000	7,500	—
1909 ЭБ	—	BV+20%	280	300	330	400
1910 ЭБ	200,000	BV+20%	280	300	330	400
1911 ЭБ	100,000	BV+20%	300	330	450	700
1901-11 Common date proof	—	Value: 2,500				

Y# 64   10 ROUBLES

8.6026 g., 0.9000 Gold 0.2489 oz. AGW   **Ruler:** Nicholas II
Obv: Head left **Rev:** Crowned double-headed imperial eagle, ribbons on crown **Note:** Without mint mark. Moneyer's initials on edge.

Date	Mintage	F	VF	XF	Unc	BU
1901 ФЗ	2,377,000	BV+20%	370	400	450	600
1901 АР	Inc. above	BV+20%	370	400	450	600
1902 АР	2,019,000	BV+20%	370	400	450	600
1903 АР	2,817,000	BV+20%	370	400	450	600
1904 АР	1,025,000	BV+20%	370	400	450	600
1906 ЭБ Proof	10	Value: 15,000				
1909 ЭБ	50,000	BV+30%	370	400	500	700
1910 ЭБ	100,000	BV+30%	370	400	500	700
1911 ЭБ	50,000	BV+30%	370	400	500	700
1901-11 Common date proof	—	Value: 4,500				

Y# A65   25 ROUBLES

32.2500 g., 0.9000 Gold 0.9331 oz. AGW   **Ruler:** Nicholas II
Obv: Head left **Rev:** Crowned double imperial eagle, ribbons on crown, within circle flanked by rosettes **Rev. Leg.:** 2-1/2 ИМПЕРІАЛЪА (IMPERIALS) **Note:** Struck at St. Petersburg without mint mark.

Date	Mintage	F	VF	XF	Unc	BU
1908	150	—	—	70,000	90,000	—
1908 Proof	25	Value: 95,000				

Y# B65a   37 ROUBLES 50 KOPEKS

Copper-Nickel   **Ruler:** Nicholas II **Obv:** Head left **Rev:** Crowned double headed imperial eagle within beaded circle **Rev. Insc.:** Letter "P" after "1902 G" **Edge:** Plain **Note:** Gold plated specimens were done outside the mint.

Date	Mintage	F	VF	XF	Unc	BU
1902 (1991) P Restrike	—	—	—	—	35.00	—

Y# B65   37 ROUBLES 50 KOPEKS

32.2500 g., 0.9000 Gold 0.9331 oz. AGW   **Ruler:** Nicholas II
Obv: Head left **Rev:** Crowned double-headed imperial eagle within beaded circle **Rev. Leg.:** 100 ФРАНКОВЪ **Note:** Without mint mark.

Date	Mintage	F	VF	XF	Unc	BU
1902	225	—	—	—	75,000	—
	Note: UBS sale #67 9-06, near Unc realized $68,750.					
1902 Proof	—	Value: 75,000				
	Note: Impaired Proofs are valued at approximately $60,000.					

GOLD MINE INGOTS

During the late 19th and early 20th century, Russian law provided that gold mine owners who supplied gold to the mints should receive back whatever silver was recovered during refining of the gold. The silver was returned in the form of circular ingots of various weights which resembled coins. These pieces have often been erroneously described as Russian trade coins for use in Mongolia, China, and Turkestan.

Note: Both the Doyla and the Zolotnik are weights, not denominations.

KM# 1   24 DOLYA

1.0664 g., 0.9900 Silver 0.0339 oz. ASW   **Ruler:** Nicholas II
Obv: Crowned double headed eagle within circle **Rev:** Value

Date	Mintage	F	VF	XF	Unc	BU
ND(1901)	—	—	350	450	650	—

KM# 2   ZOLOTNIK

4.2656 g., 0.9900 Silver 0.1358 oz. ASW   **Ruler:** Nicholas II
Obv: Crowned double headed eagle within small circle **Rev:** Value

Date	Mintage	F	VF	XF	Unc	BU
ND(1901)	—	—	300	400	600	—

KM# 3   3 ZOLOTNIKS

12.7969 g., 0.9900 Silver 0.4073 oz. ASW   **Ruler:** Nicholas II
Obv: Crowned double headed eagle within small circle **Rev:** Value

Date	Mintage	F	VF	XF	Unc	BU
ND(1901)	—	—	1,000	1,500	2,000	—

KM# 4   10 ZOLOTNIKS

42.6563 g., 0.9900 Silver 1.3577 oz. ASW   **Ruler:** Nicholas II
Obv: Crowned double headed eagle within small circle **Rev:** Value

Date	Mintage	F	VF	XF	Unc	BU
ND(1901)	—	—	350	550	900	—

РСФСР (R.S.F.S.R.)
(Russian Soviet Federated Socialist Republic)

STANDARD COINAGE

Y# 80   10 KOPEKS

1.8000 g., 0.5000 Silver 0.0289 oz. ASW   **Obv:** National arms **Rev:** Value and date within beaded circle, star on top divides wreath

Date	Mintage	F	VF	XF	Unc	BU
1921	950,000	10.00	20.00	35.00	70.00	—
1921 Proof	—	Value: 375				
1922	18,640,000	3.00	5.00	15.00	25.00	—
1922 Proof	—	Value: 275				
1923	33,424,000	2.00	5.00	10.00	20.00	—
1923 Proof	—	Value: 225				

Y# 81   15 KOPEKS

2.7000 g., 0.5000 Silver 0.0434 oz. ASW   **Obv:** National arms within circle **Rev:** Value and date within beaded circle, star on top divides wreath

Date	Mintage	F	VF	XF	Unc	BU
1921	933,000	10.00	20.00	40.00	80.00	—
1921 Proof	—	Value: 400				
1922	13,633,000	5.00	10.00	15.00	30.00	—
1922 Proof	—	Value: 250				
1923	28,504,000	3.00	5.00	10.00	20.00	—
1923 Proof	—	Value: 200				

Y# 82   20 KOPEKS

3.6000 g., 0.5000 Silver 0.0579 oz. ASW   **Obv:** National arms within circle **Rev:** Value and date within beaded circle, star on top divides wreath **Note:** Varieties exist.

Date	Mintage	F	VF	XF	Unc	BU
1921	825,000	10.00	20.00	40.00	80.00	—
1921 Proof	—	Value: 500				
1922	14,220,000	5.00	10.00	20.00	40.00	—
1922 Proof	—	Value: 275				
1923	27,580,000	4.00	7.00	12.00	25.00	—
1923 Proof	—	Value: 225				

Y# 83   50 KOPEKS

9.9980 g., 0.9000 Silver 0.2893 oz. ASW   **Obv:** National arms within beaded circle **Rev:** Value in center of star within beaded circle **Edge:** Mintmaster's initials

Date	Mintage	F	VF	XF	Unc	BU
1921 АГ	1,400,000	10.00	15.00	30.00	50.00	—
1921 АГ Proof	—	Value: 750				
1922 АГ	8,224,000	10.00	15.00	30.00	50.00	—
1922 АГ Proof	—	Value: 950				
1922 ПЛ	Inc. above	10.00	15.00	30.00	50.00	—
1922 ПЛ Proof	—	Value: 650				

Y# 84   ROUBLE

19.9960 g., 0.9000 Silver 0.5786 oz. ASW   **Obv:** National arms within beaded circle **Rev:** Value in center of star within beaded circle **Edge:** Mintmaster's initials **Note:** Varieties exist.

Date	Mintage	F	VF	XF	Unc	BU
1921 АГ	1,000,000	20.00	30.00	60.00	120	140
1921 АГ Proof	—	Value: 2,250				
1922 АГ	2,050,000	25.00	40.00	90.00	160	200
1922 АГ Proof	—	Value: 3,000				
1922 ПЛ	Inc. above	25.00	40.00	90.00	160	200
1922 ПЛ Proof	—	Value: 2,750				

TRADE COINAGE

Y# 85 CHERVONETZ (10 Roubles)
8.6026 g., 0.9000 Gold 0.2489 oz. AGW **Obv:** National arms, PCØCP below arms **Rev:** Standing figure with head right **Edge:** Mintmaster's initials

Date	Mintage	F	VF	XF	Unc	BU
1923 ПЛ	2,751,000	275	400	600	750	1,250
1923 ПЛ Proof	—	Value: 8,000				
1975	250,000	—	—	—	BV+10%	—
1976 ЛМД	1,000,000	—	—	—	BV+10%	—
1976 Rare	—	—	—	—	—	—
1977 ММД	1,000,000	—	—	—	BV+10%	—
1977 ЛМД	1,000,000	—	—	—	BV+10%	—
1978 ММД	350,000	—	—	—	BV+10%	—
1979 ММД	1,000,000	—	—	—	BV+10%	—
1980 ЛМД	900,000	—	—	—	BV+10%	—
1980 ММД	—	—	—	—	—	—
1980 ММД Proof	100,000	Value: 195				
1981 ММД	1,000,000	—	—	—	BV+10%	—
1981 ЛМД Rare	—	—	—	—	—	—
1982 ММД	65,000	—	—	—	BV+10%	—
1982 ЛМД Rare	—	—	—	—	—	—

Y# A86 CHERVONETZ (10 Roubles)
8.6026 g., 0.9000 Gold 0.2489 oz. AGW **Obv:** National arms with CCCP below **Rev:** Standing figure with head right

Date	Mintage	F	VF	XF	Unc	BU
1925 Unique	600,000	—	—	—	—	—

Note: Chervonetz were first struck in 1923 under the R.S.F.S.R. government; in 1925 the U.S.S.R. government attempted a new issue of these coins, of which only one remaining coin is known; from 1975 to 1982 the U.S.S.R. government continued striking the original type with new dates

CCCP (U.S.S.R.)
(Union of Soviet Socialist Republics)

STANDARD COINAGE

Y# 75 1/2 KOPEK
Copper **Obv:** CCCP within circle **Rev:** Value and date

Date	Mintage	F	VF	XF	Unc	BU
1925	45,380,000	15.00	30.00	40.00	70.00	—
1927	45,380,000	15.00	30.00	40.00	70.00	—
1927 Proof	—	Value: 350				
1928	—	51.00	30.00	40.00	80.00	—

Y# 76 KOPEK
3.2000 g., Bronze **Obv:** National arms within circle **Rev:** Value and date within oat sprigs

Date	Mintage	F	VF	XF	Unc	BU
1924	34,705,000	10.00	15.00	30.00	60.00	—
Note: Reeded edge						
1924 Proof	—	Value: 400				
Note: Reeded edge						
1924	Inc. above	50.00	100	150	500	—
Note: Plain edge						
1925	141,806,000	80.00	150	200	350	—

Y# 91 KOPEK
1.0300 g., Aluminum-Bronze, 15 mm. **Obv:** National arms within circle **Rev:** Value and date within oat sprigs **Note:** Varieties exist.

Date	Mintage	F	VF	XF	Unc	BU
1926	87,915,000	2.00	3.00	5.00	10.00	—
1926 Proof	—	Value: 200				
1927	—	2.00	3.00	5.00	10.00	—
1928	—	1.00	2.00	4.00	8.00	—
1929	95,950,000	1.00	2.00	4.00	8.00	—

Date	Mintage	F	VF	XF	Unc	BU
1930	85,351,000	3.00	6.00	10.00	15.00	—
1931	106,100,000	1.00	2.00	4.00	8.00	—
1932	56,900,000	1.00	2.00	4.00	8.00	—
1933	111,257,000	1.00	2.00	4.00	8.00	—
1934	100,245	2.00	5.00	10.00	15.00	—
1935	66,405,000	1.00	2.00	5.00	10.00	—

Y# 98 KOPEK
Aluminum-Bronze **Obv:** National arms **Rev:** Value and date within oat sprigs

Date	Mintage	F	VF	XF	Unc	BU
1935	—	7.00	10.00	15.00	20.00	—
Note: Mintage inc.Y91						
1936	132,204,000	2.00	3.00	5.00	10.00	—

Y# 105 KOPEK
0.9400 g., Aluminum-Bronze, 15.20 mm. **Obv:** National arms **Rev:** Value and date within oat sprigs **Note:** Varieties exist.

Date	Mintage	F	VF	XF	Unc	BU
1937	—	1.00	2.00	3.00	6.00	—
1938	—	1.00	2.00	3.00	6.00	—
1939	—	1.00	2.00	3.00	6.00	—
1940	—	1.00	2.00	3.00	6.00	—
1941	—	2.00	3.00	5.00	10.00	—
1945	—	2.00	3.00	5.00	10.00	—
1946	—	2.00	3.00	5.00	10.00	—

Y# 112 KOPEK
1.0000 g., Aluminum-Bronze **Obv:** National arms **Rev:** Value and date within oat sprigs **Note:** Varieties exist.

Date	Mintage	F	VF	XF	Unc	BU
1948	—	2.00	3.00	5.00	10.00	—
1949	—	2.00	3.00	5.00	10.00	—
1950	—	2.00	3.00	5.00	12.00	—
1951	—	2.00	3.00	5.00	12.00	—
1952	—	1.00	2.00	3.00	5.00	—
1953	—	1.00	2.00	3.00	5.00	—
1954	—	1.00	2.00	3.00	4.00	—
1955	—	1.00	2.00	3.00	4.00	—
1956	—	1.00	2.00	3.00	4.00	—
1957 Rare	—	—	—	—	—	—

Y# 119 KOPEK
Aluminum-Bronze **Obv:** National arms **Rev:** Value and date within oat sprigs

Date	Mintage	F	VF	XF	Unc	BU
1957	—	2.00	4.00	8.00	16.00	—

Y# 126 KOPEK
Copper-Nickel **Obv:** National arms **Rev:** Value and date within oat sprigs

Date	Mintage	F	VF	XF	Unc	BU
1958	30,265,000	—	—	—	300	—

Note: Never officially released for circulation; majority of mintage remelted

Y# 126a KOPEK
1.0000 g., Brass, 15.05 mm. **Obv:** National arms **Rev:** Value and date above spray **Note:** Varieties exist.

Date	Mintage	F	VF	XF	Unc	BU
1961	—	0.10	0.25	0.50	2.00	—
1962	—	0.10	0.30	0.50	1.00	—
1963	—	0.10	0.30	0.50	1.00	—

Date	Mintage	F	VF	XF	Unc	BU
1964	—	0.20	0.50	1.00	3.00	—
1965	—	0.10	0.30	0.50	1.00	—
1966	—	0.10	0.30	0.50	1.00	—
1967	—	0.10	0.30	0.50	1.00	—
1968	—	0.10	0.30	0.50	1.00	—
1969	—	0.10	0.30	0.50	1.00	—
1970	—	0.10	0.30	0.50	1.00	—
1971	—	0.10	0.30	0.50	1.00	—
1972	—	0.20	0.30	0.50	1.00	—
1973	—	0.20	0.30	0.50	1.00	—
1974	—	0.20	0.30	0.50	1.00	—
1975	—	0.20	0.30	0.50	1.00	—
1976	—	0.20	0.30	0.50	1.00	—
1977	—	0.20	0.30	0.50	1.00	—
1978	—	0.20	0.30	0.50	1.00	—
1979	—	0.20	0.30	0.50	1.00	—
1980	—	0.20	0.30	0.50	1.00	—
1981	—	0.20	0.30	0.50	1.00	—
1982	—	0.20	0.30	0.50	1.00	—
1983	—	0.20	0.30	0.50	1.00	—
1984	—	0.20	0.30	0.50	1.00	—
1985	—	0.20	0.30	0.50	1.00	—
1986	—	0.20	0.30	0.50	1.00	—
1987	—	0.20	0.30	0.50	1.00	—
1988	—	0.20	0.30	0.50	1.00	—
1989	—	0.10	0.20	0.30	0.50	—
1990	—	0.10	0.20	0.30	0.50	—
1991 M	—	0.10	0.20	0.30	0.50	—
1991 Л	—	0.10	0.20	0.30	0.50	—

Y# 77 2 KOPEKS
Bronze **Obv:** National arms **Rev:** Value and date within oat sprigs **Note:** Varieties exist.

Date	Mintage	F	VF	XF	Unc	BU
1924	119,996,000	15.00	30.00	50.00	100	—
Note: Reeded edge						
1924	Inc. above	50.00	80.00	150	550	—
Note: Plain edge						
1925 Rare	Inc. above	—	—	—	800	—

Y# 92 2 KOPEKS
2.0000 g., Aluminum-Bronze **Obv:** National arms within circle **Rev:** Value and date within oat sprigs **Note:** Varieties exist.

Date	Mintage	F	VF	XF	Unc	BU
1926	105,053,000	2.00	3.00	5.00	10.00	—
1926 Proof	—	Value: 200				
1927 Rare	—	—	—	—	800	—
1928	—	2.00	3.00	5.00	10.00	—
1929	80,000,000	2.00	3.00	5.00	8.00	—
1930	134,186,000	2.00	3.00	5.00	8.00	—
1931	99,523,000	2.00	3.00	5.00	8.00	—
1932	39,573,000	2.00	3.00	5.00	8.00	—
1933	54,874,000	4.00	8.00	10.00	14.00	—
1934	61,574,000	2.00	3.00	4.00	8.00	—
1935	81,121,000	2.00	3.00	4.00	8.00	—

Y# 99 2 KOPEKS
Aluminum-Bronze **Obv:** National arms **Rev:** Value and date within oat sprigs **Note:** Varieties exist.

Date	Mintage	F	VF	XF	Unc	BU
1935	—	3.00	4.00	8.00	15.00	—
1936	94,354,000	2.00	3.00	5.00	10.00	—

Y# 106 2 KOPEKS
2.0000 g., Aluminum-Bronze **Obv:** National arms **Rev:** Value and date within oat sprigs

Date	Mintage	F	VF	XF	Unc	BU
1937	—	2.00	3.00	4.00	7.00	—
1938	—	2.00	3.00	4.00	7.00	—

Date	Mintage	F	VF	XF	Unc	BU
1939	—	2.00	3.00	4.00	7.00	—
1940	—	2.00	3.00	4.00	7.00	—
1941	—	2.00	3.00	4.00	7.00	—
1945	—	2.00	3.00	5.00	9.00	—
1946	—	2.00	3.00	4.00	7.00	—
1948	—	40.00	70.00	130	225	—

Note: Five ribbons on each wreath

Y# 113   2 KOPEKS
1.8000 g., Aluminum-Bronze **Obv:** National arms **Rev:** Value and date within oat sprigs **Note:** Varieties exist.

Date	Mintage	F	VF	XF	Unc	BU
1948	—	1.00	3.00	4.00	5.00	—
1949	—	1.00	3.00	4.00	5.00	—
1950	—	1.00	3.00	4.00	5.00	—
1951	—	2.00	3.00	4.00	8.00	—
1952	—	1.00	2.00	3.00	9.00	—
1953	—	1.00	2.00	3.00	9.00	—
1954	—	1.00	2.00	3.00	9.00	—
1955	—	1.00	2.00	3.00	9.00	—
1956	—	1.00	2.00	3.00	9.00	—

Y# 120   2 KOPEKS
Aluminum-Bronze **Obv:** National arms **Rev:** Value and date within oat sprigs

Date	Mintage	F	VF	XF	Unc	BU
1957	—	2.00	5.00	8.00	15.00	—

Y# 127   2 KOPEKS
Copper-Nickel **Obv:** National arms **Rev:** Value and date within sprays

Date	Mintage	F	VF	XF	Unc	BU
1958	39,591,000				300	—

Note: Never officially released for circulation; majority of mintage remelted

Y# 127a   2 KOPEKS
2.0000 g., Brass, 18 mm. **Obv:** National arms **Rev:** Value and date within sprays **Note:** Varieties exist.

Date	Mintage	F	VF	XF	Unc	BU
1961	—	0.10	0.15	0.25	0.50	—
1962	—	0.10	0.15	0.25	0.50	—
1963	—	0.10	0.15	0.25	0.50	—
1964	—	0.15	0.25	0.50	1.00	—
1965	—	0.10	0.15	0.25	0.50	—
1966	—	0.10	0.15	0.25	0.50	—
1967	—	0.10	0.15	0.25	0.50	—
1968	—	0.10	0.15	0.25	0.50	—
1969	—	0.10	0.15	0.25	0.50	—
1970	—	0.10	0.15	0.25	0.50	—
1971	—	0.10	0.15	0.25	0.50	—
1972	—	0.10	0.15	0.25	0.50	—
1973	—	0.10	0.15	0.25	0.50	—
1974	—	0.10	0.15	0.25	0.50	—
1975	—	0.10	0.15	0.25	0.50	—
1976	—	0.10	0.15	0.25	0.50	—
1977	—	0.10	0.15	0.25	0.50	—
1978	—	0.10	0.15	0.25	0.50	—
1979	—	0.10	0.15	0.25	0.50	—
1980	—	0.10	0.15	0.25	0.50	—
1981	—	0.10	0.15	0.25	0.50	—
1982	—	0.10	0.15	0.25	0.50	—
1983	—	0.10	0.15	0.25	0.50	—
1984	—	0.10	0.15	0.25	0.50	—
1985	—	0.10	0.15	0.25	0.50	—
1986	—	0.10	0.15	0.25	0.50	—
1987	—	0.10	0.15	0.25	0.50	—
1988	—	0.10	0.15	0.25	0.50	—
1989	—	0.10	0.15	0.20	0.50	—
1990	—	0.10	0.15	0.20	0.50	—
1991 M	—	0.10	0.15	0.20	0.50	—
1991 Л	—	0.10	0.15	0.20	0.50	—

Y# 78   3 KOPEKS
Bronze **Obv:** National arms within circle **Rev:** Value and date within oat sprigs **Note:** Varieties exist.

Date	Mintage	F	VF	XF	Unc	BU
1924	101,283,000	50.00	100	200	300	—

Note: Reeded edge

Date	Mintage	F	VF	XF	Unc	BU
1924	Inc. above	10.00	20.00	40.00	80.00	—

Note: Plain edge

Y# 93   3 KOPEKS
3.0900 g., Aluminum-Bronze, 22 mm. **Obv:** National arms within circle **Rev:** Value and date within oat sprigs **Note:** Varieties exist.

Date	Mintage	F	VF	XF	Unc	BU
1926	19,940,000	3.00	5.00	8.00	15.00	—
1926 Proof		Value: 225				
1926 Rare						

Note: Obverse of Y#100

1927	—	7.00	12.00	25.00	50.00	—
1928	—	2.00	4.00	8.00	10.00	—
1929	50,150,000	2.00	4.00	7.00	14.00	—
1930	74,159,000	1.00	3.00	4.00	8.00	—
1931	121,168,000	1.00	3.00	4.00	8.00	—
1931 Rare	—	—	—	—	—	—

Note: Without CCCP obverse

1932	37,718,000	2.00	3.00	4.00	6.00	—
1933	44,764,000	2.00	3.00	4.00	8.00	—
1934	44,529,000	2.00	3.00	4.00	8.00	—
1935	58,303,000	2.00	3.00	5.00	8.00	—
1937 Rare						

Y# 100   3 KOPEKS
Aluminum-Bronze **Obv:** National arms **Rev:** Value and date within oat sprigs **Note:** Varieties exist.

Date	Mintage	F	VF	XF	Unc	BU
1935	—	2.00	4.00	8.00	16.00	—
1936	62,757,000	2.00	4.00	7.00	14.00	—

Y# 107   3 KOPEKS
3.0000 g., Aluminum-Bronze **Obv:** National arms **Rev:** Value and date within oat sprigs **Note:** Varieties exist.

Date	Mintage	F	VF	XF	Unc	BU
1937	—	2.00	3.00	4.00	8.00	—
1938	—	2.00	3.00	4.00	8.00	—
1939	—	2.00	3.00	4.00	8.00	—
1940	—	2.00	3.00	4.00	12.00	—
1941	—	2.00	3.00	4.00	8.00	—
1943	—	2.00	3.00	4.00	8.00	—
1945	—	4.00	5.00	10.00	18.00	—
1946	—	2.00	3.00	4.00	8.00	—
1948 Five ribbons on each wreath	—	40.00	70.00	130	225	—

Y# 114   3 KOPEKS
Aluminum-Bronze **Obv:** National arms **Rev:** Value and date within oat sprigs **Note:** Varieties exist.

Date	Mintage	F	VF	XF	Unc	BU
1946 Rare						
1948	—	2.00	3.00	4.00	8.00	—
1949	—	2.00	3.00	4.00	5.00	—
1950	—	2.00	3.00	4.00	5.00	—

Date	Mintage	F	VF	XF	Unc	BU
1951	—	2.00	3.00	4.00	9.00	—
1952	—	2.00	3.00	4.00	5.00	—
1953	—	2.00	3.00	4.00	5.00	—
1954	—	2.00	3.00	4.00	5.00	—
1955	—	2.00	3.00	4.00	5.00	—
1956	—	2.00	3.00	4.00	5.00	—
1957	—	10.00	15.00	40.00	60.00	—

Y# 121   3 KOPEKS
Aluminum-Bronze **Obv:** National arms **Rev:** Value and date within oat sprigs

Date	Mintage	F	VF	XF	Unc	BU
1957	—	2.00	3.00	6.00	12.00	—

Y# 128   3 KOPEKS
Copper-Zinc **Obv:** National arms **Rev:** Value and date within sprigs

Date	Mintage	F	VF	XF	Unc	BU
1958	26,676,000				300	—

Note: Never officially released for circulation; majority of mintage remelted

Y# 128a   3 KOPEKS
3.0000 g., Aluminum-Bronze, 22.05 mm. **Obv:** National arms **Rev:** Value and date within sprigs **Note:** Varieties exist.

Date	Mintage	F	VF	XF	Unc	BU
1961	—	0.10	0.15	0.25	0.60	—
1962	—	0.25	0.50	1.00	2.00	—
1965	—	0.25	0.50	1.00	2.00	—
1966	—	0.10	0.15	0.25	0.60	—
1967	—	0.10	0.15	0.25	0.60	—
1968	—	0.10	0.15	0.25	0.60	—
1969	—	0.10	0.15	0.25	0.60	—
1970	—	0.10	0.15	0.25	0.60	—
1971	—	0.10	0.15	0.25	0.60	—
1972	—	0.10	0.15	0.25	0.60	—
1973	—	0.10	0.15	0.25	0.60	—
1974	—	0.10	0.15	0.25	0.60	—
1975	—	0.10	0.15	0.25	0.60	—
1976	—	0.10	0.15	0.25	0.60	—
1977	—	0.10	0.15	0.25	0.60	—
1978	—	0.10	0.15	0.25	0.60	—
1979	—	0.10	0.15	0.25	0.60	—
1980	—	0.10	0.15	0.25	0.60	—
1981	—	0.10	0.15	0.25	0.60	—
1982	—	0.10	0.15	0.25	0.60	—
1983	—	0.10	0.15	0.25	0.60	—
1984	—	0.10	0.15	0.25	0.60	—
1985	—	0.10	0.15	0.25	0.60	—
1986	—	0.10	0.15	0.25	0.60	—
1987	—	0.10	0.15	0.25	0.60	—
1988	—	0.10	0.15	0.25	0.60	—
1989	—	0.10	0.15	0.20	0.40	—
1990	—	0.10	0.15	0.20	0.40	—
1991 M	—	0.10	0.15	0.20	0.40	—
1991 Л	—	0.10	0.15	0.20	0.40	—

Y# 79   5 KOPEKS
Bronze **Obv:** National arms within circle **Rev:** Value and date within oat sprigs **Note:** Varieties exist.

Date	Mintage	F	VF	XF	Unc	BU
1924	88,510,000	50.00	100	200	300	—

Note: Reeded edge

Date	Mintage	F	VF	XF	Unc	BU
1924	Inc. above	15.00	30.00	50.00	100	—

Note: Plain edge

Y# 94   5 KOPEKS
5.0000 g., Aluminum-Bronze **Obv:** National arms **Rev:** Value and date **Note:** Varieties exist.

Date	Mintage	F	VF	XF	Unc	BU
1926	14,697,000	5.00	10.00	15.00	30.00	—
1926 Proof	—	Value: 250				
1927	—	30.00	80.00	120	170	—
1928	—	5.00	10.00	15.00	20.00	—
1929	20,220,000	7.00	12.00	18.00	25.00	—
1930	44,490,000	3.00	4.00	7.00	10.00	—
1931	89,540,000	3.00	4.00	7.00	10.00	—
1932	65,100,000	3.00	4.00	7.00	10.00	—
1933	18,135,000	25.00	50.00	100	300	—
1934	5,354,000	25.00	50.00	90.00	120	—
1935	11,735,000	5.00	10.00	15.00	50.00	—

Y# 101   5 KOPEKS
Aluminum-Bronze **Obv:** National arms **Rev:** Value and date within oat sprigs **Note:** Varieties exist.

Date	Mintage	F	VF	XF	Unc	BU
1935	—	5.00	10.00	15.00	30.00	—
1936	5,242,000	5.00	10.00	15.00	30.00	—

Y# 108   5 KOPEKS
5.2100 g., Aluminum-Bronze, 25.1 mm. **Obv:** National arms **Rev:** Value and date within oat sprigs **Note:** Varieties exist.

Date	Mintage	F	VF	XF	Unc	BU
1937	—	5.00	9.00	15.00	30.00	—
1938	—	2.00	3.00	6.00	10.00	—
1939	—	2.00	3.00	6.00	10.00	—
1940	—	2.00	3.00	6.00	10.00	—
1941	—	2.00	3.00	6.00	10.00	—
1943	—	2.00	3.00	6.00	10.00	—
1945	—	5.00	8.00	15.00	20.00	—
1946	—	2.00	3.00	5.00	10.00	—

Y# 115   5 KOPEKS
4.8000 g., Aluminum-Bronze **Obv:** National arms **Rev:** Value and date withing oat sprigs **Note:** Varieties exist.

Date	Mintage	F	VF	XF	Unc	BU
1948	—	1.00	2.00	4.00	6.00	—
1949	—	1.00	2.00	4.00	6.00	—
1950	—	1.00	2.00	4.00	6.00	—
1951	—	4.00	6.00	10.00	15.00	—
1952	—	1.00	2.00	4.00	6.00	—
1953	—	1.00	2.00	4.00	6.00	—
1954	—	1.00	2.00	4.00	6.00	—
1955	—	1.00	2.00	4.00	6.00	—
1956	—	1.00	2.00	4.00	6.00	—

Y# 122   5 KOPEKS
4.9000 g., Aluminum-Bronze **Obv:** National arms **Rev:** Value and date within oat sprigs **Note:** Varieties exist.

Date	Mintage	F	VF	XF	Unc	BU
1957	—	3.00	6.00	10.00	15.00	—

Y# 129   5 KOPEKS
Copper-Zinc **Obv:** National arms **Rev:** Value and date within sprigs

Date	Mintage	F	VF	XF	Unc	BU
1958	61,119,000	—	—	—	600	—

Note: Never officially released for circulation; majority of mintage remelted

Y# 129a   5 KOPEKS
5.0000 g., Aluminum-Bronze, 25.1 mm. **Obv:** National arms **Rev:** Value and date within sprigs **Note:** Varieties exist.

Date	Mintage	F	VF	XF	Unc	BU
1961	—	0.20	0.30	0.50	1.00	—
1962	—	0.20	0.30	0.50	1.00	—
1965	—	3.00	5.00	8.00	12.00	—
1966	—	2.00	4.00	7.00	12.00	—
1967	—	0.50	1.00	1.50	3.00	—
1968	—	0.50	1.00	1.50	3.00	—
1969	—	2.00	4.00	6.00	10.00	—
1970	—	10.00	15.00	35.00	60.00	—
1971	—	2.00	4.00	6.00	10.00	—
1972	—	2.00	4.00	6.00	10.00	—
1973	—	1.00	1.50	2.00	3.00	—
1974	—	0.10	0.20	0.50	1.00	—
1975	—	0.10	0.20	0.50	1.00	—
1976	—	0.10	0.15	0.30	0.75	—
1977	—	0.10	0.15	0.30	0.75	—
1978	—	0.10	0.15	0.30	0.75	—
1979	—	0.10	0.15	0.30	0.75	—
1980	—	0.10	0.15	0.30	0.75	—
1981	—	0.10	0.15	0.30	0.75	—
1982	—	0.10	0.15	0.30	0.70	—
1983	—	0.10	0.15	0.30	0.75	—
1984	—	0.10	0.15	0.30	0.75	—
1985	—	0.10	0.15	0.30	0.75	—
1986	—	0.10	0.15	0.30	0.75	—
1987	—	0.10	0.15	0.30	0.75	—
1988	—	0.10	0.15	0.30	0.75	—
1989	—	0.10	0.15	0.25	0.50	—
1990	—	0.15	0.25	0.45	1.25	—
1990M	—	7.00	10.00	20.00	30.00	—
1991M	—	0.10	0.15	0.25	0.50	—
1991	—	0.10	0.15	0.25	0.50	—

Y# 86   10 KOPEKS
1.8000 g., 0.5000 Silver 0.0289 oz. ASW **Obv:** National arms within circle **Rev:** Value and date within oat sprigs **Note:** Varieties exist.

Date	Mintage	F	VF	XF	Unc	BU
1924	67,351,000	3.00	5.00	10.00	15.00	—
1924 Proof	—	Value: 450				
1925	101,013,000	3.00	5.00	10.00	15.00	—
1925 Proof	—	Value: 225				
1927	—	3.00	5.00	10.00	15.00	—
1927 Proof	—	Value: 225				
1928	—	3.00	5.00	10.00	15.00	—
1929	64,900,000	3.00	5.00	10.00	15.00	—
1930	163,424,000	3.00	5.00	10.00	15.00	—
1931 Rare	8,791,000	—	—	—	—	—

Y# 95   10 KOPEKS
1.8200 g., Copper-Nickel, 17.4 mm. **Obv:** National arms within circle **Rev:** Value on shield held by figure at left looking right **Note:** Varieties exist.

Date	Mintage	F	VF	XF	Unc	BU
1931	122,511,000	4.00	8.00	10.00	20.00	—
1932	171,641,000	2.00	3.00	4.00	8.00	—
1933	163,125,000	2.00	3.00	4.00	8.00	—
1934	104,059,000	2.00	3.00	4.00	8.00	—

Y# 102   10 KOPEKS
1.8000 g., Copper-Nickel **Obv:** National arms **Rev:** Value within octagon flanked by sprigs with date below

Date	Mintage	F	VF	XF	Unc	BU
1935	79,628,000	2.00	3.00	5.00	10.00	—
1936	122,260,000	2.00	3.00	4.00	8.00	—

Y# 109   10 KOPEKS
1.6900 g., Copper-Nickel, 17.5 mm. **Obv:** National arms **Rev:** Value within octagon flanked by sprigs with date below **Note:** Varieties exist.

Date	Mintage	F	VF	XF	Unc	BU
1937	—	2.00	3.00	5.00	10.00	—
1938	—	2.00	3.00	4.00	8.00	—
1939	—	2.00	3.00	4.00	8.00	—
1940	—	2.00	3.00	4.00	8.00	—
1941	—	2.00	3.00	4.00	8.00	—
1942	—	20.00	40.00	75.00	100	—
1943	—	2.00	3.00	4.00	8.00	—
1944	—	8.00	15.00	25.00	45.00	—
1945	—	2.00	3.00	4.00	8.00	—
1946	—	2.00	3.00	4.00	8.00	—

Y# A110   10 KOPEKS
Copper-Nickel **Obv:** National arms **Rev:** Value within octagon flanked by sprigs **Note:** Mule.

Date	Mintage	F	VF	XF	Unc	BU
1946 Rare	—	—	—	—	—	—

Y# 116   10 KOPEKS
1.8000 g., Copper-Nickel **Obv:** National arms, 8 and 7 ribbons on wreath **Rev:** Value within octagon flanked by sprigs with date below **Note:** Varieties exist.

Date	Mintage	F	VF	XF	Unc	BU
1948	—	2.00	3.00	4.00	7.00	—
1949	—	2.00	3.00	4.00	7.00	—
1950	—	2.00	3.00	4.00	7.00	—
1951	—	2.00	3.00	4.00	7.00	—
1952	—	2.00	3.00	4.00	7.00	—
1953	—	1.00	2.00	3.00	4.00	—
1954	—	1.00	2.00	3.00	4.00	—
1955	—	1.00	2.00	3.00	4.00	—
1956	—	1.00	2.00	3.00	4.00	—
1956	—	25.00	40.00	60.00	100	—

Note: Reverse of Y#123

Y# 123   10 KOPEKS
1.8000 g., Copper-Nickel **Obv:** National arms, 7 and 7 ribbons on wreath **Rev:** Value within octagon flanked by sprigs with date below

Date	Mintage	F	VF	XF	Unc	BU
1957	—	20.00	30.00	60.00	100	—

Note: Reverse of Y#116

1957	—	2.00	3.00	4.00	8.00	—

Y# A130 10 KOPEKS

Copper-Nickel **Obv:** National arms **Rev:** Value and date within sprigs

Date	Mintage	F	VF	XF	Unc	BU
1958	108,023,000	—	—	—	300	—

Note: Never officially released for circulation; majority of mintage remelted

Y# 130 10 KOPEKS

1.6000 g., Copper-Nickel-Zinc, 17.35 mm. **Obv:** National arms **Rev:** Value and date flanked by sprigs

Date	Mintage	F	VF	XF	Unc	BU
1961	—	0.20	0.30	0.50	1.00	—
1962	—	0.20	0.30	0.50	1.00	—
1965	—	3.00	5.00	10.00	15.00	—
1966	—	1.00	2.50	5.00	10.00	—
1967	—	0.50	0.80	1.50	3.00	—
1968	—	0.10	0.20	0.35	0.75	—
1969	—	0.10	0.20	0.35	0.75	—
1970	—	0.10	0.20	0.35	0.75	—
1971	—	0.10	0.20	0.35	0.75	—
1972	—	0.10	0.20	0.35	0.75	—
1973	—	0.10	0.20	0.35	0.75	—
1974	—	0.10	0.20	0.35	0.75	—
1975	—	0.10	0.20	0.35	0.75	—
1976	—	0.10	0.20	0.35	0.75	—
1977	—	0.10	0.20	0.35	0.75	—
1978	—	0.10	0.20	0.35	0.75	—
1979	—	0.10	0.20	0.35	0.75	—
1980	—	0.10	0.20	0.35	0.75	—
1981	—	0.10	0.20	0.35	0.75	—
1982	—	0.10	0.20	0.35	0.75	—
1983	—	0.10	0.20	0.35	0.75	—
1984	—	0.10	0.20	0.35	0.75	—
1985	—	0.10	0.20	0.35	0.75	—
1986	—	0.10	0.20	0.35	0.75	—
1987	—	0.10	0.20	0.35	0.75	—
1988	—	0.10	0.20	0.35	0.75	—
1989	—	0.10	0.20	0.30	0.50	—
1990	—	0.25	0.50	1.00	2.50	—
1990 Л	—	0.10	0.20	0.30	0.50	—
1990 M	—	4.00	7.50	12.50	20.00	—
1991	—	0.15	0.25	0.50	1.25	—
1991 Л	—	0.10	0.20	0.30	0.50	—
1991 M	—	0.10	0.20	0.30	0.50	—

Y# 136 10 KOPEKS

Copper-Nickel-Zinc, 17 mm. **Subject:** 50th Anniversary of Revolution **Obv:** National arms within radiant circle with dates at right **Rev:** Value above radiant sun and design

Date	Mintage	F	VF	XF	Unc	BU
1967	49,789,000	—	0.50	1.00	2.00	—
1967 Prooflike	211,000	—	—	—	—	—

Y# 87 15 KOPEKS

2.7000 g., 0.5000 Silver 0.0434 oz. ASW **Obv:** National arms within circle **Rev:** Value and date within oat sprigs **Note:** Varieties exist.

Date	Mintage	F	VF	XF	Unc	BU
1924	72,426,000	3.00	4.00	8.00	15.00	—
1924 Proof	—	Value: 450				
1925	112,709,000	3.00	4.00	7.00	14.00	—
1925 Proof	—	Value: 225				
1927	—	3.00	4.00	7.00	14.00	—
1927 Proof	—	Value: 225				
1928	—	3.00	4.00	7.00	14.00	—
1929	46,400,000	3.00	4.00	7.00	14.00	—
1930	79,868,000	3.00	4.00	7.00	14.00	—
1931 Rare	5,099,000	—	—	—	—	—

Y# 96 15 KOPEKS

Copper-Nickel, 20 mm. **Obv:** National arms within circle **Rev:** Value on shield held by figure at left looking right **Note:** Varieties exist.

Date	Mintage	F	VF	XF	Unc	BU
1931	75,859,000	3.00	5.00	7.00	12.00	—
1932	136,046,000	2.00	3.00	4.00	7.00	—
1933	127,591,000	2.00	3.00	4.00	7.00	—
1934	58,367,000	3.00	4.00	5.00	9.00	—

Y# 103 15 KOPEKS

2.7000 g., Copper-Nickel, 20 mm. **Obv:** National arms **Rev:** Value within octagon flanked by sprigs with date below

Date	Mintage	F	VF	XF	Unc	BU
1935	51,308,000	3.00	4.00	5.00	9.00	—
1936	52,183,000	3.00	4.00	5.00	9.00	—

Y# 110 15 KOPEKS

2.6800 g., Copper-Nickel, 20 mm. **Obv:** National arms **Rev:** Value within octagon flanked by sprigs with date below **Note:** Varieties exist.

Date	Mintage	F	VF	XF	Unc	BU
1937	—	3.00	4.00	5.00	9.00	—
1938	—	2.00	3.00	4.00	7.00	—
1939	—	2.00	3.00	4.00	7.00	—
1940	—	2.00	3.00	4.00	7.00	—
1941	—	2.00	3.00	4.00	7.00	—
1942	—	25.00	60.00	80.00	100	—
1943	—	2.00	3.00	5.00	8.00	—
1944	—	3.00	5.00	9.00	15.00	—
1945	—	2.00	3.00	4.00	7.00	—
1946	—	2.00	3.00	4.00	7.00	—

Y# 117 15 KOPEKS

2.7000 g., Copper-Nickel, 20 mm. **Obv:** National arms, 8 and 7 ribbons on wreath **Rev:** Value within octagon flanked by sprigs with date below **Note:** Varieties exist.

Date	Mintage	F	VF	XF	Unc	BU
1948	—	2.00	3.00	4.00	7.00	—
1949	—	2.00	3.00	4.00	7.00	—
1950	—	1.00	2.00	3.00	5.00	—
1951	—	2.00	3.00	5.00	10.00	—
1952	—	1.00	2.00	3.00	5.00	—
1953	—	1.00	2.00	3.00	5.00	—
1954	—	1.00	2.00	3.00	5.00	—
1955	—	1.00	2.00	3.00	5.00	—
1956	—	1.00	2.00	3.00	5.00	—

Y# 124 15 KOPEKS

Copper-Nickel, 20 mm. **Obv:** National arms **Rev:** Value within octagon flanked by sprigs with date below

Date	Mintage	F	VF	XF	Unc	BU
1957	—	2.00	3.00	6.00	10.00	—

Y# A131 15 KOPEKS

Copper-Nickel, 20 mm. **Obv:** National arms **Rev:** Value and date within sprigs

Date	Mintage	F	VF	XF	Unc	BU
1958	80,052,000	—	—	—	1,000	—

Note: Never officially released for circulation; majority of mintage remelted

Y# 131 15 KOPEKS

2.5000 g., Copper-Nickel-Zinc, 19.5 mm. **Obv:** National arms **Rev:** Value and date flanked by sprigs

Date	Mintage	F	VF	XF	Unc	BU
1961	—	0.10	0.20	0.40	0.75	—
1962	—	0.10	0.20	0.40	1.00	—
1965	—	1.00	2.00	4.00	7.50	—
1966	—	1.00	2.00	4.00	7.50	—
1967	—	0.50	1.00	2.00	4.00	—
1968	—	0.25	0.50	1.00	2.00	—
1969	—	0.10	0.20	0.40	0.75	—
1970	—	15.00	25.00	40.00	75.00	—
1971	—	1.00	3.00	5.00	10.00	—
1972	—	1.00	3.00	5.00	10.00	—
1973	—	1.00	3.00	5.00	10.00	—
1974	—	0.10	0.20	0.40	0.75	—
1975	—	0.10	0.20	0.40	0.75	—
1976	—	0.10	0.20	0.40	0.75	—
1977	—	0.10	0.20	0.40	0.75	—
1978	—	0.10	0.20	0.40	0.75	—
1979	—	0.10	0.20	0.40	0.75	—
1980	—	0.10	0.20	0.40	0.75	—
1981	—	0.10	0.20	0.40	0.75	—
1982	—	0.10	0.20	0.40	0.75	—
1983	—	0.10	0.20	0.40	0.75	—
1984	—	0.10	0.20	0.40	0.75	—
1985	—	0.10	0.20	0.40	0.75	—
1986	—	0.10	0.20	0.40	0.75	—
1987	—	0.10	0.20	0.40	0.75	—
1988	—	0.10	0.20	0.40	0.75	—
1989	—	0.10	0.20	0.30	0.50	—
1990	—	0.10	0.20	0.30	0.50	—
1991 M	—	0.10	0.20	0.30	0.50	—
1991 Л	—	0.10	0.20	0.30	0.50	—

Y# 137 15 KOPEKS

Copper-Nickel-Zinc, 20 mm. **Subject:** 50th Anniversary of Revolution **Obv:** National arms above value **Rev:** Statue of Laborers and dates

Date	Mintage	F	VF	XF	Unc	BU
1967	49,789,000	0.30	0.50	1.00	2.00	—
1967 Prooflike	211,000	—	—	—	—	3.00

Y# 88 20 KOPEKS

3.6000 g., 0.5000 Silver 0.0579 oz. ASW **Obv:** National arms within circle **Rev:** Value and date within oat sprigs

Date	Mintage	F	VF	XF	Unc	BU
1924	93,810,000	5.00	10.00	15.00	25.00	—
1924 Proof	—	Value: 500				
1925	135,188,000	3.00	5.00	10.00	20.00	—
1925 Proof	—	Value: 225				
1927	—	3.00	6.00	10.00	20.00	—
1928	—	3.00	6.00	10.00	20.00	—
1929	67,250,000	3.00	6.00	10.00	20.00	—
1930	125,658,000	3.00	4.00	7.00	12.00	—
1931	9,530,000	—	—	—	800	—

Y# 97 20 KOPEKS
3.4800 g., Copper-Nickel, 22 mm. **Obv:** National arms within circle **Rev:** Value on shield held by figure at left looking right **Note:** Varieties exist.

Date	Mintage	F	VF	XF	Unc	BU
1931	82,200,000	3.00	4.00	6.00	12.00	—
1932	175,350,000	2.00	3.00	4.00	8.00	—
1933	143,927,000	2.00	3.00	4.00	8.00	—
1934	70,425,000	—				

Y# 104 20 KOPEKS
Copper-Nickel **Obv:** National arms **Rev:** Value within octagon flanked by sprigs with date below **Note:** Varieties exist.

Date	Mintage	F	VF	XF	Unc	BU
1935	125,165,000	2.00	3.00	4.00	7.00	—
1936	52,968,000	2.00	3.00	4.00	7.00	—
1941 Rare						

Y# 111 20 KOPEKS
3.6100 g., Copper-Nickel, 22.5 mm. **Obv:** National arms **Rev:** Value within octagon flanked by sprigs with date below **Note:** Varieties exist.

Date	Mintage	F	VF	XF	Unc	BU
1937	—	2.00	3.00	4.00	7.00	—
1938	—	2.00	3.00	4.00	7.00	—
1939	—	2.00	3.00	4.00	7.00	—
1940	—	2.00	3.00	4.00	7.00	—
1941	—	2.00	3.00	4.00	7.00	—
1942	—	2.00	3.00	4.00	7.00	—
1943	—	2.00	3.00	4.00	7.00	—
1944	—	2.00	3.00	4.00	7.00	—
1945	—	2.00	3.00	4.00	7.00	—
1946	—	2.00	3.00	4.00	7.00	—

Y# 118 20 KOPEKS
3.6000 g., Copper-Nickel **Obv:** National arms, 8 and 7 ribbons on wreath **Rev:** Value within octagon flanked by sprigs with date below **Note:** Varieties exist.

Date	Mintage	F	VF	XF	Unc	BU
1948	—	2.00	3.00	4.00	7.00	—
1949	—	2.00	3.00	4.00	7.00	—
1950	—	3.00	4.00	7.00	15.00	—
1951	—	2.00	3.00	4.00	10.00	—
1952	—	2.00	3.00	4.00	6.00	—
1953	—	2.00	3.00	4.00	6.00	—
1954	—	2.00	3.00	4.00	6.00	—
1955	—	2.00	3.00	4.00	6.00	—
1956	—	2.00	3.00	4.00	6.00	—

Y# 125 20 KOPEKS
Copper-Nickel **Obv:** National arms **Rev:** Value within octagon flanked by sprigs with date below

Date	Mintage	F	VF	XF	Unc	BU
1957	—	3.00	4.00	5.00	10.00	—

Y# A132 20 KOPEKS
Copper-Nickel **Obv:** National arms **Rev:** Value and date within sprigs

Date	Mintage	F	VF	XF	Unc	BU
1958	175,355,000	—	—	—	450	—

Note: Never officially released for circulation; majority of mintage remelted

Y# 132 20 KOPEKS
3.3000 g., Copper-Nickel-Zinc, 22 mm. **Obv:** National arms **Rev:** Value and date flanked by sprigs **Note:** Varieties exist.

Date	Mintage	F	VF	XF	Unc	BU
1961	—	0.30	0.50	1.00	2.00	—
1962	—	0.30	0.50	1.00	2.00	—
1965	—	1.00	3.00	5.00	10.00	—
1966	—	1.00	3.00	5.00	10.00	—
1967	—	0.50	1.00	2.00	5.00	—
1968	—	0.15	0.30	0.50	1.00	—
1969	—	0.50	1.00	2.00	4.00	—
1970	—	10.00	22.50	30.00	40.00	—
1971	—	0.50	1.00	2.00	3.00	—
1972	—	1.00	2.00	4.00	7.50	—
1973	—	10.00	15.00	25.00	40.00	—
1974	—	1.50	3.00	5.00	9.00	—
1975	—	1.00	3.00	4.00	7.50	—
1976	—	15.00	25.00	40.00	60.00	—
1977	—	0.15	0.30	0.50	1.00	—
1978	—	0.15	0.30	0.50	1.00	—
1979	—	0.15	0.30	0.50	1.00	—
1980	—	0.15	0.30	0.50	1.00	—
1981	—	0.15	0.30	0.50	1.00	—
1982	—	0.15	0.30	0.50	1.00	—
1983	—	0.15	0.30	0.50	1.00	—
1984	—	0.15	0.30	0.50	1.00	—
1985	—	0.15	0.30	0.50	1.00	—
1986	—	0.15	0.30	0.50	1.00	—
1987	—	0.15	0.30	0.50	1.00	—
1988	—	0.15	0.30	0.50	1.00	—
1989	—	0.10	0.20	0.30	0.75	—
1990	—	0.10	0.20	0.30	0.75	—
1991	—	30.00	70.00	100	300	—
1991 M	—	0.10	0.20	0.30	0.75	—
1991 Л	—	0.10	0.20	0.30	0.50	—

Y# 138 20 KOPEKS
Copper-Nickel-Zinc **Subject:** 50th Anniversary of Revolution **Obv:** National arms flanked by dates with inscription below **Rev:** Cruiser ship below value

Date	Mintage	F	VF	XF	Unc	BU
1967	49,789,000	1.00	2.00	3.00	6.00	—
1967 Prooflike	211,000	—	—	—	—	—

Y# 89.1 50 KOPEKS
9.9980 g., 0.9000 Silver 0.2893 oz. ASW **Obv:** National arms divide CCCP above inscription, circle surrounds all **Rev:** Blacksmith at anvil **Edge:** Weight shown in old Russian units

Date	Mintage	F	VF	XF	Unc	BU
1924 ПЛ	26,559,000	15.00	20.00	30.00	60.00	—
1924 ПЛ Proof	—	Value: 550				
1924 ТР	40,000,000	15.00	20.00	30.00	60.00	—

Y# 89.2 50 KOPEKS
9.9980 g., 0.9000 Silver 0.2893 oz. ASW **Obv:** National arms divide CCCP above inscription, circle surrounds all **Rev:** Blacksmith at anvil **Edge:** Weight shown in ЖУДПП (grams) only **Note:** Varieties exist.

Date	Mintage	F	VF	XF	Unc	BU
1925 ПЛ	43,558,000	15.00	20.00	30.00	60.00	—
1925 ПЛ Proof	—	Value: 400				
1926 ПЛ	24,374,000	15.00	20.00	30.00	60.00	—
1926 ПЛ Proof	—	Value: 400				
1927 ПЛ	—	20.00	30.00	40.00	70.00	—
1927 ПЛ Proof	—	Value: 500				

Y# 133 50 KOPEKS
Copper-Nickel **Obv:** National arms **Rev:** Value and date within sprigs

Date	Mintage	F	VF	XF	Unc	BU
1958	40,600,000	—	—	—	1,000	—

Note: Never officially released for circulation; majority of mintage remelted

Y# 133a.1 50 KOPEKS
4.6000 g., Copper-Nickel-Zinc **Obv:** National arms **Rev:** Value and date within sprigs **Edge:** Plain **Note:** Varieties exist.

Date	Mintage	F	VF	XF	Unc	BU
1961	—	4.00	7.00	10.00	20.00	—

Y# 133a.2 50 KOPEKS
4.4000 g., Copper-Nickel-Zinc, 24.05 mm. **Obv:** National arms **Rev:** Value and date within sprigs **Edge:** Lettered with date **Note:** Varieties exist for 1970, 1971, and 1975.

Date	Mintage	F	VF	XF	Unc	BU
1964	—	0.20	0.40	0.75	1.50	—
1965	—	0.20	0.40	0.75	1.50	—
1966	—	0.20	0.40	0.75	1.50	—
1967	—	1.00	1.50	3.00	5.00	—
1968	—	0.20	0.40	0.75	1.50	—
1969	—	0.20	0.40	0.75	1.50	—
1970	—	2.00	5.00	10.00	20.00	—
1971	—	2.00	5.00	10.00	10.00	—
1972	—	0.20	0.40	0.75	1.50	—
1973	—	0.20	0.40	0.75	1.50	—
1974	—	0.20	0.40	0.75	1.50	—
1975	—	1.00	2.50	5.00	10.00	—
1976	—	0.50	1.00	3.00	6.00	—
1977	—	0.20	0.40	0.75	1.50	—
1978	—	0.20	0.40	0.75	1.50	—
1979	—	0.20	0.40	0.75	1.50	—
1980	—	0.20	0.40	0.75	1.50	—
1981	—	0.20	0.40	0.75	1.50	—
1982	—	0.20	0.40	0.75	1.50	—
1983	—	0.20	0.40	0.75	1.50	—
1984	—	0.20	0.40	0.75	1.50	—
1985	—	0.20	0.40	0.75	1.50	—
1986	—	6.00	12.50	25.00	50.00	—

Note: With 1985 on edge

Date	Mintage	F	VF	XF	Unc	BU
1986	—	0.20	0.40	0.75	1.50	—
1987	—	0.20	0.40	0.75	1.50	—
1988	—	1.00	2.00	4.00	10.00	—

Note: With 1987 on edge

Date	Mintage	F	VF	XF	Unc	BU
1988	—	0.20	0.40	0.75	1.50	—
1989	—	6.00	12.50	25.00	50.00	—

Note: With 1988 on edge

Date	Mintage	F	VF	XF	Unc	BU
1989	—	0.15	0.25	0.50	1.00	—
1990	—	0.15	0.25	0.50	1.00	—
1990 Rare						

Note: With 1989 on edge

Date	Mintage	F	VF	XF	Unc	BU
1991 M	—	0.15	0.25	0.50	1.00	—
1991 Л	—	0.15	0.25	0.50	1.00	—

Y# 139 50 KOPEKS
Copper-Nickel-Zinc, 25 mm. **Subject:** 50th Anniversary of Revolution **Obv:** National arms **Rev:** Lenin with right arm raised facing left, star at upper left

Date	Mintage	F	VF	XF	Unc	BU
ND(1967)	49,789,000	—	3.00	4.00	8.00	—
ND(1967) Prooflike	—	—	—	—	3.00	—

Y# 90.1 ROUBLE
19.9960 g., 0.9000 Silver 0.5786 oz. ASW **Obv:** National arms divides circle with inscription within **Rev:** Two figures walking right, radiant sun rising at right **Edge:** 18 ЖУДПП (grams) (43.21d) **Note:** Varieties exist.

Date	Mintage	F	VF	XF	Unc	BU
1924 ПЛ	12,998,000	30.00	50.00	70.00	150	200
1924 ПЛ Proof	—	Value: 2,500				

Y# 90.2 ROUBLE
19.9960 g., 0.9000 Silver 0.5786 oz. ASW **Obv:** National arms divides circle holding inscription **Rev:** Two figures walking right, sun rising at right **Edge:** 4 Zolotniks 21 Dolyas

Date	Mintage	F	VF	XF	Unc	BU
1924 Rare	—	—	—	—	—	—

Y# 134 ROUBLE
Copper-Nickel **Obv:** National arms **Rev:** Value and date within sprigs

Date	Mintage	F	VF	XF	Unc	BU
1958	30,700,000	—	—	—	900	—

Note: Never officially released for circulation; majority of mintage remelted

Y# 134a.1 ROUBLE
Copper-Nickel-Zinc **Obv:** National arms within circle **Rev:** Value and date within sprigs **Edge:** Plain

Date	Mintage	F	VF	XF	Unc	BU
1961	—	5.00	10.00	15.00	25.00	—

Y# 134a.2 ROUBLE
7.4000 g., Copper-Nickel-Zinc, 27 mm. **Obv:** National arms within circle **Rev:** Value and date within sprigs **Edge:** Lettered with date

Date	Mintage	F	VF	XF	Unc	BU
1964	—	1.00	2.00	3.00	6.00	—
1965	—	1.00	2.00	3.00	6.00	—
1966	—	1.00	2.00	3.00	6.00	—
1967 Rare	—	—	—	—	—	—
Note: With 1966 on edge						
1967	—	0.50	1.00	2.00	3.00	—
1968	—	0.50	1.00	2.00	3.00	—
1969	—	0.50	1.00	2.00	3.00	—
1970	—	0.50	1.00	2.00	3.00	—
1971	—	0.50	1.00	2.00	3.00	—
1972	—	0.50	1.00	2.00	3.00	—
1973	—	0.50	1.00	2.00	3.00	—

Date	Mintage	F	VF	XF	Unc	BU
1974	—	0.50	1.00	2.00	3.00	—
1975	—	0.50	1.00	2.00	3.00	—
1976	—	0.50	1.00	2.00	3.00	—
1977	—	0.50	1.00	2.00	3.00	—
1978	—	0.50	1.00	2.00	3.00	—
1979	—	0.40	0.75	1.50	2.50	—
1980	—	0.40	0.75	1.50	2.50	—
1981	—	0.40	0.75	1.50	2.50	—
1982	—	0.40	0.75	1.50	2.50	—
1983	—	0.40	0.75	1.50	2.50	—
1984	—	0.40	0.75	1.50	2.50	—
1985	—	0.40	0.75	1.50	2.50	—
1986	—	0.40	0.75	1.50	2.50	—
1987	—	0.40	0.75	1.50	2.50	—
1988	—	0.40	0.75	1.50	2.50	—
1988	—	1.50	3.00	6.00	15.00	—
Note: With 1989 on edge						
1989	—	0.25	0.50	1.00	2.50	—
1990	—	1.50	3.00	6.00	15.00	—
Note: With 1989 on edge						
1990	—	0.25	0.50	1.00	2.50	—
1991 M	—	0.25	0.50	1.00	2.50	—
1991 Л	—	0.25	0.50	1.00	2.50	—

Y# 135.1 ROUBLE
Copper-Nickel-Zinc, 31 mm. **Subject:** 20th Anniversary of World War II Victory **Obv:** National arms divide CCCP with inscription below **Rev:** Statue by Vouchetic

Date	Mintage	F	VF	XF	Unc	BU
1965	59,989,000	—	2.00	3.00	5.00	—
1965 Prooflike	—	—	—	—	3.00	—
1965 Proof	—	Value: 30.00				

Y# 135.2 ROUBLE
Copper-Nickel-Zinc, 31 mm. **Obv:** National arms divide CCCP with inscription below **Rev:** Victory monument **Edge:** 1988.N.

Date	Mintage	F	VF	XF	Unc	BU
1965 Proof, restrike	55,000	Value: 3.50				

Y# 140.1 ROUBLE
Copper-Nickel-Zinc, 31 mm. **Subject:** 50th Anniversary of Revolution **Obv:** National arms **Rev:** Lenin with right arm raised facing left, star at upper left **Edge:** Lettered, with date

Date	Mintage	F	VF	XF	Unc	BU
1967	52,289,000	—	2.00	3.00	5.00	—
1967 Prooflike	—	—	—	—	3.00	—
1967 Proof	—	Value: 30.00				

Y# 140.2 ROUBLE
Copper-Nickel-Zinc, 31 mm. **Obv:** National arms **Rev:** Lenin with right arm raised facing left, star at upper left **Edge:** 1988.N.

Date	Mintage	F	VF	XF	Unc	BU
1967 Proof, restrike	55,000	Value: 4.00				

Y# 141 ROUBLE
Copper-Nickel-Zinc, 31 mm. **Subject:** Centennial of Lenin's Birth **Obv:** National arms divide CCCP **Rev:** Head right

Date	Mintage	F	VF	XF	Unc	BU
ND(1970)	99,889,000	—	1.00	2.00	3.00	—
ND(1970) Prooflike	—	—	—	—	3.00	—
ND(1970) Proof	—	Value: 100				

Y# 142.1 ROUBLE
Copper-Nickel-Zinc, 31 mm. **Subject:** 30th Anniversary of World War II Victory **Obv:** National arms divide CCCP **Rev:** Volgograd monument **Edge:** Date **Note:** Date appears on the edge in English and Russian as "9 March 1975". Varieties exist.

Date	Mintage	F	VF	XF	Unc	BU
1975	14,989,000	—	1.00	2.00	3.00	—
1975 Prooflike	—	—	—	—	3.00	—
1975 Proof	—	Value: 30.00				

Y# 142.2 ROUBLE
Copper-Nickel-Zinc, 31 mm. **Obv:** National arms divide CCCP, value below **Rev:** Volgograd monument **Edge:** 1988.N.

Date	Mintage	F	VF	XF	Unc	BU
ND(1975) Proof, restrike	55,000	Value: 3.50				

Y# 143.1 ROUBLE
Copper-Nickel-Zinc, 31 mm. **Subject:** 60th Anniversary of Bolshevik Revolution **Obv:** National arms divide CCCP **Rev:** Head left above ship, dates below

Date	Mintage	F	VF	XF	Unc	BU
ND(1977)	4,987,000	—	1.00	2.00	3.00	—
ND(1977) Prooflike	—	—	—	—	3.00	—
ND(1977) Proof	—	Value: 30.00				

Y# 143.2 ROUBLE
Copper-Nickel-Zinc, 31 mm. **Obv:** National arms divide CCCP, value below **Rev:** Head left above ship, dates below **Edge:** 1988.N.

Date	Mintage	F	VF	XF	Unc	BU
ND(1977) Proof, restrike	55,000	Value: 3.50				

Y# A144 ROUBLE
Copper-Nickel-Zinc, 31 mm. **Obv:** National arms divide CCCP above value **Rev:** Design with star on top with Olympic rings below **Note:** Mule

Date	Mintage	F	VF	XF	Unc	BU
1977 Rare	Inc. below	—	—	—	—	—

Y# 144 ROUBLE
Copper-Nickel-Zinc, 31 mm. **Series:** 1980 Olympics **Obv:** National arms divide CCCP above value **Rev:** Design with star on top with Olympic rings below

Date	Mintage	F	VF	XF	Unc	BU
1977	8,665,000	—	1.00	2.00	3.00	—
1977 Prooflike	—	—	—	—	3.00	—
1977 Proof	—	Value: 25.00				

Y# 153.1 ROUBLE
Copper-Nickel-Zinc, 31 mm. **Series:** 1980 Olympics **Obv:** National arms divide CCCP with value below **Rev:** Moscow Kremlin with stars on top of steeples

Date	Mintage	F	VF	XF	Unc	BU
1978	6,490,000	—	1.00	2.00	3.00	—
1978 Prooflike	—	—	—	—	3.00	—
1978 Proof	—	Value: 60.00				

Y# 153.2 ROUBLE
Copper-Nickel-Zinc, 31 mm. **Obv:** National arms divide CCCP, value below **Rev:** Clock on tower shows Roman numeral 6 (VI) instead of 4 (IV)

Date	Mintage	F	VF	XF	Unc	BU
1978	Inc. above	—	8.00	16.00	25.00	—

Y# 165 ROUBLE
Copper-Nickel-Zinc, 31 mm. **Series:** 1980 Olympics
Obv: National arms divide CCCP, value below **Rev:** Monument, Sputnik and Sojuz

Date	Mintage	F	VF	XF	Unc	BU
1979	4,665,000	—	1.00	2.00	3.00	—
1979 Prooflike	—	—	—	—	3.00	—
1979 Proof	—	Value: 25.00				

Y# 164 ROUBLE
Copper-Nickel-Zinc, 31 mm. **Series:** 1980 Olympics
Obv: National arms divide CCCP, value below **Rev:** Moscow University **Note:** Varieties in window arrangements exist.

Date	Mintage	F	VF	XF	Unc	BU
1979	4,665,000	—	1.00	2.00	3.00	—
1979 Prooflike	—	—	—	—	3.00	—
1979 Proof	—	Value: 25.00				

Y# 177 ROUBLE
Copper-Nickel, 31 mm. **Series:** 1980 Olympics **Obv:** National arms divide CCCP with value below **Rev:** Dolgorukij Monument

Date	Mintage	F	VF	XF	Unc	BU
1980	4,490,000	—	1.00	2.00	3.00	—
1980 Prooflike	—	—	—	—	3.00	—
1980 Proof	—	Value: 25.00				

Y# 178 ROUBLE
Copper-Nickel, 31 mm. **Series:** 1980 Olympics **Obv:** National arms divide CCCP, value below **Rev:** Torch

Date	Mintage	F	VF	XF	Unc	BU
1980	4,490,000	—	1.00	2.00	3.00	—
1980 Prooflike	—	—	—	—	3.00	—
1980 Proof	—	Value: 25.00				

Y# 188.1 ROUBLE
Copper-Nickel, 31 mm. **Subject:** 20th Anniversary of Manned Space Flights **Obv:** National arms divide CCCP with value below **Rev:** Cosmonaut facing flanked by rockets, hammer and sickle above

Date	Mintage	F	VF	XF	Unc	BU
ND(1981)	3,962,000	—	1.00	2.00	3.00	—
ND(1981) Proof	—	Value: 12.50				

Y# 188.2 ROUBLE
Copper-Nickel, 31 mm. **Subject:** 20th Anniversary of Manned Space Flights **Obv:** National arms divide CCCP, value below **Rev:** Cosmonaut facing flanked by rockets, hammer and sickle above **Edge:** 1988.N.

Date	Mintage	F	VF	XF	Unc	BU
ND(1981) Proof; restrike	55,000	Value: 9.00				

Y# 189.1 ROUBLE
Copper-Nickel, 31 mm. **Subject:** Russian-Bulgarian Friendship **Obv:** National arms divide CCCP with value below **Rev:** Grasped hands divide flags above and sprigs below within beaded circle **Edge:** Cyrillic lettering

Date	Mintage	F	VF	XF	Unc	BU
1981	1,984,000	—	1.00	2.00	4.00	—
1981 Proof	16,000	Value: 22.50				

Note: The same reverse die was used for both Russia 1 Rouble KM #189 and Bulgaria 1 Lev KM#119

Y# 189.2 ROUBLE
Copper-Nickel, 31 mm. **Subject:** Russian-Bulgarian Friendship **Obv:** National arms divide CCCP, value below **Rev:** Grasped hands divide flags above and sprigs below within beaded circle **Edge:** 1988.N.

Date	Mintage	F	VF	XF	Unc	BU
1981 Proof; restrike	55,000	Value: 3.50				

Note: The same reverse die was used for both Russia 1 Rouble KM#189 and Bulgaria 1 Lev KM#119

Y# 190.1 ROUBLE
Copper-Nickel, 31 mm. **Subject:** 60th Anniversary of the Soviet Union **Obv:** National arms divide CCCP with value below **Rev:** Radiant sun and standing statue facing left **Edge:** Cyrillic lettering

Date	Mintage	F	VF	XF	Unc	BU
ND(1982)	1,921,000	—	1.00	3.00	6.00	—
ND(1982) Proof	79,000	Value: 6.00				

Y# 190.2 ROUBLE
Copper-Nickel, 31 mm. **Subject:** 60th Anniversary of the Soviet Union **Obv:** National arms divide CCCP, value below **Rev:** Radiant sun back of statue **Edge:** 1988.N.

Date	Mintage	F	VF	XF	Unc	BU
ND(1982) Proof; restrike	55,000	Value: 4.50				

Y# 191.1 ROUBLE
Copper-Nickel, 31 mm. **Subject:** Death of Karl Marx Centennial **Obv:** National arms divide CCCP with value below **Rev:** Bust 3/4 left and dates **Edge:** Cyrillic lettering

Date	Mintage	F	VF	XF	Unc	BU
1983	1,921,000	—	1.00	2.00	4.00	—
1983 Proof	79,000	Value: 6.00				

Y# 191.2 ROUBLE
Copper-Nickel, 31 mm. **Subject:** Death of Karl Marx Centennial **Obv:** National arms divide CCCP, value below **Rev:** Bust 3/4 left with dates **Edge:** 1988.N.

Date	Mintage	F	VF	XF	Unc	BU
1983 Proof; restrike	55,000	Value: 4.50				

Y# 192.1 ROUBLE
12.5000 g., Copper-Nickel, 31 mm. **Subject:** 20th Anniversary of First Woman in Space **Obv:** National arms divide CCCP with value below **Rev:** Cosmonaut head facing flanked by stars

Date	Mintage	F	VF	XF	Unc	BU
1983	1,945,000	—	1.00	2.00	4.00	—
1983 Proof	55,000	Value: 6.00				

Y# 192.2 ROUBLE
Copper-Nickel, 31 mm. **Subject:** 20th Anniversary of First Woman in Space **Obv:** National arms divide CCCP, value below **Rev:** Cosmonaut head facing flanked by stars **Edge:** 1988.N.

Date	Mintage	F	VF	XF	Unc	BU
1983 Proof; restrike	55,000	Value: 3.50				

Y# 193.1 ROUBLE
Copper-Nickel, 31 mm. **Subject:** First Russian Printer **Obv:** National arms divide CCCP with value below **Rev:** Ivan Fedorov **Edge:** Cyrillic lettering

Date	Mintage	F	VF	XF	Unc	BU
1983	1,965,000	—	1.00	2.00	4.00	—
1983 Proof	35,000	Value: 7.50				

Y# 193.2 ROUBLE
Copper-Nickel, 31 mm. **Subject:** First Russian Printer **Obv:** National arms divide CCCP, value below **Rev:** Ivan Fedorov **Edge:** 1988.N.

Date	Mintage	F	VF	XF	Unc	BU
1983 Proof; restrike	55,000	Value: 3.50				

Y# 194.1 ROUBLE
Copper-Nickel, 31 mm. **Subject:** 150th Anniversary - Birth of Dmitri Ivanovich Mendeleyev **Obv:** National arms divide CCCP with value below **Rev:** Head facing and dates **Edge:** Cyrillic lettering

Date	Mintage	F	VF	XF	Unc	BU
1984	1,965,000	—	1.00	2.00	4.00	—
1984 Proof	35,000	Value: 7.50				

Y# 194.2 ROUBLE
Copper-Nickel, 31 mm. **Subject:** 150th Anniversary - birth of Dmitri Ivanovich Mendeleyev **Obv:** National arms divide CCCP, value below **Rev:** Head facing with dates at right **Edge:** 1988.N.

Date	Mintage	F	VF	XF	Unc	BU
1984 Proof; restrike	55,000	Value: 3.50				

Y# 195.1 ROUBLE
Copper-Nickel, 31 mm. **Subject:** 125th Anniversary - Birth of Alexander Popov **Obv:** National arms divide CCCP with value below **Rev:** Head facing and dates **Edge:** Cyrillic lettering

Date	Mintage	F	VF	XF	Unc	BU
1984	1,965,000	—	1.00	2.00	4.00	—
1984 Proof	35,000	Value: 6.00				

Y# 195.2 ROUBLE
Copper-Nickel, 31 mm. **Subject:** 125th Anniversary - Birth of Alexander Popov **Obv:** National arms divide CCCP, value below **Rev:** Head facing with dates at right **Edge:** 1988.N.

Date	Mintage	F	VF	XF	Unc	BU
1984 Proof; restrike	55,000	Value: 3.50				

Y# 196.1 ROUBLE
Copper-Nickel, 31 mm. **Subject:** 185th Anniversary - Birth of Alexander Sergeyevich Pushkin **Obv:** National arms divide CCCP with value below **Edge:** Cyrillic lettering

Date	Mintage	F	VF	XF	Unc	BU
1984	1,965,000	—	1.00	2.00	5.00	—
1984 Proof	35,000	Value: 7.50				

Y# 196.2 ROUBLE
Copper-Nickel, 31 mm. **Subject:** 185th Anniversary - Birth of Alexander Sergeyevich Pushkin **Obv:** National arms divide CCCP, value below **Rev:** Head left with dates at right **Edge:** 1988.N.

Date	Mintage	F	VF	XF	Unc	BU
1984 Proof; restrike	55,000	Value: 3.50				
1985 Proof; Restrike/ Error	—	Value: 50.00				

Y# 197.1 ROUBLE
Copper-Nickel, 31 mm. **Subject:** 115th Anniversary - Birth of Vladimir Lenin **Obv:** National arms divide CCCP with value below **Rev:** Bust left with dates **Edge:** Cyrillic lettering

Date	Mintage	F	VF	XF	Unc	BU
1985	1,960,000	—	1.00	3.00	6.00	—
1985 Proof	40,000	Value: 7.50				

Y# 197.2 ROUBLE
Copper-Nickel, 31 mm. **Subject:** 115th Anniversary of Vladimir Lenin **Obv:** National arms divide CCCP, value below **Rev:** Bust left with dates **Edge:** 1988.N.

Date	Mintage	F	VF	XF	Unc	BU
1985 Proof; Restrike/Error	55,000	Value: 4.50				
1988 Error	—	—	—	—	—	—

Y# 198.1 ROUBLE
Copper-Nickel, 31 mm. **Subject:** 40th Anniversary - World War II Victory **Obv:** National arms divide CCCP with value below **Rev:** Hammer and sickle within radiant star, sprig and dates below **Edge:** Cyrillic lettering

Date	Mintage	F	VF	XF	Unc	BU
1985	5,960,000	—	1.00	2.00	5.00	—
1985 Proof	40,000	Value: 6.00				

Y# 198.2 ROUBLE
Copper-Nickel, 33 mm. **Subject:** 40th Anniversary - World War II Victory **Obv:** National arms divide CCCP, value below **Rev:** Hammer and sickle within radiant star, sprig and dates below **Edge:** 1988.N.

Date	Mintage	F	VF	XF	Unc	BU
1985 Proof; restrike	55,000				Value: 3.50	

Y# 199.1 ROUBLE
Copper-Nickel, 31 mm. **Subject:** 12th World Youth Festival in Moscow **Obv:** National arms divide CCCP with value below **Rev:** Festival emblem **Edge:** Cyrillic lettering

Date	Mintage	F	VF	XF	Unc	BU
1985	5,960,000	—	1.00	2.00	5.00	—
1985 Proof	40,000				Value: 6.00	

Y# 199.2 ROUBLE
Copper-Nickel, 31 mm. **Subject:** 12th World Youth Festival in Moscow **Obv:** National arms divide CCCP, value below **Rev:** Festival emblem **Edge:** 1988.N.

Date	Mintage	F	VF	XF	Unc	BU
1985 Proof; restrike	55,000				Value: 3.50	

Y# 200.1 ROUBLE
Copper-Nickel, 31 mm. **Subject:** 165th Anniversary - Birth of Friedrich Engels **Obv:** National arms divide CCCP with value below **Rev:** Bust 3/4 left with dates

Date	Mintage	F	VF	XF	Unc	BU
1985	1,960,000	—	1.00	3.00	6.00	—
1985 Proof					Value: 6.00	

Y# 200.2 ROUBLE
Copper-Nickel, 31 mm. **Subject:** 165th Anniversary - Birth of Friedrich Engels **Obv:** National arms divide CCCP, value below **Rev:** Bust 3/4 left with dates **Edge:** 1988.N.

Date	Mintage	F	VF	XF	Unc	BU
1983 Proof; restrike					Value: 55.00	

Note: Error date

Date	Mintage	F	VF	XF	Unc	BU
1985 Proof; restrike	55,000				Value: 4.50	

Y# 201.1 ROUBLE
Copper-Nickel, 31 mm. **Subject:** International Year of Peace **Obv:** National arms divide CCCP with value below **Rev:** Hands within wreath releasing dove **Edge:** Cyrillic lettering **Note:** Rouble written with inverted "V" for ?.

Date	Mintage	F	VF	XF	Unc	BU
1986	—	—			12.00	—

Y# 201.3 ROUBLE
Copper-Nickel, 31 mm. **Subject:** International Year of Peace **Obv:** National arms divide CCCP with value below **Rev:** Hands within wreath releasing dove

Date	Mintage	F	VF	XF	Unc	BU
1986	3,955,000	—	1.00	3.00	6.00	—
1986 Proof	45,000				Value: 6.00	

Y# 201.4 ROUBLE
Copper-Nickel, 31 mm. **Subject:** International Year of Peace **Obv:** National arms divide CCCP, value below **Rev:** Hands within wreath releasing dove **Edge:** 1988.N.

Date	Mintage	F	VF	XF	Unc	BU
1986	—	—	1.00	3.00	7.00	—
1986 Proof, rare						

Y# 202.1 ROUBLE
Copper-Nickel, 31 mm. **Subject:** 275th Anniversary - Birth of Mikhail Lomonosov **Obv:** National arms divide CCCP with value below **Rev:** Bust 1/4 left **Edge:** Cyrillic lettering

Date	Mintage	F	VF	XF	Unc	BU
1986	1,965,000	—	1.00	2.00	4.00	—
1986 Proof	35,000				Value: 5.00	

Y# 202.2 ROUBLE
Copper-Nickel, 31 mm. **Subject:** 275th Anniversary - Birth of Mikhail Lomonosov **Obv:** National arms divide CCCP, value below **Rev:** Bust looking left with dates at right **Edge:** 1988.N.

Date	Mintage	F	VF	XF	Unc	BU
1984 Error						
1986 Proof; restrike	55,000				Value: 3.50	

Y# 205 ROUBLE
Copper-Nickel, 31 mm. **Subject:** 130th Anniversary - Birth of Constantin Tsiolkovsky **Obv:** National arms with CCCP and value below **Rev:** Seated figure facing left with stars and dates **Edge:** Cyrillic lettering

Date	Mintage	F	VF	XF	Unc	BU
1987	3,830,000	—	1.00	2.00	4.00	—
1987 Proof	170,000				Value: 5.00	

Y# 203 ROUBLE
Copper-Nickel, 31 mm. **Subject:** 175th Anniversary - Battle of Borodino **Obv:** National arms with CCCP and value below **Rev:** Group of soldiers **Edge:** Cyrillic lettering **Note:** Varieties with wheat in coat of arms.

Date	Mintage	F	VF	XF	Unc	BU
1987	3,780,000	—	1.00	2.00	4.00	—
1987 Proof	220,000				Value: 5.00	

Y# 204 ROUBLE
Copper-Nickel, 31 mm. **Subject:** 175th Anniversary - Battle of Borodino **Obv:** National arms with CCCP and value below **Rev:** Kutuzov Monument **Edge:** Cyrillic lettering **Note:** Varieties with wheat in coat of arms.

Date	Mintage	F	VF	XF	Unc	BU
1987	3,780,000	—	1.00	2.00	4.00	—
1987 Proof	220,000				Value: 5.00	

Y# 206 ROUBLE
Copper-Nickel, 31 mm. **Subject:** 70th Anniversary of Bolshevik Revolution **Obv:** National arms with CCCP and value below **Rev:** Hammer and sickle with ship on globe background at center of ribbon design, date and sprig below **Edge:** Cyrillic lettering **Note:** Varieties with wheat in coat of arms.

Date	Mintage	F	VF	XF	Unc	BU
1987	3,800,000	—	1.00	2.00	4.00	—
1987 Proof	200,000				Value: 6.00	

Y# 216 ROUBLE
Copper-Nickel, 31 mm. **Subject:** 160th Anniversary - Birth of Leo Tolstoi **Obv:** National arms with CCCP and value below **Rev:** Head facing **Edge:** Cyrillic lettering

Date	Mintage	F	VF	XF	Unc	BU
1987 Error						
1988	3,775,000	—	1.00	2.00	4.00	—
1988 Proof	225,000				Value: 5.00	

Y# 209 ROUBLE
Copper-Nickel, 31 mm. **Subject:** 120th Anniversary - Birth of Maxin Gorky **Obv:** National arms with CCCP and value below **Rev:** Bust 1/4 right, designs and flying bird in background **Edge:** Cyrillic lettering

Date	Mintage	F	VF	XF	Unc	BU
1988	3,775,000	—	1.00	2.00	4.00	—
1988 Proof	225,000				Value: 6.00	

Y# 220 ROUBLE
Copper-Nickel, 31 mm. **Subject:** 150th Anniversary - Birth of Musorgsky **Obv:** National arms with CCCP and value below **Rev:** Head 3/4 left divides dates **Edge:** Cyrillic lettering

Date	Mintage	F	VF	XF	Unc	BU
1989	2,700,000	—	1.00	3.00	5.00	—
1989 Proof	300,000				Value: 5.50	

Y# 228 ROUBLE
Copper-Nickel, 31 mm. **Subject:** 175th Anniversary - Birth of M.Y. Lermontov **Obv:** National arms with CCCP and value below **Rev:** Head 1/4 left, quill below, dates at right **Edge:** Cyrillic lettering

Date	Mintage	F	VF	XF	Unc	BU
1989	2,700,000	—	1.00	3.00	5.00	—
1989 Proof	300,000				Value: 6.00	

Y# 232 ROUBLE
Copper-Nickel, 31 mm. **Subject:** 100th Anniversary - Birth of Hamza Hakim-zade Niyazi **Obv:** National arms with CCCP and value below **Rev:** Bust facing, dates at right **Edge:** Cyrillic lettering

Date	Mintage	F	VF	XF	Unc	BU
1989	1,800,000	—	2.00	4.00	7.00	—
1989 Proof	200,000				Value: 6.00	

Y# 233 ROUBLE
Copper-Nickel, 31 mm. **Subject:** 100th Anniversary - Death of Mihai Eminescu **Obv:** National arms with CCCP and value below **Rev:** Head 3/4 left flanked by dates **Edge:** Cyrillic lettering

Date	Mintage	F	VF	XF	Unc	BU
1989	1,800,000	—	2.00	4.00	7.00	—
1989 Proof	200,000				Value: 6.00	

Y# 235 ROUBLE
Copper-Nickel, 31 mm. **Subject:** 175th Anniversary - Birth of T.G. Shevchenko **Obv:** National arms with CCCP and value below **Rev:** Head looking down facing 3/4 left **Edge:** Cyrillic lettering

Date	Mintage	F	VF	XF	Unc	BU
1989	2,700,000	—	1.00	3.00	5.00	—
1989 Proof	300,000				Value: 5.50	

Y# 236 ROUBLE

Copper-Nickel, 31 mm. **Subject:** 100th Anniversary - Birth of Tschaikovsky - Composer **Obv:** National arms with CCCP and value below **Rev:** Seated figure left, musical notes in background **Edge:** Cyrillic lettering

Date	Mintage	F	VF	XF	Unc	BU
1990	2,600,000	—	—	—	3.00	—
1990 Proof	400,000	Value: 6.50				

Y# 237 ROUBLE

Copper-Nickel, 31 mm. **Subject:** Anniversary - Marshal Zhukov **Obv:** National arms with CCCP and value below **Rev:** Uniformed bust left **Edge:** Cyrillic lettering

Date	Mintage	F	VF	XF	Unc	BU
1990	1,600,000	—	—	—	8.00	—
1990 Proof	400,000	Value: 7.00				

Y# 240 ROUBLE

Copper-Nickel, 31 mm. **Subject:** 130th Anniversary - Birth of Anton Chekhov **Obv:** National arms with CCCP and value below **Rev:** Head 1/4 left divides design and dates **Edge:** Cyrillic lettering

Date	Mintage	F	VF	XF	Unc	BU
1990	2,600,000	—	—	—	5.00	—
1990 Proof	400,000	Value: 6.50				

Y# 257 ROUBLE

Copper-Nickel, 31 mm. **Subject:** 125th Anniversary - Birth of Janis Rainis **Obv:** National arms with CCCP and value below **Rev:** Head facing with dates at right **Edge:** Cyrillic lettering

Date	Mintage	F	VF	XF	Unc	BU
1990	2,600,000	—	—	—	5.00	—
1990 Proof	400,000	Value: 6.50				

Y# 258 ROUBLE

Copper-Nickel, 31 mm. **Subject:** 500th Anniversary - Birth of Francisk Scorina **Obv:** National arms with CCCP and value below **Rev:** Half figure facing **Edge:** Cyrillic lettering

Date	Mintage	F	VF	XF	Unc	BU
1990	2,600,000	—	—	—	5.00	—
1990 Proof	400,000	Value: 6.50				

Y# 260 ROUBLE

Copper-Nickel, 31 mm. **Subject:** 550th Anniversary - Birth of Alisher Navoi **Obv:** National arms with CCCP and value below **Rev:** Bust with hand on chin left **Edge:** Cyrillic lettering

Date	Mintage	F	VF	XF	Unc	BU
1990 Error	—	—	—	—	—	10.00
1991 Л	2,150,000	—	—	—	6.00	—
1991 Л Proof	350,000	Value: 3.50				
1991 M	—	—	—	—	6.00	—
1991 M Proof	—	Value: 3.50				

Y# 261 ROUBLE

Copper-Nickel, 31 mm. **Subject:** 125th Anniversary - Birth of P. N. Lebedev **Obv:** National arms with CCCP and value below **Rev:** Half figure right with hand on book, designs on bottom, dates and fomulas at right **Edge:** Cyrillic lettering

Date	Mintage	F	VF	XF	Unc	BU
1990 Error, rare	—	—	—	—	—	—
1991	2,150,000	—	—	—	5.00	—
1991 Proof	350,000	Value: 5.50				

Y# 282 ROUBLE

Copper-Nickel, 31 mm. **Subject:** K.B. Ivanov **Obv:** National arms with CCCP and value below **Rev:** Head left **Edge:** Cyrillic lettering

Date	Mintage	F	VF	XF	Unc	BU
1991	3,150,000	—	—	—	5.00	—
1991 Proof	350,000	Value: 5.50				

Y# 283 ROUBLE

Copper-Nickel, 31 mm. **Subject:** Turkman Poet Makhtumkuli **Obv:** National arms with CCCP and value below **Rev:** Bust left **Edge:** Cyrillic lettering

Date	Mintage	F	VF	XF	Unc	BU
1991	2,150,000	—	—	—	6.00	—
1991 Proof	350,000	Value: 5.50				

Y# 284 ROUBLE

Copper-Nickel, 31 mm. **Subject:** 850th Anniversary - Birth of Nizami Gyanzhevi - Poet **Obv:** National arms with CCCP and value below **Rev:** Bust right writing with quill **Edge:** Cyrillic lettering

Date	Mintage	F	VF	XF	Unc	BU
1991	2,200,000	—	—	—	6.00	—
1991 Proof	300,000	Value: 5.50				

Y# 289 ROUBLE

Copper-Nickel, 31 mm. **Series:** 1992 Olympics **Obv:** National arms with CCCP and value below **Rev:** Wrestlers

Date	Mintage	F	VF	XF	Unc	BU
1991 Proof	250,000	Value: 7.50				

Y# 290 ROUBLE

Copper-Nickel, 31 mm. **Series:** 1992 Olympics **Obv:** National arms with CCCP and value below **Rev:** Javelin throwers

Date	Mintage	F	VF	XF	Unc	BU
1991 Proof	250,000	Value: 7.50				

Y# 291 ROUBLE

Copper-Nickel, 31 mm. **Series:** 1992 Olympics **Obv:** National arms with CCCP and value below **Rev:** Cyclist and charioteer

Date	Mintage	F	VF	XF	Unc	BU
1991 Proof	250,000	Value: 7.50				

Y# 299 ROUBLE

Copper-Nickel, 31 mm. **Series:** 1992 Olympics **Obv:** National arms with CCCP and value below **Rev:** Weight lifters

Date	Mintage	F	VF	XF	Unc	BU
1991 Proof	250,000	Value: 7.50				

Y# 300 ROUBLE

Copper-Nickel, 31 mm. **Series:** 1992 Olympics **Obv:** National arms with CCCP and value below **Rev:** Broad jumpers

Date	Mintage	F	VF	XF	Unc	BU
1991 Proof	250,000	Value: 7.50				

Y# 302 ROUBLE

Copper-Nickel, 31 mm. **Series:** 1992 Olympics **Obv:** National arms with CCCP and value below **Rev:** Runners

Date	Mintage	F	VF	XF	Unc	BU
1991 Proof	250,000	Value: 7.50				

Y# 263.1 ROUBLE

Copper-Nickel, 31 mm. **Subject:** 100th Birthday of Sergey Prokofiev **Obv:** National arms with CCCP and value below **Rev:** Head right **Edge:** Cyrillic lettering

Date	Mintage	F	VF	XF	Unc	BU
1991	2,150,000	—	—	—	3.00	—
1991 Proof	350,000	Value: 5.50				

Y# 263.2 ROUBLE

Copper-Nickel, 31 mm. **Subject:** 100th Birthday of Sergey Prokofiev **Obv:** National arms with CCCP and value below **Rev:** Head right, dates below **Note:** Error death date: 1952.

Date	Mintage	F	VF	XF	Unc	BU
1991 Rare	—	—	—	—	—	—

Y# A134 2 ROUBLES

Copper-Nickel **Obv:** National arms **Rev:** Value above date within wreath

Date	Mintage	F	VF	XF	Unc	BU
1958	20,976,000	—	—	—	350	—

Note: Never officially released for circulation; majority of mintage remelted

Y# B134   3 ROUBLES
Copper-Nickel **Obv:** National arms **Rev:** Value above date within wreath

Date	Mintage	F	VF	XF	Unc	BU
1958	4,050,000	—	—	—	2,300	—

Note: Never officially released for circulation; majority of mintage remelted

Y# 207   3 ROUBLES
Copper-Nickel **Subject:** 70th Anniversary - Bolshevik Revolution **Obv:** National arms with CCCP and value below **Rev:** Date above three uniformed standing figures with weapons

Date	Mintage	F	VF	XF	Unc	BU
1987	2,300,000	—	—	—	7.00	—
1987 Proof	200,000	Value: 7.50				

Y# 210   3 ROUBLES
34.5600 g., 0.9000 Silver 1.0000 oz. ASW **Subject:** 1000th Anniversary of Russian Architecture **Obv:** National arms with CCCP and value below **Rev:** Cathedral of St. Sophia in Kiev

Date	Mintage	F	VF	XF	Unc	BU
1988 (m) Proof	Est. 35,000	Value: 110				

Y# 211   3 ROUBLES
34.5600 g., 0.9000 Silver 1.0000 oz. ASW **Subject:** 1000th Anniversary of Minting in Russian **Obv:** National arms with CCCP and value below **Rev:** Coin design of St. Vladimir, 977-1015

Date	Mintage	F	VF	XF	Unc	BU
1988 (l) Proof	Est. 35,000	Value: 110				

Y# 222   3 ROUBLES
34.5600 g., 0.9000 Silver 1.0000 oz. ASW **Subject:** 500th Anniversary United Russia **Obv:** National arms with CCCP and value below **Rev:** Kremlin

Date	Mintage	F	VF	XF	Unc	BU
1989 (l) Proof	Est. 40,000	Value: 75.00				

Y# 223   3 ROUBLES
34.5600 g., 0.9000 Silver 1.0000 oz. ASW **Subject:** 500th Anniversary of the First All-Russian Coinage **Obv:** National arms with CCCP and value below **Rev:** Three ancient coins

Date	Mintage	F	VF	XF	Unc	BU
1989 (l) Proof	Est. 40,000	Value: 75.00				

Y# 234   3 ROUBLES
Copper-Nickel **Subject:** Armenian Earthquake Relief **Obv:** National arms with CCCP and value below **Rev:** Stylized hand with flame in palm, wings form mountains in background **Edge:** Cyrillic lettering

Date	Mintage	F	VF	XF	Unc	BU
1989	2,700,000	—	—	—	5.00	—
1989 Proof	300,000	Value: 6.50				

Y# 242   3 ROUBLES
34.5600 g., 0.9000 Silver 1.0000 oz. ASW **Obv:** National arms with CCCP and value below **Rev:** Captain Cook on Unalaska Island

Date	Mintage	F	VF	XF	Unc	BU
1990 (l) Proof	25,000	Value: 60.00				

Y# 247   3 ROUBLES
34.5600 g., 0.9000 Silver 1.0000 oz. ASW **Subject:** World Summit for Children **Obv:** National arms with CCCP and value below **Rev:** Baby and flower within wreath above seated figures around v-shaped design

Date	Mintage	F	VF	XF	Unc	BU
1990 (l) Proof	20,000	Value: 65.00				

Y# 248   3 ROUBLES
34.5600 g., 0.9000 Silver 1.0000 oz. ASW **Obv:** National arms with CCCP and value below **Rev:** Peter the Great's Fleet

Date	Mintage	F	VF	XF	Unc	BU
1990 (m) Proof	40,000	Value: 40.00				

Y# 249   3 ROUBLES
34.5600 g., 0.9000 Silver 1.0000 oz. ASW **Obv:** National arms with CCCP and value below **Rev:** St. Peter and Paul Fortress in Leningrad

Date	Mintage	F	VF	XF	Unc	BU
1990 (l) Proof	40,000	Value: 40.00				

Y# 262   3 ROUBLES
34.5600 g., 0.9000 Silver 1.0000 oz. ASW **Obv:** National arms with CCCP and value below **Rev:** Yuri Gagarin Monument

Date	Mintage	F	VF	XF	Unc	BU
1991 (l) Proof	35,000	Value: 45.00				

Y# 264   3 ROUBLES
34.5600 g., 0.9000 Silver 1.0000 oz. ASW **Obv:** National arms with CCCP and value below **Rev:** Fort Ross in California

Date	Mintage	F	VF	XF	Unc	BU
1991 (l) Proof	Est. 25,000	Value: 50.00				

Y# 274   3 ROUBLES
34.5600 g., 0.9000 Silver 1.0000 oz. ASW **Obv:** National arms with CCCP and value below **Rev:** Bolshoi Theater

Date	Mintage	F	VF	XF	Unc	BU
1991 (l) Proof	40,000	Value: 35.00				

Y# 275   3 ROUBLES
34.5600 g., 0.9000 Silver 1.0000 oz. ASW **Obv:** National arms with CCCP and value below **Rev:** Moscow's Arch of Triumph

Date	Mintage	F	VF	XF	Unc	BU
1991 (m) Proof	40,000	Value: 35.00				

Y# 301   3 ROUBLES

Copper-Nickel **Subject:** 50th Anniversary - Defense of Moscow
Obv: National arms with CCCP and value below **Rev:** Marching
soldiers **Edge:** Cyrillic lettering

Date	Mintage	F	VF	XF	Unc	BU
1991	2,150,000	—	—	—	7.00	—
1991 Proof	—	Value: 6.50				

Y# C134   5 ROUBLES

Copper-Nickel **Obv:** National arms **Rev:** Value and date within
sprigs

Date	Mintage	F	VF	XF	Unc	BU
1958	5,150,000	—	—	—	300	—

Note: Never officially released for circulation; majority of
mintage remelted

Y# 145   5 ROUBLES

16.6700 g., 0.9000 Silver 0.4823 oz. ASW **Series:** 1980
Olympics **Obv:** National arms flanked by CCCP with value below
Rev: Scenes of Kiev

Date	Mintage	F	VF	XF	Unc	BU
1977 (l)	250,000	—	—	—	10.00	—
1977 (l) Frosted unc.	Inc. above	—	—	—	—	—
1977 (l) Proof	121,000	Value: 10.00				
1977 (m) Proof	—	Value: 10.00				

Y# 146   5 ROUBLES

16.6700 g., 0.9000 Silver 0.4823 oz. ASW **Series:** 1980
Olympics **Obv:** National arms divide CCCP with value below
Rev: Scenes of Leningrad

Date	Mintage	F	VF	XF	Unc	BU
1977 (l)	250,000	—	—	—	10.00	—
1977 (l) Frosted unc.	Inc. above	—	—	—	—	—
1977 (l) Proof	121,000	Value: 10.00				
1977 (m)	Inc. above	—	—	—	10.00	—
1977 (m) Proof	Inc. above	Value: 10.00				

Y# 147   5 ROUBLES

16.6700 g., 0.9000 Silver 0.4823 oz. ASW **Series:** 1980
Olympics **Obv:** National arms divide CCCP with value below
Rev: Scenes of Minsk

Date	Mintage	F	VF	XF	Unc	BU
1977(l)	250,000	—	—	—	10.00	—
1977(l) Proof	121,000	Value: 10.00				
1977(m) Proof	Inc. above	Value: 10.00				

Y# 148   5 ROUBLES

16.6700 g., 0.9000 Silver 0.4823 oz. ASW **Series:** 1980
Olympics **Obv:** National arms divide CCCP with value below
Rev: Scenes of Tallinn

Date	Mintage	F	VF	XF	Unc	BU
1977(l)	252,000	—	—	—	10.00	—
1977(l) Frosted	Inc. above	—	—	—	—	—
1977(l) Proof	122,000	Value: 10.00				
1977(m)	Inc. above	—	—	—	10.00	—
1977(m) Proof	Inc. above	Value: 10.00				

Y# 154   5 ROUBLES

16.6700 g., 0.9000 Silver 0.4823 oz. ASW **Series:** 1980
Olympics **Obv:** National arms divide CCCP with value below
Rev: Runner in front of stadium

Date	Mintage	F	VF	XF	Unc	BU
1978(l)	227,000	—	—	—	10.00	—

Date	Mintage	F	VF	XF	Unc	BU
1978(m) Proof	118,000	Value: 10.00				
1978(l) Matte proof	—	Value: 30.00				

Y# 155   5 ROUBLES

16.6700 g., 0.9000 Silver 0.4823 oz. ASW **Series:** 1980
Olympics **Obv:** National arms divide CCCP with value below
Rev: Swimming

Date	Mintage	F	VF	XF	Unc	BU
1978(l)	227,000	—	—	—	10.00	—
1978(l) Frosted	Inc. above	—	—	—	—	—
1978(l) Proof	118,000	Value: 10.00				
1978(l) Matte proof	—	Value: 30.00				

Y# 156   5 ROUBLES

16.6700 g., 0.9000 Silver 0.4823 oz. ASW **Series:** 1980
Olympics **Obv:** National arms divide CCCP with value below
Rev: High jumping

Date	Mintage	F	VF	XF	Unc	BU
1978(l)	221,000	—	—	—	10.00	—
1978(l) Proof	119,000	Value: 10.00				
1978(m)	Inc. above	—	—	—	10.00	—
1978(m) Proof	Inc. above	Value: 10.00				

Y# 157   5 ROUBLES

16.6700 g., 0.9000 Silver 0.4823 oz. ASW **Series:** 1980
Olympics **Obv:** National arms divide CCCP with value below
Rev: Equestrian show jumping

Date	Mintage	F	VF	XF	Unc	BU
1978(l)	221,000	—	—	—	10.00	—
1978(l) Proof	119,000	Value: 10.00				
1978(m)	Inc. above	—	—	—	10.00	—
1978(m) Proof	Inc. above	Value: 10.00				

Y# 166   5 ROUBLES

16.6700 g., 0.9000 Silver 0.4823 oz. ASW **Series:** 1980
Olympics **Obv:** National arms divide CCCP with value below
Rev: Weight lifting

Date	Mintage	F	VF	XF	Unc	BU
1979(l)	207,000	—	—	—	10.00	—
1979(l) Proof	108,000	Value: 10.00				
1979(m)	Inc. above	—	—	—	10.00	—
1979(m) Proof	Inc. above	Value: 10.00				

Y# 167   5 ROUBLES

16.6700 g., 0.9000 Silver 0.4823 oz. ASW **Series:** 1980
Olympics **Obv:** National arms divide CCCP with value below
Rev: Hammer throw

Date	Mintage	F	VF	XF	Unc	BU
1979(l)	207,000	—	—	—	10.00	—
1979(l) Proof	119,000	Value: 10.00				
1979(m)	Inc. above	—	—	—	10.00	—
1979(m) Proof	Inc. above	Value: 10.00				

Y# 179   5 ROUBLES

16.6700 g., 0.9000 Silver 0.4823 oz. ASW **Series:** 1980 Olympics
Obv: National arms divide CCCP with value below **Rev:** Archery

Date	Mintage	F	VF	XF	Unc	BU
1980(l)	126,000	—	—	—	10.00	—
1980(l) Proof	95,000	Value: 11.00				
1980(m)	Inc. above	—	—	—	10.00	—
1980(m) Proof	Inc. above	Value: 11.00				

Y# 180   5 ROUBLES

16.6700 g., 0.9000 Silver 0.4823 oz. ASW **Series:** 1980 Olympics
Obv: National arms divide CCCP with value below **Rev:** Gymnastics

Date	Mintage	F	VF	XF	Unc	BU
1980(l)	126,000	—	—	—	12.00	—
1980(l) Proof	95,000	Value: 11.00				
1980(m)	Inc. above	—	—	—	10.00	—
1980(m) Proof	Inc. above	Value: 11.00				

Y# 181   5 ROUBLES

16.6700 g., 0.9000 Silver 0.4823 oz. ASW **Series:** 1980
Olympics **Subject:** Equestrian - Isindi **Obv:** National arms divide
CCCP with value below **Rev:** Polo players

Date	Mintage	F	VF	XF	Unc	BU
1980(l)	126,000	—	—	—	12.00	—
1980(l) Proof	96,000	Value: 11.00				

Y# 182   5 ROUBLES

16.6700 g., 0.9000 Silver 0.4823 oz. ASW **Series:** 1980
Olympics **Obv:** National arms divide CCCP with value below **Rev:**
Gorodki - stick throwing

Date	Mintage	F	VF	XF	Unc	BU
1980(l)	126,000	—	—	—	12.00	—
1980(l) Proof	96,000	Value: 11.00				

Y# 208   5 ROUBLES

Copper-Nickel **Subject:** 70th Anniversary - Bolshevik Revolution
Obv: National arms with CCCP and value below **Rev:** Head left
and date within banner

Date	Mintage	F	VF	XF	Unc	BU
1987	1,300,000	—	—	—	8.00	—
1987 Proof	200,000	Value: 7.00				

Y# 217   5 ROUBLES

Copper-Nickel, 35 mm. **Obv:** National arms with CCCP and
value below **Rev:** Leningrad - Peter the Great

Date	Mintage	F	VF	XF	Unc	BU
1988	1,675,000	—	—	—	8.00	—
1988 Proof	325,000	Value: 7.00				

Y# 218   5 ROUBLES

Copper-Nickel, 35 mm.   **Obv:** National arms with CCCP and value below **Rev:** Novgorood Monument to the Russian Millennium

Date	Mintage	F	VF	XF	Unc	BU
1988	1,675,000	—	—	—	8.00	—
1988 Proof	325,000	Value: 7.00				

Y# 219   5 ROUBLES

Copper-Nickel, 35 mm.   **Obv:** National arms with CCCP and value below **Rev:** St. Sophia Cathedral in Kiev

Date	Mintage	F	VF	XF	Unc	BU
1988	1,675,000	—	—	—	8.00	—
1988 Proof	325,000	Value: 7.00				

Y# 221   5 ROUBLES

Copper-Nickel, 35 mm.   **Obv:** National arms with CCCP and value below **Rev:** Pokrowsky Cathedral in Moscow

Date	Mintage	F	VF	XF	Unc	BU
1989	1,700,000	—	—	—	8.00	—
1989 Proof	300,000	Value: 7.00				

Y# 229   5 ROUBLES

Copper-Nickel, 35 mm.   **Obv:** National arms with CCCP and value below **Rev:** Samarkand

Date	Mintage	F	VF	XF	Unc	BU
1989	1,700,000	—	—	—	6.00	—
1989 Proof	300,000	Value: 7.00				

Y# 230   5 ROUBLES

Copper-Nickel, 35 mm.   **Obv:** National arms with CCCP and value below **Rev:** Cathedral of the Annunciation in Moscow

Date	Mintage	F	VF	XF	Unc	BU
1989	1,700,000	—	—	—	6.00	—
1989 Proof	300,000	Value: 7.00				

Y# 241   5 ROUBLES

Copper-Nickel, 35 mm.   **Obv:** National arms with CCCP and value below **Rev:** St. Petersburg Palace

Date	Mintage	F	VF	XF	Unc	BU
1990	2,600,000	—	—	—	6.00	—
1990 Proof	400,000	Value: 7.00				

Y# 246   5 ROUBLES

Copper-Nickel, 35 mm.   **Obv:** National arms with CCCP and value below **Rev:** Uspenski Cathedral **Edge:** Cyrillic lettering

Date	Mintage	F	VF	XF	Unc	BU
1990	2,600,000	—	—	—	6.00	—
1990 Proof	400,000	Value: 7.00				

Y# 259   5 ROUBLES

Copper-Nickel, 35 mm.   **Obv:** National arms with CCCP and value below **Rev:** Matenadarin Depository of Ancient Armenian Manuscripts

Date	Mintage	F	VF	XF	Unc	BU
1990	2,600,000	—	—	—	6.00	—
1990 Proof	350,000	Value: 7.00				

Y# 271   5 ROUBLES

Copper-Nickel, 35 mm.   **Obv:** National arms with CCCP and value below **Rev:** Cathedral of the Archangel Michael in Moscow **Edge:** Cyrillic lettering

Date	Mintage	F	VF	XF	Unc	BU
1991	2,150,000	—	—	—	6.00	—
1991 Proof	350,000	Value: 7.00				

Y# 272   5 ROUBLES

Copper-Nickel, 35 mm.   **Obv:** National arms with CCCP and value below **Rev:** State bank building in Moscow

Date	Mintage	F	VF	XF	Unc	BU
1991	2,600,000	—	—	—	6.00	—
1991 Proof	400,000	Value: 7.00				

Y# 273   5 ROUBLES

Copper-Nickel, 35 mm.   **Obv:** National arms with CCCP and value below **Rev:** Monument **Edge:** Cyrillic lettering

Date	Mintage	F	VF	XF	Unc	BU
1991	2,150,000	—	—	—	6.00	—
1991 Proof	350,000	Value: 7.00				

Y# 268   5 ROUBLES

7.7758 g., 0.9990 Palladium 0.2497 oz.   **Series:** Ballet **Obv:** National arms with CCCP and value below **Rev:** Ballerina

Date	Mintage	F	VF	XF	Unc	BU
1991(l)	9,000	—	—	—	—	150

Y# 149   10 ROUBLES

33.3000 g., 0.9000 Silver 0.9635 oz. ASW   **Series:** 1980 Olympics **Obv:** National arms divide CCCP with value below **Rev:** Scenes of Moscow

Date	Mintage	F	VF	XF	Unc	BU
1977(l)	250,000	—	—	—	25.00	—
1977(l) Proof	121,000	Value: 20.00				
1977(m)	Inc. above	—	—	—	25.00	—
1977(m) Proof	Inc. above	Value: 20.00				

Y# 150   10 ROUBLES

33.3000 g., 0.9000 Silver 0.9635 oz. ASW   **Series:** 1980 Olympics **Obv:** National arms divide CCCP with value below **Rev:** Map of USSR back of design above rings

Date	Mintage	F	VF	XF	Unc	BU
1977(l)	250,000	—	—	—	25.00	—
1977(l) Proof	121,000	Value: 20.00				

Y# 158.1   10 ROUBLES

33.3000 g., 0.9000 Silver 0.9635 oz. ASW   **Series:** 1980 Olympics **Obv:** National arms divide CCCP with value below **Rev:** Cycling

Date	Mintage	F	VF	XF	Unc	BU
1978(l)	227,000	—	—	—	25.00	—
1978(l) Proof	118,000	Value: 20.00				

Y# 158.2   10 ROUBLES

33.3000 g., 0.9000 Silver 0.9635 oz. ASW   **Series:** 1980 Olympics **Obv:** National arms divide CCCP with value below **Rev:** Without mint mark

Date	Mintage	F	VF	XF	Unc	BU
1978 Rare		—	—	—	—	—
1978 Proof, rare	100	—	—	—	—	—

Y# 159   10 ROUBLES

33.3000 g., 0.9000 Silver 0.9635 oz. ASW   **Series:** 1980 Olympics **Obv:** National arms divide CCCP with value below **Rev:** Canoeing

Date	Mintage	F	VF	XF	Unc	BU
1978(l) Rare	34,000	—	—	—	—	—
1978(m)	192,000	—	—	—	25.00	—
1978(m) Proof	118,000	Value: 20.00				

Y# 160   10 ROUBLES

33.3000 g., 0.9000 Silver 0.9635 oz. ASW   **Series:** 1980 Olympics **Obv:** National arms divide CCCP with value below **Rev:** Equestrian sports

Date	Mintage	F	VF	XF	Unc	BU
1978(l) Rare	34,000	—	—	—	—	—
1978(m)	192,000	—	—	—	25.00	—
1978(m) Proof	118,000	Value: 20.00				

Y# 161   10 ROUBLES

33.3000 g., 0.9000 Silver 0.9635 oz. ASW   **Series:** 1980 Olympics **Obv:** National arms divide CCCP with value below **Rev:** Pole vaulting

Date	Mintage	F	VF	XF	Unc	BU
1978(l)	221,000	—	—	—	25.00	—
1978(l) Proof	119,000	Value: 20.00				
1978(m)	Inc. above	—	—	—	25.00	—
1978(m) Proof	Inc. above	Value: 20.00				

Y# 168   10 ROUBLES
33.3000 g., 0.9000 Silver 0.9635 oz. ASW **Series:** 1980 Olympics. **Obv:** National arms divide CCCP with value below **Rev:** Basketball

Date	Mintage	F	VF	XF	Unc	BU
1979(I)	221,000	—	—	—	25.00	—
1979(I) Proof	119,000	Value: 20.00				
1979 Rare	—	—	—	—	—	—

Y# 169   10 ROUBLES
33.3000 g., 0.9000 Silver 0.9635 oz. ASW **Series:** 1980 Olympics **Obv:** National arms divide CCCP with value below **Rev:** Volleyball

Date	Mintage	F	VF	XF	Unc	BU
1979(I)	221,000	—	—	—	25.00	—
1979(I) Proof	119,000	Value: 20.00				

Y# 170   10 ROUBLES
33.3000 g., 0.9000 Silver 0.9635 oz. ASW **Series:** 1980 Olympics **Obv:** National arms divide CCCP with value below **Rev:** Boxing

Date	Mintage	F	VF	XF	Unc	BU
1979(I)	207,000	—	—	—	25.00	—
1979(I) Proof	108,000	Value: 20.00				

Y# 171   10 ROUBLES
33.3000 g., 0.9000 Silver 0.9635 oz. ASW **Series:** 1980 Olympics **Obv:** National arms divide CCCP with value below **Rev:** Judo

Date	Mintage	F	VF	XF	Unc	BU
1979(I)	207,000	—	—	—	25.00	—
1979(I) Proof	108,000	Value: 20.00				
1979(m)	Inc. above	—	—	—	25.00	—
1979(m) Proof	Inc. above	Value: 20.00				

Y# 172   10 ROUBLES
33.3000 g., 0.9000 Silver 0.9635 oz. ASW **Series:** 1980 Olympics **Obv:** National arms divide CCCP with value below **Rev:** Weight lifting

Date	Mintage	F	VF	XF	Unc	BU
1979(I)	207,000	—	—	—	25.00	—
1979(I) Proof	108,000	Value: 20.00				

Y# 183   10 ROUBLES
33.3000 g., 0.9000 Silver 0.9635 oz. ASW **Series:** 1980 Olympics **Obv:** National arms divide CCCP with value below **Rev:** Wrestlers

Date	Mintage	F	VF	XF	Unc	BU
1980(I)	126,000	—	—	—	25.00	60.00
1980(I) Proof	95,000	Value: 20.00				
1980(m)	Inc. above	—	—	—	20.00	—
1980(m) Proof	Inc. above	Value: 20.00				

Y# 184   10 ROUBLES
33.3000 g., 0.9000 Silver 0.9635 oz. ASW **Series:** 1980 Olympics **Obv:** National arms divide CCCP with value below **Rev:** Tug of war

Date	Mintage	F	VF	XF	Unc	BU
1980(I)	126,000	—	—	—	25.00	—
1980(I) Proof	95,000	Value: 20.00				

Y# 185   10 ROUBLES
33.3000 g., 0.9000 Silver 0.9635 oz. ASW **Series:** 1980 Olympics **Obv:** National arms divide CCCP with value below **Rev:** Reindeer racing

Date	Mintage	F	VF	XF	Unc	BU
1980(I)	126,000	—	—	—	25.00	—
1980(I) Proof	95,000	Value: 20.00				

Y# 238   10 ROUBLES
15.5500 g., 0.9990 Palladium 0.4994 oz. **Series:** Ballet **Obv:** National arms with CCCP and value below **Rev:** Ballerina

Date	Mintage	F	VF	XF	Unc	BU
1990(I)	Est. 15,000	—	—	—	—	250

Y# 269   10 ROUBLES
15.5500 g., 0.9990 Palladium 0.4994 oz. **Series:** Ballet **Obv:** National arms with CCCP and value below **Rev:** Ballerina

Date	Mintage	F	VF	XF	Unc	BU
1991(I)	15,000	—	—	—	—	250

Y# 285   10 ROUBLES
2.6600 g., 0.5850 Gold 0.0500 oz. AGW **Series:** Ballet **Obv:** National arms with CCCP and value below **Rev:** Ballerina

Date	Mintage	F	VF	XF	Unc	BU
1991(I)	6,000	—	—	—	—	60.00

Y# 212   25 ROUBLES
31.1000 g., 0.9990 Palladium 0.9988 oz. **Subject:** Monument to Vladimir, Grand Duke of Kiev and Millennium of Christianity in Russia **Obv:** National arms with CCCP and value below **Rev:** Monument

Date	Mintage	F	VF	XF	Unc	BU
1988(I)	7,000	—	—	—	—	450

Y# 224   25 ROUBLES
31.1000 g., 0.9990 Palladium 0.9988 oz. **Subject:** 500th Anniversary of Russian State **Obv:** National arms with CCCP and value below **Rev:** Ivan III on throne

Date	Mintage	F	VF	XF	Unc	BU
1989(I) Proof	Est. 12,000	Value: 450				

Y# 231   25 ROUBLES
31.1000 g., 0.9990 Palladium 0.9988 oz. **Series:** Ballet **Obv:** National arms with CCCP and value below **Rev:** Ballerina

Date	Mintage	F	VF	XF	Unc	BU
1989(I)	27,000	—	—	—	—	450
1989(I) Proof	3,000	Value: 500				
1989(I) Matte proof	—	Value: 500				

Y# 239   25 ROUBLES
31.1000 g., 0.9990 Palladium 0.9988 oz. **Series:** Ballet **Obv:** National arms with CCCP and value below **Rev:** Ballerina

Date	Mintage	F	VF	XF	Unc	BU
1990(I)	27,000	—	—	—	—	450
1990(I) Proof	3,000	Value: 500				

Y# 243   25 ROUBLES
31.1000 g., 0.9990 Palladium 0.9988 oz. **Subject:** 250th Anniversary - Discovery of Russian America **Obv:** National arms with CCCP and value below **Rev:** Ship, St. Peter

Date	Mintage	F	VF	XF	Unc	BU
1990(I) Proof	6,500	Value: 450				

Y# 244   25 ROUBLES
31.1000 g., 0.9990 Palladium 0.9988 oz. **Subject:** 250th Anniversary - Discovery of Russian America **Obv:** National arms with CCCP and value below **Rev:** Ship, St. Paul

Date	Mintage	F	VF	XF	Unc	BU
1990(I) Proof	6,500	Value: 450				

Y# 250   25 ROUBLES
31.1000 g., 0.9990 Palladium 0.9988 oz. **Subject:** 500th Anniversary of Russian State **Obv:** National arms with CCCP and value below **Rev:** Peter the Great

Date	Mintage	F	VF	XF	Unc	BU
1990(l) Proof	12,000		Value: 450			

Y# 265   25 ROUBLES
31.1000 g., 0.9990 Palladium 0.9988 oz. **Subject:** Three Saints Harbor - Russian settlement in America.

Date	Mintage	F	VF	XF	Unc	BU
1991(l) Proof	Est. 6,500		Value: 450			

Y# 266   25 ROUBLES
31.1000 g., 0.9990 Palladium 0.9988 oz. **Subject:** Novo Archangelsk 1799 - three-masted ship

Date	Mintage	F	VF	XF	Unc	BU
1991(l) Proof	Est. 6,500		Value: 450			

Y# 270   25 ROUBLES
31.1000 g., 0.9990 Palladium 0.9988 oz. **Series:** Ballet **Obv:** National arms with CCCP and value below **Rev:** Ballerina

Date	Mintage	F	VF	XF	Unc	BU
1991(l)	30,000	—	—	—	—	450
1991(l) Proof	30,000		Value: 450			

Y# 276   25 ROUBLES
31.1000 g., 0.9990 Palladium 0.9988 oz. **Subject:** 500th Anniversary of Russian State **Obv:** National arms with CCCP and value below **Rev:** Abolition of Serfdom in Russia

Date	Mintage	F	VF	XF	Unc	BU
1991(l) Proof	Est. 12,000		Value: 450			

Y# 286   25 ROUBLES
5.3200 g., 0.5850 Gold 0.1001 oz. AGW **Series:** Ballet **Obv:** National arms with CCCP and value below **Rev:** Ballerina

Date	Mintage	F	VF	XF	Unc	BU
1991(l)	5,000	—	—	—	—	150

Y# 286a   25 ROUBLES
3.1100 g., 0.9990 Gold 0.0999 oz. AGW **Series:** Ballet **Obv:** National arms with CCCP and value below **Rev:** Ballerina

Date	Mintage	F	VF	XF	Unc	BU
1991(l) Proof	1,500		Value: 250			

Y# 213   50 ROUBLES
8.6397 g., 0.9000 Gold 0.2500 oz. AGW **Subject:** 1000th Anniversary of Russian Architecture **Obv:** National arms divide CCCP with value below **Rev:** Cathedral of St. Sophia in Novgorod

Date	Mintage	F	VF	XF	Unc	BU
1988(m)	25,000	—	—	—	—	300

Y# 225   50 ROUBLES
8.6397 g., 0.9000 Gold 0.2500 oz. AGW **Subject:** 500th Anniversary of Russian State **Obv:** National arms with CCCP and value below **Rev:** Cathedral of the Ascension

Date	Mintage	F	VF	XF	Unc	BU
1989(m) Proof	Est. 25,000		Value: 260			

Y# 251   50 ROUBLES
8.6397 g., 0.9000 Gold 0.2500 oz. AGW **Subject:** 500th Anniversary of Russian State **Obv:** National arms with CCCP and value below **Rev:** Moscow Church of the Archangel

Date	Mintage	F	VF	XF	Unc	BU
1990(m) Proof	25,000		Value: 260			

Y# 277   50 ROUBLES
8.6440 g., 0.9000 Gold 0.2501 oz. AGW **Subject:** 500th Anniversary of Russian State **Obv:** National arms with CCCP and value below **Rev:** St. Isaac Cathedral in St. Petersburg

Date	Mintage	F	VF	XF	Unc	BU
1991(m) Proof	25,000		Value: 260			

Y# 287   50 ROUBLES
13.3000 g., 0.5850 Gold 0.2501 oz. AGW **Subject:** Bolshoi Ballet **Obv:** National arms with CCCP and value below **Rev:** Ballerina

Date	Mintage	F	VF	XF	Unc	BU
1991(l)	2,400	—	—	—	—	400

Y# 287a   50 ROUBLES
7.7800 g., 0.9990 Gold 0.2499 oz. AGW **Subject:** Bolshoi Ballet **Obv:** National arms with CCCP and value below **Rev:** Ballerina

Date	Mintage	F	VF	XF	Unc	BU
1991(l) Proof	1,500		Value: 450			

Y# A163   100 ROUBLES
17.2800 g., 0.9000 Gold 0.5000 oz. AGW **Series:** 1980 Olympics **Obv:** National arms divide CCCP with value below **Rev:** Moscow Olympic's logo, sprig within world globe, olympic rings below

Date	Mintage	F	VF	XF	Unc	BU
1977(l)	44,000	—	—	—	—	700
1977(l) Proof	38,000		Value: 500			
1977(m)	Inc. above	—	—	—	—	700
1977(m) Proof	Inc. above		Value: 500			

Y# 151   100 ROUBLES
17.2800 g., 0.9000 Gold 0.5000 oz. AGW **Series:** 1980 Olympics **Obv:** National arms divide CCCP with value below **Rev:** Lenin Stadium

Date	Mintage	F	VF	XF	Unc	BU
1978(l)	62,000	—	—	—	—	700
1978(l) Proof	45,000		Value: 500			
1978(m)	Inc. above	—	—	—	—	700
1978(m) Proof	Inc. above		Value: 500			

Y# 162   100 ROUBLES
17.2800 g., 0.9000 Gold 0.5000 oz. AGW **Series:** 1980 Olympics **Obv:** National arms divide CCCP with value below **Rev:** Waterside Grandstand

Date	Mintage	F	VF	XF	Unc	BU
1978 Rare	—	—	—	—	—	—
1978 Proof, rare	—	—	—	—	—	—
1978(l)	57,000	—	—	—	—	700
1978(l) Proof	43,000		Value: 500			
1978(m) Rare	Inc. above	—	—	—	—	—
1978(m) Proof, rare	Inc. above	—	—	—	—	—

Y# 173   100 ROUBLES
17.2800 g., 0.9000 Gold 0.5000 oz. AGW **Series:** 1980 Olympics **Obv:** National arms divide CCCP with value below **Rev:** Velodrome Building

Date	Mintage	F	VF	XF	Unc	BU
1979(l)	55,000	—	—	—	—	700
1979(l) Proof	42,000		Value: 500			
1979(m) Rare	Inc. above	—	—	—	—	—
1979(m) Proof	Inc. above		Value: 500			

Y# 174   100 ROUBLES
17.2800 g., 0.9000 Gold 0.5000 oz. AGW **Series:** 1980 Olympics **Obv:** National arms divide CCCP with value below **Rev:** Druzhba Sports Hall

Date	Mintage	F	VF	XF	Unc	BU
1979(m)	54,000	—	—	—	—	700
1979(l) Proof	38,000		Value: 500			

Y# 186   100 ROUBLES
17.2800 g., 0.9000 Gold 0.5000 oz. AGW **Series:** 1980 Olympics **Obv:** National arms divide CCCP with value below **Rev:** Torch

Date	Mintage	F	VF	XF	Unc	BU
1980(m)	25,000	—	—	—	—	700
1980(l) Proof	28,000		Value: 500			

Y# 214   100 ROUBLES
17.2800 g., 0.9000 Gold 0.5000 oz. AGW **Series:** 1980 Olympics **Subject:** 1000th Anniversary of Minting in Russia - Coin design of St. Vladimir (977-1015) **Obv:** National arms divide CCCP with value below **Rev:** Ancient coin design

Date	Mintage	F	VF	XF	Unc	BU
1988(m)	14,000	—	—	—	—	700

Y# 226   100 ROUBLES
17.2800 g., 0.9000 Gold 0.5000 oz. AGW **Series:** 1980
Olympics **Subject:** 500th Anniversary of Russian State
Obv: National arms with CCCP and value below **Rev:** Seal
of Ivan III

Date	Mintage	F	VF	XF	Unc	BU
1989(m) Proof	Est. 14,000	Value: 500				

Y# 252   100 ROUBLES
17.2800 g., 0.9000 Gold 0.5000 oz. AGW **Series:** 1980 Olympics
Subject: 500th Anniversary of Russian State **Obv:** National arms
divide CCCP with value below **Rev:** Peter the Great Monument

Date	Mintage	F	VF	XF	Unc	BU
1990(m) Proof	14,000	Value: 500				

Y# 278   100 ROUBLES
17.2800 g., 0.9000 Gold 0.5000 oz. AGW **Series:** 1980 Olympics
Subject: 500th Anniversary of Russian State **Obv:** National arms
with CCCP and value below **Rev:** Tolstoi Monument

Date	Mintage	F	VF	XF	Unc	BU
1991(m) Proof	14,000	Value: 500				

Y# 288   100 ROUBLES
26.5900 g., 0.5850 Gold 0.5001 oz. AGW **Subject:** Bolshoi
Ballet **Obv:** CCCP and value below building **Rev:** Ballerina

Date	Mintage	F	VF	XF	Unc	BU
1991(I)	1,200					800

Y# 288a   100 ROUBLES
15.5500 g., 0.9990 Gold 0.4994 oz. AGW **Subject:** Bolshoi Ballet
Obv: National arms with CCCP and value below **Rev:** Ballerina

Date	Mintage	F	VF	XF	Unc	BU
1991(I) Proof	1,500	Value: 750				

Y# 152   150 ROUBLES
15.5400 g., 0.9990 Platinum 0.4991 oz. APW **Series:** 1980
Olympics **Obv:** National arms divide CCCP with value below
Rev: Moscow Olympic's logo within wreath, Olympic rings below

Date	Mintage	F	VF	XF	Unc	BU
1977(I)	9,910	—	—	—	900	1,000
1977(I) Proof	24,000	Value: 1,000				

Y# 163   150 ROUBLES
15.5400 g., 0.9990 Platinum 0.4991 oz. APW **Series:** 1980
Olympics **Obv:** National arms divide CCCP with value below
Rev: Throwing discus

Date	Mintage	F	VF	XF	Unc	BU
1978(I)	13,000	—	—	—	900	1,000
1978(I) Proof	20,000	Value: 1,000				

Y# 175   150 ROUBLES
15.5400 g., 0.9990 Platinum 0.4991 oz. APW **Series:** 1980
Olympics **Obv:** National arms divide CCCP with value below
Rev: Greek wrestlers

Date	Mintage	F	VF	XF	Unc	BU
1979(I)	14,000	—	—	—	1,000	900
1979(I) Proof	19,000	Value: 1,000				

Y# 176   150 ROUBLES
15.5400 g., 0.9990 Platinum 0.4991 oz. APW **Series:** 1980
Olympics **Obv:** National arms divide CCCP with value below
Rev: Roman chariot racers

Date	Mintage	F	VF	XF	Unc	BU
1979(I)	9,728	—	—	—	900	1,000
1979(I) Proof	17,000	Value: 1,000				

Y# 187   150 ROUBLES
15.5400 g., 0.9990 Platinum 0.4991 oz. APW **Series:** 1980
Olympics **Obv:** National arms divide CCCP with value below
Rev: Ancient Greek runners

Date	Mintage	F	VF	XF	Unc	BU
1980(I)	7,820	—	—	—	900	1,000
1980(I) Proof	13,000	Value: 1,000				

Y# 215   150 ROUBLES
15.5500 g., 0.9990 Platinum 0.4994 oz. APW **Subject:** 1000th
Anniversary of Russian Literature **Obv:** National arms with CCCP
and value below **Rev:** Chronicler writing epic about Grand Duke Igor

Date	Mintage	F	VF	XF	Unc	BU
1988(I) Proof	16,000	Value: 850				

Y# 227   150 ROUBLES
15.5500 g., 0.9990 Platinum 0.4994 oz. APW **Subject:** 500th
Anniversary of Russian State **Obv:** National arms with CCCP
and value below **Rev:** Ugra River Encounter

Date	Mintage	F	VF	XF	Unc	BU
1989(I) Proof	Est. 16,000	Value: 1,000				

Y# 245   150 ROUBLES
15.5500 g., 0.9990 Platinum 0.4994 oz. APW **Subject:** 250th
Anniversary - Discovery of Russian America **Obv:** National arms
with CCCP and value below **Rev:** Ship - St. Gavriil

Date	Mintage	F	VF	XF	Unc	BU
1990(I) Proof	6,500	Value: 1,000				

Y# 253   150 ROUBLES
15.5500 g., 0.9990 Platinum 0.4994 oz. APW **Subject:** 500th
Anniversary of Russian State **Obv:** National arms with CCCP
and value below **Rev:** Battle of Poltava River

Date	Mintage	F	VF	XF	Unc	BU
1990(I) Proof	16,000	Value: 1,000				

Y# 267   150 ROUBLES
15.5500 g., 0.9990 Platinum 0.4994 oz. APW **Subject:** 250th
Anniversary - Discovery of Russian America **Obv:** National arms
with CCCP and value below **Rev:** Bishop Veniaminov with ship
in background

Date	Mintage	F	VF	XF	Unc	BU
1991(I) Proof	Est. 6,500	Value: 1,000				

Y# 279   150 ROUBLES
17.5000 g., 0.9990 Platinum 0.5621 oz. APW **Subject:** 500th
Anniversary of Russian State - War of Liberation Against
Napoleon **Obv:** National arms with CCCP and value below
Rev: Monument divides heads

Date	Mintage	F	VF	XF	Unc	BU
1991(I) Proof	16,000	Value: 1,100				

GOVERNMENT BANK ISSUES
1991-1992

Y# 296   10 KOPEKS
Copper Clad Steel **Obv:** Kremlin Tower and Dome **Rev:** Value
flanked by sprigs above date

Date	Mintage	F	VF	XF	Unc	BU
1991M	—	0.30	0.50	1.00	2.00	—

Y# 292   50 KOPEKS
Copper-Nickel **Obv:** Kremlin Tower and Dome **Rev:** Value
flanked by sprigs above date

Date	Mintage	F	VF	XF	Unc	BU
1991Л	—	0.25	0.50	2.00	3.00	—

Y# 293   ROUBLE
Copper-Nickel **Obv:** Kremlin Tower and Dome **Rev:** Value
flanked by sprigs above date

Date	Mintage	F	VF	XF	Unc	BU
1991Л	—	—	—	—	3.00	—
1991M	—	—	—	—	4.00	—

Y# 280   5 ROUBLES
Bi-Metallic Brass center in Copper-Nickel ring, 25 mm.
Series: Wildlife **Obv:** Value flanked by sprigs within circle
Rev: Owl flanked by grassy sprigs within circle **Edge:** Alternating
reeded and smooth

Date	Mintage	F	VF	XF	Unc	BU
1991Л	500,000	—	—	—	5.00	9.00

Y# 281 5 ROUBLES
Bi-Metallic Brass center in Copper-Nickel ring, 25 mm. **Series:** Wildlife **Obv:** Value flanked by sprigs within circle **Rev:** Mountain Goat within circle **Edge:** Alternating reeded and smooth

Date	Mintage	F	VF	XF	Unc	BU
1991Л	500,000	—	—	—	5.00	7.50

Y# 294 5 ROUBLES
Copper-Nickel, 24 mm. **Obv:** Kremlin Tower and Dome **Rev:** Value flanked by sprigs above date **Edge:** Alternating reeded and smooth

Date	Mintage	F	VF	XF	Unc	BU
1991Л	—	—	—	—	5.00	—
1991М	—	—	—	—	7.00	—

Y# 295 10 ROUBLES
5.9700 g., Bi-Metallic Copper-Nickel ring, Aluminum-Bronze center, 25 mm. **Obv:** Kremlin Tower and Dome **Rev:** Value flanked by sprigs above date **Edge:** Alternating reeded and smooth

Date	Mintage	F	VF	XF	Unc	BU
1991	—	0.50	2.00	3.00	5.00	—
1991	—	2.00	5.00	8.00	15.00	—
1992 Error	—	—	30.00	50.00	80.00	—

RUSSIAN FEDERATION
Issued by РОССИЈСКИЈ БАНК
(Russian Bank)

STANDARD COINAGE

Y# 303 ROUBLE
Copper-Nickel, 31 mm. **Subject:** Rebirth of Russian Sovereignty and Democracy **Obv:** Tower and steeples, value below **Rev:** Winged Victory and small building with flag on top

Date	Mintage	F	VF	XF	Unc	BU
1992Л	700,000	—	—	—	2.50	—
1992Л Proof	300,000	Value: 5.00				

Y# 305 ROUBLE
Copper-Nickel, 31 mm. **Subject:** 110th Anniversary - Birth of Jacob Kolas **Obv:** Tower and steeples, value below **Rev:** Head 1/4 right **Edge:** Cyrillic lettering

Date	Mintage	F	VF	XF	Unc	BU
1992Л	700,000	—	—	—	3.00	—
1992Л Proof	300,000	Value: 5.00				

Y# 306 ROUBLE
Copper-Nickel, 31 mm. **Subject:** 190th Anniversary - Birth of Admiral Nakhimov **Obv:** Tower and steeples, value below **Rev:** Uniformed bust with back facing, ship at right **Edge:** Cyrillic lettering

Date	Mintage	F	VF	XF	Unc	BU
1992Л	700,000	—	—	—	3.00	—
1992Л Proof	300,000	Value: 5.00				

Y# 311 ROUBLE
3.2500 g., Brass Clad Steel, 19.5 mm. **Obv:** Double headed eagle **Rev:** Value flanked by sprigs above date **Edge:** Plain

Date	Mintage	F	VF	XF	Unc	BU
1992	—	2.00	5.00	10.00	20.00	—
1992Л	—	—	—	—	2.00	—
1992М	—	—	—	—	2.00	—
1992(sp) (I)	—	—	—	—	3.00	—
1992(m)	—	—	—	—	3.00	—

Y# 320 ROUBLE
Copper-Nickel, 31 mm. **Obv:** Tower and steeples, value below **Rev:** Head of Yanka Kupala left **Edge:** Cyrillic lettering

Date	Mintage	F	VF	XF	Unc	BU
1992Л	1,000,000	—	—	—	3.00	—
1992Л Prooflike	200,000	—	—	—	—	—
1992Л Proof	350,000	Value: 5.00				

Y# 321 ROUBLE
Copper-Nickel, 31 mm. **Obv:** Double-headed eagle within beaded circle **Rev:** N.I. Lobachevsky 1/4 right

Date	Mintage	F	VF	XF	Unc	BU
1992М	1,000,000	—	—	—	3.00	—
1992М Prooflike	500,000	—	—	—	—	—
1992М Proof	—	Value: 5.00				

Y# 319.1 ROUBLE
Copper-Nickel, 31 mm. **Subject:** Vladimir Ivanovich Vernadsky **Obv:** Double-headed eagle within beaded circle **Rev:** Head looking down with hand on head 1/4 right

Date	Mintage	F	VF	XF	Unc	BU
1993Л	450,000	—	—	—	3.00	—
1993 Proof	15,000	Value: 3.50				
1993Л Proof	35,000	Value: 5.50				

Y# 319.2 ROUBLE
Copper-Nickel, 31 mm. **Subject:** Vladimir Ivanovich Vernadsky **Obv:** Without mint mark below eagle's claw **Rev:** Head looking down with hand on head 1/4 right

Date	Mintage	F	VF	XF	Unc	BU
1993	—	—	—	—	3.00	—
1993 Proof	—	Value: 15.00				

Y# 325 ROUBLE
Copper-Nickel, 31 mm. **Subject:** Gavrila Romanovich Derzhavin **Obv:** Double-headed eagle within beaded circle **Rev:** Bust 1/4 left above date and objects

Date	Mintage	F	VF	XF	Unc	BU
1993М	500,000	—	—	—	3.00	—
1993М Proof	—	Value: 5.00				

Y# 326 ROUBLE
Copper-Nickel, 31 mm. **Subject:** K.A. Timiryazev **Obv:** Double-headed eagle within beaded circle **Rev:** Bust facing, plant in vase at upper left

Date	Mintage	F	VF	XF	Unc	BU
1993М	500,000	—	—	—	3.00	—
1993М Proof	—	Value: 5.00				

Y# 327 ROUBLE
Copper-Nickel, 31 mm. **Subject:** V. Maikovski **Obv:** Kremlin Tower and Dome within beaded circle **Rev:** Head 1/4 left

Date	Mintage	F	VF	XF	Unc	BU
1993Л	500,000	—	—	—	3.00	—
1993М Proof	—	Value: 5.00				

Y# 335 ROUBLE
15.5500 g., 0.9000 Silver 0.4499 oz. ASW **Series:** Red Book Wildlife **Obv:** Double-headed eagle **Rev:** Tiger

Date	Mintage	F	VF	XF	Unc	BU
1993 Proof	50,000	Value: 50.00				

Y# 336 ROUBLE
15.5500 g., 0.9000 Silver 0.4499 oz. ASW **Series:** Red Book Wildlife **Obv:** Double-headed eagle **Rev:** Owl flanked by grassy designs

Date	Mintage	F	VF	XF	Unc	BU
1993 Proof	50,000	Value: 50.00				

Y# 337 ROUBLE
15.5500 g., 0.9000 Silver 0.4499 oz. ASW **Series:** Red Book Wildlife **Obv:** Double-headed eagle **Rev:** Mountain goat

Date	Mintage	F	VF	XF	Unc	BU
1993 Proof	50,000	Value: 40.00				

Y# 347 ROUBLE
Copper-Nickel, 31 mm. **Subject:** A.P. Borodin **Obv:** Double-headed eagle **Rev:** Bust facing 1/4 left, music notes and design in background

Date	Mintage	F	VF	XF	Unc	BU
1993M	500,000	—	—	—	3.00	—
1993M Proof	—	Value: 5.00				

Y# 348 ROUBLE
Copper-Nickel, 31 mm. **Subject:** I.S. Turgenev **Obv:** Double-headed eagle **Rev:** Head left

Date	Mintage	F	VF	XF	Unc	BU
1993Л	500,000	—	—	—	3.00	—
1993Л Proof	—	Value: 5.00				

Y# 372 ROUBLE
15.5500 g., 0.9000 Silver 0.4499 oz. ASW **Series:** Wildlife **Obv:** Double-headed eagle **Rev:** Red-breasted Goose

Date	Mintage	F	VF	XF	Unc	BU
1994 Proof	50,000	Value: 45.00				

Y# 373 ROUBLE
15.5500 g., 0.9000 Silver 0.4499 oz. ASW **Series:** Wildlife **Obv:** Double-headed eagle **Rev:** Asiatic Cobra

Date	Mintage	F	VF	XF	Unc	BU
1994 Proof	50,000	Value: 50.00				

Y# 374 ROUBLE
15.5500 g., 0.9000 Silver 0.4499 oz. ASW **Series:** Wildlife **Obv:** Double-headed eagle **Rev:** Asiatic black bear

Date	Mintage	F	VF	XF	Unc	BU
1994 Proof	50,000	Value: 50.00				

Y# 399 ROUBLE
Aluminum-Bronze, 19.5 mm. **Subject:** WWII Victory **Obv:** Double-headed eagle **Rev:** Mother Russia calling for volunteers

Date	Mintage	F	VF	XF	Unc	BU
1995(I) In sets only	200,000	—	—	—	2.00	—

Y# 446 ROUBLE
17.4600 g., 0.9000 Silver 0.5052 oz. ASW **Series:** Wildlife **Obv:** Double-headed eagle **Rev:** White Stork

Date	Mintage	F	VF	XF	Unc	BU
1995 Proof	50,000	Value: 50.00				

Y# 447 ROUBLE
17.4600 g., 0.9000 Silver 0.5052 oz. ASW **Series:** Wildlife **Obv:** Double-headed eagle **Rev:** Caucasian Black Grouse

Date	Mintage	F	VF	XF	Unc	BU
1995 Proof	50,000	Value: 50.00				

Y# 448 ROUBLE
17.4600 g., 0.9000 Silver 0.5052 oz. ASW **Series:** Wildlife **Obv:** Double-headed eagle **Rev:** Black Sea Dolphin

Date	Mintage	F	VF	XF	Unc	BU
1995 Proof	50,000	Value: 50.00				

Y# 492 ROUBLE
17.4600 g., 0.9000 Silver 0.5052 oz. ASW **Series:** Wildlife **Obv:** Double-headed eagle **Rev:** Peregrine Falcon

Date	Mintage	F	VF	XF	Unc	BU
1996 Proof	50,000	Value: 50.00				

Y# 493 ROUBLE
17.4600 g., 0.9000 Silver 0.5052 oz. ASW **Series:** Wildlife **Obv:** Double-headed eagle **Rev:** Turkmenistan Gecko

Date	Mintage	F	VF	XF	Unc	BU
1996 Proof	50,000	Value: 50.00				

Y# 494 ROUBLE
17.4600 g., 0.9000 Silver 0.5052 oz. ASW **Series:** Wildlife **Obv:** Double-headed eagle **Rev:** Blind Mole Rat

Date	Mintage	F	VF	XF	Unc	BU
1996 Proof	50,000	Value: 50.00				

Y# 504 ROUBLE
Brass, 19.5 mm. **Subject:** 300th Anniversary - Russian Fleet **Obv:** Double-headed eagle **Rev:** Ship

Date	Mintage	F	VF	XF	Unc	BU
1996(I) In sets only	100,000	—	—	—	1.50	—

Y# 611 ROUBLE
17.5500 g., 0.9000 Silver 0.5078 oz. ASW **Series:** Wildlife **Obv:** Double-headed eagle **Rev:** Two Lesser Flamingos

Date	Mintage	F	VF	XF	Unc	BU
1996(I) Proof	—	—	—	—	—	—
1997(I) Proof	15,000	Value: 50.00				

Y# 612 ROUBLE
17.5500 g., 0.9000 Silver 0.5078 oz. ASW **Series:** Wildlife **Obv:** Double-headed eagle within beaded circle **Rev:** Goitered Gazelle

Date	Mintage	F	VF	XF	Unc	BU
1996(I) Proof, rare	—	—	—	—	—	—
1997(I) Proof	15,000	Value: 55.00				

Y# 613 ROUBLE
17.5500 g., 0.9000 Silver 0.5078 oz. ASW **Series:** Wildlife **Obv:** Double-headed eagle **Rev:** European Bison

Date	Mintage	F	VF	XF	Unc	BU
1997 Proof	15,000	Value: 60.00				

Y# 561 ROUBLE
8.4150 g., 0.9250 Silver 0.2502 oz. ASW **Subject:** 850th Anniversary - Moscow **Obv:** Double-headed eagle within beaded circle **Rev:** Shield flanked by buildings

Date	Mintage	F	VF	XF	Unc	BU
1997 (I)	20,000	—	—	—	—	10.00
1997 (m) Proof	5,000	Value: 25.00				

Y# 562 ROUBLE
8.4150 g., 0.9250 Silver 0.2502 oz. ASW **Subject:** 850th Anniversary - Moscow **Obv:** Double-headed eagle within beaded circle **Rev:** Cathedral of the Kazan Icon of the Holy Virgin

Date	Mintage	F	VF	XF	Unc	BU
1997	20,000	—	—	—	—	10.00
1997 (m) Proof	5,000	Value: 25.00				

Y# 563 ROUBLE
8.4150 g., 0.9250 Silver 0.2502 oz. ASW **Subject:** 850th Anniversary - Moscow **Obv:** Double-headed eagle within beaded circle **Rev:** University and shield

Date	Mintage	F	VF	XF	Unc	BU
1997 (l)	20,000	—	—	—	—	10.00
1997 (m) Proof	5,000	Value: 25.00				

Y# 564 ROUBLE
8.4150 g., 0.9250 Silver 0.2502 oz. ASW **Subject:** 850th Anniversary - Moscow **Obv:** Double-headed eagle within beaded circle **Rev:** Bolshoi Theatre and shield

Date	Mintage	F	VF	XF	Unc	BU
1997 Proof	25,000	Value: 15.00				

Y# 565 ROUBLE
8.4150 g., 0.9250 Silver 0.2502 oz. ASW **Subject:** 850th Anniversary - Moscow **Obv:** Double-headed eagle within beaded circle **Rev:** Resurrection Gate on Red Square

Date	Mintage	F	VF	XF	Unc	BU
1997 Proof	25,000	Value: 15.00				

Y# 566 ROUBLE
8.4150 g., 0.9250 Silver 0.2502 oz. ASW **Subject:** 850th Anniversary - Moscow **Obv:** Double-headed eagle within beaded circle **Rev:** Temple of Christ the Savior

Date	Mintage	F	VF	XF	Unc	BU
1997 Proof	25,000	Value: 15.00				

Y# 576 ROUBLE
8.4150 g., 0.9250 Silver 0.2502 oz. ASW **Subject:** World Soccer Championship - Paris 1998 **Obv:** Double-headed eagle **Rev:** Soccer players, Eiffel Tower and 1/2 globe

Date	Mintage	F	VF	XF	Unc	BU
1997(l) Proof	20,000	Value: 15.00				

Y# 577 ROUBLE
8.4150 g., 0.9250 Silver 0.2502 oz. ASW **Subject:** 1998 Winter Olympics **Obv:** Double-headed eagle within beaded circle **Rev:** Ice Hockey

Date	Mintage	F	VF	XF	Unc	BU
1997(m) Proof	20,000	Value: 17.50				

Y# 578 ROUBLE
8.4150 g., 0.9250 Silver 0.2502 oz. ASW **Subject:** 1998 Winter Olympics - Biathalon **Obv:** Double-headed eagle within beaded circle **Rev:** Skier within snow-flake design, marksman at left

Date	Mintage	F	VF	XF	Unc	BU
1997(m) Proof	20,000	Value: 17.50				

Y# 579 ROUBLE
8.4150 g., 0.9250 Silver 0.2502 oz. ASW **Subject:** 1897 Soccer **Obv:** Double-headed eagle within beaded circle **Rev:** Three soccer players

Date	Mintage	F	VF	XF	Unc	BU
1997(l) Proof	25,000	Value: 17.50				

Y# 580 ROUBLE
8.4150 g., 0.9250 Silver 0.2502 oz. ASW **Subject:** 1945 Soccer **Obv:** Double-headed eagle within beaded circle **Rev:** Goalie

Date	Mintage	F	VF	XF	Unc	BU
1997(l) Proof	25,000	Value: 17.50				

Y# 581 ROUBLE
8.4150 g., 0.9250 Silver 0.2502 oz. ASW **Subject:** 1956 Soccer **Obv:** Double-headed eagle within beaded circle **Rev:** Soccer players and kangaroo

Date	Mintage	F	VF	XF	Unc	BU
1997(l) Proof	25,000	Value: 17.50				

Y# 582 ROUBLE
8.4150 g., 0.9250 Silver 0.2502 oz. ASW **Subject:** 1960 Soccer **Obv:** Double-headed eagle within beaded circle **Rev:** Soccer players

Date	Mintage	F	VF	XF	Unc	BU
1997(l) Proof	25,000	Value: 17.50				

Y# 583 ROUBLE
8.4150 g., 0.9250 Silver 0.2502 oz. ASW **Subject:** 1988 Soccer **Obv:** Double-headed eagle **Rev:** Three players

Date	Mintage	F	VF	XF	Unc	BU
1997(l) Proof	25,000	Value: 17.50				

Y# 342 2 ROUBLES
15.8700 g., 0.5000 Silver 0.2551 oz. ASW **Subject:** Pavel Bazhov - Author of Ural Tales **Obv:** Double-headed eagle **Rev:** Head right

Date	Mintage	F	VF	XF	Unc	BU
1994(l) Proof	250,000	Value: 12.50				

Y# 343 2 ROUBLES
15.8700 g., 0.5000 Silver 0.2551 oz. ASW **Subject:** Ivan Krylov - Author of Fables **Obv:** Double-headed eagle **Rev:** Head 1/4 left with assorted animals below

Date	Mintage	F	VF	XF	Unc	BU
1994(l) Proof	250,000	Value: 12.50				

Y# 344 2 ROUBLES
15.8700 g., 0.5000 Silver 0.2551 oz. ASW **Subject:** Nikolai Gogol - Writer **Obv:** Double-headed eagle **Rev:** Head right

Date	Mintage	F	VF	XF	Unc	BU
1994(m) Proof	250,000	Value: 12.50				

Y# 363 2 ROUBLES
15.8700 g., 0.5000 Silver 0.2551 oz. ASW **Obv:** Double-headed eagle within beaded circle **Rev:** Admiral Ushakov

Date	Mintage	F	VF	XF	Unc	BU
1994(m) Proof	250,000	Value: 12.50				

Y# 364 2 ROUBLES
15.8700 g., 0.5000 Silver 0.2551 oz. ASW **Obv:** Double-headed eagle **Rev:** Ilya Repin, painter

Date	Mintage	F	VF	XF	Unc	BU
1994(m) Proof	250,000	Value: 12.50				

Y# 377 2 ROUBLES
15.8700 g., 0.5000 Silver 0.2551 oz. ASW **Subject:** A.S. Griboyedov **Obv:** Double-headed eagle **Rev:** Bust 1/4 left divides dates

Date	Mintage	F	VF	XF	Unc	BU
1995(m) Proof	200,000	Value: 14.50				

Y# 391 2 ROUBLES
15.8700 g., 0.5000 Silver 0.2551 oz. ASW **Subject:** WWII Victory Parade **Obv:** Kremlin Tower and Dome within beaded circle **Rev:** Victory Parade

Date	Mintage	F	VF	XF	Unc	BU
1995(l) Proof	200,000			Value: 30.00		

Y# 392 2 ROUBLES
15.8700 g., 0.5000 Silver 0.2551 oz. ASW **Series:** WWII **Obv:** Kremlin Tower and Dome within beaded circle **Rev:** Marshal Zhukov on horseback

Date	Mintage	F	VF	XF	Unc	BU
1995(m) Proof	200,000			Value: 30.00		

Y# 393 2 ROUBLES
15.8700 g., 0.5000 Silver 0.2551 oz. ASW **Series:** WWII **Obv:** Kremlin Tower and Dome within beaded circle **Rev:** Nuremberg trial

Date	Mintage	F	VF	XF	Unc	BU
1995(l) Proof	200,000			Value: 30.00		

Y# 414 2 ROUBLES
15.8700 g., 0.5000 Silver 0.2551 oz. ASW **Subject:** Sergei Esenin **Obv:** Double-headed eagle **Rev:** Head 1/4 right flanked by designs

Date	Mintage	F	VF	XF	Unc	BU
1995(l) Proof	200,000			Value: 14.50		

Y# 415 2 ROUBLES
15.8700 g., 0.5000 Silver 0.2551 oz. ASW **Subject:** Field Marshal Kutuzov **Obv:** Double-headed eagle **Rev:** Bust 3/4 left

Date	Mintage	F	VF	XF	Unc	BU
1995(m) Proof	200,000			Value: 13.50		

Y# 449 2 ROUBLES
15.8700 g., 0.5000 Silver 0.2551 oz. ASW **Subject:** Ivan Bunin **Obv:** Double-headed eagle **Rev:** Bust 1/4 right divides buildings and dates

Date	Mintage	F	VF	XF	Unc	BU
1995(m) Proof	200,000			Value: 14.50		

Y# A391 2 ROUBLES
15.8700 g., 0.5000 Silver 0.2551 oz. ASW **Obv:** Double-headed eagle **Rev:** Victory Parade **Note:** Mule of 1994 eagle obverse with Y#391 Victory Parade reverse.

Date	Mintage	F	VF	XF	Unc	BU
1995 Proof	—			Value: 250		

Y# 514 2 ROUBLES
15.8700 g., 0.5000 Silver 0.2551 oz. ASW **Subject:** Nikolai Nekrasov **Obv:** Double-headed eagle **Rev:** Bust 1/4 right with building, horse in harness, book and quill

Date	Mintage	F	VF	XF	Unc	BU
1996(m) Proof	50,000			Value: 25.00		

Y# 515 2 ROUBLES
15.8700 g., 0.5000 Silver 0.2551 oz. ASW **Subject:** Fyodor Dostoevsky **Obv:** Double-headed eagle **Rev:** Bust facing with standing figure holding child, building and dates

Date	Mintage	F	VF	XF	Unc	BU
1996(l) Proof	50,000			Value: 25.00		

Y# 549 2 ROUBLES
15.8700 g., 0.5000 Silver 0.2551 oz. ASW **Subject:** N.E. Zhukovsky **Obv:** Double-headed eagle **Rev:** Head 1/4 left

Date	Mintage	F	VF	XF	Unc	BU
1997(l) Proof	50,000			Value: 25.00		

Y# 550 2 ROUBLES
15.8700 g., 0.5000 Silver 0.2551 oz. ASW **Subject:** A.N. Skryabin - Musician **Obv:** Double-headed eagle **Rev:** Bust 3/4 right divides music notes and design

Date	Mintage	F	VF	XF	Unc	BU
1997(m) Proof	50,000			Value: 25.00		

Y# 551 2 ROUBLES
15.8700 g., 0.5000 Silver 0.2551 oz. ASW **Subject:** A.L. Chizhevsky **Obv:** Double-headed eagle **Rev:** Bust with chin on hand 1/4 right, trees, sun and kneeling figure at right

Date	Mintage	F	VF	XF	Unc	BU
1997(m) Proof	10,000			Value: 80.00		

Y# 558 2 ROUBLES
15.8700 g., 0.5000 Silver 0.2551 oz. ASW **Obv:** Double-headed eagle **Rev:** Sailing ship and Afanasi Nikitin

Date	Mintage	F	VF	XF	Unc	BU
1997(m) Proof	7,500			Value: 150		

Y# 559 2 ROUBLES
15.8700 g., 0.5000 Silver 0.2551 oz. ASW **Subject:** Afanasi Nikitin - Indian Scene **Obv:** Double-headed eagle **Rev:** Head facing in center of assorted animal and ship designs

Date	Mintage	F	VF	XF	Unc	BU
1997(l) Proof	7,500			Value: 155		

Y# 584 2 ROUBLES
15.8700 g., 0.5000 Silver 0.2551 oz. ASW **Subject:** A.K. Savrasov **Obv:** Double-headed eagle **Rev:** Head facing within square at upper left of church and trees

Date	Mintage	F	VF	XF	Unc	BU
1997(m) Proof	15,000			Value: 40.00		

Y# 297 3 ROUBLES
Copper-Nickel, 33 mm. **Subject:** International Space Year **Obv:** Tower and steeples, value below **Rev:** Floating nude figure with planet at right **Edge:** Cyrillic lettering

Date	Mintage	F	VF	XF	Unc	BU
1992(m)	600,000	—	—	—	3.50	5.00
1992(m) Proof	400,000			Value: 6.50		

Y# 298   3 ROUBLES
Copper-Nickel, 33 mm. **Subject:** Battle of Chudskoye Lake
Obv: Tower and steeples, value below **Rev:** Armored figures in
battle **Edge:** Cyrillic lettering

Date	Mintage	F	VF	XF	Unc	BU
1992(I)	600,000	—	—	—	3.50	—
1992(I) Proof	400,000	Value: 5.50				

Y# 304   3 ROUBLES
Copper-Nickel, 33 mm. **Series:** WWII **Obv:** Tower and steeples,
value below **Rev:** Allied supply convoys to Murmansk

Date	Mintage	F	VF	XF	Unc	BU
1992(I) Proof	400,000	Value: 5.50				

Y# 317   3 ROUBLES
Copper-Nickel, 33 mm. **Subject:** 1st Anniversary - Defeat of
Communist Attempted Coup **Obv:** Tower and steeples, value
below **Rev:** Winged Victory holding harp-shaped shield above
sprigs, building at right

Date	Mintage	F	VF	XF	Unc	BU
1992(m)	1,000,000	—	—	—	3.50	5.00
1992(m) Prooflike		—	—	—	4.00	6.00
1992(m) Proof	—	Value: 6.50				

Y# 349   3 ROUBLES
34.5600 g., 0.9000 Silver 1.0000 oz. ASW **Obv:** Double-headed
eagle **Rev:** St. Petersburg Trinity Cathedral

Date	Mintage	F	VF	XF	Unc	BU
1992 Proof	40,000	Value: 35.00				

Y# 350   3 ROUBLES
34.5600 g., 0.9000 Silver 1.0000 oz. ASW **Obv:** Double-headed
eagle **Rev:** St. Petersburg Academy of Science and ship

Date	Mintage	F	VF	XF	Unc	BU
1992 Proof	40,000	Value: 35.00				

Y# 318   3 ROUBLES
Copper-Nickel, 33 mm. **Subject:** Battle of Stalingrad
Obv: Kremlin Tower and Dome within beaded circle **Rev:** Half
length figure looking right, monument at right

Date	Mintage	F	VF	XF	Unc	BU
1993(m)	150,000	—	—	—	3.50	—
1993(m) Prooflike		—	—	—	4.00	—
1993(m) Proof	350,000	Value: 5.50				

Y# 323   3 ROUBLES
34.5600 g., 0.9000 Silver 1.0000 oz. ASW **Subject:** Bolshoi
Ballet **Obv:** Double-headed eagle **Rev:** Ballet couple
Note: Struck at Moscow without mint mark.

Date	Mintage	F	VF	XF	Unc	BU
1993	125,000	—	—	—	25.00	—
1993 Proof	40,000	Value: 30.00				

Y# 328   3 ROUBLES
Copper-Nickel, 33 mm. **Subject:** 50th Anniversary - Battle of
Kursk **Obv:** Kremlin Tower and Dome **Rev:** Armored tank and
map **Edge:** Cyrillic lettering

Date	Mintage	F	VF	XF	Unc	BU
1993(I)	500,000	—	—	—	3.50	—
1993(I) Proof	—	Value: 5.50				

Y# 340   3 ROUBLES
Copper-Nickel, 33 mm. **Subject:** 50th Anniversary - Kiev's
Liberation from German Fascists **Obv:** Kremlin Tower and Dome
within beaded circle **Rev:** Variety of monuments

Date	Mintage	F	VF	XF	Unc	BU
1993(m)	500,000	—	—	—	3.50	—
1993(m) Proof	—	Value: 5.50				

Y# 351   3 ROUBLES
34.5600 g., 0.9000 Silver 1.0000 oz. ASW **Series:** Olympics
Obv: Double-headed eagle **Rev:** Soccer

Date	Mintage	F	VF	XF	Unc	BU
1993 Proof	40,000	Value: 32.50				

Y# 409   3 ROUBLES
34.5600 g., 0.9000 Silver 1.0000 oz. ASW **Series:** Wildlife
Obv: Double-headed eagle **Rev:** Bear

Date	Mintage	F	VF	XF	Unc	BU
1993 Proof	5,000	Value: 230				

Y# 450   3 ROUBLES
34.5600 g., 0.9000 Silver 1.0000 oz. ASW **Subject:** Ballet
Obv: Double-headed eagle **Rev:** Ballerina and building

Date	Mintage	F	VF	XF	Unc	BU
1993 Proof	45,000	Value: 50.00				

Y# 451   3 ROUBLES
34.5600 g., 0.9000 Silver 1.0000 oz. ASW **Subject:** Fedor
Schalyapin **Obv:** Double-headed eagle **Rev:** Half-length bust left
and building

Date	Mintage	F	VF	XF	Unc	BU
1993 Proof	45,000	Value: 50.00				

Y# 456   3 ROUBLES
34.5600 g., 0.9000 Silver 1.0000 oz. ASW **Obv:** Double-headed
eagle **Rev:** Vasilyblazheny Cathedral in Moscow

Date	Mintage	F	VF	XF	Unc	BU
1993 Proof	30,000	Value: 30.00				

Y# 457   3 ROUBLES
34.5600 g., 0.9000 Silver 1.0000 oz. ASW **Obv:** Double-headed
eagle **Rev:** Ivan the Great Cathedral, Moscow

Date	Mintage	F	VF	XF	Unc	BU
1993 Proof	30,000	Value: 30.00				

Y# 464 3 ROUBLES
34.5600 g., 0.9000 Silver 1.0000 oz. ASW **Obv:** Double-headed
eagle **Rev:** Ships Nadezhda and Neva on world voyage

Date	Mintage	F	VF	XF	Unc	BU
1993 Proof	25,000	Value: 32.50				

Y# 465 3 ROUBLES
34.5600 g., 0.9000 Silver 1.0000 oz. ASW **Subject:** Russo-French
Space Flight **Rev:** Cosmonauts holding flags above 1/4 globe

Date	Mintage	F	VF	XF	Unc	BU
1993 Proof	40,000	Value: 32.50				

Y# 341 3 ROUBLES
Copper-Nickel, 33 mm. **Subject:** 50th Anniversary - Battle of
Leningrad **Obv:** Kremlin Tower and Dome within beaded circle
Rev: Soldiers, monument and tower

Date	Mintage	F	VF	XF	Unc	BU
1994(l) Proof	500,000	Value: 5.50				

Y# 345 3 ROUBLES
34.5600 g., 0.9000 Silver 1.0000 oz. ASW **Obv:** Double-headed
eagle **Rev:** Cathedral of the Nativity of the Mother of God

Date	Mintage	F	VF	XF	Unc	BU
1994 Proof	30,000	Value: 30.00				

Y# 346 3 ROUBLES
Copper-Nickel **Subject:** 50th Anniversary - Liberation of Sevastopol
from German Fascists **Obv:** Kremlin Tower and Dome within beaded
circle **Rev:** Sevastopol scene, stylized soldier above

Date	Mintage	F	VF	XF	Unc	BU
1994(l) Proof	250,000	Value: 5.50				

Y# 362 3 ROUBLES
Copper-Nickel, 33 mm. **Subject:** Normandy Invasion
Obv: Kremlin Tower and Dome **Rev:** World globe with date in
center divides designs

Date	Mintage	F	VF	XF	Unc	BU
1994(m) Proof	250,000	Value: 5.50				

Y# 365 3 ROUBLES
Copper-Nickel, 33 mm. **Series:** WWII **Subject:** Partisans
Activities **Obv:** Kremlin Tower and Dome within beaded circle
Rev: Figures with weapons in bushes **Edge:** Cyrillic lettering

Date	Mintage	F	VF	XF	Unc	BU
1994(m) Proof	250,000	Value: 5.50				

Y# 366 3 ROUBLES
Copper-Nickel, 33 mm. **Series:** WWII **Subject:** Liberation of
Belgrade **Obv:** Kremlin Tower and Dome within beaded circle
Rev: Armored figures marching, building in background

Date	Mintage	F	VF	XF	Unc	BU
1994(m) Proof	250,000	Value: 5.50				

Y# 389 3 ROUBLES
34.8800 g., 0.9000 Silver 1.0092 oz. ASW **Subject:** Trans-Siberian
railway **Obv:** Double-headed eagle **Rev:** Bridge, train and map

Date	Mintage	F	VF	XF	Unc	BU
1994 Proof	25,000	Value: 35.00				

Y# 405 3 ROUBLES
34.5600 g., 0.9000 Silver 1.0000 oz. ASW **Subject:** Ballet
Obv: Double-headed eagle **Rev:** Ballet couple

Date	Mintage	F	VF	XF	Unc	BU
1994 Proof	40,000	Value: 35.00				

Y# 458 3 ROUBLES
34.5600 g., 0.9000 Silver 1.0000 oz. ASW **Obv:** Double-headed
eagle **Rev:** Pocrov Church on the Neri

Date	Mintage	F	VF	XF	Unc	BU
1994 Proof	30,000	Value: 35.00				

Y# 460 3 ROUBLES
34.5600 g., 0.9000 Silver 1.0000 oz. ASW **Series:** Wildlife
Obv: Double-headed eagle **Rev:** Sable on tree limb

Date	Mintage	F	VF	XF	Unc	BU
1994 Proof	10,000	Value: 60.00				

Y# 466 3 ROUBLES
34.5600 g., 0.9000 Silver 1.0000 oz. ASW **Subject:** Discovery
of Antarctica **Rev:** Sailing ships Vostok and Mirny

Date	Mintage	F	VF	XF	Unc	BU
1994 Proof	25,000	Value: 55.00				

Y# 513 3 ROUBLES
34.6800 g., 0.9000 Silver 1.0034 oz. ASW **Obv:** Double-headed
eagle **Rev:** Smolny Institute & Monastery - St. Petersburg

Date	Mintage	F	VF	XF	Unc	BU
1994 Proof	30,000	Value: 35.00				

Y# 520 3 ROUBLES
34.6800 g., 0.9000 Silver 1.0034 oz. ASW **Obv:** Double-headed
eagle **Rev:** Ryazin Kremlin, city view

Date	Mintage	F	VF	XF	Unc	BU
1994 Proof	30,000	Value: 35.00				

Y# 528   3 ROUBLES
34.6800 g., 0.9000 Silver 1.0034 oz. ASW   **Subject:** Vassili Ivanovich Surikov **Obv:** Double-headed eagle **Rev:** Head facing above Siberian sled scene

Date	Mintage	F	VF	XF	Unc	BU
1994 Proof	40,000				Value: 70.00	

Y# 529   3 ROUBLES
34.6800 g., 0.9000 Silver 1.0034 oz. ASW   **Subject:** Alexander Andreyevich Ivannov **Obv:** Double-headed eagle **Rev:** Head facing 1/4 right above assorted figures

Date	Mintage	F	VF	XF	Unc	BU
1994 Proof	40,000				Value: 70.00	

Y# 380   3 ROUBLES
Copper-Nickel, 33 mm.   **Series:** WWII **Subject:** Capture of Konigsberg **Obv:** Kremlin Tower and Dome within beaded circle **Rev:** Crouched soldiers in front of building

Date	Mintage	F	VF	XF	Unc	BU
1994 (m) Proof, error	—				Value: 50.00	
1995 (m) Proof	200,000				Value: 6.00	

Y# 381   3 ROUBLES
Copper-Nickel, 33 mm.   **Series:** WWII **Subject:** Capture of Vienna **Obv:** Kremlin Tower and Dome within beaded circle **Rev:** Two uniformed figures with weapons, one holding flag, building in background

Date	Mintage	F	VF	XF	Unc	BU
1995(I) Proof	200,000				Value: 6.00	

Y# 383   3 ROUBLES
Copper-Nickel, 33 mm.   **Series:** WWII **Subject:** Capture of Berlin **Obv:** Kremlin Tower and Dome within beaded circle **Rev:** Soldiers in front of building

Date	Mintage	F	VF	XF	Unc	BU
1995(I) Proof	200,000				Value: 6.00	

Y# 384   3 ROUBLES
Copper-Nickel, 33 mm.   **Series:** WWII **Subject:** German Surrender **Obv:** Kremlin Tower and Dome within beaded circle **Rev:** Seated figures at table below flags

Date	Mintage	F	VF	XF	Unc	BU
1995(I) Proof	200,000				Value: 6.00	

Y# 385   3 ROUBLES
Copper-Nickel, 33 mm.   **Series:** WWII **Subject:** Liberation of Prague **Obv:** Kremlin Tower and Dome within beaded circle **Rev:** Armored tank divides building and standing figures

Date	Mintage	F	VF	XF	Unc	BU
1995(m) Proof	200,000				Value: 6.00	

Y# 386   3 ROUBLES
Copper-Nickel, 33 mm.   **Series:** WWII **Subject:** Surrender of Japanese Army in Kwantung **Obv:** Kremlin Tower and Dome within beaded circle **Rev:** Surrender scene

Date	Mintage	F	VF	XF	Unc	BU
1995(m) Proof	200,000				Value: 6.00	

Y# 387   3 ROUBLES
Copper-Nickel, 33 mm.   **Series:** WWII **Obv:** Kremlin Tower and Dome within beaded circle **Rev:** Japanese formal surrender on Battleship U.S.S. Missouri

Date	Mintage	F	VF	XF	Unc	BU
1995(I) Proof	200,000				Value: 6.00	

Y# 388   3 ROUBLES
34.5600 g., 0.9000 Silver 1.0000 oz. ASW   **Obv:** Double-headed eagle **Rev:** Vladimir's Golden Gate

Date	Mintage	F	VF	XF	Unc	BU
1995 Proof	30,000				Value: 37.50	

Y# 394   3 ROUBLES
34.5600 g., 0.9000 Silver 1.0000 oz. ASW   **Subject:** Ballet **Obv:** Double-headed eagle **Rev:** Scene from Sleeping Beauty

Date	Mintage	F	VF	XF	Unc	BU
1995 Proof	40,000				Value: 40.00	

Y# 407   3 ROUBLES
34.5600 g., 0.9000 Silver 1.0000 oz. ASW   **Subject:** 50th Anniversary - United Nations **Obv:** Double-headed eagle **Rev:** Blacksmith, UN logo at top, building at left

Date	Mintage	F	VF	XF	Unc	BU
1995 Proof	20,000				Value: 45.00	

Y# 445   3 ROUBLES
34.5600 g., 0.9000 Silver 1.0000 oz. ASW   **Obv:** Double-headed eagle **Rev:** Smolensk Kremlin

Date	Mintage	F	VF	XF	Unc	BU
1995 Proof	30,000				Value: 37.50	

Y# 459   3 ROUBLES
34.5600 g., 0.9000 Silver 1.0000 oz. ASW   **Obv:** Double-headed eagle **Rev:** Kizhi Church on Onega Lake

Date	Mintage	F	VF	XF	Unc	BU
1995 Proof	30,000				Value: 37.50	

Y# 461   3 ROUBLES
34.5600 g., 0.9000 Silver 1.0000 oz. ASW   **Subject:** Arctic Explorers 1733-43 **Obv:** Double-headed eagle **Rev:** Busts of arctic explorers, ship, map and sled dogs

Date	Mintage	F	VF	XF	Unc	BU
1995 Proof	25,000				Value: 45.00	

Y# 462 3 ROUBLES
34.5600 g., 0.9000 Silver 1.0000 oz. ASW **Subject:** Roald Amundsen - Arctic Explorer **Obv:** Double-headed eagle **Rev:** Head left, ship and designs

Date	Mintage	F	VF	XF	Unc	BU
1995 Proof	25,000			Value: 45.00		

Y# 463 3 ROUBLES
34.5600 g., 0.9000 Silver 1.0000 oz. ASW **Subject:** 200th Anniversary - Russian National Library **Obv:** Double-headed eagle **Rev:** Book, scroll and quill in front of building

Date	Mintage	F	VF	XF	Unc	BU
1995 Proof	15,000			Value: 50.00		

Y# 467 3 ROUBLES
34.5600 g., 0.9000 Silver 1.0000 oz. ASW **Subject:** Millennium of Belgorod **Obv:** Double-headed eagle **Rev:** Scroll and building below crowned shield

Date	Mintage	F	VF	XF	Unc	BU
1995 Proof	30,000			Value: 35.00		

Y# 468 3 ROUBLES
34.5600 g., 0.9000 Silver 1.0000 oz. ASW **Subject:** Russian Millennium **Obv:** Double-headed eagle within beaded circle **Rev:** Novgorod Kremlin

Date	Mintage	F	VF	XF	Unc	BU
1995 Proof	40,000			Value: 35.00		

Y# 469 3 ROUBLES
34.5600 g., 0.9000 Silver 1.0000 oz. ASW **Subject:** Russian Millennium **Obv:** Double-headed eagle **Rev:** Spaso-Preobrazhensky Cathedral

Date	Mintage	F	VF	XF	Unc	BU
1995 Proof	40,000			Value: 30.00		

Y# 473 3 ROUBLES
34.5600 g., 0.9000 Silver 1.0000 oz. ASW **Series:** Wildlife **Obv:** Double-headed eagle **Rev:** Sable on branch

Date	Mintage	F	VF	XF	Unc	BU
1995(l) Matte	500,000	—	—	—	30.00	
1995(m) Matte	500,000	—	—	—	30.00	

Y# 474 3 ROUBLES
34.5600 g., 0.9000 Silver 1.0000 oz. ASW **Series:** Wildlife **Obv:** Double-headed eagle **Rev:** Lynx

Date	Mintage	F	VF	XF	Unc	BU
1995(l) Proof	25,000			Value: 75.00		

Y# 378 3 ROUBLES
Copper-Nickel, 33 mm. **Subject:** Liberation of Warsaw **Obv:** Kremlin Tower and Dome within beaded circle **Rev:** Standing figures holding flag

Date	Mintage	F	VF	XF	Unc	BU
1995(l) Proof	200,000			Value: 6.00		

Y# 379 3 ROUBLES
Copper-Nickel, 33 mm. **Subject:** Liberation of Budapest **Obv:** Kremlin Tower and Dome within beaded circle **Rev:** Soldiers and building

Date	Mintage	F	VF	XF	Unc	BU
1995(m) Proof	200,000			Value: 6.00		

Y# 382 3 ROUBLES
Copper-Nickel, 33 mm. **Series:** WWII **Obv:** Kremlin Tower and Dome within beaded circle **Rev:** American and Russian soldiers **Note:** 50-star U.S.A. flag.

Date	Mintage	F	VF	XF	Unc	BU
1995 (m) Proof	200,000			Value: 6.00		

Y# 470 3 ROUBLES
34.5600 g., 0.9000 Silver 1.0000 oz. ASW **Obv:** Double-headed eagle **Rev:** Ilya the Prophet's Church in Yaroslavl

Date	Mintage	F	VF	XF	Unc	BU
1996 Proof	30,000			Value: 40.00		

Y# 477 3 ROUBLES
34.5600 g., 0.9000 Silver 1.0000 oz. ASW **Subject:** Combat between Peresvet and Chelubey **Obv:** Double-headed eagle **Rev:** Two armored figures on rearing horses with swords

Date	Mintage	F	VF	XF	Unc	BU
1996 Proof	40,000			Value: 30.00		

Y# 478 3 ROUBLES
34.5600 g., 0.9000 Silver 1.0000 oz. ASW **Obv:** Double-headed eagle **Rev:** Old Testament Trinity icon

Date	Mintage	F	VF	XF	Unc	BU
1996 Proof	40,000			Value: 30.00		

Y# 482 3 ROUBLES
34.5600 g., 0.9000 Silver 1.0000 oz. ASW **Subject:** Ballet **Obv:** Double-headed eagle **Rev:** Nutcracker Ballet

Date	Mintage	F	VF	XF	Unc	BU
1996 Proof	25,000			Value: 35.00		

Y# 483 3 ROUBLES
34.5600 g., 0.9000 Silver 1.0000 oz. ASW **Subject:** Ballet - Nutcracker **Obv:** Double-headed eagle **Rev:** Duel with the Mouse King

Date	Mintage	F	VF	XF	Unc	BU
1996 Proof	25,000			Value: 35.00		

Y# 490 3 ROUBLES
34.5600 g., 0.9000 Silver 1.0000 oz. ASW **Obv:** Double-headed eagle **Rev:** Kremlin of Kazan

Date	Mintage	F	VF	XF	Unc	BU
1996 Proof	25,000			Value: 40.00		

Y# 491   3 ROUBLES
34.5600 g., 0.9000 Silver 1.0000 oz. ASW **Obv:** Double-headed eagle **Rev:** Kremlin of Tobolsk - city view

Date	Mintage	F	VF	XF	Unc	BU
1996 Proof	25,000	Value: 37.50				

Y# 510   3 ROUBLES
34.5600 g., 0.9000 Silver 1.0000 oz. ASW **Obv:** Double-headed eagle **Rev:** Alexander Column and Hermitage

Date	Mintage	F	VF	XF	Unc	BU
1996 Proof	15,000	Value: 45.00				

Y# 511   3 ROUBLES
34.5600 g., 0.9000 Silver 1.0000 oz. ASW **Subject:** 300th Anniversary - Russian Navy **Obv:** Double-headed eagle **Rev:** Icebreaker ship and bust left

Date	Mintage	F	VF	XF	Unc	BU
1996 Proof	10,000	Value: 50.00				

Y# 512   3 ROUBLES
34.5600 g., 0.9000 Silver 1.0000 oz. ASW **Subject:** 300th Anniversary - Russian Navy **Obv:** Double-headed eagle **Rev:** Carrier ship below bust facing

Date	Mintage	F	VF	XF	Unc	BU
1996 Proof	10,000	Value: 50.00				

Y# 535   3 ROUBLES
34.5600 g., 0.9000 Silver 1.0000 oz. ASW **Series:** Wildlife **Obv:** Double-headed eagle **Rev:** Tiger

Date	Mintage	F	VF	XF	Unc	BU
1996 Proof	10,000	Value: 75.00				

Y# 552   3 ROUBLES
34.5600 g., 0.9000 Silver 1.0000 oz. ASW **Subject:** 850th Anniversary - Moscow **Obv:** Double-headed eagle **Rev:** Workers building original Moscow, modern skyline behind

Date	Mintage	F	VF	XF	Unc	BU
1997 Proof	40,000	Value: 35.00				

Y# 553   3 ROUBLES
34.5600 g., 0.9000 Silver 1.0000 oz. ASW **Subject:** 850th Anniversary - Moscow **Obv:** Double-headed eagle **Rev:** Riverside city view

Date	Mintage	F	VF	XF	Unc	BU
1997 Proof	40,000	Value: 35.00				

Y# 560   3 ROUBLES
34.5600 g., 0.9000 Silver 1.0000 oz. ASW **Obv:** Double-headed eagle within beaded circle **Rev:** Monastery of the Saint Virgin in Yaroslavl

Date	Mintage	F	VF	XF	Unc	BU
1997 Proof	15,000	Value: 45.00				

Y# 567   3 ROUBLES
34.5600 g., 0.9000 Silver 1.0000 oz. ASW **Subject:** Ballet - Swan Lake **Obv:** Double-headed eagle **Rev:** Four ballerinas below crowned swan

Date	Mintage	F	VF	XF	Unc	BU
1997 Proof	10,000	Value: 50.00				

Y# 568   3 ROUBLES
34.5600 g., 0.9000 Silver 1.0000 oz. ASW **Subject:** Ballet - Swan Lake **Obv:** Double-headed eagle **Rev:** Rothbart and Prince Siegfried

Date	Mintage	F	VF	XF	Unc	BU
1997 Proof	10,000	Value: 50.00				

Y# 575   3 ROUBLES
34.5600 g., 0.9000 Silver 1.0000 oz. ASW **Subject:** First Anniversary - Russian-Belarus Treaty **Obv:** Double-headed eagle **Rev:** Two city views

Date	Mintage	F	VF	XF	Unc	BU
1997 Proof	10,000	Value: 50.00				

Y# 585   3 ROUBLES
34.5600 g., 0.9000 Silver 1.0000 oz. ASW **Subject:** Underroot Nativity of the Virgin Hermitage Monastery of Kursk **Obv:** Double-headed eagle **Rev:** Painting above monastery

Date	Mintage	F	VF	XF	Unc	BU
1997 Proof	15,000	Value: 45.00				

Y# 586   3 ROUBLES

34.5600 g., 0.9000 Silver 1.0000 oz. ASW **Subject:** Serge Julievich Witte **Obv:** Double-headed eagle **Rev:** Bust facing

Date	Mintage	F	VF	XF	Unc	BU
1997 Proof	10,000	Value: 50.00				

Y# 587   3 ROUBLES

34.5600 g., 0.9000 Silver 1.0000 oz. ASW **Subject:** Year of Reconciliation **Obv:** Double-headed eagle **Rev:** Standing figure facing holding quill and shield

Date	Mintage	F	VF	XF	Unc	BU
1997 Proof	10,000	Value: 60.00				

Y# 591   3 ROUBLES

34.5600 g., 0.9000 Silver 1.0000 oz. ASW **Obv:** Double-headed eagle **Rev:** Solovetski Monastery

Date	Mintage	F	VF	XF	Unc	BU
1997 Proof	15,000	Value: 45.00				

Y# 593   3 ROUBLES

34.5600 g., 0.9000 Silver 1.0000 oz. ASW **Series:** Wildlife **Obv:** Double-headed eagle **Rev:** Polar bear watching walrus

Date	Mintage	F	VF	XF	Unc	BU
1997 Proof	10,000	Value: 100				

Y# 312   5 ROUBLES

4.0500 g., Brass Clad Steel, 21.9 mm. **Obv:** Double-headed eagle **Rev:** Value flanked by sprigs above date

Date	Mintage	F	VF	XF	Unc	BU
1992Л	—	—	—	—	2.00	—
1992M	—	—	—	—	2.00	—

Date	Mintage	F	VF	XF	Unc	BU
1992(sp) (l)	—	—	—	—	3.00	—
1992(m)	—	—	—	—	3.00	—

Y# 322   5 ROUBLES

Copper-Nickel, 35 mm. **Obv:** Value flanked by sprigs above date **Rev:** Kazakhstan

Date	Mintage	F	VF	XF	Unc	BU
1992(l)	300,000	—	—	—	4.00	5.00
1992(l) Proof	200,000	Value: 10.00				

Y# 324   5 ROUBLES

Copper-Nickel **Subject:** Troitsk - Sergievsk Monastery **Obv:** Double-headed eagle **Rev:** Monastery

Date	Mintage	F	VF	XF	Unc	BU
1993(l)	500,000	—	—	—	6.00	7.00
1993(l) Proof	—	Value: 9.00				

Y# 339   5 ROUBLES

Copper-Nickel **Subject:** 2500 Years of Merv Minaret, Turkmenistan **Obv:** Value flanked by sprigs above date **Rev:** Building

Date	Mintage	F	VF	XF	Unc	BU
1993(l)	500,000	—	—	—	4.00	5.00
1993(l) Proof	—	Value: 10.00				

Y# 420   5 ROUBLES

7.7758 g., 0.9990 Palladium 0.2497 oz. **Subject:** Ballet **Obv:** Double-headed eagle **Rev:** Ballerina

Date	Mintage	F	VF	XF	Unc	BU
1993	6,000	—	—	—	—	300
1993 Proof	2,000	Value: 160				

Y# 431   5 ROUBLES

7.7758 g., 0.9990 Palladium 0.2497 oz. **Subject:** Ballet - Sleeping Beauty **Obv:** Double-headed eagle **Rev:** Ballerina

Date	Mintage	F	VF	XF	Unc	BU
1994	4,000	—	—	—	—	300
1994 Proof	5,000	Value: 160				

Y# 435   5 ROUBLES

7.7758 g., 0.9990 Palladium 0.2497 oz. **Obv:** Double-headed eagle **Rev:** Ballerina

Date	Mintage	F	VF	XF	Unc	BU
1995 Proof	4,000	Value: 160				

Y# 505   5 ROUBLES

4.0500 g., Brass, 21.9 mm. **Subject:** 300th Anniversary - Russian Fleet **Obv:** Double-headed eagle **Rev:** Sailing ship

Date	Mintage	F	VF	XF	Unc	BU
1996(l) In sets only	100,000	—	—	—	3.00	—

Y# 307   10 ROUBLES

5.9500 g., Bi-Metallic Aluminum-Bronze center in Copper-Nickel ring, 25 mm. **Series:** Wildlife **Obv:** Value **Rev:** Red-breasted Kazarka left **Edge:** Alternating reeded and smooth

Date	Mintage	F	VF	XF	Unc	BU
1992Л	300,000	—	—	—	4.00	9.00

Y# 308   10 ROUBLES

5.9500 g., Bi-Metallic Aluminum-Bronze center in Copper-Nickel ring, 25 mm. **Series:** Wildlife **Obv:** Value **Rev:** Tiger **Edge:** Alternating reeded and smooth

Date	Mintage	F	VF	XF	Unc	BU
1992Л	300,000	—	—	—	4.00	9.00

Y# 309   10 ROUBLES

5.9500 g., Bi-Metallic Aluminum-Bronze center in Copper-Nickel ring, 25 mm. **Series:** Wildlife **Obv:** Value **Rev:** Cobra **Edge:** Alternating reeded and smooth

Date	Mintage	F	VF	XF	Unc	BU
1992Л	300,000	—	—	—	4.00	9.00

Y# 313   10 ROUBLES

3.6500 g., Copper-Nickel, 21.1 mm. **Obv:** Double-headed eagle **Rev:** Value flanked by sprigs above date **Edge:** Reeded **Note:** St. Petersburg minted coins have a round-top 3 in date. Moscow minted coins have a flat-top 3 in date.

Date	Mintage	F	VF	XF	Unc	BU
1992Л	—	—	—	—	2.00	—
1992M	—	—	—	—	2.00	—
1993Л	—	—	—	—	2.00	—
1993M	—	—	—	—	10.00	—

Y# 313a   10 ROUBLES

3.3800 g., Copper-Nickel Clad Steel, 21.1 mm. **Obv:** Double-headed eagle **Rev:** Value flanked by sprigs **Edge:** Plain **Note:** St. Petersburg minted coins have a round-top 3 in date. Moscow minted coins have a flat-top 3 in date.

Date	Mintage	F	VF	XF	Unc	BU
1992M	—	—	—	—	12.00	—
1992(sp) (l)	—	—	—	—	2.00	—
1993Л	—	—	—	—	2.00	—
1993M	—	—	—	—	2.00	—

Y# 400   5 ROUBLES

4.0500 g., Aluminum-Bronze, 21.9 mm. **Series:** WWII **Obv:** Double-headed eagle **Rev:** Infantry officer leading attack

Date	Mintage	F	VF	XF	Unc	BU
1995(l) In sets only	200,000	—	—	—	2.00	—

Y# 352 10 ROUBLES
15.5517 g., 0.9990 Palladium 0.4995 oz. **Series:** Olympics **Obv:** Double-headed eagle **Rev:** Cubertin and Butovsky and torch

Date	Mintage	F	VF	XF	Unc	BU
1993 Proof	7,500	Value: 275				

Y# 416 10 ROUBLES
1.5552 g., 0.9990 Gold 0.0499 oz. AGW **Subject:** Ballet **Obv:** Double-headed eagle **Rev:** Ballerina

Date	Mintage	F	VF	XF	Unc	BU
1993	57,000	—	—	—	—	200
1993 Proof	11,500	Value: 60.00				

Y# 421 10 ROUBLES
15.5500 g., 0.9990 Palladium 0.4994 oz. **Subject:** Russian Ballet **Obv:** Double-headed eagle **Rev:** Ballerina

Date	Mintage	F	VF	XF	Unc	BU
1993(l)	4,000	—	—	—	—	550
1993(l) Proof	2,000	Value: 320				

Y# 424 10 ROUBLES
1.5552 g., 0.9990 Gold 0.0499 oz. AGW **Subject:** Russian Ballet **Obv:** Double-headed eagle **Rev:** Ballerina

Date	Mintage	F	VF	XF	Unc	BU
1994(m) Proof	7,000	Value: 60.00				

Y# 432 10 ROUBLES
15.5500 g., 0.9990 Palladium 0.4994 oz. **Subject:** Russian Ballet **Obv:** Double-headed eagle **Rev:** Ballerina

Date	Mintage	F	VF	XF	Unc	BU
1994(l)	3,000	—	—	—	—	550
1994(l) Proof	1,500	Value: 325				

Y# 401 10 ROUBLES
3.6500 g., Copper-Nickel, 21.1 mm. **Series:** WWII **Obv:** Double-headed eagle **Rev:** Munitions workers

Date	Mintage	F	VF	XF	Unc	BU
1995(l) In sets only	200,000	—	—	—	3.00	—

Y# 436 10 ROUBLES
15.5500 g., 0.9990 Palladium 0.4994 oz. **Subject:** Ballet - Sleeping Beauty **Obv:** Double-headed eagle **Rev:** Ballerina

Date	Mintage	F	VF	XF	Unc	BU
1995(sp) Proof	1,500	Value: 325				

Y# 438 10 ROUBLES
1.5552 g., 0.9990 Gold 0.0499 oz. AGW **Subject:** Ballet - Sleeping Beauty **Obv:** Double-headed eagle **Rev:** Ballerina

Date	Mintage	F	VF	XF	Unc	BU
1995(m) Proof	7,000	Value: 60.00				

Y# 506 10 ROUBLES
3.6500 g., Copper-Nickel, 21.1 mm. **Subject:** 300th Anniversary - Russian Fleet **Obv:** Double-headed eagle **Rev:** Cargo ship

Date	Mintage	F	VF	XF	Unc	BU
1996(l) In sets only	100,000	—	—	—	3.00	—

Y# 484 10 ROUBLES
1.5552 g., 0.9990 Gold 0.0499 oz. AGW **Subject:** Ballet - Nutcracker **Obv:** Double-headed eagle **Rev:** Nutcracker doll

Date	Mintage	F	VF	XF	Unc	BU
1996(m) Proof	7,500	Value: 60.00				

Y# 569 10 ROUBLES
1.5500 g., 0.9990 Gold 0.0498 oz. AGW **Subject:** Ballet - Swan Lake **Obv:** Double-headed eagle **Rev:** Ballerina

Date	Mintage	F	VF	XF	Unc	BU
1997(sp) Proof	2,500	Value: 65.00				

Y# 314 20 ROUBLES
5.6000 g., Copper-Nickel, 24.1 mm. **Obv:** Double-headed eagle **Rev:** Value flanked by sprigs **Edge:** Reeded and plain sections

Date	Mintage	F	VF	XF	Unc	BU
1992Л	—	—	—	—	3.00	—
1992M	—	—	—	—	3.00	—
1992Л Rare						
Note: Plain edge error						
1992M	—	—	—	—	20.00	—
Note: Plain edge error						

Y# 314a 20 ROUBLES
Copper-Nickel Clad Steel, 24.1 mm. **Obv:** Double-headed eagle **Rev:** Value flanked by sprigs **Edge:** Plain

Date	Mintage	F	VF	XF	Unc	BU
1993M	—	—	—	—	3.00	—

Y# 402 20 ROUBLES
5.6000 g., Copper-Nickel, 24.1 mm. **Series:** WWII **Obv:** Double-headed eagle **Rev:** Soldiers and tanks

Date	Mintage	F	VF	XF	Unc	BU
1995(l) In sets only	200,000	—	—	—	3.00	—

Y# 507 20 ROUBLES
5.6500 g., Copper-Nickel, 24.1 mm. **Subject:** 300th Anniversary - Russian Fleet **Obv:** Double-headed eagle **Rev:** Scientific research ship

Date	Mintage	F	VF	XF	Unc	BU
1996(l) In sets only	100,000	—	—	—	5.00	—

Y# 353 25 ROUBLES
31.1035 g., 0.9990 Palladium 0.9990 oz. **Subject:** Age of enlightenment 17th century. **Obv:** Double-headed eagle **Rev:** Catherine the Great

Date	Mintage	F	VF	XF	Unc	BU
1992(l) Proof	5,500	Value: 550				

Y# 406 25 ROUBLES
156.0400 g., 0.9990 Silver 5.0116 oz. ASW **Subject:** Russian Ballet **Obv:** Theatre within beaded circle **Rev:** Ballet couple **Note:** Illustration reduced.

Date	Mintage	F	VF	XF	Unc	BU
1993(l) Proof	Inc. above	Value: 120				
1993(m) Proof	10,000	Value: 120				

Y# 395 25 ROUBLES
3.1104 g., 0.9990 Platinum 0.0999 oz. APW **Subject:** Russian Ballet **Obv:** Double-headed eagle **Rev:** Ballerina

Date	Mintage	F	VF	XF	Unc	BU
1993(l) Proof	750	—	—	—	—	300

Y# 410 25 ROUBLES
3.1100 g., 0.9990 Gold 0.0999 oz. AGW **Series:** Wildlife **Obv:** Double-headed eagle **Rev:** Bear

Date	Mintage	F	VF	XF	Unc	BU
1993(m) Proof	2,000	Value: 125				

Y# 417 25 ROUBLES
3.1100 g., 0.9990 Gold 0.0999 oz. AGW **Subject:** Russian Ballet **Obv:** Double-headed eagle **Rev:** Ballerina

Date	Mintage	F	VF	XF	Unc	BU
1993(m)	12,500	—	—	—	—	200
1993(m) Proof	6,000	Value: 125				

Y# 422   25 ROUBLES
31.1035 g., 0.9990 Palladium 0.9990 oz. **Subject:** Russian
Ballet **Obv:** Double-headed eagle **Rev:** Ballerina

Date	Mintage	F	VF	XF	Unc	BU
1993(l)	3,000	—	—	—	—	900
1993(l) Proof	2,000	Value: 500				

Y# 452   25 ROUBLES
31.1035 g., 0.9990 Palladium 0.9990 oz. **Subject:** Russian and
World Culture **Obv:** Double-headed eagle **Rev:** M.P. Musorgsky

Date	Mintage	F	VF	XF	Unc	BU
1993(m) Proof	5,500	Value: 500				

Y# 517   25 ROUBLES
31.1035 g., 0.9990 Palladium 0.9990 oz., 37 mm. **Subject:** First
Russian Global Circumnavigation **Obv:** Double-headed eagle
Rev: Sloop Nadyezhda

Date	Mintage	F	VF	XF	Unc	BU
1993(l) Proof	2,500	Value: 500				

Y# 518   25 ROUBLES
31.1035 g., 0.9990 Palladium 0.9990 oz., 37 mm. **Series:** First
Russian Global Circumnavigation **Obv:** Double-headed eagle
Rev: Sloop Neva

Date	Mintage	F	VF	XF	Unc	BU
1993(l) Proof	25,000	Value: 500				

Y# 390   25 ROUBLES
172.8300 g., 0.9000 Silver 5.0007 oz. ASW **Subject:** 100th
Anniversary - Trans-Siberian Railroad **Rev:** Steam train, workers
laying ties on track

Date	Mintage	F	VF	XF	Unc	BU
1994(l) Proof	3,000	Value: 400				

Y# 423   25 ROUBLES
172.8300 g., 0.9000 Silver 5.0007 oz. ASW **Subject:** Russian
Ballet

Date	Mintage	F	VF	XF	Unc	BU
1994(m) Proof	7,500	Value: 225				

Y# 425   25 ROUBLES
3.1100 g., 0.9990 Gold 0.0999 oz. AGW **Subject:** Russian Ballet
Obv: Double-headed eagle **Rev:** Ballerina

Date	Mintage	F	VF	XF	Unc	BU
1994(m) Proof	5,000	Value: 125				

Y# 428   25 ROUBLES
3.1104 g., 0.9990 Platinum 0.0999 oz. APW **Subject:** Russian
Ballet **Obv:** Double-headed eagle **Rev:** Ballerina

Date	Mintage	F	VF	XF	Unc	BU
1994(l) Proof	900	Value: 220				

Y# 433   25 ROUBLES
31.1035 g., 0.9990 Palladium 0.9990 oz. **Subject:** Russian
Ballet **Obv:** Double-headed eagle **Rev:** Ballerina

Date	Mintage	F	VF	XF	Unc	BU
1994(l)	2,000	—	—	—	—	500
1994(l) Proof	1,500	Value: 550				

Y# 521   25 ROUBLES
31.1035 g., 0.9990 Palladium 0.9990 oz. **Subject:** First Russian
Antarctic Expedition, 1819-21 **Obv:** Double-headed eagle
Rev: Sloop Mirny

Date	Mintage	F	VF	XF	Unc	BU
1994 Proof	4,000	Value: 500				

Y# 522   25 ROUBLES
31.1035 g., 0.9990 Palladium 0.9990 oz. **Obv:** Double-headed
eagle **Rev:** Sloop Vostok

Date	Mintage	F	VF	XF	Unc	BU
1994 Proof	4,000	Value: 500				

Y# 524 ·25 ROUBLES
3.1103 g., 0.9990 Gold 0.0999 oz. AGW **Series:** Wildlife
Obv: Double-headed eagle **Rev:** Sable's head

Date	Mintage	F	VF	XF	Unc	BU
1994 Proof	4,000	Value: 115				

Y# 530   25 ROUBLES
31.1035 g., 0.9990 Palladium 0.9990 oz. **Obv:** Double-headed
eagle **Rev:** Andre Ruble

Date	Mintage	F	VF	XF	Unc	BU
1994 Proof	6,000	Value: 500				

Y# 534   25 ROUBLES
4.3198 g., 0.9000 Gold 0.1250 oz. AGW **Obv:** Double-headed
eagle **Rev:** Baikal railroad tunnel

Date	Mintage	F	VF	XF	Unc	BU
1994 Proof	3,000	Value: 145				

Y# 471   25 ROUBLES
155.5000 g., 0.9000 Silver 4.4993 oz. ASW **Series:** Wildlife **Obv:**
Double-headed eagle **Rev:** Lynx on log **Note:** Illustration reduced.

Date	Mintage	F	VF	XF	Unc	BU
1995 Proof	5,000	Value: 150				

Y# 472   25 ROUBLES
155.5000 g., 0.9000 Silver 4.4993 oz. ASW **Subject:** First
Station at North Pole **Obv:** Double-headed eagle **Rev:** Men, ship,
and airplane.

Date	Mintage	F	VF	XF	Unc	BU
1995 Proof	5,000	Value: 175				

Y# 437   25 ROUBLES
31.1035 g., 0.9990 Palladium 0.9990 oz. **Obv:** Double-headed
eagle **Rev:** Ballerina

Date	Mintage	F	VF	XF	Unc	BU
1995 Proof	1,500	Value: 500				

Y# 439   25 ROUBLES
3.1100 g., 0.9990 Gold 0.0999 oz. AGW **Obv:** Double-headed
eagle **Rev:** Ballerina

Date	Mintage	F	VF	XF	Unc	BU
1995 Proof	5,000	Value: 125				

Y# 442   25 ROUBLES
3.1104 g., 0.9990 Platinum 0.0999 oz. APW **Obv:** Double-
headed eagle **Rev:** Ballerina

Date	Mintage	F	VF	XF	Unc	BU
1995 Proof	900	Value: 220				

Y# 475   25 ROUBLES
31.1035 g., 0.9990 Palladium 0.9990 oz. **Obv:** Double-headed
eagle **Rev:** Alexander Nevski

Date	Mintage	F	VF	XF	Unc	BU
1995 Proof	6,000	Value: 500				

Y# 485   25 ROUBLES
155.5175 g., 0.9990 Silver 4.9948 oz. ASW **Subject:** Ballet -
Nutcracker **Obv:** Double-headed eagle **Rev:** Children dancing
around tree.

Date	Mintage	F	VF	XF	Unc	BU
1996 Proof	5,000	Value: 250				

Y# 479   25 ROUBLES
155.5000 g., 0.9000 Silver 4.4993 oz. ASW **Obv:** Double-headed
eagle **Rev:** Battle of Kulikova Plains **Note:** Illustration reduced.

Date	Mintage	F	VF	XF	Unc	BU
1996 Proof	5,000	Value: 250				

Y# 536   25 ROUBLES
172.7972 g., 0.9000 Silver 4.9998 oz. ASW **Series:** Wildlife
Obv: Double-headed eagle **Rev:** Amur Tiger.

Date	Mintage	F	VF	XF	Unc	BU
1996 Proof	3,000	Value: 250				

Y# 542   25 ROUBLES
172.7972 g., 0.9000 Silver 4.9998 oz. ASW **Obv:** Double-headed
eagle **Rev:** Battle of Gangut, 1714 **Note:** Illustration reduced.

Date	Mintage	F	VF	XF	Unc	BU
1996 Proof	3,000	Value: 300				

Y# 543   25 ROUBLES
172.7972 g., 0.9000 Silver 4.9998 oz. ASW **Subject:** Battle of
Chesme, 1770 **Obv:** Double-headed eagle **Rev:** Battle of
Chesme, 1770 **Note:** Illustration reduced.

Date	Mintage	F	VF	XF	Unc	BU
1996 Proof	3,000	Value: 300				

Y# 544   25 ROUBLES
172.7972 g., 0.9000 Silver 4.9998 oz. ASW **Obv:** Double-headed
eagle **Rev:** Battle of Corfu, 1799 **Note:** Illustration reduced.

Date	Mintage	F	VF	XF	Unc	BU
1996 Proof	3,000	Value: 300				

Y# 545   25 ROUBLES
172.7972 g., 0.9000 Silver 4.9998 oz. ASW **Obv:** Double-headed
eagle **Rev:** Battle of Sinop, 1853 **Note:** Illustration reduced.

Date	Mintage	F	VF	XF	Unc	BU
1996 Proof	3,000	Value: 300				

Y# 486   25 ROUBLES
3.1103 g., 0.9990 Gold 0.0999 oz. AGW **Subject:** Ballet -
Nutcracker **Obv:** Double headed eagle **Rev:** Figure with
nutcracker doll

Date	Mintage	F	VF	XF	Unc	BU
1996 Proof	7,500	Value: 125				

Y# 554   25 ROUBLES
172.7972 g., 0.9000 Silver 4.9998 oz. ASW **Subject:** 850th
Anniversary - Moscow **Obv:** Double-headed eagle
Rev: Monument flanked by trees

Date	Mintage	F	VF	XF	Unc	BU
1997 Proof	5,000	Value: 220				

Y# 570   25 ROUBLES
172.7972 g., 0.9000 Silver 4.9998 oz. ASW **Subject:** Ballet -
Swan Lake **Obv:** Double-headed eagle **Rev:** Prince Siegfried
dancing with Odile **Note:** Illustration reduced.

Date	Mintage	F	VF	XF	Unc	BU
1997 Proof	3,000	Value: 250				

Y# 592 25 ROUBLES
172.7972 g., 0.9000 Silver 4.9998 oz. ASW **Series:** Wildlife
Obv: Double-headed eagle **Rev:** Bear with cub **Note:** Illustration reduced.

Date	Mintage	F	VF	XF	Unc	BU
1997 Proof	1,000	Value: 350				

Y# 594 25 ROUBLES
172.7972 g., 0.9000 Silver 4.9998 oz. ASW **Series:** Wildlife
Obv: Double-headed eagle **Rev:** Polar bear, caribou, seal

Date	Mintage	F	VF	XF	Unc	BU
1997 Proof	3,000	Value: 300				

Y# 622 25 ROUBLES
173.2900 g., 0.9000 Silver 5.0141 oz. ASW **Series:** Wildlife
Obv: Double-headed eagle **Rev:** Sable in tree

Date	Mintage	F	VF	XF	Unc	BU
1997 Proof	1,000	Value: 350				

Y# 571 25 ROUBLES
3.1103 g., 0.9990 Gold 0.0999 oz. AGW **Subject:** Ballet - Swan
Lake **Obv:** Double-headed eagle **Rev:** Winged figure of Rothbart and Swan

Date	Mintage	F	VF	XF	Unc	BU
1997 Proof	2,000	Value: 175				

Y# 315 50 ROUBLES
5.9500 g., Bi-Metallic Aluminum-Bronze center in Copper-Nickel
ring, 25 mm. **Obv:** Double-headed eagle **Rev:** Value flanked by
sprigs **Note:** Off-metal strikes exist from both mints. The strike is
on the planchet reserved for Y#316, 100 Roubles.

Date	Mintage	F	VF	XF	Unc	BU
1992Л	—	0.50	0.75	1.00	3.00	—
1992M	—	0.75	1.00	1.50	4.00	—

Y# 354 50 ROUBLES
8.6397 g., 0.9000 Gold 0.2500 oz. AGW **Obv:** Double-headed
eagle **Rev:** Moscow's Pashkov Palace

Date	Mintage	F	VF	XF	Unc	BU
1992 Proof	7,500	Value: 260				

Y# 516 50 ROUBLES
8.6397 g., 0.9000 Gold 0.2500 oz. AGW **Subject:** Yakutia.
Obv: Double-headed eagle **Rev:** Chubuku (snow) ram on map

Date	Mintage	F	VF	XF	Unc	BU
1992 Proof	25,000	Value: 275				

Y# 329.1 50 ROUBLES
Aluminum-Bronze, 25 mm. **Obv:** Double-headed eagle
Rev: Value flanked by sprigs **Edge:** Alternating reeded and plain

Date	Mintage	F	VF	XF	Unc	BU
1993Л	—	—	—	—	3.00	—
1993M	—	—	—	—	3.00	—

Y# 329.2 50 ROUBLES
Brass Clad Steel, 25 mm. **Obv:** Double-headed eagle
Rev: Value **Edge:** Plain

Date	Mintage	F	VF	XF	Unc	BU
1993Л	—	—	—	—	4.00	—
1993M	—	—	—	—	3.00	—

Y# 330 50 ROUBLES
5.9500 g., Bi-Metallic Aluminum-Bronze center in Copper-Nickel
ring, 25 mm. **Series:** Wildlife **Obv:** Double-headed eagle
Rev: Black bear **Edge:** Alternating reeded and smooth

Date	Mintage	F	VF	XF	Unc	BU
1993Л	300,000	—	—	—	5.00	10.00

Y# 331 50 ROUBLES
5.9500 g., Bi-Metallic Aluminum-Bronze center in Copper-Nickel
ring, 25 mm. **Series:** Wildlife **Obv:** Double-headed eagle
Rev: Turkmenistan Gecko **Edge:** Alternating reeded and smooth

Date	Mintage	F	VF	XF	Unc	BU
1993Л	300,000	—	—	—	5.00	10.00

Y# 332 50 ROUBLES
5.9500 g., Bi-Metallic Aluminum-Bronze center in Copper-Nickel
ring, 25 mm. **Series:** Wildlife **Obv:** Double-headed eagle
Rev: Grouse **Edge:** Alternating reeded and smooth

Date	Mintage	F	VF	XF	Unc	BU
1993Л	300,000	—	—	—	5.00	10.00

Y# 333 50 ROUBLES
5.9500 g., Bi-Metallic Aluminum-Bronze center in Copper-Nickel
ring, 25 mm. **Series:** Wildlife **Obv:** Double-headed eagle
Rev: Far Eastern Stork **Edge:** Alternating reeded and smooth

Date	Mintage	F	VF	XF	Unc	BU
1993Л	300,000	—	—	—	5.00	9.00

Y# 334 50 ROUBLES
5.9500 g., Bi-Metallic Aluminum-Bronze center in Copper-Nickel
ring, 25 mm. **Series:** Wildlife **Obv:** Double-headed eagle
Rev: Black Sea Porpoise **Edge:** Alternating reeded and smooth

Date	Mintage	F	VF	XF	Unc	BU
1993Л	300,000	—	—	—	5.00	10.00

Y# 355 50 ROUBLES
8.6397 g., 0.9000 Gold 0.2500 oz. AGW **Series:** Olympics
Obv: Double-headed eagle **Rev:** Figure skater

Date	Mintage	F	VF	XF	Unc	BU
1993 Proof	7,500	Value: 260				

Y# 356 50 ROUBLES
7.7758 g., 0.9990 Platinum 0.2497 oz. APW **Series:** Olympics
Obv: Double-headed eagle **Rev:** Formal riding

Date	Mintage	F	VF	XF	Unc	BU
1993 Proof	7,500	Value: 475				

Y# 396 50 ROUBLES
7.7758 g., 0.9990 Platinum 0.2497 oz. APW **Subject:** Bolshoi
Ballet **Obv:** Double-headed eagle **Rev:** Ballerina

Date	Mintage	F	VF	XF	Unc	BU
1993 Proof	750	Value: 475				

Y# 411 50 ROUBLES
7.7800 g., 0.9990 Gold 0.2499 oz. AGW **Series:** Wildlife
Obv: Double-headed eagle **Rev:** Bear between trees and sprigs

Date	Mintage	F	VF	XF	Unc	BU
1993 Proof	1,480	Value: 270				

Y# 418 50 ROUBLES
7.7800 g., 0.9990 Gold 0.2499 oz. AGW **Subject:** Bolshoi Ballet
Obv: Double-headed eagle **Rev:** Ballerina

Date	Mintage	F	VF	XF	Unc	BU
1993	4,700	—	—	—	—	300
1993 Proof	1,500	Value: 350				

Y# 453 50 ROUBLES
7.7800 g., 0.9990 Gold 0.2499 oz. AGW **Subject:** Sergei
Rachmaninov **Obv:** Double-headed eagle **Rev:** Head right

Date	Mintage	F	VF	XF	Unc	BU
1993 Proof	7,500	Value: 260				

Y# 367 50 ROUBLES
5.9500 g., Bi-Metallic Aluminum-Bronze center in Copper-Nickel
ring, 25 mm. **Series:** Wildlife **Obv:** Double-headed eagle
Rev: Blind mole rat **Edge:** Alternating reeded and smooth

Date	Mintage	F	VF	XF	Unc	BU
1994Л	300,000	—	—	—	5.00	10.00

Y# 368   50 ROUBLES
5.9500 g., Bi-Metallic Aluminum-Bronze center in Copper-Nickel ring, 25 mm.   **Series:** Wildlife **Obv:** Double-headed eagle **Rev:** Bison **Edge:** Alternating reeded and smooth

Date	Mintage	F	VF	XF	Unc	BU
1994Л	300,000	—	—	—	5.00	7.50

Y# 369   50 ROUBLES
5.9500 g., Bi-Metallic Aluminum-Bronze center in Copper-Nickel ring, 25 mm.   **Series:** Wildlife **Obv:** Double-headed eagle **Rev:** Goitered Gazelle **Edge:** Alternating reeded and smooth

Date	Mintage	F	VF	XF	Unc	BU
1994Л	300,000	—	—	—	5.00	7.50

Y# 370   50 ROUBLES
5.9500 g., Bi-Metallic Aluminum-Bronze center in Copper-Nickel ring, 25 mm.   **Series:** Wildlife **Obv:** Double-headed eagle **Rev:** Peregrine Falcon **Edge:** Alternating reeded and smooth

Date	Mintage	F	VF	XF	Unc	BU
1994Л	300,000	—	—	—	5.00	8.00

Y# 371   50 ROUBLES
5.9500 g., Bi-Metallic Aluminum-Bronze center in Copper-Nickel ring, 25 mm.   **Series:** Wildlife **Obv:** Double-headed eagle **Rev:** Two flamingos **Edge:** Alternating reeded and smooth

Date	Mintage	F	VF	XF	Unc	BU
1994Л	300,000	—	—	—	6.00	9.00

Y# 426   50 ROUBLES
7.7759 g., 0.9990 Gold 0.2497 oz. AGW **Subject:** Bolshoi Ballet **Obv:** Double-headed eagle **Rev:** Ballerina

Date	Mintage	F	VF	XF	Unc	BU
1994 Proof	2,500	Value: 265				

Y# 429   50 ROUBLES
7.7759 g., 0.9990 Platinum 0.2497 oz. APW **Subject:** Bolshoi Ballet **Obv:** Double-headed eagle **Rev:** Ballerina

Date	Mintage	F	VF	XF	Unc	BU
1994 Proof	900	Value: 500				

Y# 525   50 ROUBLES
7.7759 g., 0.9990 Gold 0.2497 oz. AGW **Series:** Wildlife **Obv:** Double-headed eagle **Rev:** Sable in tree

Date	Mintage	F	VF	XF	Unc	BU
1994 Proof	2,500	Value: 265				

Y# 531   50 ROUBLES
7.7759 g., 0.9990 Gold 0.2497 oz. AGW **Rev:** Dmitri Grigorievich Levitsky

Date	Mintage	F	VF	XF	Unc	BU
1994 Proof	8,000	Value: 265				

Y# 403   50 ROUBLES
Aluminum-Bronze **Series:** WWII **Obv:** Double-headed eagle **Rev:** Two sailors, ship, and plane

Date	Mintage	F	VF	XF	Unc	BU
1995Л In sets only	200,000	—	—	—	5.00	—

Y# A475   50 ROUBLES
7.7800 g., 0.9990 Gold 0.2499 oz. AGW **Series:** Wildlife **Obv:** Double-headed eagle **Rev:** Lynx

Date	Mintage	F	VF	XF	Unc	BU
1995 Proof	10,000	Value: 265				

Y# 408   50 ROUBLES
7.7800 g., 0.9990 Gold 0.2499 oz. AGW **Subject:** 50th Anniversary - United Nations **Obv:** Double-headed eagle **Rev:** Blacksmith with anvil at feet, UN logo at top, building at left **Note:** Similar to 3 Roubles, Y#407.

Date	Mintage	F	VF	XF	Unc	BU
1995 Proof	5,000	Value: 260				

Y# 440   50 ROUBLES
7.7800 g., 0.9990 Gold 0.2499 oz. AGW **Subject:** Bolshoi Ballet - Sleeping Beauty **Obv:** Double-headed eagle **Rev:** Ballerina

Date	Mintage	F	VF	XF	Unc	BU
1995 Proof	2,500	Value: 350				

Y# 443   50 ROUBLES
7.7759 g., 0.9990 Platinum 0.2497 oz. APW **Subject:** Bolshoi Ballet - Sleeping Beauty **Obv:** Double-headed eagle **Rev:** Male dancer

Date	Mintage	F	VF	XF	Unc	BU
1995 Proof	900	Value: 500				

Y# 496   50 ROUBLES
8.6397 g., 0.9000 Gold 0.2500 oz. AGW **Subject:** F. Nansen and the "Fram" **Obv:** Double-headed eagle **Rev:** F. Nansen and the "Fram"

Date	Mintage	F	VF	XF	Unc	BU
1995 Proof	5,000	Value: 260				

Y# 508   50 ROUBLES
Aluminum-Bronze **Subject:** 300th Anniversary - Russian Fleet **Obv:** Double-headed eagle **Rev:** Submarine

Date	Mintage	F	VF	XF	Unc	BU
1996Л In sets only	100,000	—	—	—	10.00	—

Y# 480   50 ROUBLES
7.7800 g., 0.9990 Gold 0.2499 oz. AGW **Obv:** Double-headed eagle **Rev:** Dmitri Donskoy Monument

Date	Mintage	F	VF	XF	Unc	BU
1996 Proof	10,000	Value: 260				

Y# 487   50 ROUBLES
7.7800 g., 0.9990 Gold 0.2499 oz. AGW **Subject:** Ballet - Nutcracker **Obv:** Double-headed eagle **Rev:** Marsha and Drosselmeyer with broken doll

Date	Mintage	F	VF	XF	Unc	BU
1996 Proof	2,500	Value: 275				

Y# 501   50 ROUBLES
8.6397 g., 0.9000 Gold 0.2500 oz. AGW **Obv:** Double-headed eagle **Rev:** Church of the Savior on the Nereditza River

Date	Mintage	F	VF	XF	Unc	BU
1996 Proof	10,000	Value: 260				

Y# 537   50 ROUBLES
7.7759 g., 0.9990 Gold 0.2497 oz. AGW **Series:** Wildlife **Obv:** Double-headed eagle **Rev:** Tiger head

Date	Mintage	F	VF	XF	Unc	BU
1996 Proof	1,500	Value: 260				

Y# 546   50 ROUBLES
8.6397 g., 0.9000 Gold 0.2500 oz. AGW **Obv:** Double-headed eagle **Rev:** Cruiser Varyag 1904

Date	Mintage	F	VF	XF	Unc	BU
1996 Proof	1,500	Value: 275				

Y# 555   50 ROUBLES
8.6397 g., 0.9000 Gold 0.2500 oz. AGW **Subject:** 850th Anniversary - Moscow **Obv:** Double-headed eagle **Rev:** Shield flanked by designs

Date	Mintage	F	VF	XF	Unc	BU
1997 Proof	10,000	Value: 260				

Y# 572   50 ROUBLES
7.7759 g., 0.9990 Gold 0.2497 oz. AGW **Subject:** Ballet - Swan Lake **Obv:** Double-headed eagle **Rev:** Prince Siegfried with crossbow and swan

Date	Mintage	F	VF	XF	Unc	BU
1997 Proof	1,500	Value: 260				

Y# 595   50 ROUBLES
7.7759 g., 0.9990 Gold 0.2497 oz. AGW **Series:** Wildlife
Obv: Double-headed eagle **Rev:** Polar bear

Date	Mintage	F	VF	XF	Unc	BU
1997 Proof	1,500	Value: 265				

Y# 712   50 ROUBLES
8.7500 g., 0.9000 Gold 0.2532 oz. AGW **Series:** Three
Millenniums **Subject:** Scientific and Technical Progress
Obv: Double-headed eagle **Rev:** Icarus and space travel

Date	Mintage	F	VF	XF	Unc	BU
2000M Proof	1,000	Value: 275				

Y# 316   100 ROUBLES
6.0000 g., Bi-Metallic Copper-Nickel center in Aluminum-Bronze
ring, 25.3 mm. **Obv:** Double-headed eagle **Rev:** Value flanked
by sprigs **Note:** Off-metal strikes exist from the Moscow mint.
The strike is on the planchet reserved for Y#315, 50 Roubles.

Date	Mintage	F	VF	XF	Unc	BU
1992Л	—	0.50	1.00	2.00	4.00	—
1992M	—	1.00	2.00	3.00	5.00	—

Y# 357   100 ROUBLES
17.5000 g., 0.9000 Gold 0.5064 oz. AGW **Obv:** Double-headed
eagle **Rev:** Michael Lomonossov

Date	Mintage	F	VF	XF	Unc	BU
1992 Proof	5,700	Value: 520				

Y# 375   100 ROUBLES
17.5000 g., 0.9000 Gold 0.5064 oz. AGW **Obv:** Double-headed
eagle **Rev:** Wooly Mammoth within radiant map **Note:** Yakutia

Date	Mintage	F	VF	XF	Unc	BU
1992 Proof	14,000	Value: 520				

Y# 338   100 ROUBLES
Copper-Nickel-Zinc **Obv:** Double-headed eagle **Rev:** Value
flanked by sprigs

Date	Mintage	F	VF	XF	Unc	BU
1993Л	—	0.25	1.00	2.00	4.00	—
1993M	—	0.25	1.00	2.00	4.00	—

Y# 412   100 ROUBLES
15.5500 g., 0.9990 Gold 0.4994 oz. AGW **Series:** Wildlife
Obv: Double-headed eagle **Rev:** Black bear

Date	Mintage	F	VF	XF	Unc	BU
1993 Proof	1,400	Value: 520				

Y# 419   100 ROUBLES
15.5500 g., 0.9990 Gold 0.4994 oz. AGW **Subject:** Bolshoi
Ballet **Obv:** Double-headed eagle **Rev:** Ballerina

Date	Mintage	F	VF	XF	Unc	BU
1993	2,700					500
1993 Proof	1,500	Value: 575				

Y# 454   100 ROUBLES
17.5000 g., 0.9000 Gold 0.5064 oz. AGW **Obv:** Double-headed
eagle **Rev:** Peter Tchaikovsky

Date	Mintage	F	VF	XF	Unc	BU
1993 Proof	5,700	Value: 500				

Y# 427   100 ROUBLES
15.5500 g., 0.9990 Gold 0.4994 oz. AGW **Subject:** Bolshoi
Ballet **Obv:** Double-headed eagle **Rev:** Ballerina

Date	Mintage	F	VF	XF	Unc	BU
1994 Proof	2,500	Value: 550				

Y# 526   100 ROUBLES
15.5500 g., 0.9990 Gold 0.4994 oz. AGW **Series:** Wildlife
Obv: Double-headed eagle **Rev:** Sable in tree

Date	Mintage	F	VF	XF	Unc	BU
1994 Proof	2,500	Value: 520				

Y# 532   100 ROUBLES
15.5500 g., 0.9990 Gold 0.4994 oz. AGW **Obv:** Double-headed
eagle **Rev:** Vassili Vassilievich Kandinsky - The Blue Horse

Date	Mintage	F	VF	XF	Unc	BU
1994 Proof	6,000	Value: 500				

Y# 404   100 ROUBLES
Copper-Nickel **Series:** WWII **Obv:** Double-headed eagle
Rev: Berlin Soldier Monument

Date	Mintage	F	VF	XF	Unc	BU
1995Л In sets only	200,000	—	—	—	7.00	—

Y# 502   100 ROUBLES
17.5000 g., 0.9000 Gold 0.5064 oz. AGW **Obv:** Double-headed
eagle **Rev:** Order of Alexander Nevsky

Date	Mintage	F	VF	XF	Unc	BU
1995 Proof	5,000	Value: 525				

Y# 376   100 ROUBLES
1111.0861 g., 0.9000 Silver 32.148 oz. ASW, 100 mm.
Series: Wildlife **Obv:** Double-headed eagle **Rev:** Mother bear
with cubs **Note:** Illustration reduced.

Date	Mintage	F	VF	XF	Unc	BU
1995 Proof	500	Value: 2,500				

Y# A387   100 ROUBLES
1000.2108 g., 0.9000 Silver 28.940 oz. ASW, 103 mm.
Series: WWII **Subject:** WWII Victory **Rev:** Allied Commanders
Note: Illustration reduced.

Date	Mintage	F	VF	XF	Unc	BU
1995 Proof	1,500	Value: 1,600				

Y# 434   100 ROUBLES
912.3693 g., 0.9000 Silver 26.398 oz. ASW, 100 mm.
Subject: Ballet - Sleeping Beauty **Obv:** Building in back of
double-headed eagle **Rev:** Theater above dancers
Note: Illustration reduced.

Date	Mintage	F	VF	XF	Unc	BU
1995 Proof	1,000	Value: 1,600				

Y# 498   100 ROUBLES
912.3693 g., 0.9000 Silver 26.398 oz. ASW **Series:** Wildlife
Obv: Double-headed eagle **Rev:** Lynx with two kits.

Date	Mintage	F	VF	XF	Unc	BU
1995 Proof	500	Value: 1,350				

Y# 441   100 ROUBLES
15.5500 g., 0.9990 Gold 0.4994 oz. AGW   **Subject:** Ballet - Sleeping Beauty **Obv:** Double-headed eagle **Rev:** Ballerina

Date	Mintage	F	VF	XF	Unc	BU
1995 Proof	2,500	Value: 695				

Y# 497   100 ROUBLES
17.5000 g., 0.9000 Gold 0.5064 oz. AGW   **Obv:** Double-headed eagle **Rev:** Icebreaker "Krassin"

Date	Mintage	F	VF	XF	Unc	BU
1995 Proof	2,500	Value: 520				

Y# 499   100 ROUBLES
17.5000 g., 0.9000 Gold 0.5064 oz. AGW   **Series:** Wildlife **Obv:** Double-headed eagle **Rev:** Lynx

Date	Mintage	F	VF	XF	Unc	BU
1995 Proof	3,500	Value: 520				

Y# 509   100 ROUBLES
Copper-Nickel   **Subject:** 300th Anniversary - Russian Fleet **Obv:** Double-headed eagle **Rev:** Atlantic Icebreaker "Arctic"

Date	Mintage	F	VF	XF	Unc	BU
1996 In sets only	100,000	—	—	—	—	9.00

Y# 488   100 ROUBLES
1111.0861 g., 0.9990 Silver 35.685 oz. ASW   **Subject:** Ballet - Nutcracker **Obv:** Double-headed eagle **Rev:** Marsha cradling nutcracker doll **Note:** Illustration reduced.

Date	Mintage	F	VF	XF	Unc	BU
1996 Proof	1,000	Value: 1,500				

Y# 538   100 ROUBLES
1111.0861 g., 0.9000 Silver 32.148 oz. ASW   **Series:** Wildlife **Obv:** Double-headed eagle **Rev:** Tiger **Note:** Illustration reduced.

Date	Mintage	F	VF	XF	Unc	BU
1996 Proof	1,000	Value: 1,500				

Y# 547   100 ROUBLES
912.3693 g., 0.9000 Silver 26.398 oz. ASW   **Obv:** Double-headed eagle **Rev:** Warship Poltava, 1712 **Note:** Illustration reduced.

Date	Mintage	F	VF	XF	Unc	BU
1996 Proof	3,000	Value: 1,000				

Y# 495   100 ROUBLES
912.3693 g., 0.9000 Silver 26.398 oz. ASW   **Obv:** Double-headed eagle **Rev:** Sables around city **Note:** Photo reduced.

Date	Mintage	F	VF	XF	Unc	BU
1996 Proof	500	Value: 1,600				

Y# 481   100 ROUBLES
17.5000 g., 0.9000 Gold 0.5064 oz. AGW   **Obv:** Double-headed eagle **Rev:** All Saints Church in Kulishki

Date	Mintage	F	VF	XF	Unc	BU
1996 Proof	5,000	Value: 500				

Y# 489   100 ROUBLES
15.5517 g., 0.9990 Gold 0.4995 oz. AGW   **Subject:** Ballet - Nutcracker **Obv:** Double-headed eagle **Rev:** Dancing Prince

Date	Mintage	F	VF	XF	Unc	BU
1996 Proof	2,500	Value: 520				

Y# 539   100 ROUBLES
15.5517 g., 0.9990 Gold 0.4995 oz. AGW   **Series:** Wildlife **Obv:** Double-headed eagle **Rev:** Amur tiger

Date	Mintage	F	VF	XF	Unc	BU
1996 Proof	1,000	Value: 525				

Y# 548   100 ROUBLES
17.5000 g., 0.9000 Gold 0.5064 oz. AGW   **Subject:** Battleships of WWII **Obv:** Double-headed eagle **Rev:** Destroyers, "Gremysiy and Soobrazitelny"

Date	Mintage	F	VF	XF	Unc	BU
1996 Proof	1,000	Value: 525				

Y# 597   100 ROUBLES
1111.0861 g., 0.9000 Silver 32.148 oz. ASW   **Series:** Wildlife **Obv:** Double-headed eagle **Rev:** Two polar bears **Note:** Photo reduced.

Date	Mintage	F	VF	XF	Unc	BU
1997 Proof	1,000	Value: 1,300				

Y# 556   100 ROUBLES
1111.0861 g., 0.9000 Silver 32.148 oz. ASW   **Subject:** 850th Anniversary - Moscow **Obv:** Double-headed eagle **Rev:** Kuzma Minin and Dmitri Pozharsky Monument **Note:** Illustration reduced.

Date	Mintage	F	VF	XF	Unc	BU
1997 Proof	1,000	Value: 1,000				

Y# 573   100 ROUBLES
1111.0861 g., 0.9000 Silver 32.148 oz. ASW   **Subject:** Ballet - Swan Lake **Obv:** Double-headed eagle **Rev:** Prince Siegfried dancing with Odette **Note:** Illustration reduced.

Date	Mintage	F	VF	XF	Unc	BU
1997 Proof	1,000	Value: 1,000				

Y# 588   100 ROUBLES
1111.0861 g., 0.9000 Silver 32.148 oz. ASW   **Obv:** Double-headed eagle **Rev:** 4-Masted Ship - "The Bark Krusenstern" **Note:** Illustration reduced.

Date	Mintage	F	VF	XF	Unc	BU
1997 Proof	500	Value: 1,400				

Y# 557 100 ROUBLES
17.2890 g., 0.9000 Gold 0.5002 oz. AGW **Subject:** 850th Anniversary - Moscow **Obv:** Double-headed eagle **Rev:** Yuri Dolgoruky Monument

Date	Mintage	F	VF	XF	Unc	BU
1997 Proof	5,000	Value: 500				

Y# 574 100 ROUBLES
15.5517 g., 0.9990 Gold 0.4995 oz. AGW **Subject:** Ballet - Swan Lake **Obv:** Double-headed eagle **Rev:** Prince Siegfried and Odette'd Duet

Date	Mintage	F	VF	XF	Unc	BU
1997 Proof	1,500	Value: 520				

Y# 596 100 ROUBLES
15.5517 g., 0.9990 Gold 0.4995 oz. AGW **Series:** Wildlife **Obv:** Double-headed eagle **Rev:** Polar bear on ice flow

Date	Mintage	F	VF	XF	Unc	BU
1997 Proof	1,000	Value: 525				

Note: Notice the face on the bear's hind quarter

Y# 623 100 ROUBLES
15.7200 g., 0.9990 Gold 0.5049 oz. AGW **Obv:** Double-headed eagle **Rev:** Serge Julievech Witte

Date	Mintage	F	VF	XF	Unc	BU
1997 Proof	1,000	Value: 520				

Y# 699 100 ROUBLES
1111.1200 g., 0.9000 Silver 32.149 oz. ASW, 100 mm. **Subject:** Russian Ballet **Obv:** Double-headed eagle **Rev:** Raymonda wedding scene **Edge:** Reeded **Note:** Illustration reduced.

Date	Mintage	F	VF	XF	Unc	BU
1999(sp) Proof	1,000	Value: 1,200				

Y# 358 150 ROUBLES
15.5517 g., 0.9990 Platinum 0.4995 oz. APW **Subject:** Naval Battle of Chesme **Obv:** Double-headed eagle **Rev:** Two battle ships

Date	Mintage	F	VF	XF	Unc	BU
1992 Proof	3,000	Value: 1,000				

Y# 397 150 ROUBLES
15.5517 g., 0.9990 Platinum 0.4995 oz. APW **Subject:** Ballet **Obv:** Double-headed eagle **Rev:** Ballerina

Date	Mintage	F	VF	XF	Unc	BU
1993 Proof	750	Value: 1,000				

Y# 455 150 ROUBLES
15.5517 g., 0.9990 Platinum 0.4995 oz. APW **Obv:** Double-headed eagle **Rev:** Igor Stravinsky

Date	Mintage	F	VF	XF	Unc	BU
1993 Proof	3,000	Value: 1,000				

Y# 519 150 ROUBLES
15.5517 g., 0.9990 Platinum 0.4995 oz. APW **Subject:** First Global Circumnavigation **Obv:** Double-headed eagle **Rev:** Sloops - Nadyezdha and Neva

Date	Mintage	F	VF	XF	Unc	BU
1993 Proof	2,500	Value: 1,000				

Y# 430 150 ROUBLES
15.5517 g., 0.9990 Platinum 0.4995 oz. APW **Subject:** Bolshoi Ballet **Obv:** Double-headed eagle **Rev:** Ballerina

Date	Mintage	F	VF	XF	Unc	BU
1994 Proof	900	Value: 1,100				

Y# 523 150 ROUBLES
15.5517 g., 0.9990 Platinum 0.4995 oz. APW **Subject:** First Global Circumnavigation **Obv:** Double-headed eagle **Rev:** Sloops - "Mirny" and "Vostok"

Date	Mintage	F	VF	XF	Unc	BU
1994 Proof	4,000	Value: 1,000				

Y# 533 150 ROUBLES
15.5517 g., 0.9990 Platinum 0.4995 oz. APW **Subject:** Michail Alexandrowich Vrubel - The Demon **Obv:** Double-headed eagle **Rev:** Michail Alexandrowich Vrubel - The Demon

Date	Mintage	F	VF	XF	Unc	BU
1994 Proof	3,000	Value: 1,000				

Y# 444 150 ROUBLES
15.5517 g., 0.9990 Platinum 0.4995 oz. APW **Subject:** Ballet - Sleeping Beauty **Obv:** Double-headed eagle **Rev:** Male dancer

Date	Mintage	F	VF	XF	Unc	BU
1995 Proof	900	Value: 1,000				

Y# 503 150 ROUBLES
15.5517 g., 0.9990 Platinum 0.4995 oz. APW **Subject:** Battle of the Neva River in 1240 **Obv:** Double-headed eagle **Rev:** Armored equestrians fighting

Date	Mintage	F	VF	XF	Unc	BU
1995 Proof	3,000	Value: 1,000				

Y# 413 200 ROUBLES
31.1035 g., 0.9990 Gold 0.9990 oz. AGW **Series:** Wildlife **Obv:** Double-headed eagle **Rev:** Bear with cub

Date	Mintage	F	VF	XF	Unc	BU
1993 Proof	1,000	Value: 1,200				

Y# 527 200 ROUBLES
31.1035 g., 0.9990 Gold 0.9990 oz. AGW **Series:** Wildlife **Obv:** Double-headed eagle **Rev:** Two sables

Date	Mintage	F	VF	XF	Unc	BU
1994 Proof	2,000	Value: 1,200				

Y# 500 200 ROUBLES
31.1035 g., 0.9990 Gold 0.9990 oz. AGW **Series:** Wildlife **Obv:** Double-headed eagle **Rev:** Seated lynx

Date	Mintage	F	VF	XF	Unc	BU
1995 Proof	1,750	Value: 1,250				

Y# 540 200 ROUBLES
31.1035 g., 0.9990 Gold 0.9990 oz. AGW **Series:** Wildlife **Obv:** Double-headed eagle **Rev:** Amur tiger

Date	Mintage	F	VF	XF	Unc	BU
1996 Proof	1,000	Value: 1,200				

Y# 598   200 ROUBLES
31.1035 g., 0.9990 Gold 0.9990 oz. AGW **Series:** Wildlife
Obv: Double-headed eagle **Rev:** Seated polar bear

Date	Mintage	F	VF	XF	Unc	BU
1997 Proof	1,000	Value: 1,100				

Y# 589   1000 ROUBLES
155.5000 g., 0.9990 Gold 4.9942 oz. AGW **Obv:** Double-headed eagle **Rev:** The Bark "Krusenstern" - 4-masted ship
Note: Photo reduced.

Date	Mintage	F	VF	XF	Unc	BU
1997 Proof	250	Value: 5,000				

Y# 541   10000 ROUBLES
1111.0861 g., 0.9990 Gold 35.685 oz. AGW, 100 mm.
Series: Wildlife **Obv:** Double-headed eagle **Rev:** Amur tiger with two cubs **Note:** Illustration reduced.

Date	Mintage	F	VF	XF	Unc	BU
1996 Proof	100	Value: 35,000				

Y# 599   10000 ROUBLES
1111.0861 g., 0.9990 Gold 35.685 oz. AGW, 100 mm.
Series: Wildlife **Obv:** Double-headed eagle **Rev:** Seated polar bear with two cubs **Note:** Illustration reduced.

Date	Mintage	F	VF	XF	Unc	BU
1997 Proof	100	Value: 35,000				

REFORM COINAGE
January 1, 1998

1,000 Old Roubles = 1 New Rouble

Y# 600   KOPEK
1.5000 g., Copper-Nickel Plated Steel, 15.5 mm. **Obv:** St. George
Obv. Leg.: БАНК РОССИИ **Rev:** Value above vine sprig
Edge: Plain

Date	Mintage	F	VF	XF	Unc	BU
1997M	—	—	—	—	0.30	0.40
1997СП	—	—	—	—	0.30	0.40
1998M	—	—	—	—	0.30	0.40
1998СП	—	—	—	—	0.30	0.40
1999M	—	—	—	—	0.30	0.40
1999СП	—	—	—	—	0.30	0.40
2000M	—	—	—	—	0.30	0.40
2000СП	—	—	—	—	0.30	0.40

Y# 601   5 KOPEKS
2.5000 g., Copper-Nickel Clad Steel, 18.5 mm. **Obv:** St. George
Obv. Leg.: БАНК РОССИИ **Rev:** Value above vine sprig
Edge: Plain

Date	Mintage	F	VF	XF	Unc	BU
1997M	—	—	—	—	0.35	0.50
1997СП	—	—	—	—	0.35	0.50
1998M	—	—	—	—	0.45	0.65
1998СП	—	—	—	—	0.45	0.65
1999M	—	—	—	—	0.35	0.50
1999СП	—	—	—	—	0.35	0.50
2000M	—	—	—	—	0.35	0.50
2000СП	—	—	—	—	0.35	0.50

Y# 602   10 KOPEKS
1.9500 g., Brass, 17.5 mm. **Obv:** St. George horseback right slaying dragon **Rev:** Value above vine sprig **Edge:** Reeded

Date	Mintage	F	VF	XF	Unc	BU
1997M	—	—	—	—	0.50	0.75
1997СП	—	—	—	—	0.50	0.75
1998M	—	—	—	—	0.65	1.00
1998СП	—	—	—	—	0.65	1.00
1999M	—	—	—	—	0.50	0.75
1999СП	—	—	—	—	0.50	0.75
2000M	—	—	—	—	0.50	0.75
2000СП	—	—	—	—	0.50	0.75

Y# 603   50 KOPEKS
2.9000 g., Brass, 19.5 mm. **Obv:** St. George on horseback slaying dragon right **Rev:** Value above vine sprig **Edge:** Reeded

Date	Mintage	F	VF	XF	Unc	BU
1997M	—	—	—	—	0.75	1.00
1997СП	—	—	—	—	0.75	1.00
1998M	—	—	—	—	1.00	1.50
1998СП	—	—	—	—	1.00	1.50
1999M	—	—	—	—	0.75	1.00
1999СП	—	—	—	—	0.75	1.00

Y# 604   ROUBLE
3.2500 g., Copper-Nickel-Zinc, 20.6 mm. **Obv:** Double-headed eagle **Rev:** Value **Edge:** Reeded

Date	Mintage	F	VF	XF	Unc	BU
1997M	—	—	—	—	1.00	1.50
1997СП	—	—	—	—	1.00	1.50
1998M	—	—	—	—	1.00	1.50
1998CM	—	—	—	—	1.00	1.50
1999M	—	—	—	—	1.00	1.50
1999CM	—	—	—	—	1.00	1.50

Y# 614   ROUBLE
8.5300 g., 0.9250 Silver 0.2537 oz. ASW **Series:** World Youth Games **Obv:** Double-headed eagle **Rev:** Female tennis player

Date	Mintage	F	VF	XF	Unc	BU
1998 Proof	25,000	Value: 30.00				

Y# 615   ROUBLE
8.5300 g., 0.9250 Silver 0.2537 oz. ASW **Series:** World Youth Games **Obv:** Double headed eagle **Rev:** Female-gymnast

Date	Mintage	F	VF	XF	Unc	BU
1998 Proof	25,000	Value: 30.00				

Y# 616   ROUBLE
8.5300 g., 0.9250 Silver 0.2537 oz. ASW **Series:** World Youth Games **Obv:** Double-headed eagle **Rev:** Fencer

Date	Mintage	F	VF	XF	Unc	BU
1998 Proof	25,000	Value: 30.00				

Y# 617   ROUBLE
8.5300 g., 0.9250 Silver 0.2537 oz. ASW **Series:** World Youth Games **Obv:** Double-headed eagle **Rev:** Hammer thrower

Date	Mintage	F	VF	XF	Unc	BU
1998 Proof	25,000	Value: 30.00				

Y# 618   ROUBLE
8.5300 g., 0.9250 Silver 0.2537 oz. ASW **Series:** World Youth Games **Obv:** Double-headed eagle **Rev:** Female gymnast

Date	Mintage	F	VF	XF	Unc	BU
1998 Proof	25,000	Value: 30.00				

Y# 619   ROUBLE
8.5300 g., 0.9250 Silver 0.2537 oz. ASW **Series:** World Youth Games **Obv:** Double-headed eagle **Rev:** Volleyball player

Date	Mintage	F	VF	XF	Unc	BU
1998 Proof	25,000	Value: 30.00				

Y# 628   ROUBLE
17.5500 g., 0.9000 Silver 0.5078 oz. ASW **Series:** Wildlife
•**Obv:** Double-headed eagle **Rev:** Far Eastern Skink

Date	Mintage	F	VF	XF	Unc	BU
1998 Proof	15,000	Value: 50.00				

Y# 629   ROUBLE
17.5500 g., 0.9000 Silver 0.5078 oz. ASW **Series:** Wildlife
Obv: Double-headed eagle **Rev:** Lavtev Walrus

Date	Mintage	F	VF	XF	Unc	BU
1998 Proof	15,000	Value: 55.00				

Y# 630   ROUBLE
17.5500 g., 0.9000 Silver 0.5078 oz. ASW **Series:** Wildlife
Obv: Double-headed eagle **Rev:** Emperor Goose

Date	Mintage	F	VF	XF	Unc	BU
1998 Proof	15,000	Value: 55.00				

Y# 640   ROUBLE
Copper-Nickel-Zinc, 20.5 mm. **Obv:** Double-headed eagle
Rev: Stylized head of Pushkin left **Edge:** Reeded

Date	Mintage	F	VF	XF	Unc	BU
1999M	5,000,000	—	—	—	0.75	1.25
1999CM	5,000,000	—	—	—	0.75	1.25

Y# 641   ROUBLE
17.4400 g., 0.9000 Silver 0.5046 oz. ASW   **Series:** Wildlife
Obv: Double-headed eagle **Rev:** Daurian Hedgehog

Date	Mintage	F	VF	XF	Unc	BU
1999 Proof	15,000	Value: 55.00				

Y# 642   ROUBLE
17.4400 g., 0.9000 Silver 0.5046 oz. ASW   **Series:** Wildlife
Obv: Double-headed eagle **Rev:** Caucasian viper

Date	Mintage	F	VF	XF	Unc	BU
1999 Proof	15,000	Value: 55.00				

Y# 643   ROUBLE
17.4400 g., 0.9000 Silver 0.5046 oz. ASW   **Series:** Wildlife
Obv: Double-headed eagle **Rev:** Ross's Gull standing on shore

Date	Mintage	F	VF	XF	Unc	BU
1999 Proof	15,000	Value: 55.00				

Y# 719   ROUBLE
17.4400 g., 0.9000 Silver 0.5046 oz. ASW, 33 mm.
Subject: Wildlife **Obv:** Double-headed eagle **Rev:** Two Black-hooded cranes **Edge:** Reeded

Date	Mintage	F	VF	XF	Unc	BU
2000СП Proof	3,000	Value: 200				

Y# 720   ROUBLE
17.4400 g., 0.9000 Silver 0.5046 oz. ASW **Obv:** Double-headed eagle **Rev:** Leopard Runner snake

Date	Mintage	F	VF	XF	Unc	BU
2000СП Proof	3,000	Value: 200				

Y# 721   ROUBLE
17.4400 g., 0.9000 Silver 0.5046 oz. ASW **Obv:** Double-headed eagle **Rev:** Russian Desman

Date	Mintage	F	VF	XF	Unc	BU
2000СП Proof	3,000	Value: 200				

Y# 605   2 ROUBLES
5.1000 g., Copper-Nickel-Zinc, 23 mm. **Obv:** Double-headed eagle
Rev: Value and vine sprig **Edge:** Alternating reeded and smooth

Date	Mintage	F	VF	XF	Unc	BU
1997M	—	—	—	—	2.00	3.00
1997CM	—	—	—	—	2.00	3.00
1998M	—	—	—	—	2.00	3.00
1998CM	—	—	—	—	2.00	3.00
1999M	—	—	—	—	2.00	4.00
1999CM	—	—	—	—	2.00	4.00

Y# 607   2 ROUBLES
16.8108 g., 0.9250 Silver 0.4999 oz. ASW   **Subject:** 100th
Anniversary - Sergei Eisenstein **Obv:** Double-headed eagle
Rev: Head facing on movie screen with camera on stand at left

Date	Mintage	F	VF	XF	Unc	BU
1998	15,000	—	—	—	27.50	30.00

Y# 608   2 ROUBLES
16.8108 g., 0.9250 Silver 0.4999 oz. ASW   **Subject:** 50th
Anniversary - Sergei Eisenstein **Obv:** Double-headed eagle
Rev: Figure looking at film strip, ship in background

Date	Mintage	F	VF	XF	Unc	BU
1998	15,000	—	—	—	27.50	30.00

Y# 609   2 ROUBLES
16.8108 g., 0.9250 Silver 0.4999 oz. ASW **Obv:** Double-headed
eagle **Rev:** K.S. Stanslavski

Date	Mintage	F	VF	XF	Unc	BU
1998	15,000	—	—	—	27.50	30.00

Y# 610   2 ROUBLES
16.8108 g., 0.9250 Silver 0.4999 oz. ASW **Obv:** Double-headed
eagle **Rev:** Maxim Gorky play - Stanislavsky method

Date	Mintage	F	VF	XF	Unc	BU
1998	15,000	—	—	—	27.50	30.00

Y# 620   2 ROUBLES
17.0000 g., 0.9250 Silver 0.5055 oz. ASW **Obv:** Double-headed
eagle **Rev:** Victor Mikhailovich Vasnetsov - 3 ancient warriors

Date	Mintage	F	VF	XF	Unc	BU
1998	15,000	—	—	—	27.50	30.00

Y# 621   2 ROUBLES
17.0000 g., 0.9250 Silver 0.5055 oz. ASW **Obv:** Double-headed
eagle **Rev:** Victor Mikhailovich Vasnetsov - 3 seated figures

Date	Mintage	F	VF	XF	Unc	BU
1998	15,000	—	—	—	27.50	30.00

Y# 649   2 ROUBLES
17.0000 g., 0.9250 Silver 0.5055 oz. ASW   **Subject:** K. L.
Khetagurov 1859-1906 **Obv:** Double-headed eagle **Rev:** Portrait
with mountain tops and buildings

Date	Mintage	F	VF	XF	Unc	BU
1999 Proof	3,000	Value: 400				

Y# 650   2 ROUBLES
17.0000 g., 0.9250 Silver 0.5055 oz. ASW   **Subject:** N. K. Rerikh
1874-1947 **Obv:** Double-headed eagle **Rev:** Painter with
mountains in the background

Date	Mintage	F	VF	XF	Unc	BU
1999 Proof	15,000	Value: 25.00				

Y# 651   2 ROUBLES
17.0000 g., 0.9250 Silver 0.5055 oz. ASW   **Subject:** The Human
Acts by Rerikh. **Obv:** Double-headed eagle **Rev:** Detail from
painting, artist's portrait above

Date	Mintage	F	VF	XF	Unc	BU
1999 Proof	15,000	Value: 25.00				

Y# 652   2 ROUBLES
17.0000 g., 0.9250 Silver 0.5055 oz. ASW   **Subject:** K. P. Bryulov
1799-1852 **Obv:** Double-headed eagle **Rev:** Half length bust facing

Date	Mintage	F	VF	XF	Unc	BU
1999 Proof	15,000	Value: 20.00				

Y# 653   2 ROUBLES
17.0000 g., 0.9250 Silver 0.5055 oz. ASW   **Subject:** The Last Day of Pompei **Obv:** Double-headed eagle **Rev:** Detail from painting, portrait in exergue

Date	Mintage	F	VF	XF	Unc	BU
1999 Proof	15,000	Value: 20.00				

Y# 654   2 ROUBLES
17.0000 g., 0.9250 Silver 0.5055 oz. ASW   **Subject:** I.P. Pavlov **Obv:** Double-headed eagle **Rev:** Half bust 1/4 left, dog, books, cap, and gown

Date	Mintage	F	VF	XF	Unc	BU
1999 Proof	15,000	Value: 18.50				

Y# 655   2 ROUBLES
17.0000 g., 0.9250 Silver 0.5055 oz. ASW   **Subject:** I.P. Pavlov **Obv:** Double-headed eagle **Rev:** Seated figure left and silence tower

Date	Mintage	F	VF	XF	Unc	BU
1999 Proof	15,000	Value: 18.50				

Y# 659   2 ROUBLES
17.0000 g., 0.9250 Silver 0.5055 oz. ASW   **Subject:** Eugeny Abramovich Baratynsky **Obv:** Double-headed eagle **Rev:** Cameo to right of scenery **Edge:** Reeded

Date	Mintage	F	VF	XF	Unc	BU
2000 Proof	5,000	Value: 75.00				

Y# 660   2 ROUBLES
17.0000 g., 0.9250 Silver 0.5055 oz. ASW   **Subject:** F. A. Vassiliyev **Obv:** Double-headed eagle **Rev:** Cameo to right of scenery

Date	Mintage	F	VF	XF	Unc	BU
2000 Proof	5,000	Value: 50.00				

Y# 662   2 ROUBLES
17.0000 g., 0.9250 Silver 0.5055 oz. ASW   **Subject:** S. V. Kovaleuskaya **Obv:** Double-headed eagle **Rev:** Cameo to left of academic items

Date	Mintage	F	VF	XF	Unc	BU
2000 Proof	5,000	Value: 45.00				

Y# 663   2 ROUBLES
5.1000 g., Copper-Nickel-Zinc, 23 mm.   **Series:** World War II **Obv:** Value **Rev:** Infantry assault at Stalingrad **Edge:** Reeded and plain sections

Date	Mintage	F	VF	XF	Unc	BU
2000СП	10,000,000	—	—	—	2.00	3.00

Y# 664   2 ROUBLES
Copper-Nickel-Zinc, 23 mm.   **Obv:** Value at left of vine sprig **Rev:** Cannon manufacturing scene in Tula **Edge:** Alternating reeded and smooth

Date	Mintage	F	VF	XF	Unc	BU
2000M	10,000,000	—	—	—	2.00	3.00

Y# 665   2 ROUBLES
Copper-Nickel-Zinc, 23 mm.   **Obv:** Value at left of vine sprig **Rev:** Truck-mounted rocket launchers in Smolensk **Edge:** Alternating reeded and smooth

Date	Mintage	F	VF	XF	Unc	BU
2000M	10,000,000	—	—	—	2.00	3.00

Y# 666   2 ROUBLES
5.1000 g., Copper-Nickel-Zinc, 23 mm.   **Obv:** Value at left of vine sprig **Rev:** Murmansk ship convoy **Edge:** Alternating reeded and smooth

Date	Mintage	F	VF	XF	Unc	BU
2000M	10,000,000	—	—	—	2.00	3.00

Y# 667   2 ROUBLES
Copper-Nickel-Zinc, 23 mm.   **Obv:** Value at left of vine sprig **Rev:** Defense of Moscow scene **Edge:** Alternating reeded and smooth

Date	Mintage	F	VF	XF	Unc	BU
2000M	10,000,000	—	—	—	2.00	3.00

Y# 668   2 ROUBLES
Copper-Nickel-Zinc, 23 mm.   **Obv:** Value at left of vine sprig **Rev:** Marine landing scene in Novorusiisk **Edge:** Alternating reeded and smooth

Date	Mintage	F	VF	XF	Unc	BU
2000CM	10,000,000	—	—	—	2.00	3.00

Y# 669   2 ROUBLES
Copper-Nickel-Zinc, 23 mm.   **Obv:** Value at left of vine sprig **Rev:** Siege of Leningrad truck convoy scene **Edge:** Alternating reeded and smooth

Date	Mintage	F	VF	XF	Unc	BU
2000СП	10,000,000	—	—	—	2.00	3.00

Y# 704   2 ROUBLES
17.4400 g., 0.9250 Silver 0.5186 oz. ASW, 33 mm.   **Subject:** M.I. Chigorin **Obv:** Double-headed eagle **Rev:** Cameo to left of chess pieces **Edge:** Reeded

Date	Mintage	F	VF	XF	Unc	BU
2000(sp) Proof	5,000	Value: 45.00				

Y# 624   3 ROUBLES
34.5600 g., 0.9000 Silver 1.0000 oz. ASW   **Obv:** Double-headed eagle **Rev:** Soldier Devydov

Date	Mintage	F	VF	XF	Unc	BU
1998 Proof	15,000	Value: 50.00				

Y# 625   3 ROUBLES
34.5600 g., 0.9000 Silver 1.0000 oz. ASW   **Obv:** Double-headed eagle **Rev:** "Russian Sosaveta" sculpture

Date	Mintage	F	VF	XF	Unc	BU
1998 Proof	15,000	Value: 50.00				

Y# 626   3 ROUBLES
34.5600 g., 0.9000 Silver 1.0000 oz. ASW   **Obv:** Double-headed eagle **Rev:** Archangel's head within square

Date	Mintage	F	VF	XF	Unc	BU
1998 Proof	15,000	Value: 50.00				

Y# 627   3 ROUBLES
34.5600 g., 0.9000 Silver 1.0000 oz. ASW   **Obv:** Double-headed eagle **Rev:** Merchant woman drinking tea within square

Date	Mintage	F	VF	XF	Unc	BU
1998 Proof	15,000	Value: 50.00				

Y# 631 3 ROUBLES
34.5600 g., 0.9000 Silver 1.0000 oz. ASW **Subject:** Nilo Stolobenskaya Hermitage **Obv:** Double-headed eagle **Rev:** Monastery, ships, boats and kneeling Saint at upper left

Date	Mintage	F	VF	XF	Unc	BU
1998 Proof	15,000	Value: 75.00				

Y# 632 3 ROUBLES
34.5600 g., 0.9000 Silver 1.0000 oz. ASW **Obv:** Double-headed eagle **Rev:** Church view from bell tower

Date	Mintage	F	VF	XF	Unc	BU
1998 Proof	5,000	Value: 500				

Y# 633 3 ROUBLES
34.8800 g., 0.9000 Silver 1.0092 oz. ASW **Subject:** Russian Human Rights Year **Obv:** Double-headed eagle **Rev:** Document, people, and map **Edge:** Reeded

Date	Mintage	F	VF	XF	Unc	BU
1998 Proof	15,000	Value: 47.50				

Y# 634 3 ROUBLES
34.7700 g., 0.9000 Silver 1.0061 oz. ASW **Subject:** 275th Anniversary - St. Petersburg University **Obv:** Double-headed eagle **Rev:** Four heads facing in front of building

Date	Mintage	F	VF	XF	Unc	BU
1999 Proof	15,000	Value: 50.00				

Y# 635 3 ROUBLES
34.7300 g., 0.9000 Silver 1.0049 oz. ASW **Obv:** Double-headed eagle **Rev:** Mardjany Mosque in Kazan

Date	Mintage	F	VF	XF	Unc	BU
1999 Proof	15,000	Value: 57.50				

Y# 636 3 ROUBLES
34.7300 g., 0.9000 Silver 1.0049 oz. ASW **Subject:** 200th Birthday - A. S. Pushkin **Obv:** Double headed eagle **Rev:** Seated figure at desk facing 1/4 left

Date	Mintage	F	VF	XF	Unc	BU
1999 Proof	15,000	Value: 55.00				

Y# 637 3 ROUBLES
34.7300 g., 0.9000 Silver 1.0049 oz. ASW **Subject:** 200th Birthday - A. S. Pushkin **Obv:** Double-headed eagle **Rev:** Standing 1/2 length figure right

Date	Mintage	F	VF	XF	Unc	BU
1999 Proof	15,000	Value: 55.00				

Y# 638 3 ROUBLES
34.7300 g., 0.9000 Silver 1.0049 oz. ASW **Subject:** First Tibet Exhibition 1879-1880 **Obv:** Double-headed eagle **Rev:** Men on horseback, animals at corners

Date	Mintage	F	VF	XF	Unc	BU
1999 Proof	15,000	Value: 42.50				

Y# 639 3 ROUBLES
34.7300 g., 0.9000 Silver 1.0049 oz. ASW **Subject:** Second Tibet Exhibition 1883-1885 **Obv:** Double-headed eagle **Rev:** Camp scene

Date	Mintage	F	VF	XF	Unc	BU
1999 Proof	15,000	Value: 42.50				

Y# 644 3 ROUBLES
34.7100 g., 0.9000 Silver 1.0043 oz. ASW **Subject:** Science Academy. **Obv:** Double-headed eagle **Rev:** Allegorical figure, building, portraits, crowned double headed eagle

Date	Mintage	F	VF	XF	Unc	BU
1999 Proof	5,000	Value: 350				

Y# 645 3 ROUBLES
34.7100 g., 0.9000 Silver 1.0043 oz. ASW **Subject:** Estada Kuskovo Palace **Obv:** Double-headed eagle **Rev:** Palace from three perspectives

Date	Mintage	F	VF	XF	Unc	BU
1999 Proof	15,000	Value: 60.00				

Y# 646 3 ROUBLES
34.7100 g., 0.9000 Silver 1.0043 oz. ASW **Subject:** Juryev Monastery, Novgorod **Obv:** Double-headed eagle **Rev:** Building view and detail from interior

Date	Mintage	F	VF	XF	Unc	BU
1999 Proof	15,000	Value: 75.00				

Y# 647 3 ROUBLES
34.8800 g., 0.9000 Silver 1.0092 oz. ASW **Subject:** 50th Anniversary - Diplomacy with China **Obv:** Double-headed eagle **Rev:** Moscow Kremlin and Tiananmen Gate

Date	Mintage	F	VF	XF	Unc	BU
1999 Proof	3,000	Value: 425				

Y# 657 3 ROUBLES
34.7300 g., 0.9000 Silver 1.0049 oz. ASW **Subject:** Ballet **Obv:** Double-headed eagle **Rev:** Sword fight

Date	Mintage	F	VF	XF	Unc	BU
1999 Proof	10,000	Value: 45.00				

Y# 658 3 ROUBLES
34.7300 g., 0.9000 Silver 1.0049 oz. ASW **Subject:** Ballet **Obv:** Double-headed eagle **Rev:** Couple dancing, Arabic soldiers in background

Date	Mintage	F	VF	XF	Unc	BU
1999 Proof	10,000	Value: 45.00				

Y# 690 3 ROUBLES
34.7300 g., 0.9000 Silver 1.0049 oz. ASW, 38.8 mm. **Subject:** Ufa Friendship Monument **Obv:** Double-headed eagle **Rev:** Five figures and monument **Edge:** Reeded

Date	Mintage	F	VF	XF	Unc	BU
1999 Proof	3,000	Value: 65.00				

Y# 661 3 ROUBLES
34.8800 g., 0.9000 Silver 1.0092 oz. ASW **Subject:** World Ice Hockey Championship **Obv:** Double-headed eagle **Rev:** Two hockey players **Edge:** Reeded

Date	Mintage	F	VF	XF	Unc	BU
2000 Proof	3,000	Value: 600				

Y# 671 3 ROUBLES
34.7600 g., 0.9000 Silver 1.0058 oz. ASW **Series:** Olympics **Obv:** Double-headed eagle **Rev:** 2000 Olympic design in front of map **Edge:** Reeded

Date	Mintage	F	VF	XF	Unc	BU
2000 Proof	5,000	Value: 200				

Y# 673 3 ROUBLES
34.6700 g., 0.9990 Silver 1.1135 oz. ASW **Subject:** Soccer **Obv:** Double-headed eagle **Rev:** Two soccer players, map, and net **Edge:** Reeded

Date	Mintage	F	VF	XF	Unc	BU
2000 Proof	3,000	Value: 175				

Y# 674 3 ROUBLES
34.9400 g., 0.9000 Silver 1.0110 oz. ASW **Series:** WWII **Subject:** 55th Anniversary - WWII **Obv:** Seated soldier **Rev:** Soviet Order of Glory **Edge:** Lettered **Edge:** BANK of RUSSIA THREE ROUBLES 2000

Date	Mintage	F	VF	XF	Unc	BU
2000 Proof	5,000	Value: 70.00				

Y# 705 3 ROUBLES
34.8800 g., 0.9000 Silver 1.0092 oz. ASW, 39 mm. **Subject:** St. Nicholas Monastery **Obv:** Double-headed eagle **Rev:** Saint and buildings **Edge:** Reeded

Date	Mintage	F	VF	XF	Unc	BU
2000(m) Proof	5,000	Value: 65.00				

Y# 706 3 ROUBLES
34.8800 g., 0.9000 Silver 1.0092 oz. ASW **Subject:** Novgorod Kremlin **Obv:** Double-headed eagle **Rev:** Buildings

Date	Mintage	F	VF	XF	Unc	BU
2000(m) Proof	5,000	Value: 60.00				

Y# 707 3 ROUBLES
34.8800 g., 0.9000 Silver 1.0092 oz. ASW **Subject:** City of Pushkin **Obv:** Double-headed eagle **Rev:** Park and city view

Date	Mintage	F	VF	XF	Unc	BU
2000(m) Proof	5,000	Value: 75.00				

Y# 708 3 ROUBLES
34.8800 g., 0.9000 Silver 1.0092 oz. ASW, 39 mm. **Series:** Third Millennium **Subject:** Science **Obv:** Double-headed eagle **Rev:** Astronaut, atomic elements chart, etc. **Edge:** Reeded

Date	Mintage	F	VF	XF	Unc	BU
2000(m) Proof	5,000	Value: 45.00				

Y# 709 3 ROUBLES
34.8800 g., 0.9000 Silver 1.0092 oz. ASW **Series:** Third Millennium **Subject:** Human Role **Obv:** Double-headed eagle **Rev:** People between cog wheel and computer

Date	Mintage	F	VF	XF	Unc	BU
2000(m) Proof	5,000	Value: 45.00				

Y# 714 3 ROUBLES
34.8800 g., 0.9000 Silver 1.0092 oz. ASW **Subject:** 140th Anniversary - State Bank of Russia **Obv:** Double-headed eagle **Rev:** Seated allegorical woman

Date	Mintage	F	VF	XF	Unc	BU
2000(m) Proof	3,000	Value: 475				

Y# 716 3 ROUBLES
34.8800 g., 1.0093 Silver 1.1318 oz. ASW **Subject:** Field Marshal Suvorov in Switzerland **Obv:** Double-headed eagle **Rev:** Battle scene

Date	Mintage	F	VF	XF	Unc	BU
2000(sp) Proof	5,000	Value: 70.00				

Y# 722 3 ROUBLES
34.8800 g., 0.9000 Silver 1.0092 oz. ASW **Subject:** Snow Leopard **Obv:** Double-headed eagle **Rev:** Leopard on log

Date	Mintage	F	VF	XF	Unc	BU
2000(m) Proof	5,000	Value: 75.00				

Y# 606 5 ROUBLES
6.5000 g., Copper-Nickel Clad Copper, 25 mm. **Obv:** Double-headed eagle **Rev:** Value at left of vine sprig **Edge:** Reeded and plain sections

Date	Mintage	F	VF	XF	Unc	BU
1997M	—	—	—	—	3.00	4.00
1997СП	—	—	—	—	3.00	4.00
1998M	—	—	—	—	3.00	4.00
1998СП	—	—	—	—	3.00	4.00

Y# 695 10 ROUBLES
1.5500 g., 0.9990 Gold 0.0498 oz. AGW, 12 mm. **Subject:** Russian Ballet **Obv:** Double-headed eagle **Rev:** Standing knight within flower wreath **Edge:** Reeded

Date	Mintage	F	VF	XF	Unc	BU
1999(m) Proof	2,500	Value: 70.00				

Y# 670 10 ROUBLES
8.2600 g., Bi-Metallic Copper-Nickel center in Brass ring, 27 mm. **Series:** WWII **Subject:** 55th Anniversary - Victorious Conclusion of WWII **Obv:** Value **Rev:** Infantry officer within star design **Edge:** Reeded and lettered

Date	Mintage	F	VF	XF	Unc	BU
2000(sp)	10,000,000	—	—	—	4.00	7.00
2000(m)	10,000,000	—	—	—	4.00	7.00

Y# 691 25 ROUBLES
173.2900 g., 0.9000 Silver 5.0141 oz. ASW, 60 mm. **Subject:** Alexander Pushkin **Obv:** Double-headed eagle **Rev:** Walking figure with hat and cane **Edge:** Reeded **Note:** Illustration reduced.

Date	Mintage	F	VF	XF	Unc	BU
1999(m) Proof	3,000	Value: 225				

Y# 696 25 ROUBLES
173.2900 g., 0.9000 Silver 5.0141 oz. ASW, 60 mm. **Subject:** Russian Ballet **Obv:** Double-headed eagle **Rev:** Raymonda and the Knight dance scene **Edge:** Reeded.

Date	Mintage	F	VF	XF	Unc	BU
1999(m) Proof	3,000	Value: 225				

Y# 701 25 ROUBLES
173.2900 g., 0.9000 Silver 5.0141 oz. ASW, 60 mm.
Subject: Russian Explorers: N.M. Przhevalsky **Obv:** Double-headed eagle **Rev:** Caravan in center of other designs
Edge: Reeded **Note:** Illustration reduced.

Date	Mintage	F	VF	XF	Unc	BU
1999(sp) Proof	3,000	Value: 225				

Y# 697 25 ROUBLES
3.2000 g., 0.9990 Gold 0.1028 oz. AGW, 16 mm.
Subject: Russian Ballet **Obv:** Double-headed eagle
Rev: Dancing Saracen **Edge:** Reeded

Date	Mintage	F	VF	XF	Unc	BU
1999(sp) Proof	2,000	Value: 175				

Y# 710 25 ROUBLES
173.2900 g., 0.9000 Silver 5.0141 oz. ASW, 60 mm.
Series: Third Millennium **Subject:** Education **Obv:** Double-headed eagle **Rev:** Ancient monk and modern student
Edge: Reeded **Note:** Illustration reduced.

Date	Mintage	F	VF	XF	Unc	BU
2000(m) Proof	1,000	Value: 650				

Y# 715 25 ROUBLES
173.2900 g., 0.9000 Silver 5.0141 oz. ASW, 60 mm.
Subject: State Bank of Russia 140th Anniversary **Obv:** Double-headed eagle **Rev:** Document, portrait and building
Edge: Reeded **Note:** Illustration reduced.

Date	Mintage	F	VF	XF	Unc	BU
2000(m) Proof	1,000	Value: 1,000				

Y# 717 25 ROUBLES
173.2900 g., 0.9000 Silver 5.0141 oz. ASW, 60 mm.
Obv: Double-headed eagle **Rev:** Field Marshal Suvorov
Edge: Reeded **Note:** Illustration reduced.

Date	Mintage	F	VF	XF	Unc	BU
2000(m) Proof	1,000	Value: 700				

Y# 723 25 ROUBLES
173.2900 g., 0.9000 Silver 5.0141 oz. ASW, 60 mm.
Obv: Double-headed eagle **Rev:** Leopard on branch
Edge: Reeded **Note:** Illustration reduced.

Date	Mintage	F	VF	XF	Unc	BU
2000(m) Proof	1,000	Value: 550				

Y# 648 50 ROUBLES
8.7500 g., 0.9000 Gold 0.2532 oz. AGW **Subject:** 50th Anniversary - Diplomacy with China **Obv:** Double-headed eagle
Rev: Moscow Kremlin and Tiananmen Gate

Date	Mintage	F	VF	XF	Unc	BU
1999 Proof	1,000	Value: 400				

Y# 692 50 ROUBLES
8.7500 g., 0.9000 Gold 0.2532 oz. AGW, 22.6 mm. **Obv:**
Double-headed eagle **Rev:** Alexander Pushkin **Edge:** Reeded

Date	Mintage	F	VF	XF	Unc	BU
1999(m) Proof	1,500	Value: 265				

Y# 698 50 ROUBLES
8.7500 g., 0.9990 Gold 0.2810 oz. AGW, 22.6 mm.
Subject: Russian Ballet **Obv:** Double-headed eagle
Rev: Dancing figures **Edge:** Reeded

Date	Mintage	F	VF	XF	Unc	BU
1999(m) Proof	1,500	Value: 285				

Y# 702 50 ROUBLES
8.7500 g., 0.9000 Gold 0.2532 oz. AGW, 22.6 mm.
Subject: Russian Explorer N.M. Przhevalsky **Obv:** Double-headed eagle **Rev:** Armored bust 1/4 right **Edge:** Reeded

Date	Mintage	F	VF	XF	Unc	BU
1999(sp) Proof	1,500	Value: 265				

Y# 672 50 ROUBLES
8.7100 g., 0.9000 Gold 0.2520 oz. AGW **Series:** Olympics
Obv: Double-headed eagle **Rev:** Torch runner on map

Date	Mintage	F	VF	XF	Unc	BU
2000 Proof	1,000	Value: 300				

Y# 718 50 ROUBLES
8.7500 g., 0.9000 Gold 0.2532 oz. AGW, 22.6 mm.
Subject: Field Marshal Suvorov **Obv:** Double-headed eagle
Rev: Cameo above cannons **Edge:** Reeded

Date	Mintage	F	VF	XF	Unc	BU
2000(sp) Proof	500	Value: 300				

Y# 725 50 ROUBLES
7.8900 g., 0.9990 Gold 0.2534 oz. AGW, 22.6 mm.
Obv: Double-headed eagle **Rev:** Snow leopard head
Edge: Reeded

Date	Mintage	F	VF	XF	Unc	BU
2000(sp) Proof	1,000	Value: 300				

Y# 693 100 ROUBLES
1111.1200 g., 0.9000 Silver 32.149 oz. ASW, 100 mm.
Subject: Alexander Pushkin **Obv:** Double-headed eagle
Rev: Statue, monuments and buildings **Edge:** Reeded
Note: Illustration reduced.

Date	Mintage	F	VF	XF	Unc	BU
1999(m) Proof	1,000	Value: 1,250				

Y# 694 100 ROUBLES
17.4500 g., 0.9000 Gold 0.5049 oz. AGW, 30 mm.
Subject: Alexander Pushkin **Obv:** Double-headed eagle
Rev: Head 1/4 right, tree and scenes **Edge:** Reeded

Date	Mintage	F	VF	XF	Unc	BU
1999 Proof	1,000	Value: 520				

Y# 700 100 ROUBLES
15.7200 g., 0.9990 Gold 0.5049 oz. AGW, 30 mm.
Subject: Russian Ballet **Obv:** Double-headed eagle
Rev: Ballerina **Edge:** Reeded

Date	Mintage	F	VF	XF	Unc	BU
1999(sp) Proof	1,500	Value: 520				

Y# 703 100 ROUBLES
17.4500 g., 0.9000 Gold 0.5049 oz. AGW, 30 mm.
Subject: Russian Explorer N.M. Przhevalsky **Obv:** Double-headed eagle **Rev:** Two men viewing lake **Edge:** Reeded

Date	Mintage	F	VF	XF	Unc	BU
1999(sp) Proof	1,000	Value: 520				

Y# 724 100 ROUBLES
1111.1200 g., 0.9000 Silver 32.149 oz. ASW, 100 mm.
Obv: Double-headed eagle **Rev:** Two snow leopards
Edge: Reeded

Date	Mintage	F	VF	XF	Unc	BU
2000(sp) Proof	500	Value: 1,300				

Y# 711   100 ROUBLES
1111.1200 g., 0.9000 Silver 32.149 oz. ASW, 100 mm.
Subject: Russian State **Obv:** Double-headed eagle **Rev:** Mother Russia, mythological bird and map **Edge:** Reeded **Note:** Illustration reduced.

Date	Mintage	F	VF	XF	Unc	BU
2000(m) Proof	500	Value: 1,500				

Y# 729   100 ROUBLES
1111.1200 g., 0.9000 Silver 32.149 oz. ASW, 100 mm.
Subject: WWII Victory 55th Anniversary **Obv:** Russian soldier writing on Reichstag building pillar **Rev:** Conference scene **Edge:** Reeded **Note:** Illustration reduced.

Date	Mintage	F	VF	XF	Unc	BU
2000(sp) Proof	500	Value: 1,400				

Y# 713   100 ROUBLES
17.4500 g., 0.9000 Gold 0.5049 oz. AGW, 30 mm.
Subject: Department of Mining 300 Years **Obv:** Double-headed eagle **Rev:** Miner and equipment **Edge:** Reeded

Date	Mintage	F	VF	XF	Unc	BU
2000(m) Proof	1,000	Value: 520				

Y# 726   100 ROUBLES
15.7200 g., 0.9990 Gold 0.5049 oz. AGW, 30 mm. **Obv:** Double-headed eagle **Rev:** Snow leopard on branch **Edge:** Reeded

Date	Mintage	F	VF	XF	Unc	BU
2000(sp) Proof	1,000	Value: 525				

Y# 656   200 ROUBLES
3342.3899 g., 0.9000 Silver 96.710 oz. ASW **Subject:** 275th Anniversary - St. Petersburg Mint **Obv:** Double-headed eagle **Rev:** Peter the Great, mint view, coin designs, and medal of the Imperial Order **Note:** Illustration reduced.

Date	Mintage	F	VF	XF	Unc	BU
1999 Proof	150	Value: 2,150				

Y# 727   200 ROUBLES
31.3700 g., 0.9990 Gold 1.0075 oz. AGW, 33 mm. **Obv:** Double-headed eagle **Rev:** Snow leopard on branch **Edge:** Reeded

Date	Mintage	F	VF	XF	Unc	BU
2000(sp) Proof	500	Value: 1,100				

Y# 728   10000 ROUBLES
822.8449 g., 0.9990 Gold 26.427 oz. AGW, 100 mm.
Obv: Double-headed eagle **Rev:** Snow leopard with two cubs **Edge:** Reeded **Note:** Illustration reduced.

Date	Mintage	F	VF	XF	Unc	BU
2000(m) Proof	100	Value: 26,000				

PATTERNS
Including off metal strikes

KM#	Date	Mintage	Identification	Mkt Val
Pn160	1911	—	5 Kopeks. Nickel.	—
Pn161	1911	—	10 Kopeks. Nickel.	—
Pn162	1911	—	20 Kopeks. Nickel.	—
Pn163	1911	—	20 Kopeks. Nickel.	—
Pn164	1911	—	25 Kopeks. Nickel. Eagle, date below. 25 in circle.	—
Pn165	1916	—	Kopek. Copper. Dotted background in circle, date.	—
Pn166	1916	—	Kopek. Copper. Plain background.	—
Pn167	1916	—	Kopek. Copper. Value, date below.	—
Pn168	1916	—	2 Kopeks. Copper. Eagle in circle. 2 in circle, value, date below.	—
Pn169	1916	—	3 Kopeks. Copper. Eagle in circle. 3 in circle, value, date below.	—
Pn170	1916	—	5 Kopeks. Copper.	—
Pn171	1916	—	5 Roubles. Unknown Metal.	2,250
Pn172	1917	—	3 Kopeks. Copper. 8.2500 g. Plain edge. 1/2mm larger than 1916.	2,250
Pn173	1922	—	20 Kopeks. Bronze. Y#82	—
Pn174	1922	—	50 Kopeks. Silver. Plain edge. Y#89	—
Pn175	1923	—	20 Kopeks. Bronze. Y#82	250
Pn176	1923	—	20 Kopeks. Copper. Y#82	250
Pn202	1924	—	50 Kopeks. Copper-Nickel. Plain edge. Y#89; London Mint.	750
Pn203	1924	—	50 Kopeks. Copper-Nickel. Plain edge. Y#89	1,150
Pn177	1924	—	Kopek. Copper-Aluminum. Y#76	—
Pn178	1924	—	Kopek. Bronze. Y#76	—
Pn179	1924	—	Kopek. Aluminum. Y#76	—
Pn180	1924	—	Kopek. Copper-Nickel. Y#76	—
Pn181	1924	—	Kopek. Copper-Zinc. Y#76	—
		Note: Additional metals exist		
Pn182	1924	—	2 Kopeks. Copper-Aluminum. Y#77	—
Pn183	1924	—	2 Kopeks. Bronze. Y#77	—
Pn184	1924	—	2 Kopeks. Aluminum. Y#77	—
Pn185	1924	—	2 Kopeks. Copper-Nickel. Y#77	—
Pn186	1924	—	2 Kopeks. Copper-Zinc. Y#77	—
		Note: Additional metals exist		
Pn187	1924	—	3 Kopeks. Copper-Aluminum. Y#78	—
Pn188	1924	—	3 Kopeks. Bronze. Y#78	—
Pn189	1924	—	3 Kopeks. Aluminum. Y#78	—
Pn190	1924	—	3 Kopeks. Copper-Nickel. Y#78	—
Pn191	1924	—	3 Kopeks. Copper-Zinc. Y#78	—
		Note: Additional metals exist		
Pn192	1924	—	5 Kopeks. Unknown Metal.	—
Pn193	1924	—	5 Kopeks. Copper-Zinc. 12.0000 g. Y#79	—
Pn194	1924	—	5 Kopeks. Copper-Zinc. 18.0000 g. Y#79	—
Pn195	1924	—	5 Kopeks. Copper-Zinc. 20.0000 g. Y#79	—
Pn196	1924	—	10 Kopeks. Bronze. Y#86	—
Pn197	1924	—	15 Kopeks. Bronze. Y#87	—
Pn198	1924	—	15 Kopeks. Copper. Y#87	—
Pn199	1924	—	20 Kopeks. Bronze. Y#88	—
Pn200	1924	—	50 Kopeks. Bronze. Y#89	—
Pn201	1924	—	50 Kopeks. Unknown Metal. Y#89	—
Pn204	1924	—	Rouble. Aluminum. Y#90	—
		Note: There are additional 1924 patterns but information is sketchy at present		
Pn205	1925	—	1/2 Kopek. Copper-Aluminum. Y#75	—
Pn206	1925	—	1/2 Kopek. Aluminum. Y#75	—
Pn207	1925	—	1/2 Kopek. Copper-Nickel. Y#75	—
Pn208	1925	—	1/2 Kopek. Bronze. Y#75	—
Pn209	1925	—	1/2 Kopek. Copper-Zinc. Y#75	—
		Note: Additional metals exist		
Pn210	1925	—	10 Kopeks. Nickel. Y#86	—
Pn211	1925	—	10 Kopeks. Aluminum-Bronze. Y#86	—
Pn212	1925	—	15 Kopeks. Nickel. Y#87	—
Pn213	1925	—	15 Kopeks. Copper. Y#87	—
Pn214	1925	—	15 Kopeks. Aluminum-Bronze. Y#87	—
Pn215	1925	—	20 Kopeks. Nickel. Y#88	—
Pn216	1925	—	20 Kopeks. Copper. Y#88	—
Pn217	1925	—	20 Kopeks. Aluminum-Bronze. Y#88	—
Pn218	1925	—	50 Kopeks. Silver. Plain edge. Y#89.2	—
Pn219	1925	—	50 Kopeks. Bronze. Y#89.2	—
Pn221	1925	—	Chervonetz. Copper. Y#85	—
Pn220	1925	—	50 Kopeks. Lead. Y#89.2	275
Pn222	1926	—	3 Kopeks. Aluminum.	—
Pn223	1926	—	3 Kopeks. Aluminum.	—
Pn224	1926	—	3 Kopeks. Unknown Metal. Y#100	—
Pn225	1929	—	10 Kopeks. Nickel.	—
Pn226	1929	—	15 Kopeks. Silver. 35% Silver; Y#87	—
Pn227	1929	—	50 Kopeks. Unknown Metal.	—
Pn228	1931	—	2 Kopeks. Copper. Y#92	—
Pn229	1931	—	3 Kopeks. Copper. Y#93	—
Pn230	1931	—	10 Kopeks. Unknown Metal. Y#93	—
Pn231	1931	—	20 Kopeks. Bronze. Y#97	—
Pn232	1932	—	3 Kopeks. Copper. KM#93	—
		Note: Additional metals exist		
Pn233	1932	—	15 Kopeks. Unknown Metal. Y#96	—
Pn234	1933	—	10 Kopeks. Unknown Metal. Similar to Y#95	—
Pn235	1934	—	2 Kopeks. Copper. Y#92	—
Pn236	1934	—	3 Kopeks. Copper. Y#93	—
Pn237	1936	—	20 Kopeks. Aluminum. Y#104	—
Pn238	1937	—	20 Kopeks. Aluminum. Y#111	—
Pn239	1938	—	5 Kopeks. Unknown Metal. Y#101	—
Pn240	1938	—	15 Kopeks. Aluminum. Plain edge. Y#110	—
Pn241	1941	—	3 Kopeks. Unknown Metal. Y#107	—
Pn242	1941	—	50 Kopeks. Unknown Metal. Similar to Y#109	—
Pn243	1943	—	Rouble. Unknown Metal. Portrait Stalin.	—
Pn244	1946	—	10 Kopeks. Unknown Metal. Y#102	—
Pn245	1946	—	20 Kopeks. Unknown Metal. Y#111	—
Pn246	1947	—	Kopek. Aluminum-Bronze. Similar to Y#112; 16 bands on wreath.	—
Pn247	1947	—	2 Kopeks. Aluminum-Bronze. Similar to Y#113; 16 bands on wreath.	—
Pn248	1947	—	3 Kopeks. Unknown Metal. Similar to Y#114; 16 bands on wreath.	—
Pn249	1947	—	5 Kopeks. Aluminum-Bronze. Similar to Y#115; 16 bands on wreath.	—
Pn250	1947	—	10 Kopeks. Nickel. Similar to Y#116; 16 bands on wreath.	—
Pn251	1947	—	15 Kopeks. Unknown Metal. Similar to Y#117; 16 bands on wreath.	—
Pn252	1947	—	20 Kopeks. Nickel. Similar to Y#118; 16 bands on wreath.	—
Pn253	1949	—	Chervonetz. Copper.	—
Pn255	1953	—	Kopek. Aluminum.	—
Pn256	1953	—	Kopek. Nickel.	—
		Note: Additional metals exist		
Pn257	1953	—	Kopek. Copper-Nickel. With legend. Hammer and sickle, value above, date below.	—
Pn258	1953	—	Kopek. Aluminum.	—
Pn259	1953	—	Kopek. Nickel.	—
		Note: Additonal metals exist		
Pn261	1953	—	2 Kopeks. Aluminum.	—
Pn262	1953	—	2 Kopeks. Nickel.	—
		Note: Additional metals exist		
Pn264	1953	—	2 Kopeks. Aluminum.	—
Pn265	1953	—	2 Kopeks. Nickel.	—
		Note: Additional metals exist		
Pn267	1953	—	3 Kopeks. Aluminum.	—
Pn268	1953	—	3 Kopeks. Nickel.	—
		Note: Additional metals exist		
Pn270	1953	—	3 Kopeks. Aluminum.	—
Pn271	1953	—	3 Kopeks. Nickel.	—
		Note: Additional metals exist		
Pn272	1953	—	5 Kopeks. Aluminum. With legend.	—
Pn273	1953	—	5 Kopeks. Nickel.	—
		Note: Additional metals exist		
Pn274	1953	—	5 Kopeks. Aluminum. Without legend.	—
Pn275	1953	—	5 Kopeks. Nickel.	—
		Note: Additional metals exist		
Pn276	1953	—	10 Kopeks. Aluminum. With legend. Value and date within wreath.	—
Pn277	1953	—	10 Kopeks. Aluminum. Value, star above, date below.	—
Pn278	1953	—	10 Kopeks. Aluminum. Value, date below.	—
Pn279	1953	—	10 Kopeks. Aluminum. Value in wreath, star above date.	—
Pn280	1953	—	10 Kopeks. Aluminum. Value in wreath, date incircle at bottom.	—
Pn281	1953	—	10 Kopeks. Aluminum. Value in wreath in pellet border, date in circle at bottom.	—
Pn282	1953	—	10 Kopeks. Aluminum. Oak leaves behind value.	—
Pn283	1953	—	10 Kopeks. Aluminum. Without legend. Similar to KM#Pn276.	—
Pn284	1953	—	10 Kopeks. Aluminum. Similar to KM#Pn277.	—
Pn285	1953	—	10 Kopeks. Aluminum. Similar to KM#Pn278.	—
Pn286	1953	—	10 Kopeks. Aluminum. Similar to KM#Pn279.	—
Pn287	1953	—	10 Kopeks. Aluminum. Similar to KM#Pn280.	—
Pn288	1953	—	10 Kopeks. Aluminum. Similar to KM#Pn281.	—
Pn289	1953	—	10 Kopeks. Aluminum. Similar to KM#Pn282.	—
		Note: For Pn276-Pn289 at least four other base metal strikings exist of each		
Pn290	1953	—	15 Kopeks. Aluminum. With legend. Value and date within wreath.	—
Pn291	1953	—	15 Kopeks. Aluminum. Value, star above, date below.	—

KM#	Date	Mintage	Identification	Mkt Val
Pn292	1953	—	15 Kopeks. Aluminum. Value, date below.	—
Pn293	1953	—	15 Kopeks. Aluminum. Value in wreath, star above date in circle at bottom.	—
Pn294	1953	—	15 Kopeks. Aluminum. Value in wreath, date in circle at bottom.	—
Pn295	1953	—	15 Kopeks. Aluminum. Value in wreath, pellet border, date in circle at bottom.	—
Pn296	1953	—	15 Kopeks. Aluminum. Oak leaves behind value, date below.	—
Pn297	1953	—	15 Kopeks. Aluminum. Legend. Similar to KM#Pn290.	—
Pn298	1953	—	15 Kopeks. Aluminum. Similar to KM#Pn291.	—
Pn299	1953	—	15 Kopeks. Aluminum. Similar to KM#Pn292.	—
Pn300	1953	—	15 Kopeks. Aluminum. Similar to KM#Pn293.	—
Pn301	1953	—	15 Kopeks. Aluminum. Similar to KM#Pn294.	—
Pn302	1953	—	15 Kopeks. Aluminum. Similar to KM#Pn295.	—
Pn303	1953	—	15 Kopeks. Aluminum. Similar to KM#Pn296.	—

Note: For Pn290-Pn303 at least four other base metal strikings exist of each

KM#	Date	Mintage	Identification	Mkt Val
Pn304	1953	—	20 Kopeks. Aluminum. With legend. Value and date within wreath.	—
Pn305	1953	—	20 Kopeks. Aluminum. Value, star above, date below.	—
Pn306	1953	—	20 Kopeks. Aluminum. Value, date below.	—
Pn307	1953	—	20 Kopeks. Aluminum. Value in wreath, star above date in circle at bottom.	—
Pn308	1953	—	20 Kopeks. Aluminum. Value in wreath, date in circle at bottom.	—
Pn309	1953	—	20 Kopeks. Aluminum. Value in wreath, pellet border, date in circle at bottom.	—
Pn310	1953	—	20 Kopeks. Aluminum. Oak leaves behind value, date below.	—
Pn311	1953	—	20 Kopeks. Aluminum. Without legend. Similar to KM#Pn304.	—
Pn312	1953	—	20 Kopeks. Aluminum. Similar to KM#Pn305.	—
Pn313	1953	—	20 Kopeks. Aluminum. Similar to KM#Pn306.	—
Pn314	1953	—	20 Kopeks. Aluminum. Similar to KM#Pn307.	—
Pn315	1953	—	20 Kopeks. Aluminum. Similar to KM#Pn308.	—
Pn316	1953	—	20 Kopeks. Aluminum. Similar to KM#Pn309.	—
Pn317	1953	—	20 Kopeks. Aluminum. Similar to KM#Pn310.	—

Note: Pn304-Pn317 exist in at least four additional metals

KM#	Date	Mintage	Identification	Mkt Val
Pn318	1953	—	50 Kopeks. Bronze.	—
Pn319	1953	—	50 Kopeks. Aluminum.	—
Pn320	1953	—	50 Kopeks. Bronze.	—
Pn321	1953	—	50 Kopeks. Aluminum.	—
Pn322	1953	—	50 Kopeks. Bronze.	—
Pn323	1953	—	50 Kopeks. Aluminum.	—
Pn324	1953	—	50 Kopeks. Bronze.	—
Pn325	1953	—	50 Kopeks. Aluminum.	—

Note: Pn318-Pn325 exist in at least one other metal

KM#	Date	Mintage	Identification	Mkt Val
Pn254	1953	—	Kopek. Copper-Nickel. With legend. Hammer and sickle, value above, date below.	500
Pn260	1953	—	2 Kopeks. Copper-Nickel. With legend.	500
Pn263	1953	—	2 Kopeks. Copper-Nickel. Without legend.	500
Pn266	1953	—	3 Kopeks. Copper-Nickel. With legend.	500
Pn269	1953	—	3 Kopeks. Copper-Nickel. Without legend.	500
Pn326	1955	—	25 Kopeks. Probably copper-nickel	—
Pn327	1956	—	10 Kopeks. Nickel.	—
Pn328	1956	—	10 Kopeks. Brass.	—
Pn329	1956	—	10 Kopeks. Copper.	—
Pn330	1956	—	10 Kopeks. Aluminum.	—
Pn331	1956	—	15 Kopeks. Nickel.	—
Pn332	1956	—	15 Kopeks. Brass.	—
Pn333	1956	—	15 Kopeks. Copper.	—
Pn334	1956	—	15 Kopeks. Aluminum.	—
Pn335	1956	—	20 Kopeks. Nickel.	—
Pn336	1956	—	20 Kopeks. Brass.	—
Pn337	1956	—	20 Kopeks. Copper.	—
Pn338	1956	—	20 Kopeks. Aluminum.	—
Pn339	1956	—	50 Kopeks. Nickel.	—
Pn340	1956	—	50 Kopeks. Brass.	—
Pn341	1956	—	50 Kopeks. Copper.	—
Pn342	1956	—	50 Kopeks. Aluminum.	—
Pn343	1956	—	Rouble. Nickel.	—
Pn344	1956	—	Rouble. Brass.	—
Pn345	1956	—	Rouble. Copper.	—
Pn346	1956	—	Rouble. Aluminum.	—
Pn347	1956	—	2 Roubles. Nickel.	—
Pn348	1956	—	2 Roubles. Brass.	—
Pn349	1956	—	2 Roubles. Copper.	—
Pn350	1956	—	2 Roubles. Aluminum.	—
Pn351	1956	—	3 Roubles. Nickel.	—
Pn352	1956	—	3 Roubles. Brass.	—
Pn353	1956	—	3 Roubles. Copper.	—
Pn354	1956	—	3 Roubles. Aluminum.	—
Pn355	1956	—	5 Roubles. Nickel.	—
Pn356	1956	—	5 Roubles. Brass.	—
Pn357	1956	—	5 Roubles. Copper.	—
Pn358	1956	—	5 Roubles. Aluminum.	—
Pn359	1957	—	10 Kopeks. Copper-Nickel. Y#123	—

KM#	Date	Mintage	Identification	Mkt Val
Pn360	1957	—	10 Kopeks. Aluminum. Y#123	—
Pn361	1957	—	20 Kopeks. Copper-Nickel. Y#125	—
Pn362	1958	—	Kopek. Aluminum. Y#126	—
Pn363	1958	—	2 Kopeks. Aluminum. Y#127	—
Pn364	1958	—	3 Kopeks. Aluminum. Y#128	—
Pn365	1958	—	5 Kopeks. Aluminum. Y#129	—
Pn366	1958	—	10 Kopeks. Aluminum. Y#A130	—
Pn367	1958	—	15 Kopeks. Aluminum. Y#A131	—
Pn368	1958	—	20 Kopeks. Aluminum. Y#A132	—
Pn369	1958	—	50 Kopeks. Aluminum. Y#133	—
Pn370	1958	—	Rouble. Aluminum. Y#134	—
Pn371	1958	—	2 Roubles. Aluminum. Y#A134	—
Pn372	1958	—	3 Roubles. Aluminum. Y#B134	—
Pn373	1958	—	5 Roubles. Aluminum. Y#C134	—
Pn374	1959	—	10 Kopeks. Copper-Nickel.	—
Pn375	1959	—	15 Kopeks. Copper-Nickel.	—
Pn376	1959	—	20 Kopeks. Copper-Nickel.	—
Pn377	1961	—	1/2 Kopek. Copper.	—
Pn378	1961	—	Kopek. Copper. Y#126	—
Pn379	1961	—	2 Kopeks. Copper. Y#127	—
Pn380	1961	—	3 Kopeks. Copper. Y#128	—
Pn381	1961	—	5 Kopeks. Copper. Y#129	—
Pn382	1961	—	10 Kopeks. Copper. Y#130	—
Pn383	1961	—	15 Kopeks. Copper. Y#131	—
Pn384	1961	—	20 Kopeks. Copper. Y#132	—
Pn385	1962	—	50 Kopeks. Copper-Nickel. Y#133.1	—
Pn386	1962	—	50 Kopeks. Copper-Nickel.	—
Pn387	1962	—	Rouble. Copper-Nickel. Y#134.1	—
Pn388	1962	—	Rouble. Copper-Nickel.	—
Pn389	1963	—	50 Kopeks. Copper-Nickel.	—
Pn390	1963	—	Rouble. Copper-Nickel.	—
Pn391	1967	—	10 Kopeks. Copper-Nickel-Zinc. Arms. Ship.	250
Pn392	1967	—	10 Kopeks. Copper-Nickel-Zinc. Arms. Worker and soldier.	250
Pn393	1967	—	15 Kopeks. Unknown Metal. Uncertain 1917-67 commemorative design	—
Pn394	1967	—	20 Kopeks. Unknown Metal. Uncertain 1917-67 commemorative design	—
Pn395	1967	—	50 Kopeks. Unknown Metal. Uncertain 1917-67 commemorative design	—
Pn396	ND	—	100 Roubles. 0.9000 Gold. Y#162	—

Note: Pn390-Pn396 minor varieties exist

KM#	Date	Mintage	Identification	Mkt Val
PN397	1993	—	3 Roubles. Copper-Nickel. 34.0000 g. 38.8 mm. Same as Y-323 including silver content statement. Same as Y-323 including silver content statement. Reeded edge.	—

TRIAL STRIKES

KM#	Date	Mintage	Identification	Mkt Val
TS1	1924	—	5 Kopeks. Copper. Y#79.	350
TS2	1924	—	5 Kopeks. Copper. Y#79.	350

MINT SETS

KM#	Date	Mintage	Identification	Issue Price	Mkt Val
MS1	1957 (4)	—	Y#122-125	2.25	35.00
MS2	1961 (9)	—	Y#126-132, 133a.1, 134a.1	4.50	32.00
MS3	1962 (7)	—	Y#126-132	2.25	4.50
MS4	1964 (4)	—	Y#126, 127, 133a.2, 134a.2	2.55	4.00
MS27	Mixed dates (9)	—	Y#135, 140-143, 188-189	—	25.00
MS28	Mixed dates (8)	—	Y#135, 140-143, 188-189	—	25.00
MS5	1965 (9)	—	Y#126-132, 133a.2, 134a.2	4.50	8.00
MS6	1966 (9)	—	Y#126-132, 133a.2, 134a.2	4.50	14.00
MS7	1967 (9)	—	Y#126-132, 133a.2, 134a.2	4.50	8.00
MS8	1967 (5)	211,250	Y#136-140	6.00	8.00
MS9	1968 (9)	—	Y#126-132, 133a.2, 134a.2 and mint token	6.00	10.00
MS10	1969 (9)	—	Y#126-132, 133a.2, 134a.2	7.00	8.00
MS11	1970 (9)	—	Y#126-132, 133a.2, 134a.2	11.00	15.00
MS12	1971 (9)	—	Y#126-132, 133a.2, 134a.2	6.00	10.00
MS13	1972 (9)	10,000	Y#126-132, 133a.2, 134a.2	7.00	8.00
MS14	1973 (9)	8,000	Y#126-132, 133a.2, 134a.2	11.00	8.00
MS15	1974 (9)	27,500	Y#126-132, 133a.2, 134a.2, square mint token	11.00	8.00
MS16	1975 (9)	27,000	Y#126-132, 133a.2, 134a.2	11.00	8.00
MS17	1976 (9)	55,000	Y#126-132, 133a.2, 134a.2	11.00	10.00
MS18	1977 (9)	58,750	Y#126-132, 133a.2, 134a.2	11.00	8.00
MS19	1978 (9)	62,500	Y#126-132, 133a.2, 134a.2	11.00	8.00
MS20	1979 (9)	75,000	Y#126-132, 133a.2, 134a.2	19.00	8.00
MS21	1980 (9)	—	Y#126-132, 133a.2, 134a.2	19.00	8.00
MS22	1981 (9)	—	Y#126-132, 133a.2, 134a.2	—	8.00
MS23	1982 (9)	—	Y#126-132, 133a.2, 134a.2	—	8.00
MS24	1983 (9)	—	Y#126-132, 133a.2, 134a.2	—	8.00
MS25	1984 (9)	—	Y#126-132, 133a.2, 134a.2	—	8.00
MS26	1985 (9)	—	Y#126-132, 133a.2, 134a.2	—	8.00
MSA27	1986 (9)	—	Y#126a-129a, 130-132, 133a.2	—	14.00
MS29	1987 (9)	—	Y#126-132, 133a.2-134a.2	—	10.00
MS30	1988 (9)	—	Y#126-133, 134a.2	—	8.00
MS31	1989 (9)	—	Y#126-133, 134a.2	—	8.00
MS32	1990 (9)	—	Y#126a-129a, 130-132, 133a.2, 134a.2	—	12.00
MSA33	1991 (9)	—	Y#126a-129a, 130-132, 133a.2, 134a.2	—	10.00
MS33	1991 (3)	—	Y#268-270	245	1,950
MS34	1992 (6)	—	Y#311-316	15.00	10.00
MS36	1993 (3)	3,000	Y#420-422	—	1,950
MS35	1993 (4)	2,700	Y#416-419	—	960
MS37	1994 (3)	2,000	Y#431-433	—	1,950

KM#	Date	Mintage	Identification	Issue Price	Mkt Val
MS38	1995 (6)	200,000	Y#399-404 and medal	—	17.00
MS39	1996 (6)	100,000	Y#504-509 and medal	—	25.00
MS40	1997(SP) (7)	—	Y#600-606	—	12.50

PROOF SETS

KM#	Date	Mintage	Identification	Issue Price	Mkt Val
PS1	Mixed dates (5)	—	Y#152, 163, 175-176, 187	—	1,500
PS2	1987 (3)	—	Y#206-208	—	37.50
PS3	1990 (9)	—	Y#126a-129a, 130-132, 133a.2, 134a.2	—	15.00
PS4	1991(L) (9)	—	Y#126a-129a, 130-132, 133a.2, 134a.2	—	15.00
PS5	1991 (3)	1,500	Y#286a-288a	—	1,450
PS6	1993 (4)	1,500	Y#416-419	—	1,230
PS7	1993 (3)	750	Y#395-397	—	725
PS8	1993 (3)	2,000	Y#420-422	—	2,050
PS9	1993 (2)	10,000	Y#323, 406	—	150
PS10	1994 (4)	2,500	Y#424-427	—	1,255
PS11	1994 (3)	900	Y#428-430	—	1,360
PS13	1994 (2)	7,500	Y#405, 423	—	180
PS12	1994 (3)	1,500	Y#431-433	—	2,050
PS14	1995 (4)	2,500	Y#438-441	1,250	1,250
PS15	1995 (3)	1,500	Y#435-437	875	875
PS16	1995 (3)	900	Y#442-444	1,350	1,350

RUSSIAN CAUCASIA

Russian Caucasia, a natural area in Russia located between the Black and Caspian Seas, was a region of mystery and myth to the Ancient Greeks. It was there that Prometheus was bound for the eagle's torment and the Argonauts sought the Golden Fleece. For more than a thousand years Caucasia was the refuge for wave after wave of migrating peoples. Greeks, Romans, Persians, Turks, Huns, Mongols and finally the Russians invaded the treeless steppes and wooded highlands of this range-flanked granite bridge between Europe and Asia. Russian aggression, heroically resisted by the independent mountain races, began early in the 18th century and continued until the last opposition was stifled. The several states of Caucasia made a futile attempt to establish an independent federated republic during the Russian February Revolution of 1917, but were quickly re-conquered after the triumph of Bolshevism over the Kerensky administration.

The following area of Russian Caucasia was a coin-issuing entity of interest to numismatists.

ARMAVIR

Armavir is a city located in Krasnodar Territory, Southern Russia north of the Caucasus.

LOCAL CURRENCY UNDER THE WHITE RUSSIANS

CITY

LOCAL COINAGE

KM# 1 ROUBLE
Copper **Obv:** Double-headed eagle with monogram below tail
Rev: Value and date flanked by sprigs **Edge:** Reeded **Note:** Thin planchet.

Date	Mintage	VG	F	VF	XF	Unc
1918	—	100	150	250	475	—

KM# 2.1   3 ROUBLES
Copper, 28 mm.   **Obv:** Double-headed eagle with monogram below tail **Rev:** Value and date flanked by sprigs **Edge:** Reeded **Note:** Varieties exist.

Date	Mintage	VG	F	VF	XF	Unc
1918	—	60.00	80.00	150	275	—

KM# 2.2   3 ROUBLES
Copper, 28 mm.   **Obv:** Monogram below claw **Rev:** Value flanked by sprigs

Date	Mintage	VG	F	VF	XF	Unc
1918	—	75.00	100	175	300	—

KM# 3   5 ROUBLES
Copper, 31 mm.   **Obv:** Double-headed eagle with monogram below tail **Rev:** Value and date flanked by sprigs

Date	Mintage	VG	F	VF	XF	Unc
1918	—	150	225	400	650	—

PATTERNS
Including off metal strikes

KM#	Date	Mintage	Identification	Mkt Val
Pn1	1918	—	Rouble. Copper. 28 mm. Reeded edge. Thin planchet. Y1.	—
Pn2	1918	—	Rouble. Copper. 28 mm. Plain edge. Thin planchet. Y1.	—
Pn3	1918	—	Rouble. Copper. 28 mm. Plain edge. Thick planchet. Y1.	—
Pn3a	1918	—	Rouble. Brass.	—
Pn4	1918	—	3 Roubles. Copper. 31 mm. Monogram under tail. Y2.1.	375
Pn5	1918	—	3 Roubles. Silver. Y2.1.	700
Pn6	1918	—	5 Roubles. Aluminum. Y3.	850

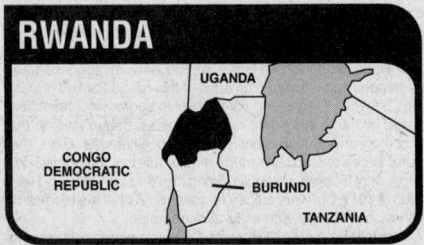

RWANDA

UGANDA

CONGO
DEMOCRATIC
REPUBLIC

BURUNDI

TANZANIA

The Republic of Rwanda, located in central Africa between the Republic of the Congo and Tanzania, has an area of 10,169 sq. mi. (26,340 sq. km.) and a population of 7.3 million. Capital: Kigali. The economy is based on agriculture and mining. Coffee and tin are exported.

German Lieutenant Count von Goetzen was the first European to visit Rwanda, 1894. Four years later the court of the Mwami (the Tutsi king of Rwanda) willingly permitted the kingdom to become a protectorate of Germany. In 1916, during the African campaigns of World War I, Belgian troops from Congo occupied Rwanda. After the war it, together with Burundi, became a Belgian League of Nations mandate under the name of the Territory of Ruanda-Urundi. Following World War II, Ruanda-Urundi became a Belgian administered U.N. trust territory. The Tutsi monarchy was deposed by the U.N. supervised election of 1961, after which Belgium granted Rwanda internal autonomy. On July 1, 1962, the U.N. terminated the Belgian trusteeship and granted full independence to both Rwanda and Burundi.

For earlier coinage see Belgian Congo, and Rwanda and Burundi.

MINT MARKS
(a) - Paris, privy marks only
(b) - Brussels, privy marks only

MONETARY SYSTEM
100 Centimes = 1 Franc

REPUBLIC
STANDARD COINAGE

KM# 9   1/2 FRANC
0.7000 g., Aluminum, 16.1 mm.   **Obv:** Value divides design within circle **Rev:** Inscription within circle

Date	Mintage	F	VF	XF	Unc	BU
1970	5,000,000	—	0.50	0.85	1.75	—

KM# 5   FRANC
Copper-Nickel, 21 mm.   **Obv:** Head 1/4 right **Rev:** Value above flag draped arms **Edge:** Plain

Date	Mintage	F	VF	XF	Unc	BU
1964(b)	3,000,000	—	5.00	10.00	20.00	—
1965(b)	4,500,000	—	0.50	0.85	1.75	—

KM# 8   FRANC
1.0900 g., Aluminum, 21.1 mm.   **Obv:** Head right **Rev:** Value above flag draped arms

Date	Mintage	F	VF	XF	Unc	BU
1969	5,000,000	—	0.50	1.50	3.50	—

KM# 12   FRANC
1.0200 g., Aluminum, 21.1 mm.   **Obv:** Millet flower **Rev:** Value above flag draped arms

Date	Mintage	F	VF	XF	Unc	BU
1974	13,000,000	—	0.20	0.50	1.00	—
1977	15,000,000	—	0.15	0.25	0.75	—
1985	—	—	0.10	0.15	0.65	—

KM# 10   2 FRANCS
1.4900 g., Aluminum, 23.5 mm.   **Series:** F.A.O. **Obv:** Seated figure facing above monogramed banner **Rev:** Value above flag draped arms

Date	Mintage	F	VF	XF	Unc	BU
1970	5,000,000	—	0.10	0.20	0.50	—

KM# 6   5 FRANCS
Bronze   **Obv:** Head 3/4 right **Rev:** Value above flag draped arms

Date	Mintage	F	VF	XF	Unc	BU
1964(b)	4,000,000	—	0.25	0.50	1.75	—
1965(b)	3,000,000	—	5.00	10.00	20.00	—

KM# 13   5 FRANCS
5.0000 g., Bronze, 26 mm.   **Obv:** Coffee tree branch **Rev:** Value above flag draped arms

Date	Mintage	F	VF	XF	Unc	BU
1974	7,000,000	—	1.00	3.00	6.00	—
1977	7,002,000	—	1.00	2.00	4.00	—
1987	—	—	0.25	0.50	1.85	—

KM# 7   10 FRANCS
10.2900 g., Copper-Nickel, 30.5 mm.   **Obv:** Head 1/4 right **Rev:** Value above flag draped arms

Date	Mintage	F	VF	XF	Unc	BU
1964(b)	6,000,000	—	1.00	2.00	4.50	—

KM# 1   10 FRANCS
3.0000 g., 0.9000 Gold 0.0868 oz. AGW   **Obv:** Value above flag draped arms **Rev:** Head 3/4 right

Date	Mintage	VG	F	VF	XF	Unc
1965	10,000					
1965 Proof	—	Value: 115				

KM# 14.1   10 FRANCS
10.5000 g., Copper-Nickel, 30.1 mm.   **Obv:** Coffee tree branch **Rev:** Value above flag draped arms

Date	Mintage	F	VF	XF	Unc	BU
1974	6,000,000	—	3.00	5.00	10.00	15.00

KM# 14.2   10 FRANCS
7.0000 g., Copper-Nickel   **Obv:** Coffee tree branch **Rev:** Value above flag draped arms **Note:** Reduced size.

Date	Mintage	F	VF	XF	Unc	BU
1985	—	—	0.50	0.85	1.85	—

KM# 15   20 FRANCS
7.9500 g., Brass, 27 mm.   **Obv:** Millet flower bud **Rev:** Value above flag draped arms

Date	Mintage	F	VF	XF	Unc	BU
1977(a)	22,000,000	—	1.00	2.00	4.00	—

KM# 2 25 FRANCS
7.5000 g., 0.9000 Gold 0.2170 oz. AGW **Obv:** Value above flag draped arms **Rev:** Head 3/4 right **Note:** Similar to 10 Francs, KM#1.

Date	Mintage	F	VF	XF	Unc	BU
1965 Proof	4,000	Value: 225				

KM# 3 50 FRANCS
15.0000 g., 0.9000 Gold 0.4340 oz. AGW **Obv:** Value above flag draped arms **Rev:** Head 3/4 right **Note:** Similar to 10 Francs, KM#1.

Date	Mintage	F	VF	XF	Unc	BU
1965 Proof	3,000	Value: 445				

KM# 16 50 FRANCS
9.9400 g., Brass, 28.88 mm. **Obv:** Leafy branch **Rev:** Value above flag draped arms

Date	Mintage	F	VF	XF	Unc	BU
1977(a)	9,000,000	—	2.50	3.50	7.00	

KM# 4 100 FRANCS
30.0000 g., 0.9000 Gold 0.8680 oz. AGW **Obv:** Value above flag draped arms **Rev:** Head 3/4 right

Date	Mintage	F	VF	XF	Unc	BU
1965 Proof	3,000	Value: 875				

KM# 18 100 FRANCS
31.2300 g., 0.9990 Silver 1.0030 oz. ASW **Subject:** Nelson Mandela **Obv:** Flag draped arms **Rev:** Head facing

Date	Mintage	F	VF	XF	Unc	BU
1990		—	—	—	32.00	35.00
1990 Proof	Est. 50,000	Value: 45.00				

KM# 21 100 FRANCS
31.1035 g., 0.9990 Silver 0.9990 oz. ASW **Subject:** Environmental Protection **Obv:** Flag draped arms **Rev:** Gorilla

Date	Mintage	F	VF	XF	Unc	BU
1993 Proof	Est. 20,000	Value: 65.00				

KM# 11 200 FRANCS
18.0000 g., 0.8000 Silver 0.4630 oz. ASW **Series:** F.A.O. **Subject:** 10th Anniversary of Independence **Obv:** Flag divides figures shaking hands **Rev:** Figure picking coffee beans, F.A.O logo within plants

Date	Mintage	F	VF	XF	Unc	BU
1972	30,000	—	—	10.00	12.50	15.00

KM# 17 1000 FRANCS
28.4700 g., 0.9250 Silver 0.8466 oz. ASW, 38.47 mm. **Subject:** 25th Anniversary of National Bank **Obv:** Bust of President Juvénal Habyarimana facing **Rev:** National bank within circle **Edge:** Reeded

Date	Mintage	F	VF	XF	Unc	BU
ND(1989)		—	—	—	42.50	47.50

KM# 19 2000 FRANCS
7.8000 g., 0.9990 Gold 0.2505 oz. AGW **Subject:** Nelson Mandela **Obv:** Flag draped arms above value **Rev:** Head facing **Note:** Similar to 5,000 Francs, KM#20.

Date	Mintage	F	VF	XF	Unc	BU
1990 Proof	Est. 50,000	Value: 265				

KM# 20 5000 FRANCS
15.5300 g., 0.9990 Gold 0.4988 oz. AGW **Subject:** Nelson Mandela **Obv:** Value below flag draped arms **Rev:** Head facing

Date	Mintage	F	VF	XF	Unc	BU
1990 Proof	3,000	Value: 525				

ESSAIS

KM#	Date	Mintage	Identification	Issue Price	Mkt Val
E1	1964(b)	—	Franc. Aluminum.	—	35.00
E2	1964(b)	—	5 Francs. Bronze. Head 1/4 right. Value above flag draped arms.	—	50.00
E3	1964(b)	—	10 Francs. Copper-Nickel.	—	65.00
E4	1977(a)	—	Franc. Aluminum.	—	20.00
E5	1977(a)	—	5 Francs. Bronze.	—	25.00
E6	1977(a)	—	20 Francs. Brass.	—	30.00
E7	1977(a)	—	50 Francs. Brass.	—	35.00

PROOF SETS

KM#	Date	Mintage	Identification	Issue Price	Mkt Val
PS1	1965(a) (4)	3,000	KM1-4	—	1,650

RWANDA-BURUNDI

Rwanda-Burundi, a Belgian League of Nations mandate and United Nations trust territory comprising the provinces of Ruanda-Urundi of the former colony of German East Africa, was located in central Africa between the present Democratic Republic of the Congo, Uganda and mainland Tanzania. The mandate-trust territory had an area of 20,916 sq. mi. (54,272 sq. km.) and a population of 4.3 million.

For specific statistics and history of Ruanda and of Urundi see individual entries.

When Rwanda and Burundi were formed into a mandate for administration by Belgium, their names were combined as Ruanda-Urundi and they were organized as an integral part of the Belgian Congo. During the mandate-trust territory period, they utilized the coinage of the Belgian Congo, which from 1954 through 1960 carried the appropriate dual identification. After the Belgian Congo acquired independence as the Democratic Republic of the Congo, the provinces of Ruanda and Urundi reverted to their former names of Rwanda and Burundi and utilized a common currency issued by a Central Bank (B.E.R.B.) established for that purpose until the time when, as independent republics, each issued its own national coinage.

For earlier coinage see Belgian Congo.

MONETARY SYSTEM
100 Centimes = 1 Franc

PROVINCES
STANDARD COINAGE

KM# 1 FRANC
Brass **Obv:** Value **Rev:** Lion

Date	Mintage	F	VF	XF	Unc	BU
1960	2,000,000	—	3.50	7.50	17.50	20.00
1961	16,000,000	—	0.50	1.00	3.50	6.00
1964	3,000,000	—	3.00	6.50	15.00	18.00

KM# 2 FRANC
Copper-Nickel **Obv:** Value **Rev:** Head left **Note:** Mule.

Date	Mintage	F	VF	XF	Unc	BU
1961	50	—	—	—	650	

ESSAIS

KM#	Date	Mintage	Identification	Issue Price	Mkt Val
E1	1960	—	Franc. Bronze. Crowned shield divides date. Palm tree divides value.	—	160
E2	1960	—	Franc. Brass. KM1.	—	60.00
E3	1960	—	Franc. Silver. KM1.	—	220

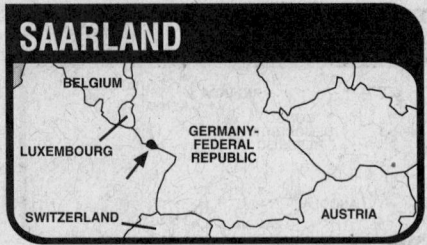

SAARLAND

The Saar, the 10th state of the German Federal Republic, is located in the coal-rich Saar basin on the Franco-German frontier, and has an area of 991 sq. mi. and a population of 1.2 million. Capital: Saarbrucken. It is an important center of mining and heavy industry.

From the late 14th century until the fall of Napoleon, the city of Saarbrucken was ruled by the counts of Nassau-Saarbrucken, but the surrounding territory was subject to the political and cultural domination of France. At the close of the Napoleonic era, the Saarland came under the control of Prussia. France was awarded the Saar coal mines following World War I, and the Saarland was made an autonomous territory of the League of Nations, its future political affiliation to be determined by referendum. The plebiscite, 1935, chose re-incorporation into Germany. France reoccupied the Saarland, 1945, establishing strong economic ties and assuming the obligation of defense and foreign affairs. After sustained agitation by West Germany, France agreed in 1955, to the return of the Saar to Germany by Jan. 1957.

MINT MARK
(a) - Paris - privy marks only

GERMAN REPUBLIC STATE
STANDARD COINAGE

KM# 1　10 FRANKEN
3.0400 g., Aluminum-Bronze, 20 mm. **Obv:** Industrial scene, arms at center **Rev:** Value and date

Date	Mintage	F	VF	XF	Unc	BU
1954(a)	11,000,000	1.00	2.00	4.00	7.00	9.00

KM# 2　20 FRANKEN
4.0000 g., Aluminum-Bronze, 23.5 mm. **Obv:** Industrial scene, arms at center **Rev:** Value and date **Edge:** Plain

Date	Mintage	F	VF	XF	Unc	BU
1954(a)	12,950,000	1.00	2.00	4.00	7.00	9.00

KM# 3　50 FRANKEN
8.0000 g., Aluminum-Bronze **Obv:** Industrial scene, arms in center **Rev:** Value and date

Date	Mintage	F	VF	XF	Unc	BU
1954(a)	5,300,000	4.00	7.00	15.00	30.00	35.00

KM# 4　100 FRANKEN
6.0400 g., Copper-Nickel, 24 mm. **Obv:** Arms within circular design **Rev:** Value and date

Date	Mintage	F	VF	XF	Unc	BU
1955(a)	11,000,000	2.00	4.00	7.00	17.50	22.50

ESSAIS
Standard metals unless otherwise noted

KM#	Date	Mintage	Identification	Issue Price	Mkt Val
E1	1954(a)	1,100	10 Franken. Aluminum-Bronze. KM1.	—	60.00
E2	1954(a)	—	10 Franken. Gold. KM1. Reported, not confirmed.	—	—
E3	1954(a)	1,100	20 Franken. Aluminum-Bronze. KM2.	—	60.00
E4	1954(a)	50	20 Franken. Gold. KM2.	—	2,000
E5	1954(a)	1,100	50 Franken. Aluminum-Bronze center. KM3.	—	60.00
E6	1954(a)	—	50 Franken. Gold. KM3. Reported, not confirmed.	—	—
E7	1955(a)	50	100 Franken. Gold. Arms within circular design. Value. KM4.	—	2,500

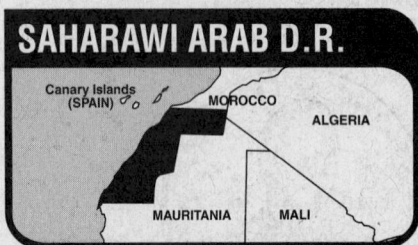

SAHARAWI ARAB D.R.

The Saharawi Arab Democratic Republic, located in northwest Africa has an area of 102,703 sq. mi. and a population (census taken 1974) of 76,425. Formerly known as Spanish Sahara, the area is bounded on the north by Morocco, on the east and southeast by Mauritania, on the northeast by Algeria, and on the west by the Atlantic Ocean. Capital: El Aaiun. Agriculture, fishing and mining are the three main industries. Exports are barley, livestock and phosphates.

A Spanish trading post was established in 1476 but was abandoned in 1524. A Spanish protectorate for the region was proclaimed in 1884. The status of the Spanish Sahara changed from a colony to an overseas province in 1958. Spain relinquished its holdings in 1975. The SADR is a "government in exile". It currently controls about 20% of its claimed territory, the former Spanish colony of Western Sahara; Morocco controls and administers the majority of the territory as its Southern Provinces. SADR claims control over a zone largely bordering Mauritania, described as "the Free Zone," although characterized by Morocco as a buffer zone.

The official languages are Spanish and an Arab dialect: The Hassaniya.

DEMOCRATIC REPUBLIC
STANDARD COINAGE

KM# 14　PESETA
2.9400 g., Copper-Nickel, 17.8 mm. **Obv:** National arms and value **Rev:** Arab and camel

Date	Mintage	F	VF	XF	Unc	BU
1992	—	—	—	—	1.25	2.50

KM# 15　2 PESETAS
3.5600 g., Copper-Nickel, 20 mm. **Obv:** National arms and value **Rev:** Arab and camel

Date	Mintage	F	VF	XF	Unc	BU
1992	—	—	—	—	1.50	3.00

KM# 16　5 PESETAS
3.9200 g., Copper-Nickel, 21.5 mm. **Obv:** National arms and value **Rev:** Arab and camel **Edge:** Plain

Date	Mintage	F	VF	XF	Unc	BU
1992	—	—	—	—	2.50	5.00

KM# 1　50 PESETAS
Copper-Nickel **Obv:** National arms and value **Rev:** Arab and camel

Date	Mintage	F	VF	XF	Unc	BU
1990	—	—	—	—	5.00	6.00

KM# 18　100 PESETAS
Copper-Nickel **Obv:** National arms and value **Rev:** Arab and sailing ship

Date	Mintage	F	VF	XF	Unc	BU
1990	—	—	—	—	10.00	11.50

KM# 20　100 PESETAS
Copper, 38 mm. **Obv:** National arms and value **Rev:** Arab and camel

Date	Mintage	F	VF	XF	Unc	BU
1990	—	—	—	—	15.00	25.00

KM# 25　100 PESETAS
Copper, 38 mm. **Obv:** National arms and value **Rev:** Arab and sailboat

Date	Mintage	F	VF	XF	Unc	BU
1990	—	—	—	—	8.00	9.00
1990 Proof	—	Value: 60.00				

KM# 7　100 PESETAS
Nickel Plated Steel　**Series:** Olympics **Obv:** National arms and value **Rev:** Equestrian event

Date	Mintage	F	VF	XF	Unc	BU
1991	5,000	—	—	—	12.00	13.50

KM# 26　100 PESETAS
Nickel Plated Steel **Obv:** National arms and value **Rev:** Ship above Canary Islands map

Date	Mintage	F	VF	XF	Unc	BU
1992	—	—	—	—	12.00	13.50

KM# 40   100 PESETAS
Copper **Subject:** Columbus' ship - Santa Maria **Obv:** National arms and value

Date	Mintage	F	VF	XF	Unc	BU
1992 Proof	78	Value: 65.00				

KM# 13   100 PESETAS
Copper-Nickel **Series:** Prehistoric Animals **Obv:** National arms and value **Rev:** Brontosaurus

Date	Mintage	F	VF	XF	Unc	BU
1992	—	—	—	—	25.00	30.00

KM# 19   100 PESETAS
Copper, 38 mm. **Series:** Prehistoric Animals **Obv:** National arms and value **Rev:** Tarbosaurus Bataar

Date	Mintage	F	VF	XF	Unc	BU
1993	—	—	—	—	25.00	30.00

KM# 17   100 PESETAS
Nickel Clad Steel **Series:** Prehistoric Animals **Obv:** National arms and value **Rev:** Triceratops

Date	Mintage	F	VF	XF	Unc	BU
1994	—	—	—	—	25.00	30.00

KM# 41   100 PESETAS
Nickel Clad Steel **Series:** Prehistoric Animals **Obv:** National arms and value **Rev:** Camarasaurus

Date	Mintage	F	VF	XF	Unc	BU
1994 Proof	100	Value: 80.00				

KM# 23   100 PESETAS
Nickel Clad Steel **Obv:** National arms and value **Rev:** WWII British Spitfire MK II, enameled

Date	Mintage	F	VF	XF	Unc	BU
1995	—	—	—	—	20.00	22.50

KM# 22   100 PESETAS
Copper, 38 mm. **Series:** Olympics **Obv:** National arms and value **Rev:** Wrestlers

Date	Mintage	F	VF	XF	Unc	BU
1996	—	—	—	—	8.50	10.00

KM# 31   200 PESETAS
Copper **Subject:** 20th Anniversary - Proclamation of Republic **Obv:** National arms and value **Rev:** Armored standing figure facing

Date	Mintage	F	VF	XF	Unc	BU
1996 Proof	—	Value: 12.50				

KM# 2   500 PESETAS
16.0000 g., 0.9990 Silver 0.5139 oz. ASW **Series:** Transportation **Obv:** National arms **Rev:** Arab walking camel

Date	Mintage	F	VF	XF	Unc	BU
1990	—	—	—	—	27.50	40.00

KM# 3   500 PESETAS
16.0000 g., 0.9990 Silver 0.5139 oz. ASW **Obv:** National arms **Rev:** Arab and sailing ship

Date	Mintage	F	VF	XF	Unc	BU
1990 Proof	—	Value: 50.00				
1990	—	—	—	—	30.00	45.00

KM# 42   500 PESETAS
Copper **Obv:** National arms **Rev:** Antique sailing ship

Date	Mintage	F	VF	XF	Unc	BU
1990 Proof	13	Value: 1,450				

KM# 4   500 PESETAS
6.0000 g., 0.9990 Silver 0.1927 oz. ASW **Series:** 1992 Olympics **Obv:** National arms **Rev:** Tennis player, skier

Date	Mintage	F	VF	XF	Unc	BU
1991	—	—	—	—	20.00	22.50

KM# 5   500 PESETAS
12.0000 g., 0.9990 Silver 0.3854 oz. ASW **Subject:** 1994 American States Games - Soccer **Obv:** National arms **Rev:** Player kicking ball

Date	Mintage	F	VF	XF	Unc	BU
1991	—	—	—	—	30.00	32.50

KM# 8   500 PESETAS
15.8400 g., 0.9990 Silver 0.5087 oz. ASW **Subject:** Soccer **Obv:** National arms **Rev:** Ball divided by inscription

Date	Mintage	F	VF	XF	Unc	BU
1991	15,000	—	—	—	25.00	27.50

KM# 9.1a   500 PESETAS
Copper **Subject:** Meeting of Two Worlds **Obv:** National arms **Rev:** Sailing ship above Canary Islands map

Date	Mintage	F	VF	XF	Unc	BU
1992	—	—	—	—	—	32.50
1992 Proof	22	Value: 1,250				

KM# 9.1   500 PESETAS
20.0000 g., 0.9990 Silver 0.6423 oz. ASW **Subject:** Meeting of Two Worlds **Obv:** National arms **Rev:** Sailing ship above Canary Islands map **Note:** Thick letters.

Date	Mintage	F	VF	XF	Unc	BU
1992	—				27.50	30.00

KM# 9.2   500 PESETAS
Copper **Subject:** Meeting of Two Worlds **Obv:** National arms **Rev:** Sailing ship above Canary Islands map **Note:** Thin letters.

Date	Mintage	F	VF	XF	Unc	BU
1992 Proof	—	Value: 35.00				

KM# 11   500 PESETAS
Copper **Subject:** Defense of Nature **Obv:** National arms **Rev:** Elephant

Date	Mintage	F	VF	XF	Unc	BU
1993	—				40.00	80.00

KM# 12   500 PESETAS
16.0000 g., 0.9990 Silver 0.5139 oz. ASW **Series:** Prehistoric Animals **Obv:** National arms **Rev:** Tarbosaurus Bataar

Date	Mintage	F	VF	XF	Unc	BU
1993	—				35.00	50.00

KM# 27   500 PESETAS
16.0000 g., 0.9990 Silver 0.5139 oz. ASW **Series:** Prehistoric Animals **Obv:** National arms **Rev:** Camarasaurus

Date	Mintage	F	VF	XF	Unc	BU
1994	—				35.00	50.00

KM# 21   500 PESETAS
20.0000 g., 0.9990 Silver 0.6423 oz. ASW **Series:** 1996 Olympics **Obv:** National arms **Rev:** Wrestlers

Date	Mintage	F	VF	XF	Unc	BU
1995 Proof	15,000	Value: 27.50				

KM# 24   500 PESETAS
20.0000 g., 0.9990 Silver 0.6423 oz. ASW **Obv:** National arms **Rev:** WWII British Spitfire MK II

Date	Mintage	F	VF	XF	Unc	BU
1995 Proof	15,000	Value: 32.50				

KM# 28   500 PESETAS
16.0000 g., 0.9990 Silver 0.5139 oz. ASW **Series:** Prehistoric Animals **Obv:** National arms **Rev:** Plateosaurus

Date	Mintage	F	VF	XF	Unc	BU
1995 Proof	—	Value: 50.00				

KM# 29   500 PESETAS
20.0000 g., 0.9990 Silver 0.6423 oz. ASW **Obv:** National arms **Rev:** Multicolor leopard

Date	Mintage	F	VF	XF	Unc	BU
1996 Proof	—	Value: 50.00				

KM# 32   500 PESETAS
20.0000 g., 0.9990 Silver 0.6423 oz. ASW **Subject:** XVI Copa Mundial - Francia 1998 - Soccer **Obv:** National arms **Rev:** Player kicking ball

Date	Mintage	F	VF	XF	Unc	BU
1996 Proof	—	Value: 50.00				

KM# 33   500 PESETAS
20.0000 g., 0.9990 Silver 0.6423 oz. ASW **Subject:** XVI Copa Mundial - Francia 1998 - Soccer **Obv:** National arms **Rev:** Multicolor player kicking ball

Date	Mintage	F	VF	XF	Unc	BU
1996 Proof	—	Value: 32.50				

KM# 34   500 PESETAS
20.0000 g., 0.9990 Silver 0.6423 oz. ASW **Series:** XXVII Olympiada - Sydney 2000 **Obv:** National arms **Rev:** Multicolor kayaker

Date	Mintage	F	VF	XF	Unc	BU
1997 Proof	—	Value: 32.50				

KM# 30   500 PESETAS
16.0000 g., 0.9990 Silver 0.5139 oz. ASW **Series:** Sydney Olympics **Obv:** National arms **Rev:** Weight lifter

Date	Mintage	F	VF	XF	Unc	BU
1997 Proof	—	Value: 37.50				

KM# 6   1000 PESETAS
3.1000 g., 0.9990 Gold 0.0996 oz. AGW **Series:** Transportation **Obv:** National arms **Rev:** Arab walking with camel **Note:** Similar to 500 Pesetas, KM#2.

Date	Mintage	F	VF	XF	Unc	BU
1991	508	—	—	—	145	165

KM# 44   1000 PESETAS
30.5000 g., 0.9990 Silver 0.9796 oz. ASW **Subject:** Thor Heyerdahl **Obv:** National arms **Rev:** Multicolor reed boats **Edge:** Plain

Date	Mintage	F	VF	XF	Unc	BU
1996	—	Value: 37.50				

KM# 53   1000 PESETAS
29.0000 g., Copper-Nickel, 38.1 mm. **Obv:** National arms
Rev: Multicolor Graf Ferdinand von Zeppelin and two Zeppelins
in flight **Edge:** Reeded

Date	Mintage	F	VF	XF	Unc	BU
ND (1997) Proof	—			Value: 50.00		

KM# 35   5000 PESETAS
33.5400 g., 0.9200 Silver 0.9920 oz. ASW **Subject:** 20th
Anniversary - Proclamation of Republic **Obv:** National arms
Rev: Female guerilla with rifle

Date	Mintage	F	VF	XF	Unc	BU
1996 Proof	—			Value: 70.00		

KM# 45   1000 PESETAS
30.5000 g., 0.9990 Silver 0.9796 oz. ASW **Subject:** Horudsch
Chaireddin **Obv:** National arms **Rev:** Multicolor pirates sailing
vessels in background

Date	Mintage	F	VF	XF	Unc	BU
1996 Proof	—			Value: 50.00		

KM# 55   1000 PESETAS
15.4800 g., 0.9990 Silver 0.4972 oz. ASW, 35 mm. **Obv:** National
arms **Rev:** Weight lifter **Edge:** Plain **Note:** Sydney Olympics

Date	Mintage	F	VF	XF	Unc	BU
1998 Proof	—			Value: 45.00		

KM# 36   5000 PESETAS
33.5400 g., 0.9200 Silver 0.9920 oz. ASW **Subject:** 20th
Anniversary - Proclamation of Republic **Obv:** National arms
Rev: Land Rover with armed guerillas

Date	Mintage	F	VF	XF	Unc	BU
1996 Proof	—			Value: 70.00		

KM# 37   1000 PESETAS
31.5000 g., 0.9990 Silver 1.0117 oz. ASW **Subject:** 15th
Anniversary - Diplomacy between Venezuela and Arabic Sahara
Obv: Pillar between national emblems **Rev:** Head facing and
equestrian

Date	Mintage	F	VF	XF	Unc	BU
1997	200	—	—	—	65.00	70.00
1997 Proof	800	Value: 55.00				

KM# 38   40000 PESETAS
15.5200 g., 0.9000 Gold 0.4491 oz. AGW **Subject:** 20th
Anniversary - Diplomacy between Venezuela and Saharawi Arab
Democratic Republic **Obv:** Arms of Venezuela and Saharawi
Arab Democratic Republic **Rev:** Bolivar and El Uali

Date	Mintage	F	VF	XF	Unc	BU
1997 Proof	90	Value: 1,000				

KM# 38a   40000 PESETAS
15.5000 g., 0.9990 Gold 0.4978 oz. AGW **Subject:** 20th
Anniversary - Diplomacy between Venezuela and Saharawi Arab
Democratic Republic **Obv:** Arms of Venezuela and Saharawi
Arab Democratic Republic **Rev:** Bolivar and El Uali

Date	Mintage	F	VF	XF	Unc	BU
1997 Proof, Rare	10	—	—	—	—	—

KM# 43   1000 PESETAS
Silver **Obv:** National emblem **Rev:** Viking ship

Date	Mintage	F	VF	XF	Unc	BU
1998 Proof	100	Value: 110				

KM# 49   1000 PESETAS
15.0000 g., 0.9990 Silver 0.4818 oz. ASW, 35 mm.
Obv: National arms **Rev:** Leonardo Da Vinci **Edge:** Plain

Date	Mintage	F	VF	XF	Unc	BU
1999 Proof	—			Value: 22.50		

KM# 50   1000 PESETAS
15.0000 g., 0.9990 Silver 0.4818 oz. ASW, 35.1 mm.
Obv: National arms **Rev:** Pedro Cabral, two sail ships and
Brazilian map **Edge:** Plain

Date	Mintage	F	VF	XF	Unc	BU
ND(2000) Proof	—			Value: 25.00		

ESSAIS

KM#	Date	Mintage	Identification	Mkt Val
E1	1997	8	1000 Pesetas. Copper. KM#37.	3,000

PATTERNS

KM#	Date	Mintage	Identification	Mkt Val
Pn2	1997	8	40000 Pesetas. Copper. KM#38.	3,000
Pn3	1997	8	40000 Pesetas. Silver. KM#38.	3,000

PIEFORTS

KM#	Date	Mintage	Identification	Mkt Val
P2	1997	8	40000 Pesetas. Gold. KM#38.	6,000
P3	1998	—	1000 Pesetas. 0.9990 Silver. 31.2000 g. 35 mm. National arms. Viking ship. Plain edge.	—

KM# 46   1000 PESETAS
14.9400 g., 0.9990 Silver 0.4798 oz. ASW, 35 mm.
Subject: World Cup Soccer **Obv:** National arms **Rev:** Soccer
ball and trophy **Edge:** Plain

Date	Mintage	F	VF	XF	Unc	BU
1997 Proof	—			Value: 30.00		

KM# 47   1000 PESETAS
15.0000 g., 0.9990 Silver 0.4818 oz. ASW, 35 mm. **Obv:** National
arms **Rev:** Multicolor Thompsons Gazelle **Edge:** Plain

Date	Mintage	F	VF	XF	Unc	BU
1997 Proof	50	Value: 50.00				

KM# 10   1000 PESETAS-10 ECU
31.0000 g., 0.9990 Silver 0.9956 oz. ASW **Subject:** European
Community **Obv:** National arms **Rev:** Knight on horse and King

Date	Mintage	F	VF	XF	Unc	BU
ND(1992) Proof	15,000	Value: 40.00				

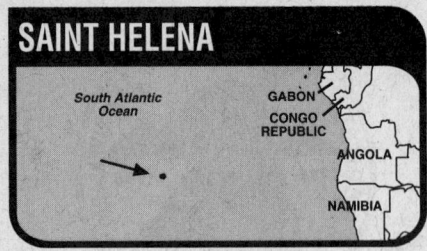

SAINT HELENA

South Atlantic Ocean

GABON
CONGO REPUBLIC
ANGOLA
NAMIBIA

Saint Helena, a British colony located about 1,150 miles (1,850 km.) from the west coast of Africa, has an area of 47 sq. mi. (410 sq. km.) and a population of *7,000. Capital: Jamestown. Flax, lace, and rope are produced for export. Ascension and Tristan da Cunha are dependencies of Saint Helena.

The island was discovered and named by the Portuguese navigator Joao de Nova Castella in 1502. The Portuguese imported livestock, fruit trees, and vegetables but established no permanent settlement. The Dutch occupied the island temporarily, 1645-51. The original European settlement was founded by representatives of the British East India Company sent to annex the island after the departure of the Dutch. The Dutch returned and captured Saint Helena from the British on New Year's Day, 1673, but were in turn ejected by a British force under Sir Richard Munden. Thereafter Saint Helena was the undisputed possession of Great Britain. The island served as the place of exile for Napoleon, several Zulu chiefs, and an ex-sultan of Zanzibar.

RULER
British

MINT MARK
PM - Pobjoy Mint

MONETARY SYSTEM
12 Pence = 1 Shilling
100 Pence = 1 Pound

BRITISH COLONY
STANDARD COINAGE

KM# 5   25 PENCE (Crown)
Copper-Nickel, 38.5 mm.   **Ruler:** Elizabeth II **Subject:** St. Helena Tercentenary **Obv:** Young bust right **Rev:** Sailing ship

Date	Mintage	VG	F	VF	XF	Unc
ND(1973)	100,000	—	—	—	—	4.00

KM# 5a   25 PENCE (Crown)
28.2800 g., 0.9250 Silver 0.8410 oz. ASW, 38.5 mm.
Ruler: Elizabeth II **Subject:** St. Helena Tercentenary
Obv: Young bust right **Rev:** Sailing ship

Date	Mintage	VG	F	VF	XF	Unc
ND(1973) Proof	10,000	Value: 22.00				

KM# 6   25 PENCE (Crown)
Copper-Nickel, 38.5 mm.   **Ruler:** Elizabeth II **Subject:** Queen Elizabeth II Silver Jubilee **Obv:** Young bust right **Rev:** Aldabra giant tortoise

Date	Mintage	VG	F	VF	XF	Unc
ND(1977)	50,000	—	—	—	—	10.00

KM# 6a   25 PENCE (Crown)
28.2800 g., 0.9250 Silver 0.8410 oz. ASW, 38.5 mm.
Ruler: Elizabeth II **Subject:** Queen Elizabeth II Silver Jubilee
Obv: Young bust right **Rev:** Aldabra giant tortoise

Date	Mintage	VG	F	VF	XF	Unc
ND(1977) Proof	25,000	Value: 20.00				

KM# 7   25 PENCE (Crown)
Copper-Nickel, 38.5 mm.   **Ruler:** Elizabeth II **Subject:** 25th Anniversary of Coronation **Obv:** Young bust right **Rev:** Crowned portrait with supporters

Date	Mintage	VG	F	VF	XF	Unc
1978PM	—	—	—	—	—	4.00

KM# 7a   25 PENCE (Crown)
28.2800 g., 0.9250 Silver 0.8410 oz. ASW, 38.5 mm.
Ruler: Elizabeth II **Subject:** 25th Anniversary of Coronation
Obv: Young bust right **Rev:** Crowned portrait with supporters

Date	Mintage	VG	F	VF	XF	Unc
1978PM	70,000	—	—	—	—	14.50
1978PM Proof	25,000	Value: 20.00				

KM# 8   25 PENCE (Crown)
Copper-Nickel, 38.5 mm.   **Ruler:** Elizabeth II **Subject:** Queen Mother's 80th Birthday **Obv:** Young bust right **Rev:** Cameo portrait above ship and hills

Date	Mintage	VG	F	VF	XF	Unc
1980	100,000	—	—	—	—	3.50

KM# 8a   25 PENCE (Crown)
28.2800 g., 0.9250 Silver 0.8410 oz. ASW, 38.5 mm.
Ruler: Elizabeth II **Subject:** Queen Mother's 80th Birthday
Obv: Young bust right **Rev:** Cameo portrait above hills

Date	Mintage	VG	F	VF	XF	Unc
1980 Proof	25,000	Value: 18.50				

KM# 9   25 PENCE (Crown)
Copper-Nickel, 38.5 mm.   **Ruler:** Elizabeth II **Subject:** Wedding of Prince Charles and Lady Diana **Obv:** Young bust right **Rev:** Nosegay separates facing heads of couple, ship above

Date	Mintage	VG	F	VF	XF	Unc
ND(1981)	50,000	—	—	—	—	3.50

KM# 9a   25 PENCE (Crown)
28.2800 g., 0.9250 Silver 0.8410 oz. ASW, 38.5 mm.
Ruler: Elizabeth II **Subject:** Wedding of Prince Charles and Lady Diana **Obv:** Young bust right **Rev:** Nosegay separates facing heads of couple, ship above

Date	Mintage	VG	F	VF	XF	Unc
ND(1981) Proof	30,000	Value: 20.00				

KM# 10   25 PENCE (Crown)
28.2800 g., 0.9250 Silver 0.8410 oz. ASW, 38.5 mm.
Ruler: Elizabeth II **Series:** International Year of the Scout **Obv:** Young bust right **Rev:** Stylized value above dates

Date	Mintage	VG	F	VF	XF	Unc
ND(1983)	10,000	—	—	—	—	30.00
ND(1983) Proof	10,000	Value: 42.50				

KM# 12   50 PENCE
28.2800 g., Copper-Nickel, 38.62 mm.   **Ruler:** Elizabeth II **Subject:** 150th Anniversary - Saint Helena Colony **Obv:** Young bust right **Rev:** Half figure above crowned shield flanked by designs **Edge:** Reeded

Date	Mintage	VG	F	VF	XF	Unc
ND(1984)	10,000	—	—	—	—	4.50

KM# 12a   50 PENCE
28.2800 g., 0.9250 Silver 0.8410 oz. ASW, 38.5 mm.
Ruler: Elizabeth II **Subject:** 150th Anniversary - Saint Helena Colony **Obv:** Young bust right **Rev:** Half figure above crowned shield flanked by designs

Date	Mintage	VG	F	VF	XF	Unc
ND(1984) Proof	5,000	Value: 28.00				

KM# 12b   50 PENCE
47.5400 g., 0.9170 Gold 1.4015 oz. AGW, 38.5 mm.
Ruler: Elizabeth II **Subject:** 150th Anniversary - Saint Helena Colony **Obv:** Young bust right **Rev:** Half figure above crowned shield flanked by designs

Date	Mintage	VG	F	VF	XF	Unc
ND(1984) Proof	150	Value: 1,400				

KM# 13   50 PENCE
Copper-Nickel, 38.5 mm.   **Ruler:** Elizabeth II **Subject:** Royal Visit of Prince Andrew **Obv:** Young bust right **Rev:** Bust left

Date	Mintage	VG	F	VF	XF	Unc
1984	125,000	—	—	—	—	3.00

KM# 13a   50 PENCE
28.2800 g., 0.9250 Silver 0.8410 oz. ASW, 38.5 mm.
Ruler: Elizabeth II **Subject:** Royal Visit of Prince Andrew **Obv:** Young bust right **Rev:** Bust left

Date	Mintage	VG	F	VF	XF	Unc
1984 Proof	5,000	Value: 30.00				

KM# 14 50 PENCE
Copper-Nickel, 38.5 mm. **Ruler:** Elizabeth II **Subject:** Queen Mother **Obv:** Crowned bust right **Rev:** Queen Mother and equestrian within circle

Date	Mintage	VG	F	VF	XF	Unc
1995	—	—	—	—	—	7.50

KM# 14a 50 PENCE
28.2800 g., 0.9250 Silver 0.8410 oz. ASW, 38.5 mm. **Ruler:** Elizabeth II **Subject:** Queen Mother **Obv:** Crowned bust right **Rev:** Queen Mother and equestrian within circle

Date	Mintage	VG	F	VF	XF	Unc
1995 Proof	10,000	Value: 35.00				

KM# 14b 50 PENCE
47.5400 g., 0.9160 Gold 1.4000 oz. AGW, 38.5 mm. **Ruler:** Elizabeth II **Subject:** Queen Mother **Obv:** Crowned bust right **Rev:** Queen Mother and equestrian within circle

Date	Mintage	VG	F	VF	XF	Unc
1995 Proof	150	Value: 1,400				

KM# 15 50 PENCE
Copper-Nickel, 38.5 mm. **Ruler:** Elizabeth II **Subject:** Queen Elizabeth II's 70th Birthday **Obv:** Crowned bust right **Rev:** Mounted guardsman

Date	Mintage	VG	F	VF	XF	Unc
1996	—	—	—	—	—	6.00

KM# 15a 50 PENCE
28.2800 g., 0.9250 Silver 0.8410 oz. ASW, 38.5 mm. **Ruler:** Elizabeth II **Subject:** Queen Elizabeth II's 70th Birthday **Obv:** Crowned bust right **Rev:** Mounted guardsman

Date	Mintage	VG	F	VF	XF	Unc
1996 Proof	5,000	Value: 50.00				

KM# 18 50 PENCE
Copper-Nickel, 38.5 mm. **Ruler:** Elizabeth II **Subject:** Elizabeth and Philip **Obv:** Crowned bust right **Rev:** Royal couple reviewing troops

Date	Mintage	VG	F	VF	XF	Unc
ND(1997)	—	—	—	—	—	6.50

KM# 16a 50 PENCE
28.2800 g., 0.9250 Silver 0.8410 oz. ASW, 38.5 mm. **Ruler:** Elizabeth II **Series:** World Wildlife Fund **Subject:** Conserving Nature **Obv:** Crowned bust right **Rev:** Three Blue Whales

Date	Mintage	VG	F	VF	XF	Unc
1998 Proof	—	Value: 45.00				

KM# 16 50 PENCE
Copper-Nickel, 38.5 mm. **Ruler:** Elizabeth II **Series:** World Wildlife Fund **Subject:** Conserving Nature **Obv:** Crowned bust right **Rev:** Three blue whales

Date	Mintage	VG	F	VF	XF	Unc
1998	—	—	—	—	—	14.00

KM# 17 50 PENCE
Copper-Nickel, 38.5 mm. **Ruler:** Elizabeth II **Series:** World Wildlife Fund **Subject:** Conserving Nature **Obv:** Crowned bust right **Rev:** Rainpiper bird, shoreline, lily

Date	Mintage	VG	F	VF	XF	Unc
1998	—	—	—	—	—	14.00

KM# 22 50 PENCE
28.2800 g., Copper-Nickel, 38.6 mm. **Ruler:** Elizabeth II **Obv:** Crowned bust right **Rev:** Crowned bust of the Queen Mother right **Edge:** Reeded

Date	Mintage	F	VF	XF	Unc	BU
ND(2000)	—	—	—	—	10.00	12.00

KM# 22a 50 PENCE
28.2800 g., 0.9250 Silver 0.8410 oz. ASW, 38.6 mm. **Ruler:** Elizabeth II **Obv:** Crowned bust right **Rev:** Crowned bust of the Queen Mother right **Edge:** Reeded

Date	Mintage	F	VF	XF	Unc	BU
ND(2000) Proof	10,000	Value: 50.00				

KM# 22b 50 PENCE
47.5400 g., 0.9166 Gold 1.4009 oz. AGW, 38.6 mm. **Ruler:** Elizabeth II **Obv:** Crowned bust right **Rev:** Crowned bust of the Queen Mother right **Edge:** Reeded

Date	Mintage	F	VF	XF	Unc	BU
ND(2000) Proof	100	Value: 1,400				

KM# 21 POUND
4.2000 g., Brass Plated Steel, 22 mm. **Ruler:** Elizabeth II **Obv:** Young bust right **Rev:** Coat of arms and value **Edge:** Reeded and plain sections

Date	Mintage	F	VF	XF	Unc	BU
1980PM	—	—	—	—	—	—

KM# 11 2 POUNDS
15.9800 g., 0.9170 Gold 0.4711 oz. AGW **Ruler:** Elizabeth II **Series:** International Year of the Scout **Obv:** Young bust right **Rev:** Scouts and tent

Date	Mintage	VG	F	VF	XF	Unc
ND(1983)	2,000	—	—	—	—	—
ND(1983) Proof	2,000	Value: 500				

PIEFORTS

KM#	Date	Mintage	Identification	Mkt Val
P1	1984	500	50 Pence. Silver. KM13a.	50.00
P2	1995	500	50 Pence. Silver. KM14a.	90.00

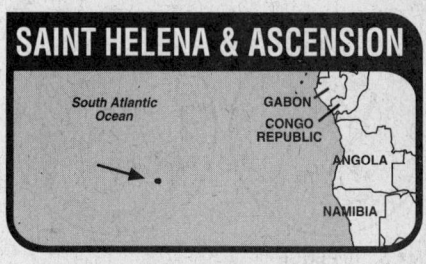

SAINT HELENA & ASCENSION

South Atlantic Ocean — GABON, CONGO REPUBLIC, ANGOLA, NAMIBIA

BRITISH OVERSEAS TERRITORY
STANDARD COINAGE

100 Pence = 1 Pound

KM# 1 PENNY
3.6000 g., Bronze, 20.32 mm. **Ruler:** Queen Elizabeth II **Obv:** Young bust right **Rev:** Tuna fish and value

Date	Mintage	F	VF	XF	Unc	BU
1984	—	—	0.20	0.50	1.25	
1984 Proof	10,000	Value: 1.50				

KM# 13 PENNY
3.6000 g., Bronze, 20.32 mm. **Ruler:** Queen Elizabeth II **Obv:** Crowned head right **Rev:** Tuna fish and value

Date	Mintage	F	VF	XF	Unc	BU
1991	—	—	0.15	0.35	1.00	

KM# 13a PENNY
3.5000 g., Copper Plated Steel Galvanized steel, 20.28 mm. **Ruler:** Queen Elizabeth II **Obv:** Crowned head right **Rev:** Tuna above value **Edge:** Plain

Date	Mintage	F	VF	XF	Unc	BU
1997	—	—	0.15	0.35	1.00	

KM# 2 2 PENCE
7.1000 g., Bronze, 25.91 mm. **Ruler:** Queen Elizabeth II **Obv:** Young bust right **Rev:** Donkey with firewood

Date	Mintage	F	VF	XF	Unc	BU
1984	—	—	0.25	0.65	1.25	
1984 Proof	10,000	Value: 2.00				

KM# 12 2 PENCE
7.1000 g., Bronze, 25.91 mm. **Ruler:** Queen Elizabeth II **Obv:** Crowned head right **Rev:** Value below donkey

Date	Mintage	F	VF	XF	Unc	BU
1991	—	—	0.20	0.60	1.50	

KM# 3 5 PENCE
5.7000 g., Copper-Nickel, 23.59 mm. **Ruler:** Queen Elizabeth II **Obv:** Young bust right **Rev:** Rainpiper

Date	Mintage	F	VF	XF	Unc	BU
1984	—	—	0.25	0.65	1.50	
1984 Proof	—	Value: 2.00				

KM# 14   5 PENCE
Copper-Nickel, 18 mm.   **Ruler:** Queen Elizabeth II
Obv: Crowned head right **Rev:** Value below rainpiper

Date	Mintage	F	VF	XF	Unc	BU
1991	—			0.20	0.75	1.50

KM# 22   5 PENCE
Copper-Nickel, 18 mm.   **Ruler:** Queen Elizabeth II
Obv: Crowned head right **Rev:** Giant tortoise

Date	Mintage	F	VF	XF	Unc	BU
1998	—			1.00	2.50	5.00

KM# 4   10 PENCE
11.3000 g., Copper-Nickel, 28.5 mm.   **Ruler:** Queen Elizabeth II
Obv: Young bust right **Rev:** Value below arum lily

Date	Mintage	F	VF	XF	Unc	BU
1984	—			0.50	1.25	2.00
1984 Proof	—	Value: 3.00				

KM# 15   10 PENCE
11.3000 g., Copper-Nickel, 28.5 mm.   **Ruler:** Queen Elizabeth II
Obv: Crowned head right

Date	Mintage	F	VF	XF	Unc	BU
1991	—	—	—	0.30	1.00	1.50

KM# 23   10 PENCE
Copper-Nickel, 24.5 mm.   **Ruler:** Queen Elizabeth II
Obv: Crowned head right **Rev:** Dolphins

Date	Mintage	F	VF	XF	Unc	BU
1998	—			2.00	4.00	6.00

KM# 21   20 PENCE
Copper-Nickel, 21.4 mm.   **Ruler:** Queen Elizabeth II
Obv: Crowned head right **Rev:** Flower

Date	Mintage	F	VF	XF	Unc	BU
1998	—			0.75	1.50	2.50

KM# 5   50 PENCE
13.5000 g., Copper-Nickel, 30 mm.   **Ruler:** Queen Elizabeth II
Obv: Young bust right **Rev:** Green sea turtle

Date	Mintage	F	VF	XF	Unc	BU
1984	—			1.75	3.75	6.00
1984 Proof	—	Value: 7.50				

KM# 7   50 PENCE
Copper-Nickel, 38.5 mm.   **Ruler:** Queen Elizabeth II
Subject: Wedding of Prince Andrew and Sarah Ferguson
Obv: Crowned bust right **Rev:** Conjoined busts of couple right
within circle

Date	Mintage	F	VF	XF	Unc	BU
ND(1986)	13,000				4.00	6.00

KM# 7a   50 PENCE
28.2800 g., 0.9250 Silver 0.8410 oz. ASW, 38.5 mm.
Ruler: Queen Elizabeth II **Subject:** Wedding of Prince Andrew
and Sarah Ferguson **Obv:** Crowned bust right **Rev:** Conjoined
busts of couple right within circle

Date	Mintage	F	VF	XF	Unc	BU
ND(1986) Proof	2,500	Value: 27.50				

KM# 7b   50 PENCE
47.5400 g., 0.9170 Gold 1.4015 oz. AGW, 38.5 mm.
Ruler: Queen Elizabeth II **Subject:** Wedding of Prince Andrew
and Sarah Ferguson **Obv:** Crowned bust right **Rev:** Conjoined
busts of couple right within circle

Date	Mintage	F	VF	XF	Unc	BU
ND(1986) Proof	50	Value: 1,450				

KM# 8   50 PENCE
Copper-Nickel, 38.5 mm.   **Ruler:** Queen Elizabeth II
Subject: 165th Anniversary of Napoleon's Death **Obv:** Crowned
bust right **Rev:** Sailing ship and 1/2 figure facing right

Date	Mintage	F	VF	XF	Unc	BU
1986	50,000				5.00	7.00

KM# 16   50 PENCE
13.5000 g., Copper-Nickel, 30 mm.   **Ruler:** Queen Elizabeth II
Obv: Crowned head right **Rev:** Green sea turtle

Date	Mintage	F	VF	XF	Unc	BU
1991	—			1.50	4.00	6.00

KM# 19   50 PENCE
Copper-Nickel, 38.5 mm.   **Ruler:** Queen Elizabeth II
Subject: Normandy Invasion **Obv:** Crowned bust right
Rev: Barbed wire above fence, artistic arrows pointing downward

Date	Mintage	F	VF	XF	Unc	BU
ND(1994)	—				6.00	8.00

KM# 19a   50 PENCE
28.2800 g., 0.9250 Silver 0.8410 oz. ASW, 38.5 mm.
Ruler: Queen Elizabeth II **Subject:** Normandy Invasion
Obv: Crowned bust right **Rev:** Barbed wire above fence, artistic
arrows pointing downward

Date	Mintage	F	VF	XF	Unc	BU
ND(1994) Proof	5,000	Value: 40.00				

KM# 6   POUND
9.5000 g., Nickel-Brass, 22.5 mm.   **Ruler:** Queen Elizabeth II
Obv: Young bust right **Rev:** Flying birds

Date	Mintage	F	VF	XF	Unc	BU
1984	—	—	—	2.50	5.50	8.00
1984 Proof	—	Value: 9.00				

KM# 6a   POUND
9.5000 g., 0.9250 Silver 0.2825 oz. ASW, 22.5 mm.
Ruler: Queen Elizabeth II **Obv:** Young bust right **Rev:** Flying
birds

Date	Mintage	F	VF	XF	Unc	BU
1984 Proof	10,000	Value: 18.00				

KM# 17   POUND
9.5000 g., Nickel-Brass, 22.5 mm.   **Ruler:** Queen Elizabeth II
Obv: Crowned head right **Rev:** Two birds in flight left

Date	Mintage	F	VF	XF	Unc	BU
1991	—			2.25	5.00	8.00

KM# 11   2 POUNDS
Copper-Nickel, 38.5 mm.   **Ruler:** Queen Elizabeth II
Subject: Queen Mother **Obv:** Crowned bust right **Rev:** Crowned
monogram flanked by flowers

Date	Mintage	F	VF	XF	Unc	BU
ND(1990)	—	—			12.00	13.50

KM# 18   2 POUNDS
28.2800 g., 0.9250 Silver 0.8410 oz. ASW, 38.5 mm.
Ruler: Queen Elizabeth II **Subject:** 40th Anniversary -
Coronation of Elizabeth II **Obv:** Crowned bust right **Rev:** Church
figures

Date	Mintage	F	VF	XF	Unc	BU
ND(1993) Proof	10,000	Value: 55.00				

KM# 24   5 POUNDS
28.2800 g., 0.9250 Silver 0.8410 oz. ASW, 38.5 mm.
Ruler: Queen Elizabeth II **Subject:** Queen Mother
Obv: Crowned bust right **Rev:** Queen Mother's monogram
Note: Prev. KM#11a.

Date	Mintage	F	VF	XF	Unc	BU
ND(1990) Proof	10,000	Value: 50.00				

KM# 9   25 POUNDS
155.0000 g., 0.9990 Silver 4.9782 oz. ASW, 65 mm.
Ruler: Queen Elizabeth II **Subject:** 165th Anniversary of Napoleon's Death **Obv:** Crowned bust right **Rev:** Sailing ship at right and 1/2 figure facing right **Note:** Illustration reduced.

Date	Mintage	F	VF	XF	Unc	BU
1986 Proof	15,000	Value: 150				

KM# 20   25 POUNDS
155.5175 g., 0.9990 Silver 4.9948 oz. ASW, 65 mm.
Ruler: Queen Elizabeth II **Subject:** 70th Birthday - Queen Elizabeth II **Obv:** Crowned bust right **Rev:** Mounted drummer and cameo head right **Note:** Illustration reduced.

Date	Mintage	F	VF	XF	Unc	BU
1996 Proof	1,000	Value: 200				

KM# 10   50 POUNDS
32.2600 g., 0.9990 Platinum 1.0361 oz. APW **Ruler:** Queen Elizabeth II **Subject:** 165th Anniversary of Napoleon's Death **Obv:** Crowned bust right **Rev:** Sailing ship at right and 1/2 figure at left looking right **Note:** Similar to KM#9.

Date	Mintage	F	VF	XF	Unc	BU
1986 Proof	5,000	Value: 2,250				

PIEFORTS
KM#	Date	Mintage	Identification	Issue Price	Mkt Val
P1	1984	2,500	Pound. Silver. KM#6a.	49.75	30.00
P2	1986	250	50 Pence. Silver. KM#7a.	74.00	75.00
P3	1994	500	50 Pence. Copper-Nickel center. KM#19.	—	60.00

MINT SETS
KM#	Date	Mintage	Identification	Issue Price	Mkt Val
MS1	1984 (6)		— KM#1-6	—	20.00

PROOF SETS
KM#	Date	Mintage	Identification	Issue Price	Mkt Val
PS1	1984 (6)		— KM#1-6	—	25.00

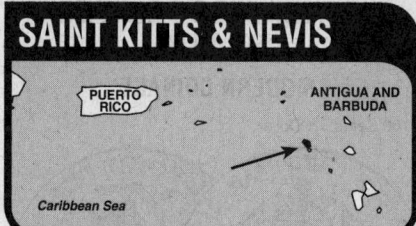

SAINT KITTS & NEVIS

This independent state, located in the Leeward Islands of the West Indies, south of Puerto Rico, comprises the islands of St. Kitts, Nevis and Anguilla. The country has an area of 101 sq. mi. (261 sq. km.) and a population of 41,000. Capital: Basseterre, on St. Kitts (as it may be called in abbreviated form). The islands export sugar, cotton, lobsters, beverages and electrical equipment.

St. Kitts was discovered by Columbus in 1493 and was settled by Thomas Warner, an Englishman, in 1623. The Treaty of Utrecht, 1713, ceded the island to the British. France protested British occupancy, and on three occasions between 1616 and 1782 seized the island and held it for short periods. St. Kitts used the coins and currency of the British Caribbean Territories (Eastern Group).

In early 1967 the Colony was, together with the islands of Nevis and Anguilla, united politically as a self-governing British Associated State. However, in June 1967 Anguilla declared its independence, severing ties with Britain and established a so-called 'Republic of Anguilla'. Britain refused to accept this and established a Commissioner to govern Anguilla; this arrangement continues to the present time.

St. Kitts and Nevis became a member of the Commonwealth of Nations on Sept. 19, 1983. Queen Elizabeth II is Head of State.

From approximately 1750-1830, billon 2 sous of the French colony of Cayenne were countermarked SK' and used on St. Kitts. They were valued at 1-1/2 Pence Sterling. (St. Kitts and Nevis now use East Caribbeah Currency.)

RULER
British

MONETARY SYSTEM
100 Cents = 1 East Caribbean Dollar

BRITISH ASSOCIATED STATE
STANDARD COINAGE
100 Cents = 1 Dollar

KM# 1   4 DOLLARS
Copper-Nickel, 38.5 mm.   **Series:** F.A.O. **Obv:** Crowned arms with supporters **Rev:** Sugar cane and banana tree branch divided by value below

Date	Mintage	F	VF	XF	Unc	BU
1970	13,000	4.00	6.00	10.00	20.00	30.00
1970 Proof	2,000	Value: 35.00				

KM# 3   10 DOLLARS
Copper-Nickel, 38.8 mm.   **Subject:** Royal Visit **Obv:** Crowned bust right **Rev:** Crowned arms with supporters

Date	Mintage	F	VF	XF	Unc	BU
1985	100,000	2.00	3.50	7.50	10.00	12.50

KM# 3a   10 DOLLARS
28.2800 g., 0.9250 Silver 0.8410 oz. ASW, 38.8 mm.
Subject: Royal Visit **Obv:** Crowned bust right **Rev:** Crowned arms with supporters

Date	Mintage	F	VF	XF	Unc	BU
1985 Proof	5,000	Value: 40.00				

KM# 3b   10 DOLLARS
47.5400 g., 0.9170 Gold 1.4015 oz. AGW, 38.8 mm.
Subject: Royal Visit **Obv:** Crowned bust right **Rev:** Crowned arms with supporters

Date	Mintage	F	VF	XF	Unc	BU
1985 Proof	250	Value: 1,400				

KM# 4   20 DOLLARS
Copper-Nickel, 38.8 mm.   **Subject:** 200th Anniversary - Battle of the Saints **Obv:** Crowned arms with supporters **Rev:** Dates above ship

Date	Mintage	F	VF	XF	Unc	BU
ND(1982)	—	—	—	—	12.50	15.00

KM# 4a   20 DOLLARS
28.2800 g., 0.9250 Silver 0.8410 oz. ASW, 38.8 mm.
Subject: 200th Anniversary - Battle of the Saints **Obv:** Crowned arms with supporters **Rev:** Dates above ship

Date	Mintage	F	VF	XF	Unc	BU
ND(1982) Proof	2,500	Value: 42.50				

KM# 2   20 DOLLARS
28.2800 g., Copper-Nickel, 38.61 mm.   **Subject:** Attainment of Independence, September 19 **Obv:** Young bust right **Rev:** Ship, map and compass

Date	Mintage	F	VF	XF	Unc	BU
1983	—	—	—	—	15.00	17.50

KM# 2a   20 DOLLARS
28.2800 g., 0.9250 Silver 0.8410 oz. ASW **Subject:** Attainment of Independence, September 19 **Obv:** Young bust right **Rev:** Compass, ship and map

Date	Mintage	F	VF	XF	Unc	BU
1983 Proof	5,000	Value: 40.00				

KM# 5   100 DOLLARS
7.9900 g., 0.9170 Gold 0.2356 oz. AGW   **Subject:** 200th Anniversary - Siege of Brimstone Hill **Rev:** Brimstone Hill

Date	Mintage	F	VF	XF	Unc	BU
ND(1982)	250	—	—	—	—	250
ND(1982) Proof	15	Value: 675				

KM# 6   100 DOLLARS
129.5900 g., 0.9250 Silver 3.8538 oz. ASW, 63 mm.
Subject: Tropical birds **Rev:** Green-throated Carib Hummingbird
Note: Illustration reduced.

Date	Mintage	F	VF	XF	Unc	BU
1988 Proof	Est. 10,000	Value: 125				

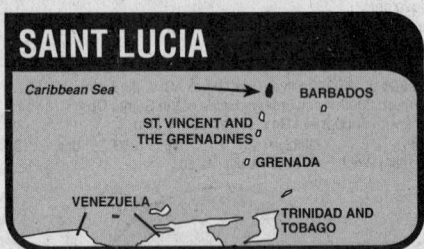

SAINT LUCIA

Caribbean Sea → BARBADOS
ST. VINCENT AND THE GRENADINES
GRENADA
VENEZUELA
TRINIDAD AND TOBAGO

Saint Lucia, an independent island nation located in the Windward Islands of the West Indies between Saint Vincent and Martinique, has an area of 238 sq. mi. (620 sq. km.) and a population of *150,000. Capital: Castries. The economy is agricultural. Bananas, copra, cocoa, sugar and logwood are exported.

Columbus discovered Saint Lucia in 1502. The first attempts at settlement undertaken by the British in 1605 and 1638 were frustrated by sickness and the determined hostility of the fierce Carib inhabitants. The French settled it in 1650 and made a treaty with the natives. Until 1814, when the island became a definite British possession, it was the scene of a continuous conflict between the British and French, which saw the island change, hands on at least 14 occasions. In 1967, under the West Indies Act, Saint Lucia was established as a British associated state, self-governing in internal affairs. Complete independence was attained on February 22, 1979. Saint Lucia is a member of the Commonwealth of Nations. Elizabeth II is Head of State as Queen of Saint Lucia.

Prior to 1950, the island used sterling, which was superseded by the currency of the British Caribbean Territories (Eastern Group) and the East Caribbean State.

RULER
British

MONETARY SYSTEM
100 Cents = 1 Dollar

BRITISH ASSOCIATED STATE

MODERN COINAGE

100 Cents = 1 Dollar

KM# 11   4 DOLLARS
Copper-Nickel, 38.5 mm. **Series:** F.A.O. **Obv:** Crowned arms with supporters **Rev:** Sugar cane and banana tree branch divided by value below

Date	Mintage	F	VF	XF	Unc	BU
1970	13,000	—	6.00	10.00	20.00	30.00
1970 Proof	2,000	Value: 35.00				

KM# 14   5 DOLLARS
Copper-Nickel **Subject:** Papal Visit - John Paul II **Obv:** Crowned arms with supporters **Obv. Leg.:** • SAINT LUCIA • FIVE DOLLARS below **Rev:** Bust left **Rev. Leg.:** • PAPAL VISIT JULY 1986 •JOHN PAUL II on shoulder

Date	Mintage	F	VF	XF	Unc	BU
1986	—	—	—	—	8.50	11.50

KM# 14a   5 DOLLARS
28.2800 g., 0.9250 Silver 0.8410 oz. ASW **Subject:** Papal Visit - John Paul II **Obv:** Crowned arms with supporters **Obv. Leg.:** • SAINT LUCIA • FIVE DOLLARS below **Rev:** Bust left **Rev. Leg.:** • PAPAL VISIT JULY 1986 • JOHN PAUL II on shoulder

Date	Mintage	F	VF	XF	Unc	BU
1986 Proof	2,120	Value: 42.50				

KM# 12   10 DOLLARS
Copper-Nickel, 38.8 mm. **Subject:** 200th Anniversary - Battle of the Saints **Obv:** Crowned arms with supporters **Rev:** Dates above battleships

Date	Mintage	F	VF	XF	Unc	BU
1982	—	—	—	—	12.50	14.50

KM# 12a   10 DOLLARS
28.2800 g., 0.9250 Silver 0.8410 oz. ASW, 38.8 mm.
Subject: 200th Anniversary - Battle of the Saints **Obv:** Crowned arms with supporters **Rev:** Dates above battleships

Date	Mintage	F	VF	XF	Unc	BU
1982 Proof	2,500	Value: 42.50				

KM# 13   10 DOLLARS
Copper-Nickel, 38.8 mm. **Subject:** Royal Visit - Queen Elizabeth II **Obv:** Crowned bust right **Rev:** Crowned arms with supporters **Rev. Leg.:** • ROYAL VISIT 1985 • TEN DOLLARS below

Date	Mintage	F	VF	XF	Unc	BU
1985	100,000	—	—	—	9.50	12.50

KM# 13a   10 DOLLARS
28.2800 g., 0.9250 Silver 0.8410 oz. ASW, 38.8 mm.
Subject: Royal Visit - Queen Elizabeth II **Obv:** Crowned bust right **Rev:** Crowned arms with supporters **Rev. Leg.:** • ROYAL VISIT 1985 • TEN DOLLARS below

Date	Mintage	F	VF	XF	Unc	BU
1985 Proof	5,000	Value: 40.00				

KM# 13b   10 DOLLARS
47.5400 g., 0.9170 Gold 1.4015 oz. AGW, 38.8 mm.
Subject: Royal Visit - Queen Elizabeth II **Obv:** Crowned bust right **Rev:** Crowned arms with supporters **Rev. Leg.:** • ROYAL VISIT 1985 • TEN DOLLARS below

Date	Mintage	F	VF	XF	Unc	BU
1985 Proof	250	Value: 1,400				

KM# 16   10 DOLLARS
28.2800 g., 0.9250 Silver 0.8410 oz. ASW
Subject: Commonwealth Finance Ministers' Meeting
Obv: Monogram flanked by sprigs within circle **Rev:** Crowned arms with supporters above lake and mountains

Date	Mintage	F	VF	XF	Unc	BU
1986 Proof	1,000	Value: 65.00				

KM# 17   100 DOLLARS
129.5900 g., 0.9250 Silver 3.8538 oz. ASW, 63 mm.
Subject: Tropical Birds **Rev:** Two amazon parrots **Note:** Illustration reduced.

Date	Mintage	F	VF	XF	Unc	BU
1988 Proof	Est. 10,000	Value: 125				

KM# 15 500 DOLLARS
15.9800 g., 0.9170 Gold 0.4711 oz. AGW **Subject:** Papal Visit
- John Paul II **Obv:** Crowned arms with supporters within circle
Rev: Bust left **Rev. Leg.:** • PAPAL VISIT JULY 1986 •

Date	Mintage	F	VF	XF	Unc	BU
1986 Proof	100	Value: 850				

ST PIERRE & MIQUELON

The Territorial Collectivity of Saint Pierre and Miquelon, a
French overseas territory located 10 miles (16 km.) off the south
coast of Newfoundland, has an area of 93 sq. mi. (242 sq. km.)
and a population of *6,000. Capital: Saint Pierre. The economy of
the barren archipelago is based on cod fishing and fur farming.
Fish and fish products, and mink and silver fox pelts are exported.

The islands were occupied by the French in 1604, then were
captured by the British in 1702 and held until 1763, at which time
they were returned to the possession of France and employed as a
fishing station. They passed between France and England on
six more occasions between 1778 and 1814 when the Treaty of
Paris awarded them permanently to France. The rugged, soil-
poor granite islands, which will support only evergreen shrubs,
are all that remain of France's extensive North American colonies.
In 1958 Saint Pierre and Miquelon voted in favor of the new constitution of the Fifth Republic of France, thereby choosing to
remain within the new French Community.

RULER
French

MINT MARK
(a) - Paris, privy marks only

MONETARY SYSTEM
100 Centimes = 1 Franc

FRENCH OVERSEAS DEPARTMENT
STANDARD COINAGE

KM# 1 FRANC
1.3200 g., Aluminum, 22.56 mm. **Obv:** Winged Liberty head left
Rev: Ship above value **Edge:** Plain

Date	Mintage	F	VF	XF	Unc	BU
1948(a)	600,000	1.00	2.00	4.00	10.00	15.00

KM# 2 2 FRANCS
2.1400 g., Aluminum, 26.95 mm. **Obv:** Winged Liberty head left
Rev: Ship above value **Edge:** Plain

Date	Mintage	F	VF	XF	Unc	BU
1948(a)	300,000	1.00	2.00	4.00	10.00	15.00

ESSAIS
Standard metals unless otherwise noted

KM#	Date	Mintage	Identification	Issue Price	Mkt Val
E1a	1948(a)	2,000	Franc. Copper-Nickel.	—	40.00
E2a	1948(a)	2,000	2 Francs. Copper-Nickel.	—	45.00

PIEFORTS WITH ESSAIS
Double thickness, standard metals unless otherwise noted

KM#	Date	Mintage	Identification	Issue Price	Mkt Val
PE1	1948(a)	104	Franc.	—	120
PE2	1948(a)	104	2 Francs.	—	150

SAINT THOMAS & PRINCE

The Democratic Republic of St. Thomas & Prince (São Tomé
e Príncipe) is located in the Gulf of Guinea 150 miles (241 km.)
off the western coast of Africa. It has an area of 372 sq. mi. (960
sq. km.) and a population of *121,000. Capital: São Tomé. The
economy of the islands is based on cocoa, copra and coffee.

Saint Thomas and Saint Prince were uninhabited when discovered by Portuguese navigators Joao de Santarem and Pedro
de Escobar in 1470. After the failure of their initial settlement of
1485, the Portuguese successfully colonized St. Thomas with a
colony of prisoners and exiled Jews in 1493. An initial prosperity
based on the sugar trade gave way to a time of misfortune, 1567-
1709, that saw the colony attacked and occupied or plundered
by the French and Dutch, ravaged by the slave revolt of 1595; and
finally rendered destitute by the transfer of the world sugar trade
to Brazil. In the late 1800s, the colony turned from the production
of sugar to cocoa, the basis of its present economy

The islands were designated a Portuguese overseas province
in 1951. On April 25, 1974, the government of Portugal was seized
by a military junta, which reached agreements providing for independence for the Portuguese overseas provinces of Portuguese
Guinea (Guinea-Bissau), Mozambique, Cape Verde Islands,
Angola, and Saint Thomas and Prince Islands. The Democratic
Republic of São Tomé and Principe was declared on July 12, 1975.

RULERS
Portuguese, until 1975

MINT MARKS
R – Rio

MONETARY SYSTEM
100 Centavos = 1 Escudo

PORTUGUESE COLONY
REFORM COINAGE

100 Centavos = 1 Escudo

KM# 2 10 CENTAVOS
Nickel-Bronze **Obv:** Liberty head left **Rev:** Shield within globe
above value

Date	Mintage	F	VF	XF	Unc	BU
1929	500,000	2.00	6.00	20.00	50.00	—

KM# 15 10 CENTAVOS
Bronze **Obv:** Value **Rev:** Shield within crowned globe

Date	Mintage	F	VF	XF	Unc	BU
1962	500,000	0.50	1.25	4.50	12.00	—

KM# 15a 10 CENTAVOS
Aluminum **Obv:** Value **Rev:** Shield within crowned globe

Date	Mintage	F	VF	XF	Unc	BU
1971	1,000,000	0.35	0.65	1.25	3.50	—

KM# 3 20 CENTAVOS
Nickel-Bronze **Obv:** Liberty head left **Rev:** Shield within globe
above value

Date	Mintage	F	VF	XF	Unc	BU
1929	250,000	2.50	6.50	22.50	55.00	—

KM# 16.1 20 CENTAVOS
Bronze, 18 mm. **Obv:** Value **Rev:** Shield within crowned globe

Date	Mintage	F	VF	XF	Unc	BU
1962	250,000	0.50	1.25	5.50	15.00	—

KM# 16.2 20 CENTAVOS
Bronze, 16 mm. **Obv:** Value **Rev:** Shield within crowned globe

Date	Mintage	F	VF	XF	Unc	BU
1971	750,000	0.35	0.75	1.50	4.00	—

KM# 1 50 CENTAVOS
Nickel-Bronze **Obv:** Liberty head left **Rev:** Shield within globe
above value

Date	Mintage	F	VF	XF	Unc	BU
1928	—	30.00	90.00	350	900	—
1929	400,000	4.00	12.00	50.00	150	—

KM# 8 50 CENTAVOS
Nickel-Bronze **Obv:** Value **Rev:** Shield within crowned globe

Date	Mintage	F	VF	XF	Unc	BU
1948	80,000	10.00	30.00	100	265	—

KM# 10 50 CENTAVOS
4.4500 g., Copper-Nickel, 22.64 mm. **Obv:** Value **Rev:** Shield
within crowned globe

Date	Mintage	F	VF	XF	Unc	BU
1951	48,000	1.75	3.50	25.00	70.00	—

KM# 17.1 50 CENTAVOS
3.9500 g., Bronze, 20 mm. **Obv:** Value **Rev:** Shield within
crowned globe

Date	Mintage	F	VF	XF	Unc	BU
1962	480,000	0.25	0.50	2.50	5.00	—

KM# 17.2   50 CENTAVOS
Bronze, 22 mm. **Obv:** Value **Rev:** Shield within crowned globe

Date	Mintage	F	VF	XF	Unc	BU
1971	600,000	0.20	0.35	1.50	3.00	—

KM# 4   ESCUDO
Copper-Nickel **Obv:** Value **Rev:** Shield within crowned globe

Date	Mintage	F	VF	XF	Unc	BU
1939	100,000	9.00	25.00	100	285	—

KM# 9   ESCUDO
Nickel-Bronze **Obv:** Value **Rev:** Shield within crowned globe

Date	Mintage	F	VF	XF	Unc	BU
1948	60,000	12.50	40.00	120	275	350

KM# 11   ESCUDO
Copper-Nickel **Obv:** Value **Rev:** Shield within crowned globe

Date	Mintage	F	VF	XF	Unc	BU
1951	18,000	3.50	12.00	60.00	175	—

KM# 18   ESCUDO
7.8500 g., Bronze, 26 mm. **Obv:** Value **Rev:** Shield within crowned globe

Date	Mintage	F	VF	XF	Unc	BU
1962	160,000	0.75	2.50	15.00	35.00	—
1971	350,000	0.35	0.75	1.50	3.50	—

KM# 5   2-1/2 ESCUDOS
3.5000 g., 0.6500 Silver 0.0731 oz. ASW **Obv:** Shield within globe on cross **Rev:** Shield within crowned globe

Date	Mintage	F	VF	XF	Unc	BU
1939	80,000	10.00	30.00	100	300	—
1948	120,000	15.00	35.00	100	300	—

KM# 12   2-1/2 ESCUDOS
3.5000 g., 0.6500 Silver 0.0731 oz. ASW **Obv:** Shield within globe on cross **Rev:** Shield within crowned globe

Date	Mintage	F	VF	XF	Unc	BU
1951	64,000	2.50	6.00	30.00	100	—

KM# 19   2-1/2 ESCUDOS
Copper-Nickel **Obv:** Shield within globe on cross **Rev:** Shield within crowned globe

Date	Mintage	F	VF	XF	Unc	BU
1962	140,000	0.75	1.50	5.00	15.00	—
1971	250,000	0.50	1.00	2.50	7.00	—

KM# 6   5 ESCUDOS
7.0000 g., 0.6500 Silver 0.1463 oz. ASW **Obv:** Shield within globe on cross **Rev:** Shield within crowned globe

Date	Mintage	F	VF	XF	Unc	BU
1939	60,000	12.50	35.00	100	300	—
1948	100,000	18.00	45.00	110	300	—

KM# 13   5 ESCUDOS
7.0000 g., 0.6500 Silver 0.1463 oz. ASW, 25 mm. **Obv:** Shield within globe on cross **Rev:** Shield within crowned globe

Date	Mintage	F	VF	XF	Unc	BU
1951	72,000	3.50	7.00	20.00	45.00	—

KM# 20   5 ESCUDOS
4.0000 g., 0.6000 Silver 0.0772 oz. ASW, 22 mm. **Obv:** Shield within globe **Rev:** Shield within crowned globe

Date	Mintage	F	VF	XF	Unc	BU
1962	88,000	1.50	2.50	6.00	12.50	—

KM# 22   5 ESCUDOS
Copper-Nickel **Obv:** Shield within globe on cross **Rev:** Shield within crowned globe

Date	Mintage	F	VF	XF	Unc	BU
1971	100,000	0.75	1.50	3.50	8.00	—

KM# 7   10 ESCUDOS
12.5000 g., 0.8350 Silver 0.3356 oz. ASW **Obv:** Shield within globe on cross **Rev:** Shield within crowned globe

Date	Mintage	F	VF	XF	Unc	BU
1939	40,000	12.00	25.00	65.00	250	—

KM# 14   10 ESCUDOS
12.5000 g., 0.7200 Silver 0.2893 oz. ASW **Obv:** Shield within globe on cross **Rev:** Shield within crowned globe

Date	Mintage	F	VF	XF	Unc	BU
1951	40,000	6.00	9.00	16.50	35.00	—

KM# 23   10 ESCUDOS
Copper-Nickel **Obv:** Shield within globe on cross **Rev:** Shield within crowned globe

Date	Mintage	F	VF	XF	Unc	BU
1971	100,000	1.25	2.50	5.50	12.50	—

KM# 24   20 ESCUDOS
Nickel **Obv:** Shield within globe **Rev:** Shield within circle

Date	Mintage	F	VF	XF	Unc	BU
1971	75,000	1.50	3.00	6.00	13.50	—

KM# 21   50 ESCUDOS
18.0000 g., 0.6500 Silver 0.3761 oz. ASW **Subject:** 500th Anniversary of Discovery **Obv:** Cross within designed circle **Rev:** Double shields flanked by dates, star design at top

Date	Mintage	F	VF	XF	Unc	BU
1970	150,000	—	—	—	8.00	10.00
1970 Matte proof	Est. 200	—	—	—	—	—

Note: Produced at the Lisbon Mint on private contract.

DEMOCRATIC REPUBLIC

STANDARD COINAGE

100 Centimos = 1 Dobra

KM# 25 50 CENTIMOS
Brass, 17 mm. **Series:** F.A.O. **Obv:** Arms with supporters **Rev:** Fish above value

Date	Mintage	F	VF	XF	Unc	BU
1977	2,000,000	—	0.10	0.20	0.75	1.00
1977 Proof	2,500	Value: 3.00				

KM# 26 DOBRA
Brass, 20 mm. **Series:** F.A.O. **Obv:** Arms with supporters **Rev:** Cocoa beans on stem and value

Date	Mintage	F	VF	XF	Unc	BU
1977	1,500,000	—	0.15	0.25	1.00	1.25
1977 Proof	2,500	Value: 3.00				

KM# 27 2 DOBRAS
Copper-Nickel, 18.5 mm. **Series:** F.A.O. **Obv:** Arms with supporters **Rev:** Goats

Date	Mintage	F	VF	XF	Unc	BU
1977	1,000,000	—	0.25	0.40	1.50	1.75
1977 Proof	2,500	Value: 3.50				

KM# 28 5 DOBRAS
Copper-Nickel, 24 mm. **Series:** F.A.O. **Obv:** Arms with supporters **Rev:** Corn and value

Date	Mintage	F	VF	XF	Unc	BU
1977	750,000	—	0.35	0.65	2.00	2.50
1977 Proof	2,500	Value: 5.00				

KM# 29 10 DOBRAS
6.4000 g., Copper-Nickel, 26 mm. **Series:** F.A.O. **Obv:** Arms with supporters **Rev:** Chickens with eggs in cartons

Date	Mintage	F	VF	XF	Unc	BU
1977	300,000	—	0.60	1.25	4.00	5.00
1977 Proof	2,500	Value: 7.00				

KM# 29a 10 DOBRAS
Copper-Nickel Clad Steel, 26 mm. **Series:** F.A.O. **Obv:** Arms with supporters **Rev:** Chickens with eggs in cartons

Date	Mintage	F	VF	XF	Unc	BU
1990	—	—	0.60	1.25	4.00	5.00

KM# 30 20 DOBRAS
7.9000 g., Copper-Nickel Clad Steel, 29 mm. **Series:** F.A.O. **Obv:** Arms with supporters **Rev:** Logo and value to right of various plants and produce

Date	Mintage	F	VF	XF	Unc	BU
1977	500,000	—	1.00	2.00	6.00	7.00
1977 Proof	2,500	Value: 10.00				

KM# 52 50 DOBRAS
Copper-Nickel Clad Steel **Series:** F.A.O. **Obv:** Arms with supporters **Rev:** Value within octogon design with bird above and snake below

Date	Mintage	F	VF	XF	Unc	BU
1990	—	—	—	—	6.00	9.00

KM# 41 100 DOBRAS
Copper-Nickel **Subject:** World Fisheries Conference **Obv:** Arms with supporters **Rev:** Figure standing in boat with fish net

Date	Mintage	F	VF	XF	Unc	BU
ND(1984)	1,000,000	—	—	—	9.00	10.00

KM# 41a 100 DOBRAS
28.2800 g., 0.9250 Silver 0.8410 oz. ASW **Subject:** World Fisheries Conference **Obv:** Arms with supporters **Rev:** Figure standing in boat with fish net

Date	Mintage	F	VF	XF	Unc	BU
ND(1984) Proof	20,000	Value: 40.00				

KM# 41b 100 DOBRAS
47.5400 g., 0.9170 Gold 1.4015 oz. AGW **Subject:** World Fisheries Conference **Obv:** Arms with supporters **Rev:** Figure standing in boat with fish net

Date	Mintage	F	VF	XF	Unc	BU
ND(1984) Proof	100	Value: 1,450				

KM# 42 100 DOBRAS
Copper-Nickel **Subject:** 10th Anniversary of Independence **Obv:** Arms with supporters **Rev:** Value, stars and map

Date	Mintage	F	VF	XF	Unc	BU
ND(1985)	—	—	—	—	6.50	7.50

KM# 42a 100 DOBRAS
28.2800 g., 0.9250 Silver 0.8410 oz. ASW **Subject:** 10th Anniversary of Independence **Obv:** Arms with supporters **Rev:** Value, stars and map

Date	Mintage	F	VF	XF	Unc	BU
ND(1985) Proof	1,000	Value: 42.50				

KM# 42b 100 DOBRAS
47.5400 g., 0.9170 Gold 1.4015 oz. AGW **Subject:** 10th Anniversary of Independence **Obv:** Arms with supporters **Rev:** Value, stars and map

Date	Mintage	F	VF	XF	Unc	BU
ND(1985) Proof	50	Value: 1,500				

KM# 87 100 DOBRAS
Chrome Clad Steel, 17.5 mm. **Obv:** Arms with supporters **Rev:** Value below bird

Date	Mintage	F	VF	XF	Unc	BU
1997	—	—	—	—	1.25	1.75

KM# 31 250 DOBRAS
17.4000 g., 0.9250 Silver 0.5174 oz. ASW **Subject:** Independence **Obv:** Arms with supporters **Rev:** World population

Date	Mintage	F	VF	XF	Unc	BU
1977	450	—	—	—	42.50	47.50
1977 Proof	750	Value: 40.00				

KM# 32 250 DOBRAS
17.4000 g., 0.9250 Silver 0.5174 oz. ASW **Subject:** Independence **Obv:** Arms with supporters **Rev:** World friendship

Date	Mintage	F	VF	XF	Unc	BU
1977	450	—	—	—	42.50	47.50
1977 Proof	800	Value: 40.00				

KM# 33 250 DOBRAS
17.4000 g., 0.9250 Silver 0.5174 oz. ASW **Subject:** Independence **Obv:** Arms with supporters **Rev:** Folklore statue

Date	Mintage	F	VF	XF	Unc	BU
1977	300	—	—	—	42.50	47.50
1977 Proof	600	Value: 40.00				

KM# 34 250 DOBRAS
17.4000 g., 0.9250 Silver 0.5174 oz. ASW **Subject:** Independence **Obv:** Arms with supporters **Rev:** World unity emblems

Date	Mintage	F	VF	XF	Unc	BU
1977	400	—	—	—	42.50	47.50
1977 Proof	700	Value: 40.00				

KM# 35   250 DOBRAS
17.4000 g., 0.9250 Silver 0.5174 oz. ASW **Subject:** Independence
Obv: Arms with supporters **Rev:** Mother and child

Date	Mintage	F	VF	XF	Unc	BU
1977	350	—	—	—	42.50	47.50
1977 Proof	700	Value: 40.00				

KM# 88   250 DOBRAS
Chrome Clad Steel **Obv:** Arms with supporters **Rev:** Value above bird

Date	Mintage	F	VF	XF	Unc	BU
1997	—	—	—	—	1.50	3.00

KM# 70   500 DOBRAS
Copper-Nickel **Obv:** Arms with supporters **Rev:** Elvis Presley

Date	Mintage	F	VF	XF	Unc	BU
1993	—	—	—	—	12.50	14.50

KM# 89   500 DOBRAS
Chrome Clad Steel **Obv:** Arms with supporters **Rev:** Monkey in trees

Date	Mintage	F	VF	XF	Unc	BU
1997	—	—	—	—	2.00	3.00

KM# 44   1000 DOBRAS
23.3300 g., 0.9250 Silver 0.6938 oz. ASW **Subject:** Soccer
Obv: Arms with supporters **Rev:** 2 players

Date	Mintage	F	VF	XF	Unc	BU
1990 Proof	15,000	Value: 30.00				

KM# 45   1000 DOBRAS
23.3300 g., 0.9250 Silver 0.6938 oz. ASW **Subject:** Soccer
Obv: Arms with supporters **Rev:** 2 players running

Date	Mintage	F	VF	XF	Unc	BU
1990 Proof	15,000	Value: 30.00				

KM# 47   1000 DOBRAS
25.9600 g., 0.9990 Silver 0.8338 oz. ASW **Subject:** Soccer
Obv: Arms with supporters **Rev:** Soccer player

Date	Mintage	F	VF	XF	Unc	BU
1990 Proof	—	Value: 45.00				

KM# 48   1000 DOBRAS
25.9600 g., 0.9990 Silver 0.8338 oz. ASW **Subject:** Soccer
Obv: Arms with supporters **Rev:** Soccer players

Date	Mintage	F	VF	XF	Unc	BU
1990 Proof	—	Value: 45.00				

KM# 49   1000 DOBRAS
20.0000 g., 0.9990 Silver 0.6423 oz. ASW **Subject:** National
independence **Obv:** Arms with supporters **Rev:** Cheering figures

Date	Mintage	F	VF	XF	Unc	BU
1990 Proof	—	Value: 40.00				

KM# 50   1000 DOBRAS
20.0000 g., 0.9990 Silver 0.6423 oz. ASW **Subject:** Vasco de
Gama **Obv:** Arms with supporters **Rev:** Cameo to right of ship

Date	Mintage	F	VF	XF	Unc	BU
1990 Proof	—	Value: 37.50				

KM# 53   1000 DOBRAS
20.0000 g., 0.9990 Silver 0.6423 oz. ASW **Subject:** Olympics and
Discovery of America **Obv:** Arms with supporters **Rev:** Seated
figure, partial map and ship, book with olympic circles on cover

Date	Mintage	F	VF	XF	Unc	BU
1990 Proof	—	Value: 35.00				

KM# 73   1000 DOBRAS
23.7400 g., 0.9250 Silver 0.7060 oz. ASW **Series:** 1992 Olympics
Obv: Arms with supporters **Rev:** Date below flames and mountains

Date	Mintage	F	VF	XF	Unc	BU
1990 Proof	10,000	Value: 32.50				

KM# 74   1000 DOBRAS
23.7400 g., 0.9250 Silver 0.7060 oz. ASW **Series:** 1992
Olympics **Obv:** Arms with supporters **Rev:** Diver

Date	Mintage	F	VF	XF	Unc	BU
1990 Proof	10,000	Value: 27.50				

KM# 54   1000 DOBRAS
Copper-Nickel **Series:** Atlanta Olympics **Obv:** Arms with
supporters **Rev:** Wrestling

Date	Mintage	F	VF	XF	Unc	BU
ND(1993) Proof	—	Value: 28.50				

KM# 63   1000 DOBRAS
Copper-Nickel **Series:** Atlanta Olympics **Obv:** Arms with
supporters **Rev:** Swimmers

Date	Mintage	F	VF	XF	Unc	BU
ND(1993) Proof	—	Value: 28.50				

KM# 55   1000 DOBRAS
Copper-Nickel **Series:** Atlanta Olympics **Obv:** Arms with
supporters **Rev:** Soccer players

Date	Mintage	F	VF	XF	Unc	BU
ND(1993) Proof	—	Value: 28.50				

KM# 56   1000 DOBRAS
Copper-Nickel **Series:** Atlanta Olympics **Obv:** Arms with
supporters **Rev:** Boxer

Date	Mintage	F	VF	XF	Unc	BU
ND(1993) Proof	—	Value: 28.50				

KM# 57 1000 DOBRAS
Copper-Nickel **Series:** Atlanta Olympics **Obv:** Arms with supporters **Rev:** Bicyclist

Date	Mintage	F	VF	XF	Unc	BU
ND(1993) Proof	—	Value: 28.50				

KM# 58 1000 DOBRAS
Copper-Nickel **Series:** Atlanta Olympics **Obv:** Arms with supporters **Rev:** Karate competition

Date	Mintage	F	VF	XF	Unc	BU
ND(1993) Proof	—	Value: 28.50				

KM# 59 1000 DOBRAS
Copper-Nickel **Series:** Atlanta Olympics **Obv:** Arms with supporters **Rev:** Runner

Date	Mintage	F	VF	XF	Unc	BU
ND(1993) Proof	—	Value: 28.50				

KM# 60 1000 DOBRAS
Copper-Nickel **Series:** Atlanta Olympics **Obv:** Arms with supporters **Rev:** Field hockey players

Date	Mintage	F	VF	XF	Unc	BU
ND(1993) Proof	—	Value: 28.50				

KM# 61 1000 DOBRAS
Copper-Nickel **Series:** Atlanta Olympics **Obv:** Arms with supporters **Rev:** Four track and field events

Date	Mintage	F	VF	XF	Unc	BU
ND(1993) Proof	—	Value: 28.50				

KM# 62 1000 DOBRAS
Copper-Nickel **Series:** Atlanta Olympics **Obv:** Arms with supporters **Rev:** Surfer

Date	Mintage	F	VF	XF	Unc	BU
ND(1993) Proof	—	Value: 25.00				

KM# 64 1000 DOBRAS
Copper-Nickel **Series:** Atlanta Olympics **Obv:** Arms with supporters **Rev:** Three gymnastic events

Date	Mintage	F	VF	XF	Unc	BU
ND(1993) Proof	—	Value: 28.50				

KM# 65 1000 DOBRAS
Copper-Nickel **Series:** Atlanta Olympics **Obv:** Arms with supporters **Rev:** Tennis players

Date	Mintage	F	VF	XF	Unc	BU
ND(1993) Proof	—	Value: 28.50				

KM# 71 1000 DOBRAS
25.0000 g., 0.9250 Silver 0.7435 oz. ASW **Obv:** Arms with supporters **Rev:** Elvis Presley

Date	Mintage	F	VF	XF	Unc	BU
1993 Proof	—	Value: 32.50				

KM# 76 1000 DOBRAS
25.0000 g., 0.9250 Silver 0.7435 oz. ASW **Obv:** Arms with supporters **Rev:** Black Kite **Note:** Enamel.

Date	Mintage	F	VF	XF	Unc	BU
1995 Proof	15,000	Value: 47.00				

KM# 77 1000 DOBRAS
25.0000 g., 0.9250 Silver 0.7435 oz. ASW **Obv:** Arms with supporters **Rev:** Porcelain rose **Note:** Enamel.

Date	Mintage	F	VF	XF	Unc	BU
1995 Proof	15,000	Value: 55.00				

KM# 78 1000 DOBRAS
25.0000 g., 0.9250 Silver 0.7435 oz. ASW **Obv:** Arms with supporters **Rev:** Seahorse and crab **Note:** Enamel.

Date	Mintage	F	VF	XF	Unc	BU
1995 Proof	15,000	Value: 55.00				

KM# 85a 1000 DOBRAS
31.1035 g., 0.9990 Silver 0.9990 oz. ASW **Subject:** Diana - Queen of the Hearts **Obv:** Arms with supporters **Rev:** Bust with hat left **Note:** Prev. KM#85.1.

Date	Mintage	F	VF	XF	Unc	BU
1997 Proof	5,000	Value: 32.50				

KM# 102 1000 DOBRAS
1.2500 g., 0.9990 Gold 0.0401 oz. AGW **Subject:** Diana - Queen of the Hearts **Obv:** Arms with supporters **Rev:** Bust with hat left **Note:** Prev. KM#85.2.

Date	Mintage	F	VF	XF	Unc	BU
1997 Proof	3,000	Value: 60.00				

KM# 90 1000 DOBRAS
6.3000 g., Chrome Clad Steel **Obv:** Arms with supporters **Rev:** Flowers and value

Date	Mintage	F	VF	XF	Unc	BU
1997	—	—	—	—	2.75	3.75

KM# 92 1000 DOBRAS
Copper-Nickel **Subject:** Heidiland **Obv:** Arms with supporters **Rev:** Girl with goats

Date	Mintage	F	VF	XF	Unc	BU
1998	15,000	—	—	—	10.00	12.00

KM# 114 1000 DOBRAS
15.1000 g., 0.9990 Silver 0.4850 oz. ASW, 30 mm. **Obv:** Arms with supporters **Rev:** Empress Elizabeth of Austria (1837-1898) **Edge:** Reeded

Date	Mintage	F	VF	XF	Unc	BU
1998 Proof	—	Value: 30.00				

KM# 93 1000 DOBRAS
25.0000 g., 0.9250 Silver 0.7435 oz. ASW **Subject:** Heidiland **Obv:** Arms with supporters **Rev:** Girl holding hat and flowers, bird, trees and mountains

Date	Mintage	F	VF	XF	Unc	BU
1998 Proof	10,000	Value: 32.50				

KM# 79 1000 DOBRAS
31.1035 g., 0.9990 Silver 0.9990 oz. ASW **Obv:** Arms with supporters **Rev:** Peacock hologram

Date	Mintage	F	VF	XF	Unc	BU
1998(1997) Prooflike	10,000	—	—	—	—	75.00

KM# 80   1000 DOBRAS
31.1035 g., 0.9990 Silver 0.9990 oz. ASW **Obv:** Arms with supporters **Rev:** Hummingbird hologram

Date	Mintage	F	VF	XF	Unc	BU
1998(1997) Prooflike	10,000	—	—	—	—	75.00

KM# 94   1000 DOBRAS
25.1400 g., 0.9250 Silver 0.7476 oz. ASW **Subject:** World Cup Soccer - France 1998 **Obv:** Arms with supporters **Rev:** Soccer players and goalie net

Date	Mintage	F	VF	XF	Unc	BU
1998 Proof	10,000	Value: 35.00				

KM# 82   1000 DOBRAS
31.1035 g., 0.9990 Silver 0.9990 oz. ASW **Obv:** Arms with supporters **Rev:** Butterfly hologram

Date	Mintage	F	VF	XF	Unc	BU
1998(1997) Prooflike	10,000	—	—	—	—	75.00

KM# 81   1000 DOBRAS
31.1035 g., 0.9990 Silver 0.9990 oz. ASW **Obv:** Arms with supporters **Rev:** Fish hologram

Date	Mintage	F	VF	XF	Unc	BU
1998(1997) Prooflike	10,000	—	—	—	—	70.00

KM# 99   1000 DOBRAS
36.5500 g., , 34.9 mm. **Subject:** Millennium **Obv:** Arms with supporters **Rev:** Perforated gold insert exposing digital clock **Edge:** Reeded **Note:** Silver shell with gold insert encased digital clock. 8.1mm thick.

Date	Mintage	F	VF	XF	Unc	BU
1999 Proof	—	Value: 32.50				

KM# 91   2000 DOBRAS
Chrome Clad Steel **Obv:** Arms with supporters **Rev:** Tropical food plants within circle

Date	Mintage	F	VF	XF	Unc	BU
1997	—	—	—	—	3.75	5.00

KM# 86   2000 DOBRAS
25.0000 g., 0.9250 Silver 0.7435 oz. ASW **Subject:** Third Christian millennium **Obv:** Arms with supporters **Rev:** Year 2000 CE calendar

Date	Mintage	F	VF	XF	Unc	BU
1998 Proof	5,000	Value: 28.00				

KM# 86a   2000 DOBRAS
Copper-Nickel **Subject:** Third Christian millennium **Obv:** Arms with supporters **Rev:** Year 2000 CE calendar **Note:** Calendar detailing is acid etched, not struck.

Date	Mintage	F	VF	XF	Unc	BU
1998 Prooflike	—	—	—	—	10.00	12.00

KM# 98   2000 DOBRAS
31.1600 g., 0.9990 Silver 1.0008 oz. ASW, 27.1x47.2 mm. **Subject:** Pseudo - Millennium **Obv:** Arms with supporters **Rev:** Multicolor world and year split **Edge:** Plain

Date	Mintage	VG	F	VF	XF	Unc
1998 Proof	—	Value: 47.50				

KM# 36   2500 DOBRAS
6.4800 g., 0.9000 Gold 0.1875 oz. AGW **Subject:** Independence **Obv:** Arms with supporters **Rev:** World friendship

Date	Mintage	F	VF	XF	Unc	BU
1977	100	—	—	—	225	250
1977 Proof	170	Value: 200				

KM# 37   2500 DOBRAS
6.4800 g., 0.9000 Gold 0.1875 oz. AGW **Subject:** Independence - World Population **Obv:** Arms with supporters **Rev:** World population

Date	Mintage	F	VF	XF	Unc	BU
1977	100	—	—	—	225	250
1977 Proof	170	Value: 200				

KM# 38   2500 DOBRAS
6.4800 g., 0.9000 Gold 0.1875 oz. AGW **Subject:** Independence **Obv:** Arms with supporters **Rev:** Folklore monument

Date	Mintage	F	VF	XF	Unc	BU
1977	100	—	—	—	225	250
1977 Proof	170	Value: 200				

KM# 39   2500 DOBRAS
6.4800 g., 0.9000 Gold 0.1875 oz. AGW **Subject:** Independence **Obv:** Arms with supporters **Rev:** World unity

Date	Mintage	F	VF	XF	Unc	BU
1977	100	—	—	—	225	250
1977 Proof	170	Value: 200				

KM# 40   2500 DOBRAS
6.4800 g., 0.9000 Gold 0.1875 oz. AGW **Subject:** Independence **Obv:** Arms with supporters **Rev:** Mother and child

Date	Mintage	F	VF	XF	Unc	BU
1977	100	—	—	—	225	250
1977 Proof	170	Value: 200				

KM# 83   2500 DOBRAS
6.2207 g., 0.9999 Gold 0.2000 oz. AGW **Obv:** Arms with supporters **Rev:** Hummingbird hologram **Note:** Similar to 1,000 Dobras, KM#80.

Date	Mintage	F	VF	XF	Unc	BU
1998(1997) Proof	2,500	Value: 250				

KM# 84   2500 DOBRAS
6.2207 g., 0.9999 Gold 0.2000 oz. AGW **Obv:** Arms with supporters **Rev:** Butterfly hologram **Note:** Similar to 1,000 Dobras, KM#82.

Date	Mintage	F	VF	XF	Unc	BU
1998(1997) Proof	2,500	Value: 250				

KM# 46   3500 DOBRAS
136.0800 g., 0.9250 Silver 4.0468 oz. ASW, 63 mm. **Subject:** Wildlife Protection **Obv:** Arms with supporters **Rev:** Sea turtle **Note:** Illustration reduced.

Date	Mintage	F	VF	XF	Unc	BU
1990 Proof	750	Value: 175				

KM# 100   5000 DOBRAS
168.5600 g., 0.9990 5.4137 oz. **Subject:** Millennium **Obv:** Arms with supporters **Rev:** Perforated silver insert exposing digital clock **Edge:** Reeded **Note:** Silver shell with encased digital clock. 9mm thick.

Date	Mintage	F	VF	XF	Unc	BU
1999 Proof	—	Value: 100				

KM# 51   10000 DOBRAS
7.7750 g., 0.9000 Gold 0.2250 oz. AGW **Obv:** Arms with supporters **Rev:** Sea turtle

Date	Mintage	F	VF	XF	Unc	BU
1992 Proof	500	Value: 325				

KM# 72   25000 DOBRAS
15.5500 g., 0.9990 Gold 0.4994 oz. AGW **Obv:** Arms with supporters **Rev:** Elvis Presley

Date	Mintage	F	VF	XF	Unc	BU
1993 Proof	— Value: 550					

DUAL DENOMINATED COINAGE

KM# 67   500 DOBRAS- 1 ECU
Copper-Nickel **Subject:** 15th Anniversary of Association With European Common Market **Obv:** Arms with supporters **Rev:** Circular star design above ships and city view

Date	Mintage	F	VF	XF	Unc	BU
1993	20,000				11.50	13.50

KM# 68   2500 DOBRAS-5 ECU
25.0000 g., 0.9250 Silver 0.7435 oz. ASW **Subject:** 15th Anniversary of Association With European Common Market **Obv:** Arms with supporters **Rev:** Circular star design above ships and city view

Date	Mintage	F	VF	XF	Unc	BU
1993 Proof	12,000 Value: 32.50					

KM# 69   25000 DOBRAS-50 ECU
6.7200 g., 0.9000 Gold 0.1944 oz. AGW **Subject:** 15th Anniversary of Association With European Common Market **Obv:** Arms with supporters **Rev:** Old harbor scene **Note:** Similar to 2500 Dobras, 5 Ecu, KM#68.

Date	Mintage	F	VF	XF	Unc	BU
1993 Proof	1,000 Value: 220					

KM# 95   2000 DOBRAS-1 EURO
Copper-Nickel **Obv:** Arms with supporters **Rev:** Head left and multicolor Swiss flag in circle of stars, value at lower left

Date	Mintage	F	VF	XF	Unc	BU
1997 Proof	5,000 Value: 12.50					

KM# 103   2000 DOBRAS-1 EURO
31.1000 g., 0.9250 Silver The Belgian one franc coin adds 2.74g for a total weight of 33.85g 0.9249 oz. ASW, 38.6 mm. **Subject:** Year of the Euro **Obv:** Arms with supporters **Rev:** Map with inset Belgian 1 franc coin **Edge:** Reeded

Date	Mintage	F	VF	XF	Unc	BU
1999 Proof	— Value: 45.00					

KM# 104   2000 DOBRAS-1 EURO
31.2100 g., 0.9250 Silver The Italian 50 lire adds 4.46g for a total weight of 35.67 0.9281 oz. ASW, 38.6 mm. **Subject:** Year of the Euro **Obv:** Arms with supporters **Rev:** Map with inset Italian 50 lire coin **Edge:** Reeded

Date	Mintage	F	VF	XF	Unc	BU
1999 Proof	— Value: 45.00					

KM# 105   2000 DOBRAS-1 EURO
30.9500 g., 0.9250 Silver The French 1/2 franc adds 4.5g for a total weight of 35.45g 0.9204 oz. ASW, 38.6 mm. **Subject:** Year of the Euro **Obv:** Arms with supporters **Rev:** Map with inset French 1/2 franc coin **Edge:** Reeded

Date	Mintage	F	VF	XF	Unc	BU
1999 Proof	— Value: 45.00					

KM# 110   2000 DOBRAS-1 EURO
31.1000 g., 0.9250 Silver 0.9249 oz. ASW, 38.5 mm. **Subject:** Year of the Euro **Obv:** Arms with supporters **Rev:** Luxembourg 25 centimes KM-45a.1 glued to map design **Edge:** Reeded **Note:** Total weight 31.83g with Luxembourg coin

Date	Mintage	F	VF	XF	Unc	BU
1999 Proof	— Value: 45.00					

KM# 112   2000 DOBRAS-1 EURO
31.1000 g., 0.9250 Silver 0.9249 oz. ASW, 38.5 mm. **Subject:** Year of the Euro **Obv:** Arms with supporters **Rev:** Portuguese 1 escudo KM-631 glued to map design **Edge:** Reeded **Note:** Total weight 32.82g with Portuguese coin

Date	Mintage	F	VF	XF	Unc	BU
1999 Proof	— Value: 45.00					

KM# 107   2000 DOBRAS-1 EURO
31.1000 g., 0.9250 Silver 0.9249 oz. ASW, 38.5 mm. **Subject:** Year of the Euro **Obv:** Arms with supporters **Rev:** Finnland 10 penni KM-65 glued to map design **Edge:** Reeded **Note:** Total weight 32.84g with Finnish coin

Date	Mintage	F	VF	XF	Unc	BU
1999 Proof	— Value: 45.00					

KM# 113   2000 DOBRAS-1 EURO
31.1000 g., 0.9250 Silver 0.9249 oz. ASW, 38.5 mm. **Subject:** Year of the Euro **Obv:** Arms with supporters **Rev:** Spanish 5 pesetas KM-833 glued to map design **Edge:** Reeded **Note:** Total weight 34.14g with Spanish coin

Date	Mintage	F	VF	XF	Unc	BU
1999 Proof	— Value: 45.00					

KM# 108   2000 DOBRAS-1 EURO
31.1000 g., 0.9250 Silver 0.9249 oz. ASW, 38.5 mm. **Subject:** Year of the Euro **Obv:** Arms with supporters **Rev:** German 5 pfennig KM-107 glued to map design **Edge:** Reeded **Note:** Total weight 34.1g with German coin

Date	Mintage	F	VF	XF	Unc	BU
1999 Proof	— Value: 45.00					

KM# 111   2000 DOBRAS-1 EURO
31.1000 g., 0.9250 Silver 0.9249 oz. ASW, 38.5 mm. **Subject:** Year of the Euro **Obv:** Arms with supporters **Rev:** Netherlands 25 cents KM-183 glued to map design **Edge:** Reeded **Note:** Total weight 34.2g with Dutch coin

Date	Mintage	F	VF	XF	Unc	BU
1999 Proof	— Value: 45.00					

KM# 109   2000 DOBRAS-1 EURO
31.1000 g., 0.9250 Silver 0.9249 oz. ASW, 38.5 mm. **Subject:** Year of the Euro **Obv:** Arms with supporters **Rev:** Irish 5 pence KM-28.1 glued to map design **Edge:** Reeded **Note:** Total weight 34.33g with Irish coin

Date	Mintage	F	VF	XF	Unc	BU
1999 Proof	— Value: 45.00					

KM# 106   2000 DOBRAS-1 EURO
31.1000 g., 0.9250 Silver 0.9249 oz. ASW, 38.5 mm. **Subject:** Year of the Euro **Obv:** Arms with supporters **Rev:** Austrian 50 groschen KM-2885 glued to map design **Edge:** Reeded **Note:** Total weight with Austrian coin 34.1g

Date	Mintage	F	VF	XF	Unc	BU
1999	— Value: 45.00					

KM# 96   10000 DOBRAS-5 EURO
25.0000 g., 0.9250 Silver 0.7435 oz. ASW **Obv:** Arms with supporters **Rev:** Head left and Swiss flag in star circle, date at lower left

Date	Mintage	F	VF	XF	Unc	BU
1998 Proof	5,000 Value: 35.00					

KM# 101   15000 DOBRAS-7.5 EURO
25.0000 g., Silver, 38.55 mm. **Subject:** Switzerland and the European Union **Obv:** Arms with supporters **Rev:** Helvetia viewing a Swiss flag within a circle of stars **Edge:** Reeded

Date	Mintage	F	VF	XF	Unc	BU
1997 Proof	— Value: 40.00					

PATTERNS

KM#	Date	Mintage	Identification	Mkt Val
Pn1	ND(1994)	—	1000 Dobras. Copper-Nickel. 1 player.	55.00
Pn2	ND(1994)	—	1000 Dobras. Copper-Nickel. With denticles.	55.00
Pn3	ND(1994)	—	1000 Dobras. 0.9990 Silver. 19.7100 g. With 999 CuNi in error.	65.00
Pn4	ND(1994)	—	1000 Dobras. Copper-Nickel. 2 soccer players and E.P. 999.	55.00
Pn5	ND(1994)	—	1000 Dobras. 0.9990 Silver. 21.0000 g. E.P. 999.	65.00

PIEFORTS

KM#	Date	Mintage	Identification	Mkt Val
P1	1984	500	100 Dobras. Silver.	65.00

PROVAS

Standard metals; stamped 'PROVA' in field

KM#	Date	Mintage	Identification	Mkt Val
Pr1	1928	—	50 Centavos. Nickel-Bronze. KM1.	200
Pr2	1929	—	10 Centavos. Nickel-Bronze center. KM2.	50.00
Pr3	1929	—	20 Centavos. Nickel-Bronze. KM3.	50.00
Pr4	1929	—	50 Centavos. Nickel-Bronze. KM1.	125
Pr5	1939	—	Escudo. Silver. KM5.	225
Pr6	1939	—	2-1/2 Escudos. Silver. KM5.	165
Pr7	1939	—	5 Escudos. Silver. KM6.	175
Pr8	1939	—	10 Escudos. Silver. KM7.	300
Pr9	1948	—	50 Centavos. Nickel-Bronze. KM8.	65.00
Pr10	1948	—	Escudo. Nickel-Bronze. KM9.	65.00
Pr11	1948	—	2-1/2 Escudos. Silver. KM5.	75.00
Pr12	1948	—	5 Escudos. Silver. KM6.	80.00
Pr13	1951	—	50 Centavos. Copper-Nickel. KM10.	85.00
Pr14	1951	—	Escudo. Copper-Nickel. KM11.	125
Pr15	1951	—	2-1/2 Escudos. Silver. KM12.	45.00
Pr16	1951	—	5 Escudos. Silver center. KM13.	65.00
Pr17	1951	—	10 Escudos. Silver. KM14.	125
Pr18	1962	—	10 Centavos. Bronze. KM15.	20.00
Pr19	1962	—	20 Centavos. Bronze. KM16.	22.50
Pr20	1962	—	50 Centavos. Bronze. KM17.	22.50
Pr21	1962	—	Escudo. Bronze. KM18.	25.00
Pr22	1962	—	2-1/2 Escudos. Copper-Nickel. KM19.	27.50
Pr23	1962	—	5 Escudos. Silver. KM20.	45.00
Pr24	1970	—	50 Escudos. Silver. KM21.	75.00
Pr25	1971	—	10 Centavos. Aluminum. KM15a.	20.00
Pr26	1971	—	20 Centavos. Bronze. KM16.2.	20.00
Pr27	1971	—	50 Centavos. Bronze. KM17.2.	20.00
Pr28	1971	—	Escudo. Bronze. KM18.	20.00
Pr29	1971	—	2-1/2 Escudos. Copper-Nickel. KM19.	22.50
Pr30	1971	—	5 Escudos. Copper-Nickel. KM22.	25.00
Pr31	1971	—	10 Escudos. Copper-Nickel. KM23.	27.50
Pr32	1971	—	20 Escudos. Nickel. KM24.	30.00

MINT SETS

KM#	Date	Mintage	Identification	Issue Price	Mkt Val
MS1	1977 (5)	—	KM31-35	71.00	235
MS2	1977 (5)	100	KM36-40	655	1,250

PROOF SETS

KM#	Date	Mintage	Identification	Issue Price	Mkt Val
PS1	1977 (5)	—	KM31-35	93.50	200
PS2	1977 (5)	170	KM36-40	805	1,000

SAINT VINCENT

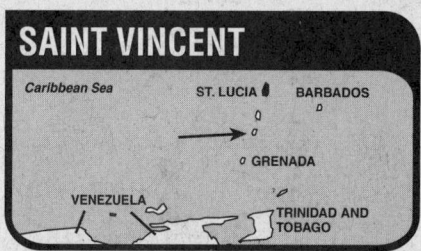

Saint Vincent and the Grenadines, consisting of the island of Saint Vincent and the northern Grenadines (a string of islets stretching southward from Saint Vincent), is located in the Windward Islands of the West Indies, West of Barbados and south of Saint Lucia. The tiny nation has an area of 150sq. mi. (340 sq. km.) and a population of *105,000. Capital: Kingstown. Arrowroot, cotton, sugar, molasses, rum and cocoa are exported. Tourism is a principal industry.

Saint Vincent was discovered by Columbus on Jan. 22,1498, but was left undisturbed for more than a century. The British began colonization early in the 18th century against bitter and prolonged Carib resistance. The island was taken by the French in 1779, but was restored to the British in 1783, at the end of the American Revolution. Saint Vincent and the northern Grenadines became a British associated state in Oct. 1969. Independence under the name of Saint Vincent and the Grenadines was attained at midnight of Oct. 26, 1979. The new nation chose to become a member of the Commonwealth of Nations with Elizabeth II as Head of State and Queen of Saint Vincent.

A local coinage was introduced in 1797, with the gold withdrawn in 1818 and the silver in 1823. This was replaced by sterling. From the mid-1950's, Saint Vincent used the currency of the British Caribbean Territories (Eastern Group), then that of the East Caribbean States.

RULER
British

MONETARY SYSTEM
Commencing 1979
100 Cents = 1 Dollar

BRITISH COLONY
MODERN COINAGE

KM# 13   4 DOLLARS
Copper-Nickel, 38.5 mm. **Series:** F.A.O. **Obv:** Flower above
shield with banner and date below **Rev:** Value below divides
sugar cane plant and banana tree branch

Date	Mintage	F	VF	XF	Unc	BU
1970	13,000	4.00	6.00	10.00	20.00	30.00
1970 Proof	2,000	Value: 35.00				

KM# 14   10 DOLLARS
Copper-Nickel **Subject:** Royal Visit **Obv:** Crowned bust right
Rev: Flower above shield within circle

Date	Mintage	F	VF	XF	Unc	BU
1985	100,000	5.00	7.50	10.00	20.00	32.50

KM# 14a   10 DOLLARS
28.2800 g., 0.9250 Silver 0.8410 oz. ASW **Subject:** Royal Visit
Obv: Crowned bust right **Rev:** Flower above shield within circle

Date	Mintage	F	VF	XF	Unc	BU
1985 Proof	5,000	Value: 60.00				

KM# 14b   10 DOLLARS
47.5400 g., 0.9170 Gold 1.4015 oz. AGW **Subject:** Royal Visit
Obv: Crowned bust right **Rev:** Flower above shield within circle

Date	Mintage	F	VF	XF	Unc	BU
1985 Proof	250	Value: 1,400				

KM# 15   100 DOLLARS
129.5900 g., 0.9250 Silver 3.8538 oz. ASW, 63 mm.
Subject: Tropical Birds - Pelican **Obv:** Coat of arms **Rev:** Pelican
Note: Illustration reduced.

Date	Mintage	F	VF	XF	Unc	BU
1988 Proof	Est. 10,000	Value: 145				

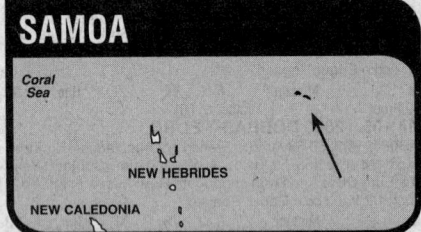

SAMOA

Coral Sea

NEW HEBRIDES

NEW CALEDONIA

The Independent State of Samoa (formerly Western Samoa),
located in the Pacific Ocean 1,600 miles (2,574 km.) northeast of New
Zealand, has an area of 1,097 sq. mi. (2,860 sq. km.) and a population
of *182,000. Capital: Apia. The economy is based on agriculture, fishing and tourism. Copra, cocoa and bananas are exported.

The first European to sight the Samoan group of islands was
the Dutch navigator Jacob Roggeveen in 1722. Great Britain, the
United States and Germany established consular representation
at Apia in 1847, 1853 and 1861 respectively. The conflicting interests of the three powers produced the Berlin agreement of 1889,
which declared Samoa neutral and had the effect of establishing
a tripartite protectorate over the islands. A further agreement,
1899, recognized the rights of the United States in those islands
east of 171 deg. west longitude (American Samoa) and of Germany in the other islands (Western Samoa). New Zealand occupied Western Samoa at the start of World War I and administered
it as a League of Nations mandate and U. N. trusteeship until Jan.
1, 1962, when it became an independent state.

Samoa is a member of the Commonwealth of Nations. The
Chief Executive is Chief of State. The prime minister is the Head
of Government. The present Head of State, Malietoa Tanumafili
II, holds his position for life. The Legislative Assembly will elect
future Heads of State for 5-year terms.

Samoa, which had used New Zealand coinage, converted to
a decimal coinage in 1967.

RULERS
British, until 1962
Malietoa Tanumafili II, 1962—

MONETARY SYSTEM
100 Sene = 1 Tala

CONSTITUTIONAL MONARCHY
Commonwealth of Nations
STANDARD COINAGE

KM# 1   SENE
1.7500 g., Bronze, 17.5 mm. **Obv:** Head left **Rev:** Stars and
value within wreath

Date	Mintage	F	VF	XF	Unc	BU
1967	915,000	—	0.10	0.15	0.30	—
1967 Proof	15,000	Value: 0.50				

KM# 12   SENE
1.7500 g., Bronze, 17.5 mm. **Obv:** Head left **Rev:** Stars and
value within wreath

Date	Mintage	F	VF	XF	Unc	BU
1974	3,380,000	—	—	0.10	0.25	—
1987	—	—	—	0.10	0.25	—
1988	—	—	—	0.10	0.25	—
1993	—	—	—	0.10	0.25	—
1996	—	—	—	0.10	0.25	—

KM# 12a   SENE
1.9500 g., 0.9250 Silver 0.0580 oz. ASW, 17.5 mm. **Obv:** Head
left **Rev:** Stars and value within wreath

Date	Mintage	F	VF	XF	Unc	BU
1974 Proof	5,578	Value: 1.25				

KM# 2   2 SENE
3.2500 g., Bronze, 21.1 mm. **Obv:** Head left **Rev:** Stars and
value within wreath

Date	Mintage	F	VF	XF	Unc	BU
1967	465,000	—	0.10	0.20	0.40	—
1967 Proof	15,000	Value: 0.50				

KM# 13   2 SENE
3.2500 g., Bronze, 21.1 mm. **Obv:** Head left **Rev:** Value below
nut sprig

Date	Mintage	F	VF	XF	Unc	BU
1974	1,640,000	—	0.10	0.15	0.30	—
1988	—	—	0.10	0.15	0.30	—
1996	—	—	0.10	0.15	0.30	—

KM# 13a   2 SENE
3.8000 g., 0.9250 Silver 0.1130 oz. ASW, 21.1 mm. **Obv:** Head
left **Rev:** Value below nut sprig

Date	Mintage	F	VF	XF	Unc	BU
1974 Proof	5,578	Value: 2.25				

KM# 122   2 SENE
3.9400 g., Bronze, 19.25 mm. **Series:** F.A.O. **Obv:** Head left
Rev: Stars and value within wreath **Edge:** Plain

Date	Mintage	F	VF	XF	Unc	BU
1999	—	—	—	—	0.35	—
2000	—	—	—	—	0.35	—

KM# 3   5 SENE
2.8000 g., Copper-Nickel, 19.4 mm. **Obv:** Head left **Rev:** Value
and stars

Date	Mintage	F	VF	XF	Unc	BU
1967	495,000	—	0.15	0.25	0.50	—
1967 Proof	15,000	Value: 1.00				

KM# 14   5 SENE
2.8000 g., Copper-Nickel, 19.4 mm. **Obv:** Head left
Rev: Pineapple and value

Date	Mintage	F	VF	XF	Unc	BU
1974	1,736,000	—	0.10	0.20	0.40	—
1987	—	—	0.10	0.20	0.40	—
1988	—	—	0.10	0.20	0.40	—
1993	—	—	0.10	0.20	0.40	—
1996	—	—	0.10	0.20	0.40	—
2000	—	—	0.10	0.20	0.40	—

KM# 14a   5 SENE
3.2500 g., 0.9250 Silver 0.0966 oz. ASW, 19.4 mm. **Obv:** Head
left **Rev:** Pineapple and value

Date	Mintage	F	VF	XF	Unc	BU
1974 Proof	5,578	Value: 2.50				

KM# 4   10 SENE
5.6500 g., Copper-Nickel, 23.6 mm. **Obv:** Head left
Rev: National arms

Date	Mintage	F	VF	XF	Unc	BU
1967	400,000	—	0.20	0.35	0.70	—
1967 Proof	15,000	Value: 1.00				

KM# 15   10 SENE
5.6500 g., Copper-Nickel, 23.6 mm. **Obv:** Head left **Rev:** Value to lower left of leafy plants

Date	Mintage	F	VF	XF	Unc	BU
1974	1,580,000	—	0.15	0.30	0.60	—
1987	—	—	0.15	0.30	0.60	—
1988	—	—	0.15	0.30	0.60	—
1993	—	—	0.15	0.30	0.60	—
1996	—	—	0.15	0.30	0.60	—
2000	—	—	0.15	0.30	0.60	—

KM# 15a   10 SENE
6.3700 g., 0.9250 Silver 0.1894 oz. ASW, 23.6 mm. **Obv:** Head left **Rev:** Value to lower left of leafy plants

Date	Mintage	F	VF	XF	Unc	BU
1974 Proof	5,578	Value: 3.25				

KM# 5   20 SENE
11.3000 g., Copper-Nickel, 28.5 mm. **Obv:** Head left **Rev:** National arms

Date	Mintage	F	VF	XF	Unc	BU
1967	400,000	—	0.25	0.50	1.00	—
1967 Proof	15,000	Value: 1.50				

KM# 16   20 SENE
11.3000 g., Copper-Nickel, 28.5 mm. **Obv:** Head left **Rev:** Breadfruit and value

Date	Mintage	F	VF	XF	Unc	BU
1974	1,380,000	—	0.20	0.40	0.80	—
1987	—	—	0.20	0.40	0.80	—
1988	—	—	0.20	0.40	0.80	—
1993	—	—	0.20	0.40	0.80	—
1996	—	—	0.20	0.40	0.80	—
2000	—	—	0.20	0.40	0.80	—

KM# 16a   20 SENE
12.7000 g., 0.9250 Silver 0.3777 oz. ASW, 28.5 mm. **Obv:** Head left **Rev:** Breadfruit and value

Date	Mintage	F	VF	XF	Unc	BU
1974 Proof	5,578	Value: 6.00				

KM# 6   50 SENE
14.0000 g., Copper-Nickel, 32.4 mm. **Obv:** Head left **Rev:** National arms

Date	Mintage	F	VF	XF	Unc	BU
1967	80,000	—	0.75	1.25	2.00	—
1967 Proof	15,000	Value: 2.50				

KM# 17   50 SENE
14.0000 g., Copper-Nickel, 32.4 mm. **Obv:** Head left **Rev:** Banana tree and value

Date	Mintage	F	VF	XF	Unc	BU
1974	50,000	—	0.75	1.25	2.00	—
1988	—	—	0.75	1.25	2.00	—
1996	—	—	0.75	1.25	2.00	—
2000	—	—	0.75	1.25	2.00	—

KM# 17a   50 SENE
15.4000 g., 0.9250 Silver 0.4580 oz. ASW, 32.4 mm. **Obv:** Head left **Rev:** Banana tree and value

Date	Mintage	F	VF	XF	Unc	BU
1974 Proof	5,578	Value: 7.00				

KM# 80   50 SENE
14.0000 g., Copper-Nickel, 32.4 mm. **Subject:** 25th Anniversary of Independence **Obv:** Head left **Rev:** National arms

Date	Mintage	F	VF	XF	Unc	BU
1987	—	—	—	—	2.25	—

KM# 7   TALA
26.8500 g., Copper-Nickel, 38.71 mm. **Obv:** Head of Malietoa Tanumafili II left **Rev:** National arms, value **Edge:** Lettered **Edge:** DECIMAL CURRENCY INTRODUCED 10 JULY 1967

Date	Mintage	F	VF	XF	Unc	BU
1967	20,000	—	—	1.50	2.50	3.50
1967 Proof	15,000	Value: 5.00				

KM# 8   TALA
Copper-Nickel, 38.8 mm. **Subject:** 75th Anniversary - Death of Robert Louis Stevenson **Obv:** National arms **Rev:** Reclining figure holding pen and paper left

Date	Mintage	F	VF	XF	Unc	BU
1969	25,000	—	—	—	2.50	3.50
1969 Proof	1,500	Value: 5.00				

KM# 9   TALA
Copper-Nickel, 38.8 mm. **Subject:** 200th Anniversary - Capt. Cook voyages **Obv:** National arms **Rev:** Head right

Date	Mintage	F	VF	XF	Unc	BU
1970	32,000	—	—	—	2.50	3.50
1970 Proof	3,000	Value: 5.00				

KM# 10   TALA
Copper-Nickel, 38.8 mm. **Subject:** Visit of Pope Paul VI **Obv:** National arms **Rev:** Bust right

Date	Mintage	F	VF	XF	Unc	BU
1970	35,000	—	—	—	3.00	4.00
1970 Proof	3,000	Value: 6.00				

KM# 11   TALA
Copper-Nickel, 38.8 mm. **Subject:** Roggeveen's Pacific voyage **Obv:** National arms **Rev:** Sailing ship

Date	Mintage	F	VF	XF	Unc	BU
1972	35,000	—	—	—	3.00	4.00
1972 Proof	3,000	Value: 6.50				

KM# 18   TALA
Copper-Nickel, 38.8 mm. **Subject:** 10th British Commonwealth Games **Obv:** National arms **Rev:** Boxing match

Date	Mintage	F	VF	XF	Unc	BU
1974	40,000	—	—	—	3.50	4.50

KM# 18a   TALA
27.7000 g., 0.9250 Silver 0.8237 oz. ASW, 38.8 mm. **Subject:** 10th British Commonwealth Games **Obv:** National arms **Rev:** Boxing match

Date	Mintage	F	VF	XF	Unc	BU
1974 Proof	1,500	Value: 16.00				

KM# 19 TALA
Copper-Nickel, 38.8 mm. **Obv:** Head of Malietoa Tanumafili II left **Rev:** Coconut palm and value

Date	Mintage	F	VF	XF	Unc	BU
1974	24,000	—	—	—	2.50	3.50

KM# 19a TALA
31.1500 g., 0.9250 Silver 0.9263 oz. ASW, 38.8 mm. **Obv:** Head of Malietoa Tanumafili II left **Rev:** Coconut palm and value

Date	Mintage	F	VF	XF	Unc	BU
1974 Proof	11,000	Value: 15.00				

KM# 20 TALA
Copper-Nickel, 38.8 mm. **Subject:** U.S. Bicentennial **Obv:** Head of Malietoa Tanumafili II left **Rev:** Equestrian and USA map

Date	Mintage	F	VF	XF	Unc	BU
ND(1976)	40,000	—	—	—	2.50	3.50

KM# 20a TALA
30.4000 g., 0.9250 Silver 0.9040 oz. ASW, 38.8 mm. **Subject:** U.S. Bicentennial **Obv:** Head of Malietoa Tanumafili II left **Rev:** Equestrian and USA map

Date	Mintage	F	VF	XF	Unc	BU
ND(1976) Proof	4,127	Value: 14.50				

KM# 22 TALA
Copper-Nickel, 38.8 mm. **Series:** Montreal Olympics **Obv:** National arms **Rev:** Weight lifter

Date	Mintage	F	VF	XF	Unc	BU
1976	40,000	—	—	—	3.00	4.00

KM# 22a TALA
30.4000 g., 0.9250 Silver 0.9040 oz. ASW, 38.8 mm. **Series:** Montreal Olympics **Obv:** National arms **Rev:** Weight lifter

Date	Mintage	F	VF	XF	Unc	BU
1976 Proof	6,000	Value: 14.50				

KM# 24 TALA
Copper-Nickel, 38.8 mm. **Subject:** Queen's Silver Jubilee **Obv:** National arms **Rev:** Cameo flanked by palm trees

Date	Mintage	F	VF	XF	Unc	BU
1977	27,000	—	—	—	2.50	3.50

KM# 24a TALA
30.4000 g., 0.9250 Silver 0.9040·oz. ASW, 38.8 mm. **Subject:** Queen's Silver Jubilee **Obv:** National arms **Rev:** Cameo flanked by palm trees

Date	Mintage	F	VF	XF	Unc	BU
1977 Proof	6,171	Value: 14.50				

KM# 26 TALA
Copper-Nickel, 38.8 mm. **Subject:** Lindbergh's New York to Paris flight **Obv:** National arms **Rev:** Bust of Lindbergh at left, plane above, Eiffel tower at right, Statue of Liberty at left, ocean in background

Date	Mintage	F	VF	XF	Unc	BU
1977	17,000	—	—	—	3.00	4.00

KM# 26a TALA
30.4000 g., 0.9250 Silver 0.9040 oz. ASW, 38.8 mm. **Subject:** Lindbergh's New York to Paris flight **Obv:** National arms **Rev:** Bust of Lindbergh at left, plane above, Eiffel tower at right, Statue of Liberty at left, ocean in background

Date	Mintage	F	VF	XF	Unc	BU
1977 Proof	4,522	Value: 15.00				

KM# 28 TALA
Copper-Nickel, 38.8 mm. **Subject:** 50th Anniversary - First Transpacific Flight **Obv:** National arms **Rev:** Head left, map, plane and date

Date	Mintage	F	VF	XF	Unc	BU
1978	20,000	—	—	—	3.00	4.00

KM# 28a TALA
30.4000 g., 0.9250 Silver 0.9040 oz. ASW, 38.8 mm. **Subject:** 50th Anniversary - First Transpacific Flight **Obv:** National arms **Rev:** Head left, map, plane and date

Date	Mintage	F	VF	XF	Unc	BU
1978 Proof	5,000	Value: 14.50				

KM# 30 TALA
Copper-Nickel, 38.8 mm. **Subject:** XI Commonwealth Games **Obv:** National arms **Rev:** Runners

Date	Mintage	F	VF	XF	Unc	BU
1978	7,710	—	—	—	3.00	4.00

KM# 30a TALA
30.4000 g., 0.9250 Silver 0.9040 oz. ASW, 38.8 mm. **Subject:** XI Commonwealth Games **Obv:** National arms **Rev:** Runners

Date	Mintage	F	VF	XF	Unc	BU
1978 Proof	5,000	Value: 14.50				

KM# 32 TALA
Copper-Nickel, 38.8 mm. **Subject:** Bicentenary - Death of Capt. James Cook **Obv:** National arms **Rev:** Head right and sailing ship

Date	Mintage	F	VF	XF	Unc	BU
1979	5,000	—	—	—	2.50	3.50

KM# 35 TALA
Copper-Nickel, 38.8 mm. **Series:** 1980 Olympics **Obv:** National arms **Rev:** Hurdles event

Date	Mintage	F	VF	XF	Unc	BU
1980	5,000	—	—	—	3.00	5.00

KM# 38 TALA
Copper-Nickel, 38.8 mm. **Series:** F.A.O. **Obv:** National arms **Rev:** Coconut palm and value

Date	Mintage	F	VF	XF	Unc	BU
1980	10,000	—	—	—	2.50	4.00

KM# 40 TALA
Copper-Nickel, 38.8 mm. **Subject:** Gov. Wilhelm Solf **Obv:** National arms **Rev:** Armored bust left flanked by palm trees

Date	Mintage	F	VF	XF	Unc	BU
1980	5,000	—	—	—	3.00	5.00

KM# 43 TALA
Copper-Nickel, 38.8 mm. **Subject:** Wedding of Prince Charles and Lady Diana **Obv:** National arms **Rev:** Conjoined heads left

Date	Mintage	F	VF	XF	Unc	BU
1981	12,000	—	—	—	2.50	3.00

KM# 47 TALA

Copper-Nickel, 38.8 mm. Subject: IYDP - President Franklin Roosevelt Obv: National arms Rev: Seated figure in wheelchair facing

Date	Mintage	F	VF	XF	Unc	BU
1981	8,000	—	—	—	2.50	3.00

KM# 50 TALA

Copper-Nickel, 38.8 mm. Subject: Commonwealth Games Obv: National arms Rev: Javelin thrower

Date	Mintage	F	VF	XF	Unc	BU
1982	6,000	—	—	—	3.00	4.00

KM# 53 TALA

Copper-Nickel, 38.8 mm. Subject: South Pacific Games Obv: National arms Rev: Runner

Date	Mintage	F	VF	XF	Unc	BU
1983	8,000	—	—	—	3.00	4.00

KM# 57 TALA

9.5000 g., Aluminum-Bronze, 30.6 mm. Subject: Circulation coinage Obv: Head left Rev: National arms

Date	Mintage	F	VF	XF	Unc	BU
1984	1,000,000	—	0.50	0.75	1.00	1.50

KM# 57a TALA

27.2200 g., Copper-Nickel, 30 mm. Obv: Head left Rev: National arms Edge: Plain

Date	Mintage	F	VF	XF	Unc	BU
1984	5,000	—	—	—	5.00	6.50

KM# 58 TALA

Copper-Nickel, 38.8 mm. Series: Summer Olympics Obv: National arms Rev: Boxing match

Date	Mintage	F	VF	XF	Unc	BU
1984	8,000	—	—	—	3.50	5.00

KM# 63 TALA

Copper-Nickel, 38.8 mm. Subject: Prince Andrew and Sarah Ferguson's Marriage Obv: National arms Rev: Conjoined busts

Date	Mintage	F	VF	XF	Unc	BU
1986	10,000	—	—	—	2.50	4.00

KM# 74 TALA

Copper-Nickel, 38.8 mm. Subject: 25th Anniversary of World Wildlife Fund Obv: National arms Rev: Samoan Fantail bird

Date	Mintage	F	VF	XF	Unc	BU
1986	—	—	—	—	9.00	12.00

KM# 88 TALA

Copper-Nickel, 38.8 mm. Subject: 40th Anniversary - Reign of Queen Elizabeth II Obv: National arms Rev: Cross in center circle, equestrians and chariot around border

Date	Mintage	F	VF	XF	Unc	BU
ND(1992)	—	—	—	—	3.00	4.50

KM# 111 TALA

Copper-Nickel, 38.8 mm. Subject: Queen Mother Obv: National arms Rev: Glamis Castle within beaded circle

Date	Mintage	F	VF	XF	Unc	BU
1995	Est. 30,000	—	—	—	3.00	4.50

KM# 112 TALA

10.0000 g., 0.5000 Silver 0.1607 oz. ASW Series: Olympics Obv: National arms Rev: Gymnast and pommel horse

Date	Mintage	F	VF	XF	Unc	BU
1996	Est. 10,000	—	—	—	7.50	10.00

KM# 120 2 TALA

42.4139 g., 0.9250 Silver 1.2613 oz. ASW Obv: National arms Rev: Value and three scenes Note: Part of a tri-national, three-coin matching set with Cook Islands and Fiji.

Date	Mintage	F	VF	XF	Unc	BU
1998 Proof	Est. 20,000	Value: 35.00				

KM# 125 5 TALA

19.8300 g., Copper Nickel, 38.7 mm. Subject: Robert Louis Stevenson Obv: National arms Rev: Ship, portrait and pirate scene Edge: Reeded

Date	Mintage	F	VF	XF	Unc	BU
ND(1994)	100,000	—	—	—	5.00	6.50

KM# 115 5 TALA

15.5518 g., 0.9250 Silver 0.4625 oz. ASW Subject: War and peace Obv: National arms Rev: Arrows and sword Note: 1/2 of 2-part coin, combined with Kiribati KM#22, issued in sets only. Value is determined by combining the 2 parts.

Date	Mintage	F	VF	XF	Unc	BU
ND(1997) Proof	Est. 10,000	Value: 22.50				

KM# 116 5 TALA

15.5518 g., 0.9250 Silver 0.4625 oz. ASW Subject: Epoch - making events Obv: National arms Rev: Helmet and crowns Note: 1/2 of 2-part coin, combined with Kiribati KM#23, issued in sets only. Value is determined by combining the 2 parts.

Date	Mintage	F	VF	XF	Unc	BU
ND(1997) Proof	Est. 10,000	Value: 22.50				

KM# 117 5 TALA

15.5518 g., 0.9250 Silver 0.4625 oz. ASW Subject: Tempora Mutantur Obv: National arms Rev: Man with torch Note: 1/2 of 2-part coin, combined with Kiribati KM#24, issued in sets only. Value is determined by combining the 2 parts.

Date	Mintage	F	VF	XF	Unc	BU
ND(1997) Proof	Est. 10,000	Value: 22.50				

KM# 117a 5 TALA

Copper-Nickel Subject: Tempora Mutantur Obv: National arms Rev: Man with torch Note: 1/2 of 2-part coin, combined with Kiribati KM#24a, issued in pairs only. Value is determined by combining the 2 parts.

Date	Mintage	F	VF	XF	Unc	BU
ND(1997)	—	—	—	—	10.00	12.50

KM# 118 5 TALA
15.5518 g., 0.9250 Silver 0.4625 oz. ASW **Subject:** People and buildings **Obv:** National arms **Rev:** Working hands **Note:** 1/2 of 2-part coin, combined with Kiribati KM#25, issued in sets only. Value is determined by combining the 2 parts.

Date	Mintage	F	VF	XF	Unc	BU
ND(1997) Proof	Est. 10,000				Value: 22.50	

KM# 138 5 TALA
14.8000 g., 0.9250 Silver 0.4401 oz. ASW, 24.5 mm.
Subject: Epoch Making Events **Obv:** National arms **Rev:** Topless Marianne and Guru **Edge:** Pain

Date	Mintage	F	VF	XF	Unc	BU
ND(1998) Proof	—				Value: 22.50	

KM# 33 10 TALA
31.3300 g., 0.5000 Silver 0.5036 oz. ASW **Subject:** Bicentenary - Death of Capt. James Cook **Obv:** National arms **Rev:** Head right and ship

Date	Mintage	F	VF	XF	Unc	BU
1979	3,000	—	—	—	8.50	10.00

KM# 33a 10 TALA
31.4700 g., 0.9250 Silver 0.9359 oz. ASW **Subject:** Bicentenary - Death of Capt. James Cook **Obv:** National arms **Rev:** Head right and ship

Date	Mintage	F	VF	XF	Unc	BU
1979 Proof	5,000				Value: 16.00	

KM# 36 10 TALA
31.3300 g., 0.5000 Silver 0.5036 oz. ASW **Series:** 1980 Olympics **Obv:** National arms **Rev:** Hurdles event

Date	Mintage	F	VF	XF	Unc	BU
1980	3,000	—	—	—	8.50	10.00

KM# 36a 10 TALA
31.4700 g., 0.9250 Silver 0.9359 oz. ASW **Series:** 1980 Olympics **Obv:** National arms **Rev:** Hurdles event

Date	Mintage	F	VF	XF	Unc	BU
1980 Proof	4,000				Value: 16.00	

KM# 39 10 TALA
31.3300 g., 0.5000 Silver 0.5036 oz. ASW, 38.8 mm.
Series: F.A.O. **Obv:** National arms **Rev:** Palm tree with coconuts

Date	Mintage	F	VF	XF	Unc	BU
1980 Proof	3,000				Value: 16.00	

KM# 41 10 TALA
31.3300 g., 0.5000 Silver 0.5036 oz. ASW **Subject:** Gov. Wilhelm Solf **Obv:** National arms **Rev:** Uniformed bust left flanked by palm trees

Date	Mintage	F	VF	XF	Unc	BU
1980	3,000	—	—	—	8.50	10.00

KM# 41a 10 TALA
31.4700 g., 0.9250 Silver 0.9359 oz. ASW **Subject:** Gov. Wilhelm Solf **Obv:** National arms **Rev:** Uniformed bust left flanked by palm trees

Date	Mintage	F	VF	XF	Unc	BU
1980 Proof	4,000				Value: 16.00	

KM# 44 10 TALA
31.4700 g., 0.9250 Silver 0.9359 oz. ASW **Subject:** Wedding of Prince Charles and Lady Diana **Obv:** National arms **Rev:** Conjoined busts left

Date	Mintage	F	VF	XF	Unc	BU
1981 Proof	5,000				Value: 16.00	

KM# 48 10 TALA
31.4700 g., 0.9250 Silver 0.9359 oz. ASW **Subject:** IYDP - President Franklin Roosevelt **Obv:** National arms **Rev:** Seated figure in wheelchair facing

Date	Mintage	F	VF	XF	Unc	BU
1981 Proof	5,000				Value: 16.00	

KM# 51 10 TALA
31.4700 g., 0.9250 Silver 0.9359 oz. ASW **Subject:** Commonwealth Games **Obv:** National arms **Rev:** Javelin thrower

Date	Mintage	F	VF	XF	Unc	BU
1982 Proof	4,000				Value: 16.00	

KM# 54 10 TALA
31.4700 g., 0.9250 Silver 0.9359 oz. ASW **Subject:** South Pacific Games **Obv:** National arms **Rev:** Runner

Date	Mintage	F	VF	XF	Unc	BU
1983 Proof	3,000				Value: 16.00	

KM# 59 10 TALA
31.4700 g., 0.9250 Silver 0.9359 oz. ASW **Series:** Summer Olympics **Obv:** National arms **Rev:** Boxing match

Date	Mintage	F	VF	XF	Unc	BU
1984 Proof	3,000				Value: 22.50	

KM# 64 10 TALA
31.4700 g., 0.9359 oz. ASW **Subject:** Prince Andrew and Sara Ferguson's Marriage **Obv:** National arms **Rev:** Conjoined busts left **Note:** Similar to Tala, KM#63.

Date	Mintage	F	VF	XF	Unc	BU
1986 Proof	2,500				Value: 16.00	

KM# 72 10 TALA
31.4700 g., 0.9250 Silver 0.9359 oz. ASW **Subject:** 25th Anniversary of World Wildlife Fund **Obv:** National arms **Rev:** Samoan Fantail bird

Date	Mintage	F	VF	XF	Unc	BU
1986 Proof	25,000				Value: 25.00	

KM# 66 10 TALA
31.1000 g., 0.9990 Silver 0.9988 oz. ASW **Subject:** America's Cup Race - 1987 Perth **Obv:** The Cup **Rev:** Sailing scene

Date	Mintage	F	VF	XF	Unc	BU
1987 Proof	50,000				Value: 17.50	

KM# 70 10 TALA
31.1000 g., 0.9990 Silver 0.9988 oz. ASW **Series:** 1988 Olympics **Obv:** National arms **Rev:** Three torches and athletes

Date	Mintage	F	VF	XF	Unc	BU
1988	20,000	—	—	—	16.50	18.50

KM# 75 10 TALA
31.1030 g., 0.9990 Silver 0.9989 oz. ASW **Obv:** National arms **Rev:** Kon-Tiki raft and map

Date	Mintage	F	VF	XF	Unc	BU
1988 Proof	Est. 16,500				Value: 17.50	

KM# 79 10 TALA
31.4700 g., 0.9250 Silver 0.9359 oz. ASW, 38.7 mm.
Series: Save the Children Fund **Obv:** National arms **Rev:** Two children flanked by palms leaves **Edge:** Reeded

Date	Mintage	F	VF	XF	Unc	BU
1990 Proof	Est. 20,000				Value: 16.50	

KM# 82   10 TALA
31.4700 g., 0.9250 Silver 0.9359 oz. ASW **Series:** Summer Olympics **Obv:** National arms **Rev:** Shot putter

Date	Mintage	F	VF	XF	Unc	BU
1991 Proof	Est. 70,000				Value: 16.00	

KM# 83   10 TALA
31.1030 g., 0.9250 Silver 0.9249 oz. ASW **Subject:** RA expeditions **Obv:** National arms **Rev:** Map within circle to right of ship

Date	Mintage	F	VF	XF	Unc	BU
1991 Proof	15,000				Value: 18.50	

KM# 85   10 TALA
31.4700 g., 0.9250 Silver 0.9359 oz. ASW **Series:** Olympics **Obv:** National arms **Rev:** Javelin thrower

Date	Mintage	F	VF	XF	Unc	BU
1991 Proof	Est. 70,000				Value: 15.00	

KM# 86   10 TALA
31.4700 g., 0.9250 Silver 0.9359 oz. ASW **Series:** Olympics **Obv:** National arms **Rev:** Hammer thrower

Date	Mintage	F	VF	XF	Unc	BU
1992 Proof	Est. 70,000				Value: 15.00	

KM# 89   10 TALA
31.8600 g., 0.9250 Silver 0.9475 oz. ASW **Subject:** World Cup Soccer **Obv:** National arms **Rev:** Arena behind player's legs kicking ball

Date	Mintage	F	VF	XF	Unc	BU
1992 Proof	Est. 20,000				Value: 18.00	

KM# 93   10 TALA
31.4700 g., 0.9250 Silver 0.9359 oz. ASW **Subject:** Jakob Roggeveen **Obv:** National arms

Date	Mintage	F	VF	XF	Unc	BU
1992 Proof	15,000				Value: 16.00	

KM# 98   10 TALA
31.3500 g., 0.9250 Silver 0.9323 oz. ASW **Series:** Endangered Wildlife **Obv:** National arms **Rev:** Pair of birds

Date	Mintage	F	VF	XF	Unc	BU
1992 Proof	Est. 20,000				Value: 35.00	

KM# 99   10 TALA
31.7700 g., 0.9250 Silver 0.9448 oz. ASW **Obv:** National arms **Rev:** Roggeveen's fleet

Date	Mintage	F	VF	XF	Unc	BU
1992 Proof	Est. 15,000				Value: 16.00	

KM# 109   10 TALA
31.4700 g., 0.9250 Silver 0.9359 oz. ASW **Subject:** 40th Anniversary - Reign of Queen Elizabeth II **Obv:** National arms **Rev:** Royal carriage and guard around Order of the Garter

Date	Mintage	F	VF	XF	Unc	BU
1992 Proof	Est. 5,000				Value: 22.50	

KM# 97   10 TALA
31.8100 g., 0.9250 Silver 0.9460 oz. ASW **Series:** 1996 Olympics **Obv:** National arms **Rev:** Gymnast on pommel horse

Date	Mintage	F	VF	XF	Unc	BU
1993 Proof	50,000				Value: 15.00	

KM# 91   10 TALA
31.8100 g., 0.9250 Silver 0.9460 oz. ASW **Series:** Olympics **Obv:** National arms **Rev:** Diver

Date	Mintage	F	VF	XF	Unc	BU
1994 Proof	Est. 50,000				Value: 15.00	

KM# 121   10 TALA
31.2300 g., 0.9250 Silver 0.9287 oz. ASW, 38.6 mm. **Obv:** National arms **Rev:** Seated Robert Louis Stephenson **Edge:** Reeded

Date	Mintage	F	VF	XF	Unc	BU
1994 Proof	10,000				Value: 30.00	

KM# 94   10 TALA
31.1035 g., 0.9250 Silver 0.9250 oz. ASW **Subject:** Tigris Expedition **Obv:** National arms **Rev:** Pyramid behind boat

Date	Mintage	F	VF	XF	Unc	BU
1994 Proof	10,000				Value: 25.00	

KM# 95   10 TALA
31.1035 g., 0.9250 Silver 0.9250 oz. ASW **Subject:** Tigris Expedition **Obv:** National arms **Rev:** Burning Tigris

Date	Mintage	F	VF	XF	Unc	BU
1994 Proof	10,000				Value: 25.00	

KM# 100   10 TALA
31.7700 g., 0.9250 Silver 0.9448 oz. ASW **Obv:** National arms **Rev:** Two figures sighting land

Date	Mintage	F	VF	XF	Unc	BU
1994 Proof	10,000				Value: 17.50	

KM# 101   10 TALA
31.2300 g., 0.9250 Silver 0.9287 oz. ASW **Series:** Endangered Wildlife **Obv:** National arms **Rev:** Flying bat

Date	Mintage	F	VF	XF	Unc	BU
1994 Proof	Est. 20,000				Value: 45.00	

KM# 102   10 TALA
31.4700 g., 0.9250 Silver 0.9359 oz. ASW **Subject:** Comte de la Perouse **Obv:** National arms **Rev:** World globe on stand flanked by figures, ship and date above

Date	Mintage	F	VF	XF	Unc	BU
1994 Proof	Est. 20,000				Value: 17.50	

KM# 103   10 TALA
31.4700 g., 0.9250 Silver 0.9359 oz. ASW **Subject:** Protect Our World **Obv:** National arms **Rev:** Flowers

Date	Mintage	F	VF	XF	Unc	BU
1994 Proof	Est. 10,000	Value: 18.50				

KM# 104   10 TALA
31.4700 g., 0.9250 Silver 0.9359 oz. ASW **Subject:** Queen Mother **Obv:** National arms **Rev:** Glamis Castle within beaded circle

Date	Mintage	F	VF	XF	Unc	BU
1994 Proof	Est. 30,000	Value: 17.50				

KM# 105   10 TALA
31.4700 g., 0.9250 Silver 0.9359 oz. ASW **Subject:** Edmond Halley **Obv:** National arms **Rev:** Bust 1/4 right

Date	Mintage	F	VF	XF	Unc	BU
1995 Proof	10,000	Value: 18.50				

KM# 124   10 TALA
31.6200 g., 0.9250 Silver 0.9403 oz. ASW, 38.5 mm.
Subject: Queen Elizabeth - Queen Mother **Obv:** National arms **Rev:** Young Lady sitting on horse **Edge:** Reeded

Date	Mintage	F	VF	XF	Unc	BU
1995 Proof	—	Value: 25.00				

KM# 144   10 TALA
1.2600 g., 0.9999 Gold 0.0405 oz. AGW, 13.75 mm.
Obv: National arms **Obv. Leg.:** SAMOA - SISIFO **Rev:** Sailing ship "The Endeavour" **Edge:** Reeded

Date	Mintage	F	VF	XF	Unc	BU
1995 Proof	25,000	Value: 55.00				

KM# 113   10 TALA
1.2442 g., 0.9999 Gold 0.0400 oz. AGW **Series:** Olympics
Obv: National arms **Rev:** Discus thrower

Date	Mintage	F	VF	XF	Unc	BU
1995	Est. 25,000	—	—	—	—	45.00

KM# 114   10 TALA
31.7000 g., 0.9250 Silver 0.9427 oz. ASW **Subject:** Jakob le Maire **Obv:** National arms **Rev:** Sailing ship

Date	Mintage	F	VF	XF	Unc	BU
1996 Proof	—	Value: 20.00				

KM# 127   10 TALA
31.8000 g., 0.9250 Silver 0.9457 oz. ASW, 38.6 mm.
Subject: Victorian Age **Obv:** National arms **Rev:** Queen Victoria and family within circle **Edge:** Reeded

Date	Mintage	F	VF	XF	Unc	BU
1996 Proof	—	Value: 30.00				

KM# 145   10 TALA
1.2300 g., Gold, 13..91 mm. **Subject:** The Gold of Captain Flint - Treasure Island **Obv:** National arms **Obv. Leg.:** SAMOA **Rev:** Treasure map **Edge:** Reeded

Date	Mintage	F	VF	XF	Unc	BU
1997 Proof	25,000	Value: 55.00				

KM# 128   10 TALA
31.8000 g., 0.9250 Silver 0.9457 oz. ASW, 38.6 mm.
Subject: Queen Mother **Obv:** National arms **Rev:** Queen Mother presenting shamrocks to the Irish Guards **Edge:** Reeded

Date	Mintage	F	VF	XF	Unc	BU
1998 Proof	—	Value: 30.00				

KM# 123   10 TALA
31.5000 g., 0.9250 Silver 0.9368 oz. ASW, 38.6 mm.
Subject: Princess Diana **Obv:** National arms **Rev:** Diana holding child **Edge:** Reeded

Date	Mintage	F	VF	XF	Unc	BU
1998 Proof	—	Value: 18.50				

KM# 129   10 TALA
31.4200 g., 0.9250 Silver 0.9344 oz. ASW, 38.6 mm.
Subject: Olympics **Obv:** National arms **Rev:** Two volleyball players **Edge:** Reeded

Date	Mintage	F	VF	XF	Unc	BU
2000 Proof	—	Value: 35.00				

KM# 62   25 TALA
155.5000 g., 0.9990 Silver 4.9942 oz. ASW, 65 mm. **Subject:** Kon-Tiki **Obv:** National arms **Rev:** Sailing ship **Note:** Illustration reduced.

Date	Mintage	F	VF	XF	Unc	BU
1986 Proof	25,000	Value: 85.00				

KM# 67   25 TALA
155.5000 g., 0.9990 Silver 4.9942 oz. ASW, 65 mm.
Subject: America's Cup Race **Obv:** National arms **Rev:** Sailing ship **Note:** Illustration reduced.

Date	Mintage	F	VF	XF	Unc	BU
1987 Proof	35,000	Value: 95.00				

KM# 76   50 TALA
31.1030 g., 0.9990 Palladium 0.9989 oz. **Subject:** Kon-Tiki **Obv:** National arms **Rev:** Raft and bamboo poles

Date	Mintage	F	VF	XF	Unc	BU
1988 Proof	6,500	Value: 425				

KM# 78   50 TALA
7.7700 g., 0.9990 Gold 0.2496 oz. AGW **Subject:** Trans-Antarctica Expedition **Obv:** Sled dogs and musher and single dog head facing left **Rev:** Six doves above snake on rock, value at upper left

Date	Mintage	F	VF	XF	Unc	BU
1988 Proof	30,000	Value: 250				

KM# 90   50 TALA
7.7760 g., 0.5833 Gold 0.1458 oz. AGW **Series:** 1996 Olympics
Obv: National arms **Rev:** Discus thrower

Date	Mintage	F	VF	XF	Unc	BU
1993 Proof	7,500	Value: 150				

KM# 92 50 TALA
7.7760 g., 0.5833 Gold 0.1458 oz. AGW **Subject:** World Cup Soccer **Obv:** National arms **Rev:** Soccer players

Date	Mintage	F	VF	XF	Unc	BU
1993 Proof	Est. 3,000				Value: 150	

KM# 106 50 TALA
7.7760 g., 0.5833 Gold 0.1458 oz. AGW **Obv:** National arms **Rev:** Portrait

Date	Mintage	F	VF	XF	Unc	BU
1993 Proof	Est. 3,000				Value: 145	

KM# 107 50 TALA
7.7760 g., 0.5833 Gold 0.1458 oz. AGW **Subject:** The Endeavor **Obv:** National arms **Rev:** Sailing ship within radiant sun

Date	Mintage	F	VF	XF	Unc	BU
1994 Proof	Est. 2,500				Value: 150	

KM# 108 50 TALA
7.7760 g., 0.5833 Gold 0.1458 oz. AGW **Series:** Endangered Wildlife **Obv:** National arms **Rev:** Dolphins

Date	Mintage	F	VF	XF	Unc	BU
1995 Proof	Est. 2,500				Value: 150	

KM# 119 50 TALA
3.8875 g., 0.9990 Gold 0.1249 oz. AGW **Subject:** Tempora Mutantur **Obv:** National arms **Rev:** Man with torch **Note:** 1/2 of 2-part coin, combined with Kiribati KM#26, issued in sets only; Value is determined by combining the 2 parts.

Date	Mintage	F	VF	XF	Unc	BU
ND(1997) Proof	Est. 2,500				Value: 175	

KM# 21 100 TALA
15.5500 g., 0.9170 Gold 0.4584 oz. AGW **Subject:** U.S. Bicentennial **Obv:** National arms **Rev:** Equestrian and USA map

Date	Mintage	F	VF	XF	Unc	BU
1976 Proof	2,000				Value: 450	

KM# 23 100 TALA
15.5500 g., 0.9170 Gold 0.4584 oz. AGW **Series:** Montreal Olympics **Obv:** National arms **Rev:** Weight lifter

Date	Mintage	F	VF	XF	Unc	BU
1976 Proof	2,500				Value: 450	

KM# 25 100 TALA
15.5500 g., 0.9170 Gold 0.4584 oz. AGW **Subject:** Queen's Silver Jubilee

Date	Mintage	F	VF	XF	Unc	BU
1977 Proof	2,500				Value: 450	

KM# 27 100 TALA
15.5500 g., 0.9170 Gold 0.4584 oz. AGW **Subject:** Lindbergh's New York to Paris flight **Obv:** National arms **Rev:** Bust 1/4 right, plane, statue of Liberty, Eiffel tower and dates

Date	Mintage	F	VF	XF	Unc	BU
1977 Proof	660				Value: 450	

KM# 29 100 TALA
15.5500 g., 0.9170 Gold 0.4584 oz. AGW **Subject:** 50th Anniversary - Transpacific Flight **Obv:** National arms **Rev:** Globe with plane flying across Pacific Ocean, portrait of Lindbergh facing left

Date	Mintage	F	VF	XF	Unc	BU
1978 Proof	1,500				Value: 450	

KM# 31 100 TALA
15.5500 g., 0.9170 Gold 0.4584 oz. AGW **Subject:** XI Commonwealth Games **Obv:** National arms **Rev:** Runners

Date	Mintage	F	VF	XF	Unc	BU
1978 Proof	1,000				Value: 450	

KM# 34 100 TALA
12.5000 g., 0.9170 Gold 0.3685 oz. AGW **Subject:** Bicentenary - death of Capt. James Cook **Obv:** National arms **Rev:** Portrait of Cook at left of sailing ship

Date	Mintage	F	VF	XF	Unc	BU
1979 Proof	1,000				Value: 375	

KM# 37 100 TALA
7.5000 g., 0.9170 Gold 0.2211 oz. AGW **Series:** 1980 Moscow Olympics **Obv:** National arms **Rev:** Hurdles event, Moscow Olympic logo below

Date	Mintage	F	VF	XF	Unc	BU
1980	250	—	—	—	—	235
1980 Proof	1,000				Value: 225	

KM# 42 100 TALA
7.5000 g., 0.9170 Gold 0.2211 oz. AGW **Subject:** Gov. Wilhelm Solf **Obv:** National arms **Rev:** Uniformed bust left flanked by huts and palm trees

Date	Mintage	F	VF	XF	Unc	BU
1980	250	—	—	—	—	235
1980 Proof	1,000				Value: 225	

KM# 45 100 TALA
7.5000 g., 0.9170 Gold 0.2211 oz. AGW **Subject:** Wedding of Prince Charles and Lady Diana **Obv:** National arms **Rev:** Conjoined busts left

Date	Mintage	F	VF	XF	Unc	BU
1981	250	—	—	—	—	235
1981 Proof	1,500				Value: 225	

KM# 49 100 TALA
7.5000 g., 0.9170 Gold 0.2211 oz. AGW **Subject:** IYDP - President Franklin Roosevelt **Obv:** National arms **Rev:** Seated figure in wheelchair facing

Date	Mintage	F	VF	XF	Unc	BU
1981	250	—	—	—	—	235
1981 Proof	1,500				Value: 225	

KM# 52 100 TALA
7.5000 g., 0.9170 Gold 0.2211 oz. AGW **Subject:** Commonwealth Games **Obv:** National arms **Rev:** Javelin thrower

Date	Mintage	F	VF	XF	Unc	BU
1982	250	—	—	—	—	235
1982 Proof	1,000				Value: 225	

KM# 55 100 TALA
7.5000 g., 0.9170 Gold 0.2211 oz. AGW **Subject:** South Pacific Games **Obv:** National arms **Rev:** Runner

Date	Mintage	F	VF	XF	Unc	BU
1983	—	—	—	—	—	235
1983 Proof	1,000				Value: 225	

KM# 60 100 TALA
7.5000 g., 0.9170 Gold 0.2211 oz. AGW **Series:** Summer Olympics **Obv:** National arms **Rev:** Boxing match

Date	Mintage	F	VF	XF	Unc	BU
1984	200	—	—	—	—	235
1984 Proof	500				Value: 225	

KM# 68 100 TALA
7.5000 g., 0.9000 Gold 0.2170 oz. AGW **Subject:** America's Cup Race **Obv:** National arms **Rev:** Ship

Date	Mintage	F	VF	XF	Unc	BU
1987 Proof	5,000				Value: 225	

KM# 77 100 TALA
7.5000 g., 0.9000 Gold 0.2170 oz. AGW **Subject:** Kon-Tiki **Obv:** National arms **Rev:** Boat and inscription

Date	Mintage	F	VF	XF	Unc	BU
1988 Proof	1,500				Value: 225	

KM# 81 100 TALA
7.5000 g., 0.9170 Gold 0.2211 oz. AGW **Series:** Save the Children **Obv:** National arms **Rev:** Children playing

Date	Mintage	F	VF	XF	Unc	BU
1990 Proof	3,000				Value: 225	

KM# 84 100 TALA
7.5000 g., 0.9170 Gold 0.2211 oz. AGW **Subject:** RA expeditions **Obv:** National arms **Rev:** Ship (RA II)

Date	Mintage	F	VF	XF	Unc	BU
1991 Proof	5,000				Value: 225	

KM# 87 100 TALA
7.5000 g., 0.9000 Gold 0.2170 oz. AGW **Series:** Olympics **Obv:** National arms **Rev:** Torch runner

Date	Mintage	F	VF	XF	Unc	BU
1991 Proof	6,000				Value: 225	

KM# 96 100 TALA
7.5000 g., 0.9170 Gold 0.2211 oz. AGW **Subject:** Tigris Expedition **Obv:** National arms **Rev:** Tigris sailing

Date	Mintage	F	VF	XF	Unc	BU
1994 Proof	2,000				Value: 225	

KM# 126 100 TALA
7.5000 g., 0.9160 Gold 0.2209 oz. AGW, 28.5 mm. **Subject:** Robert Louis Stevenson **Obv:** National arms **Rev:** Ship and portrait **Edge:** Reeded

Date	Mintage	F	VF	XF	Unc	BU
ND(1994) Proof	2,000				Value: 225	

KM# 130 200 TALA
14.7000 g., 0.9990 Gold 0.4721 oz. AGW, 38.7x22.85 mm. **Subject:** People and Buildings **Obv:** National arms, value and dates **Rev:** Statue of Liberty **Edge:** Plain

Date	Mintage	F	VF	XF	Unc	BU
1999-2000 Proof	—				Value: 475	

KM# 136 500 TALA
69.8200 g., 0.9990 Gold 2.2424 oz. AGW, 36.4 mm. **Obv:** National arms **Rev:** Dove and sword handle above two soldiers **Edge:** Plain **Note:** Jagged coin half matching with Kiribati KM#36

Date	Mintage	F	VF	XF	Unc	BU
2000 Proof	99				Value: 2,250	

KM# 46 1000 TALA
33.9500 g., 0.9170 Gold 1.0009 oz. AGW **Subject:** Wedding of Prince Charles and Lady Diana **Obv:** National arms **Rev:** Conjoined busts left

Date	Mintage	F	VF	XF	Unc	BU
1981 Proof	100				Value: 950	

KM# 56 1000 TALA
31.1000 g., 0.9170 Gold 0.9169 oz. AGW **Subject:** South Pacific Games **Obv:** National arms **Rev:** Runner

Date	Mintage	F	VF	XF	Unc	BU
1983 Proof	100				Value: 1,000	

KM# 61   1000 TALA
31.1000 g., 0.9170 Gold 0.9169 oz. AGW **Series:** 1984 Olympics **Obv:** National arms **Rev:** Boxing match

Date	Mintage	F	VF	XF	Unc	BU
1984 Proof	100	Value: 925				

KM# 65   1000 TALA
33.9500 g., 0.9170 Gold 1.0009 oz. AGW **Subject:** Prince Andrew and Sarah Fereguson's Marriage **Obv:** National arms **Rev:** Conjoined busts left

Date	Mintage	F	VF	XF	Unc	BU
1986 Proof	50	Value: 1,000				

KM# 110   1000 TALA
33.9500 g., 0.9170 Gold 1.0009 oz. AGW **Subject:** 40th Anniversary - Reign of Queen Elizabeth II **Obv:** National arms **Rev:** Royal carriage and guard around Order of the Garter

Date	Mintage	F	VF	XF	Unc	BU
1992 Proof	Est. 150	Value: 975				

PIEFORTS

KM#	Date	Mintage	Identification	Mkt Val
P1	1984	3,000	Tala. 0.9250 Silver. KM57.	22.00
P2	1992	—	Tala. 0.9250 Silver. KM109.	50.00

COMBINED PROOF SETS (CPS)

KM#	Date	Mintage	Identification	Issue Price	Mkt Val
CPS1	1997 (8)	10,000	West Samoa KM#115-118, Kiribati KM#22-25	—	225

MINT SETS

KM#	Date	Mintage	Identification	Issue Price	Mkt Val
MS1	1967 (6)	—	KM1-6	—	2.50
MS2	1974 (7)	10,740	KM12-17, 19	5.30	5.00

PROOF SETS

KM#	Date	Mintage	Identification	Issue Price	Mkt Val
PS1	1967 (7)	15,000	KM1-7	10.00	7.00
PS2	1974 (7)	5,578	KM12a-17a, 19a	53.00	30.00
PS3	1988 (3)	—	KM75-77	—	650
PS4	1991 (2)	1,000	KM83-84	—	175
PS5	1994 (3)	500	KM94-96	—	245

SAN MARINO

The Republic of San Marino, the oldest and smallest republic in the world is located in north central Italy entirely surrounded by the Province of Emilia-Romagna. It has an area of 24 sq. mi. (60 sq. km.) and a population of *23,000. Capital: San Marino. The principal economic activities are farming, livestock raising, cheese making, tourism and light manufacturing. Building stone, lime, wheat, hides and baked goods are exported. The government derives most of its revenue from the sale of postage stamps for philatelic purposes.

According to tradition, San Marino was founded about 350AD by a Christian stonecutter as a refuge against religious persecution. While gradually acquiring the institutions of an independent state, it avoided the factional fights of the Middle Ages and, except for a brief period in fief to Cesare Borgia, retained its freedom despite attacks on its sovereignty by the Papacy, the Lords of Rimini, Napoleon and Mussolini. In 1862 San Marino established a customs union with, and put itself under the protection of, Italy. A Communist-Socialist coalition controlled the Government for 12 years after World War II. The Christian Democratic Party has been the core of government since 1957. In 1978 a Communist-Socialist coalition again came into power and remained in control until 1991.

San Marino has its own coinage, but Italian and Vatican City coins and currency are also in circulation.

MINT MARKS
M - Milan
R – Rome

MONETARY SYSTEM
100 Centesimi = 1 Lira

REPUBLIC

STANDARD COINAGE

KM# 12   5 CENTESIMI
3.2000 g., Bronze **Obv:** Crowned pointed arms within wreath **Rev:** Value and date

Date	Mintage	F	VF	XF	Unc	BU
1935R	800,000	1.25	2.00	12.00	32.00	—
1936R	400,000	1.25	2.00	12.00	32.00	—
1937R	200,000	2.00	6.00	19.00	38.00	—
1938R	200,000	2.00	6.00	19.00	38.00	—

KM# 13   10 CENTESIMI
5.4000 g., Bronze **Obv:** Crowned pointed arms within wreath **Rev:** Value and date

Date	Mintage	F	VF	XF	Unc	BU
1935R	600,000	2.00	6.00	15.00	30.00	—
1936R	300,000	2.00	6.00	15.00	30.00	—
1937R	400,000	2.00	6.00	15.00	30.00	—
1938R	400,000	2.00	6.00	15.00	30.00	—

KM# 4   LIRA
5.0000 g., 0.8350 Silver 0.1342 oz. ASW· **Obv:** Crowned arms within wreath **Obv. Leg.:** RESPVBLICA S. MARINI **Rev:** Value, date within wreath

Date	Mintage	F	VF	XF	Unc	BU
1906R	30,000	15.00	22.50	40.00	228	—

KM# 14   LIRA
Aluminum **Obv:** Bust of Saint 1/4 left **Rev:** Value above arms without shield

Date	Mintage	F	VF	XF	Unc	BU
1972	291,000	—	—	0.10	0.20	—

KM# 22   LIRA
Aluminum **Obv:** Crowned shield **Rev:** Girl with national flag

Date	Mintage	F	VF	XF	Unc	BU
1973	291,000	—	—	0.10	0.20	—

KM# 30   LIRA
Aluminum **Obv:** Smoking towers within circle **Rev:** Ant

Date	Mintage	F	VF	XF	Unc	BU
1974	276,000	—	—	0.25	1.25	2.50

KM# 40   LIRA
Aluminum **Obv:** Smoking towers within circle **Rev:** Spiders in web

Date	Mintage	F	VF	XF	Unc	BU
1975	291,000	—	—	0.25	1.25	2.50

KM# 51   LIRA
Aluminum **Obv:** Smoking towers **Rev:** Crossed flags flanked by hands

Date	Mintage	F	VF	XF	Unc	BU
1976	195,000	—	—	0.10	0.20	—

KM# 63   LIRA
0.6500 g., Aluminum **Series:** F.A.O. **Obv:** Smoking towers within circle **Rev:** Globe in center of star wreath

Date	Mintage	F	VF	XF	Unc	BU
1977	1,180,000	—	—	0.10	0.20	—

KM# 76   LIRA
Aluminum **Obv:** Value below smoking towers **Rev:** Sitting figure within spider web

Date	Mintage	F	VF	XF	Unc	BU
1978	130,000	—	—	0.15	0.30	—

KM# 89   LIRA
Aluminum **Obv:** Crowned shield **Rev:** Sword handle divides value

Date	Mintage	F	VF	XF	Unc	BU
1979	125,000	—	—	0.15	0.30	—

KM# 102   LIRA
Aluminum **Series:** 1980 Olympics **Obv:** Olympic circles and date to left of smoking towers **Rev:** Ballerina

Date	Mintage	F	VF	XF	Unc	BU
1980	125,000	—	—	0.15	0.30	—

KM# 116   LIRA
Aluminum **Obv:** Crowned shield **Rev:** Value within design

Date	Mintage	F	VF	XF	Unc	BU
1981R	100,000	—	—	0.15	0.30	—

KM# 131   LIRA
Aluminum **Subject:** Social conquest **Obv:** Crown above smoking towers **Rev:** Back of standing figure divides date and value

Date	Mintage	F	VF	XF	Unc	BU
1982R	78,000	—	—	0.15	0.30	—

KM# 145 LIRA
Aluminum **Subject:** Nuclear war threat **Obv:** Crowned shield above sprig **Rev:** Beast of war

Date	Mintage	F	VF	XF	Unc	BU
1983R	72,000	—	—	0.20	0.40	—

KM# 159 LIRA
Aluminum **Obv:** Castle **Rev:** Bust facing flanked by value and caduceus

Date	Mintage	F	VF	XF	Unc	BU
1984R	65,000	—	—	0.20	0.40	—

KM# 173 LIRA
Aluminum **Subject:** War on drugs **Obv:** Shield **Rev:** Supine male 1/2 length figure below value and date

Date	Mintage	F	VF	XF	Unc	BU
1985R	60,000	—	—	0.10	0.25	—

KM# 187 LIRA
Aluminum **Subject:** Revolution of technology **Obv:** Crown above smoking towers on rock **Rev:** Footprints on the moon

Date	Mintage	F	VF	XF	Unc	BU
1986R	50,000	—	—	0.10	0.25	—

KM# 201 LIRA
Aluminum **Subject:** 15th Anniversary - Resumption of Coinage **Obv:** Crowned pointed arms within sprigs **Rev:** Tree flanked by value

Date	Mintage	F	VF	XF	Unc	BU
1987R	83,000	—	—	0.10	0.25	—

KM# 218 LIRA
Aluminum **Subject:** Fortifications **Obv:** Crowned ornate arms on shield **Rev:** Corner Tower

Date	Mintage	F	VF	XF	Unc	BU
1988R	38,000	—	—	0.10	0.25	—

KM# 231 LIRA
Aluminum **Subject:** History **Obv:** Crowned shield **Rev:** Stone Age tool

Date	Mintage	F	VF	XF	Unc	BU
1989R	37,000	—	—	0.10	0.25	—

KM# 248 LIRA
Aluminum **Subject:** 1,600 Years of History **Obv:** Stylized towers **Rev:** Stylized Saint

Date	Mintage	F	VF	XF	Unc	BU
1990R	36,000	—	—	0.10	0.25	—

KM# 261 LIRA
Aluminum **Obv:** Date to upper left of smoking towers **Rev:** Hands holding hammer and chisel below value

Date	Mintage	F	VF	XF	Unc	BU
1991R		—	—	0.10	0.25	—

KM# 278 LIRA
Aluminum **Subject:** Columbus **Obv:** Towers with feather-like designs above within circle **Rev:** Potatoes and plant within design with value at left

Date	Mintage	F	VF	XF	Unc	BU
ND(1992)R		—	—	0.10	0.25	—

KM# 293 LIRA
Aluminum **Obv:** Stylized smoking towers **Rev:** Seedling divides date and value

Date	Mintage	F	VF	XF	Unc	BU
1993R		—	—	0.10	0.25	—

KM# 306 LIRA
Aluminum **Obv:** Bust facing with arms holding hammer and chisel, smoking towers at left **Rev:** Mother and child

Date	Mintage	F	VF	XF	Unc	BU
1994R	40,000	—	—	0.10	0.25	—

KM# 322 LIRA
Aluminum **Obv:** Banner around design **Rev:** Child on broken sword divides sprig and value

Date	Mintage	F	VF	XF	Unc	BU
1995R		—	—	0.10	0.25	—

KM# 349 LIRA
Aluminum **Subject:** Talete - Child of the Universe **Obv:** Bust facing with flame within hands **Rev:** Value and date at left of head facing

Date	Mintage	F	VF	XF	Unc	BU
1996R	32,000	—	—	0.10	0.25	—

KM# 359 LIRA
Aluminum **Subject:** The Arts - Prehistoric **Obv:** Bust facing with flame within hands **Rev:** Elk

Date	Mintage	F	VF	XF	Unc	BU
1997R	28,000	—	—	0.10	0.25	0.75

KM# 5 2 LIRE
10.0000 g., 0.8350 Silver 0.2684 oz. ASW, 27 mm.
Obv: Crowned arms within wreath **Obv. Leg.:** RESPVBLICA S. MARINI **Rev:** Value, date within wreath

Date	Mintage	F	VF	XF	Unc	BU
1906R	15,000	25.00	40.00	175	380	—

KM# 15 2 LIRE
Aluminum, 18 mm. **Obv:** Value above stylized smoking towers **Rev:** Bust of Saint 1/4 right

Date	Mintage	F	VF	XF	Unc	BU
1972	291,000	—	—	0.10	0.30	—

KM# 23 2 LIRE
Aluminum, 18 mm. **Obv:** Crowned shield **Rev:** Pelican

Date	Mintage	F	VF	XF	Unc	BU
1973	291,000	—	—	0.20	1.00	2.25

KM# 31 2 LIRE
Aluminum, 18 mm. **Obv:** Smoking towers within circle **Rev:** Beetle

Date	Mintage	F	VF	XF	Unc	BU
1974	276,000	—	—	0.25	1.25	2.50

KM# 41 2 LIRE
Aluminum, 18 mm. **Obv:** Smoking towers **Rev:** Seahorses

Date	Mintage	F	VF	XF	Unc	BU
1975	291,000	—	—	0.25	1.25	2.25

KM# 52 2 LIRE
Aluminum, 18 mm. **Obv:** Smoking towers **Rev:** Stylized sun, hills and sitting figure

Date	Mintage	F	VF	XF	Unc	BU
1976	195,000	—	—	0.10	0.30	0.50

KM# 64 2 LIRE
Aluminum, 18 mm. **Obv:** Value and smoking towers within circle **Rev:** Stars above wave-like designs within circle

Date	Mintage	F	VF	XF	Unc	BU
1977	180,000	—	—	0.10	0.30	—

KM# 77   2 LIRE
Aluminum, 18 mm.   **Obv:** Value below smoking towers
Rev: Standing figure working

Date	Mintage	F	VF	XF	Unc	BU
1978	130,000	—	—	0.10	0.30	—

KM# 90   2 LIRE
Aluminum, 18 mm.   **Obv:** Crowned shield **Rev:** Bugle with banner divides value

Date	Mintage	F	VF	XF	Unc	BU
1979	125,000	—	—	0.10	0.30	—

KM# 103   2 LIRE
Aluminum, 18 mm.   **Series:** 1980 Olympics **Obv:** Olympic rings and date to left of smoking towers **Rev:** Soccer player

Date	Mintage	F	VF	XF	Unc	BU
1980	125,000	—	—	0.25	0.75	—

KM# 117   2 LIRE
Aluminum, 18 mm.   **Obv:** Crowned shield **Rev:** Small head and hand left, date and value at upper left

Date	Mintage	F	VF	XF	Unc	BU
1981R	100,000	—	—	0.10	0.30	—

KM# 132   2 LIRE
Aluminum, 18 mm.   **Subject:** Social Conquests **Obv:** Crown above smoking towers **Rev:** Value below stylized design

Date	Mintage	F	VF	XF	Unc	BU
1982R	78,000	—	—	0.10	0.30	—

KM# 146   2 LIRE
Aluminum, 18 mm.   **Subject:** Nuclear war threat **Obv:** Crowned shield above sprig **Rev:** Two reaching arms

Date	Mintage	F	VF	XF	Unc	BU
1983R	72,000	—	—	0.20	0.40	—

KM# 160   2 LIRE
Aluminum, 18 mm.   **Obv:** Castle **Rev:** Head facing

Date	Mintage	F	VF	XF	Unc	BU
1984R	65,000	—	—	0.20	0.40	—

KM# 174   2 LIRE
Aluminum, 18 mm.   **Subject:** War on Drugs **Obv:** Shield
Rev: Clenched fist

Date	Mintage	F	VF	XF	Unc	BU
1985R	60,000	—	—	0.10	0.25	—

KM# 188   2 LIRE
Aluminum, 18 mm.   **Subject:** Revolution of Technology
Obv: Crown above smoking towers on rock **Rev:** Astronaut walking in space

Date	Mintage	F	VF	XF	Unc	BU
1986R	50,000	—	—	0.10	0.25	—

KM# 202   2 LIRE
Aluminum, 18 mm.   **Subject:** 15th Anniversary - Resumption of Coinage **Obv:** Crowned pointed shield within sprigs **Rev:** Flower designs

Date	Mintage	F	VF	XF	Unc	BU
1987R	83,000	—	—	0.10	0.25	—

KM# 219   2 LIRE
Aluminum, 18 mm.   **Subject:** Fortifications **Obv:** Crowned ornate arms on shield **Rev:** Fortified archway

Date	Mintage	F	VF	XF	Unc	BU
1988R	38,000	—	—	0.10	0.25	—

KM# 232   2 LIRE
Aluminum, 18 mm.   **Subject:** History **Obv:** Crowned shield
Rev: Value divides wheat stalk and olive branch

Date	Mintage	F	VF	XF	Unc	BU
1989R	37,000	—	—	0.10	0.25	—

KM# 249   2 LIRE
Aluminum, 18 mm.   **Subject:** 1,600 Years of History
Obv: Stylized towers **Rev:** Stylized figure with spear

Date	Mintage	F	VF	XF	Unc	BU
1990R	36,000	—	—	0.10	0.25	—

KM# 262   2 LIRE
Aluminum, 18 mm.   **Obv:** Date to upper left of smoking towers
Rev: Hands with interlocked fingers below value

Date	Mintage	F	VF	XF	Unc	BU
1991R	—	—	—	0.10	0.25	—

KM# 279   2 LIRE
Aluminum, 18 mm.   **Subject:** Columbus **Obv:** Towers with feather-like designs on top within circle **Rev:** Ear of corn to left of value within design

Date	Mintage	F	VF	XF	Unc	BU
ND(1992)R	—	—	—	0.10	0.25	—

KM# 294   2 LIRE
Aluminum, 18 mm.   **Obv:** Smoking towers **Rev:** Rose

Date	Mintage	F	VF	XF	Unc	BU
1993R	—	—	—	0.10	0.25	—

KM# 307   2 LIRE
Aluminum, 18 mm.   **Obv:** Head with hands holding hammer and chisel, towers at left **Rev:** Standing stonecutter at work

Date	Mintage	F	VF	XF	Unc	BU
1994R	40,000	—	—	0.10	0.25	—

KM# 323   2 LIRE
Aluminum, 18 mm.   **Obv:** Banner around bottom of design
Rev: Child with toy castle

Date	Mintage	F	VF	XF	Unc	BU
1995R	—	—	—	0.10	0.25	—

KM# 350   2 LIRE
Aluminum, 18 mm.   **Obv:** Bust facing with flame within hands
Rev: Head of Socrates

Date	Mintage	F	VF	XF	Unc	BU
1996R	32,000	—	—	0.10	0.25	—

KM# 360   2 LIRE
Aluminum, 18 mm.   **Subject:** The Arts - Literature **Obv:** Bust facing with flame within hands **Rev:** Dante holding Divine Comedy

Date	Mintage	F	VF	XF	Unc	BU
1997R	28,000	—	—	0.10	0.25	—

KM# 9   5 LIRE
5.0000 g., 0.8350 Silver 0.1342 oz. ASW, 23 mm.   **Obv:** Bust left within beaded circle **Rev:** Plant divides value above plow

Date	Mintage	F	VF	XF	Unc	BU
1931R	50,000	3.50	5.50	10.00	100	—
1932R	50,000	3.50	5.50	10.00	100	—
1933R	50,000	3.50	5.50	8.50	30.00	—
1935R	200,000	3.50	5.50	8.50	20.00	—
1936R	100,000	3.50	5.50	8.50	50.00	—
1937R	100,000	3.50	5.50	8.50	50.00	—
1938R	120,000	3.50	5.50	8.50	50.00	—

KM# 16 5 LIRE
Aluminum, 20 mm. **Obv:** Bust of Saint 1/4 left **Rev:** Value above stylized smoking towers

Date	Mintage	F	VF	XF	Unc	BU
1972	291,000	—	—	0.10	0.35	—

KM# 24 5 LIRE
Aluminum, 20 mm. **Obv:** Crowned shield **Rev:** Heads within small circle on globe, radiant star border

Date	Mintage	F	VF	XF	Unc	BU
1973	291,000	—	—	0.10	0.35	—

KM# 32 5 LIRE
Aluminum, 20 mm. **Obv:** Smoking towers within circle **Rev:** Porcupine

Date	Mintage	F	VF	XF	Unc	BU
1974	276,000	—	—	0.25	1.25	2.50

KM# 42 5 LIRE
Aluminum, 20 mm. **Obv:** Smoking towers **Rev:** Hedgehogs

Date	Mintage	F	VF	XF	Unc	BU
1975	291,000	—	—	0.20	1.00	2.50

KM# 53 5 LIRE
Aluminum, 20 mm. **Series:** F.A.O. **Obv:** Stylized smoking towers **Rev:** Stylized standing figures within design

Date	Mintage	F	VF	XF	Unc	BU
1976	695,000	—	—	0.10	0.25	—

KM# 65 5 LIRE
Aluminum, 20 mm. **Obv:** Value below smoking towers within circle **Rev:** Stars within circle

Date	Mintage	F	VF	XF	Unc	BU
1977	180,000	—	—	0.10	0.35	—

KM# 78 5 LIRE
Aluminum, 20 mm. **Obv:** Value below smoking towers **Rev:** Standing figure holding water hose

Date	Mintage	F	VF	XF	Unc	BU
1978	130,000	—	—	0.10	0.35	—

KM# 91 5 LIRE
Aluminum, 20 mm. **Obv:** Crowned shield **Rev:** Crossbow divides value

Date	Mintage	F	VF	XF	Unc	BU
1979	125,000	—	—	0.10	0.35	—

KM# 104 5 LIRE
Aluminum, 20 mm. **Series:** 1980 Olympics **Obv:** Olympic rings and date to left of smoking towers **Rev:** Running figure right

Date	Mintage	F	VF	XF	Unc	BU
1980	125,000	—	—	0.25	0.75	—

KM# 118 5 LIRE
Aluminum, 20 mm. **Obv:** Crowned shield **Rev:** Goat divides value and date

Date	Mintage	F	VF	XF	Unc	BU
1981R	100,000	—	—	0.25	0.75	2.50

KM# 133 5 LIRE
Aluminum, 20 mm. **Subject:** Social Conquests **Obv:** Crown above smoking towers **Rev:** Stylized boats and plane

Date	Mintage	F	VF	XF	Unc	BU
1982R	78,000	—	—	0.10	0.30	—

KM# 147 5 LIRE
Aluminum, 20 mm. **Subject:** Nuclear War Threat **Obv:** Crown above shield and sprig **Rev:** Pair of reaching arms within barred window

Date	Mintage	F	VF	XF	Unc	BU
1983R	72,000	—	—	0.20	0.40	—

KM# 161 5 LIRE
Aluminum, 20 mm. **Obv:** Castle **Rev:** Bust of Galileo facing

Date	Mintage	F	VF	XF	Unc	BU
1984R	65,000	—	—	0.20	0.40	—

KM# 175 5 LIRE
Aluminum, 20 mm. **Subject:** War on Drugs **Obv:** Shield **Rev:** Face of addict

Date	Mintage	F	VF	XF	Unc	BU
1985R	60,000	—	—	0.10	0.30	—

KM# 189 5 LIRE
Aluminum, 20 mm. **Subject:** Revolution of Technology **Obv:** Crown above smoking towers on rock **Rev:** Human figure operating larger robot

Date	Mintage	F	VF	XF	Unc	BU
1986R	50,000	—	—	0.10	0.30	—

KM# 203 5 LIRE
Aluminum, 20 mm. **Subject:** 15th Anniversary - Resumption of Coinage **Obv:** Crowned pointed shield within sprigs **Rev:** Flowers in designed vase divide value

Date	Mintage	F	VF	XF	Unc	BU
1987R	83,000	—	—	0.10	0.30	—

KM# 220 5 LIRE
Aluminum, 20 mm. **Subject:** Fortification **Obv:** Crowned ornate arms on shield **Rev:** Round corner tower

Date	Mintage	F	VF	XF	Unc	BU
1988R	38,000	—	—	0.10	0.30	—

KM# 233 5 LIRE
Aluminum, 20 mm. **Subject:** History **Obv:** Crowned shield **Rev:** Cluster of grapes divide value

Date	Mintage	F	VF	XF	Unc	BU
1989R	37,000	—	—	0.10	0.30	—

KM# 250 5 LIRE
Aluminum, 20 mm. **Subject:** 1,600 Years of History **Obv:** Stylized towers above design **Rev:** Two stylized facing figures

Date	Mintage	F	VF	XF	Unc	BU
1990R	36,000	—	—	0.10	0.30	—

KM# 263 5 LIRE
Aluminum, 20 mm. **Obv:** Date at upper left of smoking towers **Rev:** Hand holding quill below value

Date	Mintage	F	VF	XF	Unc	BU
1991R	—	—	—	0.10	0.30	—

KM# 280 5 LIRE
Aluminum, 20 mm. **Subject:** Columbus **Obv:** Towers with feather-like designs on top within circle **Rev:** Cotton plants and value within design

Date	Mintage	F	VF	XF	Unc	BU
ND(1992)R	—	—	—	0.10	0.30	—

KM# 295   5 LIRE
Aluminum, 20 mm.   **Obv:** Stylized smoking towers **Rev:** Spade and hoe

Date	Mintage	F	VF	XF	Unc	BU
1993R	—			0.10	0.30	—

KM# 308   5 LIRE
Aluminum, 20 mm.   **Obv:** Stone cutter holding hammer and chisel, towers at left **Rev:** Standing figures with tools

Date	Mintage	F	VF	XF	Unc	BU
1994R	40,000			0.10	0.30	—

KM# 324   5 LIRE
Aluminum, 20 mm.   **Obv:** Banner wrapped around quills **Rev:** Child with 2 deer

Date	Mintage	F	VF	XF	Unc	BU
1995R	—			0.10	0.30	—

KM# 351   5 LIRE
Aluminum, 20 mm.   **Obv:** Bust facing with flame within hands **Rev:** Plato

Date	Mintage	F	VF	XF	Unc	BU
1996R	32,000	—		0.10	0.30	—

KM# 361   5 LIRE
Aluminum, 20 mm.   **Subject:** The Arts - Theater **Obv:** Bust facing with flame within hands **Rev:** Hamlet with skull

Date	Mintage	F	VF	XF	Unc	BU
1997R	28,000			0.10	0.30	—

KM# 7   10 LIRE
3.2258 g., 0.9000 Gold 0.0933 oz. AGW **Obv:** Smoking towers within circle **Rev:** Standing Saint facing divides value **Note:** 16,000 coins melted at the mint.

Date	Mintage	F	VF	XF	Unc	BU
1925R	20,000	175	500	800	1,250	—

KM# 10   10 LIRE
10.0000 g., 0.8350 Silver 0.2684 oz. ASW **Obv:** Nine sided shield divides value within circle, crown at top divides circle **Rev:** Facing figure holding crown divides date within circle

Date	Mintage	F	VF	XF	Unc	BU
1931R	25,000	8.50	15.00	35.00	80.00	—
1932R	25,000	8.50	15.00	35.00	80.00	—

Date	Mintage	F	VF	XF	Unc	BU
1933R	25,000	8.50	15.00	35.00	80.00	—
1935R	30,000	6.50	10.00	25.00	65.00	—
1936R	15,000	10.00	18.00	40.00	95.00	—
1937R	20,000	6.50	10.00	25.00	65.00	—
1938R	10,000	12.00	20.00	50.00	200	—

KM# 17   10 LIRE
1.6000 g., Aluminum, 23.3 mm.   **Obv:** Stylized smoking towers **Rev:** Cow nursing calf

Date	Mintage	F	VF	XF	Unc	BU
1972	291,000	—	0.10	0.20	0.50	2.50

KM# 25   10 LIRE
1.6000 g., Aluminum, 23.3 mm.   **Obv:** Crowned shield **Rev:** Man fighting four-headed dragon

Date	Mintage	F	VF	XF	Unc	BU
1973	291,000	—	0.10	0.15	0.40	—

KM# 33   10 LIRE
1.6000 g., Aluminum, 23.3 mm.   **Series:** F.A.O. **Obv:** Smoking towers within circle **Rev:** Bee

Date	Mintage	F	VF	XF	Unc	BU
1974	1,276,000	—	—	0.15	0.45	1.50

KM# 43   10 LIRE
1.6000 g., Aluminum, 23.3 mm.   **Obv:** Smoking towers **Rev:** Rats divide value

Date	Mintage	F	VF	XF	Unc	BU
1975	291,000	—	0.10	0.25	1.00	2.50

KM# 54   10 LIRE
1.6000 g., Aluminum, 23.3 mm.   **Obv:** Stylized smoking towers **Rev:** Fetus within circle, standing baby at left

Date	Mintage	F	VF	XF	Unc	BU
1976	195,000	—	0.10	0.15	0.40	—

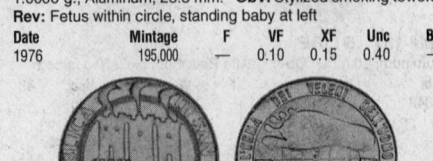

KM# 66   10 LIRE
1.6000 g., Aluminum, 23.3 mm.   **Obv:** Stylized smoking towers within circle **Rev:** Foot above 1/2 designed star wreath

Date	Mintage	F	VF	XF	Unc	BU
1977	180,000	—	0.10	0.15	0.40	—

KM# 79   10 LIRE
1.6000 g., Aluminum, 23.3 mm.   **Obv:** Smoking towers above value **Rev:** Seated figure

Date	Mintage	F	VF	XF	Unc	BU
1978	130,000	—	0.10	0.15	0.40	—

KM# 92   10 LIRE
1.6000 g., Aluminum, 23.3 mm.   **Obv:** Crowned shield **Rev:** Date flanked by two crowned shields on stands

Date	Mintage	F	VF	XF	Unc	BU
1979	125,000	—	0.10	0.15	0.40	—

KM# 105   10 LIRE
1.6000 g., Aluminum, 23.3 mm.   **Series:** 1980 Olympics **Obv:** Olympic rings and date to left of smoking towers **Rev:** Jumping equestrian

Date	Mintage	F	VF	XF	Unc	BU
1980	125,000	—	0.25	0.50	0.80	1.50

KM# 119   10 LIRE
1.6000 g., Aluminum, 23.3 mm.   **Obv:** Crowned shield **Rev:** Value surrounded by nude figure

Date	Mintage	F	VF	XF	Unc	BU
1981R	100,000	—	0.10	0.20	0.50	—

KM# 134   10 LIRE
1.6000 g., Aluminum, 23.3 mm.   **Subject:** Social Conquests **Obv:** Crown above smoking towers **Rev:** Stylized figures

Date	Mintage	F	VF	XF	Unc	BU
1982R	78,000	—	0.10	0.20	0.50	—

KM# 148   10 LIRE
1.6000 g., Aluminum, 23.3 mm.   **Subject:** Nuclear War Threat **Obv:** Crown above shield and sprig **Rev:** Vertical line within square divides reaching arms

Date	Mintage	F	VF	XF	Unc	BU
1983R	72,000	—	0.10	0.25	0.75	—

KM# 162 10 LIRE
1.6000 g., Aluminum, 23.3 mm. **Subject:** Alessandro Volta
Obv: Castle **Rev:** Bust 3/4 right

Date	Mintage	F	VF	XF	Unc	BU
1984R	65,000	—	0.10	0.25	0.75	—

KM# 176 10 LIRE
1.6000 g., Aluminum, 23.3 mm. **Subject:** War on Drugs
Obv: Shield **Rev:** Mother lecturing son

Date	Mintage	F	VF	XF	Unc	BU
1985R	60,000	—	—	0.10	0.35	—

KM# 190 10 LIRE
1.6000 g., Aluminum, 23.3 mm. **Subject:** Revolution of
Technology **Obv:** Crown above smoking towers on rock
Rev: Radio receiver

Date	Mintage	F	VF	XF	Unc	BU
1986R	50,000	—	—	0.10	0.35	—

KM# 204 10 LIRE
1.6000 g., Aluminum, 23.3 mm. **Subject:** 15th Anniversary -
Resumption of Coinage **Obv:** Crowned pointed shield within
sprigs **Rev:** Tower divides value

Date	Mintage	F	VF	XF	Unc	BU
1987R	83,000	—	—	0.10	0.35	—

KM# 221 10 LIRE
1.6000 g., Aluminum, 23.3 mm. **Subject:** Fortifications
Obv: Crowned ornate arms on shield **Rev:** Sloping fortress wall

Date	Mintage	F	VF	XF	Unc	BU
1988R	38,000	—	—	0.10	0.35	—

KM# 234 10 LIRE
1.6000 g., Aluminum, 23.3 mm. **Subject:** History **Obv:** Crowned
shield **Rev:** Ancient pottery divides value

Date	Mintage	F	VF	XF	Unc	BU
1989R	37,000	—	—	0.10	0.35	—

KM# 251 10 LIRE
1.6000 g., Aluminum, 23.3 mm. **Subject:** 1,600 Years of History
Obv: Stylized towers above design **Rev:** Stylized soldier

Date	Mintage	F	VF	XF	Unc	BU
1990R	36,000	—	—	0.10	0.35	—

KM# 264 10 LIRE
1.6000 g., Aluminum, 23.3 mm. **Obv:** Date at left of smoking
towers **Rev:** Value above hand holding castle tower

Date	Mintage	F	VF	XF	Unc	BU
1991R	—	—	—	0.10	0.35	—

KM# 281 10 LIRE
1.6000 g., Aluminum, 23.3 mm. **Subject:** Columbus
Obv: Towers with feather-like designs on top within circle
Rev: Dolphin, ship and value within globe design

Date	Mintage	F	VF	XF	Unc	BU
ND(1992)R	—	—	—	0.20	0.75	2.00

KM# 296 10 LIRE
1.6000 g., Aluminum, 23.3 mm. **Obv:** Smoking towers
Rev: Value above corinthian column

Date	Mintage	F	VF	XF	Unc	BU
1993R	—	—	—	0.10	0.35	—

KM# 309 10 LIRE
1.6000 g., Aluminum, 23.3 mm. **Obv:** Stone cutter holding
hammer and chisel, towers at left **Rev:** Marino and Leo working

Date	Mintage	F	VF	XF	Unc	BU
1994R	40,000	—	—	0.10	0.35	—

KM# 325 10 LIRE
1.6000 g., Aluminum, 23.3 mm. **Obv:** Banner wrapped around
bottom of design **Rev:** Child holding two urns within square

Date	Mintage	F	VF	XF	Unc	BU
1995R	—	—	—	0.10	0.35	—

KM# 352 10 LIRE
1.6000 g., Aluminum, 23.3 mm. **Obv:** Bust facing with flame
within hands **Rev:** Aristotle

Date	Mintage	F	VF	XF	Unc	BU
1996R	28,000	—	—	0.10	0.35	—

KM# 362 10 LIRE
1.6000 g., Aluminum, 23.3 mm. **Subject:** The Arts - Architecture
Obv: Bust facing with flame within hands **Rev:** Building on pillars

Date	Mintage	F	VF	XF	Unc	BU
1997R	28,000	—	—	0.10	0.35	—

KM# 378 10 LIRE
1.6000 g., Aluminum, 23.3 mm. **Subject:** Mathematics
Rev: Hand and geometric shape

Date	Mintage	F	VF	XF	Unc	BU
1998R	—	—	—	0.10	0.35	—

KM# 389 10 LIRE
1.6000 g., Aluminum, 23.3 mm. **Subject:** Exploration
Obv: Crowned shield **Rev:** Earth flat, as once envisioned

Date	Mintage	F	VF	XF	Unc	BU
1999R	—	—	—	0.10	0.35	—

KM# 399 10 LIRE
1.6000 g., Aluminum, 23.3 mm. **Subject:** Love **Obv:** Bust facing
with flame within hands **Rev:** Child within poinsettia and globe
design **Edge:** Plain **Note:** Struck at Rome.

Date	Mintage	F	VF	XF	Unc	BU
2000R	—	—	—	—	0.35	—

KM# 8 20 LIRE
6.4516 g., 0.9000 Gold 0.1867 oz. AGW **Obv:** Smoking towers
Rev: Standing Saint figure divides value **Note:** 7,334 coins were
melted at the mint.

Date	Mintage	F	VF	XF	Unc	BU
1925R	9,334	400	700	1,200	2,300	—

KM# 11   20 LIRE
15.0000 g., 0.8000 Silver 0.3858 oz. ASW **Obv:** Upright stylized
feathers above value with crown above **Rev:** Half length figure
holding smoking towers within circle

Date	Mintage	F	VF	XF	Unc	BU
1931R	10,000	25.00	45.00	90.00	200	—
1932R	10,000	35.00	60.00	110	235	—
1933R	10,000	30.00	50.00	100	220	—
1935R	10,000	30.00	50.00	100	220	—
1936R	5,000	60.00	125	200	425	—

KM# 11a   20 LIRE
20.0000 g., 0.8000 Silver 0.5144 oz. ASW **Obv:** Stylized upright
feathers above value with crown above **Rev:** Half length figure
holding smoking towers within circle

Date	Mintage	F	VF	XF	Unc	BU
1935R Rare	2	—	—	—	—	—
1937R	5,100	100	200	435	775	—
1938R	2,500	200	400	850	1,325	—

KM# 18   20 LIRE
3.6000 g., Aluminum-Bronze, 21.25 mm. **Obv:** Stylized feathers
within towers **Rev:** Standing figures

Date	Mintage	F	VF	XF	Unc	BU
1972	291,000	—	0.10	0.25	0.60	—

KM# 26   20 LIRE
3.6000 g., Aluminum-Bronze, 21.25 mm. **Obv:** Crowned shield
Rev: Man rescuing old man and baby from fire

Date	Mintage	F	VF	XF	Unc	BU
1973	291,000	—	0.10	0.25	0.60	—

KM# 34   20 LIRE
3.6000 g., Aluminum-Bronze, 21.25 mm. **Obv:** Smoking towers
within circle **Rev:** Lobster

Date	Mintage	F	VF	XF	Unc	BU
1974	276,000	—	0.10	0.30	1.50	2.50

KM# 44   20 LIRE
3.6000 g., Aluminum-Bronze, 21.25 mm. **Series:** F.A.O.
Obv: Smoking towers **Rev:** Bird feeding babies

Date	Mintage	F	VF	XF	Unc	BU
1975	291,000	—	0.10	0.30	0.75	1.25

KM# 55   20 LIRE
3.6000 g., Aluminum-Bronze, 21.25 mm. **Obv:** Smoking towers
Rev: Design flanked by stylized hands

Date	Mintage	F	VF	XF	Unc	BU
1976	195,000	—	0.10	0.25	0.60	—

KM# 67   20 LIRE
3.6000 g., Aluminum-Bronze, 21.25 mm. **Obv:** Smoking towers
Rev: Circular pattern within stylized hand

Date	Mintage	F	VF	XF	Unc	BU
1977	180,000	—	0.10	0.25	0.60	—

KM# 80   20 LIRE
3.6000 g., Aluminum-Bronze, 21.25 mm. **Obv:** Value below
smoking towers **Rev:** Kneeling figure

Date	Mintage	F	VF	XF	Unc	BU
1978	130,000	—	0.10	0.25	0.60	—

KM# 93   20 LIRE
3.6000 g., Aluminum-Bronze, 21.25 mm. **Obv:** Crowned shield
Rev: Crowned skeleton keys divide value

Date	Mintage	F	VF	XF	Unc	BU
1979	125,000	—	0.10	0.30	0.60	—

KM# 106   20 LIRE
3.6000 g., Aluminum-Bronze, 21.25 mm. **Series:** 1980
Olympics **Obv:** Olympic rings and date to left of smoking towers
Rev: Pole vaulter

Date	Mintage	F	VF	XF	Unc	BU
1980	125,000	—	0.25	0.50	1.00	—

KM# 120   20 LIRE
3.6000 g., Aluminum-Bronze, 21.25 mm. **Obv:** Crowned shield
Rev: Value above bird

Date	Mintage	F	VF	XF	Unc	BU
1981R	100,000	—	0.10	0.30	0.75	2.00

KM# 135   20 LIRE
3.6000 g., Aluminum-Bronze, 21.25 mm. **Subject:** Social
conquests **Obv:** Crown above smoking towers **Rev:** Standing
figures within design

Date	Mintage	F	VF	XF	Unc	BU
1982R	78,000	—	0.10	0.25	0.60	—

KM# 149   20 LIRE
3.6000 g., Aluminum-Bronze, 21.25 mm. **Subject:** Nuclear war
threat **Obv:** Crown above shield and sprig **Rev:** Torch above man

Date	Mintage	F	VF	XF	Unc	BU
1983R	72,000	—	0.10	0.30	0.75	—

KM# 163   20 LIRE
3.6000 g., Aluminum-Bronze, 21.25 mm. **Obv:** Castle **Rev:** Bust
of Louis Pasteur facing

Date	Mintage	F	VF	XF	Unc	BU
1984R	65,000	—	0.10	0.30	0.75	—

KM# 177   20 LIRE
3.6000 g., Aluminum-Bronze, 21.25 mm. **Subject:** War on drugs
Obv: Shield **Rev:** Open hand flanked by value and date

Date	Mintage	F	VF	XF	Unc	BU
1985R	60,000	—	—	0.15	0.55	—

KM# 191   20 LIRE
3.6000 g., Aluminum-Bronze, 21.25 mm. **Subject:** Revolution
of technology **Obv:** Crown above smoking towers on rock
Rev: Stylized figure at lower right of computer flanked by value
and date

Date	Mintage	F	VF	XF	Unc	BU
1986R	50,000	—	—	0.15	0.55	—

KM# 205   20 LIRE
3.6000 g., Aluminum-Bronze, 21.25 mm. **Subject:** 15th
Anniversary - Resumption of Coinage **Obv:** Crowned pointed
arms within sprigs **Rev:** Volcanoes

Date	Mintage	F	VF	XF	Unc	BU
1987R	83,000	—	—	0.15	0.55	—

KM# 222 20 LIRE
3.6000 g., Aluminum-Bronze, 21.25 mm. **Subject:** Fortifications
Obv: Crowned ornate arms on shield **Rev:** Small fortified gate

Date	Mintage	F	VF	XF	Unc	BU
1988R	38,000	—	—	0.15	0.55	—

KM# 235 20 LIRE
3.6000 g., Aluminum-Bronze, 21.25 mm. **Subject:** History
Obv: Crowned shield **Rev:** Sword with value within flag

Date	Mintage	F	VF	XF	Unc	BU
1989R	37,000	—	—	0.15	0.55	—

KM# 252 20 LIRE
3.6000 g., Aluminum-Bronze, 21.25 mm. **Subject:** 1,600 Years
of History **Obv:** Stylized towers above design **Rev:** Stylized large
figure straddling value

Date	Mintage	F	VF	XF	Unc	BU
1990R	96,000	—	—	0.15	0.55	—

KM# 265 20 LIRE
3.6000 g., Aluminum-Bronze, 21.25 mm. **Obv:** Date at upper
left of smoking towers **Rev:** Value above gloved hand rejecting
cardinal ring

Date	Mintage	F	VF	XF	Unc	BU
1991R	—	—	—	0.15	0.55	—

KM# 282 20 LIRE
3.6000 g., Aluminum-Bronze, 21.25 mm. **Obv:** Towers with feather-
like designs on top within circle **Rev:** Columbus landing on Hispaniola

Date	Mintage	F	VF	XF	Unc	BU
1992R	—	—	—	0.10	0.55	—

KM# 297 20 LIRE
3.6000 g., Aluminum-Bronze, 21.25 mm. **Rev:** Scroll and arch

Date	Mintage	F	VF	XF	Unc	BU
1993R	—	—	—	0.10	0.55	—

KM# 310 20 LIRE
3.6000 g., Aluminum-Bronze, 21.25 mm. **Obv:** Stone cutter
Rev: Workers pulling stone

Date	Mintage	F	VF	XF	Unc	BU
1994R	40,000	—	—	0.10	0.55	—

KM# 326 20 LIRE
3.6000 g., Aluminum-Bronze, 21.25 mm. **Obv:** Banner wrapped
around quills **Rev:** Child straddling cornucopia

Date	Mintage	F	VF	XF	Unc	BU
1995R	—	—	—	0.10	0.55	—

KM# 353 20 LIRE
3.6000 g., Aluminum-Bronze, 21.25 mm. **Obv:** Bust of Saint
Thomas facing

Date	Mintage	F	VF	XF	Unc	BU
1996R	32,000	—	—	0.10	0.55	—

KM# 363 20 LIRE
3.6000 g., Aluminum-Bronze, 21.25 mm. **Subject:** The Arts -
Cinema **Obv:** Bust facing with flame within hands **Rev:** Film strips

Date	Mintage	F	VF	XF	Unc	BU
1997R	28,000	—	—	0.10	0.55	—

KM# 379 20 LIRE
3.6000 g., Aluminum-Bronze, 21.25 mm. **Subject:**
Communications **Rev:** Two profiles in silhouette left

Date	Mintage	F	VF	XF	Unc	BU
1998R	—	—	—	0.10	0.55	—

KM# 390 20 LIRE
3.6000 g., Aluminum-Bronze, 21.25 mm. **Subject:** Exploration
Obv: Crowned shield **Rev:** Earth as known today

Date	Mintage	F	VF	XF	Unc	BU
1999R	—	—	—	0.10	0.55	—

KM# 400 20 LIRE
3.6000 g., Aluminum-Bronze, 21.22 mm. **Subject:** Solidarity
Obv: Bust facing with flame within hands **Rev:** Two hands about
to grasp, globe design in background **Edge:** Plain

Date	Mintage	F	VF	XF	Unc	BU
2000R	—	—	—	0.10	0.55	—

KM# 19 50 LIRE
6.2000 g., Aluminum-Bronze, 21.25 mm. **Obv:** Stylized feathers within towers
Rev: Female kneeling before St. Marinus

Date	Mintage	F	VF	XF	Unc	BU
1972	291,000	0.15	0.25	0.50	1.00	—

KM# 27 50 LIRE
6.2000 g., Steel, 24.8 mm. **Obv:** Crowned shield **Rev:** Stylized
standing figure with sword and scale **Note:** Depicts the balance
of man, not as an individual but as a race

Date	Mintage	F	VF	XF	Unc	BU
1973	291,000	0.15	0.25	0.50	1.00	—

KM# 35 50 LIRE
6.2000 g., Steel, 24.8 mm. **Obv:** Smoking towers within circle
Rev: Stylized chicken

Date	Mintage	F	VF	XF	Unc	BU
1974	276,000	0.15	0.25	0.60	1.25	2.50

KM# 45 50 LIRE
6.2000 g., Steel, 24.8 mm. **Obv:** Smoking towers **Rev:** Cluster
of fish

Date	Mintage	F	VF	XF	Unc	BU
1975	831,000	0.15	0.25	0.60	1.25	2.50

KM# 56 50 LIRE
6.2000 g., Steel, 24.8 mm. **Obv:** Stylized smoking towers
Rev: Face forward within triangle flanked by pair of scales

Date	Mintage	F	VF	XF	Unc	BU
1976	195,000	0.15	0.25	0.50	1.00	—

KM# 68 50 LIRE
6.2000 g., Steel, 24.8 mm. **Obv:** Value below smoking towers
within circle **Rev:** Fingers in center of circle of stars

Date	Mintage	F	VF	XF	Unc	BU
1977	180,000	0.15	0.25	0.50	1.00	—

KM# 81   50 LIRE
6.2000 g., Steel, 24.8 mm. **Obv:** Value below smoking towers **Rev:** Flowering plant below seated mother and child at desk

Date	Mintage	F	VF	XF	Unc	BU
1978	130,000	0.15	0.25	0.50	1.00	—

KM# 94   50 LIRE
6.2000 g., Steel, 24.8 mm. **Obv:** Crowned shield **Rev:** Liberty bell in front of building

Date	Mintage	F	VF	XF	Unc	BU
1979	125,000	0.15	0.25	0.50	1.00	—

KM# 107   50 LIRE
6.2000 g., Steel, 24.8 mm. **Series:** 1980 Olympics **Obv:** Olympic rings and date to upper left of smoking towers **Rev:** Downhill skier

Date	Mintage	F	VF	XF	Unc	BU
1980	125,000	0.25	0.50	1.00	2.00	—

KM# 121   50 LIRE
6.2000 g., Steel, 24.8 mm. **Obv:** Crowned shield **Rev:** Value at left of dancing figure

Date	Mintage	F	VF	XF	Unc	BU
1981R	100,000	0.15	0.25	0.50	1.00	—

KM# 136   50 LIRE
6.2000 g., Steel, 24.8 mm. **Subject:** Social conquests **Obv:** Crown above smoking towers **Rev:** Standing figures within design

Date	Mintage	F	VF	XF	Unc	BU
1982R	78,000	0.15	0.25	0.50	1.00	—

KM# 150   50 LIRE
6.2000 g., Steel, 24.8 mm. **Subject:** Nuclear war threat **Obv:** Crown above shield and sprig **Rev:** Beast of war above woman

Date	Mintage	F	VF	XF	Unc	BU
1983R	72,000	0.20	0.40	0.80	1.50	—

KM# 164   50 LIRE
6.2000 g., Steel, 24.8 mm. **Obv:** Castle **Rev:** Pierre and Marie Curie

Date	Mintage	F	VF	XF	Unc	BU
1984R	65,000	0.20	0.40	0.80	1.50	—

KM# 178   50 LIRE
6.2000 g., Steel, 24.8 mm. **Subject:** War on drugs **Obv:** Shield **Rev:** Stylized figures

Date	Mintage	F	VF	XF	Unc	BU
1985R	110,000	—	0.10	0.20	0.85	—

KM# 192   50 LIRE
6.2000 g., Steel, 24.8 mm. **Subject:** Revolution of technology **Obv:** Crown above smoking towers on rock **Rev:** Splitting the atom

Date	Mintage	F	VF	XF	Unc	BU
1986R	50,000	—	0.10	0.20	0.85	—

KM# 206   50 LIRE
6.2000 g., Steel, 24.8 mm. **Subject:** 15th Anniversary - Resumption of Coinage **Obv:** Crowned pointed shield within sprigs **Rev:** Animal in front of rock with tower at top

Date	Mintage	F	VF	XF	Unc	BU
1987R	93,000	—	0.10	0.20	0.85	—

KM# 223   50 LIRE
6.2000 g., Steel, 24.8 mm. **Subject:** Fortifications **Obv:** Crowned ornate arms on shield **Rev:** Ramp leading to gate house

Date	Mintage	F	VF	XF	Unc	BU
1988R	38,000	—	0.10	0.20	0.85	—

KM# 236   50 LIRE
6.2000 g., Steel, 24.8 mm. **Subject:** History **Obv:** Crowned shield **Rev:** Crossbow divides value

Date	Mintage	VG	F	VF	XF	Unc
1989R	87,000	—	—	0.10	0.20	0.85

KM# 253   50 LIRE
Steel, 17 mm. **Subject:** 1,600 Years of History **Obv:** Stylized towers above design **Rev:** Stylized bird

Date	Mintage	F	VF	XF	Unc	BU
1990R	52,000	—	0.10	0.20	0.85	—

KM# 266   50 LIRE
Steel, 17 mm. **Obv:** Date at upper left of smoking towers **Rev:** Value above hand holding cannon barrels and wheat stalks

Date	Mintage	F	VF	XF	Unc	BU
1991R	—	—	0.10	0.20	0.85	—

KM# 283   50 LIRE
Steel, 17 mm. **Subject:** Columbus **Obv:** Towers with feather-like designs on top within circle **Rev:** Flying seagulls within radiant sun flanked by dates

Date	Mintage	F	VF	XF	Unc	BU
1992R	—	—	0.10	0.20	0.85	1.25

KM# 298   50 LIRE
Steel, 17 mm. **Obv:** Stylized feathers within towers **Rev:** Wheat growing through barbed wire

Date	Mintage	F	VF	XF	Unc	BU
1993R	—	—	0.10	0.20	0.85	—

KM# 311   50 LIRE
Stainless Steel, 17 mm. **Obv:** Stonecutter holding hammer and chisel, smoking towers at left **Rev:** Two stonecutters

Date	Mintage	F	VF	XF	Unc	BU
1994R	40,000	—	0.10	0.20	0.85	—

KM# 327   50 LIRE
Stainless Steel, 17 mm. **Obv:** Banner wrapped around bottom of design **Rev:** Child hugging bird

Date	Mintage	F	VF	XF	Unc	BU
1995R	—	—	0.10	0.20	0.85	—

KM# 354   50 LIRE
Stainless Steel, 17 mm. **Obv:** Bust facing with flame within hands **Rev:** Descartes

Date	Mintage	F	VF	XF	Unc	BU
1996R	32,000	—	0.10	0.20	0.85	—

KM# 364 50 LIRE
Stainless Steel, 19 mm. **Subject:** The Arts - Sculpture **Obv:** Bust facing with flame within hands **Rev:** Han Dynasty Horse statue

Date	Mintage	F	VF	XF	Unc	BU
1997R	28,000	—	0.15	0.25	1.00	2.00

KM# 380 50 LIRE
Copper-Nickel, 19 mm. **Subject:** Engineering **Rev:** Cogwheel mind

Date	Mintage	F	VF	XF	Unc	BU
1998R	—	—	0.10	0.20	0.85	—

KM# 391 50 LIRE
Copper-Nickel, 19 mm. **Subject:** Exploration **Obv:** Crowned shield **Rev:** Ship sail, sun and waves

Date	Mintage	F	VF	XF	Unc	BU
1999R	—	—	0.10	0.20	0.85	—

KM# 401 50 LIRE
4.5000 g., Copper-Nickel, 19.2 mm. **Subject:** Equality **Obv:** Bust facing with flame within hands **Rev:** Five different plant leaves on 1 stem **Edge:** Plain **Note:** Struck at Rome.

Date	Mintage	F	VF	XF	Unc	BU
2000R	—	—	0.10	0.20	0.85	—

KM# 20 100 LIRE
8.0000 g., Steel, 27.8 mm. **Obv:** Three smoking towers **Rev:** St. Marinus in a small boat

Date	Mintage	F	VF	XF	Unc	BU
1972	291,000	0.15	0.30	0.60	1.50	—

KM# 28 100 LIRE
8.0000 g., Steel, 27.8 mm. **Obv:** Crowned shield **Rev:** Ulysses passing the pillars of Hercules

Date	Mintage	F	VF	XF	Unc	BU
1973	291,000	0.15	0.30	0.60	1.50	—

KM# 36 100 LIRE
8.0000 g., Steel, 27.8 mm. **Obv:** Smoking towers within circle **Rev:** Goat

Date	Mintage	F	VF	XF	Unc	BU
1974	276,000	0.15	0.30	0.65	1.75	3.00

KM# 46 100 LIRE
8.0000 g., Steel, 27.8 mm. **Obv:** Smoking towers **Rev:** Dog and cat lying together

Date	Mintage	F	VF	XF	Unc	BU
1975	821,000	0.15	0.30	0.65	1.75	3.50

KM# 57 100 LIRE
8.0000 g., Steel, 27.8 mm. **Obv:** Smoking towers **Rev:** Stylized seated figures within arch of building

Date	Mintage	F	VF	XF	Unc	BU
1976	1,853,000	0.15	0.30	0.60	1.50	—

KM# 69 100 LIRE
8.0000 g., Steel, 27.8 mm. **Obv:** Value below smoking towers within circle **Rev:** Design within circular star wreath

Date	Mintage	F	VF	XF	Unc	BU
1977	565,000	0.15	0.30	0.60	1.50	—

KM# 70 100 LIRE
8.0000 g., Steel, 27.8 mm. **Obv:** Value below smoking towers within circle **Rev:** Stylized fish

Date	Mintage	F	VF	XF	Unc	BU
1977	565,000	0.15	0.30	0.60	2.00	—

KM# 82 100 LIRE
8.0000 g., Steel, 27.8 mm. **Series:** F.A.O. **Obv:** Value below smoking towers **Rev:** Standing figure using sickle

Date	Mintage	F	VF	XF	Unc	BU
1978	875,000	0.15	0.30	0.60	1.50	—

KM# 95 100 LIRE
8.0000 g., Steel, 27.8 mm. **Obv:** Crowned shield **Rev:** Design in center with assorted shields around border

Date	Mintage	F	VF	XF	Unc	BU
1979	665,000	0.15	0.30	0.60	1.50	—

KM# 108 100 LIRE
8.0000 g., Steel, 27.8 mm. **Series:** 1980 Olympics **Obv:** Olympic rings and date to upper left of smoking towers **Rev:** Archery

Date	Mintage	F	VF	XF	Unc	BU
1980	350,000	0.25	0.50	1.00	2.00	—

KM# 122 100 LIRE
8.0000 g., Steel, 27.8 mm. **Obv:** Crowned shield **Rev:** Stylized draped figure to left of value

Date	Mintage	F	VF	XF	Unc	BU
1981R	512,000	0.15	0.30	0.60	1.50	—

KM# 137 100 LIRE
8.0000 g., Steel, 27.8 mm. **Obv:** Crown above smoking towers **Rev:** Social conquests

Date	Mintage	F	VF	XF	Unc	BU
1982R	178,000	0.15	0.30	0.60	1.50	—

KM# 151 100 LIRE
8.0000 g., Steel, 27.8 mm. **Subject:** Nuclear War Threat **Obv:** Crown above shield and sprig **Rev:** Beast of war above man and woman

Date	Mintage	F	VF	XF	Unc	BU
1983R	172,000	0.15	0.30	0.60	1.50	—

KM# 165 100 LIRE
8.0000 g., Steel, 27.8 mm. **Obv:** Castle **Rev:** Bust of Guglielmo Marconi left

Date	Mintage	F	VF	XF	Unc	BU
1984R	165,000	0.15	0.30	0.60	1.50	—

KM# 179   100 LIRE
8.0000 g., Steel, 27.8 mm.   **Subject:** War on Drugs **Obv:** Shield
Rev: Three figures in discussion

Date	Mintage	F	VF	XF	Unc	BU
1985R	210,000	—	—	0.35	1.25	—

KM# 193   100 LIRE
8.0000 g., Steel, 27.8 mm.   **Subject:** Revolution of Technology
Obv: Crown above smoking towers on rock **Rev:** Satellite and
receiving dishes divide date and value

Date	Mintage	F	VF	XF	Unc	BU
1986R	150,000	—	—	0.35	1.25	—

KM# 207   100 LIRE
8.0000 g., Steel, 27.8 mm.   **Subject:** 15th Anniversary -
Resumption of Coinage **Obv:** Crowned pointed shield within
sprigs **Rev:** Sprig divides value

Date	Mintage	F	VF	XF	Unc	BU
1987R	143,000	—	—	0.35	1.25	—

KM# 224   100 LIRE
8.0000 g., Steel, 27.8 mm.   **Subject:** Fortifications
Obv: Crowned ornate arms on shield **Rev:** Gate tower

Date	Mintage	F	VF	XF	Unc	BU
1988R	38,000	—	—	0.35	1.25	—

KM# 237   100 LIRE
8.0000 g., Steel, 27.8 mm.   **Subject:** History **Obv:** Crowned
shield **Rev:** Teacher and student

Date	Mintage	F	VF	XF	Unc	BU
1989R	37,000	—	—	0.35	1.25	—

KM# 254   100 LIRE
Steel, 18 mm.   **Subject:** 1,600 Years of History **Obv:** Towers
above design **Rev:** Balance scales

Date	Mintage	F	VF	XF	Unc	BU
1990R	1,086,000	—	—	0.35	1.25	—

KM# 267   100 LIRE
Steel, 18 mm.   **Obv:** Date at upper left of smoking towers
Rev: Value above clasped hands

Date	Mintage	F	VF	XF	Unc	BU
1991R	—	—	—	0.35	1.25	—

KM# 284   100 LIRE
Steel, 18 mm.   **Subject:** Columbus **Obv:** Towers with feather-like
designs on top within circle **Rev:** Value below three sailing ships

Date	Mintage	F	VF	XF	Unc	BU
1992R	—	—	—	0.35	1.25	—

KM# 299   100 LIRE
Copper-Nickel, 22 mm.   **Obv:** Three towers above dentiled
design **Rev:** Pan swallow above western Europe

Date	Mintage	F	VF	XF	Unc	BU
1993R	—	—	—	0.35	1.50	—

KM# 312   100 LIRE
Copper-Nickel, 22 mm.   **Obv:** Stonecutter holding hammer and
chisel, smoking towers at left **Rev:** Two stonecutters

Date	Mintage	F	VF	XF	Unc	BU
1994R	40,000	—	—	0.35	1.25	—

KM# 328   100 LIRE
Copper-Nickel, 22 mm.   **Obv:** Banner wrapped around quills
Rev: Three children

Date	Mintage	F	VF	XF	Unc	BU
1995R	—	—	—	0.35	1.25	—

KM# 355   100 LIRE
Copper-Nickel, 22 mm.   **Obv:** Bust facing with flame within hands
Rev: Head of Rousseau 1/4 right

Date	Mintage	F	VF	XF	Unc	BU
1996R	32,000	—	—	0.35	1.25	—

KM# 365   100 LIRE
Copper-Nickel, 22 mm.   **Subject:** The Arts - Dance **Obv:** Bust
facing with flame within hands **Rev:** Ballet dancers

Date	Mintage	F	VF	XF	Unc	BU
1997R	28,000	—	—	0.35	1.25	—

KM# 381   100 LIRE
Copper-Nickel, 22 mm.   **Subject:** Physics **Rev:** Human, crossbow

Date	Mintage	F	VF	XF	Unc	BU
1998R	—	—	—	0.35	1.25	—

KM# 392   100 LIRE
Copper-Nickel, 22 mm.   **Subject:** Exploration **Obv:** Crowned
shield **Rev:** Submarine below Arctic ice-cap

Date	Mintage	F	VF	XF	Unc	BU
1999R	—	—	—	0.35	1.25	—

KM# 402   100 LIRE
4.5000 g., Copper-Nickel, 22 mm.   **Subject:** Ecology **Obv:** Bust
facing with flame within hands **Rev:** Outline of house in center of
leaf design, globe design in background **Edge:** Reeded and plain
sectioned

Date	Mintage	F	VF	XF	Unc	BU
2000R	—	—	—	0.35	1.25	—

KM# 83   200 LIRE
5.0000 g., Aluminum-Bronze, 24 mm.   **Obv:** Value below
smoking towers **Rev:** Seated figure weaving

Date	Mintage	F	VF	XF	Unc	BU
1978	530,000	—	0.25	0.75	1.75	—

KM# 96   200 LIRE
5.0000 g., Aluminum-Bronze, 24 mm.   **Series:** F.A.O.
Obv: Crowned shield **Rev:** Nude figure fighting lion flanked by
value and date, F.A.O logo at upper right

Date	Mintage	F	VF	XF	Unc	BU
1979	675,000	—	0.25	0.75	1.75	2.50

KM# 109   200 LIRE
5.0000 g., Aluminum-Bronze, 24 mm.   **Series:** 1980 Olympics
Obv: Olympic rings and date at upper left of smoking towers
Rev: Wrestlers

Date	Mintage	F	VF	XF	Unc	BU
1980	675,000	—	0.50	1.00	2.50	—

KM# 123   200 LIRE
5.0000 g., Aluminum-Bronze, 24 mm.   **Series:** F.A.O.
Obv: Crowned shield **Rev:** Stylized animal divides date and value

Date	Mintage	F	VF	XF	Unc	BU
1981R	700,000	—	0.25	0.75	1.75	2.50

KM# 138   200 LIRE
5.0000 g., Aluminum-Bronze, 24 mm.   **Subject:** Social Conquests **Obv:** Crown above smoking towers **Rev:** Stylized figure within design

Date	Mintage	F	VF	XF	Unc	BU
1982R	178,000	—	0.25	0.75	1.75	—

KM# 225   200 LIRE
5.0000 g., Aluminum-Bronze, 24 mm.   **Subject:** Fortifications **Obv:** Crowned ornate arms on shield **Rev:** Tower divides value

Date	Mintage	F	VF	XF	Unc	BU
1988R	38,000	—	—	0.40	1.50	—

KM# 313   200 LIRE
5.0000 g., Aluminum-Bronze, 24 mm.   **Obv:** Stonecutter holding hammer and chisel, smoking towers at left **Rev:** Man and bear

Date	Mintage	F	VF	XF	Unc	BU
1994R	40,000	—	—	0.40	1.50	—

KM# 152   200 LIRE
5.0000 g., Aluminum-Bronze, 24 mm.   **Subject:** Nuclear War Threat **Obv:** Crown above shield and sprig **Rev:** Rider spearing victim

Date	Mintage	F	VF	XF	Unc	BU
1983R	172,000	—	0.25	0.75	1.75	—

KM# 238   200 LIRE
5.0000 g., Aluminum-Bronze, 24 mm.   **Subject:** History **Obv:** Crowned shield **Rev:** Stylized view of San Marino

Date	Mintage	F	VF	XF	Unc	BU
1989R	1,037,000	—	—	0.40	1.50	—

KM# 329   200 LIRE
5.0000 g., Aluminum-Bronze, 24 mm.   **Obv:** Banner wrapped around quills **Rev:** Two children playing

Date	Mintage	F	VF	XF	Unc	BU
1995R	—	—	—	0.40	1.50	—

KM# 166   200 LIRE
5.0000 g., Aluminum-Bronze, 24 mm.   **Obv:** Castle **Rev:** Bust of Enrico Fermi facing

Date	Mintage	F	VF	XF	Unc	BU
1984R	165,000	—	0.25	0.75	1.75	—

KM# 255   200 LIRE
5.0000 g., Aluminum-Bronze, 24 mm.   **Subject:** 1,600 Years of History **Obv:** Towers above design **Rev:** Stylized head left

Date	Mintage	F	VF	XF	Unc	BU
1990R	36,000	—	—	0.40	1.50	—

KM# 356   200 LIRE
5.0000 g., Aluminum-Bronze, 24 mm.   **Subject:** Kant **Obv:** Bust facing with flame within hands **Rev:** Head of Kant right within square above value

Date	Mintage	F	VF	XF	Unc	BU
1996R	32,000	—	—	0.40	1.50	—

KM# 180   200 LIRE
5.0000 g., Aluminum-Bronze, 24 mm.   **Subject:** War on Drugs **Obv:** Shield **Rev:** Family group

Date	Mintage	F	VF	XF	Unc	BU
1985R	210,000	—	—	0.40	1.50	—

KM# 268   200 LIRE
5.0000 g., Aluminum-Bronze, 24 mm.   **Obv:** Date at upper left of smoking towers **Rev:** Value above hand holding coin die

Date	Mintage	F	VF	XF	Unc	BU
1991R	—	—	—	0.40	1.50	—

KM# 366   200 LIRE
5.0000 g., Aluminum-Bronze, 24 mm.   **Subject:** The Arts - Painting **Obv:** Bust facing with flame within hands **Rev:** Seated figure painting portrait of standing figure at left

Date	Mintage	F	VF	XF	Unc	BU
1997R	28,000	—	—	0.40	1.50	—

KM# 194   200 LIRE
5.0000 g., Aluminum-Bronze, 24 mm.   **Subject:** Revolution of Technology **Obv:** Crown above smoking towers on rock **Rev:** Stylized hand holding microchip

Date	Mintage	F	VF	XF	Unc	BU
1986R	150,000	—	—	0.40	1.50	—

KM# 285   200 LIRE
5.0000 g., Aluminum-Bronze, 24 mm.   **Obv:** Stylized feathers on top of towers within circle **Rev:** Columbus navigating by the stars

Date	Mintage	F	VF	XF	Unc	BU
ND(1992)R	—	—	—	0.40	1.50	—

KM# 382   200 LIRE
5.0000 g., Aluminum-Bronze, 24 mm.   **Subject:** Zoology **Rev:** Stylized dolphins

Date	Mintage	F	VF	XF	Unc	BU
1998R	—	—	—	0.40	2.50	—

KM# 208   200 LIRE
5.0000 g., Aluminum-Bronze, 24 mm.   **Subject:** 15th Anniversary - Resumption of Coinage **Obv:** Crowned pointed shield within sprigs **Rev:** Building in front of smoking towers

Date	Mintage	F	VF	XF	Unc	BU
1987R	143,000	—	—	0.40	1.50	—

KM# 300   200 LIRE
5.0000 g., Aluminum-Bronze, 24 mm.   **Rev:** Door and arches

Date	Mintage	F	VF	XF	Unc	BU
1993R	—	—	—	0.40	1.50	—

KM# 393   200 LIRE
5.0000 g., Aluminum-Bronze, 24 mm.   **Subject:** Exploration **Obv:** Crowned shield **Rev:** Stonehenge beneath the sun and stars

Date	Mintage	F	VF	XF	Unc	BU
1999R	—	—	—	0.40	1.50	—

KM# 403   200 LIRE
5.0000 g., Aluminum-Bronze, 24 mm. **Subject:** Knowledge
Obv: Bust facing with flame within hands **Rev:** Allegorical female head left within globe design **Edge:** Reeded **Note:** Struck at Rome.

Date	Mintage	F	VF	XF	Unc	BU
2000R	—	—	—	0.40	1.50	—

KM# 21   500 LIRE
11.0000 g., 0.8350 Silver 0.2953 oz. ASW, 29 mm. **Obv:** Three towers **Rev:** Mother lifting child in air **Note:** 22,374 coins melted at the mint.

Date	Mintage	F	VF	XF	Unc	BU
1972	291,000	—	—	6.50	11.50	—

KM# 29   500 LIRE
11.0000 g., 0.8350 Silver 0.2953 oz. ASW, 29 mm.
Obv: Crowned shield **Rev:** Child holding dove **Note:** 6,544 coins melted at the mint.

Date	Mintage	F	VF	XF	Unc	BU
1973	291,000	—	—	6.50	11.50	—

KM# 37   500 LIRE
11.0000 g., 0.8350 Silver 0.2953 oz. ASW, 29 mm.
Obv: Smoking towers within circle **Rev:** Two stylized pigeons **Note:** 6,295 coins melted at the mint.

Date	Mintage	F	VF	XF	Unc	BU
1974	276,000	—	—	7.00	14.00	17.00

KM# 47   500 LIRE
11.0000 g., 0.8350 Silver 0.2953 oz. ASW, 29 mm.
Obv: Smoking towers **Rev:** Seagulls flying over barbed wire **Note:** 119,743 coins melted at the mint.

Date	Mintage	F	VF	XF	Unc	BU
1975	291,000	—	—	7.00	14.00	17.00

KM# 48   500 LIRE
11.0000 g., 0.8350 Silver 0.2953 oz. ASW, 29 mm.
Subject: Numismatic Agency opening **Obv:** Value and date below smoking towers **Rev:** Ancient stonecutter **Note:** 47,495 coins melted at the mint.

Date	Mintage	F	VF	XF	Unc	BU
1975	200,000	—	—	6.50	11.50	—

KM# 58   500 LIRE
11.0000 g., 0.8350 Silver 0.2953 oz. ASW, 29 mm. **Obv:** Smoking towers **Rev:** Design **Note:** 40,509 coins melted at the mint.

Date	Mintage	F	VF	XF	Unc	BU
1976	195,000	—	—	6.50	11.50	—

KM# 59   500 LIRE
11.0000 g., 0.8350 Silver 0.2953 oz. ASW, 29 mm. **Subject:** Social Security **Obv:** Stylized smoking towers **Rev:** Standing figure holding blanket to cover man **Note:** 106,604 coins melted at the mint.

Date	Mintage	F	VF	XF	Unc	BU
1976	195,000	—	—	6.50	11.50	—

KM# 71   500 LIRE
11.0000 g., 0.8350 Silver 0.2953 oz. ASW, 29 mm. **Obv:** Value below stylized smoking towers within circle **Rev:** Stylized upside-down bird among stars within circle **Note:** 45,483 coins melted at the mint.

Date	Mintage	F	VF	XF	Unc	BU
1977	180,000	—	—	6.50	11.50	—

KM# 84   500 LIRE
11.0000 g., 0.8350 Silver 0.2953 oz. ASW, 29 mm. **Obv:** Value below smoking towers **Rev:** Group of figures holding flags **Note:** 16,297 coins melted at the mint.

Date	Mintage	F	VF	XF	Unc	BU
1978	130,000	—	—	6.50	11.50	—

KM# 97   500 LIRE
11.0000 g., 0.8350 Silver 0.2953 oz. ASW, 29 mm. **Obv:** Half length figure holding three smoking towers **Rev:** Victory in a biga **Note:** 33,278 coins melted at the mint.

Date	Mintage	F	VF	XF	Unc	BU
1979	125,000	—	—	7.00	12.50	15.00

KM# 110   500 LIRE
11.0000 g., 0.8350 Silver 0.2953 oz. ASW, 29 mm. **Series:** 1980 Olympics **Obv:** Olympic rings and date at upper left of smoking towers **Rev:** Boxers **Note:** 47,724 coins melted at the mint.

Date	Mintage	F	VF	XF	Unc	BU
1980	125,000	—	—	7.00	12.50	—

KM# 124   500 LIRE
11.0000 g., 0.8350 Silver 0.2953 oz. ASW, 29 mm.
Subject: 2000th Anniversary - Virgil's Death **Obv:** Crowned shield within sprigs **Rev:** Seated figure playing flute under tree **Note:** 9,122 coins melted at the mint.

Date	Mintage	F	VF	XF	Unc	BU
1981	75,000	—	—	7.00	12.50	—

KM# 125   500 LIRE
11.0000 g., 0.8350 Silver 0.2953 oz. ASW, 29 mm.
Subject: 2,000th Anniversary - Virgil's Death **Obv:** Crowned shield within sprigs **Rev:** The seed sower **Note:** 9,122 coins melted at the mint.

Date	Mintage	F	VF	XF	Unc	BU
1981	75,000	—	—	7.00	12.50	—

KM# 126   500 LIRE
11.0000 g., 0.8350 Silver 0.2953 oz. ASW, 29 mm.
Obv: Crowned shield **Rev:** Value flanked by hands below head right **Note:** 21,124 coins melted at the mint.

Date	Mintage	F	VF	XF	Unc	BU
1981R	100,000	—	—	7.00	12.50	—

KM# 139 500 LIRE
11.0000 g., 0.8350 Silver 0.2953 oz. ASW, 29 mm.
Subject: Centennial - Death of Garibaldi **Obv:** Crowned design above towers **Rev:** Head facing **Note:** 112 uncirculated and 369 proof coins melted at the mint.

Date	Mintage	F	VF	XF	Unc	BU
ND(1982)R	48,000	—	—	7.00	12.50	—
ND(1982)R Proof	13,000	Value: 22.50				

KM# 140 500 LIRE
6.8000 g., Bi-Metallic Aluminum-Bronze center in Stainless Steel ring, 25.8 mm. **Subject:** Social Conquests **Obv:** Crown above smoking towers within circle **Rev:** Stylized figures within circle

Date	Mintage	F	VF	XF	Unc	BU
1982R	1,900,000	—	—	2.00	4.00	—

KM# 153 500 LIRE
6.8000 g., Bi-Metallic Aluminum-Bronze center in Stainless Steel ring, 25.8 mm. **Subject:** Nuclear War Threat **Obv:** Crown above shield and sprig **Rev:** Three horses above two people

Date	Mintage	F	VF	XF	Unc	BU
1983R	1,922,000	—	—	2.00	4.00	—

KM# 154 500 LIRE
11.0000 g., 0.8350 Silver 0.2953 oz. ASW, 29 mm. **Subject:** 500th Anniversary - Birth of Artist Raphael **Obv:** Head 3/4 right, smoking towers at top and to right **Rev:** Seated figure looking at portrait **Note:** 80 uncirculated and 1,939 proof coins melted at the mint.

Date	Mintage	F	VF	XF	Unc	BU
1983R	42,000	—	—	7.00	12.50	—
1983R Proof	12,000	Value: 22.50				

KM# 167 500 LIRE
6.8000 g., Bi-Metallic Aluminum-Bronze center in Stainless Steel ring, 25.8 mm. **Obv:** Castle within circle **Rev:** Bust of Albert Einstein facing within circle

Date	Mintage	F	VF	XF	Unc	BU
1984R	2,633,000	—	—	2.00	4.00	—

KM# 168 500 LIRE
11.0000 g., 0.8350 Silver 0.2953 oz. ASW, 29 mm. **Series:** 1984 Summer Olympics **Obv:** Stylized smoking towers **Rev:** Entwined vertical figures to left of Olympic rings, date and value **Note:** 2,920 uncirculated and 20 proof coins melted at the mint.

Date	Mintage	F	VF	XF	Unc	BU
1984R	52,000	—	—	6.50	11.50	—
1984R Proof	15,000	Value: 13.50				

KM# 181 500 LIRE
6.8000 g., Bi-Metallic Aluminum-Bronze center in Stainless Steel ring, 25.8 mm. **Subject:** War on Drugs **Obv:** Stylized bending figure within circle **Rev:** Cured addict within circle

Date	Mintage	F	VF	XF	Unc	BU
1985R	2,647,000	—	—	2.00	4.00	—

KM# 182 500 LIRE
11.0000 g., 0.8350 Silver 0.2953 oz. ASW, 29 mm.
Subject: European Music Year, Bach Tercentenary **Rev:** Music seated at organ **Note:** 6,704 uncirculated and 122 proof coins melted at the mint.

Date	Mintage	F	VF	XF	Unc	BU
1985R	40,000	—	—	7.00	12.50	—
1985R Proof	12,000	Value: 15.00				

KM# 195 500 LIRE
6.8000 g., Bi-Metallic Aluminum-Bronze center in Stainless Steel ring, 25.8 mm. **Subject:** Revolution of Technology **Obv:** Crown above smoking towers on rock **Rev:** Human figure seated on console control panel

Date	Mintage	F	VF	XF	Unc	BU
1986R	3,111,000	—	—	2.00	4.00	—

KM# 196 500 LIRE
11.0000 g., 0.8350 Silver 0.2953 oz. ASW, 29 mm.
Subject: Soccer **Obv:** Head left **Rev:** Field design **Note:** 5,212 uncirculated and 60 proof coins melted at the mint.

Date	Mintage	F	VF	XF	Unc	BU
1986R	45,000	—	—	—	12.50	—
1986R Proof	12,000	Value: 15.00				

KM# 209 500 LIRE
6.8000 g., Bi-Metallic Aluminum-Bronze center in Stainless Steel ring, 25.8 mm. **Subject:** 15th Anniversary - Resumption of Coinage **Obv:** Crowned pointed shield within sprigs **Rev:** Smoking towers

Date	Mintage	F	VF	XF	Unc	BU
1987R	3,063,000	—	—	2.00	4.00	—

KM# 213 500 LIRE
11.0000 g., 0.8350 Silver 0.2953 oz. ASW, 29 mm.
Subject: Zagreb University Games **Rev:** Runner **Note:** 9,208 uncirculated and 1,206 proof coins melted at the mint.

Date	Mintage	F	VF	XF	Unc	BU
1987R	35,000	—	—	—	12.50	—
1987R Proof	10,000	Value: 15.00				

KM# 216 500 LIRE
11.0000 g., 0.8350 Silver 0.2953 oz. ASW, 29 mm.
Series: Winter Olympics **Obv:** Stylized smoking towers **Rev:** Downhill skier, oak leaf and Olympic rings **Note:** 146 uncirculated and 3 proof coins melted at the mint.

Date	Mintage	F	VF	XF	Unc	BU
1988R	32,000	—	—	—	9.00	—
1988R Proof	9,600	Value: 15.00				

KM# 226 500 LIRE
6.8000 g., Bi-Metallic Aluminum-Bronze center in Stainless Steel ring, 25.8 mm. **Subject:** Fortifications **Obv:** Crowned ornate arms on shield **Rev:** Hilltop fortification

Date	Mintage	F	VF	XF	Unc	BU
1988R	3,526,000	—	—	2.00	4.00	—

KM# 239 500 LIRE
6.8000 g., Bi-Metallic Aluminum-Bronze center in Stainless Steel ring, 25.8 mm. **Subject:** History **Obv:** Crowned shield **Rev:** Stone carver

Date	Mintage	F	VF	XF	Unc	BU
1989R	3,145,000	—	—	2.00	4.00	—

KM# 243   500 LIRE
11.0000 g., 0.8350 Silver 0.2953 oz. ASW, 29 mm.   **Subject:** San Marino Grand Prix **Obv:** Stylized smoking towers **Rev:** Vertical horse and rider above car **Note:** 5,180 coins melted at the mint.

Date	Mintage	F	VF	XF	Unc	BU
1989R	30,000	—	—	—	10.00	—
1989R Proof	8,000	Value: 25.00				

KM# 246   500 LIRE
11.0000 g., 0.8350 Silver 0.2953 oz. ASW, 29 mm.   **Subject:** World Cup Soccer Championship Game **Obv:** Patterned design surrounds oval shield at center **Rev:** Cluster of stylized running figures

Date	Mintage	F	VF	XF	Unc	BU
1990R	40,000	—	—	—	10.00	—
1990R Proof	19,000	Value: 20.00				

KM# 256   500 LIRE
6.8000 g., Bi-Metallic Aluminum-Bronze center in Stainless Steel ring, 25.8 mm.   **Subject:** 1,600 Years of History **Obv:** Towers above design **Rev:** Birds and stamp

Date	Mintage	F	VF	XF	Unc	BU
1990R	Est. 60,000	—	—	2.00	4.00	—

KM# 269   500 LIRE
6.8000 g., Bi-Metallic Aluminum-Bronze center in Stainless Steel ring, 25.8 mm.   **Obv:** Date at left of smoking towers within circle **Rev:** Value above hand holding flowers within circle

Date	Mintage	F	VF	XF	Unc	BU
1991R	3,580,563	—	—	2.00	4.00	—

KM# 271   500 LIRE
11.0000 g., 0.8350 Silver 0.2953 oz. ASW, 29 mm.   **Series:** Barcelona Olympics **Obv:** Seated Saint facing with hammer in hand **Rev:** Priestess lighting fire with sun beam

Date	Mintage	F	VF	XF	Unc	BU
1991R	Est. 60,000	—	—	—	9.00	—
1991R Proof	Est. 8,000	Value: 20.00				

KM# 276   500 LIRE
11.0000 g., 0.8350 Silver 0.2953 oz. ASW, 29 mm.   **Series:** Olympics **Obv:** Three smoking towers **Rev:** Chariot

Date	Mintage	F	VF	XF	Unc	BU
1992R	Est. 70,000	—	—	—	12.00	15.00
1992R Proof	—	Value: 20.00				

KM# 286   500 LIRE
6.8000 g., Bi-Metallic Aluminumn-Bronze center in Steel ring, 25.8 mm.   **Subject:** Columbus **Obv:** Towers with feather-like designs on top within circle **Rev:** Winds blowing ship within circle

Date	Mintage	F	VF	XF	Unc	BU
1992R	4,554,864	—	—	—	3.50	—

KM# 291   500 LIRE
11.0000 g., 0.8350 Silver 0.2953 oz. ASW, 29 mm.   **Subject:** Wildlife protection **Obv:** Crowned pointed shield within sprigs **Rev:** Two European polecats

Date	Mintage	F	VF	XF	Unc	BU
1993R	Est. 35,000	—	—	—	12.50	18.00
1993R Proof	—	Value: 25.00				

KM# 301   500 LIRE
6.8000 g., Bi-Metallic Aluminum-Bronze center in Stainless Steel ring, 25.8 mm.   **Obv:** Smoking towers within circle **Rev:** Growth from a tree stump

Date	Mintage	F	VF	XF	Unc	BU
1993R	4,200,000	—	—	—	3.50	—

KM# 314   500 LIRE
6.8000 g., Bi-Metallic Aluminum-Bronze center in Stainless Steel ring, 25.8 mm.   **Obv:** Stonecutter holding hammer and chisel, smoking towers at left, all within circle **Rev:** St. Marino receiving Mount Titano within circle

Date	Mintage	F	VF	XF	Unc	BU
1994R	40,000	—	—	—	3.50	—

KM# 317   500 LIRE
11.0000 g., 0.8350 Silver 0.2953 oz. ASW, 29 mm.   **Subject:** World Cup Soccer **Obv:** Crowned pointed shield within sprigs **Rev:** Fallen soccer player

Date	Mintage	F	VF	XF	Unc	BU
1994R Proof	—	Value: 15.00				

KM# 330   500 LIRE
6.8000 g., Bi-Metallic Aluminum-Bronze center in Stainless Steel ring, 25.8 mm.   **Series:** F.A.O. **Subject:** 50th Anniversary - F.A.O. **Obv:** Banner wrapped around bottom of design **Rev:** Kneeling figure under sprig

Date	Mintage	F	VF	XF	Unc	BU
1995R	3,000,000	—	—	—	3.50	—

KM# 357   500 LIRE
6.8000 g., Bi-Metallic Aluminum-Bronze center in Stainless Steel ring, 25.8 mm.   **Obv:** Bust facing with flame within hands within circle **Rev:** Face within triangle and circle design

Date	Mintage	F	VF	XF	Unc	BU
1996R	3,911,288	—	—	—	3.50	—

KM# 367   500 LIRE
6.8000 g., Bi-Metallic Aluminum-Bronze center in Stainless Steel ring, 25.8 mm.   **Subject:** The Arts - Music **Obv:** Bust facing with flame within hands within circle **Rev:** Woman playing pipes within circle

Date	Mintage	F	VF	XF	Unc	BU
1997R	28,000	—	—	—	3.50	—

Note: In mint sets only

KM# 383   500 LIRE
6.8000 g., Bi-Metallic Aluminum-Bronze center in Stainless Steel ring, 25.8 mm.   **Subject:** Chemistry **Obv:** Bust facing with flame within hands within circle **Rev:** Laboratory

Date	Mintage	F	VF	XF	Unc	BU
1998R	1,300,000	—	—	—	3.50	—

KM# 394   500 LIRE
6.8000 g., Bi-Metallic Aluminum-Bronze center in Stainless Steel ring, 25.86 mm.   **Subject:** Exploration **Obv:** Bust facing with flame within hands within circle **Rev:** Moon's surface, radio waves and Saturn **Edge:** segmented reeding

Date	Mintage	F	VF	XF	Unc	BU
1999R	2,000,000	—	—	—	3.00	4.00

KM# 404   500 LIRE
6.8000 g., Bi-Metallic Aluminum-Bronze center in Stainless Steel ring, 25.8 mm.   **Subject:** Work **Obv:** Bust facing with flames within hands within circle **Rev:** Spinning wheel design within circle **Edge:** Reeded and plain sections

Date	Mintage	VG	F	VF	XF	Unc
2000R	28,000	—	—	—	—	4.00

Note: In mint sets only

KM# 72   1000 LIRE
14.6000 g., 0.8350 Silver 0.3919 oz. ASW, 31.4 mm.   **Subject:** 600th Anniversary - Birth of Brunelleschi- architect, author **Obv:** Standing figures on railed platform **Rev:** Head 3/4 left facing **Note:** 38,145 coins melted at the mint.

Date	Mintage	F	VF	XF	Unc	BU
ND(1977)	180,000	—	—	—	10.00	—

KM# 85   1000 LIRE
14.6000 g., 0.8350 Silver 0.3919 oz. ASW, 31.4 mm.   **Subject:** 150th Anniversary - Birth of Tolstoy **Obv:** Smoking towers **Rev:** Head left **Note:** 17,892 coins melted at the mint.

Date	Mintage	F	VF	XF	Unc	BU
ND(1978)	130,000	—	—	—	10.00	—

KM# 98   1000 LIRE
14.6000 g., 0.8350 Silver 0.3919 oz. ASW, 31.4 mm.   **Subject:** European Unity **Obv:** Crown above stylized smoking towers **Rev:** Seagulls above figure facing right **Note:** 14,945 coins melted at the mint.

Date	Mintage	F	VF	XF	Unc	BU
1979	125,000	—	—	—	16.50	—

KM# 112   1000 LIRE
14.6000 g., 0.8350 Silver 0.3919 oz. ASW, 31.4 mm.   **Subject:** 1,500th Anniversary - Birth of St. Benedict **Obv:** Smoking towers **Rev:** Bust facing **Note:** 49,095 coins melted at the mint.

Date	Mintage	F	VF	XF	Unc	BU
1980	125,000	—	—	—	15.00	—

KM# 127   1000 LIRE
14.6000 g., 0.8350 Silver 0.3919 oz. ASW, 31.4 mm.   **Subject:** 200th Anniversary - Virgil's Death **Obv:** Crowned shield within sprigs **Rev:** Armored figure on horse **Note:** 9,122 coins melted at the mint.

Date	Mintage	F	VF	XF	Unc	BU
1981	75,000	—	—	—	15.00	—

KM# 141   1000 LIRE
14.6000 g., 0.8350 Silver 0.3919 oz. ASW, 31.4 mm.   **Subject:** Centennial - Garibaldi's Death **Obv:** Crowned design above towers **Rev:** Large head facing **Note:** 112 uncirculated and 369 proof coins melted at the mint.

Date	Mintage	F	VF	XF	Unc	BU
ND(1982)R	48,000	—	—	—	15.00	—
ND(1982)R Proof	13,000	Value: 25.00				

KM# 155   1000 LIRE
14.6000 g., 0.8350 Silver 0.3919 oz. ASW, 31.4 mm.   **Subject:** 500th Anniversary - Birth of Artist Raphael **Obv:** Head 1/4 right, towers at top and right **Rev:** Standing figure facing divides date and value **Note:** 80 uncirculated and 1,939 proof coins melted at the mint.

Date	Mintage	F	VF	XF	Unc	BU
1983R	42,000	—	—	—	15.00	—
1983R Proof	12,000	Value: 25.00				

KM# 169   1000 LIRE
14.6000 g., 0.8350 Silver 0.3919 oz. ASW, 31.4 mm.   **Series:** 1984 Summer Olympics **Obv:** Stylized smoking towers **Rev:** Figures reaching wings of bird divide date and value with olympic rings below **Note:** 2,920 uncirculated and 20 proof coins melted at the mint.

Date	Mintage	F	VF	XF	Unc	BU
1984R	52,000	—	—	—	12.50	—
1984R Proof	15,000	Value: 22.50				

KM# 183   1000 LIRE
14.6000 g., 0.8350 Silver 0.3919 oz. ASW, 31.4 mm.   **Subject:** European Music Year, Bach Tercentenary **Obv:** Smoking towers within crowned shield **Rev:** J.S. Bach **Note:** 6,704 uncirculated and 122 proof coins melted at the mint.

Date	Mintage	F	VF	XF	Unc	BU
1985R	40,000	—	—	—	15.00	—
1985R Proof	12,000	Value: 25.00				

KM# 197   1000 LIRE
14.6000 g., 0.8350 Silver 0.3919 oz. ASW, 31.4 mm.   **Subject:** Soccer **Obv:** Head left **Rev:** Stylized flags **Note:** 5,212 uncirculated and 60 proof coins melted at the mint.

Date	Mintage	F	VF	XF	Unc	BU
1986R	45,000	—	—	—	16.00	—
1986R Proof	12,000	Value: 30.00				

KM# 210   1000 LIRE
14.6000 g., 0.8350 Silver 0.3919 oz. ASW, 31.4 mm.   **Subject:** 15th Anniversary - Resumption of Coinage **Obv:** Crowned pointed shield within sprigs **Rev:** Standing Saint figure facing **Note:** 13 coins melted at the mint.

Date	Mintage	F	VF	XF	Unc	BU
1987R	43,000	—	—	—	18.00	—

KM# 214   1000 LIRE
14.6000 g., 0.8350 Silver 0.3919 oz. ASW, 31.4 mm.
Subject: Zagreb University Games **Rev:** Pole vaulter
Note: 9,207 uncirculated and 1,206 proof coins melted at the mint.

Date	Mintage	F	VF	XF	Unc	BU
1987R	35,000	—	—	—	16.00	—
1987R Proof	10,000	Value: 30.00				

KM# 217   1000 LIRE
14.6000 g., 0.8350 Silver 0.3919 oz. ASW, 31.4 mm.
Series: Summer Olympics **Obv:** Stylized smoking towers
Rev: Diver **Note:** 146 uncirculated and 3 proof coins melted at the mint.

Date	Mintage	F	VF	XF	Unc	BU
1988R	32,000	—	—	—	17.50	—
1988R Proof	9,600	Value: 30.00				

KM# 227   1000 LIRE
14.6000 g., 0.8350 Silver 0.3919 oz. ASW, 31.4 mm.
Subject: Fortifications **Obv:** Crowned ornate arms on shield
Rev: Walls and towers

Date	Mintage	F	VF	XF	Unc	BU
1988R	38,000	—	—	—	20.00	—

KM# 240   1000 LIRE
14.6000 g., 0.8350 Silver 0.3919 oz. ASW, 31.4 mm. **Subject:**
History **Obv:** Crowned shield **Rev:** Two men standing in boat

Date	Mintage	F	VF	XF	Unc	BU
1989R	32,000	—	—	—	20.00	—

KM# 244   1000 LIRE
14.6000 g., 0.8350 Silver 0.3919 oz. ASW, 31.4 mm. **Subject:**
San Marino Grand Prix **Obv:** Stylized smoking towers **Rev:** Date
and value below race car **Note:** 5,180 coins melted at the mint.

Date	Mintage	F	VF	XF	Unc	BU
1989R	30,000	—	—	—	20.00	—
1989R Proof	8,000	Value: 35.00				

KM# 247   1000 LIRE
14.6000 g., 0.8350 Silver 0.3919 oz. ASW, 31.4 mm.
Subject: World Cup Soccer Championship Games
Obv: Patterned design surrounds oval shield at center
Rev: Winged Victory divides value

Date	Mintage	F	VF	XF	Unc	BU
1990R	40,000	—	—	—	20.00	—
1990R Proof	19,000	Value: 30.00				

KM# 257   1000 LIRE
14.6000 g., 0.8350 Silver 0.3919 oz. ASW, 31.4 mm.
Subject: 1,600 Years of History **Obv:** Towers above design
Rev: Stylized hand and two figures

Date	Mintage	F	VF	XF	Unc	BU
1990R	36,000	—	—	—	20.00	—

KM# 270   1000 LIRE
14.6000 g., 0.8350 Silver 0.3919 oz. ASW, 31.4 mm. **Obv:** Date
at upper left of smoking towers **Rev:** Large value above hand
holding dove

Date	Mintage	F	VF	XF	Unc	BU
1991R	—	—	—	—	20.00	—

KM# 272   1000 LIRE
14.6000 g., 0.8350 Silver 0.3919 oz. ASW, 31.4 mm. **Series:**
Barcelona Olympics **Rev:** Stylized runner and Olympic rings

Date	Mintage	F	VF	XF	Unc	BU
1991R	Est. 60,000	—	—	—	20.00	—
1991R Proof	Est. 8,000	Value: 32.50				

KM# 277   1000 LIRE
14.6000 g., 0.8350 Silver 0.3919 oz. ASW, 31.4 mm.
Series: Olympics **Obv:** Stylized smoking towers **Rev:** Athletes

Date	Mintage	F	VF	XF	Unc	BU
1992R	Est. 70,000	—	—	—	20.00	—
1992R Proof	—	Value: 32.50				

KM# 287   1000 LIRE
14.6000 g., 0.8350 Silver 0.3919 oz. ASW, 31.4 mm.
Obv: Towers with feather-like designs at top within circle
Rev: Columbus studying chart within circle

Date	Mintage	F	VF	XF	Unc	BU
ND(1992)R	—	—	—	—	22.50	—

KM# 292   1000 LIRE
14.6000 g., 0.8350 Silver 0.3919 oz. ASW, 31.4 mm.
Series: Wildlife Protection **Obv:** Crowned pointed shield within
sprigs **Rev:** Falcon and Woodpecker

Date	Mintage	F	VF	XF	Unc	BU
1993R	Est. 35,000	—	—	—	20.00	—
1993R Proof	—	Value: 30.00				

KM# 302   1000 LIRE
14.6000 g., 0.8350 Silver 0.3919 oz. ASW, 31.4 mm.
Obv: Smoking towers **Rev:** Wing above globe

Date	Mintage	F	VF	XF	Unc	BU
1993R	—	—	—	—	22.50	—

KM# 315   1000 LIRE
14.6000 g., 0.8350 Silver 0.3919 oz. ASW, 31.4 mm.
Subject: Founder Building First San Marino Church
Obv: Stonecutter holding hammer and chisel, smoking towers at left
Rev: Seated stone cutter

Date	Mintage	F	VF	XF	Unc	BU
1994R	40,000	—	—	—	22.50	—

KM# 316   1000 LIRE
14.6000 g., 0.8350 Silver 0.3919 oz. ASW, 31.4 mm.
Series: Olympics **Obv:** Crowned pointed shield within sprigs
Rev: Ski jumper

Date	Mintage	F	VF	XF	Unc	BU
1994R Proof	—	Value: 18.50				

KM# 318   1000 LIRE
14.6000 g., 0.8350 Silver 0.3919 oz. ASW, 31.4 mm.
Subject: World Cup Soccer **Obv:** Crowned pointed shield within sprigs **Rev:** Soccer players

Date	Mintage	F	VF	XF	Unc	BU
1994R Proof	—			Value: 27.50		

KM# 331   1000 LIRE
14.6000 g., 0.8350 Silver 0.3919 oz. ASW, 31.4 mm. **Obv:** Banner wrapped around quills **Rev:** Pyramid of children within value

Date	Mintage	F	VF	XF	Unc	BU
1995R	—	—	—	—	22.50	—

KM# 332   1000 LIRE
14.6000 g., 0.8350 Silver 0.3919 oz. ASW, 31.4 mm.
Series: 1996 Olympics **Obv:** Crowned pointed shield within sprigs **Rev:** Pole vaulting and discus

Date	Mintage	F	VF	XF	Unc	BU
1995R Proof	50,000			Value: 30.00		

KM# 358   1000 LIRE
14.6000 g., 0.8350 Silver 0.3919 oz. ASW, 31.4 mm. **Obv:** Bust facing with flame within hands **Rev:** Head of Popper facing

Date	Mintage	F	VF	XF	Unc	BU
1996R	32,000	—	—	—	20.00	—

KM# 368   1000 LIRE
8.8200 g., Bi-Metallic Copper-Nickel center in Aluminum-Bronze ring, 27 mm. **Subject:** Millennium of building of the castle **Obv:** Heraldic lion within circle **Rev:** Statue, building and value within circle

Date	Mintage	F	VF	XF	Unc	BU
1997R	2,232,541	—	—	—	8.00	—

KM# 369   1000 LIRE
14.6000 g., 0.8350 Silver 0.3919 oz. ASW, 31.4 mm. **Subject:** The Arts - Interplanetary Communication **Obv:** Bust facing with flame within hands **Rev:** Nude couple from Pioneer 10 space probe plaque

Date	Mintage	F	VF	XF	Unc	BU
1997R	28,000	—	—	—	25.00	—

KM# 384   1000 LIRE
Bi-Metallic Copper-Nickel center in Aluminum-Bronze ring, 27 mm. **Subject:** Geology **Obv:** Child of the Universe **Rev:** Family standing on earth

Date	Mintage	F	VF	XF	Unc	BU
1998R	2,061,275	—	—	—	8.00	—

KM# 395   1000 LIRE
Bi-Metallic Copper-Nickel center in Aluminum-Bronze ring, 27 mm. **Subject:** Exploration **Obv:** Child of the Universe **Rev:** Radiant north star design

Date	Mintage	F	VF	XF	Unc	BU
1999R	1,836,495	—	—	—	8.00	—

KM# 405   1000 LIRE
Bi-Metallic Copper-Nickel center in Aluminum-Bronze ring, 27 mm. **Subject:** Liberty **Obv:** Child of the Universe **Rev:** Barn Swallow flying over world globe **Edge:** Reeded and plain sectioned **Note:** Struck at Rome.

Date	Mintage	F	VF	XF	Unc	BU
2000R	2,898,805	—	—	—	10.00	—

KM# 333   5000 LIRE
18.0000 g., 0.8350 Silver 0.4832 oz. ASW **Subject:** Sail Training Ship "Amerigo Vespucci" **Obv:** Crowned pointed shield within sprigs **Rev:** Sailing ship

Date	Mintage	F	VF	XF	Unc	BU
1995R Proof	Est. 35,000			Value: 17.50		

KM# 340   5000 LIRE
18.0000 g., 0.8350 Silver 0.4832 oz. ASW **Series:** Wildlife Protection **Obv:** Crowned pointed shield within sprigs **Rev:** Falcons

Date	Mintage	F	VF	XF	Unc	BU
1996 Proof	Est. 35,000			Value: 50.00		

KM# 370   5000 LIRE
18.0000 g., 0.8350 Silver 0.4832 oz. ASW **Obv:** Crowned pointed shield within sprigs **Rev:** Sailing ship and map of Africa **Rev. Leg.:** VASCO DA GAMA 1497

Date	Mintage	F	VF	XF	Unc	BU
1997R Proof	—			Value: 17.50		

KM# 385   5000 LIRE
18.0000 g., 0.8350 Silver 0.4832 oz. ASW **Subject:** Medicine **Obv:** Child of the Universe **Rev:** Emblem within circle of face outline left

Date	Mintage	F	VF	XF	Unc	BU
1998R	—	—	—	—	18.00	—

KM# 386   5000 LIRE
18.0000 g., 0.8350 Silver 0.4832 oz. ASW, 32 mm.
Subject: Europe in the New Millennium **Obv:** Crowned pointed shield within sprigs **Rev:** Euro bridge with ivy, olive and oak trees **Edge:** Lettered **Edge:** RELINQUO VOS LIBEROS **Note:** Struck at Rome.

Date	Mintage	F	VF	XF	Unc	BU
1998R Proof	—			Value: 20.00		

KM# 396   5000 LIRE
18.0000 g., 0.8350 Silver 0.4832 oz. ASW **Subject:** Exploration **Obv:** Crowned shield **Rev:** Solar system, European map and dish in human mind

Date	Mintage	F	VF	XF	Unc	BU
1999R	—	—	—	—	18.00	—

KM# 410   5000 LIRE
18.0000 g., 0.8350 Silver 0.4832 oz. ASW **Subject:** European Union **Obv:** Crowned pointed shield within sprigs **Rev:** Value above flags **Edge:** Lettered **Edge:** RELINQUO VOS LIBEROS

Date	Mintage	F	VF	XF	Unc	BU
1999R Proof	—	Value: 30.00				

KM# 406   5000 LIRE
18.0000 g., 0.8350 Silver 0.4832 oz. ASW, 32 mm.
Subject: Peace **Obv:** Child of the Universe **Rev:** Hawk and dove with same olive branch in their beaks **Edge:** Reeded and plain sectioned **Note:** Struck at Rome.

Date	Mintage	F	VF	XF	Unc	BU
2000R	—	—	—	—	25.00	—

KM# 421   5000 LIRE
18.0000 g., 0.8350 Silver 0.4832 oz. ASW **Subject:** First Holy Year Jubilee **Obv:** Crowned pointed shield within sprigs **Rev:** Pope Boniface VIII with two aides **Edge:** Lettered **Edge:** RELINQUO VOS LIBEROS

Date	Mintage	F	VF	XF	Unc	BU
2000R Proof	—	Value: 20.00				

KM# 334   10000 LIRE
22.0000 g., 0.8350 Silver 0.5906 oz. ASW **Subject:** Amerigo Vespucci **Obv:** Crowned pointed shield within sprigs **Rev:** Cameo to upper left of ship

Date	Mintage	F	VF	XF	Unc	BU
1995R Proof	Est. 35,000	Value: 22.50				

KM# 341   10000 LIRE
22.0000 g., 0.8350 Silver 0.5906 oz. ASW **Series:** Wildlife Protection **Obv:** Crowned pointed shield within sprigs **Rev:** Wolves

Date	Mintage	F	VF	XF	Unc	BU
1996 Proof	Est. 35,000	Value: 60.00				

KM# 342   10000 LIRE
22.0000 g., 0.8350 Silver 0.5906 oz. ASW **Subject:** Euro **Obv:** Crowned pointed shield within sprigs **Rev:** Parliament building and map

Date	Mintage	F	VF	XF	Unc	BU
1996 Proof	—	Value: 30.00				

KM# 371   10000 LIRE
22.0000 g., 0.8350 Silver 0.5906 oz. ASW **Subject:** Giovanni Caboto 1497 **Obv:** Crowned pointed shield within sprigs **Rev:** Ship and Atlantic map

Date	Mintage	F	VF	XF	Unc	BU
1997R Proof	—	Value: 28.00				

KM# 372   10000 LIRE
22.0000 g., 0.8350 Silver 0.5906 oz. ASW **Subject:** Euro - "Libertas" **Obv:** National arms above the 9 Casteli arms **Rev:** Head left within oval star design

Date	Mintage	F	VF	XF	Unc	BU
1997R Proof	—	Value: 32.00				

KM# 376   10000 LIRE
22.0000 g., 0.8350 Silver 0.5906 oz. ASW **Subject:** Soccer World Championship **Obv:** Crowned pointed shield within sprigs **Rev:** Soccer players

Date	Mintage	F	VF	XF	Unc	BU
1998R Proof	—	Value: 30.00				

KM# 377   10000 LIRE
22.0000 g., 0.8350 Silver 0.5906 oz. ASW, 34 mm.
Subject: 50th Anniversary - Ferrari **Obv:** Crowned pointed shield within sprigs **Rev:** Race cars **Edge:** Reeded and plain sections

Date	Mintage	F	VF	XF	Unc	BU
1998R Proof	30,000	Value: 27.50				

KM# 387   10000 LIRE
22.0000 g., 0.8350 Silver 0.5906 oz. ASW **Subject:** Europe in the New Millennium **Obv:** Crowned pointed shield within sprigs **Rev:** Child with flags

Date	Mintage	F	VF	XF	Unc	BU
1998R Proof	—	Value: 28.50				

KM# 397   10000 LIRE
22.0000 g., 0.8350 Silver 0.5906 oz. ASW **Subject:** III Millennium **Obv:** Crowned pointed shield within sprigs **Rev:** Allegorical portrait of DNA unraveling from human mind

Date	Mintage	F	VF	XF	Unc	BU
1999R Proof	Est. 25,000	Value: 30.00				

KM# 398   10000 LIRE
22.0000 g., 0.8350 Silver 0.5906 oz. ASW **Series:** 2000 Olympics **Obv:** Crowned pointed shield within sprigs **Rev:** Prone shooter

Date	Mintage	F	VF	XF	Unc	BU
1999R Proof	Est. 35,000	Value: 27.50				

KM# 411 10000 LIRE
22.0000 g., 0.8350 Silver 0.5906 oz. ASW **Subject:** European Union **Obv:** Crowned pointed shield within sprigs **Rev:** Circle of paper dolls above value

Date	Mintage	F	VF	XF	Unc	BU
1999R Proof	—	Value: 35.00				

KM# 419 10000 LIRE
22.0000 g., 0.8350 Silver 0.5906 oz. ASW, 34 mm. **Subject:** 17th Centennial of the Republic **Obv:** Crowned pointed shield within sprigs **Rev:** Bust of St. Marino facing

Date	Mintage	F	VF	XF	Unc	BU
2000R Proof	18,000	Value: 22.50				

KM# 422 10000 LIRE
22.0000 g., 0.8350 Silver 0.5906 oz. ASW, 34 mm. **Subject:** Holy Year **Obv:** Crowned pointed shield within sprigs **Rev:** Pope kneeling before an open door **Edge:** Reeded and plain sections

Date	Mintage	F	VF	XF	Unc	BU
2000R Proof	—	Value: 30.00				

KM# 423 10000 LIRE
22.0000 g., 0.8350 Silver 0.5906 oz. ASW, 34 mm. **Obv:** Crowned pointed shield within sprigs **Rev:** Michelangelo's Sacred Family Painting **Edge:** Reeded and plain sections

Date	Mintage	F	VF	XF	Unc	BU
2000R Proof	—	Value: 30.00				

KM# 416 1/2 SCUDO
1.6100 g., 0.9000 Gold 0.0466 oz. AGW, 14 mm. **Subject:** Ilcenacolo **Obv:** Crowned pointed shield within sprigs **Rev:** Bearded bust facing **Edge:** Reeded **Note:** 1,915 coins melted at the mint.

Date	Mintage	F	VF	XF	Unc	BU
1998 Proof	8,000	Value: 50.00				

KM# 413 1/2 SCUDO
1.6100 g., 0.9000 Gold 0.0466 oz. AGW **Subject:** Ritratto di Agnolo Doni **Obv:** Crowned pointed shield within sprigs **Rev:** Head 3/4 right

Date	Mintage	F	VF	XF	Unc	BU
1999 Proof	8,000	Value: 50.00				

KM# 407 1/2 SCUDO
1.6100 g., 0.9000 Gold 0.0466 oz. AGW **Subject:** Ritratto di Giovane Donna **Obv:** Crowned pointed shield within sprigs **Rev:** Head left

Date	Mintage	F	VF	XF	Unc	BU
2000 Proof	6,000	Value: 50.00				

KM# 38 SCUDO
3.0000 g., 0.9170 Gold 0.0884 oz. AGW **Obv:** Crowned pointed shield within sprigs **Rev:** Standing Saint facing **Note:** 2,491 coins melted at the mint.

Date	Mintage	F	VF	XF	Unc	BU
1974	87,000	—	—	—	—	90.00

KM# 49 SCUDO
3.0000 g., 0.9170 Gold 0.0884 oz. AGW **Obv:** Crowned pointed shield within sprigs **Rev:** Value and date within wreath **Note:** 37,668 coins melted at the mint.

Date	Mintage	F	VF	XF	Unc	BU
1975	90,000	—	—	—	—	90.00

KM# 60 SCUDO
3.0000 g., 0.9170 Gold 0.0884 oz. AGW **Obv:** Smoking towers **Rev:** Laureate head right **Note:** 30,026 coins melted at the mint.

Date	Mintage	F	VF	XF	Unc	BU
1976	65,000	—	—	—	—	90.00

KM# 73 SCUDO
3.0000 g., 0.9170 Gold 0.0884 oz. AGW **Obv:** Smoking towers **Rev:** Democrazia **Note:** 1,839 coins melted at the mint.

Date	Mintage	F	VF	XF	Unc	BU
1977	35,000	—	—	—	—	90.00

KM# 86 SCUDO
3.0000 g., 0.9170 Gold 0.0884 oz. AGW **Obv:** Smoking towers **Rev:** Miss Liberta **Note:** 9,021 coins melted at the mint.

Date	Mintage	F	VF	XF	Unc	BU
1978	38,000	—	—	—	—	90.00

KM# 99 SCUDO
3.0000 g., 0.9170 Gold 0.0884 oz. AGW **Obv:** Value within upright feathers **Rev:** Peace **Note:** 4,152 coins melted at the mint.

Date	Mintage	F	VF	XF	Unc	BU
1979	38,000	—	—	—	—	90.00

KM# 113 SCUDO
3.0000 g., 0.9170 Gold 0.0884 oz. AGW **Rev:** Head on hands facing, dove at left **Note:** 10,309 coins melted at the mint.

Date	Mintage	F	VF	XF	Unc	BU
1980R	38,000	—	—	—	—	90.00

KM# 128 SCUDO
3.0000 g., 0.9170 Gold 0.0884 oz. AGW **Subject:** World Food Day **Obv:** Crowned pointed shield within sprigs above inscription **Rev:** Seated figure reading **Note:** 196 coins melted at the mint.

Date	Mintage	F	VF	XF	Unc	BU
1981R	31,000	—	—	—	—	90.00

KM# 142 SCUDO
3.0000 g., 0.9170 Gold 0.0884 oz. AGW **Obv:** Crowned shield **Rev:** Head left **Note:** 1,192 coins melted at the mint.

Date	Mintage	F	VF	XF	Unc	BU
1982R	17,000	—	—	—	—	90.00

KM# 156 SCUDO
2.0000 g., 0.9170 Gold 0.0590 oz. AGW **Rev:** Perpetual Liberty **Note:** 917 coins melted at the mint.

Date	Mintage	F	VF	XF	Unc	BU
1983R	14,000	—	—	—	—	65.00

KM# 170 SCUDO
2.0000 g., 0.9170 Gold 0.0590 oz. AGW **Subject:** Peace **Obv:** Crowned shield in front of city scene **Rev:** Half-figure holding laurel branch left **Note:** 979 coins melted at the mint.

Date	Mintage	F	VF	XF	Unc	BU
1984R	11,000	—	—	—	—	65.00

KM# 184 SCUDO
2.0000 g., 0.9170 Gold 0.0590 oz. AGW **Subject:** International Year for Youth **Rev:** Head left **Note:** 1,162 coins melted at the mint.

Date	Mintage	F	VF	XF	Unc	BU
1985R	10,000	—	—	—	—	90.00

KM# 198 SCUDO
3.3920 g., 0.9170 Gold 0.1000 oz. AGW **Subject:** Insects at Work **Rev:** Large ant **Note:** 1,308 coins melted at the mint.

Date	Mintage	F	VF	XF	Unc	BU
1986R	9,000	—	—	—	—	100

KM# 211 SCUDO
3.3920 g., 0.9170 Gold 0.1000 oz. AGW **Subject:** European Year for Environment **Obv:** Robe-like design with seagull at right **Rev:** Nude children under sprig **Note:** 962 coins melted at the mint.

Date	Mintage	F	VF	XF	Unc	BU
1987R	8,000	—	—	—	—	100

KM# 228 SCUDO
3.3920 g., 0.9170 Gold 0.1000 oz. AGW **Subject:** Disarmament
Obv: Smoking towers **Rev:** Design within globe **Note:** 873 coins
melted at the mint.

Date	Mintage	F	VF	XF	Unc	BU
1988R	7,000	—	—	—	—	100

KM# 241 SCUDO
3.2258 g., 0.9000 Gold 0.0933 oz. AGW **Subject:** French
Revolution **Rev:** Standing figure holding flag **Note:** 731 coins
melted at the mint.

Date	Mintage	F	VF	XF	Unc	BU
1989R	7,500	—	—	—	—	100

KM# 258 SCUDO
3.2258 g., 0.9000 Gold 0.0933 oz. AGW **Subject:** San Marino's
Presidency of the European Council **Obv:** Crowned pointed
shield within sprigs **Rev:** Bust facing

Date	Mintage	F	VF	XF	Unc	BU
1990R	7,300	—	—	—	—	100

KM# 273 SCUDO
3.2258 g., 0.9000 Gold 0.0933 oz. AGW **Subject:** Peace
Obv: Crowned pointed shield within sprigs **Rev:** Child fleeing

Date	Mintage	F	VF	XF	Unc	BU
1991R Proof	Est. 7,500	Value: 100				

KM# 288 SCUDO
3.2258 g., 0.9000 Gold 0.0933 oz. AGW **Subject:** San Marino's
Entry Into the United Nations **Obv:** Crowned shield within sprigs
Rev: UN logo

Date	Mintage	F	VF	XF	Unc	BU
1992R Proof	8,500	Value: 100				

KM# 303 SCUDO
3.2258 g., 0.9000 Gold 0.0933 oz. AGW **Series:** International
Monetary Fund **Rev:** Three standing figures within pointed oblong
design **Note:** 455 coins melted at the mint.

Date	Mintage	F	VF	XF	Unc	BU
1993R Proof	7,500	Value: 100				

KM# 319 SCUDO
3.2258 g., 0.9000 Gold 0.0933 oz. AGW **Series:** International Year
of the Family **Obv:** Crowned shield within sprigs **Rev:** Couple facing
each other **Note:** Sets only. 648 coins melted at the mint.

Date	Mintage	F	VF	XF	Unc	BU
1994R Proof	7,500	Value: 100				

KM# 335 SCUDO
3.2258 g., 0.9000 Gold 0.0933 oz. AGW **Series:** 50th
Anniversary - United Nations **Obv:** Crowned shield within sprigs
Note: Sets only. 494 coins melted at the mint.

Date	Mintage	F	VF	XF	Unc	BU
1995R Proof	6,500	Value: 100				

KM# 338 SCUDO
3.2258 g., 0.9000 Gold 0.0933 oz. AGW **Series:** 1996 Olympics
Rev: Boxers **Note:** 664 coins melted at the mint.

Date	Mintage	F	VF	XF	Unc	BU
1996 Proof	7,000	Value: 100				

KM# 373 SCUDO
3.2258 g., 0.9000 Gold 0.0933 oz. AGW **Rev:** Michelangelo's
"Kneeling Angel" **Note:** 412 coins melted at the mint.

Date	Mintage	F	VF	XF	Unc	BU
1997 Proof	6,500	Value: 100				

KM# 417 SCUDO
3.2258 g., 0.9000 Gold 0.0933 oz. AGW, 15.9 mm.
Subject: Canone Delle Proporzioni **Obv:** Crowned pointed shield
within sprigs **Rev:** Anatomical drawing **Edge:** Reeded **Note:** 312
coins melted at the mint.

Date	Mintage	F	VF	XF	Unc	BU
1998 Proof	6,000	Value: 75.00				

KM# 414 SCUDO
3.2258 g., 0.9000 Gold 0.0933 oz. AGW **Subject:** La Velata
Obv: Crowned shield **Rev:** Head facing 1/4 left

Date	Mintage	F	VF	XF	Unc	BU
1999 Proof	8,000	Value: 100				

KM# 408 SCUDO
3.2258 g., 0.9000 Gold 0.0933 oz. AGW **Obv:** Crowned shield
Rev: La Primavera

Date	Mintage	F	VF	XF	Unc	BU
2000 Proof	—	Value: 100				

KM# 39 2 SCUDI
6.0000 g., 0.9170 Gold 0.1769 oz. AGW **Obv:** Crowned pointed
shield within wreath **Rev:** Standing figure facing **Note:** 1,637
coins melted at the mint.

Date	Mintage	F	VF	XF	Unc	BU
1974	77,000	—	—	—	—	175

KM# 50 2 SCUDI
6.0000 g., 0.9170 Gold 0.1769 oz. AGW **Obv:** Crowned pointed
shield within wreath **Rev:** Value and date within wreath
Note: 3,373 coins melted at the mint.

Date	Mintage	F	VF	XF	Unc	BU
1975	80,000	—	—	—	—	175

KM# 61 2 SCUDI
6.0000 g., 0.9170 Gold 0.1769 oz. AGW **Obv:** Smoking towers
Rev: Head 3/4 right **Note:** 20,246 coins melted at the mint.

Date	Mintage	F	VF	XF	Unc	BU
1976	55,000	—	—	—	—	175

KM# 74 2 SCUDI
6.0000 g., 0.9170 Gold 0.1769 oz. AGW **Obv:** Date at right of
smoking towers **Rev:** Democrazia **Note:** 912 coins melted at the
mint.

Date	Mintage	F	VF	XF	Unc	BU
1977	34,000	—	—	—	—	175

KM# 87 2 SCUDI
6.0000 g., 0.9170 Gold 0.1769 oz. AGW **Obv:** Value at upper
left of smoking towers **Rev:** Libertas **Note:** 8,120 coins melted at
the mint.

Date	Mintage	F	VF	XF	Unc	BU
1978	37,000	—	—	—	—	175

KM# 100 2 SCUDI
6.0000 g., 0.9170 Gold 0.1769 oz. AGW **Subject:** Peace
Obv: Three upright feathers **Rev:** Clasped hands **Note:** 3,238
coins melted at the mint.

Date	Mintage	F	VF	XF	Unc	BU
1979	37,000	—	—	—	—	175

KM# 114 2 SCUDI
6.0000 g., 0.9170 Gold 0.1769 oz. AGW **Subject:** Justice
Obv: Smoking towers **Rev:** Mother holding 2 children **Note:** 9,340
coins melted at the mint.

Date	Mintage	F	VF	XF	Unc	BU
1980R	37,000	—	—	—	—	175

KM# 129 2 SCUDI
6.0000 g., 0.9170 Gold 0.1769 oz. AGW **Series:** World Food Day **Obv:** Crowned pointed arms within wreath above sprigs **Rev:** Seated nude figure with knees bent upright **Note:** 196 coins melted at the mint.

Date	Mintage	F	VF	XF	Unc	BU
1981R	30,000	—	—	—	—	175

KM# 143 2 SCUDI
6.0000 g., 0.9170 Gold 0.1769 oz. AGW **Obv:** Crown above smoking towers flanked by sprig and design **Rev:** Stylized seated nude right **Note:** 244 coins melted at the mint.

Date	Mintage	F	VF	XF	Unc	BU
1982R	16,000	—	—	—	—	175

KM# 157 2 SCUDI
4.0000 g., 0.9170 Gold 0.1179 oz. AGW **Subject:** Perpetual Liberty **Obv:** Inscription above crowned shield and sprig **Rev:** Smoking towers on top of head left **Note:** 17 coins melted at the mint.

Date	Mintage	F	VF	XF	Unc	BU
1983R	13,000	—	—	—	—	115

KM# 171 2 SCUDI
4.0000 g., 0.9170 Gold 0.1179 oz. AGW **Subject:** Liberty **Obv:** Crowned shield in front of city scene **Rev:** Standing figure with arms outstretched left **Note:** 12 coins melted at the mint.

Date	Mintage	F	VF	XF	Unc	BU
1984R	10,000	—	—	—	—	115

KM# 185 2 SCUDI
4.0000 g., 0.9170 Gold 0.1179 oz. AGW **Series:** International Year for Youth **Obv:** Crown above smoking towers on rock flanked by sprigs **Rev:** Head right divides flower and date **Note:** 200 coins melted at the mint.

Date	Mintage	F	VF	XF	Unc	BU
1985R	9,000	—	—	—	—	115

KM# 199 2 SCUDI
6.7840 g., 0.9170 Gold 0.2000 oz. AGW **Obv:** Crowned shield above view **Rev:** Spider within web divides 2S **Note:** 329 coins melted at the mint.

Date	Mintage	F	VF	XF	Unc	BU
1986R	8,000	—	—	—	—	200

KM# 212 2 SCUDI
6.7840 g., 0.9170 Gold 0.2000 oz. AGW **Subject:** European Year for Envrionment **Rev:** Sprig divides dancing figures **Note:** 14 coins melted at the mint.

Date	Mintage	F	VF	XF	Unc	BU
1987R	7,000	—	—	—	—	200

KM# 229 2 SCUDI
6.7840 g., 0.9170 Gold 0.2000 oz. AGW **Subject:** Disarmament **Rev:** Value above sprig within clasped hands, all within world globe design **Note:** 7 coins melted at the mint.

Date	Mintage	F	VF	XF	Unc	BU
1988R	6,000	—	—	—	—	200

KM# 242 2 SCUDI
6.4516 g., 0.9000 Gold 0.1867 oz. AGW **Subject:** French Revolution **Rev:** Dates above fortress

Date	Mintage	F	VF	XF	Unc	BU
1989R	6,500	—	—	—	—	185

KM# 259 2 SCUDI
6.4516 g., 0.9000 Gold 0.1867 oz. AGW **Subject:** San Marino's Presidency of the European Council **Obv:** Crowned shield within wreath **Rev:** World globe

Date	Mintage	F	VF	XF	Unc	BU
1990R	6,800	—	—	—	—	185

KM# 274 2 SCUDI
6.4516 g., 0.9000 Gold 0.1867 oz. AGW **Subject:** Peace **Obv:** Crowned shield within wreath **Rev:** New shoots growing from stump

Date	Mintage	F	VF	XF	Unc	BU
1991R Proof	Est. 6,500	Value: 185				

KM# 289 2 SCUDI
6.4516 g., 0.9000 Gold 0.1867 oz. AGW **Subject:** San Marino's Entry Into the United Nations **Obv:** Crowned shield within wreath **Rev:** UN logo above inscription

Date	Mintage	F	VF	XF	Unc	BU
1992R Proof	7,500	Value: 185				

KM# 304 2 SCUDI
6.4516 g., 0.9000 Gold 0.1867 oz. AGW **Series:** International Monetary Fund **Obv:** Crowned shield within wreath **Rev:** Two stylized figures within globe design **Note:** 106 coins melted at the mint.

Date	Mintage	F	VF	XF	Unc	BU
1993R Proof	6,500	Value: 185				

KM# 320 2 SCUDI
6.4516 g., 0.9000 Gold 0.1867 oz. AGW **Series:** International Year of the Family **Obv:** Crowned shield within wreath **Rev:** Family divides value **Note:** Sets only. 252 coins melted at the mint.

Date	Mintage	F	VF	XF	Unc	BU
1994R Proof	6,500	Value: 185				

KM# 336 2 SCUDI
6.4516 g., 0.9000 Gold 0.1867 oz. AGW **Series:** 50th Anniversary - United Nations **Obv:** Crowned shield within wreath **Rev:** Seated figure with arms outstretched below value within triangular design **Note:** Sets only.

Date	Mintage	F	VF	XF	Unc	BU
1995R Proof	Est. 7,000	Value: 185				

KM# 339 2 SCUDI
6.4516 g., 0.9000 Gold 0.1867 oz. AGW **Series:** 1996 Olympics **Subject:** Track and Field **Obv:** Crowned shield within wreath **Rev:** Three athletes standing left **Note:** 1 coin melted at the mint.

Date	Mintage	F	VF	XF	Unc	BU
1996 Proof	6,000	Value: 185				

KM# 374 2 SCUDI
6.4516 g., 0.9000 Gold 0.1867 oz. AGW **Rev:** Michelangelo's "David" **Note:** 124 coins melted at the mint.

Date	Mintage	F	VF	XF	Unc	BU
1997 Proof	5,800	Value: 185				

KM# 418 2 SCUDI
6.4516 g., 0.9000 Gold 0.1867 oz. AGW, 21 mm. **Subject:** Vergine Delle Rocce **Obv:** Crowned shield within wreath **Rev:** Female Saint facing **Edge:** Reeded **Note:** 334 coins melted at the mint.

Date	Mintage	F	VF	XF	Unc	BU
1998R Proof	5,500	Value: 185				

KM# 415   2 SCUDI
6.4516 g., 0.9000 Gold 0.1867 oz. AGW **Subject:** Sposalizio
Della Vergine **Obv:** Crowned shield within wreath **Rev:** Three
seated figures

Date	Mintage	F	VF	XF	Unc	BU
1999 Proof	8,000	Value: 185				

KM# 409   2 SCUDI
6.4516 g., 0.9000 Gold 0.1867 oz. AGW **Subject:** Madonna
Della Melagrna **Obv:** Crowned shield within wreath
Rev: Madonna and child

Date	Mintage	F	VF	XF	Unc	BU
2000 Proof	6,000	Value: 185				

KM# 62   5 SCUDI
15.0000 g., 0.9170 Gold 0.4422 oz. AGW **Obv:** Value below
smoking towers **Rev:** Head left **Note:** 25 coins melted at mint.

Date	Mintage	F	VF	XF	Unc	BU
1976	8,000	—	—	—	—	625

KM# 75   5 SCUDI
15.0000 g., 0.9170 Gold 0.4422 oz. AGW **Subject:** Democrazia
Obv: Value below smoking towers **Rev:** Stylized head left
Note: 29 coins melted at mint.

Date	Mintage	F	VF	XF	Unc	BU
1977	16,000	—	—	—	—	445

KM# 101   5 SCUDI
15.0000 g., 0.9170 Gold 0.4422 oz. AGW **Subject:** Peace
Obv: Value within upright feathers **Rev:** Stylized hands and arms
Note: 161 coins melted at mint.

Date	Mintage	F	VF	XF	Unc	BU
1979	24,000	—	—	—	—	445

KM# 115   5 SCUDI
15.0000 g., 0.9170 Gold 0.4422 oz. AGW **Subject:** Justice
Obv: Smoking towers **Rev:** Head at upper right of birds
Note: 1,428 coins melted at mint.

Date	Mintage	F	VF	XF	Unc	BU
1980R	24,000	—	—	—	—	445

KM# 130   5 SCUDI
15.0000 g., 0.9170 Gold 0.4422 oz. AGW **Series:** World Food Day
Obv: Crowned shield on sprigs above inscription **Rev:** Seated nude
figure with knees bent upright **Note:** 33 coins melted at mint.

Date	Mintage	F	VF	XF	Unc	BU
1981R	24,000	—	—	—	—	445

KM# 144   5 SCUDI
15.0000 g., 0.9170 Gold 0.4422 oz. AGW **Subject:** Defense of
Liberty **Obv:** Crown above smoking towers flanked by sprig and
design **Rev:** Value above stylized hands **Note:** 19 coins melted
at mint.

Date	Mintage	F	VF	XF	Unc	BU
1982R	15,000	—	—	—	—	445

KM# 158   5 SCUDI
10.0000 g., 0.9170 Gold 0.2948 oz. AGW **Subject:** Perpetual
Liberty **Obv:** Inscription above crowned shield and sprig
Rev: Standing figure and child walking right **Note:** 25 coins
melted at mint.

Date	Mintage	F	VF	XF	Unc	BU
1983R	11,000	—	—	—	—	295

KM# 172   5 SCUDI
10.0000 g., 0.9170 Gold 0.2948 oz. AGW **Subject:** Justice
Obv: Crowned shield in front of castle view **Rev:** Liberty walking
on parapet of castle **Note:** 28 coins melted at mint.

Date	Mintage	F	VF	XF	Unc	BU
1984R	9,000	—	—	—	—	300

KM# 186   5 SCUDI
10.0000 g., 0.9170 Gold 0.2948 oz. AGW **Subject:** Libertas
Obv: Crown above smoking towers on rock flanked by sprigs
Rev: Three nude dancing figures **Note:** 13 coins melted at mint.

Date	Mintage	F	VF	XF	Unc	BU
1985R	7,400	—	—	—	—	400

KM# 200   5 SCUDI
16.9500 g., 0.9170 Gold 0.4997 oz. AGW **Subject:** Work
Obv: Crowned shield above view **Rev:** Bee within honey comb
design divides value **Note:** 14 coins melted at mint.

Date	Mintage	F	VF	XF	Unc	BU
1986R	7,000	—	—	—	—	485

KM# 215   5 SCUDI
16.9500 g., 0.9170 Gold 0.4997 oz. AGW **Subject:** United
Nations **Obv:** Crowned shield within wreath **Rev:** Value to left of
building and tower **Note:** 49 coins melted at mint.

Date	Mintage	F	VF	XF	Unc	BU
1987R	6,000	—	—	—	—	485

KM# 230   5 SCUDI
16.9500 g., 0.9170 Gold 0.4997 oz. AGW **Subject:** Human
Rights **Obv:** Crowned shield within wreath **Rev:** Stylized flame
within wreath, value at upper left **Note:** 11 coins melted at mint.

Date	Mintage	F	VF	XF	Unc	BU
1988R	5,000	—	—	—	—	485

KM# 245   5 SCUDI
16.9500 g., 0.9170 Gold 0.4997 oz. AGW **Subject:** Entrance of
San Marino in Common Market

Date	Mintage	F	VF	XF	Unc	BU
1989R	6,000	—	—	—	—	485

KM# 260   5 SCUDI
16.9500 g., 0.9170 Gold 0.4997 oz. AGW **Subject:** Founding
of the Republic **Obv:** Doves in front of smoking towers **Rev:** Three
kneeling figures to right of standing figure

Date	Mintage	F	VF	XF	Unc	BU
1990R Proof	6,500	Value: 485				

KM# 275   5 SCUDI
16.9500 g., 0.9170 Gold 0.4997 oz. AGW **Subject:** Peace and
Freedom **Obv:** Crowned shield within wreath **Rev:** Tree divides
family

Date	Mintage	F	VF	XF	Unc	BU
1991R Proof	7,000	Value: 485				

KM# 290 5 SCUDI
16.9500 g., 0.9170 Gold 0.4997 oz. AGW **Subject:** Customer Agreement with European Economic Community **Obv:** Crowned shield within wreath **Rev:** Value and oat sprig within center of circle of stars

Date	Mintage	F	VF	XF	Unc	BU
1992R Proof	Est. 6,500	Value: 485				

KM# 305 5 SCUDI
16.9500 g., 0.9170 Gold 0.4997 oz. AGW **Series:** International Monetary Fund **Obv:** Crowned shield within wreath **Rev:** Stylized figure holding scale above shield **Note:** 68 coins melted at the mint.

Date	Mintage	F	VF	XF	Unc	BU
1993R Proof	5,500	Value: 485				

KM# 321 5 SCUDI
16.9500 g., 0.9170 Gold 0.4997 oz. AGW **Series:** International Year of the Family **Obv:** Crowned shield within wreath **Rev:** Family divides value **Note:** 207 coins melted at the mint.

Date	Mintage	F	VF	XF	Unc	BU
1994R Proof	5,500	Value: 485				

KM# 337 5 SCUDI
16.9500 g., 0.9170 Gold 0.4997 oz. AGW **Series:** 50th Anniversary - United Nations **Obv:** Crowned shield within wreath **Rev:** Seated nude figure and squirrel flanked by dates above value **Note:** 65 coins melted at the mint.

Date	Mintage	F	VF	XF	Unc	BU
1995R Proof	5,000	Value: 485				

KM# 343 5 SCUDI
16.9500 g., 0.9170 Gold 0.4997 oz. AGW **Obv:** Crowned shield within wreath **Rev:** The Pieta, Mary receives Jesus' body **Note:** 19 coins melted at the mint.

Date	Mintage	F	VF	XF	Unc	BU
1996 Proof	5,840	Value: 485				

KM# 375 5 SCUDI
16.9500 g., 0.9170 Gold 0.4997 oz. AGW **Subject:** The Annunciation **Obv:** Crowned shield within wreath **Rev:** Angel **Note:** 469 coins melted at the mint.

Date	Mintage	F	VF	XF	Unc	BU
1997 Proof	5,500	Value: 485				

KM# 412 5 SCUDI
16.9590 g., 0.9170 Gold 0.5000 oz. AGW **Subject:** Madonna Della Seggiola **Obv:** Crowned shield within wreath **Rev:** Woman with 2 children **Note:** 1,151 coins melted at the mint.

Date	Mintage	F	VF	XF	Unc	BU
1998R Proof	5,000	Value: 485				

KM# 388 5 SCUDI
16.9590 g., 0.9170 Gold 0.5000 oz. AGW **Subject:** Birth of Venus **Obv:** Crowned shield within wreath **Rev:** Venus standing in shell

Date	Mintage	F	VF	XF	Unc	BU
1999R Proof	Est. 5,500	Value: 485				

KM# 420 5 SCUDI
16.9590 g., 0.9170 Gold 0.5000 oz. AGW **Subject:** Tiziano's painting "Rape of Europa" **Obv:** Crowned shield within wreath **Rev:** Europa on a bull's (Zeus) back

Date	Mintage	F	VF	XF	Unc	BU
2000R Proof	4,500	—	—	—	—	485

KM# 88 10 SCUDI
30.0000 g., 0.9170 Gold 0.8844 oz. AGW **Obv:** Smoking towers within circle **Rev:** Head left **Note:** 54 coins melted at the mint.

Date	Mintage	F	VF	XF	Unc	BU
1978 Proof	20,000	Value: 875				

PROVAS

KM#	Date	Mintage	Identification	Mkt Val
Pr1	1925R	75	20 Lire. Gold. KM8.	3,300
Pr2	1931R	—	5 Lire. Silver. KM9.	265
Pr3	1931R	—	10 Lire. Silver. KM10.	225
Pr4	1931R	—	20 Lire. Silver. KM11.	525
Pr5	1932R	—	5 Lire. Silver. KM9.	900
Pr6	1932R	—	10 Lire. Silver. KM10.	525
Pr7	1933	—	5 Lire. Silver. KM9.	175
Pr8	1933	—	10 Lire. Silver. KM10.	185
Pr9	1933	—	20 Lire. Silver. KM11.	200
Pr10	1935R	—	5 Lire. Silver. KM9.	525
Pr11	1935R	—	20 Lire. Silver. KM11.	575
PrA12	1936R	—	5 Lire. Silver. KM#9.	—
Pr12	1937R	—	10 Lire. Silver. KM10.	400
Pr13	1938R	—	10 Lire. 0.8350 Silver. 10.0000 g. 27 mm. Crowned arms. Allegorical woman. Lettered edge.	—

MINT SETS

KM#	Date	Mintage	Identification	Issue Price	Mkt Val
MS1	1972 (8)	—	KM14-21	5.00	12.50
MS2	1973 (8)	—	KM22-29	6.00	12.50
MS3	1974 (8)	60,000	KM30-37	9.00	15.00
MS4	1974 (2)	60,000	KM38-39	—	185
MS5	1975 (8)	—	KM40-47	6.50	15.00
MS6	1975 (5)	—	KM40-44	—	—
MS7	1975 (2)	90,000	KM49-50	—	185
MS8	1976 (8)	—	KM51-58	6.00	12.50
MS9	1976 (2)	40,000	KM60-61	—	185
MS10	1977 (9)	—	KM63-71	—	15.00
MS11	1977 (2)	30,000	KM73-74	—	185
MS12	1978 (9)	—	KM76-84	—	15.00
MS13	1978 (2)	—	KM86-87	—	160
MS14	1979 (9)	—	KM89-98	—	15.00
MS15	1979 (2)	—	KM99-100	—	160
MS16	1980 (9)	—	KM102-110	—	15.00
MS17	1980 (2)	—	KM113-114	—	160
MS18	1981 (9)	—	KM116-123, 126	—	15.00
MS19	1981 (3)	—	KM124-125, 127	—	—
MS20	1981 (2)	—	KM128-129	—	160
MS21	1982 (9)	—	KM131-138, 140	6.00	8.50
MS22	1982 (2)	—	KM139, 141	—	27.50
MS23	1982 (2)	—	KM142-143	—	170
MS24	1983 (2)	—	KM145-153	5.50	8.50
MS25	1983 (2)	—	KM154-155	—	27.50
MS26	1983 (2)	—	KM156-157	—	175
MS27	1984 (9)	—	KM159-167	—	—
MS28	1984 (9)	—	KM168-169	—	22.00
MS29	1984 (2)	—	KM170-171	—	175
MS30	1985 (9)	—	KM173-181	—	8.50
MS31	1985 (2)	—	KM182-183	—	22.00
MS32	1985 (2)	—	KM184-185	—	200
MS33	1986 (2)	—	KM187-195	7.00	8.50
MS34	1986 (2)	—	KM196-197	—	30.00
MS35	1986 (2)	—	KM198-199	—	190
MS36	1987 (10)	43,000	KM201-210	—	25.00
MS37	1987 (2)	—	KM213-214	—	30.00
MS38	1987 (2)	—	KM211-212	—	190
MS39	1988 (10)	80,000	KM218-227	22.00	26.00
MS40	1988 (2)	—	KM216-217	—	30.00
MS41	1988 (2)	—	KM228-229	—	190
MS42	1989 (10)	32,000	KM231-240	—	28.00
MS43	1989 (2)	30,000	KM243-244	—	30.00
MS44	1989 (2)	6,500	KM241-242	—	170
MS45	1990 (2)	36,000	KM248-257	—	35.00
MS46	1990 (2)	40,000	KM246-247	—	175
MS47	1990 (2)	6,800	KM258-259	—	175
MS48	1991 (2)	36,000	KM261-270	—	32.00
MS49	1991 (2)	25,000	KM271-272	—	32.00
MS50	1992 (10)	45,000	KM278-287	—	32.00
MS51	1992 (2)	—	KM276-277	34.00	40.00
MS52	1993 (10)	—	KM293-302	18.00	28.00
MS53	1993 (2)	35,000	KM291-292	26.00	30.00
MS54	1994 (2)	40,000	KM307-315	18.00	30.00
MS55	1995 (10)	—	KM322-331	—	30.00
MS56	1996 (2)	32,000	KM344, 349-357	18.00	30.00
MS57	1997 (10)	28,000	KM358-367	18.00	30.00
MS58	1998 (8)	—	KM378-385	18.00	25.00
MS59	1999 (8)	—	KM389-396	18.00	25.00
MS60	2000 (8)	28,000	KM399-406	18.00	25.00

PROOF SETS

KM#	Date	Mintage	Identification	Issue Price	Mkt Val
PS1	1989 (2)	8,000	KM243-244	55.00	60.00
PS2	1990 (2)	18,800	KM246-247	55.00	60.00
PS3	1991 (2)	8,000	KM271-272	55.00	60.00
PS4	1991 (2)	6,800	KM273-274	—	175
PS5	1993 (2)	—	KM303-304	158	160
PS6	1994 (2)	7,500	KM319-320	—	200
PS7	1995 (2)	—	KM333-334	31.00	45.00
PS8	1995 (2)	7,000	KM335-336	161	175
PS9	1996 (2)	—	KM340-341	35.00	45.00
PS10	1997 (2)	—	KM370-371	35.00	45.00
PSA11	1998 (2)	—	KM#386-387	—	—
PS11	1999 (2)	—	KM410-411	—	60.00
PS12	1999 (3)	8,000	KM413-415	179	180
PS13	2000 (3)	6,000	KM407-409	179	180

SARAWAK

Sarawak is a former British protectorate located on the north-west coast of Borneo. The Japanese occupation during World War II so thoroughly devastated the economy that Rajah Sir Charles V. Brooke ceded it to Great Britain on July 1, 1946. In September, 1963 the colony joined the Federation of Malaysia. The capital is Kuching.

RULERS
Charles J. Brooke, Rajah, 1868-1917
Charles V. Brooke, Rajah, 1917-1946

MINT MARKS
H - Heaton, Birmingham

MONETARY SYSTEM
100 Cents = 1 Dollar

BRITISH PROTECTORATE

STANDARD COINAGE
100 Cents = 1 Dollar

KM# 20 1/2 CENT
Bronze 0 **Ruler:** Charles V. Brooke Rajah **Obv:** Head right **Rev:** Value within wreath

Date	Mintage	F	VF	XF	Unc	BU
1933H	2,000,000	6.00	10.00	25.00	35.00	—
1933H Proof	—	Value: 400				

KM# 12 CENT
Copper-Nickel **Ruler:** Charles V. Brooke Rajah **Obv:** Head right **Rev:** Value within wreath

Date	Mintage	F	VF	XF	Unc	BU
1920H	5,000,000	6.00	10.00	25.00	40.00	80.00

KM# 18 CENT
Bronze **Ruler:** Charles V. Brooke Rajah **Obv:** Head right **Rev:** Value within wreath

Date	Mintage	F	VF	XF	Unc	BU
1927H	5,000,000	1.25	3.00	8.00	18.00	—
1929H	2,000,000	1.25	3.00	8.00	18.00	—
1930H	3,000,000	1.25	3.00	8.00	18.00	—
1937H	3,000,000	1.25	3.00	8.00	18.00	—
1937H Proof	—	Value: 400				
1941H	3,000,000	400	800	1,200	1,800	—

Note: Estimate 50 pieces exist

KM# 8 5 CENTS
1.3500 g., 0.8000 Silver 0.0347 oz. ASW **Ruler:** Charles J. Brooke Rajah **Obv:** Head left **Obv. Leg.:** C. BROOKE RAJAH **Rev:** Value within roped wreath

Date	Mintage	F	VF	XF	Unc	BU
1908H	40,000	60.00	150	250	400	—
1908H Proof	—	Value: 700				
1911H	40,000	60.00	150	250	400	—
1913H	100,000	60.00	110	220	330	—
1913H Proof	—	Value: 700				
1915H	100,000	60.00	110	220	330	—
1915H Proof	—	Value: 700				

KM# 13 5 CENTS
1.3500 g., 0.4000 Silver 0.0174 oz. ASW **Ruler:** Charles V. Brooke Rajah **Obv:** Head right **Rev:** Value within roped wreath

Date	Mintage	F	VF	XF	Unc	BU
1920H	100,000	80.00	160	250	450	—
1920H Proof	—	Value: 700				

KM# 14 5 CENTS
Copper-Nickel **Ruler:** Charles V. Brooke Rajah **Obv:** Head right **Rev:** Value within wreath

Date	Mintage	F	VF	XF	Unc	BU
1920H	400,000	2.00	4.00	10.00	25.00	—
1927H	600,000	2.00	4.00	10.00	22.00	—
1927H Proof	—	Value: 450				

KM# 9 10 CENTS
2.7100 g., 0.8000 Silver 0.0697 oz. ASW **Ruler:** Charles J. Brooke Rajah **Obv:** Head left **Obv. Leg.:** C. BROOKE RAJAH **Rev:** Value within roped wreath

Date	Mintage	F	VF	XF	Unc	BU
1906H	50,000	50.00	60.00	120	280	—
1906H Proof	—	Value: 700				
1910H	50,000	50.00	60.00	120	280	—
1910H Proof	—	Value: 700				
1911H Proof	—	Value: 700				
1911H	100,000	35.00	55.00	100	250	—
1913H	100,000	35.00	55.00	100	250	—
1913H Proof	—	Value: 700				
1915H	100,000	80.00	150	220	450	—
1915H Proof	—	Value: 700				

KM# 15 10 CENTS
2.7100 g., 0.4000 Silver 0.0348 oz. ASW **Ruler:** Charles V. Brooke Rajah **Obv:** Head right **Rev:** Value within roped wreath

Date	Mintage	F	VF	XF	Unc	BU
1920H	150,000	40.00	80.00	150	220	—
1920H Proof	—	Value: 650				

KM# 16 10 CENTS
Copper-Nickel **Ruler:** Charles V. Brooke Rajah **Obv:** Head right **Rev:** Value within wreath

Date	Mintage	F	VF	XF	Unc	BU
1920H	800,000	2.00	4.00	10.00	25.00	—
1927H	1,000,000	2.00	3.00	9.00	25.00	—
1927H Proof	—	Value: 450				
1934H	2,000,000	2.00	3.00	9.00	25.00	—
1934H Proof	—	Value: 450				

KM# 10 20 CENTS
5.4300 g., 0.8000 Silver 0.1397 oz. ASW **Ruler:** Charles J. Brooke Rajah **Obv:** Head left **Obv. Leg.:** C. BROOKE RAJAH **Rev:** Value within roped wreath

Date	Mintage	F	VF	XF	Unc	BU
1906H	25,000	70.00	150	350	650	—
1906H Proof	—	Value: 1,100				
1910H	25,000	70.00	150	350	650	—
1910H Proof	—	Value: 1,100				
1911H	15,000	70.00	150	350	650	—
1913H	25,000	70.00	150	350	650	—
1913H Proof	—	Value: 1,100				
1915H	25,000	350	500	800	1,200	—
1915H Proof	—	Value: 1,800				

KM# 17 20 CENTS
5.4300 g., 0.4000 Silver 0.0698 oz. ASW **Ruler:** Charles V. Brooke Rajah **Obv:** Head right **Rev:** Value within roped wreath

Date	Mintage	F	VF	XF	Unc	BU
1920H	25,000	160	300	500	800	—
1920H Proof	—	Value: 1,300				

KM# 17a 20 CENTS
5.0800 g., 0.4000 Silver 0.0653 oz. ASW **Ruler:** Charles V. Brooke Rajah **Obv:** Head right **Rev:** Value within roped wreath

Date	Mintage	F	VF	XF	Unc	BU
1927H	250,000	20.00	40.00	100	200	—
1927H Proof	—	Value: 750				

KM# 11 50 CENTS
13.5700 g., 0.8000 Silver 0.3490 oz. ASW **Ruler:** Charles V. Brooke Rajah **Obv:** Head left **Obv. Leg.:** C. BROOKE RAJAH **Rev:** Value within roped wreath

Date	Mintage	F	VF	XF	Unc	BU
1906H	10,000	600	800	1,300	2,200	—
1906H Proof	—	Value: 3,300				

KM# 19 50 CENTS
10.3000 g., 0.5000 Silver 0.1656 oz. ASW **Ruler:** Charles V. Brooke Rajah **Obv:** Head right **Rev:** Value within roped wreath

Date	Mintage	F	VF	XF	Unc	BU
1927H	200,000	40.00	80.00	200	280	—
1927H Proof	—	Value: 750				

SAUDI ARABIA

The Kingdom of Saudi Arabia, an independent and absolute hereditary monarchy comprising the former sultanate of Nejd, the old kingdom of Hejaz, Asir and Al Hasa, occupies four-fifths of the Arabian peninsula. The kingdom has an area of 830,000 sq. mi. (2,149,690 sq. km.) and a population of *16.1 million. Capital: Riyadh. The economy is based on oil, which provides 85 percent of Saudi Arabia's revenue.

Mohammed united the Arabs in the 7th century and his followers founded a great empire with its capital at Medina. The Turks established nominal rule over much of Arabia in the 16th and 17th centuries, and in the 18th century divided it into principalities.

The Kingdom of Saudi Arabia was created by King Abd Al-Aziz Bin Saud (1882-1953), a descendant of earlier Wahhabi rulers of the Arabian peninsula. In 1901 he seized Riyadh, capital of the Sultanate of Nejd, and in 1905 established himself as Sultan. In 1913 he captured the Turkish province of Al Hasa; took the Hejaz in 1925 and by 1926 most of Asir. In 1932 he combined Nejd and Hejaz into the single kingdom of Saudi Arabia. Asir was incorporated into the kingdom a year later.

TITLES

العربية السعودية

Al-Arabiya(t) as-Sa'udiya(t)

المملكة العربية السعودية

Al-Mamlaka(t) al-'Arabiya(t) as-Sa'udiya(t)

RULERS
al Sa'ud Dynasty
Abd Al-Aziz Bin Sa'ud, (Ibn Sa'ud), AH1344-1373/1926-1953AD
Sa'ud Bin Abd Al-Aziz, AH1373-1383/1953-1964AD
Faisal Bin Abd Al-Aziz, AH1383-1395/1964-1975AD
Khalid Bin Abd Al-Aziz, AH1395-1403/1975-1982AD
Fahad Bin Abd Al-Aziz, AH1403-/1982AD

MONETARY SYSTEM
Until 1960
20-22 Ghirsh = 1 Riyal
40 Riyals = 1 Guinea
NOTE: Copper-nickel, reeded-edge coins dated AH1356 and silver coins dated AH1354 were struck at the U. S. Mint in Philadelphia between 1944-1949.

HEJAZ & NEJD

Mecca, the metropolis of Islam and the capital of Hejaz, is located inland from the Red Sea due east of the port of Jidda. A center of non-political commercial, cultural and religious activities, Mecca remained virtually independent until 1259. Two centuries of Egyptian rule were followed by four centuries of Turkish rule which lasted until the Arab revolts which extinguished pretensions to sovereignty over any part of the Arabian peninsula.

MINT NAME
Makkah, Mecca

RULERS
Sharifs of Mecca
Ghalib b. Ma'sud, AH1219-1229
Yahya b. Surer, AH1230-1240
Abdul Muttalib and Ibn Awn,
  AH1240-1248

KINGDOM AND SULTANATE
Abd Al-Aziz bin Sa'ud as King of Hejaz and Sultan of Nejd
TRANSITIONAL COINAGE

Struck at the Mecca Mint during the occupation by Abd Al-Aziz Bin Sa'ud while establishing his kingdom.

KM# 1   1/4 GHIRSH
Copper Or Bronze   **Obv:** Toughra **Rev:** Inscription

Date	Mintage	Good	VG	F	VF	XF
AH1343	—	—	60.00	125	175	325

Note: Several varieties exist, including reeded and plain edges; Some specimens struck over bronze Hejaz 1/4 and 1/2 Piastres (KM#23 and KM#26), and some occur with a light silver wash

KM# 2.1   1/2 GHIRSH
Copper Or Bronze   **Obv:** Toughra **Obv. Insc.:** Al-Faisal al Saud **Rev:** Inscription

Date	Mintage	Good	VG	F	VF	XF
AH1343	—	—	20.00	40.00	60.00	125

KM# 2.2   1/2 GHIRSH
Copper Or Bronze   **Obv:** Toughra **Obv. Insc.:** Al-Faisal **Rev:** Inscription

Date	Mintage	Good	VG	F	VF	XF
AH1343	—	—	75.00	150	300	500

KM# A3   1/2 GHIRSH
Bronze

Date	Mintage	Good	VG	F	VF	XF
AH1344//2	—	—	15.00	30.00	50.00	100

REGULAR COINAGE

KM# 4   1/4 GHIRSH
Copper-Nickel   **Obv:** Legend **Rev:** Value and date below legend

Date	Mintage	Good	VG	F	VF	XF
AH1344	—	—	4.00	8.00	12.00	40.00
AH1344 Proof	—	Value: 750				

KM# 5   1/2 GHIRSH
Copper-Nickel   **Obv:** Legend **Rev:** Value and date below legend

Date	Mintage	Good	VG	F	VF	XF
AH1344	—	—	8.00	15.00	30.00	75.00
AH1344 Proof	—	Value: 750				

KM# 6   GHIRSH
Copper-Nickel   **Obv:** Legend **Rev:** Value and date below legend

Date	Mintage	Good	VG	F	VF	XF
AH1344	—	—	6.00	12.00	25.00	60.00
AH1344 Proof	—	Value: 750				

HEJAZ & NEJD SULTANATE
KINGDOM
REGULAR COINAGE

KM# 7   1/4 GHIRSH
Copper-Nickel   **Obv:** Legend **Rev:** Value and date below legend

Date	Mintage	VG	F	VF	XF	Unc
AH1346	3,000,000	6.00	10.00	15.00	40.00	

KM# 13   1/4 GHIRSH
Copper-Nickel   **Obv:** Legend **Rev:** Value and date below legend

Date	Mintage	VG	F	VF	XF	Unc
AH1348	—	12.00	20.00	40.00	75.00	
AH1348 Proof	1,000					

KM# 8   1/2 GHIRSH
Copper-Nickel

Date	Mintage	VG	F	VF	XF	Unc
AH1346	3,000,000	10.00	15.00	25.00	60.00	

KM# 14   1/2 GHIRSH
Copper-Nickel   **Obv:** Legend **Rev:** Value and date below legend

Date	Mintage	VG	F	VF	XF	Unc
AH1348	—	12.00	25.00	40.00	100	
AH1348 Proof	1,000					

KM# 9   GHIRSH
Copper-Nickel   **Obv:** Legend **Rev:** Value and date below legend

Date	Mintage	VG	F	VF	XF	Unc
AH1346	3,000,000	3.00	5.00	10.00	35.00	

KM# 15   GHIRSH
Copper-Nickel   **Obv:** Legend **Rev:** Value and date below inscription

Date	Mintage	VG	F	VF	XF	Unc
AH1348	—	12.00	20.00	30.00	75.00	
AH1348 Proof	1,000					

KM# 10   1/4 RIYAL
6.0500 g., 0.9170 Silver 0.1784 oz. ASW, 24 mm. **Obv:** Inscription within beaded circle, legend above, crossed swords below within design flanked by palms trees **Rev:** Inscription within beaded circle, legend above, value below within design flanked by palm trees

Date	Mintage	VG	F	VF	XF	Unc
AH1346	400,000	40.00	60.00	100	200	—
AH1346 Proof	—	Value: 750				
AH1348	200,000	60.00	90.00	150	350	*
AH1348 Proof	1,500	—	—	—	—	*

KM# 11 1/2 RIYAL
12.1000 g., 0.9170 Silver 0.3567 oz. ASW, 27 mm.
Obv: Inscription within beaded circle, legend above, crossed swords below within design flanked by palm trees **Rev:** Inscription within beaded circle, legend above, value below within design flanked by palm trees and swords

Date	Mintage	VG	F	VF	XF	Unc
AH1346	200,000	100	175	250	500	—
AH1346 Proof	—	Value: 1,250				
AH1348	100,000	125	200	350	750	—
AH1348 Proof	2,000	—	—	—	—	—

KM# 12 RIYAL
24.1000 g., 0.9170 Silver 0.7105 oz. ASW, 37 mm. **Obv:** Inscription within beaded circle, legend above, crossed swords below within design flanked by palm trees **Rev:** Inscription within beaded circle, legend above, value below within design flanked by palm trees

Date	Mintage	VG	F	VF	XF	Unc
AH1346	800,000	40.00	60.00	90.00	150	—
AH1346 Proof	—	Value: 1,500				
AH1348	400,000	50.00	75.00	150	250	—
AH1348 Proof	2,000	—	—	—	—	—

UNITED KINGDOMS
KINGDOM
STANDARD COINAGE

KM# 19.1 1/4 GHIRSH
Copper-Nickel **Obv:** Legend **Rev:** Value and date below legend **Edge:** Plain

Date	Mintage	VG	F	VF	XF	Unc
AH1356 (1937)	1,000,000	2.00	5.00	10.00	35.00	—

KM# 19.2 1/4 GHIRSH
Copper-Nickel **Obv:** Legend **Rev:** Value and date below legend **Edge:** Reeded

Date	Mintage	VG	F	VF	XF	Unc
AH1356 (1937)	21,500,000	0.25	0.50	1.00	2.50	7.50

Note: Struck in 1947 (AH1366-67) at Philadelphia

KM# 20.1 1/2 GHIRSH
Copper-Nickel **Obv:** Legend **Rev:** Value and date below legend **Edge:** Plain

Date	Mintage	VG	F	VF	XF	Unc
AH1356 (1937)	1,000,000	3.00	8.00	20.00	45.00	—

KM# 20.2 1/2 GHIRSH
Copper-Nickel **Obv:** Legend **Rev:** Value and date below legend **Edge:** Reeded

Date	Mintage	VG	F	VF	XF	Unc
AH1356 (1937)	10,850,000	0.20	0.50	1.50	3.00	10.00

Note: Struck in 1947 (AH1366-67) at Philadelphia

KM# 21.1 GHIRSH
Copper-Nickel **Obv:** Legend **Rev:** Value and date below legend **Edge:** Plain

Date	Mintage	VG	F	VF	XF	Unc
AH1356 (1937)	4,000,000	3.00	8.00	15.00	40.00	—

KM# 21.2 GHIRSH
Copper-Nickel **Obv:** Legend **Rev:** Value and date below legend **Edge:** Reeded

Date	Mintage	VG	F	VF	XF	Unc
AH1356 (1937)	7,150,000	0.50	1.00	2.50	5.00	12.50

Note: Struck in 1947 (AH1366-67) at Philadelphia

KM# 40 GHIRSH
3.0000 g., Copper-Nickel, 22 mm. **Obv:** Palm above crossed swords at center of legend **Rev:** Value and date below legend **Edge:** Reeded

Date	Mintage	F	VF	XF	Unc	BU
AH1376 (1957)	10,000,000	0.15	0.25	0.50	3.00	—
AH1378 (1958)	50,000,000	0.15	0.25	0.50	2.00	—

KM# 41 2 GHIRSH
Copper-Nickel, 27 mm. **Obv:** Crossed swords below palm at center of legend **Rev:** Value and date below legend **Edge:** Reeded

Date	Mintage	F	VF	XF	Unc	BU
AH1376 (1957)	50,000,000	0.10	0.35	0.75	5.00	—
AH1379 (1959)	28,110,000	0.10	0.35	0.70	3.50	—

KM# 42 4 GHIRSH
Copper-Nickel, 30 mm. **Obv:** Crossed swords below palm at center of legend **Rev:** Value and date below legend **Edge:** Reeded

Date	Mintage	F	VF	XF	Unc	BU
AH1376 (1956)	49,100,000	0.25	0.50	1.00	6.00	—
AH1378 (1958)	10,000,000	0.25	0.50	1.00	5.00	—

KM# 16 1/4 RIYAL
3.1000 g., 0.9170 Silver 0.0914 oz. ASW. **Obv:** Inscription within beaded circle, legend above, crossed swords below within design flanked by palm trees **Rev:** Inscription within beaded circle, legend above, value below within design flanked by palm trees

Date	Mintage	F	VF	XF	Unc	BU
AH1354 (1935)	900,000	1.75	2.50	3.00	5.50	—
AH1354 (1935) Proof	—	Value: 250				

KM# 37 1/4 RIYAL
2.9500 g., 0.9170 Silver 0.0870 oz. ASW **Obv:** Inscription within beaded circle, legend above, crossed swords below within design flanked by palm trees **Rev:** Inscription within beaded circle, legend above, value below within design flanked by palm trees

Date	Mintage	F	VF	XF	Unc	BU
AH1374 (1954)	4,000,000	BV	1.50	3.00	5.50	—

KM# 17 1/2 RIYAL
5.8500 g., 0.9170 Silver 0.1725 oz. ASW **Obv:** Inscription within beaded circle, legend above, crossed swords below within design flanked by palm trees **Rev:** Inscription within beaded circle, legend above, value below within design flanked by palm trees

Date	Mintage	F	VF	XF	Unc	BU
AH1354 (1935)	950,000	BV	3.00	8.00	20.00	—
AH1354 (1935) Proof	—	Value: 250				

KM# 38 1/2 RIYAL
5.9500 g., 0.9170 Silver 0.1754 oz. ASW **Obv:** Inscription within beaded circle, legend above, crossed swords below within design flanked by palm trees **Rev:** Inscription within beaded circle, legend above, value below within design flanked by palm trees

Date	Mintage	F	VF	XF	Unc	BU
AH1374 (1954)	2,000,000	BV	3.00	4.50	15.00	—

KM# 18 RIYAL
11.6000 g., 0.9170 Silver 0.3420 oz. ASW **Obv:** Inscription within beaded circle, legend above, crossed swords below within design flanked by palm trees **Rev:** Inscription within beaded circle, legend above, value below within design flanked by palm trees

Date	Mintage	F	VF	XF	Unc	BU
AH1354 (1935)	60,000,000	BV	5.50	6.50	12.50	—
AH1354 (1935) Proof	20,000,000	Value: 300				
AH1367 (1947)	Inc. above	BV	5.50	6.50	15.00	—
AH1370 (1950)		BV	5.50	6.50	17.50	—

KM# 39 RIYAL
11.6000 g., 0.9170 Silver 0.3420 oz. ASW **Obv:** Inscription within beaded circle, legend above, crossed swords below within design flanked by palm trees **Rev:** Inscription within beaded circle, legend above, value below within design flanked by palm trees

Date	Mintage	F	VF	XF	Unc	BU
AH1374 (1954)	48,000,000	BV	5.75	7.00	17.50	—

COUNTERMARKED COINAGE

70 = 65 Countermark

The following pieces are countermarked examples of earlier types bearing the Arabic numerals 65. They were countermarked in a move to break money changers' monopoly on small coins in AH1365 (1946AD). These countermarks vary in size and are found with the Arabic numbers raised in a circle. Incuse countermarks are considered a recent fabrication.

KM# 22   1/4 GHIRSH

Countermark: "65" **Note:** Countermark in Arabic numerals on 1/4 Ghirsh, KM#4.

CM Date	Host Date	Good	VG	F	VF	XF
AH1365	AH1344	6.00	12.00	30.00	65.00	—

KM# 23   1/4 GHIRSH

Countermark: "65" **Obv:** Countermark at center of legend **Rev:** Value and date below legend **Note:** Countermark in Arabic numerals on 1/4 Ghirsh, KM#7.

CM Date	Host Date	Good	VG	F	VF	XF
AH1365	AH1346	6.00	12.00	30.00	65.00	—

KM# 24   1/4 GHIRSH

Countermark: "65" **Note:** Countermark in Arabic numerals on 1/4 Ghirsh, KM#13.

CM Date	Host Date	Good	VG	F	VF	XF
AH1365	AH1348	20.00	30.00	50.00	100	—

KM# 25   1/4 GHIRSH

Countermark: "65" **Obv:** Countermark at center of legend **Rev:** Value and date below legend **Edge:** Plain **Note:** Countermark in Arabic numerals on 1/4 Ghirsh, KM#19.

CM Date	Host Date	Good	VG	F	VF	XF
AH1365	AH1356	2.50	5.00	15.00	30.00	—

KM# 26   1/2 GHIRSH

Countermark: "65" **Obv:** Countermark at center of legend **Rev:** Date below legend **Note:** Countermark in Arabic numerals on 1/2 Ghirsh, KM#5.

CM Date	Host Date	Good	VG	F	VF	XF
AH1365	AH1344	6.00	12.00	25.00	60.00	—

KM# 27   1/2 GHIRSH

Countermark: "65" **Obv:** Countermark at center of legend **Rev:** Date below legend **Note:** Countermark in Arabic numerals on 1/2 Ghirsh, KM#8.

CM Date	Host Date	Good	VG	F	VF	XF
AH1365	AH1346	6.00	12.00	25.00	60.00	—

KM# 28   1/2 GHIRSH

Countermark: "65" **Note:** Countermark in Arabic numerals on 1/2 Ghirsh, KM#14.

CM Date	Host Date	Good	VG	F	VF	XF
AH1365	AH1348	6.00	12.00	25.00	60.00	—

KM# 29   1/2 GHIRSH

Copper-Nickel **Countermark:** "65" **Obv:** Countermark at center of legend **Rev:** Date below legend **Edge:** Plain **Note:** Countermark in Arabic numerals on 1/2 Ghirsh, KM#20.1.

CM Date	Host Date	Good	VG	F	VF	XF
AH1365	AH1356	5.00	10.00	25.00	40.00	—

KM# 30   GHIRSH

Countermark: "65" **Obv:** Countermark at center of legend **Rev:** Value and date below legend **Note:** Countermark in Arabic numerals on 1 Ghirsh, KM#6.

CM Date	Host Date	Good	VG	F	VF	XF
AH1365	AH1344	6.00	12.00	35.00	65.00	—

KM# 31   GHIRSH

Countermark: "65" **Note:** Countermark in Arabic numerals on 1 Ghirsh, KM#9.

CM Date	Host Date	Good	VG	F	VF	XF
AH1365	AH1346	6.00	12.00	30.00	65.00	—

KM# 32   GHIRSH

Countermark: "65" **Obv:** Countermark at center of legend **Rev:** Value and date below legend **Note:** Countermark in Arabic numerals on 1 Ghirsh, KM#15.

CM Date	Host Date	Good	VG	F	VF	XF
AH1365	AH1348	10.00	20.00	35.00	65.00	—

KM# 33   GHIRSH

Copper-Nickel **Countermark:** "65" **Edge:** Plain **Note:** Countermark in Arabic numerals on 1 Ghirsh, KM#21.

CM Date	Host Date	Good	VG	F	VF	XF
AH1365	AH1356	6.00	10.00	20.00	30.00	—

REFORM COINAGE

5 Halala = 1 Ghirsh; 100 Halala = 1 Riyal

KM# 44   HALALA

Bronze **Obv:** Crossed swords and palm tree at center, legend above and below **Rev:** Value and date below legend

Date	Mintage	F	VF	XF	Unc	BU
AH1383 (1963)	5,000,000	0.50	0.60	0.85	3.00	—

KM# 60   HALALA

Bronze **Obv:** Different legend **Rev:** Value and date below legend

Date	Mintage	F	VF	XF	Unc	BU
AH1397 (1979)	—	—	—	—	—	175

Note: Not released for circulation

KM# 45   5 HALALA (Ghirsh)

2.5000 g., Copper-Nickel, 19.5 mm. **Obv:** Crossed swords and palm tree at center, legend above and below **Rev:** Legend above inscription in circle dividing value, date below

Date	Mintage	F	VF	XF	Unc	BU
AH1392 (1972)	130,000,000	0.10	0.15	0.30	0.50	—

KM# 53   5 HALALA (Ghirsh)

2.5000 g., Copper-Nickel, 19.5 mm. **Obv:** Crossed swords and palm tree at center, legend above and below **Rev:** Legend above inscription in circle dividing value, date below **Edge:** Reeded

Date	Mintage	F	VF	XF	Unc	BU
AH1397 (1976)	20,000,000	0.15	0.25	0.60	2.00	—
AH1400 (1979)	—	0.15	0.25	0.60	2.00	—

KM# 57   5 HALALA (Ghirsh)

2.5000 g., Copper-Nickel, 19.5 mm. **Series:** F.A.O. **Obv:** Crossed swords and palm tree at center, legend above and below **Rev:** Legend above inscription in circle dividing value, date below

Date	Mintage	F	VF	XF	Unc	BU
AH1398-1978	1,500,000	—	0.30	0.50	1.00	—

KM# 61   5 HALALA (Ghirsh)

2.5000 g., Copper-Nickel, 19.5 mm. **Obv:** National emblem at center, legend above and below **Rev:** Legend above inscription in circle dividing value, date below

Date	Mintage	F	VF	XF	Unc	BU
AH1408 (1987)	80,000,000	—	0.15	0.30	0.75	1.00
AH1408 (1987) Proof	5,000	Value: 5.00				

KM# 46   10 HALALA (2 Ghirsh)

4.0000 g., Copper-Nickel, 21 mm. **Obv:** Crossed swords and palm tree at center, legend above and below **Rev:** Legend above inscription in circle dividing value, date below **Edge:** Reeded

Date	Mintage	F	VF	XF	Unc	BU
AH1392 (1972)	55,000,000	0.10	0.20	0.35	0.50	—

KM# 54   10 HALALA (2 Ghirsh)

4.0000 g., Copper-Nickel, 21 mm. **Obv:** Crossed swords and palm tree at center, legend above and below **Rev:** Legend above inscription in circle dividing value, date below

Date	Mintage	F	VF	XF	Unc	BU
AH1397 (1976)	50,000,000	0.15	0.25	1.00	2.50	—
AH1400 (1979)	29,500,000	0.25	0.75	1.00	3.00	—

KM# 58   10 HALALA (2 Ghirsh)
4.0000 g., Copper-Nickel, 21 mm. **Series:** F.A.O. **Obv:** Crossed swords and palm tree at center, legend above and below **Rev:** Legend above inscription in circle dividing value, date below

Date	Mintage	F	VF	XF	Unc	BU
AH1398-1978	1,000,000	—	0.25	0.50	1.00	—

KM# 62   10 HALALA (2 Ghirsh)
4.0000 g., Copper-Nickel, 21 mm. **Ruler:** Fahad Bin Abd Al-Aziz AH1403-1426/1982-2005AD **Obv:** National emblem at center, legend above and below **Rev:** Legend above inscription in circle dividing value, date below

Date	Mintage	F	VF	XF	Unc	BU
AH1408 (1987)	100,000,000	—	0.15	0.35	0.90	1.20
AH1408 (1987) Proof	5,000	Value: 6.00				

KM# 49   25 HALALA (1/4 Riyal)
5.0000 g., Copper-Nickel, 23 mm. **Series:** F.A.O. **Obv:** Crossed swords and palm tree at center, legend above and below **Rev:** Legend above inscription in circle dividing value, date below

Date	Mintage	F	VF	XF	Unc	BU
AH1392-1973	200,000	—	0.20	0.50	1.00	—

KM# 48   25 HALALA (1/4 Riyal)
5.0000 g., Copper-Nickel, 23 mm. **Obv:** Crossed swords and palm tree at center, legend above and below **Rev:** Legend above inscription in circle dividing value, date below **Note:** Corrected denomination; feminine gender.

Date	Mintage	F	VF	XF	Unc	BU
AH1392 (1972)	Inc. above	0.25	0.50	1.00	2.00	—

KM# 47   25 HALALA (1/4 Riyal)
5.0000 g., Copper-Nickel, 23 mm. **Obv:** Crossed swords and palm tree at center, legend above and below **Rev:** Legend above inscription in circle dividing value, date below **Note:** Error. Denomination in masculine gender.

Date	Mintage	F	VF	XF	Unc	BU
AH1392 (1972)	48,465,000	1.00	2.00	6.00	25.00	30.00

KM# 55   25 HALALA (1/4 Riyal)
5.0000 g., Copper-Nickel, 23 mm. **Obv:** Crossed swords and palm tree at center, legend above and below **Rev:** Legend above inscription in circle dividing value, date below

Date	Mintage	F	VF	XF	Unc	BU
AH1397 (1976)	20,000,000	0.35	0.50	1.00	3.00	—
AH1400 (1979)	57,000,000	0.35	0.50	0.85	2.50	—

KM# 63   25 HALALA (1/4 Riyal)
5.0000 g., Copper-Nickel, 23 mm. **Ruler:** Fahad Bin Abd Al-Aziz AH1403-1426/1982-2005AD **Obv:** National emblem at center, legend above and below **Rev:** Legend above inscription in circle dividing value, date below

Date	Mintage	F	VF	XF	Unc	BU
AH1408 (1987)	100,000,000	—	0.20	0.45	1.10	1.50
AH1408 (1987) Proof	5,000	Value: 7.50				

KM# 50   50 HALALA (1/2 Riyal)
6.5000 g., Copper-Nickel, 26 mm. **Series:** F.A.O. **Obv:** Crossed swords and palm tree at center, legend above and below **Rev:** Legend above inscription in circle dividing value, date below

Date	Mintage	F	VF	XF	Unc	BU
AH1392 (1972)	500,000	—	0.30	0.60	2.50	—

KM# 51   50 HALALA (1/2 Riyal)
6.5000 g., Copper-Nickel, 26 mm. **Obv:** Crossed swords and palm tree at center, legend above and below **Rev:** Legend above inscription in circle dividing value, date below

Date	Mintage	F	VF	XF	Unc	BU
AH1392 (1972)	16,000,000	0.20	0.35	0.60	2.00	—

KM# 56   50 HALALA (1/2 Riyal)
6.5000 g., Copper-Nickel, 26 mm. **Obv:** Crossed swords and palm tree at center, legend above and below **Rev:** Legend above inscription in circle dividing value, date below **Edge:** Reeded

Date	Mintage	F	VF	XF	Unc	BU
AH1397 (1976)	20,000,000	0.50	0.75	1.00	3.00	—
AH1400 (1979)	21,600,000	0.75	1.00	1.50	3.50	—

KM# 64   50 HALALA (1/2 Riyal)
6.5000 g., Copper-Nickel, 26 mm. **Ruler:** Fahad Bin Abd Al-Aziz AH1403-1426/1982-2005AD **Obv:** National emblem at center, legend above and below **Rev:** Legend above inscription in circle dividing value, date below

Date	Mintage	F	VF	XF	Unc	BU
AH1408 (1987)	70,000,000	0.15	0.30	0.75	1.50	2.00
AH1408 (1987) Proof	5,000	Value: 15.00				

KM# 52   100 HALALA (1 Riyal)
10.0000 g., Copper-Nickel, 30 mm. **Obv:** Crossed swords and palm tree at center, legend above and below **Rev:** Legend above inscription in circle dividing value, date below

Date	Mintage	F	VF	XF	Unc	BU
AH1396 (1976)	250,000	—	0.65	1.00	3.50	—
AH1400 (1980)	30,000,000	—	0.65	1.00	3.00	—

KM# 59   100 HALALA (1 Riyal)
10.0000 g., Copper-Nickel, 30 mm. **Series:** F.A.O. **Obv:** Crossed swords and palm tree at center flanked by dates, legend above and below **Rev:** Legend above inscription in circle dividing value, date below

Date	Mintage	F	VF	XF	Unc	BU
AH1397 - 1977	—	—	150	275	325	

Note: AH1397 date was struck as samples for the Saudi Arabia government by the British Royal Mint, but some escaped into circulation

Date	Mintage	F	VF	XF	Unc	BU
AH1398 - 1978	10,000,000	—	0.75	1.50	3.50	

KM# 65   100 HALALA (1 Riyal)
10.0000 g., Copper-Nickel, 30 mm. **Obv:** National emblem at center, legend above and below **Rev:** Legend above inscription in circle dividing value, date below

Date	Mintage	F	VF	XF	Unc	BU
AH1408 (1987)	40,000,000	—	0.60	1.20	3.00	4.00
AH1408 (1987) Proof	5,000	Value: 22.00				
AH1414 (1993)	5,000	—	0.60	1.20	3.00	4.00

KM# 66   100 HALALA (1 Riyal)
Bi-Metallic Brass center in Copper-Nickel ring, 23 mm. **Ruler:** Fahad Bin Abd Al-Aziz AH1403-1426/1982-2005AD **Obv:** National emblem at center, legend above and below **Rev:** Inscription at center, value at left, legend above, date below **Edge:** Reeded

Date	Mintage	F	VF	XF	Unc	BU
AH1419 (1998)	—	—	1.00	2.50	5.00	—

KM# 67   100 HALALA (1 Riyal)
Bi-Metallic Brass center in Copper-Nickel ring, 23 mm. **Ruler:** Fahad Bin Abd Al-Aziz AH1403-1426/1982-2005AD **Subject:** Centennial of Kingdom **Obv:** National emblem at center **Rev:** Inscription at center, legend above, value at left, date below **Edge:** Reeded

Date	Mintage	F	VF	XF	Unc	BU
AH1419 (1998)	—	—	1.50	3.50	6.50	—
AH1419 (1998) Proof	—	Value: 12.50				

TRADE COINAGE

KM# 36 GUINEA
7.9881 g., 0.9170 Gold 0.2355 oz. AGW **Obv:** Inscription within beaded circle, legend above, crossed swords below within design flanked by palm trees **Rev:** Inscription within beaded circle, legend above, value below within design flanked by palm trees

Date	Mintage	F	VF	XF	Unc	BU
AH1370 (1950)	2,000,000	—	—	BV	240	250

KM# 43 GUINEA
7.9881 g., 0.9170 Gold 0.2355 oz. AGW

Date	Mintage	F	VF	XF	Unc	BU
AH1377 (1957)	1,579,000	—	—	BV	240	265

BULLION COINAGE
Post WWII Issues

KM# 35 SOVEREIGN (Pound)
7.9881 g., 0.9170 Gold 0.2355 oz. AGW **Obv:** Eagle with wings open **Rev:** Three lined inscription within horizontal bars **Note:** KM#35 was struck at the Philadelphia Mint for a concession payment for oil to the Saudi Government. Most were melted into bullion.

Date	Mintage	F	VF	~XF	Unc	BU
ND(1947)	123,000	—	300	500	750	—

KM# 34 4 POUNDS
31.9500 g., 0.9170 Gold 0.9419 oz. AGW **Obv:** Eagle with wings open **Rev:** Three lined inscription within horizontal bars **Note:** KM#34 was struck at the Philadelphia Mint for a concession payment for oil to the Saudi Government. Most were melted into bullion.

Date	Mintage	F	VF	XF	Unc	BU
ND(1945-46)	91,000	—	—	BV	900	1,200

PATTERNS
Including off metal strikes

KM#	Date	Mintage	Identification			Mkt Val
Pn1	AH1373	—	1/4 Riyal. 0.9170 Silver. 2.9500 g. As KM37			—
Pn2	AH1373	—	1/2 Riyal. 0.9170 Silver. 5.9500 g. As KM38			—
Pn3	AH1373	—	Riyal. 0.9170 Silver. 11.6000 g. As KM39			—
Pn4	AH1370	—	Guinea. Aluminum. KM#36.			1,500
Pn5	AH1370	—	Guinea. Bronze. KM#36, reeded edge, with Paris privy marks.			3,500
Pn6	AH1370	—	Guinea. Gold. KM#36, reeded edge, with Paris privy marks, Rare.			—

MINT SETS

KM#	Date	Mintage	Identification	Issue Price	Mkt Val
MS1	AH1408(1988) (5)	—	KM#61-65	20.00	45.00

PROOF SETS

KM#	Date	Mintage	Identification	Issue Price	Mkt Val
PS1	AH1408(1988) (5)	5,000	KM#61-65	40.00	75.00

SENEGAL

The Republic of Senegal, located on the bulge of West Africa between Mauritania and Guinea-Bissau, has an area of 75,750 sq. mi. (196,190 sq. km.) and a population of *7.5 million. Capital: Dakar. The economy is primarily agricultural. Peanuts and products, phosphates, and canned fish are exported.

An abundance of megalithic remains indicates that Senegal was inhabited in prehistoric times. The Portuguese had some trading stations on the banks of the Senegal River in the 15th century. French commercial establishments date from the 17th century. The French gradually acquired control over the interior regions, which were administered as a protectorate until 1920, and as a colony thereafter. After the 1958 French constitutional referendum, Senegal became a member of the French Community with virtual autonomy. In 1959 Senegal and the French Soudan merged to form the Mali Federation, which became fully independent on June 20, 1960. (April 4, the date the transfer of power agreement was signed with France, is celebrated as Senegal's independence day). The Federation broke up on Aug. 20, 1960, when Senegal seceded and proclaimed the Republic of Senegal. Soudan became the Republic of Mali a month later.

Senegal is a member of a monetary union of autonomous republics called the Monetary Union of West African States (*Union Monetaire Ouest-Africaine*). The other members are Ivory Coast, Benin, Burkina Faso (Upper Volta), Niger, Mauritania and Togo. Mali was a member, but seceded in 1962. Some of the member countries have issued coinage in addition to the common currency issued by the Monetary Union of West African States.

REPUBLIC
STANDARD COINAGE

KM# 1 10 FRANCS
3.2000 g., 0.9000 Gold 0.0926 oz. AGW **Subject:** 8th Anniversary of Independence **Obv:** Star above shield within wreath **Rev:** Stars above value and date

Date	Mintage	F	VF	XF	Unc	BU
1968 Proof	—	Value: 110				

KM# 2 25 FRANCS
8.0000 g., 0.9000 Gold 0.2315 oz. AGW **Subject:** 8th Anniversary of Independence **Obv:** Star above shield within wreath **Rev:** Stars above value and date

Date	Mintage	F	VF	XF	Unc	BU
1968 Proof	—	Value: 250				

KM# 3 50 FRANCS
16.0000 g., 0.9000 Gold 0.4630 oz. AGW **Subject:** 8th Anniversary of Independence **Obv:** Star above shield within wreath **Rev:** Stars above value and date

Date	Mintage	F	VF	XF	Unc	BU
1968 Proof	—	Value: 475				

KM# 5 50 FRANCS
28.2800 g., 0.9250 Silver 0.8410 oz. ASW **Subject:** 25th Anniversary of Eurafrique Program **Obv:** Sailboat at upper left of value and map **Rev:** Bust facing

Date	Mintage	F	VF	XF	Unc	BU
1975	1,968	—	—	—	220	270
1975 Proof	18,032	Value: 210				

KM# 4 100 FRANCS
32.0000 g., 0.9000 Gold 0.9259 oz. AGW **Subject:** 8th Anniversary of Independence **Obv:** Star above shield within wreath **Rev:** Stars above value and date

Date	Mintage	F	VF	XF	Unc	BU
1968 Proof	—	Value: 925				

KM# 6 150 FRANCS
79.9700 g., 0.9250 Silver 2.3782 oz. ASW **Subject:** 25th Anniversary of Eurafrique Program **Obv:** Flying stork above value and map **Rev:** Bust facing

Date	Mintage	F	VF	XF	Unc	BU
1975	1,075	—	—	—	250	300
1975 Proof	18,925	Value: 245				

KM# 7 250 FRANCS
3.9800 g., 0.9170 Gold 0.1173 oz. AGW **Subject:** 25th Anniversary of Eurafrique Program **Obv:** Star above shield within wreath **Rev:** Bust facing

Date	Mintage	F	VF	XF	Unc	BU
1975	1,000	—	—	—	—	135
1975 Proof	1,250	Value: 140				

KM# 8   500 FRANCS
7.9600 g., 0.9170 Gold 0.2347 oz. AGW **Subject:** 25th Anniversary of Eurafrique Program **Obv:** Star above shield within wreath **Rev:** Bust facing

Date	Mintage	F	VF	XF	Unc	BU
1975	500	—	—	—	—	265
1975 Proof	1,250	Value: 260				

KM# 9   1000 FRANCS
15.9500 g., 0.9160 Gold 0.4697 oz. AGW **Subject:** 25th Anniversary of Eurafrique Program **Obv:** Star above shield within wreath **Rev:** Bust facing

Date	Mintage	F	VF	XF	Unc	BU
1975	217	—	—	—	—	500
1975 Proof	1,250	Value: 485				

KM# 10   2500 FRANCS
39.9300 g., 0.9160 Gold 1.1759 oz. AGW **Subject:** 25th Anniversary of Eurafrique Program **Obv:** Star above shield within wreath **Rev:** Bust facing

Date	Mintage	F	VF	XF	Unc	BU
1975	195	—	—	—	—	1,200
1975 Proof	1,250	Value: 1,175				

TOKEN COINAGE

KM# Tn2   5 CENTIMES
Aluminum **Issuer:** Dakar, Chamber of Commerce

Date	Mintage	VG	F	VF	XF	Unc
1920	—	50.00	70.00	125	200	400

KM# Tn7   5 CENTIMES
Aluminum **Issuer:** Kayes, Upper Senegal-Niger Chamber of Commerce

Date	Mintage	VG	F	VF	XF	Unc
1920	—	75.00	125	180	225	—

KM# Tn12   5 CENTIMES
Aluminum **Issuer:** Rufisque, Chamber of Commerce

Date	Mintage	VG	F	VF	XF	Unc
1920	—	50.00	70.00	125	200	400

KM# Tn3   10 CENTIMES
Aluminum **Issuer:** Dakar, Chamber of Commerce

Date	Mintage	VG	F	VF	XF	Unc
1920	—	40.00	60.00	100	150	—

KM# Tn4   10 CENTIMES
Brass **Issuer:** Dakar, Chamber of Commerce

Date	Mintage	VG	F	VF	XF	Unc
1920	—	50.00	70.00	125	200	—

KM# Tn8   10 CENTIMES
Aluminum **Issuer:** Kayes, Upper Senegal-Niger Chamber of Commerce

Date	Mintage	VG	F	VF	XF	Unc
1920	—	100	150	200	300	550

KM# Tn13   10 CENTIMES
Aluminum **Issuer:** Rufisque, Chamber of Commerce

Date	Mintage	VG	F	VF	XF	Unc
1920	—	45.00	65.00	125	175	—

KM# Tn5   25 CENTIMES
Aluminum **Issuer:** Dakar, Chamber of Commerce

Date	Mintage	VG	F	VF	XF	Unc
1920	—	45.00	65.00	115	180	350

KM# Tn9   25 CENTIMES
Aluminum **Issuer:** Kayes, Upper Senegal-Niger Chamber of Commerce

Date	Mintage	VG	F	VF	XF	Unc
1920	—	150	225	275	425	—

KM# Tn10   25 CENTIMES
Copper-Nickel **Issuer:** Kayes, Upper Senegal-Niger Chamber of Commerce

Date	Mintage	VG	F	VF	XF	Unc
1920	—	150	200	300	400	—

KM# Tn14   25 CENTIMES
Aluminum **Issuer:** Rufisque, Chamber of Commerce

Date	Mintage	VG	F	VF	XF	Unc
1920	—	60.00	80.00	150	250	—

KM# Tn6   50 CENTIMES
Aluminum **Issuer:** Dakar, Chamber of Commerce

Date	Mintage	VG	F	VF	XF	Unc
1920	—	60.00	80.00	150	250	—

KM# Tn11   50 CENTIMES
Aluminum **Issuer:** Kayes, Upper Senegal-Niger Chamber of Commerce

Date	Mintage	VG	F	VF	XF	Unc
1920	—	150	200	300	500	750

KM# Tn15   50 CENTIMES
Aluminum **Issuer:** Rufisque, Chamber of Commerce

Date	Mintage	VG	F	VF	XF	Unc
1920	—	60.00	80.00	150	250	—

KM# Tn16   50 CENTIMES
Brass **Issuer:** Rufisque, Chamber of Commerce

Date	Mintage	VG	F	VF	XF	Unc
1920	—	70.00	95.00	180	295	—

KM# Tn17   50 CENTIMES
Brass **Issuer:** Ziguinchor, Chamber of Commerce

Date	Mintage	VG	F	VF	XF	Unc
1921	—	70.00	95.00	180	300	600

KM# Tn18   FRANC
Brass **Issuer:** Ziguinchor, Chamber of Commerce

Date	Mintage	VG	F	VF	XF	Unc
1921	—	75.00	125	225	325	—

KM# Tn19   FRANC
Aluminum **Issuer:** Ziguinchor, Chamber of Commerce

Date	Mintage	VG	F	VF	XF	Unc
1921	—	40.00	80.00	175	350	500

ESSAIS
Standard metals unless otherwise noted

KM#	Date	Mintage	Identification	Mkt Val
E1	1920	—	25 Centimes. Kayes. KM#Tn10.	250
E2	1921	—	50 Centimes. Brass. Zinguinchor. KMTn17.	300
E3	1921	—	Franc. Brass. Zinguinchor. KMTn18.	320

MINT SETS

KM#	Date	Mintage	Identification	Issue Price	Mkt Val
MS1	1975 (4)	195	KM#7-10	—	1,550

PROOF SETS

KM#	Date	Mintage	Identification	Issue Price	Mkt Val
PS1	1968 (4)	—	KM#1-4	—	1,225
PS2	1975 (2)	—	KM#5-6	—	450

SERBIA

Serbia, a former inland Balkan kingdom has an area of 34,116 sq. mi. (88,361 sq. km.). Capital: Belgrade.

Serbia emerged as a separate kingdom in the 12th century and attained its greatest expansion and political influence in the mid-14th century. After the Battle of Kosovo, 1389, Serbia became a vassal principality of Turkey and remained under Turkish suzerainty until it was re-established as an independent kingdom by the 1878 Treaty of Berlin. Following World War I, which had its immediate cause in the assassination of Austrian Archduke Francis Ferdinand by a Serbian nationalist, Serbia joined with the Croats and Slovenes to form the new Kingdom of the South Slavs with Peter I of Serbia as King. The name of the kingdom was later changed to Yugoslavia. Invaded by Germany during World War II, Serbia emerged as a constituent republic of the Socialist Federal Republic of Yugoslavia.

RULERS
Alexander I, 1889-1902
Peter I, 1903-1918

MINT MARKS
A - Paris
(a) - Paris, privy mark only
(g) - Gorham Mfg. Co., Providence, R.I.
H - Birmingham
V - Vienna
БП - (BP) Budapest

MONETARY SYSTEM
100 Para = 1 Dinara

DENOMINATIONS
ПАРА = Para
ПАРЕ = Pare
ДИНАР = Dinar
ДИНАРА = Dinara

KINGDOM

STANDARD COINAGE

KM# 23   2 PARE
2.0000 g., Bronze, 20 mm. **Ruler:** Peter I **Obv:** Crowned double-headed eagle **Rev:** Value **Note:** Medallic die alignment.

Date	Mintage	F	VF	XF	Unc	BU
1904	12,500,000	2.00	6.00	18.00	38.00	—

KM# 18   5 PARA
3.0000 g., Copper-Nickel, 17 mm. **Ruler:** Milan I as Prince **Obv:** Crowned double-headed eagle **Rev:** Value **Note:** Medallic die alignment.

Date	Mintage	F	VF	XF	Unc	BU
1904	8,000,000	1.25	3.00	10.00	20.00	—
1904 Proof	Inc. above	Value: 200				
1912	10,500,032	1.00	2.00	6.00	14.00	—
1912 Proof	—	Value: 140				
1917(g)	5,000,000	5.00	12.00	24.00	40.00	—

KM# 19 10 PARA

4.0000 g., Copper-Nickel, 20 mm. **Ruler:** Milan I as King **Obv:** Crowned double-headed eagle **Rev:** Value **Note:** Medallic die alignment.

Date	Mintage	F	VF	XF	Unc	BU
1904 Proof	—	Value: 350				
1912	7,700,032	0.75	1.50	4.50	15.00	—
1912 Proof	—	Value: 140				
1917(g)	5,000,000	4.00	10.00	20.00	30.00	—
1917(g) Proof	—	Value: 220				

KM# 20 20 PARA

6.0000 g., Copper-Nickel, 22 mm. **Ruler:** Milan I as King **Obv:** Crowned double-headed eagle **Rev:** Value **Note:** Medallic die alignment.

Date	Mintage	F	VF	XF	Unc	BU
1904 Proof	—	Value: 400				
1912	5,650,035	0.75	2.00	7.00	16.00	—
1912 Proof	—	Value: 140				
1917(g)	5,000,000	1.00	4.00	12.00	28.00	—

KM# 24.1 50 PARA

2.5000 g., 0.8350 Silver 0.0671 oz. ASW, 18 mm. **Ruler:** Peter I **Obv:** Head right with designer name **Rev:** Crown above value and date within wreath **Note:** Medallic die alignment.

Date	Mintage	F	VF	XF	Unc	BU
1904	1,400,031	2.50	8.00	16.00	40.00	—
1904 Proof	—	Value: 220				
1912	800,000	2.50	7.50	18.00	38.00	—
1915(a)	12,137,928	1.25	2.50	5.00	13.00	—

KM# 24.3 50 PARA

2.4000 g., Silver **Ruler:** Peter I **Obv:** With designer's signature **Rev:** Crown above value and date within wreath **Note:** Coin die alignment.

Date	Mintage	F	VF	XF	Unc	BU
A	—	—	—	—	—	—
1915	—	—	—	—	—	—

KM# 24.2 50 PARA

2.5000 g., 0.8350 Silver 0.0671 oz. ASW **Ruler:** Peter I **Obv:** Without designer's name **Rev:** Crown above value and date within wreath **Note:** Medallic die alignment

Date	Mintage	F	VF	XF	Unc	BU
1915(a)	1,862,071	8.00	14.00	36.00	96.00	—

KM# 24.4 50 PARA

Silver **Ruler:** Peter I **Obv:** Without designer name **Rev:** Crown above value and date within wreath **Note:** Coin die alignment

Date	Mintage	F	VF	XF	Unc	BU
1915(a)	—	—	—	—	—	—

KM# 24.5 50 PARA

Silver **Ruler:** Peter I **Obv:** With designer's signature **Rev:** Crown above value and date within wreath **Note:** Coin die alignment.

Date	Mintage	F	VF	XF	Unc	BU
1915(a)	—	—	—	—	—	—

KM# 25.1 DINAR

5.0000 g., 0.8350 Silver 0.1342 oz. ASW **Ruler:** Peter I **Obv:** Head right with designer's name below neck **Rev:** Crown above value and date within wreath **Note:** Medallic die alignment

Date	Mintage	F	VF	XF	Unc	BU
1904	2,000,086	4.50	13.00	26.00	76.00	—
1904 Proof	—	Value: 260				
1912	8,000,000	3.00	6.00	15.00	38.00	—
1915(a)	10,688,711	2.25	4.50	9.00	18.00	—

KM# 25.2 DINAR

5.0000 g., 0.8350 Silver 0.1342 oz. ASW **Ruler:** Peter I **Obv:** Without designer's name **Rev:** Crown above value and date within wreath **Note:** Medallic die alignment.

Date	Mintage	F	VF	XF	Unc	BU
1915	2,312,304	5.00	15.00	35.00	100	—

KM# 25.3 DINAR

Silver **Ruler:** Peter I **Obv:** With designer name **Rev:** Crown above value and date within wreath **Note:** Coin die alignment

Date	Mintage	F	VF	XF	Unc	BU
1915(a)	—	—	—	—	—	—

KM# 25.4 DINAR

Silver **Ruler:** Peter I **Obv:** Without designer name **Rev:** Crown above value and date within wreath **Note:** Coin die alignment

Date	Mintage	F	VF	XF	Unc	BU
1915(a)	—	—	—	—	—	—

KM# 26.1 2 DINARA

10.0000 g., 0.8350 Silver 0.2684 oz. ASW **Ruler:** Peter I **Obv:** Head right with designer's name below neck **Rev:** Crown above value and date within wreath **Note:** Medallic die alignment

Date	Mintage	F	VF	XF	Unc	BU
1904	1,150,044	7.50	15.00	32.00	90.00	—
1904 Proof	—	Value: 325				
1912	800,016	8.00	16.00	35.00	95.00	—
1915(a)	4,174,142	6.00	12.00	20.00	38.00	—

KM# 26.2 2 DINARA

10.0000 g., 0.8350 Silver 0.2684 oz. ASW **Ruler:** Peter I **Obv:** Without designer's name **Rev:** Crown above value and date within wreath **Note:** Medallic die alignment.

Date	Mintage	F	VF	XF	Unc	BU
1915(a)	825,858	9.00	24.00	52.00	140	—

KM# 26.3 2 DINARA

10.0000 g., 0.8350 Silver 0.2684 oz. ASW **Ruler:** Peter I **Obv:** Without designer's signature **Rev:** Crown above value and date within wreath **Note:** Coin die alignment.

Date	Mintage	VG	F	VF	XF	Unc
1915(a)	Inc. above	—	5.00	10.00	18.00	36.00
1915A						

KM# 27 5 DINARA

25.0000 g., 0.9000 Silver 0.7234 oz. ASW, 37 mm. **Ruler:** Peter I **Subject:** 100th Anniversary - Karageorgevich Dynasty **Obv:** Conjoined heads right with designer name below neck **Rev:** Crowned double-headed eagle on shield within crowned mantle **Edge:** Lettered, Type I **Edge:** • БОГ • ЧУВА • СРБИЈУ • **Note:** Edge lettered in Cyrillic: God Protect Serbia

Date	Mintage	F	VF	XF	Unc	BU
1904	200,000	35.00	80.00	240	700	—
1904 Proof	—	Value: 2,200				

KM# 28 5 DINARA

25.0000 g., 0.9000 Silver 0.7234 oz. ASW, 37 mm. **Ruler:** Peter I **Subject:** 100th Anniversary - Karageorgevich Dynasty **Edge:** Lettered, Type II **Edge:** • БОГ • СРБИЈУ • ЧУВА • **Note:** Edge lettered in Cyrillic: God Serbia Protect

Date	Mintage	F	VF	XF	Unc	BU
1904	Inc. above	150	300	700	1,800	—

GERMAN OCCUPATION
World War II
OCCUPATION COINAGE

KM# 30 50 PARA

Zinc **Obv:** Double-headed eagle **Rev:** Value and date within oat sprigs

Date	Mintage	F	VF	XF	Unc	BU
1942БП (BP)	20,000,000	2.00	4.50	10.00	22.00	—

KM# 31 DINAR

Zinc **Obv:** Double headed eagle **Rev:** Value and date within oat sprigs

Date	Mintage	F	VF	XF	Unc	BU
1942БП (BP)	50,000,000	0.70	2.00	7.50	18.00	—

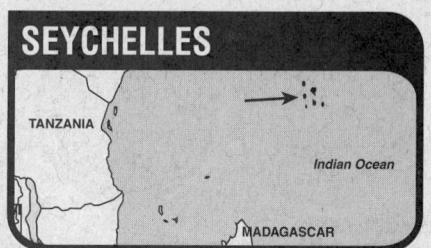

KM# 32 2 DINARA

Zinc **Obv:** Double-headed eagle **Rev:** Value and date within oat sprigs

Date	Mintage	F	VF	XF	Unc	BU
1942БП (BP)	40,000,000	0.70	2.00	8.00	20.00	—

KM# 33 10 DINARA

Zinc **Obv:** Double-headed eagle **Rev:** Value and date within oat sprigs

Date	Mintage	F	VF	XF	Unc	BU
1943БП (BP)	50,000,000	1.00	2.50	9.00	22.00	—

PATTERNS
Including off metal strikes

KM#	Date	Mintage	Identification	Mkt Val
PnC6	1904	—	2 Dinara. Bronze.	1,500
PnD6	1904	4	5 Dinara. Gold. 44.5000 g.	—
Pn6	1917	—	5 Para. Gold.	—
Pn7	1917	—	10 Para. Gold.	—
Pn8	1917	—	20 Para. Gold.	—
Pn9	1917	—	20 Dinara. Gold.	—

SEYCHELLES

TANZANIA

Indian Ocean

MADAGASCAR

The Republic of Seychelles, an archipelago of 85 granite and coral islands situated in the Indian Ocean 600 miles (965 km.) northeast of Madagascar, has an area of 156 sq. mi. (455 sq. km.) and a population of *70,000. Among these islands are the Aldabra Islands, the Farquhar Group, and Ile Desroches, which the United Kingdom ceded to the Seychelles upon its independence. Capital: Victoria, on Mahe. The economy is based on fishing, a plantation system of agriculture, and tourism. Copra, cinnamon and vanilla are exported.

Although the Seychelles is marked on Portuguese charts of the early 16th century, the first recorded visit to the islands, by an English ship, occurred in 1609. The Seychelles were annexed to France by Captain Lazare Picault in 1743 and permanently settled in 1768, with the intention of establishing spice plantations to compete with the Dutch monopoly of the spice trade. British troops seized the islands in 1810, during the Napoleonic Wars; the Treaty of Paris, 1814, formally ceded them to Britain. The Seychelles was a dependency of Mauritius until Aug. 31, 1903, when they became a separate British Crown Colony. The colony was granted limited internal self-government in 1970, and attained independence on June 28, 1976, becoming Britain's last African possession to do so. Seychelles is a member of the Commonwealth of Nations. The president is the Head of State and of Government.

RULER
British, until 1976

MINT MARKS

(sa) - M in oval – South African Mint Co.
    On coins dated 2000 and up in
    Place of PM

PM - Pobjoy Mint
None - British Royal Mint

MONETARY SYSTEM
100 Cents = 1 Rupee

BRITISH CROWN COLONY

STANDARD COINAGE

KM# 5 CENT
Bronze **Obv:** Crowned head left **Rev:** Value within beaded circle

Date	Mintage	F	VF	XF	Unc	BU
1948	300,000	—	0.25	0.50	1.25	—
1948 Proof	—	Value: 50.00				

KM# 14 CENT
Bronze **Obv:** Crowned head right **Rev:** Value within beaded circle

Date	Mintage	F	VF	XF	Unc	BU
1959	30,000	—	0.75	1.50	3.00	—
1959 Proof	—	—	—	—	—	—
1961	30,000	—	0.50	1.00	2.25	—
1961 Proof	—	—	—	—	—	—
1963	40,000	—	0.50	1.00	1.50	—
1963 Proof	—	—	—	—	—	—
1965	20,000	—	2.00	3.00	5.00	—
1969	Est. 5,000	15.00	20.00	30.00	65.00	—

Note: Latest reports indicate only 5,000 circulation strikes have been releasesd to date in addition to proof issues

1969 Proof	—	Value: 5.00				

KM# 17 CENT
0.7000 g., Aluminum, 16 mm. **Series:** F.A.O. **Obv:** Young bust right **Rev:** Cow head **Edge:** Plain

Date	Mintage	F	VF	XF	Unc	BU
1972	2,350,000	—	—	0.10	0.25	1.00

KM# 6 2 CENTS
Bronze **Obv:** Crowned head left **Rev:** Value within beaded circle

Date	Mintage	F	VF	XF	Unc	BU
1948	350,000	—	0.35	0.60	1.50	—
1948 Proof	—	Value: 75.00				

KM# 15 2 CENTS
Bronze **Obv:** Crowned head right **Rev:** Value within beaded circle

Date	Mintage	F	VF	XF	Unc	BU
1959	30,000	—	0.50	1.00	2.75	—
1959 Proof	—	—	—	—	—	—
1961	30,000	—	0.50	1.00	2.75	—
1961 Proof	—	—	—	—	—	—
1963	40,000	—	0.75	1.25	2.50	—
1963 Proof	—	—	—	—	—	—
1965	20,000	—	2.00	3.00	4.50	—
1968	20,000	—	2.00	3.00	5.50	—
1969 Proof	5,000	Value: 4.00				

KM# 7 5 CENTS
Bronze **Obv:** Crowned head left **Rev:** Value within circle

Date	Mintage	F	VF	XF	Unc	BU
1948	300,000	—	0.40	0.80	3.00	—
1948 Proof	—	Value: 100				

KM# 16 5 CENTS
Bronze **Obv:** Crowned head right **Rev:** Value within beaded circle

Date	Mintage	F	VF	XF	Unc	BU
1964	20,000	—	1.50	3.00	6.00	—
1964 Proof	—	—	—	—	—	—
1965	40,000	—	1.50	2.50	5.50	—
1967	20,000	—	2.50	5.00	9.00	—
1968	40,000	—	1.00	2.00	7.00	—
1969	100,000	—	0.50	1.00	5.00	—
1969 Proof	—	Value: 4.00				
1971	25,000	—	0.50	1.50	2.50	—

KM# 18 5 CENTS
0.7700 g., Aluminum, 18.5 mm. **Series:** F.A.O. **Obv:** Young bust right **Rev:** Cabbage head

Date	Mintage	F	VF	XF	Unc	BU
1972	2,200,000	—	—	0.10	0.25	—
1975	1,200,000	—	—	0.10	0.25	—

KM# 1 10 CENTS
Copper-Nickel **Obv:** Crowned head left **Rev:** Value within sprig above date

Date	Mintage	F	VF	XF	Unc	BU
1939	36,000	—	10.00	35.00	70.00	—
1939 Proof	—	Value: 150				
1943	36,000	—	10.00	22.00	40.00	—
1944	36,000	—	10.00	22.00	40.00	—
1944 Proof	—	Value: 175				

KM# 8 10 CENTS
Copper-Nickel **Obv:** Crowned head left **Rev:** Value within sprig above date

Date	Mintage	F	VF	XF	Unc	BU
1951	36,000	—	6.00	15.00	30.00	—
1951 Proof	—	Value: 135				

KM# 10 10 CENTS
6.0400 g., Nickel-Brass, 21.57 mm. **Obv:** Crowned head right **Rev:** Value within sprig above date

Date	Mintage	F	VF	XF	Unc	BU
1953	130,000	—	0.50	1.00	3.00	—
1953 Proof	—	Value: 100				
1965	40,000	—	1.00	1.50	5.00	—
1967	20,000	—	4.00	7.50	15.00	—
1968	50,000	—	1.00	4.00	12.50	—
1969	60,000	—	1.00	2.00	7.00	—
1969 Proof	—	Value: 2.00				
1970	75,000	—	0.50	1.00	4.50	—
1971	100,000	—	0.50	1.00	1.75	—
1972	120,000	—	0.30	0.50	1.00	—
1973	100,000	—	0.15	0.25	1.00	—
1974	100,000	—	0.15	0.25	0.75	—

KM# 2 25 CENTS
2.9200 g., 0.5000 Silver 0.0469 oz. ASW **Obv:** Crowned head left **Rev:** Value within sprig above date

Date	Mintage	F	VF	XF	Unc	BU
1939	36,000	—	7.50	35.00	125	—
1939 Proof	—	Value: 200				
1943	36,000	—	5.00	25.00	100	—
1944	36,000	—	3.50	20.00	85.00	—
1944 Proof	—	Value: 300				

KM# 9 25 CENTS
Copper-Nickel **Obv:** Crowned head left **Rev:** Value within sprig above date

Date	Mintage	F	VF	XF	Unc	BU
1951	36,000	—	3.00	10.00	35.00	—
1951 Proof	—	Value: 160				

KM# 11 25 CENTS
3.0000 g., Copper-Nickel **Obv:** Crowned head right **Rev:** Value within sprig above date

Date	Mintage	F	VF	XF	Unc	BU
1954	124,000	—	0.75	1.25	3.50	—
1954 Proof	—	Value: 120				
1960	40,000	—	0.75	1.25	2.00	—
1960 Proof	—	—	—	—	—	—
1964	40,000	—	1.00	2.00	5.00	—
1965	40,000	—	1.00	2.00	5.00	—
1966	10,000	—	4.50	12.00	30.00	—
1967	20,000	—	2.50	4.00	15.00	—
1968	20,000	—	2.50	4.00	15.00	—
1969	100,000	—	1.00	2.00	4.00	—
1969 Proof	—	Value: 3.00				
1970	40,000	—	1.50	3.00	10.00	—
1972	120,000	—	0.50	0.75	1.50	—
1973	100,000	—	0.50	0.75	1.50	—
1974	100,000	—	0.50	0.75	1.50	—

KM# 3 1/2 RUPEE
5.8300 g., 0.5000 Silver 0.0937 oz. ASW **Obv:** Crowned head left **Rev:** Value within sprig above date

Date	Mintage	F	VF	XF	Unc	BU
1939	36,000	—	22.00	80.00	175	—
1939 Proof	—	Value: 250				

KM# 12 1/2 RUPEE
Copper-Nickel **Obv:** Crowned head right **Rev:** Value within sprig above date

Date	Mintage	F	VF	XF	Unc	BU
1954	72,000	—	0.50	1.25	3.75	—
1954 Proof	—	Value: 150				
1960	60,000	—	0.50	3.00	6.00	—
1960 Proof	—	Value: 150				
1966	15,000	—	2.00	10.00	25.00	—
1967	20,000	—	3.00	12.00	25.00	—
1968	20,000	—	3.00	15.00	30.00	—
1969	60,000	—	0.75	5.00	12.00	—
1969 Proof	—	Value: 3.00				
1970	50,000	—	0.75	3.00	8.00	—
1971	100,000	—	0.75	2.00	6.00	—

Date	Mintage	F	VF	XF	Unc	BU
1972	120,000	—	0.50	0.75	1.00	—
1974	100,000	—	0.50	0.75	1.00	—

KM# 4 RUPEE
11.6600 g., 0.5000 Silver 0.1874 oz. ASW, 30 mm. **Obv:** Crowned head left **Rev:** Value within sprig above date **Edge:** Reeded

Date	Mintage	F	VF	XF	Unc	BU
1939	90,000	12.00	25.00	95.00	165	—
1939 Proof	—	Value: 400				

KM# 13 RUPEE
11.6400 g., Copper-Nickel, 30 mm. **Obv:** Crowned head right **Rev:** Value within sprig above date

Date	Mintage	F	VF	XF	Unc	BU
1954	150,000	—	0.50	1.00	3.00	—
1954 Proof	—	Value: 200				
1960	60,000	—	0.75	1.25	3.50	—
1960 Proof						
1966	45,000	—	1.25	2.25	8.50	—
1967	10,000	—	6.00	12.50	30.00	—
1968	40,000	—	2.50	10.00	20.00	—
1969	50,000	—	1.50	5.00	12.50	—
1969 Proof	—	Value: 5.00				
1970	50,000	—	1.50	3.50	10.00	—
1971	100,000	—	0.75	1.50	5.00	—
1972	120,000	—	0.75	1.50	2.00	—
1974	100,000	—			1.50	—

KM# 19 5 RUPEES
Copper-Nickel, 30 mm. **Obv:** Young bust right **Rev:** Palm tree, sailboats,giant tortoise and value **Edge:** Plain

Date	Mintage	F	VF	XF	Unc	BU
1972	220,000	—	1.50	2.50	5.00	6.00

KM# 19a 5 RUPEES
15.5000 g., 0.9250 Silver 0.4609 oz. ASW, 30 mm. **Obv:** Young bust right **Rev:** Palm tree, boats and value

Date	Mintage	F	VF	XF	Unc	BU
1972 Proof	2,500	Value: 25.00				
1974 Proof	5,000	Value: 17.50				

KM# 20 10 RUPEES
Copper-Nickel, 38.5 mm. **Obv:** Young bust right **Rev:** Sea turtle and value

Date	Mintage	F	VF	XF	Unc	BU
1974	—	—	2.00	4.00	12.00	14.00

KM# 20a 10 RUPEES
28.2800 g., 0.9250 Silver 0.8410 oz. ASW **Obv:** Young bust right **Rev:** Green sea turtle

Date	Mintage	F	VF	XF	Unc	BU
1974 Proof	25,000	Value: 20.00				

REPUBLIC
STANDARD COINAGE

KM# 21 CENT
Aluminum, 16 mm. **Subject:** Declaration of Independence **Obv:** Head right **Rev:** Boueteur fish and value

Date	Mintage	F	VF	XF	Unc	BU
1976	109,000	—	0.10	0.20	0.75	1.00
1976 Proof	8,500	Value: 1.50				

KM# 30 CENT
0.7000 g., Aluminum, 16 mm. **Obv:** Arms with supporters **Rev:** Boueteur fish and value

Date	Mintage	F	VF	XF	Unc	BU
1977	—	—	0.15	0.75	1.00	

KM# 46.1 CENT
Brass **Obv:** Arms with supporters **Rev:** Mud Crab and value

Date	Mintage	F	VF	XF	Unc	BU
1982	500,000	—	0.15	0.50	1.50	
1982 Proof	—	Value: 2.25				

KM# 46.2 CENT
1.4300 g., Brass, 16.03 mm. **Obv:** Altered coat of arms **Rev:** Mud Crab **Edge:** Plain

Date	Mintage	F	VF	XF	Unc	BU
1990PM	—	—	0.15	0.45	0.60	
1992PM	—	—	0.15	0.45	0.60	
1992PM Proof	—	Value: 2.25				
1997	—	—	0.15	0.40	0.50	

KM# 22 5 CENTS
Aluminum **Subject:** Declaration of Independence **Obv:** Head right **Rev:** Fish above value and sprigs **Note:** Varieties exist.

Date	Mintage	F	VF	XF	Unc	BU
1976	209,000	—	0.10	0.20	0.75	1.25
1976 Proof	8,500	Value: 1.50				

KM# 31 5 CENTS
Aluminum **Series:** F.A.O. **Obv:** Arms with supporters **Rev:** Fish above value and sprigs

Date	Mintage	F	VF	XF	Unc	BU
1977	300,000	—	0.15	0.75	1.25	

KM# 43 5 CENTS
1.9500 g., Brass, 18 mm. **Series:** World Food Day **Obv:** Arms with supporters **Rev:** Value at lower left of tapioca plant

Date	Mintage	F	VF	XF	Unc	BU
1981	720,000	—	0.15	0.45	1.00	

KM# 47.1 5 CENTS
1.9500 g., Brass, 18 mm. **Obv:** Arms with supporters **Rev:** Value at lower left of tapioca plant

Date	Mintage	F	VF	XF	Unc	BU
1982	1,500,000	—	0.10	0.30	0.50	
1982 Proof	Inc. above	Value: 2.50				

KM# 47.2 5 CENTS
1.9500 g., Brass, 18 mm. **Obv:** Altered coat of arms **Rev:** Tapioca plant

Date	Mintage	F	VF	XF	Unc	BU
1990PM	—	—	0.10	0.30	0.50	
1992PM	—	—	0.10	0.30	0.50	
1992PM Proof	—	Value: 2.50				
1995PM	—	—	0.10	0.30	0.50	
1997PM	—	—	0.10	0.30	0.50	
1997PM Proof	—	Value: 2.50				
2000 (sa)	—	—	0.10	0.30	0.50	

KM# 23 10 CENTS
Nickel-Brass, 21 mm. **Subject:** Declaration of Independence **Obv:** Head right **Rev:** Sailfish and value **Edge:** Plain

Date	Mintage	F	VF	XF	Unc	BU
1976	209,000	—	0.20	0.50	1.50	2.50
1976 Proof	8,500	Value: 2.50				

KM# 32 10 CENTS
Nickel-Brass, 21 mm. **Series:** F.A.O. **Obv:** Arms with supporters **Rev:** Sailfish and value

Date	Mintage	F	VF	XF	Unc	BU
1977	125,000	—	0.10	0.35	1.50	2.50

KM# 44 10 CENTS
3.2500 g., Brass, 21 mm. **Series:** World Food Day **Obv:** Arms with supporters **Rev:** Yellowfin tuna and value

Date	Mintage	F	VF	XF	Unc	BU
1981	145,000	—	0.10	0.25	1.00	1.50

KM# 48.1   10 CENTS
3.2500 g., Brass, 21 mm. **Obv:** Arms with supporters
Rev: Yellowfin tuna and value

Date	Mintage	F	VF	XF	Unc	BU
1982	1,000,000	—	0.10	0.25	1.00	1.50
1982 Proof	Inc. above	Value: 2.75				

KM# 48.2   10 CENTS
3.2500 g., Brass, 21 mm. **Obv:** Altered coat of arms
Rev: Yellowfin tuna **Edge:** Plain

Date	Mintage	F	VF	XF	Unc	BU
1990PM	—		0.10	0.25	1.00	1.50
1992PM	—		0.10	0.25	1.00	1.50
1992PM Proof	—	Value: 2.75				
1994PM	—		0.10	0.35	1.00	1.50
1997PM	—		0.10	0.35	1.00	1.50
2000 (sa)	—		0.10	0.35	1.00	1.50

KM# 24   25 CENTS
2.9000 g., Copper-Nickel, 19 mm. **Subject:** Declaration of
Independence **Obv:** Head right **Rev:** Black Parrot and value

Date	Mintage	F	VF	XF	Unc	BU
1976	209,000	—	0.50	1.00	3.00	4.50
1976 Proof	8,500	Value: 3.50				

KM# 33   25 CENTS
2.9000 g., Copper-Nickel, 19 mm. **Obv:** Arms with supporters
Rev: Black Parrot and value

Date	Mintage	F	VF	XF	Unc	BU
1977	—		0.25	0.75	3.00	4.50

KM# 49.1   25 CENTS
2.9000 g., Copper-Nickel, 19 mm. **Obv:** Arms with supporters
Rev: Black Parrot and value **Edge:** Reeded

Date	Mintage	F	VF	XF	Unc	BU
1982	375,000	—	0.25	0.75	2.50	3.00
1982 Proof	Inc. above	Value: 4.00				

KM# 49.2   25 CENTS
2.9000 g., Copper-Nickel, 19 mm. **Obv:** Arms with supporters
Rev: Black Parrot and value

Date	Mintage	F	VF	XF	Unc	BU
1989	1,500,000	—	0.25	0.75	2.25	4.00
1992PM	—		0.25	0.75	2.25	4.00
1992PM Proof	—	Value: 5.00				

KM# 49a   25 CENTS
2.9700 g., Nickel Clad Steel, 18.9 mm. **Obv:** National arms
Rev: Black Parrot and value **Edge:** Plain

Date	Mintage	F	VF	XF	Unc	BU
1993PM	—		0.25	0.60	1.50	2.00
1997PM	—		0.25	0.60	1.50	2.00

KM# 49b   25 CENTS
Stainless Steel, 19 mm. **Obv:** Arms with supporters **Rev:** Black
Parrot and value

Date	Mintage	F	VF	XF	Unc	BU
2000 (sa)	—			0.40	1.00	1.25

KM# 25   50 CENTS
5.8000 g., Copper-Nickel, 23.6 mm. **Subject:** Declaration of
Independence **Obv:** Head right **Rev:** Orchid and value
Edge: Reeded

Date	Mintage	F	VF	XF	Unc	BU
1976	209,000	—	0.50	1.00	2.50	3.50
1976 Proof	8,500	Value: 5.00				

KM# 34   50 CENTS
5.8000 g., Copper-Nickel, 23.6 mm. **Obv:** Arms with supporters
Rev: Orchid and value

Date	Mintage	F	VF	XF	Unc	BU
1977	—		0.20	0.45	1.00	1.50

KM# 26   RUPEE
11.6500 g., Copper-Nickel, 30 mm. **Subject:** Declaration of
Independence **Obv:** Head right **Rev:** Triton Conch shell and value
Edge: Reeded

Date	Mintage	F	VF	XF	Unc	BU
1976	259,000	—	0.75	1.00	1.75	2.50
1976 Proof	8,500	Value: 3.50				

KM# 35   RUPEE
11.6500 g., Copper-Nickel, 30 mm. **Obv:** Arms with supporters
Rev: Triton Conch shell and value

Date	Mintage	F	VF	XF	Unc	BU
1977	—		0.50	0.75	1.75	3.00

KM# 50.1   RUPEE
6.0500 g., Copper-Nickel, 25.3 mm. **Obv:** Arms with supporters
Rev: Triton Conch shell and value

Date	Mintage	F	VF	XF	Unc	BU
1982	2,000,000	—	0.25	0.50	2.00	3.50
1982 Proof	Inc. above	Value: 5.00				
1983	—		0.50	1.00	2.00	3.50

KM# 50.2   RUPEE
6.1800 g., Copper-Nickel, 25.46 mm. **Obv:** Altered coat of arms
Rev: Triton Conch Shell **Edge:** Reeded

Date	Mintage	F	VF	XF	Unc	BU
1992PM	—		0.25	0.60	1.50	2.00
1992PM Proof	—	Value: 5.00				
1995PM	—		0.25	0.60	1.50	2.00
1997PM	—		0.25	0.60	1.50	2.00

KM# 85   RUPEE
Copper-Nickel   **Series:** Queen Elizabeth The Queen Mother
Subject: Wedding of Lady Elizabeth Bowes-Lyon: The Duke of York,
1923 **Obv:** Arms with supporters **Rev:** Royal couple facing on steps

Date	Mintage	F	VF	XF	Unc	BU
1995	Est. 30,000	—	—	—	10.00	12.00

KM# 27   5 RUPEES
13.5000 g., Copper-Nickel, 30 mm. **Subject:** Declaration of
Independence **Obv:** Head right **Rev:** Palm tree and value

Date	Mintage	F	VF	XF	Unc	BU
1976	50,000	—	1.25	1.75	3.00	4.50

KM# 27a   5 RUPEES
15.5000 g., 0.9250 Silver 0.4609 oz. ASW, 30 mm.
Subject: Declaration of Independence **Obv:** Head right
Rev: Palm tree and value

Date	Mintage	F	VF	XF	Unc	BU
1976 Proof	8,500	Value: 12.50				

KM# 36   5 RUPEES
13.5000 g., Copper-Nickel, 30 mm. **Obv:** Arms with supporters
Rev: Palm tree and value

Date	Mintage	F	VF	XF	Unc	BU
1977	—		1.00	1.50	2.25	3.50

KM# 51.1   5 RUPEES
13.5000 g., Copper-Nickel, 30 mm. **Obv:** Arms with supporters
Rev: Palm tree and value

Date	Mintage	F	VF	XF	Unc	BU
1982	300,000	—	1.00	1.50	2.00	3.00
1982 Proof	Inc. above	Value: 5.00				

KM# 51.2   5 RUPEES
8.9700 g., Copper-Nickel, 28.8 mm. **Obv:** Altered arms
Rev: Fruit tree divides value **Edge:** Reeded

Date	Mintage	F	VF	XF	Unc	BU
1992PM	—		0.35	0.80	2.00	2.75
1992PM Proof	—	Value: 5.00				
1997PM	—		0.35	0.80	2.00	2.75
2000 (sa) Thicker lettering	—		0.35	0.80	2.00	2.75

KM# 89 5 RUPEES
Copper-Nickel **Series:** 50th Anniversary United Nations **Obv:** Arms with supporters **Rev:** Dove in flight over UN's logo, large 50 at right

Date	Mintage	F	VF	XF	Unc	BU
ND(1995)	—	—	—	—	10.00	12.00

KM# 109 5 RUPEES
Copper-Nickel **Subject:** Marriage of Prince Edward **Obv:** Arms with supporters **Rev:** Tied initials and birds **Note:** Similar to 25 Rupees, KM#110.

Date	Mintage	F	VF	XF	Unc	BU
1999	—	—	—	—	9.00	11.00

KM# 112 5 RUPEES
Copper-Nickel **Subject:** Millennium **Obv:** Arms with supporters **Rev:** Latent image of 1999-2000 dates **Note:** Similar to 25 Rupees, KM#113.

Date	Mintage	F	VF	XF	Unc	BU
2000(sa) (sa)	—	—	—	—	9.00	11.00

KM# 114 5 RUPEES
Copper-Nickel **Subject:** British Queen Mother **Obv:** Arms with supporters **Rev:** Head with hat 1/4 right, dates at right **Edge:** Reeded

Date	Mintage	F	VF	XF	Unc	BU
2000(sa) (sa)	—	—	—	—	9.00	11.00

KM# 28 10 RUPEES
18.1000 g., Copper-Nickel, 34.5 mm. **Subject:** Declaration of Independence **Obv:** Head right **Rev:** Green sea turtle and value

Date	Mintage	F	VF	XF	Unc	BU
1976	50,000	—	2.00	2.75	6.00	10.00

KM# 28a 10 RUPEES
28.2800 g., 0.9250 Silver 0.8410 oz. ASW, 34.5 mm.
Subject: Declaration of Independence **Obv:** Head right
Rev: Green sea turtle and value

Date	Mintage	F	VF	XF	Unc	BU
1976 Proof	29,000	Value: 17.50				

KM# 37 10 RUPEES
18.1000 g., Copper-Nickel, 34.5 mm. **Series:** F.A.O. **Obv:** Arms with supporters **Rev:** Green sea turtle and value

Date	Mintage	F	VF	XF	Unc	BU
1977	—	—	2.00	3.00	6.00	12.00
1977 Proof	—	Value: 12.00				

KM# 64 10 RUPEES
10.0000 g., 0.9250 Silver 0.2974 oz. ASW **Series:** Endangered Wildlife **Obv:** Arms with supporters **Rev:** Magpie Robin **Note:** Similar to 25 Rupees, KM#65.

Date	Mintage	F	VF	XF	Unc	BU
1993 Proof	Est. 20,000	Value: 20.00				

KM# 87 10 RUPEES
10.0000 g., 0.5000 Silver 0.1607 oz. ASW **Subject:** 1996 Olympics **Obv:** Arms with supporters **Rev:** Cyclist

Date	Mintage	F	VF	XF	Unc	BU
1996	Est. 10,000	—	—	—	27.50	30.00

KM# 52 20 RUPEES
Copper-Nickel **Subject:** 5th Anniversary of Central Bank **Obv:** Arms with supporters **Rev:** Turtle at center of symbols of commerce

Date	Mintage	F	VF	XF	Unc	BU
1983	—	—	4.00	5.00	6.00	8.00

KM# 52a 20 RUPEES
19.4400 g., 0.9250 Silver 0.5781 oz. ASW **Subject:** 5th Anniversary of Central Bank **Obv:** Arms with supporters **Rev:** Turtle at center of symbols of commerce

Date	Mintage	F	VF	XF	Unc	BU
1983 Proof	5,000	Value: 50.00				

KM# 52b 20 RUPEES
33.9000 g., 0.9170 Gold 0.9994 oz. AGW **Subject:** 5th Anniversary of Central Bank **Obv:** Arms with supporters **Rev:** Turtle at center of symbols of commerce

Date	Mintage	F	VF	XF	Unc	BU
1983 Proof	50	Value: 1,000				

KM# 38 25 RUPEES
28.2800 g., 0.5000 Silver 0.4546 oz. ASW **Subject:** Queen's Silver Jubilee **Obv:** Head right **Rev:** Royal Orb at center of legends

Date	Mintage	F	VF	XF	Unc	BU
ND(1977)	17,000	—	—	—	9.00	11.50

KM# 38a 25 RUPEES
28.2800 g., 0.9250 Silver 0.8410 oz. ASW **Subject:** Queen's Silver Jubilee **Obv:** Head right **Rev:** Royal Orb at center of legends

Date	Mintage	F	VF	XF	Unc	BU
ND(1977) Proof	15,000	Value: 16.50				

KM# 53 25 RUPEES
Copper-Nickel **Series:** F.A.O. **Subject:** World Fisheries Conference **Obv:** Arms with supporters **Rev:** Fish trap

Date	Mintage	F	VF	XF	Unc	BU
1983	100,000	—	5.00	6.00	9.00	12.00

KM# 53a 25 RUPEES
28.2800 g., 0.9250 Silver 0.8410 oz. ASW **Series:** F.A.O. **Subject:** World Fisheries Conference **Obv:** Arms with supporters **Rev:** Fish trap

Date	Mintage	F	VF	XF	Unc	BU
1983 Proof	20,000	Value: 37.50				

KM# 53b 25 RUPEES
47.5400 g., 0.9170 Gold 1.4015 oz. AGW **Series:** F.A.O. **Subject:** World Fisheries Conference **Obv:** Arms with supporters **Rev:** Fish trap

Date	Mintage	F	VF	XF	Unc	BU
1983 Proof	100	Value: 1,400				

KM# 63 25 RUPEES
31.4700 g., 0.9250 Silver 0.9359 oz. ASW **Subject:** 40th Anniversary of Queen Elizabeth's Coronation **Obv:** Arms with supporters **Rev:** Royal carriage

Date	Mintage	F	VF	XF	Unc	BU
1993 Proof	Est. 10,000	Value: 45.00				

KM# 65 25 RUPEES
28.2800 g., 0.9250 Silver 0.8410 oz. ASW **Series:** Endangered Wildlife **Obv:** Arms with supporters **Rev:** Magpie Robin

Date	Mintage	F	VF	XF	Unc	BU
1993 Proof	Est. 20,000	Value: 30.00				

KM# 67 25 RUPEES
31.4600 g., 0.9250 Silver 0.9356 oz. ASW **Subject:** World Cup Soccer **Obv:** Arms with supporters **Rev:** Goalie at net

Date	Mintage	F	VF	XF	Unc	BU
1993 Proof	Est. 15,000	Value: 28.00				

KM# 68   25 RUPEES
31.4600 g., 0.9250 Silver 0.9356 oz. ASW **Obv:** Arms with
supporters **Rev:** Space shuttle

Date	Mintage	F	VF	XF	Unc	BU
1993 Proof	Est. 10,000		Value: 25.00			

KM# 69   25 RUPEES
31.4600 g., 0.9250 Silver 0.9356 oz. ASW **Subject:** First French
Landing **Obv:** Arms with supporters **Rev:** Figure with flag in boat,
ships in background

Date	Mintage	F	VF	XF	Unc	BU
1993 Proof	Est. 10,000		Value: 22.50			

KM# 70   25 RUPEES
31.4600 g., 0.9250 Silver 0.9356 oz. ASW **Series:** 1992 Olympics
Obv: Arms with supporters **Rev:** Balance beam gymnasts

Date	Mintage	F	VF	XF	Unc	BU
1993 Proof	Est. 40,000		Value: 15.00			

KM# 71   25 RUPEES
31.4600 g., 0.9250 Silver 0.9356 oz. ASW **Series:** Protect Our
World **Obv:** Arms with supporters **Rev:** Fish and coral

Date	Mintage	F	VF	XF	Unc	BU
1993 Proof	Est. 10,000		Value: 35.00			

KM# 72   25 RUPEES
19.4400 g., 0.9250 Silver 0.5781 oz. ASW **Subject:** 15th
Anniversary - Central Bank **Obv:** Arms with supporters
Rev: Turtle flanked by dates

Date	Mintage	F	VF	XF	Unc	BU
1993 Proof	Est. 1,000		Value: 80.00			

KM# 74   25 RUPEES
19.4400 g., 0.9250 Silver 0.5781 oz. ASW **Series:** Endangered
Wildlife **Obv:** Arms with supporters **Rev:** Butterfly and value

Date	Mintage	F	VF	XF	Unc	BU
1994PM Proof	20,000		Value: 35.00			

KM# 79   25 RUPEES
31.4700 g., 0.9250 Silver 0.9359 oz. ASW **Series:** Queen
Elizabeth The Queen Mother **Subject:** Wedding of Lady
Elizabeth Bowes-Lyon: The Duke of York, 1923 **Obv:** Arms with
supporters **Rev:** Royal couple on steps

Date	Mintage	F	VF	XF	Unc	BU
1994 Proof	50,000		Value: 25.00			

KM# 78   25 RUPEES
28.2800 g., 0.9250 Silver 0.8410 oz. ASW **Series:** Endangered
Wildlife **Obv:** Arms with supporters **Rev:** Kestrel

Date	Mintage	F	VF	XF	Unc	BU
1995 Proof	Est. 20,000		Value: 35.00			

KM# 80   25 RUPEES
28.2800 g., 0.9250 Silver 0.8410 oz. ASW **Series:** Olympics
Obv: Arms with supporters **Rev:** Figures sailing

Date	Mintage	F	VF	XF	Unc	BU
1995 Proof	Est. 30,000		Value: 25.00			

KM# 81   25 RUPEES
28.2800 g., 0.9250 Silver 0.8410 oz. ASW **Subject:** Vasco da
Gama **Obv:** Arms with supporters **Rev:** Horizontal line divides
ship and palms from standing ship captain **Edge:** Reeding over
lettering **Edge:** EXPLORERS OF THE WORLD

Date	Mintage	F	VF	XF	Unc	BU
1995 Proof	Est. 10,000		Value: 37.50			

KM# 108   25 RUPEES
28.2800 g., 0.9250 Silver 0.8410 oz. ASW **Series:** 50th
Anniversary U.N. **Obv:** Arms with supporters **Rev:** Flying bird
above UN logo and numeral 50

Date	Mintage	F	VF	XF	Unc	BU
1995 Proof	—		Value: 35.00			

KM# 97   25 RUPEES
31.4700 g., 0.9250 Silver 0.9359 oz. ASW **Series:** 1996 Olympic
Games **Obv:** Arms with supporters **Rev:** Cyclist

Date	Mintage	F	VF	XF	Unc	BU
1995 Proof	—		Value: 25.00			

KM# 88   25 RUPEES
31.4700 g., 0.9250 Silver 0.9359 oz. ASW **Subject:** Foundation of the Commonwealth **Obv:** Arms with supporters **Rev:** Crown and assorted flags

Date	Mintage	F	VF	XF	Unc	BU
1996	40,000	—	—	—	30.00	32.50

KM# 124   25 RUPEES
28.2800 g., 0.9250 Silver 0.8410 oz. ASW, 39 mm. **Obv:** National arms **Rev:** Victoria Cross above advancing infantry **Edge:** Reeded

Date	Mintage	F	VF	XF	Unc	BU
1996 Proof	—	Value: 25.00				

KM# 83   25 RUPEES
28.2800 g., 0.9250 Silver 0.8410 oz. ASW **Series:** Endangered Wildlife **Obv:** Arms with supporters **Rev:** Flycatcher bird feeding babies

Date	Mintage	F	VF	XF	Unc	BU
1996 Proof	Est. 20,000	Value: 45.00				

KM# 92   25 RUPEES
1.2400 g., 0.9990 Gold 0.0398 oz. AGW **Subject:** Diana - The People's Princess **Obv:** Arms with supporters **Rev:** Head 1/4 right **Note:** Similar to KM#91.

Date	Mintage	F	VF	XF	Unc	BU
1997 Proof	Est. 10,000	Value: 50.00				

KM# 117   25 RUPEES
19.4400 g., 0.9250 Silver 0.5781 oz. ASW, 36 mm.
Subject: UNICEF **Obv:** Arms with supporters **Rev:** Boy fishing **Edge:** Reeded

Date	Mintage	F	VF	XF	Unc	BU
1997 Proof	25,000	Value: 25.00				

KM# 91   25 RUPEES
28.2800 g., 0.9250 Silver 0.8410 oz. ASW **Subject:** Diana - The People's Princess **Obv:** Arms with supporters **Rev:** Head 1/4 right

Date	Mintage	F	VF	XF	Unc	BU
1997 Proof	Est. 10,000	Value: 40.00				

KM# 95   25 RUPEES
28.2800 g., 0.9250 Silver 0.8410 oz. ASW **Subject:** Diana - The People's Princess **Obv:** Arms with supporters **Rev:** Diana holding baby Prince William

Date	Mintage	F	VF	XF	Unc	BU
1997 Proof	Est. 10,000	Value: 30.00				

KM# 96   25 RUPEES
1.2400 g., 0.9990 Gold 0.0398 oz. AGW **Subject:** Diana - The People's Princess **Obv:** Arms with supporters **Rev:** Diana holding baby Prince William

Date	Mintage	F	VF	XF	Unc	BU
1997 Proof	Est. 10,000	Value: 55.00				

KM# 99   25 RUPEES
28.2800 g., 0.9250 Silver 0.8410 oz. ASW **Subject:** Diana - The People's Princess **Obv:** Arms with supporters **Rev:** Bust left holding young cancer patient

Date	Mintage	F	VF	XF	Unc	BU
1997 Proof	Est. 10,000	Value: 40.00				

KM# 100   25 RUPEES
1.2400 g., 0.9990 Gold 0.0398 oz. AGW **Subject:** Diana - The People's Princess **Obv:** Arms with supporters **Rev:** Diana holding young cancer patient

Date	Mintage	F	VF	XF	Unc	BU
1997 Proof	Est. 10,000	Value: 55.00				

KM# 103   25 RUPEES
28.2800 g., 0.9250 Silver 0.8410 oz. ASW **Subject:** Diana - The People's Princess **Obv:** Arms with supporters **Rev:** Diana in summer clothes

Date	Mintage	F	VF	XF	Unc	BU
1998 Proof	Est. 10,000	Value: 42.50				

KM# 104   25 RUPEES
1.2441 g., 0.9999 Gold 0.0400 oz. AGW **Subject:** Diana - The People's Princess **Obv:** Arms with supporters **Rev:** Diana in summer clothes

Date	Mintage	F	VF	XF	Unc	BU
1998 Proof	Est. 10,000	Value: 60.00				

KM# 110   25 RUPEES
28.2800 g., 0.9250 Silver 0.8410 oz. ASW **Subject:** Marriage of Prince Edward and Miss Sophie Rhys-Jones **Obv:** Arms with supporters **Rev:** Tied vertical monograms flanked by doves

Date	Mintage	F	VF	XF	Unc	BU
1999 Proof	Est. 10,000	Value: 40.00				

KM# 113   25 RUPEES
1.2441 g., 0.9999 Gold 0.0400 oz. AGW **Subject:** Millennium **Obv:** Arms with supporters **Rev:** Latent image of 1999-2000 dates

Date	Mintage	F	VF	XF	Unc	BU
2000 Proof	Est. 10,000	Value: 50.00				

KM# 115   25 RUPEES
1.2441 g., 0.9999 Gold 0.0400 oz. AGW **Subject:** 100th Birthday - British Queen Mother **Obv:** Arms with supporters **Rev:** Head with hat 1/4 right **Edge:** Reeded

Date	Mintage	F	VF	XF	Unc	BU
2000 Proof	Est. 10,000	Value: 50.00				

KM# 39   50 RUPEES
28.2800 g., 0.9250 Silver 0.8410 oz. ASW **Subject:** Conservation **Obv:** Arms with supporters **Rev:** Squirrel fish, coral and value

Date	Mintage	F	VF	XF	Unc	BU
1978	4,453	—	—	—	20.00	22.50
1978 Proof	4,281	Value: 27.50				

KM# 42   50 RUPEES
19.4400 g., 0.9250 Silver 0.5781 oz. ASW **Series:** UNICEF and International Year of the Child **Obv:** Arms with supporters **Rev:** Figures below palm tree flanked by UNICEF logos

Date	Mintage	F	VF	XF	Unc	BU
1980 Proof	10,000	Value: 17.50				

KM# 54   50 RUPEES
19.4400 g., 0.9250 Silver 0.5781 oz. ASW **Series:** Decade for Women **Obv:** Arms with supporters **Rev:** Map flanked by figures above value

Date	Mintage	F	VF	XF	Unc	BU
1985 Proof	500	Value: 28.00				

KM# 75   50 RUPEES
1.2440 g., 0.9999 Gold 0.0400 oz. AGW **Series:** Endangered Wildlife **Obv:** Arms with supporters **Rev:** Milkweed Butterfly **Note:** Similar to 25 Rupees, KM#74.

Date	Mintage	F	VF	XF	Unc	BU
1994PM Prooflike	—	—	—	—	—	45.00

KM# 107   50 RUPEES
3.1100 g., 0.5833 Gold 0.0583 oz. AGW **Series:** Olympics Games 2000 **Obv:** Arms with supporters **Rev:** Two divers

Date	Mintage	F	VF	XF	Unc	BU
1997 Proof	5,000	Value: 65.00				

KM# 40   100 RUPEES
31.6500 g., 0.9250 Silver 0.9412 oz. ASW **Subject:** Conservation **Obv:** Arms with supporters **Rev:** White-tailed Tropic bird

Date	Mintage	F	VF	XF	Unc	BU
1978	4,453	—	—	—	22.50	25.00
1978 Proof	4,075	Value: 32.50				

KM# 45   100 RUPEES
31.6500 g., 0.9250 Silver 0.9412 oz. ASW **Series:** World Food Day **Obv:** Arms with supporters **Rev:** Value and coconuts below seated figure flanked by palm trees

Date	Mintage	F	VF	XF	Unc	BU
1981	6,000	—	—	—	25.00	27.50
1981 Proof	5,000	Value: 37.50				

KM# 45a   100 RUPEES
35.0000 g., 0.5000 Silver 0.5626 oz. ASW **Subject:** World Food Day **Obv:** Arms with supporters **Rev:** Value and coconuts below seated figure flanked by palm trees

Date	Mintage	F	VF	XF	Unc	BU
1981 Proof	10,000	Value: 25.00				

KM# 55   100 RUPEES
19.4400 g., 0.9250 Silver 0.5781 oz. ASW **Subject:** 10th Anniversary of Independence **Obv:** Arms with supporters **Rev:** Design above shark tail design dividing dates

Date	Mintage	F	VF	XF	Unc	BU
ND(1986) Proof	1,000	Value: 45.00				

KM# 57   100 RUPEES
19.4400 g., 0.9250 Silver 0.5781 oz. ASW **Subject:** 10th Anniversary of Liberation **Obv:** Arms with supporters **Rev:** Standing figure divides dates

Date	Mintage	F	VF	XF	Unc	BU
ND(1987)PM Proof	1,000	Value: 40.00				

KM# 59   100 RUPEES
19.4000 g., 0.9170 Silver 0.5719 oz. ASW **Subject:** 10th Anniversary of Central Bank **Obv:** Arms with supporters **Rev:** Sea Turtle, dates below

Date	Mintage	F	VF	XF	Unc	BU
ND(1988)PM Proof	—	Value: 100				

KM# 60   100 RUPEES
1.7000 g., 0.9170 Gold 0.0501 oz. AGW **Subject:** 10th Anniversary of Central Bank **Obv:** Arms with supporters **Rev:** Sea turtle

Date	Mintage	F	VF	XF	Unc	BU
ND(1988)PM Proof	—	Value: 100				

KM# 76   100 RUPEES
3.1103 g., 0.9999 Gold 0.1000 oz. AGW **Series:** Endangered Wildlife **Obv:** Arms with supporters **Rev:** Milkweed Butterfly

Date	Mintage	F	VF	XF	Unc	BU
1994PM Prooflike	—	—	—	—	—	100

KM# 82   100 RUPEES
7.7760 g., 0.5830 Gold 0.1457 oz. AGW **Series:** Olympics **Obv:** Arms with supporters **Rev:** Sailboats

Date	Mintage	F	VF	XF	Unc	BU
1995 Proof	Est. 3,000	Value: 150				

KM# 86   100 RUPEES
7.7760 g., 0.5830 Gold 0.1457 oz. AGW **Subject:** British Queen Mother **Obv:** Arms with supporters **Rev:** Wedding portrait

Date	Mintage	F	VF	XF	Unc	BU
1995 Proof	Est. 5,000	Value: 150				

KM# 93   100 RUPEES
7.7760 g., 0.5830 Gold 0.1457 oz. AGW **Subject:** Diana - The People's Princess **Obv:** Arms with supporters **Rev:** Bust facing

Date	Mintage	F	VF	XF	Unc	BU
1997 Proof	Est. 7,500	Value: 150				

KM# A97   100 RUPEES
7.7760 g., 0.5830 Gold 0.1457 oz. AGW **Subject:** Diana - The People's Princess **Obv:** Arms with supporters **Rev:** Diana holding newborn Prince William

Date	Mintage	F	VF	XF	Unc	BU
1997 Proof	7,500	Value: 150				

KM# 101   100 RUPEES
7.7760 g., 0.5830 Gold 0.1457 oz. AGW **Subject:** Diana - The People's Princess **Obv:** Arms with supporters **Rev:** Diana holding young cancer patient

Date	Mintage	F	VF	XF	Unc	BU
1997 Proof	Est. 7,500	Value: 150				

KM# 105   100 RUPEES
7.7760 g., 0.5830 Gold 0.1457 oz. AGW **Subject:** Diana - The People's Princess **Obv:** Arms with supporters **Rev:** Diana in summer clothes

Date	Mintage	F	VF	XF	Unc	BU
1998 Proof	Est. 7,500	Value: 150				

KM# 111   100 RUPEES
6.2200 g., 0.9999 Gold 0.1999 oz. AGW **Subject:** Marriage of Prince Edward **Obv:** Arms with supporters **Rev:** Tied monograms and birds

Date	Mintage	F	VF	XF	Unc	BU
1999 Proof	Est. 2,000	Value: 210				

KM# 116   100 RUPEES
6.2200 g., 0.9999 Gold 0.1999 oz. AGW, 22 mm. **Subject:** 100th Birthday Queen Mother **Obv:** Arms with supporters **Rev:** Queen Mother's portrait **Edge:** Reeded

Date	Mintage	F	VF	XF	Unc	BU
2000 Proof	2,000	Value: 210				

KM# 66   250 RUPEES
6.2200 g., 0.9990 Gold 0.1998 oz. AGW **Series:** Endangered Wildlife **Obv:** Arms with supporters **Rev:** Magpie Robin

Date	Mintage	F	VF	XF	Unc	BU
1993 Proof	—	Value: 210				

KM# 77   250 RUPEES
6.2200 g., 0.9990 Gold 0.1998 oz. AGW **Series:** Endangered Wildlife **Obv:** Arms with supporters **Rev:** Milkweed Butterfly

Date	Mintage	F	VF	XF	Unc	BU
1993 Proof	—	Value: 210				
1994PM Proof	—	Value: 210				
1996PM Proof	5,000	Value: 210				

KM# 84   250 RUPEES
6.2200 g., 0.9990 Gold 0.1998 oz. AGW **Series:** Endangered Wildlife **Obv:** Arms with supporters **Rev:** Paradise Flycatcher Bird

Date	Mintage	F	VF	XF	Unc	BU
1996 Proof	Est. 5,000	Value: 210				

KM# 98   250 RUPEES
6.2200 g., 0.9990 Gold 0.1998 oz. AGW **Subject:** Diana - The People's Princess **Obv:** Arms with supporters **Rev:** Diana holding newborn Prince William

Date	Mintage	F	VF	XF	Unc	BU
1997 Proof	Est. 5,000	Value: 210				

KM# 102   250 RUPEES
6.2200 g., 0.9990 Gold 0.1998 oz. AGW **Subject:** Diana - The People's Princess **Obv:** Arms with supporters **Rev:** Diana holding young cancer patient

Date	Mintage	F	VF	XF	Unc	BU
1997 Proof	Est. 5,000	Value: 210				

KM# 94   250 RUPEES
6.2200 g., 0.9990 Gold 0.1998 oz. AGW **Subject:** Diana - The People's Princess **Obv:** Arms with supporters **Rev:** Bust facing **Note:** Similar to 25 Rupees, KM#91.

Date	Mintage	F	VF	XF	Unc	BU
1997 Proof	Est. 5,000	Value: 210				

KM# 106 250 RUPEES

6.2200 g., 0.9990 Gold 0.1998 oz. AGW **Subject:** Diana - The People's Princess **Obv:** Arms with supporters **Rev:** Diana in summer dress

Date	Mintage	F	VF	XF	Unc	BU
1998 Proof	Est. 5,000	Value: 210				

KM# 62 500 RUPEES

7.1300 g., 0.9000 Gold 0.2063 oz. AGW **Series:** Decade for Women **Obv:** Arms with supporters **Rev:** Value below standing figures

Date	Mintage	F	VF	XF	Unc	BU
1985 Proof	500	Value: 220				

KM# 29 1000 RUPEES

15.9800 g., 0.9170 Gold 0.4711 oz. AGW **Subject:** Declaration of Independence **Obv:** President Mancham **Rev:** Tortoise, date, value

Date	Mintage	F	VF	XF	Unc	BU
1976	5,000	—	—	—	—	475
1976 Proof	1,000	Value: 490				

KM# 56 1000 RUPEES

15.9800 g., 0.9170 Gold 0.4711 oz. AGW **Subject:** 10th Anniversary of Independence **Obv:** Arms with supporters **Rev:** Design above shark tail design dividing dates

Date	Mintage	F	VF	XF	Unc	BU
ND(1986) Proof	100	Value: 475				

KM# 58 1000 RUPEES

15.9800 g., 0.9170 Gold 0.4711 oz. AGW **Subject:** 10th Anniversary of Liberation **Obv:** Arms with supporters **Rev:** Standing figure divides dates

Date	Mintage	F	VF	XF	Unc	BU
ND(1987)PM Proof	100	Value: 475				

KM# 61 1000 RUPEES

15.9400 g., 0.9170 Gold 0.4699 oz. AGW **Subject:** 100th Anniversary of Central Bank **Obv:** Arms with supporters **Rev:** Sea turtle

Date	Mintage	F	VF	XF	Unc	BU
ND(1988)PM Proof	Est. 5,000	Value: 465				

KM# 73 1000 RUPEES

15.9800 g., 0.9170 Gold 0.4711 oz. AGW **Subject:** Central Banking

Date	Mintage	F	VF	XF	Unc	BU
1993 Proof	Est. 200	Value: 475				

KM# 41 1500 RUPEES

33.4370 g., 0.9000 Gold 0.9675 oz. AGW **Subject:** Conservation **Obv:** Arms with supporters **Rev:** Flycatcher birds

Date	Mintage	F	VF	XF	Unc	BU
1978	683	—	—	—	—	950
1978 Proof	201	Value: 1,000				

PATTERNS

Including off metal strikes

KM#	Date	Mintage	Identification	Mkt Val
Pn1	1974	—	10 Rupees. Brass. KM#20.	—
Pn2	1974	—	10 Rupees. Bronze. KM#20.	—
Pn3	1974	—	10 Rupees. Copper-Nickel. KM#20.	—
Pn4	1974	—	10 Rupees. Silver. KM#20.	—
Pn5	1976	—	10 Cents. Silver. KM#23, thick planchet.	250
Pn6	1976	—	1000 Rupees. Bronze. KM#29.	—

PIEFORTS

KM#	Date	Mintage	Identification	Mkt Val
P1	1980	78	50 Rupees. Silver. KM#42.	90.00
P2	1983	500	50 Rupees.	65.00
P3	1984	500	50 Rupees. 0.9250 Silver.	65.00
P4	1984	100	50 Rupees. 0.9000 Gold.	1,500

MINT SETS

KM#	Date	Mintage	Identification	Issue Price	Mkt Val
MS1	1972 (7)	—	KM#10-13, 17-19	—	8.50
MS2	1974 (5)	—	KM#10-13, 20	—	8.50
MS3	1976 (8)	—	KM#21-28	—	16.00
MS4	1977 (8)	—	KM#30-37	—	11.50
MS5	1982 (6)	—	KM#46.1-51.1	—	5.00
MS6	1992 (6)	—	KM#46.2, 47.2, 48.2, 49.2, 50.2, 51.2	12.00	12.00
MS7	Mixed dates (6)	—	KM#46.2 (1990), 47.2-51.2 (1997)	—	8.50

PROOF SETS

KM#	Date	Mintage	Identification	Issue Price	Mkt Val
PS1	1939 (4)	—	KM#1-4	—	1,000
PS2	1969 (7)	5,000	KM#10-16	8.40	20.00
PS3	1974 (2)	5,000	KM#19-a, 20a	37.00	32.50
PS4	1976 (9)	1,000	KM#21-26, 27a, 28a, 29	375	375
PS5	1976 (8)	7,500	KM#21-26, 27a, 28a	42.50	42.50
PS6	1982 (6)	5,000	KM#46.1-51.1	29.95	20.00
PS7	1992 (6)	—	KM#46.2-51.2	—	20.00

SHARJAH

Ras Al Khaimah
Umm Al-Qaiwain
Ajman
OMAN
QATAR
Sharjah
Fujairah
Persian Gulf
Dubai
Gulf of Oman
Abu-Dhabi
SAUDI ARABIA
OMAN

Sharjah is the only one of the emirates that shares boundaries with all of the others plus Oman. It has an area of 1,000 sq. mi. (2,600 sq. km.) and a population of 40,000. Sharjah was an important pirate base in the 18th and early 19th centuries. Most of the treaties and diplomatic relations were with Great Britain.

TITLE
Ash-Sharqa(t)

RULERS
Saqr Bin Khalid al-Qasimi, 1883-1914
Khalid Bin Ahmad al-Qasimi, 1914-1924
Sultan Bin Saqr al-Qasimi, 1924-1951
Saqr Bin Sultan al-Qasimi, 1951-1965
Khalid Bin Muhammad al-Qasimi, 1965-1972
Sultan Bin Muhammad al-Qasimi,1972-

EMIRATE

NON-CIRCULATING LEGAL TENDER COINAGE

KM# 2 RIYAL

3.0000 g., 1.0000 Silver 0.0964 oz. ASW **Ruler:** Khalid bin Muhammad al-Qasimi **Subject:** Mona Lisa **Obv:** National arms **Rev:** Bust facing

Date	Mintage	F	VF	XF	Unc	BU
AH1389-1970 Proof	3,850	Value: 17.50				

KM# 3 2 RIYALS

6.0000 g., 1.0000 Silver 0.1929 oz. ASW **Ruler:** Khalid bin Muhammad al-Qasimi **Subject:** Mexico World Soccer Cup **Obv:** National arms **Rev:** World soccer cup within globe design

Date	Mintage	F	VF	XF	Unc	BU
AH1389-1970 Proof	4,500	Value: 27.50				

KM# 4 5 RIYALS

15.0000 g., 1.0000 Silver 0.4822 oz. ASW **Ruler:** Khalid bin Muhammad al-Qasimi **Subject:** Napoleon **Obv:** National arms **Rev:** Uniformed bust facing 1/4 left divides logo and dates

Date	Mintage	F	VF	XF	Unc	BU
AH1389-1970 Proof	2,500	Value: 37.50				

KM# 5 10 RIYALS

30.0000 g., 1.0000 Silver 0.9645 oz. ASW **Ruler:** Khalid bin Muhammad al-Qasimi **Subject:** Bolivar **Obv:** National arms **Rev:** Head right

Date	Mintage	F	VF	XF	Unc	BU
AH1389-1970 Proof	3,200	Value: 65.00				

KM# 7 25 RIYALS

5.1800 g., 0.9000 Gold 0.1499 oz. AGW **Ruler:** Khalid bin Muhammad al-Qasimi **Subject:** Mona Lisa **Obv:** National arms **Rev:** Bust facing

Date	Mintage	F	VF	XF	Unc	BU
AH1389-1970 Proof	6,775	Value: 175				

KM# 8 50 RIYALS

10.3600 g., 0.9000 Gold 0.2998 oz. AGW **Ruler:** Khalid bin Muhammad al-Qasimi **Subject:** Mexico World Soccer Cup **Obv:** National arms **Rev:** World soccer cup within globe design

Date	Mintage	F	VF	XF	Unc	BU
AH1389-1970 Proof	1,815	Value: 325				

KM# 9   100 RIYALS
20.7300 g., 0.9000 Gold 0.5998 oz. AGW **Ruler:** Khalid bin
Muhammad al-Qasimi **Subject:** Bicentennial - Napoleon
Obv: National arms **Rev:** Uniformed bust facing 1/4 left divides
logo and dates

Date	Mintage	F	VF	XF	Unc	BU
AH1389-1970 Proof	—	Value: 600				

KM# 10   100 RIYALS
20.7300 g., 0.9000 Gold 0.5998 oz. AGW **Ruler:** Khalid bin
Muhammad al-Qasimi **Subject:** Bolivar **Obv:** National arms
Rev: Head right

Date	Mintage	F	VF	XF	Unc	BU
AH1389-1970 Proof	—	Value: 600				

KM# 11   200 RIYALS
41.4600 g., 0.9000 Gold 1.1996 oz. AGW **Ruler:** Khalid bin
Muhammad al-Qasimi **Subject:** Khalid III **Obv:** National arms
Rev: Head facing

Date	Mintage	F	VF	XF	Unc	BU
AH1389-1970 Proof	435	Value: 1,200				

PROOF SETS

KM#	Date	Mintage	Identification	Issue Price	Mkt Val
PS1	1970 (9)	—	KM#2-5, 7-11	—	3,150
PS2	1970 (5)	—	KM#7-11	—	3,000
PS3	1970 (4)	2,500	KM#2-5	25.30	150

SIERRA LEONE

The Republic of Sierra Leone is located in western Africa
between Guinea and Liberia, has an area of 27,699 sq. mi.
(71,740 sq. km.) and a population of *4.1 million. Capital: Freetown. The economy is predominantly agricultural but mining con-
tributes significantly to export revenues. Diamonds, iron ore,
palm kernels, cocoa, and coffee are exported.

The coast of Sierra Leone was first visited by Portuguese
and British slavers in the 15th and 16th centuries. The first settlement, at Freetown, 1787, was established as a refuge for freed
slaves within the British Empire, runaway slaves from the United
States and Negroes discharged from the British armed forces.
The first settlers were virtually wiped out by tribal attacks and disease. The colony was re-established under the auspices of the
Sierra Leone Company and transferred to the British Crown in
1807. The interior region was secured and established as a protectorate in 1896. Sierra Leone became independent on April 27,
1961, and adopted a republican constitution ten years later. It is
a member of the Commonwealth of Nations. The president is
Chief of State and Head of Government.

For similar coinage refer to British West Africa.

RULER
British, until 1961

MONETARY SYSTEM
Beginning 1964
100 Cents = 1 Leone
NOTE: Sierra Leone's official currency is the Leone. For pre-
viously listed Dollar Denominated Coinage, see the 5th Edition of
Unusual World Coins.

REPUBLIC
STANDARD COINAGE

KM# 16   1/2 CENT
2.8500 g., Bronze, 20.2 mm. **Obv:** Value divides fish **Rev:** Head
of right Sir Milton Margai **Edge:** Plain

Date	Mintage	F	VF	XF	Unc	BU
1964	600,000	—	—	0.15	0.25	0.75
1964 Proof	10,000	Value: 1.00				

KM# 16a   1/2 CENT
2.8300 g., 0.9250 Silver 0.0842 oz. ASW, 20.2 mm. **Obv:** Value
divides fish **Rev:** Head of right Sir Milton Margai

Date	Mintage	F	VF	XF	Unc	BU
1964 Proof	22	Value: 650				

KM# 31   1/2 CENT
2.8500 g., Bronze, 20.2 mm. **Obv:** Value above arms **Rev:** Head
of Dr. Siaka Stevens right

Date	Mintage	F	VF	XF	Unc	BU
1980	—	—	0.15	0.30	1.00	
1980 Proof	10,000	Value: 1.50				

KM# 17   CENT
5.7000 g., Bronze, 25.45 mm. **Obv:** Value within palm sprigs
Rev: Head of Sir Milton Margai right **Edge:** Plain

Date	Mintage	F	VF	XF	Unc	BU
1964	35,000,000	—	—	0.15	0.25	
1964 Proof	10,000	Value: 1.25				

KM# 17a   CENT
5.6700 g., 0.9250 Silver 0.1686 oz. ASW, 25.45 mm.
Obv: Value within palm sprigs **Rev:** Head of Sir Milton Margai
right

Date	Mintage	F	VF	XF	Unc	BU
1964 Proof	22	Value: 650				

KM# 32   CENT
5.7000 g., Bronze, 25.45 mm. **Obv:** Value above arms
Rev: Head of Sir Milton Margai right

Date	Mintage	F	VF	XF	Unc	BU
1980	—	—	0.15	0.30	1.00	
1980 Proof	10,000	Value: 1.50				

KM# 18   5 CENTS
2.5000 g., Copper-Nickel, 17.8 mm. **Obv:** Tree divides date
within circle **Rev:** Head of right Sir Milton Margai

Date	Mintage	F	VF	XF	Unc	BU
1964	900,000	—	0.15	0.25	0.50	—
1964 Proof	10,000	Value: 1.50				

KM# 18a   5 CENTS
2.4900 g., 0.9250 Silver 0.0740 oz. ASW, 17.8 mm. **Obv:** Tree
divides date within circle **Rev:** Head of right Sir Milton Margai

Date	Mintage	F	VF	XF	Unc	BU
1964 Proof	22	Value: 650				

KM# 33   5 CENTS
2.5000 g., Copper-Nickel, 17.8 mm. **Obv:** Value above arms
Rev: Head of Dr. Siaka Stevens right

Date	Mintage	F	VF	XF	Unc	BU
1980	—	—	0.15	0.30	0.75	—
1980 Proof	10,000	Value: 2.50				
1984	—	—	0.15	0.30	0.75	—

KM# 19   10 CENTS
4.9000 g., Copper-Nickel, 22.9 mm. **Obv:** Value within cocoa
bean wreath **Rev:** Head of right Sir Milton Margai

Date	Mintage	F	VF	XF	Unc	BU
1964	24,000,000	—	0.25	0.40	0.65	—
1964 Proof	10,000	Value: 1.25				

KM# 19a   10 CENTS
4.9200 g., 0.9250 Silver 0.1463 oz. ASW, 22.9 mm. **Obv:** Value
within cocoa bean wreath **Rev:** Head of right Sir Milton Margai

Date	Mintage	F	VF	XF	Unc	BU
1964 Proof	22	Value: 650				

KM# 34   10 CENTS
4.9000 g., Copper-Nickel, 22.9 mm. **Obv:** Value above arms
Rev: Head of Dr. Siaka Stevens right

Date	Mintage	F	VF	XF	Unc	BU
1978	200,000	—	0.25	0.50	1.00	—
1980	—	—	0.20	0.40	0.75	—
1980 Proof	10,000	Value: 5.00				
1984	—	—	0.20	0.40	0.75	—

KM# 20   20 CENTS
8.2500 g., Copper-Nickel, 26.95 mm. **Obv:** Lion walking left
Rev: Head of Sir Milton Margai right **Edge:** Reeded

Date	Mintage	F	VF	XF	Unc	BU
1964	11,000,000	—	0.35	0.60	1.25	—
1964 Proof	10,000	Value: 2.00				

KM# 20a   20 CENTS
8.2200 g., 0.9250 Silver 0.2444 oz. ASW, 26.95 mm. **Obv:** Lion
walking right **Rev:** Head of right Sir Milton Margai

Date	Mintage	F	VF	XF	Unc	BU
1964 Proof	22	Value: 650				

KM# 30 20 CENTS

8.2500 g., Copper-Nickel, 26.95 mm. **Obv:** Value above arms
Rev: Head of Dr. Siaka Stevens right

Date	Mintage	F	VF	XF	Unc	BU
1978	2,375,000	—	0.35	0.65	1.50	—
1980	—	—	0.35	0.60	1.25	—
1980 Proof	10,000	Value: 7.00				
1984	—	—	0.35	0.60	1.25	—

KM# 25 50 CENTS

11.6000 g., Copper-Nickel, 30 mm. **Obv:** Value above arms
Rev: Head of Dr. Siaka Stevens right

Date	Mintage	F	VF	XF	Unc	BU
1972	1,000,000	—	1.00	1.75	3.00	—
1972 Proof	2,000	Value: 5.00				
1980	—	—	1.00	1.50	2.75	—
1980 Proof	10,000	Value: 10.00				
1984	—	—	1.00	1.50	2.75	—

KM# 21 LEONE

Copper-Nickel **Obv:** Value above arms **Rev:** Head of right Sir
Milton Margai

Date	Mintage	F	VF	XF	Unc	BU
1964 Proof	10,000	Value: 10.00				

KM# 21a LEONE

22.6220 g., 0.9250 Silver 0.6727 oz. ASW **Obv:** Value above
arms **Rev:** Head of right Sir Milton Margai

Date	Mintage	F	VF	XF	Unc	BU
1964 Proof	12	Value: 1,000				

KM# 21b LEONE

0.9170 Gold **Obv:** Value above arms **Rev:** Head of right Sir
Milton Margai

Date	Mintage	F	VF	XF	Unc	BU
1964 Proof	10	Value: 2,600				

KM# 26 LEONE

Copper-Nickel **Subject:** 10 Anniversary of Bank **Obv:** Lion right
within circle **Rev:** Head of Dr. Siaka Stevens right

Date	Mintage	F	VF	XF	Unc	BU
ND(1974)	103,000	—	1.50	2.50	6.00	7.50

KM# 26a LEONE

28.2800 g., 0.9250 Silver 0.8410 oz. ASW **Obv:** Head of Dr.
Siaka Stevens right **Rev:** Lion right within circle

Date	Mintage	F	VF	XF	Unc	BU
ND(1974) Proof	22,000	Value: 17.50				

KM# 26b LEONE

Gold **Subject:** 10 Anniversary of Bank **Obv:** Head of Dr. Siaka
Stevens right **Rev:** Lion right within circle

Date	Mintage	F	VF	XF	Unc	BU
ND(1974	100	—	—	—	1,350	—

KM# 36 LEONE

Copper-Nickel **Subject:** O.A.U. Summit Conference **Obv:** Map
within circle **Rev:** Head of Dr. Siaka Stevens right

Date	Mintage	F	VF	XF	Unc	BU
1980	75,000	—	1.75	2.75	6.00	—

KM# 36a LEONE

28.2800 g., 0.9250 Silver 0.8410 oz. ASW **Obv:** Map within
circle **Rev:** Head of Dr. Siaka Stevens right

Date	Mintage	F	VF	XF	Unc	BU
1980 Proof	15,000	Value: 20.00				

KM# 40 LEONE

9.5000 g., 0.9250 Silver 0.2825 oz. ASW **Subject:** Freetown
Bicentennial **Obv:** Numeral 200 within design **Rev:** Bust of Dr.
Joseph Saidu Momoh left

Date	Mintage	F	VF	XF	Unc	BU
1987 Proof	3,000	Value: 25.00				

KM# 40a LEONE

16.0000 g., 0.9170 Gold 0.4717 oz. AGW **Subject:** Freetown
Bicentennial **Obv:** Numeral 200 within design **Rev:** Bust of Dr.
Joseph Saidu Momoh left

Date	Mintage	F	VF	XF	Unc	BU
1987 Proof	1,250	Value: 475				

KM# 43 LEONE

Nickel-Bronze **Obv:** Value above arms **Rev:** Bust of Dr. Joseph
Saidu Momoh left

Date	Mintage	F	VF	XF	Unc	BU
1987	—	—	0.50	0.75	1.50	2.50
1988	—	—	0.50	0.75	1.50	2.50

KM# 29 2 LEONES

Copper-Nickel, 30 mm. **Series:** F.A.O. **Subject:** Regional
Conference for Africa **Obv:** Farmer tilling field **Rev:** Head of Dr.
Siaka Stevens right **Edge:** Plain

Date	Mintage	F	VF	XF	Unc	BU
1976	20,000	—	1.00	2.50	5.50	6.50

KM# 38 10 LEONES

28.2800 g., 0.9250 Silver 0.8410 oz. ASW **Series:** Year of the
Scout **Obv:** Seated figure with hat within plants **Rev:** Head of Dr.
Siaka Stevens right

Date	Mintage	F	VF	XF	Unc	BU
ND(1983)	10,000	—	—	—	35.00	—
ND(1983) Proof	10,000	Value: 47.50				

KM# 41 10 LEONES

28.2800 g., 0.9250 Silver 0.8410 oz. ASW **Series:** World Wildlife
Fund **Obv:** Pygmy Hippopotamus **Rev:** Bust of Dr. Joseph Saidu
Momoh left

Date	Mintage	F	VF	XF	Unc	BU
1987 Proof	25,000	Value: 27.50				

KM# 44 10 LEONES

2.5000 g., Nickel-Bonded Steel, 17.99 mm. **Obv:** Value divides
fish **Rev:** Bust of Mammy Yoko facing within circle **Edge:** Plain

Date	Mintage	F	VF	XF	Unc	BU
1996	—	—	—	—	0.75	1.00

KM# 45 50 LEONES

Nickel-Bonded Steel **Obv:** Building above value **Rev:** Bust of
Sir Henry Lightfoot facing

Date	Mintage	F	VF	XF	Unc	BU
1996	—	—	—	—	1.25	1.50

KM# 39 100 LEONES

15.9800 g., 0.9170 Gold 0.4711 oz. AGW **Series:** Year of the Scout
Obv: Lion within shield **Rev:** Head of Dr. Siaka Stevens right

Date	Mintage	F	VF	XF	Unc	BU
ND(1983)	2,000	—	—	—	—	485
ND(1983) Proof	2,000	Value: 485				

KM# 46   100 LEONES
Nickel-Bonded Steel **Obv:** Cocoa pods and value within beaded
circle **Rev:** Head of Naimbana facing within beaded circle

Date	Mintage	F	VF	XF	Unc	BU
1996	—	—	—	—	1.75	2.00

KM# 22   1/4 GOLDE
13.6360 g., 0.9000 Gold 0.3946 oz. AGW, 24 mm. **Subject:** 5th
Anniversary of Independence **Obv:** Value within map **Rev:** Lion
head facing

Date	Mintage	F	VF	XF	Unc	BU
ND(1966)	5,000	—	—	—	—	400

KM# 22a   1/4 GOLDE
15.0000 g., 0.9160 Gold 0.4417 oz. AGW **Subject:** 5th Anniversary
of Independence **Obv:** Value within map **Rev:** Lion head facing

Date	Mintage	F	VF	XF	Unc	BU
ND(1966) Proof	600	Value: 425				

KM# 22b   1/4 GOLDE
10.3150 g., Palladium **Subject:** 5th Anniversary of
Independence **Obv:** Value within map **Rev:** Lion head facing

Date	Mintage	F	VF	XF	Unc	BU
ND(1966) Proof	100	Value: 325				

KM# 23   1/2 GOLDE
27.2730 g., 0.9000 Gold 0.7891 oz. AGW, 32 mm. **Subject:** 5th
Anniversary of Independence **Obv:** Value within map **Rev:** Lion
head facing

Date	Mintage	F	VF	XF	Unc	BU
ND(1966)	2,500	—	—	—	—	800

KM# 23a   1/2 GOLDE
30.0000 g., 0.9160 Gold 0.8835 oz. AGW **Subject:** 5th Anniversary
of Independence **Obv:** Value within map **Rev:** Lion head facing

Date	Mintage	F	VF	XF	Unc	BU
ND(1966) Proof	600	Value: 850				

KM# 23b   1/2 GOLDE
20.6290 g., Palladium **Subject:** 5th Anniversary of
Independence **Obv:** Value within map **Rev:** Lion head facing

Date	Mintage	F	VF	XF	Unc	BU
ND(1966) Proof	100	Value: 650				

KM# 24   GOLDE
54.5450 g., 0.9000 Gold 1.5782 oz. AGW, 48 mm. **Subject:** 5th
Anniversary of Independence **Obv:** Value within map **Rev:** Lion
head facing

Date	Mintage	F	VF	XF	Unc	BU
ND(1966)	1,500	—	—	—	—	1,600

KM# 24a   GOLDE
60.0000 g., 0.9160 Gold 1.7669 oz. AGW **Subject:** 5th Anniversary
of Independence **Obv:** Value within map **Rev:** Lion head facing

Date	Mintage	F	VF	XF	Unc	BU
ND(1966) Proof	400	Value: 1,800				

KM# 24b   GOLDE
41.2590 g., Palladium **Subject:** 5th Anniversary of
Independence **Obv:** Value within map **Rev:** Lion head facing

Date	Mintage	F	VF	XF	Unc	BU
ND(1966) Proof	100	Value: 1,500				

KM# 24c   GOLDE
41.2590 g., Platinum APW **Subject:** 5th Anniversary of
Independence **Obv:** Value within map **Rev:** Lion head facing

Date	Mintage	F	VF	XF	Unc	BU
ND(1966) Proof	—	Value: 2,000				

KM# 37   5 GOLDE
15.9800 g., 0.9170 Gold 0.4711 oz. AGW **Subject:** O.A.U.
Summit Conference **Obv:** Head of Dr. Siaka Stevens right
Rev: Map within circle

Date	Mintage	F	VF	XF	Unc	BU
1980	457	—	—	—	450	
1980 Proof	325	Value: 475				

KM# 42   5 GOLDE
15.9980 g., 0.9170 Gold 0.4716 oz. AGW **Series:** World Wildlife
Fund **Obv:** Bust of Dr. Joseph Saidu Momoh left **Rev:** Duiker Zebra

Date	Mintage	F	VF	XF	Unc	BU
1987 Proof	5,000	Value: 475				

KM# 28   10 GOLDE
57.6000 g., 0.9160 Gold 1.6963 oz. AGW **Subject:** 70th Birthday
- Dr. Siaka Stevens **Obv:** Lion facing right **Rev:** Head right

Date	Mintage	F	VF	XF	Unc	BU
ND(1975)	727	—	—	—	—	1,650
ND(1975) Proof	307	Value: 1,700				

DOLLAR DENOMINATED COINAGE

KM# 47   DOLLAR
Copper-Nickel **Obv:** Arms **Rev:** Crowned lion

Date	Mintage	F	VF	XF	Unc	BU
1997	—	—	—	—	7.50	9.00

KM# 48   DOLLAR
Copper-Nickel **Obv:** Arms **Rev:** Unicorn

Date	Mintage	F	VF	XF	Unc	BU
1997	—	—	—	—	7.50	9.00

KM# 53   DOLLAR
Copper-Nickel **Subject:** Golden Wedding Anniversary
Obv: Arms **Rev:** E and P monogram

Date	Mintage	F	VF	XF	Unc	BU
1997	—	—	—	—	10.00	12.00

KM# 56   DOLLAR
Copper-Nickel **Subject:** Golden Wedding Anniversary
Obv: Arms **Rev:** Royal yacht

Date	Mintage	F	VF	XF	Unc	BU
1997	—	—	—	—	7.00	8.50

KM# 59   DOLLAR
Copper-Nickel **Subject:** Golden Wedding Anniversary
Obv: Arms **Rev:** Royal couple

Date	Mintage	F	VF	XF	Unc	BU
1997	—	—	—	—	7.00	8.50

KM# 62   DOLLAR
Copper-Nickel **Subject:** Golden Wedding Anniversary
Obv: Arms **Rev:** Fireworks above palace

Date	Mintage	F	VF	XF	Unc	BU
1997	—	—	—	—	7.00	8.50

KM# 65   DOLLAR
Copper-Nickel **Subject:** Golden Wedding Anniversary
Obv: Arms **Rev:** Queen with two children

Date	Mintage	F	VF	XF	Unc	BU
1997	—	—	—	—	7.00	8.50

KM# 68   DOLLAR
Copper-Nickel **Subject:** Golden Wedding Anniversary
Obv: Arms **Rev:** Royal couple with two children

Date	Mintage	F	VF	XF	Unc	BU
1997	—	—	—	—	7.00	8.50

KM# 71   DOLLAR
Copper-Nickel **Subject:** Diana - The Peoples' Princess
Obv: Arms **Rev:** Head 1/4 right

Date	Mintage	F	VF	XF	Unc	BU
1997	—	—	—	—	8.00	9.00

KM# 77   DOLLAR
Copper-Nickel **Subject:** Diana - The Peoples' Princess
Obv: Arms **Rev:** Diana with Mother Theresa

Date	Mintage	F	VF	XF	Unc	BU
1997	—	—	—	—	9.00	10.00

KM# 83   DOLLAR
Copper-Nickel **Subject:** Diana - The Peoples' Princess
Obv: Arms **Rev:** Diana and AIDS patient

Date	Mintage	F	VF	XF	Unc	BU
1997	—	—	—	—	8.00	9.00

KM# 89 DOLLAR
Copper-Nickel **Subject:** Diana - The Peoples' Princess
Obv: Arms **Rev:** Diana with sons William and Harry

Date	Mintage	F	VF	XF	Unc	BU
1997	—	—	—	—	8.00	9.00

KM# 95 DOLLAR
Copper-Nickel **Subject:** Jurassic Park **Obv:** Arms
Rev: Velociraptor

Date	Mintage	F	VF	XF	Unc	BU
1997	—	—	—	—	15.00	—

KM# 103 DOLLAR
Copper-Nickel **Subject:** In Memoriam, Diana - The Peoples'
Princess **Obv:** Arms **Rev:** Head 1/4 left

Date	Mintage	F	VF	XF	Unc	BU
1998	—	—	—	—	8.00	9.00

KM# 109 DOLLAR
Copper-Nickel **Subject:** Dr. Livingston **Obv:** Arms **Rev:** Half
length bust of David Livingstone at right above natives in longboat

Date	Mintage	F	VF	XF	Unc	BU
1998	—	—	—	—	8.00	9.00

KM# 118 DOLLAR
Copper-Nickel **Subject:** China 2000 Series **Obv:** Arms
Rev: Kneeling terracotta warrior

Date	Mintage	F	VF	XF	Unc	BU
1999	—	—	—	—	8.50	10.00

KM# 112 DOLLAR
Copper-Nickel **Subject:** Amerigo Vespucci **Obv:** Arms
Rev: Ship and mountainous portrait

Date	Mintage	F	VF	XF	Unc	BU
1999	—	—	—	—	8.00	9.00

KM# 115 DOLLAR
Copper-Nickel **Subject:** Charles Darwin **Obv:** Arms **Rev:** Ship
at left, bust at right

Date	Mintage	F	VF	XF	Unc	BU
1999	—	—	—	—	8.00	9.00

KM# 121 DOLLAR
Copper-Nickel **Subject:** China 2000 Series - Ming Dynasty
Obv: Arms **Rev:** Temple of Heaven

Date	Mintage	F	VF	XF	Unc	BU
1999	—	—	—	—	8.50	10.00

KM# 124 DOLLAR
Copper-Nickel **Subject:** China 2000 Series **Obv:** Arms
Rev: Portion of the Great Wall

Date	Mintage	F	VF	XF	Unc	BU
1999	—	—	—	—	8.50	10.00

KM# 127 DOLLAR
Copper-Nickel **Subject:** China 2000 Series **Obv:** Arms
Rev: Bronze chariot

Date	Mintage	F	VF	XF	Unc	BU
1999	—	—	—	—	8.50	10.00

KM# 130 DOLLAR
Copper-Nickel **Subject:** China 2000 Series **Obv:** Arms
Rev: First century armillary sphere

Date	Mintage	F	VF	XF	Unc	BU
1999	—	—	—	—	8.50	10.00

KM# 133 DOLLAR
Copper-Nickel **Subject:** China 2000 Series **Obv:** Arms
Rev: Tang Dynasty Royal Horse

Date	Mintage	F	VF	XF	Unc	BU
1999	—	—	—	—	8.50	10.00

KM# 136 DOLLAR
Copper-Nickel **Subject:** Macau returns to China **Obv:** Arms
Rev: Church, car, roulette wheel, and hands shaking

Date	Mintage	F	VF	XF	Unc	BU
1999	—	—	—	—	9.50	11.00

KM# 139 DOLLAR
Copper-Nickel **Subject:** Prince Edward's Wedding **Obv:** Arms
Rev: Symbolic wedding design

Date	Mintage	F	VF	XF	Unc	BU
1999	—	—	—	—	8.50	10.00

KM# 152 DOLLAR
28.4300 g., Copper-Nickel, 38.7 mm. **Obv:** Arms **Rev:** Chinese
unicorn within circle **Edge:** Reeded

Date	Mintage	F	VF	XF	Unc	BU
2000	—	—	—	—	10.00	12.00
1999	—	—	—	—	10.00	12.00

Note: Reported as an error date resulting from muled dies

KM# 142 DOLLAR
Copper-Nickel **Subject:** Year of the Dragon **Obv:** Arms
Rev: Dragon

Date	Mintage	F	VF	XF	Unc	BU
2000	—	—	—	—	10.00	14.00

KM# 150 DOLLAR
28.2800 g., Copper-Nickel **Obv:** Arms **Rev:** Two Phoenix birds
Edge: Reeded

Date	Mintage	F	VF	XF	Unc	BU
2000	—	—	—	—	10.00	14.00

KM# 151 DOLLAR
Copper-Nickel **Obv:** Arms **Rev:** Chinese dragon

Date	Mintage	F	VF	XF	Unc	BU
2000	—	—	—	—	10.00	14.00

KM# 174 DOLLAR
Copper-Nickel **Subject:** Buddha **Obv:** Arms **Rev:** Seated Buddha

Date	Mintage	F	VF	XF	Unc	BU
2000	—	—	—	—	8.50	10.00

KM# 175 DOLLAR
Copper-Nickel **Obv:** Arms **Rev:** Goddess of Mercy

Date	Mintage	F	VF	XF	Unc	BU
2000	—	—	—	—	8.50	10.00

KM# 176 DOLLAR
Copper-Nickel **Obv:** Arms **Rev:** Tzai-yen holding scroll

Date	Mintage	F	VF	XF	Unc	BU
2000	—	—	—	—	10.00	12.00

KM# 98 5 DOLLARS
15.5517 g., 0.9990 Silver 0.4995 oz. ASW **Subject:** Shanghai Coin
and Stamp Exposition **Obv:** Arms **Rev:** Standing crowned lion right

Date	Mintage	F	VF	XF	Unc	BU
1997 Proof	Est. 10,000			Value: 30.00		

KM# 99 5 DOLLARS
15.5517 g., 0.9990 Silver 0.4995 oz. ASW **Subject:** Shanghai Coin
and Stamp Exposition **Obv:** Arms **Rev:** Standing unicorn left

Date	Mintage	F	VF	XF	Unc	BU
1997 Proof	Est. 10,000			Value: 30.00		

KM# 101 5 DOLLARS
15.5517 g., 0.9990 Silver 0.4995 oz. ASW **Subject:** Visit of
President Clinton to China **Obv:** Arms **Rev:** Bust 1/4 right, tower
at right

Date	Mintage	F	VF	XF	Unc	BU
1998 Proof	Est. 10,000			Value: 30.00		

KM# 102 5 DOLLARS
15.5517 g., 0.9990 Silver 0.4995 oz. ASW **Subject:** Visit of
President Clinton to Beijing **Obv:** Arms **Rev:** Great Wall at left,
bust 1/4 left

Date	Mintage	F	VF	XF	Unc	BU
1998 Proof	Est. 10,000			Value: 30.00		

KM# 49   10 DOLLARS
28.2800 g., 0.9250 Silver 0.8410 oz. ASW **Obv:** Arms
Rev: Standing crowned lion right

Date	Mintage	F	VF	XF	Unc	BU
1997 Proof	Est. 10,000	Value: 45.00				

KM# 50   10 DOLLARS
28.2800 g., 0.9250 Silver 0.8410 oz. ASW **Obv:** Arms
Rev: Standing unicorn left

Date	Mintage	F	VF	XF	Unc	BU
1997 Proof	Est. 10,000	Value: 45.00				

KM# 54   10 DOLLARS
28.2800 g., 0.9250 Silver 0.8410 oz. ASW **Subject:** Golden
Wedding Anniversary **Obv:** Arms **Rev:** E and P monogram within
flower circle

Date	Mintage	F	VF	XF	Unc	BU
1997 Proof	Est. 10,000	Value: 47.50				

KM# 57   10 DOLLARS
28.2800 g., 0.9250 Silver 0.8410 oz. ASW **Subject:** Golden
Wedding Anniversary **Obv:** Arms **Rev:** Royal Yacht with cameo
head facing at upper left

Date	Mintage	F	VF	XF	Unc	BU
1997 Proof	Est. 10,000	Value: 47.50				

KM# 60   10 DOLLARS
28.2800 g., 0.9250 Silver 0.8410 oz. ASW **Subject:** Golden
Wedding Anniversary **Obv:** Arms **Rev:** Royal couple

Date	Mintage	F	VF	XF	Unc	BU
1997 Proof	Est. 10,000	Value: 47.50				

KM# 63   10 DOLLARS
28.2800 g., 0.9250 Silver 0.8410 oz. ASW **Subject:** Golden
Wedding Anniversary **Obv:** Arms **Rev:** Fireworks above palace

Date	Mintage	F	VF	XF	Unc	BU
1997 Proof	Est. 10,000	Value: 47.50				

KM# 66   10 DOLLARS
28.2800 g., 0.9250 Silver 0.8410 oz. ASW **Subject:** Golden
Wedding Anniversary **Obv:** Arms **Rev:** Queen with two children

Date	Mintage	F	VF	XF	Unc	BU
1997 Proof	Est. 10,000	Value: 47.50				

KM# 69   10 DOLLARS
28.2800 g., 0.9250 Silver 0.8410 oz. ASW **Subject:** Golden
Wedding Anniversary **Obv:** Arms **Rev:** Royal couple with two
children

Date	Mintage	F	VF	XF	Unc	BU
1997 Proof	Est. 10,000	Value: 47.50				

KM# 72   10 DOLLARS
28.2800 g., 0.9250 Silver 0.8410 oz. ASW **Subject:** Diana - The
Peoples' Princess **Obv:** Arms **Rev:** Head facing

Date	Mintage	F	VF	XF	Unc	BU
1997 Proof	Est. 10,000	Value: 30.00				

KM# 78   10 DOLLARS
28.2800 g., 0.9250 Silver 0.8410 oz. ASW **Subject:** Diana - The
Peoples' Princess **Obv:** Arms **Rev:** Diana with Mother Theresa

Date	Mintage	F	VF	XF	Unc	BU
1997	Est. 10,000	Value: 42.50				

KM# 84   10 DOLLARS
28.2800 g., 0.9250 Silver 0.8410 oz. ASW **Subject:** Diana - The
Peoples' Princess **Obv:** Arms **Rev:** Diana and AIDS patient

Date	Mintage	F	VF	XF	Unc	BU
1997 Proof	Est. 10,000	Value: 25.00				

KM# 90   10 DOLLARS
28.2800 g., 0.9250 Silver 0.8410 oz. ASW **Subject:** Diana - The
Peoples' Princess **Obv:** Arms **Rev:** Diana with sons William and
Harry

Date	Mintage	F	VF	XF	Unc	BU
1997 Proof	Est. 10,000	Value: 27.50				

KM# 96 10 DOLLARS
28.2800 g., 0.9250 Silver 0.8410 oz. ASW **Subject:** Jurassic
Park **Obv:** Arms **Rev:** Velociraptor

Date	Mintage	F	VF	XF	Unc	BU
1997 Proof	Est. 10,000			Value: 45.00		

KM# 104 10 DOLLARS
28.2800 g., 0.9250 Silver 0.8410 oz. ASW **Subject:** In Memoriam,
Diana - The Peoples' Princess **Obv:** Arms **Rev:** Head 1/4 left

Date	Mintage	F	VF	XF	Unc	BU
1998 Proof	Est. 10,000			Value: 37.50		

KM# A110 10 DOLLARS
28.2800 g., 0.9250 Silver 0.8410 oz. ASW **Subject:** Dr.
Livingstone **Obv:** Arms **Rev:** Standing figures rowing ancient
boat, bust 1/4 left at upper right **Note:** Prev. KM#110.

Date	Mintage	F	VF	XF	Unc	BU
1998 Proof	Est. 10,000			Value: 50.00		

KM# 113 10 DOLLARS
28.2800 g., 0.9250 Silver 0.8410 oz. ASW **Subject:** Amerigo
Vespucci **Obv:** Arms **Rev:** Ship and Vespucci portrait

Date	Mintage	F	VF	XF	Unc	BU
1999 Proof	Est. 10,000			Value: 50.00		

KM# 116 10 DOLLARS
28.2800 g., 0.9250 Silver 0.8410 oz. ASW **Subject:** Charles
Darwin **Obv:** Arms **Rev:** Ship and bust facing at upper right

Date	Mintage	F	VF	XF	Unc	BU
1999 Proof	Est. 10,000			Value: 50.00		

KM# 119 10 DOLLARS
28.2800 g., 0.9250 Silver 0.8410 oz. ASW **Subject:** China 2000
Series **Obv:** Arms **Rev:** Kneeling Terracotta warrior

Date	Mintage	F	VF	XF	Unc	BU
1999 Proof	Est. 10,000			Value: 47.50		

KM# 122 10 DOLLARS
28.2800 g., 0.9250 Silver 0.8410 oz. ASW **Subject:** China 2000
Series - Ming Dynasty **Obv:** Arms **Rev:** Temple of Heaven

Date	Mintage	F	VF	XF	Unc	BU
1999 Proof	Est. 10,000			Value: 47.50		

KM# 125 10 DOLLARS
28.2800 g., 0.9250 Silver 0.8410 oz. ASW **Subject:** China 2000
Series **Obv:** Arms **Rev:** Portion of the Great Wall

Date	Mintage	F	VF	XF	Unc	BU
1999 Proof	Est. 10,000			Value: 47.50		

KM# 128 10 DOLLARS
28.2800 g., 0.9250 Silver 0.8410 oz. ASW **Subject:** China 2000
Series **Obv:** Arms **Rev:** Bronze chariot

Date	Mintage	F	VF	XF	Unc	BU
1999 Proof	Est. 10,000			Value: 47.50		

KM# 131 10 DOLLARS
28.2800 g., 0.9250 Silver 0.8410 oz. ASW **Subject:** China 2000
Series **Obv:** Arms **Rev:** First century armillary sphere

Date	Mintage	F	VF	XF	Unc	BU
1999 Proof	Est. 10,000			Value: 47.50		

KM# 134 10 DOLLARS
28.2800 g., 0.9250 Silver 0.8410 oz. ASW **Subject:** China 2000
Series **Obv:** Arms **Rev:** Tang Dynasty royal horse

Date	Mintage	F	VF	XF	Unc	BU
1999 Proof	Est. 10,000			Value: 47.50		

KM# 137 10 DOLLARS
28.2800 g., 0.9250 Silver 0.8410 oz. ASW **Subject:** Macau
Return to China **Obv:** Arms **Rev:** Church, car, roulette wheel and
clasped hands below

Date	Mintage	F	VF	XF	Unc	BU
1999 Proof	Est. 10,000			Value: 50.00		

KM# 140   10 DOLLARS
28.2800 g., 0.9250 Silver 0.8410 oz. ASW   **Subject:** Prince Edward's Wedding **Obv:** Arms **Rev:** Symbolic wedding design

Date	Mintage	F	VF	XF	Unc	BU
1999 Proof	Est. 10,000			Value: 50.00		

KM# 143   10 DOLLARS
28.2800 g., 0.9250 Silver 0.8410 oz. ASW   **Subject:** Year of the Dragon **Obv:** Arms **Rev:** Dragon

Date	Mintage	F	VF	XF	Unc	BU
2000 Proof	Est. 25,000			Value: 45.00		

KM# 153   10 DOLLARS
28.2800 g., 0.9250 Silver 0.8410 oz. ASW **Obv:** Arms **Rev:** Two Phoenix birds

Date	Mintage	F	VF	XF	Unc	BU
2000 Proof	Est. 10,000			Value: 45.00		

KM# 154   10 DOLLARS
28.2800 g., 0.9250 Silver 0.8410 oz. ASW   **Obv:** Arms **Rev:** Chinese dragon

Date	Mintage	F	VF	XF	Unc	BU
2000 Proof	Est. 10,000			Value: 45.00		

KM# 155   10 DOLLARS
28.2800 g., 0.9250 Silver 0.8410 oz. ASW   **Obv:** Arms **Rev:** Chinese unicorn within circle

Date	Mintage	F	VF	XF	Unc	BU
2000 Proof	Est. 10,000			Value: 45.00		

KM# 177   10 DOLLARS
28.2800 g., 0.9250 Silver 0.8410 oz. ASW   **Obv:** Arms **Rev:** Seated Buddha

Date	Mintage	F	VF	XF	Unc	BU
2000 Proof	Est. 25,000			Value: 47.50		

KM# 178   10 DOLLARS
28.2800 g., 0.9250 Silver 0.8410 oz. ASW   **Obv:** Arms **Rev:** Goddess of Mercy

Date	Mintage	F	VF	XF	Unc	BU
2000 Proof	Est. 25,000			Value: 47.50		

KM# 179   10 DOLLARS
28.2800 g., 0.9250 Silver 0.8410 oz. ASW   **Obv:** Arms **Rev:** Tzai-yen holding scroll

Date	Mintage	F	VF	XF	Unc	BU
2000 Proof	Est. 25,000			Value: 47.50		

KM# 73   20 DOLLARS
1.2441 g., 0.9990 Gold 0.0400 oz. AGW   **Subject:** Diana - The Peoples' Princess **Obv:** Arms **Rev:** Head facing

Date	Mintage	F	VF	XF	Unc	BU
1997 Proof	Est. 101,000			Value: 47.50		

KM# 79   20 DOLLARS
1.2441 g., 0.9990 Gold 0.0400 oz. AGW   **Subject:** Diana - The Peoples' Princess **Obv:** Arms **Rev:** Lady Diana and Mother Theresa

Date	Mintage	F	VF	XF	Unc	BU
1997 Proof	Est. 101,000			Value: 55.00		

KM# 85   20 DOLLARS
1.2441 g., 0.9990 Gold 0.0400 oz. AGW   **Subject:** Diana - The Peoples' Princess **Obv:** Arms **Rev:** Lady Diana and AIDS patient

Date	Mintage	F	VF	XF	Unc	BU
1997 Proof	Est. 101,000			Value: 45.00		

KM# 91   20 DOLLARS
1.2441 g., 0.9990 Gold 0.0400 oz. AGW   **Subject:** Diana - The Peoples' Princess **Obv:** Arms **Rev:** With sons William and Harry

Date	Mintage	F	VF	XF	Unc	BU
1997 Proof	Est. 101,000			Value: 45.00		

KM# 105   20 DOLLARS
1.2441 g., 0.9990 Gold 0.0400 oz. AGW   **Subject:** In Memorium **Obv:** Arms **Rev:** Lady Diana

Date	Mintage	F	VF	XF	Unc	BU
1998 Proof	Est. 10,000			Value: 50.00		

KM# 144   20 DOLLARS
1.2441 g., 0.9990 Gold 0.0400 oz. AGW   **Subject:** Year of the Dragon **Obv:** Arms **Rev:** Dragon

Date	Mintage	F	VF	XF	Unc	BU
2000 Proof	Est. 15,000			Value: 55.00		

KM# 180   20 DOLLARS
1.2400 g., 0.9990 Gold 0.0398 oz. AGW   **Subject:** Buddha **Obv:** Arms **Rev:** Seated Buddha **Edge:** Reeded **Note:** Struck at Pobjoy Mint.

Date	Mintage	F	VF	XF	Unc	BU
2000 Proof	Est. 5,000			Value: 55.00		

KM# 181   20 DOLLARS
1.2400 g., 0.9990 Gold 0.0398 oz. AGW   **Obv:** Arms **Rev:** Goddess of Mercy

Date	Mintage	F	VF	XF	Unc	BU
2000 Proof	Est. 5,000			Value: 55.00		

KM# 182   20 DOLLARS
1.2400 g., 0.9990 Gold 0.0398 oz. AGW   **Obv:** Arms **Rev:** Tzai-yen holding scroll

Date	Mintage	F	VF	XF	Unc	BU
2000 Proof	Est. 5,000			Value: 55.00		

KM# 74   50 DOLLARS
3.1100 g., 0.9990 Gold 0.0999 oz. AGW   **Subject:** Diana - The Peoples' Princess **Obv:** Arms **Rev:** Portrait of Lady Diana

Date	Mintage	F	VF	XF	Unc	BU
1997 Proof	Est. 7,500			Value: 100		

KM# 80   50 DOLLARS
3.1100 g., 0.9990 Gold 0.0999 oz. AGW   **Subject:** Diana - The Peoples' Princess **Obv:** Arms **Rev:** Lady Diana and Mother Theresa

Date	Mintage	F	VF	XF	Unc	BU
1997 Proof	Est. 7,500			Value: 100		

KM# 86   50 DOLLARS
3.1100 g., 0.9990 Gold 0.0999 oz. AGW   **Subject:** Diana - The Peoples' Princess **Obv:** Arms **Rev:** Lady Diana and AIDS patient

Date	Mintage	F	VF	XF	Unc	BU
1997 Proof	Est. 7,500			Value: 100		

KM# 92   50 DOLLARS
3.1100 g., 0.9990 Gold 0.0999 oz. AGW   **Subject:** Diana - The Peoples' Princess **Obv:** Arms **Rev:** With sons William and Harry

Date	Mintage	F	VF	XF	Unc	BU
1997 Proof	Est. 7,500			Value: 100		

KM# 106   50 DOLLARS
3.1100 g., 0.9990 Gold 0.0999 oz. AGW   **Subject:** Diana - The Peoples' Princess **Obv:** Arms **Rev:** Portrait of Lady Diana

Date	Mintage	F	VF	XF	Unc	BU
1998 Proof	Est. 7,500			Value: 100		

KM# 184   50 DOLLARS
3.1100 g., 0.9990 Gold 0.0999 oz. AGW   **Obv:** Arms **Rev:** Goddess of Mercy

Date	Mintage	F	VF	XF	Unc	BU
2000 Proof	Est. 5,000			Value: 100		

KM# 145   50 DOLLARS
3.1100 g., 0.9990 Gold 0.0999 oz. AGW   **Subject:** Year of the Dragon **Obv:** Arms **Rev:** Dragon

Date	Mintage	F	VF	XF	Unc	BU
2000 Proof	Est. 20,000			Value: 100		

KM# 183   50 DOLLARS
3.1100 g., 0.9990 Gold 0.0999 oz. AGW   **Obv:** Arms **Rev:** Seated Buddha **Edge:** Reeded

Date	Mintage	F	VF	XF	Unc	BU
2000 Proof	Est. 5,000			Value: 100		

KM# 185   50 DOLLARS
3.1100 g., 0.9990 Gold 0.0999 oz. AGW   **Obv:** Arms **Rev:** Tzai-yen holding scroll

Date	Mintage	F	VF	XF	Unc	BU
2000 Proof	Est. 5,000			Value: 100		

KM# 51   100 DOLLARS
6.2200 g., 0.9999 Gold 0.1999 oz. AGW   **Subject:** Shanghai Coin and Stamp Exposition **Obv:** Arms **Rev:** Crowned lion

Date	Mintage	F	VF	XF	Unc	BU
1997 Proof	Est. 5,000			Value: 200		

KM# 52   100 DOLLARS
6.2200 g., 0.9999 Gold 0.1999 oz. AGW   **Subject:** Shanghai Coin and Stamp Exposition **Obv:** Arms **Rev:** Crowned lion

Date	Mintage	F	VF	XF	Unc	BU
1997 Proof	Est. 5,000			Value: 200		

KM# 55   100 DOLLARS
6.2200 g., 0.9999 Gold 0.1999 oz. AGW   **Subject:** Golden Wedding Anniversary **Obv:** Arms **Rev:** E and P monogram

Date	Mintage	F	VF	XF	Unc	BU
1997 Proof	Est. 3,500			Value: 200		

KM# 58 100 DOLLARS
6.2200 g., 0.9999 Gold 0.1999 oz. AGW **Subject:** Golden Wedding Anniversary **Obv:** Arms **Rev:** Yacht

Date	Mintage	F	VF	XF	Unc	BU
1997 Proof	Est. 3,500				Value: 200	

KM# 61 100 DOLLARS
6.2200 g., 0.9999 Gold 0.1999 oz. AGW **Subject:** Golden Wedding Anniversary **Obv:** Arms **Rev:** Royal couple

Date	Mintage	F	VF	XF	Unc	BU
1997 Proof	Est. 10,000				Value: 200	

KM# 64 100 DOLLARS
6.2200 g., 0.9999 Gold 0.1999 oz. AGW **Subject:** Golden Wedding Anniversary **Obv:** Arms **Rev:** Fireworks above palace

Date	Mintage	F	VF	XF	Unc	BU
1997 Proof	Est. 3,500				Value: 200	

KM# 67 100 DOLLARS
6.2200 g., 0.9999 Gold 0.1999 oz. AGW **Subject:** Golden Wedding Anniversary **Obv:** Arms **Rev:** Queen with two children

Date	Mintage	F	VF	XF	Unc	BU
1997 Proof	Est. 3,500				Value: 200	

KM# 70 100 DOLLARS
6.2200 g., 0.9999 Gold 0.1999 oz. AGW **Subject:** Golden Wedding Anniversary **Obv:** Arms **Rev:** Royal couple with two children

Date	Mintage	F	VF	XF	Unc	BU
1997 Proof	Est. 3,500				Value: 200	

KM# 75 100 DOLLARS
6.2200 g., 0.9999 Gold 0.1999 oz. AGW **Subject:** Diana - The Peoples' Princess **Obv:** Arms **Rev:** Portrait of Lady Diana

Date	Mintage	F	VF	XF	Unc	BU
1997 Proof	Est. 5,000				Value: 200	

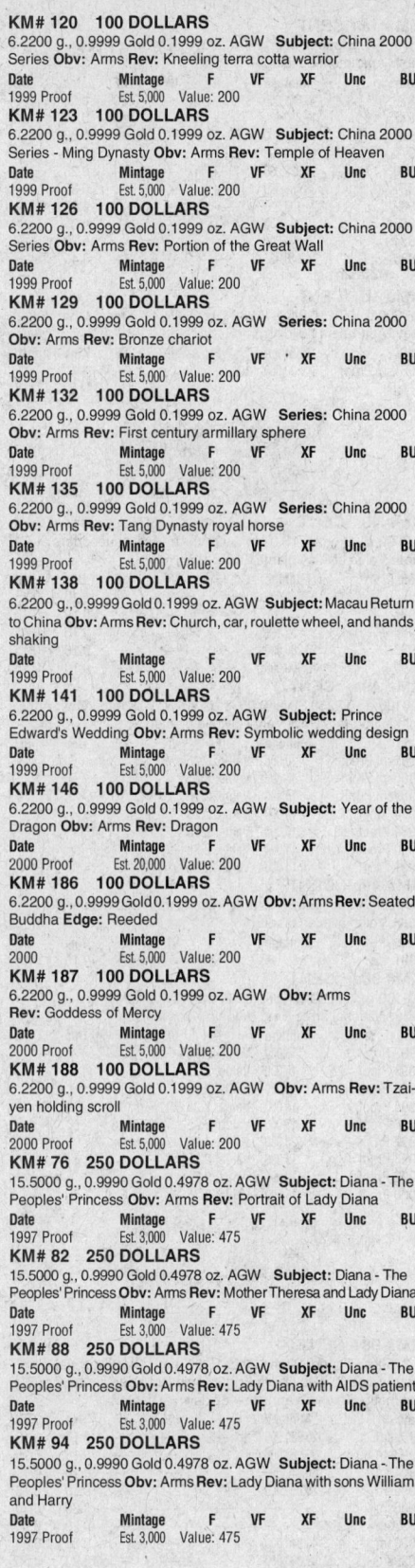

KM# 81 100 DOLLARS
6.2200 g., 0.9999 Gold 0.1999 oz. AGW **Subject:** Diana - The Peoples' Princess **Obv:** Arms with supporters **Rev:** Diana with Mother Theresa

Date	Mintage	F	VF	XF	Unc	BU
1997 Proof	Est. 5,000				Value: 200	

KM# 87 100 DOLLARS
6.2200 g., 0.9999 Gold 0.1999 oz. AGW **Subject:** Diana - The Peoples' Princess **Obv:** Arms **Rev:** Lady Diana and AIDS patient

Date	Mintage	F	VF	XF	Unc	BU
1997 Proof	Est. 5,000				Value: 200	

KM# 93 100 DOLLARS
6.2200 g., 0.9999 Gold 0.1999 oz. AGW **Subject:** Diana - The Peoples' Princess **Obv:** Arms **Rev:** With sons William and Harry

Date	Mintage	F	VF	XF	Unc	BU
1997 Proof	Est. 5,000				Value: 200	

KM# 97 100 DOLLARS
6.2200 g., 0.9999 Gold 0.1999 oz. AGW **Subject:** Jurassic Park **Obv:** Arms **Rev:** Velociraptor

Date	Mintage	F	VF	XF	Unc	BU
1997 Proof	Est. 5,000				Value: 200	

KM# 100 100 DOLLARS
6.2200 g., 0.9999 Gold 0.1999 oz. AGW **Subject:** Queen Victoria's Diamond Jubilee Centennial **Obv:** Arms **Rev:** Crowned bust with diamond necklace facing

Date	Mintage	F	VF	XF	Unc	BU
1997 Proof	Est. 3,500				Value: 200	

KM# 107 100 DOLLARS
6.2200 g., 0.9999 Gold 0.1999 oz. AGW **Subject:** Diana - The People's Princess **Obv:** Arms **Rev:** Head half left

Date	Mintage	F	VF	XF	Unc	BU
1998 Proof	Est. 5,000				Value: 200	

KM# 111 100 DOLLARS
6.2200 g., 0.9999 Gold 0.1999 oz. AGW **Subject:** Dr. Livingstone **Obv:** Arms **Rev:** Dr. Livingstone above figures in boat

Date	Mintage	F	VF	XF	Unc	BU
1998 Proof	Est. 5,000				Value: 200	

KM# 114 100 DOLLARS
6.2200 g., 0.9999 Gold 0.1999 oz. AGW **Subject:** Amerigo Vespucci **Obv:** Arms **Rev:** Ship and mountainous portrait

Date	Mintage	F	VF	XF	Unc	BU
1999 Proof	Est. 5,000				Value: 200	

KM# 117 100 DOLLARS
6.2200 g., 0.9999 Gold 0.1999 oz. AGW **Subject:** Charles Darwin **Obv:** Arms **Rev:** Ship and portrait

Date	Mintage	F	VF	XF	Unc	BU
1999 Proof	Est. 5,000				Value: 200	

KM# 120 100 DOLLARS
6.2200 g., 0.9999 Gold 0.1999 oz. AGW **Subject:** China 2000 Series **Obv:** Arms **Rev:** Kneeling terra cotta warrior

Date	Mintage	F	VF	XF	Unc	BU
1999 Proof	Est. 5,000				Value: 200	

KM# 123 100 DOLLARS
6.2200 g., 0.9999 Gold 0.1999 oz. AGW **Subject:** China 2000 Series - Ming Dynasty **Obv:** Arms **Rev:** Temple of Heaven

Date	Mintage	F	VF	XF	Unc	BU
1999 Proof	Est. 5,000				Value: 200	

KM# 126 100 DOLLARS
6.2200 g., 0.9999 Gold 0.1999 oz. AGW **Subject:** China 2000 Series **Obv:** Arms **Rev:** Portion of the Great Wall

Date	Mintage	F	VF	XF	Unc	BU
1999 Proof	Est. 5,000				Value: 200	

KM# 129 100 DOLLARS
6.2200 g., 0.9999 Gold 0.1999 oz. AGW **Series:** China 2000 **Obv:** Arms **Rev:** Bronze chariot

Date	Mintage	F	VF	XF	Unc	BU
1999 Proof	Est. 5,000				Value: 200	

KM# 132 100 DOLLARS
6.2200 g., 0.9999 Gold 0.1999 oz. AGW **Series:** China 2000 **Obv:** Arms **Rev:** First century armillary sphere

Date	Mintage	F	VF	XF	Unc	BU
1999 Proof	Est. 5,000				Value: 200	

KM# 135 100 DOLLARS
6.2200 g., 0.9999 Gold 0.1999 oz. AGW **Series:** China 2000 **Obv:** Arms **Rev:** Tang Dynasty royal horse

Date	Mintage	F	VF	XF	Unc	BU
1999 Proof	Est. 5,000				Value: 200	

KM# 138 100 DOLLARS
6.2200 g., 0.9999 Gold 0.1999 oz. AGW **Subject:** Macau Return to China **Obv:** Arms **Rev:** Church, car, roulette wheel, and hands shaking

Date	Mintage	F	VF	XF	Unc	BU
1999 Proof	Est. 5,000				Value: 200	

KM# 141 100 DOLLARS
6.2200 g., 0.9999 Gold 0.1999 oz. AGW **Subject:** Prince Edward's Wedding **Obv:** Arms **Rev:** Symbolic wedding design

Date	Mintage	F	VF	XF	Unc	BU
1999 Proof	Est. 5,000				Value: 200	

KM# 146 100 DOLLARS
6.2200 g., 0.9999 Gold 0.1999 oz. AGW **Subject:** Year of the Dragon **Obv:** Arms **Rev:** Dragon

Date	Mintage	F	VF	XF	Unc	BU
2000 Proof	Est. 20,000				Value: 200	

KM# 186 100 DOLLARS
6.2200 g., 0.9999 Gold 0.1999 oz. AGW **Obv:** Arms **Rev:** Seated Buddha **Edge:** Reeded

Date	Mintage	F	VF	XF	Unc	BU
2000	Est. 5,000				Value: 200	

KM# 187 100 DOLLARS
6.2200 g., 0.9999 Gold 0.1999 oz. AGW **Obv:** Arms **Rev:** Goddess of Mercy

Date	Mintage	F	VF	XF	Unc	BU
2000 Proof	Est. 5,000				Value: 200	

KM# 188 100 DOLLARS
6.2200 g., 0.9999 Gold 0.1999 oz. AGW **Obv:** Arms **Rev:** Tzai-yen holding scroll

Date	Mintage	F	VF	XF	Unc	BU
2000 Proof	Est. 5,000				Value: 200	

KM# 76 250 DOLLARS
15.5000 g., 0.9990 Gold 0.4978 oz. AGW **Subject:** Diana - The Peoples' Princess **Obv:** Arms **Rev:** Portrait of Lady Diana

Date	Mintage	F	VF	XF	Unc	BU
1997 Proof	Est. 3,000				Value: 475	

KM# 82 250 DOLLARS
15.5000 g., 0.9990 Gold 0.4978 oz. AGW **Subject:** Diana - The Peoples' Princess **Obv:** Arms **Rev:** Mother Theresa and Lady Diana

Date	Mintage	F	VF	XF	Unc	BU
1997 Proof	Est. 3,000				Value: 475	

KM# 88 250 DOLLARS
15.5000 g., 0.9990 Gold 0.4978 oz. AGW **Subject:** Diana - The Peoples' Princess **Obv:** Arms **Rev:** Lady Diana with AIDS patient

Date	Mintage	F	VF	XF	Unc	BU
1997 Proof	Est. 3,000				Value: 475	

KM# 94 250 DOLLARS
15.5000 g., 0.9990 Gold 0.4978 oz. AGW **Subject:** Diana - The Peoples' Princess **Obv:** Arms **Rev:** Lady Diana with sons William and Harry

Date	Mintage	F	VF	XF	Unc	BU
1997 Proof	Est. 3,000				Value: 475	

KM# 240 250 DOLLARS
15.5500 g., 0.9999 Gold 0.4999 oz. AGW, 29.9 mm. **Subject:** Centennial of Queen Victoria's Diamond Jubilee **Obv:** Arms **Rev:** Crowned bust with diamond necklace facing **Edge:** Reeded **Note:** The entire issue is reported to have been commissioned by and sold to a single purchaser.

Date	Mintage	F	VF	XF	Unc	BU
1997 Proof	Est. 1,000				Value: 475	

KM# 108 250 DOLLARS
15.5000 g., 0.9990 Gold 0.4978 oz. AGW **Subject:** Diana - The Peoples' Princess **Obv:** Arms **Rev:** Head half left

Date	Mintage	F	VF	XF	Unc	BU
1998 Proof	Est. 3,000				Value: 475	

KM# 147 250 DOLLARS
15.5000 g., 0.9990 Gold 0.4978 oz. AGW **Subject:** Year of the Dragon **Obv:** Arms **Rev:** Dragon

Date	Mintage	F	VF	XF	Unc	BU
2000 Proof	Est. 5,000				Value: 475	

KM# 189 250 DOLLARS
15.5000 g., 0.9990 Gold 0.4978 oz. AGW **Obv:** Arms **Rev:** Seated Buddha

Date	Mintage	F	VF	XF	Unc	BU
2000 Proof	Est. 5,000				Value: 475	

KM# 190 250 DOLLARS
15.5500 g., 0.9990 Gold 0.4994 oz. AGW **Obv:** Arms **Rev:** Goddess of Mercy

Date	Mintage	F	VF	XF	Unc	BU
2000 Proof	Est. 5,000				Value: 475	

KM# 191 250 DOLLARS
15.5500 g., 0.9990 Gold 0.4994 oz. AGW **Obv:** Arms **Rev:** Tzai-yen holding scroll

Date	Mintage	F	VF	XF	Unc	BU
2000 Proof	Est. 5,000				Value: 475	

KM# 148 500 DOLLARS
31.1035 g., 0.9990 Gold 0.9990 oz. AGW **Subject:** Year of Dragon **Obv:** Arms **Rev:** Dragon **Note:** Similar to 10 Dollars, KM#143.

Date	Mintage	F	VF	XF	Unc	BU
2000 Proof	Est. 1,000				Value: 975	

KM# 192 500 DOLLARS
31.1035 g., 0.9990 Gold 0.9990 oz. AGW **Obv:** Arms **Rev:** Seated Buddha **Edge:** Reeded

Date	Mintage	F	VF	XF	Unc	BU
2000 Proof	Est. 5,000				Value: 975	

KM# 193 500 DOLLARS
31.1035 g., 0.9990 Gold 0.9990 oz. AGW **Obv:** Arms **Rev:** Goddess of Mercy

Date	Mintage	F	VF	XF	Unc	BU
2000 Proof	Est. 5,000				Value: 975	

KM# 194 500 DOLLARS
31.1035 g., 0.9990 Gold 0.9990 oz. AGW **Obv:** Arms **Rev:** Tzai-yen holding scroll

Date	Mintage	F	VF	XF	Unc	BU
2000 Proof	Est. 5,000				Value: 975	

KM# 149 2500 DOLLARS
155.5175 g., 0.9990 Gold 4.9948 oz. AGW **Subject:** Year of the Dragon **Obv:** Arms **Rev:** Dragon

Date	Mintage	F	VF	XF	Unc	BU
2000 Proof	250				Value: 4,750	

KM# 195 2500 DOLLARS
155.5175 g., 0.9990 Gold 4.9948 oz. AGW **Obv:** Arms **Rev:** Seated Buddha **Edge:** Reeded

Date	Mintage	F	VF	XF	Unc	BU
2000 Proof	Est. 250				Value: 4,750	

KM# 196 2500 DOLLARS
155.5175 g., 0.9990 Gold 4.9948 oz. AGW **Obv:** Arms **Rev:** Goddess of Mercy

Date	Mintage	F	VF	XF	Unc	BU
2000 Proof	Est. 250				Value: 4,750	

KM# 197 2500 DOLLARS
155.5175 g., 0.9990 Gold 4.9948 oz. AGW **Obv:** Arms **Rev:** Tzai-yen holding scroll

Date	Mintage	F	VF	XF	Unc	BU
2000 Proof	Est. 250				Value: 4,750	

TRIAL STRIKES

KM# Date	Mintage	Identification	Mkt Val
TS1 ND	—	5 Centesimos. Steel. Portrait of Milton Margai, Prime Minster. Uruguay 5 Centavos design with MBLAT top, HA in number 5. Reeded edge.	135
TS2 ND(1964)	—	10 Cents. Brass. Head right. Value within wreath.	125
TS3 ND(1964)	—	10 Cents. Aluminum. Reverse of KM#19. Uruguay 10 Centesimos.	125

MINT SETS

KM#	Date	Mintage	Identification	Issue Price	Mkt Val
MS1	1966 (3)	—	KM#22-24	—	1,650

PROOF SETS

KM#	Date	Mintage	Identification	Issue Price	Mkt Val
PS1	1964 (6)	10,000	KM#16-21	—	16.50
PS2	1964 (6)	12	KM#16a-20a, 21b	—	5,750
PS3	1964 (6)	10	KM#16a-21a	—	4,250
PS4	1966 (3)	400	KM#22a-24a	—	1,950
PS5	1972 (2)	1,000	KM25 (2 pieces with 50 cent bank note (0 serial#) in plush case	—	20.00
PS6	1980 (6)	10,000	KM25, 30-34	34.00	28.00

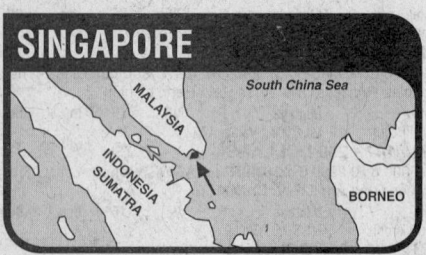

SINGAPORE

The Republic of Singapore, a member of the Commonwealth of Nations situated off the southern tip of the Malay peninsula, has an area of 224 sq. mi. (633 sq. km.) and a population of *2.7 million. Capital: Singapore. The economy is based on entrepôt trade, manufacturing and oil. Rubber, petroleum products, machinery and spices are exported.

Singapore's modern history - it was an important shipping center in the 14th century before the rise of Malacca and Penang - began in 1819 when Sir Thomas Stamford Raffles, an agent for the British East India Company, founded the town of Singapore. By 1825 its trade exceeded that of Malacca and Penang combined. The opening of the Suez Canal (1869) and the demand for rubber and tin created by the automobile and packaging industries combined to make Singapore one of the major ports of the world. In 1826 Singapore, Penang and Malacca were combined to form the Straits Settlements, which was made a Crown Colony in 1867. Singapore became a separate Crown Colony in 1946 when the Straits Settlements was dissolved. It joined in the formation of Malaysia in 1963, but broke away on Aug. 9, 1965, to become an independent republic. The President is Chief of State. The prime minister is Head of Government.

For earlier coinage see Straits Settlements, Malaya, Malaya and British Borneo.

MINT MARK
sm = "*sm*" - Singapore Mint monogram

MONETARY SYSTEM
100 Cents = 1 Dollar

REPUBLIC

STANDARD COINAGE
100 Cents = 1 Dollar

KM# 1   CENT
2.0000 g., Bronze, 17.8 mm.   **Obv:** Value **Rev:** Apartment building **Edge:** Plain

Date	Mintage	F	VF	XF	Unc	BU
1967	7,500,000	—	—	0.30	0.60	—
1967 Proof	2,000	Value: 2.25				
1968	2,969,000	—	—	0.30	0.60	—
1968 Proof	5,000	Value: 2.00				
1969	7,220,000	—	—	1.20	2.00	—
1969 Proof	3,000	Value: 10.00				
1970	1,402,000	—	0.25	1.00	2.00	—
1971	9,731,000	—	—	0.25	0.60	—
1972	1,665,000	—	—	0.30	0.70	—
1972 Proof	749	Value: 40.00				
1973	6,377,000	—	—	0.20	0.30	—
1973 Proof	1,000	Value: 5.00				
1974	9,421,000	—	—	—	0.30	—
1974 Proof	1,500	Value: 4.00				
1975	24,226,000	—	—	—	0.30	—
1975 Proof	3,000	Value: 1.50				
1976	2,500,000	—	—	0.20	1.00	2.00
1976sm Proof	3,500	Value: 1.25				
1977sm Proof	3,500	Value: 1.25				
1978sm Proof	4,000	Value: 1.25				
1979sm Proof	3,500	Value: 1.25				
1980sm Proof	14,000	Value: 1.00				
1982sm Proof	20,000	Value: 1.00				
1983sm Proof	15,000	Value: 1.00				
1984sm Proof	15,000	Value: 1.00				

KM# 1a   CENT
1.7500 g., Copper Clad Steel, 17.8 mm.   **Obv:** Value **Rev:** Apartment building

Date	Mintage	F	VF	XF	Unc	BU
1976	13,665,000	—	—	0.20	0.30	—
1977	13,940,000	—	—	0.20	0.30	—
1978	5,931,000	—	—	—	0.30	—
1979	11,986,000	—	—	—	0.25	—
1980	19,922,000	—	—	—	0.25	—
1981	38,084,000	—	—	—	0.25	—
1982	24,105,000	—	—	—	0.25	—
1983	2,204,000	—	—	—	0.25	—
1984	5,695,000	—	—	—	0.25	—
1985	148,424	—	—	—	0.45	—

Note: In sets only

KM# 1b   CENT
2.9200 g., 0.9250 Silver 0.0868 oz. ASW, 17.8 mm.   **Obv:** Value **Rev:** Apartment building

Date	Mintage	F	VF	XF	Unc	BU
1981sm Proof	30,000	Value: 5.00				

KM# 49   CENT
1.7500 g., Bronze, 17.8 mm.   **Obv:** Arms with supporters **Rev:** Value divides plants **Edge:** Plain

Date	Mintage	F	VF	XF	Unc	BU
1986	20,000,000	—	—	—	0.10	0.15
1987	—	—	—	—	0.10	0.15
1988	—	—	—	—	0.10	0.15
1989	20,080,000	—	—	—	0.10	0.15
1990	10,000,000	—	—	—	0.10	0.15

KM# 49a   CENT
1.8100 g., 0.9250 Silver 0.0538 oz. ASW, 17.8 mm.   **Obv:** Arms with supporters **Rev:** Value divides plants

Date	Mintage	F	VF	XF	Unc	BU
1985sm Proof	20,000	Value: 2.25				
1986sm Proof	15,000	Value: 2.25				
1987sm Proof	15,000	Value: 2.25				
1988 Proof	15,000	Value: 2.25				
1989 Proof	15,000	Value: 2.25				
1990 Proof	15,000	Value: 2.25				
1991 Proof	15,000	Value: 2.25				

KM# 49b   CENT
Copper Plated Zinc, 17.8 mm.   **Obv:** Arms with supporters **Rev:** Value divides plants

Date	Mintage	F	VF	XF	Unc	BU
1991	—	—	—	—	0.10	0.15

KM# 98a   CENT
1.8100 g., 0.9250 Silver 0.0538 oz. ASW, 17.8 mm.   **Obv:** National arms **Rev:** Value divides plants

Date	Mintage	F	VF	XF	Unc	BU
1992 Proof	15,000	Value: 2.25				
1993 Proof	15,000	Value: 2.25				
1994 Proof	10,000	Value: 2.25				
1995 Proof	10,000	Value: 2.25				
1996 Proof	17,000	Value: 2.25				
1997 Proof	20,000	Value: 2.25				
1998 Proof	16,800	Value: 2.25				
1999 Proof	10,000	Value: 2.25				
2000 Proof	16,800	Value: 2.25				

KM# 98   CENT
1.2750 g., Copper Plated Zinc, 15.96 mm.   **Obv:** National arms **Rev:** Value divides plants **Edge:** Plain **Note:** Similar to KM#49 but motto ribbon on arms curves down at center.

Date	Mintage	F	VF	XF	Unc	BU
1992sm	20,000,000	—	—	—	0.10	0.15
1993sm	39,920,000	—	—	—	0.10	0.15
1994sm	130,810,000	—	—	—	0.10	0.15
1995sm	220,000,000	—	—	—	0.10	0.15
1996sm	—	—	—	—	0.20	0.30
1997sm	—	—	—	—	0.20	0.30
1998sm	48,940,000	—	—	—	0.20	0.30
1999sm	49,090,000	—	—	—	0.20	0.30
2000sm	52,360,000	—	—	—	0.20	0.15

KM# 2   5 CENTS
1.4000 g., Copper-Nickel, 16.25 mm.   **Obv:** Value and date **Rev:** Great White Egret **Edge:** Reeded

Date	Mintage	F	VF	XF	Unc	BU
1967 Proof	2,000	Value: 3.25				
1967	28,000,000	—	—	0.20	0.35	0.75

Date	Mintage	F	VF	XF	Unc	BU
1968 Proof	5,000	Value: 3.00				
1968	4,217,000	—	—	0.25	0.40	0.80
1969 Proof	3,000	Value: 15.00				
1969	14,778,000	—	—	0.10	0.35	0.75
1970	4,065,000	—	—	0.20	0.40	0.80
1971	13,202,000	—	—	0.10	0.35	0.75
1972 Proof	749	Value: 50.00				
1972	9,817,000	—	—	0.10	0.35	0.75
1973 Proof	1,000	Value: 7.50				
1973	2,980,000	—	0.50	1.50	2.25	—
1974 Proof	1,500	Value: 6.50				
1974	10,868,000	—	—	0.10	0.35	0.75
1975 Proof	3,000	Value: 2.50				
1975	1,729,000	—	—	0.40	1.00	1.25
1976sm Proof	3,500	Value: 2.25				
1976	15,541,000	—	—	0.10	0.35	0.75
1977sm Proof	3,500	Value: 2.25				
1977	9,956,000	—	—	0.10	0.35	0.75
1978sm Proof	4,000	Value: 2.25				
1978	5,956,000	—	—	0.10	0.35	0.75
1979sm Proof	3,500	Value: 2.25				
1979	9,974,000	—	—	—	0.35	0.75
1980sm Proof	14,000	Value: 2.00				
1980	20,534,000	—	—	—	0.35	0.75
1981	23,866,000	—	—	—	0.35	0.75
1982sm Proof	20,000	Value: 2.00				
1982	24,413,000	—	—	—	0.35	0.75
1983sm Proof	15,000	Value: 2.00				
1983	4,016,000	—	—	—	0.35	0.75
1984sm Proof	15,000	Value: 2.00				
1984	18,880,000	—	—	—	0.35	0.75
1985 In sets only	148,424	—	—	—	0.50	0.85

KM# 8   5 CENTS
1.2700 g., Aluminum, 22 mm.   **Series:** F.A.O. **Obv:** Value and date **Rev:** Pomfret fish **Edge:** Plain

Date	Mintage	F	VF	XF	Unc	BU
1971	3,049,000	—	0.10	0.30	1.00	1.25

KM# 2a   5 CENTS
1.3000 g., Copper-Nickel Clad Steel, 16.25 mm.   **Obv:** Value **Rev:** Great White Egret **Edge:** Reeded

Date	Mintage	F	VF	XF	Unc	BU
1980	12,001,000	—	—	—	0.35	0.50
1981	23,866,000	—	—	—	0.35	0.50
1982	24,413,000	—	—	—	0.35	0.50
1983	4,016,000	—	—	—	0.35	0.50
1984	—	—	—	—	0.35	0.50

KM# 2b   5 CENTS
1.6500 g., 0.9250 Silver 0.0491 oz. ASW, 16.25 mm.   **Obv:** Value **Rev:** Great White Egret

Date	Mintage	F	VF	XF	Unc	BU
1981 Proof	30,000	Value: 5.00				

KM# 50   5 CENTS
Aluminum-Bronze, 16.25 mm.   **Obv:** Arms with supporters **Rev:** Fruit salad plant **Edge:** Reeded

Date	Mintage	F	VF	XF	Unc	BU
1985	14,840,000	—	—	—	0.20	0.30
1986	15,480,000	—	—	—	0.20	0.30
1987	31,040,000	—	—	—	0.20	0.30
1988	45,180,000	—	—	—	0.20	0.30
1989	69,988,000	—	—	—	0.20	0.30
1990	26,052,000	—	—	—	0.20	0.30
1991	—	—	—	—	0.20	0.30

KM# 50a   5 CENTS
2.0000 g., 0.9250 Silver 0.0595 oz. ASW, 16.25 mm.   **Obv:** Arms with supporters **Rev:** Fruit salad plant

Date	Mintage	F	VF	XF	Unc	BU
1985sm Proof	20,000	Value: 2.50				
1986sm Proof	15,000	Value: 2.50				
1987sm Proof	15,000	Value: 2.50				
1988 Proof	15,000	Value: 2.50				
1989 Proof	15,000	Value: 2.50				
1990 Proof	15,000	Value: 2.50				
1991 Proof	15,000	Value: 2.50				

KM# 99a   5 CENTS
2.0000 g., 0.9250 Silver 0.0595 oz. ASW, 16.25 mm.   **Obv:** National arms **Rev:** Fruit salad plant

Date	Mintage	F	VF	XF	Unc	BU
1992sm Proof	15,000	Value: 2.50				
1993sm Proof	15,000	Value: 2.50				
1994sm Proof	10,000	Value: 2.50				
1995sm Proof	10,000	Value: 2.50				
1996sm Proof	17,000	Value: 2.50				

Date	Mintage	F	VF	XF	Unc	BU
1997sm Proof	20,000	Value: 2.50				
1998sm Proof	16,800	Value: 2.50				
1999sm Proof	10,000	Value: 2.50				
2000sm Proof	16,800	Value: 2.50				

KM# 99 5 CENTS
1.6000 g., Aluminum-Bronze, 16.25 mm. **Obv:** National arms **Rev:** Fruit salad plant **Edge:** Reeded **Note:** Similar to KM#50 but motto ribbon on arms curves down at center.

Date	Mintage	F	VF	XF	Unc	BU
1992sm	—	—	—	—	0.20	0.30
1993sm	5,996,000	—	—	—	0.20	0.30
1994sm	—	—	—	—	0.20	0.30
1995sm	90,000,000	—	—	—	0.20	0.30
1996sm	—	—	—	—	0.20	0.30
1997sm	60,000,000	—	—	—	0.20	0.30
1998sm	31,005,000	—	—	—	0.20	0.30
1999sm	35,630,000	—	—	—	0.20	0.30
2000sm	32,550,000	—	—	—	0.20	0.30

KM# 3 10 CENTS
2.8500 g., Copper-Nickel, 19.4 mm. **Obv:** Value and date **Rev:** Stylized Great Crowned Seahorse **Edge:** Reeded

Date	Mintage	F	VF	XF	Unc	BU
1967	40,000,000	—	—	0.15	0.65	1.50
1967 Proof	2,000	Value: 5.00				
1968	36,261,000	—	—	0.20	0.65	1.50
1968 Proof	5,000	Value: 5.00				
1969	25,000,000	—	—	0.10	0.65	1.50
1969 Proof	3,000	Value: 20.00				
1970	21,304,000	—	—	0.20	0.65	1.50
1971	33,040,999	—	—	0.10	0.50	1.50
1972	2,675,000	—	0.20	0.75	1.50	2.00
1972 Proof	749	Value: 60.00				
1973	14,290,000	—	—	0.10	0.65	1.50
1973 Proof	1,000	Value: 10.00				
1974	13,450,000	—	—	0.10	0.65	1.50
1974 Proof	1,500	Value: 7.50				
1975	828,000	—	0.50	1.25	2.25	3.00
1975 Proof	3,000	Value: 4.00				
1976	29,718,000	—	—	0.15	0.35	1.50
1976sm Proof	3,500	Value: 3.50				
1977	11,776,000	—	—	0.10	0.35	1.50
1977sm Proof	3,500	Value: 3.50				
1978	5,936,000	—	—	0.10	0.35	1.50
1978sm Proof	4,000	Value: 3.50				
1979	12,001,000	—	—	0.10	0.35	1.50
1979sm Proof	3,500	Value: 3.50				
1980	40,299,000	—	—	0.10	0.35	1.50
1980sm Proof	14,000	Value: 3.00				
1981	58,600,000	—	—	0.10	0.35	1.50
1982	48,514,000	—	—	0.10	0.35	1.50
1982sm Proof	20,000	Value: 3.00				
1983	10,415,000	—	—	0.10	0.35	1.50
1983sm Proof	15,000	Value: 3.00				
1984	29,700,000	—	—	0.10	0.35	1.50
1984sm Proof	15,000	Value: 3.00				
1985 In sets only	148,424	—	—	0.10	0.35	1.50

KM# 3a 10 CENTS
3.3500 g., 0.9250 Silver 0.0996 oz. ASW, 19.4 mm. **Obv:** Value and date **Rev:** Stylized Great Crowned Seahorse

Date	Mintage	F	VF	XF	Unc	BU
1981sm Proof	30,000	Value: 9.00				

KM# 51 10 CENTS
2.8500 g., Copper-Nickel, 19.4 mm. **Obv:** Arms with supporters **Rev:** Star Jasmine plant above value **Edge:** Reeded

Date	Mintage	F	VF	XF	Unc	BU
1985	45,040,000	—	—	—	0.20	0.30
1986	113,000,000	—	—	—	0.20	0.30
1987	90,000,000	—	—	—	0.20	0.30
1988	54,455,000	—	—	—	0.20	0.30
1989	134,190,000	—	—	—	0.20	0.30
1990	51,720,000	—	—	—	0.20	0.30
1991	159,770,000	—	—	—	0.20	0.30

KM# 51a 10 CENTS
3.0500 g., 0.9250 Silver 0.0907 oz. ASW, 19.4 mm. **Obv:** Arms with supporters **Rev:** Star Jasmine plant above value

Date	Mintage	F	VF	XF	Unc	BU
1985sm Proof	20,000	Value: 4.00				
1986sm Proof	15,000	Value: 4.00				
1987sm Proof	15,000	Value: 4.00				
1988 Proof	15,000	Value: 4.00				
1989 Proof	15,000	Value: 4.00				
1990 Proof	15,000	Value: 4.00				
1991 Proof	15,000	Value: 4.00				

KM# 100a 10 CENTS
3.0500 g., 0.9250 Silver 0.0907 oz. ASW, 19.4 mm. **Obv:** National arms **Rev:** Star Jasmine plant **Edge:** Reeded

Date	Mintage	F	VF	XF	Unc	BU
1992 Proof	15,000	Value: 4.00				
1993 Proof	15,000	Value: 4.00				
1994 Proof	10,000	Value: 4.00				
1995 Proof	10,000	Value: 4.00				
1996 Proof	17,000	Value: 4.00				
1997 Proof	20,000	Value: 4.00				
1998 Proof	16,800	Value: 4.00				
1999 Proof	10,000	Value: 4.00				
2000 Proof	16,800	Value: 4.00				

KM# 100 10 CENTS
2.8500 g., Copper-Nickel, 19.4 mm. **Obv:** National arms **Rev:** Star Jasmine plant **Edge:** Reeded **Note:** Similar to KM#51 but motto ribbon on arms curves down at center.

Date	Mintage	F	VF	XF	Unc	BU
1992sm	—	—	—	—	0.20	0.30
1993sm	89,855,000	—	—	—	0.20	0.30
1994sm	—	—	—	—	0.20	0.30
1995sm	—	—	—	—	0.20	0.30
1996sm	—	—	—	—	0.20	0.30
1997sm	—	—	—	—	0.20	0.30
1998sm	89,840,000	—	—	—	0.20	0.30
1999sm	97,350,000	—	—	—	0.20	0.30
2000sm	80,370,000	—	—	—	0.20	0.30

KM# 4 20 CENTS
5.6500 g., Copper-Nickel, 23.6 mm. **Obv:** Value and date **Rev:** Swordfish **Edge:** Reeded

Date	Mintage	F	VF	XF	Unc	BU
1967	36,500,000	—	0.15	0.35	0.75	1.50
1967 Proof	2,000	Value: 7.00				
1968	10,934,000	—	0.15	0.35	0.75	1.50
1968 Proof	5,000	Value: 6.00				
1969	8,460,000	—	0.15	0.35	0.75	1.50
1969 Proof	3,000	Value: 30.00				
1970	3,250,000	—	0.15	0.30	0.80	1.50
1971	1,732,000	—	0.15	0.70	2.00	3.00
1972	9,107,000	—	0.15	0.30	0.80	1.50
1972 Proof	749	Value: 70.00				
1973	8,838,000	—	0.15	0.30	0.80	1.50
1973 Proof	1,000	Value: 17.50				
1974	4,567,000	—	0.15	0.30	0.75	1.50
1974 Proof	1,500	Value: 12.50				
1975	1,546,000	0.15	0.35	1.20	2.00	2.50
1975 Proof	3,000	Value: 6.50				
1976	19,760,000	—	0.20	0.50	0.85	1.50
1976sm Proof	3,500	Value: 6.00				
1977	7,074,000	—	0.15	0.50	0.85	1.50
1977sm Proof	3,500	Value: 6.00				
1978	4,450,000	—	0.15	0.50	0.85	1.50
1978sm Proof	4,000	Value: 6.00				
1979	14,865,000	—	0.15	0.50	0.85	1.50
1979sm Proof	3,500	Value: 6.00				
1980	27,903,000	—	—	0.25	0.60	1.50
1980sm Proof	14,000	Value: 5.00				
1981	46,997,000	—	—	0.25	0.60	1.50
1982	25,234,000	—	—	0.25	0.60	1.50
1982sm Proof	20,000	Value: 4.00				
1983	6,424,000	—	—	0.25	0.60	1.50
1983sm Proof	15,000	Value: 4.00				
1984	9,290,000	—	—	0.25	0.60	1.50
1984sm Proof	15,000	Value: 4.00				
1985	148,424	—	—	—	0.60	1.50

Note: In sets only

KM# 4a 20 CENTS
6.5100 g., 0.9250 Silver 0.1936 oz. ASW, 23.6 mm. **Obv:** Value and date **Rev:** Swordfish

Date	Mintage	F	VF	XF	Unc	BU
1981sm Proof	30,000	Value: 12.50				

KM# 52 20 CENTS
5.6500 g., Copper-Nickel, 23.6 mm. **Obv:** Arms with supporters **Rev:** Powder-puff plant above value

Date	Mintage	F	VF	XF	Unc	BU
1985	25,980,000	—	—	0.20	0.50	1.00
1986	47,560,000	—	—	0.20	0.50	1.00
1987	80,010,000	—	—	0.20	0.50	1.00
1988	35,783,000	—	—	0.20	0.50	1.00
1989	51,890,000	—	—	0.20	0.50	1.00
1990	49,958,000	—	—	0.20	0.50	1.00
1991	60,000,000	—	—	0.20	0.50	1.00

KM# 52a 20 CENTS
5.2400 g., 0.9250 Silver 0.1558 oz. ASW, 23.6 mm. **Obv:** Arms with supporters **Rev:** Powder puff plant above value

Date	Mintage	F	VF	XF	Unc	BU
1985sm Proof	20,000	Value: 6.50				
1986sm Proof	15,000	Value: 6.50				
1987sm Proof	15,000	Value: 6.50				
1988 Proof	15,000	Value: 6.50				
1989 Proof	15,000	Value: 6.50				
1990 Proof	15,000	Value: 6.50				
1991 Proof	15,000	Value: 6.50				

KM# 101a 20 CENTS
5.2400 g., 0.9250 Silver 0.1558 oz. ASW, 23.6 mm. **Obv:** National arms **Rev:** Powder puff plant above value **Edge:** Reeded

Date	Mintage	F	VF	XF	Unc	BU
1992 Proof	15,000	Value: 6.50				
1993 Proof	15,000	Value: 6.50				
1994 Proof	10,000	Value: 6.50				
1995 Proof	10,000	Value: 6.50				
1996 Proof	17,000	Value: 6.50				
1997 Proof	20,000	Value: 6.50				
1998 Proof	16,800	Value: 6.50				
1999 Proof	10,000	Value: 6.50				
2000 Proof	16,800	Value: 6.50				

KM# 101 20 CENTS
5.6500 g., Copper-Nickel, 23.6 mm. **Obv:** National arms **Rev:** Powder puff plant above value **Edge:** Reeded **Note:** Similar to KM#52 but motto ribbon on arms curves down at center.

Date	Mintage	F	VF	XF	Unc	BU
1992sm	—	—	—	—	0.60	0.85
1993sm	24,998,000	—	—	—	0.50	0.70
1994sm	—	—	—	—	0.60	0.85
1995sm	—	—	—	—	0.60	0.85
1996sm	45,000,000	—	—	—	0.50	0.70
1997sm	90,000,000	—	—	—	0.50	0.70
1998sm	62,600,000	—	—	—	0.60	0.85
1999sm	64,590,000	—	—	—	0.60	0.85
2000sm	54,670,000	—	—	—	0.60	0.85

KM# 5 50 CENTS
9.3500 g., Copper-Nickel, 27.75 mm. **Obv:** Value and date **Rev:** Lion fish **Edge:** Reeded

Date	Mintage	F	VF	XF	Unc	BU
1967 Proof	2,000	Value: 10.00				
1967	11,000,000	—	0.30	0.65	2.00	2.50
1968 Proof	5,000	Value: 8.50				
1968	3,189,000	—	0.30	0.80	2.00	2.50
1969 Proof	3,000	Value: 35.00				
1969	2,008,000	—	0.30	1.00	2.00	2.50
1970	3,102,000	—	0.30	0.65	2.00	2.50
1971	3,933,000	—	0.30	0.65	1.80	2.00
1972 Proof	749	Value: 90.00				
1972	5,427,000	—	0.30	0.65	1.60	2.00
1973 Proof	1,000	Value: 30.00				
1973	4,474,000	—	0.30	0.60	1.10	1.50
1974 Proof	1,500	Value: 22.50				
1974	11,550,000	—	0.30	0.60	1.10	1.50
1975 Proof	3,000	Value: 10.00				
1975	1,432,000	0.25	0.30	2.00	3.00	4.00

Date	Mintage	F	VF	XF	Unc	BU
1976sm Proof	3,500	Value: 8.50				
1976	5,728,000	—	0.30	0.65	1.20	1.75
1977sm Proof	3,500	Value: 8.50				
1977	6,953,000	—	—	0.65	1.20	1.75
1978sm Proof	4,000	Value: 8.50				
1978	3,934,000	—	—	0.65	1.20	1.75
1979sm Proof	3,500	Value: 8.50				
1979	8,461,000	—	—	0.65	1.20	1.75
1980sm Proof	14,000	Value: 7.00				
1980	14,717,000	—	—	0.65	1.20	1.75
1981	29,542,000	—	—	0.60	1.10	1.75
1982sm Proof	20,000	Value: 5.00				
1982	13,756,000	—	—	0.60	1.10	1.75
1983sm Proof	15,000	Value: 5.00				
1983	4,482,000	—	—	0.85	1.50	1.85
1984sm Proof	15,000	Value: 5.00				
1984	3,658,000	—	—	0.85	1.50	1.85
1985	148,424	—	—	—	1.50	1.85

Note: In sets only

KM# 5a 50 CENTS
10.8200 g., 0.9250 Silver 0.3218 oz. ASW, 27.75 mm.
Obv: Value and date **Rev:** Lion fish

Date	Mintage	F	VF	XF	Unc	BU
1981sm Proof	30,000	Value: 15.00				

KM# 53.1 50 CENTS
Copper-Nickel **Obv:** Arms with supporters within designed circle
Rev: Yellow Allamanda plant above value **Edge:** Reeded

Date	Mintage	F	VF	XF	Unc	BU
1985	14,960,000	—	—	0.60	1.10	1.35
1986	15,022,000	—	—	0.60	1.10	1.35
1987	30,000,000	—	—	0.60	1.10	1.35
1988	25,000,000	—	—	0.60	1.10	1.35

KM# 53.1a 50 CENTS
8.5600 g., 0.9250 Silver 0.2546 oz. ASW **Obv:** Arms with
supporters within designed circle **Rev:** Yellow Allamanda plant
above value

Date	Mintage	F	VF	XF	Unc	BU
1985sm Proof	20,000	Value: 12.00				
1986sm Proof	15,000	Value: 12.00				
1987sm Proof	15,000	Value: 12.00				
1988 Proof	15,000	Value: 12.00				

KM# 53.2 50 CENTS
Copper-Nickel **Obv:** Arms with supporters **Rev:** Yellow Allamanda
plant above value **Edge:** REPUBLIC OF SINGAPORE (lion's head)

Date	Mintage	F	VF	XF	Unc	BU
1989	20,046,000	—	—	0.45	0.85	2.00
1990	19,740,000	—	—	0.45	0.75	1.50
1991	19,946,000	—	—	0.45	0.75	1.50

KM# 53.2a 50 CENTS
8.5600 g., 0.9250 Silver 0.2546 oz. ASW **Obv:** Arms with
supporters **Rev:** Yellow Allamanda plant above value

Date	Mintage	F	VF	XF	Unc	BU
1989 Proof	15,000	Value: 12.00				
1990 Proof	—	Value: 12.00				
1991 Proof	—	Value: 12.00				

KM# 102a 50 CENTS
8.5600 g., 0.9250 Silver 0.2546 oz. ASW **Obv:** National arms
Rev: Yellow Allamanda plant above value

Date	Mintage	F	VF	XF	Unc	BU
1992 Proof	15,000	Value: 12.00				
1993 Proof	15,000	Value: 12.00				
1994 Proof	10,000	Value: 12.00				
1995 Proof	10,000	Value: 12.00				
1996 Proof	17,000	Value: 12.00				
1997 Proof	20,000	Value: 12.00				
1998 Proof	16,800	Value: 12.00				
1999 Proof	10,000	Value: 12.00				
2000 Proof	16,800	Value: 12.00				

KM# 102 50 CENTS
7.1900 g., Copper-Nickel, 24 mm. **Obv:** National arms
Rev: Yellow Allamanda plant above value **Edge:** Plain
Edge: REPUBLIC OF SINGAPORE (lion's head) **Note:** Similar
to KM#53 but motto ribbon on arms curves down at center.

Date	Mintage	F	VF	XF	Unc	BU
1992sm	—	—	—	—	0.75	1.00
1993sm	4,878,000	—	—	—	0.75	1.00
1994sm	—	—	—	—	0.75	1.00

Date	Mintage	F	VF	XF	Unc	BU
1995sm	49,440,000	—	—	—	0.75	1.00
1996sm	—	—	—	—	0.75	1.00
1997sm	30,000,000	—	—	—	0.75	1.00
1998sm	27,590,000	—	—	—	0.75	1.00
1999sm	28,960,000	—	—	—	0.75	1.00
2000sm	29,780,000	—	—	—	0.75	1.00

KM# 6 DOLLAR
16.8500 g., Copper-Nickel, 33.3 mm. **Obv:** Value and date
Rev: Statue flanked by sprigs **Edge:** Reeded

Date	Mintage	F	VF	XF	Unc	BU
1967	3,000,000	—	0.65	1.50	3.00	—
1967 Proof	2,000	Value: 22.50				
1968	2,194,000	—	0.65	1.50	3.00	—
1968 Proof	5,000	Value: 20.00				
1969	1,871,000	—	0.65	1.75	3.25	—
1969 Proof	3,000	Value: 75.00				
1970	560,000	—	0.65	1.75	3.25	—
1971	900,000	—	0.65	1.75	3.25	—
1972	458,000	—	0.75	2.00	5.00	—
1972 Proof	749	Value: 150				
1973	341,000	—	0.75	2.00	3.50	—
1973 Proof	1,000	Value: 50.00				
1974	352,000	—	0.75	2.00	3.50	—
1974 Proof	1,500	Value: 40.00				
1975	430,000	—	0.75	2.00	3.50	—
1975 Proof	3,000	Value: 20.00				
1976	165,000	—	2.00	3.00	6.00	—
1976sm Proof	3,500	Value: 13.50				
1977	132,000	—	2.00	4.00	8.00	—
1977sm Proof	3,500	Value: 13.50				
1978	37,000	—	5.00	10.00	20.00	—
1978sm Proof	4,000	Value: 13.50				
1979	100,000	—	—	4.00	8.00	—
1979sm Proof	3,500	Value: 13.50				
1980	166,000	—	—	2.25	4.00	—
1980sm Proof	14,000	Value: 11.50				
1981	1,230,000	—	—	2.25	4.00	—
1982	1,080,000	—	—	2.25	4.00	—
1983	101,000	—	—	3.00	5.25	—
1984	170,000	—	—	3.00	4.50	—
1985	148,424	—	—	0.65	1.25	—

Note: In sets only

KM# 6a DOLLAR
18.0500 g., 0.9250 Silver 0.5368 oz. ASW, 33.3 mm.
Obv: Value and date **Rev:** Statue flanked by sprigs

Date	Mintage	F	VF	XF	Unc	BU
1975 Proof	3,000	Value: 140				
1976sm Proof	10,000	Value: 65.00				
1977sm Proof	10,000	Value: 65.00				
1978sm Proof	10,000	Value: 85.00				
1979sm Proof	8,000	Value: 75.00				
1980sm Proof	10,000	Value: 65.00				
1981sm Proof	30,000	Value: 12.50				
1982sm Proof	20,000	Value: 15.00				
1983sm Proof	15,000	Value: 12.50				
1984sm Proof	15,000	Value: 12.50				

KM# 54 DOLLAR
Copper-Nickel **Obv:** Arms with supporters **Rev:** Periwinkle flower

Date	Mintage	F	VF	XF	Unc	BU
1985	—	—	—	—	1.75	2.50
1986	120,000	—	—	—	1.75	2.50
	Note: In sets only					
1987	120,000	—	—	—	1.75	2.50
	Note: In sets only					

KM# 54a DOLLAR
9.9700 g., 0.9250 Silver 0.2965 oz. ASW **Obv:** Arms with
supporters **Rev:** Periwinkle flower

Date	Mintage	F	VF	XF	Unc	BU
1985sm Proof	20,000	Value: 15.00				
1986sm Proof	15,000	Value: 15.00				

KM# 54b DOLLAR
Aluminum-Bronze, 22.3 mm. **Obv:** Arms with supporters
Rev: Periwinkle flower **Edge:** REPUBLIC OF SINGAPORE
(lion's head)

Date	Mintage	F	VF	XF	Unc	BU
1987	21,772,000	—	—	0.75	1.50	2.25
1988	59,332,000	—	—	0.75	1.50	2.25
1989	62,586,000	—	—	0.75	1.50	2.25
1990	37,608,000	—	—	0.75	1.50	2.25
1991	—	—	—	0.75	1.50	2.25

KM# 54c DOLLAR
8.4273 g., 0.9250 Silver 0.2506 oz. ASW **Obv:** Arms with
supporters **Rev:** Periwinkle flower

Date	Mintage	F	VF	XF	Unc	BU
1987sm Proof	15,000	Value: 15.00				
1988 Proof	15,000	Value: 15.00				
1989 Proof	15,000	Value: 15.00				
1990 Proof	15,000	Value: 15.00				
1991 Proof	15,000	Value: 15.00				

KM# 103a DOLLAR
8.4273 g., 0.9250 Silver 0.2506 oz. ASW **Obv:** National arms
Rev: Periwinkle flower

Date	Mintage	F	VF	XF	Unc	BU
1992 Proof	15,000	Value: 15.00				
1993 Proof	15,000	Value: 15.00				
1994 Proof	10,000	Value: 15.00				
1995 Proof	10,000	Value: 15.00				
1996 Proof	17,000	Value: 15.00				
1997 Proof	20,000	Value: 15.00				
1998 Proof	16,800	Value: 15.00				
1999 Proof	10,000	Value: 15.00				
2000 Proof	17,000	Value: 15.00				

KM# 103 DOLLAR
6.2900 g., Aluminum-Bronze, 22.3 mm. **Obv:** National arms
Rev: Periwinkle flower **Edge:** Reeded **Note:** Similar to KM#54
but motto ribbon on arms curves down at center.

Date	Mintage	F	VF	XF	Unc	BU
1992sm	—	—	—	—	1.50	2.25
1993sm	—	—	—	—	1.50	2.25
1994sm	5,008,000	—	—	—	1.50	2.25
1995sm	65,000,000	—	—	—	1.50	2.25
1996sm	—	—	—	—	1.50	2.25
1997sm	129,856,000	—	—	—	1.50	2.25
1998sm	40,880,000	—	—	—	1.50	2.25
1999sm	38,300,000	—	—	—	1.50	2.25
2000sm	35,690,000	—	—	—	1.50	2.25

KM# 156 2 DOLLARS
20.0000 g., 0.9250 Silver 0.5948 oz. ASW **Series:** UNICEF
Obv: Arms with supporters **Rev:** Children using computer below
UNICEF logo within circle

Date	Mintage	F	VF	XF	Unc	BU
1997 Proof	25,000	Value: 60.00				

KM# 10   5 DOLLARS

25.0000 g., 0.5000 Silver 0.4019 oz. ASW **Subject:** 7th Southeast Asia Peninsular Games **Obv:** Arms with supporters **Rev:** Games logo above stadium

Date	Mintage	F	VF	XF	Unc	BU
1973 Proof	5,000	Value: 160				
1973	250,000	—	—	—	25.00	—

KM# 19   5 DOLLARS

Copper-Nickel, 33.5 mm. **Obv:** Arms with supporters **Rev:** Changi Airport **Edge:** Reeded

Date	Mintage	F	VF	XF	Unc	BU
1981	220,000	—	—	6.00	10.00	—

KM# 19a   5 DOLLARS

18.0500 g., 0.9250 Silver 0.5368 oz. ASW, 33.5 mm. **Obv:** Arms with supporters **Rev:** Changi airport

Date	Mintage	F	VF	XF	Unc	BU
1981sm Proof	20,000	Value: 75.00				

KM# 22   5 DOLLARS

Copper-Nickel, 33.5 mm. **Obv:** Arms with supporters **Rev:** Benjamin Shears Bridge

Date	Mintage	F	VF	XF	Unc	BU
1982	260,000	—	—	6.00	10.00	—

KM# 22a   5 DOLLARS

18.0500 g., 0.9250 Silver 0.5368 oz. ASW, 33.5 mm. **Obv:** Arms with supporters **Rev:** Benjamin Shears Bridge

Date	Mintage	F	VF	XF	Unc	BU
1982sm Proof	20,000	Value: 75.00				

KM# 25   5 DOLLARS

Copper-Nickel **Subject:** 12th SEA Games **Obv:** Arms with supporters **Rev:** Games logo above waves within circle, athletes around outer top half

Date	Mintage	F	VF	XF	Unc	BU
1983	270,000	—	—	6.00	10.00	—

KM# 25a   5 DOLLARS

20.0000 g., 0.9250 Silver 0.5948 oz. ASW **Obv:** Arms with supporters **Rev:** Games logo above waves within circle, athletes around outer top half

Date	Mintage	F	VF	XF	Unc	BU
1983sm Proof	20,000	Value: 75.00				

KM# 32   5 DOLLARS

Copper-Nickel **Subject:** 25 Years of Nation - Building **Obv:** Arms with supporters **Rev:** Value above flowered sprigs

Date	Mintage	F	VF	XF	Unc	BU
ND(1984)	270,000	—	—	—	6.00	10.00

KM# 32a   5 DOLLARS

20.0000 g., 0.9250 Silver 0.5948 oz. ASW **Subject:** 25 Years of Nation - Building **Obv:** Arms with supporters **Rev:** Value above flower sprigs

Date	Mintage	F	VF	XF	Unc	BU
ND(1984)sm Proof	20,000	Value: 75.00				

KM# 48   5 DOLLARS

Copper-Nickel **Subject:** 25 Years of Public Housing **Obv:** Arms with supporters and legend **Rev:** Figures in front of buildings

Date	Mintage	F	VF	XF	Unc	BU
1985	117,000	—	—	—	6.00	10.00

KM# 48a   5 DOLLARS

20.0000 g., 0.9250 Silver 0.5948 oz. ASW **Obv:** Arms with supporters and legend **Rev:** Figures in front of buildings

Date	Mintage	F	VF	XF	Unc	BU
1985sm Proof	20,000	Value: 75.00				

KM# 68   5 DOLLARS

Copper-Nickel **Subject:** 100th Anniversary of National Museum **Obv:** Arms with supporters **Rev:** Museum building

Date	Mintage	F	VF	XF	Unc	BU
ND(1987)	70,000	—	—	—	10.00	—

KM# 68a   5 DOLLARS

20.0000 g., 0.9250 Silver 0.5948 oz. ASW **Subject:** 100th Anniversary of National Museum **Obv:** Arms with supporters **Rev:** Museum building

Date	Mintage	F	VF	XF	Unc	BU
ND(1987)sm Proof	25,000	Value: 75.00				

KM# 70   5 DOLLARS

Copper-Nickel **Subject:** 100th Anniversary of Singapore Fire Brigade **Obv:** Arms with supporters **Rev:** Pair of horses pulling wagon with equipment within circle

Date	Mintage	F	VF	XF	Unc	BU
ND(1988)	50,000	—	—	—	13.50	15.00

KM# 70a   5 DOLLARS

20.0000 g., 0.9250 Silver 0.5948 oz. ASW **Subject:** 100th Anniversary of Singapore Fire Brigade **Obv:** Arms with supporters **Rev:** Pair of horses pulling wagon with equipment within circle

Date	Mintage	F	VF	XF	Unc	BU
ND(1988)sm Proof	25,000	Value: 75.00				

KM# 74   5 DOLLARS

Copper-Nickel **Subject:** Rapid Transit System **Obv:** Arms with supporters **Rev:** Train in city

Date	Mintage	F	VF	XF	Unc	BU
1989	60,000	—	—	—	10.00	12.00

KM# 74a   5 DOLLARS

20.0000 g., 0.9250 Silver 0.5948 oz. ASW **Subject:** Rapid Transit System **Obv:** National arms **Rev:** Train in city

Date	Mintage	F	VF	XF	Unc	BU
1989 Proof	30,000	Value: 62.50				

KM# 77   5 DOLLARS

20.0000 g., 0.9250 Silver 0.5948 oz. ASW, 38.7 mm. **Series:** Save the Children Fund **Obv:** Arms with supporters **Rev:** Children, kayak, palm tree and value **Edge:** Reeded

Date	Mintage	F	VF	XF	Unc	BU
1989 Proof	20,000	Value: 52.50				

KM# 94   5 DOLLARS

Copper-Aluminum-Nickel **Subject:** 25th Anniversary of Independence **Obv:** Arms with supporters **Rev:** City view from water

Date	Mintage	F	VF	XF	Unc	BU
1990	1,000,000	—	—	—	7.00	—

KM# 86   5 DOLLARS

Copper-Nickel **Subject:** Civil Defense **Obv:** Arms with supporters **Rev:** Working figures within circle

Date	Mintage	F	VF	XF	Unc	BU
1991	55,000	—	—	—	9.00	—
1991 Proof	10,000	Value: 50.00				

KM# 86a   5 DOLLARS

20.0000 g., 0.9250 Silver 0.5948 oz. ASW **Subject:** Civil Defense **Obv:** Arms with supporters **Rev:** Working figures within circle

Date	Mintage	F	VF	XF	Unc	BU
1991 Proof	20,000	Value: 50.00				

KM# 104.1   5 DOLLARS
Bi-Metallic Aluminum-Bronze center in Copper-Nickel ring **Subject:** Vanda Miss Joaquim **Obv:** National arms, date and BCCS logo **Rev:** Flower and value within beaded circle

Date	Mintage	F	VF	XF	Unc	BU
1992sm	—	—	—	—	—	15.00
Note: In mint sets only						
1993sm	—	—	—	—	—	15.00
Note: In mint sets only						
1994sm	—	—	→	—	—	15.00
Note: In mint sets only						
1995sm	—	—	—	—	—	15.00
Note: In mint sets only						
1996sm	—	—	—	—	—	15.00
Note: In mint sets only						
1997sm	—	—	—	—	—	15.00
Note: In mint sets only						
1998sm	—	—	—	—	—	15.00
Note: In mint sets only						

KM# 104.1a   5 DOLLARS
8.2500 g., 0.9250 Silver 0.2453 oz. ASW **Subject:** Vanda Miss Joaquim **Obv:** National arms, date and BCCS logo **Rev:** Flower and value within beaded circle

Date	Mintage	F	VF	XF	Unc	BU
1992sm Proof	15,000	Value: 25.00				
1994sm Proof	10,000	Value: 25.00				
1995sm Proof	10,000	Value: 25.00				
1996sm Proof	17,000	Value: 25.00				
1997sm Proof	19,970	Value: 25.00				
1998sm Proof	16,800	Value: 25.00				

KM# 115   5 DOLLARS
Copper-Nickel **Subject:** XVII Sea Games **Obv:** Arms with supporters **Rev:** Martial arts

Date	Mintage	F	VF	XF	Unc	BU
1993	23,000	—	—	—	9.00	—
1993 Proof	2,000	Value: 35.00				

KM# 115a   5 DOLLARS
20.0000 g., 0.9250 Silver 0.5948 oz. ASW **Subject:** XVII Sea Games **Obv:** Arms with supporters **Rev:** Martial arts

Date	Mintage	F	VF	XF	Unc	BU
1993 Proof	10,000	Value: 62.50				

KM# 124   5 DOLLARS
Copper-Nickel **Subject:** Year of the Family **Obv:** Arms with supporters **Rev:** Stylized family and value

Date	Mintage	F	VF	XF	Unc	BU
1994	20,000	—	—	—	14.00	—

KM# 124a   5 DOLLARS
20.0000 g., 0.9250 Silver 0.5948 oz. ASW **Subject:** Year of the Family **Obv:** Arms with supporters **Rev:** Stylized family and value

Date	Mintage	F	VF	XF	Unc	BU
1994 Proof	40,000	Value: 62.50				

KM# 138   5 DOLLARS
Bi-Metallic Aluminum-Bronze center in Copper-Nickel ring **Series:** 50th Anniversary - United Nations **Obv:** Arms with supporters within beaded circle **Rev:** UN logo within artistic design

Date	Mintage	F	VF	XF	Unc	BU
1995	500,000	—	—	—	10.00	12.00

KM# 139   5 DOLLARS
20.0000 g., 0.9250 Silver 0.5948 oz. ASW **Series:** 50th Anniversary - United Nations **Obv:** Arms with supporters **Rev:** UN logo within artistic design

Date	Mintage	F	VF	XF	Unc	BU
1995 Proof	9,000	Value: 70.00				

KM# 150   5 DOLLARS
Copper-Nickel **Subject:** 30th Anniversary - Singapore's Independence **Obv:** Arms with supporters **Rev:** Globe on map

Date	Mintage	F	VF	XF	Unc	BU
1995	20,000	—	—	—	12.00	15.00

KM# 150a   5 DOLLARS
20.0000 g., 0.9250 Silver 0.5948 oz. ASW **Subject:** 30th Anniversary - Singapore's Independence **Obv:** Arms with supporters **Rev:** Globe on map

Date	Mintage	F	VF	XF	Unc	BU
1995 Proof	8,000	Value: 70.00				

KM# 149   5 DOLLARS
Copper-Nickel **Subject:** World Trade Organization Conference **Obv:** Arms with supporters **Rev:** Value within stylized lion head

Date	Mintage	F	VF	XF	Unc	BU
1996	23,800	—	—	—	8.00	—

KM# 149a   5 DOLLARS
20.0000 g., 0.9250 Silver 0.5948 oz. ASW **Subject:** World Trade Organization Conference **Obv:** Arms with supporters with mintmark **Rev:** Value within stylized lion head

Date	Mintage	F	VF	XF	Unc	BU
1996 Proof	16,800	Value: 62.50				

KM# 151   5 DOLLARS
Copper-Nickel **Subject:** 50th Anniversary - Singapore Airlines **Obv:** Arms with supporters with no mint mark **Rev:** Plane in front of numeral 50

Date	Mintage	F	VF	XF	Unc	BU
1997	20,800	—	—	—	17.00	—

KM# 151a   5 DOLLARS
20.0000 g., 0.9250 Silver 0.5948 oz. ASW **Subject:** 50th Anniversary - Singapore Airlines **Obv:** Arms with supporters with mint mark **Rev:** Plane in front of numeral 50

Date	Mintage	F	VF	XF	Unc	BU
1997 Proof	14,112	Value: 62.50				

KM# 157   5 DOLLARS
7.7760 g., 0.9999 Gold 0.2500 oz. AGW **Series:** UNICEF **Obv:** Arms with supporters **Rev:** Children using computer

Date	Mintage	F	VF	XF	Unc	BU
1997 Proof	10,000	Value: 350				

KM# 163   5 DOLLARS
Copper-Nickel **Subject:** Charity Work in Singapore **Obv:** Arms with supporters **Rev:** Two hands holding heart-shaped fruit

Date	Mintage	F	VF	XF	Unc	BU
1998	9,200	—	—	—	21.50	—

KM# 163a   5 DOLLARS
20.0000 g., 0.9250 Silver 0.5948 oz. ASW **Subject:** Charity Work in Singapore **Obv:** Arms with supporters **Rev:** Two hands holding heart-shaped fruit

Date	Mintage	F	VF	XF	Unc	BU
1998 Proof	12,000	Value: 95.00				

KM# 173   5 DOLLARS
20.0000 g., Copper-Nickel **Subject:** Parliament **Obv:** Arms with supporters **Rev:** Parliament building **Edge:** Reeded

Date	Mintage	F	VF	XF	Unc	BU
1999	10,000	—	—	—	20.00	—
1999 Proof	10,000	Value: 60.00				

KM# 104.2   5 DOLLARS
Bi-Metallic **Ring:** Copper-Nickel **Center:** Aluminum-Bronze **Obv:** National arms, date and MAS logo **Rev:** Flower above value **Edge:** Plain

Date	Mintage	F	VF	XF	Unc	BU
1999sm	—	—	—	—	—	12.00
Note: In mint sets only						
2000sm	—	—	—	—	—	12.00
Note: In mint sets only						

KM# 104.2a   5 DOLLARS
8.2500 g., 0.9250 Silver 0.2453 oz. ASW **Obv:** National arms, date and MAS logo **Rev:** Flower above value **Edge:** Plain

Date	Mintage	F	VF	XF	Unc	BU
1999sm Proof	10,000	Value: 25.00				
2000sm Proof	16,800	Value: 25.00				

KM# 173a   5 DOLLARS
20.0000 g., 0.9250 Silver 0.5948 oz. ASW **Obv:** Arms with supporters **Rev:** Parliament building

Date	Mintage	F	VF	XF	Unc	BU
1999 Proof	10,000	Value: 55.00				

KM# 171   5 DOLLARS
Bi-Metallic Aluminum-Bronze center in Copper-Nickel ring **Obv:** Arms with supporters above latent date within beaded circle **Rev:** Millennium design **Edge:** Scalloped

Date	Mintage	F	VF	XF	Unc	BU
2000	406,000	—	—	—	6.50	10.00

KM# 172 5 DOLLARS
31.1030 g., 0.9990 Gold 0.9989 oz. AGW **Subject:** Millennium
Obv: Arms with supporters above latent date within beaded circle
Rev: Millennium design **Edge:** Scalloped

Date	Mintage	F	VF	XF	Unc	BU
2000 Proof	3,000	Value: 1,000				

KM# 9.1 10 DOLLARS
31.1000 g., 0.9000 Silver 0.8999 oz. ASW **Obv:** Arms with
supporters **Obv. Leg.:** SINGAPORE inverted **Rev:** Hawk
descending

Date	Mintage	F	VF	XF	Unc	BU
1972	80,000	—	—	—	30.00	35.00
1972 Proof	3,000	Value: 175				

KM# 9.2 10 DOLLARS
31.1000 g., 0.9000 Silver 0.8999 oz. ASW **Obv:** Arms with
supporters **Rev:** Hawk descending

Date	Mintage	F	VF	XF	Unc	BU
1973	80,000	—	—	—	25.00	30.00
1973 Proof	5,000	Value: 170				

KM# 9.2a 10 DOLLARS
31.1000 g., 0.5000 Silver 0.4999 oz. ASW **Obv:** Arms with
supporters **Rev:** Hawk descending

Date	Mintage	F	VF	XF	Unc	BU
1974	100,000	—	—	—	20.00	22.50
1974 Proof	6,000	Value: 120				

KM# 11 10 DOLLARS
31.1000 g., 0.5000 Silver 0.4999 oz. ASW **Subject:** 10th
Anniversary of Independence **Obv:** Arms with supporters
Rev: Value above ship

Date	Mintage	F	VF	XF	Unc	BU
ND(1975)	200,000	—	—	—	12.50	15.00
ND(1975) Proof	10,000	Value: 70.00				

KM# 15 10 DOLLARS
31.1000 g., 0.5000 Silver 0.4999 oz. ASW, 40 mm.
Subject: 10th Anniversary of Independence **Obv:** Arms with
supporters **Rev:** Ship in port

Date	Mintage	F	VF	XF	Unc	BU
1976	150,000	—	—	—	12.50	15.00
1976sm Proof	10,000	Value: 70.00				
1977	150,000	—	—	—	12.50	15.00
1977sm Proof	10,000	Value: 70.00				

KM# 16 10 DOLLARS
31.1000 g., 0.5000 Silver 0.4999 oz. ASW **Subject:** ASEAN
10th Anniversary **Obv:** Arms with supporters **Rev:** Cluster of
hands holding circled map

Date	Mintage	F	VF	XF	Unc	BU
ND(1977)	200,000	—	—	—	12.50	15.00
ND(1977)sm Proof	10,000	Value: 70.00				

KM# 17.1 10 DOLLARS
31.1000 g., 0.5000 Silver 0.4999 oz. ASW **Obv:** Arms with
supporters **Rev:** Communications Satellites

Date	Mintage	F	VF	XF	Unc	BU
1978	167,000	—	—	—	12.50	15.00
1978sm Proof	10,000	Value: 70.00				
1979	168,000	—	—	—	12.50	15.00
1979sm Proof	9,000	Value: 70.00				

KM# 17.1a 10 DOLLARS
Nickel **Obv:** Arms with supporters **Rev:** Communications Satellites

Date	Mintage	F*	VF	XF	Unc	BU
1980	120,000	—	—	—	13.50	16.50

KM# 17.2 10 DOLLARS
Nickel **Obv:** Arms with supporters **Rev:** Communications Satellites

Date	Mintage	F	VF	XF	Unc	BU
1980sm Proof	15,000	Value: 70.00				

KM# 20 10 DOLLARS
Nickel **Subject:** Year of the Rooster **Obv:** Arms with supporters
Rev: Rooster within circle, value below, various animals border

Date	Mintage	F	VF	XF	Unc	BU
1981	180,000	—	—	—	68.00	75.00

KM# 20a 10 DOLLARS
31.1000 g., 0.5000 Silver 0.4999 oz. ASW **Obv:** Arms with
supporters **Rev:** Rooster within circle, value below, various
animals border

Date	Mintage	F	VF	XF	Unc	BU
1981sm Proof	20,000	Value: 220				

KM# 23 10 DOLLARS
Nickel **Subject:** Year of the Dog **Obv:** Arms with supporters
Rev: Dog within circle, value below, various animals border

Date	Mintage	F	VF	XF	Unc	BU
1982	210,000	—	—	—	35.00	50.00

KM# 23a 10 DOLLARS
31.1000 g., 0.5000 Silver 0.4999 oz. ASW **Obv:** Arms with
supporters **Rev:** Dog within circle, value below, various animals
border

Date	Mintage	F	VF	XF	Unc	BU
1982sm Proof	20,000	Value: 150				

KM# 26 10 DOLLARS
Nickel **Subject:** Year of the Pig **Obv:** Arms with supporters
Rev: Pig within circle, value below, various animals border

Date	Mintage	F	VF	XF	Unc	BU
1983	307,000	—	—	—	20.00	30.00

KM# 26a 10 DOLLARS
31.1000 g., 0.5000 Silver 0.4999 oz. ASW **Obv:** Arms with
supporters **Rev:** Pig within circle, value below, various animals
border

Date	Mintage	F	VF	XF	Unc	BU
1983sm Proof	20,000	Value: 130				

KM# 33 10 DOLLARS
Nickel **Subject:** Year of the Rat **Obv:** Arms with supporters
Rev: Rat within circle, value below, various animals border

Date	Mintage	F	VF	XF	Unc	BU
1984	300,000	—	—	—	20.00	30.00

KM# 33a 10 DOLLARS
31.1000 g., 0.5000 Silver 0.4999 oz. ASW **Obv:** Arms with
supporters **Rev:** Rat within circle, value below, various animals
border

Date	Mintage	F	VF	XF	Unc	BU
1984sm Proof	20,000	Value: 100				

KM# 44 10 DOLLARS
Nickel **Subject:** Year of the Ox **Obv:** Arms with supporters
Rev: Ox within circle, value below, various animals border

Date	Mintage	F	VF	XF	Unc	BU
1985	307,000	—	—	—	20.00	30.00

KM# 44a 10 DOLLARS
31.1000 g., 0.5000 Silver 0.4999 oz. ASW **Obv:** Arms with
supporters **Rev:** Ox within circle, value below, various animals
border

Date	Mintage	F	VF	XF	Unc	BU
1985sm Proof	20,000	Value: 110				

KM# 59   10 DOLLARS
Nickel   **Subject:** Year of the Tiger **Obv:** Arms with supporters
Rev: Tiger within circle, value below, various animals border

Date	Mintage	F	VF	XF	Unc	BU
1986	300,000	—	—	—	20.00	30.00

KM# 59a   10 DOLLARS
31.1000 g., 0.5000 Silver 0.4999 oz. ASW   **Obv:** Arms with
supporters **Rev:** Tiger within circle, value below, various animals
border

Date	Mintage	F	VF	XF	Unc	BU
1986 Proof	20,000	Value: 100				

KM# 66   10 DOLLARS
Nickel   **Subject:** Year of the Rabbit **Obv:** Arms with supporters
Rev: Rabbit within circle, value below, various animals border

Date	Mintage	F	VF	XF	Unc	BU
1987	300,000	—	—	—	15.00	30.00

KM# 66a   10 DOLLARS
31.1000 g., 0.5000 Silver 0.4999 oz. ASW   **Obv:** Arms with
supporters **Rev:** Rabbit within circle, value below, various animals
border

Date	Mintage	F	VF	XF	Unc	BU
1987sm Proof	25,000	Value: 70.00				

KM# 67   10 DOLLARS
Copper-Nickel   **Subject:** Association of Southeast Asian Nations
Obv: Arms with supporters above 1967-1987 **Rev:** ASEAN logo
within legend above value

Date	Mintage	F	VF	XF	Unc	BU
1987	80,000	—	—	—	8.50	12.50

KM# 67a   10 DOLLARS
31.1030 g., 0.5000 Silver 0.5000 oz. ASW   **Subject:** Association
of Southeast Asian Nations **Obv:** Arms with supporters above
1967-1987 **Rev:** ASEAN logo within legend above value

Date	Mintage	F	VF	XF	Unc	BU
1987sm Proof	25,000	Value: 60.00				

KM# 69   10 DOLLARS
Nickel   **Subject:** Year of the Dragon **Obv:** Arms with supporters
Rev: Dragon within circle, value below, various animals border

Date	Mintage	F	VF	XF	Unc	BU
1988	300,000	—	—	—	25.00	30.00

KM# 69a   10 DOLLARS
31.1030 g., 0.5000 Silver 0.5000 oz. ASW   **Subject:** Year of the
Dragon **Obv:** Arms with supporters **Rev:** Dragon within circle,
value below, various animals border

Date	Mintage	F	VF	XF	Unc	BU
1988 Proof	25,000	Value: 120				

KM# 71   10 DOLLARS
Nickel   **Subject:** Year of the Snake **Obv:** Arms with supporters
Rev: Snake within circle, value below, various animals border

Date	Mintage	F	VF	XF	Unc	BU
1989	250,000	—	—	—	20.00	30.00

KM# 71a   10 DOLLARS
31.1030 g., 0.9250 Silver 0.9249 oz. ASW   **Subject:** Year of the
Snake **Obv:** Arms with supporters **Rev:** Snake within circle, value
below, various animals border

Date	Mintage	F	VF	XF	Unc	BU
1989 Proof	25,000	Value: 95.00				

KM# 75   10 DOLLARS
Nickel   **Subject:** Year of the Horse **Obv:** Arms with supporters
Rev: Horse within circle with value and assorted animal border

Date	Mintage	F	VF	XF	Unc	BU
1990	330,000	—	—	—	20.00	25.00

KM# 75a   10 DOLLARS
31.1030 g., 0.9250 Silver 0.9249 oz. ASW   **Subject:** Year of the
Horse **Obv:** Arms with supporters **Rev:** Horse within circle, value
below, various animals border

Date	Mintage	F	VF	XF	Unc	BU
1990sm Proof	30,000	Value: 70.00				

KM# 95   10 DOLLARS
31.1030 g., 0.9250 Silver 0.9249 oz. ASW   **Subject:** 25th
Anniversary of Independence **Obv:** Arms with supporters **Rev:**
Stylized numeral 25 above city view and dates with value at right

Date	Mintage	F	VF	XF	Unc	BU
1990 Proof	50,000	Value: 70.00				

KM# 84   10 DOLLARS
Nickel   **Subject:** Year of the Goat **Obv:** Arms with supporters
Rev: Goat within circle, value below, various animals border

Date	Mintage	F	VF	XF	Unc	BU
1991	300,000	—	—	—	20.00	30.00

KM# 84a   10 DOLLARS
31.1030 g., 0.9250 Silver 0.9249 oz. ASW   **Subject:** Year of the
Goat **Obv:** Arms with supporters **Rev:** Goat within circle, value
below, various animals border

Date	Mintage	F	VF	XF	Unc	BU
1991sm Proof	30,000	Value: 70.00				

KM# 92   10 DOLLARS
Nickel   **Subject:** Year of the Monkey **Obv:** Arms with supporters
Rev: Monkey below value **Note:** Similar to 500 Dollars, KM#93.

Date	Mintage	F	VF	XF	Unc	BU
1992	300,000	—	—	—	20.00	30.00

KM# 92a   10 DOLLARS
31.1030 g., 0.9250 Silver 0.9249 oz. ASW   **Obv:** Arms with
supporters **Rev:** Monkey below value

Date	Mintage	F	VF	XF	Unc	BU
1992 Proof	30,000	Value: 75.00				

KM# 105   10 DOLLARS
0.9250 Silver   **Subject:** 25th Anniversary - Board of
Commissioners of Currency **Obv:** Arms with supporters
Rev: Stylized dollar sign within circle

Date	Mintage	F	VF	XF	Unc	BU
1992 Proof	15,000	Value: 85.00				

KM# 113   10 DOLLARS
Copper-Nickel   **Subject:** Year of the Rooster **Obv:** Arms with
supporters **Rev:** Stylized rooster

Date	Mintage	F	VF	XF	Unc	BU
1993 Prooflike	209,000	—	—	—	25.00	30.00

KM# 113a   10 DOLLARS
62.2070 g., 0.9990 Silver 1.9979 oz. ASW   **Subject:** Year of the
Rooster **Obv:** Arms with supporters **Rev:** Stylized rooster

Date	Mintage	F	VF	XF	Unc	BU
1993 Proof	40,000	Value: 85.00				

KM# 122 10 DOLLARS
Copper-Nickel **Subject:** Year of the Dog **Obv:** Arms with supporters **Rev:** Stylized dog within designs

Date	Mintage	F	VF	XF	Unc	BU
1994 Prooflike	215,000	—	—	—	28.00	30.00

KM# 122a 10 DOLLARS
62.2070 g., 0.9990 Silver 1.9979 oz. ASW **Subject:** Year of the Dog **Obv:** Arms with supporters **Rev:** Stylized dog within designs

Date	Mintage	F	VF	XF	Unc	BU
1994 Proof	35,000	Value: 85.00				

KM# 125 10 DOLLARS
Copper-Nickel **Subject:** Year of the Pig **Obv:** Arms with supporters **Rev:** Stylized pig

Date	Mintage	F	VF	XF	Unc	BU
1995 Prooflike	210,000	—	—	—	17.50	25.00

KM# 125a 10 DOLLARS
62.2070 g., 0.9990 Silver 1.9979 oz. ASW **Subject:** Year of the Pig **Obv:** Arms with supporters **Rev:** Stylized pig

Date	Mintage	F	VF	XF	Unc	BU
1995 Proof	8,000	Value: 90.00				

KM# 141 10 DOLLARS
Copper-Nickel **Subject:** Year of the Rat **Obv:** Arms with supporters **Rev:** Stylized rat within designs

Date	Mintage	F	VF	XF	Unc	BU
1996 Prooflike	245,000	—	—	—	16.00	25.00

KM# 141a 10 DOLLARS
62.2070 g., 0.9990 Silver 1.9979 oz. ASW **Subject:** Year of the Rat **Obv:** Arms with supporters **Rev:** Stylized rat within designs

Date	Mintage	F	VF	XF	Unc	BU
1996 Proof	35,000	Value: 90.00				

KM# 154 10 DOLLARS
62.2070 g., 0.9990 Silver 1.9979 oz. ASW **Subject:** Year of the Ox **Obv:** Arms with supporters **Rev:** Stylized Ox within designs

Date	Mintage	F	VF	XF	Unc	BU
1997 Proof	38,000	Value: 95.00				

KM# 153 10 DOLLARS
Copper-Nickel **Subject:** Year of the Ox **Obv:** Arms with supporters **Rev:** Stylized ox within designs **Note:** Similar to KM#154.

Date	Mintage	F	VF	XF	Unc	BU
1997 Prooflike	251,000	—	—	—	15.00	20.00

KM# 164 10 DOLLARS
Copper-Nickel **Subject:** Year of the Tiger **Obv:** Arms with supporters **Rev:** Stylized tiger **Note:** Similar to KM#165.

Date	Mintage	F	VF	XF	Unc	BU
1998 Prooflike	220,000	—	—	—	16.00	25.00

KM# 165 10 DOLLARS
62.2070 g., 0.9990 Silver 1.9979 oz. ASW **Subject:** Year of the Tiger **Obv:** Arms with supporters **Rev:** Stylized tiger within designs

Date	Mintage	F	VF	XF	Unc	BU
1998 Proof	38,000	Value: 90.00				

KM# 167 10 DOLLARS
28.0000 g., Copper-Nickel **Subject:** Year of the Rabbit **Obv:** Arms with supporters **Rev:** Stylized rabbit within designs **Edge:** Reeded

Date	Mintage	F	VF	XF	Unc	BU
1999	—	—	—	—	15.00	25.00

KM# 168 10 DOLLARS
62.2070 g., 0.9990 Silver 1.9979 oz. ASW **Subject:** Year of the Rabbit **Obv:** Arms with supporters **Rev:** Rabbit

Date	Mintage	F	VF	XF	Unc	BU
1999 Proof	38,000	Value: 100				

KM# 174 10 DOLLARS
Copper-Nickel **Subject:** Year of the Dragon **Obv:** Arms with supporters **Rev:** Dragon **Edge:** Reeded

Date	Mintage	F	VF	XF	Unc	BU
2000 Prooflike	225,000	—	—	—	20.00	25.00

KM# 175 10 DOLLARS
62.2060 g., 0.9990 Silver 1.9979 oz. ASW, 40.7 mm. **Subject:** Year of the Dragon **Obv:** Arms with supporters **Rev:** Dragon **Edge:** Reeded **Note:** Piefort thickness.

Date	Mintage	F	VF	XF	Unc	BU
2000 Proof	38,000	Value: 100				

KM# 18 50 DOLLARS
31.1000 g., 0.5000 Silver 0.4999 oz. ASW **Subject:** International Financial Center **Obv:** Arms with supporters **Rev:** Stylized letters and dollar sign

Date	Mintage	F	VF	XF	Unc	BU
1980	25,000	—	—	—	45.00	
1980sm Proof	15,000	Value: 90.00				
1981	50,000	—	—	—	45.00	
1981sm Proof	20,000	Value: 90.00				

KM# 78 50 DOLLARS
10.0000 g., 0.9160 Gold 0.2945 oz. AGW **Series:** Save the Children Fund **Obv:** Arms with supporters **Rev:** Children, kayak, palm tree and value

Date	Mintage	F	VF	XF	Unc	BU
1989 Proof	3,000	Value: 420				

KM# 140 50 DOLLARS
31.1035 g., 0.9999 Gold 0.9999 oz. AGW **Series:** 50th Anniversary - United Nations **Obv:** Arms with supporters **Rev:** UN logo within design

Date	Mintage	F	VF	XF	Unc	BU
1995 Proof	1,000	Value: 1,100				

KM# 152 50 DOLLARS
31.1035 g., 0.9999 Gold 0.9999 oz. AGW **Subject:** 50th Anniversary - Singapore Airlines **Obv:** Arms with supporters **Rev:** Airplane in front of numeral 50

Date	Mintage	F	VF	XF	Unc	BU
1997 Proof	1,800	Value: 1,200				

KM# 170 50 DOLLARS
31.1035 g., 0.9999 Gold 0.9999 oz. AGW **Subject:** Parliament **Obv:** Arms with supporters **Rev:** Parliament buildings

Date	Mintage	F	VF	XF	Unc	BU
1999 Proof	1,000	Value: 1,480				

KM# 12 100 DOLLARS
6.9119 g., 0.9000 Gold 0.2000 oz. AGW **Subject:** 10th Anniversary of Independence **Obv:** Arms with supporters **Rev:** Building

Date	Mintage	F	VF	XF	Unc	BU
1975	100,000	—	—	—	—	200
1975 Proof	3,000	Value: 330				

KM# 106   100 DOLLARS
31.1000 g., 0.9990 Gold 0.9988 oz. AGW **Subject:** 25th Anniversary - Board of Commissioners of Currency **Obv:** Arms with supporters **Rev:** Stylized dollar sign and value within circle

Date	Mintage	F	VF	XF	Unc	BU
1992 Proof	800	Value: 1,050				

KM# 7   150 DOLLARS
24.8830 g., 0.9160 Gold 0.7328 oz. AGW **Subject:** 150th Anniversary - Founding of Singapore **Obv:** Arms with supporters **Rev:** Lighthouse and value

Date	Mintage	F	VF	XF	Unc	BU
ND(1969)	198,000	—	—	—	—	750
ND(1969) Proof	500	Value: 2,400				

KM# 107   200 DOLLARS
31.1035 g., 0.9990 Platinum 0.9990 oz. APW **Subject:** 25th Anniversary - Board of Commissioners of Currency **Obv:** Arms with supporters **Rev:** Stylized dollar sign and value within circle **Note:** Similar to KM#106.

Date	Mintage	F	VF	XF	Unc	BU
1992 Proof	300	Value: 1,700				

KM# 13   250 DOLLARS
17.2797 g., 0.9000 Gold 0.5000 oz. AGW **Subject:** 10th Anniversary of Independence **Obv:** Arms with supporters **Rev:** Four grasped hands below value

Date	Mintage	F	VF	XF	Unc	BU
ND(1975)	30,000	—	—	—	—	485
ND(1975) Proof	2,000	Value: 830				

KM# 96   250 DOLLARS
31.1040 g., 0.9990 Gold 0.9990 oz. AGW **Subject:** 25th Anniversary of Independence **Obv:** Arms with supporters **Rev:** Stylized numeral 25 above city view with value at lower right

Date	Mintage	F	VF	XF	Unc	BU
1990 Proof	6,000	Value: 975				

KM# 114   250 DOLLARS
31.1035 g., 0.9990 Gold 0.9990 oz. AGW **Subject:** Year of the Rooster **Obv:** Arms with supporters **Rev:** Stylized rooster

Date	Mintage	F	VF	XF	Unc	BU
1993 Proof	10,000	Value: 1,150				

KM# 123   250 DOLLARS
31.1035 g., 0.9990 Gold 0.9990 oz. AGW **Subject:** Year of the Dog **Obv:** Arms with supporters **Rev:** Stylized dog within designs

Date	Mintage	F	VF	XF	Unc	BU
1994 Proof	7,500	Value: 1,100				

KM# 127   250 DOLLARS
31.1035 g., 0.9990 Gold 0.9990 oz. AGW **Subject:** Year of the Pig **Obv:** Arms with supporters **Rev:** Stylized pig within design

Date	Mintage	F	VF	XF	Unc	BU
1995 Proof	7,500	Value: 1,100				

KM# 143   250 DOLLARS
31.1035 g., 0.9990 Gold 0.9990 oz. AGW **Subject:** Year of the Rat **Obv:** Arms with supporters **Rev:** Stylized rat within designs

Date	Mintage	F	VF	XF	Unc	BU
1996 Proof	7,500	Value: 1,100				

KM# 155   250 DOLLARS
31.1035 g., 0.9990 Gold 0.9990 oz. AGW **Subject:** Year of the Ox **Obv:** Arms with supporters **Rev:** Stylized ox within designs

Date	Mintage	F	VF	XF	Unc	BU
1997 Proof	7,800	Value: 975				

KM# 166   250 DOLLARS
31.1035 g., 0.9990 Gold 0.9990 oz. AGW **Subject:** Year of the Tiger **Obv:** Arms with supporters **Rev:** Stylized tiger

Date	Mintage	F	VF	XF	Unc	BU
1998 Proof	7,600	Value: 1,000				

KM# 169   250 DOLLARS
31.1035 g., 0.9990 Gold 0.9990 oz. AGW **Obv:** Arms with supporters **Rev:** Stylized rabbit within designs **Edge:** Reeded

Date	Mintage	F	VF	XF	Unc	BU
1999 Proof	7,600	Value: 1,100				

KM# 176   250 DOLLARS
31.1035 g., 0.9990 Gold 0.9990 oz. AGW, 32.12 mm. **Subject:** Year of the Dragon **Obv:** Arms with supporters **Rev:** Stylized dragon **Edge:** Reeded

Date	Mintage	F	VF	XF	Unc	BU
2000 Proof	7,600	Value: 1,300				

KM# 14   500 DOLLARS
34.5590 g., 0.9000 Gold 0.9999 oz. AGW **Subject:** 10th Anniversary of Independence **Obv:** Arms with supporters **Rev:** Lion head

Date	Mintage	F	VF	XF	Unc	BU
ND(1975)	30,000	—	—	—	950	1,000
ND(1975) Proof	2,000	Value: 2,150				

KM# 21   500 DOLLARS
16.9650 g., 0.9160 Gold 0.4996 oz. AGW **Subject:** Year of the Rooster **Obv:** Arms with supporters **Rev:** Rooster

Date	Mintage	F	VF	XF	Unc	BU
1981sm Proof	12,000	Value: 1,100				

KM# 24   500 DOLLARS
16.9650 g., 0.9160 Gold 0.4996 oz. AGW **Subject:** Year of the Dog **Obv:** Arms with supporters **Rev:** Dog

Date	Mintage	F	VF	XF	Unc	BU
1982sm Proof	5,500	Value: 1,000				

KM# 27   500 DOLLARS
16.9650 g., 0.9160 Gold 0.4996 oz. AGW **Subject:** Year of the Pig **Obv:** Arms with supporters **Rev:** Pig

Date	Mintage	F	VF	XF	Unc	BU
1983sm Proof	5,000	Value: 1,100				

KM# 34   500 DOLLARS
16.9650 g., 0.9160 Gold 0.4996 oz. AGW **Subject:** Year of the Rat **Obv:** Arms with supporters **Rev:** Rat

Date	Mintage	F	VF	XF	Unc	BU
1984sm Proof	4,000	Value: 1,100				

KM# 45   500 DOLLARS
16.9650 g., 0.9160 Gold 0.4996 oz. AGW **Subject:** Year of the Ox **Obv:** Arms with supporters **Rev:** Ox

Date	Mintage	F	VF	XF	Unc	BU
1985sm Proof	4,000	Value: 900				

KM# 60   500 DOLLARS
16.9650 g., 0.9160 Gold 0.4996 oz. AGW **Subject:** Year of the Tiger **Obv:** Arms with supporters **Rev:** Tiger

Date	Mintage	F	VF	XF	Unc	BU
1986sm Proof	3,000	Value: 1,500				

KM# 64   500 DOLLARS
16.9650 g., 0.9160 Gold 0.4996 oz. AGW **Subject:** Year of the Rabbit **Obv:** Arms with supporters **Rev:** Rabbit

Date	Mintage	F	VF	XF	Unc	BU
1987sm Proof	2,400	Value: 2,650				

KM# 73   500 DOLLARS
16.9650 g., 0.9160 Gold 0.4996 oz. AGW **Subject:** Year of the Dragon **Obv:** Arms with supporters **Rev:** Dragon

Date	Mintage	F	VF	XF	Unc	BU
1988sm Proof	4,000	Value: 1,330				

KM# 72   500 DOLLARS
16.9650 g., 0.9160 Gold 0.4996 oz. AGW **Subject:** Year of the Snake **Obv:** Arms with supporters **Rev:** Snake

Date	Mintage	F	VF	XF	Unc	BU
1989sm Proof	2,500	Value: 2,000				

KM# 76   500 DOLLARS
16.9650 g., 0.9160 Gold 0.4996 oz. AGW **Subject:** Year of the Horse **Obv:** Arms with supporters **Rev:** Horse

Date	Mintage	F	VF	XF	Unc	BU
1990sm Proof	5,000	Value: 1,000				

KM# 97   500 DOLLARS
31.1040 g., 0.9990 Platinum 0.9990 oz. APW **Subject:** 25th Anniversary of Independence **Obv:** Arms with supporters **Rev:** Numeral 25 and value above city view

Date	Mintage	F	VF	XF	Unc	BU
1990 Proof	2,000	Value: 1,750				

KM# 85   500 DOLLARS
16.9650 g., 0.9160 Gold 0.4996 oz. AGW **Subject:** Year of the Goat **Obv:** Arms with supporters **Rev:** Goat

Date	Mintage	F	VF	XF	Unc	BU
1991sm Proof	5,000	Value: 930				

KM# 93   500 DOLLARS
16.9650 g., 0.9160 Gold 0.4996 oz. AGW **Subject:** Year of the Monkey **Obv:** Arms with supporters **Rev:** Monkey

Date	Mintage	F	VF	XF	Unc	BU
1992sm Proof	5,000	Value: 930				

BULLION COINAGE

KM# 28   DOLLAR
3.1100 g., 0.9990 Gold 0.0999 oz. AGW **Obv:** National arms **Rev:** Carp and lotus flower

Date	Mintage	F	VF	XF	Unc	BU
1983	20,000	—	—	—	BV+15%	—
1984	10,000	—	—	—	BV+15%	—

KM# 144   DOLLAR
1.5552 g., 0.9999 Gold 0.0500 oz. AGW, 13.92 mm. **Series:** Lunar **Subject:** Year of the Rat **Obv:** National arms **Rev:** Stylized lion's head right, rat privy mark at lower left

Date	Mintage	F	VF	XF	Unc	BU
1996 Proof	2,688	BV+25%				

KM# 158   DOLLAR
1.5552 g., 0.9999 Gold 0.0500 oz. AGW, 13.92 mm. **Series:** Lunar **Subject:** Year of the Ox **Obv:** National arms **Rev:** Stylized lion's head right, ox privy mark at lower left

Date	Mintage	F	VF	XF	Unc	BU
1997 Proof	Est. 2,200	BV+25%				

KM# 197   DOLLAR
1.5550 g., 0.9999 Gold 0.0500 oz. AGW, 13.92 mm. **Series:** Lunar **Subject:** Year of the Tiger **Obv:** National arms **Rev:** Stylized lion's head right, tiger privy mark at lower left

Date	Mintage	F	VF	XF	Unc	BU
1998 Proof	—	BV+25%				

KM# 202   DOLLAR
1.5550 g., 0.9999 Gold 0.0500 oz. AGW, 13.92 mm. **Series:** Lunar **Subject:** Year of the Rabbit **Obv:** National arms **Rev:** Stylized lion's head right, rabbit privy mark at lower left

Date	Mintage	F	VF	XF	Unc	BU
1999 Proof	—	BV+25%				

KM# 207   DOLLAR
1.5550 g., 0.9999 Gold 0.0500 oz. AGW, 13.92 mm. **Series:** Lunar **Subject:** Year of the Dragon **Obv:** National arms **Rev:** Stylized lion's head right, dragon privy mark at lower left

Date	Mintage	F	VF	XF	Unc	BU
2000 Proof	—	BV+25%				

KM# 29   2 DOLLARS
7.7750 g., 0.9990 Gold 0.2497 oz. AGW **Obv:** National arms **Rev:** Qilin

Date	Mintage	F	VF	XF	Unc	BU
1983	20,000	—	—	—	BV+12%	—
1984	10,000	—	—	—	BV+12%	—

KM# 30   5 DOLLARS
15.5500 g., 0.9990 Gold 0.4994 oz. AGW **Obv:** National arms **Rev:** Phoenix

Date	Mintage	F	VF	XF	Unc	BU
1983	10,000	—	—	—	BV+9%	—
1984	10,000	—	—	—	BV+9%	—

KM# 79   5 DOLLARS
1.5550 g., 0.9999 Gold 0.0500 oz. AGW, 13.92 mm. **Obv:** National arms **Rev:** Stylized lion's head right

Date	Mintage	F	VF	XF	Unc	BU
1990	8,000	—	—	—	—	BV+20%
1990 Proof	Est. 2,000	BV+20%				

KM# 87   5 DOLLARS
1.5550 g., 0.9999 Gold 0.0500 oz. AGW, 13.92 mm. **Series:** Lunar **Subject:** Year of the Goat **Obv:** National arms **Rev:** Stylized lion's head right, goat privy mark at lower left

Date	Mintage	F	VF	XF	Unc	BU
1991	8,000	—	—	—	—	BV+20%
1991 Proof	2,500	BV+20%				

KM# 108   5 DOLLARS
1.5550 g., 0.9990 Gold 0.0500 oz. AGW, 13.92 mm. **Series:** Lunar **Subject:** Year of the Monkey **Obv:** National arms **Rev:** Stylized lion's head right, monkey privy mark at lower left

Date	Mintage	F	VF	XF	Unc	BU
1992	6,500	—	—	—	—	BV+20%
1992 Proof	2,000	BV+20%				

KM# 117   5 DOLLARS
1.5550 g., 0.9999 Gold 0.0500 oz. AGW, 13.92 mm. **Series:** Lunar **Subject:** Year of the Rooster **Obv:** National arms **Rev:** Stylized lion's head right, rooster privy mark at lower left

Date	Mintage	F	VF	XF	Unc	BU
1993	3,400	—	—	—	—	BV+20%
1993 Proof	Est. 1,500	BV+20%				

KM# 128   5 DOLLARS
1.5550 g., 0.9999 Gold 0.0500 oz. AGW, 13.92 mm. **Series:** Lunar **Subject:** Year of the Dog **Obv:** National arms **Rev:** Stylized lion's head right, dog privy mark at lower left

Date	Mintage	F	VF	XF	Unc	BU
1994	—	—	—	—	—	BV+20%
1994 Proof	Est. 1,500	BV+20%				

KM# 133   5 DOLLARS
1.5550 g., 0.9999 Gold 0.0500 oz. AGW, 13.92 mm. **Series:** Lunar **Subject:** Year of the Boar **Obv:** National arms **Rev:** Stylized lion's head right, boar privy mark at lower left

Date	Mintage	F	VF	XF	Unc	BU
1995	—	—	—	—	—	BV+20%
1995 Proof	1,500	BV+20%				

KM# 145   5 DOLLARS
3.1103 g., 0.9999 Gold 0.1000 oz. AGW, 17.95 mm. **Series:** Lunar **Subject:** Year of the Rat **Obv:** National arms **Rev:** Stylized lion's head right, rat privy mark at lower left

Date	Mintage	F	VF	XF	Unc	BU
1996 Proof	1,600	BV+20%				

KM# 159   5 DOLLARS
3.1103 g., 0.9999 Gold 0.1000 oz. AGW, 17.95 mm. **Series:** Lunar **Subject:** Year of the Ox **Obv:** National arms **Rev:** Stylized lion's head right, ox privy mark at lower left

Date	Mintage	F	VF	XF	Unc	BU
1997 Proof	Est. 1,000	BV+20%				

KM# 198   5 DOLLARS
3.1100 g., 0.9999 Gold 0.1000 oz. AGW, 17.95 mm. **Series:** Lunar **Subject:** Year of the Tiger **Obv:** National arms **Rev:** Stylized lion's head right, tiger privy mark at lower left

Date	Mintage	F	VF	XF	Unc	BU
1998 Proof	—	BV+20%				

KM# 203   5 DOLLARS
3.1100 g., 0.9999 Gold 0.1000 oz. AGW, 17.95 mm. **Series:** Lunar **Subject:** Year of the Rabbit **Obv:** National arms **Rev:** Stylized lion's head right, rabbit privy mark at lower left

Date	Mintage	F	VF	XF	Unc	BU
1999 Proof	—	BV+20%				

KM# 208   5 DOLLARS
3.1100 g., 0.9999 Gold 0.1000 oz. AGW, 17.95 mm. **Series:** Lunar **Subject:** Year of the Dragon **Obv:** National arms **Rev:** Stylized lion's head right, dragon privy mark at lower left

Date	Mintage	F	VF	XF	Unc	BU
2000 Proof	—	BV+20%				

KM# 31   10 DOLLARS
31.1000 g., 0.9990 Gold 0.9988 oz. AGW **Obv:** National arms **Rev:** Dragon

Date	Mintage	F	VF	XF	Unc	BU
1983	10,000	—	—	—	—	BV+10%
1984 Proof	10,000	BV+10%				

KM# 80   10 DOLLARS
3.1103 g., 0.9999 Gold 0.1000 oz. AGW, 17.95 mm. **Obv:** National arms **Rev:** Stylized lion's head right

Date	Mintage	F	VF	XF	Unc	BU
1990	Est. 5,000	—	—	—	—	BV+15%
1990 Proof	Est. 2,000	BV+15%				

KM# 88   10 DOLLARS
3.1103 g., 0.9999 Gold 0.1000 oz. AGW, 17.95 mm.
Series: Lunar **Subject:** Year of the Goat **Obv:** National arms
Rev: Stylized lion's head right, goat privy mark at lower left

Date	Mintage	F	VF	XF	Unc	BU
1991	5,500	—	—	—	—	BV+15%
1991 Proof	2,500	BV+15%				

KM# 109   10 DOLLARS
3.1103 g., 0.9999 Gold 0.1000 oz. AGW, 17.95 mm.
Series: Lunar **Subject:** Year of the Monkey **Obv:** National arms
Rev: Stylized lion's head right, monkey privy mark at lower left

Date	Mintage	F	VF	XF	Unc	BU
1992	4,000	—	—	—	—	BV+15%
1992 Proof	2,000	BV+15%				

KM# 118   10 DOLLARS
3.1103 g., 0.9999 Gold 0.1000 oz. AGW, 17.95 mm.
Series: Lunar **Subject:** Year of the Rooster **Obv:** National arms
Rev: Stylized lion's head right, rooster privy mark at lower left

Date	Mintage	F	VF	XF	Unc	BU
1993	3,100	—	—	—	—	BV+15%
1993 Proof	Est. 1,500	BV+15%				

KM# 129   10 DOLLARS
3.1103 g., 0.9999 Gold 0.1000 oz. AGW, 17.95 mm.
Series: Lunar **Subject:** Year of the Dog **Obv:** National arms
Rev: Stylized lion's head right, dog privy mark at lower left

Date	Mintage	F	VF	XF	Unc	BU
1994	—	—	—	—	—	BV+15%
1994 Proof	Est. 1,500	BV+15%				

KM# 134   10 DOLLARS
3.1103 g., 0.9999 Gold 0.1000 oz. AGW, 17.95 mm.
Series: Lunar **Subject:** Year of the Boar **Obv:** National arms
Rev: Stylized lion's head right, boar privy mark at lower left

Date	Mintage	F	VF	XF	Unc	BU
1995	—	—	—	—	—	BV+15%
1995 Proof	—	BV+20%				

KM# 146   10 DOLLARS
7.7759 g., 0.9999 Gold 0.2500 oz. AGW, 21.96 mm. **Series:** Lunar
Subject: Year of the Rat **Obv:** National arms **Rev:** Stylized lion's
head right, rat privy mark at lower left **Note:** Year of the Rat privy mark.

Date	Mintage	F	VF	XF	Unc	BU
1996 Proof	2,688	BV+10%				

KM# 160   10 DOLLARS
7.7759 g., 0.9999 Gold 0.2500 oz. AGW, 21.96 mm.
Series: Lunar **Subject:** Year of the ox **Obv:** National arms
Rev: Stylized lion's head right, ox privy mark at lower left

Date	Mintage	F	VF	XF	Unc	BU
1997 Proof	Est. 2,200	BV+10%				

KM# 199   10 DOLLARS
7.7760 g., 0.9999 Gold 0.2500 oz. AGW, 21.96 mm.
Series: Lunar **Subject:** Year of the Tiger **Obv:** National arms
Rev: Stylized lion's head right, tiger privy mark at lower left

Date	Mintage	F	VF	XF	Unc	BU
1998 Proof	—	BV+10%				

KM# 204   10 DOLLARS
7.7750 g., 0.9999 Gold 0.2499 oz. AGW, 21.96 mm.
Series: Lunar **Subject:** Year of the Rabbit **Obv:** National arms
Rev: Stylized lion's head right, rabbit privy mark at lower left

Date	Mintage	F	VF	XF	Unc	BU
1999 Proof	—	BV+10%				

KM# 209   10 DOLLARS
7.7750 g., 0.9999 Gold 0.2499 oz. AGW, 21.96 mm.
Series: Lunar **Subject:** Year of the Dragon **Obv:** National arms
Rev: Stylized lion's head right, dragon privy mark at lower left

Date	Mintage	F	VF	XF	Unc	BU
2000 Proof	—	BV+10%				

KM# 147   20 DOLLARS
15.5517 g., 0.9999 Gold 0.4999 oz. AGW, 27 mm. **Series:** Lunar
Subject: Year of the Rat **Obv:** National arms **Rev:** Stylized lion's
head right, rat privy mark at lower left

Date	Mintage	F	VF	XF	Unc	BU
1996 Proof	2,688	BV+10%				

KM# 161   20 DOLLARS
15.5517 g., 0.9999 Gold 0.4999 oz. AGW, 27 mm. **Series:** Lunar
Subject: Year of the Ox **Obv:** National arms **Rev:** Stylized lion's
head right, ox privy mark at lower left

Date	Mintage	F	VF	XF	Unc	BU
1997 Proof	Est. 2,200	BV+12%				

KM# 200   20 DOLLARS
15.5520 g., 0.9999 Gold 0.4999 oz. AGW, 27 mm. **Series:** Lunar
Subject: Year of the Tiger **Obv:** National arms **Rev:** Stylized
lion's head right, tiger privy mark at lower left

Date	Mintage	F	VF	XF	Unc	BU
1998 Proof	—	BV+12%				

KM# 205   20 DOLLARS
15.5520 g., 0.9999 Gold 0.4999 oz. AGW, 27 mm. **Series:** Lunar
Subject: Year of the Rabbit **Obv:** National arms **Rev:** Stylized
lion's head right, rabbit privy mark at lower left

Date	Mintage	F	VF	XF	Unc	BU
1999 Proof	—	BV+12%				

KM# 210   20 DOLLARS
15.5520 g., 0.9999 Gold 0.4999 oz. AGW **Series:** Lunar
Subject: Year of the Dragon **Obv:** National arms **Rev:** Stylized
lion's head right, dragon privy mark at lower left

Date	Mintage	F	VF	XF	Unc	BU
2000 Proof	—	BV+12%				

KM# 81   25 DOLLARS
7.7757 g., 0.9999 Gold 0.2500 oz. AGW, 21.96 mm.
Obv: National arms **Rev:** Stylized lion's head right

Date	Mintage	F	VF	XF	Unc	BU
1990	Est. 5,000	—	—	—	—	BV+12%
1990 Proof	Est. 2,000	BV+12%				

KM# 89   25 DOLLARS
7.7757 g., 0.9999 Gold 0.2500 oz. AGW, 21.96 mm.
Series: Lunar **Subject:** Year of the Goat **Obv:** National arms
Rev: Stylized lion's head right, goat privy mark at lower left

Date	Mintage	F	VF	XF	Unc	BU
1991	5,500	—	—	—	—	BV+12%
1991 Proof	2,500	BV+12%				

KM# 110   25 DOLLARS
7.7757 g., 0.9999 Gold 0.2500 oz. AGW, 21.96 mm.
Series: Lunar **Subject:** Year of the Monkey **Obv:** National arms
Rev: Stylized lion's head right, monkey privy mark at lower left

Date	Mintage	F	VF	XF	Unc	BU
1992	4,000	—	—	—	—	BV+12%
1992 Proof	2,000	BV+12%				

KM# 119   25 DOLLARS
7.7757 g., 0.9999 Gold 0.2500 oz. AGW, 21.96 mm.
Series: Lunar **Subject:** Year of the Rooster **Obv:** National arms
Rev: Stylized lion's head right, rooster privy mark at lower left

Date	Mintage	F	VF	XF	Unc	BU
1993	3,000	—	—	—	—	BV+12%
1993 Proof	Est. 1,500	BV+12%				

KM# 130   25 DOLLARS
7.7757 g., 0.9999 Gold 0.2500 oz. AGW, 21.96 mm.
Series: Lunar **Subject:** Year of the Dog **Obv:** National arms
Rev: Stylized lion's head right, dog privy mark at lower left

Date	Mintage	F	VF	XF	Unc	BU
1994	—	—	—	—	—	BV+12%
1994 Proof	Est. 1,500	BV+12%				

KM# 135   25 DOLLARS
7.7757 g., 0.9999 Gold 0.2500 oz. AGW, 21.96 mm.
Series: Lunar **Subject:** Year of the Boar **Obv:** National arms
Rev: Stylized lion's head right, boar privy mark at lower left

Date	Mintage	F	VF	XF	Unc	BU
1995	—	—	—	—	—	BV+12%
1995 Proof	1,500	BV+12%				

KM# 82   50 DOLLARS
15.5500 g., 0.9999 Gold 0.4999 oz. AGW, 27 mm.
Obv: National arms **Rev:** Stylized lion's head right

Date	Mintage	F	VF	XF	Unc	BU
1990 Proof	Est. 2,000	BV+10%				

KM# 90   50 DOLLARS
15.5500 g., 0.9999 Gold 0.4999 oz. AGW, 27 mm. **Series:** Lunar
Subject: Year of the Goat **Obv:** National arms **Rev:** Stylized
lion's head right, goat privy mark at lower left

Date	Mintage	F	VF	XF	Unc	BU
1991	5,500	—	—	—	—	BV+10%
1991 Proof	2,500	BV+10%				

KM# 111   50 DOLLARS
15.5500 g., 0.9999 Gold 0.4999 oz. AGW, 27 mm. **Series:** Lunar
Subject: Year of the Monkey **Obv:** National arms **Rev:** Stylized
lion's head right, monkey privy mark at lower left

Date	Mintage	F	VF	XF	Unc	BU
1992	4,000	—	—	—	—	BV+10%
1992 Proof	2,000	BV+10%				

KM# 120   50 DOLLARS
15.5500 g., 0.9999 Gold 0.4999 oz. AGW, 27 mm. **Series:** Lunar
Subject: Year of the Rooster **Obv:** National arms **Rev:** Stylized
lion's head right, rooster privy mark at lower left

Date	Mintage	F	VF	XF	Unc	BU
1993	2,600	—	—	—	—	BV+10%
1993 Proof	Est. 1,500	BV+10%				

KM# 131   50 DOLLARS
15.5500 g., 0.9999 Gold 0.4999 oz. AGW, 27 mm. **Series:** Lunar
Subject: Year of the Dog **Obv:** National arms **Rev:** Stylized lion's
head right, dog privy mark at lower left

Date	Mintage	F	VF	XF	Unc	BU
1994	—	—	—	—	—	BV+10%
1994 Proof	Est. 1,500	BV+10%				

KM# 136   50 DOLLARS
15.5500 g., 0.9999 Gold 0.4999 oz. AGW, 27 mm. **Series:** Lunar
Subject: Year of the Boar **Obv:** National arms **Rev:** Stylized lion's
head right, boar privy mark at lower left

Date	Mintage	F	VF	XF	Unc	BU
1995	—	—	—	—	—	BV+10%
1995 Proof	1,500	BV+10%				

KM# 148   50 DOLLARS
31.1035 g., 0.9999 Gold 0.9999 oz. AGW, 32.12 mm.
Series: Lunar **Subject:** Year of the Rat **Obv:** National arms
Rev: Stylized lion's head right, rat privy mark at lower left

Date	Mintage	F	VF	XF	Unc	BU
1996 Proof	2,688	BV+9%				

KM# 162   50 DOLLARS
31.1035 g., 0.9999 Gold 0.9999 oz. AGW, 32.12 mm.
Series: Lunar **Subject:** Year of the Ox **Obv:** National arms
Rev: Stylized lion's head right, ox privy mark at lower left

Date	Mintage	F	VF	XF	Unc	BU
1997 Proof	Est. 2,200	BV+9%				

KM# 201   50 DOLLARS
31.1030 g., 0.9999 Gold 0.9998 oz. AGW, 32.12 mm.
Series: Lunar **Subject:** Year of the Tiger **Obv:** National arms
Rev: Stylized lion's head right, tiger privy mark at lower left

Date	Mintage	F	VF	XF	Unc	BU
1998 Proof	—	BV+9%				

KM# 206   50 DOLLARS
31.1030 g., 0.9999 Gold 0.9998 oz. AGW, 32.12 mm.
Series: Lunar **Subject:** Year of the Rabbit **Obv:** National arms
Rev: Stylized lion's head right, rabbit privy mark at lower left

Date	Mintage	F	VF	XF	Unc	BU
1999 Proof	—	BV+9%				

KM# 211   50 DOLLARS
31.1030 g., 0.9999 Gold 0.9998 oz. AGW, 32.12 mm.
Series: Lunar **Subject:** Year of the Dragon **Obv:** National arms
Rev: Stylized lion's head right, dragon privy mark at lower left

Date	Mintage	F	VF	XF	Unc	BU
2000 Proof	—	BV+9%				

KM# 83 100 DOLLARS
31.1000 g., 0.9999 Gold 0.9997 oz. AGW, 32.12 mm.
Obv: National arms **Rev:** Stylized lion's head right

Date	Mintage	F	VF	XF	Unc	BU
1990	Est. 5,000	—	—	—	—	BV+7%
1990 Proof	Est. 2,000	BV+7%				

KM# 91 100 DOLLARS
31.1000 g., 0.9999 Gold 0.9997 oz. AGW, 32.12 mm.
Series: Lunar **Subject:** Year of the Goat **Obv:** National arms
Rev: Stylized lion's head right, goat privy mark at lower left

Date	Mintage	F	VF	XF	Unc	BU
1991	13,000	—	—	—	—	BV+7%
1991 Proof	2,500	BV+7%				

KM# 112 100 DOLLARS
31.1000 g., 0.9999 Gold 0.9997 oz. AGW, 32.12 mm.
Series: Lunar **Subject:** Year of the Monkey **Obv:** National arms
Rev: Stylized lion's head right, monkey privy mark at lower left

Date	Mintage	F	VF	XF	Unc	BU
1992	4,000	—	—	—	—	BV+7%
1992 Proof	2,000	BV+7%				

KM# 121 100 DOLLARS
31.1000 g., 0.9999 Gold 0.9997 oz. AGW, 32.12 mm.
Series: Lunar **Subject:** Year of the Rooster **Obv:** National arms
Rev: Stylized lion's head right, rooster privy mark at lower left

Date	Mintage	F	VF	XF	Unc	BU
1993	3,100	—	—	—	—	BV+7%
1993 Proof	Est. 1,500	BV+7%				

KM# 132 100 DOLLARS
31.1000 g., 0.9999 Gold 0.9997 oz. AGW, 32.12 mm.
Series: Lunar **Subject:** Year of the Dog **Obv:** National arms
Rev: Stylized lion's head right, dog privy mark at lower left

Date	Mintage	F	VF	XF	Unc	BU
1994	—	—	—	—	—	BV+7%
1994 Proof	Est. 1,500	BV+7%				

KM# 137 100 DOLLARS
31.1000 g., 0.9999 Gold 0.9997 oz. AGW, 32.12 mm.
Series: Lunar **Subject:** Year of the Boar **Obv:** National arms
Rev: Stylized lion's head right, boar privy mark at lower left

Date	Mintage	F	VF	XF	Unc	BU
1995	—	—	—	—	—	BV+7%
1995 Proof	1,500	BV+7%				

MINT SETS

KM#	Date	Mintage	Identification	Issue Price	Mkt Val
MS1	1967 (6)	8,000	KM#1-6	1.50	45.00
MS2	1968 (6)	16,000	KM#1-6	1.50	40.00
MS3	1969 (6)	14,000	KM#1-6	1.50	45.00
MS4	1970 (6)	13,000	KM#1-6	1.50	80.00
MS5	1970 (6)	27,000	KM#1-6 Issued only in package of 3 sets plus KM#11, each set in plastic wallet for Expo'97 Osaka Japan	1.75	80.00
MS7	1972 (6)	13,000	KM#1-6	3.00	95.00
MS8	1973 (6)	15,000	KM#1-6	2.00	20.00
MS9	1974 (6)	20,000	KM#1-6	2.00	40.00
MS10	1975 (6)	30,000	KM#1-6	12.00	20.00
MS11	1975 (3)	30,000	KM#12-14	—	1,100
MS12	1976 (6)	35,000	KM#1-6	2.00	13.00
MS13	1977 (6)	40,000	KM#1a, 2-6	2.00	13.00
MS14	1978 (6)	55,000	KM#1a, 2-6	—	25.00
MS15	1979 (6)	65,000	KM#1a, 2-6	—	12.00
MS16	1980 (6)	70,000	KM#1a, 2-6	—	10.00
MS17	1981 (6)	110,000	KM#1a, 2-6	5.00	7.50
MS18	1982 (6)	160,000	KM#1a, 2-6	5.00	7.50
MS19	1983 (6)	40,000	KM#1a, 2-6 with Medallion, I.A.P.N.	—	9.00
MS20	1983 (6)	150,000	KM#1a, 2-6	5.00	8.00
MS21	1984 (6)	160,000	KM#1a, 2-6	3.75	7.50
MS22	1985 (6)	148,424	KM#1a, 2-6	—	22.00
MS23	1986 (6)	120,000	KM#49-52, 53.1, 54	—	14.50
MS24	1987 (6)	120,000	KM#49-52, 53.1, 54	—	15.00
MS25	1988 (6)	120,000	KM#49-52, 53.1, 54b	—	7.50
MS26	1989 (6)	100,000	KM#49-52, 53.2, 54b	—	7.50
MS27	1990 (6)	100,000	KM#49-52, 53.2, 54b	—	7.50
MS28	1990 (5)	5,000	KM#79-83	—	900
MS29	1991 (7)	70,000	KM#49b, 50-52, 53.2, 54b (1991), 94 (1990)	—	12.00
MS30	1992 (7)	55,000	KM#98-104	—	12.00
MS32	1994 (7)	100,000	KM#98-104	—	12.00
MS33	1995 (7)	124,000	KM#98-104	—	12.00
MS34	1996 (7)	180,000	KM#98-104	—	12.00
MS35	1997 (7)	—	KM#98-104	—	12.00
MS36	1998 (7)	—	KM#98-104	—	12.00
MS37	1999 (7)	—	KM#98-104.1	—	12.00
MS38	2000 (7)	—	KM#98-104.1	—	12.00

PROOF SETS

KM#	Date	Mintage	Identification	Issue Price	Mkt Val
PS1	1967 (6)	2,000	KM#1-6	25.00	85.00
PS2	1968 (6)	5,000	KM#1-6	25.00	65.00
PS3	1969 (6)	3,000	KM#1-6	25.00	280
PS4	1972 (6)	749	KM#1-6	25.00	475
PS5	1973 (6)	1,000	KM#1-6	32.00	200
PS6	1974 (6)	1,500	KM#1-6	34.00	170
PS7	1975 (6)	3,000	KM#1-6	35.00	60.00
PS8	1975 (3)	2,000	KM#12-14	—	1,600
PS9	1976 (6)	3,500	KM#1-6	37.00	60.00
PS10	1977 (6)	3,500	kM#1-6	—	60.00
PS11	1978 (6)	4,000	KM#1-6	—	60.00
PS12	1979 (7)	3,500	KM#1-6, 17.1	—	120
PS13	1980 (7)	14,000	KM#1-6, 17.2	64.00	60.00
PS14	1981 (6)	30,000	KM#1b-2b, 3a-6a, .925 Silver	82.00	80.00
PS15	1982 (6)	20,000	KM#1-5, 6a	52.00	55.00
PS16	1983 (6)	15,000	KM#1-5, 6a	52.00	50.00
PS17	1984 (6)	15,000	KM#1-5, 6a	52.00	50.00
PS18	1985 (6)	20,000	KM#49a-52a, 53.1a, 54a	40.00	50.00
PS19	1986 (6)	15,000	KM#49a-52a, 53.1a, 54a	—	48.00
PS20	1987 (6)	15,000	KM#49a-52a, 53.1a, 54c	42.00	48.00
PS21	1987 (6)	1,000	KM-MB28-MB32	1,400	1,650
PS22	1988 (6)	15,000	KM#49a-52a, 53.1a, 54c	—	45.00
PS23	1988 (5)	500	KM-MB41-45	—	1,650
PS24	1989 (6)	15,000	KM#49a-52a, 53.2a, 54c	—	60.00
PS25	1989 (5)	200	KM-MB51-55	—	1,975
PS26	1990 (6)	15,000	KM#49a-52a, 53.2a, 54c	—	55.00
PS27	1990 (5)	2,000	KM#79-83	—	850
PSA28	1990 (3)	1,000	KM#95-97	—	1,700
PS28	1991 (7)	15,000	KM#49a-52a, 53.2a, 54c, 86a	—	65.00
PS29	1991 (5)	2,500	KM#87-91	—	850
PS30	1991 (2)	5,000	KM#86, 86a	—	65.00
PS31	1992 (7)	15,000	KM#98a-104a	—	80.00
PS32	1992 (5)	2,000	KM#108-112 Ingot	—	850
PS33	1992 (3)	200	KM#105-107	—	1,600
PS34	1993 (7)	15,000	KM#98a-104a	—	80.00
PS35	1993 (5)	1,500	KM#117-121 Ingot	—	875
PS36	1993 (2)	2,000	KM#115, 115a	—	85.00
PS37	1994 (7)	10,000	KM#98a-104a	—	80.00
PS38	1994 (5)	1,500	KM#128-132 Ingot	—	875
PS39	1995 (7)	10,000	KM#98a-104a	—	75.00
PS41	1995 (5)	1,500	KM#133-137 Ingot	1,718	875
PS42	1995 (3)	2,689	KM#138-140	1,052	750
PS43	1996 (7)	17,000	KM#98a-104a Ingot	—	75.00
PS44	1996 (5)	2,688	KM#144-148 Ingot	—	900
PS45	1996 (2)	2,800	KM#149, 149a	66.00	70.00
PS46	1997 (7)	20,000	KM#98a-104a Ingot	90.00	120
PS47	1997 (2)	3,800	KM#151, 151a Ingot	—	65.00
PS48	1997 (3)	888	KM#151, 151a, 152 Ingot	—	625
PS49	1997 (5)	2,200	KM#158-162	—	1,000
PS50	1998 (3)	1,998	KM#164-166 Ingot	—	1,100
PS51	1998 (7)	—	KM#98a-104a	—	100
PS52	1998 (4)	1,000	KM#197-200	—	—
PS53	1998 (6)	500	KM#197-201 plus ingot	—	—
PS54	1999 (7)	—	KM#98a-104.1a	—	100
PS55	1999 (4)	1,000	KM#202-205	—	—
PS56	1999 (5)	500	KM#202-206 plus ingot	—	—
PS57	2000 (4)	—	KM#207-210	—	—
PS58	2000 (5)	—	KM#207-211	—	—
PS59	2000 (7)	17,000	KM#98a-104.1a	74.25	100
PS60	2000 (3)	2,000	KM#174-176, plus Ingot	—	1,400

SLOVAKIA

The Republic of Slovakia has an area of 18,923 sq. mi. (49,035 sq. km.) and a population of 4.9 million. Capital: Bratislava. Textiles, steel, and wood products are exported.

The Slovak lands were united with the Czechs and the Czechoslovak State came into existence on Oct. 28, 1918 upon the dissolution of Austro-Hungarian Empire at the close of World War I. In March 1939, the German-influenced Slovak government proclaimed Slovakia independent and Germany incorporated the Czech lands into the Third Reich as the "Protectorate of Bohemia and Moravia". A Czechoslovak government-in-exile was setup in London in July 1940. The Soviet and USA forces liberated the area by May, 1945. At the close of World War II, Communist influence increased steadily while pressure for liberalization culminated in the overthrow of the Stalinist leader Antonin Novotny and his associates in 1968. The Communist Party then introduced far reaching reforms which received warnings from Moscow, followed by occupation by Warsaw Pact forces resulting in stationing of Soviet forces. Mass civilian demonstrations for reform began in Nov.1989 and the Federal Assembly abolished the Communist Party's sole right to govern. New governments followed on Dec. 3 and Dec. 10 and the Czech and Slovak Federal Republic was formed. The Movement for Democratic Slovakia was apparent in the June 1992 elections with the Slovak National Council adopting a declaration of sovereignty. Later, a constitution for an independent Slovakia with the Federal Assembly voting for the dissolution of the Republic came into effect on Dec. 31, 1992, and two new republics came into being on Jan. 1, 1993.

MINT MARK

Kremnica Mint

REPUBLIC
1939-45

STANDARD COINAGE
100 Halierov = 1 Koruna Slovenska (Ks)

KM# 8 5 HALIEROV
0.9400 g., Zinc, 14 mm. **Obv:** Double cross within shield
Rev: Large value **Edge:** Plain

Date	Mintage	F	VF	XF	Unc	BU
1942	1,000,000	3.00	5.00	15.00	30.00	—

KM# 1 10 HALIEROV
1.6600 g., Bronze, 16 mm. **Obv:** Double cross within shield above sprigs **Rev:** Castle and large value

Date	Mintage	F	VF	XF	Unc	BU
1939	15,000,000	1.50	2.00	4.00	8.00	—
1942	7,000,000	3.00	2.00	8.00	16.00	—

KM# 4 20 HALIEROV
2.5000 g., Bronze, 18 mm. **Obv:** Double cross on shield within flower sprig **Rev:** Nitra Castle, large value **Edge:** Plain

Date	Mintage	F	VF	XF	Unc	BU
1940	10,972,000	1.25	2.00	3.00	6.00	—
1941	4,028,000	2.50	6.00	10.00	30.00	—
1942	6,474,000	10.00	15.00	30.00	60.00	—

KM# 4a 20 HALIEROV
0.6500 g., Aluminum, 18 mm. **Obv:** Double cross on shield within flower sprigs **Rev:** Nitra castle and large value **Edge:** Plain
Note: Varieties exist.

Date	Mintage	F	VF	XF	Unc	BU
1942	Inc. above	1.00	1.50	4.00	9.00	—
1943	15,000,000	1.00	1.50	4.00	9.00	—

KM# 5 50 HALIEROV
3.3300 g., Copper-Nickel, 20 mm. **Obv:** Double cross on shield and date **Rev:** Value above plow **Edge:** Plain

Date	Mintage	F	VF	XF	Unc	BU
1940	Inc. above	30.00	40.00	50.00	100	—
1941	8,000,000	1.00	2.00	3.00	6.00	—

KM# 5a 50 HALIEROV
1.0000 g., Aluminum, 20 mm. **Obv:** Double cross on shield and date **Rev:** Value above plow **Edge:** Milled

Date	Mintage	F	VF	XF	Unc	BU
1943	4,400,000	1.00	1.50	2.50	5.00	—
1944	2,621,000	5.00	10.00	15.00	30.00	—

KM# 6 KORUNA
5.0000 g., Copper-Nickel, 22 mm. **Obv:** Double cross on shield within circle above date **Rev:** Value within oat sprigs and stalks **Edge:** Milled **Note:** Open and closed 4.

Date	Mintage	F	VF	XF	Unc	BU
1940	2,350,000	0.75	1.25	2.25	6.00	—
1941	11,650,000	0.50	1.00	2.00	5.00	—
1942	6,000,000	0.50	1.00	2.00	5.00	—

Date	Mintage	F	VF	XF	Unc	BU
Note: Varieties exist of 1942, in the numeral 4						
1944	884,000	10.00	15.00	30.00	60.00	—
1945	3,321,000	0.75	1.25	2.25	6.00	—

KM# 2   5 KORUN
Nickel, 27 mm. **Obv:** Double cross on shield within wheat sprigs below value with date below **Rev:** Head left **Edge:** Milled **Note:** Pointed top or flat top to the letter A in NAROD.

Date	Mintage	F	VF	XF	Unc	BU
1939	5,101,000	1.50	2.00	3.50	12.00	—
Note: Approximately 2,000,000 pieces were melted down by the Czechoslovak National Bank in 1947						

KM# 9.1   10 KORUN
7.0000 g., 0.5000 Silver 0.1125 oz. ASW, 29 mm. **Obv:** Double cross on shield within radiant circle **Rev:** Standing figures facing divide value **Edge:** Plain **Note:** Variety 1 - Cross atop church held by left figure.

Date	Mintage	F	VF	XF	Unc	BU
1944	1,381,000	2.00	4.00	5.00	12.00	—

KM# 9.2   10 KORUN
7.0000 g., 0.5000 Silver 0.1125 oz. ASW **Obv:** Double cross on shield within radiant circle **Rev:** Standing figure facing divides value **Note:** Variety 2 - Without cross atop church held by left figure.

Date	Mintage	F	VF	XF	Unc	BU
1944	Inc. above	2.50	5.00	7.00	15.00	—

KM# 3   20 KORUN
15.0000 g., 0.5000 Silver 0.2411 oz. ASW, 31 mm. **Obv:** Double cross on shield within wreath flanked by value **Rev:** Head right **Edge:** Milled

Date	Mintage	F	VF	XF	Unc	BU
1939	200,000	5.00	10.00	20.00	40.00	—

KM# 7.1   20 KORUN
15.0000 g., 0.5000 Silver 0.2411 oz. ASW, 31 mm. **Subject:** St. Kyrill and St. Methodius **Obv:** Double cross on shield within sprigs **Rev:** Standing figures flanked by value **Edge:** Milled

Date	Mintage	F	VF	XF	Unc	BU
1941	2,500,000	4.00	5.00	7.00	16.00	—

KM# 7.2   20 KORUN
15.0000 g., 0.5000 Silver 0.2411 oz. ASW **Subject:** St. Kyrill and St. Methodius **Obv:** Double cross on shield within sprigs **Rev:** Variety 2 - Double bar cross

Date	Mintage	F	VF	XF	Unc	BU
1941	Inc. above	4.50	6.50	20.00	50.00	—

KM# 10   50 KORUN
16.5000 g., 0.7000 Silver 0.3713 oz. ASW, 34 mm. **Subject:** 5th Anniversary of Independence **Obv:** Double cross on shield within wreath flanked by value **Rev:** Head right **Edge:** Milled

Date	Mintage	F	VF	XF	Unc	BU
1944	2,000,000	6.00	7.00	9.00	18.00	—

REPUBLIC

STANDARD COINAGE
100 Halierov = 1 Slovak Koruna (Sk)

KM# 17   10 HALIEROV
0.7200 g., Aluminum, 17 mm. **Obv:** Double cross on shield above inscription **Rev:** Church steeple **Edge:** Plain

Date	Mintage	F	VF	XF	Unc	BU
1993	32,200,000	—	—	—	0.35	—
Note: Varieties of cross on state emblem						
1994	89,130,000	—	—	—	0.35	—
1995 In sets only	23,990,000	—	—	—	1.00	—
1996	31,540,000	—	—	—	0.35	—
1997	10,000,000	—	—	—	0.35	—
1998	30,260,000	—	—	—	0.35	—
1999	31,420,000	—	—	—	0.35	—
1999	11,500	Value: 5.00				
2000	30,600,000	—	—	—	0.35	—
2000 Proof	12,500	Value: 5.00				

KM# 18   20 HALIEROV
0.9500 g., Aluminum, 19.5 mm. **Obv:** Double cross on shield above inscription **Rev:** Mountain peak and value **Edge:** Reeded

Date	Mintage	F	VF	XF	Unc	BU
1993	37,410,000	—	—	—	0.45	—
1994	71,020,000	—	—	—	0.45	—
1995	32,390,000	—	—	—	0.45	—
1996	19,800,000	—	—	—	0.45	—
1997	10,000,000	—	—	—	0.45	—
1998	21,000,000	—	—	—	0.45	—
1999	15,710,000	—	—	—	0.45	—
1999 Proof	11,500	Value: 5.00				
2000	31,120,000	—	—	—	0.45	—
2000 Proof	12,500	Value: 5.00				

KM# 15   50 HALIEROV
1.2000 g., Aluminum, 22 mm. **Obv:** Double cross on shield above inscription **Rev:** Watch tower and value **Edge:** Plain

Date	Mintage	F	VF	XF	Unc	BU
1993	35,130,000	—	—	—	0.55	—
1994	19,020,000	—	—	—	1.50	—
1995 In sets only	12,000	—	—	—	1.50	—

KM# 35   50 HALIEROV
2.8000 g., Copper Plated Steel, 18.7 mm. **Obv:** Double cross on shield above inscription **Rev:** Watch tower and value **Edge:** Milled and plain

Date	Mintage	F	VF	XF	Unc	BU
1996	39,640,000	—	—	—	0.60	—
1997 In sets only	11,500	—	—	—	1.50	—

Date	Mintage	F	VF	XF	Unc	BU
1998	15,000,000	—	—	—	0.60	—
1999 In sets only	11,500	—	—	—	1.50	—
2000	20,212,000	—	—	—	0.60	—
2000 Proof	12,500	Value: 5.00				

KM# 12   KORUNA
3.8500 g., Bronze Clad Steel, 21 mm. **Subject:** 15th Century of Madonna and Child **Obv:** Double cross on shield above inscription **Rev:** Madonna holding child and value **Edge:** Milled

Date	Mintage	F	VF	XF	Unc	BU
1993	58,930,000	—	—	—	0.75	—
1994	44,320,000	—	—	—	0.75	—
1995	28,030,000	—	—	—	0.75	—
1996 In sets only	15,000	—	—	—	1.50	—
1997 In sets only	15,000	—	—	—	1.50	—
1998 In sets only	12,000	—	—	—	1.50	—
1999 In sets only	11,500	—	—	—	1.50	—
2000 In sets only	12,500	—	—	—	1.50	—
2000 Proof	900	Value: 10.00				

KM# 13   2 KORUNA
4.4000 g., Nickel Clad Steel, 21.5 mm. **Obv:** Double cross on shield above inscription **Rev:** Venus statue and value

Date	Mintage	F	VF	XF	Unc	BU
1993	36,810,000	—	—	—	0.85	—
Note: Varieties of artist's initials						
1994	24,720,000	—	—	—	0.85	—
1995	30,510,000	—	—	—	0.85	—
1996 In sets only	15,000	—	—	—	2.00	—
1997 In sets only	15,000	—	—	—	2.00	—
1998 In sets only	12,000	—	—	—	2.00	—
1999 In sets only	11,500	—	—	—	2.00	—
2000 In sets only	12,500	—	—	—	2.00	—
2000 Proof	900	Value: 10.00				

KM# 14   5 KORUNA
5.4000 g., Nickel Clad Steel, 24.75 mm. **Obv:** Double cross on shield above inscription **Rev:** Celtic coin of BIATEC at upper left of value **Edge:** Milled

Date	Mintage	F	VF	XF	Unc	BU
1993	36,200,000	—	—	—	1.25	—
Note: Varieties in artist's initials						
1994	26,140,000	—	—	—	1.25	—
1995	16,530,000	—	—	—	1.25	—
1996 In sets only	15,000	—	—	—	2.00	—
1997 In sets only	15,000	—	—	—	2.00	—
1998 In sets only	11,500	—	—	—	2.00	—
1999 In sets only	12,500	—	—	—	2.00	—
2000 In sets only	12,500	—	—	—	2.00	—
2000 Proof	900	Value: 20.00				

KM# 11.1   10 KORUNA
6.6000 g., Brass, 26.5 mm. **Obv:** Double cross on shield above inscription **Rev:** Bronze cross and value

Date	Mintage	F	VF	XF	Unc	BU
1993	40,934,000	—	—	—	2.50	—
1994	14,360,000	—	—	—	2.50	—
1995	42,204,000	—	—	—	2.50	—
1996 In sets only	15,000	—	—	—	4.00	—
1997 In sets only	15,000	—	—	—	4.00	—
1998 In sets only	12,000	—	—	—	4.00	—
1999 In sets only	11,500	—	—	—	4.00	—

Date	Mintage	F	VF	XF	Unc	BU
2000 In sets only	12,500	—	—	—	4.00	—
2000 Proof	900	Value: 35.00				

KM# 11.2   10 KORUNA
8.5000 g., 0.7500 Silver 0.2050 oz. ASW, 26.5 mm. **Obv:** Double cross on shield abov inscription **Rev:** Bronze cross and value

Date	Mintage	F	VF	XF	Unc	BU
1993 Proof	1,000	Value: 350				

Note: These coins are numbered and punched with an R

KM# 16   100 KORUN
13.0000 g., 0.7500 Silver 0.3135 oz. ASW, 29 mm.
Subject: National Independence **Obv:** Double cross on shield above inscription and value **Rev:** Three doves below double cross within clouds **Edge:** Milled **Note:** 7,450 uncirculated pieces melted in 2002.

Date	Mintage	F	VF	XF	Unc	BU
1993MK	65,000	—	—	—	9.00	—
1993MK Proof	5,000	Value: 18.00				

KM# 20   200 KORUN
20.0000 g., 0.7500 Silver 0.4822 oz. ASW, 34 mm. **Subject:** 200th Anniversary - Birth of Jan Kollar **Obv:** Double cross on shield above inscription, value at left **Rev:** Windswept head facing, name and dates at bottom **Edge:** SLAVME SLAVNE SLAVU SLAVOV SLAVNYCH **Note:** 10,065 uncirculated pieces melted in 2002.

Date	Mintage	F	VF	XF	Unc	BU
1993MK	35,000	—	—	—	15.00	—
1993MK Proof	2,000	Value: 35.00				

KM# 19   200 KORUN
20.0000 g., 0.7500 Silver 0.4822 oz. ASW, 34 mm.
Subject: 150th Anniversary of Slovak Language **Obv:** Double cross on shield above value **Rev:** Three heads facing above dates **Edge:** Plain with ornament **Note:** 6,182 uncirculated pieces melted.

Date	Mintage	F	VF	XF	Unc	BU
1993MK	35,000	—	—	—	15.00	—
1993MK Proof	2,000	Value: 30.00				

KM# 23   200 KORUN
20.0000 g., 0.7500 Silver 0.4822 oz. ASW, 34 mm. **Subject:** 50th Anniversary - D-Day **Obv:** Double cross on shield within stylized leaves flanked by dates and value **Rev:** Crowned emblem within v-shaped design divides dates and symbol **Edge:** SLOVACI PROTI FASIZMU **Note:** 10,550 uncirculated pieces melted..

Date	Mintage	F	VF	XF	Unc	BU
1994	35,000	—	—	—	20.00	—
1994 Proof	2,600	Value: 100				

KM# 21   200 KORUN
20.0000 g., 0.7500 Silver 0.4822 oz. ASW, 34 mm.
Subject: 100th Anniversary - Olympic Committee **Obv:** Olympic rings and double cross on shield within design, dates at upper left **Rev:** Value, hockey player and snow flake design below **Edge:** Snowflakes **Note:** 16,475 uncirculated pieces melted.

Date	Mintage	F	VF	XF	Unc	BU
1994	45,000	—	—	—	15.00	—
1994 Proof	3,000	Value: 32.50				

KM# 22   200 KORUN
20.0000 g., 0.7500 Silver 0.4822 oz. ASW, 34 mm.
Subject: 100th Anniversary - Birth of Poet and Painter Janko Alexy **Obv:** Small double cross on shield below value and head of young girl in winter **Rev:** Head 3/4 right **Edge:** Plain with ornament **Note:** 13,100 uncirculated pieces melted.

Date	Mintage	F	VF	XF	Unc	BU
1994MK	34,000	—	—	—	15.00	—
1994MK Proof	2,500	Value: 35.00				

KM# 26   200 KORUN
20.0000 g., 0.7500 Silver 0.4822 oz. ASW, 34 mm.
Subject: European Environmental Protection **Obv:** Double cross on shield above woodpecker feeding young **Rev:** Two storks and a flying swallow at right of flowers above value **Edge:** ENCY 1995 (3 fish) **Note:** 11,400 uncirculated pieces melted.

Date	Mintage	F	VF	XF	Unc	BU
1995	28,000	—	—	—	25.00	30.00
1995 Proof	2,000	Value: 50.00				

KM# 25   200 KORUN
20.0000 g., 0.7500 Silver 0.4822 oz. ASW, 34 mm. **Subject:** 100th Anniversary - Birth of Mikulas Galanda **Obv:** Double cross on shield to left of mother with child **Rev:** Head facing 3/4 right, dates diagonally at right, value at lower right **Edge:** MIKULAS GALANDA - MALIAR A GRAFIK **Note:** 10,700 uncirculated pieces melted.

Date	Mintage	F	VF	XF	Unc	BU
1995	25,000	—	—	—	15.00	—
1995 Proof	1,500	Value: 30.00				

KM# 24   200 KORUN
20.0000 g., 0.7500 Silver 0.4822 oz. ASW, 34 mm.
Subject: 200th Anniversary - Birth of Pavol Jozef Safarik **Obv:** Double cross on shield in center of inscription **Rev:** Head facing within inscription, value at bottom, dates diagonally at left **Edge:** ZAKLADATEL VEDECKEJ SLAVISTIKY **Note:** 8,700 uncirculated pieces melted in 2002.

Date	Mintage	F	VF	XF	Unc	BU
1995MK	23,500	—	—	—	15.00	—
1995MK Proof	1,500	Value: 37.50				

KM# 27   200 KORUN
20.0000 g., 0.7500 Silver 0.4822 oz. ASW, 34 mm.
Subject: Centennial of Bratislava Electric Tram **Obv:** Double cross on shield and date in center of inscription and value as a triangular design **Rev:** Two tram cars within triangular design **Edge:** HLAVNE NADRAZIE TEREZIANSKA STVRT **Note:** 9,300 uncirculated pieces melted.

Date	Mintage	F	VF	XF	Unc	BU
1995	25,000	—	—	—	15.00	—
1995 Proof	1,600	Value: 40.00				

KM# 34   200 KORUN
20.0000 g., 0.7500 Silver 0.4822 oz. ASW, 34 mm. **Subject:** 200th Anniversary - Birth of Moric Benovsky **Obv:** Small double cross on shield at left of ship **Rev:** Bust facing **Edge:** IN ADVERSIS ET PROSPERIS **Note:** 5,050 uncirculated pieces melted in 2002.

Date	Mintage	F	VF	XF	Unc	BU
1996	21,400	—	—	—	15.00	—
1996 Proof	2,000	Value: 40.00				

KM# 33   200 KORUN
20.0000 g., 0.7500 Silver 0.4822 oz. ASW, 34 mm.
Subject: Centennial - Mountain Railway to Strba Lake **Obv:** Double cross on shield above value, inscription and date **Rev:** Train and passenger car above dates and inscription **Edge:** VYSOKE TATRY VYSOKE TATRY **Note:** 6,050 uncirculated pieces melted.

Date	Mintage	F	VF	XF	Unc	BU
1996	22,000	—	—	—	15.00	—
1996 Proof	1,600	Value: 32.50				

KM# 30   200 KORUN
20.0000 g., 0.7500 Silver 0.4822 oz. ASW, 34 mm.
Subject: 200th Anniversary - Birth of Samuel Jurkovic
Obv: Double cross on shield to left of design within lined square
Rev: Half of head facing at left of lined square design **Edge:** V
SLUZBACH NARODA **Note:** 11,100 uncirculated pieces melted.

Date	Mintage	F	VF	XF	Unc	BU
1996MK	26,000	—	—	—	15.00	—
1996MK Proof	1,600	Value: 37.50				

KM# 31   200 KORUN
20.0000 g., 0.7500 Silver 0.4822 oz. ASW, 34 mm.
Subject: Olympic Games **Obv:** Double cross on shield and Olympic
rings within square, date and inscription below **Rev:** Greek column
within oval track, value below **Edge:** V DUCHU ODKAZU PIERRA
DE COUBERTINA **Note:** 7,700 uncirculated pieces melted.

Date	Mintage	F	VF	XF	Unc	BU
1996MK	23,000	—	—	—	16.50	—
1996MK Proof	1,700	Value: 35.00				

KM# 32   200 KORUN
20.0000 g., 0.7500 Silver 0.4822 oz. ASW, 34 mm.
Subject: 100th Anniversary - Birth of Jozef Ciger Hronsky
Obv: Small double cross on shield within last O of value within
square **Rev:** Half face with glasses and stylized sun within small
squares flanked by dates and inscription **Edge:** NIET KRAJSICH
SLOV AKO SKUTKY **Note:** 7,750 uncirculated pieces melted.

Date	Mintage	F	VF	XF	Unc	BU
1996MK	20,500	—	—	—	15.00	—
1996MK Proof	1,500	Value: 32.50				

KM# 40   200 KORUN
20.0000 g., 0.7500 Silver 0.4822 oz. ASW, 34 mm.
Subject: 200th Anniversary - Birth of Stefan Moyzes, 1797-1997
Obv: Stylized double cross in tree form with small double cross
on shield below **Rev:** Head with glasses facing within circle above
book and value **Edge:** PRVY PREDSEDA MATICE
SLOVENSKEJ **Note:** 2,900 pieces melted.

Date	Mintage	F	VF	XF	Unc	BU
1997	14,900	—	—	—	15.00	—
1997 Proof	1,500	Value: 35.00				

KM# 38   200 KORUN
20.0000 g., 0.7500 Silver 0.4822 oz. ASW, 34 mm.
Subject: Banska Stiavnica - UNESCO **Obv:** Small double cross on
shield at right of tower **Rev:** Baroque buildings **Edge:** PATRIMOINE
MODIAL - WORLD HERITAGE **Note:** 1,900 Uncirculated pieces
melted.

Date	Mintage	F	VF	XF	Unc	BU
1997	16,500	—	—	—	15.00	—
1997 Proof	1,700	Value: 37.50				

KM# 37   200 KORUN
20.0000 g., 0.7500 Silver 0.4822 oz. ASW, 34 mm.
Subject: 150th Anniversary - Birth of Svetozar Hurban Vajansky
1847-1916 **Obv:** Double cross on shield **Rev:** Large head with
beard and mustache **Edge:** POLITIK SPISOVATEL KRITIK
NOVINAR **Note:** 4,600 uncirculated pieces melted.

Date	Mintage	F	VF	XF	Unc	BU
1997	17,400	—	—	—	15.00	—
1997 Proof	1,800	Value: 35.00				

KM# 43   200 KORUN
20.0000 g., 0.7500 Silver 0.4822 oz. ASW **Subject:** 150th
Anniversary - Slovak Revolt of 1848 **Obv:** Small double cross on
shield divides date above emblem within circle flanked by vertical
inscriptions **Rev:** Standing figure flanked by vertical inscriptions and
dates **Edge:** ZA NARODNU SLOBODU **Note:** 1,900 pieces melted.

Date	Mintage	F	VF	XF	Unc	BU
1998	13,400	—	—	—	15.00	—
1998 Proof	1,500	Value: 37.50				

KM# 42   200 KORUN
20.0000 g., 0.7500 Silver 0.4822 oz. ASW **Subject:** 150th
Anniversary - 1st Railroad in Slovakia **Obv:** Small double cross
on shield to right of train emerging from tunnel **Rev:** Bratislava
Castle and locomotive **Edge:** 150 ROKOV ZELEZNIC NA
SLOVENSKU **Note:** 200 pieces melted.

Date	Mintage	F	VF	XF	Unc	BU
1998	14,000	—	—	—	15.00	—
1998 Proof	1,800	Value: 32.50				

KM# 45   200 KORUN
20.0000 g., 0.7500 Silver 0.4822 oz. ASW, 34 mm.
Subject: Centennial - Birth of Jan Smrek **Obv:** Stylized seated
female figure **Rev:** Half figure outline facing left **Edge:** BASNIK
JAN SMREK 100 VYROCIE NARODENIA **Note:** 2,300 pieces
melted.

Date	Mintage	F	VF	XF	Unc	BU
1998	13,400	—	—	—	15.00	—
1998 Proof	1,500	Value: 35.00				

KM# 41   200 KORUN
20.0000 g., 0.7500 Silver 0.4822 oz. ASW, 34 mm. **Subject:** 50th
Anniversary - Slovak National Gallery **Obv:** Crowned Madonna and
child **Rev:** Daughters of King Lycomed **Edge:** GOTIKA A BAROK
V ZBIERKACH SNG **Note:** 700 pieces melted.

Date	Mintage	F	VF	XF	Unc	BU
1998	15,000	—	—	—	15.00	—
1998 Proof	1,600	Value: 30.00				

KM# 44   200 KORUN
20.0000 g., 0.7500 Silver 0.4822 oz. ASW, 34 mm.
Subject: UNESCO World Heritage site **Obv:** Cathedral towers
Rev: Castle and gothic window arch **Edge:** PATRIMONIE
MONDIAL WORLD HERITAGE **Note:** 700 pieces melted.

Date	Mintage	F	VF	XF	Unc	BU
1998	13,500	—	—	—	15.00	—
1998 Proof	1,500	Value: 35.00				

KM# 49   200 KORUN
20.0000 g., 0.7500 Silver 0.4822 oz. ASW, 34 mm.
Subject: 50th Anniversary - Slovac Philharmonic **Obv:** Pipe
organ above double cross on shield flanked by value and date
Rev: Reduta building bay window **Edge:** HUDBA-
UNIVERZALNA REC LUDSTVA **Note:** 300 pieces melted.

Date	Mintage	F	VF	XF	Unc	BU
1999MK	12,700	—	—	—	15.00	—
1999MK Proof	1,400	Value: 35.00				

KM# 48 200 KORUN
20.0000 g., 0.7500 Silver 0.4822 oz. ASW, 34 mm.
Subject: 150th Anniversary - Birth of Pavol Orszagh Hviezdoslav
Obv: Portrait of face made with treetops **Rev:** Portrait of the artist
Edge: HEROLD SVITAJUCICH CASOV **Note:** 800 pieces
melted.

Date	Mintage	F	VF	XF	Unc	BU
1999	12,700	—	—	—	15.00	—
1999 Proof	1,400	Value: 35.00				

KM# 55 200 KORUN
20.0000 g., 0.7500 Silver 0.4822 oz. ASW, 33.9 mm. **Subject:** Juraj
Fandly **Obv:** Radiant book above double cross on shield within
design **Rev:** Half figure writing in book facing right **Edge:** NIE SILOU
ANI MOCOU, ALE MOJIM DUCHOM **Note:** 700 pieces melted.

Date	Mintage	F	VF	XF	Unc	BU
2000	10,600	—	—	—	15.00	—
2000 Proof	1,600	Value: 35.00				

KM# 28 500 KORUN
33.6300 g., 0.9250 Silver 1.0000 oz. ASW, 40 mm.
Subject: Slovensky Raj National Park **Obv:** Double cross on
shield, date, value and flowers **Rev:** Waterfall **Edge:** OCHRANA
PRIRODY A. KRAJINY **Note:** 11,800 Uncirculated pieces melted
in 2002.

Date	Mintage	F	VF	XF	Unc	BU
1994	27,500	—	—	—	35.00	—
1994 Proof	2,400	Value: 45.00				

KM# 39 500 KORUN
33.6300 g., 0.9250 Silver 1.0000 oz. ASW, 40 mm.
Subject: Pieninsky National Park **Obv:** Double cross on shield
above butterfly within circle **Rev:** Park scene in circle within
butterfly wings **Edge:** OCHRANA PRIRODY A KRAJINY
Note: 2700 pieces uncirculated melted.

Date	Mintage	F	VF	XF	Unc	BU
1997	14,500	—	—	—	60.00	—
1997 Proof	1,700	Value: 125				

KM# 47 500 KORUN
33.6300 g., 0.9250 Silver 1.0000 oz. ASW, 40 mm.
Subject: Tatransky National Park **Obv:** Value, mountains,
flowers and dates **Rev:** Chamois above flowers, date and double
cross on shield **Edge:** OCHRANA PRIRODY A KRAJINY

Date	Mintage	F	VF	XF	Unc	BU
1999	12,000	—	—	—	45.00	—
	Note: 700 pieces uncirculated melted.					
1999 Proof	1,400	Value: 250				

KM# 50 500 KORUN
33.6300 g., 0.9250 Silver 1.0000 oz. ASW, 40 mm.
Subject: 500th Anniversary - First Thalers of Kremnica
Obv: Mining scene within beaded circle **Rev:** Old coin designs
and city view within beaded circle **Edge:** GULDINER-
PREDCHODCA TOLIARA

Date	Mintage	F	VF	XF	Unc	BU
1999	12,000	—	—	—	45.00	—
1999 Proof	1,400	Value: 400				

KM# 53 500 KORUN
33.6300 g., 0.9250 Silver 1.0000 oz. ASW, 40 mm.
Subject: 250th Anniversary - Death of Samuel Mikovini **Obv:**
Armored bust right and cartographic instruments **Rev:** Allegorical
scene and map **Edge:** KARTOGRAF - MATEMATIK - STAVITEL

Date	Mintage	F	VF	XF	Unc	BU
2000	10,100	—	—	—	37.50	—
2000 Proof	1,500	Value: 60.00				

KM# 51 2000 KORUN
124.4140 g., 0.9990 Silver 3.9958 oz. ASW, 65 mm. **Subject:** 2000
Bi-millennium **Obv:** Small double cross on shield, value and historical
scenes **Rev:** Jesus within churches and value **Edge:** Plain

Date	Mintage	F	VF	XF	Unc	BU
MM(2000) Proof	3,000	Value: 450				

KM# 29 5000 KORUN
7.0000 g., 0.9000 Gold 0.2025 oz. AGW, 24 mm.
Subject: 1100th Anniversary - Death of Moravian King Svatopluk
Obv: Double cross on shield, value and date **Rev:** Head of
Svatopluk and ruin of castle Devin **Edge:** Milled

Date	Mintage	F	VF	XF	Unc	BU
1994 Proof	5,000	Value: 500				

KM# 36 5000 KORUN
9.5000 g., 0.9000 Gold 0.2749 oz. AGW, 26 mm.
Subject: Banska Stiavnica Mines - UNESCO historic site
Obv: Double cross on shield, value, date and upright design
Rev: Steepled buildings **Edge:** Milled

Date	Mintage	F	VF	XF	Unc	BU
1997 Proof	8,000	Value: 325				

KM# 46 5000 KORUN
9.5000 g., 0.9000 Gold 0.2749 oz. AGW, 26 mm.
Subject: Spissky Castle - UNESCO historic site **Obv:** Double
cross on shield and lion within design above date **Rev:** Scenic
design and value **Edge:** Milled

Date	Mintage	F	VF	XF	Unc	BU
1998 Proof	6,000	Value: 325				

KM# 54 5000 KORUN
9.5000 g., 0.9000 Gold 0.2749 oz. AGW, 26 mm. **Subject:** 500th
Anniversary - Kremnica Mint **Obv:** Hungarian coin design
Rev: Hungarian coin design **Edge:** Reeded

Date	Mintage	F	VF	XF	Unc	BU
ND(1999) Proof	5,500	Value: 325				

KM# 52 10000 KORUN
19.0000 g., 0.9000 Gold 0.5498 oz. AGW, 34 mm.
Subject: 2000 Bi-millennium **Obv:** Double cross on shield, value
and historical scenes **Rev:** Jesus with churches **Edge:** Milled
Note: Similar to 2000 Korun, KM#51.

Date	Mintage	F	VF	XF	Unc	BU
MM(2000) Proof	3,500	Value: 600				

ESSAIS

KM#	Date	Mintage Identification				Mkt Val
E1	1939	— 20 Korun. 0.5000 Silver. KM#7				—
E2	1941	— 10 Korun. 0.5000 Silver. KM#9.1				—

MINT SETS

KM#	Date	Mintage Identification	Issue Price	Mkt Val
MS1	1993 (7)	28,800 KM#11.1-15, 17-18, plus medal	—	12.00
MS2	1994 (7)	19,000 KM#11.1-15, 17-18, plus medal	—	12.00
MS3	1995 (7)	12,000 KM#11.1-15, 17-18, plus medal	—	12.00
MS4	1996 (7)	15,000 KM#11.1-14, 17-18, 35, plus medal	—	12.00
MS5	1997 (7)	15,000 KM#11.1-14, 17-18, 35, plus medal	—	12.00
MS6	1998 (7)	12,000 KM#11.1-14, 17-18, 35, plus medal	—	12.00
MS7	1999 (7)	11,500 KM#11.1-14, 17-18, 35, plus medal	—	12.00
MS8	2000 (7)	13,000 KM#11.1-14, 17-18, 35, plus medal	—	12.00

PROOF SETS

KM#	Date	Mintage Identification	Issue Price	Mkt Val
PS1	2000 (7)	900 KM#11.1-14, 17-18, 35	—	85.00

SLOVENIA

The Republic of Slovenia is located northwest of Yugoslavia in the valleys of the Danube River. It has an area of 7,819 sq. mi. and a population of *1.9 million. Capital: Ljubljana. Agriculture is the main industry with large amounts of hops and fodder crops grown as well as many varieties of fruit trees. Sheep raising, timber production and the mining of mercury from one of the country's oldest mines are also very important to the economy.

Slovenia was important as a land route between Europe and the eastern Mediterranean region. The Roman Catholic Austro-Hungarian Empire gained control of the area during the 14th century and retained its dominance until World War I. The United Kingdom of the Serbs, Croats and Slovenes (Yugoslavia) was founded in 1918 and consisted of various groups of South Slavs.

In 1929, King Alexander declared his assumption of power temporarily, however he was assassinated in 1934. His son Peter's regent, Prince Paul tried to settle internal problems, however, the Slovenes denounced the agreement he made. He resigned in 1941 and Peter assumed the throne. Peter was forced to flee when Yugoslavia was occupied. Slovenia was divided between Germany and Italy. Even though Yugoslavia attempted to remain neutral, the Nazis occupied the country and were resisted by guerilla armies, most notably Marshal Josif Broz Tito.

Under Marshal Tito, the Constitution of 1946 established 6 constituent republics which made up Yugoslavia. Each republic was permitted Liberties under supervision of the Communist Party.

In Oct. 1989 the Slovene Assembly voted a constitutional amendment giving it the right to secede from Yugoslavia. A referendum on Dec. 23, 1990 resulted in a majority vote for independence, which was formally declared on Dec. 26.

On June 25 Slovenia declared independence, but agreed to suspend this for 3 months at peace talks sponsored by the EC. Federal troops moved into Slovenia on June 27 to secure Yugoslavia's external borders, but after some fighting withdrew by the end of July. The 3-month moratorium agreed at the EC having expired, Slovenia (and Croatia) declared their complete independence of the Yugoslav federation on Oct.8, 1991.

MINT MARKS
Based on last digit in date.
(K) - Kremnitz (Slovakia): open 4, upturned 5
(BP) - Budapest (Hungary): closed 4, downturned 5

MONETARY SYSTEM
100 Stotinov = 1 Tolar

REPUBLIC
STANDARD COINAGE
100 Stotinow = 1 Tolar

KM# 7   10 STOTINOV
0.5500 g., Aluminum, 16 mm. **Obv:** Value within square **Rev:** Olm salamander **Edge:** Plain **Note:** Varieties exist.

Date	Mintage	F	VF	XF	Unc	BU
1992	2,515,000	—	—	—	0.35	0.75
1992 Proof	1,000	Value: 5.00				

Date	Mintage	F	VF	XF	Unc	BU
1993	2,515,000	—	—	—	0.35	0.75
1993 Proof	1,000	Value: 5.00				
1994 In sets only	1,000	—	—	—	—	3.00
1994 Proof	1,000	Value: 5.00				
1995 In sets only	1,000	—	—	—	—	3.00
1995 Proof	1,000	Value: 5.00				
1996 In sets only	1,000	—	—	—	—	3.00
1996 Proof	800	Value: 5.00				
1997 In sets only	1,000	—	—	—	—	3.00
1997 Proof	800	Value: 5.00				
1998 In sets only	1,000	—	—	—	—	3.00
1998 Proof	800	Value: 5.00				
1999 In sets only	1,000	—	—	—	—	3.00
1999 Proof	800	Value: 5.00				
2000 In sets only	1,000	—	—	—	—	3.00
2000 Proof	800	Value: 5.00				

KM# 8   20 STOTINOV
0.7000 g., Aluminum, 18 mm. **Obv:** Value within square **Rev:** Barn owl and value **Edge:** Plain

Date	Mintage	F	VF	XF	Unc	BU
1992	2,515,000	—	—	—	0.50	1.00
Note: Minor reverse varieties exist						
1992 Proof	1,000	Value: 6.00				
1993	2,515,000	—	—	—	0.50	1.00
Note: Minor reverse varieties exist						
1993 Proof	1,000	Value: 6.00				
1994 In sets only	1,000	—	—	—	—	4.00
1994 Proof	1,000	Value: 6.00				
1995 In sets only	1,000	—	—	—	—	4.00
1995 Proof	1,000	Value: 6.00				
1996 In sets only	1,000	—	—	—	—	4.00
1996 Proof	800	Value: 6.00				
1997 In sets only	1,000	—	—	—	—	4.00
1997 Proof	800	Value: 6.00				
1998 In sets only	1,000	—	—	—	—	4.00
1998 Proof	800	Value: 6.00				
1999 In sets only	1,000	—	—	—	—	4.00
1999 Proof	800	Value: 6.00				
2000 In sets only	1,000	—	—	—	—	4.00
2000 Proof	800	Value: 6.00				

KM# 3   50 STOTINOV
0.8500 g., Aluminum, 19.9 mm. **Obv:** Value within square **Rev:** Bee and value **Edge:** Plain

Date	Mintage	F	VF	XF	Unc	BU
1992	5,015,000	—	—	0.10	0.50	0.75
Note: Minor reverse varieties exist						
1992 Proof	1,000	Value: 7.50				
1993	18,315,000	—	—	0.10	0.50	0.75
1993 Proof	1,000	Value: 7.50				
1994 In sets only	1,000	—	—	—	—	6.00
1994 Proof	1,000	Value: 7.50				
1995	3,000,000	—	—	0.10	0.50	0.75
1995 In sets only	1,000	—	—	—	—	6.00
1995 Proof	1,000	Value: 7.50				
1996	3,000,000	—	—	0.10	0.50	0.75
1996 Proof	Est. 500	Value: 7.50				
1997 In sets only	1,000	—	—	—	—	6.00
1997 Proof	500	Value: 7.50				
1998 In sets only	1,000	—	—	—	—	6.00
1998 Proof	500	Value: 7.50				
1999 In sets only	1,000	—	—	—	—	6.00
1999 Proof	500	Value: 7.50				
2000 In sets only	1,000	—	—	—	—	6.00
2000 Proof	800	Value: 7.50				

KM# 4   TOLAR
4.5000 g., Brass, 21.9 mm. **Obv:** Value within circle **Rev:** Three brown trout **Edge:** Reeded **Note:** Date varieties exist: 1994 = closed or open "4"; 1995 = serif up and serif down in "5".

Date	Mintage	F	VF	XF	Unc	BU
1992	10,015,000	—	—	0.20	0.85	1.50
1992 Proof	1,000	Value: 7.50				
1993	30,015,000	—	—	0.20	0.85	1.50
1993 Proof	1,000	Value: 7.50				

Date	Mintage	F	VF	XF	Unc	BU
1994 (K)	10,000,000	—	—	—	0.75	1.50
Note: 4 open to the top						
1994 (K) Proof	1,000	Value: 7.50				
Note: 4 open to right						
1994 (BP)	5,000,000	—	—	—	0.75	1.50
1995 (K)	10,000,000	—	—	—	0.75	1.50
1995 (K) In sets only	1,000	—	—	—	—	5.00
1995 (K) Proof	1,000	Value: 7.50				
1995 (BP)	10,000,000	—	—	—	0.75	1.50
1996	Est. 21,800,000	—	—	—	0.75	1.50
1996 Proof	Est. 3,000	Value: 7.50				
1997	8,000,000	—	—	—	0.75	1.50
1997 Proof	500	Value: 10.00				
1998	12,000,000	—	—	—	0.75	1.50
1998 Proof	500	Value: 10.00				
1999	8,000,000	—	—	—	0.75	1.50
1999 Proof	500	Value: 10.00				
2000	15,001,000	—	—	—	0.75	1.50
2000 Proof	800	Value: 7.50				

KM# 5   2 TOLARJA
5.4000 g., Brass, 24 mm. **Obv:** Value within circle **Rev:** Barn swallow in flight **Edge:** Reeded **Note:** Date varieties exist: 1994 = closed or open "4"; 1995 = serif up and serif down in "5".

Date	Mintage	F	VF	XF	Unc	BU
1992	5,015,000	—	—	0.25	0.85	1.75
1992 Proof	1,000	Value: 8.50				
1993	10,015,000	—	—	0.25	0.85	1.75
1993 Proof	1,000	Value: 8.50				
1994 (K)	10,000,000	—	—	—	0.75	1.75
Note: 4 open to the top						
1994 (K) In sets only	1,000	—	—	—	—	7.00
Note: 4 open to right						
1994 (K) Proof	1,000	Value: 8.50				
Note: 4 open to right						
1994 (BP)	5,000,000	—	—	—	0.75	1.75
1995 (K)	10,000,000	—	—	—	0.75	1.75
1995 (K) In sets only	1,000	—	—	—	—	7.00
1995 (K) Proof	1,000	Value: 8.50				
1995 (BP)	10,000,000	—	—	—	0.75	1.75
1996	Est. 16,600,000	—	—	—	0.75	1.75
1996 Proof	1,000	Value: 8.50				
1997	6,060,000	—	—	—	0.75	1.75
1997 Proof	500	Value: 12.00				
1998	5,000,000	—	—	—	0.75	1.75
1998 Proof	500	Value: 12.00				
1999	5,200,000	—	—	—	0.75	1.75
1999 Proof	500	Value: 12.00				
2000	15,001,000	—	—	—	0.75	1.75
2000 Proof	800	Value: 8.50				

KM# 6   5 TOLARJEV
6.3900 g., Brass, 26 mm. **Obv:** Value within circle **Rev:** Head and horns of ibex **Edge:** Reeded **Note:** Date varieties exist: 1994 = closed or open "4"; 1995 = serif up and serif down in "5".

Date	Mintage	F	VF	XF	Unc	BU
1992	10,015,000	—	—	0.35	1.00	2.00
1992 Proof	1,000	Value: 10.00				
1993 Proof	1,000	Value: 10.00				
1993	10,015,000	—	—	0.35	1.00	2.00
1994 (K)	10,000,000	—	—	—	0.85	2.00
Note: 4 open to the top						
1994 (K) In sets only	1,000	—	—	—	—	8.00
Note: 4 open to right						
1994 (K) Proof	1,000	Value: 10.00				
Note: 4 open to right						
1994 (BP)	5,000,000	—	—	—	0.85	2.00
1995 2 tip	—	—	—	—	0.85	2.00
1995	5,000,000	—	—	—	0.85	2.00
1996	6,000,000	—	—	—	0.85	2.00
1996 Proof	Est. 3,000	Value: 10.00				
1997	8,000,000	—	—	—	0.85	2.00
1997 Proof	500	Value: 15.00				
1998	10,000,000	—	—	—	0.85	2.00
1998 Proof	500	Value: 15.00				
1999	6,403,000	—	—	—	0.85	2.00
1999 Proof	500	Value: 15.00				

Date	Mintage	F	VF	XF	Unc	BU
2000	15,001,000	—	—	—	0.85	2.00
2000 Proof	800	Value: 10.00				

KM# 9   5 TOLARJEV
6.4000 g., Brass, 26 mm.   **Subject:** 400th Anniversary - Battle of Sisek **Obv:** Value and date **Rev:** City view, arms, date, Andrej G. Turjaski **Edge:** Reeded

Date	Mintage	F	VF	XF	Unc	BU
1993	100,000	—	—	—	1.65	2.25

KM# 12   5 TOLARJEV
6.4000 g., Brass, 26 mm.   **Subject:** 300th Anniversary - Establishment of Operosorum Labacensium Academy **Obv:** Value and date **Rev:** Beehive and bees **Edge:** Reeded

Date	Mintage	F	VF	XF	Unc	BU
1993	100,000	—	—	—	2.00	5.00

KM# 15   5 TOLARJEV
Brass, 26 mm.   **Subject:** 50th Anniversary - Slovenian Bank **Obv:** Value and date **Rev:** Linden leaf and seed pod **Edge:** Reeded

Date	Mintage	F	VF	XF	Unc	BU
1994	100,000	—	—	—	1.65	2.25

KM# 16   5 TOLARJEV
Brass, 26 mm.   **Subject:** 1,000th Anniversary - Glagolitic Alphabet **Obv:** Value and date **Rev:** Feather **Edge:** Reeded

Date	Mintage	F	VF	XF	Unc	BU
1994	200,000	—	—	—	1.65	2.25

KM# 21   5 TOLARJEV
Brass, 26 mm.   **Series:** F.A.O. **Subject:** 50th Anniversary - F.A.O. **Obv:** Value within circle **Rev:** Hands holding F.A.O. logo **Edge:** Reeded

Date	Mintage	F	VF	XF	Unc	BU
ND(1995)	500,000	—	—	—	1.65	2.25

KM# 22   5 TOLARJEV
Brass, 26 mm.   **Subject:** 50th Anniversary - Defeat of Fascism **Obv:** Value **Rev:** Vertical chain link design and dates **Edge:** Reeded

Date	Mintage	F	VF	XF	Unc	BU
1995	200,000	—	—	—	1.65	2.25

KM# 26   5 TOLARJEV
Brass, 26 mm.   **Subject:** Aljazev Stolp **Obv:** Value within triangle design **Rev:** Head facing in front of mountains **Edge:** Reeded

Date	Mintage	F	VF	XF	Unc	BU
1995	200,000	—	—	—	1.65	2.25

KM# 29   5 TOLARJEV
Brass, 26 mm.   **Subject:** 150th Anniversary - First Railway in Slovenia **Obv:** Date within design at upper right, value at far left **Rev:** Dates above train **Edge:** Reeded

Date	Mintage	F	VF	XF	Unc	BU
1996	Est. 300,000	—	—	—	1.65	2.25
1996 Proof	Inc. above	Value: 8.00				

KM# 32   5 TOLARJEV
Brass, 26 mm.   **Subject:** 5th Anniversary of Independence **Obv:** Value and date at left **Rev:** Pink Carnation and dates **Edge:** Reeded

Date	Mintage	F	VF	XF	Unc	BU
1996	200,000	—	—	—	1.65	2.25
1996 Proof	—	Value: 8.00				

KM# 33   5 TOLARJEV
Brass, 26 mm.   **Series:** Olympics **Subject:** Olympics Centennial **Obv:** Value above olympic rings and flag **Rev:** Gymnast above dates **Edge:** Reeded

Date	Mintage	F	VF	XF	Unc	BU
1996	200,000	—	—	—	1.65	2.25
1996 Proof	Est. 3,000	Value: 8.00				

KM# 38   5 TOLARJEV
Brass, 26 mm.   **Subject:** Ziga Zois **Obv:** Value and date **Rev:** Zois ziga written within outline of face above dates **Edge:** Reeded

Date	Mintage	F	VF	XF	Unc	BU
1997	200,000	—	—	—	1.65	2.25
1997 Proof	—	—	—	—	—	—

KM# 41   10 TOLARJEV
5.7500 g., Copper Nickel, 22 mm.   **Obv:** Value within circle **Rev:** Stylized rearing horse **Edge:** Reeded

Date	Mintage	F	VF	XF	Unc	BU
2000	10,001,000	—	—	—	1.00	2.00
2000 Proof	800	Value: 12.00				

KM# 1   500 TOLARJEV
15.0000 g., 0.9250 Silver 0.4461 oz. ASW   **Subject:** 1st Anniversary of Independence **Obv:** Value within circle at left, date at right **Rev:** Leaf, design and value **Note:** Eight minor obverse and reverse varieties exist.

Date	Mintage	F	VF	XF	Unc	BU
1991 Proof	15,000	Value: 35.00				

KM# 10   500 TOLARJEV
15.0000 g., 0.9250 Silver 0.4461 oz. ASW, 32 mm.   **Subject:** Battle of Sisek **Obv:** Value and date **Rev:** City view, arms and date

Date	Mintage	F	VF	XF	Unc	BU
1993 Proof	5,000	Value: 28.50				

KM# 13   500 TOLARJEV
15.0000 g., 0.9250 Silver 0.4461 oz. ASW, 32 mm.   **Subject:** 300th Anniversary - Establishment of Operasorum Labacensium Academy **Obv:** Value and date **Rev:** Dates above angel

Date	Mintage	F	VF	XF	Unc	BU
1993 Proof	5,000	Value: 28.50				

KM# 17   500 TOLARJEV
15.0000 g., 0.9250 Silver 0.4461 oz. ASW, 32 mm. **Subject:** 50th Anniversary - Slovenian Bank **Obv:** Value **Rev:** Leaf and dates

Date	Mintage	F	VF	XF	Unc	BU
1994 Proof	5,000	Value: 28.50				

KM# 19   500 TOLARJEV
15.0000 g., 0.9250 Silver 0.4461 oz. ASW **Subject:** 1000th Anniversary - Bishop Abraham - Glagolistic Alphabet **Obv:** Value and date **Rev:** Feather and dates

Date	Mintage	F	VF	XF	Unc	BU
1994 Proof	3,000	Value: 28.50				

KM# 23   500 TOLARJEV
15.0000 g., 0.9250 Silver 0.4461 oz. ASW, 32 mm. **Subject:** 50th Anniversary - Defeat of Fascism **Obv:** Stylized design **Rev:** Stylized design, dates and value

Date	Mintage	F	VF	XF	Unc	BU
1995 Proof	3,000	Value: 28.50				

KM# 25   500 TOLARJEV
15.0000 g., 0.9250 Silver 0.4461 oz. ASW, 25 mm.
Series: F.A.O. **Subject:** 50th Anniversary - F.A.O. **Obv:** Vertical value **Rev:** F.A.O. logo above weeds

Date	Mintage	F	VF	XF	Unc	BU
1995 Proof	3,000	Value: 28.50				

KM# 27   500 TOLARJEV
15.0000 g., 0.9250 Silver 0.4461 oz. ASW, 32 mm. **Subject:** 100th Anniversary - Aljazev Stolp **Obv:** Value within triangle design below date **Rev:** Head facing in front of mountains

Date	Mintage	F	VF	XF	Unc	BU
1995 Proof	3,000	Value: 28.50				

KM# 30   500 TOLARJEV
15.0000 g., 0.9250 Silver 0.4461 oz. ASW, 32 mm. **Subject:** 150th Anniversary - First Railway in Slovenia **Obv:** Large value **Rev:** Design within wheel designed circle

Date	Mintage	F	VF	XF	Unc	BU
1996 Proof	4,000	Value: 28.50				

KM# 34   500 TOLARJEV
15.0000 g., 0.9250 Silver 0.4461 oz. ASW, 32 mm. **Subject:** 5th Anniversary of Independence **Obv:** Map of Slovenia divides date and value **Rev:** World globe and dates

Date	Mintage	F	VF	XF	Unc	BU
1996 Proof	3,000	Value: 28.50				

KM# 36   500 TOLARJEV
15.0000 g., 0.9250 Silver 0.4461 oz. ASW, 32 mm.
Series: Olympics **Obv:** Value above olympic rings and flag **Rev:** Gymnast and dates

Date	Mintage	F	VF	XF	Unc	BU
1996 Proof	3,000	Value: 27.50				

KM# 39   500 TOLARJEV
15.0000 g., 0.9250 Silver 0.4461 oz. ASW, 32 mm.
Subject: Zois Ziga

Date	Mintage	F	VF	XF	Unc	BU
1997 Proof	3,000	Value: 28.50				

KM# 2.1   5000 TOLARJEV
7.0000 g., 0.9000 Gold 0.2025 oz. AGW **Subject:** 1st Anniversary of Independence **Obv:** Value within circle at left, date at right **Rev:** Bird's beak at center of spiral

Date	Mintage	F	VF	XF	Unc	BU
1991 Proof	2,000	Value: 235				

KM# 2.2   5000 TOLARJEV
7.0000 g., 0.9000 Gold 0.2025 oz. AGW **Obv:** Value within circle at left, date at right **Rev:** Bird's beak below center of spiral

Date	Mintage	F	VF	XF	Unc	BU
1991 Proof	Inc. above	Value: 215				

KM# 11   5000 TOLARJEV
7.0000 g., 0.9000 Gold 0.2025 oz. AGW, 24 mm. **Subject:** Battle of Sisek **Obv:** Value below date **Rev:** City view, arms and date

Date	Mintage	F	VF	XF	Unc	BU
1993 Proof	2,000	Value: 215				

KM# 14   5000 TOLARJEV
7.0000 g., 0.9000 Gold 0.2025 oz. AGW, 24 mm. **Subject:** 300th Anniversary - Establishment of Operosorum Labacensium Academy **Obv:** Value below date **Rev:** Beehive among bees

Date	Mintage	F	VF	XF	Unc	BU
1993 Proof	2,000	Value: 225				

KM# 18   5000 TOLARJEV
7.0000 g., 0.9000 Gold 0.2025 oz. AGW, 24 mm. **Subject:** 50th Anniversary - Slovenian Bank **Obv:** Value and vertical date **Rev:** Leaf and dates

Date	Mintage	F	VF	XF	Unc	BU
1994 Proof	2,000	Value: 215				

KM# 20   5000 TOLARJEV
7.0000 g., 0.9000 Gold 0.2025 oz. AGW **Subject:** 1000th Anniversary - Bishop Abraham - Glagolitic Alphabet **Obv:** Value **Rev:** Feather

Date	Mintage	F	VF	XF	Unc	BU
1994 Proof	1,000	Value: 215				

KM# 24   5000 TOLARJEV
7.0000 g., 0.9000 Gold 0.2025 oz. AGW, 24 mm. **Subject:** 50th Anniversary - Defeat of Fascism **Obv:** Value **Rev:** Vertical chain link design and dates

Date	Mintage	F	VF	XF	Unc	BU
1995 Proof	1,000	Value: 215				

KM# 28   5000 TOLARJEV
7.0000 g., 0.9000 Gold 0.2025 oz. AGW, 24 mm. **Subject:** Aljazev Stolp and Mountain Summit **Obv:** Value within triangle design **Rev:** Head facing in front of mountains

Date	Mintage	F	VF	XF	Unc	BU
1995 Proof	1,000	Value: 215				

KM# 31 5000 TOLARJEV
7.0000 g., 0.9000 Gold 0.2025 oz. AGW, 24 mm. **Subject:** 100th Anniversary - First Railway in Slovenia **Obv:** Date within design at upper right, value at left **Rev:** Train below dates

Date	Mintage	F	VF	XF	Unc	BU
1996 Proof	1,000	Value: 220				

KM# 35 5000 TOLARJEV
7.0000 g., 0.9000 Gold 0.2025 oz. AGW, 24 mm. **Subject:** 5th Anniversary of Independence **Obv:** Value above date **Rev:** Pink carnation above dates

Date	Mintage	F	VF	XF	Unc	BU
1996 Proof	1,000	Value: 215				

KM# 37 5000 TOLARJEV
7.0000 g., 0.9000 Gold 0.2025 oz. AGW, 24 mm. **Series:** Olympics **Obv:** Value above olympic rings and flag **Rev:** Gymnast above dates

Date	Mintage	F	VF	XF	Unc	BU
1996 Proof	1,000	Value: 225				

KM# 40 5000 TOLARJEV
7.0000 g., 0.9000 Gold 0.2025 oz. AGW, 24 mm. **Subject:** Zois Ziga

Date	Mintage	F	VF	XF	Unc	BU
1997 Proof	1,000	Value: 215				

MINT SETS

KM#	Date	Mintage	Identification	Issue Price	Mkt Val
MS1	1992 (6)	—	KM#3-8	—	8.00
MS2	1992 (5)	15,000	KM#4-8	—	7.00
MS3	1993 (6)	—	KM#3-8	—	8.00
MS4	1993 (5)	15,000	KM#4-8	—	7.00
MS5	1996 (9)	300	KM#4-6, 29-30, 32-34, 36	—	45.00
MS6	1994	1,000	KM#3-8	—	35.00
MS7	1995	1,000	KM#3-8	—	35.00

PROOF SETS

KM#	Date	Mintage	Identification	Issue Price	Mkt Val
PS1	1991 (2)	—	KM#1, 2.2	—	325
PS2	1992 (6)	1,000	KM#3-8	—	35.00
PS3	1992 (5)	1,000	KM#4-8	—	30.00
PS4	1993 (6)	1,000	KM#3-8	—	35.00
PS5	1993 (5)	1,000	KM#4-8	—	30.00
PS6	1994 (6)	1,000	KM#3-8	—	35.00
PS7	1995 (6)	1,000	KM#3-8	—	35.00
PS8	1996 (9)	3,000	KM#4-6, 29-30, 32-34, 36	—	125
PS19	1996-1997-1998-1999 (28)	—	1996-1999 KM#3-8, 1996 KM#29, 32, 33, 1997 KM# 38	—	—
PS12	2000 (7)	—	KM#3, 4, 5, 6, 7, 8, 41	—	45.00

SOLOMON ISLANDS

The Solomon Islands are made up of approximately 200 islands. They are located in the southwest Pacific east of Papua New Guinea, have an area of 10,983 sq. mi. (28,450 sq. km.) and a population of *552,000. Capital: Honiara. The most important islands of the Solomon chain are Guadalcanal (scene of some of the fiercest fighting of World War II), Malaitia, New Georgia, Flor-ida, Vella Lavella, Choiseul, Rendova, San Cristobal, the Lord Howe group, the Santa Cruz islands, and the Duff group. Copra is the only important cash crop but it is hoped that timber will become an economic factor.

The Solomon Islands were discovered by Spanish navigator Alvaro de Mendana in 1567, and in 1569 he made an unsuc-cessful attempt to colonize them. European knowledge of the group would not be completed until the end of the 19th century. Germany declared a protectorate over the northern Solomon's in 1885. The British protectorate over the southern Solomons was established in 1893. In 1899 Germany transferred its claim to all Solomon Islands except Buka and Bougainville to Great Britain in exchange for recognition of German claims in Western Samoa. Australia occupied the two German islands in 1914, and admin-istered them after 1920.

The Japanese invaded the Solomons during 1942-43, but were driven out by an American counteroffensive after a series of bloody clashes.

Following World War II, the islands returned to the status of a British protectorate. In 1976 the protectorate was abolished, and the Solomons became a self-governing dependency. Full independence was achieved on July 7,1978. Solomon Islands is a member of the Commonwealth of Nations. Queen Elizabeth II is Head of State, as Queen of the Solomon Islands.

RULER
British, until 1978
Queen Elizabeth II (see above)

MINT MARK
FM - Franklin Mint, U.S.A.*

NOTE: From 1977-1985 the Franklin Mint produced coinage in up to 3 different qualities. Qualities of issue are designated in ( ) after each date and are defined as follows:

(M) MATTE - Normal circulation strike or a dull finish pro-duced by sandblasting special uncirculated (polish finish) or proof quality dies.

(U) SPECIAL UNCIRCULATED - Polished or proof-like in appearance without any frosted features.

(P) PROOF - The highest quality obtainable having mirror-like fields and frosted features.

MONETARY SYSTEM
100 Cents = 1 Dollar

COMMONWEALTH NATION
STANDARD COINAGE

KM# 1 CENT
2.6000 g., Bronze, 17.53 mm. **Ruler:** Elizabeth II **Series:** F.A.O. **Obv:** Young bust right **Obv. Leg.:** ELIZABETH II - SOLOMON ISLANDS **Rev:** Food bowl divides value **Edge:** Plain

Date	Mintage	F	VF	XF	Unc	BU
1977	1,828,000	—	—	0.10	0.15	0.35
1977FM (M)	6,000	—	—	—	0.50	0.75
1977FM (U)	—	—	—	—	1.25	2.00
1977FM (P)	14,000	Value: 1.00				
1978FM (M)	6,000	—	—	—	0.50	0.75
1978FM (U)	544	—	—	—	1.25	2.00
1978FM (P)	5,122	Value: 1.00				
1979FM (M)	6,000	—	—	—	0.50	0.75
1979FM (U)	677	—	—	—	1.25	2.00
1979FM (P)	2,845	Value: 1.50				
1980FM (M)	6,000	—	—	—	0.50	0.75
1980FM (U)	624	—	—	—	1.25	2.00
1980FM (P)	1,031	Value: 1.50				
1981	—	—	—	—	0.50	0.75
1981FM (M)	6,000	—	—	—	0.50	0.75
1981FM (U)	212	—	—	—	2.00	3.00
1981FM (P)	448	Value: 1.50				
1982FM (U)	—	—	—	—	1.25	2.00
1982FM (P)	—	Value: 1.50				
1983FM (M)	—	—	—	—	0.50	0.75
1983FM (U)	200	—	—	—	2.00	3.00
1983FM (P)	—	Value: 1.50				

KM# 1a CENT
Bronze Plated Steel, 17.53 mm. **Series:** F.A.O. **Obv:** Young bust right **Rev:** Food bowl divides value **Edge:** Plain

Date	Mintage	F	VF	XF	Unc	BU
1985	—	—	—	—	0.25	0.50

KM# 24 CENT
2.3000 g., Bronze Plated Steel, 17.53 mm. **Ruler:** Elizabeth II **Obv:** Crowned head right **Obv. Leg.:** ELIZABETH II - SOLOMON ISLANDS **Rev:** Food bowl divides value **Edge:** Plain

Date	Mintage	F	VF	XF	Unc	BU
1987	—	—	—	—	0.35	0.75

Date	Mintage	F	VF	XF	Unc	BU
1989	—	—	—	—	0.35	0.75
1996	—	—	—	—	0.35	0.75

KM# 2 2 CENTS
5.2000 g., Bronze, 21.59 mm. **Subject:** Eagle Spirit of Malaita **Obv:** Young bust right **Rev:** Eagle spirit below value **Edge:** Plain

Date	Mintage	F	VF	XF	Unc	BU
1977	2,400,000	—	—	0.10	0.25	0.50
1977FM (M)	6,000	—	—	—	0.75	1.25
1977FM (U)	—	—	—	—	1.50	2.50
1977FM (P)	14,000	Value: 1.50				
1978FM (M)	6,000	—	—	—	0.75	1.25
1978FM (U)	544	—	—	—	1.50	2.50
1978FM (P)	5,122	Value: 1.50				
1979FM (M)	6,000	—	—	—	0.75	1.25
1979FM (U)	677	—	—	—	1.50	2.50
1979FM (P)	2,845	Value: 1.75				
1980FM (M)	6,000	—	—	—	0.75	1.25
1980FM (U)	624	—	—	—	1.50	2.50
1980FM (P)	1,031	—	—	—	1.25	2.00
1981FM (M)	6,000	—	—	—	0.75	1.25
1981FM (U)	212	—	—	—	1.50	2.50
1981FM (P)	448	Value: 2.00				
1982FM (U)	—	—	—	—	1.50	2.50
1982FM (P)	—	Value: 2.00				
1983FM (M)	—	—	—	—	0.75	1.25
1983FM (U)	200	—	—	—	1.50	2.50
1983FM (P)	—	Value: 2.00				

KM# 2a 2 CENTS
Bronze Plated Steel Galvanized steel planchet, 21.6 mm. **Ruler:** Elizabeth II **Subject:** Eagle Spirit of Malaita **Obv:** Crowned young bust right **Obv. Leg.:** ELIZABETH II - SOLOMON ISLANDS **Rev:** Eagle spirit below value **Edge:** Plain

Date	Mintage	F	VF	XF	Unc	BU
1985	—	—	0.75	1.50	2.75	4.00

KM# 25 2 CENTS
Bronze Plated Steel, 21.6 mm. **Ruler:** Elizabeth II **Obv:** Crowned head right **Obv. Leg.:** ELIZABETH II - SOLOMON ISLANDS **Rev:** Eagle spirit below value **Edge:** Plain

Date	Mintage	F	VF	XF	Unc	BU
1987	—	—	—	—	0.35	0.75
1989	—	—	—	—	0.35	0.75
1996	—	—	—	—	0.35	0.75

KM# 3 5 CENTS
2.8000 g., Copper-Nickel, 19.4 mm. **Subject:** Santa Ysabel **Obv:** Young bust right **Rev:** Native mask and value **Edge:** Reeded

Date	Mintage	F	VF	XF	Unc	BU
1977	1,200,000	—	—	0.15	0.35	0.75
1977FM (U)	—	—	—	—	1.50	2.50
1977FM (M)	6,000	—	—	—	1.00	1.50
1977FM (P)	14,000	Value: 1.75				
1978FM (M)	6,000	—	—	—	1.00	1.50
1978FM (U)	544	—	—	—	1.50	2.50
1978FM (P)	5,122	Value: 2.00				
1979FM (M)	6,000	—	—	—	1.00	1.50
1979FM (U)	677	—	—	—	1.50	2.50
1979FM (P)	2,845	Value: 2.00				
1980	—	—	—	—	—	—
1980FM (M)	6,000	—	—	—	1.00	1.50
1980FM (U)	624	—	—	—	1.50	2.50
1980FM (P)	1,031	Value: 2.50				
1981	—	—	—	—	—	—
1981FM (M)	6,000	—	—	—	1.00	1.50
1981FM (U)	212	—	—	—	1.50	2.50
1981FM (P)	448	Value: 2.50				
1982FM (U)	—	—	—	—	1.50	2.50
1982FM (P)	—	Value: 2.50				
1983FM (M)	—	—	—	—	1.00	1.50
1983FM (U)	200	—	—	—	2.00	3.50
1983FM (P)	—	Value: 2.50				
1985	—	—	—	—	0.30	0.50

KM# 26   5 CENTS
2.8000 g., Copper-Nickel, 19.4 mm. **Ruler:** Elizabeth II
Obv: Crowned head right **Obv. Leg.:** ELIZABETH II - SOLOMON
ISLANDS **Rev:** Native mask and value **Edge:** Reeded

Date	Mintage	F	VF	XF	Unc	BU
1987	—	—	—	—	0.50	1.00
1988	—	—	—	—	0.50	1.00
1989	—	—	—	—	0.50	1.00

KM# 26a   5 CENTS
Nickel Plated Steel Galvanized steel planchet., 18.40 mm.
Ruler: Elizabeth II **Obv:** Crowned bust right **Obv. Leg.:**
ELIZABETH II - SOLOMON ISLANDS **Rev:** Value at left, native
mask at center right

Date	Mintage	F	VF	XF	Unc	BU
1993	—	—	—	—	0.50	1.00
1996	—	—	—	—	0.50	1.00

KM# 4   10 CENTS
5.6500 g., Copper-Nickel, 23.6 mm. **Subject:** Ngorieru
Obv: Young bust right **Rev:** Sea spirit divides value
Edge: Reeded

Date	Mintage	F	VF	XF	Unc	BU
1977	3,600,000	—	—	0.20	0.50	0.75
1977FM (M)	6,000	—	—	—	1.25	2.00
1977FM (U)	—	—	—	—	2.50	4.00
1977FM (P)	14,000	Value: 2.50				
1978FM (M)	6,000	—	—	—	1.25	2.00
1978FM (U)	544	—	—	—	2.50	4.00
1978FM (P)	5,122	Value: 2.75				
1979FM (M)	6,000	—	—	—	1.25	2.00
1979FM (U)	677	—	—	—	2.50	4.00
1979FM (P)	2,845	Value: 3.50				
1980FM (M)	6,000	—	—	—	1.25	2.00
1980FM (U)	624	—	—	—	2.50	4.00
1980FM (P)	1,031	Value: 4.00				
1981FM (M)	6,000	—	—	—	1.25	2.00
1981FM (U)	212	—	—	—	2.50	4.00
1981FM (P)	448	Value: 4.00				
1982FM (U)	—	—	—	—	2.50	4.00
1982FM (P)	—	Value: 4.00				
1983FM (M)	—	—	—	—	1.25	2.00
1983FM (U)	200	—	—	—	3.50	5.00
1983FM (P)	—	Value: 4.00				

KM# 27   10 CENTS
5.6500 g., Copper-Nickel, 23.6 mm. **Subject:** Ngorieru
Obv: Crowned head right **Rev:** Sea spirit divides value
Edge: Reeded

Date	Mintage	F	VF	XF	Unc	BU
1988	—	—	—	—	0.65	1.00

KM# 27a   10 CENTS
Nickel Plated Steel Galvanized steel planchet., 23.6 mm.
Ruler: Elizabeth II **Subject:** Ngorieru **Obv:** Crowned head right
Obv. Leg.: ELIZABETH II - SOLOMON ISLANDS **Rev:** Sea spirit
divides value **Edge:** Reeded

Date	Mintage	F	VF	XF	Unc	BU
1990	—	—	—	—	0.65	1.00
1993	—	—	—	—	0.65	1.00
1996	—	—	—	—	0.65	1.00
2000	—	—	—	—	0.65	1.00

KM# 5   20 CENTS
11.2500 g., Copper-Nickel, 28.5 mm. **Obv:** Young bust right
Rev: Malaita pendant design within circle, denomination appears
twice in legend **Edge:** Reeded

Date	Mintage	F	VF	XF	Unc	BU
1977	3,000,000	—	0.15	0.35	0.80	1.25
1977FM (M)	5,000	—	—	—	2.50	3.50
1977FM (P)	14,000	Value: 3.50				
1978	293,000	—	0.25	0.50	1.00	1.75
1978FM (M)	5,000	—	—	—	2.50	3.50
1978FM (U)	544	—	—	—	3.50	5.50
1978FM (P)	5,122	Value: 3.75				
1979FM (M)	5,000	—	—	—	2.50	3.50
1979FM (U)	677	—	—	—	3.50	5.00
1979FM (P)	2,845	Value: 3.75				
1980FM (M)	5,000	—	—	—	2.50	3.50
1980FM (U)	624	—	—	—	3.50	5.00
1980FM (P)	1,031	Value: 3.75				
1981FM (M)	5,000	—	—	—	2.50	3.50
1981FM (U)	212	—	—	—	4.00	6.00
1981FM (P)	448	Value: 4.00				
1982FM (U)	—	—	—	—	4.00	6.00
1982FM (P)	—	Value: 4.00				
1983FM (M)	—	—	—	—	2.50	3.50
1983FM (U)	200	—	—	—	5.00	7.00
1983FM (P)	—	Value: 4.00				

KM# 28   20 CENTS
11.2500 g., Nickel Plated Steel Galvanized steel planchet.,
28.5 mm. **Ruler:** Elizabeth II **Obv:** Crowned head right
Obv. Leg.: ELIZABETH II _ SOLOMON ISLANDS **Rev:** Malaita
pendant design within circle, denomination appears twice in
legend **Edge:** Reeded

Date	Mintage	F	VF	XF	Unc	BU
1987	—	—	—	—	0.85	1.25
1989	—	—	—	—	0.85	1.25
1993	—	—	—	—	0.85	1.25
1996	—	—	—	—	0.85	1.25
1997	—	—	—	—	0.85	1.25
2000	—	—	—	—	0.85	1.25

KM# 82   20 CENTS
Copper-Nickel, 26 mm. **Subject:** FAO **Obv:** Crowned bust right
Rev: Native woman with basket on head **Edge:** Reeded

Date	Mintage	F	VF	XF	Unc	BU
1995	20,200	—	—	—	3.00	4.00

KM# 23   50 CENTS
Copper-Nickel, 29.5 mm. **Subject:** 10th Anniversary of
Independence **Obv:** Crowned head right **Rev:** Arms with
supporters **Edge:** Plain

Date	Mintage	F	VF	XF	Unc	BU
1988	—	—	—	—	2.00	3.00

KM# 29   50 CENTS
10.0000 g., Copper-Nickel, 29.5 mm. **Ruler:** Elizabeth II
Obv: Crowned head right **Obv. Leg.:** ELIZABETH II - SOLOMON
ISLANDS **Rev:** Arms with supporters **Edge:** Plain
Note: Circulation type.

Date	Mintage	F	VF	XF	Unc	BU
1990	—	—	—	—	2.00	3.00
1995	—	—	—	—	2.00	3.00
1996	—	—	—	—	2.00	3.00
1997	—	—	—	—	2.00	3.00

KM# 6   DOLLAR
13.4000 g., Copper-Nickel, 30 mm. **Subject:** Nusu-Nusu head
Obv: Young bust right **Rev:** Sea spirit statue divides value
Edge: Plain

Date	Mintage	F	VF	XF	Unc	BU
1977	1,500,000	—	—	1.00	2.00	3.00
1977FM (M)	3,000	—	—	—	3.00	5.00
1977FM (P)	14,000	Value: 4.50				
1978FM (M)	3,000	—	—	—	3.00	5.00
1978FM (U)	544	—	—	—	4.50	6.00
1978FM (P)	5,122	Value: 4.50				
1979FM (M)	3,000	—	—	—	3.00	5.00
1979FM (U)	677	—	—	—	4.50	6.00
1979FM (P)	2,845	Value: 5.00				
1980FM (M)	3,000	—	—	—	3.00	5.00
1980FM (U)	624	—	—	—	4.50	6.00
1980FM (P)	1,031	Value: 5.50				
1981FM (M)	3,000	—	—	—	3.00	5.00
1981FM (U)	212	—	—	—	7.00	10.00
1981FM (P)	448	Value: 6.00				
1982FM (U)	—	—	—	—	4.50	6.00
1982FM (P)	—	Value: 6.00				
1983FM (M)	—	—	—	—	3.00	5.00
1983FM (U)	200	—	—	—	7.00	10.00
1983FM (P)	—	Value: 5.50				

KM# 19   DOLLAR
Copper-Nickel **Series:** 1984 Olympics **Obv:** Young bust right
Rev: Runners above torch and value

Date	Mintage	F	VF	XF	Unc	BU
1984	5,000	—	—	—	4.50	6.00

KM# 30   DOLLAR
Copper-Nickel **Subject:** 50th Anniversary of Pearl Harbor
Obv: Crowned head right **Rev:** Pearl Harbor war scene within
circle

Date	Mintage	F	VF	XF	Unc	BU
1991	—	—	—	—	3.00	5.00

KM# 30a   DOLLAR
28.2800 g., 0.9250 Silver 0.8410 oz. ASW **Subject:** 50th
Anniversary of Pearl Harbor **Obv:** Crowned head right **Rev:** Pearl
Harbor war scene

Date	Mintage	F	VF	XF	Unc	BU
1991 Proof	Est. 25,000	Value: 14.50				

KM# 35 DOLLAR
Copper-Nickel **Subject:** 50th Anniversary - Battle of the Coral Sea
Obv: Crowned head right **Rev:** Planes bombing ship within circle

Date	Mintage	F	VF	XF	Unc	BU
1992	—	—	—	—	3.00	5.00

KM# 35a DOLLAR
28.2800 g., 0.9250 Silver 0.8410 oz. ASW **Subject:** 50th
Anniversary - Battle of the Coral Sea **Obv:** Crowned head right
Rev: War planes bombing ships within circle

Date	Mintage	F	VF	XF	Unc	BU
1992 Proof	Est. 25,000	Value: 16.00				

KM# 41 DOLLAR
Copper-Nickel **Subject:** 50th Anniversary - Battle of Guadalcanal
Obv: Crowned head right **Rev:** Uniformed soldiers within circle

Date	Mintage	F	VF	XF	Unc	BU
1992	—	—	—	—	4.00	6.00

KM# 41a DOLLAR
28.2800 g., 0.9250 Silver 0.8410 oz. ASW **Subject:** 50th
Anniversary - Battle of Guadalcanal **Obv:** Crowned head right
Rev: Uniformed soldiers within circle

Date	Mintage	F	VF	XF	Unc	BU
1992 Proof	Est. 25,000	Value: 15.00				

KM# 77 DOLLAR
28.3000 g., Copper-Nickel, 38.6 mm. **Subject:** Queen Mother
Obv: Crowned head right **Rev:** Queen Mother's Coronation
within beaded circle **Edge:** Reeded

Date	Mintage	F	VF	XF	Unc	BU
1995	30,000	—	—	—	6.00	8.00

KM# 89 DOLLAR
28.2800 g., 0.9250 Silver 0.8410 oz. ASW, 38 mm.
Ruler: Elizabeth II **Series:** FAO - FOOD FOR ALL **Obv:** Bust
right **Rev:** 2 palm trees on island divide value, FAO symbol above,
inscription below **Edge:** Reeded

Date	Mintage	F	VF	XF	Unc	BU
1995	—	—	—	—	—	—

KM# 72 DOLLAR
13.4500 g., Copper-Nickel, 30 mm. **Ruler:** Elizabeth II
Obv: Crowned head right **Obv. Leg.:** ELIZABETH II - SOLOMON
ISLANDS **Rev:** Sea spirit statue divides value **Edge:** Plain

---

Date	Mintage	F	VF	XF	Unc	BU
1996	—	—	—	—	2.50	4.00
1997	—	—	—	—	2.50	4.00

KM# 64 DOLLAR
Copper-Nickel **Subject:** World Wildlife Fund - Conserving
Nature **Obv:** Crowned head right **Rev:** Eagle descending on fish

Date	Mintage	F	VF	XF	Unc	BU
1998	—	—	—	—	7.50	10.00

KM# 64a DOLLAR
28.2800 g., 0.9250 Silver 0.8410 oz. ASW **Subject:** World
Wildlife Fund - Conserving Nature **Obv:** Crowned head right
Rev: Eagle descending on fish

Date	Mintage	F	VF	XF	Unc	BU
1998 Proof	—	Value: 22.00				

KM# 65 DOLLAR
32.5500 g., Copper-Nickel, 38.62 mm. **Ruler:** Elizabeth II
Series: Olympics 2000 **Obv:** Head with tiara right **Rev:** Multicolor
koala swimming below torch within map **Edge:** Reeded

Date	Mintage	F	VF	XF	Unc	BU
2000 Proof	50,000	Value: 13.50				

KM# 66 DOLLAR
32.5500 g., Copper-Nickel, 38.62 mm. **Ruler:** Elizabeth II
Series: Olympics 2000 **Obv:** Head with tiara right **Rev:** Multicolor
kangaroo sail boarding **Edge:** Reeded

Date	Mintage	F	VF	XF	Unc	BU
2000 Proof	50,000	Value: 13.50				

KM# 7 5 DOLLARS
28.2800 g., 0.9250 Silver 0.8410 oz. ASW, 40 mm. **Obv:** Young
bust right **Rev:** Fossilized clam shell on top of circle **Edge:** Reeded

Date	Mintage	F	VF	XF	Unc	BU
1977FM (U)	200	—	—	—	40.00	—
1977FM (P)	15,000	Value: 13.50				
1978FM (P)	5,148	Value: 15.00				
1979FM (P)	2,845	Value: 16.00				
1980FM (P)	1,031	Value: 18.00				

Date	Mintage	F	VF	XF	Unc	BU
1981FM (P)	448	Value: 22.50				
1983FM (P)	339	Value: 25.00				

KM# 7a 5 DOLLARS
Copper-Nickel **Obv:** Young bust right **Rev:** Fossilized
clam shell on top of circle **Edge:** Reeded

Date	Mintage	F	VF	XF	Unc	BU
1978FM (M)	200	—	—	—	25.00	—
1978FM (U)	544	—	—	—	15.00	—
1979FM (M)	200	—	—	—	25.00	—
1979FM (U)	677	—	—	—	14.00	—
1980FM (M)	200	—	—	—	25.00	—
1980FM (U)	624	—	—	—	14.00	—
1981FM (M)	200	—	—	—	25.00	—
1981FM (U)	212	—	—	—	25.00	—
1983FM (U)	202	—	—	—	25.00	—

KM# 8 5 DOLLARS
28.2800 g., 0.9250 Silver 0.8410 oz. ASW **Subject:** Coronation
Jubilee **Obv:** Young bust right **Rev:** Crown flanked by supporters

Date	Mintage	F	VF	XF	Unc	BU
1978	8,886	Value: 14.50				

KM# 13 5 DOLLARS
Copper-Nickel, 40 mm. **Subject:** Battle of Guadalcanal
Obv: Young bust right **Rev:** Uniformed soldiers

Date	Mintage	F	VF	XF	Unc	BU
1982FM (U)	—	—	—	—	10.00	12.00

KM# 13a 5 DOLLARS
28.2800 g., 0.9250 Silver 0.8410 oz. ASW, 40 mm. **Subject:** Battle
of Guadalcanal **Obv:** Young bust right **Rev:** Uniformed soldiers

Date	Mintage	F	VF	XF	Unc	BU
1982FM (P)	1,368	Value: 22.00				

KM# 15 5 DOLLARS
30.2800 g., 0.5000 Silver 0.4867 oz. ASW **Subject:** 30th
Anniversary of Coronation **Obv:** Young bust right **Rev:** Crossed
scepters divides dates, crown and cross on globe design

Date	Mintage	F	VF	XF	Unc	BU
1983FM (P)	2,944	Value: 9.00				

KM# 16 5 DOLLARS
28.2800 g., 0.9250 Silver 0.8410 oz. ASW **Series:** International Year of the Child **Obv:** Young bust right **Rev:** Figures rowing boat divides emblems

Date	Mintage	F	VF	XF	Unc	BU
1983 Proof	5,775	Value: 14.50				

KM# 22 5 DOLLARS
28.2800 g., 0.9250 Silver 0.8410 oz. ASW **Series:** Decade for Women **Obv:** Crowned head right **Rev:** Teacher and student reading within circle

Date	Mintage	F	VF	XF	Unc	BU
1985 Proof	1,050	Value: 17.50				

KM# 63 5 DOLLARS
10.0000 g., 0.5000 Silver 0.1607 oz. ASW **Subject:** Alvaro Mendana de Neyra **Obv:** Crowned head right **Rev:** Bust with hat facing, palm tree and ancient boat at left

Date	Mintage	F	VF	XF	Unc	BU
1994 Proof	Est. 20,000	Value: 7.00				

KM# 54 5 DOLLARS
Copper-Nickel **Subject:** MacArthur Accepting Japanese Surrender **Obv:** Crowned head right **Rev:** Uniformed bust left at far right

Date	Mintage	F	VF	XF	Unc	BU
1995	—	—	—	—	5.00	7.00

KM# 54a 5 DOLLARS
28.2800 g., 0.9250 Silver 0.8410 oz. ASW **Subject:** MacArthur Accepting Japanese Surrender **Obv:** Crowned head right **Rev:** Uniformed bust left at far right **Note:** Similar to 50 Dollars, KM#57.

Date	Mintage	F	VF	XF	Unc	BU
1995 Proof	Est. 10,000	Value: 17.50				

KM# 78 5 DOLLARS
28.2000 g., 0.9250 Silver 0.8386 oz. ASW, 38.6 mm. **Subject:** Queen's 70th Birthday **Obv:** Crowned bust right **Rev:** Royal yacht **Edge:** Reeded

Date	Mintage	F	VF	XF	Unc	BU
1996 Proof	—	Value: 22.00				

KM# 80 5 DOLLARS
9.9400 g., 0.5250 Silver 0.1678 oz. ASW, 29.9 mm. **Obv:** Crowned head right **Rev:** Queen and Diana at the races **Edge:** Reeded

Date	Mintage	F	VF	XF	Unc	BU
1998 Proof	—	Value: 8.00				

KM# 69 5 DOLLARS
20.1000 g., 0.8000 Silver 0.5170 oz. ASW, 33.9 mm. **Subject:** Ship of Death **Obv:** Crowned head right **Rev:** Sailing ship **Edge:** Reeded

Date	Mintage	F	VF	XF	Unc	BU
1999 Proof	Est. 20,000	Value: 10.00				

KM# 70 5 DOLLARS
32.2000 g., Copper-Nickel, 38.6 mm. **Obv:** Head with tiara right **Obv. Insc.:** Portrait from dies of Solomon Islands KM# 67-68 **Rev:** Pied Cormorant **Rev. Insc.:** From dies from New Zealand KM#125 **Edge:** Reeded **Note:** Mule.

Date	Mintage	F	VF	XF	Unc	BU
2000 Proof	—	Value: 650				

Note: This coin is included in a New Zealand Proof set dated 2000

KM# 67 5 DOLLARS
24.9100 g., 0.9250 Silver 0.7408 oz. ASW, 38.7 mm. **Series:** Olympics 2000 **Obv:** Head with tiara right **Rev:** Stylized multicolor koala tennis player below torch within map **Edge:** Reeded **Note:** Struck at Valcambi.

Date	Mintage	F	VF	XF	Unc	BU
2000 Proof	15,000	Value: 14.00				

KM# 68 5 DOLLARS
24.9100 g., 0.9250 Silver 0.7408 oz. ASW **Series:** Olympics 2000 **Obv:** Crowned head right **Rev:** Stylized multicolored kangaroo bicyclist below torch within map

Date	Mintage	F	VF	XF	Unc	BU
2000 Proof	15,000	Value: 14.00				

KM# 10 10 DOLLARS
Copper-Nickel, 45 mm. **Obv:** Young bust right **Rev:** Flying frigate bird above value **Edge:** Reeded

Date	Mintage	F	VF	XF	Unc	BU
1979FM (M)	100	—	—	—	35.00	—
1979FM (U)	777	—	—	—	16.00	—
1980FM (M)	100	—	—	—	35.00	—
1980FM (U)	624	—	—	—	16.00	—
1981FM (M)	100	—	—	—	35.00	—
1981FM (U)	212	—	—	—	18.50	—
1982FM (U)	—	—	—	—	16.00	—

KM# 10a 10 DOLLARS
42.2700 g., 0.9250 Silver 1.2570 oz. ASW, 45 mm. **Obv:** Young bust right **Rev:** Frigate bird above value **Edge:** Reeded

Date	Mintage	F	VF	XF	Unc	BU
1979FM (P)	4,670	Value: 20.00				
1980FM (P)	1,569	Value: 22.50				
1981FM (P)	593	Value: 32.50				
1982FM (P)	579	Value: 32.50				

KM# 17 10 DOLLARS
Copper-Nickel, 45 mm. **Subject:** 5th Anniversary of Independence **Obv:** Young bust right **Rev:** Arms with supporters in front of flag

Date	Mintage	F	VF	XF	Unc	BU
1983FM (U)	202	—	—	—	16.50	—

KM# 17a 10 DOLLARS
40.5000 g., 0.9250 Silver 1.2044 oz. ASW, 45 mm. **Subject:** 5th Anniversary of Independence **Obv:** Young bust right **Rev:** Arms with supporters in front of flag

Date	Mintage	F	VF	XF	Unc	BU
1983FM (P)	425	Value: 32.50				

KM# 20 10 DOLLARS
33.4400 g., 0.9250 Silver 0.9944 oz. ASW **Series:** 1984 Olympics
Obv: Young bust right **Rev:** Runners above torch and value

Date	Mintage	F	VF	XF	Unc	BU
1984 Proof	2,500	Value: 20.00				

KM# 47 10 DOLLARS
31.8000 g., 0.9250 Silver 0.9457 oz. ASW **Subject:** Alvaro de
Neyra **Obv:** Crowned head right **Rev:** Half figure with hat facing

Date	Mintage	F	VF	XF	Unc	BU
1991 Proof	—	Value: 17.50				

KM# 31 10 DOLLARS
3.1300 g., 0.9990 Gold 0.1005 oz. AGW, 16.5 mm.
Subject: 50th Anniversary of Pearl Harbor **Obv:** Crowned head
right **Rev:** Map of Pearl Harbor

Date	Mintage	F	VF	XF	Unc	BU
1991 Proof	Est. 500	Value: 110				

KM# 48 10 DOLLARS
31.4200 g., 0.9250 Silver 0.9344 oz. ASW **Series:** 1992
Olympics **Obv:** Crowned head right **Rev:** Runner

Date	Mintage	F	VF	XF	Unc	BU
1991 Proof	Est. 40,000	Value: 14.50				

KM# 36 10 DOLLARS
3.1300 g., 0.9990 Gold 0.1005 oz. AGW, 16.5 mm.
Subject: 50th Anniversary - Battle of the Coral Sea **Rev:** Planes
dropping bombs within circle

Date	Mintage	F	VF	XF	Unc	BU
1992 Proof	500	Value: 110				

KM# 40 10 DOLLARS
31.4700 g., 0.9250 Silver 0.9359 oz. ASW **Subject:** First Lunar
Vehicle **Obv:** Crowned head right **Rev:** First lunar vehicle with
astronaut

Date	Mintage	F	VF	XF	Unc	BU
1992 Proof	Est. 10,000	Value: 16.00				

KM# 42 10 DOLLARS
3.1300 g., 0.9990 Gold 0.1005 oz. AGW, 16.5 mm. **Subject:** 50th
Anniversary - Battle of Guadalcanal **Rev:** Battle scene within circle

Date	Mintage	F	VF	XF	Unc	BU
1992 Proof	500	Value: 110				

KM# 46 10 DOLLARS
31.4700 g., 0.9250 Silver 0.9359 oz. ASW **Subject:** 40th
Anniversary - Queen Elizabeth's Coronation **Obv:** Crowned head
right **Rev:** Crowned figure on throne facing

Date	Mintage	F	VF	XF	Unc	BU
1992 Proof	Est. 50,000	Value: 15.00				

KM# 50 10 DOLLARS
31.4700 g., 0.9250 Silver 0.9359 oz. ASW **Series:** 1992
Olympics **Obv:** Crowned head right **Rev:** Boxer

Date	Mintage	F	VF	XF	Unc	BU
1992 Proof	40,000	Value: 14.50				

KM# 51 10 DOLLARS
31.4700 g., 0.9250 Silver 0.9359 oz. ASW **Series:** Endangered
Wildlife **Obv:** Crowned head right **Rev:** Saltwater crocodile

Date	Mintage	F	VF	XF	Unc	BU
1992 Proof	Est. 10,000	Value: 35.00				

KM# 49 10 DOLLARS
28.2800 g., 0.9250 Silver 0.8410 oz. ASW **Subject:** 100 Years
as British Protectorate **Obv:** Crowned head right **Rev:** Cameo to
upper left of ship

Date	Mintage	F	VF	XF	Unc	BU
1993 Proof	5,000	Value: 22.00				

KM# 59 10 DOLLARS
31.4700 g., 0.9250 Silver 0.9359 oz. ASW **Subject:** Protect Our
World **Obv:** Crowned head right **Rev:** Orchid and butterfly

Date	Mintage	F	VF	XF	Unc	BU
1993 Proof	Est. 10,000	Value: 18.50				

KM# 52 10 DOLLARS
28.2800 g., 0.9250 Silver 0.8410 oz. ASW **Subject:** Sailing ship
"Swallow" **Obv:** Crowned head right **Rev:** Ship divides cameos

Date	Mintage	F	VF	XF	Unc	BU
1994 Proof	Est. 15,000	Value: 14.50				

KM# 53 10 DOLLARS
28.2800 g., 0.9250 Silver 0.8410 oz. ASW **Series:** 1996
Olympics **Obv:** Crowned head right **Rev:** Relay runners

Date	Mintage	F	VF	XF	Unc	BU
1994 Proof	Est. 30,000	Value: 13.50				

KM# 55 10 DOLLARS
3.1300 g., 0.9990 Gold 0.1005 oz. AGW, 16.5 mm. **Rev:** Marine
and armored tank within circle

Date	Mintage	F	VF	XF	Unc	BU
1995 Proof	Est. 500	Value: 110				

KM# 71 10 DOLLARS
31.4400 g., 0.9250 Silver 0.9350 oz. ASW, 38.5 mm.
Subject: Queen Mother **Obv:** Crowned head right
Rev: Coronation scene within beaded circle **Edge:** Reeded

Date	Mintage	F	VF	XF	Unc	BU
1995 Proof	—	Value: 16.50				

KM# 79   10 DOLLARS
31.6000 g., 0.9250 Silver 0.9397 oz. ASW, 38.6 mm.
Obv: Crowned head right **Rev:** Queen Elizabeth and Diana at the races **Edge:** Reeded

Date	Mintage	F	VF	XF	Unc	BU
1998 Proof	—				Value: 18.50	

KM# 73   10 DOLLARS
28.3200 g., 0.9250 Silver with gilt outer ring 0.8422 oz. ASW, 38.5 mm. **Subject:** Queen Mother **Obv:** Crowned head right within beaded circle **Rev:** Inspecting the bombing of Buckingham Palace **Edge:** Reeded

Date	Mintage	F	VF	XF	Unc	BU
2000 Proof	—				Value: 17.50	

KM# 74   10 DOLLARS
31.5500 g., 0.9250 Silver 0.9382 oz. ASW, 38.7 mm.
Obv: Crowned head right **Rev:** Missionary ship **Edge:** Reeded

Date	Mintage	F	VF	XF	Unc	BU
2000 Proof	—				Value: 20.00	

KM# 88   10 DOLLARS
1.2000 g., Gold, 13.91 mm. **Ruler:** Elizabeth II **Obv:** Crowned head right **Rev:** Statue of Nguzunguzu **Edge:** Reeded

Date	Mintage	F	VF	XF	Unc	BU
2000 Proof	—				Value: 55.00	

KM# 32   25 DOLLARS
7.8100 g., 0.9990 Gold 0.2508 oz. AGW, 22 mm. **Subject:** 50th Anniversary - Pearl Harbor **Obv:** Crowned head right **Rev:** Pearl Harbor battle scene within circle

Date	Mintage	F	VF	XF	Unc	BU
1991 Proof	Est. 3,000				Value: 260	

KM# 37   25 DOLLARS
7.8100 g., 0.9990 Gold 0.2508 oz. AGW, 22 mm. **Subject:** 50th Anniversary - Battle of the Coral Sea **Rev:** Pearl Harbor battle scene within circle

Date	Mintage	F	VF	XF	Unc	BU
1992 Proof	Est. 3,000				Value: 260	

KM# 43   25 DOLLARS
7.8100 g., 0.9990 Gold 0.2508 oz. AGW, 22 mm. **Subject:** 50th Anniversary - Battle of Guadalcanal **Rev:** Uniformed soldiers and armored tank in woods within circle

Date	Mintage	F	VF	XF	Unc	BU
1992 Proof	Est. 3,000				Value: 260	

KM# 56   25 DOLLARS
7.8100 g., 0.9990 Gold 0.2508 oz. AGW, 22 mm. **Subject:** 50th Anniversary - Iwo Jima Flag Raising **Rev:** Uniformed soldiers raising flag within circle

Date	Mintage	F	VF	XF	Unc	BU
1995 Proof	Est. 2,500				Value: 260	

KM# 81   25 DOLLARS
500.0000 g., 0.9990 Silver 16.058 oz. ASW, 89 mm.
Subject: Discovery of the Solomon Islands by Kermadec
Obv: Crowned head right **Rev:** Sailing ship **Edge:** Reeded

Date	Mintage	F	VF	XF	Unc	BU
2000 Proof	—				Value: 245	

KM# 33   50 DOLLARS
15.6000 g., 0.9990 Gold 0.5010 oz. AGW, 27 mm.
Subject: 50th Anniversary - Pearl Harbor **Obv:** Crowned head right **Rev:** Pearl Harbor battle scene within circle

Date	Mintage	F	VF	XF	Unc	BU
1991 Proof	Est. 500				Value: 485	

KM# 38   50 DOLLARS
15.6000 g., 0.9990 Gold 0.5010 oz. AGW, 27 mm.
Subject: 50th Anniversary - Battle of the Coral Sea **Rev:** Planes bombing ship within circle

Date	Mintage	F	VF	XF	Unc	BU
1992 Proof	Est. 500				Value: 485	

KM# 44   50 DOLLARS
15.6000 g., 0.9990 Gold 0.5010 oz. AGW, 27 mm.
Subject: 50th Anniversary - Battle of Guadalcanal
Rev: Uniformed soldiers within circle

Date	Mintage	F	VF	XF	Unc	BU
1992 Proof	Est. 500				Value: 485	

KM# 60   50 DOLLARS
7.7600 g., 0.5830 Gold 0.1454 oz. AGW **Series:** Endangered Wildlife **Obv:** Crowned head right **Rev:** Descending eagle

Date	Mintage	F	VF	XF	Unc	BU
1993 Proof	Est. 3,000				Value: 160	

KM# 61   50 DOLLARS
155.5175 g., 0.9990 Silver 4.9948 oz. ASW, 65 mm.
Subject: Johannes Kepler **Obv:** Crowned bust right **Rev:** Bust 1/4 right **Note:** Illustration reduced.

Date	Mintage	F	VF	XF	Unc	BU
1994 Proof	Est. 2,000				Value: 90.00	

KM# 62   50 DOLLARS
31.4700 g., 0.9250 Silver 0.9359 oz. ASW. **Rev:** MacArthur accepting Japanese surrender **Note:** Similar to 5 Dollars, KM#54.

Date	Mintage	F	VF	XF	Unc	BU
1995 Proof	—				Value: 27.50	

KM# 57 50 DOLLARS
15.6100 g., 0.9990 Gold 0.5014 oz. AGW, 27 mm.
Rev: MacArthur accepting Japanese surrender

Date	Mintage	F	VF	XF	Unc	BU
1995 Proof	500	Value: 485				

KM# 9 100 DOLLARS
9.3700 g., 0.9000 Gold 0.2711 oz. AGW **Subject:** Attainment of Sovereignty **Obv:** Young bust right **Rev:** Arms with supporters

Date	Mintage	F	VF	XF	Unc	BU
1978FM (M)	50	—	—	—	—	280
1978FM (U)	213	—	—	—	—	275
1978FM (P)	3,159	Value: 265				

KM# 11 100 DOLLARS
7.6400 g., 0.5000 Gold 0.1228 oz. AGW **Subject:** Native Art **Obv:** Young bust right **Rev:** Artistic design in center of designed circles

Date	Mintage	F	VF	XF	Unc	BU
1980FM (U)	50	—	—	—	—	185
1980FM (P) Proof	7,500	Value: 125				

KM# 12 100 DOLLARS
7.6400 g., 0.5000 Gold 0.1228 oz. AGW **Obv:** Young bust right **Rev:** Shark

Date	Mintage	F	VF	XF	Unc	BU
1981 Proof	675	Value: 150				

KM# 14 100 DOLLARS
9.3700 g., 0.9000 Gold 0.2711 oz. AGW **Subject:** Battle of Guadalcanal **Obv:** Young bust right **Rev:** Uniformed soldiers

Date	Mintage	F	VF	XF	Unc	BU
1982FM (P)	311	Value: 275				

KM# 18 100 DOLLARS
9.3700 g., 0.9000 Gold 0.2711 oz. AGW **Subject:** 5th Anniversary of Independence **Obv:** Young bust right within circle, radiant border **Rev:** Arms with supporters in front of flag within circle, radiant border

Date	Mintage	F	VF	XF	Unc	BU
1983FM (P)	268	Value: 275				

KM# 21 100 DOLLARS
7.5000 g., 0.9170 Gold 0.2211 oz. AGW **Series:** 1984 Olympics **Rev:** Weightlifter

Date	Mintage	F	VF	XF	Unc	BU
1984 Proof	500	Value: 225				

KM# 34 100 DOLLARS
31.2100 g., 0.9990 Gold 1.0024 oz. AGW, 32.7 mm. **Subject:** 50th Anniversary of Pearl Harbor **Obv:** Crowned head right **Rev:** Pearl Harbor battle scene within circle

Date	Mintage	F	VF	XF	Unc	BU
1991 Proof	Est. 500	Value: 975				

KM# 39 100 DOLLARS
31.2100 g., 0.9990 Gold 1.0024 oz. AGW, 32.7 mm. **Subject:** 50th Anniversary - Battle of Coral Sea **Rev:** Soldiers in lifeboats, burning building and boat, all within circle

Date	Mintage	F	VF	XF	Unc	BU
1992 Proof	Est. 500	Value: 975				

KM# 45 100 DOLLARS
31.2100 g., 0.9990 Gold 1.0024 oz. AGW, 32.69 mm. **Subject:** 50th Anniversary - Battle of Guadalcanal **Rev:** Planes bombing ship within circle

Date	Mintage	F	VF	XF	Unc	BU
1992 Proof	Est. 500	Value: 975				

KM# 58 100 DOLLARS
31.2100 g., 0.9990 Gold 1.0024 oz. AGW, 32.69 mm. **Rev:** B-25 bomber and mushroom cloud within circle

Date	Mintage	F	VF	XF	Unc	BU
1995 Proof	Est. 500	Value: 975				

PIEFORTS

KM#	Date	Mintage	Identification	Mkt Val
P1	1983	62	5 Dollars. Silver. KM16.	100

PATTERNS
Including off metal strikes

KM#	Date	Mintage	Identification	Mkt Val
Pn1	2000	1	Dollar. Copper-Nickel. 32.3000 g. 38.6 mm. Head with tiara right with italic legends. Cartoon kangaroo on sailboard. Reeded edge.	—
Pn2	2000	30	Dollar. Copper-Nickel. 32.3000 g. 38.6 mm. Head with tiara right italic legends. Cartoon kangaroo on sailboard. Reeded edge.	—
Pn3	2000	—	Dollar. Copper-Nickel. 32.3000 g. 38.6 mm. Head with tiara right with italic legend. Multicolor cartoon kangaroo on sailboard. Reeded edge.	—

Note: Mintage included in Pn2

Pn4	2000	30	Dollar. Copper-Nickel. 32.3000 g. 38.6 mm. Head with tiara right with italic legends. Cartoon koala swimming. Reeded edge.	—
Pn5	2000	—	Dollar. Copper-Nickel. 32.3000 g. 38.6 mm. Head with tiara right. Multicolor cartoon koala swimming. Reeded edge.	—

Note: mintage included with Pn4

Pn6	2000	1	5 Dollars. Copper-Nickel. 32.3000 g. 38.6 mm. Head with tiara right with italic legends. Cartoon koala playing tennis. Reeded edge.	—
Pn7	2000	30	5 Dollars. 0.9250 Silver. 32.0000 g. 38.6 mm. Head with tiara right. Cartoon koala playing tennis. Reeded edge.	—
Pn8	2000	—	5 Dollars. 0.9250 Silver. 32.0000 g. 38.6 mm. Head with tiara right with italic legends. Multicolor cartoon koala playing tennis. Reeded edge.	—

Note: mintage included with Pn7

Pn9	2000	30	5 Dollars. 0.9250 Silver. 32.0000 g. 38.6 mm. Head with tiara right with italic legends. Cartoon kangaroo on bicycle. Reeded edge.	—
Pn10	2000	—	5 Dollars. 0.9250 Silver. 32.0000 g. 38.6 mm. Head with tiara right with italic legends. Multicolor cartoon kangaroo on bicycle. Reeded edge.	—

Note: mintage included with Pn9

Pn11	2000	30	50 Dollars. 0.5833 Gold. 7.7600 g. 25 mm. Head with tiara right with italic legends. Multicolor cartoon emu running. Reeded edge.	—

MINT SETS

KM#	Date	Mintage	Identification	Issue Price	Mkt Val
MS1	1978 (7)	544	KM#1-6, 7a	22.00	32.50
MS2	1979 (8)	677	KM#1-6, 7a, 10	31.00	42.50
MS3	1980 (8)	624	KM#1-6, 7a, 10	35.00	50.00
MS4	1981 (8)	212	KM#1-6, 7a, 10	36.00	60.00
MS5	1982 (8)	—	KM#1-6, 10, 13	36.00	65.00
MS6	1983 (8)	192	KM#1-6, 7a, 17	36.00	72.00

PROOF SETS

KM#	Date	Mintage	Identification	Issue Price	Mkt Val
PS1	1977 (7)	72,748	KM#1-7	40.00	28.00
PSA2	1977 (6)	—	KM#1-6	—	16.50
PS2	1978 (7)	5,122	KM#1-7	45.00	32.50
PS3	1979 (8)	2,845	KM#1-7, 10a	77.00	65.00
PS4	1980 (8)	1,031	KM#1-7, 10a	135	70.00
PS5	1981 (8)	448	KM#1-7, 10a	137	80.00
PS6	1982 (8)	—	KM#1-6, 10a, 13a	87.00	100
PS7	1983 (8)	334	KM#1-7, 17a	137	95.00
PS8	1991 (4)	500	KM#31-34	1,650	1,250
PS9	1991 (2)	—	KM#30a, 32	—	185
PS10	1992 (4)	500	KM#36-39	1,595	1,250
PS11	1992 (4)	500	KM#42-45	1,595	1,250
PS12	1995 (4)	500	KM#55-58	1,595	1,275

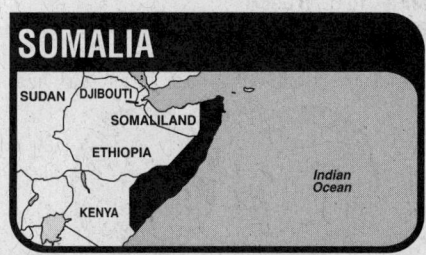

SOMALIA

The Somali Democratic Republic, comprised of the former Italian Somaliland, is located on the coast of the eastern projection of the African continent commonly referred to as the "Horn". It has an area of 178,201 sq. mi. (461,657 sq. km.) and a population of *8.2 million. Capital: Mogadishu. The economy is pastoral and agricultural. Livestock, bananas and hides are exported.

The area of the British Somaliland Protectorate was known to the Egyptians at least 1,500 years B.C., and was occupied by the Arabs and Portuguese before British sea captains obtained trading and anchorage rights in 1827. The land of sandy clay and sporadic rainfall acquired a strategic importance with the opening of the Suez Canal in 1869. After negotiating treaties with the tribes, Britain declared the area a protectorate in 1888. Italy acquired Italian Somaliland in 1895 by purchase from the Sultan of Zanzibar.

Britain occupied Italian Somaliland in 1941 and administered it until April 1, 1950, when it was returned to Italy as a U.N. trusteeship. The British Somaliland protectorate became independent on June 26, 1960. Five days later it joined with Italian Somaliland to form the Somali Republic. The country was under a revolutionary military regime installed Oct. 21, 1969. After eleven years of civil war rebel forces fought their way into the capital. A.M. Muhammad became president in Aug. 1991, but inter-factional fighting continued. A UN-sponsored truce was signed in March 1992 and a peace plan and pact was signed Jan. 15, 1993.

The Northern Somali National Movement (SNM) declared a secession of the northwestern Somaliland Republic on May 17, 1991, which is not recognized by the Somali Democratic Republic.

TITLE
Al-Jumhuriya(t)as - Somaliya(t)

RULERS
Italian, until 1941
British, until 1950

MINT MARKS
Az - Arezzo (Italy)
R – Rome

U. N. TRUSTEESHIP UNDER ITALY
STANDARD COINAGE

100 Centesimi = 1 Scellino

KM# 1   CENTESIMO
3.0000 g., Copper, 21 mm. **Obv:** African elephant **Rev:** Value within circle with star flanked by crescents above **Edge:** Plain

Date	Mintage	F	VF	XF	Unc	BU
AH1369-1950	4,000,000	—	0.20	0.50	2.00	4.00

KM# 2   5 CENTESIMI
Copper **Obv:** African elephant **Rev:** Value within circle with star flanked by crescents above

Date	Mintage	F	VF	XF	Unc	BU
AH1369-1950	6,800,000	—	0.30	1.00	3.50	7.50

KM# 3   10 CENTESIMI
Copper **Rev:** Value within circle with star flanked by crescents above **Edge:** African elephant

Date	Mintage	F	VF	XF	Unc	BU
AH1369-1950	7,400,000	—	0.50	2.00	6.00	12.00

KM# 4   50 CENTESIMI
3.8000 g., 0.2500 Silver 0.0305 oz. ASW **Obv:** Star flanked by crescents above lion **Rev:** Value within beaded circle

Date	Mintage	F	VF	XF	Unc	BU
AH1369-1950	1,800,000	—	1.25	3.75	10.00	15.00

KM# 5   SOMALO
7.6000 g., 0.2500 Silver 0.0611 oz. ASW **Obv:** Star flanked by crescents above lion **Rev:** Value within beaded circle

Date	Mintage	F	VF	XF	Unc	BU
AH1369-1950	11,480,000	—	2.25	4.75	12.50	20.00

SOMALI REPUBLIC
STANDARD COINAGE

100 Centesimi = 1 Scellino

KM# 6   5 CENTESIMI
2.5000 g., Brass **Obv:** Crowned arms with supporters **Rev:** Value and star within circle

Date	Mintage	F	VF	XF	Unc	BU
1967	10,000,000	—	—	0.20	0.60	1.00

KM# 7   10 CENTESIMI
Brass **Obv:** Crowned arms with supporters **Rev:** Value and star within circle

Date	Mintage	F	VF	XF	Unc	BU
1967	15,000,000	—	0.15	0.25	0.70	1.25

KM# 8   50 CENTESIMI
Copper-Nickel **Obv:** Crowned arms with supporters **Rev:** Value and star within beaded circle

Date	Mintage	F	VF	XF	Unc	BU
1967	5,100,000	—	0.50	1.00	2.50	4.00

KM# 9   SCELLINO / SHILLING
7.6300 g., Copper-Nickel, 26.7 mm. **Obv:** Arms with supporters **Rev:** Value within beaded circle

Date	Mintage	F	VF	XF	Unc	BU
1967	8,150,000	—	1.00	3.00	6.00	9.00

KM# 10   20 SHILLINGS / SCELLINI
2.8000 g., 0.9000 Gold 0.0810 oz. AGW **Subject:** 5th Anniversary of Independence **Obv:** Bust facing **Rev:** Crowned arms with supporters

Date	Mintage	F	VF	XF	Unc	BU
1965Az Proof	6,325	Value: 90.00				
1966Az Proof	—	Value: 90.00				

KM# 11   50 SHILLINGS
7.0000 g., 0.9000 Gold 0.2025 oz. AGW **Subject:** 5th Anniversary of Independence **Obv:** Bust facing **Rev:** Crowned arms with supporters

Date	Mintage	F	VF	XF	Unc	BU
1965Az Proof	6,325	Value: 220				
1966Az Proof	—	Value: 220				

KM# 12   100 SHILLINGS
14.0000 g., 0.9000 Gold 0.4051 oz. AGW **Subject:** 5th Anniversary of Independence **Obv:** Bust facing **Rev:** Crowned arms with supporters

Date	Mintage	F	VF	XF	Unc	BU
1965Az Proof	6,325	Value: 425				
1966Az Proof	—	Value: 425				

KM# 13   200 SHILLINGS
28.0000 g., 0.9000 Gold 0.8102 oz. AGW **Subject:** 5th Anniversary of Independence **Obv:** Bust facing **Rev:** Arms with supporters **Note:** Similar to 100 Shillings, KM#12.

Date	Mintage	F	VF	XF	Unc	BU
1965Az Proof	6,325	Value: 850				
1966Az Proof	—	Value: 850				

KM# 14   500 SHILLINGS
70.0000 g., 0.9000 Gold 2.0254 oz. AGW **Subject:** 5th Anniversary of Independence **Obv:** Bust facing **Rev:** Arms with supporters **Note:** Similar to 100 Shillings, KM#12.

Date	Mintage	F	VF	XF	Unc	BU
1965Az Proof	6,325	Value: 1,950				
1966Az Proof	—	Value: 1,950				

DEMOCRATIC REPUBLIC
STANDARD COINAGE

100 Centesimi = 1 Scellino

KM# 15   5 SHILLINGS
Copper-Nickel, 38 mm. **Subject:** 2nd F.A.O. Conference **Obv:** Crowned arms with supporters **Rev:** Cow and goats **Edge:** Reeded

Date	Mintage	F	VF	XF	Unc	BU
1970	100,000	—	1.50	2.50	6.00	7.50
1970 Proof	1,000	Value: 16.50				

KM# 16   20 SHILLINGS
2.8000 g., 0.9000 Gold 0.0810 oz. AGW **Subject:** 10th Anniversary of Independence **Obv:** Crowned arms with supporters **Rev:** Star-like design within circle

Date	Mintage	F	VF	XF	Unc	BU
ND(1970) Proof	8,000	Value: 95.00				

KM# 17   50 SHILLINGS
7.0000 g., 0.9000 Gold 0.2025 oz. AGW **Subject:** 10th Anniversary of Independence **Obv:** Crowned arms with supporters **Rev:** Half-figure with bowl right

Date	Mintage	F	VF	XF	Unc	BU
ND(1970) Proof	8,000	Value: 210				

KM# 18   50 SHILLINGS
7.0000 g., 0.9000 Gold 0.2025 oz. AGW **Subject:** 1st Anniversary of 1969 Revolution **Obv:** Crowned arms with supporters **Rev:** Wheat sprig

Date	Mintage	F	VF	XF	Unc	BU
ND(1970) Proof	—	Value: 210				

KM# 19   100 SHILLINGS
14.0000 g., 0.9000 Gold 0.4051 oz. AGW **Subject:** 10th Anniversary of Independence **Obv:** Crowned arms with supporters flanked by dates **Rev:** Bust with headscarf and fruit basket on back left

Date	Mintage	F	VF	XF	Unc	BU
ND(1970) Proof	8,000	Value: 420				

KM# 20   100 SHILLINGS
14.0000 g., 0.9000 Gold 0.4051 oz. AGW **Subject:** 1st Anniversary of the 1969 Revolution **Obv:** Crowned arms with supporters **Rev:** Hand, helmet and gun in front of design

Date	Mintage	F	VF	XF	Unc	BU
ND(1970) Proof	—	Value: 420				

KM# 21   200 SHILLINGS
28.0000 g., 0.9000 Gold 0.8102 oz. AGW **Subject:** 10th Anniversary of Independence **Obv:** Crowned arms with supporters **Rev:** Supplies on camel

Date	Mintage	F	VF	XF	Unc	BU
ND(1970) Proof	8,000	Value: 825				

KM# 22   200 SHILLINGS
28.0000 g., 0.9000 Gold 0.8102 oz. AGW **Subject:** 1st Anniversary of 1969 Revolution **Obv:** Crowned arms with supporters **Rev:** Monument

Date	Mintage	F	VF	XF	Unc	BU
ND(1970) Proof	—	Value: 825				

KM# 23   500 SHILLINGS
70.0000 g., 0.9000 Gold 2.0254 oz. AGW **Subject:** 10th Anniversary of Independence **Obv:** Crowned arms with supporters **Rev:** Building within map

Date	Mintage	F	VF	XF	Unc	BU
ND(1970) Proof	8,000	Value: 1,950				

REFORM COINAGE
100 Senti = 1 Shilling

KM# A24   5 SENTI
Aluminum **Series:** F.A.O. **Obv:** Value within circle **Rev:** Corn ears and flower flanked by dates

Date	Mintage	F	VF	XF	Unc	BU
1976	—	—	—	—	200	—

KM# 24   5 SENTI
0.8700 g., Aluminum, 20 mm. **Series:** F.A.O. **Obv:** Crowned arms with supporters **Rev:** Value above fruit, grains and bread

Date	Mintage	F	VF	XF	Unc	BU
1976	18,500,000	—	0.10	0.20	0.35	0.50

KM# 25   10 SENTI
1.3900 g., Aluminum, 23.5 mm. **Series:** F.A.O. **Obv:** Crowned arms with supporters **Rev:** Lamb flanked by dates below value **Edge:** Plain

Date	Mintage	F	VF	XF	Unc	BU
1976	40,500,000	—	0.10	0.20	0.50	1.00

KM# 26   50 SENTI
3.8500 g., Copper-Nickel, 21 mm. **Series:** F.A.O. **Obv:** Crowned arms with supporters **Rev:** Value above grains and dates

Date	Mintage	F	VF	XF	Unc	BU
1976	10,080,000	—	0.15	0.25	0.75	1.00

KM# 26a   50 SENTI
3.8100 g., Nickel Plated Steel, 21 mm. **Series:** F.A.O. **Obv:** Crowned arms with supporters **Rev:** Value above grains and dates

Date	Mintage	F	VF	XF	Unc	BU
1984	—	—	1.00	2.00	5.00	—

KM# 27   SHILLING
6.2200 g., Copper-Nickel, 25.5 mm. **Series:** F.A.O. **Obv:** Crowned arms with supporters **Rev:** Lamb flanked by dates below value

Date	Mintage	F	VF	XF	Unc	BU
1976	20,040,000	—	0.35	0.65	2.25	2.50

KM# 27a   SHILLING
6.1900 g., Nickel Plated Steel, 25.42 mm. **Series:** F.A.O. **Obv:** Crowned arms with supporters **Rev:** Lamb flanked by dates below value

Date	Mintage	F	VF	XF	Unc	BU
1984	—	—	2.00	4.00	10.00	—

KM# 28   10 SHILLINGS
Copper-Nickel **Subject:** 10th Anniversary of Republic **Obv:** Crowned arms with supporters **Rev:** Workers

Date	Mintage	F	VF	XF	Unc	BU
ND(1979)	—	—	—	—	7.00	8.00

KM# 28a   10 SHILLINGS
28.2800 g., 0.9250 Silver 0.8410 oz. ASW **Subject:** 10th Anniversary of Republic **Obv:** Crowned arms with supporters **Rev:** Workers

Date	Mintage	F	VF	XF	Unc	BU
ND(1979) Proof	Est. 5,000	Value: 37.50				

KM# 29   10 SHILLINGS
Copper-Nickel **Subject:** 10th Anniversary of Republic
Obv: Crowned arms with supporters **Rev:** Seated figures in front
of tents

Date	Mintage	F	VF	XF	Unc	BU
ND(1979)	—	—	—	—	7.00	8.00

KM# 29a   10 SHILLINGS
28.2800 g., 0.9250 Silver 0.8410 oz. ASW **Subject:** 10th
Anniversary of Republic **Obv:** Crowned arms with supporters
Rev: Seated figures in front of tents

Date	Mintage	F	VF	XF	Unc	BU
ND(1979) Proof	Est. 5,000	Value: 38.50				

KM# 30   10 SHILLINGS
Copper-Nickel **Subject:** 10th Anniversary of Republic
Obv: Crowned arms with supporters **Rev:** Lab workers

Date	Mintage	F	VF	XF	Unc	BU
ND(1979)	—	—	—	—	7.00	8.00

KM# 30a   10 SHILLINGS
28.2800 g., 0.9250 Silver 0.8410 oz. ASW **Subject:** 10th
Anniversary of Republic **Obv:** Crowned arms with supporters
Rev: Lab workers

Date	Mintage	F	VF	XF	Unc	BU
ND(1979) Proof	Est. 5,000	Value: 36.50				

KM# 31   10 SHILLINGS
Copper-Nickel **Subject:** 10th Anniversary of Republic
Obv: Crowned arms with supporters **Rev:** Dancers

Date	Mintage	F	VF	XF	Unc	BU
ND(1979)	—	—	—	—	7.00	8.00

KM# 31a   10 SHILLINGS
28.2800 g., 0.9250 Silver 0.8410 oz. ASW **Subject:** 10th
Anniversary of Republic **Obv:** Crowned arms with supporters
Rev: Dancers

Date	Mintage	F	VF	XF	Unc	BU
ND(1979) Proof	Est. 5,000	Value: 37.50				

KM# 32   10 SHILLINGS
Copper-Nickel **Subject:** 10th Anniversary of Republic
Obv: Crowned arms with supporters **Rev:** Man and woman

Date	Mintage	F	VF	XF	Unc	BU
ND(1979)	—	—	—	—	7.00	8.00

KM# 32a   10 SHILLINGS
28.2800 g., 0.9250 Silver 0.8410 oz. ASW **Subject:** 10th
Anniversary of Republic **Obv:** Crowned arms with supporters
Rev: Man and woman

Date	Mintage	F	VF	XF	Unc	BU
ND(1979) Proof	Est. 5,000	Value: 37.50				

KM# 40   25 SHILLINGS
Copper-Nickel **Subject:** World Fisheries Conference
Obv: Crowned arms with supporters **Rev:** Green sea turtle

Date	Mintage	F	VF	XF	Unc	BU
ND(1984)	100,000	—	—	12.00	35.00	45.00

KM# 40a   25 SHILLINGS
28.2800 g., 0.9250 Silver 0.8410 oz. ASW **Subject:** World
Fisheries Conference **Obv:** Crowned arms with supporters
Rev: Green sea turtle

Date	Mintage	F	VF	XF	Unc	BU
ND(1984) Proof	20,000	Value: 75.00				

KM# 40b   25 SHILLINGS
47.5400 g., 0.9170 Gold 1.4015 oz. AGW **Subject:** World
Fisheries Conference **Obv:** Crowned arms with supporters
Rev: Green sea turtle

Date	Mintage	F	VF	XF	Unc	BU
ND(1984) Proof	200	Value: 1,400				

KM# 38   150 SHILLINGS
28.2800 g., 0.9250 Silver 0.8410 oz. ASW **Series:** International
Year of Disabled Persons **Obv:** Crowned arms with supporters
Rev: Head left, emblem at lower left

Date	Mintage	F	VF	XF	Unc	BU
1983	5,500	—	—	—	40.00	45.00
1983 Proof	5,500	Value: 50.00				

KM# 33   1500 SHILLINGS
15.9800 g., 0.9170 Gold 0.4711 oz. AGW **Subject:** 10th
Anniversary of Republic **Obv:** Crowned arms with supporters
Rev: Workers facing

Date	Mintage	F	VF	XF	Unc	BU
ND(1979)	500	—	—	—	—	465
ND(1979) Proof	500	Value: 475				

KM# 34   1500 SHILLINGS
15.9800 g., 0.9170 Gold 0.4711 oz. AGW **Subject:** 10th
Anniversary of Republic **Obv:** Crowned arms with supporters
Rev: Seated figures in front of tents

Date	Mintage	F	VF	XF	Unc	BU
ND(1979)	500	—	—	—	—	465
ND(1979) Proof	500	Value: 475				

KM# 35   1500 SHILLINGS
15.9800 g., 0.9170 Gold 0.4711 oz. AGW **Subject:** 10th
Anniversary of Republic **Obv:** Crowned arms with supporters
Rev: Lab workers

Date	Mintage	F	VF	XF	Unc	BU
ND(1979)	500	—	—	—	—	465
ND(1979) Proof	500	Value: 475				

KM# 36   1500 SHILLINGS
15.9800 g., 0.9170 Gold 0.4711 oz. AGW **Subject:** 10th
Anniversary of Republic **Obv:** Crowned arms with supporters
Rev: Dancers

Date	Mintage	F	VF	XF	Unc	BU
ND(1979)	500	—	—	—	—	465
ND(1979) Proof	500	Value: 475				

KM# 37   1500 SHILLINGS
15.9800 g., 0.9170 Gold 0.4711 oz. AGW **Subject:** 10th
Anniversary of Republic **Obv:** Crowned arms with supporters
Rev: Man and woman

Date	Mintage	F	VF	XF	Unc	BU
1979	500	—	—	—	—	465
1979 Proof	500	Value: 475				

KM# 39   1500 SHILLINGS
15.9800 g., 0.9170 Gold 0.4711 oz. AGW **Series:** International
Year of Disabled Persons **Obv:** Crowned arms with supporters
Rev: Emblem above busts facing

Date	Mintage	F	VF	XF	Unc	BU
1983	—	—	—	—	—	465
1983 Proof	—	Value: 475				

REPUBLIC OF SOMALIA

STANDARD COINAGE

100 Centesimi = 1 Scellino

KM# 45 5 SHILLING / SCELLINI
1.2900 g., Aluminum, 21 mm. **Series:** F.A.O. **Obv:** Crowned arms with supporters **Rev:** Elephant **Edge:** Plain

Date	Mintage	F	VF	XF	Unc	BU
2000	—	—	—	—	1.50	1.75

KM# 46 10 SHILLINGS / SCELLINI
1.2900 g., Aluminum, 21.92 mm. **Series:** F.A.O. **Obv:** Crowned arms with supporters **Rev:** Camel **Edge:** Plain

Date	Mintage	F	VF	XF	Unc	BU
1999	—	—	—	—	2.00	2.25
2000	—	—	—	—	2.00	2.25

KM# 90 10 SHILLINGS / SCELLINI
4.8200 g., Nickel Clad Steel, 24.9 mm. **Series:** Asian Astrology **Obv:** National arms **Rev:** Rat **Edge:** Plain

Date	Mintage	F	VF	XF	Unc	BU
2000	—	—	—	—	1.00	1.25

KM# 91 10 SHILLINGS / SCELLINI
4.8200 g., Nickel Clad Steel, 25 mm. **Series:** Asian Astrology **Obv:** National arms **Rev:** Ox **Edge:** Plain

Date	Mintage	F	VF	XF	Unc	BU
2000	—	—	—	—	1.00	1.25

KM# 92 10 SHILLINGS / SCELLINI
4.8200 g., Nickel Clad Steel, 25 mm. **Series:** Asian Astrology **Obv:** National arms **Rev:** Tiger **Edge:** plain

Date	Mintage	F	VF	XF	Unc	BU
2000	—	—	—	—	1.00	1.25

KM# 93 10 SHILLINGS / SCELLINI
4.8200 g., Nickel Clad Steel, 25 mm. **Series:** Asian Astrology **Obv:** National arms **Rev:** Rabbit **Edge:** Plain

Date	Mintage	F	VF	XF	Unc	BU
2000	—	—	—	—	1.00	1.25

KM# 94 10 SHILLINGS / SCELLINI
4.8200 g., Nickel Clad Steel, 25 mm. **Series:** Asian Astrology **Obv:** National arms **Rev:** Dragon **Edge:** Plain

Date	Mintage	F	VF	XF	Unc	BU
2000	—	—	—	—	1.25	1.50

KM# 95 10 SHILLINGS / SCELLINI
4.8200 g., Nickel Clad Steel, 25 mm. **Series:** Asian Astrology **Obv:** National arms **Rev:** Snake **Edge:** Plain

Date	Mintage	F	VF	XF	Unc	BU
2000	—	—	—	—	1.00	1.25

KM# 96 10 SHILLINGS / SCELLINI
4.8200 g., Nickel Clad Steel, 25 mm. **Series:** Asian Astrology **Obv:** National arms **Rev:** Horse **Edge:** Plain

Date	Mintage	F	VF	XF	Unc	BU
2000	—	—	—	—	1.25	1.50

KM# 97 10 SHILLINGS / SCELLINI
4.8200 g., Nickel Clad Steel, 25 mm. **Series:** Asian Astrology **Obv:** National arms **Rev:** Goat **Edge:** Plain

Date	Mintage	F	VF	XF	Unc	BU
2000	—	—	—	—	1.00	1.25

KM# 98 10 SHILLINGS / SCELLINI
4.8200 g., Nickel Clad Steel, 25 mm. **Series:** Asian Astrology **Obv:** National arms **Rev:** Monkey **Edge:** Plain

Date	Mintage	F	VF	XF	Unc	BU
2000	—	—	—	—	1.00	1.25

KM# 99 10 SHILLINGS / SCELLINI
4.8200 g., Nickel Clad Steel, 25 mm. **Series:** Asian Astrology **Obv:** National arms **Rev:** Rooster **Edge:** Plain

Date	Mintage	F	VF	XF	Unc	BU
2000	—	—	—	—	1.00	1.25

KM# 100 10 SHILLINGS / SCELLINI
4.8200 g., Nickel Clad Steel, 25 mm. **Series:** Asian Astrology **Obv:** National arms **Rev:** Dog **Edge:** Plain

Date	Mintage	F	VF	XF	Unc	BU
2000	—	—	—	—	1.00	1.25

KM# 101 10 SHILLINGS / SCELLINI
4.8200 g., Nickel Clad Steel, 25 mm. **Series:** Asian Astrology **Obv:** National arms **Rev:** Pig **Edge:** Plain

Date	Mintage	F	VF	XF	Unc	BU
2000	—	—	—	—	1.00	1.25

KM# 107 10 SHILLINGS / SCELLINI
Silver **Obv:** Crowned arms with supporters **Rev:** Multicolored dragon

Date	Mintage	F	VF	XF	Unc	BU
2000 Proof	—	Value: 35.00				

KM# 41 25 SHILLINGS
Copper-Nickel **Subject:** History of World Shipping - Sinking of Titanic **Obv:** Crowned arms with supporters **Rev:** Multi-color inner circle design with partially submerged ship **Rev. Leg.:** Inner legend reads "THE TITANIC SINKS - APRIL 15, 1912"

Date	Mintage	F	VF	XF	Unc	BU
1998 Proof	—	Value: 10.00				

KM# 47 25 SHILLINGS
2.0000 g., Copper-Nickel, 37.9 mm. **Subject:** Wildlife of Somalia **Obv:** Crowned arms with supporters **Rev:** Multicolored hippopotamus **Edge:** Plain

Date	Mintage	F	VF	XF	Unc	BU
1998	—	—	—	—	15.00	

KM# 50 25 SHILLINGS
Copper-Nickel **Subject:** History of World Shipping - Cutty Sark **Obv:** Crowned arms with supporters **Rev:** Multicolored Ship **Edge:** Plain **Note:** Weight varies 18.42-20.2g.

Date	Mintage	F	VF	XF	Unc	BU
1998 Proof	—	Value: 10.00				

KM# 51 25 SHILLINGS
Copper-Nickel **Subject:** History of World Shipping - Caravel Nina **Obv:** Crowned arms with supporters **Rev:** Multicolored ship

Date	Mintage	F	VF	XF	Unc	BU
1998 Proof	—	Value: 10.00				

KM# 52 25 SHILLINGS
Copper-Nickel **Subject:** History of World Shipping **Obv:** Crowned arms with supporters **Rev:** Multicolored Greek Trireme **Note:** Weight varies 18.42-20.2g.

Date	Mintage	VG	F	VF	XF	Unc
1998 Proof	—	Value: 10.00				

KM# 53 25 SHILLINGS
Copper-Nickel **Subject:** History of World Shipping **Obv:** Crowned arms with supporters **Rev:** Multicolored Roman merchant ship **Note:** Weight varies 18.42-20.2g.

Date	Mintage	F	VF	XF	Unc	BU
1998 Proof	—	Value: 10.00				

KM# 54 25 SHILLINGS
Copper-Nickel **Subject:** History of World Shipping **Obv:** Crowned arms with supporters **Rev:** Multicolored Hansa Trading Cog **Note:** Weight varies 18.42-20.2g.

Date	Mintage	F	VF	XF	Unc	BU
1998 Proof	—	Value: 10.00				

KM# 55 25 SHILLINGS
Copper-Nickel **Subject:** History of World Shipping **Obv:** Crowned arms with supporters **Rev:** Multicolored Titanic **Note:** Weight varies 18.42-20.2g.

Date	Mintage	F	VF	XF	Unc	BU
1998 Proof	—	Value: 10.00				

KM# 56 25 SHILLINGS
Copper-Nickel **Subject:** Wildlife of Somalia **Obv:** Crowned arms with supporters **Rev:** Multicolored Ostrich **Note:** Weight varies 18.42-20.2g.

Date	Mintage	F	VF	XF	Unc	BU
1998	—	—	—	—	17.50	25.00

KM# 57   25 SHILLINGS
Copper-Nickel **Subject:** Wildlife of Somalia **Obv:** Crowned arms with supporters **Rev:** Multicolored running Eland **Note:** Weight varies 18.42-20.2g.

Date	Mintage	F	VF	XF	Unc	BU
1998	—	—	—	—	17.50	25.00

KM# 58   25 SHILLINGS
Copper-Nickel **Subject:** Wildlife of Somalia **Obv:** Crowned arms with supporters **Rev:** Multicolored Spurfowl in grass **Note:** Weight varies 18.42-20.2g.

Date	Mintage	F	VF	XF	Unc	BU
1998	—	—	—	—	17.50	25.00

KM# 59   25 SHILLINGS
Copper-Nickel **Subject:** Wildlife of Somalia **Obv:** Crowned arms with supporters **Rev:** Multicolored Leopard **Note:** Weight varies 18.42-20.2g.

Date	Mintage	F	VF	XF	Unc	BU
1998	—	—	—	—	17.50	25.00

KM# 60   25 SHILLINGS
Copper-Nickel **Subject:** Wildlife of Somalia **Obv:** Crowned arms with supporters **Rev:** Multicolored bird on branch **Note:** Weight varies 18.42-20.2g.

Date	Mintage	F	VF	XF	Unc	BU
1998	—	—	—	—	17.50	25.00

KM# 61   25 SHILLINGS
Copper-Nickel **Subject:** Wildlife of Somalia **Obv:** Crowned arms with supporters **Rev:** Multicolored variable sunbird on branch **Note:** Weight varies 18.42-20.2g.

Date	Mintage	F	VF	XF	Unc	BU
1998	—	—	—	—	17.50	25.00

KM# 62   25 SHILLINGS
Copper-Nickel **Subject:** Wildlife of Somalia **Obv:** Crowned arms with supporters **Rev:** Multicolored starling on broken branch **Note:** Weight varies 18.42-20.2g.

Date	Mintage	F	VF	XF	Unc	BU
1998	—	—	—	—	17.50	25.00

KM# 141   25 SHILLINGS
20.0000 g., Copper-Nickel, 38 mm. **Subject:** 100th Birthday - British Queen Mother **Obv:** Crowned arms with supporters above value **Rev:** Queen Mother **Edge:** Plain

Date	Mintage	F	VF	XF	Unc	BU
ND (1999)	—	—	—	—	10.00	12.00

KM# 106   25 SHILLINGS
Copper-Nickel **Subject:** Fall of Berlin Wall **Obv:** Crowned arms with supporters **Rev:** Berlin wall destruction scene

Date	Mintage	F	VF	XF	Unc	BU
1999	—	—	—	—	8.00	10.00

KM# 108   25 SHILLINGS
Copper-Nickel **Obv:** Crowned arms with supporters **Rev:** Multicolored penguins

Date	Mintage	F	VF	XF	Unc	BU
2000 Proof	—	Value: 30.00				

KM# 70   25 SHILLINGS
Copper-Nickel, 38 mm. **Subject:** Winston Churchill **Obv:** Crowned arms with supporters **Rev:** Bust facing **Edge:** Plain

Date	Mintage	F	VF	XF	Unc	BU
2000	—	—	—	—	5.00	6.00

KM# 71   25 SHILLINGS
Copper-Nickel, 38 mm. **Subject:** Pope John Paul II **Obv:** Crowned arms with supporters **Rev:** Bust facing **Edge:** Plain

Date	Mintage	F	VF	XF	Unc	BU
2000	—	—	—	—	5.00	6.00

KM# 72   25 SHILLINGS
20.0000 g., Copper-Nickel, 38 mm. **Subject:** Nelson Mandela **Obv:** Crowned arms with supporters **Rev:** Bust facing **Edge:** Reeded

Date	Mintage	F	VF	XF	Unc	BU
2000	—	—	—	—	5.00	6.00

KM# 73   25 SHILLINGS
Copper-Nickel **Subject:** Che Guevara **Obv:** Crowned arms with supporters **Rev:** Bust with hat facing

Date	Mintage	F	VF	XF	Unc	BU
2000	—	—	—	—	5.00	6.00

KM# 74   25 SHILLINGS
Copper-Nickel, 37.9 mm. **Subject:** Emperor Hirohito **Obv:** Crowned arms with supporters **Rev:** Bust facing **Edge:** Plain

Date	Mintage	F	VF	XF	Unc	BU
2000 Prooflike	—	—	—	—	7.00	8.50

KM# 75 25 SHILLINGS
Copper-Nickel **Subject:** Mao Tse-Tung **Obv:** Crowned arms with supporters **Rev:** Bust facing

Date	Mintage	F	VF	XF	Unc	BU
2000 Prooflike	—	—	—	—	7.00	8.50

KM# 76 25 SHILLINGS
Copper-Nickel **Subject:** Berlin **Obv:** Crowned arms with supporters **Rev:** Berlin wall destruction scene

Date	Mintage	F	VF	XF	Unc	BU
ND(2000) Prooflike	—	—	—	—	7.00	8.50

KM# 77 150 SHILLINGS
14.8100 g., 0.9990 Silver 0.4757 oz. ASW, 34.25 mm.
Subject: Christopher Columbus **Obv:** Crowned arms with supporters **Rev:** Cameo above 3 ships **Edge:** Reeded

Date	Mintage	F	VF	XF	Unc	BU
2000 Proof	—	Value: 25.00				

KM# 113 150 SHILLINGS
15.0000 g., 0.9990 Silver 0.4818 oz. ASW, 34.25 mm.
Subject: Millennium **Obv:** Crowned arms with supporters **Rev:** World globe **Edge:** Reeded

Date	Mintage	F	VF	XF	Unc	BU
2000	—	Value: 25.00				

KM# 42 250 SHILLINGS
23.5000 g., 0.9250 Silver 0.6988 oz. ASW **Subject:** History of World Shipping - Sinking of Titanic **Obv:** Crowned arms with supporters **Rev:** Multicolored sinking ship

Date	Mintage	F	VF	XF	Unc	BU
1998 Proof	20,000	Value: 35.00				

KM# 42a 250 SHILLINGS
Bi-Metallic Copper-Nickel center in Brass ring **Subject:** Historic Ships **Obv:** Crowned arms with supporters **Rev:** Multicolor sinking ship

Date	Mintage	F	VF	XF	Unc	BU
1998	—	—	—	—	22.50	

KM# 48 250 SHILLINGS
23.7000 g., 0.9250 Silver 0.7048 oz. ASW, 38.1 mm.
Subject: Wildlife of Somalia **Obv:** Crowned arms with supporters **Rev:** Multicolored Hippopotamus **Edge:** Reeded

Date	Mintage	F	VF	XF	Unc	BU
1998 Proof	—	Value: 25.00				

KM# 48a 250 SHILLINGS
Bi-Metallic Copper-Nickel center in Brass ring, 38 mm.
Subject: Wildlife of Somalia **Obv:** Crowned arms with supporters **Rev:** Multicolored Hippopotamus **Edge:** Reeded

Date	Mintage	F	VF	XF	Unc	BU
1998	—	—	—	—	25.00	

KM# 49 250 SHILLINGS
23.7000 g., 0.9250 Silver 0.7048 oz. ASW **Subject:** Wildlife of Somalia **Obv:** Crowned arms with supporters **Rev:** Multicolored Ostrich

Date	Mintage	F	VF	XF	Unc	BU
1998 Proof	—	Value: 35.00				

KM# 49a 250 SHILLINGS
Bi-Metallic Brass center in Copper-nickel ring, 38 mm.
Subject: Wildlife of Somalia **Obv:** Crowned arms with supporters **Rev:** Multicolored Ostrich

Date	Mintage	F	VF	XF	Unc	BU
1998	—	—	—	—	30.00	

KM# 64 250 SHILLINGS
24.8300 g., 0.9000 Silver 0.7184 oz. ASW, 37.2 mm.
Subject: Wildlife of Somalia **Obv:** Crowned arms with supporters **Rev:** Multicolored Yellow-necked Spurfowl in grass
Edge: Reeded

Date	Mintage	F	VF	XF	Unc	BU
1998 Proof	—	Value: 30.00				

KM# 64a 250 SHILLINGS
Bi-Metallic Brass center in Copper-nickel ring, 38 mm.
Subject: Wildlife of Somalia **Obv:** Crowned arms with supporters **Rev:** Multicolored Yellow-necked Spurfowl in grass

Date	Mintage	F	VF	XF	Unc	BU
1998	—	—	—	—	30.00	

KM# 65 250 SHILLINGS
24.8300 g., 0.9000 Silver 0.7184 oz. ASW **Subject:** Wildlife of Somalia **Obv:** Crowned arms with supporters **Rev:** Multicolored running Eland

Date	Mintage	F	VF	XF	Unc	BU
1998 Proof	—	Value: 32.50				

KM# 66 250 SHILLINGS
24.8300 g., 0.9000 Silver 0.7184 oz. ASW **Subject:** Wildlife of Somalia **Obv:** Crowned arms with supporters **Rev:** Multicolored Leopard

Date	Mintage	F	VF	XF	Unc	BU
1998 Proof	—	Value: 35.00				

KM# 66a 250 SHILLINGS
Bi-Metallic Brass center in Copper-nickel ring, 38 mm.
Subject: Wildlife of Somalia **Obv:** Crowned arms with supporters **Rev:** Multicolored Leopard

Date	Mintage	F	VF	XF	Unc	BU
1998	—	—	—	—	24.00	

KM# 67 250 SHILLINGS
24.8300 g., 0.9000 Silver 0.7184 oz. ASW **Subject:** Wildlife of Somalia **Obv:** Crowned arms with supporters **Rev:** Multicolored Golden Palm Weaver on branch

Date	Mintage	F	VF	XF	Unc	BU
1998 Proof	—	Value: 35.00				

KM# 67a 250 SHILLINGS
Bi-Metallic Brass center in Copper-nickel ring **Ring:** Copper-Nickel, 38 mm. **Subject:** Wildlife of Somalia **Obv:** Crowned arms with supporters **Rev:** Multicolored Golden Palm Weaver on branch

Date	Mintage	F	VF	XF	Unc	BU
1998	—	—	—	—	30.00	

KM# 68   250 SHILLINGS
24.8300 g., 0.9000 Silver 0.7184 oz. ASW **Subject:** Wildlife of Somalia **Obv:** Crowned arms with supporters **Rev:** Multicolored variable sunbird on branch

Date	Mintage	F	VF	XF	Unc	BU
1998 Proof	—	Value: 35.00				

KM# 68a   250 SHILLINGS
Bi-Metallic Brass center in Copper-nickel ring, 38 mm. **Subject:** Wildlife of Somalia **Obv:** Crowned arms with supporters **Rev:** Multicolored variable sunbird on branch

Date	Mintage	F	VF	XF	Unc	BU
1998	—	—	—	—	35.00	—

KM# 69   250 SHILLINGS
24.8300 g., 0.9000 Silver 0.7184 oz. ASW **Subject:** Wildlife of Somalia **Obv:** Crowned arms with supporters **Rev:** Milticolored starling on broken branch

Date	Mintage	F	VF	XF	Unc	BU
1998 Proof	—	Value: 35.00				

KM# 69a   250 SHILLINGS
Bi-Metallic Copper-Nickel center in Brass ring, 38 mm. **Subject:** Wildlife of Somalia **Obv:** Crowned arms with supporters **Rev:** Multicolored starling on broken branch

Date	Mintage	F	VF	XF	Unc	BU
1998	—	—	—	—	30.00	—

KM# 78   250 SHILLINGS
Bi-Metallic Brass center in Copper-nickel ring, 38 mm. **Subject:** History of World Shipping **Obv:** Crowned arms with supporters **Rev:** Multicolored Titanic

Date	Mintage	F	VF	XF	Unc	BU
1998	—	—	—	—	22.50	—

KM# 79   250 SHILLINGS
Bi-Metallic Brass center in Copper-nickel ring, 38 mm. **Subject:** History of World Shipping **Obv:** Crowned arms with supporters **Rev:** Multicolored Greek trirema

Date	Mintage	F	VF	XF	Unc	BU
1998	—	—	—	—	22.50	—

KM# 80   250 SHILLINGS
Bi-Metallic Brass center in Copper-nickel ring, 38 mm. **Subject:** History of World Shipping **Obv:** Crowned arms with supporters **Rev:** Multicolored Roman merchant ship

Date	Mintage	F	VF	XF	Unc	BU
1998	—	—	—	—	22.50	—

KM# 81   250 SHILLINGS
Bi-Metallic Brass center in Copper-nickel ring, 38 mm. **Subject:** History of World Shipping **Obv:** Crowned arms with supporters **Rev:** Multicolored Hanseatic Trading Cog

Date	Mintage	F	VF	XF	Unc	BU
1998	—	—	—	—	22.50	—

KM# 82   250 SHILLINGS
Bi-Metallic Brass center in Copper-nickel ring, 38 mm. **Subject:** History of World Shipping **Obv:** Crowned arms with supporters **Rev:** Multicolored Caravel "Nina" **Edge:** Reeded

Date	Mintage	F	VF	XF	Unc	BU
1998	—	—	—	—	22.50	—

KM# 83   250 SHILLINGS
Bi-Metallic Brass center in Copper-nickel ring, 38 mm. **Subject:** History of World Shipping **Obv:** Crowned arms with supporters **Rev:** Multicolored Clipper "Cutty Sark"

Date	Mintage	F	VF	XF	Unc	BU
1998	—	—	—	—	22.50	—

KM# 102   250 SHILLINGS
24.0000 g., 0.9000 Silver 0.6944 oz. ASW, 38.1 mm. **Subject:** Olympics **Obv:** Crowned arms with supporters **Rev:** Multicolor skier **Edge:** Reeded

Date	Mintage	F	VF	XF	Unc	BU
1998 Proof	—	Value: 40.00				

KM# 142   250 SHILLINGS
22.0000 g., Tri-Metallic Gold Plated Brass center in Silver Plated Brass inner ring within a Gold Plated Brass outer ring, 38 mm. **Subject:** 100th Birthday - British Queen Mother **Obv:** Crowned arms with supporters above value **Rev:** Queen Mother **Edge:** Reeded

Date	Mintage	F	VF	XF	Unc	BU
ND (1999)	—	—	—	—	35.00	40.00

KM# 105   250 SHILLINGS
23.1000 g., 0.9250 Silver 0.6870 oz. ASW, 38.6 mm. **Obv:** Crowned arms with supporters **Rev:** Two giraffes **Edge:** Reeded

Date	Mintage	F	VF	XF	Unc	BU
1999 Proof	—	Value: 35.00				

KM# 114   250 SHILLINGS
23.0000 g., 0.9250 Silver 0.6840 oz. ASW, 38 mm. **Subject:** Winston Churchill **Obv:** Crowned arms with supporters **Rev:** Bust facing **Edge:** Reeded

Date	Mintage	F	VF	XF	Unc	BU
2000	—	—	—	—	40.00	42.50

KM# 63   250 SHILLINGS
24.8300 g., 0.9000 Silver 0.7184 oz. ASW, 37.2 mm. **Subject:** Marine Life Protection **Obv:** Crowned arms with supporters **Rev:** Multicolor penguins **Edge:** Reeded

Date	Mintage	F	VF	XF	Unc	BU
2000 Proof	—	Value: 45.00				

KM# 115   250 SHILLINGS
23.0000 g., 0.9250 Silver 0.6840 oz. ASW, 38 mm. **Subject:** Pope John Paul II **Obv:** Crowned arms with supporters **Rev:** Bust facing **Edge:** Reeded

Date	Mintage	F	VF	XF	Unc	BU
2000	—	—	—	—	40.00	42.50

KM# 116 250 SHILLINGS
21.9000 g., Tri-Metallic Brass center, Copper-Nickel inner ring,
brass outer ring **Subject:** Millennium Icons - Nelson Mandela
Obv: Crowned arms with supporters **Obv. Leg.:** REPUBLIC OF
SOMALIA **Rev:** Bust facing

Date	Mintage	F	VF	XF	Unc	BU
2000	—	—	—	—	—	30.00

KM# 116a 250 SHILLINGS
23.0000 g., 0.9250 Silver 0.6840 oz. ASW, 38 mm.
Subject: Millennium Icons - Nelson Mandela **Obv:** Crowned arms
with supporters **Obv. Leg.:** REPUBLIC OF SOMALIA **Rev:** Bust
facing **Edge:** Reeded

Date	Mintage	F	VF	XF	Unc	BU
2000 Proof	—	Value: 45.00				

KM# 117 250 SHILLINGS
21.9000 g., Tri-Metallic Brass center, Copper-Nickel inner ring,
Brass outer ring **Subject:** Millennium Icons - Emperor Hirohito
Obv: Crowned arms with supporters **Obv. Leg.:** REPUBLIC OF
SOMALIA **Rev:** Bust facing

Date	Mintage	F	VF	XF	Unc	BU
2000	—	—	—	—	—	30.00

KM# 117a 250 SHILLINGS
23.0000 g., 0.9250 Silver 0.6840 oz. ASW, 38 mm.
Subject: Millennium Icons - Emperor Hirohito **Obv:** Crowned
arms with supporters **Obv. Leg.:** REPUBLIC OF SOMALIA
Rev: Bust facing **Edge:** Reeded

Date	Mintage	F	VF	XF	Unc	BU
2000 Proof	—	Value: 45.00				

KM# 118 250 SHILLINGS
21.9000 g., Tri-Metallic Brass center, Copper-Nickel inner ring,
Brass outer ring, 38 mm. **Subject:** Millennium Icons - Mao Tse-
tung **Obv:** Crowned arms with supporters **Obv. Leg.:** REPUBLIC
OF SOMALIA **Rev:** Head right **Edge:** Reeded

Date	Mintage	F	VF	XF	Unc	BU
2000	—	—	—	—	30.00	—

KM# 119 250 SHILLINGS
21.9000 g., Tri-Metallic Brass center in Copper-Nickel inner ring,
Brass outer ring, 38 mm. **Subject:** Millennium Icons - Che
Guevara **Obv:** Crowned arms with supporters **Obv. Leg.:**
REPUBLIC OF SOMALIA **Rev:** Bust facing **Edge:** Reeded

Date	Mintage	F	VF	XF	Unc	BU
2000	—	—	—	—	—	30.00

KM# 119a 250 SHILLINGS
23.0000 g., 0.9250 Silver 0.6840 oz. ASW, 38 mm.
Subject: Millennium Icons - Che Guevara **Obv:** Crowned arms
with supporters **Obv. Leg.:** REPUBLIC OF SOMALIA **Rev:** Bust
facing **Edge:** Reeded

Date	Mintage	F	VF	XF	Unc	BU
2000 Proof	—	Value: 45.00				

KM# 84 5000 SHILLINGS / SCELLINI
7.0600 g., 0.9990 Silver 0.2267 oz. ASW, 29.7 mm.
Subject: Tall Ship Series: Amerigo Vespucci **Obv:** Crowned
arms with supporters **Rev:** Sailing ship **Edge:** Plain

Date	Mintage	F	VF	XF	Unc	BU
1998 Proof	—	Value: 25.00				

KM# 85 5000 SHILLINGS / SCELLINI
7.0600 g., 0.9990 Silver 0.2267 oz. ASW **Subject:** Tall Ships
Series: Sedov **Obv:** Crowned arms with supporters **Rev:** Sailing ship

Date	Mintage	F	VF	XF	Unc	BU
1998 Proof	—	Value: 25.00				

KM# 86 5000 SHILLINGS / SCELLINI
7.0600 g., 0.9990 Silver 0.2267 oz. ASW **Subject:** Tall Ships
Series: Gorch Fock **Obv:** Crowned arms with supporters
Rev: Sailing ship

Date	Mintage	F	VF	XF	Unc	BU
1998 Proof	—	Value: 25.00				

KM# 87 5000 SHILLINGS / SCELLINI
7.0600 g., 0.9990 Silver 0.2267 oz. ASW **Subject:** Tall Ships
Series: Libertad **Obv:** Crowned arms with supporters **Rev:** Sailing
ship

Date	Mintage	F	VF	XF	Unc	BU
1998 Proof	—	Value: 25.00				

KM# 88 5000 SHILLINGS / SCELLINI
7.0600 g., 0.9990 Silver 0.2267 oz. ASW **Subject:** Tall Ships
Series: Alexander von Humboldt **Obv:** Crowned arms with
supporters **Rev:** Sailing ship

Date	Mintage	F	VF	XF	Unc	BU
1998 Proof	—	Value: 25.00				

KM# 89 5000 SHILLINGS / SCELLINI
7.0600 g., 0.9990 Silver 0.2267 oz. ASW **Subject:** Tall Ship Series:
Eagle **Obv:** Crowned arms with supporters **Rev:** Sailing ship

Date	Mintage	F	VF	XF	Unc	BU
1998 Proof	—	Value: 25.00				

KM# 43 10000 SHILLINGS / SCELLINI
15.0000 g., 0.9990 Silver 0.4818 oz. ASW **Subject:** Fauna of
Africa **Obv:** Crowned arms with supporters **Rev:** Ostriches

Date	Mintage	F	VF	XF	Unc	BU
1998 Proof	—	Value: 45.00				

KM# 44 10000 SHILLINGS / SCELLINI
15.0000 g., 0.9990 Silver 0.4818 oz. ASW **Subject:** Fauna of Africa
Obv: Crowned arms with supporters **Rev:** Three Dammah Oryx

Date	Mintage	F	VF	XF	Unc	BU
1998 Proof	—	Value: 50.00				

PIEFORTS

KM#	Date	Mintage	Identification	Mkt Val
P1	1983	500	150 Shillings. 0.9250 Silver.	115
P2	1983	—	1500 Shillings. Gold. KM39.	875
P3	ND(1984)	500	25 Shillings. 0.9250 Silver.	100
P4	1998	2,500	250 Shillings. 0.9250 Silver. 47.5400 g. Skier.	135
P5	1998	—	250 Shillings. Silver. Titanic. KM42.	70.00
P6	1998	—	250 Shillings. 0.9250 Silver. Ostrich. KM49.	50.00

PROVAS

KM#	Date	Mintage	Identification	Mkt Val
Pr1	1950	—	Centesimo.	50.00
Pr2	1950	—	5 Centesimi.	50.00
Pr3	1950	—	10 Centesimi.	50.00
Pr4	1950	—	50 Centesimi.	75.00
Pr5	1950	—	Somalo.	100

MINT SETS

KM#	Date	Mintage	Identification	Issue Price	Mkt Val
MS1	1979 (5)	—	KM33-37	2,375	1,750

PROOF SETS

KM#	Date	Mintage	Identification	Issue Price	Mkt Val
PS1	1965 (5)	6,325	KM10-14	—	2,250
PS2	1965 (5)	—	KM10-14. Gilt copper nickel.	—	—
PS3	1970 (5)	8,000	KM16, 17, 19, 21, 23	335	2,700
PS4	1970 (3)	14,500	KM18, 20, 22	—	1,120
PS5	1979 (5)	5,000	KM28a-32a	325	150
PS6	1979 (5)	—	KM33-37	3,125	1,800

SOMALILAND

The Somaliland Republic, comprised of the former British Somaliland Protectorate is located on the coast of the northeastern projection of the African continent commonly referred to as the "Horn" on the southwestern end of the Gulf of Aden.

Bordered by Ethiopia to west and south and Somalia to the east. It has an area of 68,000* sq. mi. (176,000* sq. km). Capital: Hargeysa. It is mostly arid and mountainous except for the gulf shoreline.

The Protectorate of British Somaliland was established in 1888 and from 1905 a commissioner under the British Colonial Office administered the territory. Italian Somaliland was administered as a colony from 1893 to 1941, when British forces occupied the territory. In 1950 the United Nations allowed Italy to resume control of Italian Somaliland under a trusteeship. In 1960 British and Italian Somaliland were united as Somalia, an independent republic outside the Commonwealth.

Civil war erupted in the late 1970's and continued until the capital of Somalia was taken in 1990. The United Nations provided aid and peacekeeping. A UN sponsored truce was signed in March 1992 and a peace plan and pact was signed Jan. 15, 1993. The northern Somali National Movement (SNM) declared a secession of the Somaliland Republic on May 17, 1991, which is not recognized by the Somali Democratic Republic.

The currency issued by the East African Currency Board was used in British Somaliland from 1945 to 1961; Somali currency was used later until 1995.

REPUBLIC

SHILLING COINAGE

KM# 1 SHILLING
1.0700 g., Aluminum, 20.5 mm. **Issuer:** Bank of Somaliland **Obv:** Bird **Obv. Leg.:** REPUBLIC OF SOMALILAND **Rev:** Value **Rev. Leg.:** • BAANKA SOMALILAND • **Edge:** Reeded

Date	Mintage	F	VF	XF	Unc	BU
1994PM	—	—	—	1.50	3.00	5.00

SOUTH AFRICA

The Republic of South Africa, located at the southern tip of Africa, has an area of 471,445 sq. mi. (1,221,043 sq. km.) and a population of *30.2 million. Capitals: Administrative, Pretoria; Legislative, Cape Town; Judicial, Bloemfontein. Manufacturing, mining and agriculture are the principal industries. Exports include wool, diamonds, gold, and metallic ores.

Portuguese navigator Bartholomew Diaz became the first European to sight the region of South Africa when he rounded the Cape of Good Hope in 1488, but throughout the 16th century the only white men to come ashore were the survivors of ships wrecked while attempting the stormy Cape passage. Jan van Riebeeck of the Dutch East India Company established the first permanent settlement in 1652. In subsequent decades additional Dutch, German and Huguenot refugees from France settled in the Cape area to form the Afrikaner segment of today's population.

Great Britain captured the Cape colony in 1795, and again in 1806, receiving permanent title in 1814. To escape British political rule and cultural dominance, many Afrikaner farmers (Boers) migrated northward (the Great Trek) beginning in 1836, and established the independent Boer Republics of the Transvaal (the South African Republic, Zuid Afrikaansche Republic) in 1852, and the Orange Free State in 1854. British political intrigues against the two republics, coupled with the discovery of diamonds and gold in the Boer-settled regions, led to the bitter Boer Wars (1880-81, 1899-1902) and the incorporation of the Boer republics into the British Empire.

On May 31, 1910, the two former Boer Republics (Transvaal and Orange Free State) were joined with the British colonies of Cape of Good Hope and Natal to form the Union of South Africa, a dominion of the British Empire. In 1934 the Union achieved status as a sovereign state within the British Empire.

Political integration of the various colonies did not still the conflict between the Afrikaners and the English-speaking groups, which continued to have a significant impact on political developments. A resurgence of Afrikaner nationalism in the 1940s and 1950s led to a referendum in the white community authorizing the relinquishment of dominion status and the establishment of a republic. The decision took effect on May 31, 1961. The Republic of South Africa withdrew from the British Commonwealth in Oct. 1961.

The apartheid era ended April 27, 1994 with the first democratic election for all people of South Africa. Nelson Mandela was inaugurated President May 10, 1994, and South Africa was readmitted into the Commonwealth of Nations. Walvis Bay, former enclave of Cape Province, transferred to Namibia.

South African coins and currency bear inscriptions in tribal languages, Afrikaans and English.

RULERS
British, until 1934

MONETARY SYSTEM
Until 1961
12 Pence = 1 Shilling
2 Shillings = 1 Florin
20 Shillings = 1 Pound (Pond)
Commencing 1961
100 Cents = 1 Rand

REPUBLIK
Zuid-Afrikaansche Republiek

MONETARY SYSTEM
12 Pence = 1 Shilling
20 Shillings = 1 Pond

Beware of counterfeit double shafts. Aside from there being two shafts on the wagon in the coat of arms (reverse), the two wheels of the wagon must be the same size. On single-shaft wagons, the rear wheel is noticeably larger than the front wheel.

STANDARD COINAGE
12 Pence = 1 Shilling; 20 Shillings = 1 Pond

KM# 11 1/2 POND
0.9990 Gold **Subject:** Veld-Boer War Siege Issue **Obv:** Monogram and date **Rev:** Inscription

Date	Mintage	F	VF	XF	Unc	BU
1902	986	750	1,350	2,750	5,000	

UNION OF SOUTH AFRICA
Dominion under Great Britain

STANDARD COINAGE
12 Pence = 1 Shilling; 2 Shillings = 1 Florin; 20 Shillings 1 Pound

KM# 12.1 1/4 PENNY (Farthing)
Bronze, 20.20 mm. **Ruler:** George V **Obv:** Crowned bust left **Rev:** Wheat sprig and berries divide birds within circle **Edge:** Plain

Date	Mintage	F	VF	XF	Unc	BU
1923	33,000	1.50	5.00	10.00	20.00	—
1923 Proof	1,402	Value: 285				
1924	95,000	1.50	3.50	9.00	20.00	—

KM# 12.2 1/4 PENNY (Farthing)
Bronze **Ruler:** George V **Obv:** Crowned bust left **Rev:** Oat sprigs and berries divide birds within circle

Date	Mintage	F	VF	XF	Unc	BU
1926 Proof	16	Value: 20,500				
	Note: Only 5 examples currently known					
1928	64,000	1.50	3.00	5.00	12.50	—
1930	6,560	30.00	60.00	120	200	—
1930 Proof	14	Value: 1,200				
1931	154,000	1.00	1.50	4.00	6.00	—

KM# 12.3 1/4 PENNY (Farthing)
Bronze **Ruler:** George V **Obv:** Crowned bust left **Rev:** Oat sprig and berries divide birds within circle

Date	Mintage	F	VF	XF	Unc	BU
1931	Inc. above	5.00	10.00	15.00	35.00	—
1931 Proof	62	Value: 200				
1932	105,000	1.00	1.50	3.50	7.00	—
1932 Proof	12	Value: 375				
1933	76	750	1,450	2,200	3,250	—
1933 Proof	20	Value: 4,000				
1934	52	750	1,450	2,200	3,250	—
1934 Proof	24	Value: 3,750				
1935	61,000	1.00	1.50	3.50	8.00	—
1935 Proof	20	Value: 3,000				
1936	43	350	750	1,100	2,000	—
1936 Proof	40	Value: 3,000				

KM# 23 1/4 PENNY (Farthing)
2.8400 g., Bronze, 20 mm. **Ruler:** George VI **Obv:** Head left **Rev:** Oat sprig and berries divide birds within circle

Date	Mintage	F	VF	XF	Unc	BU
1937	38,000	1.50	3.00	6.00	12.50	—
1937 Proof	116	Value: 40.00				
1938	51,000	1.00	2.00	4.00	8.00	—

Date	Mintage	F	VF	XF	Unc	BU
1938 Proof	44	Value: 100				
1939	102,000	0.50	1.50	3.00	7.50	—
1939 Proof	30	Value: 125				
1941	91,000	0.50	1.50	3.00	7.50	—
1942	3,756,000	0.25	0.50	1.00	2.00	—
1943	9,918,000	0.25	0.50	0.75	1.50	—
1943 Proof	104	Value: 40.00				
1944	4,468,000	0.25	0.50	0.75	2.00	—
1944 Proof	150	Value: 35.00				
1945	5,297,000	0.25	0.50	1.50	3.00	—
1945 Proof	150	Value: 35.00				
1946	4,378,000	0.25	0.50	1.50	4.00	—
1946 Proof	150	Value: 35.00				
1947	3,895,000	0.25	0.50	1.50	4.00	—
1947 Proof	2,600	Value: 4.00				

KM# 32.1 1/4 PENNY (Farthing)
Bronze Ruler: George VI Obv: Head left Rev: Oat sprig and berries divide birds within circle

Date	Mintage	F	VF	XF	Unc	BU
1948	2,415,000	0.25	0.50	1.00	2.00	—
1948 Proof	1,120	Value: 3.00				
1949	3,568,000	0.25	0.50	1.00	2.50	—
1949 Proof	800	Value: 5.00				
1950	8,694,000	0.25	0.50	0.75	1.50	—
1950 Proof	500	Value: 8.00				

KM# 32.2 1/4 PENNY (Farthing)
2.7000 g., Bronze, 20.5 mm. Ruler: George VI Obv: Head left Rev: Oat sprig and berries divide birds within circle Rev. Leg.: SUID AFRIKA-SOUTH AFRICA

Date	Mintage	F	VF	XF	Unc	BU
1951	3,511,000	0.15	0.35	0.75	2.50	—
1951 Proof	2,000	Value: 2.00				
1952	2,805,000	0.15	0.35	0.75	2.00	—
1952 Proof	16,000	Value: 2.00				

KM# 44 1/4 PENNY (Farthing)
2.8000 g., Bronze Ruler: Elizabeth II Obv: Laureate head right Rev: Oat sprig and berries divide birds within circle

Date	Mintage	F	VF	XF	Unc	BU
1953	7,193,000	0.15	0.25	0.50	1.50	—
1953 Proof	5,000	Value: 2.00				
1954	6,568,000	0.15	0.25	0.50	1.50	—
1954 Proof	3,150	Value: 2.00				
1955	11,798,000	0.15	0.25	0.50	1.50	—
1955 Proof	2,850	Value: 2.00				
1956	1,287,000	0.15	0.25	0.50	2.50	—
1956 Proof	1,700	Value: 3.00				
1957	3,065,000	0.15	0.25	0.50	1.50	—
1957 Proof	1,130	Value: 4.00				
1958	5,452,000	0.15	0.25	0.50	1.50	—
1958 Proof	985	Value: 5.00				
1959	1,567,000	0.15	0.25	0.50	1.50	—
1959 Proof	900	Value: 6.00				
1960	1,022,999	0.15	0.25	0.50	2.00	—
1960 Proof	3,360	Value: 1.50				

KM# 13.1 1/2 PENNY
Bronze Ruler: George V Subject: Dromedaris (ship) Obv: Crowned bust left Rev: Sailing ship

Date	Mintage	F	VF	XF	Unc	BU
1923	12,000	25.00	40.00	70.00	100	—
1923 Proof	1,402	Value: 100				
1924	64,000	7.50	12.50	30.00	60.00	—

Date	Mintage	F	VF	XF	Unc	BU
1925	69,000	7.50	12.50	30.00	80.00	—
1926	65,000	10.00	15.00	35.00	100	—

KM# 13.2 1/2 PENNY
Bronze Ruler: George V Subject: Dromedaris (ship) Obv: Crowned bust left Rev: Sailing ship

Date	Mintage	F	VF	XF	Unc	BU
1928	105,000	5.00	12.50	35.00	75.00	—
1929	272,000	2.50	5.00	15.00	35.00	—
1930	147,000	3.50	7.00	20.00	40.00	—
1930 Proof	14	Value: 400				
1930	Inc. above	4.00	8.00	25.00	50.00	—
Note: Without star after date						
1931	145,000	3.50	7.00	25.00	50.00	—

KM# 13.3 1/2 PENNY
Bronze Ruler: George V Subject: Dromedaris (ship) Obv: Crowned bust left Rev: Sailing ship

Date	Mintage	F	VF	XF	Unc	BU
1931 Proof	62	Value: 1,000				
1932	106,000	5.00	10.00	30.00	75.00	—
1932 Proof	12	Value: 1,000				
1933	63,000	8.00	25.00	55.00	100	—
1933 Proof		Value: 500				
1934	326,000	1.50	5.00	15.00	45.00	—
1934 Proof	24	Value: 500				
1935	405,000	1.50	5.00	15.00	40.00	—
1935 Proof	20	Value: 500				
1936	407,000	1.50	5.00	15.00	30.00	—
1936 Proof	40	Value: 200				

KM# 24 1/2 PENNY
Bronze Ruler: George VI Subject: Dromedaris (ship) Obv: Head left Rev: Sailing ship

Date	Mintage	F	VF	XF	Unc	BU
1937	638,000	1.00	2.00	9.00	15.00	—
1937 Proof	116	Value: 50.00				
1938	560,000	1.00	2.00	6.00	15.00	—
1938 Proof	44	Value: 125				
1939	271,000	2.50	5.00	10.00	20.00	—
1939 Proof	30	Value: 175				
1940	1,535,000	0.30	0.75	3.00	8.00	—
1941	2,053,000	0.30	0.75	3.00	8.00	—
1942	8,382,000	0.25	0.60	2.00	6.00	—
1943	5,135,000	0.25	0.60	2.00	6.00	—
1943 Proof	104	Value: 45.00				
1944	3,920,000	0.25	0.75	3.00	8.00	—
1944 Proof	150	Value: 35.00				
1945	2,357,000	0.25	0.60	2.50	7.00	—
1945 Proof	150	Value: 35.00				
1946	1,022,000	0.25	0.75	3.00	9.00	—
1946 Proof	150	Value: 35.00				
1947	258,000	1.00	3.00	6.00	17.50	—
1947 Proof	2,600	Value: 10.00				

KM# 33 1/2 PENNY
Bronze, 25 mm. Ruler: George VI Subject: Dromedaris (ship) Obv: Head left Rev: Sailing ship

Date	Mintage	F	VF	XF	Unc	BU
1948	685,000	0.50	1.00	4.00	9.00	—
1948 Proof	1,120	Value: 15.00				

Date	Mintage	F	VF	XF	Unc	BU
1949	1,850,000	0.25	0.50	1.75	4.00	—
1949 Proof	800	Value: 15.00				
1950	2,186,000	0.25	0.50	1.50	3.00	—
1950 Proof	500	Value: 6.00				
1951	3,746,000	0.25	0.50	1.25	3.00	—
1951 Proof	2,000	Value: 5.00				
1952	4,174,000	0.25	0.50	1.00	2.50	—
1952 Proof	1,550	Value: 4.00				

KM# 45 1/2 PENNY
5.6000 g., Bronze Ruler: Elizabeth II Subject: Dromedaris (ship) Obv: Laureate head right Rev: Sailing ship

Date	Mintage	F	VF	XF	Unc	BU
1953	5,572,000	0.15	0.35	1.00	3.00	—
1953 Proof	5,000	Value: 4.00				
1954	101,000	2.00	4.00	7.50	12.50	—
1954 Proof	3,150	Value: 15.00				
1955	3,774,000	0.15	0.35	1.00	3.00	—
1955 Proof	2,850	Value: 4.00				
1956	1,305,000	0.15	0.35	1.00	3.00	—
1956 Proof	1,700	Value: 4.00				
1957	2,025,000	0.15	0.35	1.00	3.00	—
1957 Proof	1,130	Value: 4.00				
1958	2,171,000	0.15	0.35	1.00	2.50	—
1958 Proof	985	Value: 5.00				
1959	2,397,000	0.15	0.25	0.75	2.00	—
1959 Proof	900	Value: 6.00				
1960	2,552,000	0.15	0.25	0.75	2.00	—
1960 Proof	3,360	Value: 1.50				

KM# 14.1 PENNY
Bronze, 30.8 mm. Ruler: George V Subject: Dromedaris (ship) Obv: Crowned bust left Rev: Sailing ship

Date	Mintage	F	VF	XF	Unc	BU
1923	91,000	3.00	7.00	17.50	35.00	—
1923 Proof	1,402	Value: 50.00				
1924	134,000	4.00	10.00	25.00	50.00	—

KM# 14.2 PENNY
Bronze, 30.8 mm. Ruler: George V Subject: Dromedaris (ship) Obv: Crowned bust left Rev: Sailing ship

Date	Mintage	F	VF	XF	Unc	BU
1926	393,000	3.00	10.00	40.00	100	—
1926 Proof	16	Value: 600				
1927	285,000	3.00	10.00	40.00	90.00	—
1928	386,000	3.00	10.00	40.00	90.00	—
1929	1,093,000	1.00	5.00	15.00	35.00	—
1930	754,000	1.00	5.00	20.00	40.00	—
1930 Proof	14	Value: 600				

KM# 14.3   PENNY
9.5000 g., Bronze, 30.8 mm. **Ruler:** George V **Subject:** Dromedaris (ship) **Obv:** Crowned bust left **Rev:** Sailing ship

Date	Mintage	F	VF	XF	Unc	BU
1931	284,000	1.00	5.00	17.50	40.00	—
1931 Proof	62	Value: 400				
1932	260,000	1.00	5.00	20.00	50.00	—
1932 Proof	12	Value: 800				
1933	225,000	2.00	10.00	30.00	45.00	—
1933 Proof	20	Value: 500				
1933	Inc. above	4.00	10.00	30.00	50.00	—
Note: Without star after date						
1934	2,089,999	0.50	1.50	8.00	22.50	—
1934 Proof	24	Value: 600				
1935	2,295,000	.0.50	1.50	8.00	22.50	—
1935 Proof	20	Value: 600				
1936	1,819,000	0.35	1.50	20.00	—	
1936 Proof	40	Value: 300				

KM# 25   PENNY
9.3000 g., Bronze, 30.8 mm. **Ruler:** George VI **Subject:** Dromedaris (ship) **Obv:** Head left **Rev:** Sailing ship

Date	Mintage	F	VF	XF	Unc	BU
1937	3,281,000	0.50	1.50	10.00	25.00	—
1937 Proof	116	Value: 75.00				
1938	1,840,000	0.50	1.50	8.00	30.00	—
1938 Proof	44	Value: 100				
1939	1,506,000	0.50	1.50	10.00	25.00	—
1939 Proof	30	Value: 175				
1940	3,592,000	0.35	1.00	4.00	10.00	—
1940	Inc. above	1.50	3.00	6.00	15.00	—
Note: Without star after date						
1941	7,871,000	0.25	0.75	2.50	7.00	—
1942	14,428,000	0.25	0.75	2.00	6.00	—
1942	Inc. above	3.00	6.00	12.50	30.00	—
Note: Without star after date						
1943	4,010,000	0.25	0.75	2.50	6.00	—
1943 Proof	104	Value: 55.00				
1944	6,425,000	0.25	0.75	2.50	7.00	—
1944 Proof	150	Value: 45.00				
1945	4,810,000	0.25	0.75	2.50	7.00	—
1945 Proof	150	Value: 45.00				
1946	2,605,000	0.25	0.75	3.00	8.00	—
1946 Proof	150	Value: 45.00				
1947	135,000	2.50	4.00	7.50	17.50	—
1947 Proof	2,600	Value: 7.00				

KM# 34.1   PENNY
Bronze, 30.8 mm. **Ruler:** George VI **Subject:** Dromedaris (ship) **Obv:** Head left **Rev:** Sailing ship

Date	Mintage	F	VF	XF	Unc	BU
1948	2,398,000	0.25	0.75	2.50	6.00	—
1948 Proof	1,120	Value: 5.00				
1948	Inc. above	1.00	2.00	5.00	10.00	—
Note: Without star after date						
1949	3,634,000	0.25	0.75	2.00	6.00	—
1949 Proof	800	Value: 12.00				
1950	4,890,000	0.25	0.75	2.00	5.00	—
1950 Proof	500	Value: 10.00				

KM# 34.2   PENNY
Bronze, 30.8 mm. **Ruler:** George VI **Subject:** Dromedaris (ship) **Obv:** Head left **Rev:** Sailing ship **Rev. Leg.:** SUID AFRIKA-SOUTH AFRICA

Date	Mintage	F	VF	XF	Unc	BU
1951	3,787,000	0.25	0.75	1.50	4.00	—
1951 Proof	2,000	Value: 5.00				
1952	12,674,000	0.25	0.50	1.00	2.50	—
1952 Proof	16,000	Value: 4.00				

KM# 46   PENNY
9.6000 g., Bronze, 30.8 mm. **Ruler:** Elizabeth II **Subject:** Dromedaris (ship) **Obv:** Laureate head right **Rev:** Sailing ship

Date	Mintage	F	VF	XF	Unc	BU
1953	5,491,000	0.20	0.35	0.75	2.00	—
1953 Proof	5,000	Value: 2.00				
1954	6,665,000	1.00	2.00	5.00	10.00	—
1954 Proof	3,150	Value: 15.00				
1955	6,508,000	0.20	0.35	0.75	3.00	—
1955 Proof	2,850	Value: 2.00				
1956	4,390,000	0.20	0.35	1.00	4.00	—
1956 Proof	1,700	Value: 3.00				
1957	3,973,000	0.20	0.35	0.75	3.00	—
1957 Proof	1,130	Value: 5.00				
1958	5,311,000	0.20	0.35	0.75	3.00	—
1958 Proof	985	Value: 6.00				
1959	5,066,000	0.20	0.35	0.75	2.00	—
1959 Proof	900	Value: 7.00				
1960	5,106,000	0.20	0.35	0.75	2.00	—
1960 Proof	3,360	Value: 2.00				

KM# 15A   3 PENCE
1.4100 g., 0.8000 Silver 0.0363 oz. ASW, 16.5 mm. **Ruler:** George V **Obv:** Crowned bust left **Rev:** Value within wreath

Date	Mintage	F	VF	XF	Unc	BU
1923	302,000	4.00	8.00	20.00	45.00	—
1923 Proof	1,402	Value: 50.00				
1924	501,000	4.00	10.00	25.00	50.00	—
1925		10.00	35.00	200	475	

KM# 15.1   3 PENCE
1.4100 g., 0.8000 Silver 0.0363 oz. ASW, 16.5 mm. **Ruler:** George V **Obv:** Crowned bust left **Rev:** Protea flower in center, value as 3 PENCE

Date	Mintage	F	VF	XF	Unc	BU
1925	358,000	5.00	25.00	90.00	175	—
1926	1,572,000	1.00	3.50	20.00	50.00	—
1926 Proof	16	Value: 2,000				
1927	2,285,000	1.00	2.50	15.00	45.00	—
1928	919,000	1.50	3.50	20.00	50.00	—
1929	1,948,000	1.00	2.50	15.00	45.00	—
1930	981,000	1.00	3.50	20.00	50.00	—
1930 Proof	14	Value: 800				

KM# 15.2   3 PENCE
1.4100 g., 0.8000 Silver 0.0363 oz. ASW, 16.5 mm. **Ruler:** George V **Obv:** Crowned bust left **Rev:** Protea flower in center, value as 3D

Date	Mintage	F	VF	XF	Unc	BU
1931	66	750	1,000	1,750	3,500	—
1931 Proof	62	Value: 3,500				
1932	2,622,000	1.00	2.50	15.00	30.00	—
1932 Proof	12	Value: 1,000				
1933	5,135,000	1.00	2.50	15.00	30.00	—
1933 Proof	20	Value: 1,000				
1934	2,357,000	1.00	2.50	15.00	30.00	—
1934 Proof	24	Value: 1,000				
1935	1,655,000	1.00	2.50	15.00	30.00	—
1935 Proof	20	Value: 1,000				
1936	1,095,000	1.00	2.50	15.00	35.00	—
1936 Proof	40	Value: 250				

KM# 26   3 PENCE
1.4100 g., 0.8000 Silver 0.0363 oz. ASW, 16.5 mm. **Ruler:** George VI **Obv:** Head left **Rev:** Protea flower in center of designed bars shaped as a triangle

Date	Mintage	F	VF	XF	Unc	BU
1937	3,576,000	0.60	1.00	3.00	10.00	—
1937 Proof	116	Value: 80.00				
1938	2,394,000	0.60	1.50	7.00	20.00	—
1938 Proof	44	Value: 100				
1939	3,224,000	0.60	1.50	5.00	12.50	—
1939 Proof	30	Value: 250				
1940	4,887,000	0.60	1.00	3.00	12.50	—
1941	8,968,000	0.60	1.00	3.00	9.00	—
1942	8,055,999	0.60	1.00	3.00	9.00	—
1943	14,827,000	0.60	1.00	2.50	6.00	—
1943 Proof	104	Value: 70.00				
1944	3,331,000	0.60	1.00	3.00	9.00	—
1944 Proof	150	Value: 60.00				
1945/3	4,094,000	1.00	3.00	10.00	20.00	—
1945	Inc. above	0.60	1.00	3.00	9.00	—
1945 Proof	150	Value: 60.00				
1946	2,219,000	0.60	1.00	3.00	10.00	—
1946 Proof	150	Value: 65.00				
1947	1,127,000	0.60	1.00	2.50	8.00	—
1947 Proof	2,600	Value: 8.00				

KM# 35.1   3 PENCE
1.4100 g., 0.8000 Silver 0.0363 oz. ASW, 16.5 mm. **Ruler:** George VI **Obv:** Head left **Rev:** Protea flower in center of designed bars shaped as a triangle

Date	Mintage	F	VF	XF	Unc	BU
1948	2,720,000	0.60	1.00	3.00	7.00	—
1948 Proof	1,120	Value: 5.00				
1949	1,904,000	0.60	1.00	3.00	7.00	—
1949 Proof	800	Value: 5.00				
1950	4,096,000	0.60	1.00	2.50	5.00	—
1950 Proof	500	Value: 7.00				

KM# 35.2   3 PENCE
1.4100 g., 0.5000 Silver 0.0227 oz. ASW, 16.5 mm. **Ruler:** George VI **Obv:** Head left **Rev:** Protea flower in center of designed bars shaped as a triangle **Note:** Many varieties exist of George VI 3 Pence.

Date	Mintage	F	VF	XF	Unc	BU
1951	6,323,000	BV	0.50	1.00	3.00	—
1951 Proof	2,000	Value: 4.00				
1952	13,057,000	BV	0.50	1.00	2.00	—
1952 Proof	16,000	Value: 2.00				

KM# 47   3 PENCE
1.4100 g., 0.5000 Silver 0.0227 oz. ASW, 16.5 mm.
Ruler: Elizabeth II **Obv:** Laureate head right **Rev:** Protea flower in center of designed bars shaped as a triangle

Date	Mintage	F	VF	XF	Unc	BU
1953	5,483,000	BV	0.50	1.00	3.00	—
1953 Proof	5,000	Value: 3.00				
1954	3,898,000	BV	0.50	1.00	3.50	—
1954 Proof	3,150	Value: 4.00				
1955	4,720,000	BV	0.50	1.00	3.00	—
1955 Proof	2,850	Value: 3.00				
1956	6,189,000	BV	0.50	1.00	3.00	—
1956 Proof	1,700	Value: 4.00				
1957	1,893,000	BV	0.50	1.00	3.00	—
1957 Proof	1,130	Value: 5.00				
1958	3,227,000	BV	0.50	1.00	3.00	—
1958 Proof	985	Value: 6.00				
1959	2,552,000	BV	0.50	1.00	2.00	—
1959 Proof	900	Value: 7.00				
1959	Inc. above	2.00	3.00	5.00	10.00	
Note: No K-G on reverse						
1960	18,000	1.00	2.50	4.00	7.00	
1960 Proof	3,360	Value: 3.00				

KM# 16A   6 PENCE
2.8300 g., 0.8000 Silver 0.0728 oz. ASW, 19.5 mm.
Ruler: George V **Obv:** Crowned bust left **Rev:** Value within wreath

Date	Mintage	F	VF	XF	Unc	BU
1923	208,000	4.00	15.00	35.00	80.00	—
1923 Proof	1,402	Value: 80.00				
1924	326,000	3.50	12.50	30.00	70.00	—

KM# 16.1   6 PENCE
2.8300 g., 0.8000 Silver 0.0728 oz. ASW, 19.5 mm.
Ruler: George V **Obv:** Crowned bust left **Rev:** Protea flower in center, value as 6 PENCE

Date	Mintage	F	VF	XF	Unc	BU
1925	79,000	5.00	15.00	55.00	125	—
1926	722,000	2.00	10.00	45.00	100	—
1926 Proof	16	Value: 3,000				
1927	1,548,000	1.50	9.00	25.00	50.00	—
1929	784,000	2.00	8.00	30.00	60.00	—
1930	448,000	2.00	8.00	35.00	70.00	—
1930 Proof	14	Value: 1,000				

KM# 16.2   6 PENCE
2.8300 g., 0.8000 Silver 0.0728 oz. ASW, 19.5 mm.
Ruler: George V **Obv:** Crowned bust left **Rev:** Protea flower in center, value as 6D

Date	Mintage	F	VF	XF	Unc	BU
1931	4,743	75.00	150	250	550	—
1931 Proof	62	Value: 1,000				
1932	1,525,000	1.50	5.00	17.50	35.00	—
1932 Proof	12	Value: 1,200				
1933	2,819,000	1.50	5.00	17.50	35.00	—
1933 Proof	20	Value: 1,200				
1934	1,519,000	1.50	7.00	20.00	40.00	—
1934 Proof	24	Value: 1,200				
1935	573,000	2.00	8.00	30.00	100	—
1935 Proof	20	Value: 1,200				
1936	627,000	1.50	7.00	20.00	40.00	—
1936 Proof	40	Value: 275				

KM# 27   6 PENCE
2.8300 g., 0.8000 Silver 0.0728 oz. ASW, 19.5 mm.
Ruler: George VI **Obv:** Head left **Rev:** Protea flower in center of designed bars

Date	Mintage	F	VF	XF	Unc	BU
1937	1,696,000	1.20	2.00	7.00	17.50	—
1937 Proof	116	Value: 90.00				
1938	1,725,000	1.20	2.00	7.00	17.50	—
1938 Proof	44	Value: 125				
1939 Proof	30	Value: 3,750				
1940	1,629,000	1.20	1.50	5.00	10.00	—
1941	2,263,000	1.20	1.50	5.00	10.00	—
1942	4,936,000	BV	1.25	3.00	8.00	—
1943	3,776,000	BV	1.25	3.00	8.00	—
1943 Proof	104	Value: 85.00				
1944	228,000	2.00	7.00	15.00	30.00	—
1944 Proof	150	Value: 75.00				
1945	420,000	1.50	5.00	15.00	35.00	—
1945 Proof	150	Value: 75.00				
1946	290,000	1.50	6.00	15.00	30.00	—
1946 Proof	150	Value: 80.00				
1947	577,000	1.20	1.50	5.00	10.00	—
1947 Proof	2,600	Value: 10.00				

KM# 36.1   6 PENCE
2.8300 g., 0.8000 Silver 0.0728 oz. ASW, 19.5 mm.
Ruler: George VI **Obv:** Head left **Rev:** Protea flower in center of designed bars

Date	Mintage	F	VF	XF	Unc	BU
1948	2,266,000	BV	1.25	2.50	6.00	—
1948 Proof	1,120	Value: 10.00				
1949	196,000	3.00	7.50	15.00	30.00	—
1949 Proof	800	Value: 15.00				
1950	2,122,000	BV	1.20	2.00	5.00	—
1950 Proof	500	Value: 15.00				

KM# 36.2   6 PENCE
2.8300 g., 0.5000 Silver 0.0455 oz. ASW, 19.5 mm.
Ruler: George VI **Obv:** Head left **Rev:** Protea flower in center of designed bars

Date	Mintage	F	VF	XF	Unc	BU
1951	2,602,000	BV	1.00	2.00	4.00	—
1951 Proof	2,000	Value: 4.00				
1952	4,265,000	BV	0.75	1.25	3.00	—
1952 Proof	16,000	Value: 2.00				

KM# 48   6 PENCE
2.8300 g., 0.5000 Silver 0.0455 oz. ASW, 19 mm.
Ruler: Elizabeth II **Obv:** Laureate head right **Rev:** Protea flower in center of designed bars

Date	Mintage	F	VF	XF	Unc	BU
1953	2,496,000	BV	0.75	1.75	4.50	—
1953 Proof	5,000	Value: 3.00				
1954	2,196,000	BV	1.00	2.00	4.50	—
1954 Proof	3,150	Value: 4.00				
1955	1,969,000	BV	1.00	2.00	4.50	—
1955 Proof	2,850	Value: 3.00				
1956	1,772,000	BV	1.00	2.00	5.00	—
1956 Proof	1,700	Value: 4.00				
1957	3,288,000	BV	0.75	1.75	4.50	—
1957 Proof	1,130	Value: 6.00				
1958	1,172,000	BV	1.00	2.00	4.50	—
1958 Proof	985	Value: 6.00				
1959	261,000	1.00	2.00	4.00	12.00	—
1959 Proof	900	Value: 8.00				
1960	1,587,000	BV	0.75	1.25	2.50	—
1960 Proof	3,360	Value: 2.50				

KM# 17.1   SHILLING
5.6600 g., 0.8000 Silver 0.1456 oz. ASW, 23.5 mm.
Ruler: George V **Obv:** Crowned bust left **Rev:** Value as 1 SHILLING 1

Date	Mintage	F	VF	XF	Unc	BU
1923	808,000	4.00	15.00	35.00	75.00	—
1923 Proof	1,402	Value: 80.00				
1924	1,269,000	3.50	12.50	30.00	75.00	—

KM# 17.2   SHILLING
5.6600 g., 0.8000 Silver 0.1456 oz. ASW, 23.5 mm.
Ruler: George V **Obv:** Crowned bust left **Rev:** Value as SHILLING

Date	Mintage	F	VF	XF	Unc	BU
1926	238,000	15.00	75.00	400	1,150	—
1926 Proof	16	Value: 3,000				
1927	488,000	10.00	25.00	150	375	—
1928	889,000	8.00	25.00	100	250	—
1929	926,000	5.00	10.00	30.00	175	—
1930	422,000	6.00	15.00	60.00	150	—
1930 Proof	14	Value: 1,000				

KM# 17.3   SHILLING
5.6600 g., 0.8000 Silver 0.1456 oz. ASW, 23.5 mm.
Ruler: George V **Obv:** Crowned bust left **Rev:** Standing female figure leaning on large anchor

Date	Mintage	F	VF	XF	Unc	BU
1931	6,541	80.00	165	375	600	—
1931 Proof	62	Value: 1,200				
1932	2,537,000	2.50	5.00	15.00	50.00	—
1932 Proof	12	Value: 1,400				
1933	1,463,000	3.50	7.00	30.00	70.00	—
1933 Proof	20	Value: 1,400				
1934	821,000	3.50	7.00	35.00	80.00	—
1934 Proof	24	Value: 1,400				
1935	685,000	4.00	8.50	45.00	90.00	—
1935 Proof	20	Value: 1,400				
1936	693,000	3.50	7.00	25.00	60.00	—
1936 Proof	40	Value: 500				

KM# 28   SHILLING
5.6600 g., 0.8000 Silver 0.1456 oz. ASW, 23.5 mm.
Ruler: George VI **Obv:** Head left **Rev:** Standing female figure leaning on large anchor

Date	Mintage	F	VF	XF	Unc	BU
1937	1,194,000	BV	3.00	10.00	25.00	—
1937 Proof	116	Value: 120				
1938	1,160,000	BV	3.00	10.00	25.00	—
1938 Proof	44	Value: 250				
1939 Proof	30	Value: 4,000				
1940	1,365,000	BV	2.50	7.50	17.50	—
1941	1,826,000	BV	2.50	7.50	17.50	—
1942	3,867,000	BV	2.50	7.50	17.50	—
1943	4,187,999	BV	2.00	5.00	10.00	—
1943 Proof	104	Value: 165				
1944	48,000	8.00	20.00	40.00	70.00	—
1944 Proof	160	Value: 150				
1945	54,000	8.00	20.00	40.00	70.00	—
1945 Proof	150	Value: 150				
1946	27,000	10.00	30.00	60.00	120	—
1946 Proof	150	Value: 165				
1947	7,184	10.00	20.00	35.00	65.00	—
1947 Proof	2,600	Value: 70.00				

KM# 37.1 SHILLING
5.6600 g., 0.8000 Silver 0.1456 oz. ASW, 23.5 mm.
Ruler: George VI **Obv:** Head left **Rev:** Standing female figure leaning on large anchor

Date	Mintage	F	VF	XF	Unc	BU
1948	4,974	10.00	20.00	35.00	65.00	
1948 Proof	1,120	Value: 70.00				
1949 Proof	800	Value: 225				
1950	1,704,000	BV	2.50	4.00	8.00	—
1950 Proof	500	Value: 40.00				

KM# 37.2 SHILLING
5.6600 g., 0.5000 Silver 0.0910 oz. ASW, 23.5 mm.
Ruler: George VI **Obv:** Head left **Rev:** Standing female figure, value as 1S

Date	Mintage	F	VF	XF	Unc	BU
1951	2,405,000	BV	1.50	4.00	8.00	—
1951 Proof	2,000	Value: 4.00				
1952	1,934,000	BV	1.50	3.50	7.00	—
1952 Proof	1,550	Value: 3.00				

KM# 49 SHILLING
5.6600 g., 0.5000 Silver 0.0910 oz. ASW, 23.5 mm.
Ruler: Elizabeth II **Obv:** Laureate head right **Rev:** Standing female figure leaning on large anchor

Date	Mintage	F	VF	XF	Unc	BU
1953	2,672,000	BV	1.50	2.50	5.50	—
1953 Proof	5,000	Value: 4.00				
1954	3,576,000	BV	1.50	2.50	5.50	—
1954 Proof	3,150	Value: 4.00				
1955	2,206,000	BV	1.50	2.50	5.50	—
1955 Proof	2,850	Value: 5.50				
1956	2,142,000	BV	1.50	2.50	6.00	—
1956 Proof	1,700	Value: 6.00				
1957	791,000	BV	2.50	5.00	10.00	—
1957 Proof	1,130	Value: 6.00				
1958	4,067,000	BV	1.50	2.50	5.50	—
1958 Proof	985	Value: 8.00				
1959	205,000	1.50	3.00	5.00	10.00	—
1959 Proof	900	Value: 10.00				
1960	2,187,000	BV	1.50	2.50	5.50	—
1960 Proof	3,360	Value: 3.00				

KM# 18 FLORIN
11.3100 g., 0.8000 Silver 0.2909 oz. ASW, 28.3 mm.
Ruler: George V **Obv:** Crowned bust left **Rev:** Shield divides date

Date	Mintage	F	VF	XF	Unc	BU
1923	695,000	6.00	20.00	40.00	80.00	—
1923 Proof	1,402	Value: 120				
1924	1,513,000	5.00	15.00	40.00	150	—
1925	50,000	125	350	1,000	2,200	—
1926	324,000	7.50	40.00	250	650	—
1927	399,000	7.50	35.00	200	600	—
1928	1,092,000	5.00	10.00	100	200	—
1929	648,000	6.00	15.00	120	225	—
1930	267,000	6.00	15.00	75.00	150	—
1930 Proof	14	Value: 1,200				

KM# 22 2 SHILLINGS
11.3100 g., 0.8000 Silver 0.2909 oz. ASW, 28.3 mm.
Ruler: George V **Obv:** Crowned bust left **Rev:** Shield divides date

Date	Mintage	F	VF	XF	Unc	BU
1931	383	250	450	700	1,200	—
1931 Proof	62	Value: 1,500				
1932	1,315,000	BV	6.00	18.00	75.00	—
1932 Proof	12	Value: 2,000				
1933	891,000	4.75	8.00	25.00	85.00	—
1933 Proof	20	Value: 2,000				
1934	559,000	4.75	8.00	25.00	60.00	—
1934 Proof	24	Value: 1,650				
1935	554,000	5.00	8.00	25.00	90.00	—
1935 Proof	20	Value: 1,650				
1936	669,000	4.75	8.00	25.00	65.00	—
1936 Proof	40	Value: 650				

KM# 29 2 SHILLINGS
11.3100 g., 0.8000 Silver 0.2909 oz. ASW, 28.3 mm.
Ruler: George VI **Obv:** Head left **Rev:** Shield divides date

Date	Mintage	F	VF	XF	Unc	BU
1937	1,495,000	BV	5.00	10.00	30.00	—
1937 Proof	116	Value: 150				
1938	214,000	5.00	10.00	20.00	50.00	—
1938 Proof	44	Value: 325				
1939	279,000	5.00	10.00	20.00	50.00	—
1939 Proof	30	Value: 1,000				
1940	2,600,000	BV	4.75	8.00	20.00	—
1941	1,764,000	BV	4.75	8.00	20.00	—
1942	2,847,000	—	BV	5.00	10.00	—
1943	3,125,000	—	BV	5.00	10.00	—
1943 Proof	104	Value: 135				
1944	225,000	4.75	7.00	17.50	40.00	—
1945	473,000	BV	6.00	15.00	35.00	—
1945 Proof	150	Value: 120				
1946	14,000	7.50	20.00	40.00	90.00	—
1946 Proof	150	Value: 135				
1947	2,892	15.00	25.00	40.00	85.00	—
1947 Proof	2,600	Value: 70.00				

KM# 38.1 2 SHILLINGS
11.3100 g., 0.8000 Silver 0.2909 oz. ASW, 28.3 mm.
Ruler: George VI **Obv:** Head left **Rev:** Shield divides date

Date	Mintage	F	VF	XF	Unc	BU
1948	6,773	10.00	15.00	30.00	70.00	—
1948 Proof	1,120	Value: 70.00				
1949	203,000	5.00	10.00	15.00	35.00	—
1949 Proof	800	Value: 60.00				
1950	4,945	20.00	40.00	80.00	140	—
1950 Proof	500	Value: 160				

KM# 38.2 2 SHILLINGS
11.3100 g., 0.5000 Silver 0.1818 oz. ASW, 28.3 mm.
Ruler: George VI **Obv:** Head left **Rev:** Shield, value as 2S

Date	Mintage	F	VF	XF	Unc	BU
1951	730,000	BV	3.50	5.00	10.00	—
1951 Proof	2,000	Value: 15.00				

Date	Mintage	F	VF	XF	Unc	BU
1952	3,570,000	—	BV	3.50	6.50	—
1952 Proof	16,000	Value: 8.00				

KM# 50 2 SHILLINGS
11.3100 g., 0.5000 Silver 0.1818 oz. ASW, 28.3 mm.
Ruler: Elizabeth II **Obv:** Laureate head right **Rev:** Shield

Date	Mintage	F	VF	XF	Unc	BU
1953	3,274,000	BV	3.00	5.00	8.50	—
1953 Proof	5,000	Value: 6.50				
1954	5,866,000	BV	3.00	4.00	7.00	—
1954 Proof	3,150	Value: 6.50				
1955	3,745,000	BV	3.00	4.00	7.50	—
1955 Proof	2,850	Value: 6.50				
1956	2,549,000	BV	3.00	5.00	9.00	—
1956 Proof	1,700	Value: 7.50				
1957	2,507,000	BV	3.00	5.00	10.00	—
1957 Proof	1,130	Value: 7.50				
1958	2,821,000	BV	3.00	5.00	10.00	—
1958 Proof	985	Value: 15.00				
1959	1,219,000	BV	3.00	5.00	10.00	—
1959 Proof	900	Value: 20.00				
1960	1,951,000	BV	3.00	4.00	6.00	—
1960 Proof	3,360	Value: 4.00				

KM# 19.1 2-1/2 SHILLINGS
14.1400 g., 0.8000 Silver 0.3637 oz. ASW, 32.3 mm.
Ruler: George V **Obv:** Crowned bust left **Rev:** Value as 2-1/2 SHILLINGS 2-1/2 **Rev. Leg.:** ZUID-AFRIKA

Date	Mintage	F	VF	XF	Unc	BU
1923	1,227,000	6.00	15.00	35.00	70.00	—
1923 Proof	1,402	Value: 125				
1924	2,556,000	BV	10.00	50.00	120	—
1925	460,000	9.00	30.00	180	600	—

KM# 19.2 2-1/2 SHILLINGS
14.1400 g., 0.8000 Silver 0.3637 oz. ASW, 32.3 mm.
Ruler: George V **Obv:** Crowned bust left **Rev:** Value as 2-1/2 SHILLINGS

Date	Mintage	F	VF	XF	Unc	BU
1926	205,000	10.00	40.00	250	650	—
1926 Proof	16	Value: 4,000				
1927	194,000	10.00	40.00	350	850	—
1928	984,000	6.50	25.00	125	325	—
1929	617,000	6.50	25.00	175	350	—
1930	324,000	6.50	15.00	100	250	—
1930 Proof	14	Value: 1,650				

KM# 19.3 2-1/2 SHILLINGS
14.1400 g., 0.8000 Silver 0.3637 oz. ASW, 32.3 mm.
Ruler: George V **Obv:** Crowned bust left **Rev:** Crowned shield divides date **Rev. Leg.:** SUID. AFRIKA

Date	Mintage	F	VF	XF	Unc	BU
1931	790	225	450	700	1,300	—
1931 Proof	62	Value: 1,800				
1932	1,028,999	6.00	8.00	22.50	85.00	—
1932 Proof	12	Value: 2,400				
1933	136,000	9.00	40.00	185	300	—
1933 Proof	20	Value: 2,400				
1934	416,000	6.00	9.00	30.00	100	—
1934 Proof	24	Value: 1,650				
1935	345,000	6.50	12.50	32.50	125	—
1935 Proof	20	Value: 1,650				
1936	553,000	6.00	8.50	25.00	90.00	—
1936 Proof	40	Value: 800				

KM# 30 2-1/2 SHILLINGS
14.1400 g., 0.8000 Silver 0.3637 oz. ASW, 32.3 mm.
Ruler: George VI **Obv:** Head left **Rev:** Crowned shield divides date

Date	Mintage	F	VF	XF	Unc	BU
1937	1,154,000	BV	6.00	15.00	32.50	—
1937 Proof	116	Value: 175				
1938	534,000	6.00	8.00	20.00	60.00	—
1938 Proof	44	Value: 400				
1939	133,000	7.00	15.00	40.00	80.00	—
1939 Proof	30	Value: 800				
1940	2,976,000	BV	6.00	8.00	20.00	—
1941	1,988,000	BV	6.00	8.00	20.00	—
1942	3,180,000	BV	6.00	8.00	20.00	—
1943	2,098,000	BV	6.00	8.00	20.00	—
1943 Proof	104	Value: 150				
1944	1,360,000	BV	6.50	10.00	25.00	—
1944 Proof	150	Value: 130				
1945	183,000	BV	8.00	25.00	60.00	—
1945 Proof	150	Value: 130				
1946	11,000	15.00	30.00	50.00	90.00	—
1946 Proof	150	Value: 150				
1947	3,582	20.00	35.00	60.00	100	—
1947 Proof	2,600	Value: 110				

KM# 39.1 2-1/2 SHILLINGS
14.1400 g., 0.8000 Silver 0.3637 oz. ASW, 32.3 mm.
Ruler: George VI **Obv:** Head left **Rev:** Crowned shield divides date

Date	Mintage	F	VF	XF	Unc	BU
1948	1,600	25.00	45.00	75.00	100	—
1948 Proof	1,120	Value: 110				
1949	1,891	25.00	45.00	75.00	110	—
1949 Proof	800	Value: 120				
1950	5,076	25.00	45.00	75.00	140	—
1950 Proof	500	Value: 200				

KM# 39.2 2-1/2 SHILLINGS
14.1400 g., 0.5000 Silver 0.2273 oz. ASW, 32.3 mm.
Ruler: George VI **Obv:** Head left **Rev:** Crowned shield, value as 2-1/2 S

Date	Mintage	F	VF	XF	Unc	BU
1951	783,000	3.75	4.50	6.00	15.00	—
1951 Proof	2,000	Value: 9.00				
1952	1,996,000	BV	3.75	4.50	8.50	—
1952 Proof	16,000	Value: 5.00				

KM# 51 2-1/2 SHILLINGS
14.1400 g., 0.5000 Silver 0.2273 oz. ASW, 32.3 mm.
Ruler: Elizabeth II **Obv:** Laureate head right **Rev:** Crowned shield

Date	Mintage	F	VF	XF	Unc	BU
1953	2,513,000	BV	3.75	4.50	8.50	—
1953 Proof	6,000	Value: 6.00				
1954	4,249,000	BV	3.75	4.50	8.50	—
1954 Proof	3,150	Value: 7.50				
1955	3,863,000	BV	3.75	4.50	8.50	—
1955 Proof	2,850	Value: 7.50				
1956	2,437,000	BV	3.75	4.50	8.50	—
1956 Proof	1,700	Value: 8.50				
1957	2,137,000	BV	3.75	4.50	8.50	—
1957 Proof	1,130	Value: 8.50				
1958	2,260,000	BV	3.75	4.50	9.00	—
1958 Proof	985	Value: 14.00				
1959	46,000	3.75	4.50	7.00	12.50	—
1959 Proof	900	Value: 18.00				
1960	12,000	3.75	5.00	7.50	12.50	—
1960 Proof	3,360	Value: 5.00				

KM# 31 5 SHILLINGS
28.2800 g., 0.8000 Silver 0.7273 oz. ASW, 38.8 mm.
Ruler: George VI **Subject:** Royal Visit **Obv:** Head left **Rev:** Springbok

Date	Mintage	F	VF	XF	Unc	BU
1947	300,000	BV	12.50	15.00	20.00	—
1947 Proof	5,600	Value: 45.00				

KM# 40.1 5 SHILLINGS
28.2800 g., 0.8000 Silver 0.7273 oz. ASW, 38.8 mm.
Ruler: George VI **Obv:** Head left **Rev:** Springbok

Date	Mintage	F	VF	XF	Unc	BU
1948	780,000	—	BV	13.50	20.00	—
1948 Prooflike	1,000	—	—	—	22.50	—
1948 Proof	1,120	Value: 30.00				
1949	535,000	—	BV	13.50	20.00	—
1949 Prooflike	2,000	—	—	—	35.00	—
1949 Proof	800	Value: 50.00				
1950	83,000	BV	15.00	17.50	25.00	—
1950 Prooflike	1,200	—	—	—	60.00	—
1950 Proof	500	Value: 75.00				

KM# 40.2 5 SHILLINGS
28.2800 g., 0.5000 Silver 0.4546 oz. ASW, 38.8 mm.
Ruler: George VI **Obv:** Head left **Rev:** Springbok

Date	Mintage	F	VF	XF	Unc	BU
1951	363,000	BV	7.50	10.00	18.00	—
1951 Prooflike	1,483	—	—	—	25.00	—
1951 Proof	2,000	Value: 35.00				

KM# 41 5 SHILLINGS
28.2800 g., 0.5000 Silver 0.4546 oz. ASW, 38.8 mm.
Ruler: George VI **Subject:** 300th Anniversary - Founding of Capetown **Obv:** Head left **Rev:** Schooner in harbor **Edge:** Reeded

Date	Mintage	F	VF	XF	Unc	BU
ND(1952)	1,698,000	BV	7.50	9.00	12.00	—
ND(1952) Prooflike	12,000	—	—	—	13.50	—
ND(1952) Proof	16,000	Value: 16.50				

KM# 52 5 SHILLINGS
28.2800 g., 0.5000 Silver 0.4546 oz. ASW, 38.8 mm.
Ruler: Elizabeth II **Obv:** Laureate head right **Rev:** Springbok

Date	Mintage	F	VF	XF	Unc	BU
1953	250,000	BV	7.50	10.00	16.00	—
1953 Prooflike	8,000	—	—	—	18.00	—
1953 Proof	5,000	Value: 22.00				
1953 Matte Proof	—	Value: 700				
1954	10,000	BV	8.50	12.50	20.00	—
1954 Prooflike	3,890	—	—	—	22.50	—
1954 Proof	3,150	Value: 25.00				
1955	40,000	BV	7.50	10.00	16.00	—
1955 Prooflike	2,230	—	—	—	20.00	—
1955 Proof	2,850	Value: 22.50				
1956	100,000	BV	7.00	9.00	12.50	—
1956 Prooflike	2,200	—	—	—	20.00	—
1956 Proof	1,700	Value: 25.00				
1957	154,000	BV	7.00	9.00	12.50	—
1957 Prooflike	1,600	—	—	—	25.00	—
1957 Proof	1,130	Value: 30.00				
1958	233,000	BV	7.00	9.00	12.50	—
1958 Prooflike	1,500	—	—	—	25.00	—
1958 Proof	985	Value: 30.00				
1959	2,989	20.00	35.00	65.00	100	—
1959 Prooflike	2,200	—	—	—	110	—
1959 Proof	950	Value: 120				

KM# 55 5 SHILLINGS
28.2800 g., 0.5000 Silver 0.4546 oz. ASW, 38.8 mm.
Ruler: Elizabeth II **Subject:** 50th Anniversary - South African Union **Obv:** Shield **Rev:** Building and ship divides dates
Edge: Reeded **Note:** Many varieties exist of letters HM below building.

Date	Mintage	F	VF	XF	Unc	BU
1960	396,000	BV	7.00	8.50	11.50	—
1960 Prooflike	22,000	—	—	—	13.50	—
1960 Proof	3,360	Value: 16.50				

KM# 20 1/2 SOVEREIGN
3.9940 g., 0.9170 Gold 0.1177 oz. AGW **Ruler:** George V
Obv: Head left **Rev:** Armored figure on rearing horse **Note:** British type with Pretoria mint mark: SA.

Date	Mintage	F	VF	XF	Unc	BU
1923 Proof	655	Value: 525				
1925	947,000	—	—	BV	150	—
1926	809,000	—	—	BV	150	—

KM# 42 1/2 POUND
3.9940 g., 0.9170 Gold 0.1177 oz. AGW **Ruler:** George V
Obv: Head left **Rev:** Springbok

Date	Mintage	F	VF	XF	Unc	BU
1952	4,002	—	—	—	BV	110
1952 Proof	12,000	Value: 115				

KM# 53 1/2 POUND
3.9940 g., 0.9170 Gold 0.1177 oz. AGW **Ruler:** Elizabeth II
Obv: Laureate head right

Date	Mintage	F	VF	XF	Unc	BU
1953 Proof	4,000	Value: 115				
1954 Proof	1,275	Value: 115				
1955 Proof	900	Value: 120				
1956 Proof	508	Value: 210				
1957 Proof	560	Value: 180				
1958 Proof	515	Value: 195				
1959	500	—	—	—	BV	110
1959 Proof	630	Value: 165				
1960	1,052	—	—	—	BV	110
1960 Proof	1,950	Value: 115				

KM# 21 SOVEREIGN
7.9881 g., 0.9170 Gold 0.2355 oz. AGW **Ruler:** George V
Obv: Head left **Rev:** Armored figure on rearing horse **Note:** British type with Pretoria mint mark: SA.

Date	Mintage	F	VF	XF	Unc	BU
1923	64	BV	300	400	700	—
1923 Proof	655	Value: 650				
1924	3,184	700	1,350	2,250	4,500	—
1925	6,086,000	—	—	—	BV	230

Date	Mintage	F	VF	XF	Unc	BU
1926	11,108,000	—	—	—	BV	230
1927	16,379,999	—	—	—	BV	230
1928	18,235,000	—	—	—	BV	230

KM# A22 SOVEREIGN
7.9881 g., 0.9170 Gold 0.2355 oz. AGW **Ruler:** George V
Obv: Modified effigy, slightly smaller bust

Date	Mintage	F	VF	XF	Unc	BU
1929	12,024,000	—	—	—	BV	230
1930	10,028,000	—	—	—	BV	230
1931	8,512,000	—	—	—	BV	230
1932	1,067,000	—	—	—	BV	230

KM# 43 POUND
7.9881 g., 0.9170 Gold 0.2355 oz. AGW **Ruler:** George VI
Obv: Head left **Rev:** Springbok

Date	Mintage	F	VF	XF	Unc	BU
1952	4,508	—	—	—	BV	230
1952 Proof	12,000	Value: 235				

KM# 54 POUND
7.9881 g., 0.9170 Gold 0.2355 oz. AGW **Ruler:** Elizabeth II
Obv: Laureate head right **Rev:** Springbok

Date	Mintage	F	VF	XF	Unc	BU
1953 Proof	4,000	Value: 235				
1954 Proof	1,275	Value: 235				
1955 Proof	900	Value: 235				
1956 Proof	508	Value: 250				
1957 Proof	560	Value: 235				
1958 Proof	515	Value: 240				
1959	502	—	—	—	BV	230
1959 Proof	630	Value: 235				
1960	1,161	—	—	—	BV	230
1960 Proof	1,950	Value: 235				

REPUBLIC

STANDARD COINAGE
100 Cents = 1 Rand

KM# 56 1/2 CENT
5.6000 g., Brass **Obv:** Oat sprig and berries divide birds
Rev: Bust facing 1/4 right

Date	Mintage	F	VF	XF	Unc	BU
1961	39,189,000	—	0.15	0.25	1.25	2.00
1961 Proof	7,530	Value: 1.00				
1962	17,895,000	—	0.15	0.25	1.25	2.00
1962 Proof	3,844	Value: 1.00				
1963	11,611,000	—	0.15	0.25	2.00	2.50
1963 Proof	4,025	Value: 1.00				
1964	9,258,000	—	0.15	0.25	1.25	2.00
1964 Proof	16,000	Value: 2.00				

KM# 81 1/2 CENT
Bronze **Obv:** Arms with supporters **Rev:** Sparrows below value
Note: Bilingual.

Date	Mintage	F	VF	XF	Unc	BU
1970	Est. 57,721,000	—	0.10	0.25	0.50	—

Note: Coins dated 1970 were also struck for circulation in 1971, 1972 and 1973.

Date	Mintage	F	VF	XF	Unc	BU
1970 Proof	10,000	Value: 2.50				
1971	8,000	—	—	—	2.50	
1971 Proof	12,000	Value: 2.50				
1972	8,000	—	—	—	2.50	
1972 Proof	12,000	Value: 2.50				
1973	20,000	—	—	0.10	0.20	2.50
1973 Proof	11,000	Value: 2.50				

Date	Mintage	F	VF	XF	Unc	BU
1974	20,000	—	0.20	0.40	2.50	—
1974 Proof	15,000	Value: 2.50				
1975	20,000	—	—	0.10	0.20	2.50
1975 Proof	18,000	Value: 2.50				
1977	20,000	—	—	0.10	0.20	2.50
1977 Proof	19,000	Value: 2.50				
1978	18,000	—	—	0.10	0.20	2.50
1978 Proof	19,000	Value: 2.50				
1980 Proof	15,000	Value: 2.50				
1981 Proof	10,000	Value: 2.50				
1983 Proof	14,000	Value: 2.50				

KM# 90 1/2 CENT
Bronze **Obv:** President Fouche left **Rev:** Birds on branches
Note: Similar to 1 Cent, KM#91.

Date	Mintage	F	VF	XF	Unc	BU
1976	20,000	—	—	—	1.00	—
1976 Proof	21,000	Value: 1.50				

KM# 97 1/2 CENT
Bronze **Obv:** Head of President Diederichs left **Rev:** Sparrows below value

Date	Mintage	F	VF	XF	Unc	BU
1979	18,000	—	—	—	1.00	—
1979 Proof	17,000	Value: 1.50				

KM# 108 1/2 CENT
Bronze **Obv:** Head of President Vorster 1/4 right **Rev:** Sparrows below value

Date	Mintage	F	VF	XF	Unc	BU
1982 Proof	12,000	Value: 1.50				

KM# 57 CENT
9.4200 g., Brass **Obv:** Covered wagon **Rev:** Bust 1/4 right

Date	Mintage	F	VF	XF	Unc	BU
1961	52,266,000	—	0.15	0.40	1.50	—
1961 Proof	7,530	Value: 0.75				
1962	21,929,000	—	0.15	0.40	1.50	—
1962 Proof	3,844	Value: 1.00				
1963	9,081,000	—	0.15	0.50	3.00	—
1963 Proof	4,025	Value: 1.00				
1964	14,265,000	—	0.15	0.40	1.50	—
1964 Proof	16,000	Value: 2.00				

KM# 65.1 CENT
3.0000 g., Bronze, 19 mm. **Obv:** Head of Jan van Riebeeck right
Obv. Leg.: English legend **Rev:** Sparrows below value

Date	Mintage	F	VF	XF	Unc	BU
1965	26,000	—	—	—	2.00	—
1965 Proof	25,000	Value: 2.50				
1966	50,157,000	—	—	0.10	0.50	—
1967	21,114,000	—	—	0.10	0.50	—
1969	10,196,000	—	—	0.10	0.50	—

KM# 65.2 CENT
3.0000 g., Bronze, 19 mm. **Obv:** Head of Jan van Riebeeck right
Obv. Leg.: Afrikaans legend **Rev:** Sparrows below value

Date	Mintage	F	VF	XF	Unc	BU
1965	846	—	100	200	300	—
1965 Proof	185	Value: 350				

Date	Mintage	F	VF	XF	Unc	BU
1966	50,157,000	—	—	0.10	0.50	—
1966 Proof	25,000	Value: 1.00				
1967	21,114,000	—	—	0.10	0.50	—
1967 Proof	25,000	Value: 1.00				
1969	10,196,000	—	—	0.10	0.50	—
1969 Proof	12,000	Value: 1.50				

KM# 74.1 CENT
3.0000 g., Bronze, 19 mm. **Subject:** President Charles Swart **Obv:** Head left **Obv. Leg.:** English legend **Rev:** Sparrows below value

Date	Mintage	F	VF	XF	Unc	BU
1968	6,000,000	—	—	0.10	0.50	—
1968 Proof	25,000	Value: 1.00				

KM# 74.2 CENT
3.0000 g., Bronze, 19 mm. **Subject:** President Charles Swart **Obv:** Head left **Obv. Leg.:** Afrikaans legend **Rev:** Sparrows below value

Date	Mintage	F	VF	XF	Unc	BU
1968	6,000,000	—	—	0.10	0.50	—

KM# 82 CENT
3.0000 g., Bronze, 19 mm. **Obv:** Arms with supporters **Obv. Leg.:** Bilingual legend **Rev:** Sparrows below value

Date	Mintage	F	VF	XF	Unc	BU
1970	37,072,000	—	—	—	0.30	0.50
1970 Proof	10,000	Value: 1.00				
1971	34,053,000	—	—	—	0.30	0.50
1971 Proof	12,000	Value: 1.00				
1972	35,662,000	—	—	—	0.30	0.50
1972 Proof	10,000	Value: 1.00				
1973	35,898,000	—	0.10	0.20	0.40	0.60
1973 Proof	11,000	Value: 1.00				
1974	54,940,000	—	—	—	0.25	0.50
1974 Proof	15,000	Value: 1.00				
1975	62,982,000	—	—	—	0.25	0.50
1975 Proof	18,000	Value: 1.00				
1977	72,444,000	—	—	—	0.25	0.50
1977 Proof	19,000	Value: 1.00				
1978	70,152,000	—	—	—	0.25	0.50
1978 Proof	17,000	Value: 0.50				
1980	63,432,000	—	—	—	0.25	0.50
1980 Proof	15,000	Value: 0.50				
1981	63,444,000	—	—	—	0.25	0.50
1981 Proof	10,000	Value: 0.50				
1983	182,131,000	—	—	—	0.25	0.50
1983 Proof	14,000	Value: 0.50				
1984	107,155,000	—	—	—	0.25	0.50
1984 Proof	11,000	Value: 0.50				
1985	186,042,000	—	—	—	0.25	0.50
1985 Proof	9,859	Value: 0.50				
1986	169,734,000	—	—	—	0.25	0.50
1986 Proof	7,000	Value: 0.50				
1987	120,674,000	—	—	—	0.25	0.50
1987 Proof	6,781	Value: 0.50				
1988	240,272,000	—	—	—	0.25	0.50
1988 Proof	7,250	Value: 0.50				
1989	—	—	—	—	0.25	0.50
1989 Proof	—	Value: 0.50				

KM# 91 CENT
3.0000 g., Bronze, 19 mm. **Obv:** Head of President Fouche right **Rev:** Sparrows below value

Date	Mintage	F	VF	XF	Unc	BU
1976	91,860,000	—	—	0.30	0.50	—
1976 Proof	21,000	Value: 0.75				

KM# 98 CENT
3.0000 g., Bronze, 19 mm. **Obv:** Head of President Diederichs left **Rev:** Sparrows below value

Date	Mintage	F	VF	XF	Unc	BU
1979	63,432,000	—	—	0.30	0.50	—
1979 Proof	15,000	Value: 0.75				

KM# 109 CENT
3.0000 g., Bronze, 19 mm. **Obv:** Head of President Vorster 1/4 right **Rev:** Sparrows below value

Date	Mintage	F	VF	XF	Unc	BU
1982	145,954,000	—	—	0.30	0.50	—
1982 Proof	12,000	Value: 0.75				

KM# 132 CENT
1.5000 g., Copper-Plated-Steel, 15 mm. **Obv:** Arms with supporters **Rev:** Value divides sparrows

Date	Mintage	F	VF	XF	Unc	BU
1990	—	—	—	—	0.25	0.50
1990 Proof	—	Value: 0.50				
1991	—	—	—	—	0.25	0.50
1991 Proof	—	Value: 0.50				
1992	—	—	—	—	0.25	0.50
1992 Proof	—	Value: 0.50				
1993	—	—	—	—	0.25	0.50
1993 Proof	7,790	Value: 0.50				
1994	—	—	—	—	0.25	0.50
1994 Proof	5,804	Value: 0.50				
1995	—	—	—	—	0.25	0.50
1995 Proof	—	Value: 0.50				

KM# 158 CENT
1.5000 g., Copper-Plated-Steel, 15 mm. **Obv:** Arms with supporters **Obv. Leg.:** Zulu legend **Rev:** Value divides sparrows **Edge:** Plain

Date	Mintage	F	VF	XF	Unc	BU
1996	—	—	—	—	0.25	0.50
1996 Proof	10,000	Value: 0.50				

KM# 170 CENT
1.5000 g., Copper Plated Steel, 15 mm. **Obv:** Arms with supporters **Obv. Leg.:** Ndebele legend **Rev:** Value divides sparrows

Date	Mintage	F	VF	XF	Unc	BU
1997	—	—	—	—	0.25	0.50
1997 Proof	3,596	Value: 0.50				
1998	—	—	—	—	0.25	0.50
1998 Proof	—	Value: 0.50				
1999	—	—	—	—	0.25	0.50
1999 Proof	—	Value: 0.50				
2000	—	Value: 0.25				

KM# 221 CENT
1.5000 g., Copper Plated Steel, 15 mm. **Obv:** New national arms **Obv. Leg.:** ISEWULA - AFRIKA **Rev:** Value divides two sparrows **Edge:** Plain

Date	Mintage	F	VF	XF	Unc	BU
2000	—	—	—	0.15	0.35	0.50

KM# 66.1 2 CENTS
4.0000 g., Bronze, 22.45 mm. **Obv:** English legend **Rev:** Black Wildebeest

Date	Mintage	F	VF	XF	Unc	BU
1965	29,887,000	—	—	0.10	0.35	1.00
1966	9,267,000	—	—	0.10	0.40	1.00
1966 Proof	25,000	Value: 0.50				
1967	11,862,000	—	—	0.10	0.35	1.00
1967 Proof	25,000	Value: 0.50				
1969	5,817,000	—	—	0.10	0.40	1.00
1969 Proof	12,000	Value: 0.50				

KM# 66.2 2 CENTS
4.0000 g., Bronze, 22.45 mm. **Obv:** Afrikaans legend **Rev:** Black Wildebeest

Date	Mintage	F	VF	XF	Unc	BU
1965	29,887,000	—	—	0.10	0.35	1.00
1965 Proof	25,000	Value: 0.50				
1966	9,267,000	—	—	0.10	0.35	1.00
1967	11,862,000	—	—	0.10	0.35	1.00
1969	5,817,000	—	—	0.10	0.40	1.00

KM# 75.1 2 CENTS
4.0000 g., Bronze, 22.45 mm. **Obv:** Head of President Charles Swart left **Obv. Leg.:** English legend **Rev:** Wildebeest

Date	Mintage	F	VF	XF	Unc	BU
1968	5,500,000	—	—	0.20	0.50	1.00

KM# 75.2 2 CENTS
4.0000 g., Bronze, 22.45 mm. **Obv:** Head of President Charles Swart left **Obv. Leg.:** Afrikaans legend **Rev:** Wildebeest

Date	Mintage	F	VF	XF	Unc	BU
1968	5,525,000	—	—	0.20	0.50	1.00
1968 Proof	25,000	Value: 1.00				

KM# 83 2 CENTS
4.0000 g., Bronze, 22.45 mm. **Obv:** Arms with supporters **Obv. Leg.:** Bilingual legend **Rev:** Wildebeest

Date	Mintage	F	VF	XF	Unc	BU
1970	35,217,000	—	—	0.15	0.50	1.00
1970 Proof	10,000	Value: 0.75				
1971	24,093,000	—	—	0.15	0.50	1.00
1971 Proof	12,000	Value: 0.75				
1972	7,304,000	—	—	0.15	0.50	1.00
1972 Proof	10,000	Value: 0.75				
1973	18,685,000	—	—	0.15	0.50	1.00
1973 Proof	11,000	Value: 0.75				
1974	25,301,000	—	—	0.15	0.50	1.00
1974 Proof	15,000	Value: 0.75				
1975	24,982,000	—	—	0.15	0.50	1.00
1975 Proof	18,000	Value: 0.75				
1977	45,116,000	—	—	0.15	0.50	1.00
1977 Proof	19,000	Value: 0.75				
1978	50,527,000	—	—	0.15	0.50	1.00
1978 Proof	17,000	Value: 0.75				
1980	37,795,000	—	—	0.15	0.50	1.00

Date	Mintage	F	VF	XF	Unc	BU
1980 Proof	15,000	Value: 0.75				
1981	79,350,000	—	—	0.15	0.50	1.00
1981 Proof	10,000	Value: 0.75				
1983	112,575,000	—	—	0.15	0.50	1.00
1983 Proof	14,000	Value: 0.75				
1984	101,497,000	—	—	0.15	0.50	1.00
1984 Proof	11,000	Value: 0.75				
1985	102,708,000	—	—	0.15	0.50	1.00
1985 Proof	9,859	Value: 0.75				
1986	683,294,000	—	—	0.15	0.50	1.00
1986 Proof	7,100	Value: 0.75				
1987	104,981,000	—	—	0.15	0.50	1.00
1987 Proof	6,781	Value: 0.75				
1988	182,036,000	—	—	0.15	0.50	1.00
1988 Proof	7,250	Value: 0.75				
1989	—	—	—	0.15	0.50	1.00
1989 Proof	—	Value: 0.75				
1990	215,192,000	—	—	0.15	0.50	1.00

KM# 92   2 CENTS
4.0000 g., Bronze, 22.45 mm. **Obv:** Head of President Fouche right **Rev:** Wildebeest

Date	Mintage	F	VF	XF	Unc	BU
1976	51,474,000	—	—	0.25	0.50	1.00
1976 Proof	21,000	Value: 0.75				

KM# 99   2 CENTS
4.0000 g., Bronze, 22.45 mm. **Obv:** Head of President Diederichs left **Rev:** Wildebeest

Date	Mintage	F	VF	XF	Unc	BU
1979	40,043,000	—	—	0.25	0.50	1.00
1979 Proof	15,000	Value: 0.75				

KM# 110   2 CENTS
4.0000 g., Bronze, 22.45 mm. **Obv:** Head of President Vorster 1/4 right **Rev:** Wildebeest

Date	Mintage	F	VF	XF	Unc	BU
1982	53,962,000	—	—	0.25	0.50	1.00
1982 Proof	12,000	Value: 0.75				

KM# 133   2 CENTS
3.0000 g., Copper-Plated-Steel, 18 mm. **Obv:** Arms with supporters **Rev:** Eagle with fish in talons divides value

Date	Mintage	F	VF	XF	Unc	BU
1990	—	—	—	—	1.50	1.75
1990 Proof	—	Value: 2.00				
1991	—	—	—	—	1.50	1.75
1991 Proof	12,000	Value: 2.00				
1992	—	—	—	—	0.50	0.75
1992 Proof	—	Value: 2.00				
1993	—	—	—	—	0.50	0.75
1993 Proof	7,790	Value: 2.00				
1994	—	—	—	—	0.50	0.75
1994 Proof	5,804	Value: 2.00				
1995	—	—	—	—	0.50	0.75
1995 Proof	—	Value: 2.00				

KM# 159   2 CENTS
3.0000 g., Copper-Plated-Steel, 18 mm. **Obv:** Arms with supporters **Obv. Leg.:** AFURIKA TSHIPEMBE, Venda legend **Rev:** Eagle with fish in talons divides value

Date	Mintage	F	VF	XF	Unc	BU
1996	—	—	—	—	0.50	0.75
1996 Proof	—	Value: 1.00				
1997	—	—	—	—	0.50	0.75
1997 Proof	3,596	Value: 1.00				
1998	—	—	—	—	0.50	0.75
1998 Proof	—	Value: 1.00				
1999	—	—	—	—	0.50	0.75
1999 Proof	—	Value: 1.00				
2000	—	—	—	—	0.50	0.75

KM# 222   2 CENTS
3.0000 g., Copper Plated Steel, 18 mm. **Obv:** New national arms **Obv. Leg.:** AFURIKA - TSHIPEMBE **Rev:** Eagle with fish in talons divides value **Edge:** Plain

Date	Mintage	F	VF	XF	Unc	BU
2000	—	—	—	—	0.50	0.75

KM# 58   2-1/2 CENTS
1.4100 g., 0.5000 Silver 0.0227 oz. ASW **Obv:** Protea flower **Rev:** Bust facing

Date	Mintage	F	VF	XF	Unc	BU
1961	292,000	—	0.50	1.00	2.00	—
1961 Proof	7,530	Value: 4.00				
1962	8,745	—	2.00	4.00	8.00	—
1962 Proof	3,844	Value: 8.00				
1963	33,000	—	1.50	2.50	4.00	—
1963 Proof	4,025	Value: 6.00				
1964	14,000	—	2.00	4.00	6.00	—
1964 Proof	16,000	Value: 4.00				

KM# 174   2-1/2 CENTS
1.4140 g., 0.9250 Silver 0.0420 oz. ASW **Obv:** Protea flower **Rev:** Knysna seahorse below value

Date	Mintage	F	VF	XF	Unc	BU
1997 Proof	Est. 2,627	Value: 25.00				

KM# 176   2-1/2 CENTS
1.4140 g., 0.9250 Silver 0.0420 oz. ASW **Obv:** Protea flower **Rev:** Jackass Penguin

Date	Mintage	F	VF	XF	Unc	BU
1998 Proof	Est. 5,000	Value: 30.00				

KM# 217   2-1/2 CENTS
1.4100 g., 0.9250 Silver 0.0419 oz. ASW **Obv:** Protea flower **Rev:** Great White Shark

Date	Mintage	F	VF	XF	Unc	BU
1999 Proof	5,000	Value: 25.00				

KM# 233   2-1/2 CENTS
1.4140 g., 0.9250 Silver 0.0420 oz. ASW, 16.3 mm. **Obv:** Protea flower **Rev:** Octopus **Edge:** Reeded

Date	Mintage	F	VF	XF	Unc	BU
2000 Proof	—	Value: 30.00				

KM# 59   5 CENTS
2.8300 g., 0.5000 Silver 0.0455 oz. ASW, 17.35 mm. **Obv:** Protea flower in center of designed bars **Rev:** Bust 1/4 right

Date	Mintage	F	VF	XF	Unc	BU
1961	1,479,000	—	BV	1.00	2.00	—
1961 Proof	7,530	Value: 2.50				
1962	4,187,999	—	BV	0.85	1.50	—
1962 Proof	3,844	Value: 3.00				
1963	8,054,000	—	BV	0.75	1.25	—
1963 Proof	4,025	Value: 3.00				
1964	3,567,000	—	BV	0.75	1.25	—
1964 Proof	16,000	Value: 1.50				

KM# 67.1   5 CENTS
2.5000 g., Nickel, 17.35 mm. **Obv:** English legend **Rev:** Blue Crane

Date	Mintage	F	VF	XF	Unc	BU
1965	32,689,999	—	—	0.15	0.75	1.25
1965 Proof	25,000	Value: 0.80				
1966	4,101,000	—	—	0.15	0.75	1.25
1967	4,590,000	—	—	0.15	0.75	1.25
1969	5,020,000	—	—	0.15	0.75	1.25

KM# 67.2   5 CENTS
2.5000 g., Nickel, 17.35 mm. **Obv:** Afrikaans legend **Rev:** Blue Crane

Date	Mintage	F	VF	XF	Unc	BU
1965	32,689,999	—	—	0.15	0.75	1.25
1966	4,101,000	—	—	0.15	0.75	1.25
1966 Proof	25,000	Value: 0.80				
1967	4,590,000	—	—	0.15	0.75	1.25
1967 Proof	25,000	Value: 0.80				
1969	5,020,000	—	—	0.15	0.75	1.25
1969 Proof	12,000	Value: 0.80				

KM# 76.1   5 CENTS
2.5000 g., Nickel, 17.35 mm. **Subject:** President Charles Swart **Obv:** Head left **Obv. Leg.:** English legend **Rev:** Blue Crane

Date	Mintage	F	VF	XF	Unc	BU
1968	6,000,000	—	—	0.15	0.75	1.00
1968 Proof	25,000	Value: 0.80				

KM# 76.2   5 CENTS
2.5000 g., Nickel, 17.35 mm. **Subject:** President Charles Swart **Obv:** Afrikaans legend **Rev:** Blue Crane

Date	Mintage	F	VF	XF	Unc	BU
1968	6,000,000	—	—	0.15	0.75	1.00

KM# 84   5 CENTS
2.5000 g., Nickel, 17.35 mm. **Obv:** Arms with supporters **Obv. Leg.:** Bilingual legend **Rev:** Blue Crane

Date	Mintage	F	VF	XF	Unc	BU
1970	6,652,000	—	—	0.15	0.75	1.00
1970 Proof	10,000	Value: 0.80				
1971	20,329,000	—	—	0.15	0.75	1.00
1971 Proof	12,000	Value: 0.80				
1972	3,117,000	—	—	0.15	0.75	1.00

Date	Mintage	F	VF	XF	Unc	BU
1972 Proof	9,000	Value: 0.80				
1973	17,092,000	—	—	0.15	0.75	1.00
1973 Proof	11,000	Value: 0.80				
1974	19,978,000	—	—	0.15	0.75	1.00
1974 Proof	15,000	Value: 0.80				
1975	21,982,000	—	—	0.15	0.75	1.00
1975 Proof	18,000	Value: 0.80				
1977	51,729,000	—	—	0.15	0.75	1.00
1977 Proof	19,000	Value: 0.80				
1978	30,050,000	—	—	0.15	0.75	1.00
1978 Proof	19,000	Value: 0.80				
1980	46,665,000	—	—	0.15	0.75	1.00
1980 Proof	15,000	Value: 0.80				
1981	40,351,000	—	—	0.15	0.75	1.00
1981 Proof	10,000	Value: 0.80				
1983	57,487,000	—	—	0.15	0.75	1.00
1983 Proof	14,000	Value: 0.80				
1984	67,345,000	—	—	0.15	0.75	1.00
1984 Proof	11,000	Value: 0.80				
1985	57,167,000	—	—	0.15	0.75	1.00
1985 Proof	9,859	Value: 0.80				
1986	54,226,000	—	—	0.15	0.75	1.00
1986 Proof	7,100	Value: 0.80				
1987	42,786,000	—	—	0.15	0.75	1.00
1987 Proof	5,297	Value: 0.80				
1988	110,164,000	—	—	0.15	0.75	1.00
1988 Proof	7,250	Value: 0.80				
1989	35,540,000	—	—	0.15	0.75	1.00
1989 Proof	Inc. above	Value: 1.50				

KM# 93 5 CENTS
2.5000 g., Nickel, 17.35 mm. **Obv:** Head of President Fouche right **Rev:** Blue Crane

Date	Mintage	F	VF	XF	Unc	BU
1976	48,972,000	—	—	0.30	0.75	1.00
1976 Proof	19,000	Value: 1.50				

KM# 100 5 CENTS
2.5000 g., Nickel, 17.35 mm. **Obv:** Head of President Diederichs left **Rev:** Blue Crane

Date	Mintage	F	VF	XF	Unc	BU
1979	17,533,000	—	—	0.30	0.75	1.00
1979 Proof	17,000	Value: 1.50				

KM# 111 5 CENTS
2.5000 g., Nickel, 17.35 mm. **Obv:** Head of President Vorster 1/4 right **Rev:** Blue Crane

Date	Mintage	F	VF	XF	Unc	BU
1982	47,236,000	—	—	0.30	0.75	1.00
1982 Proof	12,000	Value: 1.50				

KM# 134 5 CENTS
4.5000 g., Copper-Plated-Steel, 21 mm. **Obv:** Arms with supporters **Rev:** Blue crane

Date	Mintage	F	VF	XF	Unc	BU
1990	—	—	—	0.15	1.00	—
1990 Proof	—	Value: 1.25				
1991	—	—	—	0.15	1.00	—
1991 Proof	12,000	Value: 1.25				
1992	—	—	—	0.15	1.00	—
1992 Proof	—	Value: 1.25				
1993	—	—	—	0.15	1.00	—
1993 Proof	7,790	Value: 1.25				
1994	—	—	—	0.15	1.00	—
1994 Proof	5,804	Value: 1.25				
1995	—	—	—	0.15	1.00	—
1995 Proof	—	Value: 1.25				

KM# 160 5 CENTS
4.5000 g., Copper Plated Steel, 21 mm. **Obv:** Arms with supporters **Obv. Leg.:** AFRIKA DZONGA, Tsonga legend **Rev:** Blue crane

Date	Mintage	F	VF	XF	Unc	BU
1996	—	—	—	0.15	0.75	1.00
1996 Proof	—	Value: 1.25				
1997	—	—	—	0.15	0.75	1.00
1997 Proof	3,596	Value: 1.25				
1998	—	—	—	0.15	0.75	1.00
1998 Proof	—	Value: 1.50				
1999	—	—	—	0.15	0.75	1.00
1999 Proof	—	Value: 1.50				
2000	—	—	—	0.15	0.75	1.00

KM# 223 5 CENTS
4.4300 g., Copper Plated Steel, 21 mm. **Obv:** New national arms **Obv. Leg.:** AFRIKA- DZONGA **Rev:** Value and Blue crane **Edge:** Plain

Date	Mintage	F	VF	XF	Unc	BU
2000	—	—	0.10	0.25	0.65	1.00
2000 Proof	—	Value: 5.00				

KM# 234 5 CENTS
8.4560 g., 0.9250 Silver 0.2515 oz. ASW, 26.7 mm.
Series: Wildlife - Predator **Obv:** Lion's head 3/4 right **Rev:** Lions, value **Edge:** Reeded

Date	Mintage	F	VF	XF	Unc	BU
2000 Proof	2,158	Value: 30.00				

KM# 60 10 CENTS
5.6600 g., 0.5000 Silver 0.0910 oz. ASW **Obv:** Standing female figure leaning on large anchor **Rev:** Bust 1/4 right

Date	Mintage	F	VF	XF	Unc	BU
1961	1,136,000	—	BV	1.50	2.50	—
1961 Proof	7,530	Value: 2.50				
1962	2,447,000	—	BV	1.50	2.50	—
1962 Proof	3,844	Value: 3.50				
1963	3,327,000	—	BV	1.50	2.50	—
1963 Proof	4,025	Value: 3.50				
1964	4,152,999	—	BV	1.50	2.00	—
1964 Proof	16,000	Value: 2.50				

KM# 68.1 10 CENTS
4.0000 g., Nickel, 20.7 mm. **Obv:** Head of Jan van Riebeeck right **Rev:** Aloe plant and value

Date	Mintage	F	VF	XF	Unc	BU
1965	29,210,000	—	—	0.10	0.35	—
1966	3,685,000	—	—	0.10	0.45	—
1966 Proof	25,000	Value: 0.60				
1967	50,000	—	—	—	1.00	—
1967 Proof	25,000	Value: 0.60				
1969	558,000	—	—	0.10	0.50	—
1969 Proof	12,000	Value: 1.00				

KM# 68.2 10 CENTS
4.0000 g., Nickel, 20.7 mm. **Obv:** Head of Jan van Riebeeck right **Rev:** Aloe plant and value

Date	Mintage	F	VF	XF	Unc	BU
1965	29,210,000	—	—	0.10	0.35	—
1965 Proof	25,000	Value: 0.60				

Date	Mintage	F	VF	XF	Unc	BU
1966	3,685,000	—	—	0.10	0.45	—
1967	50,000	—	—	—	1.00	—
1969	558,000	—	0.10	0.20	2.50	—

KM# 77.1 10 CENTS
4.0000 g., Nickel, 20.7 mm. **Obv:** Head of President Charles Swart left **Rev:** Aloe plant and value

Date	Mintage	F	VF	XF	Unc	BU
1968	50,000	—	—	—	2.00	—

KM# 77.2 10 CENTS
4.0000 g., Nickel, 20.7 mm. **Obv:** Afrikaans legend **Rev:** Aloe plant and value

Date	Mintage	F	VF	XF	Unc	BU
1968	50,000	—	—	—	1.50	—
1968 Proof	25,000	Value: 0.60				

KM# 85 10 CENTS
4.0000 g., Nickel, 20.7 mm. **Obv:** Arms with supporters **Rev:** Aloe plant and value

Date	Mintage	F	VF	XF	Unc	BU
1970	7,598,000	—	—	0.10	0.35	—
1970 Proof	10,000	Value: 0.60				
1971	6,440,000	—	—	0.10	0.35	—
1971 Proof	12,000	Value: 0.60				
1972	10,028,000	—	—	0.10	0.35	—
1972 Proof	10,000	Value: 0.60				
1973	1,760,000	—	—	0.10	0.35	—
1973 Proof	11,000	Value: 0.60				
1974	9,897,000	—	—	0.10	0.35	—
1974 Proof	15,000	Value: 0.60				
1975	12,982,000	—	—	0.10	0.35	—
1975 Proof	18,000	Value: 0.60				
1977	28,851,000	—	—	0.10	0.35	—
1977 Proof	19,000	Value: 0.60				
1978	25,008,000	—	—	0.10	0.35	—
1978 Proof	19,000	Value: 0.60				
1980	5,040,000	—	—	0.10	0.35	—
1980 Proof	15,000	Value: 0.60				
1981	9,604,000	—	—	0.10	0.35	—
1981 Proof	10,000	Value: 0.60				
1983	26,495,000	—	—	0.10	0.35	—
1983 Proof	14,000	Value: 0.60				
1984	35,465,000	—	—	0.10	0.35	—
1984 Proof	11,000	Value: 0.60				
1985	29,270,000	—	—	0.10	0.35	—
1985 Proof	9,859	Value: 0.60				
1986	24,480,000	—	—	0.10	0.35	—
1986 Proof	7,100	Value: 0.60				
1987	43,234,000	—	—	0.10	0.35	—
1987 Proof	6,781	Value: 0.60				
1988	48,267,000	—	—	0.10	0.35	—
1988 Proof	-7,250	Value: 0.60				
1989	—	—	—	—	0.35	—
1989 Proof	—	Value: 0.60				

KM# 94 10 CENTS
4.0000 g., Nickel, 20.7 mm. **Obv:** Head of President Fouche right **Rev:** Aloe plant and value

Date	Mintage	F	VF	XF	Unc	BU
1976	30,986,000	—	—	0.40	1.00	—
1976 Proof	21,000	Value: 1.50				

KM# 101   10 CENTS
4.0000 g., Nickel, 20.7 mm. **Obv:** Head of President Diederichs left **Rev:** Aloe plant and value

Date	Mintage	F	VF	XF	Unc	BU
1979	5,042,000	—	—	0.40	1.00	—
1979 Proof	17,000	Value: 1.50				

KM# 112   10 CENTS
4.0000 g., Nickel, 20.7 mm. **Obv:** Head of President Vorster 1/4 right **Rev:** Aloe plant and value

Date	Mintage	F	VF	XF	Unc	BU
1982	15,806,000	—	—	0.40	1.00	—
1982 Proof	12,000	Value: 1.50				

KM# 135   10 CENTS
2.0000 g., Brass Plated Steel, 16 mm. **Obv:** Arms with supporters **Rev:** Arum lily and value

Date	Mintage	F	VF	XF	Unc	BU
1990	—	—	—	—	0.40	—
1990 Proof	—	Value: 0.60				
1991	—	—	—	—	0.40	—
1991 Proof	12,000	Value: 0.60				
1992	—	—	—	—	0.40	—
1992 Proof	—	Value: 0.60				
1993	—	—	—	—	0.40	—
1993 Proof	7,790	Value: 0.60				
1994	—	—	—	—	0.40	—
1994 Proof	5,804	Value: 0.60				
1995	—	—	—	—	0.40	—
1995 Proof	—	Value: 0.60				

KM# 161   10 CENTS
2.0000 g., Brass Plated Steel, 16 mm. **Obv:** English legend **Rev:** Arum lily and value

Date	Mintage	F	VF	XF	Unc	BU
1996	—	—	—	—	0.40	0.60
1996 Proof	—	Value: 0.75				
1997	—	—	—	—	0.40	0.60
1997 Proof	3,596	Value: 0.75				
1998	—	—	—	—	0.40	0.60
1998 Proof	—	Value: 1.75				
1999	—	—	—	—	0.40	0.60
1999 Proof	—	Value: 1.75				
2000	—	—	—	—	0.40	0.60

KM# 224   10 CENTS
2.0000 g., Bronze Plated Steel, 16 mm. **Obv:** New national arms **Obv. Leg.:** South Africa **Rev:** Arum Lily and value **Edge:** Reeded

Date	Mintage	F	VF	XF	Unc	BU
2000	—	—	—	0.30	0.75	1.00

KM# 235   10 CENTS
16.8630 g., 0.9250 Silver 0.5015 oz. ASW, 32.7 mm.
Series: Wildlife - Predator **Obv:** Lion's head 3/4 right **Rev:** Lions, value **Edge:** Reeded

Date	Mintage	F	VF	XF	Unc	BU
2000 Proof	2,139	Value: 45.00				

KM# 61   20 CENTS
11.3100 g., 0.5000 Silver 0.1818 oz. ASW. **Obv:** Shield **Rev:** Bust of Jan van Riebeeck 1/4 right

Date	Mintage	F	VF	XF	Unc	BU
1961	2,954,000	—	BV	3.00	3.50	—
1961 Proof	7,530	Value: 4.00				
1962 Small 2	3,568,000	—	BV	3.00	3.50	—
1962 Large 2	Inc. above	—	—	—	—	—
1962 Small 2; Proof	3,844	Value: 5.00				
1963	4,380,000	—	BV	3.00	3.50	—
1963 Proof	4,025	Value: 5.00				
1964	4,335,000	—	BV	3.00	3.50	—
1964 Proof	16,000	Value: 3.50				

KM# 69.1   20 CENTS
6.0000 g., Nickel, 24.2 mm. **Obv:** Head of Jan van Riebeeck, English legend **Obv. Leg.:** English legend **Rev:** Protea flower within sprigs, value at left

Date	Mintage	F	VF	XF	Unc	BU
1965	29,210,000	—	0.15	0.20	0.40	—
1965 Proof	25,000	Value: 0.60				
1966	4,049,000	—	0.15	0.20	0.50	—
1967	58,000	—	—	—	1.00	—
1969	9,952	—	—	—	10.00	—

KM# 69.2   20 CENTS
6.0000 g., Nickel, 24.2 mm. **Obv:** Head of Jan van Riebeeck, Africaans legend **Obv. Leg.:** Afrikaans legend **Rev:** Protea flower within sprigs, value at left

Date	Mintage	F	VF	XF	Unc	BU
1965	29,210,000	—	0.15	0.20	0.40	—
1966	4,049,000	—	0.15	0.20	0.50	—
1966 Proof	25,000	Value: 0.60				
1967	58,000	—	—	—	1.00	—
1967 Proof	25,000	Value: 0.60				
1969	9,952	—	—	—	6.00	—
1969 Proof	12,000	Value: 4.00				

KM# 78.1   20 CENTS
6.0000 g., Nickel, 24.2 mm. **Obv:** Head of President Charles Swart left, English legend **Rev:** Protea flower within sprigs, value at left

Date	Mintage	F	VF	XF	Unc	BU
1968	50,000	—	—	—	3.00	—
1968 Proof	25,000	Value: 0.60				

KM# 78.2   20 CENTS
6.0000 g., Nickel, 24.2 mm. **Obv:** Africaans legend **Rev:** Protea flower within sprigs, value at left

Date	Mintage	F	VF	XF	Unc	BU
1968	50,000	—	—	—	3.50	—

KM# 86   20 CENTS
6.0000 g., Nickel, 24.2 mm. **Obv:** Arms with supporters, bilingual legend **Obv. Leg.:** Bilingual legend **Rev:** Protea flower within sprigs, value at left **Note:** Varieties exist.

Date	Mintage	F	VF	XF	Unc	BU
1970	14,000	—	—	—	10.00	—
1970 Proof	10,000	Value: 1.50				
1971	5,893,000	—	0.15	0.25	0.60	—
1971 Proof	12,000	Value: 1.50				
1972	9,069,000	—	0.15	0.25	0.60	—
1972 Proof	10,000	Value: 1.50				
1973	20,000	—	—	—	5.00	—
1973 Proof	11,000	Value: 1.50				
1974	2,436,000	—	0.15	0.35	0.75	—
1974 Proof	15,000	Value: 1.50				
1975	12,982,000	—	—	0.20	0.60	—
1975 Proof	18,000	Value: 1.00				
1977	30,650,000	—	—	0.20	0.60	—
1977 Proof	19,000	Value: 0.75				
1978	10,049,000	—	—	0.20	0.60	—
1978 Proof	19,000	Value: 0.75				
1980	13,335,000	—	—	0.20	0.60	—
1980 Proof	15,000	Value: 0.75				
1981	8,534,000	—	—	0.20	0.60	—
1981 Proof	10,000	Value: 0.75				
1983	25,667,000	—	—	0.20	0.60	—
1983 Proof	14,000	Value: 0.75				
1984	31,607,000	—	—	0.20	0.60	—
1984 Proof	11,000	Value: 0.75				
1985	29,329,000	—	—	0.20	0.60	—
1985 Proof	9,859	Value: 0.75				
1986	11,408,000	—	—	0.20	0.60	—
1986 Proof	7,100	Value: 0.75				
1987	36,904,000	—	—	0.20	0.60	—
1987 Proof	6,781	Value: 0.75				
1988	43,115,000	—	—	0.20	0.60	—
1988 Proof	7,250	Value: 0.75				
1989	—	—	—	0.20	0.60	—
1989 Proof	—	Value: 0.75				
1990	98,512,000	—	—	0.20	0.60	—

KM# 95   20 CENTS
6.0000 g., Nickel, 24.2 mm. **Obv:** Head of President Fouche right **Rev:** Protea flower within sprigs, value at left

Date	Mintage	F	VF	XF	Unc	BU
1976	18,826,000	—	—	0.70	1.50	—
1976 Proof	21,000	Value: 2.50				

KM# 102   20 CENTS
6.0000 g., Nickel, 24.2 mm. **Obv:** Head of President Diederichs left **Rev:** Protea flower within sprigs, value at left

Date	Mintage	F	VF	XF	Unc	BU
1979	5,032,000	—	—	0.70	1.50	—
1979 Proof	15,000	Value: 2.50				

KM# 113   20 CENTS
6.0000 g., Nickel, 24.2 mm. **Obv:** Head of President Vorster 1/4 right **Rev:** Protea flower within sprigs, value at left

Date	Mintage	F	VF	XF	Unc	BU
1982	18,083,000	—	—	0.70	1.50	—
1982 Proof	12,000	Value: 2.50				

KM# 136 20 CENTS
3.5000 g., Brass Plated Steel, 19 mm. **Obv:** Arms with supporters **Rev:** Protea flower within sprigs, value at upper right

Date	Mintage	F	VF	XF	Unc	BU
1990	—	—	—	—	4.00	—
1990 Proof	—	Value: 8.00				
1991	—	—	—	—	4.00	—
1991 Proof	11,800	Value: 8.00				
1992	—	—	—	—	0.60	—
1992 Proof	—	Value: 8.00				
1993	—	—	—	—	0.60	—
1993 Proof	7,790	Value: 8.00				
1994	—	—	—	—	0.60	—
1994 Proof	5,804	Value: 8.00				
1995	—	—	—	—	0.60	—
1995 Proof	—	Value: 8.00				

KM# 162 20 CENTS
3.5000 g., Brass Plated Steel, 19 mm. **Obv:** Arms with supporters **Obv. Leg.:** AFERIKA BORWA, Tswana legend above arms **Rev:** Protea flower within sprigs, value at upper right

Date	Mintage	F	VF	XF	Unc	BU
1996	—	—	—	—	0.60	0.85
1996 Proof	—	Value: 4.00				
1997	—	—	—	—	0.60	0.85
1997 Proof	3,596	Value: 4.00				
1998	—	—	—	—	0.60	0.85
1998 Proof	—	Value: 4.00				
1999	—	—	—	—	0.60	0.85
1999 Proof	—	Value: 4.00				
2000	—	—	—	—	0.60	0.85

KM# 225 20 CENTS
3.5000 g., Bronze Plated Steel, 19 mm. **Obv:** New national arms **Obv. Leg.:** Aferika - Borwa **Rev:** Protea flower and value **Edge:** Reeded

Date	Mintage	F	VF	XF	Unc	BU
2000	—	—	—	0.35	0.90	1.20

KM# 236 20 CENTS
33.7260 g., 0.9250 Silver 1.0030 oz. ASW, 38.3 mm. **Series:** Wildlife - Predator **Obv:** Lion's head 3/4 right **Rev:** Lions, value **Edge:** Reeded

Date	Mintage	F	VF	XF	Unc	BU
2000 Proof	2,270	Value: 60.00				

KM# 62 50 CENTS
28.2800 g., 0.5000 Silver 0.4546 oz. ASW **Obv:** Springbok **Rev:** Bust of Jan van Riebeeck 1/4 right **Note:** Varieties exist with narrow, high relief and wide, low letters.

Date	Mintage	F	VF	XF	Unc	BU
1961	26,000	—	BV	7.50	10.00	—
1961 Prooflike	20,000	—	—	—	10.00	—
1961 Proof	8,530	Value: 18.00				
1962	15,000	—	BV	7.50	10.00	—
1962 Prooflike	6,024	—	—	—	12.50	—
1962 Proof	3,844	Value: 20.00				
1963	143,000	—	BV	7.50	10.00	—
1963 Prooflike	10,000	—	—	—	12.50	—
1963 Proof	4,025	Value: 20.00				
1964	86,000	—	BV	7.50	9.00	—
1964 Prooflike	25,000	—	—	—	10.00	—
1964 Proof	16,000	Value: 10.00				

KM# 70.1 50 CENTS
9.5000 g., Nickel, 27.8 mm. **Obv:** Head of Jan van Riebeeck right, English legend **Rev:** Flower and value

Date	Mintage	F	VF	XF	Unc	BU
1965 Proof	—	Value: 3,500				
1966	8,055,999	—	—	0.50	2.50	—
1966 Proof	25,000	Value: 4.00				
1967 In sets only	52,000	—	—	—	1.50	—
1967 Proof	25,000	Value: 4.00				
1969 In sets only	7,968	—	—	—	10.00	—
1969 Proof	12,000	Value: 10.00				

KM# 70.2 50 CENTS
9.5000 g., Nickel, 27.8 mm. **Obv:** Head of Jan van Riebeeck right, Afrikaans legend **Rev:** Flower and value

Date	Mintage	F	VF	XF	Unc	BU
1965	28,000	—	—	—	6.00	—
1965 Proof	25,000	Value: 6.00				
1966	8,055,999	—	—	0.50	2.50	—
1967 In sets only	52,000	—	—	—	3.50	—
1969 In sets only	7,968	—	—	—	15.00	—

KM# 79.1 50 CENTS
9.5000 g., Nickel, 27.8 mm. **Obv:** Head of President Charles Swart left, English legend **Rev:** Flowers and value

Date	Mintage	F	VF	XF	Unc	BU
1968	750,000	—	—	0.50	1.50	—

KM# 79.2 50 CENTS
9.5000 g., Nickel, 27.8 mm. **Obv:** Head of President Charles Swart left, Afrikaans legend **Rev:** Flowers and value

Date	Mintage	F	VF	XF	Unc	BU
1968	750,000	—	—	0.50	2.00	—
1968 Proof	25,000	Value: 3.50				

KM# 87 50 CENTS
9.5000 g., Nickel, 27.8 mm. **Obv:** Arms with supporters, bilingual legend **Rev:** Flowers and value **Note:** Varieties exist.

Date	Mintage	F	VF	XF	Unc	BU
1970	4,098,000	—	—	0.50	1.50	—
1970 Proof	10,000	Value: 2.00				
1971	5,062,000	—	—	0.50	1.50	—
1971 Proof	12,000	Value: 2.00				
1972	771,000	—	—	0.50	1.50	—
1972 Proof	10,000	Value: 2.00				

Date	Mintage	F	VF	XF	Unc	BU
1973	1,042,999	—	—	0.50	1.50	—
1973 Proof	11,000	Value: 2.00				
1974	1,942,000	—	—	0.50	1.50	—
1974 Proof	15,000	Value: 2.00				
1975	4,888,000	—	—	0.50	1.50	—
1975 Proof	18,000	Value: 2.00				
1977	10,196,000	—	—	0.50	1.50	—
1977 Proof	19,000	Value: 2.00				
1978	5,071,000	—	—	0.50	1.50	—
1978 Proof	17,000	Value: 2.00				
1980	4,268,000	—	—	0.50	1.50	—
1980 Proof	15,000	Value: 2.00				
1981	5,681,000	—	—	0.50	1.50	—
1981 Proof	10,000	Value: 2.00				
1983	5,150,000	—	—	0.40	1.00	—
1983 Proof	14,000	Value: 1.50				
1984	9,687,000	—	—	0.40	1.00	—
1984 Proof	11,000	Value: 1.50				
1985	13,339,000	—	—	0.40	1.00	—
1985 Proof	9,859	Value: 1.50				
1986	2,294,000	—	—	0.40	1.00	—
1986 Proof	7,100	Value: 1.50				
1987	19,071,000	—	—	0.40	1.00	—
1987 Proof	6,781	Value: 1.50				
1988	27,698,000	—	—	0.40	1.00	—
1988 Proof	7,250	Value: 1.50				
1989	—	—	—	0.40	1.00	—
1989 Proof	—	Value: 1.50				
1990	29,442,000	—	—	0.40	1.00	—

KM# 96 50 CENTS
9.5000 g., Nickel, 27.8 mm. **Obv:** Head of President Fouche right **Rev:** Flowers and value

Date	Mintage	F	VF	XF	Unc	BU
1976	9,632,000	—	0.75	1.50	3.00	—
1976 Proof	21,000	Value: 5.00				

KM# 103 50 CENTS
9.5000 g., Nickel, 27.8 mm. **Obv:** Head of President Diederichs left **Rev:** Flowers and value

Date	Mintage	F	VF	XF	Unc	BU
1979	5,051,000	—	0.75	1.50	3.50	—
1979 Proof	15,000	Value: 5.00				

KM# 114 50 CENTS
9.5000 g., Nickel, 27.8 mm. **Obv:** Head of President Vorster 1/4 right **Rev:** Flowers and value

Date	Mintage	F	VF	XF	Unc	BU
1982	2,069,999	—	0.75	1.50	3.50	—
1982 Proof	12,000	Value: 5.00				

KM# 137 50 CENTS
5.0000 g., Brass Plated Steel, 22 mm. **Obv:** Arms with supporters **Rev:** Plant and value

Date	Mintage	F	VF	XF	Unc	BU
1990	—	—	—	—	5.00	—
1990 Proof	—	Value: 10.00				
1991	—	—	—	—	5.00	—

Date	Mintage	F	VF	XF	Unc	BU
1991 Proof	12,000	Value: 10.00			—	—
1992	—	—	—	—	1.00	—
1992 Proof	—	Value: 10.00			—	—
1993	—	—	—	—	1.00	—
1993 Proof	7,790	Value: 10.00			—	—
1994	—	—	—	—	1.00	—
1994 Proof	5,804	Value: 10.00			—	—
1995	—	—	—	—	1.00	—
1995 Proof	—	Value: 10.00			—	—

KM# 163   50 CENTS
5.0000 g., Bronze Plated Steel, 22 mm. **Obv:** Arms with supporters
Obv. Leg.: AFRIKA BORWA, Sotho legend **Rev:** Plant and value

Date	Mintage	F	VF	XF	Unc	BU
1996	—	—	—	—	1.00	1.25
1996 Proof	—	Value: 5.00			—	—
1997	—	—	—	—	1.00	1.25
1997 Proof	—	Value: 5.00			—	—
1998	—	—	—	—	1.00	1.25
1998 Proof	—	Value: 5.00			—	—
1999	—	—	—	—	1.00	1.25
1999 Proof	—	Value: 5.00			—	—
2000	—	—	—	—	1.00	1.25

KM# 226   50 CENTS
5.0000 g., Bronze-Plated Steel, 22 mm. **Obv:** New national arms
Obv. Leg.: AFERIKA - BORWA **Rev:** Strelitzia plant, value
Edge: Reeded

Date	Mintage	F	VF	XF	Unc	BU
2000	—	—	—	0.50	1.20	1.60

KM# 237   50 CENTS
76.4020 g., 0.9250 Silver 2.2721 oz. ASW, 50 mm. **Series:** Wildlife
- Predator **Obv:** Lion's head 3/4 right **Rev:** Lion, value **Edge:** Reeded

Date	Mintage	F	VF	XF	Unc	BU
2000 Proof	2,122	Value: 75.00				

KM# 63   RAND
3.9940 g., 0.9170 Gold 0.1177 oz. AGW **Obv:** Springbok
Rev: Bust of Jan van Riebeeck 1/4 right

Date	Mintage	F	VF	XF	Unc	BU
1961	4,246	—	—	—	—BV+15%	
1961 Proof	4,932	BV+20%			—	—
1962	3,955	—	—	—	—BV+15%	
1962 Proof	2,344	BV+20%			—	—
1963	4,023	—	—	—	—BV+15%	
1963 Proof	2,508	BV+20%			—	—
1964	5,866	—	—	—	—BV+15%	
1964 Proof	4,000	BV+20%			—	—
1965	10,000	—	—	—	—BV+15%	
1965 Proof	6,024	BV+20%			—	—
1966	10,000	—	—	—	—BV+15%	
1966 Proof	11,000	BV+20%			—	—
1967	10,000	—	—	—	—BV+15%	
1967 Proof	11,000	BV+20%			—	—
1968	10,000	—	—	—	—BV+15%	
1968 Proof	11,000	BV+20%			—	—
1969	10,000	—	—	—	—BV+15%	
1969 Proof	8,000	BV+20%			—	—
1970	10,000	—	—	—	—BV+15%	
1970 Proof	7,000	BV+20%			—	—
1971	10,000	—	—	—	—BV+15%	
1971 Proof	7,650	BV+20%			—	—
1972	12,000	—	—	—	—BV+15%	
1972 Proof	7,500	BV+20%			—	—
1973	15,000	—	—	—	—BV+15%	
1973 Proof	12,000	BV+20%			—	—
1974	23,000	—	—	—	—BV+15%	
1974 Proof	17,000	BV+20%			—	—
1975	12,000	—	—	—	—BV+15%	
1975 Proof	18,000	BV+20%			—	—
1976	12,000	—	—	—	—BV+15%	
1976 Proof	21,000	BV+20%			—	—
1977	27,000	—	—	—	—BV+15%	
1977 Proof	20,000	BV+20%			—	—

Date	Mintage	F	VF	XF	Unc	BU
1978	13,000	—	—	—	—BV+15%	
1978 Proof	19,000	BV+20%			—	—
1979	17,000	—	—	—	—BV+15%	
1979 Proof	17,000	BV+20%			—	—
1980	14,000	—	—	—	—BV+15%	
1980 Proof	18,000	BV+20%			—	—
1981	9,274	—	—	—	—BV+15%	
1981 Proof	10,000	BV+20%			—	—
1982	14,000	—	—	—	—BV+15%	
1983	15,000	—	—	—	—BV+15%	

KM# 71.1   RAND
15.0000 g., 0.8000 Silver 0.3858 oz. ASW **Obv:** Head of Jan
van Riebeeck right **Rev:** Springbok above value

Date	Mintage	F	VF	XF	Unc	BU
1965	—	—	—	BV	7.00	—
1965 Proof	25,000	Value: 20.00			—	—
1966	1,434,000	—	—	BV	6.50	—
1966 Proof	20	Value: 1,250			—	—
1968 In sets only	50,000	—	—	BV	6.50	—
1968 Proof	25,000	Value: 6.50			—	—

KM# 71.2   RAND
15.0000 g., 0.8000 Silver 0.3858 oz. ASW **Obv:** Head of Jan van
Riebeeck right, Afrikaans legend **Rev:** Springbok above value

Date	Mintage	F	VF	XF	Unc	BU
1965 V.I.P. Proof	—	Value: 1,000			—	—
1966	1,434,000	—	—	BV	6.50	—
1966 Proof	25,000	Value: 7.00			—	—
1968 In sets only	50,000	—	—	—	8.00	—
1968 Proof	Est. 20	Value: 1,250			—	—

KM# 72.1   RAND
15.0000 g., 0.8000 Silver 0.3858 oz. ASW **Subject:** 1st
Anniversary - Death of Dr. Verwoerd **Obv:** Bust right, English
legend **Rev:** Springbok above value

Date	Mintage	F	VF	XF	Unc	BU
1967	1,544,000	—	—	BV	6.50	—
1967 Proof	Est. 20	Value: 1,250			—	—

KM# 72.2   RAND
15.0000 g., 0.8000 Silver 0.3858 oz. ASW **Subject:** 1st
Anniversary - Death of Dr. Verwoerd **Obv:** Bust right, Afrikaans
legend **Rev:** Springbok above value

Date	Mintage	F	VF	XF	Unc	BU
1967	1,544,000	—	—	BV	6.50	—
1967 Proof	25,000	Value: 7.50			—	—

KM# 80.1   RAND
15.0000 g., 0.8000 Silver 0.3858 oz. ASW, 32.6 mm.
Subject: Dr. T.E. Donges **Obv:** Bust right, English legend
Rev: Springbok above value **Note:** The South African mint does
not acknowledge the existence of these 1 Rand pieces struck in
proof.

Date	Mintage	F	VF	XF	Unc	BU
1969	506,000	—	—	BV	6.50	—
1969 Proof	Est. 20	Value: 1,250			—	—

KM# 80.2   RAND
15.0000 g., 0.8000 Silver 0.3858 oz. ASW, 32.6 mm.
Subject: Dr. T.E. Donges **Obv:** Bust right, Afrikaans legend
Rev: Springbok above value

Date	Mintage	F	VF	XF	Unc	BU
1969	506,000	—	—	BV	6.50	—
1969 Proof	12,000	Value: 7.50			—	—

KM# 89   RAND
15.0000 g., 0.8000 Silver 0.3858 oz. ASW **Subject:** 50th
Anniversary of Pretoria Mint **Obv:** Arms with supporters **Rev:** 4
Coin designs surround brick door at center

Date	Mintage	F	VF	XF	Unc	BU
1974	20,000	—	—	—	12.50	—
1974 Proof	15,000	Value: 15.00			—	—

KM# 88   RAND
15.0000 g., 0.8000 Silver 0.3858 oz. ASW **Obv:** Arms with
supporters, bilingual legend **Rev:** Springbok

Date	Mintage	F	VF	XF	Unc	BU
1970	14,000	—	—	BV	6.50	—
1970 Proof	10,000	Value: 8.00			—	—
1971	20,000	—	—	BV	6.50	—
1971 Proof	12,000	Value: 8.00			—	—
1972	20,000	—	—	BV	6.50	—
1972 Proof	10,000	Value: 8.00			—	—
1973	20,000	—	—	BV	6.50	—
1973 Proof	11,000	Value: 8.00			—	—
1975	20,000	—	—	BV	6.50	—
1975 Proof	18,000	Value: 8.00			—	—
1976	20,000	—	—	BV	6.50	—
1976 Proof	21,000	Value: 8.00			—	—
1977	19,000	—	—	—	9.00	—
1978 Proof	17,000	Value: 9.00			—	—
1979 Proof	15,000	Value: 9.00			—	—
1980 Proof	15,000	Value: 9.00			—	—
1981 Proof	12,000	Value: 12.50			—	—

Date	Mintage	F	VF	XF	Unc	BU
1982 Proof	10,000	Value: 12.50				
1983 Proof	14,000	Value: 12.50				
1984 Proof	11,000	Value: 12.50				
1987	4,526	—		BV	15.00	—
1987 Proof	13,000	Value: 12.50				
1988	21	—				
1988 Proof	7,250	Value: 15.00				
1989	3,684	—		BV	15.00	—
1989 Proof	15,000	Value: 12.50				
1990 Proof	—	Value: 25.00				

KM# 88a RAND
12.0000 g., Nickel, 31 mm. **Obv:** Arms with supporters, bilingual legend **Rev:** Springbok above value

Date	Mintage	F	VF	XF	Unc	BU
1977	29,871,000	—	—	0.75	2.00	—
1977 Proof	10	Value: 1,500				
1978	12,021,000	—	—	0.75	2.00	—
1978 Proof	10	Value: 1,500				
1980	2,690,000	—	—	0.75	2.00	—
1981	2,035,000	—	—	0.75	2.00	—
1983	7,182,000	—	—	0.75	2.00	—
1983 Proof	10	Value: 1,500				
1984	5,736,000	—	—	0.75	2.00	—
1984 Proof	11,000	Value: 5.00				
1986	1,570,000	—	—	0.75	2.00	—
1986 Proof	7,000	Value: 5.00				
1987	12,152,000	—	—	0.75	2.00	—
1987 Proof	6,781	Value: 5.00				
1988	21,335,000	—	—	0.75	2.00	—
1988 Proof	7,250	Value: 5.00				
1989	—	—	—	—	2.00	—
1989 Proof	—	Value: 5.00				

KM# 104 RAND
12.0000 g., Nickel, 31 mm. **Obv:** Head of President Diederichs left **Rev:** Springbok above value

Date	Mintage	F	VF	XF	Unc	BU
1979	13,466,000	—	2.00	4.00	10.00	—
1979 Proof	5	Value: 2,000				

KM# 115 RAND
Nickel **Obv:** Head of President Vorster 1/4 right **Rev:** Springbok above value

Date	Mintage	F	VF	XF	Unc	BU
1982	7,685,000	—	2.50	5.00	10.00	—
1982 Proof	15	Value: 1,500				

KM# 116 RAND
15.0000 g., 0.8000 Silver 0.3858 oz. ASW **Subject:** 75th Anniversary of Parliament **Obv:** Crossed scepters divides shield and lion **Rev:** Parliament building

Date	Mintage	F	VF	XF	Unc	BU
1985	8,731	—	—	—	11.50	—
1985 Proof	26,000	Value: 18.50				

KM# 117 RAND
Nickel **Obv:** Head of President Marais Viljoen left **Rev:** Springbok above value

Date	Mintage	F	VF	XF	Unc	BU
1985	3,983,000	—	2.50	5.00	10.00	—
1985 Proof	9,859	Value: 5.00				

KM# 119 RAND
15.0000 g., 0.8000 Silver 0.3858 oz. ASW **Subject:** 100th Anniversary of Johannesburg **Obv:** Arms with supporters **Rev:** View of city

Date	Mintage	F	VF	XF	Unc	BU
1986	7,501	—	—	—	13.50	—
1986 Proof	5,683	Value: 22.50				

KM# 120 RAND
15.0000 g., 0.8000 Silver 0.3858 oz. ASW **Series:** Year of the Disabled **Obv:** Arms with supporters **Rev:** Stylized standing figure and figure in wheelchair, value at left

Date	Mintage	F	VF	XF	Unc	BU
1986	1,005	—	—	—	40.00	—
1986 Proof	5,150	Value: 22.50				

KM# 122 RAND
15.0000 g., 0.8000 Silver 0.3858 oz. ASW **Subject:** Bartolomeu Dias **Obv:** Arms with supporters **Rev:** Crown above point of star design to left of map

Date	Mintage	F	VF	XF	Unc	BU
1988	7,091	—	—	—	12.50	—
1988 Proof	9,640	Value: 16.50				

KM# 125 RAND
15.0000 g., 0.8000 Silver 0.3858 oz. ASW **Subject:** Huguenots **Obv:** Arms with supporters **Rev:** Descending dove and design divide dates below small cross, all within circle

Date	Mintage	F	VF	XF	Unc	BU
1988	5,497	—	—	—	12.50	—
1988 Proof	9,028	Value: 16.50				

KM# 128 RAND
15.0000 g., 0.8000 Silver 0.3858 oz. ASW **Subject:** The Great Trek **Obv:** Arms with supporters **Rev:** Stylized wheel and arrow design

Date	Mintage	F	VF	XF	Unc	BU
1988	6,555	—	—	—	12.50	—
1988 Proof	7,941	Value: 17.50				

KM# 141 RAND
Nickel **Obv:** Head of President Botha facing **Rev:** Springbok above value

Date	Mintage	F	VF	XF	Unc	BU
1990	25,323,000	—	—	1.75	3.50	—
1990 Proof	15,000	Value: 10.00				

KM# 148 RAND
4.0000 g., Nickel Plated Copper, 20 mm. **Obv:** Head of President Botha facing **Rev:** Springbok below value

Date	Mintage	F	VF	XF	Unc	BU
1990 Proof	10,000	Value: 15.00				
1990	12,000	—	—	—	10.00	—

KM# 138 RAND
4.0000 g., Nickel Plated Copper, 20 mm. **Obv:** Arms with supporters **Rev:** Springbok below value

Date	Mintage	F	VF	XF	Unc	BU
1991	20,765,000	—	—	—	2.50	—
1991 Proof	12,000	Value: 15.00				
1992	59,571,000	—	—	—	2.50	—
1992 Proof	10,000	Value: 15.00				
1993	37,977,000	—	—	—	2.50	—
1993 Proof	7,790	Value: 20.00				
1994	54,633,000	—	—	—	2.50	—
1994 Proof	5,804	Value: 20.00				
1995	28,012,000	—	—	—	2.50	—
1995 Proof	5,816	Value: 20.00				

KM# 142 RAND
14.9700 g., 0.9250 Silver 0.4452 oz. ASW, 32.7 mm.
Subject: South African Nursing Schools **Obv:** Protea flower
Rev: Aladdin lamp divides dates within cross design
Edge: Reeded

Date	Mintage	F	VF	XF	Unc	BU
1991	13,576	—	—	—	12.50	—
1991 Proof	8,675	Value: 17.50				

KM# 143 RAND
14.9700 g., 0.9250 Silver 0.4452 oz. ASW, 32.7 mm.
Subject: Coinage Centennial **Obv:** Protea flower **Rev:** Assorted
coin designs **Edge:** Reeded

Date	Mintage	F	VF	XF	Unc	BU
1992	13,920	—	—	—	12.50	—
1992 Proof	8,094	Value: 17.50				

KM# 168 RAND
14.9700 g., 0.9250 Silver 0.4452 oz. ASW, 32.7 mm.
Subject: 200 Years of Banking **Obv:** Protea flower **Rev:** Tower
divides lion head and coin designs **Edge:** Reeded

Date	Mintage	F	VF	XF	Unc	BU
1993	7,584	—	—	—	15.00	—
1993 Proof	3,907	Value: 22.50				

KM# 149 RAND
15.0000 g., 0.9250 Silver 0.4461 oz. ASW, 32.7 mm.
Subject: Presidential Inauguration **Obv:** National arms
Rev: Building below value **Edge:** Reeded

Date	Mintage	F	VF	XF	Unc	BU
1994 Proof	6,269	Value: 100				

KM# 167 RAND
15.0000 g., 0.9250 Silver 0.4461 oz. ASW, 32.7 mm.
Subject: Conservation **Obv:** Protea flower **Rev:** Assorted
animals within stylized design **Edge:** Reeded

Date	Mintage	F	VF	XF	Unc	BU
1994	11,190	—	—	—	15.00	—
1994 Proof	4,706	Value: 22.50				

KM# 152 RAND
15.0000 g., 0.9250 Silver 0.4461 oz. ASW, 32.7 mm.
Subject: Railway Centennial **Obv:** Protea flower **Rev:** Train and
value **Edge:** Reeded

Date	Mintage	F	VF	XF	Unc	BU
1995	8,006	—	—	—	15.00	—
1995 Proof	4,491	Value: 22.50				

KM# 164 RAND
4.0000 g., Nickel Plated Copper, 20 mm. **Obv:** Arms with
supporters, Afrikaans legend **Rev:** Springbok and value

Date	Mintage	F	VF	XF	Unc	BU
1996	12,199,000	—	—	—	1.75	—
1996 Proof	4,827	Value: 6.00				
1997	38,876,000	—	—	—	1.75	—
1997 Proof	3,596	Value: 6.00				
1998	—	—	—	—	1.75	—
1998 Proof	—	Value: 6.00				
1999	—	—	—	—	1.75	—
1999 Proof	—	Value: 6.00				
2000	—	—	—	—	1.75	—

KM# 169 RAND
15.0000 g., 0.9250 Silver 0.4461 oz. ASW, 32.7 mm.
Subject: Constitution **Obv:** Protea flower **Rev:** Hand writing in
book **Edge:** Reeded

Date	Mintage	F	VF	XF	Unc	BU
1996	5,059	—	—	—	15.00	—
1996 Proof	2,931	Value: 25.00				

KM# 181 RAND
15.0000 g., 0.9250 Silver 0.4461 oz. ASW, 32.7 mm.
Subject: Women of South Africa **Obv:** Protea flower
Rev: Stylized 1/2 head facing within map **Edge:** Reeded

Date	Mintage	F	VF	XF	Unc	BU
1997	3,312	—	—	—	17.50	—
1997 Proof	2,329	Value: 28.50				

KM# 182 RAND
3.1103 g., 0.9999 Gold 0.1000 oz. AGW, 16.5 mm.
Subject: 30th Anniversary - First Heart Transplant **Obv:** National
arms **Obv. Leg.:** SOUTH AFRICA **Rev:** Doctor working on
stylized heart **Edge:** Reeded

Date	Mintage	F	VF	XF	Unc	BU
1997 Proof	1,000	Value: 115				

KM# 177 RAND
15.0000 g., 0.9250 Silver 0.4461 oz. ASW, 32.7 mm.
Obv: Protea flower **Rev:** Assorted designs divided into 16
sections **Edge:** Reeded

Date	Mintage	F	VF	XF	Unc	BU
1998	2,673	—	—	—	16.50	—
1998 Proof	1,999	Value: 28.00				

KM# 178 RAND
3.1103 g., 0.9999 Gold 0.1000 oz. AGW, 16.5 mm. **Series:** Cultural
Subject: San Tribe **Obv:** National arms **Obv. Leg.:** SOUTH
AFRICA **Rev:** Tribesman hunting in Kalahari desert **Edge:** Reeded

Date	Mintage	F	VF	XF	Unc	BU
1998 Proof	559	Value: 115				

KM# 219 RAND
3.1103 g., 0.9999 Gold 0.1000 oz. AGW, 16.5 mm.
Series: Cultural **Obv:** National arms **Obv. Leg.:** ININGIZIMU
AFRIKA / SOUTH AFRICA **Rev:** Zulu warrior **Edge:** Reeded

Date	Mintage	F	VF	XF	Unc	BU
1999 Proof	664	Value: 115				

KM# 232 RAND
15.0000 g., 0.9250 Silver 0.4461 oz. ASW, 32.7 mm.
Obv: Protea flower **Rev:** Mine tower outline **Edge:** Reeded

Date	Mintage	F	VF	XF	Unc	BU
1999	6,277	—	—	—	30.00	—
1999 Proof	2,617	Value: 40.00				

KM# 238 RAND
15.0000 g., 0.9250 Silver 0.4461 oz. ASW, 32.7 mm. **Obv:** Protea flower **Rev:** Wine barrels, grapes and leaves **Edge:** Reeded

Date	Mintage	F	VF	XF	Unc	BU
2000	2,131	—	—	—	30.00	—
2000 Proof	1,519	Value: 40.00				

KM# 239 RAND
3.1103 g., 0.9999 Gold 0.1000 oz. AGW, 16.5 mm. **Series:** Cultural **Obv:** National arms **Obv. Leg.:** UMZANTSI AFRIKA / SOUTH AFRICA **Rev:** Three Xhosa tribe members **Edge:** Reeded

Date	Mintage	F	VF	XF	Unc	BU
2000 Proof	564	Value: 115				

KM# 378 RAND
3.1103 g., 0.9999 Gold 0.1000 oz. AGW, 16.5 mm. **Series:** Cultural **Obv:** New national arms **Obv. Leg.:** UMZANTSI AFRIKA - SOUTH AFRICA **Rev:** Three Xhosa tribe members **Edge:** Reeded

Date	Mintage	F	VF	XF	Unc	BU
2000 Proof	395	Value: 180				

KM# 227 RAND
4.0000 g., Nickel Plated Copper, 20 mm. **Obv:** New national arms **Obv. Leg.:** SUID- AFRIKA **Rev:** Springbok, value **Edge:** Segmented reeding

Date	Mintage	F	VF	XF	Unc	BU
2000	—	—	—	0.60	1.50	2.00

KM# 64 2 RAND
7.9881 g., 0.9170 Gold 0.2355 oz. AGW **Obv:** Springbok **Rev:** Bust of Jan van Riebeeck 1/4 right

Date	Mintage	F	VF	XF	Unc	BU
1961	3,014	—	—	—BV+10%	—
1961 Proof	3,932	—	—	—BV+15%	—
1962	10,000	—	—	—BV+10%	—
1962 Proof	2,344	—	—	—BV+15%	—
1963	3,179	—	—	—BV+10%	—
1963 Proof	2,508	—	—	—BV+15%	—
1964	3,994	—	—	—BV+10%	—
1964 Proof	4,000	—	—	—BV+15%	—
1965	10,000	—	—	—BV+10%	—
1965 Proof	6,024	—	—	—BV+15%	—
1966	10,000	—	—	—BV+10%	—
1966 Proof	11,000	—	—	—BV+15%	—
1967	10,000	—	—	—BV+10%	—
1967 Proof	11,000	—	—	—BV+15%	—
1968	10,000	—	—	—BV+10%	—
1968 Proof	11,000	—	—	—BV+15%	—
1969	10,000	—	—	—BV+10%	—
1969 Proof	8,000	—	—	—BV+15%	—
1970	10,000	—	—	—BV+10%	—
1970 Proof	7,000	—	—	—BV+15%	—
1971	10,000	—	—	—BV+10%	—
1971 Proof	7,650	—	—	—BV+15%	—
1972	18,000	—	—	—BV+10%	—
1972 Proof	7,500	—	—	—BV+15%	—
1973	14,000	—	—	—BV+10%	—
1973 Proof	13,000	—	—	—BV+15%	—
1974	13,000	—	—	—BV+10%	—
1974 Proof	17,000	—	—	—BV+15%	—
1975	12,000	—	—	—BV+10%	—
1975 Proof	18,000	—	—	—BV+15%	—
1976	12,000	—	—	—BV+10%	—
1976 Proof	21,000	—	—	—BV+15%	—

Date	Mintage	F	VF	XF	Unc	BU
1977	12,000	—	—	—BV+10%	—
1977 Proof	20,000	—	—	—BV+15%	—
1978	11,000	—	—	—BV+10%	—
1978 Proof	19,000	—	—	—BV+15%	—
1979	12,000	—	—	—BV+10%	—
1979 Proof	20,000	—	—	—BV+15%	—
1980	12,000	—	—	—BV+10%	—
1980 Proof	18,000	—	—	—BV+15%	—
1981	8,538	—	—	—BV+10%	—
1981 Proof	10,000	—	—	—BV+15%	—
1982	2,030	—	—	—BV+10%	—
1982 Proof	12,000	—	—	—BV+15%	—
1983	15,000	—	—	—BV+15%	—

KM# 139 2 RAND
5.5000 g., Nickel Plated Copper, 23 mm. **Obv:** Arms with supporters **Rev:** Greater Kudu

Date	Mintage	F	VF	XF	Unc	BU
1989	65,233,000	—	—	—	2.00	—
1989 Proof	13,000	Value: 10.00				
1990	70,655,000	—	—	—	2.00	—
1990 Proof	10,000	Value: 7.50				
1991	39,243,000	—	—	—	2.00	—
1991 Proof	12,000	Value: 7.50				
1992	2,115,000	—	—	—	2.00	—
1992 Proof	10,000	Value: 7.50				
1993	92,000	—	—	—	2.00	—
1993 Proof	7,790	Value: 7.50				
1994	994,000	—	—	—	2.00	—
1994 Proof	5,804	Value: 7.50				
1995	13,213,000	—	—	—	2.00	—
1995 Proof	5,816	Value: 7.50				

KM# 147 2 RAND
33.6260 g., 0.9250 Silver 1.0000 oz. ASW, 38.7 mm. **Series:** Barcelona Olympics **Obv:** Arms holding torch with outlined map behind **Rev:** Three event athletes **Edge:** Reeded **Note:** 1,670 used in jewelry mountings.

Date	Mintage	F	VF	XF	Unc	BU
1992 Proof	16,523	Value: 27.50				

KM# 145 2 RAND
33.6260 g., 0.9250 Silver 1.0000 oz. ASW, 38.7 mm. **Subject:** Coin Minting **Obv:** National arms **Rev:** Assorted coins and design above value **Edge:** Reeded **Note:** 50 pieces used in jewelry mountings.

Date	Mintage	F	VF	XF	Unc	BU
1992 Proof	6,738	Value: 35.00				

KM# 151 2 RAND
33.6260 g., 0.9250 Silver 1.0000 oz. ASW, 38.7 mm. **Subject:** Peace **Obv:** National arms **Rev:** Stylized doves and figures within globe design **Edge:** Reeded **Note:** 828 pieces used in jewelry.

Date	Mintage	F	VF	XF	Unc	BU
1993 Proof	5,628	Value: 42.50				

KM# 156 2 RAND
33.6260 g., 0.9250 Silver 1.0000 oz. ASW, 38.7 mm. **Subject:** World Cup Soccer **Obv:** Stylized figure and soccer ball **Rev:** Soccer ball and North American map **Edge:** Reeded **Note:** 288 pieces used in jewelry.

Date	Mintage	F	VF	XF	Unc	BU
1994 Proof	3,498	Value: 40.00				

KM# 153 2 RAND
33.6260 g., 0.9250 Silver 1.0000 oz. ASW, 38.7 mm. **Subject:** Rugby World Cup **Obv:** National arms **Rev:** Three players running **Edge:** Reeded **Note:** 215 pieces used in jewelry.

Date	Mintage	F	VF	XF	Unc	BU
1995 Proof	4,196	Value: 40.00				

KM# 154 2 RAND
33.6260 g., 0.9250 Silver 1.0000 oz. ASW **Subject:** 50th Anniversay F. A. O. **Obv:** National arms **Rev:** Man with child in bird nest, sparrow and F.A.O. logo

Date	Mintage	F	VF	XF	Unc	BU
1995 Proof	1,743	Value: 45.00				

KM# 155   2 RAND
33.6260 g., 0.9250 Silver 1.0000 oz. ASW, 38.7 mm. **Subject:** 50th Anniversary United Nations **Obv:** National arms **Rev:** Numeral 50 and UN emblem above world globe and map **Edge:** Reeded

Date	Mintage	F	VF	XF	Unc	BU
1995 Proof	1,412	Value: 42.50				

KM# 157   2 RAND
33.6260 g., 0.9250 Silver 1.0000 oz. ASW, 38.7 mm. **Subject:** African Cup **Obv:** Arms with supporters **Rev:** Soccer player within soccerball design **Edge:** Reeded

Date	Mintage	F	VF	XF	Unc	BU
1996 Proof	2,690	Value: 40.00				

KM# 165   2 RAND
5.5000 g., Nickel Plated Copper, 23 mm. **Obv:** Arms with supporters **Obv. Leg.:** UMZANSTI AFRIKA, Xhosa legend **Rev:** Greater Kudu

Date	Mintage	F	VF	XF	Unc	BU
1996	123,000	—	—	—	2.50	—
1996 Proof	4,827	Value: 8.00				
1997	1,804,000	—	—	—	2.50	—
1997 Proof	3,596	Value: 8.00				
1998	—	—	—	—	2.50	—
1998 Proof	—	Value: 8.00				
1999	—	—	—	—	2.50	—
1999 Proof	—	Value: 8.00				
2000	—	—	—	—	2.50	—

KM# 175   2 RAND
33.6260 g., 0.9250 Silver 1.0000 oz. ASW, 38.7 mm. **Obv:** National arms **Rev:** Knysna Seahorse **Edge:** Reeded

Date	Mintage	F	VF	XF	Unc	BU
1997 Proof	3,000	Value: 45.00				

KM# 183   2 RAND
7.0000 g., 0.9999 Gold 0.2250 oz. AGW, 22 mm. **Subject:** Early Man **Obv:** National arms **Rev:** Australopithecus Africanus - walking at left, skull at lower right **Edge:** Reeded

Date	Mintage	F	VF	XF	Unc	BU
1997 Proof	1,000	Value: 275				

KM# 179   2 RAND
33.6260 g., 0.9250 Silver 1.0000 oz. ASW, 38.7 mm. **Obv:** National arms **Rev:** Jackass Penguin **Edge:** Reeded

Date	Mintage	F	VF	XF	Unc	BU
1998 Proof	Est. 2,053	Value: 45.00				

KM# 180   2 RAND
7.7770 g., 0.9999 Gold 0.2500 oz. AGW, 22 mm. **Obv:** National arms **Rev:** Coelacanth fish and fossil **Edge:** Reeded

Date	Mintage	F	VF	XF	Unc	BU
1998 Proof	386	Value: 320				

KM# 218   2 RAND
33.6260 g., 0.9250 Silver 1.0000 oz. ASW, 38.7 mm. **Obv:** National arms **Rev:** Great white shark **Edge:** Reeded

Date	Mintage	F	VF	XF	Unc	BU
1999 Proof	1,982	Value: 60.00				

KM# 220   2 RAND
7.7770 g., 0.9999 Gold 0.2500 oz. AGW, 22 mm. **Obv:** National arms **Rev:** Thrinaxodon dinosaur **Edge:** Reeded

Date	Mintage	F	VF	XF	Unc	BU
1999 Proof	292	Value: 320				

KM# 228   2 RAND
5.5000 g., Nickel Plated Copper, 23 mm. **Obv:** New national arms **Obv. Leg.:** UMZANSTI - AFRIKA **Rev:** Greater Kudu, value **Edge:** Segmented reeding

Date	Mintage	F	VF	XF	Unc	BU
2000	—	—	—	0.80	2.00	3.00

KM# 240   2 RAND
33.6260 g., 0.9250 Silver 1.0000 oz. ASW, 38.7 mm. **Obv:** National arms **Rev:** Octopus **Edge:** Reeded

Date	Mintage	F	VF	XF	Unc	BU
2000 Proof	3,344	Value: 60.00				

KM# 241   2 RAND
7.7770 g., 0.9999 Gold 0.2500 oz. AGW, 22 mm. **Obv:** National arms **Rev:** "Little Foot" skeleton find **Edge:** Reeded

Date	Mintage	F	VF	XF	Unc	BU
2000 Proof	394	Value: 320				

KM# 140   5 RAND
7.0000 g., Nickel Plated Copper, 26 mm. **Obv:** Arms with supporters **Rev:** Wildebeest

Date	Mintage	F	VF	XF	Unc	BU
1994	45,212,000	—	—	—	4.50	5.50
1994 Proof	5,804	Value: 10.00				
1995	41,238,000	—	—	—	4.50	5.50
1995 Proof	5,816	Value: 10.00				

KM# 150   5 RAND
7.0000 g., Nickel Plated Copper, 26 mm. **Subject:** Presidential Inauguration **Obv:** Arms with supporters **Rev:** Building below value

Date	Mintage	F	VF	XF	Unc	BU
1994	10,095,000	—	—	—	5.50	6.50
1994 Proof	10,000	Value: 8.50				

KM# 166   5 RAND
7.0000 g., Nickel Plated Copper, 26 mm. **Obv:** Arms with supporters **Obv. Leg.:** ININGIZIMU AFRIKA, Zulu/Swati legend **Rev:** Wildebeest

Date	Mintage	F	VF	XF	Unc	BU
1996	15,435,000	—	—	—	4.50	—
1996 Proof	4,827	Value: 10.00				
1997	1,276,000	—	—	—	4.50	—
1997 Proof	3,596	Value: 10.00				
1998	—	—	—	—	4.50	—
1998 Proof	—	Value: 10.00				
1999	—	—	—	—	4.50	—
1999 Proof	—	Value: 10.00				
2000	—	—	—	—	4.50	—

KM# 230   5 RAND
7.0000 g., Nickel Plated Steel, 26 mm. **Obv:** Head of Nelson Mandela 1/4 right **Obv. Leg.:** ININGIZIMU AFRIKA, Zulu legend **Rev:** Wildebeest **Edge:** Reeded and plain sections

Date	Mintage	F	VF	XF	Unc	BU
2000	—	—	—	—	4.50	5.50
2000 Proof	—	Value: 10.00				

KM# 229   5 RAND
7.0000 g., Nickel Plated Copper, 26 mm. **Obv:** New national arms **Obv. Leg.:** ININGIZIMU AFRIKA **Rev:** Wildebeest, value **Edge:** Segmented reeding

Date	Mintage	F	VF	XF	Unc	BU
2000	—	—	—	1.20	3.75	5.00

BULLION COINAGE

Mint mark: GRC - Gold Reef City

KM# 105   1/10 KRUGERRAND
3.3930 g., 0.9170 Gold .1000 AGW 0.1000 oz. AGW, 16.50 mm. **Obv:** Bust of Paul Kruger left **Rev:** Springbok walking right divides date **Edge:** Reeded **Edge:** 180 serrations for uncirculated. 220 serrations for proof

Date	Mintage	F	VF	XF	Unc	BU
1980	856,915	—	—	—	BV+15%	
1980 Proof	60	Value: 2,500				
1981	1,313,522	—	—	—	BV+15%	
1981 Proof	7,500	Value: 115				
1982	1,053,539	—	—	—	BV+15%	
1982 Proof	11,270	Value: 115				
1983	495,445	—	—	—	BV+15%	
1983 Proof	12,075	Value: 115				
1984	885,250	—	—	—	BV+15%	
1984 Proof	13,020	Value: 115				
1985	275,548	—	—	—	BV+15%	

Date	Mintage	F	VF	XF	Unc	BU
1985 Proof	6,700	Value: 115				
1986	87,000	—	—	—	BV+15%	—
1986 Proof	8,612	Value: 115				
1987	53,400	—	—	—	BV+15%	—
1987 Proof	4,939	Value: 115				
1987 GRC Proof	1,126	Value: 400				
1988	87,433	—	—	—	BV+15%	—
1988 Proof	1,913	Value: 115				
1988 GRC Proof	949	Value: 400				
1989	—	—	—	—	BV+15%	—
1989 Proof	2,939	Value: 115				
1989 GRC Proof	377	Value: 1,000				
1990	9,500	—	—	—	BV+15%	—
1990 Proof	2,363	Value: 115				
1990 GRC Proof	1,096	Value: 275				
1991	82,274	—	—	—	BV+15%	—
1991 Proof	3,098	Value: 115				
1991 GRC Proof	426	Value: 275				
1992 Proof	1,789	Value: 115				
1993	53,535	—	—	—	BV+15%	—
1993 Proof	3,811	Value: 115				
1994	85,753	—	—	—	BV+15%	—
1994 Proof	2,215	Value: 115				
1995	24,788	—	—	—	BV+15%	—
1995 Proof	1,612	Value: 125				
1996	8,945	—	—	—	BV+15%	—
1996 Proof	2,891	Value: 115				
1997	19,496	—	—	—	BV+15%	—
1997 Proof	2,440	Value: 115				
1997 Proof	30	Value: 300				

Note: 30th Anniversary of Krugerrand privy mark

Date	Mintage	F	VF	XF	Unc	BU
1998	15,452	—	—	—	BV+15%	—
1998 Proof	1,799	Value: 115				
1999	28,643	—	—	—	BV+15%	—
1999 Proof	—	Value: 115				
2000	64,759	—	—	—	BV+15%	—
2000 Proof	4,603	Value: 115				

KM# 106 1/4 KRUGERRAND

8.4820 g., 0.9170 Gold 0.2501 oz. AGW, 22 mm. **Obv:** Bust of Paul Kruger left **Obv. Leg.:** SUID — AFRIKA • SOUTH AFRICA **Rev:** Springbok bounding right divides date **Edge:** Reeded
Edge: 180 serrations for uncirculated, 220 serrations for proof

Date	Mintage	F	VF	XF	Unc	BU
1980	533,818	—	—	—	BV+10%	—
1980 Proof	60	Value: 3,000				
1981	718,928	—	—	—	BV+10%	—
1981 Proof	7,500	Value: 275				
1982	1,259,898	—	—	—	BV+10%	—
1982 Proof	11,270	Value: 275				
1983	51,612	—	—	—	BV+10%	—
1983 Proof	12,075	Value: 275				
1984	489,351	—	—	—	BV+10%	—
1984 Proof	13,020	Value: 275				
1985	587,193	—	—	—	BV+10%	—
1985 Proof	6,700	Value: 275				
1986 Proof	8,613	Value: 275				
1987 Proof	4,929	Value: 275				
1987 GRC Proof	1,121	Value: 500				
1988	5,946	—	—	—	BV+10%	—
1988 Proof	2,027	Value: 275				
1988 GRC Proof	835	Value: 500				
1989	5,943	—	—	—	BV+10%	—
1989 Proof	2,998	Value: 275				
1989 GRC Proof	318	Value: 1,400				
1990 Proof	1,084	Value: 275				
1990 GRC Proof	1,066	Value: 400				
1991 Proof	1,200	Value: 275				
1991 GRC Proof	426	Value: 400				
1992 Proof	1,629	Value: 275				
1993 Proof	3,061	Value: 275				
1994	38,747	—	—	—	BV+10%	—
1994 Proof	1,874	Value: 275				
1995	12,865	—	—	—	BV+10%	—
1995 Proof	1,095	Value: 275				
1996 Proof	1,853	Value: 275				
1997 Proof	1,440	Value: 275				
1997 Proof	30	Value: 500				

Note: 30th Anniversary of Krugerrand privy mark

Date	Mintage	F	VF	XF	Unc	BU
1998	3,937	—	—	—	BV+10%	—
1998 Proof	1,701	Value: 275				
1999	34,844	—	—	—	BV+10%	—
1999 Proof	1,990	Value: 275				
2000	30,282	—	—	—	BV+10%	—
2000 Proof	3,600	Value: 275				

KM# 107 1/2 KRUGERRAND

16.9650 g., 0.9170 Gold 0.5001 oz. AGW, 27 mm. **Obv:** Bust of Paul Kruger left **Obv. Leg.:** SUID ? AFRIKA ? SOUTH AFRICA **Rev:** Springbok walking right divides date **Edge:** Reeded
Edge: 180 serrations for uncirculated, 220 serrations for proof

Date	Mintage	F	VF	XF	Unc	BU
1980	374,313	—	—	—	BV+8%	—
1980 Proof	60	Value: 3,500				
1981	169,014	—	—	—	BV+8%	—
1981 Proof	9,000	Value: 525				
1982	416,390	—	—	—	BV+8%	—
1982 Proof	13,000	Value: 525				
1983	46,805	—	—	—	BV+8%	—
1983 Proof	13,600	Value: 525				
1984	176,760	—	—	—	BV+8%	—
1984 Proof	9,900	Value: 525				
1985	97,689	—	—	—	BV+8%	—
1985 Proof	5,945	Value: 525				
1986 Proof	8,002	Value: 525				
1987 Proof	4,203	Value: 525				
1987 GRC Proof	1,186	Value: 850				
1988	5,454	—	—	—	BV+8%	—
1988 Proof	2,062	Value: 525				
1988 GRC Proof	1,026	Value: 850				
1989	4,980	—	—	—	BV+8%	—
1989 Proof	3,328	Value: 525				
1989 GRC Proof	399	Value: 1,500				
1990 Proof	1,784	Value: 525				
1990 GRC Proof	1,066	Value: 550				
1991 Proof	3,033	Value: 525				
1991 GRC Proof	426	Value: 550				
1992 Proof	1,501	Value: 525				
1993	10,800	—	—	—	BV+8%	—
1993 Proof	2,439	Value: 525				
1994	15,910	—	—	—	BV+8%	—
1994 Proof	2,146	Value: 525				
1995	10,417	—	—	—	BV+8%	—
1995 Proof	1,012	Value: 525				
1996	3,311	—	—	—	BV+8%	—
1996 Proof	1,788	Value: 525				
1997	10,598	—	—	—	BV+8%	—
1997 Proof	2,030	Value: 525				
1997 Proof	30	Value: 575				

Note: 30th Anniversary of Krugerrand privy mark

Date	Mintage	F	VF	XF	Unc	BU
1998 Proof	1,303	Value: 525				
1999	23,971	—	—	—	BV+8%	—
1999 Proof	1,924	Value: 525				
2000	23,851	—	—	—	BV+8%	—
2000 Proof	3,453	Value: 525				

KM# 73 KRUGERRAND

33.9300 g., 0.9170 Gold 1.0003 oz. AGW, 32.7 mm. **Obv:** Bust of Paul Kruger left **Obv. Leg.:** SUID — AFRIKA • SOUTH AFRICA **Rev:** Springbok walking right divides date **Edge:** Reeded
Edge: 180 serrations for uncirculated, 220 serrations for proof

Date	Mintage	F	VF	XF	Unc	BU
1967	40,000	—	—	—	BV+5%	—
1967 Proof	10,000	Value: 1,000				
1968	20,000	—	—	—	BV+5%	—
1968 Proof	1,044	Value: 1,100				

Note: Frosted bust and frosted reverse

Date	Mintage	F	VF	XF	Unc	BU
1968 Proof	8,956	Value: 1,000				
1969	20,000	—	—	—	BV+5%	—
1969 Proof	10,000	Value: 1,000				
1970	211,018	—	—	—	BV+5%	—
1970 Proof	10,000	Value: 1,000				
1971	550,200	—	—	—	BV+5%	—
1971 Proof	6,000	Value: 1,000				
1972	553,700	—	—	—	BV+5%	—
1972 Proof	6,625	Value: 1,000				
1973	859,300	—	—	—	BV+5%	—
1973 Proof	10,000	Value: 1,000				
1974	3,203,000	—	—	—	BV+5%	—
1974 Proof	6,352	Value: 1,000				
1975	4,803,925	—	—	—	BV+5%	—
1975 Proof	5,600	Value: 1,000				
1976	3,004,945	—	—	—	BV+5%	—

Date	Mintage	F	VF	XF	Unc	BU
1976 Proof	6,600	Value: 1,000				
1977	3,331,344	—	—	—	BV+5%	—

Note: 188 serrations on edge

Date	Mintage	F	VF	XF	Unc	BU
1977 Proof	8,500	Value: 1,000				

Note: 188 serrations on edge

Date	Mintage	F	VF	XF	Unc	BU
1977	Inc. above	—	—	—	BV+5%	—

Note: 220 serrations on edge

Date	Mintage	F	VF	XF	Unc	BU
1977 Proof	Inc. above	Value: 1,000				

Note: 220 serrations on edge

Date	Mintage	F	VF	XF	Unc	BU
1978	6,012,293	—	—	—	BV+5%	—
1978 Proof	10,000	Value: 1,000				
1979	4,940,755	—	—	—	BV+5%	—
1979 Proof	11,800	Value: 1,000				
1980	3,049,396	—	—	—	BV+5%	—
1980 Proof	12,000	Value: 1,000				
1981	3,185,827	—	—	—	BV+5%	—
1981 Proof	12,900	Value: 1,000				
1982	2,668,506	—	—	—	BV+5%	—
1982 Proof	16,960	Value: 1,000				
1983	3,349,061	—	—	—	BV+5%	—
1983 Proof	19,100	Value: 1,000				
1984	2,055,689	—	—	—	BV+5%	—
1984 Proof	14,000	Value: 1,000				
1985	864,995	—	—	—	BV+5%	—
1985 Proof	10,224	Value: 1,000				
1986 Proof	21,040	Value: 1,000				
1987	19,798	—	—	—	BV+5%	—
1987 Proof	10,196	Value: 1,000				
1987 GRC Proof	1,160	Value: 1,250				
1988	614,673	—	—	—	BV+5%	—
1988 Proof	3,854	Value: 1,000				
1988 GRC Proof	1,220	Value: 1,250				
1989	194,319	—	—	—	BV+5%	—
1989 Proof	4,083	Value: 1,000				
1989 GRC Proof	987	Value: 1,650				
1990	391,393	—	—	—	BV+5%	—
1990 Proof	1,966	Value: 1,000				
1990 GRC Proof	1,066	Value: 1,650				
1991	283,184	—	—	—	BV+5%	—
1991 Proof	1,755	Value: 1,000				
1991 GRC Proof	426	Value: 1,650				
1992	1,803	—	—	—	BV+5%	—
1992 Proof	2,067	Value: 1,000				
1993	162,340	—	—	—	BV+5%	—
1993 Proof	3,963	Value: 1,000				
1994	129,530	—	—	—	BV+5%	—
1994 Proof	1,761	Value: 1,000				
1995	58,630	—	—	—	BV+5%	—
1995 Proof	1,678	Value: 1,000				
1996	9,874	—	—	—	BV+5%	—
1996 Proof	2,188	Value: 1,000				
1997 Proof	1,663	Value: 1,000				
1997 SS Proof	72	Value: 1,000				
1997 Proof	30	Value: 1,400				

Note: 30th Anniversary of Krugerrand privy mark

Date	Mintage	F	VF	XF	Unc	BU
1998	7,097	—	—	—	BV+5%	—
1998 Proof	1,179	Value: 1,000				
1999	17,051	—	—	—	BV+5%	—
1999 Proof	2,787	Value: 1,000				
2000	34,850	—	—	—	BV+5%	—
2000 Proof	3,143	Value: 1,000				

KM# 118 OUNCE

33.9305 g., 0.9170 Gold 1.0003 oz. AGW, 32.7 mm. **Subject:** 75th Anniversary of Parliament **Obv:** Crossed Parliamentary maces divide lion and shield **Rev:** Parliament building **Edge:** Reeded

Date	Mintage	F	VF	XF	Unc	BU
1985 Proof	3,019	Value: 1,200				

KM# 184 OUNCE

31.1070 g., 0.9999 Gold 1.0000 oz. AGW, 32.7 mm. **Subject:** Presidential Inauguration **Obv:** National arms **Rev:** Union buildings in Pretoria **Edge:** Reeded

Date	Mintage	F	VF	XF	Unc	BU
1994 Proof	1,742	Value: 975				

KM# 185 OUNCE

31.1070 g., 0.9999 Gold 1.0000 oz. AGW, 32.69 mm. **Subject:** Rugby World Cup **Obv:** National arms **Rev:** Three players running **Edge:** Reeded

Date	Mintage	F	VF	XF	Unc	BU
1995 Proof	406	Value: 975				

KM# 131 1/10 PROTEA

3.3900 g., 0.9170 Gold 0.0999 oz. AGW, 16.5 mm. **Subject:** 100th Anniversary of Johannesburg **Obv:** Protea flower **Rev:** Miner, mine shaft tower with modern skyline in background **Edge:** Reeded

Date	Mintage	F	VF	XF	Unc	BU
1986 Proof	5,212	Value: 115				

KM# 123 1/10 PROTEA
3.3900 g., 0.9170 Gold 0.0999 oz. AGW, 16.5 mm.
Subject: 400th Anniversary Bartolomeu Dias Discovery of Cape **Obv:** Protea plant **Rev:** Compass at left, caravel and map of Africa and southern Europe at right **Edge:** Reeded

Date	Mintage	F	VF	XF	Unc	BU
1988	134	—	—	—	—	—
1988 Proof	2,199	Value: 115				

KM# 126 1/10 PROTEA
3.3900 g., 0.9170 Gold 0.0999 oz. AGW, 16.5 mm.
Subject: 300th Anniversary of Huguenots **Obv:** Protea flowers **Rev:** Descending dove and design divide dates below small cross, all within circle **Edge:** Reeded

Date	Mintage	F	VF	XF	Unc	BU
1988	90	—	—	—	—	—
1988 Proof	2,060	Value: 115				

KM# 129 1/10 PROTEA
3.3900 g., 0.9170 Gold 0.0999 oz. AGW, 16.5 mm.
Subject: The Great Trek **Obv:** Protea flower **Rev:** Stylized wheel and arrow design **Edge:** Reeded

Date	Mintage	F	VF	XF	Unc	BU
1988	—	—	—	—	—	—
1988 Proof	2,999	Value: 115				

KM# 171 1/10 PROTEA
3.3900 g., 0.9170 Gold 0.0999 oz. AGW, 16.5 mm.
Subject: South African Nursing Schools **Obv:** Protea Flower **Rev:** Aladdin lamp divides dates within cross
Rev. Leg.: VERPLEGING PROTEA NURSING **Edge:** Reeded

Date	Mintage	F	VF	XF	Unc	BU
1991 Proof	3,950	Value: 115				

KM# 144 1/10 PROTEA
3.3900 g., 0.9170 Gold 0.0999 oz. AGW, 16.5 mm.
Subject: Coinage Centennial **Obv:** Protea flower **Rev:** 4 assorted coin designs **Rev. Leg.:** SOLI DEO GLORIA **Edge:** Reeded

Date	Mintage	F	VF	XF	Unc	BU
1992 Proof	2,503	Value: 115				

KM# 172 1/10 PROTEA
3.3900 g., 0.9170 Gold 0.0999 oz. AGW, 16.50 mm. **Subject:** 200 Years of Banking **Obv:** Protea flower **Rev:** 2 coins, stack of coins, Reserve Bank building, lion's head **Edge:** BANKWESE BANKING **Edge:** Reeded **Note:** 828 pieces used in jewelry.

Date	Mintage	F	VF	XF	Unc	BU
1993 Proof	5,064	Value: 115				

KM# 187 1/10 PROTEA
3.3900 g., 0.9170 Gold 0.0999 oz. AGW, 16.5 mm.
Subject: Conservation **Obv:** Protea flower **Rev:** Outlined map with big 5 animal heads **Rev. Leg.:** BEWARING PROTEA CONSERVATION **Edge:** Reeded **Note:** 342 pieces used in jewelry.

Date	Mintage	F	VF	XF	Unc	BU
1994 Proof	1,905	Value: 125				

KM# 193.1 1/10 PROTEA
3.3900 g., 0.9170 Gold 0.0999 oz. AGW, 16.5 mm.
Subject: Centennial Delagoabay Railways **Obv:** Protea flower **Rev:** Train passing through NZASM tunnel, filled window and door in cab of locomotive **Edge:** Reeded

Date	Mintage	F	VF	XF	Unc	BU
1995 Proof	Inc. below	Value: 125				

KM# 199 1/10 PROTEA
3.3900 g., 0.9170 Gold 0.0999 oz. AGW, 16.5 mm.
Subject: Constitution **Obv:** Protea flower **Rev:** Hand writing in open book **Edge:** Reeded

Date	Mintage	F	VF	XF	Unc	BU
1996 Proof	1,292	Value: 125				

KM# 205 1/10 PROTEA
3.3900 g., 0.9170 Gold 0.0999 oz. AGW, 16.5 mm.
Subject: Women of South Africa **Obv:** Protea flower **Rev:** Partial woman's head at left, South African countryside, Mother Earth flowing into Sister Moon at right **Edge:** Reeded

Date	Mintage	F	VF	XF	Unc	BU
1997 Proof	792	Value: 130				

KM# 211 1/10 PROTEA
3.3900 g., 0.9170 Gold 0.0999 oz. AGW, 16.5 mm. **Subject:** Year of the Child **Obv:** Protea flower **Rev:** Life's puzzle **Edge:** Reeded

Date	Mintage	F	VF	XF	Unc	BU
1998 Proof	568	Value: 130				

KM# 193.2 1/10 PROTEA
3.3900 g., 0.9170 Gold 0.0999 oz. AGW, 16.5 mm. **Subject:** Protea flower **Rev:** Train passing through NZASM tunnel. open window and door in locomotive cab **Edge:** Reeded **Note:** 222 pieces used in jewelry

Date	Mintage	F	VF	XF	Unc	BU
1998 Proof	1,217	Value: 110				

KM# 250.1 1/10 PROTEA
3.1107 g., 0.9999 Gold 0.1000 oz. AGW, 16.5 mm. **Obv:** Protea flower **Rev:** Gold miner horizontal drilling **Edge:** Reeded **Note:** With initials "P B" above drill at lower right.

Date	Mintage	F	VF	XF	Unc	BU
1999 Proof	461	Value: 115				

KM# 250.2 1/10 PROTEA
3.1107 g., 0.9999 Gold 0.1000 oz. AGW, 16.5 mm. **Obv:** Protea flower **Rev:** Gold miner horizontal drilling **Edge:** Reeded **Note:** Without initials "P B" above drill at lower right.

Date	Mintage	F	VF	XF	Unc	BU
1999 Proof	Inc. above	Value: 115				

KM# 256 1/10 PROTEA
3.1107 g., 0.9999 Gold 0.1000 oz. AGW, 16.5 mm.
Subject: Wine Industry **Obv:** Protea flower **Rev:** Cape Dutch farmstead **Rev. Insc.:** PROTEA **Edge:** Reeded

Date	Mintage	F	VF	XF	Unc	BU
2000 Proof	444	Value: 115				

KM# 121 PROTEA
33.9300 g., 0.9170 Gold 1.0003 oz. AGW, 32.69 mm.
Subject: 100th Anniversary of Johannesburg **Obv:** Protea flower **Rev:** Miner, mine shaft tower with modern skyline in background **Edge:** Reeded

Date	Mintage	F	VF	XF	Unc	BU
1986 Proof	4,701	Value: 975				

KM# 124.2 PROTEA
33.9300 g., 0.9170 Gold 1.0003 oz. AGW, 32.69 mm.
Subject: 400th Anniversary Bartolomeu Dias Discovery of Cape **Obv:** Protea plant **Rev:** Compass at left, caravel and map of Africa and modified southern Europe at right **Edge:** Reeded

Date	Mintage	F	VF	XF	Unc	BU
1988	26	—	—	—	1,800	—
1988 Proof	3,776	Value: 975				

KM# 124.1 PROTEA
33.9310 g., 0.9170 Gold 1.0003 oz. AGW, 32.69 mm.
Subject: 400th Anniversary Bartolomeu Dias Discovery of Cape **Obv:** Protea plant **Rev:** Compass at left, caravel and map of Africa and southern Europe at right **Edge:** Reeded **Note:** "ID Protea" struck for Mossel Bat festival.

Date	Mintage	F	VF	XF	Unc	BU
1988	Est. 160	Value: 1,000				

KM# 127 PROTEA
33.9300 g., 0.9170 Gold 1.0003 oz. AGW, 32.69 mm.
Subject: 300th Anniversary of Huguenots **Obv:** Protea flowers **Rev:** Descending dove and design divide dates below small cross, all within circle **Edge:** Reeded

KM# 130 PROTEA
33.9300 g., 0.9170 Gold 1.0003 oz. AGW, 32.69 mm.
Subject: The Great Trek **Obv:** Protea flower **Rev:** Wheel and arrow design **Edge:** Reeded

Date	Mintage	F	VF	XF	Unc	BU
1988	—	Value: 1,800				
1988 Proof	2,956	Value: 975				

KM# 186 PROTEA
33.9300 g., 0.9170 Gold 1.0003 oz. AGW, 32.69 mm.
Subject: South Africa Nursing Schools **Obv:** Protea flower **Rev:** Alladin lamp divides dates within cross **Rev. Leg.:** VERPLEGING PROTEA NURSING **Edge:** Reeded

Date	Mintage	F	VF	XF	Unc	BU
1991 Proof	3,004	Value: 975				

KM# 146 PROTEA
33.9300 g., 0.9170 Gold 1.0003 oz. AGW, 32.69 mm.
Subject: Coinage Centennial **Obv:** Protea flower **Rev:** 4 assorted coin designs **Rev. Leg.:** SOLI DEO GLORIA **Edge:** Reeded

Date	Mintage	F	VF	XF	Unc	BU
1992 Proof	1,752	Value: 975				

KM# 173 PROTEA
33.9300 g., 0.9170 Gold 1.0003 oz. AGW, 32.69 mm.
Subject: 200 Years of Banking **Obv:** Protea flower **Rev:** 2 coins, stack of coins, Reserve Bank building, lion's head **Rev. Leg.:** BANKWESE BANKING **Edge:** Reeded

Date	Mintage	F	VF	XF	Unc	BU
1993 Proof	2,032	Value: 975				
1993 GRC Proof	500	Value: 1,000				

KM# 188 PROTEA
33.9300 g., 0.9170 Gold 1.0003 oz. AGW, 32.69 mm.
Subject: Conservation **Obv:** Protea flower **Rev:** Outlined map with big 5 animal heads **Rev. Leg.:** BEWARING PROTEA CONSERVATION **Edge:** Reeded

Date	Mintage	F	VF	XF	Unc	BU
1994 Proof	1,187	Value: 975				
1994 PTA ZOO Proof	660	Value: 1,000				
Note: PTA.ZOO						

KM# 194.1 PROTEA
33.9300 g., 0.9170 Gold 1.0003 oz. AGW, 32.69 mm.
Subject: Centennial Delagoabay Railways **Obv:** Protea flower **Rev:** Train passing through NZASM tunnel, filled window and door in locomotive cab **Edge:** Reeded

Date	Mintage	F	VF	XF	Unc	BU
1995 Proof	Inc. below	Value: 1,000				

KM# 194.2 PROTEA
33.9300 g., 0.9170 Gold 1.0003 oz. AGW, 32.69 mm.
Subject: Centennial Delagoabay Railways **Obv:** Protea flower **Rev:** Train passing through NZASM tunnel, open window and door in locomotive cab **Edge:** Reeded

Date	Mintage	F	VF	XF	Unc	BU
1995 Proof	694	Value: 975				

KM# 200 PROTEA
33.9300 g., 0.9170 Gold 1.0003 oz. AGW, 32.69 mm.
Subject: Constitution **Obv:** Protea flower **Rev:** Hand writing in open book **Edge:** Reeded

Date	Mintage	F	VF	XF	Unc	BU
1996 Proof	987	Value: 975				

KM# 206 PROTEA
33.9300 g., 0.9170 Gold 1.0003 oz. AGW, 32.69 mm.
Subject: Women of South Africa **Obv:** Protea flower **Rev:** Partial woman's head at left, South Africa countryside, Mother Earth, Flowing into Sister Moon at right **Edge:** Reeded

Date	Mintage	F	VF	XF	Unc	BU
1997 Proof	351	Value: 1,050				

(top right table)

Date	Mintage	F	VF	XF	Unc	BU
1988	20	—	—	—	—	—
1988 Proof	3,391	Value: 975				

KM# 212 PROTEA
33.9300 g., 0.9170 Gold 1.0003 oz. AGW, 32.69 mm.
Subject: Year of the Child **Obv:** Protea flower **Rev:** Life's puzzle
Edge: Reeded

Date	Mintage	F	VF	XF	Unc	BU
1998 Proof	298	Value: 950				

KM# 251 PROTEA
31.1070 g., 0.9999 Gold 1.0000 oz. AGW, 32.69 mm.
Obv: Protea flower **Rev:** Gold miner horizontal drilling
Edge: Reeded

Date	Mintage	F	VF	XF	Unc	BU
1999 Proof	253	Value: 975				
1999 GRC Proof	198	Value: 1,000				

KM# 257 PROTEA
31.1070 g., 0.9999 Gold 1.0000 oz. AGW, 32.69 mm.
Subject: Wine Industry **Obv:** Protea flower **Rev:** Woman carrying
basket of grapes at right, Table Mountain in background
Rev. Insc.: PROTEA **Edge:** Reeded

Date	Mintage	F	VF	XF	Unc	BU
2000 Proof	330	Value: 975				
2000 CW Proof	52	Value: 2,250				
2000 WM Proof	100	Value: 3,000				

NATURA GOLD BULLION COINAGE

KM# 189 1/10 OUNCE
3.1104 g., 0.9990 Gold 0.0999 oz. AGW, 16.5 mm. **Series:**
Natura **Obv:** Lion's head right **Rev:** Male and female lions drinking
Edge: Reeded **Note:** Matte finish restrikes exist used in jewelry.

Date	Mintage	F	VF	XF	Unc	BU
1994 Proof	6,660	Value: 115				

KM# 195 1/10 OUNCE
3.1107 g., 0.9990 Gold 0.0999 oz. AGW, 16.5 mm.
Series: Natura **Obv:** Rhinoceros walking facing **Rev:**
Rhinocerous drinking **Edge:** Reeded **Note:** 222 pieces used in
jewelry and matte finish restrikes exist also used in jewelry.

Date	Mintage	F	VF	XF	Unc	BU
1995 Proof	2,834	Value: 115				

KM# 201 1/10 OUNCE
3.1104 g., 0.9990 Gold 0.0999 oz. AGW, 16.5 mm.
Series: Natura **Obv:** Elephant's head **Rev:** Elephant walking
carrying uprooted tree **Edge:** Reeded

Date	Mintage	F	VF	XF	Unc	BU
1996 Proof	9,014	Value: 115				

KM# 207 1/10 OUNCE
3.1104 g., 0.9990 Gold 0.0999 oz. AGW, 16.5 mm.
Series: Natura **Obv:** Buffalo's head **Rev:** Buffalo drinking water
Edge: Reeded **Note:** Matte finish restrikes exist used in jewelry.

Date	Mintage	F	VF	XF	Unc	BU
1997 Proof	3,590	Value: 115				

KM# 213 1/10 OUNCE
3.1107 g., 0.9990 Gold 0.0999 oz. AGW, 16.5 mm. **Series:** Natura
Obv: Leopard's head **Rev:** Leopard drinking water **Edge:** Reeded

Date	Mintage	F	VF	XF	Unc	BU
1998 Proof	4,405	Value: 115				

KM# 252.1 1/10 OUNCE
3.1107 g., 0.9999 Gold 0.1000 oz. AGW, 16.5 mm. **Series:** Natura
Obv: Greater Kudu's head **Rev:** Kudu herd drinking **Edge:** Reeded

Date	Mintage	F	VF	XF	Unc	BU
1999 Proof	4,930	Value: 115				

KM# 252.2 1/10 OUNCE
3.1107 g., 0.9999 Gold 0.1000 oz. AGW, 16.5 mm. **Series:** Natura
Subject: President Mbeki's Inauguration **Obv:** Greater Kudu's
head **Rev:** Kudu herd drinking **Rev. Insc.:** INAUGURATION 1999
Edge: Reeded

Date	Mintage	F	VF	XF	Unc	BU
1999 Proof	600	Value: 225				

KM# 258 1/10 OUNCE
3.1107 g., 0.9999 Gold 0.1000 oz. AGW, 16.5 mm. **Series:** Natura
Obv: Sable bull's head **Rev:** Sable drinking **Edge:** Reeded

Date	Mintage	F	VF	XF	Unc	BU
2000 Proof	3,782	Value: 115				

KM# 190 1/4 OUNCE
7.7770 g., 0.9999 Gold 0.2500 oz. AGW, 22 mm. **Series:** Natura
Obv: Lion's head right **Rev:** Family of lions at a kill **Edge:** Reeded

Date	Mintage	F	VF	XF	Unc	BU
1994 Proof	4,159	Value: 250				

KM# 196 1/4 OUNCE
7.7770 g., 0.9999 Gold 0.2500 oz. AGW, 22 mm. **Series:** Natura
Obv: Rhinoceros walking facing **Rev:** Rhinoceros standing in
bush field **Edge:** Reeded

Date	Mintage	F	VF	XF	Unc	BU
1995 Proof	1,752	Value: 250				

KM# 202 1/4 OUNCE
7.7770 g., 0.9999 Gold 0.2500 oz. AGW, 22 mm. **Series:** Natura
Obv: Elephant's head **Rev:** Mother and baby elephants walking
3/4 right **Edge:** Reeded

Date	Mintage	F	VF	XF	Unc	BU
1996 Proof	3,740	Value: 250				

KM# 208 1/4 OUNCE
7.7770 g., 0.9999 Gold 0.2500 oz. AGW, 22 mm. **Series:** Natura
Obv: Buffalo's head **Rev:** Buffalo family resting **Edge:** Reeded

Date	Mintage	F	VF	XF	Unc	BU
1997 Proof	2,164	Value: 250				

KM# 214 1/4 OUNCE
7.7770 g., 0.9999 Gold 0.2500 oz. AGW, 22 mm. **Series:** Natura
Obv: Leopard's head **Rev:** Leopard mother and cub playing
Edge: Reeded

Date	Mintage	F	VF	XF	Unc	BU
1998 Proof	2,752	Value: 250				

KM# 253 1/4 OUNCE
7.7770 g., 0.9999 Gold 0.2500 oz. AGW, 22 mm. **Series:** Natura
Obv: Kudu's head **Rev:** Two Kudu jousting **Edge:** Reeded

Date	Mintage	F	VF	XF	Unc	BU
1999 Proof	3,019	Value: 250				

KM# 259 1/4 OUNCE
7.7770 g., 0.9999 Gold 0.2500 oz. AGW, 22 mm. **Series:** Natura
Obv: Sable bull's head **Rev:** Two Sable bulls facing off
Edge: Reeded

Date	Mintage	F	VF	XF	Unc	BU
2000 Proof	2,128	Value: 250				

KM# 191 1/2 OUNCE
15.5530 g., 0.9999 Gold 0.5000 oz. AGW, 27 mm.
Series: Natura **Obv:** Lion's head right **Rev:** Two lionesses
attacking a bull Kudu **Edge:** Reeded

Date	Mintage	F	VF	XF	Unc	BU
1994 Proof	3,999	Value: 485				

KM# 197 1/2 OUNCE
15.5530 g., 0.9999 Gold 0.5000 oz. AGW, 27 mm.
Series: Natura **Obv:** Rhinoceros walking facing **Rev:** Mother
rhinocerous and offspring grazing in the veld **Edge:** Reeded

Date	Mintage	F	VF	XF	Unc	BU
1995 Proof	1,551	Value: 485				

KM# 203 1/2 OUNCE
15.5530 g., 0.9999 Gold 0.5000 oz. AGW, 27 mm.
Series: Natura **Obv:** Elephant' head **Rev:** Two elephants drinking
water **Edge:** Reeded

Date	Mintage	F	VF	XF	Unc	BU
1996 Proof	3,457	Value: 485				

KM# 209 1/2 OUNCE
15.5530 g., 0.9999 Gold 0.5000 oz. AGW, 27 mm.
Series: Natura **Obv:** Buffalo's head **Rev:** Herd of buffalo moving
through veld **Edge:** Reeded

Date	Mintage	F	VF	XF	Unc	BU
1997 Proof	1,912	Value: 485				

KM# 215 1/2 OUNCE
15.5530 g., 0.9999 Gold 0.5000 oz. AGW, 27 mm.
Series: Natura **Obv:** Leopard's head **Rev:** Leopard in tree eating
it's prey **Edge:** Reeded

Date	Mintage	F	VF	XF	Unc	BU
1998 Proof	2,257	Value: 485				

KM# 254 1/2 OUNCE
15.5518 g., 0.9990 Gold 0.4995 oz. AGW, 27 mm.
Series: Natura **Obv:** Greater Kudu's head **Rev:** Kudu attacked
by lioness **Edge:** Reeded

Date	Mintage	F	VF	XF	Unc	BU
1999 Proof	2,787	Value: 485				

KM# 260 1/2 OUNCE
15.5530 g., 0.9999 Gold 0.5000 oz. AGW, 27 mm. **Series:** Natura
Obv: Sable bull's head **Rev:** Sable family resting **Edge:** Reeded

Date	Mintage	F	VF	XF	Unc	BU
2000 Proof	1,964	Value: 485				

KM# 192 OUNCE
31.1070 g., 0.9999 Gold 1.0000 oz. AGW, 32.69 mm.
Series: Natura **Obv:** Lion's head right **Rev:** Family of lions
Edge: Reeded

Date	Mintage	F	VF	XF	Unc	BU
1994 Proof	2,902	Value: 975				
1994 PTA ZOO Proof	775	Value: 975				

KM# 198 OUNCE
31.1070 g., 0.9999 Gold 1.0000 oz. AGW, 32.69 mm.
Series: Natura **Obv:** Rhinoceros walking facing **Rev:** Two
rhinoceros grazing in the veld **Edge:** Reeded

Date	Mintage	F	VF	XF	Unc	BU
1995 Proof	1,800	Value: 975				
1995 Hluhuwe Proof	350	Value: 975				

KM# 204 OUNCE
31.1070 g., 0.9999 Gold 1.0000 oz. AGW, 32.69 mm.
Series: Natura **Obv:** Elephant's head **Rev:** Four elephants
drinking at river **Edge:** Reeded **Note:** CW/e logo - CW monogram
on elephant.

Date	Mintage	F	VF	XF	Unc	BU
1996 Proof	4,472	Value: 975				
1996 CW/e logo Proof	300	Value: 2,250				

KM# 210 OUNCE
31.1070 g., 0.9999 Gold 1.0000 oz. AGW, 32.69 mm.
Series: Natura **Obv:** Buffalo's head **Rev:** Buffalo defending itself
from attacking lioness **Edge:** Reeded **Note:** SS - Sabi Sabi

Date	Mintage	F	VF	XF	Unc	BU
1997 Proof	2,472	Value: 1,100				
1997 SS Proof	220	Value: 2,250				

KM# 216 OUNCE
31.1070 g., 0.9999 Gold 1.0000 oz. AGW, 32.69 mm.
Series: Natura **Obv:** Leopard's head **Rev:** Leopard resting on
tree branch **Edge:** Reeded **Note:** "L" - Londo Lozi

Date	Mintage	F	VF	XF	Unc	BU
1998 Proof	2,645	Value: 1,100				
1998 L Proof	300	Value: 1,500				

KM# 255 OUNCE
31.1070 g., 0.9999 Gold 1.0000 oz. AGW, 32.69 mm.
Series: Natura **Obv:** Greater Kudu's head **Rev:** Kudu eating tree
leaves **Edge:** Reeded **Note:** SS - Sabi Sabi

Date	Mintage	F	VF	XF	Unc	BU
1999 Proof	2,682	Value: 1,100				
1999 SS Proof	247	Value: 1,500				

KM# 261 OUNCE
31.1070 g., 0.9999 Gold 1.0000 oz. AGW, 32.69 mm.
Series: Natura **Obv:** Sable bull's head Left **Rev:** Sable bull's
head 3/4 right **Edge:** Reeded

Date	Mintage	F	VF	XF	Unc	BU
2000 Proof	1,514	Value: 1,100				
2000 PTA ZOO	591	Value: 1,500				

PATTERNS
Including off metal strikes

KM#	Date	Mintage	Identification	Mkt Val
Pn1	1925	—	1/4 Penny. Lead.	—
Pn3	1942	—	1/4 Penny. Bronze. Smaller head of George VI.	—

TRIAL STRIKES

KM#	Date	Mintage	Identification	Mkt Val
TS1	1925	—	2 Shilling 6 Pence. Lead. Uniface. 2s6d.	—

MINT SETS

KM#	Date	Mintage	Identification	Issue Price	Mkt Val
MS1	1967 (7)	50,000	KM#65.1-70.1, 72.1	7.50	10.00
MS2	1967 (7)	50,000	KM#65.2-70.2, 72.2	7.50	8.00
MS3	1968 (7)	50,000	KM#71.1, 74.1-79.1	7.50	12.00
MS4	1968 (7)	50,000	KM#71.2, 74.2-79.2	7.50	12.00
MS5	1969 (7)	7,500	KM#65.1-70.1, 80.1	7.50	50.00
MS6	1969 (7)	7,500	KM#65.2-70.2, 80.2	7.50	50.00
MS7	1970 (8)	16,000	KM#81-88	7.50	12.00
MS8	1971 (8)	20,000	KM#81-88	7.50	8.00
MS9	1972 (8)	20,000	KM#81-88	7.50	8.00
MS10	1973 (8)	20,000	KM#81-88	7.50	8.00
MS11	1974 (8)	20,000	KM#81-87, 89	7.50	17.50
MS12	1975 (8)	20,000	KM#81-88	7.50	8.00
MS13	1976 (8)	20,000	KM#88, 90-96	5.65	8.00
MS14	1977 (8)	20,000	KM#81-87, 88a	—	8.00
MS15	1978 (8)	20,000	KM#81-87, 88a	—	8.00
MS16	1979 (8)	20,000	KM#97-104	—	25.00
MS17	1980 (7)	20,000	KM#82-87, 88a	—	8.00
MS18	1981 (7)	10,000	KM#82-87, 88a	—	10.00
MS19	1982 (7)	10,000	KM#109-115	—	25.00
MS20	1983 (7)	23,000	KM#82-87, 88a	—	8.00
MS21	1984 (7)	13,875	KM#82-87, 88a	—	10.00
MS22	1985 (7)	10,200	KM#82-87, 117	—	17.50
MS23	1986 (7)	9,100	KM#82-87, 88a	—	12.00
MS24	1987 (7)	7,642	KM#82-87, 88a	—	12.00
MS25	1988 (7)	6,250	KM#82-87, 88a	—	25.00
MS26	1989 (7)	13,000	KM#82-87, 88a	—	15.00
MS27	1990 (8)	12,000	KM#132-137, 139, 148	—	30.00
MS28	1991 (8)	15,000	KM#132-139	—	30.00
MSA29	1992 (8)	15,000	KM#132-139	—	30.00
MS29	1993 (8)	11,000	KM#132-139	—	30.00
MS30	1994 (9)	6,786	KM#132-140	—	35.00
MS31	1995 (9)	8,477	KM#132-140 Plastic holder	—	35.00
MS32	1995 (9)	—	KM#132-140 Cardboard holder	—	30.00
MS33	1996 (9)	12,000	KM#158-166	12.50	15.00
MS34	1997 (9)	7,515	KM#159-166, 170	—	30.00
MS35	1998 (9)	—	KM#159-166, 170	—	30.00
MS36	1999 (9)	10,000	KM#159-166, 170	19.50	30.00
MS37	2000 (9)	—	KM#159-166, 170	—	30.00

PROOF SETS

KM#	Date	Mintage	Identification	Issue Price	Mkt Val
PS1	1923 (10)	655	KM#12.1-17.1, 18, 19.1, 20-21	—	2,150
PS2	1923 (8)	747	KM#12.1-17.1, 18, 19.1	—	1,000

KM#	Date	Mintage	Identification	Issue Price	Mkt Val
PS3	1926 (6)	3	KM#12.2, 14-2-17.2, 19.2	—	33,500
PS4	1930 (8)	14	KM#12.2-17.2, 18, 19.2	—	8,000
PS5	1930 (8)	—	KM#12.2 (dated 1928), 13.2-17.2, 18, 19.2	—	15,000
PS6	1931 (8)	62	KM#12.3-17.3, 19.3, 22	—	10,000
PS7	1932 (8)	12	KM#12.3-17.3, 19.3, 22	—	10,000
PS8	1933 (8)	20	KM#12.3-17.3, 19.3, 22	—	13,000
PS9	1934 (8)	24	KM#12.3-17.3, 19.3, 22	—	11,750
PS10	1935 (8)	20	KM#12.3-17.3, 19.3, 22	—	11,000
PS11	1936 (8)	40	KM#12.3-17.3, 19.3, 22	—	6,000
PS12	1937 (8)	116	KM#23-30	—	800
PS13	1938 (8)	44	KM#23-30	—	1,500
PS14	1939 (8)	30	KM#23-30	—	10,000
PS15	1943 (8)	104	KM#23-30	—	750
PS16	1944 (8)	150	KM#23-30	—	650
PS17	1945 (8)	150	KM#23-30	—	650
PS18	1946 (8)	150	KM#23-30	—	700
PS19	1947 (8)	2,600	KM#23-31	—	300
PS20	1948 (9)	1,120	KM#32.1, 33, 34.1-40.1	—	325
PS21	1949 (9)	800	KM#32.1, 33, 34.1-40.1	—	500
PS22	1950 (9)	500	KM#32.1, 33, 34.1-40.1	—	525
PS23	1951 (9)	2,000	KM#32.2, 33, 34.2-40.2	—	80.00
PS24	1952 (11)	12,000	KM#32.2, 33, 34.2-39.2, 41-43	—	400
PS25	1952 (9)	3,500	KM#32.2, 33, 34.2-39.2, 41	—	45.00
PS26	1953 (11)	3,000	KM#44-54	29.40	400
PS27	1953 (9)	2,000	KM#44-52	4.35	50.00
PS28	1953 (2)	1,000	KM#53-54	25.20	350
PS29	1954 (11)	875	KM#44-54	29.40	435
PS30	1954 (9)	2,275	KM#44-52	4.35	80.00
PS31	1954 (2)	350	KM#53-54	25.20	350
PS32	1955 (11)	600	KM#44-54	29.40	400
PS33	1955 (9)	2,250	KM#44-52	4.35	55.00
PS34	1955 (2)	300	KM#53-54	25.20	350
PS35	1956 (11)	350	KM#44-54	29.40	525
PS36	1956 (9)	1,350	KM#44-52	4.35	65.00
PS37	1956 (2)	158	KM#53-54	25.20	450
PS38	1957 (11)	380	KM#44-54	29.40	500
PS39	1957 (9)	750	KM#44-52	4.35	75.00
PS40	1957 (2)	180	KM#53-54	25.20	415
PS41	1958 (11)	360	KM#44-54	29.40	530
PS42	1958 (9)	625	KM#44-52	4.35	95.00
PS43	1958 (2)	155	KM#53-54	25.20	435
PS44	1959 (11)	390	KM#44-54	29.40	600
PS45	1959 (9)	560	KM#44-52	4.35	225
PS46	1959 (2)	240	KM#53-54	25.20	400
PS47	1960 (11)	1,500	KM#44-51, 53-55	29.40	300
PS48	1960 (9)	1,860	KM#44-51, 55	4.35	20.00
PS49	1960 (2)	450	KM#53-54	25.20	275
PS50	1961 (9)	3,139	KM#56-64	—	200
PS51	1961 (7)	4,391	KM#56-62	—	20.00
PS52	1961 (2)	793	KM#63-64 BV + 20%	—	—
PS53	1962 (9)	1,544	KM#56-64	—	210
PS54	1962 (7)	2,300	KM#56-62	—	15.00
PS55	1962 (2)	800	KM#63-64 BV+20%	—	—
PS56	1963 (9)	1,500	KM#56-64	—	200
PS57	1963 (7)	2,525	KM#56-62	—	12.00
PS58	1963 (2)	1,008	KM#63-64 BV+20%	—	—
PS59	1964 (9)	3,000	KM#56-64	—	190
PS60	1964 (7)	13,000	KM#56-62	—	10.00
PS61	1964 (2)	1,000	KM#63-64 BV+20%	—	—
PS62	1965 (9)	5,099	KM#63-64, 65.1, 66.2, 67.1, 68.2, 69.1, 70.2, 71.1	23.50	185
PS63	1965 (9)	85	KM#63-64, 65.1-66.2, 67.1, 68.2, 69.1, 70.2, 71.2 V.I.P.	—	1,200
PS64	1965 (7)	19,889	KM#65.1, 66.2, 67.1, 68.2, 69.1, 70.2, 71.1	5.00	12.00
PS65	1965 (2)	925	KM#63-64 BV+20%	18.15	—
PS66	1966 (9)	10,000	KM#63-64, 65.2, 66.1, 67.2, 68.1, 69.2, 70.1, 71.2	24.10	185
PS67	1966 (7)	15,000	KM#65.2, 66.1, 67.2, 68.1, 69.2, 70.1, 71.2	5.00	8.00
PS68	1966 (2)	1,000	KM#63-64 BV+20%	18.15	—
PS69	1967 (9)	10,000	KM#63-64, 65.2, 66.1, 67.2, 68.1, 69.2, 70.1, 72.2	24.10	185
PS70	1967 (7)	15,000	KM#65.2, 66.1, 67.2, 68.1, 69.2, 70.1, 72.2	5.00	8.00
PS71	1967 (2)	1,000	KM#63-64 BV+20%	18.15	—
PS72	1968 (9)	10,000	KM#63-64, 71.1, 74.1, 75.2, 76.1, 77.2, 78.1, 79.2	35.00	185
PS73	1968 (7)	15,000	KM#71.1, 74.1, 75.2, 76.1, 77.2, 78.1, 79.2	16.00	8.00
PS74	1968 (2)	1,000	KM#63-64 BV+20%	28.00	—
PS75	1969 (9)	7,000	KM#63-64, 65.2, 66.1, 67.2, 68.1, 69.2, 70.1, 80.2	34.85	185
PS76	1969 (7)	5,000	KM#65.2, 66.1, 67.2, 68.1, 69.2, 70.1, 80.2	13.95	8.00
PS77	1969 (2)	1,000	KM#63-64 BV+20%	27.85	—
PS78	1970 (10)	6,000	KM#63-64, 81-88	35.05	185
PS79	1970 (8)	4,000	KM#81-88	14.00	9.00
PS80	1970 (2)	1,000	KM#63-64 BV+20%	28.05	—
PS81	1971 (10)	7,000	KM#63-64, 81-88	35.00	185
PS82	1971 (8)	5,000	KM#81-88	14.00	9.00
PS83	1971 (2)	650	KM#63-64 BV+20%	28.00	—
PS84	1972 (10)	6,000	KM#63-64, 81-88	32.80	185
PS85	1972 (8)	4,000	KM#81-88	13.10	9.00
PS86	1972 (2)	1,500	KM#63-64 BV+20%	26.25	—
PS87	1973 (10)	6,850	KM#63-64, 81-88	32.00	185
PS88	1973 (8)	4,000	KM#81-88	12.80	9.00
PS89	1973 (2)	6,088	KM#63-64 BV+20%	25.60	—
PS90	1974 (10)	11,000	KM#63-64, 81-87, 89	52.50	185
PS91	1974 (8)	4,000	KM#81-87, 89	15.00	9.00
PS92	1974 (2)	5,600	KM#63-64 BV+20%	45.00	—

KM#	Date	Mintage	Identification	Issue Price	Mkt Val
PS93	1975 (10)	12,500	KM#63-64, 81-87, 88	116	185
PS94	1975 (8)	5,500	KM#81-88	14.55	9.00
PS95	1975 (2)	7,000	KM#63-64 BV+20%	102	—
PS96	1976 (10)	14,000	KM#63-64, 88, 90-96	92.00	185
PS97	1976 (8)	7,000	KM#88, 90-96	11.50	9.00
PS98	1976 (2)	8,000	KM#63-64 BV+20%	80.50	—
PS99	1977 (10)	12,000	KM#63-64, 81-88	92.00	185
PS100	1977 (8)	7,000	KM#81-88	11.50	12.00
PS101	1977 (2)	8,000	KM#63-64 BV+20%	80.50	—
PS102	1978 (10)	10,000	KM#63-64, 81-88	—	185
PS103	1978 (8)	7,000	KM#81-88	—	12.00
PS104	1978 (2)	9,000	KM#63-64 BV+20%	—	—
PS106	1979 (8)	5,000	KM#88, 97-103	—	22.00
PS105	1979 (10)	10,000	KM#63-64, 97-103, 104a	—	185
PS107	1979 (2)	10,000	KM#63-64 BV+20%	—	—
PS108	1980 (10)	10,000	KM#63-64, 81-88	—	185
PS109	1980 (8)	5,000	KM#81-88	—	22.00
PS110	1980 (2)	8,000	KM#63-64 BV+20%	—	—
PS111	1980 (2)	8,000	KM#63-64	—	—
PS112	1980 (3)	60	KM#105-107	—	9,000
PS113	1981 (10)	6,000	KM#63-64, 81-88	—	185
PS114	1981 (8)	4,900	KM#81-88	—	22.00
PS115	1981 (2)	6,238	KM#63-64 BV+20%	—	—
PS116	1982 (10)	7,100	KM#63-64, 108-115	—	190
PS117	1982 (8)	4,900	KM#88, 108-114	—	22.00
PS118	1982 (2)	6,930	KM#63-64 BV+20%	—	—
PS119	1983 (10)	7,300	KM#63-64, 81-88	—	185
PS120	1983 (8)	6,835	KM#81-88	—	22.00
PS121	1983 (2)	7,300	KM#63-64 BV+20%	—	—
PS122	1984 (8)	11,250	KM#82-88, 88a	—	15.00
PS123	1985 (8)	9,859	KM#82-87, 116, 117	—	25.00
PS124	1986 (8)	7,000	KM#82-87, 88a, 119	—	25.00
PS125	1986 (2)	428	KM#73, 121 Plus large gold plated Silver #1	—	1,400
PS126	1986 (2)	750	KM#121, 131	—	700
PS127	1986 (2)	500	KM#119, 121, 131	—	725
PS128	1987 (8)	6,781	KM#82-88, 88a	—	25.00
PS129	1987 (2)	750	KM#73, 105-107	—	1,050
PS130	1987 GRC (4)	1,121	KM#73, 105-107	—	2,900
PS131	1988 (8)	7,250	KM#82-88, 88a	—	50.00
PS132	1988 (4)	806	KM#73, 105-107	—	1,050
PS133	1988 GRC (4)	835	KM#73, 105-107	—	2,900
PS134	1988 (3)	3,388	KM#122, 125, 128	—	70.00
PS135	1988 (3)	600	KM#124, 127, 130	—	2,750
PS136	1989 (8)	9,571	KM#82-88, 88a	—	50.00
PS137	1989 (4)	—	KM#73, 105-107	—	1,050
PS138	1989 GRC (4)	318	KM#73, 105-107	—	5,500
PS139	1990 (8)	10,000	KM#132-137, 139, 148	—	70.00
PS140	1990 (4)	—	KM#73, 105-107	—	1,050
PS141	1990 GRC (4)	1,066	KM#73, 105-107	—	2,775
PS142	1991 (8)	12,000	KM#132-139	—	70.00
PSA143	1991 GRC (4)	426	KM#73, 105-107	—	2,775
PS143	1992 (8)	10,000	KM#132-139	—	50.00
PS144	1993 (8)	—	KM#132-139	—	50.00
PS145	1994 (9)	5,804	KM#132-140	—	60.00
PS146	1994 (4)	166	KM#189-192 Wood case	—	1,200
PS147	1994 (4)	1,750	KM#189-192 Velvet case	—	1,175
PS148	1994 (3)	420	KM#167, 187-188	—	750
PS149	1995 (9)	5,816	KM#132-140	—	65.00
PS150	1995 (4)	750	KM#73, 105-107	—	1,400
PS151	1995	—	KM#73, 105-107 Wooden box	—	1,425
PS152	1995 (4)	89	KM#195-198 Wood case	—	1,200
PS153	1995 (4)	926	KM#195-198 Velvet case	—	1,175
PS154	1995 (3)	210	KM#152, 193-194	—	755
PS155	1996 (9)	4,827	KM#158-166	30.00	36.00
PS156	1996 (4)	368	KM#201-204, Wood case	—	1,200
PS157	1996 (4)	1,677	KM#201-204 Velvet case	—	1,175
PS158	1996 (3)	346	KM#169, 199-200	—	760
PS159	1997 (4)	500	KM#73, 105-107	—	1,100
PS160	1997 (4)	500	KM#207-210 Wood case	—	1,200
PS161	1997 (4)	1,015	KM#207-210, Velvet case	—	1,175
PS162	1997 (3)	144	KM#181, 205-206	—	780
PS163	1997 (4)	30	KM#73, 105-107, 30 Year Wine set with privy marks	—	2,550
PS164	1997 (9)	3,596	KM#159-166, 170	—	40.00
PS165	1998 (9)	—	KM#159-166, 170	—	40.00
PS166	1998 (4)	—	KM#213-216 Wood case	—	1,200
PS167	1998 (4)	—	KM#213-216 Velvet case	—	1,175
PS168	1998 (3)	—	KM#177, 211-212	—	780
PS169	1999 (9)	6,000	KM#159-166, 170	39.50	40.00
PS220	1999 (4)	509	KM#252.1, 253-255, prestige	—	1,325
PS221	1999 (4)	1,046	KM#252.1, 253-255, leatherette-2.5	—	1,950
PS222	1999 (4)	537	KM#252.1, 253-255, special	—	2,250
PS191	2000 (4)	236	KM#234-237, wood case	—	65.00
PS192	2000 (4)	1,140	KM#234-237, velvet lined case	—	300

SPECIMEN SETS (SS)

KM#	Date	Mintage	Identification	Issue Price	Mkt Val
SS1	1994 (9)	5,508	KM#132-140	—	25.00
SS2	1995 (9)	4,956	KM#132-140	—	25.00
SS3	1996 (9)	5,766	KM#158-166	19.50	25.00
SS4	1997 (9)	4,236	KM#159-166, 170	—	25.00
SS5	1998 (9)	—	KM#159-166, 170	—	25.00

KM#	Date	Mintage	Identification	Issue Price	Mkt Val
SS6	1999 (9)	—	KM#159-166, 170	—	25.00

SOUTH ARABIA

Fifteen of the sixteen Western Protectorate States, the Wahidi State of the Eastern Protectorate, and Aden Colony joined to form the Federation of South Arabia.

In 1959, Britain agreed to prepare South Arabia for full independence, which was achieved on Nov. 30, 1967, at which time South Arabia, including Aden, changed its name to the Peoples Republic of Southern Yemen. On Dec. 1, 1970, following the overthrow of the new government by the National Liberation Front, Southern Yemen changed its name to the Peoples Democratic Republic of Yemen.

TITLE
Al-Junubiya(t) al-Arabiya(t)

MONETARY SYSTEM
1000 Fils = 1 Dinar

FEDERATION

STANDARD COINAGE

KM# 1   FILS
Aluminum, 20 mm. **Obv:** Snowflake design **Rev:** Crossed swords

Date	Mintage	F	VF	XF	Unc	BU
1964	10,000,000	—	0.10	0.15	0.25	
1964 Proof	—	Value: 1.50				

KM# 2   5 FILS
Bronze **Obv:** Snowflake design **Rev:** Crossed swords

Date	Mintage	F	VF	XF	Unc	BU
1964	10,000,000	—	0.15	0.25	0.50	0.65
1964 Proof	—	Value: 2.00				

KM# 3   25 FILS
Copper-Nickel **Obv:** Snowflake design **Rev:** Sailboat

Date	Mintage	F	VF	XF	Unc	BU
1964	4,000,000	—	0.25	0.45	0.85	1.00
1964 Proof	—	Value: 2.75				

KM# 4   50 FILS
Copper-Nickel **Obv:** Snowflake design **Rev:** Sailboat

Date	Mintage	F	VF	XF	Unc	BU
1964	6,000,000	—	0.45	0.65	1.25	1.50
1964 Proof	—	Value: 3.75				

PROOF SETS

KM#	Date	Mintage	Identification	Issue Price	Mkt Val
PS1	1964 (4)	10,500	KM1-4	9.90	10.00

S. GEORGIA & THE S. SANDWICH IS.

ARGENTINA — SOUTH GEORGIA ISLAND — SOUTH SANDWICH ISLANDS — Scotia Sea

South Georgia and the South Sandwich Islands are a dependency of the Falkland Islands, and located about 800 miles east of them. South Georgia is 1,450 sq. mi. (1,770 sq. km.), and the South Sandwich Islands are 120 sq. mi. (311 sq. km.) Fishing and Antarctic research are the main industries. The islands were claimed for Great Britain in 1775 by Captain James Cook.

RULER
British since 1775

BRITISH OVERSEAS TERRITORY

STANDARD COINAGE

KM# 1 2 POUNDS
28.2800 g., Copper-Nickel, 38.7 mm. Subject: 100th Birthday - Queen Mother Obv: Crowned bust of Queen Elizabeth II right Rev: Crowned arms with supporters Edge: Reeded Mint: Pobjoy

Date	Mintage	F	VF	XF	Unc	BU
2000	—	—	—	—	10.00	12.00

KM# 1a 2 POUNDS
28.2800 g., 0.9250 Silver 0.8410 oz. ASW Subject: 100th Birthday - Queen Mother Obv: Crowned bust of Queen Elizabeth II right Rev: Crowned arms with supporters Edge: Reeded Mint: Pobjoy

Date	Mintage	F	VF	XF	Unc	BU
2000 Proof	—	Value: 50.00				

KM# 1a.1 2 POUNDS
28.2800 g., 0.9250 Silver 0.8410 oz. ASW, 38.6 mm. Subject: Queen Mother Obv: Bust with tiara right Rev: Crowned arms with supporters with a tiny black sapphire mounted below Edge: Reeded Mint: Pobjoy

Date	Mintage	F	VF	XF	Unc	BU
2000 Proof	1,000	Value: 55.00				

KM# 3 2 POUNDS
28.2800 g., Copper-Nickel, 38.6 mm. Obv: Crowned bust of Queen Elizabeth II right Rev: Standing figure on deck of ship within inner circle Edge: Reeded Mint: Pobjoy

Date	Mintage	F	VF	XF	Unc	BU
2000	—	—	—	—	8.50	10.00

KM# 3a 2 POUNDS
28.2800 g., 0.9250 Silver 0.8410 oz. ASW, 38.7 mm. Obv: Crowned bust of Queen Elizabeth II right Rev: Standing figure on the deck of the ship within inner circle Edge: Reeded Mint: Pobjoy

Date	Mintage	F	VF	XF	Unc	BU
2000 Proof	—	Value: 47.50				

KM# 4 2 POUNDS
28.2800 g., Copper-Nickel Subject: 225th Anniversary - Possession by Captain Cook Obv: Crowned bust of Queen Elizabeth II right Rev: Bust right Mint: Pobjoy

Date	Mintage	F	VF	XF	Unc	BU
2000	—	—	—	—	8.50	10.00

KM# 4a 2 POUNDS
28.2800 g., 0.9250 Silver 0.8410 oz. ASW Subject: 225th Anniversary - Possession by Captain Cook Obv: Crowned bust of Queen Elizabeth II right Rev: Bust right Mint: Pobjoy

Date	Mintage	F	VF	XF	Unc	BU
2000 Proof	—	Value: 47.50				

KM# 5 20 POUNDS
6.2200 g., 0.9999 oz. AGW, 22 mm. Obv: Crowned bust of Queen Elizabeth II right Rev: Standing figure on the deck of the ship within circle Edge: Reeded Mint: Pobjoy

Date	Mintage	F	VF	XF	Unc	BU
2000 Proof	—	Value: 210				

KM# 6 20 POUNDS
6.2200 g., 0.9999 Gold 0.1999 oz. AGW Subject: 225th Anniversary - Possession by Captain Cook Obv: Crowned bust of Queen Elizabeth II right Rev: Bust right Mint: Pobjoy

Date	Mintage	F	VF	XF	Unc	BU
2000 Proof	—	Value: 210				

KM# 2.1 20 POUNDS
6.2200 g., 0.9999 Gold 0.1999 oz. AGW Subject: 100th Birthday - Queen Mother Obv: Crowned bust of Queen Elizabeth II right Rev: Crowned arms with supporters Edge: Reeded Mint: Pobjoy

Date	Mintage	F	VF	XF	Unc	BU
2000 Proof	—	Value: 210				

KM# 2.2 20 POUNDS
6.2200 g., 0.9990 Gold 0.1998 oz. AGW, 22 mm. Obv: Crowned bust of Queen Elizabeth II right Rev: Crowned arms with supporters with a tiny black sapphire mounted below Edge: Reeded Mint: Pobjoy

Date	Mintage	F	VF	XF	Unc	BU
2000 Proof	1,000	Value: 210				

SOUTHERN RHODESIA

BELGIAN CONGO — TANGANYIKA TERRITORY — NYASALAND PROT. — ANGOLA — NORTHERN RHODESIA — MOZAMBIQUE — SOUTH WEST AFRICA — SOUTHERN RHODESIA — Mozambique Channel — BECHUANALAND PROT. — UNION OF SOUTH AFRICA

Colonization of Rhodesia began in 1890 when settlers forcibly acquired Shona lands and then Ndebele lands in 1893. It was named as Rhodesia, after Cecil Rhodes who led the build-up of the Colony.

Rhodesia became a self-governing colony under the name of Southern Rhodesia in 1923. Consequent upon later political difficulties and disagreement with the British authorities over common emancipation of the people, a unilateral declaration of independence (UDI) was declared on November 11, 1965.

Following United Nations sanctions against the country, various renamings as Rhodesia and Rhodesia-Zimbabwe, and elections in February 1980, the country became independent on April 18, 1980, as the Republic of Zimbabwe as a member of the Commonwealth of Nations.

RULER
British, until 1966

MONETARY SYSTEM
12 Pence = 1 Shilling
2 Shillings = 1 Florin
5 Shillings = 1 Crown
20 Shillings = 1 Pound

BRITISH COLONY

POUND COINAGE

KM# 6 1/2 PENNY
Copper-Nickel Ruler: George V Obv: Crowned flower design within circle, hole in center Rev: Value written within sprigs, hole in center

Date	Mintage	F	VF	XF	Unc	BU
1934	240,000	1.00	3.50	15.00	40.00	—
1934 Proof	—	Value: 125				
1936	240,000	5.00	25.00	60.00	150	—
1936 Proof	—	—	—	—	—	—

KM# 14 1/2 PENNY
Copper-Nickel Ruler: George VI Obv: Crowned flower design within circle, hole in center Rev: Value written within sprigs, hole in center

Date	Mintage	F	VF	XF	Unc	BU
1938	240,000	0.75	1.75	7.00	20.00	30.00
1938 Proof	—	—	—	—	—	—
1939	480,000	1.00	2.00	20.00	60.00	85.00
1939 Proof	—	—	—	—	—	—

KM# 14a 1/2 PENNY
Bronze Ruler: George VI Obv: Crowned flower design within circle, hole in center Rev: Value within sprigs, hole in center

Date	Mintage	F	VF	XF	Unc	BU
1942	480,000	0.60	1.50	9.50	25.00	—
1942 Proof	—	—	—	—	—	—
1943	960,000	0.35	0.75	1.50	6.50	18.00
1944	960,000	0.35	0.75	1.75	8.00	20.00
1944 Proof	—	—	—	—	—	—

KM# 26 1/2 PENNY
Bronze Ruler: George VI Obv: Crowned flower design within circle, hole in center Obv. Leg.: KING GEORGE THE SIXTH Rev: Value written within sprigs, hole in center

Date	Mintage	F	VF	XF	Unc	BU
1951	480,000	0.75	1.25	2.25	6.50	18.00
1951 Proof	—	—	—	—	—	—
1952	480,000	0.75	1.25	5.00	10.00	22.00
1952 Proof	—	—	—	—	—	—

KM# 28 1/2 PENNY
Bronze Ruler: Elizabeth II Obv: Crowned flower design within circle, hole in center Rev: Value written within sprigs, hole in center

Date	Mintage	F	VF	XF	Unc	BU
1954	960,000	0.75	2.00	25.00	65.00	—
1954 Proof	20	Value: 350				

KM# 7 PENNY
Copper-Nickel **Ruler:** George V **Obv:** Crowned flower design within circle, hole in center **Rev:** Value written within sprigs, hole in center

Date	Mintage	F	VF	XF	Unc	BU
1934	360,000	0.75	1.50	9.50	25.00	50.00
1934 Proof	—	Value: 125				
1935	492,000	1.50	15.00	55.00	125	250
1935 Proof	—	—	—	—	—	—
1936	1,044,000	0.60	1.25	10.00	30.00	60.00
1936 Proof	—	—	—	—	—	—

KM# 8 PENNY
Copper-Nickel **Ruler:** George VI **Obv:** Crowned flower design within circle, hole in center **Rev:** Value written within sprigs, hole in center

Date	Mintage	F	VF	XF	Unc	BU
1937	908,000	0.60	1.25	9.50	25.00	—
1937 Proof	—	Value: 300				
1938	240,000	1.50	3.00	20.00	50.00	—
1938 Proof	—	—	—	—	—	—
1939	1,284,000	0.45	1.00	16.50	37.50	—
1939 Proof	—	—	—	—	—	—
1940	1,080,000	0.45	1.00	16.50	37.50	—
1940 Proof	—	—	—	—	—	—
1941	720,000	0.50	1.25	17.50	40.00	—
1941 Proof	—	—	—	—	—	—
1942	960,000	0.50	1.25	27.50	65.00	—
1942 Proof	—	—	—	—	—	—

KM# 8a PENNY
Bronze **Ruler:** George VI **Obv:** Crowned flower design within circle, hole in center **Rev:** Written value within sprigs, hole in center

Date	Mintage	F	VF	XF	Unc	BU
1942	480,000	Value: 200				
1942 Proof	—	Value: 400				
1943	3,120,000	0.50	0.80	4.50	15.00	30.00
1944	2,400,000	0.50	0.80	6.00	20.00	40.00
1944 Proof	—	—	—	—	—	—
1947	3,600,000	0.75	1.25	6.00	20.00	40.00
1947 Proof	—	—	—	—	—	—

KM# 25 PENNY
Bronze **Ruler:** George VI **Obv:** Crowned flower design within circle, hole in center **Rev:** Value written within sprigs, hole in center

Date	Mintage	F	VF	XF	Unc	BU
1949	1,440,000	0.50	1.00	8.50	25.00	50.00
1949 Proof	—	Value: 125				
1950	720,000	1.00	1.75	17.50	40.00	80.00
1950 Proof	—	Value: 125				
1951	4,896,000	0.50	0.75	2.25	10.00	18.00
1951 Proof	—	Value: 125				
1952	2,400,000	0.50	0.75	1.50	12.50	25.00
1952 Proof	—	—	—	—	—	—

KM# 29 PENNY
Bronze **Ruler:** Elizabeth II **Obv:** Crowned flower design within circle, hole in center **Rev:** Value written within sprigs, hole in center

Date	Mintage	F	VF	XF	Unc	BU
1954	960,000	4.00	16.50	85.00	250	350
1954 Proof	20	Value: 450				

KM# 1 3 PENCE
1.4100 g., 0.9250 Silver 0.0419 oz. ASW, 16 mm. **Ruler:** George V **Obv:** Crowned bust left **Rev:** Three spearheads divide date

Date	Mintage	F	VF	XF	Unc	BU
1932	688,000	Value: 60.00				
1932 Proof	—	—	—	—	—	—
1934	628,000	Value: 120				
1934 Proof	—	—	—	—	—	—
1935	840,000	Value: 65.00				
1935 Proof	—	—	—	—	—	—
1936	1,052,000	0.85	2.00	20.00	45.00	65.00
1936 Proof	—	—	—	—	—	—

KM# 9 3 PENCE
1.4100 g., 0.9250 Silver 0.0419 oz. ASW, 16 mm. **Ruler:** George VI **Obv:** Crowned head left **Rev:** Three spearheads divide date

Date	Mintage	F	VF	XF	Unc	BU
1937	1,228,000	0.85	2.00	15.00	40.00	60.00
1937 Proof	—	Value: 225				

KM# 16 3 PENCE
1.4100 g., 0.9250 Silver 0.0419 oz. ASW, 16 mm. **Ruler:** George VI **Obv:** Crowned head left **Rev:** Three spearheads divide date

Date	Mintage	F	VF	XF	Unc	BU
1939	160,000	6.00	10.00	55.00	150	—
1939 Proof	—	Value: 300				
1940	1,200,000	0.85	2.00	20.00	40.00	—
1940 Proof	—	—	—	—	—	—
1941	600,000	2.50	5.00	22.50	50.00	—
1941 Proof	—	—	—	—	—	—
1942	2,000,000	0.75	1.50	12.50	30.00	—
1942 Proof	—	—	—	—	—	—

KM# 16a 3 PENCE
1.4100 g., 0.5000 Silver 0.0227 oz. ASW, 16 mm. **Ruler:** George VI **Obv:** Crowned head left **Rev:** Three spearheads divide date **Edge:** Plain

Date	Mintage	F	VF	XF	Unc	BU
1944	1,600,000	0.65	1.50	22.50	60.00	—
1945	800,000	1.00	3.00	15.00	65.00	—
1945 Proof	—	—	—	—	—	—
1946	2,400,000	0.65	1.50	12.50	35.00	—
1946 Proof	—	—	—	—	—	—

KM# 16b 3 PENCE
Copper-Nickel, 16 mm. **Ruler:** George VI **Obv:** Crowned head left **Rev:** Three spearheads divide date

Date	Mintage	F	VF	XF	Unc	BU
1947	8,000,000	0.40	0.80	8.00	20.00	—
1947 Proof	—	Value: 250				

KM# 20 3 PENCE
Copper-Nickel, 16 mm. **Ruler:** George VI **Obv:** Crowned head left **Rev:** Three spearheads divide date

Date	Mintage	F	VF	XF	Unc	BU
1948	2,000,000	0.40	2.00	9.50	30.00	45.00
1948 Proof	—	—	—	—	—	—
1949	4,000,000	Value: 40.00				
1949 Proof	—	Value: 150				

Date	Mintage	F	VF	XF	Unc	BU
1951	5,600,000	0.40	5.00	25.00	75.00	125
1951 Proof	—	—	—	—	—	—
1952	4,800,000	0.40	5.00	22.50	60.00	110
1952 Proof	—	Value: 150				

KM# 2 6 PENCE
2.8300 g., 0.9250 Silver 0.0842 oz. ASW **Ruler:** George V **Obv:** Crowned bust left **Rev:** Crossed axes divide date and value

Date	Mintage	F	VF	XF	Unc	BU
1932	544,000	2.00	8.00	20.00	55.00	—
1932 Proof	—	Value: 65.00				
1934	214,000	3.00	10.00	38.00	90.00	—
1935	380,000	2.00	9.50	32.50	75.00	—
1935 Proof	—	—	—	—	—	—
1936	675,000	1.50	8.00	25.00	60.00	—
1936 Proof	—	—	—	—	—	—

KM# 10 6 PENCE
2.8300 g., 0.9250 Silver 0.0842 oz. ASW **Ruler:** George VI **Obv:** Crowned head left **Rev:** Crossed axes divide date and value

Date	Mintage	F	VF	XF	Unc	BU
1937	823,000	2.50	9.00	22.50	55.00	—
1937 Proof	—	Value: 300				

KM# 17 6 PENCE
2.8300 g., 0.9250 Silver 0.0842 oz. ASW **Ruler:** George VI **Obv:** Crowned head left **Rev:** Crossed axes divide date and value

Date	Mintage	F	VF	XF	Unc	BU
1939	200,000	3.00	16.50	90.00	200	300
1939 Proof	—	Value: 450				
1940	600,000	Value: 150				
1940 Proof	—	—	—	—	—	—
1941	300,000	Value: 125				
1941 Proof	—	—	—	—	—	—
1942	1,200,000	1.50	7.50	20.00	55.00	120
1942 Proof	—	Value: 200				

KM# 17a 6 PENCE
2.8300 g., 0.5000 Silver 0.0455 oz. ASW **Ruler:** George VI **Obv:** Crowned head left **Rev:** Crossed axes divide date and value

Date	Mintage	F	VF	XF	Unc	BU
1944	800,000	1.25	2.50	38.00	90.00	150
1945	400,000	10.00	20.00	60.00	150	300
1945 Proof	—	—	—	—	—	—
1946	1,600,000	1.25	7.50	25.00	60.00	135
1946 Proof	—	—	—	—	—	—

KM# 17b 6 PENCE
Copper-Nickel **Ruler:** George VI **Obv:** Crowned head left **Rev:** Crossed axes divide date and value

Date	Mintage	F	VF	XF	Unc	BU
1947	5,000,000	0.50	1.00	10.00	20.00	50.00
1947 Proof	—	Value: 250				

KM# 21 6 PENCE
Copper-Nickel **Ruler:** George VI **Obv:** Crowned head left **Rev:** Crossed axes divide date and value

Date	Mintage	F	VF	XF	Unc	BU
1948	1,000,000	0.50	1.25	10.00	27.50	50.00
1948 Proof	—	—	—	—	—	—
1949	2,000,000	0.50	5.00	12.50	30.00	60.00
1949 Proof	—	Value: 250				
1950	2,000,000	0.50	6.00	16.50	55.00	95.00
1950 Proof	—	Value: 250				
1951	2,800,000	0.50	1.00	5.00	27.50	50.00
1951 Proof	—	—	—	—	—	—
1952	1,200,000	0.50	1.50	15.00	45.00	80.00
1952 Proof	—	—	—	—	—	—

KM# 3 SHILLING
5.6600 g., 0.9250 Silver 0.1683 oz. ASW **Ruler:** George V
Obv: Crowned bust left **Rev:** Bird sculpture divides date

Date	Mintage	F	VF	XF	Unc	BU
1932	896,000	2.75	12.00	30.00	80.00	—
1932 Proof	—	Value: 90.00				
1934	333,000	4.00	25.00	70.00	175	—
1935	830,000	2.75	15.00	50.00	120	—
1935 Proof	—	Value: 220				
1936	1,663,000	2.75	18.50	42.50	115	—
1936 Proof	—	—	—	—	—	—

KM# 11 SHILLING
5.6600 g., 0.9250 Silver 0.1683 oz. ASW **Ruler:** George VI
Obv: Crowned head left **Rev:** Bird sculpture divides date

Date	Mintage	F	VF	XF	Unc	BU
1937	1,700,000	2.75	15.00	38.00	90.00	—
1937 Proof	—	Value: 300				

KM# 18 SHILLING
5.6600 g., 0.9250 Silver 0.1683 oz. ASW **Ruler:** George VI
Obv: Crowned head left **Rev:** Bird sculpture divides date

Date	Mintage	F	VF	XF	Unc	BU
1939	420,000	7.00	27.50	110	275	—
1939 Proof	—	Value: 500				
1940	750,000	5.50	22.00	65.00	165	—
1940 Proof	—	—	—	—	—	—
1941	800,000	6.50	20.00	55.00	140	—
1941 Proof	—	—	—	—	—	—
1942	2,100,000	2.50	3.50	17.50	55.00	—
1942 Proof	—	—	—	—	—	—

KM# 18a SHILLING
5.6600 g., 0.5000 Silver 0.0910 oz. ASW **Ruler:** George VI
Obv: Crowned head left **Rev:** Bird sculpture divides date

Date	Mintage	F	VF	XF	Unc	BU
1944	1,600,000	2.00	14.00	45.00	80.00	—
1946	1,700,000	3.50	18.00	70.00	120	—
1946 Proof	—	—	—	—	—	—

KM# 18b SHILLING
Copper-Nickel **Ruler:** George VI **Obv:** Crowned head left
Rev: Bird sculpture divides date

Date	Mintage	F	VF	XF	Unc	BU
1947	8,000,000	0.75	1.50	16.50	40.00	80.00
1947 Proof	—	Value: 300				

KM# 22 SHILLING
Copper-Nickel **Ruler:** George VI **Obv:** Crowned head left
Rev: Bird sculpture divides date

Date	Mintage	F	VF	XF	Unc	BU
1948	1,500,000	0.75	1.50	12.00	30.00	60.00
1948 Proof	—	—	—	—	—	—
1949	4,000,000	0.75	5.00	12.50	35.00	65.00
1949 Proof	—	Value: 250				
1950	2,000,000	1.00	8.00	22.00	55.00	90.00
1950 Proof	—	Value: 225				
1951	3,000,000	0.75	2.50	10.00	20.00	40.00
1951 Proof	—	—	—	—	—	—
1952	2,600,000	0.75	5.00	22.00	55.00	90.00
1952 Proof	—	—	—	—	—	—

KM# 4 2 SHILLINGS
11.3100 g., 0.9250 Silver 0.3363 oz. ASW **Ruler:** George V
Obv: Crowned bust left **Rev:** Sable antelope

Date	Mintage	F	VF	XF	Unc	BU
1932	498,000	5.50	12.00	37.50	110	200
1932 Proof	—	Value: 125				
1934	154,000	12.50	25.00	100	225	425
1935	365,000	6.50	15.00	50.00	120	200
1935 Proof	—	—	—	—	—	—
1936	683,000	5.50	15.00	45.00	120	200
1936 Proof	—	—	—	—	—	—

KM# 12 2 SHILLINGS
11.3100 g., 0.9250 Silver 0.3363 oz. ASW **Ruler:** George VI
Obv: Crowned head left **Rev:** Sable antelope

Date	Mintage	F	VF	XF	Unc	BU
1937	552,000	7.50	18.00	55.00	135	—
1937 Proof	—	Value: 400				

KM# 19 2 SHILLINGS
11.3100 g., 0.9250 Silver 0.3363 oz. ASW **Ruler:** George VI
Obv: Crowned head left **Rev:** Sable antelope

Date	Mintage	F	VF	XF	Unc	BU
1939	120,000	50.00	135	325	650	—
1939 Proof	—	Value: 750				
1940	525,000	8.00	32.50	110	250	—
1940 Proof	—	—	—	—	—	—
1941	400,000	7.00	15.00	125	300	—
1941 Proof	—	—	—	—	—	—
1942	850,000	5.50	9.00	32.50	90.00	—

KM# 19a 2 SHILLINGS
11.3100 g., 0.5000 Silver 0.1818 oz. ASW **Ruler:** George VI
Obv: Crowned head left **Rev:** Sable antelope

Date	Mintage	F	VF	XF	Unc	BU
1944	1,300,000	6.00	15.00	45.00	135	—
1946	700,000	100	180	280	650	—
1946 Proof	—	—	—	—	—	—

KM# 19b 2 SHILLINGS
Copper-Nickel **Ruler:** George VI **Obv:** Crowned head left
Rev: Sable antelope

Date	Mintage	F	VF	XF	Unc	BU
1947	3,750,000	1.75	4.00	22.50	45.00	90.00
1947 Proof	—	Value: 300				

KM# 23 2 SHILLINGS
Copper-Nickel **Ruler:** George VI **Obv:** Crowned head left
Rev: Sable antelope

Date	Mintage	F	VF	XF	Unc	BU
1948	750,000	1.00	3.00	22.50	60.00	110
1948 Proof	—	—	—	—	—	—
1949	2,000,000	1.00	3.00	22.50	80.00	180
1949 Proof	—	Value: 350				
1950	1,000,000	1.00	4.00	25.00	115	225
1950 Proof	—	Value: 350				
1951	2,600,000	1.00	3.00	12.00	47.00	90.00
1951 Proof	—	—	—	—	—	—
1952	1,800,000	1.00	3.00	28.00	75.00	175
1952 Proof	—	—	—	—	—	—

KM# 30 2 SHILLINGS
Copper-Nickel **Ruler:** Elizabeth II **Obv:** Laureate bust right
Rev: Sable antelope

Date	Mintage	F	VF	XF	Unc	BU
1954	300,000	25.00	35.00	275	900	—
1954 Proof	20	Value: 1,250				

KM# 5 1/2 CROWN
14.1400 g., 0.9250 Silver 0.4205 oz. ASW, 32 mm.
Ruler: George V **Obv:** Crowned bust left **Rev:** Crowned shield

Date	Mintage	F	VF	XF	Unc	BU
1932	634,000	Value: 200				
1932 Proof	—	Value: 125				
1934	419,000	Value: 450				
1934 Proof	—	—	—	—	—	—
1935	512,000	Value: 300				
1935 Proof	—	—	—	—	—	—
1936	518,000	7.00	16.00	50.00	145	260
1936 Proof	—	—	—	—	—	—

KM# 13 1/2 CROWN
14.1400 g., 0.9250 Silver 0.4205 oz. ASW, 32 mm.
Ruler: George VI **Obv:** Crowned head left **Rev:** Crowned shield

Date	Mintage	F	VF	XF	Unc	BU
1937	1,174,000	7.00	20.00	50.00	130	200
1937 Proof	—	Value: 350				

KM# 15   1/2 CROWN
14.1400 g., 0.9250 Silver 0.4205 oz. ASW, 32 mm.
Ruler: George VI **Obv:** Crowned head left **Rev:** Crowned shield

Date	Mintage	F	VF	XF	Unc	BU
1938	400,000	7.00	20.00	55.00	150	260
1938 Proof	—	—	—	—	—	—
1939	224,000	10.00	20.00	115	300	550
1939 Proof	—	Value: 500				
1940	800,000	Value: 160				
1940 Proof	—	—	—	—	—	—
1941	1,240,000	Value: 125				
1941 Proof	—	—	—	—	—	—
1942	2,008,000	BV	7.00	25.00	70.00	140
1942 Proof	—	—	—	—	—	—

KM# 15a   1/2 CROWN
14.1400 g., 0.5000 Silver 0.2273 oz. ASW **Ruler:** George VI
Obv: Crowned head left **Rev:** Crowned shield

Date	Mintage	F	VF	XF	Unc	BU
1944	800,000	3.75	6.00	25.00	90.00	165
1946	1,400,000	4.00	8.00	55.00	135	200
1946 Proof	—	—	—	—	—	—

KM# 15b   1/2 CROWN
Copper-Nickel, 32 mm. **Ruler:** George VI **Obv:** Crowned head left **Rev:** Crowned shield

Date	Mintage	F	VF	XF	Unc	BU
1947	6,000,000	1.25	2.50	5.00	20.00	50.00
1947 Proof	—	Value: 300				

KM# 24   1/2 CROWN
Copper-Nickel, 32 mm. **Ruler:** George VI **Obv:** Crowned head left **Rev:** Crowned shield

Date	Mintage	F	VF	XF	Unc	BU
1948	800,000	Value: 100				
1948 Proof	—	—	—	—	—	—
1949	1,600,000	Value: 110				
1949 Proof	—	Value: 450				
1950	1,200,000	Value: 125				
1950 Proof	—	Value: 450				
1951	3,200,000	1.25	2.50	20.00	50.00	90.00
1951 Proof	—	Value: 350				
1952	2,800,000	1.25	2.50	22.50	70.00	100
1952 Proof	—	Value: 350				

KM# 31   1/2 CROWN
Copper-Nickel, 32 mm. **Ruler:** Elizabeth II **Obv:** Laureate bust right **Rev:** Crowned shield

Date	Mintage	F	VF	XF	Unc	BU
1954	1,200,000	8.00	12.50	35.00	95.00	130
1954 Proof	20	Value: 450				

KM# 27   CROWN
28.2800 g., 0.5000 Silver 0.4546 oz. ASW, 38.5 mm.
Ruler: Elizabeth II **Subject:** Birth of Cecil Rhodes Centennial
Obv: Larueate bust right **Rev:** Cameo flanked by sprigs with ribbon above assorted shields **Edge:** 1853 OUT OF VISION CAME REALITY 1953 **Note:** Both upright and inverted edge varieties exist.

Date	Mintage	F	VF	XF	Unc	BU
1953	124,000	7.50	12.50	20.00	40.00	60.00
1953 Proof	1,500	Value: 125				
1953 Matte Proof	—	Value: 350				

TRIAL STRIKES

KM#	Date	Mintage	Identification	Mkt Val
TS1	1932	—	3 Pence. White Metal. Plain edge. Rev. KM#1.	550
TS2	1932	—	6 Pence. White Metal. Plain edge. Rev. KM#2.	550
TS3	1932	—	Shilling. White Metal. Plain edge. Rev. KM#3.	650
TS4	1932	—	Florin. White Metal. Plain edge. Rev. KM#4.	850
TS5	1932	—	1/2 Crown. White Metal. Plain edge. Rev. KM#5.	1,150
TS6	1934	—	3 Pence. White Metal. Plain edge. Rev. KM#1. Thick flan.	550
TS7	1934	—	1/2 Crown. White Metal. Plain edge. Rev. KM#5. Thick flan.	1,150

PROOF SETS

KM#	Date	Mintage	Identification	Issue Price	Mkt Val
PS1	1932 (5)	496	KM#1-5	—	450
PS2	1937 (6)	40	KM#8-13	—	2,000
PS3	1939 (5)	10	KM#15-19	—	2,500
PS6	1947 (5)	10	KM#15b-19b	—	1,500
PS4	1953 (2)	3	KM#27 Double set; Rare	—	—
PS5	1954 (4)	20	KM#28-31	—	2,500

SPAIN

North Atlantic Ocean — FRANCE — ANDORRA — PORTUGAL — Santander — Bilbao — Burgos — Pamplona — Segovia — Barcelona — Madrid — Cuenca — Toledo — Valencia — Sevilla — Cadiz — Mediterranean Sea — MOROCCO — ALGERIA

The Spanish State, forming the greater part of the Iberian Peninsula of southwest Europe, has an area of 195,988 sq. mi. (504,714 sq. km.) and a population of 39.4 million including the Balearic and the Canary Islands. Capital: Madrid. The economy is based on agriculture, industry and tourism. Machinery, fruit, vegetables and chemicals are exported.

Discontent against the mother country increased after 1808 as colonists faced new imperialist policies from Napoleon or Spanish liberals. The revolutionary movement was established which resulted in the eventual independence of the Vice-royalties of New Spain, New Granada and Rio de la Plata within 2 decades.

The doomed republic was trapped in a tug-of-war between the right and left wing forces inevitably resulting in the Spanish Civil War of 1936-38. The leftist Republicans were supported by the U.S.S.R. and the International Brigade, which consisted of mainly communist volunteers from all over the western world. The right wing Nationalists were supported by the Fascist governments of Italy and Germany. Under the leadership of Gen. Francisco Franco, the Nationalists emerged victorious and immediately embarked on a program of reconstruction and neutrality as dictated by the new "Caudillo"(leader) Franco.

The monarchy was reconstituted in 1947 under the regency of General Francisco Franco; the king designate to be crowned after Franco's death. Franco died on Nov. 20, 1975. Two days after his passing, Juan Carlos de Borbon, the grandson of Alfonso XIII, was proclaimed King of Spain.

RULERS
Alfonso XIII, 1886-1931
 2nd Republic and Civil War, 1931-1939
Francisco Franco, 1939-1947
 as Caudillo and regent, 1947-1975
Juan Carlos I, 1975-
NOTE: From 1868 to 1982, two dates may be found on most Spanish coinage. The larger date is the year of authorization and the smaller date incused on the two 6-pointed-stars found on most types is the year of issue. The latter appears in parentheses in these listings.

MINT MARKS
Until 1980
6-pointed star - Madrid

NOTE: Letters after date are initials of mint officials.
After 1982
Crowned M – Madrid

KINGDOM
THIRD DECIMAL COINAGE
10 Milesimas = 1 Centimo

100 Centesimos = 1 Peseta

KM# 724   20 PESETAS
6.4516 g., 0.9000 Gold 0.1867 oz. AGW **Obv:** Head right **Rev:** Crowned and mantled shield **Note:** Mint mark: 6-pointed star.

Date	Mintage	F	VF	XF	Unc	BU
1904 (04) SM-V	3,814	850	1,650	2,250	3,000	—

DECIMAL COINAGE
Peseta System
100 Centimos = 1 Peseta

KM# 726   CENTIMO
Bronze **Ruler:** Alfonso XIII **Obv:** Head right **Rev:** Crowned shield divides value within beaded circle **Note:** Mint mark: 6-pointed star.

Date	Mintage	F	VF	XF	Unc	BU
1906 (6) SL-V	7,500,000	0.35	0.75	1.50	5.00	6.00
1906 (6) SM-V	Inc. above	350	650	800	1,050	1,200

KM# 731   CENTIMO
Bronze **Ruler:** Alfonso XIII **Obv:** Head left **Rev:** Crowned shield divides value within beaded circle **Note:** Mint mark: 6-pointed star.

Date	Mintage	F	VF	XF	Unc	BU
1911 (1) PC-V	1,462,000	45.00	75.00	110	130	150
1912 (2) PC-V	2,109,000	2.00	3.50	7.00	15.00	20.00
1913 (3) PC-V	1,429,000	3.50	6.50	13.50	25.00	30.00

KM# 722   2 CENTIMOS
Copper **Ruler:** Alfonso XIII **Obv:** Head right **Rev:** Crowned shield divides value within beaded circle **Note:** Mint mark: 6-pointed star.

Date	Mintage	F	VF	XF	Unc	BU
1904 (04) SM-V	10,000,000	0.65	2.00	6.00	15.00	20.00
1905 (05) SM-V	5,000,000	0.75	3.00	8.00	20.00	25.00

KM# 732   2 CENTIMOS
Copper **Ruler:** Alfonso XIII **Obv:** Head left **Rev:** Crowned shield divides value within beaded circle **Note:** Mint mark: 6-pointed star.

Date	Mintage	F	VF	XF	Unc	BU
1911 (11) PC-V	2,284,000	0.65	1.75	6.00	15.00	20.00
1912 (12) PC-V	5,216,000	0.65	1.75	5.00	14.00	18.00

KM# 740   25 CENTIMOS
7.0000 g., Copper-Nickel, 25 mm. **Ruler:** Alfonso XIII
Obv: Sailing ship **Obv. Leg.:** ESPAÑA 1927 **Rev:** Crowned value flanked by sprigs **Edge:** plain

Date	Mintage	F	VF	XF	Unc	BU
1925 PC-S	8,001,000	0.50	1.50	12.00	50.00	75.00

KM# 742   25 CENTIMOS
7.0000 g., Copper-Nickel, 25.2 mm. **Ruler:** Alfonso XIII **Obv:** Vine entwined on cross, crown and date, hole in center **Rev:** Value above oat sprigs, hole in center

Date	Mintage	F	VF	XF	Unc	BU
1927 PC-S	12,000,000	0.50	1.00	10.00	50.00	75.00

KM# 723   50 CENTIMOS
2.5000 g., 0.8350 Silver 0.0671 oz. ASW **Ruler:** Alfonso XIII
Obv: Head left **Rev:** Crowned shield flanked by pillars with banner **Note:** Mint mark: 6-pointed star.

Date	Mintage	F	VF	XF	Unc	BU
1904 (04) SM-V	4,851,000	2.50	3.50	7.00	15.00	20.00
1904 (10) PC-V	1,303,000	2.75	4.00	8.00	20.00	25.00

KM# 730   50 CENTIMOS
2.5000 g., 0.8350 Silver 0.0671 oz. ASW **Ruler:** Alfonso XIII
Obv: Head left **Rev:** Crowned shield flanked by pillars with banner **Note:** Mint mark: 6-pointed star.

Date	Mintage	F	VF	XF	Unc	BU
1910 (10) PC-V	4,526,000	2.75	4.00	8.00	24.00	30.00

KM# 741   50 CENTIMOS
2.5000 g., 0.8350 Silver 0.0671 oz. ASW **Ruler:** Alfonso XIII
Obv: Head left **Rev:** Crowned shield within wreath

Date	Mintage	F	VF	XF	Unc	BU
1926 PC-S	4,000,000	2.75	3.50	6.50	12.00	16.00

KM# 706   PESETA
5.0000 g., 0.8350 Silver 0.1342 oz. ASW **Ruler:** Alfonso XIII
Obv: Child's head left **Obv. Leg.:** ALFONSO XIII... **Rev:** Crowned arms, pillars, value below **Rev. Leg.:** REYCONST... **Note:** Mint mark: 6-pointed star. Prices are for coins with full right star dates. Partial right star dates sell for less. Examples with no visable right star date have limited collector appeal.

Date	Mintage	F	VF	XF	Unc	BU
1901 (01) SM-V	8,449,000	5.00	16.00	55.00	125	145
1902 (02) SM-V	2,599,000	25.00	80.00	175	350	400

KM# 721   PESETA
5.0000 g., 0.8350 Silver 0.1342 oz. ASW **Ruler:** Alfonso XIII
Obv: Head left **Rev:** Crowned shield flanked by pillars with banner **Note:** Mint mark 6-pointed star.

Date	Mintage	F	VF	XF	Unc	BU
1903 (03) SM-V	10,602,000	4.00	14.00	40.00	90.00	100
1904 (04) SM-V	5,294,000	5.00	15.00	45.00	95.00	125
1905 (05) SM-V	492,000	45.00	135	550	950	1,100

KM# 725   2 PESETAS
10.0000 g., 0.8350 Silver 0.2684 oz. ASW **Ruler:** Alfonso XIII
Obv: Head left **Rev:** Crowned shield flanked by pillars with banner **Note:** Mint mark: 6-pointed star.

Date	Mintage	F	VF	XF	Unc	BU
1905 (05) SM-V	3,589,000	4.50	15.00	25.00	50.00	55.00

REPUBLIC
1931 - 1939
DECIMAL COINAGE
Peseta System

100 Centimos = 1 Peseta

KM# 752   5 CENTIMOS
Iron **Obv:** Head left **Rev:** Value and date within wreath

Date	Mintage	F	VF	XF	Unc	BU
1937	10,000,000	0.35	1.00	2.00	5.00	10.00

KM# 756   10 CENTIMOS
Iron **Obv:** Crowned shield **Rev:** Value and date within wreath

Date	Mintage	F	VF	XF	Unc	BU
1938	1,000	—	600	1,050	2,100	3,000

Note: This coin was never released into circulation

KM# 751   25 CENTIMOS
Copper-Nickel **Obv:** Bust right holding sprig, hole in center **Rev:** Value above oat sprig and gear, hole in center

Date	Mintage	F	VF	XF	Unc	BU
1934	12,272,000	0.30	0.75	3.50	20.00	25.00

KM# 753   25 CENTIMOS
7.1100 g., Copper-Nickel, 25 mm. **Obv:** Inscription, date and arrow design, hole in center **Rev:** Crowned shield, value and sprig, hole in center

Date	Mintage	F	VF	XF	Unc	BU
1937 Proof	—	Value: 500				
1937	42,000,000	0.20	0.40	1.00	4.00	5.00

Note: This coin was issued by way of decree April 5, 1938, by the Governmant in Burgos. Franco and the Nationalist forces controlled the majority of Spain by this point in time

KM# 757   25 CENTIMOS
Copper **Obv:** Chain links around center hole **Rev:** Value and center hole divide sprigs

Date	Mintage	F	VF	XF	Unc	BU
1938	45,500,000	0.75	1.50	5.00	10.00	15.00

KM# 754.1   50 CENTIMOS
5.8000 g., Copper **Obv:** Seated figure holding sprig **Rev:** Value within beaded circle **Note:** Mint mark: 6-pointed star. Several varieties exist.

Date	Mintage	F	VF	XF	Unc	BU
1937 (34)	50,000,000	0.50	1.00	5.00	15.00	25.00
1937 (36)	1,000,000	0.65	1.50	5.00	11.00	20.00

KM# 754.2   50 CENTIMOS
Copper **Obv:** Seated allegorical figure left **Rev:** Border of rectangles **Note:** Mint mark: 6-pointed star.

Date	Mintage	F	VF	XF	Unc	BU
1937 (36)	Inc. above	1.50	3.00	8.00	20.00	30.00

KM# 750 PESETA
5.0000 g., 0.8350 Silver 0.1342 oz. ASW **Obv:** Seated figure holding sprig **Rev:** Crowned shield flanked by pillars with banner **Note:** Mint mark: 6-pointed star.

Date	Mintage	F	VF	XF	Unc	BU
1933 (3-4)	2,000,000	5.00	15.00	21.00	30.00	35.00

Note: Rotated reverse varieties exist, with values increasing by the degree of rotation.

KM# 755 PESETA
Brass **Obv:** Head left **Rev:** Value and grapes on vine

Date	Mintage	F	VF	XF	Unc	BU
1937	50,000,000	0.35	0.85	2.00	7.50	10.00

NATIONALIST GOVERNMENT
1939 - 1947
DECIMAL COINAGE
Peseta System
100 Centimos = 1 Peseta

KM# 765 5 CENTIMOS
Aluminum **Obv:** Armored figure on rearing horse **Rev:** Crowned shield within eagle flanked by pillars with banner **Note:** Mint mark: 6-pointed star. To realize the values below all Unc. and BU coins must have full strike including letters.

Date	Mintage	F	VF	XF	Unc	BU
1940 PLVS	175,000,000	1.50	5.00	15.00	40.00	55.00
1941	202,107,000	1.00	2.50	3.50	15.00	18.00
1945	221,500,000	—	1.00	3.00	9.00	12.00
1953	31,573,000	12.00	30.00	40.00	70.00	85.00

KM# 766 10 CENTIMOS
8.0700 g., Aluminum, 23 mm. **Obv:** Armored figure on rearing horse **Rev:** Crowned shield within eagle flanked by pillars with banner **Edge:** Coarse reeding **Note:** Varieties exist. To realize the values below all Unc. and BU coins must have full strike including letters.

Date	Mintage	F	VF	XF	Unc	BU
1940 PLUS	225,000,000	0.40	2.00	11.00	45.00	60.00
1940 PLVS	Inc. above	20.00	40.00	80.00	200	250
1941 PLUS	247,981,000	0.50	2.00	5.00	12.50	16.50
1941 PLVS	Inc. above	10.00	20.00	45.00	80.00	100
1945	250,000,000	—	0.60	3.00	11.00	14.00
1953	865,850,000	—	0.35	2.50	6.00	8.00

KM# 767 PESETA
Aluminum-Bronze **Obv:** Crowned shield within eagle flanked by pillars with banner **Rev:** Value in center of design **Note:** To realize the values below all Unc. and BU coins must have full strike including letters.

Date	Mintage	F	VF	XF	Unc	BU
1944	150,000,000	—	0.45	5.00	30.00	40.00

KINGDOM
1949 - Present
DECIMAL COINAGE
Peseta System
100 Centimos = 1 Peseta

KM# 790 10 CENTIMOS
Aluminum, 18 mm. **Ruler:** Caudillo and regent **Obv:** Head right **Rev:** Value within designed wreath **Edge:** Reeded

Date	Mintage	F	VF	XF	Unc	BU
1959	900,000,000	—	—	—	0.25	0.35
1959 Proof	101,000	Value: 3.00				

KM# 776 50 CENTIMOS
Copper-Nickel, 21 mm. **Ruler:** Caudillo and regent **Obv:** Anchor, date and part of captains wheel, hole in center **Rev:** Value, design with arrows pointing down and hole in center divide assorted shields **Edge:** Plain **Note:** Mint mark: 6-pointed star.

Date	Mintage	F	VF	XF	Unc	BU
1949 (51)	990,000	5.00	10.00	15.00	30.00	35.00

Note: Minting date "51" in incused star

KM# 777 50 CENTIMOS
Copper-Nickel, 21 mm. **Ruler:** Caudillo and regent **Obv:** Anchor, date and part of captains wheel, hole in center **Rev:** Value, design with arrows pointing up and hole in center divide assorted shields **Edge:** Plain **Note:** Mint mark: 6-pointed star.

Date	Mintage	F	VF	XF	Unc	BU
1949 (51)	8,010,000	—	2.00	3.00	18.50	25.00
1949 (E51)	Est. 5,000	—	—	—	600	750

Note: Issued to commemorate the 1st Ibero-American Numismatic Exposition December 2, 1951; An "E" replaces the "19" on the lower star

Date	Mintage	F	VF	XF	Unc	BU
1949 (52)	18,567,000	—	0.25	2.00	15.00	20.00
1949 (53)	17,500,000	—	0.50	5.00	25.00	30.00
1949 (54)	37,000,000	—	0.60	4.00	15.00	20.00
1949 (56)	38,000,000	—	0.15	2.00	12.00	15.00
1949 (62)	31,000,000	—	0.20	1.50	7.00	10.00
1963 (63)	4,000,000	1.50	5.50	9.00	30.00	35.00
1963 (64)	20,000,000	—	0.10	0.25	2.50	3.50
1963 (65)	14,000,000	—	0.10	0.20	1.50	2.50

KM# 795 50 CENTIMOS
1.1000 g., Aluminum, 20.1 mm. **Ruler:** Caudillo and regent **Obv:** Head right **Rev:** Sprig divides value **Edge:** Reeded **Note:** Mint mark: 6-pointed star. These coins generally suffer from oxidation and the values given are for perfect proof specimens.

Date	Mintage	F	VF	XF	Unc	BU
1966 (67)	80,000,000	—	—	0.15	0.75	1.00
1966 (68)	100,000,000	—	—	0.15	0.60	1.00
1966 (69)	50,000,000	—	—	0.25	2.50	3.00
1966 (70) Prooflike, in sets only	—	—	—	—	125	175
1966 (71)	99,000,000	—	—	0.15	0.35	0.75
1966 (72)	2,283,000	—	—	0.25	2.50	3.00
1966 (72) Proof	30,000	Value: 5.00				
1966 (73)	10,000,000	—	—	0.15	0.35	0.50
1966 (73) Proof	25,000	Value: 3.50				
1966 (74) Proof	23,000	Value: 50.00				
1966 (75) Proof	75,000	Value: 10.00				

KM# 805 50 CENTIMOS
Copper-Nickel **Ruler:** Juan Carlos I **Obv:** Head left **Rev:** Sprig divides value **Note:** Mint mark: 6-pointed star.

Date	Mintage	F	VF	XF	Unc	BU
1975 (76)	4,060,000	—	—	0.10	0.20	0.50
1975 (76) Proof	—	Value: 0.85				

KM# 815 50 CENTIMOS
Aluminum, 20 mm. **Ruler:** Juan Carlos I **Subject:** World Cup Soccer Games **Obv:** Head left **Rev:** Soccer ball and globe above value **Edge:** Reeded **Note:** Mint mark: 6-pointed star.

Date	Mintage	F	VF	XF	Unc	BU
1980 (80)	15,000,000	—	—	0.10	0.20	0.35
1980 (80) Proof	—	Value: 0.75				

KM# 775 PESETA
Aluminum-Bronze, 21 mm. **Ruler:** Francisco Franco, caudillo **Obv:** Head right **Rev:** Crowned shield within eagle flanked by pillars with banner **Edge:** Reeded **Note:** Mint mark: 6-pointed star.

Date	Mintage	F	VF	XF	Unc	BU
1946 (48)	Est. 5,000	1,000	1,500	2,000	3,000	—
1947 (48)	15,000,000	—	1.00	15.00	150	200
1947 (49)	27,600,000	—	0.75	15.00	150	175
1947 (50)	4,000,000	1.50	6.00	50.00	500	750
1947 (51)	9,185,000	2.00	4.00	40.00	300	500
1947 (E51)	Est. 5,000	—	—	—	600	800

Note: Issued to commemorate the 2nd National Numismatic Exposition December 2, 1951; An "E" replaces the "19" on the lower star

Date	Mintage	F	VF	XF	Unc	BU
1947 (52)	19,195,000	—	1.00	10.00	75.00	150
1947 (53)	34,000,000	—	0.75	10.00	70.00	150
1947 (54)	50,000,000	—	1.00	15.00	75.00	200
1947 (56)	—	10.00	30.00	100	600	1,000
1953 (54)	40,272,000	—	3.00	30.00	250	325
1953 (56)	118,000,000	—	0.10	1.00	5.00	8.00
1953 (60)	45,160,000	—	0.70	10.50	75.00	125
1953 (61)	25,830,000	—	0.60	10.00	50.00	90.00
1953 (62)	66,252,000	—	0.10	1.00	3.00	7.00
1953 (63)	37,000,000	—	0.25	1.50	15.00	30.00
1963 (63)	36,000,000	—	0.35	2.25	20.00	25.00
1963 (64)	80,000,000	—	0.10	1.00	3.00	5.00
1963 (65)	70,000,000	—	0.10	1.00	3.00	5.00
1963 (66)	63,000,000	—	0.10	1.00	5.00	10.00
1963 (67)	11,300,000	—	2.00	10.00	50.00	100

KM# 796 PESETA
Aluminum-Bronze, 21 mm. **Ruler:** Caudillo and regent **Obv:** Head right **Rev:** Crowned shield within eagle flanked by pillars with banner **Edge:** Reeded **Note:** Mint mark: 6-pointed star.

Date	Mintage	F	VF	XF	Unc	BU
1966 (67)	59,000,000	—	0.15	0.30	1.50	4.50
1966 (68)	120,000,000	—	0.10	0.20	1.00	1.50
1966 (69)	120,000,000	—	0.10	0.20	1.00	1.50
1966 (70)	75,000,000	—	0.10	0.20	2.00	3.00
1966 (71)	115,270,000	—	0.10	0.15	0.75	1.50
1966 (72)	106,000,000	—	—	0.10	0.50	0.75
1966 (72) Proof	30,000	Value: 1.50				
1966 (73)	152,000,000	—	—	0.10	0.35	0.65
1966 (73) Proof	25,000	Value: 1.50				
1966 (74)	181,000,000	—	—	0.10	0.35	0.65
1966 (74) Proof	23,000	Value: 1.50				
1966 (75)	227,580,000	—	—	0.10	0.25	0.35
1966 (75) Proof	75,000	Value: 1.00				

KM# 806 PESETA
Aluminum-Bronze, 21 mm. **Ruler:** Juan Carlos I **Obv:** Head left **Rev:** Crowned shield within eagle flanked by pillars with banner **Edge:** Reeded

Date	Mintage	F	VF	XF	Unc	BU
1975 (76)	170,380,000	—	—	0.10	0.25	0.35
1975 (76) Proof			Value: 0.75			
1975 (77)	243,380,000	—	—	0.10	0.25	0.35
1975 (77) Proof			Value: 0.75			
1975 (78)	Est. 603,320,000	—	—	0.10	0.25	0.35
1975 (79)	507,000,000	—	—	0.10	0.25	0.35

Note: Two varieties of tilde size for the n in España exist of this date; Large is Madrid mint, small is Santiago de Chile

1975 (79) Proof			Value: 0.75			
1975 (80)	590,000,000	—	—	0.10	0.25	0.50

KM# 816 PESETA
Aluminum-Bronze, 21 mm. **Ruler:** Juan Carlos I **Subject:** World Cup Soccer Games **Obv:** Head left **Rev:** Small crowned shield within eagle at left of value

Date	Mintage	F	VF	XF	Unc	BU
1980 (80)	—	—	—	0.10	0.15	0.30
1980 (80) Proof			Value: 0.75			
1980 (81)	385,000,000	—	—	0.10	0.25	0.35
1980 (82)	333,000,000	—	—	0.10	0.25	0.35

KM# 821 PESETA
1.2000 g., Aluminum, 21 mm. **Ruler:** Juan Carlos I **Obv:** Head left **Rev:** Crowned shield flanked by pillars with banner to right of value

Date	Mintage	F	VF	XF	Unc	BU
1982	—	—	—	0.10	0.20	0.35

Note: Mintage included in KM#816, 1980 (82)

1983	52,000,000	—	—	0.10	0.50	0.75
1984	131,000,000	—	—	0.10	0.20	0.35
1985	220,065,000	—	—	0.10	0.20	0.35
1986	299,960,000	—	—	0.10	0.20	0.35
1987	299,550,000	—	—	0.10	0.20	0.35
1988	223,460,000	—	—	0.10	0.20	0.35
1989	—	—	—	0.10	0.60	1.00

Note: Mintage included in KM#832, 1989

KM# 828 PESETA
Aluminum, 21 mm. **Ruler:** Juan Carlos I **Subject:** 3rd National Numismatic Exposition - Madrid **Obv:** Head left **Rev:** Crowned shield flanked by pillars with banner at right of value

Date	Mintage	F	VF	XF	Unc	BU
1987/E-87 Proof	60,000	Value: 50.00				

KM# 832 PESETA
Aluminum, 14 mm. **Ruler:** Juan Carlos I **Obv:** Vertical line divides head left from value **Rev:** Crowned shield flanked by pillars with banner **Edge:** Plain

Date	Mintage	F	VF	XF	Unc	BU
1989	198,415,000	—	—	0.10	0.25	0.50
1990	197,700,000	—	—	0.10	0.25	0.50
1991	173,780,000	—	—	0.10	0.25	0.50
1992	168,870,000	—	—	0.10	0.20	0.25
1993	300,013,000	—	—	0.10	0.20	0.25
1994	162,860,000	—	—	0.10	0.20	0.25
1995	183,175,000	—	—	0.10	0.20	0.25
1996	101,885,000	—	—	0.10	0.20	0.25

Date	Mintage	F	VF	XF	Unc	BU
1997	342,620,000	—	—	0.10	0.20	0.25
1998	411,614,000	—	—	0.10	0.20	0.25
1999	84,946,000	—	—	0.10	0.20	0.25
2000	—	—	—	0.10	0.20	0.25

KM# 822 2 PESETAS
2.0000 g., Aluminum, 24 mm. **Ruler:** Juan Carlos I **Obv:** Head left **Rev:** Value within map

Date	Mintage	F	VF	XF	Unc	BU
1982	21,500,000	—	—	0.20	0.50	0.75
1984	47,650,000	—	—	0.20	0.45	0.65

KM# 785 2-1/2 PESETAS
Aluminum-Bronze **Ruler:** Caudillo and regent **Obv:** Head right **Rev:** Crowned shield within eagle flanked by pillars with banner

Date	Mintage	F	VF	XF	Unc	BU
1953 (54)	22,729,000	—	0.25	1.00	5.00	10.00
1953 (56)	30,322,000	—	0.25	1.00	5.00	10.00
1953 (56) Proof			Value: 100			
1953 (68)	1,000	—	—	—	—	1,500
	Note: In sets only					
1953 (69)	2,000	—	—	—	—	1,250
	Note: In sets only					
1953 (70)	6,000	—	—	—	—	140
	Note: In sets only					
1953 (71)	10,000	—	—	—	—	150
	Note: In sets only					

KM# 778 5 PESETAS
Nickel, 32 mm. **Ruler:** Caudillo and regent **Obv:** Head right **Rev:** Crowned shield within eagle flanked by pillars with banner **Edge:** Reeded

Date	Mintage	F	VF	XF	Unc	BU
1949 (49)	612,000	—	2.50	10.00	20.00	30.00
1949 (50)	21,000,000	—	0.85	2.00	5.00	10.00
1949 (E51)	Est. 6,000	—	—	—	1,500	2,250

Note: Issued to commemorate the Second National Numismatic Exposition December 2, 1951; An "E" replaces the "19" on the lower star

1949 (51) Rare	145,000	—	—	—	—	—
1949 (52) Rare	Est. 200,000	—	—	—	—	—

KM# 786 5 PESETAS
5.7500 g., Copper-Nickel, 23 mm. **Ruler:** Caudillo and regent **Obv:** Head right **Rev:** Crowned shield within flying bird **Edge:** Reeded **Note:** Values in uncirculated drop by 50% or more when the PLUS in legend is not readable. This defect is most often seen on coins struck before 1968.

Date	Mintage	F	VF	XF	Unc	BU
1957 BA	Est. 43,000	—	100	150	225	300

Note: Issued to commemorate the 1958 2nd Ibero-American Numismatic Exposition in Barcelona with "BA" replacing the star on left side of reverse

1957 (58)	13,000,000	—	—	0.45	3.00	50.00	100
1957 (59)	107,000,000	—	—	0.10	1.00	25.00	30.00
1957 (60)	26,000,000	—	—	0.10	1.00	10.00	20.00
1957 (61)	78,992,000	—	—	0.15	3.50	25.00	35.00
1957 (62)	40,963,000	—	—	0.10	1.00	10.00	20.00
1957 (63)	50,000,000	—	—	2.00	15.00	125	175

Date	Mintage	F	VF	XF	Unc	BU
1957 (64)	51,000,000	—	0.10	1.00	10.00	20.00
1957 (65)	25,000,000	—	0.15	0.75	8.00	15.00
1957 (66)	28,000,000	—	0.15	3.50	25.00	35.00
1957 (67)	30,000,000	—	0.15	0.75	5.00	10.00
1957 (68)	60,000,000	—	0.20	0.60	3.00	4.00
1957 (69)	40,000,000	—	0.20	0.60	3.00	5.00
1957 (70)	43,000,000	—	0.20	0.60	3.00	9.00
1957 (71)	77,000,000	—	0.20	0.60	1.50	3.00
1957 (72)	70,000,000	—	—	0.55	3.00	4.00
1957 (72) Proof	30,000	Value: 5.00				
1957 (73)	78,000,000	—	—	0.10	0.75	2.00
1957 (73) Proof	25,000	Value: 2.50				
1957 (74)	100,000,000	—	—	0.10	0.45	1.00
1957 (74) Proof	23,000	Value: 2.50				
1957 (75)	139,047,000	—	—	0.10	0.25	0.50
1957 (75) Proof	75,000	Value: 1.00				

KM# 811 5 PESETAS
Copper-Nickel **Ruler:** Juan Carlos I **Obv:** Head left **Rev:** World globe, soccerball, value and star with numeral 80 **Note:** Mule.

Date	Mintage	F	VF	XF	Unc	BU
1975 (80)	Est. 30,000	—	—	200	300	350

KM# 807 5 PESETAS
5.7500 g., Copper-Nickel, 23 mm. **Ruler:** Juan Carlos I **Obv:** Head left **Rev:** Crossed scepters and shield within wreath divides value, crown on top **Edge:** Reeded

Date	Mintage	F	VF	XF	Unc	BU
1975 (76)	150,560,000	—	—	0.10	0.25	0.35
1975 (76) Proof	—	Value: 1.00				
1975 (77)	154,982,000	—	—	0.10	0.25	0.35
1975 (77) Proof	Inc. above	Value: 1.00				
1975 (78)	412,610,000	—	—	0.10	0.35	0.50
1975 (79)	436,000,000	—	—	0.10	0.25	0.35
1975 (79) Proof	—	Value: 1.00				
1975 (80)	322,000,000	—	—	0.10	0.50	1.00

KM# 817 5 PESETAS
5.7500 g., Copper-Nickel, 23 mm. **Ruler:** Juan Carlos I **Subject:** World Cup Soccer Games **Obv:** Head left **Rev:** Numeral 82 on world globe, soccer ball above value

Date	Mintage	F	VF	XF	Unc	BU
1980 (80)	75,000,000	—	—	0.10	0.25	0.35
1980 (80) Proof	—	Value: 1.00				
1980 (81)	294,000,000	—	—	0.10	0.25	0.50
1980 (82)	291,000,000	—	—	0.10	0.25	0.50

KM# 823 5 PESETAS
5.7500 g., Copper-Nickel, 23 mm. **Ruler:** Juan Carlos I **Obv:** Head left **Rev:** Crossed scepters and shield within wreath divide value, crown on top **Note:** Mint mark: Crowned M.

Date	Mintage	F	VF	XF	Unc	BU
1982	—	—	—	0.10	1.00	1.50

Note: Mintage included in KM#817, 1980 (82)

1983	200,000,000	—	—	0.10	0.50	0.65
1984	169,000,000	—	—	0.10	0.60	0.80
1989	—	—	—	0.10	0.75	1.00

KM# 833 5 PESETAS
3.0500 g., Aluminum-Bronze, 18 mm. **Ruler:** Juan Carlos I **Obv:** Stylized design and date **Rev:** Value above stylized sailboats **Edge:** Plain

Date	Mintage	F	VF	XF	Unc	BU
1989	109,270,000	—	—	0.10	0.30	0.50
1990	191,740,000	—	—	0.10	0.50	1.00

Date	Mintage	F	VF	XF	Unc	BU
1991	313,820,000	—	—	0.10	0.45	0.85
1992	493,224,000	—	—	0.10	0.35	0.50
1998	923,978,000	—	—	0.10	0.25	0.35
2000	—	—	—	0.10	0.25	0.35

KM# 919 5 PESETAS
Nickel-Brass, 17.5 mm. **Ruler:** Juan Carlos I **Subject:** Jacobeo **Obv:** Standing figure with staff at left of design **Rev:** Value, dates and design **Edge:** Plain **Note:** Coins with extra metal in the denomination 5 sell for a premium.

Date	Mintage	F	VF	XF	Unc	BU
1993	372,746,000	—	—	—	0.25	0.35

KM# 931 5 PESETAS
Nickel-Brass, 17.5 mm. **Ruler:** Juan Carlos I **Subject:** Aragon **Obv:** Front view of building **Rev:** Ballerina **Edge:** Plain **Note:** Wide rim variety exists.

Date	Mintage	F	VF	XF	Unc	BU
1994	199,678,000	—	—	—	0.25	0.40

KM# 946 5 PESETAS
Aluminum-Bronze, 17.5 mm. **Ruler:** Juan Carlos I **Subject:** Asturias **Obv:** Cross and date **Rev:** Value and design **Edge:** Plain

Date	Mintage	F	VF	XF	Unc	BU
1995	301,756,000	—	—	—	0.25	0.40

KM# 960 5 PESETAS
Aluminum-Bronze, 17.5 mm. **Ruler:** Juan Carlos I **Subject:** La Rioja **Obv:** Front view of building **Rev:** Figure on stilts, value and grapes **Edge:** Plain

Date	Mintage	F	VF	XF	Unc	BU
1996	674,168,000	—	—	—	0.15	0.25

KM# 981 5 PESETAS
Brass, 17.5 mm. **Ruler:** Juan Carlos I **Subject:** Balearic Islands **Obv:** Stone monument **Rev:** Figure on rearing horse **Edge:** Plain

Date	Mintage	F	VF	XF	Unc	BU
1997	709,006,000	—	—	—	0.15	0.25

KM# 1008 5 PESETAS
Brass, 17.5 mm. **Ruler:** Juan Carlos I **Obv:** Crowned shield with supporters on arch **Rev:** Murcia waterwheel **Edge:** Plain

Date	Mintage	F	VF	XF	Unc	BU
1999	216,230,000	—	—	—	0.15	0.25

KM# 827 10 PESETAS
4.0000 g., Copper-Nickel, 18.5 mm. **Ruler:** Juan Carlos I **Obv:** Head left **Rev:** Crowned shield flanked by pillars with banner **Note:** Denomination "DIEZ".

Date	Mintage	F	VF	XF	Unc	BU
1983	149,000,000	—	—	0.25	0.35	0.40

Date	Mintage	F	VF	XF	Unc	BU
1984	66,000,000	—	—	0.25	0.40	0.50
1985	45,706,000	—	—	0.25	0.50	0.60

KM# 903 10 PESETAS
4.0000 g., Copper-Nickel, 18.5 mm. **Ruler:** Juan Carlos I **Obv:** Head left **Rev:** Crowned shield flanked by pillars with banner **Edge:** Reeded

Date	Mintage	F	VF	XF	Unc	BU
1992	51,820,000	—	—	0.25	0.40	0.50

KM# 918 10 PESETAS
4.0000 g., Copper-Nickel, 18.5 mm. **Ruler:** Juan Carlos I **Subject:** Juan Miro **Obv:** Value, dates and inscription **Rev:** Head 3/4 right **Edge:** Plain

Date	Mintage	F	VF	XF	Unc	BU
1993	53,845,000	—	—	0.25	0.60	1.00

KM# 932 10 PESETAS
4.0000 g., Copper-Nickel, 18.5 mm. **Ruler:** Juan Carlos I **Subject:** Musician P. Sarasate **Obv:** Head right **Rev:** Violin **Edge:** Reeded

Date	Mintage	F	VF	XF	Unc	BU
1994	3,050,000	—	—	0.35	1.25	2.00

KM# 947 10 PESETAS
4.0000 g., Copper-Nickel, 18.5 mm. **Ruler:** Juan Carlos I **Subject:** Don Francisco de Quevedo **Obv:** Bust 1/4 left **Rev:** Quill in ink, book, glasses and value **Edge:** Reeded

Date	Mintage	F	VF	XF	Unc	BU
1995	1,050,000	—	—	1.00	4.00	5.00

KM# 961 10 PESETAS
4.0000 g., Copper-Nickel, 18.5 mm. **Ruler:** Juan Carlos I **Subject:** Emilia Pardo Bazan **Obv:** Monument and value **Rev:** Half length figure facing **Edge:** Reeded

Date	Mintage	F	VF	XF	Unc	BU
1996	1,060,000	—	—	0.30	1.75	2.50

KM# 982 10 PESETAS
4.0000 g., Copper-Nickel, 18.5 mm. **Ruler:** Juan Carlos I **Subject:** Seneca **Obv:** Head facing **Rev:** Castle gate

Date	Mintage	F	VF	XF	Unc	BU
1997	—	—	—	0.25	0.40	0.50

KM# 1012 10 PESETAS
4.0000 g., Copper-Nickel, 18.5 mm. **Ruler:** Juan Carlos I **Obv:** Head left **Rev:** Value above national arms **Edge:** Reeded **Note:** Older portrait.

Date	Mintage	F	VF	XF	Unc	BU
1998	14,965,000	—	—	0.25	0.75	1.00
1999	2,125,000	—	—	0.35	0.85	1.00
2000	—	—	—	0.25	0.65	0.75

KM# 787 25 PESETAS
8.5000 g., Copper-Nickel, 26.5 mm. **Ruler:** Caudillo and regent **Obv:** Head right **Rev:** Crowned shield within flying bird **Edge:** UNA GRANDE LIBRE **Note:** Values in uncirculated drop by 50% or more when the "PLUS" in legend is not readable. This defect is most often seen on coins struck before 1968.

Date	Mintage	F	VF	XF	Unc	BU
1957 (58)	8,635,000	—	0.35	7.00	70.00	100
1957(BA)	43,000	—	25.00	55.00	85.00	100

Note: Issued to commemorate the 1958 Barcelona Exposition with "BA" replacing the star on left side of the reverse

Date	Mintage	F	VF	XF	Unc	BU
1957 (59)	42,185,000	—	0.30	1.50	30.00	50.00
1957 (61)	24,120,000	—	2.00	20.00	160	200
1957 (64)	42,200,000	—	0.15	1.50	20.00	30.00
1957 (65)	20,000,000	—	0.20	1.00	8.00	15.00
1957 (66)	15,000,000	—	0.20	1.00	10.00	15.00
1957 (67)	20,000,000	—	0.15	1.50	20.00	30.00
1957 (68)	30,000,000	—	0.20	1.00	2.50	5.00
1957 (69)	24,000,000	—	0.30	0.75	2.00	4.00
1957 (70)	25,000,000	—	0.20	1.00	5.00	7.00
1957 (71)	7,800,000	—	1.00	5.00	35.00	60.00
1957 (72)	4,733,000	—	0.20	0.75	4.00	8.00
1957 (72) Proof	30,000	Value: 10.00				
1957 (73) Proof	25,000	Value: 80.00				
1957 (74)	5,000,000	—	0.30	0.65	5.00	8.00
1957 (74) Proof	23,000	Value: 10.00				
1957 (75)	10,270,000	—	0.30	0.65	2.25	3.00
1957 (75) Proof	75,000	Value: 3.50				

KM# 808 25 PESETAS
8.5000 g., Copper-Nickel, 26.5 mm. **Ruler:** Juan Carlos I **Obv:** Head left **Rev:** Crown above value **Edge:** UNA GRANDE LIBRE

Date	Mintage	F	VF	XF	Unc	BU
1975 (76)	35,707,000	—	0.20	0.25	0.75	1.00
1975 (76) Proof	—	Value: 1.00				
1975 (77)	46,690,000	—	0.20	0.25	0.75	1.00
1975 (77) Proof	Inc. above	Value: 1.00				
1975 (78)	97,555,000	—	0.20	0.25	2.00	3.00
1975 (79)	172,000,000	—	0.20	0.25	0.75	1.00
1975 (79) Proof	—	Value: 1.00				
1975 (80)	136,000,000	—	0.20	0.25	2.50	5.00

KM# 818 25 PESETAS
8.5000 g., Copper-Nickel, 26.5 mm. **Ruler:** Juan Carlos I **Subject:** World Cup Soccer Games **Obv:** Head left **Rev:** Soccer ball on net above value **Edge:** UNA GRANDE LIBRE

Date	Mintage	F	VF	XF	Unc	BU
1980 (80)	35,000,000	—	0.20	0.30	0.60	0.75
1980 (80) Proof	—	Value: 1.50				
1980 (81)	117,000,000	—	0.20	0.30	0.75	1.00
1980 (82)	100,000,000	—	0.20	0.30	1.00	2.00

KM# 824 25 PESETAS
8.5000 g., Copper-Nickel, 26.5 mm. **Ruler:** Juan Carlos I **Obv:** Head left **Rev:** Crown above value **Edge:** Reeded **Note:** Mint mark: Crowned M; Similar to KM#808.

Date	Mintage	F	VF	XF	Unc	BU
1982	146,000,000	—	0.20	0.30	2.00	3.00

Date	Mintage	F	VF	XF	Unc	BU
1983	248,000,000	—	0.30	0.45	1.50	2.25
1984	242,000,000	—	0.20	0.30	3.50	5.00

KM# 850 25 PESETAS
Nickel-Bronze, 19.5 mm. Ruler: Juan Carlos I Subject: 1992 Olympics Obv: Discus thrower to right of center hole Rev: Center hole divides value, Olympic rings below

Date	Mintage	F	VF	XF	Unc	BU
1990	150,000,000	—	0.25	0.30	1.25	1.50
1991	Inc. above	—	0.20	0.25	3.50	6.50

KM# 851 25 PESETAS
Nickel-Bronze, 19.5 mm. Ruler: Juan Carlos I Subject: 1992 Olympics Obv: Center hole divides letters and bust left Rev: High jumper to upper right of center hole Edge: Plain

Date	Mintage	F	VF	XF	Unc	BU
1990	Inc. above	—	—	—	0.95	1.50
1991	87,000,000	—	—	—	2.50	3.00

KM# 904 25 PESETAS
Nickel-Bronze, 19.5 mm. Ruler: Juan Carlos I Subject: Giralda Tower of Sevilla Obv: Center hole divides letters and bust left Rev: Center hole divides tower and value

Date	Mintage	F	VF	XF	Unc	BU
1992	179,833,000	—	—	—	2.50	3.00

KM# 905 25 PESETAS
Nickel-Bronze, 19.5 mm. Ruler: Juan Carlos I Subject: Tower of Gold in Seville Obv: Globe design around center hole Rev: Center hole divides tower and vertical letters Edge: Plain

Date	Mintage	F	VF	XF	Unc	BU
1992	Inc. above	—	—	—	1.00	1.25

KM# 920 25 PESETAS
Nickel-Bronze, 19.5 mm. Ruler: Juan Carlos I Subject: Vasc Country Obv: Center hole divides inscription, date and design Rev: Center hole divides value and buildings

Date	Mintage	F	VF	XF	Unc	BU
1993	150,012,000	—	—	—	0.80	1.00

KM# 933 25 PESETAS
Nickel-Bronze, 19.5 mm. Ruler: Juan Carlos I Subject: Canary Islands Obv: Center hole divides inscription, date and flowers Rev: Center hole divides value, design and inscription Edge: Plain

Date	Mintage	F	VF	XF	Unc	BU
1994	242,566,000	—	—	—	0.60	0.75

KM# 948 25 PESETAS
Brass, 19.5 mm. Ruler: Juan Carlos I Subject: Castilla and Leon Obv: Center hole divides tower and inscription Rev: Center hole divides stylized animal figures, value and inscription Edge: Plain

Date	Mintage	F	VF	XF	Unc	BU
1995 without Y	Inc. above	—	—	45.00	75.00	100
1995	221,963,000	—	—	—	1.00	1.25

KM# 962 25 PESETAS
Copper-Zinc-Nickel, 19.5 mm. Ruler: Juan Carlos I Subject: Castilla - La Mancha - Don Quiote Obv: Center hole divides figure on horse, design and inscription Rev: Center hole divides design, inscription and value Edge: Plain

Date	Mintage	F	VF	XF	Unc	BU
1996	37,403,000	—	—	—	0.45	0.70

KM# 983 25 PESETAS
Brass, 19.5 mm. Ruler: Juan Carlos I Subject: Melilla Obv: Center hole divides towered buildings Rev: Center hole divides ancient amphora and dates Edge: Plain

Date	Mintage	F	VF	XF	Unc	BU
1997	461,688,000	—	—	—	0.45	0.70

KM# 990 25 PESETAS
Copper-Zinc-Nickel, 19.5 mm. Ruler: Juan Carlos I Subject: Ceuta Obv: Center hole right of ornamented building corner Rev: Center hole divides statue on wall shelf and value Edge: Plain

Date	Mintage	F	VF	XF	Unc	BU
1998	184,360,000	—	—	—	0.50	0.80

KM# 1007 25 PESETAS
4.3000 g., Nickel-Brass, 19.5 mm. Ruler: Juan Carlos I Subject: Navarra Obv: Center hole between castle towers Rev: Man running from bull, value and shield, all around center hole Edge: Plain

Date	Mintage	F	VF	XF	Unc	BU
1999	2,130,000	—	—	—	1.50	2.00

KM# 1013 25 PESETAS
4.2000 g., Nickel-Brass, 19.5 mm. Ruler: Juan Carlos I Subject: Navarra Obv: Center hole divides bust left and vertical letters Rev: Crowned above center hole, order collar at right, value at left Edge: Plain

Date	Mintage	F	VF	XF	Unc	BU
2000	—	—	—	—	1.00	1.50

KM# 788 50 PESETAS
12.3500 g., Copper-Nickel, 30 mm. Ruler: Caudillo and regent Obv: Head right Rev: Crowned shield within flying bird Edge: UNA GRANDE LIBRE

Date	Mintage	F	VF	XF	Unc	BU
1957 (BA)	Est. 43,000	—	30.00	60.00	80.00	125

Note: Issued to commemorate the 1958 Barcelona Exposition with "BA" replacing the star on left side of reverse

1957 (58)	21,471,000	—	0.50	0.75	2.50	3.50
1957 (58)	Inc. above	100	200	350	600	700

Note: Edge variety with UNA - LIBRE - GRANDE

1957 (59)	28,000,000	—	0.50	0.75	2.50	3.50
1957 (60)	24,800,000	—	0.50	0.75	2.50	3.50
1957 (67)	850,000	—	0.50	2.00	8.00	10.00
1957 (68)	1,000	—	—	—	—	1,500

Note: In sets only

1957 (69)	1,200	—	—	—	—	1,250

Note: In sets only

1957 (70)	19,000	—	—	—	—	250

Note: In sets only

1957(71)	4,400,000	—	0.65	2.50	18.50	35.00
1957 (72) Proof	23,000	Value: 35.00				
1957 (73) Proof	28,000	Value: 60.00				
1957 (74) Proof	25,000	Value: 60.00				
1957 (75) Proof	75,000	Value: 15.00				

KM# 809 50 PESETAS
12.3500 g., Copper-Nickel, 30 mm. Ruler: Juan Carlos I Obv: Head left Rev: Crossed scepters and shield within order collar, crown above

Date	Mintage	F	VF	XF	Unc	BU
1975 (78)	17,555,000	—	0.50	0.75	2.50	3.00
1975 (79)	33,000,000	—	0.50	0.60	1.00	1.50
1975 (79) Proof	—	Value: 2.00				
1975 (80)	34,000,000	—	0.50	0.60	3.50	4.50
1975 (81)	4,400,000	—	0.50	0.60	1.00	1.25
1975 (76) Proof	—	Value: 2.00				

KM# 819 50 PESETAS
12.3500 g., Copper-Nickel, 30 mm. Ruler: Juan Carlos I Subject: World Cup Soccer Games Obv: Head left Rev: Soccer ball above value Edge: UNA GRANDE LIBRE

Date	Mintage	F	VF	XF	Unc	BU
1980 (80)	15,000,000	—	0.50	0.60	0.75	0.85
1980 (80) Proof	—	Value: 2.00				
1980 (81)	38,300,000	—	0.50	0.60	1.35	1.50
1980 (82)	30,950,000	—	0.50	0.60	2.00	2.50

KM# 825 50 PESETAS
12.3500 g., Copper-Nickel, 30 mm. Ruler: Juan Carlos I Obv: Head left Rev: Crossed scepters and shield within order collar, crown above Note: Mint mark: Crowned M.

Date	Mintage	F	VF	XF	Unc	BU
1982	27,000,000	—	0.50	1.00	2.50	4.50

Date	Mintage	F	VF	XF	Unc	BU
1983	93,000,000	—	0.50	1.00	2.00	3.00
1984	17,500,000	5.00	12.00	20.00	40.00	70.00

KM# 852   50 PESETAS
Copper-Nickel, 20.3 mm. **Ruler:** Juan Carlos I **Subject:** Expo '92 **Obv:** Bust left **Rev:** Globe and value **Edge:** Notched

Date	Mintage	F	VF	XF	Unc	BU
1990	25,234,000	—	—	—	1.00	1.25

KM# 853   50 PESETAS
Copper-Nickel, 20.3 mm. **Ruler:** Juan Carlos I **Subject:** Expo '92 **Obv:** City view **Rev:** Globe and value **Edge:** Notched

Date	Mintage	F	VF	XF	Unc	BU
1990	7,916,000	—	—	—	1.00	1.25

KM# 906   50 PESETAS
Copper-Nickel, 20.3 mm. **Ruler:** Juan Carlos I **Subject:** 1992 Olympics **Obv:** "La Pedrera" building **Rev:** Pointed designs above Olympic rings, value at left **Edge:** Notched

Date	Mintage	F	VF	XF	Unc	BU
1992	40,370,000	—	—	—	1.00	1.25

KM# 907   50 PESETAS
Copper-Nickel, 20.3 mm. **Ruler:** Juan Carlos I **Subject:** 1992 Olympics **Obv:** Bust left **Rev:** Cathedral Sagrada Familia (Gaudi) **Edge:** Notched

Date	Mintage	F	VF	XF	Unc	BU
1992	Inc. above	—	—	—	1.00	1.25

KM# 921   50 PESETAS
Copper-Nickel, 20.3 mm. **Ruler:** Juan Carlos I **Subject:** Extremadura **Obv:** Bridge **Rev:** Tower **Edge:** Notched

Date	Mintage	F	VF	XF	Unc	BU
1993	24,314,000	—	—	—	1.00	1.25

KM# 934   50 PESETAS
Copper-Nickel, 20.3 mm. **Ruler:** Juan Carlos I **Subject:** Altamira Cave Paintings **Obv:** Building **Rev:** Stylized design above value **Edge:** Notched

Date	Mintage	F	VF	XF	Unc	BU
1994	3,002,000	—	—	—	2.25	3.00

KM# 949   50 PESETAS
Copper-Nickel, 20.3 mm. **Ruler:** Juan Carlos I **Subject:** Alcala Gate **Obv:** Partial building and date **Rev:** Steepled buildings **Edge:** Notched

Date	Mintage	F	VF	XF	Unc	BU
1995	1,001,000	—	—	—	4.00	5.00

KM# 963   50 PESETAS
Copper-Nickel, 20.3 mm. **Ruler:** Juan Carlos I **Subject:** Philip V **Obv:** Head facing **Rev:** Shield divides value and letters, crown above divides date **Edge:** Notched

Date	Mintage	F	VF	XF	Unc	BU
1996	11,047,000	—	—	—	0.75	1.00

KM# 985   50 PESETAS
Copper-Nickel, 20.3 mm. **Ruler:** Juan Carlos I **Subject:** Juan De Herrera **Obv:** Head left **Rev:** Escorial Monastery **Edge:** Notched

Date	Mintage	F	VF	XF	Unc	BU
1997	17,496,000	—	—	—	1.00	1.25

KM# 991   50 PESETAS
Copper-Nickel, 20.3 mm. **Ruler:** Juan Carlos I **Obv:** Bust left **Rev:** Crossed scepters and shield within order chain, crown above, value at left **Edge:** Notched

Date	Mintage	F	VF	XF	Unc	BU
1998	17,496,000	—	—	—	1.00	1.50
1999	2,100,000	—	—	—	2.25	3.00
2000		—	—	—	2.00	2.50

KM# 797   100 PESETAS
19.0000 g., 0.8000 Silver 0.4887 oz. ASW **Ruler:** Caudillo and regent **Obv:** Head right **Rev:** Assorted emblems within flower design, crown on top **Edge:** UNA GRANDE LIBRE

Date	Mintage	F	VF	XF	Unc	BU
1966 (66)	15,045,000	—	BV	BV	7.50	9.00
1966 (67)	15,000,000	—	BV	BV	7.50	9.00
1966 (68)	24,000,000	—	BV	BV	7.50	9.00
1966 (69)	1,000,000	—	—	175	400	500

Note: 69 with straight 9 in star

1966 (69)	Inc. above	—	—	75.00	150	175

Note: 69 with curved 9 in star

1966 (70)	995,000	BV	7.50	10.00	20.00	25.00

Note: 1966(69) coins heavily altered; authentication recommended

KM# 810   100 PESETAS
Copper-Nickel **Ruler:** Juan Carlos I **Obv:** Head left **Rev:** Crowned shield flanked by pillars with banner

Date	Mintage	F	VF	XF	Unc	BU
1975 (76)	4,400,000	—	0.75	1.00	1.50	2.00
1975 (76) Proof	—	Value: 3.00				

KM# 820   100 PESETAS
Copper-Nickel **Ruler:** Juan Carlos I **Subject:** World Cup Soccer Games - Spain '82 **Obv:** Head left **Rev:** Value in center of assorted emblems

Date	Mintage	F	VF	XF	Unc	BU
1980 (80)	20,000,000	—	—	0.75	1.00	1.50
1980 (80) Proof	—	Value: 3.00				

KM# 826   100 PESETAS
9.3000 g., Aluminum-Bronze, 24.5 mm. **Ruler:** Juan Carlos I **Obv:** Head left **Rev:** Crowned shield flanked by pillars with banner **Edge:** Fleur-de-lis repeated

Date	Mintage	F	VF	XF	Unc	BU
1982	117,600,000	—	0.75	1.25	3.50	5.00
1982 Proof	—	Value: 5.00				
1983		—	0.75	1.25	30.00	45.00
1984	208,000,000	—	0.75	1.25	8.00	10.00
1985	118,000,000	—	0.75	1.25	10.00	15.00
1986	160,000,000	—	0.75	1.25	3.00	4.00
1988	125,674,000	—	0.75	1.25	4.00	6.00
1989	80,877,000	—	0.75	1.25	2.50	3.00
1990	25,636,000	—	0.75	1.25	6.00	8.00

Note: Varieties exist

KM# 834   100 PESETAS
1.6800 g., 0.9250 Silver 0.0500 oz. ASW **Ruler:** Juan Carlos I **Subject:** Discovery of America **Obv:** Crown within beaded circle **Rev:** Mayan pyramid within beaded circle

Date	Mintage	F	VF	XF	Unc	BU
1989	43,000	—	—	—	—	8.00
1989 Proof	57,000	Value: 8.00				

KM# 854   100 PESETAS
1.6800 g., 0.9250 Silver 0.0500 oz. ASW **Ruler:** Juan Carlos I **Obv:** Bust of Brother Juniper Serra 3/4 right **Rev:** Mission ruins within legend

Date	Mintage	F	VF	XF	Unc	BU
1990	24,000	—	—	—	—	9.00
1990 Proof	27,000	Value: 9.00				

KM# 882 100 PESETAS
1.6800 g., 0.9250 Silver 0.0500 oz. ASW **Ruler:** Juan Carlos I
Obv: bust of Celestino Mutis 1/4 right **Rev:** Flower plant within beaded circle

Date	Mintage	F	VF	XF	Unc	BU
1991	14,000	—	—	—	—	10.00
1991 Proof	—	Value: 10.00				

KM# 908 100 PESETAS
9.3000 g., Aluminum-Bronze, 24.5 mm. **Ruler:** Juan Carlos I
Rev: Crowned shield flanked by pillars with banner

Date	Mintage	F	VF	XF	Unc	BU
1992	22,661,000	—	—	—	4.00	5.00

Note: Edge varieties exist with positioning of fleur-de-lis

KM# 993 100 PESETAS
1.6800 g., 0.9250 Silver 0.0500 oz. ASW **Ruler:** Juan Carlos I
Subject: Seville Expo '92 **Obv:** Arched bridge **Rev:** Bridge

Date	Mintage	F	VF	XF	Unc	BU
1992	16,000	—	—	—	—	9.50
1992 Proof	16,000	Value: 10.00				

KM# 922 100 PESETAS
9.3000 g., Nickel-Brass, 24.5 mm. **Ruler:** Juan Carlos I
Subject: European unity **Obv:** Value within map **Rev:** Radiant sun within star circle

Date	Mintage	F	VF	XF	Unc	BU
1993	39,723,000	—	—	—	3.00	5.00

KM# 935 100 PESETAS
9.3000 g., Nickel-Brass, 24.5 mm. **Ruler:** Juan Carlos I
Subject: Museo del Prado **Obv:** Head left **Rev:** Statue in front of museum **Edge:** Fleur-de-lis repeated

Date	Mintage	F	VF	XF	Unc	BU
1994	24,853,000	—	—	—	2.50	3.50

KM# 950 100 PESETAS
9.3000 g., Copper-Nickel, 24.5 mm. **Ruler:** Juan Carlos I
Series: F.A.O. **Obv:** Head left **Rev:** Oat sprig, value and F.A.O. logo **Edge:** Fleur-de-lis repeated

Date	Mintage	F	VF	XF	Unc	BU
1995	71,957,000	—	—	—	2.00	3.00

KM# 964 100 PESETAS
9.3000 g., Copper-Zinc-Nickel, 24.5 mm. **Ruler:** Juan Carlos I
Obv: Head left **Rev:** National Library **Edge:** Fleur-de-lis repeated

Date	Mintage	F	VF	XF	Unc	BU
1996	21,466,000	—	—	—	2.50	3.50

KM# 984 100 PESETAS
9.3000 g., Copper-Zinc-Nickel, 24.5 mm. **Ruler:** Juan Carlos I
Subject: Royal Theatre **Obv:** Head left **Rev:** Building

Date	Mintage	F	VF	XF	Unc	BU
1997	29,480,000	—	—	—	2.00	3.00

KM# 989 100 PESETAS
9.3000 g., Aluminum-Bronze, 24.5 mm. **Ruler:** Juan Carlos I
Obv: Head left **Rev:** Crowned shield flanked by pillars with banner **Edge:** Fleur-de-lis repeated

Date	Mintage	F	VF	XF	Unc	BU
1998	—	—	—	—	1.50	2.00
2000	—	—	—	—	2.00	2.50

KM# 1006 100 PESETAS
9.3000 g., Brass, 24.5 mm. **Ruler:** Juan Carlos I **Obv:** Head left **Rev:** Design above sprig and value **Edge:** Fleur-de-lis repeated

Date	Mintage	F	VF	XF	Unc	BU
1999	60,332,000	—	—	—	1.50	2.00

KM# 829 200 PESETAS
Copper-Nickel, 21.7 mm. **Ruler:** Juan Carlos I **Obv:** Head left **Rev:** Value divides sprigs

Date	Mintage	F	VF	XF	Unc	BU
1986	43,576,000	—	—	2.00	6.00	8.00
1987	66,718,000	—	—	2.00	12.00	16.00
1988	37,190,000	—	—	2.00	12.00	16.00

KM# 830 200 PESETAS
Copper-Nickel, 21.7 mm. **Ruler:** Juan Carlos I **Subject:** Madrid Numismatic Exposition **Obv:** Head left **Rev:** Value divides sprigs

Date	Mintage	F	VF	XF	Unc	BU
1987 (E87) Proof	60,000	Value: 60.00				

KM# 835 200 PESETAS
3.3700 g., 0.9250 Silver 0.1002 oz. ASW **Ruler:** Juan Carlos I
Subject: Discovery of America **Obv:** Crown above monogram within beaded circle **Rev:** Astrolobe within beaded circle

Date	Mintage	F	VF	XF	Unc	BU
1989	43,000	—	—	—	—	9.00
1989 Proof	57,000	Value: 9.00				

KM# 855 200 PESETAS
Copper-Nickel, 25.5 mm. **Ruler:** Juan Carlos I **Obv:** Conjoined busts of King and Crown Prince right **Rev:** Pair of lions pulling seated figure on barrel within circle

Date	Mintage	F	VF	XF	Unc	BU
1990	8,000,000	—	—	—	4.00	5.00

KM# 856 200 PESETAS
3.3700 g., 0.9250 Silver 0.1002 oz. ASW **Ruler:** Juan Carlos I
Subject: History in Common-Alonso de Frcilla **Obv:** Bust left **Rev:** Hand writing in a book within inner circle

Date	Mintage	F	VF	XF	Unc	BU
1990	24,000	—	—	—	—	10.00
1990 Proof	27,000	Value: 10.00				

KM# 883 200 PESETAS
3.3700 g., 0.9250 Silver 0.1002 oz. ASW **Ruler:** Juan Carlos I
Subject: Las Casas **Obv:** Bust left within beaded circle **Rev:** 3 Indian figures within beaded circle

Date	Mintage	F	VF	XF	Unc	BU
1991	14,000	—	—	—	—	11.00
1991 Proof	14,000	Value: 11.00				

KM# 884 200 PESETAS
Copper-Nickel, 25.5 mm. **Ruler:** Juan Carlos I **Subject:** Madrid - European Culture Capital **Obv:** Conjoined busts of King and Crown Prince right **Rev:** Pair of lions pulling seated figure on barrel within circle

Date	Mintage	F	VF	XF	Unc	BU
1991	11,400,000	—	—	—	2.00	3.00

KM# 884a 200 PESETAS
12.2500 g., 0.9250 Silver 0.3643 oz. ASW **Ruler:** Juan Carlos I
Subject: Madrid - European Culture Capital **Obv:** Conjoined busts of King and Crown Prince right **Rev:** Pair of lions pulling seated figure on barrel within circle

Date	Mintage	F	VF	XF	Unc	BU
1992 Proof	38,000	Value: 150				

KM# 909 200 PESETAS
Copper-Nickel, 25.5 mm. **Ruler:** Juan Carlos I **Subject:** Madrid - European Culture Capital **Obv:** Conjoined busts of King and Crown Prince right **Rev:** Equestrian within circle

Date	Mintage	F	VF	XF	Unc	BU
1992	Inc. above	—	—	—	3.00	3.50

KM# 910   200 PESETAS
Copper-Nickel, 25.5 mm. **Ruler:** Juan Carlos I **Subject:** Madrid - European Culture Capital **Obv:** Conjoined busts of King and Crown Prince right **Rev:** Upright bear by tree within circle

Date	Mintage	F	VF	XF	Unc	BU
1992	Inc. above	—	—	—	3.00	3.50

KM# 994   200 PESETAS
3.3700 g., 0.9250 Silver 0.1002 oz. ASW **Ruler:** Juan Carlos I **Subject:** Seville Expo '92 **Obv:** Hydro-electric dam within beaded circle **Rev:** Tower of Seville within beaded circle

Date	Mintage	F	VF	XF	Unc	BU
1992	16,000	Value: 12.50				
1992	17,000	—	—	—	—	12.00

KM# 923   200 PESETAS
Copper-Nickel, 25.5 mm. **Ruler:** Juan Carlos I **Subject:** Juan Luis Vives **Obv:** Feather and designs within circle **Rev:** Bust facing and crowned design within circle

Date	Mintage	F	VF	XF	Unc	BU
1993	2,811,000	—	—	—	6.00	7.00

KM# 936   200 PESETAS
Copper-Nickel, 25.5 mm. **Ruler:** Juan Carlos I **Subject:** Velasquez and Goya Paintings **Obv:** Three figures within circle **Rev:** Kneeling figures with umbrella within circle

Date	Mintage	F	VF	XF	Unc	BU
1994	2,997,000	—	—	—	4.00	5.00

KM# 951   200 PESETAS
Copper-Nickel, 25.5 mm. **Ruler:** Juan Carlos I **Subject:** Murillo and El Greco paintings **Obv:** Standing figures within circle **Rev:** Child and lamb within circle

Date	Mintage	F	VF	XF	Unc	BU
1995	1,022,000	—	—	—	20.00	30.00

KM# 965   200 PESETAS
Copper-Nickel, 25.5 mm. **Ruler:** Juan Carlos I **Subject:** Fortuny and Balleau paintings **Obv:** Seated figure blowing on instrument within circle **Rev:** Seated figure playing guitar within circle

Date	Mintage	F	VF	XF	Unc	BU
1996	9,206,000	—	—	—	2.00	3.00

KM# 986   200 PESETAS
Copper-Nickel, 25.5 mm. **Ruler:** Juan Carlos I **Subject:** Jacinto Benavente **Obv:** Stylized books within circle **Rev:** Bust left within circle

Date	Mintage	F	VF	XF	Unc	BU
1997	6,845,000	—	—	—	3.00	4.00

KM# 992   200 PESETAS
Copper-Nickel, 25.5 mm. **Ruler:** Juan Carlos I **Obv:** Conjoined busts of King and Crown Prince right **Rev:** Value within circle

Date	Mintage	F	VF	XF	Unc	BU
1998	5,008,000	—	—	—	2.00	3.50
1999	—	—	—	—	4.00	6.00
2000	—	—	—	—	5.00	7.00

KM# 831   500 PESETAS
Copper-Aluminum-Nickel **Ruler:** Juan Carlos I **Obv:** Conjoined heads of Juan Carlos and Sofia left **Rev:** Crowned shield flanked by pillars with banner, vertical value at right

Date	Mintage	F	VF	XF	Unc	BU
1987 Proof	Inc. above	Value: 10.00				
1987	400,000,000	—	—	3.50	10.00	12.00
1988	81,309,000	—	—	3.50	9.00	11.00
1989	103,861,000	—	—	3.50	5.00	6.00
1990	28,372,000	—	—	2.25	7.00	12.00

KM# 836   500 PESETAS
6.7500 g., 0.9250 Silver 0.2007 oz. ASW **Ruler:** Juan Carlos I **Subject:** Discovery of America - Juego De Pelota Game **Obv:** Head facing within beaded circle **Rev:** Kneeling masked figure within beaded circle

Date	Mintage	F	VF	XF	Unc	BU
1989	43,000	—	—	—	—	12.00
1989 Proof	57,000	Value: 12.00				

KM# 857   500 PESETAS
6.7500 g., 0.9250 Silver 0.2007 oz. ASW **Ruler:** Juan Carlos I **Subject:** Juan de la Cosa **Obv:** Bust with hat facing within beaded circle **Rev:** Ocean navigation map within legend

Date	Mintage	F	VF	XF	Unc	BU
1990	24,000	—	—	—	—	12.00
1990 Proof	27,000	Value: 12.00				

KM# 885   500 PESETAS
6.7500 g., 0.9250 Silver 0.2007 oz. ASW **Ruler:** Juan Carlos I **Obv:** Bust of Jorge Juan 1/4 left within beaded circle **Rev:** World globe map within beaded circle

Date	Mintage	F	VF	XF	Unc	BU
1991	14,000	—	—	—	—	18.00
1991 Proof	14,000	Value: 18.00				

KM# 995   500 PESETAS
6.7500 g., 0.9250 Silver 0.2007 oz. ASW **Ruler:** Juan Carlos I **Subject:** Seville Expo '92 **Obv:** Church within beaded circle **Rev:** Palace portal within beaded circle

Date	Mintage	F	VF	XF	Unc	BU
1992	17,000	—	—	—	—	20.00
1992 Proof	16,000	Value: 20.00				

KM# 924   500 PESETAS
11.9000 g., Copper-Aluminum-Nickel **Ruler:** Juan Carlos I **Obv:** Conjoined heads of Juan Carlos and Sofia left **Rev:** Crowned shield flanked by pillars with banner, vertical value at right

Date	Mintage	F	VF	XF	Unc	BU
1993	3,059,000	—	—	—	30.00	40.00
1994	3,041,000	—	—	—	35.00	45.00
1995	1,015,000	—	—	—	30.00	40.00
1996	1,031,000	—	—	—	15.00	20.00
1997	4,881,000	—	—	—	12.00	15.00
1998	5,161,000	—	—	—	12.00	15.00
1999	2,030,000	—	—	—	12.00	15.00
2000	—	—	—	—	12.00	15.00

KM# 837   1000 PESETAS
13.5000 g., 0.9250 Silver 0.4015 oz. ASW **Ruler:** Juan Carlos I **Subject:** Discovery of America - Capture of Granada **Obv:** Standing figure divides date and beaded circle **Rev:** Armored figures on horses within beaded circle

Date	Mintage	F	VF	XF	Unc	BU
1989 Proof	57,000	Value: 15.00				
1989	43,000	—	—	—	—	15.00

KM# 858   1000 PESETAS
13.5000 g., 0.9250 Silver 0.4015 oz. ASW **Ruler:** Juan Carlos I **Subject:** Magallanes and Elcano **Obv:** Busts facing above ships wheel **Rev:** Primitive global world map within legend

Date	Mintage	F	VF	XF	Unc	BU
1990	24,000	—	—	—	—	15.00
1990 Proof	27,000	Value: 15.00				

KM# 886 1000 PESETAS
13.5000 g., 0.9250 Silver 0.4015 oz. ASW **Ruler:** Juan Carlos I
Subject: Simon Bolivar and San Martin **Obv:** Figure on horse
within beaded circle **Rev:** Bust facing within beaded circle

Date	Mintage	F	VF	XF	Unc	BU
1991	14,000	—	—	—	—	20.00
1991 Proof	14,000	Value: 20.00				

KM# 996 1000 PESETAS
13.5000 g., 0.9250 Silver 0.4015 oz. ASW **Ruler:** Juan Carlos I
Subject: Seville Expo '92 **Obv:** Expo buildings within beaded
circle **Rev:** India's archives building within beaded circle

Date	Mintage	F	VF	XF	Unc	BU
1992	17,000	—	—	—	—	25.00
1992 Proof	16,000	Value: 25.00				

KM# 952 1000 PESETAS
13.6600 g., 0.9250 Silver 0.4062 oz. ASW **Ruler:** Juan Carlos I
Subject: 1996 Olympics **Obv:** Head left **Rev:** Stylized figure,
torch and value

Date	Mintage	F	VF	XF	Unc	BU
1995 Proof	67,743	Value: 25.00				

KM# 973 1000 PESETAS
13.6600 g., 0.9250 Silver 0.4062 oz. ASW **Ruler:** Juan Carlos I
Subject: Olympics **Obv:** Head left **Rev:** Three divers

Date	Mintage	F	VF	XF	Unc	BU
1996 Proof	30,000	Value: 25.00				

KM# 988 1000 PESETAS
13.5000 g., 0.9250 Silver 0.4015 oz. ASW **Ruler:** Juan Carlos I
Subject: Soccer World Championship - France '98 **Obv:** Head
left **Rev:** Two soccer players

Date	Mintage	F	VF	XF	Unc	BU
1998 Proof	30,000	Value: 30.00				

KM# 1000 1000 PESETAS
13.5000 g., 0.9250 Silver 0.4015 oz. ASW **Ruler:** Juan Carlos I
Subject: Expo '98 Lisbon **Obv:** Head left **Rev:** Sailing ship

Date	Mintage	F	VF	XF	Unc	BU
1998 Proof	50,000	Value: 22.50				

KM# 1034 1000 PESETAS
13.5000 g., 0.9250 Silver 0.4015 oz. ASW, 32.9 mm.
Ruler: Juan Carlos I **Subject:** Constitution **Obv:** Head left
Rev: Building **Edge:** Reeded

Date	Mintage	F	VF	XF	Unc	BU
1998 Proof	75,000	Value: 25.00				

KM# 1009 1000 PESETAS
13.5000 g., 0.9250 Silver 0.4015 oz. ASW **Ruler:** Juan Carlos I
Subject: Olympics - Sidney 2000 **Obv:** Head left **Rev:** Water
polo players **Edge:** Plain

Date	Mintage	F	VF	XF	Unc	BU
1999 Proof	50,000	Value: 22.50				

KM# 1010 1500 PESETAS
19.8300 g., 0.9250 Silver 0.5897 oz. ASW **Ruler:** Juan Carlos I
Subject: Millennium **Obv:** Head left within beaded border
Rev: Space walking astronaut above Columbus's ships
Edge: Plain

Date	Mintage	F	VF	XF	Unc	BU
1999 Proof	50,000	Value: 25.00				

KM# 1039 1500 PESETAS
20.0000 g., 0.9250 Silver 0.5948 oz. ASW, 33 mm.
Ruler: Juan Carlos I **Subject:** Millennium **Obv:** Head left
Rev: Dove above Atlantic Ocean **Edge:** Plain

Date	Mintage	F	VF	XF	Unc	BU
2000 Proof	30,000	Value: 30.00				

KM# 1035 1500 PESETAS
20.0000 g., 0.9250 Silver 0.5948 oz. ASW, 33 mm.
Ruler: Juan Carlos I **Subject:** Printing **Obv:** Head left
Rev: Antique printing press **Edge:** Plain

Date	Mintage	F	VF	XF	Unc	BU
2000 Proof	30,000	Value: 30.00				

KM# 838 2000 PESETAS
27.0000 g., 0.9250 Silver 0.8029 oz. ASW **Ruler:** Juan Carlos I
Subject: Discovery of America **Obv:** Busts facing each other within
beaded circle **Rev:** Head of Columbus 1/4 left within beaded circle

Date	Mintage	F	VF	XF	Unc	BU
1989	43,000	—	—	—	—	22.50
1989 Proof	57,000	Value: 22.50				

KM# 859 2000 PESETAS
27.0000 g., 0.9250 Silver 0.8029 oz. ASW **Ruler:** Juan Carlos I
Subject: 1992 Olympics **Obv:** Conjoined busts of King and
Crown Prince right **Rev:** Symbols

Date	Mintage	F	VF	XF	Unc	BU
1990	52,524	—	—	—	—	20.00
1990 Proof	130,993	Value: 20.00				

Note: See note below KM#914

KM# 861 2000 PESETAS
26.7000 g., 0.9250 Silver 0.7940 oz. ASW **Ruler:** Juan Carlos I
Subject: 1992 Olympics **Obv:** Conjoined busts of King and
Crown Prince right **Rev:** Archer

Date	Mintage	F	VF	XF	Unc	BU
1990	26,843	—	—	—	—	20.00
1990 Proof	87,655	Value: 20.00				

Note: Uncirculated strikes have medallic die alignment and
edges with reeded and plain sections; Proof strikes
have coin die alignment and reeded edges

KM# 862 2000 PESETAS
26.7000 g., 0.9250 Silver 0.7940 oz. ASW **Ruler:** Juan Carlos I
Subject: 1992 Olympics **Obv:** Conjoined busts of King and
Crown Prince right **Rev:** Soccer player

Date	Mintage	F	VF	XF	Unc	BU
1990	Est. 19,638	—	—	—	—	20.00
1990 Proof	Est. 104,351	Value: 20.00				

Note: Uncirculated strikes have medallic die alignment and
edges with reeded and plain sections; Proof strikes
have coin die alignment and reeded edges

KM# 863   2000 PESETAS
26.7000 g., 0.9250 Silver 0.7940 oz. ASW **Ruler:** Juan Carlos I
Subject: 1992 Olympics **Obv:** Conjoined busts of King and
Crown Prince right **Rev:** Human pyramid

Date	Mintage	F	VF	XF	Unc	BU
1990	Est. 16,332	—	—	—	—	22.50
1990 Proof	Est. 73,510	Value: 22.50				

Note: Uncirculated strikes have medallic die alignment and
edges with reeded and plain sections; Proof strikes
have coin die alignment and reeded edges

KM# 864   2000 PESETAS
26.7000 g., 0.9250 Silver 0.7940 oz. ASW **Ruler:** Juan Carlos I
Subject: 1992 Olympics **Obv:** Conjoined busts of King and
Crown Prince right **Rev:** Greek runner

Date	Mintage	F	VF	XF	Unc	BU
1990	Est. 15,407	—	—	—	—	25.00
1990 Proof	Est. 73,469	Value: 25.00				

Note: Uncirculated strikes have medallic die alignment and
edges with reeded and plain sections; Proof strikes
have coin die alignment and reeded edges

KM# 865   2000 PESETAS
26.7000 g., 0.9250 Silver 0.7940 oz. ASW **Ruler:** Juan Carlos I
Subject: 1992 Olympics **Obv:** Conjoined busts of King and
Crown Prince right **Rev:** Ancient boat

Date	Mintage	F	VF	XF	Unc	BU
1990	Est. 14,223	—	—	—	—	25.00
1990 Proof	Est. 53,835	Value: 25.00				

Note: Uncirculated strikes have medallic die alignment and
edges with reeded and plain sections; Proof strikes
have coin die alignment and reeded edges

KM# 866   2000 PESETAS
26.7000 g., 0.9250 Silver 0.7940 oz. ASW **Ruler:** Juan Carlos I
Subject: 1992 Olympics **Obv:** Conjoined busts of King and
Crown Prince right **Rev:** Basketball players

Date	Mintage	F	VF	XF	Unc	BU
1990	Est. 14,395	—	—	—	—	25.00
1990 Proof	Est. 56,356	Value: 25.00				

Note: Uncirculated strikes have medallic die alignment and
edges with reeded and plain sections; Proof strikes
have coin die alignment and reeded edges

KM# 867   2000 PESETAS
26.7000 g., 0.9250 Silver 0.7940 oz. ASW **Ruler:** Juan Carlos I
Subject: 1992 Olympics **Obv:** Conjoined busts of King and
Crown Prince right **Rev:** Pelota player

Date	Mintage	F	VF	XF	Unc	BU
1990 Proof	Est. 45,219	Value: 25.00				

Note: Uncirculated strikes have medallic die alignment and
edges with reeded and plain sections; Proof strikes
have coin die alignment and reeded edges

Date	Mintage	F	VF	XF	Unc	BU
1990	Est. 12,554	—	—	—	—	25.00

KM# 868   2000 PESETAS
26.7000 g., 0.9250 Silver 0.7940 oz. ASW **Ruler:** Juan Carlos I
Subject: Hidalgo, Morelos and Juarez **Obv:** Three busts facing
Rev: Aztec pictorial design within legend

Date	Mintage	F	VF	XF	Unc	BU
1990	24,000	—	—	—	—	27.50
1990 Proof	27,000	Value: 27.50				

KM# 860   2000 PESETAS
26.7000 g., 0.9250 Silver 0.7940 oz. ASW **Ruler:** Juan Carlos I
Counterstamp: INUTILIZACION/OCTOBRE 1992
Obv: Conjoined busts of King and Crown Prince right **Rev:** Symbols
and Olympic rings **Note:** Counterstamp on reverse below Olympic
rings

Date	Mintage	F	VF	XF	Unc	BU
1990 "1992"; Proof	—	Value: 35.00				

Note: Uncirculated strikes have medallic die alignment and
edges with reeded and plain sections; Proof strikes
have coin die alignment and reeded edges

KM# 887   2000 PESETAS
26.7000 g., 0.9250 Silver 0.7940 oz. ASW **Ruler:** Juan Carlos I
Subject: Olympics **Obv:** Conjoined busts of King and Crown
Prince right **Rev:** Torch, flag and Olympic rings

Date	Mintage	F	VF	XF	Unc	BU
1991	18,545	—	—	—	—	40.00
1991 Proof	78,192	Value: 40.00				

KM# 888   2000 PESETAS
26.7000 g., 0.9250 Silver 0.7940 oz. ASW **Ruler:** Juan Carlos I
Subject: Olympics **Obv:** Conjoined busts of King and Crown
Prince right **Rev:** Tennis player

Date	Mintage	F	VF	XF	Unc	BU
1991	12,350	—	—	—	—	40.00
1991 Proof	38,905	Value: 40.00				

Note: Medal rotation

KM# 889   2000 PESETAS
26.7000 g., 0.9250 Silver 0.7940 oz. ASW **Ruler:** Juan Carlos I
Subject: Olympics **Obv:** Conjoined busts of King and Crown
Prince right **Rev:** Medieval rider

Date	Mintage	F	VF	XF	Unc	BU
1991	15,056	—	—	—	—	40.00
1991 Proof	31,317	Value: 40.00				

Note: Medal rotation

KM# 890   2000 PESETAS
26.7000 g., 0.9250 Silver 0.7940 oz. ASW **Ruler:** Juan Carlos I
Subject: Olympics **Obv:** Conjoined busts of King and Crown
Prince right **Rev:** Bowling

Date	Mintage	F	VF	XF	Unc	BU
1991	10,561	—	—	—	—	40.00
1991 Proof	35,447	Value: 40.00				

Note: Medal rotation

KM# 891 2000 PESETAS
26.7000 g., 0.9250 Silver 0.7940 oz. ASW **Ruler:** Juan Carlos I
Subject: Ibero - American Series **Obv:** Crowned shield flanked
by pillars with banner in center of assorted shields **Rev:** Crown
divides beaded circle with assorted designs in center

Date	Mintage	F	VF	XF	Unc	BU
(19)91 Proof	20,000	Value: 90.00				

KM# 892 2000 PESETAS
26.7000 g., 0.9250 Silver 0.7940 oz. ASW **Ruler:** Juan Carlos I
Subject: Federman, Quesada and Benalcazar **Obv:** Armored
busts left within beaded circle **Rev:** Standing figures around
armored figure on horse within beaded circle

Date	Mintage	F	VF	XF	Unc	BU
1991 Proof	14,000	Value: 25.00				
1991	14,000	—	—	—	—	25.00

KM# 911 2000 PESETAS
26.7000 g., 0.9250 Silver 0.7940 oz. ASW **Ruler:** Juan Carlos I
Subject: Olympics **Obv:** Conjoined busts of King and Crown
Prince right **Rev:** Tug-of-war

Date	Mintage	F	VF	XF	Unc	BU
1992	9,043	—	—	—	—	50.00
1992 Proof	33,980	Value: 50.00				

Note: Uncirculated strikes have medallic die alignment and
edges with reeded and plain sections; Proof strikes
have coin die alignment and reeded edges

KM# 912 2000 PESETAS
26.7000 g., 0.9250 Silver 0.7940 oz. ASW **Ruler:** Juan Carlos I
Subject: Olympics **Obv:** Conjoined busts of King and Crown
Prince right **Rev:** Wheelchair basketball

Date	Mintage	F	VF	XF	Unc	BU
1992	8,997	—	—	—	—	50.00
1992 Proof	27,886	Value: 50.00				

Note: Uncirculated strikes have medallic die alignment and
edges with reeded and plain sections; Proof strikes
have coin die alignment and reeded edges

KM# 913 2000 PESETAS
26.7000 g., 0.9250 Silver 0.7940 oz. ASW **Ruler:** Juan Carlos I
Subject: Olympics **Obv:** Conjoined busts of King and Crown
Prince right **Rev:** Sprinters

Date	Mintage	F	VF	XF	Unc	BU
1992	16,000	—	—	—	—	40.00
1992 Proof	42,000	Value: 40.00				

Note: Uncirculated strikes have medallic die alignment and
edges with reeded and plain sections; Proof strikes
have coin die alignment and reeded edges

KM# 914 2000 PESETAS
26.7000 g., 0.9250 Silver 0.7940 oz. ASW **Ruler:** Juan Carlos I
Subject: Olympics **Obv:** Conjoined busts of King and Crown
Prince right **Rev:** Chariot racing

Date	Mintage	F	VF	XF	Unc	BU
1992 Proof	37,000	Value: 50.00				

Note: Uncirculated strikes have medallic die alignment and
edges with reeded and plain sections; Proof strikes
have coin die alignment and reeded edges

1992	13,000	—	—	—	—	50.00

KM# 980 2000 PESETAS
26.7000 g., 0.9250 Silver 0.7940 oz. ASW **Ruler:** Juan Carlos I
Subject: Seville Expo '92 **Obv:** Exposition building and date
within beaded circle **Rev:** Tower of Seville within beaded circle

Date	Mintage	F	VF	XF	Unc	BU
1992	17,000	—	—	—	—	35.00
1992 Proof	16,000	Value: 35.00				

KM# 925 2000 PESETAS
26.7000 g., 0.9250 Silver 0.7940 oz. ASW **Ruler:** Juan Carlos I
Subject: Holy Jacobean Year **Obv:** Head left **Rev:** German
Jacobean Pilgrims within square and beaded circle

Date	Mintage	F	VF	XF	Unc	BU
1993 Proof	10,000	Value: 75.00				

KM# 926 2000 PESETAS
26.7000 g., 0.9250 Silver 0.7940 oz. ASW **Ruler:** Juan Carlos I
Subject: Holy Jacobean Year **Obv:** Head left **Rev:** Santiago
cross and scallop shell within beaded circle

Date	Mintage	F	VF	XF	Unc	BU
1993 Proof	17,000	Value: 75.00				

KM# 937 2000 PESETAS
18.0000 g., 0.9250 Silver 0.5353 oz. ASW **Ruler:** Juan Carlos I
Subject: International Monetary Fund and Bank **Obv:** Head left
Rev: Designs above building

Date	Mintage	F	VF	XF	Unc	BU
1994	8,669,000	—	—	—	20.00	22.00

KM# 938 2000 PESETAS
27.0000 g., 0.9250 Silver 0.8029 oz. ASW **Ruler:** Juan Carlos I
Subject: Courtyard of the Lions **Rev:** Courtyard scene

Date	Mintage	F	VF	XF	Unc	BU
1994 Proof	7,312	Value: 40.00				

KM# 939   2000 PESETAS
27.0000 g., 0.9250 Silver 0.8029 oz. ASW **Ruler:** Juan Carlos I
Subject: Environmental Protection **Rev:** Spanish lynx within circle

Date	Mintage	F	VF	XF	Unc	BU
1994 Proof	20,000	Value: 100				

KM# 940   2000 PESETAS
27.0000 g., 0.9250 Silver 0.8029 oz. ASW **Ruler:** Juan Carlos I
Obv: Head left **Rev:** Purple herons in swamp

Date	Mintage	F	VF	XF	Unc	BU
1994 Proof	6,555	Value: 53.00				

KM# 941   2000 PESETAS
27.0000 g., 0.9250 Silver 0.8029 oz. ASW **Ruler:** Juan Carlos I
Obv: Head left **Rev:** Two bulls fighting

Date	Mintage	F	VF	XF	Unc	BU
1994 Proof	10,388	Value: 50.00				

KM# 953   2000 PESETAS
27.0000 g., 0.9250 Silver 0.8029 oz. ASW **Ruler:** Juan Carlos I
Obv: Head left **Rev:** Capercaillie bird

Date	Mintage	F	VF	XF	Unc	BU
1995 Proof	13,859	Value: 50.00				

KM# 954   2000 PESETAS
27.0000 g., 0.9250 Silver 0.8029 oz. ASW **Ruler:** Juan Carlos I
Subject: Presidential Council - V.E **Obv:** Head left **Rev:** Designs
above building

Date	Mintage	F	VF	XF	Unc	BU
1995	—	—	—	—	20.00	22.00

KM# 955   2000 PESETAS
27.0000 g., 0.9250 Silver 0.8029 oz. ASW **Ruler:** Juan Carlos I
Subject: 50th Anniversary - United Nations **Obv:** Head left **Rev:**
Numeral 50 and UN logo above design

Date	Mintage	F	VF	XF	Unc	BU
1995 Proof	26,049	Value: 110				

KM# 966   2000 PESETAS
27.0000 g., 0.9250 Silver 0.8029 oz. ASW **Ruler:** Juan Carlos I
Obv: Head left **Rev:** Wolves

Date	Mintage	F	VF	XF	Unc	BU
1996 Proof	35,000	Value: 75.00				

KM# 967   2000 PESETAS
27.0000 g., 0.9250 Silver 0.8029 oz. ASW **Ruler:** Juan Carlos I
Obv: Head left **Rev:** Bears

Date	Mintage	F	VF	XF	Unc	BU
1996 Proof	35,000	Value: 60.00				

KM# 968   2000 PESETAS
18.0000 g., 0.9250 Silver 0.5353 oz. ASW **Ruler:** Juan Carlos I
Subject: Francisco de Goya **Obv:** Head left **Rev:** Reclining nude
female figure

Date	Mintage	F	VF	XF	Unc	BU
1996	—	—	—	—	20.00	22.00

KM# 974   2000 PESETAS
27.0000 g., 0.9250 Silver 0.8029 oz. ASW **Ruler:** Juan Carlos I
Series: Patrimonio de la Humanidad **Obv:** UNESCO logo
Rev: Taj Mahal, India

Date	Mintage	F	VF	XF	Unc	BU
1996 Proof	30,000	Value: 35.00				

KM# 975   2000 PESETAS
27.0000 g., 0.9250 Silver 0.8029 oz. ASW **Ruler:** Juan Carlos I
Series: Patrimonio de la Humanidad **Obv:** Crowned shield with
value as II **Rev:** Djenne, Mali

Date	Mintage	F	VF	XF	Unc	BU
1996 Proof	30,000	Value: 35.00				

KM# 976   2000 PESETAS
27.0000 g., 0.9250 Silver 0.8029 oz. ASW **Ruler:** Juan Carlos I
Series: Patrimonio de la Humanidad **Obv:** Crowned shield with
value as II **Rev:** Abu Simbel, Egypt

Date	Mintage	F	VF	XF	Unc	BU
1996 Proof	30,000	Value: 35.00				

KM# 977   2000 PESETAS
27.0000 g., 0.9250 Silver 0.8029 oz. ASW **Ruler:** Juan Carlos I **Series:** Patrimonio de la Humanidad **Obv:** Crowned shield with value as II **Rev:** Palenque, Mexico

Date	Mintage	F	VF	XF	Unc	BU
1996 Proof	30,000	Value: 35.00				

KM# 978   2000 PESETAS
27.0000 g., 0.9250 Silver 0.8029 oz. ASW **Ruler:** Juan Carlos I **Series:** Patrimonio de la Humanidad **Obv:** Crowned shield with value as II **Rev:** Merida, Spain

Date	Mintage	F	VF	XF	Unc	BU
1996 Proof	30,000	Value: 35.00				

KM# 999   2000 PESETAS
18.0000 g., 0.9250 Silver 0.5353 oz. ASW **Ruler:** Juan Carlos I **Subject:** Don Quixote **Obv:** Head left **Rev:** Quixote and friend plus cameo of Cervantes

Date	Mintage	F	VF	XF	Unc	BU
1997	—	—	—	—	20.00	22.00

KM# 1018   2000 PESETAS
27.0000 g., 0.9250 Silver 0.8029 oz. ASW, 40 mm. **Ruler:** Juan Carlos I **Series:** "Patrimono de la Humanidad" UNESCO **Obv:** UNESCO logo **Rev:** Abomey lion **Edge:** Reeded

Date	Mintage	F	VF	XF	Unc	BU
1997 Proof	30,000	Value: 30.00				

KM# 1019   2000 PESETAS
27.0000 g., 0.9250 Silver 0.8029 oz. ASW **Ruler:** Juan Carlos I **Series:** "Patrimono de la Humanidad" UNESCO **Obv:** UNESCO logo **Rev:** Easter Island statues

Date	Mintage	F	VF	XF	Unc	BU
1997 Proof	30,000	Value: 30.00				

KM# 1020   2000 PESETAS
27.0000 g., 0.9250 Silver 0.8029 oz. ASW **Ruler:** Juan Carlos I **Series:** "Patrimono de la Humanidad" UNESCO **Obv:** UNESCO logo **Rev:** Temple at Petra

Date	Mintage	F	VF	XF	Unc	BU
1997 Proof	30,000	Value: 30.00				

KM# 1021   2000 PESETAS
27.0000 g., 0.9250 Silver 0.8029 oz. ASW **Ruler:** Juan Carlos I **Series:** "Patrimono de la Humanidad" UNESCO **Obv:** UNESCO logo **Rev:** Acropolis

Date	Mintage	F	VF	XF	Unc	BU
1997 Proof	30,000	Value: 30.00				

KM# 1022   2000 PESETAS
27.0000 g., 0.9250 Silver 0.8029 oz. ASW **Ruler:** Juan Carlos I **Series:** "Patrimono de la Humanidad" UNESCO **Obv:** UNESCO logo **Rev:** Horyu-Ji pagoda

Date	Mintage	F	VF	XF	Unc	BU
1997 Proof	30,000	Value: 30.00				

KM# 1024   2000 PESETAS
27.0000 g., 0.9250 Silver 0.8029 oz. ASW, 40 mm. **Ruler:** Juan Carlos I **Subject:** House of Borbon **Obv:** Bust of Philip V facing within beaded border **Rev:** Figural sculpture within beaded border **Edge:** Reeded

Date	Mintage	F	VF	XF	Unc	BU
1997 Proof	—	Value: 30.00				

KM# 1025   2000 PESETAS
27.0000 g., 0.9250 Silver 0.8029 oz. ASW **Ruler:** Juan Carlos I **Subject:** House of Borbon **Obv:** Bust of Louis I left within beaded border **Rev:** Crowned arms in order chain within beaded border

Date	Mintage	F	VF	XF	Unc	BU
1997 Proof	—	Value: 30.00				

KM# 1026   2000 PESETAS
27.0000 g., 0.9250 Silver 0.8029 oz. ASW **Ruler:** Juan Carlos I **Subject:** House of Borbon **Obv:** Bust of Ferdinand VI 1/4 right within beaded circle **Rev:** Spanish galleon within beaded circle

Date	Mintage	F	VF	XF	Unc	BU
1997 Proof	—	Value: 30.00				

KM# 1036   2000 PESETAS
27.3000 g., 0.9250 Silver 0.8119 oz. ASW, 39.9 mm. **Ruler:** Juan Carlos I **Subject:** House of Borbon **Obv:** Bust of Ferdinand VII 1/4 right **Rev:** Prado Museum **Edge:** Reeded

Date	Mintage	F	VF	XF	Unc	BU
1998 Proof	30,000	Value: 30.00				

KM# 987   2000 PESETAS

18.0000 g., 0.9250 Silver 0.5353 oz. ASW **Ruler:** Juan Carlos I
Subject: Philip II **Obv:** Head left within beaded circle **Rev:** Head
left, design above steepled building within beaded circle

Date	Mintage	F	VF	XF	Unc	BU
1998	—	—	—	—	20.00	22.00

KM# 1011   2000 PESETAS

18.0000 g., 0.9250 Silver 0.5353 oz. ASW **Ruler:** Juan Carlos I
Subject: St. Jacob **Obv:** Head left within beaded circle **Rev:** St.
Jacob, value and dagger

Date	Mintage	F	VF	XF	Unc	BU
1999	—	—	—	—	32.00	35.00

KM# 1029   2000 PESETAS

27.0000 g., 0.9250 Silver 0.8029 oz. ASW **Ruler:** Juan Carlos I
Subject: Barcelona City Government 750 Years **Obv:** Head left
Rev: Stylized city arms

Date	Mintage	F	VF	XF	Unc	BU
1999 Proof	30,000	Value: 30.00				

KM# 1031   2000 PESETAS

27.0000 g., 0.9250 Silver 0.8029 oz. ASW **Ruler:** Juan Carlos I
Obv: House of Borbon **Obv:** Head of Alfonso XII 1/4 right
within beaded circle **Rev:** Train within beaded circle

Date	Mintage	F	VF	XF	Unc	BU
1999 Proof	—	Value: 32.50				

KM# 1032   2000 PESETAS

27.0000 g., 0.9250 Silver 0.8029 oz. ASW **Ruler:** Juan Carlos I
Subject: House of Borbon - Alfonso XIII **Obv:** Childhood portrait
of Alfonso XIII within circle and beaded border

Date	Mintage	F	VF	XF	Unc	BU
1999 Proof	—	Value: 30.00				

KM# 1033   2000 PESETAS

27.0000 g., 0.9250 Silver 0.8029 oz. ASW **Ruler:** Juan Carlos I
Subject: House of Borbon - Alfonso XIII **Obv:** Adult portrait of
Alfonso XIIII within beaded border

Date	Mintage	F	VF	XF	Unc	BU
1999 Proof	—	Value: 30.00				

KM# 1037   2000 PESETAS

27.0000 g., 0.9250 Silver 0.8029 oz. ASW, 40 mm.
Ruler: Juan Carlos I **Obv:** Head left **Rev:** Bilbao city arms
Edge: Reeded

Date	Mintage	F	VF	XF	Unc	BU
2000 Proof	30,000	Value: 30.00				

KM# 1030   2000 PESETAS

27.0000 g., 0.9250 Silver 0.8029 oz. ASW **Ruler:** Juan Carlos I
Subject: House of Borbon **Obv:** Bust of Isabel II 1/4 right within
beaded circle

Date	Mintage	F	VF	XF	Unc	BU
1999 Proof	—	Value: 30.00				

KM# 1015   2000 PESETAS

18.0000 g., 0.9250 Silver 0.5353 oz. ASW, 33 mm.
Ruler: Juan Carlos I **Subject:** Charles V **Obv:** Head left within
beaded border **Rev:** Laureate Head right within beaded border
Edge: Plain

Date	Mintage	F	VF	XF	Unc	BU
2000	—	—	—	—	32.00	35.00

KM# 839   5000 PESETAS

54.0000 g., 0.9250 Silver 1.6059 oz. ASW **Ruler:** Juan Carlos I
Subject: Discovery of America **Obv:** Crowned shield flanked by
pillars with banner within beaded circle **Rev:** Santa Maria

Date	Mintage	F	VF	XF	Unc	BU
1989	24,000	—	—	—	—	45.00
1989 Proof	33,000	Value: 45.00				

KM# 840   5000 PESETAS

1.6800 g., 0.9990 Gold 0.0540 oz. AGW **Ruler:** Juan Carlos I
Subject: Discovery of America **Obv:** Crown within beaded circle
Rev: Crown above compass face within beaded circle

Date	Mintage	F	VF	XF	Unc	BU
1989	6,000	—	—	—	—	65.00
1989 Proof	8,000	Value: 65.00				

KM# 869   5000 PESETAS

54.0000 g., 0.9250 Silver 1.6059 oz. ASW **Ruler:** Juan Carlos I
Subject: Cortes, Montezuma and Marina **Obv:** Three busts facing
within beaded circle **Rev:** Scene from Aztec mythology within legend

Date	Mintage	F	VF	XF	Unc	BU
1990	11,000	—	—	—	—	60.00
1990 Proof	13,000	Value: 60.00				

KM# 870   5000 PESETAS

1.6800 g., 0.9990 Gold 0.0540 oz. AGW **Ruler:** Juan Carlos I
Obv: Bust of Philip V facing **Rev:** Compass face

Date	Mintage	F	VF	XF	Unc	BU
1990	3,000	—	—	—	—	70.00
1990 Proof	4,000	Value: 70.00				

KM# 893   5000 PESETAS

54.0000 g., 0.9250 Silver 1.6059 oz. ASW **Ruler:** Juan Carlos I
Obv: Pizarro and Atahualpa facing right within circle **Rev:** Incan
ruins in mountains within beaded circle

Date	Mintage	F	VF	XF	Unc	BU
1991	8,000	—	—	—	—	85.00
1991 Proof	8,145	Value: 85.00				

KM# 894 5000 PESETAS
1.6800 g., 0.9990 Gold 0.0540 oz. AGW **Ruler:** Juan Carlos I
Obv: Bust of Fernando VI 1/4 right **Rev:** Crown above compass
face within beaded circle

Date	Mintage	F	VF	XF	Unc	BU
1991	1,000	—	—	—	—	90.00
1991 Proof	2,000	Value: 90.00				

KM# 997 5000 PESETAS
54.0000 g., 0.9250 Silver 1.6059 oz. ASW **Ruler:** Juan Carlos I
Subject: Seville Expo '92 **Obv:** Mint building within beaded circle
Rev: Old coin press within beaded circle

Date	Mintage	F	VF	XF	Unc	BU
1992	8,000	—	—	—	—	100
1992 Proof	7,000	Value: 100				

KM# 1001 5000 PESETAS
54.0000 g., 0.9250 Silver 1.6059 oz. ASW **Ruler:** Juan Carlos I
Obv: Crown within beaded circle **Rev:** Screw press

Date	Mintage	F	VF	XF	Unc	BU
1992	1,000	—	—	—	—	110
1992 Proof	—	Value: 110				

KM# 942 5000 PESETAS
54.0000 g., 0.9250 Silver 1.6059 oz. ASW **Ruler:** Juan Carlos I
Rev: Imperial Eagle

Date	Mintage	F	VF	XF	Unc	BU
1994 Proof	30,000	Value: 70.00				

KM# 956 5000 PESETAS
54.0000 g., 0.9250 Silver 1.6059 oz. ASW **Ruler:** Juan Carlos I
Rev: Spanish Ibex

Date	Mintage	F	VF	XF	Unc	BU
1995 Proof	25,000	Value: 75.00				

KM# 969 5000 PESETAS
54.0000 g., 0.9250 Silver 1.6059 oz. ASW **Ruler:** Juan Carlos I
Rev: Gaudi sculpture

Date	Mintage	F	VF	XF	Unc	BU
1996 Proof	Est. 20,000	Value: 65.00				

KM# 842 10000 PESETAS
3.3700 g., 0.9990 Gold 0.1082 oz. AGW **Ruler:** Juan Carlos I
Subject: Discovery of America **Obv:** Crown above monogram
within beaded circle **Rev:** Armillary sphere within beaded circle

Date	Mintage	F	VF	XF	Unc	BU
1989	5,000	—	—	—	—	115
1989 Proof	7,000	Value: 115				

KM# 841 10000 PESETAS
168.7500 g., 0.9250 Silver 5.0183 oz. ASW, 73 mm.
Ruler: Juan Carlos I **Subject:** Regional Autonomy **Obv:** Royal
family depicted in circular frames **Rev:** Crowned arms at center
of crowned provincial arms **Note:** Illustration reduced.

Date	Mintage	F	VF	XF	Unc	BU
1989	47,000	—	—	—	—	120
1989 Proof	—	Value: 120				

KM# 873 10000 PESETAS
168.7500 g., 0.9250 Silver 5.0183 oz. ASW, 73 mm.
Ruler: Juan Carlos I **Subject:** Spanish Royal Family **Obv:** Royal
family depicted in circular frames within beaded circle
Rev: Center circle depicts men holding up world within beaded
circle, busts of discoverers and liberators surround
Note: Illustration reduced.

Date	Mintage	F	VF	XF	Unc	BU
1990	26,000	—	—	—	—	140
1990 Proof	—	Value: 140				

KM# 871 10000 PESETAS
3.3700 g., 0.9990 Gold 0.1082 oz. AGW **Ruler:** Juan Carlos I
Series: 1992 Olympics **Obv:** Bust right **Rev:** Stylized field hockey
player

Date	Mintage	F	VF	XF	Unc	BU
1990	3,000	—	—	—	—	115
1990 Proof	5,000	Value: 115				

Note: Uncirculated strikes have medallic die alignment and
edges with reeded and plain sections; Proof strikes
have coin die alignment and reeded edges

KM# 872 10000 PESETAS
3.3700 g., 0.9990 Gold 0.1082 oz. AGW **Ruler:** Juan Carlos I
Series: 1992 Olympics **Obv:** Bust right **Rev:** Stylized gymnast

Date	Mintage	F	VF	XF	Unc	BU
1990	2,000	—	—	—	—	120
1990 Proof	3,000	Value: 120				

Note: Uncirculated strikes have medallic die alignment and
edges with reeded and plain sections; Proof strikes
have coin die alignment and reeded edges

KM# 874 10000 PESETAS
3.3700 g., 0.9990 Gold 0.1082 oz. AGW **Ruler:** Juan Carlos I
Obv: Quauchtemoc within beaded circle **Rev:** Crown above
compass face within beaded circle

Date	Mintage	F	VF	XF	Unc	BU
1990	9,000	—	—	—	—	120
1990 Proof	2,000	Value: 120				

KM# 895 10000 PESETAS
3.3700 g., 0.9990 Gold 0.1082 oz. AGW **Ruler:** Juan Carlos I
Series: Olympics **Obv:** Bust 3/4 right within circle **Rev:** Tae Kwon
Do participant within circle

Date	Mintage	F	VF	XF	Unc	BU
1991	2,000	—	—	—	—	180
1991 Proof	3,000	Value: 180				

Note: Uncirculated strikes have medallic die alignment and
edges with reeded and plain sections; Proof strikes
have coin die alignment and reeded edges.

KM# 897 10000 PESETAS
3.3700 g., 0.9990 Gold 0.1082 oz. AGW **Ruler:** Juan Carlos I
Obv: Tupac Amaru II within beaded circle **Rev:** Armillary sphere
within beaded circle

Date	Mintage	F	VF	XF	Unc	BU
1991	1,000	—	—	—	—	150
1991 Proof	2,000	Value: 150				

KM# 896   10000 PESETAS

168.7500 g., 0.9250 Silver 5.0183 oz. ASW, 73 mm. **Ruler:** Juan Carlos I **Subject:** Discoverers and Liberators **Obv:** Royal family depicted in circular frames within beaded circle **Rev:** Center circle depicts men holding up world within beaded circle, busts of discoverers and liberators surround **Note:** Illustration reduced.

Date	Mintage	F	VF	XF	Unc	BU
1991	17,000	—	—	—	—	175
1991 Proof	—	Value: 175				

KM# 1002   10000 PESETAS

3.3700 g., 0.9990 Gold 0.1082 oz. AGW **Ruler:** Juan Carlos I **Obv:** Crowned monogram **Rev:** Worker operating screw press

Date	Mintage	F	VF	XF	Unc	BU
1992 Proof	—	Value: 180				
1992	1,000					180

KM# 915   10000 PESETAS

3.3700 g., 0.9990 Gold 0.1082 oz. AGW **Ruler:** Juan Carlos I **Series:** Olympics **Obv:** Bust 1/4 right within circle **Rev:** Baseball player within circle

Date	Mintage	F	VF	XF	Unc	BU
1992	1,000				—	180
1992 Proof	6,000	Value: 180				

Note: Uncirculated strikes have medallic die alignment and edges with reeded and plain sections; Proof strikes have coin die alignment and reeded edges

KM# 998   10000 PESETAS

168.7500 g., 0.9250 Silver 5.0183 oz. ASW **Ruler:** Juan Carlos I **Series:** Seville Expo '92 - Nobel Prize winners **Obv:** Royal family depicted in circular frames **Rev:** Nobel winners depicted in oval frames, hand with quill encircled below

Date	Mintage	F	VF	XF	Unc	BU
1992 Proof	14,000	Value: 235				

KM# 928   10000 PESETAS

168.7500 g., 0.9250 Silver 5.0183 oz. ASW, 75 mm. **Ruler:** Juan Carlos I **Subject:** Holy Jacobean Year **Obv:** Crowned cameo above cathedral within beaded circle **Rev:** Pilgrims within beaded circle, crown at top **Note:** Illustration reduced.

Date	Mintage	F	VF	XF	Unc	BU
1993 Proof	7,000	Value: 265				

KM# 943   10000 PESETAS

167.7500 g., 0.9250 Silver 4.9886 oz. ASW, 73 mm. **Ruler:** Juan Carlos I **Subject:** Goya's paintings **Obv:** "The Parasol" **Rev:** Bull fighting scene **Note:** Illustration reduced.

Date	Mintage	F	VF	XF	Unc	BU
1994 Proof	15,000	Value: 200				

KM# 957   10000 PESETAS

168.7500 g., 0.9250 Silver 5.0183 oz. ASW, 73 mm. **Ruler:** Juan Carlos I **Subject:** Velazquez's paintings **Obv:** Cameo to right of figure on horse **Rev:** Radiant sun and three standing figures **Note:** Illustration reduced.

Date	Mintage	F	VF	XF	Unc	BU
1995 Proof	5,368	Value: 185				

KM# 970   10000 PESETAS

168.7500 g., 0.9250 Silver 5.0183 oz. ASW **Ruler:** Juan Carlos I **Subject:** Velazguez's paintings **Obv:** "The Naked Maja" **Rev:** Family picking flowers

Date	Mintage	F	VF	XF	Unc	BU
1996 Proof	15,000	Value: 150				

KM# 1027   10000 PESETAS

168.7500 g., 0.9250 Silver 5.0183 oz. ASW, 73 mm. **Ruler:** Juan Carlos I **Subject:** House of Borbon - Juan Carlos I **Obv:** King standing and Queen seated **Rev:** Crowned provincial arms within circle at center of family heads separated by fleur de lis **Edge:** Reeded **Note:** Illustration reduced.

Date	Mintage	F	VF	XF	Unc	BU
1997 Proof	10,000	Value: 150				

KM# 1068   10000 PESETAS
169.1000 g., 0.9250 Silver 5.0287 oz. ASW, 73 mm.
Ruler: Juan Carlos I **Subject:** 500th Birthday of Charles I
Obv: Uniformed half-figure facing **Rev:** Uniformed figure seated
on an eagle with pillars in background **Edge:** Plain

Date	Mintage	F	VF	XF	Unc	BU
ND (2000) Proof	—	Value: 150				

KM# 843   20000 PESETAS
6.7500 g., 0.9990 Gold 0.2168 oz. AGW **Ruler:** Juan Carlos I
Subject: Discovery of America **Obv:** Head facing within beaded
circle **Rev:** Pinzon Brother within beaded circle

Date	Mintage	F	VF	XF	Unc	BU
1989	5,000	—	—	—	—	250
1989 Proof	6,500	Value: 250				

KM# 875   20000 PESETAS
6.7500 g., 0.9990 Gold 0.2168 oz. AGW **Ruler:** Juan Carlos I
Subject: 1992 Olympics - La Sagrada Familia **Obv:** Bust 1/4 right
within beaded circle **Rev:** Cathedral towers within beaded circle

Date	Mintage	F	VF	XF	Unc	BU
1990	4,000	—	—	—	—	250
1990 Proof	10,000	Value: 250				

Note: Uncirculated strikes have medallic die alignment and
edges with reeded and plain sections; Proof strikes
have coin die alignment and reeded edges

KM# 876   20000 PESETAS
6.7500 g., 0.9990 Gold 0.2168 oz. AGW **Ruler:** Juan Carlos I
Series: 1992 Olympics **Obv:** Bust 1/4 right within beaded circle
Rev: Ruins of Empuries within beaded circle

Date	Mintage	F	VF	XF	Unc	BU
1990	2,000	—	—	—	—	250

Date	Mintage	F	VF	XF	Unc	BU
1990 Proof	4,000	Value: 250				

Note: Uncirculated strikes have medallic die alignment and
edges with reeded and plain sections; Proof strikes
have coin die alignment and reeded edges

KM# 877   20000 PESETAS
6.7500 g., 0.9990 Gold 0.2168 oz. AGW **Ruler:** Juan Carlos I
Subject: Tupac Amaru I **Obv:** Bust 1/4 right within beaded circle
Rev: Stylized standing figure with hat and scepter within beaded
circle

Date	Mintage	F	VF	XF	Unc	BU
1990	2,000	—	—	—	—	250
1990 Proof	3,000	Value: 250				

KM# 898   20000 PESETAS
6.7500 g., 0.9990 Gold 0.2168 oz. AGW **Ruler:** Juan Carlos I
Series: Olympics **Obv:** Bust 1/4 right within circle **Rev:** Montjuic
Stadium within circle

Date	Mintage	F	VF	XF	Unc	BU
1991	2,000	—	—	—	—	270
1991 Proof	3,000	Value: 270				

Note: Uncirculated strikes have medallic die alignment and
edges with reeded and plain sections; Proof strikes
have coin die alignment and reeded edges

KM# 899   20000 PESETAS
6.7500 g., 0.9990 Gold 0.2168 oz. AGW **Ruler:** Juan Carlos I
Subject: Huascar **Obv:** Bust facing within beaded circle
Rev: Armored bust with spear within beaded circle

Date	Mintage	F	VF	XF	Unc	BU
1991	1,000	—	—	—	—	250
1991 Proof	2,000	Value: 250				

KM# 916   20000 PESETAS
6.7500 g., 0.9990 Gold 0.2168 oz. AGW **Ruler:** Juan Carlos I
Series: Olympics **Obv:** Bust 1/4 right within circle **Rev:** Dome
building within circle

Date	Mintage	F	VF	XF	Unc	BU
1992	1,000	—	—	—	—	270
1992 Proof	3,000	Value: 270				

Note: Uncirculated strikes have medallic die alignment and
edges with reeded and plain sections; Proof strikes
have coin die alignment and reeded edges

KM# 1003   20000 PESETAS
6.7500 g., 0.9990 Gold 0.2168 oz. AGW **Ruler:** Juan Carlos I
Obv: Bust facing within beaded circle **Rev:** Worker feeding
screw press

Date	Mintage	F	VF	XF	Unc	BU
1992	1,000	—	—	—	—	270
1992 Proof	—	Value: 270				

KM# 929   20000 PESETAS
6.7500 g., 0.9990 Gold 0.2168 oz. AGW **Ruler:** Juan Carlos I
Subject: Holy Jacobean Year **Rev:** Conveyance of Santiago's body

Date	Mintage	F	VF	XF	Unc	BU
1993 Proof	2,000	Value: 250				

Date	Mintage	F	VF	XF	Unc	BU
1990 Proof	4,000	Value: 250				

Note: Uncirculated strikes have medallic die alignment and
edges with reeded and plain sections; Proof strikes
have coin die alignment and reeded edges

KM# 944   20000 PESETAS
6.7500 g., 0.9990 Gold 0.2168 oz. AGW **Ruler:** Juan Carlos I
Subject: Paleolithic Cave Painting **Rev:** Stylized animal cave
paintings

Date	Mintage	F	VF	XF	Unc	BU
1994 Proof	8,000	Value: 260				

KM# 958   20000 PESETAS
6.7500 g., 0.9990 Gold 0.2168 oz. AGW **Ruler:** Juan Carlos I
Subject: Ancient Sculpture - Dama de Elche **Rev:** Hooded bust left

Date	Mintage	F	VF	XF	Unc	BU
1995 Proof	8,000	Value: 250				

KM# 971   20000 PESETAS
6.7500 g., 0.9990 Gold 0.2168 oz. AGW **Ruler:** Juan Carlos I
Rev: Pillars and arches

Date	Mintage	F	VF	XF	Unc	BU
1996 Proof	Est. 6,000	Value: 250				

KM# 844   40000 PESETAS
13.5000 g., 0.9990 Gold 0.4336 oz. AGW **Ruler:** Juan Carlos I
Subject: Discovery of America **Obv:** Standing figure divides date
and beaded circle **Rev:** Sea monster attacking ship within beaded
circle

Date	Mintage	F	VF	XF	Unc	BU
1989	4,500	—	—	—	—	475
1989 Proof	6,000	Value: 425				

KM# 878   40000 PESETAS
13.5000 g., 0.9990 Gold 0.4336 oz. AGW **Ruler:** Juan Carlos I
Subject: Felipe II **Obv:** Standing figure divides date and beaded
circle **Rev:** King seated on throne within beaded circle

Date	Mintage	F	VF	XF	Unc	BU
1990	2,000	—	—	—	—	475
1990 Proof	3,000	Value: 425				

KM# 900   40000 PESETAS
13.5000 g., 0.9990 Gold 0.4336 oz. AGW **Ruler:** Juan Carlos I
Obv: Standing figure divides beaded circle and dates
Rev: Imperial double eagle

Date	Mintage	F	VF	XF	Unc	BU
1991	1,000	—	—	—	—	550
1991 Proof	2,000	Value: 550				

KM# 1004   40000 PESETAS
13.5000 g., 0.9990 Gold 0.4336 oz. AGW **Ruler:** Juan Carlos I
Obv: Standing figure divides beaded circle and dates
Rev: Horse-powered coin press

Date	Mintage	F	VF	XF	Unc	BU
1992	1,000	—	—	—	—	600
1992 Proof	—	Value: 600				

KM# 979   40000 PESETAS
13.5000 g., 0.9990 Gold 0.4336 oz. AGW **Ruler:** Juan Carlos I
Subject: Patrimonio de la Humanidad **Obv:** UNESCO logo
Rev: Statues at Abu Simbel

Date	Mintage	F	VF	XF	Unc	BU
1996 Proof	4,000	Value: 475				

KM# 1023   40000 PESETAS
13.5000 g., 0.9990 Gold 0.4336 oz. AGW; 30 mm.
Ruler: Juan Carlos I **Series:** "Patrimonio de la Humanidad -
UNESCO" **Obv:** UNESCO logo **Rev:** Horyu-Ji pagoda
Edge: Reeded

Date	Mintage	F	VF	XF	Unc	BU
1997 Proof	4,000	Value: 475				

KM# 845   80000 PESETAS
27.0000 g., 0.9990 Gold 0.8672 oz. AGW **Ruler:** Juan Carlos I
Subject: Discovery of America **Obv:** Crowned busts of Juan Carlos
and Sofia facing each other within beaded circle **Rev:** Crowned busts
of Ferdinand and Isabella facing each other within circle

Date	Mintage	F	VF	XF	Unc	BU
1989	6,000	—	—	—	—	850
1989 Proof	7,000	Value: 850				

KM# 879   80000 PESETAS
27.0000 g., 0.9990 Gold 0.8672 oz. AGW **Ruler:** Juan Carlos I
Series: 1992 Olympics **Obv:** Royal family facing within circle
Rev: Discus thrower within circle

Date	Mintage	F	VF	XF	Unc	BU
1990	3,000	—	—	—	—	850
1990 Proof	5,000	Value: 850				

> **Note:** Uncirculated strikes have medallic die alignment and
> edges with reeded and plain sections; Proof strikes
> have coin die alignment and reeded edges

KM# 880   80000 PESETAS
27.0000 g., 0.9990 Gold 0.8672 oz. AGW **Ruler:** Juan Carlos I
Series: 1992 Olympics **Obv:** Royal family facing **Rev:** Prince
Balthasar Carlos on horseback

Date	Mintage	F	VF	XF	Unc	BU
1990	1,000	—	—	—	—	850
1990 Proof	4,000	Value: 850				

> **Note:** Uncirculated strikes have medallic die alignment and
> edges with reeded and plain sections; Proof strikes
> have coin die alignment and reeded edges

KM# 881   80000 PESETAS
27.0000 g., 0.9990 Gold 0.8672 oz. AGW **Ruler:** Juan Carlos I
Subject: Carlos V **Obv:** Crowned heads of Juan Carlos and Sofia
facing each other within beaded circle **Rev:** Armored half-figure
facing within beaded circle

Date	Mintage	F	VF	XF	Unc	BU
1990	2,000	—	—	—	—	850
1990 Proof	3,000	Value: 850				

KM# 901   80000 PESETAS
27.0000 g., 0.9990 Gold 0.8672 oz. AGW **Ruler:** Juan Carlos I
Series: Olympics **Obv:** Royal family facing **Rev:** Women tossing
man on blanket within circle

Date	Mintage	F	VF	XF	Unc	BU
1991	1,000	—	—	—	—	1,000
1991 Proof	2,000	Value: 1,000				

> **Note:** Uncirculated strikes have medallic die alignment and
> edges with reeded and plain sections; Proof strikes
> have coin die alignment and reeded edges

KM# 902   80000 PESETAS
27.0000 g., 0.9990 Gold 0.8672 oz. AGW **Ruler:** Juan Carlos I
Subject: Carlos III **Obv:** Crowned busts of Juan Carlos and Sofia
facing each other within beaded circle **Rev:** Armored bust right
within beaded circle

Date	Mintage	F	VF	XF	Unc	BU
1991	1,000	—	—	—	—	1,000
1991 Proof	2,000	Value: 1,000				

KM# 917   80000 PESETAS
27.0000 g., 0.9990 Gold 0.8672 oz. AGW **Ruler:** Juan Carlos I
Series: Olympics **Rev:** Two children playing within circle

Date	Mintage	F	VF	XF	Unc	BU
1992	1,000	—	—	—	—	1,000
1992 Proof	2,000	Value: 1,000				

> **Note:** Uncirculated strikes have medallic die alignment and
> edges with reeded and plain sections; Proof strikes
> have coin die alignment and reeded edges

KM# 1005   80000 PESETAS
27.0000 g., 0.9990 Gold 0.8672 oz. AGW **Ruler:** Juan Carlos I
Obv: Crowned busts of Juan Carlos and Sofia facing each other
within beaded circle **Rev:** Hammer minting scene

Date	Mintage	F	VF	XF	Unc	BU
1992	1,000	—	—	—	—	1,000
1992 Proof	—	Value: 1,000				

KM# 930   80000 PESETAS
27.0000 g., 0.9990 Gold 0.8672 oz. AGW **Ruler:** Juan Carlos I
Subject: Holy Jacobean Year **Obv:** Head left **Rev:** French
Fraternity of Santiago Medallion within beaded circle

Date	Mintage	F	VF	XF	Unc	BU
1993 Proof	1,500	Value: 1,000				

KM# 945   80000 PESETAS
27.0000 g., 0.9990 Gold 0.8672 oz. AGW **Ruler:** Juan Carlos I
Rev: Iberian Lynx

Date	Mintage	F	VF	XF	Unc	BU
1994 Proof	5,000	Value: 1,000				

KM# 959   80000 PESETAS
27.0000 g., 0.9990 Gold 0.8672 oz. AGW **Ruler:** Juan Carlos I
Rev: Leda and the Swan

Date	Mintage	F	VF	XF	Unc	BU
1995 Proof	5,000 Value: 1,000					

KM# 972   80000 PESETAS
27.0000 g., 0.9990 Gold 0.8672 oz. AGW **Ruler:** Juan Carlos I
Rev: Folk dancers

Date	Mintage	F	VF	XF	Unc	BU
1996 Proof	Est. 3,500 Value: 1,000					

KM# 1028   80000 PESETAS
27.0000 g., 0.9990 Gold 0.8672 oz. AGW, 38 mm.
Ruler: Juan Carlos I **Subject:** House of Borbon **Obv:** Head of
Ferdinand VI right within circle and beaded border **Rev:** Crowned
shield within circle and beaded border **Edge:** Reeded

Date	Mintage	F	VF	XF	Unc	BU
1997 Proof	4,000 Value: 1,000					

EURO COINAGE
European Union Issues

KM# 1040   EURO CENT
2.2700 g., Copper Plated Steel, 16.2 mm. **Ruler:** Juan Carlos I
Obv: Cathedral of Santiago de Compostela **Rev:** Value and globe
Edge: Plain

Date	Mintage	F	VF	XF	Unc	BU
1999(M)	721,000,000	—	—	—	0.25	0.35
2000(M)	83,400,000	—	—	—	1.00	1.25

KM# 1041   2 EURO CENT
3.0300 g., Copper Plated Steel, 18.7 mm. **Ruler:** Juan Carlos I
Obv: Cathedral of Santiago de Compostela **Rev:** Value and globe
Edge: Grooved

Date	Mintage	F	VF	XF	Unc	BU
1999(M)	291,700,000	—	—	—	0.75	1.00
2000(M)	711,300,000	—	—	—	0.25	0.35

KM# 1042   5 EURO CENT
3.8600 g., Copper Plated Steel, 21.2 mm. **Ruler:** Juan Carlos I
Obv: Cathedral of Santiago de Compostela **Rev:** Value and globe
Edge: Plain

Date	Mintage	F	VF	XF	Unc	BU
1999(M)	483,500,000	—	—	—	0.65	0.75
2000(M)	399,900,000	—	—	—	0.65	0.75

KM# 1043   10 EURO CENT
4.0700 g., Brass, 19.7 mm. **Ruler:** Juan Carlos I **Obv:** Head of
Cervantes with ruffed collar 1/4 left within star border **Rev:** Value
and map **Edge:** Reeded

Date	Mintage	F	VF	XF	Unc	BU
1999(M)	588,100,000	—	—	—	0.65	0.75
2000(M)	243,900,000	—	—	—	0.65	0.75

KM# 1044   20 EURO CENT
5.7300 g., Brass, 22.1 mm. **Ruler:** Juan Carlos I **Obv:** Head of
Cervantes with ruffed collar 1/4 left within star border **Rev:** Value
and map **Edge:** Notched

Date	Mintage	F	VF	XF	Unc	BU
1999(M)	762,300,000	—	—	—	0.85	1.00
2000(M)	29,300,000	—	—	—	2.75	3.50

KM# 1045   50 EURO CENT
7.8100 g., Brass, 24.2 mm. **Ruler:** Juan Carlos I **Obv:** Head of
Cervantes with ruffed collar 1/4 left within star border **Rev:** Value
and map **Edge:** Reeded

Date	Mintage	F	VF	XF	Unc	BU
1999(M)	371,000,000	—	—	—	1.50	1.75
2000(M)	519,600,000	—	—	—	1.25	1.50

KM# 1046   EURO
7.5000 g., Bi-Metallic Copper-Nickel center in Brass ring, 23.2 mm.
Ruler: Juan Carlos I **Obv:** Head 1/4 left within circle and star border
Rev: Value and map within circle **Edge:** Reeded and plain sections

Date	Mintage	F	VF	XF	Unc	BU
1999(M)	100,200,000	—	—	—	3.00	3.50
2000(M)	89,300,000	—	—	—	4.00	4.50

KM# 1047   2 EURO
8.5200 g., Bi-Metallic Brass center in Copper-Nickel ring, 25.7 mm.
Ruler: Juan Carlos I **Obv:** Head 1/4 left within circle and star border
Rev: Value and map within circle **Edge:** Reeded **Edge:** 2's and stars

Date	Mintage	F	VF	XF	Unc	BU
1999(M)	60,500,000	—	—	—	5.00	6.00
2000(M)	36,600,000	—	—	—	5.00	6.00

TRIAL STRIKES

KM#	Date	Mintage	Identification	Mkt Val
TS1	1987	—	500 Pesetas. Silver. Conjoined heads left. Inscription divides crown, letter and star. KM#831.	12.50
TS2	1987	—	500 Pesetas. Stainless Steel.	10.00
TS3	1987	—	500 Pesetas. Silver. Inscription divides crown, letter and star. Crown above monogram within banner.	12.50
TS4	1987	—	500 Pesetas. Stainless Steel. Inscription divides crown, letter and star. Value above design and crown.	10.00
TS5	ND	—	2000 Pesetas. Silver. KM#859.	175

PATTERNS
Including off metal strikes

KM#	Date	Mintage	Identification	Mkt Val
Pn16	1937	—	10 Centimos. Zinc. Denomination. Crowned arms on eagle. III Año Triunfal.	1,000
Pn17	ND	—	5 Euro Cent. Bronze. 4.7200 g. 23.4 mm. Sumpol, mint mark and denomination. Denomination. Plain edge.	*
Pn18	ND	—	10 Euro Cent. Brass. 4.6400 g. 23 mm. Symbol, mint mark and denomination. Denomination. Plain edge.	*

MINT SETS

KM#	Date	Mintage	Identification	Issue Price	Mkt Val
MS1	1949 (E51) (3)	5,000	KM#776, 777-778	—	3,500
MSA2	1962 (7)	—	KM785-788, 790, 795-796, in Carton	—	100
MSB2	1963 (7)	—	KM785-788, 790, 795-796, in carton, 2.5 peseta struck from rusty dies with new alloy onlu found in this set.	—	100
MS2	1958Ba (3)	—	KM#786-788	—	400
MS3	1964 (7)	—	KM#785-788, 790, 795-796; Set contains KM#790, dated 1959. Mixed dates, 1964 latest date, 1 peseta proof. In cardboard holder.	3.60	100
MS4	1965 (7)	—	KM#785-788, 790, 795-796; Set contains KM#790, dated 1959. 1965 1 peseta proof. Mixed dates, 1965 latest date. In cardboard holder.	3.60	150
MSA5	1966 (7)	—	KM775, 777, 785-788, 790, 1 peseta & 2.5 peseta proofs	—	150
MS5	1966 (8)	—	KM#775, 777, 785-788, 790, 797; Set contains KM#790, dated 1959. Mixed date, 1966 1 peseta & 1956 2.5 peseta proof, 1966 latest date. In cardboard holder.	—	200
MS6	1966 (8)	—	KM#775, 777, 785-788, 790, 797; Set contains KM#790, dated 1959. Mixed dates, 1peseta & 2.5 peseta proof, 1966 latest date. In plastic sleeve.	—	200
MSA7	1967 (7)	—	KM786-788, 790, 795-797; Prooflike in plastic sleeve, all * 67, except 25 pesetas * 66.	—	250
MS7	1968 (8)	1,000	KM#785-788, 790, 795-797; Set contains KM#790, dated 1959 with added 'strike date' to match the set	3.60	3,000
MS8	1969 (8)	1,200	KM#785-788, 790, 795-797; Set contains KM#790, dated 1959 with added 'strike date' to match the set	3.60	2,500
MS9	1970 (8)	6,000	KM#785-788, 790, 795-797; Set contains KM#790, dated 1959 with added 'strike date' to match the set	3.60	400
MS10	1971 (7)	10,000	KM#785-788, 790, 795-797; Set contains KM#790, dated 1959 with added 'strike date' to match the set. KM797 is *70.	3.60	225
MS11	1980//82 (4)	—	KM#816, 817, 818, 819. Unofficial Tourist set.	—	6.50
MS12	1982 (4)	—	KM#823, 824, 825, 826. Unofficial Tourist set.	—	15.00
MS13	1990 (U) (5)	—	KM#854, 856-858, 868	—	60.00
MS15	1991 (U) (5)	—	KM#882-883, 885-886, 892	—	85.00
MS18	1992 (10)	—	KM#832-833, 903-910	12.00	60.00
MS19	1993 (8)	—	KM#832, 918-919, 920-924, labeled as proof	15.00	45.00
MS20	1994 (8)	—	KM#832, 924, 931-936	12.00	70.00
MS21	1995 (8)	—	KM#832, 924, 946-951	13.50	200
MS22	1996 (8)	—	KM#832, 924, 960-965	14.00	50.00
MS23	1997 (8)	—	KM#832, 924, 981-986	15.50	20.00
MS24	1998 (8)	—	KM#832-833, 924, 989-992, 1012	15.50	25.00
MS25	1999 (8)	49,030	KM#832-833, 924, 991-992, 1006-1008, 1012	15.50	35.00
MS26	2000 (8)	49,600	KM#832-833, 924, 991-992, 1012-1013	15.50	45.00
MS27	2000-2001 (8)	49,426	KM#832-833, 924, 991-992 (both dated 2000), 1012-1013, 1016	15.50	20.00

PROOF SETS

KM#	Date	Mintage	Identification	Issue Price	Mkt Val
PS1	1972 (6)	30,000	KM#786-788, 790, 795-796	5.00	45.00
PS2	1973 (6)	25,000	KM#786-788, 790, 795-796	5.00	140
PS3	1974 (6)	23,000	KM#786-788, 790, 795-796	5.00	100
PS4	1975 (6)	75,000	KM#786-788, 790, 795-796	5.00	18.50
PS5	1976 (6)	400,000	KM#805-810	5.00	3.50
PS6	1977 (3)	300,000	KM#806-808	0.35	1.50
PS7	1979 (4)	300,000	KM#806-809	0.90	1.75
PSA8	1980 (80) (6)	—	KM#815-820 Set labeled "Fabrica National de Moneda y Timbre"	—	7.50
PS8	1987 (6)	—	KM#831, Pn4, Pn4a, Pn5-6	25.00	35.00
PS9	1987 (2)	—	KM#828, 830	—	120
PS10	1989 (7)	—	KM#834-839, 841	—	250
PS11	1989 (5)	—	KM#M1-M5	—	950
PS12	1989 (5)	—	KM#840, 842-845	3,177	1,775
PS13	1990 (7)	—	KM#854, 856-858, 868-869, 873	—	250
PS14	1991 (7)	—	KM#882-883, 885-886, 892-893, 896	—	375
PS15	1992 (7)	—	KM#980, 993-998	—	450
PS16	1995 (5)	—	I.A. KM#938, 953, 956-959	—	1,550
PS17	1995 (4)	25,000	KM#938, 953, 956-959	—	300
PS18	1996 (6)	—	KM#966-967, 969-972	1,675	1,600
PS19	1996 (5)	—	KM#966-967, 969-972	1,650	1,600
PS20	1996 (4)	—	KM#966-967, 969-970	—	350
PS21	1996 (4)	—	KM#966-967, 969-970	—	350
PS22	1996 (5)	—	KM#973-978	198	160
PS23	1996 (7)	—	KM#973-979	702	675

SPAIN-Civil War

With the loss of her American empire, Spain drifted into chaotic times. Stung by their defeats in Cuba, the army blamed the Socialists for what they considered to be mismanagement at home. Additional political complications were derived from the successful Russian Revolution which gave impetus to an already thriving Socialist party and trade union movement. Finally, King Alphonso XIII committed the fatal mistake of encouraging a reckless general to start a campaign in Morocco that ended in the virtual extermination of the Spanish army. Fearing that the inevitable parliamentary investigation would incriminate the crown, he offered no objection when General Primo de Rivera seized the government and established himself as dictator in 1926. Rivera fell from power in 1930, and the government was taken over by an alliance of Liberals and Socialists who tried to separate the Church and State, take the army out of politics, and introduce effective labor and agrarian reforms despite numerous strikes and street riots. The election of 1936 brought to power a coalition of Socialists, Liberals and Communists, to the dismay of the traditionalists and landowners.

A number of right-wing generals, including the young and clever Francisco Franco, began preparations for a military coup which erupted into a civil war in July of 1936. The destructive conflict, in which more than a million died, lasted three years. During the struggle, areas under control of both the Nationalists (rebels) and the Republicans (Loyalists) issued coinages that circulated to whatever extent the political and military situation permitted. The war ended defeat for the Loyalists when Madrid fell to Franco on March 28, 1939.

During the Spanish Civil War (1936-1939) a great many coins and tokens were minted in the provincial districts. The coins are grouped here under the heading of the district in which they most commonly circulated.

CAUTIONARY NOTE: Many counterfeits of the Civil War coinage exist. Authentication has been recommended by leading experts in this field.

AMETLLA DEL VALLES

A town in the province of Tarragona in northeastern Spain. The town adopted the name L'Ametlla del Valles in 1933. Before that the name was La Ametlla.

REPUBLICAN ZONE

DECIMAL COINAGE

KM# 1   25 CENTIMOS
Brass, 25 mm.

Date	Mintage	F	VF	XF	Unc	BU
ND (1937)	50,000	12.00	25.00	35.00	50.00	—

KM# 2.1   50 CENTIMOS
Aluminum, 20 mm.

Date	Mintage	F	VF	XF	Unc	BU
ND (1937)	3,000	100	200	250	300	—

KM# 2.2   50 CENTIMOS
Aluminum, 20 mm. **Obv:** Without legend

Date	Mintage	F	VF	XF	Unc	BU
ND (1937)	30,000	25.00	50.00	70.00	100	—

KM# 3.1   PESETA
Aluminum, 26 mm.

Date	Mintage	F	VF	XF	Unc	BU
ND (1937)	3,000	75.00	100	125	150	—

KM# 3.2   PESETA
Aluminum, 26 mm. **Obv:** Without legend

Date	Mintage	F	VF	XF	Unc	BU
ND (1937)	30,000	15.00	30.00	40.00	50.00	—

ARAHAL

A town 30 miles east of Seville. Issued 3 undated types of coins in 1936.

NATIONALIST ZONE

DECIMAL COINAGE

KM# 1   50 CENTIMOS
Brass, 19 mm. **Obv:** Value within legend **Note:** Uniface.

Date	Mintage	F	VF	XF	Unc	BU
ND (1936)	3,000	50.00	100	200	300	—

Note: Forgeries exist

KM# 2   PESETA
Brass, 25 mm. **Obv:** Value within legend **Note:** Uniface.

Date	Mintage	F	VF	XF	Unc	BU
ND (1936)	10,000	20.00	30.00	50.00	75.00	—

Note: Forgeries exist

KM# 3   2 PESETAS
Brass, 30 mm. **Obv:** Value within legend **Note:** Uniface.

Date	Mintage	F	VF	XF	Unc	BU
ND (1936)	10,000	20.00	30.00	50.00	75.00	—

Note: Forgeries exist

ARENYS DE MAR

A resort village on the Mediterranean shore that is 20 miles north of Barcelona. One of the villages in the area of operations of General Mola at the beginning of the war.

REPUBLICAN ZONE

DECIMAL COINAGE

KM# 1   50 CENTIMOS
Aluminum, 21 mm. **Obv:** Shield divides value **Note:** Uniface.

Date	Mintage	F	VF	XF	Unc	BU
ND (1937)	6,000	50.00	90.00	110	150	—

Note: Forgeries exist

KM# 2   PESETA
Aluminum, 29 mm. **Obv:** Shield divides value **Note:** Uniface.

Date	Mintage	F	VF	XF	Unc	BU
ND (1937)	3,500	55.00	100	120	160	—

Note: Forgeries exist

ASTURIAS AND LEON

Asturias is a province on the northern coast of Spain with the province of Leon just to its south. The councils of these adjoining provinces decided to mint coins in 1937 for use in the area due to lack of other circulating coins in the north.

REPUBLICAN ZONE

DECIMAL COINAGE

KM# 1   50 CENTIMOS
Copper-Nickel, 21 mm. **Obv:** Crossed tools and gear in back of upright design **Rev:** Value and date

Date	Mintage	F	VF	XF	Unc	BU
1937	200,000	15.00	20.00	30.00	35.00	40.00

KM# 2   PESETA
Copper, 23 mm. **Obv:** Standing figure with hat facing left **Rev:** Value and date

Date	Mintage	F	VF	XF	Unc	BU
1937	100,000	15.00	25.00	35.00	50.00	—

KM# 3   2 PESETAS
Copper-Nickel **Obv:** Standing figure with hand on gear **Rev:** Value and date **Note:** Varieties exist with differences in the leaves.

Date	Mintage	F	VF	XF	Unc	BU
1937	400,000	5.00	7.50	10.00	20.00	25.00

CAZALLA DE LA SIERRA

A town 43 miles north of Seville that issued a 10 Centimos in brass in 1936 (undated).

NATIONALIST ZONE

DECIMAL COINAGE

KM# 1 10 CENTIMOS
Brass, 23 mm. **Obv:** Crowned shield to right of legend
Rev: Legend and value, single sprig at left

Date	Mintage	F	VF	XF	Unc	BU
ND (1936)	10,000	30.00	45.00	70.00	125	—

EUZKADI

Euzkadi or the Viscayan Republic was located in north central Spain adjoining the southeast corner of France. It was made up of 3 provinces - Guipuzcoa, Alava, and Viscaya. These Basque provinces declared autonomy on October 8, 1936. The 2 nickel coins were made in Brussels, Belgium and saw some circulation before the end of the Republic on June 18, 1937.

VISCAYAN REPUBLIC

DECIMAL COINAGE

KM# 1 PESETA
Nickel, 22 mm. **Obv:** Liberty head right **Rev:** Value and date within wreath

Date	Mintage	F	VF	XF	Unc	BU
1937	7,000,000	2.50	5.00	7.00	10.00	12.50

KM# 2 2 PESETAS
Nickel, 26 mm. **Obv:** Liberty head right **Rev:** Value and date within wreath

Date	Mintage	F	VF	XF	Unc	BU
1937	6,000,000	3.00	6.00	8.00	12.00	15.00

GRATALLOPS

REPUBLICAN ZONE

DECIMAL COINAGE

KM# 1 5 CENTIMOS
Zinc **Issuer:** Ayuntamiento de Gratallops **Note:** Stamped 5-C/G. Size 21x21mm.

Date	Mintage	F	VF	XF	Unc	BU
ND(1937)	—	150	200	300	—	—

KM# 2 10 CENTIMOS
Zinc **Issuer:** Ayuntamiento de Gratallops **Note:** Stamped 10-C/G. Size 26x26mm.

Date	Mintage	F	VF	XF	Unc	BU
ND(1937)	—	150	200	300	—	—

KM# 3 25 CENTIMOS
Zinc **Issuer:** Ayuntamiento de Gratallops **Note:** Stamped 25-C/G. Size 31x22mm.

Date	Mintage	F	VF	XF	Unc	BU
ND(1937)	—	150	200	300	—	—

KM# 4 50 CENTIMOS
Zinc, 23 mm. **Issuer:** Ayuntamiento de Grattalops
Note: Stamped 50/C.

Date	Mintage	F	VF	XF	Unc	BU
ND(1937)	—	150	225	350	—	—

KM# 5 PESO
Zinc, 25 mm. **Issuer:** Ayuntamiento de Gratallops
Note: Stamped 1-P/G.

Date	Mintage	F	VF	XF	Unc	BU
ND(1937)	—	150	225	350	—	—

IBI

A village north and west of Alicante on the east coast of Spain. The isolation of the area in comparison with other contending areas made the maintaining of this area during the war very difficult.

REPUBLICAN ZONE

DECIMAL COINAGE

KM# 1.1 25 CENTIMOS
Copper, 24 mm. **Obv:** Legend and value **Rev:** Liberty head left flanked by sprigs **Note:** Varieties exist.

Date	Mintage	F	VF	XF	Unc	BU
1937	30,000	20.00	35.00	50.00	60.00	—

KM# 1.2 25 CENTIMOS
Copper, 24 mm. **Obv:** Value and map of Spain in field
Rev: Liberty head left flanked by sprigs

Date	Mintage	F	VF	XF	Unc	BU
1937	7,000	65.00	100	150	200	—

KM# 2 PESETA
Nickel-Brass, 24 mm. **Obv:** Legend and date **Rev:** Value

Date	Mintage	F	VF	XF	Unc	BU
1937	5,000	50.00	85.00	125	200	—

LORA DEL RIO

A town 35 miles northeast of Seville. Issued an undated 25 Centimos in 1936.

NATIONALIST ZONE

DECIMAL COINAGE

KM# 1 25 CENTIMOS
Brass, 23 mm. **Obv:** Crowned shield within cross **Rev:** Legend and value, wheat sprig at right

Date	Mintage	F	VF	XF	Unc	BU
ND (1936)	1,500	225	375	450	950	—

MARCHENA

A village 30 miles east of Seville. It was the last issuer in Seville province. Two varieties of undated coins were produced in 1936.

NATIONALIST ZONE

DECIMAL COINAGE

KM# 1.1 25 CENTIMOS
Brass, 40 mm. **Obv:** Value at center of Legend **Note:** Uniface; denomination: 25C.

Date	Mintage	F	VF	XF	Unc	BU
ND (1936)	5,000	30.00	75.00	125	225	—

KM# 1.2 25 CENTIMOS
Brass, 40 mm. **Obv:** Value at center of legend **Note:** Uniface; denomination: 025C.

Date	Mintage	F	VF	XF	Unc	BU
ND (1936)	500	400	600	900	1,200	—

Note: Forgeries exist

MENORCA

Menorca is the smaller of the 2 major islands in the Balearic Islands. A serious coin and supply shortage developed during the war because of the isolation of the island from the mainland.

REPUBLICAN ZONE

DECIMAL COINAGE

KM# 1 5 CENTIMOS
Brass, 13 mm. **Obv:** Emblem within beaded circle **Rev:** Value above star, single sprig at left **Note:** Varieties exist.

Date	Mintage	F	VF	XF	Unc	BU
1937	42,000	—	40.00	50.00	60.00	—

KM# 2 10 CENTIMOS
Brass, 16 mm. **Obv:** Emblem within beaded circle **Rev:** Value above star, single sprig at left **Note:** Varieties exist.

Date	Mintage	F	VF	XF	Unc	BU
1937	32,000	—	25.00	35.00	45.00	—

KM# 3 25 CENTIMOS
Brass, 18 mm. **Obv:** Emblem within beaded circle **Rev:** Value above star, single sprig at left

Date	Mintage	F	VF	XF	Unc	BU
1937	38,000	—	20.00	25.00	30.00	—

KM# 4   PESETA
Brass, 20 mm. **Obv:** Emblem within beaded circle **Rev:** Value above star, single sprig at left

Date	Mintage	F	VF	XF	Unc	BU
1937	37,000	—	20.00	25.00	30.00	—

KM# 5   2-1/2 PESETAS
Brass, 22 mm. **Obv:** Emblem within beaded circle **Rev:** Value above star, single sprig at left

Date	Mintage	F	VF	XF	Unc	BU
1937	24,000	—	60.00	100	125	—

NULLES

Nulles is a mountain village in the province of Tarragona. The mountainous terrain of the area isolated the village from friendly forces and normal commerce. Therefore, in 1937, an undated series of 5 denominations were issued.

REPUBLICAN ZONE

DECIMAL COINAGE

KM# 1   5 CENTIMOS
Zinc, 23 mm. **Obv:** Value at center of legend **Note:** Uniface, legends similar to 10 Centimos, KM#2.

Date	Mintage	F	VF	XF	Unc	BU
ND (1937)	5,000	200	350	500	650	—

KM# 2   10 CENTIMOS
Zinc, 21 mm. **Obv:** Value at center of legend **Note:** Uniface.

Date	Mintage	F	VF	XF	Unc	BU
ND (1937)	3,000	250	400	600	900	—

KM# 3   25 CENTIMOS
Brass, 20 mm. **Obv:** Value at center of legend **Note:** Uniface. Legends similar to 10 Centimos, KM#2.

Date	Mintage	F	VF	XF	Unc	BU
ND (1937)	5,000	200	350	500	600	—

KM# 4   50 CENTIMOS
Brass, 22 mm. **Obv:** Value at center of legend **Note:** Uniface, legends similar to 10 Centimos, KM#2.

Date	Mintage	F	VF	XF	Unc	BU
ND (1937)	1,000	250	400	550	700	—

KM# 5   PESETA
Brass, 22 mm. **Obv:** Value at center of legend **Note:** Uniface.

Date	Mintage	F	VF	XF	Unc	BU
ND (1937)	5,000	150	200	250	350	—

OLOT

A village in the province of Gerona in northeastern Spain near the French border. The village council authorized 2 denominations of coins on September 24, 1937.

REPUBLICAN ZONE

DECIMAL COINAGE

KM# 1   10 CENTIMOS
Iron, 24 mm. **Obv:** Vertical lines and eagle wing within design **Rev:** Caduceus divides value

Date	Mintage	F	VF	XF	Unc	BU
1937	25,000	45.00	65.00	100	175	—

KM# 2   15 CENTIMOS
Iron, 30 mm. **Obv:** Vertical lines and eagle wing within design **Rev:** Stylized factory scene and value

Date	Mintage	F	VF	XF	Unc	BU
1937	100	1,600	1,850	3,700	7,400	—
Note: Forgeries exist						

PUEBLA DE CAZALLA

A village only a few miles east of El Arahal and some 40 miles from Sevilla. Undated coins of 2 values were issued in 1936.

NATIONALIST ZONE

DECIMAL COINAGE

KM# 1   10 CENTIMOS
Brass, 23 mm. **Obv:** Tied arrows with banner to left of legend **Rev:** Value **Note:** Counterstamped varieties exist.

Date	Mintage	F	VF	XF	Unc	BU
ND (1936)	1,500	175	350	450	650	—

KM# 2   25 CENTIMOS
Brass, 25 mm. **Obv:** Tied arrows with banner to left of legend **Rev:** Value **Note:** Counterstamped varieties exist.

Date	Mintage	F	VF	XF	Unc	BU
ND (1936)	5,000	150	325	425	600	—

SANTANDER, PALENCIA & BURGOS

REPUBLICAN ZONE

DECIMAL COINAGE

KM# 1.1   50 CENTIMOS
Copper-Nickel, 20 mm. **Obv:** Standing 1/2 length figure with hammer **Rev:** Value above crossed sprigs

Date	Mintage	F	VF	XF	Unc	BU
1937	100,000	—	25.00	35.00	45.00	55.00

KM# 1.2   50 CENTIMOS
Copper-Nickel, 20 mm. **Obv:** Blacksmith with factory in background **Rev:** Letters PR or PJR below CTS

Date	Mintage	F	VF	XF	Unc	BU
1937	10,000	—	30.00	40.00	50.00	60.00

KM# 2   PESETA
Copper-Nickel, 23 mm. **Obv:** Crowned shield to left of legend **Rev:** Value within 1/2 wreath

Date	Mintage	F	VF	XF	Unc	BU
1937	300,000	—	15.00	20.00	30.00	—

SEGARRA DE GAIA

A village in the southern part of the province of Tarragona. A single denomination of coin was authorized in 1937.

REPUBLICAN ZONE

DECIMAL COINAGE

KM# 2   PESETA
Aluminum, 24 mm. **Obv:** C.M. SEGARRA = DE GAIA = above, 1pta. below, numerals stamped at center **Note:** Uniface

Date	Mintage	F	VF	XF	Unc	BU
ND(1937)	—	150	225	350	—	—

KM# 1   PESETA
Copper-Nickel, 23 mm. **Obv:** Value over bars of Aragon in circle

Date	Mintage	F	VF	XF	Unc	BU
ND(1937)	5,000	15.00	25.00	35.00	40.00	—

KM# 1a   PESETA
Copper, 23 mm. **Obv:** Value over bars of Aragon in circle **Note:** Uniface. Value over bars of Aragon in circle.

Date	Mintage	F	VF	XF	Unc	BU
ND(1937)	20,000	75.00	125	150	200	—

SPITZBERGEN

Spitzbergen (Svalbard), a Norwegian territory, is a group of mountainous islands in the Arctic Ocean 360 miles (579 km.) north of Norway. The islands have an area of 23,957 sq. mi. (62,050 sq. km.) and a population of about 4,000. West Spitzbergen, the largest island, is the seat of administration. Sealing and fishing are economically important. Despite rich carboniferous and tertiary coal deposits, coal mining, which was started on a commercial scale by the Arctic Coal Co. of Boston, Mass. in 1904, produces only small quantities.

Spitzbergen was probably discovered in 1194, but modern knowledge of it dates from its discovery by William Barents in 1596. Quarrels among the various nationalities involved in the whaling industry, which was set up in 1611, resulted in a de facto division of the coast, but despite diverse interests in, and claims to the islands by British, Dutch, Norwegians, Swedes, Danes, Russians and Americans, the question of sovereignty was not resolved until 1920, when a treaty agreed to by the claimants awarded the islands to Norway.

In 1932, the Russian mining company Arktikugol began operations in the islands. The tokens listed here were minted in Leningrad for use by the company in Spitzbergen.

RULER
Norwegian, 1920-

LEGENDS

= Spitzbergen

= Artikugol = Arctic Coal Co.

= Exchange Tokens

NORWEGIAN TERRITORY

TOKEN COINAGE
Artic Coal Issues

KM# Tn1 10 KOPEKS
Aluminum-Bronze **Obv:** Star below date, legend around **Rev:** Value, legend

Date	Mintage	F	VF	XF	Unc	BU
1946	—	18.00	30.00	65.00	125	—

KM# Tn2 15 KOPEKS
Aluminum-Bronze **Obv:** Star below date, legend around **Rev:** Value, legend

Date	Mintage	F	VF	XF	Unc	BU
1946	—	22.00	35.00	70.00	140	—

KM# Tn3 20 KOPEKS
Copper-Nickel **Obv:** Star below date, legend around **Rev:** Value, legend

Date	Mintage	F	VF	XF	Unc	BU
1946	—	25.00	45.00	75.00	150	—

KM# Tn4.1 50 KOPEKS
Copper-Nickel **Obv:** Larger star below date, legend around **Rev:** Value, legend

Date	Mintage	F	VF	XF	Unc	BU
1946	—	30.00	50.00	80.00	160	—

KM# Tn4.2 50 KOPEKS
Copper-Nickel **Obv:** Smaller star below date, legend around **Rev:** Value, legend

Date	Mintage	F	VF	XF	Unc	BU
1946	—	30.00	50.00	80.00	160	—

KM# Tn5 10 ROUBLES
Copper-Nickel Clad Steel **Obv:** Polar bear seated on 1/2 world globe **Rev:** Value within circle, legend around with date below

Date	Mintage	F	VF	XF	Unc	BU
1993	—	—	—	—	3.50	5.00

KM# Tn6 25 ROUBLES
Copper-Nickel Clad Steel **Obv:** Polar bear seated on 1/2 world globe **Rev:** Value within circle, legend around with date below

Date	Mintage	F	VF	XF	Unc	BU
1993	—	—	—	—	4.50	6.00

KM# Tn7 50 ROUBLES
Copper-Nickel Clad Steel **Obv:** Polar bear seated on 1/2 world globe **Rev:** Value within circle, legend around with date below

Date	Mintage	F	VF	XF	Unc	BU
1993	—	—	—	—	6.50	8.00

KM# Tn8 100 ROUBLES
Aluminum-Bronze **Obv:** Polar bear seated on 1/2 world globe **Rev:** Value within circle, legend around with date below

Date	Mintage	F	VF	XF	Unc	BU
1993	—	—	—	—	9.00	12.00

SRI (SHRI) LANKA

The Democratic Socialist Republic of Sri Lanka (formerly Ceylon) situated in the Indian Ocean 18 miles (29 km.) southeast of India, has an area of 25,332 sq. mi. (65,610 sq. km.) and a population of *16.9 million. Capital: Colombo. The economy is chiefly agricultural. Tea, coconut products and rubber are exported.

Sri Lanka is a member of the Commonwealth of Nations. The president is Chief of State. The prime minister is Head of Government. The present leaders of the country have reverted the country name back to Sri Lanka.

RULER
British, 1796-1948

DEMOCRATIC SOCIALIST REPUBLIC

DECIMAL COINAGE

100 Cents = 1 Rupee

KM# 137 CENT
Aluminum **Obv:** Value above designs within wreath **Rev:** National arms

Date	Mintage	F	VF	XF	Unc	BU
1975	52,778,000	—	—	0.10	0.25	0.45
1978	34,006,000	—	—	0.10	0.25	0.45
1978 Proof	20,000	Value: 2.50				
1989	6,000,000	—	—	0.10	0.25	0.45
1994	5,000,000	—	—	0.10	0.25	0.45

KM# 138 2 CENTS
0.7600 g., Aluminum, 18.5 mm. **Obv:** Value above designs within wreath **Rev:** National arms

Date	Mintage	F	VF	XF	Unc	BU
1975	62,503,000	—	—	0.10	0.25	0.45
1978 Proof	20,000	Value: 3.00				
1978	23,425,000	—	—	0.10	0.25	0.45

KM# 139 5 CENTS
3.3000 g., Nickel-Brass **Obv:** Value above designs within wreath **Rev:** National arms

Date	Mintage	F	VF	XF	Unc	BU
1975	19,584,000	—	—	0.10	0.25	0.45

KM# 139a 5 CENTS
1.0000 g., Aluminum **Obv:** Value above designs within wreath **Rev:** National arms

Date	Mintage	F	VF	XF	Unc	BU
1978	272,308,000	—	—	0.10	0.25	0.45
1978 Proof	20,000	Value: 3.00				
1988	40,000,000	—	—	0.10	0.25	0.45
1991	50,000,000	—	—	0.10	0.25	0.45

KM# 140 10 CENTS
4.1000 g., Nickel-Brass **Obv:** Value above designs within wreath **Rev:** National arms

Date	Mintage	F	VF	XF	Unc	BU
1975	10,800,000	—	—	0.10	0.25	0.45

KM# 140a 10 CENTS
1.2700 g., Aluminum, 23 mm. **Obv:** Value above designs within wreath **Rev:** National arms

Date	Mintage	F	VF	XF	Unc	BU
1978	188,820,000	—	—	0.10	0.25	0.45
1978 Proof	20,000	Value: 3.50				
1988	40,000,000	—	—	0.10	0.25	0.45
1991	50,000,000	—	—	0.10	0.25	0.45

KM# 141.1 25 CENTS
Copper-Nickel **Obv:** Value above designs within wreath
Rev: National arms **Edge:** Security

Date	Mintage	F	VF	XF	Unc	BU
1975	39,600,000	—	—	0.10	0.25	0.45
1975 Proof	1,431	Value: 4.00				
1978	65,009,000	—	—	0.10	0.25	0.45
1978 Proof	20,000	Value: 3.50				

KM# 141.2 25 CENTS
Copper-Nickel **Obv:** Value above designs within wreath
Rev: National arms **Edge:** Reeded

Date	Mintage	F	VF	XF	Unc	BU
1982	90,000,000	—	—	0.10	0.25	0.45
1989	45,000,000	—	—	0.10	0.25	0.45
1991	50,000,000	—	—	0.10	0.25	0.45
1994	50,000,000	—	—	0.10	0.25	0.45

KM# 141a 25 CENTS
Nickel Clad Steel **Obv:** National arms **Rev:** Value **Edge:** Reeded

Date	Mintage	F	VF	XF	Unc	BU
1996	50,000,000	—	—	0.10	0.25	0.45

KM# 135.1 50 CENTS
Copper-Nickel **Obv:** Value above designs within wreath
Rev: National arms **Edge:** Security

Date	Mintage	F	VF	XF	Unc	BU
1972	11,000,000	—	0.15	0.30	0.75	1.25
1975	34,000,000	—	0.15	0.30	0.75	1.25
1978	66,010,000	—	0.15	0.30	0.75	1.25
1978 Proof	20,000	Value: 4.50				

KM# 135.2 50 CENTS
5.5000 g., Copper-Nickel **Obv:** Value above designs within wreath **Rev:** National arms **Edge:** Reeded

Date	Mintage	F	VF	XF	Unc	BU
1982	65,000,000	—	0.10	0.25	0.65	1.00
1991	40,000,000	—	0.10	0.25	0.65	1.00
1994	40,000,000	—	0.10	0.25	0.65	1.00

KM# 135a 50 CENTS
Nickel Clad Steel **Obv:** National arms **Rev:** Value **Edge:** Reeded

Date	Mintage	F	VF	XF	Unc	BU
1996	50,000,000	—	0.10	0.25	0.65	1.00

KM# 136.1 RUPEE
Copper-Nickel **Obv:** Inscription below designs within wreath
Rev: National arms **Edge:** Security

Date	Mintage	F	VF	XF	Unc	BU
1972	7,000,000	—	0.30	0.60	1.25	1.75
1975	31,500,000	—	0.25	0.50	1.00	1.50
1978	37,018,000	—	0.25	0.50	1.00	1.50
1978 Proof	20,000	Value: 6.50				

KM# 136.2 RUPEE
Copper-Nickel **Obv:** Inscriptions below designs within wreath
Rev: National arms **Edge:** Reeded

Date	Mintage	F	VF	XF	Unc	BU
1982	75,000,000	—	0.25	0.50	1.00	1.50
1994	50,000,000	—	0.25	0.50	1.00	1.50

KM# 136a RUPEE
Nickel Clad Steel **Obv:** National arms **Rev:** Value **Edge:** Reeded

Date	Mintage	F	VF	XF	Unc	BU
1996	50,000,000	—	0.25	0.50	1.00	1.50
2000	30,000,000	—	0.25	0.50	1.00	1.50

KM# 144 RUPEE
Copper-Nickel **Subject:** Inauguration of President Jayewardene
Obv: National arms **Rev:** Head left

Date	Mintage	F	VF	XF	Unc	BU
1978	1,997,400	—	0.30	0.60	1.25	1.75
1978	2,600	—	—	—	—	50.00

Note: Right shoulder straight

Date	Mintage	F	VF	XF	Unc	BU
1978 Proof	20,000	Value: 6.50				

KM# 144a RUPEE
Gold **Subject:** Inauguration of President Jayawardene
Obv: National arms **Rev:** Head left

Date	Mintage	F	VF	XF	Unc	BU
1978 Proof	40	—	—	—	—	—

KM# 151 RUPEE
Copper-Nickel **Subject:** 3rd Anniversary of 2nd Executive
President Premadusa **Obv:** Facing lions with swords above
rectangular design **Rev:** Bust facing within wreath

Date	Mintage	F	VF	XF	Unc	BU
1992	25,000,000	—	0.30	0.65	1.75	2.50
1992 Proof	2,000	Value: 10.00				

KM# 151a RUPEE
0.9250 Silver **Subject:** 3rd Anniversary of 2nd Executive
President Premadusa **Obv:** Facing lions with swords above
rectangular design **Rev:** Bust facing within wreath

Date	Mintage	F	VF	XF	Unc	BU
1992 Frosted proof	2,500	Value: 50.00				

KM# 151b RUPEE
0.9167 Gold **Subject:** 3rd Anniversary of 2nd Executive
President Premadusa **Obv:** Lions with swords above rectangular
design **Rev:** Bust facing within wreath

Date	Mintage	F	VF	XF	Unc	BU
1992 Proof	100	—	—	—	—	—

KM# 157 RUPEE
Copper-Nickel **Subject:** UNICEF 50th Anniversary
Obv: Inscription and value below designs within wreath
Rev: Numeral 50 and UNICEF logo within circle

Date	Mintage	F	VF	XF	Unc	BU
1996	5,000,000	—	—	—	1.75	2.50

KM# 162 RUPEE
7.1300 g., Nickel Plated Steel, 25.4 mm. **Subject:** Army's 50th
Anniversary **Obv:** National arms above crossed swords above dates
within beaded circle **Rev:** Soldier giving dove to boy **Edge:** Reeded

Date	Mintage	F	VF	XF	Unc	BU
1999 Prooflike	127,000	—	—	—	—	6.00
1999 Proof	8,000	Value: 10.00				

KM# 164 RUPEE
7.1300 g., Nickel Plated Steel, 25.4 mm. **Subject:** Sri Lankan
Navy 50 Years **Obv:** National arms within circle **Rev:** Patrol boat
within circle **Edge:** Reeded

Date	Mintage	F	VF	XF	Unc	BU
2000	20,000	—	—	—	—	6.00

KM# 164a RUPEE
Copper Nickel, 25.4 mm. **Subject:** Sri Lankan Navy 50 Years
Obv: National arms within circle **Rev:** Patrol boat within circle
Edge: Reeded

Date	Mintage	F	VF	XF	Unc	BU
2000 Proof	2,000	Value: 10.00				

KM# 142 2 RUPEES
Copper-Nickel, 30 mm. **Subject:** Non-Aligned Nations
Conference **Obv:** Value within inscription, legend around border
Rev: Conference building **Edge:** Plain

Date	Mintage	F	VF	XF	Unc	BU
1976	2,000,000	—	0.50	1.50	2.25	3.50
1976 Proof	500	Value: 10.00				

KM# 145 2 RUPEES
Copper-Nickel **Subject:** Mahaweli Dam **Obv:** Numeral value
within inscription, legend around border **Rev:** Dam within circle

Date	Mintage	F	VF	XF	Unc	BU
1981	45,000,000	—	0.35	0.75	2.50	3.75

KM# 147 2 RUPEES
Copper-Nickel **Obv:** National arms **Rev:** Value

Date	Mintage	F	VF	XF	Unc	BU
1984	25,000,000	—	0.25	0.50	1.00	1.50
1993	40,000,000	—	0.30	0.60	1.35	1.75
1996	50,000,000	—	0.30	0.60	1.35	1.75

KM# 155 2 RUPEES
Copper-Nickel **Series:** F.A.O. **Subject:** F.A.O. 50th Anniversary
Obv: Value within inscription, legend around border **Rev:** F.A.O.
logo and dates within circle

Date	Mintage	F	VF	XF	Unc	BU
1995	40,000,000	—	—	—	2.25	3.25

KM# 143   5 RUPEES
13.7000 g., Nickel   **Subject:** Non-Aligned Nations Conference **Obv:** Value within inscription, legend around border **Rev:** Conference building

Date	Mintage	F	VF	XF	Unc	BU
1976	1,000,000	—	0.75	1.50	3.00	4.50
1976 Proof	500	Value: 12.00				

KM# 146   5 RUPEES
Copper-Nickel   **Subject:** 50th Anniversary - Universal Adult Franchise **Obv:** Value within inscription, legend around border **Rev:** Building with flag

Date	Mintage	F	VF	XF	Unc	BU
1981	2,000,000	—	0.75	1.50	3.00	4.50

KM# 148.1   5 RUPEES
Aluminum-Bronze   **Obv:** National arms **Rev:** Value within inscription, legend around border **Edge:** Lettered **Edge:** CBC - Central Bank of Ceylon

Date	Mintage	F	VF	XF	Unc	BU
1984	25,000,000	—	0.35	0.75	2.25	3.00

KM# 148.2   5 RUPEES
9.5000 g., Aluminum-Bronze   **Obv:** National arms **Rev:** Value **Edge:** Lettered **Edge:** CBSL - Central Bank of Sri Lanka

Date	Mintage	F	VF	XF	Unc	BU
1986	60,000,000	—	0.35	0.75	2.25	3.00
1991	40,000,000	—	0.35	0.75	2.25	3.00
1994	50,000,000	—	0.35	0.65	2.00	2.75

KM# 156   5 RUPEES
Aluminum-Bronze   **Subject:** 50th Anniversary - United Nations **Obv:** Value within inscription, legend around border **Rev:** Numeral 50 and UN logo within circle

Date	Mintage	F	VF	XF	Unc	BU
1995 Proof	5,000	—	—	—	—	—
1995	50,000,000	—	—	—	2.50	3.50

KM# 161   5 RUPEES
Aluminum-Bronze   **Subject:** World Cricket Champions **Obv:** Trophy **Rev:** Batsman within circle

Date	Mintage	F	VF	XF	Unc	BU
1999	50,000,000	—	—	—	2.75	4.00

KM# 149   10 RUPEES
Copper-Nickel   **Subject:** International Year of Shelter for Homeless **Obv:** Value within inscription, legend around border **Rev:** Logo, legend around border

Date	Mintage	F	VF	XF	Unc	BU
1987 Proof	200	—	—	—	—	—
1987	2,000,000	—	—	—	3.50	5.00

KM# 158   10 RUPEES
8.9500 g., Bi-Metallic Brass center in Copper-Nickel ring, 27 mm.   **Subject:** 50th Anniversary of Independence **Obv:** Value and dates within designed wreath **Rev:** Building within and outside of circle **Edge:** CBSL, (4 times) reeded

Date	Mintage	F	VF	XF	Unc	BU
1998	50,000,000	—	—	—	4.50	5.50

KM# 152   100 RUPEES
10.2000 g., 0.9250 Silver 0.3033 oz. ASW   **Subject:** 5th South Asian Federation Games **Obv:** Sunface above lion, elephant and rabbit, crescent below **Rev:** Logo above inscription, date and value

Date	Mintage	F	VF	XF	Unc	BU
1991 Proof	20,000	Value: 35.00				

KM# 150   500 RUPEES
28.2800 g., 0.9250 Silver 0.8410 oz. ASW, 38.6 mm.   **Subject:** 40th Anniversary of Central Bank **Obv:** National arms within circle **Rev:** Central Bank building within circle **Edge:** Reeded

Date	Mintage	F	VF	XF	Unc	BU
1990	10,000	—	—	—	—	32.50
1990 Proof	2,200	Value: 60.00				

KM# 153   500 RUPEES
1.6000 g., 0.5000 Gold 0.0257 oz. AGW   **Subject:** 5th South Asian Federation Games **Obv:** Stylized seated figure **Rev:** Value above logo and inscription

Date	Mintage	F	VF	XF	Unc	BU
1991 Proof	8,000	Value: 50.00				

KM# 154   500 RUPEES
28.2800 g., 0.9250 Silver 0.8410 oz. ASW   **Subject:** 2,300th Anniversary - Buddha's Teachings in Sri Lanka **Obv:** Large stylized leaf within circle **Rev:** Kneeling figure praying within forest, design above, all within circle **Note:** This is the only coin on which the country name SHRI LANKA appears. Shri Lanka was used only from June 1992 to December 1993, without constitutional authority, by decision of President Premadasa.

Date	Mintage	F	VF	XF	Unc	BU
1993 Proof	30,000	Value: 55.00				

KM# 159   1000 RUPEES
28.2800 g., 0.9250 Silver 0.8410 oz. ASW   **Subject:** 50 Years of Independence **Obv:** Flag and value within wreath **Rev:** Lion statue within circle

Date	Mintage	F	VF	XF	Unc	BU
1998 Proof	25,000	Value: 60.00				

KM# 163   1000 RUPEES
28.2800 g., 0.9250 Silver 0.8410 oz. ASW, 38.6 mm.   **Subject:** 1996 Cricket Champions **Obv:** Trophy **Rev:** Two players **Edge:** Reeded **Note:** Struck at British Royal Mint.

Date	Mintage	F	VF	XF	Unc	BU
1999 Proof	25,000	Value: 45.00				

KM# 165   1000 RUPEES
28.2800 g., 0.9250 Silver 0.8410 oz. ASW, 38.6 mm.
Subject: Central Bank 50 Years **Obv:** Sunface in center circle
of designs **Rev:** Building and value within circle **Edge:** Milled

Date	Mintage	F	VF	XF	Unc	BU
2000 Proof	10,000	Value: 50.00				

KM# 160   5000 RUPEES
7.9800 g., 0.9167 Gold 0.2352 oz. AGW **Subject:** 50 Years of
Independence **Obv:** Flag and value within wreath
Rev: Avalokitheshvara, an aspirant Buddha, seated in a graceful
stance within circle

Date	Mintage	F	VF	XF	Unc	BU
1998 Proof	5,000	Value: 260				

PATTERNS
Including off metal strikes

KM#	Date	Mintage Identification	Mkt Val
Pn1	1971	— 5 Cents. Nickel-Brass Plated Steel. Similar to KM#129, with TRIAL in raised letters on obverse.	—
Pn2	1971	— 5 Cents. Steel. Similar to KM#129, with TRIAL in raised letters on obverse.	—
Pn3	1971	— 5 Cents. Aluminum. Similar to #KM129, with TRIAL in raised letters on obverse.	—
Pn4	1971	— 10 Cents. Nickel-Brass Plated Steel. Similar to KM#130, with TRIAL in raised letters on obverse.	—
Pn5	1971	— 10 Cents. Steel. Similar to KM#130, with TRIAL in raised letters on obverse.	—
Pn6	1971	— 10 Cents. Aluminum. Similar to KM#130, with TRIAL in raised letters on obverse.	—
Pn7	1975	— 5 Cents. Aluminum. KM#139a	—
Pn8	1975	— 10 Cents. Aluminum. KM#140a	—

PROOF SETS

KM#	Date	Mintage Identification	Issue Price	Mkt Val
PS1	1978 (8)	20,000 KM135.1, 136.1, 137, 138, 139a, 140a, 141.1, 144	26.00	35.00

STRAITS SETTLEMENTS

[Map: THAILAND, PERLIS, KEDAH, PENANG, PERAK, KELANTAN, South China Sea, TRENGGANU, PAHANG, SELANGOR, NEGRI SEMBILAN, MALACCA, JOHORE, SINGAPORE, SUMATRA, Indian Ocean]

Straits Settlements, a former British crown colony situated on the Malay Peninsula of Asia, was formed in 1826 by combining the territories of Singapore, Penang and Malacca. The colony was administered by the East India Company until its abolition in 1858. Straits Settlements was a part of British India from 1858 to 1867 at which time it became a Crown Colony.

The Straits Settlements coinage gradually became acceptable legal tender in the neighboring Federated as well as the Unfederated Malay States. The Straits Settlements were dissolved in 1946, while the coinage continued to circulate until demonetized at the end of 1952.

RULER
British

MINT MARKS
H - Heaton, Birmingham
W - Soho Mint
B - Bombay

MONETARY SYSTEM
100 Cents = 1 Dollar

BRITISH CROWN COLONY
1867-1942

STANDARD COINAGE

KM# 14   1/4 CENT
Bronze **Ruler:** Victoria **Obv:** Crowned head left
Obv. Leg.: VICTORIA QUEEN **Rev:** Value within beaded circle
Rev. Leg.: STRAITS SETTLEMENTS.. **Edge:** Reeded

Date	Mintage	F	VF	XF	Unc	BU
1901	2,000,000	12.00	25.00	110	380	—

KM# 17   1/4 CENT
Bronze **Ruler:** Edward VII **Obv:** Crowned bust right **Rev:** Value within beaded circle

Date	Mintage	F	VF	XF	Unc	BU
1904 Proof	—	Value: 2,200				
	Note: Plain edge					
1905	2,008,000	15.00	35.00	100	250	—
1905 Proof	—	Value: 2,000				
1908	1,200,000	15.00	35.00	100	250	—

KM# 27   1/4 CENT
Bronze **Ruler:** George V **Obv:** Crowned bust left **Rev:** Value within beaded circle

Date	Mintage	F	VF	XF	Unc	BU
1916	4,000,000	8.00	15.00	30.00	60.00	—
1916 Proof	—	Value: 650				

KM# 18   1/2 CENT
Bronze **Ruler:** Edward VII **Obv:** Crowned bust right **Rev:** Value within beaded circle

Date	Mintage	F	VF	XF	Unc	BU
1904 Proof	—	Value: 3,600				
1908	2,000,000	20.00	40.00	100	300	—

KM# 28   1/2 CENT
Bronze **Ruler:** George V **Obv:** Crowned bust left **Rev:** Value within beaded circle

Date	Mintage	F	VF	XF	Unc	BU
1916	3,000,000	8.00	15.00	25.00	50.00	—
1916 Proof	—	Value: 660				

KM# 37   1/2 CENT
Bronze **Ruler:** George V **Rev:** Value within beaded circle
Edge: Crowned bust left

Date	Mintage	F	VF	XF	Unc	BU
1932	5,000,000	5.00	8.00	20.00	40.00	—
1932 Proof	—	Value: 520				

KM# 16   CENT
Bronze **Ruler:** Victoria **Obv:** Crowned head left
Obv. Leg.: VICTORIA QUEEN **Rev:** Value within beaded circle
Rev. Leg.: STRAITS SETTLEMENTS **Edge:** Reeded

Date	Mintage	F	VF	XF	Unc	BU
1901	15,230,000	3.00	15.00	100	350	—

KM# 19   CENT
Bronze **Ruler:** Edward VII **Obv:** Crowned bust right **Rev:** Value within beaded circle

Date	Mintage	F	VF	XF	Unc	BU
1903	7,053,000	3.00	15.00	100	310	—
1903 Proof, Rare	—					
1904	6,647,000	3.00	15.00	100	310	—
1904 Proof, Rare	—					
1906	7,504,000	15.00	80.00	200	500	—
1907	5,015,000	5.00	15.00	100	300	—
1908 Proof, Rare	—					
1908	Inc. above	4.00	10.00	55.00	220	—

KM# 32   CENT
Bronze, 21 mm. **Obv:** Crowned bust left **Rev:** Value within beaded circle **Edge:** Plain

Date	Mintage	F	VF	XF	Unc	BU
1919	20,165,000	0.50	1.50	15.00	55.00	—
1919 Proof	—	Value: 500				
1920	55,000,000	0.50	1.50	10.00	40.00	—
1920 Proof	—	Value: 500				
1926	5,000,000	0.50	1.50	15.00	80.00	—

KM# 10   5 CENTS
1.3600 g., 0.8000 Silver 0.0350 oz. ASW **Ruler:** Victoria
Obv: Crowned head left **Obv. Leg.:** VICTORIA QUEEN
Rev: Value within beaded circle **Rev. Leg.:** STRAITS
SETTLEMENTS

Date	Mintage	F	VF	XF	Unc	BU
1901	3,000,000	10.00	15.00	70.00	350	—
1901 Proof	—	Value: 1,200				

KM# 20   5 CENTS
1.3600 g., 0.8000 Silver 0.0350 oz. ASW **Ruler:** Edward VII
Obv: Crowned bust right **Rev:** Value within beaded circle

Date	Mintage	F	VF	XF	Unc	BU
1902	1,920,000	10.00	25.00	180	280	—
1902 Proof	—	Value: 1,200				
1903	2,270,000	10.00	25.00	180	280	—
1903 Proof	—	Value: 1,200				

KM# 20a 5 CENTS
1.3600 g., 0.6000 Silver 0.0262 oz. ASW, 15.4 mm. **Ruler:**
Edward VII **Obv:** Crowned bust right **Rev:** Value within beaded circle

Date	Mintage	F	VF	XF	Unc	BU
1910B	13,012,000	2.00	8.00	20.00	60.00	—
1910B Proof	—	Value: 1,200				

KM# 31 5 CENTS
1.3600 g., 0.4000 Silver 0.0175 oz. ASW **Ruler:** George V
Obv: Crowned bust left **Rev:** Value within beaded circle

Date	Mintage	F	VF	XF	Unc	BU
1918	3,100,000	1.50	3.00	28.00	50.00	—
1919	6,900,000	1.50	3.00	28.00	50.00	—
1920	4,000,000	600	1,300	2,500	7,500	—

KM# 34 5 CENTS
Copper-Nickel **Ruler:** George V **Obv:** Crowned bust left
Rev: Value within beaded circle

Date	Mintage	F	VF	XF	Unc	BU
1920	20,000,000	1.50	25.00	110	220	—
1920 Proof, Rare	—	—	—	—	—	—

KM# 36 5 CENTS
1.3600 g., 0.6000 Silver 0.0262 oz. ASW **Ruler:** George V
Obv: Smaller bust, broader rim **Rev:** Value within beaded circle

Date	Mintage	F	VF	XF	Unc	BU
1926 Proof	—	Value: 2,200				
1926	10,000,000	1.00	2.00	10.00	25.00	—
1935	3,000,000	1.00	2.00	6.00	20.00	—
1935 Proof	—	Value: 2,200				

KM# 11 10 CENTS
2.7100 g., 0.8000 Silver 0.0697 oz. ASW **Ruler:** Victoria **Obv:**
Crowned head left **Obv. Leg.:** VICTORIA QUEEN **Rev:** Value
within beaded circle **Rev. Leg.:** STRAITS SETTLEMENTS

Date	Mintage	F	VF	XF	Unc	BU
1901	2,700,000	10.00	15.00	80.00	250	—

KM# 21 10 CENTS
2.7100 g., 0.8000 Silver 0.0697 oz. ASW **Ruler:** Edward VII
Obv: Crowned bust right **Rev:** Value within beaded circle

Date	Mintage	F	VF	XF	Unc	BU
1902	6,118,000	10.00	25.00	110	350	—
1902 Proof, Rare	—	—	—	—	—	—
1903	1,401,000	10.00	30.00	150	300	—
1903 Proof, Rare	—	—	—	—	—	—

KM# 21a 10 CENTS
2.7100 g., 0.6000 Silver 0.0523 oz. ASW **Ruler:** Edward VII
Obv: Crowned bust right **Rev:** Value within beaded circle

Date	Mintage	F	VF	XF	Unc	BU
1909B	11,088,000	15.00	40.00	120	400	—

Date	Mintage	F	VF	XF	Unc	BU
1910B	1,657,000	2.00	5.00	20.00	50.00	
1910B Proof, Rare						

KM# 29 10 CENTS
2.7100 g., 0.6000 Silver 0.0523 oz. ASW **Ruler:** George V
Obv: Crowned bust left **Rev:** Value within beaded circle

Date	Mintage	F	VF	XF	Unc	BU
1916	600,000	5.00	12.00	80.00	180	
1917	5,600,000	1.00	2.00	22.00	130	

KM# 29a 10 CENTS
2.7100 g., 0.4000 Silver 0.0348 oz. ASW **Ruler:** George V
Obv: Crowned bust left **Rev:** Value within beaded circle

Date	Mintage	F	VF	XF	Unc	BU
1918	7,500,000	1.00	2.50	22.00	130	
1919	11,500,000	1.00	2.50	22.00	130	
1920	4,000,000	16.00	50.00	220	600	

KM# 29b 10 CENTS
2.7100 g., 0.6000 Silver 0.0523 oz. ASW **Ruler:** George V
Obv: Crowned bust left **Rev:** Value within beaded circle

Date	Mintage	F	VF	XF	Unc	BU
1926	20,000,000	1.50	2.00	10.00	28.00	
1926 Proof	—	Value: 650				
1927	23,000,000	1.50	2.00	5.00	10.00	
1927 Proof	—	Value: 650				

KM# 12 20 CENTS
5.4300 g., 0.8000 Silver 0.1397 oz. ASW, 23 mm. **Ruler:** Victoria
Obv: Crowned head left **Obv. Leg.:** VICTORIA QUEEN **Rev:** Value
within beaded circle **Rev. Leg.:** STRAITS SETTLEMENTS

Date	Mintage	F	VF	XF	Unc	BU
1901	600,000	8.00	15.00	50.00	320	

KM# 22 20 CENTS
5.4300 g., 0.8000 Silver 0.1397 oz. ASW, 23 mm.
Ruler: Edward VII **Obv:** Crowned bust right **Rev:** Value within
beaded circle

Date	Mintage	F	VF	XF	Unc	BU
1902	1,105,000	20.00	40.00	200	550	
1902 Proof, Rare	—	—	—	—	—	
1903	1,150,000	20.00	40.00	200	550	
1903 Proof, Rare	—	—	—	—	—	

KM# 22a 20 CENTS
5.4300 g., 0.6000 Silver 0.1047 oz. ASW, 23 mm.
Ruler: Edward VII **Obv:** Crowned bust right **Rev:** Value within
beaded circle

Date	Mintage	F	VF	XF	Unc	BU
1910B	3,276,000	7.00	12.00	60.00	180	
1910B Proof, Rare	—	—	—	—	—	

KM# 30 20 CENTS
5.4300 g., 0.6000 Silver 0.1047 oz. ASW, 23 mm. **Ruler:** George V
Obv: Crowned bust left **Rev:** Value within beaded circle

Date	Mintage	F	VF	XF	Unc	BU
1916B	545,000	10.00	22.00	130	300	
1916B Proof, Rare	—	—	—	—	—	
1917B	652,000	4.50	12.00	80.00	190	

KM# 30a 20 CENTS
5.4300 g., 0.4000 Silver 0.0698 oz. ASW, 23 mm. **Ruler:** George V
Obv: Crowned bust left **Rev:** Value within beaded circle

Date	Mintage	F	VF	XF	Unc	BU
1919B	2,500,000	3.00	8.00	50.00	180	
1919B Proof, Rare	—	—	—	—	—	

KM# 30b 20 CENTS
5.4300 g., 0.6000 Silver 0.1047 oz. ASW, 23 mm. **Ruler:** George V
Obv: Crowned bust left **Rev:** Value within beaded circle

Date	Mintage	F	VF	XF	Unc	BU
1926	2,500,000	2.00	5.00	22.00	120	
1926 Proof, Rare	—	—	—	—	—	
1927	3,000,000	2.00	5.00	12.00	30.00	
1927 Proof, Rare	—	—	—	—	—	
1935 Round-top 3	1,000,000	2.50	4.00	12.00	18.00	
1935 Flat-top 3	Inc. above	2.50	4.00	12.00	18.00	

KM# 13 50 CENTS
13.5769 g., 0.8000 Silver 0.3492 oz. ASW **Ruler:** Victoria
Obv: Crowned head left **Obv. Leg.:** VICTORIA QUEEN
Rev: Value within beaded circle **Rev. Leg.:** STRAITS
SETTLEMENTS

Date	Mintage	F	VF	XF	Unc	BU
1901	120,000	52.00	80.00	350	1,500	—

KM# 23 50 CENTS
13.5769 g., 0.8000 Silver 0.3492 oz. ASW, 31 mm. **Ruler:**
Edward VII **Obv:** Crowned bust right **Rev:** Value within beaded circle

Date	Mintage	F	VF	XF	Unc	BU
1902	148,000	100	200	600	1,100	—
1902 Proof, Rare	—	—	—	—	—	—
1903	193,000	100	200	600	1,200	—
1903 Proof, Rare	—	—	—	—	—	—
1905B Raised	498,000	95.00	180	450	700	—
1905B Proof, raised, Rare	—	—	—	—	—	—
1905B Proof, incuse, Rare	—	—	—	—	—	—

KM# 24 50 CENTS
10.1000 g., 0.9000 Silver 0.2922 oz. ASW, 28 mm.
Ruler: Edward VII **Obv:** Crowned bust right **Rev:** Value within beaded circle

Date	Mintage	F	VF	XF	Unc	BU
1907	464,000	20.00	35.00	100	220	—
1907H	2,667,000	20.00	35.00	100	220	—
1908	2,869,000	20.00	35.00	100	220	—
1908H	Inc. above	20.00	40.00	120	230	—

Note: Mintage included with 1907H

KM# 35.1 50 CENTS
8.4200 g., 0.5000 Silver 0.1353 oz. ASW **Ruler:** George V
Obv: Crowned bust left **Rev:** Value within beaded circle

Date	Mintage	F	VF	XF	Unc	BU
1920	3,900,000	5.00	7.50	12.00	22.00	—
1920 Proof, Rare	—	—	—	—	—	—
1921	2,579,000	5.00	8.00	15.00	28.00	—
1921 Proof, Rare	—	—	—	—	—	—

KM# 35.2 50 CENTS
8.4200 g., 0.5000 Silver 0.1353 oz. ASW **Ruler:** George V
Obv: Crowned bust left with dot below bust **Rev:** Value within beaded circle

Date	Mintage	F	VF	XF	Unc	BU
1920	Inc. above	250	420	650	1,300	—

KM# 25 DOLLAR
26.9500 g., 0.9000 Silver 0.7798 oz. ASW, 37 mm. **Ruler:**
Edward VII **Obv:** Crowned bust right **Rev:** Artistic design within circle

Date	Mintage	F	VF	XF	Unc	BU
1903 Proof, Rare	—	—	—	—	—	—
1903B Incuse	15,010,000	40.00	80.00	180	320	—
1903B Raised	Inc. above	140	250	600	1,200	—
1903B Proof, raised, Rare	—	—	—	—	—	—
1904B	20,365,000	30.00	40.00	110	220	—
1904B Proof, Rare	—	—	—	—	—	—

KM# 26 DOLLAR
20.2100 g., 0.9000 Silver 0.5848 oz. ASW, 34.5 mm.
Ruler: Edward VII **Obv:** Crowned bust right **Rev:** Artistic design within circle **Note:** Reduced size.

Date	Mintage	F	VF	XF	Unc	BU
1907	6,842,000	12.00	25.00	70.00	120	—
1907H	4,000,000	12.00	25.00	70.00	120	—
1907H Proof, Rare	—	—	—	—	—	—
1908	4,152,000	10.00	20.00	55.00	120	—
1908 Proof, Rare	—	—	—	—	—	—

Date	Mintage	F	VF	XF	Unc	BU
1909	1,014,000	15.00	30.00	80.00	250	—
1909 Proof, Rare	—	—	—	—	—	—

KM# 33 DOLLAR
16.8500 g., 0.5000 Silver 0.2709 oz. ASW **Ruler:** George V
Obv: Crowned bust left **Rev:** Artistic design within circle

Date	Mintage	F	VF	XF	Unc	BU
1919	6,000,000	60.00	120	250	400	—
1919 Proof		Value: 250				
Note: Restrike						
1920	8,164,000	25.00	50.00	120	220	—
1920 Proof		Value: 250				
Note: Restrike						
1925	—	—	—	10,000	—	—
1925 Proof, Rare	—	—	—	—	—	—
1925 Proof, Rare	—	—	—	—	—	—
Note: Restrike						
1926	—	—	—	6,500	—	—
1926 Proof		Value: 10,000				
1926 Proof, Rare	—	—	—	—	—	—
Note: Restrike						

SUDAN

The Democratic Republic of the Sudan, located in northeast Africa on the Red Sea between Egypt and Ethiopia, has an area of 967,500 sq. mi. (2,505,810 sq. km.) and a population of *24.5 million. Capital: Khartoum. Agriculture and livestock raising are the chief occupations. Cotton, gum arabic and peanuts are exported.

The Sudan, site of the powerful Nubian kingdom of Roman times, was a collection of small independent states from the 14th century until 1820-22 when it was conquered and united by Mohammed Ali, Pasha of Egypt. Egyptian forces were driven from the area during the Mahdist revolt, 1881-98, but the Sudan was retaken by Anglo-Egyptian expeditions, 1896-98, and established as an Anglo-Egyptian condominium in 1899. Britain supplied the administrative apparatus and personnel, but the appearance of joint Anglo-Egyptian administration was continued until Jan. 9, 1954, when the first Sudanese self-government parliament was inaugurated. The Sudan achieved independence on Jan. 1, 1956 with the consent of the British and Egyptian government.

TITLES

جمهورية السودان

Jumhuriya(t) as-Sudan

الجمهورية السودان الديمقراطية

Al-Arabiya(t) as-Sa'udiya(t)al-Jumhuriya(t) as-Sudan ad-Dimiqratiya(t)

MINT NAME

مالناپور

Omdurman

REPUBLIC
STANDARD COINAGE

KM# 29.1 MILLIM
1.7800 g., Bronze **Obv:** Large legend and value above flower sprigs **Rev:** Camel with rider running left

Date	Mintage	F	VF	XF	Unc	BU
AH1376-1956	5,000,000	—	—	0.15	0.30	0.75
AH1379-1960	1,300,000	—	—	0.15	0.35	0.75
AH1386-1966 Proof	—	—	—	—	—	—
AH1387-1967	—	—	—	0.15	0.30	0.75
AH1388-1968	—	—	—	0.15	0.30	0.75
AH1389-1969	—	—	—	0.15	0.30	0.75

KM# 29.2 MILLIM
Bronze **Obv:** Small legend and value above flower sprigs **Rev:** Camel with rider running left **Note:** Except for proof sets, mintage figures have generally not been released since 1967.

Date	Mintage	F	VF	XF	Unc	BU
AH1387-1967 Proof	7,834	Value: 1.00				
AH1388-1968 Proof	5,251	Value: 1.00				
AH1389-1969 Proof	2,149	Value: 1.00				

KM# 39 MILLIM
Bronze **Obv:** New Arabic legend and value above flower sprigs **Rev:** Camel with rider running left

Date	Mintage	F	VF	XF	Unc	BU
AH1390-1970	—	—	—	—	—	—
AH1390-1970 Proof	1,646	Value: 1.00				
AH1391-1971 Proof	1,772	Value: 1.00				

KM# 30.1 2 MILLIM
Bronze **Obv:** Large written value with legend above flower sprigs **Rev:** Camel with rider running left **Edge:** Plain

Date	Mintage	F	VF	XF	Unc	BU
AH1376-1956	5,000,000	—	—	0.15	0.50	1.00
AH1386-1966 Proof	—	Value: 1.00				
AH1387-1967	—	—	—	0.15	0.50	1.00
AH1388-1968	—	—	—	0.15	0.50	1.00
AH1389-1969	—	—	—	0.15	0.50	1.00

KM# 30.2 2 MILLIM
Bronze, 20.5 mm. **Obv:** Small written value with legend above flower sprigs **Rev:** Camel with rider running left **Edge:** Plain

Date	Mintage	F	VF	XF	Unc	BU
AH1387-1967 Proof	7,834	Value: 1.00				
AH1388-1968 Proof	5,251	Value: 1.00				
AH1389-1969 Proof	2,149	Value: 1.25				

KM# 40 2 MILLIM
Bronze **Obv:** New Arabic legend and value above flower sprigs **Rev:** Camel with rider running left

Date	Mintage	F	VF	XF	Unc	BU
AH1390-1970 Proof	1,646	Value: 1.50				
AH1391-1971 Proof	1,772	Value: 1.50				

KM# 31.1 5 MILLIM
3.9500 g., Bronze **Obv:** Thin legend and narrow 5 **Rev:** Camel with rider running left **Note:** Camel and rider, date size varieties exist, and with or without outlined bare line.

Date	Mintage	F	VF	XF	Unc	BU
AH1376-1956	30,000,000	—	0.10	0.20	0.50	1.00
AH1382-1962	6,000,000	—	0.10	0.20	0.50	1.00
AH1386-1966	4,000,000	—	0.10	0.15	0.50	1.00
AH1386-1966 Proof	—	—	—	—	—	—
AH1387-1967	4,000,000	—	0.10	0.15	0.35	1.00
AH1388-1968	—	—	0.10	0.15	0.35	1.00
AH1389-1969	—	—	0.10	0.15	0.35	1.00

KM# 31.2 5 MILLIM
Bronze **Obv:** Thick legend and small value **Rev:** Camel with rider running left

Date	Mintage	F	VF	XF	Unc	BU
AH1387-1967 Proof	7,834	Value: 1.00				
AH1388-1968 Proof	5,251	Value: 1.25				
AH1389-1969 Proof	2,149	Value: 1.50				

KM# 41.1 5 MILLIM
Bronze **Obv:** New large Arabic legend narrow 5 **Rev:** Camel with rider running left **Note:** Date heighth and size varieties exist

Date	Mintage	F	VF	XF	Unc	BU
AH1390-1970	—	—	0.20	0.45	1.25	1.75
AH1391-1971	3,000,000	—	0.20	0.45	1.25	1.75

KM# 41.2 5 MILLIM
Bronze **Obv:** Small legend and wide 5 **Rev:** Camel with rider running left

Date	Mintage	F	VF	XF	Unc	BU
AH1390-1970 Proof	1,646	Value: 2.50				
AH1391-1971 Proof	1,772	Value: 2.50				

KM# 47 5 MILLIM
Bronze **Subject:** 2nd Anniversary of Revolution **Obv:** Legend and value above flower sprigs **Rev:** Eagle divides dates below legend

Date	Mintage	F	VF	XF	Unc	BU
AH1391-1971	500,000	—	0.15	0.25	0.50	1.00

KM# 53 5 MILLIM
3.3200 g., Bronze, 21.5 mm. **Series:** F.A.O. **Obv:** Legend and value above flower sprigs **Rev:** Eagle divides dates below legend **Edge:** Plain

Date	Mintage	F	VF	XF	Unc	BU
AH1392-1972	6,000,000	—	—	0.15	0.35	—
AH1393-1973	9,000,000	—	—	0.15	0.35	—

KM# 54a.1 5 MILLIM
Brass **Obv:** Thick legend and written value **Rev:** Ribbon with 3 equal sections

Date	Mintage	F	VF	XF	Unc	BU
AH1395-1975	4,132,000	—	—	0.20	0.40	—
AH1398-1978	—	—	—	0.20	0.40	—

KM# 54 5 MILLIM
Bronze **Obv:** Legend and value **Rev:** Eagle divides AH and CE dates **Note:** Similar to 10 Millim, KM#55, but round.

Date	Mintage	F	VF	XF	Unc	BU
AH1392-1972	—	—	—	0.20	0.45	—

KM# 60 5 MILLIM
Brass **Series:** F.A.O. **Obv:** Legend and value above flower sprigs **Rev:** Eagle within sprigs divide legend and dates **Note:** Size varies 21.4 - 22.5 mm.

Date	Mintage	F	VF	XF	Unc	BU
AH1396-1976	7,868,000	—	—	0.10	0.20	—
AH1398-1978	7,000,000	—	—	0.10	0.20	—

KM# 94 5 MILLIM
Brass **Subject:** 20th Anniversary of Independence **Obv:** Legend and value above flower sprigs **Rev:** Eagle divides dates below legend

Date	Mintage	F	VF	XF	Unc	BU
AH1396-1976	—	—	0.15	0.20	0.25	—

KM# 54a.2 5 MILLIM
Brass **Obv:** Large legend and large 5 **Rev:** Eagle divides dates, ribbon with long center section

Date	Mintage	F	VF	XF	Unc	BU
AH1398-1978	—	—	—	0.20	0.40	—

KM# 54a.3 5 MILLIM
Brass **Obv:** Thin legend and narrow 5, different style **Rev:** Eagle divides dates, ribbon with 3 equal sections

Date	Mintage	F	VF	XF	Unc	BU
AH1400-1980 Proof	—	Value: 1.00				

KM# 32.1 10 MILLIM
Bronze **Obv:** Large written value **Rev:** Camel with rider running left **Note:** Camel, rider and date size varieties exist.

Date	Mintage	F	VF	XF	Unc	BU
AH1376-1956	15,000,000	—	0.15	0.25	0.85	1.25
AH1380-1960	12,250,000	—	0.15	0.20	0.75	1.00
AH1381-1962 High date	—	—	0.15	0.20	0.75	1.00

Date	Mintage	F	VF	XF	Unc	BU
AH1381-1962 Low date	—	—	0.15	0.20	0.75	1.00
AH1386-1966	1,000,000	—	0.15	0.25	0.85	1.50
AH1386-1966 Proof	—	—	—	—	—	—
AH1387-1967	1,000,000	—	0.15	0.20	0.75	1.00
AH1388-1968	—	—	0.15	0.20	0.75	1.50
AH1389-1969	—	—	0.15	0.20	0.75	1.50

KM# 32.2 10 MILLIM
Bronze **Obv:** Small written value **Rev:** Camel with rider running left

Date	Mintage	F	VF	XF	Unc	BU
AH1387-1967 Proof	7,834	Value: 1.50				
AH1388-1968 Proof	5,251	Value: 3.00				
AH1389-1969 Proof	2,149	Value: 3.00				

KM# 42.1 10 MILLIM
Bronze **Obv:** New large Arabic legend and written value **Rev:** Camel with rider running left

Date	Mintage	F	VF	XF	Unc	BU
AH1390-1970	—	—	0.20	0.40	1.00	1.50
AH1391-1971	3,000,000	—	0.20	0.40	1.00	1.50

KM# 42.2 10 MILLIM
Bronze **Obv:** Small legend and written value **Rev:** Camel with rider running left

Date	Mintage	F	VF	XF	Unc	BU
AH1390-1970 Proof	1,646	Value: 2.00				
AH1391-1971 Proof	1,772	Value: 2.00				

KM# 48 10 MILLIM
Bronze **Subject:** 2nd Anniversary of the Revolution **Obv:** Legend and value above flower sprigs **Rev:** Eagle divides dates below legend

Date	Mintage	F	VF	XF	Unc	BU
AH1391-1971	500,000	—	10.00	15.00	25.00	—

KM# 55a.1 10 MILLIM
Brass **Obv:** Large legend and written value **Rev:** Ribbon with three equal sections

Date	Mintage	F	VF	XF	Unc	BU
AH1395-1975	12,000,000	—	0.25	0.35	0.75	—
AH1398-1978	9,410,000	—	0.25	0.45	1.00	—

KM# 55a.3 10 MILLIM
Brass **Obv:** Small legend and written value **Rev:** Eagle divides dates, ribbon with 3 equal sections

Date	Mintage	F	VF	XF	Unc	BU
AH1400-1980	2,490,000	—	0.25	0.45	1.00	—
AH1400-1980 Proof	—	Value: 2.50				

KM# 55   10 MILLIM
Bronze Obv: Legend and value above flower sprigs Rev: Eagle divides dates

Date	Mintage	F	VF	XF	Unc	BU
AH1392-1972	6,500,000	—	0.15	0.25	0.50	—

KM# 55a.2   10 MILLIM
Brass, 25.5 mm. Obv: Large legend Rev: Ribbon with long center section, eagle divides AH and CE dates Edge: Plain

Date	Mintage	F	VF	XF	Unc	BU
AH1398-1978	—	—	0.75	1.75	4.25	—

KM# 61   10 MILLIM
Brass Series: F.A.O. Obv: Legend and value above flower sprigs Rev: Eagle within sprigs divides date and legend

Date	Mintage	F	VF	XF	Unc	BU
AH1396-1976	3,000,000	—	0.10	0.15	0.25	—
AH1398-1978	—	—	0.10	0.15	0.25	—

KM# 62   10 MILLIM
Brass Subject: 20th Anniversary of Independence Obv: Legend and value above flower sprigs Rev: Eagle divides dates below legend

Date	Mintage	F	VF	XF	Unc	BU
AH1396-1976	3,610,000	—	0.10	0.20	0.40	—

KM# 111   10 MILLIM
Brass, 24.5 mm. Obv: Legend and value above flower sprigs Rev: Eagle divides dates

Date	Mintage	F	VF	XF	Unc	BU
AH1400-1980	—	—	1.25	3.75	7.50	—

KM# 97   GHIRSH
Brass Obv: Legend and value above flower sprigs Rev: Eagle divides dates, ribbon with 3 equal sections

Date	Mintage	F	VF	XF	Unc	BU
AH1403-1983	1,140,000	—	0.25	0.65	2.00	—

KM# 99   GHIRSH
Aluminum-Bronze Obv: Legend and value above flower sprigs Rev: Building above inscription and crossed sprigs

Date	Mintage	F	VF	XF	Unc	BU
AH1408-1987	—	—	0.30	0.80	3.00	—

KM# 33   2 GHIRSH
Copper-Nickel, 17.5 mm. Obv: Legend and value above flower sprigs Rev: Camel with rider running left

Date	Mintage	F	VF	XF	Unc	BU
AH1376-1956	5,000,000	—	0.15	0.35	0.75	1.50
AH1381-1962	—	—	0.15	0.35	0.75	1.50

KM# 36   2 GHIRSH
Copper-Nickel, 20 mm. Obv: Legend and value above flower sprigs Rev: Camel with rider running left

Date	Mintage	F	VF	XF	Unc	BU
AH1382-1963	1,250,000	—	0.15	0.35	0.75	1.50
AH1386-1966 Proof	—	—	—	—	—	—
AH1387-1967	7,834	—	0.15	0.35	0.75	1.50
AH1387-1967 Proof	7,834	Value: 1.50				
AH1388-1968	5,251	—	0.15	0.35	0.75	1.50
AH1388-1968 Proof	5,251	Value: 1.50				
AH1389-1969	2,149	—	0.15	0.35	0.75	1.50
AH1389-1969 Proof	2,149	Value: 1.75				

KM# 43.1   2 GHIRSH
Copper-Nickel Obv: New large Arabic legend and written value Rev: Camel with rider running left

Date	Mintage	F	VF	XF	Unc	BU
AH1390-1970	—	—	0.30	0.60	1.25	2.00

KM# 43.2   2 GHIRSH
Copper-Nickel Obv: New small legend and written value Rev: Camel with rider running left

Date	Mintage	F	VF	XF	Unc	BU
AH1390-1970 Proof	1,646	Value: 2.00				
AH1391-1971 Proof	1,772	Value: 2.00				

KM# 49   2 GHIRSH
Copper-Nickel Subject: 2nd Anniversary of Revolution Obv: Legend and value above flower sprigs Rev: Eagle divides dates below legend

Date	Mintage	F	VF	XF	Unc	BU
AH1391-1971	500,000	—	0.25	0.45	0.80	—

KM# 57.1   2 GHIRSH
Copper-Nickel Obv: Thick legend and value above flower sprigs Rev: Eagle divides dates, ribbon with 3 equal sections

Date	Mintage	F	VF	XF	Unc	BU
AH1395-1975	1,000,000	—	0.20	0.35	0.75	—
AH1398-1978	1,250,000	—	0.20	0.35	0.75	—

KM# 57.2   2 GHIRSH
Copper-Nickel Obv: Large legend Rev: Ribbon with long center section, eagle divides AH and AD dates

Date	Mintage	F	VF	XF	Unc	BU
AH1398-1978	—	—	0.20	0.35	0.75	—
AH1400-1980	—	—	0.20	0.35	0.75	—

KM# 57.3   2 GHIRSH
Copper-Nickel, 20 mm. Obv: Thin legend and value above flower sprig Rev: Eagle divides dates, ribbon with 3 equal sections Edge: Reeded

Date	Mintage	F	VF	XF	Unc	BU
AH1399-1979	2,000,000	—	0.20	0.35	0.75	—
AH1400-1980	6,825,000	—	0.20	0.35	0.75	—
AH1400-1980 Proof	Inc. above	Value: 2.00				

KM# 57.2a   2 GHIRSH
Brass Obv: Legend with different style and value above flower sprigs Rev: Eagle divides dates

Date	Mintage	F	VF	XF	Unc	BU
AH1403-1983	100,000	—	0.75	1.50	3.50	—

KM# 63.1   2 GHIRSH
Copper-Nickel Series: F.A.O. Obv: Thick value Rev: Eagle within sprigs divides dates and legend

Date	Mintage	F	VF	XF	Unc	BU
AH1396-1976	500,000	—	0.20	0.35	0.75	—
AH1398-1978	Inc. above	—	0.20	0.35	0.75	—

KM# 64   2 GHIRSH
Copper-Nickel Subject: 20th Anniversary of Independence Obv: Legend and value above flower sprigs Rev: Eagle divides dates below legend

Date	Mintage	F	VF	XF	Unc	BU
AH1396-1976	1,750,000	—	0.20	0.30	0.60	—

KM# 63.2   2 GHIRSH
Copper-Nickel Series: F.A.O. Obv: Thin value Rev: Eagle divides AH and AD dates Note: Like KM#63.1.

Date	Mintage	F	VF	XF	Unc	BU
AH1398-1978	Inc. above	—	5.00	7.00	10.00	—

KM# 34.1   5 GHIRSH
Copper-Nickel, 24 mm. Obv: Large written value Rev: Camel with rider running left Edge: Reeded

Date	Mintage	F	VF	XF	Unc	BU
AH1376-1956	40,000,000	—	0.20	0.40	1.20	1.50
AH1386-1966 Proof	—	Value: 2.00				
AH1387-1967	—	—	0.20	0.30	1.00	1.50
AH1388-1968	—	—	0.20	0.30	1.00	1.50
AH1389-1969	—	—	0.20	0.30	1.00	1.50

KM# 34.2   5 GHIRSH
Copper-Nickel Obv: Small written value Rev: Camel with rider running left

Date	Mintage	F	VF	XF	Unc	BU
AH1387-1967 Proof	7,834	Value: 2.00				

Date	Mintage	F	VF	XF	Unc	BU
AH1388-1968 Proof	5,251	Value: 1.75				
AH1389-1969 Proof	2,149	Value: 2.50				

KM# 44 5 GHIRSH
Copper-Nickel **Obv:** New Arabic legend, value above flower sprigs **Rev:** Camel with rider running left

Date	Mintage	F	VF	XF	Unc	BU
AH1390-1970 Proof	1,646	Value: 2.50				
AH1391-1971 Proof	1,772	Value: 2.50				

KM# 51 5 GHIRSH
Copper-Nickel **Subject:** 2nd Anniversary of Revolution **Obv:** Legend and value above flower sprigs **Rev:** Eagle divides dates below legend

Date	Mintage	F	VF	XF	Unc	BU
AH1391-1971	500,000	—	0.30	0.60	1.20	—

KM# 58.3 5 GHIRSH
Copper-Nickel, 23.5 mm. **Obv:** Small legend with different style and value above flower sprigs **Rev:** Ribbon with 3 equal sections, eagle divides dates **Edge:** Reeded

Date	Mintage	F	VF	XF	Unc	BU
AH1397-1977	2,000,000	—	0.25	0.45	0.85	—
AH1398-1978	1,000,000	—	0.25	0.45	0.85	—
AH1400-1980	1,000,000	—	0.25	0.45	0.85	—
AH1400-1980 Proof	Inc. above	Value: 3.00				

KM# 58.1 5 GHIRSH
Copper-Nickel **Obv:** Large legend and value **Rev:** Eagle divides dates, ribbon with 3 equal sections

Date	Mintage	F	VF	XF	Unc	BU
AH1395-1975	1,600,000	—	0.25	0.45	0.85	—

KM# 58.2 5 GHIRSH
Copper-Nickel **Obv:** Large legend style change, small value **Rev:** Eagle divides dates, ribbon with long center section **Note:** Edge varieties exist.

Date	Mintage	F	VF	XF	Unc	BU
AH1400-1980	—	—	0.25	0.45	0.85	—

Note: Mintage included with KM#58.1.

KM# 58.4 5 GHIRSH
Copper-Nickel **Obv:** Large legend in different style **Rev:** Ribbon with long center section, eagle divides AH and AD dates **Note:** Edge varieties exist.

Date	Mintage	F	VF	XF	Unc	BU
AH1400-1980	—	—	0.25	0.45	0.85	—

Note: Mintage included with KM#58.1.

KM# 65 5 GHIRSH
Copper-Nickel **Series:** F.A.O. **Obv:** Legend and value above flower sprigs **Rev:** Eagle within sprigs divides dates and legend

Date	Mintage	F	VF	XF	Unc	BU
AH1396-1976	500,000	—	0.20	0.30	0.65	—
AH1398-1978		—	0.20	0.30	0.65	—

KM# 66 5 GHIRSH
Copper-Nickel **Subject:** 20th Anniversary of Independence **Obv:** Legend and value above flower sprigs **Rev:** Eagle divides dates below legend

Date	Mintage	F	VF	XF	Unc	BU
AH1396-1976	3,940,000	—	0.25	0.50	1.00	—

KM# 74 5 GHIRSH
Copper-Nickel **Subject:** Council of Arab Economic Unity **Obv:** Clasped hands and legend within wreath **Rev:** Eagle divides dates **Note:** Edge varieties exist.

Date	Mintage	F	VF	XF	Unc	BU
AH1398-1978	5,040,000	—	0.15	0.25	0.50	—

KM# 84 5 GHIRSH
Copper-Nickel **Series:** F.A.O. **Obv:** Cow and calf flanked by designs **Rev:** Eagle divides dates **Note:** Edge varieties exist.

Date	Mintage	F	VF	XF	Unc	BU
AH1401-1981	1,000,000	—	0.20	0.40	0.75	—

KM# 110.1 5 GHIRSH
Brass **Obv:** Large value **Rev:** Ribbon with three equal sections, eagle divides AH and AD dates

Date	Mintage	F	VF	XF	Unc	BU
AH1403-1983	—	—	0.25	0.60	1.55	—

KM# 110.2 5 GHIRSH
Brass **Obv:** Legend and value above flower sprigs **Rev:** Eagle divides dates, ribbon with long center section

Date	Mintage	F	VF	XF	Unc	BU
AH1403-1983	—	—	0.50	1.25	2.25	—

KM# 110.3 5 GHIRSH
Brass **Obv:** Small value, legend in different style **Rev:** Ribbon with three equal sections, eagle divides AH and AD dates

Date	Mintage	F	VF	XF	Unc	BU
AH1403-1983	—	—	5.00	7.00	10.00	—

KM# 110.4 5 GHIRSH
Brass **Obv:** Large value and legend **Rev:** Ribbon with long center section, eagle divides AH and AD dates

Date	Mintage	F	VF	XF	Unc	BU
AH1403-1983	—	—	1.50	4.50	7.50	—

KM# 100 5 GHIRSH
Aluminum-Bronze **Obv:** Legend and value above flower sprigs **Rev:** Central bank building above inscription and crossed sprigs

Date	Mintage	F	VF	XF	Unc	BU
AH1408-1987	—	—	0.40	1.00	2.00	—

KM# 35.1 10 GHIRSH
Copper-Nickel, 28 mm. **Obv:** Large written value **Rev:** Camel with rider running left

Date	Mintage	F	VF	XF	Unc	BU
AH1376-1956	15,000,000	—	0.35	0.75	2.00	3.00
AH1386-1966 Proof						
AH1387-1967	—	—	0.30	0.60	1.50	2.50
AH1388-1968	—	—	0.30	0.60	1.50	2.50
AH1389-1969	—	—	0.30	0.60	1.50	2.50

KM# 35.2 10 GHIRSH
Copper-Nickel, 28 mm. **Obv:** Small written value **Rev:** Camel with rider running left

Date	Mintage	F	VF	XF	Unc	BU
AH1387-1967 Proof	7,834	Value: 3.00				
AH1388-1968 Proof	5,251	Value: 3.00				
AH1389-1969 Proof	2,149	Value: 3.50				

KM# 45.1 10 GHIRSH
Copper-Nickel, 28 mm. **Obv:** New large Arabic legend and written value **Rev:** Camel with rider running left

Date	Mintage	F	VF	XF	Unc	BU
AH1390-1970	—	—	0.60	1.25	3.00	—
AH1391-1971	385,000	—	0.60	1.25	3.00	—

KM# 45.2 10 GHIRSH
Copper-Nickel, 28 mm. **Obv:** New small Arabic legend and written value **Rev:** Camel with rider running left

Date	Mintage	F	VF	XF	Unc	BU
AH1390-1970 Proof	1,646	Value: 3.00				
AH1391-1971 Proof	1,772	Value: 3.00				

KM# 52   10 GHIRSH
Copper-Nickel, 28 mm. **Subject:** 2nd Anniversary of Revolution **Obv:** Legend and value above flower sprigs **Rev:** Eagle divides dates below legend

Date	Mintage	F	VF	XF	Unc	BU
AH1391-1971	500,000	—	0.60	1.25	3.00	—

KM# 59.5   10 GHIRSH
Copper-Nickel, 28 mm. **Obv:** Thin legend, different style and value above flower sprigs **Rev:** Eagle divides dates **Edge:** Reeded

Date	Mintage	F	VF	XF	Unc	BU
AH1397-1977	1,000,000	—	0.50	1.00	2.75	—
AH1400-1980	2,965,000	—	0.50	1.00	2.75	—
AH1400-1980 Proof	—	Value: 4.50				

KM# 59.1   10 GHIRSH
Copper-Nickel, 28 mm. **Obv:** Legend and value above flower sprigs **Rev:** Eagle divides dates, ribbon with 3 equal sections **Edge:** Reeded

Date	Mintage	F	VF	XF	Unc	BU
AH1395-1975	1,000,000	—	0.50	1.00	2.50	—

KM# 59.2   10 GHIRSH
Copper-Nickel, 28 mm. **Obv:** Legend and value above flower sprigs **Rev:** Eagle divides dates, ribbon with long center section **Note:** Edge varieties exist.

Date	Mintage	F	VF	XF	Unc	BU
AH1400-1980	—	—	0.50	1.00	2.50	—

KM# 59.3   10 GHIRSH
Copper-Nickel **Obv:** Legend and value above flower sprigs **Rev:** Eagle divides dates **Note:** Reduced size. Edge varieties exist.

Date	Mintage	F	VF	XF	Unc	BU
AH1403-1983	—	—	0.50	1.00	2.50	—

KM# 59.4   10 GHIRSH
Copper-Nickel **Obv:** Value within flower sprigs below legend **Rev:** Ribbon with three equal sections, eagle divides AH and AD dates

Date	Mintage	F	VF	XF	Unc	BU
AH1403-1983	1,100,000	—	7.00	10.00	20.00	—

KM# 67   10 GHIRSH
Copper-Nickel, 28 mm. **Series:** F.A.O. **Obv:** Legend and value above flower sprigs **Rev:** Eagle within sprigs divides dates and legend

Date	Mintage	F	VF	XF	Unc	BU
AH1396-1976	500,000	—	0.30	0.65	1.50	—
AH1398-1978	—	—	0.30	0.65	1.50	—

KM# 68   10 GHIRSH
Copper-Nickel, 28 mm. **Subject:** 20th Anniversary of Independence **Obv:** Legend and value above flower sprigs **Rev:** Eagle divides dates below legend **Edge:** Reeded **Note:** Edge varieties exist.

Date	Mintage	F	VF	XF	Unc	BU
AH1396-1976	5,540,000	—	0.25	0.60	1.25	—

KM# 95   10 GHIRSH
Copper-Nickel, 28 mm. **Subject:** Council of Arab Economic Unity **Obv:** Clasped hands below inscription within wreath **Rev:** Eagle divides dates **Note:** Edge varieties exist.

Date	Mintage	F	VF	XF	Unc	BU
AH1398-1978	1,000,000	—	0.60	1.25	2.50	—

KM# 85   10 GHIRSH
Copper-Nickel, 28 mm. **Series:** F.A.O. **Obv:** Cow and calf flanked by designs **Rev:** Eagle divides dates **Edge:** Reeded **Note:** Edge varieties exist.

Date	Mintage	F	VF	XF	Unc	BU
AH1401-1981	1,000,000	—	0.60	1.25	2.50	—

KM# 107   10 GHIRSH
Aluminum-Bronze **Obv:** Legend and value above flower sprigs **Rev:** Central bank building above inscription and crossed sprigs

Date	Mintage	F	VF	XF	Unc	BU
AH1408-1987	—	—	0.75	1.50	3.00	—

KM# 37   20 GHIRSH
Copper-Nickel **Obv:** Legend and value above flower sprigs **Rev:** Camel with rider running left

Date	Mintage	F	VF	XF	Unc	BU
AH1387-1967 Proof	7,834	Value: 5.00				
AH1388-1968 Proof	5,251	Value: 5.00				
AH1389-1969 Proof	2,149	Value: 7.00				

KM# 46   20 GHIRSH
Copper-Nickel **Obv:** New Arabic legend and value above flower sprigs **Rev:** Camel with rider running left

Date	Mintage	F	VF	XF	Unc	BU
AH1390-1970 Proof	1,646	Value: 10.00				
AH1391-1971 Proof	1,772	Value: 10.00				

KM# 98   20 GHIRSH
Copper-Nickel, 26.5 mm. **Obv:** Legend and value above flower sprigs **Rev:** Eagle divides dates

Date	Mintage	F	VF	XF	Unc	BU
AH1403-1983	72,000	—	—	—	5.00	—

KM# 96   20 GHIRSH
Copper-Nickel **Series:** F.A.O. **Obv:** Designs, value and F.A.O. letters **Rev:** Eagle divides dates

Date	Mintage	F	VF	XF	Unc	BU
AH1405-1985	—	—	—	—	3.00	—

KM# 101.1   20 GHIRSH
Aluminum-Bronze **Obv:** Small value **Rev:** Central bank building above inscription and crossed sprigs **Note:** Denomination is 8mm high.

Date	Mintage	F	VF	XF	Unc	BU
AH1408-1987	—	—	0.60	1.25	2.50	—

KM# 101.2   20 GHIRSH
Aluminum-Bronze **Obv:** Large value **Rev:** Central bank building **Note:** Denomination is 9.5 mm high.

Date	Mintage	F	VF	XF	Unc	BU
AH1408-1987	—	—	0.60	1.25	2.50	—

KM# 38   25 GHIRSH
Copper-Nickel   **Series:** F.A.O. **Obv:** Legend and value above flower sprigs **Rev:** Camel with rider running left

Date	Mintage	F	VF	XF	Unc	BU
AH1388-1968	Inc. below	—	—	—	35.00	—
AH1388-1968 Prooflike	224,000	—	—	—	—	15.00

KM# 102.1   25 GHIRSH
Aluminum-Bronze   **Obv:** Legend and value above flower sprigs **Rev:** Central bank building, inner ring of dashes only visible on the corners

Date	Mintage	F	VF	XF	Unc	BU
AH1408-1987	—	—	0.85	1.75	3.50	—

KM# 102.2   25 GHIRSH
Aluminum-Bronze   **Obv:** Value **Rev:** Inner ring of dashes completely visible

Date	Mintage	F	VF	XF	Unc	BU
AH1408-1987	—	—	1.00	2.00	4.00	—

KM# 108   25 GHIRSH
Copper-Nickel Plated Steel   **Obv:** Legend, value and dates **Rev:** Central bank building

Date	Mintage	F	VF	XF	Unc	BU
AH1409-1989	—	—	0.50	1.00	2.25	—

KM# 56.1   50 GHIRSH
Copper-Nickel   **Series:** F.A.O. **Obv:** Eagle divides dates **Rev:** Large design

Date	Mintage	F	VF	XF	Unc	BU
AH1392-1972	1,000,000	—	1.50	3.00	6.50	—

KM# 56.2   50 GHIRSH
Copper-Nickel   **Series:** F.A.O. **Obv:** Eagle divides dates **Rev:** Small design **Note:** Struck in 1976.

Date	Mintage	F	VF	XF	Unc	BU
AH1392-1972	30,000	—	5.00	10.00	20.00	—

KM# 69   50 GHIRSH
Copper-Nickel   **Subject:** Establishment of Arab Cooperative **Obv:** Shield and value **Rev:** Legend above eagle and dates

Date	Mintage	F	VF	XF	Unc	BU
AH1396-1976	—	—	1.00	2.25	4.50	—

KM# 73   50 GHIRSH
Copper-Nickel   **Subject:** 8th Anniversary of 1969 Revolt **Obv:** Eagle divides dates **Rev:** Cogwheel design with inscription on circular design at bottom

Date	Mintage	F	VF	XF	Unc	BU
AH1397-1977	100,000	—	1.00	2.25	4.50	—

KM# 103   50 GHIRSH
Aluminum-Bronze   **Obv:** Legend and value above flower sprigs **Rev:** Central bank building above inscription and crossed sprigs

Date	Mintage	F	VF	XF	Unc	BU
AH1408-1987	—	—	0.75	1.75	3.75	—

KM# 105   50 GHIRSH
Aluminum-Bronze   **Subject:** 33rd Anniversary of Independence **Obv:** Legend and value above flower sprigs **Rev:** Inscription within map flanked by dates, designs below and legend above

Date	Mintage	F	VF	XF	Unc	BU
AH1409-1989	—	—	0.75	1.75	3.75	—

KM# 109   50 GHIRSH
Copper-Nickel Plated Steel   **Obv:** Value **Rev:** Central Bank building

Date	Mintage	F	VF	XF	Unc	BU
AH1409-1989	—	—	0.65	1.25	2.75	—

KM# 75   POUND
Copper-Nickel   **Series:** F.A.O. **Subject:** Rural women **Obv:** Eagle divides dates **Rev:** Stylized designs

Date	Mintage	F	VF	XF	Unc	BU
AH1398-1978	456,000	—	2.50	4.00	8.00	—

KM# 104   POUND
Aluminum-Bronze   **Obv:** Legend and value above flower sprigs **Rev:** Central bank building

Date	Mintage	F	VF	XF	Unc	BU
AH1408-1987	—	—	2.00	3.00	7.00	—

KM# 106   POUND
Copper-Nickel Plated Steel   **Obv:** Value **Rev:** Central Bank building

Date	Mintage	F	VF	XF	Unc	BU
AH1409-1989	—	—	0.75	1.50	3.75	—

KM# 70   2-1/2 POUNDS
28.2800 g., 0.9250 Silver 0.8410 oz. ASW   **Subject:** Conservation **Obv:** Eagle divides date **Rev:** Shoebill Stork

Date	Mintage	F	VF	XF	Unc	BU
AH1396-1976	5,183	—	—	—	22.50	25.00
AH1396-1976 Proof	5,590	Value: 30.00				

KM# 71   5 POUNDS
35.0000 g., 0.9250 Silver 1.0408 oz. ASW   **Subject:** Conservation **Obv:** Eagle divides dates **Rev:** Hippopotamus with calf

Date	Mintage	F	VF	XF	Unc	BU
AH1396-1976	5,087	—	—	—	25.00	30.00
AH1396-1976 Proof	5,393	Value: 35.00				

KM# 76   5 POUNDS
17.5000 g., 0.9250 Silver 0.5204 oz. ASW   **Subject:** Khartoum meeting of O.A.U. **Obv:** Eagle divides value **Rev:** African map within circle

Date	Mintage	F	VF	XF	Unc	BU
AH1398-1978	21	—	—	—	—	—
AH1398-1978 Proof	1,423	Value: 22.50				

Note: Without countermarks

AH1398-1978 Proof	2,000	Value: 16.50				

Note: AH1398 with countermarks of B23 in hexagon and bell between dates

KM# 80 5 POUNDS
17.5000 g., 0.9250 Silver 0.5204 oz. ASW **Subject:** 1,400th Anniversary of Islam **Obv:** Eagle divides value below legend **Rev:** Monument

Date	Mintage	F	VF	XF	Unc	BU
AH1400-1980	7,500	—	—	—	17.50	20.00
AH1400-1980 Proof	5,500	Value: 22.50				

KM# 86 5 POUNDS
28.2800 g., 0.9250 Silver 0.8410 oz. ASW **Subject:** 25th Anniversary of Independence **Obv:** Bust 3/4 right **Rev:** Monument

Date	Mintage	F	VF	XF	Unc	BU
AH1401-1981	20,000	—	—	—	45.00	50.00
AH1401-1981 Proof	20,000	Value: 60.00				

KM# 87 5 POUNDS
19.4400 g., 0.9250 Silver 0.5781 oz. ASW **Series:** UNICEF, International Year of the Child **Obv:** Eagle divides value **Rev:** Children playing in front of building with logos below

Date	Mintage	F	VF	XF	Unc	BU
AH1401-1981 Proof	35,000	Value: 15.00				

KM# 92 5 POUNDS
19.4400 g., 0.9250 Silver 0.5781 oz. ASW **Series:** Decade for Women **Obv:** Eagle divides value **Rev:** Dancing female within map

Date	Mintage	F	VF	XF	Unc	BU
AH1404-1984 Proof	20,000	Value: 25.00				

KM# 77 10 POUNDS
35.0000 g., 0.9250 Silver 1.0408 oz. ASW **Subject:** Khartoum Meeting of O.A.U. **Obv:** Eagle divides value **Rev:** African map within circle

Date	Mintage	F	VF	XF	Unc	BU
AH1398-1978	21	—	—	—	—	350
AH1398-1978 Proof	1,417	Value: 45.00				

Note: Without countermarks

| AH1398-1978 Proof | 2,000 | Value: 37.50 | | | | |

Note: AH1398 with countermarks of B23 in hexagon and bell between dates

KM# 81 10 POUNDS
35.0000 g., 0.9250 Silver 1.0408 oz. ASW **Subject:** 1,400th Anniversary of Islam **Obv:** Eagle divides value **Rev:** Buildings and upright design

Date	Mintage	F	VF	XF	Unc	BU
AH1400-1980	3,000	—	—	—	37.50	40.00
AH1400-1980 Proof	2,000	Value: 45.00				

KM# 88 10 POUNDS
28.2800 g., 0.9250 Silver 0.8410 oz. ASW **Series:** Year of the Disabled Person **Obv:** Eagle divides legend and dates **Rev:** Rope entwined on post and tree trunk

Date	Mintage	F	VF	XF	Unc	BU
AH1401-1981	Est. 10,000	—	—	—	35.00	37.50
AH1401-1981 Proof	10,000	Value: 42.50				

KM# 78 25 POUNDS
8.2500 g., 0.9170 Gold 0.2432 oz. AGW **Subject:** Khartoum Meeting of O.A.U. **Obv:** Eagle divides value **Rev:** African map within circle

Date	Mintage	F	VF	XF	Unc	BU
AH1398-1978	15	—	—	—	600	—
AH1398-1978 Proof	467	Value: 275				

Note: Without countermarks

| AH1398-1978 Proof | 350 | Value: 265 | | | | |

Note: With countermarks of B23 in hexagon and bell between dates

KM# 82 25 POUNDS
8.2500 g., 0.9170 Gold 0.2432 oz. AGW **Subject:** 1,400th Anniversary of Islam **Obv:** Eagle divides value **Rev:** Buildings and upright design

Date	Mintage	F	VF	XF	Unc	BU
AH1400-1980	7,500	—	—	—	235	245
AH1400-1980 Proof	5,500	Value: 260				

KM# 79 50 POUNDS
17.5000 g., 0.9170 Gold 0.5159 oz. AGW **Subject:** Khartoum Meeting of O.A.U. **Obv:** Eagle divides value **Rev:** African map within circle

Date	Mintage	F	VF	XF	Unc	BU
AH1398-1978	11	—	—	—	1,500	—
AH1398-1978 Proof	211	Value: 550				

Note: Without countermarks

| AH1398-1978 Proof | 350 | Value: 500 | | | | |

Note: With countermarks of B23 in hexagon and bell between dates

KM# 83 50 POUNDS
17.5000 g., 0.9170 Gold 0.5159 oz. AGW **Subject:** 1,400th Anniversary of Islam **Obv:** Eagle divides value **Rev:** Buildings and upright design

Date	Mintage	F	VF	XF	Unc	BU
AH1400-1979	3,000	—	—	—	485	500
AH1400-1979 Proof	2,000	Value: 525				

KM# 89 50 POUNDS
7.9900 g., 0.9170 Gold 0.2356 oz. AGW **Subject:** 25th Anniversary of Independence

Date	Mintage	F	VF	XF	Unc	BU
AH1401-1981	5,000	—	—	—	235	245
AH1401-1981 Proof	5,000	Value: 260				

KM# 72 100 POUNDS
33.4370 g., 0.9000 Gold 0.9675 oz. AGW **Subject:** Conservation **Obv:** Eagle divides dates **Rev:** Scimitar-horned oryx

Date	Mintage	F	VF	XF	Unc	BU
AH1396-1976	872	—	—	—	925	945
AH1396-1976 Proof	251	Value: 975				

KM# 90 100 POUNDS
15.9800 g., 0.9170 Gold 0.4711 oz. AGW **Subject:** 25th Anniversary of Independence

Date	Mintage	F	VF	XF	Unc	BU
AH1401-1981	2,500	—	—	—	450	465
AH1401-1981 Proof	2,500	Value: 485				

KM# 91 100 POUNDS
15.9800 g., 0.9170 Gold 0.4711 oz. AGW **Series:** Year of the Disabled Person **Obv:** Eagle **Rev:** Stylized arrowhead within wreath

Date	Mintage	F	VF	XF	Unc	BU
AH1401-1981	2,000	—	—	—	475	500
AH1401-1981 Proof	2,000	Value: 550				

KM# 93   100 POUNDS
8.1000 g., 0.9170 Gold 0.2388 oz. AGW **Series:** Decade for Women **Obv:** Eagle divides value **Rev:** Half female figure facing right

Date	Mintage	F	VF	XF	Unc	BU
AH1404-1984 Proof	513	Value: 250				

REFORM COINAGE

100 Qurush (Piastres) = 1 Dinar

10 Pounds = 1 Dinar

KM# 117   1/4 DINAR
3.0000 g., Brass Plated Steel, 18 mm. **Obv:** Value **Rev:** Central Bank building **Edge:** Plain

Date	Mintage	F	VF	XF	Unc	BU
AH1415-1994 Rare						

KM# 118   1/2 DINAR
4.0000 g., Brass Plated Steel, 20 mm. **Obv:** Value **Rev:** Central Bank building **Edge:** Plain

Date	Mintage	F	VF	XF	Unc	BU
AH1415-1994 Rare						

KM# 112   DINAR
5.1400 g., Brass, 22.2 mm. **Obv:** Value **Rev:** Central Bank building **Edge:** Plain

Date	Mintage	F	VF	XF	Unc	BU
AH1415-1994	—	—	0.25	0.50	1.00	2.00

KM# 113   2 DINAR
Brass Plated Steel **Obv:** Value **Rev:** Central Bank building **Edge:** Plain **Note:** Varieties exist with finely spaced and widely spaced shading to the number "2" in the denomination.

Date	Mintage	F	VF	XF	Unc	BU
AH1415-1994	—	—	0.45	0.75	1.00	3.00

KM# 114   5 DINARS
Brass **Obv:** Value **Rev:** Central Bank building **Edge:** Plain

Date	Mintage	F	VF	XF	Unc	BU
AH1417-1996	—	—	1.00	2.00	4.50	7.00

KM# 115.1   10 DINARS
Brass **Obv:** Legend and value above designs **Rev:** Central Bank building, thin inscription below **Edge:** Plain

Date	Mintage	F	VF	XF	Unc	BU
AH1417-1996	—	—	1.00	2.00	3.50	6.00

KM# 115.2   10 DINARS
Brass **Obv:** Legend and value **Rev:** Central Bank building, thick inscription below **Edge:** Plain

Date	Mintage	F	VF	XF	Unc	BU
AH1417-1996	—	—	1.00	2.00	3.50	6.00

KM# 116.1   20 DINARS
Copper-Nickel, 22 mm. **Obv:** Value **Rev:** Central Bank building, "a" to right of "n" at the left end of the Arabic inscription, 72 border beads **Edge:** Plain

Date	Mintage	F	VF	XF	Unc	BU
AH1417-1996	—	—	1.25	2.25	4.00	7.00

KM# 116.2   20 DINARS
4.6100 g., Copper-Nickel, 22.17 mm. **Obv:** Legend and value **Rev:** Smaller Central Bank building, "a" above "n" at the left end of the Arabic inscription, 64 border beads **Edge:** Plain

Date	Mintage	F	VF	XF	Unc	BU
AH1419-1999	—	—	1.25	2.25	4.00	7.00

PATTERNS
Including off metal strikes

KM#	Date	Mintage	Identification	Mkt Val
Pn1	1956AD-1375AH	—	Millim. Copper. 19.6 mm. "HAKUMAT AS-SUDAN"	
Pn2	1956AD-1375AH	5	Millim. Copper. 24.9 mm. "HAKUMAT AS-SUDAN"	
Pn3	1956AD-1375AH	5	Ghirsh. Copper-Nickel. 23.9 mm. "HAKUMAT AS-SUDAN"	
Pn4	1956AD-1375AH	—	10 Ghirsh. Copper-Nickel. 30.9 mm. "HAKUMAT AS-SUDAN"	

ESSAIS

KM#	Date	Mintage	Identification	Mkt Val
E1	1978	25	5 Pounds. Aluminum.	40.00
E2	1978	15	5 Pounds. Copper.	85.00
E3	1978	25	10 Pounds. Aluminum. 40.6 mm.	40.00
E4	1978	21	10 Pounds. Copper. KM77.	125
E5	1978	25	25 Pounds. Aluminum.	40.00
E6	1978	21	25 Pounds. Copper.	75.00
E7	1978	25	50 Pounds. Aluminum.	40.00
E8	1978	21	50 Pounds. Copper.	85.00
E9	1979	15	5 Pounds. Copper. KM817.	85.00
E10	1979	40	10 Pounds. Aluminum. 40.7 mm. KM81.	40.00
E11	1979	21	10 Pounds. Copper. KM81.	125
E12	1979	21	50 Pounds. Copper. KM83.	85.00
E13	1980	25	5 Pounds. Aluminum.	40.00
E14	1980	15	5 Pounds. Copper.	85.00
E15	1980	25	10 Pounds. Aluminum.	40.00
E16	1980	21	10 Pounds. Copper.	125
E17	1980	25	25 Pounds. Aluminum.	40.00
E18	1980	20	25 Pounds. Copper.	75.00
E19	1980	25	50 Pounds. Aluminum.	40.00
	1980	25	50 Pounds. Aluminum.	40.00
E20	1980	21	50 Pounds. Copper.	85.00

PIEFORTS

KM#	Date	Mintage	Identification	Mkt Val
P1	1978	5	5 Pounds. Copper. KM76.	185
P2	1978	10	5 Pounds. 0.9250 Silver. KM76.	—
P3	1978	5	10 Pounds. Copper.	225
P4	1978	10	10 Pounds. 0.9250 Silver. KM77.	—
P5	1978	5	25 Pounds. Copper.	185
P6	1979	5	5 Pounds. Copper. KM80.	185
P7	1979	10	5 Pounds. 0.9250 Silver. KM80.	—
P8	1979	5	10 Pounds. Copper. KM81.	225
P9	1979	10	10 Pounds. 0.9250 Silver. KM81.	—
P10	1979	—	25 Pounds. Brass. KM83.	185
P11	1979	10	25 Pounds. Silver. 22.5 mm. KM83.	185
PA12	1979	—	50 Pounds. Silver. 26.1 mm. KM#83.	—
P12	1979	—	50 Pounds. Copper. KM83. Gold plated.	—
P13	1980	5	5 Pounds. Copper.	185
P14	1980	5	10 Pounds. Copper.	225
P15	1980	5	25 Pounds. Copper.	185
P16	1979	—	50 Pounds. Gold. KM83.	1,350
P17	1981	2,587	5 Pounds. Silver. KM87.	40.00
P18	1981	1,000	10 Pounds. Silver. KM88.	75.00
P19	1981	—	100 Pounds. Gold. KM91.	1,500

MINT SETS

KM#	Date	Mintage	Identification	Issue Price	Mkt Val
MS1	1976 (2)	—	KM70-71	—	50.00

PROOF SETS

KM#	Date	Mintage	Identification	Issue Price	Mkt Val
PS1	1967 (8)	7,834	KM29-32, 34-37	12.25	7.50
PS2	1968 (8)	5,251	KM29-32, 34-37	15.25	8.00
PS3	1969 (8)	2,149	KM29-32, 34-37	15.25	10.00
PS4	1970 (8)	1,646	KM39-46	15.25	15.00
PS5	1971 (8)	1,772	KM39-46	15.25	15.00
PS6	1976 (2)	—	KM70-71	—	65.00
PS7	1978 (4)	—	KM76-79	—	900
PS9	1980 (4)	—	KM80-83	—	825
PS8	1980 (5)	—	KM54, 55a, 57-59	12.00	13.50

DARFUR

Darfur had been an independent Sultanate until taken over by Egypt in 1874, and subsequently by the Mahdists. After the latter's defeat in 1898 by the British, 'Ali Dinar re-established the Sultanate which ended in 1916 with his demise. His coins copied the Ottoman coins of Egypt. The mint was located at El Fasher, the Sultanate capital, and was active from 1909 to 1914.

MINT

الفشير

al-Fasher

RULER
Ali Dinar, AH1316-1335/1898-1916AD

SULTANATE
HAMMERED COINAGE

KM# 4   1/2 PIASTRE
Billon **Ruler:** Ali Dinar AH1316-35/1898-1916AD **Obv:** Toughra within circle **Rev:** Value and date within circle

Date	Mintage	Good	VG	F	VF	XF
AH1328/8 Rare						

Note: Due to the low denomination and little demand, this coin was only struck for a very short time, though varieties do exist

KM# 1   PIASTRE
Copper-Nickel-Zinc **Obv:** Toughra within circle **Rev:** Inscription, date and value within circle

Date	Mintage	Good	VG	F	VF	XF
AH1223 (sic)/23 Rare	—	—	—	—	—	—
AH1223 (sic)/13 Rare	—	—	—	—	—	—

Note: Due to a shortage of small change, debased, unmilled imitations of Egyptian Qirsh (Piastre) KM#181, which had been produced outside of Sudan were brought into circulation in Darfur from AH1323-1325/1905-1907AD, privately struck in agreement with the Sultan

KM# 2   PIASTRE
Billon **Obv:** Toughra within circle **Rev:** Inscription, date and value within circle **Note:** Struck at al-Fasher mint from 1909-1914. Flan size varies and most appear crude due to thinness of flan. Off center and double strikes exist. Those bearing the date AH1327, regnal year 17 are probably the sultan's approved type. Other hejira and regnal years are engraving errors of filled dies.

Date	Mintage	Good	VG	F	VF	XF
AH1227(sic)/5	—	—	—	—	—	—
AH1237(sic)/71	—	—	—	—	—	—

Note: With retrograde 3

Date	Mintage	Good	VG	F	VF	XF
AH1321(sic)/71	—	—	—	—	—	—
AH1323(sic)/65	—	—	—	—	—	—
AH1327/7	—	—	—	—	—	—

Date	Mintage	Good	VG	F	VF	XF
AH1327/17	—	30.00	80.00	160	190	—
AH1327/26	—	—	—	—	—	—
AH3127/71	—	—	—	—	—	—
AH1327/71	—	15.00	30.00	45.00	60.00	—
AH1327/71	—	—	—	—	—	—
Note: Retrograde 3						
AH1327/76	—	—	—	—	—	—
AH1327/77	—	—	—	—	—	—
AHx321(sic)/17	—	—	—	—	—	—
AH3167/7x	—	—	—	—	—	—
AH1387(sic)/17	—	—	—	—	—	—
AH7132(sic)/x	—	—	—	—	—	—

KM# 5 5 PIASTRES
Copper-Nickel-Zinc **Ruler:** Ali Dinar AH1316-35/1898-1916AD **Obv:** Toughra within design **Rev:** Inscription, value and date within design **Note:** Size varies: 21.6-24.4 mm.

Date	Mintage	Good	VG	F	VF	XF
AH1328 Rare	—	—	—	—	—	—

Note: Copied from Ottoman Mejidiye coinage; about 800 are reported having been put into circulation; further striking was discontinued as the coin was unpopular due to low silver content. Specimens dated 8231 are contemporary forgeries.

COUNTERMARKED COINAGE

KM# 3 PIASTRE
Copper-Nickel-Zinc **Countermark:** "Ali" 1312 **Obv:** Inscription, date and value within circle **Rev:** Toughra within circle **Note:** Countermark on KM#1.

CM Date	Host Date	Good	VG	F	VF	XF
ND	AH1223/13 Rare	—	—	—	—	—

Note: In a move to control import and circulation of KM#1, the Sultan ordered the countermarking; AH1312 is the year 'Ali Dinar used as the official beginning of his Sultanate. The countermark can be on the obverse or reverse. Counterfeit (contemporary) may exist. AH1327/17 approximates 1312, the year 'Ali Dinar officially used as the beginning of his dynasty as per noted historian O'Fahey.

ND	AH1223/23 Rare	—	—	—	—	—

SURINAME

VENEZUELA
GUYANA
Atlantic Ocean
FRENCH GUIANA
BRAZIL

The Republic of Suriname also known as Dutch Guiana, located on the north central coast of South America between Guyana and French Guiana has an area of 63,037 sq. mi. (163,270 sq. km.) and a population of *433,000. Capital: Paramaribo. The country is rich in minerals and forests, and self-sufficient in rice, the staple food crop. The mining, processing and exporting of bauxite is the principal economic activity.

Lieutenants of Amerigo Vespucci sighted the Guiana coast in 1499. Spanish explorers of the 16th century, disappointed at finding no gold, departed leaving the area to be settled by the British in 1652. The colony prospered and the Netherlands acquired it in 1667 in exchange for the Dutch rights in Nieuw Nederland (state of New York). During the European wars of the 18th and 19th centuries, which were fought in part in the new world, Suriname was occupied by the British from 1781-1784 and 1796-1814.Suriname became an autonomous part of the Kingdom of the Netherlands on Dec. 15, 1954. Full independence was achieved on Nov. 25, 1975. In 1980, a coup installed a military government, which has since been dissolved.

RULER
Dutch, until 1975

MINT MARKS
(B) - British Royal Mint, no mint mark

FM - Franklin Mint, U.S.A.**
P - Philadelphia, U.S.A.
S - Sydney
(u) - Utrecht (privy marks only)

NOTE: From 1975-1985 the Franklin Mint produced coinage in up to 3 different qualities. Qualities of issue are designated in ( ) after each date and are defined as follows:

(M) MATTE - Normal circulation strike or a dull finish produced by sandblasting special uncirculated (polish finish) or proof quality dies.

(U) SPECIAL UNCIRCULATED - Polished or prooflike in appearance without any frosted features.

(P) PROOF - The highest quality obtainable having mirror-like fields and frosted features.

MONETARY SYSTEM
100 Cents = 1 Gulden (Guilders)

After January, 2004
1 Dollar = 100 Cents

DUTCH ADMINISTRATION
WORLD WAR II COINAGE

The 1942-1943 issues that follow are homeland coinage types of the Netherlands. KM#152, KM#163 and KM#164 were executed expressly for use in Suriname. Related issues produced for use in Curacao and Suriname are listed under Curacao. They are distinguished by a palm tree (acorn on homeland issues) and a mint mark (P-Philadelphia, D-Denver, S-San Francisco) flanking the date. See the Netherlands for similar issues. See Curacao for similar coins dated 1941-P, 1942-P and 1943-P.

KM# 10 CENT
2.5000 g., Brass, 18 mm. **Obv:** Upright lion with sword within beaded circle **Rev:** Value within 'orange wreath **Edge:** Reeded

Date	Mintage	F	VF	XF	Unc	BU
1943P Palm	4,000,000	0.85	3.75	7.50	15.00	20.00

KM# 10a CENT
2.5000 g., Bronze, 19 mm. **Obv:** Upright lion with sword within beaded circle **Rev:** Value within orange wreath **Edge:** Reeded

Date	Mintage	F	VF	XF	Unc	BU
1957(u)	1,200,000	—	1.00	2.00	4.50	7.00
1957(u) Proof	—	Value: 30.00				
1959(u)	1,800,000	—	1.00	2.00	4.50	7.00
1959(u) Proof	—	Value: 30.00				
1960(u)	1,200,000	—	1.00	2.00	4.50	7.00
1960(u) Proof	—	Value: 30.00				

KM# 9 10 CENTS
1.4000 g., 0.6400 Silver 0.0288 oz. ASW **Obv:** Head of Queen Wilhelmina left **Obv. Leg.:** Value and date within orange wreath **Edge:** Reeded

Date	Mintage	F	VF	XF	Unc	BU
1942P Palm	1,500,000	6.00	12.50	15.00	30.00	35.00

REPUBLIC
MODERN COINAGE

KM# 11 CENT
2.5500 g., Bronze, 18 mm. **Obv:** Arms with supporters within wreath **Rev:** Value divides date within circle **Edge:** Plain

Date	Mintage	F	VF	XF	Unc	BU
1962(u) Fish	6,000,000	—	0.25	0.50	1.00	2.00
1962(u) S Proof	650	Value: 28.00				
1966(u)	6,500,000	—	0.25	0.50	1.00	2.00
1966(u) Proof	—	Value: 42.00				
1970(u) Cock	5,000,000	—	0.25	0.50	1.00	2.00
1972(u)	6,000,000	—	0.25	0.50	1.00	2.00

KM# 11a CENT
0.8000 g., Aluminum, 18 mm. **Obv:** Arms with supporters within wreath **Rev:** Value divides date within circle **Edge:** Plain

Date	Mintage	F	VF	XF	Unc	BU
1972 Proof	—	Value: 45.00				
1974(u)	1,000,000	—	0.10	0.25	0.50	1.00
1975(u)	1,000,000	—	0.10	0.25	0.50	1.00
1976 Proof	Est. 10	Value: 55.00				
1976(u)	3,000,000	—	0.10	0.25	0.50	1.00
1977(u)	10,000,000	—	—	0.25	0.50	1.00
1978(u)	6,000,000	—	—	0.25	0.50	1.00
1979(u)	10,000,000	—	—	0.25	0.50	1.00
1980(u)	8,000,000	—	—	0.25	0.50	1.00
Note: Cock and star privy marks						
1982(u) Anvil	8,000,000	—	—	0.25	0.50	1.00
1984	5,000,000	—	—	0.25	0.50	1.00
1985	2,000,000	—	—	0.25	0.50	1.00
1986	3,000,000	—	—	0.25	0.50	1.00

KM# 11b CENT
2.5000 g., Copper Plated Steel, 18 mm. **Obv:** Arms with supporters within wreath **Rev:** Value divides date within circle **Edge:** Plain

Date	Mintage	F	VF	XF	Unc	BU
1987(B)	—	—	—	0.20	0.80	1.25
1988(B)	—	—	—	0.20	0.80	1.25
1988(B) Proof	Est. 1,500	Value: 2.00				
1989(B)	—	—	—	0.20	0.80	1.25

KM# 12.1 5 CENTS
4.0000 g., Nickel-Brass, 22 mm. **Obv:** Arms with supporters within circle **Rev:** Value divides date within circle

Date	Mintage	F	VF	XF	Unc	BU
1962(u) Fish	2,200,000	—	0.50	1.00	2.00	4.00
1962(u) S Proof	650	Value: 25.00				
1966(u)	2,300,000	—	0.50	1.00	2.00	4.00
Note: With mint mark and mintmaster's mark						
1966(u) Proof	—	Value: 50.00				
1966(u)	400,000	—	1.75	3.50	7.00	10.00
Note: Without mint mark and mint master's mark						
1971(u) Cock	500,000	—	1.25	2.50	5.00	10.00
1972(u)	1,500,000	—	0.50	1.00	2.00	4.00

KM# 12.2 5 CENTS
4.0000 g., Nickel-Brass, 18 mm. **Obv:** Arms with supporters within circle **Rev:** Value divides date within circle **Note:** Medal turn.

Date	Mintage	F	VF	XF	Unc	BU
1966(u)	—	4.00	8.00	20.00	40.00	75.00
1966(u) Proof	—	Value: 450				

KM# 12.1a 5 CENTS
1.2000 g., Aluminum, 18 mm. **Obv:** Arms with supporters within circle **Rev:** Value divides date within circle

Date	Mintage	F	VF	XF	Unc	BU
1976(u)	5,500,000	—	0.10	0.25	0.50	1.00
1976 Proof	Est. 10	Value: 75.00				
1978(u)	3,000,000	—	0.10	0.25	0.50	1.00
1979(u)	2,000,000	—	0.10	0.25	0.50	1.00
1980(u)	1,000,000	—	0.10	0.25	0.50	1.00
Note: Cock and star privy marks						
1982(u) Anvil	1,000,000	—	0.10	0.25	0.50	1.00
1985(u)	1,000,000	—	0.10	0.25	0.50	1.00
1986(u)	1,500,000	—	0.10	0.25	0.50	1.00

KM# 12.1b 5 CENTS
3.0000 g., Copper Plated Steel, 18 mm. **Obv:** Arms with supporters within circle **Rev:** Value divides date within circle **Edge:** Plain

Date	Mintage	F	VF	XF	Unc	BU
1987(B)	—	—	—	0.30	0.60	1.00
1988(B)	—	—	—	0.30	0.60	1.00
1988(B) Proof	Est. 1,500	Value: 2.00				
1989(B)	—	—	—	0.30	0.60	1.00

KM# 13 10 CENTS
2.0000 g., Copper-Nickel, 16 mm. **Obv:** Arms with supporters within wreath **Rev:** Value and date within circle

Date	Mintage	F	VF	XF	Unc	BU
1962(u) Fish	3,000,000	—	0.25	0.50	1.00	2.00
1962(u) S Proof	650	Value: 25.00				
1966(u)	2,500,000	—	0.25	0.50	1.00	2.00
1966(u) Proof	—	Value: 50.00				
1971(u) Cock	500,000	—	0.75	1.50	3.00	4.00
1972(u)	1,500,000	—	0.25	0.50	1.00	2.00
1974(u)	1,500,000	—	0.25	0.50	1.00	2.00
1976(u)	5,000,000	—	0.15	0.30	0.60	1.50
1976 Proof	Est. 10	Value: 100				
1978(u)	2,000,000	—	0.15	0.30	0.60	1.50
1979(u)	2,000,000	—	0.15	0.30	0.60	1.50
1982(u) Anvil	1,000,000	—	0.15	0.30	0.60	1.50
1985(u)	1,000,000	—	0.15	0.30	0.60	1.50
1986(u)	1,500,000	—	0.15	0.30	0.60	1.50

KM# 13a 10 CENTS
2.0000 g., Nickel Plated Steel, 16 mm. **Obv:** Arms with supporters within wreath **Rev:** Value and date within circle **Edge:** Reeded

Date	Mintage	F	VF	XF	Unc	BU
1987(B)	—	—	0.15	0.35	0.75	1.50
1988(B) Proof	Est. 1,500	Value: 3.00				
1989(B)	—	—	0.10	0.35	0.75	1.50

KM# 14 25 CENTS
3.5000 g., Copper-Nickel, 20 mm. **Obv:** Arms with supporters within wreath **Rev:** Value and date within circle **Edge:** Reeded

Date	Mintage	F	VF	XF	Unc	BU
1962(u) Fish	2,300,000	0.25	0.30	0.50	1.00	2.00
1962(u) S Proof	650	Value: 20.00				
1966(u)	2,300,000	0.25	0.30	0.50	1.00	2.00
1966(u) Proof	—	Value: 50.00				
1972(u) Cock	1,800,000	0.25	0.30	0.50	1.00	2.50
1974(u)	1,500,000	0.30	0.30	0.50	1.00	2.50
1976(u)	5,000,000	0.25	0.30	0.50	1.00	2.50
1976 Proof	Est. 10	Value: 125				
1979(u)	2,000,000	0.20	0.30	0.50	1.00	2.00
1982(u) Anvil	2,000,000	0.20	0.30	0.50	1.00	2.00
1985(u)	1,000,000	0.20	0.30	0.50	1.00	2.50
1986(u)	1,500,000	0.20	0.30	0.50	1.00	2.50

KM# 14a 25 CENTS
3.5000 g., Nickel Plated Steel, 20 mm. **Obv:** Arms with supporters within wreath **Rev:** Value and date within circle **Edge:** Reeded

Date	Mintage	F	VF	XF	Unc	BU
1987(B)	—	0.20	0.30	0.50	1.00	2.00
1988(B)	—	0.20	0.30	0.50	1.00	2.00
1988(B) Proof	Est. 1,500	Value: 5.00				
1989(B)	—	0.20	0.35	0.65	1.25	2.50

KM# 15 GULDEN
10.0000 g., 0.7200 Silver 0.2315 oz. ASW, 28 mm. **Obv:** Head of Queen Juliana right **Rev:** Arms with supporters within wreath **Edge:** JUSTITIA * PIETAS * FIDES *

Date	Mintage	F	VF	XF	Unc	BU
1962(u)	150,000	—	BV	6.00	10.00	15.00
1962(u) S Proof	650	Value: 50.00				
1966(u)	100,000	15.00	40.00	100	135	170
Note: Never officially released to circulation						
1966(u) Proof	—	Value: 250				

KM# 23 100 CENTS
Copper-Nickel, 23 mm. **Obv:** Arms with supporters within wreath **Rev:** Value and date within circle **Edge:** Reeded

Date	Mintage	F	VF	XF	Unc	BU
1987(B)	—	—	0.40	0.80	1.75	3.00
1988(B)	—	—	0.40	0.80	1.75	3.00
1988(B) Proof	Est. 1,500	Value: 12.00				
1989(B)	—	—	0.40	0.80	1.75	3.00

KM# 24 250 CENTS
9.5700 g., Copper-Nickel, 28 mm. **Obv:** Arms with supporters within wreath **Rev:** Value and date within circle

Date	Mintage	F	VF	XF	Unc	BU
1987(B)	—	—	0.80	1.75	3.50	5.00
1988(B)	—	—	0.80	1.75	3.50	5.00
1988(B) Proof	Est. 1,500	Value: 17.50				
1989(B)	—	—	0.80	1.75	3.50	5.00

KM# 16 10 GULDEN
15.9500 g., 0.9250 Silver 0.4743 oz. ASW **Subject:** 1st Anniversary of Independence **Obv:** Flag, Surinam map, rising sun **Rev:** Arms with supporters divide date **Edge:** JUSTITIA * PIETAS * FIDES *

Date	Mintage	F	VF	XF	Unc	BU
1976(u)	100,000	—	—	—	12.50	13.50
1976(u) Proof	5,711	Value: 15.00				

KM# 17 25 GULDEN
26.2000 g., 0.9250 Silver 0.7791 oz. ASW **Subject:** 1st Anniversary of Independence **Obv:** Flag, Surinam map, rising sun **Rev:** Arms with supporters divide date

Date	Mintage	F	VF	XF	Unc	BU
1976(u)	75,000	—	—	—	17.50	20.00
1976(u) F Proof	5,503	Value: 20.00				

KM# 19 25 GULDEN
15.5000 g., 0.9250 Silver 0.4609 oz. ASW **Subject:** 1st Anniversary of Revolution **Obv:** Revolution monument **Rev:** Allegorical group of revolutionaries **Edge:** Reeded

Date	Mintage	F	VF	XF	Unc	BU
1981FM (U)	10,000	—	—	—	30.00	35.00
1981FM (P)	800	Value: 85.00				

KM# 21 25 GULDEN
25.1000 g., 0.9250 Silver 0.7464 oz. ASW **Subject:** 5th Anniversary of Revolution **Obv:** Peace dove, flag superimposed on Surinam map **Rev:** Stylized fist and 5 on star within designed circle **Edge:** JUSTITIA * PIETAS * FIDES *

Date	Mintage	F	VF	XF	Unc	BU
ND(1985)(u)	4,800	—	—	—	60.00	65.00
ND(1985)(u) Proof	200	Value: 100				

KM# 32 25 GUILDER
28.2800 g., 0.9250 Silver 0.8410 oz. ASW **Subject:** World Cup Soccer **Obv:** Arms with supporters within wreath **Rev:** Player R. Gullit, stadium and half globe

Date	Mintage	F	VF	XF	Unc	BU
1990(B) Proof	50,000	Value: 60.00				

KM# 36 25 GUILDER
28.2800 g., 0.9250 Silver 0.8410 oz. ASW, 38.61 mm. **Series:** Save the Children **Obv:** Arms with supporters **Rev:** Children **Edge:** Reeded

Date	Mintage	F	VF	XF	Unc	BU
1991 Proof	30,000	Value: 50.00				
1992 Reported, not confirmed						

KM# 27 30 GULDEN
14.3000 g., 0.9250 Silver 0.4253 oz. ASW **Subject:** 30th Anniversary of Central Bank **Obv:** Arms with supporters divide date **Rev:** Central Bank building

Date	Mintage	F	VF	XF	Unc	BU
1987(u)	7,000	—	—	30.00	40.00	55.00

KM# 28   50 GUILDER

28.2800 g., 0.9250 Silver 0.8410 oz. ASW **Series:** Seoul
Olympics **Subject:** Anthony Nesty, Butterfly gold medalist
Obv: Arms with supporters within wreath **Rev:** Conjoined
swimmers left within circle **Edge:** Reeded

Date	Mintage	F	VF	XF	Unc	BU
1988(B) Proof	Est. 25,000				Value: 45.00	

KM# 30   50 GUILDER

28.2800 g., 0.9250 Silver 0.8410 oz. ASW **Subject:** 125th
Anniversary of De Surinaamsche Bank **Obv:** Arms with
supporters within wreath **Rev:** Designs and horizontal lines within
circle **Edge:** Reeded

Date	Mintage	F	VF	XF	Unc	BU
ND(1990)(B) Proof	Est. 7,500				Value: 50.00	

KM# 34   50 GUILDER

26.0000 g., 0.9250 Silver 0.7732 oz. ASW **Subject:** 15th
Anniversary of Independence **Obv:** Arms with supporters
Rev: Stylized design **Edge:** Reeded **Note:** Similar to 500
Guilders, KM#35.

Date	Mintage	F	VF	XF	Unc	BU
ND(1990)(B) Proof	Est. 5,000				Value: 55.00	

KM# 38   50 GUILDER

26.0000 g., 0.9250 Silver 0.7732 oz. ASW **Subject:** 35th
Anniversary of Central Bank **Obv:** Arms with supporters within
wreath **Rev:** Geometric arrow design divides date at top and
bottom within circle **Edge:** Reeded

Date	Mintage	F	VF	XF	Unc	BU
ND(1992) Proof	Est. 1,500				Value: 60.00	

KM# 18a   100 GULDEN

6.7200 g., 0.9000 Yellow Gold 0.1944 oz. AGW **Subject:** 1st
Anniversary of Independence **Obv:** Flag, Surinam map, rising
sun within circle **Rev:** Arms with supporters divide date

Date	Mintage	F	VF	XF	Unc	BU
1976(u)	19,100	—	—	—	—	185
1976(u) Proof	4,749				Value: 200	

KM# 18b   100 GULDEN

6.7200 g., 0.9000 Red Gold 0.1944 oz. AGW **Subject:** 1st
Anniversary of Independence **Obv:** Flag, Surinam map, rising
sun within circle **Rev:** Arms with supporters divide date

Date	Mintage	F	VF	XF	Unc	BU
1976(u)	900				200	220

KM# 52   100 GULDEN

20.0000 g., 0.9990 Silver 0.6423 oz. ASW, 36.9 mm.
Subject: 700th Anniversary of the Helvetic Confederation and
125th Anniversary of the Red Cross **Obv:** Arms with supporters
Rev: Wilhelm Tell, maps, flags and arms **Edge:** Reeded

Date	Mintage	F	VF	XF	Unc	BU
ND(1991) Proof	—				Value: 100	

KM# 40.2   100 GUILDER

20.0000 g., 0.9990 Silver 0.6423 oz. ASW **Series:** Barcelona
Olympics **Subject:** Basketball **Obv:** Arms with supporters within
wreath **Rev:** Four basketball players within circle with .999
Edge: Reeded **Note:** Struck at Nova Mint, Barcelona

Date	Mintage	F	VF	XF	Unc	BU
1992 Proof	15,000				Value: 70.00	

KM# 40.1   100 GUILDER

20.0000 g., 0.9990 Silver 0.6423 oz. ASW **Series:** Barcelona
Olympics **Subject:** Basketball **Obv:** Arms with supporters within
wreath **Rev:** Four basketball players within circle **Edge:** Reeded
Note: Struck at Nova Mint, Barcelona.

Date	Mintage	F	VF	XF	Unc	BU
1992 Proof	Est. 15,000				Value: 70.00	

KM# 41   100 GUILDER

20.0000 g., 0.9990 Silver 0.6423 oz. ASW **Series:** Barcelona
Olympics **Subject:** Cyclists **Obv:** Arms with supporters **Rev:** Three
cyclists **Edge:** Reeded **Note:** Struck at Nova Mint, Barcelona.

Date	Mintage	F	VF	XF	Unc	BU
1992 Proof	Est. 15,000				Value: 70.00	

KM# 42.1   100 GUILDER

20.0000 g., 0.9990 Silver 0.6423 oz. ASW **Series:** Barcelona
Olympics **Subject:** Anthony Nesty **Obv:** Arms with supporters
Rev: Swimmer within circle **Edge:** Reeded **Note:** Struck at
Kaapstad (Capetown, South Africa).

Date	Mintage	F	VF	XF	Unc	BU
ND(1992) Proof	2,500				Value: 95.00	

KM# 42.2   100 GUILDER

20.0000 g., 0.9990 Silver 0.6423 oz. ASW **Series:** Barcelona
Olympics **Obv:** Arms with supporters **Rev:** Swimmer Antony
Nesty, "200 M" above swimmer **Edge:** Reeded **Note:** Struck at
Kaapstad (Capetown, South Africa)

Date	Mintage	F	VF	XF	Unc	BU
ND(1992) Proof	2,500				Value: 95.00	

KM# 42.1a   100 GUILDER

30.0000 g., 0.9990 Silver 0.9635 oz. ASW **Series:** Barcelona
Olympics **Subject:** Anthony Nesty **Obv:** Arms with supporters
Rev: Swimer within circle **Edge:** Reeded **Note:** Struck at
Kaapstad (Capetown, South Africa)

Date	Mintage	F	VF	XF	Unc	BU
ND (1992) Proof	2,500				Value: 95.00	

KM# 42.2a   100 GUILDER

30.0000 g., 0.9990 Silver 0.9635 oz. ASW **Series:** Barcelona
Olympics **Obv:** Arms with supporters **Rev:** Swimmer Antony
Nesty, "200 M" above swimmer **Edge:** Reeded **Note:** Struck at
Kaapstad (Capetown, South Africa)

Date	Mintage	F	VF	XF	Unc	BU
ND (1992) Proof	2,500				Value: 95.00	

KM# 43.1   100 GUILDER

19.7000 g., 0.9990 Silver 0.6327 oz. ASW **Subject:** World Cup
soccer **Obv:** Arms with supporters **Rev:** 2 soccer players, "999
E.P." at right **Edge:** Reeded

Date	Mintage	F	VF	XF	Unc	BU
ND(1994) Proof	—				Value: 50.00	

KM# 43.2   100 GUILDER

19.7000 g., 0.9990 Silver 0.6327 oz. ASW **Subject:** World Cup
soccer **Obv:** Arms with supporters **Rev:** 2 soccer players, "999
E.P." at left **Edge:** Reeded

Date	Mintage	F	VF	XF	Unc	BU
ND(1994) Proof	—				Value: 85.00	

KM# 44   100 GUILDER

20.0000 g., 0.9990 Silver 0.6423 oz. ASW **Subject:** World Cup
soccer **Obv:** Arms with supporters within wreath **Rev:** Soccer player
in stadium, Brazil winner **Edge:** Reeded **Note:** Struck at Capetown.

Date	Mintage	F	VF	XF	Unc	BU
ND(1994) Proof	—				Value: 45.00	

KM# 46 100 GUILDER
28.5000 g., Copper-Nickel **Obv:** Arms with supporters **Rev:** 1956 Ford Thunderbird **Edge:** Reeded

Date	Mintage	F	VF	XF	Unc	BU
1996 Proof	500	Value: 75.00				

KM# 47 100 GUILDER
28.5000 g., Copper-Nickel **Obv:** Arms with supporters **Rev:** 1957 Ford Thunderbird **Edge:** Reeded

Date	Mintage	F	VF	XF	Unc	BU
1996 Proof	500	Value: 75.00				

KM# 49 100 GUILDER
28.3000 g., 0.9990 Copper-Nickel 0.9089 oz. **Series:** Olympics **Obv:** Arms with supporters within wreath **Rev:** Discus thrower flanked by sprigs within pillars **Edge:** Reeded

Date	Mintage	F	VF	XF	Unc	BU
1996 Proof	—	Value: 140				

KM# 20 200 GULDEN
7.1200 g., 0.5000 Gold 0.1145 oz. AGW **Subject:** 1st Anniversary of Revolution **Obv:** Revolution monument **Rev:** Allegorical group of revolutionaries **Edge:** Reeded

Date	Mintage	F	VF	XF	Unc	BU
1981FM (U)	11,000	—	—	—	135	—
1981FM (P) Proof	1,363	Value: 180				

KM# 22 250 GULDER
6.7200 g., 0.9000 Gold 0.1944 oz. AGW **Subject:** 5th Anniversary of Revolution **Obv:** Dove and "10" on map-shaped flag **Rev:** Stylized fist on star design **Edge:** Reeded

Date	Mintage	F	VF	XF	Unc	BU
1985(u)	5,000	—	—	—	190	210
1985(u) Proof	200	Value: 255				

KM# 33 250 GULDER
7.9800 g., 0.9170 Gold 0.2353 oz. AGW **Subject:** World Cup Soccer **Obv:** Arms with supporters within wreath **Rev:** Soccer player R. Gullit, stadium and half-globe **Edge:** Reeded

Date	Mintage	F	VF	XF	Unc	BU
1990(B) Proof	1,000	Value: 245				

KM# 37 250 GUILDER
7.9800 g., 0.9170 Gold 0.2353 oz. AGW **Series:** Save the Children **Obv:** Arms with supporters within wreath **Rev:** Children looking at spider web **Edge:** Reeded

Date	Mintage	F	VF	XF	Unc	BU
1991 Proof	3,000	Value: 235				
1992	—	—	—	225	—	

KM# 25 500 GUILDER
7.9800 g., 0.9170 Gold 0.2353 oz. AGW **Subject:** 43rd General Assembly, Military Sports Organization CISM **Obv:** Arms with supporters **Rev:** Globe, laurel wreath, rings and sword within flower design **Edge:** Reeded

Date	Mintage	F	VF	XF	Unc	BU
ND(1988)(B) Proof	2,500	Value: 235				

KM# 29 500 GUILDER
7.9800 g., 0.9170 Gold 0.2353 oz. AGW **Series:** Seoul Olympics **Subject:** Anthony Nesty, butterfly gold medalist **Obv:** Arms with supporters within wreath **Rev:** Swimmer within circle **Edge:** Reeded

Date	Mintage	F	VF	XF	Unc	BU
1988(B) Proof	Est. 2,000	Value: 250				

KM# 31 500 GUILDER
7.9800 g., 0.9170 Gold 0.2353 oz. AGW **Subject:** 125th Anniversary - De Surinaamsche Bank **Obv:** Arms with supporters **Rev:** Abstract design **Edge:** Reeded

Date	Mintage	F	VF	XF	Unc	BU
1990(B) Proof	Est. 2,000	Value: 280				

KM# 35 500 GUILDER
7.9800 g., 0.9170 Gold 0.2353 oz. AGW **Subject:** 15th Anniversary of Independence **Obv:** Arms with supporters within wreath **Rev:** Floral design **Edge:** Reeded

Date	Mintage	F	VF	XF	Unc	BU
ND(1990)(B) Proof	Est. 1,250	Value: 350				

KM# 39 500 GUILDER
7.9800 g., 0.9170 Gold 0.2353 oz. AGW **Subject:** 35th Anniversary of Central Bank **Obv:** Arms with supporters **Rev:** Symetric arrow design and dates within circle and legend **Edge:** Reeded

Date	Mintage	F	VF	XF	Unc	BU
1992(B) Proof	Est. 300	Value: 375				

KM# 26 1000 GUILDER
15.9800 g., 0.9170 Gold 0.4711 oz. AGW **Subject:** 40th Anniversary - Military Sports Organization CISM **Obv:** Arms with supporters **Rev:** Globe, laurel wreath, rings and sword within flower design **Edge:** Reeded

Date	Mintage	F	VF	XF	Unc	BU
ND(1988)(B) Proof	1,250	Value: 500				

KM# 48 1000 GUILDER
Brass **Series:** Olympics **Obv:** Arms with supporters **Rev:** Three cyclists **Edge:** Reeded **Note:** Struck at Capetown.

Date	Mintage	F	VF	XF	Unc	BU
1992	—	—	—	—	—	

KM# 48b 1000 GUILDER
4.8000 g., Gold Plated Brass **Series:** Olympics **Obv:** Arms with supporters **Rev:** Three cyclists **Edge:** Reeded **Note:** Struck at Capetown.

Date	Mintage	F	VF	XF	Unc	BU
1992	—	—	—	—	—	

KM# 48c 1000 GUILDER
7.9800 g., 0.9170 Gold 0.2353 oz. AGW **Series:** Olympics **Obv:** Arms with supporters **Rev:** Three cyclists **Edge:** Reeded **Note:** Struck at Capetown.

Date	Mintage	F	VF	XF	Unc	BU
1992 Proof	400	Value: 275				

KM# 50 12500 GULDEN
28.2800 g., 0.9250 Silver 0.8410 oz. ASW **Subject:** Hindu Immigration **Obv:** Arms with supporters within wreath **Rev:** Standing figures in front of ship **Edge:** Reeded

Date	Mintage	F	VF	XF	Unc	BU
ND(1999)(B) Proof	Est. 1,000	Value: 90.00				

KM# 51 50000 GULDEN
7.9800 g., 0.9170 Gold 0.2353 oz. AGW **Subject:** Hindu Immigration **Obv:** Arms with supporters **Rev:** Hindu couple with ship in background **Edge:** Reeded

Date	Mintage	F	VF	XF	Unc	BU
ND(1998)(B) Proof	Est. 1,000	Value: 350				

KM# 53 75000 GULDEN
7.9800 g., 0.9170 Gold 0.2353 oz. AGW **Subject:** Coppename Bridge **Edge:** Reeded

Date	Mintage	F	VF	XF	Unc	BU
1999 Proof	1,000	Value: 400				

KM# 54 100000 GULDEN
7.9800 g., 0.9170 Gold 0.2353 oz. AGW **Subject:** 25th Anniversary of Independence **Obv:** Arms with supporters **Edge:** Reeded

Date	Mintage	F	VF	XF	Unc	BU
2000 Proof	1,000	Value: 500				

KM# 55 100000 GULDEN
7.9800 g., 0.9170 Gold 0.2353 oz. AGW **Subject:** River Bridge **Obv:** Arms with supporters **Rev:** Bridge over Suriam River **Edge:** Reeded

Date	Mintage	F	VF	XF	Unc	BU
2000 Proof	1,000	Value: 500				

KM# 56 100000 GULDEN
7.9800 g., 0.9170 Gold 0.2353 oz. AGW **Subject:** Millennium 2000-2001 **Obv:** Arms with supporters **Rev:** Circles **Edge:** Reeded

Date	Mintage	F	VF	XF	Unc	BU
2000 Proof	1,500	Value: 450				

KM# 57 125,000 GULDEN
15.0000 g., 0.5850 Gold 0.2821 oz. AGW **Subject:** Millennium 2000-2001 **Obv:** Arms with supporters **Rev:** Circles **Edge:** Reeded

Date	Mintage	F	VF	XF	Unc	BU
2000 Proof	2,500	Value: 500				

PATTERNS
Including off metal strikes

KM#	Date	Mintage	Identification		Mkt Val
Pn1	1962	—	Gulden. Bronze. KM#15. Nickel coated.		60.00
Pn2	ND(1994)	—	100 Guilder. Copper-Nickel. KM#44.		60.00
Pn3	ND(1994)	—	100 Guilder. Silver. KM#44.		80.00

TRIAL STRIKES

KM#	Date	Mintage	Identification	Mkt Val
TS1	1984	—	10 Guilders. Silver. Arms with supporters. Shot put thrower and torch.	

PROOF SETS

KM#	Date	Mintage	Identification	Issue Price	Mkt Val
PS1	1962 (5)	650	KM11-15	—	170
PS2	1966 (5)	—	KM11-15	—	440
PS3	1976 (4)	10	KM11a, 12.1a, 13, 14	—	300
PS4	1976 (3)	—	KM16-18	145	160
PS5	1976 (2)	—	KM16-17	50.00	35.00
PS6	1988 (6)	1,500	KM11b, 12.1b, 13a, 14a, 23, 24	42.00	50.00

SWAZILAND

MOZAMBIQUE

SOUTH AFRICA

Indian Ocean

LESOTHO

The Kingdom of Swaziland, located in southeastern Africa, has an area of 6,704 sq. mi. (17,360 sq. km.) and a population of *756,000. Capital: Mbabane (administrative); Lobamba (legislative). The diversified economy includes mining, agriculture, and light industry. Asbestos, iron ore, wood pulp, and sugar are exported.

The people of the present Swazi nation established themselves in an area including what is now Swaziland in the early 1800s. The first Swazi contact with the British came early in the reign of the extremely able Swazi leader Mswati when he asked the British for aid against Zulu raids into Swaziland. The British and Transvaal responded by guaranteeing the independence of Swaziland, 1881. South Africa assumed the power of protection and administration in 1894 and Swaziland continued under this administration until the conquest of the Transvaal during the Anglo-Boer War, when administration was transferred to the British government. After World War II, Britain began to prepare Swaziland for independence, which was achieved on Sept. 6, 1968. The Kingdom is a member of the Commonwealth of Nations. King Mswati III is Head of State. The prime minister is Head of Government.

RULERS
Sobhuza II, 1968-1982
Queen Dzeliwe, Regent for
Prince Makhosetive, 1982-1986
King Msawati III, 1986-

MONETARY SYSTEM
100 Cents = 1 Luhlanga
25 Luhlanga = 1 Lilangeni
(plural - Emalangeni)

KINGDOM

STANDARD COINAGE

100 Cents = 1 Luhlanga; 25 Luhlanga = 1 Lilangeni

KM# 1   5 CENTS
2.7500 g., 0.8000 Silver 0.0707 oz. ASW   **Ruler:** Sobhuza II
Subject: Independence Commemorative **Obv:** Head 3/4 left
Rev: Shield and three spears

Date	Mintage	F	VF	XF	Unc	BU
1968 Proof	10,000	Value: 5.00				

KM# 2   10 CENTS
4.3800 g., 0.8000 Silver 0.1127 oz. ASW   **Ruler:** Sobhuza II
Subject: Independence Commemorative **Obv:** Head 3/4 left
Rev: Shield and three spears

Date	Mintage	F	VF	XF	Unc	BU
1968 Proof	10,000	Value: 7.00				

KM# 3   20 CENTS
6.6300 g., 0.8000 Silver 0.1705 oz. ASW   **Ruler:** Sobhuza II
Subject: Independence Commemorative **Obv:** Head 3/4 left
Rev: Shield and three spears

Date	Mintage	F	VF	XF	Unc	BU
1968 Proof	10,000	Value: 8.00				

KM# 4   50 CENTS
10.3900 g., 0.8000 Silver 0.2672 oz. ASW   **Ruler:** Sobhuza II
Subject: Independence Commemorative **Obv:** Head 3/4 left
Rev: Shield and three spears

Date	Mintage	F	VF	XF	Unc	BU
1968 Proof	10,000	Value: 10.00				

KM# 5   LUHLANGA
15.0000 g., 0.8000 Silver 0.3858 oz. ASW   **Ruler:** Sobhuza II
Subject: Independence Commemorative **Obv:** Head 3/4 left
Rev: Shield with three spears divides date

Date	Mintage	VG	F	VF	XF	Unc
1968 Proof	10,000	Value: 15.00				

KM# 6   LILANGENI
33.9305 g., 0.9170 Gold 1.0003 oz. AGW   **Ruler:** Sobhuza II
Subject: Independence Commemorative **Obv:** Head 3/4 left
Rev: Arms with supporters **Note:** Approximately 1,450 melted.

Date	Mintage	F	VF	XF	Unc	BU
1968 Proof	2,000	Value: 975				

DECIMAL COINAGE

100 Cents = 1 Lilangeni (plural emelangeni)

KM# 7   CENT
2.0000 g., Bronze, 18.3 mm.   **Ruler:** Sobhuza II **Obv:** Head 1/4 right **Rev:** Pineapple and value

Date	Mintage	F	VF	XF	Unc	BU
1974	6,002,000	—	—	0.10	0.20	—
1974 Proof	13,000	Value: 0.75				
1979	500,000	—	—	0.10	0.25	—
1979 Proof	10,000	Value: 0.75				
1982	—			0.10	0.25	—
1983	1,100,000			0.10	0.25	—

KM# 21   CENT
2.0000 g., Bronze, 18.3 mm.   **Ruler:** Sobhuza II **Series:** F.A.O.
Obv: Head 1/4 right **Rev:** Pineapple and value

Date	Mintage	F	VF	XF	Unc	BU
1975	2,500,000	—	—	0.10	0.25	—

KM# 39   CENT
Copper Plated Steel   **Ruler:** Queen Dzeliwe Regent for Prince Makhosetive **Obv:** Bust facing **Rev:** Pineapple

Date	Mintage	F	VF	XF	Unc	BU
1986	12,000,000				0.10	0.25

KM# 39a   CENT
Bronze   **Ruler:** Queen Dzeliwe Regent for Prince Makhosetive **Obv:** Bust facing **Rev:** Pineapple

Date	Mintage	F	VF	XF	Unc	BU
1986	—			1.00	2.50	

KM# 51   CENT
Bronze   **Ruler:** King Msawati III **Obv:** Head 1/4 right
Rev: Pineapple and value

Date	Mintage	F	VF	XF	Unc	BU
1995	—				0.25	—

KM# 8   2 CENTS
2.8000 g., Bronze, 18.6 mm.   **Ruler:** Sobhuza II **Obv:** Head 1/4 right **Rev:** Trees and value

Date	Mintage	F	VF	XF	Unc	BU
1974	2,252,000			0.15	0.30	—
1974 Proof	13,000	Value: 0.75				
1979	1,000,000			0.15	0.30	—
1979 Proof	10,000	Value: 1.00				
1982	500,000			0.15	0.30	—

KM# 22   2 CENTS
2.8000 g., Bronze, 18.6 mm.   **Ruler:** Sobhuza II **Series:** F.A.O.
Obv: Head 1/4 right **Rev:** Trees and value **Edge:** Plain

Date	Mintage	F	VF	XF	Unc	BU
1975	1,500,000			0.15	0.30	—

KM# 9   5 CENTS
2.1500 g., Copper-Nickel, 18.5 mm.   **Ruler:** Sobhuza II
Obv: Head 1/4 right **Rev:** Arum lily and value

Date	Mintage	F	VF	XF	Unc	BU
1974	1,252,000	—	0.10	0.20	0.40	—
1974 Proof	13,000	Value: 1.00				
1975	1,500,000		0.10	0.20	0.40	—
1979	1,680,000		0.10	0.20	0.40	—
1979 Proof	10,000	Value: 1.75				

KM# 40.1   5 CENTS
2.1500 g., Copper-Nickel, 18.5 mm.   **Ruler:** Queen Dzeliwe Regent for Prince Makhosetive **Obv:** Bust facing **Rev:** Arum lily and value **Edge:** Plain

Date	Mintage	F	VF	XF	Unc	BU
1986	—		0.15	0.25	0.50	—

KM# 40.2   5 CENTS
Nickel Plated Steel, 18.5 mm.   **Ruler:** King Msawati III **Obv:** Bust facing **Rev:** Arum lily **Edge:** Plain

Date	Mintage	F	VF	XF	Unc	BU
1992	—		0.15	0.25	0.50	—

KM# 48 5 CENTS
2.1000 g., Copper-Nickel, 18.5 mm. **Ruler:** King Msawati III
Obv: Bust 3/4 right **Rev:** Arum lily and value **Edge:** Plain

Date	Mintage	F	VF	XF	Unc	BU
1995	—	—	—	0.20	0.50	0.75
1996	—	—	—	0.20	0.50	0.75
1998	—	—	—	0.20	0.50	0.75
1999	—	—	—	0.20	0.50	0.75
2000	—	—	—	0.20	0.50	0.75
Note: Thick inscription						
2000	—	—	—	0.20	0.50	0.75
Note: Thin inscription						

KM# 48a 5 CENTS
Copper-Nickel, 18.5 mm. **Ruler:** King Msawati III **Obv:** Bust 1/4 right **Rev:** Arum lily and value

Date	Mintage	F	VF	XF	Unc	BU
1999	—	—	—	—	0.50	0.75

KM# 10 10 CENTS
Copper-Nickel, 22 mm. **Ruler:** Sobhuza II **Obv:** Head 1/4 right **Rev:** Sugar cane and value

Date	Mintage	F	VF	XF	Unc	BU
1974	752,000	—	0.15	0.25	0.50	—
1974 Proof	13,000	Value: 1.00				
1979	500,000	—	0.15	0.25	0.50	—
1979 Proof	4,231	Value: 2.50				

KM# 23 10 CENTS
Copper-Nickel, 22 mm. **Ruler:** Sobhuza II **Series:** F.A.O. **Obv:** Head 1/4 right **Rev:** Sugar cane and value

Date	Mintage	F	VF	XF	Unc	BU
1975	1,500,000	—	0.15	0.25	0.50	—

KM# 41 10 CENTS
3.6000 g., Copper-Nickel, 22 mm. **Ruler:** King Msawati III
Obv: Head facing **Rev:** Sugar cane and value **Edge:** Plain

Date	Mintage	F	VF	XF	Unc	BU
1986	—	—	0.15	0.25	0.50	—
1992	—	—	0.15	0.25	0.50	—

KM# 49 10 CENTS
3.6000 g., Copper-Nickel, 22 mm. **Ruler:** King Msawati III
Obv: Bust 3/4 right **Rev:** Sugar cane and value **Edge:** Plain

Date	Mintage	F	VF	XF	Unc	BU
1995	—	—	—	0.30	0.75	1.00
1996	—	—	—	0.30	0.75	1.00
1998	—	—	—	0.30	0.75	1.00
2000	—	—	—	0.30	0.75	1.00

KM# 11 20 CENTS
5.6000 g., Copper-Nickel, 25.2 mm. **Ruler:** Sobhuza II
Obv: Head 1/4 right **Rev:** Elephant head and value

Date	Mintage	F	VF	XF	Unc	BU
1974	502,000	—	0.35	0.75	2.50	4.50
1974 Proof	13,000	Value: 3.00				
1975	1,000,000	—	0.35	0.75	2.50	4.50
1979	—	—	0.35	0.75	2.50	4.50
1979 Proof	—	Value: 4.00				

KM# 31 20 CENTS
5.6000 g., Copper-Nickel, 25.2 mm. **Ruler:** Sobhuza II
Series: F.A.O. **Obv:** Head 1/4 right **Rev:** Sprigs and logo

Date	Mintage	F	VF	XF	Unc	BU
1981	150,000	—	0.40	0.80	1.75	—

KM# 42 20 CENTS
5.6000 g., Copper-Nickel, 25.2 mm. **Ruler:** Queen Dzeliwe Regent for Prince Makhosetive **Obv:** Head facing **Rev:** Elephant head and value **Edge:** Plain

Date	Mintage	F	VF	XF	Unc	BU
1986	—	—	0.40	0.80	3.00	5.00

KM# 50.1 20 CENTS
5.6000 g., Copper-Nickel, 25.2 mm. **Ruler:** King Msawati III
Obv: Large bust 3/4 right **Rev:** Elephant head and value **Edge:** Plain

Date	Mintage	F	VF	XF	Unc	BU
1996	—	—	0.40	0.90	2.25	3.00
2000	—	—	0.40	0.90	2.25	3.00

KM# 50.2 20 CENTS
5.5200 g., Copper-Nickel, 25.2 mm. **Ruler:** King Msawati III
Obv: Small bust 3/4 right **Rev:** Elephant head, value **Edge:** Plain

Date	Mintage	F	VF	XF	Unc	BU
1998	—	—	—	0.45	1.10	1.50

KM# 12 50 CENTS
8.9000 g., Copper-Nickel, 29.45 mm. **Ruler:** Sobhuza II
Obv: Head 1/4 right **Rev:** Arms with supporters

Date	Mintage	F	VF	XF	Unc	BU
1974	252,000	—	1.00	1.50	2.75	—
1974 Proof	13,000	Value: 3.00				
1975	500,000	—	1.00	1.50	2.75	—
1979	—	—	0.50	1.00	2.50	—
1979 Proof	10,000	Value: 5.00				
1981	1,150,000	—	0.50	1.00	2.50	—

KM# 43 50 CENTS
8.9000 g., Copper-Nickel, 29.45 mm. **Ruler:** King Msawati III
Obv: Head facing **Rev:** Arms with supporters **Edge:** Plain

Date	Mintage	F	VF	XF	Unc	BU
1986	1,000,000	—	0.50	1.50	3.50	—
1993	—	—	0.50	1.50	3.50	—

KM# 52 50 CENTS
8.9000 g., Copper-Nickel, 29.45 mm. **Ruler:** King Msawati III
Obv: Head 1/4 right **Rev:** Arms with supporters

Date	Mintage	F	VF	XF	Unc	BU
1996	—	—	—	—	3.75	4.50
1998	—	—	—	—	3.75	4.50

KM# 13 LILANGENI
11.6500 g., Copper-Nickel, 30 mm. **Ruler:** Sobhuza II
Obv: Head 1/4 right **Rev:** Female and child facing

Date	Mintage	F	VF	XF	Unc	BU
1974	127,000	—	1.50	2.50	4.50	—
1974 Proof	13,000	Value: 6.00				
1979	—	—	1.00	2.00	4.50	—
1979 Proof	110,000	Value: 7.50				

KM# 24 LILANGENI
Copper-Nickel, 30.5 mm. **Ruler:** Sobhuza II **Series:** F.A.O., International Women's Year **Obv:** Head 1/4 right **Rev:** Female and child facing

Date	Mintage	F	VF	XF	Unc	BU
1975	100,000	—	1.50	2.75	6.50	—

KM# 28 LILANGENI
11.6500 g., Copper-Nickel, 30 mm. **Ruler:** Sobhuza II
Series: F.A.O. **Obv:** Head 1/4 right **Rev:** Female and child facing

Date	Mintage	F	VF	XF	Unc	BU
1976	100,000	—	1.50	2.75	6.50	—

KM# 29.1 LILANGENI
15.5500 g., 0.9990 Gold 0.4994 oz. AGW **Ruler:** Sobhuza II
Subject: 80th Anniversary - Birth of King Sobhuza II **Obv:** Head
1/4 right **Rev:** Arms with supporters

Date	Mintage	F	VF	XF	Unc	BU
ND(1979)	1,250	—	—	—	475	—
ND(1979) Proof	Inc. above	Value: 500				

KM# 29.2 LILANGENI
15.5500 g., 0.9990 Gold 0.4994 oz. AGW **Ruler:** Sobhuza II
Subject: 80th Anniversary - Birth of King Sobhuza II **Obv:** Head
1/4 right **Rev:** Dates 1923-1979 above arms with supporters

Date	Mintage	F	VF	XF	Unc	BU
ND(1979)	—	—	—	—	550	—

KM# 32 LILANGENI
11.6500 g., Copper-Nickel, 30 mm. **Ruler:** Sobhuza II
Series: F.A.O. **Obv:** Head 1/4 right **Rev:** Half length figure
husking corn

Date	Mintage	F	VF	XF	Unc	BU
1981	871,000	—	1.50	3.00	7.00	—

KM# 32a LILANGENI
11.6600 g., 0.9250 Silver 0.3467 oz. ASW **Ruler:** Sobhuza II
Series: F.A.O. **Obv:** Head 1/4 right **Rev:** Half length figure
husking corn

Date	Mintage	F	VF	XF	Unc	BU
1981	5,000	—	—	—	22.50	—
1981 Proof	5,000	Value: 32.50				

KM# 44.1 LILANGENI
9.5000 g., Nickel-Brass, 22.5 mm. **Ruler:** Queen Dzeliwe
Regent for Prince Makhosetive **Obv:** Head facing **Rev:** Bust
facing **Edge:** Reeded

Date	Mintage	F	VF	XF	Unc	BU
1986	1,025,000	—	—	2.00	4.00	—

KM# 44.2 LILANGENI
Nickel-Brass Plated Steel, 22.5 mm. **Ruler:** King Msawati III
Obv: Head facing **Rev:** Bust facing **Edge:** Reeded

Date	Mintage	F	VF	XF	Unc	BU
1992	—	—	—	1.50	3.50	—

KM# 45 LILANGENI
9.5000 g., Brass, 22.5 mm. **Ruler:** King Msawati III **Obv:** Head
1/4 right **Rev:** Bust facing

Date	Mintage	F	VF	XF	Unc	BU
1995	—	—	—	1.50	3.50	4.00
1996	—	—	—	1.50	3.50	4.00
1998	—	—	—	1.50	3.50	4.00

KM# 33 2 EMALANGENI
17.0000 g., 0.9250 Silver 0.5055 oz. ASW, 34 mm.
Ruler: Sobhuza II **Subject:** Diamond Jubilee of King Sobhuza II
Obv: Head 1/4 right **Rev:** Lilies and value

Date	Mintage	F	VF	XF	Unc	BU
1981 Proof	—	Value: 32.50				

KM# 33a 2 EMALANGENI
Copper-Nickel **Ruler:** Sobhuza II **Subject:** Diamond Jubilee of
King Sobhuza II **Obv:** Head 1/4 right **Rev:** Lilies and value

Date	Mintage	F	VF	XF	Unc	BU
1981	50,000	—	2.00	3.50	7.50	—

KM# 46 2 EMALANGENI
5.0000 g., Brass **Ruler:** King Msawati III **Obv:** Head 1/4 right
Rev: Lilies and value

Date	Mintage	F	VF	XF	Unc	BU
1995 lg. bust	—	—	—	—	3.75	4.25
1996 sm. bust	—	—	—	—	3.75	4.25
1998 lg. bust	—	—	—	—	3.75	4.25

KM# 14 5 EMALANGENI
10.3000 g., 0.9250 Silver 0.3063 oz. ASW **Ruler:** Sobhuza II
Subject: 75th Anniversary - Birth of King Sobhuza II **Obv:** Head
1/4 right **Rev:** Building and emblem

Date	Mintage	F	VF	XF	Unc	BU
1974 Proof	—	Value: 55.00				

KM# 15 5 EMALANGENI
5.5600 g., 0.9000 Gold 0.1609 oz. AGW **Ruler:** Sobhuza II
Subject: 75th Anniversary - Birth of King Sobhuza II **Obv:** Head
1/4 right **Rev:** Arms with supporters within circle

Date	Mintage	F	VF	XF	Unc	BU
1974 Proof	60,000	Value: 175				

KM# 47 5 EMALANGENI
7.6000 g., Brass **Ruler:** King Msawati III **Obv:** Head 1/4 right
Rev: Arms with supporters above value that divides date

Date	Mintage	F	VF	XF	Unc	BU
1995 sm. bust	—	—	—	—	6.00	7.00
1996 sm. bust	—	—	—	—	6.00	7.00
1998 lg. bust	—	—	—	—	6.00	7.00
1999	—	—	—	—	6.00	7.00

KM# 53 5 EMALANGENI
Brass **Ruler:** King Msawati III **Subject:** Central Bank's 25th
Anniversary **Obv:** Head 1/4 right **Rev:** Bank seal within circle

Date	Mintage	F	VF	XF	Unc	BU
ND(1999)	—	—	—	—	5.50	6.50

KM# 16 7-1/2 EMALANGENI
16.2000 g., 0.9250 Silver 0.4818 oz. ASW **Ruler:** Sobhuza II
Subject: 75th Anniversary - Birth of King Sobhuza II **Obv:** Head
1/4 right **Rev:** Bird

Date	Mintage	F	VF	XF	Unc	BU
1974 Proof	—	Value: 65.00				

KM# 17 10 EMALANGENI
11.1200 g., 0.9000 Gold 0.3218 oz. AGW **Ruler:** Sobhuza II
Subject: 75th Anniversary - Birth of King Sobhuza II **Obv:** Head
1/4 right **Rev:** Standing figure divides date and value within circle

Date	Mintage	F	VF	XF	Unc	BU
1974 Proof	Est. 40,000	Value: 345				

KM# 25 10 EMALANGENI
25.5000 g., 0.9250 Silver 0.7583 oz. ASW **Ruler:** Sobhuza II
Subject: 75th Anniversary - Birth of King Sobhuza II **Obv:** Head
1/4 right **Rev:** Heron

Date	Mintage	F	VF	XF	Unc	BU
1975	Est. 1,000	—	—	—	50.00	55.00
1975 Proof	Est. 1,500	Value: 60.00				

KM# 18 15 EMALANGENI

32.6000 g., 0.9250 Silver 0.9695 oz. ASW **Ruler:** Sobhuza II
Subject: 75th Anniversary - Birth of King Sobhuza II **Obv:** Head
1/4 right **Rev:** Uniformed bust right saluting army with flags

Date	Mintage	F	VF	XF	Unc	BU
1974 Proof	—	Value: 95.00				

KM# 19 20 EMALANGENI

22.2300 g., 0.9000 Gold 0.6432 oz. AGW **Ruler:** Sobhuza II
Subject: 75th Anniversary - Birth of King Sobhuza II **Obv:** Head
1/4 right **Rev:** Child facing and UNICEF emblem

Date	Mintage	F	VF	XF	Unc	BU
1974 Proof	Est. 25,000	Value: 625				

KM# 20 25 EMALANGENI

27.7800 g., 0.9000 Gold 0.8038 oz. AGW **Ruler:** Sobhuza II
Subject: 75th Anniversary - Birth of King Sobhuza II **Obv:** Head
1/4 right **Rev:** Conjoined busts facing within circle

Date	Mintage	F	VF	XF	Unc	BU
1974	Est. 15,000	—	—	—	—	800

KM# 34 25 EMALANGENI

28.2800 g., 0.9250 Silver 0.8410 oz. ASW, 38.61 mm.
Ruler: Sobhuza II **Subject:** Diamond Jubilee of King Sobhuza II
Obv: Head 1/4 right **Rev:** Bird and value

Date	Mintage	F	VF	XF	Unc	BU
1981	Est. 10,000	—	—	—	35.00	40.00
1981 Proof	Est. 10,000	Value: 50.00				

KM# 37 25 EMALANGENI

28.2800 g., 0.9250 Silver 0.8410 oz. ASW **Ruler:** King
Msawati III **Subject:** Accession of King Makhosetive **Obv:** Bust
facing **Rev:** Bust facing

Date	Mintage	F	VF	XF	Unc	BU
ND(1986) Proof	Est. 2,500	Value: 45.00				

KM# 26 50 EMALANGENI

4.3100 g., 0.9000 Gold 0.1247 oz. AGW **Ruler:** Sobhuza II
Subject: 75th Anniversary - Birth of King Sobhuza II **Obv:** Head
1/4 right **Rev:** Antelope

Date	Mintage	F	VF	XF	Unc	BU
1975	3,510	—	—	—	125	135
1975 Proof	3,262	Value: 150				

KM# 27 100 EMALANGENI

8.6400 g., 0.9000 Gold 0.2500 oz. AGW **Ruler:** Sobhuza II
Subject: 75th Anniversary - Birth of King Sobhuza II **Obv:** Head
1/4 right **Rev:** Bust 1/4 left

Date	Mintage	F	VF	XF	Unc	BU
ND(1975)	1,000	—	—	—	250	275
ND(1975) Proof	—	Value: 300				

KM# 35 250 EMALANGENI

15.9800 g., 0.9170 Gold 0.4711 oz. AGW **Ruler:** Sobhuza II
Subject: Diamond Jubilee of King Sobhuza II **Obv:** Head 1/4
right **Rev:** Elephant

Date	Mintage	F	VF	XF	Unc	BU
1981	2,000	—	—	—	450	475
1981 Proof	2,000	Value: 500				

KM# 38 250 EMALANGENI

15.9800 g., 0.9170 Gold 0.4711 oz. AGW **Ruler:** King Msawati III
Subject: Accession of King Makhosetive **Obv:** Bust facing
Rev: Bust facing

Date	Mintage	F	VF	XF	Unc	BU
ND(1986)	250	—	—	—	460	485
ND(1986) Proof	250	Value: 525				

GOLD BULLION COINAGE

KM# 30 2 EMALANGENI

31.1000 g., 0.9990 Gold 0.9988 oz. AGW **Ruler:** Sobhuza II
Subject: 80th Anniversary - Birth of King Sobhuza II **Obv:** Head
1/4 right **Rev:** Young bust of Queen Elizabeth II right

Date	Mintage	F	VF	XF	Unc	BU
ND(1979)	1,250	—	—	—	950	975
ND(1979) Proof	Inc. above	Value: 1,000				

KM# 36 5 EMALANGENI

31.1000 g., 0.9990 Gold 0.9988 oz. AGW **Ruler:** Sobhuza II
Subject: Queen Elizabeth II's Silver Jubilee **Obv:** Head 1/4 right
within circle **Rev:** Crowned bust of Queen Elizabeth II facing
divides dates within circle

Date	Mintage	F	VF	XF	Unc	BU
ND(1978) Proof	—	Value: 1,000				

MINT SETS

KM#	Date	Mintage	Identification	Issue Price	Mkt Val
MS1	1974 (7)	—	KM7-13	10.00	10.00
MS2	1975 (3)	1,000	KM25-27	—	445
MS3	1986 (6)	—	KM39, 40.1, 41-43, 44.1	—	8.00

PROOF SETS

KM#	Date	Mintage	Identification	Issue Price	Mkt Val
PS1	1968 (5)	10,000	KM1-5	25.80	45.00
PS2	1974 (7)	20,000	KM7-13	18.00	16.00
PS3	1974 (4)	—	KM15, 17, 19, 20	745	1,300
PS4	1974 (3)	—	KM14, 16, 17	70.00	440
PS5	1975 (3)	—	KM25-27	—	490
PS6	1975 (2)	—	KM26-27	252	430
PS7	1979 (7)	3,231	KM7-13	34.00	22.50
PS8	1979 (2)	—	KM29.1, 30	1,172	1,450

SWEDEN

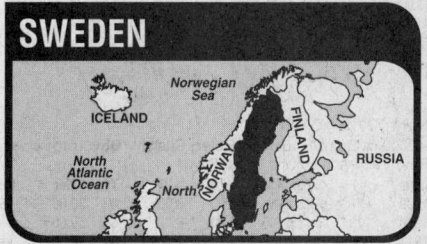

The Kingdom of Sweden, a limited constitutional monarchy
located in northern Europe between Norway and Finland, has an
area of 173,732 sq. mi. (449,960 sq. km.) and a population of *8.5
million. Capital: Stockholm. Mining, lumbering and a specialized
machine industry dominate the economy. Machinery, paper, iron
and steel, motor vehicles and wood pulp are exported.

Olaf Skottkonung founded Sweden as a Christian stronghold late in the 10th century. After conquering Finland late in the
13th century, Sweden, together with Norway, came under the
rule of Denmark, 1397-1523, in an association known as the
Union of Kalmar. Modern Sweden had its beginning in 1523 when
Gustaf Vasa drove the Danes out of Sweden and was himself
chosen king. Under Gustaf Adolphus II and Charles XII, Sweden
was one of the great powers of 17th century Europe – until
Charles invaded Russia in 1708, and was defeated at the Battle
of Pultowa in June, 1709. Early in the 18th century, a coalition of
Russia, Poland and Denmark took away Sweden's Baltic empire
and in 1809 Sweden was forced to cede Finland to Russia. The
Treaty of Kiel ceded Norway to Sweden in January 1814. The
Norwegians resisted for a time but later signed the Act of Union
at the Convention of Moss in August 1814. The Union was dissolved in 1905 and Norway became independent. A new constitution that took effect on Jan. 1, 1975, restricts the function of
the king largely to a ceremonial role.

RULERS
Oscar II, 1872-1907
Gustaf V, 1907-1950
Gustaf VI, 1950-1973
Carl XVI Gustaf, 1973-

MINT OFFICIALS' INITIALS

Letter	Date	Name
AL	1898-1916	Adolf Lindberg, engraver
B	1992-2005	Stefan Ingves
D	1986-1992	Bengt Dennis
EB	1876-1908	Emil Brusewitz
EL	1916-1944	Erik Lindberg, engraver
G	1927-1945	Alf Grabe
LH	1944-1974	Leo Holmberg, engraver
SI	2005-	Stefan Ingves
TS	1945-1961	Torsten Swensson
U	1961-1986	Benkt Ulvfot
W	1908-1927	Karl-August Wallroth

MONETARY SYSTEM
100 Ore = 1 Krona

KINGDOM

REFORM COINAGE
1873 - present

KM# 750 ORE
2.0000 g., Bronze, 16 mm. **Ruler:** Oscar II **Obv:** Monogram within crowned shield, legend lengthened **Rev:** Value and date flanked by 3 crowns

Date	Mintage	F	VF	XF	Unc	BU
1901	3,074,700	1.00	2.50	4.50	20.00	—
1902	2,685,400	1.00	2.50	4.50	22.50	—
1903	2,695,600	1.00	2.50	4.50	22.50	—
1904	2,032,700	1.00	2.50	4.50	20.00	—
1905	3,556,000	0.85	2.25	3.50	16.50	—

KM# 768 ORE
Bronze, 16 mm. **Ruler:** Oscar II **Obv:** Crowned shield **Rev:** Value and date flanked by crowns

Date	Mintage	F	VF	XF	Unc	BU
1906	1,783,300	2.00	4.00	10.00	65.00	—
1907	8,250,500	0.20	0.50	2.00	12.50	—

KM# 777.1 ORE
Bronze, 16 mm. **Ruler:** Gustaf V **Obv:** Crowned monogram with small cross on crown **Rev:** Value and crowns

Date	Mintage	F	VF	XF	Unc	BU
1909	3,805,600	6.00	9.00	18.00	100	—

KM# 777.2 ORE
2.0000 g., Bronze, 16 mm. **Ruler:** Gustaf V **Obv:** Large cross **Rev:** Value and crowns **Edge:** Plain

Date	Mintage	F	VF	XF	Unc	BU
1909	Inc. above	2.00	3.00	8.00	30.00	—
1910	1,582,600	3.00	6.00	10.00	50.00	—
1911	3,149,000	0.75	1.50	3.00	15.00	—
1912/1	3,170,000	8.50	20.00	47.50	250	—
1912	Inc. above	0.75	1.50	3.00	15.00	—
1913/12	3,197,300	4.00	10.00	22.50	125	—
1913	Inc. above	0.75	1.50	3.00	15.00	—
	Note: Long and short-tailed 9					
1914 Open 4	2,214,050	35.00	60.00	125	435	—
1914 Closed 4	Inc. above	0.75	1.50	5.00	30.00	—
1915/3	4,471,300	2.25	6.00	10.00	37.50	—
1915	Inc. above	0.25	0.50	1.75	7.00	—
1916 Short 6	7,615,500	0.25	0.50	1.75	7.00	—
1916 Long 6	Inc. above	0.30	0.70	2.50	10.00	—
1919 Unique	—	—	—	—	—	—
1920	5,547,600	0.25	0.50	1.25	5.00	—
1921	7,441,510	0.25	0.50	1.25	5.00	—
1922	1,165,700	2.00	4.00	6.00	30.00	—
1923	4,511,800	0.35	0.75	1.75	7.00	—
1924	2,578,900	0.25	0.75	1.75	8.00	—
1925	4,714,900	0.15	0.35	0.60	3.00	—
1926	7,739,300	0.15	0.35	*0.60	3.00	—
1927	3,601,600	0.15	0.35	0.60	3.00	—
1928	2,380,800	0.25	0.75	2.50	10.00	—
1929 Curved 2	6,090,500	0.20	0.35	0.85	4.00	—
1929 Straight 2	Inc. above	0.40	0.60	2.00	9.00	—
1930	5,477,300	0.20	0.35	0.85	4.00	—
1931	5,678,500	0.20	0.35	0.85	4.00	—
1932	3,339,000	—	0.45	1.75	7.00	—
1933	3,426,800	—	0.45	0.85	5.00	—
1934	6,120,500	—	0.30	0.60	3.00	—
1935	4,599,800	—	0.30	0.60	3.00	—
1936 Long 6	6,166,100	0.20	0.45	1.25	3.50	—
1936 Short 6	Inc. above	0.10	0.30	0.60	3.00	—
1937	7,738,200	0.10	0.25	0.60	1.75	—
1938	6,992,900	0.10	0.25	0.60	1.75	—
1939	6,562,300	0.10	0.25	0.60	1.75	—
1940	4,059,900	0.10	0.25	0.50	1.50	—
1941	11,599,090	0.10	0.25	0.50	1.50	—
1942	3,992,000	0.10	0.25	0.60	1.75	—
1950	22,421,200	0.10	0.25	0.50	1.50	—

KM# 789 ORE
Iron, 16 mm. **Ruler:** Gustaf V **Obv:** Crowned monogram divides date **Rev:** Value and crowns **Note:** World War I issues.

Date	Mintage	F	VF	XF	Unc	BU
1917	8,127,700	0.50	1.50	4.00	20.00	—
1918	9,706,100	1.00	2.25	6.50	27.50	—
1919	7,169,500	1.50	3.00	8.00	40.00	—

KM# 810 ORE
1.7000 g., Iron, 16 mm. **Ruler:** Gustaf V **Obv:** Crowned monogram divides date **Rev:** Value and crowns **Note:** World War II issues. Similar to KM#777.

Date	Mintage	F	VF	XF	Unc	BU
1942	10,053,000	0.10	0.25	0.75	3.50	—
1943	10,714,000	0.10	0.25	0.85	4.50	—
1944	8,648,500	0.10	0.25	0.75	4.50	—
1945	9,527,000	0.10	0.25	0.75	4.50	—
1945 Serif 4	Inc. above	3.50	6.50	15.00	30.00	—
1946	6,611,000	—	0.25	0.50	1.50	—
1947	14,244,500	—	0.20	0.40	1.50	—
1948	15,442,000	—	0.20	0.40	1.50	—
1949	11,778,900	—	0.20	0.40	1.50	—
1950	14,431,500	—	0.20	0.40	1.50	—

KM# 820 ORE
2.0000 g., Bronze, 16 mm. **Ruler:** Gustaf VI **Obv:** Crown above inscription **Rev:** Value within circle divides date below crown **Edge:** Plain **Note:** Varieties exist.

Date	Mintage	F	VF	XF	Unc	BU
1952 TS	3,819,000	—	0.20	0.75	3.50	—
1953 TS	22,635,800	—	—	0.30	2.00	—
1954 TS	15,492,000	—	—	0.30	2.00	—
1955 TS	24,008,000	—	—	0.30	2.00	—
1956 TS	20,792,000	—	—	0.30	2.00	—
1957 TS	21,018,500	—	—	0.30	2.00	—
1958 TS	20,220,000	—	—	0.30	2.00	—
1959 TS	14,027,500	—	—	0.30	2.00	—
1960 TS	21,840,000	—	—	0.25	2.00	—
1961 TS	11,457,500	—	—	0.35	2.25	—
1961 U	4,927,500	—	0.20	0.50	3.50	—
1962 U	19,692,500	—	—	0.30	2.00	—
1963 U	26,070,000	—	—	0.15	0.65	—
1964 U	19,290,000	—	—	0.15	0.65	—
1965 U	22,335,000	—	—	0.15	0.65	—
1966 U	24,092,500	—	—	0.15	0.30	—
1967 U	30,420,000	—	—	0.10	0.30	—
1968 U	20,760,000	—	—	0.10	0.30	—
1969 U	20,197,500	—	—	0.10	0.30	—
1970 U	44,400,000	—	—	0.10	0.30	—
1971 U	16,490,000	—	—	0.10	0.30	—

KM# 746 2 ORE
3.9100 g., Bronze, 21 mm. **Ruler:** Oscar II **Obv:** Large lettering **Rev:** Value, date and crowns within circle

Date	Mintage	F	VF	XF	Unc	BU
1901	1,415,200	0.50	1.25	3.50	22.50	—
1902	2,035,550	0.50	1.25	3.50	22.50	—

Date	Mintage	F	VF	XF	Unc	BU
1904	698,050	0.50	1.25	4.50	30.00	—
1905	1,429,900	0.50	1.25	3.50	22.50	—

KM# 769 2 ORE
Bronze, 21 mm. **Ruler:** Oscar II **Obv:** Crowned shield **Rev:** Value, date and crowns within circle

Date	Mintage	F	VF	XF	Unc	BU
1906/5	994,250	100	200	420	875	—
1906	Inc. above	2.75	8.00	25.00	90.00	—
1907	3,807,350	0.30	0.60	2.50	15.00	—

KM# 778 2 ORE
4.0000 g., Bronze, 21 mm. **Ruler:** Gustaf V **Obv:** Crowned monogram divides date **Rev:** Value and crowns

Date	Mintage	F	VF	XF	Unc	BU
1909	1,584,550	0.50	2.00	8.00	47.50	—
1910	809,400	2.00	8.00	22.50	90.00	—
1912	445,750	2.50	10.00	32.50	100	—
1913	805,650	0.30	2.00	10.00	47.50	—
1914	1,196,900	0.30	2.00	10.00	47.50	—
1915/4	813,850	4.50	12.50	35.00	110	—
1915	Inc. above	0.30	2.00	10.00	47.50	—
1916/5	2,815,450	2.75	8.00	27.50	90.00	—
1916 Short 6	Inc. above	0.25	0.60	5.00	30.00	—
1916 Long 6	Inc. above	0.25	0.60	5.00	30.00	—
1919	1,202,700	0.25	0.60	4.00	22.50	—
1920	3,464,750	0.30	0.50	2.00	10.00	—
1921	2,958,250	0.30	0.50	1.75	10.00	—
1922	521,600	0.70	1.75	6.00	37.50	—
1923	769,200	1.00	2.50	7.00	47.50	—
1924	1,283,000	0.30	0.75	3.50	27.50	—
1925	3,903,350	0.20	0.50	1.75	15.00	—
1926	3,573,950	0.20	0.50	1.75	15.00	—
1927	2,190,250	0.20	0.50	1.75	15.00	—
1928	832,250	0.40	1.00	4.00	30.00	—
1929	2,384,350	0.20	0.30	1.75	10.00	—
1930	2,589,850	0.20	0.30	1.75	10.00	—
1931	2,295,200	0.20	0.30	1.75	10.00	—
1932	1,179,150	0.35	0.85	4.00	30.00	—
1933	1,721,300	0.20	0.35	1.75	10.00	—
1934	1,794,950	0.20	0.35	1.75	10.00	—
1935	3,677,750	0.20	0.30	1.25	7.00	—
1936 Short 6	2,244,100	0.20	0.30	1.00	6.00	—
1936 Long 6	Inc. above	0.65	1.25	3.75	18.50	—
1937	2,980,950	0.10	0.25	1.25	6.00	—
1938	3,224,800	0.10	0.25	0.75	6.00	—
1939	4,014,200	0.10	0.25	0.75	4.50	—
1940	3,304,750	0.10	0.25	0.75	4.50	—
1941	7,337,198	0.10	0.25	0.75	4.50	—
1942	1,614,000	0.30	0.75	1.50	10.00	—
1950	5,823,000	0.10	0.20	0.65	4.50	—

KM# 790 2 ORE
Iron, 21 mm. **Ruler:** Gustaf V **Obv:** Crowned monogram divides date **Rev:** Value and crowns **Note:** World War I issues. Similar to KM#553.

Date	Mintage	F	VF	XF	Unc	BU
1917	4,576,200	2.00	3.00	8.50	42.50	—
1918	4,981,750	2.50	5.00	12.50	57.50	—
1919	2,923,100	6.50	12.50	27.50	90.00	—
1920	1	—	—	—	—	—

KM# 811 2 ORE
3.5000 g., Iron, 21 mm. **Ruler:** Gustaf V **Obv:** Crowned monogram divides date **Rev:** Value and crowns **Note:** World War II issues.

Date	Mintage	F	VF	XF	Unc	BU
1942	9,343,350	0.15	0.30	1.50	10.00	—
1943	6,999,300	0.15	0.30	1.50	10.00	—

Date	Mintage	F	VF	XF	Unc	BU
1944	6,125,900	0.15	0.30	1.50	10.00	—
1945	4,773,400	0.20	0.40	1.50	11.50	—
1946	5,854,000	0.15	0.30	1.50	10.00	—
1947	9,535,750	0.15	0.30	0.75	7.00	—
1948	11,424,250	0.15	0.30	0.75	7.00	—
1949 Long 9	10,599,750	0.15	0.30	0.75	7.00	—
1949 Short 9	Inc. above	0.15	0.30	0.75	7.00	—
1950	13,323,000	0.15	0.30	0.75	7.00	—

KM# 821 2 ORE
Bronze, 21 mm. **Ruler:** Gustaf VI **Obv:** Crown above inscription **Rev:** Value within circle divides date below crown **Edge:** Plain **Note:** Varieties exist.

Date	Mintage	F	VF	XF	Unc	BU
1952 TS	3,011,000	0.20	0.50	0.85	6.00	—
1953 TS	15,619,900	0.10	0.20	0.75	4.50	—
1954 TS	10,086,000	0.10	0.20	0.75	4.50	—
1955 TS	12,963,400	0.10	0.20	0.75	4.50	—
1956 TS	13,890,250	0.10	0.20	0.75	4.50	—
1957 TS	9,991,300	0.10	0.20	0.75	4.50	—
1958 TS	10,105,500	0.10	0.20	0.75	4.50	—
1959 TS	11,571,750	0.10	0.20	0.75	4.50	—
1960 TS	11,092,500	0.10	0.20	0.75	4.50	—
1961 TS	9,672,500	0.10	0.20	0.75	4.50	—
1961 U	1,075,000	0.70	1.50	3.00	15.00	—
1962 U	9,568,750	—	0.10	0.45	2.00	—
1963 U	13,337,500	—	0.10	0.45	2.00	—
1964 U	19,346,250	—	0.10	0.20	2.00	—
1964 U	Inc. above	0.60	1.25	2.50	10.00	—

Note: O in crown: first dot in crown on left with hollow center

1965 U	23,356,000	—	0.10	0.20	0.75	—
1966 U	18,278,000	—	0.10	0.20	0.75	—
1967 U	23,931,000	—	—	0.10	0.45	—
1968 U	26,238,000	—	—	0.10	0.45	—
1969 U	16,843,000	—	—	0.10	0.45	—
1970 U	31,254,000	—	—	0.10	0.45	—
1971 U	19,179,000	—	—	0.10	0.45	—

KM# 757 5 ORE
Bronze, 27 mm. **Ruler:** Oscar II **Obv:** Large lettering **Rev:** Value, date and crowns within beaded circle

Date	Mintage	F	VF	XF	Unc	BU
1901	441,660	1.00	4.00	12.50	60.00	—
1902	652,420	1.00	4.00	12.50	60.00	—
1903	243,000	1.75	5.00	18.00	70.00	—
1904	414,240	1.00	4.00	12.50	50.00	—
1905	545,080	1.00	4.00	15.00	55.00	—

KM# 770 5 ORE
Bronze, 27 mm. **Ruler:** Oscar II **Obv:** Crowned shield **Rev:** Value, date and crowns within beaded circle

Date	Mintage	F	VF	XF	Unc	BU
1906	565,280	0.75	3.50	12.50	47.50	—
1907	1,953,260	0.50	2.00	6.00	25.00	—

KM# 779.1 5 ORE
8.0000 g., Bronze, 27 mm. **Ruler:** Gustaf V **Obv:** Small cross above crowned monograms **Rev:** Value above crowns

Date	Mintage	F	VF	XF	Unc	BU
1909	917,230	2.00	6.00	30.00	175	—

KM# 779.2 5 ORE
7.9400 g., Bronze, 27 mm. **Ruler:** Gustaf V **Obv:** Large cross above crowned monogram **Rev:** Value above crowns **Note:** Varieties exist.

Date	Mintage	F	VF	XF	Unc	BU
1909	Inc. above	7.00	45.00	265	875	—
1910	30,630	115	265	545	1,325	—
1911	778,000	0.85	3.50	25.00	135	—

Note: Narrow base mint mark

1911	Inc. above	3.00	12.00	50.00	200	—

Note: Wide base mint mark

1912	547,480	—	3.50	35.00	190	—
1913	761,780	0.85	2.25	22.50	125	—
1914	400,100	2.50	5.50	42.50	235	—
1915	1,122,820	0.50	2.50	18.50	65.00	—
1916/5	955,440	10.00	20.00	40.00	165	—
1916 Short 6	Inc. above	0.50	2.50	15.00	70.00	—
1916 Long 6	Inc. above	0.50	2.50	15.00	70.00	—
1917	1	—	—	—	—	—
1919	1,129,380	0.25	1.00	13.50	60.00	—
1920	2,360,920	0.25	1.00	8.00	35.00	—
1921	1,878,500	0.20	0.75	12.00	50.00	—
1922	763,420	0.25	2.50	27.50	125	—
1923	505,580	0.85	4.50	65.00	245	—
1924	899,500	0.25	1.50	17.50	90.00	—
1925	1,943,500	0.20	0.75	8.50	50.00	—
1926	1,742,100	0.20	0.75	8.50	50.00	—
1927	36,380	80.00	175	525	1,200	—
1928	987,900	0.20	1.00	12.00	65.00	—
1929	1,668,560	0.20	0.50	8.50	50.00	—
1930	1,716,040	0.20	0.50	8.50	50.00	—
1931	1,130,960	0.20	0.50	8.50	55.00	—
1932	1,165,220	0.20	0.50	8.50	55.00	—
1933	574,340	0.65	2.50	27.50	135	—
1934	1,710,260	0.20	0.40	5.00	37.50	—
1935	1,682,020	0.20	0.40	5.00	37.50	—
1936 Short 6	1,625,700	0.20	0.40	6.00	37.50	—
1936	Inc. above	0.25	0.75	7.00	47.50	—
1937	2,637,260	—	0.30	4.00	22.50	—
1938	2,354,240	—	0.30	4.00	22.50	—
1939	2,591,500	—	0.45	6.00	22.50	—
1940	2,729,580	—	0.35	3.50	20.00	—
1940 Serif 4	Inc. above	—	0.45	4.00	25.00	—
1941	2,054,540	—	0.35	2.50	17.50	—
1942	395,400	2.00	4.00	22.50	90.00	—
1950	12,559,100	—	0.25	0.75	6.00	—

KM# 791 5 ORE
Iron **Ruler:** Gustaf V **Obv:** Crowned monogram **Rev:** Value above crowns **Note:** World War I issues

Date	Mintage	F	VF	XF	Unc	BU
1917	2,953,320	4.00	8.00	18.00	70.00	—
1918	2,457,840	10.00	20.00	32.50	125	—
1919	2,302,480	10.00	20.00	32.50	120	—

KM# 812 5 ORE
7.0000 g., Iron, 27 mm. **Ruler:** Gustaf V **Obv:** Crowned monogram divides date **Rev:** Value above crowns **Note:** World War II issues.

Date	Mintage	F	VF	XF	Unc	BU
1942	4,343,420	0.20	0.75	4.00	30.00	—
1943	5,570,180	0.20	0.75	4.00	30.00	—
1944	4,561,980	0.20	0.75	4.00	30.00	—
1945	3,771,100	0.20	0.75	4.00	30.00	—
1946	2,375,080	—	0.50	3.00	20.00	—
1947	6,034,840	—	0.50	3.00	20.00	—
1948	6,246,000	—	0.50	3.00	20.00	—
1949	7,839,640	—	0.50	2.00	16.50	—
1950	5,289,500	—	0.50	2.00	16.50	—

KM# 822 5 ORE
8.0000 g., Bronze, 27 mm. **Ruler:** Gustaf VI **Obv:** Crown above inscription **Rev:** Value within circle divides date below crown **Edge:** Plain

Date	Mintage	F	VF	XF	Unc	BU
1952 TS	3,065,400	0.20	0.50	1.75	8.50	—
1953 TS	12,329,320	0.20	0.50	1.75	8.50	—
1954 TS	7,232,100	0.20	0.50	1.75	8.50	—
1955 TS	8,464,620	0.20	0.50	1.75	8.50	—
1956 TS	7,997,120	0.20	0.50	1.75	9.00	—
1957 TS	6,275,600	0.20	0.50	1.75	8.50	—

Date	Mintage	F	VF	XF	Unc	BU
1958 TS	9,498,400	0.20	0.50	2.00	9.00	—
1959 TS	8,370,500	0.20	0.50	2.00	9.00	—
1960 TS	10,542,300	0.20	0.40	1.25	7.50	—
1961 TS	3,909,000	0.20	0.40	1.25	7.50	—
1961 U	2,451,500	0.20	0.50	1.25	8.50	—
1962 U	22,305,500	—	0.10	0.50	3.50	—
1963 U	17,156,500	—	0.10	0.50	3.50	—
1964 U	10,922,500	—	0.10	0.75	7.00	—
1964 U	Inc. above	2.75	5.50	11.50	30.00	—

Note: O in crown: first dot in crown on left with hollow center

1965 U	22,635,000	—	0.10	0.20	1.00	—
1966 U	18,213,000	—	0.10	0.20	1.00	—
1967 U	20,776,000	—	0.10	0.20	1.00	—
1968 U	27,093,500	—	0.10	0.20	1.00	—
1969 U	26,886,500	—	0.10	0.20	1.00	—
1970 U	29,419,500	—	0.10	0.20	1.00	—
1971 U	15,749,000	—	0.10	0.20	1.00	—

KM# 845 5 ORE
2.7000 g., Bronze, 18 mm. **Ruler:** Gustaf VI **Obv:** Large crown above smaller crown **Rev:** Value divides date

Date	Mintage	F	VF	XF	Unc	BU
1972 U	107,894,000	—	—	0.10	0.25	0.60
1973 U	193,037,580	—	—	0.10	0.25	0.60

KM# 849 5 ORE
Copper-Tin-Zinc, 18 mm. **Ruler:** Carl XVI Gustaf **Obv:** Value **Rev:** Crowned monogram divides date **Edge:** Plain

Date	Mintage	F	VF	XF	Unc	BU
1976 U	4,672,350	—	—	0.10	0.40	0.60
1977 U	31,037,129	—	—	0.10	0.30	0.60
1978 U	46,021,707	—	—	0.10	0.30	0.60
1979 U	65,833,193	—	—	0.10	0.25	0.60
1980 U	60,996,699	—	—	0.10	0.25	0.60
1981 U	19,791,000	—	—	0.10	0.25	0.60

KM# 849a 5 ORE
Copper-Zinc, 18 mm. **Ruler:** Carl XVI Gustaf **Obv:** Value **Rev:** Crowned monogram divides date

Date	Mintage	F	VF	XF	Unc	BU
1981 U	34,960,593	—	—	0.10	0.20	0.60
1982 U	40,471,115	—	—	0.10	0.20	0.60
1983 U	36,304,042	—	—	0.10	0.20	0.60
1984 U	13,449,245	—	—	0.10	0.20	0.60

KM# 755 10 ORE
1.4500 g., 0.4000 Silver 0.0186 oz. ASW, 15 mm. **Ruler:** Oscar II **Obv:** Large lettering **Rev:** Value, date **Note:** Varieties exist.

Date	Mintage	F	VF	XF	Unc	BU
1902 EB	1,945,600	1.00	3.50	12.50	32.50	—
1903 EB	1,508,930	1.00	3.50	12.50	32.50	—
1904 EB	3,279,520	0.75	1.50	8.50	25.00	—

KM# 774 10 ORE
1.4500 g., 0.4000 Silver 0.0186 oz. ASW, 15 mm. **Ruler:** Oscar II **Obv:** Crowned shield flanked by crowns **Rev:** Value and date

Date	Mintage	F	VF	XF	Unc	BU
1907 EB	7,319,040	0.45	1.25	5.00	20.00	—

KM# 780 10 ORE
1.4500 g., 0.4000 Silver 0.0186 oz. ASW, 15 mm. **Ruler:** Gustaf V **Obv:** Three small crowns within crowned shield divides date **Rev:** Value

Date	Mintage	F	VF	XF	Unc	BU
1909 W	1,610,400	1.25	4.00	13.50	70.00	—
1911 W	3,180,650	0.35	2.00	8.50	32.50	—
1913 W	1,580,910	1.00	2.50	11.50	50.00	—

Date	Mintage	F	VF	XF	Unc	BU
1914 W	1,571,330	0.75	3.00	8.50	32.50	—
1914 Serif 4	Inc. above	0.75	2.25	10.00	50.00	—
1915 W	1,546,950	0.50	2.25	8.00	47.50	—
1916/5 W	3,034,880	2.50	7.00	22.50	110	—
1916 W	Inc. above	0.75	1.75	6.50	32.50	—
1917 W	4,996,139	0.35	0.75	2.50	18.50	—
1918 W	4,114,180	0.35	0.75	2.50	18.50	—
1919 W	5,737,020	0.35	0.75	2.50	18.50	—
1927 W	2,509,590	0.30	0.60	2.50	22.50	—
1928 G	2,901,150	0.30	0.60	2.50	22.50	—
1929 G	5,505,200	0.30	0.60	1.75	11.50	—
1930 G	3,222,710	0.30	0.60	1.75	11.50	—
1931 G	4,272,073	0.30	0.60	1.75	11.50	—
1933 G	1,948,090	0.80	1.75	3.25	25.00	—
1934 G	4,059,293	0.30	0.50	1.25	6.50	—
1935 G	2,426,283	0.30	0.50	1.25	6.50	—
1936 G Short 6	5,099,270	1.75	4.50	20.00	60.00	—
1936 G Long 6	Inc. above	0.30	0.45	1.50	9.00	—
1937 G	5,116,920	0.30	0.40	1.00	6.50	—
1938 G	7,428,140	0.30	0.40	1.00	6.50	—
1938 G Proof	—	Value: 12.50				—
1939/29 G	2,020,670	3.75	8.00	22.00	55.00	—
1939 G	Inc. above	0.30	0.60	2.25	13.50	—
1939 G Proof	—	Value: 17.50				—
1940 G	3,017,320	0.30	0.50	1.25	6.00	—
1941 G	9,106,380	0.30	0.50	1.25	6.00	—
1942 G	3,691,640	0.30	0.50	1.25	6.00	—

KM# 795   10 ORE
1.5000 g., Nickel-Bronze, 15 mm. **Ruler:** Gustaf V **Obv:** Crowned monogram divides date **Rev:** Value

Date	Mintage	F	VF	XF	Unc	BU
1920 W	3,612,250	0.50	1.00	5.00	40.00	—
1920 W Large W	Inc. above	13.50	28.00	60.00	300	—
1921 W	2,269,950	0.50	1.25	6.00	40.00	—
1923 W	2,143,560	0.50	1.25	7.00	50.00	—
1924 W	1,600,000	0.50	1.50	8.00	70.00	—
1925 W	1,472,340	0.75	3.25	16.50	85.00	—
1940 G	3,373,200	0.20	0.50	2.00	16.00	—
1941	815,880	0.75	1.50	4.00	30.00	—
1946 TS	4,115,940	0.10	0.30	0.75	6.00	—
1947 TS	4,132,950	0.10	0.30	0.75	6.00	—

KM# 813   10 ORE
1.4400 g., 0.4000 Silver 0.0185 oz. ASW, 15 mm. **Ruler:** Gustaf V **Obv:** Crown **Rev:** Value **Note:** Varieties exist.

Date	Mintage	F	VF	XF	Unc	BU
1942 G	1,600,000	0.25	0.40	1.25	6.50	—
1942 G Proof	—	Value: 35.00				—
1943 G	7,661,100	0.25	0.40	1.25	6.50	—
1944 G	12,276,900	BV	0.35	0.85	5.00	—
1945 G	11,702,510	BV	0.35	0.85	5.00	—
1945 TS	Inc. above	BV	0.35	0.85	5.00	—
1945 TS/G	Inc. above	BV	0.35	1.25	6.50	—
1946/5 TS Open 6	3,575,500	5.50	13.00	25.00	70.00	—
1946 TS Open 6	Inc. above	0.30	0.75	2.50	22.50	—
1946 TS Closed 6	Inc. above	BV	0.35	1.75	12.50	—
1947 TS	7,293,250	BV	0.30	0.85	5.00	—
1948 TS	10,418,650	BV	0.30	0.75	5.00	—
1949 TS	12,044,000	BV	0.30	0.75	5.00	—
1950 TS	31,823,870	BV	0.30	0.75	4.00	—

KM# 823   10 ORE
1.4400 g., 0.4000 Silver 0.0185 oz. ASW, 15 mm. **Ruler:** Gustaf VI **Obv:** Crown **Rev:** Value

Date	Mintage	F	VF	XF	Unc	BU
1952 TS	4,659,700	BV	0.40	0.85	4.50	—
1953 TS	28,484,040	—	BV	0.85	4.50	—
1954 TS	15,913,250	—	BV	0.85	4.50	—
1955 TS	16,687,200	—	BV	0.85	4.50	—
1956 TS	21,985,600	—	BV	0.60	3.50	—
1957 TS	21,294,400	—	BV	0.60	3.50	—
1958 TS	19,605,400	—	BV	0.60	3.50	—
1959 TS	18,523,000	—	BV	0.60	3.50	—
1960 TS	16,605,000	—	BV	0.60	3.50	—
1961 TS	8,283,000	—	BV	0.60	3.50	—
1961 U	7,843,000	—	BV	0.60	3.50	—
1962 U	8,619,000	—	BV	0.60	3.50	—

KM# 835   10 ORE
1.4000 g., Copper-Nickel, 15 mm. **Ruler:** Gustaf VI **Obv:** Crowned monogram divides date **Rev:** Value

Date	Mintage	F	VF	XF	Unc	BU
1962 U	8,814,000	0.10	0.25	0.60	3.50	7.50
1963 U	28,170,000	—	—	0.15	0.60	3.50
1964 U	36,895,000	—	—	0.15	0.60	3.50
1965 U	29,870,000	—	—	0.15	0.60	3.50
1966 U	20,435,000	—	—	0.15	0.60	3.50
1967 U	18,245,000	—	—	0.15	0.60	3.50
1968 U	51,490,000	—	—	0.15	0.50	3.50
1969 U	55,880,000	—	—	0.15	0.50	1.75
1970 U	60,910,000	—	—	0.15	0.50	1.75
1971 U	27,075,000	—	—	0.15	0.50	1.75
1972 U	36,766,500	—	—	0.15	0.25	1.00
1973 U	160,740,000	—	—	0.15	0.25	1.00

KM# 850   10 ORE
1.4500 g., Copper-Nickel, 14.54 mm. **Ruler:** Carl XVI Gustaf **Obv:** Crowned monogram divides date **Rev:** Value **Edge:** Plain

Date	Mintage	F	VF	XF	Unc	BU
1976 U	4,172,790	—	—	0.15	0.50	1.00
1977 U	44,517,287	—	—	0.10	0.35	0.75
1978 U	74,341,720	—	—	0.10	0.35	0.75
1979 U	75,305,608	—	—	0.10	0.15	0.40
1980 U	108,293,811	—	—	0.10	0.15	0.40
1981 U	102,453,931	—	—	0.10	0.15	0.30
1982 U	103,905,592	—	—	0.10	0.15	0.30
1983 U	773,149,400	—	—	0.10	0.15	0.30
1984 U	122,128,092	—	—	0.10	0.15	0.30
1985 U	79,154,951	—	—	0.10	0.15	0.30
1986 U	48,945,396	—	—	0.10	0.15	0.40
1986 D	48,945,220	—	—	0.10	0.15	0.40
1987 D	146,877,318	—	—	0.10	0.15	0.40
1988 D	194,986,479	—	—	0.10	0.15	0.30
1989 D	245,180,644	—	—	0.10	0.15	0.30
1990 D	139,298,404	—	—	0.10	0.15	0.30
1991 D	5,176,842	—	—	0.15	0.50	1.00

KM# 739   25 ORE
2.4200 g., 0.6000 Silver 0.0467 oz. ASW, 17 mm. **Ruler:** Oscar II **Obv:** Large lettering **Rev:** Value within wreath, date below

Date	Mintage	F	VF	XF	Unc	BU
1902 EB	1,259,039	2.00	7.00	22.50	80.00	—
1904 EB	691,888	2.00	7.00	22.50	82.00	—
1905 EB	732,000	1.75	5.50	18.50	70.00	—

KM# 775   25 ORE
2.4200 g., 0.6000 Silver 0.0467 oz. ASW, 17 mm. **Ruler:** Oscar II **Obv:** Crowned shield flanked by crowns **Rev:** Value within wreath

Date	Mintage	F	VF	XF	Unc	BU
1907 EB	3,222,580	0.80	2.00	6.00	42.50	—

KM# 785   25 ORE
2.4200 g., 0.6000 Silver 0.0467 oz. ASW, 17 mm. **Ruler:** Gustaf V **Obv:** Small crowns within crowned shield divides date **Rev:** Value above sprigs

Date	Mintage	F	VF	XF	Unc	BU
1910 W Large cross	2,043,936	0.75	2.00	6.00	50.00	—
1910 W Small cross	Inc. above	7.00	27.50	75.00	475	—
1912 W	1,013,740	0.75	2.75	15.00	70.00	—
1914 W	3,719,232	0.75	2.75	15.00	40.00	—
1916 W	1,269,120	0.75	2.75	15.00	70.00	—
1917 W	1,657,312	0.75	2.25	5.50	40.00	—

Date	Mintage	F	VF	XF	Unc	BU
1918 W Small 8	2,364,784	0.75	2.25	7.50	50.00	—
1918 W Wide 8	Inc. above	0.75	2.25	9.50	58.00	—
1919 W	3,205,164	0.75	1.50	5.00	35.00	—
1927 W	1,687,984	0.75	1.75	5.00	35.00	—
1928 G	836,899	0.75	2.00	9.50	58.00	—
1929 G	1,124,932	0.75	1.75	6.00	40.00	—
1930 G	3,489,628	BV	1.50	3.00	18.50	—
1931 G	1,391,938	BV	1.50	3.00	18.50	—
1932 G	1,133,344	BV	1.50	3.00	18.50	—
1933 G	964,340	BV	1.50	8.00	35.00	—
1934 G	1,403,648	BV	1.50	3.00	11.50	—
1936 G	1,852,000	BV	1.50	3.00	11.50	—
1937 G Large G	Inc. above	0.75	2.00	4.50	18.50	—
1937 G Proof	Inc. above	Value: 20.00				—
1937 G Small G	3,258,956	BV	1.50	4.50	12.50	—
1938	3,678,876	BV	1.25	2.75	7.50	—
1939	2,136,600	BV	1.00	2.75	7.50	—
1940	2,301,788	BV	1.00	2.50	7.00	—
1941	1,995,200	BV	1.00	2.50	7.00	—

KM# 798   25 ORE
2.4000 g., Nickel-Bronze, 17 mm. **Ruler:** Gustaf V **Obv:** Crowned monogram divides date **Rev:** Value within oat sprigs

Date	Mintage	F	VF	XF	Unc	BU
1921 W	1,354,656	1.50	3.00	13.50	85.00	—
1940 G	2,333,040	0.15	0.50	3.00	18.50	—
1941 G	1,056,680	0.15	0.50	3.00	27.50	—
1946 TS	2,066,048	0.15	0.30	1.25	9.00	—
1947 TS	1,594,200	0.15	0.30	1.25	9.00	—

KM# 816   25 ORE
2.3200 g., 0.4000 Silver 0.0298 oz. ASW, 17 mm. **Ruler:** Gustaf V **Obv:** Crown **Rev:** Value and date

Date	Mintage	F	VF	XF	Unc	BU
1943 G	9,854,640	BV	0.50	1.25	7.50	—
1944 G	9,532,148	BV	0.50	1.25	7.50	—
1945 G	5,362,800	BV	0.50	1.25	7.50	—
1945 TS	Inc. above	BV	0.75	1.25	11.50	—
1945 G/TS	Inc. above	BV	0.60	3.50	16.50	—
1946 TS	2,249,600	—	BV	2.50	11.50	—
1946 TS serif 6	Inc. above	2.00	4.00	14.50	42.50	—
1947 TS	5,332,800	—	BV	1.25	4.50	—
1948 TS	3,191,000	—	BV	1.25	4.50	—
1949 TS	5,812,180	—	BV	1.25	4.50	—
1950 TS	12,059,144	—	BV	1.25	3.50	—

KM# 824   25 ORE
2.3200 g., 0.4000 Silver 0.0298 oz. ASW, 17 mm. **Ruler:** Gustaf VI **Obv:** Value and date **Rev:** Crown

Date	Mintage	F	VF	XF	Unc	BU
1952 TS	2,113,890	—	BV	1.25	4.50	—
1953 TS	18,177,420	—	BV	1.00	2.50	—
1954 TS	9,491,740	—	BV	1.00	2.50	—
1955 TS	7,663,100	—	BV	1.25	4.00	—
1956 TS	10,930,800	—	BV	1.00	3.50	—
1957 TS	12,497,200	—	BV	1.00	3.50	—
1958 TS	6,883,940	—	BV	1.00	3.50	—
1959 TS	4,772,000	—	BV	1.00	3.50	—
1960 TS	4,374,000	BV	0.50	2.00	10.00	—
1961 TS	8,380,800	—	BV	1.00	3.50	—

KM# 836   25 ORE
2.2900 g., Copper-Nickel, 16.94 mm. **Ruler:** Gustaf VI **Obv:** Crowned monogram divides date **Rev:** Value **Edge:** Plain

Date	Mintage	F	VF	XF	Unc	BU
1962 U	4,426,000	—	0.25	1.00	3.25	—
1963 U	26,710,000	—	0.20	0.50	2.50	—
1964 U	17,300,000	—	0.20	0.50	2.50	—
1965 U	6,884,000	—	0.20	0.50	2.50	—
1966 U	12,932,000	—	—	0.25	1.25	—
1967 U	28,038,000	—	—	0.20	0.65	—
1968 U	14,366,000	—	—	0.20	0.65	—

Date	Mintage	F	VF	XF	Unc	BU
1969 U	20,214,000	—	—	0.20	0.65	—
1970 U	23,780,000	—	—	0.20	0.65	—
1971 U	8,606,000	—	—	0.20	0.65	—
1972 U	1,323,200	—	—	0.20	0.65	—
1973 U	76,993,000	—	—	0.15	0.45	—

KM# 851 25 ORE
2.2000 g., Copper-Nickel, 17 mm. **Ruler:** Carl XVI Gustaf **Obv:** Crowned monogram divides date **Rev:** Value

Date	Mintage	F	VF	XF	Unc	BU
1976 U	2,515,285	—	—	0.15	0.65	—
1977 U	5,509,491	—	—	0.15	0.50	—
1978 U	54,593,293	—	—	0.10	0.30	—
1979 U	48,423,422	—	—	0.10	0.30	—
1980 U	38,889,325	—	—	0.10	0.30	—
1981 U	46,371,204	—	—	0.10	0.30	—
1982 U	43,212,638	—	—	0.10	0.30	—
1983 U	28,954,257	—	—	0.10	0.30	—
1984 U	7,293,722	—	—	0.10	0.30	—

KM# 771 50 ORE
5.0000 g., 0.6000 Silver 0.0964 oz. ASW, 22 mm.
Ruler: Oscar II **Obv:** Crowned shield flanked by crowns
Rev: Value and date within wreath

Date	Mintage	F	VF	XF	Unc	BU
1906 EB	319,452	2.75	8.00	35.00	190	—
1907 EB	803,340	2.00	5.00	32.50	125	—

KM# 788 50 ORE
5.0000 g., 0.6000 Silver 0.0964 oz. ASW, 22 mm.
Ruler: Gustaf V **Obv:** Three small crowns within crowned shield divides date **Rev:** Value above sprigs

Date	Mintage	F	VF	XF	Unc	BU
1911 W	472,534	3.25	7.00	28.00	140	—
1912 W	483,062	4.50	8.50	30.00	165	—
1914 W	378,448	4.50	8.50	30.00	165	—
1916 W	536,718	3.25	7.00	25.00	135	—
1919 W	458,296	3.25	7.00	28.00	120	—
1927 W	671,596	1.50	3.00	15.00	80.00	—
1928 G	1,135,054	BV	2.00	7.00	45.00	—
1929 G	470,990	1.50	3.00	15.00	80.00	—
1930 G	547,920	1.50	3.00	15.00	75.00	—
1931 G	671,457	BV	2.00	12.50	55.00	—
1933 G	547,606	BV	2.00	12.50	55.00	—
1934 G	613,124	BV	2.00	7.00	40.00	—
1935 G	690,792	BV	2.00	7.00	40.00	—
1936 G Short 6	823,176	BV	2.00	7.00	40.00	—
1936 G Long 6	Inc. above	BV	3.50	12.50	70.00	—
1938 G	441,546	BV	1.50	4.50	25.00	—
1939 G	921,750	—	BV	2.50	18.00	—
1939 G Proof	—	Value: 35.00				

KM# 796 50 ORE
Nickel-Bronze, 22 mm. **Ruler:** Gustaf V **Obv:** Crowned monogram divides date **Rev:** Value within oat sprigs
Note: Varieties exist.

Date	Mintage	F	VF	XF	Unc	BU
1920 W Oval 0	479,500	1.75	8.00	40.00	200	—
1920 W Round 0	Inc. above	35.00	70.00	230	645	—
1921 W	214,922	2.75	20.00	110	385	—
1924 W	645,368	1.25	10.00	45.00	275	—
1940 G	1,340,750	0.25	1.00	4.50	35.00	—
1940 G large G	Inc. above	5.50	15.00	40.00	90.00	—
1946 TS	1,425,990	0.25	1.00	4.00	20.00	—
1947 TS	1,031,800	0.25	1.00	4.00	20.00	—

KM# 817 50 ORE
4.8000 g., 0.4000 Silver 0.0617 oz. ASW, 22 mm.
Ruler: Gustaf V **Obv:** Crown **Rev:** Value and date

Date	Mintage	F	VF	XF	Unc	BU
1943 G	784,700	1.50	3.00	10.00	55.00	—
1944 G	1,540,296	BV	1.00	2.00	12.00	—
1945 G	2,584,800	BV	1.00	2.00	12.00	—
1946 TS	1,091,000	BV	1.00	2.00	12.00	—
1947 TS	1,770,500	BV	1.00	2.00	12.00	—
1948 TS	1,731,400	BV	1.00	2.00	12.00	—
1949 TS	1,883,100	BV	1.00	2.00	12.00	—
1950 TS	3,353,620	BV	1.00	1.50	10.00	—

KM# 825 50 ORE
4.8000 g., 0.4000 Silver 0.0617 oz. ASW, 22 mm.
Ruler: Gustaf VI **Obv:** Value and date **Rev:** Crown

Date	Mintage	F	VF	XF	Unc	BU
1952 TS	1,197,760	BV	1.00	3.00	22.50	—
1953 TS	4,395,620	BV	1.00	2.50	20.00	—
1954 TS	5,778,850	BV	1.00	2.50	20.00	—
1955 TS	2,699,700	BV	1.00	4.00	18.50	—
1956 TS	7,056,670	—	BV	1.50	8.50	—
1957 TS	2,404,700	—	BV	2.50	18.50	—
1958 TS	1,659,800	—	BV	2.50	18.50	—
1961 TS	2,775,000	—	BV	1.50	11.50	—

KM# 837 50 ORE
4.5000 g., Copper-Nickel, 22 mm. **Ruler:** Gustaf VI
Obv: Crowned monogram divides date **Rev:** Value

Date	Mintage	F	VF	XF	Unc	BU
1962 U	1,400,000	0.50	0.75	3.25	21.50	—
1963 U	5,808,000	0.15	0.25	1.25	11.50	—
1964 U	5,325,000	0.15	0.25	1.25	11.50	—
1965 U	6,453,000	0.15	0.25	0.60	7.50	—
1966 U	6,309,000	0.15	0.25	0.50	6.00	—
1967 U	7,890,000	0.15	0.25	0.50	6.00	—
1968 U	9,198,000	—	0.15	0.25	1.25	—
1969 U	7,265,000	—	0.15	0.25	1.25	—
1970 U	9,426,000	—	0.15	0.25	1.25	—
1971 U	7,218,000	—	0.15	0.25	1.25	—
1972 U	7,388,000	—	0.15	0.25	1.25	—
1973 U	52,467,000	—	0.15	0.20	0.60	—

KM# 855 50 ORE
4.5000 g., Copper-Nickel, 22 mm. **Ruler:** Carl XVI Gustaf
Obv: Crowned monogram divides date **Rev:** Value **Edge:** Plain

Date	Mintage	F	VF	XF	Unc	BU
1976 U	2,588,575	—	0.15	0.25	1.00	—
1977 U	10,359,708	—	—	0.15	0.40	—
1978 U	33,282,476	—	—	0.15	0.40	—
1979 U	30,723,730	—	—	0.15	0.40	—
1980 U	28,665,662	—	—	0.15	0.40	—
1981 U	15,516,559	—	—	0.15	0.40	—
1982 U	14,778,358	—	—	0.15	0.40	—
1983 U	17,528,777	—	—	0.15	0.40	—
1984 U	27,527,534	—	—	0.15	0.40	—
1985 U	14,078,477	—	—	0.15	0.40	—
1986 U	937,214	—	—	0.20	0.75	—
1987 D	1,077,317	—	—	0.20	0.70	—
1988 D	531,669	—	—	0.20	0.75	—
1989 D	605,780	—	—	0.20	0.75	—
1990 D	31,934,675	—	—	0.10	0.20	—
1991 D	16,315,160	—	—	0.10	0.20	—

KM# 878 50 ORE
3.7000 g., Bronze, 18.7 mm. **Ruler:** Carl XVI Gustaf **Obv:** Value
Rev: Three crowns and date **Edge:** Reeded

Date	Mintage	F	VF	XF	Unc	BU
1992 D	39,531,000	—	—	0.15	0.30	—
1992 B	39,531,000	—	—	0.15	0.40	—
1992 B	39,530,810	—	—	0.15	0.40	0.50
1993 B	643,520	—	—	0.20	0.65	0.85
1993 D	—	—	—	0.20	0.65	0.85
1994 B	517,575	—	—	0.20	0.65	0.85
1995 W	486,538	—	—	0.10	0.20	0.35
1996 B	247,620	—	—	0.10	0.20	0.35
1997 B	69,995	—	—	0.10	0.20	0.35
1998 B	5,064,956	—	—	0.10	0.15	0.25
1999 B	22,076,128	—	—	0.10	0.15	0.25
2000 B	33,060,252	—	—	0.10	0.15	0.25

KM# 760 KRONA
7.5000 g., 0.8000 Silver 0.1929 oz. ASW **Ruler:** Oscar II
Obv: Head left **Obv. Leg.:** OSCAR II SVERIGES... **Rev:** Crowned arms with supporters

Date	Mintage	F	VF	XF	Unc	BU
1901/898 EB	270,960	9.00	30.00	150	560	—
1901 EB	Inc. above	7.00	28.00	140	485	—
1903 EB	473,386	6.00	25.00	95.00	365	—
1904 EB	563,586	5.00	15.00	90.00	325	—

KM# 772 KRONA
7.5000 g., 0.8000 Silver 0.1929 oz. ASW **Ruler:** Oscar II
Obv: Head left **Rev:** Crowned arms with supporters

Date	Mintage	F	VF	XF	Unc	BU
1906 EB	426,939	5.00	20.00	85.00	270	—
1907 EB	1,058,286	3.50	14.00	60.00	245	—

KM# 786.1 KRONA
7.5000 g., 0.8000 Silver 0.1929 oz. ASW **Ruler:** Gustaf V
Obv: Head left **Rev:** Crowned arms within order chain

Date	Mintage	F	VF	XF	Unc	BU
1910 W	643,065	3.25	12.50	45.00	175	—
1912 W	303,420	7.00	22.50	110	420	—
1913 W	353,051	3.50	12.50	42.50	190	—
1914 W	622,217	3.25	11.50	40.00	180	—
1915 W	1,415,956	3.00	7.00	25.00	145	—
1916/5 W	1,139,245	4.00	13.50	55.00	230	—
1916 W	Inc. above	3.25	11.50	40.00	190	—
1918 W	258,091	3.25	8.50	30.00	200	—
1923 W	746,277	3.00	8.00	27.50	135	—
1924 W	2,066,155	BV	6.50	17.50	100	—

KM# 786.2 KRONA
7.5000 g., 0.8000 Silver 0.1929 oz. ASW **Ruler:** Gustaf V
Obv: Head left **Rev:** Crowned arms within order chain

Date	Mintage	F	VF	XF	Unc	BU
1924 W	Inc. above	BV	4.50	22.50	90.00	—
1925 W	369,919	3.00	8.50	45.00	200	—
1926 W	465,467	3.00	7.50	28.00	135	—
1927 G	401,167	3.00	8.00	40.00	180	—
1928 G	739,189	BV	3.50	22.50	80.00	—
1929 G	1,345,647	BV	3.00	12.50	50.00	—
1930 G	1,743,783	—	BV	6.50	37.50	—
1931 G	1,007,523	—	BV	6.50	37.50	—
1932 G	1,035,877	—	BV	6.50	37.50	—

Date	Mintage	F	VF	XF	Unc	BU
1933 G	1,044,634	—	BV	6.50	37.50	—
1934 G	585,673	—	3.00	12.50	60.00	—
1935 G	1,604,343	—	BV	3.00	12.50	—
1936 G	3,222,312	—	BV	3.00	10.00	—
1937 G	2,666,998	—	BV	3.00	10.00	—
1938 G	1,911,464	—	BV	3.00	10.00	—
1938 G Proof	—	Value: 25.00				
1939 G	7,589,316	—	BV	3.00	6.00	—
1940 G	6,917,460	—	BV	3.00	6.00	—
1941/4 G	2,183,338	BV	6.00	18.00	45.00	—
1941 G	Inc. above	—	BV	3.50	10.00	—
1942 G	240,000	20.00	40.00	90.00	345	—

KM# 814 KRONA
7.0000 g., 0.4000 Silver 0.0900 oz. ASW, 25 mm. **Ruler:** Gustaf V
Obv: Head left **Rev:** Crowned arms within order chain divide value

Date	Mintage	F	VF	XF	Unc	BU
1942 G	5,644,990	—	BV	3.00	18.50	—
1943 G Plain 4	7,915,850	—	BV	3.00	18.50	—
1943 G Crosslet 4	Inc. above	—	BV	3.00	18.50	—
1944 G	7,423,463	—	BV	2.00	8.00	—
1945 G	7,359,360	—	BV	2.00	8.00	—
1945 TS	Inc. above	BV	1.50	2.75	15.00	—
1945 TS/G	Inc. above	BV	1.60	3.00	20.00	—
1946 TS	19,170,454	—	BV	1.75	6.00	—
1947 TS	9,124,335	—	BV	1.75	6.00	—
1948 TS	10,430,588	—	BV	1.75	6.00	—
1949 TS	7,981,162	—	BV	1.75	6.00	—
1950 TS	5,310,141	—	BV	1.75	8.00	—

KM# 826 KRONA
7.0000 g., 0.4000 Silver 0.0900 oz. ASW, 25 mm.
Ruler: Gustaf VI **Obv:** Head left **Rev:** Crowned shield divides value

Date	Mintage	F	VF	XF	Unc	BU
1952 TS	1,101,625	—	BV	3.00	22.50	—
1953/2 TS	Inc. above	BV	1.50	4.50	20.00	—
1953 TS	3,305,843	—	BV	3.00	20.00	—
1954 TS	6,460,770	—	BV	3.00	15.00	—
1955 TS	4,140,904	—	BV	3.00	15.00	—
1956 TS	6,226,705	—	BV	3.00	8.00	—
1957 TS	3,544,268	—	BV	3.00	9.00	—
1958 TS	1,438,940	BV	1.50	4.50	20.00	—
1959 TS	1,187,000	1.50	2.75	7.50	35.00	—
1960 TS	4,085,250	—	BV	2.00	6.00	—
1961 TS	4,283,000	—	BV	2.00	6.00	—
1961 U	2,973,275	BV	1.50	3.00	20.00	—
1962 U	6,838,550	—	BV	2.00	6.00	—
1963 U	14,227,500	—	BV	1.50	3.50	—
1964 U	15,972,500	—	BV	1.50	3.00	—
1965 U	18,638,500	—	BV	1.50	3.00	—
1966 U	22,396,500	—	—	BV	2.25	—
1967 U	17,234,500	—	—	BV	2.25	—
1968 U	12,325,500	—	—	BV	2.25	—

KM# 826a KRONA
7.0000 g., Copper-Nickel Clad Copper, 25 mm. **Ruler:** Gustaf VI
Obv: Head left **Rev:** Crowned shield divides value

Date	Mintage	F	VF	XF	Unc	BU
1968 U	5,177,000	—	0.30	1.00	3.50	—
1969 U	30,855,500	—	0.30	0.40	1.50	—
1970 U	25,314,500	—	0.30	0.40	1.50	—
1971 U	18,342,000	—	0.30	0.40	1.50	—
1972 U	21,941,000	—	0.30	0.40	1.50	—
1973 U	142,000,000	—	0.30	0.40	1.50	—

KM# 852 KRONA
7.0000 g., Copper-Nickel Clad Copper, 25 mm.
Ruler: Carl XVI Gustaf **Obv:** Head left **Rev:** Three small crowns within crowned shield

Date	Mintage	F	VF	XF	Unc	BU
1976 U	4,320,811	—	0.30	0.50	1.25	—
1977 U	80,477,822	—	0.30	0.40	0.75	—
1978 U	81,407,892	—	0.30	0.40	0.75	—
1979 U	47,450,148	—	0.30	0.40	0.75	—
1980 U	51,694,323	—	0.30	0.40	0.75	—
1981 U	62,078,991	—	0.30	0.40	0.75	—

KM# 852a KRONA
7.0000 g., Copper-Nickel, 25 mm. **Ruler:** Carl XVI Gustaf
Obv: Head left **Rev:** Three small crowns within crowned shield
Edge: Reeded

Date	Mintage	F	VF	XF	Unc	BU
1982 U	24,836,789	—	—	0.30	0.65	—
1983 U	23,530,222	—	—	0.30	0.65	—
1984 U	37,811,592	—	—	0.30	0.65	—
1985 U	4,909,279	—	—	0.30	0.70	—
1986 U	901,095	—	—	0.50	1.25	—
1987 D	21,543,317	—	—	0.30	0.65	—
1988 D	30,341,842	—	—	0.30	0.45	—
1989 D	55,963,148	—	—	—	0.30	—
1990 D	54,469,545	—	—	—	0.30	—
1991 D	34,249,994	—	—	—	0.30	—
1992 B	16,770,810	—	—	—	0.30	—
1993 B	407,208	—	0.30	0.50	1.00	—
1994 B	567,137	—	0.30	0.50	1.00	—
1995 B	499,758	—	0.30	0.50	1.00	—
1996 B	323,656	—	—	1.00	2.00	—
1997 B	25,042,398	—	—	—	0.25	—
1998 B	39,747,941	—	—	—	0.25	—
1999 B	55,018,508	—	—	—	0.25	—
2000 B	104,213,074	—	—	—	0.25	—

KM# 897 KRONA
6.9800 g., Copper-Nickel, 24.9 mm. **Ruler:** Carl XVI Gustaf
Subject: Millennium **Obv:** Head left **Rev:** Crowned monogram
Edge: Reeded

Date	Mintage	F	VF	XF	Unc	BU
2000	2,978,113	—	—	—	2.00	3.00

KM# 761 2 KRONOR
15.0000 g., 0.8000 Silver 0.3858 oz. ASW, 31 mm.
Ruler: Oscar II **Obv:** Head left **Obv. Leg.:** OSCAR II SVERIGES... **Rev:** Crowned arms with supporters

Date	Mintage	F	VF	XF	Unc	BU
1903 EB	64,308	25.00	85.00	240	865	—
1904 EB	175,029	12.00	40.00	145	465	—

KM# 773 2 KRONOR
15.0000 g., 0.8000 Silver 0.3858 oz. ASW, 31 mm.
Ruler: Oscar II **Obv:** Head left **Rev:** Crowned arms with supporters

Date	Mintage	F	VF	XF	Unc	BU
1906 EB	112,468	9.00	22.50	90.00	320	—
1907 EB	300,573	6.50	18.50	75.00	320	—

KM# 776 2 KRONOR
15.0000 g., 0.8000 Silver 0.3858 oz. ASW, 31 mm.
Ruler: Oscar II **Subject:** Golden Wedding Anniversary
Obv: Busts of King Oscar II and Queen Sofia right **Rev:** Crowned arms within order chain **Edge:** Reeded

Date	Mintage	F	VF	XF	Unc	BU
1907	251,000	BV	6.50	11.50	22.50	—

KM# 787 2 KRONOR
15.0000 g., 0.8000 Silver 0.3858 oz. ASW, 31 mm.
Ruler: Gustaf V **Obv:** Head left **Rev:** Crowned arms within order chain

Date	Mintage	F	VF	XF	Unc	BU
1910 W Initial far from date	374,725	6.00	16.00	70.00	220	—
1910 W	Inc. above	37.50	100	365	900	—
1912 W	156,912	6.50	25.00	90.00	320	—
1913 W	304,616	BV	10.00	50.00	220	—
1914 W	191,905	6.00	13.50	68.00	240	—
1915 W	155,965	6.00	18.00	70.00	245	—
1922 W	201,821	BV	7.00	30.00	110	—
1924 W	199,314	BV	8.00	30.00	120	—
1926 W	221,577	BV	6.50	25.00	100	—
1928 G	160,319	BV	7.00	30.00	175	—
1929 G	184,458	BV	6.50	25.00	110	—
1930 G	178,387	BV	6.00	20.00	95.00	—
1931 G	210,576	—	BV	10.00	30.00	—
1934 G	273,419	—	BV	10.00	30.00	—
1935 G	211,059	—	BV	10.00	30.00	—
1936 G	491,296	—	BV	8.00	20.00	—
1937 G Proof	—	Value: 200				
1937 G	129,760	—	BV	16.50	70.00	—
1938 G	638,970	—	BV	7.00	18.00	—
1938 G Proof	—	Value: 30.00				
1939 G	1,200,329	—	BV	6.00	14.00	—
1939 G Proof	—	Value: 30.00				
1940 G	517,740	—	BV	7.00	15.00	—
1940 G Serif 4	Inc. above	BV	6.00	9.00	30.00	—

KM# 799 2 KRONOR
15.0000 g., 0.8000 Silver 0.3858 oz. ASW, 31 mm.
Ruler: Gustaf V **Subject:** 400th Anniversary of Political Liberty
Obv: Head right within decorative inner circle **Rev:** Crowned shield divides date within decorative inner circle

Date	Mintage	F	VF	XF	Unc	BU
1921 W	265,943	BV	6.50	8.50	20.00	—

KM# 805 2 KRONOR
15.0000 g., 0.8000 Silver 0.3858 oz. ASW, 31 mm.
Ruler: Gustaf V **Subject:** 300th Anniversary - Death of Gustaf II Adolf **Obv:** Inscription within square with three small crowns within shield below **Rev:** Laureate bust right

Date	Mintage	F	VF	XF	Unc	BU
1932 G	253,770	BV	6.50	10.00	27.50	—

KM# 807 2 KRONOR
15.0000 g., 0.8000 Silver 0.3858 oz. ASW, 31 mm.
Ruler: Gustaf V **Subject:** 300th Anniversary - Settlement of Delaware **Obv:** Head left **Rev:** The ship "Calmare Nyckel"

Date	Mintage	F	VF	XF	Unc	BU
ND(1938) G	508,815	BV	6.50	9.00	20.00	—

KM# 815 2 KRONOR
14.0000 g., 0.4000 Silver 0.1800 oz. ASW **Ruler:** Gustaf V
Obv: Head left **Rev:** Crowned arms divides value

Date	Mintage	F	VF	XF	Unc	BU
1942 G	200,000	BV	3.75	6.50	32.50	—
1943 G	271,824	3.00	5.50	14.50	70.00	—
1944 G	627,200	BV	3.00	5.00	20.00	—
1945 G	969,675	BV	2.75	4.00	15.00	—
1945 G	Inc. above	6.50	13.50	28.00	90.00	—
Note: Without dots in motto						
1945 TS	Inc. above	BV	3.00	5.00	20.00	—
1945 TS/G	Inc. above	BV	3.50	7.00	27.50	—
1946 TS	978,000	—	BV	3.50	14.50	—
1947 TS	1,465,975	—	BV	3.50	14.50	—
1948 TS	281,660	BV	3.00	5.00	20.00	—
1949 TS	331,715	BV	3.00	5.00	20.00	—
1950/1 TS	3,727,465	—	BV	3.50	14.50	—
1950 TS	Inc. above	—	BV	3.50	8.50	—

KM# 827 2 KRONOR
14.0000 g., 0.4000 Silver 0.1800 oz. ASW **Ruler:** Gustaf VI
Obv: Head left **Rev:** Crowned shield divides value

Date	Mintage	F	VF	XF	Unc	BU
1952 TS	315,325	BV	2.75	4.00	16.50	—
1953 TS	1,009,380	—	BV	3.00	8.00	—
1954 TS	2,300,835	—	BV	3.00	7.00	—
1955 TS	1,137,734	—	BV	3.50	9.00	—
1956 TS	1,709,468	—	BV	3.00	7.00	—
1957 TS	688,900	—	BV	3.50	15.00	—
1958 TS	1,104,555	—	BV	3.00	7.00	—
1959 TS	581,330	—	BV	3.50	15.00	—
1961 TS	533,220	—	BV	3.00	13.50	—
1963 U	1,468,750	—	—	BV	5.00	—
1964 U	1,212,750	—	—	BV	4.50	—
1965 U	1,189,500	—	—	BV	4.50	—
1966 U	989,250	—	—	BV	5.00	—

KM# 827a 2 KRONOR
Copper-Nickel **Ruler:** Gustaf VI **Obv:** Head left **Rev:** Crowned shield divides value

Date	Mintage	F	VF	XF	Unc	BU
1968 U	1,170,750	0.45	0.55	1.25	4.00	—
1969 U	1,148,250	0.45	0.55	0.70	2.25	—
1970 U	1,159,000	0.45	0.55	0.70	2.25	—
1971 U	1,213,250	0.45	0.55	0.85	2.75	—

KM# 766 5 KRONOR
2.2402 g., 0.9000 Gold 0.0648 oz. AGW **Ruler:** Oscar II
Obv: Head right **Rev:** Value and crowns within wreath

Date	Mintage	F	VF	XF	Unc	BU
1901 EB	109,186	BV	65.00	80.00	100	—

KM# 797 5 KRONOR
2.2402 g., 0.9000 Gold 0.0648 oz. AGW **Ruler:** Gustaf V
Obv: Head right **Rev:** Value and crowns above sprigs

Date	Mintage	F	VF	XF	Unc	BU
1920 W	103,000	BV	65.00	80.00	100	—

KM# 806 5 KRONOR
25.0000 g., 0.9000 Silver 0.7234 oz. ASW, 36 mm. **Ruler:** Gustaf V
Subject: 500th Anniversary of Riksdag **Obv:** Head left **Rev:** Three small crowns within shield in center of cross design

Date	Mintage	F	VF	XF	Unc	BU
ND(1935) G	663,819	BV	11.50	14.50	22.50	—

KM# 828 5 KRONOR
22.7000 g., 0.4000 Silver 0.2919 oz. ASW, 36 mm. **Ruler:** Gustaf VI
Subject: 70th Birthday of Gustaf VI Adolf **Obv:** Head left
Rev: Crowned monogram divides value **Edge:** Plain

Date	Mintage	F	VF	XF	Unc	BU
ND(1952) TS	219,237	4.50	7.50	13.50	30.00	—

KM# 829 5 KRONOR
18.0000 g., 0.4000 Silver 0.2315 oz. ASW, 34 mm.
Ruler: Gustaf VI **Obv:** Head left **Rev:** Crowned shield divides value **Edge:** PLIKTEN FRAMFOR ALLT **Note:** Regular issue.

Date	Mintage	F	VF	XF	Unc	BU
1954 TS	1,510,316	—	BV	3.75	7.00	—
1955 TS	3,568,985	—	BV	3.50	6.00	—
1971 U	712,500	—	BV	3.50	6.00	—

KM# 830 5 KRONOR
18.0000 g., 0.4000 Silver 0.2315 oz. ASW, 34 mm.
Ruler: Gustaf VI **Subject:** Constitution Sesquicentennial
Obv: Head left **Rev:** Standing figures with hats facing

Date	Mintage	F	VF	XF	Unc	BU
1959 TS	504,150	—	BV	4.50	8.50	—

KM# 838 5 KRONOR
18.0000 g., 0.4000 Silver 0.2315 oz. ASW, 34 mm.
Ruler: Gustaf VI **Subject:** 80th Birthday of Gustaf VI Adolf
Obv: Head left **Rev:** Pallas Athena left holding shield and owl

Date	Mintage	F	VF	XF	Unc	BU
ND(1962) U	256,000	4.00	7.50	13.50	35.00	—
Note: An additional 96,525 melted						

KM# 839 5 KRONOR
18.0000 g., 0.4000 Silver 0.2315 oz. ASW, 34 mm.
Ruler: Gustaf VI **Subject:** 100th Anniversary of Constitution Reform **Obv:** Head left **Rev:** Inscription within square flanked by sprigs **Edge:** Horizontal wavy lines

Date	Mintage	F	VF	XF	Unc	BU
1966 U	1,023,500	—	BV	3.50	6.00	—

KM# 846   5 KRONOR
Copper-Nickel Clad Nickel   **Ruler:** Gustaf VI **Obv:** Head left
Rev: Crowned shield divides value

Date	Mintage	F	VF	XF	Unc	BU
1972 U	21,736,000	—	—	1.25	2.00	—
1973 U	1,139,000	—	1.25	1.50	2.75	—

KM# 853   5 KRONOR
9.5000 g., Copper-Nickel, 28.5 mm.   **Ruler:** Carl XVI Gustaf
Obv: Crowned monogram **Rev:** Value

Date	Mintage	F	VF	XF	Unc	BU
1976 U	2,252,923	—	—	1.00	1.75	—
1977 U	3,985,381	—	—	1.00	1.75	—
1978 U	3,952,352	—	—	1.00	1.75	—
1979 U	3,164,051	—	—	1.00	1.75	—
1980 U	2,221,846	—	—	1.00	1.75	—
1981 U	5,507,222	—	—	1.00	1.75	—
1982 U	36,603,696	—	—	0.75	1.25	—
1983 U	31,364,320	—	—	0.85	1.50	—
1984 U	27,689,251	—	—	0.85	1.50	—
1985 U	10,603,060	—	—	0.75	1.25	—
1986 U	714,132	—	—	1.25	4.00	—
1987 D	15,117,317	—	—	0.75	1.25	—
1988 D	18,643,957	—	—	0.85	1.50	—
1989 D	960,667	—	—	1.25	3.50	—
1990 D	10,557,882	—	—	0.75	1.25	—
1991 D	15,792,139	—	—	0.75	1.25	—
1991 U	Est. 25,000	16.50	27.50	55.00	110	—
1992 D	5,350,810	—	—	1.00	1.50	—

KM# 853a   5 KRONOR
9.6000 g., Copper-Nickel Clad Nickel, 28.5 mm.
Ruler: Carl XVI Gustaf **Obv:** Crowned monogram **Rev:** Value

Date	Mintage	F	VF	XF	Unc	BU
1993 B	274,932	—	—	—	1.75	2.00
1994 B	173,438	—	—	—	2.00	2.25
1995 B	186,687	—	—	—	1.00	1.25
1996 B	180,405	—	—	—	1.00	1.25
1997 B	174,455	—	—	—	1.00	1.25
1998 B	84,991	—	—	—	1.00	1.25
1999 B	96,035	—	—	—	1.00	1.25
2000 B	3,851,326	—	—	—	1.00	1.25

KM# 885   5 KRONOR
Copper-Nickel Clad Nickel, 28.5 mm.   **Ruler:** Carl XVI Gustaf
Subject: 50th Anniversary - United Nations **Obv:** Crowned
monogram **Rev:** Numeral 50 and UN emblem

Date	Mintage	F	VF	XF	Unc	BU
ND(1995) B	300,000	—	—	1.00	3.50	4.50

KM# 767   10 KRONOR
4.4803 g., 0.9000 Gold 0.1296 oz. AGW   **Ruler:** Oscar II
Obv: Large head right **Rev:** Crowned and mantled arms

Date	Mintage	F	VF	XF	Unc	BU
1901 EB	213,286	—	BV	125	140	—
1901 EB Proof	Inc. above	Value: 525				

KM# 847   10 KRONOR
18.0000 g., 0.8300 Silver 0.4803 oz. ASW, 32 mm.
Ruler: Gustaf VI **Subject:** 90th Birthday of Gustaf VI Adolf
Obv: Head left **Rev:** Inscription and value

Date	Mintage	F	VF	XF	Unc	BU
1972 U	2,000,000	—	BV	7.50	9.50	—

Note: 652,907 were returned to the mint.

KM# 877   10 KRONOR
6.6700 g., Copper-Aluminum-Zinc, 20.46 mm.   **Ruler:** Carl XVI
Gustaf **Obv:** Head left **Rev:** Three crowns within value

Date	Mintage	F	VF	XF	Unc	BU
1991 D Medal	106,548,000	—	—	2.00	3.00	—
1991 D Coin	Inc. above	20.00	30.00	40.00	60.00	—
1992 D	42,506,792	—	—	—	1.75	—
1993 B	20,107,110	—	—	—	1.75	—
1994 B	573,243	—	—	—	2.00	—
1995 B	523,685	—	—	—	2.00	—
1996 B	295,053	—	—	—	2.00	—
1997 B	332,450	—	—	—	2.00	—
1998 B	332,000	—	—	—	2.00	—
1999 B	81,430	—	—	—	2.00	—
2000 B	8,520,983	—	—	—	1.75	—

KM# 765   20 KRONOR
8.9606 g., 0.9000 Gold 0.2593 oz. AGW   **Ruler:** Oscar II
Obv: Head right **Obv. Leg.:** OSCAR II SVERIGES...
Rev: Crowned and mantled arms

Date	Mintage	F	VF	XF	Unc	BU
1901 EB	226,679	—	BV	235	250	—
1902 EB	113,810	—	BV	245	275	—

KM# 800   20 KRONOR
8.9606 g., 0.9000 Gold 0.2593 oz. AGW   **Ruler:** Gustaf V
Obv: Head right **Rev:** Crowned arms within order chain divide
value

Date	Mintage	F	VF	XF	Unc	BU
1925 W	387,257	250	325	465	765	—

KM# 848   50 KRONOR
27.0000 g., 0.9250 Silver 0.8029 oz. ASW   **Ruler:** Carl XVI Gustaf
Subject: Constitutional Reform **Obv:** Three crowns above value
Rev: Flaming torch divides date within cluster of reaching hands, all
within inner circle

Date	Mintage	F	VF	XF	Unc	BU
1975 U	500,000	—	BV	12.50	15.00	—

KM# 854   50 KRONOR
27.0000 g., 0.9250 Silver 0.8029 oz. ASW   **Ruler:** Carl XVI Gustaf
Subject: Wedding of King Carl XVI Gustaf and Queen Silvia
Obv: Heads facing **Rev:** Crowned arms with supporters

Date	Mintage	F	VF	XF	Unc	BU
ND(1976) U	2,000,000	—	BV	12.50	14.50	—

KM# 861   100 KRONOR
16.0000 g., 0.9250 Silver 0.4758 oz. ASW   **Ruler:** Carl XVI Gustaf
Subject: Parliament **Obv:** Front view of radiant arched building
Rev: Three crowns within brick designed circle

Date	Mintage	F	VF	XF	Unc	BU
1983	400,000	—	—	—	18.50	20.00

KM# 863   100 KRONOR
16.0000 g., 0.9250 Silver 0.4758 oz. ASW   **Ruler:** Carl XVI Gustaf
Subject: Stockholm Conference **Obv:** Three crowns on thin upright
branch within waved circle **Rev:** Design and arch within circle

Date	Mintage	F	VF	XF	Unc	BU
1984	300,000	—	—	—	18.50	20.00

KM# 864 100 KRONOR

16.0000 g., 0.9250 Silver 0.4758 oz. ASW **Ruler:** Carl XVI
Gustaf **Subject:** International Youth Year **Obv:** Three small
crowns within crowned shield **Rev:** Three conjoined lined profiles
left within wreath, inner circle surrounds

Date	Mintage	F	VF	XF	Unc	BU
1985	120,000	—	—	—	20.00	22.50

KM# 865 100 KRONOR

16.0000 g., 0.9250 Silver 0.4758 oz. ASW **Ruler:** Carl XVI Gustaf
Subject: European Music Year **Obv:** Three crowns at upper left of
music notes **Rev:** Stylized profile left within circle of stars

Date	Mintage	F	VF	XF	Unc	BU
1985	120,000	—	—	—	20.00	22.50

KM# 866 100 KRONOR

16.0000 g., 0.9250 Silver 0.4758 oz. ASW **Ruler:** Carl XVI
Gustaf **Subject:** International Year of the Forest **Obv:** Three
crowns on tree ring design **Rev:** Standing figures under tree within
circle flanked by small trees

Date	Mintage	F	VF	XF	Unc	BU
1985	120,000	—	—	—	22.50	25.00

KM# 867.1 100 KRONOR

16.0000 g., 0.9250 Silver 0.4758 oz. ASW **Ruler:** Carl XVI Gustaf
Subject: 350th Anniversary of Swedish Colony in Delaware
Obv: Large head left **Rev:** Three small crowns, map and ship

Date	Mintage	F	VF	XF	Unc	BU
ND(1988)	32,000	—	—	—	27.50	30.00

KM# 867.2 100 KRONOR

16.0000 g., 0.9250 Silver 0.4758 oz. ASW **Ruler:** Carl XVI Gustaf
Subject: 350th Anniversary of Swedish Colony in Delaware
Obv: Small head left **Rev:** Three small crowns, map and ship

Date	Mintage	F	VF	XF	Unc	BU
ND(1988)	118,000	—	—	—	22.50	25.00

KM# 860 200 KRONOR

27.0000 g., 0.9250 Silver 0.8029 oz. ASW **Ruler:** Carl XVI
Gustaf **Subject:** Swedish Royal Succession Law **Obv:** Head left
Rev: Inscription, date and value

Date	Mintage	F	VF	XF	Unc	BU
1980 U Prooflike	500,000	—	—	—	30.00	40.00

KM# 862 200 KRONOR

27.0000 g., 0.9250 Silver 0.8029 oz. ASW **Ruler:** Carl XVI Gustaf
Subject: 10th Anniversary of Reign **Obv:** Head left **Rev:** Crowned
arms with supporters

Date	Mintage	F	VF	XF	Unc	BU
1983	100,000	—	—	—	35.00	42.50

KM# 869 200 KRONOR

27.0000 g., 0.9250 Silver 0.8029 oz. ASW **Ruler:** Carl XVI
Gustaf **Subject:** Ice Hockey **Obv:** Three small crowns within
patterned circle **Rev:** Hockey goalie within circle

Date	Mintage	F	VF	XF	Unc	BU
1989	Est. 80,000	—	—	—	32.50	40.00

KM# 875 200 KRONOR

27.0000 g., 0.9250 Silver 0.8029 oz. ASW **Ruler:** Carl XVI
Gustaf **Subject:** Warship - Vasa **Obv:** Head left **Rev:** Ship

Date	Mintage	F	VF	XF	Unc	BU
1990	50,000	—	—	—	35.00	40.00

KM# 879 200 KRONOR

27.0000 g., 0.9250 Silver 0.8029 oz. ASW **Ruler:** Carl XVI
Gustaf **Subject:** 200th Anniversary - Death of Gustaf III
Obv: Three small crowns within mantle **Rev:** Head right

Date	Mintage	F	VF	XF	Unc	BU
ND(1992)	50,000	—	—	—	35.00	40.00

KM# 881 200 KRONOR

27.0000 g., 0.9250 Silver 0.8029 oz. ASW **Ruler:** Carl XVI Gustaf
Subject: 20th Anniversary of Reign **Obv:** Head left **Rev:** Crown

Date	Mintage	F	VF	XF	Unc	BU
1993	50,000	—	—	—	35.00	40.00

KM# 882 200 KRONOR

27.0000 g., 0.9250 Silver 0.8029 oz. ASW **Ruler:** Carl XVI
Gustaf **Subject:** 50th Birthday of Queen Silvia **Obv:** Crowned
head right **Rev:** Crowned arms with supporters

Date	Mintage	F	VF	XF	Unc	BU
ND(1993)	49,000	—	—	—	35.00	40.00
ND(1993) Prooflike	1,000	—	—	—	—	75.00

KM# 886 200 KRONOR

27.0000 g., 0.9250 Silver 0.8029 oz. ASW **Ruler:** Carl XVI
Gustaf **Subject:** 1000th Anniversary - Swedish Coinage
Obv: Head left **Rev:** Coin designs within circle

Date	Mintage	F	VF	XF	Unc	BU
ND(1995)	49,000	—	—	—	35.00	40.00
ND(1995) Prooflike	1,000	—	—	—	—	75.00

KM# 888   200 KRONOR
27.0000 g., 0.9250 Silver 0.8029 oz. ASW **Ruler:** Carl XVI
Gustaf **Subject:** 50th Birthday - King Carl XVI Gustaf **Obv:** Head
left **Rev:** Crowned arms with supporters

Date	Mintage	F	VF	XF	Unc	BU
ND(1996)	49,000	—	—	—	35.00	40.00
ND(1996) Prooflike	1,000	—	—	—	—	75.00

KM# 890   200 KRONOR
27.0000 g., 0.9250 Silver 0.8029 oz. ASW **Ruler:** Carl XVI
Gustaf **Subject:** Kalmar Union **Obv:** Head left **Rev:** Queen
Margareta's head left and castle

Date	Mintage	F	VF	XF	Unc	BU
1997	Est. 50,000	—	—	—	35.00	45.00

KM# 892   200 KRONOR
27.0000 g., 0.9250 Silver 0.8029 oz. ASW **Ruler:** Carl XVI Gustaf
Subject: 25th Anniversary - Reign of Carl XVI **Obv:** Head 1/4 left
Rev: Crown above sceptre, crowned monogram and orb

Date	Mintage	F	VF	XF	Unc	BU
1998	50,000	—	—	—	35.00	40.00

KM# 898   200 KRONOR
27.0300 g., 0.9250 Silver 0.8038 oz. ASW, 36 mm.
Ruler: Carl XVI Gustaf **Subject:** Millennium **Obv:** Conjoined
heads of King Gustaf and Crown Princess Victoria left
Rev: Crowned and mantled arms **Edge:** Plain

Date	Mintage	F	VF	XF	Unc	BU
1999 Prooflike	2,000	—	—	—	—	40.00
1999	98,000	—	—	—	30.00	—

KM# 868   1000 KRONOR
5.8000 g., 0.9000 Gold 0.1678 oz. AGW **Ruler:** Carl XVI Gustaf
Subject: 350th Anniversary of Swedish Colony in Delaware
Obv: Head left **Rev:** Ship at sea

Date	Mintage	F	VF	XF	Unc	BU
ND(1988)	10,000	—	—	—	235	285

KM# 870   1000 KRONOR
5.8000 g., 0.9000 Gold 0.1678 oz. AGW **Ruler:** Carl XVI Gustaf
Subject: Ice Hockey **Obv:** Three small crowns within designed
circle **Rev:** Hockey goalie within circle

Date	Mintage	F	VF	XF	Unc	BU
1989	20,000	—	—	—	185	225

KM# 876   1000 KRONOR
5.8000 g., 0.9000 Gold 0.1678 oz. AGW **Ruler:** Carl XVI Gustaf
Subject: The Vasa - Arms **Obv:** Head left **Rev:** The Vasa - Arms

Date	Mintage	F	VF	XF	Unc	BU
1990	15,000	—	—	—	200	250

KM# 880   1000 KRONOR
5.8000 g., 0.9000 Gold 0.1678 oz. AGW **Ruler:** Carl XVI Gustaf
Subject: 200th Anniversary - Death of Gustaf III **Obv:** Crowned
arms within order chain **Rev:** Head right

Date	Mintage	F	VF	XF	Unc	BU
ND(1992)	15,000	—	—	—	200	250

KM# 883   1000 KRONOR
5.8000 g., 0.9000 Gold 0.1678 oz. AGW **Ruler:** Carl XVI Gustaf
Subject: 20th Anniversary of Reign **Obv:** Head left **Rev:** Crown

Date	Mintage	F	VF	XF	Unc	BU
1993	15,000	—	—	—	175	225

KM# 884   1000 KRONOR
5.8000 g., 0.9000 Gold 0.1678 oz. AGW **Ruler:** Carl XVI Gustaf
Subject: 50th Birthday of Queen Silvia **Obv:** Crowned head right
Rev: Crowned arms with supporters

Date	Mintage	F	VF	XF	Unc	BU
ND(1993)	14,000	—	—	—	185	225
ND(1993) Prooflike	1,000	—	—	—	—	385

KM# 887   1000 KRONOR
5.8000 g., 0.9000 Gold 0.1678 oz. AGW **Ruler:** Carl XVI Gustaf
Subject: 100th Anniversary - Swedish Coinage **Obv:** Head left
Rev: Coin designs within circle

Date	Mintage	F	VF	XF	Unc	BU
ND(1995)	14,000	—	—	—	185	225
ND(1995) Prooflike	1,000	—	—	—	—	350

KM# 889   1000 KRONOR
5.8000 g., 0.9000 Gold 0.1678 oz. AGW **Ruler:** Carl XVI Gustaf
Subject: 50th Birthday - King Carl XVI Gustaf **Obv:** Head left
Rev: Crowned arms with supporters

Date	Mintage	F	VF	XF	Unc	BU
ND(1996)	14,000	—	—	—	185	225
ND(1996) Prooflike	1,000	—	—	—	—	350

KM# 891   1000 KRONOR
5.8000 g., 0.9000 Gold 0.1678 oz. AGW **Ruler:** Carl XVI Gustaf
Subject: Kalmar Union - Queen Margareta **Obv:** Head left
Rev: Crowned head left and shield

Date	Mintage	F	VF	XF	Unc	BU
1997	Est. 15,000	—	—	—	170	200

KM# 893   1000 KRONOR
5.8000 g., 0.9000 Gold 0.1678 oz. AGW **Ruler:** Carl XVI Gustaf
Subject: 25th Anniversary - Reign of King Carl XVI **Obv:** Head
1/4 left **Rev:** Crown above sceptre, crowned monogram and orb

Date	Mintage	F	VF	XF	Unc	BU
1998	15,000	—	—	—	—	200
1998 Proof	—	Value: 225				

KM# 899   2000 KRONOR
13.0000 g., 0.9000 Gold 0.3761 oz. AGW, 26 mm.
Ruler: Carl XVI Gustaf **Subject:** Millennium **Obv:** Conjoined
heads of King Gustaf and Crown Princess Victoria left
Rev: Crowned mantled arms **Edge:** Plain

Date	Mintage	F	VF	XF	Unc	BU
1999 Prooflike	2,000	—	—	—	—	385
1999	30,000	—	—	—	365	—

PATTERNS
Including off metal strikes

KM#	Date	Mintage	Identification	Mkt Val
Pn99	1901	—	2 Ore. Iron. KM#716	—
Pn100	1901	—	5 Kronor. Bronze. KM#766	—
Pn101	1909	—	2 Ore. Bronze. Flat-based 2	—
Pn102	1909	—	5 Ore. Bronze. Flat-based 5	—
Pn103	1913	—	2 Kronor. Bronze. KM#787	—
Pn104	1916	—	Ore. Iron. KM#777.2	—
Pn105	1916	—	2 Ore. Iron. KM#778	—
Pn106	1916	—	5 Ore. Iron. KM#779.2	—
Pn107	1918 W	—	10 Ore. Iron. Center hole	—
Pn108	1918 W	—	25 Ore. Iron. Center hole	—
Pn109	1918 W	—	25 Ore. Silver. Center hole	—
Pn110	1918 W	—	50 Ore. Iron. Center hole	—
Pn111	1918 W	—	50 Ore. Silver. Center hole	—
Pn112	1918 W	—	Krona. Iron. Center hole	—
Pn113	1918 W	—	Krona. Nickel. Center hole	—
Pn114	1918 W	—	Krona. Silver. Center hole	—
Pn115	1918	—	5 Kronor. Nickel. KM#797	—
Pn116	1919	—	Ore. Bronze. Center hole	—
Pn117	1919	—	5 Ore. Iron. Center hole	—
Pn118	1919	—	5 Ore. Bronze. Center hole	—
Pn119	1919	—	10 Ore. Nickel. KM#780	—
Pn120	1919	—	2 Kronor. Bronze. KM#787	—
Pn121	1920	—	2 Ore. Bronze. Copper hole	—
Pn122	1920	—	5 Ore. Bronze. Center hole	—
Pn123	1920 W	—	50 Ore. Silver.	—
Pn124	1921	—	2 Kronor. Bronze. KM#787	—
Pn125	1949	—	5 Ore. Bronze. "PROV"	—
PnA126	1949	—	50 Ore. Aluminum. "PROV"	—
Pn126	1950	—	Ore. Copper Plated Iron. KM#810	—
Pn127	1950	—	Ore. Copper Plated Iron. "PROV"	—

KM#	Date	Mintage	Identification	Mkt Val
Pn128	1950	—	2 Ore. Copper Plated Iron. KM#811	—
Pn129	1950	—	2 Ore. Copper Plated Iron. "PROV"	—
Pn130	1950	—	5 Ore. Tombac Plated Iron. KM#812	—
Pn131	1950	—	5 Ore. Copper Plated Iron. "PROV"	—
Pn132	1950	—	10 Ore. Nickel Plated Iron. "PROV"	—
Pn133	1950	—	25 Ore. Nickel Plated Iron. "PROV"	—
Pn134	1951	—	2 Ore. Bronze. "PROV"	—
Pn135	1951	—	2 Ore. Iron. "PROV"	—
Pn136	1951	—	50 Ore. Silver. "PROV"	—
Pn137	1951	—	Krona. Silver. Plain edge. "PROV"	—
Pn138	1951	—	Krona. Silver. Reeded edge. "PROV"	—
Pn139	1951 TS	—	Krona. Silver. "PROV"	—
Pn140	1951 TS	—	5 Kronor. Silver. "PROV"	—
Pn141	1952 TS	—	5 Ore. Bronze. "PROV"	—
Pn142	1952 TS	—	10 Ore. Silver. "PROV"	—
Pn143	1952 TS	—	10 Ore. Copper-Nickel. "PROV"	—
Pn144	1952 TS	—	10 Ore. Silver. "PROV"	—
Pn145	1952 TS	—	25 Ore. Silver. "PROV"	—
Pn146	1952 TS	—	50 Ore. Silver. "PROV", high relief	—
Pn147	1952 TS	—	50 Ore. Silver. "PROV", low relief	—
Pn148	1952 TS	—	Krona. Silver. "PROV"	—
Pn149	1952 TS	—	Krona. Silver. "PROV"; different head	—
Pn150	1952 TS	—	5 Kronor. Silver. Plain edge. "PROV"	—
Pn151	1952 TS	—	5 Kronor. Silver. Reeded edge. "PROV"	—
Pn152	1953 TS	—	5 Kronor. Silver. Plain edge. "PROV"	—
Pn153	1953 TS	—	5 Kronor. Silver. Reeded edge. "PROV"	—
Pn154	1953 TS	—	5 Kronor. Silver. "PROV"; small value	—
Pn155	1953 TS	—	5 Kronor. Silver. "PROV"; large value	—
Pn156	1954 TS	—	5 Kronor. Silver. "PROV"	—
Pn157	1970 U	—	Ore. Iron. 1.5000 g. KM#820	175

MINT SETS

KM#	Date	Mintage	Identification	Issue Price	Mkt Val
MS1	1973 (6)	20,000	KM#826a, 835-837, 845, 846	5.00	22.50
MS2	1976 (6)	61,234	KM#849-853, 855 Swedish - soft plastic case	5.00	11.00
MS3	1976 (6)	10,000	KM#849-853, 855 English - soft plastic case	5.00	11.00
MS4	1977 (6)	43,346	KM#849-853, 855 Swedish - soft plastic case	5.00	12.00
MS5	1977 (6)	5,800	KM#849-853, 855 English - soft plastic case	5.00	13.50
MS6	1978 (6)	20,115	KM#849-853, 855 Swedish - soft plastic case	5.00	20.00
MS7	1978 (6)	1,500	KM#849-853, 855 English - soft plastic case	5.00	22.50
MS8	1978 (6)	31,245	KM#849-853, 855 Swedish - soft plastic case	5.00	27.50
MS9	1979 (6)	10,200	KM#849-853, 855 Swedish - soft plastic case	5.00	12.00
MS10	1979 (6)	1,900	KM#849-853, 855 English - soft plastic case	5.00	17.50
MS11	1979 (6)	38,957	KM#849-853, 855 Swedish - soft plastic case	5.00	16.50
MS12	1979 (6)	9,871	KM#849-853, 855 English - soft plastic case	5.00	25.00
MS13	1980 (6)	10,140	KM#849-853, 855 Swedish - soft plastic case	5.00	12.00
MS14	1980 (6)	2,000	KM#849-853, 855 English - soft plastic case	5.00	17.50
MS15	1980 (6)	45,495	KM#849-853, 855 Swedish - soft plastic case	5.50	15.00
MS16	1980 (6)	9,880	KM#849-853, 855 English - soft plastic case	5.50	25.00
MS17	1981 (6)	11,927	KM#849a, 850-853, 855 Swedish - soft plastic case	5.50	12.00
MS18	1981 (6)	2,000	KM#849a, 850-853, 855 English - soft plastic case	5.50	17.50
MS19	1981 (6)	65,338	KM#849a, 850-853, 855 Swedish - hard plastic case	5.50	10.00
MS20	1981 (6)	5,000	KM#849a, 850-853, 855 English - hard plastic case	5.50	30.00
MS21	1982 (5)	9,463	KM#849a, 850-851, 852a, 853 Swedish - soft plastic case	5.50	12.00
MS22	1982 (5)	2,300	KM#849a, 850-851, 852a, 853 English - soft plastic case	5.50	13.50
MS23	1982 (5)	58,772	KM#849a, 850-851, 852a, 853 Swedish - hard plastic case	5.50	10.00
MS24	1982 (5)	4,978	KM#849a, 850-851, 852a, 853 English - hard plastic case	5.50	30.00
MS25	1983 (5)	10,300	KM#849a, 850-851, 852a, 853 Swedish - soft plastic case	6.00	12.00
MS26	1983 (5)	2,750	KM#849a, 850-851, 852a, 853 English - soft plastic case	6.00	13.50
MS27	1983 (6)	57,205	KM#849a, 850-851, 852a, 853 Swedish - hard plastic case	6.00	10.00
MS28	1983 (6)	5,017	KM#849a, 850-851, 852a, 853 English - hard plastic case	6.00	30.00
MS29	1984 (6)	10,100	KM#849a, 850-851, 852a, 853, 855 Swedish - soft plastic case	6.00	10.00
MS30	1984 (6)	1,600	KM#849a, 850-851, 852a, 853, 855 English - soft plastic case	6.00	22.50
MS31	1984 (6)	70,849	KM#849a, 850-851, 852a, 853, 855 Swedish - hard plastic case	6.00	10.00
MS32	1984 (6)	4,271	KM#849a, 850-851, 852a, 853, 855 English - hard plastic case	6.00	35.00
MS33	1985 (4)	8,000	KM#850, 852a, 853, 855 Swedish - soft plastic case	6.50	11.50
MS34	1985 (4)	1,445	KM#850, 852a, 853, 855 English - soft plastic case	6.50	22.50
MS35	1985 (4)	52,462	KM#850, 852a, 853, 855 Swedish - hard plastic case	6.50	10.00
MS36	1985 (4)	2,717	KM#850, 852a, 853, 855 English - hard plastic case	6.50	45.00
MS37	1986 (4)	16,265	KM#850, 852a, 853, 855 Swedish - hard plastic case	6.50	16.50
MS38	1986 (4)	1,880	KM#850, 852a, 853, 855 English - soft plastic case	6.50	22.50
MS39	1986 (4)	54,890	KM#850, 852a, 853, 855 Swedish - hard plastic case	6.50	20.00
MS40	1986 (4)	967	KM#850, 852a, 853, 855 English - hard plastic case	6.50	100
MS85	1996 (4)	5,481	KM#852a, 853a, 877, 878 Souvenir folder	11.05	14.50
MS41	1987 (4)	5,600	KM#850, 852a, 853, 855 Swedish - soft plastic case	6.50	10.00
MS42	1987 (4)	1,100	KM#850, 852a, 853, 855 English - soft plastic case	6.55	25.00
MS43	1987 (4)	70,060	KM#850, 852a, 853, 855 Swedish - hard plastic case	6.50	10.00
MS44	1987 (4)	557	KM#850, 852a, 853, 855 Swedish and English - hard plastic case	6.50	200
MS45	1988 (4)	4,815	KM#850, 852a, 853, 855 Swedish - soft plastic case	6.50	15.00
MS46	1988 (4)	2,456	KM#850, 852a, 853, 855 English - hard plastic case	6.50	16.50
MS47	1988 (4)	56,753	KM#850, 852a, 853, 855 Swedish - hard plastic case	6.50	15.00
MS48	1988 (4)	1,777	KM#850, 852a, 853, 855 English - hard plastic case	6.50	47.50
MS49	1989 (4)	7,170	KM#850, 852a, 853, 855 Swedish - soft plastic case	6.50	16.00
MS50	1989 (4)	56,895	KM#850, 852a, 853, 855 Swedish - hard plastic case	6.50	15.00
MS51	1989 (4)	2,780	KM#850, 852a, 853, 855 English - hard plastic case	—	17.50
MS52	1989 (4)	1,000	KM#850, 852a, 853, 855 English - hard plastic case	—	32.50
MS53	1990 (4)	6,503	KM#850, 852a, 853, 855 Swedish - soft plastic case	6.50	12.50
MS54	1990 (4)	55,265	KM#850, 852a, 853, 855 Swedish - hard plastic case	6.50	13.50
MS55	1990 (4)	2,440	KM#850, 852a, 853, 855 English - hard plastic case	—	13.50
MS56	1990 (4)	2,492	KM#850, 852a, 853, 855 English - hard plastic case	—	11.50
MS57	1991 (5)	8,079	KM#850, 852a, 853, 855, 877 Swedish - soft plastic case	—	17.50
MS58	1991 (5)	1,680	KM#850, 852a, 853, 855, 877 English - soft plastic case	—	17.50
MS59	1991 (5)	62,517	KM#850, 852a, 853, 855, 877 Swedish - hard plastic case	—	18.50
MS60	1991 (5)	2,884	KM#850, 852a, 853, 855, 877 English - hard plastic case	—	20.00
MS61	1991 (5)	5,000	KM#850 (3), 855 (2), medal	—	12.00
MS62	1992 (4)	5,600	KM#852a, 853, 877-878 Swedish - soft plastic case	6.50	11.50
MS63	1992 (4)	1,840	KM#852a, 853, 877-878 English - soft plastic case	6.50	11.50
MS64	1992 (4)	61,183	KM#852a, 853, 877-878 Swedish - hard plastic case	6.50	11.00
MS65	1992 (4)	2,187	KM#852a, 853, 877-878 English - hard plastic case	6.50	13.50
MS66	1993 (4)	4,784	KM#852a, 853a, 877, 878 Swedish - soft plastic case	6.50	16.50
MS67	1993 (4)	2,016	KM#852a, 853a, 877, 878 English - soft plastic case	6.50	11.00
MS68	1993 (4)	57,700	KM#852a, 853a, 877, 878 Swedish - hard plastic case	6.50	16.50
MS69	1993 (4)	2,164	KM#852a, 853a, 877, 878 English - hard plastic case	6.50	17.50
MS70	1993 (4)	4,956	KM#852a, 853a, 877, 878 Souvenir folder	—	22.50
MS71	1994 (4)	5,360	KM#852a, 853a, 877, 878 Swedish - soft plastic case	—	16.50
MS72	1994 (4)	2,240	KM#852a, 853a, 877, 878 English - soft plastic case	—	15.00
MS73	1994 (4)	48,881	KM#852a, 853a, 877, 878, mint medal Swedish - hard plastic case	—	16.50
MS74	1994 (4)	1,966	KM#852a, 853a, 877, 878, mint medal English - hard plastic case	—	17.50
MS75	1994 (4)	9,950	KM#852a, 853a, 877, 878, mint medal Souvenir folder	—	13.50
MS76	1995 (4)	10,000	KM#852a, 853a, 877, 878, 885 Swedish - hard plastic case	14.00	32.50
MS77	1995 (4)	45,836	KM#852a, 877, 878, 885, medal Swedish - hard plastic case	20.00	16.50
MS78	1995 (4)	4,650	KM#852a, 853a, 877, 878, 885 English - soft plastic case	—	15.00
MS79	1995 (4)	2,479	KM#852a, 853a, 877, 878, 885, medal English - hard plastic case	—	18.50
MS80	1995 (4)	5,000	KM#852a, 877, 878, 885, medal Souvenir folder	—	32.50
MS81	1996 (4)	42,729	KM#852a, 853a, 877, 878 Swedish - hard plastic case	11.05	13.50
MS82	1996 (4)	2,000	KM#852a, 853a, 877, 878 English - hard plastic case	11.05	16.50
MS83	1996 (4)	7,100	KM#852a, 853a, 877, 878 Swedish - soft plastic case	7.55	11.50
MS84	1996 (4)	2,500	KM#852a, 853a, 877, 878 English - soft plastic case	7.55	12.50
MS86	1997 (4)	39,470	KM#852a, 853a, 877, 878 Swedish - hard plastic case	11.05	18.50
MS87	1997 (4)	1,997	KM#852a, 853a, 877, 878 English - hard plastic case	11.05	22.50
MS88	1997 (4)	5,100	KM#852a, 853a, 877, 878 Swedish - soft plastic case	7.55	15.00
MS89	1997 (4)	2,200	KM#852a, 853a, 877, 878 English - soft plastic case	7.55	16.50
MS90	1997 (4)	4,954	KM#852a, 853a, 877, 878 Souvenir folder	11.05	16.50
MS91	1998 (4)	7,067	KM#852a, 853a, 877, 878 Souvenir folder	13.34	13.50
MS92	1998 (4)	5,170	KM#852a, 853a, 877, 878 Swedish - soft plastic case	—	15.00
MS93	1998 (4)	2,000	KM#852a, 853a, 877, 878 English - soft plastic case	—	16.50
MS94	1998 (4)	34,750	KM#852a, 853a, 877, 878 Swedish - hard plastic case	—	18.50
MS95	1998 (4)	1,980	KM#852a, 853a, 877, 878 English - hard plastic case	—	20.00
MS100	1999 (4)	8,045	KM#852a, 853a, 877, 878 Souvenir folder	—	13.50
MS96	1999 (4)	4,480	KM#852a, 853a, 877, 878 Swedish - hard plastic case	—	11.50
MS97	1999 (4)	2,080	KM#852a, 853a, 877, 878 English - soft plastic case	—	12.50
MS98	1999 (4)	33,334	KM#852a, 853a, 877, 878 Swedish - hard plastic case	—	16.50
MS99	1999 (4)	1,970	KM#852a, 853a, 877, 878 English - hard plastic case	—	17.50
MS101	2000 (4)	5,000	KM#852a, 853a, 877, 878 Swedish - hard plastic case	—	8.00
MS102	2000 (4)	1,000	KM#852a, 853a, 877, 878 English - soft plastic case	—	8.00
MS103	2000 (4)	30,912	KM#852a, 853a, 877, 878 Swedish - hard plastic case	—	13.50
MS104	2000 (4)	1,801	KM#852a, 853a, 877, 878 English - hard plastic case	—	13.50
MS105	2000 (4)	7,209	KM#852a, 853a, 877, 878 Souvenir folder	—	13.50
MS106	2000 (4)	14,300	KM#852a, 853a, 877, 878 Special Millennium set	—	20.00

PROOF-LIKE SETS (PL)

KM#	Date	Mintage	Identification	Issue Price	Mkt Val
PL1	1993 (2)	1,000	KM#882, 884	—	460
PL2	1995 (2)	1,000	KM#886, 887	—	425
PL3	ND(1996) (2)	1,000	KM#888, 889	—	425
PL4	1999 (2)	2,000	KM#898-899	—	300

SWITZERLAND

The Swiss Confederation, located in central Europe north of Italy and south of Germany, has an area of 15,941 sq. mi. (41,290 sq. km.) and a population of *6.6 million. Capital: Bern. The economy centers about a well developed manufacturing industry. Machinery, chemicals, watches and clocks, and textiles are exported.

Switzerland, the habitat of lake dwellers in prehistoric times, was peopled by the Celtic Helvetians when Julius Caesar made it a part of the Roman Empire in 58 B.C. After the decline of Rome, Switzerland was invaded by Teutonic tribes, who established small temporal holdings which in the Middle Ages, became a federation of fiefs of the Holy Roman Empire. As a nation, Switzerland originated in 1291 when the districts of Nidwalden, Schwyz and Uri united to defeat Austria and attain independence as the Swiss Confederation. After acquiring new cantons in the 14th century, Switzerland was made independent from the Holy Roman Empire by the 1648 Treaty of Westphalia. The revolutionary armies of Napoleonic France occupied Switzerland and set up the Helvetian Republic, 1798-1803. After the fall of Napoleon, the Congress of Vienna, 1815, recognized the independence of Switzerland and guaranteed its neutrality. The Swiss Constitutions of 1848 and 1874 established a union modeled upon that of the United States.

MINT MARKS
B - Bern
BA - Basel
BB - Strasbourg
S – Solothurn

NOTE: The coinage of Switzerland has been struck at the Bern Mint since 1853 with but a few exceptions. All coins minted there carry a B mint mark through 1969, except for the 2-Centime and 2-Franc values where the mint mark was discontinued after 1968. In 1968 and 1969 some issues were struck at both Bern (B) and in London (no mint mark).

NOTE: The Swiss Shooting Fest coins, KM#S18-S68 previously listed here are actually medallic issues without legal tender status and as such are now listed in *Unusual World Coins, 5th Edition*, by Krause Publications.

CONFEDERATION

Confoederatio Helvetica

MONETARY SYSTEM
100 Rappen (Centimes) = 1 Franc

DECIMAL COINAGE

KM# 3.2　RAPPEN
1.5000 g., Bronze, 16 mm. **Obv:** Thin cross in shield within sprigs
Rev: Value within wreath

Date	Mintage	F	VF	XF	Unc	BU
1902B	950,000	35.00	65.00	125	200	350
1903B	1,000,000	22.00	35.00	55.00	85.00	140
1904B	1,000,000	22.00	35.00	60.00	85.00	140
1905B	2,000,000	5.00	13.00	19.00	30.00	40.00
1906B	1,000,000	16.00	30.00	45.00	70.00	135
1907B	2,000,000	5.00	9.00	12.50	30.00	45.00
1908B	3,000,000	4.50	7.50	12.50	18.00	27.00
1909B	1,000,000	12.50	20.00	30.00	45.00	70.00
1910B	1,500,000	9.00	15.00	22.00	30.00	40.00
1911B	1,500,000	9.00	15.00	22.00	30.00	40.00
1912B	2,000,000	4.00	8.50	12.50	20.00	30.00
1913B	3,000,000	1.25	4.00	6.00	9.00	15.00
1914B	3,500,000	1.75	4.50	9.50	22.00	35.00
1915B	3,000,000	2.50	6.00	11.00	30.00	45.00
1917B	2,000,000	3.50	8.50	16.00	28.00	40.00
1918B	3,000,000	1.50	3.00	5.00	13.00	30.00
1919B	3,000,000	1.50	3.50	6.00	13.00	30.00
1920B	1,000,000	3.00	8.00	13.00	18.00	30.00
1921B	3,000,000	1.50	4.00	5.50	18.00	27.00
1924B	2,000,000	3.00	8.00	18.00	22.00	28.00
1925/4B	2,500,000	2.50	6.00	15.00	30.00	40.00
1925B	Inc. above	2.00	4.50	9.00	13.00	22.00
1926B	2,000,000	2.00	4.50	9.00	18.00	30.00
1927B	1,500,000	4.00	9.00	13.00	17.00	30.00
1928B	2,000,000	2.00	5.00	7.50	13.00	25.00
1929B	4,000,000	0.55	1.25	2.00	7.50	15.00
1930B	2,500,000	1.75	3.50	6.50	10.00	25.00
1931B	5,000,000	0.55	1.00	1.50	6.50	12.50
1932B	5,000,000	0.55	1.00	1.50	6.50	12.50
1933B	3,000,000	0.75	1.50	3.00	9.00	18.00
1934B	3,000,000	0.75	1.50	2.50	9.00	18.00
1936B	2,000,000	1.50	3.50	9.00	13.00	25.00
1937B	2,400,000	0.75	1.50	2.50	6.50	9.00
1938B	5,300,000	0.75	1.50	2.50	6.50	9.00
1939B	10,000	18.00	45.00	50.00	75.00	100
1940B	3,027,000	1.50	4.50	5.00	13.50	22.00
1941B	12,794,000	—	0.50	1.00	5.00	7.00

KM# 3a　RAPPEN
Zinc, 16 mm. **Obv:** Cross in shield **Rev:** Value within wreath

Date	Mintage	F	VF	XF	Unc	BU
1942B	17,969,000	—	0.50	1.50	9.50	16.00
1943B	8,647,000	0.55	1.25	3.00	9.50	19.00
1944B	11,825,000	—	0.50	2.50	-9.50	16.00
1945B	2,800,000	4.00	9.50	15.00	30.00	50.00
1946B	12,063,000	—	0.50	1.50	6.50	12.50

KM# 46　RAPPEN
1.5400 g., Bronze, 15.95 mm. **Obv:** Cross **Rev:** Value and oat sprig **Edge:** Plain

Date	Mintage	F	VF	XF	Unc	BU
1948B	10,500,000	—	0.25	0.35	3.00	11.00
1949B	11,100,000	—	0.25	0.35	3.00	11.00
1950B	3,610,000	—	1.25	2.50	5.00	13.00
1951B	22,624,000	—	0.20	0.30	3.00	11.00
1952B	11,520,000	—	0.20	0.30	3.00	11.00
1953B	5,947,000	—	0.25	0.60	3.00	11.00
1954B	5,175,000	—	0.25	0.60	3.00	11.00
1955B	5,282,000	—	0.55	1.00	3.00	11.00
1956B	4,960,000	—	0.25	0.60	3.00	8.50
1957B	15,226,000	—	0.10	0.25	1.00	4.00
1958B	20,142,000	—	0.10	0.25	1.00	4.00
1959B	5,582,000	—	0.20	0.35	1.25	4.50
1962B	5,010,000	—	0.20	0.35	1.25	4.50
1963B	15,920,000	—		0.15	0.90	1.25
1966B	5,030,000	—		0.20	0.90	1.25
1967B	3,020,000	—		0.30	0.90	1.25
1968B	4,920,000	—		0.20	0.50	1.00
1969B	4,810,000	—		0.20	0.50	1.00
1970	7,810,000	—		0.10	0.50	1.00
1971	5,030,100	—		0.10	0.50	1.00
1973	3,000,000	—		0.10	0.50	1.00
1974	3,007,000	—		0.10	0.50	1.00
1974 Proof	2,400	Value: 35.00				
1975	3,010,000	—		0.10	0.50	1.00
1975 Proof	10,000	Value: 2.50				

Date	Mintage	F	VF	XF	Unc	BU
1976	3,005,000	—		0.10	0.50	1.00
1976 Proof	5,130	Value: 3.00				
1977	2,007,000	—	—	0.10	0.50	1.00
1977 Proof	7,030	Value: 3.00				
1978	2,010,000	—	—	0.10	0.50	1.00
1978 Proof	10,000	Value: 2.50				
1979	1,025,000	—	—	0.10	0.50	1.00
1979 Proof	10,000	Value: 2.50				
1980	1,030,000	—	—	0.10	0.50	1.00
1980 Proof	10,000	Value: 2.50				
1981	4,935,000	—	—	0.10	0.50	1.00
1981 Proof	10,000	Value: 2.50				
1982	6,655,000	—	—	0.10	0.50	1.00
1982 Proof	10,000	Value: 2.50				
1983	4,031,000	—	—	0.10	0.50	1.00
1983 Proof	11,000	Value: 2.50				
1984	3,995,000	—	—	0.10	0.50	1.00
1984 Proof	14,000	Value: 2.50				
1985	3,027,000	—	—	0.10	0.50	1.00
1985 Proof	12,000	Value: 2.50				
1986B	2,031,000	—	—	0.10	0.50	1.00
1986B Proof	10,000	Value: 2.50				
1987B	1,028,000	—	—	0.10	0.50	1.00
1987B Proof	8,800	Value: 3.00				
1988B	2,029,000	—	—	0.10	0.50	1.00
1988B Proof	9,000	Value: 3.00				
1989B	2,031,000	—	—	0.10	0.50	1.00
1989B Proof	8,800	Value: 3.00				
1990B	1,032,000	—	—	—	0.50	1.00
1990B Proof	8,900	Value: 3.00				
1991B	536,000	—	—	—	1.50	2.50
1991B Proof	9,900	Value: 3.00				
1992B	528,000	—	—	—	1.50	2.50
1992B Proof	7,450	Value: 3.00				
1993B	523,000	—	—	—	1.50	2.50
1993B Proof	6,200	Value: 3.00				
1994B	2,023,000	—	—	—	0.50	1.00
1994B Proof	6,100	Value: 3.00				
1995B	6,024,000	—	—	—	0.50	1.00
1995B Proof	6,100	Value: 3.00				
1996B	1,023,000	—	—	—	0.50	1.00
1996B Proof	6,100	Value: 3.00				
1997B	1,022,000	—	—	—	0.50	1.00
1997B Proof	5,500	Value: 3.00				
1998B	1,021,000	—	—	—	0.50	1.00
1998B Proof	4,800	Value: 3.00				
1999B	1,021,000	—	—	—	0.50	1.00
1999B Proof	5,000	Value: 3.00				
2000B	1,026,000	—	—	—	0.50	1.00
2000B Proof	5,500	Value: 3.00				

KM# 4.2　2 RAPPEN
3.0000 g., Bronze, 20 mm. **Obv:** Cross in shield within sprigs
Rev: Value within wreath

Date	Mintage	F	VF	XF	Unc	BU
1902B	500,000	21.00	45.00	85.00	140	250
1903B	500,000	18.00	35.00	60.00	100	150
1904B	500,000	16.00	35.00	50.00	70.00	125
1906B	500,000	16.00	35.00	45.00	70.00	150
1907B	1,000,000	2.50	12.00	16.00	22.00	45.00
1908B	1,000,000	2.50	9.50	15.00	22.00	35.00
1909B	1,000,000	2.50	6.00	13.00	18.00	32.00
1910B	500,000	18.00	35.00	50.00	70.00	100
1912B	1,000,000	6.50	11.00	19.00	23.00	35.00
1913B	1,000,000	6.50	16.00	21.00	45.00	70.00
1914B	1,000,000	6.50	16.00	21.00	28.00	65.00
1915B	1,000,000	5.00	12.50	19.00	25.00	45.00
1918B	1,000,000	5.00	9.50	12.00	14.00	25.00
1919B	2,000,000	1.75	3.50	5.00	13.00	20.00
1920B	500,000	23.00	45.00	65.00	75.00	145
1925B	1,250,000	1.00	2.50	4.00	7.00	18.00
1926B	750,000	12.50	28.00	45.00	75.00	100
1927B	500,000	18.00	35.00	50.00	75.00	100
1928B	500,000	16.00	30.00	45.00	65.00	100
1929B	750,000	5.00	11.00	16.00	27.00	35.00
1930B	1,000,000	5.00	11.00	16.00	27.00	32.00
1931B	1,288,000	3.50	9.00	13.00	26.00	32.00
1932B	1,500,000	1.00	3.00	4.50	9.50	15.00
1933B	1,000,000	2.50	6.00	9.50	15.00	25.00
1934B	500,000	8.50	19.00	25.00	40.00	65.00
1936B	500,000	4.00	9.00	15.00	25.00	32.00
1937B	1,200,000	2.00	4.50	6.00	9.50	15.00
1938B	1,369,000	2.50	6.50	11.00	15.00	25.00
1941B	3,448,000	—	1.00	1.50	2.50	6.50

KM# 4.2a　2 RAPPEN
2.4000 g., Zinc, 20 mm. **Obv:** Cross on shield within sprigs
Rev: Value within wreath

Date	Mintage	F	VF	XF	Unc	BU
1942B	8,954,000	—	0.75	1.50	7.00	15.00
1943B	4,499,000	—	2.50	6.00	16.00	30.00
1944B	8,086,000	—	0.75	1.50	7.00	15.00
1945B	3,640,000	2.00	4.00	12.00	25.00	45.00
1946B	1,393,000	7.50	22.00	35.00	45.00	70.00

KM# 47　2 RAPPEN
3.0200 g., Bronze, 20 mm. **Obv:** Cross **Rev:** Value and oat sprig

Date	Mintage	F	VF	XF	Unc	BU
1948B	10,197,000	—	0.25	0.50	5.00	11.00
1951B	9,622,000	—	0.25	0.50	5.00	11.00
1952B	1,916,000	—	0.50	1.75	7.00	17.00
1953B	2,007,000	—	0.50	1.75	5.00	14.00
1954B	2,539,000	—	0.50	1.00	4.50	9.00
1955B	2,493,000	—	0.25	1.00	4.50	9.00
1957B	8,099,000	—	0.10	0.25	2.50	5.50
1958B	6,078,000	—	0.10	0.25	2.50	5.50
1963B	10,065,000	—	0.10	0.25	1.50	2.50
1966B	2,510,000	—	0.10	0.25	1.50	2.00
1967B	1,510,000	—	0.20	0.95	1.50	2.25
1968B	2,865,000	—	0.10	0.25	0.75	1.50
1969	6,200,000	—	0.10	0.20	0.50	1.00
1970	3,115,000	—	0.10	0.20	0.50	1.00
1974	3,540,000	—	0.10	0.20	0.50	1.00
1974 Proof	2,400	Value: 50.00				

KM# 26　5 RAPPEN
2.0000 g., Copper-Nickel, 17.1 mm. **Obv:** Crowned head right
Obv. Leg.: CONFOEDERATIO HELVETICA **Rev:** Value within
wreath **Edge:** Plain

Date	Mintage	F	VF	XF	Unc	BU
1901B	3,000,000	0.50	3.00	5.00	25.00	50.00
1902B	9.00	15.00	60.00	125	250
Note: "T" over "L" in HELVETICA						
1902B	1,000,000	7.50	10.00	40.00	100	165
1902B	Inc. above	7.50	10.00	45.00	100	225
Note: "I" over tilted "I" in Helvetica						
1903B	2,000,000	1.00	2.50	12.00	65.00	100
1904B	1,000,000	4.00	10.00	30.00	120	200
1905B	1,000,000	3.00	7.00	12.00	60.00	120
1906B	3,000,000	0.50	2.50	9.50	20.00	40.00
1907B	5,000,000	0.50	2.50	6.00	13.00	25.00
1908B	3,000,000	0.50	2.50	6.00	13.00	30.00
1909B	2,000,000	0.50	2.50	6.00	15.00	35.00
1910B	1,000,000	2.00	5.00	10.00	50.00	90.00
1911B	2,000,000	0.50	1.00	3.00	13.00	30.00
1912B	3,000,000	0.50	1.00	3.00	13.00	30.00
1913B	3,000,000	0.50	1.00	3.00	13.00	30.00
1914B	3,000,000	0.50	1.00	7.00	75.00	150
1915B	3,000,000	0.50	1.00	12.50	150	250
1917B	1,000,000	1.50	2.50	10.00	125	200
1919B	6,000,000	—	0.50	2.50	23.00	35.00
1920B	5,000,000	—	0.50	2.50	13.00	30.00
1921B	3,000,000	—	0.50	2.50	13.00	30.00
1922B	4,000,000	—	0.50	1.75	12.00	22.00
1925B	3,000,000	—	0.50	2.00	13.00	25.00
1926B	3,000,000	—	0.50	2.00	13.00	25.00
1927B	2,000,000	—	0.50	4.50	14.00	35.00
1928B	2,000,000	—	0.50	2.50	13.00	30.00
1929B	2,000,000	—	0.50	1.75	13.00	30.00
1930B	3,000,000	—	0.50	1.75	13.00	30.00
1931B	5,037,000	—	0.50	1.75	13.00	20.00
1940B	1,416,000	—	7.00	60.00	125	
1942B	5,078,000	—	0.25	0.50	12.50	26.00
1943B	6,591,000	—	0.25	0.50	12.50	26.00
1944B	9,981,000	—	0.25	0.50	12.50	26.00
1945B	985,000	—	1.00	12.00	100	325
1946B	6,179,000	—	0.25	0.50	12.50	25.00
1947B	5,125,000	—	0.25	0.50	12.50	25.00
1948B	4,710,000	—	0.25	0.50	7.00	9.50
1949B	4,589,000	—	0.50	0.50	5.00	7.00
1950B	920,000	—	0.50	1.50	6.00	8.50
1951B	2,141,000	—	0.50	2.50	35.00	60.00
1952B	4,690,000	—	0.20	0.35	3.50	8.00
1953B	9,131,000	—	0.20	0.35	3.00	8.00
1954B	8,038,000	—	0.20	0.35	6.00	16.00
1955B	19,943,000	—	0.20	0.30	2.25	11.00
1957B	10,147,000	—	0.20	0.30	2.25	11.00
1958B	10,217,000	—	0.20	0.30	2.25	11.00
1959B	11,085,000	—	0.20	0.30	2.25	11.00
1962B	23,840,000	—	0.10	0.20	0.90	7.50
1963B	29,730,000	—	0.10	0.20	0.50	4.00
1964B	17,080,000	—	0.10	0.20	0.50	3.50
1965B	1,430,000	—	0.25	1.00	1.50	3.00
1966B	10,010,000	—		0.15	0.50	1.00
1967B	13,010,000	—		0.55	1.25	1.75
1968B	10,020,000	—		0.15	0.50	1.00
1969B	32,990,000	—		0.10	0.50	1.00
1970	34,800,000	—		0.10	0.50	1.00
1971	40,020,000	—		0.10	0.50	1.00
1974 Proof	2,400	Value: 35.00				
1974	30,002,000	—		0.10	0.50	1.00

Date	Mintage	F	VF	XF	Unc	BU
1975 Proof	10,000	Value: 3.00				
1975	34,005,000	—	—	0.10	0.50	1.00
1976 Proof	5,130	Value: 4.00				
1976	12,005,000	—	—	0.10	0.50	1.00
1977 Proof	7,030	Value: 4.00				
1977	14,012,000	—	—	0.10	0.50	1.00
1978 Proof	10,000	Value: 3.00				
1978	16,415,000	—	—	0.10	0.50	1.00
1979 Proof	10,000	Value: 3.00				
1979	27,010,000	—	—	0.10	0.50	1.00
1980 Proof	10,000	Value: 3.00				
1980	15,500,000	—	—	0.10	0.50	1.00

KM# 26a 5 RAPPEN
Brass, 17.1 mm. Obv: Crowned head right Rev: Value within wreath

Date	Mintage	F	VF	XF	Unc	BU
1918B	6,000,000	4.00	7.00	20.00	30.00	40.00

KM# 26b 5 RAPPEN
Nickel, 17.1 mm. Obv: Crowned head right Rev: Value within wreath Edge: Plain Note: Retired legal tender status as of January 1, 2004, removed from circulation.

Date	Mintage	F	VF	XF	Unc	BU
1932B	6,000,000	—	0.50	1.50	10.00	15.00
1933B	3,000,000	—	0.50	1.50	10.00	15.00
1934B	4,000,000	—	0.50	1.50	10.00	15.00
1936B	1,000,000	—	0.75	2.50	11.00	20.00
1937B	2,000,000	—	0.50	1.00	12.00	22.00
1938B	1,000,000	—	0.50	1.50	11.00	20.00
1939B	10,048,000	—	0.50	1.00	10.00	15.00
1941B	3,087,000	—	1.75	5.00	60.00	90.00

KM# 26c 5 RAPPEN
2.0000 g., Aluminum-Brass, 17.1 mm. Obv: Crowned head right Rev: Value within wreath Edge: Plain

Date	Mintage	F	VF	XF	Unc	BU
1981	79,020,000	—	—	—	0.50	1.00
1981 Proof	10,000	Value: 3.00				
1982	75,340,000	—	—	—	0.50	1.00
1982 Proof	10,000	Value: 3.00				
1983	92,746,000	—	—	—	0.50	1.00
1983 Proof	11,000	Value: 3.00				
1984	69,960,000	—	—	—	0.50	1.00
1984 Proof	14,000	Value: 3.00				
1985	60,032,000	—	—	—	0.50	1.00
1985 Proof	12,000	Value: 3.00				
1986B	55,041,000	—	—	—	0.50	1.00
1986B Proof	10,000	Value: 3.00				
1987B	39,828,000	—	—	—	0.50	1.00
1987B Proof	8,800	Value: 4.00				
1988B	55,044,000	—	—	—	0.50	1.00
1988B Proof	9,000	Value: 4.00				
1989B	45,031,000	—	—	—	0.50	1.00
1989B Proof	8,800	Value: 4.00				
1990B	16,042,000	—	—	—	0.50	1.00
1990B Proof	8,900	Value: 4.00				
1991B	35,036,000	—	—	—	0.50	1.00
1991B Proof	9,900	Value: 3.00				
1992B	35,028,000	—	—	—	0.50	1.00
1992B Proof	7,450	Value: 4.00				
1993B	38,023,000	—	—	—	0.50	1.00
1993B Proof	6,200	Value: 4.00				
1994B	35,023,000	—	—	—	0.50	1.00
1994B Proof	6,100	Value: 4.00				
1995B	20,024,000	—	—	—	0.50	1.00
1995B Proof	6,100	Value: 4.00				
1996B	25,023,000	—	—	—	0.50	1.00
1996B Proof	6,100	Value: 4.00				
1997B	25,022,000	—	—	—	0.50	1.00
1997B Proof	5,500	Value: 4.00				
1998B	10,021,000	—	—	—	0.50	1.00
1998B Proof	4,800	Value: 4.00				
1999B	8,021,000	—	—	—	0.50	1.00
1999B Proof	5,000	Value: 4.00				
2000B	5,026,000	—	—	—	0.50	1.00
2000B Proof	5,500	Value: 4.00				

KM# 27 10 RAPPEN
3.0000 g., Copper-Nickel, 19.1 mm. Obv: Crowned head right Obv. Leg.: CONFOEDERATIO HELVETICA Rev: Value within wreath Edge: Plain

Date	Mintage	F	VF	XF	Unc	BU
1901B	1,000,000	1.50	6.50	19.00	65.00	140
1902B	1,000,000	1.50	6.50	12.00	60.00	125
1903B	1,000,000	1.50	6.50	10.00	90.00	150
1904B	1,000,000	1.50	5.00	26.00	175	350
1906B	1,000,000	1.50	5.00	10.00	40.00	80.00
1907B	2,000,000	1.00	2.00	5.00	24.00	60.00
1908B	2,000,000	1.00	2.00	5.00	24.00	60.00
1909B	2,000,000	1.00	2.00	5.00	24.00	60.00
1911B	1,000,000	1.50	3.00	8.00	40.00	80.00
1912B	1,500,000	0.50	1.50	5.00	38.00	85.00
1913B	2,000,000	0.50	1.00	5.00	50.00	100
1914B	2,000,000	0.50	1.50	8.00	80.00	175
1915B	1,200,000	1.00	2.00	30.00	225	400
1919B	3,000,000	—	0.50	3.00	27.00	55.00
1920B	3,500,000	—	0.50	3.00	25.00	40.00
1921B	3,000,000	—	0.50	3.00	25.00	40.00
1922B	2,000,000	—	0.50	3.00	35.00	55.00
1924B	2,000,000	—	0.50	3.00	35.00	60.00
1925B	3,000,000	—	0.50	3.00	16.00	30.00
1926B	3,000,000	—	0.50	3.00	16.00	30.00
1927B	2,000,000	—	0.50	3.00	16.00	35.00
1928B	2,000,000	—	0.50	3.00	16.00	35.00
1929B	2,000,000	—	0.50	3.00	26.00	40.00
1930B	2,000,000	—	0.50	3.00	30.00	50.00
1931B	2,244,000	—	0.50	3.00	30.00	50.00
1940B	2,000,000	—	0.75	15.00	85.00	150
1942B	2,110,000	—	0.75	10.00	50.00	100
1943B	3,176,000	—	0.50	5.00	40.00	75.00
1944B	6,133,000	—	0.50	2.50	16.00	25.00
1945B	993,000	—	1.00	15.00	150	250
1946B	4,010,000	—	0.50	2.50	24.00	50.00
1947B	3,152,000	—	0.50	2.50	24.00	55.00
1948B	1,000,000	0.50	1.00	18.00	200	350
1949B	2,269,000	—	0.50	1.00	30.00	50.00
1950B	3,200,000	—	0.35	0.70	2.50	6.00
1951B	3,430,000	—	0.35	0.70	7.00	20.00
1952B	4,451,000	—	0.35	0.70	7.00	20.00
1953B	6,149,000	—	0.35	0.70	7.00	20.00
1954B	3,200,000	—	0.35	0.70	18.00	35.00
1955B	11,795,000	—	0.35	0.70	7.00	12.00
1957B	10,092,000	—	0.35	0.70	10.00	20.00
1958B	10,040,000	—	0.35	0.70	7.00	15.00
1959B	13,053,000	—	0.35	0.70	6.00	12.00
1960B	4,040,000	—	0.35	0.70	6.00	10.00
1961B	7,949,000	—	—	0.50	2.00	4.00
1962B	34,965,000	—	—	0.20	1.00	3.00
1964B	16,340,000	—	—	0.20	1.00	3.00
1965B	14,190,000	—	—	0.20	1.00	3.00
1966B	4,025,000	—	—	0.50	1.00	1.50
1967B	10,000,000	—	—	0.50	1.00	1.50
1968B	14,065,000	—	—	0.25	0.50	1.00
1969B	28,855,000	—	—	0.25	0.50	1.00
1970	40,020,000	—	—	0.25	0.50	1.00
1972	7,877,000	—	—	0.25	0.50	1.00
1973	30,350,000	—	—	—	0.50	1.00
1974	30,007,000	—	—	—	0.50	1.00
1974 Proof	2,400	Value: 60.00				
1975	25,002,000	—	—	—	0.50	1.00
1975 Proof	10,000	Value: 4.00				
1976	19,012,000	—	—	—	0.50	1.00
1976 Proof	5,130	Value: 5.00				
1977	10,007,000	—	—	—	0.50	1.00
1977 Proof	7,030	Value: 5.00				
1978	19,957,000	—	—	—	0.50	1.00
1978 Proof	10,000	Value: 4.00				
1979	18,010,000	—	—	—	0.50	1.00
1979 Proof	10,000	Value: 4.00				
1980	18,005,000	—	—	—	0.50	1.00
1980 Proof	10,000	Value: 4.00				
1981	30,140,000	—	—	—	0.50	1.00
1981 Proof	10,000	Value: 4.00				
1982	50,110,000	—	—	—	0.50	1.00
1982 Proof	10,000	Value: 4.00				
1983	40,033,000	—	—	—	0.50	1.00
1983 Proof	11,000	Value: 4.00				
1984	22,022,000	—	—	—	0.50	1.00
1984 Proof	14,000	Value: 4.00				
1985	3,032,000	—	—	—	0.50	1.00
1985 Proof	12,000	Value: 4.00				
1986B	2,324,000	—	—	—	0.50	1.00
1986B Proof	10,000	Value: 4.00				
1987B	5,028,000	—	—	—	0.50	1.00
1987B Proof	8,800	Value: 5.00				
1988B	5,029,000	—	—	—	0.50	1.00
1988B Proof	9,000	Value: 5.00				
1989B	41,031,000	—	—	—	0.50	1.00
1989B Proof	8,800	Value: 5.00				
1990B	40,032,000	—	—	—	0.50	1.00
1990B Proof	8,900	Value: 5.00				

Date	Mintage	F	VF	XF	Unc	BU
1991B	35,046,000	—	—	—	0.50	1.00
1991B Proof	9,900	Value: 4.00				
1992B	18,028,000	—	—	—	0.50	1.00
1992B Proof	7,450	Value: 5.00				
1993B	27,022,000	—	—	—	0.50	1.00
1993B Proof	6,200	Value: 5.00				
1994B	18,023,000	—	—	—	0.50	1.00
1994B Proof	6,100	Value: 5.00				
1995B	5,024,000	—	—	—	0.50	1.00
1995B Proof	6,100	Value: 5.00				
1996B	18,023,000	—	—	—	0.50	1.00
1996B Proof	6,100	Value: 5.00				
1997B	15,022,000	—	—	—	0.50	1.00
1997B Proof	5,500	Value: 5.00				
1998B	10,021,000	—	—	—	0.50	1.00
1998B Proof	4,800	Value: 5.00				
1999B	7,021,000	—	—	—	0.50	1.00
1999B Proof	5,000	Value: 5.00				
2000B	5,026,000	—	—	—	0.50	1.00
2000B Proof	5,500	Value: 5.00				

KM# 27a 10 RAPPEN
Brass, 19.1 mm. Obv: Crowned head right Rev: Value within wreath

Date	Mintage	F	VF	XF	Unc	BU
1918B	6,000,000	7.50	12.00	20.00	35.00	60.00
1919B	3,000,000	35.00	75.00	95.00	125	200

KM# 27b 10 RAPPEN
Nickel, 19.1 mm. Obv: Crowned head right Rev: Value within wreath Edge: Plain Note: Retired legal tender status as of January 1, 2004, removed from circulation.

Date	Mintage	F	VF	XF	Unc	BU
1932B	3,500,000	—	0.50	1.00	13.00	25.00
1933B	2,000,000	—	0.50	1.00	13.00	40.00
1934B	3,000,000	—	0.50	1.00	15.00	40.00
1936B	1,500,000	—	0.50	1.00	15.00	40.00
1937B	1,000,000	0.40	0.75	1.50	20.00	55.00
1938B	1,000,000	0.40	0.75	1.50	13.00	25.00
1939B	10,022,000	—	0.50	1.00	13.00	25.00

KM# 29 20 RAPPEN
4.0000 g., Nickel, 21 mm. Obv: Crowned head right Obv. Leg.: CONFOEDERATIO HELVETICA Rev: Value within wreath Note: Retired legal tender status as of January 1, 2004, removed from circulation.

Date	Mintage	F	VF	XF	Unc	BU
1901B	1,000,000	0.50	1.00	8.00	150	300
1902B	1,000,000	0.50	1.00	8.00	75.00	150
1903B	1,000,000	0.50	1.00	8.00	65.00	120
1906B	1,000,000	0.50	1.00	8.00	55.00	110
1907B	1,000,000	0.50	1.00	7.00	32.00	60.00
1908B	1,500,000	0.50	1.00	5.00	45.00	85.00
1909B	2,000,000	0.50	1.00	5.00	32.00	60.00
1911B	1,000,000	0.50	1.00	6.00	75.00	150
1912B	2,000,000	0.35	0.75	5.00	65.00	125
1913B	1,500,000	0.35	0.75	5.00	100	190
1919B	1,500,000	0.35	0.75	5.00	38.00	80.00
1920B	3,100,000	—	0.50	2.00	30.00	55.00
1921B	2,500,000	—	0.50	2.00	22.00	50.00
1924B	1,100,000	—	0.50	2.00	65.00	125
1925B	1,500,000	—	0.50	2.00	20.00	45.00
1926B	1,500,000	—	0.50	2.00	22.00	50.00
1927B	500,000	1.00	2.50	12.00	110	225
1929B	2,000,000	—	0.50	1.00	18.00	40.00
1930B	2,000,000	—	0.50	1.00	18.00	45.00
1931B	2,250,000	—	0.50	1.00	18.00	45.00
1932B	2,000,000	—	0.50	1.00	81.00	45.00
1933B	1,500,000	—	0.50	1.00	28.00	70.00
1934B	2,000,000	—	0.50	1.00	25.00	55.00
1936B	1,000,000	0.50	1.00	2.00	32.00	80.00
1938B	2,805,000	—	0.50	1.50	32.00	80.00

KM# 29a 20 RAPPEN
4.2000 g., Copper-Nickel, 21 mm. Obv: Crowned head right Rev: Value within wreath Edge: Plain

Date	Mintage	F	VF	XF	Unc	BU
1939B	8,100,000	—	0.50	18.00	150	300
1943B	10,173,000	—	0.50	1.00	28.00	60.00
1944B	7,139,000	—	0.50	1.00	10.00	25.00
1945B	1,992,000	—	1.00	10.00	60.00	150
1947B	5,131,000	—	0.50	0.75	25.00	45.00
1947B	Inc. above	1.00	2.00	4.00	30.00	70.00
Note: Dot over 4 in date						
1950B	5,970,000	—	0.50	0.75	6.00	15.00

Date	Mintage	F	VF	XF	Unc	BU
1951B	3,640,000	—	0.50	0.75	13.00	30.00
1952B	3,075,000	—	0.50	0.75	13.00	30.00
1953B	6,958,000	—	0.50	0.75	6.00	15.00
1954B	1,504,000	—	1.00	4.00	40.00	100
1955B	9,103,000	—	0.50	0.75	12.00	25.00
1956B	5,111,000	—	0.50	0.75	12.00	20.00
1957B	2,535,000	—	0.50	1.25	30.00	75.00
1958B	5,037,000	—	0.50	0.75	12.00	25.00
1959B	10,136,000	—	—	0.50	3.50	10.00
1960B	15,469,000	—	—	0.50	3.50	9.00
1961B	8,234,000	—	—	0.50	3.50	9.00
1962B	30,145,000	—	—	0.50	3.00	8.00
1963B	9,020,000	—	—	0.50	3.50	9.00
1964B	14,370,000	—	—	0.50	2.00	6.00
1965B	15,005,000	—	—	0.50	2.00	6.00
1966B	10,785,000	—	—	0.50	1.00	2.00
1967B	8,995,000	—	—	0.50	1.50	3.50
1968B	10,540,000	—	—	0.50	1.00	2.00
1969B	39,875,000	—	—	0.40	1.00	2.00
1970	45,605,000	—	—	—	1.00	2.00
1971	25,160,000	—	—	—	1.00	2.00
1974	30,025,000	—	—	—	1.00	2.00
1974 Proof	2,400	Value: 75.00				
1975	50,060,000	—	—	—	1.00	2.00
1975 Proof	10,000	Value: 5.00				
1976	23,150,000	—	—	—	1.00	2.00
1976 Proof	5,130	Value: 6.00				
1977	14,012,000	—	—	—	1.00	2.00
1977 Proof	7,030	Value: 6.00				
1978	14,815,000	—	—	—	1.00	2.00
1978 Proof	10,000	Value: 5.00				
1979	18,378,000	—	—	—	1.00	2.00
1979 Proof	10,000	Value: 5.00				
1980	24,560,000	—	—	—	1.00	2.00
1980 Proof	10,000	Value: 5.00				
1981	22,020,000	—	—	—	1.00	2.00
1981 Proof	10,000	Value: 5.00				
1982	25,035,000	—	—	—	1.00	2.00
1982 Proof	10,000	Value: 5.00				
1983	10,026,000	—	—	—	1.00	2.00
1983 Proof	11,000	Value: 5.00				
1984	22,055,000	—	—	—	1.00	2.00
1984 Proof	14,000	Value: 5.00				
1985	40,027,000	—	—	—	1.00	2.00
1985 Proof	12,000	Value: 5.00				
1986B	10,299,000	—	—	—	1.00	2.00
1986B Proof	10,000	Value: 5.00				
1987B	10,028,000	—	—	—	1.00	2.00
1987B Proof	8,800	Value: 6.00				
1988B	25,029,000	—	—	—	1.00	2.00
1988B Proof	9,000	Value: 6.00				
1989B	20,031,000	—	—	—	1.00	2.00
1989B Proof	8,800	Value: 6.00				
1990B	6,534,000	—	—	—	1.00	2.00
1990B Proof	8,900	Value: 6.00				
1991B	48,076,000	—	—	—	1.00	2.00
1991B Proof	9,900	Value: 6.00				
1992B	12,628,000	—	—	—	1.00	2.00
1992B Proof	7,450	Value: 6.00				
1993B	32,523,000	—	—	—	1.00	2.00
1993B Proof	6,200	Value: 6.00				
1994B	20,023,000	—	—	—	1.00	2.00
1994B Proof	6,100	Value: 6.00				
1995B	8,024,000	—	—	—	1.00	2.00
1995B Proof	6,100	Value: 6.00				
1996B	4,023,000	—	—	—	1.00	2.00
1996B Proof	6,100	Value: 6.00				
1997B	6,022,000	—	—	—	1.00	2.00
1997B Proof	5,500	Value: 6.00				
1998B	7,021,000	—	—	—	1.00	2.00
1998B Proof	4,800	Value: 6.00				
1999B	4,021,000	—	—	—	1.00	2.00
1999B Proof	5,000	Value: 6.00				
2000B	3,026,000	—	—	—	1.00	2.00
2000B Proof	5,500	Value: 6.00				

KM# 23   1/2 FRANC
2.5000 g., 0.8350 Silver 0.0671 oz. ASW, 18.1 mm.
Obv: Standing Helvetia with lance and shield within star border
Rev: Value, date within wreath **Edge:** Reeded

Date	Mintage	F	VF	XF	Unc	BU
1901B	200,000	15.00	60.00	225	900	1,800
1901B Specimen	—	—	—	—	—	5,000
1903B	800,000	1.00	3.00	15.00	110	175
1903B Specimen	—	—	—	—	—	2,000
1904B	400,000	2.00	6.00	100	750	1,500
1904B Specimen	—	—	—	—	—	5,000
1905B	600,000	1.00	3.00	23.00	150	275
1905B Specimen	—	—	—	—	—	2,000
1906B	1,000,000	1.00	3.00	23.00	150	250
1906B Specimen	—	—	—	—	—	2,000
1907B	1,200,000	1.00	3.00	15.00	125	210
1907B Specimen	—	—	—	—	—	1,800
1908B	800,000	1.00	3.00	18.00	125	210

Date	Mintage	F	VF	XF	Unc	BU
1908B Specimen	—	—	—	—	—	1,600
1909B	1,000,000	1.00	3.00	12.00	110	175
1909B Specimen	—	—	—	—	—	1,500
1910B	1,000,000	1.00	3.00	12.00	75.00	150
1910B Specimen	—	—	—	—	—	1,500
1913B	800,000	1.00	3.00	7.50	70.00	140
1913B Specimen	—	—	—	—	—	1,000
1914B	2,000,000	1.00	3.00	6.00	40.00	70.00
1914B Specimen	—	—	—	—	—	600
1916B	800,000	1.00	3.00	5.00	100	175
1916B Specimen	—	—	—	—	—	1,200
1920B	5,400,000	1.00	3.00	5.00	20.00	35.00
1920B Specimen	—	—	—	—	—	450
1921B	6,000,000	1.00	3.00	5.00	20.00	35.00
1921B Specimen	—	—	—	—	—	450
1928B	1,000,000	1.00	3.00	9.50	70.00	150
1928B Specimen	—	—	—	—	—	600
1929B	2,000,000	1.00	3.00	6.00	20.00	35.00
1929B Specimen	—	—	—	—	—	300
1931B	1,000,000	1.00	2.00	9.50	40.00	80.00
1931B Specimen	—	—	—	—	—	500
1932B	1,000,000	1.00	2.00	6.50	35.00	60.00
1932B Specimen	—	—	—	—	—	400
1934B	2,000,000	1.00	2.00	6.50	20.00	35.00
1934B Specimen	—	—	—	—	—	250
1936B	400,000	1.50	3.00	9.50	45.00	85.00
1936B Specimen	—	—	—	—	—	450
1937B	1,000,000	1.00	2.00	6.00	20.00	35.00
1937B Specimen	—	—	—	—	—	275
1939B	1,001,000	1.00	2.00	6.00	20.00	40.00
1939B Specimen	—	—	—	—	—	200
1940B	2,002,000	—	2.00	5.00	15.00	30.00
1940B Specimen	—	—	—	—	—	120
1941B	200,000	1.50	3.00	8.00	25.00	45.00
1941B Specimen	—	—	—	—	—	90.00
1942B	2,969,000	—	1.50	3.00	6.00	12.00
1942B Specimen	—	—	—	—	—	90.00
1943B	4,573,000	—	1.50	3.00	6.00	12.00
1943B Specimen	—	—	—	—	—	90.00
1944B	7,455,000	—	1.50	2.50	5.00	10.00
1944B Specimen	—	—	—	—	—	90.00
1945B	4,928,000	—	1.50	2.50	5.00	10.00
1945B Specimen	—	—	—	—	—	90.00
1946B	6,817,000	—	1.50	2.50	5.00	8.00
1946B	Inc. above	50.00	110	175	250	600

Note: Medal alignment

Date	Mintage	F	VF	XF	Unc	BU
1946B Specimen	—	—	—	—	—	90.00
1948B	6,113,000	—	1.50	2.50	5.00	9.00
1948B Specimen	—	—	—	—	—	90.00
1950	7,148,000	—	1.50	2.50	5.00	9.00
1950B Specimen	—	—	—	—	—	90.00
1951B	8,530,000	—	1.50	2.50	4.00	7.00
1951B Specimen	—	—	—	—	—	90.00
1952B	14,023,000	—	1.50	2.50	4.00	7.00
1952B Specimen	—	—	—	—	—	75.00
1953B	3,567,000	—	1.50	2.50	5.00	9.00
1953B Specimen	—	—	—	—	—	90.00
1955B	1,320,000	—	1.50	3.00	10.00	15.00
1955B Specimen	—	—	—	—	—	110
1956B	4,250,000	—	1.50	2.50	5.00	9.00
1956B Specimen	—	—	—	—	—	60.00
1957B	12,085,000	—	1.50	2.50	4.00	7.00
1957B Specimen	—	—	—	—	—	30.00
1958B	11,558,000	—	1.50	2.50	4.00	7.00
1958B Specimen	—	—	—	—	—	30.00
1959B	12,581,000	—	1.50	2.50	4.00	7.00
1959B Specimen	—	—	—	—	—	30.00
1960B	14,528,000	—	1.50	2.50	4.00	7.00
1960B Specimen	—	—	—	—	—	30.00
1961B	6,906,000	—	1.50	2.50	4.00	7.00
1961B Specimen	—	—	—	—	—	30.00
1962B	18,272,000	—	1.50	2.50	4.00	7.00
1962B Specimen	—	—	—	—	—	30.00
1963B	25,168,000	—	1.50	2.50	4.00	7.00
1963B Specimen	—	—	—	—	—	30.00
1964B	22,720,000	—	1.50	2.50	4.00	7.00
1964B Specimen	—	—	—	—	—	30.00
1965B	17,920,000	—	1.50	2.50	4.00	7.00
1965B Specimen	—	—	—	—	—	30.00
1966B	10,008,000	—	1.50	2.50	4.00	7.00
1966B Specimen	—	—	—	—	—	30.00
1967B	16,096,000	—	1.50	2.50	4.00	7.00
1967B Specimen	—	—	—	—	—	30.00

KM# 23a.1   1/2 FRANC
2.2000 g., Copper-Nickel, 18.1 mm. **Obv:** Standing Helvetia with lance and shield within star border **Rev:** Value within wreath

Date	Mintage	F	VF	XF	Unc	BU
1968	20,000,000	—	—	—	2.50	4.00
1968B	44,920,000	—	—	—	2.50	4.00
1969	31,400,000	—	—	—	2.50	4.00
1969B	51,704,000	—	—	—	2.50	4.00
1970	52,620,000	—	—	—	2.50	4.00
1971	34,472,000	—	—	—	2.50	4.00

Date	Mintage	F	VF	XF	Unc	BU
1972	9,996,000	—	—	—	2.50	4.00
1973	5,000,000	—	—	—	4.00	7.00
1974	45,006,000	—	—	—	2.50	4.00
1974 Proof	2,400	Value: 85.00				
1975	27,234,000	—	—	—	2.50	3.50
1975 Proof	10,000	Value: 6.00				
1976	10,009,000	—	—	—	2.50	3.50
1976 Proof	5,130	Value: 6.00				
1977	19,011,000	—	—	—	2.50	3.50
1977 Proof	7,030	Value: 6.00				
1978	20,818,000	—	—	—	2.50	3.50
1978 Proof	10,000	Value: 6.00				
1979	27,014,000	—	—	—	2.50	3.50
1979 Proof	10,000	Value: 6.00				
1980	31,064,000	—	—	—	2.50	3.50
1980 Proof	10,000	Value: 6.00				
1981	30,155,000	—	—	—	2.50	3.50
1981 Proof	10,000	Value: 6.00				

KM# 23a.2   1/2 FRANC
2.2000 g., Copper-Nickel, 18.1 mm. **Obv:** 22 Stars around figure **Rev:** Value within wreath **Note:** Medal alignment.

Date	Mintage	F	VF	XF	Unc	BU
1982	30,151,000	—	—	—	2.50	3.50
1982 Proof	10,000	Value: 6.00				

KM# 23a.3   1/2 FRANC
2.2000 g., Copper-Nickel, 18.1 mm. **Obv:** 23 Stars around figure **Rev:** Value within wreath **Edge:** Reeded

Date	Mintage	F	VF	XF	Unc	BU
1983	22,020,000	—	—	—	2.00	3.00
1983 Proof	11,000	Value: 6.00				
1984	22,036,000	—	—	—	2.00	3.00
1984 Proof	14,000	Value: 6.00				
1985	6,026,000	—	—	—	2.50	3.50
1985 Proof	12,000	Value: 6.00				
1986B	5,031,000	—	—	—	2.50	3.50
1986B Proof	10,000	Value: 6.00				
1987B	10,028,000	—	—	—	2.00	3.00
1987B Proof	8,800	Value: 6.00				
1988B	5,029,000	—	—	—	2.50	3.50
1988B Proof	9,000	Value: 6.00				
1989B	10,031,000	—	—	—	2.00	3.00
1989B Proof	8,800	Value: 6.00				
1990B	20,032,000	—	—	—	2.00	3.00
1990B Proof	8,900	Value: 6.00				
1991B	10,036,000	—	—	—	2.00	3.00
1991B Proof	9,900	Value: 6.00				
1992B	30,028,000	—	—	—	2.00	3.00
1992B Proof	7,450	Value: 7.00				
1993B	13,023,000	—	—	—	2.00	3.00
1993B Proof	6,200	Value: 7.00				
1994B	15,023,000	—	—	—	2.00	3.00
1994B Proof	6,100	Value: 7.00				
1995B	10,024,000	—	—	—	2.00	3.00
1995B Proof	6,000	Value: 7.00				
1996B	8,023,000	—	—	—	2.50	3.50
1996B Proof	6,100	Value: 7.00				
1997B	6,022,000	—	—	—	2.50	3.50
1997B Proof	5,500	Value: 8.00				
1998B	6,021,000	—	—	—	2.50	3.50
1998B Proof	4,800	Value: 8.00				
1999B	5,021,000	—	—	—	2.50	3.50
1999B Proof	5,000	Value: 8.00				
2000B	4,026,000	—	—	—	2.50	3.50
2000B Proof	5,500	Value: 8.00				

KM# 24   FRANC
5.0000 g., 0.8350 Silver 0.1342 oz. ASW, 23.5 mm.
Obv: Standing Helvetia with lance and shield within star border
Rev: Value, date within wreath **Edge:** A. Bovy

Date	Mintage	F	VF	XF	Unc	BU
1901B	400,000	4.00	10.00	100	500	1,000
1901B Specimen	—	—	—	—	—	4,000
1903B	1,000,000	2.00	3.50	20.00	150	300
1903B Specimen	—	—	—	—	—	2,000
1904B	400,000	5.00	12.00	200	1,300	2,500
1904B Specimen	—	—	—	—	—	5,000
1905B	700,000	2.00	3.50	30.00	225	400
1905B Specimen	—	—	—	—	—	2,000
1906B	700,000	2.00	3.50	50.00	350	700
1906B Specimen	—	—	—	—	—	2,500
1907B	800,000	2.00	3.50	40.00	325	650
1907B Specimen	—	—	—	—	—	2,250
1908B	1,200,000	2.00	3.50	12.00	150	275
1908B Specimen	—	—	—	—	—	1,750
1909B	900,000	2.00	3.50	12.00	150	275
1909B Specimen	—	—	—	—	—	1,750
1910B	1,000,000	2.00	3.50	11.00	95.00	175
1910B Specimen	—	—	—	—	—	1,500
1911B	1,200,000	2.00	3.50	11.00	95.00	175
1911B Specimen	—	—	—	—	—	1,500
1912B	1,200,000	2.00	3.50	6.00	75.00	135

Date	Mintage	F	VF	XF	Unc	BU
1912B Specimen	—	—	—	—	—	1,250
1913B	1,200,000	2.00	3.50	6.00	70.00	125
1913B Specimen	—	—	—	—	—	1,250
1914B	4,200,000	2.00	3.50	5.00	30.00	60.00
1914B Specimen	—	—	—	—	—	750
1916B	1,000,000	2.00	3.50	7.00	100	175
1916B Specimen	—	—	—	—	—	1,500
1920B	3,300,000	2.00	3.00	5.00	30.00	50.00
1920B Specimen	—	—	—	—	—	450
1921B	3,800,000	2.00	3.00	5.00	30.00	50.00
1921B Specimen	—	—	—	—	—	450
1928B	1,500,000	2.00	3.00	5.00	20.00	35.00
1928B Specimen	—	—	—	—	—	400
1931B	1,000,000	2.00	3.00	5.00	40.00	65.00
1931B Specimen	—	—	—	—	—	350
1932B	500,000	2.00	3.00	7.00	85.00	140
1932B Specimen	—	—	—	—	—	750
1934B	500,000	2.00	3.00	9.50	85.00	140
1934B Specimen	—	—	—	—	—	700
1936B	500,000	2.00	3.00	9.50	65.00	125
1936B Specimen	—	—	—	—	—	650
1937B	1,000,000	2.00	3.00	5.00	25.00	50.00
1937B Specimen	—	—	—	—	—	300
1939B	2,106,000	2.00	3.00	5.00	13.00	23.00
1939B Specimen	—	—	—	—	—	175
1940B	2,003,000	2.00	3.00	5.00	13.00	23.00
1940B Specimen	—	—	—	—	—	150
1943B	3,526,000	2.00	3.00	5.00	9.00	18.00
1943B Specimen	—	—	—	—	—	150
1944B	6,225,000	2.00	3.00	5.00	9.00	16.00
1944B Specimen	—	—	—	—	—	150
1945B	7,794,000	2.00	3.00	5.00	9.00	18.00
1945B Specimen	—	—	—	—	—	150
1946B	2,539,000	2.00	3.00	5.00	13.00	22.00
1946B Specimen	—	—	—	—	—	150
1947B	624,000	2.50	3.00	7.00	20.00	32.00
1947B Specimen	—	—	—	—	—	150
1952B	2,853,000	2.00	3.00	5.00	8.00	12.00
1952B Specimen	—	—	—	—	—	120
1953B	786,000	2.50	3.00	7.00	20.00	32.00
1953B Specimen	—	—	—	—	—	120
1955B	194,000	3.00	4.00	12.00	28.00	45.00
1955B Specimen	—	—	—	—	—	150
1956B	2,500,000	—	—	3.00	6.50	10.00
1956B Specimen	—	—	—	—	—	90.00
1957B	6,421,000	—	—	3.00	6.50	10.00
1957B Specimen	—	—	—	—	—	45.00
1958B	3,580,000	—	—	3.00	6.50	10.00
1958B Specimen	—	—	—	—	—	45.00
1959B	1,859,000	—	—	3.00	6.50	10.00
1959B Specimen	—	—	—	—	—	45.00
1960B	3,523,000	—	—	2.00	6.00	10.00
1960B Specimen	—	—	—	—	—	45.00
1961B	6,549,000	—	—	2.50	6.50	10.00
1961B Specimen	—	—	—	—	—	45.00
1962B	6,220,000	—	—	2.50	6.00	10.00
1962B Specimen	—	—	—	—	—	45.00
1963B	13,476,000	—	—	2.50	6.00	9.00
1963B Specimen	—	—	—	—	—	45.00
1964B	12,560,000	—	—	2.50	6.00	9.00
1964B Specimen	—	—	—	—	—	45.00
1965B	5,032,000	—	—	2.50	6.00	9.00
1965B Specimen	—	—	—	—	—	45.00
1966B	3,032,000	—	—	2.50	6.00	9.00
1966B Specimen	—	—	—	—	—	45.00
1967B	2,088,000	—	—	2.50	6.00	9.00
1967B Specimen	—	—	—	—	—	45.00

KM# 24a.1 FRANC
4.4000 g., Copper-Nickel, 23.1 mm. **Obv:** Standing Helvetia with lance and shield within star border **Rev:** Value within wreath **Edge:** Reeded

Date	Mintage	F	VF	XF	Unc	BU
1968	15,000,000	—	—	1.00	3.00	5.00
1968B	40,864,000	—	—	—	3.00	5.00
1969B	37,598,000	—	—	—	3.00	5.00
1970	24,240,000	—	—	—	3.00	5.00
1971	11,496,000	—	—	—	3.00	5.00
1973	5,000,000	—	—	—	4.00	7.00
1974	15,012,000	—	—	—	3.00	5.00
1974 Proof	2,400	Value: 85.00				
1975	13,012,000	—	—	—	3.00	5.00
1975 Proof	10,000	Value: 7.00				
1976	5,009,000	—	—	—	4.00	7.00
1976 Proof	5,130	Value: 8.00				
1977	6,019,000	—	—	—	4.00	7.00
1977 Proof	7,030	Value: 8.00				
1978	13,548,000	—	—	—	3.00	5.00
1978 Proof	10,000	Value: 7.00				
1979	10,800,000	—	—	—	3.00	5.00
1979 Proof	10,000	Value: 7.00				
1980	11,002,000	—	—	—	3.00	5.00

Date	Mintage	F	VF	XF	Unc	BU
1980 Proof	10,000	Value: 7.00				
1981	18,013,000	—	—	—	3.00	5.00
1981 Proof	10,000	Value: 7.00				

KM# 24a.2 FRANC
4.4000 g., Copper-Nickel, 23.1 mm. **Obv:** 22 Stars around figure **Rev:** Value and date within wreath **Note:** Medal alignment.

Date	Mintage	F	VF	XF	Unc	BU
1982	15,039,000	—	—	—	3.50	6.00
1982 Proof	10,000	Value: 8.00				

KM# 24a.3 FRANC
4.4000 g., Copper-Nickel, 23.1 mm. **Obv:** 23 Stars around figure **Rev:** Value and date within wreath **Edge:** Reeded

Date	Mintage	F	VF	XF	Unc	BU
1983	7,018,000	—	—	—	3.00	5.00
1983 Proof	11,000	Value: 7.00				
1984	3,028,000	—	—	—	3.00	5.00
1984 Proof	14,000	Value: 7.00				
1985	20,042,000	—	—	—	3.00	5.00
1985 Proof	12,000	Value: 7.00				
1986B	17,997,000	—	—	—	3.00	5.00
1986B Proof	10,000	Value: 7.00				
1987B	17,028,000	—	—	—	3.00	5.00
1987B Proof	8,800	Value: 7.00				
1988B	18,029,000	—	—	—	3.00	5.00
1988B Proof	9,000	Value: 7.00				
1989B	15,031,000	—	—	—	3.00	5.00
1989B Proof	8,800	Value: 7.00				
1990B	2,032,000	—	—	—	4.00	7.00
1990B Proof	8,900	Value: 7.00				
1991B	9,036,000	—	—	—	3.00	5.00
1991B Proof	9,900	Value: 7.00				
1992B	12,028,000	—	—	—	3.00	5.00
1992B Proof	7,450	Value: 7.00				
1993B	12,023,000	—	—	—	3.00	5.00
1993B Proof	6,200	Value: 8.00				
1994B	10,023,000	—	—	—	3.00	5.00
1994B Proof	6,100	Value: 8.00				
1995B	13,024,000	—	—	—	3.00	5.00
1995B Proof	6,100	Value: 8.00				
1996B	3,023,000	—	—	—	3.50	6.00
1996B Proof	6,100	Value: 8.00				
1997B	3,022,000	—	—	—	3.50	6.00
1997B Proof	5,500	Value: 8.00				
1998B	3,021,000	—	—	—	3.50	6.00
1998B Proof	4,800	Value: 8.00				
1999B	3,021,000	—	—	—	3.50	6.00
1999B Proof	5,000	Value: 8.00				
2000B	4,026,000	—	—	—	3.50	6.00
2000B Proof	5,500	Value: 8.00				

KM# 21 2 FRANCS
10.0000 g., 0.8350 Silver 0.2684 oz. ASW, 27.5 mm. **Obv:** Standing Helvetia with lance and shield within star border **Rev:** Value, date within wreath **Edge:** Reeded

Date	Mintage	F	VF	XF	Unc	BU
1901B	50,000	80.00	150	2,000	7,500	11,000
1901B Specimen	—	—	—	—	—	50,000
1903B	300,000	4.50	10.00	100	700	1,200
1903B Specimen	—	—	—	—	—	4,000
1904B	200,000	8.00	20.00	275	1,400	2,300
1904B Specimen	—	—	—	—	—	7,500
1905B	300,000	4.50	10.00	85.00	700	1,200
1905B Specimen	—	—	—	—	—	4,500
1906B	400,000	4.00	8.00	125	650	1,000
1906B Specimen	—	—	—	—	—	4,000
1907B	400,000	4.50	12.00	200	1,250	2,000
1907B Specimen	—	—	—	—	—	6,000
1908B	200,000	6.00	15.00	450	1,600	2,700
1908B Specimen	—	—	—	—	—	8,000
1909B	300,000	5.00	12.00	75.00	450	850
1909B Specimen	—	—	—	—	—	5,000
1910B	250,000	5.00	9.00	175	800	1,400
1910B Specimen	—	—	—	—	—	6,000
1911B	400,000	5.00	7.00	60.00	275	500
1911B Specimen	—	—	—	—	—	2,500
1912B	400,000	5.00	7.00	60.00	175	300
1912B Specimen	—	—	—	—	—	2,000
1913B	300,000	5.00	7.00	70.00	250	400
1913B Specimen	—	—	—	—	—	2,500

Date	Mintage	F	VF	XF	Unc	BU
1914B	1,000,000	5.00	6.00	25.00	175	250
1914B Specimen	—	—	—	—	—	2,000
1916B	250,000	5.00	9.00	165	600	1,000
1916B Specimen	—	—	—	—	—	3,000
1920B	2,300,000	5.00	6.00	12.00	40.00	75.00
1920B Specimen	—	—	—	—	—	750
1921B	2,000,000	5.00	6.00	10.00	40.00	75.00
1921B Specimen	—	—	—	—	—	750
1922B	400,000	5.00	6.00	35.00	275	450
1922B Specimen	—	—	—	—	—	2,000
1928B	750,000	5.00	6.00	12.00	40.00	75.00
1928B Specimen	—	—	—	—	—	750
1931B	500,000	5.00	6.00	15.00	40.00	90.00
1931B Specimen	—	—	—	—	—	700
1932B	250,000	5.00	6.00	35.00	250	500
1932B Specimen	—	—	—	—	—	1,200
1936B	250,000	5.00	6.00	24.00	150	250
1936B Specimen	—	—	—	—	—	750
1937B	250,000	5.00	6.00	18.00	100	165
1937B Specimen	—	—	—	—	—	600
1939B	1,455,000	BV	5.00	9.00	15.00	25.00
1939B Specimen	—	—	—	—	—	1,250
1940B	2,503,000	BV	5.00	9.00	15.00	25.00
1940B Specimen	—	—	—	—	—	180
1941B	1,192,000	BV	5.00	9.00	20.00	32.00
1941B Specimen	—	—	—	—	—	180
1943B	2,089,000	BV	5.00	9.00	20.00	32.00
1943B Specimen	—	—	—	—	—	180
1944B	6,276,000	BV	5.00	9.00	13.00	20.00
1944B Specimen	—	—	—	—	—	180
1945B	1,134,000	BV	5.00	15.00	30.00	50.00
1945B Specimen	—	—	—	—	—	180
1946B	1,629,000	BV	5.00	15.00	25.00	45.00
1946B Specimen	—	—	—	—	—	180
1947B	500,000	BV	6.00	15.00	40.00	65.00
1947B Specimen	—	—	—	—	—	180
1948B	920,000	BV	5.00	14.00	20.00	30.00
1948B Specimen	—	—	—	—	—	180
1953B	438,000	BV	5.00	14.00	45.00	70.00
1953B Specimen	—	—	—	—	—	200
1955B	1,032,000	BV	5.00	8.00	15.00	27.00
1955B Specimen	—	—	—	—	—	150
1957B	2,298,000	BV	5.00	8.00	12.00	21.00
1957B Specimen	—	—	—	—	—	60.00
1958B	650,000	BV	5.00	8.00	12.00	21.00
1958B Specimen	—	—	—	—	—	60.00
1959B	2,905,000	BV	5.00	8.00	12.00	22.00
1959B Specimen	—	—	—	—	—	60.00
1960B	1,980,000	BV	5.00	8.00	12.00	22.00
1960B Specimen	—	—	—	—	—	60.00
1961B	4,653,000	BV	5.00	7.50	8.00	13.00
1961B Specimen	—	—	—	—	—	60.00
1963B	8,030,000	BV	5.00	7.50	8.00	13.00
1963B Specimen	—	—	—	—	—	60.00
1964B	4,558,000	BV	5.00	7.50	8.00	13.00
1964B Specimen	—	—	—	—	—	60.00
1965B	8,526,000	BV	5.00	7.50	8.00	13.00
1965B Specimen	—	—	—	—	—	60.00
1967B	4,132,000	BV	5.00	7.50	8.00	13.00
1967B Specimen	—	—	—	—	—	60.00

KM# 21a.1 2 FRANCS
8.8000 g., Copper-Nickel, 27.4 mm. **Obv:** Standing Helvetia with lance and shield within star border **Rev:** Value within wreath **Edge:** Reeded

Date	Mintage	F	VF	XF	Unc	BU
1968	10,000,000	—	—	—	5.00	8.00
1968B	31,588,000	—	—	—	5.00	8.00
1969B	17,296,000	—	—	—	5.00	8.00
1970	10,350,000	—	—	—	5.00	8.00
1972	5,003,000	—	—	—	5.00	8.00
1973	5,996,000	—	—	—	5.00	8.00
1974	15,009,000	—	—	—	5.00	8.00
1974 Proof	2,400	Value: 85.00				
1975	7,061,000	—	—	—	5.00	8.00
1975 Proof	10,000	Value: 12.00				
1976	5,011,000	—	—	—	5.00	8.00
1976 Proof	5,130	Value: 15.00				
1977	2,010,000	—	—	—	6.00	10.00
1977 Proof	7,030	Value: 15.00				
1978	12,812,000	—	—	—	5.00	8.00
1978 Proof	10,000	Value: 12.00				
1979	10,995,000	—	—	—	5.00	8.00
1979 Proof	10,000	Value: 12.00				
1980	10,001,000	—	—	—	5.00	8.00
1980 Proof	10,000	Value: 12.00				
1981	13,852,000	—	—	—	5.00	8.00
1981 Proof	10,000	Value: 12.00				

KM# 21a.2   2 FRANCS
8.8000 g., Copper-Nickel, 27.4 mm. **Obv:** 22 Stars around figure
Rev: Value within wreath **Note:** Medal alignment.

Date	Mintage	F	VF	XF	Unc	BU
1982	5,912,000	—	—	—	5.00	8.00
1982 Proof	10,000	Value: 15.00				

KM# 21a.3   2 FRANCS
8.8000 g., Copper-Nickel, 27.4 mm. **Obv:** 23 Stars around figure
Rev: Value within wreath **Edge:** Reeded

Date	Mintage	F	VF	XF	Unc	BU
1983	3,023,000	—	—	—	5.00	8.00
1983 Proof	11,000	Value: 12.00				
1984	2,029,000	—	—	—	5.00	8.00
1984 Proof	14,000	Value: 12.00				
1985	2,022,000	—	—	—	5.00	8.00
1985 Proof	12,000	Value: 12.00				
1986B	3,032,000	—	—	—	5.00	8.00
1986B Proof	10,000	Value: 12.00				
1987B	8,028,000	—	—	—	5.00	8.00
1987B Proof	8,800	Value: 15.00				
1988B	10,029,000	—	—	—	5.00	8.00
1988B Proof	9,000	Value: 12.00				
1989B	8,031,000	—	—	—	5.00	8.00
1989B Proof	8,800	Value: 12.00				
1990B	5,045,000	—	—	—	5.00	8.00
1990B Proof	8,900	Value: 12.00				
1991B	12,036,000	—	—	—	4.00	7.00
1991B Proof	9,900	Value: 12.00				
1992B	10,028,000	—	—	—	4.00	7.00
1992B Proof	7,450	Value: 15.00				
1993B	13,050,000	—	—	—	4.00	7.00
1993B Proof	6,200	Value: 15.00				
1994B	16,023,000	—	—	—	4.00	7.00
1994B Proof	6,100	Value: 15.00				
1995B	7,024,000	—	—	—	4.00	7.00
1995B Proof	6,100	Value: 15.00				
1996B	5,023,000	—	—	—	5.00	8.00
1996B Proof	6,100	Value: 15.00				
1997B	5,022,000	—	—	—	5.00	8.00
1997B Proof	5,500	Value: 15.00				
1998B	4,021,000	—	—	—	5.00	8.00
1998B Proof	4,800	Value: 15.00				
1999B	3,021,000	—	—	—	5.00	8.00
1999B Proof	5,000	Value: 15.00				
2000B	3,026,000	—	—	—	5.00	8.00
2000B Proof	5,500	Value: 15.00				

KM# 34   5 FRANCS
25.0000 g., 0.9000 Silver 0.7234 oz. ASW, 37 mm.
Obv: Laureate head left **Obv. Leg.:** CONFOEDERATIO
HELVETICA **Rev:** Shield divides value within wreath, star above

Date	Mintage	F	VF	XF	Unc	BU
1904B	40,000	350	700	1,500	3,500	6,000
1904B Specimen	—	—	—	—	—	10,000
1907B	277,000	75.00	150	300	850	1,400
1907B Specimen	—	—	—	—	—	5,000
1908B	200,000	125	160	400	900	1,500
1908B Specimen	—	—	—	—	—	5,000
1909B	120,000	175	250	450	1,200	2,000
1909B Specimen	—	—	—	—	—	5,000
1912B	11,000	2,000	3,500	4,500	7,000	12,500
1912B Specimen	—	—	—	—	—	17,500

Date	Mintage	F	VF	XF	Unc	BU
1916B	22,000	700	1,300	1,900	2,600	4,000
1916B Specimen	—	—	—	—	—	9,000

KM# 37   5 FRANCS
25.0000 g., 0.9000 Silver 0.7234 oz. ASW, 37 mm. **Obv:** William
Tell right **Rev:** Shield flanked by sprigs

Date	Mintage	F	VF	XF	Unc	BU
1922B	2,400,000	50.00	75.00	110	250	400
1922B	Inc. above	—	—	1,500	2,250	3,000
	Note: Dot between Confoederatio and Helvetica					
1922B Specimen	—	—	—	—	—	3,000
1923B	11,300,000	30.00	50.00	95.00	175	350
1923B Specimen	—	—	—	—	—	3,000

KM# 38   5 FRANCS
25.0000 g., 0.9000 Silver 0.7234 oz. ASW, 37 mm. **Obv:** William
Tell right **Rev:** Shield flanked by sprigs

Date	Mintage	F	VF	XF	Unc	BU
1924B	182,000	250	350	650	1,000	1,800
1924B Specimen	—	—	—	—	—	3,500
1925B	2,830,000	50.00	90.00	115	225	400
1925B Specimen	—	—	—	—	—	1,500
1926B	2,000,000	60.00	120	160	275	450
1926B Specimen	—	—	—	—	—	1,500
1928B	24,000	4,000	8,000	12,000	15,000	20,000
1928B Specimen; Rare	—	—	—	—	—	—

KM# 40   5 FRANCS
15.0000 g., 0.8350 Silver 0.4027 oz. ASW, 31.5 mm.
Obv: William Tell right **Rev:** Shield flanked by sprigs
Edge: Lettered; two variations **Edge:** Lettering starts with vertical
dividing line and group of three stars. Type I; "3 stars/DOMINUS/
PROVIDEBIT/10 stars" Type II; "3 stars/DOMINUS/10 stars/
PROVIDEBIT" **Note:** Raised edge lettering.

Date	Mintage	F	VF	XF	Unc	BU
1931B	3,520,000	BV	8.00	28.00	80.00	150
	Note: Edge lettering type I starts at 6 o'clock					
1931B	Inc. above	—	50.00	90.00	250	400
	Note: Edge lettering type II starts at 6 o'clock					
1931B Specimen	Inc. above	—	—	—	—	2,000
	Note: Edge lettering type I starts at 6 o'clock					
1931B	Inc. above	—	16.00	45.00	80.00	150
	Note: Edge lettering type I starts at 2 o'clock					
1931B	Inc. above	—	1,200	1,500	2,000	3,000
	Note: Edge lettering type II starts at 10 o'clock					
1932B	10,580,000	BV	8.00	12.00	26.00	45.00
1932B Specimen	—	—	—	—	—	600
1933B	5,900,000	BV	8.00	13.00	26.00	45.00
1933B Specimen	—	—	—	—	—	600
1935B	3,000,000	BV	9.00	18.00	45.00	65.00
1935B Specimen	—	—	—	—	—	650
1937B	645,000	BV	9.00	18.00	60.00	85.00
1937B Specimen	—	—	—	—	—	900
1939B	2,197,000	BV	9.00	15.00	26.00	40.00
1939B Specimen	—	—	—	—	—	500
1940B	1,601,000	BV	9.00	20.00	50.00	80.00
1940B Specimen	—	—	—	—	—	750

Date	Mintage	F	VF	XF	Unc	BU
1948B	416,000	BV	10.00	22.00	60.00	85.00
1948B Specimen	—	—	—	—	—	700
1949B	407,000	BV	10.00	22.00	65.00	100
1949B Specimen	—	—	—	—	—	700
1950B	482,000	BV	10.00	22.00	50.00	80.00
1950B Specimen	—	—	—	—	—	600
1951B	1,096,000	BV	9.00	16.00	35.00	55.00
1951B Specimen	—	—	—	—	—	350
1952B	155,000	20.00	40.00	80.00	150	250
1952B Specimen	—	—	—	—	—	800
1953B	3,403,000	BV	8.00	15.00	18.00	25.00
1953B Specimen	—	—	—	—	—	150
1954B	6,600,000	BV	8.00	12.00	16.00	22.00
1954B Specimen	—	—	—	—	—	150
1965B	5,021,000	BV	8.00	10.00	13.00	20.00
1965B Specimen	—	—	—	—	—	120
1966B	9,016,000	BV	7.00	8.00	10.00	14.00
1966B Specimen	—	—	—	—	—	120
1967B	13,817,000	BV	7.00	8.00	10.00	14.00
	Note: Edge lettering type I starts at 6 o'clock					
1967B Specimen	—	—	—	—	—	120
	Note: Edge lettering type I starting at 6 o'clock					
1967B	Inc. above	35.00	70.00	100	165	250
	Note: Edge lettering type II starts at 2 o'clock					
1969B	8,637,000	BV	7.00	8.00	10.00	14.00
1969B Specimen	—	—	—	—	—	120

KM# A48   5 FRANCS
Gold

Date	Mintage	F	VF	XF	Unc	BU
1948B	Est. 50	—	—	—	15,000	

KM# 40a.1   5 FRANCS
13.2000 g., Copper-Nickel, 31.3 mm. **Obv:** William Tell right
Rev: Shield flanked by sprigs **Edge:** DOMINUS PROVIDEBIT

Date	Mintage	F	VF	XF	Unc	BU
1968B	33,871,000	—	—	—	8.00	12.00
1970	6,306,000	—	—	—	8.00	12.00
1973	5,002,000	—	—	—	8.00	12.00
1974	6,007,000	—	—	—	8.00	12.00
1974 Proof	2,400	Value: 125				
1975	4,015,000	—	—	—	8.00	12.00
1975 Proof	10,000	Value: 20.00				
1976	3,007,000	—	—	—	8.00	12.00
1976 Proof	5,130	Value: 20.00				
1977	2,009,000	—	—	—	8.00	12.00
1977 Proof	7,030	Value: 20.00				
1978	4,411,000	—	—	—	8.00	12.00
1978 Proof	10,000	Value: 16.00				
1979	4,011,000	—	—	—	8.00	12.00
1979 Proof	10,000	Value: 16.00				
1980	4,026,000	—	—	—	8.00	12.00
1980 Proof	10,000	Value: 16.00				
1981	6,018,000	—	—	—	8.00	12.00
1981 Proof	10,000	Value: 16.00				

KM# 40a.2   5 FRANCS
13.2000 g., Copper-Nickel, 31.3 mm. **Obv:** William Tell right
Rev: Cross on shield flanked by sprigs **Note:** Medal alignment.

Date	Mintage	F	VF	XF	Unc	BU
1982	5,050,000	—	—	—	8.00	12.00
1982 Proof	10,000	Value: 20.00				
1983	4,033,000	—	—	—	8.00	12.00
1983 Proof	11,000	Value: 20.00				
1984	3,953,000	—	—	—	8.00	12.00
1984 Proof	14,000	Value: 16.00				

KM# 40a.3   5 FRANCS
13.2000 g., Copper-Nickel, 31.3 mm. **Obv:** William Tell right
Rev: Shield flanked by sprigs **Note:** Incuse edge lettering. Retired
legal tender status as of January 1, 2004, 1985-1993 removed
from circulation.

Date	Mintage	F	VF	XF	Unc	BU
1985	4,050,000	—	—	—	8.00	12.00
1985 Proof	12,000	Value: 16.00				
1986B	7,083,000	—	—	—	8.00	12.00
1986B Proof	10,000	Value: 16.00				
1987B	7,028,000	—	—	—	8.00	12.00
1987B Proof	8,800	Value: 20.00				
1988B	7,029,000	—	—	—	8.00	12.00
1988B Proof	9,000	Value: 20.00				
1989B	5,031,000	—	—	—	8.00	12.00
1989B Proof	8,800	Value: 20.00				
1990B	1,049,000	—	—	—	8.00	12.00
1990B Proof	8,900	Value: 20.00				
1991B	26,100	—	—	—	—	150
	Note: In sets only; 5,000,000 were minted and destroyed					
1991B Proof	9,900	Value: 175				
1992B	5,035,000	—	—	—	8.00	12.00
1992B Proof	7,450	Value: 20.00				

Date	Mintage	F	VF	XF	Unc	BU
1993B Variety 1 closed shirt	16,400	—	—	—	—	150

Note: In sets only; 5,000,000 were minted and destroyed

Date	Mintage	F	VF	XF	Unc	BU
1993B Variety 2 open shirt	Inc. above	—	—	—	—	150
1993B Proof	6,200	Value: 175				

KM# 40a.4   5 FRANCS
13.2000 g., Copper-Nickel, 31.3 mm.   **Obv:** William Tell right **Rev:** Shield flanked by sprigs **Edge:** DOMINUS PROVIDEBIT and 13 stars raised

Date	Mintage	F	VF	XF	Unc	BU
1994B	12,023,000	—	—	—	8.00	12.00
1994B Proof	6,100	Value: 20.00				
1995B	12,024,000	—	—	—	8.00	12.00
1995B Proof	6,100	Value: 20.00				
1996B	12,023,000	—	—	—	8.00	12.00
1996B Proof	6,100	Value: 20.00				
1997B	9,022,000	—	—	—	8.00	12.00
1997B Proof	5,500	Value: 20.00				
1998B	9,021,000	—	—	—	8.00	12.00
1998B Proof	4,800	Value: 22.50				
1999B	9,021,000	—	—	—	8.00	12.00
1999B Proof	5,000	Value: 22.50				
2000B	7,026,000	—	—	—	8.00	12.00
2000B Proof	5,500	Value: 20.00				

KM# 36   10 FRANCS
3.2258 g., 0.9000 Gold 0.0933 oz. AGW   **Obv:** Young bust left **Rev:** Radiant cross above date and sprigs

Date	Mintage	F	VF	XF	Unc	BU
1911B	100,000	125	225	325	400	600
1912B	200,000	BV	115	120	165	180
1913B	600,000	BV	85.00	100	130	150
1914B	200,000	BV	100	115	135	160
1915B	400,000	BV	95.00	110	130	155
1916B	130,000	BV	115	120	165	190
1922B	1,020,000	—	—	BV	95.00	110

KM# 35.1   20 FRANCS
6.4516 g., 0.9000 Gold 0.1867 oz. AGW   **Obv:** Young head left **Obv. Leg.:** HELVETIA **Rev:** Shield within oak branches divides value

Date	Mintage	F	VF	XF	Unc	BU
1901B	500,000	—	BV	170	185	210
1902B	600,000	—	BV	170	185	210
1903B	200,000	BV	170	185	210	235
1904B	100,000	—	195	215	245	325
1905B	100,000	—	190	210	235	325
1906B	100,000	BV	180	185	215	235
1907B	150,000	—	BV	175	195	220
1908B	355,000	—	BV	170	180	210
1909B	400,000	—	BV	170	180	210
1910B	375,000	—	BV	170	180	210
1911B	350,000	—	BV	170	180	210
1912B	450,000	—	BV	170	180	210
1913B	700,000	—	BV	170	180	200
1914B	700,000	—	BV	170	180	200
1915B	750,000	—	BV	170	180	200
1916B	300,000	—	BV	170	180	210
1922B	2,783,678	—	—	BV	170	190
1925B	400,000	—	BV	170	180	200
1926B	50,000	—	175	195	210	235
1927B	5,015,000	—	—	BV	170	190
1930B	3,371,764	—	—	BV	170	190
1935B	175,000	—	165	175	185	215
1935L-B	20,008,813	—	—	BV	160	180

Note: The 1935L-B issue was struck in 1945, 1946 and 1947

KM# 35.2   20 FRANCS
6.4516 g., 0.9000 Gold 0.1867 oz. AGW   **Obv:** Bust left **Rev:** Shield within oak branches divides value **Edge:** AD LEGEM ANNI MCMXXXI

Date	Mintage	F	VF	XF	Unc	BU
1947B	9,200,000	—	—	BV	170	190
1949B	10,000,000	—	—	BV	170	190

KM# 49   25 FRANCS
5.6450 g., 0.9000 Gold 0.1633 oz. AGW   **Obv:** Value above small cross **Rev:** William Tell with bow **Note:** Not available in commercial channels.

Date	Mintage	F	VF	XF	Unc	BU
1955B	5,000,000	—	—	—	—	—
1958B	5,000,000	—	—	—	—	—
1959B	5,000,000	—	—	—	—	—

KM# 50   50 FRANCS
11.2900 g., 0.9000 Gold 0.3267 oz. AGW   **Obv:** Value above small cross **Rev:** Three standing figures facing **Note:** Not available in commercial channels.

Date	Mintage	F	VF	XF	Unc	BU
1955B	2,000,000	—	—	—	—	—
1958B	2,000,000	—	—	—	—	—
1959B	2,000,000	—	—	—	—	—

KM# 39   100 FRANCS
32.2581 g., 0.9000 Gold 0.9334 oz. AGW   **Obv:** Young bust left **Rev:** Radiant cross above value, date and sprigs

Date	Mintage	F	VF	XF	Unc	BU
1925B	5,000	—	6,000	7,500	9,000	12,500

COMMEMORATIVE COINAGE

KM# 41   5 FRANCS
15.0000 g., 0.8350 Silver 0.4027 oz. ASW, 31 mm.   **Subject:** Confederation Armament Fund **Obv:** Kneeling female figure holding sword and dove right **Rev:** Inscription within square flanked by oak leaves **Edge:** DOMINUS PROVIDEBIT (stars)

Date	Mintage	F	VF	XF	Unc	BU
1936B	130,000	—	10.00	15.00	25.00	40.00
1936B Specimen	—	—	—	—	—	300

KM# 42   5 FRANCS
15.0000 g., 0.8350 Silver 0.4027 oz. ASW, 31 mm.   **Subject:** 600th Anniversary - Battle of Laupen **Obv:** Seated hooded figure facing right **Rev:** Cross, date and value **Edge:** DOMINUS PROVIDEBIT (stars)

Date	Mintage	F	VF	XF	Unc	BU
1939B	30,600	—	250	350	400	500

KM# 43   5 FRANCS
15.0000 g., 0.8350 Silver 0.4027 oz. ASW, 31 mm.   **Subject:** Zurich Exposition **Obv:** Small cross on shield above inscription **Rev:** Shaking hands below standing figures with horse

Date	Mintage	F	VF	XF	Unc	BU
1939B	60,000	—	35.00	60.00	80.00	120
Note: Minted at Huguenin, Le Locle						
1939 Specimen	—	—	—	—	—	900
1939B Matte	Est. 250	—	—	1,750	2,150	2,450

KM# 44   5 FRANCS
15.0000 g., 0.8350 Silver 0.4027 oz. ASW, 31 mm.   **Subject:** 650th Anniversary of Confederation **Obv:** Three standing figures representing the original cantons of Uri, Schwyz and Unterwalden **Rev:** Small cross divides dates above inscription **Edge:** DOMINUS PROVIDEBIT (stars)

Date	Mintage	F	VF	XF	Unc	BU
ND(1941)B	100,150	—	—	25.00	40.00	55.00	75.00
ND(1941)B Specimen	—	—	—	—	—	360

KM# 45   5 FRANCS
15.0000 g., 0.8350 Silver 0.4027 oz. ASW, 31 mm.   **Subject:** 500th Anniversary - Battle of St. Jakob An Der Birs **Obv:** Kneeling figure looking right **Rev:** Small cross above inscription **Edge:** DOMINUS PROVIDEBIT (stars)

Date	Mintage	F	VF	XF	Unc	BU
1944B	101,680	—	20.00	30.00	50.00	70.00
1944B Specimen	—	—	—	—	—	360

KM# 48   5 FRANCS
15.0000 g., 0.8350 Silver 0.4027 oz. ASW, 31 mm.
Subject: Swiss Constitution Centennial **Obv:** Seated woman and child facing left **Rev:** Small cross divides date below inscription

Date	Mintage	F	VF	XF	Unc	BU
1948B	500,400	—	8.00	10.00	15.00	20.00
1948B Specimen	—	—	—	—	—	150

KM# 51   5 FRANCS
Silver, 31 mm.   **Subject:** Red Cross Centennial **Obv:** Value **Rev:** Nurse standing, patient on stretcher, motif forming a cross

Date	Mintage	F	VF	XF	Unc	BU
ND(1963)B	623,000	—	8.00	10.00	15.00	20.00
ND(1963)B Specimen	—	—	—	—	—	120

KM# 52   5 FRANCS
13.2000 g., Copper-Nickel, 31.3 mm.   **Subject:** 100th Anniversary - Revision of Constitution **Obv:** Dates flanked by vertical inscriptions **Rev:** Three standing female figures and cross

Date	Mintage	F	VF	XF	Unc	BU
ND(1974)	3,709,000	—	—	—	7.00	9.00
ND(1974) Proof	130,000	Value: 16.00				

KM# 53   5 FRANCS
13.2000 g., Copper-Nickel, 31.3 mm.   **Subject:** European Monument Protection Year **Obv:** Value and inscription **Rev:** Date above inscription flanked by hands

Date	Mintage	F	VF	XF	Unc	BU
1975	2,500,000	—	—	—	8.00	10.00
1975 Proof	60,000	Value: 26.00				

KM# 54   5 FRANCS
13.2000 g., Copper-Nickel, 31.3 mm.   **Subject:** 500th Anniversary - Battle of Murten **Obv:** Value **Rev:** Stylized figures

Date	Mintage	F	VF	XF	Unc	BU
1976	1,506,000	—	—	—	8.00	11.00
1976 Proof	100,900	Value: 22.00				

KM# 55   5 FRANCS
13.2000 g., Copper-Nickel, 31.3 mm.   **Subject:** 150th Anniversary - Death of Johann Pestalozzi **Obv:** Value and cross at center **Rev:** Hooded head left

Date	Mintage	F	VF	XF	Unc	BU
1977	802,000	—	—	—	9.00	12.00
1977 Proof	50,260	Value: 22.00				

KM# 56   5 FRANCS
13.2000 g., Copper-Nickel, 31.3 mm.   **Subject:** 150th Anniversary - Birth of Henry Dunant, founder of the International Red Cross **Obv:** Value and date **Rev:** Head facing

Date	Mintage	F	VF	XF	Unc	BU
1978	903,000	—	—	—	8.00	11.00
1978 Proof	60,000	Value: 22.00				

KM# 57   5 FRANCS
13.2000 g., Copper-Nickel, 31.3 mm.   **Subject:** Centennial - Birth of Albert Einstein **Obv:** Inscription, value and date **Rev:** Head facing

Date	Mintage	F	VF	XF	Unc	BU
1979	900,000	—	—	—	10.00	14.00
1979 Proof	35,000	Value: 45.00				

KM# 58   5 FRANCS
13.2000 g., Copper-Nickel, 31.3 mm.   **Subject:** Centennial - Birth of Albert Einstein **Obv:** Inscription above value **Rev:** Formulas

Date	Mintage	F	VF	XF	Unc	BU
1979	902,000	—	—	—	10.00	14.00
1979 Proof	35,000	Value: 45.00				

KM# 59   5 FRANCS
13.2000 g., Copper-Nickel, 31.3 mm.   **Subject:** Ferdinand Hodler - Painter **Obv:** Value above legend and date **Rev:** Head facing

Date	Mintage	F	VF	XF	Unc	BU
1980	951,000	—	—	—	12.00	20.00
1980 Proof	50,000	Value: 20.00				

KM# 60   5 FRANCS
13.2000 g., Copper-Nickel, 31.3 mm.   **Subject:** 500th Anniversary - Stans Convention of 1481 **Obv:** Value and date **Rev:** Stylized design

Date	Mintage	F	VF	XF	Unc	BU
1981	950,000	—	—	—	10.00	16.00
1981 Proof	50,260	Value: 14.00				

KM# 61   5 FRANCS
13.2000 g., Copper-Nickel, 31.3 mm.   **Subject:** 100th Anniversary - Gotthard Railway **Obv:** Value and date above sprigs **Rev:** Stylized design **Edge:** Lettering in relief **Edge:** DOMINUS PROVIDEBIT (stars)

Date	Mintage	F	VF	XF	Unc	BU
1982	1,105,000	—	—	—	8.00	11.00
1982 Proof	65,110	Value: 16.00				

KM# 62   5 FRANCS
13.2000 g., Copper-Nickel, 31.3 mm.   **Subject:** 100th Anniversary - Birth of Ernest Ansermet **Obv:** Value and date **Rev:** Music notes within head right

Date	Mintage	F	VF	XF	Unc	BU
1983	951,000	—	—	—	8.00	11.00
1983 Proof	60,160	Value: 17.00				

KM# 63   5 FRANCS
13.2000 g., Copper-Nickel, 31.3 mm.   **Subject:** Centennial - Birth of Auguste Piccard **Obv:** Value and date **Rev:** Stylized designs

Date	Mintage	F	VF	XF	Unc	BU
1984	1,012,000	—	—	—	8.00	11.00
1984 Proof	75,000	Value: 16.00				

KM# 64   5 FRANCS
13.2000 g., Copper-Nickel, 31.3 mm. **Subject:** European Year of Music **Obv:** Value and vertical inscription **Rev:** Sphere design **Edge:** DOMINUS PROVIDEBIT (stars)

Date	Mintage	F	VF	XF	Unc	BU
1985	1,156,000	—	—	—	7.00	9.00
1985 Proof	84,000	Value: 14.00				

KM# 65   5 FRANCS
13.2000 g., Copper-Nickel, 31.3 mm. **Subject:** 500th Anniversary - Battle of Sempach **Obv:** Cross above inscription and date **Rev:** Stylized design

Date	Mintage	F	VF	XF	Unc	BU
1986B	1,082,000	—	—	—	7.00	9.00
1986B Proof	75,000	Value: 14.00				

KM# 66   5 FRANCS
13.2000 g., Copper-Nickel, 31.3 mm. **Subject:** 100th Anniversary - Birth of Le Corbusier **Obv:** Value within diamond shape **Rev:** Standing figure within squared design

Date	Mintage	F	VF	XF	Unc	BU
1987B	960,000	—	—	—	8.00	12.00
1987B Proof	62,000	Value: 17.00				

KM# 67   5 FRANCS
13.2000 g., Copper-Nickel, 31.3 mm. **Subject:** Olympics - Dove and Rings **Obv:** Value within entwined circles **Rev:** Stylized dove and circles

Date	Mintage	F	VF	XF	Unc	BU
1988B	1,026,000	—	—	—	8.00	12.00
1988B Proof	68,500	Value: 16.00				

KM# 68   5 FRANCS
13.2000 g., Copper-Nickel, 31.3 mm. **Subject:** General Guisan - 1939 Mobilization **Obv:** Value within cluster of small crosses **Rev:** Stylized head with cap facing 1/4 left

Date	Mintage	F	VF	XF	Unc	BU
1989B	1,270,000	—	—	—	8.00	12.00
1989B Proof	69,000	Value: 16.00				

KM# 69   5 FRANCS
13.2000 g., Copper-Nickel, 31.3 mm. **Subject:** Gottfried Keller **Obv:** Value, inscription and date **Rev:** Bust left

Date	Mintage	F	VF	XF	Unc	BU
1990B	1,100,000	—	—	—	7.00	10.00
1990B Proof	69,400	Value: 16.00				

KM# 86   5 FRANCS
14.9100 g., Bi-Metallic Brass center in Copper-Nickel ring, 33 mm. **Subject:** Wine Festival **Obv:** Value and inscription within circle, assorted rodents around border **Rev:** Grapes within circle

Date	Mintage	F	VF	XF	Unc	BU
1999B	160,000	—	—	—	8.00	12.00
1999B Proof	16,000	Value: 24.00				

KM# 89   5 FRANCS
15.0000 g., Bi-Metallic Brass center in Copper-Nickel ring, 33 mm. **Subject:** Basler Fasnacht **Obv:** Value within circle **Rev:** Costumed flutists within circle **Edge:** Reeded

Date	Mintage	F	VF	XF	Unc	BU
2000B	170,000	—	—	—	8.00	12.00
2000B Proof	20,000	Value: 24.00				

KM# 91   5 FRANCS
15.0000 g., Bi-Metallic Gold center in Copper-Nickel ring, 33 mm. **Subject:** Swiss National Coinage, 150 Years **Obv:** Value within detailed leaf surface showing vein structure **Rev:** Honeycomb design within circle **Edge:** Reeded

Date	Mintage	F	VF	XF	Unc	BU
2000B	150,000	—	—	—	8.00	12.00
2000B Proof	15,000	Value: 22.00				

KM# 70   20 FRANCS
20.0000 g., 0.8350 Silver 0.5369 oz. ASW **Subject:** 700 Years of Confederation **Obv:** Value **Rev:** Dates and designs

Date	Mintage	F	VF	XF	Unc	BU
1991B	672,650	—	—	—	20.00	25.00
1991B Proof	99,800	Value: 28.00				

KM# 72   20 FRANCS
20.0000 g., 0.8350 Silver 0.5369 oz. ASW **Subject:** Gertrud Kurz **Obv:** Vertical inscription and date divides value **Rev:** Horizontal dates and inscription divides barbed wire

Date	Mintage	F	VF	XF	Unc	BU
1992B	188,542	—	—	—	20.00	25.00
1992B Proof	36,000	Value: 28.00				

KM# 73   20 FRANCS
20.0000 g., 0.8350 Silver 0.5369 oz. ASW **Subject:** 500th Anniversary - Birth of Paracelsus **Obv:** Value and date **Rev:** Head 1/4 left

Date	Mintage	F	VF	XF	Unc	BU
1993B	185,120	—	—	—	22.00	28.00
1993B Proof	29,530	Value: 32.00				

KM# 74   20 FRANCS
20.0000 g., 0.8350 Silver 0.5369 oz. ASW **Subject:** Devil's Bridge - Teufelsbrucke **Obv:** Value and date at center of large cross **Rev:** Stylized devil within trees **Edge:** DOMINUS PROVIDEBIT

Date	Mintage	F	VF	XF	Unc	BU
1994B	184,868	—	—	—	22.00	28.00
1994B Proof	32,195	Value: 32.00				

KM# 75   20 FRANCS
20.0000 g., 0.8350 Silver 0.5369 oz. ASW **Subject:** Mythological White Snake Queen **Obv:** Value and date at center of large cross **Rev:** Crowned snake **Edge:** DOMINUS PROVIDEBIT (13 stars)

Date	Mintage	F	VF	XF	Unc	BU
1995B	159,262	—	—	—	22.00	28.00
1995B Proof	30,381	Value: 32.00				

KM# 76   20 FRANCS
20.0000 g., 0.8350 Silver 0.5369 oz. ASW **Subject:** Mythological Giant Boy **Obv:** Value and date at center of large cross **Rev:** Giant's bust facing above trees

Date	Mintage	F	VF	XF	Unc	BU
1996B	118,076	—	—	—	30.00	35.00
1996B Proof	29,424	Value: 35.00				

KM# 77   20 FRANCS
20.0000 g., 0.8350 Silver 0.5369 oz. ASW **Subject:** Mythological Dragon of Breno **Obv:** Value and date at center of large cross **Rev:** Dragon above mountains and water

Date	Mintage	F	VF	XF	Unc	BU
1996B	102,997	—	—	—	22.00	28.00
1996B Proof	26,367	Value: 35.00				

KM# 78   20 FRANCS
20.0000 g., 0.8350 Silver 0.5369 oz. ASW **Subject:** 150th Anniversary - Swiss Railway **Obv:** Modern train wheel **Rev:** Ancient train wheel

Date	Mintage	F	VF	XF	Unc	BU
1997B	166,416	—	—	—	30.00	35.00
1997B Proof	18,997	Value: 45.00				

KM# 79   20 FRANCS
20.0000 g., 0.8350 Silver 0.5369 oz. ASW **Subject:** 200th Anniversary - Birth of Jeremias Gotthelf **Obv:** Stylized numeral value and date **Rev:** Bust facing

Date	Mintage	F	VF	XF	Unc	BU
1997B	104,070	—	—	—	30.00	35.00
1997B Proof	19,494	Value: 45.00				

KM# 80   20 FRANCS
20.0000 g., 0.8350 Silver 0.5369 oz. ASW **Subject:** 200th Anniversary - Helvetian Republic **Obv:** Value and boxed crosses design **Rev:** 1798 coin design within square, crosses flank

Date	Mintage	F	VF	XF	Unc	BU
1998B	72,115	—	—	—	24.00	30.00
1998B Proof	15,284	Value: 50.00				

KM# 82   20 FRANCS
20.0000 g., 0.8350 Silver 0.5369 oz. ASW **Subject:** 150th Anniversary - Confederation **Obv:** Boxed crosses design and value **Rev:** 1848 coin design within square flanked by crosses

Date	Mintage	F	VF	XF	Unc	BU
1998B	75,358	—	—	—	24.00	30.00
1998B Proof	15,500	Value: 50.00				

KM# 84   20 FRANCS
20.0000 g., 0.8350 Silver 0.5369 oz. ASW **Subject:** Death of C.F. Meyer **Obv:** Value and date **Rev:** Large head 3/4 right with signature across face

Date	Mintage	F	VF	XF	Unc	BU
1998B	71,181	—	—	—	24.00	30.00
1998B Proof	14,411	Value: 50.00				

KM# 85   20 FRANCS
20.0000 g., 0.8350 Silver 0.5369 oz. ASW **Subject:** 150th Anniversary Swiss Postal Service **Obv:** Value, country name and date within wreath **Rev:** Cartoon-like postal carrier on top half of globe

Date	Mintage	F	VF	XF	Unc	BU
1999B	138,998	—	—	—	24.00	30.00
1999B Proof	10,325	Value: 50.00				

KM# 87   20 FRANCS
20.0000 g., 0.8350 Silver 0.5369 oz. ASW **Subject:** Battle of Dornach **Obv:** Value and cross design **Rev:** Sword splitting an eagle, boxed crosses around border **Edge:** DOMINUS PROVIDEBIT (13 stars)

Date	Mintage	F	VF	XF	Unc	BU
1999B	64,547	—	—	—	25.00	30.00
1999B Proof	11,000	Value: 50.00				

KM# 90   20 FRANCS
20.0000 g., 0.8350 Silver 0.5369 oz. ASW, 32.7 mm. **Subject:** Year 2000 - Peace on Earth **Obv:** Olive branch **Rev:** Angel floating above people

Date	Mintage	F	VF	XF	Unc	BU
2000B	58,772	—	—	—	30.00	35.00
2000B Proof	9,635	Value: 50.00				

KM# 97   20 FRANCS
20.0000 g., 0.8350 Silver 0.5369 oz. ASW, 32.7 mm. **Subject:** Lumen Christi **Obv:** Inscription above value **Rev:** Jesus preaching within design

Date	Mintage	F	VF	XF	Unc	BU
2000B	45,537	—	—	—	25.00	30.00
2000B Proof	8,111	Value: 50.00				

KM# 81   100 FRANCS
22.5800 g., 0.9000 Gold 0.6533 oz. AGW **Subject:** 200th Anniversary of Helvetian Republic **Obv:** Value and boxed crosses design **Rev:** 1798 coin design within square flanked by crosses

Date	Mintage	F	VF	XF	Unc	BU
1998B Proof	2,500	Value: 900				

KM# 83   100 FRANCS
22.5800 g., 0.9000 Gold 0.6533 oz. AGW **Subject:** 150th Anniversary of Swiss Confederation **Obv:** Value and boxed crosses design **Rev:** 1848 coin design within square flanked by crosses

Date	Mintage	F	VF	XF	Unc	BU
1998B Proof	2,500	Value: 1,000				

KM# 88 100 FRANCS
22.5800 g., 0.9000 Gold 0.6533 oz. AGW **Subject:** Wine Festival **Obv:** Value and small fox looking up at grapes **Rev:** Small fox eating grapes and cresent

Date	Mintage	F	VF	XF	Unc	BU
1999B Proof	3,000	Value: 750				

KM# 96 100 FRANCS
22.5800 g., 0.9000 Gold 0.6533 oz. AGW, 28 mm. **Subject:** 2000 Years of Christianity **Obv:** Inscription and date divides value **Rev:** Stylized baby **Edge:** Lettered

Date	Mintage	F	VF	XF	Unc	BU
2000B Proof	2,130	Value: 750				

KM# 71.1 250 FRANCS
8.0000 g., 0.9000 Gold 0.2315 oz. AGW **Subject:** 700 Years of Confederation **Obv:** Diagonal and horizontal inscription to right of value **Rev:** Dates **Edge:** Plus sign (+) between dates

Date	Mintage	F	VF	XF	Unc	BU
1991B	296,741	—	—	—	235	275

Note: 200,000 recalled and melted due to poor quality

KM# 71.2 250 FRANCS
8.0000 g., 0.9000 Gold 0.2315 oz. AGW **Subject:** 700 Years of Confederation **Edge:** Elongated plus sign between dates

Date	Mintage	F	VF	XF	Unc	BU
1991B	193,259	—	—	—	235	275

COMMEMORATIVE COINAGE
Shooting Festival

The listings which follow have traditionally been categorized in many catalogs as Swiss Shooting Thalers. Technically, all are medallic issues rather than coins, excepting the Solothurn issue of 1855. According to the Swiss Federal Finance Department, the issue was legally equal to the then current-silver 5 Francs issue to which it was identical in design, aside from bearing an edge inscription which read, EIDGEN FREISCHIESSEN SOLOTHURN (National Shooting Fest Solothurn).

For the silver issues of 1855-1885, the presence of the denomination was only intended to indicate these coins were of the same weight and fineness as prescribed for legal tender coins.

Beginning with the issues of 1934, denominations and sizes were no longer the same as regular Swiss legal tender issues. These coins all have legends indicating that they could only be redeemed during and at the shooting fest of issue.

Exceptional quality BU examples for 1934 and 1939 will command a premium over the prices listed.

X# S18 5 FRANCS
0.8350 Silver **Subject:** Federal Festival in Fribourg **Note:** Prev. KM#S18.

Date	Mintage	F	VF	XF	Unc	BU
1934B Matte	650	—	200	300	450	650
1934B Specimen	—	—	—	—	—	180
1934B	40,000	—	20.00	35.00	60.00	90.00

X# S20 5 FRANCS
0.8350 Silver **Subject:** Federal Festival in Lucerne **Note:** Prev. KM#S20.

Date	Mintage	F	VF	XF	Unc	BU
1939B	40,000	—	20.00	30.00	50.00	75.00
1939B Specimen	—	—	—	—	—	250

X# S54 5 FRANCS
Copper-Nickel **Subject:** Albisgütli Centennial (Zurich City) **Note:** Prev. KM#S54.

Date	Mintage	F	VF	XF	Unc	BU
1998 Proof	2,500	Value: 60.00				

X# S55 20 FRANCS
25.0000 g., 0.9990 Silver 0.8029 oz. ASW **Subject:** Albisgutli Centennial (Zurich City) **Note:** Prev. KM#S55.

Date	Mintage	F	VF	XF	Unc	BU
1998 Proof	1,000	Value: 165				

X# S22 50 FRANCS
25.0000 g., 0.9000 Silver 0.7234 oz. ASW **Subject:** Zurich "Field Shoot" in Oberhasli **Note:** Prev. KM#S22.

Date	Mintage	F	VF	XF	Unc	BU
1984	6,000	—	—	—	60.00	85.00
1984 Proof	200	Value: 650				

X# S24 50 FRANCS
25.0000 g., 0.9000 Silver 0.7234 oz. ASW **Subject:** Uri Festival in Altdorf **Note:** Prev. KM#S24.

Date	Mintage	F	VF	XF	Unc	BU
1985 Proof	3,500	Value: 165				

X# S26 50 FRANCS
25.0000 g., 0.9000 Silver 0.7234 oz. ASW **Subject:** Federal Festival in Appenzell **Note:** Prev. KM#S26.

Date	Mintage	F	VF	XF	Unc	BU
1986 Proof	3,700	Value: 125				

X# S28 50 FRANCS
25.0000 g., 0.9000 Silver 0.7234 oz. ASW **Subject:** Federal "Battle Shoot" in Galarus **Note:** Prev. KM#S28.

Date	Mintage	F	VF	XF	Unc	BU
1987 Proof	3,200	Value: 125				

X# S30 50 FRANCS
25.0000 g., 0.9000 Silver 0.7234 oz. ASW **Subject:** Aargau Festival in Brugg **Note:** Prev. KM#S30.

Date	Mintage	F	VF	XF	Unc	BU
1988 Proof	3,000	Value: 200				

X# S32 50 FRANCS
25.0000 g., 0.9000 Silver 0.7234 oz. ASW **Subject:** Zug Festival in Menzingen **Note:** Prev. KM#S32.

Date	Mintage	F	VF	XF	Unc	BU
1989 Proof	2,200	Value: 190				

X# S34 50 FRANCS
25.0000 g., 0.9000 Silver 0.7234 oz. ASW **Subject:** Federal Festival in Winterthur (Zurich) **Note:** Prev. KM#S34.

Date	Mintage	F	VF	XF	Unc	BU
1990 Proof	5,000		Value: 90.00			

X# S38 50 FRANCS
25.0000 g., 0.9000 Silver 0.7234 oz. ASW **Series:** Bern Festival in Langenthal **Rev:** William Tell with rifle and flag **Note:** Prev. KM#S38.

Date	Mintage	F	VF	XF	Unc	BU
1991 Proof	4,000		Value: 150			

X# S40 50 FRANCS
25.0000 g., 0.9000 Silver 0.7234 oz. ASW **Subject:** Zurich Festival in Dielsdorf **Note:** Prev. KM#S40.

Date	Mintage	F	VF	XF	Unc	BU
1992 Proof	1,750		Value: 185			

X# S42 50 FRANCS
25.0000 g., 0.9000 Silver 0.7234 oz. ASW **Subject:** Thurgau Festival in Weinfelden **Note:** Prev. KM#S42.

Date	Mintage	F	VF	XF	Unc	BU
1993 Proof	2,000		Value: 135			

X# S44 50 FRANCS
25.0000 g., 0.9000 Silver 0.7234 oz. ASW **Subject:** St. Gallen Festival **Note:** Prev. KM#S44.

Date	Mintage	F	VF	XF	Unc	BU
1994 Proof	2,200		Value: 85.00			

X# S46 50 FRANCS
25.0000 g., 0.9000 Silver 0.7234 oz. ASW **Issuer:** Thun in Bern **Subject:** Federal Festival in Thun (Bern) **Note:** Prev. KM#S46.

Date	Mintage	F	VF	XF	Unc	BU
1995 Proof	5,000		Value: 150			

X# S48 50 FRANCS
25.0000 g., 0.9000 Silver 0.7234 oz. ASW **Subject:** Sempach "Battle Shoot" (Lucerne) **Note:** Prev. KM#S48.

Date	Mintage	F	VF	XF	Unc	BU
1996 Proof	1,500		Value: 110			

X# S50 50 FRANCS
25.0000 g., 0.9000 Silver 0.7234 oz. ASW **Subject:** Schaffhausen Festival **Note:** Prev. KM#S50.

Date	Mintage	F	VF	XF	Unc	BU
1997 Proof	1,500		Value: 150			

X# S52 50 FRANCS
25.0000 g., 0.9000 Silver 0.7234 oz. ASW **Issuer:** Schwyz **Note:** Prev. KM#S52.

Date	Mintage	F	VF	XF	Unc	BU
1998 Proof	1,500		Value: 165			

X# S57 50 FRANCS
25.0000 g., 0.9000 Silver 0.7234 oz. ASW **Subject:** Wallis Festival in Sion **Note:** Prev. KM#S57.

Date	Mintage	F	VF	XF	Unc	BU
1999 Proof	1,500		Value: 125			

X# S59 50 FRANCS
25.0000 g., 0.9000 Silver 0.7234 oz. ASW **Subject:** Federal Festival in Biere (Vaud) **Note:** Prev. KM#S59.

Date	Mintage	F	VF	XF	Unc	BU
2000 Proof	3,000		Value: 90.00			

X# S19 100 FRANCS
25.9000 g., 0.9000 Gold 0.7494 oz. AGW **Subject:** Federal Festival in Fribourg **Note:** Prev. KM#S19.

Date	Mintage	F	VF	XF	Unc	BU
1934B	2,000	—	1,750	2,400	2,800	3,200

X# S21 100 FRANCS
17.5000 g., 0.9000 Gold 0.5064 oz. AGW **Subject:** Federal Festival in Lucerne **Note:** Prev. KM#S21.

Date	Mintage	F	VF	XF	Unc	BU
1939B	6,000	—	—	500	600	750

X# S56 200 FRANCS
13.9600 g., 0.9860 Gold 0.4425 oz. AGW **Subject:** Albisgutli Centennial (Zurich City) **Note:** Prev. KM#S56.

Date	Mintage	F	VF	XF	Unc	BU
1998 Matte Proof	100		Value: 1,750			

X# S47 500 FRANCS
13.0000 g., 0.9990 Gold 0.4175 oz. AGW **Subject:** Federal Festival in Thun (Bern) **Note:** Prev. KM#S47.

Date	Mintage	F	VF	XF	Unc	BU
1995 Proof	500		Value: 1,100			

X# S49 500 FRANCS
13.0000 g., 0.9000 Gold 0.3761 oz. AGW **Subject:** Sempach "Battle Shoot" (Lucerne) **Note:** Prev. KM#S49.

Date	Mintage	F	VF	XF	Unc	BU
1996 Proof	96		Value: 1,600			

X# S51 500 FRANCS
13.0000 g., 0.9990 Gold 0.4175 oz. AGW **Subject:** Schaffhausen
Festival **Note:** Prev. KM#S51.

Date	Mintage	F	VF	XF	Unc	BU
1997 Proof	97	Value: 1,600				

X# S53 500 FRANCS
13.0000 g., 0.9990 Gold 0.4175 oz. AGW **Subject:** Schwyz
Festival **Note:** Prev. KM#S53.

Date	Mintage	F	VF	XF	Unc	BU
1998 Proof	98	Value: 1,600				

X# S58 500 FRANCS
13.0000 g., 0.9990 Gold 0.4175 oz. AGW **Subject:** Wallis
Festival in Sion **Note:** Prev. KM#S58.

Date	Mintage	F	VF	XF	Unc	BU
1999 Proof	99	Value: 1,600				

X# S60 500 FRANCS
13.0000 g., 0.9990 Gold 0.4175 oz. AGW **Subject:** Federal
Festival in Biere (Vaud) **Note:** Prev. KM#S60.

Date	Mintage	F	VF	XF	Unc	BU
2000 Proof	300	Value: 1,300				

X# S23 1000 FRANCS
26.0000 g., 0.9000 Gold 0.7523 oz. AGW **Subject:** Zurich "Field
Shoot" in Oberhasli **Note:** Prev. KM#S23.

Date	Mintage	F	VF	XF	Unc	BU
1984 Proof	300	Value: 1,550				

X# S25 1000 FRANCS
26.0000 g., 0.9000 Gold 0.7523 oz. AGW **Subject:** Uri Festival
in Altdorf **Note:** Prev. KM#S25.

Date	Mintage	F	VF	XF	Unc	BU
1985 Proof	300	Value: 1,350				

X# S27 1000 FRANCS
26.0000 g., 0.9000 Gold 0.7523 oz. AGW **Subject:** Federal
Festival in Appenzell **Note:** Prev. KM#S27.

Date	Mintage	F	VF	XF	Unc	BU
1986 Proof	350	Value: 1,100				

X# S29 1000 FRANCS
26.0000 g., 0.9000 Gold 0.7523 oz. AGW **Subject:** Federal
"Battle Shoot" in Glarus **Note:** Prev. KM#S29.

Date	Mintage	F	VF	XF	Unc	BU
1987 Proof	300	Value: 1,400				

X# S31 1000 FRANCS
26.0000 g., 0.9000 Gold 0.7523 oz. AGW **Subject:** Aargau
Festival in Brugg **Note:** Prev. KM#S31.

Date	Mintage	F	VF	XF	Unc	BU
1988 Proof	400	Value: 1,400				

X# S33 1000 FRANCS
26.0000 g., 0.9000 Gold 0.7523 oz. AGW **Subject:** Zug Festival
in Menzingen **Note:** Prev. KM#S33.

Date	Mintage	F	VF	XF	Unc	BU
1989 Proof	250	Value: 1,400				

X# S35 1000 FRANCS
26.0000 g., 0.9000 Gold 0.7523 oz. AGW **Subject:** Federal
Festival in Winterthur (Zurich) **Note:** Prev. KM#S35.

Date	Mintage	F	VF	XF	Unc	BU
1990 Proof	400	Value: 1,200				

X# S75 1000 FRANCS
26.0000 g., 0.9000 Gold 0.7523 oz. AGW **Subject:** Federal
Festival Winter Thur (Z&#65533;rich) **Note:** Prev. KM#S75.

Date	Mintage	F	VF	XF	Unc	BU
1990	Est. 400	Value: 1,200				

X# S39 1000 FRANCS
26.0000 g., 0.9000 Gold 0.7523 oz. AGW **Subject:** Bern Festival
in Langenthal **Rev:** William Tell with rifle and flag **Note:** Prev.
KM#S39.

Date	Mintage	F	VF	XF	Unc	BU
1991 Proof	400	Value: 1,350				

X# S41 1000 FRANCS
26.0000 g., 0.9000 Gold 0.7523 oz. AGW **Subject:** Zurich Festival
in Dielsdorf **Note:** Similar to 50 Francs, X#S40. Prev. KM#S41.

Date	Mintage	F	VF	XF	Unc	BU
1992 Proof	175	Value: 1,600				

X# S43 1000 FRANCS
26.0000 g., 0.9000 Gold 0.7523 oz. AGW **Subject:** Thurgau
Festival in Weinfelden **Note:** Similar to 50 Francs, X#S42. Prev.
KM#S43.

Date	Mintage	F	VF	XF	Unc	BU
1993 Proof	200	Value: 1,400				

X# S45 1000 FRANCS
26.0000 g., 0.9000 Gold 0.7523 oz. AGW **Subject:** St. Gallen
Festival **Note:** Similar to 50 Francs, X#S44. Prev. KM#S45.

Date	Mintage	F	VF	XF	Unc	BU
1994 Proof	200	Value: 1,400				

X# S36 UNZE (Ounce)
31.1030 g., 0.9990 Platinum 0.9989 oz. APW **Subject:** William
Tell and Son **Note:** Prev. X#S36.

Date	Mintage	F	VF	XF	Unc	BU
1986HF	60,000					
1986HF Proof	10,000	Value: 1,600				
1987HF	15,000					
1987HF Proof	15,000	Value: 1,600				

X# S37a UNZE (Ounce)
Brass, 32 mm. **Note:** Specimen Strike. Prev. KM#S37a.

Date	Mintage	F	VF	XF	Unc	BU
1988HF Proof	1,000	Value: 100				

X# S37 UNZE (Ounce)
31.1030 g., 0.9990 Platinum 0.9989 oz. APW **Subject:** William
Tell **Note:** Prev. KM#S37.

Date	Mintage	F	VF	XF	Unc	BU
1988HF Proof	10,000	Value: 1,600				

ESSAIS

KM#	Date	Mintage	Identification	Mkt Val
E4	1911	—	10 Francs. Gold.	35,000
E5	1925B	—	100 Francs. Bronze. 16.0800 g. Young head left. Radiant cross above value, date and sprigs.	3,500
E6	1925B	—	100 Francs. Bronze. 14.3800 g. Head left.	3,000
E17	1928B	—	100 Francs. Brass. Plain edge. Prev. KM#E5.	5,000
EA8	1930B	—	5 Francs. Silver. Hooded bust right. Cross on shield flanked by sprigs. Formerly Pn63.	12,000
E8	1930	—	Franc. Nickel.	5,000
E18	1930B	—	100 Francs. Brass. Lettered edge. Prev. KM#E6.	6,500
E7	1998	250	5 Francs. Silver.	500
E9	1998	250	20 Francs. Silver. KM#80.	550
E10	1998	250	20 Francs. Silver. KM#82.	550
E11	1998	500	20 Francs. Silver. KM#84.	360
EA12	1999	765	5 Francs. Copper-Nickel. KM#86	190
E12	2000	—	20 Francs. Silver. KM#97	250

PATTERNS
Including off metal strikes

KM#	Date	Mintage	Identification	Mkt Val
Pn40	1910	56	10 Francs. Gold. Reeded edge.	40,000
Pn41	1910	I.A.	10 Francs. Gold. Plain edge.	50,000
Pn42	1917	6	5 Rappen. Brass.	6,000
Pn43	1918	—	10 Rappen. Nickel.	—
Pn44	1922B	—	5 Francs. Silver.	3,500
Pn45	1924B	—	5 Francs.	20,000
Pn46	1925B	—	10 Francs. Silver.	6,000
Pn47	1925B	—	100 Francs. Copper.	5,000
Pn48	1927B	—	20 Rappen. Nickel.	4,500
Pn49	1928B	—	20 Rappen. Nickel.	4,500
Pn50	1928B	—	Franc. Nickel.	7,000
Pn51	1928B	—	2 Francs. Nickel.	7,500
Pn52	1928B	—	5 Francs. Silver.	20,000
Pn53	1928B	—	5 Francs. Nickel.	15,000
Pn54	1929B	—	5 Rappen. Bronze.	—
Pn55	1929B	—	50 Rappen. Nickel.	4,500
Pn56	1929	—	5 Francs. Silver.	30,000
Pn57	1930B	—	10 Rappen. Nickel.	3,000
Pn58	1930B	—	20 Rappen. Nickel.	3,000
Pn59	1930B	—	50 Rappen. Nickel.	4,500
Pn60	1930	—	50 Rappen. Nickel. Triangle.	4,000
Pn61	19xxB	—	Franc. Nickel.	—
Pn62	19xxB	—	5 Francs. Silver.	25,000
Pn64	1931	—	5 Rappen. Copper-Nickel.	—
Pn65	1931	—	50 Rappen. Nickel.	3,000
Pn66	1935	—	20 Francs. Copper.	—
Pn67	1937B	—	Franc. Copper-Nickel.	7,500
Pn68	1937B	—	2 Francs. Copper-Nickel.	7,500
Pn69	1937	—	5 Francs. Aluminum.	5,000
Pn70	1938B	—	20 Rappen. Zinc.	2,500
Pn71	1938B	—	Franc. Copper-Nickel.	3,500
Pn72	1938B	—	2 Francs. Copper-Nickel.	4,000
Pn73	1939B	—	5 Rappen. Zinc. KM#26.	1,600
Pn74	1939	—	5 Francs. Silver.	6,000
Pn75	1940B	—	5 Rappen. Aluminum. KM#26.	3,500
PnA76	1940B	—	20 Rappen. Copper-Nickel. KM#29a.	2,850
Pn76	1940B	—	10 Rappen. Zinc. KM#27.	2,000
Pn77	1940B	—	10 Rappen. Aluminum. KM#27.	4,200
Pn78	1941B	—	2 Francs. Silver-Zinc.	2,500
Pn79	1941B	—	Rappen. Aluminum. KM#3.	2,500
Pn80	1941B	—	2 Rappen. Aluminum. KM#4.	3,000
Pn81	1947	—	20 Francs. Gold.	—
Pn82	1948B	—	5 Francs. Copper Gilt.	3,500
Pn83	1955B	—	25 Francs. Silver. KM#49.	14,000
Pn84	1955B	—	50 Francs. Silver. KM#50.	14,000
Pn85	1959B	—	50 Francs. Aluminum. 4.0300 g. KM#50.	6,000
Pn86	1979	—	5 Rappen. Aluminum-Bronze. Prev. Pn.#85.	2,000

TRIAL STRIKES

KM#	Date	Mintage	Identification	Mkt Val
TS3	1935	—	20 Francs. Copper.	3,250

MINT SETS

KM#	Date	Mintage	Identification	Issue Price	Mkt Val
MS2	1970 (9)	10,000	KM#21a.1, 23a.1-24a.1, 26-27, 29a, 40a.1, 46-47	6.40	45.00
MS3	1971 (5)	5,000	KM#23a.1-24a.1, 26, 29a, 46	2.40	35.00
MS4	1972 (3)	5,000	KM#21a.1, 23a.1, 27	2.40	16.00
MS5	1973 (6)	10,000	KM#21a.1, 23a.1-24a.1, 27, 40a.1, 46	6.40	25.00
MS6	1974 (9)	10,000	KM#21a.1, 23a.1-24a.1, 26-27, 29a, 40a.1, 46-47	6.40	65.00
MS7	1975 (8)	10,000	KM#21a.1, 23a.1-24a.1, 26-27, 29a, 40a.1, 46	6.40	40.00
MS8	1976 (8)	10,000	KM#21a.1, 23a.1-24a.1, 26-27, 29a, 40a.1, 46	9.00	55.00
MS9	1977 (8)	10,000	KM#21a.1, 23a.1-24a.1, 26-27, 29a, 40a.1, 46	9.00	35.00
MS10	1978 (8)	10,000	KM#21a.1, 23a.1-24a.1, 26-27, 29a, 40a.1, 46	9.00	30.00
MS11	1979 (8)	10,000	KM#21a.1, 23a.1-24a.1, 26-27, 29a, 40a.1, 46	9.00	30.00
MS12	1980 (8)	15,000	KM#21a.1, 23a.1-24a.1, 26-27, 29a, 40a.1, 46	9.00	50.00
MS13	1981 (8)	15,000	KM#21a.1, 23a.1-24a.1, 26c, 27, 29a, 40a.1, 46	9.00	35.00
MS14	1982 (8)	15,000	KM#21a.2, 23a.2-24a.2, 26c, 27, 29a, 40a.2, 46	9.00	55.00
MS15	1983 (8)	15,740	KM#21a.3, 23a.3-24a.3, 26c, 27, 29a, 40a.2, 46	9.00	35.00
MS16	1984 (8)	20,000	KM#21a.3, 23a.3-24a.3, 26c, 27, 29a, 40a.2, 46	9.00	45.00
MS17	1985 (8)	22,140	KM#21a.3, 23a.3-24a.3, 26c, 27, 29a, 40a.3, 46	9.00	30.00
MS18	1986 (8)	21,400	KM#21a.3, 23a.3-24a.3, 26c, 27, 29a, 40a.3, 46	9.00	30.00
MS19	1987 (8)	19,100	KM#21a.3, 23a.3-24a.3, 26c, 27, 29a, 40a.3, 46	9.00	50.00
MS20	1988 (8)	20,700	KM#21a.3, 23a.3-24a.3, 26c, 27, 29a, 40a.3, 46	—	35.00
MS21	1989 (8)	22,700	KM#21a.3, 23a.3-24a.3, 26c, 27, 29a, 40a.3, 46	11.00	24.00
MS22	1990 (8)	23,100	KM#21a.3, 23a.3-24a.3, 26c, 27, 29a, 40a.3, 46	—	24.00
MS23	1991 (8)	26,100	KM#21a.3, 23a.3-24a.3, 26c, 27, 29a, 40a.3, 46	—	165
MS24	1991 (2)	110,000	KM#70-71	210	325
MS25	1992 (8)	20,300	KM#21a.3, 23a.3-24a.3, 26c, 27, 29a, 40a.3, 46	—	26.00
MS26	1993 (8)	16,200	KM#21a.3, 23a.3-24a.3, 26c, 27, 29a, 40a.3, 46	—	175
MS27	1994 (8)	17,300	KM#21a.3, 23a.3-24a.3, 26c, 27, 29a, 40a.4, 46	—	30.00
MS28	1995 (8)	18,000	KM#21a.3, 23a.3-24a.3, 26c, 27, 29a, 40a.4, 46	—	30.00
MS29	1996 (8)	17,300	KM#21a.3, 23a.3-24a.3, 26c, 27, 29a, 40a.3, 46	—	30.00
MS30	1997 (8)	16,500	KM#21a.3, 23a.3, 24a.3, 26c, 27, 29a, 40a.4, 46	—	30.00
MS31	1998 (8)	16,000	KM#21a.3, 23a.3, 24a.3, 26c, 27, 29a, 40a.4, 46	—	30.00
MS32	1999 (8)	16,000	KM#21a.3, 23a.3, 24a.3, 26c, 27, 29a, 40a.4, 46	—	60.00
MS33	2000 (9)	18,000	KM#21a.3, 23a.3, 24a.3, 26c, 27, 29a, 40a.4, 46, 89 Fasnacht	—	60.00
MS34	2000 (9)	2,000	KM#21a.3, 23a.3, 24a.3, 26c, 27, 29a, 40a.4, 46, 91 150 Years of the Swiss Franken	—	275

PROOF SETS

KM#	Date	Mintage	Identification	Issue Price	Mkt Val
PS1	1974 (9)	2,400	KM#21a.1, 23a.1, 24a.1, 26, 27, 29a, 40a.1, 46-47	12.80	550
PS2	1975 (8)	10,000	KM#21a.1, 23a.1, 24a.1, 26, 27, 29a, 40a.1, 46	16.75	45.00
PS3	1976 (8)	5,130	KM#21a.1, 23a.1, 24a.1, 26, 27, 29a, 40a.1, 46	16.75	65.00
PS4	1977 (8)	7,030	KM#21a.1, 23a.1, 24a.1, 26, 27, 29a, 40a.1, 46	16.75	45.00
PS5	1978 (8)	10,090	KM#21a.1, 23a.1, 24a.1, 26, 27, 29a, 40a.1, 46	28.00	35.00
PS6	1979 (8)	10,150	KM#21a.1, 23a.1, 24a.1, 26, 27, 29a, 40a.1, 46	28.00	35.00
PS7	1980 (8)	10,010	KM#21a.1, 23a.1, 24a.1, 26, 27, 29a, 40a.1, 46	30.00	55.00
PS8	1981 (8)	10,280	KM#21a.1, 23a.1, 24a.1, 26c, 27, 29a, 40a.1, 46	30.00	35.00
PS9	1982 (8)	10,090	KM#21a.2, 23a.2, 24a.2, 26c, 27, 29a, 40a.2, 46	30.00	65.00
PS10	1983 (8)	11,390	KM#21a.3, 23a.3, 24a.3, 26c, 27, 29a, 40a.2, 46	30.00	35.00
PS11	1984 (8)	14,100	KM#21a.3, 23a.3, 24a.3, 26c, 27, 29a, 40a.2, 46	30.00	35.00
PS12	1985 (8)	12,000	KM#21a.3, 23a.3-24a.3, 26c, 27, 29a, 40a.3, 46	30.00	35.00
PS13	1986 (8)	10,000	KM#21a.3, 23a.3, 24a.3, 26c, 27, 29a, 40a.3, 46	30.00	35.00
PS14	1987 (8)	8,800	KM#21a.3, 23a.3, 24a.3, 26c, 27, 29a, 40a.3, 46	30.00	55.00
PS15	1988 (8)	9,050	KM#21a.3, 23a.3, 24a.3, 26c, 27, 29a, 40a.3, 46	—	45.00
PS16	1989 (8)	8,800	KM#21a.3, 23a.3, 24a.3, 26c, 27, 29a, 40a.3, 46	36.50	40.00
PS17	1990 (8)	8,900	KM#21a.3, 23a.3, 24a.3, 26c, 27, 29a, 40a.3, 46	—	40.00
PS18	1991 (8)	9,900	KM#21a.3, 23a.3, 24a.3, 26c, 27, 29a, 40a.3, 46	—	195
PS19	1992 (8)	7,450	KM#21a.3, 23a.3, 24a.3, 26c, 27, 29a, 40a.3, 46	—	55.00
PS20	1993 (8)	6,300	KM#21a.3, 23a.3, 24a.3, 26c, 27, 29a, 40a.3, 46	—	200
PS21	1994 (8)	6,100	KM#21a.3, 23a.3, 24a.3, 26c, 27, 29a, 40a.4, 46	—	65.00
PS23	1994-1996 (4)	6,000	KM#74-77	—	135
PS22	1995 (8)	6,100	KM#21a.3, 23a.3, 24a.3, 26c, 27, 29a, 40a.4, 46	42.50	65.00
PS24	1996 (8)	6,100	KM#21a.3, 23a.3, 24a.3, 26c, 27, 29a, 40a.4, 46	—	65.00
PS25	1997 (8)	5,500	KM#21a.3, 23a.3, 24a.3, 26c, 27, 29a, 40a.4, 46	—	65.00
PS26	1998 (8)	4,800	KM#21a.3, 23a.3, 24a.3, 26c, 27, 29a, 40a.4, 46	—	65.00
PS27	1999 (9)	5,000	KM#21a.3, 23a.3, 24a.3, 26c, 27, 29a, 40a.4, 46, 86	—	115
PS28	2000 (9)	5,500	KM#21a.3, 23a.3, 24a.3, 26c, 27, 29a, 40a.4, 46, 89 Fasnacht	—	100
PS29	2000 (9)	500	KM#21a.3, 23a.3, 24a.3, 26c, 27, 29a, 40a.4, 46, 91 150 Years of the Swiss Franken	—	1,200

SYRIA

The Syrian Arab Republic, located in the Near East at the eastern end of the Mediterranean Sea, has an area of 71,498 sq. mi. (185,180 sq. km.) and a population of *12 million. Capital: Greater Damascus. Agriculture and animal breeding are the chief industries. Cotton, crude oil and livestock are exported.

Ancient Syria, a land bridge connecting Europe, Africa and Asia, has spent much of its history in thrall to the conqueror's whim. Its subjection by Egypt about 1500 B.C. was followed by successive conquests by the Hebrews, Phoenicians, Babylonians, Assyrians, Persians, Macedonians, Romans, Byzantines and finally, in 636 A.D., by the Moslems. The Arabs made Damascus, one of the oldest continuously inhabited cities of the world, the trade center and capital of an empire stretching from India to Spain. In 1516, following the total destruction of Damascus by the Mongols of Tamerlane, Syria fell to the Ottoman Turks and remained a part of Turkey until the end of World War I. The League of Nations gave France a mandate to the Levant states of Syria and Lebanon in 1920. In 1930, following a series of uprisings, France recognized Syria as an independent republic, but still subject to the mandate. Lebanon became fully independent on Nov. 22, 1943, and Syria on Jan. 1,1944.

TITLES

الجمهورية السورية

al-Jumhuriya(t) al-Suriya(t)

الجمهورية لعربية السورية

al-Jumhuriya(t) al-Arabiya(t) as-Suriya(t)

RULERS
Ottoman, until 1918
Faysal, 1918-1920

MINT MARK
(a)- Paris, privy marks only

MINT NAMES

دمشق

Damascus (Dimask)

حلب

Haleb (Aleppo)

KINGDOM
STANDARD COINAGE

KM# 67   DINAR
6.7000 g., Gold **Obv:** Crowned shield within sprigs **Rev:** Design within wreath

Date	Mintage	F	VF	XF	Unc	BU
AH1338 (1919)	Est. 12	—	—	—	8,500	

FRENCH PROTECTORATE
STANDARD COINAGE

KM# 68   1/2 PIASTRE
4.0000 g., Copper-Nickel **Obv:** Value within roped wreath flanked by oat sprigs **Rev:** Value within wreath

Date	Mintage	F	VF	XF	Unc	BU
1921(a)	4,000,000	0.50	2.00	5.00	15.00	—

KM# 75   1/2 PIASTRE
Nickel-Brass **Obv:** Value within roped circle **Rev:** Value within oat sprigs

Date	Mintage	F	VF	XF	Unc	BU
1935(a)	600,000	1.00	4.00	12.00	42.50	—
1936(a)	800,000	1.00	4.00	9.00	30.00	—

KM# 71   PIASTRE
5.1000 g., Nickel-Brass **Obv:** Hole in center of wreath flanked by stars **Rev:** Hole in center of sprigs flanked by lion heads

Date	Mintage	F	VF	XF	Unc	BU
1929(a)	750,000	1.00	3.00	7.00	32.50	—
1933(a)	600,000	1.50	4.00	10.00	40.00	—
1935(a)	1,900,000	0.75	2.50	5.00	22.50	—
1936(a)	1,400,000	0.75	2.50	7.00	25.00	—

KM# 71a   PIASTRE
3.5000 g., Zinc **Obv:** Hole in center of wreath flanked by stars **Rev:** Hole in center flanked by lion heads

Date	Mintage	F	VF	XF	Unc	BU
1940(a)	2,000,000	2.00	5.00	15.00	60.00	—

KM# 69   2 PIASTRES
Aluminum-Bronze **Obv:** Inscription divides dates within design **Rev:** Crossed oat sprigs divide value

Date	Mintage	F	VF	XF	Unc	BU
1926(a)	600,000	5.00	10.00	25.00	75.00	—
1926	Inc. above	5.00	10.00	25.00	75.00	—

Note: Without privy marks by date

KM# 76   2-1/2 PIASTRES
Aluminum-Bronze **Obv:** Hole in center of wreath flanked by stars **Rev:** Hole in center of sprigs flanked by lion heads

Date	Mintage	F	VF	XF	Unc	BU
1940(a)	2,000,000	1.25	4.00	8.00	27.50	—

KM# 70   5 PIASTRES
3.9000 g., Aluminum-Bronze **Obv:** Inscription divides dates within design **Rev:** Crossed oat sprigs divide value

Date	Mintage	F	VF	XF	Unc	BU
1926(a)	300,000	0.75	2.00	8.00	25.00	—
1926	600,000	0.75	3.00	12.00	35.00	—
1933(a)	1,200,000	0.40	2.00	12.50	40.00	—
1935(a)	2,000,000	0.30	1.50	8.00	25.00	—
1936(a)	900,000	0.50	2.00	10.00	30.00	—
1940(a)	500,000	0.50	1.50	4.00	15.00	—

KM# 72   10 PIASTRES
2.0000 g., 0.6800 Silver 0.0437 oz. ASW **Obv:** Star in center of flower design **Rev:** Value within circle

Date	Mintage	F	VF	XF	Unc	BU
1929	1,000,000	4.00	12.00	28.00	90.00	—

KM# 73   25 PIASTRES
5.0000 g., 0.6800 Silver 0.1093 oz. ASW **Obv:** Value within circle **Rev:** Star in center of flower design

Date	Mintage	F	VF	XF	Unc	BU
1929	1,000,000	3.00	5.00	27.50	85.00	—
1933(a)	500,000	4.00	12.00	40.00	160	—
1936(a)	897,000	3.50	7.00	30.00	100	—
1937(a)	393,000	5.00	10.00	35.00	140	—

KM# 74   50 PIASTRES
10.0000 g., 0.6800 Silver 0.2186 oz. ASW **Obv:** Value within circle **Rev:** Star in center of flower design

Date	Mintage	F	VF	XF	Unc	BU
1929	880,000	4.00	8.00	35.00	140	—
1933(a)	250,000	6.00	10.00	45.00	190	—
1936(a)	400,000	5.00	10.00	40.00	160	—
1937(a)	Inc. above	7.00	12.00	50.00	200	—

WORLD WAR II EMERGENCY COINAGE

KM# 77   PIASTRE
Brass **Obv:** English value **Rev:** Arabic value

Date	Mintage	F	VF	XF	Unc	BU
ND	—	3.00	6.00	12.00	25.00	—

KM# 78   2-1/2 PIASTRES
Aluminum **Obv:** English value **Rev:** Arabic value

Date	Mintage	F	VF	XF	Unc	BU
ND	—	10.00	20.00	40.00	75.00	—

REPUBLIC
STANDARD COINAGE

KM# 81   2-1/2 PIASTRES
Copper-Nickel **Obv:** Imperial eagle **Rev:** Inscription within rectangle below value

Date	Mintage	F	VF	XF	Unc	BU
AH1367-1948	2,500,000	0.75	1.50	3.00	6.00	—
AH1375-1956	5,000,000	0.75	1.50	3.00	6.00	—

KM# 82   5 PIASTRES
3.0000 g., Copper-Nickel **Obv:** Imperial eagle **Rev:** Value within diamond shape above design flanked by stars

Date	Mintage	F	VF	XF	Unc	BU
AH1367-1948	8,000,000	0.75	1.50	3.00	6.00	—
AH1375-1956	4,000,000	0.75	1.50	3.00	6.00	—

KM# 83   10 PIASTRES
Copper-Nickel **Obv:** Imperial eagle **Rev:** Value above 1/2 designed wreath

Date	Mintage	F	VF	XF	Unc	BU
AH1367-1948	—	0.75	1.50	3.00	6.00	—
AH1375-1956	4,000,000	0.75	1.50	3.00	6.00	—

KM# 79   25 PIASTRES
2.5000 g., 0.6000 Silver 0.0482 oz. ASW **Obv:** Imperial eagle **Rev:** Value within circle of design flanked by oat sprigs

Date	Mintage	F	VF	XF	Unc	BU
AH1366-1947	6,300,000	1.50	2.50	6.00	20.00	—

KM# 80   50 PIASTRES
5.0000 g., 0.6000 Silver 0.0964 oz. ASW **Obv:** Imperial eagle **Rev:** Value in center circle of design

Date	Mintage	F	VF	XF	Unc	BU
AH1366-1947	4,500,000	2.50	5.00	10.00	25.00	—

KM# 84   1/2 POUND
3.3793 g., 0.9000 Gold 0.0978 oz. AGW **Obv:** Imperial eagle **Rev:** Inscription within rectangle above sprigs

Date	Mintage	F	VF	XF	Unc	BU
AH1369-1950	100,000	BV	90.00	100	125	175

KM# 85   LIRA
10.0000 g., 0.6800 Silver 0.2186 oz. ASW **Obv:** Imperial eagle **Rev:** Inscription and value within center of rectangle and sprigs

Date	Mintage	F	VF	XF	Unc	BU
AH1369-1950	7,000,000	3.50	6.50	12.50	25.00	—

KM# 86   POUND
6.7586 g., 0.9000 Gold 0.1956 oz. AGW **Obv:** Imperial eagle **Rev:** Inscription and value within rectangle above sprigs

Date	Mintage	F	VF	XF	Unc	BU
AH1369-1950	250,000	—	BV	185	200	245

UNITED ARAB REPUBLIC
STANDARD COINAGE

KM# 90   2-1/2 PIASTRES
2.0000 g., Aluminum-Bronze, 17 mm. **Obv:** Imperial eagle flanked by dates **Rev:** Inscription within rectangle below value

Date	Mintage	F	VF	XF	Unc	BU
AH1380-1960	1,100,000	0.10	0.20	0.35	0.75	—

KM# 91   5 PIASTRES
3.0000 g., Aluminum-Bronze, 19 mm. **Obv:** Imperial eagle **Rev:** Value, inscription

Date	Mintage	F	VF	XF	Unc	BU
AH1380-1960	4,240,000	0.10	0.20	0.35	0.75	—

KM# 92   10 PIASTRES
4.0000 g., Aluminum-Bronze, 21 mm. **Obv:** Imperial eagle flanked by dates **Rev:** Value in center of 1/2 wreath

Date	Mintage	F	VF	XF	Unc	BU
AH1380-1960	2,800,000	0.10	0.20	0.40	1.00	—

KM# 87   25 PIASTRES
0.3500 g., 0.6000 Silver 0.0068 oz. ASW, 20.3 mm. **Obv:** Imperial eagle **Rev:** Value flanked by oat sprigs in center of gear

Date	Mintage	F	VF	XF	Unc	BU
AH1377-1958	2,300,000	1.00	2.00	3.00	7.00	—

KM# 88   50 PIASTRES
5.0000 g., 0.6000 Silver 0.0964 oz. ASW, 23.4 mm. **Obv:** Imperial eagle **Rev:** Sword divides value within wreath

Date	Mintage	F	VF	XF	Unc	BU
AH1377-1958	120,000	2.00	3.50	7.00	18.00	—

KM# 89   50 PIASTRES
5.0000 g., 0.6000 Silver 0.0964 oz. ASW **Subject:** 1st
Anniversary - Founding of United Arab Republic **Obv:** Imperial
eagle **Rev:** Value

Date	Mintage	F	VF	XF	Unc	BU
AH1378-1959	1,500,000	1.75	2.75	5.00	12.00	—

SYRIAN ARAB REPUBLIC

STANDARD COINAGE

KM# 93   2-1/2 PIASTRES
2.0000 g., Aluminum-Bronze, 17 mm. **Obv:** Imperial eagle
Rev: Inscription within rectangle below value

Date	Mintage	F	VF	XF	Unc	BU
AH1382-1962	8,000,000	—	0.10	0.20	0.50	—
AH1385-1965	8,000,000	—	0.10	0.20	0.50	—

KM# 104   2-1/2 PIASTRES
2.0000 g., Aluminum-Bronze, 17 mm. **Obv:** Imperial eagle
Rev: Inscription within rectangle below value

Date	Mintage	F	VF	XF	Unc	BU
AH1393-1973	10,000,000	—	0.10	0.15	0.25	—

KM# 94   5 PIASTRES
3.0000 g., Aluminum-Bronze, 19 mm. **Obv:** Imperial eagle
Rev: Value within diamond shape above design flanked by stars

Date	Mintage	F	VF	XF	Unc	BU
AH1382-1962	7,000,000	—	0.10	0.15	0.35	—
AH1385-1965	18,000,000	—	0.10	0.15	0.35	—

KM# 100   5 PIASTRES
3.0000 g., Aluminum-Bronze, 19 mm. **Series:** F.A.O.
Obv: Imperial eagle **Rev:** Upright oat sprig within sprigs

Date	Mintage	F	VF	XF	Unc	BU
AH1391-1971	15,000,000	—	0.10	0.15	0.25	—

KM# 105   5 PIASTRES
3.0000 g., Aluminum-Bronze, 19 mm. **Obv:** Imperial eagle
Rev: Value within diamond shape above design flanked by stars

Date	Mintage	F	VF	XF	Unc	BU
AH1394-1974	—	—	0.10	0.15	0.25	—

KM# 110   5 PIASTRES
3.0000 g., Aluminum-Bronze, 19 mm. **Series:** F.A.O. **Obv:** Imperial
eagle **Rev:** Euphrates dam within 1/2 gear and 1/2 oat sprig

Date	Mintage	F	VF	XF	Unc	BU
AH1396-1976	2,000,000	—	0.10	0.15	0.25	—

KM# 116   5 PIASTRES
3.0000 g., Aluminum-Bronze, 19 mm. **Obv:** Imperial eagle with
heavy neck feathers **Rev:** Value within diamond shape above design
flanked by stars **Note:** Similar to KM#94 but heavier neck feathers

Date	Mintage	F	VF	XF	Unc	BU
AH1399-1979	—	—	0.10	0.15	0.25	—

KM# 95   10 PIASTRES
4.0000 g., Aluminum-Bronze, 21 mm. **Obv:** Imperial eagle
Rev: Value within 1/2 designed wreath **Note:** Varieties exist with
fine (narrow) and course (widely spaced) reeding.

Date	Mintage	F	VF	XF	Unc	BU
AH1382-1962	6,000,000	—	0.10	0.20	0.45	—
AH1385-1965	22,000,000	—	0.10	0.20	0.45	—
	Note: Reeding varieties exist					

KM# 106   10 PIASTRES
4.0000 g., Aluminum-Bronze, 21 mm. **Obv:** Imperial eagle
Rev: Value within 1/2 designed wreath

Date	Mintage	F	VF	XF	Unc	BU
AH1394-1974	—	—	0.10	0.15	0.30	—

KM# 111   10 PIASTRES
4.0000 g., Brass, 21 mm. **Series:** F.A.O. **Obv:** Imperial eagle
with heavy neck feathers **Rev:** Euphrates dam within 1/2 gear
and 1/2 oat sprig **Note:** Similar to 5 Piastres, KM#110.

Date	Mintage	F	VF	XF	Unc	BU
AH1396-1976	500,000	—	0.10	0.15	0.25	—

KM# 117   10 PIASTRES
4.0000 g., Copper-Nickel, 21 mm. **Obv:** Imperial eagle
Rev: Value within 1/2 designed wreath

Date	Mintage	F	VF	XF	Unc	BU
AH1399-1979	—	—	0.10	0.15	0.30	—

KM# 96   25 PIASTRES
3.5000 g., Nickel, 20.3 mm. **Obv:** Imperial eagle **Rev:** Inscription
within rectangle flanked by dates below value

Date	Mintage	F	VF	XF	Unc	BU
AH1387-1968	15,000,000	—	0.20	0.30	0.60	—

KM# 101   25 PIASTRES
3.5000 g., Nickel, 20.3 mm. **Subject:** 25th Anniversary - Al-
Ba'ath Party **Obv:** Imperial eagle **Rev:** Flaming torch divides
value within oat sprigs

Date	Mintage	F	VF	XF	Unc	BU
AH1392-1972	—	—	0.15	0.25	0.60	—

KM# 107   25 PIASTRES
3.5000 g., Nickel, 20.3 mm. **Obv:** Imperial eagle **Rev:** Inscription
within rectangle below value

Date	Mintage	F	VF	XF	Unc	BU
AH1394-1974	—	—	0.10	0.25	0.50	—

KM# 112   25 PIASTRES
3.5000 g., Nickel, 20.5 mm. **Series:** F.A.O. **Obv:** Imperial eagle
Rev: Euphrates dam within 1/2 gear and 1/2 oat sprig

Date	Mintage	F	VF	XF	Unc	BU
AH1396-1976	1,000,000	—	0.10	0.25	0.50	—

KM# 118   25 PIASTRES
3.5000 g., Copper-Nickel, 20.3 mm. **Obv:** Imperial eagle
Rev: Inscription within rectangle below value

Date	Mintage	F	VF	XF	Unc	BU
AH1399-1979	—	—	0.10	0.25	0.50	—

KM# 97   50 PIASTRES
5.0000 g., Nickel, 23.4 mm. **Obv:** Imperial eagle **Rev:** Value in
center square of design above dates and oat sprigs

Date	Mintage	F	VF	XF	Unc	BU
AH1387-1968	10,000,000	—	0.25	0.50	0.85	—

KM# 102   50 PIASTRES
5.0000 g., Nickel, 23.4 mm. **Subject:** 25th Anniversary - Al-Ba'ath
Party **Obv:** Imperial eagle **Rev:** Inscription, dates, value and flames

Date	Mintage	F	VF	XF	Unc	BU
AH1392-1972	—	—	0.50	1.00	2.00	—

KM# 108   50 PIASTRES
5.0000 g., Nickel, 23.4 mm. **Obv:** Imperial eagle **Rev:** Value
within center square of design above sprigs

Date	Mintage	F	VF	XF	Unc	BU
AH1394-1974	—	—	0.20	0.30	0.75	—

KM# 113   50 PIASTRES
5.0000 g., Nickel, 23.4 mm.   **Series:** F.A.O.   **Obv:** Imperial eagle
Rev: Euphrates dam within 1/2 gear and 1/2 oat sprig

Date	Mintage	F	VF	XF	Unc	BU
AH1396-1976	1,000,000	—	0.20	0.50	1.00	—

KM# 119   50 PIASTRES
5.0000 g., Copper-Nickel, 23.4 mm.   **Obv:** Imperial eagle
Rev: Value in center square of design above sprigs

Date	Mintage	F	VF	XF	Unc	BU
AH1399-1979	—	—	0.20	0.30	0.75	—

KM# 98   POUND
7.5000 g., Nickel, 27 mm.   **Obv:** Imperial eagle **Rev:** Value in
diamond shape within rectangle **Edge:** Reeded

Date	Mintage	F	VF	XF	Unc	BU
AH1387-1968	10,000,000	—	0.30	0.75	1.25	—
AH1391-1971	10,000,000	—	0.30	0.75	1.25	—

KM# 99   POUND
7.5000 g., Nickel, 27 mm.   **Series:** F.A.O.   **Obv:** Imperial eagle
Rev: Hands holding rectangle, oat sprig bouquet above

Date	Mintage	F	VF	XF	Unc	BU
AH1388-1968	500,000	—	1.00	2.00	3.50	—

KM# 103   POUND
7.5000 g., Nickel, 27 mm.   **Subject:** 25th Anniversary - Al-Ba'ath
Party **Obv:** Imperial eagle **Rev:** Stylized map and flaming torch

Date	Mintage	F	VF	XF	Unc	BU
AH1392-1972	10,000,000	—	0.50	1.00	2.50	—

KM# 109   POUND
7.5000 g., Nickel, 27 mm.   **Obv:** Imperial eagle **Rev:** Value in
diamond shape at center of rectangle

Date	Mintage	F	VF	XF	Unc	BU
AH1394-1974	—	—	0.30	0.75	2.00	—

KM# 114   POUND
7.5000 g., Nickel, 27 mm.   **Series:** F.A.O.   **Obv:** Imperial eagle
Rev: Euphrates dam within 1/2 gear and 1/2 oat sprig

Date	Mintage	F	VF	XF	Unc	BU
AH1396-1976	500,000	—	0.50	1.00	2.50	—

KM# 115   POUND
7.5000 g., Nickel, 27 mm.   **Subject:** Re-election of President
Obv: Imperial eagle within circle **Rev:** Head left within circle

Date	Mintage	F	VF	XF	Unc	BU
AH1398-1978	—	—	1.50	2.50	5.00	—

KM# 120.1   POUND
7.5000 g., Copper-Nickel, 27 mm.   **Obv:** Imperial eagle **Rev:**
Value in diamond shape at center of rectangle **Edge:** Reeded

Date	Mintage	F	VF	XF	Unc	BU
AH1399-1979	—	—	0.30	0.70	1.50	—

KM# 120.2   POUND
4.9400 g., Stainless Steel, 21 mm.   **Obv:** Imperial eagle
Rev: Value in diamond shape at center of rectangle
Note: Reduced size and weight.

Date	Mintage	F	VF	XF	Unc	BU
AH1412-1991	—	—	0.30	0.70	1.50	2.00

KM# 121   POUND
5.0000 g., Stainless Steel   **Obv:** Imperial eagle **Rev:** Value in
diamond shape at center of rectangle

Date	Mintage	F	VF	XF	Unc	BU
AH1414-1994	—	—	0.30	0.70	1.50	2.00
AH1416 1996	—	—	0.30	0.75	1.50	2.00

KM# 132   POUND
5.0000 g., Stainless Steel, 25.4 mm.   **Obv:** Flowers to left of dates
below heraldic bird **Rev:** Value and ornamentation **Edge:** Reeded

Date	Mintage	F	VF	XF	Unc	BU
AH1416-1996	—	—	—	—	1.50	2.00

KM# 125   2 POUNDS
6.0000 g., Stainless Steel, 23 mm.   **Obv:** Imperial eagle flanked
by dates **Rev:** Ancient ruins and value

Date	Mintage	F	VF	XF	Unc	BU
AH1416-1996	—	—	—	0.85	1.75	2.50

KM# 123   5 POUNDS
5.0100 g., Copper-Nickel, 24.4 mm.   **Obv:** Imperial eagle within
birdhouse design **Rev:** Palace above value within birdhouse design

Date	Mintage	F	VF	XF	Unc	BU
AH1416-1996	—	—	—	1.00	2.00	3.00

KM# 124   10 POUNDS
7.0000 g., Copper-Nickel, 26.40 mm.   **Obv:** Imperial eagle within
circle **Rev:** Ancient ruins above value within circle

Date	Mintage	F	VF	XF	Unc	BU
AH1416-1996	—	—	—	1.25	2.50	3.50
AH1417-1997(a)	—	—	—	1.25	2.50	3.50

KM# 128   10 POUNDS
7.0000 g., Copper-Nickel, 26.5 mm.   **Subject:** 50th Anniversary
of Al Ba'ath Party **Obv:** Imperial eagle within circle **Rev:** Map and
flag above sprigs within circle **Edge:** Reeded

Date	Mintage	F	VF	XF	Unc	BU
AH1417-1997	100,000	—	—	1.25	2.50	3.50

KM# 122   25 POUNDS
Bi-Metallic Stainless Steel center in Aluminum-Bronze ring
Obv: Imperial eagle within circle **Rev:** Head left within circle

Date	Mintage	F	VF	XF	Unc	BU
ND(1995)	—	—	—	2.50	7.00	9.00

KM# 126   25 POUNDS
6.4500 g., Bi-Metallic Stainless Steel center in Aluminum-Bronze
ring, 25 mm.   **Obv:** Imperial eagle within designed wreath
Rev: Central Bank building within circle

Date	Mintage	F	VF	XF	Unc	BU
AH1416-1996	—	—	—	2.00	6.00	7.50

ESSAIS

KM#	Date	Mintage	Identification	Issue Price	Mkt Val
E1	1926(a)	—	2 Piastres. Aluminum-Bronze. KM69.	—	200
E2	1926(a)	—	5 Piastres. Aluminum-Bronze. KM70.	—	220
E3	1929(a)	—	Piastre. Nickel-Brass. Hole in center of wreath. Value and dates below hole in center flanked by lion heads. KM71.	—	115
E4	1929(a)	—	10 Piastres. Silver. KM72.	—	200
E5	1929(a)	—	25 Piastres. Silver. KM73.	—	250
E6	1929(a)	—	50 Piastres. Silver. Value within circle. Star in center of flower design. KM74.	—	265
E7	AH1350(a)	—	50 Piastres.	—	350
E8	1935(a)	—	1/2 Piastre. Nickel-Brass. KM75.	—	60.00

MINT SETS

KM#	Date	Mintage	Identification	Issue Price	Mkt Val
MS1	1968 (3)	—	KM96-98	—	5.50
MS2	1978-79 (6)	—	KM115 (1978), 116-120.1 (1979)	—	8.50

TAJIKISTAN

The Republic of Tajikistan (Tadjiquistan), was formed from those regions of Bukhara and Turkestan where the population consisted mainly of Tajiks. Is bordered in the north and west by Uzbekistan and Kyrgyzstan, in the east by China and in the south by Afghanistan. It has an area of 55,240 sq. miles (143,100 sq. km.) and a population of 5.95 million. It includes 2 provinces of Khudzand and Khatlon together with the Gorno-Badakhshan Autonomous Region with a population of 5,092,603. Capital: Dushanbe. Tajikistan was admitted as a constituent republic of the Soviet Union on Dec. 5, 1929. In August 1990 the Tajik Supreme Soviet adopted a declaration of republican sovereignty, and in Dec. 1991 the republic became a member of the CIS.

After demonstrations and fighting, the Communist government was replaced by a Revolutionary Coalition Council on May 7, 1992. Following further demonstrations President Nabiev was ousted on Sept. 7, 1992. Civil war broke out, and the government resigned on Nov. 10, 1992. On Nov. 30, 1992 it was announced that a CIS peacekeeping force would be sent to Tajikistan. A state of emergency was imposed in Jan. 1993. A ceasefire was signed in 1996 and a peace agreement signed in June 1997.

MONETARY SYSTEM
1 Ruble = 100 Tanga

REPUBLIC
DECIMAL COINAGE

KM# 1 20 ROUBLES
20.0000 g., 0.9250 Silver 0.5948 oz. ASW, 35.1 mm.
Subject: Medal without denomination **Obv:** Radiant Royal device within circle **Rev:** Crowned bust 1/4 right **Edge:** Reeded
Note: Medallic.

Date	Mintage	F	VF	XF	Unc	BU
1999 Proof	—	Value: 75.00				

TANNU TUVA

The Tannu-Tuva Peoples Republic (Tuva), an autonomous part of Russia located in central Asia on the northwest border of Outer Mongolia, has an area of 64,000 sq. mi. (165,760 sq. km.) and a population of about 175,000. Capital: Kyzyl. The economy is based on herding, forestry and mining.

As Urianghi, Tuva was part of Outer Mongolia of the Chinese Empire when tsarist Russia, after fomenting a separatist movement, extended its protection to the mountainous country in 1914. Tuva declared its independence as the Tannu-Tuva Peoples Republic in 1921 under the auspices of the Tuva Peoples Revolutionary Party. In 1926, following Russia's successful mediation of the resultant Tuvinian-Mongolian territorial dispute, Tannu-Tuva and Outer Mongolia formally recognized each other's independence. The Tannu-Tuva Peoples Republic became an autonomous region of the U.S.S.R. on Oct. 13, 1944.

MONETARY SYSTEM
100 Kopejek (Kopeks) = 1 Aksha

REPUBLIC
STANDARD COINAGE

KM# 1 KOPEJEK
Aluminum-Bronze **Obv:** Inscription within circle **Rev:** Value and date

Date	Mintage	VG	F	VF	XF	Unc
1934	—	20.00	30.00	50.00	90.00	

KM# 2 2 KOPEJEK
Aluminum-Bronze **Obv:** Inscription within circle **Rev:** Value and date

Date	Mintage	VG	F	VF	XF	Unc
1933	—					
1934	—	22.50	35.00	65.00	110	

KM# 3 3 KOPEJEK
Aluminum-Bronze **Obv:** Inscription within circle **Rev:** Value and date

Date	Mintage	VG	F	VF	XF	Unc
1933	—					
1934	—	20.00	30.00	50.00	90.00	

KM# 4 5 KOPEJEK
Aluminum-Bronze **Obv:** Inscription within circle **Rev:** Value and date

Date	Mintage	VG	F	VF	XF	Unc
1934	—	22.50	35.00	65.00	110	

KM# 5 10 KOPEJEK
Copper-Nickel **Obv:** Inscription within circle **Rev:** Value and date

Date	Mintage	VG	F	VF	XF	Unc
1934	—	22.50	35.00	65.00	110	

KM# 6 15 KOPEJEK
Copper-Nickel **Obv:** Inscription within circle **Rev:** Value and date

Date	Mintage	VG	F	VF	XF	Unc
1934	—	22.50	35.00	65.00	110	

KM# 7 20 KOPEJEK
Copper-Nickel **Obv:** Inscription within circle **Rev:** Value and date

Date	Mintage	VG	F	VF	XF	Unc
1934	—	22.50	35.00	65.00	110	

TANZANIA

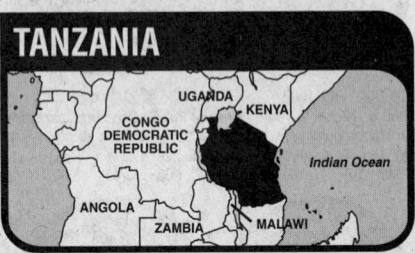

The United Republic of Tanzania, located on the east coast of Africa between Kenya and Mozambique, consists of Tanganyika and the islands of Zanzibar and Pemba. It has an area of 364,900 sq. mi. (945,090 sq. km.) and a population of *25.2 million. Capital: Dar es Salaam (Haven of Peace). The chief exports are cotton, coffee, diamonds, sisal, cloves, petroleum products, and cashew nuts.

Tanzania is a member of the Commonwealth of Nations. The President is Chief of State.

NOTE: For earlier coinage see East Africa.

REPUBLIC
STANDARD COINAGE

100 Senti = 1 Shilingi

KM# 1 5 SENTI
4.0000 g., Bronze, 22.5 mm. **Obv:** Head of President J.K. Nyerere left **Rev:** Sailfish above value

Date	Mintage	F	VF	XF	Unc	BU
1966	55,250,000	—	0.10	0.20	0.50	1.75
1966 Proof	5,500	Value: 1.25				

Date	Mintage	F	VF	XF	Unc	BU
1971	5,000,000	—	0.10	0.20	0.50	1.75
1972		—	0.10	0.20	0.50	1.75
1973	20,000,000	—	0.10	0.20	0.50	1.75
1974	12,500,000	—	0.10	0.20	0.50	1.75
1975		—	0.10	0.20	0.50	1.75
1976	37,500,000	—	0.10	0.20	0.50	1.75
1977	10,000,000	—	0.10	0.20	0.50	1.75
1979	7,200,000	—	0.10	0.20	0.50	1.75
1980	10,000,000	—	0.10	0.20	0.50	1.75
1981	13,650,000	—	0.10	0.20	0.50	1.75
1982		—	0.10	0.20	0.50	1.75
1983	18,000	—	0.10	0.20	0.50	1.75
1984		—	0.10	0.20	0.50	1.75

KM# 11   10 SENTI
4.8000 g., Nickel-Brass, 25 mm. **Obv:** Head of President J.K. Nyerere left **Rev:** Zebra running right

Date	Mintage	F	VF	XF	Unc	BU
1977	19,505,000	—	0.75	1.50	4.00	6.00
1979	8,000,000	—	0.75	1.50	4.00	6.00
1980	10,000,000	—	0.75	1.50	4.00	6.00
1981	10,000,000	—	0.75	1.50	4.00	6.00
1984		—	0.75	1.50	4.00	6.00

KM# 2   20 SENTI
5.0000 g., Nickel-Brass, 24 mm. **Obv:** Head of President J.K. Nyerere left **Rev:** Ostrich running left **Edge:** Plain

Date	Mintage	F	VF	XF	Unc	BU
1966	26,500,000	—	0.20	0.40	1.50	2.80
1966 Proof	5,500	Value: 2.25				
1970	5,000,000	—	0.20	0.40	1.50	2.80
1973	20,100,000	—	0.20	0.40	1.50	2.80
1975		—	0.20	0.40	1.50	2.80
1976	10,000,000	—	0.20	0.40	1.50	2.80
1977	10,000,000	—	0.20	0.40	1.50	2.80
1979	10,000,000	—	0.20	0.40	1.50	2.80
1980	10,000,000	—	0.20	0.40	1.50	2.80
1981	10,000,000	—	0.20	0.40	1.50	2.80
1982		—	0.20	0.40	1.50	2.80
1983	50,000	—	0.20	0.40	1.50	2.80
1984		—	0.20	0.40	1.50	2.80

KM# 3   50 SENTI
4.0000 g., Copper-Nickel, 21 mm. **Obv:** Head of President J.K. Nyerere left **Rev:** Rabbit left

Date	Mintage	F	VF	XF	Unc	BU
1966	6,250,000	—	0.20	0.40	2.00	2.50
1966 Proof	5,500	Value: 3.00				
1970	10,000,000	—	0.20	0.40	2.00	2.50
1973	10,000,000	—	0.25	0.50	2.00	2.50
1980	10,000,000	—	0.25	0.50	2.00	2.50
1981		—	0.25	0.50	2.00	2.50
1982	10,000,000	—	0.25	0.50	2.00	2.50
1983		—	0.25	0.50	2.00	2.50
1984	10,000,000	—	0.25	0.50	2.00	2.50

KM# 26   50 SENTI
4.0000 g., Nickel Clad Steel, 19.20 mm. **Obv:** President Mwinyi right flanked by flowers **Rev:** Rabbit left **Edge:** Reeded

Date	Mintage	F	VF	XF	Unc	BU
1988	10,000,000	—	0.25	0.75	1.50	2.00
1989		—	0.25	0.75	1.50	2.00
1990		—	0.25	0.75	1.50	2.00

KM# 4   SHILINGI
8.0000 g., Copper-Nickel, 27.5 mm. **Obv:** Head of President J.K. Nyerere left **Rev:** Hand holding torch

Date	Mintage	F	VF	XF	Unc	BU
1966	48,000,000	—	0.25	0.50	1.50	2.00
1966 Proof	5,500	Value: 5.00				
1972	10,000,000	—	0.25	0.50	1.50	2.00
1974	15,000,000	—	0.30	0.60	1.75	2.25
1975		—	0.30	0.60	1.75	2.25
1977	5,000,000	—	0.30	0.60	1.75	2.25
1980	10,000,000	—	0.25	0.50	1.50	2.00
1981		—	0.30	0.60	1.75	2.25
1982	10,000,000	—	0.30	0.60	1.75	2.25
1983	10,000,000	—	0.30	0.60	1.75	2.25
1984	10,000,000	—	0.30	0.60	1.75	2.25

KM# 22   SHILINGI
6.5000 g., Nickel Clad Steel, 23.5 mm. **Obv:** President Mwinyi right flanked by flowers **Rev:** Hand holding torch **Edge:** Reeded

Date	Mintage	F	VF	XF	Unc	BU
1987	5,000,000	—	0.40	0.80	2.00	2.50
1988	10,000,000	—	0.40	0.80	2.00	2.50
1989		—	0.40	0.80	2.00	2.50
1990		—	0.20	0.40	1.25	1.75
1991		—	0.20	0.40	1.25	1.75
1992		—	0.20	0.40	1.25	1.75

KM# 5   5 SHILINGI
Copper-Nickel, 31.5 mm. **Series:** F.A.O. **Subject:** 10th Anniversary of Independence **Obv:** Head of President J.K. Nyerere left **Rev:** Value in center circle, food sources in frames surround

Date	Mintage	F	VF	XF	Unc	BU
ND(1971)	1,000,000	—	0.75	1.50	3.50	4.50

KM# 6   5 SHILINGI
13.8000 g., Copper-Nickel, 31.5 mm. **Series:** F.A.O. **Obv:** Head of President J.K. Nyerere left **Rev:** Value in center circle, food sources in frames surround

Date	Mintage	F	VF	XF	Unc	BU
1972	8,000,000	—	0.75	1.50	3.50	4.00
1973	5,000,000	—	0.75	1.75	4.00	4.50
1980	5,000,000	—	0.75	1.75	4.00	4.50

KM# 10   5 SHILINGI
Copper-Nickel, 31.5 mm. **Subject:** 10th Anniversary - Bank of Tanzania **Obv:** Head of President J.K. Nyerere left **Rev:** Bank building above sprigs and value

Date	Mintage	F	VF	XF	Unc	BU
ND(1976)	1,000,000	—	0.75	1.50	3.50	4.50
ND(1976) Proof	200	Value: 40.00				

KM# 12   5 SHILINGI
Copper-Nickel, 31.5 mm. **Series:** F.A.O. **Subject:** Regional Conference for Africa **Obv:** President J.K. Nyerere left flanked by oat sprigs **Rev:** Farmer working with tractor

Date	Mintage	F	VF	XF	Unc	BU
1978	50,000	—	0.75	1.50	2.75	3.75
1978 Proof	2,000	Value: 11.50				

KM# 23   5 SHILINGI
Copper-Nickel **Obv:** Large (18mm) bust of President Mwinyi right flanked by flowers **Rev:** Value within center circle, food sources in frames surround

Date	Mintage	F	VF	XF	Unc	BU
1987	5,000,000	—	0.75	1.50	3.00	3.50
1988	10,000,000	—	0.75	1.50	3.00	3.50
1989		—	0.75	1.50	3.00	3.50

KM# 23a.1   5 SHILINGI
8.5000 g., Nickel Clad Steel, 26.5 mm. **Obv:** Small (17mm) head right flanked by flowers **Rev:** Value within center circle, food sources in frames surround **Edge:** Reeded

Date	Mintage	F	VF	XF	Unc	BU
1990		—	0.60	1.20	1.85	2.25

KM# 23a.2   5 SHILINGI
8.5000 g., Nickel Clad Steel, 26.5 mm. **Obv:** Large (18mm) head right flanked by flowers **Rev:** Value within center circle, food sources in frames surround

Date	Mintage	F	VF	XF	Unc	BU
1991		—	0.60	1.20	1.85	2.25
1992		—	0.50	1.00	1.50	2.00
1993		—	0.50	1.00	1.50	2.00

KM# 20   10 SHILINGI
9.7000 g., Copper-Nickel, 29 mm. **Obv:** President J.K. Nyerere 1/4 left within circle **Rev:** National arms

Date	Mintage	F	VF	XF	Unc	BU
1987	10,000,000	—	1.00	1.50	3.25	3.75
1988	10,000,000	—	1.00	1.50	3.25	3.75
1989		—	1.00	1.50	3.25	3.75

KM# 20a   10 SHILINGI
10.0000 g., Nickel Clad Steel, 29 mm. **Obv:** Bust of President J.K. Nyerere 1/4 left within circle **Rev:** National arms

Date	Mintage	F	VF	XF	Unc	BU
1990	—	—	1.00	1.50	2.25	2.75
1991	—	—	1.00	1.50	2.25	2.75
1992	—	—	0.85	1.25	2.00	2.50
1993	—	—	0.85	1.25	2.00	2.50

KM# 20a.1   10 SHILINGI
10.0000 g., Nickel Clad Steel, 29 mm. **Obv:** Bust of President J.K. Nyerere 1/4 left within circle **Rev:** 4 mm "10"; inscription near edge

Date	Mintage	F	VF	XF	Unc	BU
1990	—	—	0.60	1.20	1.85	2.25

KM# 20a.2   10 SHILINGI
10.0000 g., Nickel Clad Steel, 29 mm. **Obv:** Bust of President J.K. Nyerere 1/4 left within circle **Rev:** 3 mm "10"; inscription away from edge

Date	Mintage	F	VF	XF	Unc	BU
1991	—	—	0.60	1.20	1.85	2.25
1992	—	—	0.60	1.20	1.85	2.25
1993	—	—	0.60	1.20	1.85	2.25

KM# 13   20 SHILINGI
Copper-Nickel **Subject:** 20th Anniversary of Independence **Obv:** President J.K. Nyerere 1/4 left within circle **Rev:** National arms

Date	Mintage	F	VF	XF	Unc	BU
ND(1981)	997,000	—	2.50	4.50	10.00	12.00

KM# 13a   20 SHILINGI
16.0000 g., 0.9250 Silver 0.4758 oz. ASW **Obv:** Bust of President J.K. Nyerere 1/4 left within circle **Rev:** National arms

Date	Mintage	F	VF	XF	Unc	BU
ND(1981) Proof	20,000	Value: 42.50				

KM# 21   20 SHILINGI
Copper-Nickel **Subject:** 20th Anniversary of Central Bank **Obv:** President Mwinyi right **Rev:** Torch within sprigs

Date	Mintage	F	VF	XF	Unc	BU
ND(1986)	—	—	—	—	45.00	65.00

KM# 21a   20 SHILINGI
16.0000 g., 0.9250 Silver 0.4758 oz. ASW **Obv:** Head of President Mwinyi right **Rev:** Torch within sprigs

Date	Mintage	F	VF	XF	Unc	BU
ND(1986) Proof	5,000	Value: 110				

KM# 27.1   20 SHILINGI
Nickel Bonded Steel **Obv:** President Mwinyi right flanked by flowers **Rev:** Elephants

Date	Mintage	F	VF	XF	Unc	BU
1990	—	—	1.50	2.00	3.50	3.75
1991	—	—	1.50	2.00	3.50	3.75

KM# 27.2   20 SHILINGI
13.0000 g., Nickel Bonded Steel, 31 mm. **Obv:** President Mwinyi right flanked by flowers **Rev:** Elephant with calf **Note:** Reduced size.

Date	Mintage	F	VF	XF	Unc	BU
1992	—	—	1.25	1.75	3.25	5.00

KM# 7   25 SHILINGI
25.4000 g., 0.5000 Silver 0.4083 oz. ASW **Subject:** Conservation **Obv:** Head of President J.K. Nyerere left **Rev:** Giraffes running right

Date	Mintage	F	VF	XF	Unc	BU
1974	8,848	—	—	—	18.00	25.00

KM# 7a   25 SHILINGI
28.2800 g., 0.9250 Silver 0.8410 oz. ASW **Obv:** Head of President J.K. Nyerere left **Rev:** Giraffes running right

Date	Mintage	F	VF	XF	Unc	BU
1974 Proof	13,000	Value: 35.00				

KM# 30   25 SHILINGI
Copper-Nickel **Subject:** 25 Years of Independence **Obv:** President J.K. Nyerere 1/4 left within circle **Rev:** National arms

Date	Mintage	F	VF	XF	Unc	BU
ND(1985) Proof	—	Value: 270				

KM# 28   25 SHILINGI
Nickel Bonded Steel **Subject:** 25th Anniversary of Central Bank **Obv:** President Mwinyi right **Rev:** Building within sprigs

Date	Mintage	F	VF	XF	Unc	BU
ND(1991)	—	—	—	—	3.00	4.00

KM# 28a   25 SHILINGI
13.0400 g., 0.9250 Silver 0.3878 oz. ASW **Obv:** Head of President Mwinyi right **Rev:** Building within sprigs

Date	Mintage	F	VF	XF	Unc	BU
ND(1991) Proof	Est. 2,000	Value: 65.00				

KM# 8   50 SHILINGI
31.8500 g., 0.5000 Silver 0.5120 oz. ASW **Subject:** Conservation **Obv:** Head of President J.K. Nyerere left **Rev:** Black Rhinoceros facing

Date	Mintage	F	VF	XF	Unc	BU
1974	8,826	—	—	—	24.00	30.00

KM# 8a   50 SHILINGI
35.0000 g., 0.9250 Silver 1.0408 oz. ASW **Obv:** Head of President J.K. Nyerere left **Rev:** Black Rhinoceros facing

Date	Mintage	F	VF	XF	Unc	BU
1974 Proof	12,000	Value: 30.00				

KM# 33   50 SHILINGI
Brass Plated Steel **Subject:** Conservation **Obv:** Head of Ali Nassan Mwinyi right within circle **Rev:** Mother rhino and calf

Date	Mintage	F	VF	XF	Unc	BU
1996	—	—	—	—	4.00	5.00

KM# 16   100 SHILINGI
23.3300 g., 0.9250 Silver 0.6938 oz. ASW **Series:** Decade for Women **Obv:** Head of President J.K. Nyerere left **Rev:** Kneeling nurse holding baby in air

Date	Mintage	F	VF	XF	Unc	BU
1984 Proof	1,000	Value: 42.50				

KM# 18   100 SHILINGI
Copper-Nickel **Subject:** Conservation **Obv:** President J.K. Nyerere left flanked by flowers **Rev:** Elephant mother and calf

Date	Mintage	F	VF	XF	Unc	BU
1986	—	—	—	—	6.50	12.00

KM# 18a   100 SHILINGI
19.4400 g., 0.9250 Silver 0.5781 oz. ASW **Obv:** Head of President J.K. Nyerere left **Rev:** Elephant mother and calf

Date	Mintage	F	VF	XF	Unc	BU
1986 Proof	25,000	Value: 30.00				

KM# 24   100 SHILINGI
19.4400 g., 0.9250 Silver 0.5781 oz. ASW **Series:** Save the Children Fund **Rev:** Two girls with clubs mashing grain in pail within circle

Date	Mintage	F	VF	XF	Unc	BU
1990 Proof	Est. 20,000	Value: 22.50				

KM# 32 100 SHILINGI
Brass Plated Steel **Subject:** Conservation **Obv:** Bust of President J.K. Nyerere left **Rev:** Four Impalas running right

Date	Mintage	F	VF	XF	Unc	BU
1993	—	—	—	—	4.00	5.00
1994	—	—	—	—	4.00	5.00

KM# 14 200 SHILINGI
28.2800 g., 0.9250 Silver 0.8410 oz. ASW **Subject:** 20th Anniversary of Independence **Obv:** Bust of President J.K. Nyerere left **Rev:** National arms

Date	Mintage	F	VF	XF	Unc	BU
ND(1981)	110	—	—	—	135	145
ND(1981) Proof	Inc. above	Value: 160				

KM# 41 200 SHILINGI
20.0000 g., 0.5000 Silver 0.3215 oz. ASW, 34 mm.
Subject: Wildlife of Africa **Obv:** National arms **Rev:** Adult and baby rhino **Edge:** Reeded

Date	Mintage	F	VF	XF	Unc	BU
1997 Proof	—	Value: 25.00				

KM# 34 200 SHILINGI
8.0000 g., Copper-Nickel-Zinc **Obv:** Head of Sheikh Karume 1/4 left within circle **Rev:** Two lions **Edge:** Plain and reeded sections

Date	Mintage	F	VF	XF	Unc	BU
1998	—	—	—	—	5.00	8.00

KM# 40 200 SHILINGI
15.4000 g., 0.9250 Silver 0.4580 oz. ASW, 33.9 mm.
Subject: Pan Troglodytes **Obv:** National arms **Rev:** Chimpanzee family **Edge:** Reeded

Date	Mintage	F	VF	XF	Unc	BU
1999 Proof	—	Value: 35.00				

KM# 59 200 SHILINGI
15.4000 g., 0.9250 Silver 0.4580 oz. ASW, 33.9 mm.
Obv: National arms **Rev:** Water Buffalo **Edge:** Reeded

Date	Mintage	F	VF	XF	Unc	BU
1999 Proof	—	Value: 35.00				

KM# 29 250 SHILINGI
28.1600 g., 0.9250 Silver 0.8374 oz. ASW **Subject:** 25th Anniversary of Independence **Obv:** Bust of President J.K. Nyerere left **Rev:** National arms

Date	Mintage	F	VF	XF	Unc	BU
ND(1985) Proof	—	Value: 265				

KM# 57 250 SHILINGI
19.3400 g., 0.9250 Silver 0.5751 oz. ASW, 26.9 mm.
Subject: Serengeti Wildlife **Obv:** National arms **Rev:** Lion, Cheetah and Zebra **Edge:** Reeded

Date	Mintage	F	VF	XF	Unc	BU
1998 Proof	—	Value: 35.00				

KM# 47 500 SHILLINGS
31.2200 g., 0.9250 Silver 0.9284 oz. ASW, 38.5 mm.
Subject: British Queen Mother **Obv:** National arms **Rev:** Scene from Queen Mother's African tour **Edge:** Reeded

Date	Mintage	F	VF	XF	Unc	BU
1997 Proof	—	Value: 40.00				

KM# 44 500 SHILINGI
20.0000 g., 0.9990 Silver 0.6423 oz. ASW **Subject:** Visit of Richard von Weizsacker **Obv:** National arms **Rev:** Weizsacker and elephant

Date	Mintage	F	VF	XF	Unc	BU
1992 Proof	Est. 20,000	Value: 35.00				

KM# 48 500 SHILINGI
33.6300 g., 0.9250 Silver 1.0000 oz. ASW, 38.4 mm.
Subject: Serengeti Wildlife **Obv:** National arms **Rev:** Leopard head and full body portraits **Edge:** Reeded

Date	Mintage	F	VF	XF	Unc	BU
1998 Proof	—	Value: 40.00				

KM# 49 500 SHILINGI
33.6300 g., 0.9250 Silver 1.0000 oz. ASW, 38.4 mm.
Subject: Serengeti Wildlife **Obv:** National arms **Rev:** Cheetah head and full body portraits **Edge:** Reeded

Date	Mintage	F	VF	XF	Unc	BU
1998 Proof	—	Value: 40.00				

KM# 50 500 SHILINGI
33.6300 g., 0.9250 Silver 1.0000 oz. ASW, 38.4 mm.
Subject: Serengeti Wildlife **Obv:** National arms **Rev:** Hyena head and full body portraits **Edge:** Reeded

Date	Mintage	F	VF	XF	Unc	BU
1998 Proof	—	Value: 40.00				

KM# 51 500 SHILINGI
33.6300 g., 0.9250 Silver 1.0000 oz. ASW, 38.4 mm.
Subject: Serengeti Wildlife **Obv:** National arms **Rev:** Crocodile head and full body portraits **Edge:** Reeded

Date	Mintage	F	VF	XF	Unc	BU
1998 Proof	—	Value: 40.00				

KM# 43 500 SHILINGI
33.8000 g., 0.9250 Silver 1.0052 oz. ASW, 38.5 mm.
Subject: Serengeti Wildlife **Obv:** National arms **Rev:** Lions **Edge:** Reeded

Date	Mintage	F	VF	XF	Unc	BU
1998 Proof	—	Value: 40.00				

KM# 17 1000 SHILINGI
8.1000 g., 0.9000 Gold 0.2344 oz. AGW **Series:** Decade for Women **Obv:** President J.K. Nyerere left flanked by flowers **Rev:** Half figure separating grain

Date	Mintage	F	VF	XF	Unc	BU
1984 Proof	500	Value: 250				

KM# 45 1000 SHILINGI
6.0000 g., 0.9990 Gold 0.1927 oz. AGW **Subject:** Visit of Richard von Weizsacker **Obv:** National arms **Rev:** Weizsacker and elephant

Date	Mintage	F	VF	XF	Unc	BU
1992 Proof	Est. 8,000	Value: 185				

KM# 60 1000 SHILINGI
1.2440 g., 0.9990 Gold 0.0400 oz. AGW, 13.92 mm.
Obv: National arms **Rev:** Primitive gold refining scene **Edge:** Reeded

Date	Mintage	F	VF	XF	Unc	BU
1998 Proof	—	Value: 60.00				

KM# 9 1500 SHILINGI
33.4370 g., 0.9000 Gold 0.9675 oz. AGW **Subject:** Conservation **Obv:** President J.K. Nyerere left flanked by flowers **Rev:** Cheetahs

Date	Mintage	F	VF	XF	Unc	BU
1974	2,779	—	—	—	925	950
1974 Proof	866	Value: 1,000				

KM# 15 2000 SHILINGI
15.9800 g., 0.9170 Gold 0.4711 oz. AGW **Subject:** 20th Anniversary of Independence **Obv:** President J.K. Nyerere **Rev:** National arms

Date	Mintage	F	VF	XF	Unc	BU
ND(1981)	110	—	—	—	475	500
ND(1981) Proof	Inc. above	Value: 525				

KM# 19 2000 SHILINGI
15.9800 g., 0.9170 Gold 0.4711 oz. AGW **Subject:** Conservation **Obv:** President J.K. Nyerere left flanked by flowers **Rev:** Banded Green Sunbird

Date	Mintage	F	VF	XF	Unc	BU
1986 Proof	5,000	Value: 460				

KM# 25 2000 SHILINGI
10.0000 g., 0.9170 Gold 0.2948 oz. AGW **Series:** Save the Children Fund **Obv:** President Mwinyi right flanked by small sprigs **Rev:** Child and calf within circle

Date	Mintage	F	VF	XF	Unc	BU
1990 Proof	Est. 3,000	Value: 300				

KM# 46 2000 SHILINGI
10.0000 g., 0.9990 Gold 0.3212 oz. AGW **Subject:** Visit of Richard von Weizsacker **Obv:** National arms **Rev:** Weizsacker and elephant

Date	Mintage	F	VF	XF	Unc	BU
1992 Proof	Est. 5,000	Value: 325				

KM# 31   2500 SHILINGI
46.8500 g., 0.9170 Gold 1.3812 oz. AGW **Subject:** 25 Years of Independence **Obv:** President J.K. Nyerere 1/4 left within circle **Rev:** National arms

Date	Mintage	F	VF	XF	Unc	BU
ND(1985) Proof	—	Value: 1,400				

KM# 35   2500 SHILINGI
155.3600 g., 0.9990 Silver 4.9897 oz. ASW, 65 mm. **Subject:** Serengeti Wildlife **Obv:** National arms **Rev:** Zebra head and full body zebra **Edge:** Reeded **Note:** Illustration reduced.

Date	Mintage	F	VF	XF	Unc	BU
1998 Proof	—	Value: 100				

KM# 36   2500 SHILINGI
155.3600 g., 0.9990 Silver 4.9897 oz. ASW, 65 mm. **Subject:** Serengeti Wildlife **Obv:** National arms **Rev:** Giraffe head and full body giraffe **Note:** Illustration reduced.

Date	Mintage	F	VF	XF	Unc	BU
1998 Proof	—	Value: 100				

KM# 37   2500 SHILINGI
155.3600 g., 0.9990 Silver 4.9897 oz. ASW, 65 mm. **Subject:** Serengeti Wildlife **Obv:** National arms **Rev:** Cheetah head and full body portrait **Note:** Illustration reduced.

Date	Mintage	F	VF	XF	Unc	BU
1998 Proof	—	Value: 115				

KM# 38   2500 SHILINGI
155.3600 g., 0.9990 Silver 4.9897 oz. ASW, 65 mm. **Subject:** Serengeti Wildlife **Obv:** National arms **Rev:** Wildebeast herd **Note:** Illustration reduced.

Date	Mintage	F	VF	XF	Unc	BU
1998 Proof	—	Value: 110				

KM# 39   2500 SHILINGI
155.3600 g., 0.9990 Silver 4.9897 oz. ASW, 65 mm. **Subject:** Serengeti Wildlife **Obv:** National arms **Rev:** Gazelle head and full body portrait **Note:** Illustration reduced.

Date	Mintage	F	VF	XF	Unc	BU
1998 Proof	—	Value: 110				

KM# 52   2500 SHILINGI
155.3600 g., 0.9990 Silver 4.9897 oz. ASW, 65 mm. **Subject:** Serengeti Wildlife **Obv:** National arms **Rev:** Lion head and full body lion **Edge:** Reeded **Note:** Illustration reduced.

Date	Mintage	F	VF	XF	Unc	BU
1998 Proof	—	Value: 110				

KM# 53   2500 SHILINGI
155.3600 g., 0.9990 Silver 4.9897 oz. ASW, 65 mm. **Subject:** Serengeti Wildlife **Obv:** National arms **Rev:** Leopard head and full body portraits **Edge:** Reeded **Note:** Illustration reduced.

Date	Mintage	F	VF	XF	Unc	BU
1998 Proof	—	Value: 110				

KM# 54   2500 SHILINGI
155.3600 g., 0.9990 Silver 4.9897 oz. ASW, 65 mm.
Subject: Serengeti Wildlife **Obv:** National arms **Rev:** Hyena head and full body portraits **Edge:** Reeded **Note:** Illustration reduced.

Date	Mintage	F	VF	XF	Unc	BU
1998 Proof	— Value: 110					

KM# 55   2500 SHILINGI
155.3600 g., 0.9990 Silver 4.9897 oz. ASW, 65 mm.
Subject: Serengeti Wildlife **Obv:** National arms **Rev:** Crocodile head and full body portraits **Edge:** Reeded **Note:** Illustration reduced.

Date	Mintage	F	VF	XF	Unc	BU
1998 Proof	— Value: 110					

KM# 42   10000 SHILINGI
31.1035 g., 0.9999 Gold 0.9999 oz. AGW, 32.5 mm.
Subject: Serengeti Wildlife **Obv:** National arms **Rev:** Lion, Cheetah and Zebra **Edge:** Reeded

Date	Mintage	F	VF	XF	Unc	BU
1998 Proof	Est. 1,000 Value: 1,150					

KM# 58   50000 SHILINGI
155.5100 g., 0.9990 Gold 4.9946 oz. AGW **Subject:** Serengeti Wildlife **Obv:** National arms **Rev:** Lion, Cheetah and Zebra

Date	Mintage	F	VF	XF	Unc	BU
1998 Proof	— Value: 5,800					

TRIAL STRIKES

KM#	Date	Mintage	Identification	Mkt Val
TS2	1980	—	Shilingi. Copper-Nickel. KM#4.	115
TS3	1980	—	5 Senti. Copper-Nickel. KM#6.	145
TS1	1981	—	50 Senti. Copper-Nickel. KM#3.	85.00

PATTERNS
Including off metal strikes

KM#	Date	Mintage	Identification	Mkt Val
Pn1	1973	—	50 Senti. Nickel-Bronze. KM#3.	75.00

PROOF SETS

KM#	Date	Mintage	Identification	Issue Price	Mkt Val
PS1	1966 (4)	5,500	KM#1-4	10.20	10.00
PS2	1974 (2)	30,000	KM#7a-8a	50.00	75.00
PS3	1985 (3)	—	KM#29-31	—	12.00

TATARSTAN

Tatarstan, an autonomous republic in the Russian Federation, is situated between the middle of the Volga river and its tributary Kama, extends east to the Ural mountains, covering 26,500 sq. mi. (68,000 sq. km.) and as of the 1970 census, has a population of 3,743,600. Capital: Kazan. Tatarstan's economy combines its ancient traditions in the craftmanship of wood, leather, cloth, and ceramics with modern engineering, chemical, and food industries.

Colonized by the Bulgars in the 5th century, the territory of the Volga-Kama Bulgar State was inhabited by Turks. In the 13th century, Ghengis Khan conquered the area and established control until the 15th century, when residual Mongol influence left Tatarstan as the Tatar Khanate, seat of the Kazan (Tatar) Khans. In 1552, under Ivan IV (The Terrible), Russia conquered, absorbed and controlled Tatarstan until the dissolution of the U.S.S.R. in the late 20th century.

Constituted as an autonomous republic on May 27, 1990, and as a sovereign state equal with Russia April, 1992, Tatarstan, with Russia's president, signed a treaty in Feb. 1994 defining Tatarstan as a state united with Russia (Commonwealth of Independent States).

RULER
President Mintimir Shaimiev

RUSSIAN STATE

TOKEN COINAGE

KM# Tn1   KILO (Bread)
Bronze **Ruler:** President Mintimir Shaimiev **Obv:** Arms **Rev:** Wheat stalks **Edge:** Reeded

Date	Mintage	F	VF	XF	Unc	BU
ND (1993)	—	2.50	4.00	8.00	16.00	—

KM# Tn2   10 LITRES (Petrol)
Bronze **Ruler:** President Mintimir Shaimiev **Obv:** Arms **Rev:** Oil derrick **Edge:** Reeded **Note:** The bronze 10 Litres token was withdrawn from circulation because it was nickel plated in large numbers and passed off as the higher valued copper-nickel version KM-Tn3.

Date	Mintage	F	VF	XF	Unc	BU
ND (1993)	—	3.50	6.00	12.00	25.00	—

KM# Tn3   20 LITRES (Petrol)
5.2500 g., Copper-Nickel, 24.86 mm. **Ruler:** President Mintimir Shaimiev **Obv:** Arms **Rev:** Oil derrick **Edge:** Reeded **Note:** The copper-nickel Tn3 are often found with test file notches, because of the nickel plating problems of the bronze Tn2.

Date	Mintage	F	VF	XF	Unc	BU
ND (1993)	—	4.00	7.00	13.50	27.50	—

THAILAND

The Kingdom of Thailand (formerly Siam), a constitutional monarchy located in the center of mainland Southeast Asia between Burma and Laos, has an area of 198,457 mi. (514,000 sq. km.) and a population of *55.5 million. Capital: Bangkok. The economy is based on agriculture and mining. Rubber, rice, teakwood, tin and tungsten are exported.

The history of The Kingdom of Siam, the only country in south and Southeast Asia that was never colonized by an European power, dates from the 6th century A.D. when Thai people started to migrate into the area a process that accelerated with the Mongol invasion of China in the 13th century. After 400 years of sporadic warfare with the neighboring Burmese, King Taskin won the last battle in 1767. He founded a new capital, Dhonburi, on the west bank of the Chao Praya River. King Rama I moved the capital to Bangkok in 1782, thus initiating the so-called Bangkok Period of Siamese coinage characterized by Pot Duang money (bullet coins) stamped with regal symbols.

The Portuguese, who were followed by the Dutch, British and French, introduced the Thai to the Western world. Rama III of the present ruling dynasty negotiated a treaty of friendship and commerce with Britain in 1826, and in 1896 the independence of the kingdom was guaranteed by an Anglo-French accord.

In 1909 Siam ceded to Great Britain its suzerain rights over the dependencies of Kedah, Kelantan, Trengganu and Perlis, Malay states situated in southern Siam just north of British Malaya, which eliminated any British jurisdiction in Siam proper.

The absolute monarchy was changed into a constitutional monarchy in 1932.

On Dec. 8, 1941, after five hours of fighting, Thailand agreed to permit Japanese troops passage through the country to invade Northern British Malaysia. This eventually led to increased Japanese intervention and finally occupation of the country. On Jan. 25, 1942, Thailand declared war on Great Britain and the United States. A free Thai guerilla movement was soon organized to counteract the Japanese. In July 1943 Japan transferred the four northern Malay States back to Thailand. These were returned to Great Britain after peace treaties were signed in 1946.

RULERS
Rama V (Phra Maha Chulalongkorn), 1868-1910
Rama VI (Phra Maha Vajiravudh), 1910-1925
Rama VII (Phra Maha Prajadhipok), 1925-1935
Rama VIII (Phra Maha Ananda Mahidol), 1935-1946
Rama IX (Phra Maha Bhumifhol Adulyadej), 1946-

MONETARY SYSTEM
Old currency system

2 Solos = 1 Att
2 Att = 1 Sio (Pai)
2 Sio = 1 Sik
2 Sik = 1 Fuang
2 Fuang = 1 Salung (not Sal'ung)
4 Salung = 1 Baht
4 Baht = 1 Tamlung
20 Tamlung = 1 Chang

UNITS OF OLD THAI CURRENCY

Chang -	ชั่ง	Sik -	ซีก
Tamlung -	ตำลึง	Sio (Pai) -	เสี้ยว
Baht -	บาท	Att -	อัฐ
Salung -	สลึง	Solos -	โสพส
Fuang -	เฟื้อง		

MINT MARKS
H-Heaton Birmingham

DATING

Typical BE Dating

1 2 3 8   1 2 4 4

Typical CS Dating

NOTE: Sometimes the era designator *BE* or *CS* will actually appear on the coin itself.

Denomination

2 ½

2-1/2 (Satang)   RS Dating

DATE CONVERSION TABLES

B.E. date - 543 = A.D. date
Ex: 2516 - 543 = 1973
R.S. date + 1781 = A.D. date
Ex: 127 + 1781 = 1908

C.S. date + 638 = A.D. date
Ex 1238 + 638 = 1876
Primary denominations used were 1 Baht, 1/4 and 1/8 Baht up to the reign of Rama IV. Other denominations are much scarcer.

KINGDOM OF SIAM
until 1939
STANDARD COINAGE

Y# 21   1/2 ATT (1 Solot)
Bronze **Ruler:** Rama V **Obv:** Uniformed bust left **Rev:** Crowned seated figure right

Date	Mintage	F	VF	XF	Unc	BU
RS124 (1905)	—	1.50	2.50	10.00	110	—

Note: These coins were also minted in RS114, RS115, RS121 and RS122. The last year had a mintage of 5,120,000. Coins with these dates have not been observed and were probably additional mintings of coins dated RS109 and RS118. A nickel pattern dated RS114 does exist. Varieties in numeral size and rotated dies exist

Y# 22   ATT
Bronze **Ruler:** Rama V **Obv:** Uniformed bust left **Rev:** Crowned seated figure right **Note:** Full red uncirculated coins of this type carry a substantial premium.

Date	Mintage	F	VF	XF	Unc	BU
RS121 (1902)	11,251,000	3.50	5.00	40.00	200	—
RS122 (1903)	4,109,000	4.50	10.00	55.00	210	—

Note: Exists with large (greater than 1mm) and small (less than 1mm) numerals

| RS124 (1905) | — | 3.50 | 5.00 | 40.00 | 200 | — |

Y# 23   2 ATT (1/32 Baht = 1 Sio)
Bronze **Ruler:** Rama V **Obv:** Uniformed bust left **Rev:** Crowned seated figure right **Note:** Varieties in numeral size and rotated dies exist. Full red uncirculated coins of this type carry a substantial premium.

Date	Mintage	F	VF	XF	Unc	BU
RS121 (1902)	2,797,000	1.50	3.00	30.00	210	—
RS122 (1903)	2,323,000	1.50	3.00	30.00	210	—
RS124 (1905)	—	1.50	3.00	30.00	210	—

Y# 32a   FUANG (1/8 Baht)
Silver **Ruler:** Rama V **Obv:** Bust left **Rev:** National arms **Note:** Weight range: 1.7-2.01 g.

Date	Mintage	F	VF	XF	Unc	BU
RS121 (1902)	380,000	3.00	15.00	60.00	120	—
RS122 (1903)	460,000	3.00	15.00	70.00	150	—
RS123 (1904)	310,000	3.00	15.00	65.00	130	—
RS124 (1905)	410,000	3.00	15.00	65.00	135	—
RS125 (1906)	—	3.00	15.00	65.00	135	—
RS126 (1907)	—	3.00	15.00	70.00	140	—
RS127 (1908)	480,000	3.00	15.00	90.00	200	—

Y# 32c   FUANG (1/8 Baht)
Gold **Ruler:** Rama V **Obv:** Bust left **Rev:** National arms

Date	Mintage	F	VF	XF	Unc	BU
RS122 (1903)	—					
RS123 (1904)	—	1,500	3,000	5,000	7,000	
RS124 (1905)	—	1,500	3,000	5,000	7,000	
RS125 (1906)	—	1,500	3,000	5,000	7,000	
RS126 (1907)	—	1,500	3,000	5,000	7,000	
RS127 (1908)	—	1,500	3,000	5,000	7,000	
RS128 (1909)	—	1,500	3,000	5,000	7,000	
RS129 (1910)	—	1,500	3,000	5,000	7,000	

Y# 33a   SALUNG = 1/4 BAHT
Silver **Ruler:** Rama V **Obv:** Bust left **Rev:** National arms **Note:** Weight range: 3.60-4.02g.

Date	Mintage	F	VF	XF	Unc	BU
RS120 (1901)	—	100	200	300	4,000	—
RS121 (1902)	560,000	20.00	40.00	70.00	200	—
RS122 (1903)	340,000	30.00	60.00	100	400	—
RS123 (1904)	190,000	30.00	40.00	70.00	200	—
RS125 (1906)	—	20.00	40.00	70.00	200	—
RS126 (1907)	—	20.00	40.00	70.00	200	—
RS127 (1908)	270,000	20.00	60.00	90.00	220	—

Y# 43   SALUNG = 1/4 BAHT
3.7500 g., 0.8000 Silver 0.0964 oz. ASW **Ruler:** Rama VI **Obv:** Bust right **Rev:** Elephant heads flank facing elephant

Date	Mintage	F	VF	XF	Unc	BU
BE2458 (1915)	2,040,000	—	5.00	10.00	20.00	—

Y# 43a   SALUNG = 1/4 BAHT
3.7500 g., 0.6500 Silver 0.0784 oz. ASW **Ruler:** Rama VI **Obv:** Bust right **Rev:** Elephant heads flank facing elephant

Date	Mintage	F	VF	XF	Unc	BU
BE2460 (1917)	1,100,000	—	4.00	8.00	18.50	—
BE2461 (1918)	2,170,000	—	4.00	8.00	18.50	—
BE2462 (1919)	7,860,000	—	3.00	6.50	15.00	—
BE2467 (1924)	2,100,000	—	4.00	8.00	18.50	—
BE2468 (1925)	—		4.00	8.00	18.50	—

Y# 43b   SALUNG = 1/4 BAHT
3.7500 g., 0.5000 Silver 0.0603 oz. ASW **Ruler:** Rama VI **Obv:** Bust right **Rev:** Elephant heads flank facing elephant

Date	Mintage	F	VF	XF	Unc	BU
BE2462 (1919) Dot after legend	Inc. above	—	40.00	65.00	120	—

Y# 34a   BAHT
Silver, 31.5 mm. **Ruler:** Rama V **Obv:** Bust left **Rev:** National arms, flags flanking **Edge:** Plain

Date	Mintage	F	VF	XF	Unc	BU
RS120 (1901)	—	100	200	600	1,800	—
RS121 (1902)	4,070,000	20.00	40.00	100	400	—

Note: There are two varieties, large and small date

RS122 (1903)	19,150,000	30.00	50.00	90.00	250	—
RS123 (1904)	4,790,000	20.00	40.00	70.00	190	—
RS124 (1905)	6,770,000	20.00	40.00	70.00	190	—
RS125 (1906)	—	20.00	40.00	70.00	190	—
RS126 (1907)	—	40.00	60.00	170	400	—

DECIMAL COINAGE

25 Satang = 1 Salung; 100 Satang = 1 Baht

Y# 50   1/2 SATANG
Bronze **Ruler:** Rama VIII **Obv:** Hole in center divides inscription **Rev:** Hole in center of design

Date	Mintage	F	VF	XF	Unc	BU
BE2480 (1937)	—	—	0.75	1.75	3.50	—

Y# 35 SATANG
Bronze **Ruler:** Rama VI **Obv:** Hole in center divides inscription **Rev:** Hole in center of design **Edge:** Plain **Note:** Variations in lettering exist.

Date	Mintage	F	VF	XF	Unc	BU
RS127 (1908)	17,000,000	—	2.50	35.00	120	—
RS128 (1909)	150,000	—	3.50	35.00	120	—
RS129 (1910)	9,000,000	—	1.50	35.00	100	—
RS130 (1911)	30,000,000	—	1.50	25.00	50.00	—
RS132 (1913) Rare	—	—	—	—	—	—
BE2456 (1913)	10,000,000	—	1.00	1.50	4.00	—
BE2457 (1914)	1,000,000	—	2.00	4.00	12.50	—
BE2458 (1915)	5,000,000	—	0.75	1.00	2.75	—
BE2461 (1918)	18,880,000	—	0.65	1.25	3.00	—
BE2462 (1919)	6,400,000	—	0.65	1.00	2.75	—
BE2463 (1920)	17,240,000	—	1.00	1.50	3.50	—
BE2464 (1921)	6,360,000	—	15.00	25.00	100	—
BE2466 (1923)	14,000,000	—	0.75	1.00	2.75	—
BE2467 (1924)	Inc. above	—	1.00	1.50	3.50	—
BE2469 (1926)	20,000,000	—	0.50	0.75	2.50	—
BE2470 (1927)	—	—	0.50	0.75	2.50	—
BE2472 (1929)	—	—	0.50	1.00	2.75	—
BE2478 (1935)	—	—	0.50	0.70	2.00	—
BE2480 (1937)	—	—	0.50	0.70	2.00	—

Y# 51 SATANG
Bronze **Ruler:** Rama VIII **Obv:** Hole in center divides inscription **Rev:** Hole in center of design **Edge:** Plain

Date	Mintage	F	VF	XF	Unc	BU
BE2482 (1939)	24,400,000	—	1.50	3.00	6.00	—

Y# 36 5 SATANG
Nickel, 18 mm. **Ruler:** Rama VI **Obv:** Hole in center divides inscription **Rev:** Center hole within design

Date	Mintage	F	VF	XF	Unc	BU
RS127 (1908)	7,000,000	—	3.00	35.00	120	—
RS128 (1909)	4,000,000	—	3.50	35.00	100	—
RS129 (1910)	4,000,000	—	1.50	35.00	100	—
RS131 (1912)	2,000,000	—	1.50	25.00	50.00	—
RS132 (1913) Rare	—	—	—	—	—	—
BE2456 (1913)	2,000,000	—	1.50	2.50	6.00	—
BE2457 (1914)	2,000,000	—	1.50	2.50	6.00	—
BE2461 (1918)	2,000,000	—	1.50	2.50	6.00	—
BE2462 (1919)	2,000,000	—	1.00	2.00	6.00	—
BE2463 (1920)	9,900,000	—	1.00	1.50	4.50	—
BE2464 (1921)	13,000,000	—	0.60	1.25	3.00	—
BE2469 (1926)	20,000,000	—	0.60	1.25	3.00	—
BE2478 (1935)	10,000,000	—	0.60	1.25	3.00	—
BE2480 (1937)	20,000,000	—	0.60	1.25	3.00	—

Y# 37 10 SATANG
3.3000 g., Nickel **Ruler:** Rama VI **Obv:** Hole in center divides inscription **Rev:** Hole in center of design **Edge:** Plain **Note:** Variations in lettering exist.

Date	Mintage	F	VF	XF	Unc	BU
RS127 (1908)	7,000,000	—	1.50	35.00	130	—
RS129 (1910)	5,000,000	—	1.50	35.00	120	—
RS130 (1911)	500,000	—	2.00	5.00	12.00	—
RS131 (1912)	1,500,000	—	1.50	3.00	10.00	—
BE2456 (1913)	1,000,000	—	1.25	2.00	6.00	—
BE2457 (1914)	1,000,000	—	1.25	2.00	6.00	—
BE2461 (1918)	770,000	—	2.50	3.50	9.00	—
BE2462 (1919)	774,000	—	1.25	1.50	3.50	—
BE2463 (1920)	Inc. above	—	1.25	1.50	3.50	—
BE2464 (1921)	21,727,000	—	1.00	1.25	3.00	—

Date	Mintage	F	VF	XF	Unc	BU
BE2478 (1935)	5,000,000	—	1.00	1.25	3.00	—
BE2480 (1937)	5,000,000	—	0.75	1.00	2.50	—

Y# 48 25 SATANG = 1/4 BAHT
3.7500 g., 0.6500 Silver 0.0784 oz. ASW **Ruler:** Rama VII **Obv:** Uniformed bust left **Rev:** Elephant

Date	Mintage	F	VF	XF	Unc	BU
BE2472 (1929)	—	—	4.50	9.00	22.50	—

Y# 49 50 SATANG = 1/2 BAHT
7.5000 g., 0.6500 Silver 0.1567 oz. ASW **Ruler:** Rama VII **Obv:** Uniformed bust left **Rev:** Elephant

Date	Mintage	F	VF	XF	Unc	BU
BE2472 (1929)	17,008,000	—	7.00	16.50	35.00	45.00

Y# 44 2 SALUNG = 1/2 BAHT
7.5000 g., 0.8000 Silver 0.1929 oz. ASW **Ruler:** Rama VI **Obv:** Uniformed bust right **Rev:** Elephant heads flank facing elephant

Date	Mintage	F	VF	XF	Unc	BU
BE2458 (1915)	2,740,000	—	7.50	18.50	40.00	—

Y# 44b 2 SALUNG = 1/2 BAHT
7.5000 g., 0.5000 Silver 0.1206 oz. ASW **Ruler:** Rama VI **Obv:** Uniformed bust right **Rev:** Elephant heads flank facing elephant

Date	Mintage	F	VF	XF	Unc	BU
BE2462 (1919)	Inc. above	—	7.50	16.50	32.50	—
Note: Large dot after legend						
BE2462 (1919)	Inc. above	—	7.50	16.50	32.50	—
Note: Small dot after legend						

Y# 44a 2 SALUNG = 1/2 BAHT
7.5000 g., 0.6500 Silver 0.1567 oz. ASW **Ruler:** Rama VI **Obv:** Uniformed bust right **Rev:** Elephant heads flank facing elephant **Note:** Date varieties exist.

Date	Mintage	F	VF	XF	Unc	BU
BE2462 (1919)	3,230,000	—	6.00	14.00	30.00	—
BE2463 (1920)	4,970,000	—	6.00	14.00	30.00	—
BE2464 (1921)	—	—	6.00	14.00	30.00	—

Y# 39 BAHT
15.0000 g., 0.9000 Silver 0.4340 oz. ASW **Ruler:** Rama V **Obv:** Uniformed bust left **Rev:** Elephant heads flank facing elephant

Date	Mintage	F	VF	XF	Unc	BU
RS127 (1908)	1,037,000	—	2,500	3,750	6,750	—

Y# 45 BAHT
15.0000 g., 0.9000 Silver 0.4340 oz. ASW **Ruler:** Rama VI **Obv:** Uniformed bust right **Rev:** Elephant heads flank facing elephant

Date	Mintage	F	VF	XF	Unc	BU
BE2456 (1913)	2,690,000	—	12.50	18.50	40.00	—
Note: BE2456 is often found weakly struck so it does appear similar to a counterfeit						
BE2457 (1914)	490,000	—	14.50	25.00	50.00	—
BE2458 (1915)	5,000,000	—	12.50	18.50	40.00	—
BE2459 (1916)	9,080,000	—	12.50	18.50	32.00	—
BE2460 (1917)	14,340,000	—	12.50	18.50	32.00	—
BE2461 (1918)	3,840,000	—	12.50	18.50	45.00	—

Date	Mintage	F	VF	XF	Unc	BU
BE2478 (1935)	5,000,000	—	1.00	1.25	3.00	—
BE2480 (1937)	5,000,000	—	0.75	1.00	2.50	—

KINGDOM OF THAILAND
1939-
DECIMAL COINAGE
25 Satang = 1 Salung; 100 Satang = 1 Baht

Y# 54 SATANG
Bronze **Ruler:** Rama VIII **Obv:** Hole in center of design **Rev:** Hole in center of design **Edge:** Plain

Date	Mintage	F	VF	XF	Unc	BU
BE2484 (1941)	—	—	0.50	1.50	3.00	—

Y# 57 SATANG
1.5000 g., Tin **Ruler:** Rama VIII **Obv:** Center hole within design **Rev:** Center hole within design **Edge:** Plain **Note:** BE date and denomination in Thai numerals, without hole.

Date	Mintage	F	VF	XF	Unc	BU
BE2485 (1942)	20,700,000	—	0.30	0.50	1.00	—
Note: Approximately 790,000 coins were struck for circulation 1967-73						

Y# 60 SATANG
Tin **Ruler:** Rama VIII **Obv:** Hole in center of design **Rev:** Hole in center of design **Edge:** Plain **Note:** BE date and denomination in Western numerals. No hole.

Date	Mintage	F	VF	XF	Unc	BU
BE2487 (1944)	500,000	—	0.10	0.20	0.50	—

Y# 186 SATANG
0.5000 g., Aluminum, 14.58 mm. **Ruler:** Bhumipol Adulyadej (Rama IX) **Obv:** Head left **Rev:** Steepled building **Edge:** Plain

Date	Mintage	F	VF	XF	Unc	BU
BE2530 (1987)	93,000	—	—	—	0.10	—
BE2531 (1988)	200,000	—	—	—	0.10	—
BE2533 (1990)	—	—	—	—	0.10	—
BE2534 (1991)	—	—	—	—	0.10	—
BE2535 (1992)	—	—	—	—	0.10	—
BE2536 (1993)	—	—	—	—	0.10	—
BE2537 (1994)	—	—	—	—	0.10	—
BE2538 (1995)	—	—	—	—	0.10	—

Y# 342 SATANG
Aluminum **Ruler:** Bhumipol Adulyadej (Rama IX) **Subject:** 50th Anniversary - Reign of King Rama IX **Obv:** Uniformed bust facing **Rev:** Arms

Date	Mintage	F	VF	XF	Unc	BU
BE2539 (1996)	—	—	—	—	0.15	—

Y# 55 5 SATANG
1.5000 g., 0.6500 Silver 0.0313 oz. ASW **Ruler:** Rama VIII **Obv:** Center hole within design **Rev:** Center hole within design

Date	Mintage	F	VF	XF	Unc	BU
BE2484 (1941)	—	—	1.50	3.00	4.50	—

Y# 58 5 SATANG
Tin **Ruler:** Rama VIII **Obv:** Hole in center of design **Rev:** Hole in center of design **Note:** BE date and denomination in Thai numerals.

Date	Mintage	F	VF	XF	Unc	BU
BE2485 (1942)	—	—	0.50	1.50	3.00	—

Y# 61 5 SATANG
Tin **Ruler:** Rama VIII **Obv:** Hole in center of design **Rev:** Hole in center of design **Note:** Thick (2.2mm) planchet. BE date and denomination in Western numerals.

Date	Mintage	F	VF	XF	Unc	BU
BE2487 (1944)	—	—	0.50	1.25	3.00	—
BE2488 (1945)	—	—	0.50	1.25	3.00	—

Y# 61a 5 SATANG
Tin **Ruler:** Rama VIII **Obv:** Hole in center of design **Rev:** Hole in center of design **Note:** Thin (2mm) planchet.

Date	Mintage	F	VF	XF	Unc	BU
BE2488 (1945)	—	—	0.50	1.25	3.00	—

Y# 61b 5 SATANG
Tin **Ruler:** Rama VIII **Obv:** Hole in center of design **Rev:** Hole in center of design **Note:** Medium planchet.

Date	Mintage	F	VF	XF	Unc	BU
BE2488 (1945)	—	—	0.50	1.25	3.00	—

Y# 64 5 SATANG
Tin **Ruler:** Rama VIII **Obv:** King Ananda, youth head left **Rev:** Mythical creature "Garuda"

Date	Mintage	F	VF	XF	Unc	BU
BE2489 (1946)	—	—	0.50	1.00	2.00	—

Y# 68 5 SATANG
1.1000 g., Tin **Ruler:** Rama VIII **Obv:** King Ananda, youth head left **Rev:** Mythical creature "Garuda"

Date	Mintage	F	VF	XF	Unc	BU
BE2489 (1946)	24,480,000	—	0.15	0.50	1.00	—

Y# 72 5 SATANG
Tin **Ruler:** Bhumipol Adulyadej (Rama IX) **Obv:** Uniformed bust left with one medal **Rev:** Mantled arms

Date	Mintage	F	VF	XF	Unc	BU
BE2493 (1950)	Est. 6,480,000	—	0.50	0.75	1.25	—

Note: Coins bearing this date were also struck in 1954, 58, 59, and 73. Mintages are included here

Y# 72a 5 SATANG
Aluminum-Bronze **Ruler:** Bhumipol Adulyadej (Rama IX) **Obv:** Uniformed bust left **Rev:** Mantled arms **Edge:** Plain

Date	Mintage	F	VF	XF	Unc	BU
BE2493 (1950)	15,500,000	—	0.25	1.00	2.00	—

Y# 78 5 SATANG
Aluminum-Bronze **Ruler:** Bhumipol Adulyadej (Rama IX) **Obv:** Smaller head, 3 medals on uniform **Rev:** Mantled arms **Edge:** Plain

Date	Mintage	F	VF	XF	Unc	BU
BE2500 (1957)	Est. 46,440,000	—	—	0.10	0.25	—

Note: Minted without date change until 1987

Y# 78a 5 SATANG
Bronze **Ruler:** Bhumipol Adulyadej (Rama IX) **Obv:** Uniformed bust left **Rev:** Mantled arms **Edge:** Plain

Date	Mintage	F	VF	XF	Unc	BU
BE2500 (1957)	Est. 6,240,000	—	0.50	1.50	2.00	—

Y# 78b 5 SATANG
Tin **Ruler:** Bhumipol Adulyadej (Rama IX) **Obv:** Uniformed bust left **Rev:** Mantled arms

Date	Mintage	F	VF	XF	Unc	BU
BE2500 (1957)	—	—	1.75	3.00	5.00	—

Note: The above coins were struck to replace Y#72 in mint sets

Y# 208 5 SATANG
0.6000 g., Aluminum, 16 mm. **Ruler:** Bhumipol Adulyadej (Rama IX) **Obv:** Bust left **Rev:** Phra Patom Temple, Nakhon Pathom **Edge:** Plain

Date	Mintage	F	VF	XF	Unc	BU
BE2530 (1987)	—	—	—	—	25.00	—
BE2531 (1988)	704,000	—	—	—	0.10	—
BE2533 (1990)	—	—	—	—	0.10	—
BE2534 (1991)	—	—	—	—	0.10	—
BE2535 (1992)	—	—	—	—	0.10	—
BE2536 (1993)	—	—	—	—	0.10	—
BE2537 (1994)	—	—	—	—	0.10	—
BE2538 (1995)	—	—	—	—	0.10	—

Y# 343 5 SATANG
Aluminum **Ruler:** Bhumipol Adulyadej (Rama IX) **Subject:** 50th Anniversary - Reign of King Rama IX **Obv:** Bust facing **Rev:** Arms

Date	Mintage	F	VF	XF	Unc	BU
BE2539 (1996)	—	—	—	—	0.25	—

Y# 56 10 SATANG
2.5000 g., 0.6500 Silver 0.0522 oz. ASW **Ruler:** Rama VIII **Obv:** Hole in center of design **Rev:** Hole in center of design **Edge:** Plain

Date	Mintage	F	VF	XF	Unc	BU
BE2484 (1941)	—	—	2.00	4.00	8.00	—

Y# 59 10 SATANG
Tin **Ruler:** Rama VIII **Obv:** Hole in center of design **Rev:** Hole in center of design **Note:** BE date and denomination in Thai numerals.

Date	Mintage	F	VF	XF	Unc	BU
BE2485 (1942)	230,000	—	1.00	2.00	5.00	—

Y# 62 10 SATANG
Tin **Ruler:** Rama VIII **Obv:** Hole in center of design **Rev:** Hole in center of design **Note:** Thick (2.5mm) planchet. BE date and denomination in Western numerals.

Date	Mintage	F	VF	XF	Unc	BU
BE2487 (1944)	—	—	1.00	2.00	3.50	—
BE2488 (1945)	—	—	3.50	7.00	15.00	—

Y# 62a 10 SATANG
Tin **Ruler:** Bhumipol Adulyadej (Rama IX) **Obv:** Hole in center of design **Rev:** Hole in center of design **Note:** Thin (2mm) planchet.

Date	Mintage	F	VF	XF	Unc	BU
BE2488 (1945)	—	—	1.00	2.50	4.00	—

Y# 65 10 SATANG
Tin **Ruler:** Bhumipol Adulyadej (Rama IX) **Obv:** King Ananda, child head **Rev:** Mythical creature "Garuda"

Date	Mintage	F	VF	XF	Unc	BU
BE2489 (1946)	—	—	0.50	1.25	2.25	—

Y# 69 10 SATANG
Tin **Ruler:** Bhumipol Adulyadej (Rama IX) **Obv:** Youth head **Rev:** Mythical creature "Garuda" **Edge:** Plain

Date	Mintage	F	VF	XF	Unc	BU
BE2489 (1946)	40,470,000	—	0.50	1.25	2.00	—

Y# 73 10 SATANG
Tin **Ruler:** Bhumipol Adulyadej (Rama IX) **Obv:** King Bhumiphol, one medal on uniform **Rev:** Arms **Edge:** Plain

Date	Mintage	F	VF	XF	Unc	BU
BE2493 (1950)	139,695,000	—	0.40	1.00	1.50	—

Note: These coins were also struck in 1954-1973 and the mintages are also included here

Y# 73a 10 SATANG
Aluminum-Bronze **Ruler:** Bhumipol Adulyadej (Rama IX) **Obv:** King Bhumiphol left **Rev:** Arms

Date	Mintage	F	VF	XF	Unc	BU
BE2493 (1950)	4,060,000	—	0.75	1.50	2.50	—

Y# 79 10 SATANG
Aluminum-Bronze **Ruler:** Bhumipol Adulyadej (Rama IX) **Obv:** Smaller head, 3 medals on uniform **Rev:** Mantled arms with thin style legend

Date	Mintage	F	VF	XF	Unc	BU
BE2500 (1957)	Est. 55,410,000	—	0.10	0.25	0.50	—

Note: Minted without date change until 1987

Y# 79a 10 SATANG
Bronze **Ruler:** Bhumipol Adulyadej (Rama IX) **Obv:** Uniformed bust left **Rev:** Mantled arms with thick style legend **Edge:** Plain

Date	Mintage	F	VF	XF	Unc	BU
BE2500 (1957)	13,365,000	—	0.25	0.75	1.25	—
BE2501 (1958)	—	—	0.25	0.75	1.25	—

Y# 79b 10 SATANG
Tin **Ruler:** Bhumipol Adulyadej (Rama IX) **Obv:** Uniformed bust left **Rev:** Mantled arms with thick style legend

Date	Mintage	F	VF	XF	Unc	BU
BE2500 (1957)	—	—	—	—	20.00	—

Y# 79c 10 SATANG
Bronze **Ruler:** Bhumipol Adulyadej (Rama IX) **Obv:** Uniformed bust left **Rev:** Mantled arms with thin style legend

Date	Mintage	F	VF	XF	Unc	BU
BE2500 (1957)	Inc. above	—	100	200	400	—

Y# 79d 10 SATANG
Aluminum-Bronze **Ruler:** Bhumipol Adulyadej (Rama IX) **Obv:** Uniformed bust left **Rev:** Mantled arms with thick style legend **Edge:** Plain

Date	Mintage	F	VF	XF	Unc	BU
BE2500 (1957)	—	—	0.10	0.25	0.50	—

Y# 209 10 SATANG
0.8000 g., Aluminum, 16.47 mm. **Ruler:** Bhumipol Adulyadej (Rama IX) **Obv:** Young bust left **Rev:** Steepled building **Edge:** Plain

Date	Mintage	F	VF	XF	Unc	BU
BE2530 (1987)	—	—	—	—	25.00	—
BE2531 (1988)	900,000	—	—	—	0.10	—
BE2533 (1990)	—	—	—	—	0.10	—
BE2534 (1991)	—	—	—	—	0.10	—
BE2535 (1992)	—	—	—	—	0.10	—
BE2536 (1993)	—	—	—	—	0.10	—

Date	Mintage	F	VF	XF	Unc	BU
BE2537 (1994)	—	—	—	—	0.10	—
BE2538 (1995)	—	—	—	—	0.10	—

Y# 344   10 SATANG
Aluminum **Ruler:** Bhumipol Adulyadej (Rama IX) **Subject:** 50th Anniversary - Reign of King Rama IX **Obv:** Bust facing **Rev:** Arms

Date	Mintage	F	VF	XF	Unc	BU
BE2539 (1996)	—	—	—	—	0.35	—

Y# A56   20 SATANG
3.0000 g., 0.6500 Silver 0.0627 oz. ASW **Ruler:** Rama VIII **Obv:** Hole in center of design **Rev:** Hole in center of design **Note:** BE date and denomination in Thai numerals.

Date	Mintage	F	VF	XF	Unc	BU
BE2485 (1942)	—	—	3.00	6.00	12.00	—

Y# 63   20 SATANG
Tin **Ruler:** Rama VIII **Obv:** Hole in center of design **Rev:** Hole in center of design **Edge:** Plain **Note:** BE date and denomination in Western numerals.

Date	Mintage	F	VF	XF	Unc	BU
BE2488 (1945)	—	—	1.00	2.50	5.00	—

Y# 66   25 SATANG = 1/4 BAHT
Tin **Ruler:** Rama VIII **Obv:** King Ananda, childs head **Rev:** Mythical creature "Garuda"

Date	Mintage	F	VF	XF	Unc	BU
BE2489 (1946)	—	—	2.50	4.50	12.50	—

Y# 70   25 SATANG = 1/4 BAHT
Tin **Ruler:** Rama VIII **Obv:** Youth's head left **Rev:** Mythical creature "Garuda" **Edge:** Reeded

Date	Mintage	F	VF	XF	Unc	BU
BE2489 (1946)	Est. 226,348,000	—	0.20	0.40	0.75	—

Note: These coins were also struck 1954-64 and mintage figure is a total

Y# 76   25 SATANG = 1/4 BAHT
Aluminum-Bronze **Ruler:** Bhumipol Adulyadej (Rama IX) **Obv:** Young bust left, one medal on uniform **Rev:** Mantled arms

Date	Mintage	F	VF	XF	Unc	BU
BE2493 (1950)	23,170,000	—	0.75	1.75	4.00	—

Y# 80   25 SATANG = 1/4 BAHT
Aluminum-Bronze **Ruler:** Bhumipol Adulyadej (Rama IX) **Obv:** Smaller head, 3 medals on uniform **Rev:** Mantled arms **Edge:** Reeded **Note:** Dot after the letters for "Satang" are found with raised and incuse varieties.

Date	Mintage	F	VF	XF	Unc	BU
BE2500 (1957)	620,480,000	—	0.10	0.15	0.25	—

Note: Minted without date change and with and without reeded edges until 1987

Y# 109   25 SATANG = 1/4 BAHT
Brass **Ruler:** Bhumipol Adulyadej (Rama IX) **Obv:** Bust left **Rev:** Value and inscription **Note:** Date varieties exist.

Date	Mintage	F	VF	XF	Unc	BU
BE2520 (1977)	183,356,000	—	—	0.10	0.15	—

Y# 187   25 SATANG = 1/4 BAHT
1.9000 g., Aluminum-Bronze, 15.93 mm. **Ruler:** Bhumipol Adulyadej (Rama IX) **Obv:** Head left **Rev:** Steepled building **Edge:** Reeded

Date	Mintage	F	VF	XF	Unc	BU
BE2530 (1987)	5,108,000	—	—	—	0.20	—
BE2531 (1988)	42,096,000	—	—	—	0.10	—
BE2532 (1989)		—	—	—	0.10	—
BE2533 (1990)		—	—	—	0.10	—
BE2534 (1991)		—	—	—	0.10	—
BE2535 (1992)		—	—	—	0.10	—
BE2536 (1993)		—	—	—	0.10	—
BE2537 (1994)		—	—	—	0.10	—
BE2538 (1995)		—	—	—	0.10	—
BE2539 (1996)		—	—	—	0.10	—
BE2540 (1997)		—	—	—	0.10	—
BE2541 (1998)		—	—	—	0.10	—
BE2542 (1999)		—	—	—	0.10	—
BE2543 (2000)		—	—	—	0.10	—

Y# 345   25 SATANG = 1/4 BAHT
1.9000 g., Brass **Ruler:** Bhumipol Adulyadej (Rama IX) **Subject:** Golden Jubilee - Reign of King Rama IX **Obv:** Bust facing **Rev:** Arms with supporters

Date	Mintage	F	VF	XF	Unc	BU
BE2539 (1996)	—	—	—	—	0.50	—

Y# 67   50 SATANG = 1/2 BAHT
Tin **Ruler:** Rama VIII **Obv:** King Ananda, child's head left **Rev:** Mythical creature "Garuda"

Date	Mintage	F	VF	XF	Unc	BU
BE2489 (1946)	—	—	40.00	75.00	180	—

Y# 71   50 SATANG = 1/2 BAHT
Tin **Ruler:** Rama VIII **Obv:** Youth's head left **Rev:** Mythical creature "Garuda" **Edge:** Reeded

Date	Mintage	F	VF	XF	Unc	BU
BE2489 (1946)	17,008,000	—	0.75	1.50	4.00	—

Note: These coins were minted from 1954-1957 and mintage figure is a total

Y# 77   50 SATANG = 1/2 BAHT
Aluminum-Bronze **Ruler:** Bhumipol Adulyadej (Rama IX) **Obv:** Young bust left, 1 medal on uniform **Rev:** Mantled arms

Date	Mintage	F	VF	XF	Unc	BU
BE2493 (1950)	20,710,000	—	—	—	20.00	—

Y# 81   50 SATANG = 1/2 BAHT
Aluminum-Bronze **Ruler:** Bhumipol Adulyadej (Rama IX) **Obv:** Smaller head, 3 medals on uniform **Rev:** Mantled arms **Edge:** Reeded

Date	Mintage	F	VF	XF	Unc	BU
BE2500 (1957)	439,874,000	—	0.10	0.15	0.25	—

Note: Minted without date change until 1987

Y# 168   50 SATANG = 1/2 BAHT
Aluminum-Bronze **Ruler:** Bhumipol Adulyadej (Rama IX) **Obv:** Bust left **Rev:** Value and inscription **Edge:** Plain

Date	Mintage	F	VF	XF	Unc	BU
BE2523 (1980)	122,260,000	—	0.10	0.15	0.25	—

Y# 203   50 SATANG = 1/2 BAHT
2.4000 g., Brass **Ruler:** Bhumipol Adulyadej (Rama IX) **Obv:** Head left **Rev:** Steepled building divides value

Date	Mintage	F	VF	XF	Unc	BU
BE2530 (1987)		—	—	—	20.00	—
BE2531 (1988)	23,776,000	—	—	—	0.10	—
BE2532 (1989)		—	0.20	0.30	1.00	—
BE2533 (1990)		—	—	—	0.10	—
BE2534 (1991)		—	—	—	0.10	—
BE2535 (1992)		—	—	—	0.10	—
BE2536 (1993)		—	—	—	0.10	—
BE2537 (1994)		—	—	—	0.10	—
BE2538 (1995)		—	—	—	0.10	—
BE2539 (1996)		—	—	—	0.10	—
BE2540 (1997)		—	—	—	0.10	—
BE2541 (1998)		—	—	—	0.10	—
BE2542 (2000)		—	—	—	0.10	—
BE2543 (2000)		—	—	—	0.10	—

Y# 329   50 SATANG = 1/2 BAHT
Aluminum-Bronze **Ruler:** Bhumipol Adulyadej (Rama IX) **Subject:** 50th Year of Reign - King Rama IX **Obv:** Bust facing **Rev:** Arms

Date	Mintage	F	VF	XF	Unc	BU
BE2539 (1996)	—	—	—	—	0.35	—

Y# 82.1   BAHT
7.1500 g., Copper-Nickel-Silver-Zinc, 26.9 mm.   **Ruler:** Bhumipol Adulyadej (Rama IX) **Obv:** Bust left, three medals on uniform **Rev:** Mantled arms **Edge:** Reeded

Date	Mintage	F	VF	XF	Unc	BU
BE2500 (1957)	3,143,000	—	0.75	1.50	6.00	—

Note: These coins were minted from 1958-60 and mintage figure is a total

Y# 82.2   BAHT
Copper-Nickel, 26.9 mm.   **Ruler:** Bhumipol Adulyadej (Rama IX) **Obv:** Bust left, one medal on uniform **Rev:** Mantled arms

Date	Mintage	F	VF	XF	Unc	BU
BE2500 (1957)	—	—	0.75	1.50	6.00	—

Y# 82a   BAHT
Silver, 26.9 mm.   **Ruler:** Bhumipol Adulyadej (Rama IX) **Obv:** Bust left **Rev:** National arms

Date	Mintage	F	VF	XF	Unc	BU
BE2500 (1957)	—	—	—	—	—	—
Rare

Y# 83   BAHT
Copper-Nickel, 26.9 mm.   **Ruler:** Bhumipol Adulyadej (Rama IX) **Subject:** King Rama IX and Queen Sirikit return from abroad **Obv:** Conjoined busts left flanked by diamonds **Rev:** Mantled arms **Edge:** Reeded

Date	Mintage	F	VF	XF	Unc	BU
BE2504 (1961)	4,430,000	—	0.40	0.75	2.00	—

Y# 84   BAHT
Copper-Nickel, 26.9 mm.   **Ruler:** Bhumipol Adulyadej (Rama IX) **Obv:** Young bust left **Rev:** Mantled arms **Edge:** Reeded

Date	Mintage	F	VF	XF	Unc	BU
BE2505 (1962)	883,086,000	—	0.10	0.15	0.50	—

Note: These coins were minted from 1962-82 and mintage figure is a total

Y# 85   BAHT
Copper-Nickel, 26.9 mm.   **Ruler:** Bhumipol Adulyadej (Rama IX) **Subject:** 36th Birthday - King Rama IX **Obv:** Uniformed bust left **Rev:** Design in center circle of design **Edge:** Reeded

Date	Mintage	F	VF	XF	Unc	BU
ND(1963) (1963)	3,000,000	—	0.25	0.75	2.00	—

Y# 87   BAHT
Copper-Nickel, 26.9 mm.   **Ruler:** Bhumipol Adulyadej (Rama IX) **Subject:** 5th Asian Games Bangkok **Obv:** Conjoined busts right **Rev:** Star design **Edge:** Reeded

Date	Mintage	F	VF	XF	Unc	BU
BE2509 (1966)	9,000,000	—	0.25	0.75	3.00	—

Y# 91   BAHT
Copper-Nickel, 26.9 mm.   **Ruler:** Bhumipol Adulyadej (Rama IX) **Subject:** 6th Asian Games Bangkok **Obv:** Conjoined busts right **Rev:** Star design **Edge:** Reeded

Date	Mintage	F	VF	XF	Unc	BU
BE2513 (1970)	9,000,000	—	0.25	0.75	1.50	—

Y# 96   BAHT
Copper-Nickel, 26.9 mm.   **Ruler:** Bhumipol Adulyadej (Rama IX) **Series:** F.A.O. **Obv:** Head left **Rev:** State ploughing ceremony **Edge:** Reeded **Note:** Released on May 7, 1973.

Date	Mintage	F	VF	XF	Unc	BU
BE2515 (1972)	9,000,000	—	0.10	0.25	0.75	—

Y# 97   BAHT
Copper-Nickel, 26.9 mm.   **Ruler:** Bhumipol Adulyadej (Rama IX) **Subject:** Prince Vajiralongkorn Investiture **Obv:** Young head left **Rev:** Crowned monogram **Edge:** Reeded

Date	Mintage	F	VF	XF	Unc	BU
BE2515 (1972)	9,000,000	—	0.15	0.40	1.00	—

Y# 99   BAHT
Copper-Nickel, 26.9 mm.   **Ruler:** Bhumipol Adulyadej (Rama IX) **Subject:** 25th Anniversary - World Health Organization **Obv:** Head left **Rev:** Arms within wreath **Edge:** Reeded

Date	Mintage	F	VF	XF	Unc	BU
BE2516 (1973)	1,000,000	—	0.25	0.65	1.25	—

Y# 100   BAHT
Copper-Nickel, 25 mm.   **Ruler:** Bhumipol Adulyadej (Rama IX) **Obv:** Head left **Rev:** Mythical creature "Garuda" **Edge:** Reeded

Date	Mintage	F	VF	XF	Unc	BU
BE2517 (1974)	248,978,000	—	0.15	0.40	1.00	—

Y# 105   BAHT
7.0000 g., Copper-Nickel, 25 mm.   **Ruler:** Bhumipol Adulyadej (Rama IX) **Subject:** 8th SEAP Games **Obv:** Conjoined heads right **Rev:** Flower design within center circle of poinsettia design

Date	Mintage	F	VF	XF	Unc	BU
BE2518 (1975)	3,000,000	—	0.25	0.65	1.25	—

Y# 107   BAHT
7.0000 g., Copper-Nickel, 25 mm.   **Ruler:** Bhumipol Adulyadej (Rama IX) **Subject:** 75th Birthday of Princess Mother October 21st **Obv:** Bust facing **Rev:** Monogram **Edge:** Reeded

Date	Mintage	F	VF	XF	Unc	BU
BE2518 (1975)	9,000,000	—	0.15	0.40	1.00	—

Y# 110   BAHT
7.0000 g., Copper-Nickel   **Ruler:** Bhumipol Adulyadej (Rama IX) **Obv:** Head left **Rev:** Suphannahong, with Wat Aran Temple **Edge:** Reeded **Note:** Varieties exist.

Date	Mintage	F	VF	XF	Unc	BU
BE2520 (1977)	506,460,000	—	0.10	0.20	0.50	—

Y# 112   BAHT
7.0000 g., Copper-Nickel, 25 mm.   **Ruler:** Bhumipol Adulyadej (Rama IX) **Series:** F.A.O. **Obv:** Figures scattering rice **Rev:** Seated female figure left

Date	Mintage	F	VF	XF	Unc	BU
BE2520 (1977)	2,000,000	—	0.15	0.40	1.00	—

Y# 114   BAHT
7.0000 g., Copper-Nickel, 25 mm.   **Ruler:** Bhumipol Adulyadej (Rama IX) **Subject:** Princess Sirindhorn, 1st Thai Royal graduate of a great university **Obv:** Bust left **Rev:** Radiant crown **Edge:** Reeded

Date	Mintage	F	VF	XF	Unc	BU
BE2520 (1977)	8,998,000	—	0.15	0.40	1.00	—

Y# 114a BAHT

Bronze, 25 mm. **Ruler:** Bhumipol Adulyadej (Rama IX)
Subject: Princess Sirindhorn, 1st Thai Royal graduate of a great
university **Obv:** Bust left **Rev:** Radiant crown

Date	Mintage	F	VF	XF	Unc	BU
BE2520 (1977)	—	—	—	—	—	—

Y# 124 BAHT

7.0000 g., Copper-Nickel **Ruler:** Bhumipol Adulyadej
(Rama IX) **Subject:** Investiture of Princess Sirindhorn, May 12,
female counterpart to the crown prince **Obv:** Bust right
Rev: Crowned monogram

Date	Mintage	F	VF	XF	Unc	BU
BE2520 (1977)	5,000,000	—	0.15	0.40	1.00	—

Y# 127 BAHT

7.0000 g., Copper-Nickel, 25 mm. **Ruler:** Bhumipol Adulyadej
(Rama IX) **Subject:** Graduation of Crown Prince Vajiralongkorn
September 15, with the rank of "Panturi" **Obv:** Bust left
Rev: Crown within oval design **Edge:** Reeded

Date	Mintage	F	VF	XF	Unc	BU
BE2521 (1978)	5,000,000	—	0.10	0.20	0.50	—

Y# 130 BAHT

7.0000 g., Copper-Nickel, 25 mm. **Ruler:** Bhumipol Adulyadej
(Rama IX) **Subject:** 8th Asian Games **Obv:** Conjoined busts right
Rev: Small radiant sun within design **Edge:** Reeded

Date	Mintage	F	VF	XF	Unc	BU
BE2521 (1978)	5,000,000	—	0.10	0.20	0.50	—

Y# 157 BAHT

7.0000 g., Copper-Nickel, 25 mm. **Ruler:** Bhumipol Adulyadej
(Rama IX) **Series:** World Food Day October 16 **Obv:** Bust left
Rev: F.A.O. logo above wheat sprigs

Date	Mintage	F	VF	XF	Unc	BU
BE2525 (1982)	1,500,000	—	0.10	0.20	0.50	—

Y# 159.1 BAHT

7.0000 g., Copper-Nickel, 25 mm. **Ruler:** Bhumipol Adulyadej
(Rama IX) **Obv:** Large bust with collar touching hairline **Rev:** The
Grand Palace **Edge:** Reeded **Note:** 2527 and 2528 are frozen
dates, with the Thai numerals for 27 and 28 in the Finance Ministry
decal at the bottom of the reverse.

Date	Mintage	F	VF	XF	Unc	BU
BE2525 (1982)	123,585,000	—	0.10	0.20	0.50	—
BE2525 (1984)	—	—	0.10	0.20	0.50	—
BE2525 (1985)	—	—	0.10	0.20	0.50	—

Y# 159.2 BAHT

7.0000 g., Copper-Nickel **Ruler:** Bhumipol Adulyadej
(Rama IX) **Obv:** Small bust with space between collar and lower
hairline **Rev:** The Grand Palace **Edge:** Reeded

Date	Mintage	F	VF	XF	Unc	BU
BE2525 (1982)	Inc. above	—	2.50	5.00	10.00	—

Y# 183 BAHT

3.4500 g., Copper-Nickel, 20 mm. **Ruler:** Bhumipol Adulyadej
(Rama IX) **Obv:** Head left **Rev:** Palace **Edge:** Reeded
Note: Varieties exist.

Date	Mintage	F	VF	XF	Unc	BU
BE2529 (1986)	—	—	0.20	0.30	1.00	—
BE2530 (1987)	325,271,000	—	—	—	0.10	—
BE2531 (1988)	391,442,000	—	—	—	0.10	—
BE2532 (1989)	—	—	—	—	0.10	—
BE2533 (1990)	—	—	—	—	0.10	—
BE2534 (1991)	—	—	—	—	0.10	—
BE2535 (1992)	—	—	—	—	0.10	—
BE2536 (1993)	—	—	—	—	0.10	—
BE2537 (1994)	—	—	—	—	0.10	—
BE2538 (1995)	—	—	—	—	0.10	—
BE2539 (1996)	—	—	—	—	0.10	—
BE2540 (1997)	—	—	—	—	0.10	—
BE2541 (1998)	—	—	—	—	0.10	—
BE2542 (1999)	—	—	—	—	0.10	—
BE2543 (2000)	—	—	—	—	0.10	—

Y# 330 BAHT

Copper-Nickel, 20 mm. **Ruler:** Bhumipol Adulyadej (Rama IX)
Subject: 50th Anniversary - Reign of King Rama IX June 8
Obv: Bust facing **Rev:** Arms with supporters **Edge:** Reeded

Date	Mintage	F	VF	XF	Unc	BU
BE2539 (1996)	—	—	—	—	0.35	—

Y# 134 2 BAHT

Copper-Nickel, 27 mm. **Ruler:** Bhumipol Adulyadej (Rama IX)
Subject: Graduation of Princess Chulabhorn from Gusaehit
University July 19 **Obv:** Bust 1/4 left **Rev:** Design within circle
Edge: Plain **Note:** Science of Agriculture University.

Date	Mintage	F	VF	XF	Unc	BU
BE2522 (1979)	5,000,000	—	0.20	0.40	1.00	—

Y# 176 2 BAHT

Copper-Nickel Clad Copper, 22 mm. **Ruler:** Bhumipol
Adulyadej (Rama IX) **Subject:** International Youth Year **Obv:** Bust
left **Rev:** Conjoined profiles right within wreath **Edge:** Reeded

Date	Mintage	F	VF	XF	Unc	BU
BE2528 (1985)	10,000,000	—	0.20	0.40	1.00	—

Y# 177 2 BAHT

Copper-Nickel Clad Copper, 22 mm. **Ruler:** Bhumipol
Adulyadej (Rama IX) **Subject:** XII SEAP Games Bangkok
December 8-17 **Obv:** Half length bust facing **Rev:** Games logo
flanked by value **Edge:** Reeded

Date	Mintage	F	VF	XF	Unc	BU
BE2528 (1985)	5,000,000	—	0.20	0.40	1.00	—

Y# 178 2 BAHT

Copper-Nickel Clad Copper, 22 mm. **Ruler:** Bhumipol
Adulyadej (Rama IX) **Subject:** National Years of the Trees 2528-
2531 **Obv:** Bust left **Rev:** Inscription within tree flanked by
emblems below **Edge:** Reeded

Date	Mintage	F	VF	XF	Unc	BU
ND (1986)	3,000,000	—	0.50	1.00	3.50	—

Y# 180 2 BAHT

Copper-Nickel Clad Copper, 22 mm. **Ruler:** Bhumipol
Adulyadej (Rama IX) **Subject:** Year of Peace **Obv:** Bust left
Rev: Dove divides wreath below inscription **Note:** Australia,
Russia and Mongolia issued coins with identical motif.

Date	Mintage	F	VF	XF	Unc	BU
BE2529 (1986)	5,000,000	—	—	—	0.50	—

Y# 191 2 BAHT

Copper-Nickel Clad Copper, 22 mm. **Ruler:** Bhumipol
Adulyadej (Rama IX) **Subject:** Princess Chulabhorn Awarded
Einstein Medal for research October 24 **Obv:** Bust in cap and gown
1/4 left **Rev:** Head left within center circle of hexagon design

Date	Mintage	F	VF	XF	Unc	BU
BE2529 (1986)	3,000,000	—	—	—	0.50	—

Y# 188 2 BAHT

Copper-Nickel Clad Copper, 22 mm. **Ruler:** Bhumipol Adulyadej
(Rama IX) **Subject:** 100th Year of "Nairoi" Chulalongkorn Military
Academy **Obv:** Conjoined busts left **Rev:** Flagged arms

Date	Mintage	F	VF	XF	Unc	BU
BE2530 (1987)	3,000,000	—	—	—	0.50	—

Y# 194 2 BAHT

Copper-Nickel Clad Copper, 22 mm. **Ruler:** Bhumipol
Adulyadej (Rama IX) **Subject:** 60th Birthday - King Rama IX,
December 5 **Obv:** Bust facing **Rev:** Radiant crown

Date	Mintage	F	VF	XF	Unc	BU
BE2530 (1987)	10,000	—	—	—	0.50	—

Y# 204 2 BAHT

Copper-Nickel Clad Copper, 22 mm. **Ruler:** Bhumipol
Adulyadej (Rama IX) **Subject:** 72nd Anniversary of Thai
Cooperatives February 26 **Obv:** Conjoined busts left
Rev: Inscription **Edge:** Reeded

Date	Mintage	F	VF	XF	Unc	BU
BE2531 (1988)	3,000,000	—	—	—	0.50	—

THAILAND

Y# 210   2 BAHT
Copper-Nickel Clad Copper, 22 mm.   **Ruler:** Bhumipol Adulyadej (Rama IX) **Subject:** 42nd Anniversary - Reign of King Rama IX July 2 **Obv:** Bust facing **Rev:** Crowned monogram **Edge:** Reeded

Date	Mintage	F	VF	XF	Unc	BU
BE2531 (1988)	5,000,000	—	—	—	0.50	—

Y# 220   2 BAHT
Copper-Nickel Clad Copper, 22 mm.   **Ruler:** Bhumipol Adulyadej (Rama IX) **Subject:** 100th Anniversary of Siriraj Hospital April 26 **Obv:** Conjoined busts left **Rev:** Radiant crown above design

Date	Mintage	F	VF	XF	Unc	BU
BE2531 (1988)	3,412,000	—	—	—	0.50	—

Y# 222   2 BAHT
Copper-Nickel Clad Copper, 22 mm.   **Ruler:** Bhumipol Adulyadej (Rama IX) **Subject:** Crown Prince's 36th birthday **Obv:** Head 1/4 left **Rev:** Crowned monogram within lightning bolts

Date	Mintage	F	VF	XF	Unc	BU
BE2531 (1988)	2,000,000	—	—	—	0.50	—

Y# 225   2 BAHT
Copper-Nickel Clad Copper, 22 mm.   **Ruler:** Bhumipol Adulyadej (Rama IX) **Subject:** 72nd Anniversary of Chulalongkorn University March 26 **Obv:** Conjoined busts left **Rev:** Radiant crown **Edge:** Reeded

Date	Mintage	F	VF	XF	Unc	BU
BE2532 (1989)	3,000,000	—	—	—	0.50	—

Y# 230   2 BAHT
Copper-Nickel Clad Copper, 22 mm. **Ruler:** Bhumipol Adulyadej (Rama IX) **Subject:** Centennial of First Medical College, Siriraj, September 5 2433-2533 **Obv:** Conjoined uniformed busts facing **Rev:** First medical college **Edge:** Reeded

Date	Mintage	F	VF	XF	Unc	BU
BE2533 (1990)	1,000,000	—	—	—	0.50	—

Y# 232   2 BAHT
Copper-Nickel Clad Copper, 22 mm.   **Ruler:** Bhumipol Adulyadej (Rama IX) **Subject:** 90th Birthday of Queen Mother October 21 **Obv:** Crown on stand flanked by others **Rev:** Bust 1/4 left **Edge:** Reeded

Date	Mintage	F	VF	XF	Unc	BU
BE2533 (1990)	2,000,000	—	—	—	0.50	—

Y# 235   2 BAHT
Copper-Nickel Clad Copper, 22 mm.   **Ruler:** Bhumipol Adulyadej (Rama IX) **Subject:** 100th Anniversary - Office of the Comptroller General 2433-2533 **Obv:** Conjoined uniformed busts 1/4 left **Rev:** Building above computer, typewriter and phone **Edge:** Reeded

Date	Mintage	F	VF	XF	Unc	BU
BE2533 (1990)	1,000,000	—	—	—	0.50	—

Y# 243   2 BAHT
Copper-Nickel Clad Copper, 22 mm.   **Ruler:** Bhumipol Adulyadej (Rama IX) **Subject:** World Health Organization **Obv:** Bust of Queen Mother 1/4 left **Rev:** Gold medal for good health, December 17 **Edge:** Reeded

Date	Mintage	F	VF	XF	Unc	BU
BE2533 (1990)	2,000,000	—	—	—	1.00	—

Y# 237   2 BAHT
Copper-Nickel Clad Copper, 22 mm.   **Ruler:** Bhumipol Adulyadej (Rama IX) **Subject:** 36th Birthday of Princess Sirindhorn April 2 **Obv:** Uniformed bust 1/4 left **Rev:** Crowned monogram flanked by stars above sprigs **Edge:** Reeded

Date	Mintage	F	VF	XF	Unc	BU
BE2534 (1991)	2,300,000	—	—	—	0.50	—

Y# 240   2 BAHT
Copper-Nickel Clad Copper, 22 mm.   **Ruler:** Bhumipol Adulyadej (Rama IX) **Subject:** 80th Anniversary of Thai Boy Scouts July 1 2454-2534 **Obv:** Conjoined young busts 1/4 left in scout uniforms **Rev:** Scouting emblem and phrase "Better to die than to lie" **Edge:** Reeded

Date	Mintage	F	VF	XF	Unc	BU
BE2534 (1991)	2,000,000	—	—	—	1.50	—

Y# 255   2 BAHT
Copper-Nickel Clad Copper, 22 mm.   **Ruler:** Bhumipol Adulyadej (Rama IX) **Subject:** Princess Sirindhorn's Magsaysay Foundation Award for public administration August 31 **Obv:** Seated figures within circle **Rev:** Shield within sprig and circle below cameo **Edge:** Reeded

Date	Mintage	F	VF	XF	Unc	BU
BE2534 (1991)	12,000,000	—	—	—	0.50	—

Y# 248   2 BAHT
Copper-Nickel Clad Copper, 22 mm.   **Ruler:** Bhumipol Adulyadej (Rama IX) **Subject:** Centenary Celebration of Mahitorn - Father of King Rama IX, January 1 **Obv:** Head facing **Rev:** Crown on stand flanked by others **Edge:** Reeded

Date	Mintage	F	VF	XF	Unc	BU
BE2535 (1992)	2,308,000	—	—	—	0.50	—

Y# 251   2 BAHT
Copper-Nickel Clad Copper, 22 mm.   **Ruler:** Bhumipol Adulyadej (Rama IX) **Subject:** Ministry of Justice Centennial March 25 **Obv:** Conjoined busts left **Rev:** Balance scales within design **Edge:** Reeded

Date	Mintage	F	VF	XF	Unc	BU
BE2535 (1992)	1,500,000	—	—	—	0.50	—

Y# 253   2 BAHT
Copper-Nickel Clad Copper, 22 mm.   **Ruler:** Bhumipol Adulyadej (Rama IX) **Subject:** Ministry of Justice Centennial April 1 2435-2535 **Obv:** Conjoined busts facing **Rev:** Mythical animal within circle **Edge:** Reeded

Date	Mintage	F	VF	XF	Unc	BU
1992 (1992)	1,500,000	—	—	—	0.50	—

Y# 259   2 BAHT
Copper-Nickel Clad Copper, 22 mm.   **Ruler:** Bhumipol Adulyadej (Rama IX) **Subject:** Queen's 60th Birthday August 12 (Thai Mother's Day) **Obv:** Crowned bust facing **Rev:** Crowned monogram **Edge:** Reeded

Date	Mintage	F	VF	XF	Unc	BU
BE2535 (1992)	1,700,000	—	—	—	0.50	—

Y# 268   2 BAHT
Copper-Nickel Clad Copper, 22 mm.   **Ruler:** Bhumipol Adulyadej (Rama IX) **Subject:** 60th Anniversary of the National Assembly - June 28 **Obv:** Conjoined busts left **Rev:** Anatasamakhom Throne Hall **Edge:** Reeded

Date	Mintage	F	VF	XF	Unc	BU
BE2535 (1992)	1,000,000	—	—	—	0.50	—

Y# 270   2 BAHT
Copper-Nickel Clad Copper, 22 mm.   **Ruler:** Bhumipol Adulyadej (Rama IX) **Subject:** 100th Anniversary Ministry of Agriculture April 1 2435-2535 **Obv:** Conjoined busts 1/4 left **Rev:** Emblem within sprigs **Edge:** Reeded

Date	Mintage	F	VF	XF	Unc	BU
BE2535 (1992)	1,000,000	—	—	—	0.50	—

Y# 276   2 BAHT
Copper-Nickel Clad Copper, 22 mm.   **Ruler:** Bhumipol Adulyadej (Rama IX) **Subject:** Centennial of Thai Teacher Training October 12 **Obv:** Conjoined busts left **Rev:** Emblem **Edge:** Reeded

Date	Mintage	F	VF	XF	Unc	BU
BE2535 (1992)	1,200,000	—	—	—	0.50	—

Y# 277   2 BAHT
Copper-Nickel Clad Copper, 22 mm.   **Ruler:** Bhumipol Adulyadej (Rama IX) **Subject:** 50th Year of Thai National Bank December 10 **Obv:** Conjoined busts facing **Rev:** Seated figure

Date	Mintage	F	VF	XF	Unc	BU
BE2535 (1992)	1,000,000	—	—	—	0.50	—

Y# 272   2 BAHT
Copper-Nickel Clad Copper, 22 mm.   **Ruler:** Bhumipol Adulyadej (Rama IX) **Subject:** King's 64th Birthday November 18 **Obv:** Conjoined busts 1/4 left **Rev:** Crowned monograms **Edge:** Reeded **Note:** In honor of the King reaching the lifespan of his great-grandfather.

Date	Mintage	F	VF	XF	Unc	BU
BE2535 (1992)	1,000,000	—	—	—	0.50	—

Y# 278   2 BAHT
Copper-Nickel Clad Copper, 22 mm.   **Ruler:** Bhumipol Adulyadej (Rama IX) **Subject:** Centennial of Attorney General's Office April 1 2436-2536 **Obv:** Conjoined busts facing **Rev:** Crowned balance scale **Edge:** Reeded

Date	Mintage	F	VF	XF	Unc	BU
BE2536 (1993)	1,000,000	—	—	—	0.50	—

Y# 279   2 BAHT
Copper-Nickel Clad Copper, 22 mm.   **Ruler:** Bhumipol Adulyadej (Rama IX) **Subject:** Centennial of Thai Red Cross 2436-2536 **Obv:** Conjoined busts 1/4 left **Rev:** Symbols **Edge:** Reeded

Date	Mintage	F	VF	XF	Unc	BU
BE2536 (1993)	1,200,000	—	—	—	0.50	—

Y# 282   2 BAHT
Copper-Nickel Clad Copper, 22 mm.   **Ruler:** Bhumipol Adulyadej (Rama IX) **Subject:** 60th Year of the Treasury Department May 23 **Obv:** Conjoined busts left **Rev:** Emblem within circle **Edge:** Reeded

Date	Mintage	F	VF	XF	Unc	BU
BE2536 (1993)	1,200,000	—	—	—	0.50	—

Y# 288   2 BAHT
Copper-Nickel Clad Copper, 22 mm.   **Ruler:** Bhumipol Adulyadej (Rama IX) **Subject:** 100th Anniversary of Rama VII November 8 **Obv:** Bust left **Rev:** Crown and designs within oval circle **Edge:** Reeded

Date	Mintage	F	VF	XF	Unc	BU
BE2536 (1993)	1,500,000	—	—	—	0.50	—

Y# 292   2 BAHT
Copper-Nickel Clad Copper, 22 mm.   **Ruler:** Bhumipol Adulyadej (Rama IX) **Subject:** 60th Anniversary - Royal Thai Language Academy March 31 **Obv:** Conjoined busts left **Rev:** Crowned emblem **Edge:** Reeded

Date	Mintage	F	VF	XF	Unc	BU
BE2537 (1994)	1,200,000	—	—	—	0.50	—

Y# 294   2 BAHT
Copper-Nickel Clad Copper, 22 mm.   **Ruler:** Bhumipol Adulyadej (Rama IX) **Subject:** 120th Anniversary - Council of Advisors to the King - Royal decree 2417-2537 **Obv:** Conjoined busts facing **Rev:** Building **Edge:** Reeded

Date	Mintage	F	VF	XF	Unc	BU
BE2537 (1994)	1,200,000	—	—	—	0.50	—

Y# 296   2 BAHT
Copper-Nickel Clad Copper, 22 mm.   **Ruler:** Bhumipol Adulyadej (Rama IX) **Subject:** 60th Anniversary - Thammasat University June 27 **Obv:** Conjoined busts left **Rev:** University emblem within circle **Edge:** Reeded

Date	Mintage	F	VF	XF	Unc	BU
BE2537 (1994)	1,250,000	—	—	—	0.50	—

Y# 307   2 BAHT
Copper-Nickel Clad Copper, 22 mm.   **Ruler:** Bhumipol Adulyadej (Rama IX) **Series:** F.A.O. 50th Year, 1945-1995 **Obv:** Bust left **Rev:** Emblem and dates **Edge:** Reeded

Date	Mintage	F	VF	XF	Unc	BU
BE2538 (1995)		—	—	—	0.65	—

Y# 313   2 BAHT
Copper-Nickel Clad Copper, 22 mm.   **Ruler:** Bhumipol Adulyadej (Rama IX) **Subject:** Information Technology Year **Obv:** Bust 3/4 left **Rev:** Symbols on globe background **Edge:** Reeded

Date	Mintage	F	VF	XF	Unc	BU
BE2538 (1995)		—	—	—	0.50	—

Y# 315   2 BAHT
Copper-Nickel Clad Copper, 22 mm.   **Ruler:** Bhumipol Adulyadej (Rama IX) **Subject:** ASEAN Environment Year "Greenland Clean" **Obv:** Conjoined busts left **Rev:** Design within circle flanked by sprig and arrow **Edge:** Reeded

Date	Mintage	F	VF	XF	Unc	BU
BE2538 (1995)		—	—	—	0.50	—

Y# 317   2 BAHT
Copper-Nickel Clad Copper, 22 mm.   **Ruler:** Bhumipol Adulyadej (Rama IX) **Subject:** Siriraj Nursing and Midwifery School Centennial January 12 **Obv:** Bust facing **Rev:** Crowned monogram **Edge:** Reeded

Date	Mintage	F	VF	XF	Unc	BU
BE2539 (1996)		—	—	—	0.65	—

Y# 319   2 BAHT
Copper-Nickel Clad Copper, 22 mm.   **Ruler:** Bhumipol Adulyadej (Rama IX) **Subject:** King's 50th Year of Reign June 9 **Obv:** Bust facing **Rev:** National arms **Edge:** Reeded

Date	Mintage	F	VF	XF	Unc	BU
BE2539 (1996)		—	—	—	1.25	—

Y# 98   5 BAHT
Copper-Nickel   **Ruler:** Bhumipol Adulyadej (Rama IX) **Obv:** Head left **Rev:** Mythical creature "Garuda" **Edge:** Plain

Date	Mintage	F	VF	XF	Unc	BU
BE2515 (1972)	30,016,000	—	0.30	0.60	1.20	—

Y# 111   5 BAHT
Copper-Nickel Clad Copper   **Ruler:** Bhumipol Adulyadej (Rama IX) **Obv:** Head left **Rev:** Mythical creature "Garuda" **Edge:** Lettered

Date	Mintage	F	VF	XF	Unc	BU
BE2520 (1977)	27,257,000	—	0.30	0.60	1.20	—
BE2522 (1979)	72,740,000	—	0.30	0.60	1.20	—

Y# 120   5 BAHT
Copper-Nickel Clad Copper, 29.5 mm.   **Ruler:** Bhumipol Adulyadej (Rama IX) **Subject:** 50th Birthday - Rama IX December 5 **Obv:** Head left **Obv. Leg.:** PRATHET THAI **Rev:** Crowned monogram **Edge:** Reeded

Date	Mintage	F	VF	XF	Unc	BU
BE2520 (1977)	500,000	—	0.35	0.75	1.50	—

Y# 121   5 BAHT
Copper-Nickel Clad Copper, 29.5 mm. **Ruler:** Bhumipol Adulyadej (Rama IX) **Subject:** 50th Birthday - Rama IX December 5 **Obv:** Bust left **Obv. Leg.:** "SIAM MINTA" **Rev:** Crowned monogram **Edge:** Reeded **Note:** Error legend

Date	Mintage	F	VF	XF	Unc	BU
BE2520 (1977)	—	—	7.00	15.00	30.00	—

Y# 131   5 BAHT
Copper-Nickel Clad Copper, 30 mm. **Ruler:** Bhumipol Adulyadej (Rama IX) **Subject:** 8th ASEAN Games Bangkok **Obv:** Conjoined busts right **Rev:** Small radiant sun within designs **Edge:** Reeded

Date	Mintage	F	VF	XF	Unc	BU
BE2521 (1978)	500,000	—	1.50	3.50	6.50	—

Y# 132   5 BAHT
Copper-Nickel Clad Copper, 30 mm. **Ruler:** Bhumipol Adulyadej (Rama IX) **Subject:** Royal Cradle Ceremony January 11 **Obv:** Small child head right **Rev:** Inscription within designed wreath **Edge:** Reeded

Date	Mintage	F	VF	XF	Unc	BU
BE2522 (1979)	1,000,000	—	0.50	1.00	2.00	—

Y# 137   5 BAHT
Copper-Nickel Clad Copper, 30 mm. **Ruler:** Bhumipol Adulyadej (Rama IX) **Subject:** Queen's Birthday August 12 and F.A.O. Ceres Medal **Obv:** Crowned head 1/4 left **Rev:** Figures working within football-like designs **Edge:** Reeded

Date	Mintage	F	VF	XF	Unc	BU
BE2523 (1980)	9,000,000	—	0.25	0.50	1.50	—

Y# 140   5 BAHT
Copper-Nickel Clad Copper, 30 mm. **Ruler:** Bhumipol Adulyadej (Rama IX) **Subject:** 80th Birthday of King's Mother October 21 **Obv:** Bust with hat left **Rev:** Crown on stand flanked by others **Edge:** Reeded

Date	Mintage	F	VF	XF	Unc	BU
BE2523 (1980)	3,504,000	—	0.25	0.50	1.50	—

Y# 144   5 BAHT
Copper-Nickel Clad Copper, 30 mm. **Ruler:** Bhumipol Adulyadej (Rama IX) **Subject:** Rama VII Constitutional Monarchy December 10 2475-2523 **Obv:** Head left **Rev:** Crowned monogram **Edge:** Reeded

Date	Mintage	F	VF	XF	Unc	BU
BE2523 (1980)	2,113,000	—	0.25	0.50	1.50	—

Y# 142   5 BAHT
Copper-Nickel Clad Copper, 30 mm. **Ruler:** Bhumipol Adulyadej (Rama IX) **Subject:** Centennial - Birth of King Rama VI January 3 **Obv:** Bust right **Rev:** Design **Edge:** Reeded

Date	Mintage	F	VF	XF	Unc	BU
BE2524 (1981)	2,222,000	—	0.25	0.50	1.50	—

Y# 149   5 BAHT
Copper-Nickel Clad Copper, 30 mm. **Ruler:** Bhumipol Adulyadej (Rama IX) **Subject:** Bicentennial of the Chakri Dynasty **Obv:** Conjoined busts left **Rev:** Emblem **Edge:** Reeded

Date	Mintage	F	VF	XF	Unc	BU
BE2525 (1982)	5,000,000	—	0.25	0.50	1.50	—

Y# 158   5 BAHT
Copper-Nickel Clad Copper, 30 mm. **Ruler:** Bhumipol Adulyadej (Rama IX) **Series:** World Food Day **Obv:** Uniformed bust left **Rev:** Emblem above wheat sprigs **Edge:** Reeded

Date	Mintage	F	VF	XF	Unc	BU
BE2525 (1982)	400,000	—	0.35	0.75	1.50	—

Y# 161   5 BAHT
Copper-Nickel Clad Copper, 30 mm. **Ruler:** Bhumipol Adulyadej (Rama IX) **Subject:** 75th Anniversary of Boy Scouts **Obv:** Bust left in scout uniform **Rev:** Stylized banner and flag

Date	Mintage	F	VF	XF	Unc	BU
BE2525 (1982)	206,000	—	1.50	3.50	6.50	—

Y# 160   5 BAHT
12.0000 g., Copper-Nickel Clad Copper **Ruler:** Bhumipol Adulyadej (Rama IX) **Obv:** Bust left **Rev:** Mythical creature "Garuda" **Note:** 2525 is a frozen date, with the Thai numerals for the first 2 digits of the actual year (25, 28, 29) in the Finance Ministry decal at the bottom of the reverse

Date	Mintage	F	VF	XF	Unc	BU
BE2525 (25) (1982)	200,000	—	0.50	1.00	2.00	—
BE2526 (1983)	—	—	0.60	1.25	2.25	—
BE2527 (1984)	—	—	0.60	1.25	2.25	—
BE2525 (1985)	—	—	5.00	10.00	25.00	—
BE2528 (1985)	—	—	1.00	2.00	5.00	—
BE2525 (1986)	—	—	0.20	0.50	1.00	—
BE2529 (1986)	—	—	0.20	0.50	1.00	—

Y# 171   5 BAHT
Copper-Nickel Clad Copper **Ruler:** Bhumipol Adulyadej (Rama IX) **Subject:** 84th Birthday of King's Mother October 21 **Obv:** Crown on stand flanked by others **Rev:** Bust 3/4 left

Date	Mintage	F	VF	XF	Unc	BU
BE2527 (1984)	600,000	—	1.00	2.00	4.50	—

Y# 184   5 BAHT
Copper-Nickel Clad Copper, 24 mm. **Ruler:** Bhumipol Adulyadej (Rama IX) **Subject:** 200th Anniversary - Birth of Rama III 2330-2530 **Obv:** Bust facing **Rev:** Design within circle **Edge:** Reeded

Date	Mintage	F	VF	XF	Unc	BU
BE2530 (1987)	2,000,000	—	—	—	0.75	—

Y# 195   5 BAHT
Copper-Nickel Clad Copper, 30 mm. **Ruler:** Bhumipol Adulyadej (Rama IX) **Subject:** 60th Birthday - King Rama IX December 5 **Obv:** Uniformed bust facing **Rev:** Crowned emblem within lightning bolts **Edge:** Reeded

Date	Mintage	F	VF	XF	Unc	BU
BE2530 (1987)	1,500,000	—	—	—	2.00	—

Y# 185   5 BAHT
7.5000 g., Copper-Nickel Clad Copper **Ruler:** Bhumipol Adulyadej (Rama IX) **Obv:** Head left **Rev:** Suphannahong, royal grand palace **Note:** Circulation coinage.

Date	Mintage	F	VF	XF	Unc	BU
BE2530 (1987)	14,000,000	—	—	—	0.75	—
BE2531 (1988)	—	—	—	—	0.75	—

Y# 211 5 BAHT

Copper-Nickel, 30 mm. **Ruler:** Bhumipol Adulyadej (Rama IX)
Subject: 42nd Anniversary - Reign of King Rama IX July 2
Obv: Uniformed bust facing **Rev:** Crowned monogram
Edge: Reeded

Date	Mintage	F	VF	XF	Unc	BU
BE2531 (1988)	1,500,000	—	—	—	2.00	—

Y# 219 5 BAHT

7.4600 g., Copper-Nickel Clad Copper, 24 mm.
Ruler: Bhumipol Adulyadej (Rama IX) **Obv:** Head left
Rev: Penjahwat **Edge:** Coarse reeding

Date	Mintage	F	VF	XF	Unc	BU
BE2531 (1988)	—	—	—	—	0.50	—
BE2532 (1989)	—	—	—	—	0.50	—
BE2533 (1990)	—	—	—	—	0.50	—
BE2534 (1991)	—	—	—	—	0.50	—
BE2535 (1992)	—	—	—	—	0.50	—
BE2536 (1993)	—	—	—	—	0.50	—
BE2537 (1994)	—	—	—	—	0.50	—
BE2538 (1995)	—	—	—	—	0.50	—
BE2539 (1996)	—	—	—	—	0.50	—
BE2540 (1997)	—	—	—	—	0.50	—
BE2541 (1998)	—	—	—	—	0.50	—
BE2542 (1999)	—	—	—	—	0.50	—
BE2543 (2000)	—	—	—	—	0.50	—

Y# 260 5 BAHT

Copper-Nickel Clad Copper, 24 mm. **Ruler:** Bhumipol Adulyadej
(Rama IX) **Subject:** Queen's 60th Birthday August 12
Obv: Crowned bust facing **Rev:** Crowned monogram
Edge: Reeded

Date	Mintage	F	VF	XF	Unc	BU
BE2535 (1992)	1,000,000	—	—	—	1.25	—

Y# 306 5 BAHT

Copper-Nickel Clad Copper, 24 mm. **Ruler:** Bhumipol
Adulyadej (Rama IX) **Subject:** 18th SEA Games December 9-
17 held at Ching My **Obv:** Half length bust facing **Rev:** Designs
and inscription within circle above designed sprigs **Edge:** Reeded

Date	Mintage	F	VF	XF	Unc	BU
BE2538 (1995)	—	—	—	—	1.25	—

Y# 320 5 BAHT

Copper-Nickel Clad Copper, 24 mm. **Ruler:** Bhumipol
Adulyadej (Rama IX) **Subject:** King's 50th Year of Reign June 9
Obv: Bust facing **Rev:** National arms **Edge:** Reeded

Date	Mintage	F	VF	XF	Unc	BU
BE2539 (1996)	—	—	—	—	1.50	—

Y# 92 10 BAHT

5.0000 g., 0.8000 Silver 0.1286 oz. ASW, 20 mm.
Ruler: Bhumipol Adulyadej (Rama IX) **Subject:** 25th
Anniversary - Reign of King Rama IX June 9 **Obv:** Head right
Rev: Radiant crowned monogram **Edge:** Reeded

Date	Mintage	F	VF	XF	Unc	BU
BE2514 (1971)	2,000,000		BV	2.50	4.50	—

Y# 115 10 BAHT

Nickel, 32 mm. **Ruler:** Bhumipol Adulyadej (Rama IX)
Subject: Graduation of Princess Sirindhorn 1st royal graduate
Obv: Bust left **Rev:** Radiant crown **Edge:** Reeded

Date	Mintage	F	VF	XF	Unc	BU
BE2520 (1977)	2,097,000	—	0.50	1.00	2.50	—

Y# 115a 10 BAHT

Bronze, 32 mm. **Ruler:** Bhumipol Adulyadej (Rama IX)
Subject: Graduation of Princess Sirindhorn 1st royal graduate
Obv: Bust left **Rev:** Radiant crown

Date	Mintage	F	VF	XF	Unc	BU
BE2520 (1977)	—	—	—	—	20.00	—

Y# 117 10 BAHT

Nickel, 32 mm. **Ruler:** Bhumipol Adulyadej (Rama IX)
Subject: Crown Prince Vajiralongkorn and Princess Soamsawali
Wedding January 3 **Obv:** Conjoined busts right **Rev:** Crowned
monogram **Edge:** Reeded

Date	Mintage	F	VF	XF	Unc	BU
BE2520 (1977)	1,890,000	—	0.50	1.00	2.50	—

Y# 135 10 BAHT

Nickel, 32 mm. **Ruler:** Bhumipol Adulyadej (Rama IX)
Subject: Graduation of Princess Chulabhorn **Obv:** Bust 3/4 left
Rev: Graduation emblem within circle

Date	Mintage	F	VF	XF	Unc	BU
BE2522 (1979)	1,196,000	—	0.50	1.00	2.50	—

Y# 141 10 BAHT

Nickel, 32 mm. **Ruler:** Bhumipol Adulyadej (Rama IX)
Subject: 80th Birthday of King's Mother October 21 **Obv:** Bust
with hat left **Rev:** Crown on stand flanked by others **Edge:** Reeded

Date	Mintage	F	VF	XF	Unc	BU
BE2523 (1980)	1,288,000	—	0.50	1.00	2.50	—

Y# 145 10 BAHT

Nickel, 32 mm. **Ruler:** Bhumipol Adulyadej (Rama IX)
Subject: 30th Anniversary of Buddhist Fellowship **Obv:** Bust left
Rev: Design within circle and wreath **Edge:** Reeded

Date	Mintage	F	VF	XF	Unc	BU
BE2523 (1980)	1,035,000	—	0.50	1.00	2.50	—

Y# 146 10 BAHT

Nickel, 32 mm. **Ruler:** Bhumipol Adulyadej (Rama IX)
Subject: King Rama IX Anniversary of Reign, twice as long on
the throne - June 19 **Obv:** Conjoined busts left **Rev:** Crowns and
emblems **Edge:** Reeded

Date	Mintage	F	VF	XF	Unc	BU
BE2524 (1981)	2,039,000	—	0.50	1.00	2.50	—

Y# 154 10 BAHT

Nickel, 32 mm. **Ruler:** Bhumipol Adulyadej (Rama IX)
Subject: 50th Birthday of Queen Sirikit August 12 **Obv:** Crowned
head 1/4 left **Rev:** Crowned monogram **Edge:** Reeded

Date	Mintage	F	VF	XF	Unc	BU
BE2525 (1982)	500,000	—	0.75	1.50	3.50	—
BE2525 (1982) Proof	9,999	Value: 22.50				

Y# 162 10 BAHT

Nickel, 32 mm. **Ruler:** Bhumipol Adulyadej (Rama IX)
Subject: 75th Anniversary of Boy Scouts **Obv:** Bust left in
scouting uniform **Rev:** Stylized banner and flag **Edge:** Reeded
Note: Similar to 5 Baht, Y#161.

Date	Mintage	F	VF	XF	Unc	BU
BE2525 (1982)	100,000	—	1.25	2.50	5.00	—
BE2525 (1982) Proof	1,500	Value: 45.00				

Y# 163   10 BAHT
Nickel, 32 mm.   **Ruler:** Bhumipol Adulyadej (Rama IX)
Subject: 100th Anniversary of Postal Service August 4 **Obv:** Bust left **Rev:** Radiant crown above inscription

Date	Mintage	F	VF	XF	Unc	BU
BE2526 (1983)	300,000	—	0.75	1.50	3.50	—
BE2526 (1983) Proof	5,000	Value: 27.50				

Y# 181   10 BAHT
Nickel, 32 mm.   **Ruler:** Bhumipol Adulyadej (Rama IX)
Subject: 6th ASEAN Orchid Congress November 7-14 **Obv:** Bust left **Rev:** Symbols of congress meeting **Edge:** Reeded

Date	Mintage	F	VF	XF	Unc	BU
BE2529 (1986)	200,000	—	—	—	2.50	—
BE2529 (1986) Proof	3,000	Value: 37.50				

Y# 190   10 BAHT
Nickel, 32 mm.   **Ruler:** Bhumipol Adulyadej (Rama IX)
Subject: Rural Development Leadership July 21 **Obv:** Kneeling figure facing left talking to seated figures **Rev:** Emblem above inscription **Edge:** Reeded

Date	Mintage	F	VF	XF	Unc	BU
BE2530 (1987)	300,000	—	—	—	2.50	—
BE2530 (1987) Proof	2,100	Value: 45.00				

Y# 165   10 BAHT
Nickel, 32 mm.   **Ruler:** Bhumipol Adulyadej (Rama IX)
Subject: 700th Anniversary of Thai Alphabet **Obv:** Seated figure, Ramkamhaeng the Great, pre-Bangkok era **Rev:** Six-line inscription

Date	Mintage	F	VF	XF	Unc	BU
BE2526 (1983)	500,000	—	0.75	1.50	3.50	—
BE2526 (1983) Proof	5,167	Value: 25.00				

Y# 172   10 BAHT
Nickel, 32 mm.   **Ruler:** Bhumipol Adulyadej (Rama IX)
Subject: 84th Birthday of King's Mother October 21 **Obv:** Three crowns on stands **Rev:** Bust left **Note:** Similar to 5 Baht, Y#171.

Date	Mintage	F	VF	XF	Unc	BU
BE2527 (1984)	200,000	—	1.25	2.50	5.50	—
BE2527 (1984) Proof	3,492	Value: 37.50				

Y# 192   10 BAHT
Nickel, 32 mm.   **Ruler:** Bhumipol Adulyadej (Rama IX)
Subject: Princess Chulabhorn Awarded Einstein Medal October 24 **Obv:** Graduate's bust 1/4 left **Rev:** Head left within center circle of hexagon design

Date	Mintage	F	VF	XF	Unc	BU
BE2529 (1986)	200,000	—	—	—	2.50	—
BE2529 (1986) Proof	1,080	Value: 50.00				

Y# 205   10 BAHT
Nickel, 32 mm.   **Ruler:** Bhumipol Adulyadej (Rama IX)
Subject: 72nd Anniversary of Thai Cooperatives February 26 **Obv:** Conjoined busts left **Rev:** Inscription

Date	Mintage	F	VF	XF	Unc	BU
BE2531 (1988)	143,000	—	—	—	2.50	—
BE2530 (1988) Proof	3,000	Value: 32.50				

Y# 175   10 BAHT
Nickel, 32 mm.   **Ruler:** Bhumipol Adulyadej (Rama IX)
Subject: 72nd Anniversary of Government Savings Bank April 1 **Obv:** Conjoined uniformed busts 1/4 left **Rev:** Designs within sectioned circle **Edge:** Reeded

Date	Mintage	F	VF	XF	Unc	BU
BE2528 (1985)	500,000	—	0.50	1.00	2.50	—
BE2528 (1985) Proof	3,000	Value: 37.50				

Y# 196   10 BAHT
Nickel, 32 mm.   **Ruler:** Bhumipol Adulyadej (Rama IX)
Subject: 60th Birthday of King Rama IX December 5 **Obv:** Uniformed bust facing **Rev:** Crowned emblem within lightning bolts **Edge:** Reeded

Date	Mintage	F	VF	XF	Unc	BU
BE2530 (1987)	500,000	—	—	—	2.50	—
BE2530 (1987) Proof	5,000	Value: 32.50				

Y# 212   10 BAHT
Nickel, 32 mm.   **Ruler:** Bhumipol Adulyadej (Rama IX)
Subject: 42nd Anniversary - Reign of King Rama IX July 2 **Obv:** Bust facing **Rev:** Crowned monogram

Date	Mintage	F	VF	XF	Unc	BU
BE2531 (1988)	500,000	—	—	—	2.50	—
BE2531 (1988) Proof	8,110	Value: 25.00				

Y# 189   10 BAHT
Nickel, 32 mm.   **Ruler:** Bhumipol Adulyadej (Rama IX)
Subject: Chulachomklao Royal Military Academy August 5 **Obv:** Conjoined busts left **Rev:** Flagged arms

Date	Mintage	F	VF	XF	Unc	BU
BE2530 (1987)	300,000	—	—	—	2.50	—
BE2530 (1987) Proof	2,060	Value: 45.00				

Y# 221   10 BAHT
Nickel, 32 mm.   **Ruler:** Bhumipol Adulyadej (Rama IX)
Subject: 100th Anniversary of Siriraj Hospital April 26 **Obv:** Crowned busts left **Rev:** Crown above design

Date	Mintage	F	VF	XF	Unc	BU
BE2531 (1988)	290,000	—	—	—	2.50	—
BE2531 (1988) Proof	5,000	Value: 27.50				

Y# 223   10 BAHT
Nickel, 32 mm.   **Ruler:** Bhumipol Adulyadej (Rama IX)
Subject: Crown Prince's Birthday **Obv:** Head 1/4 left **Rev:** Crowned monogram within lightning bolts **Edge:** Reeded

Date	Mintage	F	VF	XF	Unc	BU
BE2531 (1988)	200,000	—	—	—	2.50	—
BE2531 (1988) Proof	3,000	Value: 32.50				

Y# 179   10 BAHT
Nickel, 32 mm.   **Ruler:** Bhumipol Adulyadej (Rama IX)
Subject: National Years of the Trees 2528-2531 **Obv:** Bust left **Rev:** Circular design below inscription within tree, emblems flank tree below

Date	Mintage	F	VF	XF	Unc	BU
ND (1986)	100,000	—	4.00	9.00	18.00	—
ND (1986) Proof	2,100	Value: 45.00				

Y# 227 10 BAHT
8.5400 g., Bi-Metallic Aluminum-bronze center in Stainless steel ring, 26 mm. **Ruler:** Bhumipol Adulyadej (Rama IX) **Obv:** Head left within circle **Rev:** Temple of the Dawn within circle **Edge:** Segmented reeding **Note:** Varieties exist.

Date	Mintage	F	VF	XF	Unc	BU
BE2531 (1988)	100,000	—	—	—	—	—
Prooflike; Rare						

Note: The BE2531 (1988) pieces were not released to general circulation and are very scarce in the numismatic community

Date	Mintage	F	VF	XF	Unc	BU
BE2532 (1989)	200,000,000	—	—	—	2.50	—
BE2533 (1990)	100	—	—	—	2,500	—
BE2534 (1991)	—	—	—	—	2.50	—
BE2535 (1992)	—	—	—	—	2.50	—
BE2536 (1993)	—	—	—	—	2.50	—
BE2537 (1994)	—	—	—	—	3.00	—
BE2538 (1995)	—	—	—	—	3.00	—
BE2539 (1996)	—	—	—	—	3.00	—

Y# 228 10 BAHT
Nickel, 32 mm. **Ruler:** Bhumipol Adulyadej (Rama IX) **Subject:** 72nd Anniversary Chulalongkorn University March 26 **Obv:** 3 Conjoined busts left **Rev:** Radiant crown

Date	Mintage	F	VF	XF	Unc	BU
BE2532 (1989)	500,000	—	—	—	2.50	—

Y# 231 10 BAHT
Copper-Nickel, 32 mm. **Ruler:** Bhumipol Adulyadej (Rama IX) **Subject:** Centennial of First Medical College September 5 2433 to September 5 2533 **Obv:** Conjoined busts facing **Rev:** Building **Edge:** Reeded

Date	Mintage	F	VF	XF	Unc	BU
BE2533 (1990)	300,000	—	—	—	2.50	—
BE2533 (1990) Proof	3,772	Value: 32.50				

Y# 233 10 BAHT
Copper-Nickel, 32 mm. **Ruler:** Bhumipol Adulyadej (Rama IX) **Subject:** 90th Birthday of the King's Mother October 21 **Obv:** Crown on stand flanked by others **Rev:** Bust 1/4 left **Edge:** Reeded

Date	Mintage	F	VF	XF	Unc	BU
BE2533 (1990)	500,000	—	—	—	2.50	—
BE2533 (1991) Proof	6,076	Value: 32.50				

Y# 236 10 BAHT
Copper-Nickel, 32 mm. **Ruler:** Bhumipol Adulyadej (Rama IX) **Subject:** 100th Anniversary - Office of Comptroller General **Obv:** Conjoined busts 1/4 left **Rev:** Building above computer, typewriter and phone

Date	Mintage	F	VF	XF	Unc	BU
BE2533 (1990)	300,000	—	—	—	2.50	—

Y# 244 10 BAHT
Copper-Nickel, 32 mm. **Ruler:** Bhumipol Adulyadej (Rama IX) **Subject:** World Health Organization December 17 **Obv:** Bust 1/4 left **Rev:** Gold medal for good health **Edge:** Reeded

Date	Mintage	F	VF	XF	Unc	BU
BE2533 (1990)	800,000	—	—	—	3.00	—
BE2533 (1990) Proof	34,041	Value: 45.00				

Y# 238 10 BAHT
Copper-Nickel, 32 mm. **Ruler:** Bhumipol Adulyadej (Rama IX) **Subject:** 36th Birthday of Princess Sirindhorn April 2 **Obv:** Uniformed bust 1/4 left **Rev:** Crowned monogram flanked by stars above sprigs **Edge:** Reeded

Date	Mintage	F	VF	XF	Unc	BU
BE2534 (1991)	1,100,000	—	—	—	2.50	—
BE2534 (1991) Proof	3,300	Value: 35.00				

Y# 241 10 BAHT
Copper-Nickel, 32 mm. **Ruler:** Bhumipol Adulyadej (Rama IX) **Subject:** 80th Anniversary of Thai Boy Scouts July 1 2454-2534 **Obv:** Conjoined busts 1/4 left in scouting uniform **Rev:** Scout emblem and motto "Better to die than to lie" **Edge:** Reeded

Date	Mintage	F	VF	XF	Unc	BU
BE2534 (1991)	650,000	—	—	—	3.00	—
BE2534 (1991) Proof	3,237	Value: 35.00				

Y# 256 10 BAHT
Copper-Nickel, 32 mm. **Ruler:** Bhumipol Adulyadej (Rama IX) **Subject:** Princess Sirindhorn's Magsaysay Foundation Award August 31 **Obv:** Seated and kneeling figures within circle **Rev:** Foundation Award medal below cameo **Edge:** Reeded

Date	Mintage	F	VF	XF	Unc	BU
BE2534 (1991)	800,000	—	—	—	2.50	—
BE2534 (1991) Proof	2,111	Value: 37.50				

Y# 249 10 BAHT
Copper-Nickel, 32 mm. **Ruler:** Bhumipol Adulyadej (Rama IX) **Subject:** Centenary Celebration - Father of King Rama IX Mahidon - January 1 **Obv:** Crown on stand flanked by others **Rev:** Bust facing **Edge:** Reeded

Date	Mintage	F	VF	XF	Unc	BU
BE2535 (1992)	800,000	—	—	—	2.50	—
BE2535 (1992) Proof	5,314	Value: 25.00				

Y# 252 10 BAHT
Copper-Nickel, 32 mm. **Ruler:** Bhumipol Adulyadej (Rama IX) **Subject:** Ministry of Justice Centennial March 25 **Obv:** Conjoined busts left **Rev:** Balance scales within design **Edge:** Reeded

Date	Mintage	F	VF	XF	Unc	BU
BE2535 (1992)	800,000	—	—	—	2.50	—
BE2535 (1992) Proof		Value: 22.50				

Y# 254 10 BAHT
Copper-Nickel, 32 mm. **Ruler:** Bhumipol Adulyadej (Rama IX) **Subject:** Ministry of Interior Centennial April 1 2435 to 2535 **Obv:** Conjoined uniformed busts facing **Rev:** Mythical animal within circle **Edge:** Reeded

Date	Mintage	F	VF	XF	Unc	BU
BE2535 (1992)	800,000	—	—	—	2.50	—
BE2535 (1992) Proof	10,000	Value: 17.50				

Y# 261 10 BAHT
Copper-Nickel, 32 mm. **Ruler:** Bhumipol Adulyadej (Rama IX) **Subject:** Queen's 60th Birthday August 12 (Thai Mother's Day) **Obv:** Crowned bust facing **Rev:** Crowned monogram **Edge:** Reeded

Date	Mintage	F	VF	XF	Unc	BU
BE2535 (1992)	1,100,000	—	—	—	3.00	—
BE2535 (1992) Proof	18,000	Value: 17.50				

Y# 269   10 BAHT
Copper-Nickel, 32 mm.   **Ruler:** Bhumipol Adulyadej (Rama IX)
Subject: 60th Anniversary of National Assembly June 28
Obv: Conjoined busts left **Rev:** Ratasapa - Paraliment building
Edge: Reeded

Date	Mintage	F	VF	XF	Unc	BU
BE2535 (1992)	44,000	—	—	—	2.50	—

Y# 271   10 BAHT
Copper-Nickel, 32 mm.   **Ruler:** Bhumipol Adulyadej (Rama IX)
Subject: Ministry of Agriculture April 1 **Obv:** Conjoined busts 1/4
left **Rev:** Emblem above designed sprigs **Edge:** Reeded

Date	Mintage	F	VF	XF	Unc	BU
BE2535 (1992)	550,000	—	—	—	2.50	—
BE2535 (1992) Proof		Value: 25.00				

Y# 284   10 BAHT
Copper-Nickel, 32 mm.   **Ruler:** Bhumipol Adulyadej (Rama IX)
Subject: Centennial of Thai Teacher Training October 12
Obv: Conjoined busts left **Rev:** Emblem **Edge:** Reeded

Date	Mintage	F	VF	XF	Unc	BU
BE2535 (1992)	700,000	—	—	—	2.50	—

Y# 285   10 BAHT
Copper-Nickel, 32 mm.   **Ruler:** Bhumipol Adulyadej (Rama IX)
Subject: Centennial of Thai National Bank December 10
Obv: Conjoined busts facing **Rev:** Seated figure **Edge:** Reeded

Date	Mintage	F	VF	XF	Unc	BU
BE2535 (1992)	700,000	—	—	—	2.50	—
BE2535 (1992) Proof	6,927	Value: 20.00				

Y# 273   10 BAHT
Copper-Nickel, 32 mm.   **Ruler:** Bhumipol Adulyadej (Rama IX)
Subject: King's 64th Birthday November 18 **Obv:** Conjoined
busts 1/4 left **Rev:** Crowned monograms **Edge:** Reeded
Note: In honor of the King reaching the life span of his great
grandfather.

Date	Mintage	F	VF	XF	Unc	BU
BE2535 (1992)	550,000	—	—	—	2.50	—
BE2535 (1992) Proof	3,711	Value: 25.00				

Y# 280   10 BAHT
Copper-Nickel, 32 mm.   **Ruler:** Bhumipol Adulyadej (Rama IX)
Subject: Centennial of Thai Red Cross 2436-2536
Obv: Conjoined busts 1/4 left **Rev:** Symbols **Edge:** Reeded

Date	Mintage	F	VF	XF	Unc	BU
BE2536 (1993)	700,000	—	—	—	2.50	—
BE2535 (1993) Proof	14,000	Value: 18.50				

Y# 283   10 BAHT
Copper-Nickel, 32 mm.   **Ruler:** Bhumipol Adulyadej (Rama IX)
Subject: 60th Anniversary Treasury Department May 23
Obv: Conjoined busts left **Rev:** Emblem within circle
Edge: Reeded

Date	Mintage	F	VF	XF	Unc	BU
BE2536 (1993)	600,000	—	—	—	2.50	—
BE2535 (1993) Proof	10,000	Value: 22.50				

Y# 286   10 BAHT
Copper-Nickel, 32 mm.   **Ruler:** Bhumipol Adulyadej (Rama IX)
Subject: Centennial of Attorney General's Office April 1 2436-
2536 **Obv:** Conjoined busts facing **Rev:** Crowned balance scales
above sprigs **Edge:** Reeded

Date	Mintage	F	VF	XF	Unc	BU
BE2536 (1993)	700,000	—	—	—	2.50	—

Y# 289   10 BAHT
Copper-Nickel, 32 mm.   **Ruler:** Bhumipol Adulyadej (Rama IX)
Subject: 100th Anniversary of Rama VII November 8 **Obv:** Bust
left **Rev:** Crown and designs within oval circle **Edge:** Reeded

Date	Mintage	F	VF	XF	Unc	BU
BE2536 (1993)	800,000	—	—	—	2.50	—
BE2536 (1993) Proof	10,000	Value: 22.50				

Y# 293   10 BAHT
Copper-Nickel, 32 mm.   **Ruler:** Bhumipol Adulyadej (Rama IX)
Subject: 60th Anniversary - Royal Thai Language Academy March
31 **Obv:** Conjoined busts left **Rev:** Crowned emblem **Edge:** Reeded

Date	Mintage	F	VF	XF	Unc	BU
BE2537 (1994)	700,000	—	—	—	2.50	—
BE2537 (1994) Proof	10,000	Value: 22.50				

Y# 295   10 BAHT
Copper-Nickel, 32 mm.   **Ruler:** Bhumipol Adulyadej (Rama IX)
Subject: 120th Anniversary Council of Advisors to the King -
Royal decree 2417-2537 **Obv:** Conjoined busts facing
Rev: Building **Edge:** Reeded

Date	Mintage	F	VF	XF	Unc	BU
BE2537 (1994)	800,000	—	—	—	2.50	—
BE2537 (1994) Proof	12,000	Value: 22.50				

Y# 297   10 BAHT
Copper-Nickel, 32 mm.   **Ruler:** Bhumipol Adulyadej (Rama IX)
Subject: 60th Anniversary - Thammasat University June 27
Obv: Conjoined busts left **Rev:** Emblem within circle and wreath
Edge: Reeded

Date	Mintage	F	VF	XF	Unc	BU
BE2537 (1994)	800,000	—	—	—	2.50	—
BE2537 (1994) Proof	12,000	Value: 22.50				

Y# 339   10 BAHT
8.4200 g., Bi-Metallic Brass center in Copper-Nickel ring, 26 mm.
Ruler: Bhumipol Adulyadej (Rama IX) **Subject:** International Rice
Award June 5 **Obv:** Half length figure with camera left within circle
Rev: Rice plant within circle **Edge:** Alternating reeded and plain

Date	Mintage	F	VF	XF	Unc	BU
BE2538 (1996)	—	—	—	—	3.50	—

Y# 328.1   10 BAHT
Bi-Metallic Brass center in Copper-Nickel ring, 26 mm.
Ruler: Bhumipol Adulyadej (Rama IX) **Subject:** 50th
Anniversary - Reign of King Rama IX June 9 **Obv:** Bust facing
within circle **Rev:** National arms within circle **Edge:** Alternating
reeded and plain

Date	Mintage	F	VF	XF	Unc	BU
BE2539 (1996)	—	—	—	—	3.00	—

Y# 328.2   10 BAHT
Bi-Metallic Brass center in Copper-Nickel ring, 26 mm.
Ruler: Bhumipol Adulyadej (Rama IX) **Subject:** 50th
Anniversary - Reign of King Rama IX June 9 **Obv:** Bust facing
within circle **Rev:** National arms within circle **Edge:** Alternating
reeded and plain

Date	Mintage	F	VF	XF	Unc	BU
BE2539 (1996)	—	—	—	—	3.00	—

Y# 334   10 BAHT
Bi-Metallic Brass center in Copper-Nickel ring, 26 mm.
Ruler: Bhumipol Adulyadej (Rama IX) **Subject:** F.A.O. World
Summit December 2 **Obv:** Bust left within circle **Rev:** Seated and
kneeling figures within circle **Edge:** Alternating reeded and plain

Date	Mintage	F	VF	XF	Unc	BU
BE2538 (1996)	—	—	—	—	3.50	—

Y# 347   10 BAHT
Bi-Metallic Brass center in Copper-Nickel ring, 26 mm.
Ruler: Bhumipol Adulyadej (Rama IX) **Subject:** 100th
Anniversary of Chulalongkorn's European Tour **Obv:** Bust right
within circle **Rev:** Design and inscription divides circle
Edge: Alternating reeded and plain

Date	Mintage	F	VF	XF	Unc	BU
BE2540 (1997)	—	—	—	—	2.50	—

Y# 346   10 BAHT
Bi-Metallic Brass center in Copper-Nickel ring, 26 mm.
Ruler: Bhumipol Adulyadej (Rama IX) **Subject:** 100th
Anniversary - Central General Hospital - Medication Office 2441-
2541 **Obv:** Conjoined busts facing within circle **Rev:** Figure
seated on facing elephant within circle **Edge:** Alternating reeded
and plain

Date	Mintage	F	VF	XF	Unc	BU
BE2541 (1998)	—	—	—	—	4.00	—

Y# 348   10 BAHT
Bi-Metallic Brass center in Copper-Nickel ring, 26 mm.
Ruler: Bhumipol Adulyadej (Rama IX) **Subject:** 13th Asian
Games Bangkok December 6-20 **Obv:** Bust left within circle
Rev: Symbols within circle **Edge:** Alternating reeded and plain

Date	Mintage	F	VF	XF	Unc	BU
BE2541 (1998)	10,000,000	—	—	—	2.50	—

Y# 352   10 BAHT
Bi-Metallic Brass center in Copper-Nickel ring, 26 mm.
Ruler: Bhumipol Adulyadej (Rama IX) **Subject:** Rama III
honored with the title "Great" March 31 **Obv:** Head facing within
circle **Rev:** Crowned arms within circle **Edge:** Alternating reeded
and plain

Date	Mintage	F	VF	XF	Unc	BU
BE2541 (1998)	—	—	—	—	2.50	—

Y# 349   10 BAHT
Bi-Metallic Brass center in Copper-Nickel ring, 26 mm.
Ruler: Bhumipol Adulyadej (Rama IX) **Subject:** 125th
Anniversary of the Customer's Department July 4 **Obv:** Conjoined
busts 1/4 right **Rev:** Buildings below emblem **Edge:** Alternating
reeded and plain

Date	Mintage	F	VF	XF	Unc	BU
BE2542 (1999)	—	—	—	—	2.50	—

Y# 350   10 BAHT
Bi-Metallic Brass center in Copper-Nickel ring, 26 mm.
Ruler: Bhumipol Adulyadej (Rama IX) **Subject:** King's 72nd
Birthday December 5 **Obv:** Head left within circle **Rev:** Crowned
emblem within circle **Edge:** Alternating reeded and plain

Date	Mintage	F	VF	XF	Unc	BU
BE2542 (1999)	10,000,000	—	—	—	1.75	—

Y# 354   10 BAHT
Bi-Metallic Brass center in Copper-Nickel ring, 26 mm.
Ruler: Bhumipol Adulyadej (Rama IX) **Subject:** 100th Anniversary
Army Medical Department January 7 2443-2543 **Obv:** Conjoined
busts facing **Rev:** Emblem within circle **Edge:** Alternating reeded
and plain

Date	Mintage	F	VF	XF	Unc	BU
ND (2000)	—	—	—	—	2.00	—

Y# 358   10 BAHT
8.4900 g., Bi-Metallic Brass center in Copper-Nickel ring, 26 mm.
Ruler: Bhumipol Adulyadej (Rama IX) **Subject:** 80th
Anniversary - Commerce Ministry August 20 **Obv:** Head facing
within circle **Rev:** Ministry logo within square and circle
Edge: Segmented reeding

Date	Mintage	F	VF	XF	Unc	BU
BE2543 (2000)	—	—	—	—	2.00	—

Y# 361   10 BAHT
Bi-Metallic Brass center in Copper-Nickel ring, 26 mm.
Ruler: Bhumipol Adulyadej (Rama IX) **Subject:** 100th Birthday
- King's Mother October 21 **Obv:** Bust left within circle
Rev: Emblem within circle **Edge:** Alternating reeded and plain

Date	Mintage	F	VF	XF	Unc	BU
BE2543 (2000)	—	—	—	—	2.00	—

Y# 371   10 BAHT
8.4500 g., Bi-Metallic Brass center in Copper-Nickel ring, 26 mm.
Ruler: Bhumipol Adulyadej (Rama IX) **Subject:** National Economic
and Social Development Board February 15 **Obv:** Bust 3/4 left
Rev: Three seated figures within circle **Edge:** Segmented reeding

Date	Mintage	F	VF	XF	Unc	BU
BE2543(2000)	—	—	—	—	2.00	—

Y# 86   20 BAHT
19.6000 g., 0.7500 Silver 0.4726 oz. ASW, 34.5 mm.
Ruler: Bhumipol Adulyadej (Rama IX) **Subject:** 36th Birthday -
Rama IX **Obv:** Uniformed bust left **Rev:** Crown and emblem
divided by crossed scepter and spear

Date	Mintage	F	VF	XF	Unc	BU
ND (1963)	1,000,000	—	—	8.00	10.00	13.50

Y# 298   20 BAHT
Copper-Nickel, 32 mm. **Ruler:** Bhumipol Adulyadej (Rama IX)
Subject: 120th Anniversary - Ministry of Finance 2418-2538
Obv: Conjoined busts right **Rev:** Stylized eagle **Edge:** Reeded

Date	Mintage	F	VF	XF	Unc	BU
BE2538 (1995)	800,000	—	—	—	3.50	—
BE2538 (1995) Proof	1,920	Value: 35.00				

Y# 300   20 BAHT
Copper-Nickel, 32 mm. **Ruler:** Bhumipol Adulyadej (Rama IX)
Subject: 108th Anniversary - Ministry of Defense April 8
Obv: Conjoined uniformed busts facing **Rev:** Mythical animal within circle **Edge:** Reeded

Date	Mintage	F	VF	XF	Unc	BU
BE2538 (1995)	800,000	—	—	—	3.50	—
BE2538 (1995) Proof	2,000	Value: 35.00				

Y# 302   20 BAHT
Copper-Nickel, 32 mm. **Ruler:** Bhumipol Adulyadej (Rama IX)
Subject: 120th Anniversary - Ministry of Foreign Affairs April 14
Obv: Conjoined busts facing **Rev:** Seated figure within designed circle and wreath **Edge:** Reeded

Date	Mintage	F	VF	XF	Unc	BU
BE2538 (1995)	—	—	—	—	3.50	—
BE2538 (1995)	800,000	—	—	—	3.50	—
BE2538 (1995) Proof	740	Value: 55.00				

Y# 304   20 BAHT
Copper-Nickel, 32 mm. **Ruler:** Bhumipol Adulyadej (Rama IX)
Subject: 72nd Birthday of Princess May 6 **Obv:** Uniformed bust 3/4 facing **Rev:** Crowned arms **Edge:** Reeded

Date	Mintage	F	VF	XF	Unc	BU
BE2538 (1995)	800,000	—	—	—	3.50	—
BE2538 (1995) Proof	1,560	Value: 27.50				

Y# 308   20 BAHT
Copper-Nickel, 32 mm. **Ruler:** Bhumipol Adulyadej (Rama IX)
Series: F.A.O. 1945-1995 **Obv:** Bust left **Rev:** F.A.O. logo and dates **Edge:** Reeded

Date	Mintage	F	VF	XF	Unc	BU
BE2538 (1995)	400,000	—	—	—	3.50	—
BE2538 (1995) Proof	—	Value: 25.00				

Y# 309   20 BAHT
Copper-Nickel **Ruler:** Bhumipol Adulyadej (Rama IX)
Subject: 80th Anniversary - Department of Revenue September 2 **Obv:** Conjoined busts 1/4 left **Rev:** Seated figure within circle **Edge:** Reeded

Date	Mintage	F	VF	XF	Unc	BU
BE2538 (1995)	800,000	—	—	—	3.50	—
BE2538 (1995) Proof	—	Value: 20.00				

Y# 311   20 BAHT
Copper-Nickel, 32 mm. **Ruler:** Bhumipol Adulyadej (Rama IX)
Subject: 120th Anniversary - Audit Council 2418-2538
Obv: Conjoined uniformed busts facing **Rev:** Balance scales **Edge:** Reeded

Date	Mintage	F	VF	XF	Unc	BU
BE2538 (1995)	800,000	—	—	—	3.50	—
BE2538 (1995) Proof	—	Value: 20.00				

Y# 314   20 BAHT
Copper-Nickel, 32 mm. **Ruler:** Bhumipol Adulyadej (Rama IX)
Subject: Information Technology Year **Obv:** Bust left
Rev: Design and inscription within world globe **Edge:** Reeded

Date	Mintage	F	VF	XF	Unc	BU
BE2538 (1995)	—	—	—	—	3.50	—
BE2538 (1995) Proof	—	Value: 20.00				

Y# 316   20 BAHT
Copper-Nickel, 32 mm. **Ruler:** Bhumipol Adulyadej (Rama IX)
Subject: Asean Environment Year **Obv:** Conjoined busts right
Rev: Symbol within center circle, grain sprig and arrow surround

Date	Mintage	F	VF	XF	Unc	BU
BE2538 (1995)	—	—	—	—	3.50	—
BE2538 (1995) Proof	—	Value: 20.00				

Y# 331   20 BAHT
Copper-Nickel, 32 mm. **Ruler:** Bhumipol Adulyadej (Rama IX)
Subject: Ministry of Commerce **Obv:** Conjoined uniformed busts facing **Rev:** Seal within circle **Edge:** Reeded

Date	Mintage	F	VF	XF	Unc	BU
BE2538 (1995)	—	—	—	—	4.00	—

Y# 338   20 BAHT
Copper-Nickel, 32 mm. **Ruler:** Bhumipol Adulyadej (Rama IX)
Subject: 50 Years of Peace August 16 **Obv:** Uniformed busts of Rama VIII and Rama IX facing **Rev:** Busts left with flag and doves within center circle **Edge:** Reeded

Date	Mintage	F	VF	XF	Unc	BU
ND(BE2538) (1995)	—	—	—	—	3.50	—

Y# 318   20 BAHT
Copper-Nickel, 32 mm. **Ruler:** Bhumipol Adulyadej (Rama IX)
Subject: Siriraj Nursing and Midwife School Centennial January 12 **Obv:** Uniformed bust facing **Rev:** Crowned monogram flanked by sprigs **Edge:** Reeded

Date	Mintage	F	VF	XF	Unc	BU
BE2539 (1996)	—	—	—	—	3.50	—

Y# 321.1   20 BAHT
Copper-Nickel, 32 mm. **Ruler:** Bhumipol Adulyadej (Rama IX)
Subject: 50th Anniversary - Reign of King Rama IX June 9
Obv: Bust facing **Rev:** National arms **Edge:** Reeded

Date	Mintage	F	VF	XF	Unc	BU
BE2539 (1996)	—	—	—	—	4.00	—
BE2539 (1996) Proof	—	Value: 30.00				

Y# 321.2   20 BAHT
Copper-Nickel, 32 mm. **Ruler:** Bhumipol Adulyadej (Rama IX)
Subject: 50th Anniversary - Reign of King Rama IX June 9
Obv: Bust facing **Rev:** Crowned arms with supporters

Date	Mintage	F	VF	XF	Unc	BU
BE2539 (1996)	—	—	—	—	4.00	—
BE2539 (1996) Proof	—	Value: 30.00				

Y# 335   20 BAHT
Copper-Nickel, 32 mm. **Ruler:** Bhumipol Adulyadej (Rama IX)
Subject: F.A.O. World Food Summit **Obv:** Bust left within circle
Rev: Seated and kneeling figures within circle **Edge:** Reeded

Date	Mintage	F	VF	XF	Unc	BU
BE2539 (1996)	—	—	—	—	3.50	—
BE2539 (1996) Proof	—	Value: 25.00				

Y# 340   20 BAHT
Copper-Nickel, 32 mm. **Ruler:** Bhumipol Adulyadej (Rama IX)
Subject: International Rice Award June 5 **Obv:** Half length bust left
within circle **Rev:** Inscription and sprigs within circle **Edge:** Reeded

Date	Mintage	F	VF	XF	Unc	BU
BE2539 (1996)	—	—	—	—	3.50	—
BE2539 (1996) Proof	—	Value: 25.00				

Y# 332   20 BAHT
Copper-Nickel, 32 mm. **Ruler:** Bhumipol Adulyadej (Rama IX)
Subject: 100th Anniversary - Thai Railway March 26
Obv: Conjoined busts 1/4 left **Rev:** Radiant crown above stylized
eagle **Edge:** Reeded

Date	Mintage	F	VF	XF	Unc	BU
BE2540 (1997)	—	—	—	—	3.50	—
BE2540 (1997) Proof	—	Value: 30.00				

Y# 333   20 BAHT
Copper-Nickel, 32 mm. **Ruler:** Bhumipol Adulyadej (Rama IX)
Subject: 90th Anniversary - Thai Savings Bank April 1
Obv: Uniformed bust facing **Rev:** Designs within sectioned circle
Edge: Reeded

Date	Mintage	F	VF	XF	Unc	BU
BE2540 (1997)	—	—	—	—	3.50	—
BE2540 (1997) Proof	—	Value: 28.00				

Y# 341   20 BAHT
Copper-Nickel, 32 mm. **Ruler:** Bhumipol Adulyadej (Rama IX)
Subject: 50th Anniversary - Thai Veterans Organization;
Veteran's Day February 3 **Obv:** Uniformed bust facing
Rev: Armored figures within circle **Edge:** Reeded

Date	Mintage	F	VF	XF	Unc	BU
BE2541 (1998)	—	—	—	—	3.50	—
BE2541 (1998) Proof	—	Value: 18.50				

Y# 351   20 BAHT
Copper Nickel, 32 mm. **Ruler:** Bhumipol Adulyadej (Rama IX)
Subject: 72nd Birthday of the King December 5 **Obv:** Bust left
Rev: Crowned emblem **Edge:** Reeded

Date	Mintage	F	VF	XF	Unc	BU
BE2542 (1999)	—	—	—	—	2.50	—
BE2542 (1999) Proof	5,000	Value: 17.50				

Y# 355   20 BAHT
14.9100 g., Copper Nickel, 32 mm. **Ruler:** Bhumipol
Adulyadej (Rama IX) **Subject:** 84th Anniversary - Audit Council
Bureau September 18 **Obv:** Uniformed bust facing **Rev:** Balance
scale **Edge:** Reeded

Date	Mintage	F	VF	XF	Unc	BU
BE2542 (1999)	—	—	—	—	3.50	—

Y# 376   20 BAHT
15.0000 g., Copper-Nickel, 32 mm. **Ruler:** Bhumipol
Adulyadej (Rama IX) **Subject:** The 9th King reaches the age of
the 1st King May 23 **Obv:** Conjoined busts facing **Rev:** Two royal
symbols **Edge:** Reeded

Date	Mintage	F	VF	XF	Unc	BU
BE2543(2000)	—	—	—	—	3.50	—

Y# 357   20 BAHT
Copper-Nickel, 32 mm. **Ruler:** Bhumipol Adulyadej (Rama IX)
Subject: Asian Development Bank Board Meeting **Obv:** Bust 1/4
right **Rev:** Chieng money illustration **Edge:** Reeded

Date	Mintage	F	VF	XF	Unc	BU
ND (2000)	—	—	—	—	4.00	—

Y# 362   20 BAHT
Copper-Nickel, 32 mm. **Ruler:** Bhumipol Adulyadej (Rama IX)
Subject: 100th Birthday - King's Mother **Obv:** Bust left
Rev: Emblem divides date **Edge:** Reeded

Date	Mintage	F	VF	XF	Unc	BU
BE2543 (2000)	—	—	—	—	3.50	—
BE2543 (2000) Proof	—	Value: 17.50				

Y# 95   50 BAHT
24.7000 g., 0.9000 Silver 0.7147 oz. ASW, 40 mm.
Ruler: Bhumipol Adulyadej (Rama IX) **Subject:** 20th Year
Buddhist Fellowship **Obv:** Bust 1/4 left **Rev:** The Buddhist wheel
of law, Dhamachakr **Edge:** Reeded

Date	Mintage	F	VF	XF	Unc	BU
BE2514 (1971)	200,000	—	BV	12.50	15.00	—
BE2514 (1971) Prooflike	60,000	—	—	—	—	22.50

Y# 101   50 BAHT
24.8500 g., 0.4000 Silver 0.3196 oz. ASW **Ruler:** Bhumipol
Adulyadej (Rama IX) **Subject:** National Museum Centennial
Obv: Conjoined busts left **Rev:** Crowns within designed wreath

Date	Mintage	F	VF	XF	Unc	BU
BE2517 (1974)	200,000	—	—	10.00	15.00	—

Y# 102   50 BAHT
25.5500 g., 0.5000 Silver 0.4107 oz. ASW **Ruler:** Bhumipol
Adulyadej (Rama IX) **Series:** Conservation **Obv:** Bust 1/4 left
Rev: Sumatran Rhinoceros

Date	Mintage	F	VF	XF	Unc	BU
BE2517 (1974)	20,000	—	—	—	32.00	35.00

Y# 102a   50 BAHT
28.2800 g., 0.9250 Silver 0.8410 oz. ASW **Ruler:** Bhumipol
Adulyadej (Rama IX) **Series:** Conservation **Obv:** Bust 1/4 left
Rev: Rhinoceros

Date	Mintage	F	VF	XF	Unc	BU
BE2517 (1974) Proof	9,885	Value: 60.00				

Y# 336   50 BAHT
Nickel, 36 mm. **Ruler:** Bhumipol Adulyadej (Rama IX)
Subject: F.A.O. World Food Summit December 2 **Obv:** Bust left
within circle **Rev:** Seated and kneeling figures within circle
Edge: Reeded **Note:** Similar to 20 Baht, Y#335.

Date	Mintage	F	VF	XF	Unc	BU
BE2538 (1995)	—	—	—	—	12.50	—

Y# 363   50 BAHT

20.0000 g., 0.9250 Silver 0.5948 oz. ASW, 38.7 mm.
Ruler: Bhumipol Adulyadej (Rama IX) **Subject:** Year of the Dragon
Obv: Bust 1/4 left **Rev:** Dragon and latent image date pearl
Edge: Reeded

Date	Mintage	F	VF	XF	Unc	BU
BE2543 (2000)	8,500	Value: 55.00				
Proof						

Y# 364   50 BAHT

20.0000 g., 0.9250 Silver 0.5948 oz. ASW **Ruler:** Bhumipol
Adulyadej (Rama IX) **Subject:** Year of the Dragon **Obv:** Bust 1/4
left **Rev:** Two dragons with pearl hologram

Date	Mintage	F	VF	XF	Unc	BU
BE2543 (2000)	8,500	Value: 150				
Proof						

Y# 365   50 BAHT

20.0000 g., 0.9250 Silver 0.5948 oz. ASW **Ruler:** Bhumipol
Adulyadej (Rama IX) **Subject:** Year of the Dragon **Obv:** Bust 1/4
left **Rev:** Dragon with gold-plated pearl

Date	Mintage	F	VF	XF	Unc	BU
BE2543 (2000)	8,500	Value: 55.00				
Proof						

Y# 103   100 BAHT

31.9000 g., 0.5000 Silver 0.5128 oz. ASW. **Ruler:** Bhumipol
Adulyadej (Rama IX) **Series:** Conservation **Obv:** Bust 1/4 left
Rev: Brown-antlered deer

Date	Mintage	F	VF	XF	Unc	BU
BE2517 (1974)	20,000	—	—	—	37.50	40.00

Y# 103a   100 BAHT

35.0000 g., 0.9250 Silver 1.0408 oz. ASW **Ruler:** Bhumipol
Adulyadej (Rama IX) **Series:** Conservation **Obv:** Bust 1/4 left
Rev: Brown-antlered deer

Date	Mintage	F	VF	XF	Unc	BU
BE2517 (1974)	9,294	Value: 70.00				
Proof						

Y# 106   100 BAHT

25.0000 g., 0.9000 Silver 0.7234 oz. ASW **Ruler:** Bhumipol
Adulyadej (Rama IX) **Subject:** 100th Anniversary - Ministry of
Finance **Obv:** Conjoined busts facing **Rev:** Building within circle

Date	Mintage	F	VF	XF	Unc	BU
BE2518 (1975)	30,000	—	—	13.50	20.00	

Y# 242   100 BAHT

Copper-Nickel, 38 mm. **Ruler:** Bhumipol Adulyadej (Rama IX)
Subject: World Bank - International Monetary Fund
Obv: Conjoined busts right **Rev:** Emblem

Date	Mintage	F	VF	XF	Unc	BU
BE2534 (1991)	500,000	—	—	—	12.50	
BE2534 (1991)	60,000	Value: 27.50				
Proof						

Y# 287   100 BAHT

Copper-Nickel, 38 mm. **Ruler:** Bhumipol Adulyadej (Rama IX)
Subject: 33rd World Scount Conference **Obv:** Conjoined busts
right **Rev:** Crowned emblem

Date	Mintage	F	VF	XF	Unc	BU
BE2536 (1993)	200,000	—	—	—	17.50	
BE2536 (1993)	30,000	Value: 32.50				
Proof						

Y# 359   100 BAHT

15.0000 g., 0.9250 Silver 0.4461 oz. ASW, 30 mm.
Ruler: Bhumipol Adulyadej (Rama IX) **Series:** World Wildlife
Fund **Obv:** Bust left **Rev:** Tiger head and value **Note:** Thickness
of coin is 4.7mm.

Date	Mintage	F	VF	XF	Unc	BU
BE2540 (1997)	50,000	Value: 25.00				
Proof						

Y# 366   100 BAHT

7.7759 g., 0.9999 Gold 0.2500 oz. AGW, 22 mm. **Ruler:** Bhumipol
Adulyadej (Rama IX) **Subject:** Year of the Dragon **Obv:** Bust 1/4
left **Rev:** Dragon with golden plated pearl **Edge:** Reeded

Date	Mintage	F	VF	XF	Unc	BU
BE2543 (2000)	1,800	Value: 275				
Proof						

Y# 88   150 BAHT

3.7500 g., 0.9000 Gold 0.1085 oz. AGW **Ruler:** Bhumipol
Adulyadej (Rama IX) **Subject:** Queen Sirikit 36th Birthday
Obv: Bust right **Rev:** Crowned monogram

Date	Mintage	F	VF	XF	Unc	BU
BE2511 (1968)	202,000	—	—	—	125	—

Y# 108   150 BAHT

22.0000 g., 0.9250 Silver 0.6542 oz. ASW **Ruler:** Bhumipol
Adulyadej (Rama IX) **Subject:** 75th Birthday of King's Mother
October 21 **Obv:** Bust with hat facing **Rev:** Emblem

Date	Mintage	F	VF	XF	Unc	BU
BE2518 (1975)	200,000	—	—	12.00	18.50	—

Y# 113   150 BAHT

22.0000 g., 0.9250 Silver 0.6542 oz. ASW **Ruler:** Bhumipol
Adulyadej (Rama IX) **Series:** F.A.O. **Obv:** Standing half length
figures scattering rice **Rev:** Elephants within circle

Date	Mintage	F	VF	XF	Unc	BU
BE2520 (1977)	50,000	—	—	12.00	22.00	27.50

Y# 118   150 BAHT

22.0000 g., 0.9250 Silver 0.6542 oz. ASW **Ruler:** Bhumipol
Adulyadej (Rama IX) **Subject:** Crown Prince Vajiralongkorn and
Princess Soamsawali Wedding January 3 **Obv:** Conjoined busts
right **Rev:** Crowned monogram within designs

Date	Mintage	F	VF	XF	Unc	BU
BE2520 (1977)	200,000	—	—	11.50	15.00	—

Y# 116   150 BAHT

22.0000 g., 0.9250 Silver 0.6542 oz. ASW **Ruler:** Bhumipol
Adulyadej (Rama IX) **Subject:** Graduation of Princess
Sirindhorn; 1st royal graduate of a Thai University **Obv:** Bust left
Rev: Radiant crown

Date	Mintage	F	VF	XF	Unc	BU
BE2520 (1977)	100,000	—	—	11.50	15.00	—

Y# 125 150 BAHT
22.0000 g., 0.9250 Silver 0.6542 oz. ASW **Ruler:** Bhumipol Adulyadej (Rama IX) **Subject:** Investiture of Princess Sirindhorn May 12 **Obv:** Bust right **Rev:** Crowned monogram

Date	Mintage	F	VF	XF	Unc	BU
BE2520 (1977)	50,000	—	—	13.50	28.50	—

Y# 123 150 BAHT
22.0000 g., 0.9250 Silver 0.6542 oz. ASW **Ruler:** Bhumipol Adulyadej (Rama IX) **Subject:** 9th World Orchid Conference **Obv:** Uniformed bust 1/4 left **Rev:** Orchids

Date	Mintage	F	VF	XF	Unc	BU
BE2521 (1978)	30,000	—	—	12.50	25.00	—

Y# 128 150 BAHT
22.0000 g., 0.9250 Silver 0.6542 oz. ASW **Ruler:** Bhumipol Adulyadej (Rama IX) **Subject:** Graduation of Crown Prince Vajiralongkorn **Obv:** Bust left **Rev:** Crowned elephant head facing within frame

Date	Mintage	F	VF	XF	Unc	BU
BE2521 (1978)	50,000	—	—	12.00	18.50	—

Y# 197 150 BAHT
7.5000 g., 0.9250 Silver 0.2230 oz. ASW **Ruler:** Bhumipol Adulyadej (Rama IX) **Subject:** 60th Birthday - King Rama IX **Obv:** Uniformed bust facing **Rev:** Crowned radiant emblem **Note:** Similar to 6000 Baht, Y#202.

Date	Mintage	F	VF	XF	Unc	BU
BE2530 (1987)	12,000	—	—	—	25.00	—
BE2530 (1987) Proof	1,100	Value: 125				

Y# 213 150 BAHT
7.5000 g., 0.9250 Silver 0.2230 oz. ASW **Ruler:** Bhumipol Adulyadej (Rama IX) **Subject:** 42nd Anniversary - Reign of King Rama IX **Obv:** Uniformed bust facing **Rev:** Crowned monogram **Note:** Similar to 10 Baht, Y#212.

Date	Mintage	F	VF	XF	Unc	BU
BE2531 (1988)	20,000	—	—	—	25.00	—
BE2531 (1988) Proof	2,454	Value: 135				

Y# 262 150 BAHT
7.5000 g., 0.9250 Silver 0.2230 oz. ASW **Ruler:** Bhumipol Adulyadej (Rama IX) **Subject:** Queen's 60th Birthday **Obv:** Crowned bust facing **Rev:** Crowned monogram **Note:** Similar to 10 Baht, Y#261.

Date	Mintage	F	VF	XF	Unc	BU
BE2535 (1992)	25,000	—	—	—	25.00	—
BE2535 (1992) Proof	5,600	Value: 45.00				

Y# 322 150 BAHT
7.5000 g., 0.9250 Silver 0.2230 oz. ASW **Ruler:** Bhumipol Adulyadej (Rama IX) **Subject:** 50th Anniversary - Reign of King Rama IX **Obv:** Bust facing **Rev:** National arms **Note:** Similar to 20 Baht, Y#321.1.

Date	Mintage	F	VF	XF	Unc	BU
BE2539 (1996)	—	—	—	—	17.50	—
BE2539 (1996) Proof	—	Value: 45.00				

Y# 133 200 BAHT
22.0000 g., 0.9250 Silver 0.6542 oz. ASW **Ruler:** Bhumipol Adulyadej (Rama IX) **Subject:** Royal Cradle Ceremony **Obv:** Infant head 1/4 right **Rev:** Inscription within designed wreath

Date	Mintage	F	VF	XF	Unc	BU
BE2522 (1979)	50,000	—	—	11.50	16.50	—

Y# 152 200 BAHT
23.3200 g., 0.9250 Silver 0.6935 oz. ASW **Ruler:** Bhumipol Adulyadej (Rama IX) **Series:** International Year of the Child **Obv:** Bust left **Rev:** Dancing figure flanked by emblems below

Date	Mintage	F	VF	XF	Unc	BU
BE2524 (1981) Proof	9,525	Value: 65.00				

Y# 206 200 BAHT
23.1800 g., 0.9250 Silver 0.6893 oz. ASW **Ruler:** Bhumipol Adulyadej (Rama IX) **Series:** 25th Anniversary of World Wildlife Fund **Obv:** Bust left **Rev:** Siamese Fireback pheasant

Date	Mintage	F	VF	XF	Unc	BU
BE2530 (1987) Proof	25,000	Value: 30.00				

Y# 379 200 BAHT
23.3300 g., 0.9250 Silver 0.6938 oz. ASW, 38.6 mm. **Ruler:** Bhumipol Adulyadej (Rama IX) **Subject:** UNICEF **Obv:** Bust left **Rev:** Three seated children **Edge:** Reeded

Date	Mintage	F	VF	XF	Unc	BU
BE2540-1997 Proof	2,900	Value: 27.50				

Y# 399 200 BAHT
23.2600 g., 0.9250 Silver 0.6917 oz. ASW, 38.5 mm. **Ruler:** Bhumipol Adulyadej (Rama IX) **Subject:** World Wildlife Fund **Obv:** Bust left **Rev:** Elephants right **Edge:** Reeded

Date	Mintage	F	VF	XF	Unc	BU
BE2541-1998 Proof	—	Value: 125				

Y# 360 200 BAHT
23.1800 g., 0.9250 Silver 0.6893 oz. ASW, 38.5 mm. **Ruler:** Bhumipol Adulyadej (Rama IX) **Series:** World Wildlife Fund **Obv:** Bust left **Rev:** Two tigers above value **Edge:** Reeded **Note:** Thickness of coin is 4.7mm.

Date	Mintage	F	VF	XF	Unc	BU
BE2541-1998 Proof	15,000	Value: 75.00				

Y# 372 200 BAHT
23.1800 g., 0.9250 Silver 0.6893 oz. ASW **Ruler:** Bhumipol Adulyadej (Rama IX) **Series:** World Wildlife Fund **Obv:** Bust left **Rev:** Elephants

Date	Mintage	F	VF	XF	Unc	BU
BE2541-1998 Proof	—	Value: 60.00				

Y# 367 200 BAHT
155.5175 g., 0.9250 Silver 4.6248 oz. ASW, 65 mm. **Ruler:** Bhumipol Adulyadej (Rama IX) **Subject:** Year of the Dragon **Obv:** Bust left **Rev:** Two dragons around silver pearl within orange circle **Edge:** Reeded

Date	Mintage	F	VF	XF	Unc	BU
BE2543-2000 Proof	2,000	Value: 185				

Y# 169   250 BAHT
28.2800 g., 0.9250 Silver 0.8410 oz. ASW **Ruler:** Bhumipol Adulyadej (Rama IX) **Series:** International Year of Disabled Persons **Obv:** Bust left **Rev:** Emblem within sprigs

Date	Mintage	F	VF	XF	Unc	BU
BE2526 (1983)	307	—	—	—	275	—
BE2526 (1983) Proof	233	Value: 550				

Y# 368   250 BAHT
15.5510 g., 0.9999 Gold 0.4999 oz. AGW, 27 mm.
Ruler: Bhumipol Adulyadej (Rama IX) **Subject:** Year of the Dragon **Obv:** Bust left **Rev:** Dragon with latent image pearl **Edge:** Reeded

Date	Mintage	F	VF	XF	Unc	BU
BE2543-2000 Proof	2,800	Value: 550				

Y# 89   300 BAHT
7.5000 g., 0.9000 Gold 0.2170 oz. AGW **Ruler:** Bhumipol Adulyadej (Rama IX) **Subject:** Queen Sirikit 36th Birthday **Obv:** Bust right **Rev:** Crowned monogram

Date	Mintage	F	VF	XF	Unc	BU
BE2511 (1968)	101,000	—	—	—	245	—

Y# 136   300 BAHT
22.0000 g., 0.9250 Silver 0.6542 oz. ASW **Ruler:** Bhumipol Adulyadej (Rama IX) **Subject:** Graduation of Princess Chulabhorn **Obv:** Bust 1/4 left **Rev:** Graduation emblem within circle **Note:** Similar to 10 Baht, Y#135.

Date	Mintage	F	VF	XF	Unc	BU
BE2522 (1979)	20,000	—	—	15.00	20.00	—

Y# 198   300 BAHT
15.0000 g., 0.9250 Silver 0.4461 oz. ASW **Ruler:** Bhumipol Adulyadej (Rama IX) **Subject:** 60th Birthday - King Rama IX **Obv:** Uniformed bust facing **Rev:** Radiant crowned emblem

Date	Mintage	F	VF	XF	Unc	BU
BE2530 (1987)	6,680	—	—	—	25.00	—
BE2530 (1987) Proof	800	Value: 50.00				

Y# 214   300 BAHT
15.0000 g., 0.9250 Silver 0.4461 oz. ASW **Ruler:** Bhumipol Adulyadej (Rama IX) **Subject:** 42nd Anniversary - Reign of King Rama IX **Obv:** Uniformed bust facing **Rev:** Crowned monogram

Date	Mintage	F	VF	XF	Unc	BU
BE2531 (1988)	11,000	—	—	—	20.00	—
BE2531 (1988) Proof	2,391	Value: 50.00				

Y# 263   300 BAHT
15.0000 g., 0.9250 Silver 0.4461 oz. ASW **Ruler:** Bhumipol Adulyadej (Rama IX) **Subject:** Queen's 60th Birthday **Obv:** Crowned bust facing **Rev:** Crowned monogram

Date	Mintage	F	VF	XF	Unc	BU
BE2535 (1992)	25,000	—	—	—	35.00	—
BE2535 (1992) Proof	4,000	Value: 45.00				

Y# 323   300 BAHT
15.0000 g., 0.9250 Silver 0.4461 oz. ASW **Ruler:** Bhumipol Adulyadej (Rama IX) **Subject:** 50th Anniversary - Reign of King Rama IX **Obv:** Bust facing **Rev:** National arms

Date	Mintage	F	VF	XF	Unc	BU
BE2539 (1996)	—	—	—	—	22.50	—
BE2539 (1996) Proof	—	Value: 50.00				

Y# 93   400 BAHT
10.0000 g., 0.9000 Gold 0.2893 oz. AGW **Ruler:** Bhumipol Adulyadej (Rama IX) **Subject:** 25th Anniversary - Reign of King Rama IX **Obv:** Head right **Rev:** Radiant crowned monogram

Date	Mintage	F	VF	XF	Unc	BU
BE2514 (1971)	47,000	—	—	—	300	325

Y# 90   600 BAHT
15.0400 g., 0.9000 Gold 0.4352 oz. AGW, 26.95 mm.
Ruler: Bhumipol Adulyadej (Rama IX) **Subject:** Queen Sirikit 36th Birthday **Obv:** Crowned bust right **Rev:** Crowned monogram within wreath **Edge:** Reeded

Date	Mintage	F	VF	XF	Unc	BU
BE2511 (1968)	46,000	—	—	—	450	500

Y# 138   600 BAHT
14.9000 g., 0.9250 Silver 0.4431 oz. ASW **Ruler:** Bhumipol Adulyadej (Rama IX) **Subject:** Queen's Anniversary and F.A.O. Ceres Medal **Obv:** Crowned bust 1/4 left **Rev:** Figures working within football-like frames

Date	Mintage	F	VF	XF	Unc	BU
BE2523 (1980)	23,000	—	—	18.00	28.00	—

Y# 143   600 BAHT
14.9000 g., 0.9250 Silver 0.4431 oz. ASW **Ruler:** Bhumipol Adulyadej (Rama IX) **Subject:** Centennial - Birth of Rama VI **Obv:** Bust right **Rev:** Emblem

Date	Mintage	F	VF	XF	Unc	BU
BE2524 (1981)	19,000	—	—	15.00	25.00	—

Y# 147   600 BAHT
22.0000 g., 0.9250 Silver 0.6542 oz. ASW **Ruler:** Bhumipol Adulyadej (Rama IX) **Subject:** 35th Anniversary - Reign of King Rama IX **Obv:** Conjoined busts left **Rev:** Crowns and emblem

Date	Mintage	F	VF	XF	Unc	BU
BE2524 (1981)	15,000	—	—	20.00	30.00	—

Y# 150   600 BAHT
22.0000 g., 0.9250 Silver 0.6542 oz. ASW **Ruler:** Bhumipol Adulyadej (Rama IX) **Subject:** Bicentennial of Bangkok **Obv:** Conjoined busts left **Rev:** Emblem

Date	Mintage	F	VF	XF	Unc	BU
BE2525 (1982)	15,000	—	—	20.00	30.00	—

Y# 155   600 BAHT
22.0000 g., 0.9250 Silver 0.6542 oz. ASW **Ruler:** Bhumipol Adulyadej (Rama IX) **Subject:** 50th Birthday of Queen Sirikit **Obv:** Crowned bust 1/4 left **Rev:** Crowned monogram

Date	Mintage	F	VF	XF	Unc	BU
BE2525 (1982)	3,895	—	—	28.00	55.00	—
BE2525 (1982) Proof	1,011	Value: 225				

Y# 164   600 BAHT
22.0000 g., 0.9250 Silver 0.6542 oz. ASW **Ruler:** Bhumipol Adulyadej (Rama IX) **Subject:** 100th Anniversary of Postage Stamps **Obv:** Conjoined busts left **Rev:** Stamps

Date	Mintage	F	VF	XF	Unc	BU
BE2526 (1983)	5,000	—	—	28.00	55.00	—
BE2526 (1983) Proof	1,400	Value: 160				

Y# 166   600 BAHT
22.0000 g., 0.9250 Silver 0.6542 oz. ASW **Ruler:** Bhumipol Adulyadej (Rama IX) **Subject:** 700th Anniversary of Thai Alphabet **Obv:** Seated figure left **Rev:** Inscription

Date	Mintage	F	VF	XF	Unc	BU
BE2526 (1983)	4,300	—	—	28.00	55.00	—
BE2526 (1983) Proof	1,000	Value: 200				

Y# 173   600 BAHT
22.0000 g., 0.9250 Silver 0.6542 oz. ASW **Ruler:** Bhumipol Adulyadej (Rama IX) **Subject:** 84th Birthday of Princess Mother **Obv:** Bust 1/4 left **Rev:** Crown on stand flanked by others

Date	Mintage	F	VF	XF	Unc	BU
BE2527 (1984)	3,530	—	—	28.00	45.00	—
BE2527 (1984) Proof	520	Value: 260				

Y# 193   600 BAHT
22.0000 g., 0.9250 Silver 0.6542 oz. ASW **Ruler:** Bhumipol Adulyadej (Rama IX) **Subject:** Princess Chulabhorn Awarded Einstein Medal **Obv:** Head of Albert Einstein left within circle at center of hexagon **Rev:** Graduate's bust left **Note:** Similar to 10 Baht, Y#192.

Date	Mintage	F	VF	XF	Unc	BU
BE2529 (1986)	2,400	—	—	—	55.00	—
BE2529 (1986) Proof	212	Value: 225				

Y# 182   600 BAHT
22.0000 g., 0.9250 Silver 0.6542 oz. ASW **Ruler:** Bhumipol Adulyadej (Rama IX) **Subject:** 6th ASEAN Orchid Congress **Obv:** Uniformed bust left **Rev:** Symbols of congress **Note:** Similar to 10 Baht, Y#181.

Date	Mintage	F	VF	XF	Unc	BU
BE2529 (1986)	5,000	—	—	—	45.00	—
BE2529 (1986) Proof	300	Value: 200				

Y# 229   600 BAHT
30.0000 g., 0.9250 Silver 0.8921 oz. ASW **Ruler:** Bhumipol Adulyadej (Rama IX) **Subject:** Asian Institute of Technology **Obv:** Kneeling figure left with students **Rev:** Symbol above inscription **Note:** Similar to 10 Baht, Y#190.

Date	Mintage	F	VF	XF	Unc	BU
BE2530 (1987)	2,700	—	—	—	40.00	—
BE2530 (1987) Proof	400	Value: 175				

Y# 199   600 BAHT
30.0000 g., 0.9250 Silver 0.8921 oz. ASW **Ruler:** Bhumipol Adulyadej (Rama IX) **Subject:** 60th Birthday - King Rama IX **Obv:** Uniformed bust facing **Rev:** Radiant crowned emblem **Note:** Similar to 6000 Baht, Y#202.

Date	Mintage	F	VF	XF	Unc	BU
BE2530 (1987)	5,000	—	—	—	100	—
BE2530 (1987) Proof	750	Value: 350				

Y# 215   600 BAHT
30.0000 g., 0.9250 Silver 0.8921 oz. ASW **Ruler:** Bhumipol Adulyadej (Rama IX) **Subject:** 42nd Anniversary - Reign of King Rama IX **Obv:** Uniformed bust facing **Rev:** Crowned monogram **Note:** Similar to 10 Baht, Y#212.

Date	Mintage	F	VF	XF	Unc	BU
BE2531 (1988)	8,840	—	—	—	45.00	—
BE2531 (1988) Proof	1,110	Value: 135				

Y# 224   600 BAHT
30.0000 g., 0.9250 Silver 0.8921 oz. ASW **Ruler:** Bhumipol Adulyadej (Rama IX) **Subject:** Crown Prince's Birthday **Obv:** Head 1/4 left **Rev:** Crowned monogram within lightning bolts

Date	Mintage	F	VF	XF	Unc	BU
BE2531 (1988)	5,000	—	—	—	45.00	—
BE2531 (1988) Proof	1,000	Value: 145				

Y# 226   600 BAHT
30.0000 g., 0.9000 Silver 0.8680 oz. ASW **Ruler:** Bhumipol Adulyadej (Rama IX) **Subject:** 72nd Anniversary of Chulalongkorn University **Obv:** Conjoined busts left **Rev:** Radiant crown

Date	Mintage	F	VF	XF	Unc	BU
BE2532 (1989)	10,000	—	—	—	50.00	—

Y# 234   600 BAHT
30.0000 g., 0.9250 Silver 0.8921 oz. ASW **Ruler:** Bhumipol Adulyadej (Rama IX) **Subject:** 90th Birthday of Princess Mother **Obv:** Bust 1/4 left **Rev:** Crown on stand flanked by others

Date	Mintage	F	VF	XF	Unc	BU
BE2533 (1990)	20,000	—	—	—	32.50	—
BE2533 (1990) Proof	2,000	Value: 95.00				

Y# 245   600 BAHT
30.0000 g., 0.9250 Silver 0.8921 oz. ASW **Ruler:** Bhumipol Adulyadej (Rama IX) **Subject:** World Health Organization **Obv:** Bust facing **Rev:** Medal with small emblem above **Note:** Similar to 10 Baht, Y#244.

Date	Mintage	F	VF	XF	Unc	BU
BE2533 (1990)	25,000	—	—	—	32.50	—
BE2533 (1990) Proof	596	Value: 275				

Y# 239   600 BAHT
30.0000 g., 0.9000 Silver 0.8680 oz. ASW **Ruler:** Bhumipol Adulyadej (Rama IX) **Subject:** 36th Birthday of Princess Sirindhorn **Obv:** Uniformed bust 1/4 left **Rev:** Crowned monogram flanked by stars above sprigs

Date	Mintage	F	VF	XF	Unc	BU
BE2534 (1991)	30,000	—	—	—	32.50	—
BE2534 (1991) Proof	2,583	Value: 85.00				

Y# 264   600 BAHT
30.0000 g., 0.9250 Silver 0.8921 oz. ASW **Ruler:** Bhumipol Adulyadej (Rama IX) **Subject:** Queen's 60th Birthday **Obv:** Crowned bust facing **Rev:** Crowned monogram

Date	Mintage	F	VF	XF	Unc	BU
BE2535 (1992)	25,000	—	—	—	32.50	—
BE2535 (1992) Proof	3,500	Value: 80.00				

Y# 274   600 BAHT
30.0000 g., 0.9250 Silver 0.8921 oz. ASW **Ruler:** Bhumipol Adulyadej (Rama IX) **Subject:** 64th Birthday - King Rama IX **Obv:** Conjoined busts 1/4 left **Rev:** Crowned monograms

Date	Mintage	F	VF	XF	Unc	BU
BE2535 (1992)	10,000	—	—	—	37.50	—
BE2535 (1992) Proof	511	Value: 320				

Y# 250   600 BAHT
30.0000 g., 0.9250 Silver 0.8921 oz. ASW **Ruler:** Bhumipol Adulyadej (Rama IX) **Subject:** Centenary Celebration - Father of King Rama IX **Obv:** Three crowns on stands **Rev:** Bust facing

Date	Mintage	F	VF	XF	Unc	BU
BE2535 (1992)	19,000	—	—	—	32.50	—
BE2535 (1992) Proof	11,000	Value: 75.00				

Y# 281   600 BAHT
30.0000 g., 0.9250 Silver 0.8921 oz. ASW **Ruler:** Bhumipol Adulyadej (Rama IX) **Subject:** Centennial of Thai Red Cross **Obv:** Conjoined busts 1/4 left **Rev:** Emblems

Date	Mintage	F	VF	XF	Unc	BU
BE2536 (1993)	13,000	—	—	—	32.50	—

Y# 290   600 BAHT
30.0000 g., 0.9250 Silver 0.8921 oz. ASW **Ruler:** Bhumipol Adulyadej (Rama IX) **Subject:** 100th Anniversary of Rama VII **Obv:** Uniformed bust left **Rev:** Crown and designs within oval

Date	Mintage	F	VF	XF	Unc	BU
BE2536 (1993)	12,000	—	—	—	32.50	—
BE2536 (1993) Proof	1,000	Value: 100				

Y# 299   600 BAHT
22.1500 g., 0.9250 Silver 0.6587 oz. ASW **Ruler:** Bhumipol Adulyadej (Rama IX) **Subject:** 120th Anniversary - Ministry of Finance **Obv:** Conjoined busts right **Rev:** Stylized eagle within circle

Date	Mintage	F	VF	XF	Unc	BU
BE2538 (1995)	17,000	—	—	—	32.50	—
BE2538 (1995) Proof	491	Value: 85.00				

Y# 257   600 BAHT
30.0000 g., 0.9250 Silver 0.8921 oz. ASW **Ruler:** Bhumipol Adulyadej (Rama IX) **Subject:** Princess Sirindhorn's Magsaysay Foundation Award **Obv:** Seated and kneeling figures within circle **Rev:** Inscription within sprigs and circle below cameo

Date	Mintage	F	VF	XF	Unc	BU
BE2534 (1991)	15,000	—	—	—	35.00	—
BE2534 (1991) Proof	10,000	Value: 75.00				

Y# 301   600 BAHT
22.1500 g., 0.9250 Silver 0.6587 oz. ASW **Ruler:** Bhumipol Adulyadej (Rama IX) **Subject:** Ministry of Defense **Obv:** Conjoined uniformed busts facing **Rev:** Mythical animal within circle

Date	Mintage	F	VF	XF	Unc	BU
BE2538 (1995)	18,000	—	—	—	32.50	—
BE2538 (1995) Proof	2,960	Value: 70.00				

Y# 303   600 BAHT
22.1500 g., 0.9250 Silver 0.6587 oz. ASW   **Ruler:** Bhumipol Adulyadej (Rama IX) **Subject:** Ministry of Foreign Affairs **Obv:** Conjoined busts facing **Rev:** Seated figure within designed circle and wreath

Date	Mintage	F	VF	XF	Unc	BU
BE2538 (1995)	14,000	—	—	—	32.50	—
BE2538 (1995) Proof	627	Value: 85.00				

Y# 305   600 BAHT
22.1500 g., 0.9250 Silver 0.6587 oz. ASW   **Ruler:** Bhumipol Adulyadej (Rama IX) **Subject:** 72nd Birthday of Princess **Obv:** Uniformed bust 3/4 facing **Rev:** Crowned arms

Date	Mintage	F	VF	XF	Unc	BU
BE2538 (1995)	12,000	—	—	—	32.50	—
BE2538 (1995) Proof	600	Value: 75.00				

Y# 310   600 BAHT
22.0000 g., 0.9250 Silver 0.6542 oz. ASW   **Ruler:** Bhumipol Adulyadej (Rama IX) **Subject:** 80th Anniversary - Department of Revenue **Obv:** Conjoined busts 1/4 left **Rev:** Seated figure within circle

Date	Mintage	F	VF	XF	Unc	BU
BE2538 (1995)	4,000	—	—	—	37.50	—
BE2538 (1995) Proof	—	Value: 75.00				

Y# 312   600 BAHT
22.0000 g., 0.9250 Silver 0.6542 oz. ASW   **Ruler:** Bhumipol Adulyadej (Rama IX) **Subject:** 120th Anniversary - Audit Council **Obv:** Conjoined busts facing **Rev:** Balance scale

Date	Mintage	F	VF	XF	Unc	BU
BE2538 (1995)	6,000	—	—	—	35.00	—
BE2538 (1995) Proof	—	Value: 75.00				

Y# 324   600 BAHT
30.0000 g., 0.9250 Silver 0.8921 oz. ASW   **Ruler:** Bhumipol Adulyadej (Rama IX) **Subject:** 50th Anniversary - Reign of King Rama IX **Obv:** Bust facing **Rev:** National arms **Note:** Similar to 20 Baht, Y#321.1.

Date	Mintage	F	VF	XF	Unc	BU
BE2539 (1996)	—	—	—	—	32.50	—
BE2539 (1996) Proof	—	Value: 75.00				

Y# 356   600 BAHT
22.1500 g., 0.9250 Silver 0.6587 oz. ASW, 35 mm.   **Ruler:** Bhumipol Adulyadej (Rama IX) **Subject:** King's 6th Cycle Birthday Anniversary **Obv:** Bust facing **Rev:** Radiant arms **Edge:** Reeded

Date	Mintage	F	VF	XF	Unc	BU
BE2542 (1999)	100,000	—	—	—	20.00	—
BE2542 (1999) Proof	30,000	Value: 35.00				

Y# 377   600 BAHT
22.1500 g., 0.9250 Silver 0.6587 oz. ASW, 35 mm.
Ruler: Bhumipol Adulyadej (Rama IX) **Subject:** King's 72nd Birthday **Obv:** King and Rama I portraits **Rev:** Two royal symbols **Edge:** Reeded

Date	Mintage	F	VF	XF	Unc	BU
BE2543(2000) Proof	—	Value: 95.00				

Y# 94   800 BAHT
20.0000 g., 0.9000 Gold 0.5787 oz. AGW   **Ruler:** Bhumipol Adulyadej (Rama IX) **Subject:** 25th Anniversary - Reign of King Rama IX **Obv:** Head right **Rev:** Radiant crowned monogram flanked by sprigs

Date	Mintage	F	VF	XF	Unc	BU
BE2514 (1971)	22,000	—	—	—	600	650

Y# 200   1500 BAHT
3.7500 g., 0.9000 Gold 0.1085 oz. AGW   **Ruler:** Bhumipol Adulyadej (Rama IX) **Subject:** 60th Birthday - King Rama IX **Obv:** Bust facing **Rev:** Radiant crowned emblem

Date	Mintage	F	VF	XF	Unc	BU
BE2530 (1987)	5,000	—	—	—	125	—
BE2530 (1987) Proof	400	Value: 200				

Y# 216   1500 BAHT
3.7500 g., 0.9000 Gold 0.1085 oz. AGW   **Ruler:** Bhumipol Adulyadej (Rama IX) **Subject:** 42nd Anniversary - Reign of King Rama IX **Obv:** Bust facing **Rev:** Crowned monogram

Date	Mintage	F	VF	XF	Unc	BU
BE2531 (1988)	11,000	—	—	—	125	—
BE2531 (1988) Proof	995	Value: 180				

Y# 265   1500 BAHT
3.7500 g., 0.9000 Gold 0.1085 oz. AGW   **Ruler:** Bhumipol Adulyadej (Rama IX) **Subject:** Queen's 60th Birthday **Obv:** Crowned bust facing **Rev:** Crowned monogram **Note:** Similar to 10 Baht, Y#261.

Date	Mintage	F	VF	XF	Unc	BU
BE2535 (1992)	10,000	—	—	—	125	—
BE2535 (1992) Proof	1,500	Value: 165				

Y# 380   2000 BAHT
6.2200 g., 0.9990 Gold 0.1998 oz. AGW, 22 mm.
Ruler: Bhumipol Adulyadej (Rama IX) **Subject:** UNICEF **Obv:** Bust 3/4 left **Rev:** Girl with Thai desk **Edge:** Reeded

Date	Mintage	F	VF	XF	Unc	BU
BE2540-1997 (1997) Proof	1,700	Value: 225				

Y# 119   2500 BAHT
15.0000 g., 0.9000 Gold 0.4340 oz. AGW   **Ruler:** Bhumipol Adulyadej (Rama IX) **Subject:** Crown Prince Vajiralongkorn and Princess Soamsawali Wedding **Obv:** Conjoined busts right **Rev:** Crowned monogram within lightning bolts

Date	Mintage	F	VF	XF	Unc	BU
BE2520 (1977)	20,000	—	—	—	450	475

Y# 126   2500 BAHT
15.0000 g., 0.9000 Gold 0.4340 oz. AGW   **Ruler:** Bhumipol Adulyadej (Rama IX) **Subject:** Investiture of Princess Sirindhorn **Obv:** Bust 1/4 right **Rev:** Crowned monogram

Date	Mintage	F	VF	XF	Unc	BU
BE2520 (1977)	5,000	—	—	—	475	500

Y# 170   2500 BAHT
15.0000 g., 0.9000 Gold 0.4340 oz. AGW   **Ruler:** Bhumipol Adulyadej (Rama IX) **Series:** International Year of Disabled Persons **Obv:** Bust left **Rev:** Emblem within sprigs

Date	Mintage	F	VF	XF	Unc	BU
BE2526 (1983)	92	—	—	—	—	1,400
BE2526 (1983) Proof	793	Value: 1,250				

Y# 207   2500 BAHT
15.9800 g., 0.9000 Gold 0.4624 oz. AGW   **Ruler:** Bhumipol Adulyadej (Rama IX) **Series:** 25th Anniversary of World Wildlife Fund **Obv:** Bust left **Rev:** Elephant left within circle

Date	Mintage	F	VF	XF	Unc	BU
BE2530 (1987) Proof	Est. 5,000	Value: 500				

Y# 325   2500 BAHT
3.7500 g., 0.9000 Gold 0.1085 oz. AGW   **Ruler:** Bhumipol Adulyadej (Rama IX) **Subject:** 50th Anniversary - Reign of King Rama IX **Obv:** Bust facing **Rev:** National arms **Note:** Similar to 20 Baht, Y#321.1.

Date	Mintage	F	VF	XF	Unc	BU
BE2539 (1996)	—	—	—	—	125	—
BE2539 (1996) Proof	—	Value: 150				

Y# 369   2500 BAHT
155.5175 g., 0.9999 Gold 4.9993 oz. AGW, 55 mm.
Ruler: Bhumipol Adulyadej (Rama IX) **Subject:** Year of the Dragon **Obv:** Bust left **Rev:** Two dragons with pearl hologram **Edge:** Reeded

Date	Mintage	F	VF	XF	Unc	BU
BE2543 (2000) Proof	500	Value: 5,000				

Note: In sets only

Y# 129   3000 BAHT
15.0000 g., 0.9000 Gold 0.4340 oz. AGW   **Ruler:** Bhumipol Adulyadej (Rama IX) **Subject:** Graduation of Crown Prince Vijiralongkorn **Obv:** Bust left **Rev:** Crowned elephant head facing within frame

Date	Mintage	F	VF	XF	Unc	BU
BE2521 (1978)	10,000	—	—	—	475	500

Y# 201   3000 BAHT
7.5000 g., 0.9000 Gold 0.2170 oz. AGW   **Ruler:** Bhumipol Adulyadej (Rama IX) **Subject:** 60th Birthday - King Rama IX **Obv:** Uniformed bust facing **Rev:** Radiant crowned emblem

Date	Mintage	F	VF	XF	Unc	BU
BE2530 (1987)	3,000	—	—	—	245	—
BE2530 (1987) Proof	400	Value: 350				

Y# 217   3000 BAHT
7.5000 g., 0.9000 Gold 0.2170 oz. AGW   **Ruler:** Bhumipol zAdulyadej (Rama IX) **Subject:** 42nd Anniversary - Reign of King Rama IX **Obv:** Uniformed bust facing **Rev:** Radiant crowned monogram

Date	Mintage	F	VF	XF	Unc	BU
BE2531 (1988)	7,904	—	—	—	250	—
BE2531 (1988) Proof	780	Value: 375				

Y# 266   3000 BAHT
7.5000 g., 0.9000 Gold 0.2170 oz. AGW   **Ruler:** Bhumipol Adulyadej (Rama IX) **Subject:** Queen's 60th Birthday **Obv:** Crowned bust facing **Rev:** Crowned monogram

Date	Mintage	F	VF	XF	Unc	BU
BE2535 (1992)	7,000	—	—	—	250	—
BE2535 (1992) Proof	1,100	Value: 375				

Y# 326   3000 BAHT
7.5000 g., 0.9000 Gold 0.2170 oz. AGW   **Ruler:** Bhumipol Adulyadej (Rama IX) **Subject:** 50th Anniversary - Reign of King Rama IX **Obv:** Uniformed bust facing **Rev:** National arms

Date	Mintage	F	VF	XF	Unc	BU
BE2539 (1996)	—	—	—	—	260	—
BE2539 (1996) Proof	—	Value: 380				

Y# 153   4000 BAHT
17.1700 g., 0.9000 Gold 0.4968 oz. AGW   **Ruler:** Bhumipol Adulyadej (Rama IX) **Series:** International Year of the Child **Obv:** Bust left **Rev:** Two children playing

Date	Mintage	F	VF	XF	Unc	BU
BE2524 (1981) Proof	3,963	Value: 550				

Y# 104   5000 BAHT
33.4370 g., 0.9000 Gold 0.9675 oz. AGW   **Ruler:** Bhumipol Adulyadej (Rama IX) **Series:** Conservation **Obv:** Bust 1/4 left **Rev:** White-eyed River Martin

Date	Mintage	F	VF	XF	Unc	BU
BE2517 (1974)	2,602	—	—	—	1,100	1,150
BE2517 (1974) Proof	623	Value: 1,750				

Y# 122   5000 BAHT
30.0000 g., 0.9000 Gold 0.8680 oz. AGW   **Ruler:** Bhumipol Adulyadej (Rama IX) **Subject:** 50th Birthday - King Rama IX **Obv:** Bust left **Rev:** Radiant crowned monogram

Date	Mintage	F	VF	XF	Unc	BU
BE2520 (1977)	6,400	—	—	—	875	900

Y# 156   6000 BAHT
15.0000 g., 0.9000 Gold 0.4340 oz. AGW   **Ruler:** Bhumipol Adulyadej (Rama IX) **Subject:** 50th Birthday - Queen Sirikit **Obv:** Crowned bust 1/4 left **Rev:** Crowned monogram

Date	Mintage	F	VF	XF	Unc	BU
BE2525 (1982)	1,471	—	—	—	500	550
BE2525 (1982) Proof	99	Value: 4,000				

Y# 167   6000 BAHT
15.0000 g., 0.9000 Gold 0.4340 oz. AGW   **Ruler:** Bhumipol Adulyadej (Rama IX) **Subject:** 700th Anniversary - Thai Alphabet **Obv:** Seated figure left **Rev:** Inscription

Date	Mintage	F	VF	XF	Unc	BU
BE2526 (1983)	700	—	—	—	475	500
BE2526 (1983) Proof	235	Value: 675				

Y# 174   6000 BAHT
15.0000 g., 0.9000 Gold 0.4340 oz. AGW   **Ruler:** Bhumipol Adulyadej (Rama IX) **Subject:** 84th Birthday - Princess Mother **Obv:** Bust left **Rev:** Crown on stand flanked by others

Date	Mintage	F	VF	XF	Unc	BU
BE2527 (1984)	835	—	—	—	475	500
BE2527 (1984) Proof	246	Value: 700				

Y# 202   6000 BAHT
15.0000 g., 0.9000 Gold 0.4340 oz. AGW   **Ruler:** Bhumipol Adulyadej (Rama IX) **Subject:** 60th Birthday - King Rama IX **Obv:** Uniformed bust facing **Rev:** Radiant crowned emblem

Date	Mintage	F	VF	XF	Unc	BU
BE2530 (1987)	2,000	—	—	—	450	500
BE2530 (1987) Proof	350	Value: 600				

Y# 247   6000 BAHT
15.0000 g., 0.9000 Gold 0.4340 oz. AGW   **Ruler:** Bhumipol Adulyadej (Rama IX) **Subject:** Asian Institute of Technology **Obv:** Kneeling and seated figures within circle **Rev:** Emblem

Date	Mintage	F	VF	XF	Unc	BU
BE2530 (1987)	700	—	—	—	475	500
BE2530 (1987) Proof	100	Value: 700				

Y# 218   6000 BAHT
15.0000 g., 0.9000 Gold 0.4340 oz. AGW   **Ruler:** Bhumipol Adulyadej (Rama IX) **Subject:** 42nd Anniversary - Reign of King Rama IX **Obv:** Uniformed bust facing **Rev:** Radiant crowned monogram

Date	Mintage	F	VF	XF	Unc	BU
BE2531 (1988)	6,067	—	—	—	450	500
BE2531 (1988) Proof	670	Value: 600				

Y# 246   6000 BAHT
15.0000 g., 0.9000 Gold 0.4340 oz. AGW   **Ruler:** Bhumipol Adulyadej (Rama IX) **Subject:** World Health Organization

Date	Mintage	F	VF	XF	Unc	BU
BE2534 (1991)	5,000	—	—	—	475	500
BE2534 (1991) Proof	591	Value: 675				

Y# 258   6000 BAHT
15.0000 g., 0.9000 Gold 0.4340 oz. AGW   **Ruler:** Bhumipol Adulyadej (Rama IX) **Subject:** Princess Sirindhorn's Magsaysay Foundation Award **Obv:** Princess seated with children **Rev:** Obverse of medal above larger reverse with inscription

Date	Mintage	F	VF	XF	Unc	BU
BE2535 (1992)	1,600	—	—	—	475	500
BE2535 (1992) Proof	500	Value: 700				

Y# 267   6000 BAHT
15.0000 g., 0.9000 Gold 0.4340 oz. AGW   **Ruler:** Bhumipol Adulyadej (Rama IX) **Subject:** Queen's 60th Birthday **Obv:** Crowned bust facing **Rev:** Crowned monogram

Date	Mintage	F	VF	XF	Unc	BU
BE2535 (1992)	7,000	—	—	—	475	500
BE2535 (1992) Proof	1,200	Value: 575				

Y# 275   6000 BAHT
15.0000 g., 0.9000 Gold 0.4340 oz. AGW   **Ruler:** Bhumipol Adulyadej (Rama IX) **Subject:** 64th Birthday - King Rama IX **Obv:** Conjoined busts left **Rev:** Crowned monograms

Date	Mintage	F	VF	XF	Unc	BU
BE2535 (1992)	3,000	—	—	—	475	500
BE2535 (1992) Proof	500	Value: 700				

Y# 291   6000 BAHT
15.0000 g., 0.9000 Gold 0.4340 oz. AGW   **Ruler:** Bhumipol Adulyadej (Rama IX) **Subject:** 100th Anniversary of Rama VII **Obv:** Bust left **Rev:** Royal crown and accoutrements

Date	Mintage	F	VF	XF	Unc	BU
BE2536 (1993)	2,484	—	—	—	475	500
BE2536 (1993) Proof	300	Value: 700				

Y# 327   6000 BAHT
15.0000 g., 0.9000 Gold 0.4340 oz. AGW   **Ruler:** Bhumipol Adulyadej (Rama IX) **Subject:** King's 50th Year of Reign **Obv:** Uniformed bust facing **Rev:** National arms

Date	Mintage	F	VF	XF	Unc	BU
BE2539 (1996)	—	—	—	—	475	500
BE2539 (1996) Proof	—	Value: 650				

Y# 337   6000 BAHT
15.0000 g., 0.9000 Gold 0.4340 oz. AGW   **Ruler:** Bhumipol Adulyadej (Rama IX) **Series:** F.A.O. **Subject:** 50th Anniversary - Reign of King Rama IX and World Food Summit **Obv:** Bust left within circle **Rev:** King planting seedlings before adoring crowd

Date	Mintage	F	VF	XF	Unc	BU
BE2539 (1996)	—	—	—	—	475	500
BE2539 (1996) Proof	—	Value: 650				

Y# 370   6000 BAHT

15.0000 g., 0.9000 Gold 0.4340 oz. AGW **Ruler:** Bhumipol Adulyadej (Rama IX) **Subject:** King's 72nd Birthday **Obv:** King's portrait **Rev:** Crowned emblem

Date	Mintage	F	VF	XF	Unc	BU
BE2542 (1999)	20,000	—	—	—	475	500
BE2542 (1999) Proof	10,000	Value: 550				

Y# 378   6000 BAHT

15.0000 g., 0.9000 Gold 0.4340 oz. AGW, 26 mm.
Ruler: Bhumipol Adulyadej (Rama IX) **Subject:** King's 72nd Birthday **Obv:** King and Rama I portraits **Rev:** Two royal symbols **Edge:** Reeded

Date	Mintage	F	VF	XF	Unc	BU
BE2543(2000) Proof	—	Value: 500				

Y# 139   9000 BAHT

12.0000 g., 0.9000 Gold 0.3472 oz. AGW **Ruler:** Bhumipol Adulyadej (Rama IX) **Series:** F.A.O. Ceres Medal **Subject:** Queen's Anniversary **Obv:** Crowned bust 3/4 facing **Rev:** Medal design

Date	Mintage	F	VF	XF	Unc	BU
BE2523 (1980)	3,900	—	—	—	425	450

Y# A143   9000 BAHT

12.0000 g., 0.9000 Gold 0.3472 oz. AGW **Ruler:** Bhumipol Adulyadej (Rama IX) **Subject:** Centennial - Birth of King Rama VI **Obv:** Uniformed bust right **Rev:** Radiant crown on stand flanked by others

Date	Mintage	F	VF	XF	Unc	BU
BE2524 (1981)	2,600	—	—	—	425	450

Y# 148   9000 BAHT

15.0000 g., 0.9000 Gold 0.4340 oz. AGW **Ruler:** Bhumipol Adulyadej (Rama IX) **Subject:** King Rama IX Anniversary of Reign

Date	Mintage	F	VF	XF	Unc	BU
BE2524 (1981)	4,000	—	—	—	425	450

Y# 151   9000 BAHT

15.0000 g., 0.9000 Gold 0.4340 oz. AGW **Ruler:** Bhumipol Adulyadej (Rama IX) **Subject:** Bicentennial of Bangkok **Obv:** Uniformed conjoined busts left **Rev:** Emblem

Date	Mintage	F	VF	XF	Unc	BU
BE2525 (1982)	3,290	—	—	—	425	450

OCCUPATION COINAGE

These coins were to be circulated in the four occupied provinces of Malaya during World War II. They were not put into circulation there but were later used in Japanese military service clubs in Bangkok before Japan's surrender in 1945.

KM# 5   SEN

Tin **Ruler:** Rama VIII **Obv:** Mythical creature "Garuda" **Rev:** Value

Date	Mintage	F	VF	XF	Unc	BU
BE2486	—	—	—	7,000	—	—

KM# 10   5 SEN

Tin **Ruler:** Rama VIII **Obv:** Mythical creature "Garuda" **Rev:** Value within beaded circle

Date	Mintage	F	VF	XF	Unc	BU
BE2486	—	—	—	5,000	—	—

KM# 15   10 SEN

Tin **Ruler:** Rama VIII **Obv:** Mythical creature "Garuda" **Rev:** Value within beaded circle

Date	Mintage	F	VF	XF	Unc	BU
BE2486	—	—	—	4,000	—	—

BULLION COINAGE

In 1943, the government of Thailand made an internal loan by virtue of the Royal Act of Internal Loan related regulation of the Ministry of Finance, both dated 17th May, 1943.

Eight years later another Regulation of the Ministry of Finance dated 11th June, 1951 related to the actual redemption of the loan above mentioned was proclaimed with the following effect: Bond holders have the choice to be paid either in gold coins or gold bars or in other forms, all of which should bear the Garuda emblem and the specific inscription as to its weight and gold purity.

KM# 1   50 BAHT

8.6930 g., 0.9950 Gold 0.2781 oz. AGW **Ruler:** Bhumipol Adulyadej (Rama IX) **Obv:** Mythical creature "Garuda" flanked by sprigs **Rev:** Inscription

Date	Mintage	F	VF	XF	Unc	BU
ND(1951)	—	—	300	375	500	—

KM# 2   100 BAHT

17.3870 g., 0.9950 Gold 0.5562 oz. AGW **Ruler:** Bhumipol Adulyadej (Rama IX) **Obv:** Mythical creature "Garuda" flanked by sprigs **Rev:** Inscription

Date	Mintage	F	VF	XF	Unc	BU
ND(1951)	—	—	575	650	800	—

KM# 3   1000 BAHT

173.8790 g., 0.9950 Gold 5.5622 oz. AGW **Ruler:** Bhumipol Adulyadej (Rama IX) **Obv:** Mythical creature "Garuda" flanked by sprigs **Rev:** Inscription

Date	Mintage	F	VF	XF	Unc	BU
ND(1951)	—	—	6,500	9,500	14,500	—

TRIAL STRIKES

KM#	Date	Mintage	Identification	Mkt Val
TS1	ND (1963)	—	20 Baht. Copper. Trial strike in copper of 20 Baht, Y#86.	—

ESSAIS

KM#	Date	Mintage	Identification	Mkt Val
E1	RS127	—	Baht. Silver. Y#39.	23,000
E2	RS128	—	1/4 Baht. Silver.	10,000
E3	RS129	—	1/2 Baht. Silver.	—

Note: Struck at the Paris Mint. Taisei-Baldwin-Gillio Hong Kong sale 25 9-97 BU realized $23,000. Spink-Taisei Singapore Auction 14 3-93 Unc set of E 1, 2 and 3 realized $190,000

PATTERNS

Including off metal strikes

KM#	Date	Mintage	Identification	Mkt Val
Pn47	RS124	—	2 Att. Copper. Facing bust.	10,000
Pn48	RS126	—	Baht. Silver. Y#39. Vishnu and Garuda.	40,000
Pn49	RS127	—	Satang. Nickel. Y#35.	3,000
Pn50	RS127	—	Satang. Gold. Y#35a.	10,000
	RS127	—	Satang. Gold. Y#35a.	10,000
Pn51	RS127	—	5 Satang. Gold. Y#36a.	10,000
	RS127	—	5 Satang. Gold. Y#36a.	10,000
Pn52	RS127	—	10 Satang. Gold. Y#37a.	10,000
	RS127	—	10 Satang. Gold. Y#37a.	10,000
Pn53	RS129	—	Baht. Silver. Y#39.	—
PnA54	BE2488	—	Baht. Tin. 10.0000 g. 30 mm. "Child's head" of King Rama VIII (Ananda Mahidol) facing left. National arms.	—
Pn54	BE2489	—	Baht. Tin. Y#67.	—
Pn55	BE2505	—	Baht. Copper-Nickel. Y#84.	—
Pn56	BE2515	—	5 Baht. Copper-Nickel. Small bust, Y#28.	—
Pn57	BE2515	—	5 Baht. Copper-Nickel. Royal parasol.	—
Pn58	BE2515	—	5 Baht. Copper-Nickel. Different bust.	100

PIEFORTS

KM#	Date	Mintage	Identification	Mkt Val
P1	BE2524	126	200 Baht. I.Y.O.C.	1,100
P2	BE2524	61	4000 Baht. Gold. I.Y.O.C.	2,400
P3	BE2526	500	250 Baht. 0.9250 Silver. I.Y.D.P.	1,250
P4	BE2526	—	2500 Baht. Gold. I.Y.D.P.	6,500
P5	BE2540	—	100 Baht. 0.9250 Silver. 30.0000 g. WWF Tiger.	75.00
P6	BE2541	—	200 Baht. 0.9250 Silver. 46.3600 g. WWF Tigers.	110
P7	BE2541	—	200 Baht. 0.9250 Silver. 46.3600 g. WWF Elephants.	125

MINT SETS

KM#	Date	Mintage	Identification	Issue Price	Mkt Val
MS2	Mixed (32)	—	Two each Y#57, 70, 72, 73, 78a, 78-87, 91	22.00	45.00
MS3	Mixed (30)	100,000	Two each Y#60, 70, 72, 73, 78, 78a, 79, 79a, 80-86	20.00	30.00
MS4	Mixed (10)	—	Y#70, 72, 73, 78, 78a, 79, 79a, 80-82	—	12.00
MS5	Mixed (10)	—	Y#70, 78, 78a, 78b, 79a, 79b, 79d, 80, 81, 82	—	12.00
MS6	Mixed (8)	—	Y#83, 85-87, 91, 92, 95, 97	11.00	35.00
MS7	1975 (2)	—	Y#102-103	32.50	70.00
MS8	1988 (7)	—	Y#183, 185-187, 203, 208-209	—	3.50
MS9	1991 (8)	—	Y#183, 186-187, 203, 208-209, 219, 227	4.00	10.00
MS10	1992 (8)	—	Y#183, 186-187, 203, 208-209, 219, 227	—	10.00
MS11	1993 (8)	—	Y#183, 186-187, 203, 208-209, 219, 227	—	10.00
MS12	1994 (8)	—	Y#183, 186-187, 203, 208-209, 219, 227	—	10.00
MS13	Mixed (34)	—	Two each Y#57, 70, 72-73, 78, 78a, 79, 79a, 80-87, 91	—	60.00
MS14	Mixed (29)	—	Y#86 plus two each Y#57, 68, 73, 78, 78a, 79, 79a, 80-85, 87	—	35.00

PROOF SETS

KM#	Date	Mintage	Identification	Issue Price	Mkt Val
PS1	1974 (2)	—	Y#102a-103a	50.00	160
PS2	2000 (3)	3,500	Y#363-365	115	260
PS3	2000 (5)	500	Y#363-365, 367, 369	3,480	5,300
PS4	2000 (2)	1,800	Y#366, 368	446	635

TIBET

Tibet, an autonomous region of China located in central Asia between the Himalayan and Kunlun Mountains. has an area of 471,660 sq. mi. (1,221,599 sq. km.) and a population of *1.9 million. Capital: Lhasa. The economy is based on agriculture and livestock. Wool, livestock, salt and hides are exported.

Lamaism, a form of Buddhism, developed in Tibet in the 8th century. From that time until the 1900s, the Tibetan rulers virtually isolated the country from the outside world. The British in India achieved some influence in the early 20th century. British troops were sent with the F. E. Younghusband mission to extend trade in the north of India in December 1903; leaving during September

1904. The 13th Dalai Lama had fled to Urga where he remained until 1907. In April 1905 a revolt broke out and spread through southwestern Szechuan and northwestern Yunnan. Chao Erh-feng was appointed to subdue this rebellion and entered Lhasa in January 1910 with 2,000 troops. The Dalai Lama fled to India until he returned in June 1912. The British encouraged Tibet to declare its independence from China in 1913. The Communist revolution in China marked a new era in Tibetan history. Chinese Communist troops invaded Tibet in October 1950. After a token resistance, Tibet signed an agreement with China in which China recognized the spiritual and temporal leadership of the Dalai Lama, and Tibet recognized the suzerainty of China. In 1959, a nationwide revolt triggered by Communist-initiated land reform broke out. The revolt was ruthlessly crushed. The Dalai Lama fled to India, and on Sept. 1,1965, the Chinese made Tibet an autonomous region of China.

The first coins to circulate in Tibet were those of neighboring Nepal from about 1570. Shortly after 1720, the Nepalese government began striking specific issues for use in Tibet. These coins had a lower silver content than those struck for use in Nepal and were exchanged with the Tibetans for an equal weight in silver bullion. Around 1763 the Tibetans struck their own coins for the first time in history. The number of coins struck at that time must have been very small. Larger quantities of coins were struck by the Tibetan government mint, which opened in 1791 with the permission of the Chinese. Operations of this mint however were suspended two years later. The Chinese opened a second mint in Lhasa in 1792. It produced a coinage until 1836. Shortly thereafter, the Tibetan mint was reopened and the government of Tibet continued to strike coins until 1953.

DATING

Based on the Tibetan calendar, Tibetan coins are dated by the cycle which contains 60 years. To calculate the western date use the following formula: Number of cycles -1, x 60 + number of years + 1026. Example 15th cycle 25th year = 1891 AD. Example: 15th cycle, 25th year 15 - 1 x 60 + 25 + 1026 = 1891AD.

13/30 = 1776	14/30 = 1836	15/30 = 1896
13/40 = 1786	14/40 = 1846	15/40 = 1906
13/50 = 1796	14/50 = 1856	15/50 = 1916
13/60 = 1806	14/60 = 1866	15/60 = 1926
14/10 = 1816	15/10 = 1876	16/10 = 1936
14/20 = 1826	15/20 = 1886	16/20 = 1946

Certain Sino-Tibetan issues are dated in the year of reign of the Emperor of China.

Tibetan Currency Units

Tibet had a dual and therefore complicated system of currency units. One was imported from Nepal and its basic unit is the "tangka" (also called 'trangks', 'tam' or 'tamga', equivalent to about 5.4 to 5.6 grams of alloyed silver) and the other was imported from China and its basic unit is the "srang" (Chinese liang, , equivalent to 37.3 grams of silver). These two systems were used in Tibet concurrently from about 1640 until 1959. The respective value was calculated as follows:
1 Srang = 6-2/3 Tangkas
1 Tangka = 1-1/2 Sho = 15 Skar
½ Tangka = 7-1/2 Skar
1 Sho = 2/3 Tangka = 10 Skar
The subdivisions of the Srang were as follows:
1 Srang = 10 Zho = 100 Skar
1 Sho = 10 Skar
1 srang was called *Srang Gang*
1 Sho was called *Zho Gang*
2 Sho were called *Zho Do*
1 Skar was called *Skar Gang*
In the 20th century the following units were struck:
Copper:
½ Skar (Skar Che)
1 Skar (Skar Gang)
1/8 Sho
¼ Sho
2-1/2 Skar (Skar Phyed Gsum or Kha Gang)
5 Skar (Skar Inga)
7-1/2 Skar (Skar Phyed Brgyad)
1 Sho
3 Sho
5 Sho
Silver or billon:
1 Tangka
1 Sho (Zho Gang)
2 Sho (Zho Do)
5 Sho (Zho Inga)
1 Srang (Srang Gang)
1-1/2 Srang (Srang Gang Zho Inga)
3 Srang (Srang Sum)
5 Srang (in limited numbers; this coin was also struck in copper)
10 Srang (Srang Bcu)
Gold
20 Srang (Gser Tam)

TANGKA

16(th)CYCLE 2(nd)YEAR = 1928AD

"CYCLE"

7   16
(YEAR)   (CYCLE)
16(th) CYCLE 7(th) YEAR = 1933AD

NUMERALS

1	?	གཅིག་
2	༢	གཉིས་
3	༣	གསུམ་
4	༤	བཞི་
5	༥	ལྔ་
6	༦	དྲུག་
7	༧	བདུན་
8	༨	བརྒྱད་
9	༩	དགུ་
10	༡༠	བཅུ་ or བཅུ་ཐམ་པ་
11	༡༡	བཅུག་ or བཅུ་གཅིག་
12	༡༢	བཅུས་ or བཅུ་གཉིས་
13	༡༣	བཅུ་མ་ or བཅུ་གསུམ་
14	༡༤	བཅུ་བཞི་
15	༡༥	བཅོ་ལྔ་

16	༡༦	བཅུ་དྲུག་
17	༡༧	བཅུ་བདུན་
18	༡༨	བཅོ་བརྒྱད་
19	༡༩	བཅུ་དགུ་
20	༢༠	ཉི་ཤུ་
21	༢༡	ཉི་ཤུ་རྩ་གཅིག་ or ཉེར་གཅིག་
22	༢༢	ཉེར་གཉིས་
23	༢༣	ཉེར་གསུམ་
24	༢༤	ཉེར་བཞི་
25	༢༥	ཉེར་ལྔ་
26	༢༦	ཉེར་དྲུག་
27	༢༧	ཉེར་བདུན་
28	༢༨	ཉེར་བརྒྱད་

TIBETAN AUTHORITY
TRADE COINAGE

Y# A1.3 RUPEE
11.6700 g., Silver **Ruler:** Hsüan-t'ung **Obv:** Similar to Y#A1.1.
Rev: Tibetan legend in the inner circle engraved in revers, legends between the inner and outer circle are engraved inverted (upside down). The inner circle consists of 38 beads

Date	Mintage	Good	VG	F	VF	XF
ND(1902-02)	—	—	—	—	—	—

TIBETAN TANGKA COINAGE

The legend of this Tangka appears to be in ornamental Lantsa (Ranjana)script and has yet to be deciphered. The type is a copy of the Nepalese debased Tangka of Pratap Simha. Struck unofficially by Nepalese traders in Tibet between 1880 and 1912, it was legal tender, due to an edict issued in 1881 ordering that no distinction be made between false and genuine coins. The Tangka, C#27 was cut in parts of 3, 4, and 5 petals to make change and the resulting fractions are occasionally encountered.

C# 27.1 RANJANA TANGKA
Silver **Obv:** Crescent and sun at top **Note:** Weight varies: 3.60-5.40 grams. Diameter varies: 28.2-28.8mm. 2 varieties exist with large or small circle around lotus. Varieties of ornamentation as well as style of inscription exist. Prev. #C27.

Date	Mintage	Good	VG	F	VF	XF
BE15-40 (1906)	—	8.00	15.00	25.00	40.00	70.00

Note: In addition to the meaningful dates, the following meaningless ones exist: 13-16, 13-31, 13-92, 15-40, 16-16, 16-61, 16-64, 16-69, 16-92, 16-93, 92-34, 92-39, 96-61 (sixes may be reversed threes and nines reversed ones).

GA-DEN TANGKA COINAGE
Hammered

The Ga-den Tangkas are among the most common and perhaps most beautiful of all Tibetan silver coins. The obverse shows a stylized Lotus flower within a circle surrounded by the 8 Buddhist lucky symbols in radiating petals. The reverse shows an 8-petalled wheel (flower) within a star surrounded by a Tibetan inscription (reading Ga-den Palace, victorious in all directions), which is broken up into 8 oval frames. The Ga-den Palace is the former residence of the Dala Lamas, located in Drepung Monastery near Lhasa. On Tibetan coins the name "Ga-den Palace" is used as epithet for "Tibetan Government". Compass directions indicate the location of the Buddhist emblems.

Numbers for Obverse Types A & B

Numbers for Obverse Types C thru H

1. Umbrella of sovereignty.
2. Two golden fish of good fortune.
3. Amphora of ambrosia.
4. Lotus.
5. Conch shell.
6. Emblem of endless birth.
7. Banner of victory.
8. Wheel of empire.

Reverse - All Types

དགའ	dGa'	"Ga-"
ལྡན	lDan	"den"
ཕོ	Pho	Po-
བྲང	Braṅ	dang
ཕྱོགས	Phyogs	Tschog-
ལས	Las	le
རྣམ	rNam	Nam-
རྒྱལ	rGyal	gyel

Based on the ornamentation in the outer angles between the petals on both sides of the coin, the Ga-Den Tangkas can be differentiated in the following 8 types, A-H.

Type	Outer Obv.	Water-line	Outer Rev.	Rev. Ctr.
A	∴	None	〰	Pellet
B	∴	2 lines	〰	3 Crescents
C	∴	1 line	〰	2 Crescents
D	∴	1 line	∴	2 Crescents
E	〰	1 line	∴	2 Crescents
F	•	1 line	∴	2 Crescents
G	None	1 line	None	2 Crescents
H	•	1 line	•	3 Crescents

Within these types, changes in the order, design, and style of the 8 lucky signs or significant errors constitute subtypes. The sutypes appearing in this catalog are not the only ones. Some subtypes show a wide range of styles and die varieties. Weights given include 95 percent of the indicated types.

Error strikes with muled reverses exist. Specimens of Types D, E, and F with lumps are known, reportedly containing gold, probably used by high lamas in their offerings.

Obverse   Reverse

Obverse has wavy water line in outer angles. New style lotus without three small leaves to left and right. Reverse has three dots in outer angles, wheel with spokes.

Y# E13.1   TANGKA
Silver **Obv:** Dot to left and right of lotus **Edge:** Plain **Note:** Weight varies: 4.60-4.80 grams. Prev. Y#13.4.

Date	Mintage	VG	F	VF	XF	Unc
ND(ca.1899-1907)	—	3.00	4.00	7.00	12.00	35.00

Y# E13.2   TANGKA
Silver **Obv:** Dot to left and right of lotus **Edge:** Plain

Date	Mintage	Good	VG	F	VF	XF
ND(ca.1899-1907)	—	150	250	400	600	1,000

Y# E13.3   TANGKA
Silver **Obv:** Four dots (NE), one dot (E) **Edge:** Plain **Note:** Weight varies: 3.80-5.70 grams. Similar to Y#E13.1 but obverse emblems rotated by one position clockwise (error).

Date	Mintage	Good	VG	F	VF	XF
ND(ca.1899-1907)	—	75.00	100	150	200	300

Y# E13.4   TANGKA
3.8000 g., Silver **Obv:** 7.5-8.0mm lotus circle, no dot at left and right of lotus **Edge:** Plain **Note:** Prev. Y#E13.8 (Y#13.5).

Date	Mintage	VG	F	VF	XF	Unc
ND(ca.1904)	—	60.00	85.00	120	180	250

Obverse   Reverse

Obverse has one dot in outer angles.
The reverse has three dots in outer edges.

Y# F13.1   TANGKA
Billon **Obv:** Nine dots within lotus circle **Rev:** Flower buds full or outlined **Edge:** Plain **Note:** Six varieties exist. Weight varies: 4.10-4.70 grams. Prev. Y#13.6.

Date	Mintage	VG	F	VF	XF	Unc
ND(ca.1907-09)	—	4.00	6.00	10.00	16.00	40.00

Y# F13.2   TANGKA
Billon **Obv:** Northwest symbol circle with dots; no dot at left and right of lotus; lotus circle varies 10-12mm **Rev:** Central lotus buds hollow **Edge:** Plain **Note:** Weight varies: 4.10-4.70. Four varieties exist.

Date	Mintage	Good	VG	F	VF	XF
ND(1910-15)	—	6.00	9.00	15.00	25.00	45.00

Y# F13.3   TANGKA
Billon **Obv:** 11mm lotus circle **Rev:** Solid lotus buds **Edge:** Plain **Note:** Machine struck. Similar to Y#F13.2 and 2 Tangka, Y#15. Weight varies: 5.20-5.60 grams.

Date	Mintage	Good	VG	F	VF	XF
ND(ca.1912)	—	100	150	200	275	500

Y# F13.6   TANGKA
Billon, 27 mm. **Obv:** Dots to left and right of base of lotus in the water line; northwest symbol a circle with dots; northeast symbol two fish with dots; south symbol very ornate with two side hooks and a dot **Edge:** Plain **Note:** Weight varies: 4.10-4.70 grams.

Date	Mintage	Good	VG	F	VF	XF
ND(ca.1909)	—	8.00	12.00	18.00	30.00	50.00

Y# F13.5   TANGKA
Billon **Obv:** Dot to left and right of lotus; northeast symbol double hook between two fish and dots; northwest symbol circle with two hooks, dots south symbol has three dots **Edge:** Plain **Note:** Weight varies: 4.10-4.70 grams. Varieties exist including 34-78 dots for outer circle. Prev. Y#13.8.

Date	Mintage	Good	VG	F	VF	XF
ND(1912-22)	—	8.00	12.00	20.00	32.00	60.00

Y# F13.4   TANGKA
Billon **Obv:** Dot to left and right of lotus; northeast symbol two fish with dots; south symbol with 3 dots; northwest symbol circle with 4 dots around center dot **Edge:** Plain **Note:** Weight varies: 4.10-4.70 grams. Varieties exist including 34-78 dots for outer circles. Prev. Y#13.7.

Date	Mintage	VG	F	VF	XF	Unc
ND(ca.1912-22)	—	8.00	12.00	20.00	32.00	60.00

The obverse and reverse have no outer angle symbols.
The petals are joined on the obverse.

Y# G13 TANGKA
Billon **Rev:** No outer angles at inner circle **Edge:** Plain
Note: Weight varies: 3.30-4.60 grams. Prev. Y#13.9.

Date	Mintage	VG	F	VF	XF	Unc
ND (ca.1921)	—	4.00	6.00	9.00	15.00	45.00

Y# F13.7 TANGKA
Billon, 31 mm. **Edge:** Plain **Note:** Similar to Y#F13.6.

Date	Mintage	Good	VG	F	VF	XF
ND (ca.1924-25) Rare	—	—	—	—	—	—

The obverse and reverse have one dot in outer angles.
The obverse petals are joined.

Y# H13.1 TANGKA
Billon **Obv:** Dot between symbols at inner circle, lotus petals joined **Rev:** Dot between characters at inner circle **Edge:** Plain
Note: Weight varies: 4.00-4.20 grams. Two minor die varieties exist. Prev. Y#13.10.

Date	Mintage	VG	F	VF	XF	Unc
ND (1929)	—	10.00	14.00	20.00	30.00	50.00

Y# H13.2 TANGKA
Billon **Obv:** Similar to Y#H13.1 **Rev:** Similar to Y#H13.1 but Northeast character in retrograde **Edge:** Plain **Note:** Weight varies: 4.00-4.20 grams. Machine struck.

Date	Mintage	VG	F	VF	XF	Unc
ND (ca.1929-30)	—	60.00	90.00	120	150	—

Y# 15 2 TANGKA
Billon **Note:** Weight varies: 7.80-10.50 grams. Varieties exist.

Date	Mintage	VG	F	VF	XF	Unc
ND (ca.1912)	—	125	200	400	500	—

PRESENTATION TANGKA COINAGE

Y# 14 TANGKA
Silver **Obv:** Fifteen obverse varieties exist with combinations of none or up to two dots inside trapezoids enclosing the legend **Rev:** 2 crescents in center point clock or counter-clockwise **Edge:** Plain **Note:** Weight varies: 2.70-5.00 grams. Struck for presentation to monks.

Date	Mintage	VG	F	VF	XF	Unc
ND (1910)	600,000	10.00	15.00	25.00	50.00	60.00

Note: Cut pieces in 4 and 5 petals exist but are considered dubious since cut pieces usually were done in the 19th century before Y14 was struck

Y# 31 TANGKA
0.9000 Silver **Edge:** Reeded **Note:** Weight varies: 3.10-5.30 grams. Varieties exist, the two "commas" in central circle are in either vertical or horizontal alignment.

Date	Mintage	VG	F	VF	XF	Unc
ND(1953)	331,292	7.00	10.00	15.00	22.00	40.00

Note: Struck for presentation to Monks; Circulated later but briefly with value of 5 and then 10 Srang

SHO-SRANG COINAGE

Y# A7 1/8 SHO
4.0000 g., Copper, 22 mm. **Ruler:** Hsüan-t'ung **Note:** Two reverse varieties exist, one with a dot between the upper two syllables of the legend, the other is without a dot.

Date	Mintage	Good	VG	F	VF	XF
CD1 (1909)	—	85.00	150	225	350	—

Note: A silver striking of this type exists (rare), possibly a pattern

Y# B7 1/4 SHO
Copper, 26 mm. **Ruler:** Hsüan-t'ung

Date	Mintage	Good	VG	F	VF	XF
CD1(1909)	—	50.00	100	150	250	—

Note: This coin struck in silver is a forgery; Modern forgeries struck in copper and copper-nickel exist

Y# 10 2-1/2 SKAR
Copper, 22 mm. **Obv:** Lion standing left, looking backwards **Edge:** Plain **Note:** Lion varieties exist as do counterfeits.

Date	Mintage	Good	VG	F	VF	XF
BE15-43 (1909)	—	150	250	350	500	—

Y# 16.1 2-1/2 SKAR
Copper **Obv:** Lion crouching and looking upwards **Edge:** Plain **Note:** Weight varies: 3.70-6.00 grams. Varieties and overstrikes exist.

Date	Mintage	Good	VG	F	VF	XF
BE15-47 (1913)	—	5.00	12.00	20.00	50.00	—
BE15-48 (1914)	—	5.00	12.00	20.00	50.00	—
BE15-49 (1915)	—	15.00	30.00	60.00	120	—
BE15-50 (1916)	—	8.00	16.00	30.00	70.00	—
BE15-51 (1917)	—	30.00	60.00	120	240	—
BE15-52 (1918)	—	6.50	14.00	25.00	60.00	—

Y# 16.2 2-1/2 SKAR
Copper **Obv:** Lion standing left looking backwards with and without rays from sun **Edge:** Plain **Note:** Weight varies: 3.70-6.00 grams. Varieties exist, one with retrograde u-sign on reverse top in the word "gsum" (three)(error); the other variety has the letter corrected. With and without rays from sun.

Date	Mintage	Good	VG	F	VF	XF
BE15-48 (1914)	—	8.00	16.00	30.00	70.00	—

KM# 16.3 2-1/2 SKAR
Copper **Obv:** Crouching lion looking backwards

Date	Mintage	Good	VG	F	VF	XF
BE15-48(1914)	—	10.00	15.00	35.00	60.00	—

Y# A19 2-1/2 SKAR
Copper **Obv:** Lion standing left, looking back and upwards **Note:** Forgeries exist.

Date	Mintage	Good	VG	F	VF	XF
BE15-52 (1918)	—	50.00	85.00	110	150	—
BE15-53 (1919)	—	50.00	90.00	120	165	—
BE15-55 (1921)	—	100	150	200	250	—

Y# A10 5 SKAR
Copper, 25 mm. **Obv:** Lion standing left, looking back and upwards **Edge:** Plain **Note:** Counterfeits exist.

Date	Mintage	Good	VG	F	VF	XF
BE15-43 (1909)	—	150	250	350	500	—

Y# 17 5 SKAR
Copper **Obv:** Lion standing left and looking upward **Edge:** Plain **Note:** Overstrikes exist.

Date	Mintage	Good	VG	F	VF	XF
BE15-47 (1913)	—	6.00	10.00	25.00	55.00	—
BE15-48 (1914)	—	4.00	7.00	15.00	35.00	—
BE15-49 (1915)	—	5.00	8.00	18.00	40.00	—
BE15-50 (1916)	—	5.00	8.00	18.00	40.00	—
BE15-51 (1917)	—	3.50	6.00	12.00	30.00	—
BE15-52 (1918)	—	25.00	55.00	120	250	—

Y# 17.1 5 SKAR
Copper **Obv:** Lion standing left, looking back **Edge:** Plain **Note:** Size of obverse circle and weight of coin vary considerably. Inscription varieties exist plus in dots.

Date	Mintage	Good	VG	F	VF	XF
BE15-48 (1914)	—	4.00	7.00	15.00	32.00	—
BE15-48 (1915)	—	4.00	7.00	15.00	32.00	—

Note: Inscription varieties exist.

BE15-49 (1915)	—	4.00	7.00	15.00	32.00	—

Note: Obverse varieties (lion) exist

BE15-50 (1916)	—	4.00	7.00	15.00	32.00	—
BE15-51 (1917)	—	4.00	7.00	15.00	32.00	—
BE15-52 (1918)	—	5.00	8.00	18.00	40.00	—

Y# 17.2   5 SKAR
Copper   Obv: Lion standing left looking back and upwards
Edge: Plain

Date	Mintage	Good	VG	F	VF	XF
BE15-48 (1914)	—	5.00	9.00	20.00	45.00	
Note: 2-line varieties exist of 15-48.						
BE15-49 (1915)	—	8.00	14.00	35.00	70.00	

Y# 17.3   5 SKAR
Copper   Obv: Lion standing left looking back and sideways
Rev: Flower with eight petals rather than wheel with eight spokes
Edge: Plain

Date	Mintage	Good	VG	F	VF	XF
BE15-48 (1914)	—	6.00	10.00	25.00	55.00	

Y# 19   5 SKAR
Copper   Obv: Lion standing left   Edge: Reeded   Note: Varieties exist.

Date	Mintage	Good	VG	F	VF	XF
BE15-52 (1918)	—	2.25	3.50	6.00	12.00	
BE15-53 (1919)	—	2.00	3.00	5.50	11.00	
BE15-54 (1920)	—	1.50	2.50	5.00	10.00	
Note: 2 varieties of 4 in 54 exist						
BE15-55 (1921)	—	5.00	10.00	20.00	40.00	
BE15-56 (1922)	—	1.50	2.50	5.00	10.00	
BE56-15 (1922) Error	—	25.00	40.00	70.00	110	
Note: Reverse inscription reads counterclockwise on error date coin						

Y# 19.1   5 SKAR
Copper   Obv: Lion standing left   Rev: Dot added above center
Edge: Reeded

Date	Mintage	Good	VG	F	VF	XF
BE15-55 (1921)	—	10.00	20.00	35.00	65.00	
BE15-56 (1922)	—	4.00	8.00	15.00	25.00	

Y# 11   7-1/2 SKAR
Copper, 28 mm.   Obv: Lion standing left, looking back and upwards   Edge: Plain   Note: Modern counterfeits.

Date	Mintage	Good	VG	F	VF	XF
BE15-43 (1909)	—	150	250	350	500	

Y# 20   7-1/2 SKAR
Copper   Edge: Plain   Note: Some 15-52, 15-53, 15-54, and 15-55 specimens have the reverse central pinwheel fishes in a counterclockwise direction. Many varieties exist with size of inner circle on reverse.

Date	Mintage	Good	VG	F	VF	XF
BE15-52 (1918)	—	2.00	3.00	5.00	8.50	
BE15-53 (1919)	—	1.50	2.50	4.00	7.00	
BE15-54 (1920)	—	1.50	2.50	4.00	7.00	
BE15-55 (1921)	—	1.50	2.50	4.00	7.00	
BE15-57 (1922)	—	1.50	2.50	4.00	7.00	
BE15-60 (1926)	—	20.00	30.00	50.00	100	
Note: 5 varieties exist						

Y# 21.1a   SHO
Copper, 24 mm.   Obv: Lion standing left, looking backwards, with dots in obverse angles   Rev: Without dots in reverse arabesques   Note: Weight varies: 3.95-7.13 grams. Varieties exist and also in planchet thickness and size of circles

Date	Mintage	Good	VG	F	VF	XF
BE15-52 (1918)	—	1.50	2.00	3.25	7.00	—
BE15-53/52 (1919)	—					—
BE15-53 (1919)	—	1.00	1.50	2.50	5.00	—
BE15-54 (1920)	—	1.00	1.50	2.50	5.00	—
BE15-55 (1921)	—	1.00	1.50	2.50	5.00	—
BE15-56 (1922)	—	1.00	1.50	2.50	5.00	—
BE15-57 (1923)	—	1.50	2.00	3.25	7.00	—
BE15-58 (1924)	—	1.00	1.50	2.50	5.00	—
BE15-59 (1925)	—	1.00	1.50	2.50	5.00	—
BE15-60 (1926)	—	1.00	1.50	2.50	5.00	—
BE16-1 (1927)	—	1.00	1.50	2.50	5.00	—
BE16-2 (1928) w/retrograde 2 (error)	—	1.00	1.50	2.50	5.00	—
BE16-2 (1928)	—	1.00	1.50	2.50	5.00	—

Y# 21b   SHO
Copper   Obv: Lion standing left looking backwards   Rev: Central legend horizontal   Note: Large size 25.6 mm.

Date	Mintage	Good	VG	F	VF	XF
BE15-52 (1918)	—	40.00	60.00	80.00	140	—

Y# 21   SHO
Copper   Obv: Lion standing left, looking upwards   Rev: Central legend horizontal   Note: Large size 25.6 mm.

Date	Mintage	Good	VG	F	VF	XF
BE15-52 (1918)	—	30.00	45.00	75.00	120	—

KM# 21.1b   SHO
Copper, 24 mm.   Obv: W/o dots in obverse angles   Rev: W/o dots in reverse arabesques   Note: Weight varies: 3.95-7.13 grams. Varieties exist.

Date	Mintage	Good	VG	F	VF	XF
BE15-53 (1919)	—	5.00	10.00	20.00	30.00	—
BE15-57 (1923)	—	5.00	10.00	20.00	30.00	—
BE15-58 (1924)	—	20.00	30.00	50.00	80.00	—
BE15-59 (1925)	—	5.00	10.00	20.00	30.00	—

Y# 21.2   SHO
Copper   Obv: Lion standing left looking upwards,   Rev: Dots in reverse arabesques   Note: Weight varies: 3.31-7.27 g. Varieties exist including size of circles.

Date	Mintage	Good	VG	F	VF	XF
BE51-54 (1920) (error) 51 instead of 15	—	—	—	—	—	—
BE15-54 (1920)	—	2.00	3.00	5.00	9.00	—

Date	Mintage	Good	VG	F	VF	XF
Note: Specimens dated 15-54 may all be contemporary forgeries						
BE15-54 (1920) "year" retrograde	—	—	—	—	—	—
BE15-54 (1920) (error) "year" and 15 transposed	—	—	—	—	—	—
Note: 2 lion varieties exist of 15-54.						
BE51-15 (1920) (error) cycle and 15 transposed	—	25.00	40.00	65.00	100	—
BE54-15 (1920) (error) cycle and 15 transposed	—	25.00	40.00	65.00	100	—
BE15-55 (1921)	—	1.50	2.50	4.50	7.00	—
BE15-55 (1921) (error) "year" and 15 transposed	—					—
BE55-15 (1921) (error) cycle and 15 transposed	—	25.00	40.00	65.00	100	—
BE15-56/5 (1921)	—	1.00	1.50	2.50	5.00	—
BE15-56 (1922)	—	1.00	1.50	2.50	5.00	—
BE15-57 (1923)	—	1.25	1.75	3.25	7.00	—
BE15-57 (1923) "year" and 15 transposed	—					—
BE15-57 (1923) (error) "year" and 15 transposed	—					—
BE15-58 (1924)	—	1.00	1.50	2.50	5.00	—
BE15-58 (1924) "year" and 15 transposed	—					—
BE15-59 (1925)	—	1.00	1.50	2.50	5.00	—
BE15-6 (1926) (error) for 15-60	—					—
BE15-60 (1926)	—	1.00	1.50	2.50	5.00	—
BE16-1/15-60 (1927)	—	15.00	25.00	40.00	65.00	—
BE16-1 (1927) dot below syllable "rab"	—	1.00	1.50	2.50	5.00	—
BE16-2/1 (1928)	—	1.00	1.50	2.50	5.00	—
BE16-2 (1928)	—	1.00	1.50	2.50	5.00	—

Y# 21a   SHO
Copper   Rev: Central legend vertical   Note: Two varieties (lion) exist for each of the following dates: 15-56, 15-57, 15-58, and 16-2. Overstrikes on 5 Skar, Y#17 exist. Varieties exist. Weight varies: 3.48-4.78 g.

Date	Mintage	VG	F	VF	XF	Unc
BE15-56 (1922)	—	8.00	13.50	20.00	30.00	—
BE15-57 (1923)	—	2.00	3.50	6.00	10.00	—
BE15-57 (1923) Error; "year" and 15 transposed	—	25.00	40.00	65.00	100	—
BE15-58 (1924)	—	2.00	3.50	6.00	10.00	—
BE15-59/8 (1925)	—	1.25	2.25	4.00	8.00	—
BE15-59 (1925)	—	1.25	2.25	4.00	8.00	—
BE15-60 (1925)	—	1.25	2.25	4.00	8.00	—
BE15-60/59 (1926)	—	1.25	2.25	4.00	8.00	—
BE16-1 (1927)	—	1.25	2.25	4.00	8.00	—
BE16-1 (1927) Dot below syllable rab	—	1.25	2.25	4.00	8.00	—
BE16-2 (1928)	—	2.00	3.50	6.00	10.00	—
Note: A scarce 16-2 variety features a reversed 2						

The following marks are located in the position indicated by the arrow:

b: ●   c: ✚   d: ↓   e: ∨   f: ❤   g:

Y# 23   SHO
Copper   Edge: Reeded   Note: Weight varies: 4.02-6.09 grams. Dates 16-10, 16-11, 16-12, and 16-16 exist struck on thin planchets, many lion obverse varieties.

Date	Mintage	VG	F	VF	XF	Unc
BE16-6 (1932) (a)	6,000,000	3.00	5.00	9.00	15.00	—
BE16-7 (1933) (a)	Inc. above	3.00	5.00	9.00	15.00	—
BE16-8 (1934) (a)	Inc. above	3.00	5.00	9.00	15.00	—
Note: Two varieties exist						
BE16-9 (1935) (a)	Inc. above	2.00	3.50	6.00	11.00	—
Note: Two varieties exist						
BE16-9 (1935) (b)	Inc. above	1.50	3.00	5.00	10.00	—
Note: A scarce 16-9 variety features a hook ("bird") on the Sengi's (lion's) back						
BE16-10 (1936) (a)	Inc. above	5.00	10.00	15.00	25.00	—
BE16-10 (1936) (b)	Inc. above	5.00	10.00	15.00	25.00	—
BE16-10 (1936) (c)	Inc. above	1.50	3.00	5.00	10.00	—
BE16-11 (1937) (a)	Inc. above	2.50	4.00	9.00	15.00	—
BE16-11 (1937) (b)	Inc. above	5.00	10.00	15.00	25.00	—
BE16-11 (1937) (c)	Inc. above	2.50	4.00	9.00	15.00	—

Date	Mintage	VG	F	VF	XF	Unc

Note: A variety exists with stars at 4:00 and 8:00 close to inner reverse circle

Date	Mintage	VG	F	VF	XF	Unc
BE16-11 (1937) (d)	Inc. above	2.50	4.00	9.00	15.00	—
BE16-11 (1937) (e)	Inc. above	1.50	3.00	5.00	10.00	—
BE16-11 (1937) (f)	Inc. above	5.00	10.00	15.00	25.00	—
BE16-11 (1937) (g)	Inc. above	5.00	10.00	15.00	25.00	—
BE16-12 (1938) (c)	Inc. above	5.00	10.00	15.00	25.00	—
BE16-12 (1938) (d)	Inc. above	5.00	10.00	15.00	25.00	—
BE16-12 (1938) (f)	Inc. above	4.00	8.00	12.00	20.00	—
BE16-12 (1938) (g)	Inc. above	4.00	8.00	12.00	20.00	—
BE16-16 (1942) (f)	Inc. above	—	—	—	—	—
Rare						

Y# 27.1 3 SHO
Copper **Obv:** Single cloud line **Rev:** Four varieties of conch shell on reverse **Note:** Variety with line or cloud (scarcer) right of right obverse mountain.

Date	Mintage	VG	F	VF	XF	Unc
BE16-20 (1946)	—	8.00	15.00	25.00	50.00	—

Y# 27.2 3 SHO
Copper **Obv:** Double cloud line

Date	Mintage	VG	F	VF	XF	Unc
BE16-20 (1946)	—	15.00	30.00	50.00	85.00	—

Y# 8 5 SHO
Silver **Ruler:** Hsüan-t'ung **Edge:** Reeded **Note:** Weight varies: 9.4-9.7 grams.

Date	Mintage	VG	F	VF	XF	Unc
CD1 (1909)	—	600	1,200	2,000	2,500	—

Note: Forgeries exist: some of the stars blundered and letters inaccurate, modern ones of larger size struck in base metals

Y# 18 5 SHO
Silver **Obv:** Lion looking upwards **Edge:** Reeded **Note:** Weight varies: 8.4-11.4 grams.

Date	Mintage	VG	F	VF	XF	Unc
BE15-47 (1913)	—	50.00	70.00	100	150	—
BE15-48 (1914)	—	35.00	50.00	80.00	125	—
BE15-49 (1915)	—	35.00	50.00	80.00	125	—
BE15-50 (1916)	—	35.00	50.00	80.00	125	—

Note: Two BE15-50 varieties exist; small and large lions, or 13.5mm vs. 14.5mm obverse circle, short or long flowers on reverse

Date	Mintage	VG	F	VF	XF	Unc
BE15-58 (1924)	—	—	—	—	—	—
Rare						
BE15-59 (1925)	—	200	300	500	700	—
BE15-60 (1926)	—	180	280	525	750	—

Y# 18.1 5 SHO
Silver **Obv:** Lion looking backwards **Edge:** Reeded **Note:** Weight varies: 7.40-9.80 grams. Varieties exist.

Date	Mintage	VG	F	VF	XF	Unc
BE15-49 (1915)	—	35.00	50.00	80.00	125	—
BE15-50 (1916)	—	35.00	50.00	80.00	125	—
BE15-51 (1917)	—	35.00	50.00	80.00	125	—
BE15-52 (1918)	—	35.00	50.00	80.00	125	—
BE15-53 (1919)	—	100	175	275	400	—
BE15-56 (1922)	—	100	175	275	400	—
BE15-59 (1925)	—	500	600	750	1,250	—
BE15-60 (1926)	—	400	550	700	1,200	—
BE16-1 (1927)	—	125	225	350	500	—

Y# 18.1a 5 SHO
Copper **Note:** Some specimens are silver plated or silver washed.

Date	Mintage	VG	F	VF	XF	Unc
BE15-53 (1919)	—	225	300	400	500	—
BE15-56 (1922)	—	225	300	400	500	—

Y# 18.2 5 SHO
Silver **Edge:** Reeded **Note:** Weight varies: 8.00-9.70 grams.

Date	Mintage	VG	F	VF	XF	Unc
BE15-52 (1920)	—	125	175	250	350	—

a. C̬ "CYCLE"

b. ॐ "YEAR"

c. ꠳ "16"

Y# 28 5 SHO
Copper **Obv:** Two mountains with two suns **Edge:** Reeded **Note:** Three lion die varieties exist. Modern counterfiets made of yellowish copper exist.

Date	Mintage	VG	F	VF	XF	Unc
BE16-21 (1947)	—	4.00	7.50	10.00	20.00	—

Y# 28.1 5 SHO
Copper **Obv:** Three mountains with two suns **Edge:** Reeded **Note:** Die varieties involving lion's tail hairs (5-8), leg hairs (2-5) and yin-yang features (S, reversed S or the incuse of either) include 5 of 16-21, 38 of 16-22 and 30 of 16-23.

Date	Mintage	VG	F	VF	XF	Unc
BE16-21 (1947)	—	2.00	3.50	6.00	10.00	—

Note: A modern medallic series dated 16-21 (1947) exists struck in copper, silver, and gold which were authorized by the Dalai Lama while in exile; Refer to Unusual World Coins, 5th edition, KP Books, 2007

Date	Mintage	VG	F	VF	XF	Unc
BE16-21 (1947) dots a and b	—	2.50	4.00	7.50	12.50	—
BE16-22 (1948) dots a, b, and c	—	23.00	30.00	40.00	50.00	—
BE16-23 (1949) dots	—	5.00	8.00	14.00	25.00	—

Note: With 8, 9, 10 or 12 sunrays

Date	Mintage	VG	F	VF	XF	Unc
BE16-23 (1949) dots a, b, and c	—	1.50	3.00	5.00	8.50	—

Note: Unclear overdates and varieties of BE16-23 exist

Date	Mintage	VG	F	VF	XF	Unc
BE16-24 (1950) dots a and b	—	30.00	40.00	50.00	65.00	—
BE16-24/3 (1950) dots a and b	—	40.00	60.00	80.00	100	—

Y# 28.2 5 SHO
Copper **Obv:** Cloud above middle mountain missing **Edge:** Reeded

Date	Mintage	VG	F	VF	XF	Unc
BE16-22 (1948)	—	35.00	60.00	95.00	150	—

Y# 28a 5 SHO
Copper **Obv:** Moon and sun above 3 mountains **Edge:** Reeded **Note:** Lion and edge varieties exist.

Date	Mintage	VG	F	VF	XF	Unc
BE16-23 (1949) dots a and b	—	20.00	28.00	38.00	50.00	—
BE16-24 (1950) dot b						
BE16-24/3 (1950) dots a and b	—	40.00	60.00	80.00	100	—
BE16-24 (1950) dots a and b	—	2.00	3.50	6.50	11.00	—

Note: Unclear overdates of 15-24 exist

Date	Mintage	VG	F	VF	XF	Unc
BE16-24 (1950) dots a and b	—	10.00	15.00	22.00	30.00	—

Note: Cloud merged with mountain as in illustration

Date	Mintage	VG	F	VF	XF	Unc
BE16-24 (1950) dots a and b	—	15.00	22.00	30.00	40.00	—

Note: Moon engraved over sun

Date	Mintage	VG	F	VF	XF	Unc
BE16-25 (1951) dot a and b (tiny)	—	—	—	—	—	—
BE16-25/24 (1951) dot a and b	—	4.00	7.00	12.50	20.00	—
BE16-25 (1951) dot a	—	2.00	3.50	6.50	11.00	—
BE16-25 (1951) dot a and b	—	6.00	10.00	16.00	25.00	—

Note: Moon engraved over sun; Unclear overdates exist for BE16-25

Date	Mintage	VG	F	VF	XF	Unc
BE16-26 (1952) dot a	—	4.00	7.00	12.00	20.00	—

Note: Without dot after "26"

Date	Mintage	VG	F	VF	XF	Unc
BE16-26 (1952) dot a and b	—	4.00	7.00	12.00	20.00	—
BE16-27 (1953)	—	6.00	10.00	18.00	30.00	—
BE16-27 (1953) dot a	—	23.00	30.00	40.00	50.00	—

Y# 9   SRANG

Silver   **Ruler:** Hsüan-t'ung **Edge:** Reeded **Note:** 17.2-19.9 g.
Reverse varieties exist

Date	Mintage	VG	F	VF	XF	Unc
CD1 (1909)	—	125	185	275	425	—

Y# 12   SRANG

Silver   **Obv:** Lion standing left, looking backwards **Edge:** Plain
Note: Weight varies: 18.00-18.30 grams. Varieties exist.

Date	Mintage	VG	F	VF	XF	Unc
BE15-43 (1909)	—	140	225	325	475	—

Y# A18   SRANG

18.1000 g., Silver   **Obv:** Lion standing left looking back and
upwards **Edge:** Reeded

Date	Mintage	VG	F	VF	XF	Unc
BE15-48 (1914)	—	800	1,000	1,500	2,000	—

Y# A18.1   SRANG

Silver   **Obv:** Lion standing left looking backwards **Edge:** Reeded
Note: Weight varies: 17.80-18.30 grams

Date	Mintage	VG	F	VF	XF	Unc
BE15-52 (1918)	—	350	650	850	1,200	—
BE15-53 (1919)	—	275	450	700	1,000	—

Date	Mintage	F	VF	XF	Unc	BU
BE16-12 (1938)	—	3.50	6.00	10.00	20.00	—
BE16-20 (1946)	—	20.00	40.00	70.00	90.00	—

Y# 25   3 SRANG

11.3000 g., Silver   **Edge:** Reeded **Note:** Dates are written in
words, not numerals. Varieties exist in lion.

Date	Mintage	F	VF	XF	Unc	BU
BE16-7 (1933)	—	8.00	12.00	20.00	35.00	—
Note: 7 or 8-tail plume variety						
BE16-8 (1934)	—	8.00	12.00	20.00	35.00	—

Y# 26   3 SRANG

Silver   **Edge:** Reeded **Note:** Dates are written in words, not
numerals. Obverse and reverse varieties exist.

Date	Mintage	F	VF	XF	Unc	BU
BE16-9 (1935)	—	7.00	10.00	18.00	30.00	—
BE16-10 (1936)	—	6.00	9.00	15.00	25.00	—
BE16-10/9 (1936)	—	7.00	10.00	18.00	30.00	—
BE16-11 (1937)	—	6.00	9.00	15.00	25.00	—
BE16-12 (1938)	—	6.00	9.00	15.00	25.00	—
BE16-20 (1946)	—	20.00	40.00	70.00	110	—
BE16-20 (1946) dot after date	—	—	—	—	—	—

Y# 29   10 SRANG

Billon   **Obv:** Two suns **Rev:** Numerals for denomination at center
right **Edge:** Reeded

Date	Mintage	F	VF	XF	Unc	BU
BE(16)-22 (1948)	—	4.50	9.00	18.00	40.00	—

Y# 29a   10 SRANG

Billon   **Obv:** Moon and sun **Rev:** Value written in words at center
right **Edge:** Reeded **Note:** The "dot" is after the denomination.
No cycle written. Refer to "Unusual World Coins", 5th edition, KP
Books, 2007.

Date	Mintage	F	VF	XF	Unc	BU
BE(16)-23 (1949)	—	20.00	45.00	100	175	—
Note: With dot						
BE(16)-24/23 (1950)	—	7.00	15.00	30.00	60.00	—
Note: With dot						
BE(16)-24/23 (1950)	—	20.00	40.00	80.00	140	—
Note: With dot and moon cut over sun						
BE(16)-24/22 (1950) with dot	—	9.00	18.00	35.00	70.00	—
Note: A modern medallic series dated 16-24 (1950) exists struck in copper-nickel, silver, and gold which were authorized by the Dalai Lama while in exile.						
BE(16)-24 (1950)	—	10.00	20.00	40.00	70.00	—
Note: With dot and moon cut over sun						
BE(16)-24 (1950)	—	12.00	22.00	50.00	90.00	—
Note: With dot						

Date	Mintage	F	VF	XF	Unc	BU
BE(16)-25 (1951) w/o dot	—	—	—	—	—	—
BE(16)-25/24 (1951)	—	7.00	15.00	30.00	60.00	—
Note: With dot						
BE(16)-25/24 (1951)	—	10.00	20.00	40.00	70.00	—
Note: Without dot						
BE(16)-25 (1951)	—	7.00	15.00	30.00	60.00	—
Note: Without dot						
BE(16)-26/25 (1952)	—	7.00	15.00	30.00	60.00	—
Note: Without dot						
BE(16)-26 (1952)	—	7.00	15.00	30.00	60.00	—
Note: With dot						

Y# 29.1   10 SRANG

Billon   **Obv:** 2 suns **Rev:** Words for denomination at center right
Note: No cycle written.

Date	Mintage	F	VF	XF	Unc	BU
BE(16)-23 (1949)	—	6.00	10.00	20.00	40.00	—
Note: With dot before and after ten						
BE(16)-23 (1949)	—	6.00	10.00	20.00	40.00	—
Note: Without dot after ten						
BE(16)-23/22 (1949)	—	12.00	20.00	35.00	70.00	—

Y# 30   10 SRANG

Billon   **Rev:** Cycle and year in words **Edge:** Reeded **Note:** Said
to be struck for payment of Tibetan Army members

Date	Mintage	F	VF	XF	Unc	BU
BE16-24 (1950)	—	6.00	12.00	25.00	55.00	—
Note: Without dot after year						
BE16-24 (1950)	—	7.00	15.00	30.00	65.00	—
Note: With dot						
BE16-25/4 (1951)	—	5.00	10.00	20.00	45.00	—
Note: With dot						
BE16-25 (1951)	—	5.00	10.00	20.00	45.00	—
Note: With dot						

Y# 22   20 SRANG

Gold   **Obv:** Eight Buddhist lucky symbols in outer circle
Rev: Varieties with 2.8mm, 2.5 mm, and 2.2 mm central rev. circle
Edge: Reeded

Date	Mintage	F	VF	XF	Unc	BU
BE15-52 (1918)	—	—	—	—	—	—
Note: w/o dot in rev. center						
BE15-52 (1918)	—	475	600	850	1,150	—
Note: With dot in reverse center						
BE15-53 (1919)	—	475	600	850	1,150	—
Note: With small circle in reverse center						
BE15-53 (1919)	—	475	600	850	1,150	—
Note: With small circle in reverse center; Silver strikings for 15-53 exist and are forgeries						
BE15-54 (1920)	—	475	600	850	1,100	—
Note: Silver strikings for 15-54 exist and are believed to be forgeries; Deceptive forgeries struck in high grade gold also exist; without dot in reverse center						
BE15-54 (1920)	—	475	600	850	1,150	—
Note: With dot in reverse center						
BE15-55 (1921)	—	700	1,000	1,500	2,000	—
Note: w/o dot in rev. center						

Y# 24   1-1/2 SRANG

5.0000 g., Silver   **Edge:** Reeded **Note:** Dates are written in
words, not numerals. Obverse and reverse varieties exist.

Date	Mintage	F	VF	XF	Unc	BU
BE16-10 (1936) coin and medal rotations exist	—	—	—	—	—	—
BE16-10 (1936)	—	3.50	6.00	10.00	20.00	—
BE16-11 (1937)	—	3.00	5.00	9.00	17.00	—

TRADE COINAGE

1 Rupee = 3 Tangka

Rupees (Y#3) due to their inscription and first mint also called Szechuan Rupees. Total mintage of the 1 Rupee between 1902 and 1942 (with decreasing fineness) was between 25.5 and 27.5 million according to Chinese sources. In addition to the types illustrated above, large quantities of the following coins also circulated in Tibet: China Dollars, Y#318a, 329, and 345 plus Szechuan issues Y#449 and 459, and Indian Rupees, KM#473, 492, and 508.

Rupees exist with local merchant countermarks in Chinese, Tibetan, and other scripts. Examples of crown-size rupees struck in silver (26.30-27.90 grams) and gold (36.30 grams) are considered fantasies and are listed in Unusual World Coins, 5th edition, Krause Publications, 2007.

Y# 1   1/4 RUPEE
2.8000 g., 0.9350 Silver 0.0842 oz. ASW, 19 mm.
Edge: Reeded **Note:** Varieties exist as do modern forgeries.

Date	Mintage	F	VF	XF	Unc	BU
ND(1904-05, 1912)	120,000	45.00	65.00	100	175	—

Y# 1a   1/4 RUPEE
5.4500 g., Gold **Note:** Deceptive forgeries exist.

Date	Mintage	F	VF	XF	Unc	BU
ND(1905)	—	1,150	1,900	2,650	3,450	—

Y# 2   1/2 RUPEE
5.6000 g., 0.9350 Silver 0.1683 oz. ASW, 24 mm.
Edge: Reeded **Note:** Varieties exist

Date	Mintage	F	VF	XF	Unc	BU
ND(1904-05, 1907, 1912)	130,000	60.00	85.00	145	250	—

Y# 2a   1/2 RUPEE
9.3800 g., Gold

Date	Mintage	F	VF	XF	Unc	BU
ND(1905)	—	1,250	2,000	2,750	3,500	—

Y# A1.1   RUPEE
11.5000 g., Silver **Ruler:** Hsüan-t'ung **Edge:** Plain **Note:** Prev. #C20.

Date	Mintage	Good	VG	F	VF	XF
ND(1902-03)	—	750	1,000	1,500	2,250	—

Note: Struck in or near Kangding (Tachienlu) and known as Lu Kuan Rupee. It was meant to replace the Indian Rupee which was used in eastern Tibet and western Szechuan (Sichuan) in the 19th century and is considered the forerunner of the Szechuan Rupee (Y#3).

Y# A1.2   RUPEE
Silver **Ruler:** Hsüan-t'ung **Obv:** Similar to Y#A1.1. **Rev:** Different inscription w/o inner beaded circle **Note:** Kann#1285

Date	Mintage	Good	VG	F	VF	XF
ND(1902-03)	—	750	1,000	1,500	2,250	—

Y# 3   RUPEE
11.4000 g., Silver **Obv:** Small bust without collar **Rev:** Vertical rosette **Edge:** Reeded **Note:** Two reverse varieties exist. Finenesses vary: .8800-.9350.

Date	Mintage	F	VF	XF	Unc	BU
ND(1902-11)	—	30.00	50.00	80.00	125	—

Y# 3.1   RUPEE
11.4000 g., Silver **Obv:** Small bust w/o collar **Rev:** Horizontal rosette **Edge:** Reeded **Note:** Two reverse varieties exist. Finenesses vary: .880-.835.

Date	Mintage	F	VF	XF	Unc	BU
ND(1902-11)	—	20.00	40.00	60.00	100	—

Y# 3.2a   RUPEE
20.6700 g., Gold **Obv:** Small bust w/o collar **Rev:** Vertical rosette

Date	Mintage	F	VF	XF	Unc	BU
ND(ca. 1903-05)	—	900	1,200	1,750	—	—

Note: An example with two obverses exists (20.40 grams).

Y# 3.2   RUPEE
0.7000 Silver **Obv:** Small bust with collar, varieties with missing base of bust exist **Rev:** Vertical rosette **Note:** Two reverse varieties exist. Weight varies .700-.740 g.

Date	Mintage	F	VF	XF	Unc	BU
ND(1911-16, 1930-33)	—	15.00	25.00	45.00	75.00	—

Note: An example with two obverses exists

Y# 3b   RUPEE
23.1500 g., Gold **Obv:** Large bust with collar **Rev:** Vertical rosette

Date	Mintage	F	VF	XF	Unc	BU
ND(ca.1930)	—	800	1,200	1,750	—	—

Y# 3.3   RUPEE
Silver **Obv:** Large bust with collar **Rev:** Vertical rosette **Note:** Finenesses vary .420-.500. Varieties exist.

Date	Mintage	F	VF	XF	Unc	BU
ND(1939-42)	—	20.00	35.00	65.00	110	—

Y# 3.5   RUPEE
Silver **Obv:** Small bust with collar **Rev:** Horizontal rosette **Note:** Weight varies .420-.500. Varieties exist.

Date	Mintage	F	VF	XF	Unc	BU
ND(1933-39)	—	30.00	50.00	90.00	160	—

Y# 3.4   RUPEE
Silver **Obv:** Small bust with flat nose and collar, revised non-floral gown and solid line separating nose and lips sections from face **Rev:** Vertical rosette **Note:** Weight varies: .500-.650

Date	Mintage	F	VF	XF	Unc	BU
ND(1933-39)	—	20.00	35.00	65.00	110	—

Y# 3a   RUPEE
Debased Silver/Billon **Obv:** Large bust with collar **Rev:** Vertical rosette **Note:** Fineness .220 or less.

Date	Mintage	F	VF	XF	Unc	BU
ND(1939-42)	—	10.00	20.00	40.00	70.00	—

Note: Coins with copper base and silver wash exist

CUT COINAGE

The Tangka C#27 was cut in parts of 3, 4, and 5 petals to make change and the resulting fraactions are occasionally encountered. Cut pieces of the presentation Tangka Y#14 in 4 and 5 petals exist but are considered dubious. Tibetan Rupees (Y3) due to their inscriptions also called Szechuan Rupees, have been cut in half and quarter for use as small change. The process of cutting the rupee frequently allowed customers to chip away from the coin's middle. In 1934 the treasury made cutting of the rupee illegal. To enforce this decree, all official payments had to be made with uncut coins; payment of smaller values was to be made with copper coins. However, the shortage of coinage made this decree impractical.

Y# A5   1/4 RUPEE
Silver **Note:** 1/4 segment of 1 Rupee, Y#3.

Date	Mintage	VG	F	VF	XF	Unc
ND (1902-42)	—	—	—	—	—	—

Y# B5   1/2 RUPEE
Silver **Note:** 1/2 segment of 1 Rupee, of all types Y#3.

Date	Mintage	VG	F	VF	XF	Unc
ND (1902-42)	—	15.00	20.00	35.00	60.00	—

TOKEN COINAGE

KM# Tn1   TAEL / (SRANG)
Copper **Note:** 8.23-8.98 grams. Struck over 3 Sho, Y#27 and 5 Sho, Y#28a and Y#28.1. This token was issued by the Lhasa Motor Car Repair Factory and was good for 4 Taels of grain (=200 g).

Date	Mintage	F	VF	XF	Unc	BU
ND(1959-60) Rare	—	75.00	100	200	400	600

JOINT CHINESE AND TIBETAN AUTHORITY

SINO-TIBETAN COINAGE

Struck in the name of the Chinese Emperor

Y# A4   1/2 SKAR
Copper **Ruler:** Hsüan-t'ung **Edge:** Plain **Note:** Weight varies: 3.10-3.60 grams.

Date	Mintage	Good	VG	F	VF	XF
ND(1910)	—	300	500	700	1,000	—

Y# 4   SKAR
Copper, 27 mm. **Ruler:** Hsüan-t'ung **Rev. Insc.:** Hsüan-t'ung.... **Edge:** Plain **Note:** Weight varies: 5.40-6.60 grams. Varieties in dragon and spacing of inscription exist. Modern counterfeits exist.

Date	Mintage	Good	VG	F	VF	XF
ND(1910)	—	90.00	150	250	400	—

Y# 5   SHO
Silver, 22 mm. **Ruler:** Hsüan-t'ung **Rev. Insc.:** Hsüan-t'ung.... **Edge:** Reeded **Note:** Weight varies: 3.30-4.10 grams. Varieties exist, one having the inner circle of dots, on the Chinese side, connected by lines. Modern counterfeits in copper and base metals exist.

Date	Mintage	Good	VG	F	VF	XF
ND(1910)	—	20.00	30.00	50.00	75.00	125

Y# 6   2 SHO

Silver, 25 mm. **Ruler:** Hsüan-t'ung **Rev. Insc.:** Hsüan-t'ung....
Edge: Reeded **Note:** Weight varies: 5.20-8.40 grams. Varieties with different dragon claws and lotus exist. Modern counterfeits exist.

Date	Mintage	Good	VG	F	VF	XF
ND(1910)	—	25.00	40.00	80.00	125	175

TIBETAN TANGKA COINAGE

The legend of this Tangka appears to be in ornamental Lantsa (Ranjana)script and has yet to be deciphered. The type is a copy of the Nepalese debased Tangka of Pratap Simha. Struck unofficially by Nepalese traders in Tibet between 1880 and 1912, it was legal tender, due to an edict issued in 1881 ordering that no distinction be made between false and genuine coins. The Tangka, C#27 was cut in parts of 3, 4, and 5 petals to make change and the resulting fractions are occasionally encountered.

C# 27.2   RANJANA TANGKA

4.5000 g., Silver **Obv:** Crescent and swastika at top **Note:** See note for C#27.1.

Date	Mintage	Good	VG	F	VF	XF
BE15-46 (1912)	—	60.00	80.00	100	150	225

PATTERNS

Including off metal strikes

KM#	Date	Mintage	Identification	Mkt Val
Pn3	ND (1909)	—	10 Tam. Silver. 27.6700 g.	—
Pn4	ND (1910)	—	Shokang. Silver. 3.6000 g. Y5	—
Pn5	BE15-57 (1923)	—	Sho. Copper.	—
Pn6	BE15-57 (1923)	—	Sho. Brass.	—
Pn8	BE15-57 (1923)	—	20 Srang. Brass. 7.2300 g.	—
Pn9	BE16-1 (1928)	—	Sho. Brass. 5.2600 g.	—
Pn10	ND (1928)	—	Srang. Silver.	—
Pn11	ND (1928)	—	10 Tam. Silver. 12.6100 g.	—
PnA12	ND(1928-29)	—	5 Sho. Silver. Reeded edge. Weight varies: 5.43-6.55g. Two obverse varieties exist.	1,500
Pn12	ND (1929-30)	—	10 Tam. Silver. 8.3000 g.	—
Pn13	BE16-4 (1931)	—	5 Sho. Silver. 5.0000 g.	—
Pn14	Yr.925 (1951)	—	25 Srang. Silver. 13.5200 g.	—
Pn15	Yr.925 (1951)	—	50 Srang. Copper. 17.3000 g.	—
Pn16	Yr.925 (1951)	—	50 Srang. Silver. 26.0000 g.	—
Pn17	Yr.925 (1951)	—	50 Srang. Silver. 26.0000 g.	—
Pn18	ND (1951)	—	50 Srang. Silver. 25.1000 g.	—
Pn17	Yr.925 (1951)	—	50 Srang. Silver. 26.0000 g.	—
Pn20	Yr.927 (1953)	—	5 Srang. Copper. 6.2000 g.	600

Note: Some specimens of Pn20 seem to have entered circulation.

Pn21	Yr. 927 (1953)	—	5 Srang. Silver. 5.0000 g.	—

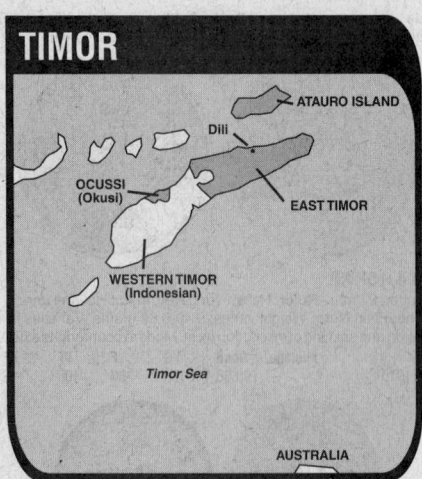

TIMOR

(East Timor)

Timor is an island between the Savu and Timor Seas. It has an area, including the former colony of Portuguese Timor, of 11,883 sq. mi. (30,775 sq. km.) and a population of 1.5 million. Western Timor is administered as part of Nusa Tenggara Timur (East Nusa Tenggara) province. Capital: Kupang. The eastern half of the island, the former Portuguese colony, forms a single province, Timor Timur (East Timor). Originally the Portuguese colony also included the area around Ocussi-Ambeno and the small island of Atauro (Pulau Kambing) located north of Dili. Capital: Dili. Timor exports sandalwood, coffee, tea, hides, rubber and copra.

Portuguese traders reached Timor about 1520, and moved to the north and east when the Dutch established themselves in

Kupang, a sheltered bay at the southwestern tip in 1613. Treaties effective in 1860 and 1914 established the boundaries between the two colonies. Japan occupied the entire island during World War II. The former Dutch colony in the western part of the island became part of Indonesia in 1950.

For later coinage see East Timor.

MONETARY SYSTEM
100 Avos = 1 Pataca

PORTUGUESE COLONY

MILLED COINAGE
100 Avos = 1 Pataca

KM# 5   10 AVOS

Bronze, 20 mm. **Obv:** Small circles within cross design **Obv. Leg.:** REPUBLICA PORTUGUESA **Rev:** Value above sprigs **Rev. Leg.:** COLONIA DE TIMOR

Date	Mintage	F	VF	XF	Unc	BU
1945	50,000	120	220	400	1,000	—
1948	500,000	3.50	8.00	17.00	35.00	—
1951	6,250,000	1.50	3.50	7.50	15.00	—

KM# 6   20 AVOS

Nickel-Bronze, 23 mm. **Obv:** Laureate liberty head right **Obv. Leg.:** REPUBLICA PORTUGUESA **Rev:** Shield within globe and wreath **Rev. Leg.:** COLONIA DE TIMOR

Date	Mintage	F	VF	XF	Unc	BU
1945	50,000	16.00	35.00	70.00	175	—

KM# 7   50 AVOS

3.5000 g., 0.6500 Silver 0.0731 oz. ASW, 20.5 mm. **Obv:** Shield within globe on maltese cross **Obv. Leg.:** REPUBLICA PORTUGUESA **Rev:** Value above sprigs **Rev. Leg.:** COLONIA DE TIMOR

Date	Mintage	F	VF	XF	Unc	BU
1945	100,000	45.00	90.00	135	275	—
1948	500,000	3.00	5.50	12.00	30.00	—
1951	6,250,000	2.00	4.00	9.00	18.00	—

1958 REFORM COINAGE
100 Centavos = 1 Escudo

KM# 10   10 CENTAVOS

Bronze, 18 mm. **Obv:** Value **Obv. Leg.:** REPUBLICA PORTUGUESA **Rev:** Shield within crowned globe, flowers in legend, date below **Rev. Leg.:** TIMOR

Date	Mintage	F	VF	XF	Unc	BU
1958	1,000,000	1.00	3.00	15.00	35.00	—

KM# 17   20 CENTAVOS

Bronze **Obv:** Value **Obv. Leg.:** REPUBLICA PORTUGUESA **Rev:** Shield within crowned globe, flowers in legend, date below **Rev. Leg.:** TIMOR

Date	Mintage	F	VF	XF	Unc	BU
1970	1,000,000	0.45	1.00	2.50	5.00	7.50

KM# 11   30 CENTAVOS

Bronze, 22 mm. **Obv:** Value **Obv. Leg.:** REPUBLICA PORTUGUESA **Rev:** Shield within crowned globe, flowers in legend, date below **Rev. Leg.:** TIMOR

Date	Mintage	F	VF	XF	Unc	BU
1958	2,000,000	0.75	1.50	12.00	30.00	—

KM# 18   50 CENTAVOS

4.0000 g., Bronze, 19.8 mm. **Obv:** Value **Obv. Leg.:** REPUBLICA PORTUGUESA **Rev:** Shield within crowned globe, flowers in legend, date below **Rev. Leg.:** TIMOR

Date	Mintage	F	VF	XF	Unc	BU
1970	1,000,000	0.45	1.00	2.00	4.50	6.50

KM# 12   60 CENTAVOS

Copper-Nickel-Zinc, 23 mm. **Obv:** Shield within globe on maltese cross, date below **Obv. Leg.:** REPUBLICA PORTUGUESA **Rev:** Shield within crowned globe, flowers in legend, value below **Rev. Leg.:** TIMOR

Date	Mintage	F	VF	XF	Unc	BU
1958	1,000,000	1.25	2.75	12.00	30.00	—

KM# 13   ESCUDO

Copper-Nickel-Zinc, 26.5 mm. **Obv:** Shield within globe on maltese cross, date below **Obv. Leg.:** REPUBLICA PORTUGUESA **Rev:** Shield within crowned globe, flowers in legend, value below **Rev. Leg.:** TIMOR

Date	Mintage	F	VF	XF	Unc	BU
1958	1,200,000	2.00	4.00	40.00	75.00	—

KM# 19   ESCUDO

7.8700 g., Bronze, 25.7 mm. **Obv:** Value **Obv. Leg.:** REPUBLICA PORTUGUESA **Rev:** Shield within crowned globe, flowers in legend, date below **Rev. Leg.:** TIMOR

Date	Mintage	F	VF	XF	Unc	BU
1970	1,200,000	1.50	3.00	7.00	15.00	—

KM# 20   2-1/2 ESCUDOS

Copper-Nickel **Obv:** Shield within globe on maltese cross, date below **Obv. Leg.:** REPUBLICA PORTUGUESA **Rev:** Shield within crowned globe, flowers in legend, value below **Rev. Leg.:** TIMOR

Date	Mintage	F	VF	XF	Unc	BU
1970	1,000,000	0.75	1.50	3.50	8.00	14.00

KM# 14 3 ESCUDOS
3.5000 g., 0.6500 Silver 0.0731 oz. ASW, 20 mm. **Obv:** Shield within globe on maltese cross, date below **Obv. Leg.:** REPUBLICA PORTUGUESA **Rev:** Shield within crowned globe, flowers in legend, value below **Rev. Leg.:** TIMOR

Date	Mintage	F	VF	XF	Unc	BU
1958	1,000,000	3.00	5.00	10.00	25.00	—

KM# 21 5 ESCUDOS
6.9300 g., Copper-Nickel, 24 mm. **Obv:** Shield within globe on maltese cross, date below **Obv. Leg.:** REPUBLICA PORTUGUESA **Rev:** Shield within crowned globe, flowers in legend, value below **Rev. Leg.:** TIMOR

Date	Mintage	F	VF	XF	Unc	BU
1970	1,200,000	1.50	3.00	6.50	12.00	—

KM# 15 6 ESCUDOS
7.0000 g., 0.6500 Silver 0.1463 oz. ASW, 25 mm. **Obv:** Shield within globe on maltese cross, date below **Obv. Leg.:** REPUBLICA PORTUGUESA **Rev:** Shield within crowned globe, flowers in legend, value below **Rev. Leg.:** TIMOR

Date	Mintage	F	VF	XF	Unc	BU
1958	1,000,000	3.50	6.00	12.50	25.00	—

KM# 16 10 ESCUDOS
7.0000 g., 0.6500 Silver 0.1463 oz. ASW **Obv:** Shield within globe on maltese cross, date below **Obv. Leg.:** REPUBLICA PORTUGUESA **Rev:** Shield within crowned globe, flowers in legend, value below **Rev. Leg.:** TIMOR

Date	Mintage	F	VF	XF	Unc	BU
1964	600,000	3.50	6.00	12.50	25.00	—

KM# 22 10 ESCUDOS
9.0000 g., Copper-Nickel, 28 mm. **Obv:** Shield within globe on maltese cross, date below **Obv. Leg.:** REPUBLICA PORTUGUESA **Rev:** Shield within crowned globe, flowers in legend, value below **Rev. Leg.:** TIMOR

Date	Mintage	F	VF	XF	Unc	BU
1970	700,000	3.00	5.50	12.00	24.00	—

PROVAS
Raised or stamped "PROVA" in field

KM#	Date	Mintage	Identification	Mkt Val
Pr1	1948	—	10 Avos. Bronze. KM#5.	
Pr2	1948	—	50 Avos. Silver. KM#7.	

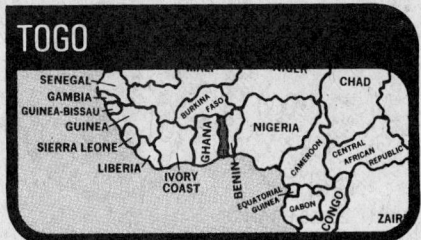

TOGO

The Republic of Togo (formerly part of German Togoland), situated on the Gulf of Guinea in West Africa between Ghana and Dahomey, has an area of 21,622 sq.mi. (56,790 sq. km.) and a population of *3.4 million. Capital: Lome. Agriculture and herding, the production of dyewoods, and the mining of phosphates and iron ore are the chief industries. Copra, phosphates and coffee are exported.

Although Brazilians were the first traders to settle in Togo, Germany achieved possession, in 1884, by inducing coastal chiefs to place their territories under German protection. The German protectorate was extended international recognition at the Berlin conference of 1885 and its ultimate boundaries delimited by treaties with France in 1897 and with Britain in 1904. Anglo-French forces occupied Togoland in 1914, subsequently becoming a League of Nations mandate and a U.N. trusteeship divided, for administrative purpose, between Great Britain and France. The British portion voted in 1957 for incorporation with Ghana. The French portion became the independent Republic of Togo on April 27, 1960.

RULERS
German, 1884-1914
Anglo - French, 1914-1957
French, 1957-1960

MINT MARK
(a) - Paris, privy marks only

MONETARY SYSTEM
100 Centimes = 1 Franc

FRENCH MANDATE
U.N. Trusteeship
STANDARD COINAGE
100 Centimes = 1 Franc

KM# 1 50 CENTIMES
Aluminum-Bronze **Obv:** Laureate head left **Rev:** Value within upright sprigs

Date	Mintage	F	VF	XF	Unc	BU
1924(a)	3,691,000	4.00	20.00	50.00	80.00	—
1925(a)	2,064,000	5.00	22.00	55.00	100	—
1926(a)	445,000	20.00	50.00	100	300	—

KM# 2 FRANC
Aluminum-Bronze **Obv:** Laureat head left **Rev:** Value within upright sprigs

Date	Mintage	F	VF	XF	Unc	BU
1924(a)	3,472,000	3.50	27.50	60.00	125	—
1925(a)	2,768,000	4.00	19.00	65.00	140	—

KM# 4 FRANC
Aluminum **Obv:** Winged head left **Rev:** Slender-horned gazelle head divides value within sprigs

Date	Mintage	F	VF	XF	Unc	BU
1948(a)	5,000,000	5.00	12.00	30.00	70.00	125

KM# 3 2 FRANCS
Aluminum-Bronze **Obv:** Laureate head left **Rev:** Value within upright sprigs

Date	Mintage	F	VF	XF	Unc	BU
1924(a)	750,000	6.00	35.00	110	250	—
1925(a)	580,000	7.00	38.00	120	275	—

KM# 5 2 FRANCS
2.1000 g., Aluminum **Obv:** Winged head left **Rev:** Slender-horned gazelle head divides value within sprigs **Note:** Similar to 1 Franc, KM#4.

Date	Mintage	F	VF	XF	Unc	BU
1948(a)	5,000,000	6.00	15.00	35.00	80.00	150

KM# 6 5 FRANCS
Aluminum-Bronze, 20 mm. **Obv:** Head left **Rev:** Slender-horned gazelle head divides value within sprigs

Date	Mintage	F	VF	XF	Unc	BU
1956(a)	10,000,000	3.00	6.00	12.00	25.00	—

REPUBLIC
STANDARD COINAGE
100 Centimes = 1 Franc

KM# 13 500 FRANCS
7.0000 g., 0.9990 Silver 0.2248 oz. ASW, 30 mm. **Obv:** Arms with supporters **Rev:** Apollo 11 launch scene **Edge:** Plain

Date	Mintage	F	VF	XF	Unc	BU
ND(1999) Proof		—	Value: 35.00			

KM# 14 500 FRANCS
7.0000 g., 0.9990 Silver 0.2248 oz. ASW **Obv:** Arms with supporters **Rev:** Three astronauts, moon and space capsule

Date	Mintage	F	VF	XF	Unc	BU
ND(1999) Proof		—	Value: 35.00			

KM# 15 500 FRANCS
7.0000 g., 0.9990 Silver 0.2248 oz. ASW **Obv:** Arms with supporters **Rev:** Moon-walking astronaut

Date	Mintage	F	VF	XF	Unc	BU
ND(1999) Proof		—	Value: 35.00			

KM# 18 500 FRANCS
6.9300 g., 0.9990 Silver 0.2226 oz. ASW, 29.7 mm. **Obv:** National arms **Obv. Leg.:** REPUBLIQUE TOGOLAISE **Rev:** German Naval sailing ship **Rev. Leg.:** GORCH FOCK **Edge:** Plain

Date	Mintage	F	VF	XF	Unc	BU
ND(2000) Proof	5,000	Value: 35.00				

KM# 19   500 FRANCS
6.9300 g., 0.9990 Silver 0.2226 oz. ASW, 27.9 mm. **Obv:** Arms with supporters **Rev:** Head of Albert Einstein facing **Edge:** Plain

Date	Mintage	F	VF	XF	Unc	BU
ND Proof	—	Value: 35.00				

KM# 16   1000 FRANCS
14.9700 g., 0.9990 Silver 0.4808 oz. ASW, 35 mm. **Obv:** Arms with supporters **Rev:** Bust of Martin Luther 3/4 right **Edge:** Plain

Date	Mintage	F	VF	XF	Unc	BU
1999 Proof	—	Value: 50.00				

KM# 28   1000 FRANCS
14.9500 g., 0.9990 Silver 0.4802 oz. ASW, 35 mm. **Obv:** Arms with supporters **Rev:** Lion **Edge:** Plain

Date	Mintage	F	VF	XF	Unc	BU
2000 Proof	5,000	Value: 45.00				

KM# 8   5000 FRANCS
24.3600 g., 0.9250 Silver 0.7244 oz. ASW **Subject:** 10th Year of General Gnassingbe Eyadema as President **Obv:** Arms with supporters **Rev:** Head left

Date	Mintage	F	VF	XF	Unc	BU
1977 Proof	150	Value: 250				

KM# 9   10000 FRANCS
49.3200 g., 0.9250 Silver 1.4667 oz. ASW **Subject:** 10th Year of General Gnassingbe Eyadema as President **Obv:** Arms with supporters **Rev:** Head left

Date	Mintage	F	VF	XF	Unc	BU
1977 Proof	150	Value: 350				

KM# 10   15000 FRANCS
4.4800 g., 0.9170 Gold 0.1321 oz. AGW **Subject:** 10th Year of General Gnassingbe Eyadema as President **Obv:** Arms with supporters **Rev:** Head facing

Date	Mintage	F	VF	XF	Unc	BU
1977 Proof	75	Value: 200				

KM# 11   25000 FRANCS
9.0000 g., 0.9170 Gold 0.2653 oz. AGW **Subject:** 10th Year of General Gnassingbe Eyadema as President **Obv:** Arms with supporters **Rev:** Head facing

Date	Mintage	F	VF	XF	Unc	BU
1977 Proof	75	Value: 375				

KM# 12   50000 FRANCS
18.0000 g., 0.9170 Gold 0.5307 oz. AGW **Subject:** 10th Year of General Gnassingbe Eyadema as President **Obv:** Arms with supporters **Rev:** Head facing **Note:** Similar to 25,000 Francs, KM#11.

Date	Mintage	F	VF	XF	Unc	BU
1977 Proof	50	Value: 750				

ESSAIS

KM#	Date	Mintage	Identification	Mkt Val
E1	1924(a)	—	50 Centimes. Aluminum-Bronze. KM#1.	150
E2	1924(a)	—	Franc. Aluminum-Bronze. Head laureate left. Value within upright sprigs. KM#2.	150
E3	1924(a)	—	2 Francs. Aluminum-Bronze. KM#3.	200
E4	1948(a)	2,000	Franc. Copper-Nickel. KM#4.	30.00
E5	1948(a)	2,000	2 Francs. Copper-Nickel. KM#5.	37.50
E6	1956(a)	2,300	5 Francs. Aluminum-Bronze. KM#6.	15.00
E7	1956(a)	2,300	10 Francs. KM#7.	37.50
E8	1956(a)	2,300	25 Francs.	45.00
E9	1977	25	5000 Francs. Aluminum. KM#8.	200
E10	1977	20	5000 Francs. Copper. KM#8.	200
E11	1977	25	10000 Francs. Aluminum. KM#9.	275
E12	1977	20	10000 Francs. Copper. KM#9.	275
E13	1977	25	15000 Francs. Aluminum. KM#10.	100
E14	1977	20	15000 Francs. Copper. KM#10.	100
E15	1977	25	25000 Francs. Aluminum. KM#11.	150
E16	1977	20	25000 Francs. Copper. KM#11.	150

PIEFORTS

KM#	Date	Mintage	Identification	Mkt Val
P1	1977	5	5000 Francs. Copper. KM#8.	400
P2	1977	10	5000 Francs. Silver. 48.7200 g. KM#8.	400
P3	1977	5	10000 Francs. Copper. KM#9.	500
P3a	1977	10	10000 Francs. Silver. KM#9.	500
P4	1977	5	15000 Francs. Copper. KM#10.	325
P4a	1977	10	15000 Francs. Silver. KM#10.	200
P4b	1977	2	15000 Francs. Gold. KM#10.	800
P5	1977	5	25000 Francs. Copper. KM#11.	300
P5a	1977	10	25000 Francs. Silver. KM#11.	300
P5b	1977	2	25000 Francs. Gold. KM#11.	1,000
P6	1977	—	25000 Francs. Gold. KM#11.	900

PIEFORTS WITH ESSAIS

KM#	Date	Mintage	Identification	Mkt Val
PE1	1948(a)	104	Franc. Aluminum. KM#4.	85.00
PE2	1948(a)	104	2 Francs. Aluminum. KM#5.	95.00

TRIAL STRIKES

KM#	Date	Mintage	Identification	Mkt Val
TS1	1977	10	5000 Francs. Copper. Obverse of KM#8. PRUEBA.	200
TS2	1977	10	5000 Francs. Copper. Reverse of KM#8. PRUEBA.	200
TS3	1977	10	5000 Francs. Silver. Obverse of KM#8. PRUEBA.	250
TS4	1977	10	5000 Francs. Silver. Reverse of KM#8. PRUEBA.	250
TS5	1977	10	10000 Francs. Copper. Obverse of KM#9. PRUEBA.	250
TS6	1977	10	10000 Francs. Copper. Reverse of KM#9. PRUEBA.	250
TS7	1977	10	10000 Francs. Silver. Obverse of KM#9. PRUEBA.	300
TS8	1977	10	10000 Francs. Silver. Reverse of KM#9. PRUEBA.	300
TS9	1977	10	15000 Francs. Copper. Obverse of KM#10. PRUEBA.	100
TS10	1977	10	15000 Francs. Copper. Reverse of KM#10. PRUEBA.	100
TS11	1977	10	15000 Francs. Silver. Obverse of KM#10. PRUEBA.	125
TS12	1977	10	15000 Francs. Silver. Reverse of KM#10. PRUEBA.	125
TS13	1977	10	25000 Francs. Copper. Obverse of KM#11. PRUEBA.	150
TS14	1977	10	25000 Francs. Copper. Reverse of KM11. PRUEBA.	150
TS15	1977	10	25000 Francs. Silver. Obverse of KM#11. PRUEBA.	175
TS16	1977	10	25000 Francs. Silver. Reverse of KM#11. PRUEBA.	175

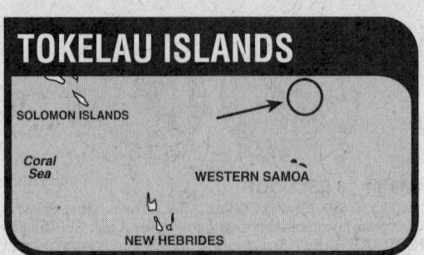

TOKELAU ISLANDS

Tokelau or Union Islands, a New Zealand Territory located in the South Pacific 2,100 miles (3,379 km.) northeast of New Zealand and 300 miles (483 km.) north of Samoa, has an area of 4 sq. mi. (10 sq. km.) and a population of *2,000. Geographically, the group consists of four atolls - Atafu, Nukunono, Fakaofo and Swains – but the last belongs to American Samoa (and the United States claims the other three). The people are of Polynesian origin; Samoan is the official language. The New Zealand Minister for Foreign Affairs governs the islands; councils of family elders handle local government at the village level. The chief settlement is Fenuafala, on Fakaofo. It is connected by wireless with the offices of the New Zealand Administrative Center, located at Apia, Western Samoa. Subsistence farming and the production of copra for export are the main occupations. Revenue is also derived from the sale of postage stamps and, since 1978, coins.

Great Britain annexed the group of islands in 1889. They were added to the Gilbert and Ellice Islands colony in 1916. In 1926, they were brought under the jurisdiction of Western Samoa, which was held as a mandate of the League of Nations by New Zealand. They were declared a part of New Zealand in 1948. Tokelau Islands issued its first coin in 1978, a "$1 TahiTala," Tokelauan for "One Dollar."

RULER
British

MINT MARK
PM - Pobjoy

NEW ZEALAND TERRITORY
STANDARD COINAGE

KM# 1   TALA
Copper-Nickel, 38.5 mm. **Ruler:** Elizabeth II **Obv:** Young bust right **Rev:** Coconut and value **Edge:** Reeded

Date	Mintage	F	VF	XF	Unc	BU
1978	10,000	—	—	3.00	12.00	17.50

KM# 1a   TALA
27.2500 g., 0.9250 Silver 0.8104 oz. ASW, 38.5 mm. **Ruler:** Elizabeth II **Obv:** Young bust right **Rev:** Coconut and value

Date	Mintage	F	VF	XF	Unc	BU
1978 Proof	5,000	Value: 22.50				

KM# 2   TALA
Copper-Nickel, 38.5 mm. **Ruler:** Elizabeth II **Obv:** Young bust right **Rev:** V-shaped tool, bucket, rope and value

Date	Mintage	F	VF	XF	Unc	BU
1979	—	—	—	2.50	10.00	15.00

KM# 2a TALA
27.2500 g., 0.9250 Silver 0.8104 oz. ASW, 38.5 mm.
Ruler: Elizabeth II **Obv:** Young bust right **Rev:** V-shaped tool, bucket, rope and value

Date	Mintage	F	VF	XF	Unc	BU
1979 Proof	—	Value: 20.00				

KM# 3 TALA
Copper-Nickel **Ruler:** Elizabeth II **Obv:** Young bust right
Rev: Coconut crab and value **Edge:** Reeded

Date	Mintage	F	VF	XF	Unc	BU
1980	10,000	—	—	4.00	15.00	20.00

KM# 3a TALA
27.2500 g., 0.9250 Silver 0.8104 oz. ASW, 38.5 mm. **Ruler:** Elizabeth II **Obv:** Young bust right **Rev:** Coconut Crab and value

Date	Mintage	F	VF	XF	Unc	BU
1980 Proof	6,004	Value: 24.00				

KM# 4 TALA
Copper-Nickel **Ruler:** Elizabeth II **Obv:** Young bust right **Rev:** Frigate bird and value

Date	Mintage	F	VF	XF	Unc	BU
1981	6,500	—	—	4.00	15.00	20.00

KM# 4a TALA
27.2500 g., 0.9250 Silver 0.8104 oz. ASW, 38.5 mm. **Ruler:** Elizabeth II **Obv:** Arnold Machin **Rev:** Frigate bird and value

Date	Mintage	F	VF	XF	Unc	BU
1981 Proof	6,500	Value: 27.10				

KM# 5 TALA
Copper-Nickel, 38.5 mm. **Ruler:** Elizabeth II **Obv:** Young bust right **Rev:** Outrigger canoe **Edge:** Reeded

Date	Mintage	F	VF	XF	Unc	BU
1982	10,000	—	—	5.00	18.00	22.50

KM# 5a TALA
27.2500 g., 0.9250 Silver 0.8104 oz. ASW, 38.5 mm.
Ruler: Elizabeth II **Obv:** Young bust right **Rev:** Outrigger canoe

Date	Mintage	F	VF	XF	Unc	BU
1982 Proof	5,000	Value: 27.50				

KM# 6 TALA
Copper-Nickel, 38.5 mm. **Ruler:** Elizabeth II **Subject:** Water Conservation **Obv:** Young bust right **Rev:** Seated and standing figure next to ancient water barrel

Date	Mintage	F	VF	XF	Unc	BU
1983	2,000	—	—	—	30.00	50.00

KM# 7 5 TALA
28.2800 g., 0.9250 Silver 0.8410 oz. ASW **Ruler:** Elizabeth II **Subject:** Water Conservation **Obv:** Young bust right **Rev:** Seated and standing figure next to ancient water barrel **Note:** Similar to 1 Tala, KM#6.

Date	Mintage	F	VF	XF	Unc	BU
1983 Proof	1,000	Value: 65.00				

KM# 8.1 5 TALA
27.0500 g., 0.9250 Silver 0.8044 oz. ASW **Ruler:** Elizabeth II **Obv:** Young bust right **Rev:** Fishermen in sailboat **Edge:** Plain

Date	Mintage	F	VF	XF	Unc	BU
1984	1,500	—	—	—	35.00	55.00

KM# 8.2 5 TALA
27.0500 g., 0.9250 Silver 0.8044 oz. ASW **Ruler:** Elizabeth II **Obv:** Young bust right **Rev:** Fishermen in sailboat **Edge:** Reeded

Date	Mintage	F	VF	XF	Unc	BU
1984 Proof	500	Value: 75.00				

KM# 10 5 TALA
27.0500 g., 0.9250 Silver 0.8044 oz. ASW **Ruler:** Elizabeth II **Series:** Olympics **Obv:** Young bust right **Rev:** Javelin thrower

Date	Mintage	F	VF	XF	Unc	BU
1988	20,000	—	—	—	15.00	17.50

KM# 9 5 TALA
27.2100 g., 0.9250 Silver 0.8092 oz. ASW **Ruler:** Elizabeth II **Obv:** Crowned head right **Rev:** Captain John Byron and HMS Dolphin **Edge:** Reeded

Date	Mintage	F	VF	XF	Unc	BU
1989 Proof	500	Value: 30.00				

KM# 11 5 TALA
Copper-Nickel **Ruler:** Elizabeth II **Subject:** 50th Anniversary of Attack on Pearl Harbor **Obv:** Crowned bust right **Rev:** Pearl Harbor scene within circle

Date	Mintage	F	VF	XF	Unc	BU
1991 Prooflike	—	—	—	—	5.00	7.00

KM# 13 5 TALA
Copper-Nickel **Ruler:** Elizabeth II **Obv:** Crowned bust right **Rev:** Battle of Guadal canal scene within circle

Date	Mintage	F	VF	XF	Unc	BU
1991 Proof-like	—	—	—	—	5.00	7.00

KM# 14 5 TALA
Copper-Nickel **Ruler:** Elizabeth II **Obv:** Crowned bust right **Rev:** General Dwight Eisenhower saluting left

Date	Mintage	F	VF	XF	Unc	BU
1991 Proof-like	—	—	—	—	5.00	7.00

KM# 15   5 TALA
Copper-Nickel **Ruler:** Elizabeth II **Obv:** Crowned bust right
Rev: Raising the flag on Iwo Jima scene

Date		Mintage	F	VF	XF	Unc	BU
1991 Proof-like	•	—	—	—	—	5.00	7.00

KM# 16   5 TALA
31.4700 g., 0.9250 Silver 0.9359 oz. ASW **Ruler:** Elizabeth II
Obv: Crowned head right **Rev:** Scene of first lunar orbit

Date	Mintage	F	VF	XF	Unc	BU
1993 Proof	10,000	Value: 30.00				

KM# 17   5 TALA
31.4700 g., 0.9250 Silver 0.9359 oz. ASW **Ruler:** Elizabeth II
Series: Endangered Wildlife **Obv:** Crowned head right
Rev: Steindachner's Emo Skink

Date	Mintage	F	VF	XF	Unc	BU
1993 Proof	15,000	Value: 30.00				

KM# 18   5 TALA
31.4700 g., 0.9250 Silver 0.9359 oz. ASW **Ruler:** Elizabeth II
Obv: Crowned head right **Rev:** H.M.S. Pandora

Date	Mintage	F	VF	XF	Unc	BU
1993 Proof	15,000	Value: 28.00				

KM# 19   5 TALA
31.4700 g., 0.9250 Silver 0.9359 oz. ASW **Ruler:** Elizabeth II
Series: Olympics **Obv:** Crowned head right **Rev:** Swimmers

Date	Mintage	F	VF	XF	Unc	BU
1994 Proof	40,000	Value: 22.50				

KM# 20   5 TALA
31.4700 g., 0.9250 Silver 0.9359 oz. ASW **Ruler:** Elizabeth II
Subject: World Cup Soccer **Obv:** Crowned head right
Rev: Soccer player and flying bird within globe design

Date	Mintage	F	VF	XF	Unc	BU
1994 Proof	25,000	Value: 20.00				

KM# 21   5 TALA
31.4700 g., 0.9250 Silver 0.9359 oz. ASW **Ruler:** Elizabeth II
Series: Protect Our World **Obv:** Crowned head right **Rev:** Swamp
scene

Date	Mintage	F	VF	XF	Unc	BU
1994 Proof	10,000	Value: 20.00				

KM# 22   5 TALA
31.4700 g., 0.9250 Silver 0.9359 oz. ASW **Ruler:** Elizabeth II
Series: Olympics **Obv:** Crowned head right **Rev:** Sailboarding

Date	Mintage	F	VF	XF	Unc	BU
1994 Proof	50,000	Value: 25.00				

KM# 23   5 TALA
31.4700 g., 0.9250 Silver 0.9359 oz. ASW **Ruler:** Elizabeth II
Series: Queen Elizabeth The Queen Mother **Obv:** Crowned head
right **Rev:** Queen Mother, daughter and son

Date	Mintage	F	VF	XF	Unc	BU
1995 Proof	30,000	Value: 22.50				

KM# 27   5 TALA
31.5500 g., 0.9250 Silver 0.9382 oz. ASW, 38.5 mm.
Ruler: Elizabeth II **Series:** Queen Elizabeth The Queen Mother
Subject: VE Day Celebrations, 8th of May **Obv:** Crowned head
right **Rev:** 1/2 Figures of royal couple facing within beaded circle
Edge: Reeded

Date	Mintage	F	VF	XF	Unc	BU
1997 Proof	—	Value: 25.00				

KM# 25   5 TALA
31.4700 g., 0.9250 Silver 0.9359 oz. ASW, 38.5 mm.
Ruler: Elizabeth II **Obv:** Crowned head right **Rev:** H.M.S. Dolphin
Edge: Reeded

Date	Mintage	F	VF	XF	Unc	BU
1998 Proof	—	Value: 30.00				

KM# 29   5 TALA
31.5200 g., 0.9250 Silver 0.9373 oz. ASW, 38.6 mm.
Ruler: Elizabeth II **Subject:** Diana Princess Of Wales
Obv: Crowned head right **Rev:** Diana and young dancers
Edge: Reeded

Date	Mintage	F	VF	XF	Unc	BU
1999 Proof	—	Value: 35.00				

KM# 26 5 TALA
28.1200 g., 0.9250 Silver 0.8362 oz. ASW, 38.4 mm.
Ruler: Elizabeth II **Subject:** Queen Mother **Obv:** Crowned head right **Rev:** Queen Mother celebrating "VE" day **Edge:** Reeded

Date	Mintage		VF	XF	Unc	BU
2000 Proof	10,000	Value: 25.00				

Note: With gold gilt outer ring

KM# 12 50 TALA
31.1030 g., 0.9990 Silver 0.9989 oz. ASW **Ruler:** Elizabeth II **Subject:** 50th Anniversary of Attack on Pearl Harbor **Obv:** Crowned bust right **Rev:** Pearl Harbor scene

Date	Mintage	F	VF	XF	Unc	BU
1991 Proof	50,000	Value: 35.00				

KM# 34 50 TALA
31.1000 g., Silver **Ruler:** Elizabeth II **Obv:** Crowned bust right **Obv. Leg.:** TOKELAU **Rev:** Battle of Guadalcanal

Date	Mintage	F	VF	XF	Unc	BU
1991 Proof	50,000	Value: 35.00				

KM# 35 50 TALA
31.1000 g., Silver **Ruler:** Elizabeth II **Obv:** Crowned bust right **Obv. Leg.:** TOKELAU **Rev:** Mount Sirubachi and Iwo Jima battle scene

Date	Mintage	F	VF	XF	Unc	BU
1991 Proof	50,000	Value: 35.00				

KM# 36 50 TALA
31.1000 g., Silver **Ruler:** Elizabeth II **Obv:** Crowned bust right **Obv. Leg.:** TOKELAU **Rev:** General Dwight D. Eisenhower and troups

Date	Mintage	F	VF	XF	Unc	BU
1991 Proof	50,000	Value: 35.00				

KM# 28 50 TALA
31.2500 g., 0.9990 Silver 1.0037 oz. ASW, 38.6 mm.
Ruler: Elizabeth II **Subject:** Anne Frank **Obv:** Crowned bust right **Rev:** Building arch and head facing within circle **Edge:** Reeded

Date	Mintage	F	VF	XF	Unc	BU
1993 Proof	—	Value: 30.00				

KM# 37 50 TALA
31.1000 g., 0.9990 Silver 0.9988 oz. ASW **Ruler:** Elizabeth II **Series:** World War II **Obv:** Crowned bust right **Obv. Leg.:** TOKELAU **Rev:** Three airplanes and carrier **Rev. Leg.:** • CARRIERS • THE STRIKE FORCE • **Edge:** Reeded

Date	Mintage	F	VF	XF	Unc	BU
1993 Proof	—	Value: 30.00				

KM# 38 50 TALA
31.1000 g., 0.9990 Silver 0.9988 oz. ASW **Ruler:** Elizabeth II **Series:** World War II **Obv:** Crowned bust right **Obv. Leg.:** TOKELAU **Rev:** Bust of pilot 3/4 right, three planes at right in background **Rev. Leg.:** • TUSKEGEE AIRMEN • **Edge:** Reeded

Date	Mintage	F	VF	XF	Unc	BU
1993 Proof	—	Value: 30.00				

KM# 39 50 TALA
31.1000 g., 0.9990 Silver 0.9988 oz. ASW **Ruler:** Elizabeth II **Series:** World War II **Obv:** Crowned bust right **Obv. Leg.:** TOKELAU **Rev:** Headdress at left, bust of Navajo soldier at right on radio **Rev. Leg.:** NATIVE AMERICAN CODE TALKERS **Edge:** Reeded

Date	Mintage	F	VF	XF	Unc	BU
1993 Proof	—	Value: 30.00				

KM# 40 50 TALA
31.1000 g., 0.9990 Silver 0.9988 oz. ASW **Ruler:** Elizabeth II **Series:** World War II **Obv:** Crowned bust right **Obv. Leg.:** TOKELAU **Rev:** Bust of WAC facing saluting **Rev. Leg.:** WOMEN IN THE ARMED FORCES **Edge:** Reeded

Date	Mintage	F	VF	XF	Unc	BU
1993 Proof	—	Value: 30.00				

KM# 41 50 TALA
31.1000 g., 0.9990 Silver 0.9988 oz. ASW **Ruler:** Elizabeth II **Series:** World War II **Obv:** Crowned bust right **Obv. Leg.:** TOKELAU **Rev:** 1/2 length bust of Polish soldier at left, patroling soldiers in background **Rev. Leg.:** POLISH FREEDOM FIGHTERS **Edge:** Reeded

Date	Mintage	F	VF	XF	Unc	BU
1993 Proof	—	Value: 30.00				

KM# 42 50 TALA
31.1000 g., 0.9990 Silver 0.9988 oz. ASW **Ruler:** Elizabeth II **Series:** World War II **Obv:** Crowned bust right **Obv. Leg.:** TOKELAU **Rev:** P. O. W. camp, guard tower **Rev. Leg.:** M. I. A.s + P. O. W.s **Edge:** Reeded

Date	Mintage	F	VF	XF	Unc	BU
1993 Proof	—	Value: 30.00				

KM# 44 50 TALA
7.7800 g., 0.5833 Gold 0.1459 oz. AGW, 24.5 mm.
Ruler: Elizabeth II **Subject:** 50th Anniversary Birth of Prince Charles **Obv:** Crowned head right **Obv. Leg.:** TOKELAU **Rev:** Queen Mother and Princess Elizabeth seated holding Prince Charles **Rev. Leg.:** QUEEN ELIZABETH THE QUEEN MOTHER **Edge:** Reeded

Date	Mintage	F	VF	XF	Unc	BU
1998 Proof	—	Value: 250				

KM# 31 10 TALA
1.2440 g., 0.9990 Gold 0.0400 oz. AGW, 13.92 mm.
Ruler: Elizabeth II **Obv:** Elizabeth II **Rev:** Ship, the Golden Hind above value **Edge:** Reeded

Date	Mintage	F	VF	XF	Unc	BU
1997 Proof	—	Value: 52.50				

KM# 43 10 TALA
1.2400 g., 0.9990 Gold 0.0398 oz. AGW **Ruler:** Elizabeth II **Obv:** Crowned head right **Obv. Leg.:** TOKELAU **Rev:** Sailing ship **Rev. Leg.:** GOLDEN HIND **Edge:** Reeded

Date	Mintage	F	VF	XF	Unc	BU
1997 Proof	25,000	Value: 70.00				

KM# 45 10 TALA
1.2400 g., 0.9990 Gold 0.0398 oz. AGW **Ruler:** Elizabeth II **Obv:** Crowned head right **Obv. Leg.:** TOKELAU **Rev:** Sea maiden and turtle **Edge:** Reeded

Date	Mintage	F	VF	XF	Unc	BU
1999 Proof	25,000	Value: 55.00				

KM# 24 100 TALA
1000.0000 g., 0.9990 Silver 32.117 oz. ASW, 100 mm.
Ruler: Elizabeth II **Subject:** Warships; H.M.S. Dolphin, Pandora and General Jackson **Obv:** Crowned head right **Rev:** Three sailing warships and compass face **Note:** Illustration reduced.

Date	Mintage	F	VF	XF	Unc	BU
1996 Proof	1,500	Value: 850				

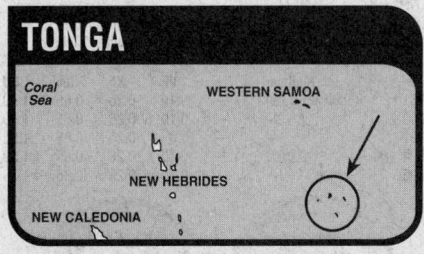

TONGA

Coral Sea

WESTERN SAMOA

NEW HEBRIDES

NEW CALEDONIA

The Kingdom of Tonga (or Friendly Islands) is an archipelago situated in the southern Pacific Ocean south of Western Samoa and east of Fiji comprised of 150 islands. Tonga has an area of 270 sq. mi. (748 sq. km.) and a population of *100,000. Capital: Nuku'alofa. Primarily agricultural, the kingdom exports bananas and copra.

Dutch navigators Willem Schouten and Jacob Lemaire were the first Europeans to visit Tonga in 1616. The noted Dutch explorer Abel Tasman who visited the Tongatapu group in 1643 followed them. No further European contact was made until 1773 when British navigator Capt. James Cook arrived and, impressed by the peaceful deportment of the natives, named the islands the Friendly Islands. Within a few years of Cook's visit, Tonga was embroiled in a civil war that lasted until the great chief Taufa'ahau, who reigned as Siasoi Tupou I (1845-93), was converted to Christianity and brought unity and peace to the islands. Tonga became a self-governing protectorate of Great Britain in 1900 and a fully independent state on June 4, 1970. The monarchy is a member of the Commonwealth of Nations. King Taufa'ahau is Head of State and Government.

RULERS
Queen Salote, 1918-1965
King Taufa'ahau IV, 1967—2006

KINGDOM
STANDARD COINAGE

16 Pounds = 1 Koula

KM# 1 1/4 KOULA
8.1250 g., 0.9160 Gold 0.2393 oz. AGW **Ruler:** Queen Salote **Obv:** Head right **Rev:** Crowned arms

Date	Mintage	F	VF	XF	Unc	BU
1962	—	—	—	—	—	250
1962 Proof	6,300	Value: 265				

KM# 1a 1/4 KOULA
Platinum APW **Ruler:** Queen Salote **Obv:** Head right **Rev:** Crowned arms

Date	Mintage	F	VF	XF	Unc	BU
1962 Proof	—	Value: 600				

KM# 2 1/2 KOULA
16.2500 g., 0.9160 Gold 0.4785 oz. AGW **Ruler:** Queen Salote **Obv:** Crowned arms **Rev:** Standing female half left

Date	Mintage	F	VF	XF	Unc	BU
1962	—	—	—	—	—	480
1962 Proof	3,000	Value: 500				

KM# 2a 1/2 KOULA
Platinum APW **Ruler:** Queen Salote **Obv:** Crowned arms **Rev:** Standing female half left

Date	Mintage	F	VF	XF	Unc	BU
1962 Proof	—	Value: 850				

KM# 3 KOULA
32.5000 g., 0.9160 Gold 0.9571 oz. AGW **Ruler:** Queen Salote **Obv:** Crowned arms below value **Rev:** Standing figure half left

Date	Mintage	F	VF	XF	Unc	BU
1962	1,500	—	—	—	—	950
1962 Proof	—	Value: 970				

KM# 3a KOULA
Platinum APW **Ruler:** Queen Salote **Obv:** Crowned arms below value **Rev:** Standing figure half left

Date	Mintage	F	VF	XF	Unc	BU
1962 Proof	—	Value: 1,350				

DECIMAL COINAGE

100 Senti = 1 Pa'anga; 100 Pa'anga = 1 Hau

KM# 4 SENITI
1.8500 g., Bronze, 17.5 mm. **Ruler:** King Taufa'ahau Tupou IV **Obv:** Head right **Rev:** Giant Tortoise **Edge:** Plain

Date	Mintage	F	VF	XF	Unc	BU
1967	500,000	—	0.10	0.15	1.00	2.50
1967 Proof	—	Value: 2.00				

KM# 27   SENITI
1.8500 g., Bronze, 17.5 mm. **Ruler:** King Taufa'ahau Tupou IV
Obv: Head right **Rev:** Giant tortoise **Edge:** Plain

Date	Mintage	F	VF	XF	Unc	BU
1968	500,000	—	0.10	0.15	1.00	2.00
1968 Proof	—	Value: 2.50				

KM# 27a   SENITI
1.6900 g., Brass, 17.5 mm. **Ruler:** King Taufa'ahau Tupou IV
Obv: Head right **Rev:** Giant tortoise **Edge:** Plain

Date	Mintage	F	VF	XF	Unc	BU
1974	500,000	—	0.10	0.15	0.75	1.50

KM# 42   SENITI
1.8500 g., Bronze, 17.5 mm. **Series:** F.A.O. **Obv:** Ear of corn **Rev:** Sow right **Edge:** Plain

Date	Mintage	F	VF	XF	Unc	BU
1975	1,000,000	—	—	0.10	0.45	1.25
1979	1,000,000	—	—	0.10	0.45	1.25

KM# 66   SENITI
1.8000 g., Bronze, 16.51 mm. **Ruler:** King Taufa'ahau Tupou IV
Series: World Food Day **Obv:** Ear of corn **Rev:** Vanilla plant
Edge: Plain

Date	Mintage	F	VF	XF	Unc	BU
1981	1,544,000	—	—	0.10	0.45	0.80
1990	—	—	—	0.10	0.35	0.75
1991	—	—	—	0.10	0.35	0.75
1994	500,000	—	—	0.10	0.35	0.75
1996	—	—	—	0.10	0.35	0.75

KM# 5   2 SENITI
3.9000 g., Bronze, 21 mm. **Ruler:** King Taufa'ahau Tupou IV
Obv: Head right **Rev:** Giant Tortoise **Edge:** Plain

Date	Mintage	F	VF	XF	Unc	BU
1967	500,000	—	0.10	0.20	1.50	3.00
1967 Proof	—	Value: 3.00				

KM# 28   2 SENITI
3.9000 g., Bronze, 21 mm. **Ruler:** King Taufa'ahau Tupou IV
Obv: Head right **Rev:** Giant tortoise **Edge:** Plain

Date	Mintage	F	VF	XF	Unc	BU
1968	200,000	—	0.10	0.20	1.75	3.00
1968 Proof	—	Value: 3.80				
1974	25,000	—	0.10	0.20	1.75	3.00

KM# 43   2 SENITI
3.9000 g., Bronze, 21 mm. **Ruler:** King Taufa'ahau Tupou IV
Series: F.A.O. **Obv:** Two watermelons **Rev:** Paper doll cutouts
form design in center circle of wreath **Edge:** Plain

Date	Mintage	F	VF	XF	Unc	BU
1975	400,000	—	—	0.15	0.65	1.50
1979	500,000	—	—	0.15	0.65	1.50

KM# 67   2 SENITI
3.8700 g., Bronze, 19.46 mm. **Ruler:** King Taufa'ahau Tupou IV
Series: World Food Day **Obv:** Taro Plants **Rev:** Paper doll
cutouts form design in center circle of wreath **Edge:** Plain

Date	Mintage	F	VF	XF	Unc	BU
1981	1,102,000	—	—	0.15	0.65	1.35
1990	—	—	—	0.15	0.50	1.25
1991	—	—	—	0.15	0.50	1.25
1994	250,000	—	—	0.15	0.50	1.25
1996	—	—	—	0.15	0.50	1.25

KM# 6   5 SENITI
2.8000 g., Copper-Nickel, 19.5 mm. **Ruler:** King Taufa'ahau
Tupou IV **Obv:** Head right **Rev:** Value and stars flanked by sprigs
Edge: Plain

Date	Mintage	F	VF	XF	Unc	BU
1967	300,000	—	0.10	0.25	1.75	2.50
1967 Proof	—	Value: 3.50				

KM# 29   5 SENITI
2.8000 g., Copper-Nickel, 19.5 mm. **Ruler:** King Taufa'ahau
Tupou IV **Obv:** Head right **Rev:** Value and stars flanked by sprigs

Date	Mintage	F	VF	XF	Unc	BU
1968	100,000	—	0.10	0.25	1.50	2.25
1968 Proof	—	Value: 2.50				
1974	75,000	—	0.10	0.25	1.50	2.25

KM# 44   5 SENITI
2.8000 g., Copper-Nickel, 19.5 mm. **Ruler:** King Taufa'ahau
Tupou IV **Series:** F.A.O. **Obv:** Hen with chicks **Rev:** Banana bunch

Date	Mintage	F	VF	XF	Unc	BU
1975	100,000	—	0.10	0.25	1.00	1.75
1977	110,000	—	0.10	0.25	1.00	1.75
1979	100,000	—	0.10	0.25	1.00	1.75

KM# 68   5 SENITI
2.8000 g., Copper-Nickel, 19.5 mm. **Ruler:** King Taufa'ahau
Tupou IV **Series:** World Food Day **Obv:** Hen with chicks
Rev: Coconuts above sprig **Edge:** Reeded

Date	Mintage	F	VF	XF	Unc	BU
1981	941,000	—	0.10	0.25	0.85	1.50
1990	—	—	0.10	0.25	0.85	1.50
1991	—	—	—	0.25	0.85	1.50
1994	200,000	—	0.10	0.25	0.85	1.50
1996	—	—	—	0.25	0.75	1.25

KM# 7   10 SENITI
5.6500 g., Copper-Nickel, 23.5 mm. **Ruler:** King Taufa'ahau
Tupou IV **Obv:** Head right **Rev:** Value and stars flanked by sprigs

Date	Mintage	F	VF	XF	Unc	BU
1967	300,000	—	0.20	0.35	1.85	2.50
1967 Proof	—	Value: 3.50				

KM# 30   10 SENITI
5.6500 g., Copper-Nickel, 23.5 mm. **Ruler:** King Taufa'ahau
Tupou IV **Obv:** Head right **Rev:** Value and stars flanked by sprigs

Date	Mintage	F	VF	XF	Unc	BU
1968	100,000	—	0.20	0.40	1.75	2.25
1968 Proof	—	Value: 3.00				
1974	50,000	—	0.25	0.30	1.75	2.25

KM# 45   10 SENITI
5.6500 g., Copper-Nickel, 23.5 mm. **Ruler:** King Taufa'ahau
Tupou IV **Series:** F.A.O. **Obv:** Uniformed bust facing **Rev:** Cows
in pasture

Date	Mintage	F	VF	XF	Unc	BU
1975	75,000	—	0.20	0.30	1.25	2.00
1977	25,000	—	0.20	0.30	1.25	2.00
1979	100,000	—	0.20	0.30	1.25	2.00

KM# 69   10 SENITI
5.6500 g., Copper-Nickel, 23.5 mm. **Ruler:** King Taufa'ahau
Tupou IV **Series:** World Food Day **Obv:** Uniformed bust facing
Rev: Banana tree **Edge:** Reeded

Date	Mintage	F	VF	XF	Unc	BU
1981	712,000	—	0.20	0.30	1.25	2.00
1990	—	—	0.20	0.30	1.00	1.75
1991	—	—	0.20	0.30	1.00	1.75
1994	140,000	—	0.20	0.30	1.00	1.75
1996	—	—	0.20	0.30	1.00	1.75

KM# 8   20 SENITI
11.3000 g., Copper-Nickel, 28.5 mm. **Ruler:** King Taufa'ahau
Tupou IV **Obv:** Head right **Rev:** Crowned arms

Date	Mintage	F	VF	XF	Unc	BU
1967	150,000	—	0.25	0.50	2.25	3.50
1967 Proof	—	Value: 4.50				

KM# 13   20 SENITI
11.3000 g., Copper-Nickel, 28.5 mm. **Ruler:** King Taufa'ahau
Tupou IV **Subject:** Coronation of Taufa'ahau Tupou IV
Obv: Head right, small crowns around border **Rev:** Crowned
arms **Edge:** Reeded

Date	Mintage	F	VF	XF	Unc	BU
ND(1967)	15,000	—	0.50	1.25	2.25	3.50
ND(1967) Proof	—	Value: 3.50				

KM# 31 20 SENITI
11.3000 g., Copper-Nickel, 28.5 mm. **Ruler:** King Taufa'ahau Tupou IV **Obv:** Head right **Rev:** Crowned arms

Date	Mintage	F	VF	XF	Unc	BU
1968	35,000	—	0.25	0.50	2.00	2.75
1968 Proof	—	Value: 3.00				
1974	50,000	—	0.25	0.50	2.00	2.75

KM# 46 20 SENITI
11.3000 g., Copper-Nickel, 28.5 mm. **Ruler:** King Taufa'ahau Tupou IV **Series:** F.A.O. **Obv:** Uniformed bust facing **Rev:** Box hive and 20 bees

Date	Mintage	F	VF	XF	Unc	BU
1975	75,000	—	0.25	0.60	2.00	4.00
1977	25,000	—	0.25	0.60	2.00	4.00
1979	50,000	—	0.25	0.60	2.00	4.00

KM# 70 20 SENITI
11.3000 g., Copper-Nickel, 28.5 mm. **Ruler:** King Taufa'ahau Tupou IV **Series:** World Food Day **Obv:** Uniformed bust facing **Obv. Leg.:** TONGA **Rev:** Yams **Rev. Leg.:** FAKALAHI ME'AKAI **Edge:** Reeded

Date	Mintage	F	VF	XF	Unc	BU
1981	610,000	—	0.25	0.50	1.50	2.50
1990	610,000	—	0.25	0.50	1.25	2.25
1991	—	—	0.25	0.50	1.25	2.25
1994	680,000	—	0.25	0.50	1.25	2.00
1996	—	—	0.25	0.50	1.25	2.00

KM# 9 50 SENITI
18.0000 g., Copper-Nickel, 34.5 mm. **Ruler:** King Taufa'ahau Tupou IV **Obv:** Head right **Rev:** Crowned arms

Date	Mintage	F	VF	XF	Unc	BU
1967	75,000	—	0.75	1.25	2.75	4.00
1967 Proof	—	Value: 5.00				

KM# 15 50 SENITI
Copper-Nickel, 34.5 mm. **Ruler:** King Taufa'ahau Tupou IV **Subject:** Coronation of Taufa'ahau Tupou IV **Obv:** Head right **Rev:** Crowned arms

Date	Mintage	F	VF	XF	Unc	BU
ND(1967)	15,000	—	1.00	1.75	3.00	4.50
ND(1967) Proof	—	Value: 6.00				

KM# 32 50 SENITI
17.8000 g., Copper-Nickel, 34.5 mm. **Ruler:** King Taufa'ahau Tupou IV **Obv:** Head right **Rev:** Crowned arms

Date	Mintage	F	VF	XF	Unc	BU
1968	25,000	—	0.75	1.25	2.25	3.50
1968 Proof	—	Value: 4.00				

KM# 41 50 SENITI
14.6000 g., Copper-Nickel, 32.5 mm. **Ruler:** King Taufa'ahau Tupou IV **Obv:** Head right **Rev:** Crowned arms **Edge:** Plain

Date	Mintage	F	VF	XF	Unc	BU
1974	50,000	—	0.75	1.25	2.00	3.50

KM# 47 50 SENITI
14.6000 g., Copper-Nickel, 32.5 mm. **Ruler:** King Taufa'ahau Tupou IV **Series:** F.A.O. **Obv:** Uniformed bust facing **Rev:** 50 Fish swimming in circle formation **Edge:** Plain

Date	Mintage	F	VF	XF	Unc	BU
1975	40,000	—	0.50	1.00	2.25	4.00
1977	20,000	—	0.75	1.25	2.75	5.00
1978	60,000	—	0.50	1.00	2.25	4.00

KM# 71 50 SENITI
14.6000 g., Copper-Nickel, 32.5 mm. **Ruler:** King Taufa'ahau Tupou IV **Series:** World Food Day **Obv:** Uniformed bust facing **Obv. Leg.:** TONGA **Rev:** Tomato plants **Rev. Leg.:** FAKALAHI ME'AKAI **Edge:** Plain

Date	Mintage	F	VF	XF	Unc	BU
1981	555,000	—	0.45	0.75	1.75	3.00
1990	—	—	0.45	0.75	1.50	3.00
1991	—	—	0.45	0.75	1.50	2.75
1994	41,000	—	0.45	0.75	1.50	2.75
1996	—	—	0.45	0.75	1.50	2.50

KM# 82 50 SENITI
Copper-Nickel, 38.5 mm. **Ruler:** King Taufa'ahau Tupou IV **Subject:** 100th Anniversary of Automobile Industry **Obv:** Head right **Rev:** Silver Ghost and Camargue by Rolls-Royce **Edge:** Reeded

Date	Mintage	F	VF	XF	Unc	BU
1985	Est. 20,000	—	—	—	3.50	4.00

KM# 83 50 SENITI
Copper-Nickel, 38.5 mm. **Ruler:** King Taufa'ahau Tupou IV **Subject:** 100th Anniversary of Automobile Industry **Obv:** Head right **Rev:** Range Rover and Land Rover **Edge:** Reeded

Date	Mintage	F	VF	XF	Unc	BU
1985	Est. 20,000	—	—	—	3.50	4.00

KM# 84 50 SENITI
Copper-Nickel, 38.5 mm. **Ruler:** King Taufa'ahau Tupou IV **Subject:** 100th Anniversary of Automobile Industry **Obv:** Head right **Rev:** Cowley Touring Car and Morris Mini **Edge:** Reeded

Date	Mintage	F	VF	XF	Unc	BU
1985	Est. 20,000	—	—	—	3.50	4.00

KM# 85 50 SENITI
Copper-Nickel, 38.5 mm. **Ruler:** King Taufa'ahau Tupou IV **Subject:** 100th Anniversary of Automobile Industry **Obv:** Head right **Rev:** MGB GT and MG TA **Edge:** Reeded

Date	Mintage	F	VF	XF	Unc	BU
1985	Est. 20,000	—	—	—	3.50	4.00

KM# 98 50 SENITI
Copper-Nickel, 38.5 mm. **Ruler:** King Taufa'ahau Tupou IV **Subject:** 85th Birthday of Queen Mother **Obv:** Head right **Rev:** Queen Mother as a young girl **Edge:** Reeded

Date	Mintage	F	VF	XF	Unc	BU
1985	Est. 20,000	—	—	—	3.00	3.50

KM# 99   50 SENITI
Copper-Nickel, 38.5 mm.   **Ruler:** King Taufa'ahau Tupou IV
Subject: 85th Birthday of Queen Mother **Obv:** Head right
Rev: Wedding of King George VI and Elizabeth **Edge:** Reeded

Date	Mintage	F	VF	XF	Unc	BU
1985	Est. 20,000	—	—	—	3.00	3.50

KM# 100   50 SENITI
Copper-Nickel, 38.5 mm.   **Ruler:** King Taufa'ahau Tupou IV
Subject: 85th Birthday of Queen Mother **Obv:** Head right
Rev: King George VI and Elizabeth **Edge:** Reeded

Date	Mintage	F	VF	XF	Unc	BU
1985	Est. 20,000	—	—	—	3.00	3.50

KM# 101   50 SENITI
Copper-Nickel, 38.5 mm.   **Ruler:** King Taufa'ahau Tupou IV
Subject: 85th Birthday of Queen Mother **Obv:** Head right
Rev: Queen Mother holding Queen Elizabeth II **Edge:** Reeded

Date	Mintage	F	VF	XF	Unc	BU
1985	Est. 20,000	—	—	—	3.00	3.50

KM# 102   50 SENITI
Copper-Nickel, 38.5 mm.   **Ruler:** King Taufa'ahau Tupou IV
Subject: 85th Birthday of Queen Mother **Obv:** Head right
Rev: Queen Mother facing **Edge:** Reeded

Date	Mintage	F	VF	XF	Unc	BU
1985	Est. 20,000	—	—	—	3.00	3.50

KM# 171   50 SENITI
20.0000 g., 0.9250 Silver 0.5948 oz. ASW, 34 mm.
Ruler: King Taufa'ahau Tupou IV **Subject:** Olympics
Obv: Crowned arms within circle **Rev:** Boxer within circle
Edge: Reeded

Date	Mintage	F	VF	XF	Unc	BU
1998 Proof	50,000	Value: 16.50				

KM# 11   PA'ANGA
Copper-Nickel, 38.5 mm.   **Ruler:** King Taufa'ahau Tupou IV
Obv: Head right **Rev:** Crowned arms **Edge:** Reeded

Date	Mintage	F	VF	XF	Unc	BU
1967	78,000	—	1.00	2.00	3.75	5.00
1967 Proof	—	Value: 6.00				

KM# 17   PA'ANGA
Copper-Nickel, 38.5 mm.   **Ruler:** King Taufa'ahau Tupou IV
Subject: Coronation of Taufa'ahau Tupou IV **Obv:** Head right,
small crowns around border **Rev:** Crowned arms **Edge:** Reeded

Date	Mintage	F	VF	XF	Unc	BU
ND(1967)	13,000	—	1.00	2.00	4.00	5.50
ND(1967) Proof	1,923	Value: 6.50				

KM# 33   PA'ANGA
Copper-Nickel, 38.5 mm.   **Ruler:** King Taufa'ahau Tupou IV
Obv: Head right **Rev:** Crowned arms **Edge:** Reeded

Date	Mintage	F	VF	XF	Unc	BU
1968	14,000	—	1.00	2.00	4.00	5.50
1968 Proof	—	Value: 6.50				
1974	10,000	—	1.00	2.00	4.00	4.00

KM# 48   PA'ANGA
Copper-Nickel, 38.5 mm.   **Ruler:** King Taufa'ahau Tupou IV
Series: F.A.O. **Obv:** Uniformed bust facing **Rev:** 100 Palm trees
Edge: Reeded

Date	Mintage	F	VF	XF	Unc	BU
1975	13,000	—	1.25	2.50	4.50	6.00

KM# 57   PA'ANGA
Copper-Nickel, 48x27 mm.   **Ruler:** King Taufa'ahau Tupou IV
Series: F.A.O **Obv:** Uniformed bust facing **Rev:** 100 Palm trees
Edge: Plain

Date	Mintage	F	VF	XF	Unc	BU
1977	25,000	—	2.00	3.50	7.50	12.50

KM# 58   PA'ANGA
Copper-Nickel, 48x27 mm.   **Ruler:** King Taufa'ahau Tupou IV
Series: F.A.O. **Subject:** 60th Birthday **Obv:** Uniformed bust facing
flanked by stars and dates **Rev:** 100 Palm trees **Edge:** Plain

Date	Mintage	F	VF	XF	Unc	BU
1978	10,000	—	2.00	3.50	7.50	12.50

KM# 58a   PA'ANGA
24.5000 g., 0.9990 Silver 0.7869 oz. ASW, 48x27 mm.
Ruler: King Taufa'ahau Tupou IV **Obv:** Uniformed bust facing
flanked by stars and dates **Rev:** 100 Palm trees

Date	Mintage	F	VF	XF	Unc	BU
1978 Proof	750	Value: 25.00				

KM# 60   PA'ANGA
Copper-Nickel, 48x27 mm.   **Ruler:** King Taufa'ahau Tupou IV
Series: F.A.O. **Subject:** Technical Cooperation Program
Obv: Uniformed bust facing divides circular inscriptions **Rev:** 100
Palm trees

Date	Mintage	F	VF	XF	Unc	BU
1979	26,000	—	1.50	3.00	5.50	8.50

KM# 60a PA'ANGA
24.5000 g., 0.9990 Silver 0.7869 oz. ASW, 48x27 mm.
Ruler: King Taufa'ahau Tupou IV **Obv:** Uniformed bust facing divides circular inscriptions **Rev:** 100 Palm trees

Date	Mintage	F	VF	XF	Unc	BU
1979 Proof	850	Value: 20.00				

KM# 62 PA'ANGA
Copper-Nickel, 48x27 mm. **Ruler:** King Taufa'ahau Tupou IV
Series: F.A.O. **Subject:** Rural Women's Advancement **Obv:** Bust facing **Rev:** Kneeling figure in front of hut and palm trees **Edge:** Plain

Date	Mintage	F	VF	XF	Unc	BU
1980	8,000	—	—	2.50	5.50	8.50

KM# 62a PA'ANGA
24.5000 g., 0.9990 Silver 0.7869 oz. ASW, 48x27 mm.
Ruler: King Taufa'ahau Tupou IV **Subject:** Rural Women's Andancement **Obv:** Bust facing **Rev:** Kneeling figure in front of hut and palm trees **Rev. Leg.:** F.A.O.

Date	Mintage	F	VF	XF	Unc	BU
1980 Proof	2,200	Value: 17.50				

KM# 72 PA'ANGA
Copper-Nickel, 48x27 mm. **Ruler:** King Taufa'ahau Tupou IV
Series: World Food Day **Obv:** Uniformed bust facing
Rev: Sailboat **Edge:** Plain

Date	Mintage	F	VF	XF	Unc	BU
1981	485,000	—	—	2.50	5.50	8.50

KM# 72a PA'ANGA
24.5000 g., 0.9990 Silver 0.7869 oz. ASW, 48x27 mm.
Ruler: King Taufa'ahau Tupou IV **Subject:** World Food Day
Obv: Uniformed bust facing **Rev:** Sailboat

Date	Mintage	F	VF	XF	Unc	BU
1981 Proof	3,500	Value: 17.50				

KM# 77 PA'ANGA
Copper-Nickel, 30 mm. **Ruler:** King Taufa'ahau Tupou IV
Subject: Christmas **Obv:** Head right **Rev:** Praying hands
Edge: Plain

Date	Mintage	F	VF	XF	Unc	BU
1982	5,000	—	—	1.00	3.00	4.00
1982 Proof	—	Value: 5.00				

KM# 77a PA'ANGA
15.5000 g., 0.9250 Silver 0.4609 oz. ASW, 30 mm.
Ruler: King Taufa'ahau Tupou IV **Subject:** Christmas
Obv: Head right **Rev:** Praying hands

Date	Mintage	F	VF	XF	Unc	BU
1982 Proof	2,500	Value: 8.50				

KM# 77b PA'ANGA
26.0000 g., 0.9170 Gold 0.7665 oz. AGW, 30 mm. **Ruler:** King Taufa'ahau Tupou IV **Subject:** Christmas **Obv:** Head right
Rev: Praying hands

Date	Mintage	F	VF	XF	Unc	BU
1982 Proof	250	Value: 775				

KM# 77c PA'ANGA
30.4000 g., 0.9500 Platinum 0.9285 oz. APW, 30 mm.
Ruler: King Taufa'ahau Tupou IV **Subject:** Christmas
Obv: Head right **Rev:** Praying hands

Date	Mintage	F	VF	XF	Unc	BU
1982 Proof	25	Value: 2,000				

KM# 80 PA'ANGA
Copper-Nickel, 30 mm. **Ruler:** King Taufa'ahau Tupou IV
Subject: Christmas **Obv:** Head right **Rev:** Kneeling Joseph and Mary **Edge:** Plain

Date	Mintage	F	VF	XF	Unc	BU
1983	5,000	—	—	1.00	3.00	4.00

KM# 80a PA'ANGA
15.5000 g., 0.9250 Silver 0.4609 oz. ASW, 30 mm. **Ruler:** King Taufa'ahau Tupou IV **Subject:** Christmas **Obv:** Head right
Rev: Kneeling Joseph and Mary

Date	Mintage	F	VF	XF	Unc	BU
1983 Proof	2,500	Value: 8.50				

KM# 80b PA'ANGA
26.0000 g., 0.9170 Gold 0.7665 oz. AGW, 30 mm. **Ruler:** King Taufa'ahau Tupou IV **Subject:** Christmas **Obv:** Head right
Rev: Kneeling Joseph and Mary

Date	Mintage	F	VF	XF	Unc	BU
1983 Proof	250	Value: 775				

KM# 80c PA'ANGA
30.4000 g., 0.9500 Platinum 0.9285 oz. APW, 30 mm.
Ruler: King Taufa'ahau Tupou IV **Subject:** Christmas
Obv: Head right **Rev:** Kneeling Joseph and Mary

Date	Mintage	F	VF	XF	Unc	BU
1983 Proof	25	Value: 2,000				

KM# 81 PA'ANGA
Copper-Nickel, 30 mm. **Ruler:** King Taufa'ahau Tupou IV
Subject: Christmas **Obv:** Head right **Rev:** After Bellini's Madonna & Child **Edge:** Plain

Date	Mintage	F	VF	XF	Unc	BU
1984	5,000	—	—	1.00	3.00	4.00

KM# 81a PA'ANGA
15.5000 g., 0.9250 Silver 0.4609 oz. ASW, 30 mm. **Ruler:** King Taufa'ahau Tupou IV **Subject:** Christmas **Obv:** Head right
Rev: After Bellini's Madonna & Child

Date	Mintage	F	VF	XF	Unc	BU
1984 Proof	2,500	Value: 8.50				

KM# 81b PA'ANGA
26.0000 g., 0.9170 Gold 0.7665 oz. AGW, 30 mm. **Ruler:** King Taufa'ahau Tupou IV **Subject:** Christmas **Obv:** Head right
Rev: After Bellini's Madonna & Child

Date	Mintage	F	VF	XF	Unc	BU
1984 Proof	250	Value: 775				

KM# 81c PA'ANGA
30.4000 g., 0.9500 Platinum 0.9285 oz. APW, 30 mm.
Ruler: King Taufa'ahau Tupou IV **Subject:** Christmas
Obv: Head right **Rev:** After Bellini's Madonna & Child

Date	Mintage	F	VF	XF	Unc	BU
1984 Proof	25	Value: 2,000				

KM# 86 PA'ANGA
Silver Clad Copper-Nickel **Ruler:** King Taufa'ahau Tupou IV
Subject: 100th Anniversary of Automobile Industry **Obv:** Head right **Rev:** Rolls-Royce and Silver Ghost

Date	Mintage	F	VF	XF	Unc	BU
1985 Proof	—	Value: 5.00				

KM# 86a PA'ANGA
28.2800 g., 0.9250 Silver 0.8410 oz. ASW **Ruler:** King Taufa'ahau Tupou IV **Subject:** 100th Anniversary of Automobile Industry
Obv: Head right **Rev:** Rolls Royce and Silver Ghost

Date	Mintage	F	VF	XF	Unc	BU
1985 Proof	5,000	Value: 22.50				

KM# 87 PA'ANGA
Silver Clad Copper-Nickel **Ruler:** King Taufa'ahau Tupou IV
Subject: 100th Anniversary of Automobile Industry **Obv:** Head right **Rev:** Range Rover and Land Rover

Date	Mintage	F	VF	XF	Unc	BU
1985 Proof	—	Value: 5.00				

KM# 87a PA'ANGA
28.2800 g., 0.9250 Silver 0.8410 oz. ASW **Ruler:** King Taufa'ahau Tupou IV **Subject:** 100th Anniversary of Automobile Industry **Obv:** Head right **Rev:** Range Rover and Land Rover

Date	Mintage	F	VF	XF	Unc	BU
1985 Proof	5,000	Value: 16.50				

KM# 88 PA'ANGA
Silver Clad Copper-Nickel **Ruler:** King Taufa'ahau Tupou IV
Subject: 100th Anniversary of Automobile Industry **Obv:** Head right **Rev:** Mini Morris Cowley and Touring Car

Date	Mintage	F	VF	XF	Unc	BU
1985 Proof	—	Value: 5.00				

KM# 88a PA'ANGA
28.2800 g., 0.9250 Silver 0.8410 oz. ASW **Ruler:** King Taufa'ahau Tupou IV **Subject:** 100th Anniversary of Automobile Industry **Obv:** Head right **Rev:** Mini Morris Cowley and Touring Car

Date	Mintage	F	VF	XF	Unc	BU
1985 Proof	5,000	Value: 16.50				

KM# 89 PA'ANGA
Silver Clad Copper-Nickel **Ruler:** King Taufa'ahau Tupou IV
Subject: 100th Anniversary of Automobile Industry **Obv:** Head right **Rev:** MGB GT and MG TA **Note:** Similar to 50 Seniti, KM#85.

Date	Mintage	F	VF	XF	Unc	BU
1985 Proof	—	Value: 5.00				

KM# 89a PA'ANGA
28.2800 g., 0.9250 Silver 0.8410 oz. ASW **Ruler:** King Taufa'ahau Tupou IV **Subject:** 100th Anniversary of Automobile Industry **Obv:** Head right **Rev:** MGB GT and MG TA

Date	Mintage	F	VF	XF	Unc	BU
1985 Proof	5,000	Value: 16.50				

KM# 103 PA'ANGA
Silver Clad Copper-Nickel **Ruler:** King Taufa'ahau Tupou IV
Subject: 85th Birthday of Queen Mother **Obv:** Head right
Rev: Queen Mother as a young girl **Note:** Similar to 50 Seniti, KM#98.

Date	Mintage	F	VF	XF	Unc	BU
1985 Proof	—	Value: 4.50				

KM# 103a PA'ANGA
28.2800 g., 0.9250 Silver 0.8410 oz. ASW **Ruler:** King Taufa'ahau Tupou IV **Subject:** 85th Birthday of Queen Mother
Obv: Head right **Rev:** Queen Mother as a young girl

Date	Mintage	F	VF	XF	Unc	BU
1985 Proof	5,000	Value: 13.50				

KM# 104 PA'ANGA
Silver Clad Copper-Nickel **Ruler:** King Taufa'ahau Tupou IV
Subject: 85th Birthday of Queen mother **Obv:** Head right
Rev: Wedding of King George VI and Elizabeth **Note:** Similar to 50 Seniti, KM#99.

Date	Mintage	F	VF	XF	Unc	BU
1985 Proof	—	Value: 4.50				

KM# 104a PA'ANGA
28.2800 g., 0.9250 Silver 0.8410 oz. ASW **Ruler:** King Taufa'ahau Tupou IV **Subject:** 85th Birthday of Queen Mother **Obv:** Head right **Rev:** Wedding of King George VI and Elizabeth

Date	Mintage	F	VF	XF	Unc	BU
1985 Proof	5,000	Value: 13.50				

KM# 105 PA'ANGA
Silver Clad Copper-Nickel **Ruler:** King Taufa'ahau Tupou IV **Subject:** 85th Birthday of Queen Mother **Obv:** Head right **Rev:** King George VI and Elizabeth **Note:** Similar to 50 Seniti, KM#100.

Date	Mintage	F	VF	XF	Unc	BU
1985 Proof	—	Value: 4.50				

KM# 105a PA'ANGA
28.2800 g., 0.9250 Silver 0.8410 oz. ASW **Ruler:** King Taufa'ahau Tupou IV **Subject:** 85th Birthday of Queen mother **Obv:** Head right **Rev:** King George VI and Elizabeth

Date	Mintage	F	VF	XF	Unc	BU
1985 Proof	5,000	Value: 13.50				

KM# 106 PA'ANGA
Silver Clad Copper-Nickel **Ruler:** King Taufa'ahau Tupou IV **Subject:** 85th Birthday of Queen Mother **Obv:** Head right **Rev:** Queen Mother holding Queen Elizabeth II **Note:** Similar to 50 Seniti, KM#101.

Date	Mintage	F	VF	XF	Unc	BU
1985 Proof	—	Value: 4.50				

KM# 106a PA'ANGA
28.2800 g., 0.9250 Silver 0.8410 oz. ASW **Ruler:** King Taufa'ahau Tupou IV **Subject:** 85th Birthday of Queen Mother **Obv:** Head right **Rev:** Queen Mother holding Queen Elizabeth II

Date	Mintage	F	VF	XF	Unc	BU
1985 Proof	5,000	Value: 13.50				

KM# 107 PA'ANGA
Silver Clad Copper-Nickel **Ruler:** King Taufa'ahau Tupou IV **Subject:** 85th Birthday of Queen Mother **Obv:** Head right **Rev:** Queen Mother facing **Note:** Similar to 50 Seniti, KM#102.

Date	Mintage	F	VF	XF	Unc	BU
1985 Proof	—	Value: 4.50				

KM# 107a PA'ANGA
28.2800 g., 0.9250 Silver 0.8410 oz. ASW **Ruler:** King Taufa'ahau Tupou IV **Subject:** 85th Birthday of the Queen Mother **Obv:** Head right **Rev:** Queen Mother facing

Date	Mintage	F	VF	XF	Unc	BU
1985 Proof	5,000	Value: 13.50				

KM# 118 PA'ANGA
Copper-Nickel, 30 mm. **Ruler:** King Taufa'ahau Tupou IV **Subject:** Christmas **Obv:** Head right **Rev:** Dove with laurel branch **Edge:** Plain

Date	Mintage	F	VF	XF	Unc	BU
1985	—	—	—	1.00	2.75	5.00

KM# 118a PA'ANGA
15.5000 g., 0.9250 Silver 0.4609 oz. ASW **Ruler:** King Taufa'ahau Tupou IV **Subject:** Christmas **Obv:** Head right **Rev:** Dove with laurel branch

Date	Mintage	F	VF	XF	Unc	BU
1985 Proof	250	Value: 17.50				

KM# 118b PA'ANGA
26.0000 g., 0.9170 Gold 0.7665 oz. AGW **Ruler:** King Taufa'ahau Tupou IV **Subject:** Christmas **Obv:** Head right **Rev:** Dove with laurel branch

Date	Mintage	F	VF	XF	Unc	BU
1985 Proof	250	Value: 775				

KM# 118c PA'ANGA
30.4000 g., 0.9500 Platinum 0.9285 oz. APW **Ruler:** King Taufa'ahau Tupou IV **Subject:** Christmas **Obv:** Head right **Rev:** Dove with laurel branch

Date	Mintage	F	VF	XF	Unc	BU
1985 Proof	—	Value: 2,000				

KM# 123 PA'ANGA
Copper-Nickel **Ruler:** King Taufa'ahau Tupou IV **Subject:** Christmas **Obv:** Head right **Rev:** Three Wise Men

Date	Mintage	F	VF	XF	Unc	BU
1986	—	—	—	1.00	2.75	4.00

KM# 123a PA'ANGA
15.5000 g., 0.9250 Silver 0.4609 oz. ASW **Ruler:** King Taufa'ahau Tupou IV **Subject:** Christmas **Obv:** Head right **Rev:** Three Wise Men

Date	Mintage	F	VF	XF	Unc	BU
1986 Proof	—	Value: 16.50				

KM# 123b PA'ANGA
26.0000 g., 0.9170 Gold 0.7665 oz. AGW **Ruler:** King Taufa'ahau Tupou IV **Subject:** Christmas **Obv:** Head right **Rev:** Three Wise Men

Date	Mintage	F	VF	XF	Unc	BU
1986 Proof	—	Value: 775				

KM# 123c PA'ANGA
30.4000 g., 0.9500 Platinum 0.9285 oz. APW **Ruler:** King Taufa'ahau Tupou IV **Subject:** Christmas **Obv:** Head right **Rev:** Three Wise Men

Date	Mintage	F	VF	XF	Unc	BU
1986 Proof	—	Value: 2,000				

KM# 128 PA'ANGA
Copper-Nickel **Ruler:** King Taufa'ahau Tupou IV **Series:** 25th Anniversary of World Wildlife Fund **Obv:** Head right **Rev:** Humpback whale cow and calf within circle **Edge:** Reeded

Date	Mintage	F	VF	XF	Unc	BU
1986	—	—	—	—	7.00	14.00

KM# 139 PA'ANGA
Copper-Nickel **Ruler:** King Taufa'ahau Tupou IV **Subject:** Christmas **Obv:** Head right **Rev:** Madonna and child

Date	Mintage	F	VF	XF	Unc	BU
1987	—	—	—	—	2.75	4.00
1987 Proof	—	Value: 5.00				

KM# 127 PA'ANGA
Copper-Nickel, 30 mm. **Ruler:** King Taufa'ahau Tupou IV **Subject:** Christmas **Obv:** Head right **Rev:** After Albrecht Durer, Madonna and child **Edge:** Plain

Date	Mintage	F	VF	XF	Unc	BU
1988	—	—	—	—	2.75	4.00
1988 Proof	—	Value: 5.00				

KM# 127a PA'ANGA
15.5000 g., 0.9250 Silver 0.4609 oz. ASW **Ruler:** King Taufa'ahau Tupou IV **Subject:** Christmas **Obv:** Head right **Rev:** After Albrecht Durer, Madonna and child

Date	Mintage	F	VF	XF	Unc	BU
1988 Proof	—	Value: 16.50				

KM# 127b PA'ANGA
26.0000 g., 0.9170 Gold 0.7665 oz. AGW **Ruler:** King Taufa'ahau Tupou IV **Subject:** Christmas **Obv:** Head right **Rev:** After Albrecht Durer, Madonna and child

Date	Mintage	F	VF	XF	Unc	BU
1988 Proof	—	Value: 775				

KM# 127c PA'ANGA
30.4000 g., 0.9500 Platinum 0.9285 oz. APW **Ruler:** King Taufa'ahau Tupou IV **Subject:** Christmas **Obv:** Head right **Rev:** After Albrecht Durer, Madonna and child

Date	Mintage	F	VF	XF	Unc	BU
1988 Proof	—	Value: 2,000				

KM# 133 PA'ANGA
31.7300 g., 0.9250 Silver 0.9436 oz. ASW **Ruler:** King Taufa'ahau Tupou IV **Series:** Olympics **Obv:** Head right **Rev:** Javelin thrower within circle

Date	Mintage	F	VF	XF	Unc	BU
1988 Proof	—	Value: 17.50				

KM# 134 PA'ANGA
31.7300 g., 0.9250 Silver 0.9436 oz. ASW **Ruler:** King Taufa'ahau Tupou IV **Series:** Olympics **Obv:** Head right **Rev:** Swimmers within circle

Date	Mintage	F	VF	XF	Unc	BU
1988 Proof	—	Value: 17.50				

KM# 135 PA'ANGA
31.7300 g., 0.9250 Silver 0.9436 oz. ASW **Ruler:** King Taufa'ahau Tupou IV **Series:** Olympics **Obv:** Head right **Rev:** Boxers

Date	Mintage	F	VF	XF	Unc	BU
1988 Proof	—	Value: 17.50				

KM# 136 PA'ANGA
31.7300 g., 0.9250 Silver 0.9436 oz. ASW **Ruler:** King Taufa'ahau Tupou IV **Series:** Olympics **Obv:** Head right **Rev:** Discus thrower within circle

Date	Mintage	F	VF	XF	Unc	BU
1988 Proof	—	Value: 17.50				

KM# 137 PA'ANGA
31.7300 g., 0.9250 Silver 0.9436 oz. ASW **Ruler:** King Taufa'ahau Tupou IV **Series:** Olympics **Obv:** Head right **Rev:** Shotput thrower

Date	Mintage	F	VF	XF	Unc	BU
1988 Proof	—	Value: 17.50				

KM# 138 PA'ANGA
31.7300 g., 0.9250 Silver 0.9436 oz. ASW **Ruler:** King
Taufa'ahau Tupou IV **Series:** Olympics **Obv:** Head right
Rev: Runners within circle

Date	Mintage	F	VF	XF	Unc	BU
1988 Proof	—	Value: 17.50				

KM# 145 PA'ANGA
31.7300 g., 0.9250 Silver 0.9436 oz. ASW **Ruler:** King
Taufa'ahau Tupou IV **Series:** Olympics **Obv:** Head right
Rev: Bicycling within circle

Date	Mintage	F	VF	XF	Unc	BU
1988 Proof	—	Value: 17.50				

KM# 146 PA'ANGA
31.7300 g., 0.9250 Silver 0.9436 oz. ASW **Ruler:** King
Taufa'ahau Tupou IV **Series:** Olympics **Obv:** Head right
Rev: Gymnast on rings within circle

Date	Mintage	F	VF	XF	Unc	BU
1988 Proof	—	Value: 17.50				

KM# 147 PA'ANGA
31.7300 g., 0.9250 Silver 0.9436 oz. ASW **Ruler:** King
Taufa'ahau Tupou IV **Series:** Olympics **Obv:** Head right **Rev:** Diver

Date	Mintage	F	VF	XF	Unc	BU
1988 Proof	—	Value: 22.50				

KM# 148 PA'ANGA
31.7300 g., 0.9250 Silver 0.9436 oz. ASW **Ruler:** King
Taufa'ahau Tupou IV **Series:** Olympics **Obv:** Head right **Rev:** Judo

Date	Mintage	F	VF	XF	Unc	BU
1988 Proof	—	Value: 17.50				

KM# 149 PA'ANGA
31.7300 g., 0.9250 Silver 0.9436 oz. ASW **Ruler:** King
Taufa'ahau Tupou IV **Series:** Olympics **Obv:** Head right
Rev: Broad jumper

Date	Mintage	F	VF	XF	Unc	BU
1988 Proof	—	Value: 17.50				

KM# 150 PA'ANGA
31.7300 g., 0.9250 Silver 0.9436 oz. ASW **Ruler:** King
Taufa'ahau Tupou IV **Series:** Olympics **Obv:** Head right
Rev: Weight lifter

Date	Mintage	F	VF	XF	Unc	BU
1988 Proof	—	Value: 17.50				

KM# 175 PA'ANGA
31.8000 g., 0.9250 Silver 0.9457 oz. ASW **Ruler:** King
Taufa'ahau Tupou IV **Subject:** 25th Anniversary of Reign
Obv: Crowned arms **Rev:** Radiant sun rising through stone
structure

Date	Mintage	F	VF	XF	Unc	BU
ND(1990) Proof	—	Value: 20.00				

KM# 140 PA'ANGA
31.6000 g., 0.9250 Silver 0.9397 oz. ASW **Ruler:** King
Taufa'ahau Tupou IV **Series:** Olympics **Obv:** National arms
Rev: Diver

Date	Mintage	F	VF	XF	Unc	BU
1991 Proof	Est. 40,000	Value: 16.00				

KM# 141 PA'ANGA
31.6000 g., 0.9250 Silver 0.9397 oz. ASW **Ruler:** King
Taufa'ahau Tupou IV **Subject:** Explorers **Rev:** William Schouten
and Jakob LeMaire and ship

Date	Mintage	F	VF	XF	Unc	BU
1991 Proof	Est. 10,000	Value: 16.50				

KM# 143 PA'ANGA
31.6000 g., 0.9250 Silver 0.9397 oz. ASW **Ruler:** King
Taufa'ahau Tupou IV **Subject:** Endangered Wildlife
Rev: Pritchard's Megapode Birds

Date	Mintage	F	VF	XF	Unc	BU
1991 Proof	—	Value: 17.50				

KM# 156 PA'ANGA
31.6000 g., 0.9250 Silver 0.9397 oz. ASW **Ruler:** King
Taufa'ahau Tupou IV **Series:** 1996 Olympics **Obv:** National arms
Rev: Sailing

Date	Mintage	F	VF	XF	Unc	BU
1992 Proof	40,000	Value: 16.00				

KM# 157 PA'ANGA
31.6000 g., 0.9250 Silver 0.9397 oz. ASW **Ruler:** King
Taufa'ahau Tupou IV **Subject:** Soccer **Rev:** Players

Date	Mintage	F	VF	XF	Unc	BU
1992 Proof	10,000	Value: 16.50				

KM# 158 PA'ANGA
31.6000 g., 0.9250 Silver 0.9397 oz. ASW **Ruler:** King
Taufa'ahau Tupou IV **Subject:** Space Flight **Obv:** National arms
within circle **Rev:** Saturn V on launchpad at right, US map at left

Date	Mintage	F	VF	XF	Unc	BU
1992 Proof	10,000	Value: 16.50				

KM# 168 PA'ANGA
31.6000 g., 0.9250 Silver 0.9397 oz. ASW **Ruler:** King
Taufa'ahau Tupou IV **Subject:** 25th Anniversary - Coronation of
Tupou IV **Obv:** National arms within circle **Rev:** Coronation scene

Date	Mintage	F	VF	XF	Unc	BU
1992 Proof	Est. 5,000	Value: 17.50				

KM# 144 PA'ANGA
31.4700 g., 0.9250 Silver 0.9359 oz. ASW **Ruler:** King
Taufa'ahau Tupou IV **Subject:** 40th Anniversary of Queen
Elizabeth's Coronation **Obv:** National arms within circle
Rev: Symbols of royalty

Date	Mintage	F	VF	XF	Unc	BU
1993 Proof	Est. 10,000	Value: 16.00				

KM# 151 PA'ANGA
31.4700 g., 0.9250 Silver 0.9359 oz. ASW **Ruler:** King
Taufa'ahau Tupou IV **Subject:** Hermann Oberth 1894-1989
Obv: Crowned arms within circle **Rev:** Bust facing left to right of
standing figures and rockets

Date	Mintage	F	VF	XF	Unc	BU
1993 Proof	Est. 10,000	Value: 16.50				

KM# 152 PA'ANGA
31.4700 g., 0.9250 Silver 0.9359 oz. ASW **Ruler:** King
Taufa'ahau Tupou IV **Subject:** Johannes Gutenberg 1400-1468
Obv: Crowned arms within circle **Rev:** Half-length bust at left,
stack of printed pages and press at right

Date	Mintage	F	VF	XF	Unc	BU
1993 Proof	Est. 10,000	Value: 16.50				

KM# 153 PA'ANGA
31.4700 g., 0.9250 Silver 0.9359 oz. ASW **Ruler:** King
Taufa'ahau Tupou IV **Subject:** Protect Our World **Obv:** Crowned
arms within circle **Rev:** Alexander von Humboldt

Date	Mintage	F	VF	XF	Unc	BU
1993 Proof	Est. 10,000	Value: 16.50				

KM# 154 PA'ANGA
31.4700 g., 0.9250 Silver 0.9359 oz. ASW **Ruler:** King
Taufa'ahau Tupou IV **Obv:** Crowned arms within circle
Rev: Sailing ship - "La Princesa"

Date	Mintage	F	VF	XF	Unc	BU
1993 Proof	Est. 15,000	Value: 16.50				
1994 Proof	—	Value: 16.50				

KM# 160 PA'ANGA
31.4700 g., 0.9250 Silver 0.9359 oz. ASW **Ruler:** King
Taufa'ahau Tupou IV **Subject:** Richard Wagner **Obv:** Crowned
arms within circle **Rev:** Bust at right, dancers at upper left

Date	Mintage	F	VF	XF	Unc	BU
1993 Proof	Est. 10,000	Value: 16.50				

KM# 169 PA'ANGA
31.4700 g., 0.9250 Silver 0.9359 oz. ASW **Ruler:** King
Taufa'ahau Tupou IV **Subject:** 75th Birthday, July 4, 1993
Obv: Uniformed bust facing **Rev:** Siu'a'alo rowers

Date	Mintage	F	VF	XF	Unc	BU
1993 Proof	Est. 2,000	Value: 18.00				

KM# 159.1 PA'ANGA
31.5500 g., 0.9250 Silver 0.9382 oz. ASW **Ruler:** King
Taufa'ahau Tupou IV **Series:** 1996 Olympics **Obv:** Crowned arms
within circle **Rev:** Javelin thrower within circle **Note:** Prev. KM#159.

Date	Mintage	F	VF	XF	Unc	BU
1994 Proof	40,000	Value: 16.00				

KM# 159.2 PA'ANGA

31.4700 g., 0.9250 Silver 0.9359 oz. ASW, 38.7 mm. **Ruler:** King Taufa'ahau Tupou IV **Subject:** Olympics **Obv:** Crowned arms within circle **Rev:** Javelin thrower within circle **Edge:** Reeded **Note:** Smaller letters in legend than the KM-159.1 version

Date	Mintage	F	VF	XF	Unc	BU
1994 Proof	—	Value: 30.00				

KM# 161 PA'ANGA

31.4700 g., 0.9250 Silver 0.9359 oz. ASW **Ruler:** King Taufa'ahau Tupou IV **Subject:** World Cup Soccer **Obv:** Crowned arms within circle **Rev:** Two soccer players

Date	Mintage	F	VF	XF	Unc	BU
1994 Proof	Est. 10,000	Value: 17.50				

KM# 162 PA'ANGA

31.4700 g., 0.9250 Silver 0.9359 oz. ASW **Ruler:** King Taufa'ahau Tupou IV **Series:** Endangered Wildlife **Obv:** Crowned arms within circle **Rev:** Humpback whale cow and calf

Date	Mintage	F	VF	XF	Unc	BU
1994 Proof	Est. 10,000	Value: 35.00				

KM# 180 PA'ANGA

31.1100 g., 0.9250 Silver 0.9249 oz. ASW, 38.5 mm. **Ruler:** King Taufa'ahau Tupou IV **Subject:** 50 Years - FAO **Obv:** Bust facing at left, TONGA at right **Rev:** FAO emblem, value above, date at right **Edge:** Reeded

Date	Mintage	F	VF	XF	Unc	BU
1995 Proof	—	—	—	—	—	—

KM# 177 PA'ANGA

31.4100 g., 0.9250 Silver 0.9341 oz. ASW, 38.6 mm. **Ruler:** King Taufa'ahau Tupou IV **Series:** Queen Elizabeth The Queen Mother **Subject:** The Coronation of Elizabeth **Obv:** Crowned arms within circle **Rev:** Queen seated on throne within beaded circle **Edge:** Reeded

Date	Mintage	F	VF	XF	Unc	BU
1996 Proof	—	Value: 22.50				

KM# 166 PA'ANGA

31.4700 g., 0.9250 Silver 0.9359 oz. ASW **Ruler:** King Taufa'ahau Tupou IV **Series:** Queen Elizabeth The Queen Mother **Obv:** Crowned arms within circle **Rev:** Crown within beaded circle

Date	Mintage	F	VF	XF	Unc	BU
1996	Est. 40,000	—	—	—	16.00	—

KM# 170 PA'ANGA

31.4700 g., 0.9250 Silver 0.9359 oz. ASW **Ruler:** King Taufa'ahau Tupou IV **Subject:** 70th Birthday - Queen Mata'aho, May 25, 1996 **Obv:** National arms within circle **Rev:** Crown above bust of Queen Mata'aho facing within wreath

Date	Mintage	F	VF	XF	Unc	BU
1996 Proof	Est. 5,000	Value: 18.00				

KM# 174 PA'ANGA

31.4700 g., 0.9250 Silver 0.9359 oz. ASW **Ruler:** King Taufa'ahau Tupou IV **Obv:** National arms within circle **Rev:** Polynesian sailing catamaran

Date	Mintage	F	VF	XF	Unc	BU
1998 Proof	20,000	Value: 17.50				

KM# 176 PA'ANGA

31.1100 g., 0.9250 Silver 0.9252 oz. ASW, 35.5 mm. **Ruler:** King Taufa'ahau Tupou IV **Subject:** Millennium 2000 **Obv:** Crowned arms within circle and beaded border **Rev:** Stone archway **Edge:** Reeded

Date	Mintage	F	VF	XF	Unc	BU
1999 Proof	—	Value: 35.00				

KM# 19 2 PA'ANGA

Copper-Nickel, 44.5 mm. **Ruler:** King Taufa'ahau Tupou IV **Subject:** Coronation of Taufa'ahau Tupou IV **Obv:** Head right **Rev:** National arms

Date	Mintage	F	VF	XF	Unc	BU
ND(1967)	10,000	—	1.25	2.75	5.50	6.50
ND(1967) Proof	—	Value: 10.00				

KM# 37 2 PA'ANGA

Copper-Nickel, 44.5 mm. **Ruler:** King Taufa'ahau Tupou IV **Obv:** Head right **Rev:** National arms **Edge:** Reeded

Date	Mintage	F	VF	XF	Unc	BU
1968 Proof	—	Value: 8.00				
1968	14,000	—	1.25	2.25	5.00	6.00
1974	10,000	—	1.25	3.00	5.50	6.50

KM# 49 2 PA'ANGA

Copper-Nickel, 44.5 mm. **Ruler:** King Taufa'ahau Tupou IV **Series:** F.A.O. **Obv:** Uniformed bust facing **Rev:** Palm tree in center of assorted animals, grains and fruit **Edge:** Reeded

Date	Mintage	F	VF	XF	Unc	BU
1975	13,000	—	1.25	2.75	5.50	6.50
1977	12,000	—	1.25	2.75	5.50	6.50

KM# 59 2 PA'ANGA

Copper-Nickel, 44.5 mm. **Ruler:** King Taufa'ahau Tupou IV **Series:** F.A.O. **Subject:** 60th Birthday **Obv:** Uniformed bust facing **Rev:** Palm tree in center of assorted animals and grains **Edge:** Reeded

Date	Mintage	F	VF	XF	Unc	BU
1978	10,000	—	1.25	2.75	5.50	6.50

KM# 59a 2 PA'ANGA

42.1000 g., 0.9990 Silver 1.3521 oz. ASW, 44.5 mm. **Ruler:** King Taufa'ahau Tupou IV **Series:** F.A.O. **Subject:** 60th Birthday **Obv:** Uniformed bust facing **Rev:** Palm tree in center of assorted animals and grains

Date	Mintage	F	VF	XF	Unc	BU
1978 Proof	750	Value: 27.50				

KM# 61 2 PA'ANGA

Copper-Nickel, 44.5 mm. **Ruler:** King Taufa'ahau Tupou IV **Series:** F.A.O. **Subject:** SEA Resource Management **Obv:** Uniformed bust facing **Rev:** Humpback whale - bull in breach **Edge:** Reeded

Date	Mintage	F	VF	XF	Unc	BU
1979	8,000	—	—	3.00	7.00	12.00

KM# 61a 2 PA'ANGA

42.1000 g., 0.9990 Silver 1.3521 oz. ASW, 44.5 mm. **Ruler:** King Taufa'ahau Tupou IV **Series:** F.A.O. **Subject:** SEA Resource Management **Obv:** Uniformed bust facing **Rev:** Humpback whale - bull in breach

Date	Mintage	F	VF	XF	Unc	BU
1979 Proof	850	Value: 27.50				

KM# 121   2 PA'ANGA
28.2800 g., 0.9250 Silver 0.8410 oz. ASW, 38.61 mm.
Ruler: King Taufa'ahau Tupou IV **Subject:** Wildlife
Obv: Uniformed bust facing **Rev:** Humpback whales - cow and calf within circle

Date	Mintage	F	VF	XF	Unc	BU
1986 Proof	25,000	Value: 30.00				

KM# 50   5 PA'ANGA
31.0000 g., 0.9990 Silver 0.9956 oz. ASW **Ruler:** King Taufa'ahau Tupou IV **Subject:** Constitution Centennial
Obv: Uniformed bust left above open scroll **Rev:** Crowned arms

Date	Mintage	F	VF	XF	Unc	BU
ND(1975)	2,118	—	—	—	16.00	17.50
ND(1975) Proof	418	Value: 25.00				

KM# 63   2 PA'ANGA
Copper-Nickel, 44.5 mm.   **Ruler:** King Taufa'ahau Tupou IV
Series: F.A.O. **Subject:** SEA Resource Management
Obv: Uniformed bust facing **Rev:** Humpback whale - bull in breach **Edge:** Reeded

Date	Mintage	F	VF	XF	Unc	BU
1980	8,000	—	—	3.00	7.00	10.00

KM# 63a   2 PA'ANGA
42.1000 g., 0.9990 Silver 1.3521 oz. ASW, 44.5 mm.
Ruler: King Taufa'ahau Tupou IV **Series:** F.A.O. **Subject:** SEA Resource Management **Obv:** Uniformed bust facing
Rev: Humpback whale - bull in breach

Date	Mintage	F	VF	XF	Unc	BU
1980 Proof	2,200	Value: 25.00				

KM# 124   2 PA'ANGA
155.5200 g., 0.9990 Silver 4.9949 oz. ASW, 65 mm.
Ruler: King Taufa'ahau Tupou IV **Subject:** America's Cup
Rev: Sailing ship in front of map within circle **Note:** Illustration reduced.

Date	Mintage	F	VF	XF	Unc	BU
1987 Proof	7,500	Value: 90.00				

KM# 51   10 PA'ANGA
62.0000 g., 0.9990 Silver 1.9913 oz. ASW **Ruler:** King Taufa'ahau Tupou IV **Subject:** Constitution Centennial
Obv: Uniformed bust left above stone arch **Rev:** Crowned arms

Date	Mintage	F	VF	XF	Unc	BU
ND(1975)	1,116	—	—	—	32.00	35.00
ND(1975) Proof	420	Value: 40.00				

KM# 64   10 PA'ANGA
0.4000 g., 0.9170 Gold 0.0118 oz. AGW **Ruler:** King Taufa'ahau Tupou IV **Series:** F.A.O. **Subject:** Rural Women's Advancement **Obv:** Queen Salote **Rev:** Female symbol on dove

Date	Mintage	F	VF	XF	Unc	BU
1980	750	—	—	—	—	135
1980 Proof	2,000	Value: 125				

KM# 73   2 PA'ANGA
Copper-Nickel, 44.5 mm.   **Ruler:** King Taufa'ahau Tupou IV
Series: World Food Day **Obv:** Uniformed bust facing **Rev:** Pigs, chickens and nursing calf, logo at top **Edge:** Reeded

Date	Mintage	F	VF	XF	Unc	BU
1981	485,000	—	—	1.75	4.50	8.00

KM# 73a   2 PA'ANGA
42.1000 g., 0.9990 Silver 1.3521 oz. ASW, 44.5 mm.
Ruler: King Taufa'ahau Tupou IV **Series:** World Food Day
Obv: Uniformed bust facing **Rev:** Chickens, pig and nursing calf, logo at top

Date	Mintage	F	VF	XF	Unc	BU
1981 Proof	3,500	Value: 25.00				

KM# 129   2 PA'ANGA
155.5200 g., 0.9990 Silver 4.9949 oz. ASW, 65 mm.
Ruler: King Taufa'ahau Tupou IV **Series:** Olympics **Obv:** Head right **Rev:** Swimmers within circle **Note:** Illustration reduced.

Date	Mintage	F	VF	XF	Unc	BU
1988 Proof	2,000	Value: 125				

KM# 78   10 PA'ANGA
28.2800 g., 0.9250 Silver 0.8410 oz. ASW, 38.61 mm.
Ruler: King Taufa'ahau Tupou IV **Subject:** Commonwealth Games **Obv:** Head right **Rev:** Two runners at finish line
Edge: Reeded

Date	Mintage	F	VF	XF	Unc	BU
1982	500	—	—	—	14.50	17.50
1982 Proof	1,000	Value: 22.50				

KM# 90   10 PA'ANGA
5.1000 g., 0.3750 Gold 0.0615 oz. AGW **Ruler:** King Taufa'ahau Tupou IV **Subject:** 100th Anniversary of Automobile Industry **Obv:** Head right **Rev:** Rolls Royce and Silver Ghost
Note: Similar to 50 Seniti, KM#82

Date	Mintage	F	VF	XF	Unc	BU
1985 Proof	1,000	Value: 70.00				

KM# 90a   10 PA'ANGA
7.9600 g., 0.9170 Gold 0.2347 oz. AGW **Ruler:** King Taufa'ahau Tupou IV **Subject:** 100th Anniversary of Automobile Industry **Obv:** Head right **Rev:** Rolls Royce and Silver Ghost

Date	Mintage	F	VF	XF	Unc	BU
1985 Proof	500	Value: 245				

KM# 120   2 PA'ANGA
28.2800 g., 0.5000 Silver 0.4546 oz. ASW, 38.61 mm.
Ruler: King Taufa'ahau Tupou IV **Subject:** Commonwealth Games **Obv:** Head right **Rev:** Boxing match

Date	Mintage	F	VF	XF	Unc	BU
1986	50,000	—	—	BV	8.50	10.00

KM# 120a   2 PA'ANGA
28.2800 g., 0.9250 Silver 0.8410 oz. ASW, 38.61 mm.
Ruler: King Taufa'ahau Tupou IV **Subject:** Commonwealth Games **Obv:** Head right **Rev:** Boxing match

Date	Mintage	F	VF	XF	Unc	BU
1986 Proof	20,000	Value: 17.50				

KM# 91   10 PA'ANGA
5.1000 g., 0.3750 Gold 0.0615 oz. AGW **Ruler:** King
Taufa'ahau Tupou IV **Subject:** 100th Anniversary of Automobile
Industry **Obv:** Head right **Rev:** Range Rover and Land Rover
Note: Similar to 50 Seniti, KM#83.2

Date	Mintage	F	VF	XF	Unc	BU
1985 Proof	1,000	Value: 70.00				

KM# 91a   10 PA'ANGA
7.9600 g., 0.9170 Gold 0.2347 oz. AGW **Ruler:** King
Taufa'ahau Tupou IV **Subject:** 100th Anniversary of Automobile
Industry **Obv:** Head right **Rev:** Range Rover and Land Rover

Date	Mintage	F	VF	XF	Unc	BU
1985 Proof	500	Value: 245				

KM# 92   10 PA'ANGA
5.1000 g., 0.3750 Gold 0.0615 oz. AGW **Ruler:** King
Taufa'ahau Tupou IV **Subject:** 100th Anniversary of Automobile
Industry **Obv:** Head right **Rev:** Mini Morris Cowley and Touring
Car **Note:** Similar to 50 Seniti, KM#84.

Date	Mintage	F	VF	XF	Unc	BU
1985 Proof	1,000	Value: 70.00				

KM# 92a   10 PA'ANGA
7.9600 g., 0.9170 Gold 0.2347 oz. AGW **Ruler:** King
Taufa'ahau Tupou IV **Subject:** 100th Anniversary of Automobile
Industry **Obv:** Head right **Rev:** Mini Morris Cowley and Touring Car

Date	Mintage	F	VF	XF	Unc	BU
1985 Proof	500	Value: 245				

KM# 93   10 PA'ANGA
5.1000 g., 0.3750 Gold 0.0615 oz. AGW **Ruler:** King
Taufa'ahau Tupou IV **Subject:** 100th Anniversary of Automobile
Industry **Obv:** Head right **Rev:** MGB GT and MG TA **Note:** Similar
to 50 Seniti, KM#85.

Date	Mintage	F	VF	XF	Unc	BU
1985 Proof	1,000	Value: 70.00				

KM# 93a   10 PA'ANGA
7.9600 g., 0.9170 Gold 0.2347 oz. AGW **Ruler:** King
Taufa'ahau Tupou IV **Subject:** 100th Anniversary of Automobile
Industry **Obv:** Head right **Rev:** MGB GT and MG TA

Date	Mintage	F	VF	XF	Unc	BU
1985 Proof	500	Value: 245				

KM# 108   10 PA'ANGA
5.1000 g., 0.3750 Gold 0.0615 oz. AGW **Ruler:** King
Taufa'ahau Tupou IV **Subject:** 85th Birthday of Queen Mother
Obv: Head right **Rev:** Queen Mother as a young girl **Note:** Similar
to 50 Seniti, KM#98.

Date	Mintage	F	VF	XF	Unc	BU
1985 Proof	1,000	Value: 70.00				

KM# 108a   10 PA'ANGA
7.9600 g., 0.9170 Gold 0.2347 oz. AGW **Ruler:** King
Taufa'ahau Tupou IV **Subject:** 85th Birthday of Queen Mother
Obv: Head right **Rev:** Queen Mother as a young girl

Date	Mintage	F	VF	XF	Unc	BU
1985 Proof	500	Value: 245				

KM# 109   10 PA'ANGA
5.1000 g., 0.3750 Gold 0.0615 oz. AGW **Ruler:** King
Taufa'ahau Tupou IV **Subject:** 85th Birthday of Queen Mother
Obv: Head right **Rev:** Wedding of King George VI and Elizabeth
Note: Similar to 50 Seniti, KM#99.

Date	Mintage	F	VF	XF	Unc	BU
1985 Proof	1,000	Value: 70.00				

KM# 109a   10 PA'ANGA
7.9600 g., 0.9170 Gold 0.2347 oz. AGW **Ruler:** King
Taufa'ahau Tupou IV **Subject:** 85th Birthday of Queen Mother
Obv: Head right **Rev:** Wedding of King George VI and Elizabeth

Date	Mintage	F	VF	XF	Unc	BU
1985 Proof	500	Value: 245				

KM# 110   10 PA'ANGA
5.1000 g., 0.3750 Gold 0.0615 oz. AGW **Ruler:** King Taufa'ahau
Tupou IV **Subject:** 85th Birthday of Queen Mother **Obv:** Head
right **Rev:** King George VI and Elizabeth **Note:** Similar to 50
Seniti, KM#100.

Date	Mintage	F	VF	XF	Unc	BU
1985 Proof	1,000	Value: 70.00				

KM# 110a   10 PA'ANGA
7.9600 g., 0.9170 Gold 0.2347 oz. AGW **Ruler:** King
Taufa'ahau Tupou IV **Subject:** 85th Birthday of Queen Mother
Obv: Head right **Rev:** King George VI and Elizabeth

Date	Mintage	F	VF	XF	Unc	BU
1985 Proof	500	Value: 245				

KM# 111   10 PA'ANGA
5.1000 g., 0.3750 Gold 0.0615 oz. AGW **Ruler:** King
Taufa'ahau Tupou IV **Subject:** 85th Birthday of Queen Mother
Obv: Head right **Rev:** Queen Mother holding Queen Elizabeth II
Note: Similar to 50 Seniti, KM#101.

Date	Mintage	F	VF	XF	Unc	BU
1985 Proof	1,000	Value: 70.00				

KM# 111a   10 PA'ANGA
7.9600 g., 0.9170 Gold 0.2347 oz. AGW **Ruler:** King
Taufa'ahau Tupou IV **Subject:** 85th Birthday of Queen Mother
Obv: Head right **Rev:** Queen Mother holding Queen Elizabeth II

Date	Mintage	F	VF	XF	Unc	BU
1985 Proof	500	Value: 245				

KM# 112   10 PA'ANGA
5.1000 g., 0.3750 Gold 0.0615 oz. AGW **Ruler:** King
Taufa'ahau Tupou IV **Subject:** 85th Birthday of Queen Mother
Obv: Head right **Rev:** Queen Mother facing **Note:** Similar to 50
Seniti, KM#102.

Date	Mintage	F	VF	XF	Unc	BU
1985 Proof	1,000	Value: 70.00				

KM# 112a   10 PA'ANGA
7.9600 g., 0.9170 Gold 0.2347 oz. AGW **Ruler:** King
Taufa'ahau Tupou IV **Subject:** 85th Birthday of Queen Mother
Obv: Head right **Rev:** Queen Mother facing

Date	Mintage	F	VF	XF	Unc	BU
1985 Proof	500	—	—	—	—	—

KM# 126   10 PA'ANGA
Copper-Nickel **Ruler:** King Taufa'ahau Tupou IV
Subject: America's Cup **Obv:** Head right **Rev:** National flags and
sailboat

Date	Mintage	F	VF	XF	Unc	BU
1987	—	—	—	—	5.00	6.00

KM# 126a   10 PA'ANGA
31.1030 g., 0.9990 Palladium 0.9989 oz. **Ruler:** King
Taufa'ahau Tupou IV **Subject:** America's Cup **Obv:** Head right
Rev: National flags and sailboat

Date	Mintage	F	VF	XF	Unc	BU
1987 Proof	25,000	Value: 500				

KM# 125   10 PA'ANGA
311.0400 g., 0.9990 Silver 9.9897 oz. ASW, 75 mm.
Ruler: King Taufa'ahau Tupou IV **Subject:** America's Cup
Obv: Head right **Rev:** Sailboat and map **Note:** Illustration
reduced.

Date	Mintage	F	VF	XF	Unc	BU
1987 Proof	5,000	Value: 170				

KM# 130   10 PA'ANGA
15.5500 g., 0.9990 Gold 0.4994 oz. AGW **Ruler:** King
Taufa'ahau Tupou IV **Subject:** Summer Olympics **Obv:** Head
right **Rev:** Boxing match within circle

Date	Mintage	F	VF	XF	Unc	BU
1988 Proof	Est. 2,000	Value: 525				

KM# 131   10 PA'ANGA
31.1000 g., 0.9990 Palladium 0.9988 oz. **Ruler:** King Taufa'ahau
Tupou IV **Series:** Summer Olympics **Obv:** Head right **Rev:** Shot
putter within circle

Date	Mintage	F	VF	XF	Unc	BU
1988 Proof	Est. 2,000	Value: 500				

KM# 132   10 PA'ANGA
15.6300 g., 0.9500 Palladium 0.4774 oz. **Ruler:** King Taufa'ahau
Tupou IV **Series:** Summer Olympics **Obv:** Head right **Rev:** Discus
thrower within circle

Date	Mintage	F	VF	XF	Unc	BU
1988 Proof	Est. 2,000	Value: 250				

KM# 173   10 PA'ANGA
1.2441 g., 0.9999 Gold 0.0400 oz. AGW, 13.92 mm.
Ruler: King Taufa'ahau Tupou IV **Subject:** Destruction of the
English Privateer "Port-au-Prince" **Obv:** Crowned arms
Rev: Looted shipwreck and native **Edge:** Reeded

Date	Mintage	F	VF	XF	Unc	BU
1998 Proof	—	Value: 50.00				

KM# 172   10 PA'ANGA
1.2441 g., 0.9999 Gold 0.0400 oz. AGW, 13.92 mm.
Ruler: King Taufa'ahau Tupou IV **Subject:** King's 80th Birthday
July 3, 1998 **Obv:** National arms within circle **Rev:** Bust 3/4 left
Edge: Reeded **Note:** Struck at Valcambi Mint.

Date	Mintage	F	VF	XF	Unc	BU
1998 Proof	—	Value: 50.00				

KM# 52   20 PA'ANGA
140.0000 g., 0.9990 Silver 4.4964 oz. ASW **Ruler:** King
Taufa'ahau Tupou IV **Subject:** Constitution Centennial
Obv: Heads of various Monarchs **Rev:** National arms

Date	Mintage	F	VF	XF	Unc	BU
1975	1,170	—	—	—	80.00	90.00
1975 Proof	800	Value: 100				

KM# 65 20 PA'ANGA
0.8000 g., 0.9170 Gold 0.0236 oz. AGW **Ruler:** King Taufa'ahau Tupou IV **Series:** F.A.O. **Subject:** Rural Women's Advancement **Obv:** Head of Queen Salote right **Rev:** Female symbol on dove

Date	Mintage	F	VF	XF	Unc	BU
1980	750	—	—	—	—	35.00
1980 Proof	2,000	Value: 30.00				

KM# 53 25 PA'ANGA
5.0000 g., 0.9170 Gold 0.1474 oz. AGW **Ruler:** King Taufa'ahau Tupou IV **Subject:** Constitution Centennial **Obv:** Head facing **Rev:** National arms

Date	Mintage	F	VF	XF	Unc	BU
1975	405	—	—	—	—	160
1975 Proof	105	Value: 165				

KM# 54 50 PA'ANGA
10.0000 g., 0.9170 Gold 0.2948 oz. AGW **Ruler:** King Taufa'ahau Tupou IV **Subject:** Constitution Centennial **Obv:** Head facing **Rev:** National arms

Date	Mintage	F	VF	XF	Unc	BU
1975	205	—	—	—	—	325
1975 Proof	105	Value: 350				

KM# 55 75 PA'ANGA
15.0000 g., 0.9170 Gold 0.4422 oz. AGW **Ruler:** King Taufa'ahau Tupou IV **Subject:** Constitution Centennial **Obv:** Queen Salote Tupou III **Rev:** National arms

Date	Mintage	F	VF	XF	Unc	BU
1975	204	—	—	—	—	450
1975 Proof	105	Value: 470				

KM# 56 100 PA'ANGA
20.0000 g., 0.9170 Gold 0.5896 oz. AGW **Ruler:** King Taufa'ahau Tupou IV **Subject:** Constitution Centennial **Obv:** Uniformed bust left **Rev:** National arms

Date	Mintage	F	VF	XF	Unc	BU
ND(1975)	205	—	—	—	—	600
ND(1975) Proof	105	Value: 625				

KM# 167 100 PA'ANGA
17.7000 g., 0.5833 Gold 0.3319 oz. AGW **Ruler:** King Taufa'ahau Tupou IV **Subject:** 25th Jubilee of Accession **Obv:** Head left at center of circle with dove, crown and stars **Rev:** National arms within circle

Date	Mintage	F	VF	XF	Unc	BU
ND(1990) Proof	Est. 5,000	Value: 360				

KM# 155 100 PA'ANGA
17.7000 g., 0.5833 Gold 0.3319 oz. AGW **Ruler:** King Taufa'ahau Tupou IV **Series:** Olympics **Obv:** Crowned arms within circle **Rev:** Gymnast on rings

Date	Mintage	F	VF	XF	Unc	BU
1993 Proof	3,000	Value: 350				

KM# 163 100 PA'ANGA
17.7000 g., 0.5833 Gold 0.3319 oz. AGW **Ruler:** King Taufa'ahau Tupou IV **Subject:** World Cup Soccer **Obv:** Crowned arms within circle **Rev:** Goalie

Date	Mintage	F	VF	XF	Unc	BU
1994 Proof	Est. 3,000	Value: 350				

KM# 164 100 PA'ANGA
17.7000 g., 0.5833 Gold 0.3319 oz. AGW **Ruler:** King Taufa'ahau Tupou IV **Series:** 1996 Olympic Games **Obv:** Crowned arms within circle **Rev:** High jumper

Date	Mintage	F	VF	XF	Unc	BU
1994 Proof	Est. 3,000	Value: 350				

KM# 165 100 PA'ANGA
17.7000 g., 0.5833 Gold 0.3319 oz. AGW **Ruler:** King Taufa'ahau Tupou IV **Series:** Endangered Wildlife **Obv:** Crowned arms within circle **Rev:** Banded iguana

Date	Mintage	F	VF	XF	Unc	BU
1994 Proof	Est. 2,000	Value: 350				

KM# 21 1/4 HAU
16.0000 g., 0.9800 Palladium 0.5041 oz. **Ruler:** King Taufa'ahau Tupou IV **Subject:** Coronation of Taufa'ahau Tupou IV **Obv:** Head right, small crowns around border **Edge:** HISTORICALLY THE FIRST PALLADIUM COINAGE

Date	Mintage	F	VF	XF	Unc	BU
1967	1,700	—	—	—	—	275

KM# 23 1/2 HAU
32.0000 g., 0.9800 Palladium 1.0082 oz. **Ruler:** King Taufa'ahau Tupou IV **Subject:** Coronation of Taufa'ahau Tupou IV **Rev:** National arms **Edge:** HISTORICALLY THE FIRST PALLADIUM COINAGE

Date	Mintage	F	VF	XF	Unc	BU
1967	1,650	—	—	—	—	525

KM# 74 1/2 HAU
28.2800 g., 0.9250 Silver 0.8410 oz. ASW **Ruler:** King Taufa'ahau Tupou IV **Subject:** Wedding and Treaty of Friendship **Obv:** Head right **Rev:** Wedding of Prince Charles and Lady Diana

Date	Mintage	F	VF	XF	Unc	BU
1981	1,000	—	—	—	22.50	—
1981 Proof	15,000	Value: 18.50				

KM# 122 1/2 HAU
10.0000 g., 0.9170 Gold 0.2948 oz. AGW **Ruler:** King Taufa'ahau Tupou IV **Subject:** Wildlife **Obv:** Head right **Rev:** Ground dwelling birds

Date	Mintage	F	VF	XF	Unc	BU
1986 Proof	5,000	Value: 320				

KM# 25 HAU
64.0000 g., 0.9800 Palladium 2.0164 oz. **Ruler:** King Taufa'ahau Tupou IV **Subject:** Coronation of Taufa'ahau Tupou IV **Obv:** Head right, small crowns around border **Rev:** National arms **Edge:** HISTORICALLY THE FIRST PALLADIUM COINAGE

Date	Mintage	F	VF	XF	Unc	BU
1967	1,500	—	—	—	—	950

KM# 75 HAU
7.9900 g., 0.9170 Gold 0.2356 oz. AGW **Ruler:** King Taufa'ahau Tupou IV **Subject:** Wedding and Treaty of Friendship **Obv:** Head right **Rev:** Wedding of Prince Charles and Lady Diana

Date	Mintage	F	VF	XF	Unc	BU
1981	500	—	—	—	—	260
1981 Proof	2,500	Value: 245				

KM# 79 HAU
7.9900 g., 0.9170 Gold 0.2356 oz. AGW **Ruler:** King Taufa'ahau Tupou IV **Subject:** Commonwealth Games **Obv:** Head right **Rev:** Runners and emblem

Date	Mintage	F	VF	XF	Unc	BU
1982	500	—	—	—	—	235
1982 Proof	500	Value: 250				

KM# 94 HAU
52.0000 g., 0.9500 Platinum 1.5882 oz. APW **Ruler:** King Taufa'ahau Tupou IV **Subject:** 100th Anniversary of Automobile Industry **Obv:** Head right **Rev:** Rolls Royce and Silver Ghost **Note:** Similar to 50 Seniti, KM#82.

Date	Mintage	F	VF	XF	Unc	BU
1985 Proof	—	Value: 3,000				

KM# 95 HAU
52.0000 g., 0.9500 Platinum 1.5882 oz. APW **Ruler:** King Taufa'ahau Tupou IV **Subject:** 100th Anniversary of Automobile Industry **Obv:** Head right **Rev:** Range Rover and Land Rover **Note:** Similar to 50 Seniti, KM#83.

Date	Mintage	F	VF	XF	Unc	BU
1985 Proof	—	Value: 3,000				

KM# 96 HAU
52.0000 g., 0.9500 Platinum 1.5882 oz. APW **Ruler:** King Taufa'ahau Tupou IV **Subject:** 100th Anniversary of Automobile Industry **Obv:** Head right **Rev:** Mini Morris Cowley and Touring Car **Note:** Similar to 50 Seniti, KM#84.

Date	Mintage	F	VF	XF	Unc	BU
1985 Proof	—	Value: 3,000				

KM# 97 HAU
52.0000 g., 0.9500 Platinum 1.5882 oz. APW **Ruler:** King Taufa'ahau Tupou IV **Subject:** 100th Anniversary of Automobile Industry **Obv:** Head right **Rev:** MGB GT and MG TA **Note:** Similar to 50 Seniti, KM#85.

Date	Mintage	F	VF	XF	Unc	BU
1985 Proof	—	Value: 3,000				

KM# 113 HAU
52.0000 g., 0.9500 Platinum 1.5882 oz. APW **Ruler:** King Taufa'ahau Tupou IV **Subject:** 85th Birthday of Queen Mother **Obv:** Head right **Rev:** Queen Mother as a young girl **Note:** Similar to 50 Seniti, KM#98.

Date	Mintage	F	VF	XF	Unc	BU
1985 Proof	—	Value: 3,000				

KM# 114 HAU
52.0000 g., 0.9500 Platinum 1.5882 oz. APW **Ruler:** King Taufa'ahau Tupou IV **Subject:** 85th Birthday of Queen Mother **Obv:** Head right **Rev:** Wedding of King George VI and Elizabeth **Note:** Similar to 50 Seniti, KM#99.

Date	Mintage	F	VF	XF	Unc	BU
1985 Proof	—	Value: 3,000				

KM# 115 HAU
52.0000 g., 0.9500 Platinum 1.5882 oz. APW **Ruler:** King Taufa'ahau Tupou IV **Subject:** 85th Birthday of Queen Mother **Obv:** Head right **Rev:** King George VI and Elizabeth **Note:** Similar to 50 Seniti, KM#100.

Date	Mintage	F	VF	XF	Unc	BU
1985 Proof	—	Value: 3,000				

KM# 116 HAU
52.0000 g., 0.9500 Platinum 1.5882 oz. APW **Ruler:** King Taufa'ahau Tupou IV **Subject:** 85th Birthday of Queen Mother **Obv:** Head right **Rev:** Queen Mother holding Queen Elizabeth II **Note:** Similar to 50 Seniti, KM#101.

Date	Mintage	F	VF	XF	Unc	BU
1985 Proof	—	Value: 3,000				

KM# 117 HAU
52.0000 g., 0.9500 Platinum 1.5882 oz. APW **Ruler:** King Taufa'ahau Tupou IV **Subject:** 85th Birthday of Queen Mother **Obv:** Head right **Rev:** Queen Mother facing **Note:** Similar to 50 Seniti, KM#102.

Date	Mintage	F	VF	XF	Unc	BU
1985 Proof	—	Value: 3,000				

KM# 76   5 HAU
15.9800 g., 0.9170 Gold 0.4711 oz. AGW **Ruler:** King
Taufa'ahau Tupou IV **Subject:** Wedding and Treaty of Friendship
Obv: Head right **Rev:** Wedding of Prince Charles and Lady Diana

Date	Mintage	F	VF	XF	Unc	BU
1981	250	—	—	—	—	525
1981 Proof	1,000	Value: 500				

COUNTERMARKED
COMMEMORATIVE COINAGE

Commemorative coins which contain a countermark
creating a new commemorative representation. The Date
listed refers to the original date the coin was struck.

KM# 14   20 SENITI
Copper-Nickel, 28.5 mm. **Ruler:** King Taufa'ahau Tupou IV
Countermark: 1918/TTIV/1968 **Obv:** Head right, small crowns
around border **Note:** Countermark on KM#13.

Date	Mintage	F	VF	XF	Unc	BU
ND(1967) Proof	1,577	Value: 6.00				

KM# 10   50 SENITI
Copper-Nickel, Gold Plated, 34.5 mm. **Ruler:** King
Taufa'ahau Tupou IV **Countermark:** IN MEMORIAM/1965 +1970
Obv: Head right **Edge:** Reeded **Note:** Countermark on KM#10.

Date	Mintage	F	VF	XF	Unc	BU
1967	Inc. above	—	—	—	5.00	—

KM# 16   50 SENITI
Copper-Nickel, 34.5 mm. **Ruler:** King Taufa'ahau Tupou IV
Countermark: 1918/TTIV/1968 **Obv:** Head right, small crowns
around border **Note:** Countermark on KM#15.

Date	Mintage	F	VF	XF	Unc	BU
ND(1967) Proof	1,577	Value: 7.00				

KM# 12   PA'ANGA
Copper-Nickel, Gold Plated, 38.5 mm. **Ruler:** King Taufa'ahau
Tupou IV **Countermark:** IN MEMORIAM/1965 + 1970
Obv: Head right **Note:** Countermark on KM#11.

Date	Mintage	F	VF	XF	Unc	BU
1967	Inc. above	—	—	—	6.50	—

KM# 18   PA'ANGA
Copper-Nickel, 38.5 mm. **Ruler:** King Taufa'ahau Tupou IV
Countermark: 1918/TTIV/1968 **Obv:** Head right, small crowns
around border **Note:** Countermark on KM#17.

Date	Mintage	F	VF	XF	Unc	BU
1967 Proof	1,577	Value: 8.00				

KM# 34   PA'ANGA
Copper-Nickel, Gold Plated, 38.5 mm. **Ruler:** King Taufa'ahau
Tupou IV **Countermark:** Oil rig 1969 OIL SEARCH **Obv:** Head right
Edge: Reeded **Note:** Countermark on KM#17.

Date	Mintage	F	VF	XF	Unc	BU
1968	5,017	—	1.50	2.50	5.50	—

KM# 35   PA'ANGA
Copper-Nickel, Gold Plated, 38.5 mm.
Countermark: COMMONWEALTH MEMBER/1970 **Obv:** Head
right **Edge:** Reeded **Note:** Countermark on KM#17.

Date	Mintage	F	VF	XF	Unc	BU
1968	3,000	—	1.50	3.00	6.50	—

KM# 36   PA'ANGA
Copper-Nickel, Gold Plated, 38.5 mm. **Ruler:** King
Taufa'ahau Tupou IV **Countermark:** INVESTITURE/1971
Obv: Head right **Edge:** Reeded **Note:** Countermark on KM#17.

Date	Mintage	F	VF	XF	Unc	BU
1968	3,000	—	1.50	3.00	6.50	—
1968 Proof	1,000	Value: 9.00				

KM# 20   2 PA'ANGA
Copper-Nickel, 44.5 mm. **Ruler:** King Taufa'ahau Tupou IV
Countermark: 1918/TTIV/1968 **Obv:** Head right, small crowns
around border **Note:** Countermark on KM#19.

Date	Mintage	F	VF	XF	Unc	BU
ND(1967) Proof	1,577	Value: 10.00				

KM# 38   2 PA'ANGA
Copper-Nickel, Gold Plated, 44.5 mm. **Ruler:** King
Taufa'ahau Tupou IV **Countermark:** Oil rig 1969 OIL SEARCH
Obv: Head right **Edge:** Reeded **Note:** Countermark on KM#37.

Date	Mintage	F	VF	XF	Unc	BU
1968	5,039	—	2.00	4.00	7.50	—

KM# 39   2 PA'ANGA
Copper-Nickel, Gold Plated, 44.5 mm. **Ruler:** King Taufa'ahau
Tupou IV **Countermark:** COMMONWEALTH MEMBER/1970
Obv: Head right **Edge:** Reeded **Note:** Countermark on KM#37.

Date	Mintage	F	VF	XF	Unc	BU
1968	3,006	—	2.00	4.50	8.50	—

KM# 40   2 PA'ANGA
Copper-Nickel, Gold Plated, 44.5 mm. **Ruler:** King Taufa'ahau
Tupou IV **Countermark:** INVESTITURE/1971 **Obv:** Head right
Note: Countermark on KM#37.

Date	Mintage	F	VF	XF	Unc	BU
1968	3,000	—	2.00	4.50	8.50	—
1968 Proof	1,000	Value: 15.00				

KM# 22   1/4 HAU
16.0000 g., 0.9800 Palladium 0.5041 oz. **Ruler:** King Taufa'ahau
Tupou IV **Countermark:** 1918/TTIV/1968 **Edge:** HISTORICALLY
THE FIRST PALLADIUM COINAGE **Note:** Countermark on KM#21.

Date	Mintage	F	VF	XF	Unc	BU
1967	400	—	—	—	—	275

KM# 24   1/2 HAU
32.0000 g., 0.9800 Palladium 1.0082 oz. **Ruler:** King Taufa'ahau
Tupou IV **Countermark:** 1918/TTIV/1968 **Obv:** Head right, small
crowns around border **Rev:** Crowned arms **Edge:** HISTORICALLY
THE FIRST PALLADIUM COINAGE **Note:** Countermark on KM#23.

Date	Mintage	F	VF	XF	Unc	BU
ND(1967)	513	—	—	—	—	475

KM# 26   HAU
64.0000 g., 0.9800 Palladium 2.0164 oz. **Ruler:** King Taufa'ahau
Tupou IV **Countermark:** 1918/TTIV/1968 **Edge:** HISTORICALLY
THE FIRST PALLADIUM COINAGE **Note:** Countermark on KM#25.

Date	Mintage	F	VF	XF	Unc	BU
ND(1967)	400	—	—	—	—	950

MINT SETS

KM#	Date	Mintage	Identification	Issue Price	Mkt Val
MS1	1962 (3)	—	KM#1-3	—	1,000
MS2	1967 (3)	1,500	KM#21, 23, 25	207	1,275
MS3	1968 (3)	400	KM#22, 24, 26	—	1,700
MS4	1970 (2)	10,000	KM#10, 12	2.30	11.50
MS5	1969 (2)	10,000	KM#34, 38	13.68	12.50
MS6	1970 (2)	3,000	KM#35, 39	13.68	15.00
MS7	1971 (2)	3,000	KM#36, 40	4.80	15.00
MS8	1974 (8)	10,000	KM#27-33, 37	7.60	20.00
MS9	1975 (8)	—	KM#42-49	7.75	18.00
MS10	1975 (3)	—	KM#53-56	385	885
MS11	1975 (3)	—	KM#50-52	59.60	85.00
MS12	1977 (5)	—	KM#44-47	0.85	7.00
MS13	1977 (2)	—	KM#49, 57	3.00	10.00
MS14	1978 (2)	—	KM#58-59	3.00	11.50
MS15	1978 (5)	—	KM#42-46	—	5.50
MS16	1979 (2)	8,008	KM#60-61	3.00	10.00
MS17	1980 (2)	8,000	KM#62-63	3.00	12.00
MS18	1980 (2)	750	KM#64-65, Gold	30.00	45.00
MS19	1981 (8)	15,000	KM#66-73	5.38	35.00
MS20	1985 (5)	20,000	KM#98-102	25.25	10.00
MS21	1985 (4)	20,000	KM#82-85. Auto Industry.	21.00	15.00
MS22	1991 (6)	—	KM#66-71	—	6.00

PROOF SETS

KM#	Date	Mintage	Identification	Issue Price	Mkt Val
PS1	1962 (3)	250	KM#1-3	—	1,070
PS2	1962 (3)	25	KM#1a-3a. Platinum.	—	2,400
PS3	1967 (7)	5,000	KM#4-9, 11	15.00	22.50
PS4	1967 (4)	1,923	KM#13, 15, 17, 19	17.25	25.00
PS5	1968 (8)	2,500	KM#27-33, 37	22.50	30.00
PS6	1968 (4)	1,577	KM#14, 16, 18, 20	22.80	32.50
PS8	1971 (2)	1,000	KM#36, 40	13.40	25.00
PS9	1975 (3)	418	KM#50-52	82.00	120
PS10	1975 (4)	105	KM#53-56	538	950
PS11	1978 (2)	750	KM#58a-59a	—	55.00
PS12	1979 (2)	854	KM#60a-61a	45.00	50.00
PS13	1980 (2)	400	KM#62a-63a	80.00	40.00
PS14	1980 (2)	200	KM#64-65	60.00	45.00
PS15	1981 (2)	3,500	KM#72a-73a	88.00	40.00
PSA15		—	KM#74-76	—	450
PS16	1985 (5)	20,000	KM#98-102, Copper-nickel	26.25	18.00
PS17	1985 (5)	10,000	KM#103-107, Silver clad copper-nickel	55.00	22.00
PS18	1985 (5)	5,000	KM#103a-107a, .925 Silver	180	75.00
PS19	1985 (5)	1,000	KM#108-112, .374 Gold	315	200
PS20	1985 (5)	500	KM#108a-112a, .917 Gold	775	725
PS21	1985 (5)	50	KM#113-117, .950 Platinum. BV+15%.	5,850	—
PS22	1985 (4)	10,000	KM#86-89	44.00	20.00
PS23	1985 (4)	5,000	KM#86a-89a, .925 Silver	144	75.00
PS24	1985 (4)	1,000	KM#90-93, .374 Gold	252	170
PS25	1985 (4)	500	KM#90a-93a, .917 Gold	620	580
PS26	1985 (4)	50	KM#94-97, .950 Platinum. BV+15%.	4,680	—
PS28	1988 (4)	2,000	KM#129-132	—	950

VIET NAM-TONKIN

Tonkin (North Viet Nam), a former French protectorate in North Indo-China, comprises the greater part of present North Viet Nam. It had an area of 44,672 sq. mi. (75,700 sq. km.) and a population of about 4 million. Capital: Hanoi. The initial value of Tonkin to France was contained in the access it afforded to the trade of China's Yunnan province.

France established a protectorate over Annam and Tonkin by the treaties of Tientsin and Hue negotiated in 1884. Tonkin was incorporated in the independent state of Viet Nam (within the French Union) and upon the defeat of France by the Viet Minh became the body of *North Viet Nam*.

MINT MARK
(a) - Paris, privy marks only

FRENCH PROTECTORATE
MILLED COINAGE

KM# 1   1/600 PIASTRE
2.1000 g., Zinc   **Obv:** Legend around square center hole
Obv. Leg.: PROTECTORAT DU TONKIN **Rev:** Value above and below, "Thong-bao" at left and right **Note:** 0.9 mm thick planchet.

Date	Mintage	F	VF	XF	Unc	BU
1905(a)	60,000,000	4.50	8.50	20.00	50.00	—

ESSAIS

KM#	Date	Mintage	Identification	Mkt Val
E1	1905(a)	—	1/600 Piastre. Zinc. 2.1000 g. Legend around center squared hole. PROTECTORAT DU TONKIN. Value above and below squared hole in center flanked by thong-bao. 0.9 mm thick planchet.	300

PIEFORTS

KM#	Date	Mintage	Identification	Mkt Val
P1	1905(a)	—	1/600 Piastre. Zinc. 4.8000 g. PROTECTORAT DU TONKIN. Value above and below, "Thong-bao" at left and right. 1.5 mm thick planchet.	700

TRANSNISTRIA

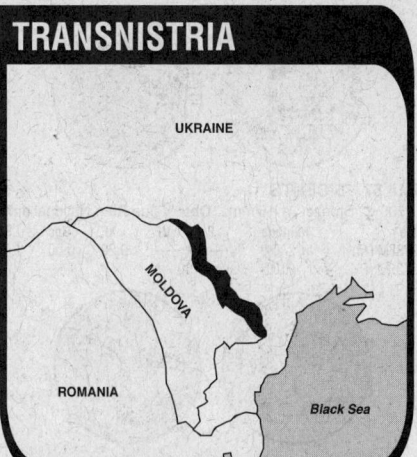

The Pridnestrovskaia Moldavskaia Respublica was formed in 1990, even before the separation of Moldavia from Russia. It has an area of 11,544 sq. mi. (29,900 sq. km.) and a population of 555,000. Capital: Tiraspol.

The area was conquered from the Turks in the last half of the 18th century, and in 1792 the capital city of Bessarabia (present Moldova and part of the Ukraine) became part of the Russian Empire. During the Russian Revolution, in 1918, the area was taken by Romanian troops, and in 1924 the Moldavian Autonomous SSR was formed on the left bank of the Dniester River. On June 22, 1941, Romania declared war on the U.S.S.R. and Romanian troops fought alongside the Germans up to Stalingrad. A Romanian occupation area between the Dniester and Bug Rivers called Transnistria was established in October 1941. Its center was the port of Odessa.

Once the Moldavian SSR declared independence in August 1991, Transnistria did not want to be part of Moldavia. In 1992, Moldova tried to solve the issue militarily with battles in Bendery and Doubossary. The conflict was ended with Russian mediation and Russian peacekeeping forces were stationed there.

Transnistria (or Transdniestra) has a president, parliament, army and police forces, but as yet it is lacking international recognition.

MOLDAVIAN REPUBLIC
STANDARD COINAGE
1 Rublei = 100 Kopeek

KM# 1   KOPEEK
0.6200 g., Aluminum, 15.9 mm.   **Obv:** National arms
Obv. Leg.: ПРИДНЕСТРОВСКАЯ МОЛДАВСКАЯ
РЕСПУБЛИКА **Rev:** Value between wheat stalks **Edge:** Plain

Date	Mintage	F	VF	XF	Unc	BU
2000	—	—	0.10	0.30	0.40	

KM# 2   5 KOPEEK
0.7000 g., Aluminum, 17.9 mm.   **Obv:** National arms
Obv. Leg.: ПРИДНЕСТРОВСКАЯ МОЛДАВСКАЯ
РЕСПУБЛИКА **Rev:** Value flanked by wheat stalks **Edge:** Plain

Date	Mintage	F	VF	XF	Unc	BU
2000	—	—	0.20	0.50	0.65	

KM# 3   10 KOPEEK
1.0000 g., Aluminum, 20 mm.   **Obv:** National arms
Obv. Leg.: ПРИДНЕСТРОВСКАЯ МОЛДАВСКАЯ
РЕСПУБЛИКА **Rev:** Value flanked by wheat stalks **Edge:** Plain

Date	Mintage	F	VF	XF	Unc	BU
2000	—	—	0.25	0.65	0.90	

KM# 4   50 KOPEEK
2.6000 g., Aluminum-Bronze, 18.86 mm.   **Obv:** National arms
Obv. Leg.: ПРИДНЕСТРОВСКАЯ МОЛДАВСКАЯ
РЕСПУБЛИКА **Rev:** Value within sprays **Edge:** Plain

Date	Mintage	F	VF	XF	Unc	BU
2000	—	—	0.15	0.45	1.10	1.50

KM# 6   50 RUBLEI
14.3700 g., Copper-Nickel, 32.75 mm.   **Subject:** 10th Anniversary
Obv: State arms above value **Rev:** Statue **Edge:** Plain

Date	Mintage	F	VF	XF	Unc	BU
(ND)2000 Proof	—	Value: 40.00				

TRINIDAD & TOBAGO

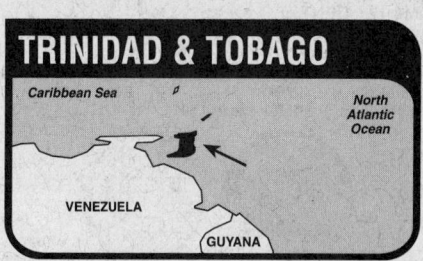

The Republic of Trinidad and Tobago is situated 7 miles (11 km.) off the coast of Venezuela, has an area of 1,981 sq. mi. (5,130 sq. km.) and a population of *1.2 million. Capital: Port-of-Spain. The island of Trinidad contains the world's largest natural asphalt bog. Birds of Paradise live on little Tobago, the only place outside of their native New Guinea where they can be found in a wild state. Petroleum and petroleum products are the mainstay of the economy. Petroleum products, crude oil and sugar are exported.

Columbus discovered Trinidad and Tobago in 1498. Trinidad remained under Spanish rule from the time of its settlement in 1592 until its capture by the British in 1797. It was ceded to the British in 1802. Tobago was occupied at various times by the French, Dutch and English before being ceded to Britain in 1814. Trinidad and Tobago were merged into a single colony in 1888. The colony was part of the Federation of the West Indies until Aug. 31, 1962, when it became independent. A new constitution establishing a republican form of government was adopted on Aug. 1, 1976. Trinidad and Tobago is a member of the Commonwealth of Nations. The President is Chief of State. The Prime Minister is Head of Government.

RULER
British, until 1976
MINT MARKS
FM - Franklin Mint, U.S.A.*
   *NOTE: From 1975-1985 the Franklin Mint produced coinage in up to 3 different qualities. Qualities of issue are designated in ( ) after each date and are defined as follows:
   (M) MATTE - Normal circulation strike or a dull finish produced by sandblasting special uncirculated (polish finish) or proof quality dies.
   (U) SPECIAL UNCIRCULATED - Polished or proof-like in appearance without any frosted features.
   (P) PROOF - The highest quality obtainable having mirror-like fields and frosted features.
MONETARY SYSTEM
100 Cents = 1 Dollar

BRITISH COLONIAL
STANDARD COINAGE

KM# 1   CENT
1.9500 g., Bronze, 17.8 mm.   **Obv:** Value **Rev:** National arms
Edge: Plain

Date	Mintage	F	VF	XF	Unc	BU
1966	24,500,000	—	—	0.10	0.15	0.30
1966 Proof	8,000	Value: 1.00				

Date	Mintage	F	VF	XF	Unc	BU
1967	4,000,000	—	—	0.10	0.25	0.50
1968	5,000,000	—	—	0.10	0.25	0.50
1970	5,000,000	—	—	0.10	0.25	0.50
1970 Proof	2,104	Value: 1.50				
1971	10,600,000	—	—	0.10	0.15	0.30
1971FM (M)	286,000	—	—	0.10	0.20	0.40
1971FM (P)	12,000	Value: 0.50				
1972	16,500,000	—	—	0.10	0.20	0.30
1973	10,000,000	—	—	0.10	0.20	0.30

KM# 9   CENT
1.9500 g., Bronze, 17.8 mm. **Subject:** 10th Anniversary of Independence **Obv:** Value and date **Rev:** National arms **Edge:** Plain

Date	Mintage	F	VF	XF	Unc	BU
1972	5,000,000	—	—	0.10	0.15	0.30
1972FM (M)	125,000	—	—	0.10	0.25	0.50
1972FM (P)	16,000	Value: 0.50				

KM# 17   CENT
1.9500 g., Bronze, 17.8 mm. **Obv:** Value and date **Rev:** National arms **Edge:** Plain

Date	Mintage	F	VF	XF	Unc	BU
1973FM (M)	127,000	—	—	0.20	0.50	1.00
1973FM (P)	20,000	Value: 1.50				

KM# 25   CENT
1.9500 g., Bronze, 17.8 mm. **Obv:** National arms **Rev:** Hummingbird and value **Edge:** Plain

Date	Mintage	F	VF	XF	Unc	BU
1974FM (M)	128,000	—	—	0.20	0.50	1.00
1974FM (P)	14,000	Value: 0.80				
1975	10,000,000	—	—	0.20	0.50	1.00
1975FM (M)	125,000	—	—	0.20	0.50	1.00
1975FM (U)	1,111	—	—	0.50	1.25	2.50
1975FM (P)	24,000	Value: 0.80				
1976	15,050,000	—	—	0.20	0.50	1.00

KM# 2   5 CENTS
3.2500 g., Bronze, 21.15 mm. **Obv:** Value **Rev:** National arms

Date	Mintage	F	VF	XF	Unc	BU
1966	7,500,000	—	—	0.10	0.25	0.50
1966 Proof	8,000	Value: 1.25				
1967	3,000,000	—	—	0.10	0.50	1.00
1970 Proof	2,104	Value: 1.75				
1971	2,400,000	—	—	0.10	0.50	1.00
1971FM (M)	57,000	—	—	—	0.15	0.30
1971FM (P)	12,000	Value: 0.75				
1972	2,250,000	—	—	0.10	0.50	1.00

KM# 10   5 CENTS
3.2500 g., Bronze, 21.15 mm. **Subject:** 10th Anniversary of Independence **Obv:** Value and date **Rev:** National arms

Date	Mintage	F	VF	XF	Unc	BU
1972	15,000	—	—	0.15	0.35	0.70
1972FM (M)	25,000	—	—	0.15	0.25	0.50
1972FM (P)	16,000	Value: 0.75				

KM# 57   5 CENTS
3.2500 g., Bronze, 21.15 mm. **Obv:** Value **Rev:** National arms

Date	Mintage	F	VF	XF	Unc	BU
1973FM (M)	27,000	—	—	0.20	0.50	1.00
1973FM (P)	20,000	Value: 1.50				

KM# 26   5 CENTS
3.2500 g., Bronze, 21.15 mm. **Obv:** National arms **Rev:** Bird of Paradise and value

Date	Mintage	F	VF	XF	Unc	BU
1974FM (M)	28,000	—	—	0.20	0.50	1.00
1974FM (P)	14,000	Value: 0.75				
1975	1,500,000	—	—	0.10	0.45	0.90
1975FM (M)	25,000	—	—	0.20	0.45	0.90
1975FM (U)	1,111	—	—	1.00	2.50	5.00
1975FM (P)	24,000	Value: 0.75				
1976	7,500,000	—	—	0.10	0.45	0.90

KM# 3   10 CENTS
1.4000 g., Copper-Nickel, 16.3 mm. **Obv:** Value and date **Rev:** National arms **Edge:** Reeded

Date	Mintage	F	VF	XF	Unc	BU
1966	7,800,000	—	—	0.10	0.30	0.60
1966 Proof	8,000	Value: 1.50				
1967	4,000,000	—	—	0.10	0.45	0.90
1970 Proof	2,104	Value: 2.00				
1971	—	—	—	0.10	0.45	0.90
1971FM (M)	29,000	—	—	—	0.35	0.70
1971FM (P)	12,000	Value: 1.00				
1972	4,000,000	—	—	0.10	0.30	0.60

KM# 11   10 CENTS
1.4000 g., Copper-Nickel, 16.3 mm. **Subject:** 10th Anniversary of Independence **Obv:** Value **Rev:** National arms **Edge:** Reeded

Date	Mintage	F	VF	XF	Unc	BU
1972	41,000	—	—	—	0.40	0.80
1972FM (M)	13,000	—	—	—	0.60	1.20
1972FM (P)	16,000	Value: 1.00				

KM# 58   10 CENTS
1.4000 g., Copper-Nickel, 16.3 mm. **Obv:** Value **Rev:** National arms **Edge:** Reeded

Date	Mintage	F	VF	XF	Unc	BU
1973FM (M)	14,000	—	—	—	1.00	2.00
1973FM (P)	20,000	Value: 2.50				

KM# 27   10 CENTS
1.4000 g., Copper-Nickel, 16.3 mm. **Obv:** National arms **Rev:** Flaming Hibiscus and value **Edge:** Reeded

Date	Mintage	F	VF	XF	Unc	BU
1974FM (M)	16,000	—	—	0.50	1.00	2.00
1974FM (P)	14,000	Value: 1.00				
1975	4,000,000	—	—	0.10	0.25	0.50
1975FM (M)	13,000	—	—	0.25	0.50	1.00
1975FM (U)	1,111	—	—	1.00	2.50	5.00
1975FM (P)	24,000	Value: 1.00				
1976	14,720,000	—	—	0.10	0.20	0.40

KM# 4   25 CENTS
3.5000 g., Copper-Nickel, 20 mm. **Obv:** Value **Rev:** National arms **Edge:** Reeded

Date	Mintage	F	VF	XF	Unc	BU
1966	7,200,000	—	0.10	0.15	0.35	0.70
1966 Proof	8,000	Value: 1.75				
1967	1,800,000	—	0.10	0.15	0.50	1.00
1970 Proof	2,014	Value: 2.50				
1971	1,500,000	—	0.10	0.15	0.50	1.00
1971FM (M)	11,000	—	—	0.30	0.65	1.30
1971FM (P)	12,000	Value: 1.25				
1972	3,000,000	—	0.10	0.15	0.35	0.70

KM# 12   25 CENTS
3.5000 g., Copper-Nickel, 20 mm. **Subject:** 10th Anniversary of Independence **Obv:** Value and date **Rev:** National arms **Edge:** Reeded

Date	Mintage	F	VF	XF	Unc	BU
1972	14,000	—	0.20	0.65	1.00	2.00
1972FM (M)	5,000	—	—	0.50	1.50	3.00
1972FM (P)	16,000	Value: 1.25				

KM# 59   25 CENTS
3.5000 g., Copper-Nickel, 20 mm. **Obv:** Value **Rev:** National arms **Edge:** Reeded

Date	Mintage	F	VF	XF	Unc	BU
1973FM (M)	6,575	—	—	0.50	2.25	4.50
1973FM (P)	20,000	Value: 3.00				

KM# 28   25 CENTS
3.5000 g., Copper-Nickel, 20 mm. **Obv:** National arms **Rev:** Chaconia and value **Edge:** Reeded

Date	Mintage	F	VF	XF	Unc	BU
1974FM (M)	8,258	—	—	0.50	1.75	3.50
1974FM (P)	14,000	Value: 1.25				
1975	3,000,000	—	0.10	0.15	0.30	0.60
1975FM (M)	5,000	—	—	0.50	1.50	3.00
1975FM (U)	1,111	—	—	0.75	2.00	4.00
1975FM (P)	24,000	Value: 1.25				
1976	9,000,000	—	0.10	0.15	0.30	0.60

KM# 5   50 CENTS
7.0000 g., Copper-Nickel, 26 mm. **Obv:** Value **Rev:** National arms **Edge:** Reeded

Date	Mintage	F	VF	XF	Unc	BU
1966	975,000	—	0.25	0.60	1.50	3.00
1966 Proof	8,000	Value: 2.50				
1967	750,000	—	0.25	0.50	1.25	2.50
1970 Proof	2,104	Value: 3.00				
1971FM (M)	5,714	—	—	0.75	2.50	5.00
1971FM (P)	12,000	Value: 1.75				

KM# 13 50 CENTS
7.0000 g., Copper-Nickel, 26 mm. **Subject:** 10th Anniversary of Independence **Obv:** Value **Rev:** National arms **Edge:** Reeded

Date	Mintage	F	VF	XF	Unc	BU
1972	375,000	—	0.50	0.75	1.50	3.00
1972FM (M)	2,500	—	—	1.50	5.00	10.00
1972FM (P)	16,000	Value: 1.75				

KM# 22 50 CENTS
7.0000 g., Copper-Nickel, 26 mm. **Obv:** National arms **Rev:** Kettle drums and value **Edge:** Reeded

Date	Mintage	F	VF	XF	Unc	BU
1973FM (M)	4,075	—	—	1.00	2.50	5.00
1973FM (P)	20,000	Value: 2.25				
1974FM (M)	5,758	—	—	1.00	2.50	5.00
1974FM (P)	14,000	Value: 2.25				
1975FM (M)	2,500	—	—	1.25	4.00	8.00
1975FM (U)	1,111	—	—	1.00	2.50	5.00
1975FM (P)	24,000	Value: 2.00				
1976	750,000	—	0.50	0.75	1.50	3.00

KM# 6 DOLLAR
12.7000 g., Nickel, 32 mm. **Series:** F.A.O. **Obv:** National arms **Rev:** Value in front of leaves

Date	Mintage	F	VF	XF	Unc	BU
1969	250,000	—	0.75	1.50	3.50	7.00

KM# 7 DOLLAR
12.7000 g., Copper-Nickel, 32 mm. **Obv:** Value **Rev:** National arms

Date	Mintage	F	VF	XF	Unc	BU
1971 (M)	2,857	—	—	2.00	5.00	10.00
1971 (P)	12,000	Value: 3.00				

KM# 7a DOLLAR
Nickel, 36 mm. **Obv:** Value **Rev:** National arms

Date	Mintage	F	VF	XF	Unc	BU
1970 Proof	2,014	Value: 6.00				

KM# 14 DOLLAR
Copper-Nickel, 36 mm. **Subject:** 10th Anniversary of Independence **Obv:** National arms **Rev:** Bird on branch and value

Date	Mintage	F	VF	XF	Unc	BU
1972	9,700	—	—	2.00	6.00	12.00
1972FM (M)	1,250	—	—	4.00	12.50	20.00
1972FM (P)	16,000	Value: 4.00				

KM# 23 DOLLAR
Copper-Nickel, 36 mm. **Obv:** National arms **Rev:** Bird on branch and value

Date	Mintage	F	VF	XF	Unc	BU
1973FM (M)	2,825	—	—	2.00	5.50	10.00
1973FM (P)	20,000	Value: 4.00				
1974FM (M)	4,508	—	—	2.00	5.50	10.00
1974FM (P)	14,000	Value: 4.00				
1975FM (M)	1,250	—	—	2.50	6.50	12.00
1975FM (U)	1,111	—	—	2.50	6.50	12.00
1975FM (P)	24,000	Value: 4.00				

KM# 8 5 DOLLARS
29.7000 g., 0.9250 Silver 0.8832 oz. ASW, 40 mm. **Obv:** National arms **Rev:** Scarlet Ibis and value

Date	Mintage	F	VF	XF	Unc	BU
1971FM (M)	571	—	—	15.00	25.00	30.00
1971FM (P)	11,000	Value: 17.50				
1973FM (M)	1,825	—	—	12.50	20.00	25.00
1973FM (P)	25,000	Value: 17.50				
1974FM (P)	16,000	Value: 17.50				
1975FM (P)	26,000	Value: 17.50				

KM# 8a 5 DOLLARS
Copper-Nickel, 40 mm. **Obv:** National arms **Rev:** Scarlet Ibis and value

Date	Mintage	F	VF	XF	Unc	BU
1974FM (M)	3,508	—	—	5.00	10.00	15.00
1975FM (M)	250	—	—	7.00	20.00	25.00
1975FM (U)	1,111	—	—	5.00	10.00	12.50

KM# 15 5 DOLLARS
29.7000 g., 0.9250 Silver 0.8832 oz. ASW, 40 mm. **Subject:** 10th Anniversary of Independence **Obv:** National arms **Rev:** Scarlet Ibis and value

Date	Mintage	F	VF	XF	Unc	BU
1972	10,000	—	—	7.00	16.00	17.50
1972FM	250	—	—	20.00	40.00	45.00
1972FM Proof	19,000	Value: 15.00				

KM# 16 10 DOLLARS
35.0000 g., 0.9250 Silver 1.0408 oz. ASW, 42 mm. **Subject:** 10th Anniversary of Independence **Obv:** National arms **Rev:** Fish, ship, map and value within waves

Date	Mintage	F	VF	XF	Unc	BU
1972	—	—	—	8.00	17.50	20.00
1972FM (M)	125	—	—	100	125	130
1972FM (P)	26,000	Value: 18.00				

KM# 24a 10 DOLLARS
35.0000 g., 0.9250 Silver 1.0408 oz. ASW, 42 mm. **Obv:** National arms **Rev:** Fish, ship, map and value within waves

Date	Mintage	F	VF	XF	Unc	BU
1973FM (M)	1,700	—	—	10.00	22.50	25.00
1973FM (U)	—	—	—	10.00	20.00	22.50
1973FM (P)	24,000	Value: 18.50				
1974FM (P)	21,000	Value: 18.50				
1975FM (P)	28,000	Value: 18.50				

KM# 24 10 DOLLARS
Copper-Nickel, 42 mm. **Obv:** National arms **Rev:** Fish, ship, map and value within waves

Date	Mintage	F	VF	XF	Unc	BU
1974FM (M)	3,632	—	—	6.50	12.50	15.00
1975FM (M)	125	—	—	30.00	50.00	60.00
1975FM (U)	1,111	—	—	9.50	15.00	20.00

REPUBLIC

STANDARD COINAGE

KM# 29 CENT
1.9500 g., Bronze, 17.76 mm. **Obv:** National arms **Rev:** Hummingbird and value **Edge:** Plain

Date	Mintage	F	VF	XF	Unc	BU
1976FM (M)	150,000	—	—	0.20	0.35	1.00
1976	—	—	—	0.20	0.35	1.00
1976FM (U)	582	—	—	1.00	2.50	3.50
1976FM (P)	10,000	Value: 0.60				
1977FM	25,000,000	—	—	0.20	0.35	1.00
1977FM (M)	150,000	—	—	0.20	0.35	1.00
1977FM (U)	633	—	—	1.00	2.50	3.50
1977FM (P)	5,337	Value: 0.60				
1978FM	12,500,000	—	—	0.20	0.35	1.00
1978FM (M)	150,000	—	—	0.20	0.35	1.00
1978FM (U)	472	—	—	1.00	2.50	3.50
1978FM (P)	4,845	Value: 1.00				
1979FM	30,200,000	—	—	0.20	0.35	1.00
1979FM (M)	150,000	—	—	0.20	0.35	1.00
1979FM (U)	518	—	—	1.00	2.50	3.50
1979FM (P)	3,270	Value: 1.00				
1980FM	12,500,000	—	—	0.20	0.35	1.00
1980FM (M)	75,000	—	—	0.20	0.35	1.00
1980FM (U)	796	—	—	1.00	2.50	3.50
1980FM (P)	2,393	Value: 1.00				
1981FM	—	—	—	0.20	0.35	1.00
1981FM (M)	—	—	—	0.20	0.35	1.00
1981FM (U)	—	—	—	1.00	2.50	3.50
1981FM (P)	—	Value: 1.00				
1982FM	—	—	—	0.20	0.35	1.00
1983FM	—	—	—	0.20	0.35	1.00
1984FM	—	—	—	0.20	0.35	1.00
1985FM	25,400,000	—	—	0.20	0.35	1.00
1986FM	10,000,000	—	—	0.20	0.35	1.00
1987FM	10,000,000	—	—	0.20	0.35	1.00
1988FM	5,000,000	—	—	0.20	0.35	1.00
1989FM	—	—	—	0.20	0.35	1.00
1990FM	—	—	—	0.20	0.35	1.00
1991FM	—	—	—	0.20	0.35	1.00
1993FM	—	—	—	0.20	0.35	1.00
1994FM	—	—	—	0.20	0.35	1.00
1995FM	—	—	—	0.20	0.35	1.00
1996FM	—	—	—	0.20	0.35	1.00
1997FM	—	—	—	0.20	0.35	1.00

Date	Mintage	F	VF	XF	Unc	BU
1998	—	—	—	0.20	0.35	1.00
1999 Proof	3,000	Value: 0.60				
1999	—	—	—	0.20	0.35	1.00
2000	—	—	—	0.20	0.35	1.00

KM# 29a CENT
2.0000 g., 0.9250 Silver 0.0595 oz. ASW, 17.8 mm.
Obv: National arms **Rev:** Hummingbird and value

Date	Mintage	F	VF	XF	Unc	BU
1981FM (P)	898	Value: 10.00				

KM# 42 CENT
1.9500 g., Bronze, 17.8 mm. **Subject:** 20th Anniversary of Independence **Obv:** National arms **Rev:** Flaming hibiscus and value **Edge:** Plain

Date	Mintage	F	VF	XF	Unc	BU
1982FM (M)	—	—	—	0.10	0.15	0.30
1982FM (U)	—	—	—	0.75	1.50	3.00
1982FM (P)	—	Value: 1.00				

KM# 42a CENT
2.0000 g., 0.9250 Silver 0.0595 oz. ASW, 17.8 mm.
Obv: National arms **Rev:** Flaming hibiscus and value

Date	Mintage	F	VF	XF	Unc	BU
1982FM (P)	699	Value: 10.00				

KM# 51 CENT
1.9500 g., Bronze, 17.8 mm. **Obv:** National arms **Rev:** Flaming hibiscus and value **Edge:** Plain

Date	Mintage	F	VF	XF	Unc	BU
1983FM (M)	—	—	—	—	1.50	3.00
1983FM (P)	—	Value: 1.00				
1984FM (P)	—	Value: 1.00				

KM# 51a CENT
2.0000 g., 0.9250 Silver 0.0595 oz. ASW, 17.8 mm.
Obv: National arms **Rev:** Flaming hibiscus and value

Date	Mintage	F	VF	XF	Unc	BU
1983FM (P)	1,344	Value: 10.00				
1984FM (P)	—	Value: 10.00				

KM# 30 5 CENTS
3.3100 g., Bronze, 21.2 mm. **Obv:** National arms **Rev:** Bird of paradise and value **Edge:** Plain

Date	Mintage	F	VF	XF	Unc	BU
1976FM (M)	30,000	—	—	0.10	0.25	1.00
1976FM (U)	582	—	—	0.80	1.75	3.50
1976FM (P)	10,000	Value: 0.75				
1977	12,000,000	—	—	0.10	0.25	1.00
1977FM (M)	30,000	—	—	0.10	0.25	1.00
1977FM (U)	633	—	—	0.55	1.75	3.50
1977FM (P)	5,337	Value: 0.75				
1978	1,500,000	—	—	0.10	0.25	1.00
1978FM (M)	30,000	—	—	0.10	0.25	1.00
1978FM (U)	472	—	—	0.65	1.75	3.50
1978FM (P)	4,845	Value: 1.25				
1979	—	—	—	0.10	0.25	1.00
1979FM (M)	30,000	—	—	0.10	0.25	1.00
1979FM (U)	518	—	—	0.65	1.75	3.50
1979FM (P)	3,270	Value: 1.25				
1980	15,000,000	—	—	0.10	0.25	1.00
1980FM (M)	15,000	—	—	0.10	0.25	1.00
1980FM (U)	796	—	—	1.25	5.00	7.50
1980FM (P)	2,393	Value: 1.25				
1981	—	—	—	0.10	0.25	1.00
1981FM (M)	—	—	—	0.10	0.25	1.00
1981FM (U)	—	—	—	0.65	1.75	2.50
1981FM (P)	—	Value: 1.25				
1983	—	—	—	0.10	0.25	1.00
1984	4,094,999	—	—	0.10	1.00	1.25
1988	20,000,000	—	—	0.10	0.25	1.00
1990	—	—	—	0.10	0.25	1.00
1992	—	—	—	0.10	0.25	1.00
1995	—	—	—	0.10	0.25	1.00
1996	—	—	—	0.10	0.25	1.00
1997	—	—	—	0.10	0.25	1.00
1998	—	—	—	0.10	0.25	1.00
1999 Proof	3,000	Value: 1.00				
1999	—	—	—	0.10	0.25	1.00
2000	—	—	—	0.10	0.25	1.00

KM# 30a 5 CENTS
3.5000 g., 0.9250 Silver 0.1041 oz. ASW, 21.15 mm.
Obv: National arms **Rev:** Bird of paradise and value

Date	Mintage	F	VF	XF	Unc	BU
1981FM (P)	898	Value: 13.50				

KM# 43 5 CENTS
3.2500 g., Bronze, 21.15 mm. **Subject:** 20th Anniversary of Independence **Obv:** National arms **Rev:** Butterfly and value

Date	Mintage	F	VF	XF	Unc	BU
1982FM (M)	—	—	—	—	1.50	5.00
1982FM (U)	—	—	—	—	3.00	6.00
1982FM (P)	—	Value: 5.00				

KM# 43a 5 CENTS
3.5000 g., 0.9250 Silver 0.1041 oz. ASW, 21.15 mm.
Obv: National arms **Rev:** Butterfly and value

Date	Mintage	F	VF	XF	Unc	BU
1982FM (P)	699	Value: 15.00				

KM# 52 5 CENTS
3.2500 g., Bronze, 21.15 mm. **Obv:** National arms **Rev:** Butterfly

Date	Mintage	F	VF	XF	Unc	BU
1983FM (M)	—	—	—	1.00	2.50	5.00
1983FM (P)	—	Value: 6.00				
1984FM (P)	—	Value: 6.00				

KM# 52a 5 CENTS
3.5000 g., 0.9250 Silver 0.1041 oz. ASW, 21.15 mm.
Obv: National arms **Rev:** Butterfly and value

Date	Mintage	F	VF	XF	Unc	BU
1983FM (P)	1,324	Value: 17.50				
1984FM (P)	—	Value: 17.50				

KM# 31 10 CENTS
1.4000 g., Copper-Nickel, 16.2 mm. **Obv:** National arms **Rev:** Hibiscus and value **Edge:** Reeded

Date	Mintage	F	VF	XF	Unc	BU
1976FM (M)	15,000	—	—	—	0.50	1.00
1976FM (U)	582	—	—	5.00	7.50	10.00
1976FM (P)	10,000	Value: 1.00				
1977	17,280,000	—	—	0.10	0.20	0.40
1977FM (M)	15,000	—	—	—	0.50	1.00
1977FM (U)	633	—	—	5.00	7.50	10.00
1977FM (P)	5,337	Value: 1.00				
1978	10,000,000	—	—	0.10	0.20	0.40
1978FM (M)	15,000	—	—	—	0.50	1.00
1978FM (U)	472	—	—	5.00	7.50	9.00
1978FM (P)	4,845	Value: 1.50				
1979	1,970,000	—	—	0.10	0.30	0.60
1979FM (M)	15,000	—	—	—	0.50	1.00
1979FM (U)	518	—	—	5.00	7.50	9.00
1979FM (P)	3,270	Value: 1.50				
1980	20,000,000	—	—	0.10	0.30	0.60
1980FM (M)	7,500	—	—	—	0.50	1.00
1980FM (U)	796	—	—	5.00	7.50	9.00
1980FM (P)	2,393	Value: 1.50				
1981	—	—	—	0.10	0.30	0.60
1981FM (M)	—	—	—	—	0.50	1.00
1981FM (U)	—	—	—	5.00	7.50	9.00
1981FM (P)	—	Value: 1.50				
1990	—	—	—	0.10	0.30	0.60
1997	—	—	—	0.20	0.50	1.00
1998	—	—	—	0.20	0.50	1.00
1999 Proof	—	Value: 2.00				
1999	—	—	—	0.20	0.50	1.00
2000	—	—	—	0.20	0.50	1.00

KM# 31a 10 CENTS
1.5000 g., 0.9250 Silver 0.0446 oz. ASW, 16.3 mm.
Obv: National arms **Rev:** Hibiscus and value

Date	Mintage	F	VF	XF	Unc	BU
1981FM (P)	898	Value: 15.00				

KM# 44 10 CENTS
1.4000 g., Copper-Nickel, 16.3 mm. **Subject:** 20th Anniversary of Independence **Obv:** National arms **Rev:** Hummingbird and value **Edge:** Reeded

Date	Mintage	F	VF	XF	Unc	BU
1982FM (M)	—	—	—	1.00	3.00	7.00
1982FM (U)	—	—	—	1.25	4.00	7.00
1982FM (P)	—	Value: 2.50				

KM# 44a 10 CENTS
1.5000 g., 0.9250 Silver 0.0446 oz. ASW, 16.3 mm.
Obv: National arms **Rev:** Hummingbird and value

Date	Mintage	F	VF	XF	Unc	BU
1982FM (P)	699	Value: 15.00				

KM# 53 10 CENTS
1.4000 g., Copper-Nickel, 16.3 mm. **Obv:** National arms **Rev:** Hummingbird and value

Date	Mintage	F	VF	XF	Unc	BU
1983FM (M)	—	—	—	1.50	3.00	6.00
1983FM (P)	—	Value: 2.00				
1984FM (P)	—	Value: 2.00				

KM# 53a 10 CENTS
1.5000 g., 0.9250 Silver 0.0446 oz. ASW, 16.3 mm.
Obv: National arms **Rev:** Hummingbird and value

Date	Mintage	F	VF	XF	Unc	BU
1983FM (P)	—	Value: 10.00				
1984FM (P)	—	Value: 10.00				

KM# 32 25 CENTS
3.5700 g., Copper-Nickel, 20 mm. **Obv:** National arms **Rev:** Chaconia and value **Edge:** Reeded

Date	Mintage	F	VF	XF	Unc	BU
1976FM (M)	6,000	—	—	0.50	1.00	2.00
1976FM (U)	582	—	—	5.00	7.50	10.00
1976FM (P)	10,000	Value: 1.25				
1977	9,000,000	—	0.10	0.15	0.30	0.60
1977FM (M)	6,000	—	—	0.50	1.00	2.00
1977FM (U)	633	—	—	5.00	7.50	10.00
1977FM (P)	5,337	Value: 1.25				
1978	5,470,000	—	0.10	0.15	0.30	0.60
1978FM (M)	6,000	—	—	0.50	1.00	2.00
1978FM (U)	472	—	—	5.00	7.50	10.00
1978FM (P)	4,845	Value: 1.75				
1979	—	—	0.10	0.15	0.40	0.80
1979FM (M)	6,000	—	—	0.90	1.00	2.00
1979FM (U)	518	—	—	5.00	7.50	10.00
1979FM (P)	3,270	Value: 2.00				
1980	15,000,000	—	0.10	0.15	0.40	0.80
1980FM (M)	3,000	—	—	0.50	1.00	2.00
1980FM (U)	796	—	—	5.00	7.50	10.00
1980FM (P)	2,393	Value: 2.00				
1981	—	—	0.10	0.15	0.40	0.80
1981FM (M)	—	—	—	0.50	1.00	2.00
1981FM (U)	—	—	—	5.00	7.50	10.00
1981FM (P)	—	Value: 2.00				
1983	—	—	0.10	0.15	0.40	0.80
1983FM (M)	—	—	—	0.60	2.00	4.00
1983FM (P)	—	Value: 2.00				
1984	—	—	0.10	0.15	0.40	0.80
1984	—	Value: 2.00				
1993	—	—	—	0.15	0.40	0.80
1997	—	—	—	0.15	0.40	0.80
1998	—	—	—	0.15	0.40	0.80
1999	—	—	—	0.15	0.40	0.80
1999 Proof	—	Value: 3.00				

KM# 32a 25 CENTS
3.6000 g., 0.9250 Silver 0.1071 oz. ASW, 20 mm. **Obv:** National arms **Rev:** Chaconia and value

Date	Mintage	F	VF	XF	Unc	BU
1981FM (P)	898	Value: 12.00				
1983FM (P)	—	Value: 12.00				
1984FM (P)	—	Value: 12.00				

KM# 45   25 CENTS
3.5000 g., Copper-Nickel, 20 mm.   **Subject:** 20th Anniversary of Independence **Obv:** National arms **Rev:** Chaconia and value **Edge:** Reeded

Date	Mintage	F	VF	XF	Unc	BU
1982FM (M)	—	—	—	0.50	1.00	2.00
1982FM (U)	—	—	—	1.00	2.25	4.50
1982FM (P)	—	Value: 2.00				

KM# 45a   25 CENTS
3.6000 g., 0.9250 Silver 0.1071 oz. ASW, 20 mm.   **Obv:** National arms **Rev:** Chaconia and value

Date	Mintage	F	VF	XF	Unc	BU
1982FM (P)	699	Value: 15.00				

KM# 33   50 CENTS
7.0000 g., Copper-Nickel, 26 mm.   **Obv:** National arms **Rev:** Kettle drums and value **Edge:** Reeded

Date	Mintage	F	VF	XF	Unc	BU
1976FM (M)	3,000	—	—	1.00	3.25	5.00
1976FM (U)	582	—	—	5.00	7.50	15.00
1976FM (P)	10,000	Value: 1.50				
1977	1,500,000	—	0.25	0.50	1.00	2.00
1977FM (M)	3,000	—	—	1.50	3.00	6.00
1977FM (U)	633	—	—	5.00	7.50	15.00
1977FM (P)	5,337	Value: 1.50				
1978	563,000	—	0.50	0.75	1.50	3.50
1978FM (M)	3,000	—	—	1.50	3.00	6.00
1978FM (U)	472	—	—	5.00	7.50	15.00
1978FM (P)	4,845	Value: 2.00				
1979	750,000	—	0.50	0.75	1.50	3.50
1979FM (M)	3,000	—	—	1.50	3.25	6.00
1979FM (U)	518	—	—	5.00	7.50	15.00
1979FM (P)	3,270	Value: 2.00				
1980	3,750,000	—	0.25	0.50	1.00	2.00
1980FM (M)	1,500	—	—	1.50	3.00	6.00
1980FM (U)	796	—	—	5.00	7.50	15.00
1980FM (P)	2,393	Value: 2.00				
1981FM (M)	—	—	—	1.50	3.00	6.00
1981FM (U)	—	—	—	5.00	7.50	10.00
1981FM (P)	—	Value: 2.00				
1999	—	—	—	1.00	2.00	4.00
1999 Proof	3,000	Value: 4.00				

KM# 33a   50 CENTS
7.2500 g., 0.9250 Silver 0.2156 oz. ASW, 26 mm.   **Obv:** National arms **Rev:** Kettle drums and value

Date	Mintage	F	VF	XF	Unc	BU
1981FM (P)	898	Value: 18.00				

KM# 46   50 CENTS
7.0000 g., Copper-Nickel, 26 mm.   **Subject:** 20th Anniversary of Independence **Obv:** National arms **Rev:** Kettle drums and player **Edge:** Reeded

Date	Mintage	F	VF	XF	Unc	BU
1982FM (M)	—	—	—	1.50	3.00	6.00
1982FM (U)	—	—	—	1.00	2.50	5.00
1982FM (P)	—	Value: 2.00				

KM# 46a   50 CENTS
7.2500 g., 0.9250 Silver 0.2156 oz. ASW, 26 mm.   **Obv:** National arms **Rev:** Kettle drums and player

Date	Mintage	F	VF	XF	Unc	BU
1982FM (P)	699	Value: 20.00				

KM# 54   50 CENTS
7.0000 g., Copper-Nickel, 26 mm.   **Obv:** National arms **Rev:** Kettle drums and player

Date	Mintage	F	VF	XF	Unc	BU
1983FM (M)	—	—	—	1.75	4.00	8.00
1983FM (P)	—	Value: 2.00				
1984FM (P)	—	Value: 2.00				

KM# 54a   50 CENTS
7.2500 g., 0.9250 Silver 0.2156 oz. ASW, 26 mm.   **Obv:** National arms **Rev:** Kettle drums and player

Date	Mintage	F	VF	XF	Unc	BU
1983FM (P)	1,325	Value: 17.00				
1984FM (P)	—	Value: 17.00				

KM# 34   DOLLAR
Copper-Nickel, 36 mm.   **Obv:** National arms **Rev:** Bird on branch and value

Date	Mintage	F	VF	XF	Unc	BU
1976FM (M)	1,500	—	—	3.00	6.00	10.00
1976FM (U)	582	—	—	8.00	10.00	15.00
1976FM (P)	10,000	Value: 2.00				
1977FM (M)	1,500	—	—	2.00	6.00	10.00
1977FM (U)	633	—	—	8.00	10.00	15.00
1977FM (P)	5,337	Value: 2.00				
1978FM (M)	1,500	—	—	2.00	6.00	10.00
1978FM (U)	472	—	—	8.00	10.00	15.00
1978FM (P)	4,845	Value: 3.00				
1979FM (M)	1,500	—	—	2.00	6.00	10.00
1979FM (U)	518	—	—	8.00	10.00	15.00
1979FM (P)	3,270	Value: 3.00				
1980FM (M)	750	—	—	8.00	10.00	15.00
1980FM (U)	796	—	—	8.00	10.00	15.00
1980FM (P)	2,393	Value: 5.00				
1981FM (M)	—	—	—	1.75	5.00	10.00
1981FM (U)	—	—	—	1.00	3.00	6.00
1981FM (P)	—	Value: 2.50				
1983FM (M)	—	—	—	2.00	6.00	10.00
1983FM (P)	—	Value: 2.50				
1984FM (P)	—	Value: 2.50				

KM# 38   DOLLAR
12.7000 g., Copper Nickel, 32 mm.   **Series:** F.A.O. **Obv:** National arms **Rev:** Value in front of leaves

Date	Mintage	F	VF	XF	Unc	BU
1979	—	—	0.75	1.50	3.50	6.50

KM# 34a   DOLLAR
18.6000 g., 0.9250 Silver 0.5531 oz. ASW, 36 mm.   **Obv:** National arms **Rev:** Bird on branch and value

Date	Mintage	F	VF	XF	Unc	BU
1981FM (P)	898	Value: 20.00				
1983FM (P)	2,544	Value: 16.50				
1984FM (P)	—	Value: 16.50				

KM# 47   DOLLAR
Copper-Nickel, 36 mm.   **Subject:** 20th Anniversary of Independence **Obv:** National arms **Rev:** Bird on branch and value within circle

Date	Mintage	F	VF	XF	Unc	BU
1982FM (M)	—	—	—	3.00	9.00	12.50
1982FM (U)	—	—	—	2.00	6.00	9.00
1982FM (P)	—	Value: 5.00				

KM# 47a   DOLLAR
18.6000 g., 0.9250 Silver 0.5531 oz. ASW, 36 mm. **Obv:** National arms **Rev:** Bird on branch and value within circle

Date	Mintage	F	VF	XF	Unc	BU
1982FM (P)	699	Value: 20.00				

KM# 61   DOLLAR
8.4000 g., Copper-Nickel   **Subject:** 50th Anniversary - F.A.O. **Obv:** National arms **Rev:** Sprig, value and logo

Date	Mintage	F	VF	XF	Unc	BU
1995	—	—	—	1.00	1.75	2.75
1999	—	—	—	1.00	1.75	2.75
1999 Proof	3,000	Value: 5.00				

KM# 35a   5 DOLLARS
29.7000 g., 0.9250 Silver 0.8832 oz. ASW, 40 mm. **Obv:** National arms **Rev:** Bird on branch and value

Date	Mintage	F	VF	XF	Unc	BU
1976 (P)	11,000	Value: 15.00				
1977 (P)	6,107	Value: 16.50				
1978 (P)	5,460	Value: 16.50				
1979 (P)	3,755	Value: 18.50				
1980 (P)	2,393	Value: 20.00				
1981 (P)	—	Value: 30.00				
1983 (P)	—	Value: 30.00				
1984 (P)	—	Value: 30.00				

KM# 35   5 DOLLARS
Copper-Nickel, 40 mm.   **Obv:** National arms **Rev:** Bird on branch and value

Date	Mintage	F	VF	XF	Unc	BU
1976FM (M)	300	—	—	7.00	20.00	25.00
1976FM (U)	582	—	—	7.00	20.00	25.00
1977FM (M)	300	—	—	7.00	20.00	25.00
1977FM (U)	633	—	—	6.50	17.00	20.00
1978FM (M)	300	—	—	7.00	20.00	25.00
1978FM (U)	472	—	—	7.00	20.00	25.00
1979FM (M)	300	—	—	7.00	20.00	25.00
1979FM (U)	518	—	—	7.00	20.00	25.00
1980FM (M)	150	—	—	8.00	25.00	30.00
1980FM (U)	796	—	—	6.50	17.00	20.00
1981FM (M)	—	—	—	7.00	20.00	25.00
1981FM (U)	—	—	—	6.50	17.00	20.00
1981FM (P)	—	Value: 20.00				
1983FM (M)	—	—	—	7.00	20.00	25.00
1983FM (P)	1,312	Value: 20.00				
1984FM (P)	—	Value: 20.00				

KM# 35a.1   5 DOLLARS
11.0000 g., Copper Nickel, 30 mm.   **Obv:** National arms **Rev:** Bird on branch and value **Note:** Reduced size.

Date	Mintage	F	VF	XF	Unc	BU
1999 Proof	—	Value: 20.00				

KM# 48   5 DOLLARS
Copper-Nickel, 40 mm.   **Subject:** 20th Anniversary of Independence **Obv:** National arms **Rev:** Bird on branch and value

Date	Mintage	F	VF	XF	Unc	BU
1982FM (M)	—	—	—	7.00	20.00	25.00
1982FM (U)	—	—	—	5.00	12.50	15.00
1982FM (P)	—	Value: 17.00				

KM# 48a   5 DOLLARS
30.0000 g., 0.9250 Silver 0.8921 oz. ASW, 40 mm.
Obv: National arms **Rev:** Bird on branch and value

Date	Mintage	F	VF	XF	Unc	BU
1982FM (P)	699	Value: 30.00				

KM# 36a   10 DOLLARS
35.0000 g., 0.9250 Silver 1.0408 oz. ASW, 42 mm.
Obv: National arms **Rev:** Fish, ship, map and value within waves

Date	Mintage	F	VF	XF	Unc	BU
1976FM (P)	13,000	Value: 16.00				
1977FM (P)	6,643	Value: 17.50				
1978FM (P)	7,449	Value: 17.50				
1979FM (P)	4,994	Value: 22.00				
1980FM (P)	3,726	Value: 25.00				

KM# 36   10 DOLLARS
Copper-Nickel, 42 mm.   **Obv:** National arms **Rev:** Fish, ship, value and map within waves

Date	Mintage	F	VF	XF	Unc	BU
1976FM (M)	150	—	—	—	40.00	45.00
1976FM (U)	582	—	—	—	30.00	35.00
1977FM (M)	150	—	—	—	40.00	45.00
1977FM (U)	633	—	—	10.00	30.00	35.00
1978FM (M)	150	—	—	—	12.00	40.00
1978FM (U)	472	—	—	10.00	30.00	35.00
1979FM (M)	150	—	—	—	12.00	40.00
1979FM (U)	518	—	—	10.00	30.00	35.00
1980FM (M)	—	—	—	—	12.00	40.00	45.00
1980FM (U)	—	—	—	10.00	30.00	35.00

KM# 40   10 DOLLARS
Copper-Nickel, 42 mm. **Subject:** 5th Anniversary of the Republic **Obv:** National arms **Rev:** Fish, ship, map and value in waves within circle

Date	Mintage	F	VF	XF	Unc	BU
1981FM (U)	—	—	—	7.00	20.00	25.00

KM# 40a   10 DOLLARS
35.0000 g., 0.9250 Silver 1.0408 oz. ASW, 42 mm. **Obv:** National arms **Rev:** Fish, boat, map and value in waves within circle

Date	Mintage	F	VF	XF	Unc	BU
1981FM (P)	2,374	Value: 27.50				

KM# 49   10 DOLLARS
Copper-Nickel, 42 mm.   **Subject:** 20th Anniversary of Independence **Obv:** National arms **Rev:** Flag and value

Date	Mintage	F	VF	XF	Unc	BU
1982FM (M)	—	—	—	7.00	20.00	25.00
1982FM (U)	—	—	—	7.00	20.00	25.00
1982FM (P)	—	Value: 20.00				

KM# 49a   10 DOLLARS
35.0000 g., 0.9250 Silver 1.0408 oz. ASW, 42 mm.
Obv: National arms **Rev:** Flag and value

Date	Mintage	F	VF	XF	Unc	BU
1982FM (P)	1,682	Value: 37.50				

KM# 55   10 DOLLARS
Copper-Nickel, 42 mm.   **Obv:** National arms **Rev:** Ships and value

Date	Mintage	F	VF	XF	Unc	BU
1983FM (U)	288	—	—	16.50	55.00	65.00

KM# 55a   10 DOLLARS
35.0000 g., 0.9250 Silver 1.0408 oz. ASW, 42 mm.
Obv: National arms **Rev:** Ships and value

Date	Mintage	F	VF	XF	Unc	BU
1983FM (P)	1,565	Value: 40.00				
1984FM (P)	—	Value: 40.00				

KM# 60   10 DOLLARS
28.2800 g., 0.9250 Silver 0.8410 oz. ASW, 38.61 mm.
Subject: 30th Anniversary - Central Bank **Obv:** National arms **Rev:** Bird and sprigs

Date	Mintage	F	VF	XF	Unc	BU
1994 Proof	Est. 5,000	Value: 40.00				

KM# 62   10 DOLLARS
Bi-Metallic Silver center in Gold-plated ring, 28.4 mm.
Subject: Central Bank 35 Years **Obv:** National arms within circle **Rev:** Bank building within circle **Edge:** Reeded

Date	Mintage	F	VF	XF	Unc	BU
1999 Proof	6,500	Value: 42.50				

KM# 39   25 DOLLARS
30.2800 g., 0.5000 Silver 0.4867 oz. ASW **Subject:** 10th Anniversary of Caribbean Development Bank **Obv:** National arms **Rev:** Map on globe above flag, beaded border

Date	Mintage	F	VF	XF	Unc	BU
ND(1980)FM (P)	3,039	Value: 20.00				

KM# 37   100 DOLLARS
6.2100 g., 0.5000 Gold 0.0998 oz. AGW   **Obv:** National arms **Rev:** Flying birds and value

Date	Mintage	F	VF	XF	Unc	BU
1976FM (M)	200	—	—	—	120	130
1976FM (P)	29,000	Value: 115				

KM# 41   100 DOLLARS
6.2100 g., 0.5000 Gold 0.0998 oz. AGW **Subject:** 5th Anniversary of the Republic **Obv:** National arms **Rev:** Hummingbird and flower **Edge:** Reeded

Date	Mintage	F	VF	XF	Unc	BU
1981FM (U)	100	—	—	—	175	195
1981FM (P)	400	Value: 150				

KM# 50   100 DOLLARS
6.2100 g., 0.5000 Gold 0.0998 oz. AGW **Subject:** 20th Anniversary of Independence **Obv:** National arms **Rev:** Building within circle

Date	Mintage	F	VF	XF	Unc	BU
1982FM (P)	1,380	Value: 115				

KM# 56   200 DOLLARS
11.1700 g., 0.5000 Gold 0.1796 oz. AGW **Subject:** 20th Anniversary of Central Bank **Obv:** National arms **Rev:** Building below value

Date	Mintage	F	VF	XF	Unc	BU
1984FM (P)	1,200	Value: 200				

MINT SETS

KM#	Date	Mintage	Identification	Issue Price	Mkt Val
MS1	1973 (8)	1,575	KM#8, 18-24	24.00	22.00
MS2	1974 (8)	3,258	KM#8a, 22-23, 24a, 25-28	25.00	15.00
MS3	1975 (8)	1,111	KM#8a, 22-23, 24a, 25-28	27.50	20.00
MS4	1976 (8)	582	KM#29-34, 35a-36a	27.50	30.00
MS5	1977 (8)	632	KM#29-34, 35a-36a	27.50	30.00
MS6	1978 (8)	472	KM#29-34, 35a-36a	27.50	30.00
MS7	1979 (8)	518	KM#29-34, 35a-36a	28.50	40.00
MS8	1980 (8)	796	KM#29-34, 35a-36a	28.50	30.00
MS9	1981 (8)	—	KM#29-34, 35a, 40	28.50	45.00
MS10	1982 (8)	—	KM#42-49	28.50	45.00
MS11	1983 (8)	281	KM#32, 34, 35a, 51-55	37.00	80.00
MS12	1999 (6)	—	KM#29-33, 61	35.00	35.00

PROOF SETS

KM#	Date	Mintage	Identification	Issue Price	Mkt Val
PS1	1966 (5)	8,000	KM#1-5	12.50	10.00
PS2	1970 (6)	2,104	KM#1-5, 7	15.25	12.50
PS3	1971 (7)	11,039	KM#1-5, 7a, 8	21.00	15.00
PS4	1971 (6)	488	KM#1-6	15.00	12.50
PS5	1972 (8)	13,874	KM#9-16	35.00	20.00
PS6	1972 (7)	15,957	KM#9-15	22.00	12.50
PS7	1973 (8)	14,615	KM#8, 17, 22-23, 24a, 57-59	35.00	20.00
PS8	1973 (8)	5,050	KM#8,17,22-23, 57-59	22.00	15.00
PS9	1974 (8)	13,991	KM#8, 22-28	50.00	20.00
PS10	1975 (8)	24,472	KM#8, 22-28	55.00	22.00
PS24	1999 (6)	3,000	KM#29-33, 35a.1, 61-62	90.00	95.00
PS11	1976 (8)	10,099	KM#29-36	55.00	25.00
PS12	1977 (8)	5,337	KM#29-36	55.00	35.00
PS13	1978 (8)	4,845	KM#29-36	55.00	35.00
PS14	1979 (8)	3,270	KM#29-36	57.00	40.00
PS15	1980 (8)	2,393	KM#29-36	66.00	55.00
PS16	1981 (8)	—	KM#29-34, 35a, 40a	87.00	65.00
PS17	1981 (8)	—	KM#29a-34a, 35, 40a	222	125
PS19	1982 (8)	—	KM#42a-49a	222	135
PS18	1982 (8)	—	KM#42-49	87.00	65.00
PS20	1983 (8)	461	KM#32, 34, 35a, 51-54, 55a	87.00	85.00
PS21	1983 (8)	753	KM#32a, 34a, 35, 51a-55a	197	100
PS22	1984 (8)	—	KM#32, 34, 35a, 51-54, 55a	87.00	75.00
PS23	1984 (8)	—	KM#32a, 34a, 35, 51a-55a	197	100

TRISTAN DA CUNHA

South Atlantic *Ocean*

NAMIBIA

SOUTH AFRICA

Tristan da Cunha is the principal island and group name of a small cluster of volcanic islands located in the South Atlantic midway between the Cape of Good Hope and South America, and 1,500 miles (2,414 km.) south-southwest of the British colony of St. Helena. The other islands are Inaccessible, Gough, and the three Nightingale Islands. The group, which comprises a dependency of St. Helena, has a total area of 40 sq. mi. (104 sq. km.) and a population of less than 300. There is a village of 60 houses called Edinburgh. Potatoes are the staple subsistence crop.

Portuguese admiral Tristao da Cunha discovered Tristan da Cunha in 1506. Unsuccessful attempts to colonize the islands were made by the Dutch in 1656, but the first permanent inhabitant didn't arrive until 1810. During the exile of Napoleon on St. Helena, Britain placed a temporary garrison on Tristan da Cunha to prevent any attempt to rescue Napoleon from his island prison. The islands were formally annexed to Britain in 1816 and became a dependency of St. Helena in 1938.

RULER
British

MINT MARK
PM - Pobjoy Mint

MONETARY SYSTEM
25 Pence = 1 Crown
100 Pence = 1 Pound

ST. HELENA DEPENDENCY
STANDARD COINAGE

KM# 1   25 PENCE
Copper-Nickel, 38.5 mm. **Ruler:** Elizabeth II **Subject:** Queen's Silver Jubilee **Obv:** Young bust right **Rev:** Boat and rock **Edge:** Reeded

Date	Mintage	F	VF	XF	Unc	BU
ND(1977)	50,000	—	1.00	2.00	5.00	6.00

KM# 1a   25 PENCE
28.2800 g., 0.9250 Silver 0.8410 oz. ASW, 38.61 mm.
Ruler: Elizabeth II **Subject:** Queen's Silver Jubilee **Obv:** Young bust right **Rev:** Boat and rock **Edge:** Reeded

Date	Mintage	F	VF	XF	Unc	BU
ND(1977) Proof	25,000	Value: 14.50				

KM# 3   25 PENCE
Copper-Nickel, 38.5 mm. **Ruler:** Elizabeth II **Subject:** 80th Birthday of Queen Mother **Obv:** Young bust right **Rev:** Queen Mother 1/4 left above sprig **Edge:** Reeded

Date	Mintage	F	VF	XF	Unc	BU
ND(1980)	65,000	—	1.00	1.75	3.50	4.50

KM# 3a   25 PENCE
28.2800 g., 0.9250 Silver 0.8410 oz. ASW, 38.5 mm.
Ruler: Elizabeth II **Subject:** 80th Birthday of Queen Mother **Obv:** Young bust right **Rev:** Queen Mother 1/4 left above sprig

Date	Mintage	F	VF	XF	Unc	BU
ND(1980) Proof	25,000	Value: 14.50				

KM# 4   25 PENCE
Copper-Nickel, 38.5 mm. **Ruler:** Elizabeth II **Subject:** Wedding of Prince Charles and Lady Diana **Obv:** Young bust right **Rev:** Design in center divides cameo heads facing each other **Edge:** Reeded

Date	Mintage	F	VF	XF	Unc	BU
ND(1981)PM	—	—	1.00	1.75	3.50	4.50

KM# 4a   25 PENCE
28.2800 g., 0.9250 Silver 0.8410 oz. ASW, 38.5 mm.
Ruler: Elizabeth II **Subject:** Wedding of Prince Charles and Lady Diana **Obv:** Young bust right **Rev:** Design in center divides cameo heads facing each other

Date	Mintage	F	VF	XF	Unc	BU
ND(1981)PM Proof	30,000	Value: 17.50				

KM# 5   25 PENCE
28.2800 g., 0.9250 Silver 0.8410 oz. ASW, 38.5 mm.
Ruler: Elizabeth II **Series:** International Year of the Scout **Obv:** Young bust right **Rev:** Scouting emblem within roped wreath

Date	Mintage	F	VF	XF	Unc	BU
ND(1983)	10,000			—	32.50	35.00
ND(1983) Proof	10,000	Value: 47.50				

KM# 7   50 PENCE
28.2800 g., 0.9250 Silver 0.8410 oz. ASW, 38.5 mm.
Ruler: Elizabeth II **Subject:** 40th Wedding Anniversary of Queen Elizabeth and Prince Philip **Obv:** Crowned bust right **Rev:** Crowned initials at center of flower design **Edge:** Reeded

Date	Mintage	F	VF	XF	Unc	BU
ND(1987) Proof	2,000	Value: 25.00				

KM# 7a   50 PENCE
47.5400 g., 0.9170 Gold 1.4015 oz. AGW, 38.5 mm.
Ruler: Elizabeth II **Subject:** 40th Wedding Anniversary of Queen Elizabeth and Prince Philip **Obv:** Crowned head right **Rev:** Crowned initials at center of flower design

Date	Mintage	F	VF	XF	Unc	BU
ND(1987) Proof	75	Value: 1,450				

KM# 7b   50 PENCE
Copper-Nickel, 38.5 mm. **Ruler:** Elizabeth II **Subject:** 40th Wedding Anniversary of Queen Elizabeth and Prince Philip **Obv:** Crowned bust right **Rev:** Crowned initials at center of flower design

Date	Mintage	F	VF	XF	Unc	BU
ND(1987)	—	—	—	—	4.50	6.00

KM# 9   50 PENCE
28.2800 g., Copper-Nickel, 38.6 mm. **Ruler:** Elizabeth II **Subject:** Winston Churchill **Obv:** Crowned bust right **Rev:** Uniformed bust 1/4 left and two fighter planes **Edge:** Reeded **Note:** Struck at British Royal Mint.

Date	Mintage	F	VF	XF	Unc	BU
1999	—	—	—	—	7.00	9.00

KM# 9a   50 PENCE
28.2800 g., 0.9250 Silver 0.8410 oz. ASW, 38.6 mm.
Subject: Winston Churchill **Obv:** Crowned head right **Rev:** Uniformed bust 1/4 left and two fighter planes

Date	Mintage	F	VF	XF	Unc	BU
1999 Proof	2,500	Value: 42.50				

KM# 9b   50 PENCE
47.5400 g., 0.9170 Gold 1.4015 oz. AGW, 38.6 mm.
Ruler: Elizabeth II **Subject:** Winston Churchill **Obv:** Crowned bust right **Rev:** Uniformed bust 1/4 left and two fighter planes

Date	Mintage	F	VF	XF	Unc	BU
1999	Est. 125	Value: 1,450				

KM# 10 50 PENCE
28.6400 g., Copper-Nickel, 38.6 mm. **Ruler:** Elizabeth II
Subject: Queen Mother's Centennial Birthday **Obv:** Crowned
bust right **Rev:** Bust of Queen Mother right **Edge:** Reeded

Date	Mintage	F	VF	XF	Unc	BU
ND(2000)	—	—	—	—	6.50	7.50

KM# 10a 50 PENCE
28.4000 g., 0.9250 Silver 0.8446 oz. ASW, 38.6 mm.
Ruler: Elizabeth II **Subject:** Queen Mother's Centennial Birthday
Obv: Crowned bust right **Rev:** Bust of Queen Mother right

Date	Mintage	F	VF	XF	Unc	BU
ND(2000)	—					
ND(2000) Proof	10,000	Value: 50.00				

KM# 10b 50 PENCE
47.5400 g., 0.9166 Gold 1.4009 oz. AGW, 38.6 mm.
Ruler: Elizabeth II **Subject:** Queen Mother's 100th Birthday
Obv: Crowned bust right **Rev:** Bust of Queen Mother right
Edge: Reeded

Date	Mintage	F	VF	XF	Unc	BU
ND(2000) Proof	100	Value: 1,450				

KM# 11 50 PENCE
28.6400 g., Copper-Nickel, 38.6 mm. **Ruler:** Elizabeth II
Subject: Princess Anne's 50th Birthday **Obv:** Crowned bust right
Rev: Bust of Princess Anne facing **Edge:** Reeded

Date	Mintage	F	VF	XF	Unc	BU
ND(2000)	—	—	—	—	6.50	7.50

KM# 11a 50 PENCE
28.2800 g., 0.9250 Silver 0.8410 oz. ASW, 38.6 mm.
Ruler: Elizabeth II **Subject:** Princess Anne's 50th Birthday
Obv: Crowned bust right **Rev:** Bust of Princess Anne facing
Edge: Reeded

Date	Mintage	F	VF	XF	Unc	BU
ND(2000) Proof	2,500	Value: 50.00				

KM# 11b 50 PENCE
47.5400 g., 0.9166 Gold 1.4009 oz. AGW, 38.6 mm. **Ruler:**
Elizabeth II **Subject:** Princess Anne's 50th Birthday **Obv:** Crowned
bust right **Rev:** Bust of Princess Anne facing **Edge:** Reeded

Date	Mintage	F	VF	XF	Unc	BU
ND(2000) Proof	50	Value: 1,450				

KM# 2 CROWN
Copper-Nickel, 38.5 mm. **Ruler:** Elizabeth II **Subject:** 25th
Anniversary of Coronation **Obv:** Young bust right **Rev:** Tristan
rock lobster on coat of arms **Edge:** Reeded

Date	Mintage	F	VF	XF	Unc	BU
1978PM	—	—	1.00	1.75	3.50	4.50

KM# 2a CROWN
28.2800 g., 0.9250 Silver 0.8410 oz. ASW, 38.5 mm.
Ruler: Elizabeth II **Obv:** Young bust right **Rev:** Tristan rock
lobster on coat of arms

Date	Mintage	F	VF	XF	Unc	BU
1978PM	70,000			—	13.50	15.00
1978PM Proof	25,000	Value: 18.50				

KM# 6 2 POUNDS
15.9800 g., 0.9170 Gold 0.4711 oz. AGW **Ruler:** Elizabeth II
Series: International Year of the Scout **Obv:** Young bust right
Rev: Sailboat

Date	Mintage	F	VF	XF	Unc	BU
1983	2,000					500
1983 Proof	2,000	Value: 525				

KM# 8 2 POUNDS
Copper-Nickel, 38.5 mm. **Ruler:** Elizabeth II **Subject:** 90th
Anniversary of Queen Mother **Obv:** Crowned bust right
Rev: Crowned monogram flanked by flower sprigs **Edge:** Reeded

Date	Mintage	F	VF	XF	Unc	BU
ND(1990)	—	—	—	—	12.50	13.50

KM# 8a 2 POUNDS
28.2800 g., 0.9250 Silver 0.8410 oz. ASW, 38.5 mm.
Ruler: Elizabeth II **Subject:** 90th Anniversary of Queen Mother
Obv: Crowned bust right **Rev:** Crowned monogram flanked by
flower sprigs

Date	Mintage	F	VF	XF	Unc	BU
ND(1990) Proof	Est. 10,000	Value: 55.00				

TUNISIA

ITALY

Mediterranean Sea

ALGERIA

LIBYA

The Republic of Tunisia, located on the northern coast of
Africa between Algeria and Libya, has an area of 63,170sq. mi.
(163,610 sq. km.) and a population of *7.9 million. Capital: Tunis.
Agriculture is the backbone of the economy. Crude oil, phosphates, olive oil, and wine are exported.

Tunisia, settled by the Phoenicians in the 12th century B.C.,
was the center of the seafaring Carthaginian Empire. After the
total destruction of Carthage, Tunisia became part of Rome's African province. It remained a part of the Roman Empire (except for
the 439-533 interval of Vandal conquest) until taken by the Arabs,
648, who administered it until the Turkish invasion of 1570. Under
Turkish control, the public revenue was heavily dependent upon
the piracy of Mediterranean shipping, an endeavor that wasn't
abandoned until 1819 when a coalition of powers threatened
appropriate reprisal. Deprived of its major source of income, Tunisia underwent a financial regression that ended in bankruptcy,
enabling France to establish a protectorate over the country in
1881. National agitation and guerrilla fighting forced France to
grant Tunisia internal autonomy in 1955 and to recognize Tunisian independence on March 20, 1956. Tunisia abolished the
monarchy and established a republic on July 25, 1957.

TITLES

المملكة التونسية

al-Mamlaka al-Tunisiya

الجمهورية العراقية

al-Jumhuriya al-Tunisiya

al-Amala al-Tunisiya
(Tunisian Protectorate)

MINT MARKS
A - Paris, AH1308/1891-AH1348/1928
(a) - Paris, privy marks,
   AH1349/1929-AH1376/1957
FM - Franklin Mint, Franklin Center, PA
   Numismatic Italiana, Arezzo, Italy

TUNISIA

FRENCH PROTECTORATE

Ali Bey
"Struck in his name"

DECIMAL COINAGE
100 Centimes = 1 Franc

The following coins all bear French inscriptions on one
side, Arabic on the other, and usually have both AH and AD
dates. Except for KM#246-48, they are struck in the name
of the Tunisian Bey.

KM# 223 50 CENTIMES
2.5000 g., 0.8350 Silver 0.0671 oz. ASW **Obv:** Legend flanked
by sprigs **Obv. Leg.:** ALI **Rev:** Value, date in center circle of
ornate design

Date	Mintage	F	VF	XF	Unc	BU
AH1319/1901A	1,000	—	—	150	250	—
AH1320/1902A	1,000	—	—	150	250	—

KM# 224 FRANC
5.0000 g., 0.8350 Silver 0.1342 oz. ASW **Obv:** Legend flanked
by sprigs **Obv. Leg.:** ALI **Rev:** Value, date in center circle of
ornate design

Date	Mintage	F	VF	XF	Unc	BU
AH1319/1901A	700	—	—	175	275	—
AH1320/1902A	703	—	—	175	275	—

KM# 225 2 FRANCS
10.0000 g., 0.8350 Silver 0.2684 oz. ASW **Obv:** Legend flanked
by sprigs **Obv. Leg.:** ALI **Rev:** Value, date within center circle of
ornate design

Date	Mintage	F	VF	XF	Unc	BU
AH1319/1901A	300	—	—	200	350	—
AH1320/1902A	300	—	—	200	350	—

KM# 226 10 FRANCS
3.2258 g., 0.9000 Gold 0.0933 oz. AGW **Obv:** Legend flanked
by sprigs **Obv. Leg.:** ALI **Rev:** Value, date in center circle of
ornate design

Date	Mintage	F	VF	XF	Unc	BU
AH1319/1901A	80	—	—	450	850	—
AH1319/1901A	80	—	—	450	850	—
AH1320/1902A	83	—	—	450	850	—

KM# 227   20 FRANCS
6.4516 g., 0.9000 Gold 0.1867 oz. AGW **Obv:** Legend flanked by sprigs **Obv. Leg.:** ALI **Rev:** Value, date in center circle of ornate design

Date	Mintage	F	VF	XF	Unc	BU
AH1319/1901A	150,000	—	—	BV	195	—
AH1319/1901A	150,000	—	—	BV	200	—
AH1320/1902A	20	—	—	550	1,000	—

Muhammad al-Hadi Bey
"Struck in his name"

DECIMAL COINAGE
100 Centimes = 1 Franc

The following coins all bear French inscriptions on one side, Arabic on the other, and usually have both AH and AD dates. Except for KM#246-48, they are struck in the name of the Tunisian Bey.

KM# 228   5 CENTIMES
Bronze **Obv:** Inscription within sprigs **Obv. Leg.:** MUHAMMAD AL-HADI **Rev:** Value and date within center circle

Date	Mintage	F	VF	XF	Unc	BU
AH1321/1903A	500,000	—	8.00	12.00	25.00	—
AH1322/1904A	1,000,000	—	8.00	12.00	25.00	—

KM# 229   10 CENTIMES
Bronze **Obv:** Inscription within sprigs **Obv. Leg.:** MUHAMMAD AL-HADI **Rev:** Value and date within center circle

Date	Mintage	F	VF	XF	Unc	BU
AH1321/1903A	250,000	—	10.00	20.00	30.00	—
AH1322/1904A	500,000	—	10.00	20.00	30.00	—

KM# 230   50 CENTIMES
2.5000 g., 0.8350 Silver 0.0671 oz. ASW **Obv. Leg.:** MUHAMMAD AL-HADI

Date	Mintage	F	VF	XF	Unc	BU
AH1321/1903A	1,003	—	—	150	250	—
AH1322/1904A	1,003	—	—	150	250	—
AH1323/1905A	1,003	—	—	150	250	—
AH1324/1906A	1,003	—	—	150	250	—

KM# 231   FRANC
5.0000 g., 0.8350 Silver 0.1342 oz. ASW **Obv. Leg.:** MUHAMMAD AL-HADI

Date	Mintage	F	VF	XF	Unc	BU
AH1321/1903A	703	—	—	150	250	—
AH1322/1904A	300,000	—	75.00	100	150	—
AH1323/1905A	703	—	—	150	250	—
AH1324/1906A	703	—	—	150	250	—

KM# 232   2 FRANCS
10.0000 g., 0.8350 Silver 0.2684 oz. ASW **Obv. Leg.:** MUHAMMAD AL-HADI

Date	Mintage	F	VF	XF	Unc	BU
AH1321/1903A	303	—	—	150	250	—
AH1322/1904A	150,000	—	100	150	220	—
AH1323/1905A	303	—	—	150	250	—
AH1324/1906A	303	—	—	150	250	—

KM# 233   10 FRANCS
3.2258 g., 0.9000 Gold 0.0933 oz. AGW **Obv. Leg.:** MUHAMMAD AL-HADI

Date	Mintage	F	VF	XF	Unc	BU
AH1321/1903A	83	—	—	450	900	—
AH1322/1904A	83	—	—	450	900	—
AH1323/1905A	83	—	—	450	900	—
AH1324/1906A	83	—	—	450	900	—

KM# 234   20 FRANCS
6.4516 g., 0.9000 Gold 0.1867 oz. AGW **Obv:** Inscription within sprigs **Obv. Leg.:** MUHAMMAD AL-HADI **Rev:** Value and date within center circle

Date	Mintage	F	VF	XF	Unc	BU
AH1321/1903A	300,000	—	—	BV	200	—
AH1321/1904A	600,000	—	—	BV	200	—
AH1322/1904A	Inc. above	—	—	BV	200	—
AH1323/1905A	23	—	—	550	1,000	—
AH1324/1906A	23	—	—	550	1,000	—

Muhammad al-Nasir Bey
"Struck in his name"

DECIMAL COINAGE
100 Centimes = 1 Franc

The following coins all bear French inscriptions on one side, Arabic on the other, and usually have both AH and AD dates. Except for KM#246-48, they are struck in the name of the Tunisian Bey.

KM# 235   5 CENTIMES
Bronze, 26 mm. **Obv:** Inscription within sprigs **Obv. Leg.:** MUHAMMAD AL-NASIR **Rev:** Value and date within center circle **Edge:** Plain

Date	Mintage	F	VF	XF	Unc	BU
AH1325/1907A	1,000,000	—	3.00	6.00	17.00	—
AH1326/1908A	1,000,000	—	3.00	6.00	17.00	—
AH1330/1912A	1,000,000	—	3.00	6.00	17.00	—
AH1332/1914A	1,000,000	—	3.00	6.00	17.00	—
AH1334/1916A	2,000,000	—	3.00	6.00	12.00	—
AH1336/1917A	2,021,000	—	3.00	6.00	12.00	—

KM# 242   5 CENTIMES
Nickel-Bronze, 19 mm. **Obv:** Hole in center of inscription **Obv. Leg.:** MOHAMMED AL-NASIR **Rev:** Value above hole in center, date and sprigs

Date	Mintage	F	VF	XF	Unc	BU
AH1337/1918(a)	1,549,000	—	4.00	10.00	25.00	—
AH1337/1919(a)	4,451,000	—	3.00	8.00	20.00	—
AH1338/1920(a)	Inc. above	—	3.00	8.00	20.00	—
AH1338/6/1920(a)	2,206,000	—	4.00	10.00	25.00	—
AH1338/7/1920(a)	Inc. above	—	4.00	10.00	25.00	—
AH1339/1920(a)	Inc. above	—	3.00	8.00	20.00	—

KM# 245   5 CENTIMES
Nickel-Bronze, 17 mm. **Obv:** Hole in center of inscription **Rev:** Value above hole in center, date and sprigs **Note:** Reduced size.

Date	Mintage	F	VF	XF	Unc	BU
AH1339/1920(a)	1,794,000	—	20.00	40.00	75.00	—

KM# 236   10 CENTIMES
9.4000 g., Bronze **Obv:** Inscription within sprigs **Obv. Leg.:** MUHAMMAD AL-NASIR **Rev:** Value and date within center circle

Date	Mintage	F	VF	XF	Unc	BU
AH1325/1907A	500,000	—	3.00	8.00	20.00	—
AH1326/1908A	500,000	—	3.00	8.00	20.00	—
AH1329/1911A	500,000	—	3.00	8.00	20.00	—
AH1330/1912A	500,000	—	3.00	8.00	20.00	—
AH1332/1914A	500,000	—	3.00	8.00	20.00	—
AH1334/1916A	1,000,000	—	3.00	8.00	20.00	—
AH1336/1917A	1,050,000	—	3.00	8.00	20.00	—

KM# 243   10 CENTIMES
Nickel-Bronze **Obv:** Hole in center of inscription **Obv. Leg.:** MUHAMMAD AL-NASIR **Rev:** Value above hole in center, date and sprigs

Date	Mintage	F	VF	XF	Unc	BU
AH1337/1918(a)	1,288,000	—	3.00	8.00	25.00	—
AH1337/1919(a)	2,712,000	—	3.00	8.00	20.00	—
AH1338/1920(a)	3,000,000	—	3.00	8.00	20.00	—

KM# 244   25 CENTIMES
Nickel-Bronze **Obv:** Hole in center of inscription **Obv. Leg.:** MUHAMMAD AL-NASIR **Rev:** Value above hole in center, date and sprigs

Date	Mintage	F	VF	XF	Unc	BU
AH1337/1918(a)	2,000,000	—	5.00	12.00	35.00	—
AH1337/1919(a)	Inc. above	—	4.00	10.00	25.00	—
AH1338/1920(a)	2,000,000	—	4.00	10.00	25.00	—

KM# 237   50 CENTIMES
2.5000 g., 0.8350 Silver 0.0671 oz. ASW **Obv:** Inscription within sprigs **Obv. Leg.:** MUHAMMAD AL-NASIR **Rev:** Value and date within center circle

Date	Mintage	F	VF	XF	Unc	BU
AH1325/1907A	201,000	—	10.00	20.00	40.00	—
AH1326/1908A	2,006	—	—	100	150	—
AH1327/1909A	1,003	—	—	100	175	—
AH1328/1910A	1,003	—	—	100	175	—
AH1329/1911A	1,003	—	—	100	175	—
AH1330/1912A	201,000	—	10.00	20.00	40.00	—
AH1331/1913A	1,003	—	—	100	175	—
AH1332/1914A	201,000	—	10.00	20.00	40.00	—
AH1334/1915A	707,000	—	8.00	15.00	30.00	—
AH1334/1916A	3,614,000	—	7.00	12.00	25.00	—
AH1335/1916A	Inc. above	—	7.00	12.00	25.00	—
AH1335/1917A	2,139,000	—	7.00	12.00	25.00	—
AH1336/1917A	Inc. above	—	7.00	12.00	25.00	—
AH1337/1918A	1,003	—	—	100	175	—
AH1338/1919A	1,003	—	—	100	175	—
AH1339/1920A	1,003	—	—	100	175	—
AH1340/1921A	1,003	—	—	100	175	—

KM# 238   FRANC
5.0000 g., 0.8350 Silver 0.1342 oz. ASW **Obv:** Inscription within sprigs **Obv. Leg.:** MUHAMMAD AL-NASIR **Rev:** Value and date within center circle

Date	Mintage	F	VF	XF	Unc	BU
AH1325/1907A	301,000	—	10.00	20.00	35.00	—
AH1326/1908A	401,000	—	10.00	15.00	35.00	—
AH1327/1909A	703	—	—	135	225	—
AH1328/1910A	703	—	—	135	225	—
AH1329/1911A	1,051,000	—	7.00	12.00	30.00	—
AH1330/1912A	501,000	—	8.00	15.00	30.00	—
AH1331/1913A	703	—	—	135	225	—
AH1332/1914A	201,000	—	8.00	15.00	25.00	—
AH1333/1914A	Inc. above	—	8.00	15.00	25.00	—
AH1334/1915A	1,060,000	—	7.00	12.00	20.00	—
AH1334/1916A	3,270,000	—	7.00	12.00	20.00	—
AH1335/1916A	Inc. above	—	7.00	12.00	20.00	—
AH1335/1917A	1,628,000	—	7.00	12.00	20.00	—
AH1336/1918A	804,000	—	7.00	12.00	18.00	—
AH1337/1918A	Inc. above	—	7.00	12.00	18.00	—
AH1338/1919A	703	—	—	135	225	—
AH1339/1920A	703	—	—	135	225	—
AH1340/1921A	703	—	—	135	225	—

KM# 239   2 FRANCS
10.0000 g., 0.8350 Silver 0.2684 oz. ASW **Obv:** Inscription within sprigs **Obv. Leg.:** MUHAMMAD AL-NASIR **Rev:** Value and date within center circle

Date	Mintage	F	VF	XF	Unc	BU
AH1325/1907A	306	—	—	150	250	—
AH1326/1908A	101,000	—	20.00	40.00	100	—
AH1327/1909A	303	—	—	150	250	—
AH1328/1910A	303	—	—	150	250	—
AH1329/1911A	475,000	—	20.00	30.00	50.00	—
AH1330/1912A	200,000	—	20.00	30.00	50.00	—
AH1331/1913A	303	—	—	150	250	—
AH1332/1914A	100,000	—	20.00	30.00	50.00	—
AH1333/1914A	Inc. above	—	20.00	30.00	50.00	—
AH1334/1915A	408,000	—	20.00	30.00	50.00	—
AH1334/1916A	1,000,000	—	20.00	30.00	50.00	—
AH1335/1916A	Inc. above	—	20.00	30.00	50.00	—
AH1336/1917A	303	—	—	150	250	—
AH1337/1918A	303	—	—	150	250	—
AH1338/1919A	303	—	—	150	250	—
AH1339/1920A	303	—	—	150	250	—
AH1340/1921A	303	—	—	150	250	—

KM# 240   10 FRANCS
3.2258 g., 0.9000 Gold 0.0933 oz. AGW **Obv. Leg.:** MUHAMMAD AL-NASIR

Date	Mintage	F	VF	XF	Unc	BU
AH1325/1907A	36	—	—	500	900	—
AH1326/1908A	166	—	—	300	500	—
AH1327/1909A	83	—	—	450	850	—
AH1328/1910A	83	—	—	450	850	—
AH1329/1911A	83	—	—	450	850	—
AH1330/1912A	83	—	—	450	850	—
AH1331/1913A	83	—	—	450	850	—
AH1332/1914A	83	—	—	450	850	—
AH1334/1915A	83	—	—	450	850	—
AH1334/1916A	83	—	—	450	850	—
AH1336/1917A	83	—	—	450	850	—
AH1337/1918A	83	—	—	450	850	—
AH1338/1919A	83	—	—	450	850	—
AH1339/1920A	83	—	—	450	850	—
AH1340/1921A	83	—	—	450	850	—

KM# 241   20 FRANCS
6.4516 g., 0.9000 Gold 0.1867 oz. AGW **Obv. Leg.:** MUHAMMAD AL-NASIR

Date	Mintage	F	VF	XF	Unc	BU
AH1325/1907A	26	—	—	550	1,000	—
AH1326/1908A	46	—	—	450	850	—
AH1327/1909A	23	—	—	550	1,000	—
AH1328/1910A	23	—	—	550	1,000	—
AH1329/1911A	23	—	—	550	1,000	—
AH1330/1912A	23	—	—	550	1,000	—
AH1331/1913A	23	—	—	550	1,000	—
AH1332/1914A	23	—	—	550	1,000	—
AH1334/1915A	23	—	—	550	1,000	—
AH1334/1916A	23	—	—	550	1,000	—
AH1336/1917A	23	—	—	550	1,000	—

Date	Mintage	F	VF	XF	Unc	BU
AH1337/1918A	23	—	—	550	1,000	—
AH1338/1919A	23	—	—	550	1,000	—
AH1339/1920A	23	—	—	550	1,000	—
AH1340/1921A	23	—	—	550	1,000	—

Muhammad al-Habib Bey
"Struck in his name"
DECIMAL COINAGE
100 Centimes = 1 Franc

The following coins all bear French inscriptions on one side, Arabic on the other, and usually have both AH and AD dates. Except for KM#246-48, they are struck in the name of the Tunisian Bey.

KM# 254   10 CENTIMES
4.0000 g., Nickel-Bronze **Obv:** Hole in center of inscription **Obv. Leg.:** MUHAMMAD AL-HABIB **Rev:** Value above hole in center, date and sprigs

Date	Mintage	F	VF	XF	Unc	BU
AH1345/1926(a)	1,000,000	—	20.00	50.00	100	—

KM# 249   50 CENTIMES
2.5000 g., 0.8350 Silver 0.0671 oz. ASW **Obv:** Inscription within sprigs **Obv. Leg.:** MUHAMMAD AL-HABIB **Rev:** Value and date within center circle

Date	Mintage	F	VF	XF	Unc	BU
AH1341/1922A	1,003	—	—	100	200	—
AH1342/1923A	2,009	—	—	100	200	—
AH1343/1924A	1,003	—	—	100	200	—
AH1344/1925A	1,003	—	—	100	200	—
AH1345/1926A	1,003	—	—	100	200	—
AH1346/1927A	1,003	—	—	100	200	—
AH1347/1928A	1,003	—	—	100	200	—

KM# 250   FRANC
5.0000 g., 0.8350 Silver 0.1342 oz. ASW **Obv. Leg.:** MUHAMMAD AL-HABIB

Date	Mintage	F	VF	XF	Unc	BU
AH1341/1922A	703	—	—	135	275	—
AH1342/1923A	1,409	—	—	100	250	—
AH1343/1924A	703	—	—	135	275	—
AH1344/1925A	703	—	—	135	275	—
AH1345/1926A	703	—	—	135	275	—
AH1346/1927A	703	—	—	135	275	—
AH1347/1928A	703	—	—	135	275	—

KM# 250a   FRANC
5.5000 g., 0.8350 Silver 0.1476 oz. ASW

Date	Mintage	F	VF	XF	Unc	BU
AH1347/1928A	Inc. above	—	—	135	275	—

KM# 251   2 FRANCS
10.0000 g., 0.8350 Silver 0.2684 oz. ASW **Obv. Leg.:** MUHAMMAD AL-HABIB

Date	Mintage	F	VF	XF	Unc	BU
AH1341/1922A	303	—	—	150	325	—
AH1342/1923A	690	—	—	135	275	—
AH1343/1924A	303	—	—	150	325	—
AH1344/1925A	303	—	—	150	325	—
AH1345/1926A	303	—	—	150	325	—
AH1346/1927A	303	—	—	150	325	—

KM# 251a   2 FRANCS
8.6000 g., 0.8350 Silver 0.2309 oz. ASW

Date	Mintage	F	VF	XF	Unc	BU
AH1347/1928A	303	—	—	150	325	—

KM# 252   10 FRANCS
3.2258 g., 0.9000 Gold 0.0933 oz. AGW **Obv. Leg.:** MUHAMMAD AL-HABIB BEY

Date	Mintage	F	VF	XF	Unc	BU
AH1341/1922A	83	—	—	450	850	—
AH1342/1923A	169	—	—	300	500	—
AH1343/1924A	83	—	—	450	850	—
AH1344/1925A	83	—	—	450	850	—
AH1345/1926A	83	—	—	450	850	—
AH1346/1927A	83	—	—	450	850	—
AH1347/1928A	83	—	—	450	850	—

KM# 253   20 FRANCS
6.4516 g., 0.9000 Gold 0.1867 oz. AGW **Obv. Leg.:** MUHAMMAD AL-HABIB

Date	Mintage	F	VF	XF	Unc	BU
AH1341/1922A	23	—	—	650	1,100	—
AH1342/1923A	49	—	—	450	850	—
AH1343/1924A	23	—	—	550	1,000	—
AH1344/1925A	23	—	—	550	1,000	—

Ahmad Pasha Bey
"Struck in his name"
DECIMAL COINAGE
100 Centimes = 1 Franc

The following coins all bear French inscriptions on one side, Arabic on the other, and usually have both AH and AD dates. Except for KM#246-48, they are struck in the name of the Tunisian Bey.

KM# 258   5 CENTIMES
2.0000 g., Nickel-Bronze **Obv:** Hole in center of inscription **Obv. Leg.:** AHMAD **Rev:** Value above hole in center, date and sprigs

Date	Mintage	F	VF	XF	Unc	BU
AH1350/1931(a)	2,000,000	—	4.00	10.00	25.00	—
AH1352/1933(a)	1,000,000	—	5.00	12.00	30.00	—
AH1357/1938(a)	1,200,000	—	4.00	10.00	25.00	—

KM# 259   10 CENTIMES
Nickel-Bronze **Obv:** Hole in center of inscription **Obv. Leg.:** AHMAD **Rev:** Value above hole in center, date and sprigs

Date	Mintage	F	VF	XF	Unc	BU
AH1350/1931(a)	750,000	—	6.00	15.00	35.00	—
AH1352/1933(a)	1,000,000	—	6.00	15.00	35.00	—

Note: Wide and narrow dates

Date	Mintage	F	VF	XF	Unc	BU
AH1357/1938(a)	1,200,000	—	—	5.00	12.00	25.00

KM# 267   10 CENTIMES
2.5000 g., Zinc **Obv. Leg.:** AHMAD

Date	Mintage	F	VF	XF	Unc	BU
AH1360/1941(a)	5,000,000	—	2.50	6.00	25.00	—
AH1361/1942(a)	10,000,000	—	1.50	4.00	20.00	—

KM# 268   20 CENTIMES
3.6000 g., Zinc **Obv:** Hole in center of inscription **Obv. Leg.:** AHMAD **Rev:** Value above hole in center, date and sprigs

Date	Mintage	F	VF	XF	Unc	BU
AH1361/1942A	5,000,000	—	20.00	35.00	50.00	—

KM# 260   25 CENTIMES
5.0000 g., Nickel-Aluminum-Bronze **Obv:** Hole in center of inscription **Obv. Leg.:** AHMAD **Rev:** Value above hole in center, date and sprigs

Date	Mintage	F	VF	XF	Unc	BU
AH1350/1931(a)	300,000	—	8.00	15.00	35.00	—
AH1352/1933(a)	400,000	—	8.00	15.00	35.00	—
AH1357/1938(a)	480,000	—	4.00	10.00	25.00	—

KM# 261 5 FRANCS
5.0000 g., 0.6800 Silver 0.1093 oz. ASW **Obv:** Inscription and date within sprigs **Obv. Leg.:** AHMAD **Rev:** Value flanked by designs

Date	Mintage	F	VF	XF	Unc	BU
AH1353 (1934) (a)	2,000,000	—	10.00	18.00	25.00	—
AH1355 (1936) (a)	2,000,000	—	10.00	18.00	25.00	—

KM# 264 5 FRANCS
5.0000 g., 0.6800 Silver 0.1093 oz. ASW **Obv:** Inscription and date within sprigs **Obv. Leg.:** AHMAD **Rev:** Value in center of circular inscription and design

Date	Mintage	F	VF	XF	Unc	BU
AH1358/1939(a)	1,600,000	—	15.00	25.00	40.00	—

KM# 255 10 FRANCS
10.0000 g., 0.6800 Silver 0.2186 oz. ASW **Obv:** Inscription within oblong design flanked by sprigs **Obv. Leg.:** AHMAD **Rev:** Value and date within center circle of design

Date	Mintage	F	VF	XF	Unc	BU
AH1349/1930(a)	60,000	—	45.00	70.00	110	—
AH1350/1931(a)	1,103	—	150	250	350	—
AH1351/1932(a)	60,000	—	60.00	100	200	—
AH1352/1933(a)	1,103	—	150	250	350	—
AH1353/1934(a)	30,000	—	45.00	70.00	110	—

KM# 262 10 FRANCS
10.0000 g., 0.6800 Silver 0.2186 oz. ASW **Obv:** Inscription and date within sprigs **Rev:** Value flanked by designs

Date	Mintage	F	VF	XF	Unc	BU
AH1353 (1934) (a)	1,501,000	—	10.00	20.00	35.00	—
AH1354 (1935) (a)	1,103	—	—	225	350	—
AH1355 (1936) (a)	2,006	—	—	225	350	—
AH1356 (1937) (a)	1,103	—	—	225	350	—
AH1357 (1938)	—	—	—	400	600	—
AH1358 (1939)	—	—	—	400	600	—

KM# 265 10 FRANCS
10.0000 g., 0.6800 Silver 0.2186 oz. ASW **Obv:** Inscription and date within sprigs **Rev:** Value and date within circular inscription and design

Date	Mintage	F	VF	XF	Unc	BU
AH1358/1939(a)	501,000	—	7.00	15.00	35.00	—
AH1359/1940(a)	—	—	—	225	350	—
AH1360/1941(a)	1,103	—	—	225	350	—
AH1361/1942(a)	1,103	—	—	225	350	—

KM# 256 20 FRANCS
20.0000 g., 0.6800 Silver 0.4372 oz. ASW **Obv:** Inscription within oblong design flanked by sprigs **Obv. Leg.:** AHMAD **Rev:** Value and date within center circle of design

Date	Mintage	F	VF	XF	Unc	BU
AH1349/1930(a)	20,000	—	60.00	100	175	—
AH1350/1931(a)	53	—	200	300	500	—
AH1351/1932(a)	20,000	—	75.00	150	275	—
AH1352/1933(a)	53	—	200	300	500	—
AH1353/1934(a)	9,500	—	60.00	100	175	—

Note: It is believed that an additional number of coins dated AH1353/1934(a) were struck and included in mintage figures of KM#263 of the same date

KM# 263 20 FRANCS
20.0000 g., 0.6800 Silver 0.4372 oz. ASW **Obv:** Inscription and date within sprigs **Rev:** Value flanked by designs

Date	Mintage	F	VF	XF	Unc	BU
AH1353 (1934) (a)	1,250,000	—	12.00	25.00	60.00	—
AH1354 (1935)	53	—	—	275	450	—
AH1355 (1936)	106	—	—	225	375	—
AH1356 (1937) (a)	53	—	—	275	450	—

KM# 266 20 FRANCS
20.0000 g., 0.6800 Silver 0.4372 oz. ASW **Obv:** Inscription and date within sprigs **Rev:** Value and date within circular inscription and design

Date	Mintage	F	VF	XF	Unc	BU
AH1358/1939(a)	100,000	—	20.00	40.00	90.00	—
AH1359/1940(a)	—					

Note: Reported, not confirmed

Date	Mintage	F	VF	XF	Unc	BU
AH1360/1941(a)	53	—	—	275	450	—
AH1361/1942(a)	53	—	—	275	450	—

KM# 257 100 FRANCS
6.5500 g., 0.9000 Gold 0.1895 oz. AGW **Obv:** Inscription within oblong design flanked by sprigs **Obv. Leg.:** AHMAD **Rev:** Value and date within center circle of design

Date	Mintage	F	VF	XF	Unc	BU
AH1349/1930(a)	3,000	—	—	500	900	—
AH1350/1931(a)	33	—	—	500	900	—
AH1351/1932(a)	3,000	—	—	500	900	—
AH1352/1933(a)	33	—	—	500	900	—
AH1353/1934(a)	133	—	—	500	900	—
AH1354/1935(a)	3,000	—	—	500	900	—
AH1355/1936(a)	33	—	—	500	900	—
AH1356/1937(a)	33	—	—	500	900	—

Muhammad al-Amin Bey
"Struck in his name"
DECIMAL COINAGE
100 Centimes = 1 Franc

The following coins all bear French inscriptions on one side, Arabic on the other, and usually have both AH and AD dates. Except for KM#246-48, they are struck in the name of the Tunisian Bey.

KM# 271 10 CENTIMES
1.6000 g., Nickel-Aluminum-Bronze **Obv:** Hole in center of inscription **Obv. Leg.:** MUHAMMAD AL AMIN **Rev:** Value above hole in center, date and sprigs

Date	Mintage	F	VF	XF	Unc	BU
AH1364/1945(a)	10,000,000	—	40.00	75.00	140	—

Note: Most were probably melted

KM# 272 20 CENTIMES
Zinc **Obv:** Hole in center of inscription **Obv. Leg.:** MUHAMMAD AL-AMIN **Rev:** Value above hole in center, date and sprigs

Date	Mintage	F	VF	XF	Unc	BU
AH1364/1945(a)	5,205,000	—	60.00	120	200	—

Note: A large quantity was remelted

KM# 273 5 FRANCS
Aluminum-Bronze **Obv:** Inscription and date within sprigs **Obv. Leg.:** MUHAMMAD AL-AMIN **Rev:** Value and date within circular inscription and design

Date	Mintage	F	VF	XF	Unc	BU
AH1365/1946(a)	10,000,000	—	1.50	5.00	10.00	—

KM# 277 5 FRANCS
Copper-Nickel **Obv:** Dates within crescent below design **Rev:** Value and date within upper circle

Date	Mintage	F	VF	XF	Unc	BU
AH1373/1954(a)	18,000,000	—	1.00	2.50	5.00	—
AH1376/1957(a)	4,000,000	—	2.00	4.00	7.00	—

KM# 269 10 FRANCS
10.0000 g., 0.6800 Silver 0.2186 oz. ASW **Obv:** Inscription and date within sprigs **Rev:** Value and date within circular inscription and design

Date	Mintage	F	VF	XF	Unc	BU
AH1363/1943(a)	1,503	—	—	225	350	—
AH1364/1944(a)	2,206	—	—	200	300	—

KM# 270 20 FRANCS
20.0000 g., 0.6800 Silver 0.4372 oz. ASW **Obv. Leg.:** MUHAMMAD AL-AMIN

Date	Mintage	F	VF	XF	Unc	BU
AH1363/1943(a)	103	—	—	300	500	—
AH1364/1944(a)	106	—	—	300	500	—

KM# 274   20 FRANCS
Copper-Nickel **Obv:** Dates within crescent below design
Rev: Value and date within upper circle

Date	Mintage	F	VF	XF	Unc	BU
AH1370/1950(a)	10,000,000	—	0.60	2.25	6.50	—
AH1376/1957(a)	4,000,000	—	0.45	1.25	4.50	—

KM# 275   50 FRANCS
Copper-Nickel **Obv:** Dates within crescent below design
Obv. Leg.: MUHAMMAD AL-AMIN **Rev:** Value and date within upper circle

Date	Mintage	F	VF	XF	Unc	BU
AH1370/1950(a)	5,000,000	—	0.60	2.25	6.50	—
AH1376/1957(a)	600,000	—	1.25	2.75	6.50	—

KM# 276   100 FRANCS
Copper-Nickel **Obv:** Dates within crescent below design
Obv. Leg.: MUHAMMAD AL-AMIN **Rev:** Value and date within upper circle

Date	Mintage	F	VF	XF	Unc	BU
AH1370/1950(a)	8,000,000	—	2.25	5.50	11.50	—
AH1376/1957(a)	1,000,000	—	2.25	4.50	10.00	—

Anonymous
TOKEN COINAGE

KM# 246   50 CENTIMES
1.9500 g., Aluminum-Bronze, 18 mm. **Obv:** Date within wreath
Rev: Value within wreath **Rev. Insc.:** BON POUR (Good For) 50 CENTIMES

Date	Mintage	F	VF	XF	Unc	BU
AH1340/1921(a)	4,000,000	—	2.00	7.00	20.00	—
AH1345/1926(a)	1,000,000	—	3.00	10.00	25.00	—
AH1352/1933(a)	500,000	—	6.00	17.00	50.00	—
AH1360/1941(a)	4,646,000	—	1.00	3.00	10.00	—
AH1364/1945(a)	11,180,000	—	1.00	2.00	10.00	—

KM# 246a   50 CENTIMES
1.9500 g., Aluminum-Bronze Gold-plated, 18 mm. **Obv:** Date within wreath **Rev:** Value within wreath **Rev. Insc.:** BON POUR (Good For) 50 CENTIMES **Note:** Exists in gilt only.

Date	Mintage	F	VF	XF	Unc	BU
AH1347/1928	—	—	—	—	—	—

KM# 247   FRANC
Aluminum-Bronze, 23.5 mm. **Obv:** Date within wreath **Rev:** Value within wreath **Rev. Insc.:** BON POUR (Good For) 1 FRANC

Date	Mintage	F	VF	XF	Unc	BU
AH1340/1921(a)	5,000,000	—	2.00	7.00	20.00	—
AH1344/1926(a)	1,000,000	—	2.00	15.00	35.00	—

Date	Mintage	F	VF	XF	Unc	BU
AH1345/1926(a)	1,000,000	—	4.00	17.00	40.00	—
AH1360/1941(a)	6,612,000	—	1.00	4.00	10.00	—
AH1364/1945(a)	10,699,000	—	1.00	3.00	10.00	—

KM# 247a   FRANC
Aluminum-Bronze Gold-plated, 23.5 mm. **Obv:** Date within wreath **Rev:** Value within wreath **Rev. Insc.:** BON POUR (Good For) 1 FRANC **Note:** Exists in gilt only.

Date	Mintage	F	VF	XF	Unc	BU
AH1347/1928	—	—	—	—	—	—

KM# 248   2 FRANCS
8.1000 g., Aluminum-Bronze **Obv:** Date within wreath **Rev:** Value within wreath **Rev. Insc.:** BON POUR (Good For) 2 FRANCS

Date	Mintage	F	VF	XF	Unc	BU
AH1340/1921(a)	1,500,000	—	3.00	15.00	35.00	—
AH1343/1924(a)	500,000	—	8.00	20.00	50.00	—
AH1345/1926(a)	500,000	—	8.00	20.00	50.00	—
AH1360/1941(a)	1,976,000	—	3.00	8.00	15.00	—
AH1364/1945(a)	6,464,000	—	3.00	6.00	15.00	—

KM# 248a   2 FRANCS
8.1000 g., Aluminum-Bronze Gold-plated. **Obv:** Date within wreath **Rev:** Value within wreath **Rev. Insc.:** BON POUR (Good For) 2 FRANCS **Note:** Exists in gilt only.

Date	Mintage	F	VF	XF	Unc	BU
AH1347/1928	—	—	—	—	—	—

REPUBLIC
DECIMAL COINAGE
1000 Millim = 1 Dinar

KM# 280   MILLIM
0.6500 g., Aluminum, 18 mm. **Obv:** Oak tree and date
Rev: Value within sprigs

Date	Mintage	F	VF	XF	Unc	BU
1960	—	—	—	0.10	0.25	—

KM# 349   MILLIM
1.2000 g., Aluminum **Series:** F.A.O. **Obv:** Oak tree and date
Rev: Value within sprigs

Date	Mintage	F	VF	XF	Unc	BU
1999	—	—	—	—	0.75	—
2000	—	—	—	—	0.75	—

KM# 281   2 MILLIM
1.0000 g., Aluminum, 21 mm. **Obv:** Oak tree and date
Rev: Value within sprigs

Date	Mintage	F	VF	XF	Unc	BU
1960	—	—	—	0.10	0.25	—

KM# 282   5 MILLIM
1.5000 g., Aluminum, 24 mm. **Obv:** Oak tree and date
Rev: Value within sprigs

Date	Mintage	F	VF	XF	Unc	BU
1960	—	—	—	0.10	0.25	—
1983	—	—	—	0.10	0.25	—

Date	Mintage	F	VF	XF	Unc	BU
1993	—	—	—	0.10	0.25	—
1996	—	—	—	0.10	0.25	—

KM# 348   5 MILLIM
1.4900 g., Aluminum, 24 mm. **Obv:** Oak tree and dates
Rev: Value within sprigs

Date	Mintage	F	VF	XF	Unc	BU
AH1418-1997	—	—	—	—	0.50	—

KM# 306   10 MILLIM
3.5000 g., Brass, 19 mm. **Obv:** Inscription and dates within inner circle of design **Rev:** Value in center of design **Edge:** Reeded

Date	Mintage	F	VF	XF	Unc	BU
AH1380-1960	—	—	0.15	0.25	0.50	—
AH1414-1993	—	—	0.15	0.25	0.50	—
AH1416-1996	—	—	0.15	0.25	0.50	—
AH1418-1997	—	—	0.15	0.25	0.50	—

KM# 307   20 MILLIM
4.5000 g., Brass, 22 mm. **Obv:** Inscription and dates within center circle of design **Rev:** Value within center of design

Date	Mintage	F	VF	XF	Unc	BU
AH1380-1960	—	—	0.30	0.50	0.80	—
AH1403-1983	—	—	0.30	0.50	0.80	—
Note: Large and small date varieties exist.						
AH1414-1993	—	—	0.30	0.50	0.80	—
AH1416-1996	—	—	0.30	0.50	0.80	—
AH1418-1997	—	—	0.30	0.50	0.80	—

KM# 308   50 MILLIM
6.0000 g., Brass, 25 mm. **Obv:** Inscription and dates within center circle of design **Rev:** Value in center of design

Date	Mintage	F	VF	XF	Unc	BU
AH1380-1960	—	—	0.65	0.85	1.25	—
AH1403-1983	—	—	0.65	0.85	1.25	—
Note: Large and small date varieties exist.						
AH1414-1993	—	—	0.65	0.85	1.25	—
AH1416-1996	—	—	0.65	0.85	1.25	—
AH1418-1997	—	—	0.65	0.85	1.25	—

KM# 309   100 MILLIM
7.5000 g., Brass, 27 mm. **Obv:** Inscription and dates within center circle of design **Rev:** Value in center of design

Date	Mintage	F	VF	XF	Unc	BU
AH1380-1960	—	—	1.25	1.50	2.00	—
AH1403-1983	—	—	1.25	1.50	2.00	—
Note: Large and small date varieties exist.						
AH1414-1993	—	—	1.25	1.50	2.00	—
AH1416-1996	—	—	1.25	1.50	2.00	—
AH1418-1997	—	—	1.25	1.50	2.00	—
AH1421-2000	—	—	1.25	1.50	2.00	—

KM# 291 1/2 DINAR
Nickel **Obv:** Head left **Rev:** Value and date

Date	Mintage	F	VF	XF	Unc	BU
1968(a)	500,000	—	1.00	2.00	4.50	—

KM# 303 1/2 DINAR
Copper-Nickel **Series:** F.A.O. **Obv:** Head left **Rev:** 2 Hands with fruit and wheat sprig

Date	Mintage	F	VF	XF	Unc	BU
1976	700,000	—	1.50	3.50	6.50	—
Note: Variations exist with large and small designer's name						
1983	400,000	—	1.50	3.50	6.50	—

KM# 318 1/2 DINAR
Copper-Nickel **Series:** F.A.O. **Obv:** Map and date **Rev:** 2 Hands with fruit and wheat sprig

Date	Mintage	F	VF	XF	Unc	BU
1988	—	—	1.00	3.00	5.50	—
1990	300,000	—	1.00	3.00	5.50	—

KM# 346 1/2 DINAR
Copper-Nickel **Obv:** Shield within circle **Rev:** 2 hands with fruit and wheat sprig **Note:** Rim width varieties exist.

Date	Mintage	F	VF	XF	Unc	BU
AH1416-1996	5,000,000	—	1.00	2.50	4.50	—
AH1418-1997	—	—	1.00	2.50	4.50	—

KM# 292 DINAR
20.0000 g., 0.9250 Silver 0.5948 oz. ASW **Obv:** Head of Habib Bourguiba left **Rev:** Standing armored figure of Hannibal among elephant heads and designs

Date	Mintage	F	VF	XF	Unc	BU
1969 NI Proof	5,000	Value: 42.50					
1969FM NI Proof	15,000	Value: 17.50					

KM# 293 DINAR
20.0000 g., 0.9250 Silver 0.5948 oz. ASW **Obv:** Head of Habib Bourguiba left **Rev:** Stylized armored figure on horse and head of Masinissa left

Date	Mintage	F	VF	XF	Unc	BU
1969FM NI Proof	15,000	Value: 13.50					
1969 NI Proof	5,000	Value: 40.00					

KM# 294 DINAR
20.0000 g., 0.9250 Silver 0.5948 oz. ASW **Obv:** Head of Habib Bourguiba left **Rev:** Stylized head of Jugurtha left in center of balance scale

Date	Mintage	F	VF	XF	Unc	BU
1969FM NI Proof	15,000	Value: 13.50					
1969 NI Proof	5,000	Value: 40.00					

KM# 295 DINAR
20.0000 g., 0.9250 Silver 0.5948 oz. ASW **Obv:** Head of Habib Bourguiba left **Rev:** Seated figure of Virgil flanked by standing figures

Date	Mintage	F	VF	XF	Unc	BU
1969FM NI Proof	15,000	Value: 13.50					
1969 NI Proof	5,000	Value: 40.00					

KM# 296 DINAR
20.0000 g., 0.9250 Silver 0.5948 oz. ASW **Obv:** Head of Habib Bourguiba left **Rev:** Seated figure of St. Augustine at desk and bust facing

Date	Mintage	F	VF	XF	Unc	BU
1969FM NI Proof	15,000	Value: 12.00					
1969 NI Proof	5,000	Value: 40.00					

KM# 297 DINAR
20.0000 g., 0.9250 Silver 0.5948 oz. ASW **Obv:** Head of Habib Bourguiba left **Rev:** Phoenician Ship

Date	Mintage	F	VF	XF	Unc	BU
1969FM NI Proof	15,000	Value: 18.50					
1969 NI Proof	5,000	Value: 50.00					

KM# 298 DINAR
20.0000 g., 0.9250 Silver 0.5948 oz. ASW **Obv:** Head of Habib Bourguiba left **Rev:** Standing Neptune surrounded by mermaids and sea horses

Date	Mintage	F	VF	XF	Unc	BU
1969FM NI Proof	15,000	Value: 14.00					
1969 NI Proof	5,000	Value: 40.00					

KM# 299 DINAR
20.0000 g., 0.9250 Silver 0.5948 oz. ASW **Obv:** Head of Habib Bourguiba left **Rev:** Venus, with the ribbon of love

Date	Mintage	F	VF	XF	Unc	BU
1969FM NI Proof	15,000	Value: 17.50					
1969 NI Proof	5,000	Value: 50.00					

KM# 300 DINAR
20.0000 g., 0.9250 Silver 0.5948 oz. ASW **Obv:** Head of Habib Bourguiba left **Rev:** Thysdrus-El Djem, Africa's Colosseum

Date	Mintage	F	VF	XF	Unc	BU
1969FM NI Proof	15,000	Value: 13.50					
1969 NI Proof	5,000	Value: 40.00					

KM# 301   DINAR
20.0000 g., 0.9250 Silver 0.5948 oz. ASW **Obv:** Head of Habib Bourguiba left **Rev:** Building - Sbeitla-Sufetula

Date	Mintage	F	VF	XF	Unc	BU
1969FM NI Proof	15,000	Value: 13.50				
1969 NI Proof	5,000	Value: 40.00				

KM# 302   DINAR
18.0000 g., 0.6800 Silver 0.3935 oz. ASW **Series:** F.A.O. **Obv:** Head of Habib Bourguiba left **Rev:** Coconut tree, oxen and figure, tractor in background at left

Date	Mintage	F	VF	XF	Unc	BU
1970(a)	100,000	—	7.00	9.00	13.50	—
1970(a) Proof	1,250	Value: 40.00				

KM# 304   DINAR
Copper-Nickel **Series:** F.A.O. **Obv:** Head of Habib Bourguiba left **Rev:** Female half figure right **Note:** Varieties exist. Coins dated 1976 exist with or without dots (error) below iy of Tunisiya.

Date	Mintage	F	VF	XF	Unc	BU
1976	12,000,000	—	2.00	4.00	8.00	—
1983	4,000,000	—	2.00	4.00	8.00	—

KM# 319   DINAR
Copper-Nickel **Series:** F.A.O. **Obv:** Map and date **Rev:** Female half figure right

Date	Mintage	F	VF	XF	Unc	BU
1988	—	—	2.00	4.00	8.00	—
1990	8,000,000	—	2.00	4.00	8.00	—

KM# 351   DINAR
18.0000 g., 0.6800 Silver 0.3935 oz. ASW, 32 mm.
Subject: F.A.O. 50th Anniversary **Obv:** F.A.O. logo **Rev:** Orchard workers with ladder **Edge:** Reeded

Date	Mintage	F	VF	XF	Unc	BU
ND (1995) Proof	5,000	Value: 40.00				

KM# 347   DINAR
Copper-Nickel **Series:** F.A.O. **Obv:** Shield within circle **Rev:** Female half figure right

Date	Mintage	F	VF	XF	Unc	BU
AH1416-1996	—	—	2.00	4.00	7.50	—
AH1418-1997	—	—	2.00	4.00	7.50	—

KM# 286   2 DINARS
3.8000 g., 0.9000 Gold 0.1100 oz. AGW **Subject:** 10th Anniversary **Obv:** Head of Habib Bourguiba left **Rev:** Towered building flanked by dates

Date	Mintage	F	VF	XF	Unc	BU
ND(1967) NI Proof	7,259	Value: 150				

KM# 283   5 DINARS
11.7900 g., 0.9000 Gold 0.3411 oz. AGW, 25 mm. **Obv:** Head of Habib Bourguiba left, French legend **Rev:** Coat of arms with flags above sprigs, value and banner, French legend

Date	Mintage	F	VF	XF	Unc	BU
1959 Proof	—	Value: 700				
1960 Proof	—	Value: 700				
1962 Proof	—	Value: 700				

KM# 320   5 DINARS
11.7900 g., 0.9000 Gold 0.3411 oz. AGW, 25 mm. **Obv:** Arabic legends **Rev:** Arabic legends, coat of arms with flags

Date	Mintage	F	VF	XF	Unc	BU
1960-1380 Proof	—	Value: 700				
1962-1382 Proof	—	Value: 700				

KM# 284   5 DINARS
11.7900 g., 0.9000 Gold 0.3411 oz. AGW, 25 mm. **Obv:** Head of Habib Bourguiba left, French legends **Rev:** Coat of arms w/o flags above value, French legends

Date	Mintage	F	VF	XF	Unc	BU
1963 Proof	—	Value: 700				
1964 Proof	—	Value: 700				

KM# 321   5 DINARS
11.7900 g., 0.9000 Gold 0.3411 oz. AGW, 25 mm. **Obv:** Arabic legends **Rev:** Arabic legends, coat of arms w/o flags

Date	Mintage	F	VF	XF	Unc	BU
1963-1383 Proof	—	Value: 700				
1964-1384 Proof	—	Value: 700				
1966-1386 Proof	—	Value: 700				

KM# 287   5 DINARS
9.5000 g., 0.9000 Gold 0.2749 oz. AGW **Subject:** 10th Anniversary of Republic **Obv:** Head of Habib Bourguiba left **Rev:** Minaret

Date	Mintage	F	VF	XF	Unc	BU
ND(1967) NI Proof	7,259	Value: 325				

KM# 326   5 DINARS
9.4060 g., 0.9000 Gold 0.2722 oz. AGW, 22 mm. **Obv:** Coat of arms, Arabic legends **Rev:** Arabic legends

Date	Mintage	F	VF	XF	Unc	BU
1967-1387 Proof	550	Value: 400				
1968-1388 Proof	550	Value: 400				
1969-1389 Proof	550	Value: 400				
1972-1392 Proof	550	Value: 400				
1974-1394 Proof	550	Value: 400				
1976-1396 Proof	550	Value: 400				
1978-1398 Proof	550	Value: 400				
1979-1399 Proof	550	Value: 400				

Date	Mintage	F	VF	XF	Unc	BU
1980-1400 Proof	1,450	Value: 400				
1981-1401 Proof	1,450	Value: 400				
1982-1402 Proof	725	Value: 400				

KM# 325a   5 DINARS
9.4060 g., 0.9000 Gold 0.2722 oz. AGW, 22 mm. **Obv:** Head of Habib Bourguiba left, French legends **Rev:** Coat of arms above value, French legends

Date	Mintage	F	VF	XF	Unc	BU
1972 Proof	—	Value: 500				
1973 Proof	—	Value: 500				
1974 Proof	—	Value: 500				
1975 Proof	—	Value: 500				
1976 Proof	—	Value: 500				
1979 Proof	—	Value: 500				
1980 Proof	1,450	Value: 500				
1981 Proof	1,450	Value: 500				
1982 Proof	725	Value: 500				

KM# 305   5 DINARS
24.0000 g., 0.6800 Silver 0.5247 oz. ASW **Subject:** 20th Anniversary of Independence **Obv:** Head of Habib Bourguiba left **Rev:** Design and value

Date	Mintage	F	VF	XF	Unc	BU
ND(1976)	200,000	—	—	—	25.00	—

KM# 313   5 DINARS
27.2200 g., 0.9250 Silver 0.8095 oz. ASW **Series:** International Year of the Child **Obv:** Head of Habib Bourguiba left **Rev:** Seated child playing

Date	Mintage	F	VF	XF	Unc	BU
1982 Proof	1,108	Value: 22.50				

KM# 327   5 DINARS
9.4060 g., 0.9000 Gold 0.2722 oz. AGW **Subject:** 25th Anniversary of Republic **Obv:** French legends **Rev:** Coat of arms, French legends **Rev. Insc.:** President de la Republique

Date	Mintage	F	VF	XF	Unc	BU
1983 Proof	—	Value: 400				
1984 Proof	—	Value: 400				
1985 Proof	—	Value: 400				
1986 Proof	—	Value: 400				

KM# 328   5 DINARS
9.4060 g., 0.9000 Gold 0.2722 oz. AGW **Subject:** 25th Anniversary of Republic **Obv:** Arabic legends **Rev:** Coat of arms, Arabic legends **Note:** Similar to 10 Dinars, KM#335.

Date	Mintage	F	VF	XF	Unc	BU
1983-1403 Proof	—	Value: 400				
1984-1404 Proof	—	Value: 400				
1985-1405 Proof	—	Value: 400				
1985-1406 Proof	—	Value: 400				
1986-1406 Proof	—	Value: 400				

KM# 355   5 DINARS
9.4060 g., 0.9000 Gold 0.2722 oz. AGW **Obv:** Country map **Rev:** Coat of arms **Note:** Arabic legends.

Date	Mintage	F	VF	XF	Unc	BU
1987-1407	—	—	—	—	400	—

KM# 329   5 DINARS
9.4060 g., 0.9000 Gold 0.2722 oz. AGW **Subject:** 1st Anniversary of 7 Nov 1987 **Obv:** Map **Rev:** Allegorical design **Note:** French legends vary by year.

Date	Mintage	F	VF	XF	Unc	BU
1988-1409	250	—	—	—	400	—
1989-1410	125	—	—	—	400	—
1990-1411	—	—	—	—	400	—

KM# 330   5 DINARS
9.4060 g., 0.9000 Gold 0.2722 oz. AGW **Subject:** 1st Anniversary of 7 Nov 1987 **Obv:** Map **Rev:** Allegorical design **Note:** Arabic legends vary by year.

Date	Mintage	F	VF	XF	Unc	BU
1989-1410	125	—	—	—	400	—

Date	Mintage	F	VF	XF	Unc	BU
1988-1409	250	—	—	—	400	—
1990-1411	—	—	—	—	400	—

KM# 322 10 DINARS
23.4800 g., 0.9000 Gold 0.6794 oz. AGW, 31 mm. **Obv:** French legends **Rev:** Coat of arms with flags, French legends

Date	Mintage	F	VF	XF	Unc	BU
1959 Proof	—	Value: 1,100				
1960 Proof	—	Value: 1,100				
1962 Proof	—	Value: 1,100				

KM# 285 10 DINARS
23.4800 g., 0.9000 Gold 0.6794 oz. AGW, 31 mm. **Obv:** Head of Habib Bourguiba left, Arabic legends **Rev:** Coat of arms with flags above value, Arabic legends

Date	Mintage	F	VF	XF	Unc	BU
1959-1379 Proof	—	Value: 1,100				
1960-1380 Proof	—	Value: 1,100				
1962-1382 Proof	—	Value: 1,100				

KM# 360 10 DINARS
23.4800 g., 0.9000 Gold 0.6794 oz. AGW, 31 mm. **Obv:** Head of Bourguiba left **Rev:** National arms without flags **Note:** Arabic legends.

Date	Mintage	F	VF	XF	Unc	BU
1963-1383 Proof	—	Value: 1,100				
1964-1384 Proof	—	Value: 1,100				

KM# 359 10 DINARS
23.9800 g., 0.9000 Gold 0.6938 oz. AGW, 31 mm. **Obv:** Head of Bourguiba left **Rev:** National arms without flags **Note:** French legends.

Date	Mintage	F	VF	XF	Unc	BU
1963 Proof	—	Value: 1,100				

KM# 288 10 DINARS
19.0000 g., 0.9000 Gold 0.5498 oz. AGW **Subject:** 10th Anniversary of Republic **Obv:** Head of Habib Bourguiba left **Rev:** Towered building flanked by dates

Date	Mintage	F	VF	XF	Unc	BU
ND(1967) NI Proof	6,480	Value: 600				

KM# 332 10 DINARS
18.7700 g., 0.5431 Gold 0.3277 oz. AGW **Obv:** Head of President Bourguisa left **Rev:** Coat of arms without flags **Note:** Arabic legends.

Date	Mintage	F	VF	XF	Unc	BU
1971-1391 Proof	—	Value: 650				
1973-1393 Proof	—	Value: 650				
1974-1394 Proof	—	Value: 650				
1976-1396 Proof	—	Value: 650				
1977-1397 Proof	—	Value: 650				
1979-1399 Proof	—	Value: 650				
1980-1400 Proof	—	Value: 650				
1981-1401 Proof	1,400	Value: 650				
1982-1402 Proof	700	Value: 650				

KM# 331 10 DINARS
18.7700 g., 0.9000 Gold 0.5431 oz. AGW **Obv:** Head of President Bourguiba left, date below **Rev:** Coat of arms without flags, value below **Note:** French legends.

Date	Mintage	F	VF	XF	Unc	BU
1971 Proof	—	Value: 650				
1972 Proof	—	Value: 650				
1973 Proof	—	Value: 650				
1974 Proof	—	Value: 650				
1975 Proof	—	Value: 650				
1977 Proof	—	Value: 650				
1979 Proof	—	Value: 650				
1980 Proof	—	Value: 650				
1981 Proof	2,000	Value: 650				
1982 Proof	700	Value: 650				

KM# 361 10 DINARS
18.7700 g., 0.9000 Gold 0.5431 oz. AGW **Subject:** 20th Anniversary - Victory and Return of Bourguiba **Obv:** Head of Bourguiba **Rev:** Boats in harbor

Date	Mintage	F	VF	XF	Unc	BU
ND(1975)	2,000	—	—	—	750	—

KM# 324 10 DINARS
18.7700 g., 0.9000 Gold 0.5431 oz. AGW **Subject:** 20th Anniversary of Independence - 20. March 1956 **Obv:** Head of Habib Bourguiba left **Rev:** Coat of arms without flags

Date	Mintage	F	VF	XF	Unc	BU
ND(1976)	2,000	—	—	—	750	—

KM# 343 10 DINARS
18.7700 g., 0.9000 Gold 0.5431 oz. AGW **Subject:** 20th Anniversary of Republic **Obv:** Head of President Habib Bourguiba left **Rev:** Dates in wreath

Date	Mintage	F	VF	XF	Unc	BU
ND(1977)	2,000	—	—	—	750	—

KM# 362 10 DINARS
18.7700 g., 0.9000 Gold 0.5431 oz. AGW **Subject:** 20th Anniversary of Republic

Date	Mintage	F	VF	XF	Unc	BU
ND(1977)	2,000	—	—	—	750	—

KM# 356 10 DINARS
38.0000 g., 0.9000 Silver 1.0995 oz. ASW, 40 mm. **Subject:** 20th Anniversary - Central Bank **Obv:** Head of President Bourguiba right **Rev:** Mosque of El Zituna

Date	Mintage	F	VF	XF	Unc	BU
ND(1978)	—	—	—	—	100	—
ND(1978) Proof	—	Value: 150				

KM# 344 10 DINARS
38.0000 g., 0.9000 Silver 1.0995 oz. ASW, 40 mm. **Subject:** 20th Anniversary - Central Bank **Obv:** Head of Habib Bourguiba left **Rev:** Sadiki College building

Date	Mintage	F	VF	XF	Unc	BU
ND(1978)	—	—	—	—	100	—
ND(1978) Proof	—	Value: 150				

KM# 345 10 DINARS
38.0000 g., 0.9000 Silver 1.0995 oz. ASW, 40 mm. **Subject:** 20th Anniversary - Central Bank **Obv:** Head of President Habib Bourguiba left **Rev:** Tunis Central Bank building

Date	Mintage	F	VF	XF	Unc	BU
ND(1978)	—	—	—	—	100	—
ND(1978) Proof	—	Value: 150				

KM# 345a 10 DINARS
18.8080 g., 0.9000 Gold 0.5442 oz. AGW, 28 mm. **Subject:** 20th Anniversary - Central Bank

Date	Mintage	F	VF	XF	Unc	BU
ND(1978)	2,000	—	—	—	700	—

KM# 311 10 DINARS
18.8240 g., 0.9000 Gold 0.5447 oz. AGW **Subject:** 25th Anniversary of President's Return **Obv:** Habib Bourguiba

Date	Mintage	F	VF	XF	Unc	BU
1980 Proof	2,000	Value: 650				

KM# 312 10 DINARS
18.7700 g., 0.9000 Gold 0.5431 oz. AGW **Subject:** 25th Anniversary of Independence **Obv:** Head of Habib Bourguiba left **Rev:** Stylized silhouette of girl leaping with large veil overhead

Date	Mintage	F	VF	XF	Unc	BU
ND(1981) Proof	2,000	Value: 650				

KM# 333 10 DINARS
18.7700 g., 0.9000 Gold 0.5431 oz. AGW **Subject:** 25th Anniversary of the Republic **Rev:** Tunisian girl

Date	Mintage	F	VF	XF	Unc	BU
ND(1982) Proof	2,000	Value: 650				

KM# 334 10 DINARS
18.7700 g., 0.9000 Gold 0.5431 oz. AGW **Subject:** 25th Anniversary of Republic **Obv:** "President" added to inscription, head left **Obv. Insc.:** President de la Republique **Rev:** Coat of arms without flags, value below **Note:** French legends.

Date	Mintage	F	VF	XF	Unc	BU
1983 Proof	—	Value: 650				
1984 Proof	—	Value: 650				
1985 Proof	—	Value: 650				
1986 Proof	—	Value: 650				

KM# 335 10 DINARS
18.7700 g., 0.9000 Gold 0.5431 oz. AGW **Subject:** 25th Anniversary of Republic **Obv:** Head of president left **Rev:** Coat of arms without flags **Note:** Arabic legends.

Date	Mintage	F	VF	XF	Unc	BU
1983-1403 Proof	—	Value: 650				
1984-1404 Proof	—	Value: 650				
1985-1405 Proof	—	Value: 650				
1986-1406 Proof	—	Value: 650				

KM# 314 10 DINARS
38.0000 g., 0.9000 Silver 1.0995 oz. ASW **Subject:** 25th Anniversary - Central Bank **Obv:** Head left **Rev:** Gabes branch bank building

Date	Mintage	F	VF	XF	Unc	BU
ND(1983)	—	—	—	—	100	—
ND(1983) Proof	2,500	Value: 150				

KM# 315 10 DINARS
38.0000 g., 0.9000 Silver 1.0995 oz. ASW **Subject:** 25th Anniversary - Central Bank **Obv:** Head left **Rev:** Nabeul branch bank building

Date	Mintage	F	VF	XF	Unc	BU
ND(1983)	—	—	—	—	100	—
ND(1983) Proof	1,000	Value: 150				

KM# 316 10 DINARS
38.0000 g., 0.9000 Silver 1.0995 oz. ASW **Subject:** 25th Anniversary - Central Bank **Obv:** Head left **Rev:** Sfax branch bank building

Date	Mintage	F	VF	XF	Unc	BU
ND(1983)	—	—	—	—	100	—
ND(1983) Proof	1,000	Value: 150				

KM# 336 10 DINARS
18.7700 g., 0.9000 Gold 0.5431 oz. AGW **Subject:** 50th Anniversary of the Socialist Party (DESTUR)

Date	Mintage	F	VF	XF	Unc	BU
ND(1984) Proof	—	Value: 450				

KM# 323 10 DINARS
18.7700 g., 0.9000 Gold 0.5431 oz. AGW **Subject:** 30th Anniversary - Return of Bourguiba **Obv:** Head left **Rev:** Statue of Bourghiba

Date	Mintage	F	VF	XF	Unc	BU
ND(1985-1405) Proof	2,000	Value: 650				

KM# 337 10 DINARS
18.7700 g., 0.9000 Gold 0.5431 oz. AGW **Subject:** 30th Anniversary of Independence **Obv:** Head left **Rev:** Stylized horse and rider

Date	Mintage	F	VF	XF	Unc	BU
ND(1986) Proof	—	Value: 650				

KM# 338 10 DINARS
18.7700 g., 0.9000 Gold 0.5431 oz. AGW **Subject:** 30th Anniversary of Republic

Date	Mintage	F	VF	XF	Unc	BU
1987 Proof	2,000	Value: 550				

KM# 363 10 DINARS
18.7700 g., 0.9000 Gold 0.5431 oz. AGW **Obv:** Country map **Rev:** National arms without flags **Note:** Arabic legends.

Date	Mintage	F	VF	XF	Unc	BU
AH1407-1987	—	—	—	—	700	—

KM# 340 10 DINARS
18.7700 g., 0.9000 Gold 0.5431 oz. AGW **Subject:** 1st Anniversary - 7 Nov 1987 **Obv:** Map **Rev:** Allegorical design **Note:** French legends vary by year.

Date	Mintage	F	VF	XF	Unc	BU
1988-1409	250	—	—	—	750	—
1989-1410	150	—	—	—	650	—
1990-1411	—	—	—	—	650	—

KM# 339 10 DINARS
38.0000 g., 0.9000 Silver 1.0995 oz. ASW **Subject:** 30th Anniversary - Central Bank **Obv:** Map of country **Rev:** Kasserin branch bank building

Date	Mintage	F	VF	XF	Unc	BU
ND(1988) Proof	4,000	Value: 150				
ND(1988)	—	—	—	—	100	—

KM# 364 10 DINARS
38.0000 g., 0.9000 Silver 1.0995 oz. ASW **Subject:** 30th Anniversary - Central Bank **Rev:** Gafsa branch bank building

Date	Mintage	F	VF	XF	Unc	BU
ND(1988)	—	—	—	—	100	—
ND(1988) Proof	—	Value: 150				

KM# 365 10 DINARS
38.0000 g., 0.9000 Silver 1.0995 oz. ASW **Subject:** 30th Anniversary - Central Bank **Obv:** Country map **Rev:** Kairuan branch bank building

Date	Mintage	F	VF	XF	Unc	BU
ND(1988)	—	—	—	—	100	—
ND(1988) Proof	—	Value: 150				

KM# 341   10 DINARS
18.7700 g., 0.9000 Gold 0.5431 oz. AGW **Subject:** 1st Anniversary - 7 Nov 1987 **Obv:** Map of country **Rev:** Allegorical design **Note:** Arabic legends vary by year.

Date	Mintage	F	VF	XF	Unc	BU
1989-1409	250	—	—	—	750	—
1989-1410	150	—	—	—	750	—
1990-1411	—	—	—	—	750	—

KM# 368   10 DINARS
38.0000 g., 0.9000 Silver 1.0995 oz. ASW **Subject:** 6th Anniversary - 7 Nov 1987 **Obv:** National arms **Rev:** Allegorical design over country map

Date	Mintage	F	VF	XF	Unc	BU
AH1414-1993	—	—	—	—	250	—

KM# 369   10 DINARS
38.0000 g., 0.9000 Silver 1.0995 oz. ASW **Subject:** 7th Anniversary of 7 Nov 87

Date	Mintage	F	VF	XF	Unc	BU
AH1415-1994	—	—	—	—	250	—

KM# 370   10 DINARS
38.0000 g., 0.9000 Silver 1.0995 oz. ASW **Subject:** 8th Anniversary - 7 Nov 87

Date	Mintage	F	VF	XF	Unc	BU
AH1416-1995	—	—	—	—	250	—

KM# 371   10 DINARS
38.0000 g., 0.9000 Silver 1.0995 oz. ASW **Subject:** 9th Anniversary - 7 Nov 1987

Date	Mintage	F	VF	XF	Unc	BU
AH1417-1996	—	—	—	—	250	—

KM# 372   10 DINARS
38.0000 g., 0.9000 Silver 1.0995 oz. ASW **Subject:** 40th Anniversary - Central Bank **Obv:** National arms **Rev:** Monastir branch bank building

Date	Mintage	F	VF	XF	Unc	BU
ND(1998) Proof	—	Value: 150				

KM# 375   10 DINARS
38.0000 g., 0.9000 Silver 1.0995 oz. ASW **Subject:** 11th Anniversary 7 Nov 1987 **Note:** Arabic legends.

Date	Mintage	F	VF	XF	Unc	BU
AH1419-1998	—	—	—	—	250	—

KM# 373   10 DINARS
38.0000 g., 0.9000 Silver 1.0995 oz. ASW **Subject:** 40th Anniversary - Central Bank **Obv:** National arms **Rev:** Sfax branch bank building **Note:** Arabic legend

Date	Mintage	F	VF	XF	Unc	BU
ND(1998) Proof	—	Value: 150				

KM# 374   10 DINARS
38.0000 g., 0.9000 Silver 1.0995 oz. ASW **Subject:** 40th Anniversary - Central Bank **Obv:** National arms **Rev:** Sfax branch bank building **Note:** French legends.

Date	Mintage	F	VF	XF	Unc	BU
ND(1998) Proof	—	Value: 150				

KM# A350   10 DINARS
38.0000 g., 0.9000 Silver 1.0995 oz. ASW **Subject:** 12th Anniversary of 7 Nov 87 and Millennium **Obv:** National arms **Rev:** Stylized design with 2000 above

Date	Mintage	F	VF	XF	Unc	BU
1999-1420	—	—	—	—	250	—

KM# 377   10 DINARS
38.0000 g., 0.9000 Silver 1.0995 oz. ASW **Subject:** 13th Anniversary of 7 Nov 1987 and 21st Century

Date	Mintage	F	VF	XF	Unc	BU
AH1421-2000	—	—	—	—	250	—

KM# 289   20 DINARS
38.0000 g., 0.9000 Gold 1.0995 oz. AGW **Subject:** 10th Anniversary of Republic **Rev:** Minaret

Date	Mintage	F	VF	XF	Unc	BU
ND(1967) NI	3,536	—	—	—	1,250	—

KM# 290   40 DINARS
76.0000 g., 0.9000 Gold 2.1990 oz. AGW **Subject:** 10th Anniversary of Republic **Obv:** Head left **Rev:** Minaret **Note:** Similar to 20 Dinars, KM#289.

Date	Mintage	F	VF	XF	Unc	BU
ND(1967) NI Proof	3,031	Value: 2,500				

KM# 384   50 DINARS
21.0000 g., 0.9000 Gold 0.6076 oz. AGW, 34 mm. **Subject:** 5th Anniversary of 7 Nov 1987 **Edge:** Reeded

Date	Mintage	F	VF	XF	Unc	BU
AH1413-1992 Proof	400	Value: 850				

KM# 385   50 DINARS
21.0000 g., 0.9000 Gold 0.6076 oz. AGW, 34 mm. **Subject:** 6th Anniversary 7 Nov 1987 **Edge:** Reeded

Date	Mintage	F	VF	XF	Unc	BU
AH1414-1993 Proof	—	Value: 850				

KM# 386   50 DINARS
21.0000 g., 0.9000 Gold 0.6076 oz. AGW, 34 mm. **Subject:** 7th Anniversary of 7 Nov 87 **Edge:** Reeded

Date	Mintage	F	VF	XF	Unc	BU
AH1415-1994 Proof	400	Value: 850				

KM# 387   50 DINARS
21.0000 g., 0.9000 Gold 0.6076 oz. AGW, 34 mm. **Subject:** 8th Anniversary of 7 Nov 1987 **Obv:** National arms **Rev:** Stylized 7 with dove in flight **Edge:** Reeded

Date	Mintage	F	VF	XF	Unc	BU
AH1416-1995 Proof	400	Value: 850				

KM# 388   50 DINARS
21.0000 g., 0.9000 Gold 0.6076 oz. AGW, 34 mm. **Subject:** 20th Soccer Africa Cup plus 9th Anniversary of 7 Nov 87 **Edge:** Reeded

Date	Mintage	F	VF	XF	Unc	BU
AH1417-1996 Proof	—	Value: 850				

KM# 390   50 DINARS
21.0000 g., 0.9000 Gold 0.6076 oz. AGW, 34 mm. **Subject:** 10th Anniversary of 7 Nov 1987 **Rev:** Head of Zine El Abdine Ben Ali **Edge:** Reeded **Note:** Arabic legends.

Date	Mintage	F	VF	XF	Unc	BU
AH1418-1997 Proof	—	Value: 850				

KM# 389   50 DINARS
21.0000 g., 0.9000 Gold 0.6076 oz. AGW, 34 mm. **Subject:** 10th Anniversary of 7 Nov 1987 **Obv:** National arms **Rev:** Head of Zine El Abdine Ben Ali **Edge:** Reeded **Note:** French legends.

Date	Mintage	F	VF	XF	Unc	BU
AH1418-1997 Proof	—	Value: 850				

KM# 391   50 DINARS
21.0000 g., 0.9000 Gold 0.6076 oz. AGW, 34 mm. **Subject:** 11th Anniversary of 7 Nov 1987 **Obv:** National arms **Edge:** Reeded **Note:** French legends.

Date	Mintage	F	VF	XF	Unc	BU
AH1419-1998 Proof	—	Value: 850				

KM# 392   50 DINARS
21.0000 g., 0.9000 Gold 0.6076 oz. AGW, 34 mm. **Subject:** 11th Anniversary of 7 Nov 1987 **Obv:** National arms **Edge:** Reeded **Note:** Arabic legends.

Date	Mintage	F	VF	XF	Unc	BU
AH1419-1998 Proof	550	Value: 850				

KM# 394   50 DINARS
21.0000 g., 0.9000 Gold 0.6076 oz. AGW, 34 mm. **Subject:** 12th Anniversary of 7 Nov 1987 plus The Millennium **Obv:** National arms **Edge:** Reeded **Note:** Arabic legends.

Date	Mintage	F	VF	XF	Unc	BU
AH1420-1999 Proof	—	Value: 850				

KM# 393   50 DINARS
21.0000 g., 0.9000 Gold 0.6076 oz. AGW, 34 mm. **Subject:** 12th Anniversary of 7 Nov 1987 plus the Millennium **Obv:** National arms **Edge:** Reeded **Note:** French legends.

Date	Mintage	F	VF	XF	Unc	BU
AH1420-1999 Proof	—	Value: 850				

KM# 395   50 DINARS
21.0000 g., 0.9000 Gold 0.6076 oz. AGW, 34 mm. **Subject:** 13th Anniversary 7 Nov 1987 plus 21st Century **Obv:** National arms **Rev:** Two interlocked currycombs, each with the number 21 **Edge:** Reeded **Note:** Arabic legends.

Date	Mintage	F	VF	XF	Unc	BU
AH1421-2000 Proof	—	Value: 850				

KM# 353   50 DINARS
0.9000 Gold, 34 mm. **Subject:** 13th Anniversary of 7 Nov 1987 plus 21st Century **Obv:** National arms **Rev:** Two interlocked currycombs, each with the number 21 **Note:** French legends.

Date	Mintage	F	VF	XF	Unc	BU
2000-1421 Proof	—	Value: 750				

KM# 317   75 DINARS
15.5500 g., 0.9000 Gold 0.4499 oz. AGW **Series:** International Year of the Child **Obv:** Head of Habib Bourguiba left **Rev:** Standing figures facing left

Date	Mintage	F	VF	XF	Unc	BU
1982 Proof	4,518	Value: 485				

KM# 399   100 DINARS
38.0000 g., 0.9000 Gold 1.0995 oz. AGW, 40 mm. **Subject:** 5th Anniversary of 7 Nov 1987

Date	Mintage	F	VF	XF	Unc	BU
AH1413-1992 Proof	250	Value: 1,650				

KM# A401   100 DINARS
38.0000 g., 0.9000 Gold 1.0995 oz. AGW **Subject:** 6th Anniversary of 7 Nov 1987 **Obv:** National arms **Note:** Arabic legends.

Date	Mintage	F	VF	XF	Unc	BU
AH1414-1993 Proof	250	—	—	—	—	—

KM# 401   100 DINARS
38.0000 g., 0.9000 Gold 1.0995 oz. AGW **Subject:** 7th Anniversary of 7 Nov 1987

Date	Mintage	F	VF	XF	Unc	BU
AH1415-1994 Proof	250	Value: 1,650				

KM# 402   100 DINARS
38.0000 g., 0.9000 Gold 1.0995 oz. AGW **Subject:** 8th Anniversary of 7 Nov 1987

Date	Mintage	F	VF	XF	Unc	BU
AH1416-1995 Proof	—	Value: 1,650				

KM# 403   100 DINARS
38.0000 g., 0.9000 Gold 1.0995 oz. AGW **Subject:** 9th Anniversary of 7 Nov 1987 and 20th Soccer Africa Cup

Date	Mintage	F	VF	XF	Unc	BU
AH1417-1996 Proof	—	Value: 1,650				

KM# 405   100 DINARS
38.0000 g., 0.9000 Gold 1.0995 oz. AGW **Subject:** 10th Anniversary of 7 Nov 1987 **Obv:** National arms **Rev:** Bust of Zine El Abdine Ben Ali **Note:** Arabic legends.

Date	Mintage	F	VF	XF	Unc	BU
AH1418-1997 Proof	—	Value: 1,650				

KM# 404   100 DINARS
38.0000 g., 0.9000 Gold 1.0995 oz. AGW **Subject:** 10th Anniversary of 7 Nov 1987 **Obv:** National arms **Rev:** Bust of Zine El Abdine Ben Ali right **Note:** French legends.

Date	Mintage	F	VF	XF	Unc	BU
AH1418-1997 Proof	—	Value: 1,650				

KM# 406   100 DINARS
38.0000 g., 0.9000 Gold 1.0995 oz. AGW **Subject:** 11th Anniversary of 7 Nov 1987 **Note:** French legends.

Date	Mintage	F	VF	XF	Unc	BU
AH1419-1998 Proof	—	Value: 1,650				

KM# 407   100 DINARS
38.0000 g., 0.9000 Gold 1.0995 oz. AGW **Subject:** 11th Anniversary of 7 Nov 1987 **Note:** Arabic legends.

Date	Mintage	F	VF	XF	Unc	BU
AH1419-1998 Proof	—	Value: 1,650				

KM# 409   100 DINARS
38.0000 g., 0.9000 Gold 1.0995 oz. AGW **Subject:** 12th Anniversary of 7 Nov 1987 and The Millennium **Obv:** National arms **Note:** Arabic legends.

Date	Mintage	F	VF	XF	Unc	BU
AH1420-1999 Proof	—	Value: 1,650				

KM# 408   100 DINARS
38.0000 g., 0.9000 Gold 1.0995 oz. AGW **Subject:** 12th Anniversary of 7 Nov 1987 and The Millennium **Note:** French legends.

Date	Mintage	F	VF	XF	Unc	BU
AH1420-1999 Proof	—	Value: 1,650				

KM# 410   100 DINARS
Subject: 13th Anniversary of 7 Nov 1987 and 21st Century **Note:** French legends.

Date	Mintage	F	VF	XF	Unc	BU
AH1421-2000 Proof	—	Value: 1,650				

KM# 411   100 DINARS
38.0000 g., 0.9000 Gold 1.0995 oz. AGW **Subject:** 13th Anniversary of 7 Nov 1987 and 21st Century **Obv:** National arms **Note:** Arabic legends.

Date	Mintage	F	VF	XF	Unc	BU
AH1421-2000 Proof	—	Value: 1,650				

ESSAIS
Standard metals unless otherwise noted

KM#	Date	Mintage	Identification	Mkt Val
E1	1918(a)	—	5 Centimes. Nickel-Bronze. KM#242.	80.00
E2	1918(a)	—	10 Centimes. Nickel-Bronze. KM#243.	85.00
E3	1918(a)	—	25 Centimes. Nickel-Bronze. KM#244.	90.00
E4	1920(a)	—	5 Centimes. Nickel-Bronze. KM#245.	125
E5	1921(a)	—	50 Centimes. Alum.-Bronze. KM#246.	90.00
E6	1921(a)	—	Franc. Aluminum-Bronze. KM#247.	120
E7	1921(a)	—	Franc. Aluminum. KM#247.	130
E8	1928A	—	Franc. Nickel-Bronze. KM#250a.	250
E9	1928	—	2 Francs. Silver-Bronze. KM#251.	260
E10	1930(a)	—	10 Francs. Silver. KM#255, uniface.	170
E11	1930(a)	—	20 Francs. Silver. KM#256, uniface.	350
E12	1930(a)	—	100 Francs. Gold. KM#257, uniface.	375
E13	1931(a)	—	5 Centimes. Nickel-Bronze. KM#258.	75.00
E14	1931(a)	—	10 Centimes. Nickel-Bronze. KM#259.	80.00
E15	1931(a)	—	25 Centimes. Nickel-Aluminum-Bronze. KM#260.	85.00
E16	AH1353(a)	—	5 Francs. Silver. KM#261.	90.00
E17	AH1353(a)	—	10 Francs. Silver. KM#255.	100
E18	AH1353(a)	—	20 Francs. Silver. KM#256.	175
EA19	AH1354(a)	—	100 Francs. Gilt Bronze. KM#257.	—
E19	1938(a)	—	100 Francs. Gilt Bronze. KM-M1.	110
E20	1938(a)	—	100 Francs. Gold. KM-M1.	950
E21	1939(a)	—	5 Francs. Silver. KM#264.	60.00
E22	1939(a)	—	10 Francs. Silver. KM#265.	80.00
E23	1939(a)	—	20 Francs. Silver. KM#266.	150
E24	1942(a)	—	20 Centimes. Zinc. KM#268.	50.00
E25	1945(a)	1,100	10 Centimes. Nickel-Aluminum-Bronze. KM#271.	50.00
E26	1945(a)	1,100	20 Centimes. Zinc. KM#272.	60.00

KM#	Date	Mintage	Identification	Mkt Val
E27	1946(a)	1,100	5 Francs. Aluminum-Bronze. Inscription and date within sprigs. Value and date within circular inscription and design. KM#273.	35.00
E28	1950(a)	1,100	20 Francs. Copper-Nickel. KM#274.	35.00
E29	1950(a)	1,100	50 Francs. Copper-Nickel. KM#275.	35.00
E30	1950(a)	1,100	100 Francs. Copper-Nickel. KM#276.	35.00
E31	1954(a)	1,100	5 Francs. Copper-Nickel. KM#277.	20.00
EA32	1967	—	2 Dinars. Aluminum. KM#286.	20.00
EB32	1967	—	5 Dinars. Aluminum. KM#287.	20.00
EC32	1967	—	10 Dinars. Aluminum. KM#288.	20.00
ED32	1967	—	20 Dinars. Aluminum. KM#289.	20.00
EE32	1967	—	40 Dinars. Aluminum. KM#290.	20.00
E32	1968(a)	1,260	1/2 Dinar. Nickel. KM#291.	35.00
E33	1968(a)	70	1/2 Dinar. Gold.	550
E34	1970(a)	1,250	Dinar. Silver. Head left. Coconut tree in center of oxen, tractor and figure. KM#302.	45.00
E35	1976	2,050	1/2 Dinar. Copper-Nickel. KM#303.	30.00
E36	1976	2,050	Dinar. Copper-Nickel. KM#304.	40.00

PIEFORTS

Double thickness; standard metals unless otherwise noted

KM#	Date	Mintage	Identification	Issue Price	Mkt Val
P1	1968(a)	500	1/2 Dinar. Nickel. KM#291.	—	35.00
P2	1982	96	5 Dinars. Silver. KM#313.	—	165
P3	1982	55	75 Dinars. Gold. KM#317.	—	1,250

PIEFORTS WITH ESSAI

Double thickness

KM#	Date	Mintage	Identification	Mkt Val
PE1	1945(a)	104	20 Centimes. Zinc. KM#272.	100
PE2	1945(a)	104	50 Centimes. Alum.-Bronze. KM#246.	100
PE3	1945(a)	104	Franc. Aluminum-Bronze. KM#247.	100
PE4	1945(a)	104	2 Francs. Aluminum-Bronze. Date within wreath. Value flanked by sprigs. KM#248.	100
PE5	1946(a)	104	5 Francs. Alum.-Bronze. KM#273.	120
PE6	1954(a)	104	5 Francs. Copper-Nickel. KM#277.	90.00

MINT SETS

KM#	Date	Mintage	Identification	Issue Price	Mkt Val
MS1	1960 (7)	—	KM#280-282, 306-309	—	5.50
MS2	1996 (7)	—	KM#282, 306-309, 346-347	—	16.50

PROOF SETS

KM#	Date	Mintage	Identification	Issue Price	Mkt Val
PS2	1967 (5)	3,031	KM#286-290	—	3,500
PS3	1969FM-NI (10)	15,202	KM#292-301 Many sets were ruined while in storage.	77.00	120
PS4	1969NI (10)	5,000	KM#292-301	—	450

TURKEY

The Republic of Turkey, a parliamentary democracy of the Near East located partially in Europe and partially in Asia between the Black and the Mediterranean Seas, has an area of 301,382 sq. mi. (780,580 sq. km.) and a population of *55.4 million. Capital: Ankara. Turkey exports cotton, hazelnuts, and tobacco, and enjoys a virtual monopoly in meerschaum.

The Ottoman Turks, a tribe from Central Asia, first appeared in the early 13th century, and by the 17th century had established the Ottoman Empire which stretched from the Persian Gulf to the southern frontier of Poland, and from the Caspian Sea to the Algerian plateau. The defeat of the Turkish navy by the Holy League in 1571, and of the Turkish forces besieging Vienna in 1683, began the steady decline of the Ottoman Empire which, accelerated by the rise of nationalism, contracted its European border, and by the end of World War I deprived it of its Arab lands. The present Turkish boundaries were largely fixed by the Treaty of Lausanne in 1923. The sultanate and caliphate, the political and spiritual ruling institutions of the old empire, were separated and the sultanate abolished in 1922. On Oct. 29, 1923, Turkey formally became a republic.

RULERS

Abdul Hamid II, AH1293-1327/1876-1909AD
Muhammad V, AH1327-1336/1909-1918AD
Muhammad VI, AH1336-1341/1918-1923AD
Republic, AH1341/AD1923-

MINT NAMES

Constantinople
(Qustantiniyah)

Misr
See Egypt

MONETARY EQUIVALENTS

3 Akche = 1 Para
5 Para = Beshlik (Beshparalik)
10 Para = Onluk
20 Para = Yirmilik
30 Para = Zolota
40 Para = Kurush (Piastre)
1-1/2 Kurush (Piastres) = Altmishlik

MONETARY SYSTEM

Silver Coinage
40 Para = 1 Kurush (Piastre)
2 Kurush (Piastres) = 1 Ikilik
2-1/2 Kurush (Piastres) = Yuzluk
3 Kurush (Piastres) = Uechlik
5 Kurush (Piastres) = Beshlik
6 Kurush (Piastres) = Altilik
Gold Coinage
100 Kurush (Piastres) = 1 Turkish Pound (Lira)

This system has remained essentially unchanged since its introduction by Ahmad III in 1688, except that the Asper and Para have long since ceased to be coined. The Piastre, established as a crown-sized silver coin approximately equal to the French Ecu of Louis XIV, has shrunk to a tiny copper coin, worth about 1/15 of a U.S. cent. Since the establishment of the Republic in 1923, the Turkish terms, Kurus and Lira, have replaced the European names Piastres and Turkish Pounds.

MINT VISIT ISSUES

From time to time, certain cities of the Ottoman Empire, such as Bursa, Edirne, Kosova, Manistir and Salonika were honored by having special coins struck at Istanbul, but with inscriptions stating that they were struck in the city of honor. These were produced on the occasion of the Sultan's visit to that city. The coins were struck in limited, but not small quantities, and were probably intended for distribution to the notables of the city and the Sultan's own followers. Because they were of the same size and type as the regular circulation issues struck at Istanbul, many specimens found their way into circulation and worn or mounted specimens are found today, although some have been preserved in XF or better condition. Mintage statistics are not known.

MONNAIE DE LUXE

In the 23rd year of the reign of Abdul Hamid II, two parallel series of gold coins were produced, regular mint issues and monnaies de luxe', which were intended primarily for presentation and jewelry purposes. The Monnaie de Luxe' were struck to a slightly less weight and the same fineness as regular issues, but were broader and thinner, and from more ornate dies.

Coins are listed by type, followed by a list of reported years. Most of the reported years have never been confirmed and other years may also exist. Mintage figures are known for the AH1293 and 1327 series, but are unreliable and of little utility.

Although some years are undoubtedly much rarer than others, there is at present no date collecting of Ottoman gold and therefore little justification for higher prices for rare dates.

There is no change in design in the regular series. Only the toughra, accessional date and regnal year vary. The deluxe series show ornamental changes. The standard coins generally do not bear the denomination.

HONORIFIC TITLES

El Ghazi   Reshat

The first coinage of Abdul Hamid II has a flower right of the toughra while the second coinage has el Ghazi (The Victorious). The first coinage of Mohammad Reshat Vhas Reshat right of the toughra while his second coinage has el Ghazi.

SULTANATE

Abdul Hamid II
AH1293-1327/1876-1909AD
STANDARD COINAGE

KM# 743 5 PARA

1.0023 g., 0.1000 Silver 0.0032 oz. ASW Obv: Toughra; "el-Ghazi" to right Rev: Text within crescent below value, date and star Mint: Qustantiniyah

Date	Mintage	VG	F	VF	XF	Unc
AH1293//27 (1901)	—	0.25	0.50	1.25	4.00	—
AH1293//28 (1902)	—	0.50	1.00	3.00	12.00	—
AH1293//30 (1904)	—	6.00	12.00	20.00	40.00	—

KM# 744 10 PARA

2.0046 g., 0.1000 Silver 0.0064 oz. ASW Obv: Toughra; "el-Ghazi" to right Rev: Text within crescent below date, value and star Mint: Qustantiniyah

Date	Mintage	VG	F	VF	XF	Unc
AH1293//27 (1901)	—	0.25	0.50	1.00	4.00	—
Note: Varieties exist in size of regnal year 27						
AH1293//28 (1902)	—	0.25	0.50	1.50	6.00	—
AH1293//30 (1904)	—	1.00	2.00	5.00	15.00	—

KM# 735 KURUSH

1.2027 g., 0.8300 Silver 0.0321 oz. ASW Obv: Toughra; "el-Ghazi" to right Rev: Text, value and date within circle of stars Mint: Qustantiniyah Note: Varieties exist in the size of year and inscription.

Date	Mintage	VG	F	VF	XF	Unc
AH1293//27 (1901)	9,945,000	1.00	2.00	3.00	5.00	—
AH1293//28 (1902)	16,139,000	1.00	2.00	3.00	5.00	—
AH1293//29 (1903)	7,076,000	1.00	2.00	3.00	5.00	—
AH1293//30 (1904)	707,000	2.00	4.00	8.00	15.00	—
AH1293//31 (1905)	1,366,000	1.00	2.00	3.00	5.00	—
AH1293//32 (1906)	1,140,000	1.00	2.00	3.00	5.00	—
AH1293//33 (1907)	1,700,000	1.00	2.00	3.00	5.00	—
AH1293//34 (1908)	—	150	200	230	260	—

KM# 736 2 KURUSH

2.4055 g., 0.8300 Silver 0.0642 oz. ASW Obv: Toughra; "el-Ghazi" to right Rev: Text, value and date within circle of stars Mint: Qustantiniyah Note: Varieties exist in the size of toughra and year.

Date	Mintage	VG	F	VF	XF	Unc
AH1293//27 (1901)	4,689,000	1.50	2.00	4.00	7.00	—
AH1293//28 (1902)	7,567,000	1.50	2.00	4.00	7.00	—
AH1293//29 (1903)	7,775,000	1.50	2.00	4.00	7.00	—
AH1293//30 (1904)	1,366,000	1.50	2.00	4.00	7.00	—
AH1293//31 (1905)	3,014,000	1.50	2.00	4.00	7.00	—
AH1293//32 (1906)	1,625,000	1.50	2.00	4.00	7.00	—
AH1293//33 (1907)	2,173,000	1.50	2.00	4.00	7.00	—
AH1293//34 (1908)	—	150	225	250	300	—

KM# 737 5 KURUSH

6.0130 g., 0.8300 Silver 0.1605 oz. ASW Obv: Toughra; "el-Ghazi" to right Rev: Text, value and date within circle of stars and crescent border Mint: Qustantiniyah Note: Varieties exist in the size of toughra, inscription, and date.

Date	Mintage	VG	F	VF	XF	Unc
AH1293//27 (1901)	16,000	15.00	30.00	45.00	75.00	—
AH1293//28 (1902)	6,000	100	150	175	200	—
AH1293//29 (1903)	7,000	100	150	175	200	—
AH1293//30 (1904)	38,000	5.00	10.00	15.00	30.00	—
AH1293//31 (1905)	Inc. above		4.50	7.00	15.00	—
		3.50				
AH1293//31/0 (1905)	3,175,000	6.00	13.00	25.00	35.00	—
AH1293//32 (1906)	3,334,000	2.50	3.75	5.00	9.50	—
AH1293//33 (1907)	907,000	3.00	5.00	9.00	16.00	—
AH1293//34 (1908)	—	200	225	275	350	—

KM# 738 10 KURUSH

12.0270 g., 0.8300 Silver 0.3209 oz. ASW Obv: Toughra; "el-Ghazi" to right Rev: Text, value and date within circle of stars and crescent border

Date	Mintage	VG	F	VF	XF	Unc
AH1293//31 (1905)	51,000	60.00	100	120	150	—
AH1293//32 (1906)	575,000	7.50	12.50	18.00	30.00	—
AH1293//33 (1907)	274,000	6.50	11.50	20.00	35.00	—

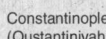

MILLED COINAGE

Gold Issues

KM# 745 12-1/2 KURUSH
0.8770 g., 0.9170 Gold 0.0259 oz. AGW   **Series:** Monnaie de Luxe **Obv:** Toughra **Mint:** Qustantiniyah

Date	Mintage	VG	F	VF	XF	Unc
AH1293//27	720	—	—	—	—	—
AH1293//28	800	45.00	150	250	350	—
AH1293//29	11,696	35.00	100	180	300	—
AH1293//30	13,208	35.00	100	180	300	—
AH1293//31	24,504	35.00	100	180	300	—
AH1293//32	14,392	35.00	100	180	300	—
AH1293//33	13,032	35.00	100	180	300	—
AH1293//34	—	45.00	180	250	400	—

KM# 729 25 KURUSH
1.8040 g., 0.9170 Gold 0.0532 oz. AGW   **Obv:** Toughra; "el-Ghazi" to right **Rev:** Text, value and date within wreath, star above **Mint:** Qustantiniyah

Date	Mintage	VG	F	VF	XF	Unc
AH1293//27	99,500	—	BV	75.00	115	—
AH1293//28	77,300	—	BV	75.00	115	—
AH1293//29	101,548	—	BV	75.00	115	—
AH1293//30	156,280	—	BV	75.00	115	—
AH1293//31	58,404	—	BV	75.00	115	—
AH1293//32	112,000	—	BV	75.00	115	—
AH1293//33	15,535	—	BV	75.00	115	—
AH1293//34	115,484	—	BV	75.00	115	—

KM# 739 25 KURUSH
1.7540 g., 0.9170 Gold 0.0517 oz. AGW   **Series:** Monnaie de Luxe **Obv:** Toughra; "el-Ghazi" to right **Rev:** Text, value and date in beaded circle within circular text **Mint:** Qustantiniyah

Date	Mintage	VG	F	VF	XF	Unc
AH1293//27	7,620	60.00	75.00	150	220	—
AH1293//28	9,268	60.00	75.00	150	220	—
AH1293//29	29,056	60.00	75.00	150	220	—
AH1293//30	27,964	60.00	75.00	150	220	—
AH1293//31	39,192	60.00	75.00	150	220	—
AH1293//32	41,696	60.00	75.00	150	220	—
AH1293//33	17,728	60.00	75.00	150	220	—
AH1293//34	—	60.00	95.00	180	250	—

KM# 731 50 KURUSH
3.6080 g., 0.9170 Gold 0.1064 oz. AGW   **Obv:** Toughra; "el-Ghazi" to right **Rev:** Text, value and date within wreath, star above **Mint:** Qustantiniyah

Date	Mintage	VG	F	VF	XF	Unc
AH1293//27	14,200	—	BV	115	150	—
AH1293//28	33,450	—	BV	115	150	—
AH1293//29	24,244	—	BV	115	150	—
AH1293//30	66,000	—	BV	115	150	—
AH1293//31	58,612	—	BV	115	150	—
AH1293//32	48,000	—	BV	115	150	—
AH1293//33	16,145	—	BV	115	150	—
AH1293//34	6,276	BV	115	150	220	—

KM# 740 50 KURUSH
3.5080 g., 0.9170 Gold 0.1034 oz. AGW   **Series:** Monnaie de Luxe **Obv:** Toughra; "el-Ghazi" to right **Rev:** Text, value and date in beaded circle within circular text **Mint:** Qustantiniyah

Date	Mintage	VG	F	VF	XF	Unc
AH1293//27	6,630	—	BV	150	220	—
AH1293//28	8,660	—	BV	150	220	—
AH1293//29	14,924	—	BV	150	220	—
AH1293//30	18,812	—	BV	150	220	—
AH1293//31	22,460	—	BV	150	220	—

Date	Mintage	VG	F	VF	XF	Unc
AH1293//32	27,542	—	BV	150	220	
AH1293//33	12,886	—	BV	150	220	
AH1293//34		—	BV	250	350	

KM# 730 100 KURUSH
7.2160 g., 0.9170 Gold 0.2127 oz. AGW   **Obv:** Toughra; "el-Ghazi" to right **Rev:** Text, value and date within wreath, star above **Mint:** Qustantiniyah

Date	Mintage	VG	F	VF	XF	Unc
AH1293//27	48,200	—	—	215	250	—
AH1293//28	865,011	—	—	BV	230	—
AH1293//29	1,026,275	—	—	BV	230	—
AH1293//30	1,643,795	—	—	BV	230	—
AH1293//31	2,748,448	—	—	BV	230	—
AH1293//32	1,951,611	—	—	BV	230	—
AH1293//33	962,672	—	—	BV	230	—
AH1293//34	1,715,274	—	BV	300	450	—

Note: Combined mintage total, with 100 Kurush KM#754, AH1327//1

KM# 741 100 KURUSH
7.0160 g., 0.9170 Gold 0.2068 oz. AGW   **Series:** Monnaie de Luxe **Obv:** Toughra; "el-Ghazi" to right **Rev:** Text, value and date in beaded circle within circular text **Mint:** Qustantiniyah

Date	Mintage	VG	F	VF	XF	Unc
AH1293//27	9,580	—	BV	215	285	—
AH1293//28	13,638	—	BV	215	285	—
AH1293//29	18,129	—	BV	215	285	—
AH1293//30	22,796	—	BV	215	285	—
AH1293//31	31,126	—	BV	215	285	—
AH1293//32	42,662	—	BV	215	285	—
AH1293//33	18,716	—	BV	215	285	—
AH1293//34	—	BV	210	250	350	—

KM# 732 250 KURUSH
18.0400 g., 0.9170 Gold 0.5318 oz. AGW   **Obv:** Toughra; "el-Ghazi" to right **Rev:** Text, value and date within wreath, star above **Mint:** Qustantiniyah

Date	Mintage	VG	F	VF	XF	Unc
AH1293//27	1,450	—	BV	575	650	—
AH1293//28	7,027	—	BV	575	650	—
AH1293//29	7,522	—	BV	575	650	—
AH1293//30	4,900	—	BV	575	650	—
AH1293//31	8,552	—	BV	575	650	—
AH1293//32	8,729	—	BV	575	650	—
AH1293//33	2,669	—	BV	575	650	—
AH1293//34	6,478	—	BV	650	800	—

KM# 742 250 KURUSH
17.5400 g., 0.9170 Gold 0.5171 oz. AGW   **Series:** Monnaie de Luxe **Obv:** Toughra; "el-Ghazi" to right **Rev:** Text, value and date within beaded circle, designed wreath **Mint:** Qustantiniyah

Date	Mintage	VG	F	VF	XF	Unc
AH1293//27	1,770	—	BV	675	850	—
AH1293//28	1,520	—	BV	675	850	—
AH1293//29	1,631	—	BV	675	850	—
AH1293//30	1,922	—	BV	675	850	—
AH1293//31	1,778	—	BV	675	850	—
AH1293//32	2,650	—	BV	675	850	—
AH1293//33	931	BV	675	1,000	1,500	—
AH1293//34 Rare						

KM# 733 500 KURUSH
36.0800 g., 0.9170 Gold 1.0637 oz. AGW   **Obv:** Toughra; "el-Ghazi" to right **Rev:** Text, value and date within wreath, star above **Mint:** Qustantiniyah

Date	Mintage	VG	F	VF	XF	Unc
AH1293//27	22,450	—	BV	1,150	1,250	—
AH1293//28	35,918	—	BV	1,150	1,250	—
AH1293//29	16,621	—	BV	1,150	1,250	—
AH1293//30	33,129	—	BV	1,150	1,250	—
AH1293//31	40,953	—	BV	1,150	1,250	—
AH1293//32	32,516	—	BV	1,150	1,250	—
AH1293//33	16,403	—	BV	1,150	1,250	—
AH1293//34	39,028	—	BV	1,150	1,250	—

KM# 746 500 KURUSH
35.0800 g., 0.9170 Gold 1.0342 oz. AGW   **Series:** Monnaie de Luxe **Obv:** Radiant Toughra above crossed flags, ornamental base **Rev:** Inscription and date within star and designed border **Mint:** Qustantiniyah

Date	Mintage	VG	F	VF	XF	Unc
AH1293//27	1,428	—	BV	1,200	1,500	—
AH1293//28	858	—	BV	1,200	1,500	—
AH1293//29	804	—	BV	1,200	1,500	—
AH1293//30	1,204	—	BV	1,200	1,500	—
AH1293//31	1,021	—	BV	1,200	1,500	—
AH1293//32	1,334	—	BV	1,200	1,500	—
AH1293//33	812	—	BV	1,200	1,500	—
AH1293//34	—	—	BV	1,200	1,500	—

Muhammad V
AH1327-36/1909-18AD

STANDARD COINAGE

KM# 759 5 PARA
Nickel **Obv:** Toughra; "Reshat" to right **Rev:** Value within beaded circle above sprigs **Mint:** Qustantiniyah

Date	Mintage	Good	VG	F	VF	XF
AH1327//2 (1910)	1,664,000	—	2.00	4.00	6.00	9.00
AH1327//3 (1911)	21,760,000	—	0.50	1.00	2.00	4.00
AH1327//4 (1912)	21,392,000	—	0.50	1.00	2.00	4.00
AH1327//5 (1913)	30,579,000	—	0.50	1.00	2.00	4.00
AH1327//6 (1914)	15,751,000	—	0.50	1.00	2.00	4.00
AH1327//7 (1915)	2,512,000	—	10.00	15.00	20.00	30.00

KM# 767 5 PARA
Nickel **Obv:** Toughra; "el-Ghazi" to right **Rev:** Value within beaded circle above sprigs **Mint:** Qustantiniyah

Date	Mintage	Good	VG	F	VF	XF
AH1327//7 (1915)	740,000	—	10.00	12.50	15.00	20.00

KM# 760 10 PARA
2.6000 g., Nickel **Obv:** Toughra; "Reshat" to right **Rev:** Value within beaded circle above sprigs **Mint:** Qustantiniyah

Date	Mintage	Good	VG	F	VF	XF
AH1327//2 (1910)	2,576,000	—	0.25	0.50	2.00	5.00
AH1327//3 (1911)	18,992,000	—	0.15	0.25	1.00	3.00
AH1327//4 (1912)	18,576,000	—	0.15	0.25	1.00	3.00
AH1327//5 (1913)	31,799,000	—	0.15	0.25	1.00	3.00
AH1327//6 (1914)	17,024,000	—	0.15	0.25	1.00	3.00
AH1327//7 (1915)	21,680,000	—	0.30	0.65	1.50	4.00

KM# 768 10 PARA
2.6000 g., Nickel **Obv:** Toughra; "el-Ghazi" to right **Rev:** Value within beaded circle above sprigs **Mint:** Qustantiniyah

Date	Mintage	Good	VG	F	VF	XF
AH1327//7 (1915)	—	—	0.30	0.60	1.50	4.00
Note: Mintage included in KM760						
AH1327//8 (1916)	7,590,000	—	0.50	1.00	4.00	10.00

KM# 761 20 PARA
Nickel **Obv:** Toughra; "Reshat" to right **Rev:** Value within beaded circle above sprigs **Mint:** Qustantiniyah

Date	Mintage	Good	VG	F	VF	XF
AH1327 (1909) No regnal year	—	—	5.00	8.50	15.00	25.00
AH1327//2 (1910)	1,524,000	—	0.25	0.50	2.00	8.00
AH1327//3 (1911)	11,418,000	—	0.15	0.35	1.50	6.00
AH1327//4 (1912)	10,848,000	—	0.15	0.25	1.00	5.00
AH1327//5 (1913)	24,350,000	—	0.15	0.25	1.00	5.00
AH1327//6 (1914)	20,663,000	—	0.15	0.25	1.00	5.00
AH1327//7 (1915) Rare	—	—	500	700	900	1,200

KM# 769 20 PARA
Nickel **Obv:** Toughra; "el-Ghazi" to right **Mint:** Qustantiniyah

Date	Mintage	Good	VG	F	VF	XF
AH1327//7 (1915) Rare	—	—	400	600	750	1,000

KM# 766 40 PARA
5.9200 g., Nickel **Obv:** Toughra; "Reshat" to right **Mint:** Qustantiniyah **Note:** Struck at Qustantiniyah.

Date	Mintage	Good	VG	F	VF	XF
AH1327//3 (1910)	1,992,000	—	0.50	1.00	3.00	10.00
AH1327//4 (1911)	8,716,000	—	0.15	0.30	2.00	5.00
AH1327//5 (1912)	9,248,000	—	0.15	0.30	2.00	5.00

KM# 779 40 PARA
Copper-Nickel **Obv:** Toughra; "el-Ghazi" to right **Rev:** Value within beaded circle above sprigs **Mint:** Qustantiniyah

Date	Mintage	Good	VG	F	VF	XF
AH1327//8 (1916)	16,339,000	—	0.15	0.30	2.00	5.00
AH1327//9 (1917)	3,034,000	—	1.00	2.00	10.00	25.00

KM# 748 KURUSH
1.2027 g., 0.8300 Silver 0.0321 oz. ASW **Obv:** Toughra within star border **Rev:** Inscription and date within star border **Mint:** Qustantiniyah

Date	Mintage	Good	VG	F	VF	XF
AH1327//1 (1909)	1,270,000	—	1.25	2.50	3.50	6.00
AH1327//2 (1910)	8,770,000	—	1.00	2.00	3.00	5.00
AH1327//3 (1911)	840,000	—	1.50	3.00	6.00	12.50

KM# 749 2 KURUSH
2.4055 g., 0.8300 Silver 0.0642 oz. ASW **Obv:** Toughra; "Reshat" to right **Rev:** Inscription and date within star border **Mint:** Qustantiniyah **Note:** Varieties exist in the size of date.

Date	Mintage	Good	VG	F	VF	XF
AH1327//1 (1909)	5,157,000	—	1.75	2.25	3.50	7.50
AH1327//2 (1910)	11,120,000	—	1.50	2.00	3.00	6.50
AH1327//3 (1911)	6,110,000	—	1.50	2.00	3.00	6.50
AH1327//4 (1912)	4,031,000	—	1.50	2.00	3.00	6.50
AH1327//5 (1913)	301,000	—	2.50	5.00	10.00	20.00
AH1327//6 (1914)	1,884,000	—	2.00	2.50	4.00	8.00
AH1327//6/2 (1914)	Inc. above	—	2.00	2.50	4.00	8.00

KM# 770 2 KURUSH
2.4055 g., 0.8300 Silver 0.0642 oz. ASW **Obv:** Toughra; "el-Ghazi" to right **Rev:** Inscription and date within star border **Mint:** Qustantiniyah **Note:** Varieties exist in the size of date.

Date	Mintage	Good	VG	F	VF	XF
AH1327//7 (1915)	17,000	—	12.50	25.00	40.00	75.00
AH1327//8 (1916)	398,000	—	20.00	30.00	50.00	100
AH1327//9 (1917)	8,000	—	250	350	450	600

KM# 750 5 KURUSH
6.0130 g., 0.8300 Silver 0.1605 oz. ASW **Obv:** Toughra; "Reshat" to right **Rev:** Inscription and date within star border and design **Mint:** Qustantiniyah

Date	Mintage	Good	VG	F	VF	XF
AH1327//1 (1909)	1,558,000	—	BV	3.50	6.00	10.00
AH1327//2 (1910)	1,886,000	—	BV	3.50	6.00	10.00
AH1327//3 (1911)	1,273,000	—	BV	3.50	6.00	10.00
AH1327//4 (1912)	1,635,000	—	BV	3.50	6.00	10.00
AH1327//5 (1913)	194,000	—	6.00	9.00	15.00	28.00
AH1327//6 (1914)	664,000	—	3.00	3.50	5.00	9.00
AH1327//7 (1915)	834,000	—	3.00	3.50	5.00	9.00

KM# 771 5 KURUSH
6.0130 g., 0.8300 Silver 0.1605 oz. ASW **Obv:** Toughra; "el-Ghazi" to right **Rev:** Inscription and date within star border and design **Mint:** Qustantiniyah

Date	Mintage	Good	VG	F	VF	XF
AH1327//7 (1915)	—	—	3.50	4.50	7.00	10.00
Note: Mintage included in KM750						
AH1327//8 (1916)	648,000	—	4.00	7.00	10.00	20.00
AH1327//9 (1917)	3,938	—	100	200	250	350

KM# 751 10 KURUSH
12.0270 g., 0.8300 Silver 0.3209 oz. ASW **Obv:** Toughra; "Reshat" to right **Rev:** Inscription and date within star border and design **Mint:** Qustantiniyah

Date	Mintage	Good	VG	F	VF	XF
AH1327//1 (1909)	110,000	—	12.50	25.00	50.00	100
AH1327//2 (1910)	Inc. above	—	10.00	20.00	50.00	100
AH1327//3 (1911)	8,000	—	70.00	125	1,000	1,600
AH1327//4 (1912)	96,000	—	550	8.00	15.00	25.00
AH1327//5 (1913)	34,000	—	10.00	20.00	50.00	100
AH1327//6 (1914)	81,000	—	7.50	12.50	17.50	30.00
AH1327//7 (1915)	582,000	—	6.50	10.00	16.50	32.00

KM# 772 10 KURUSH
12.0270 g., 0.8300 Silver 0.3209 oz. ASW **Obv:** Toughra; "el-Ghazi" to right **Rev:** Inscription and date within star border and design **Mint:** Qustantiniyah

Date	Mintage	Good	VG	F	VF	XF
AH1327//7 (1915)	—	—	5.50	8.00	15.00	28.00
Note: Mintage included in KM751						
AH1327//8 (1916)	408,000	—	7.00	9.00	17.50	32.00
AH1327//9 (1917)	299,000	—	10.00	20.00	35.00	50.00
AH1327//10 (1918)	666,000	—	12.50	25.00	50.00	85.00

KM# 780 20 KURUSH
24.0550 g., 0.8300 Silver 0.6419 oz. ASW **Obv:** Toughra within star border and crescent wreath **Rev:** Inscription and date within star border and crescent wreath **Mint:** Qustantiniyah

Date	Mintage	Good	VG	F	VF	XF
AH1327//8 (1916)	713,000	—	11.50	13.50	20.00	35.00
AH1327//9 (1917)	5,962,000	—	BV	11.50	15.00	30.00
AH1327//10 (1918)	11,025,000	—	11.50	13.50	20.00	35.00

MILLED COINAGE
Gold Issues

KM# 762   12-1/2 KURUSH
0.9020 g., 0.9170 Gold 0.0266 oz. AGW **Series:** Monnaie de Luxe **Obv:** Toughra; "Reshat" to right **Rev:** Value and date within designed wreath **Mint:** Qustantiniyah

Date	Mintage	VG	F	VF	XF	Unc
AH1327//2	43,568	30.00	50.00	100	180	—
AH1327//3	50,368	30.00	50.00	100	180	—
AH1327//4	19,344	30.00	50.00	100	180	—
AH1327//5	9,160	30.00	50.00	100	180	—
AH1327//6	11,880	30.00	50.00	100	180	—

KM# 752   25 KURUSH
1.8040 g., 0.9170 Gold 0.0532 oz. AGW **Obv:** Toughra; "Reshat" to right **Rev:** Inscription and date within wreath, star on top **Mint:** Qustantiniyah

Date	Mintage	VG	F	VF	XF	Unc
AH1327//1	115,484	—	BV	60.00	75.00	—
AH1327//2	194,740	—	BV	60.00	75.00	—
AH1327//3	249,416	—	BV	60.00	75.00	—
AH1327//4	338,172	—	BV	60.00	75.00	—
AH1327//5	167,592	—	BV	60.00	75.00	—
AH1327//6	72,872	—	BV	60.00	75.00	—

KM# 763   25 KURUSH
1.7540 g., 0.9170 Gold 0.0517 oz. AGW **Series:** Monnaie de Luxe **Obv:** Toughra within designed wreath **Rev:** Inscription and date within designed wreath **Mint:** Qustantiniyah

Date	Mintage	VG	F	VF	XF	Unc
AH1327//2	47,788	BV	60.00	110	150	—
AH1327//3	70,775	BV	60.00	110	150	—
AH1327//4	47,088	BV	60.00	110	150	—
AH1327//5	25,964	55.00	80.00	130	180	—
AH1327//6	23,348	55.00	80.00	130	180	—

KM# 773   25 KURUSH
1.8040 g., 0.9170 Gold 0.0532 oz. AGW **Obv:** Toughra; "el-Ghazi" to right **Rev:** Inscription and date within wreath, star on top **Mint:** Qustantiniyah

Date	Mintage	VG	F	VF	XF	Unc
AH1327//7	22,420	—	BV	75.00	110	—
AH1327//8	5,926	—	BV	75.00	110	—
AH1327//9	4,060	—	BV	85.00	130	—
AH1327//10	53,524	1,000	1,500	2,000	2,500	—

KM# 774   25 KURUSH
1.7540 g., 0.9170 Gold 0.0517 oz. AGW **Series:** Monnaie de Luxe **Obv:** Toughra **Mint:** Qustantiniyah

Date	Mintage	VG	F	VF	XF	Unc
AH1327//8	10,612	1,750	2,500	3,500	5,000	—

KM# 753   50 KURUSH
3.6080 g., 0.9170 Gold 0.1064 oz. AGW **Obv:** Toughra; "Reshat" to right **Rev:** Inscription and date within wreath, star on top **Mint:** Qustantiniyah

Date	Mintage	VG	F	VF	XF	Unc
AH1327//1	6,276	1,000	1,500	2,000	3,000	—
AH1327//2	89,712	—	BV	115	150	—
AH1327//3	75,442	—	BV	115	150	—
AH1327//4	96,030	—	BV	115	150	—
AH1327//5	40,618	—	BV	115	150	—
AH1327//6	26,408	—	BV	115	150	—

KM# 764   50 KURUSH
3.5080 g., 0.9170 Gold 0.1034 oz. AGW **Series:** Monnaie de Luxe **Obv:** Toughra within designed wreath **Rev:** Inscription and date within designed wreath **Mint:** Qustantiniyah

Date	Mintage	VG	F	VF	XF	Unc
AH1327//2	25,224	—	BV	180	210	—
AH1327//3	23,971	—	BV	180	210	—
AH1327//4	15,716	—	BV	180	210	—
AH1327//5	17,118	—	BV	180	210	—
AH1327//6	8,706	—	BV	220	300	—

KM# 775   50 KURUSH
3.6080 g., 0.9170 Gold 0.1064 oz. AGW **Obv:** Toughra; "el-Ghazi" to right **Mint:** Qustantiniyah

Date	Mintage	VG	F	VF	XF	Unc
AH1327//7	9,175	—	BV	180	280	—
AH1327//8	7,330	—	BV	180	280	—
AH1327//9	2,000	—	BV	180	280	—
AH1327//10	53,524	1,000	1,500	2,000	3,000	—

KM# 781   50 KURUSH
3.5080 g., 0.9170 Gold 0.1034 oz. AGW **Series:** Monnaie de Luxe **Obv:** Toughra **Mint:** Qustantiniyah

Date	Mintage	VG	F	VF	XF	Unc
AH1327//8	3,291	250	500	950	1,500	—

KM# 754   100 KURUSH
7.2160 g., 0.9170 Gold 0.2127 oz. AGW **Obv:** Toughra; "Reshat" to right **Rev:** Inscription and date within wreath, star on top **Mint:** Qustantiniyah

Date	Mintage	VG	F	VF	XF	Unc
AH1327//1	1,715,274	—	—	BV	210	—

Note: Combined mintage total, with 100 Kurush KM#730, AH1293//34

AH1327//2	3,376,679	—	—	BV	235	—
AH1327//3	4,627,115	—	—	BV	235	—
AH1327//4	3,591,676	—	—	BV	235	—
AH1327//5	881,895	—	—	BV	235	—
AH1327//6	3,769,100	—	—	BV	235	—
AH1327//7	2,989,609	—	—	BV	235	—

KM# 755   100 KURUSH
7.0160 g., 0.9170 Gold 0.2068 oz. AGW **Series:** Monnaie de Luxe **Obv:** Toughra within designed wreath **Rev:** Inscription and date within designed wreath

Date	Mintage	VG	F	VF	XF	Unc
AH1327//1	—	—	BV	220	250	—
AH1327//2	37,110	—	BV	220	250	—
AH1327//3	53,738	—	BV	220	250	—
AH1327//4	41,507	—	BV	220	250	—
AH1327//5	58,819	—	BV	220	250	—
AH1327//6	19,768	—	BV	220	250	—

KM# 776   100 KURUSH
7.2160 g., 0.9170 Gold 0.2127 oz. AGW **Obv:** Toughra; "el-Ghazi" to right **Rev:** Inscription and date within wreath, star on top **Mint:** Qustantiniyah

Date	Mintage	VG	F	VF	XF	Unc
AH1327//7	1,232,090	—	—	BV	235	—
AH1327//8	Inc. above	—	—	BV	235	—
AH1327//9	3,582,005	—	—	BV	235	—
AH1327//10		—	—	BV	235	—

KM# 782   100 KURUSH
7.0160 g., 0.9170 Gold 0.2068 oz. AGW **Series:** Monnaie de Luxe **Obv:** Toughra **Mint:** Qustantiniyah

Date	Mintage	Good	VG	F	VF	XF
AH1327//8 (1916)	13,250	—	250	400	600	1,000

KM# 756   250 KURUSH
18.0400 g., 0.9170 Gold 0.5318 oz. AGW **Obv:** Toughra; "Reshat" to right **Rev:** Inscription and date within wreath, star on top **Mint:** Qustantiniyah

Date	Mintage	VG	F	VF	XF	Unc
AH1327//1	6,878	—	BV	575	675	—
AH1327//2	9,207	—	BV	575	675	—
AH1327//3	9,990	—	BV	575	675	—
AH1327//4	13,400	—	BV	575	675	—
AH1327//5	18,143	—	BV	575	675	—
AH1327//6	6,155	—	BV	575	675	—

KM# 757   250 KURUSH
17.5400 g., 0.9170 Gold 0.5171 oz. AGW **Series:** Monnaie de Luxe **Obv:** Toughra within designed wreath **Rev:** Inscription and date within designed wreath **Mint:** Qustantiniyah

Date	Mintage	VG	F	VF	XF	Unc
AH1327//1	—	BV	550	650	800	—
AH1327//2	6,995	BV	550	650	800	—
AH1327//3	12,084	BV	550	650	800	—
AH1327//4	10,250	BV	550	650	800	—
AH1327//5	16,879	BV	550	650	800	—
AH1327//6	9,039	BV	550	650	800	—

KM# 777   250 KURUSH
18.0400 g., 0.9170 Gold 0.5318 oz. AGW **Obv:** Toughra; "el-Ghazi" to right **Rev:** Inscription and date within wreath, star on top **Mint:** Qustantiniyah

Date	Mintage	VG	F	VF	XF	Unc
AH1327//7	30	1,250	1,750	2,800	4,000	—
AH1327//8	21	1,750	2,500	3,500	5,000	—
AH1327//9	28	1,750	2,500	3,500	5,000	—

KM# 783   250 KURUSH
17.5400 g., 0.9170 Gold 0.5171 oz. AGW **Series:** Monnaie de Luxe **Obv:** Toughra within designed wreath **Rev:** Inscription and date within designed wreath **Mint:** Qustantiniyah

Date	Mintage	VG	F	VF	XF	Unc
AH1327//8	3,107	1,250	1,750	2,500	3,500	—

KM# 758   500 KURUSH

17.5400 g., 0.9170 Gold 0.5171 oz. AGW **Obv:** Toughra; "Reshat" to right **Rev:** Inscription and date within wreath, star on top **Mint:** Qustantiniyah

Date	Mintage	VG	F	VF	XF	Unc
AH1327//1	39,028	—	BV	675	950	—
AH1327//2	37,474	—	BV	675	950	—
AH1327//3	53,900	—	BV	675	950	—
AH1327//4	41,863	—	BV	675	950	—
AH1327//5	36,996	—	BV	675	950	—
AH1327//6	17,792	—	BV	675	950	—

KM# 765   500 KURUSH

35.0800 g., 0.9170 Gold 1.0342 oz. AGW **Series:** Monnaie de Luxe **Obv:** Radiant Toughra above crossed flags, ornamental base **Rev:** Inscription and date within designed wreath **Mint:** Qustantiniyah

Date	Mintage	VG	F	VF	XF	Unc
AH1327//2	1,718	—	BV	1,150	150	—
AH1327//3	4,631	—	BV	1,150	1,500	—
AH1327//4	3,887	—	BV	1,150	1,500	—
AH1327//5	5,145	—	BV	1,150	1,500	—
AH1327//6	2,401	—	BV	1,150	1,500	—

KM# 784   500 KURUSH

36.0800 g., 0.9170 Gold 1.0637 oz. AGW **Obv:** Toughra; "el-Ghazi" to right **Rev:** Inscription and date within wreath, star on top **Mint:** Qustantiniyah

Date	Mintage	VG	F	VF	XF	Unc
AH1327//7	484	1,750	2,500	3,500	5,000	—
AH1327//8	19	1,750	2,750	4,250	6,000	—
AH1327//9	22	1,750	2,750	4,250	6,000	—
AH1327//10	—	1,750	2,500	3,500	5,000	—

KM# 778   500 KURUSH

35.0800 g., 0.9170 Gold 1.0342 oz. AGW **Series:** Monnaie de Luxe **Obv:** Radiant Toughra above crossed flags, ornamental base **Rev:** Inscription and date within designed wreath **Mint:** Qustantiniyah **Note:** Struck at Qustantiniyah.

Date	Mintage	VG	F	VF	XF	Unc
AH1327//7	295	1,250	1,750	2,500	3,500	—
AH1327//8	1,618	1,150	1,500	2,200	3,000	—

MILLED COINAGE
Gold Mint Visit Issues

Muhammad V's visit to Bursa

KM# 787   25 KURUSH

1.8040 g., 0.9170 Gold 0.0532 oz. AGW **Obv:** Toughra in center of sprigs and stars **Rev:** Inscription and date within wreath, star on top **Mint:** Bursa

Date	Mintage	F	VF	XF	Unc	BU
AH1327//1	—	185	350	600	950	—

KM# 788   50 KURUSH

3.6080 g., 0.9170 Gold 0.1064 oz. AGW **Obv:** Toughra in center of sprigs and stars **Rev:** Inscription and date within wreath, star on top **Mint:** Bursa

Date	Mintage	F	VF	XF	Unc	BU
AH1327//1	—	165	275	350	650	—

KM# 789   100 KURUSH

7.2160 g., 0.9170 Gold 0.2127 oz. AGW **Obv:** Toughra in center of sprigs and stars **Rev:** Inscription and date within wreath, star on top **Mint:** Bursa

Date	Mintage	F	VF	XF	Unc	BU
AH1327//1	—	225	325	400	700	—

MILLED COINAGE
Gold Mint Visit Issues

Muhammad V visit to Edirne

KM# 793   50 KURUSH

3.6080 g., 0.9170 Gold 0.1064 oz. AGW **Obv:** Toughra in center of sprigs and stars **Rev:** Inscription and date within wreath, star on top **Mint:** Edirne

Date	Mintage	F	VF	XF	Unc	BU
AH1327//2	—	200	275	350	600	—

KM# 794   100 KURUSH

7.2160 g., 0.9170 Gold 0.2127 oz. AGW **Obv:** Toughra in center of sprigs and stars **Rev:** Inscription and date within wreath, star on top **Mint:** Edirne

Date	Mintage	F	VF	XF	Unc	BU
AH1327//2	—	250	350	475	700	—

KM# 795   500 KURUSH

36.0800 g., 0.9170 Gold 1.0637 oz. AGW **Obv:** Toughra in center of sprigs and stars **Rev:** Inscription and date within wreath, star on top **Mint:** Edirne

Date	Mintage	F	VF	XF	Unc	BU
AH1327//2	—	1,500	2,500	3,500	4,000	—

MILLED COINAGE
Gold Mint Visit Issues

Muhammad Vs visit to Kosova

KM# 799   50 KURUSH

3.6080 g., 0.9170 Gold 0.1064 oz. AGW **Obv:** Toughra in center of sprigs and stars **Rev:** Inscription and date within wreath, star on top **Mint:** Kosova

Date	Mintage	F	VF	XF	Unc	BU
AH1327//3	1,200	225	275	400	700	—

KM# 800   100 KURUSH

7.2160 g., 0.9170 Gold 0.2127 oz. AGW **Obv:** Toughra in center of stars and sprigs **Rev:** Inscription and date within wreath, star on top **Mint:** Kosova

Date	Mintage	F	VF	XF	Unc	BU
AH1327//3	750	250	300	450	750	—

KM# 801   500 KURUSH

36.0800 g., 0.9170 Gold 1.0637 oz. AGW **Obv:** Toughra in center of stars and sprigs **Rev:** Inscription and date within wreath, star on top **Mint:** Kosova

Date	Mintage	F	VF	XF	Unc	BU
AH1327//3	20	3,000	4,000	5,000	6,000	—

MILLED COINAGE
Gold Mint Visit Issues

Muhammad V's visit to Manastir

KM# 805   50 KURUSH
3.6080 g., 0.9170 Gold 0.1064 oz. AGW **Obv:** Toughra in center of sprigs and stars **Rev:** Inscription and date within wreath, star on top **Mint:** Manastir

Date	Mintage	F	VF	XF	Unc	BU
AH1327//3	1,200	200	325	450	700	—

KM# 806   100 KURUSH
7.2160 g., 0.9170 Gold 0.2127 oz. AGW **Obv:** Toughra in center of sprigs and stars **Rev:** Inscription and date within wreath, star on top **Mint:** Manastir

Date	Mintage	F	VF	XF	Unc	BU
AH1327//3	750	245	350	450	750	—

KM# 807   500 KURUSH
36.0800 g., 0.9170 Gold 1.0637 oz. AGW **Obv:** Toughra in center of sprigs and stars **Rev:** Inscription and date within wreath, star on top **Mint:** Manastir

Date	Mintage	F	VF	XF	Unc	BU
AH1327//3	20	2,750	4,000	5,000	6,250	—

MILLED COINAGE
Gold Mint Visit Issues

Muhammad V's visit to Salonika

KM# 811   50 KURUSH
3.6080 g., 0.9170 Gold 0.1064 oz. AGW **Obv:** Toughra in center of sprigs and stars **Rev:** Inscription and date within wreath, star on top **Mint:** Salonika

Date	Mintage	F	VF	XF	Unc	BU
AH1327//3	1,200	200	325	400	700	—

KM# 812   100 KURUSH
7.2160 g., 0.9170 Gold 0.2127 oz. AGW **Obv:** Toughra in center of sprigs and stars **Rev:** Inscription and date within wreath, star on top **Mint:** Salonika

Date	Mintage	F	VF	XF	Unc	BU
AH1327//3	750	245	350	450	750	—

KM# 813   500 KURUSH
36.0800 g., 0.9170 Gold 1.0637 oz. AGW **Obv:** Toughra in center of sprigs and stars **Rev:** Inscription and date within wreath, star on top **Mint:** Salonika

Date	Mintage	F	VF	XF	Unc	BU
AH1327//3	20	2,750	4,250	5,250	6,750	—

MINT VISIT COINAGE

KM# 785   2 KURUSH
2.4055 g., 0.8300 Silver 0.0642 oz. ASW **Obv:** Toughra within star border **Rev:** Inscription and date within star border **Mint:** Bursa

Date	Mintage	F	VF	XF	Unc	BU
AH1327//1 (1909)	—	15.00	30.00	75.00	125	—

KM# 790   2 KURUSH
2.4055 g., 0.8300 Silver 0.0642 oz. ASW **Obv:** Toughra within star border **Rev:** Inscription and date within star border **Mint:** Edirne

Date	Mintage	F	VF	XF	Unc	BU
AH1327//2 (1910)	—	15.00	30.00	75.00	125	—

KM# 796   2 KURUSH
2.4055 g., 0.8300 Silver 0.0642 oz. ASW **Obv:** Toughra within star border **Rev:** Inscription and date within star border **Mint:** Kosova

Date	Mintage	F	VF	XF	Unc	BU
AH1327//3 (1911)	13,000	15.00	30.00	100	150	—

KM# 802   2 KURUSH
2.4055 g., 0.8300 Silver 0.0642 oz. ASW **Obv:** Toughra within star border **Rev:** Inscription and date within star border **Mint:** Manastir

Date	Mintage	F	VF	XF	Unc	BU
AH1327//3 (1911)	13,000	15.00	30.00	100	150	—

KM# 808   2 KURUSH
2.4055 g., 0.8300 Silver 0.0642 oz. ASW **Obv:** Toughra within star border **Rev:** Inscription and date within star border **Mint:** Salonika

Date	Mintage	F	VF	XF	Unc	BU
AH1327//3 (1911)	13,000	15.00	30.00	100	150	—

KM# 786   5 KURUSH
6.0130 g., 0.8300 Silver 0.1605 oz. ASW **Obv:** Toughra within star border and design **Rev:** Inscription and date within star border and design **Mint:** Bursa

Date	Mintage	F	VF	XF	Unc	BU
AH1327//1 (1909)	—	20.00	40.00	90.00	165	—

KM# 791   5 KURUSH
6.0130 g., 0.8300 Silver 0.1605 oz. ASW **Obv:** Toughra within star border and design **Rev:** Inscription and date within star border and design **Mint:** Edirne

Date	Mintage	F	VF	XF	Unc	BU
AH1327//2 (1910)	—	20.00	40.00	90.00	165	—

KM# 797   5 KURUSH
6.0130 g., 0.8300 Silver 0.1605 oz. ASW **Obv:** Toughra within star border and design **Rev:** Inscription and date within star border and design **Mint:** Kosova

Date	Mintage	F	VF	XF	Unc	BU
AH1327//3 (1911)	3,000	20.00	40.00	125	185	—

KM# 803   5 KURUSH
6.0130 g., 0.8300 Silver 0.1605 oz. ASW **Obv:** Toughra within star border and design **Rev:** Inscription and date within star border and design **Mint:** Manastir

Date	Mintage	F	VF	XF	Unc	BU
AH1327//3 (1911)	3,000	20.00	40.00	125	185	—

KM# 809   5 KURUSH
6.0130 g., 0.8300 Silver 0.1605 oz. ASW **Obv:** Toughra within star border and design **Rev:** Inscription and date within star border and design **Mint:** Salonika

Date	Mintage	F	VF	XF	Unc	BU
AH1327//3 (1911)	3,000	20.00	40.00	125	185	—

KM# 792   10 KURUSH
12.0270 g., 0.8300 Silver 0.3209 oz. ASW **Obv:** Toughra within star border and design **Rev:** Inscription and date within star border and design **Mint:** Edirne

Date	Mintage	F	VF	XF	Unc	BU
AH1327//2 (1910)	—	90.00	150	250	455	—

Date	Mintage	VG	F	VF	XF	Unc
AH1336//3	447	150	200	250	500	—
AH1336//4	200	250	450	750	1,500	—
AH1336//5	204	200	300	450	1,000	—

KM# 798   10 KURUSH
12.0270 g., 0.8300 Silver 0.3209 oz. ASW **Obv:** Toughra within star border and crescent wreath **Rev:** Inscription and date within star border and crescent wreath **Mint:** Kosova

Date	Mintage	F	VF	XF	Unc	BU
AH1327//3 (1911)	1,500	100	175	300	525	—

KM# 804   10 KURUSH
12.0270 g., 0.8300 Silver 0.3209 oz. ASW **Obv:** Toughra within star border and design **Rev:** Inscription and date within star border and design **Mint:** Manastir

Date	Mintage	F	VF	XF	Unc	BU
AH1327//3 (1911)	1,500	100	200	350	550	—

KM# 810   10 KURUSH
12.0270 g., 0.8300 Silver 0.3209 oz. ASW **Obv:** Toughra within star border and design **Rev:** Inscription and date within star border and design **Mint:** Salonika

Date	Mintage	F	VF	XF	Unc	BU
AH1327//3 (1911)	1,500	100	200	350	550	—

Muhammad VI
AH1336-41/1918-23AD
STANDARD COINAGE

KM# 828   40 PARA
Copper-Nickel **Obv:** Toughra within beaded circle above sprigs **Rev:** Value within beaded circle above sprigs **Mint:** Qustantiniyah

Date	Mintage	Good	VG	F	VF	XF
AH1336//4 (1920)	6,520,000	—	1.75	2.50	4.00	10.00

KM# 815   2 KURUSH
2.4055 g., 0.8300 Silver 0.0642 oz. ASW **Obv:** Toughra within star border **Rev:** Inscription and date within star border **Mint:** Qustantiniyah

Date	Mintage	Good	VG	F	VF	XF
AH1336//1 (1918)	25,000	—	50.00	100	150	220
AH1336//2 (1918)	3,000	—	75.00	125	200	350

KM# 816   5 KURUSH
6.0130 g., 0.8300 Silver 0.1605 oz. ASW **Obv:** Toughra within star border and crescent wreath **Rev:** Inscription and date within star border and crescent wreath **Mint:** Qustantiniyah

Date	Mintage	Good	VG	F	VF	XF
AH1336//1 (1917)	10,000	—	50.00	125	175	265
AH1336//2 (1918)	2,000	—	75.00	150	225	385

KM# 817   10 KURUSH
12.0270 g., 0.8300 Silver 0.3209 oz. ASW **Obv:** Toughra within star border and crescent wreath **Rev:** Inscription and date within star border and crescent wreath **Mint:** Qustantiniyah

Date	Mintage	Good	VG	F	VF	XF
AH1336//1 (1917)	10,000	—	120	250	400	600
AH1336//2 (1918)	2,000	—	200	400	600	1,000

KM# 818   20 KURUSH
24.0550 g., 0.8300 Silver 0.6419 oz. ASW **Obv:** Toughra within star bordr and crescent wreath **Rev:** Inscription and date within star border and crescent wreath **Mint:** Qustantiniyah

Date	Mintage	Good	VG	F	VF	XF
AH1336//1 (1917)	—	—	30.00	60.00	125	185
AH1336//2 (1918)	1,530	—	350	525	650	925

MILLED COINAGE
Gold Issues

KM# 819   25 KURUSH
1.8040 g., 0.9170 Gold 0.0532 oz. AGW **Obv:** Toughra in center of sprigs and stars **Rev:** Inscription and date within wreath, star on top **Mint:** Qustantiniyah

Date	Mintage	VG	F	VF	XF	Unc
AH1336//1	53,524	60.00	80.00	110	175	—
AH1336//2	62,253	60.00	80.00	110	175	—
AH1336//3	52,421	60.00	80.00	180	275	—
AH1336//4	400	75.00	180	280	450	—
AH1336//5	819	80.00	180	300	450	—

KM# 825   25 KURUSH
1.7540 g., 0.9170 Gold 0.0517 oz. AGW **Series:** Monnaie de Luxe **Obv:** Toughra **Mint:** Qustantiniyah

Date	Mintage	VG	F	VF	XF	Unc
AH1336//2	8,400	65.00	100	180	280	—
AH1336//3	11,179	65.00	100	180	280	—

KM# 820   50 KURUSH
3.6080 g., 0.9170 Gold 0.1064 oz. AGW **Obv:** Toughra in center of sprigs and stars **Rev:** Inscription and date within wreath, star on top **Mint:** Qustantiniyah

Date	Mintage	VG	F	VF	XF	Unc
AH1336//1	162,363	115	130	150	300	—
AH1336//2	346	115	130	150	300	—

KM# 821   100 KURUSH
7.2160 g., 0.9170 Gold 0.2127 oz. AGW **Obv:** Toughra in center of sprigs and stars **Rev:** Inscription and date within wreath, star on top **Mint:** Qustantiniyah

Date	Mintage	VG	F	VF	XF	Unc
AH1336//1	5,036,830	—	—	BV	225	—
AH1336//2	37,634	—	—	BV	225	—
AH1336//3	30,313	—	BV	240	450	—
AH1336/4	200	400	600	800	1,000	—
AH1336//5	—	400	600	800	1,000	—

KM# 826   100 KURUSH
7.0160 g., 0.9170 Gold 0.2068 oz. AGW **Series:** Monnaie de Luxe **Obv:** Toughra in center of legend **Rev:** Inscription and date in center of legend **Mint:** Qustantiniyah

Date	Mintage	VG	F	VF	XF	Unc
AH1336//2	33,077	250	300	400	500	—
AH1336//3	20,248	250	300	400	500	—

KM# 822   250 KURUSH
18.0400 g., 0.9170 Gold 0.5318 oz. AGW **Obv:** Toughra in center of sprigs and stars **Rev:** Inscription and date within wreath, star on top **Mint:** Qustantiniyah

Date	Mintage	VG	F	VF	XF	Unc
AH1336//1	39	1,750	3,000	4,500	6,500	—
AH1336//2	26	1,750	3,000	4,500	6,500	—
AH1336//3	31	1,750	3,000	4,500	6,500	—
AH1336/4	20	1,750	3,000	4,500	6,500	—
AH1336/5	21	1,750	3,000	4,500	6,500	—

KM# 827   250 KURUSH
17.5400 g., 0.9170 Gold 0.5171 oz. AGW **Series:** Monnaie de Luxe **Obv:** Toughra within beaded circle **Rev:** Inscription and date within beaded circle **Mint:** Qustantiniyah

Date	Mintage	VG	F	VF	XF	Unc
AH1336//2	5,995	BV	600	800	1,200	—
AH1336//3	12,739	BV	600	800	1,200	—

KM# 824   500 KURUSH
35.0800 g., 0.9170 Gold 1.0342 oz. AGW **Series:** Monnaie de Luxe **Obv:** Radiant Toughra above crossed flags, ornamental base **Rev:** Inscription and date within designed wreath **Mint:** Qustantiniyah

Date	Mintage	VG	F	VF	XF	Unc
AH1336//1	—	1,100	1,250	1,750	2,400	—
AH1336//2	—	BV	1,100	1,350	—
AH1336//3	5,207	BV	1,100	1,350	—
AH1336//4	88	1,500	2,000	2,500	3,200	—

KM# 823   500 KURUSH
36.0800 g., 0.9170 Gold 1.0637 oz. AGW **Obv:** Toughra in center of sprigs and stars **Rev:** Inscription and date within wreath, star on top **Mint:** Qustantiniyah **Note:** Beware of counterfeits

Date	Mintage	VG	F	VF	XF	Unc
AH1336//1	26,984	1,100	1,250	1,450	1,800	—
AH1336//2	22,192	1,100	1,250	1,450	1,800	—
AH1336//3	16,424	1,100	1,250	1,450	1,800	—
AH1336//4	23	2,000	4,000	6,000	8,000	—
AH1336//5	22	2,000	4,000	6,000	8,000	—

REPUBLIC

STANDARD COINAGE
Old Monetary System

KM# 830   100 PARA
2.0000 g., Aluminum-Bronze **Obv:** Inscription and date to left of oat sprig **Rev:** Value to left of sprig, crescent and star at top

Date	Mintage	F	VF	XF	Unc	BU
AH1340 (1921)	1,798,026	3.00	5.00	10.00	60.00	—
AH1341 (1922)	5,582,846	1.00	2.50	5.00	30.00	—

KM# 834   100 PARA
Aluminum-Bronze **Obv:** Inscription and date to left of oat sprig **Rev:** Value to left of sprig, crescent and star on top

Date	Mintage	F	VF	XF	Unc	BU
1926	4,388,266	1.00	2.50	6.00	32.00	—
1928	4,000	150	225	400	600	—

KM# 831   5 KURUS
4.0000 g., Aluminum-Bronze **Obv:** Inscription and date to left of oat sprig **Rev:** Value to left of sprig, crescent and star on top

Date	Mintage	F	VF	XF	Unc	BU
AH1340 (1921)	5,023,238	1.00	2.50	7.00	32.00	—
AH1341 (1922)	23,544,591	1.00	2.50	7.00	32.00	—

KM# 835   5 KURUS
Aluminum-Bronze **Obv:** Inscription and date to left of oat sprig **Rev:** Value to left of sprig, crescent and star on top

Date	Mintage	F	VF	XF	Unc	BU
1926	355,910	1.00	2.50	7.00	32.00	—
1928	2,000	175	250	500	700	—

KM# 832   10 KURUS
Aluminum-Bronze **Obv:** Inscription and date to left of oat sprig **Rev:** Value to left of sprig, crescent and star on top **Note:** Varieties exist.

Date	Mintage	F	VF	XF	Unc	BU
AH1340 (1921)	4,836,483	1.50	3.00	8.00	35.00	—
AH1341 (1922)	14,223,098	1.50	3.00	8.00	35.00	—

KM# 836   10 KURUS
Aluminum-Bronze **Obv:** Inscription and date to left of oat sprig **Rev:** Value to left of sprigs, crescent and star on top

Date	Mintage	F	VF	XF	Unc	BU
1926	855,982	1.50	3.00	8.00	35.00	—
1928	1,000	125	200	375	575	—

KM# 833   25 KURUS
Nickel **Obv:** Inscription and date to left of oat sprig **Rev:** Value to left of sprigs, crescent and star on top

Date	Mintage	F	VF	XF	Unc	BU
AH1341 (1922)	4,972,686	2.00	4.00	10.00	30.00	—

KM# 837   25 KURUS
Nickel **Obv:** Inscription and date to left of sprigs, crescent and star on top **Note:** Varieties exist.

Date	Mintage	F	VF	XF	Unc	BU
1926	26,869	175	275	475	675	—
1928	5,794,000	1.50	3.00	8.00	30.00	—

KM# 840   25 KURUSH
1.8040 g., 0.9170 Gold 0.0532 oz. AGW **Obv:** Inscription and date within wreath **Rev:** Star divides inner circle above inscription and date

Date	Mintage	F	VF	XF	Unc	BU
1926	4,539	BV	75.00	140	175	235
1927	14,000	BV	75.00	120	150	200
1928	8,424	BV	75.00	130	165	220
1929	—	BV	75.00	120	150	200

KM# 844   25 KURUSH
1.7540 g., 0.9170 Gold 0.0517 oz. AGW, 23 mm. **Series:** Monnaie de Luxe **Obv:** Radiant star and crescent above inscription within sprigs **Rev:** Value and date within designed wreath

Date	Mintage	F	VF	XF	Unc	BU
1927	4,103	BV	80.00	150	200	—
1928	4,549	BV	80.00	150	200	—

KM# 841   50 KURUSH
3.6080 g., 0.9170 Gold 0.1064 oz. AGW **Obv:** Inscription and date within wreath **Rev:** Star divides circle above inscription and date

Date	Mintage	F	VF	XF	Unc	BU
1926	2,168	BV	150	200	275	325
1927	2,116	BV	150	200	275	325
1928	2,431	BV	150	200	275	325
1929	—	BV	150	200	275	325

KM# 845   50 KURUSH
3.5080 g., 0.9170 Gold 0.1034 oz. AGW, 28 mm. **Series:** Monnaie de Luxe **Obv:** Radiant star and crescent above inscription within sprigs **Rev:** Inscription and date within designed wreath

Date	Mintage	F	VF	XF	Unc	BU
1927	3,903	BV	150	250	375	—
1928	3,620	BV	150	250	375	—

KM# 842   100 KURUSH
7.2160 g., 0.9170 Gold 0.2127 oz. AGW **Obv:** Inscription and date within wreath **Rev:** Star divides circle above inscription and date

Date	Mintage	F	VF	XF	Unc	BU
1926	1,073	—	BV	250	350	400
1927	—	—	BV	250	350	400
1928	920	—	BV	250	350	400
1929	—	—	BV	250	350	400

KM# 846   100 KURUSH
7.0160 g., 0.9170 Gold 0.2068 oz. AGW, 35 mm. **Series:** Monnaie de Luxe

Date	Mintage	F	VF	XF	Unc	BU
1927	8,676	—	BV	250	350	—
1928	6,092	—	BV	250	350	—

KM# 843 250 KURUSH
18.0400 g., 0.9170 Gold 0.5318 oz. AGW **Obv:** Inscription and date within wreath **Rev:** Star divides circle above inscription and date

Date	Mintage	F	VF	XF	Unc	BU
1926	604	—	BV	600	750	950
1927	886	—	BV	600	750	950
1928	110	—	BV	600	750	—
1929	—	—	BV	600	750	—

KM# 847 250 KURUSH
17.5400 g., 0.9170 Gold 0.5171 oz. AGW, 45 mm. **Series:** Monnaie de Luxe **Obv:** Radiant star and crescent above inscription within sprigs **Rev:** Inscription and date within designed wreath

Date	Mintage	F	VF	XF	Unc	BU
1927	7,411	—	BV	550	675	—
1928	5,045	—	BV	550	675	—

KM# 839 500 KURUSH
36.0800 g., 0.9170 Gold 1.0637 oz. AGW **Obv:** Inscription and date within wreath **Rev:** Star divides circle above inscription and date

Date	Mintage	F	VF	XF	Unc	BU
1925	226	—	BV	1,100	1,500	—
1926	2,268	—	—	BV	1,100	—
1927	4,011	—	—	BV	1,100	—
1928	375	—	BV	1,100	1,500	—
1929	—	—	—	BV	1,100	1,500	—

KM# 848 500 KURUSH
35.0800 g., 0.9170 Gold 1.0342 oz. AGW, 49 mm. **Series:** Monnaie de Luxe **Obv:** Radiant star and crescent above inscription within sprigs **Rev:** Inscription and date within designed wreath

Date	Mintage	F	VF	XF	Unc	BU
1927	5,097	—	—	BV	1,100	—
1928	2,242	—	—	BV	1,100	—

DECIMAL COINAGE
Western numerals and Latin alphabet

40 Para = 1 Kurus; 100 Kurus = 1 Lira

Mintage figures of the 1930s and early 1940s may not be exact. It is suspected that in some cases, figures for a particular year may include quantities struck with the previous year's date.

KM# 868 10 PARA (1/4 Kurus)
Aluminum-Bronze **Obv:** Crescent and star **Rev:** Value and date

Date	Mintage	VG	F	VF	XF	Unc
1940	30,800,000	0.25	0.75	2.50	5.00	—
1941	22,400,000	0.25	0.75	2.50	5.00	—
1942	26,800,000	0.25	0.75	2.50	5.00	—

KM# 884 1/2 KURUS (20 Para)
Brass **Obv:** Center hole and date **Rev:** Center hole divides oat sprig and value

Date	Mintage	F	VF	XF	Unc	BU
1948	150	—	—	800	1,000	—

Note: Not released to circulation

KM# 884a 1/2 KURUS (20 Para)
3.9000 g., 0.9160 Gold 0.1149 oz. AGW, 16 mm. **Series:** Nostalgia **Obv:** Center hole and date **Rev:** Center hole divides value and sprig **Edge:** Plain **Mint:** Istanbul

Date	Mintage	F	VF	XF	Unc	BU
1948	441	—	—	—	135	—

KM# 861 KURUS
Copper-Nickel **Obv:** Star above crescent **Rev:** Value within designed sprigs

Date	Mintage	VG	F	VF	XF	Unc
1935	784,000	2.00	4.00	6.00	15.00	—
1936	5,300,000	2.50	3.50	5.00	10.00	—
1937	4,500,000	2.50	3.50	5.00	10.00	—

KM# 867 KURUS
2.4000 g., Copper-Nickel **Obv:** Star above crescent **Rev:** Value within designed sprigs

Date	Mintage	VG	F	VF	XF	Unc
1938	16,400,000	0.25	0.50	1.50	4.00	—
1939	21,600,000	0.25	0.50	1.50	4.00	—
1940	8,800,000	0.50	1.00	2.00	8.00	—
1941	6,700,000	0.25	0.75	1.75	5.00	—
1942	10,800,000	0.25	0.50	1.50	4.00	—
1943	4,000,000	0.25	0.75	1.75	5.00	—
1944	6,000,000	0.25	0.75	1.75	5.00	—

KM# 881 KURUS
2.2000 g., Brass, 18.5 mm. **Obv:** Date below hole in center **Rev:** Hole in center flanked by oat sprig and value **Edge:** Plain

Date	Mintage	F	VF	XF	Unc	BU
1947	890,000	1.00	1.50	2.50	5.00	—
1948	35,470,000	0.15	0.25	0.50	1.50	—
1949	29,530,000	0.15	0.25	0.50	1.25	—
1950	32,800,000	0.15	0.25	0.50	1.25	—
1951	6,310,000	0.15	0.30	0.75	2.25	—

KM# 881a KURUS
4.9000 g., 0.9160 Gold 0.1443 oz. AGW, 18 mm. **Series:** Nostalgia **Obv:** Date below hole in center **Rev:** Hole in center flanked by oat sprig and value **Edge:** Plain **Mint:** Istanbul

Date	Mintage	F	VF	XF	Unc	BU
1949	441	—	—	—	165	—

KM# 895 KURUS
1.0000 g., Brass **Obv:** Crescent and star **Rev:** Olive branch divides value and date

Date	Mintage	F	VF	XF	Unc	BU
1961	1,180,000	—	—	0.10	5.00	—
1962	3,620,000	—	—	0.10	5.00	—
1963	1,085,000	—	—	0.10	5.00	—

KM# 895a KURUS
1.0000 g., Bronze, 14 mm. **Obv:** Crescent and star **Rev:** Olive branch divides value and date **Edge:** Plain

Date	Mintage	F	VF	XF	Unc	BU
1963	1,180,000	—	—	0.10	1.50	—
1964	2,520,000	—	—	0.10	1.50	—
1965	1,860,000	—	—	0.10	1.50	—
1966	1,820,000	—	—	0.10	1.50	—
1967	2,410,000	—	—	0.10	1.50	—
1968	1,040,000	—	—	0.10	1.50	—
1969	900,000	—	—	0.10	1.50	—
1970	1,960,000	—	—	0.10	1.50	—
1971	2,940,000	—	—	0.10	1.50	—
1972	720,000	—	—	0.10	1.50	—
1973	540,000	—	—	0.10	1.50	—
1974	510,000	—	—	0.10	1.50	—

KM# 895b KURUS
Aluminum, 14 mm. **Obv:** Crescent and star **Rev:** Olive branch divides date and value

Date	Mintage	F	VF	XF	Unc	BU
1975	690,000	—	0.10	0.25	1.00	—
1976	200,000	—	0.10	0.25	1.50	—
1977	110,000	—	0.10	0.25	4.00	—

KM# 924   KURUS
Bronze Series: F.A.O. Obv: Anatolic bride's head left Rev: Olive branch divides value and date

Date	Mintage	F	VF	XF	Unc	BU
1979	15,000	—	0.25	1.00	3.00	—

KM# 924a   KURUS
Aluminum Series: F.A.O. Obv: Head left Rev: Olive branch divides date and value

Date	Mintage	F	VF	XF	Unc	BU
1979	15,000	—	0.25	1.00	3.00	—

KM# 885   2-1/2 KURUS
3.2000 g., Brass, 21 mm. Obv: Date below center hole Rev: Center hole divides oat sprig and value

Date	Mintage	F	VF	XF	Unc	BU
1948	24,720,000	0.25	0.50	1.00	3.00	—
1949	23,720,000	0.25	0.50	1.00	3.00	—
1950	11,560,000	3.00	5.00	8.00	15.00	—
1951	2,000,000	12.50	25.00	50.00	100	—

KM# 885a   2-1/2 KURUS
6.9000 g., 0.9160 Gold 0.2032 oz. AGW, 21 mm. Series: Nostalgia Obv: Date below center hole Rev: Hole in center divides oat sprig and value Edge: Plain Mint: Istanbul

Date	Mintage	F	VF	XF	Unc	BU
1950	441	—	—	—	240	—

KM# 862   5 KURUS
4.0000 g., Copper-Nickel Obv: Star within crescent Rev: Value within designed sprigs

Date	Mintage	VG	F	VF	XF	Unc
1935	100,000	2.00	5.00	10.00	50.00	100
1936	2,900,000	0.50	1.00	2.00	8.00	25.00
1937	4,060,000	0.30	0.75	1.50	8.00	22.50
1938	13,380,000	0.25	0.50	1.00	5.00	12.50
1939	12,520,000	0.25	0.50	1.00	5.00	12.50
1940	4,340,000	0.30	0.75	1.50	5.00	15.00
1942	10,160,000	0.20	0.40	1.00	5.00	12.50
1943	15,360,000	0.20	0.40	1.00	5.00	12.50

KM# 887   5 KURUS
Brass, 16.3 mm. Obv: Crescent, star and date Rev: Value within wreath Edge: TURMITE CUMHURITETI

Date	Mintage	F	VF	XF	Unc	BU
1949	4,500,000	0.25	0.50	1.00	4.00	—
1950	45,900,000	0.15	0.35	0.75	3.00	—
1951	29,600,000	0.15	0.35	0.75	3.00	—
1955	15,300,000	0.15	0.35	0.75	3.00	—
1956	21,380,000	0.15	0.35	0.75	3.00	—
1957	3,320,000	0.25	0.50	1.00	4.00	—

KM# 890.1   5 KURUS
2.5000 g., Bronze, 17 mm. Obv: Crescent and star Rev: Oak branch divides value and date

Date	Mintage	F	VF	XF	Unc	BU
1958	25,870,000	0.10	0.25	0.50	20.00	—
1959	21,580,000	—	—	0.10	20.00	—
1960	17,150,000	—	—	0.10	15.00	—
1961	11,110,000	—	—	0.10	15.00	—
1962	15,280,000	—	—	0.10	6.00	—
1963	17,680,000	—	—	0.10	6.00	—
1964	18,190,000	—	—	0.10	5.00	—
1965	19,170,000	—	—	0.10	3.00	—
1966	19,840,000	—	—	0.10	3.00	—

Date	Mintage	F	VF	XF	Unc	BU
1967	16,170,000	—	—	0.10	2.00	—
1968	26,050,000	—	—	0.10	2.00	—

KM# 890.2   5 KURUS
2.0000 g., Bronze Obv: Crescent and star Rev: Oak branch divides value and date Note: Reduced weight.

Date	Mintage	F	VF	XF	Unc	BU
1969	33,630,000	—	—	0.10	2.00	—
1970	29,360,000	—	—	0.10	1.00	—
1971	17,440,000	—	—	0.10	1.00	—
1972	22,670,000	—	—	0.10	1.00	—
1973	17,370,000	—	—	0.10	1.00	—

KM# 890.3   5 KURUS
1.3500 g., Bronze Obv: Crescent and star Rev: Oak branch divides value and date Note: Varieties exist.

Date	Mintage	F	VF	XF	Unc	BU
1974	13,540,000	—	—	0.10	1.00	—
1974 Unconiferous	Inc. above	—	—	50.00	125	—

KM# 890a   5 KURUS
1.6900 g., Aluminum, 21 mm. Obv: Crescent and star Rev: Oak branch divides value and date

Date	Mintage	F	VF	XF	Unc	BU
1975	1,560,000	—	—	0.10	1.00	—
1976	1,321,000	—	—	0.10	1.00	—
1977	190,000	—	0.10	0.20	5.00	—

KM# 906   5 KURUS
0.9100 g., Aluminum, 17 mm. Series: F.A.O. Obv: Anatolic bride's head left Rev: Oak branch divides date and value

Date	Mintage	F	VF	XF	Unc	BU
1975	1,019,000	—	0.50	1.50	3.00	—

KM# 907   5 KURUS
Aluminum Series: F.A.O. Obv: Mother breastfeeding infant Rev: Oak branch divides value and date

Date	Mintage	F	VF	XF	Unc	BU
1976	17,000	—	0.50	1.50	10.00	—

KM# 934   5 KURUS
Bronze Series: F.A.O. Obv: Fisherman within flounder Rev: Oak branch divides value and date

Date	Mintage	F	VF	XF	Unc	BU
1980	13,000	—	0.25	0.75	7.00	—

KM# 863   10 KURUS
5.8000 g., Copper-Nickel Obv: Star within crescent Rev: Star above value and date within designed sprigs

Date	Mintage	VG	F	VF	XF	Unc
1935	60,000	2.00	5.00	8.00	20.00	—
1936	3,580,000	0.75	2.00	5.00	12.50	—
1937	3,020,000	0.50	1.00	4.00	8.00	—
1938	6,610,000	0.50	1.00	4.00	8.00	—
1939	4,610,000	0.50	1.00	2.50	5.00	—
1940	6,960,000	0.50	1.00	2.50	5.00	—

KM# 888   10 KURUS
Brass Obv: Star, crescent and date Rev: Value within wreath

Date	Mintage	F	VF	XF	Unc	BU
1949	27,000,000	0.10	0.25	0.75	3.00	—
1951	6,200,000	0.10	0.25	0.75	3.00	—
1955	10,090,000	0.10	0.25	0.75	3.00	—
1956	9,910,000	0.10	0.25	0.75	3.00	—

KM# 891.1   10 KURUS
4.0000 g., Bronze, 21.3 mm. Obv: Star and crescent Rev: Oat stalks divide date and value

Date	Mintage	F	VF	XF	Unc	BU
1958	14,770,000	—	0.10	0.25	30.00	—
1959	11,160,000	—	—	0.10	30.00	—
1960	9,450,000	—	—	0.10	20.00	—
1961	5,370,000	—	—	0.10	20.00	—
1962	9,250,000	—	—	0.10	10.00	—
1963	10,390,000	—	—	0.10	4.00	—
1964	9,890,000	—	—	0.10	4.00	—
1965	10,480,000	—	—	0.10	3.00	—
1966	12,200,000	—	—	0.10	3.00	—
1967	11,410,000	—	—	0.10	2.00	—
1968	1,862,000	—	—	0.10	2.00	—

KM# 891a   10 KURUS
1.3800 g., Aluminum Obv: Star and crescent Rev: Oat stalks divide date and value

Date	Mintage	F	VF	XF	Unc	BU
1975	2,165,000	—	—	0.10	1.00	—
1976	559,000	—	0.10	0.20	1.00	—
1977	106,000	—	0.10	0.50	10.00	—

KM# 891.2   10 KURUS
3.5000 g., Bronze Obv: Star and crescent Rev: Oat stalks divide date and value Note: Reduced weight.

Date	Mintage	F	VF	XF	Unc	BU
1969	21,190,000	—	—	0.10	2.00	—
1970	19,930,000	—	—	0.10	1.00	—
1971	14,780,000	—	—	0.10	1.00	—
1972	17,960,000	—	—	0.10	1.00	—
1973	11,930,000	—	—	0.10	1.00	—

KM# 891.3   10 KURUS
2.5000 g., Bronze Obv: Star and crescent Rev: Oat stalks divide date and value Note: Varieties exist.

Date	Mintage	F	VF	XF	Unc	BU
1974	9,280,000	—	—	1.00	1.50	—
1974 Open 4	Inc. above	—	—	40.00	75.00	—

KM# 898.1   10 KURUS
3.5000 g., Bronze Series: F.A.O. Obv: Atatürk driving a tractor Rev: Oat stalks divide value and date

Date	Mintage	F	VF	XF	Unc	BU
1971	1,140,000	—	0.50	1.00	2.00	—
1972	500,000	—	1.00	2.00	4.00	—
1973	10,000	—	.100	250	500	—

KM# 898.2   10 KURUS
2.5000 g., Bronze Obv: Atatürk driving tractor Rev: Oat stalks divide value and date

Date	Mintage	F	VF	XF	Unc	BU
1974	605,000	—	1.00	2.00	4.00	—

KM# 898a   10 KURUS
Aluminum **Obv:** Atatürk driving tractor **Rev:** Oat stalks divide date and value

Date	Mintage	F	VF	XF	Unc	BU
1975	517,000	—	0.50	1.00	2.00	—

KM# 908   10 KURUS
Aluminum **Series:** F.A.O. **Obv:** Mother breastfeading infant **Rev:** Oat stalks divide value and date

Date	Mintage	F	VF	XF	Unc	BU
1976	17,000	—	0.50	2.00	10.00	—

KM# 935   10 KURUS
Bronze **Series:** F.A.O. **Obv:** Anatolic bride's head left **Rev:** Oat stalks divide date and value

Date	Mintage	F	VF	XF	Unc	BU
1980	13,000	—	0.25	1.00	6.00	—

KM# 864   25 KURUS
3.0000 g., 0.8300 Silver 0.0801 oz. ASW **Obv:** Head of Kemal Atatürk left **Rev:** Oat sprig divides date, value at left

Date	Mintage	VG	F	VF	XF	Unc
1935	888,000	1.35	2.25	6.00	15.00	—
1936	10,576,000	1.35	2.50	10.00	20.00	—
1937	8,536,000	1.35	2.50	10.00	20.00	—

KM# 880   25 KURUS
2.8700 g., Nickel-Bronze **Obv:** Crescent and star **Rev:** Oat sprig divides date, value at left

Date	Mintage	VG	F	VF	XF	Unc
1944	20,000,000	0.25	0.50	1.00	2.50	—
1945	5,328,000	0.50	1.00	1.50	3.00	—
1946	2,672,000	0.50	1.25	2.00	4.00	—

KM# 886   25 KURUS
Brass **Obv:** Crescent and star **Rev:** Value within wreath

Date	Mintage	F	VF	XF	Unc	BU
1948	18,000,000	0.10	0.20	0.40	1.25	—
1949	21,000,000	0.10	0.20	0.40	1.25	—
1951	2,000,000	5.00	10.00	25.00	50.00	—
1955	9,624,000	0.10	0.20	0.40	1.25	—
1956	14,376,000	0.10	0.20	0.40	1.25	—

KM# 886a   25 KURUS
10.0000 g., 0.9160 Gold 0.2945 oz. AGW, 22.6 mm.
Series: Nostalgia **Obv:** Crescent and star **Rev:** Value within wreath **Edge:** Plain **Mint:** Istanbul

Date	Mintage	F	VF	XF	Unc	BU
1951	441	—	—	—	320	—

KM# 892.1   25 KURUS
5.0000 g., Stainless Steel, 22.5 mm. **Obv:** Smooth ground under standing figure facing **Rev:** Value within wreath

Date	Mintage	F	VF	XF	Unc	BU
1959	21,864,000	0.10	0.15	0.30	10.00	—

KM# 892.2   25 KURUS
5.0000 g., Stainless Steel, 22.5 mm. **Obv:** Rough ground under standing figure facing **Rev:** Value within wreath

Date	Mintage	F	VF	XF	Unc	BU
1960	14,778,000	—	0.10	0.15	10.00	—
1961	7,248,000	—	0.10	0.15	15.00	—
1962	10,722,000	—	0.10	0.15	10.00	—
1963	11,016,000	—	0.10	0.15	10.00	—
1964	13,962,000	—	0.10	0.15	8.00	—
1965	9,816,000	—	0.10	0.15	5.00	—
1966	2,424,000	—	0.10	0.15	5.00	—

KM# 892.3   25 KURUS
4.0000 g., Stainless Steel **Obv:** Standing figure facing **Rev:** Value within wreath **Note:** Reduced weight

Date	Mintage	F	VF	XF	Unc	BU
1966	7,596,000	—	—	0.10	5.00	—
1967	17,022,000	—	—	0.10	4.00	—
1968	31,482,000	—	—	0.10	3.00	—
1969	34,566,000	—	—	0.10	3.00	—
1970	32,960,000	—	—	0.10	2.00	—
1973	20,496,000	—	—	0.10	2.00	—
1974	16,602,000	—	—	0.10	1.00	—
1977	10,204,000	—	—	0.10	1.00	—
1978	185,000	0.35	0.75	1.25	3.00	—

KM# 865   50 KURUS
6.0000 g., 0.8300 Silver 0.1601 oz. ASW **Obv:** Head of Kemal Atatürk left **Rev:** Oat sprig divides date, value at left

Date	Mintage	VG	F	VF	XF	Unc
1935	630,000	3.25	6.50	10.00	25.00	—
1936	5,082,000	2.75	5.00	8.00	17.00	—
1937	4,270,000	12.00	30.00	50.00	100	—

KM# 882   50 KURUS
4.0000 g., 0.6000 Silver 0.0772 oz. ASW **Obv:** Crescent, star and date **Rev:** Value within wreath **Note:** Edge varieties exist.

Date	Mintage	F	VF	XF	Unc	BU
1947	9,296,000	1.50	2.50	3.50	6.00	—
1948	12,704,000	1.50	2.50	3.50	6.00	—

KM# 899   50 KURUS
Stainless Steel, 24 mm. **Obv:** Anatolic bride's head left **Rev:** Value within wreath

Date	Mintage	F	VF	XF	Unc	BU
1971	16,756,000	—	0.10	0.15	1.00	—
1972	22,152,000	—	0.10	0.15	1.00	—
1973	18,928,000	—	0.10	0.15	1.00	—
1974	14,480,000	—	0.10	0.15	1.00	—
1975	27,714,000	—	0.10	0.15	1.00	—
1976	27,476,000	—	0.10	0.15	1.00	—
1977	5,062,000	—	0.10	0.15	1.00	—
1979	3,714,000	—	0.10	0.15	1.00	—

KM# 913   50 KURUS
Stainless Steel, 24 mm. **Series:** F.A.O. **Obv:** Mother breastfeeding child **Rev:** Value and date within wreath

Date	Mintage	F	VF	XF	Unc	BU
1978	10,000	—	2.00	4.00	6.00	—

KM# 925   50 KURUS
Stainless Steel, 24 mm. **Series:** F.A.O. **Obv:** Atatürk driving tractor **Rev:** Value and date within wreath

Date	Mintage	F	VF	XF	Unc	BU
1979	20,000	—	2.00	4.00	6.00	—

KM# 936   50 KURUS
Stainless Steel, 24 mm. **Series:** F.A.O. **Obv:** Anatolic bride's head left **Rev:** Value and date within wreath

Date	Mintage	F	VF	XF	Unc	BU
1980	13,000	—	2.00	4.00	6.00	—

KM# 860.2   100 KURUS (Lira)
12.0000 g., 0.8300 Silver 0.3202 oz. ASW **Obv:** Head of Kemal Atatürk left **Rev:** Low star above value within crescent, date below

Date	Mintage	VG	F	VF	XF	Unc
1934	Inc. above	15.00	30.00	50.00	80.00	—

KM# 860.1   100 KURUS (Lira)
12.0000 g., 0.8300 Silver 0.3202 oz. ASW **Obv:** Head of Kemal Atatürk left **Rev:** High star above value within crescent, date below

Date	Mintage	VG	F	VF	XF	Unc
1934	718,000	30.00	40.00	75.00	150	—

KM# 860.1a   100 KURUS (Lira)
13.5000 g., 0.9250 Silver 0.4015 oz. ASW, 29.5 mm.
Series: Nostalgia **Obv:** Head of Kemal Atatürk left **Rev:** High star above value within crescent, date below **Edge:** Plain **Mint:** Istanbul

Date	Mintage	F	VF	XF	Unc	BU
1934 Matte	684	—	—	—	40.00	—

KM# 941   1/2 LIRA
7.8600 g., 0.9250 Silver 0.2337 oz. ASW **Subject:** 100th Anniversary of Atatürk's Birth **Obv:** Crescent and star at top of mountain, signature above globe below **Rev:** Head of Kemal Atatürk right

Date	Mintage	F	VF	XF	Unc	BU
ND(1981)	7,555	—	—	—	20.00	—

KM# 941a   1/2 LIRA
8.0000 g., 0.9170 Gold 0.2358 oz. AGW **Subject:** 100th Anniversary of Atatürk's Birth **Obv:** Crescent and star at top of mountain, signature above globe below **Rev:** Head of Kemal Atatürk right

Date	Mintage	F	VF	XF	Unc	BU
ND(1981)	25,000	—	—	—	250	—

KM# 866   LIRA
12.0000 g., 0.8300 Silver 0.3202 oz. ASW **Obv:** Head of Kemal Atatürk left **Rev:** Value and date within crescent below star

Date	Mintage	VG	F	VF	XF	Unc
1937	1,624,000	5.50	10.00	15.00	32.00	—
1938	8,282,000	25.00	50.00	75.00	150	—
1939	376,000	5.50	10.00	15.00	32.00	—

KM# 869   LIRA
12.0000 g., 0.8300 Silver 0.3202 oz. ASW **Obv:** Head of Ismet Inonu left **Rev:** Star above value and date within crescent

Date	Mintage	VG	F	VF	XF	Unc
1940	253,000	7.50	12.50	15.00	25.00	—
1941	6,167,000	5.00	10.00	12.50	22.50	—

KM# 883   LIRA
7.5000 g., 0.6000 Silver 0.1447 oz. ASW **Obv:** Crescent, star and date **Rev:** Value within wreath **Note:** Edge varieties exist.

Date	Mintage	F	VF	XF	Unc	BU
1947	11,104,000	BV	3.50	5.00	8.50	—
1948	16,896,000	BV	3.00	4.00	7.50	—

KM# 889   LIRA
Copper-Nickel **Obv:** Head of Kemal Atatürk left **Rev:** Value and date within wreath

Date	Mintage	F	VF	XF	Unc	BU
1957	25,000,000	0.25	0.50	1.00	7.00	—

KM# 889a.1   LIRA
8.0000 g., Stainless Steel **Obv:** Head of Kemal Atatürk left **Rev:** Value and date within wreath

Date	Mintage	F	VF	XF	Unc	BU
1959	7,452,000	—	0.10	0.20	25.00	—
1960	11,436,000	—	0.10	0.20	25.00	—
1961	2,100,000	—	0.10	0.20	75.00	—
1962	4,228,000	—	0.10	0.20	20.00	—
1963	4,316,000	—	0.10	0.20	20.00	—
1964	4,976,000	—	0.10	0.20	15.00	—
1965	5,348,000	—	0.10	0.20	10.00	—
1966	8,040,000	—	0.10	0.20	10.00	—
1967	—	—	25.00	50.00	80.00	—

KM# 889a.2   LIRA
7.0000 g., Stainless Steel, 27 mm. **Obv:** Head of Kemal Atatürk left **Rev:** Value and date within wreath **Note:** Reduced weight.

Date	Mintage	F	VF	XF	Unc	BU
1967	10,444,000	—	0.10	0.20	10.00	—
1968	12,728,000	—	0.10	0.20	5.00	—
1969	6,612,000	—	0.10	0.20	5.00	—
1970	8,652,000	—	0.10	0.20	3.00	—
1971	10,504,000	—	0.10	0.20	3.00	—
1972	26,512,000	—	0.10	0.20	3.00	—
1973	12,596,000	—	0.10	0.20	3.00	—
1974	11,596,000	—	0.10	0.20	3.00	—
1975	20,348,000	—	0.10	0.20	2.00	—
1976	23,144,000	—	0.10	0.20	1.00	—
1977	30,244,000	—	0.10	0.20	1.00	—
1978	22,156,000	—	0.10	0.20	1.00	—
1979	9,289,000	—	0.10	0.20	1.00	—
1980	3,585,000	—	0.10	0.20	1.00	—

KM# 914   LIRA
8.0000 g., Stainless Steel **Series:** F.A.O. **Obv:** Mother breastfeeding infant **Rev:** Value and date within wreath

Date	Mintage	F	VF	XF	Unc	BU
1978	20,000	—	2.00	4.00	6.00	—

KM# 926   LIRA
8.0000 g., Stainless Steel **Series:** F.A.O. **Obv:** Atatürk driving tractor **Rev:** Value and date within wreath

Date	Mintage	F	VF	XF	Unc	BU
1979	20,000	—	2.00	4.00	6.00	—

KM# 937   LIRA
8.0000 g., Stainless Steel **Series:** F.A.O. **Obv:** Anatolic bride's head left **Rev:** Value and date within wreath

Date	Mintage	F	VF	XF	Unc	BU
1980	13,000	—	2.00	4.00	6.00	—

KM# 942   LIRA
16.0000 g., 0.9250 Silver 0.4758 oz. ASW **Subject:** 100th Anniversary of Ataturk's Birth **Obv:** Crescent and star at top of mountain, signature above globe below **Rev:** Head of Kemal Atatürk right

Date	Mintage	F	VF	XF	Unc	BU
ND(1981)	7,580	—	—	—	30.00	—

KM# 942a   LIRA
16.0000 g., 0.9170 Gold 0.4717 oz. AGW **Subject:** 100th Anniversary of Ataturk's Birth **Obv:** Crescent and star at top of mountain, signature above globe below **Rev:** Head of Kemal Atatürk right

Date	Mintage	F	VF	XF	Unc	BU
ND(1981)	25,000	—	—	—	500	—

KM# 943   LIRA
1.1000 g., Aluminum, 17 mm. **Obv:** Head of Kemal Atatürk left **Rev:** Value and date within wreath

Date	Mintage	F	VF	XF	Unc	BU
1981	14,432,000	—	—	0.10	0.50	—

KM# 990   LIRA
1.1000 g., Aluminum, 17 mm. **Obv:** Head of Kemal Atatürk left **Rev:** Crescent opens right with thin "1"

Date	Mintage	F	VF	XF	Unc	BU
1982	799,000	—	—	1.00	2.00	—

KM# 962.1   LIRA
1.1000 g., Aluminum, 17 mm. **Obv:** Head of Kemal Atatürk left **Rev:** Large (5mm) "1"

Date	Mintage	F	VF	XF	Unc	BU
1984	498,000	—	—	0.10	0.50	—

KM# 962.2   LIRA
1.1000 g., Aluminum, 17 mm. **Obv:** Head of Kemal Atatürk left **Rev:** Small (3.5mm) "1" **Note:** Varieties exist.

Date	Mintage	F	VF	XF	Unc	BU
1985	712,000	—	—	0.10	0.50	—
1986	504,000	—	—	0.10	0.50	—
1987	500,000	—	—	0.10	0.50	—
1988	75,000	—	—	0.10	0.50	—
1989	10,000	—	—	0.10	4.00	—

KM# 893.1   2-1/2 LIRA
12.0000 g., Stainless Steel, 30 mm. **Obv:** Standing figure facing right **Rev:** Value and date within wreath

Date	Mintage	F	VF	XF	Unc	BU
1960	4,015,000	—	0.25	1.00	100	—
1961	1,222,000	—	0.25	1.00	150	—
1962	3,636,000	—	0.25	1.00	150	—
1963	3,108,000	—	0.25	1.00	100	—
1964	2,710,000	—	0.25	1.00	50.00	—
1965	1,246,000	—	0.25	1.00	10.00	—
1966	1,788,000	—	0.25	1.00	40.00	—
1967	5,333,000	—	0.25	1.00	20.00	—
1968	2,707,000	—	0.25	1.00	10.00	—

KM# 893.1a   2-1/2 LIRA
11.8000 g., 0.9250 Silver 0.3509 oz. ASW, 30 mm.
Series: Nostalgia **Obv:** Standing figure facing right **Rev:** Value and date within wreath **Edge:** Plain **Mint:** Istanbul

Date	Mintage	F	VF	XF	Unc	BU
1965	684	—	—	—	20.00	—

KM# 893.2   2-1/2 LIRA
9.0000 g., Stainless Steel, 30 mm. **Obv:** Standing figure facing right **Rev:** Value and date within wreath **Note:** Reduced weight. Varieties exist with landscape and number of beads in laurel.

Date	Mintage	F	VF	XF	Unc	BU
1969	1,378,000	—	0.15	0.75	10.00	—
1970	3,777,000	—	0.15	0.75	5.00	—
1971	2,170,000	—	0.15	0.75	4.00	—
1972	9,147,000	—	0.15	0.50	4.00	—
1973	4,348,000	—	0.15	0.50	4.00	—
1974	3,816,000	—	0.15	0.50	4.00	—
1975	9,811,000	—	0.15	0.50	2.50	—
1976	3,952,000	—	0.15	0.50	2.50	—
1977	21,473,000	—	0.10	0.25	2.00	—
1978	15,738,000	—	0.10	0.25	2.00	—
1979	6,074,000	—	0.10	0.25	2.00	—
1980	2,621,000	—	0.10	0.25	2.00	—

KM# 896   2-1/2 LIRA
9.0000 g., Stainless Steel, 30 mm. **Series:** F.A.O. **Obv:** Atatürk driving tractor **Rev:** Value and date within wreath

Date	Mintage	F	VF	XF	Unc	BU
1970	200,000	—	0.75	1.00	1.50	—

KM# 910   2-1/2 LIRA
Stainless Steel, 30 mm. **Series:** F.A.O. **Obv:** Stylized standing figures **Rev:** Value and date within wreath

Date	Mintage	F	VF	XF	Unc	BU
1977	25,000	—	1.00	1.50	2.00	—

KM# 915   2-1/2 LIRA
Stainless Steel, 30 mm. **Series:** F.A.O. **Obv:** Mother breastfeeding infant **Rev:** Value and date within wreath

Date	Mintage	F	VF	XF	Unc	BU
1978	10,000	—	2.50	5.00	10.00	—

KM# 927   2-1/2 LIRA
Stainless Steel, 30 mm. **Series:** F.A.O. **Obv:** Head of Kemal Atatürk left **Rev:** Value and date within wreath

Date	Mintage	F	VF	XF	Unc	BU
1979	20,000	—	4.00	6.00	8.00	—

KM# 938   2-1/2 LIRA
Stainless Steel, 30 mm. **Series:** F.A.O. **Obv:** Fisherman within flounder **Rev:** Value and date within wreath

Date	Mintage	F	VF	XF	Unc	BU
1980	13,000	—	3.00	5.00	10.00	12.00

KM# 905   5 LIRA
11.1000 g., Stainless Steel, 32.5 mm. **Obv:** Atatürk on horseback **Rev:** Value and date within wreath

Date	Mintage	F	VF	XF	Unc	BU
1974	2,842,000	—	0.15	0.75	5.00	—
1975	10,855,000	—	0.15	0.25	2.00	—
1976	17,532,000	—	0.15	0.25	2.00	—
1977	6,172,000	—	0.15	0.75	3.00	—
1978	76,000	1.50	2.50	3.50	8.00	—
1979	6,054,000	—	0.15	0.30	1.00	—

KM# 905a   5 LIRA
14.7000 g., 0.9250 Silver 0.4372 oz. ASW, 32.5 mm.
Series: Nostalgia **Obv:** Atatürk on horseback **Rev:** Value and date within wreath **Edge:** Plain **Mint:** Istanbul

Date	Mintage	F	VF	XF	Unc	BU
1975	684	—	—	—	20.00	—

KM# 909   5 LIRA
Stainless Steel **Series:** International Women's Year; F.A.O. **Obv:** Mother breastfeeding infant **Rev:** Value and date within wreath

Date	Mintage	F	VF	XF	Unc	BU
1976	17,000	—	3.00	6.00	12.00	—

KM# 911   5 LIRA
Stainless Steel **Series:** F.A.O. **Obv:** Stylized standing figures **Rev:** Value and date within wreath

Date	Mintage	F	VF	XF	Unc	BU
1977	25,000	—	1.75	2.50	3.50	—

KM# 916   5 LIRA
Stainless Steel **Series:** F.A.O. **Obv:** Atatürk driving tractor **Rev:** Value and date within wreath

Date	Mintage	F	VF	XF	Unc	BU
1978	10,000	—	5.00	8.00	12.00	—

KM# 928   5 LIRA
Stainless Steel **Series:** F.A.O. **Obv:** Anatolic bride's head left **Rev:** Value and date within wreath

Date	Mintage	F	VF	XF	Unc	BU
1979	20,000	—	3.00	6.00	12.00	—

KM# 939   5 LIRA
Stainless Steel **Series:** F.A.O. **Obv:** Fisherman within flounder **Rev:** Value and date within wreath

Date	Mintage	F	VF	XF	Unc	BU
1980	13,000	—	6.00	8.00	12.00	15.00

KM# 944   5 LIRA
Aluminum **Obv:** Atatürk on horseback **Rev:** Crescent opens left

Date	Mintage	F	VF	XF	Unc	BU
1981	61,605,000	—	—	0.15	1.00	—

KM# 949.1   5 LIRA
1.7000 g., Aluminum, 19.42 mm. **Obv:** Atatürk on horseback **Rev:** Crescent opens right **Edge:** Reeded

Date	Mintage	F	VF	XF	Unc	BU
1982	69,975,000	—	—	0.15	1.00	—

KM# 949.2   5 LIRA
Aluminum **Obv:** Atatürk on horseback **Rev:** Smaller, bolder "5"

Date	Mintage	F	VF	XF	Unc	BU
1983	90,310,000	—	—	0.15	1.00	—

KM# 963 5 LIRA
1.6700 g., Aluminum, 19.46 mm. **Obv:** Head left **Rev:** Value and date within wreath **Edge:** Reeded **Note:** Varieties exist.

Date	Mintage	F	VF	XF	Unc	BU
1984	17,316,000	—	—	0.15	1.00	—
1985	9,405,000	—	—	0.15	1.00	—
1986	9,575,000	—	—	0.20	1.00	—
1987	500,000	—	—	0.20	1.00	—
1988	100,000	—	—	0.20	1.00	—
1989	10,000	—	—	0.20	4.00	—

KM# 894 10 LIRA
15.0000 g., 0.8300 Silver 0.4003 oz. ASW **Subject:** 27th May Revolution **Obv:** Head of Atatürk left **Rev:** Radiant crescent and star above torch, balance scales, crossed flag and wing

Date	Mintage	F	VF	XF	Unc	BU
ND(1960)	4,000,000	—	BV	7.00	10.00	—
ND(1960) Prooflike	—	—	—	—	12.50	—

KM# 945 10 LIRA
Aluminum **Obv:** Half-length figure right **Rev:** Value and date within wreath, crescent opens left

Date	Mintage	F	VF	XF	Unc	BU
1981	25,520,000	—	0.10	0.25	0.50	—

KM# 950.1 10 LIRA
Aluminum **Obv:** Half-length figure right **Rev:** Value and date within wreath, crescent opens right

Date	Mintage	F	VF	XF	Unc	BU
1982	17,092,000	—	0.10	0.25	0.50	—

KM# 950.2 10 LIRA
Aluminum **Obv:** Half-length figure right **Rev:** Value and date within wreath

Date	Mintage	F	VF	XF	Unc	BU
1983	2,228,000	—	0.10	1.00	4.00	—

KM# 964 10 LIRA
2.3000 g., Aluminum, 25 mm. **Obv:** Head of Atatürk left **Rev:** Value and date within wreath **Note:** Varieties exist.

Date	Mintage	F	VF	XF	Unc	BU
1984	23,360,000	—	0.10	0.25	0.50	—
1985	41,736,000	—	—	0.15	0.50	—
1986	78,224,000	—	—	0.15	0.50	—
1987	62,340,000	—	—	0.15	0.50	—
1988	17,620,000	—	—	0.15	1.00	—
1989	10,000	—	—	0.15	4.00	—

KM# 946 20 LIRA
Aluminum **Series:** World Food Day **Obv:** Value and date within wreath **Rev:** Stylized design below sprig

Date	Mintage	F	VF	XF	Unc	BU
1981	10,000	—	—	2.50	4.00	—

KM# 965 20 LIRA
7.2000 g., Copper-Nickel **Obv:** Head of Atatürk left **Rev:** Value and date within wreath

Date	Mintage	F	VF	XF	Unc	BU
1984	1,644,000	—	0.10	0.25	2.00	—
1989	—	—	0.10	0.25	2.00	—

KM# 897 25 LIRA
14.6000 g., 0.8300 Silver 0.3896 oz. ASW **Subject:** 50th Anniversary of National Assembly in Ankara **Obv:** Bust facing **Rev:** Building above value

Date	Mintage	F	VF	XF	Unc	BU
ND(1970)	23,000	—	—	8.50	12.00	—
ND(1970) Proof	Inc. above	—	Value: 14.00			

KM# 975 25 LIRA
2.8500 g., Aluminum, 27 mm. **Obv:** Head of Atatürk left **Rev:** Value and date within wreath **Note:** Varieties exist.

Date	Mintage	F	VF	XF	Unc	BU
1985	37,014,000	—	—	0.15	0.50	—
1986	49,611,000	—	—	0.15	0.50	—
1987	61,335,000	—	—	0.15	0.50	—
1988	39,540,000	—	—	0.15	1.00	—
1989	10,000	—	—	0.15	4.00	—

KM# 900 50 LIRA
19.0000 g., 0.8300 Silver 0.5070 oz. ASW **Subject:** 900th Anniversary - Battle of Malazgirt, Alparslan **Obv:** Armored bust 1/4 left **Rev:** Map of Turkey

Date	Mintage	F	VF	XF	Unc	BU
ND(1971)	33,000	—	—	10.00	13.00	—
ND(1971) Proof	Inc. above	—	Value: 15.00			

KM# 901 50 LIRA
20.1000 g., 0.8300 Silver 0.5363 oz. ASW **Subject:** Kemal Atatürk's Entry into Smyrna **Obv:** Atatürk on horse left **Rev:** Uniformed figures in battle

Date	Mintage	F	VF	XF	Unc	BU
ND(1972)	172,000	—	—	9.00	12.00	—
ND(1972) Proof	—	Value: 13.50				

KM# 902 50 LIRA
13.0000 g., 0.9000 Silver 0.3761 oz. ASW **Subject:** 50th Anniversary of Republic **Obv:** Radiant head on torch facing divides profiles **Rev:** Cascading star within flower at upper right of inscription

Date	Mintage	F	VF	XF	Unc	BU
ND(1973)	70,000	—	—	7.50	10.00	—
ND(1973) Proof	Inc. above	Value: 12.00				

KM# 912 50 LIRA
8.8500 g., 0.8300 Silver 0.2362 oz. ASW **Series:** F.A.O. **Obv:** Stylized standing figures **Rev:** Value and date within wreath

Date	Mintage	F	VF	XF	Unc	BU
1977	25,000	—	—	7.50	11.50	—

KM# 966 50 LIRA
Copper-Nickel-Zinc, 26.8 mm. **Obv:** Head of Atatürk left **Rev:** Value and date within wreath **Edge:** Reeded **Note:** Varieties exist.

Date	Mintage	F	VF	XF	Unc	BU
1984	14,731,000	—	0.10	0.25	0.60	—
1985	52,658,000	—	0.10	0.20	0.50	—
1986	80,656,000	—	0.10	0.20	0.50	—
1987	32,078,000	—	0.10	0.20	0.50	—

KM# 987 50 LIRA
3.2500 g., Aluminum-Bronze, 18.7 mm. **Obv:** Head of Atatürk left **Rev:** Value and date within wreath **Note:** Varieties exist.

Date	Mintage	F	VF	XF	Unc	BU
1988	3,396,000	—	—	—	0.15	—
1989	25,463,000	—	—	—	0.15	—
1990	500,000	—	—	—	0.15	—
1991	10,000	—	—	—	0.15	—
1992	10,000	—	—	—	0.15	—
1993	5,000	—	—	—	0.35	—
1994	2,500	—	—	—	0.50	—

KM# 903   100 LIRA
22.0000 g., 0.9000 Silver 0.6366 oz. ASW **Subject:** 50th Anniversary of Republic **Obv:** Radiant head on torch facing divides profiles **Rev:** Cascading star within flower to upper right of inscription

Date	Mintage	F	VF	XF	Unc	BU
1973	65,000	—	—	12.00	18.00	—
1973 Prooflike	—	—	—	—	25.00	—

KM# 951   100 LIRA
Copper-Nickel, 38.5 mm. **Subject:** World Championship Soccer - Madrid **Obv:** Soccer player **Rev:** Date within soccer ball

Date	Mintage	F	VF	XF	Unc	BU
1982	100,000	0.75	1.50	3.00	6.00	—

KM# 967   100 LIRA
11.0500 g., Copper-Nickel-Zinc, 29.65 mm. **Obv:** Head of Atatürk left **Rev:** Value and date within wreath **Note:** Varieties exist.

Date	Mintage	F	VF	XF	Unc	BU
1984	758,000	—	0.20	0.40	0.85	—
1985	866,000	—	0.20	0.40	0.85	—
1986	12,064,000	—	0.20	0.40	0.85	—
1987	91,400,000	—	0.15	0.25	0.65	—
1988	16,184,000	—	0.15	0.25	0.65	—

KM# 988   100 LIRA
4.1500 g., Aluminum-Bronze, 20.8 mm. **Obv:** Head of Atatürk left **Rev:** Value and date within wreath **Note:** Varieties exist.

Date	Mintage	F	VF	XF	Unc	BU
1988	10,000,000	—	—	—	0.20	—
1989	233,750,000	—	—	—	0.20	—
1990	152,230,000	—	—	—	0.20	—
1991	49,160,000	—	—	—	0.20	—
1992	22,930,000	—	—	—	0.20	—
1993	3,700,000	—	—	—	0.20	—
1994	2,500	—	—	—	0.50	—

KM# 988a   100 LIRA
5.1000 g., 0.9250 Silver 0.1517 oz. ASW, 21 mm. **Obv:** Head of Atatürk left **Rev:** Value and date within wreath **Edge:** Reeded **Mint:** Mexico City

Date	Mintage	F	VF	XF	Unc	BU
1988 Proof	998	Value: 75.00				

KM# 917   150 LIRA
9.0000 g., 0.8000 Silver 0.2315 oz. ASW **Subject:** World Cup Soccer Championship **Obv:** Soccer player and net **Rev:** Various maps divide emblem and value

Date	Mintage	F	VF	XF	Unc	BU
1978	5,000	—	—	—	30.00	—

KM# 918.1   150 LIRA
9.0000 g., 0.8000 Silver 0.2315 oz. ASW **Series:** F.A.O. **Obv:** Atatürk driving tractor **Rev:** Value and date within wreath **Edge:** Reeded

Date	Mintage	F	VF	XF	Unc	BU
1978	10,000	—	—	—	15.00	—

KM# 918.2   150 LIRA
9.0000 g., 0.8000 Silver 0.2315 oz. ASW **Series:** F.A.O. **Obv:** Atatürk driving tractor **Rev:** Value and date within wreath **Edge:** Lettered

Date	Mintage	F	VF	XF	Unc	BU
1978 Proof	2,500	Value: 80.00				

KM# 929.1   150 LIRA
9.0000 g., 0.8000 Silver 0.2315 oz. ASW **Series:** F.A.O. **Obv:** Anatolic bride's head left **Rev:** Value and date within wreath **Edge:** Reeded

Date	Mintage	F	VF	XF	Unc	BU
1979	10,000	—	—	—	15.00	—

KM# 929.2   150 LIRA
9.0000 g., 0.8000 Silver 0.2315 oz. ASW **Series:** F.A.O. **Obv:** Anatolic bride's head left **Rev:** Value and date within wreath **Edge:** Lettered

Date	Mintage	F	VF	XF	Unc	BU
1979 Proof	2,500	Value: 40.00				

KM# 919   200 LIRA
9.0000 g., 0.8300 Silver 0.2402 oz. ASW **Subject:** 705th Anniversary - Death of Jalaladdin Rumi, Poet **Obv:** Bust with headdress facing 1/4 left **Rev:** Steepled and dome buildings

Date	Mintage	F	VF	XF	Unc	BU
1978	10,000	—	—	—	17.50	—
1978 Proof	1,000	Value: 35.00				

KM# 904   500 LIRA
6.0000 g., 0.9170 Gold 0.1769 oz. AGW **Subject:** 50th Anniversary of Republic **Obv:** Bust facing **Rev:** Cascading star within flower to upper right of inscription

Date	Mintage	F	VF	XF	Unc	BU
1973	30,000	—	—	—	190	200

KM# 920   500 LIRA
8.0000 g., 0.9170 Gold 0.2358 oz. AGW **Series:** F.A.O. **Obv:** Mother breastfeeding infant **Rev:** Value and date within wreath

Date	Mintage	F	VF	XF	Unc	BU
1978 Proof	650	Value: 950				

KM# 921   500 LIRA
8.0000 g., 0.9170 Gold 0.2358 oz. AGW **Subject:** 705th Anniversary - Death of Jalaladdin Rumi, Poet

Date	Mintage	F	VF	XF	Unc	BU
1978 Proof	900	Value: 950				

KM# 930   500 LIRA
8.0000 g., 0.9170 Gold 0.2358 oz. AGW **Series:** F.A.O.

Date	Mintage	F	VF	XF	Unc	BU
1979 Proof	783	Value: 950				

KM# 931   500 LIRA
23.3300 g., 0.9250 Silver 0.6938 oz. ASW **Subject:** UNICEF and I.Y.C. **Obv:** Value within wreath **Rev:** Multiracial children dancing, city view above, logos and date below

Date	Mintage	F	VF	XF	Unc	BU
1979(1981) Proof	10,000	Value: 30.00				

KM# 940.1   500 LIRA
9.0000 g., 0.9000 Silver 0.2604 oz. ASW **Series:** F.A.O. **Obv:** Mother breastfeeding infant **Rev:** Value and date within wreath **Edge:** Reeded

Date	Mintage	F	VF	XF	Unc	BU
1980	13,000	—	—	—	15.00	—

KM# 940.2   500 LIRA
9.0000 g., 0.9000 Silver 0.2604 oz. ASW **Obv:** Mother breastfeeding infant **Rev:** Value and date within wreath **Edge:** Lettered

Date	Mintage	F	VF	XF	Unc	BU
1980 Proof	4,000	Value: 40.00				

KM# 952   500 LIRA
23.3300 g., 0.9250 Silver 0.6938 oz. ASW **Subject:** World Championship Soccer - Madrid **Obv:** Soccer player **Rev:** Soccer ball and map in front of lined globe design

Date	Mintage	F	VF	XF	Unc	BU
1982 Proof	12,000	Value: 30.00				

KM# 953   500 LIRA
23.3300 g., 0.9250 Silver 0.6938 oz. ASW **Subject:** World Championship Soccer - Madrid **Obv:** Soccer ball in inner circle **Rev:** Goalie blocking shot

Date	Mintage	F	VF	XF	Unc	BU
1982 Proof	12,000	Value: 20.00				

KM# 957   500 LIRA
Copper-Nickel   **Subject:** Lydia - First Coin in the World
Obv: Value and date within oat sprigs **Rev:** Animal heads at center of circular inscriptions

Date	Mintage	F	VF	XF	Unc	BU
1983	3,542	—	—	6.50	12.50	—

KM# 968   500 LIRA
Copper-Nickel   **Series:** F.A.O. **Subject:** World Fisheries
Conference **Obv:** Value **Rev:** Turbot fish

Date	Mintage	F	VF	XF	Unc	BU
ND(1984)	3,000	—	—	10.00	25.00	—

KM# 968a   500 LIRA
28.2800 g., 0.9250 Silver 0.8410 oz. ASW   **Series:** World
Fisheries Conference **Obv:** Value **Rev:** Turbot fish

Date	Mintage	F	VF	XF	Unc	BU
ND(1984) Proof	763	Value: 75.00				

KM# 968b   500 LIRA
47.5400 g., 0.9170 Gold 1.4015 oz. AGW   **Subject:** World
Fisheries Conference **Obv:** Value **Rev:** Turbot fish

Date	Mintage	F	VF	XF	Unc	BU
ND(1984) Proof	74	Value: 1,500				

KM# 979   500 LIRA
Copper-Nickel   **Subject:** 40th Anniversary of F.A.O. **Obv:** Value
within wreath **Rev:** Leafy produce in bowl in front of FAO logo,
dates on bottom

Date	Mintage	F	VF	XF	Unc	BU
ND(1986) Proof	3,000	Value: 12.00				

KM# 989a   500 LIRA
7.6000 g., 0.9250 Silver 0.2260 oz. ASW, 24 mm.   **Obv:** Head
of Atatürk left **Rev:** Value and date within wreath **Edge:** Reeded
Mint: Mexico City

Date	Mintage	F	VF	XF	Unc	BU
1989 Proof	998	Value: 75.00				

KM# 989   500 LIRA
6.1500 g., Aluminum-Bronze, 24 mm.   **Obv:** Head of Atatürk left
Rev: Value and date within wreath **Edge:** Reeded **Note:** Varieties
exist.

Date	Mintage	F	VF	XF	Unc	BU
1989	141,813,000	—	—	—	0.60	—
1990	100,114,000	—	—	—	0.60	—
1991	30,006,000	—	—	—	0.60	—
1992	10,000	—	—	—	0.60	—
1993	5,000	—	—	—	0.75	—
1994	2,500	—	—	—	0.85	—
1995	2,500	—	—	—	0.85	—
1996	10,000	—	—	—	0.60	—
1997	—	—	—	—	0.60	—

KM# 922   1000 LIRA
16.0000 g., 0.9170 Gold 0.4717 oz. AGW   **Series:** F.A.O.
Obv: Anatolic bride's head left **Rev:** Value and date within wreath

Date	Mintage	F	VF	XF	Unc	BU
1978 Proof	650	Value: 1,450				

KM# 923   1000 LIRA
16.0000 g., 0.9170 Gold 0.4717 oz. AGW   **Subject:** 705th
Anniversary - Death of Jalaladdin Rumi, Poet

Date	Mintage	F	VF	XF	Unc	BU
1978 Proof	450	Value: 1,450				

KM# 932   1000 LIRA
16.0000 g., 0.9170 Gold 0.4717 oz. AGW   **Series:** F.A.O.

Date	Mintage	F	VF	XF	Unc	BU
1979 Proof	900	Value: 1,200				

KM# 985   1000 LIRA
Nickel-Bronze   **Subject:** Peace **Obv:** Value within wreath
Rev: Doves within diamond shape

Date	Mintage	F	VF	XF	Unc	BU
1986 Proof	—	Value: 12.50				

KM# 980   1000 LIRA
Copper-Nickel   **Subject:** Shelter for the Homeless **Obv:** Value
within wreath **Rev:** Emblem within center of window design

Date	Mintage	F	VF	XF	Unc	BU
ND(1987) Proof	—	Value: 12.50				

KM# 991   1000 LIRA
Copper-Nickel   **Subject:** 400th Anniversary - Death of Architect
Sinan **Obv:** Value within wreath **Rev:** Arched city view

Date	Mintage	F	VF	XF	Unc	BU
ND(1988) Proof	—	Value: 15.00				

KM# 996   1000 LIRA
Copper-Zinc-Nickel, 25.8 mm.   **Subject:** Environmental
Protection **Obv:** Value and date within oat sprigs **Rev:** Fence
surrounds tree trunk

Date	Mintage	F	VF	XF	Unc	BU
1990	500,000	—	—	—	8.50	—

KM# 997   1000 LIRA
Copper-Zinc-Nickel, 25.8 mm.   **Obv:** Head of Atatürk left
Rev: Value and date within oat sprigs **Edge:** Reeded

Date	Mintage	F	VF	XF	Unc	BU
1990	136,480,000	—	0.15	0.25	2.00	—
1991	110,245,000	—	0.15	0.25	2.00	—
1992	15,820,000	—	0.15	0.25	2.00	—
1993	11,675,000	—	0.15	0.25	2.00	—
1994	61,515,000	—	0.15	0.25	2.00	—

KM# 1028   1000 LIRA
3.0700 g., Bronze Clad Brass, 16.93 mm.   **Obv:** Head of Atatürk
left **Rev:** Value and date within oat sprigs

Date	Mintage	F	VF	XF	Unc	BU
1995	36,820,000	—	—	—	1.00	—
1996	3,900,000	—	—	—	1.00	—
1997	—	—	—	—	1.00	—

KM# 947   1500 LIRA
16.0000 g., 0.9250 Silver 0.4758 oz. ASW   **Series:** F.A.O.
Obv: Value and date within wreath **Rev:** Stylized design below
sprig

Date	Mintage	F	VF	XF	Unc	BU
1981	6,000	—	—	—	18.50	—
1982	500	—	—	—	47.50	—

KM# 958   1500 LIRA
16.0000 g., 0.9250 Silver 0.4758 oz. ASW   **Series:** World Food
Day **Obv:** Value and date within wreath **Rev:** Nursing goat within
designed wreath

Date	Mintage	F	VF	XF	Unc	BU
1983 Proof	1,552	Value: 45.00				

KM# 1015   2500 LIRA
Nickel-Bronze, 26.5 mm.   **Obv:** Head of Atatürk left **Rev:** Value
to lower right of oak leaf branch **Edge:** TURKIYE CUMHURIYETI

Date	Mintage	F	VF	XF	Unc	BU
1991	22,938,000	0.10	0.25	0.50	3.00	—
1992	48,784,000	0.10	0.25	0.50	3.00	—
1993	2,310,000	0.10	0.25	0.50	3.00	—
1994	2,500	0.10	0.25	0.50	4.50	—
1995	2,500	0.10	0.25	0.50	4.50	—
1996	10,000	0.10	0.25	0.50	3.00	—
1997	—	0.10	0.25	0.50	3.00	—

KM# 948   3000 LIRA
28.2800 g., 0.9250 Silver 0.8410 oz. ASW   **Series:** International
Year of Disabled Persons **Obv:** Stylized design divides top and
bottom emblems **Rev:** Value within wreath

Date	Mintage	F	VF	XF	Unc	BU
1981	14,000	—	—	—	45.00	—
1981 Proof	16,000	Value: 55.00				

KM# 959 3000 LIRA
28.2800 g., 0.9250 Silver 0.8410 oz. ASW **Series:** International Year of the Scout **Obv:** Value within wreath **Rev:** Mountain campsite scene

Date	Mintage	F	VF	XF	Unc	BU
ND(1982)	12,000	—	—	—	45.00	—
ND(1982) Proof	14,000	Value: 55.00				

KM# 960 3000 LIRA
16.0000 g., 0.9250 Silver 0.4758 oz. ASW **Subject:** 60th Anniversary of the Republic **Obv:** Head of Atatürk left within circle **Rev:** Stylized reaching and standing figures within circle

Date	Mintage	F	VF	XF	Unc	BU
ND(1983) Proof	4,000	Value: 35.00				

KM# 954 5000 LIRA
7.1300 g., 0.5000 Gold 0.1146 oz. AGW **Subject:** World Championship Soccer - Madrid **Obv:** Soccer player kicking the ball **Rev:** Soccer ball as world globe with SPANYA'82 across middle

Date	Mintage	F	VF	XF	Unc	BU
ND(1982) Proof	2,400	Value: 145				

KM# 969 5000 LIRA
23.3300 g., 0.9250 Silver 0.6938 oz. ASW **Subject:** Decade for Women **Obv:** Value and date within wreath **Rev:** Stylized woman holding dove

Date	Mintage	F	VF	XF	Unc	BU
1984 Proof	20,000	Value: 35.00				

KM# 970 5000 LIRA
23.3300 g., 0.9250 Silver 0.6938 oz. ASW **Series:** 1984 Summer Olympics **Obv:** Value within wreath **Rev:** Olympic athletes around center circle with stylized flame

Date	Mintage	F	VF	XF	Unc	BU
ND(1984) Proof	5,343	Value: 40.00				

KM# 971 5000 LIRA
23.3300 g., 0.9250 Silver 0.6938 oz. ASW **Series:** 1984 Winter Olympics **Obv:** Value within wreath **Rev:** Stylized slalom, bobsledder, ski jumper, and figure skater in inner circle, legend around

Date	Mintage	F	VF	XF	Unc	BU
1984 Proof	4,657	Value: 50.00				

KM# 972 5000 LIRA
23.3300 g., 0.9250 Silver 0.6938 oz. ASW **Subject:** 50th Anniversary of Women's Suffrage **Obv:** Value within wreath **Rev:** Three standing women facing in front of building

Date	Mintage	F	VF	XF	Unc	BU
ND(1984) Proof	1,000	Value: 80.00				

KM# 976 5000 LIRA
23.3300 g., 0.9250 Silver 0.6938 oz. ASW **Subject:** 500th Anniversary of Turkish Navy **Obv:** Value within wreath **Rev:** Bust with Turkish headdress at right, fleet of masted ships at left

Date	Mintage	F	VF	XF	Unc	BU
ND(1985) Proof	1,000	Value: 80.00				

KM# 977 5000 LIRA
23.3300 g., 0.9250 Silver 0.6938 oz. ASW **Subject:** Forestry Conference - Mexico **Obv:** Value within wreath **Rev:** Trees

Date	Mintage	F	VF	XF	Unc	BU
1985 Proof	2,000	Value: 45.00				

KM# 978 5000 LIRA
23.3300 g., 0.9250 Silver 0.6938 oz. ASW **Subject:** Youth Year **Obv:** Value within wreath **Rev:** Stylized head facing

Date	Mintage	F	VF	XF	Unc	BU
1985 Proof	2,000	Value: 40.00				

KM# 1011 5000 LIRA
23.3300 g., 0.9250 Silver 0.6938 oz. ASW **Subject:** Architect - Sinan

Date	Mintage	F	VF	XF	Unc	BU
ND(1988) Proof	—	Value: 40.00				

KM# 1005 5000 LIRA
Copper-Nickel **Subject:** Yunus Emre Sevgi Yili **Obv:** Value within wreath **Rev:** Inscription and arched design

Date	Mintage	F	VF	XF	Unc	BU
1991 Proof	—	Value: 7.50				

KM# 1018 5000 LIRA
Copper-Nickel **Subject:** Turkish Jews **Obv:** Value within wreath **Rev:** Standing figures below ship

Date	Mintage	F	VF	XF	Unc	BU
ND(1992) Proof	—	Value: 8.50				

KM# 1025 5000 LIRA
Nickel-Bronze, 28.5 mm. **Obv:** Head of Atatürk left **Rev:** Flower sprigs to left of value and date **Edge:** TURKIYE CUMHURIYETI

Date	Mintage	F	VF	XF	Unc	BU
1992	24,904,000	0.10	0.25	0.50	3.00	—
1992 Proof	—	Value: 6.50				
1993	15,872,000	0.10	0.25	0.50	3.00	—
1994	69,504,000	0.10	0.25	0.50	3.00	—

KM# 1029.1 5000 LIRA
5.9800 g., Brass, 19.5 mm. **Obv:** Head of Atatürk left **Rev:** Flower sprigs to left of value and date

Date	Mintage	F	VF	XF	Unc	BU
1995 Large date	69,550,000	—	—	—	1.50	—
1995 Small date	Inc. above	—	—	—	0.75	—
1996	80,506,000	—	—	—	0.75	—
1997	—	—	—	—	0.75	—
1998	—	—	—	—	0.75	—

KM# 1029.2   5000 LIRA
3.4800 g., Brass, 19.5 mm. **Obv:** Head of Atatürk left
Rev: Flower sprigs to left of value and date **Edge:** Reeded
Note: Reduced weight version of KM#1029.1

Date	Mintage	F	VF	XF	Unc	BU
1998	—	—	—	—	0.75	—
1999	—	—	—	—	0.75	—

KM# 933   10000 LIRA (10 Lira)
17.1700 g., 0.9000 Gold 0.4968 oz. AGW **Subject:** UNICEF
and I.Y.C. **Obv:** Value within wreath **Rev:** Multiracial children
dancing, city view above, logos and date below **Note:** Similar to
500 Lira, KM#931

Date	Mintage	F	VF	XF	Unc	BU
1979(1981) Proof	4,450	Value: 550				

KM# 986   10000 LIRA (10 Bin Lira)
23.3300 g., 0.9250 Silver 0.6938 oz. ASW **Subject:** 1986 World
Cup Soccer - Mexico **Rev:** Soccer player in center of soccer ball

Date	Mintage	F	VF	XF	Unc	BU
1986 Proof	5,000	Value: 22.50				

KM# 1009   10000 LIRA (10 Bin Lira)
23.3300 g., 0.9250 Silver 0.6938 oz. ASW **Subject:** 1986 World
Cup Soccer **Rev:** Cactus

Date	Mintage	F	VF	XF	Unc	BU
1986 Proof	7,000	Value: 20.00				

KM# 1010   10000 LIRA (10 Bin Lira)
23.3300 g., 0.9250 Silver 0.6938 oz. ASW **Subject:** A. Ersoy - Poet

Date	Mintage	F	VF	XF	Unc	BU
1986 Proof	—	Value: 35.00				

KM# 1022   10000 LIRA (10 Bin Lira)
23.3300 g., 0.9250 Silver 0.6938 oz. ASW **Subject:** World Peace
Obv: Value within wreath **Rev:** Doves within diamond shape

Date	Mintage	F	VF	XF	Unc	BU
1986 Proof	Est. 1,200	Value: 60.00				

KM# 981   10000 LIRA (10 Bin Lira)
22.9700 g., 0.9250 Silver 0.6831 oz. ASW **Subject:** Shelter for
the Homeless **Obv:** Value within wreath **Rev:** Emblem within
center of window design

Date	Mintage	F	VF	XF	Unc	BU
ND(1987) Proof	—	Value: 35.00				

KM# 982   10000 LIRA (10 Bin Lira)
22.9700 g., 0.9250 Silver 0.6831 oz. ASW **Subject:** 130 Years
of Turkish Forestry **Obv:** Value within wreath **Rev:** Bird on top of
globe design above pine trees

Date	Mintage	F	VF	XF	Unc	BU
ND(1987) Proof	5,000	Value: 40.00				

KM# 983   10000 LIRA (10 Bin Lira)
23.3300 g., 0.9250 Silver 0.6938 oz. ASW **Series:** Winter
Olympics **Obv:** Value within wreath **Rev:** Stylized upright bear
holding torch at left of totem pole

Date	Mintage	F	VF	XF	Unc	BU
1988 Proof	Est. 10,000	Value: 40.00				

KM# 984   10000 LIRA (10 Bin Lira)
23.3300 g., 0.9250 Silver 0.6938 oz. ASW **Series:** 1988 Summer
Olympics **Obv:** Value within wreath **Rev:** Stylized torch and designs

Date	Mintage	F	VF	XF	Unc	BU
1988	1,000	—	—	—	35.00	—
1988 Proof	Est. 10,000	Value: 40.00				

KM# 1027.1   10000 LIRA (10 Bin Lira)
9.7500 g., Copper-Nickel-Zinc, 23.5 mm. **Obv:** Head of Kemal
Atat?rk left **Rev:** Value to left of flower sprig, large lettering
Edge: Reeded with legend **Edge:** TURKIYE CUMHURIYETI,
dates 1994 and 1995

Date	Mintage	F	VF	XF	Unc	BU
1994	17,319,000	—	0.10	0.25	3.00	—
1995	56,584,000	—	0.10	0.25	3.00	—
1996	119,572,000	—	0.10	0.25	3.00	—
1997	—	—	0.10	0.25	3.00	—

KM# 1042   10000 LIRA (10 Bin Lira)
9.7500 g., Copper-Nickel-Zinc, 23.5 mm. **Series:** 1994 Olympics
Obv: Value to left of flower sprig **Rev:** Radiant Olympic rings

Date	Mintage	F	VF	XF	Unc	BU
1994	500,000	—	—	—	3.75	—

KM# 1027.2   10000 LIRA (10 Bin Lira)
9.7500 g., Copper-Nickel-Zinc, 23.5 mm. **Obv:** Head of Kemal
Atatürk left **Rev:** Value to left of flower sprig, small lettering
Edge: Reeded with incuse legend **Edge:** TURKIYE
CUMHURIYETI, dates 1996 and 1997 **Note:** Thin planchet. Edge
varieties exist.

Date	Mintage	F	VF	XF	Unc	BU
1997	—	—	0.10	0.25	3.00	—
1998	—	—	0.10	0.25	3.00	—
1999	—	—	0.10	0.25	3.00	—

KM# 1027.3   10000 LIRA (10 Bin Lira)
6.7500 g., Copper-Nickel-Zinc, 23.5 mm. **Obv:** Head of Kemal
Atatürk left **Rev:** Value to left of flower sprig, small lettering
Edge: "T.C." 6 times separated by vertical line pattern
Note: Thinner planchet, edge varieties exist, dates 1998 and
1999.

Date	Mintage	F	VF	XF	Unc	BU
1998						

KM# 998   20000 LIRA (20 Bin Lira)
23.3200 g., 0.9250 Silver 0.6935 oz. ASW **Subject:** Environmental
Protection **Obv:** Value within wreath **Rev:** Designs

Date	Mintage	F	VF	XF	Unc	BU
1988 Proof	Est. 5,000	Value: 40.00				

KM# 1001   20000 LIRA (20 Bin Lira)
23.3200 g., 0.9250 Silver 0.6935 oz. ASW **Subject:** 400th
Anniversary - Death of Architect Sinan **Obv:** Value within wreath
Rev: City view

Date	Mintage	F	VF	XF	Unc	BU
ND(1988) Proof	1,239	Value: 37.50				

KM# 1003   20000 LIRA (20 Bin Lira)
23.3200 g., 0.9250 Silver 0.6935 oz. ASW **Subject:** Teacher's Day
Obv: Value within wreath **Rev:** Stylized design divides date below

Date	Mintage	F	VF	XF	Unc	BU
1989 Proof	1,013	Value: 37.50				

KM# 1013   20000 LIRA (20 Bin Lira)
23.3200 g., 0.9250 Silver 0.6935 oz. ASW **Subject:** Istanbul
Metro **Obv:** Value within wreath **Rev:** City view

Date	Mintage	F	VF	XF	Unc	BU
ND(1989) Proof	Est. 5,000	Value: 75.00				

KM# 992   20000 LIRA (20 Bin Lira)
23.3200 g., 0.9250 Silver 0.6935 oz. ASW **Subject:** 1990 World
Cup Soccer **Obv:** Value within wreath **Rev:** Stylized football
player kicking ball **Rev. Leg.:** 1990 DUNYA FUTBOL
SAMPIYONASI ITALYA

Date	Mintage	F	VF	XF	Unc	BU
1990 Proof	12,959	Value: 35.00				

KM# 993   20000 LIRA (20 Bin Lira)
23.3200 g., 0.9250 Silver 0.6935 oz. ASW **Subject:** 75th
Anniversary - Battle of Gallipoli **Obv:** Value within wreath
Rev: Armored figure facing, holding flag and weapon in front of
monument

Date	Mintage	F	VF	XF	Unc	BU
ND(1990) Proof	1,963	Value: 40.00				

KM# 995   20000 LIRA (20 Bin Lira)
23.3200 g., 0.9250 Silver 0.6935 oz. ASW **Subject:** Soccer
Obv: Value within wreath **Rev:** Soccer ball above stylized wolf

Date	Mintage	F	VF	XF	Unc	BU
1990 Proof	8,796	Value: 37.50				

KM# 1014   20000 LIRA (20 Bin Lira)
23.3200 g., 0.9250 Silver 0.6935 oz. ASW **Subject:** 70th
Anniversary of Parliament **Rev:** Parliament building

Date	Mintage	F	VF	XF	Unc	BU
1990 Proof	1,163	Value: 40.00				

KM# 1057   20000 LIRA (20 Bin Lira)
23.3200 g., 0.9250 Silver 0.6935 oz. ASW **Series:** Summer
Olympics **Obv:** Value within wreath **Rev:** Bicyclist

Date	Mintage	F	VF	XF	Unc	BU
ND(1990) Proof	—	Value: 40.00				

KM# 1077   20000 LIRA (20 Bin Lira)
23.4200 g., 0.9250 Silver 0.6965 oz. ASW **Series:** Olympics
Subject: Speed Skating **Obv:** Value within wreath **Rev:** Speed
skater

Date	Mintage	F	VF	XF	Unc	BU
ND(1990) Proof	—	Value: 30.00				

KM# 1041   25000 LIRA (25 Bin Lira)
Copper-Nickel-Zinc, 26.5 mm. **Obv:** Head of Atatürk left
Rev: Value to left of rose **Edge:** Lettered TC and flower five times

Date	Mintage	F	VF	XF	Unc	BU
1995	13,740,000	0.20	0.30	0.50	3.00	—
1996	59,742,000	0.20	0.30	0.50	3.00	—
1997	—	0.20	0.30	0.50	3.00	—
1998	—	0.20	0.30	0.50	3.00	—
1999	—	0.20	0.30	0.50	3.00	—
2000	—	0.20	0.30	0.50	3.00	—

KM# 1043   25000 LIRA (25 Bin Lira)
11.1400 g., Copper-Nickel-Zinc, 26.5 mm. **Series:**
Environmental Protection **Obv:** Small head facing divides profiles
with birds and nest on top of heads **Rev:** Value to left of rose

Date	Mintage	F	VF	XF	Unc	BU
1995	500,000	—	—	—	5.00	—

KM# 955   30000 LIRA
15.9800 g., 0.9170 Gold 0.4711 oz. AGW **Series:** International
Year of Disabled Persons **Obv:** Value within wreath **Rev:** Stylized
seated figure missing legs and globe design

Date	Mintage	F	VF	XF	Unc	BU
1981	140	—	—	—	—	525
1981 Proof	3,000	Value: 550				

KM# 961   30000 LIRA
15.9800 g., 0.9170 Gold 0.4711 oz. AGW **Series:** International
Year of the Scout **Obv:** Value within wreath **Rev:** Emblems within
circle

Date	Mintage	F	VF	XF	Unc	BU
ND(1983)	2,000	—	—	—	—	525
ND(1983) Proof	2,000	Value: 550				

KM# 973   50000 LIRA (50 Bin Lira)
7.1300 g., 0.9000 Gold 0.2063 oz. AGW **Series:** Decade for
Women **Obv:** Value and date within wreath **Rev:** Half-figure of
female facing

Date	Mintage	F	VF	XF	Unc	BU
1984 Proof	800	Value: 225				

KM# 999   50000 LIRA (50 Bin Lira)
28.2800 g., 0.9250 Silver 0.8410 oz. ASW **Series:** Winter
Olympics **Obv:** Value within wreath **Rev:** Speed skater

Date	Mintage	F	VF	XF	Unc	BU
ND(1990) Proof	15,000	Value: 30.00				

KM# 1000   50000 LIRA (50 Bin Lira)
28.2800 g., 0.9250 Silver 0.8410 oz. ASW **Series:** 1990
Summer Olympics **Obv:** Value within wreath **Rev:** Bicyclist

Date	Mintage	F	VF	XF	Unc	BU
ND(1990) Proof	15,000	Value: 30.00				

KM# 1006   50000 LIRA (50 Bin Lira)
22.8700 g., 0.9250 Silver 0.6801 oz. ASW **Subject:** Yunus Emre
Sevgi Yili **Obv:** Value within wreath **Rev:** Inscription and arched
brick facade

Date	Mintage	F	VF	XF	Unc	BU
1991 Proof	1,578	Value: 40.00				

KM# 1007 50000 LIRA (50 Bin Lira)
22.8700 g., 0.9250 Silver 0.6801 oz. ASW **Subject:** Mozart
Opera **Obv:** Value within wreath **Rev:** Cameo within curtains
above theater, circle surrounds all

Date	Mintage	F	VF	XF	Unc	BU
ND(1991) Proof	1,614	Value: 40.00				

KM# 1019 50000 LIRA (50 Bin Lira)
22.7700 g., 0.9250 Silver 0.6771 oz. ASW **Subject:** Ahmet
Adnan Saygun - Musician **Obv:** Value within wreath **Rev:** Bust
facing in front of music sheet

Date	Mintage	F	VF	XF	Unc	BU
ND(1991) Proof	1,021	Value: 45.00				

KM# 1016 50000 LIRA (50 Bin Lira)
23.3300 g., 0.9250 Silver 0.6938 oz. ASW **Subject:** Turkish Jews
Obv: Value within wreath **Rev:** Similar to 5000 Lira, KM#1018

Date	Mintage	F	VF	XF	Unc	BU
ND(1992) Proof	2,813	Value: 60.00				

KM# 1023 50000 LIRA (50 Bin Lira)
23.0800 g., 0.9250 Silver 0.6864 oz. ASW **Subject:** 200th
Birthday of Rossini **Obv:** Value within wreath **Rev:** Bust 1/4 right
to left of building within circle

Date	Mintage	F	VF	XF	Unc	BU
ND(1992) Proof	945	Value: 70.00				

KM# 1136 50000 LIRA (50 Bin Lira)
23.1600 g., 0.9250 Silver 0.6887 oz. ASW, 38.6 mm. **Subject:** 30th
Anniversary - Constitution **Obv:** Value within wreath **Rev:** Flame
above open book within circle **Edge:** Reeded **Mint:** Istanbul

Date	Mintage	F	VF	XF	Unc	BU
ND(1992) Proof	1,134	Value: 65.00				

KM# 1020 50000 LIRA (50 Bin Lira)
23.0800 g., 0.9250 Silver 0.6864 oz. ASW **Subject:** 1994 World
Cup Soccer **Obv:** Value within wreath **Rev:** Soccer ball on top of
torch

Date	Mintage	F	VF	XF	Unc	BU
ND(1993) Proof	3,724	Value: 30.00				

KM# 1021.1 50000 LIRA (50 Bin Lira)
23.0800 g., 0.9250 Silver 0.6864 oz. ASW **Subject:** 1994 World
Cup Soccer **Obv:** Value within wreath **Rev:** Bridge behind soccer
player, fuzzy looking rock under bridge

Date	Mintage	F	VF	XF	Unc	BU
ND(1993)	6,038	—	—	75.00	—	
ND(1993) Proof	Inc. above	Value: 25.00				

KM# 1021.2 50000 LIRA (50 Bin Lira)
23.0800 g., 0.9250 Silver 0.6864 oz. ASW **Subject:** 1994 World
Cup Soccer **Obv:** Value within wreath **Rev:** Sharp looking rock
under bridge

Date	Mintage	F	VF	XF	Unc	BU
ND(1993) Proof	550	Value: 45.00				

KM# 1044 50000 LIRA (50 Bin Lira)
23.0800 g., 0.9250 Silver 0.6864 oz. ASW **Subject:** 125 Years
- Turkish Supreme Court **Obv:** Value within wreath **Rev:** Balance
scales within circle

Date	Mintage	F	VF	XF	Unc	BU
ND(1993) Proof	1,052	Value: 40.00				

KM# 1024 50000 LIRA (50 Bin Lira)
23.0800 g., 0.9250 Silver 0.6864 oz. ASW **Subject:** 25th
Anniversary of Turkish Red Crescent **Obv:** Value within wreath
Rev: Aerial country view below world globe

Date	Mintage	F	VF	XF	Unc	BU
ND(1993) Proof	938	Value: 70.00				

KM# 1026 50000 LIRA (50 Bin Lira)
22.8400 g., 0.9250 Silver 0.6792 oz. ASW **Series:** Olympics
Obv: Value within wreath **Rev:** Flag and Olympic rings

Date	Mintage	F	VF	XF	Unc	BU
ND(1994) Proof	1,821	Value: 60.00				

KM# 1030 50000 LIRA (50 Bin Lira)
31.4700 g., 0.9250 Silver 0.9359 oz. ASW **Series:** Endangered
Wildlife **Obv:** Value within wreath **Rev:** Bald Ibis

Date	Mintage	F	VF	XF	Unc	BU
ND(1994) Proof	6,807	Value: 45.00				

KM# 1031 50000 LIRA (50 Bin Lira)
23.3300 g., 0.9250 Silver 0.6938 oz. ASW **Subject:** Tschaikovsky
Obv: Value within wreath **Rev:** Head facing at upper right of ballet
scene

Date	Mintage	F	VF	XF	Unc	BU
ND(1994) Proof	1,237	Value: 35.00				

KM# 1033   50000 LIRA (50 Bin Lira)
23.3300 g., 0.9250 Silver 0.6938 oz. ASW **Subject:** 75th
Anniversary - Turkish National Assembly **Obv:** Value within
wreath **Rev:** Upright designs above building

Date	Mintage	F	VF	XF	Unc	BU
1995 Proof	3,000	Value: 25.00				

KM# 1035   50000 LIRA (50 Bin Lira)
23.3300 g., 0.9250 Silver 0.6938 oz. ASW **Subject:** 150th
Anniversary - National Police **Obv:** Value within wreath
Rev: Police badge above dates

Date	Mintage	F	VF	XF	Unc	BU
1995 Proof	1,262	Value: 45.00				

KM# 1037   50000 LIRA (50 Bin Lira)
Brass **Obv:** Value within wreath **Rev:** Swimming sea turtle
Note: Oxidized finish.

Date	Mintage	F	VF	XF	Unc	BU
1995	1,235	—	—	—	40.00	—

KM# 1037a   50000 LIRA (50 Bin Lira)
23.3300 g., 0.9250 Silver 0.6938 oz. ASW **Obv:** Value within
wreath **Rev:** Swimming sea turtle

Date	Mintage	F	VF	XF	Unc	BU
1995 Proof	2,961	Value: 45.00				

KM# 1038   50000 LIRA (50 Bin Lira)
23.3300 g., 0.9250 Silver 0.6938 oz. ASW **Obv:** Value within
wreath **Rev:** Sailing ship - "Piri Reis"

Date	Mintage	F	VF	XF	Unc	BU
1995 Proof	13,923	Value: 40.00				

KM# 1040   50000 LIRA (50 Bin Lira)
23.3300 g., 0.9250 Silver 0.6938 oz. ASW **Series:** 50th
Anniversary - F.A.O. **Obv:** Value within wreath **Rev:** Anniversary
date above logo within design

Date	Mintage	F	VF	XF	Unc	BU
1995 Proof	3,798	Value: 22.50				

KM# 1045   50000 LIRA (50 Bin Lira)
31.4700 g., 0.9250 Silver 0.9359 oz. ASW **Series:** Summer
Olympics **Obv:** Value and date within wreath **Rev:** Wrestlers

Date	Mintage	F	VF	XF	Unc	BU
1995 Proof	12,476	Value: 30.00				

KM# 1050   50000 LIRA (50 Bin Lira)
11.7800 g., Copper-Nickel-Zinc, 28 mm. **Series:** F.A.O.
Obv: Globe within center of designs, single sprig at left
Rev: Value **Edge:** "T.C." and four fleur-de-lis repeated four times

Date	Mintage	F	VF	XF	Unc	BU
ND(1996)	500,000	—	—	—	4.50	—

KM# 1056   50000 LIRA (50 Bin Lira)
11.6000 g., Copper-Nickel-Zinc, 28 mm. **Obv:** Head of Atatürk
left **Rev:** Value

Date	Mintage	F	VF	XF	Unc	BU
1996	11,916,000	—	—	—	3.50	—
1997	—	—	—	—	3.50	—
1998	—	—	—	—	3.50	—
1999	—	—	—	—	3.50	—
2000	—	—	—	—	3.50	—

KM# 1103   50000 LIRA (50 Bin Lira)
1.5000 g., Aluminum, 20 mm. **Series:** F.A.O **Obv:** .Value and date
within wreath **Rev:** Ancient vintner **Edge:** Plain **Mint:** Istanbul

Date	Mintage	F	VF	XF	Unc	BU
1999	—	—	—	—	1.00	2.00

KM# 956   100000 LIRA (100 Bin Lira)
33.8200 g., 0.9170 Gold 0.9970 oz. AGW **Subject:** Islamic
World 15th Century **Rev:** City view above value within circle

Date	Mintage	F	VF	XF	Unc	BU
1982 Proof	12,000	Value: 1,100				

KM# 1078   100000 LIRA (100 Bin Lira)
Copper-Nickel-Zinc **Subject:** 75th Anniversary of Republic
Obv: Value below crescent and star **Rev:** Bust of Mustafa Kemal
Atatürk left

Date	Mintage	F	VF	XF	Unc	BU
1999	—	—	—	—	3.00	—
2000	—	—	—	—	3.00	—

KM# 1079   100000 LIRA (100 Bin Lira)
Copper-Nickel-Zinc **Subject:** 75th Anniversary of Republic
Obv: Value below crescent and star **Rev:** Anniversary logo and
dates

Date	Mintage	F	VF	XF	Unc	BU
1999	—	—	—	—	4.00	—
2000	—	—	—	—	4.00	—

KM# 974   200000 LIRA
33.8200 g., 0.9170 Gold 0.9970 oz. AGW **Subject:** 50th
Anniversary of Women's Suffrage

Date	Mintage	F	VF	XF	Unc	BU
ND(1984) Proof	62	Value: 1,850				

KM# 1002   200000 LIRA
7.2160 g., 0.9170 Gold 0.2127 oz. AGW **Subject:** 400th
Anniversary - Death of Architect Sinan **Obv:** Value within wreath
Rev: Arched city view

Date	Mintage	F	VF	XF	Unc	BU
ND(1988) Proof	244	Value: 325				

KM# 1004   200000 LIRA
7.2160 g., 0.9170 Gold 0.2127 oz. AGW **Subject:** Teacher's
Day **Obv:** Value within wreath **Rev:** Stylized design divides date

Date	Mintage	F	VF	XF	Unc	BU
1989 Proof	197	Value: 350				

KM# 994   200000 LIRA
7.2160 g., 0.9170 Gold 0.2127 oz. AGW **Subject:** 75th
Anniversary - Battle of Gallipoli

Date	Mintage	F	VF	XF	Unc	BU
ND(1990) Proof	Est. 494	Value: 325				

KM# 1051   400000 LIRA
Bronze **Subject:** Habitat II **Obv:** City view **Rev:** Conference logo

Date	Mintage	F	VF	XF	Unc	BU
1996	2,402	—	—	—	12.50	—

KM# 1008   500000 LIRA
7.1300 g., 0.9000 Gold 0.2063 oz. AGW **Subject:** Yunus Emre **Obv:** Value within wreath **Rev:** Inscription and arched brick facade

Date	Mintage	F	VF	XF	Unc	BU
1991 Proof	288	Value: 320				

KM# 1017   500000 LIRA
7.1400 g., 0.9000 Gold 0.2066 oz. AGW **Subject:** 100 Years of Peace and Harmony - Turkish Jews **Obv:** Value within wreath **Rev:** Standing figures next to ship

Date	Mintage	F	VF	XF	Unc	BU
ND(1992) Proof	485	Value: 320				

KM# 1032   500000 LIRA
7.2160 g., 0.9166 Gold 0.2126 oz. AGW **Subject:** Southeast Anatolian Project **Obv:** Value within wreath **Rev:** Design within wreath

Date	Mintage	F	VF	XF	Unc	BU
ND(1994) Proof	950	Value: 300				

KM# 1034   500000 LIRA
7.2160 g., 0.9166 Gold 0.2126 oz. AGW **Subject:** 75th Anniversary - Turkish National Assembly **Obv:** Value and date within wreath **Rev:** Building in front of upright designs

Date	Mintage	F	VF	XF	Unc	BU
1995 Proof	255	Value: 300				

KM# 1036   500000 LIRA
7.2160 g., 0.9166 Gold 0.2126 oz. AGW **Subject:** Istanbul Gold Exchange **Obv:** Value and date within wreath **Rev:** AR above inscription and date

Date	Mintage	F	VF	XF	Unc	BU
1995 Proof	271	Value: 300				

KM# 1039   500000 LIRA
7.2160 g., 0.9166 Gold 0.2126 oz. AGW **Obv:** Value and date within wreath **Rev:** Sailing ship - "Piri Reis"

Date	Mintage	F	VF	XF	Unc	BU
1995 Proof	1,904	Value: 300				

KM# 1138   500000 LIRA
12.1000 g., Copper Nickel, 32 mm. **Subject:** Lira to Euro Transition **Obv:** Value and date within wreath **Rev:** Head of Atatürk left **Edge:** Reeded **Mint:** Istanbul **Note:** Dual denomination: 500,000 lira-2 euro

Date	Mintage	F	VF	XF	Unc	BU
1998	12,660	—	—	—	15.00	—

KM# 1081   500000 LIRA
11.9100 g., Copper-Nickel **Subject:** Trojan Horse **Obv:** Value and date within wreath **Rev:** Ancient Greek soldier and wooden horse **Edge:** Reeded **Note:** Struck at Istanbul.

Date	Mintage	F	VF	XF	Unc	BU
1999	6,243	—	—	—	15.00	—

KM# 1046   750000 LIRA
31.4700 g., 0.9250 Silver 0.9359 oz. ASW **Subject:** Europa **Obv:** Value and date within wreath **Rev:** Various landmarks

Date	Mintage	F	VF	XF	Unc	BU
1996 Proof	Est. 35,000	Value: 30.00				

KM# 1048.1   750000 LIRA
23.2000 g., 0.9250 Silver 0.6899 oz. ASW **Series:** F.A.O. **Obv:** Value within wreath **Rev:** World globe with corn stalks at left

Date	Mintage	F	VF	XF	Unc	BU
1996 Proof	—	Value: 20.00				

KM# 1048.2   750000 LIRA
23.2000 g., 0.9250 Silver 0.6899 oz. ASW **Series:** F.A.O. **Obv:** Value within wreath **Rev:** World globe with corn stalks at right

Date	Mintage	F	VF	XF	Unc	BU
1996 Proof	2,010	Value: 22.50				

KM# 1049   750000 LIRA
23.4100 g., 0.9250 Silver 0.6962 oz. ASW **Subject:** Turkish European Customs Union **Obv:** Flying plane and hills **Rev:** Clasped hands divide circle of stars

Date	Mintage	F	VF	XF	Unc	BU
1996 Proof	3,947	Value: 22.50				

KM# 1052   750000 LIRA
23.3700 g., 0.9250 Silver 0.6950 oz. ASW **Subject:** Nasreddin Hoca **Obv:** Stylized figure with headdress on donkey facing **Rev:** Stylized figure with headdress on donkey walking away

Date	Mintage	F	VF	XF	Unc	BU
1996 Proof	4,300	Value: 20.00				

KM# 1063   750000 LIRA
31.4700 g., 0.9250 Silver 0.9359 oz. ASW **Subject:** World Cup Soccer **Obv:** Value and date within wreath **Rev:** Goalie catching ball

Date	Mintage	F	VF	XF	Unc	BU
1996 Proof	6,848	Value: 30.00				

KM# 1058   750000 LIRA
Bronze **Subject:** First World Air Games - Manned Flight
Obv: Value within wreath **Rev:** Figure with bat-like wings flying
over city, all within circle

Date	Mintage	F	VF	XF	Unc	BU
1997	1,733	—	—	—	10.00	—

KM# 1059   750000 LIRA
Bronze **Subject:** XI World Forestry Congress **Obv:** Value within
wreath **Rev:** Stylized dove left below tree

Date	Mintage	F	VF	XF	Unc	BU
1997	1,778	—	—	—	12.50	—

KM# 1068   750000 LIRA
Bronze **Subject:** Forestry - "TEMA" **Obv:** Value within wreath
Rev: Wheel of trees design

Date	Mintage	F	VF	XF	Unc	BU
1998	1,950	—	—	—	12.50	—

KM# 1047   1000000 LIRA
31.7200 g., 0.9250 Silver 0.9433 oz. ASW **Series:** Endangered
Wildlife **Obv:** Ocean view within circle **Rev:** Mediterranean seal

Date	Mintage	F	VF	XF	Unc	BU
1996 Proof	3,594	Value: 35.00				

KM# 1053   1000000 LIRA
31.4600 g., 0.9250 Silver 0.9356 oz. ASW **Series:** Endangered
Wildlife **Obv:** Value and date within wreath **Rev:** Galathus Elwesii
flowers

Date	Mintage	F	VF	XF	Unc	BU
1996 Proof	3,100	Value: 25.00				

KM# 1054   1000000 LIRA
31.4600 g., 0.9250 Silver 0.9356 oz. ASW **Subject:** Habitat II
Obv: Steepled buildings **Rev:** Conference logo

Date	Mintage	F	VF	XF	Unc	BU
1996 Proof	3,968	Value: 25.00				

KM# 1055   1000000 LIRA
31.7700 g., 0.9250 Silver 0.9448 oz. ASW **Obv:** Value and date
within oat sprigs **Rev:** Bust of Hulusi Behcet facing

Date	Mintage	F	VF	XF	Unc	BU
1996 Proof	2,250	Value: 22.50				

KM# 1060   1000000 LIRA
31.5700 g., 0.9250 Silver 0.9388 oz. ASW **Subject:** Chinese
History - Excavation of the Terra Cotta Army **Obv:** Great Wall of
China **Rev:** Excavation site

Date	Mintage	F	VF	XF	Unc	BU
1997	4,273	—	—	—	22.50	—

Note: This coin does not have any national identification
other than the mintmark and denomination

KM# 1066   1000000 LIRA
1.2441 g., 0.9990 Gold 0.0400 oz. AGW **Obv:** Value in wreath **Rev:**
Head of King Croesus of Lydia right **Edge:** Reeded **Mint:** Istanbul

Date	Mintage	F	VF	XF	Unc	BU
1997 Proof	10,465	Value: 45.00				

KM# 1067   1000000 LIRA
1.2441 g., 0.9990 Gold 0.0400 oz. AGW **Obv:** Value and date
within wreath **Rev:** Ancient Lydian coin portraying lion

Date	Mintage	F	VF	XF	Unc	BU
1997 Proof	3,848	Value: 45.00				

KM# 1069   1000000 LIRA
31.4400 g., 0.9250 Silver 0.9350 oz. ASW **Subject:** Mehmed
Akif Ersoy **Obv:** Spiral inscription **Rev:** Bust facing

Date	Mintage	F	VF	XF	Unc	BU
1997 Proof	Est. 2,250	Value: 30.00				

KM# 1098   1000000 LIRA
1.2200 g., 0.9990 Gold 0.0392 oz. AGW, 13.9 mm. **Obv:** Value
and date within wreath **Rev:** Sailing ship - "Piri Reis"
Edge: Reeded **Mint:** Istanbul

Date	Mintage	F	VF	XF	Unc	BU
1997 Proof	10,655	Value: 45.00				

KM# 1061   1500000 LIRA
31.4400 g., 0.9250 Silver 0.9350 oz. ASW **Subject:** First World
Air Games - Manned Flight **Obv:** Value and date within wreath
Rev: Figure with bat-like wings flying over city

Date	Mintage	F	VF	XF	Unc	BU
1997 Proof	2,300	Value: 28.00				

KM# 1062   1500000 LIRA
31.4400 g., 0.9250 Silver 0.9350 oz. ASW **Subject:** XI World
Forestry Conference **Obv:** Value within wreath **Rev:** Stylized
dove left below tree

Date	Mintage	F	VF	XF	Unc	BU
1997 Proof	2,255	Value: 28.00				

KM# 1082   1500000 LIRA
31.3300 g., 0.9250 Silver 0.9317 oz. ASW **Subject:** Barbaros
Hayreddin **Obv:** Value and date within wreath **Rev:** Two war ships
Edge: Reeded **Mint:** Istanbul

Date	Mintage	F	VF	XF	Unc	BU
1997 Proof	7,062	Value: 30.00				

KM# 1100   1500000 LIRA
31.3700 g., 0.9250 Silver 0.9329 oz. ASW, 38.6 mm.
Subject: Myra'li Aziz Noel Baba and Euro **Obv:** Value and date
within wreath **Rev:** Statue and tower within 1/2 star wreath
Edge: Reeded **Mint:** Istanbul

Date	Mintage	F	VF	XF	Unc	BU
1997 Proof	10,492	Value: 25.00				

KM# 1064   2500000 LIRA
31.1500 g., 0.9250 Silver 0.9263 oz. ASW **Obv:** Value and date
within wreath **Rev:** Bust of Hasan-Ali Yücel 1/4 right

Date	Mintage	F	VF	XF	Unc	BU
1998 Proof	2,030	Value: 37.50				

KM# 1065   2500000 LIRA
31.5800 g., 0.9250 Silver 0.9391 oz. ASW **Subject:** Forestry -
"TEMA" **Obv:** Value and date within wreath **Rev:** Wheel of trees
design, similar to 750000 Lira, KM#1068

Date	Mintage	F	VF	XF	Unc	BU
1998 Proof	Est. 4,537	Value: 22.50				

KM# 1070   2500000 LIRA
31.4400 g., 0.9250 Silver 0.9350 oz. ASW **Subject:** 75 Years
of Peace **Obv:** Value and date within wreath **Rev:** Doves, treaty,
and radiant sun

Date	Mintage	F	VF	XF	Unc	BU
1998 Proof	2,394	Value: 30.00				

KM# 1084   2500000 LIRA
23.3000 g., 0.9250 Silver 0.6929 oz. ASW **Obv:** Value and date
within wreath **Rev:** Head of Atatürk left **Edge:** Reeded **Mint:** Istanbul

Date	Mintage	F	VF	XF	Unc	BU
1998 Proof	4,694	Value: 30.00				

KM# 1083   2500000 LIRA
31.3500 g., 0.9250 Silver 0.9323 oz. ASW **Series:** 2000
Olympics **Obv:** Value and date within wreath **Rev:** Weight lifter
and mosque **Edge:** Reeded **Note:** Struck at Istanbul.

Date	Mintage	F	VF	XF	Unc	BU
1998 Proof	4,983	Value: 27.50				

KM# 1071   3000000 LIRA
31.3233 g., 0.9250 Silver 0.9315 oz. ASW **Subject:** 75 Years
of Peace **Obv:** 75th Anniversary logo above inscription, value
below flanked by sprigs **Rev:** Doves, treaty, and radiant sun

Date	Mintage	F	VF	XF	Unc	BU
ND(1998) Proof	4,352	Value: 30.00				

KM# 1072   3000000 LIRA
31.3233 g., 0.9250 Silver 0.9315 oz. ASW **Subject:** 75th
Anniversary Republic **Obv:** 75th Anniversary logo **Rev:** Atatürk's
revolution

Date	Mintage	F	VF	XF	Unc	BU
ND(1998) Proof	3,513	Value: 32.50				

KM# 1073   3000000 LIRA
31.3233 g., 0.9250 Silver 0.9315 oz. ASW **Subject:** 75th
Anniversary of Republic **Obv:** 75th Anniversary logo **Rev:** Couple
dancing, people in background

Date	Mintage	F	VF	XF	Unc	BU
ND(1998) Proof	4,150	Value: 30.00				

KM# 1074   3000000 LIRA
31.3233 g., 0.9250 Silver 0.9315 oz. ASW **Obv:** 75th
Anniversary logo **Rev:** Ataturk with children

Date	Mintage	F	VF	XF	Unc	BU
ND(1998) Proof	3,701	Value: 32.50				

KM# 1075   3000000 LIRA
31.3233 g., 0.9250 Silver 0.9315 oz. ASW **Obv:** 75th
Anniversary logo **Rev:** Atatürk with cane before crowd

Date	Mintage	F	VF	XF	Unc	BU
ND(1998) Proof	6,199	Value: 30.00				

KM# 1076   3000000 LIRA
31.3233 g., 0.9250 Silver 0.9315 oz. ASW **Obv:** 75th
Anniversary logo **Rev:** Depictions of arts and sciences in Turkey

Date	Mintage	F	VF	XF	Unc	BU
ND(1998) Proof	3,522	Value: 30.00				

KM# 1086   3000000 LIRA
31.3600 g., 0.9250 Silver 0.9326 oz. ASW **Subject:** Galata
Kulesi **Obv:** Value and date within wreath **Rev:** Tower and city
view above "EURO"

Date	Mintage	F	VF	XF	Unc	BU
1998 Proof	7,843	Value: 30.00				

KM# 1087   4000000 LIRA
31.4000 g., 0.9250 Silver 0.9338 oz. ASW **Subject:** Fethiye
Obv: Value within wreath **Rev:** Two sailing ships **Edge:** Reeded
Mint: Istanbul

Date	Mintage	F	VF	XF	Unc	BU
1999 Proof	3,857	Value: 35.00				

KM# 1091   4000000 LIRA
31.4000 g., 0.9250 Silver 0.9338 oz. ASW **Subject:** Solar Eclipse
Obv: Value and date within wreath **Rev:** People watching eclipse

Date	Mintage	F	VF	XF	Unc	BU
1999 Proof	2,327	Value: 50.00				

KM# 1080   3000000 LIRA
31.3600 g., 0.9250 Silver 0.9326 oz. ASW
Subject: Dolmabahce Sarayi Palace **Obv:** Value within wreath
Rev: Building above "EURO" with stars above **Edge:** Reeded
Note: Struck at Istanbul.

Date	Mintage	F	VF	XF	Unc	BU
1998 Proof	1,710	Value: 50.00				

KM# 1088   4000000 LIRA
31.4000 g., 0.9250 Silver 0.9338 oz. ASW **Subject:** 80th
Anniversary - Atatürk's Landing at Samsun **Obv:** Value and date
within wreath **Rev:** Bust right above steamship

Date	Mintage	F	VF	XF	Unc	BU
1999 Proof	1,632	Value: 45.00				

KM# 1092   4000000 LIRA
31.4000 g., 0.9250 Silver 0.9338 oz. ASW **Subject:** Silk Road
Obv: Scroll design with landmarks **Rev:** Mounted archer hunting
lion **Note:** Antiqued finish.

Date	Mintage	F	VF	XF	Unc	BU
1999 Proof	1,263	Value: 55.00				

KM# 1107   3000000 LIRA
31.4700 g., 0.9250 Silver 0.9359 oz. ASW, 38.6 mm.
Series: Olympics **Obv:** Value and date within wreath **Rev:** Long
jumper and logo **Edge:** Reeded **Mint:** Istanbul

Date	Mintage	F	VF	XF	Unc	BU
1999 Proof	31,000	Value: 32.50				

KM# 1089   4000000 LIRA
31.4000 g., 0.9250 Silver 0.9338 oz. ASW **Subject:** Istanbul
Culture Capital **Obv:** Value and date within wreath **Rev:** Capital
building

Date	Mintage	F	VF	XF	Unc	BU
1999 Proof	1,180	Value: 55.00				

KM# 1093   4000000 LIRA
31.4000 g., 0.9250 Silver 0.9338 oz. ASW **Subject:** Osman Gazi
Obv: Value within wreath **Rev:** Turbaned 1/2-length bust facing

Date	Mintage	F	VF	XF	Unc	BU
1999 Proof	2,408	Value: 50.00				

KM# 1108   4000000 LIRA
31.4700 g., 0.9250 Silver 0.9359 oz. ASW, 38.6 mm.
Subject: Ataturk **Obv:** Value and date within wreath **Rev:** Half
length bust right below "EURO" flanked by stars **Edge:** Reeded
Mint: Istanbul

Date	Mintage	F	VF	XF	Unc	BU
1999 Proof	4,596	Value: 32.50				

KM# 1090   4000000 LIRA
31.4000 g., 0.9250 Silver 0.9338 oz. ASW **Subject:** Solar
Eclipse **Obv:** Value within wreath **Rev:** Eclipse stages above map

Date	Mintage	F	VF	XF	Unc	BU
1999 Proof	2,520	Value: 50.00				

KM# 1094   4000000 LIRA
31.4000 g., 0.9250 Silver 0.9338 oz. ASW **Obv:** Value within
wreath **Rev:** Gazi leading mounted troops

Date	Mintage	F	VF	XF	Unc	BU
1999 Proof	2,483	Value: 45.00				

KM# 1095   4000000 LIRA
31.4000 g., 0.9250 Silver 0.9338 oz. ASW   **Obv:** Value within
wreath **Rev:** Mounted archers and prey

Date	Mintage	F	VF	XF	Unc	BU
1999 Proof	2,336	Value: 45.00				

KM# 1099   4000000 LIRA
31.4100 g., 0.9250 Silver 0.9341 oz. ASW, 38.6 mm.
Subject: Lacerta Clarkorum **Obv:** Value and date within wreath
Rev: Two Clark's lizards **Edge:** Reeded **Mint:** Istanbul

Date	Mintage	F	VF	XF	Unc	BU
1999 Proof	2,608	Value: 55.00				

KM# 1096   4000000 LIRA
31.4000 g., 0.9250 Silver 0.9338 oz. ASW   **Obv:** Value within
wreath **Rev:** 700-year-old Islamic coin design

Date	Mintage	F	VF	XF	Unc	BU
1999 Proof	2,483	Value: 45.00				

KM# 1109   4000000 LIRA
31.4700 g., 0.9250 Silver 0.9359 oz. ASW, 38.6 mm.
Subject: "Bogazici" (Bosphorus) **Obv:** Value within wreath
Rev: Water front mosque above "EURO" **Edge:** Reeded
Mint: Istanbul

Date	Mintage	F	VF	XF	Unc	BU
1999 Proof	5,692	Value: 35.00				

KM# 1097   60000000 LIRA
15.0000 g., 0.9167 Gold 0.4421 oz. AGW **Subject:** 700th
Anniversary - The Ottoman Empire **Obv:** Value within wreath
Rev: Ottoman coat of arms **Edge:** Reeded **Mint:** Istanbul

Date	Mintage	F	VF	XF	Unc	BU
1999 Proof	1,904	Value: 475				

KM# 1101   7500000 LIRA
31.4000 g., 0.9250 Silver 0.9338 oz. ASW, 38.6 mm. **Subject:** 34th
World Chess Olympiad **Obv:** World globe with chess pieces within
circle **Rev:** Logo and horse head **Edge:** Reeded **Mint:** Istanbul

Date	Mintage	F	VF	XF	Unc	BU
2000 Proof	1,318	Value: 62.50				

KM# 1102   7500000 LIRA
23.3300 g., 0.9250 Silver 0.6938 oz. ASW, 38.6 mm.
Subject: UNICEF **Obv:** Value within wreath **Rev:** Two children
candle dancing **Edge:** Reeded **Mint:** Istanbul

Date	Mintage	F	VF	XF	Unc	BU
2000 Proof	—	Value: 50.00				

KM# 1111   7500000 LIRA
31.4700 g., 0.9250 Silver 0.9359 oz. ASW, 38.6 mm.
Subject: Ephesus' Celcius Library **Obv:** Mint logo and value
within circle **Rev:** Building **Edge:** Reeded **Mint:** Istanbul

Date	Mintage	F	VF	XF	Unc	BU
2000 Matte	1,042				40.00	
2000 Proof	1,171	Value: 40.00				

KM# 1112   7500000 LIRA
31.4700 g., 0.9250 Silver 0.9359 oz. ASW **Subject:** Traditional
Turkish Theater **Obv:** Mint logo and value within circle
Rev: Marionette theater scene **Mint:** Istanbul

Date	Mintage	F	VF	XF	Unc	BU
2000 Proof	1,183	Value: 40.00				

KM# 1113   7500000 LIRA
31.4700 g., 0.9250 Silver 0.9359 oz. ASW   **Subject:** United
Nations Summit **Obv:** Coiled rope design within circle **Rev:** UN
logo and stylized 2000 **Mint:** Istanbul

Date	Mintage	F	VF	XF	Unc	BU
2000 Proof	1,026	Value: 40.00				

KM# 1114   7500000 LIRA
31.4700 g., 0.9250 Silver 0.9359 oz. ASW   **Subject:** Turkish
European Union Candidacy **Obv:** Inscription within circular
design **Rev:** Cluster of flags behind star and crescent within star
border **Mint:** Istanbul

Date	Mintage	F	VF	XF	Unc	BU
2000 Proof	1,202	Value: 40.00				

KM# 1115   7500000 LIRA
31.4700 g., 0.9250 Silver 0.9359 oz. ASW **Subject:** First Female
Pilots **Obv:** Turkish pilot's badge within circle **Rev:** Early female
pilot saluting **Mint:** Istanbul

Date	Mintage	F	VF	XF	Unc	BU
2000 Proof	1,148	Value: 40.00				

KM# 1116   7500000 LIRA

31.4700 g., 0.9990 Silver 1.0107 oz. ASW **Subject:** President Clinton's Turkish Visit **Obv:** Mint logo within circle **Rev:** Clinton holding baby

Date	Mintage	F	VF	XF	Unc	BU
2000 Proof	1,490	Value: 40.00				

KM# 1186   10000000 LIRA

1.2400 g., 0.9990 Gold 0.0398 oz. AGW, 14.03 mm. **Subject:** Turkey in Europe **Obv:** Value within sprays **Rev:** Statue of Nikolas von Myra with children at center, tower at right **Edge:** Reeded

Date	Mintage	F	VF	XF	Unc	BU
2000 Proof	3,147	Value: 55.00				

KM# 1119   150000000 LIRA

Bi-Metallic 0.916 Gold center in 0.925 Silver ring, 38.6 mm. **Subject:** President Clinton's Turkish Visit **Obv:** Mint logo **Rev:** Clinton holding baby **Edge:** Reeded **Mint:** Istanbul

Date	Mintage	F	VF	XF	Unc	BU
2000 Proof	444	Value: 775				

GOLD BULLION COINAGE

Since 1943, the Turkish government has issued regular and deluxe gold coins in five denominations corresponding to the old traditional 25, 50, 100, 250, and 500 Kurus of the Ottoman period. The regular coins are all dated 1923, plus the year of the republic (e.g. 1923/40 = 1963), de Luxe coins bear actual AD dates. For a few years, 1944-1950, the bust of Ismet Inonu replaced that of Kemal Ataturk.

KM# 850   25 KURUSH

1.8041 g., 0.9170 Gold 0.0532 oz. AGW, 15 mm. **Obv:** Head of Ismet Inonu

Date	Mintage	F	VF	XF	Unc	BU
1923/20	—	BV	60.00	70.00	90.00	—
1923/22	3,228	BV	60.00	80.00	120	—
1923/23	2,757	BV	60.00	80.00	120	—
1923/24	46,000	BV	60.00	70.00	90.00	—
1923/25	20,000	BV	60.00	75.00	110	—
1923/26	16,000	BV	60.00	75.00	110	—

KM# 851   25 KURUSH

1.8041 g., 0.9170 Gold 0.0532 oz. AGW **Obv:** Head of Ataturk left **Rev:** Legend and date within wreath

Date	Mintage	F	VF	XF	Unc	BU
1923/20	14,000	—	—	BV	60.00	70.00
1923/27	18,000	—	—	BV	60.00	70.00
1923/28	15,000	—	—	BV	60.00	70.00
1923/29	15,000	—	—	BV	60.00	70.00
1923/30	17,000	—	—	BV	60.00	70.00
1923/31	19,000	—	—	BV	60.00	70.00
1923/32	5,455	—	—	BV	60.00	70.00
1923/33	11,000	—	—	BV	60.00	70.00
1923/34	20,000	—	—	BV	60.00	70.00
1923/35	25,000	—	—	BV	60.00	70.00
1923/36	34,000	—	—	BV	60.00	70.00
1923/37	31,000	—	—	BV	60.00	70.00
1923/38	35,000	—	—	BV	60.00	70.00
1923/39	46,000	—	—	BV	60.00	70.00
1923/40	49,000	—	—	BV	60.00	70.00
1923/41	59,000	—	—	BV	60.00	70.00
1923/42	74,000	—	—	BV	60.00	70.00
1923/43	90,000	—	—	BV	60.00	70.00
1923/44	85,000	—	—	BV	60.00	70.00
1923/45	73,000	—	—	BV	60.00	70.00
1923/46	89,000	—	—	BV	60.00	70.00
1923/47	119,000	—	—	BV	60.00	70.00
1923/48	112,000	—	—	BV	60.00	70.00
1923/49	112,000	—	—	BV	60.00	70.00
1923/50	67,000	—	—	BV	60.00	70.00
1923/51	40,000	—	—	BV	60.00	70.00
1923/52	71,000	—	—	BV	60.00	70.00
1923/53	124,000	—	—	BV	60.00	70.00
1923/54	196	—	—	BV	60.00	70.00
1923/55	112,000	—	—	BV	60.00	70.00
1923/56	—	—	—	BV	60.00	70.00
1923/57	—	—	—	BV	60.00	70.00
1923/60	—	—	—	BV	60.00	70.00
1923/64	—	—	—	BV	60.00	70.00
1923/65	—	—	—	BV	60.00	70.00
1923/66	—	—	—	BV	60.00	70.00

KM# 870   25 KURUSH

1.7540 g., 0.9170 Gold 0.0517 oz. AGW **Series:** Monnaie de Luxe **Obv:** Head of Ataturk left **Rev:** Country name and date in ornate monogram within circle of stars, floral border surrounds

Date	Mintage	F	VF	XF	Unc	BU
1942	138	—	55.00	75.00	150	—
1943	386	—	55.00	75.00	125	—
1944	811	—	55.00	75.00	125	—
1946	235	—	55.00	75.00	150	—
1950	2,053	—	—	BV	60.00	80.00
1951	2,035	—	—	BV	60.00	80.00
1952	3,374	—	—	BV	60.00	80.00
1953	1,944	—	—	BV	60.00	80.00
1954	2,244	—	—	BV	60.00	80.00
1955	2,573	—	—	BV	60.00	80.00
1956	4,004	—	—	BV	60.00	80.00
1957	8,842	—	—	BV	60.00	80.00
1958	9,546	—	—	BV	60.00	80.00
1959	17,000	—	—	BV	55.00	75.00
1960	19,000	—	—	BV	55.00	75.00
1961	35,000	—	—	BV	55.00	75.00
1962	31,000	—	—	BV	55.00	75.00
1963	47,000	—	—	BV	55.00	75.00
1964	57,000	—	—	BV	55.00	75.00
1965	78,000	—	—	BV	55.00	75.00
1966	106,000	—	—	BV	55.00	75.00
1967	114,000	—	—	BV	55.00	75.00
1968	152,000	—	—	BV	55.00	75.00
1969	163,000	—	—	BV	55.00	75.00
1970	224,000	—	—	BV	55.00	75.00
1971	306,000	—	—	BV	55.00	75.00
1972	271,000	—	—	BV	55.00	75.00
1973	162,000	—	—	BV	55.00	75.00
1974	141,000	—	—	BV	55.00	75.00
1975	202,000	—	—	BV	55.00	75.00
1976	583,000	—	—	BV	55.00	75.00
1977	1,089,000	—	—	BV	55.00	75.00
1978	238,000	—	—	BV	55.00	75.00
1980	—	—	—	BV	55.00	75.00
1998	—	—	—	BV	55.00	75.00

KM# 875   25 KURUSH

1.7540 g., 0.9170 Gold 0.0517 oz. AGW **Series:** Monnaie de Luxe **Obv:** Head of Ismet Inonu left

Date	Mintage	F	VF	XF	Unc	BU
1943	—	70.00	90.00	140	200	—

Note: Mintage included in KM#870

1944	—	70.00	90.00	140	200	

Note: Mintage included in KM#870

1945	592	70.00	90.00	140	200	—
1946	—	70.00	90.00	140	200	—

Note: Mintage included in KM#870

1947	3,443	70.00	90.00	125	185	—
1948	714	70.00	90.00	140	200	—
1949	552	70.00	90.00	140	200	—

KM# 852   50 KURUSH

3.6083 g., 0.9170 Gold 0.1064 oz. AGW, 18 mm. **Obv:** Head of Ismet Inonu left

Date	Mintage	F	VF	XF	Unc	BU
1923/20	—	BV	110	125	175	—
1923/22	1,093	BV	110	125	175	—
1923/23	897	BV	120	140	200	—
1923/24	11,000	BV	110	125	175	—
1923/25	3,004	BV	110	125	175	—
1923/26	817	BV	120	140	200	—
1923/27	5,228	BV	110	125	175	—

KM# 853   50 KURUSH

3.6083 g., 0.9170 Gold 0.1064 oz. AGW **Obv:** Head of Ataturk left **Rev:** Legend and date within wreath

Date	Mintage	F	VF	XF	Unc	BU
1923/20	12,000	—	—	BV	115	125
1923/27	Inc. above	—	—	BV	115	125
1923/28	3,300	—	—	BV	115	125
1923/29	6,384	—	—	BV	115	125
1923/30	4,590	—	—	BV	115	125
1923/31	9,068	—	—	BV	115	125
1923/32	4,344	—	—	BV	115	125
1923/33	3,958	—	—	BV	115	125
1923/34	9,499	—	—	BV	115	125
1923/35	9,307	—	—	BV	115	125
1923/36	12,000	—	—	BV	115	125
1923/37	9,049	—	—	BV	115	125
1923/38	9,854	—	—	BV	115	125
1923/39	11,000	—	—	BV	115	125
1923/40	13,000	—	—	BV	115	125
1923/41	13,000	—	—	BV	115	125
1923/42	18,000	—	—	BV	115	125
1923/43	26,000	—	—	BV	115	125
1923/44	26,000	—	—	BV	115	125
1923/45	25,000	—	—	BV	115	125
1923/46	28,000	—	—	BV	115	125
1923/47	38,000	—	—	BV	115	125
1923/48	35,000	—	—	BV	115	125
1923/49	28,000	—	—	BV	115	125
1923/50	16,000	—	—	BV	115	125
1923/51	8,000	—	—	BV	115	125
1923/52	14,000	—	—	BV	115	125
1923/53	28,000	—	—	BV	115	125
1923/54	54,000	—	—	BV	115	125
1923/55	16,000	—	—	BV	115	125
1923/57	—	—	—	BV	115	125
1923/64	—	—	—	BV	115	125
1923/65	—	—	—	BV	115	125
1923/66	—	—	—	BV	115	125

KM# 871   50 KURUSH

3.5080 g., 0.9170 Gold 0.1034 oz. AGW **Series:** Monnaie de Luxe **Obv:** Head of Kemal Ataturk left within circle of stars, wreath surrounds **Rev:** Country name and date in ornate monogram within circle of stars, floral border surrounds

Date	Mintage	F	VF	XF	Unc	BU
1942	115	110	150	200	250	—
1943	91	110	150	200	250	—
1944	950	BV	120	140	175	—
1946	565	BV	120	140	175	—
1950	1,971	—	BV	110	140	—
1951	1,780	—	BV	110	140	—
1952	2,557	—	BV	110	140	—
1953	2,392	—	BV	110	140	—
1954	1,714	—	BV	110	140	—
1955	4,143	—	BV	110	120	—
1956	2,956	—	BV	110	120	—
1957	6,855	—	BV	110	120	—
1958	6,381	—	BV	100	120	—
1959	12,000	—	—	BV	110	120
1960	12,000	—	—	BV	110	120
1961	15,000	—	—	BV	110	120
1962	22,000	—	—	BV	110	120
1963	29,000	—	—	BV	110	120
1964	34,000	—	—	BV	110	120
1965	44,000	—	—	BV	110	120
1966	58,000	—	—	BV	110	120
1967	64,000	—	—	BV	110	120
1968	82,000	—	—	BV	110	120
1969	79,000	—	—	BV	110	120
1970	109,000	—	—	BV	110	120
1971	154,000	—	—	BV	110	120
1972	110,000	—	—	BV	110	120
1973	73,000	—	—	BV	110	120
1974	45,000	—	—	BV	110	120
1975	72,000	—	—	BV	110	120
1976	196,000	—	—	BV	110	120
1977	361,000	—	—	BV	110	120
1978	161,000	—	—	BV	110	120
1980	—	—	—	BV	110	120

KM# 876   50 KURUSH

3.5080 g., 0.9170 Gold 0.1034 oz. AGW **Series:** Monnaie de Luxe **Obv:** Head of Ismet Inonu left

Date	Mintage	F	VF	XF	Unc	BU
1943	—	—	150	200	250	—

Note: Mintage included in KM#871

1944	—	—	120	170	220	—

Note: Mintage included in KM#871

1946	—	—	BV	140	190	—

Note: Mintage included in KM#871

1947	3,481	—	BV	140	190	—
1948	773	—	BV	140	190	—
1949	582	—	BV	140	190	—

KM# 872   100 KURUSH
7.0160 g., 0.9170 Gold 0.2068 oz. AGW   **Series:** Monnaie de Luxe **Obv:** Head of Atatürk left within circle of stars, wreath surrounds **Rev:** Country name and date in ornate monogram within circle of stars, floral border surrounds

Date	Mintage	F	VF	XF	Unc	BU
1942	8,659	—	—	BV	230	—
1943	6,594	—	—	BV	230	—
1944	7,160	—	—	BV	230	—
1948	14,000	—	—	BV	215	—
1950	25,000	—	—	BV	215	—
1951	35,000	—	—	BV	215	—
1952	41,000	—	—	BV	215	—
1953	32,000	—	—	BV	215	—
1954	24,000	—	—	BV	215	—
1955	4,881	—	—	BV	215	—
1956	11,000	—	—	—	BV	215
1957	49,000	—	—	—	BV	215
1958	67,000	—	—	—	BV	215
1959	89,000	—	—	—	BV	215
1960	57,000	—	—	—	BV	210
1961	77,000	—	—	—	BV	215
1962	108,000	—	—	—	BV	215
1963	146,000	—	—	—	BV	215
1964	128,000	—	—	—	BV	215
1965	157,000	—	—	—	BV	215
1966	190,000	—	—	—	BV	215
1967	177,000	—	—	—	BV	215
1968	143,000	—	—	—	BV	215
1969	206,000	—	—	—	BV	215
1970	253,000	—	—	—	BV	215
1971	293,000	—	—	—	BV	215
1972	222,000	—	—	—	BV	215
1973	140,000	—	—	—	BV	215
1974	82,000	—	—	—	BV	215
1975	142,000	—	—	—	BV	215
1976	265,000	—	—	—	BV	215
1977	277,000	—	—	—	BV	215
1978	86,000	—	—	—	BV	215
1980		—	—	—	BV	215

KM# 877   100 KURUSH
7.0160 g., 0.9170 Gold 0.2068 oz. AGW, 22 mm.
Series: Monnaie de Luxe **Obv:** Head of Ismet Inonu left

Date	Mintage	F	VF	XF	Unc	BU
1943	—	BV	220	265	325	—

Note: Mintage included in KM#872

| 1944 | — | BV | 220 | 265 | 375 | — |

Note: Mintage included in KM#872

1945	2,202	BV	220	265	400	—
1946	8,863	BV	220	265	325	—
1947	28,000	BV	220	265	325	—
1948	—	BV	220	265	325	—

Note: Mintage included in KM#872

| 1949 | 6,578 | BV | 220 | 265 | 325 | — |
| 1950 | — | BV | 220 | 265 | 325 | — |

Note: Mintage included in KM#872

KM# 854   100 KURUSH
7.2160 g., 0.9170 Gold 0.2127 oz. AGW   **Obv:** Head of Ismet Inonu left **Rev:** legend and date within wreath

Date	Mintage	F	VF	XF	Unc	BU
1923/20	—	—	—	BV	220	235
1923/22 Rare	3	—	—	—	—	—
1923/23	381,000	—	—	BV	220	235
1923/24	2,274	—	BV	220	235	—
1923/25	28,000	—	—	BV	220	235
1923/26	2,097	—	BV	220	235	—
1923/27	17,000	—	—	BV	220	235

KM# 855   100 KURUSH
7.2160 g., 0.9170 Gold 0.2127 oz. AGW   **Obv:** Head of Atatürk left **Rev:** Legend and date within wreath

Date	Mintage	F	VF	XF	Unc	BU
1923/20	—	—	—	BV	215	230
1923/27	Inc. above	—	—	BV	215	230
1923/28 Rare	3	—	—	—	—	—
1923/29	2,111	—	—	BV	215	230
1923/30	13,000	—	—	BV	215	230
1923/31	109,000	—	—	BV	215	230
1923/32	134,000	—	—	BV	215	230

Date	Mintage	F	VF	XF	Unc	BU
1923/33	216,000	—	—	BV	215	230
1923/34	463,000	—	—	BV	215	230
1923/35	405,000	—	—	BV	215	230
1923/36	25,000	—	—	BV	215	230
1923/37	131,000	—	—	BV	215	230
1923/38	159,000	—	—	BV	215	230
1923/39	85,000	—	—	BV	215	230
1923/40	10,000	—	—	BV	215	230
1923/41	164,000	—	—	BV	215	230
1923/42	63,000	—	—	BV	215	230
1923/43	56,000	—	—	BV	215	230
1923/44	198,000	—	—	BV	215	230
1923/45	176,000	—	—	BV	215	230
1923/46	1,290,000	—	—	BV	215	230
1923/47	513,000	—	—	BV	215	230
1923/48	600	—	—	BV	215	230
1923/49	1,300	—	—	BV	215	230
1923/50	47,000	—	—	BV	215	230
1923/51	240,000	—	—	BV	215	230
1923/52	1,046,999	—	—	BV	215	230
1923/53	550,000	—	—	BV	215	230
1923/54	18,000	—	—	BV	215	230
1923/55	309,000	—	—	BV	215	230
1923/57	—	—	—	BV	215	230
1923/58	—	—	—	BV	215	230
1923/59	—	—	—	BV	215	230
1923/60	—	—	—	BV	215	230
1923/61	—	—	—	BV	215	230
1923/62	—	—	—	BV	215	230
1923/63	—	—	—	BV	215	230
1923/64	—	—	—	BV	215	230
1923/65	—	—	—	BV	215	230

KM# 873   250 KURUSH
17.5400 g., 0.9170 Gold 0.5171 oz. AGW   **Series:** Monnaie de Luxe **Obv:** Head of Atatürk left within circle of stars, wreath surrounds **Rev:** Country name and date in ornate monogram within circle of stars, floral border surrounds

Date	Mintage	F	VF	XF	Unc	BU
1942	10,000	—	—	BV	625	—
1943	11,000	—	—	BV	625	—
1944	15,000	—	BV	650	900	—
1946	16,000	—	BV	650	900	—
1947	42,000	—	—	BV	625	—
1948	13,000	—	—	BV	625	—
1950	45,000	—	—	BV	625	—
1951	41,000	—	—	BV	525	525
1952	59,000	—	—	BV	525	525
1953	45,000	—	—	BV	525	525
1954	40,000	—	—	BV	525	525
1955	7,067	—	—	BV	525	525
1956	14,000	—	—	BV	525	525
1957	47,000	—	—	BV	525	525
1958	75,000	—	—	BV	525	525
1959	93,000	—	—	BV	525	550
1960	50,000	—	—	BV	525	550
1961	65,000	—	—	BV	525	550
1962	99,000	—	—	BV	525	550
1963	137,000	—	—	BV	525	550
1964	152,000	—	—	BV	525	550
1965	194,000	—	—	BV	525	550
1966	218,000	—	—	BV	525	550
1967	201,000	—	—	BV	525	550
1968	150,000	—	—	BV	525	550
1969	262,000	—	—	BV	525	550
1970	301,000	—	—	BV	525	550
1971	356,000	—	—	BV	525	550
1972	305,000	—	—	BV	525	550
1973	198,000	—	—	BV	525	550
1974	142,000	—	—	BV	525	550
1975	223,000	—	—	BV	525	550
1976	345,000	—	—	BV	525	550
1977	227,000	—	—	BV	525	550
1978	311,000	—	—	BV	525	550
1980		—	—	BV	525	550

KM# 878   250 KURUSH
17.5400 g., 0.9170 Gold 0.5171 oz. AGW, 27 mm.
Series: Monnaie de Luxe **Obv:** Head of Ismet Inonu left

Date	Mintage	F	VF	XF	Unc	BU
1943	—	—	—	BV	525	550

Note: Mintage included in KM#873

| 1944 | — | — | — | BV | 525 | 550 |

Note: Mintage included in KM#873

| 1945 | 4,135 | — | — | 525 | 550 | — |
| 1946 | — | — | — | BV | 525 | 550 |

Note: Mintage included in KM#873

| 1947 | — | — | — | BV | 525 | 550 |

Note: Mintage included in KM#873

| 1948 | — | — | — | BV | 525 | 550 |

Note: Mintage included in KM#873

| 1949 | 11,000 | — | — | BV | 525 | 550 |
| 1950 | — | — | — | BV | 525 | 550 |

Note: Mintage included in KM#873

KM# 856   250 KURUSH
18.0400 g., 0.9170 Gold 0.5318 oz. AGW   **Obv:** Head of Ismet Inonu left

Date	Mintage	F	VF	XF	Unc	BU
1923/20	—	—	BV	550	575	—
1923/23	14,000	—	BV	550	575	—
1923/24	60	—	BV	550	575	—

KM# 857   250 KURUSH
18.0400 g., 0.9170 Gold 0.5318 oz. AGW   **Obv:** Head of Atatürk left

Date	Mintage	F	VF	XF	Unc	BU
1923/20	10,000	—	—	BV	550	—
1923/29 Rare	3	—	—	—	—	—
1923/30	130	—	550	700	900	—
1923/31	—	—	550	700	900	—
1923/38	245	—	BV	550	625	—
1923/39	389	—	BV	550	625	—
1923/40	435	—	BV	550	625	—
1923/41	349	—	BV	550	625	—
1923/42	460	—	BV	550	625	—
1923/43	1,008	—	—	BV	550	—
1923/44	712	—	—	BV	550	—
1923/45	1,034	—	—	BV	550	—
1923/46	1,035	—	—	BV	550	—
1923/47	1,408	—	—	BV	550	—
1923/48	904	—	—	BV	550	—
1923/49	1,066	—	—	BV	550	—
1923/50	975	—	—	BV	550	—
1923/51	298	—	—	BV	550	—
1923/52	610	—	—	BV	550	—
1923/53	586	—	—	BV	550	—
1923/54	289	—	—	BV	550	—
1923/55	267	—	—	BV	550	—
1923/57		—	—	BV	550	—
1923/70		—	—	BV	550	—

KM# 858   500 KURUSH
36.0800 g., 0.9170 Gold 1.0637 oz. AGW, 35 mm.   **Obv:** Head of Ismet Inonu left **Rev:** Legend and date within wreath

Date	Mintage	F	VF	XF	Unc	BU
1923/20	—	—	—	BV	1,100	—
1923/23	9,006	—	—	BV	1,100	—
1923/24	7,923	—	—	BV	1,100	—
1923/25	272	—	—	BV	1,150	—

KM# 859   500 KURUSH

36.0800 g., 0.9170 Gold 1.0637 oz. AGW **Obv:** Head of Atatürk left **Rev:** Legend and date within wreath

Date	Mintage	F	VF	XF	Unc	BU
1923/20	12,000	—	BV	1,100	1,150	—
1923/27	615	—	BV	1,100	1,150	—
1923/28	34	—	BV	1,100	1,150	—
1923/29	137	—	BV	1,100	1,150	—
1923/30	45	—	BV	1,100	1,150	—
1923/31	100	—	BV	1,100	1,150	—
1923/32	74	—	BV	1,100	1,150	—
1923/33	268	—	BV	1,100	1,150	—
1923/34	758	—	BV	1,100	1,150	—
1923/35	1,586	—	—	BV	1,100	1,150
1923/36	765	—	—	BV	1,100	1,150
1923/37	983	—	—	BV	1,100	1,150
1923/38	1,738	—	—	BV	1,100	1,150
1923/39	2,629	—	—	BV	1,100	1,150
1923/40	2,763	—	—	BV	1,100	1,150
1923/41	3,440	—	—	BV	1,100	1,150
1923/42	3,335	—	—	BV	1,100	1,150
1923/43	4,914	—	—	BV	1,100	1,150
1923/44	4,308	—	—	BV	1,100	1,150
1923/45	3,488	—	—	BV	1,100	1,150
1923/46	5,636	—	—	BV	1,100	1,150
1923/47	7,588	—	—	BV	1,100	1,150
1923/48	6,060	—	—	BV	1,100	1,150
1923/49	4,235	—	—	BV	1,100	1,150
1923/50	4,733	—	—	BV	1,100	1,150
1923/51	2,757	—	—	BV	1,100	1,150
1923/52	2,041	—	—	BV	1,100	1,150
1923/53	4,819	—	—	BV	1,100	1,150
1923/54	1,401	—	—	BV	1,100	1,150
1923/55	1,484	—	—	BV	1,100	1,150
1923/57	—	—	—	BV	1,100	1,150
1923/69	—	—	—	BV	1,100	1,150

KM# 874   500 KURUSH

35.0800 g., 0.9170 Gold 1.0342 oz. AGW **Series:** Monnaie de Luxe **Obv:** Head of Atatürk left within circle of stars, wreath surrounds **Rev:** Country name and date in ornate monogram within circle of stars, floral border surrounds

Date	Mintage	F	VF	XF	Unc	BU
1942	2,949	—	—	BV	1,000	1,050
1943	1,210	—	—	BV	1,000	1,050
1944	1,254	—	—	BV	1,000	1,050
1947	3,699	—	—	BV	1,000	1,050
1950	59	—	—	BV	1,000	1,050
1951	21	—	—	BV	1,000	1,050
1952	26	—	—	BV	1,000	1,050
1953	35	—	—	BV	1,000	1,050
1954	182	—	—	BV	1,000	1,050
1955	14	—	—	BV	1,000	1,050
1956	13	—	—	BV	1,000	1,050
1957	68	—	—	BV	1,000	1,050
1958	121	—	—	BV	1,000	1,050

Date	Mintage	F	VF	XF	Unc	BU
1959	294	—	—	BV	1,000	1,050
1960	208	—	—	BV	1,000	1,050
1961	619	—	—	BV	1,000	1,050
1962	1,228	—	—	BV	1,000	1,050
1963	1,985	—	—	BV	1,000	1,050
1964	2,787	—	—	BV	1,000	1,050
1965	4,631	—	—	BV	1,000	1,050
1966	5,572	—	—	BV	1,000	1,050
1967	6,637	—	—	BV	1,000	1,050
1968	5,983	—	—	BV	1,000	1,050
1969	7,152	—	—	BV	1,000	1,050
1970	11,000	—	—	BV	1,000	1,050
1971	15,000	—	—	BV	1,000	1,050
1972	15,000	—	—	BV	1,000	1,050
1973	7,939	—	—	BV	1,000	1,050
1974	5,412	—	—	BV	1,000	1,050
1975	6,205	—	—	BV	1,000	1,050
1976	11,000	—	—	BV	1,000	1,050
1977	6,931	—	—	BV	1,000	1,050
1978	5,740	—	—	BV	1,000	1,050
1980	—	—	—	BV	1,000	1,050

KM# 879   500 KURUSH

35.0800 g., 0.9170 Gold 1.0342 oz. AGW **Series:** Monnaie de Luxe **Obv:** Head of Ismet Inonu left within circle of stars **Rev:** Country name and date in ornate monogram within circle of stars, floral border surrounds

Date	Mintage	F	VF	XF	Unc	BU
1943	—	—	—	BV	1,100	1,150

Note: Mintage included in KM#874.

| 1944 | — | — | — | BV | 1,100 | 1,150 |

Note: Mintage included in KM#874.

1945	115	—	—	BV	1,100	1,150
1946	298	—	—	BV	1,100	1,150
1947	—	—	—	BV	1,100	1,150

Note: Mintage included in KM#874.

| 1948 | 40 | — | — | BV | 1,100 | 1,150 |

PATTERNS
Including off metal strikes

KM#	Date	Mintage	Identification	Mkt Val
Pn9	1948	—	5 Kurus. Brass. KM#887. Prev. KM#Pn2.	500
Pn10	1948	—	10 Kurus. Brass. KM#888. Prev. KM#Pn3.	500

PIEFORTS

KM#	Date	Mintage	Identification	Mkt Val
P1	1981	2,500	500 Lira. 0.9250 Silver. KM#931	165
P2	1981	1,200	3000 Lira. 0.9250 Silver. KM#948	180
P3	1981	—	30000 Lira. Gold. KM#955	1,350
P4	1982	600	3000 Lira. 0.9250 Silver. KM#959	125

MINT SETS

KM#	Date	Mintage	Identification	Issue Price	Mkt Val
MSA1	1949 (8)	—	KM#881-888	—	—
MS1	1962 (7)	—	KM#889a.1, 890.1, 891.1, 892.2, 893.1, 894 (1960), 895	—	—
MSA2	1963 (6)	—	KM#889a.1, 890.1, 891.1, 892.2, 893.1, 895a	—	—
MS2	1964 (6)	—	KM#889a.1, 890.1, 891.1, 892.2, 893.1, 895a	—	4.50
MS3	1965 (6)	—	KM#889a.1, 890.1, 891.1, 892.2, 893.1, 895a	—	4.50
MS4	1966 (6)	—	KM#889a.1, 890.1, 891.1, 892.2, 893.1, 895a	—	4.50
MSA5	1967 (6)	—	KM#889a.2, 890.1, 891.1, 892.3, 893.1, 895a	—	—
MS5	1968 (6)	—	KM#889a.2, 890.1, 891.1, 892.3, 893.1, 895a	—	4.50
MS6	1969 (6)	—	KM#889a.2, 890.2, 891.2, 892.3, 893.2, 895a	—	3.50
MS7	1970 (6)	—	KM#889a.2, 890.2, 891.2, 892.3, 893.2, 895a	—	3.50
MS8	1971 (6)	—	KM#889a.2, 890.2, 891.2, 893.2, 895a, 899	—	3.50

KM#	Date	Mintage	Identification	Issue Price	Mkt Val
MS9	1972 (6)	—	KM#889a.2, 890.2, 891.2, 893.2, 895a, 899	—	3.50
MS10	1973 (7)	—	KM#889a.2, 890.2, 891.2, 892.3, 893.2, 895a, 899	—	3.00
MS11	1974 (7)	—	KM#889a.2, 890.3-893.3, 893.2, 895a, 899	—	3.00
MS12	1975 (7)	—	KM#889a.2, 890a, 891a, 893.2, 895c, 899, 905	—	3.00
MS13	1976 (7)	—	KM#889a.2, 890a, 891a, 893.2, 895c, 899, 905	—	3.00
MS14	1977 (8)	—	KM#889a.2, 890a, 891a, 892.3, 893.2, 895c, 899, 905	—	3.50
MS15	1978 (4)	—	KM#889a.2, 892.3, 893.2, 905	—	3.00
MS16	1979 (4)	—	KM#889a.2, 893.2, 899, 905	—	3.00
MS17	1980 (2)	—	KM#889a.2, 893.2	—	2.00
MS18	1981 (3)	—	KM#943-945	—	3.00
MS19	1982 (3)	—	KM#943, 949.1, 950.1	—	3.00
MS20	1983 (2)	—	KM#949.2, 950.2	—	3.00
MS21	1984 (6)	—	KM#962-967	—	5.50
MS22	1985 (6)	—	KM#962-964, 966, 967, 975	—	5.00
MS23	1986 (5)	—	KM#963-967	—	4.00
MS24	1989 (7)	9,350	KM#962-964, 975, 987, 988, and medal	2.00	2.00
MS25	1990 (5)	5,300	KM#987-989, 996, 997, and medal	4.00	8.50
MS26	1991 (5)	2,250	KM#987-989, 997, 1015, and mint medal	—	20.00
MS27	1992 (6)	2,240	KM#987-989, 997, 1015, 1025, and mint medal	—	20.00
MS28	1993 (6)	1,750	KM#987-989, 997, 1015, 1025, and mint medal	—	20.00
MS29	1994 (8)	2,500	KM#987-989, 997, 1015, 1025, 1027, 1042, plus mint medal	—	20.00
MS30	1995 (7)	2,500	KM#989, 1015, 1027-1029, 1041, 1043, plus mint medal	—	15.00
MS31	1996 (8)	10,000	KM#989, 1015, 1027-1029, 1041, 1050, 1056, plus mint medal	—	8.00
MS32	1997 (7)	—	KM#989, 1015, 1027.2, 1028, 1029, 1041, 1056, plus silver mint medal	—	20.00
MS33	2000 (3)	10,000	KM#860.1a, 893.1a, 905a Mixed dates; Silver Coin Nostalgia Set	60.00	60.00
MS34	2000 (4)	25,000	KM#881a, 884a, 885a, 886a Mixed dates; Gold Coin Nostalgia Set	325	325
MS35	2000 (7)	10,000	KM#860.1a, 881a, 884a, 885a, 886a, 893.1a, 905a Mixed dates; Silver and Gold Nostalgia Set	350	350

TURKMENISTAN

The Turkmenistan Republic (formerly the Turkmen Soviet Socialist Republic) covers the territory of the Trans-Caspian Region of Turkestan, the Charjiui Vilayet of Bukhara and the part of Khiva located on the right bank of the Oxus. Bordered on the north by the Autonomous Kara-Kalpak Republic (a constituent of Uzbekistan), by Iran and Afghanistan on the south, by the Usbek Republic on the east and the Caspian Sea on the west. It has an area of 186,400 sq. mi. (488,100 sq. km.) and a population of 3.5 million. Capital: Ashkhabad (formerly Poltoratsk). Main occupation is agricultural products including cotton and maize. It is rich in minerals, oil, coal, sulphur and salt and is also famous for its carpets, Turkoman horses and Karakui sheep.

The Turkomans arrived in Trancaspia as nomadic Seluk Turks in the 11th century. It often became subjected to one of the neighboring states. Late in the 19th century the Czarist Russians invaded with their first victory at Kyzyl Arvat in 1877, arriving in Ashkhabad in 1882 resulting in submission of the Turkmen tribes. By March 18,1884 the Transcaspian province of Russian Turkestan was formed. During WW I the Czarist government tried to conscript the Turkmen; this led to a revolt in Oct. 1916 under the leadership of Aziz Chapykov. In 1918 the Turks captured Baku from the Red army and the British sent a contingent to Merv to prevent a German-Turkish offensive toward Afghanistan and India. In mid-1919 a Bureau of Turkestan Moslem Communist Organization was formed in Moscow hoping to develop one large republic including all surrounding Turkic areas within a Soviet federation. A Turkestan Autonomous Soviet Socialist Republic was formed and plans to partition Turkestan into five republics according to the principle of nationalities was quickly implemented by Joseph Stalin. On Oct. 27, 1924 Turkmenistan became a Soviet Socialist Republic and was accepted as a member of the U.S.S.R. on Jan. 29, 1925. The Bureau of T.M.C.O. was disbanded in 1934. In Aug. 1990 the Turkmen Supreme Soviet adopted a declaration of sovereignty followed by a declaration of independence in Oct. 1991 joining the Commonwealth of Independent States in Dec. A new constitution was adopted in 1992 providing for an executive presidency.

REPUBLIC

STANDARD COINAGE

100 Tenge = 1 Manat

KM# 1   TENGE
1.9000 g., Copper Plated Steel, 16 mm.   **Obv:** Value in center of flower-like design within circle **Rev:** Head of President Saparmyrat Nyyazow left **Edge:** Plain

Date	Mintage	F	VF	XF	Unc	BU
1993	—	—	—	—	0.25	0.35

KM# 2   5 TENGE
3.0000 g., Copper Plated Steel, 19.5 mm.   **Obv:** Value in center of flower-like design within circle **Rev:** Head of President Saparmyrat Nyyazow left **Edge:** Plain

Date	Mintage	F	VF	XF	Unc	BU
1993	—	—	—	—	0.35	0.45

KM# 3   10 TENGE
4.5000 g., Copper Plated Steel, 22.5 mm.   **Obv:** Value in center of designs within circle **Rev:** Head of President Saparmyrat Nyyazow left **Edge:** Plain

Date	Mintage	F	VF	XF	Unc	BU
1993	—	—	—	—	0.60	0.75

KM# 4   20 TENGE
3.6000 g., Nickel Plated Steel, 20.9 mm.   **Obv:** Value within ornate circle **Rev:** Head of President Saparmyrat Nyyazow left **Edge:** Plain

Date	Mintage	F	VF	XF	Unc	BU
1993	—	—	—	—	1.25	1.50

KM# 5   50 TENGE
4.9000 g., Nickel Plated Steel, 24 mm.   **Obv:** Value above animal leaning on horn at right **Rev:** Head of President Saparmyrat Nyyazow left **Edge:** Plain

Date	Mintage	F	VF	XF	Unc	BU
1993	—	—	—	—	2.75	3.00

KM# 6   500 MANAT
28.2800 g., 0.9250 Silver 0.8410 oz. ASW **Series:** Endangered Wildlife **Obv:** Head of President Saparmyrat Nyyazow left **Rev:** Goitered gazelle

Date	Mintage	F	VF	XF	Unc	BU
1996 Proof	Est. 5,000	Value: 70.00				

KM# 7   500 MANAT
28.2800 g., 0.9250 Silver 0.8410 oz. ASW **Series:** Endangered Wildlife **Obv:** Head of President Saparmyrat Nyyazow left **Rev:** Purple Swamphen

Date	Mintage	F	VF	XF	Unc	BU
1996 Proof	Est. 5,000	Value: 70.00				

KM# 8   500 MANAT
28.2800 g., 0.9250 Silver 0.8410 oz. ASW **Series:** Endangered Wildlife **Subject:** Kaspi Ular **Obv:** Head of President Saparmyrat Nyyazow left **Rev:** Pair of Caspian Ular snowcock

Date	Mintage	F	VF	XF	Unc	BU
1996 Proof	Est. 5,000	Value: 70.00				

KM# 9   500 MANAT
28.2800 g., 0.9250 Silver 0.8410 oz. ASW **Series:** Endangered Wildlife **Subject:** Manul **Obv:** Head of President Saparmyrat Nyyazow left **Rev:** Pallas' cat

Date	Mintage	F	VF	XF	Unc	BU
1996 Proof	Est. 5,000	Value: 78.00				

KM# 10   500 MANAT
28.2800 g., 0.9250 Silver 0.8410 oz. ASW **Series:** Endangered Wildlife **Subject:** Gulan **Obv:** Head of President Saparmyrat Nyyazow left **Rev:** Asian wild ass

Date	Mintage	F	VF	XF	Unc	BU
1996 Proof	Est. 5,000	Value: 75.00				

KM# 11   500 MANAT
28.2800 g., 0.9250 Silver 0.8410 oz. ASW **Series:** Endangered Wildlife **Obv:** Head of President Saparmyrat Nyyazow left **Rev:** Turkmenistan Gecko

Date	Mintage	F	VF	XF	Unc	BU
1996 Proof	Est. 5,000	Value: 75.00				

KM# 12   500 MANAT
Nickel Clad Steel **Obv:** Head of President Saparmyrat Nyyazow left **Rev:** Crown and value within circle **Edge:** Reeded

Date	Mintage	F	VF	XF	Unc	BU
1999	Est. 5,000	—	—	—	1.25	1.50

KM# 14   500 MANAT
28.2800 g., 0.9250 Silver 0.8410 oz. ASW **Series:** Wildlife Series **Subject:** Jaculus Turkmenicus **Obv:** Head of President Saparmyrat Nyyazow left **Rev:** Two Turkmenic Jerboa **Edge:** Reeded

Date	Mintage	F	VF	XF	Unc	BU
1999 Proof	Est. 5,000	Value: 70.00				

KM# 15   500 MANAT
28.2800 g., 0.9250 Silver 0.8410 oz. ASW **Series:** Wildlife
Series **Subject:** Chlamydotis Undulata **Obv:** Head of President
Saparmyrat Nyyazow left **Rev:** Two Houbara Bustards

Date	Mintage	F	VF	XF	Unc	BU
1999 Proof	Est. 5,000	Value: 70.00				

KM# 16   500 MANAT
28.2800 g., 0.9250 Silver 0.8410 oz. ASW **Series:** Wildlife
Series **Subject:** Falco cherrug **Obv:** Head of President
Saparmyrat Nyyazow left **Rev:** Saker falcon on branch and
falconer at left

Date	Mintage	F	VF	XF	Unc	BU
1999 Proof	Est. 5,000	Value: 70.00				

KM# 17   500 MANAT
28.2800 g., 0.9250 Silver 0.8410 oz. ASW **Series:** Wildlife
Series **Subject:** Naja Oxiana **Obv:** Head of President Saparmyrat
Nyyazow left **Rev:** Cobra

Date	Mintage	F	VF	XF	Unc	BU
1999 Proof	Est. 5,000	Value: 75.00				

KM# 18   500 MANAT
28.2800 g., 0.9250 Silver 0.8410 oz. ASW **Series:** Wildlife
Series **Subject:** Felis Caracal **Obv:** Head of President
Saparmyrat Nyyazow left **Rev:** Seated caracal

Date	Mintage	F	VF	XF	Unc	BU
1999 Proof	Est. 5,000	Value: 75.00				

KM# 19   500 MANAT
28.2800 g., 0.9250 Silver 0.8410 oz. ASW **Series:** Wildlife
Series **Subject:** Panthera tigris **Obv:** Head of President
Saparmyrat Nyyazow left **Rev:** Tiger

Date	Mintage	F	VF	XF	Unc	BU
1999 Proof	Est. 5,000	Value: 75.00				

KM# 20   500 MANAT
28.2800 g., 0.9250 Silver 0.8410 oz. ASW, 38.5 mm.
Subject: 5th Anniversary of Neutrality **Obv:** Head of President
Saparmyrat Nyyazow left within circle **Rev:** Map and monument
within sprigs and circle **Edge:** Reeded

Date	Mintage	F	VF	XF	Unc	BU
ND Proof	5,000	Value: 45.00				

KM# 21   500 MANAT
28.2800 g., 0.9250 Silver 0.8410 oz. ASW, 38.5 mm.
Subject: 5th Anniversary of Neutrality **Obv:** Head of President
Saparmyrat Nyyazow left within circle **Rev:** Astanbaba
Mausoleum within circle **Edge:** Reeded

Date	Mintage	F	VF	XF	Unc	BU
2000 Proof	5,000	Value: 55.00				

KM# 22   500 MANAT
28.2800 g., 0.9250 Silver 0.8410 oz. ASW, 38.5 mm. **Obv:** Head
of President Saparmyrat Nyyazow left within circle **Rev:** Square
based Soltan Sanjar Mausoleum within circle **Edge:** Reeded

Date	Mintage	F	VF	XF	Unc	BU
2000 Proof	5,000	Value: 55.00				

KM# 23   500 MANAT
28.2800 g., 0.9250 Silver 0.8410 oz. ASW, 38.5 mm. **Obv:** Head
of President Saparmyrat Nyyazow left within circle **Rev:** Shirkebir
Mausoleum - Mosque within circle **Edge:** Reeded

Date	Mintage	F	VF	XF	Unc	BU
2000 Proof	5,000	Value: 55.00				

KM# 24   500 MANAT
28.2800 g., 0.9250 Silver 0.8410 oz. ASW, 38.5 mm. **Obv:** Head
left within circle **Rev:** Nisa Fortress, statue with mountaintop in
background **Edge:** Reeded

Date	Mintage	F	VF	XF	Unc	BU
2000 Proof	5,000	Value: 55.00				

KM# 25   500 MANAT
28.2800 g., 0.9250 Silver 0.8410 oz. ASW, 38.5 mm.
Subject: 10th Anniversary of Independence **Obv:** Head of
President Saparmyrat Nyyazow left within circle **Rev:** Monument
divides dates within circle **Edge:** Reeded

Date	Mintage	F	VF	XF	Unc	BU
2000 Proof	5,000	Value: 55.00				

KM# 13   1000 MANAT
Nickel Clad Steel **Obv:** Head of President Saparmyrat Nyyazow
left within circle **Rev:** Value within circle **Edge:** Reeded

Date	Mintage	F	VF	XF	Unc	BU
1999 Proof	—				2.50	3.00

PROOF SETS

KM#	Date	Mintage	Identification	Issue Price	Mkt Val
PS1	1996 (6)	5,000	KM#6-11	—	370

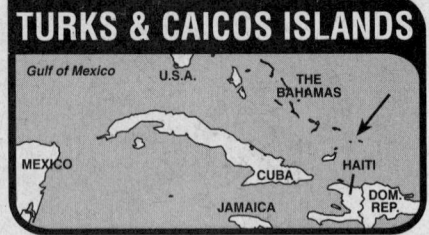

TURKS & CAICOS ISLANDS

The Colony of the Turks and Caicos Islands, a British colony situated in the West Indies at the eastern end of the Bahama Islands, has an area of 166 sq. mi. (430 sq.km.) and a population of *10,000. Capital: Cockburn Town, on Grand Turk. The principal industry of the colony is the production of salt, which is gathered by raking. Salt, crayfish, and conch shells are exported.

The Turks and Caicos Islands were discovered by Juan Ponce de Leon in 1512, but were not settled until 1678 when Bermudians arrived to rake salt from the salt ponds. The Spanish drove the British settlers from the island in 1710, during the long War of the Spanish Succession. They returned and throughout the remaining years of the war repulsed repeated attacks by France and Spain. In 1799 the islands were granted representation in the Bahamian assembly, but in 1848, on petition of the inhabitants, they were made a separate colony under Jamaica. They were annexed by Jamaica in 1873 and remained a dependency until 1959 when they became a unit territory of the Federation of the West Indies. When the Federation was dissolved in 1962, the Turks and Caicos Islands became a separate Crown Colony.

RULER
British

MONETARY SYSTEM
100 Cents = 1 East Caribbean Dollar
1 Crown = 1 Dollar U.S.A.

BRITISH COLONY

STANDARD COINAGE

KM# 51   1/4 CROWN
Copper-Nickel, 24.3 mm.   **Ruler:** Elizabeth II **Obv:** Young bust right **Rev:** Spiny Lobster

Date	Mintage	F	VF	XF	Unc	BU
1981	—	—	1.00	2.00	4.00	6.00

KM# 52   1/2 CROWN
11.3500 g., Copper-Nickel, 30.65 mm.   **Ruler:** Elizabeth II **Obv:** Young bust right **Rev:** Windmill

Date	Mintage	F	VF	XF	Unc	BU
1981	—	—	1.00	2.00	3.50	5.00

KM# 1   CROWN
Copper-Nickel, 38.5 mm.   **Ruler:** Elizabeth II **Obv:** Young bust right **Rev:** National arms

Date	Mintage	F	VF	XF	Unc	BU
1969	50,000	2.00	3.00	4.50	5.50	7.00
1969 Proof	6,000	Value: 12.50				

KM# 5   CROWN
Copper-Nickel, 36 mm.   **Ruler:** Elizabeth II **Obv:** Young bust right **Rev:** Map **Edge:** REDEEMABLE AT TURKS AND CAICOS FOR US CURRENCY

Date	Mintage	F	VF	XF	Unc	BU
1975 Matte	590	—	—	—	12.00	14.00
1975 Proof	1,370	Value: 13.50				
1976	1,960	—	—	—	7.00	9.00
1976 Proof	2,270	Value: 13.50				
1977 Proof	1,420	Value: 13.50				

KM# 60   CROWN
Copper-Nickel, 38.5 mm.   **Ruler:** Elizabeth II **Subject:** Prince Andrew's Marriage **Obv:** Young bust right **Rev:** Conjoined heads right

Date	Mintage	F	VF	XF	Unc	BU
1986	·20,000	—	—	2.00	4.50	6.50

KM# 60a   CROWN
28.2800 g., 0.9250 Silver 0.8410 oz. ASW, 38.5 mm. **Ruler:** Elizabeth II **Subject:** Prince Andrew's Marriage **Obv:** Young bust right **Rev:** Conjoined heads right

Date	Mintage	F	VF	XF	Unc	BU
1986 Proof	5,000	Value: 14.50				

KM# 122   CROWN
Copper-Nickel, 38.5 mm.   **Ruler:** Elizabeth II **Obv:** Young bust right **Rev:** National arms

Date	Mintage	F	VF	XF	Unc	BU
1986	—	—	—	2.00	4.00	5.00

KM# 64   CROWN
Copper-Nickel, 38.5 mm.   **Ruler:** Elizabeth II **Series:** World Wildlife Fund **Obv:** Young bust right **Rev:** Turk's Rock Iguana within circle

Date	Mintage	F	VF	XF	Unc	BU
1988	—	—	—	3.00	7.50	14.00

KM# 64a   CROWN
28.2800 g., 0.9250 Silver 0.8410 oz. ASW, 38.5 mm.   **Ruler:** Elizabeth II **Series:** World Wildlife Fund **Obv:** Young bust right **Rev:** Turk's Rock Iguana within circle

Date	Mintage	F	VF	XF	Unc	BU
1988 Proof	Est. 25,000	Value: 27.50				

KM# 66   CROWN
Copper-Nickel, 38.5 mm.   **Ruler:** Elizabeth II **Subject:** Queen Mother's 90th Birthday **Obv:** Crowned head right **Rev:** Crowned monogram flanked by thistle stems

Date	Mintage	F	VF	XF	Unc	BU
ND(1990)	—	—	—	2.00	5.50	6.50

KM# 66a   CROWN
28.2800 g., 0.9250 Silver 0.8410 oz. ASW, 38.5 mm. **Ruler:** Elizabeth II **Subject:** Queen Mother's 90th Birthday **Obv:** Crowned head right **Rev:** Crowned monogram flanked by thistle stems

Date	Mintage	F	VF	XF	Unc	BU
ND(1990) Proof	Est. 10,000	Value: 22.50				

KM# 74   CROWN
Copper-Nickel   **Ruler:** Elizabeth II **Subject:** Royal Birthdays **Obv:** Crowned head right **Rev:** Conjoined heads of Queen Elizabeth II and Prince Philip facing

Date	Mintage	F	VF	XF	Unc	BU
1991	—	—	—	2.00	4.50	6.50

KM# 74a   CROWN
31.1200 g., 0.9990 Silver 0.9995 oz. ASW, 39.1 mm.   **Ruler:** Elizabeth II **Subject:** Royal Birthdays **Obv:** Crowned head right **Rev:** Conjoined heads of Queen Elizabeth II and Prince Philip facing **Edge:** Reeded with plain section containing fineness

Date	Mintage	F	VF	XF	Unc	BU
1991 Proof	—	Value: 27.50				

KM# 76   CROWN
Copper-Nickel, 39.25 mm.   **Ruler:** Elizabeth II **Subject:** 10th Wedding Anniversary - Prince and Princess of Wales **Obv:** Crowned head right **Rev:** Head of Princess Diana facing **Edge:** Reeded

Date	Mintage	F	VF	XF	Unc	BU
1991	—	—	—	2.00	4.00	5.00

KM# 76a   CROWN
31.1200 g., 0.9990 Silver 0.9995 oz. ASW, 39.1 mm. **Ruler:** Elizabeth II **Subject:** 10th Wedding Anniversary - Prince Charles and Princess Diana **Obv:** Crowned head right **Rev:** Head of Princess Diana facing **Edge:** Reeded with plain section containing fineness

Date	Mintage	F	VF	XF	Unc	BU
1991 Proof	—	Value: 40.00				

KM# 121 CROWN
Copper-Nickel, 39.25 mm. **Ruler:** Elizabeth II **Subject:** 10th Wedding Anniversary - Prince and Princess of Wales **Obv:** Crowned head right **Rev:** Head of Prince Charles facing **Edge:** Reeded

Date	Mintage	F	VF	XF	Unc	BU
1991	—	—	—	2.00	4.00	5.00

KM# 121a CROWN
31.2100 g., 0.9250 Silver 0.9281 oz. ASW **Ruler:** Elizabeth II **Subject:** 10th Wedding Anniversary of Prince Charles and Princess Diana **Obv:** Crowned head right **Rev:** Head of Prince Charles facing

Date	Mintage	F	VF	XF	Unc	BU
1991 Proof	—	Value: 35.00				

KM# 143 DOLLAR
Copper-Nickel **Ruler:** Elizabeth II **Series:** Steam Locomotive **Subject:** City of Truro **Obv:** Crowned head right **Rev:** Locomotive train **Note:** Similar to 20 Dollars, KM#145.

Date	Mintage	F	VF	XF	Unc	BU
1996	—	—	—	2.00	5.00	6.50

KM# 146 DOLLAR
Copper-Nickel **Ruler:** Elizabeth II **Series:** Steam Locomotive **Subject:** Flying Scotsman **Obv:** Crowned head right **Rev:** Locomotive train **Note:** Similar to 20 Dollars, KM#148.

Date	Mintage	F	VF	XF	Unc	BU
1996	—	—	—	2.00	5.00	6.50

KM# 149 DOLLAR
Copper-Nickel **Ruler:** Elizabeth II **Series:** Steam Locomotive **Subject:** Rocket **Obv:** Crowned head right **Rev:** Locomotive train **Note:** Similar to 20 Dollars, KM#151.

Date	Mintage	F	VF	XF	Unc	BU
1996	—	—	—	2.00	5.00	6.50

KM# 152 DOLLAR
Copper-Nickel **Ruler:** Elizabeth II **Series:** Steam Locomotive **Subject:** Evening Star **Obv:** Crowned head right **Rev:** Locomotive train **Note:** Similar to 20 Dollars, KM#154.

Date	Mintage	F	VF	XF	Unc	BU
1996	—	—	—	2.00	5.00	6.50

KM# 155 DOLLAR
Copper-Nickel **Ruler:** Elizabeth II **Series:** Steam Locomotive **Subject:** Mallard **Obv:** Crowned head right **Rev:** Locomotive train **Note:** Similar to 20 Dollars, KM#157.

Date	Mintage	F	VF	XF	Unc	BU
1996	—	—	—	2.00	5.00	6.50

KM# 158 DOLLAR
Copper-Nickel **Ruler:** Elizabeth II **Series:** Steam Locomotive **Subject:** Princess Elizabeth **Obv:** Crowned head right **Rev:** Locomotive train **Note:** Similar to 20 Dollars, KM#160.

Date	Mintage	F	VF	XF	Unc	BU
1996	—	—	—	2.00	5.00	6.50

KM# 161 DOLLAR
Copper-Nickel **Ruler:** Elizabeth II **Series:** Steam Locomotive **Subject:** Southern Pacific Lines - Class GS4 **Obv:** Crowned head right **Rev:** Locomotive train **Note:** Similar to 20 Dollars, KM#163.

Date	Mintage	F	VF	XF	Unc	BU
1996	—	—	—	2.00	5.00	6.50

KM# 164 DOLLAR
Copper-Nickel **Ruler:** Elizabeth II **Series:** Steam Locomotive **Subject:** German States Railway Class 05 **Obv:** Crowned head right **Rev:** Locomotive train **Note:** Similar to 20 Dollars, KM#166.

Date	Mintage	F	VF	XF	Unc	BU
1996	—	—	—	2.00	5.00	6.50

KM# 167 DOLLAR
Copper-Nickel **Ruler:** Elizabeth II **Series:** Steam Locomotive **Subject:** Japanese National Railways Class 62 **Obv:** Crowned head right **Rev:** Locomotive train **Note:** Similar to 20 Dollars, KM#169.

Date	Mintage	F	VF	XF	Unc	BU
1996	—	—	—	2.00	5.00	6.50

KM# 170 DOLLAR
Copper-Nickel **Ruler:** Elizabeth II **Series:** Steam Locomotive **Subject:** Chinese State Railways Class RM **Obv:** Crowned head right **Rev:** Locomotive train **Note:** Similar to 20 Dollars, KM#171.

Date	Mintage	F	VF	XF	Unc	BU
1996	—	—	—	2.00	5.00	6.50

KM# 6 5 CROWNS
24.2400 g., 0.5000 Silver 0.3897 oz. ASW **Ruler:** Elizabeth II **Obv:** Young bust right **Rev:** Turks-head cactus

Date	Mintage	F	VF	XF	Unc	BU
1975 Matte	440		—	9.00	18.00	20.00
1975 Proof	1,320	Value: 13.50				
1976	1,760		—	6.50	11.50	13.50
1976 Proof	2,220	Value: 11.50				
1977 Proof	1,370	Value: 13.50				

KM# 47 5 CROWNS
14.5800 g., 0.5000 Silver 0.2344 oz. ASW **Ruler:** Elizabeth II **Subject:** Lord Mountbatten **Obv:** Young bust right **Rev:** Uniformed head left above crossed flag and sword

Date	Mintage	F	VF	XF	Unc	BU
1980 Proof	—	Value: 9.50				

KM# 75 5 CROWNS
Copper-Nickel **Ruler:** Elizabeth II **Subject:** Discovery of America **Obv:** Young bust right **Rev:** Columbus before Ferdinand and Isabella

Date	Mintage	F	VF	XF	Unc	BU
1991	—	—	—	3.00	7.50	9.00

KM# 68 5 CROWNS
Copper-Nickel **Ruler:** Elizabeth II **Series:** Olympics **Obv:** National arms **Rev:** Equestrian and 3 events

Date	Mintage	F	VF	XF	Unc	BU
1992	—	—	—	2.00	4.50	6.50

KM# 69 5 CROWNS
Copper-Nickel **Ruler:** Elizabeth II **Series:** Olympics **Obv:** National arms **Rev:** Gymnast on rings and 5 events

Date	Mintage	F	VF	XF	Unc	BU
1992	—	—	—	2.00	4.50	6.50

KM# 70 5 CROWNS
Copper-Nickel **Ruler:** Elizabeth II **Series:** Olympics **Obv:** National arms **Rev:** Weightlifting and 3 events

Date	Mintage	F	VF	XF	Unc	BU
1992	—	—	—	2.00	4.50	6.50

KM# 71 5 CROWNS
Copper-Nickel **Ruler:** Elizabeth II **Series:** Olympics **Obv:** National arms **Rev:** Rifle shooting and 3 events

Date	Mintage	F	VF	XF	Unc	BU
1992	—	—	—	2.00	4.50	6.50

KM# 72 5 CROWNS
Copper-Nickel **Ruler:** Elizabeth II **Series:** Olympics **Obv:** National arms **Rev:** Sail boarding and 3 events

Date	Mintage	F	VF	XF	Unc	BU
1992	—	—	—	2.00	4.50	6.50

KM# 73 5 CROWNS
Copper-Nickel **Ruler:** Elizabeth II **Series:** Olympics **Obv:** National arms **Rev:** Ski jumper and 4 events

Date	Mintage	F	VF	XF	Unc	BU
1992	—	—	—	2.00	4.50	6.50

KM# 77 5 CROWNS
Copper-Nickel **Ruler:** Elizabeth II **Subject:** 40th Anniversary - Reign of Elizabeth II **Obv:** National arms **Rev:** Crowned bust facing

Date	Mintage	F	VF	XF	Unc	BU
1992	—	—	—	3.00	6.75	7.25

KM# 77a 5 CROWNS
28.0400 g., 0.9250 Silver 0.8339 oz. ASW **Ruler:** Elizabeth II
Subject: 40th Anniversary - Reign of Elizabeth II **Obv:** National
arms **Rev:** Crowned bust facing

Date	Mintage	F	VF	XF	Unc	BU
1992 Proof	—	Value: 40.00				

KM# 84 5 CROWNS
Copper-Nickel **Ruler:** Elizabeth II **Subject:** 40th Anniversary -
Reign of Elizabeth II **Obv:** Crowned head right **Rev:** Conjoined
busts of Queen Elizabeth II and Prince Philip facing

Date	Mintage	F	VF	XF	Unc	BU
1992	—	—	—	3.00	6.75	7.25

KM# 84a 5 CROWNS
28.0400 g., 0.9250 Silver 0.8339 oz. ASW **Ruler:** Elizabeth II
Subject: 40th Anniversary - Reign of Elizabeth II **Obv:** Crowned
head right **Rev:** Conjoined busts of Queen Elizabeth II and Prince
Philip facing

Date	Mintage	F	VF	XF	Unc	BU
1992 Proof	—	Value: 40.00				

KM# 85 5 CROWNS
Copper-Nickel **Ruler:** Elizabeth II **Subject:** 40th Anniversary -
Reign of Elizabeth II **Obv:** Crowned head right **Rev:** Head of King
George VI facing

Date	Mintage	F	VF	XF	Unc	BU
1992	—	—	—	3.00	6.75	7.25

KM# 85a 5 CRQWNS
28.0400 g., 0.9250 Silver 0.8339 oz. ASW **Ruler:** Elizabeth II
Subject: 40th Anniversary - Reign of Elizabeth II **Obv:** Crowned
head right **Rev:** Head of King George VI facing

Date	Mintage	F	VF	XF	Unc	BU
1992 Proof	—	Value: 40.00				

KM# 86 5 CROWNS
Copper-Nickel **Ruler:** Elizabeth II **Subject:** 40th Anniversary -
Reign of Elizabeth II **Obv:** Crowned head right **Rev:** Windsor Castle

Date	Mintage	F	VF	XF	Unc	BU
1992	—	—	—	3.00	6.75	7.25

KM# 86a 5 CROWNS
28.2800 g., 0.9250 Silver 0.8410 oz. ASW **Ruler:** Elizabeth II
Subject: 40th Anniversary - Reign of Elizabeth II **Obv:** Crowned
head right **Rev:** Windsor Castle

Date	Mintage	F	VF	XF	Unc	BU
1992 Proof	—	Value: 40.00				

KM# 87 5 CROWNS
Copper-Nickel **Ruler:** Elizabeth II **Subject:** World Cup '94
Obv: Crowned head right **Rev:** Jules Rimet and trophy

Date	Mintage	F	VF	XF	Unc	BU
ND(1993)	—	—	—	3.00	6.50	7.50

KM# 88 5 CROWNS
Copper-Nickel **Ruler:** Elizabeth II **Subject:** World Cup '94 -
Uruguay Winners **Obv:** Crowned head right **Rev:** Soccer players
shaking hands

Date	Mintage	F	VF	XF	Unc	BU
ND(1993)	—	—	—	3.00	6.50	7.50

KM# 89 5 CROWNS
Copper-Nickel **Ruler:** Elizabeth II **Subject:** World Cup '94 - Italy
Winners **Obv:** Crowned head right **Rev:** Dino Zoff holding trophy

Date	Mintage	F	VF	XF	Unc	BU
ND(1993)	—	—	—	3.00	6.50	7.50

KM# 90 5 CROWNS
Copper-Nickel **Ruler:** Elizabeth II **Subject:** World Cup '94 - West
Germany winners **Obv:** Crowned head right **Rev:** Franz
Beckenbauer

Date	Mintage	F	VF	XF	Unc	BU
ND(1993)	—	—	—	3.00	6.50	7.50

KM# 91 5 CROWNS
Copper-Nickel **Ruler:** Elizabeth II **Subject:** World Cup '94 - Brazil
Winners **Obv:** Crowned head right **Rev:** Pelé with arm raised

Date	Mintage	F	VF	XF	Unc	BU
ND(1993)	—	—	—	3.00	6.50	7.50

KM# 92 5 CROWNS
Copper-Nickel **Ruler:** Elizabeth II **Subject:** World Cup '94 -
England Winners **Obv:** Crowned head right **Rev:** Bobby Moore
with trophy on teammates shoulders

Date	Mintage	F	VF	XF	Unc	BU
ND(1993)	—	—	—	3.00	6.50	7.50

KM# 93 5 CROWNS
Copper-Nickel **Ruler:** Elizabeth II **Subject:** World Cup '94 -
Argentina winners **Obv:** Crowned head right **Rev:** Mario Kempes
running right

Date	Mintage	F	VF	XF	Unc	BU
ND(1993)	—	—	—	3.00	6.50	7.50

KM# 94 5 CROWNS
Copper-Nickel **Ruler:** Elizabeth II **Subject:** World Cup '94 - USA
Host **Obv:** Crowned head right **Rev:** Stylized flag and trophy

Date	Mintage	F	VF	XF	Unc	BU
ND(1993)	—	—	—	3.00	6.50	7.50

KM# 103 5 CROWNS
Copper-Nickel **Ruler:** Elizabeth II **Subject:** 40th Anniversary of
Coronation **Obv:** Crowned head right **Rev:** Westminster Abbey

Date	Mintage	F	VF	XF	Unc	BU
ND(1993)	—	—	—	3.50	7.50	8.50

KM# 104 5 CROWNS
Copper-Nickel **Ruler:** Elizabeth II **Subject:** 40th Anniversary of
Coronation **Obv:** Crowned head right **Rev:** Crown jewels

Date	Mintage	F	VF	XF	Unc	BU
ND(1993)	—	—	—	3.50	7.50	8.50

KM# 105 5 CROWNS
Copper-Nickel **Ruler:** Elizabeth II **Subject:** 40th Anniversary of
Coronation **Obv:** Crowned head right **Rev:** Queen, clergy and
maids of honor

Date	Mintage	F	VF	XF	Unc	BU
ND(1993)	—	—	—	3.50	7.50	8.50

KM# 106   5 CROWNS
Copper-Nickel **Ruler:** Elizabeth II **Subject:** 40th Anniversary of Coronation **Obv:** Crowned head right **Rev:** Consort's Homage

Date	Mintage	F	VF	XF	Unc	BU
ND(1993)	—	—	—	3.50	7.50	8.50

KM# 107   5 CROWNS
Copper-Nickel **Ruler:** Elizabeth II **Subject:** 40th Anniversary of Coronation **Obv:** Crowned head right **Rev:** Enthroned Queen

Date	Mintage	F	VF	XF	Unc	BU
ND(1993)	—	—	—	3.50	7.50	8.50

KM# 108   5 CROWNS
Copper-Nickel **Ruler:** Elizabeth II **Subject:** 40th Anniversary of Coronation **Obv:** Crowned head right **Rev:** Queen in coach

Date	Mintage	F	VF	XF	Unc	BU
ND(1993)	—	—	—	3.50	7.50	8.50

KM# 123   5 CROWNS
Copper-Nickel **Ruler:** Elizabeth II **Series:** 1994 Winter Olympics - Lillehammer **Obv:** Crowned head right **Rev:** Speed skater within circle

Date	Mintage	F	VF	XF	Unc	BU
1993 Prooflike	—	—	—	2.00	4.75	5.50

KM# 124   5 CROWNS
Copper-Nickel **Ruler:** Elizabeth II **Series:** 1994 Winter Olympics - Lillehammer **Obv:** Crowned head right **Rev:** Figure skater

Date	Mintage	F	VF	XF	Unc	BU
1993 Prooflike	—	—	—	2.00	4.75	5.50

KM# 125   5 CROWNS
Copper-Nickel **Ruler:** Elizabeth II **Series:** 1994 Winter Olympics - Lillehammer **Obv:** Arms with supporters **Rev:** Hockey player within circle

Date	Mintage	F	VF	XF	Unc	BU
1993 Prooflike	—	—	—	2.00	4.75	5.50

KM# 126   5 CROWNS
Copper-Nickel **Ruler:** Elizabeth II **Series:** 1994 Winter Olympics - Lillehammer **Obv:** Crowned head right **Rev:** Slalom skier within circle

Date	Mintage	F	VF	XF	Unc	BU
1993 Prooflike	—	—	—	2.00	4.75	5.50

KM# 127   5 CROWNS
Copper-Nickel **Ruler:** Elizabeth II **Series:** 1994 Winter Olympics - Lillehammer **Obv:** Crowned head right **Rev:** Ski jumper

Date	Mintage	F	VF	XF	Unc	BU
1993 Prooflike	—	—	—	2.00	4.75	5.50

KM# 128   5 CROWNS
Copper-Nickel **Ruler:** Elizabeth II **Series:** 1994 Winter Olympics - Lillehammer **Obv:** Crowned head right **Rev:** Bobsled and team within circle

Date	Mintage	F	VF	XF	Unc	BU
1993 Prooflike	—	—	—	2.00	4.75	5.50

KM# 177   5 CROWNS
Copper-Nickel **Ruler:** Elizabeth II **Subject:** 25th Anniversary 1969-1994 - Apollo 11 **Obv:** Crowned head right **Rev:** Launching rocket

Date	Mintage	F	VF	XF	Unc	BU
1993	—	—	—	3.00	6.75	7.50

KM# 178   5 CROWNS
Copper-Nickel **Ruler:** Elizabeth II **Subject:** 25th Anniversary 1969-1994 - Apollo 11 **Obv:** Crowned head right **Rev:** Lunar landing

Date	Mintage	F	VF	XF	Unc	BU
1993	—	—	—	3.00	6.75	7.50

KM# 179   5 CROWNS
Copper-Nickel **Ruler:** Elizabeth II **Subject:** 25th Anniversary 1969-1994 - Apollo 11 **Obv:** Crowned head right **Rev:** Astronaut descending ladder

Date	Mintage	F	VF	XF	Unc	BU
1993	—	—	—	3.00	6.75	7.50

KM# 181   5 CROWNS
Copper-Nickel **Ruler:** Elizabeth II **Subject:** 25th Anniversary 1969-1994 - Apollo 11 **Obv:** Crowned head right **Rev:** Astronaut walking on moon

Date	Mintage	F	VF	XF	Unc	BU
1993	—	—	—	3.00	6.75	7.50

KM# 182   5 CROWNS
Copper-Nickel **Ruler:** Elizabeth II **Subject:** 25th Anniversary 1969-1994 - Apollo 11 **Obv:** Crowned head right **Rev:** Ocean recovery

Date	Mintage	F	VF	XF	Unc	BU
1993	—	—	—	3.00	6.75	7.50

KM# 180   5 CROWNS
Copper-Nickel **Ruler:** Elizabeth II **Subject:** 25th Anniversary 1969-1994 - Apollo 11 **Obv:** Crowned head right **Rev:** Astronauts raising flag on moon

Date	Mintage	F	VF	XF	Unc	BU
1993	—	—	—	3.00	6.75	7.50

KM# 234   5 CROWNS
3.1104 g., 0.9995 Platinum 0.0999 oz. APW, 16.5 mm.
Ruler: Elizabeth II **Subject:** ANA Salute to Coin Collecting **Obv:** Crowned head right **Rev:** Astronaut on the moon **Edge:** Reeded

Date	Mintage	F	VF	XF	Unc	BU
1994 Proof	200	Value: 225				

KM# 132 5 CROWNS

Copper-Nickel **Ruler:** Elizabeth II **Subject:** 25th Anniversary 1969-1994 - Apollo 11 **Obv:** Crowned head right **Rev:** Salute to ANA and coin collecting **Edge:** PEACE on a smooth section of alternating smooth and reeded

Date	Mintage	F	VF	XF	Unc	BU
1994 Prooflike	10,000	—	—	5.00	10.00	12.00

KM# 176 5 CROWNS

Copper-Nickel **Ruler:** Elizabeth II **Subject:** 50th Anniversary - Normandy Landing **Obv:** Crowned head right **Rev:** Bust of Dwight D. Eisenhower right

Date	Mintage	F	VF	XF	Unc	BU
1994	—	—	—	4.50	9.50	11.00

KM# 136 5 CROWNS

27.2000 g., Copper-Nickel, 39.14 mm. **Ruler:** Elizabeth II **Subject:** 50th Anniversary - VE Day **Obv:** National arms **Rev:** London, Washington and Paris **Edge:** Reeded

Date	Mintage	F	VF	XF	Unc	BU
1995	—	—	—	3.00	7.50	8.50

KM# 188 5 CROWNS

10.0000 g., 0.9990 Silver 0.3212 oz. ASW **Ruler:** Elizabeth II **Series:** XXVI Summer Olympics **Obv:** Crowned head right **Rev:** Hurdlers

Date	Mintage	F	VF	XF	Unc	BU
1995 Proof	—	Value: 12.50				

KM# 190 5 CROWNS

10.0000 g., 0.9990 Silver 0.3212 oz. ASW **Ruler:** Elizabeth II **Series:** XXVI Summer Olympics **Obv:** Crowned head right **Rev:** Cyclist

Date	Mintage	F	VF	XF	Unc	BU
1995 Proof	—	Value: 12.50				

KM# 173 5 CROWNS

Copper-Nickel **Ruler:** Elizabeth II **Subject:** 50th Anniversary - Normandy Landing **Obv:** Crowned head right **Rev:** Bust of Sir Bertram II Ramsay left

Date	Mintage	F	VF	XF	Unc	BU
1994	—	—	—	4.50	9.50	11.00

KM# 133 5 CROWNS

27.2000 g., Copper-Nickel, 39.14 mm. **Ruler:** Elizabeth II **Subject:** 50th Anniversary - VE Day **Obv:** National arms **Rev:** Heads of Churchill, Roosevelt and Stalin facing **Edge:** Reeded

Date	Mintage	F	VF	XF	Unc	BU
1995	—	—	—	4.50	9.50	11.00

KM# 192 5 CROWNS

10.0000 g., 0.9990 Silver 0.3212 oz. ASW **Ruler:** Elizabeth II **Series:** XXVI Summer Olympics **Obv:** Crowned head right **Rev:** Fencers

Date	Mintage	F	VF	XF	Unc	BU
1995 Proof	—	Value: 12.50				

KM# 194 5 CROWNS

10.0000 g., 0.9990 Silver 0.3212 oz. ASW **Ruler:** Elizabeth II **Series:** XXVI Summer Olympics **Obv:** Crowned head right **Rev:** Equestrian

Date	Mintage	F	VF	XF	Unc	BU
1995 Proof	—	Value: 12.50				

KM# 196 5 CROWNS

10.0000 g., 0.9990 Silver 0.3212 oz. ASW **Ruler:** George VI **Series:** XXVI Summer Olympics **Obv:** Crowned head right **Rev:** Pole vaulter

Date	Mintage	F	VF	XF	Unc	BU
1995 Proof	—	Value: 12.50				

KM# 174 5 CROWNS

Copper-Nickel **Ruler:** Elizabeth II **Subject:** 50th Aniversary - Normandy Landing **Obv:** Crowned head right **Rev:** Bust of Bernard L. Montgomery left

Date	Mintage	F	VF	XF	Unc	BU
1994	—	—	—	4.50	9.50	11.00

KM# 134 5 CROWNS

27.2000 g., Copper-Nickel, 39.14 mm. **Ruler:** Elizabeth II **Subject:** 50th Anniversary - VE Day **Obv:** National arms **Rev:** Planes **Edge:** Reeded

Date	Mintage	F	VF	XF	Unc	BU
1995	—	—	—	3.00	7.50	8.50

KM# 198 5 CROWNS

10.0000 g., 0.9990 Silver 0.3212 oz. ASW **Ruler:** Elizabeth II **Series:** XXVI Summer Olympics **Obv:** Crowned head right **Rev:** Runners

Date	Mintage	F	VF	XF	Unc	BU
1995 Proof	—	Value: 12.50				

KM# 200 5 CROWNS

10.0000 g., 0.9990 Silver 0.3212 oz. ASW **Ruler:** Elizabeth II **Series:** XXVI Summer Olympics **Obv:** Crowned head right **Rev:** Gymnast

Date	Mintage	F	VF	XF	Unc	BU
1995 Proof	—	Value: 12.50				

KM# 202 5 CROWNS

10.0000 g., 0.9990 Silver 0.3212 oz. ASW **Ruler:** Elizabeth II **Series:** XXVI Summer Olympics **Obv:** Crowned head right **Rev:** Swimmer

Date	Mintage	F	VF	XF	Unc	BU
1995 Proof	—	Value: 12.50				

KM# 204 5 CROWNS

10.0000 g., 0.9990 Silver 0.3212 oz. ASW **Ruler:** Elizabeth II **Series:** XXVI Summer Olympics **Obv:** Crowned head right **Rev:** Diver

Date	Mintage	F	VF	XF	Unc	BU
1995 Proof	—	Value: 12.50				

KM# 206 5 CROWNS

10.0000 g., 0.9990 Silver 0.3212 oz. ASW **Ruler:** Elizabeth II **Series:** XXVI Summer Olympics **Obv:** Crowned head right **Rev:** Sprinter within circle

Date	Mintage	F	VF	XF	Unc	BU
1995 Proof	—	Value: 12.50				

KM# 175 5 CROWNS

Copper-Nickel **Ruler:** Elizabeth II **Subject:** 50th Anniversary - Normandy Landing **Obv:** Crowned head right **Rev:** Bust of Omar N. Bradley right

Date	Mintage	F	VF	XF	Unc	BU
1994	—	—	—	4.50	9.50	11.00

KM# 135 5 CROWNS

27.2000 g., Copper-Nickel, 39.14 mm. **Ruler:** Elizabeth II **Subject:** 50th Anniversary - VE Day **Obv:** National arms **Rev:** U.S. and Soviet troops meet **Edge:** Reeded

Date	Mintage	F	VF	XF	Unc	BU
1995	—	—	—	3.00	7.50	8.50

KM# 225 5 CROWNS
26.2000 g., Brass, 39.1 mm. **Ruler:** Elizabeth II **Subject:** Mother Theresa **Obv:** National arms **Rev:** Bust 1/4 left and star design within globe **Edge:** Reeded

Date	Mintage	F	VF	XF	Unc	BU
1997	—	—	—	—	10.00	12.50

KM# 249 5 CROWNS
Copper-Nickel Plated Bronze **Ruler:** Elizabeth II **Subject:** 50th Wedding Anniversary **Rev:** Conjoined heads of Elizabeth and Prince Philip right

Date	Mintage	F	VF	XF	Unc	BU
1997	—	—	—	—	15.00	—

KM# 238 5 CROWNS
1.5600 g., 0.9999 Gold 0.0501 oz. AGW, 13.7 mm.
Ruler: Elizabeth II **Obv:** Crowned head right **Rev:** Two Bottle-nosed Dolphins **Edge:** Reeded

Date	Mintage	F	VF	XF	Unc	BU
1998 Proof	—	Value: 55.00				

KM# 232 5 CROWNS
26.4300 g., Copper-Nickel, 39.2 mm. **Ruler:** Elizabeth II **Subject:** Year of the Tiger **Obv:** Crowned head right **Rev:** Stylized tiger within circle **Edge:** Reeded

Date	Mintage	F	VF	XF	Unc	BU
1998	—	—	—	3.00	7.50	8.50

KM# 144 5 DOLLARS
10.0000 g., 0.9990 Silver 0.3212 oz. ASW **Ruler:** Elizabeth II **Series:** Steam Locomotive **Subject:** City of Truro **Obv:** Crowned head right **Rev:** Locomotive train **Note:** Similar to 20 Dollars, KM#145.

Date	Mintage	F	VF	XF	Unc	BU
1996 Proof	Est. 25,000	Value: 22.00				

KM# 147 5 DOLLARS
10.0000 g., 0.9990 Silver 0.3212 oz. ASW **Ruler:** Elizabeth II **Series:** Steam Locomotive **Subject:** Flying Scotsman **Obv:** Crowned head right **Rev:** Locomotive train **Note:** Similar to 20 Dollars, KM#148.

Date	Mintage	F	VF	XF	Unc	BU
1996 Proof	Est. 25,000	Value: 22.00				

KM# 150 5 DOLLARS
10.0000 g., 0.9990 Silver 0.3212 oz. ASW **Ruler:** Elizabeth II **Series:** Steam Locomotive **Subject:** Rocket **Obv:** Crowned head right **Rev:** Locomotive train **Note:** Similar to 20 Dollars, KM#151.

Date	Mintage	F	VF	XF	Unc	BU
1996 Proof	Est. 25,000	Value: 22.00				

KM# 153 5 DOLLARS
10.0000 g., 0.9990 Silver 0.3212 oz. ASW **Ruler:** Elizabeth II **Series:** Steam Locomotive **Subject:** Evening Star **Obv:** Crowned head right **Rev:** Locomotive train **Note:** Similar to 20 Dollars, KM#154.

Date	Mintage	F	VF	XF	Unc	BU
1996 Proof	Est. 25,000	Value: 22.00				

KM# 156 5 DOLLARS
10.0000 g., 0.9990 Silver 0.3212 oz. ASW **Ruler:** Elizabeth II **Series:** Steam Locomotive **Subject:** Mallard **Obv:** Crowned head right **Rev:** Locomotive train **Note:** Similar to 20 Dollars, KM#157.

Date	Mintage	F	VF	XF	Unc	BU
1996 Proof	Est. 25,000	Value: 22.00				

KM# 159 5 DOLLARS
10.0000 g., 0.9990 Silver 0.3212 oz. ASW **Ruler:** Elizabeth II **Series:** Steam Locomotive **Subject:** Princess Elizabeth **Obv:** Crowned head right **Rev:** Locomotive train **Note:** Similar to 20 Dollars, KM#160.

Date	Mintage	F	VF	XF	Unc	BU
1996 Proof	Est. 25,000	Value: 22.00				

KM# 162 5 DOLLARS
10.0000 g., 0.9990 Silver 0.3212 oz. ASW **Ruler:** Elizabeth II **Series:** Steam Locomotive **Subject:** Southern Pacific Lines - Class GS4 **Obv:** Crowned head right **Rev:** Locomotive train **Note:** Similar to 20 Dollars, KM#163.

Date	Mintage	F	VF	XF	Unc	BU
1996 Proof	Est. 25,000	Value: 22.00				

KM# 165 5 DOLLARS
10.0000 g., 0.9990 Silver 0.3212 oz. ASW **Ruler:** Elizabeth II **Series:** Steam Locomotive **Subject:** German States Railway - Class 05 **Obv:** Crowned head right **Rev:** Locomotive train **Note:** Similar to 20 Dollars, KM#166.

Date	Mintage	F	VF	XF	Unc	BU
1996 Proof	Est. 25,000	Value: 22.00				

KM# 168 5 DOLLARS
10.0000 g., 0.9990 Silver 0.3212 oz. ASW **Ruler:** Elizabeth II **Series:** Steam Locomotive **Subject:** Japanese National Railways - Class 62 **Obv:** Crowned head right **Rev:** Locomotive train **Note:** Similar to 20 Dollars, KM#169.

Date	Mintage	F	VF	XF	Unc	BU
1996 Proof	Est. 25,000	Value: 22.00				

KM# 171 5 DOLLARS
10.0000 g., 0.9990 Silver 0.3212 oz. ASW **Ruler:** Elizabeth II **Series:** Steam Locomotive **Subject:** Chinese State Railways - Class RM **Obv:** Crowned head right **Rev:** Locomotive train **Note:** Similar to 20 Dollars, KM#172.

Date	Mintage	F	VF	XF	Unc	BU
1996 Proof	Est. 25,000	Value: 22.00				

KM# 7 10 CROWNS
29.9800 g., 0.9250 Silver 0.8916 oz. ASW **Ruler:** Elizabeth II **Subject:** Age of Exploration **Obv:** Young bust right **Rev:** Spacecraft's orbital paths

Date	Mintage	F	VF	XF	Unc	BU
1975 Matte	1,250	—	—	—	16.50	20.00
1975 Proof	2,935	Value: 15.00				

KM# 12 10 CROWNS
29.9800 g., 0.9250 Silver 0.8916 oz. ASW **Ruler:** Elizabeth II **Obv:** Young bust right **Rev:** Salt windmill

Date	Mintage	F	VF	XF	Unc	BU
1976	4,185	—	—	—	14.50	16.50
1976 Proof	2,220	Value: 16.50				
1977 Proof	1,370	Value: 18.00				

KM# 45 10 CROWNS
29.7000 g., 0.9250 Silver 0.8832 oz. ASW **Ruler:** Elizabeth II **Subject:** 10th Anniversary - Prince Charles' Investiture **Obv:** Young bust right **Rev:** Head of Prince Charles left above crossed scepter and sword, with crown and ring

Date	Mintage	F	VF	XF	Unc	BU
1979 Proof	25,000	Value: 14.50				

KM# 48 10 CROWNS
23.3300 g., 0.5000 Silver 0.3750 oz. ASW **Ruler:** Elizabeth II **Subject:** Lord Mountbatten **Obv:** Young bust right **Rev:** Uniformed bust right and crowned shield

Date	Mintage	F	VF	XF	Unc	BU
1980 Proof	—	Value: 13.50				

KM# 53 10 CROWNS
29.7000 g., 0.9250 Silver 0.8832 oz. ASW **Ruler:** Elizabeth II **Subject:** Wedding of Prince Charles and Lady Diana **Obv:** Young bust right **Rev:** Conjoined busts 1/4 left **Note:** Similar to 100 Crowns, KM#54.

Date	Mintage	F	VF	XF	Unc	BU
1981 Proof	40,000	Value: 18.50				

KM# 55 10 CROWNS
23.2800 g., 0.9250 Silver 0.6923 oz. ASW **Ruler:** Elizabeth II **Series:** International Year of the Child **Obv:** Young bust right **Rev:** Child holding shell, palm trees at left and right

Date	Mintage	F	VF	XF	Unc	BU
1982 Proof	7,928	Value: 20.00				

KM# 56   10 CROWNS
23.2800 g., 0.9250 Silver 0.6923 oz. ASW **Ruler:** Elizabeth II
Subject: World Football Championship **Obv:** Young bust right
Rev: Soccer player

Date	Mintage	F	VF	XF	Unc	BU
1982 Proof	7,865	Value: 16.50				

KM# 57   10 CROWNS
23.2800 g., 0.9250 Silver 0.6923 oz. ASW **Ruler:** Elizabeth II
Subject: World Football Championship **Obv:** Young bust right
Rev: Two players

Date	Mintage	F	VF	XF	Unc	BU
1982 Proof	7,165	Value: 16.50				

KM# 58   10 CROWNS
23.2800 g., 0.9250 Silver 0.6923 oz. ASW **Ruler:** Elizabeth II
Series: Summer Olympics **Obv:** Young bust right **Rev:** Javelin
thrower

Date	Mintage	F	VF	XF	Unc	BU
1984 Proof	2,160	Value: 20.00				

KM# 63   10 CROWNS
23.2800 g., 0.9250 Silver 0.6923 oz. ASW **Ruler:** Elizabeth II
Series: Decade for Women **Obv:** Young bust right **Rev:** Female
figure facing holding shell and stylized dove within circle

Date	Mintage	F	VF	XF	Unc	BU
1985 Proof	1,001	Value: 35.00				

KM# 2   20 CROWNS
38.7000 g., 0.9250 Silver 1.1509 oz. ASW **Ruler:** Elizabeth II
Subject: Centenary - Birth of Winston Churchill **Obv:** National
arms **Rev:** Bust 1/4 left

Date	Mintage	F	VF	XF	Unc	BU
1974 Matte	268,000	—	—	—	20.00	22.00
1974 Proof	8,400	Value: 25.00				

Note: 4,100 issued individually; 4,300 issued in binational
sets with Cayman Islands 25 Dollars, KM#10.

KM# 8   20 CROWNS
38.7000 g., 0.9250 Silver 1.1509 oz. ASW **Ruler:** Elizabeth II
Subject: Age of Exploration **Obv:** Young bust right **Rev:** Bust of
Christopher Columbus right and three ships

Date	Mintage	F	VF	XF	Unc	BU
1975 Matte	1,037	—	—	—	22.00	25.00
1975 Proof	2,769	Value: 20.00				

KM# 13   20 CROWNS
38.7000 g., 0.9250 Silver 1.1509 oz. ASW **Ruler:** Elizabeth II
Subject: U.S. Bicentennial **Obv:** Young bust right **Rev:** Two
cameos facing each other below flags and crossed scepters

Date	Mintage	F	VF	XF	Unc	BU
1976 Matte	5,022	—	—	—	20.00	22.00
1976 Proof	4,474	Value: 25.00				

KM# 14   20 CROWNS
38.7000 g., 0.9250 Silver 1.1509 oz. ASW **Ruler:** Elizabeth II
Obv: Young bust right **Rev:** 4 Victoria cameos left

Date	Mintage	F	VF	XF	Unc	BU
1976	25,000	—	—	—	20.00	22.00
1976 Proof	22,000	Value: 22.00				
1977 Proof	1,934	Value: 27.50				

KM# 18   20 CROWNS
38.7000 g., 0.9250 Silver 1.1509 oz. ASW, 44.87 mm.
Ruler: Elizabeth II **Obv:** Bust with tiara right **Rev:** 4 George III
cameos right **Edge:** Plain

Date	Mintage	F	VF	XF	Unc	BU
1977	—	—	—	—	27.50	30.00
1977 Proof	1,973	Value: 32.50				

KM# 23   20 CROWNS
38.7000 g., 0.9250 Silver 1.1509 oz. ASW **Ruler:** Elizabeth II
Subject: XI Commonwealth Games **Obv:** Young bust right
Rev: Javelin thrower and runner

Date	Mintage	F	VF	XF	Unc	BU
1978 Proof	10,000	Value: 20.00				

KM# 49   20 CROWNS
29.8100 g., 0.5000 Silver 0.4792 oz. ASW, 40.02 mm.
Ruler: Elizabeth II **Subject:** Lord Mountbatten **Obv:** Bust with
tiara right **Rev:** Uniformed bust 1/4 right divides dates **Edge:** Plain

Date	Mintage	F	VF	XF	Unc	BU
1980 Proof	—	Value: 22.50				

KM# 131.1   20 CROWNS
28.0400 g., 0.9250 Silver 0.8339 oz. ASW **Ruler:** Elizabeth II
Subject: 500th Anniversary - Discovery of America **Obv:** Crude
bust right **Rev:** Columbus and Indians exchange gifts

Date	Mintage	F	VF	XF	Unc	BU
1989 Proof	—	Value: 25.00				

KM# 67.1   20 CROWNS
28.0400 g., 0.9250 Silver 0.8339 oz. ASW **Ruler:** Elizabeth II
Subject: 500th Anniversary - Discovery of America **Obv:** Crude
young bust right **Rev:** Sailing ship - Santa Maria

Date	Mintage	F	VF	XF	Unc	BU
1989 Proof	—	Value: 25.00				

KM# 67.2   20 CROWNS
28.0400 g., 0.9250 Silver 0.8339 oz. ASW   **Ruler:** Elizabeth II
Subject: 500th Anniversary - Discovery of America **Obv:** Refined young bust right **Rev:** Sailing ship - Santa Maria

Date	Mintage	F	VF	XF	Unc	BU
1991 Proof	—	Value: 27.50				

KM# 67.3   20 CROWNS
28.0400 g., 0.9250 Silver 0.8339 oz. ASW   **Ruler:** Elizabeth II
Subject: 500th Anniversary - Discovery of America **Obv:** Refined young bust right #2 **Rev:** Sailing ship - Santa Maria

Date	Mintage	F	VF	XF	Unc	BU
1992 Proof	—	Value: 27.50				

KM# 115.1   20 CROWNS
28.0400 g., 0.9250 Silver 0.8339 oz. ASW   **Ruler:** Elizabeth II
Subject: 500th Anniversary - Discovery of America **Obv:** Crude young bust right **Rev:** Ship - The Nina

Date	Mintage	F	VF	XF	Unc	BU
1989 Proof	—	Value: 25.00				

KM# 115.2   20 CROWNS
28.0400 g., 0.9250 Silver 0.8339 oz. ASW   **Ruler:** Elizabeth II
Subject: 500th Anniversary - Discovery of America **Obv:** Refined young bust right **Rev:** Ship - The Nina

Date	Mintage	F	VF	XF	Unc	BU
1991 Proof	—	Value: 27.50				

KM# 115.3   20 CROWNS
28.0400 g., 0.9250 Silver 0.8339 oz. ASW   **Ruler:** Elizabeth II
Subject: 500th Anniversary - Discovery of America **Obv:** Refined young bust #2 right **Rev:** Ship - The Nina

Date	Mintage	F	VF	XF	Unc	BU
1992 Proof	—	Value: 27.50				

KM# 116.1   20 CROWNS
28.0400 g., 0.9250 Silver 0.8339 oz. ASW   **Ruler:** Elizabeth II
Subject: 500th Anniversary - Discovery of America **Obv:** Crude young bust right **Rev:** The Pinta

Date	Mintage	F	VF	XF	Unc	BU
1989 Proof	—	Value: 25.00				

KM# 116.2   20 CROWNS
28.0400 g., 0.9250 Silver 0.8339 oz. ASW   **Ruler:** Elizabeth II
Subject: 500th Anniversary - Discovery of America **Obv:** Refined young bust right **Rev:** The Pinta

Date	Mintage	F	VF	XF	Unc	BU
1991 Proof	—	Value: 27.50				

KM# 116.3   20 CROWNS
28.0400 g., 0.9250 Silver 0.8339 oz. ASW   **Ruler:** Elizabeth II
Subject: 500th Anniversary - Discovery of America **Obv:** Refined young bust right #2 **Rev:** The Pinta

Date	Mintage	F	VF	XF	Unc	BU
1992 Proof	—	Value: 27.50				

KM# 117.1   20 CROWNS
28.0400 g., 0.9250 Silver 0.8339 oz. ASW   **Ruler:** Elizabeth II
Subject: 500th Anniversary - Discovery of America **Obv:** Crude young bust right **Rev:** Ships set sail

Date	Mintage	F	VF	XF	Unc	BU
1989 Proof	—	Value: 27.50				

KM# 117.2   20 CROWNS
28.0400 g., 0.9250 Silver 0.8339 oz. ASW   **Ruler:** Elizabeth II
Subject: 500th Anniversary - Discovery of America **Obv:** Refined young bust right **Rev:** Ships set sail

Date	Mintage	F	VF	XF	Unc	BU
1991 Proof	—	Value: 27.50				

KM# 117.3   20 CROWNS
28.0400 g., 0.9250 Silver 0.8339 oz. ASW   **Ruler:** Elizabeth II
Subject: 500th Anniversary - Discovery of America **Obv:** Refined young bust #2 right **Rev:** Ships set sail

Date	Mintage	F	VF	XF	Unc	BU
1992 Proof	—	Value: 27.50				

KM# 118.1   20 CROWNS
28.0400 g., 0.9250 Silver 0.8339 oz. ASW   **Ruler:** Elizabeth II
Subject: 500th Anniversary _ Discovery of America **Obv:** Crude young bust right **Rev:** Ships crossing the Atlantic

Date	Mintage	F	VF	XF	Unc	BU
1989 Proof	—	Value: 25.00				

KM# 118.2   20 CROWNS
28.0400 g., 0.9250 Silver 0.8339 oz. ASW   **Ruler:** Elizabeth II
Subject: 500th Anniversary _ Discovery of America **Obv:** Refined young bust right **Rev:** Ships crossing the Atlantic

Date	Mintage	F	VF	XF	Unc	BU
1991 Proof	—	Value: 27.50				

KM# 118.3   20 CROWNS
28.0400 g., 0.9250 Silver 0.8339 oz. ASW   **Ruler:** Elizabeth II
Subject: 500th Anniversary _ Discovery of America **Obv:** Refined young bust #2 right **Rev:** Ships crossing the Atlantic

Date	Mintage	F	VF	XF	Unc	BU
1992 Proof	—	Value: 27.50				

KM# 119.1   20 CROWNS
28.0400 g., 0.9250 Silver 0.8339 oz. ASW   **Ruler:** Elizabeth II
Subject: 500th Anniversary _ Discovery of America **Obv:** Crude young bust right **Rev:** Sighting land

Date	Mintage	F	VF	XF	Unc	BU
1989 Proof	—	Value: 25.00				

KM# 119.2   20 CROWNS
28.0400 g., 0.9250 Silver 0.8339 oz. ASW   **Ruler:** Elizabeth II
Subject: 500th Anniversary _ Discovery of America **Obv:** Refined young bust right **Rev:** Sighting land

Date	Mintage	F	VF	XF	Unc	BU
1991 Proof	—	Value: 27.50				

KM# 119.3   20 CROWNS
28.0400 g., 0.9250 Silver 0.8339 oz. ASW   **Ruler:** Elizabeth II
Subject: 500th Anniversary _ Discovery of America **Obv:** Refined young bust #2 right **Rev:** Sighting land

Date	Mintage	F	VF	XF	Unc	BU
1992 Proof	—	Value: 27.50				

KM# 120.1   20 CROWNS
28.0400 g., 0.9250 Silver 0.8339 oz. ASW **Ruler:** Elizabeth II
Subject: 500th Anniversary _ Discovery of America **Obv:** Crude
young bust right **Rev:** Columbus explores the Caribbean

Date	Mintage	F	VF	XF	Unc	BU
1989 Proof	—				Value: 25.00	

KM# 120.2   20 CROWNS
28.0400 g., 0.9250 Silver 0.8339 oz. ASW **Ruler:** Elizabeth II
Subject: 500th Anniversary - Discovery of America **Obv:** Refined
young bust right **Rev:** Columbus explores the Caribbean

Date	Mintage	F	VF	XF	Unc	BU
1991 Proof	—				Value: 27.50	

KM# 120.3   20 CROWNS
28.0400 g., 0.9250 Silver 0.8339 oz. ASW **Ruler:** Elizabeth II
Subject: 500th Anniversary - Discovery of America **Obv:** Refined
young bust #2 right **Rev:** Columbus explores the Caribbean

Date	Mintage	F	VF	XF	Unc	BU
1992 Proof	—				Value: 27.50	

KM# 129.1   20 CROWNS
28.0400 g., 0.9250 Silver 0.8339 oz. ASW **Ruler:** Elizabeth II
Subject: 500th Anniversary - Discovery of America **Obv:** Crude
bust right **Rev:** Columbus sights New World

Date	Mintage	F	VF	XF	Unc	BU
1989 Proof	—				Value: 25.00	

KM# 129.2   20 CROWNS
28.0400 g., 0.9250 Silver 0.8339 oz. ASW **Ruler:** Elizabeth II
Subject: 500th Anniversary - Discovery of America **Obv:** Refined
bust right **Rev:** Columbus sights New World

Date	Mintage	F	VF	XF	Unc	BU
1991 Proof	—				Value: 27.50	

KM# 129.3   20 CROWNS
28.0400 g., 0.9250 Silver 0.8339 oz. ASW **Ruler:** Elizabeth II
Subject: 500th Anniversary - Discovery of America **Obv:** Refined
bust #2 right **Rev:** Columbus sights New World

Date	Mintage	F	VF	XF	Unc	BU
1992 Proof	—				Value: 27.50	

KM# 130.1   20 CROWNS
28.0400 g., 0.9250 Silver 0.8339 oz. ASW **Ruler:** Elizabeth II
Subject: 500th Anniversary - Discovery of America **Obv:** Crude
bust right **Rev:** Columbus claims land for Spain

Date	Mintage	F	VF	XF	Unc	BU
1989 Proof	—				Value: 25.00	

KM# 130.2   20 CROWNS
28.0400 g., 0.9250 Silver 0.8339 oz. ASW **Ruler:** Elizabeth II
Subject: 500th Anniversary - Discovery of America **Obv:** Refined
bust right **Rev:** Columbus claims land for Spain

Date	Mintage	F	VF	XF	Unc	BU
1991 Proof	—				Value: 27.50	

KM# 130.3   20 CROWNS
28.0400 g., 0.9250 Silver 0.8339 oz. ASW **Ruler:** Elizabeth II
Subject: 500th Anniversary - Discovery of America **Obv:** Refined
bust #2 right **Rev:** Columbus claims land for Spain

Date	Mintage	F	VF	XF	Unc	BU
1992 Proof	—				Value: 27.50	

KM# 131.2   20 CROWNS
28.0400 g., 0.9250 Silver 0.8339 oz. ASW **Ruler:** Elizabeth II
Subject: 500th Anniversary - Discovery of America **Obv:** Refined
bust right **Rev:** Columbus and Indians exchange gifts

Date	Mintage	F	VF	XF	Unc	BU
1991 Proof	—				Value: 27.50	

KM# 226   20 CROWNS
31.1700 g., 0.9990 Silver 1.0011 oz. ASW, 38.9 mm.
Ruler: Elizabeth II **Subject:** 40th Anniversary of Accession
Obv: National arms **Rev:** Crowned bust facing **Edge:** Reeded

Date	Mintage	F	VF	XF	Unc	BU
ND(1992) Proof	—				Value: 30.00	
1993 Proof	—				Value: 30.00	

KM# 227.1   20 CROWNS
31.1700 g., 0.9990 Silver 1.0011 oz. ASW, 38.9 mm.
Ruler: Elizabeth II **Subject:** 40th Anniversary of the Accession
Obv: Crowned head right with wavy truncation **Rev:** Head of H.M.
King George VI facing **Edge:** Reeded

Date	Mintage	F	VF	XF	Unc	BU
ND(1992) Proof	—				Value: 30.00	

KM# 229.1   20 CROWNS
31.1700 g., 0.9990 Silver 1.0011 oz. ASW, 38.9 mm.
Ruler: Elizabeth II **Subject:** 40th Anniversary of the Accession
Obv: Crowned head right with wavy truncation **Rev:** Conjoined
busts of the Queen and Prince Philip facing **Edge:** Reeded

Date	Mintage	F	VF	XF	Unc	BU
ND(1992) Proof	—				Value: 30.00	

KM# 229.2   20 CROWNS
31.1700 g., 0.9990 Silver 1.0011 oz. ASW, 38.9 mm.
Ruler: Elizabeth II **Subject:** 40th Anniversary of the Accession
Obv: Crowned head right with smooth truncation **Rev:** Conjoined
busts of the Queen and Prince Philip facing **Edge:** Reeded

Date	Mintage	F	VF	XF	Unc	BU
ND(1992) Proof	—				Value: 30.00	

KM# 228.1   20 CROWNS
31.1700 g., 0.9990 Silver 1.0011 oz. ASW, 38.9 mm.
Ruler: Elizabeth II **Subject:** 40th Anniversary of the Accession
Obv: Crowned head right with wavy truncation **Rev:** Windsor
castle **Edge:** Reeded

Date	Mintage	F	VF	XF	Unc	BU
ND(1992) Proof	—				Value: 30.00	

KM# 131.3   20 CROWNS
28.0400 g., 0.9250 Silver 0.8339 oz. ASW **Ruler:** Elizabeth II
Subject: 500th Anniversary - Discovery of America **Obv:** Refined
bust #2 right **Rev:** Columbus and Indians exchange gifts

Date	Mintage	F	VF	XF	Unc	BU
1992 Proof	—				Value: 30.00	

KM# 78   20 CROWNS
31.1000 g., 0.9990 Silver 0.9988 oz. ASW, 38.95 mm.
Ruler: Elizabeth II **Series:** Olympics **Obv:** National arms
Rev: Equestrian and 3 events **Edge:** Reeded

Date	Mintage	F	VF	XF	Unc	BU
1992 Proof	20,000				Value: 21.50	

KM# 79   20 CROWNS
31.1000 g., 0.9990 Silver 0.9988 oz. ASW, 38.95 mm.
Ruler: Elizabeth II **Series:** Olympics **Obv:** National arms
Rev: Gymnast on rings and 5 events **Edge:** Reeded

Date	Mintage	F	VF	XF	Unc	BU
1992 Proof	Est. 20,000				Value: 21.50	

KM# 80   20 CROWNS
31.1000 g., 0.9990 Silver 0.9988 oz. ASW, 38.95 mm.
Ruler: Elizabeth II **Series:** Olympics **Obv:** National arms
Rev: Weightlifting and 3 events **Edge:** Reeded

Date	Mintage	F	VF	XF	Unc	BU
1992 Proof	Est. 20,000				Value: 21.50	

KM# 81   20 CROWNS
31.1000 g., 0.9990 Silver 0.9988 oz. ASW, 38.95 mm.
Ruler: Elizabeth II **Series:** Olympics **Obv:** National arms
Rev: Rifle shooting and 3 events **Edge:** Reeded

Date	Mintage	F	VF	XF	Unc	BU
1992 Proof	Est. 20,000				Value: 21.50	

KM# 82 20 CROWNS
31.1000 g., 0.9990 Silver 0.9988 oz. ASW, 38.95 mm.
Ruler: Elizabeth II **Series:** Olympics **Obv:** National arms
Rev: Sail boarding and 3 events **Edge:** Reeded

Date	Mintage	F	VF	XF	Unc	BU
1992 Proof	Est. 20,000	Value: 21.50				

KM# 83 20 CROWNS
31.1000 g., 0.9990 Silver 0.9988 oz. ASW, 38.95 mm.
Ruler: Elizabeth II **Series:** Olympics **Obv:** National arms
Rev: Ski jumper and 4 events **Edge:** Reeded

Date	Mintage	F	VF	XF	Unc	BU
1992 Proof	Est. 20,000	Value: 21.50				

KM# 184 20 CROWNS
28.0400 g., 0.9250 Silver 0.8339 oz. ASW **Ruler:** Elizabeth II
Series: Apollo II **Obv:** Crowned head right **Rev:** Lunar landing
scene

Date	Mintage	F	VF	XF	Unc	BU
1993 Proof	—	Value: 30.00				
1994 Mule?	—	—	—	—	—	—

Note: Re-engraved number 4 in date

KM# 239 20 CROWNS
28.0400 g., 0.9250 Silver 0.8339 oz. ASW **Ruler:** Elizabeth II
Series: Lillehamer Winter Olympics **Obv:** Crowned head right
Rev: Olympic skier

Date	Mintage	F	VF	XF	Unc	BU
1993 Proof	—	Value: 27.50				

KM# 187 20 CROWNS
28.0400 g., 0.9250 Silver 0.8339 oz. ASW, 38.9 mm.
Ruler: Elizabeth II **Series:** Apollo 11 **Obv:** Crowned head right
Rev: Astronaut walking on the moon **Edge:** Reeded

Date	Mintage	F	VF	XF	Unc	BU
1993 Proof	—	Value: 30.00				

KM# 95 20 CROWNS
31.1000 g., 0.9990 Silver 0.9988 oz. ASW **Ruler:** Elizabeth II
Subject: World Cup '94 **Obv:** Crowned bust right **Rev:** Bust of
Jules Rimet right and trophy

Date	Mintage	F	VF	XF	Unc	BU
ND(1993) Proof	Est. 10,000	Value: 27.50				

KM# 96 20 CROWNS
31.1000 g., 0.9990 Silver 0.9988 oz. ASW **Ruler:** Elizabeth II
Subject: World Cup '94 - Uruguay Winners **Obv:** Crowned head
right **Rev:** Two players

Date	Mintage	F	VF	XF	Unc	BU
ND(1993) Proof	Est. 10,000	Value: 30.00				

KM# 97 20 CROWNS
31.1000 g., 0.9990 Silver 0.9988 oz. ASW **Ruler:** Elizabeth II
Subject: World Cup '94 - Italy Winners **Obv:** Crowned head right
Rev: Dino Zoff

Date	Mintage	F	VF	XF	Unc	BU
ND(1993) Proof	Est. 10,000	Value: 30.00				

KM# 98 20 CROWNS
31.1000 g., 0.9990 Silver 0.9988 oz. ASW **Ruler:** Elizabeth II
Subject: World Cup '94 - West German Winners **Obv:** Crowned
head right **Rev:** Franz Breckenbauer

Date	Mintage	F	VF	XF	Unc	BU
ND(1993) Proof	Est. 10,000	Value: 30.00				

KM# 99 20 CROWNS
31.1000 g., 0.9990 Silver 0.9988 oz. ASW **Ruler:** Elizabeth II
Subject: World Cup '94 - Brazil Winners **Obv:** Crowned head
right **Rev:** Pelé

Date	Mintage	F	VF	XF	Unc	BU
ND(1993) Proof	Est. 10,000	Value: 27.50				

KM# 100 20 CROWNS
31.1000 g., 0.9990 Silver 0.9988 oz. ASW **Ruler:** Elizabeth II
Subject: World Cup '94 - England Winners **Obv:** Crowned head
right **Rev:** Bobby Moore

Date	Mintage	F	VF	XF	Unc	BU
ND(1993) Proof	Est. 10,000	Value: 30.00				

KM# 110.1 20 CROWNS
31.1000 g., 0.9990 Silver 0.9988 oz. ASW **Ruler:** Elizabeth II
Subject: 40th Anniversary of Coronation **Obv:** Crowned head
right with wavy truncation **Rev:** Crown jewels

Date	Mintage	F	VF	XF	Unc	BU
ND(1993) Proof	Est. 10,000	Value: 30.00				

KM# 110.2 20 CROWNS
31.1700 g., 0.9990 Silver 1.0011 oz. ASW, 38.9 mm.
Ruler: Elizabeth II **Subject:** 40th Anniversary of Coronation
Obv: Crowned head right with smooth truncation **Rev:** Crown
jewels **Edge:** Reeded

Date	Mintage	F	VF	XF	Unc	BU
1993 Proof	—	Value: 30.00				

KM# 101 20 CROWNS
31.1000 g., 0.9990 Silver 0.9988 oz. ASW **Ruler:** Elizabeth II
Subject: World Cup '94 - Argentina Winners **Obv:** Crowned head
right **Rev:** Mario Kempes

Date	Mintage	F	VF	XF	Unc	BU
ND(1993) Proof	Est. 10,000	Value: 30.00				

KM# 102 20 CROWNS
31.1000 g., 0.9990 Silver 0.9988 oz. ASW **Ruler:** Elizabeth II
Subject: World Cup '94 - USA Host **Obv:** Crowned head right
Rev: Trophy and flag

Date	Mintage	F	VF	XF	Unc	BU
ND(1993) Proof	Est. 10,000	Value: 27.50				

KM# 111.1 20 CROWNS
31.1000 g., 0.9990 Silver 0.9988 oz. ASW **Ruler:** Elizabeth II
Subject: 40th Anniversary of Coronation **Obv:** Crowned head
right with wavy truncation **Rev:** Queen, clergy and maids of honor

Date	Mintage	F	VF	XF	Unc	BU
ND(1993) Proof	Est. 10,000	Value: 30.00				

KM# 111.2 20 CROWNS
31.1700 g., 0.9990 Silver 1.0011 oz. ASW, 38.9 mm.
Ruler: Elizabeth II **Subject:** 40th Anniversary of Coronation
Obv: Crowned head right with smooth truncation **Rev:** Queen,
clergy and maids of honor **Edge:** Reeded

Date	Mintage	F	VF	XF	Unc	BU
1993 Proof	—	Value: 30.00				

KM# 109 20 CROWNS
31.1000 g., 0.9990 Silver 0.9988 oz. ASW **Ruler:** Elizabeth II
Subject: 40th Anniversary of Coronation **Obv:** Crowned head
right **Rev:** Westminster Abbey

Date	Mintage	F	VF	XF	Unc	BU
ND(1993) Proof	Est. 10,000	Value: 30.00				

KM# 112.1 20 CROWNS
31.1000 g., 0.9990 Silver 0.9988 oz. ASW **Ruler:** Elizabeth II
Subject: 40th Anniversary of Coronation **Obv:** Crowned head
right with wavy truncation **Rev:** Consort's homage

Date	Mintage	F	VF	XF	Unc	BU
ND(1993) Proof	Est. 10,000	Value: 30.00				

KM# 112.2 20 CROWNS
31.1700 g., 0.9990 Silver 1.0011 oz. ASW, 38.9 mm.
Ruler: Elizabeth II **Subject:** Coronation Anniversary
Obv: Crowned head right with smooth truncation **Rev:** Consort's
homage **Edge:** Reeded

Date	Mintage	F	VF	XF	Unc	BU
1993 Proof	—	Value: 30.00				

KM# 113.1 20 CROWNS
31.1000 g., 0.9990 Silver 0.9988 oz. ASW **Ruler:** Elizabeth II
Subject: 40th Anniversary of Coronation **Obv:** Crowned head right
with wavy truncation **Rev:** Enthroned Queen seated left facing

Date	Mintage	F	VF	XF	Unc	BU
ND(1993) Proof	Est. 10,000	Value: 30.00				

KM# 113.2 20 CROWNS
31.1700 g., 0.9990 Silver 1.0011 oz. ASW, 38.9 mm.
Ruler: Elizabeth II **Subject:** Coronation Anniversary
Obv: Crowned head right with smooth truncation **Rev:** Enthroned
Queen seated left facing **Edge:** Reeded

Date	Mintage	F	VF	XF	Unc	BU
1993 Proof	—	Value: 30.00				

KM# 114.1   20 CROWNS
31.1000 g., 0.9990 Silver 0.9988 oz. ASW **Ruler:** Elizabeth II
Subject: 40th Anniversary of Coronation **Obv:** Crowned head
right with wavy truncation **Rev:** Queen in coach

Date	Mintage	F	VF	XF	Unc	BU
ND(1993) Proof	Est. 10,000				Value: 30.00	

KM# 114.2   20 CROWNS
31.1700 g., 0.9990 Silver 1.0011 oz. ASW, 38.9 mm.
Ruler: Elizabeth II **Subject:** Coronation Anniversary
Obv: Crowned head right with smooth truncation **Rev:** Queen in
coach **Edge:** Reeded

Date	Mintage	F	VF	XF	Unc	BU
1993 Proof	—				Value: 30.00	

KM# 141   20 CROWNS
31.1000 g., 0.9990 Silver 0.9988 oz. ASW **Ruler:** Elizabeth II
Series: 1994 Olympics **Obv:** Crowned head right **Rev:** Bobsled
and team within circle

Date	Mintage	F	VF	XF	Unc	BU
1993 Proof	—				Value: 27.50	

KM# 142   20 CROWNS
31.1000 g., 0.9990 Silver 0.9988 oz. ASW **Ruler:** Elizabeth II
Subject: 25th Anniversary - Apollo 11 Moon Landing
Obv: Crowned head right **Rev:** Astronaut descending ladder
on moon

Date	Mintage	F	VF	XF	Unc	BU
1993 Proof	—				Value: 30.00	

KM# 183   20 CROWNS
28.0400 g., 0.9250 Silver 0.8339 oz. ASW **Ruler:** Elizabeth II
Series: Apollo II **Obv:** Crowned head right **Rev:** Rocket launch
scene **Note:** Similar to 5 Crowns, KM#177.

Date	Mintage	F	VF	XF	Unc	BU
1993 Proof	—				Value: 35.00	

KM# 185   20 CROWNS
28.0400 g., 0.9250 Silver 0.8339 oz. ASW **Ruler:** Elizabeth II
Series: Apollo II - Leaving Lunar Landing Module **Obv:** Crowned
head right **Rev:** Astronaut descending ladder

Date	Mintage	F	VF	XF	Unc	BU
1993 Proof	—				Value: 35.00	

KM# 186   20 CROWNS
28.0400 g., 0.9250 Silver 0.8339 oz. ASW **Ruler:** Elizabeth II
Series: Apollo II **Obv:** Crowned head right **Rev:** Astronauts
planting flag on moon

Date	Mintage	F	VF	XF	Unc	BU
1993 Proof	—				Value: 30.00	

KM# 228.2   20 CROWNS
31.1700 g., 0.9990 Silver 1.0011 oz. ASW, 38.9 mm.
Ruler: Elizabeth II **Subject:** 40th Anniversary of the Accession
Obv: Crowned head right with smooth truncation **Rev:** Windsor
Castle **Edge:** Reeded

Date	Mintage	F	VF	XF	Unc	BU
1993 Proof	—				Value: 30.00	

KM# 227.2   20 CROWNS
31.1700 g., 0.9990 Silver 1.0011 oz. ASW, 38.9 mm.
Ruler: Elizabeth II **Subject:** 40th Anniversary of the Accession
Obv: Crowned head right with smooth truncation **Rev:** Head of
H.M. King George VI facing **Edge:** Reeded

Date	Mintage	F	VF	XF	Unc	BU
1993 Proof	—				Value: 30.00	

KM# 218   20 CROWNS
31.1600 g., 0.9990 Silver 1.0008 oz. ASW, 39 mm.
Ruler: Elizabeth II **Series:** 50th Anniversary D-Day
Subject: General Omar Bradley **Obv:** Crowned head right
Rev: Helmeted bust 1/4 right **Edge:** Reeded

Date	Mintage	F	VF	XF	Unc	BU
1994 Proof	—				Value: 35.00	

KM# 208   20 CROWNS
21.1300 g., 0.9990 Silver 0.6786 oz. ASW **Ruler:** Elizabeth II
Series: XVII Winter Olympics **Obv:** Crowned head right
Rev: Figure skater within circle **Note:** Reportedly a mule or
pattern.

Date	Mintage	F	VF	XF	Unc	BU
1994 Proof	—				Value: 125	

KM# 219   20 CROWNS
31.1600 g., 0.9990 Silver 1.0008 oz. ASW, 39 mm.
Ruler: Elizabeth II **Series:** 50th Anniversary D-Day
Subject: General Montgomery **Obv:** Crowned head right
Rev: Uniformed bust left **Edge:** Reeded **Note:** Obverse date in
error.

Date	Mintage	F	VF	XF	Unc	BU
1991(1994) Proof	—				Value: 35.00	

KM# 220   20 CROWNS
31.1600 g., 0.9990 Silver 1.0008 oz. ASW, 39 mm.
Ruler: Elizabeth II **Series:** 50th Anniversary D-Day
Subject: Normandy Landing **Obv:** Crowned head right **Rev:** Sir
Bertram Ramsay left **Edge:** Reeded

Date	Mintage	F	VF	XF	Unc	BU
1994 Proof	—				Value: 35.00	

KM# 221   20 CROWNS
31.1600 g., 0.9990 Silver 1.0008 oz. ASW, 39 mm.
Ruler: Elizabeth II **Series:** 50th Anniversary D-Day
Subject: Normandy Landing **Obv:** Crowned head right
Rev: General Dwight Eisenhower right **Edge:** Reeded

Date	Mintage	F	VF	XF	Unc	BU
1994 Proof	—				Value: 35.00	

KM# 230   20 CROWNS
31.1700 g., 0.9990 Silver 1.0011 oz. ASW, 38.9 mm.
Ruler: Elizabeth II **Subject:** The Lady of the Century - The Queen
Mother **Obv:** Crowned head right with smooth truncation
Rev: Bust 1/4 right **Edge:** Reeded

Date	Mintage	F	VF	XF	Unc	BU
1995 Proof	—				Value: 30.00	

KM# 137   20 CROWNS
31.1035 g., 0.9990 Silver 0.9990 oz. ASW **Ruler:** Elizabeth II
Subject: 50th Anniversary - VE Day **Obv:** Arms with supporters
Rev: Heads of Churchill, Roosevelt and Stalin facing

Date	Mintage	F	VF	XF	Unc	BU
1995 Proof	15,000				Value: 32.50	

KM# 138   20 CROWNS
31.1035 g., 0.9990 Silver 0.9990 oz. ASW **Ruler:** Elizabeth II
Subject: 50th Anniversary - VE Day **Obv:** Arms with supporters
Rev: Three fighter planes

Date	Mintage	F	VF	XF	Unc	BU
1995 Proof	15,000				Value: 32.50	

KM# 139   20 CROWNS
31.1035 g., 0.9990 Silver 0.9990 oz. ASW **Ruler:** Elizabeth II
Subject: 50th Anniversary - VE Day **Obv:** Arms with supporters
Rev: U.S. and Soviet troops meet

Date	Mintage	F	VF	XF	Unc	BU
1995 Proof	15,000	Value: 32.50				

KM# 140   20 CROWNS
31.1035 g., 0.9990 Silver 0.9990 oz. ASW **Ruler:** Elizabeth II
Subject: 50th Anniversary - VE Day **Obv:** Arms with supporters
Rev: London, Washington, Moscow and Paris

Date	Mintage	F	VF	XF	Unc	BU
1995 Proof	15,000	Value: 40.00				

KM# 189   20 CROWNS
31.1035 g., 0.9990 Silver 0.9990 oz. ASW **Ruler:** Elizabeth II
Series: XXVI Summer Olympics **Obv:** Crowned head right
Rev: Hurdlers within circle

Date	Mintage	F	VF	XF	Unc	BU
1995 Proof	—	Value: 22.50				

KM# 191   20 CROWNS
31.1035 g., 0.9990 Silver 0.9990 oz. ASW **Ruler:** Elizabeth II
Series: XXVI Summer Olympics **Obv:** Crowned head right
Rev: Cyclist within circle

Date	Mintage	F	VF	XF	Unc	BU
1995 Proof	—	Value: 22.50				

KM# 193   20 CROWNS
31.1035 g., 0.9990 Silver 0.9990 oz. ASW **Ruler:** Elizabeth II
Series: XXVI Summer Olympics **Obv:** Crowned head right
Rev: Fencers within circle

Date	Mintage	F	VF	XF	Unc	BU
1995 Proof	—	Value: 22.50				

KM# 195   20 CROWNS
31.1035 g., 0.9990 Silver 0.9990 oz. ASW **Ruler:** Elizabeth II
Series: XXVI Summer Olympics **Obv:** Crowned head right
Rev: Equestrian

Date	Mintage	F	VF	XF	Unc	BU
1995 Proof	—	Value: 22.50				

KM# 197   20 CROWNS
31.1035 g., 0.9990 Silver 0.9990 oz. ASW **Ruler:** Elizabeth II
Series: XXVI Summer Olympics **Obv:** Crowned head right
Rev: Pole vaulter

Date	Mintage	F	VF	XF	Unc	BU
1995 Proof	—	Value: 22.50				

KM# 199   20 CROWNS
31.1035 g., 0.9990 Silver 0.9990 oz. ASW **Ruler:** Elizabeth II
Series: XXVI Summer Olympics **Obv:** Crowned head right
Rev: Runners within circle

Date	Mintage	F	VF	XF	Unc	BU
1995 Proof	—	Value: 22.50				

KM# 201   20 CROWNS
31.1035 g., 0.9990 Silver 0.9990 oz. ASW **Ruler:** Elizabeth II
Series: XXVI Summer Olympics **Obv:** Crowned head right
Rev: Gymnast

Date	Mintage	F	VF	XF	Unc	BU
1995 Proof	—	Value: 22.50				

KM# 203   20 CROWNS
31.1035 g., 0.9990 Silver 0.9990 oz. ASW **Ruler:** Elizabeth II
Series: XXVI Summer Olympics **Obv:** Crowned head right
Rev: Swimmer within circle

Date	Mintage	F	VF	XF	Unc	BU
1995 Proof	—	Value: 22.50				

KM# 205   20 CROWNS
31.1035 g., 0.9990 Silver 0.9990 oz. ASW **Ruler:** Elizabeth II
Series: XXVI Summer Olympics **Obv:** Crowned head right
Rev: Diver

Date	Mintage	F	VF	XF	Unc	BU
1995 Proof	—	Value: 22.50				

KM# 207   20 CROWNS
31.1035 g., 0.9990 Silver 0.9990 oz. ASW **Ruler:** Elizabeth II
Series: XXVI Summer Olympics **Obv:** Crowned head right
Rev: Sprinter within circle

Date	Mintage	F	VF	XF	Unc	BU
1995 Proof	—	Value: 22.50				

KM# 231   20 CROWNS
31.1100 g., 0.9990 Silver 0.9992 oz. ASW, 38.9 mm.
Ruler: Elizabeth II **Subject:** The 70th Birthday of H. M. Queen
Elizabeth II **Obv:** National arms **Rev:** Seated Queen with her pet
Corgi's on either side **Edge:** Reeded

Date	Mintage	F	VF	XF	Unc	BU
1996 Proof	—	Value: 30.00				

KM# 243   20 CROWNS
31.1600 g., 0.9990 Silver 1.0008 oz. ASW, 39 mm.
Ruler: Elizabeth II **Subject:** Return of Hong Kong **Obv:** Crowned
head right **Rev:** Sailing junk in harbor **Edge:** Reeded

Date	Mintage	F	VF	XF	Unc	BU
1997 Proof	—	Value: 40.00				

KM# 222   20 CROWNS
31.1035 g., 0.9990 Silver 0.9990 oz. ASW, 38.9 mm.
Ruler: Elizabeth II **Subject:** Hong Kong's Return to China
Obv: Crowned head right **Rev:** City view below flower design
Edge: Reeded

Date	Mintage	F	VF	XF	Unc	BU
1997 Proof	—	Value: 28.50				

KM# 240   20 CROWNS
31.2300 g., 0.9990 Silver 1.0030 oz. ASW, 38.9 mm.
Ruler: Elizabeth II **Obv:** Crowned head right **Rev:** Ship - R.M.S.
Titanic **Edge:** Reeded

Date	Mintage	F	VF	XF	Unc	BU
1998 Proof	—	Value: 50.00				

KM# 241   20 CROWNS
31.2300 g., 0.9990 Silver 1.0030 oz. ASW **Ruler:** Elizabeth II
Subject: 80th Anniveresary of the British Royal Air Force
Obv: Crowned head right **Rev:** Spitfire in flight **Edge:** Reeded

Date	Mintage	F	VF	XF	Unc	BU
1998 Proof	—	Value: 50.00				

KM# 217   20 CROWNS
31.2400 g., 0.9990 Silver 1.0033 oz. ASW, 39 mm.
Ruler: Elizabeth II **Obv:** Crowned head right **Rev:** Dolphins
Edge: Reeded

Date	Mintage	F	VF	XF	Unc	BU
1998 Proof	— Value: 45.00					

KM# 242   20 CROWNS
33.3700 g., 0.9990 Silver 1.0718 oz. ASW, 39.9 mm.
Ruler: Elizabeth II **Obv:** National arms **Rev:** Three marlins
jumping out of water **Edge:** Reeded

Date	Mintage	F	VF	XF	Unc	BU
1999FM Proof	— Value: 45.00					

KM# 244   20 CROWNS
31.1600 g., 0.9990 Silver 1.0008 oz. ASW, 39 mm.
Ruler: Elizabeth II **Obv:** Crowned head right **Rev:** Queen Mother
Edge: Reeded

Date	Mintage	F	VF	XF	Unc	BU
1999 Proof	— Value: 40.00					

KM# 235   20 CROWNS
31.2000 g., 0.9990 Silver 1.0021 oz. ASW, 38.9 mm.
Ruler: Elizabeth II **Subject:** Prince Edward's Wedding
Obv: Head with tiara right **Rev:** Conjoined busts of Edward and
Sophie facing **Edge:** Reeded

Date	Mintage	F	VF	XF	Unc	BU
1999 Proof	— Value: 40.00					

KM# 223   20 CROWNS
31.1035 g., 0.9990 Silver 0.9990 oz. ASW, 39.02 mm.
Ruler: Elizabeth II **Subject:** Apollo 11 **Obv:** Head with tiara right
Rev: Spacecraft in flight above world globe **Edge:** Reeded

Date	Mintage	F	VF	XF	Unc	BU
1999 Proof	— Value: 30.00					

KM# 224   20 CROWNS
31.1035 g., 0.9990 Silver 0.9990 oz. ASW, 39.02 mm.
Ruler: Elizabeth II **Subject:** Apollo 11 **Obv:** Head with tiara right
Rev: Heads of Collins, Armstrong and Aldrin left **Edge:** Reeded

Date	Mintage	F	VF	XF	Unc	BU
1999 Proof	— Value: 30.00					

KM# 145   20 DOLLARS
31.1035 g., 0.9990 Silver 0.9990 oz. ASW   **Ruler:** Elizabeth II
Subject: Steam Locomotive **Obv:** Crowned head right **Rev:** City
of Truro

Date	Mintage	F	VF	XF	Unc	BU
1996 Proof	Est. 20,000 Value: 32.50					

KM# 148   20 DOLLARS
31.1035 g., 0.9990 Silver 0.9990 oz. ASW, 38.97 mm.
Ruler: Elizabeth II **Subject:** Steam Locomotive **Obv:** Crowned
head right **Rev:** Flying Scotsman **Edge:** Reeded

Date	Mintage	F	VF	XF	Unc	BU
1996 Proof	Est. 20,000 Value: 32.50					

KM# 151   20 DOLLARS
31.1035 g., 0.9990 Silver 0.9990 oz. ASW, 38.97 mm.
Ruler: Elizabeth II **Subject:** Steam Locomotive **Obv:** Crowned
head right **Rev:** Rocket **Edge:** Reeded

Date	Mintage	F	VF	XF	Unc	BU
1996 Proof	Est. 20,000 Value: 35.00					

KM# 154   20 DOLLARS
31.1035 g., 0.9990 Silver 0.9990 oz. ASW, 38.97 mm.
Ruler: Elizabeth II **Subject:** Steam Locomotive **Obv:** Crowned
head right **Rev:** Evening Star **Edge:** Reeded

Date	Mintage	F	VF	XF	Unc	BU
1996 Proof	Est. 20,000 Value: 35.00					

KM# 157   20 DOLLARS
31.1035 g., 0.9990 Silver 0.9990 oz. ASW, 38.97 mm.
Ruler: Elizabeth II **Subject:** Steam Locomotive **Obv:** Crowned
head right **Rev:** Mallard **Edge:** Reeded

Date	Mintage	F	VF	XF	Unc	BU
1996 Proof	Est. 20,000 Value: 35.00					

KM# 160   20 DOLLARS
31.1035 g., 0.9990 Silver 0.9990 oz. ASW, 38.97 mm.
Ruler: Elizabeth II **Subject:** Steam Locomotive **Obv:** Crowned
head right **Rev:** Princess Elizabeth **Edge:** Reeded

Date	Mintage	F	VF	XF	Unc	BU
1996 Proof	Est. 20,000 Value: 32,50					

KM# 163   20 DOLLARS
31.1035 g., 0.9990 Silver 0.9990 oz. ASW, 38.97 mm.
Ruler: Elizabeth II **Subject:** Steam Locomotive **Obv:** Crowned
head right **Rev:** Southern Pacific Lines - Class GS4
Edge: Reeded

Date	Mintage	F	VF	XF	Unc	BU
1996 Proof	Est. 20,000	Value: 35.00				

KM# 166   20 DOLLARS
31.1035 g., 0.9990 Silver 0.9990 oz. ASW, 38.97 mm. **Ruler:**
Elizabeth II **Subject:** Steam Locomotive **Obv:** Crowned head
right **Rev:** German State railway - Class 05 **Edge:** Reeded

Date	Mintage	F	VF	XF	Unc	BU
1996 Proof	Est. 20,000	Value: 32.50				

KM# 169   20 DOLLARS
31.1035 g., 0.9990 Silver 0.9990 oz. ASW, 38.97 mm.
Ruler: Elizabeth II **Subject:** Steam Locomotive **Obv:** Crowned
head right **Rev:** Japanese Railway - Class 62 **Edge:** Reeded

Date	Mintage	F	VF	XF	Unc	BU
1996 Proof	Est. 20,000	Value: 35.00				

KM# 172   20 DOLLARS
31.1035 g., 0.9990 Silver 0.9990 oz. ASW, 38.97 mm.
Ruler: Elizabeth II **Subject:** Steam Locomotive **Obv:** Crowned
head right **Rev:** Chinese State Railways Class RM **Edge:** Reeded

Date	Mintage	F	VF	XF	Unc	BU
1996 Proof	Est. 20,000	Value: 35.00				

KM# 9.1   25 CROWNS
4.5000 g., 0.5000 Gold 0.0723 oz. AGW **Ruler:** Elizabeth II
Obv: Young bust right **Rev:** National arms

Date	Mintage	F	VF	XF	Unc	BU
1975	1,272	—	—	—	80.00	90.00
1975 Proof	2,096	Value: 90.00				

KM# 9.2   25 CROWNS
4.5000 g., 0.5000 Gold 0.0723 oz. AGW, 19 mm.
Ruler: Elizabeth II **Obv:** Young bust right **Rev:** National arms

Date	Mintage	F	VF	XF	Unc	BU
1976	—	—	—	—	80.00	90.00
1976 Proof	2,185	Value: 90.00				
1977 Proof	2,125	Value: 90.00				

KM# 19   25 CROWNS
43.7500 g., 0.9250 Silver 1.3010 oz. ASW **Ruler:** Elizabeth II
Subject: Queen's Silver Jubilee **Obv:** Young bust right
Rev: Crown and date within sprigs above banner

Date	Mintage	F	VF	XF	Unc	BU
1977 Matte	—	—	—	—	25.00	27.50
1977 Proof	13,000	Value: 30.00				

KM# 24   25 CROWNS
43.7500 g., 0.9250 Silver 1.3010 oz. ASW **Ruler:** Elizabeth II
Subject: 25th Anniversary of Coronation **Obv:** Young bust right
Rev: Lion of England

Date	Mintage	F	VF	XF	Unc	BU
1978 Proof	—	Value: 32.00				

KM# 25   25 CROWNS
43.7500 g., 0.9250 Silver 1.3010 oz. ASW **Ruler:** Elizabeth II
Obv: Young bust right **Rev:** Griffin of Edward III left

Date	Mintage	F	VF	XF	Unc	BU
1978 Proof	—	Value: 32.00				

KM# 26   25 CROWNS
43.7500 g., 0.9250 Silver 1.3010 oz. ASW **Ruler:** Elizabeth II
Obv: Young bust right **Rev:** Red Dragon of Wales left

Date	Mintage	F	VF	XF	Unc	BU
1978 Proof	—	Value: 32.00				

KM# 27   25 CROWNS
43.7500 g., 0.9250 Silver 1.3010 oz. ASW **Ruler:** Elizabeth II
Obv: Young bust right **Rev:** White Greyhound of Richmond left

Date	Mintage	F	VF	XF	Unc	BU
1978 Proof	—	Value: 32.00				

KM# 28   25 CROWNS
43.7500 g., 0.9250 Silver 1.3010 oz. ASW **Ruler:** Elizabeth II
Obv: Young bust right **Rev:** Unicorn of Scotland right

Date	Mintage	F	VF	XF	Unc	BU
1978 Proof	—	Value: 37.50				

KM# 29   25 CROWNS
43.7500 g., 0.9250 Silver 1.3010 oz. ASW **Ruler:** Elizabeth II
Obv: Young bust right **Rev:** The White Horse of Hannover

Date	Mintage	F	VF	XF	Unc	BU
1978 Proof	—	Value: 32.00				

KM# 30   25 CROWNS
43.7500 g., 0.9250 Silver 1.3010 oz. ASW **Ruler:** Elizabeth II
Obv: Young bust right **Rev:** Black Bull of Clarence left

Date	Mintage	F	VF	XF	Unc	BU
1978 Proof	—	Value: 32.00				

KM# 31   25 CROWNS
43.7500 g., 0.9250 Silver 1.3010 oz. ASW **Ruler:** Elizabeth II
Obv: Young bust right **Rev:** Yale of Beaufort left

Date	Mintage	F	VF	XF	Unc	BU
1978 Proof	—	Value: 32.00				

KM# 32   25 CROWNS
43.7500 g., 0.9250 Silver 1.3010 oz. ASW **Ruler:** Elizabeth II
Obv: Young bust right **Rev:** Falcon of the Plantagenets right

Date	Mintage	F	VF	XF	Unc	BU
1978 Proof	—	Value: 32.00				

KM# 33   25 CROWNS
43.7500 g., 0.9250 Silver 1.3010 oz. ASW **Ruler:** Elizabeth II
Obv: Young bust right **Rev:** White Lion of Mortimer left

Date	Mintage	F	VF	XF	Unc	BU
1978 Proof	—	Value: 32.00				

KM# 209   25 CROWNS
155.4400 g., 0.9990 Silver 4.9923 oz. ASW, 63 mm.
Ruler: Elizabeth II **Obv:** Crowned bust right **Rev:** Multicolor
purple-throated Carib bird within flowers **Note:** Illus. reduced.

Date	Mintage	F	VF	XF	Unc	BU
1995 Matte	—	—	—	—	200	225
1995 Proof	—	Value: 220				

KM# 210   25 CROWNS
155.4400 g., 0.9990 Silver 4.9923 oz. ASW, 63 mm.
Ruler: Elizabeth II **Obv:** Crowned bust right **Rev:** Multicolor
Streamertail bird **Edge:** Reeded **Note:** Illustration reduced.

Date	Mintage	F	VF	XF	Unc	BU
1995 Matte	—	—	—	—	200	225
1995 Proof	—	Value: 220				

KM# 211   25 CROWNS
155.4400 g., 0.9990 Silver 4.9923 oz. ASW, 63 mm.
Ruler: Elizabeth II **Obv:** Crowned bust right **Rev:** Multicolor
Woodstar bird **Edge:** Reeded **Note:** Illustration reduced.

Date	Mintage	F	VF	XF	Unc	BU
1995 Matte	—	—	—	—	200	225
1995 Proof	—	Value: 220				

KM# 3   50 CROWNS
9.0000 g., 0.5000 Gold 0.1447 oz. AGW **Ruler:** Elizabeth II
Subject: Centenary - Birth of Churchill **Obv:** National arms
Rev: Bust 1/4 left **Edge:** REDEEMABLE AT TURKS AND
CAICOS FOR U.S. CURRENCY

Date	Mintage	F	VF	XF	Unc	BU
1974 Matte	30,000	—	—	—	155	165
1974 Proof	4,000	Value: 165				

KM# 10   50 CROWNS
6.2200 g., 0.5000 Gold 0.1000 oz. AGW **Ruler:** Elizabeth II
Subject: Age of Exploration **Obv:** Young bust right **Rev:** Head
od Christopher Columbus right and 3 ships

Date	Mintage	F	VF	XF	Unc	BU
1975	2,863	—	—	—	110	120
1975 Proof	1,577	Value: 120				

KM# 15   50 CROWNS
6.2200 g., 0.5000 Gold 0.1000 oz. AGW **Ruler:** Elizabeth II
Subject: U.S. Bicentennial **Obv:** Young bust right **Rev:** Cameos
facing each other below flags and crossed scepter and sword

Date	Mintage	F	VF	XF	Unc	BU
1976	905	—	—	—	110	120
1976 Proof	2,421	Value: 120				

KM# 16   50 CROWNS
55.1800 g., 0.9250 Silver 1.6410 oz. ASW **Ruler:** Elizabeth II
Obv: Young bust right **Rev:** 4 Victoria cameos left

Date	Mintage	F	VF	XF	Unc	BU
1976 Matte	3,500	—	—	—	40.00	45.00
1976 Proof	2,908	Value: 45.00				
1977 Proof	940	Value: 50.00				

KM# 20   50 CROWNS
9.0000 g., 0.5000 Gold 0.1447 oz. AGW **Ruler:** Elizabeth II
Subject: Queen's Silver Jubilee **Obv:** Young bust right
Rev: Crown and date within sprigs above banner

Date	Mintage	F	VF	XF	Unc	BU
1977	—	—	—	—	155	165
1977 Proof	2,903	Value: 170				

KM# 21   50 CROWNS
55.1800 g., 0.9250 Silver 1.6410 oz. ASW **Ruler:** Elizabeth II
Obv: Young bust right **Rev:** 4 George III cameos right

Date	Mintage	F	VF	XF	Unc	BU
1977	—	—	—	—	50.00	55.00
1977 Proof	958	Value: 60.00				

KM# 34   50 CROWNS
9.0000 g., 0.5000 Gold 0.1447 oz. AGW **Ruler:** Elizabeth II
Subject: 25th Anniversary of Coronation **Obv:** Young bust right
Rev: Lion of England right

Date	Mintage	F	VF	XF	Unc	BU
1978 Proof	261	Value: 180				

KM# 35   50 CROWNS
9.0000 g., 0.5000 Gold 0.1447 oz. AGW **Ruler:** Elizabeth II
Obv: Young bust right **Rev:** Griffin of Edward III left

Date	Mintage	F	VF	XF	Unc	BU
1978 Proof	266	Value: 180				

Date	Mintage	F	VF	XF	Unc	BU
1995 Matte	—	—	—	—	200	225
1995 Proof	—	Value: 220				

KM# 36 50 CROWNS
9.0000 g., 0.5000 Gold 0.1447 oz. AGW **Ruler:** Elizabeth II
Obv: Young bust right **Rev:** Red Dragon of Wales left

Date	Mintage	F	VF	XF	Unc	BU
1978 Proof	266	Value: 180				

KM# 37 50 CROWNS
9.0000 g., 0.5000 Gold 0.1447 oz. AGW **Ruler:** Elizabeth II
Obv: Young bust right **Rev:** White Greyhound of Richmond

Date	Mintage	F	VF	XF	Unc	BU
1978 Proof	270	Value: 180				

KM# 38 50 CROWNS
9.0000 g., 0.5000 Gold 0.1447 oz. AGW **Ruler:** Elizabeth II
Obv: Young bust right **Rev:** The Unicorn of Scotland right

Date	Mintage	F	VF	XF	Unc	BU
1978 Proof	268	Value: 180				

KM# 39 50 CROWNS
9.0000 g., 0.5000 Gold 0.1447 oz. AGW **Ruler:** Elizabeth II
Obv: Young bust right **Rev:** White Horse of Hannover left

Date	Mintage	F	VF	XF	Unc	BU
1978 Proof	266	Value: 180				

KM# 40 50 CROWNS
9.0000 g., 0.5000 Gold 0.1447 oz. AGW **Ruler:** Elizabeth II
Obv: Young bust right **Rev:** Black Bull of Clarence Left

Date	Mintage	F	VF	XF	Unc	BU
1978 Proof	269	Value: 180				

KM# 41 50 CROWNS
9.0000 g., 0.5000 Gold 0.1447 oz. AGW **Ruler:** Elizabeth II
Obv: Young bust right **Rev:** Yale of Beaufort left

Date	Mintage	F	VF	XF	Unc	BU
1978 Proof	254	Value: 180				

KM# 42 50 CROWNS
9.0000 g., 0.5000 Gold 0.1447 oz. AGW **Ruler:** Elizabeth II
Obv: Young bust right **Rev:** Falcon of the Plantagenets right

Date	Mintage	F	VF	XF	Unc	BU
1978 Proof	265	Value: 180				

KM# 43 50 CROWNS
9.0000 g., 0.5000 Gold 0.1447 oz. AGW **Ruler:** Elizabeth II
Obv: Young bust right **Rev:** White Lion of Mortimer left

Date	Mintage	F	VF	XF	Unc	BU
1978 Proof	265	Value: 180				

KM# 61 50 CROWNS
136.0800 g., 0.9250 Silver 4.0468 oz. ASW, 63 mm.
Ruler: Elizabeth II **Subject:** Columbus proposes Atlantic voyage to Ferdinand and Isabella **Obv:** Young bust right **Rev:** 3 Wreathed cameos and ship **Note:** Illustration reduced.

Date	Mintage	F	VF	XF	Unc	BU
1986 Proof	20,000	Value: 95.00				

KM# 4 100 CROWNS
18.0150 g., 0.5000 Gold 0.2896 oz. AGW **Ruler:** Elizabeth II
Subject: Birth of Churchill Centenary **Obv:** National arms
Rev: Bust 1/4 left

Date	Mintage	F	VF	XF	Unc	BU
1974	4,500	—	—	—	300	320
1974 Proof	5,100	Value: 325				

KM# 11 100 CROWNS
12.4400 g., 0.5000 Gold 0.2000 oz. AGW **Ruler:** Elizabeth II
Subject: Age of Exploration **Obv:** Young bust right
Rev: Spacecraft flying around globe

Date	Mintage	F	VF	XF	Unc	BU
1975	756	—	—	—	215	225
1975 Proof	1,508	Value: 220				

KM# 17 100 CROWNS
18.0150 g., 0.5000 Gold 0.2896 oz. AGW **Ruler:** Elizabeth II
Obv: Young bust right **Rev:** 4 Victoria coin obverses

Date	Mintage	F	VF	XF	Unc	BU
1976	250	—	—	—	300	320
1976 Proof	350	Value: 325				
1977	1,655	—	—	—	300	320
1977 Proof	2,648	Value: 325				

KM# 22 100 CROWNS
18.0150 g., 0.5000 Gold 0.2896 oz. AGW **Ruler:** Elizabeth II
Obv: Young bust right **Rev:** 4 George III coin obverses

Date	Mintage	F	VF	XF	Unc	BU
1977		—	—	—	300	320
1977 Proof	844	Value: 320				

KM# 44 100 CROWNS
18.0150 g., 0.5000 Gold 0.2896 oz. AGW **Ruler:** Elizabeth II
Subject: XI Commonwealth Games

Date	Mintage	F	VF	XF	Unc	BU
1978 Proof	540	Value: 320				

KM# 46 100 CROWNS
18.0150 g., 0.5000 Gold 0.2896 oz. AGW **Ruler:** Elizabeth II
Subject: 10th Anniversary - Prince Charles' Investiture
Obv: Young bust right **Rev:** Head of Prince Charles facing left at right with crown, crossed sword and sceptre at left

Date	Mintage	F	VF	XF	Unc	BU
1979	10,000	—	—	—	300	320

KM# 50 100 CROWNS
12.9600 g., 0.5000 Gold 0.2083 oz. AGW **Ruler:** Elizabeth II
Subject: Lord Mountbatten **Obv:** Crowned bust right **Rev:** Bust 1/4 right flanked by dates

Date	Mintage	F	VF	XF	Unc	BU
1980 Proof	—	Value: 225				

KM# 54 100 CROWNS
6.4800 g., 0.9000 Gold 0.1875 oz. AGW **Ruler:** Elizabeth II
Subject: Wedding of Prince Charles and Lady Diana
Rev: Conjoined busts left

Date	Mintage	F	VF	XF	Unc	BU
1981 Proof	1,205	Value: 200				

KM# 59 100 CROWNS
6.4800 g., 0.9000 Gold 0.1875 oz. AGW **Ruler:** Elizabeth II
Subject: World Football Championship **Obv:** Young bust right
Rev: Football players

Date	Mintage	F	VF	XF	Unc	BU
1982 Proof	565	Value: 225				

KM# 62   100 CROWNS
7.1300 g., 0.9000 Gold 0.2063 oz. AGW **Ruler:** Elizabeth II
Series: Decade for Women **Rev:** Half-length figure right

Date	Mintage	F	VF	XF	Unc	BU
1985 Proof	313	Value: 275				

KM# 65   100 CROWNS
10.0000 g., 0.9170 Gold 0.2948 oz. AGW **Ruler:** Elizabeth II
Series: World Wildlife Fund **Obv:** Crowned bust right **Rev:** Spiny
lobster

Date	Mintage	F	VF	XF	Unc	BU
1988 Proof	Est. 5,000	Value: 320				

KM# 248   100 CROWNS
Silver **Ruler:** Elizabeth II **Subject:** 50th Anniversary Normandy
Landings **Obv:** Crowned bust right **Obv. Leg.:** ELIZABETH II -
TURKS AND CAICOS ISLANDS **Rev:** Field Marshall
Montgomery with planes and paratroopers in background
Rev. Leg.: D-DAY 6 JUNE '44 **Edge:** Reeded

Date	Mintage	F	VF	XF	Unc	BU
1994 Proof	—	Value: 220				

KM# 237   100 CROWNS
155.5175 g., 0.9990 Gold Plated Silver 4.9948 oz. ASW AGW,
63.7 mm. **Ruler:** Elizabeth II **Subject:** Queen's Golden Wedding
Anniversary **Obv:** National arms **Rev:** Wedding portrait of Queen
and Prince Philip **Edge:** Reeded and numbered **Note:** Illustration
reduced.

Date	Mintage	F	VF	XF	Unc	BU
1997 Proof	3,000	Value: 220				

PATTERNS
Standard metals unless noted otherwise

KM#	Date	Mintage	Identification	Issue Price	Mkt Val
Pn1	ND(1993)	50	20 Crowns. Silver. Bobsledders.	—	75.00
Pn2	ND(1993)	50	20 Crowns. Silver. Skier.	—	75.00
Pn3	ND(1993)	50	20 Crowns. Silver. Ski jumper.	—	75.00
Pn4	ND(1993)	50	20 Crowns. Silver. Figure skater.	—	75.00
Pn5	ND(1993)	50	20 Crowns. Silver. Hockey player.	—	75.00
Pn6	ND(1993)	50	20 Crowns. Silver. Speed skater.	—	75.00

PIEFORTS

KM#	Date	Mintage	Identification	Issue Price	Mkt Val
P1	1980	500	5 Crowns. Silver. KM47.	79.50	32.00
P2	1980	400	10 Crowns. Silver. KM48.	95.00	38.00
P3	1980	300	20 Crowns. Silver. KM49.	115	40.00
P4	1980	250	100 Crowns. Gold. KM50.	825	275
P5	1982	80	10 Crowns. Silver. KM55.	—	135
P6	1991	—	Crown. Silver. 61.93 g, KM76.	—	40.00
P7	1991	400	Crown. Silver. 62.08 g, KM121.	—	30.00

MINT SETS

KM#	Date	Mintage	Identification	Issue Price	Mkt Val
MS1	1975 (7)	440	KM5-11	214	350
MS2	ND(1993) (8)	—	KM87-94	67.20	45.00
MS3	ND(1993) (6)	—	KM103-108	49.95	35.00
MS4	1995 (4)	—	KM133-136	33.50	33.50
MS5	1996 (10)	—	KM143, 146, 149, 152, 155, 158, 161, 164, 167, 170	33.50	33.50

PROOF SETS

KM#	Date	Mintage	Identification	Issue Price	Mkt Val
PS1	1974 (2)	1,600	KM2, 4	—	170
PS2	1975 (7)	1,270	KM5-8, 9.1, 10-11	313	385
PS3	1976 (4)	2,185	KM5, 6, 9.2, 12	78.00	85.00
PS4	1976 (3)	—	KM14, 16, 17	280	270
PS5	1976 (2)	1,951	KM13, 15	108	115
PS6	1977 (4)	1,370	KM5, 6, 9.2, 12	87.50	100
PS7	1977 (3)	—	KM18, 21, 22	280	380
PS8	1977 (2)	—	KM14, 18	62.00	115
PS9	1978 (10)	—	KM24-33	560	320
PS10	1978 (10)	—	KM34-43	1,120	1,650
PS11	1979 (2)	—	KM45, 46	228	160
PS12	1980 (4)	—	KM47-50	458	195
PS13	1980 (3)	—	KM47-49	108	45.00
PS15	ND(1993) (8)	—	KM95-102	320	325
PS17	ND(1993) (6)	—	KM109-114	234	255
PS18	1995 (4)	15,000	KM137-140	160	160
PS19	1996 (10)	20,000	KM144, 147, 150, 153, 156, 159, 162, 165, 168, 171	220	220
PS20	1996 (10)	20,000	KM145, 148, 151, 154, 157, 160, 163, 166, 169, 172	350	350

TUVALU

SOLOMON ISLANDS

Coral Sea

VANUATU

FIJI ISLANDS

AUSTRALIA

NEW CALEDONIA

Tuvalu (formerly the Ellice or Lagoon Islands of the Gilbert and
Ellice Islands), located in the South Pacific north of the Fiji Islands,
has an area of 10 sq. mi. (26 sq.km.) and a population of *9,000.
Capital: Funafuti. The independent state includes the islands of
Nanumanga, Nanumea, Nui, Niutao, Viatupa, Funafuti, Nukufetau,
Nukulailai and Nurakita. The latter four islands were claimed by the
United States until relinquished by the Feb. 7, 1979, Treaty of
Friendship signed by the United States and Tuvalu. The principal
industries are copra production and phosphate mining.

The islands were discovered in 1764 by John Byron, a British
navigator, and annexed by Britain in 1892. In 1915 they became
part of the crown colony of the Gilbert and Ellice Islands. In 1974
the islanders voted to separate from the Gilberts, becoming on
Jan. 1, 1976, the separate constitutional dependency of Tuvalu.
Full independence was attained on Oct. 1, 1978. Tuvalu is a member of the Commonwealth of Nations. Elizabeth II is Head of State
as Queen of Tuvalu.

RULER
British, until 1978

MONETARY SYSTEM
100 Cents = 1 Dollar

CONSTITUTIONAL MONARCHY WITHIN THE COMMONWEALTH
STANDARD COINAGE

KM# 1   CENT
2.6000 g., Bronze, 17.5 mm. **Obv:** Young bust right **Rev:** Sea
shell and value

Date	Mintage	F	VF	XF	Unc	BU
1976	93,000			0.10	0.50	1.00
1976 Proof	20,000	Value: 1.00				
1981	—			0.10	0.50	1.00
1981 Proof	—	Value: 1.00				
1985	—			0.10	0.50	1.00

KM# 26   CENT
2.6000 g., Bronze, 17.5 mm. **Obv:** Crowned head right
Rev: Sea shell and value

Date	Mintage	F	VF	XF	Unc	BU
1994	—				0.50	1.00

KM# 2   2 CENTS
5.2000 g., Bronze, 21.6 mm. **Obv:** Young bust right
Rev: Stingray and value

Date	Mintage	F	VF	XF	Unc	BU
1976	51,000	—	0.10	0.15	1.00	2.50
1976 Proof	20,000	Value: 1.75				
1981	—		0.10	0.15	1.00	2.50
1981 Proof	—	Value: 1.75				
1985	—		0.10	0.15	1.00	2.50

KM# 30   2 CENTS
5.2000 g., Bronze, 21.6 mm. **Obv:** Crowned head right

Date	Mintage	F	VF	XF	Unc	BU
1994	—	—	—		1.00	2.00

KM# 3   5 CENTS
2.8000 g., Copper-Nickel, 19.4 mm. **Obv:** Young bust right
Rev: Tiger shark and value

Date	Mintage	F	VF	XF	Unc	BU
1976	26,000	—	0.10	0.25	1.50	3.50
1976 Proof	20,000	Value: 4.00				
1981	—		0.10	0.25	1.50	3.50
1981 Proof	—	Value: 4.00				
1985	—		0.10	0.25	1.50	3.50

KM# 31   5 CENTS
2.8000 g., Copper-Nickel, 19.4 mm. **Obv:** Crowned head right

Date	Mintage	F	VF	XF	Unc	BU
1994	—	—	—		1.50	4.00

KM# 4   10 CENTS
5.6000 g., Copper-Nickel, 23.5 mm. **Obv:** Young bust right
Rev: Crab and value

Date	Mintage	F	VF	XF	Unc	BU
1976	26,000	0.15	0.20	0.35	1.50	4.00
1976 Proof	20,000	Value: 4.00				
1981	—	0.15	0.20	0.35	1.50	4.00

Date	Mintage	F	VF	XF	Unc	BU
1981 Proof	—	Value: 4.00				
1985		0.15	0.20	0.35	1.50	4.00

KM# 32 10 CENTS
5.6000 g., Copper-Nickel, 23.5 mm. **Obv:** Crowned head right

Date	Mintage	F	VF	XF	Unc	BU
1994	—	—	—	—	1.50	4.00

KM# 5 20 CENTS
11.2500 g., Copper-Nickel, 28.45 mm. **Obv:** Young bust right
Rev: Flying fish and value

Date	Mintage	F	VF	XF	Unc	BU
1976	36,000	0.30	0.40	0.60	2.50	4.50
1976 Proof	20,000	Value: 6.00				
1981	—	0.30	0.40	0.60	2.50	4.50
1981 Proof	—	Value: 6.00				
1985		0.30	0.40	0.60	2.50	4.50

KM# 33 20 CENTS
11.2500 g., Copper-Nickel, 28.45 mm. **Obv:** Crowned head right

Date	Mintage	F	VF	XF	Unc	BU
1994	—	—	—	—	2.00	3.50

KM# 6 50 CENTS
15.5000 g., Copper-Nickel, 31.65 mm. **Obv:** Young bust right
Rev: Octopus and value

Date	Mintage	F	VF	XF	Unc	BU
1976	19,000	0.50	0.75	1.50	5.00	8.50
1976 Proof	20,000	Value: 8.00				
1981	—	0.50	0.75	1.50	5.00	8.50
1981 Proof	—	Value: 8.00				
1985		0.50	0.75	1.50	5.00	8.50

KM# 34 50 CENTS
15.5000 g., Copper-Nickel, 31.65 mm. **Obv:** Crowned head right

Date	Mintage	F	VF	XF	Unc	BU
1994	—	—	—	—	5.00	8.00

KM# 7 DOLLAR
16.0000 g., Copper-Nickel, 33 mm. **Obv:** Young bust right
Rev: Sea turtle and value

Date	Mintage	F	VF	XF	Unc	BU
1976	21,000	1.00	1.50	2.00	6.00	10.00
1976 Proof	20,000	Value: 11.50				
1981	—	1.00	1.50	2.00	6.00	10.00
1981 Proof	—	Value: 11.50				
1985		1.00	1.50	2.00	6.00	10.00

KM# 35 DOLLAR
16.0000 g., Copper-Nickel, 33 mm. **Obv:** Crowned head right

Date	Mintage	F	VF	XF	Unc	BU
1994	—	—	—	—	6.00	10.00

KM# 37 2 DOLLARS
10.0000 g., 0.5000 Silver 0.1607 oz. ASW, 30 mm.
Series: Olympics **Obv:** Crowned head right **Rev:** Swimmer
Edge: Reeded

Date	Mintage	F	VF	XF	Unc	BU
1996 Proof	—	Value: 7.00				

KM# 48 2 DOLLARS
15.8500 g., 0.9250 Silver 0.4714 oz. ASW, 28.3 mm.
Obv: Crowned head right **Rev:** Queen Mother receiving honorary
Doctor of Music degree **Edge:** Reeded

Date	Mintage	F	VF	XF	Unc	BU
1997 Proof	—	Value: 12.50				

KM# 8 5 DOLLARS
28.2800 g., 0.9250 Silver 0.8410 oz. ASW **Obv:** Young bust
right **Rev:** Outrigger canoe

Date	Mintage	F	VF	XF	Unc	BU
1976 Proof	20,000	Value: 15.00				

KM# 12 5 DOLLARS
Copper-Nickel **Subject:** Wedding of Prince Charles and Lady
Diana **Obv:** Young bust right **Rev:** Three plumes within crown,
value at right

Date	Mintage	F	VF	XF	Unc	BU
1981	—	—	—	—	5.00	6.50

KM# 12a 5 DOLLARS
28.2800 g., 0.9250 Silver 0.8410 oz. ASW **Subject:** Wedding
of Prince Charles and Lady Diana **Obv:** Young bust right
Rev: Three plumes within crown, value at right

Date	Mintage	F	VF	XF	Unc	BU
1981 Proof	35,000	Value: 14.50				

KM# 38 5 DOLLARS
31.6400 g., 0.9250 Silver 0.9409 oz. ASW, 38.6 mm.
Subject: Victorian Age **Obv:** Crowned head right **Rev:** 3/4
Standing figure at left, SS Great Britain in back at right
Edge: Reeded

Date	Mintage	F	VF	XF	Unc	BU
1997 Proof	—	Value: 18.50				

KM# 45 5 DOLLARS
31.5500 g., 0.9250 Silver 0.9382 oz. ASW, 38.6 mm.
Subject: Queen Mother - Opening of the Federal Parliament at
Canberra **Obv:** Crowned head right **Rev:** Cameo of the Queen
Mother and King George VI above the Australian Parliament building
Edge: Reeded

Date	Mintage	F	VF	XF	Unc	BU
1997 Proof	—	Value: 18.50				

KM# 46 5 DOLLARS
31.5500 g., 0.9250 Silver 0.9382 oz. ASW, 38.6 mm.
Subject: Queen Mother **Obv:** Crowned head right **Rev:** Queen
Mother being granted an Honorary Doctor of Music degree
Edge: Reeded

Date	Mintage	F	VF	XF	Unc	BU
1997 Proof	—	Value: 18.50				

KM# 36 5 DOLLARS
31.2200 g., 0.9250 Silver 0.9284 oz. ASW, 30.2 mm.
Subject: Millennium 2000 **Obv:** Crowned head right
Rev: Seashell, stars and stylized waves above value
Edge: Reeded, square

Date	Mintage	F	VF	XF	Unc	BU
1998 Proof	—	Value: 20.00				

KM# 47   5 DOLLARS
31.5200 g., 0.9250 Silver 0.9373 oz. ASW, 38.7 mm.
Subject: Princess Diana **Obv:** Crowned head right **Rev:** Diana
Edge: Reeded

Date	Mintage	F	VF	XF	Unc	BU
1998 Proof	—	Value: 20.00				

KM# 56   5 DOLLARS
31.0600 g., Silver, 38.74 mm. **Ruler:** Elizabeth II **Obv:** Bust right
Obv. Leg.: • QUEEN ELIZABETH II • TUVALU • **Rev:** Early
Spanish sailing ship - La Princesa **Rev. Leg.:** * NANUMAGA -
ISLA DEL COCAL * FRANCISCO MOURELLE * PRINCESA *
Edge: Reeded

Date	Mintage	F	VF	XF	Unc	BU
1999 Proof	—	—				

KM# 44   5 DOLLARS
31.2000 g., 0.9250 Silver 0.9278 oz. ASW, 30.2 mm.
Subject: Millennium **Obv:** Crowned head right **Rev:** Seashell
and value **Edge:** Reeded

Date	Mintage	F	VF	XF	Unc	BU
2000 Proof	—	Value: 18.50				

KM# 10   10 DOLLARS
35.0000 g., 0.5000 Silver 0.5626 oz. ASW **Subject:** 1st
Anniversary of Independence **Obv:** Young bust right
Rev: Brigantine "Rebecca"

Date	Mintage	F	VF	XF	Unc	BU
1979	5,000	—	—	—	12.50	14.50

KM# 10a   10 DOLLARS
35.0000 g., 0.9250 Silver 1.0408 oz. ASW **Obv:** Young bust
right **Rev:** Brigantine "Rebecca"

Date	Mintage	F	VF	XF	Unc	BU
1979 Proof	2,500	Value: 20.00				

KM# 11   10 DOLLARS
35.0000 g., 0.5000 Silver 0.5626 oz. ASW **Subject:** 80th
Birthday of Queen Mother **Obv:** Young bust right **Rev:** Crowned
bust of the Queen Mother left

Date	Mintage	F	VF	XF	Unc	BU
1980	—	—	—	—	10.00	12.00

KM# 11a   10 DOLLARS
35.0000 g., 0.9250 Silver 1.0408 oz. ASW **Obv:** Young bust
right **Rev:** Crowned bust of the Queen Mother left

Date	Mintage	F	VF	XF	Unc	BU
1980 Proof	—	Value: 18.00				

KM# 13   10 DOLLARS
35.0000 g., 0.5000 Silver 0.5626 oz. ASW **Subject:** Duke of
Edinburgh Award **Obv:** Young bust right **Rev:** Head left

Date	Mintage	F	VF	XF	Unc	BU
1981	5,000	—	—	—	10.00	12.00

KM# 13a   10 DOLLARS
35.0000 g., 0.9250 Silver 1.0408 oz. ASW **Subject:** Duke of
Edinburgh Award **Obv:** Young bust right **Rev:** Head left

Date	Mintage	F	VF	XF	Unc	BU
1981 Proof	3,000	Value: 17.50				

KM# 15   10 DOLLARS
35.0000 g., 0.5000 Silver 0.5626 oz. ASW **Subject:** Royal Visit
Obv: Young bust right **Rev:** Conjoined busts of the Queen and
Prince Philip right within circle

Date	Mintage	F	VF	XF	Unc	BU
1982	2,500	—	—	—	10.00	12.00

KM# 15a   10 DOLLARS
35.0000 g., 0.9250 Silver 1.0408 oz. ASW **Subject:** Royal Visit
Obv: Young bust right **Rev:** Conjoined busts of the Queen and
Prince Philip right within circle

Date	Mintage	F	VF	XF	Unc	BU
1982 Proof	2,500	Value: 20.00				

KM# 16   20 DOLLARS
31.4700 g., 0.9250 Silver 0.9359 oz. ASW **Subject:** 40th
Anniversary of Coronation **Obv:** Crowned head right
Rev: Coronation scene

Date	Mintage	F	VF	XF	Unc	BU
1993 Proof	10,000	Value: 16.50				

KM# 17   20 DOLLARS
31.4700 g., 0.9250 Silver 0.9359 oz. ASW **Subject:** Sir Isaac
Newton **Obv:** Crowned head right

Date	Mintage	F	VF	XF	Unc	BU
1993 Proof	10,000	Value: 16.50				

KM# 18   20 DOLLARS
31.4700 g., 0.9250 Silver 0.9359 oz. ASW **Obv:** Crowned head
right **Rev:** HMS Royalist

Date	Mintage	F	VF	XF	Unc	BU
1993 Proof	15,000	Value: 16.50				

KM# 19   20 DOLLARS
31.4700 g., 0.9250 Silver 0.9359 oz. ASW **Obv:** Crowned head
right **Rev:** Leatherback Turtle

Date	Mintage	F	VF	XF	Unc	BU
1993 Proof	Est. 10,000	Value: 35.00				

KM# 20   20 DOLLARS
31.4700 g., 0.9250 Silver 0.9359 oz. ASW **Obv:** Crowned head
right **Rev:** Dugong - Manatee-like animal

Date	Mintage	F	VF	XF	Unc	BU
1994 Proof	Est. 10,000	Value: 40.00				

KM# 22   20 DOLLARS
31.4700 g., 0.9250 Silver 0.9359 oz. ASW **Subject:** 1994 World
Cup Soccer **Obv:** Crowned head right **Rev:** Soccer ball within
circles of world flags

Date	Mintage	F	VF	XF	Unc	BU
1994 Proof	Est. 30,000	Value: 16.50				

KM# 24 20 DOLLARS
31.4700 g., 0.9250 Silver 0.9359 oz. ASW **Series:** Olympics **Obv:** Crowned head right **Rev:** Swimming event

Date	Mintage	F	VF	XF	Unc	BU
1994 Proof	Est. 50,000	Value: 16.00				

KM# 25 20 DOLLARS
31.4700 g., 0.9250 Silver 0.9359 oz. ASW **Series:** Olympics **Obv:** Crowned head right **Rev:** Javelin thrower

Date	Mintage	F	VF	XF	Unc	BU
1994 Proof	Est. 50,000	Value: 22.50				

KM# 27 20 DOLLARS
31.7000 g., 0.9250 Silver 0.9427 oz. ASW **Series:** Protect Our World **Obv:** Crowned head right **Rev:** Blue Coral seascape

Date	Mintage	F	VF	XF	Unc	BU
1994 Proof	—	Value: 17.50				

KM# 39 20 DOLLARS
155.5000 g., 0.9990 Silver 4.9942 oz. ASW, 65 mm. **Subject:** Birthday of Queen Elizabeth - The Queen Mother **Obv:** Crowned head right **Rev:** Queen Mother and grandchildren **Edge:** Reeded **Note:** Illustration reduced.

Date	Mintage	F	VF	XF	Unc	BU
1996 Proof	3,000	Value: 145				

KM# 70 20 DOLLARS
1.2400 g., 0.9990 Gold 0.0398 oz. AGW, 13.80 mm. **Ruler:** Elizabeth II **Subject:** Death of Princess Diana **Obv:** Crowned head right **Rev:** 1/2 length figure of Diana slightly right **Edge:** Reeded

Date	Mintage	F	VF	XF	Unc	BU
1997 Proof	—	Value: 55.00				

KM# 9 50 DOLLARS
15.9800 g., 0.9170 Gold 0.4711 oz. AGW **Obv:** Young bust right **Rev:** Native meeting hut

Date	Mintage	F	VF	XF	Unc	BU
1976 Proof	2,074	Value: 500				

KM# 14 50 DOLLARS
15.9800 g., 0.9170 Gold 0.4711 oz. AGW **Subject:** Wedding of Prince Charles and Lady Diana **Obv:** Young bust right **Rev:** Three plumes within crown, value at right

Date	Mintage	F	VF	XF	Unc	BU
1981 Proof	5,000	Value: 500				

KM# 29 100 DOLLARS
7.7760 g., 0.5833 Gold 0.1458 oz. AGW **Subject:** 40th Anniversary of Coronation **Obv:** Crowned head right **Rev:** Coronation scene

Date	Mintage	F	VF	XF	Unc	BU
1993 Proof	—	Value: 160				

KM# 21 100 DOLLARS
7.7760 g., 0.5833 Gold 0.1458 oz. AGW **Subject:** Todos Los Santos

Date	Mintage	F	VF	XF	Unc	BU
1994 Proof	3,000	Value: 165				

KM# 23 100 DOLLARS
7.7760 g., 0.5833 Gold 0.1458 oz. AGW **Subject:** 1994 World Cup Soccer **Obv:** Crowned head right **Rev:** Soccer ball to upper left of eagle head and wing

Date	Mintage	F	VF	XF	Unc	BU
1994 Proof	3,000	Value: 160				

MINT SETS

KM#	Date	Mintage	Identification	Issue Price	Mkt Val
MS1	1985 (7)	—	KM#1-7	10.00	20.00

PROOF SETS

KM#	Date	Mintage	Identification	Issue Price	Mkt Val
PS1	1976 (7)	20,000	KM#1-7	13.00	25.00
PS2	1981 (7)	—	KM#1-7	—	25.00

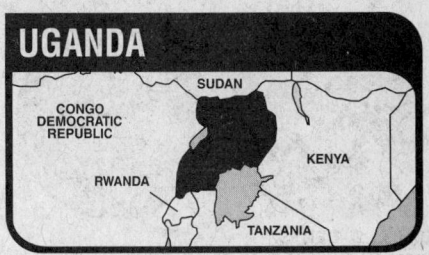

UGANDA

The Republic of Uganda, a former British protectorate located astride the equator in east-central Africa, has an area of 91,134 sq. mi. (236,040 sq. km.) and a population of *17 million. Capital: Kampala. Agriculture, including livestock, is the basis of the economy; there is some mining of copper, tin, gold and lead. Coffee, cotton, copper and tea are exported.

Uganda was first visited by Arab slavers in the 1830s. They were followed in the 1860s by British explorers searching for the headwaters of the Nile. The explorers, and the missionaries who followed them into the Lake Victoria region of south central Africa in 1877-79, found well-developed African kingdoms dating back several centuries. In 1894 the local native Kingdom of Buganda was established as a British protectorate that was extended in 1896 to encompass an area substantially the same as the present Republic of Uganda. The protectorate was given a ministerial form of government in 1955, full internal self-government on March 1, 1962, and complete independence on Oct. 9, 1962. Uganda is a member of the Commonwealth of Nations. The president is Chief of State and Head of Government.

For earlier coinage refer to East Africa.

RULER
British, until 1962

MONETARY SYSTEM
100 Cents = 1 Shilling

REPUBLIC
STANDARD COINAGE

KM# 1 5 CENTS
3.2100 g., Bronze, 20 mm. **Obv:** Value above crossed tusks within circle **Rev:** Value within circular sprig **Edge:** Plain

Date	Mintage	F	VF	XF	Unc	BU
1966	41,000,000	—	0.10	0.15	0.30	1.00
1966 Proof	—	Value: 1.00				
1974	8,624,000	—	0.20	0.30	0.75	1.00
1975	14,784,000	—	0.20	0.30	0.75	1.00

KM# 1a 5 CENTS
Copper Plated Steel **Obv:** Value above crossed tusks within circle **Rev:** Value within circular sprig

Date	Mintage	F	VF	XF	Unc	BU
1976	10,000,000	—	0.20	0.30	0.75	—

KM# 2 10 CENTS
5.0000 g., Bronze, 24.5 mm. **Obv:** Value above crossed tusks within circle **Rev:** Value within circular sprig

Date	Mintage	F	VF	XF	Unc	BU
1966	19,100,000	—	0.10	0.15	0.35	1.00
1966 Proof	—	Value: 1.00				
1968	20,000,000	—	0.10	0.15	0.35	1.00
1970	6,000,000	—	0.20	0.30	0.75	1.00
1972	6,000,000	—	0.20	0.30	0.75	1.00
1974	4,110,000	—	0.20	0.30	0.75	1.25
1975	14,000,000	—	0.20	0.30	0.75	1.25

KM# 2a 10 CENTS
Copper-Plated-Steel **Obv:** Value above crossed tusks within circle **Rev:** Value within circular sprig

Date	Mintage	F	VF	XF	Unc	BU
1976	10,000,000	—	0.20	0.30	0.75	1.25

KM# 3 20 CENTS
Bronze **Obv:** Value above crossed tusks within circle **Rev:** Value within circular sprig

Date	Mintage	F	VF	XF	Unc	BU
1966	7,000,000	—	0.30	0.70	1.65	2.00
1966 Proof	—	Value: 2.00				
1974	2,000,000	—	0.50	1.00	2.25	3.00

KM# 4 50 CENTS
Copper-Nickel **Obv:** National arms **Rev:** East African crowned crane, mountains and value

Date	Mintage	F	VF	XF	Unc	BU
1966	16,000,000	—	0.20	0.40	2.00	3.50
1966 Proof	—	Value: 3.50				
1970	3,000,000	—	0.25	0.75	3.00	3.50
1974	10,000,000	—	0.25	0.65	2.00	3.50

KM# 4a 50 CENTS
Copper-Nickel Plated Steel **Obv:** National arms **Rev:** East African crowned crane within circular sprig above value and date

Date	Mintage	F	VF	XF	Unc	BU
1976	10,000,000	—	0.25	0.65	2.00	3.00

KM# 5 SHILLING
Copper-Nickel **Obv:** National arms **Rev:** East African crowned crane within circular sprig above date and value

Date	Mintage	F	VF	XF	Unc	BU
1966	24,500,000	—	0.25	0.50	2.50	4.50
1966 Proof	—	Value: 4.50				
1968	10,000,000	—	0.35	0.85	2.75	4.50
1972	4,040,000	—	0.35	0.85	2.75	4.50
1975	15,500,000	—	0.35	0.85	2.50	4.50

KM# 5a SHILLING
Copper-Nickel Plated Steel **Obv:** National arms **Rev:** East African crowned crane within circular sprig above date and value

Date	Mintage	F	VF	XF	Unc	BU
1976	10,000,000	—	0.35	0.85	2.50	4.00

KM# 27 SHILLING
4.3000 g., Copper Plated Steel, 19.85 mm. **Obv:** National arms **Rev:** Flowers 3/4 surround value within center circle, sack below above date **Edge:** Plain

Date	Mintage	F	VF	XF	Unc	BU
1987	—	—	—	—	0.25	0.40
1987 Proof	—	Value: 2.50				

KM# 6 2 SHILLINGS
Copper-Nickel **Obv:** National arms **Rev:** East African crowned crane within circular sprig above date and value

Date	Mintage	F	VF	XF	Unc	BU
1966	4,000,000	—	1.00	2.00	5.00	7.50
1966 Proof	—	Value: 9.00				

KM# 8 2 SHILLINGS
4.0000 g., 0.9990 Silver 0.1285 oz. ASW **Subject:** Visit of Pope Paul VI **Obv:** National arms **Rev:** Head right

Date	Mintage	F	VF	XF	Unc	BU
1969 Proof	8,170	Value: 8.50				
1970 Proof	Inc. above	Value: 8.50				

KM# 28 2 SHILLINGS
8.1000 g., Copper Plated Steel, 24.37 mm. **Obv:** National arms **Rev:** Value in center circle of flowered sprigs **Edge:** Plain

Date	Mintage	F	VF	XF	Unc	BU
1987	—	—	—	—	1.00	1.50
1987 Proof	—	Value: 4.00				

KM# 7 5 SHILLINGS
Copper-Nickel, 37.8 mm. **Series:** F.A.O. **Obv:** National arms **Rev:** Cow and calf

Date	Mintage	F	VF	XF	Unc	BU
ND(1968)	100,000	—	1.50	2.50	5.00	7.00
ND(1968) Proof	5,000	Value: 8.50				

KM# 9 5 SHILLINGS
10.0000 g., 0.9990 Silver 0.3212 oz. ASW **Subject:** Visit of Pope Paul VI **Obv:** National arms **Rev:** Crested cranes within circle

Date	Mintage	F	VF	XF	Unc	BU
1969 Proof	7,670	Value: 16.50				
1970 Proof	Inc. above	Value: 16.50				

KM# 18 5 SHILLINGS
Copper-Nickel, 30 mm. **Obv:** National arms **Rev:** East African crowned crane within circular sprig **Edge:** Plain **Note:** Withdrawn from circulation. Almost entire mintage was melted.

Date	Mintage	F	VF	XF	Unc	BU
1972	Est. 8,000,000	—	25.00	45.00	90.00	125

KM# 29 5 SHILLINGS
3.5000 g., Stainless Steel, 20.23 mm. **Obv:** National arms **Rev:** Value within center circle of sprigs **Edge:** Plain

Date	Mintage	F	VF	XF	Unc	BU
1987	—	—	—	—	2.50	3.00
1987 Proof	—	Value: 6.50				

KM# 10 10 SHILLINGS
20.0000 g., 0.9990 Silver 0.6423 oz. ASW **Subject:** Visit of Pope Paul VI **Obv:** National arms **Rev:** Martyrs' shrine within circle

Date	Mintage	F	VF	XF	Unc	BU
1969 Proof	6,720	Value: 22.50				
1970 Proof	Inc. above	Value: 22.50				

KM# 21 10 SHILLINGS
Copper-Nickel **Subject:** Wedding of Prince Charles and Lady Diana **Obv:** National arms **Rev:** Conjoined heads right

Date	Mintage	F	VF	XF	Unc	BU
1981	10,000	—	—	—	7.00	8.00

KM# 30 10 SHILLINGS
5.8000 g., Stainless Steel, 25.91 mm. **Obv:** National arms **Rev:** Value in center circle of sprigs **Edge:** Plain

Date	Mintage	F	VF	XF	Unc	BU
1987	—	—	—	—	3.50	4.50
1987 Proof	—	Value: 12.50				

KM# 11 20 SHILLINGS
40.0000 g., 0.9990 Silver 1.2847 oz. ASW **Subject:** Visit of Pope
Paul VI **Obv:** National arms **Rev:** Bust right within map and circle

Date	Mintage	F	VF	XF	Unc	BU
1969 Proof	6,670	Value: 30.00				
1970 Proof	Inc. above	Value: 32.50				

KM# 12 25 SHILLINGS
50.0000 g., 0.9990 Silver 1.6059 oz. ASW **Subject:** Visit of Pope
Paul VI **Obv:** National arms **Rev:** Half-length figure facing, right
arm raised in blessing superimposed on world globe

Date	Mintage	F	VF	XF	Unc	BU
1969 Proof	6,070	Value: 32.50				
1970 Proof	Inc. above	Value: 35.00				

KM# 13 30 SHILLINGS
60.0000 g., 0.9990 Silver 1.9270 oz. ASW, 60 mm.
Subject: Visit of Pope Paul VI **Obv:** National arms **Rev:** Head
right **Note:** Illustration reduced.

Date	Mintage	F	VF	XF	Unc	BU
1969 Proof	6,720	Value: 37.50				
1970 Proof	Inc. above	Value: 40.00				

KM# 14 50 SHILLINGS
6.9100 g., 0.9000 Gold 0.1999 oz. AGW **Subject:** Visit of Pope
Paul VI **Obv:** National arms **Rev:** Martyrs' shrine within circle

Date	Mintage	F	VF	XF	Unc	BU
1969 Proof	4,390	Value: 225				
1970 Proof	Inc. above	Value: 225				

KM# 66 50 SHILLINGS
Nickel Plated Steel **Obv:** National arms **Rev:** Antelope head facing

Date	Mintage	F	VF	XF	Unc	BU
1998	—	—	—	—	1.00	1.25

KM# 15 100 SHILLINGS
13.8200 g., 0.9000 Gold 0.3999 oz. AGW **Subject:** Visit of Pope
Paul VI **Obv:** National arms **Rev:** Bust right within map and circle

Date	Mintage	F	VF	XF	Unc	BU
1969 Proof	4,190	Value: 400				
1970 Proof	Inc. above	Value: 400				

KM# 22 100 SHILLINGS
31.4700 g., 0.9250 Silver 0.9359 oz. ASW **Subject:** Wedding
of Prince Charles and Lady Diana **Obv:** National arms

Date	Mintage	F	VF	XF	Unc	BU
1981 Proof	5,000	Value: 40.00				

KM# 67 100 SHILLINGS
7.0000 g., Copper-Nickel, 26.9 mm. **Obv:** National arms
Rev: African bull **Edge:** Reeded

Date	Mintage	F	VF	XF	Unc	BU
1998	—	—	—	—	1.50	1.75

KM# 148 200 SHILLINGS
7.6000 g., Aluminum-Bronze, 27 mm. **Series:** Food For All
Subject: 50 Years - FAO **Obv:** National arms **Obv. Leg.:** BANK
OF UGANDA **Rev:** Fish

Date	Mintage	F	VF	XF	Unc	BU
1995	20,000	—	—	—	—	18.00

KM# 68 200 SHILLINGS
8.0500 g., Copper-Nickel, 24.9 mm. **Obv:** National arms
Rev: Cichlid fish above value and date **Edge:** Plain

Date	Mintage	F	VF	XF	Unc	BU
1998	—	—	—	—	2.00	2.50

KM# 16 500 SHILLINGS
69.1200 g., 0.9000 Gold 1.9999 oz. AGW **Subject:** Visit of Pope
Paul VI **Obv:** National arms **Rev:** Bust with hat facing within world
globe

Date	Mintage	F	VF	XF	Unc	BU
1969 Proof	1,680	Value: 2,150				
1970 Proof	Inc. above	Value: 2,150				

KM# 26 200 SHILLINGS
28.2800 g., 0.9250 Silver 0.8410 oz. ASW **Series:** International
Year of Disabled Persons **Obv:** National arms **Rev:** Wooden cane
divides emblem within wreath

Date	Mintage	F	VF	XF	Unc	BU
1981	10,000	—	—	—	25.00	27.50
1981 Proof	10,000	Value: 37.50				

KM# 23 500 SHILLINGS
136.0000 g., 0.5000 Silver 2.1862 oz. ASW **Series:** Wildlife
Obv: Bust of Dr. Milton Obote facing **Rev:** Elephants

Date	Mintage	F	VF	XF	Unc	BU
1981	700	—	—	—	140	160

KM# 23a 500 SHILLINGS
136.0000 g., 0.9250 Silver 4.0444 oz. ASW **Series:** Wildlife
Obv: Bust of Dr. Milton Obote facing **Rev:** Elephants

Date	Mintage	F	VF	XF	Unc	BU
1981 Proof	700	Value: 185				

KM# 69   500 SHILLINGS
9.0000 g., Aluminum-Brass, 23.5 mm. **Obv:** National arms
Rev: East African crowned crane head left **Edge:** Reeded

Date	Mintage	F	VF	XF	Unc	BU
1998	—	—	—	—	2.50	3.00

KM# 149   500 SHILLINGS
20.0000 g., Silver **Obv:** National arms **Obv. Leg.:** BANK OF
UGANDA **Rev:** Galao Matschiei animal sitting on tree branch

Date	Mintage	F	VF	XF	Unc	BU
1999 Proof	—	Value: 40.00				

KM# 17   1000 SHILLINGS
138.2400 g., 0.9000 Gold 3.9999 oz. AGW **Subject:** Visit of
Pope John Paul VI **Obv:** National arms **Rev:** Head right

Date	Mintage	F	VF	XF	Unc	BU
1969 Proof	1,390	Value: 4,250				
1970 Proof	Inc. above	Value: 4,250		*		

KM# 24   1000 SHILLINGS
10.0000 g., 0.5000 Gold 0.1607 oz. AGW **Subject:** Wedding of
Prince Charles and Lady Diana **Obv:** National arms
Rev: Conjoined busts right

Date	Mintage	F	VF	XF	Unc	BU
1981 Proof	1,500	Value: 175				

KM# 35   1000 SHILLINGS
Copper-Nickel **Series:** Famous Places **Subject:** Matterhorn
Mountain **Obv:** National arms **Rev:** Multicolor plastic applique

Date	Mintage	F	VF	XF	Unc	BU
1993	15,000	—	—	—	—	17.50

KM# 35a   1000 SHILLINGS
Silver **Series:** Famous Places **Subject:** Matterhorn Mountain
Obv: National Arms

Date	Mintage	F	VF	XF	Unc	BU
1993 Proof	—	Value: 45.00				

KM# 49   1000 SHILLINGS
Copper-Nickel **Series:** Famous Places **Subject:** Munich
Obv: National arms

Date	Mintage	F	VF	XF	Unc	BU
1994 Proof	—	Value: 17.50				

KM# 40   1000 SHILLINGS
Copper-Nickel **Series:** 50th Anniversary - United Nations
Obv: National arms **Rev:** Monument divides sprigs within circle

Date	Mintage	F	VF	XF	Unc	BU
1995 Proof	—	Value: 25.00				

KM# 50   1000 SHILLINGS
Copper-Nickel **Subject:** Year of the Pig **Obv:** Sow and piglets
left **Rev:** Stylized pig left

Date	Mintage	F	VF	XF	Unc	BU
1995 Proof	—	Value: 22.00				

KM# 41   1000 SHILLINGS
Copper-Nickel **Series:** Endangered Wildlife **Obv:** National arms
Rev: Multicolor zebra applique

Date	Mintage	F	VF	XF	Unc	BU
1996 Proof	—	Value: 25.00				

KM# 56   1000 SHILLINGS
Copper-Nickel **Subject:** Michael Schumacher **Obv:** National
arms **Rev:** Multicolor applique head facing, car and flags

Date	Mintage	F	VF	XF	Unc	BU
1996 Proof	—	Value: 22.50				
1997 Proof	—	Value: 16.50				

KM# 44   1000 SHILLINGS
Copper-Nickel **Series:** Endangered Wildlife **Obv:** National arms
Rev: Rhinoceros

Date	Mintage	F	VF	XF	Unc	BU
1996 Proof	15,000	Value: 22.50				

KM# 45   1000 SHILLINGS
Copper-Nickel **Series:** Endangered Wildlife **Obv:** National arms
Rev: Lion

Date	Mintage	F	VF	XF	Unc	BU
1996 Proof	15,000	Value: 22.50				

KM# 52   1000 SHILLINGS
Copper-Nickel **Subject:** Hong Kong's return to China
Obv: National arms **Rev:** City view

Date	Mintage	F	VF	XF	Unc	BU
1996	—	—	—	—	18.00	—

KM# 54   1000 SHILLINGS
Copper-Nickel **Subject:** Year of the rat **Obv:** Pair of rats flanking
Chinese symbol **Rev:** Multicolor rat applique

Date	Mintage	F	VF	XF	Unc	BU
1996	—	—	—	—	24.00	—

KM# 55   1000 SHILLINGS
Copper-Nickel **Subject:** Africa - Protection of Endangered
Wildlife **Obv:** National arms **Rev:** Multicolor elephant applique

Date	Mintage	F	VF	XF	Unc	BU
1996 Proof	—	Value: 25.00				

KM# 74   1000 SHILLINGS
28.5200 g., Copper-Nickel, 38.15 mm. **Subject:** Birth of Jesus
and the Modern Dating System **Obv:** National arms **Rev:** Head
of Jesus facing **Edge:** Reeded

Date	Mintage	F	VF	XF	Unc	BU
1996 Proof	—	Value: 32.50				

KM# 57   1000 SHILLINGS
Copper-Nickel **Subject:** Princess Diana - Queen of Hearts
Obv: National arms **Rev:** Multicolor applique of Princess Diana

Date	Mintage	F	VF	XF	Unc	BU
1997 Proof	—	Value: 28.00				

KM# 119   1000 SHILLINGS
28.7400 g., Copper-Nickel, 38 mm. **Obv:** National arms
Rev: Princess Diana hugging child **Edge:** Reeded

Date	Mintage	F	VF	XF	Unc	BU
1998	—	—	—	—	15.00	17.50

KM# 120   1000 SHILLINGS
28.7400 g., Copper-Nickel, 38 mm. **Obv:** National arms
Rev: Diana holding one-legged child's crutch **Edge:** Reeded

Date	Mintage	F	VF	XF	Unc	BU
1998	—	—	—	—	15.00	17.50

KM# 146   1000 SHILLINGS
19.9500 g., 0.9990 Silver 0.6407 oz. ASW, 38.3 mm.
Obv: National arms **Rev:** Lord Nelson and HMS Victory
Edge: Plain

Date	Mintage	F	VF	XF	Unc	BU
1999 Proof	—	Value: 40.00				

KM# 147   1000 SHILLINGS
19.9500 g., 0.9990 Silver 0.6407 oz. ASW, 38.3 mm.
Obv: National arms **Rev:** Albert Einstein **Edge:** Plain

Date	Mintage	F	VF	XF	Unc	BU
1999 Proof	—	Value: 40.00				

KM# 70   1000 SHILLINGS
14.9700 g., 0.9990 Silver 0.4808 oz. ASW **Series:** XXVII
Olympic Games **Obv:** National arms **Rev:** Javelin thrower

Date	Mintage	F	VF	XF	Unc	BU
1999 Proof	—	Value: 25.00				

KM# 116   1000 SHILLINGS
22.1300 g., Copper-Nickel, 38.6 mm. **Subject:** Euro Currency
Obv: National arms **Rev:** European map with paper applique
illustrating the Netherlands 10 Euro cent coin KM-237 **Edge:** Reeded

Date	Mintage	F	VF	XF	Unc	BU
1999	—	—	—	—	18.00	20.00

KM# 118   1000 SHILLINGS
31.5600 g., 0.9250 Silver 0.9385 oz. ASW, 38.7 mm.
Subject: Princess Diana **Obv:** National arms **Rev:** Charles and
Diana engagement portrait **Edge:** Reeded

Date	Mintage	F	VF	XF	Unc	BU
1999 Proof	—	Value: 45.00				

KM# 31   2000 SHILLINGS
15.9800 g., 0.9170 Gold 0.4711 oz. AGW **Series:** International
Year of Disabled Persons **Obv:** National arms **Rev:** Stylized
standing figure with cane

Date	Mintage	F	VF	XF	Unc	BU
1981	2,005	—	—	—	550	600
1981 Proof	2,005	Value: 700				

KM# 38   2000 SHILLINGS
19.8000 g., 0.9990 Silver 0.6359 oz. ASW **Subject:** World Cup
Soccer **Obv:** Arms with supporters **Rev:** Soccer player

Date	Mintage	F	VF	XF	Unc	BU
1993 Proof	—	Value: 47.50				

KM# 39   2000 SHILLINGS
19.8000 g., 0.9990 Silver 0.6359 oz. ASW **Subject:** World Cup
Soccer **Obv:** National arms **Rev:** Player kicking ball down field

Date	Mintage	F	VF	XF	Unc	BU
1993 Proof	—	Value: 47.50				

KM# 42   2000 SHILLINGS
19.9200 g., 0.9990 Silver 0.6398 oz. ASW **Series:** Famous Places
Subject: Matterhorn Mountain **Note:** With multicolor applique.

Date	Mintage	F	VF	XF	Unc	BU
1993 Proof	10,000	Value: 30.00				

KM# 64   2000 SHILLINGS
30.4600 g., 0.9990 Silver 0.9783 oz. ASW **Subject:** Protection of
the African elephant **Obv:** National arms **Rev:** Elephant head facing

Date	Mintage	F	VF	XF	Unc	BU
1993 Proof	—	Value: 50.00				

KM# 43   2000 SHILLINGS
19.9200 g., 0.9990 Silver 0.6398 oz. ASW **Series:** Famous
Places **Subject:** Munich's Frauen Kirche **Obv:** National arms
Rev: Towers

Date	Mintage	F	VF	XF	Unc	BU
1994 Proof	10,000	Value: 27.50				

KM# 53   2000 SHILLINGS
Copper-Nickel **Subject:** Nations United for Peace **Obv:** National
arms **Rev:** United Nations 50th Anniversary

Date	Mintage	F	VF	XF	Unc	BU
ND(1995)	—	—	—	—	8.50	10.00

KM# 58   2000 SHILLINGS
30.8400 g., 0.9990 Silver 0.9905 oz. ASW **Obv:** Sow and piglets
Rev: Multicolor pig applique

Date	Mintage	F	VF	XF	Unc	BU
1995 Proof	—	Value: 30.00				

KM# 46   2000 SHILLINGS
19.9200 g., 0.9990 Silver 0.6398 oz. ASW **Series:** Endangered Wildlife **Obv:** National arms **Rev:** Zebra

Date	Mintage	F	VF	XF	Unc	BU
1996 Proof	10,000		Value: 45.00			

KM# 93   2000 SHILLINGS
19.9200 g., 0.9990 Silver 0.6398 oz. ASW **Obv:** National arms **Rev:** Multicolor leaning Tower of Pisa

Date	Mintage	F	VF	XF	Unc	BU
1996 Proof	10,000		Value: 35.00			

KM# 94   2000 SHILLINGS
19.9000 g., 0.9990 Silver 0.6391 oz. ASW, 37.9 mm. **Subject:** Christian Dating System **Obv:** National arms **Rev:** Head of Jesus facing **Edge:** Reeded

Date	Mintage	F	VF	XF	Unc	BU
1996 Proof			Value: 40.00			

KM# 122   2000 SHILLINGS
31.0200 g., 0.9990 Silver 0.9963 oz. ASW, 38.5 mm. **Subject:** Wonders of the World - Leaning Tower of Pisa **Obv:** National arms **Rev:** Leaning tower within circle **Edge:** Reeded

Date	Mintage	F	VF	XF	Unc	BU
1996 Proof		—	Value: 55.00			

KM# 123   2000 SHILLINGS
31.0200 g., 0.9990 Silver 0.9963 oz. ASW, 38.5 mm. **Subject:** Wonders of the World - The Pyramids **Obv:** National arms **Rev:** Sphinx within circle **Edge:** Reeded

Date	Mintage	F	VF	XF	Unc	BU
1996 Proof		—	Value: 55.00			

KM# 124   2000 SHILLINGS
31.0200 g., 0.9990 Silver 0.9963 oz. ASW, 38.5 mm. **Subject:** Wonders of the World - The Parthenon **Obv:** National arms **Rev:** Building within circle **Edge:** Reeded

Date	Mintage	F	VF	XF	Unc	BU
1996 Proof		—	Value: 55.00			

KM# 125   2000 SHILLINGS
31.0200 g., 0.9990 Silver 0.9963 oz. ASW, 38.5 mm. **Subject:** Rome Colosseum **Obv:** National arms **Rev:** Colosseum within circle **Edge:** Reeded

Date	Mintage	F	VF	XF	Unc	BU
1996 Proof		—	Value: 55.00			

KM# 126   2000 SHILLINGS
31.0200 g., 0.9990 Silver 0.9963 oz. ASW, 38.5 mm. **Subject:** Wonders of the World - Taj Mahal **Obv:** National arms **Rev:** Taj Mahal within circle **Edge:** Reeded

Date	Mintage	F	VF	XF	Unc	BU
1996 Proof		—	Value: 55.00			

KM# 127   2000 SHILLINGS
31.0200 g., 0.9990 Silver 0.9963 oz. ASW, 38.5 mm. **Subject:** Wonders of the World - Yungang Grottoes **Obv:** National arms **Rev:** Half figures facing in front of mountain **Edge:** Reeded

Date	Mintage	F	VF	XF	Unc	BU
1996 Proof		—	Value: 55.00			

KM# 47   2000 SHILLINGS
19.9200 g., 0.9990 Silver 0.6398 oz. ASW **Series:** Endangered Wildlife **Obv:** National arms **Rev:** Rhinocerous within circle

Date	Mintage	F	VF	XF	Unc	BU
1996 Proof	10,000		Value: 50.00			

KM# 48   2000 SHILLINGS
19.9200 g., 0.9990 Silver 0.6398 oz. ASW **Series:** Endangered Wildlife **Obv:** National arms **Rev:** Lion

Date	Mintage	F	VF	XF	Unc	BU
1996 Proof	10,000		Value: 50.00			

KM# 59   2000 SHILLINGS
30.8400 g., 0.9990 Silver 0.9905 oz. ASW **Obv:** Pair of rats flanking Chinese symbols **Rev:** Multicolor rat applique

Date	Mintage	F	VF	XF	Unc	BU
1996 Proof		—	Value: 35.00			

KM# 60   2000 SHILLINGS
7.1000 g., 0.9990 Silver 0.2280 oz. ASW **Subject:** 1998 World Championship Football **Obv:** National arms **Rev:** Soccer player and Eiffel Tower within circle

Date	Mintage	F	VF	XF	Unc	BU
1996 Proof		—	Value: 22.50			

KM# 61   2000 SHILLINGS
Copper-Nickel **Series:** XXVI Summer Olympic Games **Obv:** National arms **Rev:** German Olympic stamp

Date	Mintage	F	VF	XF	Unc	BU
1996 Proof		—	Value: 20.00			

KM# 62 2000 SHILLINGS
Copper-Nickel **Series:** Olympics **Obv:** National arms
Rev: Spanish postal stamp design

Date	Mintage	F	VF	XF	Unc	BU
1996 Proof	—	Value: 20.00				

KM# 65 2000 SHILLINGS
20.2600 g., 0.9990 Silver 0.6507 oz. ASW **Series:** Endangered
Wildlife **Obv:** National arms **Rev:** Multicolor elephant

Date	Mintage	F	VF	XF	Unc	BU
1996 Proof	—	Value: 40.00				

KM# 63 2000 SHILLINGS
Copper-Nickel **Subject:** Queen's Golden Wedding Anniversary
Obv: National arms **Rev:** Queen Elizabeth and Prince Philip on
horseback

Date	Mintage	F	VF	XF	Unc	BU
ND(1997)	—	—	—	—	10.00	12.00

KM# 51 2000 SHILLINGS
19.7400 g., 0.9990 Silver 0.6340 oz. ASW **Subject:** Hong Kong's
return to China **Obv:** National arms **Rev:** City view below head left

Date	Mintage	F	VF	XF	Unc	BU
1997 Proof	—	Value: 37.50				

KM# 150 2000 SHILLINGS
6.8800 g., Silver, 30 mm. **Subject:** Death of Mother Teresa
Obv: National arms **Obv. Leg.:** BANK OF UGANDA **Rev:** Bust
of Mother Teresa with child **Rev. Leg.:** THE ANGEL OF THE
POOR **Edge:** Reeded

Date	Mintage	F	VF	XF	Unc	BU
1997 Proof	—	Value: 32.50				

KM# 95 2000 SHILLINGS
31.3200 g., 0.9990 Silver 1.0059 oz. ASW, 38.8 mm.
Subject: Zebras **Obv:** National arms **Rev:** Zebra and nursing
colt **Edge:** Reeded

Date	Mintage	F	VF	XF	Unc	BU
1999 Proof	—	Value: 45.00				

KM# 71 2000 SHILLINGS
26.0000 g., 0.9990 Silver 0.8350 oz. ASW, 40.1 mm.
Series: Olympics 2000 **Obv:** Crowned head right above national
arms **Rev:** Hurdler **Edge:** Reeded

Date	Mintage	F	VF	XF	Unc	BU
2000 Proof	5,000	Value: 32.50				

KM# 72 2000 SHILLINGS
15.7500 g., 0.9250 Silver 0.4684 oz. ASW, 45.2x23.2 mm.
Series: Millennium **Obv:** National arms above crowned head
right **Rev:** Pythagoras **Edge:** Plain

Date	Mintage	F	VF	XF	Unc	BU
2000 Proof	10,000	Value: 30.00				

KM# 73 2000 SHILLINGS
25.0000 g., 0.9250 Silver 0.7435 oz. ASW, 37.9 mm.
Subject: Wildlife protection **Obv:** National arms below crowned
head right **Rev:** Three zebras drinking in reflective water
Edge: Reeded

Date	Mintage	F	VF	XF	Unc	BU
2000 Proof	5,000	Value: 35.00				

KM# 117 4000 SHILLINGS
1.5300 g., 0.9990 Gold 0.0491 oz. AGW, 16 mm.
Subject: Famous Places **Obv:** Arms with supporters
Rev: Matterhorn Mountain within circle **Edge:** Plain

Date	Mintage	F	VF	XF	Unc	BU
ND(1997) Proof	—	Value: 75.00				

KM# 25 5000 SHILLINGS
33.9300 g., 0.9170 Gold 1.0003 oz. AGW **Subject:** Wildlife
Obv: Bust of Dr. Milton Obote facing **Rev:** East African crowned
crane

Date	Mintage	F	VF	XF	Unc	BU
1981	100	—	—	—	1,150	1,200
1981 Proof	100	Value: 1,250				

KM# 32 5000 SHILLINGS
12.0000 g., 0.9990 Silver 0.3854 oz. ASW **Subject:** Soccer
Obv: National arms **Rev:** Soccer ball and net

Date	Mintage	F	VF	XF	Unc	BU
1992	Est. 10,000	—	—	—	22.50	25.00

KM# 36 5000 SHILLINGS
500.0000 g., 0.9990 Silver 16.058 oz. ASW **Series:** Endangered
Wildlife **Obv:** African map **Rev:** 2 Leopards on branches

Date	Mintage	F	VF	XF	Unc	BU
1993 Proof	2,500	Value: 285				

Note: Underweight coins exist

KM# 36.1   5000 SHILLINGS
10.4800 g., 0.9990 Silver 0.3366 oz. ASW, 38 mm.
Subject: Reduced Size **Obv:** African map **Rev:** Two lions in tree
Edge: Reeded

Date	Mintage	F	VF	XF	Unc	BU
1993 Proof	—	Value: 35.00				

KM# 128   5000 SHILLINGS
28.2000 g., Silver, 38 mm.   **Subject:** FAO - Food for All
Obv: National arms **Rev:** Bananas

Date	Mintage	F	VF	XF	Unc	BU
1995	—	—	—	—	—	40.00

KM# 33   10000 SHILLINGS
20.0000 g., 0.9990 Silver 0.6423 oz. ASW   **Subject:** Soccer
Obv: National arms **Rev:** Mount Rushmore behind soccer players

Date	Mintage	F	VF	XF	Unc	BU
ND(1992) Proof	Est. 10,000	Value: 45.00				

KM# 34   10000 SHILLINGS
20.0000 g., 0.9990 Silver 0.6423 oz. ASW   **Subject:** Papal visit
Obv: National arms **Rev:** Half-length figure facing

Date	Mintage	F	VF	XF	Unc	BU
1993 Proof	—	Value: 37.50				

KM# 37.1   10000 SHILLINGS
12.9420 g., 0.9990 Silver 0.4157 oz. ASW, 38 mm.
Subject: Reduced Size **Obv:** African map **Rev:** Two rhinos
Edge: Reeded

Date	Mintage	F	VF	XF	Unc	BU
1993 Proof	—	Value: 35.00				

KM# 37   10000 SHILLINGS
1000.0000 g., 0.9990 Silver 32.117 oz. ASW
Series: Endangered Wildlife **Obv:** African map **Rev:** Rhinoceros

Date	Mintage	F	VF	XF	Unc	BU
1993 Proof	2,000	Value: 500				
	Note: Underweight coins exist					

KM# 92   10000 SHILLINGS
155.5000 g., 0.9990 Silver 4.9942 oz. ASW, 65 mm.
Subject: Diana Princess of Wales **Obv:** National arms **Rev:** Head
1/4 right **Edge:** Reeded **Note:** Illustration reduced.

Date	Mintage	F	VF	XF	Unc	BU
1998 Proof	2,500	Value: 150				

PATTERNS
Including off metal strikes

KM#	Date	Mintage	Identification	Mkt Val
Pn1	1994	—	1000 Shillings. Copper-Nickel. Soccer player, 999.	—
Pn2	1994	—	1000 Shillings. Copper-Nickel. 3 soccer players, 999 CuNi.	—
Pn3	1994	—	1000 Shillings. Copper-Nickel. 4 soccer players, 999.	—
Pn4	1996	—	1000 Shillings. Gilt Bronze. Surinam. 100 Guilders.	—

PIEFORTS

KM#	Date	Mintage	Identification	Mkt Val
P1	1981	—	200 Shillings. 0.9250 Silver. KM26.	75.00
P2	1981	505	2000 Shillings. 0.9170 Gold. KM31.	750

TRIAL STRIKES

KM#	Date	Mintage	Identification	Mkt Val
TS1	1969	—	500 Shillings. Goldine. KM16.	100
TS2	1970	—	1000 Shillings. Goldine. National arms. KM17.	125

MINT SETS

KM#	Date	Mintage	Identification	Issue Price	Mkt Val
MS1	1987 (4)	—	KM27-30	10.50	11.50

PROOF SETS

KM#	Date	Mintage	Identification	Issue Price	Mkt Val
PS1	1966 (6)	8,250	KM1-6	7.75	14.50
PS2	1969 (10)	1,390	KM8-17	790	6,500
PS3	1969 (6)	6,070	KM8-13	78.50	145
PS4	1970 (10)	I.A.	KM8-17, mintage included in KM-PS2	790	6,500
PS5	1970 (6)	I.A.	KM8-13, mintage included in KM-PS3	78.50	155
PS6	1987 (4)	2,500	KM27-30	25.00	27.50

UKRAINE

Ukraine (formerly the Ukrainian Soviet Socialist Republic) is bordered by Russia to the east, Russia and Belarus to the north, Poland, Slovakia and Hungary to the west, Romania and Moldova to the southwest and in the south by the Black Sea and the Sea of Azov. It has an area of 233,088 sq. mi. (603,700 sq. km.) and a population of 51.9 million. Capital: Kyiv (Kiev). Coal, grain, vegetables and heavy industrial machinery are major exports.

The territory of Ukraine has been inhabited for over 30,000 years. As the result of its location, Ukraine has served as the gateway to Europe for millennia and its early history has been recorded by Arabic, Greek, Roman, as well as Ukrainian historians.

With the disintegration of the Russian and Austro-Hungarian Empires in 1917 and 1918, Eastern Ukraine declared its full independence on January 22,1918 and Western Ukraine followed suit on November 1 of that year. On January 22, 1919 both parts united into one state that had to defend itself on three fronts: from the "Red Bolsheviks"and their puppet Ukrainian Soviet Republic formed in Kharkiv, from the "White" czarist Russian forces, and from Poland. Ukraine lost the war. In 1920 Eastern Ukraine was occupied by the

Bolsheviks and in 1922 was incorporated into the Soviet Union. There followed a brief resurgence of Ukrainian language and culture which Stalin suppressed in 1928. The artificial famine-genocide of 1932-33 killed 7-10 million Ukrainians, and Stalinist purges in the mid-1930s took a heavy toll. Western Ukraine was partitioned between Poland, Romania, Hungary and Czechoslovakia.

On August 24, 1991 Ukraine once again declared its independence. On December 1, 1991 over 90% of Ukraine's electorate approved full independence from the Soviet Union. On December 5, 1991 the Ukrainian Parliament abrogated the 1922 treaty which incorporated Ukraine into the Soviet Union. Later, Leonid Kravchuk was elected president by a 65% majority.

Ukraine is a charter member of the United Nations and has inherited the third largest nuclear arsenal in the world.

RULERS
Russian (Eastern, Northern, Southern, Central Ukraine), 1654-1917
Austrian (Western Ukraine), 1774-1918

MINT
Without mm - Lugansk; Kiev (1997-1998)

MONETARY SYSTEM
(1) Kopiyka
(2) Kopiyky КОПІЙКИ
(5 and up) Kopiyok КОПІЙОК
100 Kopiyok = 1 Hrynia ГРИВЕНЬ
100,000 Karbovanetsiv = 1 Hryni or Hryven)

REPUBLIC
STANDARD COINAGE

KM# 9   200000 KARBOVANTSIV
14.3500 g., Copper-Nickel, 33 mm. **Obv:** National arms
Rev: Bohdan Khmelnytsky Monument **Edge:** Reeded

Date	Mintage	F	VF	XF	Unc	BU
1995 Prooflike	250,000	—	—	—	6.00	10.00

KM# 10.1   200000 KARBOVANTSIV
14.3500 g., Copper-Nickel, 33 mm. **Subject:** 50th Anniversary
- End of World War II **Obv:** Ukranian letter "У" looks similar to "X"
Rev: Ukranian letter "У" looks similar to "X" **Edge:** Reeded

Date	Mintage	F	VF	XF	Unc	BU
1995 Prooflike	10,000	—	—	—	40.00	45.00

KM# 10.2   200000 KARBOVANTSIV
14.3500 g., Copper-Nickel, 33 mm. **Subject:** 50th Anniversary
- End of World War II **Obv:** Ukranian letter "У" like У/2 in legends
Rev: Ukranian letter "У" like У/2 in legends **Edge:** Reeded

Date	Mintage	F	VF	XF	Unc	BU
1995 Prooflike	240,000	—	—	—	5.00	7.50

KM# 11   200000 KARBOVANTSIV
14.3500 g., Copper-Nickel, 33 mm. **Subject:** World War II -
Monument at Kerch **Obv:** National arms **Rev:** Monument and
ship **Edge:** Reeded

Date	Mintage	F	VF	XF	Unc	BU
1995 Prooflike	50,000	—	—	—	15.00	25.00

KM# 12   200000 KARBOVANTSIV
14.3500 g., Copper-Nickel, 33 mm.   **Subject:** World War II - Monument at Odessa **Obv:** National arms **Rev:** Monument divides ship and lighthouse **Edge:** Reeded

Date	Mintage	F	VF	XF	Unc	BU
1995 Prooflike	75,000	—	—	—	7.00	10.00

KM# 13   200000 KARBOVANTSIV
14.3500 g., Copper-Nickel, 33 mm.   **Subject:** World War II - Monument at Kiev **Obv:** National arms **Rev:** Monument and city scene **Edge:** Reeded

Date	Mintage	F	VF	XF	Unc	BU
1995 Prooflike	100,000	—	—	—	6.00	7.50

KM# 14   200000 KARBOVANTSIV
14.3500 g., Copper-Nickel, 33 mm.   **Subject:** World War II - Monument at Sevastopol **Obv:** National arms **Rev:** Monuments and ship **Edge:** Reeded

Date	Mintage	F	VF	XF	Unc	BU
1995 Prooflike	75,000	—	—	—	7.00	10.00

KM# 15   200000 KARBOVANTSIV
28.2800 g., Copper-Nickel, 38.61 mm.   **Series:** 50th Anniversary - United Nations **Obv:** National arms **Rev:** Numeral 50 and emblem on top of assorted flag globe **Edge:** Reeded **Note:** Issued in March 1996

Date	Mintage	F	VF	XF	Unc	BU
1995	100,000	—	—	—	7.00	10.00

KM# 17   200000 KARBOVANTSIV
14.3500 g., Copper-Nickel, 33 mm.   **Subject:** Lesya Ukrainka **Obv:** National arms **Rev:** Half-length Poetess facing **Edge:** Reeded

Date	Mintage	F	VF	XF	Unc	BU
1996 Prooflike	100,000	—	—	—	7.00	10.00

KM# 21   200000 KARBOVANTSIV
14.3500 g., Copper-Nickel, 33 mm.   **Subject:** 10th Anniversary - Chernobyl Disaster **Obv:** National arms **Rev:** Bell with cross at top **Edge:** Reeded

Date	Mintage	F	VF	XF	Unc	BU
1996 Prooflike	250,000	—	—	—	6.00	8.00

KM# 23   200000 KARBOVANTSIV
14.3500 g., Copper-Nickel, 33 mm.   **Series:** 1st Participation in Summer Olympics **Obv:** National arms **Rev:** Athletes around octagon **Edge:** Reeded

Date	Mintage	F	VF	XF	Unc	BU
1996 Prooflike	100,000	—	—	—	6.00	8.00

KM# 24   200000 KARBOVANTSIV
14.3500 g., Copper-Nickel, 33 mm.   **Series:** Centennial of Modern Olympics **Obv:** National arms **Rev:** Flame and logo **Edge:** Reeded

Date	Mintage	F	VF	XF	Unc	BU
1996 Prooflike	100,000	—	—	—	6.00	8.00

KM# 27   200000 KARBOVANTSIV
14.3500 g., Copper-Nickel, 33 mm.   **Subject:** Mikhailo Hrushevsky - 1866-1934 **Obv:** National arms **Rev:** Half-length figure facing **Edge:** Reeded

Date	Mintage	F	VF	XF	Unc	BU
1996 Prooflike	75,000	—	—	—	7.00	10.00

KM# 16   1000000 KARBOVANETS
16.8110 g., 0.9250 Silver 0.4999 oz. ASW, 33 mm.   **Obv:** National arms **Rev:** Bohdan Khmelnytsky Monument **Edge:** Reeded

Date	Mintage	F	VF	XF	Unc	BU
1996 Proof	10,000	Value: 175				

KM# 18   1000000 KARBOVANETS
16.8110 g., 0.9250 Silver 0.4999 oz. ASW, 33 mm.
Subject: Lesya Ukrainka **Obv:** National arms **Rev:** Half-length Poetess facing **Edge:** Reeded

Date	Mintage	F	VF	XF	Unc	BU
1996 Proof	10,000	Value: 150				

KM# 20   1000000 KARBOVANETS
16.8110 g., 0.9250 Silver 0.4999 oz. ASW, 33 mm.
Subject: Hryhoriy Skovoroda **Obv:** National arms **Rev:** Bust facing **Edge:** Reeded

Date	Mintage	F	VF	XF	Unc	BU
1996 Proof	10,000	Value: 115				

KM# 32   1000000 KARBOVANETS
16.8110 g., 0.9250 Silver 0.4999 oz. ASW, 33 mm.
Subject: Mykhailo Hrushevsky **Obv:** National arms **Rev:** Half-length figure facing **Edge:** Reeded

Date	Mintage	F	VF	XF	Unc	BU
1996 Proof	10,000	Value: 125				

KM# 22   2000000 KARBOVANETS

33.6220 g., 0.9250 Silver 0.9999 oz. ASW, 38.61 mm.
Subject: 10th Anniversary - Chernobyl Disaster **Obv:** National
arms **Rev:** Bell with cross at top **Edge:** Reeded

Date	Mintage	F	VF	XF	Unc	BU
1996 Proof	10,000	Value: 75.00				

KM# 19   2000000 KARBOVANETS

33.6220 g., 0.9250 Silver 0.9999 oz. ASW, 38.61 mm.
Series: 50 Years - United Nations **Obv:** National arms
Rev: Numeral 50 and emblem on top of assorted flag globe
Edge: Reeded **Note:** Minted in 1995, issued on March 7, 1996.

Date	Mintage	F	VF	XF	Unc	BU
1996 Proof	10,000	Value: 75.00				

KM# 25   2000000 KARBOVANETS

33.6220 g., 0.9250 Silver 0.9999 oz. ASW, 38.61 mm.
Series: 1st Participation in Summer Olympics **Obv:** National
arms **Rev:** Head right within octagon surrounded by athletes
Edge: Reeded

Date	Mintage	F	VF	XF	Unc	BU
1996 Proof	10,000	Value: 65.00				

KM# 26   2000000 KARBOVANETS

33.6220 g., 0.9250 Silver 0.9999 oz. ASW, 38.61 mm.
Series: Centennial of Modern Olympics **Obv:** National arms
Rev: Olympic flame and logo **Edge:** Reeded

Date	Mintage	F	VF	XF	Unc	BU
1996 Proof	10,000	Value: 65.00				

KM# 33   2000000 KARBOVANETS

33.6220 g., 0.9250 Silver 0.9999 oz. ASW, 39 mm.
Subject: Independence **Obv:** National arms **Rev:** Standing
female figure holding sprig and wreath to left of flag and map
Edge: Reeded

Date	Mintage	F	VF	XF	Unc	BU
1996 Proof	10,000	Value: 225				

REFORM COINAGE
September 2, 1996

100,000 Karbovanets = 1 Hryvnia; 100 Kopiyok =
1 Hryvnia; The Kopiyok has replaced the Karbovanet

KM# 6   KOPIYKA

1.5300 g., Stainless Steel, 15.96 mm.   **Obv:** National arms
Rev: Value within wreath **Edge:** Plain

Date	Mintage	F	VF	XF	Unc	BU
1992	—	—	—	0.15	0.35	—
1994	—	—	—	5.00	10.00	—
1996	—	—	—	2.00	5.00	—
2000	—	—	—	0.35	0.75	—

KM# 4a   2 KOPIYKU

0.6400 g., Aluminum, 17.3 mm.   **Obv:** National arms **Rev:** Value
within wreath **Edge:** Plain **Note:** Prev. KM#4.

Date	Mintage	F	VF	XF	Unc	BU
1992	—	—	—	—	200	—
1993	—	—	0.20	0.50	1.00	—
1994	—	—	0.20	0.50	1.00	—
1996	—	—	0.40	2.00	3.00	—

KM# 7   5 KOPIYOK

4.3000 g., Stainless Steel, 23.91 mm.   **Obv:** National arms
Rev: Value within wreath **Edge:** Reeded

Date	Mintage	F	VF	XF	Unc	BU
1992	—	—	—	0.35	0.65	—
1994	—	—	—	—	100	—

KM# 1.1a   10 KOPIYOK

1.7000 g., Brass, 16.3 mm.   **Obv:** National arms **Rev:** Five dots
right of final "K" in value **Edge:** Reeded **Note:** Fine or coarse
reeded edge varieties exist. Prev. KM#1.1.

Date	Mintage	F	VF	XF	Unc	BU
1992	—	—	0.50	1.00	2.25	—
1994	—	—	0.50	1.00	2.25	—
1996	—	—	0.60	1.25	2.50	—

KM# 1.2   10 KOPIYOK

Brass **Obv:** National arms **Rev:** Six dots right of "K"

Date	Mintage	F	VF	XF	Unc	BU
1992	—	—	0.50	1.00	2.25	—

KM# 2.1a   25 KOPIYOK

2.9000 g., Brass, 20.8 mm.   **Obv:** National arms **Rev:** Value
within wreath **Note:** Prev. KM#2.1.

Date	Mintage	F	VF	XF	Unc	BU
1992	—	—	0.60	1.25	2.50	—
1994	—	—	0.60	1.25	2.50	—
1995	—	—	1.50	3.00	6.00	—
1996	—	—	0.80	2.25	4.00	—

KM# 2.2   25 KOPIYOK

Brass **Obv:** National arms **Rev:** Berries with dots inside

Date	Mintage	F	VF	XF	Unc	BU
1992	—	—	0.60	1.25	2.50	—

KM# 3.1   50 KOPIYOK

4.2000 g., Brass, 23 mm.   **Obv:** National arms **Rev:** Five dots
grouped i wreath to right of final letter "K" in value **Edge:** Reeded
sections of 16 grooves each

Date	Mintage	F	VF	XF	Unc	BU
1992	—	—	0.85	1.75	3.50	—
1994	—	—	0.85	1.75	3.50	—

KM# 3.3a   50 KOPIYOK

Brass **Obv:** National arms **Rev:** Five dots grouped in wreath to
right of final letter "K" in value **Note:** Prev. KM#3.3.

Date	Mintage	F	VF	XF	Unc	BU
1992	—	—	0.85	1.75	3.50	—
1994	—	—	0.85	1.75	3.50	—
1995	—	—	3.00	5.00	10.00	—
1996	—	—	5.00	10.00	30.00	—

KM# 3.2   50 KOPIYOK

Brass **Obv:** National arms **Rev:** Four dots grouped in wreath to
right of final letter "K" in value **Edge:** Reeded sections of seven
grooves each

Date	Mintage	F	VF	XF	Unc	BU
1992	—	—	0.85	1.75	3.50	—

KM# 8a   HRYVNIA

7.1000 g., Brass, 26 mm. **Obv:** National arms **Rev:** Value, sprigs
and designs **Note:** Prev. KM#8.

Date	Mintage	F	VF	XF	Unc	BU
1992	—	—	—	80.00	200	—
1995	—	—	—	5.00	10.00	—
1996	—	—	—	2.50	4.50	—

KM# 28   2 HRYVNI

14.3500 g., Copper-Nickel-Zinc, 33 mm. **Subject:** 200th Anniversary - Sophiyivka Dendrological Park **Obv:** National arms **Rev:** Partially overgrown stone face **Edge:** Reeded

Date	Mintage	F	VF	XF	Unc	BU
1996 Prooflike	30,000	—	—	—	—	75.00

KM# 29   2 HRYVNI

14.3500 g., Copper-Nickel-Zinc, 33 mm. **Subject:** Desiatynna Church **Obv:** National arms above Madonna and child, vines surround **Rev:** Church **Edge:** Reeded

Date	Mintage	F	VF	XF	Unc	BU
1996 Prooflike	30,000	—	—	—	—	80.00

KM# 30   2 HRYVNI

Copper-Nickel-Zinc, 31 mm. **Subject:** Modern Ukrainian coinage **Obv:** National arms within beaded circle **Rev:** Assorted coins **Edge:** Reeded

Date	Mintage	F	VF	XF	Unc	BU
1997 Prooflike	250,000	—	—	—	10.00	—

Note: 200,000 minted at Lugansk Mint in 1997 with an additional 50,000 struck at Kiev Mint in 1998

KM# 39   2 HRYVNI

14.3500 g., Copper-Nickel-Zinc, 33 mm. **Subject:** Yuri Kondratiuk **Obv:** National arms on astrological design **Rev:** Scientific drawing to right of bust facing **Edge:** Reeded

Date	Mintage	F	VF	XF	Unc	BU
1997 Prooflike	20,000	—	—	—	—	120

KM# 40   2 HRYVNI

14.3500 g., Copper-Nickel-Zinc, 33 mm. **Subject:** 1st Anniversary of the Constitution **Obv:** National arms **Rev:** Scroll below design within beaded circle **Edge:** Reeded

Date	Mintage	F	VF	XF	Unc	BU
1997 Prooflike	20,000	—	—	—	—	175

KM# 41   2 HRYVNI

14.3500 g., Copper-Nickel-Zinc, 33 mm. **Subject:** Solomiya Krushelnytska - 1872-1952 **Obv:** National arms within beaded circle **Rev:** Bust with hat left **Edge:** Reeded

Date	Mintage	F	VF	XF	Unc	BU
1997 Prooflike	20,000	—	—	—	—	110

KM# 42   2 HRYVNI

12.8000 g., Copper-Nickel-Zinc, 31 mm. **Subject:** 80 Years of Nationhood **Obv:** National arms and people above value **Rev:** Outreached arm with army on forearm to right of Cossacks **Edge:** Reeded

Date	Mintage	F	VF	XF	Unc	BU
ND(1998)	150,000	—	—	—	10.00	—
ND(1998) Prooflike	50,000	—	—	—	—	15.00

KM# 49   2 HRYVNI

12.8000 g., Copper-Nickel-Zinc, 31 mm. **Subject:** 100th Anniversary - Askania-Nova Wildlife Preserve **Obv:** National arms, value, wild animals and plants **Rev:** Standing half-length figure to lower left of animals running right **Edge:** Reeded

Date	Mintage	F	VF	XF	Unc	BU
1998	90,000	—	—	—	30.00	—
1998 Prooflike	10,000	—	—	—	—	70.00

KM# 51   2 HRYVNI

12.8000 g., Copper-Nickel-Zinc, 31 mm. **Subject:** 100th Anniversary - Kiev Polytechnical Institute **Obv:** National arms in circular design **Rev:** Building within circle **Edge:** Reeded

Date	Mintage	F	VF	XF	Unc	BU
1998	40,000	—	—	—	35.00	—
1998 Prooflike	10,000	—	—	—	—	70.00

KM# 47   2 HRYVNI

12.8000 g., Copper-Nickel-Zinc, 31 mm. **Subject:** The 80th Anniversary of the Battle of Kruty **Obv:** National arms and family group **Rev:** Soldiers on guard **Edge:** Reeded

Date	Mintage	F	VF	XF	Unc	BU
1998	150,000	—	—	—	10.00	—
1998 Prooflike	50,000	—	—	—	—	15.00

KM# 43   2 HRYVNI

12.8000 g., Copper-Nickel-Zinc, 31 mm. **Subject:** Volodimir Sosura - 1898-1965 **Obv:** National arms within beaded circle **Rev:** Head facing 1/4 left **Edge:** Reeded

Date	Mintage	F	VF	XF	Unc	BU
1998 Prooflike	20,000	—	—	—	—	100

KM# 48   2 HRYVNI

12.8000 g., Copper-Nickel-Zinc, 31 mm. **Subject:** European Bank of Reconstruction and Development **Obv:** National arms and value **Rev:** Legendary founders at Kiev monument, emblem of the ERRD **Edge:** Reeded

Date	Mintage	F	VF	XF	Unc	BU
1998	10,000	—	—	—	500	—

KM# 72   2 HRYVNI

12.8000 g., Copper-Nickel-Zinc, 31 mm. **Subject:** 50 Years - United Nations Human Rights Declaration **Obv:** National arms and value **Rev:** Logo on globe within circle **Edge:** Reeded

Date	Mintage	F	VF	XF	Unc	BU
1998	100,000	—	—	—	17.50	—

KM# 73   2 HRYVNI

12.8000 g., Copper-Nickel-Zinc, 31 mm. **Subject:** Steppe Eagle **Obv:** National arms and date divide wreath, value in center **Rev:** Eagle in flight **Edge:** Reeded

Date	Mintage	F	VF	XF	Unc	BU
1999	50,000	—	—	—	100	—

KM# 75　2 HRYVNI
12.8000 g., Copper-Nickel-Zinc, 31 mm.　**Subject:** 80th
Anniversary - Ukranian State **Obv:** National arms divides date
Rev: Seated woman in front of two shields **Edge:** Reeded

Date	Mintage	F	VF	XF	Unc	BU
1999	50,000	—	—	—	25.00	—

KM# 76　2 HRYVNI
12.8000 g., Copper-Nickel-Zinc, 31 mm.　**Subject:** Panas Myrny,
(P.Y. Rudchenko, 1849-1920), writer **Obv:** National arms within
beaded circle **Rev:** Half length figure facing divides dates divides
beaded circle **Edge:** Reeded

Date	Mintage	F	VF	XF	Unc	BU
1999 Prooflike	50,000	—	—	—	10.00	—

KM# 78　2 HRYVNI
12.8000 g., Copper-Nickel-Zinc, 31 mm.　**Subject:** Anatoliy
Solovianenko (opera singer) **Obv:** National arms within beaded
circle **Rev:** Head left **Edge:** Reeded

Date	Mintage	F	VF	XF	Unc	BU
1999 Prooflike	25,000	—	—	—	17.50	—

KM# 81　2 HRYVNI
12.8000 g., Copper-Nickel-Zinc, 31 mm.　**Subject:** Platanthera
Bifolia **Obv:** National arms and date divide wreath, value in center
Rev: Flower **Edge:** Reeded

Date	Mintage	F	VF	XF	Unc	BU
1999	50,000	—	—	—	60.00	—

KM# 82　2 HRYVNI
12.8000 g., Copper-Nickel-Zinc, 31 mm.　**Subject:** 100 Years -
Ukraine's National Mining Academy **Obv:** National arms within
beaded circle **Rev:** Building within circle **Edge:** Reeded

Date	Mintage	F	VF	XF	Unc	BU
1999	20,000	—	—	—	40.00	—

KM# 83　2 HRYVNI
12.8000 g., Copper-Nickel-Zinc, 31 mm.　**Obv:** National arms and
date divide wreath, value in center **Rev:** Mouse **Edge:** Reeded

Date	Mintage	F	VF	XF	Unc	BU
1999	50,000	—	—	—	45.00	—

KM# 79　2 HRYVNI
12.8000 g., Copper-Nickel-Zinc, 31 mm.　**Subject:** 55th
Anniversary - Freedom From Nazi Occupation **Obv:** National arms
divides date at center of grain sprig wreath **Rev:** Stylized sword
design **Edge:** Reeded

Date	Mintage	F	VF	XF	Unc	BU
1999	50,000	—	—	—	35.00	—

KM# 91　2 HRYVNI
12.8000 g., Copper-Nickel-Zinc, 31 mm.　**Subject:** 55th
Anniversary - Victory in World War II **Obv:** National arms and
ribbon divide wreath, value and date within **Rev:** Symbolic
"Peace" figure **Edge:** Reeded

Date	Mintage	F	VF	XF	Unc	BU
2000	50,000	—	—	—	15.00	—

KM# 92　2 HRYVNI
12.8000 g., Copper-Nickel-Zinc, 31 mm.　**Subject:** Archaeologist
V. Hvoika **Obv:** National arms within circles and artifacts
Rev: Head facing **Edge:** Reeded

Date	Mintage	F	VF	XF	Unc	BU
2000	20,000	—	—	—	18.00	—

KM# 93　2 HRYVNI
12.8000 g., Copper-Nickel-Zinc, 31 mm.　**Series:** Sydney 2000
Olympics **Obv:** Horizontal stylized figures divides arms and value
Rev: Stylized broad jumper **Edge:** Reeded

Date	Mintage	F	VF	XF	Unc	BU
2000	50,000	—	—	—	15.00	—

KM# 94　2 HRYVNI
12.8000 g., Copper-Nickel-Zinc　**Series:** Sydney 2000 Olympics
Obv: Horizontal stylized figures divide arms and value
Rev: Stylized gymnast on parallel bars

Date	Mintage	F	VF	XF	Unc	BU
2000	50,000	—	—	—	15.00	—

KM# 96　2 HRYVNI
12.8000 g., Copper-Nickel-Zinc, 31 mm.　**Subject:** Musician Ivan
Kozlovsky **Obv:** Head left **Rev:** Value within lyre, shield at top
divides date, all within cluster of sprigs **Edge:** Reeded

Date	Mintage	F	VF	XF	Unc	BU
2000	20,000	—	—	—	18.00	—

KM# 97　2 HRYVNI
12.8000 g., Copper-Nickel-Zinc, 31 mm.　**Series:** Sydney 2000
Olympics **Obv:** Horizontal stylized sports figures divide arms and
value **Rev:** Stylized sailing scene **Edge:** Reeded

Date	Mintage	F	VF	XF	Unc	BU
2000	50,000	—	—	—	15.00	—

KM# 98　2 HRYVNI
12.8000 g., Copper-Nickel-Zinc, 31 mm.　**Subject:** Oles' Honchar
(writer) **Obv:** National arms, flowers and value **Rev:** Head facing to
right of stylized buildings, dates below **Edge:** Reeded

Date	Mintage	F	VF	XF	Unc	BU
2000	20,000	—	—	—	20.00	—

KM# 99　2 HRYVNI
12.8000 g., Copper-Nickel-Zinc, 31 mm.　**Obv:** Arms and date
divide wreath, value within **Rev:** Crab **Edge:** Reeded

Date	Mintage	F	VF	XF	Unc	BU
2000	50,000	—	—	—	30.00	—

KM# 100 2 HRYVNI
12.8000 g., Copper-Nickel-Zinc, 31 mm. **Subject:** 125th Anniversary - Chernivtsy National University **Obv:** Arms divide circular designs **Rev:** University viewed through arch **Edge:** Reeded

Date	Mintage	F	VF	XF	Unc	BU
2000	50,000	—	—	—	18.50	—

KM# 101 2 HRYVNI
12.8000 g., Copper-Nickel-Zinc, 31 mm. **Series:** Sydney 2000 Olympics **Obv:** National arms, athletes and value **Rev:** Gymnast doing floor exercise **Edge:** Reeded

Date	Mintage	F	VF	XF	Unc	BU
2000	50,000	—	—	—	17.50	—

KM# 110 2 HRYVNI
12.8000 g., Copper-Nickel-Zinc, 31 mm. **Subject:** Kateryna Bilokour (People's Artist of Ukraine) **Obv:** Shield divides date above flowers and value **Rev:** Half-figure facing right **Edge:** Reeded

Date	Mintage	F	VF	XF	Unc	BU
2000	30,000	—	—	—	22.00	—

KM# 66 5 HRYVEN
16.5400 g., Copper-Nickel-Zinc, 35 mm. **Subject:** St. Michaels Cathedral **Obv:** Arms, value and date within beaded star **Rev:** Cathedral behind human silhouettes **Edge:** Reeded

Date	Mintage	F	VF	XF	Unc	BU
1998	200,000	—	—	—	10.00	—

KM# 69 5 HRYVEN
16.5400 g., Copper-Nickel-Zinc, 35 mm. **Subject:** Kiev-Pechersk Assumption Cathedral **Obv:** Shield, value and date within beaded star **Rev:** Cathedral behind carved ruins **Edge:** Reeded

Date	Mintage	F	VF	XF	Unc	BU
1998	200,000	—	—	—	10.00	—

KM# 74 5 HRYVEN
16.5400 g., Copper-Nickel-Zinc, 35 mm. **Subject:** 900th Anniversary - Novgorod-Siversky Principality **Obv:** Value in center of stylized sun with doves left and right **Rev:** Armored horsemen **Edge:** Reeded

Date	Mintage	F	VF	XF	Unc	BU
1999	50,000	—	—	—	75.00	—

KM# 80 5 HRYVEN
16.5400 g., Copper-Nickel-Zinc, 35 mm. **Subject:** 500th Anniversary - Kiev Magdeburg Law **Obv:** Arms above value and date in center of design **Rev:** Monument to the Law **Edge:** Reeded

Date	Mintage	F	VF	XF	Unc	BU
1999	50,000	—	—	—	30.00	—

KM# 84 5 HRYVEN
16.5400 g., Copper-Nickel-Zinc, 35 mm. **Subject:** Birth of Jesus **Obv:** National arms, value and angels **Rev:** Nativity scene **Edge:** Reeded

Date	Mintage	F	VF	XF	Unc	BU
1999	100,000	—	—	—	25.00	—

KM# 95 5 HRYVEN
16.5400 g., Copper-Nickel-Zinc, 35 mm. **Subject:** 2,500 Years - Bilgorod-Dnestrovski **Obv:** Arms above value and date within design **Rev:** Castle above city arms and ancient coins **Edge:** Reeded

Date	Mintage	F	VF	XF	Unc	BU
2000	50,000	—	—	—	20.00	—

KM# 104 5 HRYVEN
9.4000 g., Bi-Metallic Brass center in Copper-Nickel ring, 28 mm. **Subject:** Third Millennium **Obv:** National arms **Rev:** Figure sowing seeds within circle **Edge:** Reeded and plain sections

Date	Mintage	F	VF	XF	Unc	BU
2000	50,000	—	—	—	35.00	—

KM# 102 5 HRYVEN
16.5400 g., Copper-Nickel-Zinc, 35 mm. **Subject:** Russian Conversion to Christianity **Obv:** National arms and angels **Rev:** Standing bearded figure facing and crowd **Edge:** Reeded

Date	Mintage	F	VF	XF	Unc	BU
2000	100,000	—	—	—	15.00	—

KM# 103 5 HRYVEN
16.5400 g., Copper-Nickel-Zinc, 35 mm. **Subject:** Centennial - Lviv's Opera House **Obv:** Vase divides seated figures below shield **Rev:** Opera house **Edge:** Reeded

Date	Mintage	F	VF	XF	Unc	BU
2000	50,000	—	—	—	15.00	—

KM# 105 5 HRYVEN
16.5400 g., Copper-Nickel-Zinc, 35 mm. **Subject:** 2600th Anniversary - City of Kerch's **Obv:** National arms above value and bracelet **Rev:** Ancient coins above pillar **Edge:** Reeded

Date	Mintage	F	VF	XF	Unc	BU
2000	50,000	—	—	—	20.00	—

KM# 34 10 HRYVEN
16.8110 g., 0.9250 Silver 0.4999 oz. ASW, 33 mm. **Subject:** Petro Mohyla, 1596-1647 **Obv:** National arms, people and building **Rev:** Bust1/4n right holding scepter **Edge:** Reeded

Date	Mintage	F	VF	XF	Unc	BU
1996 Proof	5,000	Value: 1,000				

KM# 44 10 HRYVEN
33.6220 g., 0.9999 Silver 0.9999 oz. ASW, 38.61 mm. **Series:** Nagano Olympics **Obv:** National arms divide large snow flake designs **Rev:** Cross-country skier **Edge:** Reeded

Date	Mintage	F	VF	XF	Unc	BU
1998 Proof	7,500	Value: 46.00				

KM# 45 10 HRYVEN
33.6220 g., 0.9250 Silver 0.9999 oz. ASW, 38.61 mm. **Series:** Nagano Olympics **Obv:** National arms divide larg snowflake designs **Rev:** Biathlon shooter **Edge:** Reeded

Date	Mintage	F	VF	XF	Unc	BU
1998 Proof	7,500	Value: 46.00				

KM# 50 10 HRYVEN
33.6220 g., 0.9250 Silver 0.9999 oz. ASW, 38.61 mm. **Subject:** 100th Anniversary - Ascania National Park **Obv:** National arms within cluster of plants and animals above value **Rev:** Standing half length figure to lower left of animals running right **Edge:** Reeded

Date	Mintage	F	VF	XF	Unc	BU
1998 Proof	10,000	Value: 55.00				

KM# 52 10 HRYVEN
33.6220 g., 0.9250 Silver 0.9999 oz. ASW, 38.61 mm. **Series:** Nagano Olympics **Obv:** National arms and value **Rev:** Figure skater **Edge:** Reeded

Date	Mintage	F	VF	XF	Unc	BU
1998 Proof	7,500	Value: 46.00				

KM# 53   10 HRYVEN
33.6220 g., 0.9250 Silver 0.9999 oz. ASW, 38.61 mm.
Subject: Prince Kiy - Founder of Kiev **Obv:** Value and arms within ornamental frame **Rev:** Head facing and armored equestrians
Edge: Reeded

Date	Mintage	F	VF	XF	Unc	BU
1998 Proof	10,000	Value: 80.00				

KM# 64   10 HRYVEN
33.6220 g., 0.9250 Silver 0.9999 oz. ASW, 38.61 mm.
Subject: Prince Danylo of Halych **Obv:** National arms and value within ornamental frame **Rev:** Half-length bust holding sword, castle at left and army at right **Edge:** Reeded

Date	Mintage	F	VF	XF	Unc	BU
1998 Proof	10,000	Value: 80.00				

KM# 67   10 HRYVEN
33.6220 g., 0.9250 Silver 0.9999 oz. ASW, 38.61 mm.
Subject: St. Michael's Golden-Domed Cathedral **Obv:** Arms, value and date within ornamental frame **Rev:** Human silhouettes in front of cathedral **Edge:** Reeded

Date	Mintage	F	VF	XF	Unc	BU
1998 Proof	10,000	Value: 120				

KM# 70   10 HRYVEN
33.6220 g., 0.9250 Silver 0.9999 oz. ASW, 38.61 mm.
Subject: The Kyiv-Pechersk Assumption Cathedral **Obv:** Arms, value and date within beaded star **Rev:** Cathedral behind carved ruins **Edge:** Reeded

Date	Mintage	F	VF	XF	Unc	BU
1998 Proof	10,000	Value: 120				

KM# 77   10 HRYVEN
33.6220 g., 0.9250 Silver 0.9999 oz. ASW, 38.61 mm.
Subject: Dmytro Vyshnevetsky - BAYDA (Cossack leader)
Obv: National arms with angel and crowned lion within beaded circle **Rev:** 3/4-length figure facing with bow and arrow
Edge: Reeded

Date	Mintage	F	VF	XF	Unc	BU
1999 Proof	10,000	Value: 80.00				

KM# 85   10 HRYVEN
33.9000 g., 0.9250 Silver 1.0081 oz. ASW, 38.6 mm.
Subject: Birth of Jesus **Obv:** National arms, value and angels
Rev: Nativity scene **Edge:** Reeded

Date	Mintage	F	VF	XF	Unc	BU
1999 Proof	10,000	Value: 400				

KM# 86   10 HRYVEN
33.9000 g., 0.9250 Silver 1.0081 oz. ASW, 38.61 mm.
Subject: Prince Askold **Obv:** Shield and value within Viking carvings **Rev:** Viking and ships **Edge:** Reeded

Date	Mintage	F	VF	XF	Unc	BU
1999 Proof	10,000	Value: 80.00				

KM# 87   10 HRYVEN
33.6200 g., 0.9250 Silver 0.9998 oz. ASW, 38.61 mm.
Subject: 500th Anniversary - Magdeburg Law **Obv:** National arms, value and date within design **Rev:** Monument
Edge: Reeded

Date	Mintage	F	VF	XF	Unc	BU
1999 Proof	5,000	Value: 75.00				

KM# 88   10 HRYVEN
33.6200 g., 0.9250 Silver 0.9998 oz. ASW, 38.61 mm.
Subject: Petro Doroshenko (Cossack leader) **Obv:** National arms, angel and crowned lion within beaded circle **Rev:** Armored equestrian divides beaded circle **Edge:** Reeded

Date	Mintage	F	VF	XF	Unc	BU
1999 Proof	10,000	Value: 90.00				

KM# 89   10 HRYVEN
33.6200 g., 0.9250 Silver 0.9998 oz. ASW, 38.6 mm. **Obv:** Arms and date divide wreath with bird, value within **Rev:** Dormouse
Edge: Reeded

Date	Mintage	F	VF	XF	Unc	BU
1999 Proof	5,000	Value: 250				

KM# 90   10 HRYVEN
33.6200 g., 0.9250 Silver 0.9998 oz. ASW, 38.61 mm.
Obv: Arms and date divide wreath with bird, value within
Rev: Eagle in flight **Edge:** Reeded

Date	Mintage	F	VF	XF	Unc	BU
1999 Proof	5,000	Value: 300				

KM# 116   10 HRYVEN
33.6220 g., 0.9250 Silver 0.9999 oz. ASW, 38.61 mm.
Series: Olympics **Obv:** National arms, value and Olympic motto
Rev: Stylized broad jumper **Edge:** Reeded

Date	Mintage	F	VF	XF	Unc	BU
1999 Proof	15,000	Value: 45.00				

KM# 117   10 HRYVEN
33.6220 g., 0.9250 Silver 0.9999 oz. ASW, 38.61 mm.
Series: Olympics **Obv:** National arms, value and Olympic motto
Rev: Stylized gymnast on parallel bars **Edge:** Reeded

Date	Mintage	F	VF	XF	Unc	BU
1999 Proof	15,000	Value: 45.00				

KM# 118 10 HRYVEN
33.6220 g., 0.9250 Silver 0.9999 oz. ASW, 38.61 mm.
Subject: Platanthera Bifolia **Obv:** Arms and date divide wreath,
value within **Rev:** Flower **Edge:** Reeded

Date	Mintage	F	VF	XF	Unc	BU
1999 Proof	5,000	Value: 220				

KM# 108 10 HRYVEN
33.6220 g., 0.9250 Silver 0.9999 oz. ASW, 38.61 mm.
Subject: 55th Anniversary - End of WWII **Obv:** Arms and ribbon
divide wreath, value and date within **Rev:** Standing figure holding
palm branch above head in front of globe within 1/2 wreath
Edge: Reeded

Date	Mintage	F	VF	XF	Unc	BU
2000 Proof	3,000	Value: 550				

KM# 109 10 HRYVEN
33.6220 g., 0.9250 Silver 0.9999 oz. ASW, 38.61 mm.
Subject: Conversion of the Russ to Christianity **Obv:** Arms and
value divide angels **Rev:** Mass baptism scene **Edge:** Reeded

Date	Mintage	F	VF	XF	Unc	BU
2000 Proof	10,000	Value: 95.00				

KM# 119 10 HRYVEN
33.6220 g., 0.9250 Silver 0.9999 oz. ASW, 38.61 mm.
Subject: Princess Olga **Obv:** Arms, date and value within
ornamental frame **Rev:** Princess and court scene **Edge:** Reeded

Date	Mintage	F	VF	XF	Unc	BU
2000 Proof	10,000	Value: 100				

KM# 120 10 HRYVEN
33.6220 g., 0.9250 Silver 0.9999 oz. ASW, 38.61 mm.
Subject: Petro Sahaidachny (Cossack leader) **Obv:** National
arms, angel and crowned lion within beaded circle **Rev:** Cameo
to upper right of ship within beaded circle **Edge:** Reeded

Date	Mintage	F	VF	XF	Unc	BU
2000 Proof	10,000	Value: 80.00				

KM# 121 10 HRYVEN
33.6220 g., 0.9250 Silver 0.9999 oz. ASW, 38.61 mm.
Obv: Arms and date divide wreath with bird, value within
Rev: Crab **Edge:** Reeded

Date	Mintage	F	VF	XF	Unc	BU
2000 Proof	5,000	Value: 220				

KM# 122 10 HRYVEN
33.6220 g., 0.9250 Silver 0.9999 oz. ASW, 38.61 mm.
Subject: Prince Volodymyr the Great **Obv:** Arms divide
ornamental frame, value within **Rev:** Crowned bust with raised
hands

Date	Mintage	F	VF	XF	Unc	BU
2000 Proof	5,000	Value: 600				

KM# 123 10 HRYVEN
33.6220 g., 0.9250 Silver 0.9999 oz. ASW, 38.61 mm.
Subject: 100 Years of L'viv Opera and Ballet Theatre **Obv:** Vase
divides seated figures below shield **Rev:** Opera House
Edge: Reeded

Date	Mintage	F	VF	XF	Unc	BU
2000 Proof	3,000	Value: 270				

KM# 35 20 HRYVEN
33.6220 g., 0.9250 Silver 0.9999 oz. ASW, 38.61 mm.
Subject: The Tithe Church **Obv:** Madonna and child in center
circle, vines surround **Rev:** Church **Edge:** Reeded

Date	Mintage	F	VF	XF	Unc	BU
1996 Proof	5,000	Value: 850				

KM# 36 20 HRYVEN
33.6220 g., 0.9250 Silver 0.9999 oz. ASW, 38.61 mm.
Subject: The Savior Cathedral in Chernihiv **Obv:** Arms above
Madonna and child **Rev:** Cathedral **Edge:** Reeded

Date	Mintage	F	VF	XF	Unc	BU
1997 Proof	5,000	Value: 650				

KM# 46 20 HRYVEN
33.6220 g., 0.9250 Silver 0.9999 oz. ASW, 38.61 mm.
Subject: Severyn Nalyvaiko **Obv:** National arms **Rev:** Cossacks
in revolt **Note:** Issued Jan. 10, 1998.

Date	Mintage	F	VF	XF	Unc	BU
1997 Proof	5,000	Value: 400				

KM# 54 20 HRYVEN
33.6220 g., 0.9250 Silver 0.9999 oz. ASW, 38.61 mm.
Subject: Cossack Mamay **Obv:** National arms supported by St.
Michael and lion **Rev:** Cossack playing a bandre in center of
assorted designs **Edge:** Reeded

Date	Mintage	F	VF	XF	Unc	BU
1997 Proof	5,000	Value: 850				

KM# 57 20 HRYVEN
33.6220 g., 0.9250 Silver 0.9999 oz. ASW, 38.61 mm.
Subject: 200th Anniversary - Kiev Commodity Futures Market
Obv: National arms within center of scrolls **Rev:** Steepled building, sailboat and balance scale **Edge:** Reeded

Date	Mintage	F	VF	XF	Unc	BU
1997 Proof	5,000	Value: 450				

KM# 58 20 HRYVEN
33.6220 g., 0.9250 Silver 0.9999 oz. ASW, 38.61 mm.
Subject: 350th Anniversary - Cossack Revolt **Obv:** National arms supported by St. Michael and lion **Rev:** Cossacks attacking Polish cavalryman **Edge:** Reeded

Date	Mintage	F	VF	XF	Unc	BU
1998 Proof	10,000	Value: 90.00				

KM# 126 20 HRYVEN
Bi-Metallic Gold center in silver ring, 31 mm. **Subject:** Paleolithic Age **Obv:** Eagle on captains wheel **Rev:** Pottery and petroglyphs **Edge:** Reeded and plain sections

Date	Mintage	F	VF	XF	Unc	BU
2000 Proof	3,000	Value: 400				

KM# 127 20 HRYVEN
Bi-Metallic Gold center in silver ring **Subject:** Trypolean Culture **Obv:** Eagle on captains wheel **Rev:** Ancient sculptures **Edge:** Reeded and plain alternating

Date	Mintage	F	VF	XF	Unc	BU
2000 Proof	3,000	Value: 350				

KM# 128 20 HRYVEN
Bi-Metallic Gold center in silver ring **Subject:** The Olbian City State **Obv:** Eagle on captains wheel **Rev:** Ancient coin in center circle of Greek figures

Date	Mintage	F	VF	XF	Unc	BU
2000 Proof	3,000	Value: 400				

KM# 59 50 HRYVEN
3.1104 g., 0.9999 Gold 0.1000 oz. AGW, 16 mm. **Subject:** St. Sophia Cathedral in Kiev **Obv:** Cathedral **Rev:** Mother of God Mossaic **Edge:** Segmented reeding **Note:** Minted in 1996, issued on July 28, 1997.

Date	Mintage	F	VF	XF	Unc	BU
1996	2,000	—	—	—	4,000	

KM# 124 50 HRYVEN
17.6300 g., 0.9000 Gold 0.5101 oz. AGW, 25 mm.
Subject: Birth of Jesus **Obv:** Two angels, arms and value **Rev:** Nativity scene **Edge:** Plain

Date	Mintage	F	VF	XF	Unc	BU
1999 Proof	3,000	Value: 3,000				

KM# 125 50 HRYVEN
17.6300 g., 0.9000 Gold 0.5101 oz. AGW, 25 mm.
Subject: Conversion of the Russ to Christianity **Obv:** National arms, angels and value **Rev:** Baptism scene **Edge:** Plain

Date	Mintage	F	VF	XF	Unc	BU
2000 Proof	3,000	Value: 2,500				

KM# 63 100 HRYVEN
17.2797 g., 0.9000 Gold 0.5000 oz. AGW, 25 mm.
Subject: Kyiv Psalm book **Obv:** Open book divides shield and value **Rev:** Monk writing book **Edge:** Plain **Note:** Minted in 1997, issued in January 1998.

Date	Mintage	F	VF	XF	Unc	BU
1997 Proof	2,000	Value: 4,500				

KM# 65 100 HRYVEN
17.2797 g., 0.9000 Gold 0.5000 oz. AGW **Subject:** Poem "Eneida" by Ivan P. Kotlyarevsky **Obv:** Helmet and musical instruments divide shield and value **Rev:** Seated helmeted figure playing a bandre

Date	Mintage	F	VF	XF	Unc	BU
1998 Proof	2,000	Value: 4,500				

KM# 68 100 HRYVEN
17.2797 g., 0.9000 Gold 0.5000 oz. AGW, 25 mm. **Subject:** St. Michael's Cathedral **Obv:** Arms, value and date in center of design **Rev:** Cathedral behind human silhouettes **Edge:** Plain

Date	Mintage	F	VF	XF	Unc	BU
1998 Proof	3,000	Value: 3,500				

KM# 71 100 HRYVEN
17.2797 g., 0.9000 Gold 0.5000 oz. AGW, 25 mm. **Subject:** Kyiv-Pechersk Assumption Cathedral **Obv:** Arms, value and date within beaded star **Rev:** Cathedral behind carved ruins **Edge:** Plain

Date	Mintage	F	VF	XF	Unc	BU
1998 Proof	3,000	Value: 3,500				

KM# 60 125 HRYVEN
7.7759 g., 0.9999 Gold 0.2500 oz. AGW, 20 mm. **Obv:** St. Sophia Cathedral in Kiev **Rev:** Ornate Mosaic of the Mother of God - "Oranta" **Edge:** Segmented reeding **Note:** Minted in 1996, issued on July 28, 1997.

Date	Mintage	F	VF	XF	Unc	BU
1996	4,000	—	—	—	1,200	

KM# 37 200 HRYVEN
17.5000 g., 0.9000 Gold 0.5064 oz. AGW, 25 mm. **Obv:** National arms within beaded circle **Rev:** Bust of Taras G. Shevchenko facing **Edge:** Plain **Note:** Minted in 1996, issued on March 12, 1997.

Date	Mintage	F	VF	XF	Unc	BU
1996 Proof	10,000	Value: 750				

KM# 38 200 HRYVEN
17.5000 g., 0.9000 Gold 0.5064 oz. AGW, 25 mm.
Subject: Pecherska Lavra **Obv:** Church above date and value within beaded circle **Rev:** Standing angelic figure with radiant dove within cloud-like wings **Edge:** Plain **Note:** Minted in 1996, issued on April 10, 1997.

Date	Mintage	F	VF	XF	Unc	BU
1996 Proof	20,000	Value: 750				

KM# 61 250 HRYVEN
15.5518 g., 0.9999 Gold 0.4999 oz. AGW, 25 mm. **Obv:** St. Sophia Cathedral in Kiev **Rev:** St. Sophia **Edge:** Segmented reeding **Note:** Minted in 1996, issued on July 28, 1997.

Date	Mintage	F	VF	XF	Unc	BU
1996	3,000	—	—	—	2,500	

KM# 62 500 HRYVEN
31.1035 g., 0.9999 Gold 0.9999 oz. AGW, 32 mm. **Obv:** St. Sophia Cathedral in Kiev **Rev:** St. Sophia **Edge:** Segmented reeding **Note:** Minted in 1996, issued on July 28, 1997.

Date	Mintage	F	VF	XF	Unc	BU
1996	1,000	—	—	—	20,000	—

PATTERNS
Including off metal strikes

KM#	Date	Mintage	Identification	Mkt Val
PnA1	1992	—	Hryvnia. Brass. 26mm. KM#8a.	80.00
Pn1	1992	—	Kopiyka. Aluminum.	—
Pn2	1922	—	2 Kopiyky. Aluminum.	—
Pn3	1992	—	5 Kopiyok. White Brass.	—
Pn4	1992	—	10 Kopiyok. Brass. Incuse shield.	20.00
Pn5	1992	—	15 Kopiyok. Brass.	35.00
Pn6	1992	—	15 Kopiyok. Bronze.	35.00
Pn7	1992	—	25 Kopiyok. Brass. Incuse shield.	20.00
Pn8	1992	—	50 Kopiyok. Copper-Nickel.	—
Pn9	1992	—	50 Kopiyok. Brass. Incuse shield.	20.00
Pn10	1992	—	50 Kopiyok. Brass Clad Steel.	—
Pn11	1993	—	2 Kopiyky. Brass.	—
Pn12	1993	—	2 Kopiyky. Aluminum-Zinc.	—
Pn13	1993	—	15 Kopiyok. Aluminum.	35.00
Pn14	1994	—	Kopiyka. 0.6000 Silver. Specific gravity 9.8.	—
Pn15	1994	—	2 Kopiyky. Bronze. 3.7500 g. Piefort.	—
Pn16	1994	—	Kopiyka. 0.3500 Silver. Specific gravity: 9.43.	—
Pn17	1996	—	25 Kopiyok. Aluminum.	—
Pn18	1998	—	100 Hryvnias. Brass.	—
Pn19	ND(1998)	—	100 Hryvnias. Brass.	—
Pn20	1998	—	100 Hryvnias. Brass.	—
Pn21	ND(1998)	—	100 Hryvnias. Brass.	—
Pn22	1998	—	100 Hryvnias. Brass.	—

MINT SETS

KM# MS1	Date 1996 (8)	Mintage Identification — KM#1, 2, 3.3, 4, 6, 7, 8, 30	Issue Price —	Mkt Val 170

UMM AL QAIWAIN - U.A.E.

This emirate, one of the original members of the United Arab Emirates, is the second smallest, least developed and lowest in population. The area is 300 sq. mi. (800 sq. km.) and the population is 5,000. The first recognition by the West was in 1820. Most of the emirate is uninhabited desert. Native boat building is an important activity.

TITLE

Umm al Qaiwain

RULERS
Ahmad Bin Abdullah al-Mualla, 1872-1904
Rashid Bin Ahmad al-Mualla, 1904-1929
Ahmad Bin Rashid al-Mualla, 1929-1981
Rashid Bin Ahmad al-Mualla, 1981-

EMIRATE

NON-CIRCULATING LEGAL TENDER COINAGE

KM# 1 RIYAL
3.0000 g., 1.0000 Silver 0.0964 oz. ASW **Ruler:** Ahmad bin Rashid al-Mualla **Obv:** Dates within crossed flags, sprigs within circle **Rev:** Old cannon within wreath

Date	Mintage	F	VF	XF	Unc	BU
AH1389 (1970) Proof	2,050	Value: 45.00				

KM# 2 2 RIYALS
6.0000 g., 1.0000 Silver 0.1929 oz. ASW **Ruler:** Ahmad bin Rashid al-Mualla **Obv:** Dates within crossed flags, sprigs at left and right within circle **Rev:** Fort of the 19th Century

Date	Mintage	F	VF	XF	Unc	BU
AH1389 (1970) Proof	2,050	Value: 85.00				

KM# 3 5 RIYALS
15.0000 g., 1.0000 Silver 0.4822 oz. ASW **Ruler:** Ahmad bin Rashid al-Mualla **Obv:** Dates within crossed flags, sprigs at left and right within circle **Rev:** Two gazelles

Date	Mintage	F	VF	XF	Unc	BU
AH1389 (1970) Proof	2,100	Value: 275				

KM# 4 10 RIYALS
30.0000 g., 1.0000 Silver 0.9645 oz. ASW **Ruler:** Ahmad bin Rashid al-Mualla **Obv:** Dates within crossed flags, sprigs at left and right within circle **Rev:** Facade of the great Rock Temple

Date	Mintage	F	VF	XF	Unc	BU
AH1389 (1970) Proof	2,000	Value: 600				

KM# 6 25 RIYALS
5.1800 g., 0.9000 Gold 0.1499 oz. AGW **Ruler:** Ahmad bin Rashid al-Mualla **Obv:** Dates within crossed flags, sprigs at left and right within circle **Rev:** Old cannon within wreath

Date	Mintage	F	VF	XF	Unc	BU
AH1389 (1970) Proof	500	Value: 225				

KM# 7 50 RIYALS
10.3600 g., 0.9000 Gold 0.2998 oz. AGW **Ruler:** Ahmad bin Rashid al-Mualla **Obv:** Dates within crossed flags, sprigs at left and right within circle **Rev:** Fort of the 19th Century

Date	Mintage	F	VF	XF	Unc	BU
AH1389 (1970) Proof	420	Value: 375				

KM# 8 100 RIYALS
20.7300 g., 0.9000 Gold 0.5998 oz. AGW **Ruler:** Ahmad bin Rashid al-Mualla **Obv:** Dates within crossed flags, sprigs at left and right within circle **Rev:** Gazelles

Date	Mintage	F	VF	XF	Unc	BU
AH1389 (1970) Proof	300	Value: 750				

KM# 9 200 RIYALS
41.4600 g., 0.9000 Gold 1.1996 oz. AGW **Ruler:** Ahmad bin Rashid al-Mualla **Obv:** Dates within crossed flags, sprigs at left and right within circle **Rev:** Head of Sheik Ahmed Ben Rashid as Moalia left

Date	Mintage	F	VF	XF	Unc	BU
AH1389 (1970) Proof	230	Value: 1,350				

PROOF SETS

KM#	Date	Mintage Identification	Issue Price	Mkt Val
PS1	1970 (4)	2,000 KM#1-4	26.30	315
PS2	1970 (4)	230 KM#6-9	—	2,750
PS3	1970 (8)	— KM#1-4, 6-9	—	3,750

UNITED ARAB EMIRATES

The seven United Arab Emirates (formerly known as the Trucial Sheikhdoms or States), located along the southern shore of the Persian Gulf, are comprised of the Sheikhdoms of Abu Dhabi, Dubai, al-Sharjah, Ajman, Umm al Qaiwain, Ras al-Khaimah and al-Fujairah. They have a combined area of about 32,000 sq. mi. (83,600 sq. km.) and a population of *2.1 million. Capital: Abu Zaby (Abu Dhabi). Since the oil strikes of 1958-60, the economy has centered about petroleum.

The Trucial States came under direct British influence in 1892 when the Maritime Truce Treaty enacted after the supression of pirate activity along the Trucial Coast was enlarged to enjoin the states from disposing of any territory, or entering into any foreign agreements, without British consent in return for British protection from external aggression. In March of 1971 Britain reaffirmed its decision to terminate its treaty relationships with the Trucial Sheikhdoms, whereupon the seven states joined with Bahrain and Qatar in an effort to form a union of Arab Emirates under British protection. When the prospective members failed to agree on terms of union, Bahrain and Qatar declared their respective independence, Aug. and Sept. of 1971. Six of the sheikhdoms united to form the United Arab Emirates on Dec. 2, 1971. Ras al-Khaimah joined a few weeks later.

TITLE

الامارات العربية المتحدة

al-Imara(t) al-Arabiya(t) al-Muttahida(t)

MONETARY SYSTEM

فلسا   فلس   فلوس

Falus, Fulus   Fals, Fils   Falsan

100 Fils = 1 Dirham

UNITED EMIRATES
STANDARD COINAGE

KM# 1 FILS
1.5000 g., Bronze, 15 mm. **Series:** F.A.O. **Obv:** Value
Rev: Date palms above dates **Edge:** Plain

Date	Mintage	F	VF	XF	Unc	BU
AH1393-1973	4,000,000	—	0.10	0.20	0.45	0.75
AH1395-1975	—	—	0.20	0.30	0.50	0.75
AH1408-1988	—	—	0.20	0.30	0.50	0.75
AH1409-1989	—	—	0.20	0.30	0.50	0.75
AH1418-1997	—	—	0.20	0.30	0.50	0.75

KM# 2.1 5 FILS
3.7500 g., Bronze, 22 mm. **Series:** F.A.O. **Obv:** Value
Rev: Fish above dates **Edge:** Plain

Date	Mintage	F	VF	XF	Unc	BU
AH1393-1973	11,400,000	—	0.10	0.15	0.30	1.00
AH1402-1982	—	—	0.10	0.20	0.35	1.00
AH1407-1987	—	—	0.10	0.20	0.35	1.00
AH1408-1988	—	—	0.10	0.20	0.35	1.00
AH1409-1989	—	—	0.10	0.20	0.35	1.00

KM# 2.2 5 FILS
Bronze **Series:** F.A.O. **Obv:** Value **Rev:** Fish above dates
Note: Reduced size.

Date	Mintage	F	VF	XF	Unc	BU
AH1416-1996	—	—	0.10	0.15	0.30	1.00

KM# 3.1 10 FILS
7.5000 g., Bronze, 27 mm. **Obv:** Value **Rev:** Arab dhow above
dates

Date	Mintage	F	VF	XF	Unc	BU
AH1393-1973	6,400,000	—	0.25	0.40	0.95	1.25
AH1402-1982	—	—	0.25	0.45	1.00	1.25
AH1404-1984	—	—	0.25	0.45	1.00	1.25
AH1407-1987	—	—	0.25	0.45	1.00	1.25
AH1408-1988	—	—	0.25	0.45	1.00	1.25
AH1409-1989	—	—	0.25	0.45	1.00	1.25

KM# 3.2 10 FILS
Bronze **Obv:** Value **Rev:** Arab dhow above dates **Note:** Reduced
size.

Date	Mintage	F	VF	XF	Unc	BU
AH1416-1996 (1996)	—	—	0.20	0.35	0.80	1.20

KM# 4 25 FILS
3.5000 g., Copper-Nickel, 20 mm. **Obv:** Value **Rev:** Gazelle
above dates

Date	Mintage	F	VF	XF	Unc	BU
AH1393-1973	10,400,000	—	0.15	0.35	0.70	1.00
AH1402-1982	—	—	0.20	0.40	0.75	1.00
AH1403-1983	—	—	0.20	0.40	0.75	1.00
AH1404-1984	—	—	0.20	0.40	0.75	1.00
AH1406-1986	—	—	0.20	0.40	0.75	1.00
AH1407-1987	—	—	0.20	0.40	0.75	1.00
AH1408-1988	—	—	0.20	0.40	0.75	1.00
AH1409-1989	—	—	0.20	0.40	0.75	1.00
AH1410-1990	—	—	0.20	0.40	0.75	1.00

Date	Mintage	F	VF	XF	Unc	BU
AH1415-1995	—	—	0.20	0.40	0.75	1.00
AH1416-1996	—	—	0.20	0.40	0.75	1.00
AH1419-1998	—	—	0.20	0.40	0.75	1.00

KM# 5 50 FILS
Copper-Nickel, 24.8 mm. **Obv:** Value **Rev:** Oil derricks above
dates **Edge:** Reeded

Date	Mintage	F	VF	XF	Unc	BU
AH1393-1973	8,400,000	—	0.35	0.50	1.50	2.00
AH1402-1982	—	—	0.35	0.55	1.65	2.00
AH1404-1984	—	—	0.35	0.55	1.65	2.00
AH1407-1987	—	—	0.35	0.55	1.65	2.00
AH1408-1988	—	—	0.35	0.55	1.65	2.00
Note: Coarser edge reeding						
AH1409-1989	—	—	0.35	0.55	1.65	2.00

KM# 16 50 FILS
4.3000 g., Copper-Nickel, 21 mm. **Obv:** Value **Rev:** Oil derricks
above dates **Note:** Reduced size.

Date	Mintage	F	VF	XF	Unc	BU
AH1415-1995	—	—	0.25	0.45	1.35	1.85
AH1419-1998	—	—	0.25	0.45	1.35	1.85

KM# 6.1 DIRHAM
11.3000 g., Copper-Nickel, 28.5 mm. **Obv:** Value **Rev:** Jug
above dates **Edge:** Reeded

Date	Mintage	F	VF	XF	Unc	BU
AH1393-1973	13,000,000	—	0.50	0.75	2.00	2.50
AH1402-1982	—	—	0.50	0.80	2.25	2.75
AH1404-1984	—	—	0.50	0.80	2.25	2.75
AH1406-1986	—	—	0.50	0.80	2.25	2.75
AH1407-1987	—	—	0.50	0.80	2.25	2.75
AH1408-1988	—	—	0.50	0.80	2.25	2.75
AH1409-1989	—	—	0.50	0.80	2.25	2.75

KM# 6.2 DIRHAM
6.4000 g., Copper-Nickel, 24 mm. **Obv:** Value **Rev:** Jug above
dates **Edge:** Reeded **Note:** Reduced size.

Date	Mintage	F	VF	XF	Unc	BU
AH1415-1995	—	—	0.35	0.65	1.85	2.25
AH1419-1998	—	—	0.35	0.65	1.85	2.25

KM# 10 DIRHAM
11.3100 g., Copper-Nickel, 28.5 mm. **Subject:** 27th Chess
Olympiad in Dubai **Obv:** Value **Rev:** Chess pieces and olympic rings

Date	Mintage	F	VF	XF	Unc	BU
ND(1986)	200,000	—	2.00	4.50	9.00	

KM# 11 DIRHAM
Copper-Nickel, 28.5 mm. **Subject:** 25th Anniversary - Offshore
Oil Drilling **Obv:** Value **Rev:** Offshore oil drilling rig

Date	Mintage	F	VF	XF	Unc	BU
ND(1987)	300,000	—	2.00	4.50	9.00	

KM# 14 DIRHAM
Copper-Nickel, 28.5 mm. **Subject:** 10th Anniversary - al-Ain
University **Obv:** Value **Rev:** Emblem above map and book within
radiant design

Date	Mintage	F	VF	XF	Unc	BU
ND(1987)	200,000	—	1.75	4.00	8.00	

KM# 15 DIRHAM
Copper-Nickel, 28.5 mm. **Subject:** U.A.E. Soccer Team -
Qualification for WC - 1990 **Obv:** Value **Rev:** Stylized winged
soccer player

Date	Mintage	F	VF	XF	Unc	BU
ND(1991)	250,000	—	1.50	3.00	6.50	

KM# 32 DIRHAM
Copper-Nickel, 24 mm. **Subject:** Bank of Dubai 35th Anniversary
Obv: Value **Rev:** Towered bank building divides dates

Date	Mintage	F	VF	XF	Unc	BU
ND(1998)	500,000	—			3.50	

KM# 35 DIRHAM
Copper-Nickel, 24 mm. **Subject:** 10th Anniversary - College of
Technology **Obv:** Value **Rev:** Bird viewed through window frame

Date	Mintage	F	VF	XF	Unc	BU
ND(1998)	250,000	—			3.50	

KM# 38 DIRHAM
Copper-Nickel, 24 mm. **Subject:** 15th Anniversary - Rashid bin
Humaid Award for Culture **Obv:** Value **Rev:** Logo within circle

Date	Mintage	F	VF	XF	Unc	BU
ND(1998)	250,000	—			3.50	

KM# 39   DIRHAM
6.4000 g., Copper-Nickel, 24 mm. **Subject:** Sharjah Cultural City **Obv:** Value **Rev:** Stylized flame within beaded circle

Date	Mintage	F	VF	XF	Unc	BU
ND(1998)	200,000	—	—	—	3.50	—

KM# 40   DIRHAM
6.3700 g., Copper-Nickel, 24 mm. **Subject:** 25 Years - Oil Production on Abu Al Bukhoosh Oil Field **Obv:** Value **Rev:** Offshore oil drilling rig **Edge:** Reeded

Date	Mintage	F	VF	XF	Unc	BU
ND(1999)	200,000	—	—	—	3.50	—

KM# 41   DIRHAM
6.3700 g., Copper-Nickel, 24 mm. **Subject:** Islamic Personality of 1999 - Sheikh Zayed **Obv:** Value **Rev:** Square design

Date	Mintage	F	VF	XF	Unc	BU
ND(2000)	500,000	—	—	—	3.50	—

KM# 43   DIRHAM
6.3700 g., Copper-Nickel, 24 mm. **Subject:** 25th Anniversary - Dubai Islamic Bank **Obv:** Value **Rev:** Bank name within circle

Date	Mintage	F	VF	XF	Unc	BU
ND(2000)	250,000	—	—	—	3.50	—

KM# 46   DIRHAM
6.3700 g., Copper-Nickel, 24 mm. **Subject:** 25th Anniversary - General Women's Union (1975-2000) **Obv:** Value **Rev:** Stylized gazelle

Date	Mintage	F	VF	XF	Unc	BU
ND(2000)	500,000	—	—	—	3.50	—

KM# 9   5 DIRHAMS
Copper-Nickel **Subject:** 1500th Anniversary - al-Hegira **Obv:** Value flanked by dates **Rev:** Perched eagle

Date	Mintage	F	VF	XF	Unc	BU
AH1401-1981	2,000,000	—	2.00	4.00	15.00	—

KM# 33   25 DIRHAMS
20.0000 g., 0.9250 Silver 0.5948 oz. ASW **Subject:** Dubai National Bank - 35 Years **Obv:** Value **Rev:** Towered bank building divides dates

Date	Mintage	F	VF	XF	Unc	BU
ND(1998) Proof	5,000	Value: 45.00				

KM# 55   25 DIRHAMS
20.0000 g., 0.9250 Silver 0.5948 oz. ASW **Subject:** 25th Anniversary - Al Bukhoosh Oil Field's Production

Date	Mintage	F	VF	XF	Unc	BU
ND(1999) Proof	2,000	Value: 65.00				

KM# 44   25 DIRHAMS
20.0000 g., 0.9250 Silver 0.5948 oz. ASW, 27.9 mm. **Subject:** 25th Anniversary - Dubai Islamic Bank **Obv:** Value **Rev:** Bank name within circle **Edge:** Reeded

Date	Mintage	F	VF	XF	Unc	BU
ND(2000) Proof	1,000	Value: 45.00				

KM# 7   50 DIRHAMS
27.2200 g., 0.9250 Silver 0.8095 oz. ASW **Subject:** IYC and UNICEF **Obv:** Value **Rev:** Conjoined standing figures, emblems at sides

Date	Mintage	F	VF	XF	Unc	BU
AH1400-1980 Proof	8,031	Value: 21.50				

KM# 17   50 DIRHAMS
40.0000 g., 0.9250 Silver 1.1895 oz. ASW, 40 mm. **Subject:** Death of Shaikh Rashid Bin Saeed Al-Maktoum **Obv:** Bust facing **Rev:** International Trade Center **Edge:** Reeded

Date	Mintage	F	VF	XF	Unc	BU
ND(1992) (1990) Proof	4,000	Value: 75.00				

KM# 18   50 DIRHAMS
40.0000 g., 0.9250 Silver 1.1895 oz. ASW, 40 mm. **Subject:** 10th Anniversary - UAE Central Bank **Obv:** Bust of Shaikh Zayed Bin Sultan Al-Nahyan right **Rev:** Bank **Edge:** Reeded

Date	Mintage	F	VF	XF	Unc	BU
ND(1992) Proof	2,000	Value: 85.00				

KM# 19   50 DIRHAMS
40.0000 g., 0.9250 Silver 1.1895 oz. ASW, 40 mm. **Subject:** 50th Anniversary of the Arab League **Obv:** Eagle **Rev:** Inscription in center circle of wreath **Edge:** Reeded

Date	Mintage	F	VF	XF	Unc	BU
ND(1996) (1995) Proof	2,000	Value: 85.00				

KM# 21   50 DIRHAMS
40.0000 g., 0.9250 Silver 1.1895 oz. ASW, 40 mm. **Subject:** 25th Anniversary of the UAE - National Day Issue **Obv:** Bust of Shaikh Zayed Bin Sultan Al-Nahyan right **Rev:** Eagle within circle **Edge:** Reeded

Date	Mintage	F	VF	XF	Unc	BU
1996 (1996) Proof	8,000	Value: 70.00				

KM# 22   50 DIRHAMS
40.0000 g., 0.9250 Silver 1.1895 oz. ASW, 40 mm. **Subject:** 30th Anniversary - Reign of Shaikh Zayed **Obv:** Bust of Shaikh Zayed Bin Sultan Al-Nahyan right **Rev:** Circular design of Arabic lettering **Edge:** Reeded

Date	Mintage	F	VF	XF	Unc	BU
1996 (1996) Proof	8,000	Value: 70.00				

KM# 34   50 DIRHAMS
40.0000 g., 0.9250 Silver 1.1895 oz. ASW, 40 mm.
Subject: Dubai National Bank - 35 Years **Obv:** Value
Rev: Towered bank building divides dates **Edge:** Reeded

Date	Mintage	F	VF	XF	Unc	BU
ND(1998) Proof	5,000	Value: 75.00				

KM# 36   50 DIRHAMS
40.0000 g., 0.9250 Silver 1.1895 oz. ASW, 40 mm.
Subject: Colleges of Technology: 10 Years **Obv:** Bust of Shaikh
Zayed Bin Sultan Al-Nahyan right **Rev:** Bird viewed through
window frame **Edge:** Reeded

Date	Mintage	F	VF	XF	Unc	BU
ND(1998) Proof	6,000	Value: 75.00				

KM# 37   50 DIRHAMS
27.5000 g., 0.9250 Silver 0.8178 oz. ASW   **Series:** UNICEF
Obv: Value **Rev:** Two children, dates at left and right

Date	Mintage	F	VF	XF	Unc	BU
AH1419-1998 Proof	25,000	Value: 37.50				

KM# 88   50 DIRHAMS
40.0000 g., 0.9250 Silver 1.1895 oz. ASW, 40.mm.
Subject: Sharjah Cultural City **Obv:** Value **Rev:** Stylized flame
in beaded circle

Date	Mintage	F	VF	XF	Unc	BU
1998 Proof	4,000	Value: 70.00				

KM# 89   50 DIRHAMS
40.0000 g., 0.9250 Silver 1.1895 oz. ASW, 40 mm.
Subject: 30th Anniversary Abu Dhabi Chamber of Commerce
and Industry **Obv:** Bust of President H. H. Sheikh Zayed bin
Sultan Al Hahyan 3/4 right **Rev:** Arabic "30" / 30th

Date	Mintage	F	VF	XF	Unc	BU
ND(1999) Proof	5,000	Value: 70.00				

KM# 57   50 DIRHAMS
40.0000 g., 0.9250 Silver 1.1895 oz. ASW, 40 mm.
Subject: Sharjah Cultural City **Obv:** Value **Rev:** Stylized flame
within beaded circle **Edge:** Reeded **Note:** Similar to 1 Dirham,
KM#39.

Date	Mintage	F	VF	XF	Unc	BU
ND(1999) Proof	4,000	Value: 75.00				

KM# 56   50 DIRHAMS
40.0000 g., 0.9250 Silver 1.1895 oz. ASW, 40 mm.
Subject: 30th Anniversary - Abu Dhabi Chamber of Commerce
Edge: Reeded

Date	Mintage	F	VF	XF	Unc	BU
ND(1999) Proof	5,000	Value: 75.00				

KM# 42   50 DIRHAMS
40.2200 g., 0.9250 Silver 1.1961 oz. ASW, 40 mm.
Subject: Islamic Personality of 1999 - Sheikh Zayed **Obv:** Bust
of Shaikh Zayed Bin Sultan Al-Nahyan right **Rev:** Square design
Edge: Reeded

Date	Mintage	F	VF	XF	Unc	BU
ND(2000) Proof	5,000	Value: 90.00				

KM# 45   50 DIRHAMS
40.2200 g., 0.9250 Silver 1.1961 oz. ASW, 40 mm.
Subject: 25th Anniversary - Dubai Islamic Bank **Obv:** Value
Rev: Bank name within circle **Edge:** Reeded

Date	Mintage	F	VF	XF	Unc	BU
ND(2000) Proof	2,000	Value: 65.00				

KM# 48   50 DIRHAMS
40.0000 g., 0.9250 Silver 1.1895 oz. ASW, 40 mm.
Subject: Dubai Airport - Sheikh Rashid Terminal **Obv:** Bust
facing **Rev:** Airport scene **Edge:** Reeded

Date	Mintage	F	VF	XF	Unc	BU
ND(2001) Proof	5,000	Value: 70.00				

KM# 58   50 DIRHAMS
40.0000 g., 0.9250 Silver 1.1895 oz. ASW, 40 mm. **Subject:** 100th
Anniversary - Dubai's Dept. of Ports and Customs **Edge:** Reeded

Date	Mintage	F	VF	XF	Unc	BU
ND(2000) Proof	5,000	Value: 70.00				

KM# A58   100 DIRHAMS
40.0000 g., 0.9250 Silver 1.1895 oz. ASW   **Subject:** 100th
Anniversary - Dubai Dept. of Ports & Customs **Edge:** Reeded

Date	Mintage	F	VF	XF	Unc	BU
1999 Proof	—	Value: 95.00				

KM# 12   500 DIRHAMS
19.9700 g., 0.9170 Gold 0.5887 oz. AGW, 25 mm. **Subject:** 5th
Anniversary - United Arab Emirates **Obv:** Head /4 right,
inscription above **Rev:** Dates

Date	Mintage	F	VF	XF	Unc	BU
ND(1976) Proof	13,450	Value: 700				

KM# 23   500 DIRHAMS
19.9700 g., 0.9170 Gold 0.5887 oz. AGW, 25 mm.
Subject: Commemoration - Death of Sheikh Rashid Bin Saeed
Al Maktoum **Obv:** Bust right **Rev:** Dubai International Trade
Center **Note:** Similar to 50 Dirhams, KM#17.

Date	Mintage	F	VF	XF	Unc	BU
ND(1992) Proof	2,000	Value: 800				

KM# 24   500 DIRHAMS
19.9700 g., 0.9170 Gold 0.5887 oz. AGW, 25 mm.
Subject: 10th Anniversary - U.A.E. Central Bank **Obv:** Bust of
Shaikh Zayed Bin Sultan Al-Nahyan right **Rev:** Bank building
Note: Similar to 50 Dirhams, KM#18.

Date	Mintage	F	VF	XF	Unc	BU
ND(1992) Proof	1,000	Value: 900				

KM# 25   500 DIRHAMS
19.9700 g., 0.9170 Gold 0.5887 oz. AGW, 25 mm.
Subject: 20th Anniversary - Women's Union **Obv:** Heraldic eagle
Rev: Seal in wreath **Note:** Similar to 1000 Dirhams, KM#28.

Date	Mintage	F	VF	XF	Unc	BU
ND(1996) Proof	1,000	Value: 900				

KM# 8   750 DIRHAMS
17.1700 g., 0.9000 Gold 0.4968 oz. AGW, 25 mm.   **Subject:** IYC
and UNICEF **Obv:** Value **Rev:** Armored horseman divides emblems

Date	Mintage	F	VF	XF	Unc	BU
AH1400-1980 Proof	3,063	Value: 550				

KM# 13   1000 DIRHAMS
39.9400 g., 0.9170 Gold 1.1775 oz. AGW, 40 mm.   **Subject:** 5th
Anniversary - United Arab Emirates **Obv:** Head 1/4 right
Rev: Dates

Date	Mintage	F	VF	XF	Unc	BU
ND(1976) Proof	12,500	Value: 1,300				

KM# 26   1000 DIRHAMS
39.9400 g., 0.9170 Gold 1.1775 oz. AGW, 40 mm.
Subject: Death of Shaikh Rashid Bin Saeed Al Maktoum
Obv: Bust right **Rev:** Dubai International Trade Center
Note: Similar to 50 Dirhams, KM#17.

Date	Mintage	F	VF	XF	Unc	BU
ND(1992) Proof	2,000	Value: 1,450				

KM# 27   1000 DIRHAMS
39.9400 g., 0.9170 Gold 1.1775 oz. AGW, 40 mm.
Subject: 10th Anniversary - U.A.E. Central Bank **Obv:** Bust half
right **Rev:** Bank building **Note:** Similar to 50 Dirhams, KM#18.

Date	Mintage	F	VF	XF	Unc	BU
ND(1992) Proof	1,000	Value: 1,500				

KM# 28   1000 DIRHAMS
39.9400 g., 0.9170 Gold 1.1775 oz. AGW, 40 mm.
Subject: 20th Anniversary - General Women's Union **Obv:** Bust
right **Rev:** Seal in wreath

Date	Mintage	F	VF	XF	Unc	BU
ND(1996) Proof	1,000	Value: 1,500				

PIEFORTS

KM#	Date	Mintage	Identification	Mkt Val
P1	1980	75	50 Dirhams. 0.9250 Silver. KM#7.	75.00
P2	1981	100	750 Dirhams. 0.9000 Gold. KM#8.	900

MINT SETS

KM#	Date	Mintage	Identification	Issue Price	Mkt Val
MS1	AH1409/1989 (6)	—	KM#1, 2.1-3.1, 4-5, 6.1	—	15.00
MS2	Mixed dates (5)	—	KM#10-11 1987, KM#14 1988, KM#15 1991, KM#9 1981	—	—

UNITED STATES OF AMERICA

CIRCULATION COINAGE

CENT

Indian Head Cent

Indian head with headdress left above date obverse
Value within wreath, shield above reverse

1864 "L"

KM# 90a • 3.1100 g., **Bronze**, 19 mm. • **Obv. Legend** UNITED STATES OF AMERICA **Designer:** James B. Longacre **Notes:** The 1864 "L" variety has the designer's initial in Liberty's hair to the right of her neck.

Date	Mintage	G-4	VG-8	F-12	VF-20	XF-40	AU-50	MS-60	MS-65	Prf-65
1901	79,611,143	1.85	2.20	2.50	4.00	11.00	22.00	29.00	165	425
1902	87,376,722	1.85	2.20	2.50	4.00	10.00	22.00	28.00	165	425
1903	85,094,493	1.85	2.20	2.50	4.00	10.00	21.00	28.00	165	425
1904	61,328,015	1.75	2.20	2.50	4.00	10.00	21.00	28.00	165	475
1905	80,719,163	1.75	2.20	2.50	3.50	9.00	20.00	28.00	165	475
1906	96,022,255	1.75	2.20	2.50	3.50	9.00	21.00	28.00	165	395
1907	108,138,618	1.75	2.20	2.50	3.50	8.50	20.00	28.00	165	485
1908	32,327,987	1.75	2.30	2.50	3.50	9.00	20.00	28.00	165	395
1908S	1,115,000	58.00	61.00	70.00	83.00	160	185	285	2,650	—
1909	14,370,645	15.00	15.25	15.50	15.90	18.50	30.00	38.00	155	400
1909S	309,000	500	540	585	630	720	750	840	2,250	—

Lincoln Cent

Wheat Ears reverse

KM# 132 • 3.1100 g., **Bronze**, 19 mm. • **Designer:** Victor D. Brenner **Notes:** The 1909 "VDB" varieties have the designer's initials inscribed at the 6 o'clock position on the reverse. The initials were removed until 1918, when they were restored on the obverse • MS60 prices are for Brown coins and MS65 prices are for coins that are at least 90% original red.

Date	Mintage	G-4	VG-8	F-12	VF-20	XF-40	AU-50	MS-60	MS-65	Prf-65
1909 VDB	27,995,000	12.00	12.50	12.75	13.00	14.00	16.00	21.00	125	—
1909 VDB Doubled Die Obverse	Inc. above	—	—	55.00	75.00	100.00	120	150	1,900	—
1909S VDB	484,000	760	895	1,010	1,150	1,290	1,450	1,650	6,900	—
1909	72,702,618	4.25	4.40	4.75	5.00	6.00	12.00	15.00	85.00	520
1909S	1,825,000	115	120	130	170	245	265	360	1,325	—
1909S/S S over horizontal S	Inc. above	125	132	145	190	280	325	385	1,600	—
1910	146,801,218	.50	.60	.75	1.50	4.50	10.00	17.50	250	700
1910S	6,045,000	17.00	19.00	21.50	29.00	49.00	75.00	105	800	—
1911	101,177,787	.60	.80	2.00	2.50	7.00	11.50	20.00	375	600
1911D	12,672,000	5.25	6.00	10.00	18.50	54.00	74.00	92.00	1,550	—
1911S	4,026,000	45.00	48.00	51.00	55.00	80.00	112	180	3,300	—
1912	68,153,060	1.75	2.00	2.50	6.00	14.00	26.00	34.00	550	950
1912D	10,411,000	7.00	9.50	12.00	27.00	74.00	112	165	2,800	—
1912S	4,431,000	23.00	25.00	30.00	42.00	83.00	120	185	4,400	—
1913	76,532,352	1.00	1.20	1.75	3.40	18.50	29.50	36.00	400	550

Date	Mintage	G-4	VG-8	F-12	VF-20	XF-40	AU-50	MS-60	MS-65	Prf-65
1913D	15,804,000	3.00	3.50	4.00	11.00	50.00	65.00	98.00	2,100	—
1913S	6,101,000	13.50	17.50	20.00	32.00	56.00	108	195	6,650	—
1914	75,238,432	.75	1.10	2.25	6.50	19.00	40.00	47.50	415	600
1914D	1,193,000	220	260	400	495	975	1,475	1,975	24,000	—
1914S	4,137,000	24.50	27.00	28.00	39.00	92.00	170	295	11,500	—
1915	29,092,120	1.65	2.85	4.10	18.50	60.00	73.00	84.00	1,150	600
1915D	22,050,000	1.75	2.40	3.60	6.75	24.00	44.00	70.00	1,350	—
1915S	4,833,000	20.00	23.00	27.00	30.00	82.00	98.00	175	4,800	—
1916	131,833,677	.35	.60	1.25	2.60	8.00	13.00	18.00	385	1,650
1916D	35,956,000	1.75	2.25	3.00	6.00	15.50	36.00	72.00	3,300	—
1916S	22,510,000	2.25	3.25	4.50	7.00	25.00	38.00	84.00	8,500	—
1917	196,429,785	.35	.45	.55	2.00	5.00	13.50	16.00	480	—
1917 Doubled Die Obverse	Inc. above	100.00	125	210	375	900	1,750	2,500	25,000	—
1917D	55,120,000	1.50	1.75	2.50	5.50	39.00	45.00	62.00	3,000	—
1917S	32,620,000	.80	1.20	1.75	2.65	11.00	25.00	62.00	7,200	—
1918	288,104,634	.35	.40	.50	1.25	4.50	10.00	14.00	400	—
1918D	47,830,000	1.60	2.00	2.65	5.50	16.50	32.00	72.00	3,650	—
1918S	34,680,000	.50	1.20	1.75	3.65	11.50	32.00	61.00	8,450	—
1919	392,021,000	.30	.40	.50	.80	1.75	6.00	8.50	175	—
1919D	57,154,000	1.25	1.60	2.00	5.00	13.00	34.00	54.00	2,700	—
1919S	139,760,000	.40	.70	1.80	2.65	6.00	17.00	40.00	4,300	—
1920	310,165,000	.35	.40	.90	1.50	2.80	7.00	13.50	235	—
1920D	49,280,000	1.25	1.65	3.00	7.00	19.50	38.00	74.00	2,750	—
1920S	46,220,000	.90	1.00	1.50	2.75	13.00	38.00	112	9,350	—
1921	39,157,000	.60	1.00	1.25	3.00	13.00	22.50	44.00	375	—
1921S	15,274,000	1.25	2.10	2.85	6.00	35.00	70.00	110	6,700	—
1922D	7,160,000	17.50	20.00	22.50	25.00	38.00	76.00	108	2,450	—
1922D Weak Rev	Inc. above	16.00	17.00	20.00	22.00	32.00	63.00	90.00	1,950	—
1922D Weak D	Inc. above	32.00	45.00	65.00	110	235	300	550	—	—
1922 No D Die 2 Strong Rev	Inc. above	750	840	1,275	1,700	3,150	6,600	11,000	200,000	—
1922 No D Die 3 Weak Rev	Inc. above	300	400	685	885	1,750	3,500	8,500	—	—
1923	74,723,000	.60	.80	1.00	1.50	6.00	11.00	14.00	480	—
1923S	8,700,000	3.00	4.00	5.00	8.00	38.00	86.00	195	15,500	—
1924	75,178,000	.35	.50	.60	1.10	5.50	11.00	20.00	390	—
1924D	2,520,000	37.00	43.00	48.00	60.00	115	180	270	9,500	—
1924S	11,696,000	1.75	2.00	2.80	5.50	32.00	72.00	115	11,000	—
1925	139,949,000	.30	.40	.50	.70	2.85	7.00	10.50	100.00	—
1925D	22,580,000	1.50	2.00	3.00	6.00	16.50	30.00	62.00	5,000	—
1925S	26,380,000	1.20	1.50	2.00	3.00	12.50	32.00	90.00	10,000	—
1926	157,088,000	.25	—	.50	.70	1.65	6.00	7.75	75.00	—
1926D	28,020,000	1.50	1.70	3.50	5.50	14.50	34.00	85.00	4,350	—
1926S	4,550,000	8.50	10.00	11.50	16.00	35.00	72.00	140	10,000	—
1927	144,440,000	.20	.30	.40	.70	1.60	5.50	7.40	95.00	—
1927D	27,170,000	1.50	1.75	2.25	3.50	8.00	26.50	62.00	2,000	—
1927S	14,276,000	1.50	1.85	3.00	5.50	16.00	43.00	66.00	6,650	—
1928	134,116,000	.20	.30	.40	.70	1.25	4.25	7.50	90.00	—
1928D	31,170,000	1.10	1.40	2.25	3.75	6.50	19.50	35.00	1,100	—
1928S Small S	17,266,000	1.20	1.65	2.75	4.25	9.00	30.00	74.00	4,650	—
1928S Large S	Inc. above	2.00	2.85	4.25	6.75	16.00	44.00	140	5,500	—
1929	185,262,000	.20	.30	.40	.60	1.00	5.50	7.00	85.00	—
1929D	41,730,000	.70	1.20	1.50	2.85	6.50	14.00	24.00	625	—
1929S	50,148,000	.80	1.25	2.00	3.00	7.00	15.00	19.00	550	—
1930	157,415,000	.20	.30	.40	.60	1.25	2.75	3.75	32.50	—
1930D	40,100,000	.35	.45	.65	.90	2.00	6.00	11.00	95.00	—
1930S	24,286,000	.35	.45	.60	.80	1.50	7.00	10.00	50.00	—
1931	19,396,000	.70	.80	1.30	2.00	4.00	10.50	20.00	135	—
1931D	4,480,000	5.00	6.00	6.75	8.00	13.50	36.00	52.00	1,000	—
1931S	866,000	122	124	130	133	140	148	163	725	—
1932	9,062,000	1.75	2.00	3.00	3.50	7.00	13.50	22.00	100.00	—
1932D	10,500,000	1.40	2.00	2.50	2.85	4.15	11.00	17.50	150	—
1933	14,360,000	1.40	1.80	2.50	3.00	7.00	12.00	17.50	100.00	—
1933D	6,200,000	3.50	4.25	5.20	6.50	12.00	16.50	23.50	135	—
1934	219,080,000	.20	.30	.40	.60	1.25	4.00	8.00	30.00	—
1934D	28,446,000	.40	.60	1.00	1.65	4.00	10.00	20.00	52.00	—
1935	245,338,000	.20	.30	.40	.55	.90	1.50	3.50	28.00	—
1935D	47,000,000	.15	.20	.30	.40	.95	2.50	4.50	30.00	—
1935S	38,702,000	.25	.35	.60	1.75	3.00	5.00	12.00	55.00	—
1936 (Proof in Satin Finish)	309,637,569	.20	.30	.40	.55	.85	1.40	2.00	7.50	1,200
1936 Brilliant Proof	Inc. above	—	—	—	—	—	—	—	—	—
1936D	40,620,000	.20	.30	.40	.55	.90	1.50	3.50	22.00	—
1936S	29,130,000	.20	.30	.45	.60	1.00	1.75	3.00	18.00	—
1937	309,179,320	.20	.30	.40	.55	.85	1.40	1.60	20.00	125
1937D	50,430,000	.20	.30	.40	.60	.95	1.00	2.20	24.00	—
1937S	34,500,000	.20	.30	.40	.55	.90	1.25	2.40	22.50	—
1938	156,696,734	.20	.30	.40	.55	.85	1.20	3.00	16.50	85.00
1938D	20,010,000	.20	.30	.45	.60	1.00	1.50	3.50	17.00	—
1938S	15,180,000	.30	.40	.50	.70	1.00	2.00	2.80	26.00	—
1939	316,479,520	.20	.30	.40	.55	.75	.90	1.00	15.00	78.00
1939D	15,160,000	.35	.45	.50	.60	.85	1.90	2.50	20.00	—
1939S	52,070,000	.30	.40	.50	.60	.80	1.10	2.00	19.00	—
1940	586,825,872	.10	.20	.30	.40	.50	.75	1.00	17.00	70.00
1940D	81,390,000	.20	.30	.40	.55	.75	.50	1.20	11.50	—
1940S	112,940,000	.20	.30	.40	.55	.90	1.25	1.40	14.00	—
1941	887,039,100	.10	.20	.30	.40	.50	.70	.85	17.00	65.00
1941 Doubled Die Obv	Inc. above	35.00	50.00	70.00	80.00	95.00	135	200	2,800	—
1941D	128,700,000	.20	.30	.40	.55	.75	1.25	2.25	20.00	—
1941S	92,360,000	.20	.30	.40	.55	.75	1.75	2.75	23.50	—
1942	657,828,600	.10	.20	.30	.40	.50	.70	.85	17.00	78.00
1942D	206,698,000	.20	.25	.30	.35	.40	.50	.65	22.00	—
1942S	85,590,000	.25	.35	.45	.85	1.25	2.50	4.50	26.00	—

Wheat Ears reverse

KM# 132a • 2.7000 g., **Zinc Coated Steel**, 19 mm. • **Designer:** Victor D. Brenner

Date	Mintage	G-4	VG-8	F-12	VF-20	XF-40	AU-50	MS-60	MS-65	Prf-65
1943	684,628,670	.25	.30	.35	.45	.60	.85	1.25	4.75	—
1943D	217,660,000	.35	.40	.45	.50	.70	1.00	1.25	8.50	—
1943D/D RPM	Inc. above	30.00	38.00	50.00	65.00	90.00	125	200	—	—
1943S	191,550,000	.45	.45	.50	.65	.90	1.40	3.00	13.50	—

KM# A132 • 3.1100 g., **Copper-Zinc**, 19 mm. • **Designer:** Victor D. Brenner
Notes: KM#132 design and composition resumed • MS60 prices are for Brown coins and MS65 prices are for coins that are at least 90% original red.

Date	Mintage	XF-40	MS-65	Prf-65
1944	1,435,400,000	.40	8.00	—
1944D	430,578,000	.50	12.50	—
1944D/S Type 1	Inc. above	235	3,750	—
1944D/S Type 2	Inc. above	175	1,600	—
1944S	282,760,000	.40	12.00	—
1945	1,040,515,000	.40	15.00	—
1945D	226,268,000	.40	13.50	—
1945S	181,770,000	.40	12.00	—
1946	991,655,000	.30	13.00	—
1946D	315,690,000	.30	6.00	—
1946S	198,100,000	.30	5.50	—
1946S/D		70.00	600	—
1947	190,555,000	.45	16.00	—
1947D	194,750,000	.40	10.00	—
1947S	99,000,000	.35	12.00	—
1948	317,570,000	.40	14.00	—
1948D	172,637,000	.40	6.75	—
1948S	81,735,000	.40	6.50	—
1949	217,775,000	.40	15.00	—
1949D	153,132,000	.40	12.00	—
1949S	64,290,000	.50	10.00	—
1950	272,686,386	.40	13.50	40.00
1950D	334,950,000	.35	9.00	—
1950S	118,505,000	.40	8.00	—
1951	295,633,500	.40	14.00	40.00
1951D	625,355,000	.30	8.00	—
1951S	136,010,000	.40	10.00	—
1952	186,856,980	.40	16.00	34.00
1952D	746,130,000	.30	8.00	—
1952S	137,800,004	.60	9.00	—
1953	256,883,800	.30	18.00	28.00
1953D	700,515,000	.30	11.00	—
1953S	181,835,000	.40	11.50	—
1954	71,873,350	.25	17.50	9.00
1954D	251,552,500	.25	10.00	—
1954S	96,190,000	.25	12.00	—
1955	330,958,000	.25	15.00	13.00
1955 Doubled Die	Inc. above	1,650	43,500	—

Note: The 1955 "doubled die" has distinct doubling of the date and lettering on the obverse.

Date	Mintage	XF-40	MS-65	Prf-65
1955D	563,257,500	.20	12.00	—
1955S	44,610,000	.35	7.50	—
1956	421,414,384	.20	16.00	3.00
1956D	1,098,201,100	.20	8.00	—
1957	283,787,952	.20	9.00	2.00
1957D	1,051,342,000	.20	8.00	—
1958	253,400,652	.20	9.00	3.00
1958D	800,953,300	.20	8.00	—

Lincoln Memorial reverse

Small date   Large date

Large date   Small date

KM# 201 • 3.1100 g., **Copper-Zinc** • **Rev. Designer:** Frank Gasparro **Notes:** MS60 prices are for Brown coins and MS65 prices are for coins that are at least 90% original red. The dates were modified in 1960, 1970 and 1982, resulting in large-date and small-date varieties for those years. The 1972 "doubled die" shows doubling of "In God We Trust." The 1979-S and 1981-S Type II proofs have a clearer mint mark than the Type I proofs of those years. Some 1982 cents have the predominantly copper composition; others have the predominantly zinc composition. They can be distinguished by weight.

Date	Mintage	XF-40	MS-65	Prf-65
1959	610,864,291		18.00	1.50
1959D	1,279,760,000		16.00	—
1960 small date, low 9	588,096,602	2.10	12.00	16.00
1960 large date, high 9	Inc. above	—	10.00	1.25
1960D small date, low 9	1,580,884,000	—	10.00	—
1960D large date, high 9	Inc. above	—	11.00	—
1960D/D small over large date	Inc. above	—	300	—
1961	756,373,244		6.50	1.00

Date	Mintage	XF-40	MS-65	Prf-65
1961D	1,753,266,700		15.00	—
1962	609,263,019		8.00	1.00
1962D	1,793,148,400		14.00	—
1963	757,185,645		10.00	1.00
1963D	1,774,020,400		12.00	—
1964	2,652,525,762		6.50	1.00
1964D	3,799,071,500		7.00	—
1965	1,497,224,900		10.00	—
1965 SMS	Inc. above		7.50	—
1966	2,188,147,783		10.00	—
1966 SMS	Inc. above		8.00	—
1967	3,048,667,100		10.00	—
1967 SMS	Inc. above		8.00	—
1968	1,707,880,970		12.00	—
1968D	2,886,269,600		12.00	—
1968S	261,311,510		8.00	1.00
1969	1,136,910,000		6.50	—
1969D	4,002,832,200		10.00	—
1969S	547,309,631		8.00	1.10
1969S Doubled Die Obverse	Inc. above		—	—
1970	1,898,315,000		8.00	—
1970D	2,891,438,900		6.00	—
1970S	693,192,814		—	1.20
1970S small date, level 7	Inc. above		75.00	60.00
1970S large date, low 7	Inc. above		16.00	—
1970S Doubled Die Obverse	Inc. above		—	—
1971	1,919,490,000		25.00	—
1971D	2,911,045,600		5.50	—
1971S	528,354,192		6.00	1.20
1971S Doubled Die Obverse	—		—	—
1972	2,933,255,000		6.00	—
1972 Doubled Die Obverse	Inc. above	240	775	—
1972D	2,665,071,400		10.00	—
1972S	380,200,104		30.00	1.15
1973	3,728,245,000		8.00	—
1973D	3,549,576,588		11.00	—
1973S	319,937,634		8.00	0.80
1974	4,232,140,523		12.00	—
1974D	4,235,098,000		12.00	—
1974S	412,039,228		10.00	0.75
1975	5,451,476,142		8.00	—
1975D	4,505,245,300		13.50	—
1975S	2,845,450		—	5.50
1976	4,674,292,426		18.00	—
1976D	4,221,592,455		20.00	—
1976S	4,149,730		—	5.00
1977	4,469,930,000		14.00	—
1977D	4,149,062,300		14.00	—
1977S	3,251,152		—	3.00
1978	5,558,605,000		14.00	—
1978D	4,280,233,400		12.00	—
1978S	3,127,781		—	3.50
1979	6,018,515,000		12.00	—
1979D	4,139,357,254		8.00	—
1979S type I, proof	3,677,175		—	4.00
1979S type II, proof	Inc. above		—	4.25
1980	7,414,705,000		6.50	—
1980D	5,140,098,660		10.00	—
1980S	3,554,806		—	2.25
1981	7,491,750,000		7.50	—
1981D	5,373,235,677		9.00	—
1981S type I, proof	4,063,083		—	3.50
1981S type II, proof	Inc. above		—	60.00
1982 large date	10,712,525,000		6.00	—
1982 small date	Inc. above		8.00	—
1982D large date	6,012,979,368		6.00	—
1982S	3,857,479		—	—

KM# 201a • 2.5000 g., **Copper Plated Zinc**, 19 mm. • **Notes:** MS60 prices are for brown coins and MS65 prices are for coins that are at least 90% original red.

Date	Mintage	XF-40	MS-65	Prf-65
1982 large date	—	—	6.00	—
1982 small date	—	—	9.00	—
1982D large date	—	—	8.00	—
1982D small date	—	—	6.00	—

KM# 201b • **Copper Plated Zinc**, 19 mm. • **Notes:** MS60 prices are for brown coins and MS65 prices are for coins that are at least 90% original red. The 1983 "doubled die reverse" shows doubling of "United States of America." The 1984 "doubled die" shows doubling of Lincoln's ear on the obverse.

Date	Mintage	XF-40	MS-65	Prf-65
1982S	3,857,479		—	3.00
1983	7,752,355,000		7.00	—
1983 Doubled Die	Inc. above		400	—
1983D	6,467,199,428		5.50	—
1983S	3,279,126		—	4.00
1984	8,151,079,000		7.50	—
1984 Doubled Die	Inc. above		275	—
1984D	5,569,238,906		5.50	—
1984S	3,065,110		—	4.50
1985	5,648,489,887		4.50	—
1985D	5,287,399,926		4.50	—
1985S	3,362,821		—	6.00
1986	4,491,395,493		5.00	—

Date	Mintage	XF-40	MS-65	Prf-65
1986D	4,442,866,698	—	8.00	—
1986S	3,010,497	—	—	7.50
1987	4,682,466,931	—	8.50	—
1987D	4,879,389,514	—	6.00	—
1987S	4,227,728	—	—	5.00
1988	6,092,810,000	—	8.50	—
1988D	5,253,740,443	—	5.50	—
1988S	3,262,948	—	—	4.00
1989	7,261,535,000	—	5.00	—
1989D	5,345,467,111	—	5.00	—
1989S	3,220,194	—	—	6.00
1990	6,851,765,000	—	5.00	—
1990D	4,922,894,533	—	5.00	—
1990S	3,299,559	—	—	5.00
1990 no S, Proof only	Inc. above	—	—	2,750
1991	5,165,940,000	—	6.00	—
1991D	4,158,442,076	—	5.00	—
1991S	2,867,787	—	—	5.00
1992	4,648,905,000	—	5.50	—
1992D	4,448,673,300	—	5.50	—
1992D Close AM, Proof Reverse Die	Inc. above	—	—	—
1992S	4,176,560	—	—	5.00
1993	5,684,705,000	—	5.50	—
1993D	6,426,650,571	—	5.50	—
1993S	3,394,792	—	—	7.00
1994	6,500,850,000	—	10.00	—
1994D	7,131,765,000	—	5.50	—
1994S	3,269,923	—	—	4.00
1995	6,411,440,000	—	4.50	—
1995 Doubled Die Obverse	Inc. above	20.00	50.00	—
1995D	7,128,560,000	—	5.00	—
1995S	2,707,481	—	—	9.50
1996	6,612,465,000	—	5.00	—
1996D	6,510,795,000	—	5.00	—
1996S	2,915,212	—	—	6.50
1997	4,622,800,000	—	5.00	—
1997D	4,576,555,000	—	5.00	—
1997S	2,796,678	—	—	11.50
1998	5,032,155,000	—	5.00	—
1998 Wide AM, reverse from proof die	Inc. above	—	—	—
1998D	5,255,353,500	—	5.00	—
1998S	2,957,286	—	—	9.50
1999	5,237,600,000	—	5.00	—
1999 Wide AM, reverse from proof die	Inc. above	—	—	—
1999D	6,360,065,000	—	5.00	—
1999S	3,362,462	—	—	5.00
2000	5,503,200,000	—	4.00	—
2000 Wide AM, reverse from proof die	Inc. above	—	—	—
2000D	8,774,220,000	—	4.00	—
2000S	4,063,361	—	—	4.00

5 CENTS

Liberty Nickel

Liberty head left, within circle of stars, date below obverse
Roman numeral value within wreath, "Cents" below reverse

KM# 112 • 5.0000 g., **Copper-Nickel • Rev. Legend:** UNITED STATES OF AMERICA

Date	Mintage	G-4	VG-8	F-12	VF-20	XF-40	AU-50	MS-60	MS-65	Prf-65
1901	26,480,213	1.65	2.10	7.00	14.00	34.00	54.00	108	565	700
1902	31,480,579	1.65	2.10	4.00	14.00	31.00	54.00	105	565	700
1903	28,006,725	1.65	2.10	4.50	14.00	31.00	54.00	83.00	565	700
1904	21,404,984	1.65	2.10	4.50	11.50	30.00	54.00	100.00	565	700
1905	29,827,276	1.65	2.10	4.00	11.50	30.00	54.00	98.00	565	700
1906	38,613,725	1.65	2.10	4.00	11.50	30.00	54.00	98.00	845	700
1907	39,214,800	1.65	1.85	4.00	11.50	30.00	54.00	98.00	1,000	700
1908	22,686,177	1.65	1.85	4.00	11.50	30.00	54.00	104	1,250	700
1909	11,590,526	2.00	2.10	4.00	12.50	33.00	70.00	115	1,225	700
1910	30,169,353	1.65	1.85	4.00	10.00	30.00	40.00	68.00	565	700
1911	39,559,372	1.65	1.85	4.00	10.00	30.00	40.00	68.00	565	700
1912	26,236,714	1.65	1.85	4.00	10.00	30.00	40.00	68.00	565	700
1912D	8,474,000	2.50	3.60	11.50	38.00	74.00	175	290	2,600	—
1912S	238,000	175	245	280	500	850	1,350	1,550	7,500	—
1913 6 known	—									—

Note: 1913, Superior Sale, March 2001, Proof, $1,840,000.

Buffalo Nickel

American Bison standing on a mound reverse

KM# 133 • 5.0000 g., **Copper-Nickel**, 21.2 mm. • **Designer:** James Earle Fraser

Date	Mintage	G-4	VG-8	F-12	VF-20	XF-40	AU-50	MS-60	MS-65	Prf-65
1913	30,993,520	8.00	14.50	15.00	16.00	19.00	25.00	32.50	190	3,150
1913D	5,337,000	16.00	19.50	21.00	25.00	35.00	57.00	62.50	310	—
1913S	2,105,000	43.00	47.00	50.00	60.00	75.00	100.00	125	690	—

American Bison standing on a line reverse

1918/17D   1937D 3-legged

KM# 134 • 5.0000 g., **Copper-Nickel**, 21.2 mm. • **Designer:** James Earle Fraser
Notes: In 1913 the reverse design was modified so the ground under the buffalo was represented as a line rather than a mound. On the 1937D 3-legged variety, the buffalo's right front leg is missing, the result of a damaged die.

Date	Mintage	G-4	VG-8	F-12	VF-20	XF-40	AU-50	MS-60	MS-65	Prf-65
1913	29,858,700	8.00	12.00	13.00	14.00	19.00	25.00	34.00	355	2,500
1913D	4,156,000	125	155	180	190	265	240	285	1,450	—
1913S	1,209,000	350	400	420	435	575	675	885	3,850	—
1914	20,665,738	18.00	21.00	22.00	23.00	27.50	37.50	47.00	420	2,250
1914/3	Inc. above	150	300	425	525	700	1,050	2,850	30,000	—
1914D	3,912,000	90.00	132	165	200	335	390	475	1,600	—
1914/3D	Inc. above	115	225	335	450	625	900	3,500	—	—
1914S	3,470,000	26.00	37.50	45.00	62.50	90.00	145	165	22,350	—
1914/3S	Inc. above	250	500	750	1,000	1,450	2,260	4,300	—	—
1915	20,987,270	6.25	7.00	7.75	11.00	21.50	38.50	50.00	325	2,100
1915D	7,569,500	21.50	31.00	41.50	66.00	115	150	235	2,250	—
1915S	1,505,000	47.00	74.00	105	185	326	490	625	3,150	—
1916	63,498,066	5.50	6.40	7.00	8.00	13.50	24.00	43.50	315	3,250
1916/16	Inc. above	1,800	3,650	7,150	10,850	16,500	34,500	49,500	375,000	—
1916D	13,333,000	15.00	26.50	29.00	38.50	82.50	110	165	2,250	—
1916S	11,860,000	11.00	13.50	26.00	35.00	75.00	125	185	2,300	—
1917	51,424,029	7.50	8.00	8.75	10.00	16.00	32.50	59.00	535	—
1917D	9,910,800	26.00	31.00	55.00	80.00	135	255	345	3,250	—
1917S	4,193,000	23.00	42.00	80.00	110	180	285	395	4,850	—
1918	32,086,314	5.25	6.75	8.00	15.00	31.00	48.50	105	1,550	—
1918/17D	8,362,314	1,075	1,475	2,750	5,450	8,650	10,750	27,500	350,000	—
1918D	Inc. above	22.50	39.00	66.00	135	226	330	430	4,650	—
1918S	4,882,000	14.00	27.50	55.00	100.00	175	300	495	25,500	—
1919	60,868,000	2.60	3.50	3.90	7.00	16.00	32.00	58.00	535	—
1919D	8,006,000	15.50	31.00	66.00	115	235	335	570	6,850	—
1919S	7,521,000	8.00	26.00	50.00	110	225	360	540	24,000	—
1920	63,093,000	1.50	2.75	3.25	6.00	16.00	30.00	59.00	700	—
1920D	9,418,000	8.50	19.00	35.00	125	275	340	575	6,850	—
1920S	9,689,000	4.50	12.75	30.00	100.00	260	300	525	25,500	—
1921	10,663,000	4.00	6.25	8.50	25.00	53.50	73.00	125	800	—
1921S	1,557,000	64.00	110	192	465	825	1,150	1,575	7,350	—
1923	35,715,000	1.70	3.25	4.25	7.00	14.00	37.50	59.00	575	—
1923S	6,142,000	8.00	11.00	27.00	125	275	335	625	11,500	—
1924	21,620,000	1.25	2.40	4.50	10.00	19.00	41.00	73.50	850	—
1924D	5,258,000	8.00	12.00	30.00	90.00	215	315	375	4,950	—
1924S	1,437,000	16.50	32.00	96.00	455	1,100	1,700	2,300	12,850	—
1925	35,565,100	2.50	3.00	3.75	8.50	16.50	32.00	42.00	490	—
1925D	4,450,000	10.00	26.00	38.00	80.00	160	240	375	5,650	—
1925S	6,256,000	4.50	9.00	17.50	77.50	170	250	425	28,500	—
1926	44,693,000	1.50	2.00	2.80	5.40	11.50	26.00	31.50	235	—
1926D	5,638,000	10.00	17.50	28.50	100.00	170	295	335	5,850	—
1926S	970,000	20.00	42.00	100.00	375	875	2,450	4,950	125,000	—
1927	37,981,000	1.40	1.75	2.50	4.50	12.50	26.00	35.00	290	—
1927D	5,730,000	3.00	6.00	7.00	27.50	75.00	115	155	7,950	—
1927S	3,430,000	2.00	3.00	6.00	31.00	80.00	160	490	18,500	—
1928	23,411,000	1.40	1.75	2.50	4.50	12.50	25.00	32.50	310	—
1928D	6,436,000	1.90	2.50	3.75	16.00	40.00	46.50	53.00	685	—
1928S	6,936,000	1.75	2.35	3.00	12.00	27.50	105	225	4,750	—
1929	36,446,000	1.40	1.75	2.50	4.50	13.00	21.00	35.00	325	—
1929D	8,370,000	1.50	1.85	3.00	6.75	32.50	42.50	60.00	1,850	—
1929S	7,754,000	1.50	1.85	2.25	4.00	12.50	25.00	49.50	485	—
1930	22,849,000	1.40	1.75	2.50	4.50	12.00	21.00	32.50	235	—
1930S	5,435,000	1.50	2.00	3.00	4.50	16.00	37.50	65.00	480	—
1931S	1,200,000	15.00	16.00	17.00	19.00	31.00	46.00	59.00	300	—
1934	20,213,003	1.40	1.75	2.50	4.50	11.00	19.00	47.50	355	—
1934D	7,480,000	2.00	3.00	4.75	9.60	22.00	50.00	79.50	800	—
1935	58,264,000	1.25	1.60	2.25	3.00	4.00	11.00	20.00	145	—
1935 Double Die Rev.	Inc. above	50.00	75.00	125	250	675	1,800	4,000	75,000	—
1935D	12,092,000	1.60	2.50	3.00	9.00	26.00	48.00	72.00	415	—
1935S	10,300,000	1.35	1.75	2.50	3.50	4.50	17.50	48.50	250	—
1936	119,001,420	1.25	1.60	2.25	3.00	4.00	6.75	14.50	105	1,650
1936 Brilliant	Inc. above									2,450
1936D	24,814,000	1.35	1.75	2.75	4.00	5.35	11.50	33.50	118	—
1936D 3-1/2 leg	Inc. above	750	1,250	2,000	3,500	6,000	10,500	17,500	—	—
1935D/S	Inc. above	1.35	—	10.00	16.00	25.00	—	—	—	—
1936S	14,930,000	1.35	1.75	2.50	3.50	4.50	11.00	33.50	115	—

Date	Mintage	G-4	VG-8	F-12	VF-20	XF-40	AU-50	MS-60	MS-65	Prf-65
1937	79,485,769	1.25	1.60	2.25	3.00	4.00	6.75	14.50	69.00	2,100
1937D	17,826,000	1.35	1.75	2.50	3.50	4.50	9.00	29.00	73.00	—
1937D 3-legged	Inc. above	535	595	850	1,050	1,250	1,450	2,375	37,000	—
1937S	5,635,000	1.35	1.75	2.50	3.50	4.50	10.00	27.50	72.00	—
1938D	7,020,000	3.50	3.75	3.90	4.00	4.50	8.00	26.00	66.00	—
1938D/D	Inc. above	4.00	4.50	6.00	8.00	10.00	17.00	32.00	125	—
1938D/S	Inc. above	4.50	6.75	9.00	12.50	19.00	32.50	50.00	185	—

Jefferson Nickel

Monticello, mintmark to right side reverse

KM# 192 • 5.0000 g., Copper-Nickel, 21.2 mm. • Designer: Felix Schlag
Notes: Some 1939 strikes have doubling of the word "Monticello" on the reverse.

Date	Mintage	VG-8	F-12	VF-20	XF-40	MS-60	MS-65	-65FS	Prf-65
1938	19,515,365	.50	.75	1.00	2.00	6.00	12.00	125	130
1938D	5,376,000	1.00	1.25	1.50	2.00	10.00	20.00	95.00	—
1938S	4,105,000	1.75	2.00	2.50	3.00	5.25	12.00	165	—
1939 T I, wavy steps, Rev. of 1939	Inc. below	—	—	—	—	—	—	300	70.00
1939 T II, even steps, Rev. of 1940	120,627,535	—	.20	.25	.30	1.75	3.50	40.00	130
1939 doubled Monticello T II	Inc. above	40.00	60.00	90.00	165	300	1,250	2,000	—
1939D T IT I, wavy steps, Rev. of 1939	Inc. below	—	—	—	—	—	—	275	—
1939D T IIT II, even steps, Rev. of 1940	3,514,000	4.00	5.00	8.00	14.00	44.00	125	250	—
1939S T IT I, wavy steps, Rev. of 1939	Inc. below	—	—	—	—	—	—	250	—
1939S T IIT II, even steps, Rev. of 1940	6,630,000	.45	.60	1.50	4.00	17.00	45.00	275	—
1940	176,499,158	—	—	—	.25	1.00	3.00	35.00	135
1940D	43,540,000	—	.20	.30	.40	1.50	2.75	25.00	—
1940S	39,690,000	—	.20	.25	.50	2.50	6.00	45.00	—
1941	203,283,720	—	—	.20	.75	2.50	40.00	130	
1941D	53,432,000	—	.20	.30	.50	2.50	6.00	25.00	—
1941S	43,445,000	—	.20	.30	.50	3.75	6.75	60.00	—
1942	49,818,600	—	—	—	.40	5.00	8.50	75.00	115
1942D	13,938,000	1.00	1.50	3.00	5.00	32.00	60.00	70.00	—
1942D D over horizontal D	Inc. above	35.00	60.00	100.00	165	750	10,000	25,000	—

Note: Fully Struck Full Step nickels command higher prices. Bright, Fully Struck coins command even higher prices. 1938 thru 1989 - 5 Full Steps. 1990 to date - 6 Full Steps. Without bag marks or nicks on steps.

Monticello, mint mark above reverse

1943/2P

KM# 192a • 0.3500 Copper-Silver-Manganese, 21.2 mm. • Designer: Felix Schlag
Notes: War-time composition nickels have the mint mark above Monticello on the reverse.

Date	Mintage	VG-8	F-12	VF-20	XF-40	MS-60	MS-65	-65FS	Prf-65
1942P	57,900,600	1.20	1.30	1.50	2.00	8.00	22.50	70.00	205
1942S	32,900,000	1.20	1.30	1.50	2.50	14.00	20.00	125	—
1943P	271,165,000	1.20	1.30	1.50	2.00	4.00	15.00	35.00	—
1943/2P	Inc. above	35.00	50.00	75.00	110	250	650	1,000	—
1943D	15,294,000	1.50	1.50	1.70	2.10	5.00	13.00	30.00	—
1943S	104,060,000	1.20	1.30	1.50	2.00	6.00	13.00	55.00	—
1944P	119,150,000	1.20	1.30	1.50	2.00	10.00	22.50	100.00	—
1944D	32,309,000	1.30	1.30	1.50	2.30	10.00	17.50	30.00	—
1944S	21,640,000	1.30	1.30	1.50	2.10	7.00	14.00	185	—
1945P	119,408,100	1.20	1.30	1.50	2.00	6.00	13.50	125	—
1945D	37,158,000	1.30	1.40	1.60	2.20	5.50	13.00	40.00	—
1945S	58,939,000	1.20	1.30	1.50	2.00	5.00	14.00	250	—

Note: Fully Struck Full Step nickels command higher prices. Bright, Fully Struck coins command even higher prices. 1938 thru 1989 - 5 Full Steps. 1990 to date - 6 Full Steps. Without bag marks or nicks on steps.

Pre-war design resumed reverse

KM# A192 • 5.0000 g., Copper-Nickel, 19.53 mm. • Designer: Felix Schlag
Edge Desc: Plain Notes: KM#192 design and composition resumed. The 1979-S and 1981-S Type II proofs have clearer mint marks than the Type I proofs of those years.

Date	Mintage	VG-8	F-12	VF-20	XF-40	MS-60	MS-65	-65FS	Prf-65
1946	161,116,000	—	—	.20	.25	.80	3.50	40.00	—
1946D	45,292,200	—	—	.25	.35	.95	3.50	30.00	—

Date	Mintage	VG-8	F-12	VF-20	XF-40	MS-60	MS-65	-65FS	Prf-65
1946S	13,560,000	—	—	.30	.40	.50	2.00	45.00	—
1947	95,000,000	—	—	.20	.25	.75	2.00	30.00	—
1947D	37,822,000	—	—	.20	.30	.90	2.50	55.00	—
1947S	24,720,000	—	—	.20	.25	1.00	2.25	60.00	—
1948	89,348,000	—	—	.20	.25	.50	2.50	30.00	—
1948D	44,734,000	—	—	.25	.35	1.20	4.50	45.00	—
1948S	11,300,000	—	—	.25	.50	1.20	3.50	200	—
1949	60,652,000	—	—	.25	.30	2.25	6.00	200	—
1949D	36,498,000	—	—	.30	.40	1.25	5.00	75.00	—
1949D/S	Inc. above	—	35.00	40.00	65.00	170	325	1,750	—
1949S	9,716,000	.25	.35	.45	.90	1.50	3.50	145	—
1950	9,847,386	.20	.30	.35	.75	1.50	4.75	150	70.00
1950D	2,630,030	12.00	12.50	13.00	14.00	16.00	30.00	45.00	—
1951	28,609,500	—	—	.40	.50	1.50	9.00	90.00	70.00
1951D	20,460,000	.25	.30	.40	.50	3.00	10.00	45.00	—
1951S	7,776,000	.30	.40	.50	1.10	1.75	5.00	150	—
1952	64,069,980	—	—	.20	.25	.85	4.50	125	37.50
1952D	30,638,000	—	—	.30	.45	2.00	7.00	65.00	—
1952S	20,572,000	—	—	.20	.25	.75	3.50	195	—
1953	46,772,800	—	—	.20	.25	.40	1.50	200	37.50
1953D	59,878,600	—	—	.25	.40	1.50	100.00	—	
1953S	19,210,900	—	—	.20	.25	.60	2.50	1,750	—
1954	47,917,350	—	—	—	.20	.60	2.00	95.00	20.00
1954D	117,136,560	—	—	—	.20	.35	2.00	175	—
1954S	29,384,000	—	—	—	.25	1.00	3.00	1,000	—
1954S/D	Inc. above	—	9.00	14.00	30.00	50.00	500	—	
1955	8,266,200	.25	.35	.40	.50	.75	2.00	85.00	13.50
1955D	74,464,100	—	—	—	.15	.20	1.00	150	—
1955D/S	Inc. above	—	10.00	16.00	40.00	65.00	135	185	—
1956	35,885,384	—	—	—	.20	.30	.70	35.00	2.50
1956D	67,222,940	—	—	—	.15	.25	.60	90.00	—
1957	39,655,952	—	—	—	.15	.25	.60	40.00	1.50
1957D	136,828,900	—	—	—	.15	.25	.60	55.00	—
1958	17,963,652	—	—	.15	.25	.30	.65	80.00	7.00
1958D	168,249,120	—	—	—	.15	.25	.60	30.00	—

Note: Fully Struck Full Step nickels command higher prices. Bright, Fully Struck coins command even higher prices. 1938 thru 1989 - 5 Full Steps. 1990 to date - 6 Full Steps. Without bag marks or nicks on steps.

Date	Mintage	VG-8	F-12	VF-20	XF-40	MS-60	MS-65	-65FS	Prf-65
1959	28,397,291	—	—	—	.30	.65	30.00	1.25	
1959D	160,738,240	—	—	—	.25	.55	45.00	—	
1960	57,107,602	—	—	—	.25	2.00	60.00	1.00	
1960D	192,582,180	—	—	—	.25	.55	650	—	
1961	76,668,244	—	—	—	.25	.55	100.00	1.00	
1961D	229,342,760	—	—	—	.25	.55	800	—	
1962	100,602,019	—	—	—	.25	1.50	75.00	1.00	
1962D	280,195,720	—	—	—	.25	.55	60.00	—	
1963	178,851,645	—	—	—	.25	.55	45.00	1.00	
1963D	276,829,460	—	—	—	.25	.55	650	—	
1964	1,028,622,762	—	—	—	.25	.55	55.00	1.00	
1964D	1,787,297,160	—	—	—	.25	.55	500	—	
1965	136,131,380	—	—	—	.25	.50	225	—	
1966	156,208,283	—	—	—	.25	.50	350	—	
1967	107,325,800	—	—	—	.25	.50	275	—	
1968 none minted	—	—	—	—	—	—	—	—	
1968D	91,227,880	—	—	—	.25	.50	750	—	
1968S	103,437,510	—	—	—	.25	.50	300	0.75	
1969 none minted	—	—	—	—	—	—	—	—	
1969D	202,807,500	—	—	—	.25	.50	—	—	
1969S	123,099,631	—	—	—	.25	.50	450	0.75	
1970 none minted	—	—	—	—	—	—	—	—	
1970D	515,485,380	—	—	—	.25	.50	500	—	
1970S	241,464,814	—	—	—	.25	.50	125	0.75	
1971	106,884,000	—	—	—	.85	2.00	35.00	—	
1971D	316,144,800	—	—	—	.25	.50	25.00	—	
1971S	3,220,733	—	—	—	—	—	—	2.00	
1972	202,036,000	—	—	—	.25	.50	35.00	—	
1972D	351,694,600	—	—	—	.25	.50	25.00	—	
1972S	3,260,996	—	—	—	—	—	—	2.00	
1973	384,396,000	—	—	—	—	.50	20.00	—	
1973D	261,405,000	—	—	—	—	.50	20.00	—	
1973S	2,760,339	—	—	—	—	—	—	1.75	
1974	601,752,000	—	—	—	—	.50	75.00	—	
1974D	277,373,000	—	—	—	—	.50	50.00	—	
1974S	2,612,568	—	—	—	—	—	—	2.00	
1975	181,772,000	—	—	—	—	.75	65.00	—	
1975D	401,875,300	—	—	—	—	.50	60.00	—	
1975S	2,845,450	—	—	—	—	—	—	2.25	
1976	367,124,000	—	—	—	—	.75	150	—	
1976D	563,964,147	—	—	—	—	.60	55.00	—	
1976S	4,149,730	—	—	—	—	—	—	2.00	
1977	585,376,000	—	—	—	—	.40	65.00	—	
1977D	297,313,460	—	—	—	—	.55	35.00	—	
1977S	3,251,152	—	—	—	—	—	—	1.75	
1978	391,308,000	—	—	—	—	.40	40.00	—	
1978D	313,092,780	—	—	—	—	.40	35.00	—	
1978S	3,127,781	—	—	—	—	—	—	1.75	
1979	463,188,000	—	—	—	—	.40	95.00	—	
1979D	325,867,672	—	—	—	—	.40	35.00	—	
1979S type I, proof	3,677,175	—	—	—	—	—	—	1.50	
1979S type II, proof	Inc. above	—	—	—	—	—	—	1.75	
1980P	593,004,000	—	—	—	—	.40	30.00	—	
1980D	502,323,448	—	—	—	—	.25	.40	25.00	—
1980S	3,554,806	—	—	—	—	—	—	1.50	
1981P	657,504,000	—	—	—	—	.25	.40	70.00	—
1981D	364,801,843	—	—	—	—	.25	.40	40.00	—
1981S type I, proof	4,063,083	—	—	—	—	—	—	2.00	
1981S type II, proof	Inc. above	—	—	—	—	—	—	2.50	
1982P	292,355,000	—	—	—	—	2.00	12.50	80.00	—
1982D	373,726,544	—	—	—	—	1.50	3.50	45.00	—
1982S	3,857,479	—	—	—	—	—	—	3.50	
1983P	561,615,000	—	—	—	—	1.50	4.00	45.00	—

Date	Mintage	VG-8	F-12	VF-20	XF-40	MS-60	MS-65	-65FS	Prf-65
1983D	536,726,276	—	—	—	—	.75	2.50	35.00	—
1983S	3,279,126	—	—	—	—	—	—	—	4.00
1984P	746,769,000	—	—	—	—	1.25	3.00	65.00	—
1984D	517,675,146	—	—	—	—	.30	.85	30.00	—
1984S	3,065,110	—	—	—	—	—	—	—	5.00
1985P	647,114,962	—	—	—	—	.35	.75	60.00	—
1985D	459,747,446	—	—	—	—	.35	.75	35.00	—
1985S	3,362,821	—	—	—	—	—	—	—	4.00
1986P	536,883,483	—	—	—	—	.40	1.00	70.00	—
1986D	361,819,140	—	—	—	—	1.00	2.00	60.00	—
1986S	3,010,497	—	—	—	—	—	—	—	7.00
1987P	371,499,481	—	—	—	—	.25	.75	30.00	—
1987D	410,590,604	—	—	—	—	.25	.75	25.00	—
1987S	4,227,728	—	—	—	—	—	—	—	3.50
1988P	771,360,000	—	—	—	—	.25	.75	30.00	—
1988D	663,771,652	—	—	—	—	—	.75	25.00	—
1988S	3,262,948	—	—	—	—	—	—	—	6.50
1989P	898,812,000	—	—	—	—	.25	.75	75.00	—
1989D	570,842,474	—	—	—	—	.25	.75	25.00	—
1989S	3,220,194	—	—	—	—	—	—	—	5.50
1990P	661,636,000	—	—	—	—	.25	.75	25.00	—
1990D	663,938,503	—	—	—	—	.25	.75	25.00	—
1990S	3,299,559	—	—	—	—	—	—	—	5.50
1991P	614,104,000	—	—	—	—	.25	.75	25.00	—
1991D	436,496,678	—	—	—	—	.25	.75	25.00	—
1991S	2,867,787	—	—	—	—	—	—	—	5.00
1992P	399,552,000	—	—	—	—	.65	2.00	25.00	—
1992D	450,565,113	—	—	—	—	.25	.75	25.00	—
1992S	4,176,560	—	—	—	—	—	—	—	4.00
1993P	412,076,000	—	—	—	—	.25	.75	25.00	—
1993D	406,084,135	—	—	—	—	.25	.75	25.00	—
1993S	3,394,792	—	—	—	—	—	—	—	4.50
1994P	722,160,000	—	—	—	—	.25	.75	25.00	—
1994P matte proof	167,703	—	—	—	—	—	—	—	75.00
1994D	715,762,110	—	—	—	—	.25	.75	25.00	—
1994S	3,269,923	—	—	—	—	—	—	—	4.00
1995P	774,156,000	—	—	—	—	.25	.75	25.00	—
1995D	888,112,000	—	—	—	—	.35	.85	25.00	—
1995S	2,707,481	—	—	—	—	—	—	—	4.00
1996P	829,332,000	—	—	—	—	.25	.75	25.00	—
1996D	817,736,000	—	—	—	—	.25	.75	25.00	—
1996S	2,915,212	—	—	—	—	—	—	—	4.00
1997P	470,972,000	—	—	—	—	.25	.75	25.00	—
1997P matte proof	25,000	—	—	—	—	—	—	—	200
1997D	466,640,000	—	—	—	—	.30	2.00	25.00	—
1997S	1,975,000	—	—	—	—	.25	—	—	5.00
1998P	688,272,000	—	—	—	—	.25	.80	25.00	—
1998D	635,360,000	—	—	—	—	.25	.80	25.00	—
1998S	2,957,286	—	—	—	—	—	—	—	4.50
1999P	1,212,000,000	—	—	—	—	.25	.80	25.00	—
1999D	1,066,720,000	—	—	—	—	.25	.80	20.00	—
1999S	3,362,462	—	—	—	—	—	—	—	3.50
2000P	846,240,000	—	—	—	—	.25	.80	20.00	—
2000D	1,509,520,000	—	—	—	—	.25	.80	20.00	—
2000S	4,063,361	—	—	—	—	—	—	—	2.00

Date	Mintage	G-4	VG-8	F-12	VF-20	XF-40	AU-50	MS-60	MS-65	Prf-65
1908S	3,220,000	3.50	5.50	11.50	22.00	46.00	175	310	2,350	—
1909	10,240,650	2.25	2.75	3.50	7.25	22.00	58.00	105	695	1,485
1909D	954,000	7.25	18.50	60.00	100.00	135	225	485	3,150	—
1909O	2,287,000	4.00	7.25	12.50	22.00	50.00	92.50	185	1,650	—
1909S	1,000,000	8.75	19.50	88.00	130	182	315	525	3,150	—
1910	11,520,551	2.25	2.75	3.25	9.75	22.00	58.00	105	695	1,485
1910D	3,490,000	2.50	4.00	8.50	19.00	47.50	100.00	210	1,650	—
1910S	1,240,000	5.25	9.00	50.00	74.00	110	195	425	2,450	—
1911	18,870,543	2.25	2.75	3.25	7.00	22.00	58.00	105	695	1,485
1911D	11,209,000	2.25	2.75	3.25	7.00	22.00	58.00	105	695	—
1911S	3,520,000	3.00	4.00	8.50	18.50	39.50	105	195	1,050	—
1912	19,350,700	2.25	2.75	3.25	7.00	22.00	58.00	105	695	1,485
1912D	11,760,000	2.25	2.75	3.25	7.00	22.00	58.00	105	695	—
1912S	3,420,000	2.50	3.75	5.60	12.50	34.00	92.50	155	775	—
1913	19,760,622	2.25	2.75	3.25	7.00	22.00	58.00	105	695	1,485
1913S	510,000	35.00	50.00	120	190	240	325	480	1,375	—
1914	17,360,655	2.25	2.75	3.25	7.00	22.00	58.00	105	695	1,485
1914D	11,908,000	2.25	2.75	3.25	7.00	22.00	58.00	105	695	—
1914S	2,100,000	2.50	3.75	8.00	17.50	39.50	78.00	150	1,250	—
1915	5,620,450	2.25	2.75	3.25	7.00	22.00	58.00	105	695	1,485
1915S	960,000	7.50	11.50	34.50	49.50	66.50	135	250	1,550	—
1916	18,490,000	2.25	2.75	3.25	8.00	22.00	58.00	105	695	—
1916S	5,820,000	2.50	3.75	4.25	8.50	25.50	63.00	110	790	—

Mercury Dime

Mint mark

Full split bands

1942/41

KM# 140 • 2.5000 g., 0.9000 Silver, 0.0723 oz. ASW, 17.9 mm. • Designer: Adolph A. Weinman Notes: All specimens listed as -65FSB are for fully struck MS-65 coins with fully split and rounded horizontal bands on the fasces.

Date	Mintage	G-4	VG-8	F-12	VF-20	XF-40	MS-60	MS-65	Prf-65	-65FSB
1916	22,180,080	3.45	4.70	6.25	7.00	12.00	30.00	110	—	120
1916D	264,000	1,050	1,675	2,750	3,850	5,950	13,200	26,500	—	44,500
1916S	10,450,000	4.00	5.50	9.75	15.00	25.00	46.00	210	—	600
1917	55,230,000	1.70	2.25	2.50	5.50	8.00	28.00	155	—	400
1917D	9,402,000	4.00	6.00	11.00	26.00	51.00	120	1,100	—	6,000
1917S	27,330,000	1.90	2.40	3.50	6.50	14.00	64.00	470	—	1,150
1918	26,680,000	2.50	3.20	5.75	12.00	34.00	70.00	420	—	1,150
1918D	22,674,800	2.65	3.25	5.00	12.00	32.00	105	600	—	33,500
1918S	19,300,000	2.40	3.00	3.85	10.00	24.00	96.00	660	—	6,600
1919	35,740,000	1.90	2.50	3.00	5.50	12.00	37.00	315	—	700
1919D	9,939,000	3.50	6.50	12.00	25.00	46.00	180	2,100	—	38,500
1919S	8,850,000	2.90	3.25	8.00	17.00	42.00	180	1,250	—	13,000
1920	59,030,000	1.70	1.80	2.25	4.00	8.50	28.00	235	—	515
1920D	19,171,000	2.50	2.85	4.50	8.00	24.00	110	750	—	4,000
1920S	13,820,000	2.40	2.75	4.00	8.50	21.00	110	1,300	—	8,000
1921	1,230,000	60.00	77.00	118	265	540	1,150	3,000	—	4,400
1921D	1,080,000	80.00	120	210	365	650	1,250	2,900	—	5,600
1923	50,130,000	1.70	2.00	4.00	7.00	7.00	28.00	115	—	295
1923S	6,440,000	2.60	3.00	7.00	18.00	75.00	160	1,150	—	6,900
1924	24,010,000	1.70	2.00	2.75	4.50	13.50	42.00	175	—	520
1924D	6,810,000	3.00	4.25	6.50	22.00	63.00	175	1,050	—	1,400
1924S	7,120,000	2.90	3.75	4.25	12.00	60.00	170	1,100	—	14,000
1925	25,610,000	1.70	1.80	2.30	4.00	9.00	28.00	210	—	1,000
1925D	5,117,000	4.00	4.25	12.00	44.00	135	350	1,750	—	3,500
1925S	5,850,000	2.50	2.75	7.00	14.00	85.00	185	1,400	—	4,400
1926	32,160,000	1.70	1.80	2.30	3.00	6.00	25.00	240	—	525
1926D	6,828,000	2.90	4.00	5.00	10.00	32.00	125	550	—	2,650
1926S	1,520,000	12.50	15.00	29.00	70.00	285	865	2,750	—	6,500
1927	28,080,000	1.70	1.80	2.30	3.50	6.00	26.00	138	—	400
1927D	4,812,000	2.90	5.00	7.50	21.00	88.00	175	1,285	—	8,500
1927S	4,770,000	2.25	3.75	5.00	9.00	32.00	285	1,400	—	7,700
1928	19,480,000	1.70	1.80	2.30	3.50	4.50	27.50	120	—	300
1928D	4,161,000	3.75	4.00	9.00	22.00	55.00	175	875	—	2,500
1928S Large S	7,400,000	2.75	4.25	4.50	12.00	40.00	225	750	—	—
1928S Small S	Inc. above	2.00	2.25	3.00	6.50	19.00	125	425	—	1,900

DIME

Barber Dime

Laureate head right, date at angle below obverse
Value within wreath reverse

KM# 113 • 2.5000 g., 0.9000 Silver, 0.0723 oz. ASW, 17.9 mm. • Obv. Legend UNITED STATES OF AMERICA Designer: Charles E. Barber

Date	Mintage	G-4	VG-8	F-12	VF-20	XF-40	AU-50	MS-60	MS-65	Prf-65
1901	18,860,478	4.00	5.00	6.50	10.00	27.50	63.00	110	750	1,485
1901O	5,620,000	4.00	5.50	16.00	27.50	67.50	175	450	4,350	—
1901S	593,022	80.00	150	360	475	520	675	985	5,350	—
1902	21,380,777	4.00	5.00	5.50	8.00	23.00	63.00	110	750	1,485
1902O	4,500,000	4.00	5.50	15.00	32.50	62.50	145	350	4,500	—
1902S	2,070,000	8.00	21.00	58.00	90.00	135	195	375	3,950	—
1903	19,500,755	4.00	5.00	5.50	8.00	25.00	63.00	110	1,100	1,485
1903O	8,180,000	4.00	5.50	13.50	23.50	50.00	110	250	4,850	—
1903S	613,300	84.00	130	350	490	750	840	1,100	3,150	—
1904	14,601,027	4.00	5.00	6.25	9.75	25.00	63.00	110	1,850	1,485
1904S	800,000	45.00	75.00	165	245	335	465	725	4,500	—
1905	14,552,350	3.25	4.50	6.00	9.75	25.00	63.00	110	730	1,485
1905O	3,400,000	4.25	141	36.50	57.50	92.00	155	285	1,650	—
1905O micro O	Inc. above	35.00	50.00	75.00	140	235	375	1,750	12,500	—
1905S	6,855,199	3.50	4.25	9.00	18.50	43.50	96.00	210	775	—
1906	19,958,406	2.25	3.75	3.75	7.25	22.00	58.00	105	730	1,485
1906D	4,060,000	2.75	4.10	7.00	15.00	35.00	78.00	175	1,650	—
1906O	2,610,000	5.50	13.00	50.00	78.00	100.00	135	195	1,150	—
1906S	3,136,640	3.25	5.50	12.50	22.50	44.00	110	240	1,350	—
1907	22,220,575	2.25	2.75	3.50	7.25	22.00	58.00	105	695	1,485
1907D	4,080,000	2.75	4.25	8.75	17.50	43.50	115	275	3,950	—
1907O	5,058,000	3.25	6.75	33.50	50.00	62.50	110	210	1,350	—
1907S	3,178,470	3.25	5.50	16.00	27.50	67.50	150	410	2,450	—
1908	10,600,545	2.25	2.75	3.50	7.25	22.00	58.00	105	695	1,485
1908D	7,490,000	2.25	2.75	5.00	9.75	29.00	63.00	125	990	—
1908O	1,789,000	5.25	11.00	44.50	64.00	92.00	150	290	1,350	—

Date	Mintage	G-4	VG-8	F-12	VF-20	XF-40	MS-60	MS-65	Prf-65	-65FSB
1929	25,970,000	1.70	1.80	2.30	3.00	4.50	21.00	60.00	—	265
1929D	5,034,000	2.00	3.00	4.00	8.00	15.00	27.00	75.00	—	225
1929S	4,730,000	1.90	1.85	2.25	5.00	7.00	32.50	90.00	—	525
1929S Doubled Die Obv	Inc. above	5.00	9.00	16.00	25.00	40.00	90.00	275	—	—
1930	6,770,000	1.70	1.80	2.30	3.75	7.00	26.00	120	—	525
1930S	1,843,000	2.50	3.50	4.80	6.50	19.00	82.00	200	—	565
1931	3,150,000	2.25	3.00	3.35	4.25	12.50	33.00	135	—	—
1931D	1,260,000	9.00	11.00	15.00	20.00	46.50	100.00	285	—	350
1931 Doubled Die Obv & Rev	Inc. above	—	—	—	50.00	70.00	135	485	—	—
1931S	1,800,000	4.00	5.00	5.50	11.00	22.00	96.00	275	—	2,100
1931S Doubled Die Obv	Inc. above	7.50	10.00	13.00	25.00	35.00	140	425	—	—
1934	24,080,000	1.40	1.45	1.75	3.00	6.50	29.00	42.00	—	150
1934D	6,772,000	1.90	2.10	3.25	7.50	14.00	50.00	78.00	—	360
1935	58,830,000	—	1.35	1.50	2.15	4.25	10.00	30.00	—	70.00
1935D	10,477,000	1.50	1.90	2.85	6.50	13.00	37.00	84.00	—	600
1935S	15,840,000	1.70	1.65	2.00	3.00	5.50	24.00	37.00	—	500
1936	87,504,130	1.40	—	1.50	2.50	3.50	9.00	26.50	1,950	90.00
1936 Doubled Die Obv	Inc. above	—	—	8.00	15.00	25.00	50.00	165	—	—
1936D	16,132,000	—	1.65	2.10	4.25	8.50	28.00	53.00	—	295
1936S	9,210,000	—	1.50	1.90	3.00	6.00	20.00	33.00	—	85.00
1937	56,865,756	1.40	1.40	1.50	1.70	3.50	8.00	24.00	800	42.00
1937 Doubled Die Obv	Inc. above	—	—	—	6.00	9.00	20.00	60.00	—	—
1937D	14,146,000	1.30	1.40	1.80	3.00	6.00	22.00	43.00	—	100.00
1937S	9,740,000	—	1.50	2.00	3.00	5.50	22.00	36.00	—	195
1937S Doubled Die Obv	Inc. above	—	—	—	5.00	8.00	28.00	80.00	—	—
1938	22,198,728	1.40	—	1.50	1.70	3.75	13.00	25.00	480	80.00
1938D	5,537,000	1.75	2.25	3.25	5.00	6.00	18.00	34.00	—	65.00
1938S	8,090,000	1.50	2.00	2.75	3.25	5.00	21.00	37.00	—	135
1939	67,749,321	1.40	—	1.50	1.70	3.25	9.00	25.00	425	170
1939 Doubled Die Obv	Inc. above	—	—	—	4.00	6.00	14.00	35.00	—	—
1939D	24,394,000	1.30	1.40	1.50	2.00	3.50	7.50	26.00	—	45.00
1939S	10,540,000	1.50	1.75	2.25	3.50	6.75	25.00	50.00	—	750
1940	65,361,827	1.30	1.40	1.50	1.60	2.50	6.00	30.00	325	57.50
1940D	21,198,000	—	—	1.60	1.70	3.30	8.00	32.00	—	55.00
1940S	21,560,000	—	—	1.60	1.70	3.30	8.50	32.00	—	95.00
1941	175,106,557	1.20	1.30	1.40	1.50	2.00	6.00	30.00	325	42.00
1941 Doubled Die Obv	Inc. above	—	—	—	10.00	16.00	55.00	140	—	—
1941D	45,634,000	1.30	1.40	1.50	1.70	2.40	8.00	23.00	—	40.00
1941D Doubled Die Obv	Inc. above	—	—	—	9.00	14.00	30.00	90.00	—	—
1941S Small S	43,090,000	1.30	1.40	1.50	1.70	2.40	7.00	30.00	—	50.00
1941S Large S	Inc. above	2.50	4.00	8.00	15.00	25.00	110	250	—	—
1941S Doubled Die Rev	Inc. above	1.75	2.50	3.00	4.00	5.00	18.00	50.00	—	—
1942	205,432,329	1.20	—	1.40	1.50	2.00	6.00	24.00	325	52.50
1942/41	Inc. above	485	510	620	660	695	2,650	15,500	—	38,500
1942D	60,740,000	—	—	1.50	1.70	2.40	8.00	27.50	—	40.00
1942/41D	Inc. above	475	535	660	825	850	2,700	9,650	—	19,500
1942S	49,300,000	1.30	1.40	1.50	1.70	2.40	9.50	24.00	—	140
1943	191,710,000	1.20	1.30	1.40	1.50	2.00	6.00	31.00	—	50.00
1943D	71,949,000	1.30	1.40	1.50	1.70	2.40	7.75	30.00	—	40.00
1943S	60,400,000	1.30	1.40	1.50	1.70	2.40	9.00	26.50	—	66.00
1944	231,410,000	1.20	1.30	1.40	1.50	2.00	6.00	23.00	—	80.00
1944D	62,224,000	1.30	1.40	1.50	1.70	2.40	7.50	23.00	—	40.00
1944S	49,490,000	1.30	1.40	1.50	1.70	2.40	7.50	30.00	—	50.00
1945	159,130,000	1.20	1.30	1.40	1.50	2.00	6.00	23.00	—	8,000
1945D	40,245,000	1.30	1.40	1.50	1.70	2.40	6.50	24.00	—	40.00
1945S	41,920,000	1.30	1.40	1.50	1.70	2.40	7.00	24.00	—	135
1945S micro S	Inc. above	3.00	4.00	6.00	9.00	13.00	28.00	115	—	650

Roosevelt Dime

Mint mark 1946-64

KM# 195 • 2.5000 g., **0.9000 Silver**, 0.0723 oz. ASW, 17.9 mm. • **Designer:** John R. Sinnock

Date	Mintage	G-4	VG-8	F-12	VF-20	XF-40	AU-50	MS-60	MS-65	Prf-65
1946	225,250,000	—	—	—	—	1.50	2.00	2.00	14.00	—
1946D	61,043,500	—	—	—	—	1.50	2.20	2.25	15.00	—
1946S	27,900,000	—	—	—	—	1.50	2.25	2.35	17.00	—
1947	121,520,000	—	—	—	—	1.50	2.00	4.00	15.00	—
1947D	46,835,000	—	—	—	—	1.70	2.25	5.00	17.00	—
1947S	34,840,000	—	—	—	—	1.50	2.00	5.00	16.00	—
1948	74,950,000	—	—	—	—	1.60	2.00	4.50	15.00	—
1948D	52,841,000	—	—	—	—	1.90	2.50	6.00	17.00	—
1948S	35,520,000	—	—	—	—	1.80	2.25	5.00	14.00	—
1949	30,940,000	—	—	1.50	2.00	3.00	8.00	16.00	50.00	—
1949D	26,034,000	—	—	1.35	1.75	2.25	5.00	9.00	22.00	—
1949S	13,510,000	—	1.60	2.00	3.50	7.50	14.00	40.00	65.00	—
1950	50,181,500	—	—	—	1.75	2.25	3.50	10.00	25.00	55.00
1950D	46,803,000	—	—	—	—	—	2.50	5.00	12.00	—
1950S	20,440,000	—	1.20	1.80	2.00	3.75	9.00	32.00	60.00	—
1951	102,937,602	—	—	—	—	—	2.10	2.50	10.00	60.00
1951D	56,529,000	—	—	—	—	—	2.00	2.50	8.00	—
1951S	31,630,000	—	—	—	1.70	2.00	4.00	10.00	26.00	—
1952	99,122,073	—	—	—	—	—	1.90	2.50	9.00	40.00
1952D	122,100,000	—	—	—	—	—	1.90	2.50	10.00	—
1952S	44,419,500	—	—	—	1.75	1.90	2.75	5.50	15.00	—
1953	53,618,920	—	—	—	—	—	1.90	2.25	8.00	45.00

Date	Mintage	G-4	VG-8	F-12	VF-20	XF-40	AU-50	MS-60	MS-65	Prf-65
1953D	136,433,000	—	—	—	—	—	1.90	2.45	8.00	—
1953S	39,180,000	—	—	—	—	—	2.30	3.00	15.00	—
1954	114,243,503	—	—	—	—	—	1.90	2.10	7.00	20.00
1954D	106,397,000	—	—	—	—	—	1.90	2.10	7.00	—
1954S	22,860,000	—	—	—	—	—	1.90	2.20	10.00	—
1955	12,828,381	—	—	—	1.75	1.50	2.30	2.75	10.00	18.00
1955D	13,959,000	—	—	—	1.75	1.60	2.45	2.75	10.00	—
1955S	18,510,000	—	—	—	1.75	1.55	2.35	2.25	9.00	—
1956	109,309,384	—	—	—	—	—	1.90	2.10	9.00	8.00
1956D	108,015,100	—	—	—	—	—	1.90	2.20	10.00	—
1957	161,407,952	—	—	—	—	—	1.90	2.10	8.00	6.00
1957D	113,354,330	—	—	—	—	—	1.90	2.10	8.00	—
1958	32,785,652	—	—	—	—	—	1.90	2.10	8.50	6.00
1958D	136,564,600	—	—	—	—	—	1.90	2.10	9.00	—
1959	86,929,291	—	—	—	—	—	1.90	2.10	8.00	5.00
1959D	164,919,790	—	—	—	—	—	1.90	2.10	8.00	—
1960	72,081,602	—	—	—	—	—	1.90	2.10	7.50	5.00
1960D	200,160,400	—	—	—	—	—	1.90	2.10	7.50	—
1961	96,758,244	—	—	—	—	—	1.90	2.10	6.50	4.50
1961D	209,146,550	—	—	—	—	—	1.90	2.10	6.50	—
1962	75,668,019	—	—	—	—	—	1.90	2.10	7.00	4.50
1962D	334,948,380	—	—	—	—	—	1.90	2.10	7.00	—
1963	126,725,645	—	—	—	—	—	1.90	2.10	6.50	4.00
1963D	421,476,530	—	—	—	—	—	1.90	2.10	6.50	—
1964	933,310,762	—	—	—	—	—	1.90	2.10	6.00	4.00
1964D	1,357,517,180	—	—	—	—	—	1.90	2.10	6.00	—

Mint mark 1968- present   1982 No mint mark

KM# 195a • 2.2700 g., **Copper-Nickel Clad Copper**, 17.9 mm. • **Designer:** John R. Sinnock **Notes:** The 1979-S and 1981-S Type II proofs have clearer mint marks than the Type I proofs of those years. On the 1982 no-mint-mark variety, the mint mark was inadvertently left off.

Date	Mintage	MS-65	Prf-65	Date	Mintage	MS-65	Prf-65
1965	1,652,140,570	1.00	—	1985S	3,362,821	—	1.00
1966	1,382,734,540	1.00	—	1986P	682,649,693	2.00	—
1967	2,244,007,320	1.50	—	1986D	473,326,970	2.00	—
1968	424,470,000	1.00	—	1986S	3,010,497	—	2.75
1968D	480,748,280	1.00	—	1987P	762,709,481	1.00	—
1968S	3,041,506	—	1.00	1987D	653,203,402	1.00	—
1969	145,790,000	3.00	—	1987S	4,227,728	—	1.00
1969D	563,323,870	1.00	—	1988P	1,030,550,000	1.00	—
1969S	2,934,631	—	0.80	1988D	962,385,488	1.00	—
1970	345,570,000	1.00	—	1988S	3,262,948	—	3.00
1970S No S	—	—	1,300	1989P	1,298,400,000	1.00	—
1970D	754,942,100	1.00	—	1989D	896,535,597	1.00	—
1970S	2,632,810	—	1.00	1989S	3,220,194	—	4.00
1971	162,690,000	2.00	—	1990P	1,034,340,000	1.00	—
1971D	377,914,240	1.00	—	1990D	839,995,824	1.00	—
1971S	3,220,733	—	1.00	1990S	3,299,559	—	2.00
1972	431,540,000	1.00	—	1991P	927,220,000	1.00	—
1972D	330,290,000	1.00	—	1991D	601,241,114	1.00	—
1972S	3,260,996	—	1.00	1991S	2,867,787	—	3.00
1973	315,670,000	1.00	—	1992P	593,500,000	1.00	—
1973D	455,032,426	1.00	—	1992D	616,273,932	1.00	—
1973S	2,760,339	—	1.00	1992S	2,858,981	—	4.00
1974	470,248,000	1.00	—	1993P	766,180,000	1.00	—
1974D	571,083,000	1.00	—	1993D	750,110,166	1.50	—
1974S	2,612,568	—	1.00	1993S	2,633,439	—	7.00
1975	585,673,900	1.00	—	1994P	1,189,000,000	1.00	—
1975D	313,705,300	1.00	—	1994D	1,303,268,110	1.00	—
1975S	2,845,450	—	2.00	1994S	2,484,594	—	5.00
1976	568,760,000	1.50	—	1995P	1,125,500,000	1.50	—
1976D	695,222,774	1.00	—	1995D	1,274,890,000	2.00	—
1976S	4,149,730	—	1.00	1995S	2,010,384	—	20.00
1977	796,930,000	1.00	—	1996P	1,421,163,000	1.00	—
1977D	376,607,228	1.00	—	1996D	1,400,300,000	1.00	—
1977S	3,251,152	—	2.00	1996W	1,457,949	25.00	—
1978	663,980,000	1.00	—	1996S	2,085,191	—	2.50
1978D	282,847,540	1.00	—	1997P	991,640,000	2.00	—
1978S	3,127,781	—	1.00	1997D	979,810,000	1.00	—
1979	315,440,000	1.00	—	1997S	1,975,000	—	11.00
1979D	390,921,184	1.00	—	1998P	1,163,000,000	1.00	—
1979 type I	—	—	1.00	1998D	1,172,250,000	1.25	—
1979S type I	3,677,175	—	1.00	1998S	2,078,494	—	4.00
1979S type II	Inc. above	—	2.00	1999P	2,164,000,000	1.00	—
1980P	735,170,000	1.00	—	1999D	1,397,750,000	1.00	—
1980D	719,354,321	.70	—	1999S	2,557,897	—	4.00
1980S	3,554,806	—	1.00	2000P	1,842,500,000	1.00	—
1981P	676,650,000	1.00	—	2000D	1,818,700,000	1.00	—
1981D	712,284,143	1.00	—	2000S	3,097,440	—	1.00
1981S type I		—	1.00				
1981S type II		—	2.00				
1982P	519,475,000	8.50	—				
1982 no mint mark	Inc. above	300	—				
1982D	542,713,584	3.00	—				
1982S	3,857,479	—	2.00				
1983P	647,025,000	7.00	—				
1983D	730,129,224	2.50	—				
1983S	3,279,126	—	2.00				
1984P	856,669,000	1.00	—				
1984D	704,803,976	2.00	—				
1984S	3,065,110	—	2.00				
1985P	705,200,962	1.00	—				
1985D	587,979,970	1.00	—				

KM# 195b • 2.5000 g., 0.9000 **Silver**, 0.0723 oz. ASW, 17.9 mm. • **Designer:** John R. Sinnock

Date	Mintage	Prf-65	Date	Mintage	Prf-65
1992S	1,317,579	5.00	1997S	821,678	25.00
1993S	761,353	9.00	1998S	878,792	9.00
1994S	785,329	9.00	1999S	804,565	6.50
1995S	838,953	25.00	2000S	965,921	4.00
1996S	830,021	9.00			

QUARTER

Barber Quarter

Laureate head right, flanked by stars, date below obverse
Heraldic eagle reverse

KM# 114 • 6.2500 g., 0.9000 **Silver**, 0.1808 oz. ASW, 24.3 mm. • **Obv. Legend** IN GOD WE TRUST **Rev. Legend:** UNITED STATES OF AMERICA **Designer:** Charles E. Barber

Date	Mintage	G-4	VG-8	F-12	VF-20	XF-40	AU-50	MS-60	MS-65	Prf-65
1901	8,892,813	11.00	13.00	25.00	41.50	80.00	135	215	1,850	2,450
1901O	1,612,000	42.50	60.00	145	275	455	665	885	5,850	—
1901S	72,664	6,250	14,000	17,500	25,500	30,000	35,000	40,000	82,500	—
1902	12,197,744	6.00	8.50	19.50	32.50	65.00	120	210	1,400	2,450
1902O	4,748,000	8.50	16.00	52.50	89.00	150	245	485	5,000	—
1902S	1,524,612	14.50	22.00	55.00	95.00	170	260	525	3,750	—
1903	9,670,064	6.75	8.50	19.50	32.50	62.00	112	210	2,600	2,450
1903O	3,500,000	8.00	13.50	41.50	65.00	125	260	435	6,250	—
1903S	1,036,000	15.50	26.00	46.00	88.00	145	285	435	2,900	—
1904	9,588,813	8.00	9.75	20.00	34.50	69.00	120	220	1,500	2,450
1904O	2,456,000	11.50	21.50	62.50	120	225	460	850	3,250	—
1905	4,968,250	13.50	15.00	27.50	39.50	72.00	120	210	1,650	2,450
1905O	1,230,000	18.50	33.50	82.50	170	265	365	500	6,600	—
1905S	1,884,000	12.75	15.00	43.50	66.00	110	220	335	3,650	—
1906	3,656,435	6.75	8.50	18.50	32.50	65.00	112	205	1,400	2,450
1906D	3,280,000	7.00	8.50	25.00	42.50	69.00	155	220	2,250	—
1906O	2,056,000	7.00	13.50	41.50	60.00	110	200	290	1,700	—
1907	7,192,575	5.50	8.00	16.50	32.50	62.00	112	205	1,400	2,450
1907D	2,484,000	6.00	9.00	29.00	52.50	78.00	175	240	2,750	—
1907O	4,560,000	5.50	13.50	19.00	38.50	66.00	135	205	2,600	—
1907S	1,360,000	10.00	18.50	47.50	75.00	135	275	465	4,250	—
1908	4,232,545	5.00	6.25	18.50	33.50	66.00	112	205	1,400	2,450
1908D	5,788,000	5.00	6.25	17.50	35.00	66.00	116	240	1,750	—
1908O	6,244,000	5.00	8.50	17.50	38.50	72.00	120	205	1,400	—
1908S	784,000	18.50	40.00	90.00	165	295	500	775	4,950	—
1909	9,268,650	5.00	6.25	17.50	33.50	66.00	108	205	1,400	2,450
1909D	5,114,000	6.25	8.00	22.00	41.50	88.00	160	205	2,350	—
1909O	712,000	19.50	45.00	95.00	200	375	600	800	8,500	—
1909S	1,348,000	8.00	13.50	37.50	57.50	96.00	200	300	2,500	—
1910	2,244,551	7.75	10.00	30.00	46.00	80.00	140	205	1,400	2,450
1910D	1,500,000	8.00	11.00	47.50	75.00	130	260	375	2,250	—
1911	3,720,543	6.25	8.50	19.50	33.50	72.50	125	215	1,400	2,450
1911D	933,600	9.00	19.50	95.00	215	330	500	700	6,250	—
1911S	988,000	7.00	13.00	51.50	90.00	180	300	400	1,600	—
1912	4,400,700	5.75	8.00	17.50	33.50	70.00	108	205	1,400	2,485
1912S	708,000	9.00	13.00	46.00	84.00	130	230	390	2,750	—
1913	484,613	16.00	26.00	75.00	190	390	535	960	5,000	2,485
1913D	1,450,800	12.50	14.50	38.50	58.50	94.00	185	275	1,400	—
1913S	40,000	1,850	2,450	5,000	7,750	10,500	12,850	15,000	37,500	—
1914	6,244,610	4.50	5.75	17.00	28.00	55.00	108	205	1,400	2,550
1914D	3,046,000	4.50	5.75	17.00	28.00	55.00	108	205	1,400	—
1914S	264,000	82.00	120	235	425	620	775	1,000	3,450	—
1915	3,480,450	4.50	5.75	17.00	28.00	55.00	108	205	1,400	2,485
1915D	3,694,000	4.50	5.75	17.00	28.00	55.00	108	205	1,400	—
1915S	704,000	9.00	13.00	35.00	57.50	110	220	285	1,500	—
1916	1,788,000	4.50	5.75	17.00	28.00	55.00	108	205	1,400	—
1916D	6,540,800	4.50	5.75	17.00	28.00	55.00	108	205	1,400	—
1916D/D	Inc. above	10.00	14.00	24.00	45.00	95.00	150	400		—

Standing Liberty Quarter

Right breast exposed; Type 1 obverse

Right breast exposed

KM# 141 • 6.2500 g., 0.9000 **Silver**, 0.1808 oz. ASW, 24.3 mm. • **Designer:** Hermon A. MacNeil

Date	Mintage	G-4	VG-8	F-12	VF-20	XF-40	AU-50	MS-60	MS-65	-65FH
1916	52,000	3,500	6,350	9,500	13,000	14,500	16,500	18,500	30,000	37,500
1917	8,792,000	24.00	40.00	52.00	70.00	95.00	175	200	750	1,500
1917D	1,509,200	28.00	42.00	55.00	85.00	125	195	235	950	2,550
1917S	1,952,000	30.00	44.00	60.00	90.00	160	210	240	1,200	4,100

Right breast covered; Type 2 obverse
Three stars below eagle reverse

Right breast covered   Mint mark

KM# 145 • 6.2500 g., 0.9000 **Silver**, 0.1808 oz. ASW, 24.3 mm. • **Designer:** Hermon A. MacNeil

Date	Mintage	G-4	VG-8	F-12	VF-20	XF-40	AU-50	MS-60	MS-65	-65FH
1917	13,880,000	22.00	33.00	42.50	54.00	75.00	105	165	575	950
1917D	6,224,400	40.00	45.00	65.00	78.00	110	160	225	1,325	3,500
1917S	5,522,000	40.00	45.00	63.00	75.00	108	155	215	1,100	3,650
1918	14,240,000	17.00	21.00	29.00	35.00	46.00	80.00	135	560	1,750
1918D	7,380,000	26.00	36.00	66.00	78.00	122	195	250	1,485	4,850
1918S	11,072,000	17.00	21.00	32.00	35.00	48.00	95.00	185	1,250	13,500
1918/17S	Inc. above	1,550	2,250	3,850	5,200	7,500	13,500	17,850	110,000	320,000
1919	11,324,000	33.00	44.00	55.00	74.00	80.00	118	175	600	1,650
1919D	1,944,000	85.00	110	195	345	565	695	825	2,950	28,500
1919S	1,836,000	80.00	105	185	285	510	585	750	4,200	30,000
1920	27,860,000	15.00	18.00	25.00	37.00	51.00	90.00	165	600	2,100
1920D	3,586,400	48.00	65.00	88.00	120	160	215	325	2,250	7,200
1920S	6,380,000	19.00	25.00	30.00	37.00	57.00	110	235	2,650	24,000
1921	1,916,000	185	220	450	625	750	1,100	1,500	3,850	5,500
1923	9,716,000	15.00	18.00	35.00	37.00	55.00	95.00	155	620	4,000
1923S	1,360,000	300	425	675	985	1,250	1,650	2,300	4,750	6,500
1924	10,920,000	15.00	18.00	25.00	34.00	45.00	90.00	170	585	1,650
1924D	3,112,000	56.00	68.00	108	135	185	220	300	610	5,750
1924S	2,860,000	27.00	32.00	43.00	57.00	105	220	315	1,850	6,500
1925	12,280,000	4.00	4.75	5.70	18.50	44.00	90.00	150	575	950
1926	11,316,000	3.50	4.00	6.00	14.00	37.00	80.00	140	585	2,250
1926D	1,716,000	6.50	10.00	20.00	40.00	75.00	118	170	545	22,500
1926S	2,700,000	4.50	5.40	11.00	30.00	110	225	325	2,175	28,000
1927	11,912,000	3.50	4.00	6.00	12.00	32.00	70.00	105	550	1,300
1927D	976,400	14.00	19.00	32.00	70.00	140	210	250	600	2,650
1927S	396,000	35.00	48.00	110	285	1,000	2,650	4,750	12,000	165,000
1928	6,336,000	3.50	4.75	6.00	12.00	32.00	65.00	100.00	540	2,150
1928D	1,627,600	4.75	6.00	7.50	20.00	42.50	90.00	135	540	5,650
1928S Large S	2,644,000	6.00	7.50	10.00	25.00	65.00	115	200	—	—
1928S Small S	Inc. above	4.50	5.50	6.50	16.50	38.00	79.00	125	560	900
1929	11,140,000	3.50	4.75	6.00	12.00	32.00	65.00	100.00	540	900
1929D	1,358,000	4.25	5.50	6.75	16.00	38.50	79.00	135	540	5,850
1929S	1,764,000	4.00	5.50	6.50	15.00	34.00	75.00	120	540	875
1930	5,632,000	3.50	4.00	6.00	12.00	32.00	65.00	100.00	540	875
1930S	1,556,000	4.00	5.50	6.50	15.00	34.00	70.00	115	550	925

Washington Quarter

Mint mark 1932-64

KM# 164 • 6.2500 g., 0.9000 **Silver**, 0.1808 oz. ASW, 24.3 mm. • **Designer:** John Flanagan

Date	Mintage	G-4	VG-8	F-12	VF-20	XF-40	AU-50	MS-60	MS-65	Prf-65
1932	5,404,000	4.00	5.20	6.00	7.50	9.75	15.00	26.00	435	—
1932D	436,800	165	180	205	240	345	500	1,000	24,500	—
1932S	408,000	195	200	205	240	285	300	500	7,000	—
1934 Medium Motto	31,912,052	4.40	4.80	5.40	6.30	6.80	10.00	27.50	110	—
1934 Heavy Motto	Inc. above	4.50	5.75	7.00	12.50	18.00	30.00	50.00	225	—
1934 Light motto	Inc. above	4.00	5.00	6.00	10.00	15.00	26.00	45.00	400	—
1934 Doubled Die Obverse	Inc. above	75.00	100.00	165	200	320	450	800	8,000	—
1934D Medium Motto	3,527,200	5.00	6.00	8.50	13.50	28.00	95.00	245	1,550	—
1934D Heavy Motto	Inc. above	6.00	8.00	11.00	16.00	37.00	110	295	1,900	—
1935	32,484,000	4.10	4.20	4.40	4.80	5.00	10.00	21.50	145	—
1935D	5,780,000	4.40	4.90	7.50	14.00	30.00	130	255	975	—
1935S	5,660,000	4.40	4.90	5.00	7.50	15.00	38.50	100.00	465	—
1936	41,303,837	4.10	4.20	4.40	4.80	4.80	9.50	22.50	115	1,950
1936D	5,374,000	5.00	6.50	8.50	22.00	55.00	275	625	1,850	—
1936S	3,828,000	4.40	4.90	4.40	6.25	13.50	52.50	115	420	—
1937	19,701,542	4.10	4.20	4.40	4.80	4.50	16.00	23.50	94.00	665
1937D	7,189,600	4.40	4.90	4.40	6.25	13.50	34.00	67.00	175	—
1937S	1,652,000	4.40	5.00	7.00	15.00	34.00	100.00	170	415	—
1938	9,480,045	4.00	4.75	5.25	6.25	16.00	46.00	94.00	250	405
1938S	2,832,000	4.75	5.25	6.00	9.75	22.50	57.50	112	300	—
1939	33,548,795	4.10	4.20	4.40	4.80	4.00	7.00	16.00	56.00	345
1939D	7,092,000	4.40	4.90	4.50	5.25	11.00	20.00	45.00	125	—
1939S	2,628,000	4.00	4.40	5.25	9.00	22.00	60.00	110	375	—
1940	35,715,246	4.10	4.20	4.40	4.80	4.40	6.30	13.50	57.50	250
1940D	2,797,600	3.50	4.25	7.00	12.50	27.50	70.00	135	350	—
1940S	8,244,000	4.40	4.90	5.00	6.50	9.00	18.00	28.00	62.50	—
1941	79,047,287	—	—	—	4.00	4.40	9.75	45.00	205	
1941D	16,714,800	—	—	3.50	4.50	15.00	70.00		—	
1941S	16,080,000	—	—	3.50	6.50	12.50	31.00	70.00		—

Date	Mintage	G-4	VG-8	F-12	VF-20	XF-40	AU-50	MS-60	MS-65	Prf-65
1942	102,117,123	—	—	—	—	4.00	4.10	5.50	37.50	190
1942D	17,487,200	—	—	—	3.50	6.00	11.00	19.00	45.00	—
1942S	19,384,000	—	—	—	3.75	9.00	24.00	80.00	180	—
1943	99,700,000	—	—	—	—	4.00	4.10	5.00	44.00	—
1943D	16,095,600	—	—	—	3.75	8.00	16.50	31.00	52.50	—
1943S	21,700,000	—	—	3.00	5.00	7.50	15.00	28.00	60.00	—
1943S Double Die Obv.	Inc. above	40.00	75.00	125	175	225	275	500	3,500	—
1944	104,956,000	—	—	—	—	4.00	4.10	5.00	37.50	—
1944D	14,600,800	—	—	—	3.50	4.25	10.00	20.00	37.50	—
1944S	12,560,000	—	—	—	3.50	4.00	9.00	15.00	37.50	—
1945	74,372,000	—	—	—	—	4.00	4.10	5.00	45.00	—
1945D	12,341,600	—	—	—	3.50	6.50	11.50	19.00	47.50	—
1945S	17,004,001	—	—	—	3.50	3.75	6.00	9.00	38.50	—
1946	53,436,000	—	—	—	—	4.00	4.10	5.00	47.50	—
1946D	9,072,800	—	—	—	3.50	4.25	5.50	10.00	46.00	—
1946S	4,204,000	—	—	—	3.50	4.00	5.00	9.00	40.00	—
1947	22,556,000	—	—	—	—	4.30	5.00	11.50	47.50	—
1947D	15,338,400	—	—	—	3.50	4.10	4.50	11.00	44.00	—
1947S	5,532,000	—	—	—	3.50	4.10	4.50	10.00	40.00	—
1948	35,196,000	—	—	—	3.50	4.00	4.00	5.50	45.00	—
1948D	16,766,800	—	—	—	3.50	4.10	7.00	13.50	56.00	—
1948S	15,960,000	—	—	—	3.50	4.00	5.00	8.00	50.00	—
1949	9,312,000	—	—	—	3.50	6.50	15.00	38.50	65.00	—
1949D	10,068,400	—	—	—	3.40	5.00	10.00	18.00	51.00	—
1950	24,971,512	—	—	—	—	4.00	4.10	5.50	32.00	65.00
1950D	21,075,600	—	—	—	—	4.00	4.10	5.00	34.00	—
1950D/S	Inc. above	30.00	33.00	40.00	60.00	140	215	275	3,400	—
1950S	10,284,004	—	—	—	—	3.50	4.50	9.00	42.00	—
1950S/D	Inc. above	32.00	36.00	44.00	70.00	180	315	400	850	—
1950S/S	Inc. above									
1951	43,505,602	—	—	—	—	4.00	3.50	6.00	32.00	65.00
1951D	35,354,800	—	—	—	—	4.00	4.10	7.00	38.00	—
1951S	9,048,000	—	—	3.00	4.50	6.00	9.00	24.00	52.00	—
1952	38,862,073	—	—	—	—	4.00	4.10	5.50	36.00	46.00
1952D	49,795,200	—	—	—	—	4.00	4.10	5.00	32.00	—
1952S	13,707,800	—	—	—	4.00	7.50	12.50	22.00	47.00	—
1953	18,664,920	—	—	—	—	—	4.10	5.50	42.00	46.00
1953D	56,112,400	—	—	—	—	—	4.10	4.25	29.00	—
1953S	14,016,000	—	—	—	—	4.00	4.10	5.00	38.00	—
1954	54,645,503	—	—	—	—	—	4.10	5.00	30.00	21.00
1954D	42,305,500	—	—	—	—	—	4.10	4.75	30.00	—
1954S	11,834,722	—	—	—	—	—	4.10	4.00	26.00	—
1955	18,558,381	—	—	—	—	—	4.10	3.50	25.00	24.00
1955D	3,182,400	—	—	—	—	5.10	5.30	6.50	42.00	—
1956	44,813,384	—	—	—	—	—	4.10	4.00	24.00	23.00
1956 Double Bar 5	Inc. above	—	4.00	4.50	5.00	6.50	9.00	20.00		
1956 Type B rev, proof rev die	Inc. above	—	—	8.00	12.00	20.00	30.00	40.00	100.00	—
1956D	32,334,500	—	—	—	—	4.00	4.10	3.50	26.00	—
1957	47,779,952	—	—	—	—	—	4.10	3.50	23.00	10.00
1957 Type B rev, proof rev die	Inc. above	—	—	—	6.50	10.00	16.00	30.00	110	—
1957D	77,924,160	—	—	—	—	—	4.10	3.40	26.00	—
1958	7,235,652	—	—	—	—	4.00	4.10	4.60	20.00	6.00
1958 Type B rev, proof rev die	Inc. above	—	—	—	6.50	10.00	16.00	24.00	90.00	—
1958D	78,124,900	—	—	—	—	—	4.10	4.60	22.00	—
1959	25,533,291	—	—	—	—	—	4.10	4.60	20.00	10.00
1959 Type B rev, proof rev die	Inc. above	—	—	—	5.00	10.00	14.00	20.00	70.00	—
1959D	62,054,232	—	—	—	—	—	4.10	4.60	25.00	—
1960	30,855,602	—	—	—	—	—	4.10	4.60	17.00	8.00
1960 Type B rev, proof rev die	Inc. above	—	—	—	6.50	10.00	16.00	24.00	90.00	—
1960D	63,000,324	—	—	—	—	—	4.10	4.60	17.00	—
1961	40,064,244	—	—	—	—	—	4.10	4.60	22.50	8.00
1961 Type B rev, proof rev die	Inc. above	—	—	—	5.00	10.00	14.00	20.00	70.00	—
1961D	83,656,928	—	—	—	—	—	4.10	4.60	16.00	—
1962	39,374,019	—	—	—	—	—	4.10	4.60	18.00	6.00
1962 Type B rev, proof rev die	Inc. above	—	—	—	10.00	15.00	25.00	60.00	175	—
1962D	127,554,756	—	—	—	—	—	4.10	4.60	16.00	—
1963	77,391,645	—	—	—	—	—	4.10	4.60	15.00	6.00
1963 Type B rev, proof rev die	Inc. above	—	—	—	5.00	10.00	14.00	20.00	70.00	—
1963D	135,288,184	—	—	—	—	—	4.10	4.60	15.00	—
1964	564,341,347	—	—	—	—	—	4.10	4.60	15.00	6.00
1964 Type B rev, proof rev die	Inc. above	—	—	—	5.00	10.00	14.00	20.00	70.00	—
1964D	704,135,528	—	—	—	—	—	4.10	4.60	15.00	—
1964D Type C rev, clad rev die	Inc. above	—	—	—	40.00	55.00	75.00	125	450	—

Washington Quarter

KM# 164a • 5.6700 g., Copper-Nickel Clad Copper, 24.3 mm. • Designer: John Flanagan

Date	Mintage	MS-65	Prf-65	Date	Mintage	MS-65	Prf-65
1965	1,819,717,540	9.00	—	1971D	258,634,428	8.00	—
1965 SMS	—	7.50	—	1971S	3,220,733	—	4.00
1966	821,101,500	7.50	—	1972	215,048,000	7.50	—
1966 SMS	—	9.00	—	1972D	311,067,732	10.00	—
1967 SMS	—	10.00	—	1972S	3,260,996	—	3.50
1967	1,524,031,848	8.00	—	1973	346,924,000	10.00	—
1968	220,731,500	7.50	—	1973D	232,977,400	12.50	—
1968D	101,534,000	9.00	—	1973S	2,760,339	—	3.00
1968S	3,041,506	—	6.50	1974	801,456,000	12.00	—
1969	176,212,000	14.00	—	1974D	353,160,300	18.00	—
1969D	114,372,000	12.00	—	1974S	2,612,568	—	6.50
1969S	2,934,631	—	7.00	1975 none minted	—	—	—
1970	136,420,000	12.00	—	1975D none minted	—	—	—
1970D	417,341,364	9.50	—				
1970S	2,632,810	—	7.00	1975S none minted	—	—	—
1971	109,284,000	9.00	—				

Bicentennial design, drummer boy reverse

Mint mark 1968-present

KM# 204 • 5.6700 g., Copper-Nickel Clad Copper, 24.3 mm. • Rev. Designer: Jack L. Ahr

Date	Mintage	G-4	VG-8	F-12	VF-20	XF-40	MS-60	MS-65	Prf-65
1976	809,784,016	—	—	—	—	—	.60	10.00	—
1976D	860,118,839	—	—	—	—	—	.60	10.00	—
1976S	4,149,730	—	—	—	—	—	—	—	3.25

KM# 204a • 5.7500 g., Silver Clad, 24.3 mm. • Rev. Designer: Jack L. Ahr

Date	Mintage	G-4	VG-8	F-12	VF-20	XF-40	MS-60	MS-65	Prf-65
1976S	4,908,319	—	—	—	—	—	2.00	4.00	—
1976S	3,998,621	—	—	—	—	—	—	—	5.00

Regular design resumed reverse

KM# A164a • 5.6700 g., Copper-Nickel Clad Copper, 24.3 mm. •
Edge Desc: Reeded Notes: KM#164 design and composition resumed. The 1979-S and 1981 Type II proofs have clearer mint marks than the Type I proofs for those years.

Date	Mintage	MS-65	Prf-65	Date	Mintage	MS-65	Prf-65
1977	468,556,000	10.00	—	1987S	4,227,728	—	5.00
1977D	256,524,978	9.00	—	1988P	562,052,000	16.00	—
1977S	3,251,152	—	5.00	1988D	596,810,688	14.00	—
1978	521,452,000	10.00	—	1988S	3,262,948	—	6.50
1978D	287,373,152	11.00	—	1989P	512,868,000	18.00	—
1978S	3,127,781	—	5.00	1989D	896,535,597	5.50	—
1979	515,708,000	10.00	—	1989S	3,220,194	—	5.00
1979D	489,789,780	9.00	—	1990P	613,792,000	17.00	—
1979S T-I	—	—	4.00	1990D	927,638,181	7.00	—
1979S T-II	—	—	8.00	1990S	3,299,559	—	6.00
1980P	635,832,000	11.00	—	1991P	570,968,000	15.00	—
1980D	518,327,487	8.50	—	1991D	630,966,693	14.00	—
1980S	3,554,806	—	5.00	1991S	2,867,787	—	5.00
1981P	601,716,000	10.00	—	1992P	384,764,000	20.00	—
1981D	575,722,833	9.00	—	1992D	389,777,107	27.50	—
1981S T-I	—	—	5.00	1992S	2,858,981	—	4.50
1981S T-II	—	—	7.50	1993P	639,276,000	11.00	—
1982P	500,931,000	32.50	—	1993D	645,476,128	14.00	—
1982D	480,042,788	22.00	—	1993S	2,633,439	—	5.00
1982S	3,857,479	—	7.00	1994P	825,600,000	18.00	—
1983P	673,535,000	45.00	—	1994D	880,034,110	8.00	—
1983D	617,806,446	40.00	—	1994S	2,484,594	—	13.50
1983S	3,279,126	—	5.00	1995P	1,004,336,000	22.00	—
1984P	676,545,000	16.00	—	1995D	1,103,216,000	20.00	—
1984D	546,483,064	12.50	—	1995S	2,010,384	—	12.50
1984S	3,065,110	—	4.50	1996P	925,040,000	15.00	—
1985P	775,818,962	32.00	—	1996D	906,868,000	14.00	—
1985D	519,962,888	10.00	—	1996S		—	4.50
1985S	3,362,821	5.00	6.00	1997P	595,740,000	12.50	—
1986P	551,199,333	12.00	—	1997D	599,680,000	16.00	—
1986D	504,298,660	15.00	—	1997S	1,975,000	—	10.00
1986S	3,010,497	—	5.00	1998P	896,268,000	13.50	—
1987P	582,499,481	10.50	—	1998D	821,000,000	13.50	—
1987D	655,594,696	10.00	—	1998S		—	10.00

KM# A164b • 6.2000 g., 0.9000 Silver, 0.1794 oz. ASW •

Date	Mintage	Prf-65
1992S	1,317,579	5.00
1993S	761,353	6.50
1994S	785,329	13.50
1995S	838,953	18.00
1996S	—	16.00
1997S	—	17.00
1998S	—	10.00

50 State Quarters
Connecticut

KM# 297 • 5.6700 g., Copper-Nickel Clad Copper •

Date	Mintage	MS-63	MS-65	Prf-65
1999P	688,744,000	1.00	10.00	—
1999D	657,480,000	1.00	9.00	—
1999S	3,713,359	—	—	12.00

KM# 297a • 6.2500 g., 0.9000 Silver, 0.1808 oz. ASW •

Date	Mintage	MS-63	MS-65	Prf-65
1999S	804,565	—	—	65.00

Delaware

KM# 293 • 5.6700 g., Copper-Nickel Clad Copper, 24.3 mm. •

Date	Mintage	MS-63	MS-65	Prf-65
1999P	373,400,000	1.40	8.00	—
1999D	401,424,000	1.25	20.00	—
1999S	3,713,359	—	—	12.00

KM# 293a • 6.2500 g., 0.9000 Silver, 0.1808 oz. ASW •

Date	Mintage	MS-63	MS-65	Prf-65
1999S	804,565	—	—	65.00

Georgia

KM# 296 • 5.6700 g., Copper-Nickel Clad Copper •

Date	Mintage	MS-63	MS-65	Prf-65
1999P	451,188,000	1.20	14.00	—
1999D	488,744,000	1.20	14.00	—
1999S	3,713,359	—	—	12.00

KM# 296a • 6.2500 g., 0.9000 Silver, 0.1808 oz. ASW •

Date	Mintage	MS-63	MS-65	Prf-65
1999S	804,565	—	—	65.00

New Jersey

KM# 295 • 5.6700 g., Copper-Nickel Clad Copper •

Date	Mintage	MS-63	MS-65	Prf-65
1999P	363,200,000	1.00	10.00	—
1999D	299,028,000	1.00	9.00	—
1999S	3,713,359	—	—	12.00

KM# 295a • 6.2500 g., 0.9000 Silver, 0.1808 oz. ASW •

Date	Mintage	MS-63	MS-65	Prf-65
1999S	804,565	—	—	65.00

Pennsylvania

KM# 294 • 5.6700 g., Copper-Nickel Clad Copper, 24.3 mm. •

Date	Mintage	MS-63	MS-65	Prf-65
1999P	349,000,000	1.00	15.00	—

Date	Mintage	MS-63	MS-65	Prf-65
1999D	358,332,000	1.00	20.00	—
1999S	3,713,359	—	—	12.00

KM# 294a • 6.2500 g., 0.9000 Silver, 0.1808 oz. ASW •

Date	Mintage	MS-63	MS-65	Prf-65
1999S	804,565	—	—	65.00

Maryland

KM# 306 • 5.6700 g., Copper-Nickel Clad Copper •

Date	Mintage	MS-63	MS-65	Prf-65
2000P	678,200,000	1.00	11.00	—
2000D	556,526,000	1.00	11.00	—
2000S	4,078,747	—	—	3.50

KM# 306a • 6.2500 g., 0.9000 Silver, 0.1808 oz. ASW •

Date	Mintage	MS-63	MS-65	Prf-65
2000S	965,921	—	—	5.50

Massachusetts

KM# 305 • 5.6700 g., Copper-Nickel Clad Copper •

Date	Mintage	MS-63	MS-65	Prf-65
2000P	629,800,000	1.00	10.00	—
2000D	535,184,000	1.00	12.00	—
2000S	4,078,747	—	—	3.50

KM# 305a • 6.2500 g., 0.9000 Silver, 0.1808 oz. ASW •

Date	Mintage	MS-63	MS-65	Prf-65
2000S	965,921	—	—	5.50

New Hampshire

KM# 308 • 5.6700 g., Copper-Nickel Clad Copper •

Date	Mintage	MS-63	MS-65	Prf-65
2000P	673,040,000	1.00	12.50	—
2000D	495,976,000	1.00	10.00	—
2000S	4,078,747	—	—	3.50

KM# 308a • 6.2500 g., 0.9000 Silver, 0.1808 oz. ASW •

Date	Mintage	MS-63	MS-65	Prf-65
2000S	965,921	—	—	5.50

South Carolina

KM# 307 • 5.6700 g., Copper-Nickel Clad Copper •

Date	Mintage	MS-63	MS-65	Prf-65
2000P	742,756,000	1.40	9.00	—
2000D	566,208,000	1.40	12.00	—
2000S	4,078,747	—	—	3.50

KM# 307a • 6.2500 g., 0.9000 Silver, 0.1808 oz. ASW •

Date	Mintage	MS-63	MS-65	Prf-65
2000S	965,921	—	—	5.50

Virginia

KM# 309 • 5.6700 g., **Copper-Nickel Clad Copper** •

Date	Mintage	MS-63	MS-65	Prf-65
2000P	943,000,000	1.00	8.00	—
2000D	651,616,000	1.00	8.00	—
2000S	4,078,747	—	—	3.35

KM# 309a • 6.2500 g., 0.9000 **Silver**, 0.1808 oz. ASW •

Date	Mintage	MS-63	MS-65	Prf-65
2000S	965,921	—	—	5.50

HALF DOLLAR

Barber Half Dollar

Laureate head right, flanked by stars, date below obverse
Heraldic eagle reverse

Mint mark

KM# 116 • 12.5000 g., 0.9000 **Silver**, 0.3617 oz. ASW, 30.6 mm. • **Obv. Legend** IN GOD WE TRUST **Rev. Legend:** UNITED STATES OF AMERICA **Designer:** Charles E. Barber

Date	Mintage	G-4	VG-8	F-12	VF-20	XF-40	AU-50	MS-60	MS-65	Prf-65
1901	4,268,813	14.60	16.50	38.50	94.00	180	335	510	4,250	4,650
1901O	1,124,000	16.50	26.50	80.00	205	350	475	1,350	14,850	—
1901S	847,044	34.00	55.00	160	355	610	1,050	1,850	19,500	—
1902	4,922,777	13.10	14.50	32.50	86.00	180	335	475	4,600	4,650
1902O	2,526,000	13.50	17.00	52.50	105	225	355	725	11,500	—
1902S	1,460,670	16.00	19.00	62.50	150	260	420	750	7,750	—
1903	2,278,755	14.60	16.00	47.50	100.00	200	335	500	9,250	4,650
1903O	2,100,000	14.10	17.00	53.00	115	210	335	665	9,500	—
1903S	1,920,772	15.00	18.00	55.00	125	220	380	610	5,750	—
1904	2,992,670	13.10	14.50	33.00	85.00	180	345	475	6,450	4,650
1904O	1,117,600	20.00	30.00	80.00	220	385	590	1,100	12,500	—
1904S	553,038	38.50	75.00	260	555	1,075	1,775	9,000	41,500	—
1905	662,727	22.50	32.50	95.00	180	270	370	565	7,500	4,650
1905O	505,000	30.00	44.50	125	235	340	440	760	4,850	—
1905S	2,494,000	15.50	18.00	50.00	125	230	350	615	9,750	—
1906	2,638,675	13.10	14.50	32.00	83.00	180	335	465	3,800	4,650
1906D	4,028,000	13.10	14.50	33.00	89.00	180	335	465	4,500	—
1906O	2,446,000	13.10	14.50	44.00	98.00	190	350	600	6,350	—
1906S	1,740,154	14.60	16.50	57.50	110	215	380	590	5,950	—
1907	2,598,575	13.10	14.50	30.00	83.00	180	335	465	3,600	4,650
1907D	3,856,000	13.10	14.50	30.00	75.00	180	335	465	3,600	—
1907O	3,946,000	13.10	14.50	32.00	89.00	180	33.00	575	3,700	—
1907S	1,250,000	17.40	20.00	80.00	165	315	650	1,275	12,500	—
1908	1,354,545	13.10	14.50	30.00	80.00	180	335	465	4,350	4,650
1908D	3,280,000	13.10	14.50	30.00	80.00	180	335	485	4,250	—
1908O	5,360,000	13.10	14.50	30.00	89.00	180	345	540	3,600	—
1908S	1,644,828	18.50	25.00	72.00	160	285	435	850	6,350	—
1909	2,368,650	14.10	16.00	32.00	83.00	180	335	465	3,600	4,650
1909O	925,400	17.40	23.50	56.00	140	300	510	775	4,850	—
1909S	1,764,000	13.40	14.50	37.00	100.00	180	335	600	4,450	—
1910	418,551	20.00	28.50	90.00	170	330	445	610	3,900	4,650
1910S	1,948,000	16.60	16.50	36.00	100.00	180	355	625	6,650	—
1911	1,406,543	13.10	14.50	30.00	83.00	180	335	465	3,600	4,650
1911D	695,080	14.10	16.00	40.00	91.00	180	345	565	3,700	—
1911S	1,272,000	14.60	16.50	42.00	98.00	180	345	580	5,950	—
1912	1,550,700	13.10	14.50	30.00	83.00	180	335	465	4,100	4,650
1912D	2,300,800	13.10	14.50	30.00	81.00	180	335	465	3,600	—
1912S	1,370,000	16.40	19.50	41.50	100.00	180	335	535	5,850	—
1913	188,627	77.00	88.00	235	420	600	875	1,150	5,250	4,800
1913D	534,000	17.00	19.50	44.00	100.00	200	335	485	5,450	—
1913S	604,000	20.00	25.00	53.50	110	225	385	725	4,650	—
1914	124,610	155	175	325	550	775	1,025	1,400	11,500	5,000
1914S	992,000	16.40	19.00	41.00	98.00	190	355	575	4,950	—
1915	138,450	112	168	285	380	575	920	1,350	6,650	5,000
1915D	1,170,400	13.10	14.50	30.00	75.00	180	335	465	3,600	—
1915S	1,604,000	16.90	19.50	41.50	94.00	195	350	480	3,600	—

Walking Liberty Half Dollar

Liberty walking left wearing U.S. flag gown, sunrise at left obverse
Eagle advancing left reverse

Obverse mint mark   Reverse mint mark
1916-1917   1917-1947

KM# 142 • 12.5000 g., 0.9000 **Silver**, 0.3617 oz. ASW, 30.6 mm. • **Designer:** Adolph A. Weinman **Notes:** The mint mark appears on the obverse below the word "Trust" on 1916 and some 1917 issues. Starting with some 1917 issues and continuing through the remainder of the series, the mint mark was changed to the reverse, at about the 8 o'clock position near the rim.

Date	Mintage	G-4	VG-8	F-12	VF-20	XF-40	AU-50	MS-60	MS-65	Prf-65
1916	608,000	45.00	52.50	100.00	180	250	285	350	1,800	—
1916D	1,014,400	45.00	52.50	80.00	140	225	265	375	2,400	—
1916S	508,000	110	130	285	470	650	750	1,100	6,250	—
1917D obv. mint mark	765,400	22.00	31.50	80.00	160	235	350	640	8,000	—
1917S obv. mint mark	952,000	27.50	44.00	135	375	720	1,225	2,300	19,500	—
1917	12,292,000	5.60	5.70	9.00	20.00	44.00	75.00	135	1,000	—
1917D rev. mint mark	1,940,000	10.00	16.50	45.00	135	275	575	975	18,500	—
1917S rev. mint mark	5,554,000	5.60	6.10	16.50	33.00	65.00	160	345	13,000	—
1918	6,634,000	5.60	6.10	16.00	70.00	160	275	580	3,800	—
1918D	3,853,040	8.00	13.00	36.00	96.00	235	500	1,350	25,000	—
1918S	10,282,000	5.60	5.70	15.00	35.00	65.00	200	525	18,000	—
1919	962,000	19.00	32.50	78.50	275	550	920	1,310	7,500	—
1919D	1,165,000	18.00	38.50	100.00	325	765	1,550	6,250	130,000	—
1919S	1,552,000	17.50	30.00	75.00	325	850	1,800	3,450	20,500	—
1920	6,372,000	5.60	5.70	16.00	44.00	75.00	160	300	5,250	—
1920D	1,551,000	12.00	20.00	70.00	250	475	960	1,550	12,000	—
1920S	4,624,000	5.60	6.10	20.00	80.00	235	520	850	12,500	—
1921	246,000	185	225	350	780	1,550	2,750	4,350	18,000	—
1921D	208,000	315	390	550	940	2,200	3,400	5,300	27,500	—
1921S	548,000	46.00	70.00	220	750	4,800	8,600	14,000	105,000	—
1923S	2,178,000	8.50	11.50	27.50	115	315	700	1,400	15,000	—
1927S	2,392,000	5.60	6.10	13.50	47.50	160	415	1,050	10,000	—
1928S	1,940,000	10.00	12.50	24.00	110	300	600	1,650	—	—
1928S	Inc. above	6.75	7.25	15.00	70.00	195	450	1,000	10,750	—
1929D	1,001,200	8.00	12.00	19.00	60.00	110	210	415	3,500	—
1929S	1,902,000	5.60	6.10	12.50	28.50	115	230	425	3,550	—
1933S	1,786,000	8.50	11.00	12.50	20.00	60.00	260	625	4,500	—
1934	6,964,000	5.40	5.70	5.80	6.20	11.00	26.00	85.00	625	—
1934D	2,361,400	5.60	6.10	6.20	10.00	29.00	90.00	155	1,700	—
1934S	3,652,000	5.40	5.90	6.20	8.50	27.00	105	395	5,200	—
1935	9,162,000	5.40	5.70	5.80	6.20	8.50	22.50	45.00	585	—
1935D	3,003,800	5.40	5.90	6.20	10.00	32.50	70.00	140	3,150	—
1935S	3,854,000	5.40	5.90	6.20	8.50	29.00	100.00	295	3,700	—
1936	12,617,901	5.40	5.70	5.80	6.20	8.50	21.50	38.50	300	6,600
1936D	4,252,400	5.40	5.90	6.20	8.50	20.00	55.00	80.00	700	—
1936S	3,884,000	5.40	5.90	6.20	8.50	21.50	62.50	135	1,050	—
1937	9,527,728	5.40	5.70	5.80	6.20	8.50	22.50	40.00	335	1,700
1937D	1,676,000	5.40	6.10	8.50	14.00	33.50	110	225	850	—
1937S	2,090,000	5.40	5.90	6.20	8.50	25.50	65.00	175	850	—
1938	4,118,152	5.40	5.90	6.20	8.50	9.50	41.50	70.00	550	1,275
1938D	491,600	90.00	100.00	115	135	220	260	525	1,550	—
1939	6,820,808	5.40	5.50	6.50	7.00	8.50	22.50	42.50	230	1,150
1939D	4,267,800	5.40	5.70	5.80	6.20	8.50	26.00	47.50	275	—
1939S	2,552,000	5.40	5.90	6.20	9.00	25.00	80.00	150	370	—
1940	9,167,279	5.40	5.50	7.00	7.50	9.00	11.00	30.00	210	1,000
1940S	4,550,000	5.40	5.70	5.80	6.20	12.00	22.00	52.50	420	—
1941	24,207,412	5.40	5.50	7.00	7.50	9.00	11.00	32.50	160	850
1941D	11,248,400	5.40	5.70	5.80	6.20	10.00	18.00	38.50	200	—
1941S	8,098,000	5.40	5.70	5.80	6.20	12.00	27.50	75.00	1,175	—
1942	47,839,120	5.40	5.50	7.00	7.50	9.00	11.00	32.50	150	850
1942D	10,973,800	5.40	5.70	5.80	6.20	10.00	19.00	38.50	345	—
1942S	12,708,000	5.40	5.70	5.80	6.20	10.00	17.50	38.50	700	—
1943	53,190,000	5.40	5.50	7.00	7.50	9.00	11.00	33.50	150	—
1943D	11,346,000	5.40	5.70	5.80	6.20	10.00	25.00	43.50	330	—
1943D Double Die Obverse	—	5.60	7.50	9.00	12.00	15.00	30.00	55.00	450	—
1943S	13,450,000	5.40	5.70	5.80	6.20	10.00	18.50	43.50	485	—
1944	28,206,000	5.40	5.50	7.00	7.50	9.00	11.00	33.50	220	—
1944D	9,769,000	5.40	5.70	5.80	6.20	10.00	20.00	37.50	240	—
1944S	8,904,000	5.40	5.70	5.80	6.20	10.00	16.00	38.50	490	—
1945	31,502,000	5.40	5.50	7.00	7.50	9.00	11.00	32.50	160	—
1945D	9,966,800	5.40	5.70	5.80	6.20	10.00	19.00	34.00	160	—
1945S	10,156,000	5.40	5.70	5.80	6.20	10.00	17.50	35.00	220	—
1946	12,118,000	5.40	5.50	7.00	7.50	9.00	11.00	32.50	250	—

Date	Mintage	G-4	VG-8	F-12	VF-20	XF-40	AU-50	MS-60	MS-65	Prf-65
1946D	2,151,000	5.40	5.90	5.80	6.20	25.50	38.50	50.00	150	—
1946S	3,724,000	5.40	5.70	5.80	6.20	12.00	19.00	43.50	165	—
1947	4,094,000	5.40	7.25	7.50	6.20	11.00	22.00	52.50	230	—
1947D	3,900,600	5.40	5.90	5.80	6.20	14.00	31.50	52.50	150	—

Franklin Half Dollar

Franklin bust right obverse
Liberty Bell, small eagle at right reverse

Mint mark

KM# 199 • 12.5000 g., 0.9000 Silver, 0.3617 oz. ASW, 30.6 mm. • Designer: John R. Sinnock

Date	Mintage	G-4	VG-8	F-12	VF-20	XF-40	AU-50	MS-60	MS-65	-65FBL	-65CAM
1948	3,006,814	—	4.30	4.40	5.10	8.50	11.50	15.50	75.00	190	—
1948D	4,028,600	—	4.30	4.40	5.10	8.00	11.00	15.00	125	260	—
1949	5,614,000	—	—	—	6.30	12.00	38.50	145	250	—	—
1949D	4,120,600	—	—	—	7.30	25.00	43.50	900	1,750	—	—
1949S	3,744,000	—	—	—	5.10	11.00	30.00	62.50	160	700	—
1950	7,793,509	—	—	—	4.60	10.00	26.00	110	285	—	2,000
1950D	8,031,600	—	—	—	5.60	11.50	22.00	425	900	—	—
1951	16,859,602	—	—	—	4.30	4.70	11.00	75.00	340	—	1,450
1951D	9,475,200	—	—	—	8.60	17.50	26.00	170	540	—	—
1951S	13,696,000	—	—	—	5.30	10.00	23.50	125	750	—	—
1952	21,274,073	—	—	—	4.30	4.70	5.20	70.00	210	—	775
1952D	25,395,600	—	—	—	4.30	4.70	5.20	130	450	—	—
1952S	5,526,000	—	—	4.40	7.10	16.00	32.00	50.00	140	1,500	—
1953	2,796,920	—	—	4.40	4.60	10.00	16.00	25.00	140	1,000	475
1953D	20,900,400	—	—	—	4.30	4.70	15.00	150	400	—	—
1953S	4,148,000	—	—	—	5.30	15.00	25.00	80.00	16,000	—	—
1954	13,421,503	—	—	—	4.30	4.70	5.20	75.00	225	—	175
1954D	25,445,580	—	—	—	4.30	4.70	5.20	110	235	—	—
1954S	4,993,400	—	—	—	—	5.20	13.50	65.00	440	—	—
1955	2,876,381	—	16.00	17.00	18.00	19.00	20.00	22.00	70.00	140	120
1955 Bugs Bunny	Inc. above	—	20.00	22.00	23.00	25.00	26.00	28.00	120	750	—
1956 Type 1 rev.	4,701,384	—	4.10	4.10	4.30	4.70	5.20	13.50	55.00	125	300
1956 Type 2 rev.	Inc. above	—	—	—	—	—	—	—	—	—	40.00
1957 Type 1 rev.	6,361,952	—	—	—	4.30	4.70	5.20	63.00	95.00	—	55.00
1957 Type 2 rev.	Inc. above	—	—	—	—	—	—	—	—	—	—
1957D	19,966,850	—	—	—	4.30	4.70	5.20	60.00	100.00	—	—
1958 Type 1 rev.	4,917,652	—	—	—	4.30	4.70	5.20	55.00	110	—	60.00
1958 Type 2 rev.	Inc. above	—	—	—	12.00	20.00	26.00	—	—	—	—
1958D	23,962,412	—	—	—	4.30	4.70	5.20	55.00	80.00	—	—
1959 Type 1 rev.	7,349,291	—	—	—	4.30	4.70	5.20	110	250	—	75.00
1959 Type 2 rev.	Inc. above	—	—	—	12.00	16.00	—	115	—	—	—
1959D	13,053,750	—	—	—	4.30	4.70	5.20	125	215	—	—
1960 Type 1 rev.	7,715,602	—	—	—	4.30	4.70	5.20	110	340	—	45.00
1960 Type 2 rev.	Inc. above	—	—	—	—	—	—	—	—	—	—
1960D	18,215,812	—	—	—	4.30	4.70	5.20	400	1,350	—	—
1961 Type 1 rev.	11,318,244	—	—	—	4.30	4.70	5.20	125	1,300	—	40.00
1961 Type 2 rev.	Inc. above	—	—	—	—	—	—	—	—	—	—
1961 Double die rev.	Inc. above	—	—	—	—	—	—	—	—	—	3,500
1961D	20,276,442	—	—	—	4.30	4.70	5.20	155	875	—	—
1962 Type 1 rev.	12,932,019	—	—	—	4.30	4.70	5.20	145	1,850	—	35.00
1962 Type 2 rev.	Inc. above	—	—	—	—	—	—	—	—	—	—
1962D	35,473,281	—	—	—	4.30	4.70	5.20	175	800	—	—
1963 Type 1 rev.	25,239,645	—	—	—	4.30	4.70	5.20	55.00	1,200	—	35.00
1963 Type 2 rev.	Inc. above	—	—	—	—	—	—	—	—	—	—
1963D	67,069,292	—	—	—	4.30	4.70	5.20	75.00	165	—	—

Kennedy Half Dollar

Mint mark 1964

KM# 202 • 12.5000 g., 0.9000 Silver, 0.3617 oz. ASW, 30.6 mm. • Obv. Designer: Gilroy Roberts Rev. Designer: Frank Gasparro Edge Desc: Reeded

Date	Mintage	G-4	VG-8	F-12	VF-20	XF-40	MS-60	MS-65	Prf-65
1964	277,254,766	—	—	—	—	5.75	6.00	20.00	12.00
1964 Accented Hair	Inc. above	—	—	—	—	—	—	—	40.00
1964D	156,205,446	—	—	—	—	5.85	6.20	24.00	—

Mint mark 1968 - present

KM# 202a • 11.5000 g., 0.4000 Silver, 0.1479 oz. ASW, 30.6 mm. • Obv. Designer: Gilroy Roberts Rev. Designer: Frank Gasparro Edge Desc: Reeded

Date	Mintage	G-4	VG-8	F-12	VF-20	XF-40	MS-60	MS-65	Prf-65
1965	65,879,366	—	—	—	—	—	3.10	18.00	—
1965 SMS	2,360,000	—	—	—	—	—	—	15.00	—
1966	108,984,932	—	—	—	—	—	3.10	14.00	—
1966 SMS	2,261,583	—	—	—	—	—	—	17.00	—
1967	295,046,978	—	—	—	—	—	3.10	22.00	—
1967 SMS	18,633,440	—	—	—	—	—	—	18.00	—
1968D	246,951,930	—	—	—	—	—	3.10	18.00	—
1968S	3,041,506	—	—	—	—	—	—	—	7.00
1969D	129,881,800	—	—	—	—	—	3.10	20.00	—
1969S	2,934,631	—	—	—	—	—	—	—	7.50
1970D	2,150,000	—	—	—	—	—	13.00	38.00	—
1970S	2,632,810	—	—	—	—	—	—	—	20.00

KM# 202b • 11.3400 g., Copper-Nickel Clad Copper, 30.6 mm. • Obv. Designer: Gilroy Roberts Rev. Designer: Frank Gasparro

Date	Mintage	G-4	VG-8	F-12	VF-20	XF-40	MS-60	MS-65	Prf-65
1971	155,640,000	—	—	—	—	—	1.00	15.00	—
1971D	302,097,424	—	—	—	—	—	1.00	15.00	—
1971S	3,244,183	—	—	—	—	—	—	—	8.00
1972	153,180,000	—	—	—	—	—	1.00	20.00	—
1972D	141,890,000	—	—	—	—	—	1.00	14.00	—
1972S	3,267,667	—	—	—	—	—	—	—	7.00
1973	64,964,000	—	—	—	—	—	1.00	14.00	—
1973D	83,171,400	—	—	—	—	—	—	12.00	—
1973S	2,769,624	—	—	—	—	—	—	—	7.00
1974	201,596,000	—	—	—	—	—	1.00	18.00	—
1974D	79,066,300	—	—	—	—	—	1.00	20.00	—
1974S	2,617,350	—	—	—	—	—	—	—	5.00
1975 none minted		—	—	—	—	—	—	—	—
1975D none minted		—	—	—	—	—	—	—	—
1975S none minted		—	—	—	—	—	—	—	—

Bicentennial design, Independence Hall reverse

KM# 205 • 11.1000 g., Copper Nickel • Rev. Designer: Seth Huntington

Date	Mintage	G-4	VG-8	F-12	VF-20	XF-40	MS-60	MS-65	Prf-65
1976	234,308,000	—	—	—	—	—	1.00	22.00	—
1976D	287,565,248	—	—	—	—	—	1.00	9.00	—
1976S	7,059,099	—	—	—	—	—	—	—	4.00

KM# 205a • 11.5000 g., 0.4000 Silver, 0.1479 oz. ASW • Rev. Designer: Seth Huntington

Date	Mintage	G-4	VG-8	F-12	VF-20	XF-40	MS-60	MS-65	Prf-65
1976S	4,908,319	—	—	—	—	—	—	12.00	—
1976S	3,998,625	—	—	—	—	—	—	—	6.00

Regular design resumed reverse

KM# A202b • 11.3400 g., **Copper-Nickel Clad Copper**, 30.6 mm. •
Edge Desc: Reeded **Notes:** KM#202b design and composition resumed. The 1979-S and 1981-S Type II proofs have clearer mint marks than the Type I proofs of those years.

Date	Mintage	MS-65	Prf-65	Date	Mintage	MS-65	Prf-65
1977	43,598,000	18.00	—	1988S	3,262,948	—	6.00
1977D	31,449,106	20.00	—	1989P	24,542,000	18.00	—
1977S	3,251,152	—	4.50	1989D	23,000,216	14.00	—
1978	14,350,000	12.00	—	1989S	3,220,194	—	8.00
1978D	13,765,799	10.00	—	1990P	22,780,000	20.00	—
1978S	3,127,788	—	6.00	1990D	20,096,242	15.00	—
1979	68,312,000	11.00	—	1990S	3,299,559	—	7.00
1979D	15,815,422	9.00	—	1991P	14,874,000	15.00	—
1979S Type I	3,677,175	—	6.00	1991D	15,054,678	18.00	—
1979S Type II	Inc. above	—	20.00	1991S	2,867,787	—	16.00
1980P	44,134,000	9.00	—	1992P	17,628,000	18.00	—
1980D	33,456,449	6.50	—	1992D	17,000,106	8.00	—
1980S	3,547,030	—	6.00	1992S	2,858,981	—	8.00
1981P	29,544,000	8.00	—	1993P	15,510,000	15.00	—
1981D	27,839,533	8.50	—	1993D	15,000,006	14.00	—
1981S Type I	4,063,083	—	5.00	1993S	2,633,439	—	14.00
1981S Type II	Inc. above	—	17.50	1994P	23,718,000	8.00	—
1982P	10,819,000	10.00	—	1994D	23,828,110	8.00	—
1982P no initials FG	Inc. above	40.00	—	1994S	2,484,594	—	11.00
1982D	13,140,102	9.00	—	1995P	26,496,000	9.00	—
1982S	38,957,479	—	6.50	1995D	26,288,000	8.00	—
1983P	34,139,000	20.00	—	1995S	2,010,384	—	35.00
1983D	32,472,244	10.00	—	1996P	24,442,000	11.00	—
1983S	3,279,126	—	6.50	1996D	24,744,000	8.00	—
1984P	26,029,000	10.00	—	1996S	2,085,191	—	16.00
1984D	26,262,158	15.00	—	1997P	20,882,000	14.00	—
1984S	3,065,110	—	7.00	1997D	19,876,000	10.00	—
1985P	18,706,962	10.00	—	1997S	1,975,000	—	34.00
1985D	19,814,034	12.00	—	1998P	15,646,000	14.00	—
1985S	3,962,138	—	6.00	1998D	15,064,000	14.00	—
1986P	13,107,633	25.00	—	1998S	2,078,494	—	22.00
1986D	15,336,145	17.00	—	1999P	8,900,000	9.00	—
1986S	2,411,180	—	8.00	1999D	10,682,000	9.00	—
1987P	2,890,758	14.00	—	1999S	2,557,897	—	24.00
1987D	2,890,758	10.00	—	2000P	22,600,000	9.00	—
1987S	4,407,728	—	6.50	2000D	19,466,000	7.00	—
1988P	13,626,000	16.00	—	2000S	3,082,944	—	8.00
1988D	12,000,096	12.00	—				

KM# A202c • 12.5000 g., 0.9000 **Silver**, 0.3617 oz. ASW, 30.6 mm. • **Designer:** Gilroy Roberts

Date	Mintage	Prf-65
1992S	1,317,579	12.00
1993S	761,353	32.00
1994S	785,329	36.00
1995S	838,953	92.00
1996S	830,021	40.00
1997S	821,678	75.00
1998S	878,792	25.00
1998S Matte Proof	62,350	325
1999S	804,565	38.00
2000S	965,921	9.00

DOLLAR
Morgan Dollar
Laureate head left, date below flanked by stars obverse
Eagle within 1/2 wreath reverse

8 Tail feathers   7 Tail feathers   7/8 Tail feathers

KM# 110 • 26.7300 g., 0.9000 **Silver**, 0.7734 oz. ASW, 38.1 mm. •
Obv. Legend E.PLURIBUS.UNUM **Rev. Legend:** UNITED STATES OF AMERICA **Designer:** George T. Morgan **Notes:** "65DMPL" values are for coins grading MS-65 deep-mirror prooflike. The Pittman Act of 1918 authorized the melting of 270 Million pieces of various dates. They were not indivudually recorded.

Date	Mintage	VG-8	F-12	VF-20	XF-40	AU-50	MS-60	MS-63	MS-64	MS-65	65DMPL	Prf-65
1901	6,962,813	27.50	36.00	57.50	110	350	2,350	17,250	55,000	55.00	—	7,850
1901 doubled die reverse	Inc. above	275	450	900	2,000	3,850						
1901O	13,320,000	21.30	22.10	21.70	22.80	28.80	34.60	46.00	61.00	225	10,000	—
1901S	2,284,000	21.80	24.60	31.50	46.50	220	470	700	1,050	3,900	22,000	—
1902	7,994,777	21.80	22.10	22.70	24.80	25.00	44.00	100.00	145	525	19,500	7,350
1902O	8,636,000	21.30	22.10	21.70	22.80	25.80	33.60	46.00	59.00	192	16,000	—
1902S	1,530,000	60.00	82.00	160	220	315	425	625	1,135	3,125	15,000	—
1903	4,652,755	48.00	50.00	52.00	58.00	60.00	75.00	85.00	100.00	300	36,850	7,350
1903O	4,450,000	325	350	375	410	418	425	450	475	800	5,950	—
1903S	1,241,000	95.00	130	215	425	2,100	4,400	7,000	7,850	11,850	40,000	—
1903S Micro S	Inc. above	135	225	450	1,150	3,000	—	—	—	—	—	—
1904	2,788,650	21.00	23.00	25.00	27.00	32.00	78.00	280	645	3,700	86,500	7,350
1904O	3,720,000	21.00	23.00	25.00	27.00	29.00	37.00	46.00	58.00	163	1,165	—
1904S	2,304,000	35.00	47.50	87.00	230	570	1,075	4,350	6,250	10,500	19,000	—
1921	44,690,000	20.30	21.10	20.70	20.80	22.80	24.60	35.00	40.00	175	11,500	—
1921D	20,345,000	20.30	21.10	20.70	21.30	23.80	45.00	5,750	155	420	10,000	—
1921S	21,695,000	20.30	21.10	20.70	20.80	23.30	45.00	69.00	170	1,425	31,000	—

Peace Dollar
Liberty Head left obverse
Eagle facing right perched on rock reverse

Mint mark

KM# 150 • 26.7300 g., 0.9000 **Silver**, 0.7734 oz. ASW, 38.1 mm. • **Designer:** Anthony DeFrancisci

Date	Mintage	G-4	VG-8	F-12	VF-20	XF-40	AU-50	MS-60	MS-63	MS-64	MS-65
1921	1,006,473	100.00	125	135	140	150	170	270	525	935	2,350
1922	51,737,000	15.20	19.30	20.80	21.10	21.30	22.20	26.30	33.00	50.00	150
1922D	15,063,000	15.20	19.60	20.80	21.10	21.30	23.10	26.50	53.00	99.00	660
1922S	17,475,000	15.20	19.60	20.80	21.10	21.30	23.10	26.50	69.00	285	2,475
1923	30,800,000	15.20	19.30	20.80	21.10	21.30	22.20	26.30	33.00	50.00	150
1923D	6,811,000	15.20	16.00	16.50	17.00	18.00	22.00	52.00	135	290	1,320
1923S	19,020,000	15.20	19.60	20.80	21.10	21.30	23.10	28.50	74.00	355	8,500
1924	11,811,000	15.20	19.30	16.50	21.10	21.30	22.20	26.30	33.00	50.00	183
1924S	1,728,000	25.00	30.00	31.00	33.00	44.00	66.50	200	600	1,650	12,500

Date	Mintage	G-4	VG-8	F-12	VF-20	XF-40	AU-50	MS-60	MS-63	MS-64	MS-65
1925	10,198,000	15.20	19.30	16.50	21.10	21.30	22.20	23.00	33.00	50.00	182
1925S	1,610,000	16.10	19.50	21.00	25.00	29.00	46.00	75.00	210	1,050	27,000
1926	1,939,000	16.10	20.20	21.90	22.40	22.80	22.50	43.00	82.00	118	510
1926D	2,348,700	16.10	20.20	21.70	22.20	22.00	32.50	66.00	190	330	990
1926S	6,980,000	15.80	19.90	21.40	21.77	21.90	25.20	44.00	110	275	1,225
1927	848,000	25.00	29.00	32.00	33.00	38.00	50.00	70.00	185	525	3,650
1927D	1,268,900	24.00	28.00	30.00	31.00	34.00	80.00	148	365	1,125	6,100
1927S	866,000	24.00	28.00	31.00	32.00	35.00	80.00	148	445	1,500	11,350
1928	360,649	355	435	445	455	465	475	525	965	1,350	5,150
1928S Large S	1,632,000	30.00	36.00	40.00	46.00	54.00	90.00	220	800	2,100	29,500
1928S Small S	Inc. above	28.00	33.00	34.00	38.00	43.00	66.00	155	595	1,350	24,850
1934	954,057	16.10	19.50	21.00	21.00	22.50	46.00	120	245	440	965
1934D Large D	1,569,500	17.00	20.20	23.50	23.00	42.00	65.00	165	600	925	3,000
1934D Small D	Inc. above	16.10	20.20	21.00	21.00	36.00	46.00	135	500	790	2,150
1934S	1,011,000	26.00	31.00	48.00	85.00	200	475	1,800	3,850	5,950	8,400
1935	1,576,000	19.30	18.00	21.00	21.50	24.50	30.00	60.00	115	225	810
1935S	1,964,000	19.30	18.00	21.00	20.00	23.00	92.00	235	380	630	1,375

Eisenhower Dollar

KM# 203 • 22.6800 g., **Copper-Nickel Clad Copper**, 38.1 mm. • **Designer:** Frank Gasparro

Date	Mintage	MS-63	Prf-65	Date	Mintage	MS-63	Prf-65
1971	47,799,000	10.00	—	1973	2,000,056	14.00	—
1971D	68,587,424	8.00	—	1973D	2,000,000	15.00	—
1972 Low Relief	75,890,000	6.50	—	1973S	2,769,624	—	12.00
1972 High Relief	Inc. above	175	—	1974	27,366,000	5.50	—
1972 Modified High Relief	Inc. above	40.00	—	1974D	35,466,000	7.00	—
1972D	92,548,511	5.50	—	1974S	2,617,350	—	11.00

KM# 203a • 24.5900 g., 0.4000 **Silver**, 0.3162 oz. ASW, 38.1 mm. • **Designer:** Frank Gasparro

Date	Mintage	MS-63	Prf-65	Date	Mintage	MS-63	Prf-65
1971S	6,868,530	7.50	—	1972S	1,811,631	—	14.00
1971S	4,265,234	—	11.00	1973S	1,833,140	8.50	—
1971S Peg Leg "R" Variety	Inc. above	—	17.00	1973S	1,005,617	—	35.00
1971S Partial Peg Leg "R" Variety	Inc. above	—	18.00	1974S	1,720,000	7.50	—
1972S	2,193,056	7.50	—	1974S	1,306,579	—	14.00

Bicentennial design, moon behind Liberty Bell reverse

Type I
Squared "T"

Type II
Slant-top "T"

KM# 206 • 22.6800 g., **Copper-Nickel Clad Copper**, 38.1 mm. • **Rev. Designer:** Dennis R. Williams **Notes:** In 1976 the lettering on the reverse was changed to thinner letters, resulting in the Type II variety for that year. The Type I variety was minted 1975 and dated 1976.

Date	Mintage	MS-63	Prf-65
1976 type I	117,337,000	9.00	—
1976 type II	Inc. above	5.00	—
1976D type I	103,228,274	6.00	—
1976D type II	Inc. above	5.00	—
1976S type I	2,909,369	—	13.00
1976S type II	4,149,730	—	9.00

Bicentennial design, moon behind Liberty Bell reverse

KM# 206a • 24.5900 g., 0.4000 **Silver**, 0.3162 oz. ASW • **Rev. Designer:** Dennis R. Williams

Date	Mintage	MS-63	Prf-65	Date	Mintage	MS-63	Prf-65
1976S	4,908,319	12.50	—	1976S	3,998,621	—	20.00

Regular design resumed reverse

KM# A203 • **Copper-Nickel Clad Copper**, 38.1 mm. •

Date	Mintage	MS-63	Prf-65	Date	Mintage	MS-63	Prf-65
1977	12,596,000	7.00	—	1978	25,702,000	5.00	—
1977D	32,983,006	7.00	—	1978D	33,012,890	5.00	—
1977S	3,251,152	—	10.00	1978S	3,127,788	—	12.00

Susan B. Anthony Dollar

Susan B. Anthony bust right obverse
Eagle landing on moon, symbolic of Apollo manned moon landing reverse

KM# 207 • 8.1000 g., **Copper-Nickel Clad Copper**, 26.5 mm. • **Designer:** Frank Gasparro **Edge Desc:** Reeded **Notes:** The 1979-S and 1981-S Type II coins have a clearer mint mark than the Type I varieties for those years.

Date	Mintage	MS-63	Prf-65	Date	Mintage	MS-63	Prf-65
1979P Near date	360,222,000	70.00	—	1980S Proof	3,547,030	—	8.00
1979P	Inc. above	2.50	—	1981P	3,000,000	7.50	—
1979D	288,015,744	3.00	—	1981D	3,250,000	7.50	—
1979S Proof, Type I	3,677,175	—	8.00	1981S	3,492,000	7.50	—
1979S Proof, Type II	Inc. above	—	110	1981S Proof, Type I	4,063,083	—	8.00
1979S	109,576,000	3.00	—	1981S Proof, Type II	Inc. above	—	230
1980P	27,610,000	3.00	—	1999P	29,592,000	4.00	—
1980D	41,628,708	3.00	—	1999P Proof	Est. 750,000	—	25.00
1980S	20,422,000	3.50	—	1999D	11,776,000	4.00	—

Sacagawea Dollar

Sacagawea bust right, with baby on back obverse
Eagle in flight left reverse

KM# 310 • 8.0700 g., **Copper-Zinc-Manganese-Nickel Clad Copper**, 26.4 mm. •

Date	Mintage	MS-63	Prf-65	Date	Mintage	MS-63	Prf-65
2000P	767,140,000	2.00	—	2000S	4,048,865	—	10.00
2000D	518,916,000	2.00	—				

$2.50 (QUARTER EAGLE)

GOLD

Coronet Head

Coronet head left within circle of stars obverse
No motto above eagle reverse

KM# 72 • 4.1800 g., 0.9000 **Gold**, 0.1209 oz. AGW, 18 mm. • **Rev. Legend:** UNITED STATES OF AMERICA **Designer:** Christian Gobrecht

Date	Mintage	F-12	VF-20	XF-40	AU-50	MS-60	Prf-65
1901	91,322	150	175	200	235	275	12,500
1902	133,733	150	170	200	235	275	12,500
1903	201,257	150	170	200	235	275	13,000
1904	160,960	150	170	200	240	275	12,500
1905	217,944	150	170	200	240	275	12,500
1906	176,490	150	170	200	240	275	12,500
1907	336,448	150	170	200	240	275	12,500

Indian Head

KM# 128 • 4.1800 g., 0.9000 **Gold**, 0.1209 oz. AGW, 18 mm. • **Designer:** Bela Lyon Pratt

Date	Mintage	VF-20	XF-40	AU-50	MS-60	MS-63	MS-65	Prf-65
1908	565,057	165	220	230	275	1,800	8,500	16,000
1909	441,899	175	220	230	275	2,600	11,000	30,000
1910	492,682	175	220	230	275	2,600	12,500	18,000
1911	704,191	175	220	230	280	1,600	12,500	16,000
1911D	55,680	2,500	3,650	5,000	9,850	24,500	90,000	16,000
1912	616,197	175	220	230	275	2,800	16,000	16,000
1913	722,165	175	220	230	280	1,725	14,000	16,500
1914	240,117	175	235	260	480	8,500	34,000	16,500
1914D	448,000	175	220	230	300	2,650	40,000	23,000
1915	606,100	175	220	230	275	1,650	13,500	15,250
1925D	578,000	175	220	230	275	1,450	7,000	—
1926	446,000	175	220	230	275	1,450	7,000	—
1927	388,000	175	220	230	275	1,450	7,000	—
1928	416,000	175	220	230	275	1,450	7,000	—
1929	532,000	180	230	250	340	1,600	10,000	—

$5 (HALF EAGLE)

GOLD

Coronet Head

Coronet head, left, within circle of stars obverse "In God We Trust" above eagle reverse

KM# 101 • 8.3590 g., 0.9000 **Gold**, 0.2419 oz. AGW, 21.6 mm. •
Rev. Legend: UNITED STATES OF AMERICA **Designer:** Christian Gobrecht

Date	Mintage	VF-20	XF-40	AU-50	MS-60	MS-63	MS-65	Prf-65
1901	616,040	226	229	233	235	750	3,650	27,000
1901S	3,648,000	226	229	233	235	730	3,600	—
1902	172,562	226	229	233	235	730	4,400	27,000
1902S	939,000	226	229	233	235	730	3,600	—
1903	227,024	226	229	233	235	730	4,000	27,000
1903S	1,855,000	226	229	233	235	730	3,600	—
1904	392,136	226	229	233	235	730	3,600	27,000
1904S	97,000	233	239	277	900	3,850	9,600	—
1905	302,308	226	229	233	235	740	4,000	27,000
1905S	880,700	226	229	233	235	1,500	9,600	—
1906	348,820	226	229	233	235	745	3,600	26,000
1906D	320,000	226	229	233	235	930	3,200	—
1906S	598,000	226	229	233	240	900	4,400	—
1907	626,192	226	229	233	235	730	3,400	23,000
1907D	888,000	226	229	233	235	730	3,400	—
1908	421,874	226	229	233	235	730	3,400	—

Indian Head

KM# 129 • 8.3590 g., 0.9000 **Gold**, 0.2419 oz. AGW, 21.6 mm. • **Designer:** Bela Lyon Pratt

Date	Mintage	VF-20	XF-40	AU-50	MS-60	MS-63	MS-65	Prf-65
1908	578,012	280	290	315	545	3,400	21,500	25,500
1908D	148,000	280	290	315	545	3,400	36,500	—
1908S	82,000	355	365	410	1,275	6,000	22,250	—
1909	627,138	280	290	315	525	3,400	21,500	36,000
1909D	3,423,560	280	290	315	525	2,850	21,500	—
1909O	34,200	2,150	3,350	7,250	27,500	64,500	475,000	—
1909S	297,200	310	330	375	1,350	11,000	45,000	—
1910	604,250	280	290	315	525	3,450	21,500	37,000
1910D	193,600	280	290	315	545	4,150	39,500	—
1910S	770,200	320	345	385	975	65,000	44,000	—
1911	915,139	280	290	315	525	2,850	21,500	28,500
1911D	72,500	575	700	1,100	4,650	38,500	255,000	—
1911S	1,416,000	290	325	370	600	5,850	41,500	—
1912	790,144	280	290	315	525	2,850	21,500	28,500
1912S	392,000	325	355	460	1,675	13,500	105,000	—
1913	916,099	280	290	315	525	3,400	22,250	28,000
1913S	408,000	320	350	500	1,450	11,500	125,000	—
1914	247,125	280	290	315	545	3,550	22,500	28,500
1914D	247,000	280	290	315	545	3,450	21,500	—

Date	Mintage	VF-20	XF-40	AU-50	MS-60	MS-63	MS-65	Prf-65
1914S	263,000	325	345	410	1,375	12,850	105,000	—
1915	588,075	280	290	315	525	34,750	21,500	39,000
1915S	164,000	335	365	495	1,950	17,000	110,000	—
1916S	240,000	305	325	395	710	5,750	28,500	—
1929	662,000	7,500	10,750	11,800	14,500	31,000	50,000	—

$10 (EAGLE)

GOLD

Coronet Head

New-style head, left, within circle of stars obverse "In God We Trust" above eagle reverse

KM# 102 • 16.7180 g., 0.9000 **Gold**, 0.4837 oz. AGW, 27 mm. •
Rev. Legend: UNITED STATES OF AMERICA **Designer:** Christian Gobrecht

Date	Mintage	VF-20	XF-40	AU-50	MS-60	MS-63	MS-65	Prf-65
1901	1,718,825	534	551	561	601	1,015	5,950	43,500
1901O	72,041	562	589	599	721	3,750	12,500	—
1901S	2,812,750	534	551	561	601	1,015	6,250	—
1902	82,513	534	551	561	611	2,800	11,750	43,500
1902S	469,500	534	551	561	601	1,015	6,250	—
1903	125,926	534	551	561	611	2,450	13,500	43,500
1903O	112,771	562	589	599	711	3,250	18,000	—
1903S	538,000	534	551	561	611	1,040	5,950	—
1904	162,038	534	551	561	611	2,000	9,500	46,000
1904O	108,950	562	589	599	711	3,700	16,500	—
1905	201,078	534	551	561	601	1,450	8,500	43,500
1905S	369,250	562	584	626	1,100	5,600	22,500	—
1906	165,497	534	551	561	611	2,450	10,000	43,500
1906D	981,000	534	551	561	601	1,015	7,000	—
1906O	86,895	562	589	599	751	4,900	14,500	—
1906S	457,000	562	584	599	761	5,000	15,500	—
1907	1,203,973	534	551	561	601	1,015	5,950	43,500
1907D	1,030,000	534	551	561	611	2,250	—	—
1907S	210,500	562	584	621	801	5,450	17,000	—

Indian Head

No motto next to eagle reverse

KM# 125 • 16.7180 g., 0.9000 **Gold**, 0.4837 oz. AGW, 27 mm. • **Designer:** Augustus Saint-Gaudens **Notes:** 1907 varieties are distinguished by whether the edge is rolled or wired, and whether the legend "E Pluribus Unum" has periods between each word.

Date	Mintage	VF-20	XF-40	AU-50	MS-60	MS-63	MS-65	Prf-65
1907 wire edge, periods before and after legend	500	9,500	14,900	16,900	22,000	36,500	65,000	—
1907 same, without stars on edge, unique	—	—	—	—	—	—	—	—
1907 rolled edge, periods	42	26,000	38,500	49,000	66,500	98,500	250,000	—
1907 without periods	239,406	605	620	635	775	3,100	11,450	—
1908 without motto	33,500	590	605	620	720	4,650	14,500	—
1908D without motto	210,000	590	605	620	760	6,250	38,500	—

"In God We Trust" left of eagle reverse

KM# 130 • 16.7180 g., 0.9000 **Gold**, 0.4837 oz. AGW, 27 mm. • **Designer:** Augustus Saint-Gaudens

Date	Mintage	VF-20	XF-40	AU-50	MS-60	MS-63	MS-65	Prf-65
1908	341,486	590	605	615	700	3,150	9,450	52,500

Date	Mintage	VF-20	XF-40	AU-50	MS-60	MS-63	MS-65	Prf-65
1908D	836,500	595	610	620	705	6,850	29,000	—
1908S	59,850	605	660	670	2,950	8,650	25,500	—
1909	184,863	590	605	615	700	3,500	12,750	54,500
1909D	121,540	595	610	620	775	4,650	34,500	—
1909S	292,350	595	610	620	775	5,350	13,900	—
1910	318,704	590	605	615	700	2,350	8,950	54,500
1910D	2,356,640	585	600	615	700	2,185	8,600	—
1910S	811,000	595	610	620	705	7,450	55,000	—
1911	505,595	585	600	610	695	2,185	8,800	52,500
1911D	30,100	640	675	950	4,200	21,500	120,000	—
1911S	51,000	625	555	645	1,050	7,950	14,500	—
1912	405,083	590	605	615	700	2,350	9,650	52,500
1912S	300,000	595	610	620	705	5,850	38,500	—
1913	442,071	590	605	615	700	2,350	8,800	52,500
1913S	66,000	640	680	775	3,900	28,500	100,000	—
1914	151,050	590	605	615	700	2,400	9,850	52,500
1914D	343,500	590	605	615	700	2,650	15,500	—
1914S	208,000	600	615	625	720	6,500	32,500	—
1915	351,075	590	605	615	700	2,350	9,850	55,000
1915S	59,000	640	725	775	3,150	14,850	65,000	—
1916S	138,500	625	640	650	735	5,150	18,500	—
1920S	126,500	7,800	11,000	14,500	28,500	71,500	275,000	—
1926	1,014,000	585	600	610	695	1,650	7,450	—
1930S	96,000	7,500	10,000	13,500	21,500	41,500	68,500	—
1932	4,463,000	585	600	610	695	1,650	7,500	—
1933	312,500	110,000	140,000	150,000	185,000	245,000	650,000	—

$20 (DOUBLE EAGLE)

GOLD

Liberty

Coronet head, left, within circle of stars obverse
"Twenty Dollars" below eagle reverse

KM# 74.3 • 33.4360 g., 0.9000 Gold, 0.9675 oz. AGW • Rev. Legend: UNITED STATES OF AMERICA

Date	Mintage	VF-20	XF-40	AU-50	MS-60	MS-63	MS-65	Prf-65
1901	111,526	1,085	1,100	1,110	1,155	1,685	5,850	200,000
1901S	1,596,000	1,085	1,100	1,110	1,155	3,850	21,500	—
1902	31,254	1,085	1,295	1,050	1,400	11,250	37,500	200,000
1902S	1,753,625	1,085	1,100	1,110	1,155	2,900	23,500	—
1903	287,428	1,085	1,100	1,110	1,155	1,685	5,500	200,000
1903S	954,000	1,085	1,100	1,110	1,155	1,715	13,500	—
1904	6,256,797	1,085	1,100	1,110	1,155	1,650	4,350	200,000
1904S	5,134,175	1,085	1,100	1,110	1,155	1,650	5,400	—
1905	59,011	1,090	1,120	1,110	1,250	14,500	—	200,000
1905S	1,813,000	1,085	1,100	1,110	1,155	3,250	20,500	—
1906	69,690	1,090	1,105	1,145	1,335	6,850	26,500	200,000
1906D	620,250	1,085	1,100	1,110	1,155	3,250	22,500	—
1906S	2,065,750	1,085	1,100	1,165	1,155	2,350	19,500	—
1907	1,451,864	1,085	1,100	1,110	1,155	1,650	8,200	200,000
1907D	842,250	1,085	1,100	1,110	1,155	2,650	7,350	—
1907S	2,165,800	1,085	1,100	1,110	1,155	2,375	27,000	—

Saint-Gaudens

Roman numerals in date obverse
No motto below eagle reverse

KM# 126 • 33.4360 g., 0.9000 Gold, 0.9675 oz. AGW, 34 mm. • Designer: Augustus Saint-Gaudens Edge Desc: Plain.

Date	Mintage	VF-20	XF-40	AU-50	MS-60	MS-63	MS-65	Prf-65
MCMVII (1907) high relief, unique, AU-55, $150,000	—	—	—	—	—	—	—	—
MCMVII (1907) high relief, wire rim	11,250	7,500	8,350	10,750	13,750	24,000	52,000	—

Date	Mintage	VF-20	XF-40	AU-50	MS-60	MS-63	MS-65	Prf-65
MCMVII (1907) high relief, flat rim	Inc. above	7,750	8,850	11,750	15,000	25,500	53,500	—

Arabic numerals in date obverse
No motto below eagle reverse

KM# 127 • 33.4360 g., 0.9000 Gold, 0.9675 oz. AGW, 34 mm. • Designer: Augustus Saint-Gaudens Edge Desc: Lettered; large letters.

Date	Mintage	VF-20	XF-40	AU-50	MS-60	MS-63	MS-65	Prf-65
1907 large letters on edge, unique	—	—	—	—	—	—	—	—
1907 small letters on edge	361,667	1,100	1,110	1,140	1,190	1,365	3,350	—
1908	4,271,551	1,090	1,100	1,120	1,150	1,255	1,635	—
1908D	663,750	1,100	1,110	1,130	1,175	1,365	9,000	—

Roman numerals in date obverse
No motto below eagle reverse

KM# Pn1874 • 33.4360 g., 0.9000 Gold, 0.9675 oz. AGW, 34 mm. • Designer: Augustus Saint-Gaudens Edge Desc: Plain. Notes: The "Roman numerals" varieties for 1907 use Roman numerals for the date instead of Arabic numerals. The lettered-edge varieties have "E Pluribus Unum" on the edge, with stars between the words.

Date	Mintage	VF-20	XF-40	AU-50	MS-60	MS-63	MS-65	Prf-65
1907 extremely high relief, unique	—	—	—	—	—	—	—	—
1907 extremely high relief, lettered edge	—	—	—	—	—	—	—	—

Note: 1907 extremely high relief, lettered edge, Prf-68, private sale, 1990, $1,500,000.

"In God We Trust" below eagle reverse

KM# 131 • 33.4360 g., 0.9000 Gold, 0.9675 oz. AGW, 34 mm. • Designer: Augustus Saint-Gaudens

Date	Mintage	VF-20	XF-40	AU-50	MS-60	MS-63	MS-65	Prf-65
1908	156,359	1,095	1,105	1,130	1,200	1,750	21,500	76,500
1908 Roman finish; Prf64 Rare	—	—	—	—	—	—	—	—
1908D	349,500	1,100	1,110	1,140	1,190	1,385	5,350	—
1908S	22,000	2,450	3,150	4,850	10,650	24,500	52,000	—
1909/8	161,282	1,100	1,110	1,180	1,850	6,950	32,500	—
1909	Inc. above	1,110	1,130	1,150	1,250	3,350	42,500	92,500
1909D	52,500	1,140	1,150	1,275	3,100	8,850	39,500	—
1909S	2,774,925	1,100	1,110	1,140	1,170	1,340	5,500	—
1910	482,167	1,095	1,105	1,130	1,200	1,355	7,350	84,500
1910D	429,000	1,095	1,105	1,130	1,175	1,325	2,600	—
1910S	2,128,250	1,100	1,110	1,145	1,180	1,390	8,000	—
1911	197,350	1,100	1,110	1,150	1,190	1,875	15,500	76,500
1911D	846,500	1,095	1,105	1,130	1,175	1,325	1,735	—
1911S	775,750	1,095	1,105	1,130	1,180	1,325	6,200	—
1912	149,824	1,100	1,110	1,145	1,215	2,050	19,500	76,500
1913	168,838	1,100	1,110	1,145	1,220	2,850	37,500	82,500
1913D	393,500	1,095	1,105	1,130	1,175	1,365	5,500	—
1913S	34,000	1,150	1,160	1,180	2,000	4,350	36,500	—
1914	95,320	1,110	1,120	1,180	1,275	3,900	25,000	81,500
1914D	453,000	1,095	1,105	1,130	1,175	1,335	3,250	—
1914S	1,498,000	1,095	1,105	1,130	1,175	1,325	2,000	—
1915	152,050	1,100	1,110	1,140	1,180	2,200	28,500	125,000
1915S	567,500	1,095	1,105	1,130	1,175	1,325	2,000	—
1916S	796,000	1,100	1,110	1,140	1,215	1,355	2,700	—
1920	228,250	1,090	1,100	1,120	1,175	1,385	75,000	—
1920S	558,000	14,500	18,500	28,500	53,000	105,000	355,000	—
1921	528,500	35,000	43,500	56,500	125,000	300,000	975,000	—
1922	1,375,500	1,090	1,100	1,120	1,150	1,275	2,450	—
1922S	2,658,000	1,210	1,150	1,300	2,450	4,850	42,500	—
1923	566,000	1,090	1,100	1,120	1,150	1,275	4,750	—
1923D	1,702,250	1,100	1,110	1,130	1,160	1,275	1,735	—
1924	4,323,500	1,090	1,100	1,120	1,150	1,255	1,635	—
1924D	3,049,500	1,313	1,550	1,800	3,100	9,150	75,000	—
1924S	2,927,500	1,210	1,550	1,850	3,000	9,850	135,000	—
1925	2,831,750	1,090	1,100	1,120	1,150	1,255	1,950	—
1925D	2,938,500	1,550	2,100	2,375	4,450	11,500	110,000	—
1925S	3,776,500	1,350	1,950	3,450	9,000	24,500	145,000	—
1926	816,750	1,090	1,100	1,120	1,150	1,255	1,635	—

Date	Mintage	VF-20	XF-40	AU-50	MS-60	MS-63	MS-65	Prf-65
1926D	481,000	10,000	15,500	20,500	28,500	45,000	175,000	—
1926S	2,041,500	1,293	1,550	1,725	3,150	5,650	31,500	—
1927	2,946,750	1,090	1,100	1,120	1,150	1,255	1,635	—
1927D	180,000	155,000	200,000	245,000	325,000	1,500,000	1,750,000	—
1927S	3,107,000	6,850	8,850	13,250	26,750	56,500	170,000	—
1928	8,816,000	1,090	1,100	1,120	1,150	1,255	1,635	—
1929	1,779,750	6,950	8,450	10,850	18,500	44,500	98,500	—
1930S	74,000	35,000	41,000	49,500	70,000	118,000	225,000	—
1931	2,938,250	10,500	13,500	20,500	31,500	69,500	120,000	—
1931D	106,500	8,850	11,500	21,500	42,500	88,500	145,000	—
1932	1,101,750	12,500	14,500	17,850	26,500	73,500	—	—
1933	445,500						9,000,000	—

Note: Sotheby/Stack's Sale, July 2002. Thirteen known, only one currently available.

COMMEMORATIVE COINAGE
1892-1954

All commemorative half dollars of 1892-1954 have the following specifications: diameter -- 30.6 millimeters; weight -- 12.5000 grams; composition -- 0.9000 silver, 0.3617 ounces actual silver weight. Values for PDS sets contain one example each from the Philadelphia, Denver and San Francisco mints. Type coin prices are the most inexpensive single coin available from the date and mint-mark combinations listed.

HALF DOLLAR

PANAMA-PACIFIC EXPOSITION. KM# 135 Designer: Charles E. Barber.

Date	Mintage	AU-50	MS-60	MS-63	MS-64	MS-65
1915S	27,134	465	550	825	1,550	2,650

ILLINOIS CENTENNIAL-LINCOLN. KM# 143 Obv. Designer: George T. Morgan
Rev. Designer: John R. Sinnock.

Date	Mintage	AU-50	MS-60	MS-63	MS-64	MS-65
1918	100,058	135	155	170	250	525

MAINE CENTENNIAL. KM# 146 Designer: Anthony de Francisci.

Date	Mintage	AU-50	MS-60	MS-63	MS-64	MS-65
1920	50,028	135	165	195	310	585

PILGRIM TERCENTENARY. KM# 147.1 Designer: Cyrus E. Dallin.

Date	Mintage	AU-50	MS-60	MS-63	MS-64	MS-65
1920	152,112	85.00	110	122	160	465

ALABAMA CENTENNIAL. KM# 148.1 Designer: Laura G. Fraser. **Obverse:** "2x2" at right above stars **Notes:** "Fake 2x2" counterstamps exist.

Date	Mintage	AU-50	MS-60	MS-63	MS-64	MS-65
1921	6,006	315	330	600	950	1,975

ALABAMA CENTENNIAL. KM# 148.2 Obv. Designer: Laura G. Fraser

Date	Mintage	AU-50	MS-60	MS-63	MS-64	MS-65
1921	59,038	190	215	525	685	1,800

MISSOURI CENTENNIAL. KM# 149.1 Designer: Robert Aitken.

Date	Mintage	AU-50	MS-60	MS-63	MS-64	MS-65
1921	15,428	410	725	925	1,775	5,000

MISSOURI CENTENNIAL. KM# 149.2 Designer: Robert Aitken. **Obverse:** 2 star 4 in field at left **Notes:** "Fake "2*4" counterstamps exist.

Date	Mintage	AU-50	MS-60	MS-63	MS-64	MS-65
1921	5,000	650	800	1,100	1,900	5,000

PILGRIM TERCENTENARY. KM# 147.2 Designer: Cyrus E. Dallin. **Obverse:** 1921 date next to Pilgrim

Date	Mintage	AU-50	MS-60	MS-63	MS-64	MS-65
1921	20,053	175	200	225	285	600

GRANT MEMORIAL. KM# 151.1 Designer: Laura G. Fraser.

Date	Mintage	AU-50	MS-60	MS-63	MS-64	MS-65
1922	67,405	115	125	160	290	800

GRANT MEMORIAL. KM# 151.2 Designer: Laura G. Fraser. Obverse: Star above the word "Grant" Notes: "Fake star" counterstamps exist.

Date	Mintage	AU-50	MS-60	MS-63	MS-64	MS-65
1922	4,256	950	1,300	2,100	2,850	7,250

MONROE DOCTRINE CENTENNIAL. KM# 153 Designer: Chester Beach.

Date	Mintage	AU-50	MS-60	MS-63	MS-64	MS-65
1923S	274,077	58.00	75.00	145	525	2,950

HUGUENOT-WALLOON TERCENTENARY. KM# 154 Designer: George T. Morgan. Obverse: Huguenot leader Gaspard de Coligny and William I of Orange

Date	Mintage	AU-50	MS-60	MS-63	MS-64	MS-65
1924	142,080	135	155	175	250	550

CALIFORNIA DIAMOND JUBILEE. KM# 155 Designer: Jo Mora.

Date	Mintage	AU-50	MS-60	MS-63	MS-64	MS-65
1925S	86,594	215	240	280	520	1,125

FORT VANCOUVER CENTENNIAL. KM# 158 Designer: Laura G. Fraser.

Date	Mintage	AU-50	MS-60	MS-63	MS-64	MS-65
1925	14,994	335	415	475	600	1,450

LEXINGTON-CONCORD SESQUICENTENNIAL. KM# 156 Designer: Chester Beach.

Date	Mintage	AU-50	MS-60	MS-63	MS-64	MS-65
1925	162,013	96.00	110	120	185	485

STONE MOUNTAIN MEMORIAL. KM# 157 Designer: Gutzon Borglum.

Date	Mintage	AU-50	MS-60	MS-63	MS-64	MS-65
1925	1,314,709	70.00	77.00	85.00	90.00	285

OREGON TRAIL MEMORIAL. KM# 159 Designer: James E. and Laura G. Fraser.

Date	Mintage	AU-50	MS-60	MS-63	MS-64	MS-65
1926	47,955	140	170	190	210	335
1926S	83,055	140	170	185	205	335
Type coin	—	150	180	190	210	320
1928	6,028	220	245	280	290	390
1933D	5,008	375	400	410	420	540
1934D	7,006	205	220	230	240	365
1936	10,006	150	190	200	210	325
1936S	5,006	170	190	210	220	360
1937D	12,008	180	205	210	215	325
1938	6,006	160	175	210	215	335
1938D	6,005	160	175	215	235	335
1938S	6,006	160	175	210	220	335
1939	3,004	525	620	630	655	720
1939D	3,004	525	620	640	675	735
1939S	3,005	525	620	630	655	725

U.S. SESQUICENTENNIAL. KM# 160 Designer: John R. Sinnock.

Date	Mintage	AU-50	MS-60	MS-63	MS-64	MS-65
1926	141,120	88.00	115	150	600	4,400

VERMONT SESQUICENTENNIAL. KM# 162 Obv. Designer: Charles Keck

Date	Mintage	AU-50	MS-60	MS-63	MS-64	MS-65
1927	28,142	255	290	305	350	990

HAWAIIAN SESQUICENTENNIAL. KM# 163 Designer: Juliette M. Fraser. Notes: Counterfeits exist.

Date	Mintage	AU-50	MS-60	MS-63	MS-64	MS-65
1928	10,008	1,750	2,650	3,500	4,500	6,850

DANIEL BOONE BICENTENNIAL. KM# 165.1 Designer: Augustus Lukeman.

Date	Mintage	AU-50	MS-60	MS-63	MS-64	MS-65
1934	10,007	125	135	140	150	275

Date	Mintage	AU-50	MS-60	MS-63	MS-64	MS-65
1935	10,010	118	120	125	130	275
1935D	5,005	133	140	145	152	325
1935S	5,005	133	140	145	152	325

DANIEL BOONE BICENTENNIAL. KM# 165.2 Designer: Augustus Lukeman.
Reverse: "1934" added above the word "Pioneer."

Date	Mintage	AU-50	MS-60	MS-63	MS-64	MS-65
1935	10,008	118	120	125	130	275
Type coin	—	130	135	145	150	240
1935D	2,003	375	415	430	485	860
1935S	2,004	375	415	430	450	890
1936	12,012	118	120	125	130	275
1936D	5,005	133	140	145	152	325
1936S	5,006	133	140	145	152	325
1937	9,810	125	130	135	980	285
1937D	2,506	285	385	390	385	560
1937S	2,506	285	385	390	415	590
1938	2,100	360	395	410	415	555
1938D	2,100	360	395	410	430	545
1938S	2,100	360	395	410	415	595

MARYLAND TERCENTENARY. KM# 166 Designer: Hans Schuler.

Date	Mintage	AU-50	MS-60	MS-63	MS-64	MS-65
1934	25,015	160	180	195	215	350

TEXAS CENTENNIAL. KM# 167 Designer: Pompeo Coppini.

Date	Mintage	AU-50	MS-60	MS-63	MS-64	MS-65
1934	61,463	140	145	155	160	290
Type coin	—	145	158	163	165	260
1935	9,994	140	145	155	160	290
1935D	10,007	140	145	155	160	290
1935S	10,008	140	145	155	160	290
1936	8,911	140	145	155	160	290
1936D	9,039	140	145	155	160	290
1936S	9,055	140	145	155	160	290
1937	6,571	142	148	160	165	295
1937D	6,605	142	148	160	165	295
1937S	6,637	142	148	160	165	295
1938	3,780	240	265	275	300	500
1938D	3,775	240	265	275	300	485
1938S	3,814	240	265	275	300	485

ARKANSAS CENTENNIAL. KM# 168 Designer: Edward E. Burr.

Date	Mintage	AU-50	MS-60	MS-63	MS-64	MS-65
Type coin	—	110	115	125	130	210
1935	13,012	100.00	110	120	125	215
1935D	5,505	105	115	125	130	300
1935S	5,506	105	115	125	130	300
1936	9,660	100.00	110	120	125	230
1936D	9,660	100.00	110	120	125	230
1936S	9,662	100.00	110	120	125	230

Date	Mintage	AU-50	MS-60	MS-63	MS-64	MS-65
1937	5,505	105	115	128	135	340
1937D	5,505	105	115	128	135	330
1937S	5,506	105	115	128	135	380
1938	3,156	165	190	210	210	620
1938D	3,155	165	190	195	210	610
1938S	3,156	165	190	195	210	675
1939	2,104	330	390	400	410	1,000
1939D	2,104	330	390	400	410	980
1939S	2,105	330	390	400	410	965

CONNECTICUT TERCENTENARY. KM# 169 Designer: Henry Kreiss.

Date	Mintage	AU-50	MS-60	MS-63	MS-64	MS-65
1935	25,018	255	290	310	380	540

HUDSON, N.Y., SESQUICENTENNIAL. KM# 170 Designer: Chester Beach.

Date	Mintage	AU-50	MS-60	MS-63	MS-64	MS-65
1935	10,008	750	925	1,250	1,675	2,250

OLD SPANISH TRAIL. KM# 172 Designer: L.W. Hoffecker. Notes: Counterfeits exist.

Date	Mintage	AU-50	MS-60	MS-63	MS-64	MS-65
1935	10,008	1,250	1,375	1,700	1,900	2,250

SAN DIEGO-PACIFIC INTERNATIONAL EXPOSITION. KM# 171
Designer: Robert Aitken.

Date	Mintage	AU-50	MS-60	MS-63	MS-64	MS-65
1935S	70,132	105	130	145	150	170
1936D	30,092	105	135	150	160	170

ALBANY, N.Y., CHARTER ANNIVERSARY. KM# 173 Designer: Gertrude K. Lathrop.

Date	Mintage	AU-50	MS-60	MS-63	MS-64	MS-65
1936	17,671	320	330	380	385	470

ARKANSAS CENTENNIAL. KM# 187 Obv. Designer: Henry Kreiss
Rev. Designer: Edward E. Burr **Obverse:** Sen. Joseph T. Robinson

Date	Mintage	AU-50	MS-60	MS-63	MS-64	MS-65
1936	25,265	145	150	165	180	420

BATTLE OF GETTYSBURG 75TH ANN. KM# 181 Designer: Frank Vittor.

Date	Mintage	AU-50	MS-60	MS-63	MS-64	MS-65
1936	26,928	435	475	500	525	765

BRIDGEPORT, CONN., CENTENNIAL. KM# 175 Designer: Henry Kreiss.

Date	Mintage	AU-50	MS-60	MS-63	MS-64	MS-65
1936	25,015	140	150	190	200	315

CINCINNATI MUSIC CENTER. KM# 176 Designer: Constance Ortmayer.

Date	Mintage	AU-50	MS-60	MS-63	MS-64	MS-65
Type coin	—	335	345	375	560	700
1936	5,005	315	330	360	540	925
1936D	5,005	315	330	360	540	750
1936S	5,006	315	330	360	540	750

CLEVELAND-GREAT LAKES EXPOSITION. KM# 177 Designer: Brenda Putnam.

Date	Mintage	AU-50	MS-60	MS-63	MS-64	MS-65
1936	50,030	135	140	150	160	245

COLUMBIA, S.C., SESQUICENTENNIAL. KM# 178 Designer: A. Wolfe Davidson.

Date	Mintage	AU-50	MS-60	MS-63	MS-64	MS-65
1936	9,007	275	280	300	310	415

Date	Mintage	AU-50	MS-60	MS-63	MS-64	MS-65
Type coin	—	280	290	330	335	385
1936D	8,009	275	280	300	310	415
1936S	8,007	275	280	300	310	415

DELAWARE TERCENTENARY. KM# 179 Designer: Carl L. Schmitz.

Date	Mintage	AU-50	MS-60	MS-63	MS-64	MS-65
1936	20,993	310	325	365	385	490

ELGIN, ILL., CENTENNIAL. KM# 180 Designer: Trygve Rovelstad.

Date	Mintage	AU-50	MS-60	MS-63	MS-64	MS-65
1936	20,015	245	265	280	295	355

LONG ISLAND TERCENTENARY. KM# 182 Designer: Howard K. Weinman.

Date	Mintage	AU-50	MS-60	MS-63	MS-64	MS-65
1936	81,826	88.00	98.00	110	130	420

LYNCHBURG, VA., SESQUICENTENNIAL. KM# 183 Designer: Charles Keck.

Date	Mintage	AU-50	MS-60	MS-63	MS-64	MS-65
1936	20,013	235	265	280	295	365

NORFOLK, VA., BICENTENNIAL. KM# 184 Designer: William M. and Marjorie E. Simpson.

Date	Mintage	AU-50	MS-60	MS-63	MS-64	MS-65
1936	16,936	535	565	590	610	650

RHODE ISLAND TERCENTENARY. KM# 185 Designer: Arthur G. Carey and John H. Benson.

Date	Mintage	AU-50	MS-60	MS-63	MS-64	MS-65
1936	20,013	100.00	110	120	130	260

Date	Mintage	AU-50	MS-60	MS-63	MS-64	MS-65
Type coin	—	105	110	125	128	290
1936D	15,010	100.00	110	120	130	275
1936S	15,011	100.00	110	120	130	290

SAN FRANCISCO-OAKLAND BAY BRIDGE. KM# 174 Designer: Jacques Schnier.

Date	Mintage	AU-50	MS-60	MS-63	MS-64	MS-65
1936	71,424	170	180	220	225	375

WISCONSIN TERRITORIAL CENTENNIAL. KM# 188 Designer: David Parsons.

Date	Mintage	AU-50	MS-60	MS-63	MS-64	MS-65
1936	25,015	230	255	275	315	400

YORK COUNTY, MAINE, TERCENTENARY. KM# 189 Designer: Walter H. Rich.

Date	Mintage	AU-50	MS-60	MS-63	MS-64	MS-65
1936	25,015	135	170	195	300	590

BATTLE OF ANTIETAM 75TH ANNIVERSARY. KM# 190 Designer: William M. Simpson.

Date	Mintage	AU-50	MS-60	MS-63	MS-64	MS-65
1937	18,028	725	760	790	850	985

ROANOKE ISLAND, N.C.. KM# 186 Designer: William M. Simpson.

Date	Mintage	AU-50	MS-60	MS-63	MS-64	MS-65
1937	29,030	255	285	310	330	340

NEW ROCHELLE, N.Y.. KM# 191 Designer: Gertrude K. Lathrop.

Date	Mintage	AU-50	MS-60	MS-63	MS-64	MS-65
1938	15,266	420	445	460	470	610

BOOKER T. WASHINGTON. KM# 198 Designer: Isaac S. Hathaway. Notes: Actual mintages are higher, but unsold issues were melted to produce Washington Carver issues.

Date	Mintage	AU-50	MS-60	MS-63	MS-64	MS-65
1946	1,000,546	14.00	18.00	19.50	21.00	50.00
Type coin	—	15.00	16.00	17.50	18.50	56.00
1946D	200,113	16.00	20.00	21.00	30.00	64.00
1946S	500,729	14.00	18.00	19.50	21.00	50.00
1947	100,017	25.00	35.00	55.00	65.00	95.00
1947D	100,017	25.00	35.00	55.00	70.00	115
1947S	100,017	25.00	35.00	55.00	65.00	90.00
1948	8,005	38.00	58.00	85.00	86.00	100.00
1948D	8,005	38.00	58.00	85.00	86.00	94.00
1948S	8,005	38.00	58.00	85.00	95.00	98.00
1949	6,004	67.00	83.00	92.00	98.00	120
1949D	6,004	67.00	83.00	92.00	98.00	120
1949S	6,004	67.00	83.00	95.00	104	110
1950	6,004	45.00	65.00	78.00	88.00	98.00
1950D	6,004	45.00	65.00	75.00	88.00	96.00
1950S	512,091	15.00	20.00	24.00	28.00	52.00
1951	51,082	15.00	20.00	24.00	28.00	50.00
1951D	7,004	45.00	65.00	78.00	90.00	95.00
1951S	7,004	45.00	65.00	78.00	90.00	95.00

IOWA STATEHOOD CENTENNIAL. KM# 197 Designer: Adam Pietz.

Date	Mintage	AU-50	MS-60	MS-63	MS-64	MS-65
1946	100,057	115	120	125	130	260

BOOKER T. WASHINGTON AND GEORGE WASHINGTON CARVER. KM# 200
Designer: Isaac S. Hathaway.

Date	Mintage	AU-50	MS-60	MS-63	MS-64	MS-65
1951	110,018	26.00	34.00	53.00	54.00	290
Type coin	—	14.00	16.00	18.50	20.00	52.50
1951D	10,004	35.00	43.00	60.00	58.00	140
1951S	10,004	35.00	43.00	60.00	58.00	140
1952	2,006,292	15.00	18.00	26.50	44.00	48.00
1952D	8,006	40.00	50.00	70.00	70.00	200
1952S	8,006	40.00	50.00	80.00	70.00	160
1953	8,003	35.00	47.00	75.00	85.00	260
1953D	8,003	35.00	47.00	75.00	85.00	175
1953S	108,020	26.00	33.00	50.00	55.00	120
1954	12,006	36.00	42.00	60.00	65.00	150
1954D	12,006	36.00	42.00	60.00	65.00	200
1954S	122,024	24.00	32.00	38.00	48.00	65.00

DOLLAR

LOUISIANA PURCHASE EXPOSITION - MCKINLEY. KM# 120 0.9000 Gold 0.0484 oz. AGW. 15 mm. 1.6720 g. **Obverse:** William McKinley **Obv. Designer:** Charles E. Barber

Date	Mintage	AU-50	MS-60	MS-63	MS-64	MS-65
1903	17,500	715	765	1,080	2,150	3,300

LOUISIANA PURCHASE EXPOSITION - JEFFERSON. KM# 119 0.9000 Gold 0.0484 oz. AGW. 15 mm. 1.6720 g. **Obverse:** Jefferson **Designer:** Charles E. Barber

Date	Mintage	AU-50	MS-60	MS-63	MS-64	MS-65
1903	17,500	700	765	1,160	1,900	3,100

LEWIS AND CLARK EXPOSITION. KM# 121 0.9000 Gold 0.0484 oz. AGW. 15 mm. 1.6720 g. **Obv. Designer:** Charles E. Barber

Date	Mintage	AU-50	MS-60	MS-63	MS-64	MS-65
1904	10,025	1,050	1,350	2,550	5,900	12,250
1905	10,041	1,300	1,625	3,300	7,000	18,500

PANAMA-PACIFIC EXPOSITION. KM# 136 0.9000 Gold 0.0484 oz. AGW. 15 mm. 1.6720 g. **Obv. Designer:** Charles Keck

Date	Mintage	AU-50	MS-60	MS-63	MS-64	MS-65
1915S	15,000	650	750	950	1,500	2,450

MCKINLEY MEMORIAL. KM# 144 0.9000 Gold 0.0484 oz. AGW. 15 mm. 1.6720 g. **Obv. Designer:** Charles E. Barber **Rev. Designer:** George T. Morgan

Date	Mintage	AU-50	MS-60	MS-63	MS-64	MS-65
1916	9,977	625	685	800	1,550	2,350
1917	10,000	785	800	1,325	2,200	3,800

GRANT MEMORIAL. KM# 152.1 0.9000 Gold 0.0484 oz. AGW. 15 mm. 1.6720 g. **Obv. Designer:** Laura G. Fraser **Notes:** Without an incuse "star" above the word GRANT on the obverse.

Date	Mintage	AU-50	MS-60	MS-63	MS-64	MS-65
1922	5,000	1,875	1,900	2,350	3,650	4,900

   Star

GRANT MEMORIAL. KM# 152.2 0.9000 Gold 0.0484 oz. AGW. 15 mm. 1.6720 g. **Obv. Designer:** Laura G. Fraser **Notes:** Variety with an incuse "star" above the word GRANT on the obverse.

Date	Mintage	AU-50	MS-60	MS-63	MS-64	MS-65
1922	5,016	1,800	1,950	2,400	3,700	4,400

$2.50 (QUARTER EAGLE)

PANAMA-PACIFIC EXPOSITION. KM# 137 0.9000 Gold 0.1209 oz. AGW. 18 mm. 4.1800 g. **Obv. Designer:** Charles E. Barber **Rev. Designer:** George T. Morgan

Date	Mintage	AU-50	MS-60	MS-63	MS-64	MS-65
1915S	6,749	1,750	2,100	4,350	6,300	8,000

U.S. SESQUICENTENNIAL. KM# 161 0.9000 Gold 0.1209 oz. AGW. 18 mm. 4.1800 g. **Obv. Designer:** John R. Sinnock

Date	Mintage	AU-50	MS-60	MS-63	MS-64	MS-65
1926	46,019	525	565	850	1,700	4,200

$50

PANAMA-PACIFIC EXPOSITION OCTAGONAL. KM# 139 0.9000 Gold 2.4186 oz. AGW. 44 mm. 83.5900 g. **Obv. Designer:** Robert Aitken

Date	Mintage	AU-50	MS-60	MS-63	MS-64	MS-65
1915S	645	52,500	55,000	80,000	99,500	148,000

PANAMA-PACIFIC EXPOSITION ROUND. KM# 138 0.9000 Gold 2.4186 oz. AGW. 44 mm. 83.5900 g. **Obv. Designer:** Robert Aitken

Date	Mintage	AU-50	MS-60	MS-63	MS-64	MS-65
1915S	483	54,000	60,000	82,500	105,000	145,000

COMMEMORATIVE COINAGE
1982-PRESENT

All commemorative silver dollar coins of 1982-present have the following specifications: diameter -- 38.1 millimeters; weight -- 26.7300 grams; composition -- 0.9000 silver, 0.7736 ounces actual silver weight. All commemorative $5 coins of 1982-present have the following speciciations: diameter -- 21.6 millimeters; weight -- 8.3590 grams; composition: 0.9000 gold, 0.242 ounces actual gold weight.

Note: In 1982, after a hiatus of nearly 20 years, coinage of commemorative half dollars resumed. Those designated with a 'W' were struck at the West Point Mint. Some issues were struck in copper--nickel. Those struck in silver have the same size, weight and composition as the prior commemorative half--dollar series.

HALF DOLLAR

GEORGE WASHINGTON, 250TH BIRTH ANNIVERSARY. KM# 208 0.9000 Silver 0.3617 oz. ASW. 30.6 mm. 12.5000 g. **Obv. Designer:** Elizabeth Jones

Date	Mintage	MS-65	Prf-65	Date	Mintage	MS-65	Prf-65
1982D	2,210,458	6.50		1982S	4,894,044		6.50

STATUE OF LIBERTY CENTENNIAL. KM# 212 Copper-Nickel Clad Copper 11.3400 g. **Obv. Designer:** Edgar Z. Steever **Rev. Designer:** Sherl Joseph Winter

Date	Mintage	MS-65	Prf-65	Date	Mintage	MS-65	Prf-65
1986D	928,008	5.50	—	1986S	6,925,627	—	5.50

JAMES MADISON - BILL OF RIGHTS. KM# 240 0.9000 Silver 0.3617 oz. ASW. 12.5000 g. **Obv. Designer:** T. James Ferrell **Rev. Designer:** Dean McMullen

Date	Mintage	MS-65	Prf-65	Date	Mintage	MS-65	Prf-65
1993W	173,224	20.00	—	1993S	559,758	—	16.50

CONGRESS BICENTENNIAL. KM# 224 Copper-Nickel Clad Copper 11.3400 g. **Obv. Designer:** Patricia L. Verani **Rev. Designer:** William Woodward and Edgar Z. Steever

Date	Mintage	MS-65	Prf-65	Date	Mintage	MS-65	Prf-65
1989D	163,753	8.00	—	1989S	—	—	8.00

WORLD WAR II 50TH ANNIVERSARY. KM# 243 Copper-Nickel Clad Copper 11.3400 g. **Obv. Designer:** George Klauba **Rev. Designer:** William J. Leftwich

Date	Mintage	MS-65	Prf-65	Date	Mintage	MS-65	Prf-65
(1993)P	192,968	29.00	—	(1993)P	290,343	—	26.50

MOUNT RUSHMORE 50TH ANNIVERSARY. KM# 228 Copper-Nickel Clad Copper 11.3400 g. **Obv. Designer:** Marcel Jovine **Rev. Designer:** T. James Ferrell

Date	Mintage	MS-65	Prf-65	Date	Mintage	MS-65	Prf-65
1991D	172,754	21.50	—	1991S	—	—	20.00

1994 WORLD CUP SOCCER. KM# 246 Copper-Nickel Clad Copper 11.3400 g. **Obv. Designer:** Richard T. LaRoche **Rev. Designer:** Dean McMullen

Date	Mintage	MS-65	Prf-65	Date	Mintage	MS-65	Prf-65
1994D	168,208	9.75	—	1994P	609,354	—	8.50
1994P	122,412	10.25	—				

1992 OLYMPICS. KM# 233 Copper-Nickel Clad Copper 11.3400 g. **Obv. Designer:** William Cousins **Rev. Designer:** Steven M. Bieda

Date	Mintage	MS-65	Prf-65	Date	Mintage	MS-65	Prf-65
1992P	161,607	8.50	—	1992S	519,645	—	8.50

1996 ATLANTA OLYMPICS - BASEBALL. KM# 262 Copper-Nickel Clad Copper 11.3400 g. **Obverse:** Baseball **Obv. Designer:** Edgar Z. Steever

Date	Mintage	MS-65	Prf-65	Date	Mintage	MS-65	Prf-65
1995S	164,605	22.50	—	1995S	118,087	—	19.00

COLUMBUS VOYAGE - 500TH ANNIVERSARY. KM# 237 Copper-Nickel Clad Copper 11.3400 g. **Designer:** T. James Ferrell

Date	Mintage	MS-65	Prf-65
1992D	135,702	11.50	—
1992S	390,154	—	11.50

1996 ATLANTA OLYMPICS - BASKETBALL. KM# 257 Copper-Nickel Clad Copper 11.3400 g. **Obverse:** Basketball

Date	Mintage	MS-65	Prf-65
1995S	169,655	—	18.00
1995S	171,001	22.50	—

CIVIL WAR. KM# 254 Copper-Nickel Clad Copper 11.3400 g. **Obv. Designer:** Don Troiani **Rev. Designer:** T. James Ferrell

Date	Mintage	MS-65	Prf-65	Date	Mintage	MS-65	Prf-65
1995S	119,510	42.50	—	1995S	330,099	—	41.50

1996 ATLANTA OLYMPICS - SOCCER. KM# 271 Copper-Nickel Clad Copper 11.3400 g. **Obverse:** Soccer

Date	Mintage	MS-65	Prf-65	Date	Mintage	MS-65	Prf-65
1996S	52,836	110	—	1996S	122,412	—	105

1996 ATLANTA OLYMPICS - SWIMMING. KM# 267 Copper-Nickel Clad Copper 11.3400 g. **Obverse:** Swimming

Date	Mintage	MS-65	Prf-65	Date	Mintage	MS-65	Prf-65
1996S	49,533	165	—	1996S	114,315	—	36.00

DOLLAR

1984 LOS ANGELES OLYMPICS - DISCUS. KM# 209 Obv. Designer: Elizabeth Jones

Date	Mintage	MS-65	Prf-65
1983P	294,543	14.10	—
1983D	174,014	14.10	—
1983S	174,014	14.10	—
1983S	1,577,025	—	14.10

1984 LOS ANGELES OLYMPICS - STADIUM STATUES. KM# 210 Obv. Designer: Robert Graham

Date	Mintage	MS-65	Prf-65	Date	Mintage	MS-65	Prf-65
1984P	217,954	14.10	—	1984S	116,675	14.40	—
1984D	116,675	14.40	—	1984S	1,801,210	—	14.10

STATUE OF LIBERTY CENTENNIAL. KM# 214 Obv. Designer: John Mercanti **Rev. Designer:** John Mercanti and Matthew Peloso

Date	Mintage	MS-65	Prf-65	Date	Mintage	MS-65	Prf-65
1986P	723,635	14.10	—	1986S	6,414,638	—	14.10

CONSTITUTION BICENTENNIAL. KM# 220 Obv. Designer: Patricia L. Verani

Date	Mintage	MS-65	Prf-65	Date	Mintage	MS-65	Prf-65
1987P	451,629	14.10	—	1987S	2,747,116	—	14.10

1988 OLYMPICS. KM# 222 Obv. Designer: Patricia L. Verani **Rev. Designer:** Sherl Joseph Winter

Date	Mintage	MS-65	Prf-65
1988D	191,368	14.10	—
1988S	1,359,366	—	14.10

CONGRESS BICENTENNIAL. KM# 225 Designer: William Woodward and Chester Y. Martin.

Date	Mintage	MS-65	Prf-65	Date	Mintage	MS-65	Prf-65
1989D	135,203	16.50	—	1989S	762,198	—	18.50

USO 50TH ANNIVERSARY. KM# 232 Obv. Designer: Robert Lamb
Rev. Designer: John Mercanti

Date	Mintage	MS-65	Prf-65	Date	Mintage	MS-65	Prf-65
1991D	124,958	14.00	—	1991S	321,275	—	19.50

EISENHOWER CENTENNIAL. KM# 227 Obv. Designer: John Mercanti
Rev. Designer: Marcel Jovine and John Mercanti

Date	Mintage	MS-65	Prf-65	Date	Mintage	MS-65	Prf-65
1990W	241,669	15.50	—	1990P	638,335	—	17.00

1992 OLYMPICS - BASEBALL. KM# 234 Obv. Designer: John R. Deecken and Chester Y. Martin **Rev. Designer:** Marcel Jovine

Date	Mintage	MS-65	Prf-65	Date	Mintage	MS-65	Prf-65
1992D	187,552	24.50	—	1992S	504,505	—	26.00

KOREAN WAR - 38TH ANNIVERSARY. KM# 231 Obv. Designer: John Mercanti
Rev. Designer: T. James Ferrell

Date	Mintage	MS-65	Prf-65	Date	Mintage	MS-65	Prf-65
1991D	213,049	16.50	—	1991P	618,488	—	20.50

COLUMBUS DISCOVERY - 500TH ANNIVERSARY. KM# 238
Obv. Designer: John Mercanti **Rev. Designer:** Thomas D. Rogers, Sr.

Date	Mintage	MS-65	Prf-65	Date	Mintage	MS-65	Prf-65
1992D	106,949	29.00	—	1992P	385,241	—	39.00

MOUNT RUSHMORE 50TH ANNIVERSARY. KM# 229 Obv. Designer: Marika Somogyi **Rev. Designer:** Frank Gasparro

Date	Mintage	MS-65	Prf-65
1991P	133,139	32.50	—
1991S	738,419	—	30.00

WHITE HOUSE BICENTENNIAL. KM# 236 Obv. Designer: Edgar Z. Steever
Rev. Designer: Chester Y. Martin

Date	Mintage	MS-65	Prf-65
1992D	123,803	31.50	—
1992W	375,851	—	31.50

JAMES MADISON - BILL OF RIGHTS. KM# 241 Obv. Designer: William Krawczewicz and Thomas D. Rogers, Sr. **Rev. Designer:** Dean McMullen and Thomas D. Rogers, Sr.

Date	Mintage	MS-65	Prf-65	Date	Mintage	MS-65	Prf-65
1993D	98,383	19.50	—	1993S	534,001	—	20.00

THOMAS JEFFERSON 250TH BIRTH ANNIVERSARY. KM# 249 Designer: T. James Ferrell.

Date	Mintage	MS-65	Prf-65	Date	Mintage	MS-65	Prf-65
1993P	266,927	23.00	—	1993S	332,891	—	28.00

WORLD WAR II 50TH ANNIVERSARY. KM# 244 Designer: Thomas D. Rogers, Sr..

Date	Mintage	MS-65	Prf-65	Date	Mintage	MS-65	Prf-65
1993D	94,708	31.50	—	1993W	322,422	—	40.00

1994 WORLD CUP SOCCER. KM# 247 Obv. Designer: Dean McMullen and T. James Ferrell

Date	Mintage	MS-65	Prf-65
1994D	81,698	26.00	—
1994S	576,978	—	29.00

NATIONAL PRISONER OF WAR MUSEUM. KM# 251 Obv. Designer: Thomas Nielson and Alfred Maletsky **Rev. Designer:** Edgar Z. Steever

Date	Mintage	MS-65	Prf-65	Date	Mintage	MS-65	Prf-65
1994W	54,790	90.00	—	1994P	220,100	—	46.50

U.S. CAPITOL BICENTENNIAL. KM# 253

Date	Mintage	MS-65	Prf-65	Date	Mintage	MS-65	Prf-65
1994D	68,352	20.00	—	1994S	279,416	—	25.00

VIETNAM VETERANS MEMORIAL. KM# 250 Obv. Designer: John Mercanti **Rev. Designer:** Thomas D. Rogers, Sr.

Date	Mintage	MS-65	Prf-65	Date	Mintage	MS-65	Prf-65
1994W	57,317	85.00	—	1994P	226,262	—	69.00

WOMEN IN MILITARY SERVICE MEMORIAL. KM# 252 Obv. Designer: T. James Ferrell **Rev. Designer:** Thomas D. Rogers, Sr.

Date	Mintage	MS-65	Prf-65	Date	Mintage	MS-65	Prf-65
1994W	53,054	39.50	—	1994P	213,201	—	36.00

1996 ATLANTA OLYMPICS - CYCLING. KM# 263 Obv. Designer: John Mercanti **Obverse:** Cycling

Date	Mintage	MS-65	Prf-65	Date	Mintage	MS-65	Prf-65
1995D	19,662	150	—	1995P	118,795	—	47.50

1996 ATLANTA OLYMPICS - GYMNASTICS. KM# 260 Obverse: Gymnastics

Date	Mintage	MS-65	Prf-65	Date	Mintage	MS-65	Prf-65
1995D	42,497	75.00	—	1995P	182,676	—	58.00

1996 ATLANTA OLYMPICS - TRACK AND FIELD. KM# 264 Obv. Designer: John Mercanti **Obverse:** Track and field

Date	Mintage	MS-65	Prf-65	Date	Mintage	MS-65	Prf-65
1995D	24,796	98.00	—	1995P	136,935	—	53.00

1996 ATLANTA PARALYMPICS - BLIND RUNNER. KM# 259   Obverse: Blind runner

Date	Mintage	MS-65	Prf-65	Date	Mintage	MS-65	Prf-65
1995D	28,649	93.00	—	1995P	138,337	—	64.00

CIVIL WAR. KM# 255 Obv. Designer: Don Troiani and Edgar Z. Steever
Rev. Designer: John Mercanti

Date	Mintage	MS-65	Prf-65
1995P	45,866	74.00	
1995S	437,114		78.00

SPECIAL OLYMPICS WORLD GAMES. KM# 266 Obv. Designer: Jamie Wyeth and T. James Ferrell **Rev. Designer:** Thomas D. Rogers, Sr.

Date	Mintage	MS-65	Prf-65	Date	Mintage	MS-65	Prf-65
1995W	89,301	31.00	—	1995P	351,764	—	26.50

1996 ATLANTA OLYMPICS - HIGH JUMP. KM# A272   Rev. Designer: Thomas D. Rogers, Sr. **Obverse:** High jumper

Date	Mintage	MS-65	Prf-65	Date	Mintage	MS-65	Prf-65
1996D	15,697	400	—	1996P	124,502	—	60.00

1996 ATLANTA OLYMPICS - ROWING. KM# 272   Rev. Designer: Thomas D. Rogers, Sr. **Obverse:** Rowing

Date	Mintage	MS-65	Prf-65	Date	Mintage	MS-65	Prf-65
1996D	16,258	345	—	1996P	151,890	—	75.00

1996 ATLANTA OLYMPICS - TENNIS. KM# 269   Rev. Designer: Thomas D. Rogers, Sr. **Obverse:** Tennis

Date	Mintage	MS-65	Prf-65
1996D	15,983	330	—
1996P	92,016	—	92.00

1996 ATLANTA PARALYMPICS - WHEELCHAIR RACER. KM# 268
Rev. Designer: Thomas D. Rogers, Sr. **Obverse:** Wheelchair racer

Date	Mintage	MS-65	Prf-65	Date	Mintage	MS-65	Prf-65
1996D	14,497	385	—	1996P	84,280	—	90.00

NATIONAL LAW ENFORCEMENT OFFICERS MEMORIAL. KM# 281
Designer: Alfred Maletsky.

Date	Mintage	MS-65	Prf-65	Date	Mintage	MS-65	Prf-65
1997P	110,428	—	135	1997P	28,575	165	—

NATIONAL COMMUNITY SERVICE. KM# 275 Obv. Designer: Thomas D. Rogers, Sr. **Rev. Designer:** William C. Cousins

Date	Mintage	MS-65	Prf-65	Date	Mintage	MS-65	Prf-65
1996S	23,500	235	—	1996S	101,543	—	82.00

U.S. BOTANIC GARDENS 175TH ANNIVERSARY. KM# 278 Designer: Edgar Z. Steever.

Date	Mintage	MS-65	Prf-65	Date	Mintage	MS-65	Prf-65
1997P	57,272	45.00	—	1997P	264,528	—	44.00

SMITHSONIAN INSTITUTION 150TH ANNIVERSARY. KM# 276
Obv. Designer: Thomas D. Rogers, Sr. **Rev. Designer:** John Mercanti

Date	Mintage	MS-65	Prf-65	Date	Mintage	MS-65	Prf-65
1996D	31,230	150	—	1996P	129,152	—	69.00

BLACK REVOLUTIONARY WAR PATRIOTS. KM# 288 Obv. Designer: John Mercanti **Rev. Designer:** Ed Dwight **Obverse:** Crispus Attucks

Date	Mintage	MS-65	Prf-65	Date	Mintage	MS-65	Prf-65
1998S	37,210	175	—	1998S	75,070	—	123

JACKIE ROBINSON. KM# 279 Obv. Designer: Alfred Maletsky **Rev. Designer:** T. James Ferrell

Date	Mintage	MS-65	Prf-65
1997S	30,007	103	—
1997S	110,495	—	85.00

ROBERT F. KENNEDY. KM# 287 Obv. Designer: Thomas D. Rogers, Sr. **Rev. Designer:** James M. Peed and Thomas D. Rogers, Sr.

Date	Mintage	MS-65	Prf-65
1998S	106,422	32.50	—
1998S	99,020	—	43.00

DOLLEY MADISON. KM# 298 Designer: Tiffany & Co..

Date	Mintage	MS-65	Prf-65	Date	Mintage	MS-65	Prf-65
1999P	22,948	50.00	—	1999P	158,247	—	48.00

YELLOWSTONE. KM# 299 Obv. Designer: Edgar Z. Steever
Rev. Designer: William C. Cousins

Date	Mintage	MS-65	Prf-65	Date	Mintage	MS-65	Prf-65
1999P	23,614	56.00	—	1999P	128,646	—	58.00

LEIF ERICSON. KM# 313 Obv. Designer: John Mercanti **Rev. Designer:** T. James Ferrell

Date	Mintage	MS-65	Prf-65	Date	Mintage	MS-65	Prf-65
2000P	28,150	92.50	—	2000P	58,612	—	70.00
2000 Iceland	15,947	—	25.00				

LIBRARY OF CONGRESS BICENTENNIAL. KM# 311 Obv. Designer: Thomas D. Rogers, Sr. **Rev. Designer:** John Mercanti

Date	Mintage	MS-65	Prf-65	Date	Mintage	MS-65	Prf-65
2000P	52,771	43.00	—	2000P	196,900	—	41.00

$5 (HALF EAGLE)

STATUE OF LIBERTY CENTENNIAL. KM# 215 Designer: Elizabeth Jones.

Date	Mintage	MS-65	Prf-65	Date	Mintage	MS-65	Prf-65
1986W	95,248	226	—	1986W	404,013	—	226

CONSTITUTION BICENTENNIAL. KM# 221 Designer: Marcel Jovine.

Date	Mintage	MS-65	Prf-65	Date	Mintage	MS-65	Prf-65
1987W	214,225	226	—	1987W	651,659	—	226

1988 OLYMPICS. KM# 223 Obv. Designer: Elizabeth Jones **Rev. Designer:** Marcel Jovine

Date	Mintage	MS-65	Prf-65	Date	Mintage	MS-65	Prf-65
1988W	62,913	226	—	1988W	281,456	—	226

CONGRESS BICENTENNIAL. KM# 226 Obv. Designer: John Mercanti

Date	Mintage	MS-65	Prf-65	Date	Mintage	MS-65	Prf-65
1989W	46,899	226	—	1989W	164,690	—	226

MOUNT RUSHMORE 50TH ANNIVERSARY. KM# 230 Obv. Designer: John Mercanti **Rev. Designer:** Robert Lamb and William C. Cousins

Date	Mintage	MS-65	Prf-65	Date	Mintage	MS-65	Prf-65
1991W	31,959	285	—	1991W	111,991	—	226

1992 OLYMPICS. KM# 235 Obv. Designer: James C. Sharpe and T. James Ferrell **Rev. Designer:** James M. Peed

Date	Mintage	MS-65	Prf-65	Date	Mintage	MS-65	Prf-65
1992W	27,732	310	—	1992W	77,313	—	240

COLUMBUS QUINCENTENARY. KM# 239 Obv. Designer: T. James Ferrell **Rev. Designer:** Thomas D. Rogers, Sr.

Date	Mintage	MS-65	Prf-65	Date	Mintage	MS-65	Prf-65
1992W	79,730	—	285	1992W	24,329	320	—

JAMES MADISON - BILL OF RIGHTS. KM# 242 Obv. Designer: Scott R. Blazek
Rev. Designer: Joseph D. Peña

Date	Mintage	MS-65	Prf-65	Date	Mintage	MS-65	Prf-65
1993W	78,651	—	265	1993W	22,266	325	—

WORLD WAR II 50TH ANNIVERSARY. KM# 245 Obv. Designer: Charles J.
Madsen Rev. Designer: Edward S. Fisher

Date	Mintage	MS-65	Prf-65	Date	Mintage	MS-65	Prf-65
1993W	65,461	—	330	1993W	23,089	360	—

1994 WORLD CUP SOCCER. KM# 248 Obv. Designer: William J. Krawczewicz
Rev. Designer: Dean McMullen

Date	Mintage	MS-65	Prf-65	Date	Mintage	MS-65	Prf-65
1994W	22,464	325	—	1994W	89,619	—	265

1996 OLYMPICS - STADIUM. KM# 265 Obverse: Stadium

Date	Mintage	MS-65	Prf-65	Date	Mintage	MS-65	Prf-65
1995W	43,124	—	535	1995W	10,579	1,200	—

1996 OLYMPICS - TORCH RUNNER. KM# 261 Obverse: Torch runner

Date	Mintage	MS-65	Prf-65	Date	Mintage	MS-65	Prf-65
1995W	57,442	—	410	1995W	14,675	775	—

CIVIL WAR. KM# 256 Obv. Designer: Don Troiani Rev. Designer: Alfred Maletsky

Date	Mintage	MS-65	Prf-65	Date	Mintage	MS-65	Prf-65
1995W	12,735	900	—	1995W	55,246	—	535

1996 OLYMPICS - CAULDRON. KM# 270 Obverse: Cauldron

Date	Mintage	MS-65	Prf-65	Date	Mintage	MS-65	Prf-65
1996W	38,555	—	600	1996W	9,210	1,000	—

1996 OLYMPICS - FLAG BEARER. KM# 274 Obverse: Flag bearer

Date	Mintage	MS-65	Prf-65	Date	Mintage	MS-65	Prf-65
1996W	32,886	—	615	1996W	9,174	1,050	—

SMITHSONIAN INSTITUTION 150TH ANNIVERSARY. KM# 277
Obv. Designer: Alfred Maletsky Rev. Designer: T. James Ferrell

Date	Mintage	MS-65	Prf-65	Date	Mintage	MS-65	Prf-65
1996W	9,068	1,500	—	1996W	29,474	—	720

FRANKLIN DELANO ROOSEVELT. KM# 282 Obv. Designer: T. James Ferrell
Rev. Designer: James M. Peed and Thomas D. Rogers, Sr.

Date	Mintage	MS-65	Prf-65	Date	Mintage	MS-65	Prf-65
1997W	11,894	1,100	—	1997W	29,474	—	565

JACKIE ROBINSON. KM# 280 Obv. Designer: William C. Cousins
Rev. Designer: James M. Peed

Date	Mintage	MS-65	Prf-65	Date	Mintage	MS-65	Prf-65
1997W	5,202	5,750	—	1997W	24,546	—	900

GEORGE WASHINGTON DEATH BICENTENNIAL. KM# 300 Designer: Laura
G. Fraser.

Date	Mintage	MS-65	Prf-65	Date	Mintage	MS-65	Prf-65
1999W	22,511	475	—	1999W	41,693	—	475

$10 (EAGLE)

1984 OLYMPICS. KM# 211 0.9000 Gold 0.4837 oz. AGW. 27 mm. 16.7180 g.
Obv. Designer: James M. Peed and John Mercanti Rev. Designer: John Mercanti

Date	Mintage	MS-65	Prf-65	Date	Mintage	MS-65	Prf-65
1984W	75,886	453	—	1984S	48,551	—	453
1984P	33,309	—	453	1984W	381,085	—	453
1984D	34,533	—	453				

LIBRARY OF CONGRESS. KM# 312 Platinum-Gold-Alloy 16.2590 g.
Obv. Designer: John Mercanti Rev. Designer: Thomas D. Rogers, Sr.
Notes: Composition is 48 percent platinum, 48 percent gold, and 4 percent alloy.

Date	Mintage	MS-65	Prf-65	Date	Mintage	MS-65	Prf-65
2000W	6,683	3,600	—	2000W	27,167	—	1,350

Date	Mintage	Unc	Prf.
1998W	39,653	—	143
1999	2,750,338	102	—
1999W	48,426	—	165
1999 Die error	—	575	—
2000	569,153	138	—
2000W	50,000	—	143

AMERICAN EAGLE BULLION COINS

SILVER DOLLAR

KM# 273   0.9993 **SILVER**   0.9993 oz. ASW.   40.6mm.   31.1050 g.
Obv. Designer: Adolph A. Weinman   **Rev. Designer:** John Mercanti

Date	Mintage	Unc	Prf.
1986	5,393,005	19.40	—
1986S	1,446,778	—	38.00
1987	11,442,335	17.90	—
1987S	904,732	—	37.00
1988	5,004,646	17.90	—
1988S	557,370	—	45.00
1989	5,203,327	17.90	—
1989S	617,694	—	37.00
1990	5,840,210	17.90	—
1990S	695,510	—	37.00
1991	7,191,066	17.90	—
1991S	511,924	—	44.00
1992	5,540,068	22.50	—
1992S	498,552	—	40.00
1993	6,763,762	22.50	—
1993P	403,625	—	136
1994	4,227,319	17.90	—
1994P	372,168	—	215
1995	4,672,051	23.00	—
1995P	395,400	—	155
1995W 10th Anniversary	30,125	—	3,550
1996	3,603,386	60.00	—
1996P	473,021	—	110
1997	4,295,004	23.00	—
1997P	429,682	—	132
1998	4,847,549	22.50	—
1998P	452,319	—	44.00
1999	7,408,640	17.90	—
1999P	549,769	—	47.00
2000P	600,000	—	39.00
2000	9,239,132	22.50	—

GOLD $5

KM# 216   0.9167 **GOLD**   0.1000 oz. AGW.   16.5mm.   3.3930 g.
Obv. Designer: Augustus Saint-Gaudens   **Rev. Designer:** Miley Busiek

Date	Mintage	Unc	Prf.
MCMLXXXVI (1986)	912,609	104	—
MCMLXXXVII (1987)	580,266	104	—
MCMLXXXVIII (1988)	159,500	200	—
MCMLXXXVIII (1988)P	143,881	—	143
MCMLXXXIX (1989)	264,790	104	—
MCMLXXXIX (1989)P	82,924	—	148
MCMXC (1990)	210,210	104	—
MCMXC (1990)P	99,349	—	148
MCMXCI (1991)	165,200	108	—
MCMXCI (1991)P	70,344	—	143
1992	209,300	104	—
1992P	64,902	—	143
1993	210,709	104	—
1993P	58,649	—	143
1994	206,380	105	—
1994W	62,100	—	143
1995	223,025	104	—
1995W	62,650	—	143
1996	401,964	104	—
1996W	58,440	—	143
1997	528,515	102	—
1997W	35,000	—	143
1998	1,344,520	103	—

GOLD $10

KM# 217   0.9167 **GOLD**   0.2500 oz. AGW.   22mm.   8.4830 g.
Obv. Designer: Augustus Saint-Gaudens   **Rev. Designer:** Miley Busiek

Date	Mintage	Unc	Prf.
MCMLXXXVI (1986)	726,031	246	—
MCMLXXXVII (1987)	269,255	246	—
MCMLXXXVIII (1988)	49,000	246	—
MCMLXXXVIII (1988)P	98,028	—	265
MCMLXXXIX (1989)	81,789	246	—
MCMLXXXIX (1989)P	53,593	—	265
MCMXC (1990)	41,000	246	—
MCMXC (1990)P	62,674	—	265
MCMXCI (1991)	36,100	375	—
MCMXCI (1991)P	50,839	—	265
1992	59,546	246	—
1992P	46,290	—	265
1993	71,864	246	—
1993P	46,271	—	265
1994	72,650	246	—
1994W	47,600	—	265
1995	83,752	246	—
1995W	47,545	—	265
1996	60,318	246	—
1996W	39,190	—	265
1997	108,805	246	—
1997W	29,800	—	265
1998	309,829	246	—
1998W	29,733	—	265
1999	564,232	246	—
1999W	34,416	—	265
1999 Die error	—	900	—
2000	128,964	332	—
2000W	36,000	—	265

GOLD $25

KM# 218   0.9167 **GOLD**   0.5000 oz. AGW.   27mm.   16.9660 g.
Obv. Designer: Augustus Saint-Gaudens   **Rev. Designer:** Miley Busiek

Date	Mintage	Unc	Prf.
MCMLXXXVI (1986)	599,566	498	—
MCMLXXXVII (1987)	131,255	491	—
MCMLXXXVII (1987)P	143,398	—	644
MCMLXXXVIII (1988)	45,000	491	—
MCMLXXXVIII (1988)P	76,528	—	644
MCMLXXXIX (1989)	44,829	550	—
MCMLXXXIX (1989)P	44,264	—	644
MCMXC (1990)	31,000	750	—
MCMXC (1990)P	51,636	—	644
MCMXCI (1991)	24,100	1,350	—
MCMXCI (1991)P	53,125	—	644
1992	54,404	531	—
1992P	40,982	—	644
1993	73,324	491	—
1993P	43,319	—	644
1994	62,400	491	—
1994W	44,100	—	644
1995	53,474	491	—
1995W	45,511	—	644
1996	39,287	491	—
1996W	35,937	—	644
1997	79,605	491	—
1997W	26,350	—	644
1998	169,029	491	—
1998W	25,896	—	644
1999	263,013	491	—
1999W	30,452	—	644
1999 Die error	—	—	—
2000	79,287	644	—
2000W	32,000	—	644

GOLD $50

KM# 219 0.9167 **GOLD** 100000 oz. AGW. 32.7mm. 33.9310 g.
Obv. Designer: Augustus Saint-Gaudens **Rev. Designer:** Miley Busiek

Date	Mintage	Unc	Prf.
MCMLXXXVI (1986)	1,362,650	965	—
MCMLXXXVI (1986)W	446,290	—	1,287
MCMLXXXVII (1987)	1,045,500	965	—
MCMLXXXVII (1987)W	147,498	—	1,287
MCMLXXXVIII (1988)	465,000	965	—
MCMLXXXVIII (1988)W	87,133	—	1,287
MCMLXXXIX (1989)	—	965	—
MCMLXXXIX (1989)W	53,960	—	1,287
MCMXC (1990)	373,210	965	—
MCMXC (1990)W	62,401	—	1,287
MCMXCI (1991)	243,100	965	—
MCMXCI (1991)W	50,411	—	1,287
1992	275,000	965	—
1992W	44,835	—	1,287
1993	480,192	965	—
1993W	34,389	—	1,287
1994	221,633	965	—
1994W	36,300	—	1,287
1995	200,636	965	—
1995W	46,553	—	1,287
1996	189,148	965	—
1996W	37,302	—	1,287
1997	664,508	965	—
1997W	28,000	—	1,287
1998	1,468,530	965	—
1998W	26,060	—	1,297
1999	1,505,026	965	—
1999W	31,446	—	1,287
1999 Die error	—	1,800	—
2000	433,319	1,287	—
2000W	33,000	—	1,287

PLATINUM $10

KM# 283 0.9995 **PLATINUM** 0.0999 oz. 3.1100 g. **Obv. Designer:** John Mercanti
Rev. Designer: Thomas D. Rogers Sr

Date	Mintage	Unc	Prf.
1997	70,250	166	—
1997W	36,996	—	167
1998	39,525	110	—
1999	55,955	110	—
2000	34,027	110	—

KM# 289 0.9995 **PLATINUM** 0.0999 oz. 3.1100 g. **Obv. Designer:** John Mercanti

Date	Mintage	Unc	Prf.
1998W	19,832	—	167

KM# 301 0.9995 **PLATINUM** 0.0999 oz. 3.1100 g. **Obv. Designer:** John Mercanti

Date	Mintage	Unc	Prf.
1999W	19,123	—	167

KM# 314 0.9995 **PLATINUM** 0.0999 oz. 3.1100 g. **Obv. Designer:** John Mercanti

Date	Mintage	Unc	Prf.
2000W	15,651	—	167

PLATINUM $25

KM# 284 0.9995 **PLATINUM** 0.2502 oz. 7.7857 g. **Obv. Designer:** John Mercanti
Rev. Designer: Thomas D. Rogers Sr

Date	Mintage	Unc	Prf.
1997	27,100	272	—
1997W	18,628	—	300
1998	38,887	272	—
1999	39,734	272	—
2000	20,054	272	—

KM# 290 0.9995 **PLATINUM** 0.2502 oz. 7.7857 g. **Obv. Designer:** John Mercanti

Date	Mintage	Unc	Prf.
1998W	14,860	—	297

KM# 302 0.9995 **PLATINUM** 0.2502 oz. 7.7857 g. **Obv. Designer:** John Mercanti

Date	Mintage	Unc	Prf.
1999W	13,514	—	297

KM# 315 0.9995 **PLATINUM** 0.2502 oz. 7.7857 g. **Obv. Designer:** John Mercanti

Date	Mintage	Unc	Prf.
2000W	11,995	—	297

PLATINUM $50

KM# 285 0.9995 **PLATINUM** 0.4997 oz. 15.5520 g. **Obv. Designer:** John Mercanti
Rev. Designer: Thomas D. Rogers Sr

Date	Mintage	Unc	Prf.
1997	20,500	552	—
1997W	15,432	—	602
1998	32,415	552	—
1999	32,309	552	—
2000	18,892	552	—

KM# 291 0.9995 **PLATINUM** 0.4997 oz. 15.5520 g. **Obv. Designer:** John Mercanti

Date	Mintage	Unc	Prf.
1998W	13,821	—	602

KM# 303 0.9995 **PLATINUM** 0.4997 oz. 15.5520 g. **Obv. Designer:** John Mercanti

Date	Mintage	Unc	Prf.
1999W	11,098	—	602

KM# 316 0.9995 **PLATINUM** 0.4997 oz. 15.5520 g. **Obv. Designer:** John Mercanti

Date	Mintage	Unc	Prf.
2000W	11,049	—	602

PLATINUM $100

KM# 286 0.9995 **PLATINUM** 0.9995 oz. 31.1050 g. **Obv. Designer:** John Mercanti
Rev. Designer: Thomas D. Rogers Sr

Date	Mintage	Unc	Prf.
1997	56,000	1,062	—
1997W	15,885	—	1,140
1998	133,002	1,062	—
1999	56,707	1,062	—
2000	18,892	1,062	—

KM# 292 0.9995 **PLATINUM** 0.9995 oz. 31.1050 g. **Obv. Designer:** John Mercanti

Date	Mintage	Unc	Prf.
1998W	14,203	—	1,140

KM# 304 0.9995 **PLATINUM** 0.9995 oz. 31.1050 g. **Obv. Designer:** John Mercanti

Date	Mintage	Unc	Prf.
1999W	—	—	1,140

KM# 317 0.9995 **PLATINUM** 0.9995 oz. 31.1050 g. **Obv. Designer:** John Mercanti

Date	Mintage	Unc	Prf.
2000W	—	—	1,140

UNCIRCULATED ROLLS

Listings are for rolls containing uncirculated coins. Large date and small date varieties for 1960 and 1970 apply to the one cent coins.

Date	Cents	Nickels	Dimes	Quarters	Halves
1938	485	540	1,100	3,200	1,850
1938D	510	500	1,075	—	—
1938S	385	365	1,350	3,250	—
1938D Buffalo	—	1,150	—	—	—
1939	180	160	620	1,040	1,250
1939D	360	4,200	515	1,875	1,975
1939S	240	2,750	1,850	3,200	2,400
1940	225	145	550	1,950	1,000
1940D	250	120	780	5,500	—
1940S	375	235	685	1,275	1,200
1941	170	215	440	775	750
1941D	335	270	750	2,750	1,200
1941S	360	280	560	2,500	3,000
1942	140	270	475	485	690
1942P	—	565	—	—	—
1942D	125	2,350	800	1,060	1,350
1942S	650	525	1,100	5,500	1,475
1943	100.00	275	490	420	725
1943D	160	265	640	2,250	1,775
1943S	425	315	675	2,450	1,365
1944	30.00	720	475	425	715
1944D	30.00	680	690	750	1,250
1944S	35.00	485	695	980	1,300
1945	125	410	450	365	730
1945D	120	325	530	1,050	1,050
1945S	26.50	270	525	640	965
1946	18.00	110	95.00	375	1,050
1946D	26.50	100.00	105	385	900
1946S	27.00	55.00	130	350	900
1947	145	58.00	260	750	1,000
1947D	26.50	70.00	285	660	1,000
1947S	30.00	70.00	230	475	—
1948	52.00	80.00	195	250	485
1948D	66.00	125	330	685	425
1948S	150	90.00	265	470	—
1949	110	325	1,360	2,650	1,450
1949D	72.00	215	550	1,350	1,475
1949S	140	138	2,400	—	2,325
1950	67.00	170	740	420	900
1950D	37.00	535	245	460	875
1950S	78.00	—	1,575	850	—
1951	70.00	265	170	435	425
1951D	23.00	355	80.00	365	800
1951S	60.00	280	735	1,450	925
1952	130	215	115	565	410
1952D	17.00	260	115	315	255
1952S	400	52.00	300	1,250	1,650
1953	26.50	26.00	120	660	490
1953D	21.00	19.00	82.00	180	285
1953S	32.00	52.00	82.00	320	875
1954	19.00	66.00	70.00	200	215
1954D	18.00	39.00	70.00	220	220
1954S	19.00	66.00	70.00	160	480
1955	21.00	26.00	70.00	150	365
1955D	15.50	9.00	70.00	145	—
1955S	27.50	—	70.00	—	—
1956	13.00	8.50	70.00	175	320
1956D	12.00	8.50	70.00	165	—
1957	11.00	13.00	70.00	145	180
1957D	11.50	6.50	68.00	145	180
1958	11.00	8.00	68.00	145	165
1958D	11.00	6.50	68.00	145	160
1959	2.00	6.00	68.00	145	150
1959D	2.00	6.50	68.00	145	185
1960 large date	2.00	5.50	68.00	145	145
1960 small date	220	—	—	—	—
1960D large date	2.00	7.00	68.00	140	160
1960D small date	2.00	—	—	—	—
1961	2.00	5.50	68.00	140	144
1961D	2.00	5.50	68.00	140	144
1962	2.00	6.25	68.00	140	144
1962D	2.00	7.50	68.00	140	144
1963	2.00	5.50	68.00	140	140
1963D	2.00	6.00	68.00	140	140
1964	2.00	5.00	68.00	140	140
1964D	2.00	5.00	68.00	140	140
1965	2.25	6.00	9.00	27.00	59.00
1966	4.00	6.50	11.50	33.00	63.00

Date	Cents	Nickels	Dimes	Quarters	Halves
1967	4.25	10.50	10.25	27.00	59.00
1968	2.00	—	10.00	32.00	—
1968D	2.00	6.60	10.00	33.00	59.00
1968S	2.00	7.20	—	—	—
1969	5.00	—	44.00	100.00	—
1969D	2.00	7.00	23.00	95.00	59.00
1969S	2.00	7.50	—	—	—
1970	2.50	—	8.50	26.00	—
1970D	2.00	5.00	9.00	16.00	310
1970S	3.00	5.00	—	—	—
1970S small date	2,600	—	—	—	—
1971	5.00	29.00	16.50	42.00	28.00
1971D	3.00	8.00	10.00	24.00	17.00
1971S	3.50	—	—	—	—
1972	2.00	7.00	12.00	25.00	32.00
1972D	2.00	6.00	10.50	21.00	29.00
1972S	2.50	—	—	—	—
1973	2.00	4.50	11.50	22.00	31.00
1973D	2.00	7.00	10.00	24.00	21.00
1973S	3.00	—	—	—	—
1974	2.00	4.50	8.50	21.00	18.00
1974D	2.00	6.50	8.00	17.50	22.00
1974S	3.00	—	—	—	—
1975	2.00	13.00	10.00	—	—
1975D	2.00	5.50	12.50	—	—
1976	2.00	13.50	21.00	19.75	16.50
1976D	3.00	12.00	20.00	19.50	16.50
1977	2.00	5.50	10.50	16.50	26.00
1977D	2.50	6.00	9.75	17.50	29.00
1978	2.00	4.50	8.00	16.00	38.00
1978D	2.00	5.00	9.00	17.00	52.00
1979	2.00	4.75	8.75	17.00	24.50
1979D	2.00	5.75	8.00	23.00	26.00
1980	2.00	4.50	8.00	17.00	22.50
1980D	2.00	4.75	7.75	17.00	23.00
1981	2.00	4.25	7.50	16.50	24.50
1981D	2.00	4.75	8.00	16.50	24.50
1982	2.00	265	245	280	98.00
1982D	2.00	55.00	66.00	155	95.00
1983	3.75	80.00	235	1,075	108
1983D	11.00	37.00	39.00	410	116
1984	5.50	24.00	8.50	17.50	36.00
1984D	15.00	7.00	22.00	29.00	40.00
1985	4.00	10.00	10.00	31.00	76.00
1985D	3.50	8.00	9.50	22.00	66.00
1986	21.00	9.00	26.00	98.00	130
1986D	28.00	29.00	24.00	225	102
1987	3.00	6.50	7.75	16.00	65.00
1987D	3.50	4.50	9.00	16.00	55.00
1988	6.25	6.00	10.00	32.00	79.00
1988D	4.50	9.00	9.50	24.00	52.00
1989	3.75	6.00	13.50	22.50	44.00
1989D	3.75	8.75	13.50	21.00	34.00
1990	4.40	11.50	12.50	21.00	44.00
1990D	3.75	14.00	10.00	26.00	62.00
1991	2.75	12.50	10.00	31.00	58.00
1991D	3.50	12.50	13.00	35.00	52.00
1992	3.00	48.00	8.50	43.00	24.00
1992D	4.75	9.00	8.50	29.00	54.00
1993	3.50	13.50	9.75	40.00	62.00
1993D	4.00	17.50	14.00	37.50	24.00
1994	2.00	8.00	12.50	44.00	16.50
1994D	2.00	8.50	12.50	49.00	23.00
1995	2.25	11.00	17.50	47.00	16.00
1995D	2.25	20.00	21.00	41.00	16.00
1996	2.50	8.00	12.00	19.00	17.00
1996D	3.00	8.50	12.50	28.00	16.00
1997	2.75	14.50	31.00	23.00	17.00
1997D	3.25	62.00	12.50	40.00	16.00
1998	2.00	13.50	10.50	17.50	15.50
1998D	2.00	14.00	9.50	18.50	16.50
1999P	2.25	6.00	9.00	—	18.50
1999D	2.00	7.00	9.00	—	17.50
2000P	2.00	6.25	8.50	—	14.50
2000D	2.00	5.50	8.00	—	16.00

MINT SETS

Mint, or uncirculated, sets contain one uncirculated coin of each denomination from each mint produced for circulation that year. Values listed here are only for those sets sold by the U.S. Mint. Sets were not offered in years not listed. In years when the Mint did not offer the sets, some private companies compiled and marketed uncirculated sets. Mint sets from 1947 through 1958 contained two examples of each coin mounted in cardboard holders, which caused the coins to tarnish. Beginning in 1959, the sets have been packaged in sealed Pliofilm packets and include only one specimen of each coin struck for that year (both P & D mints). Listings for 1965, 1966 and 1967 are for "special mint sets," which were of higher quality than regular mint sets and were prooflike. They were packaged in plastic cases. The 1970 large-date and small-date varieties are distinguished by the size of the date on the coin. The 1976 three-piece set contains the quarter, half dollar and dollar with the Bicentennial design. The 1971 and 1972 sets do not include a dollar coin; the 1979 set does not include an S-mint-marked dollar. Mint sets issued prior to 1959 were double sets (containing two of each coin) packaged in cardboard with a paper overlay. Origional sets will always be toned and can bring large premiums if nicely preserved with good color.

Date	Sets Sold	Issue Price	Value
1947 Est. 5,000	—	4.87	1,375
1948 Est. 6,000	—	4.92	750
1949 Est. 5,200	—	5.45	935
1950 None issued	—	—	—
1951	8,654	6.75	900
1952	11,499	6.14	825
1953	15,538	6.14	565
1954	25,599	6.19	265
1955 flat pack	49,656	3.57	168
1956	45,475	3.34	165
1957	32,324	4.40	275
1958	50,314	4.43	150
1959	187,000	2.40	55.00
1960 large date	260,485	2.40	29.50
1961	223,704	2.40	45.00
1962	385,285	2.40	25.00
1963	606,612	2.40	25.00
1964	1,008,108	2.40	25.00
1965 Special Mint Set	2,360,000	4.00	4.00
1966 Special Mint Set	2,261,583	4.00	5.15
1967 Special Mint Set	1,863,344	4.00	9.00
1968	2,105,128	2.50	3.25
1969	1,817,392	2.50	4.00
1970 large date	2,038,134	2.50	14.00
1970 small date	Inc. above	2.50	70.00
1971	2,193,396	3.50	3.00
1972	2,750,000	3.50	3.25
1973	1,767,691	6.00	14.50
1974	1,975,981	6.00	5.90
1975	1,921,488	6.00	7.00
1976 3 coins	4,908,319	9.00	12.00
1976	1,892,513	6.00	5.75
1977	2,006,869	7.00	7.50
1978	2,162,609	7.00	6.50
1979 Type I	2,526,000	8.00	4.75
1980	2,815,066	9.00	6.50
1981 Type I	2,908,145	11.00	14.00
1982 & 1983 None issued	—	—	—
1984	1,832,857	7.00	3.65
1985	1,710,571	7.00	4.25
1986	1,153,536	7.00	8.75
1987	2,890,758	7.00	4.25
1988	1,646,204	7.00	4.50
1989	1,987,915	7.00	4.00
1990	1,809,184	7.00	4.25
1991	1,352,101	7.00	5.50
1992	1,500,143	7.00	5.00
1993	1,297,094	8.00	5.50
1994	1,234,813	8.00	4.00
1995	1,038,787	8.00	8.25
1996	1,457,949	8.00	15.00
1997	950,473	8.00	12.50
1998	1,187,325	8.00	4.00
1999 9 piece	1,421,625	14.95	14.50
2000	1,490,160	14.95	10.25

MODERN COMMEMORATIVE COIN SETS

Olympic, 1983-1984

Date	Price
1983 & 1984 3 coin set: 1983 and one 1984 uncirculated dollar and 1984W uncirculated gold $10; KM209, 210, 211.	455
1983S & 1984S 3 coin set: proof 1983 and 1984 dollar and 1984W gold $10; KM209, 210, 211.	455
1983 & 1984 6 coin set: 1983S and 1984S uncirculated and proof dollars, 1984W uncirculated and proof gold $10; KM209, 210, 211.	910
1983S & 1984S 2 coin set: proof dollars.	22.50
1983 collectors 3 coin set: 1983 PDS uncirculated dollars; KM209.	37.50
1984 collectors 3 coin set: 1984 PDS uncirculated dollars; KM210.	38.50

Statue of Liberty

Date	Price
1986 2 coin set: uncirculated silver dollar and clad half dollar; KM212, 214.	17.00
1986 2 coin set: proof silver dollar and clad half dollar; KM212, 214.	17.00
1986 3 coin set: uncirculated silver dollar, clad half dollar and gold $5; KM212, 214, 215.	225
1986 3 coin set: proof silver dollar, clad half dollar and gold $5; KM212, 214, 215.	225

Date	Price
1986 6 coin set: 1 each of the proof and uncirculated issues; KM212, 214, 215.	450

Constitution

Date	Price
1987 2 coin set: uncirculated silver dollar and gold $5; KM220, 221.	220
1987 2 coin set: proof silver dollar and gold $5; KM220, 221.	220
1987 4 coin set: silver dollar and $5 gold proof and uncirculated issues; KM220, 221.	445

Olympic, 1988

Date	Price
1988 2 coin set: uncirculated silver dollar and gold $5; KM222, 223.	220
1988 2 coin set: proof silver dollar and gold $5; KM222, 223.	220
1988 4 coin set: silver dollar and $5 gold proof and uncirculated issues; KM222, 223.	440

Congress

Date	Price
1989 2 coin set: uncirculated silver dollar and clad half dollar; KM224, 225.	20.00
1989 2 coin set: proof silver dollar and clad half dollar; KM224, 225.	21.00
1989 3 coin set: uncirculated silver dollar, clad half and gold $5; KM224, 225, 226.	220
1989 3 coin set: proof silver dollar, clad half and gold $5; KM224, 225, 226.	220
1989 6 coin set: 1 each of the proof and uncirculated issues; KM224, 225, 226.	440

Mt. Rushmore

Date	Price
1991 2 coin set: uncirculated half dollar and silver dollar; KM228, 229.	45.00
1991 2 coin set: proof half dollar and silver dollar; KM228, 229.	45.00
1991 3 coin set: uncirculated half dollar, silver dollar and gold $5; KM228, 229, 230.	300
1991 3 coin set: proof half dollar, silver dollar and gold $5; KM228, 229, 230.	225
1991 6 coin set: 1 each of proof and uncirculated issues; KM228, 229, 230.	495

Olympic, 1992

Date	Price
1992 2 coin set: uncirculated half dollar and silver dollar; KM233, 234.	28.00
1992 2 coin set: proof half dollar and silver dollar; KM233, 234.	28.00
1992 3 coin set: uncirculated half dollar, silver dollar and gold $5; KM233, 234, 235.	275
1992 3 coin set: proof half dollar, silver dollar and gold $5; KM233, 234, 235.	240
1992 6 coin set: 1 each of proof and uncirculated issues; KM233, 234, 235.	520

Columbus Quincentenary

Date	Price
1992 2 coin set: uncirculated half dollar and silver dollar; KM237, 238.	35.00
1992 2 coin set: proof half dollar and silver dollar; KM237, 238.	39.00
1992 3 coin set: uncirculated half dollar, silver dollar and gold $5; KM237, 238, 239.	320
1992 3 coin set: proof half dollar, silver dollar and gold $5; KM237, 238, 239.	265
1992 6 coin set: 1 each of proof and uncirculated issues; KM237, 238, 239.	780

Jefferson

Date	Price
1993 Jefferson: dollar, 1994 matte proof nickel and $2 note; KM249, 192.	100.00

Madison / Bill of Rights

Date	Price
1993 2 coin set: uncirculated half dollar and silver dollar; KM240, 241.	28.00
1993 2 coin set: proof half dollar and silver dollar; KM240, 241.	29.00
1993 3 coin set: uncirculated half dollar, silver dollar and gold $5; KM240, 241, 242.	320
1993 3 coin set: proof half dollar, silver dollar and gold $5; KM240, 241, 242.	250
1993 6 coin set: 1 each of proof and uncirculated issues; KM240, 241, 242.	550

World War II

Date	Price
1993 2 coin set: uncirculated half dollar and silver dollar; KM243, 244.	49.00
1993 2 coin set: proof half dollar and silver dollar; KM243, 244.	55.00
1993 3 coin set: uncirculated half dollar, silver dollar and gold $5; KM243, 244, 245.	345
1993 3 coin set: proof half dollar, silver dollar and gold $5; KM243, 244, 245.	335
1993 6 coin set: 1 each of proof and uncirculated issues; KM243, 244, 245.	665

World Cup

Date	Price
1994 2 coin set: uncirculated half dollar and silver dollar; KM246, 247.	32.00
1994 2 coin set: proof half dollar and silver dollar; KM246, 247.	37.00
1994 3 coin set: uncirculated half dollar, silver dollar and gold $5; KM246, 247, 248.	290
1994 3 coin set: proof half dollar, silver dollar and gold $5; KM246, 247, 248.	250
1994 6 coin set: 1 each of proof and uncirculated issues; KM246, 247, 248.	525

U.S. Veterans

Date	Price
1994 3 coin set: uncirculated POW, Vietnam, Women dollars; KM250, 251, 252.	170
1994 3 coin set: proof POW, Vietnam, Women dollars; KM250, 251, 252.	120

Olympic, 1995-96

Date	Price
1995 4 coin set: uncirculated basketball half, $1 gymnast & blind runner, $5 torch runner; KM257, 259, 260, 261.	715
1995 4 coin set: proof basketball half, $1 gymnast & blind runner, $5 torch runner; KM257, 259, 260, 261.	415
1995P 2 coin set: proof $1 gymnast & blind runner; KM259, 260.	105
1995P 2 coin set: proof $1 track & field, cycling; KM263, 264.	95.00
1995-96 4 coin set: proof halves, basketball, baseball, swimming, soccer; KM257, 262, 267, 271.	140
1995 & 96 8 coins in cherry wood case: proof silver dollars: blind runner, gymnast, cycling, track & field, wheelchair, tennis, rowing, high jump; KM259, 260, 263, 264, 268, 269, 272, 272A.	2,150
1995 & 96 16 coins in cherry wood case: bu and proof silver dollars: blind runner, gymnast, cycling, track & field, wheelchair, tennis, rowing, high jump; KM259, 260, 263, 264, 268, 269, 272, 272A.	2,350
1995 & 96 16 coins in cherry wood case: proof half dollars: basketball, baseball, swimming, soccer, KM257, 262, 267, 271. Proof silver dollars: blind runner, gymnast, cycling, track & field, wheelchair, tennis, rowing, high jump, KM259, 260, 263, 264, 268, 269, 272, 272A. Proof $5 gold: torch runner, stadium, cauldron, flag bearer, KM 261, 265, 270, 274.	2,400

Date	Price
1995 & 96 32 coins in cherry wood case: bu & proof half dollars: basketball, baseball, swimming, soccer, KM257, 262, 267, 271. BU & proof silver dollars: blind runner, gymnast, cycling, track & field, wheelchair, tennis, rowing, high jump, KM259, 260, 263, 264, 268, 269, 272, 272A. BU & proof $5 gold: torch runner, stadium, cauldron, flag bearer, KM261, 265, 270, 274.	6,600
1996P 2 coin set: proof $1 wheelchair & tennis; KM268, 269.	160
1996P 2 coin set: proof $1 rowing & high jump; KM272, 272A.	130

Civil War

Date	Price
1995 2 coin set: uncirculated half and dollar; KM254, 255.	90.00
1995 2 coin set: proof half and dollar; KM254, 255.	100.00
1995 3 coin set: uncirculated half, dollar and gold $5; KM254, 255, 256.	800
1995 3 coin set: proof half, dollar and gold $5; KM254, 255, 256.	500
1995 6 coin set: 1 each of proof and uncirculated issues; KM254, 255, 256.	1,275

Smithsonian

Date	Price
1996 2 coin set: proof dollar and $5 gold; KM276, 277.	615
1996 4 coin set: proof and B.U. ; KM276, 277.	2,100

Jackie Robinson

Date	Price
1997 2 coin set: proof dollar & $5 gold; KM279, 280.	800
1997 4 coin set: proof & BU; KM279, 280.	5,750
1997 legacy set.	850

Botanic Garden

Date	Price
1997 2 coin set: dollar, Jefferson nickel and $1 note; KM278, 192.	230

Franklin Delano Roosevelt

Date	Price
1997W 2 coin set: uncirculated and proof; KM282.	1,350

Kennedy

Date	Price
1998 2 coin set: proof; KM287.	70.00
1998 2 coin collectors set: Robert Kennedy dollar and John Kennedy half dollar; KM287, 202b. Matte finished.	325

Black Patriots

Date	Price
1998S 2 coin set: uncirculated and proof; KM288.	200

George Washington

Date	Price
1999 2 coin set: proof and uncirculated gold $5; KM300.	800

Dolley Madison

Date	Price
1999 2 coin set: proof and uncirculated silver dollars; KM298.	77.00

Yellowstone National Park

Date	Price
1999 2 coin set: proof and uncirculated silver dollars; KM299.	88.00

Millennium Coin & Currency

Date	Price
2000 2 coin set: uncirculated Sacagewea $1, silver Eagle & $1 note.	72.00

Leif Ericson

Date	Price
2000 2 coin set: proof and uncirculated silver dollars; KM313.	84.00

PROOF SETS

Proof coins are produced through a special process involving specially selected, highly polished planchets and dies. They usually receive two strikings from the coin press at increased pressure. The result is a coin with mirrorlike surfaces and, in recent years, a cameo effect on its raised design surfaces. Proof sets have been sold off and on by the U.S. Mint since 1858. Listings here are for sets from what is commonly called the modern era, since 1936. Values for earlier proofs are included in regular date listings. Sets were not offered in years not listed. Since 1968, proof coins have been produced at the San Francisco Mint; before that they were produced at the Philadelphia Mint. In 1942 the five-cent coin was struck in two compositions. Some proof sets for that year contain only one type (five-coin set); others contain both types. Two types of packaging were used in 1955 -- a box and a flat, plastic holder. The 1960 large-date and small-date sets are distinguished by the size of the date on the cent. Some 1968 sets are missing the mint mark on the dime, the result of an error in the preparation of an obverse die. The 1970 large-date and small-date sets are distinguished by the size of the date on the cent. Some 1970 sets are missing the mint mark on the dime, the result of an error in the preparation of an obverse die. Some 1971 sets are missing the mint mark on the five-cent piece, the result of an error in the preparation of an obverse die. The 1976 three-piece set contains the quarter, half dollar and dollar with the Bicentennial designs. The 1979 and 1981 Type II sets have clearer mint marks than the Type I sets for those years. Some 1983 sets are missing the mint mark on the dime, the result of an error in the preparation of an obverse die. Prestige sets contain the five regular-issue coins plus a commemorative silver dollar from that year. Sets issued prior to 1956 came in transparent envelopes stapled together in a small square box. In mid 1955 sets were changed to a flat clear cellophane envelope. In 1968 sets were changed to a clear hard plastic case as they still are currently issued.

Date	Sets Sold	Issue Price	Value
1936	3,837	1.89	7,500

Date	Sets Sold	Issue Price	Value	Date	Sets Sold	Issue Price	Value
1937	5,542	1.89	4,350	1984S	2,748,430	11.00	6.50
1938	8,045	1.89	1,900	1984S Prestige Set	316,680	59.00	23.00
1939	8,795	1.89	1,800	1985S	3,362,821	11.00	4.25
1940	11,246	1.89	1,475	1986S	2,411,180	11.00	5.25
1941	15,287	1.89	1,450	1986S Prestige Set	599,317	48.50	23.00
1942 6 coins	21,120	1.89	1,475	1987S	3,972,233	11.00	3.75
1942 5 coins	Inc. above	1.89	1,375	1987S Prestige Set	435,495	45.00	18.75
1950	51,386	2.10	740	1988S	3,031,287	11.00	4.25
1951	57,500	2.10	630	1988S Prestige Set	231,661	45.00	29.00
1952	81,980	2.10	285	1989S	3,009,107	11.00	6.50
1953	128,800	2.10	250	1989S Prestige Set	211,087	45.00	35.00
1954	233,300	2.10	110	1990S	2,793,433	11.00	5.25
1955 box	378,200	2.10	115	1990S no S 1¢	3,555	11.00	6,250
1955 flat pack	Inc. above	2.10	168	1990S Prestige Set	506,126	45.00	22.75
1956	669,384	2.10	65.00	1990S Prestige Set, no S 1¢	Inc. above	45.00	6,500
1957	1,247,952	2.10	27.00	1991S	2,610,833	11.00	10.50
1958	875,652	2.10	52.50	1991S Prestige Set	256,954	59.00	48.50
1959	1,149,291	2.10	25.00	1992S	2,675,618	12.00	4.50
1960 large date	1,691,602	2.10	20.50	1992S Prestige Set	183,285	59.00	57.50
1960 small date	Inc. above	2.10	32.00	1992S Silver	1,009,585	21.00	12.00
1961	3,028,244	2.10	15.50	1992S Silver premier	308,055	37.00	12.00
1962	3,218,019	2.10	15.75	1993S	2,337,819	12.50	9.50
1963	3,075,645	2.10	16.00	1993S Prestige Set	224,045	57.00	28.00
1964	3,950,762	2.10	14.75	1993S Silver	570,213	21.00	24.50
1968S	3,041,509	5.00	5.85	1993S Silver premier	191,140	37.00	24.50
1968S no mint mark dime	Inc. above	5.00	17,500	1994S	2,308,701	13.00	8.75
1969S	2,934,631	5.00	6.75	1994S Prestige Set	175,893	57.00	39.00
1970S large date	2,632,810	5.00	7.75	1994S Silver	636,009	21.00	26.00
1970S small date	Inc. above	5.00	100.00	1994S Silver premier	149,320	37.50	26.00
1970S no mint mark dime	Inc. above	5.00	1,300	1995S	2,010,384	12.50	23.00
1971S	3,224,138	5.00	3.40	1995S Prestige Set	107,112	57.00	122
1971S no mint mark nickel Est. 1,655	1,655	5.00	1,850	1995S Silver	549,878	21.00	62.50
1972S	3,267,667	5.50	3.40	1995S Silver premier	130,107	37.50	62.50
1973S	2,769,624	7.00	6.50	1996S	2,085,191	16.00	11.75
1974S	2,617,350	7.00	7.25	1996S Prestige Set	55,000	57.00	400
1975S	2,909,369	7.00	9.00	1996S Silver	623,655	21.00	34.50
1975S no mint mark dime	Inc. above	7.00	46,500	1996S Silver premier	151,366	37.50	34.50
1976S 3 coins	3,998,621	12.00	12.75	1997S	1,975,000	12.50	23.50
1976S	4,149,730	7.00	7.00	1997S Prestige Set	80,000	57.00	122
1977S	3,251,152	9.00	6.25	1997S Silver	605,473	21.00	49.50
1978S	3,127,788	9.00	7.50	1997S Silver premier	136,205	37.50	49.50
1979S Type I	3,677,175	9.00	6.75	1998S	2,078,494	12.50	12.50
1979S Type II	Inc. above	9.00	98.00	1998S Silver	638,134	21.00	19.50
1980S	3,547,030	10.00	6.25	1998S Silver premier	240,658	37.50	19.50
1981S Type I	4,063,083	11.00	6.25	1999S 9 piece	2,557,899	19.95	44.00
1981S Type II	Inc. above	11.00	335	1999S 5 quarter set	1,169,958	13.95	40.00
1982S	3,857,479	11.00	3.25	1999S Silver	804,565	31.95	295
1983S	3,138,765	11.00	5.00	2000S 10 piece	3,097,442	19.95	11.50
1983S Prestige Set	140,361	59.00	72.00	2000S 5 quarter set	995,803	13.95	6.35
1983S no mint mark dime	Inc. above	11.00	1,050	2000S Silver	965,421	31.95	27.50

URUGUAY

The Oriental Republic of Uruguay (so called because of its location on the east bank of the Uruguay River) is situated on the Atlantic coast of South America between Argentina and Brazil. This South American country has an area of 68,536 sq. mi. (176,220 sq. km.) and a population of *3 million. Capital: Montevideo. Uruguay's chief economic assets are the rich, rolling grassy plains. Meat, wool, hides and skins are exported.

Uruguay was discovered in 1516 by Juan Diaz de Solis, a Spaniard, but settled by the Portuguese who founded Colony in 1680. Spain contested Portuguese possession and, after a long struggle, gained control of the country in 1778. During the general South American struggle for independence, Uruguay 's first attempt was led by Gaucho soldier Jose Gervasio Artigas leading, the Banda Oriental. It was quelled by Spanish and Portuguese forces in 1811. The armistice was soon broken and Argentine force from Buenos Aires cast off the Spanish bond in the Plata region in 1814 only to be conquered again by the Portuguese from Brazil in the struggle of 1816-20. Revolt flared anew in 1825 and independence was reasserted in 1828 with the help of Argentina. The Uruguayan Republic was established in 1830.

MINT MARKS
A – Berlin (1901)
A – Vienna (1909 and 1936)
(a)   privy marks (torch & cornucopia): Paris
Mx, Mo - Mexico City
(p) – thunderbolt: Poissy, France
So - (Small o above S): Santiago
(u) – caduceus: Utrecht

MONETARY SYSTEM
100 Centesimo = 1 Peso
1975-1993
1000 Old Pesos = 1 Nuevo (New) Peso
Commencing 1994
1000 Nuevos Pesos = 1 Peso Uruguayo

REPUBLIC

DECIMAL COINAGE

KM# 19   CENTESIMO
2.0000 g., Copper-Nickel Obv: Radiant sun design Rev: Value within wreath

Date	Mintage	F	VF	XF	Unc	BU
1901A	6,000,000	1.00	5.00	20.00	50.00	—
1901A Proof	—	Value: 225				
1909A	5,000,000	0.50	2.00	6.00	15.00	—
1924(p)	3,000,000	0.50	2.00	8.00	20.00	—
1936A	2,000,000	0.50	2.00	8.00	20.00	—

KM# 32   CENTESIMO
1.5000 g., Copper-Nickel Obv: Artigas bust right, 'HP' below Rev: Value within wreath Note: Medal rotation.

Date	Mintage	F	VF	XF	Unc	BU
1953	5,000,000	0.25	0.50	1.00	3.00	—
1953 Proof	—	Value: 150				

KM# 20   2 CENTESIMOS
3.5000 g., Copper-Nickel, 20 mm. Obv: Radiant sun design Rev: Value within wreath

Date	Mintage	F	VF	XF	Unc	BU
1901A	7,500,000	1.00	4.00	12.00	30.00	—
1909A	10,000,000	1.00	2.00	9.00	20.00	—
1924(p)	11,000,000	1.00	2.00	7.00	15.00	—
1936A	6,500,000	1.00	3.00	11.00	25.00	—
1941So	10,000,000	1.00	2.00	10.00	22.00	—

KM# 20a   2 CENTESIMOS
3.5000 g., Copper, 20 mm. Obv: Radiant sun design Rev: Value within wreath

Date	Mintage	F	VF	XF	Unc	BU
1943So	5,000,000	0.25	1.00	3.00	10.00	—
1944So	3,500,000	0.25	1.00	3.00	10.00	—
1945So	2,500,000	0.25	1.00	3.00	10.00	—
1946So	2,500,000	0.25	0.50	3.00	10.00	—
1947So	5,000,000	0.25	0.50	1.50	7.00	—
1948So	7,500,000	0.25	0.50	1.00	6.00	—
1949So	7,400,000	0.25	0.50	1.00	6.00	—
1951So	12,500,000	0.25	0.50	1.00	6.00	—

KM# 33   2 CENTESIMOS
2.5000 g., Copper-Nickel Obv: Artigas, 'HP' below Rev: Value within wreath Note: Medal rotation.

Date	Mintage	F	VF	XF	Unc	BU
1953	50,000,000	0.15	0.30	1.00	5.00	—
1953 Proof	—	Value: 65.00				

KM# 37   2 CENTESIMOS
2.0000 g., Nickel-Brass Obv: Artigas, 'HP' below Rev: Value within wreath Note: Medal rotation.

Date	Mintage	F	VF	XF	Unc	BU
1960	17,500,000	—	0.15	0.25	1.00	—
1960 Proof	—	Value: 40.00				

KM# 21   5 CENTESIMOS
5.0000 g., Copper-Nickel, 23.3 mm. Obv: Radiant sun design Rev: Value within wreath

Date	Mintage	F	VF	XF	Unc	BU
1901A	6,000,000	1.00	4.00	12.00	30.00	—
1901A Proof	—	Value: 325				
1909A	5,000,000	1.00	3.00	10.00	22.00	—
1909A Proof	—	Value: 175				
1924(p)	5,000,000	0.50	2.00	6.00	15.00	—
1936A	3,000,000	0.50	2.00	6.00	15.00	—
1941So	2,400,000	0.25	1.00	4.00	10.00	—
1941So Proof	—	Value: 200				

KM# 21a   5 CENTESIMOS
5.0000 g., Copper, 22.8 mm. Obv: Radiant sun design Rev: Value within wreath

Date	Mintage	F	VF	XF	Unc	BU
1944So	4,000,000	0.25	1.00	3.00	10.00	—
1946So	2,000,000	0.20	1.00	4.00	12.00	—
1947So	2,000,000	0.20	1.00	4.00	12.00	—
1948So	3,000,000	0.20	0.75	3.00	10.00	—
1949So	2,800,000	0.20	0.75	3.00	10.00	—
1951So	15,000,000	0.20	0.50	2.00	7.00	—

KM# 34   5 CENTESIMOS
3.5000 g., Copper-Nickel Obv: Artigas, 'HP' below Rev: Value within wreath Note: Medal rotation.

Date	Mintage	F	VF	XF	Unc	BU
1953	17,500,000	0.20	0.30	0.50	1.00	—
1953 Proof	—	Value: 75.00				

KM# 38   5 CENTESIMOS
3.5000 g., Nickel-Brass Obv: Artigas, 'HP' below Rev: Value within wreath Note: Medal rotation.

Date	Mintage	F	VF	XF	Unc	BU
1960	88,000,000	—	0.15	0.25	1.00	—
1960 Proof	—	Value: 75.00				

KM# 25   10 CENTESIMOS
8.0000 g., Aluminum-Bronze, 27 mm. Subject: Constitutional Centennial Obv: MORLON behind neck Rev: Puma walking left in front of sun rays above value

Date	Mintage	F	VF	XF	Unc	BU
1930(a)	5,000,000	2.00	4.00	12.00	50.00	—

KM# 28   10 CENTESIMOS
6.0000 g., Aluminum-Bronze, 25 mm. Obv: Head laureate right Rev: Puma walking left in front of sunrays above value

Date	Mintage	F	VF	XF	Unc	BU
1936A	2,000,000	1.50	3.50	10.00	45.00	—

KM# 35   10 CENTESIMOS
4.5000 g., Copper-Nickel Obv: Artigas, 'HP' below Rev: Value within wreath Note: Medal rotation.

Date	Mintage	F	VF	XF	Unc	BU
1953	28,250,000	0.15	0.20	0.30	1.00	—
1953 Proof	—	Value: 75.00				
1959	10,000,000	0.20	0.30	1.00	3.00	—

KM# 39   10 CENTESIMOS
4.5000 g., Nickel-Brass Obv: Artigas, 'HP' below Rev: Value within wreath Note: Medal rotation.

Date	Mintage	F	VF	XF	Unc	BU
1960	72,500,000	0.15	0.20	0.30	1.00	—
1960 Proof	—	Value: 100				

KM# 24 20 CENTESIMOS
5.0000 g., 0.8000 Silver 0.1286 oz. ASW **Obv:** Radiant sun peeks out over arms within wreath **Rev:** Head left

Date	Mintage	F	VF	XF	Unc	BU
1920	2,500,000	2.75	5.50	12.00	35.00	—

KM# 26 20 CENTESIMOS
5.0000 g., 0.8000 Silver 0.1286 oz. ASW, 25 mm. **Subject:** Constitutional Centennial **Obv:** Seated figure left above date **Rev:** Wheat stalks divide value, mint marks flank stems

Date	Mintage	F	VF	XF	Unc	BU
1930(a)	2,500,000	2.50	4.50	10.00	30.00	—

KM# 29 20 CENTESIMOS
3.0000 g., 0.7200 Silver 0.0694 oz. ASW, 19 mm. **Obv:** Head laureate right **Rev:** Wheat stalks divide value

Date	Mintage	F	VF	XF	Unc	BU
1942So	18,000,000	1.50	2.50	4.50	7.00	—

KM# 36 20 CENTESIMOS
3.0000 g., 0.7200 Silver 0.0694 oz. ASW, 19 mm. **Obv:** Head right **Rev:** Wheat stalks divide value

Date	Mintage	F	VF	XF	Unc	BU
1954(u)	10,000,000	1.25	1.75	2.50	5.00	—

KM# 44 20 CENTESIMOS
1.4000 g., Aluminum **Obv:** Head right **Rev:** Value within wreath **Note:** Medal rotation.

Date	Mintage	F	VF	XF	Unc	BU
1965So	40,000,000	0.15	0.20	0.35	1.00	—

KM# 40 25 CENTESIMOS
3.0000 g., Copper-Nickel **Obv:** 'HP' below bust **Rev:** Radiant sun peeking out above arms within wreath, value divides circle of stars **Note:** Medal rotation.

Date	Mintage	F	VF	XF	Unc	BU
1960	48,000,000	0.20	0.35	0.50	1.00	—
1960 Proof	—	Value: 80.00				

KM# 22 50 CENTESIMOS
12.5000 g., 0.9000 Silver 0.3617 oz. ASW

Date	Mintage	F	VF	XF	Unc	BU
1916	400,000	8.50	20.00	50.00	300	—
1917	5,600,000	6.50	12.00	30.00	150	—

KM# 31 50 CENTESIMOS
7.0000 g., 0.7000 Silver 0.1575 oz. ASW **Obv:** Head right **Rev:** Date below value

Date	Mintage	F	VF	XF	Unc	BU
1943So	10,800,000	BV	3.00	5.00	12.50	—

KM# 41 50 CENTESIMOS
Copper-Nickel **Obv:** Artigas bust right, 'HP' below **Rev:** Radiant sun peeking out above arms within wreath, value divides circle of stars **Note:** Medal rotation.

Date	Mintage	F	VF	XF	Unc	BU
1960	18,000,000	0.20	0.50	1.00	2.00	—
1960 Proof	—	Value: 80.00				

KM# 45 50 CENTESIMOS
Aluminum **Obv:** Artigas head right **Rev:** Value within wreath **Note:** Medal rotation.

Date	Mintage	F	VF	XF	Unc	BU
1965So	50,000,000	0.15	0.25	0.40	1.00	—

KM# 23 PESO
25.0000 g., 0.9000 Silver 0.7234 oz. ASW **Obv:** Radiant sun peeking out above arms within wreath **Rev:** Bust left

Date	Mintage	F	VF	XF	Unc	BU
1917	2,000,000	12.50	22.50	55.00	250	—

KM# 30 PESO
9.0000 g., 0.7200 Silver 0.2083 oz. ASW **Obv:** Artigas head right **Rev:** Puma walking left, sunrays behind

Date	Mintage	F	VF	XF	Unc	BU
1942So	9,000,000	BV	5.00	10.00	40.00	—

KM# 42 PESO
Copper-Nickel **Obv:** Artigas head right, 'HP' below **Rev:** Radiant sun peeking out above arms within wreath, value divides circle of stars **Note:** Medal rotation.

Date	Mintage	F	VF	XF	Unc	BU
1960	8,000,000	0.25	0.50	0.75	2.00	—
1960 Proof	—	Value: 75.00				

KM# 46 PESO
Aluminum-Bronze **Obv:** Artigas head right **Rev:** Radiant sun peeking out above arms within wreath, value divides circle of stars **Note:** Medal rotation.

Date	Mintage	F	VF	XF	Unc	BU
1965So Proof	25	Value: 65.00				
1965So	60,000,000	—	0.15	0.35	1.00	—

KM# 49 PESO
Nickel-Brass, 17.3 mm. **Obv:** Artigas head right **Rev:** Flower and value **Note:** Medal rotation.

Date	Mintage	F	VF	XF	Unc	BU
1968So Proof	50	Value: 50.00				
1968So	103,200,000	—	0.15	0.75	—	

KM# 52 PESO
Aluminum-Brass **Obv:** Radiant sun with face **Rev:** Flower and value **Note:** Medal rotation.

Date	Mintage	F	VF	XF	Unc	BU
1969So	51,800,000	—	0.15	0.75	—	

KM# 27 5 PESOS
8.4850 g., 0.9170 Gold 0.2501 oz. AGW, 22 mm. **Subject:** Constitution Centennial **Obv:** Artigas head right, L. BAZOR in left field behind neck **Rev:** Date flanked by sprigs below value

Date	Mintage	F	VF	XF	Unc	BU
1930(a)	Est. 100,000	—	—	BV	275	300

Note: Only 14,415 were released; Remainder withheld

KM# 47 5 PESOS
Aluminum-Bronze **Obv:** Artigas head right **Rev:** Radiant sun peeking out above arms within wreath, value divides circle of stars **Note:** Medal rotation.

Date	Mintage	F	VF	XF	Unc	BU
1965So Proof	25	Value: 75.00				
1965So	18,000,000	0.20	0.30	0.50	1.00	—

KM# 50   5 PESOS
3.0000 g., Nickel-Brass **Obv:** Artigas head right **Rev:** Flower and value **Note:** Medal rotation.

Date	Mintage	F	VF	XF	Unc	BU
1968So Proof	50	Value: 65.00				
1968So	42,680,000	0.10	0.20	0.30	0.40	—

KM# 53   5 PESOS
Aluminum-Bronze **Obv:** Radiant sun with face **Rev:** Flower and value **Note:** Medal rotation.

Date	Mintage	F	VF	XF	Unc	BU
1969So	42,320,000	—	—	0.10	0.30	—

KM# 43   10 PESOS
12.5000 g., 0.9000 Silver 0.3617 oz. ASW **Subject:** Sesquicentennial of Revolution Against Spain **Obv:** M.G. Rizzello bust right with hat **Rev:** Value within wreath

Date	Mintage	F	VF	XF	Unc	BU
1961 Proof	—	Value: 600				
1961	3,000,000	—	BV	7.00	9.00	12.00

KM# 48   10 PESOS
Aluminum-Bronze **Obv:** Artigas head right **Rev:** Radiant sun peeking out above arms within wreath, value divides circle of stars **Note:** Medal rotation.

Date	Mintage	F	VF	XF	Unc	BU
1965So	18,000,000	0.15	0.20	0.35	1.00	—

KM# 51   10 PESOS
Nickel-Brass, 23 mm. **Obv:** Artigas head right **Rev:** Flower and value **Note:** Medal rotation.

Date	Mintage	F	VF	XF	Unc	BU
1968So Proof	50	Value: 80.00				
1968So	90,000,000	0.15	0.20	0.35	0.65	—

KM# 54   10 PESOS
4.1000 g., Aluminum-Bronze, 23 mm. **Obv:** Radiant sun with face **Rev:** Flower and value **Note:** Medal rotation.

Date	Mintage	F	VF	XF	Unc	BU
1969So	10,000,000	0.15	0.20	0.35	0.65	—

KM# 56   20 PESOS
Copper-Nickel **Obv:** Radiant sun peeking out above arms within wreath **Rev:** Spears of wheat and value **Note:** Medal rotation.

Date	Mintage	F	VF	XF	Unc	BU
1970So Proof	—	Value: 80.00				
1970So	50,000,000	0.15	0.25	0.40	0.75	—

KM# 57   50 PESOS
Copper-Nickel **Obv:** Radiant sun peeking out above arms within wreath **Rev:** Spears of wheat and value **Note:** Medal rotation.

Date	Mintage	F	VF	XF	Unc	BU
1970So Proof	—	Value: 80.00				
1970So	20,000,000	0.20	0.40	0.60	1.50	—

KM# 58   50 PESOS
5.2000 g., Nickel-Brass **Subject:** Centennial - Birth of Rodo **Obv:** Rodo facing **Rev:** Feather, value and date **Note:** Medal rotation.

Date	Mintage	F	VF	XF	Unc	BU
1971So	15,000,000	0.20	0.50	1.00	2.00	—

KM# 58a   50 PESOS
6.0200 g., 0.9000 Silver 0.1742 oz. ASW **Subject:** Centennial - Birth of Rodo **Obv:** Rodo facing **Rev:** Feather, value and date

Date	Mintage	F	VF	XF	Unc	BU
1971So Proof	1,000	Value: 17.50				

KM# 58b   50 PESOS
Gold **Subject:** Centennial - Birth of Rodo **Obv:** Rodo facing **Rev:** Feather, value and date

Date	Mintage	F	VF	XF	Unc	BU
1971So Proof	100	Value: 375				

KM# 59   100 PESOS
8.0000 g., Copper-Nickel **Obv:** Artigas head 1/4 left **Rev:** Value, date and sprig **Note:** Coin rotation.

Date	Mintage	F	VF	XF	Unc	BU
1973Mx	20,000,000	0.25	0.50	1.00	2.50	—

KM# 55   1000 PESOS
25.0000 g., 0.9000 Silver 0.7234 oz. ASW **Series:** F.A.O. **Obv:** Stylized radiant sun with face **Rev:** Assorted stylized designs within circle **Edge:** Lettered **Edge:** REPUBLICA ORIENTAL DEL URUGUAY **Note:** Medal rotation.

Date	Mintage	F	VF	XF	Unc	BU
1969So	500,000	—	BV	12.50	15.00	20.00
1969So Proof	350	Value: 150				

KM# 55a   1000 PESOS
Bronze **Series:** F.A.O. **Obv:** Stylized radiant sun with face **Rev:** Assorted stylized designs within circle **Edge:** Lettered **Edge:** REPUBLICA ORIENTAL DEL URUGUAY **Note:** 'So' mintmark also appears on edge.

Date	Mintage	F	VF	XF	Unc	BU
1969So	11,000	—	—	15.00	20.00	30.00

KM# 55b   1000 PESOS
Gold **Series:** F.A.O. **Obv:** Stylized radiant sun with face **Rev:** Assorted stylized designs within circle

Date	Mintage	F	VF	XF	Unc	BU
1969So	450	—	—	—	850	900

REFORM COINAGE
1000 Old Pesos = 1 Nuevo (New) Peso

KM# 71   CENTESIMO
1.0000 g., Aluminum, 19 mm. **Obv:** Radiant sun with face **Rev:** Value in front of supine wheat stalk **Note:** Medal rotation.

Date	Mintage	F	VF	XF	Unc	BU
1977So	10,000,000	—	—	0.15	0.25	—

KM# 71a   CENTESIMO
3.7000 g., 0.9000 Silver 0.1071 oz. ASW, 19 mm. **Obv:** Radiant sun with face **Rev:** Value in front of supine wheat stalk

Date	Mintage	F	VF	XF	Unc	BU
1979So Proof	202	Value: 15.00				

KM# 71b   CENTESIMO
6.2600 g., 0.9000 Gold 0.1811 oz. AGW, 19 mm. **Obv:** Radiant sun with face **Rev:** Value in front of supine wheat stalk

Date	Mintage	F	VF	XF	Unc	BU
1979So Proof	50	Value: 185				

KM# 72   2 CENTESIMOS
Aluminum, 21 mm. **Obv:** Radiant sun with face **Rev:** Value in front of supine wheat stalk **Note:** Medal rotation.

Date	Mintage	F	VF	XF	Unc	BU
1977So	17,000,000	—	—	0.15	0.25	—
1978So	3,000,000	—	—	0.15	0.25	—

KM# 72a   2 CENTESIMOS
5.2000 g., 0.9000 Silver 0.1505 oz. ASW, 21 mm. **Obv:** Radiant sun with face **Rev:** Value in front of supine wheat stalk

Date	Mintage	F	VF	XF	Unc	BU
1979So Proof	202	Value: 20.00				

KM# 72b   2 CENTESIMOS
9.2500 g., 0.9000 Gold 0.2676 oz. AGW, 21 mm. **Obv:** Radiant sun with face **Rev:** Value in front of supine wheat stalk

Date	Mintage	F	VF	XF	Unc	BU
1979So Proof	52	Value: 285				

KM# 73 5 CENTESIMOS
Aluminum, 23 mm. **Obv:** Steer left **Rev:** Value in front of supine wheat stalk **Note:** Medal rotation.

Date	Mintage	F	VF	XF	Unc	BU
1977So	11,000,000	—	—	0.15	0.50	—
1978So	19,000,000	—	—	0.15	0.50	—

KM# 73a 5 CENTESIMOS
7.4000 g., 0.9000 Silver 0.2141 oz. ASW, 23 mm. **Obv:** Steer left **Rev:** Value in front of supine wheat stalk

Date	Mintage	F	VF	XF	Unc	BU
1979So Proof	202	Value: 20.00				

KM# 73b 5 CENTESIMOS
12.5500 g., 0.9000 Gold 0.3631 oz. AGW, 23 mm. **Obv:** Steer left **Rev:** Value in front of supine wheat stalk

Date	Mintage	F	VF	XF	Unc	BU
1979So Proof	52	Value: 375				

KM# 66 10 CENTESIMOS
3.1000 g., Aluminum-Bronze, 19 mm. **Obv:** Horse left **Rev:** Value flanked by sprigs **Note:** Medal rotation.

Date	Mintage	F	VF	XF	Unc	BU
1976So	127,400,000	—	—	0.30	0.80	1.50
1976So Proof	—	—	—	—	—	—
1977So	12,700,000	—	—	0.35	0.85	1.50
1978So	19,900,000	—	—	0.35	0.85	1.50
1981So	—	—	—	0.35	0.85	1.50

KM# 66a 10 CENTESIMOS
3.8000 g., 0.9000 Silver 0.1100 oz. ASW, 19 mm. **Obv:** Horse left **Rev:** Value flanked by sprigs

Date	Mintage	F	VF	XF	Unc	BU
1976So Proof	200	Value: 20.00				
1977So Proof	200	Value: 20.00				

KM# 66b 10 CENTESIMOS
6.0000 g., 0.9000 Gold 0.1736 oz. AGW, 19 mm. **Obv:** Horse left **Rev:** Value flanked by sprigs

Date	Mintage	F	VF	XF	Unc	BU
1976So Proof	50	Value: 250				

KM# 67 20 CENTESIMOS
5.1000 g., Aluminum-Bronze, 22 mm. **Obv:** Small building on top of hill **Rev:** Value flanked by sprigs **Note:** Medal rotation.

Date	Mintage	F	VF	XF	Unc	BU
1976So	40,000,000	—	—	0.20	0.45	0.85
1976So Proof	—	—	—	—	—	—
1977So	4,700,000	—	—	0.20	0.60	1.00
1978So	15,300,000	—	—	0.20	0.45	0.85
1981So	—	—	—	0.20	0.45	0.85

KM# 67a 20 CENTESIMOS
6.4000 g., 0.9000 Silver 0.1852 oz. ASW, 22 mm. **Obv:** Small building on top of hill **Rev:** Value flanked by sprigs

Date	Mintage	F	VF	XF	Unc	BU
1976So Proof	200	Value: 22.50				
1977So Proof	200	Value: 22.50				

KM# 67b 20 CENTESIMOS
10.5000 g., 0.9000 Gold 0.3038 oz. AGW, 22 mm. **Obv:** Small building on top of hill **Rev:** Value flanked by sprigs

Date	Mintage	F	VF	XF	Unc	BU
1976So Proof	50	Value: 375				

KM# 68 50 CENTESIMOS
7.0000 g., Aluminum-Bronze, 25.5 mm. **Obv:** Scale **Rev:** Value flanked by sprigs

Date	Mintage	F	VF	XF	Unc	BU
1976So	30,000,000	—	—	0.20	0.50	1.00
1976So Proof	—	—	—	—	—	—

Date	Mintage	F	VF	XF	Unc	BU
1977So	9,800,000	—	—	0.20	0.50	1.00
1981So	200,000	—	—	0.25	0.60	1.25

KM# 68a 50 CENTESIMOS
9.0000 g., 0.9000 Silver 0.2604 oz. ASW, 25.5 mm. **Obv:** Scale **Rev:** Value flanked by sprigs

Date	Mintage	F	VF	XF	Unc	BU
1976So Proof	200	Value: 35.00				
1977So Proof	200	Value: 35.00				

KM# 68b 50 CENTESIMOS
15.0000 g., 0.9000 Gold 0.4340 oz. AGW, 25.5 mm. **Obv:** Scale **Rev:** Value flanked by sprigs

Date	Mintage	F	VF	XF	Unc	BU
1976So Proof	50	Value: 550				

KM# 69 NUEVO PESO
11.1000 g., Aluminum-Bronze, 30 mm. **Obv:** Head of Jose Gervasio Artigas left **Rev:** Value in front of supine wheat stalk **Edge:** Plain **Note:** Medal rotation.

Date	Mintage	F	VF	XF	Unc	BU
1976So	65,540,000	—	—	0.30	0.60	1.25
1976So Proof	—	—	—	—	—	—
1977So	7,360,000	—	—	0.30	0.65	1.45
1978So	27,100,000	—	—	0.30	0.65	1.45

KM# 69a NUEVO PESO
13.5000 g., 0.9000 Silver 0.3906 oz. ASW, 30 mm. **Obv:** Head of Jose Gervasio Artigas left **Rev:** Value in front of supine wheat stalk

Date	Mintage	F	VF	XF	Unc	BU
1976So Proof	200	Value: 40.00				

KM# 69b NUEVO PESO
23.0000 g., 0.9000 Gold 0.6655 oz. AGW, 30 mm. **Obv:** Head of Jose Gervasio Artigas left **Rev:** Value in front of supine wheat stalk

Date	Mintage	F	VF	XF	Unc	BU
1976So Proof	50	Value: 750				

KM# 74 NUEVO PESO
5.9000 g., Copper-Nickel, 24 mm. **Obv:** Radiant sun peeking over arms within wreath **Rev:** Flower and value **Note:** Medal rotation.

Date	Mintage	F	VF	XF	Unc	BU
1980So	50,000,000	—	—	0.20	0.35	0.65	1.00

KM# 74a NUEVO PESO
7.0000 g., 0.9000 Silver 0.2025 oz. ASW, 24 mm. **Obv:** Radiant sun peeking over arms within wreath **Rev:** Flower and value

Date	Mintage	F	VF	XF	Unc	BU
1980So Proof	300	Value: 25.00				

KM# 74b NUEVO PESO
11.6500 g., 0.9000 Gold 0.3371 oz. AGW, 24 mm. **Obv:** Radiant sun peeking over arms within wreath **Rev:** Flower and value

Date	Mintage	F	VF	XF	Unc	BU
1980So Proof	100	Value: 375				

KM# 76 NUEVO PESO
6.9400 g., 0.9000 Silver 0.2008 oz. ASW **Obv:** National flag

Date	Mintage	F	VF	XF	Unc	BU
1981 Proof	100	Value: 30.00				

KM# 95 NUEVO PESO
Stainless Steel **Obv:** Radiant sun **Rev:** Value within wreath **Note:** Medal rotation.

Date	Mintage	F	VF	XF	Unc	BU
1989	—	—	—	0.15	0.35	0.65

KM# 77 2 NUEVOS PESOS
7.1000 g., Copper-Nickel-Zinc, 25 mm. **Subject:** World Food Day **Obv:** Wheat stalks divide date and country name **Rev:** Value **Edge:** Plain

Date	Mintage	F	VF	XF	Unc	BU
1981	95,000,000	—	0.25	0.50	1.00	1.50

KM# 77a 2 NUEVOS PESOS
14.5300 g., 0.9000 Gold 0.4204 oz. AGW, 25 mm. **Subject:** World Food Day **Obv:** Wheat stalks divide date country name **Rev:** Value

Date	Mintage	F	VF	XF	Unc	BU
1981 Proof	100	Value: 450				

KM# 65 5 NUEVOS PESOS
14.4000 g., Copper-Nickel-Aluminum **Subject:** 150th Anniversary - Revolutionary Movement **Obv:** Artigas head facing within square above inscription **Rev:** Upright design **Note:** Medal rotation.

Date	Mintage	F	VF	XF	Unc	BU
ND(1975)So	3,000,000	0.50	0.75	1.25	3.50	5.00

KM# 65a 5 NUEVOS PESOS
18.4300 g., 0.9000 Silver 0.5333 oz. ASW **Subject:** 150th Anniversary - Revolutionary Movement **Obv:** Artigas head facing within square above inscription **Rev:** Upright design

Date	Mintage	F	VF	XF	Unc	BU
ND(1975)So Proof	2,000	Value: 15.00				

KM# 65b 5 NUEVOS PESOS
Gold **Subject:** 150th Anniversary - Revolutionary Movement **Obv:** Artigas head facing within square above inscription **Rev:** Upright design

Date	Mintage	F	VF	XF	Unc	BU
ND(1975)So Proof	1,000	Value: 600				

Note: 50 pieces each in aluminum, alpaca and copper are reported to have been struck

KM# 70 5 NUEVOS PESOS
Copper-Aluminum **Subject:** 250th Anniversary - Founding of Montevideo **Obv:** Head facing to left of value **Rev:** Crowned shield within wreath **Note:** Medal rotation.

Date	Mintage	F	VF	XF	Unc	BU
1976So	300,000	0.75	1.00	1.50	4.00	5.50

KM# 70a 5 NUEVOS PESOS
30.0000 g., 0.9000 Gold 0.8680 oz. AGW **Subject:** 250th Anniversary - Founding of Montevideo **Obv:** Head facing to left of value **Rev:** Crowned shield within wreath

Date	Mintage	F	VF	XF	Unc	BU
1976So Proof	100	Value: 900				

KM# 70b 5 NUEVOS PESOS
Silver **Subject:** 250th Anniversary - Founding of Montevideo **Obv:** Head facing to left of value **Rev:** Crowned shield within wreath

Date	Mintage	F	VF	XF	Unc	BU
1976So	—	—	—	—	175	—

KM# 75 5 NUEVOS PESOS
7.9000 g., Copper-Nickel, 26.15 mm. **Obv:** National flag **Rev:** Flower and value **Note:** Medal rotation.

Date	Mintage	F	VF	XF	Unc	BU
1980So	50,000,000	—	0.20	0.40	1.50	2.00
1981So	—	—	0.20	0.40	1.50	2.00

KM# 75a 5 NUEVOS PESOS
9.3000 g., 0.9000 Silver 0.2691 oz. ASW, 26.15 mm. **Obv:** National flag **Rev:** Flower and value

Date	Mintage	F	VF	XF	Unc	BU
1980So Proof	300	Value: 30.00				

KM# 75b 5 NUEVOS PESOS
15.6000 g., 0.9000 Gold 0.4514 oz. AGW, 26.15 mm. **Obv:** National flag **Rev:** Flower and value

Date	Mintage	F	VF	XF	Unc	BU
1980So Proof	100	Value: 500				

KM# 78 5 NUEVOS PESOS
9.3000 g., 0.9000 Silver 0.2691 oz. ASW **Obv:** Coat of arms

Date	Mintage	F	VF	XF	Unc	BU
1981 Proof	100	Value: 30.00				

KM# 92 5 NUEVOS PESOS
Stainless Steel **Obv:** Radiant sun **Rev:** Value and date within wreath **Note:** Medal rotation.

Date	Mintage	F	VF	XF	Unc	BU
1989	65,000,000	—	—	0.15	0.35	0.65

KM# 79   10 NUEVOS PESOS
9.8000 g., Copper-Nickel, 28 mm.   **Obv:** Bust of Jose Gervasio Artigas half left **Rev:** Flower and value **Note:** Medal rotation.

Date	Mintage	F	VF	XF	Unc	BU
1981So	—	—	0.20	0.50	1.75	2.25

KM# 79a   10 NUEVOS PESOS
11.6300 g., 0.9000 Silver 0.3365 oz. ASW, 28 mm.   **Obv:** Bust of Jose Gervasio Artigas half left **Rev:** Flower and value

Date	Mintage	F	VF	XF	Unc	BU
1981So Proof	100	Value: 35.00				

KM# 79b   10 NUEVOS PESOS
19.4800 g., 0.9000 Gold 0.5636 oz. AGW, 28 mm.   **Obv:** Bust of Jose Gervasio Artigas half left **Rev:** Flower and value

Date	Mintage	F	VF	XF	Unc	BU
1981So Proof	100	Value: 600				

KM# 93   10 NUEVOS PESOS
Stainless Steel   **Obv:** Radiant sun **Rev:** Value and date within wreath **Note:** Medal rotation.

Date	Mintage	F	VF	XF	Unc	BU
1989	79,000,000	—	0.20	0.45	0.75	

KM# 86   20 NUEVOS PESOS
Copper-Nickel, 30 mm.   **Subject:** World Fisheries Conference **Obv:** Radiant sun peeking out above arms within wreath **Rev:** Fish **Edge:** Reeded **Note:** Medal rotation.

Date	Mintage	F	VF	XF	Unc	BU
1984	3,771	—	—	—	20.00	25.00

KM# 86a   20 NUEVOS PESOS
11.6600 g., 0.9250 Silver 0.3467 oz. ASW, 30 mm.   **Subject:** World Fisheries Conference **Obv:** Radiant sun peeking out above arms within wreath **Rev:** Fish

Date	Mintage	F	VF	XF	Unc	BU
1984 Proof	25,000	Value: 32.00				

KM# 86b   20 NUEVOS PESOS
19.6000 g., 0.9170 Gold 0.5778 oz. AGW, 30 mm.   **Subject:** World Fisheries Conference **Obv:** Radiant sun peeking out above arms within wreath **Rev:** Fish

Date	Mintage	F	VF	XF	Unc	BU
1984 Proof	100	Value: 600				

KM# 94   50 NUEVOS PESOS
4.7000 g., Stainless Steel   **Obv:** Radiant sun **Rev:** Value and date within wreath **Note:** Medal rotation.

Date	Mintage	F	VF	XF	Unc	BU
1989	—	—	0.20	0.50	0.85	

KM# 80   100 NUEVOS PESOS
12.0000 g., 0.9000 Silver 0.3472 oz. ASW   **Obv:** Hydroelectric dam **Rev:** Conjoined arms with radiant sun peeking out above arms within wreath

Date	Mintage	F	VF	XF	Unc	BU
1981So	25,000	—	—	—	7.50	9.00

KM# 96   100 NUEVOS PESOS
Stainless Steel   **Obv:** Gaucho with hat right **Rev:** Value and date within wreath **Note:** Medal rotation.

Date	Mintage	F	VF	XF	Unc	BU
1989	—	—	—	0.35	0.75	1.50

KM# 97   200 NUEVOS PESOS
Copper-Nickel   **Obv:** Unchained Liberty **Rev:** Value and date within wreath **Note:** Medal rotation.

Date	Mintage	F	VF	XF	Unc	BU
1989	—	—	—	—	1.50	2.50

KM# 82   500 NUEVOS PESOS
12.0000 g., 0.9000 Silver 0.3472 oz. ASW   **Obv:** Hydroelectric dam **Rev:** Radiant sun peeking out above arms within wreath above date

Date	Mintage	F	VF	XF	Unc	BU
1983So	15,000	—	—	—	7.50	9.00

KM# 90   500 NUEVOS PESOS
12.0000 g., 0.9000 Silver 0.3472 oz. ASW   **Obv:** Head of General Leandro Gomez half left **Rev:** Building above value and date

Date	Mintage	F	VF	XF	Unc	BU
1986Mo Proof	6,000	Value: 21.50				

KM# 98   500 NUEVOS PESOS
Copper Nickel   **Obv:** Bust of Jose Gervasio Artigas half right **Rev:** Value and date within wreath **Note:** Medal rotation.

Date	Mintage	F	VF	XF	Unc	BU
1989	—	—	—	—	3.00	4.50

KM# 87   2000 NUEVOS PESOS
25.0000 g., 0.9000 Silver 0.7234 oz. ASW   **Subject:** 140th Anniversary of Silver Coinage and 25th Meeting of Inter-American Bank Governors **Obv:** Radiant sun peeking over arms in wreath within beaded circle **Rev:** Map within U-shaped design below inscription **Note:** Coin rotation.

Date	Mintage	F	VF	XF	Unc	BU
1984 Proof	15,000	Value: 18.50				

KM# 88   2000 NUEVOS PESOS
25.0000 g., 0.9000 Silver 0.7234 oz. ASW   **Subject:** 25th Meeting of Inter-American Bank Governors **Obv:** Radiant sun peeking over arms within wreath **Rev:** Map within U-shaped design below inscription **Note:** Coin rotation.

Date	Mintage	F	VF	XF	Unc	BU
1984 Proof	15,000	Value: 18.50				

KM# 81   5000 NUEVOS PESOS
12.0000 g., 0.9000 Silver 0.3472 oz. ASW   **Obv:** Hydroelectric dam **Rev:** Conjoined arms with radiant sun peeking out above arms within wreath

Date	Mintage	F	VF	XF	Unc	BU
1981So Proof	15,000	Value: 15.00				

KM# 91   5000 NUEVOS PESOS
25.0000 g., 0.9000 Silver 0.7234 oz. ASW, 37 mm.   **Subject:** 20th Anniversary of Central Bank **Obv:** National arms, sun face **Rev:** Triangular wheel design

Date	Mintage	F	VF	XF	Unc	BU
1987So Proof	10,000	Value: 16.50				

KM# 91a   5000 NUEVOS PESOS
42.7600 g., Gold   **Obv:** Double wheel design **Rev:** Snowflake design

Date	Mintage	F	VF	XF	Unc	BU
1987	—	—	—	—	—	

KM# 99 5000 NUEVOS PESOS
25.0000 g., 0.9000 Silver 0.7234 oz. ASW **Subject:** Latin America Presidents' Assembly **Obv:** Value and date within circle **Rev:** Assorted arms

Date	Mintage	F	VF	XF	Unc	BU
1988 Proof	—				Value: 20.00	

KM# 85 20000 NUEVOS PESOS
20.0000 g., 0.9000 Gold 0.5787 oz. AGW **Obv:** Hydroelectric dam **Rev:** Radiant sun peeking out above arms within wreath

Date	Mintage	F	VF	XF	Unc	BU
1983So Proof	2,500		Value: 700			

KM# 89 20000 NUEVOS PESOS
19.8700 g., 0.9000 Gold 0.5749 oz. AGW, 33.1 mm. **Subject:** 130th Anniversary of Gold Coinage and 25th Meeting of Inter-American Bank Governors **Obv:** Radiant sun peeking out above arms within wreath of assorted flags **Rev:** Map within U-shaped design below value and inscription **Edge:** Reeded

Date	Mintage	F	VF	XF	Unc	BU
1984 Proof	1,500		Value: 700			

KM# 101 25000 NUEVOS PESOS
12.5000 g., 0.9000 Silver 0.3617 oz. ASW **Subject:** 25th Anniversary of Central Bank **Obv:** Bell design above value **Rev:** Towered bank building to lower right of arms

Date	Mintage	F	VF	XF	Unc	BU
1992	—	—	—	—	16.50	18.50

KM# 100 50000 NUEVOS PESOS
27.0000 g., 0.9250 Silver 0.8029 oz. ASW **Subject:** Ibero - American Series **Obv:** Arms within center circle of value, country name and assorted arms **Rev:** Crossed flags and crowned shield divides dates **Note:** Coin rotation.

Date	Mintage	F	VF	XF	Unc	BU
1991 Proof	70,000		Value: 40.00			

REFORM COINAGE
March 1993

1,000 Nuevos Pesos = 1 Uruguayan Peso;
100 Centesimos = 1 Uruguayan Peso (UYP)

KM# 102 10 CENTESIMOS
1.6900 g., Stainless Steel, 14.48 mm. **Obv:** Artigas head right **Rev:** Value, date and sprig **Edge:** Plain **Note:** Coin rotation.

Date	Mintage	F	VF	XF	Unc	BU
1994	—	—	—	0.25	0.50	0.65

KM# 105 20 CENTESIMOS
Stainless Steel **Obv:** Artigas head right **Rev:** Value, date and sprig **Note:** Coin rotation.

Date	Mintage	F	VF	XF	Unc	BU
1994	—	—	—	0.30	0.60	0.75

KM# 106 50 CENTESIMOS
2.9400 g., Stainless Steel, 20.97 mm. **Obv:** Bust of Artigas right **Obv. Leg.:** REPUBLICA ORIENTAL DEL URUGUAY **Rev:** Value, date and sprig **Edge:** Plain **Note:** Coin rotation.

Date	Mintage	F	VF	XF	Unc	BU
1994	—	—	—	0.35	0.75	1.00
1998	—	—	—	0.35	0.75	1.00

KM# 103.1 UN PESO URUGUAYO
3.5000 g., Aluminum-Bronze, 20 mm. **Obv:** Artigas head right **Rev:** Value and date **Note:** Left point of bust shoulder points at "U" in Republic.

Date	Mintage	F	VF	XF	Unc	BU
1994	—	—	—	—	0.60	1.00

KM# 103.2 UN PESO URUGUAYO
3.5000 g., Aluminum-Bronze, 19.95 mm. **Obv:** Bust of Artigas right **Obv. Leg.:** REPUBLICA ORIENTAL DEL URUGUAY **Rev:** Value and date **Edge:** Plain **Note:** Medal rotation; left point of bust shoulder points at "P" in Republic.

Date	Mintage	F	VF	XF	Unc	BU
1998So	—	—	—	—	0.50	0.75

KM# 104.1 2 PESOS URUGUAYOS
4.5000 g., Aluminum-Bronze, 23 mm. **Obv:** Artigas head right **Rev:** Value and date **Note:** Medal rotation. Left point of bust shoulder points at "U" in "Republic".

Date	Mintage	F	VF	XF	Unc	BU
1994	—	—	—	0.75	1.50	2.00

KM# 104.2 2 PESOS URUGUAYOS
4.4900 g., Aluminum-Bronze, 23.0 mm. **Obv:** Bust of Artigas right **Obv. Leg.:** REPUBLICA ORIENTAL DEL URUGUAY **Rev:** Value and date **Edge:** Plain **Note:** Medal rotation. Left point of bust shoulder points at "P" in "Republic".

Date	Mintage	F	VF	XF	Unc	BU
1998So	—	—	—	0.75	1.50	2.00

Note: Mint mark under bust

KM# 121 10 PESOS URUGUAYOS
10.4000 g., Bi-Metallic Aluminum-Bronze center in Stainless Steel ring, 28 mm. **Obv:** Artigas head right within circle **Rev:** Value above signature within circle **Edge:** Plain

Date	Mintage	F	VF	XF	Unc	BU
2000 (RCM)	—	—	—	—	3.50	5.00

Note: 5-pointed star to each side of date, issued 2006

Date	Mintage	F	VF	XF	Unc	BU
2000	—	—	—	—	3.50	5.00

KM# 113 50 PESOS URUGUAYOS
12.5000 g., 0.9000 Silver 0.3617 oz. ASW **Subject:** Bicentennial - City of Melo **Obv:** Map and date **Rev:** City arms, value and date

Date	Mintage	F	VF	XF	Unc	BU
1996 Proof	10,000		Value: 20.00			

KM# 111 100 PESOS URUGUAYOS
25.0000 g., 0.9000 Silver 0.7234 oz. ASW **Subject:** 50th Anniversary - F.A.O. **Obv:** Wheat stalks divide value **Rev:** F.A.O logo and dates within circle

Date	Mintage	F	VF	XF	Unc	BU
ND1995 Proof	—		Value: 22.50			

KM# 112 100 PESOS URUGUAYOS
25.0000 g., 0.9000 Silver 0.7234 oz. ASW **Subject:** Centennial - Central Bank **Obv:** Radiant sun face **Rev:** Central Bank building

Date	Mintage	F	VF	XF	Unc	BU
1996 Proof	50,000		Value: 25.00			

KM# 107 200 PESOS URUGUAYOS
27.0000 g., 0.9250 Silver 0.8029 oz. ASW **Subject:** Environmental Protection **Obv:** Arms in wreath within center circle of assorted arms **Rev:** Pampas deer right

Date	Mintage	F	VF	XF	Unc	BU
1994 Proof	20,000		Value: 35.00			

KM# 116 200 PESOS URUGUAYOS
28.2800 g., 0.9250 Silver 0.8410 oz. ASW **Subject:** 50th Anniversary - United Nations

Date	Mintage	F	VF	XF	Unc	BU
1995 Proof	—		Value: 42.50			

KM# 115   200 PESOS URUGUAYOS

25.0000 g., 0.9000 Silver 0.7234 oz. ASW **Subject:** Millennium Change **Obv:** Southern Cross stars within design **Rev:** Stylized symbols of mankinds connection to the stars **Edge:** "CAMBIO DE MILENIO" twice

Date	Mintage	F	VF	XF	Unc	BU
1999	50,000	—	—	—	25.00	30.00

KM# 114   250 PESOS URUGUAYOS

27.0000 g., 0.9000 Silver 0.7812 oz. ASW **Subject:** Ibero - American Series **Obv:** Arms in wreath within center circle of assorted arms **Rev:** Standing figures leaning on wooden gate

Date	Mintage	F	VF	XF	Unc	BU
1997 Proof	11,000	Value: 47.50				

KM# 117   250 PESOS URUGUAYOS

27.0000 g., 0.9000 Silver 0.7812 oz. ASW, 40 mm. **Series:** Ibero-American **Obv:** Arms in wreath within center circle of assorted arms **Rev:** Man and woman on horseback **Edge:** Reeded

Date	Mintage	F	VF	XF	Unc	BU
2000 Proof	8,000	Value: 50.00				

GOLD BULLION COINAGE

KM# 108   1/4 GAUCHO

8.6400 g., 0.9000 Gold 0.2500 oz. AGW **Obv:** Head of Gaucho right **Rev:** Value within wreath

Date	Mintage	F	VF	XF	Unc	BU
1992 Proof	—	Value: 275				

KM# 109   1/2 GAUCHO

17.2800 g., 0.9000 Gold 0.5000 oz. AGW **Obv:** Head of Gaucho right **Rev:** Value "1/2" within wreath

Date	Mintage	F	VF	XF	Unc	BU
1992 Proof	—	Value: 550				

KM# 110   GAUCHO

34.5590 g., 0.9000 Gold 0.9999 oz. AGW **Obv:** Head of Gaucho right **Rev:** Value within wreath

Date	Mintage	F	VF	XF	Unc	BU
1992 Proof	—	Value: 1,000				

ESSAIS

KM#	Date	Mintage	Identification	Mkt Val
E5	1924(p)	12	Centesimo. Nickel. KM19.	250
E6	1924(p)	12	2 Centesimos. Nickel. KM20.	275
E7	1924(p)	12	5 Centesimos. Nickel. KM21.	300
E8	1930(a)	70	10 Centesimos. Alum.-Bronze. KM25.	100
E10	1930(a)	60	10 Centesimos. Gold. 18.3200 g. Head laureate right. Puma walking left in front of sun rays. KM25.	2,500
E11	1930(a)	—	20 Centesimos. Aluminum-Bronze. Seated figure left above date. Wheat stalks divides value. KM24.	100
EA12	1930	—	20 Centesimos. Silver. 4.9000 g.	—
E12	1930(a)	60	20 Centesimos. Gold. 8.9500 g. KM24.	2,750
E13	1930(a)	70	5 Pesos. Aluminum-Bronze. KM27.	225
E14	1930(a)	60	5 Pesos. Gold. KM27.	1,850
E15	1983	100	500 Pesos. Gold. ENSAYO, KM82.	425
E16	1983	200	2000 Pesos. Copper. KM83.	95.00
E17	1983	20	2000 Pesos. Gold. KM83	2,750
E18	1983	200	20000 Pesos. Silver. ENSAYO, KM85.	65.00
E19	1983	1,500	20000 Pesos. Gold. ENSAYO, KM85.	475
E20	1984	20,500	20 Pesos. Silver. ENSAYO, KM86a.	22.50
E21	1984	600	20 Pesos. Gold. ENSAYO, KM86b.	375
E22	1984	1,500	20000 Pesos. Gold. ENSAYO, KM89.	425

PATTERNS

Including off metal strikes

KM#	Date	Mintage	Identification	Mkt Val
Pn38	ND(1904)	—	4 Centesimos. Copper-Nickel. Radiant sun face. Value below banner in center.	275
PnA39	1916	—	50 Centesimos. Silver.	—
Pn39	1916	45	50 Centesimos. Silver.	—
Pn40	1917	20	Peso. Silver.	—
PnA41	1920	—	20 Centesimos. Copper-Nickel. Similar to KM#24.	—
Pn41	1942	10	20 Centesimos. Copper Gilt.	—
PnA42	1942	20	20 Centesimos. Silver Gilt.	—
Pn42	1942	—	20 Centesimos. Gold. KM29.	475
Pn43	1942So	—	Peso. Gold. KM30.	1,000
Pn44	1943So	—	2 Centesimos. Gold. KM20a.	950
Pn45	1943So	—	50 Centesimos. Gold. KM31	1,000
Pn46	1953	100	Centesimo. 0.9160 Gold. KM32.	—
Pn47	1953	—	2 Centesimos. Aluminum. KM33.	—
Pn48	1953	100	2 Centesimos. 0.9160 Gold. KM33.	—
Pn49	1953	100	5 Centesimos. 0.9160 Gold. KM34.	—
Pn50	1953	100	10 Centesimos. 0.9160 Gold. KM35.	—
PnB51	1953	—	Peso. Brass. Similar to PNA51.	—
PnC51	1953	—	Peso. Copper-Nickel. Similar to PNA51.	—
PnD51	1953	—	Peso. Silver. Similar to PNA51.	—
Pn51	1954	100	20 Centesimos. 0.9830 Gold. KM36.	550
Pn52	1959	—	10 Centesimos. 0.9160 Gold. KM35.	—
Pn53	1960	100	2 Centesimos. Gold. KM37.	—
Pn54	1960	100	5 Centesimos. Gold. KM38.	—
Pn55	1960	100	10 Centesimos. Gold. KM39.	—
Pn56	1960	100	25 Centesimos. Gold. KM40.	—
Pn57	1960	100	50 Centesimos. Gold. KM41.	—
Pn58	1960	—	Peso. Gold. KM42.	—
Pn59	1960	—	10 Pesos. Gold.	—
PnA54	ND(1960)	—	5 Centesimos. Nickel. Similar to KM#34 and KM#38 reverses. With a "Z" inside the base of the 5.	135
PnB54	ND(1960)	—	5 Centesimos. Aluminum. Similar to KM#34 and KM#38 reverses. With "HA" in the base of the 5 and "MBL" above the 5.	135
PnA60	1961	—	10 Pesos. Gold. KM43.	—
Pn60	1965So	10	20 Centesimos. Copper. KM44.	—
Pn61	1965So	—	20 Centesimos. Silver. KM44.	—
Pn62	1965So	—	20 Centesimos. Gold. KM44.	—
Pn63	1965So	25	50 Centesimos. Aluminum-Bronze. KM45.	—
Pn64	1965So	10	50 Centesimos. Copper. KM45.	—
Pn65	1965So	25	50 Centesimos. Copper-Nickel. KM45.	—
Pn66	1965So	—	50 Centesimos. Silver. KM45.	—
Pn67	1965So	—	50 Centesimos. Gold. KM45.	—
Pn68	1965So	10	Peso. Copper. KM46.	—
PnA69	1965	—	Peso. Aluminum-Bronze. 24 mm. Similar to KM#46. Planchet is 5 Pesos.	—
Pn69	1965So	25	Peso. Copper-Nickel. KM46.	—
Pn70	1965So	—	Peso. Silver. KM46.	—
Pn71	1965So	—	Peso. Gold. KM46.	—
Pn72	1965So	10	5 Pesos. Copper. KM47.	—

KM#	Date	Mintage	Identification	Mkt Val
Pn73	1965So	25	5 Pesos. Copper-Nickel. KM47.	—
Pn74	1965So	—	5 Pesos. Silver. KM47.	—
Pn75	1965So	—	5 Pesos. Gold. KM47.	—
Pn76	1965So	10	10 Pesos. Copper. KM48.	—
Pn77	1965So	—	10 Pesos. Silver. KM48.	—
PnA73	1965	—	5 Pesos. Copper-Nickel. 29 mm. Similar to KM#47. Planchet is 10 Pesos.	—
PnB84	1968	—	20 Pesos. Copper-Nickel. Similar to KM#56; Proof.	—
PnC84	1968	—	20 Pesos. Silver. Star. Similar to KM#56.	—
PnB85	1968	—	50 Pesos. Copper-Nickel. Similar to KM#57; Proof.	—
PnC85	1968	—	50 Pesos. Silver. Star. Similar to KM#57.	—
Pn78	1968So	100	Peso. Copper-Nickel. KM49.	35.00
Pn79	1968So	1,000	Peso. Silver. KM49.	18.00
Pn80	1968So	100	5 Pesos. Copper-Nickel. KM50.	35.00
Pn81	1968So	1,000	5 Pesos. Silver. KM50.	20.00
Pn82	1968So	100	10 Pesos. Copper-Nickel. KM51.	35.00
Pn83	1968So	1,000	10 Pesos. Silver. KM51.	22.00
PnA84	1968S	—	20 Pesos. Yellow Metal.	—
Pn84	1968So	1,000	20 Pesos. Silver.	25.00
PnA85	1968S	—	50 Pesos. Yellow Metal.	—
Pn85	1968So	1,000	50 Pesos. Silver.	30.00
Pn86	1969So	50	Peso. Copper-Nickel. KM52.	35.00
Pn87	1969So	1,000	Peso. 0.9000 Silver. KM52.	18.00
PnA88	1969So	—	Peso. 0.7500 Gold. 4.0700 g. KM52.	250
Pn88	1969So	50	5 Pesos. Copper-Nickel. KM53.	30.00
Pn89	1969So	1,000	5 Pesos. 0.9000 Silver. KM53.	18.00
PnA90	1969So	—	5 Pesos. 0.7500 Gold. 5.8600 g. KM53.	300
Pn90	1969So	50	10 Pesos. Copper-Nickel. KM54.	30.00
Pn91	1969So	1,000	10 Pesos. 0.9000 Silver. KM54.	18.00
PnA92	1969	—	10 Pesos 0.7500 Gold. 7.8700 g. 22.9 mm. Similar to KM#54; Proof.	—
Pn92	1969	20,000	1000 Pesos. Copper.	30.00
Pn93	1969	250	1000 Pesos. Silver.	45.00
Pn96	1970So	—	20 Pesos. Silver. No star on reverse. KM56.	18.00
Pn97	1970So	1,000	20 Pesos. Gold. KM56.	300
Pn98	1970So	—	50 Pesos. Silver. KM57.	18.00
Pn99	1970So	1,000	50 Pesos. Gold. KM57.	350
Pn95	1970So	—	20 Pesos. Silver. Star on reverse. KM56.	—
Pn100	1971So	—	50 Pesos. Copper Nickel. KM58.	55.00
Pn101	1971So	80	50 Pesos. Copper Nickel. With F. ORRELLANA, P., KM58	55.00
Pn102	1971So	2,000	50 Pesos. Silver. KM58.	25.00
Pn103	1971So	200	50 Pesos. Gold. KM58.	375
Pn104	1972So	3	100 Pesos.	—
Pn105	1972So	12	100 Pesos. Alpaca.	—
Pn106	1973	—	100 Pesos. Silver. KM59.	30.00
PnA107	1973	—	100 Pesos. Gold. Similar to KM#59.	—
PnB107	1973	50	100 Pesos. Aluminum.	—
PnD107	1973	50	100 Pesos. Copper.	—
PnC107	1975	50	5 Pesos. Alpaca. Similar to KM#65.	—
PnA108	1976	—	10 Centesimos. Copper. Similar to KM#66.	—
PnB108	1976	—	10 Centesimos. Aluminum. Similar to KM#66.	—
PnC108	1976	—	20 Centesimos. Copper. Similar to KM#67.	—
PnD108	1976	—	20 Centesimos. Aluminum. Similar to KM#67.	—
PnE108	1976	—	50 Centesimos. Copper. Similar to KM#68.	—
PnF108	1976	—	50 Centesimos. Aluminum. Similar to KM#68.	—
PnG108	1976	—	Nuevo Peso. Copper. Similar to KM#69.	—
PnH108	1976	—	Nuevo Peso. Aluminum. Similar to KM#69.	—
Pn107	1976	—	5 Nuevos Pesos. Aluminum. KM70.	75.00
Pn108	1976	—	5 Nuevos Pesos. Copper-Aluminum. KM70.	75.00
Pn109	1976	—	5 Nuevos Pesos. Copper-Nickel. KM70.	100
Pn110	1976	—	5 Nuevos Pesos. Silver. KM70.	150
PnA111	1977	—	Centesimo. Gold. Similar to KM#71.	—
PnB111	1977	—	Centesimo. Nickel. Similar to KM#71.	—
PnC111	1977	—	Centesimo. Copper. Similar to KM#71.	—
PnD111	1977	—	Centesimo. Aluminum-Bronze. Similar to KM#71.	—
PnE111	1977	—	2 Centesimos. Gold. Similar to KM#72.	—
PnF111	1977	—	2 Centesimos. Nickel. Similar to KM#72.	—
PnG111	1977	—	2 Centesimos. Copper. Similar to KM#72.	—
PnH111	1977	—	2 Centesimos. Aluminum-Bronze. Similar to KM#72.	—
PnI111	1977	—	5 Centesimos. Gold. Similar to KM#73.	—
PnJ111	1977	—	5 Centesimos. Nickel. Similar to KM#73.	—
PnK111	1977	—	5 Centesimos. Copper. Similar to KM#73.	—
PnL111	1977	—	5 Centesimos. Aluminum-Bronze. Similar to KM#73.	—
PnN111	1980	—	Nuevo Peso. Copper. Similar to KM#74.	—

KM#	Date	Mintage	Identification	Mkt Val
PnM111	1980	—	Nuevo Peso. Aluminum. Similar to KM#74.	—
PnB112	1980	—	5 Nuevos Pesos. Copper. Similar to KM#75.	—
PnA112	1980	—	5 Nuevos Pesos. Aluminum. Similar to KM#75.	—
Pn111	1980	—	Peso. Brass. KM74.	—
Pn112	1980	—	5 Pesos. Brass. KM75.	—
Pn113	1981	—	10 Pesos. Brass. KM79.	—
PnA114	1981So	—	100 Nuevos Pesos. 0.9000 Gold. 20.0000 g. KM80.	425
PnB114	1981So	—	5000 Nuevos Pesos. 0.9000 Gold. 20.0000 g. KM81.	375
PnA113	1981	—	2 Nuevos Pesos. Silver. Similar to KM#77; Proof.	—
PnB113	1981	—	2 Nuevos Pesos. Aluminum-Bronze. Similar to KM#77; Proof.	—
PnC113	1981	—	10 Nuevos Pesos. Copper. Similar to KM#79.	—
PnD113	1981	—	10 Nuevos Pesos. Aluminum. Similar to KM#79.	—
PnC114	1983So	—	500 Nuevos Pesos. 0.9000 Gold. 20.0000 g. KM82.	550
Pn114	1984	—	2000 Nuevos Pesos. Copper. Thick reeded edge. KM87.	—
Pn115	1984	—	2000 Nuevos Pesos. Aluminum. Thick reeded edge. KM87.	—
Pn116	1984	—	2000 Nuevos Pesos. Aluminum. Thick reeded edge. KM88.	—
Pn117	1984	—	2000 Nuevos Pesos. Aluminum. Thick reeded edge. KM88.	—
Pn118	1984	—	20000 Nuevos Pesos. Alum. KM89.	—
Pn119	1984	—	20000 Nuevos Pesos. Gold. 32.5 mm. KM89.	—
PnA118	1984	40	2000 Nuevos Pesos. Silver. 40.6 mm. Similar to KM#88. Different obverse and reverse; Proof.	—
PnA119	1984	—	20000 Nuevos Pesos. Silver. 40.6 mm. Similar to KM#89.	—
PnB119	1984	—	20000 Nuevos Pesos. Copper. Similar to KM#89.	—
PnC119	1984	—	20000 Nuevos Pesos. Brass. Similar to KM#89.	—
Pn120	1987	—	5000 Pesos. Alpaca. KM91; Alpaca	—
Pn121	1987	—	5000 Pesos. Copper. KM91.	—
Pn122	1987	—	5000 Pesos. Bronze. KM91.	—
Pn123	1988	—	5000 Nuevos Pesos. Copper. Similar to KM#99.	—
Pn124	1988	—	5000 Nuevos Pesos. Alpaca. Similar to KM#99.	—

TRIAL STRIKES

KM#	Date	Mintage	Identification	Mkt Val
TS9	1984	—	20000 Nuevos Pesos. Silver. 25.4700 g. Radiant sun peeking over shield of arms in wreath within inner circle. PRUEBA.	100
TS10	1984	—	2000 Nuevos Pesos. Silver. 25.6700 g. PRUEBA. Map of Uruguay at right, map of North and South America above rising sun at lower left.	100
TS11	1984	—	2000 Nuevos Pesos. Copper. Radiant sun peeking over shield of arms in wreath within inner circle. PRUEBA.	85.00
TS12	1984	—	2000 Nuevos Pesos. Copper. PRUEBA. Map of Uruguay at right, map of North and South America above rising sun at lower left.	85.00
TS13	1984	—	2000 Nuevos Pesos. Copper Gilt. Radiant sun peeking over shield of arms in wreath within inner circle. PRUEBA.	100
TS14	1984	—	2000 Nuevos Pesos. Copper Gilt. PRUEBA. Map of Uruguay at right, map of North and South America above rising sun at lower left.	100
TS15	1984	—	2000 Nuevos Pesos. Aluminum. Radiant sun peeking over shield of arms in wreath within inner circle. PRUEBA.	85.00
TS16	1984	—	2000 Nuevos Pesos. Aluminum. PRUEBA. Map of Uruguay at right, map of North and South America above rising sun.	85.00
TS17	1984	—	2000 Nuevos Pesos. Silver. 25.0000 g. Radiant sun peeking over shield of arms within wreath. PRUEBA.	100
TS18	1984	—	2000 Nuevos Pesos. Silver. 24.7200 g. PRUEBA. Map of Uruguay at right, map of North and South America above rising sun.	100
TS19	1984	—	2000 Nuevos Pesos. Copper. Radiant sun peeking over arms within wreath. Winged Liberty divides value.	85.00
TS20	1984	—	2000 Nuevos Pesos. Copper. PRUEBA. Map of Uruguay at right, map of North and South America above rising sun at lower left.	85.00
TS21	1984	—	2000 Nuevos Pesos. Copper Gilt. Radiant sun peeking over shield of arms within wreath. PRUEBA.	100
TS22	1984	—	2000 Nuevos Pesos. Copper Gilt. PRUEBA. Map of Uruguay at right, map of North and South America above rising sun at lower left.	100
TS23	1984	—	2000 Nuevos Pesos. Aluminum. Radiant sun peeking over shield of arms within wreath. PRUEBA.	85.00
TS24	1984	—	2000 Nuevos Pesos. Aluminum. PRUEBA. Map of Uruguay at right, map of North and South America above rising sun at lower left.	85.00

KM#	Date	Mintage	Identification	Mkt Val
TS25	1984	—	20000 Nuevos Pesos. Silver. 19.4400 g. Shield of arms flanked by flags in inner circle. PRUEBA.	110
TS26	1984	—	20000 Nuevos Pesos. Silver. 20.2700 g. PRUEBA. Map of Uruguay at right, map of North and South America above rising sun at lower left.	110
TS27	1984	—	20000 Nuevos Pesos. Copper. Shield of arms flanked by flags in inner circle. PRUEBA.	80.00
TS28	1984	—	20000 Nuevos Pesos. Copper. PRUEBA. Map of Uruguay at right, map of North and South America above rising sun at lower left.	80.00
TS29	1984	—	20000 Nuevos Pesos. Copper Gilt. Shield of arms flanked by flags in inner circle. PRUEBA.	90.00
TS30	1984	—	20000 Nuevos Pesos. Copper Gilt. PRUEBA. Map of Uruguay at right, map of North and South America above rising sun at lower left.	90.00

PIEFORTS
Double Thickness

KM#	Date	Mintage	Identification	Mkt Val
P6	1984	600	20 Pesos. Silver. KM86a.	60.00
P7	1984	—	2000 Nuevos Pesos. Silver. 50.0000 g. Plain edge. KM87.	185
P8	1984	—	2000 Nuevos Pesos. Copper. Thick plain edge. KM87.	65.00
P9	1984	—	2000 Nuevos Pesos. Copper Gilt. Thick plain edge. KM87.	75.00
P10	1984	—	2000 Nuevos Pesos. Silver. 50.4800 g. Plain edge. KM88.	125
P11	1984	—	2000 Nuevos Pesos. Copper. Thick plain edge. KM88.	65.00
P12	1984	—	2000 Nuevos Pesos. Copper Gilt. Thick plain edge. KM88.	75.00
P13	1984	—	20000 Nuevos Pesos. Silver. 20.7500 g. Reeded edge. KM89.	125
P14	1984	—	20000 Nuevos Pesos. Silver. 40.1700 g. Reeded edge. KM89.	200
P15	1984	—	20000 Nuevos Pesos. Silver. 40.4400 g. Plain edge. KM89.	200
P16	1984	—	20000 Nuevos Pesos. Copper. Thick reeded edge. KM89.	80.00
P17	1984	—	20000 Nuevos Pesos. Copper. Reeded edge. KM89.	80.00
P18	1984	—	20000 Nuevos Pesos. Copper Gilt. KM89.	100

MINT SETS

KM#	Date	Mintage	Identification	Issue Price	Mkt Val
MS1	1969/70 (5)	—	KM52-54, 56-57 KM#MS1 was issued under the law no. 13,637 of Dec. 21, 1967.	—	3.50
MS2	1969/70 (5)	—	KM52-54, 56-57 KM#MS2 was issued for the 11th Assembly of the Interamerica Bank.	—	3.50
MS3	1976 (4)	—	KM66-69	—	2.50
MS4	1976 (4)	—	KM#Pn107-110	—	400

PROOF SETS

KM#	Date	Mintage	Identification	Issue Price	Mkt Val
PS1	1953 (4)	100	KM32-35	—	275
PS2	1968 (5)	1,000	KM#Pn79, 81, 83-85	—	78.00
PS3	1968 (3)	50	KM49-51	—	200
PS4	1968 (3)	100	KM#Pn78, 80, 82	—	90.00
PS5	1969 (3)	50	KM#Pn86, 88, 90	—	75.00
PS6	1969 (3)	1,000	KM#Pn87, 89, 91	—	30.00
PS7	1969/70 (5)	1,000	KM#Pn87, 89, 91, 96, 98	—	50.00
PS8	1976 (4)	—	KM#66a-69a	—	125

UZBEKISTAN

The Republic of Uzbekistan (formerly the Uzbek S.S.R.), is bordered on the north by Kazakhstan, to the east by Kirghizia and Tajikistan, on the south by Afghanistan and on the west by Turkmenistan. The republic is comprised of the regions of Andizhan, Bukhara, Dzhizak, Ferghana, Kashkadar, Khorezm (Khiva), Namangan, Navoi, Samarkand, Surkhan-Darya, Syr-Darya, Tashkent and the Karakalpak Autonomous Republic. It has an area of 172,741 sq. mi. (447,400 sq. km.) and a population of 20.3 million. Capital: Tashkent. Crude oil, natural gas, coal, copper, and gold deposits make up the chief resources, while intensive farming, based on artificial irrigation, provides an abundance of cotton.

On June 20, 1990 the Uzbek Supreme Soviet adopted a declaration of sovereignty, and in Aug. 1991, following an unsuccessful coup, declared itself independent as the "Republic of Uzbekistan", which was confirmed by referendum in Dec. That same month Uzbekistan became a member of the CIS.

MONETARY SYSTEM
100 Tiyin = 1 Som

REPUBLIC
STANDARD COINAGE

KM# 1.1 TIYIN
1.7500 g., Brass Clad Steel, 16.9 mm. **Obv:** Arms within wreath below stars **Rev:** Value and date flanked by sprigs **Edge:** Plain

Date	Mintage	F	VF	XF	Unc	BU
1994	—	—	—	—	0.30	—

KM# 1.2 TIYIN
1.7500 g., Brass Clad Steel, 16.9 mm. **Obv:** Arms within wreath below stars **Rev:** Value and date flanked by sprigs **Edge:** Plain

Date	Mintage	F	VF	XF	Unc	BU
1994	—	—	—	—	0.25	0.35

KM# 2.1 3 TIYIN
2.7000 g., Brass Plated Steel, 19.9 mm. **Obv:** Arms within wreath below stars **Rev:** Value and date flanked by sprigs **Edge:** Reeded

Date	Mintage	F	VF	XF	Unc	BU
1994	—	—	—	—	3.00	—

KM# 2.2 3 TIYIN
2.7000 g., Brass Plated Steel, 19.9 mm. **Obv:** Arms within wreath below stars **Rev:** Value and date flanked by sprigs **Edge:** Reeded

Date	Mintage	F	VF	XF	Unc	BU
1994	—	—	—	—	1.00	—

KM# 3.1 5 TIYIN
3.4000 g., Brass Plated Steel, 21.4 mm. **Obv:** Arms within wreath below stars **Rev:** Value and date flanked by sprigs **Edge:** Reeded

Date	Mintage	F	VF	XF	Unc	BU
1994	—	—	—	—	2.00	—

KM# 3.2 5 TIYIN
3.4000 g., Brass Plated Steel, 21.4 mm. **Obv:** Arms within wreath below stars **Rev:** Value and date flanked by sprigs **Edge:** Reeded

Date	Mintage	F	VF	XF	Unc	BU
1994	—	—	—	—	0.50	—

KM# 4.1 10 TIYIN
2.8500 g., Nickel Clad Steel, 18.7 mm. **Obv:** Arms within wreath below stars **Rev:** Value and date flanked by sprigs **Edge:** Reeded
Note: Two varieties of sunray arrangements exist; die varieties exist with slightly larger or smaller denomination, plain rim.

Date	Mintage	F	VF	XF	Unc	BU
1994	—	—	—	—	0.60	—
1994PM Rare	—	—	—	—	—	—

KM# 4.2   10 TIYIN
2.8500 g., Nickel Clad Steel, 18.7 mm. **Obv:** Arms within wreath below stars **Rev:** Value and date flanked by sprigs **Edge:** Reeded **Note:** Beaded rim.

Date	Mintage	F	VF	XF	Unc	BU
1994	—	—	—	—	5.00	—

KM# 5.1   20 TIYIN
4.0000 g., Nickel Clad Steel, 22 mm. **Obv:** Arms within wreath below stars **Rev:** Date and value flanked by sprigs **Edge:** Cyrillic denomination twice

Date	Mintage	F	VF	XF	Unc	BU
1994	—	—	—	—	0.75	—

KM# 5.5   20 TIYIN
4.0000 g., Nickel Clad Steel, 22 mm. **Obv:** Arms within wreath below stars **Rev:** Date and large denomination flanked by sprigs **Edge:** Cyrillic

Date	Mintage	F	VF	XF	Unc	BU
1994	—	—	—	—	0.75	—

KM# 5.2   20 TIYIN
4.0000 g., Nickel Clad Steel, 22 mm. **Obv:** Arms within wreath below stars **Rev:** Date and value flanked by sprigs **Note:** Two sun ray varieties exist, varieties exist with wide and narrow edge lettering.

Date	Mintage	F	VF	XF	Unc	BU
1994	—	—	—	—	1.00	—
1994PM Rare	—	—	—	—	—	—

KM# 5.3   20 TIYIN
4.0000 g., Nickel Clad Steel, 22 mm. **Obv:** Arms within wreath below stars **Rev:** Date and value flanked by sprigs **Edge:** Lettering in Cyrillic **Note:** Two varieties of sunray arrangements exist.

Date	Mintage	F	VF	XF	Unc	BU
1994	—	—	—	—	0.75	—

KM# 5.4   20 TIYIN
4.0000 g., Nickel Clad Steel, 22 mm. **Obv:** Arms within wreath below stars **Rev:** Date and value flanked by sprigs **Edge:** Lettering in Cyrillic

Date	Mintage	F	VF	XF	Unc	BU
1994 Scarce	—	—	—	—	20.00	—

KM# 6.1   50 TIYIN
4.8000 g., Nickel Clad Steel, 23.9 mm. **Obv:** Arms within wreath below stars **Rev:** Small denomination and date flanked by sprigs **Edge:** Lettering in Cyrillic **Note:** 2 varieties of sunray arrangements exist; all coins show orthographic error in 1st letter of "ellik" within edge inscription.

Date	Mintage	F	VF	XF	Unc	BU
1994	—	—	—	—	1.00	—
1994PM	—	—	—	—	50.00	—

KM# 6.2   50 TIYIN
4.8000 g., Nickel Clad Steel, 23.9 mm. **Obv:** Arms within wreath below stars **Rev:** Large denomination, date flanked by sprigs **Edge:** Lettering in Cyrillic **Note:** All coins show orthographic error in 1st letter of "ellik" within edge inscription.

Date	Mintage	F	VF	XF	Unc	BU
1994	—	—	—	—	1.00	—

KM# 8   SOM
2.8000 g., Nickel Clad Steel **Obv:** Arms within wreath below stars **Rev:** Value and date flanked by sprigs **Note:** Edge varieties exist.

Date	Mintage	F	VF	XF	Unc	BU
1997	—	—	—	—	1.35	—
1998 Rare	—	—	—	—	—	—
1999	—	—	—	—	1.35	—
2000	—	—	—	—	1.35	—

KM# 12   SOM
2.8300 g., Nickel-Clad Steel, 18.8 mm. **Obv:** National arms **Rev:** Value and map **Edge:** Reeded

Date	Mintage	F	VF	XF	Unc	BU
2000	—	—	—	—	1.00	1.25

KM# 9   5 SOM
4.0000 g., Nickel Clad Steel **Obv:** Arms within wreath below stars **Rev:** Value and date flanked by sprigs

Date	Mintage	F	VF	XF	Unc	BU
1997	—	—	—	—	1.50	—
	Note: Edge varieties exist					
1998 Rare	—	—	—	—	—	—
1999	—	—	—	—	1.50	—

KM# 7   10 SOM
31.1000 g., 0.9990 Silver 0.9988 oz. ASW **Subject:** 3rd Anniversary of Independence **Obv:** Arms within wreath **Rev:** Equestrian above value

Date	Mintage	F	VF	XF	Unc	BU
1994 Proof	Est. 1,000	Value: 75.00				

KM# 10   10 SOM
4.7000 g., Nickel Clad Steel **Obv:** Arms within wreath below stars **Rev:** Value and date flanked by sprigs

Date	Mintage	F	VF	XF	Unc	BU
1997	—	—	—	—	2.00	—
	Note: Edge varieties exist					
1998 Rare	—	—	—	—	—	—
1999	—	—	—	—	2.00	—
2000	—	—	—	—	2.00	—

KM# 11   25 SOM
Nickel Clad Steel, 27 mm. **Subject:** Jaloliddin Manguberdi **Obv:** Arms within wreath **Rev:** Bust with headdress facing 1/4 right **Edge:** Plain

Date	Mintage	F	VF	XF	Unc	BU
1999	—	—	—	—	3.50	—

PATTERNS
Including off metal strikes

KM#	Date	Mintage	Identification	Mkt Val
Pn1	1994	—	Som. Gold-Plated Bronze. 15.1300 g. 31 mm. National arms. Muhammad Taragay Ulugbek (1394-1449). Reeded edge. Proof	100
Pn2	1995	—	Tiyin. 0.8000 Gold Plated Silver. 15.2200 g. 31 mm. National arms. Samarkand building. Reeded edge. Proof	200

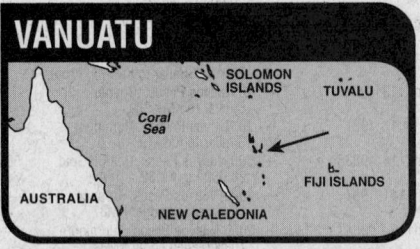

VANUATU

The Republic of Vanuatu, formerly New Hebrides Condominium, a group of islands located in the South Pacific 500 miles (800 km.) west of Fiji, were under the joint sovereignty of Great Britain and France. The islands have an area of 5,700 sq. mi. (14,760 sq. km.) and a population of 165,000, mainly Melanesians of mixed blood. Capital: Port-Vila. The volcanic and coral islands, while malarial land subject to frequent earthquakes, are extremely fertile, and produce copra, coffee, tropical fruits and timber for export.

The New Hebrides were discovered by Portuguese navigator Pedro de Quiros (sailing under orders by the King of Spain) in 1606, visited by French explorer Bougainville in 1768, and named by British navigator Capt. James Cook in 1774. Ships of all nations converged on the islands to trade for sandalwood, prompting France and Britain to relinquish their individual claims and declare the islands a neutral zone in 1878. The New Hebrides were placed under the control of a mixed Anglo-French commission of naval officers during the native uprisings of 1887, and established as a condominium under the joint sovereignty of France and Great Britain in 1906.

Vanuatu became an independent republic within the Commonwealth in July 1980. A president is Head of State and the Prime Minister is Head of Government.

MINT MARK
(a) - Paris, privy marks only

MONETARY SYSTEM
Francs until 1983
Vatu to Present

REPUBLIC
STANDARD COINAGE

KM# 3   VATU
1.9900 g., Nickel-Brass, 16.95 mm. **Obv:** National arms **Rev:** Shell and value **Edge:** Plain

Date	Mintage	F	VF	XF	Unc	BU
1983	—	—	—	0.10	0.50	0.75
1983 Proof	—	Value: 1.00				
1990	—	—	—	0.10	0.50	0.75
1999	—	—	—	0.10	0.50	0.75

KM# 4   2 VATU
3.0000 g., Nickel-Brass, 20 mm. **Obv:** National arms **Rev:** Shell and value **Edge:** Plain

Date	Mintage	F	VF	XF	Unc	BU
1983	—	—	—	0.15	0.50	1.00
1983 Proof	—	Value: 1.50				
1990	—	—	—	0.15	0.50	1.00
1995	—	—	—	0.15	0.50	1.00
1999	—	—	—	0.15	0.50	1.00

KM# 5 5 VATU

4.1000 g., Nickel-Brass, 23.5 mm. **Obv:** National arms
Rev: Shell and value **Edge:** Plain

Date	Mintage	F	VF	XF	Unc	BU
1983	—	—	—	0.20	0.75	1.50
1983 Proof	—	Value: 1.75				
1990	—	—	—	0.20	0.75	1.50
1995	—	—	—	0.20	0.75	1.50
1999	—	—	—	0.20	0.75	1.50

KM# 6 10 VATU

6.1000 g., Copper-Nickel, 23.95 mm. **Obv:** National arms
Rev: Crab and value, palm trees **Edge:** Plain

Date	Mintage	F	VF	XF	Unc	BU
1983	—	—	—	0.25	1.00	2.80
1983 Proof	—	Value: 2.00				
1990	—	—	—	0.25	1.00	2.80
1995	—	—	—	0.25	1.00	2.80
1999	—	—	—	0.25	1.00	2.80

KM# 25 10 VATU

Copper-Nickel **Subject:** End of Victorian Era - Queen Victoria
Obv: Arms **Rev:** Seated half figure of Queen Mother left within
beaded circle

Date	Mintage	F	VF	XF	Unc	BU
1995	Est. 30,000	—	—	—	2.00	3.00

KM# 28 10 VATU

10.0000 g., 0.5000 Silver 0.1607 oz. ASW **Series:** Olympics
Obv: Arms **Rev:** Gymnast

Date	Mintage	F	VF	XF	Unc	BU
1996	Est. 10,000	—	—	—	4.00	5.00

KM# 7 20 VATU

10.2000 g., Copper-Nickel, 28.45 mm. **Obv:** National arms
Rev: Crab, value, palm trees **Edge:** Reeded **Note:** Similar 10 Vatu,
KM#6.

Date	Mintage	F	VF	XF	Unc	BU
1983	—	—	—	0.35	1.50	3.00
1983 Proof	—	Value: 3.00				
1990	—	—	—	0.35	1.50	3.00

Date	Mintage	F	VF	XF	Unc	BU
1995	—	—	—	0.35	1.50	3.00
1999	—	—	—	0.35	1.50	3.00

KM# 19 20 VATU

20.0000 g., 0.5000 Silver 0.3215 oz. ASW **Subject:** Captain James
Cook **Obv:** National arms **Rev:** Seated half figure facing right

Date	Mintage	F	VF	XF	Unc	BU
1994 Proof	Est. 25,000	Value: 10.00				

KM# 20 20 VATU

20.0000 g., 0.9250 Silver 0.5948 oz. ASW **Series:** Endangered
Wildlife **Obv:** National arms **Rev:** Kingfisher

Date	Mintage	F	VF	XF	Unc	BU
1994 Proof	Est. 25,000	Value: 35.00				

KM# 1 50 VATU

15.0000 g., Nickel, 32.9 mm. **Subject:** 1st Anniversary of
Independence **Obv:** National arms **Rev:** Figures working in fields

Date	Mintage	F	VF	XF	Unc	BU
1981	—	—	—	0.75	2.00	3.00

KM# 1a 50 VATU

15.0000 g., 0.9250 Silver 0.4461 oz. ASW **Obv:** National arms
Rev: Figures working in field

Date	Mintage	F	VF	XF	Unc	BU
1981 Proof	846	Value: 18.50				

KM# 8 50 VATU

15.0000 g., Copper-Nickel, 32.9 mm. **Series:** F.A.O.
Obv: National arms **Rev:** Tubers encircled by leafy vines,
value above

Date	Mintage	F	VF	XF	Unc	BU
1983	—	—	—	0.75	2.00	3.00
1983 Proof	—	Value: 5.00				
1990	—	—	—	0.75	2.00	3.00
1995	—	—	—	0.75	2.00	3.00
1999	—	—	—	0.75	2.00	3.00

KM# 10 50 VATU

34.0000 g., 0.9250 Silver 1.0111 oz. ASW **Series:** Seoul
Olympics **Subject:** Boxing **Obv:** National arms **Rev:** Boxers

Date	Mintage	F	VF	XF	Unc	BU
1988 Proof	15,000	Value: 16.50				

KM# 11 50 VATU

31.4700 g., 0.9250 Silver 0.9359 oz. ASW **Subject:** Voyager I
Obv: National arms **Rev:** Space shuttle and planets

Date	Mintage	F	VF	XF	Unc	BU
1992 Proof	10,000	Value: 16.50				

KM# 12 50 VATU

31.4700 g., 0.9250 Silver 0.9359 oz. ASW **Subject:** Pedro
Fernandez De Quiros **Obv:** National arms **Rev:** Kneeling figure
facing, boat and ship

Date	Mintage	F	VF	XF	Unc	BU
1992 Proof	—	Value: 16.50				

KM# 13 50 VATU

31.4700 g., 0.9250 Silver 0.9359 oz. ASW **Series:** Endangered
Wildlife **Subject:** Earth Pigeons **Obv:** National arms **Rev:** Birds

Date	Mintage	F	VF	XF	Unc	BU
1992 Proof	—	Value: 25.00				

KM# 14 50 VATU
31.4700 g., 0.9250 Silver 0.9359 oz. ASW **Series:** Olympics
Subject: Canoes **Obv:** National arms **Rev:** Canoers

Date	Mintage	F	VF	XF	Unc	BU
1992 Proof	Est. 40,000				Value: 16.50	

KM# 15 50 VATU
31.4700 g., 0.9250 Silver 0.9359 oz. ASW **Subject:** 40th
Anniversary of Coronation **Obv:** National arms

Date	Mintage	F	VF	XF	Unc	BU
1993 Proof	Est. 10,000				Value: 16.50	

KM# 16 50 VATU
31.4700 g., 0.9250 Silver 0.9359 oz. ASW **Subject:** The
Boudeuse **Obv:** National arms **Rev:** Ship to left of half figure right

Date	Mintage	F	VF	XF	Unc	BU
1993 Proof	Est. 15,000				Value: 16.50	

KM# 17 50 VATU
31.4700 g., 0.9250 Silver 0.9359 oz. ASW **Subject:** Protect Our
World **Obv:** National arms **Rev:** Whale and ship

Date	Mintage	F	VF	XF	Unc	BU
1993 Proof	Est. 10,000				Value: 30.00	

KM# 18 50 VATU
31.4700 g., 0.9250 Silver 0.9359 oz. ASW **Subject:** World Cup
Soccer **Obv:** National arms **Rev:** Soccer player

Date	Mintage	F	VF	XF	Unc	BU
1994 Proof	Est. 10,000				Value: 16.50	

KM# 21 50 VATU
31.4700 g., 0.9250 Silver 0.9359 oz. ASW **Subject:** De
Bougainville **Obv:** National arms **Rev:** Bust facing at left of book,
globe and ship

Date	Mintage	F	VF	XF	Unc	BU
1994 Proof	Est. 10,000				Value: 16.50	

KM# 22 50 VATU
31.4700 g., 0.9250 Silver 0.9359 oz. ASW **Subject:** Queen
Victoria **Obv:** National arms **Rev:** Seated half figure of Queen
Mother right within beaded circle

Date	Mintage	F	VF	XF	Unc	BU
1994 Proof	Est. 20,000				Value: 16.50	

KM# 24 50 VATU
31.4700 g., 0.9250 Silver 0.9359 oz. ASW **Series:** Olympics
Obv: National arms **Rev:** Swimmers

Date	Mintage	F	VF	XF	Unc	BU
1994 Proof	Est. 40,000				Value: 16.00	

KM# 30 50 VATU
31.4700 g., 0.9250 Silver 0.9359 oz. ASW **Series:** Olympic
Games 1996 **Obv:** National arms **Rev:** Gymnast

Date	Mintage	F	VF	XF	Unc	BU
1994 Proof	40,000				Value: 16.00	

KM# 26 50 VATU
31.4700 g., 0.9250 Silver 0.9359 oz. ASW **Subject:** Birth of
Great Grandson Prince William **Obv:** National arms
Rev: Conjoined busts facing holding infant within beaded circle

Date	Mintage	F	VF	XF	Unc	BU
1995 Proof	Est. 30,000				Value: 16.50	

KM# 29 50 VATU
31.4700 g., 0.9250 Silver 0.9359 oz. ASW **Subject:** Queen
Victoria and Prince Albert **Obv:** National arms **Rev:** Conjoined
standing figures in front of building within circle

Date	Mintage	F	VF	XF	Unc	BU
1996 Proof	Est. 10,000				Value: 16.50	

KM# 44 50 VATU
1.2500 g., Gold, 13.87 mm. **Subject:** 1996 Summer Olympics
- Atlanta **Obv:** National arms **Obv. Leg.:** RIPABLIK BLONG
VANUATU **Rev:** Gymnist **Edge:** Reeded

Date	Mintage	F	VF	XF	Unc	BU
1997 Proof	—				Value: 55.00	

KM# 35 50 VATU
28.3100 g., Silver, 38.5 mm. **Subject:** 50th Anniversary -
Elizabeth and Philip **Obv:** National arms **Rev:** Family members
gazing at baby Prince Andrew **Edge:** Reeded **Note:** Gold-plated
shield on reverse reads: Prince Andrew 1960

Date	Mintage	F	VF	XF	Unc	BU
1997 Proof	—				Value: 18.00	

KM# 31 50 VATU
1.2441 g., 0.9990 Gold 0.0400 oz. AGW **Obv:** National arms
Rev: Spanish 1704 gold coin design

Date	Mintage	F	VF	XF	Unc	BU
1998 Proof	—				Value: 50.00	

KM# 32 50 VATU
1.2441 g., 0.9990 Gold 0.0400 oz. AGW **Obv:** National arms
Rev: Boar tusk necklace

Date	Mintage	F	VF	XF	Unc	BU
1998 Proof	—				Value: 45.00	

KM# 33 50 VATU
30.9700 g., 0.9250 Silver 0.9210 oz. ASW **Subject:** Millennium 2000 **Obv:** National arms **Rev:** Gold-plated shell

Date	Mintage	F	VF	XF	Unc	BU
1998 Proof	—	Value: 70.00				

KM# 36 50 VATU
31.4700 g., 0.9250 Silver 0.9359 oz. ASW, 37 mm. **Obv:** Standing native **Rev:** Three masted corvette Zelee **Edge:** Reeded

Date	Mintage	F	VF	XF	Unc	BU
1999 Proof	—	Value: 45.00				

KM# 37 50 VATU
31.4700 g., 0.9250 Silver 0.9359 oz. ASW, 37 mm. **Obv:** Standing native **Rev:** Three masted corvette Astrolabe **Edge:** Reeded

Date	Mintage	F	VF	XF	Unc	BU
1999 Proof	—	Value: 45.00				

KM# 40 50 VATU
3.1100 g., 0.5850 Gold 0.0585 oz. AGW **Subject:** XXVII Summer Olympics - Sydney 2000 **Obv:** National arms **Rev:** Sprinter

Date	Mintage	F	VF	XF	Unc	BU
1999 Proof	—	Value: 85.00				

KM# 9 100 VATU
9.5500 g., Nickel-Brass, 23.9 mm. **Obv:** National arms **Rev:** Sprouting bulbs

Date	Mintage	F	VF	XF	Unc	BU
1988	—	—	—	—	3.00	4.00
1995	—	—	—	—	3.00	4.00

KM# 23 100 VATU
7.7760 g., 0.5830 Gold 0.1457 oz. AGW **Series:** Endangered Wildlife **Obv:** National arms **Rev:** Kingfisher

Date	Mintage	F	VF	XF	Unc	BU
1994 Proof	Est. 2,000	Value: 165				

KM# 27 100 VATU
155.5000 g., 0.9250 Silver 4.6243 oz. ASW, 65 mm. **Obv:** National arms **Rev:** Crowned standing figures facing within beaded circle **Note:** Illustration reduced.

Date	Mintage	F	VF	XF	Unc	BU
1995 Proof	Est. 2,000	Value: 145				

KM# 34 100 VATU
155.5000 g., 0.9250 Silver 4.6243 oz. ASW, 65.7 mm. **Subject:** H.M.S. Resolution **Obv:** National arms **Rev:** Sailing ship and carvings **Edge:** Reeded **Note:** Illustration reduced.

Date	Mintage	F	VF	XF	Unc	BU
1996 Proof	5,000	Value: 85.00				

KM# 39 100 VATU
7.7800 g., 0.5833 Gold 0.1459 oz. AGW **Subject:** Queen Mother Elizabeth - Birth of Prince William **Obv:** National arms

Date	Mintage	F	VF	XF	Unc	BU
1997 Proof	25,000	Value: 185				

KM# 2 10000 VATU
15.9800 g., 0.9170 Gold 0.4711 oz. AGW **Subject:** 1st Anniversary of Independence **Obv:** National arms **Rev:** Crab flanked by palm trees

Date	Mintage	F	VF	XF	Unc	BU
1981	538	—	—	—	—	485
1981 Proof	1,054	Value: 480				

PROOF SETS

KM#	Date	Mintage	Identification	Issue Price	Mkt Val
PS1	1983 (6)	—	KM#3-8	—	20.00

The State of the Vatican City, a papal state on the right bank of the Tiber River within the boundaries of Rome, has an area of 0.17 sq. mi. (0.44 sq. km.) and a population of *775. Capital: Vatican City.

Vatican City State, comprising the Vatican, St. Peter's, extra-territorial right to Castel Gandolfo and 13 buildings throughout Rome, is all that remains of the extensive Papal States over which the Pope exercised temporal power in central Italy. During the struggle for Italian unification, the Papal States, including Rome, were forcibly incorporated into the Kingdom of Italy in 1870. The resultant confrontation of crozier and sword remained unresolved until the signing of the Lateran Treaty, Feb. 11, 1929, between the Vatican and the Kingdom of Italy which recognized the independence and sovereignty of the State of the Vatican City, defined the relationship between the government and the church within Italy, and financially compensated the Holy See for the territorial losses from 1870.

Today the Pope exercises supreme legislative, executive and judicial power within the Vatican City, and the State of the Vatican City is recognized by many nations as an independent sovereign state under the temporal jurisdiction of the Pope, even to the extent of ambassadorial exchange. The Pope, is of course, the head of the Roman Catholic Church.

PONTIFFS
Pius XI, 1922-1939
  Sede Vacante, Feb. 10 - Mar. 2, 1939
Pius XII, 1939-1958
  Sede Vacante, Oct. 9 - 28, 1958
John XXIII, 1958-1963
  Sede Vacante, June 3 - 21,1963
Paul VI, 1963-1978
  Sede Vacante, Aug. 6 - 26, 1978
John Paul I, Aug. 26 - Sept. 28, 1978
  Sede Vacante, Sept. 28 - Oct. 16, 1978
John Paul II, 1978-2005
  Sede Vacante, April 2 - 19, 2005
Benedict XVI, 2005-

MINT MARK
Commencing 1981
R – Rome

MONETARY SYSTEM
100 Centesimi = 1 Lira (thru 2002)
100 Euro Cent = 1 Euro

DATING
Most Vatican coins indicate the regnal year of the pope preceded by the word *Anno* (or an abbreviation), even if the *anno domini* date is omitted.

CITY STATE

Pius XI

DECIMAL COINAGE
100 Centesimi = 1 Lira

KM# 1 5 CENTESIMI
Bronze **Obv:** Crowned shield divides date **Rev:** Olive branch divides value

Date	Mintage	F	VF	XF	Unc	BU
1929/VIII	10,000	—	10.00	1,705	40.00	—
1930/IX	100,000	—	5.00	7.50	15.00	—
1931/X	100,000	—	5.00	7.50	15.00	—
1932/XI	100,000	—	5.00	7.50	15.00	—
1934/XIII	100,000	—	5.00	7.50	15.00	—
1935/XIV	44,000	—	7.50	12.50	30.00	—
1936/XV	62,000	—	5.00	7.50	15.00	—
1937/XVI	62,000	—	5.00	7.50	15.00	—
1938/XVII Rare						

KM# 11 5 CENTESIMI
Bronze, 20 mm. **Subject:** Jubilee **Obv:** Crowned shield flanked by date **Rev:** Olive branch divides value

Date	Mintage	F	VF	XF	Unc	BU
1933-34	100,000	—	7.50	12.50	30.00	—

KM# 2 10 CENTESIMI
Bronze **Obv:** Crowned shield divides date **Rev:** St. Peter bust right

Date	Mintage	F	VF	XF	Unc	BU
1929/VIII	10,000	—	10.00	17.50	40.00	—
1930/IX	90,000	—	5.00	7.50	15.00	—
1931/X	90,000	—	5.00	7.50	15.00	—
1932/XI	90,000	—	5.00	7.50	15.00	—
1934/XIII	90,000	—	5.00	7.50	15.00	—
1935/XIV	90,000	—	5.00	7.50	15.00	—
1936/XV	81,000	—	5.00	7.50	15.00	—
1937/XVI	81,000	—	5.00	7.50	15.00	—
1938/XVII		—	450	900	1,500	

KM# 12 10 CENTESIMI
Bronze, 22 mm. **Subject:** Jubilee **Obv:** Crowned shield flanked by dates **Rev:** St. Peter bust right

Date	Mintage	F	VF	XF	Unc	BU
1933-34	90,000	—	7.50	12.50	30.00	—

KM# 3   20 CENTESIMI
Nickel   Obv: Crowned Arms Rev: St. Paul bust left

Date	Mintage	F	VF	XF	Unc	BU
1929/VIII	10,000	—	10.00	17.50	40.00	—
1930/IX	80,000	—	5.00	7.50	15.00	—
1931/X	80,000	—	5.00	7.50	15.00	—
1932/XI	80,000	—	5.00	7.50	15.00	—
1934/XIII	80,000	—	5.00	7.50	15.00	—
1935/XIV	11,000	—	25.00	50.00	75.00	—
1936/XV	64,000	—	5.00	7.50	15.00	—
1937/XVI	64,000	—	5.00	7.50	15.00	—

KM# 13   20 CENTESIMI
Nickel, 21 mm.   Subject: Jubilee Obv: Crowned Arms
Rev: St. Paul bust left

Date	Mintage	F	VF	XF	Unc	BU
1933-34	80,000	—	7.50	12.50	30.00	—

KM# 4   50 CENTESIMI
Nickel   Obv: Crowned Arms Rev: Archangel Michael divides value

Date	Mintage	F	VF	XF	Unc	BU
1929/VIII	10,000	—	10.00	17.50	40.00	—
1930/IX	80,000	—	5.00	7.50	15.00	—
1931/X	80,000	—	5.00	7.50	15.00	—
1932/XI	80,000	—	5.00	7.50	15.00	—
1934/XIII	80,000	—	5.00	7.50	15.00	—
1935/XIV	14,000	—	7.50	15.00	30.00	—
1936/XV	52,000	—	5.00	7.50	15.00	—
1937/XVI	52,000	—	5.00	7.50	15.00	—

KM# 14   50 CENTESIMI
Nickel, 24 mm.   Subject: Jubilee Obv: Crowned Arms
Rev: Archangel Michael divides value

Date	Mintage	F	VF	XF	Unc	BU
1933-34	80,000	—	6.00	12.00	20.00	—

KM# 5   LIRA
Nickel   Obv: Crowned Arms Rev: Virgin Mary standing on globe
and crescent

Date	Mintage	F	VF	XF	Unc	BU
1929/VIII	10,000	—	10.00	1,705	40.00	—
1930/IX	80,000	—	5.00	7.50	15.00	—
1931/X	80,000	—	5.00	7.50	15.00	—
1932/XI	80,000	—	5.00	7.50	15.00	—
1934/XIII	80,000	—	5.00	7.50	15.00	—
1935/XIV	40,000	—	5.00	7.50	15.00	—
1936/XV	40,000	—	5.00	7.50	15.00	—
1937/XVI	70,000	—	5.00	7.50	15.00	—

KM# 15   LIRA
Nickel, 27 mm.   Subject: Jubilee Obv: Crowned Arms
Rev: Virgin Mary standing on globe and crescent
Note: Enlargement of date area.

Date	Mintage	F	VF	XF	Unc	BU
1933-34	80,000	—	7.50	12.50	30.00	—

KM# 6   2 LIRE
Nickel, 29 mm.   Obv: Crowned Arms Rev: Lamb on shoulders
of young shepard

Date	Mintage	F	VF	XF	Unc	BU
1929/VIII	10,000	—	10.00	17.50	40.00	—
1930/IX	50,000	—	5.00	7.50	15.00	—
1931/X	50,000	—	5.00	7.50	15.00	—
1932/XI	50,000	—	5.00	7.50	15.00	—
1934/XIII	50,000	—	5.00	7.50	15.00	—
1935/XIV	70,000	—	5.00	7.50	15.00	—
1936/XV	40,000	—	5.00	7.50	15.00	—
1937/XVI	70,000	—	5.00	7.50	15.00	—

KM# 16   2 LIRE
Nickel, 30 mm.   Subject: Jubilee Obv: Crowned Arms
Rev: Lamb on shoulders of young shepard

Date	Mintage	F	VF	XF	Unc	BU
1933-34	50,000	—	5.00	7.50	15.00	—

KM# 7   5 LIRE
5.0000 g., 0.8350 Silver 0.1342 oz. ASW   Obv: Bust left
Rev: St. Peter in a boat

Date	Mintage	F	VF	XF	Unc	BU
1929/VIII	10,000	—	15.00	30.00	45.00	—
1930/IX	50,000	—	7.50	12.50	30.00	—
1931/X	50,000	—	7.50	12.50	30.00	—
1932/XI	50,000	—	7.50	12.50	30.00	—
1934/XIII	30,000	—	7.50	12.50	30.00	—
1935/XIV	20,000	—	10.00	20.00	35.00	—
1936/XV	40,000	—	7.50	12.50	30.00	—
1937/XVI	40,000	—	7.50	12.50	30.00	—

KM# 17   5 LIRE
5.0000 g., 0.8350 Silver 0.1342 oz. ASW, 23 mm.
Subject: Jubilee Obv: Bust left Rev: St. Peter in a boat

Date	Mintage	F	VF	XF	Unc	BU
1933-34	50,000	—	10.00	20.00	35.00	—

KM# 8   10 LIRE
10.0000 g., 0.8350 Silver 0.2684 oz. ASW   Obv: Bust left
Rev: Mary, Queen of Peace holding infant

Date	Mintage	F	VF	XF	Unc	BU
1929/VIII	10,000	—	20.00	35.00	50.00	—
1930/IX	50,000	—	10.00	17.50	40.00	—
1931/X	50,000	—	10.00	17.50	40.00	—
1932/XI	50,000	—	10.00	17.50	40.00	—
1934/XIII	60,000	—	10.00	17.50	40.00	—
1935/XIV	50,000	—	10.00	17.50	40.00	—
1936/XV	40,000	—	10.00	17.50	40.00	—
1937/XVI	40,000	—	10.00	17.50	40.00	—

KM# 18   10 LIRE
10.0000 g., 0.8350 Silver 0.2684 oz. ASW, 27 mm.
Subject: Jubilee Obv: Bust left Rev: Seated crowned figureof
Mary, Queen of peace facing holding infant

Date	Mintage	F	VF	XF	Unc	BU
1933-34	50,000	—	10.00	17.50	40.00	—

KM# 9   100 LIRE
8.8000 g., 0.9000 Gold 0.2546 oz. AGW, 23.5 mm.   Obv: Bust
right Rev: Standing Jesus facing with child at feet

Date	Mintage	F	VF	XF	Unc	BU
1929/VIII	10,000	—	450	600	800	—
1930/IX	2,621	—	350	550	800	—
1931/X	3,343	—	BV	450	600	—
1932/XI	5,073	—	BV	450	600	—
1934/XIII	2,533	—	BV	450	600	—
1935/XIV	2,015	—	BV	450	600	—

KM# 19   100 LIRE
8.8000 g., 0.9000 Gold 0.2546 oz. AGW, 23.5 mm.
Subject: Jubilee Obv: Bust right Rev: Standing Jesus facing
with child at feet

Date	Mintage	F	VF	XF	Unc	BU
1933-34	23,000	—	BV	450	600	—

KM# 10 100 LIRE
5.1900 g., 0.9000 Gold 0.1502 oz. AGW, 20.5 mm. **Obv:** Bust right **Rev:** Standing Jesus facing with child at feet

Date	Mintage	F	VF	XF	Unc	BU
1936/XV	8,239	—	375	475	600	—
1937/XVI	2,000	—	—	2,000	3,000	—
1938 Rare	6					

Sede Vacante

KM# 20 5 LIRE
5.0000 g., 0.8350 Silver 0.1342 oz. ASW **Subject:** Sede Vacante **Obv:** Arms of Cardinal Pacelli **Rev:** Dove within 1/2 sun

Date	Mintage	F	VF	XF	Unc	BU
1939	40,000	—	20.00	35.00	50.00	—

KM# 21 10 LIRE
10.0000 g., 0.8350 Silver 0.2684 oz. ASW **Obv:** Arms of Cardinal Eugenio Pacelli **Rev:** Dove within 1/2 sun

Date	Mintage	F	VF	XF	Unc	BU
1939	30,000	—	25.00	40.00	55.00	—

Pius XII

KM# 22 5 CENTESIMI
Aluminum-Bronze **Obv:** Crowned shield divides date

Date	Mintage	F	VF	XF	Unc	BU
1939/I	62,000	—	5.00	7.50	12.50	—
1940/II	62,000	—	5.00	7.50	12.50	—
1941/III	5,000	—	10.00	17.50	40.00	—

KM# 31 5 CENTESIMI
Brass **Obv:** Bust left **Rev:** Dove

Date	Mintage	F	VF	XF	Unc	BU
1942/IV	5,000	—	30.00	50.00	75.00	—
1943/V	1,000	—	45.00	65.00	110	—
1944/VI	1,000	—	45.00	65.00	110	—
1945/VII	1,000	—	45.00	65.00	110	—
1946/VIII	1,000	—	45.00	65.00	110	—

KM# 23 10 CENTESIMI
Aluminum-Bronze **Obv:** Crowned shield divides date **Rev:** St. Peter bust right

Date	Mintage	F	VF	XF	Unc	BU
1939/I	81,000	—	5.00	7.50	12.50	—

Date	Mintage	F	VF	XF	Unc	BU
1940/II	81,000	—	5.00	7.50	12.50	—
1941/III	7,500	—	20.00	35.00	50.00	—

KM# 32 10 CENTESIMI
Brass **Obv:** Bust left **Rev:** Dove

Date	Mintage	F	VF	XF	Unc	BU
1942/IV	7,500	—	35.00	50.00	75.00	—
1943/V	1,000	—	50.00	75.00	125	—
1944/VI	1,000	—	50.00	75.00	125	—
1945/VII	1,000	—	50.00	75.00	125	—
1946/VIII	1,000	—	50.00	75.00	125	—

KM# 24 20 CENTESIMI
Nickel **Obv:** Crowned Arms **Rev:** St. Paul bust left

Date	Mintage	F	VF	XF	Unc	BU
1939/I	64,000	—	2.00	4.00	6.00	—

KM# 24a 20 CENTESIMI
Stainless Steel **Obv:** Crowned Arms **Rev:** St. Pual bust left

Date	Mintage	F	VF	XF	Unc	BU
1940/II	64,000	—	2.00	4.00	6.00	—
1941/III	125,000	—	2.00	4.00	6.00	—

KM# 33 20 CENTESIMI
Stainless Steel **Obv:** Crowned shield divides date and beaded circle **Rev:** Justice seated with tablets of the Law

Date	Mintage	F	VF	XF	Unc	BU
1942/IV	125,000	—	2.00	4.00	6.00	—
1943/V	1,000	—	50.00	75.00	125	—
1944/VI	1,000	—	50.00	75.00	125	—
1945/VII	1,000	—	50.00	75.00	125	—
1946/VIII	1,000	—	50.00	75.00	125	—

KM# 25 50 CENTESIMI
Nickel **Obv:** Crowned Arms **Rev:** Archangel Michael facing, divides value

Date	Mintage	F	VF	XF	Unc	BU
1939/I	52,000	—	2.50	4.00	6.00	—

KM# 25a 50 CENTESIMI
Stainless Steel **Obv:** Crowned Arms **Rev:** Archangel Michael facing, divides value

Date	Mintage	F	VF	XF	Unc	BU
1940/II	52,000	—	2.00	4.00	6.00	—
1941/III	180,000	—	2.00	4.00	6.00	—

KM# 34 50 CENTESIMI
Stainless Steel **Obv:** Crowned shield divides date and beaded circle **Rev:** Justice seated with tablets of the Law

Date	Mintage	F	VF	XF	Unc	BU
1942/IV	180,000	—	2.00	4.00	6.00	—
1943/V	1,000	—	50.00	75.00	125	—
1944/VII	1,000	—	50.00	75.00	125	—

Date	Mintage	F	VF	XF	Unc	BU
1945/VII	1,000	—	50.00	75.00	125	—
1946/VIII	1,000	—	50.00	75.00	125	—

KM# 26 LIRA
Nickel **Rev:** Virgin Mary standing on globe and crescent

Date	Mintage	F	VF	XF	Unc	BU
1939/I	70,000	—	5.00	10.00	20.00	—

KM# 26a LIRA
7.8600 g., Stainless Steel, 26.65 mm. **Obv:** Papal arms **Rev:** Virgin Mary standing on globe and crescent **Edge:** Reeded

Date	Mintage	F	VF	XF	Unc	BU
1940/II	70,000	—	3.00	5.00	7.50	—
1941/III	284,000	—	1.00	2.00	4.50	—

KM# 35 LIRA
Stainless Steel **Obv:** Crowned shield divides date and beaded circle **Rev:** Justice seated with tablets of the Law

Date	Mintage	F	VF	XF	Unc	BU
1942/IV	284,000	—	1.00	2.00	4.50	—
1943/V	1,000	—	50.00	75.00	125	—
1944/VI	1,000	—	50.00	75.00	125	—
1945/VII	1,000	—	50.00	75.00	125	—
1946/VIII	1,000	—	50.00	75.00	125	—

KM# 40 LIRA
Aluminum **Obv:** Crowned shield divides date and beaded circle **Rev:** Justice seated with tablet of the Law

Date	Mintage	F	VF	XF	Unc	BU
1947/IX	120,000	—	1.00	2.00	4.00	—
1948/X	10,000	—	2.00	4.00	7.00	—
1949/XI	10,000	—	2.00	4.00	7.00	—

KM# 44 LIRA
Aluminum **Subject:** Holy Year **Obv:** Crowned shield **Rev:** Holy Year Door

Date	Mintage	F	VF	XF	Unc	BU
1950	50,000	—	1.00	2.00	3.50	—

KM# 49.1 LIRA
0.6200 g., Aluminum, 17 mm. **Obv:** Crowned shield **Obv. Leg.:** ANNO **Rev:** Temperance standing pouring libation in bowl **Edge:** Plain

Date	Mintage	F	VF	XF	Unc	BU
1951/XIII	400,000	—	0.25	0.50	1.50	—
1952/XIV	400,000	—	0.25	0.50	1.50	—
1953/XV	400,000	—	0.25	0.50	1.50	—
1955/XVII	10,000	—	1.50	3.00	6.00	—
1957/XIX	30,000	—	0.75	2.00	3.50	—
1958/XX	30,000	—	0.75	2.00	3.50	—

KM# 49.2   LIRA
Aluminum, 17 mm. **Obv:** Crowned shield **Obv. Leg.:** A **Edge:** Plain

Date	Mintage	F	VF	XF	Unc	BU
1956/XVIII	10,000	—	1.50	3.00	6.00	—

KM# 27   2 LIRE
Nickel, 29 mm. **Obv:** Crowned Arms **Rev:** Lamb on shoulders of shepard

Date	Mintage	F	VF	XF	Unc	BU
1939/I	40,000	—	4.00	6.00	12.50	—

KM# 27a   2 LIRE
Stainless Steel, 29 mm. **Obv:** Crowned Arms **Rev:** Lamb on shoulders of shepard

Date	Mintage	F	VF	XF	Unc	BU
1940/II	40,000	—	0.75	2.00	4.00	—
1941/III	270,000	—	0.50	1.00	3.00	—

KM# 36   2 LIRE
Stainless Steel, 29 mm. **Obv:** Crowned shield divides date and beaded circle **Rev:** Justice seated with tablets of the Law

Date	Mintage	F	VF	XF	Unc	BU
1942/IV	270,000	—	0.50	1.00	3.00	—
1943/V	1,000	—	50.00	75.00	125	—
1944/VI	1,000	—	50.00	75.00	125	—
1945/VII	1,000	—	50.00	75.00	125	—
1946/VIII	1,000	—	50.00	75.00	125	—

KM# 41   2 LIRE
Aluminum **Obv:** Crowned shield divides date and beaded circle **Rev:** Justice seated with tablets of the Law

Date	Mintage	F	VF	XF	Unc	BU
1947/IX	65,000	—	2.00	4.00	8.00	—
1948/X	110,000	—	1.50	3.50	5.00	—
1949/XI	10,000	—	4.00	8.00	17.50	—

KM# 45   2 LIRE
Aluminum **Subject:** Holy Year **Obv:** Bust right **Rev:** Dove and St. Peter's Basilica Dome

Date	Mintage	F	VF	XF	Unc	BU
1950	50,000	—	1.25	2.50	4.00	—

KM# 50   2 LIRE
Aluminum **Obv:** Crowned shield **Rev:** Fortude standing with lion at feet

Date	Mintage	F	VF	XF	Unc	BU
1951/XIII	400,000	—	0.25	0.50	1.50	—
1952/XIV	400,000	—	0.25	0.50	1.50	—
1953/XV	400,000	—	0.25	0.50	1.50	—
1955/XVII	20,000	—	1.00	2.00	4.00	—

Date	Mintage	F	VF	XF	Unc	BU
1956/XVIII	20,000	—	1.00	2.00	4.00	—
1957/XIX	30,000	—	0.75	1.25	3.00	—
1958/XX	30,000	—	0.75	1.25	3.00	—

KM# 28   5 LIRE
5.0000 g., 0.8350 Silver 0.1342 oz. ASW **Obv:** Bust left **Rev:** St. Peter in a boat

Date	Mintage	F	VF	XF	Unc	BU
1939/I	100,000	—	4.00	10.00	20.00	—
1940/II	100,000	—	4.00	10.00	20.00	—
1941/III	4,000	—	25.00	40.00	65.00	—

KM# 37   5 LIRE
5.0000 g., 0.8350 Silver 0.1342 oz. ASW **Obv:** Bust left **Rev:** Caritas figure facing flanked by children

Date	Mintage	F	VF	XF	Unc	BU
1942/IV	4,000	—	25.00	40.00	65.00	—
1943/V	1,000	—	60.00	90.00	140	—
1944/VI	1,000	—	60.00	90.00	140	—
1945/VII	1,000	—	60.00	90.00	140	—
1946/VIII	1,000	—	60.00	90.00	140	—

KM# 42   5 LIRE
Aluminum **Obv:** Bust left **Rev:** Caritas figure facing flanked by children

Date	Mintage	F	VF	XF	Unc	BU
1947/IX	50,000	—	2.00	4.00	7.50	—
1948/X	74,000	—	2.00	4.00	7.50	—
1949/XI	74,000	—	2.00	4.00	7.50	—

KM# 46   5 LIRE
Aluminum **Subject:** Holy Year **Obv:** Bust left **Rev:** Standing Pope with staff flanked by figures within Holy Year Door

Date	Mintage	F	VF	XF	Unc	BU
1950	50,000	—	3.00	5.00	10.00	—

KM# 51.1   5 LIRE
1.0000 g., Aluminum, 20 mm. **Obv:** Bust right **Obv. Leg.:** AN **Rev:** Justice standing with sword and scales

Date	Mintage	F	VF	XF	Unc	BU
1951/XIII	1,500,000	—	0.25	0.50	1.50	—
1952/XIV	1,500,000	—	0.25	0.50	1.50	—
1953/XV	1,500,000	—	0.25	0.50	1.50	—
1955/XVII	30,000	—	0.50	0.75	2.00	—
1956/XVIII	60,000	—	0.50	0.75	2.00	—
1957/XIX	30,000	—	0.50	0.75	2.00	—
1958/XX	30,000	—	0.50	0.75	2.00	—

KM# 51.2   5 LIRE
Aluminum, 20 mm. **Obv:** Bust right **Obv. Leg.:** A

Date	Mintage	F	VF	XF	Unc	BU
1956/XVIII	30,000	—	0.50	1.00	2.50	—
1957/XIX	30,000	—	0.50	1.00	2.50	—
1958/XX	30,000	—	0.50	1.00	2.50	—

KM# 29   10 LIRE
10.0000 g., 0.8350 Silver 0.2684 oz. ASW **Obv:** Bust left **Rev:** Mary, Queen of Peace holding child

Date	Mintage	F	VF	XF	Unc	BU
1939/I	10,000	—	15.00	25.00	45.00	—
1940/II	10,000	—	15.00	25.00	45.00	—
1941/III	4,000	—	20.00	40.00	80.00	—

KM# 38   10 LIRE
10.0000 g., 0.8350 Silver 0.2684 oz. ASW **Obv:** Bust left **Rev:** Caritas figure facing flanked by children

Date	Mintage	F	VF	XF	Unc	BU
1942/IV	4,000	—	25.00	50.00	90.00	—
1943/V	1,000	—	60.00	85.00	125	—
1944/VI	1,000	—	60.00	85.00	125	—
1945/VII	1,000	—	60.00	85.00	125	—
1946/VIII	1,000	—	60.00	85.00	125	—

KM# 43   10 LIRE
Aluminum **Obv:** Bust left **Rev:** Caritas figure facing flanked by children

Date	Mintage	F	VF	XF	Unc	BU
1947/IX	50,000	—	3.00	5.00	8.00	—
1948/X	60,000	—	3.00	5.00	8.00	—
1949/XI	60,000	—	3.00	5.00	8.00	—

KM# 47   10 LIRE
Aluminum **Obv:** Bust right **Rev:** Procession thru Holy Year door

Date	Mintage	F	VF	XF	Unc	BU
1950	60,000	—	3.00	5.00	8.00	—

KM# 52.1   10 LIRE
1.0000 g., Aluminum, 23 mm. **Obv:** Bust left **Obv. Leg.:** AN **Rev:** Prudence standing and date divides value

Date	Mintage	F	VF	XF	Unc	BU
1951/XIII	1,130,000	—	0.50	0.75	1.50	—
1952/XIV	1,130,000	—	0.50	0.75	1.50	—
1953/XV	1,130,000	—	0.50	0.75	1.50	—

Date	Mintage	F	VF	XF	Unc	BU
1955/XVII	80,000	—	0.75	1.50	3.00	—
1957/XIX	—	—	0.75	1.50	3.00	—
1958/XX	—	—	0.75	1.50	3.00	—

KM# 52.2 10 LIRE
Aluminum, 23 mm. **Obv:** Bust left **Obv. Leg.:** A **Rev:** Prudence standing date divides value

Date	Mintage	F	VF	XF	Unc	BU
1956/XVIII	80,000	—	0.75	1.50	3.00	—

KM# A52.1 20 LIRE
3.6000 g., Aluminum-Bronze, 21.25 mm. **Obv:** Bust left **Obv. Leg.:** A **Rev:** Caritas standing holding child with another at feet

Date	Mintage	F	VF	XF	Unc	BU
1957/XIX	20,000	—	0.75	1.25	2.50	—

KM# A52.2 20 LIRE
5.6000 g., Aluminum-Bronze, 21.25 mm. **Obv:** Bust left **Obv. Leg.:** AN **Rev:** Caritas standing holding child with another at feet

Date	Mintage	F	VF	XF	Unc	BU
1958/XX	60,000	—	0.75	1.25	2.50	—

KM# 54.1 50 LIRE
6.2000 g., Stainless Steel, 24.8 mm. **Obv:** Bust right **Obv. Leg.:** AN **Rev:** Spes standing with large anchor which divides date and value

Date	Mintage	F	VF	XF	Unc	BU
1955/XVII	180,000	—	1.00	1.50	3.00	—
1956/XVIII	—	—	1.00	1.50	3.00	—
1957/XIX	—	—	1.00	1.50	3.00	—
1958/XX	—	—	1.00	1.50	3.00	—

KM# 54.2 50 LIRE
6.2000 g., Stainless Steel, 24.8 mm. **Obv:** Bust right **Obv. Leg.:** A **Rev:** Spes standing facing with large anchor which divides date and value

Date	Mintage	F	VF	XF	Unc	BU
1956/XVIII	180,000	—	1.00	1.50	3.00	—
1957/XIX	180,000	—	1.00	1.50	3.00	—
1958/XX	60,000	—	1.00	1.50	3.00	—

KM# 30.1 100 LIRE
5.1900 g., 0.9000 Gold 0.1502 oz. AGW **Obv:** Head right **Obv. Leg.:** AN **Rev:** Standing Jesus divides value

Date	Mintage	F	VF	XF	Unc	BU
1939/I	2,700	—	—	350	600	—
1940/II	2,000	—	—	350	600	—

KM# 30.2 100 LIRE
5.1900 g., 0.9000 Gold 0.1502 oz. AGW **Obv:** Head right **Obv. Leg.:** A **Rev:** Standing Jesus divides value

Date	Mintage	F	VF	XF	Unc	BU
1941/III	2,000	—	—	350	650	—

KM# 39 100 LIRE
5.1900 g., 0.9000 Gold 0.1502 oz. AGW **Obv:** Head right **Rev:** Caritas seated facing flanked by children

Date	Mintage	F	VF	XF	Unc	BU
1942/IV	2,000	—	—	300	550	—
1943/V	1,000	—	—	350	600	—
1944/VI	1,000	—	—	350	600	—
1945/VII	1,000	—	—	350	600	—
1946/VIII	1,000	—	—	350	600	—
1947/IX	1,000	—	—	350	600	—
1948/X	5,000	—	—	300	500	—
1949/XI	1,000	—	—	350	600	—

KM# 48 100 LIRE
5.1900 g., 0.9000 Gold 0.1502 oz. AGW **Subject:** Holy Year **Obv:** Crowned bust left **Rev:** Opening of the Holy Year Door

Date	Mintage	F	VF	XF	Unc	BU
MCML (1950)	20,000	—	—	300	500	—

KM# 53.1 100 LIRE
5.1900 g., 0.9000 Gold 0.1502 oz. AGW **Obv:** Bust right **Obv. Leg.:** AN **Rev:** Caritas standing facing holding child with another at feet

Date	Mintage	F	VF	XF	Unc	BU
1951/XIII	1,000	—	—	350	550	—
1952/XIV	1,000	—	—	350	550	—
1953/XV	1,000	—	—	350	550	—
1954/XVI	1,000	—	—	350	550	—
1955/XVII	1,000	—	—	350	550	—

KM# 53.2 100 LIRE
5.1900 g., 0.9000 Gold 0.1502 oz. AGW **Obv:** Bust right **Obv. Leg.:** A **Rev:** Caritas standing holding child with another at feet

Date	Mintage	F	VF	XF	Unc	BU
1956/XVIII	1,000	—	—	350	550	—

KM# 55 100 LIRE
8.0000 g., Stainless Steel, 27.75 mm. **Obv:** Bust left **Rev:** Fides standing with large cross divides value and date

Date	Mintage	F	VF	XF	Unc	BU
1955/XVII	1,300,000	—	0.50	1.00	2.00	—
1956/XVII	1,400,000	—	0.50	1.00	2.00	—
1957/XIX	900,000	—	0.50	1.00	2.00	—
1958/XX	852,000	—	0.50	1.00	2.00	—

KM# A53 100 LIRE
5.1900 g., 0.9000 Gold 0.1502 oz. AGW **Obv:** Bust right **Rev:** Crowned shield divides value

Date	Mintage	F	VF	XF	Unc	BU
1957/XIX	2,000	—	—	300	500	—
1958/XX	3,000	—	—	300	500	—

KM# 56 500 LIRE
11.0000 g., 0.8350 Silver 0.2953 oz. ASW, 29 mm. **Obv:** Bust left **Rev:** Crowned shield divides value

Date	Mintage	F	VF	XF	Unc	BU
1958/XX	20,000	—	7.50	15.00	25.00	—

Sede Vacante

KM# 57 500 LIRE
11.0000 g., 0.8350 Silver 0.2953 oz. ASW, 29.3 mm. **Obv:** Descending dove divides sun above value **Rev:** Arms of Cardinal Benedetto Aloisi-Masella

Date	Mintage	F	VF	XF	Unc	BU
1958	100,000	—	10.00	40.00	70.00	—

John XXIII

KM# 58.1 LIRA
Aluminum, 17 mm. **Obv:** Crowned shield **Obv. Leg.:** AN **Rev:** Temperance kneeling pouring libation into bowl **Edge:** Plain

Date	Mintage	F	VF	XF	Unc	BU
1959/I	25,000	—	1.00	3.00	6.00	—
1960/II	25,000	—	1.00	2.00	4.00	—

KM# 58.2 LIRA
Aluminum, 17 mm. **Obv:** Crowned shield **Obv. Leg.:** A **Rev:** Temperance kneeling pouring libation into bowl **Edge:** Plain

Date	Mintage	F	VF	XF	Unc	BU
1961/III	25,000	—	1.00	2.00	4.00	—
1962/IV	25,000	—	1.00	2.00	4.00	—

KM# 67 LIRA
Aluminum, 17 mm. **Subject:** Second Ecumenical Council **Obv:** Crowned shield **Rev:** Radiant dove in rays **Edge:** Plain

Date	Mintage	F	VF	XF	Unc	BU
1962/IV	50,000	—	1.00	1.50	3.00	—

KM# 59.1 2 LIRE
Aluminum, 18 mm. **Obv:** Crowned shield **Obv. Leg.:** AN **Rev:** Fortude seated facing and lion divides value and date

Date	Mintage	F	VF	XF	Unc	BU
1959/I	25,000	—	1.50	4.00	6.00	—
1960/II	25,000	—	1.50	4.00	6.00	—

KM# 59.2 2 LIRE
Aluminum, 18 mm. **Obv:** Crowned shield **Obv. Leg.:** A **Rev:** Fortude seated facing and lion divides value and date

Date	Mintage	F	VF	XF	Unc	BU
1961/III	25,000	—	1.50	4.00	6.00	—
1962/IV	25,000	—	1.50	4.00	6.00	—

KM# 68   2 LIRE
Aluminum, 18 mm.   **Subject:** Second Ecumenical Council
Obv: Crowned shield **Rev:** Radiant dove in rays

Date	Mintage	F	VF	XF	Unc	BU
1962/IV	50,000	—	1.00	1.50	3.00	—

KM# 60.1   5 LIRE
Aluminum, 20 mm.   **Obv:** Bust right **Obv. Leg.:** AN **Rev:** Kneeling
figure holding sword and scales divides value and date

Date	Mintage	F	VF	XF	Unc	BU
1959/I	25,000	—	1.50	4.00	7.00	—

KM# 60.2   5 LIRE
Aluminum, 20 mm.   **Obv:** Bust right **Obv. Leg.:** A **Rev:** Kneeling
figure holding sword and scales divides date and value

Date	Mintage	F	VF	XF	Unc	BU
1960/II	25,000	—	1.50	4.00	7.00	—
1961/III	25,000	—	1.50	4.00	7.00	—
1962/IV	25,000	—	1.00	2.00	4.00	—

KM# 69   5 LIRE
Aluminum, 20 mm.   **Subject:** Second Ecumenical Council
Obv: Bust right **Rev:** Radiant dove

Date	Mintage	F	VF	XF	Unc	BU
1962/IV	50,000	—	0.40	0.75	2.00	—

KM# 61.1   10 LIRE
Aluminum, 23 mm.   **Obv:** Bust left **Obv. Leg.:** AN **Rev:** Prudence
kneeling holding snake and object divides value and date

Date	Mintage	F	VF	XF	Unc	BU
1959/I	50,000	—	1.00	3.00	6.00	—

KM# 61.2   10 LIRE
Aluminum, 23 mm.   **Obv:** Bust left **Obv. Leg.:** A **Rev:** Prudence
kneeling

Date	Mintage	F	VF	XF	Unc	BU
1960/II	50,000	—	1.00	3.00	6.00	—
1961/III	50,000	—	1.00	3.00	6.00	—
1962/IV	50,000	—	1.00	2.00	4.00	—

KM# 70   10 LIRE
Aluminum, 23 mm.   **Subject:** Second Ecumenical Council
Obv: Bust left **Rev:** Radiant dove

Date	Mintage	F	VF	XF	Unc	BU
1962/IV	100,000	—	1.00	2.00	4.00	—

KM# 62.1   20 LIRE
3.6000 g., Aluminum-Bronze, 21.25 mm.   **Obv:** Helmeted bust
left **Obv. Leg.:** AN **Rev:** Caritas seated facing flanked by children

Date	Mintage	F	VF	XF	Unc	BU
1959/I	50,000	—	0.75	1.25	2.50	—

KM# 62.2   20 LIRE
3.6000 g., Aluminum-Bronze, 21.25 mm.   **Obv:** Capped bust left
Obv. Leg.: A **Rev:** Seated figure with children

Date	Mintage	F	VF	XF	Unc	BU
1960/II	50,000	—	0.75	1.25	2.50	—
1961/III	50,000	—	0.75	1.00	2.50	—
1962/IV	50,000	—	0.75	1.00	2.50	—

KM# 71   20 LIRE
3.6000 g., Aluminum-Bronze, 21.25 mm.   **Subject:** Second
Ecumenical Council **Obv:** Capped bust left **Rev:** Radiant dove

Date	Mintage	F	VF	XF	Unc	BU
1962/IV	100,000	—	0.75	1.00	2.00	—

KM# 63.1   50 LIRE
6.2000 g., Stainless Steel, 24.8 mm.   **Obv:** Bust right **Rev:** Spes
standing facing with large anchor divides date and value

Date	Mintage	F	VF	XF	Unc	BU
1959/I	100,000	—	1.00	2.50	6.50	—

KM# 63.2   50 LIRE
6.2000 g., Stainless Steel, 24.8 mm.   **Obv:** Bust right **Rev:** Spes
standing facing and large anchor divides date and value

Date	Mintage	F	VF	XF	Unc	BU
1960/II	100,000	—	1.00	2.50	5.50	—
1961/III	100,000	—	1.00	2.00	4.50	—
1962/IV	100,000	—	1.00	2.00	4.50	—

KM# 72   50 LIRE
6.2000 g., Stainless Steel, 24.8 mm.   **Subject:** Second
Ecumenical Council **Obv:** Bust right **Rev:** Bishops at council
meeting with radiant dove above

Date	Mintage	F	VF	XF	Unc	BU
1962/IV	200,000	—	0.50	1.25	3.00	—

KM# 66   100 LIRE
5.1900 g., 0.9000 Gold 0.1502 oz. AGW   **Obv:** Bust right
Rev: Crowned shield divides value

Date	Mintage	F	VF	XF	Unc	BU
1959/I	3,000	—	1,100	1,500	2,280	—

KM# 64.1   100 LIRE
8.0000 g., Stainless Steel, 27.75 mm.   **Obv:** Bust left **Rev:** Fides
standing, cross divides value and date

Date	Mintage	F	VF	XF	Unc	BU
1959/I	783,000	—	1.25	2.00	4.00	—

KM# 64.2   100 LIRE
8.0000 g., Stainless Steel, 27.75 mm.   **Obv:** Regnal year under
bust facing left **Rev:** Fides standing, cross divides value and date

Date	Mintage	F	VF	XF	Unc	BU
1960/II	783,000	—	1.75	3.00	6.50	—
1961/III	783,000	—	0.75	1.00	2.50	—
1962/IV	783,000	—	0.75	1.00	2.50	—

KM# 73   100 LIRE
8.0000 g., Stainless Steel, 27.75 mm.   **Subject:** Second
Ecumenical Council **Obv:** Bust left **Rev:** Bishops at council
meeting with radiant doves

Date	Mintage	F	VF	XF	Unc	BU
1962/IV	1,566,000	—	0.40	1.00	2.00	—

KM# 65.1   500 LIRE
11.0000 g., 0.8350 Silver 0.2953 oz. ASW, 29.3 mm.   **Obv:** Bust
left with continuous legend **Rev:** Crowned shield divides value

Date	Mintage	F	VF	XF	Unc	BU
1959/I	30,000	—	10.00	17.50	40.00	—

KM# 65.2   500 LIRE
11.0000 g., 0.8350 Silver 0.2953 oz. ASW, 29.3 mm.
Obv: Regnal year under bust facing left **Rev:** Crowned shield
divides value

Date	Mintage	F	VF	XF	Unc	BU
1960/II	30,000	—	10.00	20.00	35.00	—
1961/III	30,000	—	7.00	15.00	30.00	—
1962/IV	30,000	—	7.00	15.00	30.00	—

KM# 74 500 LIRE
11.0000 g., 0.8350 Silver 0.2953 oz. ASW, 29.3 mm.
Subject: Second Ecumenical Council **Obv:** Crowned bust left
Rev: Bishops at council meeting with radiant doves

Date	Mintage	F	VF	XF	Unc	BU
1962/IV	60,000	—	10.00	20.00	35.00	—

Sede Vacante

KM# 75 500 LIRE
11.0000 g., 0.8350 Silver 0.2953 oz. ASW, 29.3 mm.
Obv: Descending dove divides sun above value **Rev:** Arms of
Cardinal Benedetto Aloisi-Masella

Date	Mintage	F	VF	XF	Unc	BU
1963	200,000	—	6.00	10.00	17.50	—

Paul VI

KM# 76.1 LIRA
Aluminum, 17 mm. **Obv:** Crowned shield **Obv. Leg.:** AN
Rev: Temperance seated pouring libation divides value and date
Edge: Plain

Date	Mintage	F	VF	XF	Unc	BU
1963/I	60,000	—	0.75	2.00	3.50	—

KM# 76.2 LIRA
Aluminum, 17 mm. **Obv:** Crowned shield **Obv. Leg.:** A
Rev: Temperance seated pouring libation divides value and date
Edge: Plain

Date	Mintage	F	VF	XF	Unc	BU
1964/II	60,000	—	0.50	1.00	2.00	—
1965/III	60,000	—	0.50	1.00	2.00	—

KM# 84 LIRA
Aluminum, 17 mm. **Obv:** Crowned head left **Rev:** Sheep on
shoulders of shepard **Edge:** Plain

Date	Mintage	F	VF	XF	Unc	BU
1966/IV	90,000	—	0.25	0.75	1.25	—

KM# 92 LIRA
Aluminum, 17 mm. **Obv:** Crowned shield **Rev:** Crossed keys
within radiant sword **Edge:** Plain

Date	Mintage	F	VF	XF	Unc	BU
1967/V	100,000	—	0.25	0.75	1.25	—

KM# 100 LIRA
Aluminum, 17 mm. **Series:** F.A.O. **Obv:** Bust left **Rev:** Wheat
ears forming radiant cross **Edge:** Plain

Date	Mintage	F	VF	XF	Unc	BU
ND(1968)/VI	100,000	—	0.25	0.75	1.25	—

KM# 108 LIRA
Aluminum, 17 mm. **Series:** F.A.O. **Obv:** Crowned head 1/4 left
divides inscription **Rev:** Stylized angel in flight **Edge:** Plain

Date	Mintage	F	VF	XF	Unc	BU
1969/VII	100,000	—	0.25	0.75	1.25	—

KM# 116 LIRA
Aluminum, 17 mm. **Series:** F.A.O. **Obv:** Crowned shield
Rev: Palm sprigs

Date	Mintage	F	VF	XF	Unc	BU
1970/VIII	100,000	—	0.25	0.50	1.00	—
1971/IX	110,000	—	0.25	0.50	1.00	—
1972/X	110,000	—	0.25	0.50	1.00	—
1973/XI	132,000	—	0.25	0.50	1.00	—
1974/XII	132,000	—	0.25	0.50	1.00	—
1975/XIII	150,000	—	0.25	0.50	1.00	—
1976/XIV	150,000	—	0.25	0.50	1.00	—
1977/XV	135,000	—	0.25	0.50	1.00	—

KM# 124 LIRA
Aluminum, 17 mm. **Subject:** Holy Year - Faith in the Lord on
Part of Man Afflicted by Evil **Obv:** Crowned shield **Rev:** Mother
and child playing

Date	Mintage	F	VF	XF	Unc	BU
1975	170,000	—	0.25	0.50	1.00	—

KM# 77.1 2 LIRE
Aluminum, 18 mm. **Obv:** Crowned shield **Obv. Leg.:** AN
Rev: Fortude standing with shield, lion at side, value

Date	Mintage	F	VF	XF	Unc	BU
1963/I	60,000	—	0.75	2.00	3.00	—

KM# 77.2 2 LIRE
Aluminum, 18 mm. **Obv:** Crowned shield **Obv. Leg.:** A
Rev: Fortude standing with shield, lion at side, value

Date	Mintage	F	VF	XF	Unc	BU
1964/II	60,000	—	0.75	2.00	3.00	—
1965/III	60,000	—	0.75	3.00	3.00	—

KM# 85 2 LIRE
Aluminum, 18 mm. **Obv:** Crowned head left **Rev:** Sheep on
shoulder of shepard

Date	Mintage	F	VF	XF	Unc	BU
1966/IV	90,000	—	0.25	0.75	1.25	—

KM# 93 2 LIRE
Aluminum, 18 mm. **Obv:** Crowned shield **Rev:** Papal tiara above
inverted cross, keys flanking

Date	Mintage	F	VF	XF	Unc	BU
1967/V	100,000	—	0.25	0.75	1.25	—

KM# 101 2 LIRE
Aluminum, 18 mm. **Series:** F.A.O. **Subject:** Feeding of the 5,000
Obv: Bust right **Rev:** Standing figure flanked by others

Date	Mintage	F	VF	XF	Unc	BU
ND(1968)/VI	100,000	—	0.25	0.75	1.25	—

KM# 109 2 LIRE
Aluminum, 18 mm. **Obv:** Crowned head 1/4 left divides
inscription **Rev:** Stylized angel in flight

Date	Mintage	F	VF	XF	Unc	BU
1969/VII	100,000	—	0.25	0.75	1.25	—

KM# 117 2 LIRE
Aluminum, 18 mm. **Obv:** Crowned shield **Rev:** Lamb standing

Date	Mintage	F	VF	XF	Unc	BU
1970/VIII	100,000	—	0.25	0.50	1.00	—
1971/IX	110,000	—	0.25	0.50	1.00	—
1972/X	110,000	—	0.25	0.50	1.00	—
1973/XI	132,000	—	0.25	0.50	1.00	—
1974/XII	132,000	—	0.25	0.50	1.00	—
1975/XIII	150,000	—	0.25	0.50	1.00	—
1976/XIV	150,000	—	0.25	0.50	1.00	—
1977/XV	135,000	—	0.25	0.50	1.00	—

KM# 125 2 LIRE
Aluminum, 18 mm. **Subject:** Holy Year - Reconciliation among
brothers **Obv:** Crowned shield **Rev:** Two men embracing

Date	Mintage	F	VF	XF	Unc	BU
1975	180,000	—	0.25	0.50	1.00	—

KM# 78.1 5 LIRE
Aluminum, 20 mm. **Obv:** Bust right **Obv. Leg.:** AN **Rev:** Justice
seated with sword and scales

Date	Mintage	F	VF	XF	Unc	BU
1963/I	60,000	—	1.00	2.00	4.00	—

KM# 78.2 5 LIRE
Aluminum, 20 mm. **Obv:** Bust right **Obv. Leg.:** A **Rev:** Justice
seated with sword and scales

Date	Mintage	F	VF	XF	Unc	BU
1964/II	60,000	—	8.00	16.00	32.00	—
1965/III	60,000	—	8.00	16.00	32.00	—

KM# 86 5 LIRE
Aluminum, 20 mm. **Obv:** Crowned head left **Rev:** Sheep on
shoulder of shepard

Date	Mintage	F	VF	XF	Unc	BU
1966/IV	90,000	—	0.25	0.50	1.25	—

KM# 94   5 LIRE
Aluminum, 20 mm. **Obv:** Bust right **Rev:** Crossed keys within radiant sword

Date	Mintage	F	VF	XF	Unc	BU
1967/V	100,000	—	0.25	0.50	1.25	—

KM# 102   5 LIRE
Aluminum, 20 mm. **Series:** F.A.O. **Subject:** Lady of the Harvest **Obv:** Bust right **Rev:** Our Lady of the Harvest within wheat sprigs

Date	Mintage	F	VF	XF	Unc	BU
ND(1968)/VI	100,000	—	0.25	0.50	1.25	—

KM# 110   5 LIRE
Aluminum, 20 mm. **Obv:** Crowned head 1/4 left divides inscription **Rev:** Stylized angel in flight

Date	Mintage	F	VF	XF	Unc	BU
1969/VII	100,000	—	0.25	0.50	1.25	—

KM# 118   5 LIRE
Aluminum, 20 mm. **Obv:** Crowned shield **Rev:** Pelican feeding young

Date	Mintage	F	VF	XF	Unc	BU
1970/VIII	100,000	—	0.25	0.60	1.25	—
1971/IX	110,000	—	0.25	0.60	1.25	—
1972/X	110,000	—	0.25	0.60	1.25	—
1973/XI	132,000	—	0.25	0.60	1.25	—
1974/XII	132,000	—	0.25	0.60	1.25	—
1975/XIII	150,000	—	0.25	0.60	1.25	—
1976/XIV	150,000	—	0.25	0.60	1.25	—
1977/XV	135,000	—	0.25	0.60	1.25	—

KM# 126   5 LIRE
Aluminum, 20 mm. **Subject:** Holy Year - Redemption of the Woman of Bethany **Obv:** Crowned shield **Rev:** Female kneeling receiving blessing from seated figure

Date	Mintage	F	VF	XF	Unc	BU
1975	380,000	—	0.25	0.50	1.25	—

KM# 133   5 LIRE
Aluminum, 20 mm. **Obv:** Crowned shield **Rev:** Stylized standing figure divides value

Date	Mintage	F	VF	XF	Unc	BU
1978/XVI	120,000	—	0.25	0.50	1.25	—

KM# 79.1   10 LIRE
Aluminum, 23 mm. **Obv:** Bust left **Obv. Leg.:** AN **Rev:** Prudence standing dividing date and value

Date	Mintage	F	VF	XF	Unc	BU
1963/I	90,000	—	1.00	1.50	3.00	—

KM# 79.2   10 LIRE
Aluminum, 23 mm. **Obv:** Bust left **Obv. Leg.:** A **Rev:** Prudence standing dividing date and value

Date	Mintage	F	VF	XF	Unc	BU
1964/II	90,000	—	0.75	1.00	2.00	—
1965/III	90,000	—	0.75	1.00	2.00	—

KM# 87   10 LIRE
Aluminum, 23 mm. **Obv:** Crowned head left **Rev:** Shepard with sheep on his shoulders

Date	Mintage	F	VF	XF	Unc	BU
1966/IV	100,000	—	0.25	1.00	2.00	—

KM# 95   10 LIRE
Aluminum, 23 mm. **Obv:** Bust left **Rev:** Papal taira above inverted cross, keys flanking

Date	Mintage	F	VF	XF	Unc	BU
ND(1967)/V	110,000	—	0.25	0.75	1.25	—

KM# 103   10 LIRE
Aluminum, 23 mm. **Series:** F.A.O. **Obv:** Bust left **Rev:** Feeding of the 5,000

Date	Mintage	F	VF	XF	Unc	BU
ND(1968)/VI	110,000	—	0.25	0.75	1.50	—

KM# 111   10 LIRE
Aluminum, 23 mm. **Obv:** Crowned head 1/4 left divides inscription **Rev:** Stylized angel in flight

Date	Mintage	F	VF	XF	Unc	BU
1969/VII	110,000	—	0.25	0.50	1.25	—

KM# 119   10 LIRE
Aluminum, 23 mm. **Obv:** Crowned shield **Rev:** Fish

Date	Mintage	F	VF	XF	Unc	BU
1970/VIII	110,000	—	0.25	0.50	1.25	—
1971/IX	160,000	—	0.25	0.50	1.25	—
1972/X	160,000	—	0.25	0.50	1.25	—

Date	Mintage	F	VF	XF	Unc	BU
1973/XI	170,000	—	0.25	0.50	1.25	—
1974/XII	170,000	—	0.25	0.50	1.25	—
1975/XIII	200,000	—	0.25	0.50	1.25	—
1976/XIV	200,000	—	0.25	0.50	1.25	—
1977/XV	200,000	—	0.25	0.50	1.25	—

KM# 127   10 LIRE
Aluminum, 23 mm. **Subject:** Holy Year - Reconciliation between God and man **Obv:** Crowned shield **Rev:** Noah's ark

Date	Mintage	F	VF	XF	Unc	BU
1975	400,000	—	0.25	0.75	1.50	—

KM# 134   10 LIRE
Aluminum, 23 mm. **Obv:** Crowned shield **Rev:** Figure kneeling left

Date	Mintage	F	VF	XF	Unc	BU
1978/XVI	250,000	—	0.25	0.50	1.00	—

KM# 80.1   20 LIRE
3.6000 g., Aluminum-Bronze, 21.25 mm. **Obv:** Bust left **Obv. Leg.:** AN **Rev:** Caritas seated flanked by children

Date	Mintage	F	VF	XF	Unc	BU
1963/I	90,000	—	1.00	2.00	4.00	—
1964/II	90,000	—	1.00	2.00	4.00	—

KM# 80.2   20 LIRE
3.6000 g., Aluminum-Bronze, 21.25 mm. **Obv:** Bust left **Obv. Leg.:** A **Rev:** Caritas seated flanked by children

Date	Mintage	F	VF	XF	Unc	BU
1965/III	90,000	—	0.75	1.00	2.00	—

KM# 88   20 LIRE
3.6000 g., Aluminum-Bronze, 21.25 mm. **Obv:** Crowned head left **Rev:** Shepard with sheep on his shoulders

Date	Mintage	F	VF	XF	Unc	BU
1966/IV	100,000	—	0.25	0.75	1.25	—

KM# 96   20 LIRE
3.6000 g., Aluminum-Bronze, 21.25 mm. **Obv:** Bust right **Rev:** Saints Peter and Paul, sword between

Date	Mintage	F	VF	XF	Unc	BU
ND(1967)/V	105,000	—	0.25	0.75	1.25	—

KM# 104   20 LIRE
3.6000 g., Aluminum-Bronze, 21.25 mm. **Series:** F.A.O. **Obv:** Bust right **Rev:** Wheat ears forming radiant cross

Date	Mintage	F	VF	XF	Unc	BU
ND(1968)/VI	105,000	—	0.25	0.75	1.50	—

KM# 112   20 LIRE
3.6000 g., Aluminum-Bronze, 21.25 mm. **Obv:** Crowned head 1/4 left divides inscription **Rev:** Stylized angel in flight

Date	Mintage	F	VF	XF	Unc	BU
1969/VII	105,000	—	0.25	0.60	1.25	—

KM# 120   20 LIRE
3.6000 g., Aluminum-Bronze, 21.25 mm. **Obv:** Crowned shield **Rev:** Red deer

Date	Mintage	F	VF	XF	Unc	BU
1970/VIII	105,000	—	0.25	0.50	1.50	2.00
1971/IX	170,000	—	0.25	0.50	1.50	2.00
1972/X	170,000	—	0.25	0.50	1.50	2.00
1973/XI	—	—	0.25	0.50	1.50	2.00
1974/XII	—	—	0.25	0.50	1.50	2.00
1975/XIII	250,000	—	0.25	0.50	1.50	2.00
1976/XIV	250,000	—	0.25	0.50	1.50	2.00
1977/XV	250,000	—	0.25	0.50	1.50	2.00

KM# 128   20 LIRE
3.6000 g., Aluminum-Bronze, 21.25 mm. **Subject:** Holy Year - Man's Confidence in the Lord **Obv:** Crowned shield **Rev:** Standing figure facing right and value

Date	Mintage	F	VF	XF	Unc	BU
1975	400,000	—	0.25	0.50	1.25	—

KM# 135   20 LIRE
3.6000 g., Aluminum-Bronze, 21.25 mm. **Subject:** Prodigal Son Parable **Obv:** Crowned shield **Rev:** Standing figures facing each other above value

Date	Mintage	F	VF	XF	Unc	BU
1978/XVI	120,000	—	0.25	0.50	1.25	—

KM# 81.1   50 LIRE
6.2000 g., Stainless Steel, 24.8 mm. **Obv:** Bust right **Obv. Leg.:** AN **Rev:** Spes standing with anchor date and value are divided

Date	Mintage	F	VF	XF	Unc	BU
1963/I	120,000	—	1.00	2.00	4.00	—
1964/II	120,000	—	0.75	1.50	3.00	—

KM# 81.2   50 LIRE
6.2000 g., Stainless Steel, 24.8 mm. **Obv:** Bust right **Obv. Leg.:** A **Rev:** Spes standing with anchor, date and value divided

Date	Mintage	F	VF	XF	Unc	BU
1965/III	120,000	—	0.50	1.00	2.00	—

KM# 89   50 LIRE
6.2000 g., Stainless Steel, 24.8 mm. **Obv:** Crowned head left **Rev:** Shepard with sheep on shoulders

Date	Mintage	F	VF	XF	Unc	BU
1966/IV	150,000	—	0.50	1.00	2.00	—

KM# 97   50 LIRE
6.2000 g., Stainless Steel, 24.8 mm. **Subject:** Conversion of Saint Paul **Obv:** Bust right **Rev:** Rearing equestrian

Date	Mintage	F	VF	XF	Unc	BU
1967/V	190,000	—	0.50	1.00	2.00	—

KM# 105   50 LIRE
6.2000 g., Stainless Steel, 24.8 mm. **Series:** F.A.O. **Obv:** Bust right **Rev:** Our Lady of Harvest standing within wheat sprigs

Date	Mintage	F	VF	XF	Unc	BU
ND(1968)/VI	190,000	—	0.50	1.00	2.00	—

KM# 113   50 LIRE
6.2000 g., Stainless Steel, 24.8 mm. **Obv:** Crowned head 1/4 left divides inscription **Rev:** Stylized angel

Date	Mintage	F	VF	XF	Unc	BU
1969/VII	190,000	—	0.50	1.00	2.00	—

KM# 121   50 LIRE
6.2000 g., Stainless Steel, 24.8 mm. **Obv:** Crowned shield **Rev:** Olive branch

Date	Mintage	F	VF	XF	Unc	BU
1970/VIII	190,000	—	0.25	0.75	1.75	—
1971/IX	700,000	—	0.25	0.75	1.50	—
1972/X	700,000	—	0.25	0.75	1.50	—
1973/XI	750,000	—	0.25	0.75	1.50	—
1974/XII	750,000	—	0.25	0.75	1.50	—
1975/XIII	600,000	—	0.25	0.75	1.50	—
1976/XIV	600,000	—	0.25	0.75	1.50	—

KM# 129   50 LIRE
6.2000 g., Stainless Steel, 24.8 mm. **Subject:** Holy Year - The Peace of the Lord **Obv:** Crowned shield **Rev:** Stylized figure in fetal position within design with hand above

Date	Mintage	F	VF	XF	Unc	BU
1975	500,000	—	0.40	0.75	1.50	—

KM# A121   50 LIRE
6.2000 g., Stainless Steel, 24.8 mm. **Obv:** Crowned shield **Rev:** Wheat and grapes

Date	Mintage	F	VF	XF	Unc	BU
1977/XV	600,000	—	0.40	0.25	1.50	—

KM# 136   50 LIRE
6.2000 g., Stainless Steel, 24.8 mm. **Obv:** Crowned shield **Rev:** Child and kneeling adult

Date	Mintage	F	VF	XF	Unc	BU
1978/XVI	223,000	—	0.40	0.75	1.50	—

KM# 82.1   100 LIRE
8.0000 g., Stainless Steel, 27.75 mm. **Obv:** Bust left **Obv. Leg.:** AN **Rev:** Fides standing figure divides value and date

Date	Mintage	F	VF	XF	Unc	BU
1963/I	558,000	—	1.00	2.00	3.75	—

KM# 82.2   100 LIRE
8.0000 g., Stainless Steel, 27.75 mm. **Obv:** Bust left **Obv. Leg.:** A **Rev:** Fides standing figure divides value and date

Date	Mintage	F	VF	XF	Unc	BU
1964/II	558,000	—	0.50	1.00	2.50	—
1965/III	558,000	—	0.50	1.00	2.50	—

KM# 90   100 LIRE
8.0000 g., Stainless Steel, 27.75 mm. **Obv:** Crowned head left **Rev:** Shepard with sheep on shoulders

Date	Mintage	F	VF	XF	Unc	BU
1966/IV	388,000	—	0.50	1.00	2.50	—

KM# 98   100 LIRE
8.0000 g., Stainless Steel, 27.75 mm. **Obv:** Bust left **Rev:** St. Peter seated on throne facing

Date	Mintage	F	VF	XF	Unc	BU
1967/V	315,000	—	0.50	1.00	2.50	—

KM# 106   100 LIRE
8.0000 g., Stainless Steel, 27.75 mm. **Series:** F.A.O. **Obv:** Bust left **Rev:** Feeding of the 5,000

Date	Mintage	F	VF	XF	Unc	BU
ND(1968)/VI	315,000	—	0.50	1.00	2.50	—

KM# 114   100 LIRE
8.0000 g., Stainless Steel, 27.75 mm. **Obv:** Crowned head 1/4 left divides inscription **Rev:** Stylized angel in flight

Date	Mintage	F	VF	XF	Unc	BU
1969/VII	315,000	—	0.50	1.00	2.50	—

KM# 122   100 LIRE
8.0000 g., Stainless Steel, 27.75 mm. **Obv:** Crowned shield **Rev:** Dove in flight with olive branch

Date	Mintage	F	VF	XF	Unc	BU
1970/VIII	315,000	—	0.50	1.00	2.50	—
1971/IX	966,000	—	0.40	0.75	1.50	—
1972/X	966,000	—	0.40	0.75	1.50	—
1973/XI	830,000	—	0.40	0.75	1.50	—
1974/XII	830,000	—	0.40	0.75	1.50	—
1975/XIII	808,000	—	0.40	0.75	1.50	—
1976/XIV	808,000	—	0.40	0.75	1.50	—
1977/XV	819,000	—	0.40	0.75	1.50	—

KM# 130   100 LIRE
8.0000 g., Stainless Steel, 27.75 mm. **Subject:** Holy Year - Symbolic Baptism of Man **Obv:** Crowned shield **Rev:** Hands pulling up net filled with fish

Date	Mintage	F	VF	XF	Unc	BU
1975	605,000	—	0.75	1.50	3.50	—

KM# 137   100 LIRE
8.0000 g., Stainless Steel, 27.75 mm. **Obv:** Crowned shield **Rev:** Stylized figure standing in courtyard

Date	Mintage	F	VF	XF	Unc	BU
1978/XVI	399,000	—	0.50	1.00	2.50	—

KM# 138   200 LIRE
5.0000 g., Aluminum-Bronze, 24 mm. **Obv:** Crowned shield **Rev:** Stylized figure above value

Date	Mintage	F	VF	XF	Unc	BU
1978/XVI	355,000	—	0.50	1.00	2.50	—

KM# 83.1   500 LIRE
11.0000 g., 0.8350 Silver 0.2953 oz. ASW, 29.3 mm. **Obv:** Bust right **Obv. Leg.:** AN **Rev:** Crowned shield divides value

Date	Mintage	F	VF	XF	Unc	BU
1963/I	70,000	—	10.00	17.50	40.00	—

KM# 83.2   500 LIRE
11.0000 g., 0.8350 Silver 0.2953 oz. ASW, 29.3 mm. **Obv:** Bust right **Obv. Leg.:** A **Rev:** Crowned shield divides value

Date	Mintage	F	VF	XF	Unc	BU
1964/II	70,000	—	10.00	17.50	40.00	—
1965/III	70,000	—	10.00	17.50	40.00	—

KM# 91   500 LIRE
11.0000 g., 0.8350 Silver 0.2953 oz. ASW, 29.3 mm. **Obv:** Crowned head left **Rev:** Shepard with sheep on shoulders

Date	Mintage	F	VF	XF	Unc	BU
1966/IV	100,000	—	10.00	17.50	40.00	—

KM# 99   500 LIRE
11.0000 g., 0.8350 Silver 0.2953 oz. ASW, 29.3 mm. **Obv:** Bust left **Rev:** Saint Peter and Paul, cross between, keys below

Date	Mintage	F	VF	XF	Unc	BU
ND(1967)/V	110,000	—	10.00	17.50	40.00	—

KM# 107   500 LIRE
11.0000 g., 0.8350 Silver 0.2953 oz. ASW, 29.3 mm. **Series:** F.A.O. **Obv:** Bust left **Rev:** Wheat ears forming radiant cross

Date	Mintage	F	VF	XF	Unc	BU
ND(1968)/VI	110,000	—	10.00	17.50	40.00	—

KM# 115   500 LIRE
11.0000 g., 0.8350 Silver 0.2953 oz. ASW, 29.3 mm. **Obv:** Crowned head 1/4 left divides inscription **Rev:** Stylized angel in flight

Date	Mintage	F	VF	XF	Unc	BU
1969/VII	110,000	—	10.00	17.50	40.00	—

KM# 123   500 LIRE
11.0000 g., 0.8350 Silver 0.2953 oz. ASW, 29.3 mm. **Obv:** Crowned shield **Rev:** Wheat and grapes

Date	Mintage	F	VF	XF	Unc	BU
1970/VIII	110,000	—	—	10.00	17.50	—
1971/IX	125,000	—	—	10.00	17.50	—
1972/X	125,000	—	—	10.00	17.50	—
1973/XI	145,000	—	—	10.00	17.50	—
1974/XII	145,000	—	—	10.00	17.50	—
1975/XIII	162,000	—	—	10.00	17.50	—
1976/XIV	162,000	—	—	10.00	17.50	—

KM# 131   500 LIRE
11.0000 g., 0.8350 Silver 0.2953 oz. ASW, 29.3 mm. **Subject:** Holy Year - Forgiveness **Obv:** Crowned shield **Rev:** Stylized father embracing son

Date	Mintage	F	VF	XF	Unc	BU
1975	200,000	—	10.00	17.50	40.00	—

KM# 132   500 LIRE
11.0000 g., 0.8350 Silver 0.2953 oz. ASW, 29.3 mm. **Subject:** Book of the Evangelists **Obv:** Crowned shield **Rev:** Assorted animal heads within cross window frame

Date	Mintage	F	VF	XF	Unc	BU
1977/XV	160,000	—	—	10.00	17.50	—

KM# 139 500 LIRE
11.0000 g., 0.8350 Silver 0.2953 oz. ASW, 29.3 mm.
Obv: Crowned shield **Rev:** Stylized Jesus walking on water reaching for figure in boat

Date	Mintage	F	VF	XF	Unc	BU
1978/XVI	145,000	—	—	10.00	17.50	—

John Paul I

KM# 142 1000 LIRE
14.6000 g., 0.8350 Silver 0.3919 oz. ASW **Obv:** Bust left **Rev:** Crowned shield

Date	Mintage	F	VF	XF	Unc	BU
1978	200,000	—	—	18.00	32.00	—

Sede Vacante

KM# 140 500 LIRE
11.0000 g., 0.8350 Silver 0.2953 oz. ASW, 29.3 mm.
Obv: Descending stylized dove above value **Rev:** Arms of Cardinal Jean Villot **Rev. Leg.:** SEDE VACANTE MCMLXXVIII **Note:** First 1978 Sede Vacante issue

Date	Mintage	F	VF	XF	Unc	BU
1978	500,000	—	6.00	10.00	20.00	—

KM# 141 500 LIRE
11.0000 g., 0.8350 Silver 0.2953 oz. ASW **Obv:** Descending radiant dove **Rev:** Arms of Cardinal Jean Villot **Rev. Leg.:** SEDE VACANTE SEPTEMBER MCMLXXVIII **Note:** Second 1978 Sede Vacante issue

Date	Mintage	F	VF	XF	Unc	BU
1978		—	6.00	10.00	20.00	—

Note: Mintage included with Y#140

John Paul II

KM# 143 10 LIRE
Aluminum, 23 mm. **Obv:** Bust left **Rev:** Cardinal Virtues - Temperance

Date	Mintage	F	VF	XF	Unc	BU
1979/I	250,000		0.50	1.00	2.50	—
1980/II	170,000		0.50	1.00	2.50	—

KM# 155 10 LIRE
Aluminum, 23 mm. **Obv:** Head left **Rev:** Jesus given water at the well **Mint:** Rome

Date	Mintage	F	VF	XF	Unc	BU
1981/IIIR	170,000	—	0.50	1.00	2.50	—

KM# 161 10 LIRE
Aluminum, 23 mm. **Subject:** Creation of Woman **Obv:** Bust right **Rev:** Standing figure facing to right of value **Mint:** Rome

Date	Mintage	F	VF	XF	Unc	BU
1982/IVR	220,000	—	0.50	1.00	2.50	—

KM# 170 10 LIRE
Aluminum, 23 mm. **Subject:** Work and Teaching **Obv:** Head left at lower right of cross **Rev:** Teacher, student and value **Mint:** Rome

Date	Mintage	F	VF	XF	Unc	BU
1983/VR	110,000	—	0.50	1.00	2.50	—

KM# 177 10 LIRE
Aluminum, 23 mm. **Subject:** Year of Peace **Obv:** Bust left **Rev:** Hand holding bouquet **Mint:** Rome

Date	Mintage	F	VF	XF	Unc	BU
1984/VIR	110,000	—	0.50	1.00	2.50	—

KM# 185 10 LIRE
Aluminum, 23 mm. **Obv:** Head left **Rev:** Angel with gospel of St. Matthew

Date	Mintage	F	VF	XF	Unc	BU
1985/VII	90,000	—	0.50	1.00	2.50	—

KM# 192 10 LIRE
Aluminum, 23 mm. **Rev:** Mary seated, value

Date	Mintage	F	VF	XF	Unc	BU
1986/VIII	90,000	—	0.50	1.00	2.50	—

KM# 199 10 LIRE
Aluminum, 23 mm. **Obv:** Bust right **Rev:** Basilica behind Pieta Statue

Date	Mintage	F	VF	XF	Unc	BU
1987/IX		—	0.50	1.00	2.50	—

KM# 206 10 LIRE
Aluminum, 23 mm. **Subject:** Temptation of Adam and Eve **Obv:** Bust right **Rev:** Tree with snake divides standing figures

Date	Mintage	F	VF	XF	Unc	BU
1988/X		—	0.50	1.00	2.50	—

KM# 213 10 LIRE
Aluminum, 23 mm. **Subject:** Jesus the Teacher **Rev:** Seated figure facing standing figure

Date	Mintage	F	VF	XF	Unc	BU
1989/XI		—	0.50	1.00	2.50	—

KM# 220 10 LIRE
Aluminum, 23 mm. **Subject:** Saints Peter and Paul **Obv:** Bust 3/4 left **Rev:** Saints Peter and Paul facing

Date	Mintage	F	VF	XF	Unc	BU
1990/XII		—	0.50	1.00	2.50	—

KM# 228 10 LIRE
Aluminum, 23 mm. **Obv:** Head left **Rev:** Standing figure with book to right of value

Date	Mintage	F	VF	XF	Unc	BU
1991/XIII		—	0.50	1.00	2.50	—

KM# 236 10 LIRE
Aluminum, 23 mm. **Obv:** Bust right **Rev:** Bee on flower

Date	Mintage	F	VF	XF	Unc	BU
1992/XIV		—	0.50	1.00	2.50	—

KM# 244 10 LIRE
Aluminum, 23 mm. **Obv:** Head facing **Rev:** Sailboat divides inscription

Date	Mintage	F	VF	XF	Unc	BU
1993/XV		—	0.50	1.00	2.50	—

KM# 252 10 LIRE
Aluminum, 23 mm. **Obv:** Bust left **Rev:** Figures planting trees

Date	Mintage	F	VF	XF	Unc	BU
1994/XVI	—		0.50	1.00	2.50	—

KM# 262 10 LIRE
Aluminum, 23 mm. **Rev:** Preaching

Date	Mintage	F	VF	XF	Unc	BU
1995/XVII	—		0.50	1.00	2.50	—

KM# 272 10 LIRE
Aluminum, 23 mm. **Subject:** Child Carried to Peace **Obv:** Head left **Rev:** Stylized standing figure holding infant walking left

Date	Mintage	F	VF	XF	Unc	BU
1996/XVIII	—		0.50	1.00	3.00	—

KM# 280 10 LIRE
Aluminum, 23 mm. **Obv:** Head right **Rev:** Angel blowing horn to upper right of man sowing seeds

Date	Mintage	F	VF	XF	Unc	BU
1997/XIX	—		0.50	1.00	2.50	—

KM# 293 10 LIRE
1.6000 g., Aluminum, 23 mm. **Obv:** Bust right holding crucifix **Rev:** Standing figure flanked by seated figures

Date	Mintage	F	VF	XF	Unc	BU
1998/XX	—		0.50	1.00	3.00	—

KM# 305 10 LIRE
1.6000 g., Aluminum, 23.3 mm. **Subject:** Right to Life - Motherhood **Obv:** Bust right **Rev:** Mother with baby and child below tree **Edge:** Plain **Mint:** Rome

Date	Mintage	F	VF	XF	Unc	BU
1999/XXI	—	→	0.50	1.00	3.00	—

KM# 323 10 LIRE
1.6000 g., Aluminum, 23.2 mm. **Obv:** Papal arms within circle **Rev:** Pope lifting child **Edge:** Plain **Mint:** Rome

Date	Mintage	F	VF	XF	Unc	BU
2000/XXII	—		0.50	1.00	3.00	—

KM# 144 20 LIRE
3.6000 g., Aluminum-Bronze, 21.25 mm. **Rev:** Fortitude

Date	Mintage	F	VF	XF	Unc	BU
1979/I	120,000		0.50	1.00	3.00	—
1980/II	265,000		0.50	1.00	3.00	—

KM# 156 20 LIRE
3.6000 g., Aluminum-Bronze, 21.25 mm. **Obv:** Head left **Rev:** Open door flanked by standing figures

Date	Mintage	F	VF	XF	Unc	BU
1981/III	265,000		0.50	1.00	3.00	—

KM# 162 20 LIRE
3.6000 g., Aluminum-Bronze, 21.25 mm. **Subject:** Marriage **Obv:** Bust right **Rev:** Standing figures shaking hands

Date	Mintage	F	VF	XF	Unc	BU
1982/IV	360,000		0.50	1.00	3.00	—

KM# 171 20 LIRE
3.6000 g., Aluminum-Bronze, 21.25 mm. **Subject:** Incarnation of the Word **Obv:** Head left to lower right of cross **Rev:** Radiant dove above stylized kneeling figures within triangle shape

Date	Mintage	F	VF	XF	Unc	BU
1983/V	170,000		0.50	1.00	3.00	—

KM# 178 20 LIRE
3.6000 g., Aluminum-Bronze, 21.25 mm. **Subject:** Year of Peace **Obv:** Bust left **Rev:** Child and sheep

Date	Mintage	F	VF	XF	Unc	BU
1984/VI	170,000		0.50	1.00	3.00	—

KM# 186 20 LIRE
3.6000 g., Aluminum-Bronze, 21.25 mm. **Obv:** Head left **Rev:** Stylized eagle holding gospel of St. John

Date	Mintage	F	VF	XF	Unc	BU
1985/VII	255,000		0.50	1.00	3.00	—

KM# 193 20 LIRE
3.6000 g., Aluminum-Bronze, 21.25 mm. **Obv:** Bust right **Rev:** Stylized standing angel

Date	Mintage	F	VF	XF	Unc	BU
1986/VIII	100,000		0.50	1.00	3.00	—

KM# 200 20 LIRE
3.6000 g., Aluminum-Bronze, 21.25 mm. **Obv:** Bust right **Rev:** Assumption of Mother Mary into heaven

Date	Mintage	F	VF	XF	Unc	BU
1987/IX			0.50	1.00	3.00	—

KM# 207 20 LIRE
3.6000 g., Aluminum-Bronze, 21.25 mm. **Subject:** Temptation of Adam and Eve **Rev:** Apple tree flanked by standing figures and pair of hands **Note:** Similar to 200 Lire, KM#210.

Date	Mintage	F	VF	XF	Unc	BU
1988/X			0.50	1.00	3.00	—

KM# 214 20 LIRE
3.6000 g., Aluminum-Bronze, 21.25 mm. **Subject:** The Harvest **Rev:** Standing and kneeling figures

Date	Mintage	F	VF	XF	Unc	BU
1989/XI			0.50	1.00	3.00	—

KM# 221 20 LIRE
3.6000 g., Aluminum-Bronze, 21.25 mm. **Obv:** Bust 3/4 left **Rev:** Pope John Paul II and Eastern Rite Bishop

Date	Mintage	F	VF	XF	Unc	BU
1990/XII	—		0.50	1.00	3.00	—

KM# 229 20 LIRE
3.6000 g., Aluminum-Bronze, 21.25 mm. **Obv:** Head left **Rev:** Crane and buildings

Date	Mintage	F	VF	XF	Unc	BU
1991/XIII	—		0.50	1.00	3.00	—

KM# 237 20 LIRE
3.6000 g., Aluminum-Bronze, 21.25 mm. **Obv:** Bust right **Rev:** Three children above value

Date	Mintage	F	VF	XF	Unc	BU
1992/XIV	—		0.50	1.00	3.00	—

KM# 245 20 LIRE
3.6000 g., Aluminum-Bronze, 21.25 mm. **Obv:** Head facing **Rev:** Crucifix, as on papal croizer

Date	Mintage	F	VF	XF	Unc	BU
1993/XV	—		0.50	1.00	3.00	—

KM# 253   20 LIRE
3.6000 g., Aluminum-Bronze, 21.25 mm.   **Obv:** Bust left
Rev: Hospital patient with visitors

Date	Mintage	F	VF	XF	Unc	BU
1994/XVI	—	—	0.50	1.00	3.00	—

KM# 263   20 LIRE
3.6000 g., Aluminum-Bronze, 21.25 mm.   **Subject:** Euthanasia

Date	Mintage	F	VF	XF	Unc	BU
1995/XVII	—	—	0.50	1.00	3.00	—

KM# 273   20 LIRE
3.6000 g., Aluminum-Bronze, 21.25 mm.   **Obv:** Head left
Rev: Parents praising child

Date	Mintage	F	VF	XF	Unc	BU
1996/XVIII	—	—	0.50	1.00	3.00	—

KM# 281   20 LIRE
3.6000 g., Aluminum-Bronze, 21.25 mm.   **Obv:** Bust right
Rev: Jesus teaching with book

Date	Mintage	F	VF	XF	Unc	BU
1997/XIX	—	—	0.50	1.00	3.00	—

KM# 294   20 LIRE
3.6000 g., Aluminum-Bronze, 21.25 mm.   **Obv:** Bust right holding
crucifix **Rev:** Family and sun

Date	Mintage	F	VF	XF	Unc	BU
1998/XX	—	—	0.50	1.00	3.00	—

KM# 306   20 LIRE
3.6000 g., Aluminum-Bronze, 21.3 mm.   **Subject:** Work - The
Right to Fulfill One's Potential **Obv:** Bust right **Rev:** Workers
Edge: Plain **Mint:** Rome

Date	Mintage	F	VF	XF	Unc	BU
1999/XXI	—	—	0.50	1.00	3.00	—

KM# 324   20 LIRE
3.5700 g., Brass, 21.2 mm.   **Obv:** Papal arms within circle
Rev: Head of Pope stargazing **Edge:** Plain **Mint:** Rome

Date	Mintage	F	VF	XF	Unc	BU
2000/XXII	—	—	0.50	1.00	3.00	—

KM# 145   50 LIRE
6.2000 g., Stainless Steel, 24.8 mm.   **Obv:** Bust left **Rev:** Justice
seated right with sword and scales

Date	Mintage	F	VF	XF	Unc	BU
1979/I	223,000	—	0.50	1.00	3.00	—
1980/II	250,000	—	0.50	1.00	3.00	—

KM# 157   50 LIRE
6.2000 g., Stainless Steel, 24.8 mm.   **Obv:** Head left **Rev:** Upright
design flanked by standing figures

Date	Mintage	F	VF	XF	Unc	BU
1981/III	240,000	—	0.50	1.00	3.00	—

KM# 163   50 LIRE
6.2000 g., Stainless Steel, 24.8 mm.   **Subject:** Motherhood
Obv: Bust right **Rev:** Seated figure with infant on lap

Date	Mintage	F	VF	XF	Unc	BU
1982/IV	400,000	—	0.50	1.00	3.00	—

KM# 172   50 LIRE
6.2000 g., Stainless Steel, 24.8 mm.   **Subject:** Banishment of Adam
and Eve **Obv:** Head left to lower right of cross **Rev:** Stylized figure

Date	Mintage	F	VF	XF	Unc	BU
1983/V	300,000	—	0.50	1.00	3.00	—

KM# 179   50 LIRE
6.2000 g., Stainless Steel, 24.8 mm.   **Subject:** Year of Peace
Obv: Bust left **Rev:** Doves

Date	Mintage	F	VF	XF	Unc	BU
1984/VI	300,000	—	0.50	1.00	3.00	—

KM# 187   50 LIRE
6.2000 g., Stainless Steel, 24.8 mm.   **Obv:** Head left
Rev: Winged lion holding gospel of St. Mark

Date	Mintage	F	VF	XF	Unc	BU
1985/VII	360,000	—	0.50	1.00	3.00	—

KM# 194   50 LIRE
6.2000 g., Stainless Steel, 24.8 mm.   **Obv:** Bust right **Rev:** Moses
seated on rock

Date	Mintage	F	VF	XF	Unc	BU
1986/VIII	100,000	—	0.50	1.00	3.00	—

KM# 201   50 LIRE
6.2000 g., Stainless Steel, 24.8 mm.   **Obv:** Bust right
Rev: Mother Mary protecting kneeling sinners

Date	Mintage	F	VF	XF	Unc	BU
1987/IX	—	—	0.50	1.00	3.00	—

KM# 208   50 LIRE
6.2000 g., Stainless Steel, 24.8 mm.   **Subject:** Creation of Eve
From Adam's Rib **Obv:** Bust right **Rev:** Face profile to right of
female figure rising out of male figure on ground

Date	Mintage	F	VF	XF	Unc	BU
VS1988/X	—	—	0.50	1.00	3.00	—

KM# 215   50 LIRE
6.2000 g., Stainless Steel, 24.8 mm.   **Subject:** Human Solidarity
Rev: Standing figures

Date	Mintage	F	VF	XF	Unc	BU
1989/XI	—	—	0.50	1.00	3.00	—

KM# 222   50 LIRE
Stainless Steel, 16.3 mm.   **Obv:** Bust 3/4 left **Rev:** Radiant cross
in open door

Date	Mintage	F	VF	XF	Unc	BU
1990/XII	—	—	0.50	1.00	3.00	—

KM# 230   50 LIRE
Stainless Steel, 16.3 mm.   **Obv:** Head left **Rev:** Baptism scene

Date	Mintage	F	VF	XF	Unc	BU
1991/XIII	—	—	0.50	1.00	3.00	—

KM# 238   50 LIRE
Stainless Steel, 16.3 mm.   **Obv:** Bust right **Rev:** Cross as balance
scale between agriculture and industry

Date	Mintage	F	VF	XF	Unc	BU
1992/XIV	—	—	0.50	1.00	3.00	—

KM# 246   50 LIRE
Stainless Steel, 16.3 mm.   **Obv:** Head facing **Rev:** Chalice
divides inscription

Date	Mintage	F	VF	XF	Unc	BU
1993/XV	—	—	0.50	1.00	3.00	—

KM# 254   50 LIRE
Stainless Steel, 16.3 mm.   **Obv:** Bust left **Rev:** Hands and prison
bars

Date	Mintage	F	VF	XF	Unc	BU
1994/XVI	—	—	0.50	1.00	3.00	—

KM# 264   50 LIRE
Stainless Steel, 16.3 mm.   **Rev:** Dragon on Prone Woman
(Abortion)

Date	Mintage	F	VF	XF	Unc	BU
1995/XVII	—	—	0.50	1.00	3.00	—

KM# 274   50 LIRE
Copper-Nickel, 19.2 mm.   **Obv:** Head left **Rev:** Guardian angel
protecting child

Date	Mintage	F	VF	XF	Unc	BU
1996/XVIII	—	—	0.50	1.00	3.00	—

KM# 282   50 LIRE
Copper-Nickel, 19.2 mm.   **Obv:** Head right **Rev:** One man with
lowered sword, the other with dove

Date	Mintage	F	VF	XF	Unc	BU
1997/XIX	—	—	0.50	1.00	3.00	—

KM# 295   50 LIRE
Copper-Nickel, 19.2 mm.   **Obv:** Pope with crucifix croizer
Rev: Two figures and hand

Date	Mintage	F	VF	XF	Unc	BU
1998/XX	—	—	0.50	1.00	3.00	—

KM# 307   50 LIRE
4.4600 g., Copper-Nickel, 19.2 mm.   **Subject:** Ecosystem -
Agriculture **Obv:** Bust right **Rev:** Agricultural workers **Edge:** Plain
Mint: Rome

Date	Mintage	F	VF	XF	Unc	BU
1999/XXI	—	—	0.50	1.00	3.00	—

KM# 325   50 LIRE
4.5000 g., Copper-Nickel, 19.2 mm.   **Obv:** Papal arms within
circle **Rev:** Pope about to kiss ground **Edge:** Plain **Mint:** Rome

Date	Mintage	F	VF	XF	Unc	BU
2000/XXII	—	—	0.50	1.00	3.00	—

KM# 146   100 LIRE
8.0000 g., Stainless Steel, 27.75 mm.   **Obv:** Bust left
Rev: Prudence seated

Date	Mintage	F	VF	XF	Unc	BU
1979/I	399,000	—	0.75	1.50	3.50	—
1980/II	485,000	—	0.75	1.50	3.50	—

KM# 158   100 LIRE
8.0000 g., Stainless Steel, 27.75 mm.   **Obv:** Head left **Rev:** Angel
offering food to seated figure

Date	Mintage	F	VF	XF	Unc	BU
1981/III	550,000	—	0.75	1.50	3.50	—

KM# 164   100 LIRE
8.0000 g., Stainless Steel, 27.75 mm.   **Subject:** Family Unit
Obv: Bust right **Rev:** Standing and seated figure divides value

Date	Mintage	F	VF	XF	Unc	BU
1982/IV	656,000	—	0.75	1.50	3.50	—

KM# 173   100 LIRE
8.0000 g., Stainless Steel, 27.75 mm.   **Subject:** God Gives
World to Mankind **Obv:** Head left to lower right of cross **Rev:**
Design flanked by hand and kneeling figure

Date	Mintage	F	VF	XF	Unc	BU
1983/V	455,000	—	0.75	1.50	3.50	—

KM# 180   100 LIRE
8.0000 g., Stainless Steel, 27.75 mm.   **Subject:** Year of Peace
Obv: Bust left **Rev:** Cross divides lamb and value

Date	Mintage	F	VF	XF	Unc	BU
1984/VI	400,000	—	0.75	1.50	3.50	—

KM# 188   100 LIRE
8.0000 g., Stainless Steel, 27.75 mm.   **Obv:** Head left **Rev:** Small
airplane in flight over map

Date	Mintage	F	VF	XF	Unc	BU
1985/VII	800,000	—	0.75	1.50	3.50	—

KM# 195   100 LIRE
8.0000 g., Stainless Steel, 27.75 mm.   **Obv:** Bust right
Rev: Christ seated on rocks

Date	Mintage	F	VF	XF	Unc	BU
1986/VIII	100,000	—	0.75	1.50	3.50	—

KM# 202   100 LIRE
8.0000 g., Stainless Steel, 27.75 mm.   **Subject:** Angel and Mary,
The Annunciation **Obv:** Bust right **Rev:** Dove above angel and
seated figure

Date	Mintage	F	VF	XF	Unc	BU
1987/IX	—	—	0.75	1.50	3.50	—

KM# 209   100 LIRE
8.0000 g., Stainless Steel, 27.75 mm.   **Subject:** Adam naming
the Animals **Obv:** Bust right **Rev:** Standing figure in palm of hand
to left of assorted animals

Date	Mintage	F	VF	XF	Unc	BU
1988/X	—	—	0.75	1.50	3.50	—

KM# 216   100 LIRE
8.0000 g., Stainless Steel, 27.75 mm.   **Rev:** Pelican feeding young

Date	Mintage	F	VF	XF	Unc	BU
1989/XI	—	—	0.75	1.50	3.50	—

KM# 223   100 LIRE
Stainless Steel, 18 mm.   **Subject:** Early Bishop **Obv:** Bust 3/4
left **Rev:** Hooded half-figure facing

Date	Mintage	F	VF	XF	Unc	BU
1990/XII	—	—	0.75	1.50	3.50	—

KM# 231   100 LIRE
Stainless Steel, 18 mm. **Obv:** Head left **Rev:** Depiction of the
risen Christ

Date	Mintage	F	VF	XF	Unc	BU
1991/XIII	—	—	0.75	1.50	3.50	—

KM# 239   100 LIRE
Stainless Steel, 18 mm. **Obv:** Bust right **Rev:** Open book above
value

Date	Mintage	F	VF	XF	Unc	BU
1992/XIV	—	—	0.75	1.50	3.50	—

KM# 247   100 LIRE
Copper-Nickel, 21.8 mm. **Obv:** Head facing **Rev:** Portrait of
Jesus facing divides inscription above value

Date	Mintage	F	VF	XF	Unc	BU
1993/XV	—	—	0.75	1.50	3.50	—

KM# 255   100 LIRE
Copper-Nickel, 21.8 mm. **Obv:** Bust left **Rev:** Basketball players
with one in wheelchair

Date	Mintage	F	VF	XF	Unc	BU
1994/XVI	—	—	0.75	1.50	3.50	—

KM# 265   100 LIRE
Copper-Nickel, 21.8 mm. **Rev:** Guard and prisoners

Date	Mintage	F	VF	XF	Unc	BU
1995/XVII	—	—	0.75	1.50	3.50	—

KM# 275   100 LIRE
Copper-Nickel, 21.8 mm. **Obv:** Head left **Rev:** Women helping
children

Date	Mintage	F	VF	XF	Unc	BU
1996/XVIII	—	—	0.75	1.50	3.50	—

KM# 283   100 LIRE
Copper-Nickel, 21.8 mm. **Obv:** Bust right **Rev:** Woman filling
birdbath and doves

Date	Mintage	F	VF	XF	Unc	BU
1997/XIX	—	—	0.75	1.25	2.50	—

KM# 296   100 LIRE
Copper-Nickel, 21.8 mm. **Obv:** Pope with crucifix croizer
Rev: Female figure in front of globe

Date	Mintage	F	VF	XF	Unc	BU
1998/XX	—	—	0.75	1.50	3.50	—

KM# 308   100 LIRE
4.5000 g., Copper-Nickel, 22 mm. **Subject:** The Right to Peace
Obv: Bust right within circle **Rev:** Children of the world gathered
in peace **Edge:** Reeded and plain sections **Mint:** Rome

Date	Mintage	F	VF	XF	Unc	BU
1999/XXI	—	—	0.75	1.50	3.50	—

KM# 326   100 LIRE
4.5000 g., Copper-Nickel, 22 mm. **Obv:** Papal arms within circle
Rev: Pope resting head on hand within window frame design
Edge: Plain and reeded sections **Mint:** Rome

Date	Mintage	F	VF	XF	Unc	BU
2000/XXII	—	—	0.75	150	3.50	—

KM# 147   200 LIRE
5.0000 g., Aluminum-Bronze, 24 mm. **Obv:** Bust left **Rev:** Peace
seated flanked by value and sprig

Date	Mintage	F	VF	XF	Unc	BU
1979/I	355,000	—	0.50	1.00	2.50	—
1980/II	200,000	—	0.50	1.00	2.50	—

KM# 159   200 LIRE
5.0000 g., Aluminum-Bronze, 24 mm. **Subject:** Corporal acts
of Mercy - Bury the dead **Obv:** Head left **Rev:** Standing figures
carrying supine figure

Date	Mintage	F	VF	XF	Unc	BU
1981/III	170,000	—	0.50	1.00	3.00	—

KM# 165   200 LIRE
5.0000 g., Aluminum-Bronze, 24 mm. **Subject:** Farm labor
Obv: Bust right **Rev:** Workers and ox

Date	Mintage	F	VF	XF	Unc	BU
1982/IV	500,000	—	0.50	1.00	3.00	—

KM# 174   200 LIRE
5.0000 g., Aluminum-Bronze, 24 mm. **Subject:** Creation of Man
Obv: Head left to lower right of cross **Rev:** Stylized figure above
hands

Date	Mintage	F	VF	XF	Unc	BU
1983/V	300,000	—	0.50	1.00	3.00	—

KM# 181   200 LIRE
5.0000 g., Aluminum-Bronze, 24 mm. **Subject:** Year of Peace
Obv: Bust left **Rev:** Sailboat and cross

Date	Mintage	F	VF	XF	Unc	BU
1984/VI	250,000	—	0.50	1.00	3.00	—

KM# 189   200 LIRE
5.0000 g., Aluminum-Bronze, 24 mm. **Obv:** Head left
Rev: Winged Ox holding gospel

Date	Mintage	F	VF	XF	Unc	BU
1985/VII	300,000	—	0.50	1.00	3.00	—

KM# 196   200 LIRE
5.0000 g., Aluminum-Bronze, 24 mm. **Obv:** Bust right
Rev: Archangel Michael and value

Date	Mintage	F	VF	XF	Unc	BU
1986/VIII	100,000	—	0.50	1.00	3.00	—

KM# 203   200 LIRE
5.0000 g., Aluminum-Bronze, 24 mm. **Subject:** Mary, Queen of
Peace **Obv:** Bust right **Rev:** Seated figure in front of trees

Date	Mintage	F	VF	XF	Unc	BU
1987/IX	—	—	0.50	1.00	3.00	—

KM# 210   200 LIRE
5.0000 g., Aluminum-Bronze, 24 mm. **Subject:** Creation of
Adam **Obv:** Bust right **Rev:** Face profile at left of figure within
palm of hand

Date	Mintage	F	VF	XF	Unc	BU
1988/X	—	—	0.50	1.00	3.00	—

MB# 217   200 LIRE
5.0000 g., Aluminum-Bronze, 24 mm. **Obv:** Bust 3/4 right
Rev: Group of standing figures

Date	Mintage	F	VF	XF	Unc	BU
1989/XI	—	—	0.50	1.00	3.00	—

KM# 224   200 LIRE
5.0000 g., Aluminum-Bronze, 24 mm. **Subject:** Blessed Virgin
Mary **Obv:** Bust 3/4 left **Rev:** Standing figure facing and value

Date	Mintage	F	VF	XF	Unc	BU
1990/XII	—	—	0.50	1.00	3.00	—

KM# 232   200 LIRE
5.0000 g., Aluminum-Bronze, 24 mm. **Obv:** Head left
Rev: Stylized figure to left of city

Date	Mintage	F	VF	XF	Unc	BU
1991/XIII	—	—	0.50	1.00	3.00	—

KM# 240   200 LIRE
5.0000 g., Aluminum-Bronze, 24 mm. **Obv:** Bust right
Rev: Mother nursing child

Date	Mintage	F	VF	XF	Unc	BU
1992/XIV	—	—	0.50	1.00	3.00	—

KM# 248   200 LIRE
5.0000 g., Aluminum-Bronze, 24 mm. **Subject:** Ten
Commandments **Obv:** Head facing **Rev:** 10 commandment stone
divides name above value

Date	Mintage	F	VF	XF	Unc	BU
1993/XV	—	—	0.50	1.00	3.00	—

KM# 256   200 LIRE
5.0000 g., Aluminum-Bronze, 24 mm. **Subject:** Helping Victims
of Drug Abuse **Obv:** Bust left **Rev:** Group of standing figures

Date	Mintage	F	VF	XF	Unc	BU
1994/XVI	—	—	0.50	1.00	3.00	—

KM# 266   200 LIRE
5.0000 g., Aluminum-Bronze, 24 mm. **Rev:** Family and farming
scene

Date	Mintage	F	VF	XF	Unc	BU
1995/XVII	—	—	0.50	1.00	3.00	—

KM# 276   200 LIRE
5.0000 g., Aluminum-Bronze, 24 mm. **Obv:** Head left
Rev: Display of family togetherness

Date	Mintage	F	VF	XF	Unc	BU
1996/XVIII	—	—	0.50	1.00	3.00	—

KM# 284   200 LIRE
5.0000 g., Aluminum-Bronze, 24 mm. **Obv:** Bust right
Rev: Angel guiding two people

Date	Mintage	F	VF	XF	Unc	BU
1997/XIX	—	—	0.50	1.00	3.00	—

KM# 297   200 LIRE
5.0000 g., Aluminum-Bronze, 24 mm. **Obv:** Bust left **Rev:** Group
of standing figures

Date	Mintage	F	VF	XF	Unc	BU
1998/XX	—	—	0.50	1.00	3.00	—

KM# 309   200 LIRE
5.0000 g., Aluminum-Bronze, 24 mm. **Obv:** Bust right
Rev: Christ among the poor and outcast **Edge:** Reeded
Mint: Rome

Date	Mintage	F	VF	XF	Unc	BU
1999/XXI	—	—	0.50	1.00	3.00	—

KM# 327   200 LIRE
5.0000 g., Brass, 22 mm. **Obv:** Papal arms within circle
Rev: Pope praying **Edge:** Reeded **Mint:** Rome

Date	Mintage	F	VF	XF	Unc	BU
2000/XXII	—	—	0.50	1.00	3.00	—

KM# 148   500 LIRE
11.0000 g., 0.8350 Silver 0.2953 oz. ASW, 29.3 mm. **Obv:** Head
left **Rev:** Crowned shield

Date	Mintage	F	VF	XF	Unc	BU
1979/I	145,000	—	—	15.00	30.00	—
1980/II	184,000	—	—	15.00	30.00	—

KM# 160   500 LIRE
11.0000 g., 0.8350 Silver 0.2953 oz. ASW, 29.3 mm. **Obv:** Head
left **Rev:** Crowned shield

Date	Mintage	F	VF	XF	Unc	BU
1981/III	184,000	—	—	15.00	30.00	—

KM# 166   500 LIRE
6.8000 g., Bi-Metallic Aluminum-Bronze center in Stainless Steel
ring, 25.8 mm. **Subject:** Education **Obv:** Bust right within circle
Rev: Seated figure flanked by children within circle

Date	Mintage	F	VF	XF	Unc	BU
1982/IV	1,852,000	—	—	3.50	7.00	—

KM# 168   500 LIRE
11.0000 g., 0.8350 Silver 0.2953 oz. ASW, 29.3 mm.
Subject: Extraordinary Holy Year **Obv:** Crowned shield
Rev: Kneeling figure facing, people and buildings in background

Date	Mintage	F	VF	XF	Unc	BU
1983-84	130,000	—	—	15.00	30.00	—

KM# 175   500 LIRE
6.8000 g., Bi-Metallic Aluminum-Bronze center in Stainless Steel
ring, 25.8 mm. **Subject:** Creation of the Universe **Obv:** Head
left to lower right of cross within circle **Rev:** Hand reaching in
globe within circle

Date	Mintage	F	VF	XF	Unc	BU
1983/V	—	—	—	3.50	7.00	—

KM# 182   500 LIRE
6.8000 g., Bi-Metallic Aluminum-Bronze center in Stainless Steel
ring, 25.8 mm. **Subject:** Year of Peace **Obv:** Head left within
circle **Rev:** Sprig within clasped hands within circle

Date	Mintage	F	VF	XF	Unc	BU
1984/VI	270,000	—	—	3.50	7.00	—

KM# 184   500 LIRE
11.0000 g., 0.8350 Silver 0.2953 oz. ASW, 29.3 mm.
Subject: 2000th Anniversary - Birth of Blessed Virgin Mary
Obv: Crowned shield **Rev:** Standing and kneeling figures, crosses and domed building

Date	Mintage	F	VF	XF	Unc	BU
1984/VI	105,000	—	—	20.00	35.00	—

KM# 190   500 LIRE
6.8000 g., Bi-Metallic Aluminum-Bronze center in Stainless Steel ring, 25.8 mm. **Obv:** Head left within circle **Rev:** St. Paul in boat within circle

Date	Mintage	F	VF	XF	Unc	BU
1985/VII	300,000	—	—	3.50	7.00	—

KM# 197   500 LIRE
6.8000 g., Bi-Metallic Aluminum-Bronze center in Stainless Steel ring, 25.8 mm. **Obv:** Bust right within circle **Rev:** Seated Mary and Jesus within circle

Date	Mintage	F	VF	XF	Unc	BU
1986/VIII	300,000	—	—	3.50	7.00	—

KM# 204   500 LIRE
6.8000 g., Bi-Metallic Aluminum-Bronze center in Stainless Steel ring, 25.8 mm. **Obv:** Bust left within circle **Rev:** Mary before Crucified Jesus within circle

Date	Mintage	F	VF	XF	Unc	BU
1987/IX	—	—	—	3.50	7.00	—

KM# 211   500 LIRE
6.8000 g., Bi-Metallic Aluminum-Bronze center in Stainless Steel ring, 25.8 mm. **Obv:** Head right within circle **Rev:** Dove at center, conjoined busts within circle

Date	Mintage	F	VF	XF	Unc	BU
1988/X	—	—	—	3.50	7.00	—

KM# 218   500 LIRE
6.8000 g., Bi-Metallic Aluminum-Bronze center in Stainless Steel ring, 25.8 mm. **Obv:** Bust right within circle **Rev:** Grapevine within circle

Date	Mintage	F	VF	XF	Unc	BU
1989/XI	—	—	—	3.50	7.00	—

KM# 225   500 LIRE
6.8000 g., Bi-Metallic Aluminum-Bronze center in Stainless Steel ring, 25.8 mm. **Obv:** Bust left within circle **Rev:** Jesus flanked by kneeling figures within circle

Date	Mintage	F	VF	XF	Unc	BU
1990/XII	—	—	—	3.00	7.00	—

KM# 227   500 LIRE
11.0000 g., 0.8350 Silver 0.2953 oz. ASW, 29.3 mm.
Subject: Social doctrine **Obv:** Bust right **Rev:** Stylized figures within circle

Date	Mintage	F	VF	XF	Unc	BU
1991/XIII	—	—	—	25.00	40.00	—

KM# 233   500 LIRE
6.8000 g., Bi-Metallic Aluminum-Bronze center in Stainless Steel ring, 25.8 mm. **Obv:** Head left within circle **Rev:** Redeemer sending out missionaries within circle

Date	Mintage	F	VF	XF	Unc	BU
1991/XIII	—	—	—	2.25	5.00	—

KM# 235   500 LIRE
11.0000 g., 0.8350 Silver 0.2953 oz. ASW, 29.3 mm.
Subject: Evangelization of America **Obv:** Crowned bust left to right of world globe **Rev:** Three ships in center of map

Date	Mintage	F	VF	XF	Unc	BU
1992/XIV	—	—	—	25.00	40.00	—

KM# 241   500 LIRE
6.8000 g., Bi-Metallic Aluminum-Bronze center in Stainless Steel ring, 25.8 mm. **Obv:** Bust right within circle **Rev:** Hands holding loaf of bread within globe

Date	Mintage	F	VF	XF	Unc	BU
1992/XIV	—	—	—	2.25	5.00	—

KM# 243   500 LIRE
11.0000 g., 0.8350 Silver 0.2953 oz. ASW, 29.3 mm.
Subject: World Peace **Rev:** Seated figure with infant

Date	Mintage	F	VF	XF	Unc	BU
1993/XV	—	—	—	25.00	40.00	—

KM# 249   500 LIRE
6.8000 g., Bi-Metallic Aluminum-Bronze center in Stainless Steel ring, 25.8 mm. **Rev:** Thurible

Date	Mintage	F	VF	XF	Unc	BU
1993/XV	—	—	—	2.25	5.00	—

KM# 251   500 LIRE
11.0000 g., 0.8350 Silver 0.2953 oz. ASW, 29.3 mm.
Subject: Veritatis Splendor **Obv:** Sunrays above bust right holding crucifix **Rev:** Sunrays divide circle with standing figure within map

Date	Mintage	F	VF	XF	Unc	BU
1994/XVI	—	—	—	25.00	40.00	—
1994/XVI Proof	—	Value: 40.00				

KM# 257   500 LIRE
6.8000 g., Bi-Metallic Aluminum-Bronze center in Stainless Steel ring, 25.8 mm. **Obv:** Bust left within circle **Rev:** People meeting, Golgotha in background

Date	Mintage	F	VF	XF	Unc	BU
1994/XVI	—	—	—	2.25	5.00	—

KM# 259   500 LIRE
11.0000 g., 0.8350 Silver 0.2953 oz. ASW, 29.3 mm.
Series: International Women's Year **Obv:** Pope resting head on hand with crucifix to right of crowned shield **Rev:** 1/2-length figure holding infant to left of 1/2 designed globe
Edge: INTERNATIONALIS ANNUS MELIEREI DICATUS

Date	Mintage	F	VF	XF	Unc	BU
1995/XVII	20,000	—	—	30.00	45.00	—
1995/XVII Proof	7,000	Value: 65.00				

KM# 267   500 LIRE
6.8000 g., Bi-Metallic, 25.8 mm. **Rev:** Cain slaying Abel within circle

Date	Mintage	F	VF	XF	Unc	BU
1995/XVII	460,000	—	—	2.25	5.00	—

KM# 269   500 LIRE
11.0000 g., 0.8350 Silver 0.2953 oz. ASW, 29.3 mm.
Subject: 50th Anniversary - Ordination of Pope John Paul II
Obv: Bust right **Rev:** Sheep, lamb on shepards shoulder and
flying figure holding infant

Date	Mintage	F	VF	XF	Unc	BU
1996/XVIII	33,000	—	—	25.00	43.00	—
1996/XVIII Proof	7,000	Value: 65.00				

KM# 277   500 LIRE
6.8000 g., Bi-Metallic Aluminum-Bronze center in Stainless Steel
ring, 25.8 mm. **Obv:** Head left within circle **Rev:** Seated figures
within circle, serpent at left of circle

Date	Mintage	F	VF	XF	Unc	BU
1996/XVIII	100,000	—	—	2.25	5.00	—

KM# 279   500 LIRE
11.0000 g., 0.8350 Silver 0.2953 oz. ASW, 29.3 mm. **Subject:** XII
World Youth Conference **Obv:** Bust right **Rev:** Six children with
Jesus **Edge:** IUVENTUTIS XII UNIVERSALIS DIES PARISIIS

Date	Mintage	F	VF	XF	Unc	BU
1997/XIX	18,000	—	—	30.00	40.00	—
1997/XIX Proof		Value: 65.00				

KM# 285   500 LIRE
6.8000 g., Bi-Metallic Aluminum-Bronze center in Stainless Steel
ring, 25.8 mm. **Obv:** Head right within circle **Rev:** One man
freeing another from thorns

Date	Mintage	F	VF	XF	Unc	BU
1997/XIX	160,000	—	—	2.25	5.00	—

KM# 292   500 LIRE
11.0000 g., 0.8350 Silver 0.2953 oz. ASW, 29.3 mm.
Obv: Crowned bust right **Rev:** Shroud of Turin, head facing
Edge: SACRA SINDON OSTENTATUR AVG. TAVR.
MCMXCVIII

Date	Mintage	F	VF	XF	Unc	BU
1998/XX	23,000	—	—	30.00	45.00	—
1998R Proof		Value: 65.00				

KM# 298   500 LIRE
6.8000 g., Bi-Metallic Aluminum-Bronze center in Stainless Steel
ring, 25.8 mm. **Obv:** Bust right holding crucifix within circle
Rev: Two figures within circle

Date	Mintage	F	VF	XF	Unc	BU
1998/XX	103,500	—	—	2.25	5.00	—

KM# 310   500 LIRE
6.7000 g., Bi-Metallic Aluminum-Bronze center in Stainless Steel
ring, 25.9 mm. **Subject:** Time of Choices, Time of Hope
Obv: Bust right within circle **Rev:** God's hand above young
parent's with baby **Edge:** Reeded **Mint:** Rome

Date	Mintage	F	VF	XF	Unc	BU
1999/XXI	161,000	—	—	2.25	5.50	—

KM# 322   500 LIRE
11.0000 g., 0.8350 Silver 0.2953 oz. ASW, 29.3 mm.
Subject: 70th Anniversary - Vatican City Arms of Six Popes
Obv: Bust right **Rev:** Dates in center of assorted crowned shields

Date	Mintage	F	VF	XF	Unc	BU
1999/XXI	—	—	—	30.00	40.00	—
1999/XXI Proof		Value: 65.00				

KM# 328   500 LIRE
6.7700 g., Bi-Metallic Aluminum-Bronze center in Stainless Steel
ring, 25.7 mm. **Obv:** Papal arms within circle **Rev:** Bust right
turning a page within circle **Edge:** Reeded and plain sections
Mint: Rome

Date	Mintage	F	VF	XF	Unc	BU
2000/XXII	—	—	—	3.50	7.00	—

KM# 167   1000 LIRE
14.6000 g., 0.8350 Silver 0.3919 oz. ASW **Obv:** Bust right
Rev: Crowned shield divides value

Date	Mintage	F	VF	XF	Unc	BU
1982/IV	210,000	—	—	20.00	35.00	—

KM# 169   1000 LIRE
14.6000 g., 0.8350 Silver 0.3919 oz. ASW
Subject: Extraordinary Holy Year **Obv:** Crowned half figure left
Rev: Crowned shield divides value

Date	Mintage	F	VF	XF	Unc	BU
1983-84	130,000	—	—	20.00	35.00	—

KM# 176   1000 LIRE
14.6000 g., 0.8350 Silver 0.3919 oz. ASW **Subject:** Prayer
Obv: Crowned bust left holding crucifix **Rev:** Crowned shield

Date	Mintage	F	VF	XF	Unc	BU
1983/V	110,000	—	—	20.00	35.00	—

KM# 183   1000 LIRE
14.6000 g., 0.8350 Silver 0.3919 oz. ASW **Subject:** Year of
Peace **Obv:** Bust left **Rev:** Crowned shield

Date	Mintage	F	VF	XF	Unc	BU
1984/VI	105,000	—	—	20.00	35.00	—

KM# 191   1000 LIRE
14.6000 g., 0.8350 Silver 0.3919 oz. ASW **Obv:** Pope standing,
vestments blowing in the wind **Rev:** Crowned shield

Date	Mintage	F	VF	XF	Unc	BU
1985/VII	86,000	—	—	20.00	35.00	—

KM# 198   1000 LIRE
14.6000 g., 0.8350 Silver 0.3919 oz. ASW **Obv:** Crowned shield
Rev: Pope seated at microphone

Date	Mintage	F	VF	XF	Unc	BU
1986/VIII	80,000	—	—	20.00	35.00	—

KM# 205   1000 LIRE
14.6000 g., 0.8350 Silver 0.3919 oz. ASW **Obv:** Crowned shield
Rev: Pope in prayer and seated figure with infant

Date	Mintage	F	VF	XF	Unc	BU
1987/IX	—	—	—	20.00	35.00	—

KM# 212   1000 LIRE
14.6000 g., 0.8350 Silver 0.3919 oz. ASW **Rev:** Pope seated
at desk

Date	Mintage	F	VF	XF	Unc	BU
1988/X	—	—	—	20.00	35.00	—

KM# 219   1000 LIRE
14.6000 g., 0.8350 Silver 0.3919 oz. ASW **Obv:** Crowned shield
Rev: Pope with Prelates and worshippers

Date	Mintage	F	VF	XF	Unc	BU
1989/XI	—	—	—	20.00	35.00	—

KM# 226   1000 LIRE
14.6000 g., 0.8350 Silver 0.3919 oz. ASW **Obv:** Crowned shield
Rev: Pope walking over destroyed barbed-wire fence

Date	Mintage	F	VF	XF	Unc	BU
1990/XII	—	—	—	20.00	35.00	—

KM# 234   1000 LIRE
14.6000 g., 0.8350 Silver 0.3919 oz. ASW **Obv:** Crowned shield
Rev: Pope handing missionary cross to two young people

Date	Mintage	F	VF	XF	Unc	BU
1991/XIII	—	—	—	20.00	35.00	—

KM# 242   1000 LIRE
14.6000 g., 0.8350 Silver 0.3919 oz. ASW **Obv:** Bust right
Rev: Pope's coat-of-arms

Date	Mintage	F	VF	XF	Unc	BU
1992/XIV	—	—	—	20.00	35.00	—

KM# 250   1000 LIRE
14.6000 g., 0.8350 Silver 0.3919 oz. ASW **Obv:** Head facing
Rev: Papal coat-of-arms divides inscription

Date	Mintage	F	VF	XF	Unc	BU
1993/XV	—	—	—	20.00	35.00	—

KM# 258   1000 LIRE
14.6000 g., 0.8350 Silver 0.3919 oz. ASW **Subject:** The Good
Samaritan **Obv:** Kneeling figure reaching for standing Pope
Rev: Horse behind figures

Date	Mintage	F	VF	XF	Unc	BU
1994/XVI	—	—	—	20.00	35.00	—

KM# 268   1000 LIRE
14.6000 g., 0.8350 Silver 0.3919 oz. ASW **Obv:** Head left
Rev: Radiant Virgin Mary within stylized dragon

Date	Mintage	F	VF	XF	Unc	BU
1995/XVII	—	—	—	20.00	35.00	—

KM# 278   1000 LIRE
14.6000 g., 0.8350 Silver 0.3919 oz. ASW **Obv:** John Paul II
releasing doves from balcony **Rev:** Jesus welcomes the little
children

Date	Mintage	F	VF	XF	Unc	BU
1996/XVIII	—	—	—	20.00	35.00	—

KM# 287   1000 LIRE
14.0000 g., 0.8350 Silver 0.3758 oz. ASW **Obv:** John Paul II
teaching people **Rev:** Saint cradling ill man **Edge:** TOTVS TVVS
MCMXCVII

Date	Mintage	F	VF	XF	Unc	BU
1997/XIX	—	—	—	20.00	35.00	—

KM# 286   1000 LIRE
Bi-Metallic Stainless Steel center in Aluminum-Bronze ring, 26.9 mm.
Obv: Head right within circle **Rev:** Crowned shield within circle

Date	Mintage	F	VF	XF	Unc	BU
1997/XIX	270,000	—	—	3.50	7.00	—

KM# 299   1000 LIRE
Bi-Metallic Stainless Steel center in Aluminum-Bronze ring, 26.9 mm.
Obv: Head left within circle **Rev:** Papal coat-of-arms within circle

Date	Mintage	F	VF	XF	Unc	BU
1998/XX	306,500	—	—	3.50	8.50	—

KM# 300   1000 LIRE
14.0000 g., 0.8350 Silver 0.3758 oz. ASW **Obv:** Pope with
crucifix croizer within sun rays **Rev:** Jesus on globe **Edge:** TOTVS
TVVS MCMXCVIII

Date	Mintage	F	VF	XF	Unc	BU
1998/XX	—	—	—	20.00	35.00	—

KM# 311   1000 LIRE

8.8500 g., Bi-Metallic Stainless Steel center in Aluminum-Bronze ring, 26.9 mm. **Obv:** Pope's arms within circle **Rev:** Couple at base of Christ on cross within circle **Edge:** Reeded and plain sections **Mint:** Rome

Date	Mintage	F	VF	XF	Unc	BU
1999/XXI	126,100	—	—	4.00	8.50	—

KM# 312   1000 LIRE

14.0000 g., 0.8350 Silver 0.3758 oz. ASW **Subject:** The Right to Religous Freedom **Obv:** Bust right **Rev:** Family at altar **Edge:** TOTVS TVVS ++ ++ ++ ++ MCMXCIX ++ ++ ++ ++ **Mint:** Rome

Date	Mintage	F	VF	XF	Unc	BU
1999/XXI	—	—	—	20.00	40.00	—

KM# 329   1000 LIRE

8.8500 g., Bi-Metallic Stainless Steel center in Aluminum-Bronze ring, 26.9 mm. **Obv:** Papal arms within circle **Rev:** Pope and Eastern Orthodox Patriarch within circle **Edge:** Reeded and plain sections **Mint:** Rome

Date	Mintage	F	VF	XF	Unc	BU
2000/XXII	—	—	—	4.00	8.50	—

KM# 330   1000 LIRE

14.6000 g., 0.8350 Silver 0.3919 oz. ASW, 31.4 mm. **Obv:** Papal arms within circle **Rev:** Praying Pope divides assorted figures within circle **Edge:** TOTVS TVVS +++MM+++ **Mint:** Rome

Date	Mintage	F	VF	XF	Unc	BU
2000/XXII	—	—	—	20.00	35.00	—

KM# 313   2000 LIRE

16.0000 g., 0.8350 Silver 0.4295 oz. ASW **Subject:** Holy Year **Obv:** Pope standing by open door **Rev:** Three seated figures **Edge:** Reeded **Mint:** Rome

Date	Mintage	F	VF	XF	Unc	BU
2000	60,000	—	—	20.00	40.00	—
2000 Proof	10,000	Value: 200				

KM# 353   2000 LIRE

16.0000 g., 0.8350 Silver 0.4295 oz. ASW, 31.4 mm. **Subject:** 2000th Birthday of Jesus **Obv:** Bust of Pope in prayer **Rev:** Baby divides value **Edge:** Reeded **Mint:** Rome

Date	Mintage	F	VF	XF	Unc	BU
2000	—	—	—	20.00	35.00	—
2000R Proof	22,000	Value: 75.00				

KM# 260   10000 LIRE

22.0000 g., 0.8350 Silver 0.5906 oz. ASW **Subject:** The Annunciation **Obv:** Bust right **Rev:** Angel and seated figure below radiant dove

Date	Mintage	F	VF	XF	Unc	BU
1995	—	—	—	—	110	—
1995 Proof	30,000	Value: 80.00				

Note: Proof sets only

KM# 261   10000 LIRE

22.0000 g., 0.8350 Silver 0.5906 oz. ASW **Subject:** The Nativity **Obv:** Bust right **Rev:** Donkey heads and baby at center, standing figures at sides

Date	Mintage	F	VF	XF	Unc	BU
1995	—	—	—	30.00	45.00	—
1995 Proof	30,000	Value: 80.00				

Note: Proof sets only

KM# 270   10000 LIRE

22.0000 g., 0.8350 Silver 0.5906 oz. ASW **Subject:** Holy Year 2000 **Obv:** Bust right **Rev:** Baptism in River Jordan

Date	Mintage	F	VF	XF	Unc	BU
1996	—	—	—	—	45.00	—
1996 Proof	30,000	Value: 80.00				

Note: Proof sets only

KM# 271   10000 LIRE

22.0000 g., 0.8350 Silver 0.5906 oz. ASW **Subject:** Holy Year 2000 **Obv:** Bust right **Rev:** Jesus seated teaching above group of people

Date	Mintage	F	VF	XF	Unc	BU
1996	—	—	—	—	45.00	—
1996 Proof	30,000	Value: 80.00				

Note: Proof sets only

KM# 318   10000 LIRE

22.0000 g., 0.8350 Silver 0.5906 oz. ASW **Subject:** Cure of the Paralytic **Obv:** Bust left **Rev:** Two kneeling figures on roof above figure helping ill person

Date	Mintage	F	VF	XF	Unc	BU
1997	—	—	—	—	110	—
1997 Proof	—	Value: 80.00				

Note: Proof sets only

KM# 319   10000 LIRE

22.0000 g., 0.8350 Silver 0.5906 oz. ASW **Subject:** Calming of the Storm **Obv:** Bust left **Rev:** Figures in boat

Date	Mintage	F	VF	XF	Unc	BU
1997	—	—	—	—	110	—
1997 Proof	—	Value: 80.00				

Note: Proof sets only

KM# 290   10000 LIRE

22.0000 g., 0.8350 Silver 0.5906 oz. ASW **Obv:** Bust left **Rev:** Seated figures at long table, Last Supper

Date	Mintage	F	VF	XF	Unc	BU
1998	—	—	—	—	45.00	—
1998 Proof	30,000	Value: 80.00				

KM# 291 10000 LIRE
22.0000 g., 0.8350 Silver 0.5906 oz. ASW **Obv:** Bust left
Rev: Jesus on cross flanked by standing figures

Date	Mintage	F	VF	XF	Unc	BU
1998	—	—	—	—	45.00	—
1998 Proof	30,000	Value: 80.00				

KM# 303 10000 LIRE
22.0000 g., 0.8350 Silver 0.5906 oz. ASW, 34 mm. **Obv:** Bust
right **Rev:** Group with flames above head **Mint:** Rome

Date	Mintage	F	VF	XF	Unc	BU
1999	—	—	—	—	110	—
1999 Proof	30,000	Value: 80.00				

KM# 304 10000 LIRE
22.0000 g., 0.8350 Silver 0.5906 oz. ASW **Rev:** Jesus rising
from his tomb **Mint:** Rome

Date	Mintage	F	VF	XF	Unc	BU
1999	—	—	—	—	110	—
1999 Proof	30,000	Value: 80.00				

KM# 314 10000 LIRE
22.0000 g., 0.8350 Silver 0.5906 oz. ASW **Obv:** Bust right
Rev: Seated angel holding church above "GERUSALEMME"

Date	Mintage	F	VF	XF	Unc	BU
2000	—	—	—	—	110	—
2000 Proof	30,000	Value: 80.00				

KM# 315 10000 LIRE
22.0000 g., 0.8350 Silver 0.5906 oz. ASW **Obv:** Bust right
Rev: Seated angel holding church above "ROMA" **Mint:** Rome

Date	Mintage	F	VF	XF	Unc	BU
2000	—	—	—	—	110	—
2000 Proof	30,000	Value: 80.00				

KM# 356 50000 LIRE
7.5000 g., 0.9170 Gold 0.2211 oz. AGW **Obv:** Pope and Holy
Year Door **Rev:** John the Baptist and St. John the Evangelist
facing each other

Date	Mintage	F	VF	XF	Unc	BU
1996	—	—	—	—	325	—
1996/XVIIIR Proof	6,000	Value: 325				

KM# 288 50000 LIRE
7.5000 g., 0.9170 Gold 0.2211 oz. AGW **Obv:** Pope and Holy
Year Door **Rev:** St. Paul facing

Date	Mintage	F	VF	XF	Unc	BU
1997	—	—	—	—	325	—
1997/XIX Proof	6,000	Value: 325				

KM# 301 50000 LIRE
7.5000 g., 0.9170 Gold 0.2211 oz. AGW, 23 mm. **Obv:** Pope
and Holy Year Door **Rev:** Madonna and child **Edge:** Reeded
Mint: Rome

Date	Mintage	F	VF	XF	Unc	BU
1998/XX Proof	6,000	Value: 325				
1998	—	—	—	—	325	—

KM# 320 50000 LIRE
7.5000 g., 0.9170 Gold 0.2211 oz. AGW **Obv:** Pope and Holy
Year Door **Rev:** Statue of St. Peter

Date	Mintage	F	VF	XF	Unc	BU
1999	—	—	—	—	325	—
1999/XXI Proof	—	Value: 325				

KM# 316 50000 LIRE
7.5000 g., 0.9170 Gold 0.2211 oz. AGW **Subject:** Prodigal Son
Obv: Bust right **Rev:** Jesus on cross, standing figures at sides
Mint: Rome

Date	Mintage	F	VF	XF	Unc	BU
2000/XXII Proof	6,000	Value: 325				
2000	—	—	—	—	325	—

KM# 357 100000 LIRE
15.0000 g., 0.9170 Gold 0.4422 oz. AGW **Obv:** Pope and Holy
Year Door **Rev:** Basilica of St. John Lateran

Date	Mintage	F	VF	XF	Unc	BU
1996	—	—	—	—	600	—
1996/XVIIIR Proof	6,000	Value: 600				

KM# 289 100000 LIRE
15.0000 g., 0.9170 Gold 0.4422 oz. AGW **Obv:** Pope and Holy
Year Door **Rev:** Basilica of St. Paul outside the walls

Date	Mintage	F	VF	XF	Unc	BU
1997	—	—	—	—	600	—
1997/XIX Proof	6,000	Value: 600				

KM# 302 100000 LIRE
15.0000 g., 0.9170 Gold 0.4422 oz. AGW, 28 mm. **Obv:** Pope
and Holy Year Door **Rev:** Basilica of St. Mary Major **Edge:**
Reeded **Mint:** Rome

Date	Mintage	F	VF	XF	Unc	BU
1998	—	—	—	—	600	—
1998/XX Proof	6,000	Value: 600				

KM# 321 100000 LIRE
15.0000 g., 0.9170 Gold 0.4422 oz. AGW **Obv:** Pope and Holy
Year Door **Rev:** St. Peter's Basilica

Date	Mintage	F	VF	XF	Unc	BU
1999	—	—	—	—	600	—
1999/XXI Proof	—	Value: 600				

KM# 317 100000 LIRE
15.0000 g., 0.9170 Gold 0.4422 oz. AGW **Obv:** Bust right
Rev: Prodigal son embraced by father **Mint:** Rome

Date	Mintage	F	VF	XF	Unc	BU
2000R	—	—	—	—	600	—
2000/XXIIR Proof	6,000	Value: 600				

PROVAS

KM#	Date	Mintage	Identification	Mkt Val
Pr1	1951	103	Lira. Silver. Y#49.	75.00
Pr2	1951	103	2 Lire. Silver. Y#50.	75.00
Pr3	1951	103	5 Lire. Silver. Y#51.	110
Pr4	1951	103	10 Lire. Silver. Y#52.	125
Pr5	1952	103	Lira. Silver. Y#49.	75.00
Pr6	1952	103	2 Lire. Silver. Y#50.	75.00
Pr7	1952	103	5 Lire. Silver. Y#51.	110
Pr8	1952	103	10 Lire. Silver. Y#52.	125
Pr9	1953	103	Lira. Silver. Y#49.	75.00
Pr10	1953	103	2 Lire. Silver. Y#50.	75.00
Pr11	1953	103	5 Lire. Silver. Y#51.	110
Pr12	1953	103	10 Lire. Silver. Y#52.	125
Pr13	1955	103	Lira. Silver. Y#49.	75.00
Pr14	1955	103	2 Lire. Silver. Y#50.	75.00
Pr15	1955	103	5 Lire. Silver. Y#51.	75.00
Pr16	1955	103	10 Lire. Silver. Y#52.	95.00
Pr17	1955	103	50 Lire. Silver. Y#54.	115
Pr18	1955	103	100 Lire. Silver. Y#55.	125
Pr19	1956	103	Lira. Silver. Y#49.	75.00
Pr20	1956	103	2 Lire. Silver. Y#50.	75.00
Pr21	1956	103	5 Lire. Silver. Y#51.	75.00
Pr22	1956	103	10 Lire. Silver. Y#52.	95.00
Pr23	1956	103	50 Lire. Silver. Y#54.	115
Pr24	1956	103	100 Lire. Silver. Y#55.	125
Pr25	1957	103	Lira. Silver. Y#49.	75.00
Pr26	1957	103	2 Lire. Silver. Y#50.	75.00
Pr27	1957	103	5 Lire. Silver. Y#51.	75.00
Pr28	1957	103	10 Lire. Silver. Y#52.	75.00
Pr29	1957	103	20 Lire. Silver. Y-A52.	100
Pr30	1957	103	50 Lire. Silver. Y#54.	115
Pr31	1957	103	100 Lire. Silver. Y#55.	125
Pr32	1958	103	Lira. Silver. Y#49.	75.00
Pr33	1958	103	2 Lire. Silver. Y#50.	75.00
Pr34	1958	103	5 Lire. Silver. Y#51.	75.00
Pr35	1958	103	10 Lire. Silver. Y#52.	75.00
Pr36	1958	103	20 Lire. Silver. Y-A52.	100
Pr37	1958	103	50 Lire. Silver. Y#54.	115
Pr38	1958	103	100 Lire. Silver. Y#55.	125
Pr39	1958	103	500 Lire. Silver. Y#56.	155
Pr40	1959	103	Lira. Silver. Y#58.	75.00
Pr41	1959	103	2 Lire. Silver. Y#59.	75.00
Pr42	1959	103	5 Lire. Silver. Y#60.	75.00
Pr43	1959	103	10 Lire. Silver. Y#61.	75.00
Pr44	1959	103	20 Lire. Silver. Y#62.	100
Pr45	1959	103	50 Lire. Silver. Y#63.	115
Pr46	1959	103	100 Lire. Silver. Y#64.	125
Pr47	1959	103	500 Lire. Silver. Y#65.	155
Pr48	1960	103	Lira. Silver. Y#58.	75.00
Pr49	1960	103	2 Lire. Silver. Y#59.	75.00
Pr50	1960	103	5 Lire. Silver. Y#60.	75.00
Pr51	1960	103	10 Lire. Silver. Y#61.	75.00
Pr52	1960	103	20 Lire. Silver. Y#62.	100
Pr53	1960	103	50 Lire. Silver. Y#63.1.	115
Pr54	1960	103	100 Lire. Silver. Y#64.1.	125
Pr55	1960	103	500 Lire. Silver. Y#65.1.	155
Pr56	1961	103	Lira. Silver. Y#58.	75.00
Pr57	1961	103	2 Lire. Silver. Y#59.	75.00
Pr58	1961	103	5 Lire. Silver. Y#60.	75.00
Pr59	1961	103	10 Lire. Silver. Y#61.	75.00
Pr60	1961	103	20 Lire. Silver. Y#62.	100
Pr61	1961	103	50 Lire. Silver. Y#63.1.	115
Pr62	1961	103	100 Lire. Silver. Y#64.1.	125
Pr63	1961	103	500 Lire. Silver. Y#65.1.	155
Pr64	1962	103	Lira. Silver. Y#58.	75.00
Pr65	1962	103	2 Lire. Silver. Y#59.	75.00
Pr66	1962	103	5 Lire. Silver. Y#60.	75.00

KM#	Date	Mintage Identification	Mkt Val
Pr67	1962	103 10 Lire. Silver. Y#61.	75.00
Pr68	1962	103 20 Lire. Silver. Y#62.	100
Pr69	1962	103 50 Lire. Silver. Y#63.1.	115
Pr70	1962	103 100 Lire. Silver. Y#64.1.	125
Pr71	1962	103 500 Lire. Silver. Y#65.1.	155
Pr72	1962	103 Lira. Silver. Y#67.	75.00
Pr73	1962	103 2 Lire. Silver. Y#68.	75.00
Pr74	1962	103 5 Lire. Silver. Y#69.	75.00
Pr75	1962	103 10 Lire. Silver. Y#70.	75.00
Pr76	1962	103 20 Lire. Silver. Y#71.	100
Pr77	1962	103 50 Lire. Silver. Y#72.	115
Pr78	1962	103 100 Lire. Silver. Y#73.	125
Pr79	1962	103 500 Lire. Silver. Y#74.	155
Pr80	1963	103 Lira. Silver. Y#76.	75.00
Pr81	1963	103 2 Lire. Silver. Y#77.	75.00
Pr82	1963	103 5 Lire. Silver. Y#78.	75.00
Pr83	1963	103 10 Lire. Silver. Y#79.	75.00
Pr84	1963	103 20 Lire. Silver. Y#80.	100
Pr85	1963	103 50 Lire. Silver. Y#81.	115
Pr86	1963	103 100 Lire. Silver. Y#82.	125
Pr87	1963	103 500 Lire. Silver. Y#83.	155
Pr88	1964	103 Lira. Silver. Y#76.	75.00
Pr89	1964	103 2 Lire. Silver. Y#77.	75.00
Pr90	1964	103 5 Lire. Silver. Y#78.	75.00
Pr91	1964	103 10 Lire. Silver. Y#79.	75.00
Pr92	1964	103 20 Lire. Silver. Y#80.	100
Pr93	1964	103 50 Lire. Silver. Y#81.	115
Pr94	1964	103 100 Lire. Silver. Y#82.	125
Pr95	1964	103 500 Lire. Silver. Y#83.	155
Pr96	1965	103 Lira. Silver. Y#76.	75.00
Pr97	1965	103 2 Lire. Silver. Y#77.	75.00
Pr98	1965	103 5 Lire. Silver. Y#78.	75.00
Pr99	1965	103 10 Lire. Silver. Y#79.	75.00
Pr100	1965	103 20 Lire. Silver. Y#80.	100
Pr101	1965	103 50 Lire. Silver. Y#81.	115
Pr102	1965	103 100 Lire. Silver. Y#82.	125
Pr103	1965	103 500 Lire. Silver. Y#83.	155
Pr104	1966	103 Lira. Silver. Y#84.	75.00
Pr105	1966	103 2 Lire. Silver. Y#85.	75.00
Pr106	1966	103 5 Lire. Silver. Y#86.	75.00
Pr107	1966	103 10 Lire. Silver. Y#87.	75.00
Pr108	1966	103 20 Lire. Silver. Y#88.	100
Pr109	1966	103 50 Lire. Silver. Y#89.	115
Pr110	1966	103 100 Lire. Silver. Y#90.	125
Pr111	1966	103 500 Lire. Silver. Y#91.	155
Pr112	ND(1967)	103 Lira. Silver. Y#92.	75.00
Pr113	ND(1967)	103 2 Lire. Silver. Y#93.	75.00
Pr114	ND(1967)	103 5 Lire. Silver. Y#94.	75.00
Pr115	ND(1967)	103 10 Lire. Silver. Y#95.	75.00
Pr116	ND(1967)	103 20 Lire. Silver. Y#96.	100
Pr117	1967	103 50 Lire. Silver. Y#97.	115
Pr118	1967	103 100 Lire. Silver. Y#98.	125
Pr119	1967	103 500 Lire. Silver. Y#99.	155
Pr120	ND(1968)	103 Lira. Silver. Y#100.	75.00
Pr121	ND(1968)	103 2 Lire. Silver. Y#101.	75.00
Pr122	ND(1968)	103 5 Lire. Silver. Y#102.	75.00
Pr123	ND(1968)	103 10 Lire. Silver. Y#103.	75.00
Pr124	ND(1968)	103 20 Lire. Silver. Y#104.	100
Pr125	ND(1968)	103 50 Lire. Silver. Y#105.	115
Pr126	ND(1968)	103 100 Lire. Silver. Y#106.	125
Pr127	ND(1968)	103 500 Lire. Silver. Y#107.	155
Pr128	1969	103 Lira. Silver. Y#108.	75.00
Pr129	1969	103 2 Lire. Silver. Y#109.	75.00
Pr130	1969	103 5 Lire. Silver. Y#110.	75.00
Pr131	1969	103 10 Lire. Silver. Y#111.	75.00
Pr132	1969	103 20 Lire. Silver. Y#112.	100
Pr133	1969	103 50 Lire. Silver. Y#113.	115
Pr134	1969	103 100 Lire. Silver. Y#114.	125
Pr135	1969	103 500 Lire. Silver. Y#115.	155
Pr136	1970	103 Lira. Silver. Y#116.	75.00
Pr137	1970	103 2 Lire. Silver. Y#117.	75.00
Pr138	1970	103 5 Lire. Silver. Y#118.	75.00
Pr139	1970	103 10 Lire. Silver. Y#119.	75.00
Pr140	1970	103 20 Lire. Silver. Y#120.	100
Pr141	1970	103 50 Lire. Silver. Y#121.	115
Pr142	1970	103 100 Lire. Silver. Y#122.	125
Pr143	1970	103 500 Lire. Silver. Y#123.	155
Pr144	1971	103 Lira. Silver. Y#116.	75.00
Pr145	1971	103 2 Lire. Silver. Y#117.	75.00
Pr146	1971	103 5 Lire. Silver. Y#118.	75.00
Pr147	1971	103 10 Lire. Silver. Y#119.	75.00
Pr148	1971	103 20 Lire. Silver. Y#120.	100
Pr149	1971	103 50 Lire. Silver. Y#121.	115
Pr150	1971	103 100 Lire. Silver. Y#122.	125
Pr151	1971	103 500 Lire. Silver. Y#123.	150
Pr152	1972	103 Lira. Silver. Y#116.	75.00
Pr153	1972	103 2 Lire. Silver. Y#117.	75.00
Pr154	1972	103 5 Lire. Silver. Y#118.	75.00
Pr155	1972	103 10 Lire. Silver. Y#119.	75.00
Pr156	1972	103 20 Lire. Silver. Y#120.	100
Pr157	1972	103 50 Lire. Silver. Y#121.	115
Pr158	1972	103 100 Lire. Silver. Y#122.	125
Pr159	1972	103 500 Lire. Silver. Y#123.	155
Pr160	1973	103 Lira. Silver. Y#116.	75.00
Pr161	1973	103 2 Lire. Silver. Y#117.	75.00
Pr162	1973	103 5 Lire. Silver. Y#118.	75.00
Pr163	1973	103 10 Lire. Silver. Y#119.	75.00
Pr164	1973	103 20 Lire. Silver. Y#120.	100
Pr165	1973	103 50 Lire. Silver. Y#121.	115
Pr166	1973	103 100 Lire. Silver. Y#122.	125
Pr167	1973	103 500 Lire. Silver. Y#123.	155
Pr168	1974	103 Lira. Silver. Y#116.	75.00

KM#	Date	Mintage Identification	Mkt Val
Pr169	1974	103 2 Lire. Silver. Y#117.	75.00
Pr170	1974	103 5 Lire. Silver. Y#118.	75.00
Pr171	1974	103 10 Lire. Silver. Y#119.	75.00
Pr172	1974	103 20 Lire. Silver. Y#120.	100
Pr173	1974	103 50 Lire. Silver. Y#121.	115
Pr174	1974	103 100 Lire. Silver. Y#122.	125
Pr175	1974	103 500 Lire. Silver. Y#123.	155
Pr176	1975	103 Lira. Silver. Y#116.	75.00
Pr177	1975	103 2 Lire. Silver. Y#117.	75.00
Pr178	1975	103 5 Lire. Silver. Y#118.	75.00
Pr179	1975	103 10 Lire. Silver. Y#119.	75.00
Pr180	1975	103 20 Lire. Silver. Y#120.	100
Pr181	1975	103 50 Lire. Silver. Y#121.	115
Pr182	1975	103 100 Lire. Silver. Y#122.	125
Pr183	1975	103 500 Lire. Silver. Y#123.	155
Pr184	1975	103 Lira. Silver. Y#124.	75.00
Pr185	1975	103 2 Lire. Silver. Y#125.	75.00
Pr186	1975	103 5 Lire. Silver. Y#126.	75.00
Pr187	1975	103 10 Lire. Silver. Y#127.	75.00
Pr188	1975	103 20 Lire. Silver. Y#128.	100
Pr189	1975	103 50 Lire. Silver. Y#129.	115
Pr190	1975	103 100 Lire. Silver. Y#130.	125
Pr191	1975	103 500 Lire. Silver. Y#131.	155

MINT SETS

KM#	Date	Mintage Identification	Issue Price	Mkt Val
MS1	1929 (9)	10,000 KM#1-9	—	975
MS2	1929 (8)	10,000 KM#1-8	—	275
MS3	1930 (9)	2,621 KM#1-9	—	950
MS4	1930 (8)	50,000 KM#1-8	—	150
MS5	1931 (9)	3,343 KM#1-9	—	650
MS6	1931 (8)	50,000 KM#1-8	—	150
MS7	1932 (9)	5,073 KM#1-9	—	650
MS8	1932 (8)	50,000 KM#1-8	—	150
MS10	1933-34 (8)	50,000 KM#11-18	—	225
MS9	1933-34 (8)	23,235 KM#11-19	—	710
MS11	1934 (9)	2,533 KM#1-9	—	650
MS12	1934 (8)	30,000 KM#1-8	—	150
MS13	1935 (9)	2,105 KM#1-9	—	750
MS14	1935 (8)	9,000 KM#1-8	—	250
MS15	1936 (9)	8,239 KM#1-8, 10	—	650
MS16	1936 (8)	40,000 KM#1-8	—	150
MS17	1937 (9)	2,000 KM#1-8, 10	—	3,150
MS18	1937 (8)	20,000 KM#1-8	—	150
MS19	1938 (3)	— KM#1-2, 10 Rare	—	—
MS20	1939 (9)	2,700 KM#22-30.1	—	735
MS21	1939 (8)	10,000 KM#22-29	—	135
MS22	1939 (2)	30,000 KM#20, 21	—	95.00
MS23	1940 (9)	2,000 KM#22, 23, 24a-27a, 28-30.1	—	725
MS24	1940 (8)	10,000 KM#22, 23, 24a-27a, 28-29	—	115
MS25	1941 (9)	2,000 KM#22, 23, 24a-27a, 28-30.2	—	895
MS26	1941 (8)	4,000 KM#22, 23, 24a-27a, 28-29	—	245
MS27	1942 (9)	2,000 KM#31-39	—	875
MS28	1942 (8)	4,000 KM#31-38	—	325
MSA29	1942 (4)	— KM#33-36	—	17.50
MS29	1943 (9)	1,000 KM#31-39	—	1,575
MS30	1943 (8)	1,000 KM#31-38	—	975
MS31	1944 (9)	1,000 KM#31-39	—	1,600
MS32	1944 (8)	1,000 KM#31-38	—	1,000
MS33	1945 (9)	1,000 KM#31-39	—	1,600
MS34	1945 (8)	1,000 KM#31-38	—	1,000
MS35	1946 (9)	1,000 KM#31-39	—	1,600
MS36	1946 (8)	1,000 KM#31-38	—	1,000
MS37	1947 (5)	1,000 KM#39-43	—	630
MS38	1947 (4)	50,000 KM#40-43	—	28.00
MS39	1947 (2)	— KM#42-43	—	16.00
MS40	1948 (5)	5,000 KM#39-43	—	530
MS41	1948 (4)	10,000 KM#40-43	—	28.00
MS42	1949 (5)	1,000 KM#39-43	—	645
MS43	1949 (4)	10,000 KM#40-43	—	40.00
MS44	1950 (5)	20,000 KM#44-48	—	525
MS45	1950 (4)	50,000 KM#44-47	—	25.00
MS46	1951 (4)	1,000 KM#49.1-53.1	—	560
MS47	1951 (4)	400,000 KM#49.1, 50, 51.1-52.1	—	6.00
MS54	1956 (7)	1,000 KM#49.2-55	—	570
MS48	1952 (5)	1,000 KM#49.1-52.1, 53.1	—	560
MS49	1952 (4)	400,000 KM#49.1-52.1	—	6.00
MS50	1953 (5)	1,000 KM#49.1-52.1, 53.1	—	560
MS51	1953 (4)	400,000 KM#49.1-52.1	—	6.00
MS52	1955 (7)	1,000 KM#49.1-55	—	570
MS53	1955 (6)	10,000 KM#49.1-52.1, 54.1, 55	—	20.00
MS55	1956 (6)	10,000 KM#49.2-52.2, 54.2, 55	—	20.00
MS56	1957 (5)	2,000 KM#49.1-A52, A53, 54.2, 55	—	310
MS57	1957 (6)	20,000 KM#49.1-52.2, 54.2, 55	—	18.00
MS58	1958 (5)	3,000 KM#49.1-52.2, 54.2-57	—	320
MS59	1958 (7)	20,000 KM#49.1-52.2, 54.2-56	—	45.00
MS60	1959 (9)	3,000 KM#58.1-64.1, 65-66	—	2,350
MS61	1959 (8)	25,000 KM#58.1-64.1, 65	—	85.00
MS62	1960 (8)	25,000 KM#58.1-59.1, 60.2-64.2, 65.1	—	85.00
MS63	1961 (8)	25,000 KM#58.2-62.2, 63.2-64.2, 65.1	—	65.00
MS64	1962 (8)	25,000 KM#58.2-64.2, 65.1	—	60.00
MS65	1962 (8)	50,000 KM#67-74	—	50.00
MS66	1963 (8)	60,000 KM#76.1-83.1	—	60.00
MS68	1964 (8)	60,000 KM#76.2-79.2, 80.1-81.1, 82.2-83.2	—	75.00

KM#	Date	Mintage Identification	Issue Price	Mkt Val
MS69	1965 (8)	60,000 KM#76.2-83.2	—	70.00
MS70	1966 (8)	90,000 KM#84-91	—	37.50
MS71	1967 (8)	100,000 KM#92-99	3.25	30.00
MS72	1968 (8)	100,000 KM#100-107	4.20	30.00
MS73	1969 (8)	100,000 KM#108-115	4.20	30.00
MS74	1970 (8)	100,000 KM#116-123	5.00	25.00
MS75	1971 (8)	110,000 KM#116-123	—	25.00
MS76	1972 (8)	110,000 KM#116-123	6.00	25.00
MS77	1973 (8)	120,000 KM#116-123	6.75	25.00
MS78	1974 (8)	120,000 KM#116-123	7.25	25.00
MS79	1975 (8)	132,000 KM#116-123	9.00	25.00
MS80	1975 (8)	170,000 KM#124-131	—	28.00
MSA80	1975 (5)	— KM#126-130	—	7.50
MS81	1976 (8)	180,000 KM#116-123	—	25.00
MS82	1977 (7)	180,000 KM#116-120, 122, 132	—	25.00
MS83	1978 (7)	180,000 KM#133-139	—	27.50
MS84	1979 (6)	156,000 KM#143-148	—	37.50
MS85	1980 (5)	— KM#143-148	18.00	35.00
MS86	1981 (6)	— KM#155-160	—	37.50
MS87	1982 (7)	120,000 KM#161-167	—	47.50
MS88	1983 (7)	120,000 KM#170-176	—	47.50
MS93	1983/84 (2)	130,000 KM#168-169	—	55.00
MS89	1984 (7)	— KM#177-183	—	47.50
MS90	1985 (7)	— KM#185-191	—	45.00
MS91	1986 (7)	— KM#192-198	23.50	45.00
MS92	1987 (7)	— KM#199-205	27.00	45.00
MSA93	1987 (5)	— KM#200-204	—	18.00
MS94	1988 (7)	— KM#206-212	—	50.00
MS95	1989 (7)	— KM#213-219	30.00	45.00
MS96	1990 (7)	— KM#220-226	33.00	50.00
MS97	1991 (7)	— KM#228-234	25.00	45.00
MS98	1992 (7)	— KM#236-242	25.00	45.00
MS99	1993 (7)	— KM#244-250	—	45.00
MS100	1994 (7)	— KM#252-258	—	45.00
MS101	1995 (7)	— KM#262-268	32.50	45.00
MS102	1996 (7)	— KM#272-278	33.00	45.00
MS103	1997 (8)	— KM#280-287	—	50.00
MS104	1998 (8)	— KM#293-300	—	55.00
MS105	1999 (8)	— KM#205-312	—	70.00
MS106	2000 (8)	— KM#323-330	37.50	110

PROOF SETS

KM#	Date	Mintage Identification	Issue Price	Mkt Val
PS1	1995 (2)	30,000 KM#260-261	70.00	165
PS2	1996 (2)	30,000 KM#270-271	75.00	165
PS3	1996 (2)	— KM#356, 357	—	—
PS4	1997 (2)	6,000 KM#288-289	547	900
PS5	1997 (2)	— KM#318, 319	—	—
PS7	1998 (2)	— KM#301, 302	—	—
PS6	1998 (2)	30,000 KM#290-291	—	165
PS8	1999 (2)	— KM#303, 304	—	—
PS9	1999 (2)	— KM#320, 321	—	900
PS12	2000 (2)	— KM#316, 317	—	900
PS10	2000 (2)	— KM#314, 315	—	160
PS11	2000 (10)	30,000 KM#288, 289, 301, 302, 316, 317, 320, 321, 356, 357 Anticipation of the Holy Year 2000	—	1,800

PROVA SETS

KM#	Date	Mintage Identification	Issue Price	Mkt Val
PrS1	1951 (4)	103 Pr1-Pr4	—	385
PrS2	1952 (4)	103 Pr5-Pr8	—	385
PrS3	1953 (4)	103 Pr9-Pr12	—	385
PrS4	1955 (6)	103 Pr13-Pr18	—	565
PrS5	1956 (6)	103 Pr19-Pr24	—	565
PrS6	1957 (7)	103 Pr25-31	—	645
PrS7	1958 (8)	103 Pr32-Pr39	—	800
PrS8	1959 (8)	103 Pr40-Pr47	—	800
PrS9	1960 (8)	103 Pr48-Pr55	—	800
PrS10	1961 (8)	103 Pr56-Pr63	—	800
PrS11	1962 (8)	103 Pr64-Pr71	—	800
PrS12	1962 (8)	103 Pr72-Pr79	—	800
PrS13	1963 (8)	103 Pr80-Pr87	—	800
PrS14	1964 (8)	103 Pr88-Pr95	—	800
PrS15	1965 (8)	103 Pr96-103	—	800
PrS16	1966 (8)	103 Pr104-Pr111	—	800
PrS17	1967 (8)	103 Pr112-Pr119	—	800
PrS18	1968 (8)	103 Pr120-Pr127	—	800
PrS19	1969 (8)	103 Pr128-Pr135	—	800
PrS20	1970 (8)	103 Pr136-Pr143	—	800
PrS21	1971 (8)	103 Pr144-Pr151	—	800
PrS22	1972 (8)	103 Pr152-Pr159	—	800
PrS23	1973 (8)	103 Pr160-Pr167	—	800
PrS24	1974 (8)	103 Pr168-Pr175	—	800
PrS25	1975 (8)	103 Pr176-Pr183	—	800
PrS26	1975 (8)	103 Pr184-Pr191	—	800

VENEZUELA

The Republic of Venezuela ("Little Venice"), located on the northern coast of South America between Colombia and Guyana, has an area of 352,145 sq. mi.(912,050 sq. km.) and a population of 20 million. Capital: Caracas. Petroleum and mining provide a significant portion of Venezuela's exports. Coffee, grown on 60,000 plantations, is the chief crop. Metalurgy, refining, oil, iron and steel production are the main employment industries.

Columbus discovered Venezuela on his third voyage in 1498. Initial exploration did not reveal Venezuela to be a land of great wealth. An active pearl trade operated on the offshore islands and slavers raided the interior in search of Indians to be sold into slavery, but no significant mainland settlements were made before 1567 when Caracas was founded. Venezuela, the home of Bolivar, was among the first South American colonies to rebel against Spain in 1810. The declaration of Independence of Venezuela was signed by seven provinces which are represented by the seven stars of the Venezuelan flag. Coinage of Caracas and Margarita use the seven stars in their designs. These original provinces were: Barcelona, Barinas, Caracas, Cumana, Margarita, Merida and Trujillo. The Provinces of Coro, Guyana and Maracaibo were added to Venezuela during the Independence War. Independence was attained in 1821 but not recognized by Spain until 1845. Together with Ecuador, Panama and Colombia, Venezuela was part of "Gran Colombia" until 1830, when it became a sovereign and independent state.

RULER
Republic, 1823-present

MINT MARKS
A - Paris
(a) - Paris, privy marks only
(aa) - Altena
(b) - Berlin
(bb) - Brussels
(cc) – Canada

(c) - Caracas
(d) - Denver
H, Heaton - Heaton, Birmingham
(l) - London
(m) - Madrid
(mm) - Mexico
(o) - Ontario
(p) - Philadelphia
(s) - San Francisco
(sc) - Schwerte - Vereinigte Deutsche Nickelwerke
(w) - Werdohl - Vereinigte Deutsche Metalwerke

MONETARY SYSTEM
100 Centimos = 1 Bolívar

REPUBLIC

REFORM COINAGE
1896; 100 Centimos = 1 Bolívar

Y# 27 5 CENTIMOS
2.3000 g., Copper-Nickel **Obv:** National arms, stars above
Obv. Leg.: ESTADOS UNIDOS DE VENEZUELA **Rev:** Value within wreath

Date	Mintage	F	VF	XF	Unc	BU
1915(p)	2,000,000	1.00	4.00	50.00	150	300
1921(p)	2,000,000	0.50	4.00	70.00	200	350
1925(p)	2,000,000	0.30	1.00	10.00	20.00	40.00
1927(p)	2,000,000	0.30	1.00	10.00	20.00	40.00
1929(p)	2,000,000	0.25	1.00	10.00	20.00	40.00
1936(p)	5,000,000	0.15	0.50	4.00	10.00	20.00
1938(p)	6,000,000	0.10	0.20	4.00	10.00	20.00

Y# 29 5 CENTIMOS
2.4300 g., Brass **Obv:** National arms, stars above
Rev: Denomination within wreath

Date	Mintage	F	VF	XF	Unc	BU
1944(d)	4,000,000	0.50	1.00	6.00	20.00	60.00

Y# 29a 5 CENTIMOS
2.4000 g., Copper-Nickel, 19.1 mm. **Obv:** National arms, stars above **Rev:** Denomination within wreath

Date	Mintage	F	VF	XF	Unc	BU
1945(p)	12,000,000	0.10	0.20	0.50	4.00	6.00
1946(p)	12,000,000	0.10	0.20	0.50	4.00	6.00
1948(p)	18,000,000	0.10	0.20	0.50	3.00	5.00

Y# 38.1 5 CENTIMOS
Copper-Nickel **Obv:** National arms, stars above
Rev: Denomination within wreath

Date	Mintage	F	VF	XF	Unc	BU
1958(p)	25,000,000	—	—	—	0.75	1.25

Y# 38.2 5 CENTIMOS
2.5000 g., Copper-Nickel, 19.8 mm. **Obv:** National arms, stars above **Rev:** Denomination within wreath

Date	Mintage	F	VF	XF	Unc	BU
1964(m)	40,000,000	—	—	—	0.50	1.00
1965(m)	60,000,000	—	—	—	0.50	1.00

Y# 38.3 5 CENTIMOS
Copper-Nickel **Obv:** National arms, stars above
Rev: Denomination within wreath

Date	Mintage	F	VF	XF	Unc	BU
1971(o)	40,000,000	—	—	—	0.50	1.00

Y# 49 5 CENTIMOS
Copper Clad Steel **Obv:** National arms, stars above
Rev: Denomination below spray

Date	Mintage	F	VF	XF	Unc	BU
1974(w)	200,000,000	—	—	—	1.00	5.00
1976(w)	200,000,000	—	—	—	1.00	4.00
1977(l)	600,000,000	—	—	—	0.15	1.00

Y# 49a 5 CENTIMOS
Nickel Clad Steel **Obv:** National arms, stars above
Rev: Denomination below spray

Date	Mintage	F	VF	XF	Unc	BU
1983(w)	600,000,000	—	—	—	0.10	0.20

Y# 49b 5 CENTIMOS
Copper-Nickel Clad Steel **Obv:** National arms, stars above
Rev: Denomination below spray

Date	Mintage	F	VF	XF	Unc	BU
1986(w)	500,000,000	—	—	—	0.10	0.20

Y# A40 10 CENTIMOS
Copper-Nickel **Obv:** National arms, stars above
Rev: Denomination within wreath

Date	Mintage	F	VF	XF	Unc	BU
1971(o)	60,000,000	—	—	0.10	0.25	0.50

Y# 28 12-1/2 CENTIMOS
Copper-Nickel **Obv:** National arms, stars above
Obv. Leg.: ESTADOS UNIDOS DE VENEZUELA **Rev:** Value within wreath **Note:** Varieties exist.

Date	Mintage	F	VF	XF	Unc	BU
1925(p)	800,000	2.50	6.50	45.00	200	400
1927(p)	800,000	1.00	2.00	15.00	100	150
1929(p)	800,000	0.15	0.50	10.00	75.00	100
1936(p)	1,200,000	0.15	0.30	5.00	35.00	75.00
1938(p)	1,600,000	0.15	0.30	2.00	25.00	50.00

Y# 30 12-1/2 CENTIMOS
Brass **Obv:** National arms, stars above **Rev:** Denomination within wreath

Date	Mintage	F	VF	XF	Unc	BU
1944(d)	800,000	2.50	4.50	15.00	75.00	150

Y# 30a 12-1/2 CENTIMOS
Copper-Nickel **Obv:** National arms, stars above
Rev: Denomination within wreath

Date	Mintage	F	VF	XF	Unc	BU
1945(p)	11,200,000	0.10	0.20	0.35	9.00	15.00
1946(p)	9,200,000	0.10	0.20	0.35	12.00	20.00
1948(s)	6,000,000	0.10	0.20	0.35	12.00	20.00

Y# 39 12-1/2 CENTIMOS
Copper-Nickel **Obv:** National arms, stars above
Rev: Denomination within wreath, knobbed 2

Date	Mintage	F	VF	XF	Unc	BU
1958(p)	10,000,000	—	—	0.20	2.00	4.00

Y# A39.1 12-1/2 CENTIMOS
Copper-Nickel **Obv:** National arms, flat stars **Rev:** Denomination within wreath, plain 2

Date	Mintage	F	VF	XF	Unc	BU
1969(m)	2,000,000	—	—	—	75.00	100

Y# A39.2 12-1/2 CENTIMOS
Copper-Nickel **Obv:** National arms, raised stars
Rev: Denomination within wreath, outlined stem ends

Date	Mintage	F	VF	XF	Unc	BU
1969(m)	Inc. above				100	200

Y# A39.3 12-1/2 CENTIMOS
Copper-Nickel **Obv:** National arms, stars above
Rev: Denomination within wreath, solid stem ends

Date	Mintage	F	VF	XF	Unc	BU
1969(m)	Inc. above				100	200

Note: 1969 dated strikes were not released into circulation, but the Central Bank has been selling limited quantities on occasion

Y# 20 GR 1.250 (1/4 Bolivar)
1.2500 g., 0.8350 Silver 0.0336 oz. ASW **Obv:** National arms
Obv. Leg.: ESTADOS UNIDOS DE VENEZUELA. **Rev:** Head
left **Rev. Leg.:** BOLIVAR LIBERTADOR

Date	Mintage	F	VF	XF	Unc	BU
1901	393,000	7.00	25.00	55.00	300	600
1903(p)	400,000	6.00	20.00	50.00	200	375
1911	600,000	2.50	5.00	12.00	75.00	125
1912	800,000	3.00	6.00	15.00	100	200
1919(p)	400,000	2.50	5.00	12.00	100	300
1921(p) High 2	800,000	2.00	4.00	10.00	50.00	125
1921(p) Low 2	Inc. above	1.00	3.00	10.00	50.00	125
1924(p)	400,000	1.00	3.00	10.00	35.00	100
1929(p)	1,200,000	—	BV	1.00	6.00	15.00
1935(p)	3,400,000	—	BV	1.00	3.00	10.00
1936(p)	2,800,000	—	BV	1.00	3.00	10.00
1944(p)	1,800,000	—	BV	1.00	2.00	5.00
1945(p)	8,000,000	—	—	BV	1.50	2.50
1946(p)	8,000,000	—	—	BV	1.00	2.00
1948(s)	8,638,000	—	—	BV	1.00	2.00

Y# 35 25 CENTIMOS
1.2500 g., 0.8350 Silver 0.0336 oz. ASW **Obv:** National arms
Rev: Head of Bolivar left

Date	Mintage	F	VF	XF	Unc	BU
1954(p)	36,000,000	—	—	BV	1.00	1.50

Y# 35a 25 CENTIMOS
1.2500 g., 0.8350 Silver 0.0336 oz. ASW **Obv:** National arms
Rev: Head of Bolivar left

Date	Mintage	F	VF	XF	Unc	BU
1960	48,000,000	—	—	BV	0.75	1.50

Y# 40 25 CENTIMOS
Nickel, 17 mm. **Obv:** National arms **Rev:** Head of Bolivar left

Date	Mintage	F	VF	XF	Unc	BU
1965(l)	240,000,000			0.10	0.35	1.00

Y# 50.1 25 CENTIMOS
1.7500 g., Nickel, 17 mm. **Obv:** National arms **Rev:** Head of
Bolivar left **Note:** 1.18mm thick.

Date	Mintage	F	VF	XF	Unc	BU
1977(w)	240,000,000			0.10	0.25	0.50
1978	—			0.10	0.25	0.50

Y# 50.2 25 CENTIMOS
1.5000 g., Nickel, 17 mm. **Obv:** National arms **Rev:** Head of
Bolivar left **Note:** Dies vary for each date; thin.

Date	Mintage	F	VF	XF	Unc	BU
1977(w)	Inc. above	—	—	0.10	0.25	0.50
1978(w)	200,000,000	—	—	0.10	0.25	0.50
1987	150,000,000	—	—	0.10	0.25	0.50

Y# 50a 25 CENTIMOS
2.4800 g., Nickel Clad Steel, 16.06 mm. **Obv:** National arms
Rev: Head of Bolivar left **Edge:** Reeded **Note:** Varieties exist.

Date	Mintage	F	VF	XF	Unc	BU
1989(sc)	510,000,000	—	—	0.10	0.25	0.50
1990(mm)	400,000,000	—	—	0.10	0.25	0.50

Y# 21 GR 2.500 (1/2 Bolivar)
2.5000 g., 0.8350 Silver 0.0671 oz. ASW **Obv:** Arms within
sprigs above banner, cornucopias above **Obv. Leg.:** ESTADOS
UNIDOS DE VENEZUELA **Rev:** Head of Bolivar left
Rev. Leg.: BOLIVAR LIBERTADOR

Date	Mintage	F	VF	XF	Unc	BU
1901	600,000	20.00	50.00	175	750	1,000

Note: Privy mark placement varies with 1901

1903(p)	200,000	75.00	200	600	2,000	3,250
1911	300,000	30.00	60.00	200	600	1,200

Note: Privy mark placement varies with 1911

1912	1,920,000	5.00	15.00	50.00	300	600
1919(p)	400,000	6.00	20.00	80.00	300	800
1921(p) Normal date	600,000	2.50	7.00	16.00	100	250
1921(p) Narrow date	Inc. above	3.50	9.00	27.50	125	300
1921(p) Wide date	Inc. above	3.50	9.00	27.50	125	300
1924(p)	800,000	2.50	7.00	16.00	85.00	200
1929(p)	400,000	1.35	2.00	6.00	55.00	135
1935(p)	1,000,000	—	BV	1.35	12.00	30.00
1936(p)	600,000	BV	1.35	5.00	50.00	125

Y# 21a GR 2.500 (1/2 Bolivar)
2.5000 g., 0.8350 Silver 0.0671 oz. ASW **Obv:** National arms
above ribbon, plants flank, cornucopias above **Rev:** Head of
Bolivar left

Date	Mintage	F	VF	XF	Unc	BU
1944(d)	500,000	1.35	3.00	5.00	15.00	30.00

Note: Accent in Bolivar

1944(d)	Inc. above	1.50	5.00	10.00	25.00	50.00

Note: Without accent in Bolivar

1945(p)	4,000,000	—	BV	1.35	5.00	10.00
1946(p)	2,500,000	—	BV	1.35	5.00	10.00

Y# 36 50 CENTIMOS
2.5000 g., 0.8350 Silver 0.0671 oz. ASW, 18 mm. **Obv:** National
arms **Rev:** Head of Bolivar left

Date	Mintage	F	VF	XF	Unc	BU
1954(p)	15,000,000	—	—	BV	3.00	5.00

Y# 36a 50 CENTIMOS
2.5000 g., 0.8350 Silver 0.0671 oz. ASW, 18 mm. **Obv:** National
arms **Rev:** Head of Bolivar left

Date	Mintage	F	VF	XF	Unc	BU
1960(a)	20,000,000	—	—	BV	2.00	3.00

Y# 41 50 CENTIMOS
Nickel, 20 mm. **Obv:** National arms **Rev:** Head of Bolivar left

Date	Mintage	F	VF	XF	Unc	BU
1965(l)	180,000,000	—	0.10	0.15	0.35	1.00
1985(o)	500,000	—	0.10	0.15	0.35	1.00

Y# 41a 50 CENTIMOS
3.2000 g., Nickel Clad Steel, 20 mm. **Obv:** National arms
Rev: Head of Bolivar left

Date	Mintage	F	VF	XF	Unc	BU
1988(w)	80,000,000	—	0.10	0.15	0.30	0.50
1989(w)	260,000,000	—	0.10	0.15	0.30	0.50
1990(l)	300,000,000	—	0.10	0.15	0.30	0.50

Note: Die varieties exist for 1990 dated strikes

Y# 22 GRAM 5 (Bolivar)
5.0000 g., 0.8350 Silver 0.1342 oz. ASW **Obv:** Arms within
sprigs above banner, cornucopias above **Obv. Leg.:** ESTADOS
UNIDOS DE VENEZUELA. **Rev:** Head of Bolivar left
Rev. Leg.: BOLIVAR LIBERTADOR

Date	Mintage	F	VF	XF	Unc	BU
1901	323,000	20.00	55.00	150	650	1,000
1903(p)	800,000	5.00	15.00	90.00	350	850
1911	1,500,000	3.00	5.00	40.00	200	650
1912 Wide date	820,000	6.00	16.50	75.00	300	800
1912 Narrow date	Inc. above	6.00	16.50	75.00	300	800
1919(p)	1,000,000	2.50	3.50	12.00	60.00	150
1921(p)	1,000,000	2.50	3.50	12.00	60.00	150
1924(p)	1,500,000	BV	2.50	6.00	50.00	100
1926(p)	1,000,000	BV	2.50	6.00	50.00	100
1929(p)	2,500,000	—	BV	2.50	10.00	30.00
1935(p)	5,000,000	—	BV	2.50	5.00	12.50
1936(p)	5,000,000	—	BV	2.25	5.00	12.50

Y# 22a GRAM 5 (Bolivar)
5.0000 g., 0.8350 Silver 0.1342 oz. ASW **Obv:** National arms
above ribbon, plants flank, cornucopias above **Rev:** Head of
Bolivar left

Date	Mintage	F	VF	XF	Unc	BU
1945(p)	8,000,000	—	—	BV	3.50	5.00

Y# 37 BOLIVAR
5.0000 g., 0.8350 Silver 0.1342 oz. ASW **Obv:** National arms
above ribbon, plants flank, cornucopias above **Rev:** Head of
Bolivar left

Date	Mintage	F	VF	XF	Unc	BU
1954(p)	13,500,000	—	—	BV	2.75	4.00

Y# 37a BOLIVAR
5.0000 g., 0.8350 Silver 0.1342 oz. ASW **Obv:** National arms
above ribbon, plants flank, cornucopias above **Rev:** Head of
Bolivar left

Date	Mintage	F	VF	XF	Unc	BU
1960	30,000,000	—	—	BV	2.50	4.00

Note: Thin letters

1960	Inc. above	—	—	BV	2.50	4.00

Note: Thick letters

1965(l)	20,000,000	—	—	BV	2.50	4.00

Y# 42 BOLIVAR
Nickel, 23 mm. **Obv:** National arms above ribbon, plants flank,
cornucopias above **Rev:** Head of Bolivar left

Date	Mintage	F	VF	XF	Unc	BU
1967(l)	180,000,000	—	0.10	0.15	0.75	1.00

Y# 52 BOLIVAR

Nickel, 23 mm. **Obv:** National arms above ribbon, plants flank, cornucopias above **Rev:** Head of Bolivar left **Note:** Dies vary for each date.

Date	Mintage	F	VF	XF	Unc	BU
1977(l)	200,000,000	—	0.10	0.15	0.65	1.00
1986(w)	200,000,000	—	0.10	0.15	0.50	1.00
1986(w) Prooflike	50,000,000	—	0.10	0.15	0.60	1.50

Y# 52a.2 BOLIVAR

4.2000 g., Nickel Clad Steel, 23 mm. **Obv:** National arms above ribbon, plants flank, cornucopias above **Rev:** Head of Bolivar left **Note:** Dies vary for each date. Obverse has large letters and date

Date	Mintage	F	VF	XF	Unc	BU
1989(sc)	600,000,000	—	0.10	0.15	0.45	0.60
1990(mm)	600,000,000	—	0.10	0.15	0.45	0.60

Y# 52a.1 BOLIVAR

4.2000 g., Nickel Clad Steel, 23 mm. **Obv:** National arms above ribbon, plants flank, cornucopias above **Rev:** Head of Bolivar left **Note:** Both sides of coin have small letters and date

Date	Mintage	F	VF	XF	Unc	BU
1989(w)	370,000,000	—	0.10	0.15	0.45	0.60

Knobbed 6   Pointed 6

Y# 23 GRAM 10 (2 Bolivares)

10.0000 g., 0.8350 Silver 0.2684 oz. ASW **Obv:** Arms within sprigs above banner, cornucopias above **Obv. Leg.:** ESTADOS UNIDOS DE VENEZUELA **Rev:** Head of Bolivar left **Rev. Leg.:** BOLIVAR LIBERTADOR

Date	Mintage	F	VF	XF	Unc	BU
1902(p)	500,000	11.50	45.00	200	500	1,000
1903(p)	500,000	12.50	50.00	250	550	1,100
1904 Large 0, small 4	550,000	11.50	40.00	175	500	1,000
1904 Large 0, large 4	Inc. above	11.50	40.00	175	500	1,000
1904 Small 0, large 4	Inc. above	11.50	45.00	185	550	1,000
1904 Small 0, large slant 4	Inc. above	11.50	45.00	185	550	1,000
1904 Small 0, small 4	50,000	20.00	55.00	200	600	1,000
1905 Upright 5	750,000	4.50	16.50	100	400	800
1905 Slant 5	Inc. above	4.50	16.50	100	400	800
1911	750,000	4.50	16.50	60.00	275	650
1912	500,000	4.50	16.50	140	400	1,000
1913 Normal date	210,000	40.00	250	500	1,000	2,000
1913 Raised 3	Inc. above	40.00	250	500	1,000	2,000
1919(p)	1,000,000	BV	4.50	11.50	125	300
1922(p) Narrow date	1,000,000	BV	4.50	11.50	100	250
1922(p) Wide date	Inc. above	BV	4.50	11.50	100	250
1922(p) Low first 2	Inc. above	BV	4.50	11.50	100	250
1924(p)	1,250,000	BV	4.50	11.50	85.00	200
1926(p)	1,000,000	BV	4.50	11.50	85.00	200
1929(p)	1,500,000	—	BV	8.00	20.00	50.00
1930(p)	425,000	BV	7.00	25.00	130	300
1935(p)	3,000,000	—	BV	4.50	8.00	25.00
1936(p)	2,500,000	—	BV	4.50	8.00	25.00

Y# 23a GRAM 10 (2 Bolivares)

10.0000 g., 0.8350 Silver 0.2684 oz. ASW **Obv:** National arms above ribbon, plants flank, cornucopias above **Rev:** Head of Bolivar left

Date	Mintage	F	VF	XF	Unc	BU
1945(p)	3,000,000	—	—	BV	5.50	7.50

Y# A37 2 BOLIVARES

10.0000 g., 0.8350 Silver 0.2684 oz. ASW **Obv:** National arms above ribbon, plants flank, cornucopias above **Rev:** Head of Bolivar left

Date	Mintage	F	VF	XF	Unc	BU
1960	4,000,000	—	—	BV	5.00	6.50
1965(l)	7,170,000	—	—	BV	5.00	6.50

Y# 43 2 BOLIVARES

Nickel, 27 mm. **Obv:** National arms above ribbon, plants flank, cornucopias above **Rev:** Head of Bolivar left **Note:** Dies vary for each date.

Date	Mintage	F	VF	XF	Unc	BU
1967(l)	50,000,000	—	—	0.25	0.50	1.50
1986(w)	50,000,000	—	—	0.25	0.50	1.50
	Note: Die varieties exist for 1986 strikes					
1986(w) Prooflike		—	—	0.25	0.50	1.50
	Note: Die varieties exist for 1986 strikes					
1988(c)	80,000,000	—	—	0.25	0.50	1.50

Y# 43a.1 2 BOLIVARES

7.5000 g., Nickel Clad Steel, 27 mm. **Obv:** Small letters in legend, raised motto in ribbon, lines beneath horse, "R" in 'Libertador' 2mm away from truncation **Rev:** Head of Bolivar left, small letters

Date	Mintage	F	VF	XF	Unc	BU
1989(sc)	200,000,000	—	—	0.20	0.75	1.50
1990(c)	400,000,000	—	—	0.20	0.75	1.50
	Note: Two varieties of 1990 exist					

Y# 43a.2 2 BOLIVARES

7.5000 g., Nickel Clad Steel, 27 mm. **Obv:** Large letters in legend, no lines beneath horse, "R" in 'Libertador' touching truncation **Rev:** Head of Bolivar left, large letters

Date	Mintage	F	VF	XF	Unc	BU
1989(w)	100,000,000	—	—	0.20	0.75	1.50
1989(c)	95,000,000	—	—	0.20	0.75	1.50

Y# 24.2 GRAM 25 (5 Bolivares)

25.0000 g., 0.9000 Silver 0.7234 oz. ASW **Obv:** Date on ribbon right of arms 13 DE APRIL DE 1864, cornucopias above **Obv. Leg.:** ESTADOS UNIDOS DE VENEZUELA **Rev:** Head of Bolivar left **Rev. Leg.:** BOLIVAR LIBERTADOR

Date	Mintage	F	VF	XF	Unc	BU
1901	90,000	20.00	100	375	1,500	3,000
1902(p) Wide date	500,000	13.50	16.00	120	700	1,000
1902(p) Narrow date	Inc. above	13.50	16.00	120	700	1,000
1903(p)	200,000	13.50	16.00	120	800	1,300

Date	Mintage	F	VF	XF	Unc	BU
1904	200,000	13.50	16.00	150	1,200	3,000
1905	300,000	13.50	16.00	120	700	1,000
1910 Oval 0	13.50	16.00	85.00	450	800	
1910 Round 0	Inc. above	14.50	18.00	100	450	800
1911 Normal date	1,104,000	BV	15.00	45.00	225	500
1911 Wide date	Inc. above	BV	15.00	45.00	225	500
1911 Narrow date	Inc. above	BV	15.00	45.00	225	500
1912 Normal date	696,000	BV	15.00	45.00	225	500
1912 Wide date	Inc. above	BV	15.00	45.00	225	500
1912 Narrow date	Inc. above	BV	15.00	45.00	225	500
1919(p)	400,000	BV	14.00	30.00	175	400
1921(p) Wide date	500,000	BV	14.00	25.00	100	200
1921(p) Narrow date	Inc. above	BV	14.00	25.00	100	200
1924(p) Wide date	500,000	BV	14.00	25.00	100	200
1924(p) Narrow date	Inc. above	BV	14.00	25.00	100	200
1924(p) Low 9	Inc. above	BV	14.00	25.00	100	200
1926(p)	800,000	BV	13.50	22.50	80.00	150
1929(p) High 9	800,000	BV	13.50	22.00	60.00	120
1929(p) Low 9	Inc. above	BV	13.50	22.00	60.00	120
1935(p)	1,600,000	BV	13.50	16.50	38.00	70.00
1936(p) Normal date	2,000,000	BV	13.50	16.50	38.00	70.00
1936(p) High 3	Inc. above	BV	13.50	16.50	38.00	70.00
1936(p) Low 3	Inc. above	BV	13.50	16.50	38.00	70.00

Y# 44 5 BOLIVARES

Nickel, 31 mm. **Obv:** National arms above ribbon, plants flank, cornucopias above **Rev:** Head of Bolivar left

Date	Mintage	F	VF	XF	Unc	BU
1973(m)	20,000,000	—	0.45	0.75	1.75	15.00

Y# 53.1 5 BOLIVARES

Nickel, 31 mm. **Obv:** National arms above ribbon, plants flank, cornucopias above, six pointed stars **Rev:** Head of Bolivar left

Date	Mintage	F	VF	XF	Unc	BU
1977(m)	60,000,000	—	—	0.50	1.50	2.00

Y# 53.2 5 BOLIVARES

Nickel **Obv:** National arms above ribbon, plants flank, cornucopias above, date and denomination below, five pointed stars **Rev:** Head of Bolivar left

Date	Mintage	F	VF	XF	Unc	BU
1987(c)	25,000,000	—	—	0.50	1.50	2.00
1987(c) Prooflike	Inc. above	—	—	—	—	30.00
1988(w)	20,000,000	—	—	1.00	5.00	10.00

Y# 53a.1 5 BOLIVARES

13.3000 g., Nickel Clad Steel, 31 mm. **Obv:** National arms above ribbon, plants flank, cornucopias above, small letters **Rev:** Head of Bolivar left, large letters

Date	Mintage	F	VF	XF	Unc	BU
1989(w)	55,000,000	—	—	0.50	1.50	2.00
1989(w) Prooflike	26,000,000	—	—	1.00	2.00	3.00

Y# 53a.2 5 BOLIVARES

13.3000 g., Nickel Clad Steel, 31 mm. **Obv:** Large letters **Rev:** Small letters

Date	Mintage	F	VF	XF	Unc	BU
1989(sc)	100,000,000	—	—	0.50	1.50	3.00
1990(c)	200,000,000	—	—	0.50	1.50	3.00

Y# 53a.3   5 BOLIVARES
13.3000 g., Nickel Clad Steel, 31 mm. **Obv:** National arms above ribbon, plants flank, cornucopias above **Rev:** Head of Bolivar left **Note:** Large letters in legends.

Date	Mintage	F	VF	XF	Unc	BU
1990	—	—	—	0.65	1.75	3.00

Y# 31   GR 3.2258 (10 Bolivares)
3.2258 g., 0.9000 Gold 0.0933 oz. AGW **Obv:** National arms above ribbon, plants flank, cornucopias above **Rev:** Head of Bolivar right

Date	Mintage	F	VF	XF	Unc	BU
1930(p)	Est. 500,000	—	BV	100	115	130

Note: Only 10% of the total mintage was released; the balance remaining as part of the nation's gold reserve

Y# 45   10 BOLIVARES
30.0000 g., 0.9000 Silver 0.8680 oz. ASW **Obv:** Arms within inset at left, inscription at right **Rev:** Head of Bolivar within inset at right, inscription at left **Edge:** CENTENARIO DE LA EFIGLE DEL LIBERTADOR EN EL MONEDA

Date	Mintage	F	VF	XF	Unc	BU
1973(o)	2,000,000	—	—	—	16.50	18.50
1973(o) Proof	200	Value: 400				

Y# 75   10 BOLIVARES
Nickel Clad Steel, 17 mm. **Obv:** National arms **Rev:** Head of Bolivar left within 7-sided outline **Note:** Struck at Ceska Mincova and Budapest mints.

Date	Mintage	F	VF	XF	Unc	BU
1998	—	—	—	—	0.25	0.50

Y# 32   GR 6.4516 (20 Bolivares)
6.4516 g., 0.9000 Gold 0.1867 oz. AGW **Obv:** Arms within sprigs above banner, cornucopias above **Obv. Leg.:** ESTRADOS UNIDOS DE VENEZUELA **Rev:** Head of Bolivar right **Rev. Leg.:** BOLIVAR LIBERTADOR

Date	Mintage	F	VF	XF	Unc	BU
1904	100,000	—	BV	200	210	220
1905	100,000	—	BV	200	210	220
1910	70,000	—	BV	200	220	250

Note: Die varieties exist in the placement of dot between date and Lei, Type 1 is evenly spaced, Type 2 had dot closer to L of Lei

1911	80,000	—	BV	200	210	220

Note: Die varieties exist in the placement of dot between date and Lei, Type 1 is evenly spaced, Type 2 had dot closer to L of Lei

1912	150,000	—	BV	200	210	220

Note: Die varieties exist in the placement of the torch privy mark in relation to bust truncation; Type 1 is well below truncation, Type 2 is slightly below truncation and Type 3 is in line with the truncation

Y# 76.1   20 BOLIVARES
Nickel Clad Steel, 20 mm. **Obv:** National arms **Rev:** Head of Bolivar left within 7-sided outline **Note:** Struck at Ceska Mincova and Budapest mints.

Date	Mintage	F	VF	XF	Unc	BU
1998	—	—	—	—	0.25	0.50

Y# 76.2   20 BOLIVARES
4.3200 g., Nickel Clad Steel, 20 mm. **Obv:** National arms **Rev:** Head of Bolivar left within 7-sided outline **Edge:** Plain

Date	Mintage	F	VF	XF	Unc	BU
1999	—	—	—	0.30	0.60	0.75

Y# 46   25 BOLIVARES
28.2800 g., 0.9250 Silver 0.8410 oz. ASW **Subject:** Conservation **Obv:** National arms above ribbon, plants flank, cornucopias above **Rev:** Jaguar, denomination below

Date	Mintage	F	VF	XF	Unc	BU
1975(I)	38,000	—	—	—	25.00	35.00
1975(I) Proof	Est. 8,000	Value: 45.00				

Y# 47   50 BOLIVARES
35.0000 g., 0.9250 Silver 1.0408 oz. ASW **Subject:** Conservation **Obv:** National arms above ribbon, plants flank, cornucopias above **Rev:** Giant Armadillo

Date	Mintage	F	VF	XF	Unc	BU
1975 Proof	Est. 8,000	Value: 50.00				
1975	39,000	—	—	—	35.00	50.00

Y# 66   50 BOLIVARES
31.1000 g., 0.9000 Silver 0.8999 oz. ASW **Subject:** 50th Anniversary of Central Bank **Obv:** Flag design with initials in circle at right **Rev:** Building facade

Date	Mintage	F	VF	XF	Unc	BU
1990(c) Proof	10,000	Value: 45.00				

Y# 67   50 BOLIVARES
15.5500 g., 0.9000 Gold 0.4499 oz. AGW **Subject:** 50th Anniversary of Central Bank **Obv:** Flag design with initials in circle at right **Rev:** Building facade

Date	Mintage	F	VF	XF	Unc	BU
1990 Proof	5,000	Value: 550				

Y# 77.1   50 BOLIVARES
6.6000 g., Nickel Clad Steel **Obv:** National arms **Rev:** Head of Bolivar left within 7-sided outline **Note:** Struck at Ceska Mincova and Budapest mints.

Date	Mintage	F	VF	XF	Unc	BU
1998	—	—	—	—	0.35	0.70

Y# 77.2   50 BOLIVARES
6.6500 g., Nickel Clad Steel, 23 mm. **Obv:** National arms **Rev:** Head of Bolívar left and mint mark, in 7-sided outline **Edge:** Reeded

Date	Mintage	F	VF	XF	Unc	BU
1999	—	—	—	0.40	0.80	1.00

Y# 55   75 BOLIVARES
17.0000 g., 0.9000 Silver 0.4919 oz. ASW **Subject:** 50th Anniversary - Sucre's Death **Obv:** Body on ground at right, mountains in background, horse at left **Rev:** Head of Bolivar 3/4 facing divides dates

Date	Mintage	F	VF	XF	Unc	BU
1980(I)	500,000	—	—	—	12.50	17.50
1980(I) Proof	200	Value: 600				

Y# 56   100 BOLIVARES
22.0000 g., 0.9000 Silver 0.6366 oz. ASW **Subject:** 150th Anniversary - Bolivar's Death **Obv:** Monument **Rev:** Bust of Bolivar facing divides dates

Date	Mintage	F	VF	XF	Unc	BU
1980(I)	500,000	—	—	—	15.00	25.00
1980(I) Proof	200	Value: 600				

Y# 57   100 BOLIVARES
27.0000 g., 0.8350 Silver 0.7248 oz. ASW   **Subject:** 200th
Anniversary - Birth of Andres Bello **Obv:** Initials within circle
Rev: Head of Bolivar facing, dates below

Date	Mintage	F	VF	XF	Unc	BU
ND(1981)(w)	200	—	—	—	400	425
ND(1981)(w) Proof	500,000	Value: 12.50				

Y# 58   100 BOLIVARES
31.0000 g., 0.9000 Silver 0.8970 oz. ASW   **Subject:** 200th
Anniversary - Birth of Simon Bolivar **Obv:** Building
Rev: Bookshselves back of 3/4 figure looking left

Date	Mintage	F	VF	XF	Unc	BU
ND(1983)(w) Proof	300,000	Value: 20.00				

Y# 60   100 BOLIVARES
31.0000 g., 0.9000 Silver 0.8970 oz. ASW, 35 mm.
Subject: 200th Anniversary - Birth of Jose M. Vargas
Obv: Steepled building within circle **Rev:** Bust of Bolivar facing
within circle

Date	Mintage	F	VF	XF	Unc	BU
ND(1986)(I)	500,000	—	—	—	18.00	20.00
ND(1986)(I) Proof	500	Value: 300				

Note: Beware of some altered circulation coins to look like
proofs

Y# 78.1   100 BOLIVARES
6.8000 g., Nickel Clad Steel, 25 mm.   **Obv:** National arms
Rev: Head of Bolívar left in 7-sided outline **Note:** Struck at Ceska
Mincova and Budapest mints.

Date	Mintage	F	VF	XF	Unc	BU
1998	—	—	—	—	0.50	1.00

Y# 78.2   100 BOLIVARES
6.8200 g., Nickel-Clad Steel, 25 mm.   **Obv:** National arms
Rev: Head of Bolívar right in 7-sided outline **Edge:** Plain

Date	Mintage	F	VF	XF	Unc	BU
1999	—	—	—	0.60	1.20	1.50

Y# 54   500 BOLIVARES
18.0000 g., 0.9000 Gold 0.5208 oz. AGW, 30 mm.
Subject: Nationalization of Oil Industry **Obv:** Oil derricks within
inset at left **Rev:** Head of Bolivar left within inset

Date	Mintage	F	VF	XF	Unc	BU
1975(c) Proof	100	Value: 13,000				

Y# 64   500 BOLIVARES
31.1000 g., 0.9000 Silver 0.8999 oz. ASW   **Obv:** National arms
above ribbon, plants flank, cornucopias above **Rev:** Head of Paez
left, dates below

Date	Mintage	F	VF	XF	Unc	BU
1990(mm) Proof	30,000	Value: 25.00				

Y# 69   500 BOLIVARES
31.1000 g., 0.9000 Silver 0.8999 oz. ASW   **Subject:** Battle of
Matasiete **Obv:** National arms above ribbon, plants flank,
cornucopias above **Rev:** Monument divides dates below mountains

Date	Mintage	F	VF	XF	Unc	BU
1992(w) Proof	10,000	Value: 40.00				

Y# 71   500 BOLIVARES
31.1000 g., 0.9000 Silver 0.8999 oz. ASW   **Subject:** 50th
Anniversary - United Nations **Obv:** National arms above ribbon,
plants flank, cornucopias above **Rev:** UN logo within wreath

Date	Mintage	F	VF	XF	Unc	BU
1995 Proof	10,000	Value: 40.00				

Y# 72   500 BOLIVARES
31.1000 g., 0.9000 Silver 0.8999 oz. ASW   **Subject:** 200th
Anniversary - Sucre's Birth **Obv:** National arms above ribbon, plants
flank, cornucopias above **Rev:** Bust of Sucre facing, dates below

Date	Mintage	F	VF	XF	Unc	BU
1995 Proof	15,000	Value: 40.00				

Y# 74   500 BOLIVARES
31.1000 g., 0.9000 Silver 0.8999 oz. ASW   **Subject:** Manuel
Gual and Jose Maria Espana **Obv:** National arms above ribbon,
plants flank, cornucopias above **Rev:** Two busts above dates

Date	Mintage	F	VF	XF	Unc	BU
1997A Proof	10,000	Value: 40.00				

Y# 79.1   500 BOLIVARES
8.4000 g., Nickel Clad Steel, 28.5 mm.   **Obv:** National arms
Rev: Head of Bolívar left in 7-sided outline **Note:** Struck at Ceska
Mincova and Budapest mints.

Date	Mintage	F	VF	XF	Unc	BU
1998	—	—	—	0.50	1.20	1.60

Y# 48.1   1000 BOLIVARES
33.4370 g., 0.9000 Gold 0.9675 oz. AGW, 34 mm.
Subject: Conservation Series - Cock of the Rocks **Obv:** National
arms above ribbon, plants flank, cornucopias above **Rev:** Bird on
branch

Date	Mintage	F	VF	XF	Unc	BU
1975(I)	5,047	—	—	—	1,000	1,100
1975(I) Proof	483	Value: 1,600				

Y# 48.2   1000 BOLIVARES
33.4370 g., 0.9000 Gold 0.9675 oz. AGW, 34 mm.
Subject: Conservation Series - Cock of the Rocks **Obv:** National
arms above ribbon, plants flank, cornucopias above **Rev:** Bird
on branch with smooth wings

Date	Mintage	F	VF	XF	Unc	BU
1975(I)	Inc. above	—	—	—	1,000	1,100

Y# 68 1100 BOLIVARES
27.0000 g., 0.9250 Silver 0.8029 oz. ASW **Subject:** Ibero - American Series **Obv:** Arms at center within legend, 13 shields surround **Rev:** Statue

Date	Mintage	F	VF	XF	Unc	BU
1991(mm) Proof	30,000	Value: 60.00				

Y# 59 3000 BOLIVARES
31.1000 g., 0.9000 Gold 0.8999 oz. AGW **Subject:** 200th Anniversary - Birth of Simon Bolivar **Obv:** Building **Rev:** Bookshelves back of 3/4 figure looking left

Date	Mintage	F	VF	XF	Unc	BU
ND(1983)(w) Proof	10,000	Value: 950				

Y# 62 5000 BOLIVARES
15.5500 g., 0.9000 Gold 0.4499 oz. AGW, 27 mm. **Obv:** National arms above ribbon, plants flank, cornucopias above **Rev:** Bust of Urdaneta 3/4 left, dates below

Date	Mintage	F	VF	XF	Unc	BU
1988 Proof	25,000	Value: 475				

Y# 63 5000 BOLIVARES
15.5500 g., 0.9000 Gold 0.4499 oz. AGW, 27 mm. **Obv:** National arms above ribbon, plants flank, cornucopias above **Rev:** Bust of Marino facing, dates below

Date	Mintage	F	VF	XF	Unc	BU
1988 Proof	25,000	Value: 475				

Y# 65 5000 BOLIVARES
15.5500 g., 0.9000 Gold 0.4499 oz. AGW, 27 mm. **Obv:** National arms above ribbon, plants flank, cornucopias above **Rev:** Head of Paez right, dates below

Date	Mintage	F	VF	XF	Unc	BU
1990(mm) Proof	10,000	Value: 475				

Y# 73 5000 BOLIVARES
15.5500 g., 0.9000 Gold 0.4499 oz. AGW, 27 mm. **Subject:** 200th Anniversary - Sucre's Birth **Obv:** National arms above ribbon, plants flank, cornucopias above **Rev:** Bust of Sucre facing, dates below

Date	Mintage	F	VF	XF	Unc	BU
1995 Proof	10,000	Value: 500				

Y# 86 6000 BOLIVARES
Silver **Subject:** Founding of Maracay Mint **Obv:** Central Bank Building **Obv. Leg.:** BANCO CENTRAL DE VENEZUELA **Rev:** Mint building complex **Rev. Leg.:** CASA DE LA MONEDA VENEZUELA - MARACAY **Rev. Insc.:** FUNDADA/1999

Date	Mintage	F	VF	XF	Unc	BU
1999	—	—	—	—	—	—

Y# 61 10000 BOLIVARES
31.1000 g., 0.9000 Gold 0.8999 oz. AGW, 35 mm. **Obv:** National arms above ribbon, plants flank, cornucopias above **Rev:** Head of Bolivar right

Date	Mintage	F	VF	XF	Unc	BU
1987(c) Proof	50,000	Value: 925				

REPUBLIC
Bolivariana

Y# 80 10 BOLIVARES
2.3300 g., Nickel Clad Steel, 17 mm. **Obv:** National arms left of denomination **Obv. Leg.:** REPÚBLICA BOLIVARIANA DE VENEZUELA **Rev:** Head of Bolívar left in 7-sided outline **Rev. Leg.:** BOLÍVAR - LIBERTADOR **Edge:** Reeded

Date	Mintage	F	VF	XF	Unc	BU
2000	—	—	—	—	0.25	0.50

Y# 81 20 BOLIVARES
4.3200 g., Nickel Clad Steel, 20 mm. **Obv:** National arms left of denomination **Obv. Leg.:** REPÚBLICA BOLIVARIANA DE VENEZUELA **Rev:** Head of Bolivar left in 7-sided outline **Rev. Leg.:** BOLÍVAR - LIBERTADOR **Edge:** Plain

Date	Mintage	F	VF	XF	Unc	BU
2000	—	—	—	—	0.25	0.50

Y# 82 50 BOLIVARES
6.5800 g., Nickel Clad Steel, 23 mm. **Obv:** National arms left of denomination **Obv. Leg.:** REPÚBLICA BOLIVARIANA DE VENEZUELA **Rev:** Head of Bolivar left in 7-sided outline **Rev. Leg.:** BOLÍVAR - LIBERTADOR **Edge:** Reeded

Date	Mintage	F	VF	XF	Unc	BU
2000	—	—	—	—	0.30	0.75	1.00

Y# 79.2 500 BOLIVARES
8.4000 g., Nickel Clad Steel, 28.5 mm. **Obv:** National arms **Obv. Leg.:** REPÚBLICA BOLIVARIANA DA VENEZUELA **Rev:** Head of Bolívar left in 7-sided outline **Rev. Leg.:** BOLÍVAR - LIBERTADOR **Edge:** Segmented reeding **Note:** Prev. KM# 84.

Date	Mintage	F	VF	XF	Unc	BU
1999	—	—	0.60	1.50	2.00	

ESSAIS

KM#	Date	Mintage	Identification	Mkt Val
E18	1991(c)	—	1300 Bolivares. 0.9000 Copper. M1, thick planchet.	—
E26	1991(c)	—	1300 Bolivares. Copper. M1, thin planchet	—
E27	1991(c)	—	1300 Bolivares. Copper. M1, thick planchet.	—

PATTERNS
Including off metal strikes

KM#	Date	Mintage	Identification	Mkt Val
Pn46-47	1973(m)	—	5 Bolivares. Nickel.	700
Pn48	1977(w)	—	25 Centimos. Nickel.	100
Pn49	1977(m)	—	5 Bolivares. Nickel.	200
Pn50	1981(w)	—	100 Bolivares. Silver. Y.57, with LEY.	400
Pn51	1990(c)	—	50 Bolivares. Lead.	500
Pn52	1990(c)	—	50 Bolivares. Silver.	600
Pn53	1990(c)	—	50 Bolivares. Gold. Medal rotation.	850
Pn54	1990(c)	—	50 Bolivares. Gold. Coin rotation.	850
Pn55	1990(c)	—	50 Bolivares. Gold.	1,150
Pn56	1990	—	5000 Bolivares. Copper-Nickel. Y65.	2,000

TRIAL STRIKES

KM#	Date	Mintage	Identification	Mkt Val
TS9	1977	—	10 Bolivares. 0.9000 Silver. Uniface reverse.	1,000
TS10	1973(c)	—	10 Bolivares. Silver. 2 obverses.	400
TS12	1975(c)	—	500 Bolivares. Gold plated; Uniface reverse.	15,000
TS13	1977(m)	—	5 Bolivares. Nickel. Uniface obverse.	200
TS14	1990(c)	—	50 Bolivares. Copper. Y66, uniface obverse.	600
TS15	1990(c)	—	50 Bolivares. Copper. Y66, uniface reverse.	600
TS16	1990(c)	—	50 Bolivares. Bronze. Y66, uniface obverse.	600
TS17	1990(c)	—	50 Bolivares. Bronze. Y66, uniface reverse.	600
TS19	1990(c)	—	50 Bolivares. Y#66. Uniface.	600
TS18	1990(c)	—	50 Bolivares. Silver. Y66, uniface obverse.	1,000
TS20	1990(d)	—	50 Bolivares. Copper. Y67, uniface obverse.	600
TS21	1990(c)	—	50 Bolivares. Copper. Y67, uniface reverse.	600
TS11	1975(c)	—	500 Bolivares. Gold plated; Uniface obverse.	15,000
TS22	1991	—	1100 Bolivares. Silver. Arms at center within legend, 13 shields surround. Y68, uniface reverse.	1,000
TS23	ND (1991)	—	1100 Bolivares. Silver. Statue, two dates at right. Y68, uniface reverse.	1,000
TS24	1991(c)	—	1300 Bolivares. Copper. Numbers on and below shield, text below. Y79, uniface obverse.	350
TS25	1991(c)	—	1300 Bolivares. Copper. Two busts facing. Y79, uniface reverse.	350
TS26	1991(c)	—	1300 Bolivares. Silver. Y79, uniface obverse.	450
TS27	1991(c)	—	1300 Bolivares. Silver. Y79, uniface reverse.	450

PRIVATE PATTERNS

KM#	Date	Mintage	Identification	Mkt Val
PPn2	1973(c)	—	10 Bolivares. Silver. Arms within inset at left, legend and denomination at right. Head left within inset, name below, dates at left.	800
PPn3	1973(c)	—	10 Bolivares. Silver. Double obverse similar to KM45.	600

PRIVATE TRIAL STRIKES

KM#	Date	Mintage	Identification	Mkt Val
PTS1	1973	—	10 Bolivares. Gilt Copper center. Uniface obverse similar to KM45. (TS2)	300
PTS2	1973	—	10 Bolivares. Gilt Copper. Uniface reverse similar to KM45. (TS3)	500

MINT SETS

KM#	Date	Mintage	Identification	Issue Price	Mkt Val
MS1	1975 (3)	—	Y46-48	250	1,000

PROOF SETS

KM#	Date	Mintage	Identification	Issue Price	Mkt Val
PS1	1975 (3)	—	Y46-48	—	1,600

LEPER COLONIES

CABO BLANCO

In the late 1600's the Hospital de Lazarinos was built in Hoyada, outside of Caracas for the care and confinement of those suffering from leprosy. Early in the 1900's this hospital was relocated to Maiquetia, also near Caracas and became known as Cabo Blanco. The hospital remained in use until the early 1970's and coins were struck in 1936 for patient use within the confines of this institution.

LEPROSARIUM COINAGE

KM# L11   0.05 BOLIVAR (5 Centimos)
Brass   Note: Prev. KM#10.

Date	Mintage	VG	F	VF	XF	Unc
1936	—	3.00	6.00	10.00	20.00	—

KM# L12   0.12-1/2 BOLIVAR (12-1/2 Centimos)
Brass   Note: Prev. KM#L11.

Date	Mintage	VG	F	VF	XF	Unc
1936	—	20.00	40.00	60.00	100	—

KM# L13   0.50 BOLIVAR (50 Centimos)
Brass   Note: Prev. KM#L12.

Date	Mintage	VG	F	VF	XF	Unc
1936	—	30.00	50.00	90.00	120	—

KM# L14   BOLIVAR
Brass   Note: Prev. KM#L13.

Date	Mintage	VG	F	VF	XF	Unc
1936	—	50.00	85.00	150	250	—

KM# L15   2 BOLIVARES
Brass   Note: Prev. KM#L14.

Date	Mintage	VG	F	VF	XF	Unc
1936	—	60.00	100	165	270	—

KM# L16   5 BOLIVARES
Brass   Note: Prev. KM#L15.

Date	Mintage	VG	F	VF	XF	Unc
1936	—	80.00	140	220	375	—

KM# L17   10 BOLIVARES
Brass   Note: Prev. KM#L16.

Date	Mintage	VG	F	VF	XF	Unc
1936	—	120	200	320	500	—

KM# L18   20 BOLIVARES
Brass   Note: Prev. KM#L17.

Date	Mintage	VG	F	VF	XF	Unc
1936	—	175	300	500	900	—

ISLA DE PROVIDENCIA

Between 1916 and 1939 the name of Burro Island was changed to Isla de Providencia and the name of the colony was redesignated to match this new title. One series of coins for colony commerce use only was issued in 1939 under the name Leproserias Nacionales Isla De Providencia.

LEPROSARIUM COINAGE

KM# L19   0.05 BOLIVAR (5 Centimos)
Brass   Note: Prev. KM#L20.

Date	Mintage	VG	F	VF	XF	Unc
1939	—	2.00	4.00	8.00	16.00	—

KM# L20   0.12-1/2 BOLIVAR (12-1/2 Centimos)
Brass   Note: Prev. KM#L21.

Date	Mintage	VG	F	VF	XF	Unc
1939	—	2.50	5.00	8.00	16.00	—

KM# L20a   0.12-1/2 BOLIVAR (12-1/2 Centimos)
Copper-Nickel   Note: Prev. KM#L21a.

Date	Mintage	VG	F	VF	XF	Unc
1939 Rare	—					

KM# L21   0.50 BOLIVAR (50 Centimos)
Brass   Note: Prev. KM#L22.

Date	Mintage	VG	F	VF	XF	Unc
1939	—	20.00	40.00	75.00	125	—

KM# L22   BOLIVAR
Brass   Note: Prev. KM#L23.

Date	Mintage	VG	F	VF	XF	Unc
1939	—	25.00	50.00	90.00	150	—

KM# L23   2 BOLIVARES
Brass   Note: Prev. KM#L24.

Date	Mintage	VG	F	VF	XF	Unc
1939	—	30.00	60.00	110	185	—

KM# L24   5 BOLIVARES
Brass   Note: Prev. KM#L25.

Date	Mintage	VG	F	VF	XF	Unc
1939	—	40.00	85.00	165	275	—

KM# L25   10 BOLIVARES
Brass   Note: Prev. KM#L26.

Date	Mintage	VG	F	VF	XF	Unc
1939						

Note: Reported, not confirmed; According to records, coins with the 10 Bolivares denomination were authorized to be struck, but at present none are known to exist in the numismatic community

MARACAIBO LAZARETO NACIONAL

In 1826 Simon Bolivar authorized the establishment of Lazareto Maracaibo on Burro Island in Lake Maracaibo. Over time this became a large leper colony maintained by the Venezuelan Government, where hundreds of people suffering from Hansen's disease were cared for. To provide a monetary system and prevent regular coinage, handled by lepers, to re-circulate in the general population, the Venezuelan Government created a special currency. These coins had value only on the island until 30 years ago, when the illness was almost fully extinguished in South America and medical research revealed that little risk was involved in handling these coins. The first issues under the name Lazareto Nacional Maracaibo were struck in the late 1880's and the final series was issued in 1916.

LEPROSARIUM COINAGE

KM# L10   5 CENTIMOS
Brass   Note: Prev. KM#L8.

Date	Mintage	VG	F	VF	XF	Unc
1916	—	3.00	6.00	10.00	20.00	—

KM# L3   1/8 BOLIVAR
Brass   Note: Prev. KM#L1.

Date	Mintage	VG	F	VF	XF	Unc
1913	—	3.50	7.00	12.00	25.00	—
1916	—	20.00	40.00	80.00	145	—

KM# L3a   1/8 BOLIVAR
Copper Nickel   Note: Prev. KM#L1a.

Date	Mintage	VG	F	VF	XF	Unc
1913	—	7.00	15.00	25.00	50.00	—

KM# L4   1/2 BOLIVAR
Brass   Note: Similar to 1/8 Bolivar KM#L5. Prev. KM#L2.

Date	Mintage	VG	F	VF	XF	Unc
1913	—	20.00	35.00	75.00	135	—
1916	—	35.00	65.00	140	260	—

KM# L5   BOLIVAR
Brass   Note: Prev. KM#L3.

Date	Mintage	VG	F	VF	XF	Unc
1913	—	20.00	30.00	45.00	80.00	—
1916	—	25.00	40.00	55.00	95.00	—

KM# L6   2 BOLIVARES
Brass   Obv: Similar to 20 Bolivares, KM#L9   Note: Prev. KM#L4.

Date	Mintage	VG	F	VF	XF	Unc
1913	—	25.00	40.00	60.00	100	—
1916	—	35.00	50.00	70.00	120	—

KM# L7   5 BOLIVARES
Brass   Note: Similar to 1/8 Bolivar, KM#L3. Prev. KM#L5.

Date	Mintage	VG	F	VF	XF	Unc
1913	—	55.00	100	175	275	—
1916	—	85.00	120	200	350	—

KM# L8 10 BOLIVARES

Brass **Note:** Similar to 1/8 Bolivar, KM#L3. Prev. KM#L6.

Date	Mintage	VG	F	VF	XF	Unc
1913	—	60.00	120	200	350	—
1916	—	90.00	180	300	500	—

KM# L9 20 BOLIVARES

Brass **Rev:** Similar to 2 Bolivares, KM#L6 **Note:** Prev. KM#L7.

Date	Mintage	VG	F	VF	XF	Unc
1913	—	175	275	500	800	—
1916	—	250	350	600	1,000	—

VIET NAM

In 207 B.C. a Chinese general set up the Kingdom of Nam-Viet on the Red River. This kingdom was over-thrown by the Chinese under the Han Dynasty in 111 B.C., where upon the country became a Chinese province under the name of Giao-Chi, which was later changed to Annam or peaceful or pacified South. Chinese rule was maintained until 968, when the Vietnamese became independent until 1407 when China again invaded Viet Nam. The Chinese were driven out in 1428 and the country became independent and named Dai-Viet. Gia Long united the North and South as Dai Nam in 1802.

After the French conquered Dai Nam, they split the country into three parts. The South became the Colony of Cochin China; the North became the Protectorate of Tonkin; and the central became the Protectorate of Annam. The emperors were permitted to have their capital in Hue and to produce small quantities of their coins, presentation pieces, and bullion bars. Annam had an area of 57,840 sq. mi. (141,806 sq. km.) and a population of about 6 million. Chief products of the area are silk, cinnamon and rice. There are important mineral deposits in the mountainous inland.

EMPERORS

Thanh Thai, 1888-1907 成泰

Duy Tan, 1907-1916 維新

Khai Dinh, 1916-1925 啓定

Bao Dai, 1926-1945 保大

IDENTIFICATION

Khai 啓
Bao 寶
Thong 通
Dinh 定

CYCLICAL DATES

	庚	辛	壬	癸	甲	乙	丙	丁	戊	己
戌	1850 1910		1862 1922		1874 1934		1886 1946		1838 1898	
亥		1851 1911		1863 1923		1875 1935		1887 1947		1839 1899
子	1840 1900		1852 1912		1864 1924		1876 1936		1888 1948	
丑		1841 1901		1853 1913		1865 1925		1877 1937		1889 1949
寅	1830 1890		1842 1902		1854 1914		1866 1926		1878 1938	
卯		1831 1891		1843 1903		1855 1915		1867 1927		1879 1939
辰	1880 1940		1832 1892		1844 1904		1856 1916		1868 1928	
巳		1881 1941		1833 1893		1845 1905		1857 1917		1869 1929
午	1870 1930		1882 1942		1834 1894		1846 1906		1858 1918	
未		1871 1931		1883 1943		1835 1895		1847 1907		1859 1919
申	1860 1920		1872 1932		1884 1944		1836 1896		1848 1908	
酉		1861 1921		1873 1933		1885 1945		1837 1897		1849 1909

NOTE: This table has been adapted from *Chinese Bank Notes* by Ward Smith and Brian Matravers.

Cyclical dates consist of a pair of characters one of which indicates the animal associated with that year. Every 60 years, this pair of characters is repeated. The first character of a cyclical date corresponds to a character in the first row of the chart above. The second character is taken from the column at left. In this catalog where a cyclical date is used, the abbreviation CD appears before the A.D. date.

Annamese silver and gold coins were sometimes dated according to the year of the emperor's reign. In this case, simply add the year of reign to the year in which the reign would be 1849 (1847 plus 3 = 1850 -1 = 1849 or 1847 = 1; 1848 = 2; 1849 = 3). In this catalog the A.D. date appears in parenthesis followed by the year of reign.

NUMERALS

NUMBER	CONVENTIONAL	FORMAL	COMMERCIAL
1	一 元	壹 弌	丨
2	二	弍 貳	丨丨
3	三	叁 弎	丨丨丨
4	四	肆	Ｘ
5	五	伍	夂
6	六	陸	⊥
7	七	柒	上
8	八	捌	亠
9	九	玖	攵
10	十	拾 什	十
20	十 二 or 廿	拾貳	丨丨十
25	五十 二 or 五廿	伍拾貳	丨丨十夂
30	十 三 or 卅	拾叁	丨丨丨十
100	百 一	佰壹	丨百
1,000	千 一	仟壹	丨千
10,000	萬 一	萬壹	丨万
100,000	萬 十 億 一	萬拾 億壹	十万
1,000,000	萬 百一	萬佰壹	丨百

NOTE: This table has been adapted from *Chinese Bank Notes* by Ward Smith and Brian Matravers.

MONETARY SYSTEM

10 Dong (zinc) = 1 Dong (copper)
600 Dong (zinc) = 1 Quan (string of ¬¬cash)
Approx. 2600 Dong (zinc) = 1 Piastre
 NOTE: Ratios between metals changed frequently, therefore the above is given as an approximate relationship.

SILVER and GOLD

2-1/2 Quan = 1 Lang
10 Tien (Mace) = 1 Lang (Tael)
14 to 17 Piastres (silver) = 1 Piastre (gold)
14 to 17 Lang (silver) = 1 Lang (gold)

The real currency of Dai Nam and An Nam consisted of copper and zinc coins similar to Chinese cash-style coins and were called sapeques and dongs by the French.

The smaller gold pieces saw a limited circulation, mainly among the local merchants and foreign traders. The larger gold pieces were used mainly for hoarding, while most of these were intended as rewards and gifts. Many of these gold pieces appear to have been struck from silver coin dies or vice-versa.

 NOTE: Sch# are in reference to Albert Schroeder's *Annam, Etudes Numismatiques* or to the same numbering system used in *Gold and Silver Coins of Annam"*, by Bernard Permar and John Novak.

CHARACTER IDENTIFICATION

The Vietnamese used Chinese-style characters for official documents and coins and bars. Some were modified to their liking and will sometimes not match the Chinese character for the same word. The above identification and this table will translate most of the Vietnamese characters (Chinese-style) on their coins and bars described herein.
Chinese/French
Vietnamese/English

安 南
An Nam = name of the French protectorate

大 南
Dai Nam = name of the country under Gia Long's Nguyen dynasty

越 南
Viet Nam = name used during Minh Mang's reign and became the modern name of the country

河 內
Ha Noi = city and province in north Dai NamTonkin

內 帑
Noi Thang = court treasury in the capital of Hue

年
Nien = year

造
Tao = made

銀
Ngan = silver

金
Kim = gold

錢
Tien = a weight of about 3.78 grams

兩
Lang = a weight of about 37.78 grams

貫
Quan = a string of cash-style coins

分
Phan = a weight of about .38 grams

文
Van = cash-style coins

中平
Trung Binh = a name of weight standard

FRENCH PROTECTORATE OF ANNAM
CAST COINAGE

KM# 654   PHAN
Cast Copper Alloys   **Ruler:** Khai Dinh **Obv. Insc.:** "Khai Dinh Thong Bao" **Note:** Prev. Y#4.

Date	Mintage	Good	VG	F	VF	XF
ND(1916-25)	—	5.50	9.00	15.00	25.00	—

KM# 661   PHAN
Cast Brass   **Ruler:** Bao Dai **Obv. Insc.:** Bao-dai Thong bao **Note:** Prev. Y#6a.

Date	Mintage	Good	VG	F	VF	XF
ND(1926-45)	—	2.50	5.00	7.50	12.50	—

KM# 652   10 VAN
Cast Brass   **Ruler:** Duy Tan **Obv. Insc.:** "Duy Tan Thong Bao" **Rev. Insc.:** "10 Van" **Note:** Prev. Y#3.

Date	Mintage	Good	VG	F	VF	XF
ND(1907-16)	—	0.50	0.75	1.25	2.50	—

KM# 664   10 VAN
Copper Alloys   **Ruler:** Bao Dai **Obv. Insc.:** "Bao Dai Thong Bao" **Rev. Insc.:** "10 Van" **Note:** Prev. Y#7.

Date	Mintage	Good	VG	F	VF	XF
ND(1926-45)	—	2.00	3.50	7.50	12.50	—

MILLED COINAGE
Brass

KM# 656   PHAN
Brass   **Ruler:** Khai Dinh **Obv:** Characters slightly different **Obv. Insc.:** "Khai Dinh Thong Bao" **Note:** Prev. Y#5.2.

Date	Mintage	Good	VG	F	VF	XF
ND(1916-25)	—	2.00	3.50	6.00	10.00	—

KM# 655   PHAN
Brass   **Ruler:** Khai Dinh **Obv. Insc.:** "Khai Dinh Thong Bao" **Note:** Uniface. Prev. Y#5.1.

Date	Mintage	Good	VG	F	VF	XF
ND(1916-25)	—	1.75	2.75	4.50	7.50	—

KM# 662   PHAN
Copper Alloys, 18 mm.   **Ruler:** Bao Dai **Obv. Insc.:** "Bao Dai Thong Bao" **Note:** Prev. Y#6.

Date	Mintage	Good	VG	F	VF	XF
ND(1926-45)	—	2.50	5.00	7.50	12.50	—

BULLION SILVER BARS

All of the bars described here are inscribed with their weight, except the 10 Lang banana bars, and many contain a date or the name of the province in which they were made.

KM# 658   LANG
Silver   **Ruler:** Khai Dinh **Note:** Date on edge. Weight unknown.

Date	Mintage	VG	F	VF	XF	Unc
CD1919	—	75.00	125	185	275	—

KM# 659   LANG
Silver   **Ruler:** Khai Dinh **Note:** Date on edge. Weight unknown.

Date	Mintage	VG	F	VF	XF	Unc
CD1922	—	75.00	125	185	275	—

REBEL COMMUNIST STATE
MILLED COINAGE

KM# 1   20 XU
Aluminum   **Ruler:** Bao Dai **Obv:** Star, date below **Obv. Leg.:** VIET NAM DAN CHU CHONG HOA **Rev:** Denomination **Rev. Insc.:** 20 XU

Date	Mintage	F	VF	XF	Unc	BU
1945(v)	—	45.00	125	175	275	—

KM# 2.1   5 HAO
Aluminum   **Obv:** Ceremonial pot **Obv. Leg.:** VIET-NAM DAN-CHU CONG-HOA **Rev:** Value incused in star **Rev. Insc.:** 5 HAO

Date	Mintage	F	VF	XF	Unc	BU
1946(v)	—	4.00	10.00	20.00	60.00	—

Note: Commonly encountered with rotated dies

KM# 2.2   5 HAO
Aluminum   **Obv:** Ceremonial pot **Obv. Leg.:** VIET-NAM DAN-CHU CONG-HOA **Rev:** Value raised in star

Date	Mintage	F	VF	XF	Unc	BU
1946(v)	—	40.00	.120	200	300	—

KM# 3   DONG
Aluminum   **Obv:** Head right **Obv. Leg.:** VIET-NAM DAN-CHU CONG-HOA **Rev:** Value to right of spray **Rev. Insc.:** 1 DONG

Date	Mintage	F	VF	XF	Unc	BU
1946(v)	—	15.00	35.00	85.00	160	—

KM# 4   2 DONG
Bronze   **Obv:** Bust of Ho Chi Minh 3/4 facing **Obv. Leg.:** CHU TICH HO MIHN **Rev:** Value above and below in wreath, Nam II at bottom **Rev. Insc.:** HAI DONG **Note:** Varieties exist.

Date	Mintage	F	VF	XF	Unc	BU
1946(v)	—	7.50	15.00	40.00	150	—

NORTH VIET NAM
INDEPENDENT COMMUNIST STATE
PRESENTATION COINAGE

KM# A5   10 VIET
4.1625 g., 0.9000 Gold 0.1204 oz. AGW, 17 mm.   **Obv:** Head of Ho Chi Minh right **Obv. Leg.:** "CHU-TICH HO-CHI-MINH" **Rev:** Denomination above grain sheaves **Rev. Leg.:** "VIET-NAM DAN-CHU CONG-HOA" **Rev. Insc.:** 10 Viet

Date	Mintage	F	VF	XF	Unc	BU
1948(v)	—	—	275	375	450	

KM# B5   20 VIET
8.3250 g., 0.9000 Gold 0.2409 oz. AGW, 21 mm.   **Obv:** Head of Ho Chi Minh right **Obv. Leg.:** "CHU-TICH HO-CHI-MINH" **Rev:** Denomination above grain sheaves **Rev. Leg.:** "VIET-NAM DAN-CHU CONG-HOA" **Rev. Insc.:** "20 VIET"

Date	Mintage	F	VF	XF	Unc	BU
1948(v)	—	—	450	550	600	

KM# C5   50 VIET
16.6500 g., 0.9000 Gold 0.4818 oz. AGW, 29 mm.   **Obv:** Head of Ho Chi Minh right **Obv. Leg.:** "CHU-TICH HO-CHI-MINH" **Rev:** Denomination above grain sheaves **Rev. Insc.:** "VIET-NAM DAN-CHU CONG-HOA" **Rev. Insc.:** "50 VIET"

Date	Mintage	F	VF	XF	Unc	BU
1948(v)	—	—	650	750	800	

REFORM COINAGE

KM# 5   XU
Aluminum   **Obv:** Center hole within arms **Obv. Leg.:** "NUOC VIET NAM DAN CHU CONG HOA" **Rev:** Center hole divides date and denomination **Rev. Leg.:** "NGAN HANG QUOC GIA VIET NAM" **Rev. Insc.:** Value: "MOT XU"

Date	Mintage	F	VF	XF	Unc	BU
1958(s)	—	1.25	2.50	5.00	8.00	

KM# 6   2 XU
Aluminum   **Obv:** Center hole within arms **Obv. Leg.:** "NUOC VIET NAM DAN CHU CONG HOA" **Rev:** Center hole divides denomination and date **Rev. Leg.:** "NGAN HANG QUOC GIA VIET NAM" **Rev. Insc.:** Value: "HAI XU"

Date	Mintage	F	VF	XF	Unc	BU
1958(s)	—	1.50	3.00	6.00	10.00	

KM# 7   5 XU
Aluminum   **Obv:** Center hole within arms **Obv. Leg.:** "NUOC VIET NAM DAN CHU CONG HOA" **Rev:** Center hole divides denomination and date **Rev. Leg.:** "NGAN HANG QUOC GIA VIET NAM" **Rev. Insc.:** Value: "NAM XU"

Date	Mintage	F	VF	XF	Unc	BU
1958(s)	—	2.00	4.00	8.00	15.00	

PATTERNS
Including off metal strikes

KM#	Date	Mintage	Identification	Mkt Val
Pn1	1946(v)	—	5 Dong. Bronze. VIET NAM DAN CHU CONG HOA.	

SOCIALIST REPUBLIC
SOCIALIST REPUBLIC
STANDARD COINAGE

KM# 11 HAO
Aluminum **Obv:** Arms **Rev:** Spray divides denomination **Rev. Leg.:** "NGAN HANG NHA NUOC VIET NAM" **Rev. Insc.:** "1 HAO"

Date	Mintage	F	VF	XF	Unc	BU
1976(s)	—	1.25	2.50	5.00	10.00	—

KM# 12 2 HAO
1.4100 g., Aluminum **Obv:** Arms **Rev:** Spray divides denomination **Rev. Leg.:** "NGAN HANG NHA HUOC VIET NAM" **Rev. Insc.:** "2 HOA"

Date	Mintage	F	VF	XF	Unc	BU
1976(s)	—	1.25	2.50	5.00	10.00	—

KM# 13 5 HAO
Aluminum **Obv:** Arms **Rev:** Denomination above ornament

Date	Mintage	F	VF	XF	Unc	BU
1976	—	1.50	3.00	6.00	12.00	—

KM# 14 DONG
Aluminum **Obv:** Arms **Rev:** Ornaments flank thick denomination **Rev. Leg.:** "NGAN HANG NHA NUOC VIET NAM" **Rev. Insc.:** "1 DONG"

Date	Mintage	F	VF	XF	Unc	BU
1976(s)	—	4.00	8.00	16.00	35.00	—

KM# 36a 5 DONG
8.7700 g., 0.9000 Silver 0.2538 oz. ASW **Obv:** Arms **Obv. Leg.:** "CONG HOA XA HOI CHU NGHIA VIET NAM" **Obv. Insc.:** "5 DONG" **Rev:** Mythological bird - Phoenix flying right **Rev. Insc.:** "CHIM PHUONG"

Date	Mintage	F	VF	XF	Unc	BU
1989(L) Proof	—	Value: 12.50				

KM# 36 5 DONG
Brass **Obv:** Arms **Obv. Leg.:** "CONG HOA XA HOI CHU NGHIA VIET NAM" **Obv. Insc.:** "5 DONG" **Rev:** Mythological bird - Phoenix flying right **Rev. Leg.:** "CHIM PHUONG" **Note:** KM#36 and 36a were minted in the Leningrad (St. Petersburg) Mint (L) as gifts to the Vietnamese government and were not circulated. KM#36a was available in boxed sets of three, with KM#38a and 40a, and KM#36 and 36a were also available as encapsulated individual pieces.

Date	Mintage	F	VF	XF	Unc	BU
1989(L) Proof	—	Value: 15.00				

KM# 15 10 DONG
Copper-Nickel **Subject:** Nature **Obv:** Arms **Obv. Leg.:** "CONG HOA XA HOI CHU NGHIA VIET NAM" **Rev:** Water buffalo head left, "TRAU" below **Rev. Leg.:** "BAO VE THIEN NHIEN"

Date	Mintage	F	VF	XF	Unc	BU
1986(h)	5,000	—	—	—	14.00	25.00

KM# 16 10 DONG
Copper-Nickel **Subject:** Nature **Obv:** Arms **Obv. Leg.:** "CONG HOA XA HOI CHU NGHIA VIET NAM" **Rev:** Peacock head right, "CONG" below **Rev. Leg.:** "BAO VE THIEN NHIEN"

Date	Mintage	F	VF	XF	Unc	BU
1986(h)	5,000	—	—	—	14.00	25.00

KM# 17 10 DONG
Copper-Nickel **Subject:** Nature **Obv:** Arms **Obv. Leg.:** "CONG HOA XA HOI CHU NGHIA VIET NAM" **Rev:** Elephant head left, "VOI" below **Rev. Leg.:** "BAO VE THIEN NHIEN"

Date	Mintage	F	VF	XF	Unc	BU
1986(h)	5,000	—	—	—	22.00	35.00

KM# 28 10 DONG
Copper-Nickel **Subject:** Wildlife Preservation **Obv:** Arms **Obv. Leg.:** "CONG HOA XA HOI CHU NGHIA VIET NAM" **Rev:** Orangutan with logo **Rev. Leg.:** "BAO VE THIEN NHIEN, DUOI UOI"

Date	Mintage	F	VF	XF	Unc	BU
1987(h)	22,000	—	—	—	20.00	30.00

KM# 37.1 10 DONG
11.3100 g., Copper-Nickel, 30 mm. **Obv:** Arms **Obv. Leg.:** "CONG HOA XA HOI CHU NGHIA VIET NAM" **Rev:** Dragon ship **Rev. Leg.:** "THUYEN CO." **Edge:** Plain

Date	Mintage	F	VF	XF	Unc	BU
1988(h)	—	—	—	—	8.50	10.00

KM# 37.2 10 DONG
29.7500 g., Copper, 38 mm. **Obv:** State emblem **Rev:** Asian Dragon Ship **Edge:** Plain

Date	Mintage	F	VF	XF	Unc	BU
1988(h)	—	—	—	—	10.00	11.50

KM# 38 10 DONG
Brass **Obv:** Arms **Obv. Leg.:** "CONG HOA XA HOI CHU NGHIA VIET NAM" **Rev:** One-pillar Pagoda above water and legend **Rev. Leg.:** "CHUA MOT COT-HANOI" **Note:** KM#38 and 38a were minted in the Leningrad (St. Petersburg) Mint (L) as gifts to the Vietnamese government and were not circulated. KM#38a was available in boxed sets of three, with KM#36a and 40a, and KM#38 and 38a were also available as encapsulated individual pieces.

Date	Mintage	F	VF	XF	Unc	BU
1989(L) Proof	—	Value: 7.00				

KM# 27 10 DONG
Copper-Nickel **Subject:** Soccer - Italy **Obv:** Arms **Obv. Leg.:** "CONG HOA XA HOI CHU NGHIA VIET NAM" **Rev:** Soccer player **Rev. Leg.:** "GIAI BONGDA THE GIOI"

Date	Mintage	F	VF	XF	Unc	BU
1989(h)	—	—	—	—	10.00	12.00

KM# 38a 10 DONG
0.9000 Silver **Obv:** Arms **Obv. Leg.:** "CONG HOA XA HOI CHU NGHIA VIET NAM" **Rev:** One-pillar Pagoda above water and legend **Rev. Leg.:** "CHUA MOT COT-HANOI"

Date	Mintage	F	VF	XF	Unc	BU
1989(L) Proof	—	Value: 22.00				

KM# 33 10 DONG
Copper-Nickel **Obv:** Arms **Obv. Leg.:** "CONG HOA XA HOI CHU NGHIA VIET NAM" **Rev:** Crested Gibbons **Rev. Leg.:** "BAO VE THIEM NHIEN, DUOI UOI"

Date	Mintage	F	VF	XF	Unc	BU
1990(h)	20,000	—	—	—	35.00	50.00

KM# 39 10 DONG
Copper-Nickel **Obv:** Arms **Obv. Leg.:** "CONG HOA XA HOI CHU NGHIA VIET NAM" **Rev:** Steam and sailship - Savannah **Rev. Leg.:** "THUYEN CO SAVANNAH"

Date	Mintage	F	VF	XF	Unc	BU
1991(h)	—	—	—	—	8.50	10.00

KM# 46   10 DONG
Copper **Series:** World Cup Soccer **Obv:** Arms
Obv. Leg.: "CONG HOA XA HOI CHU NGHIA VIET NAM"
Rev: Soccer player and U.S. Capitol **Rev. Leg.:** "CUP BONG DA
THE GIOI LAN THU XV, HOA KY"

Date	Mintage	F	VF	XF	Unc	BU
1992(h)	—	—	—	—	6.50	8.50

KM# 44   10 DONG
Copper-Nickel **Series:** Prehistoric Animals **Obv:** Arms
Obv. Leg.: "CONG HOA XA HOI CHU NGHIA VIET NAM"
Rev: Diplodocus **Rev. Leg.:** "DONG VAT CO DAI"

Date	Mintage	F	VF	XF	Unc	BU
1993(h)	—	—	—	—	22.00	35.00

KM# 49   10 DONG
Copper-Nickel **Subject:** World Food Summit **Obv:** Arms
Obv. Leg.: "CONG HOA XA HOI CHU NGHIA VIET NAM"
Rev: Rice harvesting scene, logo above **Rev. Leg.:** "MOI NGHI
THUONG DINH THE GIOI VE LUOIN THUC"

Date	Mintage	F	VF	XF	Unc	BU
1996(h)	—	—	—	—	6.00	8.00

KM# 40a   20 DONG
0.9000 Silver **Obv:** Arms **Obv. Leg.:** "CONG HOA XA HOI CHU
NGHIA VIET NAM" **Rev:** Head left, dates at right **Rev. Leg.:** "HO
CHI MINH"

Date	Mintage	F	VF	XF	Unc	BU
1989(L) Proof	—	Value: 40.00				

KM# 40   20 DONG
Brass **Subject:** 100th Anniversary - Birth of Ho Chi Minh
Obv: Arms **Obv. Leg.:** "CONG HOA XA HOI CHU NGHIA VIET
NAM" **Rev:** Head left, dates at right **Rev. Leg.:** "HO CHI MINH"
Edge: Nikolay Nosov **Note:** KM#40 and 40a were minted in the
Leningrad (St. Petersburg) Mint (L) as gifts to the Vietnamese
government and were not circulated. KM#40a was available in
boxed sets of three, with KM#36a and 38a, and KM#40 and 40a
were also available as encapsulated individual pieces.

Date	Mintage	F	VF	XF	Unc	BU
1989(L) Proof	—	Value: 16.50				

KM# 18   100 DONG
12.0000 g., 0.9990 Silver 0.3854 oz. ASW **Obv:** Arms
Obv. Leg.: "CONG HOA XA HOI CHU NGHIA VIET NAM"
Rev: Junk under sail **Rev. Leg.:** "VIETNAM, THUYEN BUOM"

Date	Mintage	F	VF	XF	Unc	BU
1986(h)	2,000	—	—	—	35.00	50.00

KM# 19   100 DONG
12.0000 g., 0.9990 Silver 0.3854 oz. ASW **Subject:** Wildlife
Obv: Arms **Obv. Leg.:** "CONG HOA XA HOI CHU NGHIA VIET
NAM" **Rev:** Water buffalo right looking left **Rev. Leg.:** "BAO VE
THIEN KHIEN, TRAU"

Date	Mintage	F	VF	XF	Unc	BU
1986(h)	5,000	—	—	—	32.50	45.00

KM# 20   100 DONG
12.0000 g., 0.9990 Silver 0.3854 oz. ASW **Subject:** Wildlife
Obv: Arms **Obv. Leg.:** "CONG HOA XA HOI CHU NGHIA VIET
NAM" **Rev:** Peacock left **Rev. Leg.:** "BAO VE THIEN NHIEN,
CONG"

Date	Mintage	F	VF	XF	Unc	BU
1986(h)	5,000	—	—	—	27.50	40.00

KM# 21   100 DONG
12.0000 g., 0.9990 Silver 0.3854 oz. ASW **Subject:** Wildlife
Obv: Arms **Obv. Leg.:** "CONG HOA XA HOI CHU NGHIA VIET
NAM" **Rev:** Elephant walking right **Rev. Leg.:** "BAO VI THIEN
NHIEN, VOI"

Date	Mintage	F	VF	XF	Unc	BU
1986(h)	5,000	—	—	—	45.00	60.00

KM# 22   100 DONG
12.0000 g., 0.9990 Silver 0.3854 oz. ASW **Subject:** 100 Years
of the Automobile **Obv:** Arms **Obv. Leg.:** "CONG HOA XA HOI
CHU NGHIA VIET NAM" **Rev:** Jaguar 3/4 left **Rev. Leg.:** "100
NAN XE O TO A DOI, 1886-1986"

Date	Mintage	F	VF	XF	Unc	BU
1986(h)	2,000	—	—	—	35.00	50.00

KM# 23.1   100 DONG
6.0000 g., 0.9990 Silver 0.1927 oz. ASW, 29.5 mm.
Series: Calgary Olympics **Obv:** Arms **Obv. Leg.:** "CONG HOA
XA HOI CHU NGHIA VIET NAM" **Rev:** Skier **Rev. Leg.:** "THE
VAN HOI O-LIM-PIC MUA DONG XV, GAN-GA-RY 1986"
Edge: Plain

Date	Mintage	F	VF	XF	Unc	BU
1986(h)	5,000	—	—	—	27.50	35.00

KM# 24.2   100 DONG
12.0000 g., 0.9990 Silver 0.3854 oz. ASW, 30 mm.
Series: Seoul Olympics - Fencer **Obv:** Arms, large letters and
design **Obv. Leg.:** "CONG HOA XA HOI CHU NGHIA VIET NAM"
Rev: Fencer, reverse legend far from rim **Rev. Leg.:** "THE VAN
HOI O LIM PIC MUA HE" **Edge:** Reeded

Date	Mintage	F	VF	XF	Unc	BU
1986(h)	Inc. above	—	—	—	10.00	12.00

KM# 29.1   100 DONG
12.0000 g., 0.9990 Silver 0.3854 oz. ASW, 30 mm.
Subject: Soccer - Mexico **Obv:** Arms, small letters
Obv. Leg.: "CONG HOA XA HOI CHU NGHIA VIET NAM"
Rev: Soccer player **Rev. Leg.:** "GIAI VO DICH BONG DA THE
GIOI LAM THU XIII, ME HI CO" **Edge:** Reeded

Date	Mintage	F	VF	XF	Unc	BU
1986(h)	5,000	—	—	—	27.50	35.00

KM# 24.1   100 DONG
6.0000 g., 0.9990 Silver 0.1927 oz. ASW, 30 mm.
Series: Seoul Olympics - Fencer **Obv:** Small letters and design
Obv. Leg.: "CONG HOA XA HOI CHU NGHIA VIET NAM"
Rev: Reverse legend close to rim, fencer en garde **Edge:** Reeded

Date	Mintage	F	VF	XF	Unc	BU
1986(h)	5,000	—	—	—	10.00	12.00

KM# 23.2   100 DONG
6.0000 g., 0.9990 Silver 0.1927 oz. ASW, 29.7 mm.
Series: Calgary Olympics **Obv:** Arms, large letters
Obv. Leg.: CONG HOA XA HOI CHUNGHIA VIET NAM
Rev: Skier **Rev. Leg.:** THE VAN HOI OLIM-PIC MUA DONG XV,
GAN-GA-RAY 1986 **Edge:** Reeded

Date	Mintage	F	VF	XF	Unc	BU
1986(h)	Inc. above	—	—	—	25.00	32.50

KM# 29.2   100 DONG
6.0000 g., 0.9990 Silver 0.1927 oz. ASW, 30 mm.
Subject: Mexico Olympics - Soccer **Obv:** Arms, large letters
Obv. Leg.: CONG HOA XA HOI CHU NGHIA VIET NAM
Rev: Soccer player **Rev. Leg.:** GIAI VO DICH BONG DA THE
GIOI LAM THU XIII, ME HI CO **Edge:** Reeded

Date	Mintage	F	VF	XF	Unc	BU
1986(h)	Inc. above	—	—	—	27.50	35.00

KM# 25.1   100 DONG
15.9900 g., 0.9800 Silver 0.5038 oz. ASW **Obv:** Arms large 100
Obv. Leg.: "CONG HOA XA HOI CHU NGHIA VIET NAM"
Rev: Suphanna hong (dragon ship) **Rev. Leg.:** "THUYEN CO"

Date	Mintage	F	VF	XF	Unc	BU
1988(h)	3,000	—	—	—	20.00	22.50
1988(h) Proof	—	Value: 27.50				

KM# 25.2   100 DONG
15.9900 g., 0.9800 Silver 0.5038 oz. ASW **Obv:** Arms small 100
Obv. Leg.: "CONG HOA XA HOI CHU NGHIA VIET NAM"
Rev: Dragon ship **Rev. Leg.:** "THUYEN CO"

Date	Mintage	F	VF	XF	Unc	BU
1988(h)	—	Value: 37.50				

KM# 26   100 DONG
12.0000 g., 0.9990 Silver 0.3854 oz. ASW **Subject:** Soccer -
1988 **Obv:** Arms **Obv. Leg.:** "CONG HOA XA HOI CHU NGHIA
VIET NAM" **Rev:** Soccer players **Rev. Leg.:** "GIAI BONG DA
CHAU AU, CONG HOA LIEN BANG DUCTHUYENCO."

Date	Mintage	F	VF	XF	Unc	BU
1988(h)	1,500	—	—	—	27.50	35.00

KM# 30   100 DONG
16.0000 g., 0.9990 Silver 0.5139 oz. ASW **Subject:** Soccer -
Italy **Obv:** Arms **Obv. Leg.:** "CONG HOA XA HOI CHU NGHIA
VIET NAM" **Rev:** Soccer player **Rev. Leg.:** "GIAI BONG DA THE
GIOI, I-TA-LI-A"

Date	Mintage	F	VF	XF	Unc	BU
1989(h) Proof	10,000	Value: 28.50				

KM# 31   100 DONG
16.0000 g., 0.9990 Silver 0.5139 oz. ASW **Series:** Summer
Olympics **Subject:** Rowing **Obv:** Arms **Obv. Leg.:** "CONG HOA
XA HOI CHU NGHIA VIET NAM" **Rev:** Six people rowing
Rev. Leg.: "THE VAN HOI LAN THU XXV, BARCELONA 1992"

Date	Mintage	F	VF	XF	Unc	BU
1989(h) Proof	10,000	Value: 25.00				

KM# 32   100 DONG
16.0000 g., 0.9990 Silver 0.5139 oz. ASW **Series:** Winter
Olympics **Subject:** Hockey **Obv:** Arms **Obv. Leg.:** "CONG HOA
XA HOI CHU NGHIA VIET NAM" **Rev:** Hockey players
Rev. Leg.: "THE VAN HOI MUA DONG XVI, ALBERTVILLE
1992"

Date	Mintage	F	VF	XF	Unc	BU
1990(h) Proof	10,000	Value: 40.00				

KM# 34   100 DONG
12.0000 g., 0.9990 Silver 0.3854 oz. ASW **Subject:** Soccer
Obv: Arms **Obv. Leg.:** "CONG HOA XA HOI CHU NGHIA VIET
NAM" **Rev:** Soccer players within design **Rev. Leg.:** "CUP BONG
DA THE FIOI LAN THU XV, HOA KY 1994"

Date	Mintage	F	VF	XF	Unc	BU
1991(h)	—	—	—	—	22.50	25.00

KM# 35   100 DONG
16.0000 g., 0.9990 Silver 0.5139 oz. ASW **Obv:** Arms
Obv. Leg.: "CONG HOA XA HOI CHU NGHIA VIET NAM"
Rev: Steamship Savannah **Rev. Leg.:** "THUYEN CO
SAVANNAH"

Date	Mintage	F	VF	XF	Unc	BU
1991(h) Proof	—	Value: 30.00				

KM# 70   100 DONG
19.9000 g., 0.9990 Silver 0.6391 oz. ASW, 38.1 mm. **Obv:** Arms
Rev: Soccer player with U.S. Capital building in background
Edge: Reeded

Date	Mintage	F	VF	XF	Unc	BU
1992 Proof	—	Value: 30.00				

KM# 42   100 DONG
16.0000 g., 0.9990 Silver 0.5139 oz. ASW **Series:** Prehistoric
Animals **Obv:** Arms **Obv. Leg.:** "CONG HOA XA HOI CHU
NGHIA VIET NAM" **Rev:** Rhamphorhynchus **Rev. Leg.:** "DONG
VAT CO DAI"

Date	Mintage	F	VF	XF	Unc	BU
1993(h) Proof	—	Value: 60.00				

KM# 43   100 DONG
16.0000 g., 0.9990 Silver 0.5139 oz. ASW **Obv:** Arms
Obv. Leg.: "CONG HOA XA HOI CHU NGHIA VIET NAM"
Rev: Elephants **Rev. Leg.:** "BAO VI THIEN NHIEN - VOI"

Date	Mintage	F	VF	XF	Unc	BU
1993(h) Proof	—	Value: 45.00				

KM# 45   100 DONG
16.0000 g., 0.9990 Silver 0.5139 oz. ASW **Series:** Prehistoric
Animals **Obv:** Arms **Obv. Leg.:** "CONG HOA XA HOI CHU NGHIA
VIET NAM" **Rev:** Edaphosaurus **Rev. Leg.:** "DONG VAT CO DAI"

Date	Mintage	F	VF	XF	Unc	BU
1994(h) Proof	—	Value: 50.00				

KM# 78   100 DONG
16.0000 g., 0.9990 Silver 0.5139 oz. ASW **Obv:** National arms,
value below **Rev:** Gallimimus dinosaur **Edge:** Plain

Date	Mintage	F	VF	XF	Unc	BU
1994 Proof	—	—	—	—	—	—

KM# 47 100 DONG
20.0000 g., 0.9990 Silver 0.6423 oz. ASW **Series:** Olympics **Obv:** Arms **Obv. Leg.:** "CONG HOA XA HOI CHU NGHIA VIET NAM" **Rev:** Gymnast on pommel horse **Rev. Leg.:** "TU ATEN DEN ATLANTA"

Date	Mintage	F	VF	XF	Unc	BU
1995(h) Proof	15,000	Value: 25.00				

KM# 48 100 DONG
20.0000 g., 0.9990 Silver And Enamel 0.6423 oz. **Obv:** Arms **Obv. Leg.:** "CONG HOA XA HOI CHU NGHIA VIET NAM" **Rev:** Caracal **Rev. Leg.:** "THU AN THIT/CARACAL CARACAL"

Date	Mintage	F	VF	XF	Unc	BU
1996(h) Proof	—	Value: 60.00				

KM# 50 100 DONG
20.0000 g., 0.9990 Silver And Enamel 0.6423 oz. **Subject:** World Food Summit **Obv:** Arms **Obv. Leg.:** "CONG HOA XA HOI CHU NGHIA VIET NAM" **Rev:** Rice harvesting scene, logo above **Rev. Leg.:** "HOI NGHI THUONG DINH THE GIOI VE LUONG THUC"

Date	Mintage	F	VF	XF	Unc	BU
1996(h) Proof	—	Value: 50.00				

KM# 60 100 DONG
16.0000 g., 0.9990 Silver 0.5139 oz. ASW, 38 mm. **Subject:** UNICEF **Obv:** Arms **Rev:** Child on water buffalo **Edge:** Reeded

Date	Mintage	F	VF	XF	Unc	BU
1997 Proof	25,000	Value: 20.00				

KM# 77 100 DONG
16.0000 g., 0.9990 Silver 0.5139 oz. ASW, 35 mm. **Subject:** 2000 XXIV Olympics **Obv:** Arms **Obv. Leg.:** CONG HOA XA HOI CHU NGHIA VIET NAM **Rev:** Multicolored Steeple chase horse and rider **Rev. Leg.:** O – LIM – PIC XXVII **Edge:** Plain

Date	Mintage	F	VF	XF	Unc	BU
1998						

KM# 41 500 DONG
3.1030 g., 0.9990 Gold 0.0997 oz. AGW **Subject:** 100th Anniversary - Birth of Ho Chi Minh **Obv:** Arms **Obv. Leg.:** "CONG HOA XA HOI CHU NGHIA VIET NAM" **Note:** KM#41 were minted at the Havana Mint (h) as "Gift Coins" to the Vietnamese people and were delivered encapsulated and in presentation boxes. This piece is cataloged as A24 and illustrated in Gunter Schon's World Coins Catalogue.

Date	Mintage	F	VF	XF	Unc	BU
1989(L)	—	—	—	—	350	500

KM# 54 5000 DONG
1.2441 g., 0.9999 Gold 0.0400 oz. AGW, 13.92 mm. **Subject:** Year of the Dragon **Obv:** Arms **Obv. Leg.:** "CONG HOA XA HOI CHU NGHIA VIET NAM" **Rev:** Dragon with radiant sun **Rev. Leg.:** "RONG VIET NAM" **Edge:** Reeded

Date	Mintage	F	VF	XF	Unc	BU
2000(S)	—	Value: 55.00				

KM# 51 10000 DONG
20.0000 g., 0.9250 Silver 0.5948 oz. ASW, 38.7 mm. **Subject:** Year of the Dragon **Obv:** Arms **Obv. Leg.:** "CONG HOA XA HOI CHU NGHIA VIET NAM" **Rev:** Dragon with radiant sun **Edge:** Reeded

Date	Mintage	F	VF	XF	Unc	BU
2000(S) Proof	10,000	Value: 35.00				

KM# 52 10000 DONG
20.0000 g., 0.9250 Silver 0.5948 oz. ASW, 38.7 mm. **Subject:** Year of the Dragon **Obv:** Arms **Obv. Leg.:** "CONG HOA XA HOI CHU NGHIA VIET NAM" **Rev:** Multicolor dragon **Rev. Leg.:** "RONG VIET NAM" **Edge:** Reeded

Date	Mintage	F	VF	XF	Unc	BU
2000(S) Proof	10,000	Value: 35.00				

KM# 53 10000 DONG
20.0000 g., 0.9250 Silver 0.5948 oz. ASW, 38.7 mm. **Subject:** Year of the Dragon **Obv:** Arms **Obv. Leg.:** "CONG HOA XA HOI CHU NGHIA VIET NAM" **Rev:** Two dragons **Edge:** Reeded

Date	Mintage	F	VF	XF	Unc	BU
2000(S) Proof	10,000	Value: 35.00				

KM# 55 20000 DONG
7.7749 g., 0.9999 Gold 0.2499 oz. AGW, 22 mm. **Subject:** Year of the Dragon **Obv:** Arms **Obv. Leg.:** "CONG HOA XA HOI CHU NGHIA VIET NAM" **Rev:** Dragon and clouds **Rev. Leg.:** "RONG VIET NAM" **Edge:** Reeded

Date	Mintage	F	VF	XF	Unc	BU
2000(S) Proof	1,800	Value: 275				

KM# 56 50000 DONG
15.5518 g., 0.9999 Gold 0.4999 oz. AGW, 27 mm. **Subject:** Year of the Dragon **Obv:** Arms **Obv. Leg.:** "CONG HOA XA HOI CHU NGHIA VIET NAM" **Rev:** Dragon before radiant sun **Rev. Leg.:** "RONG VIET NAM" **Edge:** Reeded

Date	Mintage	F	VF	XF	Unc	BU
2000(S) Proof	3,800	Value: 550				

PATTERNS

KM#	Date	Mintage	Identification	Mkt Val
Pn1	1976(s)	—	Hao. Silver. Arms. "NGAN HANG NHA NUOC VIET NAM". KM#11	—
Pn2	1976(s)	—	Dong. Silver. Arms. "NGAN HANG NHA NUOC VIET NAM". KM#14	—

PIEFORTS

KM#	Date	Mintage	Identification	Mkt Val
PE1	1990(h)	110	Dong. Silver. KM#32	150

MINT SETS

KM#	Date	Mintage	Identification	Issue Price	Mkt Val
MS1	1958-1976(s) (7)	—	KM#5-7, Democratic Republic; KM#11-14, Socialist Republic	—	85.00
MS2	1975/1976(s) (4)	—	KM#8-14 NOTE: Created and sold by the Bank for Foreign Trade of Viet Nam to tourists and collectors.	—	25.00

PROOF SETS

KM#	Date	Mintage	Identification	Issue Price	Mkt Val
PS1	1989(L) (3)	—	KM#36a, 38a, 40a	—	75.00
PS2	2000(S) (3)	2,000	KM#51-53	—	100
PS3	2000(S) (2)	800	KM#55-56	—	825

STATE OF SOUTH VIET NAM
DEMOCRATIC STATE
STANDARD COINAGE

KM# 1 10 SU
Aluminum **Obv:** Three conjoined busts left **Obv. Leg.:** "QUOC-GIA VIET-NAM" **Rev:** Rice plant (oryza sativa - Gramineae) dividing value **Rev. Leg.:** "VIET-NAM"

Date	Mintage	F	VF	XF	Unc	BU
1953(a)	20,000,000	0.50	1.00	2.00	4.00	—

KM# 2 20 SU
Aluminum **Obv:** Three conjoined busts left **Obv. Leg.:** "QUOC-GIA VIET-NAM" **Rev:** Rice plant dividing value **Rev. Leg.:** "VIET-NAM"

Date	Mintage	F	VF	XF	Unc	BU
1953(a)	15,000,000	0.40	0.75	1.50	3.00	

KM# 3 50 XU
Aluminum **Obv:** Three busts; 3/4 left, facing and 3/4 right **Obv. Leg.:** "QUOC-GIA VIET-NAM" **Rev:** Dragons flank denomination **Rev. Leg.:** "VIET-NAM"

Date	Mintage	F	VF	XF	Unc	BU
1953(a)	15,000,000	3.00	6.00	12.00	25.00	

REPUBLIC OF VIET NAM

STANDARD COINAGE

KM# 4 50 SU
Aluminum **Obv:** Bust of Ngo Dihn Diem left **Obv. Leg.:** "VIET-NAM CONG-HOA" **Rev:** Bamboo plants divide denomination **Note:** The 1960 50 Su coin was minted by the Paris Mint with the French spelling Su for Xu. The coin was restruck with the correct Xu, a new date of 1963, and is cataloged as KM#6.

Date	Mintage	F	VF	XF	Unc	BU
1960(a)	10,000,000	1.00	2.00	4.00	10.00	—
1960(a) Proof			Value: 80.00			

KM# 6 50 XU
2.9400 g., Aluminum **Obv:** Bust of Ngo Dihn Diem left **Obv. Leg.:** "VIET-NAM CONG-HOA" **Rev:** Bamboo plants divide denomination

Date	Mintage	F	VF	XF	Unc	BU
1963	20,000,000	0.40	0.80	1.50	5.00	—
1963 Proof			Value: 80.00			

KM# 5 DONG
Copper-Nickel, 22 mm. **Obv:** Bust of Ngo Dihn Diem left **Obv. Leg.:** "VIET-NAM CONG-HOA" **Rev:** Bamboo plants divide denomination

Date	Mintage	F	VF	XF	Unc	BU
1960(a)	105,000,000	0.20	0.50	1.25	3.00	6.50
1960(a) Proof			Value: 80.00			

KM# 7 DONG
3.9500 g., Copper-Nickel, 22.3 mm. **Obv:** Denomination **Obv. Leg.:** "VIET-NAM CONG-HAO" **Rev:** Rice stalks

Date	Mintage	F	VF	XF	Unc	BU
1964	190,000,000	0.20	0.35	0.75	1.50	3.50
1964 Proof						

KM# 7a DONG
3.6000 g., Nickel-Clad Steel **Obv:** Denomination **Obv. Leg.:** "VIET-NAM CONG-HAO" **Rev:** Rice stalks

Date	Mintage	F	VF	XF	Unc	BU
1971	—	0.10	0.15	0.35	1.00	3.00

KM# 12 DONG
1.2000 g., Aluminum, 22.40 mm. **Series:** F.A.O. **Obv:** Denomination **Obv. Leg.:** "VIET-NAM CONG-HAO" **Rev:** Rice stalks **Rev. Leg.:** "TANG-GIA SAN-NUAT LUONG-THUC"

Date	Mintage	F	VF	XF	Unc	BU
1971	30,000,000	0.25	0.50	1.00	2.75	5.50

KM# 9 5 DONG
Copper-Nickel **Obv:** Denomination **Obv. Leg.:** "VIET-NAM CONG-HAO" **Rev:** Rice stalks **Rev. Leg.:** "NGAN-HANG VIET-NAM CONG-HOA"

Date	Mintage	F	VF	XF	Unc	BU
1966	100,000,000	0.25	0.50	1.00	2.50	4.00

KM# 9a 5 DONG
Nickel-Clad Steel **Obv:** Denomination **Obv. Leg.:** "VIET-NAM CONG-HAO" **Rev:** Rice stalks **Rev. Leg.:** "NGAN-HANG VIET-NAM CONG-HOA"

Date	Mintage	F	VF	XF	Unc	BU
1971	15,000,000	0.40	0.75	1.50	3.00	7.50

KM# 8 10 DONG
Copper-Nickel, 25.5 mm. **Obv:** Denomination **Obv. Leg.:** "VIET-NAM CONG-HAO" **Rev:** Rice stalks

Date	Mintage	F	VF	XF	Unc	BU
1964	45,000,000	0.25	0.50	1.00	2.50	6.00

KM# 8a 10 DONG
Nickel-Clad Steel **Obv:** Denomination **Obv. Leg.:** "VIET-NAM CONG-HAO" **Rev:** Rice stalks

Date	Mintage	F	VF	XF	Unc	BU
1968	30,000,000	0.25	0.50	1.00	2.50	6.00
1970	50,000,000	0.25	0.50	1.00	2.50	6.00

KM# 13 10 DONG
4.3900 g., Brass-Clad Steel, 24 mm. **Series:** F.A.O. **Obv:** Denomination **Obv. Leg.:** "VIET-NAM CONG-HAO, NGAN-HUAN QUOC-GIA VIET-NAM" **Rev:** Farmers in rice paddy **Rev. Leg.:** "TANG-GIA SAM-XUAT NONG-PHAN"

Date	Mintage	F	VF	XF	Unc	BU
1974	30,000,000	0.25	0.50	1.00	2.50	4.00

KM# 10 20 DONG
Nickel-Clad Steel **Obv:** Denomination **Obv. Leg.:** "VIET-NAM CONG-HOA" **Rev:** Farmer in rice paddy **Rev. Leg.:** "NGAN-HANG QUOC-GIA VIET-NAM"

Date	Mintage	F	VF	XF	Unc	BU
1968	—	0.75	1.50	3.00	7.00	10.00

KM# 11 20 DONG
8.7600 g., Nickel-Clad Steel, 29.6 mm. **Series:** F.A.O. **Obv:** Denomination **Obv. Leg.:** "VIET-NAM CONG-HAO" **Rev:** Farmer in rice paddy **Rev. Leg.:** "CHIEN-TICH THE-GIOI CHONG NAM DOI"

Date	Mintage	F	VF	XF	Unc	BU
1968	500,000	1.00	2.00	4.00	8.00	12.00

KM# 14 50 DONG
Nickel Clad Steel **Series:** F.A.O. **Obv:** Denomination **Obv. Leg.:** "VIET-NAM CONG-HAO, NGAN-HANG QUOC-GIA VIET-NAM" **Rev:** Farmers in rice paddy **Rev. Leg.:** "TANG-GIA SAM-XUAT NONG-PHAN"

Date	Mintage	F	VF	XF	Unc	BU
1975	1,010,000	—	—	450	650	800

Note: It is reported that all but a few examples were disposed of as scrap metal

PEOPLE'S REVOLUTIONARY GOVERNMENT

STANDARD COINAGE

KM# A8 XU
Aluminum **Obv:** Star above center hole, spray below **Obv. Leg.:** "NGAN HANG VIET NAM" **Rev:** 1 above center hole, MOT XU below, grain stalks flank

Date	Mintage	F	VF	XF	Unc	BU
ND(1975)	—	1.00	2.50	5.00	12.00	—

KM# A9 2 XU
Aluminum **Obv:** Wreath surrounds center hole, HAI XU below
Obv. Leg.: "NGAN HANG VIET NAM" **Rev:** Ornaments surround center hole, 2 above, XU below ornamentation

Date	Mintage	F	VF	XF	Unc	BU
1975	—	2.00	4.00	7.00	20.00	—

KM# A10 5 XU
Aluminum **Obv:** Denomination below center hole
Obv. Leg.: "NGAN HANG VIET NAM" **Rev:** "NAM XU" above, 5 below in stylized sprays

Date	Mintage	F	VF	XF	Unc	BU
ND(1975)	—	2.00	4.00	9.00	25.00	—

ESSAIS
Standard metals unless otherwise noted

KM#	Date	Mintage Identification	Issue Price	Mkt Val
E1	1953	1,200 10 Su. Aluminum. KM#1	—	25.00
E2	1953(a)	1,200 20 Su. Aluminum. KM#2	—	30.00
E3	1953(a)	1,200 50 Su. Aluminum. KM#3	—	35.00

PATTERNS
Including off metal strikes

KM#	Date	Mintage Identification	Mkt Val
Pn1	1963	— 50 Xu. Aluminum-Bronze.	400
Pn2	1963	— 50 Xu. Copper-Nickel.	400

PIEFORTS WITH ESSAI
Standard metals unless otherwise noted

KM#	Date	Mintage Identification	Issue Price	Mkt Val
PE1	1953(a)	104 10 Su. Aluminum. KM#1	—	200
PE2	1953(a)	104 20 Su. Aluminum. KM#2	—	200
PE3	1953(a)	104 50 Xu. Aluminum. KM#3	—	300

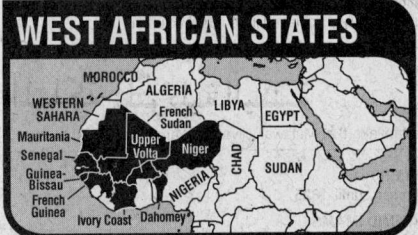

WEST AFRICAN STATES

The West African States, a former federation of eight French colonial territories on the northwest coast of Africa, has an area of 1,831,079 sq. mi. (4,742,495 sq. km.) and a population of about 17 million. Capital: Dakar. The constituent territories were Mauritania, Senegal, Dahomey, French Sudan, Ivory Coast, Upper Volta, Niger and French Guinea.

The members of the federation were overseas territories within the French Union until Sept. of 1958 when all but French Guinea approved the constitution of the Fifth French Republic, thereby electing to become autonomous members of the new French Community. French Guinea voted to become the fully independent Republic of Guinea. The other seven attained independence in 1960. The French West Africa territories were provided with a common currency, a practice which was continued as the monetary union of the West African States which provides a common currency to the autonomous republics of Dahomey (now Benin), Senegal, Upper Volta (now Burkina Faso), Ivory Coast, Mali, Togo, Niger, and Guinea-Bissau.

For earlier coinage refer to Togo, and French West Africa.

MINT MARK
(a)- Paris, privy marks only

MONETARY SYSTEM
100 Centimes = 1 Franc

FEDERATION
STANDARD COINAGE

KM# 3.1 FRANC
1.3000 g., Aluminum, 23 mm. **Obv:** Taku symbol divides denomination **Rev:** Gazelle head facing (gazella leptoceros - bovidae)

Date	Mintage	F	VF	XF	Unc	BU
1961(a)	3,000,000	—	0.15	0.30	0.60	0.85
1964(a)	10,500,000	—	0.15	0.30	0.60	0.85
1965(a)	6,000,000	—	0.15	0.30	0.60	0.85
1967(a)	2,500,000	—	0.15	0.30	0.60	0.85
1971(a)	8,000,000	—	0.15	0.30	0.60	0.85
1972(a)	4,000,000	—	0.15	0.30	0.60	0.85
1973(a)	4,500,000	—	0.15	0.30	0.60	0.85
1974(a)	4,500,000	—	0.15	0.30	0.60	0.85
1975(a)	18,000,000	—	0.15	0.30	0.60	0.85

KM# 3.2 FRANC
Aluminum, 23 mm. **Obv:** Taku symbol divides denomination
Rev: Engraver general's name

Date	Mintage	F	VF	XF	Unc	BU
1962(a)	2,000,000	—	2.00	5.00	10.00	12.00
1963(a)	4,500,000	—	1.50	4.00	7.00	9.00

KM# 8 FRANC
1.6000 g., Steel **Obv:** Taku - Ashanti gold weight **Rev:** Value and date

Date	Mintage	F	VF	XF	Unc	BU
1976(a)	8,000,000	—	—	0.10	0.35	0.60
1977(a)	14,700,000	—	—	0.10	0.35	0.60
1978(a)	21,800,000	—	—	0.10	0.35	0.60
1979(a)	16,600,000	—	—	0.10	0.35	0.60
1980(a)	13,000,000	—	—	0.10	0.35	0.60
1981(a)	2,000,000	—	—	0.10	0.35	0.60
1982(a)	6,000,000	—	—	0.10	0.35	0.60
1984(a)	33,400,000	—	—	0.10	0.35	0.60
1985(a)	26,900,000	—	—	—	—	—
1988(a)	—	—	—	0.10	0.35	0.60
1990(a)	10,000,000	—	—	0.10	0.35	0.60
1991(a)	3,500,000	—	—	0.10	0.35	0.60
1992(a)	6,000,000	—	—	0.10	0.35	0.60
1995(a)	3,000,000	—	—	0.10	0.35	0.60
1996(a)	3,000,000	—	—	0.10	0.35	0.60
1997(a)	1,500,000	—	—	0.10	0.35	0.60
1999(a)	1,000,000	—	—	0.10	0.35	0.60
2000(a)	—	—	—	0.10	0.35	0.60

KM# 2 5 FRANCS
2.9400 g., Aluminum-Bronze, 20.2 mm. **Obv:** Taku symbol divides denomination **Rev:** Gazelle head facing

Date	Mintage	F	VF	XF	Unc	BU
1960(a)	5,000,000	—	0.20	0.40	0.70	1.00

KM# 2a 5 FRANCS
3.0000 g., Aluminum-Nickel-Bronze, 20 mm. **Obv:** Taku - Ashanti gold weight divides value value **Rev:** Gazelle head facing

Date	Mintage	F	VF	XF	Unc	BU
1965(a)	12,500,000	—	0.20	0.40	0.70	1.00
1967(a)	6,500,000	—	0.20	0.40	0.70	1.00
1968(a)	6,000,000	—	0.20	0.45	0.75	1.10
1969(a)	8,000,000	—	0.20	0.40	0.70	1.00
1970(a)	10,005,000	—	0.20	0.40	0.70	1.00
1971(a)	10,000,000	—	0.20	0.40	0.70	1.00
1972(a)	5,000,000	—	0.20	0.40	0.70	1.00
1973(a)	6,000,000	—	0.20	0.45	0.75	1.10
1974(a)	13,326,000	—	0.10	0.15	0.30	0.50
1975(a)	16,840,000	—	0.20	0.40	0.70	1.00
1976(a)	20,010,000	—	0.20	0.30	0.60	0.85
1977(a)	22,000,000	—	0.20	0.30	0.60	0.85
1978(a)	40,000,000	—	0.10	0.20	0.60	0.85
1979(a)	11,000,000	—	0.10	0.20	0.40	0.60
1980(a)	18,000,000	—	0.10	0.20	0.40	0.60
1981(a)	18,000,000	—	0.10	0.20	0.40	0.60
1982(a)	25,000,000	—	0.10	0.20	0.40	0.60
1984(a)	31,700,000	—	0.10	0.20	0.40	0.60
1985(a)	16,000,000	—	0.10	0.20	0.40	0.60
1986(a)	8,000,000	—	0.10	0.20	0.40	0.60

Date	Mintage	F	VF	XF	Unc	BU
1987(a)	26,500,000	—	0.10	0.20	0.40	0.60
1989(a)	44,500,000	—	0.10	0.20	0.40	0.60
1990(a)	—	—	0.10	0.20	0.40	0.60
1991(a)	19,000,000	—	0.10	0.20	0.40	0.60
1992(a)	—	—	0.10	0.20	0.40	0.60
1993(a)	—	—	0.10	0.20	0.40	0.60
1994(a)	20,000,000	—	0.10	0.20	0.40	0.60
1995(a)	—	—	0.10	0.20	0.40	0.60
1996(a)	21,500,000	—	0.10	0.20	0.40	0.60
1997(a)	18,000,000	—	0.10	0.20	0.40	0.60
1999(a)	36,900,000	—	0.10	0.20	0.40	0.60
2000(a)	—	—	0.10	0.20	0.40	0.60

KM# 1 10 FRANCS
Aluminum-Bronze **Obv:** Taku symbol divides denomination

Date	Mintage	F	VF	XF	Unc	BU
1959(a)	10,000,000	—	0.15	0.30	0.60	0.85
1964(a)	10,000,000	—	0.20	0.40	0.70	1.00

KM# 1a 10 FRANCS
Aluminum-Nickel-Bronze **Obv:** Taku symbol divides denomination **Rev:** Gazelle head facing

Date	Mintage	F	VF	XF	Unc	BU
1966(a)	6,000,000	—	0.20	0.40	0.70	1.00
1967(a)	3,500,000	—	0.25	0.50	0.90	1.25
1968(a)	6,000,000	—	0.20	0.40	0.70	1.00
1969(a)	7,000,000	—	0.25	0.50	0.90	1.25
1970(a)	7,000,000	—	0.15	0.30	0.60	0.85
1971(a)	8,000,000	—	0.15	0.30	0.60	0.85
1972(a)	5,500,000	—	0.20	0.40	0.70	1.00
1973(a)	3,000,000	—	0.20	0.40	0.70	1.00
1974(a)	10,000,000	—	0.15	0.30	0.60	0.85
1975(a)	17,000,000	—	0.15	0.30	0.60	0.85
1976(a)	18,000,000	—	0.15	0.30	0.60	0.85
1977(a)	11,000,000	—	0.15	0.25	0.50	0.75
1978(a)	21,000,000	—	0.15	0.25	0.50	0.75
1979(a)	11,000,000	—	0.15	0.25	0.50	0.75
1980(a)	16,000,000	—	0.15	0.25	0.50	0.75
1981(a)	12,000,000	—	0.15	0.25	0.50	0.75

KM# 10 10 FRANCS
4.0000 g., Brass, 23.4 mm. **Series:** F.A.O. **Obv:** Taku - Ashanti gold weight divides value **Rev:** People getting water

Date	Mintage	F	VF	XF	Unc	BU
1981(a)	2,000,000	—	0.25	0.50	1.25	1.50
1982(a)	23,000,000	—	0.25	0.50	1.25	1.50
1983(a)	6,000,000	—	0.25	0.50	1.25	1.50
1984(a)	10,000,000	—	0.25	0.50	1.25	1.50
1985(a)	5,000,000	—	0.25	0.50	1.25	1.50
1986(a)	7,500,000	—	0.25	0.50	1.25	1.50
1987(a)	28,000,000	—	0.25	0.50	1.25	1.50
1989(a)	40,500,000	—	0.25	0.50	1.25	1.50
1990(a)	18,000,000	—	0.25	0.50	1.25	1.50
1991(a)	18,000,000	—	0.25	0.50	1.25	1.50
1992(a)	5,000,000	—	0.25	0.50	1.25	1.50
1993(a)	4,400,000	—	0.25	0.50	1.25	1.50
1994(a)	19,900,000	—	0.25	0.50	1.25	1.50
1995(a)	3,700,000	—	0.25	0.50	1.25	1.50
1996(a)	33,300,000	—	0.25	0.50	1.25	1.50
1997(a)	38,200,000	—	0.25	0.50	1.25	1.50
1999(a)	33,000,000	—	0.25	0.50	1.25	1.50
2000(a)	6,500,000	—	0.25	0.50	1.25	1.50

KM# 5 25 FRANCS
Aluminum-Bronze, 27 mm. **Obv:** Taku divides denomination **Rev:** Gazelle head facing

Date	Mintage	F	VF	XF	Unc	BU
1970(a)	7,000,000	—	0.25	0.45	1.00	1.25
1971(a)	7,000,000	—	0.50	0.75	1.25	1.50
1972(a)	2,000,000	F	1.50	2.50	4.50	6.00
1975(a)	5,035,000	—	0.25	0.45	1.00	1.25
1976(a)	3,365,000	—	0.25	0.45	1.00	1.25
1977(a)	3,288,000	—	0.25	0.45	1.00	1.25

Date	Mintage	F	VF	XF	Unc	BU
1978(a)	6,800,000	—	0.25	0.45	1.00	1.25
1979(a)	5,200,000	—	0.25	0.45	1.00	1.25

KM# 9   25 FRANCS
7.9500 g., Aluminum-Bronze, 27 mm. **Series:** F.A.O. **Obv:** Taku - Ashanti gold weight divides value **Rev:** Figure filling tube

Date	Mintage	F	VF	XF	Unc	BU
1980(a)	7,800,000	—	0.25	0.75	1.75	2.00
1981(a)	4,000,000	—	0.25	0.75	1.75	2.00
1982(a)	8,000,000	—	0.25	0.75	1.75	2.00
1984(a)	15,300,000	—	0.25	0.75	1.75	2.00
1985(a)	8,587,000	—	0.25	0.75	1.75	2.00
1987(a)	9,000,000	—	0.25	0.75	1.75	2.00
1989(a)	17,600,000	—	0.25	0.75	1.75	2.00
1990(a)	6,000,000	—	0.25	0.75	1.75	2.00
1991(a)	1,700,000	—	0.25	0.75	1.75	2.00
1992(a)	6,000,000	—	0.25	0.75	1.75	2.00
1994(a)	8,200,000	—	0.25	0.75	1.75	2.00
1995(a)	—	—	0.25	0.75	1.75	2.00
1996(a)	18,300,000	—	0.25	0.75	1.75	2.00
1997(a)	22,000,000	—	0.25	0.75	1.75	2.00
1999(a)	16,700,000	—	0.25	0.75	1.75	2.00
2000(a)	16,800,000	—	0.25	0.75	1.75	2.00

KM# 6   50 FRANCS
5.0900 g., Copper-Nickel, 22 mm. **Series:** F.A.O. **Obv:** Taku - Ashanti gold weight **Rev:** Value within mixed beans, grains and nuts

Date	Mintage	F	VF	XF	Unc	BU
1972(a)	20,000,000	—	0.35	0.50	1.25	1.50
1974(a)	3,000,000	—	0.50	0.75	1.50	1.75
1975(a)	9,000,000	—	0.25	0.40	1.00	1.25
1976(a)	6,002,000	—	0.35	0.50	1.25	1.50
1977(a)	4,832,000	—	0.35	0.50	1.25	1.50
1978(a)	7,200,000	—	0.35	0.50	1.25	1.50
1979(a)	4,200,000	—	0.35	0.50	1.25	1.50
1980(a)	7,200,000	—	0.35	0.50	1.25	1.50
1981(a)	6,000,000	—	0.35	0.50	1.25	1.50
1982(a)	12,000,000	—	0.35	0.50	1.25	1.50
1984(a)	25,500,000	—	0.35	0.50	1.25	1.50
1985(a)	4,120,000	—	0.35	0.50	1.25	1.50
1986(a)	—	—	0.35	0.50	1.25	1.50
1987(a)	10,000,000	—	0.35	0.50	1.25	1.50
1989(a)	17,000,000	—	0.35	0.50	1.25	1.50
1990(a)	7,500,000	—	0.35	0.50	1.25	1.50
1991(a)	5,600,000	—	0.35	0.50	1.25	1.50
1992(a)	7,000,000	—	0.35	0.50	1.25	1.50
1993(a)	2,800,000	—	0.35	0.50	1.25	1.50
1995(a)	40,000,000	—	0.35	0.50	1.25	1.50
1996(a)	20,500,000	—	0.35	0.50	1.25	1.50
1997(a)	25,800,000	—	0.35	0.50	1.25	1.50
1999(a)	25,200,000	—	0.35	0.50	1.25	1.50
2000(a)	14,400,000	—	0.35	0.50	1.25	1.50

KM# 4   100 FRANCS
7.0700 g., Nickel, 26 mm. **Obv:** Taku - Ashanti gold weight **Rev:** Value within flowers

Date	Mintage	F	VF	XF	Unc	BU
1967(a)	—	—	0.75	1.00	2.50	3.00
1968(a)	25,000,000	—	0.75	1.00	2.50	3.00
1969(a)	25,000,000	—	0.75	1.00	2.50	3.00
1970(a)	4,510,000	—	0.80	1.50	3.50	5.00
1971(a)	12,000,000	—	0.50	0.75	1.85	2.25
1972(a)	5,000,000	—	0.60	0.85	2.00	2.50
1973(a)	5,000,000	—	0.60	0.85	2.00	2.50
1974(a)	8,500,000	—	0.60	0.75	1.85	2.25
1975(a)	16,000,000	—	0.60	0.75	1.85	2.25
1976(a)	11,575,000	—	0.60	0.75	1.85	2.25
1977(a)	6,200,000	—	0.60	0.75	1.85	2.25
1978(a)	12,000,000	—	0.60	0.75	1.85	2.25
1979(a)	12,400,000	—	0.60	0.85	2.00	2.50
1980(a)	13,000,000	—	0.60	0.75	2.00	2.50
1981(a)	8,000,000	—	0.60	0.75	2.00	2.50

Date	Mintage	F	VF	XF	Unc	BU
1982(a)	18,000,000	—	0.60	0.75	2.00	2.50
1984(a)	2,500,000	—	0.65	0.85	2.25	2.75
1985(a)	1,460,000	—	0.65	0.85	2.25	2.75
1987(a)	9,000,000	—	0.65	0.85	2.25	2.75
1989(a)	16,500,000	—	0.65	0.85	2.25	2.75
1990(a)	6,500,000	—	0.65	0.85	2.25	2.75
1991(a)	1,000,000	—	0.65	0.85	2.25	2.75
1992(a)	4,000,000	—	0.65	0.85	2.25	2.75
1996(a)	24,000,000	—	0.65	0.85	2.25	2.75
1997(a)	69,000,000	—	0.65	0.85	2.25	2.75
2000(a)	1,800,000	—	0.60	0.85	2.25	2.75

KM# 13   250 FRANCS
Bi-Metallic Brass center in Copper-Nickel ring **Obv:** Map on globe, Taku symbol at top **Rev:** Stalks behind denomination, circle surrounds

Date	Mintage	F	VF	XF	Unc	BU
1992(a)	9,000,000	—	1.75	2.75	7.00	8.00
1993(a)	10,000,000	—	1.75	2.75	7.00	8.00
1996(a)	7,500,000	—	2.00	3.00	8.00	9.00

KM# 7   500 FRANCS
25.0000 g., 0.9000 Silver 0.7234 oz. ASW **Subject:** 10th Anniversary of Monetary Union **Obv:** Gold weight in the shape of a fish, "Taku", a symbol of prosperity **Rev:** Shields of seven states and script form circle around denomination and date

Date	Mintage	F	VF	XF	Unc	BU
1972(a) Prooflike	2,000	—	—	—	—	75.00
1972(a)	100,000	—	—	20.00	40.00	45.00

KM# 11   5000 FRANCS
24.9500 g., 0.9000 Silver 0.7219 oz. ASW **Subject:** 20th Anniversary of Monetary Union **Obv:** Gold weight in the shape of a fish, "Taku", a symbol of prosperity **Rev:** Six interlaced birds symbolizing states

Date	Mintage	F	VF	XF	Unc	BU
1982(a)	200,000	—	—	18.00	45.00	65.00

KM# 12   5000 FRANCS
14.4900 g., 0.9000 Gold 0.4193 oz. AGW **Subject:** 20th Anniversary of Monetary Union **Obv:** Gold weight in the shape of a fish, "Taku", a symbol of prosperity **Rev:** Six interlaced birds symbolizing states

Date	Mintage	F	VF	XF	Unc	BU
1982(a)	—	—	—	—	475	625

ESSAIS

KM#	Date	Mintage	Identification	Issue Price	Mkt Val
E1	1959(a)	—	10 Francs. Aluminum-Bronze. KM1.	—	17.00
E2	1960(a)	—	5 Francs. Aluminum-Bronze. KM2.	—	15.00
E3	1961(a)	—	Franc. Aluminum. KM3.	—	15.00
E4	1967(a)	1,600	100 Francs. Nickel. KM4.	—	20.00
E4a	1967(a)	100	100 Francs. Silver. KM4.	—	110
E4b	1967(a)	21	100 Francs. Gold. KM4.	—	850
E5	1970(a)	1,450	25 Francs. Aluminum-Bronze. KM5.	—	17.00
E6	1972(a)	1,750	50 Francs. Copper-Nickel. KM6.	—	15.00
E6a	1972(a)	120	50 Francs. Silver. KM6.	—	90.00
E6b	1972(a)	17	50 Francs. Gold. KM6.	—	800
E7	1972(a)	1,300	100 Francs. Silver. KM7.	—	75.00
E8	1976(a)	1,900	Franc. Steel. KM8.	—	15.00
E9	1980(a)	3,000	25 Francs. Aluminum-Bronze. Figure filling tube, date above. KM9.	—	50.00
E10	1980(a)	5	25 Francs. Gold.	—	1,800
E11	1980(a)	1,700	500 Francs.	—	40.00
E12	1981(a)	1,950	10 Francs. Brass. KM10.	—	12.00
E13	1982(a)	1,700	5000 Francs. Silver. KM11.	—	95.00
E14	1982(a)	12	5000 Francs. Gold. KM11.	—	1,500

"FDC" SETS

KM#	Date	Mintage	Identification	Issue Price	Mkt Val
SS1	1968(a) (3)	—	KM1a, 2a, 4	—	9.50

YEMEN

One of the oldest centers of civilization in the Middle East, Yemen was once part of the Minaean Kingdom and of the ancient Kingdom of Sheba, after which it was captured successively by Egyptians, Ethiopians and Romans. It was converted to Islam in 628 A.D. and administered as a caliphate until 1538, when it came under Ottoman occupation in 1849. The second Ottoman occupation which began in 1872 was maintained until 1918 when autonomy was achieved through revolution.

TITLE

المملكة المتوكلية اليمنية

al-Mamlaka(t) al-Mutawakkiliya(t) al-Yamaniya(t)

RULER
Ottoman, until 1625

QASIMID IMĀMS
al-Mansur Muhammad bin Yahya,
(Imam Mansur) AH1307-1322/1890-1904AD
al Hadi al-Hasan bin Yahya
(Counter Imam, in Sa'da) AH1322/1904AD
al-Mutawakkil Yahya bin Muhammad
(Imam Yahya) AH1322-1367/1904-1948AD
al-Nasir Ahmad bin Yahya,
(Imam Ahmad) AH1367-1382/
1948-1962AD
al-Badr Muhammad bin Ahmad,
(Imam Badr) AH1382-1388/
1962-1968AD (mostly in exile)

MINT NAME

صنعاء

San'a

MONETARY SYSTEM
After Accession of Iman Yahya
AH1322/1904AD
1 Zalat = 1/160 Riyal
2 Zalat = 1 Halala = 1/80 Riyal
2 Halala = 1 Buqsha = 1/40 Riyal
40 Buqsha = 1 Riyal
NOTE: The Riyal was called an IMADI (RIYAL) during the reign of Imam Yahya "Imadi" honorific name for Yahyawi and an AHMADI (RIYAL) during the reign of Imam Ahmad. The 1 Zalat, Y#2.1, D1, A3, A4 and all Imam Yahya gold strikes except Y#F10, bear no indication of value. Many of the Mutawakkilite coins after AH1322/1904AD bear the denomination expressed as fraction of the Riyal as follows.

BRONZE and ALUMINUM

Thumn ushr = 1/80 Riyal = 1/2 Buqsha = 1 Halala
Rub ushr = 1/40 Riyal = 1 Buqsha
Nisf ushr = 1/20 Riyal = 2 Buqsha = 1/2 Bawlah
Nisf thumn = 1/16 Riyal = 2-1/2 Buqsha
Ushr = 1/10 Riyal = 4 Buqsha = 1 Bawlah
Thumn = 1/8 Riyal = 5 Buqsha
Rub = 1/4 Riyal = 10 Buqsha
Nisf = 1/2 Riyal = 20 Buqsha
1 Riyal (Imadi, Ahmadi) = 40 Buqsha

DATING

All coins of Imam Yahya have accession date AH1322 on obverse and actual date of issue on reverse. All coins of Imam Ahmad bear accession date AH1367 on obverse and actual date on reverse.

If not otherwise noted, all coins of Imam Yahya and Imam Ahad as well as the early issues of the Republic (Y#20 through Y#A25 and Y#32), were struck at the mint in Sana'a. The Sana'a Mint was essentially a medieval mint, using hand-cut dies and crudely machined blanks. There is a large amount of variation from one die to the next in arrangement of legends and ornaments, form of crescents, number of stars, size of the circle, etc., and literally hundreds of subtypes could be identified. Types are divided only when there are changes in the inscriptions, or major variations in the basic type, such as the presence or absence of "Rabb al-Alamin" in the legend or the position of the word *Sana* (= year) in relation to the year.

NOTE: All "ZALAT" coins are without mint name or denomination.

KINGDOM

al-Mansur Muhammad bin Yahya (Imam Mansur)
AH1307-1322 / 1890-1904AD

HAMMERED COINAGE

KM# 403 HARF
Bronze **Note:** Similar to 1 Kabir, KM#410.

Date	Mintage	Good	VG	F	VF	XF
AH1320	—	—	—	—	—	—

KM# 410 KABIR
Silver, 15-16 mm. **Obv:** Similar to KM#409 **Rev:** "Allah/Abd/" date, divided by ornament, with four circular segments **Note:** Weight varies: 0.60-1.00 gram. Size varies. Varieties with three and four stars on reverse exist. Varieties of planchet thickness exist.

Date	Mintage	Good	VG	F	VF	XF
AH1319	—	15.00	30.00	50.00	150	—
AH1320	—	15.00	30.00	50.00	150	—
AH1321	—	15.00	30.00	50.00	150	—

al-Hadi al-Hasan
AH1322 / 1904AD

MILLED COINAGE

Y# C1 HALALA
1.9300 g., Bronze **Obv:** Al-Hasan/bin Yahya/Sana 1322 **Rev:** Al-Hadi/Li-din Allah

Date	Mintage	Good	VG	F	VF	XF
AH1322	—	—	—	—	—	—

al-Mutawakkil Yahya bin Muhammad (Imam Yahya)
AH1322-1367 / 1904-1948AD

MILLED COINAGE

Y# 1.1 ZALAT
Bronze **Obv:** Inscription in three lines above accession date AH1322 **Edge:** Plain **Note:** Weight varies: 0.90-1.60 grams. Obverse varieties with no stars or two stars. Reverse with eight stars. Size of inner circle varies, various planchet thicknesses.

Date	Mintage	Good	VG	F	VF	XF
AH1341	—	15.00	30.00	100	160	—
AH1342	—	5.00	12.00	30.00	50.00	—
AH1343	—	4.00	10.00	20.00	40.00	—

Note: 1343 also known with seven stars

Date	Mintage	Good	VG	F	VF	XF
AH1344	—	5.00	10.00	30.00	50.00	—

Note: 1344 also exists with traces of reeded edges

Date	Mintage	Good	VG	F	VF	XF
AH1345	—	10.00	25.00	75.00	125	—
AH1346	—	4.00	10.00	20.00	40.00	—

Y# 1.2 ZALAT
Bronze **Obv:** Inscription in two lines above accession date AH1322

Date	Mintage	Good	VG	F	VF	XF
AH1342	—	5.00	12.00	30.00	50.00	—

Note: Obverse varieties with 1, 2, and 4 stars, and reverse with 8, 11, 12, 13, 14, 15, 16, 17, 20, and 22 stars exist; Some specimens show traces of reeded edges; Various planchet thicknesses exist

Y# 1.4 ZALAT
Bronze **Obv:** Crescent below accession date AH1322

Date	Mintage	Good	VG	F	VF	XF
AH1342	—	300	425	650	1,000	—

Note: Varieties exist with 11, 14, 15, 16, and 17 stars on reverse and with 1, 2, and 4 stars on obverse; Various planchet thicknesses

Y# 1.7 ZALAT
Bronze **Obv:** Inscription in two lines above accession date AH1322 **Rev:** Date in margin at bottom

Date	Mintage	Good	VG	F	VF	XF
AH1342 Rare	—	—	—	—	—	—

Note: Obverse varieties with 1 and 2 stars, Reverse with 11 stars, various planchet thicknesses

Y# 1.8 ZALAT
Bronze **Obv:** Inscription in three lines above accession date AH1322

Date	Mintage	Good	VG	F	VF	XF
AH1344	—	—	—	—	—	—

Y# B1 ZALAT
Bronze **Obv:** Inscription in two lines above accession date AH1322 **Note:** Probably struck at Shaharah about 1925. Dies were reportedly prepared in Italy. For silver strikes, see Y#A4.

Date	Mintage	Good	VG	F	VF	XF
NDAH1322(ca.1925)	—	30.00	60.00	125	200	—

Note: This issue is believed to be a pattern

Date	Mintage	Good	VG	F	VF	XF
ND(ca.1925)	—	30.00	60.00	125	200	—

Note: Possibly a pattern

Y# 2.2 1/80 RIYAL (1/2 Buqsha)
Bronze **Obv:** Crescent below accession date AH1322 **Note:** Thin flan, 1.50-3.00 grams. The number and arrangement of stars and the size of the circle on the reverse vary as well as the exact arrangement of the legends which sometimes vary within each year. The reverse exists with 10, 12, 14, 20, 22, 24, 28, and 34 stars. Obverse varieties with 1, 2, 3 or 4 stars and without stars. Accession date: AH(1)322 or 1322. Struck at Shaharah.

Date	Mintage	Good	VG	F	VF	XF
AH1330	—	20.00	35.00	60.00	100	—
AH1331	—	20.00	35.00	75.00	150	—
AH1332	—	10.00	15.00	25.00	40.00	—
AH1333	—	10.00	15.00	25.00	40.00	—
AH1337	—	10.00	15.00	25.00	40.00	—
AH1338	—	10.00	15.00	25.00	40.00	—
AH1339	—	10.00	15.00	25.00	40.00	—

Y# D1 1/80 RIYAL (1/2 Buqsha)
Bronze **Obv:** Crescent below accession date AH1322 **Obv. Insc.:** Rabb al-Alamin **Rev:** Toughra **Note:** Without denomination or mint name.

Date	Mintage	Good	VG	F	VF	XF
ND(ca.1911) Rare;	—	—	—	—	—	—
Accessional date only						

Y# 2.1 1/80 RIYAL (1/2 Buqsha)
Bronze **Note:** Accession date AH1322 above crescent on obverse and within crescent on reverse.

Date	Mintage	Good	VG	F	VF	XF
ND(ca.1911)	—	12.50	25.00	50.00	85.00	—

Note: Probably struck at Shaharah

Y# 2.3 1/80 RIYAL (1/2 Buqsha)
Bronze **Rev:** "Duriba Bi Sana'a" added

Date	Mintage	Good	VG	F	VF	XF
AH1340	—	10.00	20.00	40.00	75.00	—

Note: AH1340 exists with 4 and 8 stars on reverse

Date	Mintage	Good	VG	F	VF	XF
AH1341	—	10.00	20.00	40.00	75.00	—

Note: AH1341 exists with 4 stars on reverse

Y# 2.4 1/80 RIYAL (1/2 Buqsha)
Bronze **Obv:** Without "Rabb al-Alamin" with crescent below accession date AH1322 **Note:** Weight and diameter varies.

Date	Mintage	Good	VG	F	VF	XF
AH1341	—	12.00	25.00	50.00	85.00	—

Note: AH1341 exists with 4 stars on reverse

Date	Mintage	Good	VG	F	VF	XF
AH1342	—	12.00	25.00	50.00	85.00	—

Note: AH1342 coins exist with 4 and 6 stars on reverse

Y# 2.5 1/80 RIYAL (1/2 Buqsha)
Bronze (Red To Yellow) **Obv:** Crescent below accession date AH1332 **Obv. Insc.:** Rabb al-alamin **Rev:** "Sana" above date **Note:** Number and arrangement of stars on reverse (4, 5, 6, 7, or 8) as well as the size of the inner circle vary. Varieties exist in the form of crescent and arrangement of legends and planchet thicknesses.

Date	Mintage	Good	VG	F	VF	XF
AH1339	—	7.00	12.00	25.00	40.00	—
AH1341	—	7.00	12.00	25.00	40.00	—
AH1342	—	2.00	5.00	12.00	20.00	—
AH1343	—	2.00	5.00	12.00	20.00	—
AH1344	—	2.00	5.00	12.00	20.00	—
AH1345	—	1.50	4.00	8.00	15.00	—
AH1346	—	1.50	3.00	6.00	12.00	—

Note: Some examples of AH1346 show the 6 re-engraved over low I

Date	Mintage	Good	VG	F	VF	XF
AH1347	—	1.50	4.00	8.00	15.00	—
AH1348	—	1.50	4.00	8.00	15.00	—
AH1349	—	1.50	4.00	8.00	15.00	—
AH1350	—	1.50	4.00	8.00	15.00	—
AH135x	—	1.50	4.00	8.00	15.00	—
AH1351	—	2.00	6.00	12.00	20.00	—
AH1352	—	2.00	6.00	12.00	20.00	—
AH1353	—	2.00	6.00	12.00	20.00	—
AH1358	—	—	—	—	—	—

Note: Reported, not confirmed

Date	Mintage	Good	VG	F	VF	XF
AH1359	—	2.50	6.00	12.00	20.00	—

Date	Mintage	Good	VG	F	VF	XF
AH1360	—	2.50	4.00	8.00	15.00	—
AH1361	—	4.00	8.00	15.00	25.00	—

Y# 2.6 1/80 RIYAL (1/2 Buqsha)
3.0000 g., Bronze **Rev:** "Sana" below date **Note:** Thin flan. Struck at Shaharah.

Date	Mintage	Good	VG	F	VF	XF
AH1333	—	80.00	100	200	300	—

Y# 2.7 1/80 RIYAL (1/2 Buqsha)
Bronze **Note:** Thick flan. Weight varies: 4-5.4 grams. Varieties with 10 and 14 stars on reverse. Obverse with 1, 2, 3, 4, or no stars. Varieties of legend distribution. Some coins occur with light silver wash. Struck at Shaharah.

Date	Mintage	Good	VG	F	VF	XF
AH1332	—	10.00	15.00	25.00	40.00	—
AH1333	—	10.00	15.00	25.00	40.00	—
AH1338	—	10.00	15.00	25.00	40.00	—

Y# 2.8 1/80 RIYAL (1/2 Buqsha)
Bronze **Note:** Mule, two obverses.

Date	Mintage	Good	VG	F	VF	XF
ND(ca.1911-21)	—	20.00	30.00	60.00	100	—

Y# A3 1/40 RIYAL (1 Buqsha)
Billon Silver **Note:** Weight varies: 0.65-1.25 grams. Size varies: 15-16 mm. Accession date: AH1322.

Date	Mintage	VG	F	VF	XF	Unc
ND(ca.1911-21)	—	275	550	1,100	1,650	—

Note: Minted at Qaflat Idhar, without mint name or denomination

Y# 3.1 1/40 RIYAL (1 Buqsha)
Bronze **Obv:** Without "Rabb al-Alamin", with crescent below accession date AH1322 **Rev:** "Sana" below date

Date	Mintage	VG	F	VF	XF	Unc
AH1341	—	10.00	20.00	40.00	80.00	—

Note: Varieties of borders, arrangement of legends, and thickness of planchets exist

Y# 3.2 1/40 RIYAL (1 Buqsha)
Bronze (Red To Yellow) **Obv:** Crescent below accession date AH1322 **Obv. Insc.:** Rabb al-Alamin **Rev:** "Sana" above date, small "Sana'a" and three leaf ornaments plus star in border legend

Date	Mintage	VG	F	VF	XF	Unc
AH1342	—	4.00	10.00	20.00	60.00	—

Note: AH1342 exists with 4 leaf ornaments and without star in border legend

AH13442	—	65.00	125	—	—	—
AH1343	—	4.00	10.00	20.00	60.00	—
AH1344	—	15.00	30.00	50.00	75.00	—

Y# 3.3 1/40 RIYAL (1 Buqsha)
Bronze (Red To Yellow) **Obv:** Crescent below accession date AH1322 **Rev:** Large "Sana'a" in legend **Note:** Varieties in arrangement of legends, ornaments, form of the crescent, and size of the circle on reverse exist; weight varies.

Date	Mintage	VG	F	VF	XF	Unc
AH1344	—	12.00	20.00	35.00	100	—
AH1345	—	12.00	20.00	35.00	100	—
AH1349	—	1.50	3.50	10.00	25.00	—

Date	Mintage	VG	F	VF	XF	Unc
AH1353	—	—	—	—	—	—

Note: Reported, not confirmed

AH1358	—	2.00	4.00	10.00	25.00	—
AH1359	—	2.00	4.00	10.00	25.00	—
AH1360	—	2.00	4.00	10.00	25.00	—
AH1361/0	—	10.00	20.00	50.00	75.00	—
AH1362/0	—	2.50	5.00	10.00	35.00	—
AH1362	—	1.50	3.50	10.00	30.00	—
AH1363	—	1.50	5.00	12.00	35.00	—
AH1364	—	1.50	5.00	12.00	35.00	—
AH1365/4	—	2.25	5.00	12.00	35.00	—
AH1365	—	2.50	5.00	12.00	35.00	—
AH1366	—	1.50	3.50	12.00	30.00	—
AH1366/x	—	2.50	5.00	12.00	35.00	—
AH1367	—	10.00	20.00	50.00	75.00	—

Y# A4 1/20 IMADI RIYAL
Silver **Obv:** Inscription in two lines above

Date	Mintage	VG	F	VF	XF	Unc
ND(1911-21)	—	60.00	120	250	400	—

Note: Dated accessionally on obverse without mint name or denomination; Probably struck at Shaharah about 1925; dies were reportedly prepared in Italy; Strikes in nickel reported; See Y#B1; This issue is believed to be a pattern

Y# B4 1/20 IMADI RIYAL
Silver **Obv:** Crescent below accession date AH1322 **Rev:** Without "Sana"

Date	Mintage	VG	F	VF	XF	Unc
AH1337 Rare	—	—	—	—	—	—

Note: Three stars on reverse

Y# 4.1 1/20 IMADI RIYAL
Silver **Obv:** Without "Rabb al-Alamin", with crescent below accession date AH1322 **Note:** Varieties in arrangement of legends, size of circle, and with 3 and 4 stars on reverse exist. Variety of Y#4 dated with 2 digits AH(13)22 of the accessional year are considered local contemporary counterfeits by leading authorities. They are reported having been produced by the Zaraing tribe at Bait Al-Faqih.

Date	Mintage	VG	F	VF	XF	Unc
AH1337	—	40.00	80.00	150	250	—
AH1338 Rare	—	—	—	—	—	—
AH1339	—	40.00	80.00	150	250	—

Note: Some strikes show accessional year as 322 only

AH1340	—	20.00	30.00	60.00	100	—

Note: Some strikes show accessional year as 322 only

AH1342	—	5.00	12.00	30.00	60.00	—
AH1343	—	4.00	10.00	25.00	50.00	—
AH1344	—	4.00	10.00	25.00	50.00	—
AH1345	—	4.00	10.00	25.00	50.00	—
AH1345/2	—	4.00	10.00	25.00	50.00	—
AH1347	—	5.00	12.00	30.00	60.00	—
AH1348	—	4.00	10.00	25.00	50.00	—
AH1349	—	4.00	10.00	25.00	50.00	—
AH1350	—	4.00	12.00	30.00	60.00	—
AH1351	—	5.00	15.00	35.00	75.00	—
AH1352	—	4.00	12.00	30.00	60.00	—
AH1353	—	4.00	12.00	30.00	60.00	—
AH1358	—	3.00	8.00	20.00	40.00	—
AH1359	—	3.00	8.00	20.00	40.00	—
AH1362/58	—	5.00	15.00	30.00	60.00	—
AH1362/59	—	5.00	15.00	30.00	60.00	—
AH1363	—	4.00	10.00	30.00	60.00	—
AH1364/46	—	3.00	8.00	20.00	40.00	—
AH1364	—	3.00	8.00	20.00	40.00	—
AHx364	—	3.00	8.00	20.00	40.00	—
AH1365	—	3.00	10.00	25.00	50.00	—
AH1366/44	—	4.00	12.00	30.00	60.00	—
AH1366	—	4.00	12.00	30.00	60.00	—

Y# 4.4 1/20 IMADI RIYAL
Silver **Rev:** Border legend shifted to left **Note:** Accession date AH1322.

Date	Mintage	VG	F	VF	XF	Unc
AH1340 Rare	—	—	—	—	—	—

Note: Three stars on reverse

Y# 4.2 1/20 IMADI RIYAL
Silver **Obv:** Crescent **Rev:** "Sana" below date, normal legend position **Note:** Four stars on reverse.

Date	Mintage	VG	F	VF	XF	Unc
AH1341	—	40.00	80.00	150	250	—
AHx341	—	40.00	80.00	150	250	—

Y# 5.1 1/10 IMADI RIYAL
Silver **Obv:** Crescent below accession date AH1322 **Obv. Insc.:** Rabb al-Alamin **Rev:** Without "Sana"

Date	Mintage	VG	F	VF	XF	Unc
AH1337	—	30.00	60.00	100	175	—

Note: Reverse varieties with 3, 4, and 5 stars. Size of circle and form of crescent varies

Y# 5.2 1/10 IMADI RIYAL
Silver **Obv:** Without "Rabb al-Alamin", with crescent below accession date AH1322

Date	Mintage	VG	F	VF	XF	Unc
AH1339	—	20.00	40.00	75.00	150	—

Note: Some AH1339 strikes show accession date as 322

AH1340	—	20.00	40.00	75.00	150	—

Note: AH1340 also exists with three stars, others with six stars on reverse

AH1341	—	20.00	40.00	75.00	150	—
AH1348	—	100	150	350	500	—

Y# 5.3 1/10 IMADI RIYAL
Silver **Obv:** Crescent below accession date AH1322 **Rev:** "Sana" above date **Note:** Varieties with three and six stars on the reverse exist.

Date	Mintage	VG	F	VF	XF	Unc
AH1341	—	20.00	40.00	75.00	150	—
AH1342	—	20.00	40.00	75.00	150	—

Y# 5.5 1/10 IMADI RIYAL
Silver **Obv:** Without "Rabb al-Alamin" **Rev:** "Sana" above date **Note:** Form of crescent, size of circle on reverse, and arrangement of legends vary. Normal reverse contains 6 stars though varieties with 7, 8, 9, 10, and 12 stars on reverse exist. Some earlier dates show varying amounts of edge reeding.

Date	Mintage	VG	F	VF	XF	Unc
AH1342	—	4.00	10.00	25.00	50.00	—
AH1343	—	4.00	10.00	25.00	50.00	—
AH1344	—	3.00	8.00	20.00	40.00	—
AH1345	—	3.00	8.00	20.00	40.00	—
AH1347	—	3.00	8.00	20.00	40.00	—
AH1348	—	3.00	8.00	20.00	35.00	—
AH1349	—	3.00	6.00	15.00	30.00	—
AH1350	—	—	—	—	—	—

Note: Reported, not confirmed

AH1351	—	4.00	10.00	25.00	40.00	—
AH1352	—	4.00	10.00	25.00	40.00	—
AH1358/49	—	3.00	8.00	15.00	30.00	—
AH1358	—	3.00	8.00	15.00	30.00	—
AH1359/3	—	3.00	8.00	15.00	30.00	—
AH1359/49	—	3.00	8.00	15.00	30.00	—
AH1362/44	—	4.00	10.00	25.00	40.00	—
AH1362/59	—	4.00	10.00	25.00	40.00	—
AH1363	—	3.00	8.00	25.00	45.00	—
AH1364/43	—	3.00	8.00	20.00	40.00	—
AH1364/3	—	3.00	8.00	25.00	45.00	—
AH1364/52	—	3.00	8.00	25.00	45.00	—
AH1364	—	3.00	8.00	15.00	35.00	—
AH1365	—	3.00	8.00	15.00	35.00	—

Date	Mintage	VG	F	VF	XF	Unc
AH1366/5	—	3.00	10.00	20.00	50.00	—
AH1366/5x	—	3.00	10.00	20.00	50.00	—

Y# 5.4 1/10 IMADI RIYAL
Silver **Obv:** Crescent below accession date AH1322
Obv. Insc.: Rabb al-Alamin **Rev:** "Sana" above date
Note: Varieties with 8, 9, and 10 stars on reverse exist.

Date	Mintage	VG	F	VF	XF	Unc
AH1342	—	20.00	40.00	75.00	150	—

Y# 8 1/8 IMADI RIYAL
Silver **Obv:** One or no stars in crescent below accession date
AH1322 **Rev:** "Thumn" in place of "Ushr" below date, 6 stars

Date	Mintage	VG	F	VF	XF	Unc
AH1339	—	325	550	1,100	1,650	—

Y# 6.1 1/4 IMADI RIYAL
Silver **Obv:** Without "Rabb al-Alamin", with crescent below
accession date AH1322 **Rev:** "Sana" below date

Date	Mintage	VG	F	VF	XF	Unc
AH1341	—	20.00	45.00	75.00	150	—
Note: AH1341 with 4 stars on reverse						
AH1342	—	25.00	50.00	100	175	—
Note: AH1342 with 4 stars on reverse and 2 stars flanking date						

Y# 6.2 1/4 IMADI RIYAL
Silver **Obv:** Crescent below accession date AH1322
Obv. Insc.: Rabb al-Alamin **Rev:** "Sana" above date, two stars
and two ornaments in border

Date	Mintage	VG	F	VF	XF	Unc
AH1342	—	70.00	100	300	450	—

Y# 6.5 1/4 IMADI RIYAL
Silver **Obv:** Crescent below accession date AH1322 **Rev:** "Sana"
below date, eight stars in border

Date	Mintage	VG	F	VF	XF	Unc
AH1342	—	100	150	300	500	—

Y# 6.6 1/4 IMADI RIYAL
Silver **Obv:** Crescent below accession date AH1322 **Rev:** "Sana"
below date, one star in border

Date	Mintage	VG	F	VF	XF	Unc
AH1342	—	100	150	300	500	—
Note: Obverse varieties with one and two stars exist						

Y# 10 1/4 IMADI RIYAL
Silver **Obv:** Crescent below accession date AH1322
Rev: Redesigned, date moved to margin **Edge:** Plain, traces of
reeding to full reeding known **Note:** The size of the reverse inner
circle varies, 12 to 16 crescents on obverse.

Date	Mintage	VG	F	VF	XF	Unc
AH1342	—	20.00	40.00	75.00	150	—
AH1343	—	20.00	60.00	100	175	—

Date	Mintage	VG	F	VF	XF	Unc
AH1344	—	4.25	10.00	25.00	75.00	—
AH1345	—	4.25	10.00	25.00	60.00	—
AH1349	—					
Note: Reported, not confirmed						
AH1351	—	20.00	30.00	50.00	100	—
AH1352	—	5.00	12.00	20.00	40.00	—
AH1358	—	3.50	5.50	15.00	35.00	—
AH1359	—	3.50	5.50	15.00	35.00	—
AH1363	—	3.50	8.00	20.00	40.00	—
AH1364/3	—	4.25	8.00	20.00	40.00	—
AH1364	—	3.50	5.00	20.00	40.00	—
AH1365/4	—	4.25	6.00	20.00	40.00	—
AH1365	—	3.50	5.00	20.00	40.00	—
AH1366	—	3.50	5.00	20.00	40.00	—

Y# 7 IMADI RIYAL
28.0700 g., Silver **Obv:** Double crescent below accession date
AH1322 **Note:** Several die varieties exist, possibly struck over a
number of years with frozen date AH1344. Edge varieties exist.

Date	Mintage	VG	F	VF	XF	Unc
AH1342	—					
Note: Reported, not confirmed						
AH1344	—	12.00	15.00	18.00	28.00	40.00
Note: Copper trial strikes dated AH1344 reported						
AH1365 Two known	—					2,000

GOLD PRESENTATION COINAGE

All Imam Yahya gold strikes are considered presentation issues which were based on the gold standard of the
Turkish Lira.

Y# A10 1/8 LIRA (1/40 Riyal)
0.9200 g., Gold **Note:** Accession date: AH1322.

Date	Mintage	VG	F	VF	XF	Unc
AH(13)44	—	—	—	—	1,350	—

Y# B10 1/4 LIRA (1/20 Riyal)
1.7000 g., Gold **Note:** Accession date: AH1322.

Date	Mintage	VG	F	VF	XF	Unc
AH(13)44	—	—	—	—	1,500	—

Y# C10 1/2 LIRA (1/10 Riyal)
3.3100 g., Gold **Note:** Accession date: AH1322.

Date	Mintage	VG	F	VF	XF	Unc
AH(13)44	—	—	—	—	1,650	—

Y# D10 LIRA (1/5 Riyal)
6.8000 g., Gold **Obv:** Crescent below accession date AH1322

Date	Mintage	VG	F	VF	XF	Unc
AH(13)44	—	—	—	—	2,000	—

Y# E10 2-1/2 LIRA (1/2 Riyal)
17.7000 g., Gold **Obv:** Crescent below accession date AH1322

Date	Mintage	VG	F	VF	XF	Unc
AH(13)44	—	—	—	—	3,500	—

Y# K10 2-1/2 LIRA (1/2 Riyal)
Gold **Note:** Weight varies: 17.44-17.82 grams. Accession date:
AH1322.

Date	Mintage	VG	F	VF	XF	Unc
AH1352	—	—	—	—	2,500	—

Y# F10 5 LIRA (1 Riyal)
35.5000 g., Gold **Note:** Similar to 1 Imadi Riyal, Y#7.

Date	Mintage	VG	F	VF	XF	Unc
AH1344 Rare	—					
Note: Dies of AH1344 Riyal silver and gold strikes are not identical						

Y# P10 5 LIRA (1 Riyal)
34.2400 g., Gold **Note:** Thin planchet strike of 10 Lira (2 Riyal),
Y#N10.

Date	Mintage	VG	F	VF	XF	Unc
AH1358 2 known	—	—	—	—	3,250	—

Y# M10 10 LIRA (2 Riyal)
69.8300 g., Gold **Obv:** Similar to Gold 2-1/2 Lira, Y#K10
Note: Accession date: AH1322.

Date	Mintage	VG	F	VF	XF	Unc
AH1352	—	—	—	—	6,500	—

Y# N10 10 LIRA (2 Riyal)
69.8300 g., Gold **Obv:** Crescent below accession date AH1322
Rev: Two crossed flags in center **Rev. Leg.:** "Duriba bi-dar al-
khilafa al-mutawakkiliya bi Sana'a 'asimat al-Yamam sana 1358"

Date	Mintage	VG	F	VF	XF	Unc
AH1358 4 known	—	—	—	—	5,500	—

al-Nasir Ahmad bin Yahya
(Imam Ahmad)
AH1367-1382 / 1948-1962AD

MILLED COINAGE

Y# 11.1 1/80 RIYAL (1 Halala = 1/2 Buqsha)
Bronze (Red To Yellow) **Obv:** Crescent below accession date
AH1367 which may vary as 1367/1267, 1367/1777, etc. **Rev:** "Sana"
above date **Note:** There is a variation in the number of stars on
reverse, as follows: AH1368 - 8 stars; AH1371-74 and some AH1381
(not overdate) - 7 stars; AH1375-81 including some AH1381, some
AH1382, and all AH1381 overdates - 8 stars. Varieties of
arrangement of legends, form of crescent, and size of circle on
reverse exist. Some earlier dates exist on thinner planchets.

Date	Mintage	VG	F	VF	XF	Unc
AH1368	—	1.00	2.00	5.00	10.00	—
AH1371	—	0.30	1.00	3.00	8.00	—
AH1372	—	0.30	1.00	3.00	8.00	—
AH1373	—	0.30	0.60	1.00	3.00	—
AH1374	—	0.30	1.00	3.00	8.00	—
AH1275 Error for 1375	—	1.00	2.00	6.00	12.00	—
AH1375						
AH1376						
AH1376/86 Error						
AH1278 Error for 1378	—	1.00	2.00	6.00	12.00	—
AH1378						
AHx379	—	1.00	2.00	6.00	12.00	—

Date	Mintage	VG	F	VF	XF	Unc
AH1379	—	0.50	1.00	2.50	5.00	
AH1380/1	—	1.00	2.00	6.00	12.00	
AH1380/79	—	0.50	1.00	2.50	5.00	
AH1380/9	—	0.50	1.00	2.50	5.00	
AH1380	—	0.50	1.00	2.50	5.00	
AH1381/80/79	—	0.40	0.85	1.50	2.50	
AH1381/79	—	0.40	0.85	1.50	2.50	
AH1381	—	0.20	0.40	0.75	1.25	
AH1382	—	5.00	10.00	15.00	20.00	

Y# 11.2   1/80 RIYAL (1 Halala = 1/2 Buqsha)
Bronze Rev: Without "Sana"

Date	Mintage	VG	F	VF	XF	Unc
AH1373 Rare	—	—	—	—	—	

Y# 11a   1/80 RIYAL (1 Halala = 1/2 Buqsha)
Aluminum Obv: Crescent below accession date AH1367
Rev: "Sana" above date Note: AH1374 and some AH1380 have 7 stars, the rest have 8 stars on reverse. Dies of 1/80 Riyal, Y#11.1, were used.

Date	Mintage	VG	F	VF	XF	Unc
AH1374	—	0.25	1.00	2.50	5.00	
AH1375	—	0.75	2.50	5.50	10.00	
AH1376	—	0.25	1.50	4.00	8.00	
AH1377	—	0.75	2.50	5.50	10.00	
AH1378	—	0.25	1.00	2.50	5.00	
AH1378/6	—	0.25	1.00	2.50	5.00	
AH1379	—	0.25	1.00	2.50	5.00	
AH1379/5	—	0.75	2.50	5.50	10.00	
AH1379/8	—	0.75	2.50	5.50	10.00	
AH1380	—	0.25	1.00	2.50	5.00	

Y# 11.3   1/80 RIYAL (1 Halala = 1/2 Buqsha)
Bronze Obv: Crescent below accession date AH1367
Note: Struck with dies of 1/4 Ahmadi Riyal, Y#15 on 1/80 Riyal planchet.

Date	Mintage	VG	F	VF	XF	Unc
AH(13)80 Rare	—	—	—	—	—	

Y# 18   1/80 RIYAL (1 Halala = 1/2 Buqsha)
Aluminum Note: Accession date: AH1367.

Date	Mintage	VG	F	VF	XF	Unc
ND	—	0.15	0.25	0.50	1.00	—

Note: Struck privately in Lebanon in 1955 and 1956 and released into circulation in 1956

Y# 12.1   1/40 RIYAL (1 Buqsha)
Bronze (Red To Yellow) Obv: Crescent below accession date AH1367 Rev: "Sana" above date, large "Sana'a" in border legend Note: Some dates exist on thinner planchets and weight varies.

Date	Mintage	VG	F	VF	XF	Unc
AH1368	—	0.50	1.00	4.00	12.00	—

Note: AH1368 also exists with accession date 13776 (error) known

AH1369	—	0.75	1.25	5.00	15.00	—
AH1370	—	0.35	0.75	3.00	6.00	—
AH1371	—	0.35	0.75	3.00	6.00	—
AH1372	—	0.35	0.75	2.00	4.00	—
AH1373/1	—	—	—	—	—	—
AH1373/2	—	0.85	1.80	3.00	6.00	—
AH1373	—	0.35	0.75	2.00	4.00	—
AH1374	—	0.35	0.75	2.00	4.00	—
AH1375/4	—	0.50	1.00	3.00	6.00	—
AH1377	—	—	—	—	—	—

Note: Reported, not confirmed

Y# 12.2   1/40 RIYAL (1 Buqsha)
Bronze (Red To Yellow) Obv: Crescent below accession date AH1367 Rev: Small "Sana'a" in legend Note: Varieties of arrangement of legends, form of crescent, and size of circle exist.

Date	Mintage	VG	F	VF	XF	Unc
AH1371	—	0.35	0.75	3.00	6.00	—
AH1374	—	0.35	0.75	2.00	4.00	—
AH1375	—	0.35	0.75	2.00	4.00	—
AH1376	—	0.50	1.00	5.00	12.00	—

Note: Exists with accession date 1376 instead of 1367 on obverse

| AH1377/6 | — | 0.85 | 1.75 | 4.00 | 8.00 | — |

Note: Exists with accession date 1376 instead of 1367 on obverse

AH1377	—	0.85	1.75	5.00	10.00	—
AH1378/5	—	—	—	—	—	—
AH1379/7	—	0.85	1.75	4.00	8.00	—
AH1380/79	—	0.85	1.75	4.00	8.00	—
AH1380	—	10.00	20.00	50.00	75.00	—

Y# 12.3   1/40 RIYAL (1 Buqsha)
Bronze (Red To Yellow) Obv: Crescent below accession date AH1367 Rev: Large "Sana'a" in legend, without "Sana" above date

Date	Mintage	VG	F	VF	XF	Unc
AH1371	—	0.50	1.00	4.00	12.00	—

Y# 12a.1   1/40 RIYAL (1 Buqsha)
Aluminum Obv: Crescent below accession date AH1367 Rev: "Sana" above date, large "Sana'a" in border legend Note: Dies of 1/40 Riyal, Y#12.1, were used.

Date	Mintage	VG	F	VF	XF	Unc
AH1371	—	0.50	1.00	4.00	10.00	—
AH1373	—	0.50	1.00	4.00	10.00	—
AH1374	—	0.50	1.00	4.00	10.00	—
AH1375	—	0.50	1.00	4.00	10.00	—
AH1377	—	15.00	30.00	50.00	90.00	—

Y# 12a.2   1/40 RIYAL (1 Buqsha)
Aluminum Obv: Crescent below accession date AH1367 Rev: Small "Sana'a" in legend Note: Dies of 1/40 Riyal, Y#12.2, were used. AH1376 and AH1377 plain dates also exist with accession date AH1376 instead of AH1367 on obverse. Varieties exist.

Date	Mintage	VG	F	VF	XF	Unc
AH1375	—	0.50	1.00	4.00	10.00	—
AH1376	—	0.50	1.00	4.00	10.00	—
AH1377/6	—	10.00	20.00	40.00	75.00	—
AH1377	—	15.00	30.00	50.00	90.00	—

Y# 19   1/40 RIYAL (1 Buqsha)
Aluminum Note: Accession date: AH1367 at bottom.

Date	Mintage	VG	F	VF	XF	Unc
ND	—	0.25	0.45	0.65	1.00	2.50

Note: Struck privately in Lebanon in 1955 and 1956 and released into circulation in 1956

Y# 13   1/16 AHMADI RIYAL
Silver Obv: Crescent below accession date AH1367
Obv. Insc.: Amir al-Mu'minin Note: Arrangement of legends and size of inner circle on reverse vary.

Date	Mintage	VG	F	VF	XF	Unc
AH1367	—	1.00	2.00	6.00	12.00	—
AH1368	—	1.00	1.75	5.00	10.00	—
AH1371	—	1.00	1.75	5.00	10.00	—
AH1374	—	1.00	1.50	4.00	8.00	—

Y# 13.1   1/16 AHMADI RIYAL
Silver Obv: Crescent below accession date AH1367, 1/8 Ahmadi Riyal, Y#14 Rev: Y#13 Note: Mule. Ends of crescents cut off on reverse.

Date	Mintage	VG	F	VF	XF	Unc
AH1374	—	20.00	40.00	100	150	—

Y# A14   1/10 AHMADI RIYAL
Silver Obv: Crescent below accession date AH1367

Date	Mintage	VG	F	VF	XF	Unc
AH1370	—	400	750	1,250	1,500	

Y# 14a   1/8 AHMADI RIYAL
Silver

Date	Mintage	VG	F	VF	XF	Unc
AH1368	—	350	650	1,250	1,850	

Y# 14   1/8 AHMADI RIYAL
Silver Obv: Crescent below accession date AH1367
Note: Pentagonal planchet. Arrangement of legends and size of inner circle on reverse vary.

Date	Mintage	VG	F	VF	XF	Unc
AH1367	—	4.00	8.00	15.00	30.00	—
AH1368	—	2.75	4.00	8.00	20.00	—
AH1370	—	2.75	4.00	8.00	20.00	—
AH1371	—	2.00	3.50	6.00	15.00	—
AH1372	—	2.00	2.75	4.00	10.00	—
AH1373	—	2.00	2.75	4.00	10.00	—
AH1374	—	2.00	3.00	5.00	15.00	—
AH1375/1	—	4.00	10.00	40.00	80.00	—
AH1379/x	—	2.00	3.00	5.00	15.00	—
AH1379/5	—	2.00	3.00	5.00	15.00	—
AH1379	—	2.00	3.50	6.00	15.00	—
AH1380	—	2.00	3.75	7.00	20.00	—

Y# 15 1/4 AHMADI RIYAL

Silver **Obv:** Crescent below accession date AH1367
Edge: Reeded **Note:** The size of inner circle as well as the arrangement of legends on reverse vary. All dates have only the final 2 digits on the coin.

Date	Mintage	VG	F	VF	XF	Unc
AH(13)67	—	3.75	5.50	7.50	15.00	—
AH(13)68	—	3.75	5.50	7.50	15.00	—
AH(13)70	—	3.25	4.50	6.00	12.00	—
AH(13)71/68	—	6.00	8.00	12.50	20.00	—
AH(13)71/0	—	4.50	6.50	9.00	15.00	—
AH(13)71	—	3.25	4.50	6.00	10.00	—
AH(13)72	—	3.25	4.50	6.00	10.00	—
AH(13)74	—	3.25	4.50	6.00	10.00	—
AH(13)75/3	—	4.50	6.50	9.00	15.00	—
AH(13)75	—	3.25	4.50	6.00	10.00	—
AH(13)77/5	—	4.50	6.50	9.00	15.00	—
AH(13)80	—	30.00	60.00	100	175	—

Y# 15a 1/4 AHMADI RIYAL

Copper

Date	Mintage	VG	F	VF	XF	Unc
AH(13)81d Rare	—	—	—	—	—	—

Note: This issue is considered a pattern

Y# 16.1 1/2 AHMADI RIYAL

Silver **Obv:** Double crescent below accession date AH1367
Rev: Full dates; denomination and mint name read inward

Date	Mintage	VG	F	VF	XF	Unc
AH1367	—	7.00	10.00	15.00	35.00	—
AH1368	—	7.00	10.00	15.00	35.00	—
AH1369	—	6.00	8.00	12.50	20.00	—
AH1370	—	8.00	12.50	20.00	40.00	—
AH1371	—	8.00	12.50	20.00	40.00	—
AH1372/68	—	7.00	10.00	15.00	30.00	—
AH1373	—	9.00	15.00	25.00	45.00	—
AH1375	—	—	—	—	—	—

Note: Reported, not confirmed

| AH(13)75 | — | 30.00 | 50.00 | 80.00 | 100 | — |
| AH1377 | — | — | — | — | — | — |

Y# 16.2 1/2 AHMADI RIYAL

Silver **Obv:** Double crescent below accession date AH1367
Rev: Full dates; denomination and mint name read outward
Edge: Reeded **Note:** Arrangement of legends and size of circle on reverse vary. These coins were struck over blanks punched from Maria Theresa Thalers. The outer rings are reported to have circulated as currency, but this is doubtful, as they are found only counterstamped "Void" in Arabic.

Date	Mintage	VG	F	VF	XF	Unc
AH1377	—	6.00	8.00	12.50	20.00	—
AH1378	—	7.00	10.00	15.00	25.00	—
AH1379	—	6.00	8.00	12.50	20.00	—
AH1380	—	17.50	30.00	40.00	75.00	—
AH1381	—	12.50	22.50	30.00	50.00	—
AH1382	—	8.00	12.50	25.00	40.00	—

Y# 16a 1/2 AHMADI RIYAL

Copper

Date	Mintage	VG	F	VF	XF	Unc
AH1381 Rare	—	—	—	—	—	—

Note: This issue is considered a pattern

Y# 17 AHMADI RIYAL

Silver, 39.5 mm. **Obv:** Double crescent below accession date AH1367 **Note:** These are usually found struck over Austrian Maria Theresa Talers and occasionally over other foreign crowns. All Y-17s have 1367 in the center obverse. The date for each piece is located in the lower left of the reverse. Varieties exist.

Date	Mintage	F	VF	XF	Unc	BU
AH1367	—	16.00	30.00	45.00	80.00	—
AH1370	—	16.00	20.00	30.00	55.00	—
AH1371	—	16.00	20.00	30.00	55.00	—
AH1372/68	—	—	—	—	—	—

Note: Reported, not confirmed

| AH1373 | — | 13.50 | 16.00 | 22.50 | 35.00 | — |

Note: Most AH1373 Riyals appear to be weakly struck from recut AH1372 dies, and the dates are easily confused

AH1374	—	14.50	16.50	25.00	45.00	—
AH1375	—	14.50	16.50	25.00	45.00	—
AH1377	—	14.00	16.50	25.00	45.00	—

Note: Reported, not confirmed

AH1378	—	14.50	16.50	25.00	45.00	—
AH1380	—	14.50	16.50	25.00	45.00	—
AH1381	—	14.50	16.50	25.00	45.00	—

GOLD COINAGE

Imam Ahmad gold strikes were based on the gold standard of the Turkish Lira (7.2164 g gold). Strikes on the British Gold Standard can have an additional countermark of an Arabic 1, 2, or 4, probably indicating the equivalence to 1, 2, or 4 British Sovereigns.

Y# G15 GOLD 1/4 RIYAL (1 Lira - Sovereign)

Gold **Obv:** Crescent below accession date AH1367
Note: Weight varies: 6.30-8.90 grams. Dies of silver 1/4 Ahmadi riyal, (Y#15) were used.

Date	Mintage	F	VF	XF	Unc	BU
AH(13)71	—	—	475	875	1,500	—
AH(13)75/3	—	—	475	875	1,500	—
AH(13)75	—	—	475	875	1,500	—
AH(13)77/5	—	—	475	875	1,500	—

Y# G16.1 GOLD 1/2 RIYAL (2-1/2 Lira - 2 Sovereigns)

Gold **Obv:** Double crescent below accession date AH1367
Rev: Full dates; denomination and mint name read inward
Note: Weight varies: 15.57-17.99 grams.

Date	Mintage	F	VF	XF	Unc	BU
AH1369 Rare	—	—	—	—	—	—

Note: Currently, one known

| AH1370 | — | BV | 675 | 1,250 | 2,000 | — |
| AH1371 | — | BV | 675 | 1,250 | 2,000 | — |

Date	Mintage	F	VF	XF	Unc	BU
AH1375	—	BV	675	1,250	2,000	—
AH(13)75	—	BV	675	1,250	2,000	—
AH1377	—	BV	675	1,250	2,000	—

Y# G16.2 GOLD 1/2 RIYAL (2-1/2 Lira - 2 Sovereigns)

Gold **Obv:** Double crescent below accession date AH1367
Rev: Full date; denomination and mint name read outward
Note: Dies of silver 1/2 Ahmadi Riyal, (Y#16) were used.

Date	Mintage	F	VF	XF	Unc	BU
AH1377	—	BV	675	1,250	2,000	—
AH1378	—	BV	675	1,250	2,000	—
AH1379	—	BV	675	1,250	2,000	—
AH1380	—	BV	675	1,250	2,000	—
AH1381	—	BV	675	1,250	2,000	—

Y# G17.1 GOLD RIYAL (5 Lira - 4 Sovereigns)

32.4860 g., 0.9000 Gold 0.9400 oz. AGW, 40 mm. **Obv:** Double crescent below accession date AH1367 with incuse Arabic number four above sword handles **Rev:** Arabic legend and inscription

Date	Mintage	F	VF	XF	Unc	BU
AH1371 Rare	—	—	—	—	—	—
AH1372 Rare	—	—	—	—	—	—

Y# G17.2 GOLD RIYAL (5 Lira - 4 Sovereigns)

32.4860 g., 0.9000 Gold 0.9400 oz. AGW, 40 mm. **Obv:** Double crescent below accession date AH1367 without incuse Arabic number four above sword handles **Rev:** Arabic legend and inscription **Note:** Weight varies: 30.46-39.06 grams. Dies of silver Ahmadi Riyal (Y#17) were used.

Date	Mintage	F	VF	XF	Unc	BU
AH1373	—	—	BV	1,100	1,850	—
AH1374	—	—	BV	1,100	1,850	—
AH1375	—	—	BV	1,100	1,850	—
AH1377	—	—	BV	1,100	1,850	—
AH1378	—	—	BV	1,100	1,850	—
AH1381	—	—	BV	1,100	1,850	—

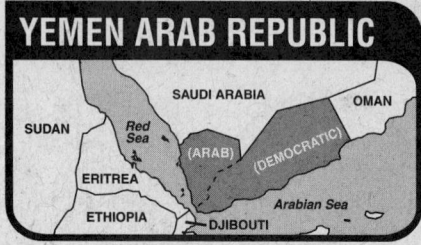

YEMEN ARAB REPUBLIC

The northwestern region of present day Yemen was dominated by Ottoman Turks until 1918. Formal boundaries were established in 1934 and a Republic was formed in 1962 leading to an eight year civil war between royalist imam and new republican forces.

REPUBLIC

MILLED COINAGE

Y# 20   1/80 RIYAL (1/2 Buqsha)
Bronze **Obv:** Denomination within circle **Rev:** Hand holding torch within circle **Note:** Varieties exist.

Date	Mintage	F	VF	XF	Unc	BU
AH1382	—	—	0.50	2.00	5.00	—

Y# 21.1   1/80 RIYAL (1/2 Buqsha)
Bronze **Obv:** Denomination within circle **Rev:** Full star between lines within circle

Date	Mintage	F	VF	XF	Unc	BU
AH1382	—	—	2.00	6.00	15.00	—

Y# 21.2   1/80 RIYAL (1/2 Buqsha)
Bronze **Obv:** Denomination within circle **Rev:** Outlined star between lines within circle **Note:** Varieties exist.

Date	Mintage	F	VF	XF	Unc	BU
AH13882 (sic)	—	—	—	—	—	—
AH1382	—	—	2.00	6.00	15.00	—

Y# 26   1/2 BUQSHA
Copper-Aluminum **Obv:** Denomination within circle **Rev:** Leafy branch within wreath **Mint:** Cairo **Note:** Varieties exist.

Date	Mintage	F	VF	XF	Unc	BU
AH1382-1963	10,000,000	—	0.15	0.20	0.35	0.75

Y# 32   1/2 BUQSHA
Bronze **Obv:** Denomination within circle **Rev:** Full star between lines within circle **Note:** Varieties exist.

Date	Mintage	F	VF	XF	Unc	BU
AH1382	—	—	3.00	5.00	9.00	—

Y# 22   1/40 RIYAL (1 Buqsha)
Brass Or Bronze **Obv:** Denomination within circle **Rev:** Hand holding torch within circle **Note:** Dated both sides; AH1382, AH1383 and AH1384/3 are dated AH1382 on obverse, actual date on reverse; AH1384 and AH1384/284 dated AH1384 on both sides. There are varieties of date size and design.

Date	Mintage	F	VF	XF	Unc	BU
AH1382	—	—	0.75	1.00	2.25	—
AH1383/282	—	—	0.75	1.00	2.25	—
AH1383	—	—	1.50	2.25	6.00	—
AH1384/284	—	—	0.75	1.00	2.25	—
AH1384/3	—	—	0.75	1.00	2.25	—
AH1384	—	—	4.00	7.50	20.00	—

Y# 27   BUQSHA
Copper-Aluminum **Obv:** Denomination within circle **Rev:** Leafy branch within wreath **Mint:** Cairo

Date	Mintage	F	VF	XF	Unc	BU
AH1382-1963	10,377,000	—	0.20	0.40	1.00	2.00

Y# 23.1   1/20 RIYAL (2 Buqsha)
0.7200 Silver **Obv:** Denomination within circle **Rev:** Three stones on top row of wall within circle **Note:** Thick variety, 1.10-1.60 grams

Date	Mintage	F	VF	XF	Unc	BU
AH1382	—	20.00	35.00	60.00	125	—

Y# 23.2   1/20 RIYAL (2 Buqsha)
0.7200 Silver **Obv:** Denomination within circle **Rev:** Two stones on top row of wall within circle **Note:** Thin variety, 0.60-0.90 grams

Date	Mintage	F	VF	XF	Unc	BU
AH1382	—	15.00	30.00	50.00	100	—

Y# A27   2 BUQSHA
4.9100 g., Copper-Aluminum, 23 mm. **Obv:** Denomination within circle **Rev:** Leafy branch within wreath

Date	Mintage	F	VF	XF	Unc	BU
AH1382-1963	—	—	0.25	0.60	1.25	2.50

Y# 24.1   1/10 RIYAL (4 Buqsha)
0.7200 Silver **Obv:** Denomination within circle **Rev:** Three or four stones in top row of wall within circle **Note:** Thick variety, 2.40-3.00 grams

Date	Mintage	F	VF	XF	Unc	BU
AH1382	—	5.00	15.00	25.00	50.00	—

Y# 24.2   1/10 RIYAL (4 Buqsha)
0.7200 Silver **Obv:** Denomination within circle **Rev:** Four stones in top row of wall within circle **Note:** Thin variety, 1.40-1.80 grams. Edge varieties, varying number of stones in wall, exist.

Date	Mintage	F	VF	XF	Unc	BU
AH1382	—	—	2.50	6.00	15.00	—

Y# 28   5 BUQSHA
0.7200 Silver **Obv:** Denomination within circle **Rev:** Leafy branch within wreath, dates below **Mint:** Cairo

Date	Mintage	F	VF	XF	Unc	BU
AH1382-1963	1,600,000	—	1.50	1.75	2.50	4.50

Y# 25.1   2/10 RIYAL (8 Buqsha)
0.7200 Silver **Obv:** Denomination within circle **Rev:** Tree and wall within circle **Note:** Thick variety, 5.80-6.50 grams.

Date	Mintage	F	VF	XF	Unc	BU
AH1382	—	6.00	15.00	25.00	50.00	—

Y# 25.2   2/10 RIYAL (8 Buqsha)
0.7200 Silver **Obv:** Denomination within circle **Rev:** Tree and wall within circle **Note:** Thin variety, 4.90-5.10 grams.

Date	Mintage	F	VF	XF	Unc	BU
AH1382	—	75.00	150	250	—	

Y# A25.1   1/4 RIYAL (10 Buqsha)
0.7200 Silver **Obv:** Denomination within circle **Rev:** Tree and wall within circle **Note:** Thick variety, 6.00-7.30 grams.

Date	Mintage	F	VF	XF	Unc	BU
AH1382	—	250	500	1,000	1,750	—

Y# A25.2   1/4 RIYAL (10 Buqsha)
0.7200 Silver **Obv:** Denomination within circle **Rev:** Tree and wall within circle **Note:** Thin variety, 4.00-4.60 grams. Overstrikes over earlier 1/4 Riyal coins exist.

Date	Mintage	F	VF	XF	Unc	BU
AH1382	—	250	500	1,000	1,750	—

Y# 29   10 BUQSHA
5.0000 g., 0.7200 Silver 0.1157 oz. ASW **Obv:** Denomination within circle **Rev:** Leafy branch within wreath

Date	Mintage	F	VF	XF	Unc	BU
AH1382-1963	1,024,000	—	2.50	3.00	5.00	8.00

Y# 30   20 BUQSHA
9.8500 g., 0.7200 Silver 0.2280 oz. ASW **Obv:** Denomination within circle **Rev:** Leafy branch within wreath

Date	Mintage	F	VF	XF	Unc	BU
AH1382-1963	1,016,000	—	4.50	6.00	8.00	12.00

Y# 31 RIYAL
19.7500 g., 0.7200 Silver 0.4572 oz. ASW **Obv:** Denomination within wreath **Rev:** Leafy branch within wreath

Date	Mintage	F	VF	XF	Unc	BU
AH1382-1963	4,614,000	—	8.00	10.00	15.00	17.50

DECIMAL COINAGE

100 Fils = 1 Riyal/Rial

Y# 33 FILS
Aluminum **Obv:** National arms **Rev:** Denomination within circle

Date	Mintage	F	VF	XF	Unc	BU
AH1394-1974	Est. 1,000,000	—	3.00	5.00	10.00	

Note: It is doubtful that the entire mintage was released for circulation

| AH1394-1974 Proof | 5,024 | Value: 1.50 |
| AH1400-1980 Proof | 10,000 | Value: 1.50 |

Y# 43 FILS
Aluminum **Series:** F.A.O. **Obv:** National arms **Rev:** Denomination within circle

Date	Mintage	F	VF	XF	Unc	BU
AH1398-1978	7,050	—	—	1.25	3.00	—

Y# 34 5 FILS
2.7500 g., Brass, 21 mm. **Obv:** National arms **Rev:** Denomination within circle

Date	Mintage	F	VF	XF	Unc	BU
AH1394-1974	10,000,000	—	0.50	1.00	2.50	—
AH1394-1974 Proof		—	Value: 2.50			
AH1400-1980 Proof		—	Value: 2.00			

Y# 38 5 FILS
2.7500 g., Brass, 21 mm. **Series:** F.A.O. **Obv:** National arms **Rev:** Denomination within circle

Date	Mintage	F	VF	XF	Unc	BU
AH1394-1974	500,000	—	—	0.10	0.25	—

Y# 35 10 FILS
4.2500 g., Brass, 23 mm. **Obv:** National arms **Rev:** Denomination within circle

Date	Mintage	F	VF	XF	Unc	BU
AH1394-1974	20,000,000	—	0.50	1.00	2.50	—
AH1394-1974 Proof	5,024	Value: 2.50				
AH1400-1980 Proof	10,000	Value: 2.00				

Y# 39 10 FILS
4.2500 g., Brass, 23 mm. **Series:** F.A.O. **Obv:** National arms **Rev:** Denomination within circle

Date	Mintage	F	VF	XF	Unc	BU
AH1394-1974	200,000	—	—	0.10	0.25	—

Y# 36 25 FILS
3.0000 g., Copper-Nickel, 20 mm. **Obv:** National arms **Rev:** Denomination within circle

Date	Mintage	F	VF	XF	Unc	BU
AH1394-1974	15,000,000	—	0.25	0.50	3.00	—
AH1394-1974 Proof	5,024	Value: 3.00				
AH1399-1979	11,000,000	—	0.25	0.50	2.00	—
AH1400-1980 Proof	10,000	Value: 2.25				

Y# 40 25 FILS
3.0000 g., Copper-Nickel, 20 mm. **Series:** F.A.O. **Obv:** National arms **Rev:** Denomination within circle

Date	Mintage	F	VF	XF	Unc	BU
AH1394-1974	40,000	—	0.20	0.40	1.00	—

Y# 37 50 FILS
5.3000 g., Copper-Nickel, 24 mm. **Obv:** National arms **Rev:** Denomination within circle

Date	Mintage	F	VF	XF	Unc	BU
AH1394-1974	10,000,000	—	0.35	0.75	2.50	—
AH1394-1974 Proof	5,024	Value: 3.50				
AH1399-1979	4,000,000	—	0.35	0.75	2.50	—
AH1400-1980 Proof	10,000	Value: 2.50				
AH1405-1985		—	0.35	0.75	2.50	—

Y# 41 50 FILS
5.3000 g., Copper-Nickel, 24 mm. **Series:** F.A.O. **Obv:** National arms **Rev:** Denomination within circle

Date	Mintage	F	VF	XF	Unc	BU
AH1394-1974	25,000	—	0.25	0.50	1.25	—

KM# 1 RIYAL
12.0000 g., 0.9250 Silver 0.3569 oz. ASW **Subject:** Qadhi Mohammed Mahmud Azzubairi Memorial **Obv:** National arms **Rev:** Figure on camel right

Date	Mintage	F	VF	XF	Unc	BU
1969 Proof	3,200	Value: 25.00				

KM# 1a RIYAL
20.4800 g., 0.9000 Gold 0.5926 oz. AGW **Subject:** Qadhi Mohammed Mahmud Azzubairi Memorial **Obv:** National arms **Rev:** Figure on camel right

Date	Mintage	F	VF	XF	Unc	BU
1969 Proof	100	Value: 650				

Y# 42 RIYAL
8.0000 g., Copper-Nickel, 28 mm. **Obv:** National arms **Rev:** Denomination within circle

Date	Mintage	F	VF	XF	Unc	BU
AH1396-1976	7,800,000	—	0.50	1.25	2.50	—
AH1400-1980 Proof	—	Value: 5.00				
AH1405-1985		—	0.50	1.25	2.50	—
AH1414-1993		—	0.50	1.25	2.50	—

Y# 44 RIYAL
8.0000 g., Copper-Nickel, 28 mm. **Series:** F.A.O. **Obv:** National arms **Rev:** Denomination within circle

Date	Mintage	F	VF	XF	Unc	BU
AH1398-1978	7,050	—	—	2.00	5.00	—

KM# 2.1 2 RIYALS
25.0000 g., 0.9250 Silver 0.7435 oz. ASW **Subject:** Apollo II - Cape Kennedy **Obv:** Eagle with shield on breast and flags on legs **Rev:** Space shuttle and launch pad **Note:** Dotted border.

Date	Mintage	F	VF	XF	Unc	BU
1969	7,583	—	—	—	28.00	—
1969 Proof	200	Value: 60.00				

KM# 2.2   2 RIYALS
25.0000 g., 0.9250 Silver 0.7435 oz. ASW **Obv:** Eagle with
shield on breast and flags on legs **Rev:** Space shuttle and launch
pad **Note:** Border of dots near rim.

Date	Mintage	F	VF	XF	Unc	BU
1969 Proof; restrike	1,000	Value: 30.00				

KM# 3.1   2 RIYALS
25.0000 g., 0.9250 Silver 0.7435 oz. ASW **Subject:** Apollo II -
Moon Landing **Obv:** Eagle with shield on breast and flags on legs
Rev: Moon landing scene **Note:** Dotted border.

Date	Mintage	F	VF	XF	Unc	BU
1969	7,583	—	—	—	28.00	—
1969 Proof	200	Value: 60.00				

KM# 3.2   2 RIYALS
25.0000 g., 0.9250 Silver 0.7435 oz. ASW **Obv:** Eagle with
shield on breast and flags on legs **Rev:** Moon landing scene
Note: Border of dots near rim.

Date	Mintage	F	VF	XF	Unc	BU
1969 Proof; restrike	1,000	Value: 30.00				

KM# 4   2 RIYALS
25.0000 g., 0.9250 Silver 0.7435 oz. ASW **Subject:** Qadhi
Mohammed Mahmud Azzubairi Memorial **Obv:** National arms
Rev: Roaring lion's head 3/4 left

Date	Mintage	F	VF	XF	Unc	BU
1969 Proof	4,200	Value: 55.00				

KM# 4a   2 RIYALS
42.2900 g., 0.9000 Gold 1.2236 oz. AGW **Subject:** Qadhi
Mohammed Mahmud Azzubairi Memorial **Obv:** National arms
Rev: Roaring lion's head 3/4 left

Date	Mintage	F	VF	XF	Unc	BU
1969 Proof	100	Value: 1,350				

KM# 14   2-1/2 RIYALS
9.0000 g., 0.9250 Silver 0.2676 oz. ASW **Subject:** Oil
Exploration **Obv:** National arms **Rev:** Oil derricks in field

Date	Mintage	F	VF	XF	Unc	BU
AH1395-1975	Est. 205,000	—	—	—	20.00	—
AH1395-1975 Proof	Est. 5,000	Value: 40.00				

KM# 6   5 RIYALS/RIALS
4.9000 g., 0.9000 Gold 0.1418 oz. AGW **Subject:** Qadhi
Mohammed Mahmud Azzubairi Memorial **Obv:** Monument
Rev: Denomination within circle

Date	Mintage	F	VF	XF	Unc	BU
1969 Proof	—	Value: 175				

KM# 15   5 RIYALS/RIALS
18.0000 g., 0.9250 Silver 0.5353 oz. ASW **Subject:** Mona Lisa
Rev: Mona Lisa within center box, chain with ornaments surrounds

Date	Mintage	F	VF	XF	Unc	BU
AH1395-1975	235,000	—	—	—	25.00	—
AH1395-1975 Proof	5,000	Value: 50.00				

KM# 7   10 RIYALS/RIALS
9.8000 g., 0.9000 Gold 0.2836 oz. AGW **Subject:** Qadhi
Mohammed Mahmud Azzubairi Memorial **Obv:** National arms
Rev: Three gazelles leaping right

Date	Mintage	F	VF	XF	Unc	BU
1969 Proof	—	Value: 350				

KM# 23   10 RIYALS/RIALS
12.0800 g., 0.9250 Silver 0.3592 oz. ASW **Obv:** Camel with
rider right **Rev:** National arms **Note:** Mule.

Date	Mintage	F	VF	XF	Unc	BU
1969 Proof	—	Value: 45.00				

KM# 16   10 RIYALS/RIALS
36.0000 g., 0.9250 Silver 1.0706 oz. ASW **Series:** Montreal
Olympics **Obv:** National arms **Rev:** Olympic events surround
central flame

Date	Mintage	F	VF	XF	Unc	BU
AH1395-1975	8,000	—	—	—	90.00	—
AH1395-1975 Proof	4,000	Value: 150				

KM# 28   10 RIYALS/RIALS
35.9000 g., 0.9250 Silver 1.0676 oz. ASW, 45.6 mm.
Subject: Montreal Olympics **Obv:** National arms **Rev:** Olympic
events surround central flame **Edge:** Plain **Mint:** Numismatica
Italiana

Date	Mintage	F	VF	XF	Unc	BU
AH1395-1975 Proof	100	Value: 400				

KM# 17   15 RIALS
54.0000 g., 0.9250 Silver 1.6059 oz. ASW **Subject:** Jerusalem
Rev: Domed buildings

Date	Mintage	F	VF	XF	Unc	BU
AH1395-1975	70,000	—	—	—	45.00	—
AH1395-1975 Proof	5,000	Value: 100				

KM# 8   20 RIYALS/RIALS
19.6000 g., 0.9000 Gold 0.5671 oz. AGW **Subject:** Apollo II -
Moon Landing **Obv:** Eagle with shield on breast and flags on legs
Rev: Capsule above astronauts on moon's surface

Date	Mintage	F	VF	XF	Unc	BU
1969 Proof	—	Value: 600				

KM# 9   20 RIYALS/RIALS
19.6000 g., 0.9000 Gold 0.5671 oz. AGW **Subject:** Qadhi
Mohammed Mahmud Azzubairi Memorial **Obv:** National arms
Rev: Camel with rider right

Date	Mintage	F	VF	XF	Unc	BU
1969 Proof	—	Value: 625				

KM# 18   20 RIYALS/RIALS
0.9000 Gold **Subject:** Albakiriah Mosque **Rev:** Mosque within oval

Date	Mintage	F	VF	XF	Unc	BU
AH1395-1975	—	—	—	—	—	350
AH1395-1975 Proof	3,500	Value: 350				

KM# 19   25 RIYALS/RIALS
0.9000 Gold **Subject:** Oil Exploration **Obv:** National arms within
rounded square **Rev:** Oil derricks in field, rounded square surrounds

Date	Mintage	F	VF	XF	Unc	BU
AH1395-1975	—	—	—	—	—	250
AH1395-1975 Proof	3,500	Value: 275				

Y# 46   25 RIYALS/RIALS
28.2800 g., 0.9250 Silver 0.8410 oz. ASW **Series:** International
Year of the Disabled Person **Obv:** National arms **Rev:** Head right

Date	Mintage	F	VF	XF	Unc	BU
AH1401-1981	10,000	—	—	—	32.50	—
AH1401-1981 Proof	Est. 10,000	Value: 50.00				

Y# 47   25 RIYALS/RIALS
28.2800 g., 0.9250 Silver 0.8410 oz. ASW **Subject:** 20th
Anniversary of the Revolution

Date	Mintage	F	VF	XF	Unc	BU
AH1402-1982 Proof	2,000	Value: 55.00				

Y# 45   25 RIYALS/RIALS
28.2500 g., 0.9250 Silver 0.8401 oz. ASW **Series:** International
Year of the Child **Obv:** National arms within wreath of leaves
Rev: Children dancing, logos flank

Date	Mintage	F	VF	XF	Unc	BU
AH1403-1983 Proof	6,604	Value: 20.00				

Y# 49   25 RIYALS/RIALS
28.2500 g., 0.9250 Silver 0.8401 oz. ASW **Series:** Decade for
Women **Obv:** National arms within wreath of leaves **Rev:** Three
half-figures of women looking left, ankh on dove cutout at left

Date	Mintage	F	VF	XF	Unc	BU
AH1405-1985 Proof	1,000	Value: 45.00				

KM# 10   30 RIYALS
29.4000 g., 0.9000 Gold 0.8507 oz. AGW **Subject:** Qadhi
Mohammed Mahmud Azzubairi Memorial **Obv:** National arms
Rev: Head 3/4 right

Date	Mintage	F	VF	XF	Unc	BU
1969 Proof	—	Value: 900				

KM# 11   50 RIYALS/RIALS
49.9700 g., Silver **Subject:** Qadhi Mohammed Mahmud
Azzubairi Memorial **Obv:** National arms **Rev:** Lion

Date	Mintage	F	VF	XF	Unc	BU
1969 Proof; restrike	—	Value: 60.00				

KM# 11a   50 RIYALS/RIALS
49.0000 g., 0.9000 Gold 1.4178 oz. AGW **Subject:** Qadhi
Mohammed Mahmud Azzubairi Memorial **Obv:** National arms
above dates and denomination

Date	Mintage	F	VF	XF	Unc	BU
1969 Proof	—	Value: 1,500				

KM# 20   50 RIYALS/RIALS
9.1000 g., 0.9000 Gold 0.2633 oz. AGW **Subject:** Mona Lisa
Rev: Mona Lisa within box, chain with ornaments surrounds

Date	Mintage	F	VF	XF	Unc	BU
AH1395-1975	—	—	—	—	—	300
AH1395-1975 Proof	3,500	Value: 375				

KM# 21   75 RIYALS
13.6500 g., 0.9000 Gold 0.3950 oz. AGW **Series:** Montreal
Olympics **Obv:** Arms **Rev:** XXI Olympiad

Date	Mintage	F	VF	XF	Unc	BU
AH1395-1975	—	—	—	—	—	450
AH1395-1975 Proof	3,500	Value: 500				

KM# 22   100 RIALS
18.2000 g., 0.9000 Gold 0.5266 oz. AGW **Obv:** National arms
Rev: Domed buildings

Date	Mintage	F	VF	XF	Unc	BU
AH1395-1975	—	—	—	—	—	575
AH1395-1975 Proof	3,500	Value: 600				

KM# 24   500 RIYALS/RIALS
15.9800 g., 0.9170 Gold 0.4711 oz. AGW **Series:** International
Year of the Disabled Person **Obv:** National arms **Rev:** Head of
Bolivar facing, tiny logos flank below

Date	Mintage	F	VF	XF	Unc	BU
AH1401-1981	—	—	—	—	—	500
AH1401-1981 Proof	—	Value: 525				

Y # 48   500 RIYALS/RIALS

15.9000 g., 0.9170 Gold 0.4687 oz. AGW **Subject:** 20th Anniversary of the Revolution **Rev:** Ship within small center circle, figures above, oil derrick at left, grain sprig at right, circle surrounds all

Date	Mintage	F	VF	XF	Unc	BU
AH1402-1982 Proof	1,000	Value: 500				

ESSAIS

KM#	Date	Mintage	Identification	Mkt Val
E1	AH1385	500	Rial. 0.7200 Silver.	27.50

PIEFORTS

KM#	Date	Mintage	Identification	Mkt Val
P1	1981	1,150	25 Riyals/Rials. Silver. I.Y.D.P.; Y#46	115
P2	1981	—	500 Riyals/Rials. Gold. I.Y.P.D.; KM#24	1,000
	1981	—	500 Riyals/Rials. Gold. I.Y.P.D.; KM#24	1,000
P3	1983	—	25 Riyals/Rials. 0.9250 Silver. 57.0000 g. Arms, legend, date. Children. I.Y.C.; Y#45	175

TRIAL STRIKES

KM#	Date	Mintage	Identification	Mkt Val
TS1	1975	—	100 Rials. Goldine. Uniface; national arms divide dates, denomination below.	

MINT SETS

KM#	Date	Mintage	Identification	Issue Price	Mkt Val
MS1	1975 (4)	—	KM#14-17	50.00	175
MS2	1975 (5)	—	KM#18-22	360	1,375

PROOF SETS

KM#	Date	Mintage	Identification	Issue Price	Mkt Val
PS1	1969 (7)	2,000	KM#1, 4, 6, 7, 9-11	375	1,350
PS2	1969 (4)	1,500	KM#1-4	—	125
PS4	1969 (3)	—	KM#2, 3, 6	78.00	175
PS5	1974 (5)	5,024	Y#33-37	15.00	12.50
PS6	1975 (5)	3,500	KM#18-22	485	1,650
PS7	1975 (4)	5,000	KM#14-17	75.00	335
PS8	1980 (6)	10,000	Y#33-37, 42	31.00	16.00

YEMEN EASTERN ADEN PROTECTORATE

Between 1200 B.C. and the 6th century A.D., what is now the Peoples Democratic Republic of Yemen was part of the Minaean kingdom. In subsequent years it was controlled by Persians, Egyptians and Turks. Aden, one of the cities mentioned in the Bible, had been a port for trade between the East and West for 2,000 years. British rule began in 1839 when the British East India Co. seized control to put an end to the piracy threatening trade with India. To protect their foothold in Aden, the British found it necessary to extend their control into the area known historically as the Hadhramaut, and to sign protection treaties with the sheiks of the hinterland.

QUATI STATE OF HADHRAMAUT

GHURFAH

A city sultanate of Eastern Aden Protectorate was an oasis settlement located in the Hadhramaut Wadi region of southern Arabia.

TITLES
al-Ghurfah

RULERS
Saleh 'Ubayd bin Abdat,
    AH1339-1358/1920-1939AD
Ubayd bin Saleh bin Abdat,
    AH1358-1365/1939-1945AD
    NOTE: The Arabic 129 in the obv. legend is an anagram for Saleh.

MINT

الغرفه

Ghurfah

Saleh 'Ubayd bin Abdat
AH1339-1358 / 1920-1939AD
STANDARD COINAGE

KM# 101   4 KHUMSI

0.6500 g., 0.9000 Silver 0.0188 oz. ASW, 11.5 mm. **Obv:** Legend within circle and wreath **Rev:** Value within circle and wreath **Note:** Prev. KM#1.

Date	Mintage	VG	F	VF	XF	Unc
AH1344	5,000	—	30.00	45.00	65.00	100

KM# 102   8 KHUMSI

1.1000 g., 0.9000 Silver 0.0318 oz. ASW, 14 mm. **Obv:** Legend within circle and wreath **Rev:** Value within circle and wreath **Note:** Prev. KM#2.

Date	Mintage	VG	F	VF	XF	Unc
AH1344	5,000	—	27.50	37.50	55.00	85.00

KM# 103   15 KHUMSI

2.0000 g., 0.9000 Silver 0.0579 oz. ASW, 18 mm. **Obv:** Legend within circle and wreath **Rev:** Value within circle and wreath **Note:** Prev. KM#3.

Date	Mintage	VG	F	VF	XF	Unc
AH1344	10,000	—	10.00	15.00	22.50	35.00

KM# 104   30 KHUMSI

3.9500 g., 0.9000 Silver 0.1143 oz. ASW, 22 mm. **Obv:** Legend within circle and wreath **Rev:** Value within circle and wreath **Note:** Prev. KM#4.

Date	Mintage	VG	F	VF	XF	Unc
AH1344	10,000	—	15.00	22.50	32.50	50.00

KM# 105   45 KHUMSI

5.9000 g., 0.9000 Silver 0.1707 oz. ASW, 24.5 mm. **Obv:** Legend within circle and wreath **Rev:** Value within circle and wreath **Note:** Prev. KM#5.

Date	Mintage	VG	F	VF	XF	Unc
AH1344	10,000	—	175	275	425	600

KM# 106   60 KHUMSI

7.8000 g., 0.9000 Silver 0.2257 oz. ASW, 27 mm. **Obv:** Legend within circle and wreath **Rev:** Value within circle and wreath **Note:** Prev. KM#6.

Date	Mintage	VG	F	VF	XF	Unc
AH1344	10,000	—	37.50	55.00	80.00	125

YEMEN REPUBLIC

The Republic of Yemen, formerly Yemen Arab Republic and Peoples Democratic Republic of Yemen, is located on the southern coast of the Arabian Peninsula. It has an area of 205,020 sq. mi. (531,000 sq. km.) and a population of 12 million. Capital: San'a. The port of Aden is the main commercial center and the area's most valuable natural resource. Recent oil and gas finds and a developing petroleum industry have improved their economic prospects. Agriculture and local handicrafts are the main industries. Cotton, fish, coffee, rock salt and hides are exported.

On May 22, 1990, the Yemen Arab Republic (North Yemen) and Peoples Democratic Republic of Yemen (South Yemen) merged into a unified Republic of Yemen. Disagreements between the two former governments simmered until civil war erupted in 1994, with the northern forces of the old Yemen Arab Republic eventually prevailing.

TITLE

دار الخلافة

Dar al-Khilafa(t)

REPUBLIC
MILLED COINAGE

KM# 25   RIYAL

2.6500 g., Stainless Steel, 19.95 mm. **Obv:** Denomination within circle **Rev:** National arms **Edge:** Multi-sided

Date	Mintage	F	VF	XF	Unc	BU
AH1414-1993	—	—	—	—	1.25	1.75

KM# 26   5 RIYALS

4.5000 g., Stainless Steel, 22.85 mm. **Obv:** Denomination within circle **Rev:** Building

Date	Mintage	F	VF	XF	Unc	BU
AH1414-1993	—	—	—	—	1.75	2.25
AH1420-2000	—	—	—	—	1.75	2.25

KM# 27   10 RIYALS

6.0500 g., Stainless Steel, 26 mm. **Obv:** Denomination within circle **Rev:** Bridge at Shaharah

Date	Mintage	F	VF	XF	Unc	BU
AH1416-1995	—	—	—	—	2.75	3.50

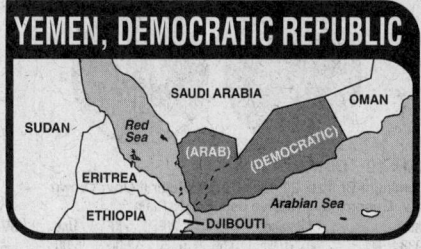

YEMEN, DEMOCRATIC REPUBLIC

The southeast region of present day Yemen was predominately controlled by the British since their occupation of Aden in 1839. Independence was declared November 30, 1967 after the collapse of the Federation of South Arabia and the withdrawal of the British.

TITLES

Al-Jumhuriya(t) al-Yamaniya(t)
ad-Dimiqratiya(t) ash-Sha'biya(t)

MONETARY SYSTEM

Falus, Fulus   Fals, Fils   Falsan, Filsan

1000 Fils = 1 Dinar

PEOPLES DEMOCRATIC REPUBLIC

DECIMAL COINAGE

KM# 3   2-1/2 FILS
0.6500 g., Aluminum, 17 mm. **Obv:** Denomination and dates
Rev: Leafy plant

Date	Mintage	F	VF	XF	Unc	BU
AH1393-1973	20,000,000	—	0.25	0.65	1.50	2.50

KM# 2   5 FILS
1.3500 g., Bronze, 23.1 mm. **Obv:** 8-sided star design
Rev: Crossed daggers

Date	Mintage	F	VF	XF	Unc	BU
1971	2,000,000	—	0.30	0.60	1.00	1.50

KM# 4   5 FILS
1.3500 g., Aluminum, 23.1 mm. **Obv:** Denomination and dates
Rev: Spiny lobster

Date	Mintage	F	VF	XF	Unc	BU
AH1393-1973	20,000,000	—	0.15	0.30	1.00	1.50
AH1404-1984	—	—	0.15	0.30	1.00	1.50

KM# 9   10 FILS
2.2000 g., Aluminum, 25.6 mm. **Obv:** Monument
Rev: Denomination within circle

Date	Mintage	F	VF	XF	Unc	BU
1981	—	—	0.35	0.75	2.00	3.00

KM# 5   25 FILS
4.5500 g., Copper-Nickel, 20 mm. **Obv:** 8-sided star design
Rev: Dhow

Date	Mintage	F	VF	XF	Unc	BU
1976	2,000,000	—	0.25	0.50	1.25	2.25
1977	1,000,000	—	0.25	0.50	1.50	2.50
1979	—	—	0.25	0.50	1.50	2.50
1982	—	—	0.25	0.50	1.50	2.50
1984	—	—	0.25	0.50	1.75	2.75

KM# 6   50 FILS
9.1000 g., Copper-Nickel, 27.8 mm. **Obv:** 8-sided star design
Rev: Dhow

Date	Mintage	F	VF	XF	Unc	BU
1976	2,000,000	—	0.35	0.75	2.50	3.50
1977	2,000,000	—	0.35	0.75	2.50	3.50
1979	—	—	0.35	0.75	2.50	3.50
1984	—	—	0.35	0.75	2.50	3.50

KM# 10   100 FILS
10.0000 g., Copper-Nickel, 23.1 mm. **Obv:** Monument
Rev: Denomination within circle

Date	Mintage	F	VF	XF	Unc	BU
1981	—	—	0.50	1.00	3.00	4.50

KM# 7   250 FILS
11.2000 g., Copper-Nickel, 31 mm. **Subject:** 10th Anniversary of Independence **Obv:** Monument **Rev:** Ship at sea with date below

Date	Mintage	F	VF	XF	Unc	BU
1977	30,000	3.00	6.00	12.00	25.00	—

KM# 11   250 FILS
11.2000 g., Copper-Nickel, 31 mm. **Obv:** Monument
Rev: Denomination within circle

Date	Mintage	F	VF	XF	Unc	BU
1981	—	—	1.50	3.00	5.50	7.00

KM# 12   2 DINARS
28.2800 g., 0.9250 Silver 0.8410 oz. ASW **Subject:** International Year of Disabled Persons - Abdulla Baradoni **Obv:** Head right **Rev:** Triangular design within wreath divides date

Date	Mintage	F	VF	XF	Unc	BU
1981	10,000	—	—	—	47.50	50.00
1981 Proof	10,000	Value: 52.50				

KM# 8   5 DINARS
12.5000 g., 0.9250 Silver 0.3717 oz. ASW **Subject:** 10th Anniversary of Independence **Obv:** Monument **Rev:** Ship at sea with date below

Date	Mintage	F	VF	XF	Unc	BU
1977 Proof	6,000	Value: 65.00				

KM# 13   50 DINARS
15.9800 g., 0.9170 Gold 0.4711 oz. AGW **Series:** International Year of Disabled Persons **Obv:** National arms **Rev:** Triangular design within wreath divides date

Date	Mintage	F	VF	XF	Unc	BU
1981	2,100	—	—	—	525	575
1981 Proof	1,100	Value: 775				

PIEFORTS

KM#	Date	Mintage	Identification	Mkt Val
P1	1981	1,050	2 Dinars. Silver. KM#12.	200
P2	1981	500	50 Dinars. Gold. KM#13.	1,500

YUGOSLAVIA

The Federal Republic of Yugoslavia, formerly the Socialist Federal Republic of Yugoslavia, a Balkan country located on the east shore of the Adriatic Sea, has an area of 39,450 sq. mi. (102,173 sq. km.) and a population of 10.5 million. Capital: Belgrade. The chief industries area agriculture, mining, manufacturing and tourism. Machinery, nonferrous metals, meat and fabrics are exported.

Yugoslavia was proclaimed on Dec. 1, 1918, after the union of the Kingdom of Serbia, Montenegro and the South Slav territories of Austria-Hungary; and changed its official name from the Kingdom of the Serbs, Croats and Slovenes to the Kingdom of Yugoslavia on Oct. 3, 1929. The republic was composed of six autonomous republics - Serbia, Croatia, Slovenia, Bosnia-Herzegovina, Macedonia and Montenegro - and two autonomous provinces within Serbia: Kosovo-Melohija and Vojvodina. The government of Yugoslavia attempted to remain neutral in World War ll but, yielding to German pressure, aligned itself with the Axis powers in March of 1941; a few days later it was overthrown by revolutionary forces and its neutrality reasserted. The Nazis occupied the country on April 6, and throughout the remaining war years were resisted by a number of guerrilla armies, notably that of Marshal Josip Broz Tito. After the defeat of the Axis powers, a leftist coalition headed by Tito abolished the monarchy and, on Jan. 31, 1946, established a "People's Republic". The collapse of the Federal Republic during 1991-1992 has resulted in the autonomous republics of Croatia, Slovenia, Bosnia-Herzegovina and Macedonia declaring their respective independence. Bosnia-Herzegovina is under military contest with the Serbian, Croat and Muslim populace opposing each other. Besides the remainder of the older Serbian sectors, a Serbian enclave in Knin located in southern Croatia has emerged called REPUBLIKE SRPSKEKRAJINE or Serbian Republic - Krajina whose capital is Knin and has also declared its independence in 1992 when the former Republics of Serbia and Montenegro became the Federal Republic of Yugoslavia.

The name Yugoslavia appears on the coinage in letters of the Cyrillic alphabet alone until formation of the Federated Peoples Republic of Yugoslavia in 1953, after which both the Cyrillic and Latin alphabets are employed. From 1965, the coin denomination appears in the 4 different languages of the federated republics in letters of both the Cyrillic and Latin alphabets.

DENOMINATIONS
Para ПАРА
Dinar, ДИНАР, Dinara ДИНАРА
Dinari ДИНАРИ, Dinarjev

RULERS
Petar I, 1918-1921
Alexander I, 1921-1934
Petar II, 1934-1945

MINT MARKS
(a) - Paris, privy marks only
(b) - Brussels
(k) - КОВНИЦА,...А.Д. = Kovnica, A.D.
(Akcionarno Drustvo) Belgrade
(l) - London
(p) - Poissy (thunderbolt)
(v) – Vienna

MONETARY SYSTEM
100 Para = 1 Dinar

KINGDOM OF THE SERBS, CROATS AND SLOVENES

STANDARD COINAGE

KM# 1 5 PARA
Zinc, 18.8 mm. **Ruler:** Petar I **Obv:** Crowned and mantled arms on shield **Rev:** Denomination above date **Edge:** Plain

Date	Mintage	F	VF	XF	Unc	BU
1920(v)	3,825,514	3.00	7.50	15.00	42.00	—

KM# 2 10 PARA
Zinc, 20.85 mm. **Ruler:** Petar I **Obv:** Crowned and mantled arms on shield **Rev:** Denomination above date **Edge:** Plain

Date	Mintage	F	VF	XF	Unc	BU
1920(v)	58,946,122	1.50	3.50	9.00	24.00	—

KM# 3 25 PARA
Nickel-Bronze, 24 mm. **Ruler:** Petar I **Obv:** Crowned and mantled arms on shield **Rev:** Denomination above date **Edge:** Plain

Date	Mintage	F	VF	XF	Unc	BU
1920(v)	48,173,138	1.50	3.50	9.50	25.00	—

KM# 4 50 PARA
Nickel-Bronze, 18 mm. **Ruler:** Alexander I **Obv:** Head left **Rev:** Denomination and date within crowned wreath **Edge:** Milled **Note:** Mint mark: lightning bolt.

Date	Mintage	F	VF	XF	Unc	BU
1925(b)	24,500,000	0.50	1.00	2.00	7.00	—
1925(p)	25,000,000	0.50	1.50	3.00	8.00	—

KM# 5 DINAR
4.9200 g., Nickel-Bronze, 23 mm. **Ruler:** Alexander I **Obv:** Head left **Rev:** Denomination and date within crowned wreath **Edge:** Milled **Note:** Mint mark: lightning bolt.

Date	Mintage	F	VF	XF	Unc	BU
1925(b)	37,000,000	0.50	1.00	2.50	7.50	—
1925(p)	37,500,410	0.75	1.50	3.00	8.00	—

KM# 6 2 DINARA
Nickel-Bronze, 27 mm. **Ruler:** Alexander I **Obv:** Head left **Rev:** Denomination and date within crowned wreath **Edge:** Milled **Note:** Mint mark: lightning bolt.

Date	Mintage	F	VF	XF	Unc	BU
1925(b)	29,500,000	1.00	2.00	5.00	13.00	—
1925(p)	25,004,177	1.00	2.50	5.50	15.00	—

KM# 7 20 DINARA
6.4516 g., 0.9000 Gold 0.1867 oz. AGW, 21 mm. **Ruler:** Alexander I **Obv:** Head left **Rev:** Denomination and date within crowned wreath **Edge:** Milled

Date	Mintage	F	VF	XF	Unc	BU
1925	1,000,000	—	BV	225	275	—
1925 Proof	—	—	—	—	—	—

KINGDOM OF YUGOSLAVIA

STANDARD COINAGE

KM# 17 25 PARA
Bronze, 20 mm. **Ruler:** Petar II **Obv:** Center hole within crowned wreath **Rev:** Center hole divides denomination **Edge:** Plain **Note:** 4 mm hole in center of coin.

Date	Mintage	F	VF	XF	Unc	BU
1938	40,000,000	1.25	2.50	5.50	14.00	—
1938 Proof	—	—	—	—	—	—

KM# 18 50 PARA
Aluminum-Bronze, 18 mm. **Ruler:** Petar II **Obv:** Crown **Rev:** Denomination above date **Edge:** Plain

Date	Mintage	F	VF	XF	Unc	BU
1938	100,000,000	0.50	1.00	2.50	7.50	—

KM# 19 DINAR
Aluminum-Bronze, 21 mm. **Ruler:** Petar II **Obv:** Crown **Rev:** Denomination above date **Edge:** Plain

Date	Mintage	F	VF	XF	Unc	BU
1938	100,000,000	0.50	0.75	2.00	6.00	—
1938 Proof	—	—	—	—	—	—

KM# 20 2 DINARA
5.1000 g., Aluminum-Bronze, 24.5 mm. **Ruler:** Petar II **Obv:** Crown **Rev:** Denomination above date, large numeral **Edge:** Plain

Date	Mintage	F	VF	XF	Unc	BU
1938	74,250,000	0.50	1.00	3.50	9.00	—
1938 Proof	—	—	—	—	—	—

KM# 21 2 DINARA
Aluminum-Bronze, 24.5 mm. **Ruler:** Petar II **Obv:** 12 mm crown **Rev:** Denomination above date, large numeral **Edge:** Plain

Date	Mintage	F	VF	XF	Unc	BU
1938	750,000	6.00	10.00	19.00	38.00	—
1938 Proof	—	—	—	—	—	—

KM# 10 10 DINARA
7.0000 g., 0.5000 Silver 0.1125 oz. ASW **Ruler:** Alexander I **Obv:** Head left **Rev:** Crowned double eagle with shield on breast **Edge:** Milled

Date	Mintage	F	VF	XF	Unc	BU
1931(l)	19,000,000	2.00	4.00	8.00	18.00	—
1931(l) Proof	—	—	—	—	—	—
1931(a)	4,000,000	3.50	7.00	15.00	32.00	—
1931(a) Proof	—	—	—	—	—	—

KM# 22 10 DINARA
Nickel, 23 mm. **Ruler:** Petar II **Obv:** Head right **Rev:** Denomination and date within crowned wreath **Edge:** Milled

Date	Mintage	F	VF	XF	Unc	BU
1938	25,000,000	0.50	1.00	2.00	4.50	—

KM# 11 20 DINARA
14.0000 g., 0.5000 Silver 0.2250 oz. ASW, 31 mm.
Ruler: Alexander I **Obv:** Head left **Rev:** Crowned double eagle with shield on breast **Edge:** Milled

Date	Mintage	F	VF	XF	Unc	BU
1931(k)	12,500,000	BV	6.00	12.50	33.00	—
1931(k) Proof	—	—	—	—	—	—

KM# 23 20 DINARA
9.0000 g., 0.7500 Silver 0.2170 oz. ASW **Ruler:** Petar II
Obv: Head left **Rev:** Crowned double eagle with shield on breast
Edge: BOG CUVA JUGOSLAVIJU ***

Date	Mintage	F	VF	XF	Unc	BU
1938	15,000,000	BV	3.75	6.50	12.50	—

KM# 16 50 DINARA
23.3300 g., 0.7500 Silver 0.5625 oz. ASW, 36 mm.
Ruler: Alexander I **Obv:** Head left **Rev:** Crowned double eagle with shield on breast **Edge:** BOG CUVA JUGOSLAVIJU
Note: Also known without the signature under the head.

Date	Mintage	F	VF	XF	Unc	BU
1932(k)	5,500,000	10.00	22.00	45.00	180	—
1932(l)	5,500,000	10.00	25.00	50.00	200	—
1932(l) Proof	—	Value: 2,200				

KM# 24 50 DINARA
15.0000 g., 0.7500 Silver 0.3617 oz. ASW, 31 mm. **Ruler:** Petar II
Obv: Head right **Rev:** Crowned double eagle with shield on breast

Date	Mintage	F	VF	XF	Unc	BU
1938	10,000,000	BV	6.50	10.00	18.00	—

TRADE COINAGE

Trade-coinage countermarks were applied by the Yugoslav Control Office for Noble Metals to confirm gold purity. The initial countermark displayed a sword, but part way through the first production year, this was retired and the second countermark, showing an ear of corn, was used.

KM# 12.1 DUKAT
3.4900 g., 0.9860 Gold 0.1106 oz. AGW **Ruler:** Alexander I
Countermark: Birds **Obv:** Head left, small legend with КОВНИЦА, А.Д. below head **Rev:** Crowned double eagle with shield on breast **Edge:** Milled

Date	Mintage	F	VF	XF	Unc	BU
1931(k)	Est. 50,000	—	BV	150	225	—
1932(k) Rare	Inc. below					

Note: The 1932(k) examples with sword countermark are believed to be mint sports

KM# 12.2 DUKAT
3.4900 g., 0.9860 Gold 0.1106 oz. AGW **Ruler:** Alexander I
Countermark: Ear of corn **Obv:** Head left **Rev:** Crowned double eagle with shield on breast **Note:** Forgeries bearing no countermark exist for 1932 and possibly other dates. Small legend on both sides

Date	Mintage	F	VF	XF	Unc	BU
1931(k)	Est. 150,000	—	BV	140	185	—
1932(k)	Est. 70,000	—	BV	145	195	—
1933(k)	Est. 40,000	—	135	185	300	—
1934(k)	Est. 2,000	—	500	850	1,250	—

KM# 12.3 DUKAT
3.4900 g., 0.9860 Gold 0.1106 oz. AGW **Ruler:** Alexander I
Countermark: Sword **Obv:** Head left **Rev:** Crowned double eagle with shield on breast **Note:** Mule.

Date	Mintage	F	VF	XF	Unc	BU
1931(k)	—	—	—	3,000	5,000	—

KM# 13.1 DUKAT
3.4900 g., 0.9860 Gold 0.1106 oz. AGW **Ruler:** Alexander I
Obv: Head left **Rev:** Crowned double eagle with shield on breast
Note: Large legend on both sides.

Date	Mintage	F	VF	XF	Unc	BU
1931(k)	2,869	—	—	3,500	5,500	—

KM# 13.2 DUKAT
3.4900 g., 0.9860 Gold 0.1106 oz. AGW **Ruler:** Alexander I
Countermark: Sword **Obv:** Head left **Rev:** Crowned double eagle with shield on breast **Note:** Large-letter varieties bear the Kovnica, A.D. mint mark but were actually struck in Vienna.

Date	Mintage	F	VF	XF	Unc	BU
1931(k)	Inc. above	—	—	4,000	6,500	—

KM# 14.2 4 DUKATA
13.9600 g., 0.9860 Gold 0.4425 oz. AGW **Ruler:** Alexander I
Countermark: Ear of corn **Obv:** Conjoined busts of royal couple left **Rev:** Crowned double eagle with shield on breast

Date	Mintage	F	VF	XF	Unc	BU
1931(k)	Est. 15,000	—	480	750	950	—

Date	Mintage	F	VF	XF	Unc	BU
1932(k)	Est. 10,000	—	480	750	1,000	—
1933(k)	Est. 2,000	—	1,000	1,600	2,500	—

KM# 14.1 4 DUKATA
13.9600 g., 0.9860 Gold 0.4425 oz. AGW **Ruler:** Alexander I
Countermark: Sword **Obv:** Conjoined busts of royal couple left **Rev:** Crowned double eagle with shield on breast **Edge:** Milled
Note: Small legend on both sides. The 1932(k) examples with birds countermark are believed to be mint sports.

Date	Mintage	F	VF	XF	Unc	BU
1931(k)	Est. 10,000	—	480	750	950	—
1932(k) Rare	Inc. below					

KM# 14.3 4 DUKATA
13.9600 g., 0.9860 Gold 0.4425 oz. AGW **Ruler:** Alexander I
Obv: Conjoined busts of royal couple left **Rev:** Crowned double eagle with shield on breast **Note:** Without countermark on either side. Only one genuine piece has been reported.

Date	Mintage	F	VF	XF	Unc	BU
1931(k) Rare						

KM# A15.1 4 DUKATA
13.9600 g., 0.9860 Gold 0.4425 oz. AGW **Ruler:** Alexander I
Obv: Conjoined busts of royal couple left **Rev:** Crowned double eagle with shield on breast **Note:** Large legend on both sides. Sword Countermark.

Date	Mintage	F	VF	XF	Unc	BU
1931(k) Rare	51	—	—	—	—	—

KM# A15.2 4 DUKATA
13.9600 g., 0.9860 Gold 0.4425 oz. AGW **Ruler:** Alexander I
Countermark: Sword **Obv:** Conjoined busts of royal couple left, large legend **Rev:** Crowned double eagle with shield on breast, large legend **Note:** Large-letter varieties bear the Kovnica, A.D. mint mark but were actually struck in Vienna.

Date	Mintage	F	VF	XF	Unc	BU
1931(k)	Inc. above					

POST WAR COINAGE

KM# 25 50 PARA
Zinc, 18 mm. **Obv:** State emblem, nine stars below
Rev: Denomination surrounded by stars **Edge:** Milled

Date	Mintage	F	VF	XF	Unc	BU
1945	40,000,000	0.50	1.00	3.00	9.00	—

KM# 26 DINAR
Zinc, 20 mm. **Obv:** State emblem, nine stars below **Rev:** Stars surround denomination **Edge:** Milled

Date	Mintage	F	VF	XF	Unc	BU
1945	90,000,000	0.50	1.00	2.50	7.00	—

KM# 27   2 DINARA
Zinc, 22 mm.   **Obv:** State emblem, nine stars below **Rev:** Stars surround denomination **Edge:** Milled

Date	Mintage	F	VF	XF	Unc	BU
1945	70,000,000	0.50	1.25	3.00	9.00	—

KM# 28   5 DINARA
Zinc, 26.5 mm.   **Obv:** State emblem, nine stars below **Rev:** Stars surround denomination **Edge:** Milled

Date	Mintage	F	VF	XF	Unc	BU
1945	50,000,000	1.00	2.00	4.00	12.00	—

FEDERAL PEOPLE'S REPUBLIC

STANDARD COINAGE

KM# 29   50 PARA
Aluminum, 17.4 mm.   **Obv:** State emblem **Rev:** Denomination divides date, seven stars above **Edge:** Plain

Date	Mintage	F	VF	XF	Unc	BU
1953	—	—	—	0.10	0.50	—

KM# 30   DINAR
Aluminum, 19.8 mm.   **Obv:** State emblem **Rev:** Denomination divides date, seven stars above **Edge:** Plain

Date	Mintage	F	VF	XF	Unc	BU
1953	—	—	0.10	0.15	0.50	—

KM# 31   2 DINARA
Aluminum, 22.2 mm.   **Obv:** State emblem **Rev:** Denomination divides date, seven stars above **Edge:** Plain

Date	Mintage	F	VF	XF	Unc	BU
1953	—	—	0.10	0.25	0.75	—

KM# 32   5 DINARA
Aluminum, 24.6 mm.   **Obv:** State emblem **Rev:** Denomination divides date, seven stars above **Edge:** Plain

Date	Mintage	F	VF	XF	Unc	BU
1953	—	—	0.10	0.25	0.50	1.00

KM# 33   10 DINARA
Aluminum-Bronze, 21 mm.   **Obv:** State emblem **Rev:** Hand holding grain stalks below head left **Edge:** Milled

Date	Mintage	F	VF	XF	Unc	BU
1955	—	0.15	0.30	0.75	1.50	—

KM# 34   20 DINARA
Aluminum-Bronze, 25.5 mm.   **Obv:** State emblem **Rev:** Head at left looking right, cogwheel lower right **Edge:** Milled

Date	Mintage	F	VF	XF	Unc	BU
1955	—	0.25	0.50	1.00	2.00	—

KM# 35   50 DINARA
Aluminum-Bronze, 25.5 mm.   **Obv:** State emblem **Rev:** Two jugate heads right, cogwheel below **Edge:** Milled

Date	Mintage	F	VF	XF	Unc	BU
1955	—	0.25	0.75	2.00	4.50	—

SOCIALIST FEDERAL REPUBLIC

STANDARD COINAGE

KM# 42   5 PARA
1.5900 g., Copper-Zinc, 16 mm.   **Obv:** State emblem **Rev:** Denomination above date within wreath, six stars above **Edge:** Milled

Date	Mintage	F	VF	XF	Unc	BU
1965	23,839,900	—	0.10	0.20	0.40	—

KM# 43   5 PARA
1.5500 g., Copper-Zinc, 16 mm.   **Obv:** State emblem **Rev:** Denomination divides date **Edge:** Milled

Date	Mintage	F	VF	XF	Unc	BU
1965	16,200,000	—	—	0.10	0.20	—
1973	36,384,000	—	—	0.10	0.15	—
1974	3,628,000	—	—	0.10	0.25	—
1975	20,272,000	—	—	0.10	0.15	—
1976	30,490,000	—	—	0.10	0.15	—
1977	10,270,000	—	—	0.10	0.15	—
1978	12,000,000	—	—	0.10	0.15	—
1979	20,414,000	—	—	0.10	0.15	—
1980	22,412,000	—	—	0.10	0.15	—
1981	630,000	—	0.10	0.25	0.50	—

KM# 44   10 PARA
2.9700 g., Copper-Zinc, 21 mm.   **Obv:** State emblem **Rev:** Denomination divides date **Edge:** Milled

Date	Mintage	F	VF	XF	Unc	BU
1965	15,400,000	—	—	0.10	0.20	—
1973	15,647,000	—	—	0.10	0.20	—

Date	Mintage	F	VF	XF	Unc	BU
1974	60,139,000	—	—	0.10	0.20	—
1975	36,139,000	—	—	0.10	0.15	—
1976	36,111,000	—	—	0.10	0.15	—
1977	40,451,000	—	—	0.10	0.15	—
1978	50,129,000	—	—	0.10	0.15	—

Note: Two varieties of "7" exist

Date	Mintage	F	VF	XF	Unc	BU
1979	89,738,000	—	—	0.10	0.15	—
1980	90,111,000	—	—	0.10	0.15	—
1981	14,090,000	—	—	0.10	0.15	—

KM# 139   10 PARA
3.1300 g., Copper-Zinc, 18.01 mm.   **Obv:** State emblem **Rev:** Denomination **Edge:** Plain

Date	Mintage	F	VF	XF	Unc	BU
1990	174,028,000	—	—	0.10	0.15	—
1991	60,828,000	—	—	0.15	0.35	—

KM# 45   20 PARA
Copper-Zinc, 23.2 mm.   **Obv:** State emblem **Rev:** Denomination divides date **Edge:** Milled **Note:** Thickness varies: 1.3-1.5 mm.

Date	Mintage	F	VF	XF	Unc	BU
1965	—	—	—	0.10	0.30	—
1973	30,448,000	—	—	0.10	0.30	—
1974	31,364,000	—	—	0.10	0.30	—
1975	44,683,000	—	—	0.10	0.30	—
1976	33,312,000	—	—	0.10	0.30	—
1977	40,782,000	—	—	0.10	0.30	—
1978	39,999,000	—	—	0.10	0.30	—
1979	49,121,000	—	—	0.10	0.30	—
1980	73,757,000	—	—	0.10	0.30	—
1981	96,144,000	—	—	0.10	0.30	—

KM# 140   20 PARA
3.8000 g., Copper-Zinc   **Obv:** State emblem **Rev:** Denomination above date

Date	Mintage	VG	F	VF	XF	Unc
1990	174,028,500	—	—	0.10	0.20	0.50
1991	60,828,000	—	—	0.10	0.20	0.50

KM# 84   25 PARA
Bronze, 17 mm.   **Obv:** State emblem **Rev:** Denomination above date **Edge:** Plain

Date	Mintage	F	VF	XF	Unc	BU
1982	185,316,000	—	—	0.10	0.25	—
1983	65,290,000	—	—	0.15	0.30	—

KM# 46.1   50 PARA
Copper-Zinc, 25.5 mm.   **Obv:** State emblem **Rev:** Denomination divides date **Edge:** Milled

Date	Mintage	F	VF	XF	Unc	BU
1965	—	—	0.10	0.20	0.65	—
1973	23,739,000	—	—	0.10	0.20	0.65	—
1974	33,000	1.00	1.50	2.50	5.00	—
1975	10,220,000	—	0.10	0.20	0.80	—
1976	8,438,000	—	0.10	0.20	1.00	—
1977	17,864,000	—	0.10	0.20	0.75	—
1978	40,177,000	—	0.10	0.20	0.65	—

Note: Two varieties of "7" exist

Date	Mintage	F	VF	XF	Unc	BU
1979	3,021,000	0.50	1.00	2.00	5.00	—

KM# 46.2 50 PARA
Copper-Zinc **Obv:** State emblem **Rev:** Denomination divides date

Date	Mintage	F	VF	XF	Unc	BU
1979	12,278,000	0.20	0.50	1.00	2.50	—
1980	24,974,000	—	0.10	0.20	0.65	—
1981	40,319,000	—	0.10	0.20	0.65	—

KM# 85 50 PARA
2.8500 g., Bronze, 19 mm. **Obv:** State emblem
Rev: Denomination above date **Edge:** Plain

Date	Mintage	F	VF	XF	Unc	BU
1982	79,584,000	—	—	0.10	0.20	—
1983	72,100,000	—	—	0.10	0.20	—
1984	59,642,000	0.25	0.50	1.00	1.50	—

KM# 141 50 PARA
Copper-Zinc **Obv:** State emblem **Rev:** Denomination

Date	Mintage	F	VF	XF	Unc	BU
1990	137,873,000	—	—	0.10	0.20	—
1991	42,152,000	—	0.20	0.40	1.00	—

KM# 36 DINAR
0.9000 g., Aluminum, 19.8 mm. **Obv:** State emblem
Rev: Denomination divides date, seven stars above **Edge:** Plain

Date	Mintage	F	VF	XF	Unc	BU
1963	—	—	—	0.10	0.15	—

KM# 47 DINAR
Copper-Nickel, 21.8 mm. **Obv:** State emblem **Rev:** Denomination
and date within wreath, six stars above **Edge:** Milled

Date	Mintage	F	VF	XF	Unc	BU
1965	75,822,000	0.10	0.15	0.30	0.60	—

KM# 48 DINAR
Copper-Nickel, 21.8 mm. **Obv:** State emblem **Rev:** Denomination
above date within wreath, six stars above **Edge:** Milled

Date	Mintage	F	VF	XF	Unc	BU
1968	35,497,000	0.10	0.20	0.40	0.80	—

KM# 59 DINAR
Copper-Nickel-Zinc, 21.8 mm. **Obv:** State emblem **Rev:** Text
surrounds denomination within wreath, six stars above **Edge:** Milled

Date	Mintage	F	VF	XF	Unc	BU
1973	18,974,000	—	0.10	0.15	0.40	—
1974	42,724,000	—	0.10	0.15	0.35	—
1975	30,260,000	—	0.10	0.15	0.35	—
1976	21,849,000	—	0.10	0.15	0.35	—
1977	30,468,000	—	0.10	0.15	0.35	—
Note: Two varieties of wreath						
1977 Proof	—	Value: 40.00				
1978	35,032,000	—	0.10	0.15	0.35	—
1979	39,844,000	—	0.10	0.15	0.35	—
1980	60,630,000	—	0.10	0.15	0.35	—
1981	56,650,000	—	0.10	0.15	0.35	—

KM# 61 DINAR
Copper-Nickel-Zinc, 21.8 mm. **Series:** F.A.O. **Obv:** State
emblem **Rev:** Text surrounds denomination, stylized grain stalks
at sides **Edge:** Milled

Date	Mintage	F	VF	XF	Unc	BU
1976	500,000	—	0.10	0.30	1.00	—

KM# 86 DINAR
3.6000 g., Nickel-Brass, 20 mm. **Obv:** State emblem **Rev:** Text
surrounds denomination **Edge:** Milled

Date	Mintage	F	VF	XF	Unc	BU
1982	70,105,000	—	—	0.10	0.30	—
1983	114,180,000	—	—	0.10	0.20	—
1984	172,185,000	—	—	0.10	0.20	—
1985	64,436,000	—	—	0.10	0.25	—
1986	122,643,000	—	—	0.10	0.20	—

KM# 142 DINAR
Copper-Nickel-Zinc **Obv:** State emblem **Rev:** Text surrounds
denomination **Edge:** Milled

Date	Mintage	F	VF	XF	Unc	BU
1990	172,105,000	—	—	0.10	0.25	—
1991	79,549,000	—	0.15	0.25	0.75	—

KM# 37 2 DINARA
Aluminum, 22.2 mm. **Obv:** State emblem **Rev:** Denomination
divides date, seven stars above **Edge:** Plain

Date	Mintage	F	VF	XF	Unc	BU
1963	—	—	0.10	0.15	0.25	—

KM# 55 2 DINARA
Copper-Nickel-Zinc, 24.5 mm. **Series:** F.A.O. **Obv:** State
emblem **Rev:** Text surrounds denomination, grain stalks at sides
Edge: Milled

Date	Mintage	F	VF	XF	Unc	BU
1970	500,000	—	0.20	0.40	1.00	—

KM# 57 2 DINARA
Copper-Nickel-Zinc, 24.5 mm. **Obv:** State emblem **Rev:** Text
encircles denomination, wreath surrounds, six stars above
Edge: Milled

Date	Mintage	F	VF	XF	Unc	BU
1971	10,413,000	—	0.10	0.30	0.70	—
1972	18,446,000	—	0.10	0.20	0.50	—
1973	31,848,000	—	0.10	0.20	0.45	—
1974	10,989,000	—	0.10	0.20	0.50	—
1975	92,000	2.00	4.00	7.50	15.00	—
1976	6,092,000	—	0.10	0.20	0.50	—
1977	19,335,000	—	0.10	0.20	0.50	—
1978	13,035,000	—	0.10	0.20	0.50	—
1979	20,069,000	—	0.10	0.20	0.45	—
1980	36,088,000	—	0.10	0.20	0.45	—
1981	42,599,000	—	0.10	0.20	0.45	—

KM# 87 2 DINARA
4.4000 g., Nickel-Brass, 22 mm. **Obv:** State emblem **Rev:** Text
surrounds denomination **Edge:** Milled

Date	Mintage	F	VF	XF	Unc	BU
1982	40,632,000	—	0.10	0.15	0.35	—
1983	35,468,000	—	0.10	0.15	0.35	—
1984	51,500,000	—	0.10	0.15	0.35	—
1985	81,100,000	—	0.10	0.15	0.35	—
1986	50,453,000	—	0.10	0.15	0.35	—

KM# 143 2 DINARA
Copper-Nickel-Zinc **Obv:** State emblem **Rev:** Text surrounds
denomination

Date	Mintage	F	VF	XF	Unc	BU
1990	15,936,000	0.15	0.30	0.60	2.00	—
1991	32,836,000	—	0.20	0.40	1.00	—
1992	14,155,000	2.50	3.50	7.00	12.50	—

KM# 38 5 DINARA
Aluminum, 24.6 mm. **Obv:** State emblem **Rev:** Denomination
divides date, seven stars above **Edge:** Plain

Date	Mintage	F	VF	XF	Unc	BU
1963	—	0.10	0.20	0.35	0.50	—

KM# 56 5 DINARA
Copper-Nickel-Zinc, 27.5 mm. **Series:** F.A.O. **Obv:** State emblem **Rev:** Text surrounds denomination, grain stalks at sides **Edge:** Milled

Date	Mintage	F	VF	XF	Unc	BU
1970	500,000	0.20	0.50	1.00	2.50	—

KM# 58 5 DINARA
6.9000 g., Copper-Nickel-Zinc, 27.5 mm. **Obv:** State emblem **Rev:** Text encircles denomination, wreath surrounds, six stars above **Edge:** Milled **Note:** Regular issue.

Date	Mintage	F	VF	XF	Unc	BU
1971	10,224,000	0.20	0.40	0.60	1.00	—
	Note: Two varieties of wreath					
1972	27,974,000	0.10	0.20	0.35	0.60	—
	Note: Two varieties of 2 in date					
1973	12,705,000	0.20	0.40	0.60	1.00	—
1974	6,054,000	0.25	0.50	1.00	2.00	—
1975	13,533,000	0.10	0.20	0.35	0.60	—
1976	4,965,383	0.10	0.25	0.40	0.80	—
1977	922,000	0.30	0.60	1.20	2.50	—
1978	1,000,000	0.10	0.25	0.50	1.50	—
1979	3,000,000	0.10	0.25	0.40	0.80	—
1980	9,977,000	0.10	0.20	0.35	0.60	—
1981	15,450,000	0.10	0.20	0.35	0.60	—

KM# 60 5 DINARA
Copper-Nickel-Zinc, 27.5 mm. **Subject:** 30th Anniversary of Nazi Defeat **Obv:** State emblem **Rev:** Denomination, six stars

Date	Mintage	F	VF	XF	Unc	BU
1975	1,020,000	0.25	0.50	1.00	2.50	—

KM# 88 5 DINARA
5.5000 g., Nickel-Brass, 24 mm. **Obv:** State emblem **Rev:** Denomination **Edge:** Milled

Date	Mintage	F	VF	XF	Unc	BU
1982	40,956,000	—	0.10	0.15	0.50	—
1983	40,156,000	—	0.10	0.15	0.50	—
1984	33,023,000	—	0.10	0.15	0.50	—
1985	94,422,000	—	0.10	0.15	0.50	—
1986	37,199,000	—	0.10	0.15	0.50	—

KM# 144 5 DINARA
Copper-Nickel-Zinc **Obv:** State emblem **Rev:** Denomination

Date	Mintage	F	VF	XF	Unc	BU
1990	9,354,000	0.25	0.45	1.00	2.50	—

Date	Mintage	F	VF	XF	Unc	BU
1991	113,420,000	—	0.25	0.50	1.25	—
1992	15,970,000	1.50	2.50	4.00	7.00	—

KM# 145 5 DINARA
Copper-Nickel-Zinc **Subject:** 1990 Chess Olympiad **Obv:** State emblem within flat bottom circle **Rev:** Logo

Date	Mintage	F	VF	XF	Unc	BU
1990 Proof	20,000	Value: 8.00				

KM# 39 10 DINARA
Aluminum-Bronze, 21 mm. **Obv:** State emblem **Rev:** Hand holding grain stalks below head left **Edge:** Milled

Date	Mintage	F	VF	XF	Unc	BU
1963	—	0.15	0.30	0.75	1.50	—

KM# 62 10 DINARA
9.8000 g., Copper-Nickel, 30 mm. **Obv:** State emblem **Rev:** Text encircles denomination, wreath surrounds, six stars above **Edge:** Milled

Date	Mintage	F	VF	XF	Unc	BU
1976	10,549,500	0.30	0.60	0.75	1.50	—
1977	39,645,000	0.30	0.60	0.75	1.25	—
	Note: Two varieties of wreath					
1978	29,834,000	0.30	0.60	0.75	1.25	—
1979	4,969,000	0.30	0.60	0.75	1.25	—
1980	10,139,000	0.30	0.60	0.75	1.25	—
1981	20,166,000	0.30	0.60	0.75	1.25	—

KM# 63 10 DINARA
Copper-Nickel-Zinc, 30 mm. **Series:** F.A.O. **Obv:** State emblem **Rev:** Text surrounds denomination, grain stalks at sides, six stars above

Date	Mintage	F	VF	XF	Unc	BU
1976	500,000	0.50	0.75	1.00	2.50	—

KM# 89 10 DINARA
5.2000 g., Copper-Nickel, 23 mm. **Obv:** State emblem **Rev:** Text surrounds denomination **Edge:** Milled

Date	Mintage	F	VF	XF	Unc	BU
1982	8,862,000	—	0.10	0.20	0.80	—
1983	42,400,000	—	0.10	0.20	0.75	—
1984	30,900,000	—	0.10	0.20	0.75	—
1985	31,647,000	—	0.10	0.20	0.75	—
1986	40,739,000	—	0.10	0.20	0.75	—
1987	104,988,000	—	0.10	0.20	0.75	—
1988	27,614,000	—	0.10	0.20	0.75	—

KM# 96 10 DINARA
Copper-Nickel, 30 mm. **Subject:** 40th Anniversary - Battle of Neretva River **Obv:** State emblem within flat bottomed circle **Rev:** Bridge over the River Neretva **Edge:** Milled

Date	Mintage	F	VF	XF	Unc	BU
ND(1983)	900,000	—	1.00	2.00	4.50	6.00
ND(1983) Proof	100,000	Value: 8.00				

KM# 97.1 10 DINARA
Copper-Nickel, 30 mm. **Subject:** 40th Anniversary - Battle of Sutjeska River **Obv:** State emblem within flat bottom circle **Rev:** Pathway divides monument **Edge:** Milled

Date	Mintage	F	VF	XF	Unc	BU
ND(1983)	900,000	—	1.00	1.50	3.50	5.00
ND(1983) Proof	100,000	Value: 7.50				

KM# 97.2 10 DINARA
Copper-Nickel **Subject:** 40th Anniversary - Battle of Sutjeska River **Obv:** State emblem within flat bottom circle **Rev:** Without pathway in front of monument

Date	Mintage	F	VF	XF	Unc	BU
ND(1983)	—	—	3.00	6.00	10.00	12.00

KM# 131 10 DINARA
Brass **Obv:** Text surrounds state emblem within square **Rev:** Denomination within square, text on four sides **Edge:** Plain

Date	Mintage	F	VF	XF	Unc	BU
1988	35,992,000	—	—	0.10	0.25	0.35
1989	75,000,000	—	—	0.10	0.25	0.35

KM# 40 20 DINARA
3.7000 g., Aluminum-Bronze, 23.2 mm. **Obv:** State emblem **Rev:** Head at left looking right, cogwheel below **Edge:** Milled

Date	Mintage	F	VF	XF	Unc	BU
1963	—	0.50	1.00	1.75	3.50	—

KM# 49 20 DINARA
9.0000 g., 0.9250 Silver 0.2676 oz. ASW, 28 mm. **Subject:** 25th Anniversary of Republic **Obv:** State emblem within circle **Rev:** Head left **Edge:** Milled **Note:** Mint mark: NI (Numismatica Italiana, Milano, Italy).

Date	Mintage	VG	F	VF	XF	Unc
1968 Proof	100,000	Value: 25.00				
1968 NI Proof	Inc. above	Value: 25.00				

KM# 112 20 DINARA
Copper-Zinc-Nickel, 25 mm. **Obv:** State emblem **Rev:** Denomination **Edge:** Milled

Date	Mintage	F	VF	XF	Unc	BU
1985	5,000,000	—	0.10	0.20	0.50	—
1986	20,235,000	—	0.10	0.15	0.35	—
1987	39,514,000	—	0.10	0.15	0.35	—

KM# 132 20 DINARA
Brass Obv: Text surrounds state emblem within square
Rev: Denomination within square, text on four sides Edge: Plain

Date	Mintage	F	VF	XF	Unc	BU
1988	29,775,000	—	—	0.10	0.25	0.35
1989	12,994,000	—	—	0.10	0.25	0.35

KM# 41 50 DINARA
Aluminum-Bronze, 25.5 mm. Obv: State emblem
Rev: Conjoined heads looking right, cogwheel below
Edge: Milled Note: Exists with filled letter in denomination. Two
varieties of the letter "P" in ANHAPA.

Date	Mintage	F	VF	XF	Unc	BU
1963	—	1.00	2.50	6.00	16.00	

KM# 50 50 DINARA
20.0000 g., 0.9250 Silver 0.5948 oz., ASW, 34 mm.
Subject: 25th Anniversary of Republic Obv: State emblem within
circle Rev: Head left within circle Note: Mint mark: NI.

Date	Mintage	F	VF	XF	Unc	BU
ND(1968) Proof	100,000	Value: 40.00				
ND(1968) NI Proof	Inc. above	Value: 40.00				

KM# 113 50 DINARA
Copper-Zinc-Nickel, 27 mm. Obv: State emblem
Rev: Denomination Edge: Milled

Date	Mintage	F	VF	XF	Unc	BU
1985	25,488,000	—	0.10	0.25	0.75	—
1986	20,353,000	—	0.10	0.25	0.75	—
1987	21,792,000	—	0.10	0.25	0.75	—
1988	28,370,000	—	0.10	0.25	0.75	—

KM# 133 50 DINARA
Brass Obv: Text surrounds state emblem within square
Rev: Denomination within square, text on four sides

Date	Mintage	F	VF	XF	Unc	BU
1988	46,973,000	—	—	0.10	0.25	0.35
1989	2,999,000	—	0.50	1.00	2.00	3.50

Note: Not issued

KM# 51 100 DINARA
7.8200 g., 0.9000 Gold 0.2263 oz. AGW Subject: 25th
Anniversary of Republic Obv: State emblem within circle
Rev: Figures with arms raised, large rock in background

Date	Mintage	F	VF	XF	Unc	BU
ND(1968) Proof	10,000	Value: 250				
ND(1968) NI Proof	Inc. above	Value: 250				

KM# 65 100 DINARA
10.0000 g., 0.9250 Silver 0.2974 oz. ASW, 28 mm.
Subject: 8th Mediterranean Games at Split Obv: Map of Split
left of emblem Rev: Bust left

Date	Mintage	F	VF	XF	Unc	BU
1978 Proof	71,000	Value: 22.50				

KM# 90 100 DINARA
13.0000 g., 0.9250 Silver 0.3866 oz. ASW, 30 mm. Series: 1984
Winter Olympics Subject: Ice Hockey Obv: Emblem and Olympic
logo on separate shields within flat bottom circle Rev: Hockey
players Edge: Milled

Date	Mintage	F	VF	XF	Unc	BU
1982 Proof	110,000	Value: 10.00				

KM# 98 100 DINARA
13.0000 g., 0.9250 Silver 0.3866 oz. ASW, 30 mm. Series: 1984
Winter Olympics Subject: Figure Skating Obv: Emblem and
Olympic logo on separate shields within flat bottom circle
Rev: Figure skater

Date	Mintage	VG	F	VF	XF	Unc
1983 Proof	110,000	Value: 10.00				

KM# 99 100 DINARA
13.0000 g., 0.9250 Silver 0.3866 oz. ASW, 30 mm. Series: 1984
Winter Olympics Subject: Bobsledding Obv: Emblem and
Olympic logo on separate shields within flat bottom circle
Rev: Bobsledders

Date	Mintage	F	VF	XF	Unc	BU
1983 Proof	110,000	Value: 10.00				

KM# 105 100 DINARA
13.0000 g., 0.9250 Silver 0.3866 oz. ASW, 30 mm. Series: 1984
Winter Olympics Subject: Speed Skating Obv: Emblem and
Olympic logo on separate shields within flat bottom circle Rev: Skater

Date	Mintage	F	VF	XF	Unc	BU
1984 Proof	110,000	Value: 10.00				

KM# 106 100 DINARA
13.0000 g., 0.9250 Silver 0.3866 oz. ASW, 30 mm. Series: 1984
Winter Olympics Subject: Pairs Figure Skating Obv: Emblem
and Olympic logo on separate shields within flat bottom circle
Rev: Figure skaters

Date	Mintage	F	VF	XF	Unc	BU
1984 Proof	110,000	Value: 10.00				

KM# 114 100 DINARA
Copper-Zinc-Nickel, 29 mm. Obv: State emblem
Rev: Denomination Edge: Milled

Date	Mintage	F	VF	XF	Unc	BU
1985	18,684,000	—	0.25	0.65	1.50	—
1986	17,905,000	—	0.20	0.50	1.00	—
1987	94,069,000	—	—	0.40	0.80	—
1988	50,294,000	—	—	0.40	0.80	—

KM# 115 100 DINARA
Copper-Nickel-Zinc Subject: 40th Anniversary - Liberation From
Fascism Obv: State emblem within flat bottom circle Rev: Head
left within circle of design

Date	Mintage	F	VF	XF	Unc	BU
ND(1985) Proof	200,000	Value: 4.00				

KM# 127.1 100 DINARA
Copper-Nickel Subject: 200th Anniversary - Birth of Karajich
Obv: State emblem Rev: Squared head right

Date	Mintage	F	VF	XF	Unc	BU
1987 Proof	Est. 200,000	Value: 4.00				

KM# 127.2   100 DINARA
Copper-Nickel   **Subject:** 200th Anniversary - Birth of Karajich
Obv: State emblem within flat bottom circle **Rev:** Squared head right

Date	Mintage	F	VF	XF	Unc	BU
1987 Proof	Inc. above				Value: 25.00	

KM# 134   100 DINARA
Brass   **Obv:** Text surrounds state emblem within square
Rev: Denomination within square, text on four sides

Date	Mintage	F	VF	XF	Unc	BU
1988	12,610,000	—	—	0.15	0.30	0.50
1989	124,260,000	—	—	0.15	0.30	0.50

KM# 146   100 DINARA
13.0000 g., 0.9250 Silver 0.3866 oz. ASW **Subject:** 1990 Chess
Olympiad **Obv:** State emblem within flat bottom circle
Rev: Petrovaradin clock tower, chessboard background

Date	Mintage	F	VF	XF	Unc	BU
1990 Proof	10,000				Value: 27.50	

KM# 66   150 DINARA
12.5000 g., 0.9250 Silver 0.3717 oz. ASW, 30 mm.
Subject: 8th Mediterranean Games at Split **Obv:** State emblem
above boats **Rev:** Head left

Date	Mintage	F	VF	XF	Unc	BU
1978 Proof	70,000				Value: 22.50	

KM# 147   150 DINARA
17.0000 g., 0.9250 Silver 0.5055 oz. ASW **Subject:** 1990 Chess
Olympiad **Obv:** State emblem within flat bottom circle
Rev: Globe, chessboard design at right

Date	Mintage	F	VF	XF	Unc	BU
1990 Proof	10,000				Value: 37.50	

KM# 52   200 DINARA
15.6400 g., 0.9000 Gold 0.4525 oz. AGW, 30 mm.
Subject: 25th Anniversary of Republic **Obv:** State emblem within
circle **Rev:** Head left

Date	Mintage	F	VF	XF	Unc	BU
ND(1968) Proof	10,000				Value: 485	
ND(1968) NI Proof	Inc. above				Value: 485	

KM# 64a   200 DINARA
15.0000 g., 0.7500 Silver 0.3617 oz. ASW **Subject:** Tito's 85th
Birthday **Obv:** State emblem at left, dates at right, denomination
below, fan background **Rev:** Head left

Date	Mintage	F	VF	XF	Unc	BU
1977 Proof	500,000				Value: 12.50	

KM# 64   200 DINARA
0.6000 g., 0.7500 Silver 0.0145 oz. ASW **Subject:** Tito's 85th
Birthday **Obv:** State emblem at left, dates at right, denomination
below, fan background **Rev:** Head left **Note:** Edge varieties with
inscription in Cyrillic, Western and alternating Cyrillic-Western exist.

Date	Mintage	F	VF	XF	Unc	BU
1977	300,000	—	—	—	8.00	10.00

KM# 67   200 DINARA
15.0000 g., 0.9250 Silver 0.4461 oz. ASW **Subject:** 8th
Mediterranean Games at Split **Obv:** State emblem at left, ancient
urn at right **Rev:** Head left

Date	Mintage	F	VF	XF	Unc	BU
1978 Proof	58,000				Value: 25.00	

KM# 68   250 DINARA
17.5000 g., 0.9250 Silver 0.5204 oz. ASW, 34 mm.
Subject: 8th Mediterranean Games at Split **Obv:** Basilica of St.
Donat in Zadar **Rev:** Head left

Date	Mintage	F	VF	XF	Unc	BU
1979 Proof	48,000				Value: 30.00	

KM# 91   250 DINARA
17.0000 g., 0.9250 Silver 0.5055 oz. ASW, 34 mm. **Series:** 1984
Winter Olympics **Obv:** Emblem and Olympic logo on separate
shields within flat bottom circle **Rev:** Sarajevo view within circle

Date	Mintage	F	VF	XF	Unc	BU
1982 Proof	110,000				Value: 12.00	

KM# 100   250 DINARA
17.0000 g., 0.9250 Silver 0.5055 oz. ASW, 34 mm. **Series:** 1984
Winter Olympics **Obv:** Emblem and Olympic logo on separate
shields within flat bottom circle **Rev:** Artifact within circle

Date	Mintage	F	VF	XF	Unc	BU
1983 Proof	110,000				Value: 12.00	

KM# 101   250 DINARA
17.0000 g., 0.9250 Silver 0.5055 oz. ASW, 34 mm. **Series:** 1984
Winter Olympics **Obv:** Emblem and Olympic logo on separate
shields within flat bottom circle **Rev:** Radimlja tombs

Date	Mintage	F	VF	XF	Unc	BU
1983 Proof	110,000				Value: 12.00	

KM# 107   250 DINARA
17.0000 g., 0.9250 Silver 0.5055 oz. ASW, 34 mm. **Series:** 1984
Winter Olympics **Obv:** Emblem and Olympic logo on separate
shields within flat bottom circle **Rev:** Jajce village

Date	Mintage	F	VF	XF	Unc	BU
1984 Proof	110,000				Value: 12.00	

KM# 108   250 DINARA
17.0000 g., 0.9250 Silver 0.5055 oz. ASW, 34 mm. **Series:** 1984
Winter Olympics **Obv:** Emblem and Olympic logo on separate
shields within flat bottom circle **Rev:** Head of Tito left

Date	Mintage	F	VF	XF	Unc	BU
1984 Proof	110,000				Value: 12.00	

KM# 69   300 DINARA
20.0000 g., 0.9250 Silver 0.5948 oz. ASW, 36 mm.
Subject: Eighth Mediterranean Games at Split **Obv:** State emblem and date above church **Rev:** Bust left

Date	Mintage	F	VF	XF	Unc	BU
1978 Proof	36,000	Value: 37.50				

KM# 70   350 DINARA
22.5000 g., 0.9250 Silver 0.6691 oz. ASW, 36 mm.
Subject: 8th Mediterranean Games at Split **Obv:** Statue divides emblem and denomination **Rev:** Head left

Date	Mintage	F	VF	XF	Unc	BU
1978 Proof	24,000	Value: 40.00				

KM# 71   400 DINARA
25.0000 g., 0.9250 Silver 0.7435 oz. ASW, 40 mm.
Subject: 8th Mediterranean Games at Split **Obv:** State emblem above pillared building **Rev:** Head left

Date	Mintage	F	VF	XF	Unc	BU
1978 Proof	24,000	Value: 40.00				

KM# 53   500 DINARA
39.1000 g., 0.9000 Gold 1.1313 oz. AGW, 45 mm.
Subject: 25th Anniversary of Republic **Obv:** State emblem **Rev:** Figures with arms raised, large rock in background

Date	Mintage	F	VF	XF	Unc	BU
ND(1968) Proof	10,000	Value: 1,250				
ND(1968) NI Proof	Inc. above	Value: 1,250				

KM# 76   500 DINARA
8.0000 g., 0.9250 Silver 0.2379 oz. ASW, 27 mm.
Subject: Vukovar Congress **Obv:** State emblem above city hall of Vukovar **Rev:** Bust 3/4 left

Date	Mintage	F	VF	XF	Unc	BU
1980 Proof	18,000	Value: 20.00				

KM# 80   500 DINARA
8.0000 g., 0.7500 Silver 0.1929 oz. ASW, 27 mm.
Subject: World Table Tennis Championship Games **Obv:** State emblem above town Novi Sad **Rev:** Stylized flower

Date	Mintage	F	VF	XF	Unc	BU
1981 Proof	18,000	Value: 25.00				

KM# 92   500 DINARA
23.0000 g., 0.9250 Silver 0.6840 oz. ASW **Series:** 1984 Winter Olympics **Subject:** Downhill Skiing **Obv:** Emblem and Olympic logo on separate shields within flat bottom circle **Rev:** Skier

Date	Mintage	F	VF	XF	Unc	BU
1982 Proof	110,000	Value: 14.00				

KM# 102   500 DINARA
23.0000 g., 0.9250 Silver 0.6840 oz. ASW, 38 mm. **Series:** 1984 Winter Olympics **Subject:** Ski Jumping **Obv:** Emblem and Olympic logo on separate shields within flat bottom circle **Rev:** Ski jumper right

Date	Mintage	F	VF	XF	Unc	BU
1983 Proof	110,000	Value: 14.00				

KM# 103   500 DINARA
23.0000 g., 0.9250 Silver 0.6840 oz. ASW, 38 mm. **Series:** 1984 Winter Olympics **Subject:** Biathalon **Obv:** Emblem and Olympic logo on separate shields within flat bottom circle **Rev:** Bi-athletes

Date	Mintage	F	VF	XF	Unc	BU
1983 Proof	110,000	Value: 14.00				

KM# 109   500 DINARA
23.0000 g., 0.9250 Silver 0.6840 oz. ASW, 38 mm. **Series:** 1984 Winter Olympics **Subject:** Cross-country Skiing **Obv:** Emblem and Olympic logo on separate shields within flat bottom circle **Rev:** Skier

Date	Mintage	F	VF	XF	Unc	BU
1984 Proof	110,000	Value: 14.00				

KM# 110   500 DINARA
23.0000 g., 0.9250 Silver 0.6840 oz. ASW, 38 mm. **Series:** 1984 Winter Olympics **Subject:** Slalom Skiing **Obv:** Emblem and Olympic logo on separate shields within flat bottom circle **Rev:** Skier

Date	Mintage	F	VF	XF	Unc	BU
1984 Proof	110,000	Value: 14.00				

KM# 116   500 DINARA
13.0000 g., 0.9250 Silver 0.3866 oz. ASW **Subject:** Ski Jumping Championship **Obv:** Similar to 10,000 Dinara, KM#123 **Rev:** Herons

Date	Mintage	F	VF	XF	Unc	BU
1985 Proof	50,000	Value: 16.50				

KM# 54   1000 DINARA
78.2000 g., 0.9000 Gold 2.2627 oz. AGW, 55 mm.
Subject: 25th Anniversary of Republic **Obv:** State emblem **Rev:** Bust of Tito left

Date	Mintage	F	VF	XF	Unc	BU
ND(1968) Proof	10,000	Value: 2,400				
ND(1968) NI Proof	Inc. above	Value: 2,400				

KM# 77   1000 DINARA
14.0000 g., 0.9250 Silver 0.4163 oz. ASW, 30 mm.
Subject: Vukovar Congress **Obv:** State emblem above city hall in Vukovar **Rev:** Bust 3/4 left

Date	Mintage	F	VF	XF	Unc	BU
1980 Proof	16,000	Value: 27.50				

KM# 78a   1000 DINARA
26.0000 g., 0.9250 Silver 0.7732 oz. ASW **Subject:** Tito's Death **Obv:** State emblem on map of Yugoslavia, globe background **Rev:** Bust 3/4 left

Date	Mintage	F	VF	XF	Unc	BU
1980 Proof	200,000	Value: 30.00				
1980 ZM Proof	Inc. above	Value: 30.00				

KM# 78   1000 DINARA
25.9000 g., 0.7500 Silver 0.6245 oz. ASW **Subject:** Tito's Death
Obv: State emblem on map of Yugoslavia, globe background
Rev: Bust 3/4 left **Note:** Eyes with and without pupils.

Date	Mintage	F	VF	XF	Unc	BU
1980	800,000				25.00	27.50

KM# 81   1000 DINARA
14.0000 g., 0.7500 Silver 0.3376 oz. ASW, 30 mm.
Subject: World Table Tennis Championship Games **Obv:** State
emblem above town Novi Sad **Rev:** Hand with racket hitting ball

Date	Mintage	F	VF	XF	Unc	BU
1981 Proof	16,000	Value: 30.00				

KM# 82   1000 DINARA
14.0000 g., 0.7500 Silver 0.3376 oz. ASW, 30 mm.
Subject: 40th Anniversary of Uprising and Revolution **Obv:** State
emblem **Rev:** Bust and dates left, stars in background

Date	Mintage	F	VF	XF	Unc	BU
1981 Proof	100,000	Value: 22.00				

KM# 93   1000 DINARA
18.0000 g., 0.9250 Silver 0.5353 oz. ASW
Subject: International Canoeing Championships **Obv:** State
emblem left of statue **Rev:** City views, bird on left

Date	Mintage	F	VF	XF	Unc	BU
1982 Proof	46,000	Value: 32.50				

KM# 117   1000 DINARA
23.0000 g., 0.9250 Silver 0.6840 oz. ASW, 38 mm.
Subject: Ski Jumping Championship **Obv:** State emblem on
shield within flat bottom circle, denomination below **Rev:** Bloudek

Date	Mintage	F	VF	XF	Unc	BU
1985 Proof	20,000	Value: 35.00				

KM# 118   1000 DINARA
23.0000 g., 0.9250 Silver 0.6840 oz. ASW, 38 mm.
Subject: Ski Jumping Championship **Obv:** Similar to 10,000
Dinara, KM#123 **Rev:** Slovenian cradle

Date	Mintage	F	VF	XF	Unc	BU
1985 Proof	20,000	Value: 35.00				

KM# 119   1000 DINARA
6.0000 g., 0.9250 Silver 0.1784 oz. ASW **Subject:** Sinjska Alka
Obv: State emblem at left of map outline **Rev:** Figures with pack
horse

Date	Mintage	F	VF	XF	Unc	BU
ND(1985) Proof	60,000	Value: 18.00				

KM# 148   1000 DINARA
3.5000 g., 0.9000 Gold 0.1013 oz. AGW **Subject:** 1990 Chess
Olympiad **Obv:** State emblem above denomination **Rev:** Logo

Date	Mintage	F	VF	XF	Unc	BU
1990 Proof	2,000	Value: 185				

KM# 72   1500 DINARA
8.8000 g., 0.9000 Gold 0.2546 oz. AGW, 24 mm.   **Subject:** 8th
Mediterranean Games at Split **Obv:** State emblem above rings
Rev: Head left

Date	Mintage	F	VF	XF	Unc	BU
1978 Proof	35,000	Value: 275				

KM# 79   1500 DINARA
22.0000 g., 0.9250 Silver 0.6542 oz. ASW, 34 mm.
Subject: Vukovar Congress **Obv:** State emblem above city hall
in Vukovar **Rev:** Bust 3/4 left

Date	Mintage	F	VF	XF	Unc	BU
1980 Proof	16,000	Value: 35.00				

KM# 83   1500 DINARA
22.0000 g., 0.7500 Silver 0.5305 oz. ASW, 34 mm.
Subject: World Table Tennis Championship Games **Obv:** State
emblem over town view **Rev:** Stylized design of city

Date	Mintage	F	VF	XF	Unc	BU
1981 Proof	16,000	Value: 35.00				

KM# 94   1500 DINARA
22.0000 g., 0.9250 Silver 0.6542 oz. ASW, 36 mm.
Subject: International Canoeing Championships **Rev:** Tito

Date	Mintage	F	VF	XF	Unc	BU
1982 Proof	36,000	Value: 32.50				

KM# 73   2000 DINARA
11.8000 g., 0.9000 Gold 0.3414 oz. AGW, 27 mm. **Subject:** 8th
Mediterranean Games at Split **Obv:** State emblem above city
view **Rev:** Head left

Date	Mintage	F	VF	XF	Unc	BU
1978 Proof	35,000	Value: 375				

KM# 120   2000 DINARA
14.0000 g., 0.9250 Silver 0.4163 oz. ASW **Subject:** Sinska Alka
Obv: State emblem left of map outline **Rev:** Three figures on
horseback

Date	Mintage	F	VF	XF	Unc	BU
ND(1985) Proof	20,000	Value: 25.00				

KM# 74   2500 DINARA
14.7000 g., 0.9000 Gold 0.4253 oz. AGW **Subject:** 8th
Mediterranean Games at Split **Obv:** State emblem above stadium
Rev: Bust left

Date	Mintage	F	VF	XF	Unc	BU
1978 Proof	35,000	Value: 475				

KM# 121 3000 DINARA

26.0000 g., 0.9250 Silver 0.7732 oz. ASW **Subject:** Sinkska Alka **Obv:** State emblem left of map outline **Rev:** Armored figures

Date	Mintage	F	VF	XF	Unc	BU
ND(1985) Proof	20,000	Value: 37.50				

KM# 128 3000 DINARA

13.0000 g., 0.9250 Silver 0.3866 oz. ASW **Subject:** 200th Anniversary - Birth of Krajich **Obv:** State emblem on shield within flat bottom circle **Rev:** Squared head right

Date	Mintage	F	VF	XF	Unc	BU
1987 Proof	50,000	Value: 32.50				

KM# 75 5000 DINARA

29.5000 g., 0.9000 Gold 0.8536 oz. AGW, 38 mm. **Subject:** 8th Mediterranean Games at Split **Obv:** State emblem above palace of Diocletian in Split **Rev:** Bust left

Date	Mintage	F	VF	XF	Unc	BU
1978 Proof	12,000	Value: 925				

KM# 95 5000 DINARA

8.0000 g., 0.9000 Gold 0.2315 oz. AGW, 24 mm. **Series:** 1984 Winter Olympics **Obv:** Emblem and Olympic logo on separate shields within flat bottom circle **Rev:** Olympic emblem within circle

Date	Mintage	F	VF	XF	Unc	BU
1982 Proof	55,000	Value: 250				

KM# 104 5000 DINARA

8.0000 g., 0.9000 Gold 0.2315 oz. AGW, 24 mm. **Series:** 1984 Winter Olympics **Obv:** Emblem and Olympic logo on separate shields within flat bottom circle **Rev:** Bust 3/4 left within circle

Date	Mintage	F	VF	XF	Unc	BU
1983 Proof	55,000	Value: 250				

KM# 111 5000 DINARA

8.0000 g., 0.9000 Gold 0.2315 oz. AGW, 24 mm. **Series:** 1984 Winter Olympics **Obv:** Emblem and Olympic logo on separate shields within flat bottom circle **Rev:** Olympic torch within circle

Date	Mintage	F	VF	XF	Unc	BU
1984 Proof	55,000	Value: 250				

KM# 122 5000 DINARA

23.5000 g., 0.9250 Silver 0.6988 oz. ASW **Subject:** 400th Anniversary - Liberation from Fascism **Note:** Similar to 100 Dinara, KM#115.

Date	Mintage	F	VF	XF	Unc	BU
1985 Proof	100,000	Value: 40.00				

KM# 129 5000 DINARA

17.0000 g., 0.9250 Silver 0.5055 oz. ASW **Subject:** 200th Anniversary - Birth of Karajich **Obv:** State emblem on shield within flat bottom circle **Rev:** Squared head right

Date	Mintage	F	VF	XF	Unc	BU
1987 Proof	Est. 50,000	Value: 35.00				

KM# 135 5000 DINARA

Copper-Zinc-Nickel **Subject:** Non-aligned Summit **Obv:** State emblem **Rev:** Symbols within circle

Date	Mintage	F	VF	XF	Unc	BU
ND(1989) Proof	50,000	Value: 4.50				

KM# 123 10000 DINARA

8.0000 g., 0.9000 Gold 0.2315 oz. AGW, 24 mm. **Subject:** World Ski Jumping Championship

Date	Mintage	F	VF	XF	Unc	BU
1985 Proof	10,000	Value: 250				

KM# 124 10000 DINARA

5.0000 g., 0.9000 Gold 0.1447 oz. AGW **Subject:** Sinjska Alka

Date	Mintage	F	VF	XF	Unc	BU
ND(1985) Proof	12,000	Value: 165				

KM# 125 20000 DINARA

8.0000 g., 0.9000 Gold 0.2315 oz. AGW **Subject:** Sinjska Alka

Date	Mintage	F	VF	XF	Unc	BU
ND(1985) Proof	8,000	Value: 265				

KM# 126 40000 DINARA

14.0000 g., 0.9000 Gold 0.4051 oz. AGW **Subject:** Sinjska Alka **Obv:** State emblem left of map outline **Rev:** Three figures on horseback

Date	Mintage	F	VF	XF	Unc	BU
ND(1985) Proof	5,000	Value: 475				

KM# 130 50000 DINARA

8.0000 g., 0.9000 Gold 0.2315 oz. AGW **Subject:** 200th Anniversary - Birth of Karajich **Obv:** State emblem on shield within flat bottom circle **Rev:** Squared head right

Date	Mintage	F	VF	XF	Unc	BU
1987 Proof	Est. 10,000	Value: 250				

KM# 136 50000 DINARA

13.0000 g., 0.9250 Silver 0.3866 oz. ASW **Subject:** Non-aligned Summit **Obv:** State emblem above denomination **Rev:** Statue left divides dates within circle

Date	Mintage	F	VF	XF	Unc	BU
ND(1989) Proof	15,000	Value: 25.00				

KM# 137 100000 DINARA

17.0000 g., 0.9250 Silver 0.5055 oz. ASW **Subject:** Non-aligned Summit **Obv:** State emblem above denomination **Rev:** Building above dates within circle

Date	Mintage	F	VF	XF	Unc	BU
ND(1989) Proof	10,000	Value: 35.00				

KM# 138 2000000 DINARA

8.0000 g., 0.9000 Gold 0.2315 oz. AGW **Subject:** Non-aligned Summit **Obv:** State emblem above denomination **Rev:** Symbols within circle

Date	Mintage	F	VF	XF	Unc	BU
ND(1989) Proof	5,000	Value: 275				

FEDERAL REPUBLIC

STANDARD COINAGE

KM# 161 PARA

Brass **Obv:** Monogram on shield **Rev:** Denomination and date

Date	Mintage	F	VF	XF	Unc	BU
1994	25,350,000	—	—	—	0.35	0.50

KM# 164.1 5 PARA

Brass **Obv:** Monogram on shield **Rev:** Denomination and date

Date	Mintage	F	VF	XF	Unc	BU
1994	30,408,000	—	—	—	0.50	0.65
1995	3,400,000	—	—	—	0.60	0.85

KM# 164.2 5 PARA

2.7200 g., Brass, 17 mm. **Obv:** Monogram on shield **Rev:** Denomination and date **Note:** Reduced size.

Date	Mintage	F	VF	XF	Unc	BU
1996	9,951,000	—	—	—	0.50	0.70

KM# 162.1 10 PARA
Copper-Nickel-Zinc **Obv:** Monogram on shield
Rev: Denomination and date

Date	Mintage	F	VF	XF	Unc	BU
1994	52,161,000	—			0.50	0.65

KM# 162.2 10 PARA
Brass **Obv:** Monogram on shield **Rev:** Denomination and date
Note: Reduced size.

Date	Mintage	F	VF	XF	Unc	BU
1995	31,041,000	—			0.65	0.85

KM# 173 10 PARA
3.3600 g., Brass **Obv:** National arms **Rev:** Denomination and date

Date	Mintage	F	VF	XF	Unc	BU
1996	18,129,000	—			0.50	0.65
1997	21,384,000	—			0.50	0.65
1998	5,153,000	—			0.50	0.70

KM# 163 50 PARA
Copper-Nickel-Zinc **Obv:** Monogram on shield **Rev:** Date and denomination

Date	Mintage	F	VF	XF	Unc	BU
1994	45,013,000	—			0.75	0.90

KM# 163a 50 PARA
Brass **Obv:** Monogram on shield **Rev:** Date and denomination

Date	Mintage	F	VF	XF	Unc	BU
1995	19,193,000	—			1.00	1.20

KM# 174 50 PARA
Brass **Obv:** National arms **Rev:** Date and denomination

Date	Mintage	F	VF	XF	Unc	BU
1996	3,520,000	—			1.00	1.25
1997	14,742,000	—			1.00	1.20
1998	20,050,000	—			1.00	1.20
1999	18,140,000	—			1.00	1.20

KM# 179 50 PARA
3.3000 g., Brass, 18 mm. **Obv:** Head 3/4 facing **Rev:** National arms above denomination **Edge:** Plain

Date	Mintage	F	VF	XF	Unc	BU
2000	23,821,000	—			0.25	0.45

KM# 165 NOVI DINAR
Copper-Nickel-Zinc **Obv:** Monogram on shield **Rev:** Date and denomination

Date	Mintage	F	VF	XF	Unc	BU
1994	47,755,000	—			1.00	1.20
1995	10,359,000	—			1.25	1.50

KM# 168 NOVI DINAR
Copper-Nickel-Zinc **Obv:** National arms **Rev:** Date and denomination **Note:** Reduced size.

Date	Mintage	F	VF	XF	Unc	BU
1996	80,122,000	—			1.00	1.20
1999	21,686,000	—			1.00	1.20

KM# 149 DINAR
Copper-Zinc **Obv:** Monogram on shield **Rev:** Date and denomination

Date	Mintage	F	VF	XF	Unc	BU
1992	49,269,000	—	0.10	0.30	0.60	0.75

KM# 154 DINAR
3.1000 g., Copper-Zinc-Nickel **Obv:** Monogram on shield **Rev:** Date and denomination

Date	Mintage	F	VF	XF	Unc	BU
1993	20,249,000	—	0.10	0.20	0.50	0.65

KM# 160 DINAR
Copper-Zinc-Nickel **Obv:** Monogram on shield **Rev:** Date and denomination

Date	Mintage	F	VF	XF	Unc	BU
1994	10,747,000	—			1.00	1.20

KM# 180 DINAR
4.4000 g., Copper-Zinc-Nickel, 20 mm. **Obv:** National arms within circle **Rev:** Building **Edge:** Reeded

Date	Mintage	F	VF	XF	Unc	BU
2000	20,076,000	—			0.25	0.50

KM# 150 2 DINARA
4.1800 g., Copper-Zinc **Obv:** Monogram on shield **Rev:** Large, thick denomination, date below

Date	Mintage	F	VF	XF	Unc	BU
1992	10,571,000	—	0.20	0.40	1.00	1.25

KM# 155 2 DINARA
3.8000 g., Copper-Zinc-Nickel **Obv:** Monogram on shield **Rev:** Denomination and date

Date	Mintage	F	VF	XF	Unc	BU
1993	10,263,000	—	0.10	0.20	0.50	0.70

KM# 181 2 DINARA
5.2000 g., Copper-Nickel-Zinc, 21.9 mm. **Obv:** National arms within circle **Rev:** Church **Edge:** Reeded

Date	Mintage	F	VF	XF	Unc	BU
2000	10,071,000	—			0.25	0.50

KM# 151 5 DINARA
5.0000 g., Copper-Zinc **Obv:** Monogram on shield **Rev:** Large, thick denomination, date below

Date	Mintage	F	VF	XF	Unc	BU
1992	26,658,000	—	0.15	0.30	0.75	0.90

KM# 156 5 DINARA
Copper-Zinc-Nickel **Obv:** Monogram on shield **Rev:** Denomination and date

Date	Mintage	F	VF	XF	Unc	BU
1993	10,135,000	—	0.10	0.20	0.50	0.65

KM# 182 5 DINARA
6.3000 g., Copper-Nickel-Zinc, 24 mm. **Obv:** National arms **Rev:** Domed building, denomination and date at left **Edge:** Reeded

Date	Mintage	F	VF	XF	Unc	BU
2000	32,762,500	—			1.25	1.50

KM# 152 10 DINARA
Copper-Zinc-Nickel **Obv:** Monogram on shield **Rev:** Large, thick denomination, date below

Date	Mintage	F	VF	XF	Unc	BU
1992	76,607,000	—	0.10	0.25	0.60	0.75

KM# 157 10 DINARA
6.0000 g., Copper-Zinc-Nickel **Obv:** Monogram on shield
Rev: Large denomination, date below

Date	Mintage	F	VF	XF	Unc	BU
1993	20,461,000	—	0.15	0.30	0.70	1.00

KM# 169 20 NOVIH DINARA
Copper-Zinc-Nickel **Subject:** Nikola Tesla **Obv:** National arms
Rev: Head 3/4 left

Date	Mintage	F	VF	XF	Unc	BU
1996 Proof	9,743	Value: 12.50				

KM# 153 50 DINARA
Copper-Zinc-Nickel **Obv:** Monogram on shield **Rev:** Large, thick
denomination, date below

Date	Mintage	F	VF	XF	Unc	BU
1992	50,571,000	—	0.25	0.50	1.00	1.25

KM# 158 50 DINARA
7.0000 g., Copper-Zinc-Nickel **Obv:** Monogram on shield
Rev: Large denomination, date below

Date	Mintage	F	VF	XF	Unc	BU
1993	10,823,000	—	0.20	0.40	0.80	1.00

KM# 159 100 DINARA
Brass **Obv:** Monogram on shield **Rev:** Denomination and date

Date	Mintage	F	VF	XF	Unc	BU
1993	14,294,500	—	0.25	0.50	1.00	1.25

KM# 166 150 NOVIH DINARA
7.8000 g., 0.9000 Gold 0.2257 oz. AGW **Subject:** 110th
Anniversary - National Bank **Obv:** National arms, building at left
Rev: Peace dove in flight

Date	Mintage	F	VF	XF	Unc	BU
ND(1995) Proof	100,000	Value: 250				

KM# 170 200 NOVIH DINARA
13.0000 g., 0.9250 Silver 0.3866 oz. ASW **Subject:** Nikola Tesla
Obv: National arms **Rev:** Head 3/4 left

Date	Mintage	F	VF	XF	Unc	BU
1996 Proof	9,847	Value: 32.00				

KM# 171 300 NOVIH DINARA
26.0000 g., 0.9250 Silver 0.7732 oz. ASW **Subject:** Nikola Tesla
Obv: National arms **Rev:** Head 3/4 left

Date	Mintage	F	VF	XF	Unc	BU
1996 Proof	9,034	Value: 45.00				

KM# 167 500 DINARA
Brass **Obv:** Monogram on shield **Rev:** Denomination and date
Note: All but 1,000 reported melted. Not released for circulation.

Date	Mintage	F	VF	XF	Unc	BU
1993	—	—	—	—	6.50	7.00

KM# 175 600 NOVIH DINARA
3.4550 g., 0.9000 Gold 0.1000 oz. AGW **Subject:** Chilander
Monastery **Obv:** Monastery **Rev:** Portraits of SS Simon and Sava

Date	Mintage	F	VF	XF	Unc	BU
1998(1999)	10,000	—	—	—	—	125

KM# 172 1000 NOVIH DINARA
8.6400 g., 0.9000 Gold 0.2500 oz. AGW **Subject:** Nikola Tesla
Obv: National arms **Rev:** Head 3/4 left

Date	Mintage	F	VF	XF	Unc	BU
1996 Proof	4,617	Value: 275				

KM# 176 1500 NOVIH DINARA
8.6400 g., 0.9000 Gold 0.2500 oz. AGW **Subject:** Chilander
Monastery **Obv:** Monastery **Rev:** Portraits of SS Simon and Sava

Date	Mintage	F	VF	XF	Unc	BU
1998(1999)	Est. 5,000	—	—	—	—	275

KM# 177 3000 NOVIH DINARA
17.2770 g., 0.9000 Gold 0.4999 oz. AGW **Subject:** Chilander
Monastery **Obv:** Monastery **Rev:** Portraits of SS Simon and Sava

Date	Mintage	F	VF	XF	Unc	BU
1998 Proof	500	Value: 550				
1999 Proof	500	Value: 550				

KM# 178 6000 NOVIH DINARA
34.5550 g., 0.9000 Gold 0.9998 oz. AGW **Subject:** Chilander
Monastery **Obv:** Monastery **Rev:** Portraits of SS Simon and Sava

Date	Mintage	F	VF	XF	Unc	BU
1998 Proof	500	Value: 1,100				
1999 Proof	500	Value: 1,100				

PATTERNS
Including off metal strikes

Patterns Pn1-Pn8 previously listed here are now listed
under Serbia.

KM#	Date	Mintage	Identification	Mkt Val
Pn9	1925	—	50 Para. Nickel. KM4. By Pattey.	700
Pn9a	1925	1	50 Para. Silver. KM4. By Pattey.	500
Pn10	1925	—	Dinar. Nickel. KM5. By Pattey.	400
Pn10a	1925	—	Dinar. Copper. KM5. By Pattey.	400
PnA11	1925	—	Dinar. Aluminum. By Pattey.	400
Pn11	1925	—	Dinar. Nickel. KM5.	400
Pn12	1925	—	2 Dinara. Nickel-Bronze. KM6. ESSAI.	1,000
Pn12a	1925	—	2 Dinara. Copper-Nickel. KM6. ESSAI. 3 millimeters thick.	1,000
Pn13	1925	—	2 Dinara. Nickel. KM6.	600
Pn14	1925(a)	—	10 Dinara. Gold.	—
Pn15	1926(k)	—	Dukat. Gold.	—
Pn16	1926	—	4 Dukata. Silver. 39.5 mm. River scene.	—
Pn17	1926(k)	—	4 Dukata. Gold. River scene.	—
Pn19	1931	—	4 Dukata. Gold. 15.0000 g. ESSAI.	—
Pn20	ND	—	4 Dukata. Silver.	—
Pn21	1932	—	50 Dinara. Bronze. Milled edge.	400
Pn21a	1932	—	50 Dinara. Copper.	400
Pn22	1938	—	10 Dinara. Copper.	200
Pn23	1938	—	20 Dinara. Copper.	250
Pn24	1938	—	50 Dinara. Copper.	300
Pn25	1953	—	25 Para. Aluminum. Hole in center.	400
Pn26	1978	20	25 Para. Aluminum.	—
Pn27	1978	19	Dinar. Copper-Nickel.	—
Pn28	1978	15	10 Dinara. Copper-Nickel.	—

PIEFORTS

KM#	Date	Mintage	Identification	Mkt Val
P1	ND(1931-1934)	—	4 Dukata. Gold. 46.4500 g. Conjoined busts.	—

TRIAL STRIKES

KM#	Date	Mintage	Identification	Mkt Val
TS1	1931(a)	—	Dukat. Gold. Uniface. ESSAI Paris/1931.	—
TS2	1931(a)	—	4 Dukata. Gold. Uniface. ESSAI Paris/1931.	—
TS3	1931	—	4 Dukata. Bronze. Uniface.	—
TS4	ND(1931)(k)	—	4 Dukata. 0.9167 Gold. 46.5000 g. Uniface obverse. KM#14 (hallmarked 22K on edge).	—
TS5	1931(k)	—	4 Dukata. Platinum. Uniface.	—
TS6	1931(k)	—	8 Dukata. Gold. Uniface.	—
TS7	1931	—	8 Dukata. 0.9000 Gold. 30.6180 g. Uniface. ESSAI/PARIS/1931.	—
TS8	1931	2	12 Dukata. 0.9000 Gold. Uniface. ESSAI/PARIS/1931. 45.875-46.45 grams.	—

MINT SETS

KM#	Date	Mintage	Identification	Issue Price	Mkt Val
MS1	1953/1955 (7)	—	KM29-35	—	5.00
MS2	1963 (6)	—	KM36-41	—	8.00
MS3	1965 (5)	—	KM42, 44-47	—	4.00
MS4	1965 (5)	—	KM43-47	—	4.00
MSA5	1976 (4)	—	KM#55-56, 62, 63	—	8.00
MS5	1982 (5)	—	KM84-89	—	3.00
MS6	1983 (6)	—	KM84-89	—	3.00
MS7	1983 (2)	—	KM96-97. Blue plastic wallet.	—	6.50
MS8	1984 (5)	—	KM85-89	—	3.00
MS9	1985 (7)	—	KM86-89, 112-114	—	3.00
MS10	1986 (7)	—	KM86-89, 112-114	—	3.00
MS11	1987 (4)	—	KM89, 112-114	—	3.00
MS12	1988 (7)	—	KM89, 113-114, 131-134	—	3.00
MS13	1989 (4)	—	KM131-134	—	6.50
MS14	1990 (6)	—	KM139-144	—	4.50
MS15	1991 (6)	—	KM139-144	—	4.00
MS16	1992 (2)	—	KM143-144	—	35.00
MS17	2000 (4)	—	KM#179-182	—	3.00

PROOF SETS

KM#	Date	Mintage	Identification	Issue Price	Mkt Val
PS1	1968 (6)	10,000	KM49-54	—	3,000
PS2	1968 (4)	10,000	KM51-54	—	2,900
PS3	1968 (2)	10,000	KM49-50	15.00	75.00
PS4	1978 (7)	6,000	KM65-71	—	185
PS5	1978 (11)	12,000	KM65-75	—	1,400
PS6	1980 (3)	—	KM76-77, 79	—	85.00
PS7	1981 (3)	—	KM80-81, 83	—	95.00
PS8	1982 (3)	—	KM90-92	—	40.00
PS9	1982 (2)	—	KM93-94	—	60.00
PS10	1983 (3)	—	KM98, 100, 102	—	40.00
PS11	1983 (3)	—	KM99, 101, 103	—	40.00
PS12	1983 (2)	100,000	KM96-97	—	15.00
PS13	1984 (3)	—	KM105, 107, 109	—	40.00
PS14	1984 (3)	—	KM106, 108, 110	—	40.00
PS15	Mixed dates (3)	—	KM95, 104, 111	—	375
PS16	1985 (6)	—	KM119-121, 124-126	—	950
PS17	1985 (4)	—	KM116-118, 123	—	250
PS18	1985 (3)	—	KM116-118	—	75.00
PS19	1985 (3)	—	KM119-121	—	60.00
PS20	1987 (3)	—	KM128-130	—	250
PS21	1987 (2)	—	KM128-129	—	70.00
PS22	1989 (3)	—	KM136-138	—	300
PS23	1989 (2)	—	KM136-137	—	60.00
PS24	1990 (3)	—	KM146-148	—	260
PS25	1990 (2)	10,000	KM146-147	—	80.00
PS26	1998(1999) (4)	—	KM#175-178	—	2,000
PS27	1998-1999 (4)	—	KM#175-176 dated 1998; KM#177-178 dated 1999	—	2,000

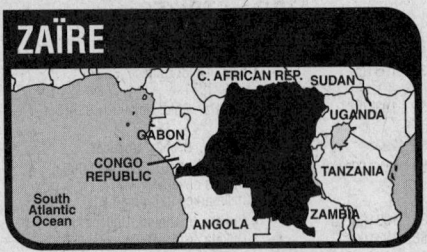

ZAÏRE

Democratic Republic of the Congo achieved independence on June 30, 1960. It followed the same monetary system as when under the Belgians. Monetary Reform of 1967 introduced new denominations and coins. The name of the country was changed to **Zaire** in 1971.

Under the command of Laurent Kabila, rebel forces overthrew ruler Sese Seko Mobutu in May of 1997. Self appointed President Kabila has officially renamed the country the Democratic Republic of Congo.

MONETARY SYSTEM
100 Makuta = 1 Zaire

1993 -
3,000,000 old Zaires = 1 Nouveau Zaire

REPUBLIC

DECIMAL COINAGE

KM# 12   5 MAKUTA
Copper-Nickel   **Obv:** Denomination **Rev:** Mobuto bust left

Date	Mintage	F	VF	XF	Unc	BU
1977	8,000,000	—	1.00	5.00	12.00	20.00

KM# 7   10 MAKUTA
8.9500 g., Copper-Nickel   **Obv:** Mobuto bust 1/4 right **Rev:** Arms below denomination

Date	Mintage	F	VF	XF	Unc	BU
1973	5,000,000	—	2.25	4.00	8.00	—
1975	—	—	2.25	4.00	8.00	—
1976	—	—	2.50	4.50	9.00	—
1978	—	—	2.50	4.50	9.00	—

KM# 8   20 MAKUTA
Copper-Nickel   **Obv:** Mobuto bust right **Rev:** Hand with torch

Date	Mintage	F	VF	XF	Unc	BU
1973	—	—	3.00	6.00	13.00	—
1976	—	—	3.50	7.00	15.00	—

KM# 13   ZAIRE
Brass   **Obv:** Denomination **Rev:** Bust facing

Date	Mintage	F	VF	XF	Unc	BU
1987 Specimen, coin rotation	—	—	—	—	—	300

Date	Mintage	F	VF	XF	Unc	BU
1987 Specimen, medal rotation	—	—	—	—	—	300
1987	—	—	0.50	1.00	2.00	—

KM# 9   2-1/2 ZAIRES
28.2800 g., 0.9250 Silver 0.8410 oz. ASW   **Subject:** Conservation **Obv:** Mobuto bust 1/4 right **Rev:** Mountain gorillas

Date	Mintage	F	VF	XF	Unc	BU
1975 Proof	6,629	Value: 40.00				
1975	5,735	—	—	—	30.00	35.00

KM# 1   5 ZAIRES
27.8401 g., 0.9250 Silver 0.8279 oz. ASW   **Obv:** Mobuto bust left **Rev:** Hotel Intercontinental

Date	Mintage	F	VF	XF	Unc	BU
1971 Proof	—	Value: 35.00				

KM# 10   5 ZAIRES
35.0000 g., 0.9250 Silver 1.0408 oz. ASW   **Subject:** Conservation **Obv:** Mobuto bust 1/4 right **Rev:** Okapi right

Date	Mintage	F	VF	XF	Unc	BU
1975 Proof	6,431	Value: 40.00				
1975	5,734	—	—	—	30.00	35.00

KM# 14   5 ZAIRES
Brass, 24 mm.   **Obv:** Denomination **Rev:** Mobuto bust facing

Date	Mintage	F	VF	XF	Unc	BU
1987	—	—	0.65	1.25	2.50	—

KM# 2   10 ZAIRES
9.9600 g., 0.9000 Gold 0.2882 oz. AGW   **Obv:** Mobuto bust left **Rev:** Hotel Intercontinental

Date	Mintage	F	VF	XF	Unc	BU
1971 Proof	—	Value: 325				

KM# 3   10 ZAIRES
6.0400 g., 0.9990 Platinum 0.1940 oz. APW   **Obv:** Mobuto bust left **Rev:** Hotel Intercontinental

Date	Mintage	F	VF	XF	Unc	BU
1971 Proof	—	Value: 425				

KM# 19   10 ZAIRES
7.9200 g., Brass   **Obv:** Denomination **Rev:** Mobuto bust facing

Date	Mintage	F	VF	XF	Unc	BU
1988	—	—	2.00	4.50	9.00	—

KM# 4   20 ZAIRES
20.9000 g., 0.9000 Gold 0.6047 oz. AGW   **Obv:** Mobuto bust left **Rev:** Hotel Intercontinental

Date	Mintage	F	VF	XF	Unc	BU
1971 Proof	—	Value: 675				

KM# 5   20 ZAIRES
3.8900 g., 0.9990 Platinum 0.1249 oz. APW   **Obv:** Mobuto bust left **Rev:** Hotel Intercontinental

Date	Mintage	F	VF	XF	Unc	BU
1971 Proof	—	Value: 275				

KM# 6   50 ZAIRES
46.9600 g., 0.9000 Gold 1.3588 oz. AGW   **Obv:** Mobuto bust 3/4 left **Rev:** Hotel Intercontinental

Date	Mintage	F	VF	XF	Unc	BU
1971 Proof	—	Value: 1,450				

KM# 11   100 ZAIRES
33.4370 g., 0.9000 Gold 0.9675 oz. AGW   **Subject:** Conservation **Obv:** Mobuto bust 1/4 right **Rev:** Leopard right

Date	Mintage	F	VF	XF	Unc	BU
1975	1,415	—	—	—	1,000	1,100
1975 Proof	279	Value: 1,200				

KM# 20 500 NOUVEAUX ZAIRES
20.0000 g., 0.5000 Silver 0.3215 oz. ASW **Subject:** Wildlife of Africa **Obv:** African map, arms at left **Rev:** Leopard on branch

Date	Mintage	F	VF	XF	Unc	BU
1996 Proof	10,000	Value: 40.00				

KM# 21 500 NOUVEAUX ZAIRES
20.0000 g., 0.5000 Silver 0.3215 oz. ASW **Subject:** Wildlife of Africa **Obv:** African map, arms at left **Rev:** Gorilla left

Date	Mintage	F	VF	XF	Unc	BU
1996 Proof	Est. 10,000	Value: 40.00				

KM# 22 500 NOUVEAUX ZAIRES
20.0000 g., 0.5000 Silver 0.3215 oz. ASW **Subject:** Wildlife of Africa **Obv:** African map, arms at left **Rev:** Two okapi

Date	Mintage	F	VF	XF	Unc	BU
1996 Proof	Est. 10,000	Value: 40.00				

KM# 23 1000 NOUVEAUX ZAIRES
29.6300 g., 0.9250 Silver 0.8811 oz. ASW **Subject:** Wildlife of Africa **Obv:** African map, arms at left **Rev:** Common hippopotamus left

Date	Mintage	F	VF	XF	Unc	BU
1997 Proof	Est. 20,000	Value: 40.00				

KM# 24 1000 NOUVEAUX ZAIRES
30.0900 g., 0.9250 Silver 0.8948 oz. ASW **Subject:** Wildlife of Africa **Obv:** African map, arms at left **Rev:** Sailing ship "Portuguese Caravel"

Date	Mintage	F	VF	XF	Unc	BU
1997 Proof	Est. 20,000	Value: 42.50				

KM# 25 5000 NOUVEAUX ZAIRES
411.4224 g., 0.9990 Silver 13.213 oz. ASW **Subject:** Wildlife of Africa **Obv:** African map, arms at left **Rev:** Leopard on branch **Edge:** Reeded

Date	Mintage	F	VF	XF	Unc	BU
1996 Proof	1,000	Value: 450				

KM# 26 10000 NOUVEAUX ZAIRES
822.8449 g., 0.9990 Silver 26.427 oz. ASW **Subject:** Wildlife of Africa **Obv:** African map, arms at left **Rev:** Gorilla left **Edge:** Reeded

Date	Mintage	F	VF	XF	Unc	BU
1996 Proof	1,000	Value: 650				

PATTERNS
Including off metal strikes

KM#	Date	Mintage Identification	Mkt Val
Pn1	1987	— Zaire. KM#13; coin rotation.	300
Pn2	1987	— Zaire. KM#13; medal rotation.	300

PROOF SETS

KM#	Date	Mintage Identification	Issue Price	Mkt Val
PS1	1971 (6)	— KM1-6	—	3,200
PS2	1975 (2)	500 KM9-10	60.00	90.00

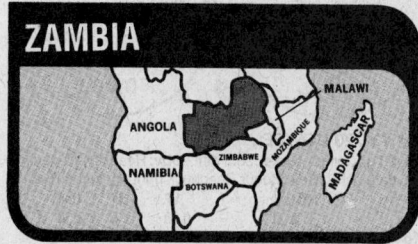

ZAMBIA

The Republic of Zambia (formerly Northern Rhodesia), a landlocked country in south-central Africa, has an area of 290,586 sq. mi. (752,610 sq. km.) and a population of*7.9 million. Capital: Lusaka. The economy of Zambia is based principally on copper, of which Zambia is the world's third largest producer. Copper, zinc, lead, cobalt and tobacco are exported.

The area that is now Zambia was brought within the British sphere of influence in 1888 by empire builder Cecil Rhodes, who obtained mining concessions in south-central Africa from indigenous chiefs. The territory was ruled by the British South Africa Company, which Rhodes established, until 1924 when its administration was transferred to the British government as a protectorate. In 1953, Northern Rhodesia was joined with Nyasaland and the colony of Southern Rhodesia to form the Federation of Rhodesia and Nyasaland. Northern Rhodesia seceded from the Federation on Oct. 24, 1964, and became the independent Republic of Zambia. Zambia is a member of the Commonwealth of Nations. The president is Chief of State.

Zambia converted to a decimal coinage on January 16, 1969. For earlier coinage refer to Rhodesia and Nyasaland.

RULER
British, until 1964

MONETARY SYSTEM
12 Pence = 1 Shilling
20 Shillings = 1 Pound

REPUBLIC
STANDARD COINAGE

KM# 5 PENNY
Bronze **Obv:** Date below center hole **Rev:** Denomination below center hole

Date	Mintage	F	VF	XF	Unc	BU
1966	7,200,000	0.25	0.45	0.85	1.75	2.75
1966 Proof	60	—	—	—	—	—

KM# 1 6 PENCE
Copper-Nickel-Zinc **Obv:** National arms divide date **Rev:** Morning Glory (Ipomoea sp. convolvulaceae), denomination below

Date	Mintage	F	VF	XF	Unc	BU
1964	3,500,000	0.15	0.30	0.60	1.20	1.50
1964 Proof	5,000	Value: 1.75				

KM# 6 6 PENCE
Copper-Nickel-Zinc **Obv:** Head of K.D. Kaunda right, date below **Rev:** Morning glory, denomination below

Date	Mintage	F	VF	XF	Unc	BU
1966	7,200,000	0.25	0.50	1.00	2.00	2.50
1966 Proof	60	—	—	—	—	—

KM# 2 SHILLING
Copper-Nickel **Obv:** National arms divides date **Rev:** Crowned Hornbill, oribi and denomination

Date	Mintage	F	VF	XF	Unc	BU
1964	3,510,000	0.25	0.50	1.00	2.00	2.50
1964 Proof	5,000	Value: 3.50				

KM# 7 SHILLING
Copper-Nickel **Obv:** Head of K.D. Kaunda right, date below **Rev:** Crowned hornbill and denomination

Date	Mintage	F	VF	XF	Unc	BU
1966	5,000,000	0.35	0.75	1.50	3.25	4.00
1966 Proof	60	—	—	—	—	—

KM# 3 2 SHILLINGS
Copper-Nickel **Obv:** National arms divides date **Rev:** Bohor Reedbuck right and denomination

Date	Mintage	F	VF	XF	Unc	BU
1964	3,770,000	0.35	0.75	1.50	3.00	5.00
1964 Proof	5,000	Value: 6.00				

KM# 8 2 SHILLINGS
Copper-Nickel **Obv:** Head of K.D. Kaunda right, date below **Rev:** Bohor Reedbuck right and denomination

Date	Mintage	F	VF	XF	Unc	BU
1966	5,000,000	0.45	1.00	2.25	4.50	5.00
1966 Proof	60	—	—	—	—	—

KM# 4 5 SHILLINGS
Copper-Nickel, 38.8 mm. **Subject:** 1st Anniversary of Independence **Obv:** National arms with supporters, denomination below **Rev:** Head of K.D. Kaunda right, date below **Edge:** ONE ZAMBIA ONE NATION * 24.10.1964 * **Note:** Two edge ltter varieties.

Date	Mintage	F	VF	XF	Unc	BU
1965	10,000	—	2.50	3.50	6.50	8.00
1965 Proof	20,000	Value: 9.00				

DECIMAL COINAGE
100 Ngwee = 1 Kwacha

KM# 9 NGWEE
2.1000 g., Bronze, 17.5 mm. **Obv:** Head of K.D. Kaunda right, date below **Rev:** Aardvark left, denomination below

Date	Mintage	F	VF	XF	Unc	BU
1968	8,000,000	—	0.10	0.30	1.50	2.50
1968 Proof	4,000	Value: 1.50				
1969	16,000,000	—	0.10	0.20	1.00	2.00
1972	21,000,000	—	0.10	0.20	1.00	2.00
1978	23,976,000	—	0.10	0.20	1.00	2.00
1978 Proof	24,000	Value: 1.50				

KM# 9a NGWEE
2.1000 g., Copper-Clad Steel, 16.47 mm. **Obv:** Head of K.D. Kaunda right, date below **Rev:** Aardvark left, denomination below **Edge:** Plain

Date	Mintage	F	VF	XF	Unc	BU
1982	10,000,000	—	0.10	0.20	1.00	1.50
1983	60,000,000	—	0.10	0.20	1.00	1.50

KM# 10 2 NGWEE
4.2000 g., Bronze, 21 mm. **Obv:** Head of K.D. Kaunda right, date below **Rev:** Martial Eagle, denomination at right

Date	Mintage	F	VF	XF	Unc	BU
1968	19,000,000	—	0.10	0.20	1.00	1.50
1968 Proof	4,000	Value: 2.00				

Date	Mintage	F	VF	XF	Unc	BU
1978	—	—	0.15	0.25	1.25	2.00
1978 Proof	24,000	Value: 2.00				

KM# 10a 2 NGWEE
4.1900 g., Copper-Clad Steel, 19.39 mm. **Obv:** Head of K.D. Kaunda right, date below **Rev:** Martial Eagle, denomination at right **Edge:** Plain

Date	Mintage	F	VF	XF	Unc	BU
1982	7,500,000	—	0.10	0.20	1.00	
1983	60,000,000	—	0.10	0.15	0.75	

KM# 11 5 NGWEE
2.8000 g., Copper-Nickel, 19.4 mm. **Obv:** Head of K.D. Kaunda right, date below **Rev:** Morning Glory, denomination below

Date	Mintage	F	VF	XF	Unc	BU
1968	12,000,000	—	0.20	0.30	0.60	—
1968 Proof	4,000	Value: 1.75				
1972	9,000,000	—	0.20	0.30	0.60	—
1978	1,976,000	—	0.20	0.30	0.60	—
1978 Proof	24,000	Value: 2.00				
1982	12,000,000	—	0.20	0.30	0.60	—
1987	10,000,000	—	0.20	0.30	0.60	—

KM# 12 10 NGWEE
5.6500 g., Copper-Nickel-Zinc, 23.6 mm. **Obv:** K.D. Kaunda head right **Rev:** Crowned Hornbill and denomination

Date	Mintage	F	VF	XF	Unc	BU
1968	1,000,000	—	0.40	0.85	1.75	—
1968 Proof	4,000	Value: 2.00				
1972	1,000,000	—	0.30	0.50	1.00	—
1978	1,976,000	—	0.30	0.50	1.00	—
1978 Proof	24,000	Value: 2.25				
1982	8,000,000	—	0.30	0.50	1.00	—
1983	2,500	—	0.30	0.50	1.00	—
1987	6,000,000	—	0.30	0.50	1.00	—

KM# 13 20 NGWEE
11.3000 g., Copper-Nickel, 28.5 mm. **Obv:** Head of K.D. Kaunda right, date below **Rev:** Bohor Reedbuck right and denomination

Date	Mintage	F	VF	XF	Unc	BU
1968	1,500,000	—	0.75	1.50	2.50	—
1968 Proof	4,000	Value: 2.75				
1972	7,500,000	—	0.50	1.00	2.00	—
1978 Proof	24,000	Value: 3.00				
1983	998,000	—	0.75	1.50	2.50	—
1987	—	—	0.50	1.00	2.00	—
1988	3,000,000	—	0.50	1.00	2.00	—

KM# 22 20 NGWEE
11.3000 g., Copper-Nickel, 28.5 mm. **Series:** F.A.O. - World Food Day **Obv:** Head of K.D. Kaunda right, date below **Rev:** Corn plant, date and denomination within inner circle

Date	Mintage	F	VF	XF	Unc	BU
1981	970,000	—	0.75	1.50	2.75	—

KM# 23 20 NGWEE
11.3000 g., Copper-Nickel, 28.5 mm. **Subject:** 20th Anniversary - Bank of Zambia **Obv:** Head of K.D. Kaunda right, date below **Rev:** Bank building divides dates, denomination above

Date	Mintage	F	VF	XF	Unc	BU
1985	—	—	0.50	1.00	1.50	—

KM# 23a 20 NGWEE
11.3100 g., 0.9250 Silver 0.3363 oz. ASW, 28.5 mm. **Subject:** 20th Anniversary - Bank of Zambia **Obv:** Head of K.D. Kaunda right, date below **Rev:** Bank building divides dates, denominaton above

Date	Mintage	F	VF	XF	Unc	BU
1985 Proof	—	Value: 7.00				

KM# 29 25 NGWEE
2.5100 g., Nickel Plated Steel, 19.93 mm. **Obv:** National arms with supporters, date below **Rev:** Crowned Hornbill and denomination **Edge:** Plain

Date	Mintage	F	VF	XF	Unc	BU
1992	—	—	—	—	1.00	—

KM# 14 50 NGWEE
11.6000 g., Copper-Nickel, 30 mm. **Series:** F.A.O. **Obv:** Head of K.D. Kaunda right, date below **Rev:** Ear of corn divides denomination

Date	Mintage	F	VF	XF	Unc	BU
ND(1969)	70,000	—	2.00	3.50	5.50	—

KM# 15 50 NGWEE
11.6000 g., Copper-Nickel, 30 mm. **Series:** F.A.O. **Obv:** Head of K.D. Kaunda right, date below **Rev:** Ear of corn divides denomination

Date	Mintage	F	VF	XF	Unc	BU
1972	510,000	—	1.25	2.50	4.50	—

KM# 16   50 NGWEE
11.6000 g., Copper-Nickel, 30 mm. **Subject:** Second Republic, 13 December 1972 **Obv:** Head of K.D. Kaunda right, date below **Rev:** National arms with supporters, denomination below

Date	Mintage	F	VF	XF	Unc	BU
1972	6,000,000	—	1.00	2.00	4.00	—
1972 Proof	2,000	Value: 14.00				
1978 Proof	24,000	Value: 8.00				
1983	998,000	—	1.00	2.00	4.00	—

KM# 24   50 NGWEE
11.6000 g., Copper-Nickel, 30 mm. **Subject:** 40th Anniversary of United Nations **Obv:** Head of K.D. Kaunda right, date below **Rev:** United Nations logo

Date	Mintage	F	VF	XF	Unc	BU
1985	—	1.00	1.25	2.50	—	

KM# 24a   50 NGWEE
11.6600 g., 0.9250 Silver 0.3467 oz. ASW **Subject:** 40th Anniversary of United Nations **Obv:** Head of K.D. Kaunda right, date below **Rev:** United Nations logo

Date	Mintage	F	VF	XF	Unc	BU
1985 Proof	—	Value: 7.50				

KM# 30   50 NGWEE
4.0500 g., Nickel Plated Steel, 22.55 mm. **Obv:** National arms with supporters, date below **Rev:** Kafue Lechwe and denomination **Edge:** Plain

Date	Mintage	F	VF	XF	Unc	BU
1992	—	—	—	—	1.50	2.00

KM# 17   KWACHA
Copper-Nickel **Subject:** 10th Anniversary of Independence **Obv:** Head of K.D. Kaunda right, date below **Rev:** National arms with supporters, denomination below

Date	Mintage	F	VF	XF	Unc	BU
ND(1974)	4,000	—	—	—	—	40.00
ND(1974) Proof	1,500	Value: 50.00				

KM# 26   KWACHA
Nickel-Brass **Obv:** Head of K.D. Kaunda right, date below **Rev:** Two falcons on branch divided by denomination

Date	Mintage	F	VF	XF	Unc	BU
1989	8,000,000	—	0.75	1.50	4.00	5.00

KM# 38   KWACHA
3.0000 g., Brass, 19.2 mm. **Obv:** National arms with supporters, date below **Rev:** Two falcons on branch divided by denomination

Date	Mintage	F	VF	XF	Unc	BU
1992	—	—	—	—	1.50	2.50

KM# 18   5 KWACHA
25.3100 g., 0.9250 Silver 0.7527 oz. ASW **Subject:** Conservation **Obv:** Head of K.D. Kaunda right, date below **Rev:** Kafue Lechwe right, denomination below

Date	Mintage	F	VF	XF	Unc	BU
1979	3,250	—	—	—	17.50	25.00

KM# 18a   5 KWACHA
28.2800 g., 0.9250 Silver 0.8410 oz. ASW **Subject:** Conservation **Obv:** Head of K.D. Kaunda right, date below **Rev:** Kafue Lechwe right, denomination below

Date	Mintage	F	VF	XF	Unc	BU
1979 Proof	3,407	Value: 30.00				

KM# 31   5 KWACHA
3.5000 g., Brass **Obv:** National arms with supporters, date below **Rev:** Oryx right and denomination

Date	Mintage	F	VF	XF	Unc	BU
1992	—	—	—	—	2.00	2.50

KM# 19   10 KWACHA
31.6500 g., 0.9250 Silver 0.9412 oz. ASW **Subject:** Conservation **Obv:** Head of K.D. Kaunda right, date below **Rev:** Taita Falcon flying right, denomination below

Date	Mintage	F	VF	XF	Unc	BU
1979	3,250	—	—	—	20.00	24.00

KM# 19a   10 KWACHA
35.0000 g., 0.9250 Silver 1.0408 oz. ASW **Subject:** Conservation **Obv:** Head of K.D. Kaunda right, date below **Rev:** Taita Falcon flying right, denomination below

Date	Mintage	F	VF	XF	Unc	BU
1979 Proof	3,256	Value: 35.00				

KM# 21   10 KWACHA
27.2200 g., 0.9250 Silver 0.8095 oz. ASW **Series:** International Year of the Child **Obv:** Head of K.D. Kaunda right, date below **Rev:** 3 children on playground equipment

Date	Mintage	F	VF	XF	Unc	BU
1980 Proof	12,000	Value: 20.00				

KM# 25   10 KWACHA
27.2200 g., 0.9250 Silver 0.8095 oz. ASW **Series:** World Wildlife Fund **Obv:** Head of K.D. Kaunda right, date below **Rev:** White-winged Flufftail, denomination below

Date	Mintage	F	VF	XF	Unc	BU
1986 Proof	25,000	Value: 30.00				

KM# 27   10 KWACHA
27.2200 g., 0.9250 Silver 0.8095 oz. ASW **Subject:** 70th Anniversary - Save the Children Fund **Obv:** Head of K.D. Kaunda right, date below **Rev:** Child holding up corn cob, denomination below

Date	Mintage	F	VF	XF	Unc	BU
1989 Proof	Est. 20,000	Value: 30.00				

KM# 32   10 KWACHA
5.1000 g., Brass **Obv:** National arms, date below **Rev:** Rhinoceros facing and denomination

Date	Mintage	F	VF	XF	Unc	BU
1992	—	—	—	—	2.50	3.00

KM# 39   10 KWACHA
20.0000 g., 0.9990 Silver 0.6423 oz. ASW **Subject:** World Cup
Soccer **Obv:** National arms with supporters divide date,
denomination below **Rev:** Player kicking ball; .999 in field

Date	Mintage	F	VF	XF	Unc	BU
1994 Proof	—	Value: 50.00				

KM# 119   10 KWACHA
27.3400 g., Copper-Nickel, 40.1 mm. **Subject:** UNICEF
Obv: National arms with supporters divide date, denomination
below **Rev:** Three boys playing soccer **Edge:** Reeded

Date	Mintage	F	VF	XF	Unc	BU
2000 Matte	—	—	—	12.00	15.00	

KM# 119a   10 KWACHA
27.2200 g., 0.9250 Silver 0.8095 oz. ASW, 40.1 mm.
Subject: UNICEF **Obv:** National arms with supporters divide date,
denomination below **Rev:** Three boys playing soccer **Edge:** Reeded

Date	Mintage	F	VF	XF	Unc	BU
2000 Proof	25,000	Value: 18.50				

KM# 33   20 KWACHA
10.1700 g., 0.9990 Silver 0.3266 oz. ASW **Series:** 1994
Olympics **Obv:** National arms **Rev:** Slalom skier

Date	Mintage	F	VF	XF	Unc	BU
1994 Proof	25,000	Value: 22.50				

KM# 51   75 KWACHA
5.0000 g., 0.9990 Silver 0.1606 oz. ASW, 22 mm.
Subject: Diana - The People's Princess **Obv:** National arms with
supporters divide date **Rev:** Bust facing

Date	Mintage	F	VF	XF	Unc	BU
1997 Proof	—	Value: 12.50				

KM# 28   100 KWACHA
28.2800 g., 0.9250 Silver 0.8410 oz. ASW **Series:** Barcelona
Summer Olympics **Subject:** Boxing **Obv:** National arms with
supporters, date below **Rev:** 2 boxers in ring fighting,
denomination above

Date	Mintage	F	VF	XF	Unc	BU
1992 Proof	Est. 50,000	Value: 27.50				

KM# 50   100 KWACHA
Copper-Nickel **Obv:** National arms with supporters
Rev: Charging bull elephant, denomination at right

Date	Mintage	F	VF	XF	Unc	BU
1997	—	—	—	—	25.00	30.00

KM# 56a   100 KWACHA
28.2800 g., 0.9990 Silver 0.9083 oz. ASW **Obv:** National arms
with supporters, date below **Rev:** Crocodile, denomination at right

Date	Mintage	F	VF	XF	Unc	BU
1998 Proof	Est. 25,000	Value: 50.00				

KM# 56   100 KWACHA
28.2800 g., Copper-Nickel **Obv:** National arms with supporters,
date below **Rev:** Crocodile, denomination at right **Edge:** Reeded

Date	Mintage	F	VF	XF	Unc	BU
1998	Est. 100,000	—	—	—	15.00	20.00

KM# 57a   100 KWACHA
28.2800 g., 0.9990 Silver 0.9083 oz. ASW **Obv:** National arms
with supporters, date below **Rev:** Leopard on branch left,
denomination below

Date	Mintage	F	VF	XF	Unc	BU
1998 Proof	Est. 25,000	Value: 60.00				

KM# 57   100 KWACHA
28.2800 g., Copper-Nickel **Obv:** National arms with supporters,
date below **Rev:** Leopard on branch left, denomination below
Edge: Reeded

Date	Mintage	F	VF	XF	Unc	BU
1998	Est. 100,000	—	—	—	15.00	20.00

KM# 58a   100 KWACHA
28.2800 g., 0.9990 Silver 0.9083 oz. ASW **Obv:** National arms
with supporters, date below **Rev:** Black Rhinoceros running right,
denomination above

Date	Mintage	F	VF	XF	Unc	BU
1998 Proof	Est. 25,000	Value: 60.00				

KM# 58   100 KWACHA
28.2800 g., Copper-Nickel **Obv:** National arms with supporters,
date below **Rev:** Rhinoceros running right, denomination above
Edge: Reeded

Date	Mintage	F	VF	XF	Unc	BU
1998	Est. 100,000	—	—	—	15.00	20.00

KM# 59a   100 KWACHA
28.2800 g., 0.9990 Silver 0.9083 oz. ASW **Obv:** National arms
with supporters, date below **Rev:** Hippopotamus and calf,
denomination above

Date	Mintage	F	VF	XF	Unc	BU
1998 Proof	Est. 25,000	Value: 60.00				

KM# 59   100 KWACHA
28.2800 g., Copper-Nickel **Obv:** National arms with supporters,
date below **Rev:** Hippopotamus and calf, denomination above
Edge: Reeded

Date	Mintage	F	VF	XF	Unc	BU
1998	Est. 100,000	—	—	—	17.00	20.00

KM# 60a   100 KWACHA
28.2800 g., 0.9990 Silver 0.9083 oz. ASW **Obv:** National arms
with supporters, date below **Rev:** Antelopes jumping over
denomination

Date	Mintage	F	VF	XF	Unc	BU
1998 Proof	Est. 25,000	Value: 55.00				

KM# 60   100 KWACHA
28.2800 g., Copper-Nickel **Obv:** National arms with supporters,
date below **Rev:** Antelopes jumping over denomination **Edge:**
Reeded

Date	Mintage	F	VF	XF	Unc	BU
1998	Est. 100,000	—	—	—	15.00	20.00

KM# 61a   100 KWACHA
28.2800 g., 0.9990 Silver 0.9083 oz. ASW **Obv:** National arms
with supporters, date below **Rev:** Pelican on branch,
denomination at right

Date	Mintage	F	VF	XF	Unc	BU
1998 Proof	Est. 25,000	Value: 65.00				

KM# 61   100 KWACHA
28.2800 g., Copper-Nickel **Obv:** National arms with supporters,
date below **Rev:** Pelican on branch, denomination at right
Edge: Reeded

Date	Mintage	F	VF	XF	Unc	BU
1998	Est. 100,000	—	—	—	17.00	25.00

KM# 62a 100 KWACHA
28.2800 g., 0.9990 Silver 0.9083 oz. ASW **Obv:** National arms with supporters, date below **Rev:** Storks left and right, denomination at right

Date	Mintage	F	VF	XF	Unc	BU
1998 Proof	Est. 25,000		Value: 50.00			

KM# 62 100 KWACHA
28.2800 g., Copper-Nickel **Obv:** National arms with supporters, date below **Rev:** Storks left and right, denomination at right **Edge:** Reeded

Date	Mintage	F	VF	XF	Unc	BU
1998	Est. 100,000	—	—	—	15.00	20.00

KM# 63a 100 KWACHA
28.2800 g., 0.9990 Silver 0.9083 oz. ASW **Obv:** National arms with supporters, date below **Rev:** Burchell's Zebra right, denomination at right

Date	Mintage	F	VF	XF	Unc	BU
1998 Proof	Est. 25,000		Value: 55.00			

KM# 63 100 KWACHA
28.2800 g., Copper-Nickel **Obv:** National arms with supporters, date below **Rev:** Zebra right, denomination at right **Edge:** Reeded

Date	Mintage	F	VF	XF	Unc	BU
1998	Est. 100,000	—	—	—	15.00	20.00

KM# 64a 100 KWACHA
28.2800 g., 0.9990 Silver 0.9083 oz. ASW **Obv:** National arms with supporters, date below **Rev:** Flamingos, denomination at left

Date	Mintage	F	VF	XF	Unc	BU
1998 Proof	Est. 25,000		Value: 50.00			

KM# 64 100 KWACHA
28.2800 g., Copper-Nickel **Obv:** National arms with supporters, date below **Rev:** Flamingo, denomination at left **Edge:** Reeded

Date	Mintage	F	VF	XF	Unc	BU
1998	Est. 100,000	—	—	—	15.00	20.00

KM# 65a 100 KWACHA
28.2800 g., 0.9990 Silver 0.9083 oz. ASW **Obv:** National arms with supporters, date below **Rev:** Giraffes, denomination at left

Date	Mintage	F	VF	XF	Unc	BU
1998 Proof	Est. 25,000		Value: 60.00			

KM# 65 100 KWACHA
28.2800 g., Copper-Nickel **Obv:** National arms with supporters, date below **Rev:** Giraffes, denomination at left **Edge:** Reeded

Date	Mintage	F	VF	XF	Unc	BU
1998	Est. 100,000	—	—	—	15.00	20.00

KM# 66a 100 KWACHA
28.2800 g., 0.9990 Silver 0.9083 oz. ASW **Obv:** National arms with supporters, date below **Rev:** Lion facing, denomination at left

Date	Mintage	F	VF	XF	Unc	BU
1998 Proof	Est. 25,000		Value: 60.00			

KM# 66 100 KWACHA
28.2800 g., Copper-Nickel **Obv:** National arms with supporters, date below **Rev:** Lion facing, denomination at left **Edge:** Reeded

Date	Mintage	F	VF	XF	Unc	BU
1998	Est. 100,000	—	—	—	17.00	25.00

KM# 67a 100 KWACHA
28.2800 g., 0.9990 Silver 0.9083 oz. ASW **Obv:** National arms with supporters, date below **Rev:** Two gazelles, denomination above

Date	Mintage	F	VF	XF	Unc	BU
1998 Proof	Est. 25,000		Value: 50.00			

KM# 67 100 KWACHA
28.2800 g., Copper-Nickel **Obv:** National arms with supporters, date below **Rev:** Gazelle, denomination above **Edge:** Reeded

Date	Mintage	F	VF	XF	Unc	BU
1998	Est. 100,000	—	—	—	15.00	20.00

Note: Please note that the copper-nickel versions were offered to the market almost two months after the silver version

KM# 52 200 KWACHA
Copper-Nickel **Subject:** Diana - The People's Princess **Obv:** National arms with supporters divide date, denomination below **Rev:** Head facing

Date	Mintage	F	VF	XF	Unc	BU
1997 Proof	—		Value: 8.00			

KM# 52a 200 KWACHA
31.1300 g., 0.9990 Silver 0.9998 oz. ASW, 35 mm. **Obv:** National arms with supporters divide date, denomination below **Rev:** Head facing **Edge:** Partially reeded with metal content from 5-7 o'clock

Date	Mintage	F	VF	XF	Unc	BU
1997 Proof	197		Value: 60.00			

KM# 20 250 KWACHA
33.6300 g., 0.9000 Gold 0.9731 oz. AGW **Subject:** Conservation **Obv:** Head of K.D. Kaunda right, date below **Rev:** African wild dog right, denomination below

Date	Mintage	F	VF	XF	Unc	BU
1979	455	—	—	—	—	1,100
1979 Proof	245		Value: 1,200			

KM# 34 250 KWACHA
136.0800 g., 0.9250 Silver 4.0468 oz. ASW, 63 mm. **Obv:** National arms with supporters, date below **Rev:** African fish eagles, one on branch and one in flight, denomination below **Note:** Illustration reduced.

Date	Mintage	F	VF	XF	Unc	BU
1993	400	—	—	—	200	225
1993 Proof	5,000		Value: 100			

KM# 35   250 KWACHA
136.0800 g., 0.9250 Silver 4.0468 oz. ASW, 63 mm.
Obv: National arms with supporters, date below **Rev:** Saddle-billed stork drinking, denomination below **Note:** Illustration reduced.

Date	Mintage	F	VF	XF	Unc	BU
1993	400	—	—	—	200	225
1993 Proof	5,000	Value: 100				

KM# 36   250 KWACHA
136.0800 g., 0.9250 Silver 4.0468 oz. ASW, 63 mm. **Obv:** National arms with supporters, date below **Rev:** Paradise Flycatchers on branch, denomination below **Note:** Illustration reduced.

Date	Mintage	F	VF	XF	Unc	BU
1993	400	—	—	—	200	225
1993 Proof	5,000	Value: 100				

KM# 37   250 KWACHA
136.0800 g., 0.9250 Silver 4.0468 oz. ASW, 63 mm.
Obv: National arms with supporters, date below **Rev:** Red-breasted Swallows facing each other on branches, denomination below **Note:** Illustration reduced.

Date	Mintage	F	VF	XF	Unc	BU
1993	400	—	—	—	200	225
1993 Proof	5,000	Value: 100				

KM# 173   250 KWACHA
136.0800 g., 0.9250 Silver 4.0468 oz. ASW, 62.9 mm.
Subject: Birds **Obv:** National arms with supporters, date below **Rev:** Two Lizard Buzzards, denomination below **Edge:** Reeded **Note:** Illustration reduced.

Date	Mintage	F	VF	XF	Unc	BU
1994 Proof	—	Value: 100				

KM# 40   500 KWACHA
31.7730 g., 0.9990 Silver 1.0205 oz. ASW   **Subject:** Equality **Obv:** National arms with supporters divide date, denomination below **Rev:** Black and white face profiles

Date	Mintage	F	VF	XF	Unc	BU
1994 Proof	—	Value: 45.00				

KM# 41   500 KWACHA
31.7730 g., 0.9990 Silver 1.0205 oz. ASW   **Subject:** Freedom of Speech **Obv:** National arms with supporters divide date, denomination below **Rev:** Perched African Fish Eagle

Date	Mintage	F	VF	XF	Unc	BU
1994 Proof	—	Value: 45.00				

KM# 42   500 KWACHA
31.7730 g., 0.9990 Silver 1.0205 oz. ASW   **Subject:** Rights of Religion and Culture **Obv:** National arms with supporters divide date, denomination below **Rev:** Books, scroll, and mask

Date	Mintage	F	VF	XF	Unc	BU
1994 Proof	—	Value: 42.50				

KM# 43   500 KWACHA
31.7730 g., 0.9990 Silver 1.0205 oz. ASW   **Subject:** Rights of Association **Obv:** National arms with supporters divide date, denomination below **Rev:** Lion cub and lamb

Date	Mintage	F	VF	XF	Unc	BU
1994 Proof	—	Value: 47.50				

KM# 44   500 KWACHA
31.7730 g., 0.9990 Silver 1.0205 oz. ASW   **Subject:** Rights to Work **Obv:** National arms with supporters divide date, denomination below **Rev:** African Masked Weaver building nest

Date	Mintage	F	VF	XF	Unc	BU
1994 Proof	—	Value: 45.00				

KM# 45   500 KWACHA
31.7730 g., 0.9990 Silver 1.0205 oz. ASW   **Subject:** Rights to Health **Obv:** National arms with supporters divide date, denomination below **Rev:** Shaman and Caduceus

Date	Mintage	F	VF	XF	Unc	BU
1994 Proof	—	Value: 45.00				

KM# 46   500 KWACHA
31.7730 g., 0.9990 Silver 1.0205 oz. ASW   **Subject:** Rights of the Disabled **Obv:** National arms divide date, denomination below **Rev:** Three elephants

Date	Mintage	F	VF	XF	Unc	BU
1994 Proof	—	Value: 47.50				

KM# 47 500 KWACHA
31.7730 g., 0.9990 Silver 1.0205 oz. ASW **Subject:** Rights to a Clean Environment **Obv:** National arms divide date, denomination below **Rev:** Two South African Shelducks

Date	Mintage	F	VF	XF	Unc	BU
1994 Proof	—				Value: 45.00	

KM# 48 500 KWACHA
31.7730 g., 0.9990 Silver 1.0205 oz. ASW **Subject:** Children's Rights **Obv:** National arms divide date, denomination below **Rev:** Fawn

Date	Mintage	F	VF	XF	Unc	BU
1994 Proof	—				Value: 45.00	

KM# 49 500 KWACHA
31.7730 g., 0.9990 Silver 1.0205 oz. ASW **Subject:** Women's Rights **Obv:** National arms divide date, denomination below **Rev:** Women with firewood

Date	Mintage	F	VF	XF	Unc	BU
1994 Proof	—				Value: 42.50	

KM# 136 500 KWACHA
223.0000 g., 0.9990 Silver 7.1621 oz. ASW, 75.15 mm.
Subject: Equality **Obv:** National arms divide date, denomination below **Rev:** Black and white facial profiles **Edge:** Reeded
Note: Illustration reduced.

Date	Mintage	F	VF	XF	Unc	BU
1995 Proof	—				Value: 275	

KM# 53 500 KWACHA
31.1035 g., 0.9990 Silver 0.9990 oz. ASW **Subject:** Diana - The People's Princess **Obv:** National arms divide date, denomination below **Rev:** Diana facing

Date	Mintage	F	VF	XF	Unc	BU
1997 Proof	Est. 13,211				Value: 22.50	

KM# 182 500 KWACHA
1.2200 g., 0.9999 Gold 0.0392 oz. AGW, 13.9 mm.
Obv: National arms **Obv. Leg.:** BANK OF ZAMBIA **Rev:** Bust of Dr. David Livingstone at lower left in front of wall **Edge:** Reeded

Date	Mintage	F	VF	XF	Unc	BU
1999 Proof	—				Value: 55.00	

KM# 179 1000 KWACHA
28.3000 g., Silver, 27.00 mm. **Subject:** Silver Jubilee, Elizabeth II and Prince Philip **Obv:** National arms **Rev:** Royal couple

Date	Mintage	F	VF	XF	Unc	BU
1997 Proof	30,000				Value: 65.00	

KM# 180 1000 KWACHA
28.0000 g., Copper Nickel, 27.00 mm. **Subject:** !st Anniversary Death of Princess Diana **Obv:** National arms **Rev:** Bust of Diana and her memorial

Date	Mintage	F	VF	XF	Unc	BU
1999 Proof	—				Value: 35.00	

KM# 91 1000 KWACHA
28.7200 g., Copper-Nickel, 38 mm. **Subject:** European Unity **Obv:** National arms divide date, denomination below **Rev:** Multicolor 20 euro note **Edge:** Plain **Note:** Deleted per contributor

Date	Mintage	F	VF	XF	Unc	BU
1999	—				Value: 20.00	

KM# 176 1000 KWACHA
19.9200 g., 0.9250 Silver 0.5924 oz. ASW, 38.4 mm.
Obv: British Queen Elizabeth II above Zambian arms **Rev:** 1st Man on the Moon **Edge:** Plain

Date	Mintage	F	VF	XF	Unc	BU
1999 Proof	—				Value: 40.00	

KM# 109 1000 KWACHA
20.0000 g., 0.9250 Silver 0.5948 oz. ASW, 38.6 mm.
Series: Sydney Olympics **Obv:** Crowned head right within circle, divides date above arms and denomination **Rev:** Discus thrower **Edge:** Plain

Date	Mintage	F	VF	XF	Unc	BU
1999 Proof	—				Value: 35.00	

KM# 120 1000 KWACHA
28.5000 g., Silver-Plated Copper-Nickel, 38 mm.
Subject: European Unity - One Currency **Obv:** National arms divide date, denomination below **Rev:** Multicolor 5 Euro note face design **Edge:** Reeded

Date	Mintage	F	VF	XF	Unc	BU
1999 Proof	—				Value: 20.00	

KM# 121 1000 KWACHA
28.5000 g., Silver-Plated Copper-Nickel, 38 mm.
Subject: European Unity - One Currency **Obv:** National arms divide date, denomination below **Rev:** Multicolor 5 Euro note back design **Edge:** Reeded

Date	Mintage	F	VF	XF	Unc	BU
1999 Proof	—				Value: 20.00	

KM# 122 1000 KWACHA
28.5000 g., Silver-Plated Copper-Nickel, 38 mm.
Subject: European Unity - One Currency **Obv:** National arms divide date, denomination below **Rev:** Multicolor 10 Euro note face design **Edge:** Reeded

Date	Mintage	F	VF	XF	Unc	BU
1999 Proof	—				Value: 20.00	

KM# 123   1000 KWACHA
28.5000 g., Silver-Plated Copper-Nickel, 38 mm.
Subject: European Unity - One Currency **Obv:** National arms divide date, denomination below **Rev:** Multicolor 10 Euro note back design **Edge:** Reeded

Date	Mintage	F	VF	XF	Unc	BU
1999 Proof	—	Value: 20.00				

KM# 124   1000 KWACHA
28.5000 g., Silver-Plated Copper-Nickel, 38 mm.
Subject: European Unity - One Currency **Obv:** National arms divide date, denomination below **Rev:** Multicolor 20 Euro note face design **Edge:** Reeded

Date	Mintage	F	VF	XF	Unc	BU
1999 Proof	—	Value: 20.00				

KM# 125   1000 KWACHA
28.5000 g., Silver-Plated Copper-Nickel, 38 mm.
Subject: European Unity - One Currency **Obv:** National arms divide date, denomination below **Rev:** Multicolor 20 Euro note back design **Edge:** Reeded

Date	Mintage	F	VF	XF	Unc	BU
1999 Proof	—	Value: 20.00				

KM# 126   1000 KWACHA
28.5000 g., Silver-Plated Copper-Nickel, 38 mm.
Subject: European Unity - One Currency **Obv:** National arms divide date, denomination below **Rev:** Multicolor 50 Euro note face design **Edge:** Reeded

Date	Mintage	F	VF	XF	Unc	BU
1999 Proof	—	Value: 22.50				

KM# 127   1000 KWACHA
28.5000 g., Silver-Plated Copper-Nickel, 38 mm.
Subject: European Unity - One Currency **Obv:** National arms divide date, denomination below **Rev:** Multicolor 50 Euro note back design **Edge:** Reeded

Date	Mintage	F	VF	XF	Unc	BU
1999 Proof	—	Value: 22.50				

KM# 128   1000 KWACHA
28.5000 g., Silver-Plated Copper-Nickel-Zinc, 38 mm.
Subject: Euro Banknotes Series **Obv:** National arms divide date, denomination below **Rev:** Multicolor 100 Euro noe face design **Edge:** Reeded

Date	Mintage	F	VF	XF	Unc	BU
1999 Proof	—	Value: 22.50				

KM# 129   1000 KWACHA
28.5000 g., Silver-Plated Copper-Nickel-Zinc, 38 mm.
Subject: Euro Banknotes Series **Obv:** National arms divide date, denomination below **Rev:** Multicolor 100 Euro note back design **Edge:** Reeded

Date	Mintage	F	VF	XF	Unc	BU
1999 Proof	—	Value: 22.50				

KM# 130   1000 KWACHA
28.5000 g., Silver-Plated Copper-Nickel-Zinc, 38 mm.
Subject: Euro Banknotes Series **Obv:** National arms divide date, denomination below **Rev:** Multicolor 200 Euro note face design **Edge:** Reeded

Date	Mintage	F	VF	XF	Unc	BU
1999 Proof	—	Value: 22.50				

KM# 131   1000 KWACHA
28.5000 g., Silver-Plated Copper-Nickel-Zinc, 38 mm.
Subject: Euro Banknotes Series **Obv:** National arms divide date, denomination below **Rev:** Multicolor 200 Euro note back design

Date	Mintage	F	VF	XF	Unc	BU
1999 Proof	—	Value: 22.50				

KM# 132   1000 KWACHA
28.5000 g., Silver-Plated Copper-Nickel-Zinc, 38 mm.
Subject: Euro Banknotes Series **Obv:** National arms divide date, denomination below **Rev:** Multicolor 500 Euro note face design **Edge:** Reeded

Date	Mintage	F	VF	XF	Unc	BU
1999 Proof	—	Value: 22.50				

KM# 133   1000 KWACHA
28.5000 g., Silver-Plated Copper-Nickel-Zinc, 38 mm.
Subject: Euro Banknotes Series **Obv:** National arms divide date, denomination below **Rev:** Multicolor 500 Euro note back design **Edge:** Reeded

Date	Mintage	F	VF	XF	Unc	BU
1999 Proof	—	Value: 22.50				

KM# 74   1000 KWACHA
29.0000 g., Copper-Nickel, 40 mm. **Obv:** Crowned head right above arms with supporters divides date **Rev:** Dated calendar within circular design

Date	Mintage	F	VF	XF	Unc	BU
2000 Proof	—	Value: 17.50				

KM# 75 1000 KWACHA
20.0000 g., Copper-Nickel, 48x30 mm. **Subject:** 100th Birthday
- Queen Mother **Obv:** Head with tiara right divides date above
arms **Rev:** Shaded bust facing **Edge:** Reeded

Date	Mintage	F	VF	XF	Unc	BU
2000 Proof	—				Value: 13.50	

KM# 76 1000 KWACHA
20.0000 g., Copper-Nickel, 48x30 mm. **Subject:** 100th Birthday
- Queen Mother **Obv:** Head with tiara right divides date above
arms **Rev:** Black and white photo of Queen Mother seated on
throne at 1937 coronation

Date	Mintage	F	VF	XF	Unc	BU
2000 Proof	50,000				Value: 13.50	

KM# 77 1000 KWACHA
20.0000 g., Copper-Nickel, 48x30 mm. **Subject:** 100th Birthday -
Queen Mother **Obv:** Head with tiara right divides date above arms
Rev: Black and white photo of Queen Mother as an elderly lady

Date	Mintage	F	VF	XF	Unc	BU
2000 Proof	50,000				Value: 13.50	

KM# 95 1000 KWACHA
Copper-Nickel, 48 x 30.1 mm. **Series:** 1,000 Years of
Exploration **Obv:** Head with tiara right divides date above arms
Rev: Multicolor portrait of Leif Ericksson and Viking ship
Edge: Reeded

Date	Mintage	F	VF	XF	Unc	BU
2000 Proof	15,000				Value: 12.00	

KM# 96 1000 KWACHA
Copper-Nickel **Series:** 1,000 Years of Exploration **Obv:** Head
with tiara right divides date above arms **Rev:** Multicolor portrait
of Marco Polo and ship

Date	Mintage	F	VF	XF	Unc	BU
2000 Proof	15,000				Value: 12.00	

KM# 97 1000 KWACHA
Copper-Nickel **Series:** 1,000 Years of Exploration **Obv:** Head
with tiara right divides date above arms **Rev:** Multicolor portrait
of Columbus and ship

Date	Mintage	F	VF	XF	Unc	BU
2000 Proof	15,000				Value: 12.00	

KM# 98 1000 KWACHA
Copper-Nickel **Series:** 1,000 Years of Exploration **Obv:** Head
with tiara right divides date above arms **Rev:** Multicolor portrait
of Sir Francis Drake and ship

Date	Mintage	F	VF	XF	Unc	BU
2000 Proof	15,000				Value: 12.00	

KM# 99 1000 KWACHA
Copper-Nickel **Series:** 1,000 Years of Exploration **Obv:** Head
with tiara right divides date above arms **Rev:** Multicolor portrait
of Captain Cook and ship

Date	Mintage	F	VF	XF	Unc	BU
2000 Proof	15,000				Value: 12.00	

KM# 100 1000 KWACHA
Copper-Nickel **Series:** 1,000 Years of Exploration **Obv:** Head
with tiara right divides date above arms **Rev:** Multicolor portrait
of Amundsen and ship

Date	Mintage	F	VF	XF	Unc	BU
2000 Proof	15,000				Value: 12.00	

KM# 147 1000 KWACHA
28.9000 g., 0.9250 Silver 0.8594 oz. ASW, 40.3 mm.
Subject: African Wildlife **Obv:** Head with tiara right divides date
above arms **Rev:** Multicolor snarling leopard under protective
acrylic, denomination below **Edge:** Reeded

Date	Mintage	F	VF	XF	Unc	BU
2000 Proof	—				Value: 55.00	

KM# 148 1000 KWACHA

28.9000 g., 0.9250 Silver 0.8594 oz. ASW, 40.3 mm.
Subject: African Wildlife **Obv:** Head with tiara right divides date above national arms **Rev:** Multicolor white stork under protective acrylic, denomination below **Edge:** Reeded

Date	Mintage	F	VF	XF	Unc	BU
2000 Proof	—				Value: 55.00	

KM# 149 1000 KWACHA

28.9000 g., 0.9250 Silver 0.8594 oz. ASW, 40.3 mm.
Subject: African Wildlife **Obv:** Head with tiara right divides date above national arms **Rev:** Multicolor cheetah under protective acrylic, denomination below **Edge:** Reeded

Date	Mintage	F	VF	XF	Unc	BU
2000 Proof	—				Value: 55.00	

KM# 137 2000 KWACHA

22.5000 g., Copper-Nickel, 38 mm. **Subject:** World Cup Soccer **Obv:** National arms with supporters divide date, denomination below **Rev:** Player kicking ball **Edge:** Reeded

Date	Mintage	F	VF	XF	Unc	BU
1994 Proof	—				Value: 20.00	

KM# 138 2000 KWACHA

22.5000 g., Copper-Nickel, 38 mm. **Subject:** World Cup Soccer **Obv:** National arms with supporters divide date, denomination below **Rev:** Two players in action **Edge:** Reeded

Date	Mintage	F	VF	XF	Unc	BU
1994 Proof	—				Value: 20.00	

KM# 139 2000 KWACHA

22.5000 g., Copper-Nickel, 38 mm. **Subject:** World Cup Soccer **Obv:** National arms with supporters divide date, denomination below **Rev:** Three players and "Winner Brazil" **Edge:** Reeded

Date	Mintage	F	VF	XF	Unc	BU
1994 Proof	—				Value: 20.00	

KM# 152 2000 KWACHA

20.2200 g., 0.9999 Silver 0.6500 oz. ASW, 38 mm.
Subject: World History **Obv:** National arms with supporters divide date, denomination below **Rev:** Human figure study **Edge:** Reeded

Date	Mintage	F	VF	XF	Unc	BU
1997 Proof	—				Value: 35.00	

KM# 54 2000 KWACHA

3.1103 g., 0.9999 Gold 0.1000 oz. AGW **Subject:** Diana - The People's Princess **Obv:** National arms with supporters divide date, denomination below **Rev:** Head facing **Note:** Similar to 200 Kwacha, KM#52.

Date	Mintage	F	VF	XF	Unc	BU
1997 Proof	—				Value: 120	

KM# 68 2000 KWACHA

15.5518 g., 0.9990 Silver 0.4995 oz. ASW **Subject:** Taipai Subway **Obv:** National arms **Rev:** Train with inset diamond headlight **Note:** Struck at Singapore Mint.

Date	Mintage	F	VF	XF	Unc	BU
1998 Proof	9,999				Value: 40.00	

KM# 146 2000 KWACHA/100 GUILDERS

25.0000 g., 0.9990 Silver 0.8029 oz. ASW, 38 mm.
Subject: World Cup Soccer **Obv:** National arms with supporters divide date, denomination below **Rev:** Two soccer players of Suriname **Edge:** Reeded **Note:** Zambia/Suriname muled dies error. Obverse is Zambia and the reverse is Suriname.

Date	Mintage	F	VF	XF	Unc	BU
1994 Proof	—				Value: 100	

KM# 55 2500 KWACHA

15.5517 g., 0.4995 Silver 0.2497 oz. ASW **Subject:** Diana - The People's Princess **Obv:** National arms with supporters divide date, denomination below **Rev:** With sons, William and Harry

Date	Mintage	F	VF	XF	Unc	BU
1997 Proof	Est. 1,997				Value: 65.00	

KM# 107 2500 KWACHA

15.5535 g., 0.9250 Silver 0.4625 oz. ASW, 36 mm.
Series: World Health Organization **Obv:** National arms with supporters divide date, denomination below **Rev:** Bust at left facing right, logo at right **Edge:** Reeded

Date	Mintage	F	VF	XF	Unc	BU
1998 Proof	—				Value: 30.00	

KM# 134 4000 KWACHA

31.1035 g., 0.9990 Silver 0.9990 oz. ASW, 38.5 mm.
Subject: Year of the Tiger **Obv:** National arms with supporters divide date, denomination below **Rev:** Gold bat disc mounted above tiger **Edge:** Reeded

Date	Mintage	F	VF	XF	Unc	BU
1997 Proof	—				Value: 125	

KM# 155 4000 KWACHA

30.3300 g., 0.9990 Silver 0.9741 oz. ASW, 38 mm.
Subject: King of Peace - King Hussein of Jordan **Obv:** National arms with supporters divide date, denomination below **Rev:** Bust at left looking right, multicolor view of Petra at right **Edge:** Reeded

Date	Mintage	F	VF	XF	Unc	BU
1998 Proof	—				Value: 50.00	

KM# 69 4000 KWACHA

31.1035 g., 0.9990 Silver 0.9990 oz. ASW **Subject:** Taipai Subway **Obv:** National arms **Rev:** Train with inset diamond headlight **Note:** Struck at Singapore Mint.

Date	Mintage	F	VF	XF	Unc	BU
1998 Proof	9,999				Value: 60.00	

KM# 161 4000 KWACHA

28.9500 g., Copper-Nickel, 37.9 mm. **Subject:** Patrons of the Ocean **Obv:** National arms divide date above "999", denomination below **Rev:** Sea Turtle and fish **Edge:** Reeded

Date	Mintage	F	VF	XF	Unc	BU
1998 Proof	—				Value: 30.00	

KM# 162 4000 KWACHA

28.9500 g., Copper-Nickel, 37.9 mm. **Subject:** Patrons of the Ocean **Obv:** National arms divide date above "999", denomination below **Rev:** Sea horse and fish **Edge:** Reeded

Date	Mintage	F	VF	XF	Unc	BU
1998 Proof	—				Value: 30.00	

KM# 163 4000 KWACHA
28.9500 g., Copper-Nickel, 37.9 mm. **Subject:** Patrons of the Ocean **Obv:** National arms divide date above "999", denomination below **Rev:** Two dolphins **Edge:** Reeded

Date	Mintage	F	VF	XF	Unc	BU
1998 Proof	—	Value: 30.00				

KM# 164 4000 KWACHA
28.9500 g., Copper-Nickel, 37.9 mm. **Subject:** Patrons of the Ocean **Obv:** National arms divide date above "999", denomination below **Rev:** Coelacanth **Edge:** Reeded

Date	Mintage	F	VF	XF	Unc	BU
1998 Proof	—	Value: 30.00				

KM# 175 4000 KWACHA
23.0000 g., 0.9990 Silver 0.7387 oz. ASW, 40 mm. **Obv:** Head with tiara right divides date above arms **Rev:** Dated calendar

Date	Mintage	F	VF	XF	Unc	BU
2000 Prooflike	—	—	—	—	—	50.00

KM# 158 4000 KWACHA
31.0000 g., 0.9990 Silver 0.9956 oz. ASW, 38.8 mm. **Subject:** African Wildlife **Obv:** Head with tiara right divides date above arms **Rev:** Leopard and two cubs, denomination below **Edge:** Reeded

Date	Mintage	F	VF	XF	Unc	BU
2000 Proof	—	Value: 40.00				

KM# 78 4000 KWACHA
20.0000 g., 0.9250 Silver 0.5948 oz. ASW, 48x30 mm. **Subject:** 100th Birthday - Queen Mother **Obv:** Head with tiara right divides date above arms **Rev:** Black and white photo of the Queen Mother as a young lady **Edge:** Reeded

Date	Mintage	F	VF	XF	Unc	BU
2000 Proof	25,000	Value: 40.00				

KM# 79 4000 KWACHA
20.0000 g., 0.9250 Silver 0.5948 oz. ASW, 48x30 mm. **Subject:** 100th Birthday - Queen Mother **Obv:** Head with tiara right divides date above arms **Rev:** Black and white photo of Queen Mother on throne at 1937 coronation

Date	Mintage	F	VF	XF	Unc	BU
2000 Proof	25,000	Value: 40.00				

KM# 80 4000 KWACHA
20.0000 g., 0.9250 Silver 0.5948 oz. ASW, 48x30 mm. **Subject:** 100th Birthday - Queen Mother **Obv:** Head with tiara right divides date above arms **Rev:** Black and white photo of an elderly Queen Mother

Date	Mintage	F	VF	XF	Unc	BU
2000 Proof	25,000	Value: 40.00				

KM# 84 4000 KWACHA
20.0000 g., 0.9250 Silver 0.5948 oz. ASW, 30.1x48 mm. **Subject:** Millennium - DNA Code **Obv:** Head with tiara right above arms and denomination **Rev:** DNA chain, date below **Edge:** Reeded

Date	Mintage	F	VF	XF	Unc	BU
2000 Proof	—	Value: 55.00				

KM# 85 4000 KWACHA
25.1000 g., 0.9250 Silver 0.7464 oz. ASW, 37.9 mm. **Series:** Wildlife Protection **Obv:** Crowned head right below arms **Rev:** Lion head hologram **Edge:** Reeded **Note:** Lighter weight and smaller diameter than official specifications

Date	Mintage	F	VF	XF	Unc	BU
2000 Proof	5,000	Value: 60.00				

KM# 101 4000 KWACHA
20.0000 g., 0.9250 Silver 0.5948 oz. ASW, 48x30.1 mm. **Series:** 1000 Years of Exploration **Obv:** Head with tiara right divides date above arms **Rev:** Multicolor portrait of Leif Eriksson and ship **Edge:** Reeded

Date	Mintage	F	VF	XF	Unc	BU
2000 Proof	5,000	Value: 47.50				

KM# 102 4000 KWACHA
20.0000 g., 0.9250 Silver 0.5948 oz. ASW **Subject:** 1000 Years of Exploration **Obv:** Head with tiara right divides date above arms **Rev:** Multicolor portrait of Marco Polo and ship

Date	Mintage	F	VF	XF	Unc	BU
2000 Proof	5,000	Value: 47.50				

KM# 103 4000 KWACHA
20.0000 g., 0.9250 Silver 0.5948 oz. ASW **Subject:** 1000 Years of Exploration **Obv:** Head with tiara right divides date above arms **Rev:** Multicolor portrait of Columbus and ship

Date	Mintage	F	VF	XF	Unc	BU
2000 Proof	5,000	Value: 47.50				

KM# 104 4000 KWACHA
20.0000 g., 0.9250 Silver 0.5948 oz. ASW **Subject:** 1000 Years of Exploration **Obv:** Head with tiara right divides date above arms **Rev:** Multicolor portrait of Sir Francis Drake and ship

Date	Mintage	F	VF	XF	Unc	BU
2000 Proof	5,000	Value: 47.50				

KM# 105 4000 KWACHA
20.0000 g., 0.9250 Silver 0.5948 oz. ASW **Subject:** 1000 Years of Exploration **Obv:** Head with tiara right divides date above arms **Rev:** Multicolor portrait of Captain Cook and ship

Date	Mintage	F	VF	XF	Unc	BU
2000 Proof	5,000	Value: 47.50				

KM# 106 4000 KWACHA
20.0000 g., 0.9250 Silver 0.5948 oz. ASW **Subject:** 1000 Years of Exploration **Obv:** Head with tiara right divides date above arms **Rev:** Multicolor portrait of Amundsen and ship

Date	Mintage	F	VF	XF	Unc	BU
2000 Proof	5,000	Value: 47.50				

KM# 144 5000 KWACHA
Silver **Rev:** Lions, map, and arms

Date	Mintage	F	VF	XF	Unc	BU
1997 Proof	2,000	Value: 210				

KM# 177 5000 KWACHA
31.2000 g., 0.9990 Silver 1.0021 oz. ASW, 40 mm.
Obv: National arms **Rev:** Asian General behind red flowers
Edge: Reeded

Date	Mintage	F	VF	XF	Unc	BU
1997 Proof	—	Value: 50.00				

KM# 70 5000 KWACHA
7.7759 g., 0.9990 Gold 0.2497 oz. AGW **Subject:** Taipai Subway **Obv:** National arms **Rev:** Train with inset diamond headlight **Note:** Struck at Singapore Mint.

Date	Mintage	F	VF	XF	Unc	BU
1998 Proof	999	Value: 350				

KM# 108 5000 KWACHA
31.2100 g., 0.9250 Silver 0.9281 oz. ASW, 40 mm.
Subject: World Health Organization **Obv:** National arms with supporters divide date, denomination below **Rev:** Bust at left facing right, logo at right **Edge:** Reeded

Date	Mintage	F	VF	XF	Unc	BU
1998 Proof	—	Value: 40.00				

KM# 157 5000 KWACHA
31.1600 g., 0.9990 Silver 1.0008 oz. ASW, 38.8 mm.
Subject: African Wildlife **Obv:** National arms with supporters divide date, denomination below **Rev:** Lions' pride, denomination above **Edge:** Reeded

Date	Mintage	F	VF	XF	Unc	BU
1999 Proof	—	Value: 40.00				

KM# 73 5000 KWACHA
31.1346 g., 0.9990 Silver 100000 oz. ASW **Subject:** African Wildlife **Obv:** National arms with supporters divide date, denomination below **Rev:** Elephant and calf in water with metal content statement

Date	Mintage	F	VF	XF	Unc	BU
1999	—	—	—	—	25.00	—
1999 Matte	—	—	—	—	30.00	—

KM# 92 5000 KWACHA
31.2100 g., 0.9990 Silver 1.0024 oz. ASW, 38.7 mm.
Subject: African Wildlife **Obv:** National arms with supporters, date below **Rev:** Elephant mother and calf right, denomination below **Edge:** Reeded

Date	Mintage	F	VF	XF	Unc	BU
1999 Proof	—	Value: 25.00				

KM# 81 5000 KWACHA
27.0000 g., 0.9990 Gold 0.8672 oz. AGW, 48x30 mm.
Subject: 100th Birthday - Queen Mother **Obv:** Head with tiara right divides date above arms **Rev:** Black and white photo of the Queen Mother as a young lady **Edge:** Reeded

Date	Mintage	F	VF	XF	Unc	BU
2000 Proof	100	Value: 975				

KM# 82 5000 KWACHA
27.0000 g., 0.9990 Gold 0.8672 oz. AGW, 48x30 mm.
Subject: 100th Birthday - Queen Mother **Obv:** Head with tiara right divides date above arms **Rev:** Black ad white photo of Queen Mother on throne at 1937 coronation

Date	Mintage	F	VF	XF	Unc	BU
2000 Proof	100	Value: 950				

KM# 83 5000 KWACHA
27.0000 g., 0.9990 Gold 0.8672 oz. AGW, 48x30 mm.
Subject: 100th Birthday - Queen Mother **Obv:** Head with tiara right divides date above arms **Rev:** Black and white photo of an elderly Queen Mother

Date	Mintage	F	VF	XF	Unc	BU
2000 Proof	100	Value: 950				

KM# 150 5000 KWACHA
31.1035 g., 0.9999 Silver 0.9999 oz. ASW, 38 mm.
Subject: Chinese Zodiac **Obv:** Dragon on Chinese map above national arms **Rev:** Cartoon rabbit within inner circle
Edge: Reeded

Date	Mintage	F	VF	XF	Unc	BU
ND Proof	—	Value: 45.00				

KM# 151 5000 KWACHA
31.1035 g., 0.9999 Silver 0.9999 oz. ASW, 38 mm.
Subject: Chinese Zodiac **Obv:** Dragon on Chinese map above national arms **Rev:** Cartoon bull within inner circle **Edge:** Reeded

Date	Mintage	F	VF	XF	Unc	BU
ND Proof	—	Value: 45.00				

KM# 141 5000 KWACHA
28.6400 g., 0.9990 Silver 0.9198 oz. ASW, 38.5 mm.
Subject: African Wildlife **Obv:** National arms **Rev:** Elephant
Edge: Reeded

Date	Mintage	F	VF	XF	Unc	BU
2000	—	Value: 40.00				